10TH EDITION - 2020

THE HOBBY'S MOST RELIABLE AND RELIED UPON SOURCE™

Prices in this guide reflect current retail rates determined just prior to printing. They do not reflect for-sale prices by the author, publisher, distributors, advertisers, or any card dealers associated with this guide. Every effort has been made to eliminate errors. Readers are invited to write us noting any errors which may be researched and corrected in subsequent printings. The publisher will not be held responsible for losses which may occur in the sale or purchase of cards because of information contained herein.

BECKETT is a registered trademark of BECKETT MEDIA LLC, DALLAS, TEXAS
Manufactured in the United States of America | Published by Beckett Media LLC

Beckett Media LLC
4635 McEwen Dr. • Dallas, TX 75244
(972) 991-6657 • beckett.com

First Printing ISBN: 978-1-936681-29-7

TABLE OF CONTENTS

BECKETT COLLECTIBLE GAMING ALMANAC

EDITORIAL
MIKE PAYNE - Editorial Director
RYAN CRACKNELL - Hobby Editor
ERIC KNAGG - Designer

COLLECTIBLES DATA PUBLISHING
BRIAN FLEISCHER - Manager, Sr. Market Analyst
LLOYD ALMONGUERA, RYAN ALTUBAR, MATT BIBLE, JEFF CAMAY, STEVE DALTON, JUSTIN GRUNERT, JUNEL MAGALE, ERIC NORTON, KRISTIAN REDULLA, ARSENIO TAN, SAM ZIMMER - Price Guide Staff

ADVERTISING
TED BARKER - Senior Sales Executive
tbarker@beckett.com 972.448.9147
ALEX SORIANO - Advertising Sales Executive
alex@beckett.com 619.392.5299

BECKETT GRADING SERVICES
JEROMY MURRAY
VP, Grading & Authentication
4635 McEwen Road, Dallas, TX 75244
jmurray@beckett.com

DALLAS OFFICE
4635 McEwen, Dallas, TX 75244
DEREK FICKEN - dficken@beckett.com • 972.448.9144

NEW YORK OFFICE
CHARLES STABILE
Northeast Regional Sales Manager
484 White Plains Rd, 2nd Floor,
Eastchester, N.Y. 10709
Office: 914.268.0533
cstabile@beckett.com

CALIFORNIA OFFICE
MICHAEL GARDNER
Western Regional Sales Manager
17890 Sky Park Circle, Suite 250,
Irvine, CA 92614
Office: 714.200.1934
mgardner@beckett.com

ASIA OFFICE
DONGWOON LEE
Asia/Pacific Sales Manager
Seoul, Korea
dongwoonl@beckett.com
Cell: +82.10.6826.6868

BECKETT AUCTION SERVICES
DANIEL MOSCOSO - Digital Studio

OPERATIONS
ALBERTO CHAVEZ
Sr. Logistics & Facilities Manager

EDITORIAL, PRODUCTION & SALES OFFICE
4635 McEwen Road, Dallas TX 75244
972.991.6657 • beckett.com

CUSTOMER SERVICE
Beckett Media, LLC
4635 McEwen Road, Dallas, TX 75244
Subscriptions, address changes, renewals, missing or damaged copies
866.287.9383 • 239.653.0225
FOREIGN INQUIRES
subscriptions@beckett.com
Back issues: beckettmedia.com
BOOKS, MERCHANDISE, REPRINTS
239.280.2380
DEALER SALES
239.280.2380 • dealers@beckett.com

BECKETT MEDIA, LLC
SANDEEP DUA: President
KEVIN ISAACSON: Vice President

Magic The Gathering Hot List

RAVNICA ALLEGIANCE – RELEASED ON: 1/25/19

Hydroid Krasis M

#2

Breeding Pool R

#3

Godless Shrine R

#4

Blood Crypt R

#5

Stomping Ground R

WAR OF THE SPARK – RELEASED ON: 5/3/19

Teferi, Time Raveler R

#2

Liliana, Dreadhorde General M

#3

Finale of Devastation M

#4

Finale of Promise M

#5

Nicol Bolas, Dragon-God M

MODERN HORIZONS – RELEASED ON: 6/14/19

#1

Wrenn and Six M

#2

Urza, Lord High Artificer M

#3

Force of Negation R

#4

Prismatic Vista L R

#5

Seasoned Pyromancer M

Magic The Gathering

GRADED CARD HOT LIST

#4

1993 Magic The Gathering Alpha Black Lotus R

1993 Magic The Gathering Alpha Mox Sapphire R

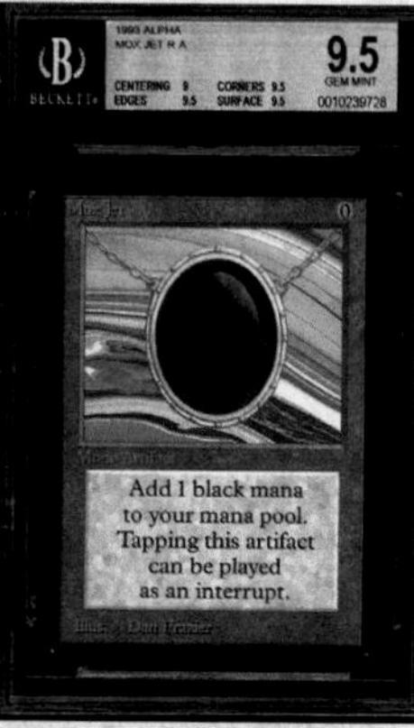

1993 Magic The Gathering Alpha Mox Jet R

1993 Magic The Gathering Alpha Time Walk R

1993 Magic The Gathering Alpha Underground Sea R

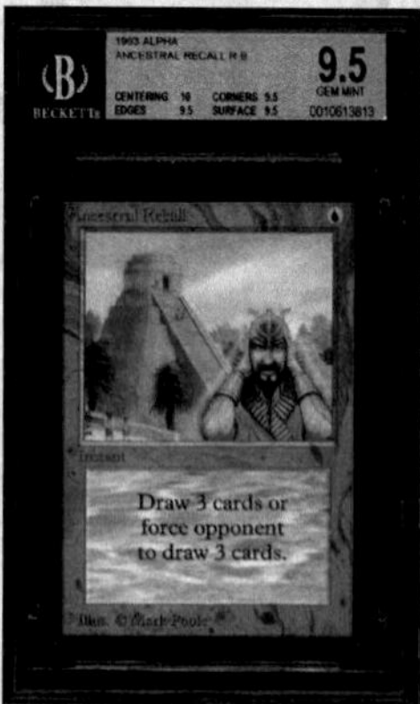

1993 Magic The Gathering Alpha Ancestral Recall R

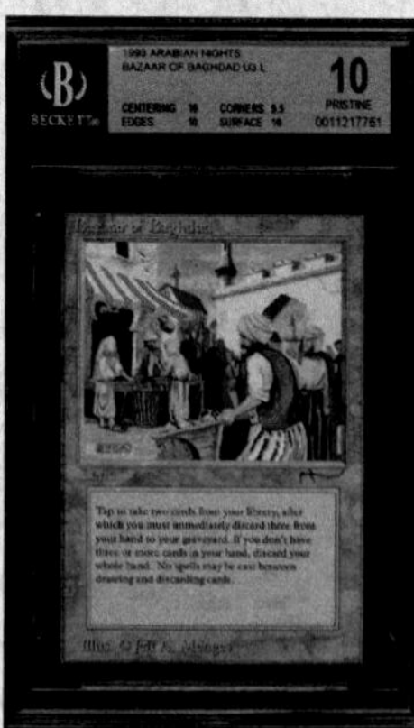

1993 Magic The Gathering Arabian Nights Bazaar of Baghdad U3

1993 Magic The Gathering Beta Volcanic Island R

1993 Magic The Gathering Alpha Chaos Orb R

1993 Magic The Gathering Time Vault R

Yu-Gi-Oh Hot List

SAVAGE STRIKE – RELEASED ON: 2/1/19

#1

Fantastical Dragon Phantazmay SCR

#2

Pot of Extravagance SCR

#3

Borreload Savage Dragon UR

#4

World Legacy Guardragon UR

#5

Cyberse Quantum Dragon UR

DARK NEOSTORM – RELEASED ON: 5/3/19

#1

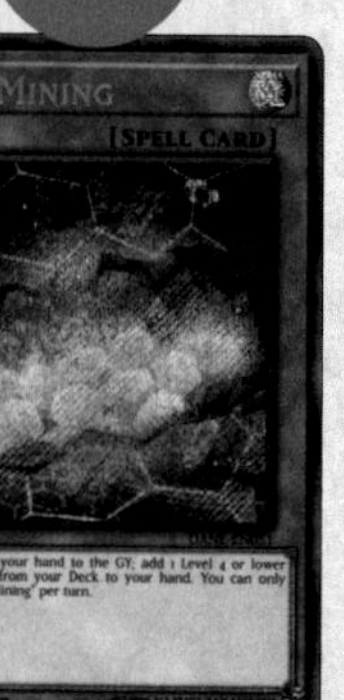

Cynet Mining SCR

#2

Gnomaterial SCR

#3

Dingirsu, the Orcust of the Evening Star UR

#4

Ib the World Chalice Justicar SCR

#5

Ghost Sister & Spooky Dogwood SCR

RISING RAMPAGE – RELEASED ON: 7/26/2019

#1

Apollousa, Bow of the Goddess SCR

#2

Marincess Coral Anemone SCR

#3

Gizmek Orochi, the Serpentron Sky Slasher SCR

#4

Get Out! SCR

#5

Marincess Sea Horse UR

Yu-Gi-Oh Graded Hot List

CORE SET 2018

2002 Yu-Gi-Oh Legend of Blue Eyes White Dragon 1st Edition Blue-Eyes White Dragon UR

#2

2003 Yu-Gi-Oh Magician's Force 1st Edition Dark Paladin Correct Art UR

#3

2002 Yu-Gi-Oh Legend of Blue Eyes White Dragon 1st Edition Gaia the Dragon Champion SCR

#4

2003 Yu-Gi-Oh Legacy of Darkness 1st Edition Injection Fairy Lily SCR

#5

2004 Yu-Gi-Oh Invasion of Chaos 1st Edition Chaos Emperor Dragon – Envoy of the End SCR

#6

2004 Yu-Gi-Oh Invasion of Chaos 1st Edition Black Luster Soldier – Envoy of the Beginning UR

#7

2002 Yu-Gi-Oh Starter Deck Kaiba 1st Edition Blue-Eyes White Dragon UR

#8

2002 Yu-Gi-Oh Dark Duel Stories Promos Blue-Eyes White Dragon SCR

#9

2003 Yu-Gi-Oh Magician's Force 1st Edition Dark Magician Girl SCR

#10

2008 Yu-Gi-Oh Crossroads of Chaos 1st Edition Black Rose Dragon GR

Dragon Ball Slayer Hot List

CLASH OF FATES

#1

Frieza, Army Reborn SCR

#2

Newfound Power Porunga SR

#3

Body Change Ginyu R

#4

Final Showdown Son Goku SR

#5

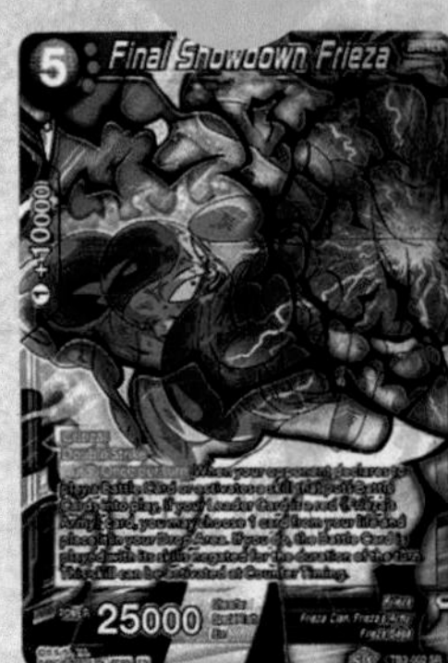

Final Showdown Frieza SR

DESTROYER KINGS

#1

Broly, Ultimate Agent of Destruction SCR

#2

Arcane Absorption Majin Buu SCR

#3

Son Goku, the Adventure Begins SR

#4

SSB Gogeta, Fusion Onslaught SR

#5

Broly, Limits Transcended SR

ASSAULT OF THE SAIYANS

#1

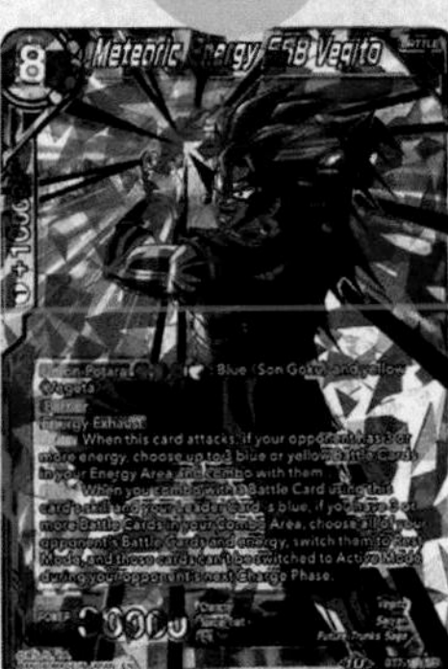

Meteoric Energy SSB Vegito SR

#2

Power of Potara – Vegito, Kefla & Zamasu SCR

#3

SS3 Scramble – Raditz, Vegeta & Broly SCR

#4

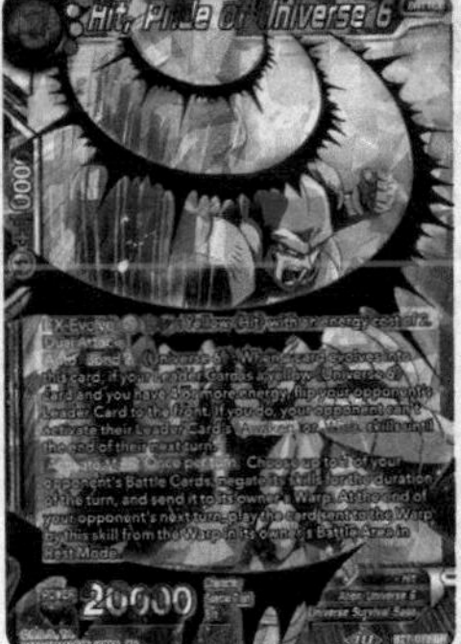

Hit, Pride of Universe 6 SR

#5

SS2 Trunks, Memories of the Past SR

2020 Beckett Collectible Gaming Almanac

WHAT'S LISTED

Products listed in the price guide typically:

- Are produced by licensed manufacturers
- Are widely available
- Have market activity on single items
- Include international releases

WHAT THE COLUMNS MEAN

The LO and HI columns reflect a range of current retail selling prices and are listed in U.S. dollars. The HI column represents the typical full retail selling price while the LO column represents the lowest price one could expect to find through extensive shopping. Both columns represent the same condition for the card listed. Keep in mind that market conditions can change quickly, up or down, based on extreme levels of demand. The published HI and LO column prices in this particular publication are a single snapshot in time and cannot be completely accurate for every card listed.

ONLY A REFERENCE

The data and pricing information contained within this publication is intended for reference only. Beckett's goal is, and always will be, to provide the most accurate and verifiable information in the industry. However, Beckett cannot guarantee the accuracy of all data published and typographical errors periodically occur. Buyers and sellers of gaming cards should be aware of this and handle their personal transactions at their own risk. If you discover an error or misprint in this publication, please notify us via email at nonsports@beckett.com

MULTIPLIERS

Some parallel sets are listed with multipliers to provide values of unlisted cards. Multiplier ranges (i.e. 1X to 2X) apply only to the HI column. Example, if basic-issue card A lists for $2 to $4, and the multiplier is "1X to 2X", then the parallel version of card A or the insert card in question is valued at $4 to $8. Please note the term "basic card" used in the price guide refers to a standard regular-issue card. A "basic card" cannot be an insert or parallel card.

CARD CONDITION

The value of your card is dependent on the condition or "grade" of your card. Prices in this issue reflect the highest raw condition (i.e. not professionally graded by a third party) of the card most commonly found at shows, shops, on the internet, and right out of the pack for brand new releases. This generally means Near Mint-Mint condition for all gaming cards. Use the following chart as a guide to estimate the value of your cards in a variety of conditions using the prices found in this issue.

CARD GRADES

Mint (MT) – A card with no wear or flaws. The card has four perfect corners, 60/40 or better centering from top to bottom and from left to right, original gloss, smooth edges, and original color borders. A Mint card does not have print spots, color or focus imperfections.

Near Mint-Mint (NRMT-MT) – A card with one minor flaw. Any one of the following would lower a Mint card to Near Mint-Mint: one corner with a slight touch of wear, barely noticeable print spots, color or focus imperfections. This card must have a 60/40 or better centering in both directions, original gloss, smooth edges, and original color borders.

Near Mint (NRMT) – A card with one minor flaw. Any one of the following would lower a Mint card to Near Mint-Mint: one very slightly scuffed corner or two or four corners with slight touches of wear, 70/30 to 60/40 centering, slightly rough edges, minor print spots, color or focus imperfections. This card must have original gloss and original color borders.

Excellent-Mint (EXMT) – A card with two or three slightly worn corners with centering no worse than 80/20. The card may have no more than two of the following slightly rough edges, very slightly discolored borders, mirror print spots, color or focus imperfections. The card must have original gloss.

Excellent (EX - aka SP or Slightly Played) – A card with four slightly worn corners and centering is no worse than 80/20. The card may have a small amount of original gloss lost, rough edges, slightly discolored borders, and minor print spots, color or focus imperfections.

Very Good (VG) – A card that has been handled but not abused slightly worn corners with slight layering, slight notching on edges, a significant amount of gloss lost from the surface but no scuffing and moderate discoloration of borders. The card may have a few light creases.

Good (G), Fair (F), Poor (P) (aka HP or Heavily Played) – A well-worn, mishandled or abused card, badly worn corners, lots of scuffing, most or all original gloss missing, seriously discolored borders, moderate or heavy creasing, and one or more serious flaws. The grade of Good, Fair or Poor depends on the severity of wear and flaws. Good, Fair, or Poor cards are generally used only as fillers.

Special Note: The most widely used grades are defined here. Obviously, many cards will not perfectly match one of the definitions. Therefore, categories between the major grades known as in-between grades are used, such as Good to Very Good (G-VG), Very Good to Excellent (VG-EX), and Excellent-Mint to Near Mint (EXMT-NRMT). Such grades indicate a card with all qualities of the lower category but with at least a few qualities of the higher category.

LEGEND

Gaming

BR	Buddy Rare
C	Common
CC	Climax Common
CLR	Climax Rare
F	Fixed
GR	Generation Rare
HOLO	Holofoil
IMR	Image Ride Rare
LIR	Legendary Idol Rare
LR	Legion Rare
NR	No Rarity
OR	Origin Rare
PR	Promo
R	Rare
RLR	Rummy Labyrinth Rare
RR	Double Rare
RRR	Triple Rare
SGR	Special Generation Rare
SP	Special Parallel
SR	Super Rare
SSP	Super Special Parallel
SVR	Special Vanguard Rare
U	Uncommon
VDR	Vanguard Deletor Rare
VR	Vanguard Rare
WSP	Wedding Special Parallel
XR	Xtra Rare
XVR	Cross Vanguard Rare
ZR	Zeroth Dragon Rare

Magic The Gathering

C	Common
C1	Common (appeared once on the press sheet)
C2	Common (appeared twice on the press sheet)
C3	Common (appeared thrice on the press sheet)
C4	Common (appeared four times on the press sheet)
M	Mythic Rare
R	Rare
TR	Timeshifted Rare
U	Uncommon
U1	Uncommon (appeared once on the press sheet)
U2	Uncommon (appeared twice on the press sheet)
U3	Uncommon (appeared thrice on the press sheet)

Pokemon

C	Common
HOLO R	Holo Rare
HOLO SR	Holo Super Rare
PR	Promo
R	Rare
U	Uncommon
UR	Ultra Rare

Yu-Gi-Oh

C	Common
GR	Ghost Rare
GUR	Gold ultra Rare
PR	Parallel Rare
R	Rare
SCR	Secret Rare
SFR	Starfoil Rare
SR	Super Rare
UR	Ultra Rare
UTR	Ultimate Rare

MAGIC THE GATHERING SETS AND SYMBOLS CHART

Core Sets

Alpha Edition
Beta Edition
Unlimited Edition
Revised Edition
Fourth Edition
Fifth Edition
Sixth Edition
Seventh Edition
Eighth Edition
Ninth Edition
Tenth Edition
Magic 2010 (M10)
Magic 2011 (M11)
Magic 2012 (M12)
Magic 2013 (M13)
Magic 2014 (M14)
Magic 2015 (M15)
Magic Origins
Magic 2019
Magic 2020

Expansion Sets

Arabian Nights
Antiquities
Legends
The Dark
Fallen Empires
Ice Age
Homelands
Alliances
Mirage
Visions
Weatherlight
Tempest
Stronghold
Exodus
Urza's Saga
Urza's Legacy
Urza's Destiny
Mercadian Masques
Nemesis
Prophecy
Invasion
Planeshift
Apocalypse
Odyssey
Torment
Judgment
Onslaught
Legions
Scourge
Mirrodin
Darksteel
Fifth Dawn
Champions of Kamigawa
Betrayers of Kamigawa
Saviors of Kamigawa
Ravnica
Guildpact
Dissension
Coldsnap
Time Spiral
Timeshifted
Planar Chaos
Future Sight
Lorwyn
Morningtide
Shadowmoor
Eventide
Shards of Alara
Conflux
Alara Reborn
Zendikar
Worldwake
Rise of the Eldrazi
Scars of Mirrodin
Mirrodin Besieged
New Phyrexia
Innistrad
Dark Ascension
Avacyn Restored
Return to Ravnica
Gatecrash
Dragon's Maze
Theros
Born of the Gods
Journey into Nyx
Khans of Tarkir
Fate Reforged
Dragons of Tarkir
Battle for Zendikar
Oath of the Gatewatch
Shadows over Innistrad
Eldritch Moon
Kaladesh
Aether Revolt
Amonkhet
Hour of Devastation
Ixalan
Rivals of Ixalan
Dominaria
Guilds of Ravnica
Ravnica Allegiance
War of the Spark

Duel Decks

Elves vs. Goblins
Jace vs. Chandra
Divine vs. Demonic
Garruk vs. Liliana
Phyrexia vs. The Coalition
Elspeth vs. Tezzeret
Knights vs. Dragons
Ajani vs. Nicol Bolas
Venser vs. Koth
Izzet vs. Golgari
Heroes vs. Monsters
Sorin vs. Tibalt
Jace vs. Vraska
Speed vs. Cunning
Elspeth vs. Kiora
Zendikar vs. Eldrazi
Blessed Vs. Cursed
Nissa Vs. Ob Nixilis
Mind Vs. Might
Merfolk vs. Goblins
Elves vs. Inventors

From the Vault

Dragons
Exiled
Relics
Legends
Realms
Twenty
Annihilation
Angels
Lore
Transform
Signature Spellbook Jace
Signature Spellbook Gideon

Special Sets

Chronicles
Vanguard
Unglued
Unhinged
Planechase 2009
Archenemy
Commander 2011
Planechase 2012
Commander's Arsenal
Modern Masters 2013
Commander 2013
Conspiracy
Commander 2014
Modern Masters 2015
Eternal Masters
Commander 2016
Planechase Anthology
Modern Masters 2017
Commander Anthology
Archenemy Nicol Bolas
Commander 2017
Iconic Masters
Unstable
Masters 25
Commander Anthology II
Battlebond
Commander 2018
Ultimate Masters
Modern Horizons
Commander 2019

Starter Sets

Portal
Portal Second Age
Portal Three Kingdoms
Starter 1999
Starter 2000

MAGIC: THE GATHERING

Magic price guide brought to you by www.pwccauctions.com

Core Sets

1993 Magic The Gathering Alpha

Item	Low	High
COMPLETE SET (295)	75000.00	100000.00
BOOSTER BOX (36 PACKS)	180000.00	300000.00
BOOSTER PACK (15 CARDS)	5000.00	8000.00
STARTER BOX (10 DECKS)	100000.00	120000.00
STARTER DECK (60 CARDS)	10000.00	12000.00

RELEASED ON AUGUST 5, 1993
LARGE ROUNDED CORNERS WITH BLACK BORDERS.
NO COPYRIGHT DATE AND NAME OF ILLUSTRATOR AT THE BOTTOM.

Card	Low	High
1 Air Elemental U :B:	20.00	30.00
2 Ancestral Recall R :B:	5000.00	7000.00
3 Animate Artifact U :B:	50.00	75.00
4 Animate Dead U :K:	250.00	400.00
5 Animate Wall R :W:	225.00	275.00
6 Ankh of Mishra R :A:	450.00	600.00
7 Armageddon R :W:	450.00	600.00
8 Aspect of Wolf R :G:	200.00	300.00
9 Bad Moon R :K:	200.00	300.00
10 Badlands R :L:	1000.00	1300.00
11 Balance R :W:	400.00	450.00
12 Basalt Monolith U :A:	300.00	500.00
13 Bayou R :L:	1500.00	2000.00
14 Benalish Hero C :W:	25.00	40.00
15 Berserk U :G:	250.00	400.00
16 Birds of Paradise R :G:	1000.00	1500.00
17 Black Knight U :K:	100.00	150.00
18 Black Lotus R :A:	20000.00	25000.00
19 Black Vise U :A:	150.00	250.00
20 Black Ward U :W:	25.00	40.00
21 Blaze of Glory R :W:	100.00	150.00
22 Blessing R :W:	100.00	150.00
23 Blue Elemental Blast C :B:	50.00	75.00
24 Blue Ward U :W:	12.00	20.00
25 Bog Wraith U :K:	10.00	15.00
26 Braingeyser R :B:	250.00	400.00
27 Burrowing U :R:	60.00	100.00
28 Camouflage U :G:	50.00	75.00
29 Castle U :W:	30.00	50.00
30 Celestial Prism U :A:	50.00	75.00
31 Channel U :G:	125.00	200.00
32 Chaos Orb R :A:	2500.00	3000.00
33 Chaoslace R :R:	75.00	125.00
34 Circle of Protection: Blue C :W:	20.00	30.00
35 Circle of Protection: Green C :W:	20.00	30.00
36 Circle of Protection: Red C :W:	20.00	30.00
37 Circle of Protection: White C :W:	15.00	25.00
38 Clockwork Beast R :A:	150.00	200.00
39 Clone U :B:	200.00	300.00
40 Cockatrice R :G:	150.00	250.00
41 Consecrate Land U :W:	75.00	125.00
42 Conservator U :A:	50.00	75.00
43 Contract from Below R :K:	600.00	1000.00
44 Control Magic U :B:	300.00	500.00
45 Conversion U :W:	40.00	60.00
46 Copper Tablet U :A:	150.00	250.00
47 Copy Artifact R :B:	1500.00	2000.00
48 Counterspell U :B:	600.00	900.00
49 Craw Wurm C :G:	50.00	75.00
50 Creature Bond C :B:	15.00	25.00
51 Crusade R :W:	300.00	450.00
52 Crystal Rod U :A:	25.00	40.00
53 Cursed Land U :K:	50.00	75.00
54 Cyclopean Tomb R :A:	500.00	800.00
55 Dark Ritual C :K:	200.00	300.00
56 Darkpact R :K:	300.00	500.00
57 Death Ward C :W:	12.00	20.00
58 Deathgrip U :K:	60.00	100.00
59 Deathlace R :K:	150.00	250.00
60 Demonic Attorney R :K:	150.00	200.00
61 Demonic Hordes R :K:	150.00	200.00
62 Demonic Tutor U :K:	200.00	250.00
63 Dingus Egg R :A:	125.00	175.00
64 Disenchant C :W:	15.00	20.00
65 Disintegrate C :R:	2.00	5.00
66 Disrupting Scepter R :A:	125.00	175.00
67 Dragon Whelp U :R:	25.00	35.00
68 Drain Life C :K:	2.00	5.00
69 Drain Power R :B:	100.00	150.00
70 Drudge Skeletons C :K:	2.00	5.00
71 Dwarven Demolition Team U :R:	12.00	16.00
72 Dwarven Warriors C :R:	2.00	5.00
73 Earth Elemental U :R:	5.00	8.00
74 Earthbind C :R:	6.00	8.00
75 Earthquake R :R:	150.00	200.00
76 Elvish Archers R :G:	250.00	300.00
77 Evil Presence U :K:	5.00	8.00
78 False Orders C :R:	2.00	5.00
79 Farmstead R :W:	150.00	200.00
80 Fastbond R :G:	350.00	400.00
81 Fear C :K:	2.00	5.00
82 Feedback U :B:	10.00	12.00
83 Fire Elemental U :R:	10.00	12.00
84 Fireball C :R:	25.00	30.00
85 Firebreathing C :R:	2.00	5.00
86 Flashfires U :R:	10.00	15.00
87 Flight C :B:	2.00	5.00
88 Fog C :G:	6.00	8.00
89 Force of Nature R :G:	325.00	375.00
90 Forcefield R :A:	800.00	1200.00
91 Forest v1 C :L:	2.00	5.00
92 Forest v2 C :L:	2.00	5.00
93 Fork R :R:	300.00	350.00
94 Frozen Shade C :K:	2.00	5.00
95 Fungusaur R :G:	175.00	225.00
96 Gaea's Liege R :G:	150.00	200.00
97 Gauntlet of Might R :A:	350.00	400.00
98 Giant Growth C :G:	10.00	15.00
99 Giant Spider C :G:	2.00	5.00
100 Glasses of Urza U :A:	8.00	11.00
101 Gloom U :K:	30.00	40.00
102 Goblin Balloon Brigade U :R:	8.00	11.00
103 Goblin King R :R:	225.00	275.00
104 Granite Gargoyle R :R:	150.00	200.00
105 Gray Ogre C :R:	2.00	5.00
106 Green Ward U :W:	5.00	8.00
107 Grizzly Bears C :G:	2.00	5.00
108 Guardian Angel C :W:	2.00	5.00
109 Healing Salve C :W:	2.00	5.00
110 Helm of Chatzuk R :A:	100.00	150.00
111 Hill Giant C :R:	2.00	5.00
112 Hive, The R :A:	175.00	225.00
113 Holy Armor C :W:	2.00	5.00
114 Holy Strength C :W:	2.00	5.00
115 Howl from Beyond C :K:	2.00	5.00
116 Howling Mine R :A:	400.00	500.00
117 Hurloon Minotaur C :R:	2.00	5.00
118 Hurricane U :G:	13.00	17.00
119 Hypnotic Specter U :K:	125.00	175.00
120 Ice Storm U :G:	30.00	40.00
121 Icy Manipulator U :A:	125.00	175.00
122 Illusionary Mask R :A:	200.00	250.00
123 Instill Energy U :G:	15.00	20.00
124 Invisibility C :B:	2.00	5.00
125 Iron Star U :A:	5.00	8.00
126 Ironclaw Orcs C :R:	2.00	5.00
127 Ironroot Treefolk C :G:	2.00	5.00
128 Island Sanctuary R :W:	75.00	125.00
129 Island v1 C :L:	2.00	5.00
130 Island v2 C :L:	2.00	5.00
131 Ivory Cup U :A:	5.00	8.00
132 Jade Monolith R :A:	100.00	150.00
133 Jade Statue U :A:	10.00	15.00
134 Jayemdae Tome R :A:	100.00	150.00
135 Juggernaut U :A:	45.00	60.00
136 Jump C :B:	2.00	5.00
137 Karma U :W:	15.00	20.00
138 Keldon Warlord U :R:	5.00	8.00
139 Kormus Bell R :A:	75.00	125.00
140 Kudzu R :G:	100.00	150.00
141 Lance U :W:	7.00	10.00
142 Ley Druid U :G:	5.00	8.00
143 Library of Leng U :A:	25.00	30.00
144 Lich R :K:	300.00	400.00
145 Lifeforce U :G:	7.00	10.00
146 Lifelace R :G:	75.00	100.00
147 Lifetap U :B:	5.00	8.00
148 Lightning Bolt C :R:	125.00	150.00
149 Living Artifact R :G:	125.00	175.00
150 Living Lands R :G:	100.00	150.00
151 Living Wall U :A:	8.00	11.00
152 Llanowar Elves C :G:	20.00	25.00
153 Lord of Atlantis R :B:	300.00	400.00
154 Lord of the Pit R :K:	300.00	350.00
155 Lure U :G:	5.00	8.00
156 Magical Hack R :B:	150.00	200.00
157 Mahamoti Djinn R :B:	275.00	325.00
158 Mana Flare R :R:	125.00	175.00
159 Mana Short R :B:	225.00	275.00
160 Mana Vault R :A:	600.00	800.00
161 Manabarbs R :R:	100.00	150.00
162 Meekstone R :A:	175.00	225.00
163 Merfolk of the Pearl Trident C :B:	2.00	5.00
164 Mesa Pegasus C :W:	2.00	5.00
165 Mind Twist R :K:	425.00	475.00
166 Mons's Goblin Raiders C :R:	2.00	5.00
167 Mountain v1 C :L:	2.00	5.00
168 Mountain v2 C :L:	2.00	5.00
169 Mox Emerald R :A:	2500.00	3500.00
170 Mox Jet R :A:	2500.00	3000.00
171 Mox Pearl R :A:	2500.00	3500.00
172 Mox Ruby R :A:	3000.00	3500.00
173 Mox Sapphire R :A:	3200.00	4000.00
174 Natural Selection R :G:	125.00	175.00
175 Nether Shadow R :K:	125.00	175.00
176 Nettling Imp U :K:	15.00	20.00
177 Nevinyrral's Disk R :A:	500.00	600.00
178 Nightmare R :K:	400.00	500.00
179 Northern Paladin R :W:	175.00	225.00
180 Obsianus Golem U :A:	5.00	8.00
181 Orcish Artillery U :R:	13.00	17.00
182 Orcish Oriflamme U :R:	35.00	40.00
183 Paralyze C :K:	2.00	5.00
184 Pearled Unicorn C :W:	2.00	5.00
185 Personal Incarnation R :W:	175.00	225.00
186 Pestilence C :K:	6.00	8.00
187 Phantasmal Forces U :B:	9.00	12.00
188 Phantasmal Terrain C :B:	2.00	5.00
189 Phantom Monster U :B:	7.00	10.00
190 Pirate Ship R :B:	150.00	200.00
191 Plague Rats C :K:	2.00	5.00
192 Plains v1 C :L:	2.00	5.00
193 Plains v2 C :L:	2.00	5.00
194 Plateau R :L:	800.00	1500.00
195 Power Leak C :B:	2.00	5.00
196 Power Sink C :B:	18.00	22.00
197 Power Surge R :R:	100.00	150.00
198 Prodigal Sorcerer C :B:	2.00	5.00
199 Psionic Blast U :B:	65.00	75.00
200 Psychic Venom C :B:	2.00	5.00
201 Purelace R :W:	75.00	125.00
202 Raging River R :R:	175.00	225.00
203 Raise Dead C :K:	2.00	5.00
204 Red Elemental Blast C :R:	35.00	45.00
205 Red Ward U :W:	5.00	8.00
206 Regeneration C :G:	2.00	5.00
207 Regrowth U :G:	45.00	55.00
208 Resurrection U :W:	10.00	15.00
209 Reverse Damage R :W:	75.00	125.00
210 Righteousness R :W:	100.00	150.00
211 Roc of Kher Ridges R :R:	125.00	175.00
212 Rock Hydra R :R:	150.00	200.00
213 Rod of Ruin U :A:	13.00	17.00
214 Royal Assassin R :K:	200.00	300.00
215 Sacrifice U :K:	5.00	8.00
216 Samite Healer C :W:	2.00	5.00
217 Savannah Lions R :W:	450.00	600.00
218 Savannah R :L:	800.00	1100.00
219 Scathe Zombies C :K:	2.00	5.00
220 Scavenging Ghoul U :K:	5.00	8.00
221 Scrubland R :L:	800.00	1300.00
222 Scryb Sprites C :G:	2.00	5.00
223 Sea Serpent C :B:	2.00	5.00
224 Sedge Troll R :R:	200.00	250.00
225 Sengir Vampire U :K:	75.00	100.00
226 Serra Angel U :W:	125.00	175.00
227 Shanodin Dryads C :G:	2.00	5.00
228 Shatter C :R:	6.00	8.00
229 Shivan Dragon R :R:	800.00	1200.00
230 Simulacrum U :K:	5.00	8.00
231 Sinkhole C :K:	50.00	65.00
232 Siren's Call U :B:	5.00	8.00
233 Sleight of Mind R :B:	150.00	200.00
234 Smoke R :R:	125.00	175.00
235 Sol Ring U :A:	175.00	225.00
236 Soul Net U :A:	7.00	10.00
237 Spell Blast C :B:	2.00	5.00
238 Stasis R :B:	200.00	250.00
239 Steal Artifact U :B:	7.00	10.00
240 Stone Giant U :R:	7.00	10.00
241 Stone Rain C :R:	8.00	10.00
242 Stream of Life C :G:	2.00	5.00
243 Sunglasses of Urza R :A:	125.00	175.00
244 Swamp v1 C :L:	4.00	6.00
245 Swamp v2 C :L:	4.00	6.00
246 Swords to Plowshares U :W:	125.00	175.00
247 Taiga R :L:	1000.00	1300.00
248 Terror C :K:	2.00	5.00
249 Thicket Basilisk U :G:	8.00	11.00
250 Thoughtlace R :B:	75.00	115.00
251 Throne of Bone U :A:	8.00	11.00
252 Timber Wolves R :G:	100.00	150.00
253 Time Vault R :A:	800.00	1100.00
254 Time Walk R :B:	3000.00	4000.00
255 Timetwister R :B:	1500.00	2000.00
256 Tranquility C :G:	2.00	5.00
257 Tropical Island R :L:	1600.00	2200.00
258 Tsunami U :G:	10.00	15.00
259 Tundra R :L:	2000.00	3000.00
260 Tunnel U :R:	5.00	8.00
261 Twiddle C :B:	6.00	8.00
262 Two-Headed Giant of Foriys R :R:	125.00	175.00
263 Underground Sea R :L:	4000.00	5500.00
264 Unholy Strength C :K:	7.00	9.00
265 Unsummon C :B:	5.00	7.00
266 Uthden Troll U :R:	5.00	8.00
267 Verduran Enchantress R :G:	150.00	200.00
268 Vesuvan Doppelganger R :B:	200.00	300.00
269 Veteran Bodyguard R :W:	100.00	150.00
270 Volcanic Eruption R :B:	100.00	150.00
271 Wall of Air U :B:	5.00	8.00
272 Wall of Bone U :K:	5.00	8.00
273 Wall of Brambles U :G:	5.00	8.00
274 Wall of Fire U :R:	7.00	10.00
275 Wall of Ice U :G:	5.00	8.00
276 Wall of Stone U :R:	5.00	8.00
277 Wall of Swords U :W:	5.00	8.00
278 Wall of Water U :B:	5.00	8.00
279 Wall of Wood C :G:	2.00	5.00
280 Wanderlust U :G:	5.00	8.00
281 War Mammoth C :G:	2.00	5.00
282 Warp Artifact R :K:	75.00	125.00
283 Water Elemental U :B:	5.00	8.00
284 Weakness C :K:	2.00	5.00
285 Web R :G:	175.00	225.00
286 Wheel of Fortune R :R:	800.00	1000.00
287 White Knight U :W:	20.00	30.00
288 White Ward U :W:	5.00	8.00
289 Wild Growth C :G:	5.00	7.00
290 Will-O'-The-Wisp R :K:	175.00	225.00
291 Winter Orb R :A:	225.00	300.00
292 Wooden Sphere U :A:	5.00	8.00
293 Word of Command R :K:	200.00	250.00
294 Wrath of God R :W:	350.00	450.00
295 Zombie Master R :K:	225.00	300.00

1993 Magic The Gathering Beta

Item	Low	High
COMPLETE SET (302)	45000.00	60000.00
BOOSTER BOX (36 PACKS)	100000.00	180000.00
BOOSTER PACK (15 CARDS)	3000.00	5000.00
STARTER BOX (10 DECKS)	50000.00	60000.00
STARTER DECK	5000.00	6000.00

RELEASED ON OCTOBER 15, 1993
BLACK BORDERS AND NO COPYRIGHT DATE
NAME OF ILLUSTRATOR AT THE BOTTOM

Card	Low	High
1 Air Elemental U :B:	5.00	8.00
2 Ancestral Recall R :B:	2500.00	3000.00
3 Animate Artifact U :B:	1.50	2.50
4 Animate Dead U :K:	40.00	50.00
5 Animate Wall R :W:	20.00	30.00
6 Ankh of Mishra R :A:	75.00	100.00
7 Armageddon R :W:	250.00	325.00
8 Aspect of Wolf R :G:	25.00	35.00
9 Bad Moon R :K:	80.00	120.00
10 Badlands R :L:	500.00	800.00
11 Balance R :W:	225.00	275.00
12 Basalt Monolith U :A:	30.00	40.00
13 Bayou R :L:	1000.00	1300.00
14 Benalish Hero C :W:	.75	2.00
15 Berserk U :G:	125.00	175.00
16 Birds of Paradise R :G:	550.00	650.00
17 Black Knight U :K:	25.00	35.00
18 Black Lotus R :A:	8000.00	11000.00
19 Black Vise U :A:	40.00	50.00
20 Black Ward U :W:	1.50	2.50
21 Blaze of Glory R :W:	45.00	55.00
22 Blessing R :W:	25.00	35.00
23 Blue Elemental Blast C :B:	6.00	8.00
24 Blue Ward U :W:	1.25	1.75
25 Bog Wraith U :K:	2.00	3.00
26 Braingeyser R :B:	175.00	225.00
27 Burrowing U :R:	1.25	1.75
28 Camouflage U :G:	20.00	25.00
29 Castle U :W:	2.50	3.50
30 Celestial Prism U :A:	1.75	2.25
31 Channel U :G:	15.00	20.00
32 Chaos Orb R :A:	500.00	800.00
33 Chaoslace R :R:	25.00	35.00
34 Circle of Protection Black C :W:	.75	2.00
35 Circle of Protection Blue C :W:	.75	2.00
36 Circle of Protection Green C :W:	.75	2.00
37 Circle of Protection Red C :W:	2.50	4.00
38 Circle of Protection White C :W:	.75	2.00
39 Clockwork Beast R :A:	20.00	30.00

40 Clone U :B:	10.00	15.00
41 Cockatrice R :G:	40.00	50.00
42 Consecrate Land U :W:	2.00	3.00
43 Conservator U :A:	1.50	2.00
44 Contract from Below R :K:	30.00	40.00
45 Control Magic U :B:	25.00	35.00
46 Conversion U :W:	1.50	2.00
47 Copper Tablet U :A:	4.00	6.00
48 Copy Artifact R :B:	225.00	275.00
49 Counterspell U :B:	100.00	150.00
50 Craw Wurm C :G:	.75	2.00
51 Creature Bond C :B:	.75	2.00
52 Crusade R :W:	175.00	225.00
53 Crystal Rod U :A:	1.50	2.00
54 Cursed Land U :K:	1.50	2.00
55 Cyclopean Tomb R :A:	65.00	80.00
56 Dark Ritual C :K:	15.00	25.00
57 Darkpact R :K:	20.00	30.00
58 Death Ward C :W:	.75	2.00
59 Deathgrip U :K:	2.00	3.00
60 Deathlace R :K:	30.00	40.00
61 Demonic Attorney R :K:	25.00	35.00
62 Demonic Hordes R :K:	65.00	80.00
63 Demonic Tutor U :K:	175.00	250.00
64 Dingus Egg R :A:	25.00	35.00
65 Disenchant C :W:	15.00	20.00
66 Disintegrate C :R:	.75	2.00
67 Disrupting Scepter R :A:	175.00	200.00
68 Dragon Whelp U :R:	10.00	12.00
69 Drain Life C :K:	2.50	4.00
70 Drain Power R :B:	40.00	50.00
71 Drudge Skeletons C :K:	.75	2.00
72 Dwarven Demolition Team U :R:	2.50	3.50
73 Dwarven Warriors C :R:	.75	2.00
74 Earth Elemental U :R:	1.50	2.00
75 Earthbind C :R:	.75	2.00
76 Earthquake R :R:	125.00	150.00
77 Elvish Archers R :G:	60.00	80.00
78 Evil Presence U :K:	2.50	3.50
79 False Orders C :R:	.75	2.00
80 Farmstead R :W:	25.00	35.00
81 Fastbond R :G:	225.00	275.00
82 Fear C :K:	.75	2.00
83 Feedback U :B:	1.50	2.00
84 Fire Elemental U :R:	3.00	3.50
85 Fireball C :R:	7.00	10.00
86 Firebreathing C :R:	.75	2.00
87 Flashfires U :R:	4.00	5.00
88 Flight C :B:	.75	2.00
89 Fog C :G:	2.50	4.00
90 Force of Nature R :G:	60.00	80.00
91 Forcefield R :A:	400.00	500.00
92 Forest (blue) C :L:	4.00	6.00
93 Forest (black) C :L:	4.00	6.00
94 Forest (with trail) v3 C :L:	4.00	6.00
95 Fork R :R:	100.00	150.00
96 Frozen Shade C :K:	.75	2.00
97 Fungusaur R :G:	20.00	30.00
98 Gaea's Liege R :G:	25.00	35.00
99 Gauntlet of Might R :A:	300.00	400.00
100 Giant Growth C :G:	3.00	5.00
101 Giant Spider C :G:	.75	2.00
102 Glasses of Urza U :A:	4.00	5.00
103 Gloom U :K:	6.00	8.00
104 Goblin Balloon Brigade U :R:	4.00	6.00
105 Goblin King R :R:	80.00	120.00
106 Granite Gargoyle R :R:	35.00	45.00
107 Gray Ogre C :R:	.75	2.00
108 Green Ward U :W:	1.75	2.25
109 Grizzly Bears C :G:	.75	2.00
110 Guardian Angel C :W:	.75	2.00
111 Healing Salve C :W:	.75	2.00
112 Helm of Chatzuk R :A:	25.00	35.00
113 Hill Giant C :R:	.75	2.00
114 Hive, The R :A:	45.00	60.00
115 Holy Armor C :W:	.75	2.00
116 Holy Strength C :W:	.75	2.00
117 Howl from Beyond C :K:	.75	2.00
118 Howling Mine R :A:	150.00	200.00
119 Hurloon Minotaur C :R:	.75	2.00
120 Hurricane U :G:	5.00	7.00
121 Hypnotic Specter U :K:	40.00	60.00
122 Ice Storm U :G:	25.00	35.00
123 Icy Manipulator U :A:	50.00	65.00
124 Illusionary Mask R :A:	175.00	225.00
125 Instill Energy U :G:	3.50	5.00
126 Invisibility C :B:	.75	2.00
127 Iron Star U :A:	1.50	2.00
128 Ironclaw Orcs C :R:	.75	2.00
129 Ironroot Treefolk C :G:	.75	2.00
130 Island Sanctuary R :W:	40.00	60.00
131 Island v1 C :L:	8.00	12.00
132 Island v2 C :L:	8.00	12.00
133 Island v3 C :L:	8.00	12.00
134 Ivory Cup U :A:	1.50	2.00
135 Jade Monolith R :A:	20.00	30.00
136 Jade Statue U :A:	7.00	10.00
137 Jayemdae Tome R :A:	300.00	400.00
138 Juggernaut U :A:	25.00	35.00
139 Jump C :B:	.75	2.00
140 Karma U :W:	4.00	6.00
141 Keldon Warlord U :R:	3.00	5.00
142 Kormus Bell R :A:	25.00	35.00
143 Kudzu R :G:	20.00	30.00
144 Lance U :W:	1.50	2.00
145 Ley Druid U :G:	1.75	2.25
146 Library of Leng U :A:	10.00	13.00
147 Lich R :K:	100.00	150.00
148 Lifeforce U :G:	2.00	3.00
149 Lifelace R :G:	20.00	30.00
150 Lifetap U :B:	1.50	2.00
151 Lightning Bolt C :R:	80.00	110.00
152 Living Artifact R :G:	30.00	40.00
153 Living Lands R :G:	25.00	35.00
154 Living Wall U :A:	4.00	5.00
155 Llanowar Elves C :G:	8.00	12.00
156 Lord of Atlantis R :B:	150.00	200.00
157 Lord of the Pit R :K:	80.00	120.00
158 Lure U :G:	2.00	3.00
159 Magical Hack R :B:	25.00	35.00
160 Mahamoti Djinn R :B:	65.00	80.00
161 Mana Flare R :R:	75.00	100.00
162 Mana Short R :B:	30.00	40.00
163 Mana Vault R :A:	500.00	600.00
164 Manabarbs R :R:	40.00	50.00
165 Meekstone R :A:	60.00	80.00
166 Merfolk of the Pearl Trident C :B:	.75	2.00
167 Mesa Pegasus C :W:	.75	2.00
168 Mind Twist R :K:	175.00	250.00
169 Mons's Goblin Raiders C :R:	.75	2.00
170 Mountain v1 C :L:	7.00	10.00
171 Mountain v2 C :L:	6.00	8.00
172 Mountain v3 C :L:	3.00	5.00
173 Mox Emerald R :A:	1000.00	1500.00
174 Mox Jet R :A:	1800.00	2500.00
175 Mox Pearl R :A:	1200.00	1800.00
176 Mox Ruby R :A:	1500.00	2000.00
177 Mox Sapphire R :A:	2000.00	2500.00
178 Natural Selection R :G:	55.00	65.00
179 Nether Shadow R :K:	65.00	80.00
180 Nettling Imp U :K:	4.00	6.00
181 Nevinyrral's Disk R :A:	150.00	175.00
182 Nightmare R :K:	80.00	110.00
183 Northern Paladin R :W:	30.00	40.00
184 Obsianus Golem U :A:	2.00	3.00
185 Orcish Artillery U :R:	2.50	3.50
186 Orcish Oriflamme U :R:	2.00	3.00
187 Paralyze C :K:	.75	2.00
188 Pearled Unicorn C :W:	.75	2.00
189 Personal Incarnation R :W:	20.00	30.00
190 Pestilence C :K:	5.00	7.00
191 Phantasmal Forces U :B:	1.75	2.25
192 Phantasmal Terrain C :B:	.75	2.00
193 Phantom Monster U :B:	2.75	3.25
194 Pirate Ship R :B:	30.00	40.00
195 Plague Rats C :K:	.75	2.00
196 Plains v1 C :L:	6.00	8.00
197 Plains v2 C :L:	4.00	6.00
198 Plains v3 C :L:	3.00	5.00
199 Plateau R :L:	450.00	600.00
200 Power Leak C :B:	.75	2.00
201 Power Sink C :B:	5.00	7.00
202 Power Surge R :R:	20.00	30.00
203 Prodigal Sorcerer C :B:	.75	2.00
204 Psionic Blast U :B:	40.00	50.00
205 Psychic Venom C :B:	.75	2.00
206 Purelace R :W:	20.00	30.00
207 Raging River R :R:	80.00	110.00
208 Raise Dead C :K:	.75	2.00
209 Red Elemental Blast C :R:	.75	2.00
210 Red Ward U :W:	1.50	2.00
211 Regeneration C :G:	.75	2.00
212 Regrowth U :G:	35.00	45.00
213 Resurrection U :W:	4.00	6.00
214 Reverse Damage R :W:	15.00	25.00
215 Righteousness R :W:	30.00	40.00
216 Roc of Kher Ridges R :R:	45.00	60.00
217 Rock Hydra R :R:	45.00	60.00
218 Rod of Ruin U :A:	2.00	2.50
219 Royal Assassin R :K:	150.00	200.00
220 Sacrifice U :K:	2.00	3.00
221 Samite Healer C :W:	.75	2.00
222 Savannah Lions R :W:	150.00	200.00
223 Savannah R :L:	900.00	1100.00
224 Scathe Zombies C :K:	.75	2.00
225 Scavenging Ghoul U :K:	2.00	2.50
226 Scrubland R :L:	800.00	950.00
227 Scryb Sprites C :G:	2.00	3.00
228 Sea Serpent C :B:	.75	2.00
229 Sedge Troll R :R:	150.00	200.00
230 Sengir Vampire U :K:	40.00	50.00
231 Serra Angel U :W:	80.00	120.00
232 Shanodin Dryads C :G:	.75	2.00
233 Shatter C :R:	2.00	3.00
234 Shivan Dragon R :R:	200.00	275.00
235 Simulacrum U :K:	2.50	3.50
236 Sinkhole C :K:	45.00	55.00
237 Siren's Call U :B:	2.00	2.50
238 Sleight of Mind R :B:	25.00	35.00
239 Smoke R :R:	30.00	40.00
240 Sol Ring U :A:	150.00	200.00
241 Soul Net U :A:	1.50	2.00
242 Spell Blast C :B:	.75	2.00
243 Stasis R :B:	125.00	150.00
244 Steal Artifact U :B:	3.50	4.50
245 Stone Giant U :R:	1.50	2.50
246 Stone Rain C :R:	8.00	12.00
247 Stream of Life C :G:	.75	2.00
248 Sunglasses of Urza R :A:	20.00	30.00
249 Swamp v1 C :L:	4.00	6.00
250 Swamp v2 C :L:	4.00	6.00
251 Swamp v3 C :L:	4.00	6.00
252 Swords to Plowshares U :W:	175.00	225.00
253 Taiga R :L:	500.00	700.00
254 Terror C :K:	3.00	5.00
255 Thicket Basilisk U :G:	3.00	3.50
256 Thoughtlace R :B:	20.00	30.00
257 Throne of Bone U :A:	1.50	2.00
258 Timber Wolves R :G:	25.00	35.00
259 Time Vault R :A:	700.00	1000.00
260 Time Walk R :B:	2500.00	3000.00
261 Timetwister R :B:	800.00	1200.00
262 Tranquility C :G:	.75	2.00
263 Tropical Island R :L:	1500.00	2000.00
264 Tsunami U :G:	8.00	12.00
265 Tundra R :L:	1200.00	1800.00
266 Tunnel U :R:	1.50	2.00
267 Twiddle C :B:	.75	2.00
268 Two-Headed Giant of Foriys R :R:	30.00	45.00
269 Underground Sea R :L:	2500.00	3000.00
270 Unholy Strength C :K:	2.50	4.00
271 Unsummon C :B:	2.00	3.00
272 Uthden Troll U :R:	3.00	5.00
273 Verduran Enchantress R :G:	65.00	80.00
274 Vesuvan Doppelganger R :B:	175.00	200.00
275 Veteran Bodyguard R :W:	20.00	30.00
276 Volcanic Eruption R :B:	30.00	40.00
277 Volcanic Island R :L:	2200.00	2700.00
278 Wall of Air U :B:	2.00	2.50
279 Wall of Bone U :K:	1.75	2.25
280 Wall of Brambles U :G:	1.50	2.00
281 Wall of Fire U :R:	1.50	2.00
282 Wall of Ice U :G:	1.75	2.25
283 Wall of Stone U :R:	2.00	2.50
284 Wall of Swords U :W:	2.00	3.00
285 Wall of Water U :B:	1.50	2.00
286 Wall of Wood C :G:	.75	2.00
287 Wanderlust U :G:	1.50	2.00
288 War Mammoth C :G:	.75	2.00
289 Warp Artifact R :K:	20.00	30.00
290 Water Elemental U :B:	1.75	2.25
291 Weakness C :K:	.75	2.00
292 Web R :G:	25.00	35.00
293 Wheel of Fortune R :R:	350.00	450.00
294 White Knight U :W:	15.00	25.00
295 White Ward U :W:	1.50	2.00
296 Wild Growth C :G:	3.00	5.00
297 Will-O'-The-Wisp R :K:	65.00	80.00
298 Winter Orb R :A:	200.00	250.00
299 Wooden Sphere U :A:	1.50	2.00
300 Word of Command R :K:	150.00	200.00
301 Wrath of God R :W:	375.00	425.00
302 Zombie Master R :K:	50.00	75.00

1993 Magic The Gathering Unlimited

COMPLETE SET (302)	20000.00	25000.00
BOOSTER BOX (36 PACKS)	25000.00	45000.00
BOOSTER PACK (15 CARDS)	700.00	1200.00
STARTER BOX (10 DECKS)	25000.00	30000.00
STARTER DECK (60 CARDS)	2500.00	3000.00

RELEASED ON DECEMBER 15, 1993
WHITE BORDERS AND NO COPYRIGHT DATE
NAME OF ILLUSTRATOR AT THE BOTTOM
EDGES ON INNER COLORED BORDERS HAVE A BEVELED LOOK TO THEM

1 Air Elemental U :B:	.40	.75
2 Ancestral Recall R :B:	1500.00	2000.00
3 Animate Artifact U :B:	.25	.40
4 Animate Dead U :K:	3.00	5.00
5 Animate Wall R :W:	1.50	2.50
6 Ankh of Mishra R :A:	15.00	20.00
7 Armageddon R :W:	40.00	60.00
8 Aspect of Wolf R :G:	3.00	5.00
9 Bad Moon R :K:	15.00	20.00
10 Badlands R :L:	150.00	200.00
11 Balance R :W:	20.00	35.00
12 Basalt Monolith U :A:	3.00	5.00
13 Bayou R :L:	250.00	300.00
14 Benalish Hero C :W:	.15	.25
15 Berserk U :G:	75.00	100.00
16 Birds of Paradise R :G:	75.00	100.00
17 Black Knight U :K:	3.00	5.00
18 Black Lotus R :A:	6000.00	8000.00
19 Black Vise U :A:	5.00	8.00
20 Black Ward U :W:	.30	.50
21 Blaze of Glory R :W:	8.00	12.00
22 Blessing R :W:	2.00	3.00
23 Blue Elemental Blast C :B:	.40	.60
24 Blue Ward U :W:	.30	.50
25 Bog Wraith U :K:	.30	.50
26 Braingeyser R :B:	50.00	75.00
27 Burrowing U :R:	.30	.50
28 Camouflage U :G:	.75	1.25
29 Castle U :W:	.30	.50
30 Celestial Prism U :A:	.30	.50
31 Channel U :G:	.75	1.25
32 Chaos Orb R :A:	200.00	250.00
33 Chaoslace R :R:	1.75	2.25
34 Circle of Protection: Black C :W:	.30	.50
35 Circle of Protection: Blue C :W:	.15	.25
36 Circle of Protection: Green C :W:	.30	.50
37 Circle of Protection: Red C :W:	.75	1.00
38 Circle of Protection: White C :W:	.30	.50
39 Clockwork Beast R :A:	2.00	2.50
40 Clone U :B:	1.50	2.00
41 Cockatrice R :G:	4.50	6.00
42 Consecrate Land U :W:	.60	1.00
43 Conservator U :A:	.30	.50
44 Contract from Below R :K:	2.75	3.25
45 Control Magic U :B:	1.50	2.00
46 Conversion U :W:	.30	.50
47 Copper Tablet U :A:	.75	1.25
48 Copy Artifact R :B:	40.00	60.00
49 Counterspell U :B:	15.00	20.00
50 Craw Wurm C :G:	.15	.25
51 Creature Bond C :B:	.15	.25
52 Crusade R :W:	20	35.00
53 Crystal Rod U :A:	.30	.50
54 Cursed Land U :K:	.30	.50
55 Cyclopean Tomb R :A:	20.00	30.00
56 Dark Ritual C :K:	2.75	3.25
57 Darkpact R :K:	1.75	2.25
58 Death Ward C :W:	.15	.25
59 Deathgrip U :K:	.30	.50
60 Deathlace R :K:	1.75	2.25
61 Demonic Attorney R :K:	1.75	2.25
62 Demonic Hordes R :K:	8.00	12.00
63 Demonic Tutor U :K:	25.00	40.00
64 Dingus Egg R :A:	2.75	3.25
65 Disenchant C :W:	.75	1.00
66 Disintegrate C :R:	.30	.50
67 Disrupting Scepter R :A:	20.00	30.00
68 Dragon Whelp U :R:	1.00	1.50
69 Drain Life C :K:	.30	.50
70 Drain Power R :B:	13.00	15.00
71 Drudge Skeletons C :K:	.15	.25
72 Dwarven Demolition Team U :R:	.30	.50
73 Dwarven Warriors C :R:	.15	.25
74 Earth Elemental U :R:	.25	.40
75 Earthbind C :R:	.15	.25
76 Earthquake R :R:	20.00	35.00
77 Elvish Archers R :G:	20.00	35.00
78 Evil Presence U :K:	.30	.50
79 False Orders C :R:	.20	.35
80 Farmstead R :W:	2.00	2.50
81 Fastbond R :G:	15.00	20.00
82 Fear C :K:	.15	.25
83 Feedback U :B:	.30	.50
84 Fire Elemental U :R:	.30	.50
85 Fireball C :R:	.50	.75
86 Firebreathing C :R:	.15	.25
87 Flashfires U :R:	.30	.50
88 Flight C :B:	.15	.25
89 Fog C :G:	.25	.40
90 Force of Nature R :G:	5.00	7.00
91 Forcefield R :A:	100.00	150.00
92 Forest v1 C :L:	.25	.40
93 Forest v2 C :L:	.50	.75
94 Forest v3 C :L:	.50	.75
95 Fork R :R:	40.00	60.00
96 Frozen Shade C :K:	.15	.25
97 Fungusaur R :G:	1.75	2.25
98 Gaea's Liege R :G:	3.50	5.00
99 Gauntlet of Might R :A:	200.00	250.00
100 Giant Growth C :G:	.30	.50
101 Giant Spider C :G:	.15	.25
102 Glasses of Urza U :A:	.30	.50
103 Gloom U :K:	.50	.75
104 Goblin Balloon Brigade U :R:	.50	.75
105 Goblin King R :R:	6.00	8.00
106 Granite Gargoyle R :R:	5.00	7.00
107 Gray Ogre C :R:	.15	.25
108 Green Ward U :W:	.25	.40
109 Grizzly Bears C :G:	.15	.25
110 Guardian Angel C :W:	.15	.25
111 Healing Salve C :W:	.15	.25
112 Helm of Chatzuk R :A:	1.50	2.00
113 Hill Giant C :R:	.15	.25
114 Hive, The R :A:	2.75	3.25
115 Holy Armor C :W:	.15	.25
116 Holy Strength C :W:	.15	.25
117 Howl from Beyond C :K:	.15	.25
118 Howling Mine R :A:	30.00	40.00
119 Hurloon Minotaur C :R:	.15	.25
120 Hurricane U :G:	.75	1.00
121 Hypnotic Specter U :K:	5.00	7.00
122 Ice Storm U :G:	8.00	12.00
123 Icy Manipulator U :A:	15.00	20.00
124 Illusionary Mask R :A:	50.00	75.00
125 Instill Energy U :G:	.75	1.00
126 Invisibility C :B:	.25	.40
127 Iron Star U :A:	.25	.40
128 Ironclaw Orcs C :R:	.15	.25
129 Ironroot Treefolk C :G:	.15	.25
130 Island Sanctuary R :W:	4.50	5.50
131 Island v1 C :L:	.75	1.00
132 Island v2 C :L:	.75	1.00
133 Island v3 C :L:	.75	1.00
134 Ivory Cup U :A:	.25	.40
135 Jade Monolith R :A:	1.75	2.25
136 Jade Statue U :A:	1.25	1.75
137 Jayemdae Tome R :A:	50.00	75.00
138 Juggernaut U :A:	2.00	2.50
139 Jump C :B:	.15	.25
140 Karma U :W:	.30	.50
141 Keldon Warlord U :R:	.50	.75
142 Kormus Bell R :A:	2.75	3.25
143 Kudzu R :G:	2.00	2.50
144 Lance U :W:	.30	.50
145 Ley Druid U :G:	.30	.50
146 Library of Leng U :A:	2.00	2.50
147 Lich R :K:	25.00	40.00
148 Lifeforce U :G:	.40	.60
149 Lifelace R :G:	1.50	2.00
150 Lifetap U :B:	.30	.50
151 Lightning Bolt C :R:	6.00	8.00
152 Living Artifact R :G:	1.75	2.25
153 Living Lands R :G:	1.75	2.25
154 Living Wall U :A:	.50	.75
155 Llanowar Elves C :G:	.75	1.25
156 Lord of Atlantis R :B:	10.00	12.00
157 Lord of the Pit R :K:	6.00	8.00
158 Lure U :G:	.30	.50
159 Magical Hack R :B:	2.50	3.00
160 Mahamoti Djinn R :B:	12.00	15.00
161 Mana Flare R :R:	6.00	8.00
162 Mana Short R :B:	5.00	7.00
163 Mana Vault R :A:	75.00	100.00
164 Manabarbs R :R:	2.00	2.50
165 Meekstone R :A:	15.00	25.00
166 Merfolk of the Pearl Trident C :B:	.15	.25
167 Mesa Pegasus C :W:	.15	.25
168 Mind Twist R :K:	30.00	50.00
169 Mons's Goblin Raiders C :R:	.15	.25
170 Mountain v1 C :L:	.50	.75
171 Mountain v2 C :L:	.50	.75
172 Mountain v3 C :L:	.50	.75
173 Mox Emerald R :A:	1000.00	1500.00
174 Mox Jet R :A:	1000.00	1500.00
175 Mox Pearl R :A:	1000.00	1500.00
176 Mox Ruby R :A:	1000.00	1500.00
177 Mox Sapphire R :A:	1500.00	2000.00
178 Natural Selection R :G:	20.00	30.00
179 Nether Shadow R :K:	7.00	10.00
180 Nettling Imp U :K:	.75	1.00
181 Nevinyrral's Disk R :A:	50.00	80.00
182 Nightmare R :K:	8.00	11.00
183 Northern Paladin R :W:	4.00	5.00
184 Obsianus Golem U :A:	.30	.50
185 Orcish Artillery U :R:	.30	.50
186 Orcish Oriflamme U :R:	.30	.50

1993 Magic The Gathering Unlimited

Card	Low	High
187 Paralyze C :K:	.15	.25
188 Pearled Unicorn C :W:	.15	.25
189 Personal Incarnation R :W:	2.00	3.00
190 Pestilence C :K:	.30	.50
191 Phantasmal Forces U :B:	.30	.50
192 Phantasmal Terrain C :B:	.15	.25
193 Phantom Monster U :B:	.30	.50
194 Pirate Ship R :B:	2.00	2.50
195 Plague Rats C :K:	.20	.35
196 Plains v1 C :L:	.50	.75
197 Plains v2 C :L:	.50	.75
198 Plains v3 C :L:	.50	.75
199 Plateau R :L:	150.00	200.00
200 Power Leak C :B:	.15	.25
201 Power Sink C :B:	.20	.35
202 Power Surge R :R:	2.00	2.50
203 Prodigal Sorcerer C :B:	.20	.35
204 Psionic Blast U :B:	12.00	15.00
205 Psychic Venom C :B:	.15	.25
206 Purelace R :W:	1.25	1.75
207 Raging River R :R:	20.00	35.00
208 Raise Dead C :K:	.15	.25
209 Red Elemental Blast C :R:	2.25	2.75
210 Red Ward U :W:	.25	.40
211 Regeneration C :G:	.15	.25
212 Regrowth U :G:	3.00	5.00
213 Resurrection U :W:	.75	1.00
214 Reverse Damage R :W:	3.50	4.25
215 Righteousness R :W:	2.75	3.25
216 Roc of Kher Ridges R :R:	3.25	3.75
217 Rock Hydra R :R:	6.00	8.00
218 Rod of Ruin U :A:	.25	.40
219 Royal Assassin R :K:	15.00	25.00
220 Sacrifice U :K:	.30	.50
221 Samite Healer C :W:	.15	.25
222 Savannah Lions R :W:	20.00	35.00
223 Savannah R :L:	150.00	200.00
224 Scathe Zombies C :K:	.15	.25
225 Scavenging Ghoul U :K:	.25	.40
226 Scrubland R :L:	175.00	225.00
227 Scryb Sprites C :G:	.15	.25
228 Sea Serpent C :B:	.15	.25
229 Sedge Troll R :R:	20.00	35.00
230 Sengir Vampire U :K:	2.50	3.50
231 Serra Angel U :W:	15.00	20.00
232 Shanodin Dryads C :G:	.15	.25
233 Shatter C :R:	.15	.25
234 Shivan Dragon R :R:	40.00	60.00
235 Simulacrum U :K:	.50	.75
236 Sinkhole C :K:	10.00	25.00
237 Siren's Call U :B:	.25	.40
238 Sleight of Mind R :B:	3.00	3.50
239 Smoke R :R:	2.75	3.25
240 Sol Ring U :A:	15.00	20.00
241 Soul Net U :A:	.30	.50
242 Spell Blast C :B:	.15	.25
243 Stasis R :B:	20.00	35.00
244 Steal Artifact U :B:	.50	.75
245 Stone Giant U :R:	.30	.50
246 Stone Rain C :R:	.30	.50
247 Stream of Life C :G:	.15	.25
248 Sunglasses of Urza R :A:	2.25	2.75
249 Swamp v1 C :L:	.50	.75
250 Swamp v2 C :L:	.50	.75
251 Swamp v3 C :L:	.50	.75
252 Swords to Plowshares U :W:	15.00	20.00
253 Taiga R :L:	150.00	200.00
254 Terror C :K:	.30	.50
255 Thicket Basilisk U :G:	.30	.50
256 Thoughtlace R :B:	1.75	2.25
257 Throne of Bone U :A:	.25	.40
258 Timber Wolves R :G:	2.00	2.50
259 Time Vault R :A:	350.00	500.00
260 Time Walk R :B:	1200.00	1600.00
261 Timetwister R :B:	600.00	1000.00
262 Tranquility C :G:	.15	.25
263 Tropical Island R :L:	300.00	350.00
264 Tsunami U :G:	.40	.60
265 Tundra R :L:	300.00	350.00
266 Tunnel U :R:	.25	.40
267 Twiddle C :B:	.15	.25
268 Two-Headed Giant of Foriys R :R:	12.00	15.00
269 Underground Sea R :L:	400.00	500.00
270 Unholy Strength C :K:	.15	.25
271 Unsummon C :B:	.15	.25
272 Uthden Troll U :R:	.30	.50
273 Verduran Enchantress R :G:	4.00	5.00
274 Vesuvan Doppelganger R :B:	15.00	20.00
275 Veteran Bodyguard R :W:	3.00	4.00
276 Volcanic Eruption R :B:	1.75	2.25
277 Volcanic Island R :L:	400.00	500.00
278 Wall of Air U :B:	.25	.40
279 Wall of Bone U :K:	.25	.40
280 Wall of Brambles U :G:	.25	.40
281 Wall of Fire U :R:	.25	.40
282 Wall of Ice U :G:	.30	.50
283 Wall of Stone U :R:	.30	.50
284 Wall of Swords U :W:	.30	.50
285 Wall of Water U :B:	.25	.40
286 Wall of Wood C :G:	.15	.25
287 Wanderlust U :G:	.25	.40
288 War Mammoth C :G:	.15	.25
289 Warp Artifact R :K:	2.50	3.00
290 Water Elemental U :B:	.25	.40
291 Weakness C :K:	.15	.25
292 Web R :G:	2.00	2.50
293 Wheel of Fortune R :R:	75.00	125.00
294 White Knight U :W:	3.00	4.00
295 White Ward U :W:	.25	.40
296 Wild Growth C :G:	.25	.40
297 Will-O'-The-Wisp R :K:	15.00	20.00
298 Winter Orb R :A:	50.00	80.00
299 Wooden Sphere U :A:	.30	.50
300 Word of Command R :K:	50.00	75.00
301 Wrath of God R :W:	50.00	75.00
302 Zombie Master R :K:	6.00	8.00

1994 Magic The Gathering Revised Edition

Card	Low	High
COMPLETE SET (306)	1200.00	600.00
BOOSTER BOX (36 PACKS)	1800.00	2500.00
BOOSTER PACK (15 CARDS)	50.00	70.00
STARTER BOX	400.00	500.00
STARTER DECK	40.00	55.00

RELEASED ON APRIL 15, 1994
ALSO KNOWN AS 3RD EDITION
WHITE BORDERS AND NO COPYRIGHT DATE
PALE COLORS AND NAME OF ILLUSTRATOR AT THE BOTTOM.
NO BEVELED EDGES INSIDE THE COLORED BORDERS.

Card	Low	High
1 Air Elemental U :B:	.15	.25
2 Aladdin's Lamp R :A:	.15	.25
3 Aladdin's Ring R :A:	.15	.25
4 Animate Artifact U :B:	.15	.25
5 Animate Dead U :K:	1.00	1.50
6 Animate Wall R :W:	.15	.25
7 Ankh of Mishra R :A:	.40	.60
8 Armageddon Clock R :A:	.15	.25
9 Armageddon R :W:	2.50	3.00
10 Aspect of Wolf R :G:	.25	.40
11 Atog C :R:	.15	.25
12 Bad Moon R :K:	1.00	1.50
13 Badlands R :L:	50.00	75.00
14 Balance R :W:	1.00	1.50
15 Basalt Monolith U :A:	.50	.75
16 Bayou R :L:	100.00	125.00
17 Benalish Hero C :W:	.15	.25
18 Birds of Paradise R :G:	6.00	8.00
19 Black Knight U :K:	.15	.25
20 Black Vise U :A:	1.00	1.25
21 Black Ward U :W:	.15	.25
22 Blessing R :W:	.25	.40
23 Blue Elemental Blast C :B:	.15	.25
24 Blue Ward U :W:	.15	.25
25 Bog Wraith U :K:	.15	.25
26 Bottle of Suleiman R :A:	.15	.25
27 Braingeyser R :B:	4.00	5.00
28 Brass Man U :A:	.15	.25
29 Burrowing U :R:	.15	.25
30 Castle U :W:	.15	.25
31 Celestial Prism U :A:	.15	.25
32 Channel U :G:	.15	.25
33 Chaoslace R :R:	.15	.25
34 Circle of Protection Black C :W:	.15	.25
35 Circle of Protection Blue C :W:	.15	.25
36 Circle of Protection Green C :W:	.15	.25
37 Circle of Protection Red C :W:	.15	.25
38 Circle of Protection White C :W:	.15	.25
39 Clockwork Beast R :A:	.15	.25
40 Clone U :B:	.15	.25
41 Cockatrice R :G:	.25	.40
42 Conservator U :A:	.15	.25
43 Contract from Below R :K:	.30	.50
44 Control Magic U :B:	.30	.50
45 Conversion U :W:	.15	.25
46 Copy Artifact R :B:	7.00	9.00
47 Counterspell U :B:	.75	1.00
48 Craw Wurm C :G:	.15	.25
49 Creature Bond C :B:	.15	.25
50 Crumble U :G:	.15	.25
51 Crusade R :W:	.50	.75
52 Crystal Rod U :A:	.15	.25
53 Cursed Land U :K:	.15	.25
54 Dancing Scimitar R :A:	.15	.25
55 Dark Ritual C :K:	.40	.60
56 Darkpact R :K:	.15	.25
57 Death Ward C :W:	.15	.25
58 Deathgrip U :K:	.15	.25
59 Deathlace R :K:	.15	.25
60 Demonic Attorney R :K:	.15	.25
61 Demonic Hordes R :K:	.50	.75
62 Demonic Tutor U :K:	18.00	22.00
63 Desert Twister U :G:	.15	.25
64 Dingus Egg R :A:	.15	.25
65 Disenchant C :W:	.15	.25
66 Disintegrate C :R:	.15	.25
67 Disrupting Scepter R :A:	.15	.25
68 Dragon Engine R :A:	.15	.25
69 Dragon Whelp U :R:	.15	.25
70 Drain Life C :K:	.15	.25
71 Drain Power R :B:	.50	.75
72 Drudge Skeletons C :K:	.15	.25
73 Dwarven Warriors C :R:	.15	.25
74 Dwarven Weaponsmith U :R:	.15	.25
75 Earth Elemental U :R:	.15	.25
76 Earthbind C :R:	.15	.25
77 Earthquake R :R:	.30	.50
78 Ebony Horse R :A:	.15	.25
79 El-Hajjaj R :K:	.15	.25
80 Elvish Archers R :G:	.25	.40
81 Energy Flux U :B:	.15	.25
82 Erg Raiders C :K:	.15	.25
83 Evil Presence U :K:	.15	.25
84 Eye for an Eye R :W:	.15	.25
85 Farmstead R :W:	.15	.25
86 Fastbond R :G:	3.50	4.25
87 Fear C :K:	.15	.25
88 Feedback U :B:	.15	.25
89 Fire Elemental U :R:	.15	.25
90 Fireball C :R:	.15	.25
91 Firebreathing C :R:	.15	.25
92 Flashfires U :R:	.15	.25
93 Flight C :B:	.15	.25
94 Flying Carpet R :A:	.15	.25
95 Fog C :G:	.15	.25
96 Force of Nature R :G:	.25	.40
97 Forest v1 C :L:	.15	.25
98 Forest v2 C :L:	.15	.25
99 Forest v3 C :L:	.15	.25
100 Fork R :R:	6.00	8.00
101 Frozen Shade C :K:	.15	.25
102 Fungusaur R :G:	.15	.25
103 Gaea's Liege R :G:	.25	.40
104 Giant Growth C :G:	.15	.25
105 Giant Spider C :G:	.15	.25
106 Glasses of Urza U :A:	.15	.25
107 Gloom U :K:	.15	.25
108 Goblin Balloon Brigade U :R:	.15	.25
109 Goblin King R :R:	1.00	1.50
110 Granite Gargoyle R :R:	.30	.50
111 Gray Ogre C :R:	.15	.25
112 Green Ward U :W:	.15	.25
113 Grizzly Bears C :G:	.15	.25
114 Guardian Angel C :W:	.15	.25
115 Healing Salve C :W:	.15	.25
116 Helm of Chatzuk R :A:	.15	.25
117 Hill Giant C :R:	.15	.25
118 Hive, The R :A:	.15	.25
119 Holy Armor C :W:	.15	.25
120 Holy Strength C :W:	.15	.25
121 Howl from Beyond C :K:	.15	.25
122 Howling Mine R :A:	2.50	3.00
123 Hurkyl's Recall R :B:	3.25	3.75
124 Hurloon Minotaur C :R:	.15	.25
125 Hurricane U :G:	.15	.25
126 Hypnotic Specter U :K:	.50	.75
127 Instill Energy U :G:	.15	.25
128 Iron Star U :A:	.15	.25
129 Ironroot Treefolk C :G:	.15	.25
130 Island Fish Jasconius R :B:	.15	.25
131 Island Sanctuary R :W:	.30	.50
132 Island v1 C :L:	.40	.60
133 Island v2 C :L:	.40	.60
134 Island v3 C :L:	.50	.75
135 Ivory Cup U :A:	.15	.25
136 Ivory Tower R :A:	1.00	1.50
137 Jade Monolith R :A:	.15	.25
138 Jandor's Ring R :A:	.15	.25
139 Jandor's Saddlebags R :A:	.15	.25
140 Jayemdae Tome R :A:	.15	.25
141 Juggernaut U :A:	.15	.25
142 Jump C :B:	.15	.25
143 Karma U :W:	.15	.25
144 Keldon Warlord U :R:	.15	.25
145 Kird Ape C :R:	.15	.25
146 Kormus Bell R :A:	.15	.25
147 Kudzu R :G:	.15	.25
148 Lance U :W:	.15	.25
149 Ley Druid U :G:	.15	.25
150 Library of Leng U :A:	.25	.40
151 Lifeforce U :G:	.15	.25
152 Lifelace R :G:	.15	.25
153 Lifetap U :B:	.15	.25
154 Lightning Bolt C :R:	2.00	2.50
155 Living Artifact R :G:	.15	.25
156 Living Lands R :G:	.15	.25
157 Living Wall U :A:	.15	.25
158 Llanowar Elves C :G:	.15	.25
159 Lord of Atlantis R :B:	4.00	5.00
160 Lord of the Pit R :K:	.30	.50
161 Lure U :G:	.15	.25
162 Magical Hack R :B:	.15	.25
163 Magnetic Mountain R :R:	.15	.25
164 Mahamoti Djinn R :B:	.30	.50
165 Mana Flare R :R:	1.50	2.00
166 Mana Short R :B:	.50	.75
167 Mana Vault R :A:	10.00	13.00
168 Manabarbs R :R:	.15	.25
169 Meekstone R :A:	1.25	1.75
170 Merfolk of the Pearl Trident C :B:	.15	.25
171 Mesa Pegasus C :W:	.15	.25
172 Mijae Djinn R :R:	.25	.40
173 Millstone R :A:	.30	.50
174 Mind Twist R :K:	2.50	3.00
175 Mishra's War Machine R :A:	.15	.25
176 Mons's Goblin Raiders C :R:	.15	.25
177 Mountain v1 C :L:	.15	.25
178 Mountain v2 C :L:	.15	.25
179 Mountain v3 C :L:	.15	.25
180 Nether Shadow R :K:	2.00	2.50
181 Nettling Imp U :K:	.15	.25
182 Nevinyrral's Disk R :A:	1.50	2.00
183 Nightmare R :K:	.50	.75
184 Northern Paladin R :W:	.25	.40
185 Obsianus Golem U :A:	.15	.25
186 Onulet R :A:	.15	.25
187 Orcish Artillery U :R:	.15	.25
188 Orcish Oriflamme U :R:	.15	.25
189 Ornithopter U :A:	.15	.25
190 Paralyze C :K:	.15	.25
191 Pearled Unicorn C :W:	.15	.25
192 Personal Incarnation R :W:	.15	.25
193 Pestilence C :K:	.15	.25
194 Phantasmal Forces U :B:	.15	.25
195 Phantasmal Terrain C :B:	.15	.25
196 Phantom Monster U :B:	.15	.25
197 Pirate Ship R :B:	.15	.25
198 Plague Rats C :K:	.15	.25
199 Plains v1 C :L:	.15	.25
200 Plains v2 C :L:	.15	.25
201 Plains v3 C :L:	.15	.25
202 Plateau R :L:	45.00	60.00
203 Power Leak C :B:	.15	.25
204 Power Sink C :B:	.15	.25
205 Power Surge R :R:	.15	.25
206 Primal Clay R :A:	.15	.25
207 Prodigal Sorcerer C :B:	.15	.25
208 Psychic Venom C :B:	.15	.25
209 Purelace R :W:	.15	.25
210 Rack, The U :A:	1.50	2.00
211 Raise Dead C :K:	.15	.25
212 Reconstruction C :B:	.15	.25
213 Red Elemental Blast C :R:	.15	.25
214 Red Ward U :W:	.15	.25
215 Regeneration C :G:	.15	.25
216 Regrowth U :G:	1.00	1.50
217 Resurrection U :W:	.15	.25
218 Reverse Damage R :W:	.15	.25
219 Reverse Polarity U :W:	.15	.25
220 Righteousness R :W:	.15	.25
221 Roc of Kher Ridges R :R:	.25	.40
222 Rock Hydra R :R:	.30	.50
223 Rocket Launcher R :A:	.15	.25
224 Rod of Ruin U :A:	.15	.25
225 Royal Assassin R :K:	1.00	1.50
226 Sacrifice U :K:	.15	.25
227 Samite Healer C :W:	.15	.25
228 Savannah Lions R :W:	.50	.75
229 Savannah R :L:	50.00	75.00
230 Scathe Zombies C :K:	.15	.25
231 Scavenging Ghoul U :K:	.15	.25
232 Scrubland R :L:	50.00	75.00
233 Scryb Sprites C :G:	.15	.25
234 Sea Serpent C :B:	.15	.25
235 Sedge Troll R :R:	.25	.40
236 Sengir Vampire U :K:	.15	.25
237 Serendib Efreet R :B:	.50	.75
238 Serra Angel U :W:	.25	.40
239 Shanodin Dryads C :G:	.15	.25
240 Shatter C :R:	.15	.25
241 Shatterstorm U :R:	1.00	1.25
242 Shivan Dragon R :R:	.50	.75
243 Simulacrum U :K:	.15	.25
244 Siren's Call U :B:	.15	.25
245 Sleight of Mind R :B:	.15	.25
246 Smoke R :R:	.40	.60
247 Sol Ring U :A:	3.75	4.25
248 Sorceress Queen R :K:	.30	.50
249 Soul Net U :A:	.15	.25
250 Spell Blast C :B:	.15	.25
251 Stasis R :B:	1.50	2.00
252 Steal Artifact U :B:	.15	.25
253 Stone Giant U :R:	.15	.25
254 Stone Rain C :R:	.15	.25
255 Stream of Life C :G:	.15	.25
256 Sunglasses of Urza R :A:	.15	.25
257 Swamp v1 C :L:	.30	.50
258 Swamp v2 C :L:	.30	.50
259 Swamp v3 C :L:	.30	.50
260 Swords to Plowshares U :W:	2.00	2.50
261 Taiga R :L:	50.00	75.00
262 Terror C :K:	.15	.25
263 Thicket Basilisk U :G:	.15	.25
264 Thoughtlace R :B:	.15	.25
265 Throne of Bone U :A:	.15	.25
266 Timber Wolves R :G:	.15	.25
267 Titania's Song R :G:	.15	.25
268 Tranquility C :G:	.15	.25
269 Tropical Island R :L:	150.00	175.00
270 Tsunami U :G:	.15	.25
271 Tundra R :L:	150.00	175.00
272 Tunnel U :R:	.15	.25
273 Underground Sea R :L:	225.00	275.00
274 Unholy Strength C :K:	.15	.25
275 Unstable Mutation C :B:	.15	.25
276 Unsummon C :B:	.15	.25
277 Uthden Troll U :R:	.15	.25
278 Verduran Enchantress R :G:	.15	.25
279 Vesuvan Doppelganger R :B:	3.00	3.50
280 Veteran Bodyguard R :W:	.25	.40
281 Volcanic Eruption R :B:	.15	.25
282 Volcanic Island R :L:	200.00	250.00
283 Wall of Air U :B:	.15	.25
284 Wall of Bone U :K:	.15	.25
285 Wall of Brambles U :G:	.15	.25
286 Wall of Fire U :R:	.15	.25
287 Wall of Ice U :G:	.15	.25
288 Wall of Stone U :R:	.15	.25
289 Wall of Swords U :W:	.15	.25
290 Wall of Water U :B:	.15	.25
291 Wall of Wood C :G:	.15	.25
292 Wanderlust U :G:	.15	.25
293 War Mammoth C :G:	.15	.25
294 Warp Artifact R :K:	.15	.25
295 Water Elemental U :B:	.15	.25
296 Weakness C :K:	.15	.25
297 Web R :G:	.15	.25
298 Wheel of Fortune R :R:	35.00	45.00
299 White Knight U :W:	.15	.25
300 White Ward U :W:	.15	.25
301 Wild Growth C :G:	.15	.25
302 Will-O'-The-Wisp R :K:	1.00	1.50
303 Winter Orb R :A:	4.00	5.00
304 Wooden Sphere U :A:	.15	.25
305 Wrath of God R :W:	4.00	5.00
306 Zombie Master R :K:	2.00	2.50

1995 Magic The Gathering 4th Edition

Card	Low	High
COMPLETE SET (378)	150.00	225.00
BOOSTER BOX (36 PACKS)	300.00	400.00
BOOSTER PACK (15 CARDS)	10.00	12.00
STARTER BOX (10 DECKS)	100.00	150.00
STARTER DECK	13.00	17.00

*ALT: 1.2X TO 3X BASIC CARDS
RELEASED ON APRIL 15, 1995
WHITE BORDERS AND A 1995 COPYRIGHT DATE

1 Abomination U :K:	.20	.35
2 Air Elemental U :B:	.20	.35
3 Alabaster Potion C :W:	.20	.35
4 Aladdin's Lamp R :A:	.20	.35
5 Aladdin's Ring R :A:	.20	.35
6 Ali Baba U :R:	.20	.35
7 Amrou Kithkin C :W:	.20	.35
8 Amulet of Kroog C :A:	.20	.35
9 Angry Mob U :W:	.20	.35
10 Animate Artifact U :B:	.20	.35
11 Animate Dead U :K:	1.00	1.50
12 Animate Wall R :W:	.20	.35
13 Ankh of Mishra R :A:	.20	.35
14 Apprentice Wizard C :B:	.20	.35
15 Armageddon R :W:	2.50	4.00
16 Armageddon Clock R :A:	.20	.35
17 Ashes to Ashes U :K:	.20	.35
18 Ashnod's Battle Gear U :A:	.20	.35
19 Aspect of Wolf R :G:	.20	.35
20 Backfire U :B:	.20	.35
21 Bad Moon R :K:	.75	1.25
22 Balance R :W:	.75	1.25
23 Ball Lightning R :R:	1.50	2.50
24 Battering Ram C :A:	.20	.35
25 Benalish Hero C :W:	.20	.35
26 Bird Maiden C :R:	.20	.35
27 Birds of Paradise R :G:	6.00	8.00
28 Black Knight U :K:	.20	.35
29 Black Mana Battery R :A:	.20	.35
30 Black Vise U :A:	.60	1.00
31 Black Ward U :W:	.20	.35
32 Blessing R :W:	.20	.35
33 Blight U :K:	.20	.35
34 Blood Lust C :R:	.20	.35
35 Blue Elemental Blast C :B:	.20	.35
36 Blue Mana Battery R :A:	.20	.35
37 Blue Ward U :W:	.20	.35
38 Bog Imp C :K:	.20	.35
39 Bog Wraith U :K:	.20	.35
40 Bottle of Suleiman R :A:	.20	.35
41 Brainwash C :W:	.20	.35
42 Brass Man U :A:	.20	.35
43 Bronze Tablet R :A:	.20	.35
44 Brothers of Fire C :R:	.20	.35
45 Brute, The C :R:	.20	.35
46 Burrowing U :R:	.20	.35
47 Carnivorous Plant C :G:	.20	.35
48 Carrion Ants U :K:	.20	.35
49 Castle U :W:	.20	.35
50 Cave People U :R:	.20	.35
51 Celestial Prism U :A:	.20	.35
52 Channel U :G:	.20	.35
53 Chaoslace R :R:	.20	.35
54 Circle of Protection Artifacts U :W:	.20	.35
55 Circle of Protection Black C :W:	.20	.35
56 Circle of Protection Blue C :W:	.20	.35
57 Circle of Protection Green C :W:	.20	.35
58 Circle of Protection Red C :W:	.20	.35
59 Circle of Protection: White C :W:	.20	.35
60 Clay Statue C :A:	.20	.35
61 Clockwork Avian R :A:	.20	.35
62 Clockwork Beast R :A:	.20	.35
63 Cockatrice R :G:	.20	.35
64 Colossus of Sardia R :A:	.20	.35
65 Conservator U :A:	.20	.35
66 Control Magic U :B:	.20	.35
67 Conversion U :W:	.20	.35
68 Coral Helm R :A:	.20	.35
69 Cosmic Horror R :K:	.20	.35
70 Counterspell U :B:	1.00	1.50
71 Craw Wurm C :G:	.20	.35
72 Creature Bond C :B:	.20	.35
73 Crimson Manticore R :R:	.20	.35
74 Crumble U :G:	.20	.35
75 Crusade R :W:	.60	1.00
76 Crystal Rod U :A:	.20	.35
77 Cursed Land U :K:	.20	.35
78 Cursed Rack U :A:	.20	.35
79 Cyclopean Mummy C :K:	.20	.35
80 Dancing Scimitar R :A:	.20	.35
81 Dark Ritual C :K:	.20	.35
82 Death Ward C :W:	.20	.35
83 Deathgrip U :K:	.20	.35
84 Deathlace R :K:	.20	.35
85 Desert Twister U :G:	.20	.35
86 Detonate U :R:	.20	.35
87 Diabolic Machine U :A:	.20	.35
88 Dingus Egg R :A:	.20	.35
89 Disenchant C :W:	.20	.35
90 Disintegrate C :R:	.20	.35
91 Disrupting Scepter R :A:	.20	.35
92 Divine Transformation U :W:	.20	.35
93 Dragon Engine R :A:	.20	.35
94 Dragon Whelp U :R:	.20	.35
95 Drain Life C :K:	.20	.35
96 Drain Power R :B:	.75	1.25
97 Drudge Skeletons C :K:	.20	.35
98 Durkwood Boars C :G:	.20	.35
99 Dwarven Warriors C :R:	.20	.35
100 Earth Elemental U :R:	.20	.35
101 Earthquake R :R:	.40	.60
102 Ebony Horse R :A:	.20	.35
103 Elder Land Wurm R :W:	.20	.35
104 El-Hajjaj R :K:	.20	.35
105 Elven Riders U :G:	.20	.35
106 Elvish Archers R :G:	.20	.35
107 Energy Flux U :B:	.20	.35
108 Energy Tap C :B:	.20	.35
109 Erg Raiders C :K:	.20	.35
110 Erosion C :B:	.20	.35
111 Eternal Warrior C :R:	.20	.35
112 Evil Presence U :K:	.20	.35
113 Eye for an Eye R :W:	.20	.35
114 Fear C :K:	.20	.35
115 Feedback U :B:	.20	.35
116 Fellwar Stone U :A:	.20	.35
117 Fire Elemental U :R:	.20	.35
118 Fireball C :R:	.20	.35
119 Firebreathing C :R:	.20	.35
120 Fissure C :R:	.20	.35
121 Flashfires U :R:	.20	.35
122 Flight C :B:	.20	.35
123 Flood C :B:	.20	.35
124 Flying Carpet R :A:	.20	.35
125 Fog C :G:	.20	.35
126 Force of Nature R :G:	.20	.35
127 Forest v1 C :L:	.20	.35
128 Forest v2 C :L:	.20	.35
129 Forest v3 C :L:	.20	.35
130 Fortified Area C :W:	.20	.35
131 Frozen Shade C :K:	.20	.35
132 Fungusaur R :G:	.20	.35
133 Gaea's Liege R :G:	.20	.35
134 Gaseous Form C :B:	.20	.35
135 Ghost Ship U :B:	.20	.35
136 Giant Growth C :G:	.20	.35
137 Giant Spider C :G:	.20	.35
138 Giant Strength C :R:	.20	.35
139 Giant Tortoise C :B:	.20	.35
140 Glasses of Urza U :A:	.20	.35
141 Gloom U :K:	.20	.35
142 Goblin Balloon Brigade U :R:	.20	.35
143 Goblin King R :R:	1.00	1.50
144 Goblin Rock Sled C :R:	.20	.35
145 Grapeshot Catapult C :A:	.20	.35
146 Gray Ogre C :R:	.20	.35
147 Greed R :K:	.40	.60
148 Green Mana Battery R :A:	.20	.35
149 Green Ward U :W:	.20	.35
150 Grizzly Bears C :G:	.20	.35
151 Healing Salve C :W:	.20	.35
152 Helm of Chatzuk R :A:	.20	.35
153 Hill Giant C :R:	.20	.35
154 Hive, The R :A:	.20	.35
155 Holy Armor C :W:	.20	.35
156 Holy Strength C :W:	.20	.35
157 Howl from Beyond C :K:	.20	.35
158 Howling Mine R :A:	2.50	4.00
159 Hurkyl's Recall R :B:	2.50	4.00
160 Hurloon Minotaur C :R:	.20	.35
161 Hurr Jackal R :R:	.20	.35
162 Hurricane U :G:	.20	.35
163 Hypnotic Specter U :K:	.75	1.25
164 Immolation C :R:	.20	.35
165 Inferno R :R:	.20	.35
166 Instill Energy U :G:	.20	.35
167 Iron Star U :A:	.20	.35
168 Ironclaw Orcs C :R:	.20	.35
169 Ironroot Treefolk C :G:	.20	.35
170 Island v1 C :L:	.20	.35
171 Island v2 C :L:	.20	.35
172 Island v3 C :L:	.20	.35
173 Island Fish Jasconius R :B:	.20	.35
174 Island Sanctuary R :W:	.20	.35
175 Ivory Cup U :A:	.20	.35
176 Ivory Tower R :A:	.50	.80
177 Jade Monolith R :A:	.20	.35
178 Jandor's Saddlebags R :A:	.20	.35
179 Jayemdae Tome R :A:	.20	.35
180 Jump C :B:	.20	.35
181 Junún Efreet U :K:	.20	.35
182 Karma U :W:	.20	.35
183 Keldon Warlord U :R:	.20	.35
184 Killer Bees U :G:	.20	.35
185 Kismet U :W:	.20	.35
186 Kormus Bell R :A:	.20	.35
187 Land Leeches C :G:	.20	.35
188 Land Tax R :W:	20.00	25.00
189 Leviathan R :B:	.20	.35
190 Ley Druid U :G:	.20	.35
191 Library of Leng U :A:	.40	.60
192 Lifeforce U :G:	.20	.35
193 Lifelace R :G:	.20	.35
194 Lifetap U :B:	.20	.35
195 Lightning Bolt C :R:	2.00	3.50
196 Living Artifact R :G:	.20	.35
197 Living Lands R :G:	.20	.35
198 Llanowar Elves C :G:	.20	.35
199 Lord of Atlantis R :B:	4.00	6.00
200 Lord of the Pit R :K:	.20	.35
201 Lost Soul C :K:	.20	.35
202 Lure U :G:	.20	.35
203 Magical Hack R :B:	.20	.35
204 Magnetic Mountain R :R:	.20	.35
205 Mahamoti Djinn R :B:	.20	.35
206 Mana Clash R :R:	.20	.35
207 Mana Flare R :R:	1.50	2.50
208 Mana Short R :B:	.20	.35
209 Mana Vault R :A:	17.00	20.00
210 Manabarbs R :R:	.20	.35
211 Marsh Gas C :K:	.20	.35
212 Marsh Viper C :G:	.20	.35
213 Meekstone R :A:	2.00	3.00
214 Merfolk of the Pearl Trident C :B:	.20	.35
215 Mesa Pegasus C :W:	.20	.35
216 Millstone R :A:	.20	.35
217 Mind Bomb U :B:	.20	.35
218 Mind Twist R :K:	2.00	3.00
219 Mishra's Factory U :L:	1.00	1.50
220 Mishra's War Machine R :A:	.20	.35
221 Mons's Goblin Raiders C :R:	.20	.35
222 Morale C :W:	.20	.35
223 Mountain v1 C :L:	.20	.35
224 Mountain v2 C :L:	.20	.35
225 Mountain v3 C :L:	.20	.35
226 Murk Dwellers C :K:	.20	.35
227 Nafs Asp C :G:	.20	.35
228 Nether Shadow R :K:	1.50	2.50
229 Nevinyrral's Disk R :A:	1.50	2.50
230 Nightmare R :K:	.20	.35
231 Northern Paladin R :W:	.20	.35
232 Oasis U :L:	.20	.35
233 Obsianus Golem U :A:	.20	.35
234 Onulet R :A:	.20	.35
235 Orcish Artillery U :R:	.20	.35
236 Orcish Oriflamme U :R:	.20	.35
237 Ornithopter U :A:	.20	.35
238 Osai Vultures U :W:	.20	.35
239 Paralyze C :K:	.20	.35
240 Pearled Unicorn C :W:	.20	.35
241 Personal Incarnation R :W:	.20	.35
242 Pestilence C :K:	.20	.35
243 Phantasmal Forces U :B:	.20	.35
244 Phantasmal Terrain C :B:	.20	.35
245 Phantom Monster U :B:	.20	.35
246 Piety C :W:	.20	.35
247 Pikemen C :W:	.20	.35
248 Pirate Ship R :B:	.20	.35
249 Pit Scorpion C :K:	.20	.35
250 Plague Rats C :K:	.20	.35
251 Plains (ver. 1) C :L:	.20	.35
252 Plains (ver. 2) C :L:	.20	.35
253 Plains (ver. 3) C :L:	.20	.35
254 Power Leak C :B:	.20	.35
255 Power Sink C :B:	.20	.35
256 Power Surge R :R:	.20	.35
257 Pradesh Gypsies C :G:	.20	.35
258 Primal Clay R :A:	.20	.35
259 Prodigal Sorcerer C :B:	.20	.35
260 Psionic Entity R :B:	.20	.35
261 Psychic Venom C :B:	.20	.35
262 Purelace R :W:	.20	.35
263 Pyrotechnics U :R:	.20	.35
264 Rack, The U :A:	1.50	2.50
265 Radjan Spirit U :G:	.20	.35
266 Rag Man R :K:	.20	.35
267 Raise Dead C :K:	.20	.35
268 Rebirth R :G:	.20	.35
269 Red Elemental Blast C :R:	.20	.35
270 Red Mana Battery R :A:	.20	.35
271 Red Ward U :W:	.20	.35
272 Regeneration C :G:	.20	.35
273 Relic Bind R :B:	.20	.35
274 Reverse Damage R :W:	.20	.35
275 Righteousness R :W:	.20	.35
276 Rod of Ruin U :A:	.20	.35
277 Royal Assassin R :K:	.75	1.25
278 Samite Healer C :W:	.20	.35
279 Sandstorm C :G:	.20	.35
280 Savannah Lions R :W:	.50	.80
281 Scathe Zombies C :K:	.20	.35
282 Scavenging Ghoul U :K:	.20	.35
283 Scryb Sprites C :G:	.20	.35
284 Sea Serpent C :B:	.20	.35
285 Seeker C :W:	.20	.35
286 Segovian Leviathan U :B:	.20	.35
287 Sengir Vampire U :K:	.20	.35
288 Serra Angel U :W:	.20	.35
289 Shanodin Dryads C :G:	.20	.35
290 Shapeshifter U :A:	.20	.35
291 Shatter C :R:	.20	.35
292 Shivan Dragon R :R:	.60	1.00
293 Simulacrum U :K:	.20	.35
294 Sindbad U :B:	.20	.35
295 Siren's Call U :B:	.20	.35
296 Sisters of the Flame C :R:	.20	.35
297 Sleight of Mind R :B:	.20	.35
298 Smoke R :R:	.60	1.00
299 Sorceress Queen R :K:	.20	.35
300 Soul Net U :A:	.20	.35
301 Spell Blast C :B:	.20	.35
302 Spirit Link U :W:	.20	.35
303 Spirit Shackle U :K:	.20	.35
304 Stasis R :B:	2.00	3.00
305 Steal Artifact U :B:	.20	.35
306 Stone Giant U :R:	.20	.35
307 Stone Rain C :R:	.20	.35
308 Stream of Life C :G:	.20	.35
309 Strip Mine U :L:	7.00	9.00
310 Sunglasses of Urza R :A:	.20	.35
311 Sunken City C :B:	.20	.35
312 Swamp v1 C :L:	.20	.35
313 Swamp v2 C :L:	.20	.35
314 Swamp v3 C :L:	.20	.35
315 Swords to Plowshares U :W:	1.50	2.50
316 Sylvan Library R :G:	15.00	17.00
317 Tawnos's Wand U :A:	.20	.35
318 Tawnos's Weaponry U :A:	.20	.35
319 Tempest Efreet R :R:	.20	.35
320 Terror C :K:	.20	.35
321 Tetravus R :A:	.20	.35
322 Thicket Basilisk U :G:	.20	.35
323 Thoughtlace R :B:	.20	.35
324 Throne of Bone U :A:	.20	.35
325 Timber Wolves R :G:	.20	.35
326 Time Elemental R :B:	.20	.35
327 Titania's Song R :G:	.20	.35
328 Tranquility C :G:	.20	.35
329 Triskelion R :A:	.50	.80
330 Tsunami U :G:	.20	.35
331 Tundra Wolves C :W:	.20	.35
332 Tunnel U :R:	.20	.35
333 Twiddle C :B:	.20	.35
334 Uncle Istvan U :K:	.20	.35
335 Unholy Strength C :K:	.20	.35
336 Unstable Mutation C :B:	.20	.35
337 Unsummon C :B:	.20	.35
338 Untamed Wilds U :G:	.20	.35
339 Urza's Avenger R :A:	.20	.35
340 Uthden Troll U :R:	.20	.35
341 Vampire Bats C :K:	.20	.35
342 Venom C :G:	.20	.35
343 Verduran Enchantress R :G:	.40	.60
344 Visions U :W:	.20	.35
345 Volcanic Eruption R :B:	.20	.35
346 Wall of Air U :B:	.20	.35
347 Wall of Bone U :K:	.20	.35
348 Wall of Brambles U :G:	.20	.35
349 Wall of Dust U :R:	.20	.35
350 Wall of Fire U :R:	.20	.35
351 Wall of Ice U :G:	.20	.35
352 Wall of Spears C :A:	.20	.35
353 Wall of Stone U :R:	.20	.35
354 Wall of Swords U :W:	.20	.35
355 Wall of Water U :B:	.20	.35
356 Wall of Wood C :G:	.20	.35
357 Wanderlust U :G:	.20	.35
358 War Mammoth C :G:	.20	.35
359 Warp Artifact R :K:	.20	.35
360 Water Elemental U :B:	.20	.35
361 Weakness C :K:	.20	.35
362 Web R :G:	.20	.35
363 Whirling Dervish U :G:	.20	.35
364 White Knight U :W:	.20	.35
365 White Mana Battery R :A:	.20	.35
366 White Ward U :W:	.20	.35
367 Wild Growth C :G:	.20	.35
368 Will-O'-The-Wisp R :K:	1.00	1.50
369 Winds of Change R :R:	5.00	7.00
370 Winter Blast U :G:	.20	.35
371 Winter Orb R :A:	3.00	4.00
372 Wooden Sphere U :A:	.20	.35
373 Word of Binding C :K:	.20	.35
374 Wrath of God R :W:	4.00	6.00
375 Xenic Poltergeist R :K:	.20	.35
376 Yotian Soldier C :A:	.20	.35
377 Zephyr Falcon C :B:	.20	.35
378 Zombie Master R :K:	2.50	3.00

1997 Magic The Gathering 5th Edition

COMPLETE SET (434)	200.00	275.00
BOOSTER BOX (36 PACKS)	200.00	300.00
BOOSTER PACK (15 CARDS)	8.00	10.00
STARTER BOX (10 DECKS)	120.00	150.00
STARTER DECK	12.00	15.00

RELEASED ON MARCH 24, 1997
WHITE BORDERS AND A 1997 COPYRIGHT DATE

1 Abbey Gargoyles U :W:	.15	.25
2 Abyssal Specter U :K:	.15	.25
3 Adarkar Wastes R :L:	4.00	6.00
4 Aether Storm U :B:	.15	.25
5 Air Elemental U :B:	.15	.25
6 Akron Legionnaire R :W:	.15	.25
7 Alabaster Potion C :W:	.15	.25
8 Aladdin's Ring R :A:	.15	.25
9 Ambush Party C :R:	.15	.25
10 Amulet of Kroog C :A:	.15	.25
11 Angry Mob U :W:	.15	.25
12 An-Havva Constable R :G:	.15	.25
13 Animate Dead U :K:	1.00	1.50
14 Animate Wall R :W:	.15	.25
15 Ankh of Mishra R :A:	.60	1.00
16 Anti-Magic Aura U :B:	.15	.25
17 Arenson's Aura U :W:	.15	.25
18 Armageddon R :W:	2.00	3.00
19 Armor of Faith C :W:	.15	.25
20 Ashes to Ashes U :K:	.15	.25
21 Ashnod's Altar U :A:	2.00	3.00
22 Ashnod's Transmogrant C :A:	.15	.25
23 Aspect of Wolf R :G:	.30	.50
24 Atog U :R:	.15	.25
25 Aurochs C :G:	.15	.25
26 Aysen Bureaucrats C :W:	.15	.25
27 Azure Drake U :B:	.15	.25
28 Bad Moon R :K:	1.00	1.50
29 Ball Lightning R :R:	1.50	2.50
30 Barbed Sextant C :A:	.15	.25
31 Barl's Cage R :A:	.15	.25
32 Battering Ram C :A:	.15	.25
33 Benalish Hero C :W:	.15	.25
34 Binding Grasp U :B:	.15	.25
35 Bird Maiden C :R:	.15	.25
36 Birds of Paradise R :G:	6.00	8.00
37 Black Knight U :K:	.15	.25
38 Blessed Wine C :W:	.15	.25
39 Blight U :K:	.15	.25
40 Blinking Spirit R :W:	.15	.25
41 Blood Lust C :R:	.15	.25
42 Bog Imp C :K:	.15	.25
43 Bog Rats C :K:	.15	.25
44 Bog Wraith U :K:	.15	.25
45 Boomerang C :B:	.15	.25
46 Bottle of Suleiman R :A:	.15	.25
47 Bottomless Vault R :L:	.60	1.00
48 Brainstorm C :B:	.60	1.00
49 Brainwash C :W:	.15	.25
50 Brassclaw Orcs C :R:	.15	.25
51 Breeding Pit U :K:	.15	.25
52 Broken Visage R :K:	.15	.25
53 Brothers of Fire C :R:	.15	.25
54 Brushland R :L:	8.00	10.00
55 Brute, The C :R:	.15	.25
56 Carapace C :G:	.15	.25
57 Caribou Range R :W:	.15	.25
58 Carrion Ants U :K:	.15	.25
59 Castle U :W:	.15	.25
60 Cat Warriors C :G:	.15	.25
61 Cave People U :R:	.15	.25
62 Chub Toad C :G:	.15	.25
63 City of Brass R :L:	3.00	5.00
64 Clay Statue C :A:	.15	.25
65 Cloak of Confusion C :K:	.15	.25
66 Clockwork Beast R :A:	.15	.25
67 Clockwork Steed U :A:	.15	.25
68 Cockatrice R :G:	.15	.25
69 Colossus of Sardia R :A:	.15	.25
70 Conquer U :R:	.15	.25

Card	Low	High
71 CoP: Artifacts U :W:	.15	.25
72 CoP: Black C :W:	.15	.25
73 CoP: Blue C :W:	.15	.25
74 CoP: Green C :W:	.15	.25
75 CoP: Red C :W:	.15	.25
76 CoP: White C :W:	.15	.25
77 Coral Helm R :A:	.15	.25
78 Counterspell C :B:	.60	1.00
79 Craw Giant U :G:	.15	.25
80 Craw Wurm C :G:	.15	.25
81 Crimson Manticore R :R:	.15	.25
82 Crown of the Ages R :A:	.15	.25
83 Crumble U :G:	.15	.25
84 Crusade R :W:	.60	1.00
85 Crystal Rod U :A:	.15	.25
86 Cursed Land U :K:	.15	.25
87 D'Avenant Archer C :W:	.15	.25
88 Dance of Many R :B:	.15	.25
89 Dancing Scimitar R :A:	.15	.25
90 Dandân C :B:	.15	.25
91 Dark Maze C :B:	.15	.25
92 Dark Ritual C :K:	.15	.25
93 Death Speakers C :W:	.15	.25
94 Death Ward C :W:	.15	.25
95 Deathgrip U :K:	.15	.25
96 Deflection R :B:	.15	.25
97 Derelor R :K:	.15	.25
98 Desert Twister U :G:	.15	.25
99 Detonate U :R:	.15	.25
100 Diabolic Machine U :A:	.15	.25
101 Dingus Egg R :A:	.15	.25
102 Disenchant C :W:	.15	.25
103 Disintegrate C :R:	.15	.25
104 Disrupting Scepter R :A:	.15	.25
105 Divine Offering C :W:	.15	.25
106 Divine Transformation U :W:	.15	.25
107 Dragon Engine R :A:	.15	.25
108 Drain Life C :K:	.15	.25
109 Drain Power R :B:	.60	1.00
110 Drudge Skeletons C :K:	.15	.25
111 Durkwood Boars C :G:	.15	.25
112 Dust to Dust U :W:	.15	.25
113 Dwarven Catapult U :R:	.15	.25
114 Dwarven Hold R :L:	.60	1.00
115 Dwarven Ruins U :L:	.15	.25
116 Dwarven Soldier C :R:	.15	.25
117 Dwarven Warriors C :R:	.15	.25
118 Earthquake R :R:	.40	.60
119 Ebon Stronghold U :L:	.15	.25
120 Elder Druid R :G:	.15	.25
121 Elkin Bottle R :A:	.15	.25
122 Elven Riders U :G:	.15	.25
123 Elvish Archers R :G:	.15	.25
124 Energy Flux U :B:	.15	.25
125 Enervate C :B:	.15	.25
126 Erg Raiders C :K:	.15	.25
127 Errantry C :R:	.15	.25
128 Eternal Warrior C :R:	.15	.25
129 Evil Eye of Orms-by-Gore U :K:	.15	.25
130 Evil Presence U :K:	.15	.25
131 Eye for an Eye R :W:	.15	.25
132 Fallen Angel U :K:	.15	.25
133 Fear C :K:	.15	.25
134 Feedback U :B:	.15	.25
135 Feldon's Cane U :A:	.30	.50
136 Fellwar Stone U :A:	.30	.50
137 Feroz's Ban R :A:	.15	.25
138 Fire Drake U :R:	.15	.25
139 Fireball C :R:	.15	.25
140 Firebreathing C :R:	.15	.25
141 Flame Spirit U :R:	.15	.25
142 Flare C :R:	.15	.25
143 Flashfires U :R:	.15	.25
144 Flight C :B:	.15	.25
145 Flood C :B:	.15	.25
146 Flying Carpet R :A:	.15	.25
147 Fog C :G:	.15	.25
148 Force of Nature R :G:	.15	.25
149 Force Spike C :B:	.15	.25
150 Forest L :L:	.15	.25
151 Forget R :B:	.15	.25
152 Fountain of Youth U :A:	.15	.25
153 Foxfire C :G:	.15	.25
154 Frozen Shade C :K:	.15	.25
155 Funeral March C :K:	.15	.25
156 Fungusaur R :G:	.15	.25
157 Fyndhorn Elder U :G:	.15	.25
158 Game of Chaos R :R:	.15	.25
159 Gaseous Form C :B:	.15	.25
160 Gauntlets of Chaos R :A:	.15	.25
161 Ghazbán Ogre C :G:	.15	.25
162 Giant Growth C :G:	.15	.25
163 Giant Spider C :G:	.15	.25
164 Giant Strength C :R:	.15	.25
165 Glacial Wall U :B:	.15	.25
166 Glasses of Urza U :A:	.15	.25
167 Gloom U :K:	.15	.25
168 Goblin Digging Team C :R:	.15	.25
169 Goblin Hero C :R:	.15	.25
170 Goblin King R :R:	1.25	2.00
171 Goblin War Drums C :R:	.15	.25
172 Goblin Warrens R :R:	.60	1.00
173 Grapeshot Catapult C :A:	.15	.25
174 Greater Realm of Preservation U :W:	.15	.25
175 Greater Werewolf U :K:	.15	.25
176 Grizzly Bears C :G:	.15	.25
177 Havenwood Battleground U :L:	.15	.25
178 Heal C :W:	.15	.25
179 Healing Salve C :W:	.15	.25
180 Hecatomb R :K:	.15	.25
181 Helm of Chatzuk R :A:	.15	.25
182 Hill Giant C :R:	.15	.25
183 Hipparion C :W:	.15	.25
184 Hive, The R :A:	.15	.25
185 Hollow Trees R :L:	.50	.80
186 Holy Strength C :W:	.15	.25
187 Homarid Warrior C :B:	.15	.25
188 Howl from Beyond C :K:	.15	.25
189 Howling Mine R :A:	2.00	3.00
190 Hungry Mist C :G:	.15	.25
191 Hurkyl's Recall R :B:	2.50	4.00
192 Hurloon Minotaur C :R:	.15	.25
193 Hurricane U :G:	.15	.25
194 Hydroblast U :B:	.40	.60
195 Icatian Phalanx U :W:	.15	.25
196 Icatian Scout C :W:	.15	.25
197 Icatian Store R :L:	.40	.60
198 Icatian Town R :W:	.15	.25
199 Ice Floe U :L:	.15	.25
200 Imposing Visage C :R:	.15	.25
201 Incinerate C :R:	.15	.25
202 Inferno R :R:	.15	.25
203 Infinite Hourglass R :A:	.15	.25
204 Initiates of the Ebon Hand C :K:	.15	.25
205 Instill Energy U :G:	.15	.25
206 Iron Star U :A:	.15	.25
207 Ironclaw Curse R :R:	.15	.25
208 Ironclaw Orcs C :R:	.15	.25
209 Ironroot Treefolk C :G:	.15	.25
210 Island L :L:	.15	.25
211 Island Sanctuary R :W:	.50	.80
212 Ivory Cup U :A:	.15	.25
213 Ivory Guardians U :W:	.15	.25
214 Jade Monolith R :A:	.15	.25
215 Jalum Tome R :A:	.15	.25
216 Jandor's Saddlebags R :A:	.15	.25
217 Jayemdae Tome R :A:	.15	.25
218 Jester's Cap R :A:	1.50	2.00
219 Johtull Wurm U :G:	.15	.25
220 Jokulhaups R :R:	2.00	3.00
221 Joven's Tools U :A:	.15	.25
222 Justice U :W:	.15	.25
223 Juxtapose R :B:	.15	.25
224 Karma U :W:	.15	.25
225 Karplusan Forest R :L:	3.00	5.00
226 Keldon Warlord U :R:	.15	.25
227 Killer Bees U :G:	.15	.25
228 Kismet U :W:	.15	.25
229 Kjeldoran Dead C :K:	.15	.25
230 Kjeldoran Royal Guard R :W:	.15	.25
231 Kjeldoran Skycaptain U :W:	.15	.25
232 Knight of Stromgald U :K:	.15	.25
233 Krovikan Fetish C :K:	.15	.25
234 Krovikan Sorcerer C :B:	.15	.25
235 Labyrinth Minotaur C :B:	.15	.25
236 Leshrac's Rite U :K:	.15	.25
237 Leviathan R :B:	.15	.25
238 Ley Druid C :G:	.15	.25
239 Lhurgoyf R :G:	.30	.50
240 Library of Leng U :A:	.50	.80
241 Lifeforce U :G:	.15	.25
242 Lifetap U :B:	.15	.25
243 Living Artifact R :G:	.15	.25
244 Living Lands R :G:	.15	.25
245 Llanowar Elves C :G:	.15	.25
246 Lord of Atlantis R :B:	3.00	5.00
247 Lord of the Pit R :K:	.15	.25
248 Lost Soul C :K:	.15	.25
249 Lure U :G:	.15	.25
250 Magical Hack R :B:	.15	.25
251 Magus of the Unseen R :B:	.30	.50
252 Mana Clash R :R:	.30	.50
253 Mana Flare R :R:	1.50	2.50
254 Mana Vault R :A:	14.00	16.00
255 Manabarbs R :R:	.15	.25
256 Marsh Viper C :G:	.15	.25
257 Meekstone R :A:	2.00	3.00
258 Memory Lapse C :B:	.15	.25
259 Merfolk of the Pearl Trident C :B:	.15	.25
260 Mesa Falcon C :W:	.15	.25
261 Mesa Pegasus C :W:	.15	.25
262 Millstone R :A:	.15	.25
263 Mind Bomb U :B:	.15	.25
264 Mind Ravel C :K:	.15	.25
265 Mind Warp U :K:	.15	.25
266 Mindstab Thrull C :K:	.15	.25
267 Mole Worms U :K:	.15	.25
268 Mons's Goblin Raiders C :R:	.15	.25
269 Mountain Goat C :R:	.15	.25
270 Mountain L :L:	.15	.25
271 Murk Dwellers C :K:	.15	.25
272 Nature's Lore C :G:	.60	1.00
273 Necrite C :K:	.15	.25
274 Necropotence R :K:	6.00	8.00
275 Nether Shadow R :K:	2.00	3.00
276 Nevinyrral's Disk R :A:	1.50	2.00
277 Nightmare R :K:	.40	.60
278 Obelisk of Undoing R :A:	.15	.25
279 Orcish Artillery U :R:	.15	.25
280 Orcish Captain U :R:	.15	.25
281 Orcish Conscripts C :R:	.15	.25
282 Orcish Farmer C :R:	.15	.25
283 Orcish Oriflamme U :R:	.15	.25
284 Orcish Squatters R :R:	.15	.25
285 Order of the Sacred Torch R :W:	.15	.25
286 Order of the White Shield U :W:	.15	.25
287 Orgg R :R:	.15	.25
288 Ornithopter U :A:	.15	.25
289 Panic C :R:	.15	.25
290 Paralyze C :K:	.15	.25
291 Pearled Unicorn C :W:	.15	.25
292 Pentagram of the Ages R :A:	.15	.25
293 Personal Incarnation R :W:	.15	.25
294 Pestilence C :K:	.15	.25
295 Phantasmal Forces U :B:	.15	.25
296 Phantasmal Terrain C :B:	.15	.25
297 Phantom Monster U :B:	.15	.25
298 Pikemen C :W:	.15	.25
299 Pirate Ship R :B:	.15	.25
300 Pit Scorpion C :K:	.15	.25
301 Plague Rats C :K:	.15	.25
302 Plains L :L:	.15	.25
303 Portent C :B:	.15	.25
304 Power Sink U :B:	.15	.25
305 Pox R :K:	.15	.25
306 Pradesh Gypsies C :G:	.15	.25
307 Primal Clay R :A:	.15	.25
308 Primal Order R :G:	.15	.25
309 Primordial Ooze U :R:	.15	.25
310 Prismatic Ward C :W:	.15	.25
311 Prodigal Sorcerer C :B:	.15	.25
312 Psychic Venom C :B:	.15	.25
313 Pyroblast U :R:	.15	.25
314 Pyrotechnics U :R:	.15	.25
315 Rabid Wombat U :G:	.15	.25
316 Radjan Spirit U :G:	.15	.25
317 Rag Man R :K:	.15	.25
318 Raise Dead C :K:	.15	.25
319 Ray of Command C :B:	.15	.25
320 Recall R :B:	.15	.25
321 Reef Pirates C :B:	.15	.25
322 Regeneration C :G:	.15	.25
323 Remove Soul C :B:	.15	.25
324 Repentant Blacksmith C :W:	.15	.25
325 Reverse Damage R :W:	.30	.50
326 Righteousness R :W:	.15	.25
327 Rod of Ruin U :A:	.15	.25
328 Ruins of Trokair U :L:	.15	.25
329 Sabretooth Tiger C :R:	.15	.25
330 Sacred Boon U :W:	.15	.25
331 Samite Healer C :W:	.15	.25
332 Sand Silos R :L:	.50	.80
333 Scaled Wurm C :G:	.15	.25
334 Scathe Zombies C :K:	.15	.25
335 Scavenger Folk C :G:	.15	.25
336 Scryb Sprites C :G:	.15	.25
337 Sea Serpent C :B:	.15	.25
338 Sea Spirit U :B:	.15	.25
339 Sea Sprite U :B:	.15	.25
340 Seasinger U :B:	.15	.25
341 Segovian Leviathan U :B:	.15	.25
342 Sengir Autocrat R :K:	.15	.25
343 Seraph R :W:	.60	1.00
344 Serpent Generator R :A:	.60	1.00
345 Serra Bestiary U :W:	.15	.25
346 Serra Paladin U :W:	.15	.25
347 Shanodin Dryads C :G:	.15	.25
348 Shapeshifter U :A:	.15	.25
349 Shatter C :R:	.15	.25
350 Shatterstorm U :R:	.60	1.00
351 Shield Bearer C :W:	.15	.25
352 Shield Wall C :W:	.15	.25
353 Shivan Dragon R :R:	.60	1.00
354 Shrink C :G:	.15	.25
355 Sibilant Spirit R :B:	.15	.25
356 Skull Catapult U :A:	.15	.25
357 Sleight of Mind R :B:	.15	.25
358 Smoke R :R:	.60	1.00
359 Sorceress Queen R :K:	.15	.25
360 Soul Barrier C :B:	.15	.25
361 Soul Net U :A:	.15	.25
362 Spell Blast C :B:	.15	.25
363 Spirit Link U :W:	.15	.25
364 Stampede R :G:	.15	.25
365 Stasis R :B:	2.00	3.00
366 Steal Artifact U :B:	.15	.25
367 Stone Giant U :R:	.15	.25
368 Stone Rain C :R:	.15	.25
369 Stone Spirit U :R:	.15	.25
370 Stream of Life C :G:	.15	.25
371 Stromgald Cabal R :K:	.15	.25
372 Sulfurous Springs R :L:	3.00	5.00
373 Svyelunite Temple U :L:	.15	.25
374 Swamp L :L:	.15	.25
375 Sylvan Library R :G:	14.00	16.00
376 Tarpan C :G:	.15	.25
377 Tawnos's Weaponry U :A:	.15	.25
378 Terror C :K:	.15	.25
379 Thicket Basilisk U :G:	.15	.25
380 Throne of Bone U :A:	.15	.25
381 Thrull Retainer U :K:	.15	.25
382 Time Bomb R :A:	.15	.25
383 Time Elemental R :B:	.15	.25
384 Titania's Song R :G:	.15	.25
385 Torture C :K:	.15	.25
386 Touch of Death C :K:	.15	.25
387 Tranquility C :G:	.15	.25
388 Truce R :W:	.15	.25
389 Tsunami U :G:	.15	.25
390 Tundra Wolves C :W:	.15	.25
391 Twiddle C :B:	.15	.25
392 Underground River R :L:	2.50	4.00
393 Unholy Strength C :K:	.15	.25
394 Unstable Mutation C :B:	.15	.25
395 Unsummon C :B:	.15	.25
396 Untamed Wilds U :G:	.15	.25
397 Updraft C :B:	.15	.25
398 Urza's Avenger R :A:	.15	.25
399 Urza's Bauble U :A:	1.50	2.00
400 Urza's Mine C :L:	2.00	3.00
401 Urza's Power Plant C :L:	2.00	3.00
402 Urza's Tower C :L:	2.00	3.00
403 Vampire Bats C :K:	.15	.25
404 Venom C :G:	.15	.25
405 Verduran Enchantress R :G:	.15	.25
406 Vodalian Soldiers C :B:	.15	.25
407 Wall of Air U :B:	.15	.25
408 Wall of Bone U :K:	.15	.25
409 Wall of Brambles U :G:	.15	.25
410 Wall of Fire U :R:	.15	.25
411 Wall of Spears C :A:	.15	.25
412 Wall of Stone U :R:	.15	.25
413 Wall of Swords U :W:	.15	.25
414 Wanderlust U :G:	.15	.25
415 War Mammoth C :G:	.15	.25
416 Warp Artifact R :K:	.15	.25
417 Weakness C :K:	.15	.25
418 Whirling Dervish U :G:	.15	.25
419 White Knight U :W:	.15	.25
420 Wild Growth C :G:	.15	.25
421 Wind Spirit U :B:	.15	.25
422 Winds of Change R :R:	4.00	6.00
423 Winter Blast U :G:	.15	.25
424 Winter Orb R :A:	3.00	5.00
425 Wolverine Pack U :G:	.15	.25
426 Wooden Sphere U :A:	.15	.25
427 Word of Blasting U :R:	.15	.25
428 Wrath of God R :W:	3.00	5.00
429 Wretched, The R :K:	.15	.25
430 Wyluli Wolf R :G:	.15	.25
431 Xenic Poltergeist R :K:	.15	.25
432 Zephyr Falcon C :B:	.15	.25
433 Zombie Master R :K:	2.50	3.50
434 Zur's Weirding R :B:	.15	.25

1999 Magic The Gathering Classic Sixth Edition

Card	Low	High
COMPLETE SET (350)	180.00	260.00
BOOSTER BOX (36 PACKS)	200.00	300.00
BOOSTER PACK (15 CARDS)	8.00	10.00
STARTER BOX (12 DECKS)	100.00	150.00
STARTER DECK	10.00	16.00
RELEASED ON APRIL 28, 1999		
1 Animate Wall R :W:	.20	.35
2 Archangel R :W:	.60	1.00
3 Ardent Militia U :W:	.20	.35
4 Armageddon R :W:	2.50	4.00
5 Armored Pegasus C :W:	.20	.35
6 Castle U :W:	.20	.35
7 Celestial Dawn R :W:	.60	1.00
8 Circle of Protection Black C :W:	.20	.35
9 Circle of Protection Blue C :W:	.20	.35
10 Circle of Protection Green C :W:	.20	.35
11 Circle of Protection Red C :W:	.20	.35
12 Circle of Protection White C :W:	.20	.35
13 Crusade R :W:	.60	1.00
14 Daring Apprentice R :B:	.20	.35
15 Dancing Scimitar R :A:	.20	.35
16 Disenchant C :W:	.20	.35
17 Divine Transformation U :W:	.20	.35
18 Ekundu Griffin C :W:	.20	.35
19 Enlightened Tutor U :W:	10.00	13.00
20 Ethereal Champion R :W:	.20	.35
21 Exile R :W:	.75	1.25
22 Healing Salve C :W:	.20	.35
23 Heavy Ballista U :W:	.20	.35
24 Hero's Resolve C :W:	.20	.35
25 Icatian Town R :W:	.20	.35
26 Infantry Veteran C :W:	.20	.35
27 Kismet U :W:	.20	.35
28 Kjeldoran Royal Guard R :W:	.20	.35
29 Light of Day U :W:	.20	.35
30 Longbow Archer U :W:	.20	.35
31 Mesa Falcon C :W:	.20	.35
32 Order of the Sacred Torch R :W:	.20	.35
33 Pacifism C :W:	.20	.35
34 Pearl Dragon R :W:	.20	.35
35 Regal Unicorn C :W:	.20	.35
36 Remedy C :W:	.20	.35
37 Reprisal U :W:	.20	.35
38 Resistance Fighter C :W:	.20	.35
39 Reverse Damage R :W:	.20	.35
40 Samite Healer C :W:	.20	.35
41 Serenity R :W:	.20	.35
42 Serra's Blessing U :W:	.20	.35
43 Spirit Link U :W:	.20	.35
44 Standing Troops C :W:	.20	.35
45 Staunch Defenders U :W:	.20	.35
46 Sunweb R :W:	.20	.35
47 Tariff R :W:	.20	.35
48 Tundra Wolves C :W:	.20	.35
49 Unyaro Griffin U :W:	.20	.35
50 Venerable Monk C :W:	.20	.35
51 Wall of Swords U :W:	.20	.35
52 Warmth U :W:	.20	.35
53 Warrior's Honor C :W:	.20	.35
54 Wrath of God R :W:	.20	.35
55 Abduction U :B:	.20	.35
56 Air Elemental U :B:	.20	.35
57 Ancestral Memories R :B:	.20	.35
58 Boomerang C :B:	.20	.35
59 Browse U :B:	.20	.35
60 Chill U :B:	.20	.35
61 Counterspell C :B:	.60	1.00
62 D'Avenant Archer C :W:	.20	.35
63 Deflection R :B:	.20	.35
64 Desertion R :B:	2.00	3.00
65 Diminishing Returns R :B:	.20	.35
66 Dream Cache C :B:	.20	.35
67 Flash R :B:	2.50	4.00
68 Flight C :B:	.20	.35
69 Fog Elemental C :B:	.20	.35
70 Forget R :B:	.20	.35
71 Gaseous Form C :B:	.20	.35
72 Glacial Wall U :B:	.20	.35
73 Harmattan Efreet U :B:	.20	.35
74 Horned Turtle C :B:	.20	.35
75 Insight U :B:	.20	.35
76 Inspiration C :B:	.20	.35
77 Juxtapose R :B:	.20	.35
78 Library of Lat-Nam R :B:	.20	.35
79 Lord of Atlantis R :B:	.20	.35
80 Mana Short R :B:	.20	.35
81 Memory Lapse C :B:	.20	.35
82 Merfolk of the Pearl Trident C :B:	.20	.35
83 Mystical Tutor U :B:	.20	.35
84 Phantasmal Terrain C :B:	.20	.35
85 Phantom Warrior U :B:	.20	.35
86 Polymorph R :B:	.20	.35
87 Power Sink U :B:	.20	.35

Card	Low	High
88 Prodigal Sorcerer C :B:	.20	.35
89 Prosperity U :B:	.20	.35
90 Psychic Transfer R :B:	.20	.35
91 Psychic Venom C :B:	.20	.35
92 Recall R :B:	.20	.35
93 Relearn U :B:	.20	.35
94 Remove Soul C :B:	.20	.35
95 Sage Owl C :B:	.20	.35
96 Sea Monster C :B:	.20	.35
97 Segovian Leviathan U :B:	.20	.35
98 Sibilant Spirit R :B:	.20	.35
99 Soldevi Sage U :B:	.20	.35
100 Spell Blast C :B:	.20	.35
101 Storm Crow C :B:	.20	.35
102 Tidal Surge C :B:	.20	.35
103 Unsummon C :B:	.20	.35
104 Vodalian Soldiers C :B:	.20	.35
105 Wall of Air U :B:	.20	.35
106 Wind Drake C :B:	.20	.35
107 Wind Spirit U :B:	.20	.35
108 Zur's Weirding R :B:	.20	.35
109 Abyssal Hunter R :K:	.20	.35
110 Abyssal Specter U :K:	.20	.35
111 Agonizing Memories U :K:	.20	.35
112 Ashen Powder R :K:	.60	1.00
113 Blight U :K:	.20	.35
114 Blighted Shaman U :K:	.20	.35
115 Blood Pet C :K:	.20	.35
116 Bog Imp C :K:	.20	.35
117 Bog Rats C :K:	.20	.35
118 Bog Wraith U :K:	.20	.35
119 Coercion C :K:	.20	.35
120 Derelor R :K:	.20	.35
121 Doomsday R :K:	3.00	4.00
122 Dread of Night U :K:	.60	.80
123 Drudge Skeletons C :K:	.20	.35
124 Dry Spell C :K:	.20	.35
125 Enfeeblement C :K:	.20	.35
126 Evil Eye of Orms-by-Gore U :K:	.20	.35
127 Fallen Angel R :K:	.20	.35
128 Fatal Blow C :K:	.20	.35
129 Fear C :K:	.20	.35
130 Feast of the Unicorn C :K:	.20	.35
131 Feral Shadow C :K:	.20	.35
132 Forbidden Crypt R :K:	.20	.35
133 Gravebane Zombie U :K:	.20	.35
134 Gravedigger C :K:	.20	.35
135 Greed R :K:	.20	.35
136 Hecatomb R :K:	.20	.35
137 Hidden Horror U :K:	.20	.35
138 Howl from Beyond C :K:	.20	.35
139 Infernal Contract R :K:	.20	.35
140 Kjeldoran Dead C :K:	.20	.35
141 Leshrac's Rite U :K:	.20	.35
142 Lost Soul C :K:	.20	.35
143 Mind Warp U :K:	.20	.35
144 Mischievous Poltergeist U :K:	.20	.35
145 Necrosavant R :K:	.20	.35
146 Nightmare R :K:	.20	.35
147 Painful Memories C :K:	.20	.35
148 Perish U :K:	.20	.35
149 Pestilence U :K:	.20	.35
150 Python C :K:	.20	.35
151 Rag Man R :K:	.20	.35
152 Raise Dead C :K:	.20	.35
153 Razortooth Rats C :K:	.20	.35
154 Scathe Zombies C :K:	.20	.35
155 Sengir Autocrat R :K:	.20	.35
156 Strands of Night U :K:	.20	.35
157 Stromgald Cabal R :K:	.20	.35
158 Stupor U :K:	.20	.35
159 Syphon Soul C :K:	.20	.35
160 Terror C :K:	.20	.35
161 Vampiric Tutor R :K:	.20	.35
162 Zombie Master R :K:	.20	.35
163 Aether Flash U :R:	.20	.35
164 Anaba Bodyguard C :R:	.20	.35
165 Anaba Shaman C :R:	.20	.35
166 Balduvian Barbarians C :R:	.20	.35
167 Balduvian Horde R :R:	.20	.35
168 Blaze U :R:	.20	.35
169 Boil U :R:	.40	.60
170 Burrowing U :R:	.20	.35
171 Conquer U :R:	.20	.35
172 Crimson Hellkite R :R:	.40	.60
173 Earthquake R :R:	.40	.60
174 Fervor R :R:	.60	1.00
175 Final Fortune R :R:	.60	1.00
176 Fire Elemental U :R:	.20	.35
177 Firebreathing C :R:	.20	.35
178 Fit of Rage C :R:	.20	.35
179 Flame Spirit C :R:	.20	.35
180 Flashfires U :R:	.20	.35
181 Giant Strength C :R:	.20	.35
182 Goblin Digging Team C :R:	.20	.35
183 Goblin Elite Infantry C :R:	.20	.35
184 Goblin Hero C :R:	.20	.35
185 Goblin King R :R:	.20	.35
186 Goblin Recruiter U :R:	.20	.35
187 Goblin Warrens R :R:	.20	.35
188 Hammer of Bogardan R :R:	.20	.35
189 Hulking Cyclops U :R:	.20	.35
190 Illicit Auction R :R:	.20	.35
191 Inferno R :R:	.20	.35
192 Jokulhaups R :R:	.20	.35
193 Lightning Blast C :R:	.20	.35
194 Manabarbs R :R:	.20	.35
195 Mountain L :L:	.20	.35
196 Orcish Artillery U :R:	.20	.35
197 Orcish Oriflamme U :R:	.20	.35
198 Pillage U :R:	.20	.35
199 Pyrotechnics C :R:	.20	.35
200 Raging Goblin C :R:	.20	.35
201 Reckless Embermage R :R:	.20	.35
202 Relentless Assault R :R:	.20	.35
203 Sabretooth Tiger C :R:	.20	.35
204 Shatter C :R:	.20	.35
205 Shatterstorm R :R:	.20	.35
206 Shock C :R:	.20	.35
207 Spitting Drake U :R:	.20	.35
208 Spitting Earth C :R:	.20	.35
209 Stone Rain C :R:	.20	.35
210 Talruum Minotaur C :R:	.20	.35
211 Tremor C :R:	.20	.35
212 Vertigo U :R:	.20	.35
213 Viashino Warrior C :R:	.20	.35
214 Volcanic Dragon R :R:	.20	.35
215 Volcanic Geyser U :R:	.20	.35
216 Wall of Fire U :R:	.20	.35
217 Birds of Paradise R :G:	6.00	8.00
218 Call of the Wild R :G:	.20	.35
219 Cat Warriors C :G:	.20	.35
220 Creeping Mold U :G:	.20	.35
221 Dense Foliage R :G:	.50	.80
222 Early Harvest R :G:	.40	.60
223 Elder Druid R :G:	.20	.35
224 Elven Cache C :G:	.20	.35
225 Elven Riders U :G:	.20	.35
226 Elvish Archers R :G:	.20	.35
227 Fallow Earth U :G:	.20	.35
228 Familiar Ground U :G:	.20	.35
229 Femeref Archers U :G:	.20	.35
230 Fog C :G:	.20	.35
231 Fyndhorn Brownie C :G:	.20	.35
232 Fyndhorn Elder U :G:	.20	.35
233 Giant Growth C :G:	.20	.35
234 Giant Spider C :G:	.20	.35
235 Gorilla Chieftain C :G:	.20	.35
236 Grizzly Bears C :G:	.20	.35
237 Hurricane R :G:	.20	.35
238 Living Lands R :G:	.20	.35
239 Llanowar Elves C :G:	.20	.35
240 Lure U :G:	.20	.35
241 Maro R :G:	.20	.35
242 Nature's Resurgence R :G:	.20	.35
243 Panther Warriors C :G:	.20	.35
244 Pradesh Gypsies C :G:	.20	.35
245 Radjan Spirit U :G:	.20	.35
246 Rampant Growth C :G:	.20	.35
247 Redwood Treefolk C :G:	.20	.35
248 Regeneration C :G:	.20	.35
249 River Boa U :G:	.20	.35
250 Rowen R :G:	.20	.35
251 Scaled Wurm C :G:	.20	.35
252 Shanodin Dryads C :G:	.20	.35
253 Stalking Tiger C :G:	.20	.35
254 Stream of Life C :G:	.20	.35
255 Summer Bloom U :G:	.20	.35
256 Thicket Basilisk U :G:	.20	.35
257 Trained Armodon C :G:	.20	.35
258 Tranquil Grove R :G:	.20	.35
259 Tranquility C :G:	.20	.35
260 Uktabi Orangutan U :G:	.20	.35
261 Uktabi Wildcats R :G:	.20	.35
262 Unseen Walker U :G:	.20	.35
263 Untamed Wilds U :G:	.20	.35
264 Verduran Enchantress R :G:	.20	.35
265 Vitalize C :G:	.20	.35
266 Waiting in the Weeds R :G:	.20	.35
267 Warthog U :G:	.20	.35
268 Wild Growth C :G:	.20	.35
269 Worldly Tutor U :G:	.20	.35
270 Wyluli Wolf R :G:	.20	.35
271 Aladdin's Ring R :A:	.20	.35
272 Amber Prison R :A:	.20	.35
273 Ankh of Mishra R :A:	.60	1.00
274 Ashnod's Altar U :A:	2.00	3.00
275 Bottle of Suleiman R :A:	.20	.35
276 Charcoal Diamond U :A:	.20	.35
277 Crystal Rod U :A:	.20	.35
278 Cursed Totem R :A:	1.50	2.50
279 Daraja Griffin U :W:	.20	.35
280 Dingus Egg R :A:	.20	.35
281 Disrupting Scepter R :A:	.20	.35
282 Dragon Engine R :A:	.20	.35
283 Dragon Mask U :A:	.20	.35
284 Fire Diamond U :A:	.20	.35
285 Flying Carpet R :A:	.20	.35
286 Fountain of Youth U :A:	.20	.35
287 Glasses of Urza U :A:	.20	.35
288 Grinning Totem R :A:	.20	.35
289 The Hive R :A:	.20	.35
290 Howling Mine R :A:	.20	.35
291 Iron Star U :A:	.20	.35
292 Ivory Cup U :A:	.20	.35
293 Jade Monolith R :A:	.20	.35
294 Jalum Tome R :A:	.20	.35
295 Jayemdae Tome R :A:	.20	.35
296 Lead Golem U :A:	.20	.35
297 Mana Prism U :A:	.20	.35
298 Marble Diamond U :A:	.20	.35
299 Meekstone R :A:	.20	.35
300 Millstone R :A:	.20	.35
301 Moss Diamond U :A:	.20	.35
302 Mystic Compass U :A:	.20	.35
303 Obsianus Golem U :A:	.20	.35
304 Ornithopter U :A:	.20	.35
305 Patagia Golem U :A:	.20	.35
306 Pentagram of the Ages R :A:	.20	.35
307 Phyrexian Vault U :A:	.20	.35
308 Primal Clay R :A:	.20	.35
309 Rod of Ruin U :A:	.20	.35
310 Skull Catapult U :A:	.20	.35
311 Sky Diamond U :A:	.20	.35
312 Snake Basket R :A:	.20	.35
313 Soul Net U :A:	.20	.35
314 Storm Cauldron R :A:	.20	.35
315 Teferi's Puzzle Box R :A:	.20	.35
316 Throne of Bone U :A:	.20	.35
317 Wand of Denial R :A:	.20	.35
318 Wooden Sphere U :A:	.20	.35
319 Adarkar Wastes R :L:	3.00	5.00
320 Brushland R :L:	5.00	7.00
321 City of Brass R :L:	4.00	6.00
322 Crystal Vein U :L:	.20	.35
323 Dwarven Ruins U :L:	.20	.35
324 Ebon Stronghold U :L:	.20	.35
325 Havenwood Battleground U :L:	.20	.35
326 Karplusan Forest R :L:	.20	.35
327 Ruins of Trokair U :L:	.20	.35
328 Sulfurous Springs R :L:	.20	.35
329 Svyelunite Temple U :L:	.20	.35
330 Underground River R :L:	.20	.35
331 Plains L :L:	.20	.35
332 Plains L :L:	.20	.35
333 Plains L :L:	.20	.35
334 Plains L :L:	.20	.35
335 Island L :L:	.20	.35
336 Island L :L:	.20	.35
337 Island L :L:	.20	.35
338 Island L :L:	.20	.35
339 Swamp L :L:	.20	.35
340 Swamp L :L:	.20	.35
341 Swamp L :L:	.20	.35
342 Swamp L :L:	.20	.35
343 Mountain Goat C :R:	.20	.35
344 Mountain L :L:	.20	.35
345 Mountain L :L:	.20	.35
346 Mountain L :L:	.20	.35
347 Forest L :L:	.20	.35
348 Forest L :L:	.20	.35
349 Forest L :L:	.20	.35
350 Forest L :L:	.20	.35

2001 Magic The Gathering Seventh Edition

Card	Low	High
COMPLETE SET (350)	175.00	240.00
BOOSTER BOX (36 PACKS)	250.00	300.00
BOOSTER PACK (15 CARDS)	5.00	8.00
STARTER DECK	6.00	10.00
THEME DECK BOX (15 DECKS)	70.00	90.00
RELEASED ON APRIL 11, 2001		
1 Angelic Page C :W:	.20	.35
2 Ardent Militia U :W:	.20	.35
3 Blessed Reversal R :W:	.20	.35
4 Breath of Life U :W:	.20	.35
5 Castle U :W:	.20	.35
6 Circle of Protection Black C :W:	.20	.35
7 Circle of Protection Blue C :W:	.20	.35
8 Circle of Protection Green C :W:	.20	.35
9 Circle of Protection Red C :W:	.20	.35
10 Circle of Protection White C :W:	.20	.35
11 Cloudchaser Eagle C :W:	.20	.35
12 Crossbow Infantry C :W:	.20	.35
13 Disenchant C :W:	.20	.35
14 Eager Cadet C :W:	.20	.35
15 Elite Archers R :W:	.20	.35
16 Gerrard's Wisdom U :W:	.20	.35
17 Glorious Anthem R :W:	.20	.35
18 Healing Salve C :W:	.20	.35
19 Heavy Ballista U :W:	.20	.35
20 Holy Strength C :W:	.20	.35
21 Honor Guard C :W:	.20	.35
22 Intrepid Hero R :W:	.20	.35
23 Kjeldoran Royal Guard R :W:	.20	.35
24 Knight Errant C :W:	.20	.35
25 Knighthood U :W:	.20	.35
26 Longbow Archer U :W:	.20	.35
27 Master Healer R :W:	.20	.35
28 Northern Paladin R :W:	.20	.35
29 Pacifism C :W:	.20	.35
30 Pariah R :W:	1.50	2.00
31 Purify R :W:	.20	.35
32 Razorfoot Griffin C :W:	.20	.35
33 Reprisal U :W:	.20	.35
34 Reverse Damage R :W:	.20	.35
35 Rolling Stones R :W:	.20	.35
36 Sacred Ground R :W:	.20	.35
37 Sacred Nectar C :W:	.20	.35
38 Samite Healer C :W:	.20	.35
39 Sanctimony U :W:	.20	.35
40 Seasoned Marshal U :W:	.20	.35
41 Serra Advocate U :W:	.20	.35
42 Serra Angel R :W:	.20	.35
43 Serra's Embrace U :W:	.20	.35
44 Shield Wall C :W:	.20	.35
45 Skyshroud Falcon C :W:	.20	.35
46 Southern Paladin R :W:	.20	.35
47 Spirit Link U :W:	.20	.35
48 Standing Troops C :W:	.20	.35
49 Starlight U :W:	.20	.35
50 Staunch Defenders U :W:	.20	.35
51 Sunweb R :W:	.20	.35
52 Sustainer of the Realm U :W:	.20	.35
53 Venerable Monk C :W:	.20	.35
54 Vengeance U :W:	.20	.35
55 Wall of Swords U :W:	.20	.35
56 Worship R :W:	4.00	6.00
57 Wrath of God R :W:	4.00	6.00
58 Air Elemental U :B:	.20	.35
59 Ancestral Memories R :B:	.20	.35
60 Arcane Laboratory U :B:	.20	.35
61 Archivist R :B:	.20	.35
62 Baleful Stare U :B:	.20	.35
63 Benthic Behemoth R :B:	.20	.35
64 Boomerang C :B:	.20	.35
65 Confiscate U :B:	.20	.35
66 Coral Merfolk C :B:	.20	.35
67 Counterspell C :B:	1.00	1.50
68 Daring Apprentice R :B:	.20	.35
69 Deflection R :B:	.20	.35
70 Delusions of Mediocrity R :B:	.20	.35
71 Equilibrium R :B:	1.50	2.00
72 Evacuation R :B:	1.00	1.50
73 Fighting Drake U :B:	.20	.35
74 Fleeting Image R :B:	.20	.35
75 Flight C :B:	.20	.35
76 Force Spike C :B:	.20	.35
77 Giant Octopus C :B:	.20	.35
78 Glacial Wall U :B:	.20	.35
79 Hibernation U :B:	.20	.35
80 Horned Turtle C :B:	.20	.35
81 Inspiration C :B:	.20	.35
82 Levitation U :B:	.20	.35
83 Lord of Atlantis R :B:	6.00	8.00
84 Mahamoti Djinn R :B:	.20	.35
85 Mana Breach U :B:	.20	.35
86 Mana Short R :B:	.20	.35
87 Mawcor R :B:	.20	.35
88 Memory Lapse C :B:	.20	.35
89 Merfolk Looter U :B:	.20	.35
90 Merfolk of the Pearl Trident C :B:	.20	.35
91 Opportunity U :B:	.20	.35
92 Opposition R :B:	2.50	4.00
93 Phantom Warrior U :B:	.20	.35
94 Prodigal Sorcerer C :B:	.20	.35
95 Remove Soul C :B:	.20	.35
96 Sage Owl C :B:	.20	.35
97 Sea Monster C :B:	.20	.35
98 Sleight of Hand C :B:	2.50	4.00
99 Steal Artifact U :B:	.20	.35
100 Storm Crow C :B:	.20	.35
101 Telepathic Spies C :B:	.20	.35
102 Telepathy U :B:	.20	.35
103 Temporal Adept R :B:	.20	.35
104 Thieving Magpie U :B:	.20	.35
105 Tolarian Winds C :B:	.20	.35
106 Treasure Trove U :B:	.20	.35
107 Twiddle C :B:	.20	.35
108 Unsummon C :B:	.20	.35
109 Vigilant Drake C :B:	.20	.35
110 Vizzerdrix R :B:	.20	.35
111 Wall of Air U :B:	.20	.35
112 Wall of Wonder R :B:	.20	.35
113 Wind Dancer U :B:	.20	.35
114 Wind Drake C :B:	.20	.35
115 Abyssal Horror R :K:	.20	.35
116 Abyssal Specter U :K:	.20	.35
117 Agonizing Memories U :K:	.20	.35
118 Befoul U :K:	.20	.35
119 Bellowing Fiend R :K:	.20	.35
120 Bereavement U :K:	.20	.35
121 Blood Pet C :K:	.20	.35
122 Bog Imp C :K:	.20	.35
123 Bog Wraith U :K:	.20	.35
124 Corrupt C :K:	.20	.35
125 Crypt Rats U :K:	2.00	3.00
126 Dakmor Lancer U :K:	.20	.35
127 Dark Banishing C :K:	.20	.35
128 Darkest Hour R :K:	1.50	2.00
129 Dregs of Sorrow R :K:	.20	.35
130 Drudge Skeletons C :K:	.20	.35
131 Duress C :K:	.20	.35
132 Eastern Paladin R :K:	.20	.35
133 Engineered Plague U :K:	.20	.35
134 Fallen Angel R :K:	.20	.35
135 Fear C :K:	.20	.35
136 Foul Imp U :K:	.20	.35
137 Fugue U :K:	.20	.35
138 Giant Cockroach C :K:	.20	.35
139 Gravedigger C :K:	.20	.35
140 Greed R :K:	.20	.35
141 Hollow Dogs C :K:	.20	.35
142 Howl from Beyond C :K:	.20	.35
143 Infernal Contract R :K:	.20	.35
144 Leshrac's Rite U :K:	.20	.35
145 Looming Shade C :K:	.20	.35
146 Megrim U :K:	.20	.35
147 Mind Rot C :K:	.20	.35
148 Nausea C :K:	.20	.35
149 Necrologia U :K:	.20	.35
150 Nightmare R :K:	.20	.35
151 Nocturnal Raid U :K:	.20	.35
152 Oppression R :K:	1.00	1.50
153 Ostracize C :K:	.20	.35
154 Persecute R :K:	.20	.35
155 Plague Beetle C :K:	.20	.35
156 Rag Man R :K:	.20	.35
157 Raise Dead C :K:	.20	.35
158 Razortooth Rats C :K:	.20	.35
159 Reprocess R :K:	.20	.35
160 Revenant R :K:	.20	.35
161 Scathe Zombies C :K:	.20	.35
162 Serpent Warrior C :K:	.20	.35
163 Soul Feast U :K:	.20	.35
164 Spineless Thug C :K:	.20	.35
165 Strands of Night U :K:	.20	.35
166 Stronghold Assassin R :K:	.20	.35
167 Tainted AEther R :K:	2.00	3.50
168 Unholy Strength C :K:	.20	.35
169 Wall of Bone U :K:	.20	.35
170 Western Paladin R :K:	.20	.35
171 Yawgmoth's Edict U :K:	.20	.35
172 AEther Flash U :R:	.20	.35
173 Balduvian Barbarians C :R:	.20	.35
174 Bedlam R :R:	.20	.35
175 Blaze U :R:	.20	.35
176 Bloodshot Cyclops R :R:	.20	.35
177 Boil U :R:	.20	.35
178 Crimson Hellkite R :R:	.20	.35
179 Disorder U :R:	.20	.35
180 Earthquake R :R:	.20	.35
181 Fervor R :R:	.20	.35
182 Final Fortune R :R:	1.00	1.50
183 Fire Elemental U :R:	.20	.35
184 Ghitu Fire-Eater U :R:	.20	.35
185 Goblin Chariot C :R:	.20	.35
186 Goblin Digging Team C :R:	.20	.35
187 Goblin Elite Infantry C :R:	.20	.35
188 Goblin Gardener C :R:	.20	.35

Card	Low	High
189 Goblin Glider U :R:	.20	.35
190 Goblin King R :R:	1.00	1.50
191 Goblin Matron U :R:	.20	.35
192 Goblin Raider C :R:	.20	.35
193 Goblin Spelunkers C :R:	.20	.35
194 Goblin War Drums U :R:	.20	.35
195 Granite Grip C :R:	.20	.35
196 Hill Giant C :R:	.20	.35
197 Impatience R :R:	.20	.35
198 Inferno R :R:	.20	.35
199 Lava Axe C :R:	.20	.35
200 Lightning Blast C :R:	.20	.35
201 Lightning Elemental C :R:	.20	.35
202 Mana Clash R :R:	.20	.35
203 Ogre Taskmaster U :R:	.20	.35
204 Okk R :R:	.20	.35
205 Orcish Artillery U :R:	.20	.35
206 Orcish Oriflamme U :R:	.20	.35
207 Pillage U :R:	.20	.35
208 Pygmy Pyrosaur C :R:	.20	.35
209 Pyroclasm U :R:	.20	.35
210 Pyrotechnics U :R:	.20	.35
211 Raging Goblin C :R:	.20	.35
212 Reckless Embermage R :R:	.20	.35
213 Reflexes C :R:	.20	.35
214 Relentless Assault R :R:	.20	.35
215 Sabretooth Tiger C :R:	.20	.35
216 Seismic Assault R :R:	2.50	4.00
217 Shatter C :R:	.20	.35
218 Shivan Dragon R :R:	.20	.35
219 Shock C :R:	.20	.35
220 Spitting Earth C :R:	.20	.35
221 Stone Rain C :R:	.20	.35
222 Storm Shaman U :R:	.20	.35
223 Sudden Impact U :R:	.20	.35
224 Trained Orgg R :R:	.20	.35
225 Tremor C :R:	.20	.35
226 Volcanic Hammer C :R:	.20	.35
227 Wall of Fire U :R:	.20	.35
228 Wildfire R :R:	.20	.35
229 Anaconda U :G:	.20	.35
230 Ancient Silverback R :G:	.20	.35
231 Birds of Paradise R :G:	6.00	8.00
232 Blanchwood Armor U :G:	.20	.35
233 Bull Hippo U :G:	.20	.35
234 Canopy Spider C :G:	.20	.35
235 Compost U :G:	.20	.35
236 Creeping Mold U :G:	.20	.35
237 Early Harvest R :G:	.20	.35
238 Elder Druid R :G:	.20	.35
239 Elvish Archers R :G:	.20	.35
240 Elvish Champion R :G:	4.00	6.00
241 Elvish Lyrist U :G:	.20	.35
242 Elvish Piper R :G:	5.00	7.00
243 Familiar Ground U :G:	.20	.35
244 Femeref Archers U :G:	.20	.35
245 Fog C :G:	.20	.35
246 Fyndhorn Elder U :G:	.20	.35
247 Gang of Elk U :G:	.20	.35
248 Giant Growth C :G:	.20	.35
249 Giant Spider C :G:	.20	.35
250 Gorilla Chieftain C :G:	.20	.35
251 Grizzly Bears C :G:	.20	.35
252 Hurricane R :G:	.20	.35
253 Llanowar Elves C :G:	.20	.35
254 Lone Wolf C :G:	.20	.35
255 Lure U :G:	.20	.35
256 Maro R :G:	.20	.35
257 Might of Oaks R :G:	.20	.35
258 Monstrous Growth C :G:	.20	.35
259 Nature's Resurgence R :G:	.20	.35
260 Nature's Revolt R :G:	.20	.35
261 Pride of Lions U :G:	.20	.35
262 Rampant Growth C :G:	.20	.35
263 Reclaim C :G:	.20	.35
264 Redwood Treefolk C :G:	.20	.35
265 Regeneration C :G:	.20	.35
266 Rowen R :G:	.20	.35
267 Scavenger Folk U :G:	.20	.35
268 Seeker of Skybreak C :G:	.20	.35
269 Shanodin Dryads C :G:	.20	.35
270 Spined Wurm C :G:	.20	.35
271 Squall C :G:	.20	.35
272 Stream of Life C :G:	.20	.35
273 Thorn Elemental R :G:	.20	.35
274 Thoughtleech U :G:	.20	.35
275 Trained Armodon C :G:	.20	.35
276 Tranquility C :G:	.20	.35
277 Treefolk Seedlings U :G:	.20	.35
278 Uktabi Wildcats R :G:	.20	.35
279 Untamed Wilds U :G:	.20	.35
280 Verduran Enchantress R :G:	.20	.35
281 Vernal Bloom R :G:	1.50	2.50
282 Wild Growth C :G:	.20	.35
283 Wing Snare U :G:	.20	.35
284 Wood Elves C :G:	.20	.35
285 Yavimaya Enchantress U :G:	.20	.35
286 Aladdin's Ring R :A:	.20	.35
287 Beast of Burden R :A:	.20	.35
288 Caltrops U :A:	.20	.35
289 Charcoal Diamond U :A:	.20	.35
290 Coat of Arms R :A:	6.00	8.00
291 Crystal Rod U :A:	.20	.35
292 Dingus Egg R :A:	.20	.35
293 Disrupting Scepter R :A:	.20	.35
294 Ensnaring Bridge R :A:	35.00	40.00
295 Feroz's Ban R :A:	.20	.35
296 Fire Diamond U :A:	.20	.35
297 Flying Carpet R :A:	.20	.35
298 Grafted Skullcap R :A:	.20	.35
299 Grapeshot Catapult U :A:	.20	.35
300 Howling Mine R :A:	2.00	3.50
301 Iron Star U :A:	.20	.35
302 Ivory Cup U :A:	.20	.35
303 Jalum Tome R :A:	.20	.35
304 Jandor's Saddlebags R :A:	.20	.35
305 Jayemdae Tome R :A:	.20	.35
306 Marble Diamond U :A:	.20	.35
307 Meekstone R :A:	2.00	3.50
308 Millstone R :A:	.20	.35
309 Moss Diamond U :A:	.20	.35
310 Patagia Golem U :A:	.20	.35
311 Phyrexian Colossus R :A:	.20	.35
312 Phyrexian Hulk U :A:	.20	.35
313 Pit Trap U :A:	.20	.35
314 Rod of Ruin U :A:	.20	.35
315 Sisay's Ring U :A:	.20	.35
316 Sky Diamond U :A:	.20	.35
317 Soul Net U :A:	.20	.35
318 Spellbook U :A:	.20	.35
319 Static Orb R :A:	5.00	7.00
320 Storm Cauldron R :A:	.20	.35
321 Teferi's Puzzle Box R :A:	4.00	6.00
322 Throne of Bone U :A:	.20	.35
323 Wall of Spears U :A:	.20	.35
324 Wooden Sphere U :A:	.20	.35
325 Adarkar Wastes R :L:	3.00	5.00
326 Brushland R :L:	5.00	7.00
327 City of Brass R :L:	5.00	7.00
328 Forest L :L:	.20	.35
329 Forest L :L:	.20	.35
330 Forest L :L:	.20	.35
331 Forest L :L:	.20	.35
332 Island L :L:	.20	.35
333 Island L :L:	.20	.35
334 Island L :L:	.20	.35
335 Island L :L:	.20	.35
336 Karplusan Forest R :L:	2.50	4.00
337 Mountain L :L:	.20	.35
338 Mountain L :L:	.20	.35
339 Mountain L :L:	.20	.35
340 Mountain L :L:	.20	.35
341 Plains L :L:	.20	.35
342 Plains L :L:	.20	.35
343 Plains L :L:	.20	.35
344 Plains L :L:	.20	.35
345 Sulfurous Springs R :L:	2.50	4.00
346 Swamp L :L:	.20	.35
347 Swamp L :L:	.20	.35
348 Swamp L :L:	.20	.35
349 Swamp L :L:	.20	.35
350 Underground River R :L:	2.00	3.50

2001 Magic The Gathering Seventh Edition Foil

Card	Low	High
COMPLETE SET (350)	600.00	900.00

2003 Magic The Gathering Eighth Edition

Card	Low	High
COMPLETE SET (356)	240.00	325.00
BOOSTER BOX (36 PACKS)	175.00	225.00
BOOSTER PACK (15 CARDS)	7.00	10.00
THEME DECK BOX	125.00	140.00
THEME DECK	8.00	10.00
RELEASED ON JULY 28, 2003		
1 Angel of Mercy U :W:	.20	.35
2 Angelic Page C :W:	.20	.35
3 Ardent Militia U :W:	.20	.35
4 Avatar of Hope R :W:	.20	.35
5 Aven Cloudchaser C :W:	.20	.35
6 Aven Flock C :W:	.20	.35
7 Blessed Reversal R :W:	.20	.35
8 Blinding Angel R :W:	1.50	2.50
9 Chastise U :W:	.20	.35
10 Circle of Protection: Black U :W:	.20	.35
11 Circle of Protection: Blue U :W:	.20	.35
12 Circle of Protection: Green U :W:	.20	.35
13 Circle of Protection: Red U :W:	.20	.35
14 Circle of Protection: White U :W:	.20	.35
15 Crossbow Infantry C :W:	.20	.35
16 Demystify C :W:	.20	.35
17 Diving Griffin C :W:	.20	.35
18 Elite Archers R :W:	.20	.35
19 Elite Javelineer U :W:	.20	.35
20 Glorious Anthem R :W:	.20	.35
21 Glory Seeker C :W:	.20	.35
22 Healing Salve C :W:	.20	.35
23 Holy Day C :W:	.20	.35
24 Holy Strength C :W:	.20	.35
25 Honor Guard C :W:	.20	.35
26 Intrepid Hero R :W:	.20	.35
27 Ivory Mask R :W:	.20	.35
28 Karma U :W:	.20	.35
29 Master Decoy C :W:	.20	.35
30 Master Healer R :W:	.20	.35
31 Noble Purpose R :W:	.20	.35
32 Oracle's Attendants R :W:	.20	.35
33 Pacifism C :W:	.20	.35
34 Peach Garden Oath U :W:	.20	.35
35 Rain of Blades U :W:	.20	.35
36 Razorfoot Griffin C :W:	.20	.35
37 Redeem C :W:	.20	.35
38 Rolling Stones R :W:	.20	.35
39 Sacred Ground R :W:	.20	.35
40 Sacred Nectar C :W:	.20	.35
41 Samite Healer C :W:	.20	.35
42 Sanctimony U :W:	.20	.35
43 Savannah Lions R :W:	.20	.35
44 Seasoned Marshal U :W:	.20	.35
45 Serra Angel R :W:	.20	.35
46 Solidarity C :W:	.20	.35
47 Spirit Link U :W:	.20	.35
48 Standing Troops C :W:	.20	.35
49 Staunch Defenders U :W:	.20	.35
50 Story Circle R :W:	.20	.35
51 Suntail Hawk C :W:	.20	.35
52 Sunweb R :W:	.20	.35
53 Sword Dancer U :W:	.20	.35
54 Tundra Wolves C :W:	.20	.35
55 Venerable Monk C :W:	.20	.35
56 Wall of Swords U :W:	.20	.35
57 Worship R :W:	4.00	6.00
58 Wrath of God R :W:	3.00	5.00
59 Air Elemental U :B:	.20	.35
60 Archivist R :B:	.20	.35
61 Aven Fisher C :B:	.20	.35
62 Balance of Power R :B:	.20	.35
63 Boomerang C :B:	.20	.35
64 Bribery R :B:	15.00	20.00
65 Catalog C :B:	.20	.35
66 Coastal Hornclaw C :B:	.20	.35
67 Coastal Piracy R :B:	3.00	5.00
68 Concentrate U :B:	.20	.35
69 Confiscate U :B:	.20	.35
70 Coral Eel C :B:	.20	.35
71 Cowardice R :B:	.20	.35
72 Curiosity U :B:	.20	.35
73 Daring Apprentice R :B:	.20	.35
74 Deflection R :B:	.20	.35
75 Dehydration C :B:	.20	.35
76 Evacuation R :B:	.20	.35
77 Fighting Drake U :B:	.20	.35
78 Flash Counter C :B:	.20	.35
79 Fleeting Image R :B:	.20	.35
80 Flight C :B:	.20	.35
81 Fugitive Wizard C :B:	.20	.35
82 Hibernation U :B:	.20	.35
83 Horned Turtle C :B:	.20	.35
84 Index C :B:	.20	.35
85 Inspiration C :B:	.20	.35
86 Intruder Alarm R :B:	6.00	8.00
87 Invisibility U :B:	.20	.35
88 Mahamoti Djinn R :B:	.20	.35
89 Mana Leak C :B:	.20	.35
90 Merchant of Secrets C :B:	.20	.35
91 Merchant Scroll U :B:	2.50	4.00
92 Mind Bend R :B:	.20	.35
93 Phantom Warrior U :B:	.20	.35
94 Puppeteer U :B:	.20	.35
95 Remove Soul C :B:	.20	.35
96 Rewind U :B:	.20	.35
97 Sage of Lat-Nam R :B:	.20	.35
98 Sage Owl C :B:	.20	.35
99 Sea Monster C :B:	.20	.35
S1 Eager Cadet C :W:	.20	.35
S2 Vengence U :W:	.20	.35
S3 Giant Octopus C :B:	.20	.35
S5 Vizzerdrix R :B:	.20	.35
S6 Enormous Baloth U :G:	.20	.35
S7 Silverback Ape U :G:	.20	.35
100 Shifting Sky R :B:	.20	.35
101 Sneaky Homunculus C :B:	.20	.35
102 Spiketail Hatchling U :B:	.20	.35
103 Steal Artifact U :B:	.20	.35
104 Storm Crow C :B:	.20	.35
105 Telepathy U :B:	.20	.35
106 Temporal Adept R :B:	.20	.35
107 Thieving Magpie U :B:	.20	.35
108 Tidal Kraken R :B:	.20	.35
109 Trade Routes R :B:	.20	.35
110 Treasure Trove U :B:	.20	.35
111 Twiddle C :B:	.20	.35
112 Unsummon C :B:	.20	.35
113 Wall of Air U :B:	.20	.35
114 Wind Drake C :B:	.20	.35
115 Wrath of Marit Lage U :B:	.20	.35
116 Zur's Weirding R :B:	.20	.35
117 Abyssal Specter U :K:	.20	.35
118 Ambition's Cost U :K:	.20	.35
119 Bog Imp C :K:	.20	.35
120 Bog Wraith U :K:	.20	.35
121 Carrion Wall U :K:	.20	.35
122 Coercion C :K:	.20	.35
123 Dark Banishing C :K:	.20	.35
124 Death Pit Offering R :K:	.20	.35
125 Death Pits of Rath R :K:	.20	.35
126 Deathgazer U :K:	.20	.35
127 Deepwood Ghoul C :K:	.20	.35
128 Diabolic Tutor U :K:	.20	.35
129 Drudge Skeletons C :K:	.20	.35
130 Dusk Imp C :K:	.20	.35
131 Eastern Paladin R :K:	.20	.35
132 Execute U :K:	.20	.35
133 Fallen Angel R :K:	.20	.35
134 Fear C :K:	.20	.35
135 Giant Cockroach C :K:	.20	.35
136 Gluttonous Zombie U :K:	.20	.35
137 Grave Pact R :K:	15.00	20.00
138 Gravedigger C :K:	.20	.35
139 Larceny R :K:	.20	.35
140 Looming Shade C :K:	.20	.35
141 Lord of the Undead R :K:	8.00	11.00
142 Maggot Carrier C :K:	.20	.35
143 Megrim U :K:	.20	.35
144 Mind Rot C :K:	.20	.35
145 Mind Slash U :K:	.20	.35
146 Mind Sludge U :K:	.20	.35
147 Murderous Betrayal R :K:	.20	.35
148 Nausea C :K:	.20	.35
149 Nekrataal U :K:	.20	.35
150 Nightmare R :K:	.20	.35
151 Persecute R :K:	.20	.35
152 Phyrexian Arena R :K:	6.00	8.00
153 Phyrexian Plaguelord R :K:	.20	.35
154 Plague Beetle C :K:	.20	.35
155 Plague Wind R :K:	1.50	2.00
156 Primeval Shambler U :K:	.20	.35
157 Raise Dead C :K:	.20	.35
158 Ravenous Rats C :K:	.20	.35
159 Royal Assassin R :K:	.20	.35
160 Scathe Zombies C :K:	.20	.35
161 Serpent Warrior C :K:	.20	.35
162 Sever Soul U :K:	.20	.35
163 Severed Legion C :K:	.20	.35
164 Slay U :K:	.20	.35
165 Soul Feast U :K:	.20	.35
166 Spineless Thug C :K:	.20	.35
167 Swarm of Rats U :K:	.20	.35
168 Underworld Dreams R :K:	2.00	3.50
169 Unholy Strength C :K:	.20	.35
170 Vampiric Spirit R :K:	.20	.35
171 Vicious Hunger C :K:	.20	.35
172 Warped Devotion R :K:	.20	.35
173 Western Paladin R :K:	.20	.35
174 Zombify U :K:	.20	.35
175 Anaba Shaman C :R:	.20	.35
176 Balduvian Barbarians C :R:	.20	.35
177 Blaze U :R:	.20	.35
178 Blood Moon R :R:	.20	.35
179 Bloodshot Cyclops R :R:	.20	.35
180 Boil U :R:	.20	.35
181 Canyon Wildcat C :R:	.20	.35
182 Cinder Wall C :R:	.20	.35
183 Demolish U :R:	.20	.35
184 Dwarven Demolition Team U :R:	.20	.35
185 Enrage U :R:	.20	.35
186 Flashfires U :R:	.20	.35
187 Furnace of Rath R :R:	.20	.35
188 Goblin Chariot C :R:	.20	.35
189 Goblin Glider U :R:	.20	.35
190 Goblin King R :R:	.20	.35
191 Goblin Raider C :R:	.20	.35
192 Guerrilla Tactics U :R:	.20	.35
193 Hammer of Bogardan R :R:	.20	.35
194 Hill Giant C :R:	.20	.35
195 Hulking Cyclops U :R:	.20	.35
196 Inferno R :R:	.20	.35
197 Lava Axe C :R:	.20	.35
198 Lava Hounds R :R:	.20	.35
199 Lesser Gargadon U :R:	.20	.35
200 Lightning Blast U :R:	.20	.35
201 Lightning Elemental C :R:	.20	.35
202 Mana Clash R :R:	.20	.35
203 Mogg Sentry R :R:	.20	.35
204 Obliterate R :R:	1.50	2.50
205 Ogre Taskmaster U :R:	.20	.35
206 Okk R :R:	.20	.35
207 Orcish Artillery U :R:	.20	.35
208 Orcish Spy C :R:	.20	.35
209 Panic Attack C :R:	.20	.35
210 Pyroclasm U :R:	.20	.35
211 Pyrotechnics U :R:	.20	.35
212 Raging Goblin C :R:	.20	.35
213 Reflexes C :R:	.20	.35
214 Relentless Assault R :R:	.20	.35
215 Ridgeline Rager C :R:	.20	.35
216 Rukh Egg R :R:	.20	.35
217 Sabretooth Tiger C :R:	.20	.35
218 Searing Wind R :R:	.20	.35
219 Seismic Assault R :R:	2.50	4.00
220 Shatter C :R:	.20	.35
221 Shivan Dragon R :R:	.20	.35
222 Shock C :R:	.20	.35
223 Shock Troops C :R:	.20	.35
224 Sizzle C :R:	.20	.35
225 Stone Rain C :R:	.20	.35
226 Sudden Impact U :R:	.20	.35
227 Thieves' Auction R :R:	1.50	2.50
228 Tremor C :R:	.20	.35
229 Two-Headed Dragon R :R:	.20	.35
230 Viashino Sandstalker U :R:	.20	.35
231 Volcanic Hammer C :R:	.20	.35
232 Wall of Stone U :R:	.20	.35
233 Birds of Paradise R :G:	6.00	8.00
234 Blanchwood Armor U :G:	.20	.35
235 Call of the Wild R :G:	.20	.35
236 Canopy Spider C :G:	.20	.35
237 Choke U :G:	2.00	3.00
238 Collective Unconscious R :G:	.20	.35
239 Craw Wurm C :G:	.20	.35
240 Creeping Mold U :G:	.20	.35
241 Elvish Champion R :G:	3.00	5.00
242 Elvish Lyrist U :G:	.20	.35
243 Elvish Pioneer C :G:	.20	.35
244 Elvish Piper R :G:	4.00	6.00
245 Elvish Scrapper U :G:	.20	.35
246 Emperor Crocodile R :G:	.20	.35
247 Fecundity U :G:	.20	.35
248 Fertile Ground C :G:	.20	.35
249 Foratog U :G:	.20	.35
250 Fungusaur R :G:	.20	.35
251 Fyndhorn Elder U :G:	.20	.35
252 Gaea's Herald R :G:	.20	.35
253 Giant Badger C :G:	.20	.35
254 Giant Growth C :G:	.20	.35
255 Giant Spider C :G:	.20	.35
256 Grizzly Bears C :G:	.20	.35
257 Horned Troll C :G:	.20	.35
258 Hunted Wumpus U :G:	.20	.35
259 Lhurgoyf R :G:	.20	.35
260 Living Terrain U :G:	.20	.35
261 Llanowar Behemoth U :G:	.20	.35
262 Lone Wolf C :G:	.20	.35
263 Lure U :G:	.20	.35
264 Maro R :G:	.20	.35
265 Might of Oaks R :G:	.20	.35
266 Monstrous Growth C :G:	.20	.35
267 Moss Monster C :G:	.20	.35
268 Nantuko Disciple C :G:	.20	.35
269 Natural Affinity R :G:	.20	.35
270 Naturalize C :G:	.20	.35
271 Norwood Ranger C :G:	.20	.35
272 Plow Under R :G:	.20	.35
273 Primeval Force R :G:	.20	.35
274 Rampant Growth C :G:	.20	.35
275 Regeneration C :G:	.20	.35
276 Revive U :G:	.20	.35
277 Rhox R :G:	.20	.35
278 Rushwood Dryad C :G:	.20	.35
279 Spined Wurm C :G:	.20	.35
280 Spitting Spider U :G:	.20	.35
281 Spreading Algae U :G:	.20	.35
282 Stream of Life U :G:	.20	.35

283 Thorn Elemental R :G: .20 .35
284 Trained Armodon C :G: .20 .35
285 Verduran Enchantress R :G: .20 .35
286 Vernal Bloom R :G: 2.00 3.00
287 Vine Trellis C :G: .20 .35
288 Wing Snare U :G: .20 .35
289 Wood Elves C :G: .20 .35
290 Yavimaya Enchantress U :G: .20 .35
291 Aladdin's Ring R :A: .20 .35
292 Beast of Burden R :A: .20 .35
293 Brass Herald R :A: .20 .35
294 Coat of Arms R :A: 6.00 8.00
295 Crystal Rod U :A: .20 .35
296 Defense Grid R :A: 4.00 6.00
297 Dingus Egg R :A: .20 .35
298 Disrupting Scepter R :A: .20 .35
299 Distorting Lens R :A: .20 .35
300 Ensnaring Bridge R :A: 35.00 40.00
301 Flying Carpet R :A: .20 .35
302 Fodder Cannon U :A: .20 .35
303 Howling Mine R :A: 2.00 3.00
304 Iron Star U :A: .20 .35
305 Ivory Cup U :A: .20 .35
306 Jayemdae Tome R :A: .20 .35
307 Millstone R :A: .20 .35
308 Patagia Golem U :A: .20 .35
309 Phyrexian Colossus R :A: .20 .35
310 Phyrexian Hulk U :A: .20 .35
311 Planar Portal R :A: 2.50 4.00
312 Rod of Ruin U :A: .20 .35
313 Skull of Orm R :A: .20 .35
314 Spellbook U :A: .20 .35
315 Star Compass U :A: .20 .35
316 Teferi's Puzzle Box R :A: 4.00 6.00
317 Throne of Bone U :A: .20 .35
318 Urza's Armor R :A: .20 .35
319 Vexing Arcanix R :A: .20 .35
320 Wall of Spears U :A: .20 .35
321 Wooden Sphere U :A: .20 .35
322 City of Brass R :L: 4.00 6.00
323 Coastal Tower U :L: .20 .35
324 Elfhame Palace U :L: .20 .35
325 Salt Marsh U :L: .20 .35
326 Shivan Oasis U :L: .20 .35
327 Urborg Volcano U :L: .20 .35
328 Urza's Mine U :L: 2.50 4.00
329 Urza's Power Plant U :L: 2.50 4.00
330 Urza's Tower U :L: 2.50 4.00
331 Plains L :L: .20 .35
332 Plains L :L: .20 .35
333 Plains L :L: .20 .35
334 Plains L :L: .20 .35
335 Island L :L: .20 .35
336 Island L :L: .20 .35
337 Island L :L: .20 .35
338 Island L :L: .20 .35
339 Swamp L :L: .20 .35
340 Swamp L :L: .20 .35
341 Swamp L :L: .20 .35
342 Swamp L :L: .20 .35
343 Mountain L :L: .20 .35
344 Mountain L :L: .20 .35
345 Mountain L :L: .20 .35
346 Mountain L :L: .20 .35
347 Forest L :L: .20 .35
348 Forest L :L: .20 .35
349 Forest L :L: .20 .35
350 Forest L :L: .20 .35

2003 Magic The Gathering Eighth Edition Foil

COMPLETE SET (350) 900.00 1300.00

2005 Magic The Gathering Ninth Edition

COMPLETE SET (350) 265.00 370.00
BOOSTER BOX (36 PACKS) 150.00 225.00
BOOSTER PACK (15 CARDS) 5.00 8.00
FAT PACK 50.00 80.00
RELEASED ON JULY 29, 2005
1 Angel of Mercy U :W: .20 .35
2 Angelic Blessing C :W: .20 .35
3 Aven Cloudchaser C :W: .20 .35
4 Aven Flock C :W: .20 .35
5 Ballista Squad U :W: .20 .35
6 Blessed Orator U :W: .20 .35
7 Blinding Angel R :W: 1.50 2.50
8 Blinking Spirit R :W: .20 .35
9 Chastise U :W: .20 .35
10 Circle of Protection: Black U :W: .20 .35
11 Circle of Protection: Red U :W: .20 .35
12 Crossbow Infantry C :W: .20 .35
13 Demystify C :W: .20 .35
14 Foot Soldiers C :W: .20 .35
15 Gift of Estates U :W: 1.50 2.00
16 Glorious Anthem R :W: .60 1.00
18 Holy Day C :W: .20 .35
19 Holy Strength C :W: .20 .35
20 Honor Guard C :W: .20 .35
21 Infantry Veteran C :W: .20 .35
22 Inspirit U :W: .20 .35
23 Ivory Mask R :W: .60 1.00
24 Kami of Old Stone U :W: .20 .35
25 Leonin Skyhunter U :W: .20 .35
26 Marble Titan R :W: .20 .35
27 Master Decoy C :W: .20 .35
28 Master Healer R :W: .20 .35
29 Mending Hands C :W: .20 .35
30 Oracle's Attendants R :W: .20 .35
31 Pacifism C :W: .20 .35
32 Paladin en-Vec R :W: .60 1.00
33 Peace of Mind U :W: .20 .35
34 Pegasus Charger C :W: .20 .35
35 Reverse Damage R :W: .20 .35
36 Righteousness R :W: .20 .35
37 Sacred Ground R :W: .20 .35
38 Sacred Nectar C :W: .20 .35
39 Samite Healer C :W: .20 .35
40 Sanctum Guardian U :W: .20 .35
41 Savannah Lions R :W: .20 .35
42 Seasoned Marshal U :W: .20 .35
43 Serra Angel R :W: .20 .35
44 Serra's Blessing U :W: .20 .35
45 Skyhunter Prowler C :W: .20 .35
46 Soul Warden U :W: .60 1.00
47 Spirit Link U :W: .20 .35
48 Story Circle R :W: .60 1.00
49 Suntail Hawk C :W: .20 .35
50 Tempest of Light U :W: .20 .35
51 Venerable Monk C :W: .20 .35
52 Veteran Cavalier C :W: .20 .35
53 Warrior's Honor C :W: .20 .35
54 Weathered Wayfarer R :W: 10.00 15.00
55 Worship R :W: 5.00 7.00
56 Wrath of God R :W: 4.00 6.00
57 Zealous Inquisitor U :W: .20 .35
58 Air Elemental U :B: .20 .35
59 Annex U :B: .20 .35
60 Archivist R :B: .20 .35
61 Aven Fisher C :B: .20 .35
62 Aven Windreader C :B: .20 .35
63 Azure Drake U :B: .20 .35
64 Baleful Stare U :B: .20 .35
65 Battle of Wits R :B: .20 .35
66 Boomerang C :B: .20 .35
67 Clone R :B: .20 .35
68 Confiscate U :B: .20 .35
69 Counsel of the Soratami C :B: .20 .35
70 Cowardice R :B: .20 .35
71 Crafty Pathmage C :B: .20 .35
72 Daring Apprentice R :B: .20 .35
73 Dehydration C :B: .20 .35
74 Dream Prowler U :B: .20 .35
75 Evacuation R :B: 1.50 2.00
76 Exhaustion U :B: .20 .35
77 Fishliver Oil C :B: .20 .35
78 Fleeting Image R :B: .20 .35
79 Flight C :B: .20 .35
80 Fugitive Wizard C :B: .20 .35
81 Horned Turtle C :B: .20 .35
82 Imaginary Pet R :B: .20 .35
83 Levitation U :B: .20 .35
84 Lumengrid Warden C :B: .20 .35
85 Mahamoti Djinn R :B: .20 .35
86 Mana Leak C :B: .20 .35
87 Mind Bend R :B: .20 .35
88 Phantom Warrior U :B: .20 .35
89 Plagiarize R :B: .20 .35
90 Polymorph R :B: 1.00 1.50
91 Puppeteer U :B: .20 .35
92 Reminisce U :B: .20 .35
93 Remove Soul C :B: .20 .35
94 Rewind U :B: .20 .35
95 Sage Aven C :B: .20 .35
96 Sea Monster C :B: .20 .35
97 Sea's Claim C :B: .20 .35
98 Sift C :B: .20 .35
99 Sleight of Hand C :B: 3.00 5.00
100 Storm Crow C :B: .20 .35
101 Telepathy U :B: .20 .35
102 Temporal Adept R :B: .20 .35
103 Thieving Magpie U :B: .20 .35
104 Thought Courier U :B: .20 .35
105 Tidal Kraken R :B: .20 .35
106 Tidings U :B: .20 .35
107 Time Ebb C :B: .20 .35
108 Trade Routes R :B: .20 .35
109 Traumatize R :B: 1.50 2.50
110 Treasure Trove U :B: .20 .35
111 Wanderguard Sentry C :B: .20 .35
112 Wind Drake C :B: .20 .35
113 Withering Gaze U :B: .20 .35
114 Zur's Weirding R :B: .20 .35
115 Blackmail U :K: 2.00 3.00
116 Glory Seeker C :W: .20 .35
116 Bog Imp C :K: .20 .35
117 Bog Wraith U :K: .20 .35
118 Coercion C :K: .20 .35
119 Consume Spirit U :K: .20 .35
120 Contaminated Bond C :K: .20 .35
121 Cruel Edict U :K: .20 .35
122 Dark Banishing C :K: .20 .35
123 Death Pits of Rath R :K: .20 .35
124 Deathgazer U :K: .20 .35
125 Diabolic Tutor U :K: .20 .35
126 Drudge Skeletons U :K: .20 .35
127 Enfeeblement C :K: .20 .35
128 Execute U :K: .20 .35
129 Fear C :K: .20 .35
130 Festering Goblin C :K: .20 .35
131 Final Punishment R :K: .20 .35
132 Foul Imp C :K: .20 .35
133 Giant Cockroach C :K: .20 .35
134 Gluttonous Zombie U :K: .20 .35
135 Grave Pact R :K: .20 .35
136 Gravedigger C :K: 15.00 20.00
137 Hell's Caretaker R :K: .20 .35
138 Highway Robber C :K: .20 .35
139 Hollow Dogs C :K: .20 .35
140 Horror of Horrors U :K: .20 .35
141 Hypnotic Specter R :K: 1.50 2.00
142 Looming Shade C :K: .20 .35
143 Lord of the Undead R :K: 8.00 12.00
144 Megrim U :K: .20 .35
145 Mind Rot C :K: .20 .35
146 Mindslicer R :K: 3.00 5.00
147 Mortivore R :K: 1.00 1.50
148 Nantuko Husk U :K: .20 .35
149 Nekrataal U :K: .20 .35
150 Nightmare R :K: .20 .35
151 Persecute R :K: .20 .35
152 Phyrexian Arena R :K: 5.00 7.00
153 Phyrexian Gargantua U :K: .20 .35
154 Plague Beetle C :K: .20 .35
155 Plague Wind R :K: 1.50 2.00
156 Raise Dead C :K: .20 .35
157 Ravenous Rats C :K: .20 .35
158 Razortooth Rats C :K: .20 .35
159 Royal Assassin R :K: .60 1.00
160 Scathe Zombies C :K: .20 .35
161 Sengir Vampire R :K: .20 .35
162 Serpent Warrior C :K: .20 .35
163 Slay U :K: .20 .35
164 Soul Feast U :K: .20 .35
165 Spineless Thug C :K: .20 .35
166 Swarm of Rats U :K: 1.00 1.50
167 Underworld Dreams R :K: 2.00 3.50
168 Unholy Strength C :K: .20 .35
169 Will-o'-the-Wisp R :K: 1.50 2.00
170 Yawgmoth Demon R :K: .20 .35
171 Zombify U :K: .20 .35
172 Anaba Shaman C :R: .20 .35
173 Anarchist U :R: .20 .35
174 Balduvian Barbarians C :R: .20 .35
175 Blaze U :R: .20 .35
176 Blood Moon R :R: 20.00 25.00
177 Bloodfire Colossus R :R: .20 .35
178 Boiling Seas U :R: .20 .35
179 Demolish U :R: .20 .35
180 Enrage U :R: .20 .35
181 Firebreathing C :R: .20 .35
182 Flame Wave U :R: .20 .35
183 Flashfires U :R: .20 .35
184 Flowstone Crusher U :R: .20 .35
185 Flowstone Shambler C :R: .20 .35
186 Flowstone Slide R :R: .20 .35
187 Form of the Dragon R :R: .20 .35
188 Furnace of Rath R :R: 1.50 2.00
189 Goblin Balloon Brigade U :R: .20 .35
190 Goblin Brigand C :R: .20 .35
191 Goblin Chariot C :R: .20 .35
192 Goblin King R :R: 2.00 3.00
193 Goblin Mountaineer C :R: .20 .35
194 Goblin Piker C :R: .20 .35
195 Goblin Sky Raider C :R: .20 .35
196 Guerrilla Tactics U :R: .20 .35
197 Hill Giant C :R: .20 .35
198 Karplusan Yeti R :R: .20 .35
199 Kird Ape U :R: 1.00 1.50
200 Lava Axe C :R: .20 .35
201 Lightning Elemental C :R: .20 .35
202 Magnivore R :R: .20 .35
203 Mana Clash R :R: .20 .35
204 Mogg Sentry R :R: .20 .35
205 Ogre Taskmaster U :R: .20 .35
206 Orcish Artillery U :R: .20 .35
207 Panic Attack C :R: .20 .35
208 Pyroclasm U :R: .20 .35
209 Raging Goblin C :R: .20 .35
210 Rathi Dragon R :R: .20 .35
211 Reflexes C :R: .20 .35
212 Relentless Assault R :R: .20 .35
213 Rogue Kavu C :R: .20 .35
214 Rukh Egg R :R: .20 .35
215 Sandstone Warrior C :R: .20 .35
216 Seething Song C :R: .20 .35
217 Shard Phoenix R :R: .20 .35
218 Shatter C :R: .20 .35
219 Shivan Dragon R :R: .20 .35
220 Shock C :R: .20 .35
221 Stone Rain C :R: .20 .35
222 Sudden Impact U :R: .20 .35
223 Threaten U :R: .20 .35
224 Thundermare R :R: .20 .35
225 Viashino Sandstalker U :R: .20 .35
226 Volcanic Hammer C :R: .20 .35
227 Whip Sergeant U :R: .20 .35
228 Wildfire R :R: .20 .35
229 Anaconda U :G: .20 .35
230 Ancient Silverback R :G: .20 .35
231 Biorhythm R :G: .20 .35
232 Blanchwood Armor U :G: .20 .35
233 Craw Wurm C :G: .20 .35
234 Creeping Mold U :G: .20 .35
235 Early Harvest R :G: .60 1.00
236 Elvish Bard U :G: .20 .35
237 Elvish Berserker C :G: .20 .35
238 Elvish Champion R :G: 4.00 6.00
239 Elvish Piper R :G: .20 .35
240 Elvish Warrior C :G: .20 .35
241 Emperor Crocodile R :G: .20 .35
242 Force of Nature R :G: .20 .35
243 Giant Growth C :G: .20 .35
244 Giant Spider C :G: .20 .35
245 Greater Good R :G: 15.00 20.00
246 Grizzly Bears C :G: .20 .35
247 Groundskeeper U :G: .20 .35
248 Hunted Wumpus U :G: .20 .35
249 Kavu Climber C :G: .20 .35
250 King Cheetah U :G: .20 .35
251 Ley Druid U :G: .20 .35
252 Llanowar Behemoth U :G: .20 .35
253 Llanowar Elves C :G: .20 .35
254 Maro R :G: .20 .35
255 Might of Oaks R :G: .20 .35
256 Natural Affinity R :G: .20 .35
257 Natural Spring C :G: .20 .35
258 Naturalize C :G: .20 .35
259 Needle Storm U :G: .20 .35
260 Norwood Ranger C :G: .20 .35
261 Order of the Sacred Bell C :G: .20 .35
262 Overgrowth C :G: .20 .35
263 Rampant Growth C :G: .20 .35
264 Reclaim C :G: .20 .35
265 Regeneration U :G: .20 .35
266 River Bear U :G: .20 .35
267 Rootbreaker Wurm U :G: .20 .35
268 Rootwalla C :G: .20 .35
269 Scaled Wurm C :G: .20 .35
270 Seedborn Muse R :G: 20.00 25.00
271 Silklash Spider R :G: .20 .35
272 Stream of Life U :G: .20 .35
273 Summer Bloom U :G: 1.50 2.00
274 Trained Armodon C :G: .20 .35
275 Tree Monkey C :G: .20 .35
276 Treetop Bracers C :G: .20 .35
277 Utopia Tree R :G: 1.50 2.00
278 Verdant Force R :G: .20 .35
279 Verduran Enchantress R :G: .20 .35
280 Viridian Shaman U :G: .20 .35
281 Web U :G: .20 .35
282 Weird Harvest R :G: .60 1.00
283 Wood Elves C :G: .20 .35
284 Yavimaya Enchantress U :G: .20 .35
285 Zodiac Monkey C :G: .20 .35
286 Aladdin's Ring R :A: .20 .35
287 Angel's Feather U :A: .20 .35
288 Beast of Burden R :A: .20 .35
289 Booby Trap R :A: .20 .35
290 Bottle Gnomes U :A: .20 .35
291 Coat of Arms R :A: 6.00 8.00
292 Dancing Scimitar U :A: .20 .35
293 Defense Grid R :A: 6.00 8.00
294 Demon's Horn U :A: .20 .35
295 Disrupting Scepter R :A: .20 .35
296 Dragon's Claw U :A: .20 .35
297 Fellwar Stone U :A: .20 .35
298 Howling Mine R :A: 2.00 3.00
299 Icy Manipulator U :A: .20 .35
300 Jade Statue R :A: .20 .35
301 Jester's Cap R :A: 2.00 3.00
302 Kraken's Eye U :A: .20 .35
303 Loxodon Warhammer R :A: .60 1.00
304 Millstone R :A: .20 .35
305 Ornithopter U :A: .20 .35
306 Phyrexian Hulk U :A: .20 .35
307 Rod of Ruin U :A: .20 .35
308 Slate of Ancestry R :A: 2.00 3.00
309 Spellbook U :A: .60 1.00
310 Storage Matrix R :A: .20 .35
311 Tanglebloom U :A: .20 .35
312 Teferi's Puzzle Box R :A: 5.00 7.00
313 Thran Golem R :A: .20 .35
314 Ur-Golem's Eye U :A: .20 .35
315 Vulshok Morningstar U :A: .20 .35
316 Wurm's Tooth U :A: .20 .35
317 Adarkar Wastes R :L: .20 .35
318 Battlefield Forge R :L: 1.00 1.50
319 Brushland R :L: 6.00 8.00
320 Caves of Koilos R :L: 1.50 2.00
321 Karplusan Forest R :L: 3.00 5.00
322 Llanowar Wastes R :L: 1.50 2.50
323 Quicksand U :L: .20 .35
324 Shivan Reef R :L: 2.50 4.00
325 Sulfurous Springs R :L: 3.00 5.00
326 Underground River R :L: 3.00 5.00
327 Urza's Mine U :L: 3.00 5.00
328 Urza's Power Plant U :L: 3.00 5.00
329 Urza's Tower U :L: 3.00 5.00
330 Yavimaya Coast R :L: 1.50 2.50
331 Plains L :L: .20 .35
332 Plains L :L: .20 .35
333 Plains L :L: .20 .35
334 Plains L :L: .20 .35
335 Island L :L: .20 .35
336 Island L :L: .20 .35
337 Island L :L: .20 .35
338 Island L :L: .20 .35
339 Swamp L :L: .20 .35
340 Swamp L :L: .20 .35
341 Swamp L :L: .20 .35
342 Swamp L :L: .20 .35
343 Mountain L :L: .20 .35
344 Mountain L :L: .20 .35
345 Mountain L :L: .20 .35
346 Mountain L :L: .20 .35
347 Forest L :L: .20 .35
348 Forest L :L: .20 .35
349 Forest L :L: .20 .35
350 Forest L :L: .20 .35
S01 Coral Eel C :B: .20 .35
S02 Eager Cadet C :W: .20 .35
S03 Enormous Baloth U :G: .20 .35
S04 Giant Octopus C :B: .20 .35
S05 Goblin Raider C :R: .20 .35
S06 Index C :B: .20 .35
S07 Spined Wurm C :G: .20 .35
S08 Vengeance U :W: .20 .35
S09 Vizzerdrix R :B: .20 .35

2007 Magic The Gathering Tenth Edition

COMPLETE SET (383) 350.00 450.00
BOOSTER BOX (36 PACKS) 200.00 250.00
BOOSTER PACK (15 CARDS) 6.00 8.00
RELEASED ON JULY 14, 2007
1 Ancestor's Chosen U :W: .30 .50
2 Angel of Mercy U :W: .30 .50

3 Angelic Chorus R :W: 4.00 5.50
4 Angelic Wall C :W: .15 .25
5 Angel's Feather U :A: .30 .50
6 Aura of Silence U :W: .30 .50
7 Aven Cloudchaser C :W: .15 .25
8 Ballista Squad U :W: .30 .50
9 Bandage C :W: .15 .25
10 Beacon of Immortality R :W: 5.00 7.00
11 Benalish Knight C :W: .15 .25
12 Cho-Manno, Revolutionary R :W: .40 .60
13 Condemn U :W: .30 .50
14 Demystify C :W: .15 .25
15 Field Marshal R :W: 4.00 6.00
16 Ghost Warden C :W: .15 .25
17 Glorious Anthem R :W: 1.00 1.50
18 Hail of Arrows U :W: .30 .50
19 Heart of Light C :W: .15 .25
20 High Ground U :W: .30 .50
21 Holy Day C :W: .40 .60
22 Holy Strength C :W: .15 .25
23 Honor Guard C :W: .15 .25
24 Icatian Priest U :W: .30 .50
25 Kjeldoran Royal Guard R :W: .30 .50
26 Loxodon Mystic C :W: .15 .25
27 Loyal Sentry R :W: .50 .75
28 Luminesce U :W: .30 .50
29 Mobilization R :W: .75 1.25
30 Nomad Mythmaker R :W: 1.75 2.00
31 Pacifism C :W: .15 .25
32 Paladin en-Vec R :W: .75 1.25
33 Pariah R :W: 2.00 2.50
34 Reviving Dose C :W: .15 .25
35 Reya Dawnbringer R :W: 1.75 2.00
36 Righteousness R :W: .30 .50
37 Rule of Law U :W: .30 .50
38 Samite Healer C :W: .30 .50
39 Serra Angel R :W: .30 .50
40 Serra's Embrace U :W: .30 .50
41 Skyhunter Patrol C :W: .15 .25
42 Skyhunter Prowler C :W: .15 .25
43 Skyhunter Skirmisher U :W: .30 .50
44 Soul Warden U :W: .30 .50
45 Spirit Link U :W: .30 .50
46 Spirit Weaver U :W: .30 .50
47 Starlight Invoker U :W: .30 .50
48 Steadfast Guard C :W: .15 .25
49 Story Circle R :W: 1.25 1.75
50 Suntail Hawk C :W: .15 .25
51 Tempest of Light U :W: .30 .50
52 Treasure Hunter U :W: .30 .50
53 True Believer R :W: 1.00 1.50
54 Tundra Wolves C :W: .15 .25
55 Venerable Monk C :W: .15 .25
56 Voice of All R :W: .40 .60
57 Wall of Swords U :W: .30 .50
58 Warrior's Honor C :W: .15 .25
59 Wild Griffin C :W: .15 .25
60 Windborn Muse R :W: 2.50 3.00
61 Wrath of God R :W: 4.00 6.00
62 Youthful Knight C :W: .15 .25
63 Academy Researchers U :B: .30 .50
64 Air Elemental U :B: .30 .50
65 Ambassador Laquatus R :B: .75 1.00
66 Arcanis the Omnipotent R :B: 2.25 2.75
67 Aura Graft U :B: .30 .50
68 Aven Fisher C :B: .15 .25
69 Aven Windreader C :B: .15 .25
70 Boomerang C :B: .15 .25
71 Cancel C :B: .15 .25
72 Cephalid Constable R :B: .50 .75
73 Clone R :B: .30 .50
74 Cloud Elemental C :B: .15 .25
75 Cloud Sprite C :B: .15 .25
76 Counsel of the Soratami C :B: .15 .25
77 Crafty Pathmage C :B: .15 .25
78 Dehydration C :B: .15 .25
79 Deluge U :B: .30 .50
80 Denizen of the Deep R :B: .30 .50
81 Discombobulate U :B: .30 .50
82 Dreamborn Muse R :B: .30 .50
83 Evacuation R :B: 1.75 2.25
84 Flashfreeze U :B: .30 .50
85 Fog Elemental U :B: .30 .50
86 Fugitive Wizard C :B: .15 .25
87 Horseshoe Crab C :B: .15 .25
88 Hurkyl's Recall R :B: 4.00 5.50
89 Lumengrid Warden C :B: .15 .25
90 Mahamoti Djinn R :B: .30 .50
91 March of the Machines R :B: .30 .50
92 Merfolk Looter C :B: .15 .25
93 Mind Bend R :B: .30 .50
94 Peek C :B: .15 .25
95 Persuasion U :B: .30 .50
96 Phantom Warrior U :B: .30 .50
97 Plagiarize R :B: .30 .50
98 Puppeteer U :B: .30 .50
99 Reminisce U :B: .30 .50
100 Remove Soul C :B: .15 .25
101 Robe of Mirrors C :B: .15 .25
102 Rootwater Commando C :B: .15 .25
103 Rootwater Matriarch R :B: .30 .50
104 Sage Owl C :B: .15 .25
105 Scalpelexis R :B: .30 .50
106 Sea Monster C :B: .15 .25
107 Shimmering Wings C :B: .15 .25
108 Sift C :B: .15 .25
109 Sky Weaver U :B: .30 .50
110 Snapping Drake C :B: .15 .25
111 Spiketail Hatchling U :B: .30 .50
112 Sunken Hope R :B: .30 .50
113 Telepathy U :B: .30 .50
114 Telling Time U :B: .30 .50
115 Thieving Magpie U :B: .30 .50
116 Tidings U :B: .30 .50
117 Time Stop R :B: 2.50 3.00
118 Time Stretch R :B: 10.00 12.00
119 Traumatize R :B: 1.25 1.75
120 Twincast R :B: 2.50 3.00
121 Twitch C :B: .15 .25
122 Unsummon C :B: .15 .25
123 Vedalken Mastermind U :B: .30 .50
124 Wall of Air U :B: .30 .50
125 Afflict C :K: .15 .25
126 Agonizing Memories U :K: .30 .50
127 Ascendant Evincar R :K: .75 1.00
128 Assassinate C :K: .15 .25
129 Beacon of Unrest R :K: 3.25 3.75
130 Bog Wraith U :K: .30 .50
131 Consume Spirit U :K: .30 .50
132 Contaminated Bond C :K: .15 .25
133 Cruel Edict U :K: .30 .50
134 Deathmark U :K: .30 .50
135 Diabolic Tutor U :K: .30 .50
136 Distress C :K: .15 .25
137 Doomed Necromancer R :K: 4.00 4.50
138 Dross Crocodile C :K: .15 .25
139 Drudge Skeletons U :K: .30 .50
140 Dusk Imp C :K: .15 .25
141 Essence Drain C :K: .15 .25
142 Fear C :K: .15 .25
143 Festering Goblin C :K: .15 .25
144 Grave Pact R :K: 9.00 11.00
145 Graveborn Muse R :K: 2.00 2.50
146 Gravedigger C :K: .15 .25
147 Hate Weaver U :K: .30 .50
148 Head Games R :K: .30 .50
149 Hidden Horror U :K: .30 .50
150 Highway Robber C :K: .15 .25
151 Hypnotic Specter R :K: 1.50 2.00
152 Knight of Dusk U :K: .30 .50
153 Looming Shade C :K: .15 .25
154 Lord of the Pit R :K: .30 .50
155 Lord of the Undead R :K: 8.00 10.00
156 Mass of Ghouls C :K: .15 .25
157 Megrim U :K: .30 .50
158 Midnight Ritual R :K: .30 .50
159 Mind Rot C :K: .15 .25
160 Mortal Combat R :K: .50 .75
161 Mortivore R :K: .75 1.25
162 Nantuko Husk U :K: .30 .50
163 Nekrataal U :K: .30 .50
164 Nightmare R :K: .30 .50
165 No Rest for the Wicked U :K: .30 .50
166 Phage the Untouchable R :K: .30 .50
167 Phyrexian Rager C :K: .15 .25
168 Plague Beetle C :K: .15 .25
169 Plague Wind R :K: 1.75 2.25
170 Rain of Tears U :K: .30 .50
171 Ravenous Rats C :K: .15 .25
172 Recover C :K: .15 .25
173 Relentless Rats U :K: .30 .50
174 Royal Assassin R :K: .50 .75
175 Scathe Zombies C :K: .15 .25
176 Sengir Vampire R :K: .30 .50
177 Severed Legion C :K: .15 .25
178 Sleeper Agent R :K: .30 .50
179 Soul Feast U :K: .30 .50
180 Spineless Thug C :K: .15 .25
181 Stronghold Discipline U :K: .30 .50
182 Terror C :K: .15 .25
183 Thrull Surgeon U :K: .15 .25
184 Underworld Dreams R :K: 2.75 3.25
185 Unholy Strength C :K: .15 .25
186 Vampire Bats C :K: .15 .25
187 Anaba Bodyguard C :R: .15 .25
188 Arcane Teachings U :R: .30 .50
189 Beacon of Destruction R :R: .30 .50
190 Blaze U :R: .30 .50
191 Bloodfire Colossus R :R: .30 .50
192 Bloodrock Cyclops C :R: .15 .25
193 Bogardan Firefiend C :R: .15 .25
194 Cone of Flame U :R: .30 .50
195 Cryoclasm U :R: .30 .50
196 Demolish C :R: .15 .25
197 Dragon Roost R :R: 1.00 1.50
198 Duct Crawler C :R: .15 .25
199 Earth Elemental U :R: .30 .50
200 Firebreathing C :R: .15 .25
201 Fists of the Anvil C :R: .15 .25
202 Flamewave Invoker U :R: .30 .50
203 Flowstone Slide R :R: .30 .50
204 Furnace of Rath R :R: .75 1.25
205 Furnace Whelp U :R: .30 .50
206 Goblin Elite Infantry C :R: .15 .25
207 Goblin King R :R: 3.50 4.25
208 Goblin Lore U :R: .30 .50
209 Goblin Piker C :R: .15 .25
210 Goblin Sky Raider C :R: .15 .25
211 Guerrilla Tactics U :R: .30 .50
212 Hill Giant C :R: .15 .25
213 Incinerate C :R: .15 .25
214 Kamahl, Pit Fighter R :R: .30 .50
215 Lava Axe C :R: .15 .25
216 Lavaborn Muse R :R: .30 .50
217 Lightning Elemental C :R: .15 .25
218 Manabarbs R :R: .30 .50
219 Mogg Fanatic U :R: .30 .50
220 Orcish Artillery U :R: .30 .50
221 Prodigal Pyromancer C :R: .15 .25
222 Pyroclasm U :R: .30 .50
223 Rage Weaver U :R: .30 .50
224 Raging Goblin C :R: .15 .25
225 Relentless Assault R :R: .40 .60
226 Rock Badger C :R: .15 .25
227 Scoria Wurm R :R: .30 .50
228 Seismic Assault R :R: 1.75 2.25
229 Shatterstorm U :R: .30 .50
230 Shivan Dragon R :R: .30 .50
231 Shivan Hellkite R :R: .30 .50
232 Shock C :R: .15 .25
233 Shunt R :R: .30 .50
234 Siege-Gang Commander R :R: 1.75 2.25
235 Smash C :R: .15 .25
236 Soulblast R :R: .30 .50
237 Spark Elemental U :R: .30 .50
238 Spitting Earth C :R: .15 .25
239 Squee, Goblin Nabob R :R: 3.25 3.75
240 Stun C :R: .15 .25
241 Sudden Impact U :R: .30 .50
242 Threaten U :R: .30 .50
243 Thundering Giant U :R: .30 .50
244 Uncontrollable Anger C :R: .15 .25
245 Viashino Runner C :R: .15 .25
246 Viashino Sandscout C :R: .15 .25
247 Wall of Fire U :R: .30 .50
248 Warp World R :R: .30 .50
249 Abundance R :G: 2.75 3.25
250 Aggressive Urge C :G: .15 .25
251 Avatar of Might R :G: .50 .75
252 Birds of Paradise R :G: 5.00 7.00
253 Blanchwood Armor U :G: .30 .50
254 Canopy Spider C :G: .15 .25
255 Civic Wayfinder C :G: .15 .25
256 Commune with Nature C :G: .15 .25
257 Craw Wurm C :G: .15 .25
258 Creeping Mold U :G: .30 .50
259 Elven Riders U :G: .30 .50
260 Elvish Berserker C :G: .15 .25
261 Elvish Champion R :G: 4.00 5.50
262 Elvish Piper R :G: 6.00 8.00
263 Enormous Baloth U :G: .30 .50
264 Femeref Archers U :G: .30 .50
265 Gaea's Herald R :G: 1.00 1.50
266 Giant Growth C :G: .15 .25
267 Giant Spider C :G: .15 .25
268 Grizzly Bears C :G: .15 .25
269 Hunted Wumpus U :G: .30 .50
270 Hurricane R :G: .30 .50
271 Joiner Adept R :G: 3.00 3.50
272 Karplusan Strider U :G: .30 .50
273 Kavu Climber C :G: .15 .25
274 Llanowar Elves C :G: .15 .25
275 Llanowar Sentinel C :G: .15 .25
276 Lure U :G: .30 .50
277 Might of Oaks R :G: .30 .50
278 Might Weaver U :G: .30 .50
279 Mirri, Cat Warrior R :G: .75 1.25
280 Molimo, Maro-Sorcerer R :G: .30 .50
281 Natural Spring C :G: .15 .25
282 Naturalize C :G: .15 .25
283 Overgrowth C :G: .15 .25
284 Overrun U :G: .30 .50
285 Pincher Beetles C :G: .15 .25
286 Primal Rage U :G: .30 .50
287 Quirion Dryad R :G: .30 .50
288 Rampant Growth C :G: .15 .25
289 Recollect U :G: .30 .50
290 Regeneration U :G: .30 .50
291 Rhox R :G: .30 .50
292 Root Maze R :G: .30 .50
293 Rootwalla C :G: .15 .25
294 Rushwood Dryad C :G: .15 .25
295 Scion of the Wild R :G: .30 .50
296 Seedborn Muse R :G: 18.00 22.00
297 Skyshroud Ranger C :G: .15 .25
298 Spined Wurm C :G: .15 .25
299 Stalking Tiger C :G: .15 .25
300 Stampeding Wildebeests U :G: .30 .50
301 Sylvan Basilisk U :G: .30 .50
302 Sylvan Scrying U :G: .30 .50
303 Tangle Spider U :G: .30 .50
304 Treetop Bracers C :G: .15 .25
305 Troll Ascetic R :G: .50 .75
306 Upwelling R :G: .30 .50
307 Verdant Force R :G: .50 .75
308 Viridian Shaman U :G: .30 .50
309 Wall of Wood C :G: .15 .25
310 Yavimaya Enchantress U :G: .30 .50
311 Angelic Blessing C :W: .15 .25
312 Bottle Gnomes U :A: .30 .50
313 Chimeric Staff R :A: .30 .50
314 Chromatic Star U :A: .30 .50
315 Citanul Flute R :A: 1.75 2.00
316 Coat of Arms R :A: 6.00 8.00
317 Colossus of Sardia R :A: .30 .50
318 Composite Golem U :A: .30 .50
319 Crucible of Worlds R :A: 55.00 60.00
320 Demon's Horn U :A: .30 .50
321 Doubling Cube R :A: 8.00 10.00
322 Dragon's Claw U :A: .30 .50
323 Fountain of Youth U :A: .30 .50
324 The Hive R :A: .30 .50
325 Howling Mine R :A: 3.50 4.00
326 Icy Manipulator U :A: .30 .50
327 Jayemdae Tome R :A: .30 .50
328 Juggernaut U :A: .30 .50
329 Kraken's Eye U :A: .30 .50
330 Legacy Weapon R :A: .75 1.25
331 Leonin Scimitar U :A: .30 .50
332 Loxodon Warhammer R :A: .75 1.25
333 Mantis Engine U :A: .30 .50
334 Millstone R :A: .30 .50
335 Mind Stone U :A: .30 .50
336 Ornithopter U :A: .30 .50
337 Phyrexian Vault U :A: .30 .50
338 Pithing Needle R :A: 2.50 3.00
339 Platinum Angel R :A: 5.00 7.00
340 Razormane Masticore R :A: .30 .50
341 Rod of Ruin U :A: .30 .50
342 Sculpting Steel R :A: 4.00 6.00
343 Spellbook U :A: .30 .50
344 Steel Golem U :A: .30 .50
345 Whispersilk Cloak U :A: .30 .50
346 Wurm's Tooth U :A: .30 .50
347 Adarkar Wastes R :L: 8.00 10.00
348 Battlefield Forge R :L: 1.75 2.25
349 Brushland R :L: 12.00 14.00
350 Caves of Koilos R :L: 2.25 2.75
351 Faerie Conclave U :L: .30 .50
352 Forbidding Watchtower U :L: .30 .50
353 Ghitu Encampment U :L: .30 .50
354 Karplusan Forest R :L: 6.00 8.00
355 Llanowar Wastes R :L: 2.50 3.00
356 Quicksand U :L: .30 .50
357 Shivan Reef R :L: 3.25 3.75
358 Spawning Pool U :L: .30 .50
359 Sulfurous Springs R :L: 4.00 5.50
360 Terramorphic Expanse C :L: .15 .25
361 Treetop Village U :L: .30 .50
362 Underground River R :L: 4.00 5.00
363 Yavimaya Coast R :L: 2.25 2.75
364 Plains :L: .15 .25
365 Plains :L: .15 .25
366 Plains :L: .15 .25
367 Plains :L: .15 .25
368 Island :L: .15 .25
369 Island :L: .15 .25
370 Island :L: .15 .25
371 Island :L: .15 .25
372 Swamp :L: .15 .25
373 Swamp :L: .15 .25
374 Swamp :L: .15 .25
375 Swamp :L: .15 .25
376 Mountain :L: .15 .25
377 Mountain :L: .15 .25
378 Mountain :L: .15 .25
379 Mountain :L: .15 .25
380 Forest :L: .15 .25
381 Forest :L: .15 .25
382 Forest :L: .15 .25
383 Forest :L: .15 .25

2007 Magic The Gathering Tenth Edition Tokens

1 Soldier .15 .25
2 Zombie .60 1.00
3 Dragon .60 1.00
4 Goblin .20 .30
5 Saproling .15 .25
6 Wasp .15 .25

2009 Magic The Gathering Magic 2010

COMPLETE SET (234) 175.00 250.00
BOOSTER BOX (36 PACKS) 150.00 200.00
BOOSTER PACK (15 CARDS) 6.00 8.00
THEME DECK 10.00 20.00
FAT PACK 60.00 120.00
RELEASED ON JULY 17, 2009
1 Ajani Goldmane M :W: 7.00 9.00
2 Angel's Mercy C :W: .15 .25
3 Armored Ascension U :W: .20 .35
4 Baneslayer Angel M :W: 7.00 9.00
5 Blinding Mage C :W: .15 .25
6 Captain of the Watch R :W: .50 .75
7 Celestial Purge U :W: .20 .35
8 Divine Verdict C :W: .15 .25
9 Elite Vanguard U :W: .20 .35
10 Excommunicate C :W: .15 .25
11 Glorious Charge C :W: .15 .25
12 Griffin Sentinel C :W: .15 .25
13 Guardian Seraph R :W: .40 .60
14 Harm's Way U :W: .20 .35
15 Holy Strength C :W: .15 .25
16 Honor of the Pure R :W: 1.75 2.00
17 Indestructibility R :W: .50 .75
18 Lifelink C :W: .15 .25
19 Lightwielder Paladin R :W: .25 .40
20 Mesa Enchantress R :W: .25 .40
21 Open the Vaults R :W: 1.50 1.75
22 Pacifism C :W: .15 .25
23 Palace Guard C :W: .15 .25
24 Planar Cleansing R :W: .25 .40
25 Razorfoot Griffin C :W: .15 .25
26 Rhox Pikemaster U :W: .20 .35
27 Righteousness U :W: .20 .35
28 Safe Passage C :W: .15 .25
29 Serra Angel U :W: .20 .35
30 Siege Mastodon C :W: .15 .25
31 Silence R :W: .75 1.15
32 Silvercoat Lion C :W: .15 .25
33 Solemn Offering C :W: .15 .25
34 Soul Warden C :W: .15 .25
35 Stormfront Pegasus C :W: .15 .25
36 Tempest of Light U :W: .20 .35
37 Undead Slayer U :W: .20 .35
38 Veteran Armorsmith C :W: .15 .25
39 Veteran Swordsmith C :W: .15 .25
40 Wall of Faith C :W: .15 .25
41 White Knight U :W: .20 .35
42 Air Elemental U :B: .20 .35
43 Alluring Siren U :B: .20 .35
44 Cancel C :B: .15 .25
45 Clone R :B: .25 .40
46 Convincing Mirage C :B: .15 .25
47 Coral Merfolk C :B: .15 .25
48 Disorient C :B: .15 .25
49 Divination C :B: .15 .25
50 Djinn of Wishes R :B: .25 .40
51 Essence Scatter C :B: .15 .25
52 Fabricate U :B: 2.00 3.50
53 Flashfreeze U :B: .20 .35
54 Hive Mind R :B: 2.00 2.50
55 Horned Turtle C :B: .15 .25
56 Ice Cage C :B: .15 .25
57 Illusionary Servant C :B: .15 .25
58 Jace Beleren M :B: 7.00 8.00
59 Jump C :B: .15 .25
60 Levitation U :B: .20 .35
61 Merfolk Looter C :B: .15 .25
62 Merfolk Sovereign R :B: .50 .75
63 Mind Control U :B: .20 .35
64 Mind Spring R :B: .25 .40

Card	Low	High
65 Negate C :B:	.15	.25
66 Phantom Warrior U :B:	.20	.35
67 Polymorph R :B:	.75	1.00
68 Ponder C :B:	.15	.25
69 Sage Owl C :B:	.15	.25
70 Serpent of the Endless Sea C :B:	.15	.25
71 Sleep U :B:	.20	.35
72 Snapping Drake C :B:	.15	.25
73 Sphinx Ambassador M :B:	3.25	3.75
74 Telepathy U :B:	.20	.35
75 Time Warp M :B:	15.00	18.00
76 Tome Scour C :B:	.15	.25
77 Traumatize R :B:	1.50	1.75
78 Twincast R :B:	2.00	3.00
79 Unsummon C :B:	.15	.25
80 Wall of Frost U :B:	.20	.35
81 Wind Drake C :B:	.15	.25
82 Zephyr Sprite C :B:	.15	.25
83 Acolyte of Xathrid C :K:	.15	.25
84 Assassinate C :K:	.15	.25
85 Black Knight U :K:	.20	.35
86 Bog Wraith U :K:	.20	.35
87 Cemetery Reaper R :K:	2.00	3.00
88 Child of Night C :K:	.15	.25
89 Consume Spirit U :K:	.20	.35
90 Deathmark U :K:	.20	.35
91 Diabolic Tutor U :K:	.20	.35
92 Disentomb C :K:	.15	.25
93 Doom Blade C :K:	.15	.25
94 Dread Warlock C :K:	.15	.25
95 Drudge Skeletons C :K:	.15	.25
96 Duress C :K:	.15	.25
97 Gravedigger C :K:	.15	.25
98 Haunting Echoes R :K:	.25	.40
99 Howling Banshee U :K:	.20	.35
100 Hypnotic Specter R :K:	1.50	1.75
101 Kelinore Bat C :K:	.15	.25
102 Liliana Vess M :K:	5.00	7.00
103 Looming Shade C :K:	.15	.25
104 Megrim U :K:	.20	.35
105 Mind Rot C :K:	.15	.25
106 Mind Shatter R :K:	.25	.40
107 Nightmare R :K:	.25	.40
108 Relentless Rats U :K:	1.25	2.00
109 Rise from the Grave U :K:	.20	.35
110 Royal Assassin R :K:	.50	.75
111 Sanguine Bond R :K:	2.00	2.50
112 Sign in Blood C :K:	.15	.25
113 Soul Bleed C :K:	.15	.25
114 Tendrils of Corruption C :K:	.15	.25
115 Underworld Dreams R :K:	2.00	3.00
116 Unholy Strength C :K:	.15	.25
117 Vampire Aristocrat C :K:	.15	.25
118 Vampire Nocturnus M :K:	3.00	5.00
119 Wall of Bone U :K:	.20	.35
120 Warpath Ghoul C :K:	.15	.25
121 Weakness C :K:	.15	.25
122 Xathrid Demon M :K:	.75	1.00
123 Zombie Goliath C :K:	.15	.25
124 Act of Treason U :R:	.20	.35
125 Ball Lightning R :R:	1.75	2.25
126 Berserkers of Blood Ridge C :R:	.15	.25
127 Bogardan Hellkite M :R:	.75	1.25
128 Burning Inquiry C :R:	.15	.25
129 Burst of Speed C :R:	.15	.25
130 Canyon Minotaur C :R:	.15	.25
131 Capricious Efreet R :R:	.25	.40
132 Chandra Nalaar M :R:	3.25	3.75
133 Dragon Whelp U :R:	.20	.35
134 Earthquake R :R:	.25	.40
135 Fiery Hellhound C :R:	.15	.25
136 Fireball U :R:	.20	.35
137 Firebreathing C :R:	.15	.25
138 Goblin Artillery U :R:	.20	.35
139 Goblin Chieftain R :R:	4.00	6.00
140 Goblin Piker C :R:	.15	.25
141 Ignite Disorder U :R:	.20	.35
142 Inferno Elemental U :R:	.20	.35
143 Jackal Familiar C :R:	.15	.25
144 Kindled Fury C :R:	.15	.25
145 Lava Axe C :R:	.15	.25
146 Lightning Bolt C :R:	.15	.25
147 Lightning Elemental C :R:	.15	.25
148 Magma Phoenix R :R:	.25	.40
149 Manabarbs R :R:	.25	.40
150 Panic Attack C :R:	.15	.25
151 Prodigal Pyromancer U :R:	.20	.35
152 Pyroclasm U :R:	.20	.35
153 Raging Goblin C :R:	.15	.25
154 Seismic Strike C :R:	.15	.25
155 Shatter C :R:	.15	.25
156 Shivan Dragon R :R:	.25	.40
157 Siege-Gang Commander R :R:	1.75	2.00
158 Sparkmage Apprentice C :R:	.15	.25
159 Stone Giant U :R:	.20	.35
160 Trumpet Blast C :R:	.15	.25
161 Viashino Spearhunter C :R:	.15	.25
162 Wall of Fire U :R:	.20	.35
163 Warp World R :R:	.25	.40
164 Yawning Fissure C :R:	.15	.25
165 Acidic Slime U :G:	.20	.35
166 Ant Queen R :G:	.50	.75
167 Awakener Druid U :G:	.20	.35
168 Birds of Paradise R :G:	5.00	7.00
169 Borderland Ranger C :G:	.15	.25
170 Bountiful Harvest C :G:	.15	.25
171 Bramble Creeper C :G:	.15	.25
172 Centaur Courser C :G:	.15	.25
173 Craw Wurm C :G:	.15	.25
174 Cudgel Troll U :G:	.20	.35
175 Deadly Recluse C :G:	.15	.25
176 Elvish Archdruid R :G:	2.00	2.50
177 Elvish Piper R :G:	5.00	7.00
178 Elvish Visionary C :G:	.15	.25
179 Emerald Oryx C :G:	.15	.25
180 Enormous Baloth U :G:	.20	.35
181 Entangling Vines C :G:	.15	.25
182 Fog C :G:	.15	.25
183 Garruk Wildspeaker M :G:	6.00	8.00
184 Giant Growth C :G:	.15	.25
185 Giant Spider C :G:	.15	.25
186 Great Sable Stag R :G:	.50	.75
187 Howl of the Night Pack U :G:	.20	.35
188 Kalonian Behemoth R :G:	.50	.75
189 Llanowar Elves C :G:	.15	.25
190 Lurking Predators R :G:	4.00	6.00
191 Master of the Wild Hunt M :G:	10.00	13.00
192 Might of Oaks R :G:	.25	.40
193 Mist Leopard C :G:	.15	.25
194 Mold Adder U :G:	.20	.35
195 Naturalize C :G:	.15	.25
196 Nature's Spiral U :G:	.20	.35
197 Oakenform C :G:	.15	.25
198 Overrun U :G:	.20	.35
199 Prized Unicorn U :G:	.20	.35
200 Protean Hydra M :G:	1.75	2.00
201 Rampant Growth C :G:	.15	.25
202 Regenerate C :G:	.15	.25
203 Runeclaw Bear C :G:	.15	.25
204 Stampeding Rhino C :G:	.15	.25
205 Windstorm U :G:	.20	.35
206 Angel's Feather U :A:	.20	.35
207 Coat of Arms R :A:	6.00	8.00
208 Darksteel Colossus M :A:	5.00	7.00
209 Demon's Horn U :A:	.20	.35
210 Dragon's Claw U :A:	.20	.35
211 Gorgon Flail U :A:	.20	.35
212 Howling Mine R :A:	2.00	3.00
213 Kraken's Eye U :A:	.20	.35
214 Magebane Armor R :A:	.25	.40
215 Mirror of Fate R :A:	.25	.40
216 Ornithopter U :A:	.20	.35
217 Pithing Needle R :A:	2.00	2.50
218 Platinum Angel M :A:	5.00	7.00
219 Rod of Ruin U :A:	.20	.35
220 Spellbook U :A:	.60	1.00
221 Whispersilk Cloak U :A:	.20	.35
222 Wurm's Tooth U :A:	.20	.35
223 Dragonskull Summit R :L:	2.00	2.50
224 Drowned Catacomb R :L:	2.00	2.75
225 Gargoyle Castle R :L:	.25	.40
226 Glacial Fortress R :L:	1.75	2.25
227 Rootbound Crag R :L:	1.50	1.75
228 Sunpetal Grove R :L:	1.75	2.25
229 Terramorphic Expanse C :L:	.15	.25
230 Plains C :L:	.15	.25
231 Plains C :L:	.15	.25
232 Plains C :L:	.15	.25
233 Plains C :L:	.15	.25
234 Island C :L:	.15	.25
235 Island C :L:	.15	.25
236 Island C :L:	.15	.25
237 Island C :L:	.15	.25
238 Swamp C :L:	.15	.25
239 Swamp C :L:	.15	.25
240 Swamp C :L:	.15	.25
241 Swamp C :L:	.15	.25
242 Mountain C :L:	.15	.25
243 Mountain C :L:	.15	.25
244 Mountain C :L:	.15	.25
245 Mountain C :L:	.15	.25
246 Forest C :L:	.10	.20
247 Forest C :L:	.15	.25
248 Forest C :L:	.15	.25
249 Forest C :L:	.15	.25

2009 Magic The Gathering Magic 2010 Tokens

Card	Low	High
1 Avatar	.60	1.00
2 Soldier	.12	.20
3 Zombie	.12	.20
4 Goblin	.15	.25
5 Beast	.20	.30
6 Insect	.25	.35
7 Wolf	.12	.20
8 Gargoyle	.12	.20

2010 Magic The Gathering Magic 2011

Card	Low	High
COMPLETE SET (249)	200.00	275.00
BOOSTER BOX (36 PACKS)	150.00	200.00
BOOSTER PACK (15 CARDS)	4.00	6.00
THEME DECK	8.00	12.00
FAT PACK	30.00	50.00
RELEASED ON JULY 16, 2010		
1 Ajani Goldmane M :W:	6.00	8.00
2 Ajani's Mantra C :W:	.15	.25
3 Ajani's Pridemate U :W:	.20	.35
4 Angelic Arbiter R :W:	1.00	1.50
5 Armored Ascension U :W:	.20	.35
6 Assault Griffin C :W:	.15	.25
7 Baneslayer Angel M :W:	7.50	9.00
8 Blinding Mage C :W:	.15	.25
9 Celestial Purge U :W:	.20	.35
10 Cloud Crusader C :W:	.15	.25
11 Condemn U :W:	.20	.35
12 Day of Judgment R :W:	2.00	2.50
13 Elite Vanguard U :W:	.20	.35
14 Excommunicate C :W:	.15	.25
15 Goldenglow Moth C :W:	.15	.25
16 Holy Strength C :W:	.15	.25
17 Honor of the Pure R :W:	1.25	1.75
18 Infantry Veteran C :W:	.15	.25
19 Inspired Charge C :W:	.15	.25
20 Knight Exemplar R :W:	2.50	3.00
21 Leyline of Sanctity R :W:	11.00	13.00
22 Mighty Leap C :W:	.15	.25
23 Pacifism C :W:	.15	.25
24 Palace Guard C :W:	.15	.25
25 Roc Egg U :W:	.20	.35
26 Safe Passage C :W:	.15	.25
27 Serra Angel U :W:	.20	.35
28 Serra Ascendant R :W:	15.00	17.00
29 Siege Mastodon C :W:	.15	.25
30 Silence R :W:	.75	1.15
31 Silvercoat Lion C :W:	.15	.25
32 Solemn Offering C :W:	.15	.25
33 Squadron Hawk C :W:	.15	.25
34 Stormfront Pegasus C :W:	.15	.25
35 Sun Titan M :W:	2.00	2.50
36 Tireless Missionaries C :W:	.15	.25
37 Vengeful Archon R :W:	.25	.40
38 Warlord's Axe U	.20	.35
39 White Knight U :W:	.20	.35
40 Wild Griffin C :W:	.15	.25
41 Aether Adept C :B:	.15	.25
42 Air Servant U :B:	.20	.35
43 Alluring Siren U :B:	.20	.35
44 Armored Cancrix C :B:	.15	.25
45 Augury Owl C :B:	.15	.25
46 Azure Drake U :B:	.20	.35
47 Call to Mind U :B:	.20	.35
48 Cancel C :B:	.15	.25
49 Clone R :B:	.25	.40
50 Cloud Elemental C :B:	.15	.25
51 Conundrum Sphinx R :B:	.25	.40
52 Diminish C :B:	.15	.25
53 Flashfreeze U :B:	.20	.35
54 Foresee C :B:	.15	.25
55 Frost Titan M :B:	.75	1.00
56 Harbor Serpent C :B:	.15	.25
57 Ice Cage C :B:	.15	.25
58 Jace Beleren M :B:	6.50	8.00
59 Jace's Erasure C :B:	.15	.25
60 Jace's Ingenuity U :B:	.20	.35
61 Leyline of Anticipation R :B:	6.50	8.00
62 Mana Leak C :B:	.15	.25
63 Maritime Guard C :B:	.15	.25
64 Mass Polymorph R :B:	.25	.40
65 Merfolk Sovereign R :B:	.50	.75
66 Merfolk Spy C :B:	.15	.25
67 Mind Control U :B:	.20	.35
68 Negate C :B:	.15	.25
69 Phantom Beast C :B:	.15	.25
70 Preordain C :B:	1.00	1.50
71 Redirect R :B:	.25	.40
72 Scroll Thief C :B:	.15	.25
73 Sleep U :B:	.20	.35
74 Stormtide Leviathan R :B:	.25	.40
75 Time Reversal M :B:	.75	1.00
76 Tome Scour C :B:	.15	.25
77 Traumatize R :B:	1.25	1.75
78 Unsummon C :B:	.15	.25
79 Wall of Frost U :B:	.20	.35
80 Water Servant U :B:	.20	.35
81 Assassinate C :K:	.15	.25
82 Barony Vampire C :K:	.15	.25
83 Black Knight U :K:	.20	.35
84 Blood Tithe C :K:	.15	.25
85 Bloodthrone Vampire C :K:	.15	.25
86 Bog Raiders C :K:	.15	.25
87 Captivating Vampire R :K:	6.00	7.50
88 Child of Night C :K:	.15	.25
89 Corrupt U :K:	.20	.35
90 Dark Tutelage R :K:	.25	.40
91 Deathmark U :K:	.20	.35
92 Demon of Death's Gate M :K:	4.00	5.00
93 Diabolic Tutor U :K:	.20	.35
94 Disentomb C :K:	.15	.25
95 Doom Blade C :K:	.15	.25
96 Duress C :K:	.15	.25
97 Grave Titan M :K:	4.50	6.00
98 Gravedigger C :K:	.15	.25
99 Haunting Echoes R :K:	.25	.40
100 Howling Banshee U :K:	.20	.35
101 Leyline of the Void R :K:	12.00	14.00
102 Liliana Vess M :K:	5.00	7.00
103 Liliana's Caress U :K:	2.00	3.50
104 Liliana's Specter C :K:	.15	.25
105 Mind Rot C :K:	.15	.25
106 Nantuko Shade R :K:	.30	.50
107 Necrotic Plague C :K:	.15	.25
108 Nether Horror C :K:	.15	.25
109 Nightwing Shade C :K:	.15	.25
110 Phylactery Lich R :K:	.25	.40
111 Quag Sickness C :K:	.15	.25
112 Rssmblng Skltn U :K:	.20	.35
113 Relentless Rats U :K:	.20	.35
114 Rise from the Grave U :K:	.20	.35
115 Rotting Legion C :K:	.15	.25
116 Royal Assassin R :K:	.50	.75
117 Sign in Blood C :K:	.15	.25
118 Stabbing Pain C :K:	.15	.25
119 Unholy Strength C :K:	.15	.25
120 Viscera Seer C :K:	.60	.25
121 Act of Treason U :R:	.20	.35
122 Ancient Hellkite R :R:	.25	.40
123 Arc Runner C :R:	.15	.25
124 Berserkers of Blood Ridge C :R:	.15	.25
125 Bloodcrazed Goblin C :R:	.15	.25
126 Canyon Minotaur C :R:	.15	.25
127 Chandra Nalaar M :R:	3.00	4.00
128 Chandra's Outrage C :R:	.15	.25
129 Chandra's Spitfire U :R:	.20	.35
130 Combust U :R:	.20	.35
131 Cyclops Gladiator R :R:	.25	.40
132 Demolish C :R:	.15	.25
133 Destructive Force R :R:	.25	.40
134 Earth Servant U :R:	.20	.35
135 Ember Hauler U :R:	.20	.35
136 Fiery Hellhound C :R:	.15	.25
137 Fire Servant U :R:	.20	.35
138 Fireball U :R:	.20	.35
139 Fling C :R:	.15	.25
140 Goblin Balloon Brigade C :R:	.15	.25
141 Goblin Chieftain R :R:	4.50	5.50
142 Goblin Piker C :R:	.15	.25
143 Goblin Tunneler C :R:	.15	.25
144 Hoarding Dragon R :R:	.25	.40
145 Incite C :R:	.15	.25
146 Inferno Titan M :R:	.75	1.25
147 Lava Axe R :R:	.25	.40
148 Leyline of Punishment R :R:	2.00	3.00
149 Lightning Bolt C :R:	1.50	2.50
150 Magma Phoenix R :R:	.25	.40
151 Manic Vandal C :R:	.15	.25
152 Prodigal Pyromancer U :R:	.20	.35
153 Pyretic Ritual C :R:	.15	.25
154 Pyroclasm U :R:	.20	.35
155 Reverberate R :R:	.50	.75
156 Shiv's Embrace U :R:	.20	.35
157 Thunder Strike C :R:	.15	.25
158 Volcanic Strength C :R:	.15	.25
159 Vulshok Berserker C :R:	.15	.25
160 Wild Evocation R :R:	.25	.40
161 Acidic Slime U :G:	.20	.35
162 Autumn's Veil U :G:	.20	.35
163 Awakener Druid U :B:	.20	.35
164 Back to Nature U :G:	.20	.35
165 Birds of Paradise R :G:	5.00	7.00
166 Brindle Boar C :G:	.15	.25
167 Cudgel Troll U :G:	.20	.35
168 Cultivate C :G:	.75	1.25
169 Dryad's Favor C :G:	.15	.25
170 Duskdale Wurm U :G:	.20	.35
171 Elvish Archdruid R :G:	2.00	2.50
172 Fauna Shaman R :G:	9.00	11.00
173 Fog C :G:	.15	.25
174 Gaea's Revenge M :G:	1.00	1.25
175 Garruk Wildspeaker M :G:	7.50	9.00
176 Garruk's Companion C :G:	.15	.25
177 Garruk's Packleader U :G:	.20	.35
178 Giant Growth C :G:	.15	.25
179 Giant Spider C :G:	.15	.25
180 Greater Basilisk C :G:	.15	.25
181 Hornet Sting C :G:	.15	.25
182 Hunters' Feast C :G:	.15	.25
183 Leyline of Vitality R :G:	.75	1.00
184 Llanowar Elves C :G:	.15	.25
185 Mitotic Slime R :G:	.25	.40
186 Naturalize C :G:	.15	.25
187 Nature's Spiral U :G:	.20	.35
188 Obstinate Baloth U :G:	.20	.35
189 Ovrwlmng Stmpd R :G:	.50	.75
190 Plummet C :G:	.15	.25
191 Primal Cocoon C :G:	.15	.25
192 Primeval Titan M :G:	7.00	9.00
193 Prized Unicorn U :G:	.20	.35
194 Protean Hydra R :G:	1.50	2.00
195 Runeclaw Bear C :G:	.15	.25
196 Sacred Wolf C :G:	.15	.25
197 Spined Wurm C :G:	.15	.25
198 Sylvan Ranger C :G:	.15	.25
199 Wall of Vines C :G:	.15	.25
200 Yavimaya Wurm C :G:	.15	.25
201 Angel's Feather U	.20	.35
202 Brittle Effigy R	.25	.40
203 Crystal Ball U	.20	.35
204 Demon's Horn U	.20	.35
205 Dragon's Claw U	.20	.35
206 Elixir of Immortality U	.20	.35
207 Gargoyle Sentinel U	.20	.35
208 Jinxed Idol R	.25	.40
209 Juggernaut U	.20	.35
210 Kraken's Eye U	.20	.35
211 Ornithopter U	.20	.35
212 Platinum Angel M	5.00	7.00
213 Sorcerer's Strongbox U	.20	.35
214 Steel Overseer R	10.00	12.00
215 Stone Golem U	.20	.35
216 Sword of Vengeance R	.75	1.00
217 Temple Bell R	.30	.50
218 Triskelion R	.30	.50
219 Voltaic Key U	.20	.35
220 War Priest of Thune U :W:	.20	.35
221 Whispersilk Cloak U	.20	.35
222 Wurm's Tooth U	.20	.35
223 Dragonskull Summit R :L:	2.00	2.50
224 Drowned Catacomb R :L:	2.50	3.00
225 Glacial Fortress R :L:	1.75	2.25
226 Mystifying Maze R :L:	1.25	1.75
227 Rootbound Crag R :L:	1.25	1.75
228 Sunpetal Grove R :L:	1.75	2.25
229 Terramorphic Expanse C :L:	.15	.25
230 Plains L :L:	.15	.25
231 Plains - B L :L:	.15	.25
232 Plains - C L :L:	.15	.25
233 Plains - D L :L:	.15	.25
234 Island L :L:	.15	.25
235 Island - B L :L:	.15	.25
236 Island - C L :L:	.15	.25
237 Island - D L :L:	.15	.25
238 Swamp L :L:	.15	.25
239 Swamp - B L :L:	.15	.25
240 Swamp - C L :L:	.15	.25
241 Swamp - D L :L:	.15	.25
242 Mountain L :L:	.15	.25
243 Mountain - B L :L:	.15	.25
244 Mountain - C L :L:	.15	.25
245 Mountain - D L :L:	.15	.25
246 Forest - A L :L:	.15	.25
247 Forest - B L :L:	.15	.25
248 Forest - C L :L:	.15	.25
249 Forest - D L :L:	.15	.25
R1 Rules Tip: Planeswalker Cards	.15	.25
R2 Rules Tip: Parts of the Turn	.15	.25
R3 Rules Tip: Deathtouch	.15	.25
R4 Rules Tip: Tokens and Counters	.15	.25
R5 Rules Tip: Building a Deck	.15	.25
R6 Rules Tip: Limited Play	.15	.25
R7 Rules Tip: The Stack	.15	.25
R8 Rules Tip: Gatherer Card Database	.15	.25
R9 Rules Tip: Leylines	.15	.25

2010 Magic The Gathering Magic 2011 Foil

COMPLETE SET (249)	150.00	300.00

2010 Magic The Gathering Magic 2011 Tokens

1 Avatar	.45	.60
2 Bird	.10	.15
3 Zombie	.10	.15
4 Beast	.10	.15
5 Ooze	.10	.15
6 Ooze	.30	.40

2011 Magic The Gathering Magic 2012

COMPLETE SET (249)	150.00	225.00
BOOSTER BOX (36 PACKS)	90.00	110.00
BOOSTER PACK (15 CARDS)	3.00	4.00
RELEASED ON JULY 15, 2011		
1 Aegis Angel R :W:	.40	.60
2 Alabaster Mage U :W:	.20	.35
3 Angelic Destiny M :W:	6.00	8.00
4 Angel's Mercy C :W:	.15	.25
5 Arbalest Elite U :W:	.20	.35
6 Archon of Justice R :W:	.25	.40
7 Armored Warhorse C :W:	.15	.25
8 Assault Griffin C :W:	.15	.25
9 Auramancer C :W:	.15	.25
10 Benalish Veteran C :W:	.15	.25
11 Celestial Purge U :W:	.20	.35
12 Day of Judgment R :W:	2.00	2.50
13 Demystify C :W:	.15	.25
14 Divine Favor C :W:	.15	.25
15 Elite Vanguard U :W:	.20	.35
16 Gideon Jura M :W:	4.00	5.50
17 Gideon's Avenger R :W:	.50	.75
18 Gideon's Lawkeeper C :W:	.15	.25
19 Grand Abolisher R :W:	3.50	5.00
20 Griffin Rider C :W:	.15	.25
21 Griffin Sentinel C :W:	.15	.25
22 Guardians' Pledge C :W:	.15	.25
23 Honor of the Pure R :W:	1.50	2.00
24 Lifelink C :W:	.15	.25
25 Mesa Enchantress R :W:	.25	.40
26 Mighty Leap C :W:	.15	.25
27 Oblivion Ring U :W:	.20	.35
28 Pacifism C :W:	.15	.25
29 Peregrine Griffin C :W:	.15	.25
30 Personal Sanctuary R :W:	.25	.40
31 Pride Guardian C :W:	.15	.25
32 Roc Egg U :W:	.20	.35
33 Serra Angel U :W:	.20	.35
34 Siege Mastodon C :W:	.15	.25
35 Spirit Mantle U :W:	.20	.35
36 Stave Off C :W:	.15	.25
37 Stonehorn Dignitary C :W:	.15	.25
38 Stormfront Pegasus C :W:	.15	.25
39 Sun Titan M :W:	2.00	2.50
40 Timely Reinforcements U :W:	.20	.35
41 AEther Adept C :B:	.15	.25
42 Alluring Siren U :B:	.20	.35
43 Amphin Cutthroat C :B:	.15	.25
44 Aven Fleetwing C :B:	.15	.25
45 Azure Mage U :B:	.20	.35
46 Belltower Sphinx U :B:	.20	.35
47 Cancel C :B:	.15	.25
48 Chasm Drake C :B:	.15	.25
49 Coral Merfolk C :B:	.15	.25
50 Divination C :B:	.15	.25
51 Djinn of Wishes R :B:	.25	.40
52 Flashfreeze U :B:	.20	.35
53 Flight C :B:	.15	.25
54 Frost Breath C :B:	.15	.25
55 Frost Titan M :B:	.50	.75
56 Harbor Serpent C :B:	.15	.25
57 Ice Cage C :B:	.15	.25
58 Jace, Memory Adept M :B:	4.00	6.00
59 Jace's Archivist R :B:	.25	.40
60 Jace's Erasure C :B:	.15	.25
61 Levitation U :B:	.20	.35
62 Lord of the Unreal R :B:	.50	.75
63 Mana Leak C :B:	.15	.25
64 Master Thief U :B:	.20	.35
65 Merfolk Looter C :B:	.15	.25
66 Merfolk Mesmerist C :B:	.15	.25
67 Mind Control U :B:	.20	.35
68 Mind Unbound R :B:	.25	.40
69 Negate C :B:	.15	.25
70 Phantasmal Bear C :B:	.15	.25
71 Phantasmal Dragon U :B:	.20	.35
72 Phantasmal Image R :B:	6.00	8.00
73 Ponder C :B:	.15	.25
74 Redirect R :B:	.25	.40
75 Skywinder Drake C :B:	.15	.25
76 Sphinx of Uthuun R :B:	.25	.40
77 Time Reversal M :B:	.75	1.00
78 Turn to Frog U :B:	.20	.35
79 Unsummon C :B:	.15	.25
80 Visions of Beyond R :B:	6.00	8.00
81 Blood Seeker C :K:	.15	.25
82 Bloodlord of Vaasgoth M :K:	1.00	1.50
83 Bloodrage Vampire C :K:	.15	.25
84 Brink of Disaster C :K:	.15	.25
85 Call to the Grave R :K:	.75	1.00
86 Cemetery Reaper R :K:	2.50	3.00
87 Child of Night C :K:	.15	.25
88 Consume Spirit U :K:	.20	.35
89 Dark Favor C :K:	.15	.25
90 Deathmark U :K:	.20	.35
91 Devouring Swarm C :K:	.15	.25
92 Diabolic Tutor U :K:	.20	.35
93 Disentomb C :K:	.15	.25
94 Distress C :K:	.15	.25
95 Doom Blade C :K:	.15	.25
96 Drifting Shade C :K:	.15	.25
97 Duskhunter Bat C :K:	.15	.25
98 Grave Titan M :K:	4.00	6.00
99 Gravedigger C :K:	.15	.25
100 Hideous Visage C :K:	.15	.25
101 Mind Rot C :K:	.15	.25
102 Monomania R :K:	.25	.40
103 Onyx Mage U :K:	.20	.35
104 Reassembling Skeleton U :K:	.20	.35
105 Royal Assassin R :K:	.40	.60
106 Rune-Scarred Demon R :K:	4.00	6.00
107 Sengir Vampire U :K:	.20	.35
108 Smallpox U :K:	.20	.35
109 Sorin Markov M :K:	14.00	16.00
110 Sorin's Thirst C :K:	.15	.25
111 Sorin's Vengeance R :K:	.75	1.25
112 Sutured Ghoul R :K:	.25	.40
113 Taste of Blood C :K:	.15	.25
114 Tormented Soul C :K:	.15	.25
115 Vampire Outcasts U :K:	.20	.35
116 Vengeful Pharaoh R :K:	.25	.40
117 Warpath Ghoul C :K:	.15	.25
118 Wring Flesh C :K:	.15	.25
119 Zombie Goliath C :K:	.15	.25
120 Zombie Infestation U :K:	.20	.35
121 Act of Treason C :R:	.15	.25
122 Blood Ogre C :R:	.15	.25
123 Bonebreaker Giant C :R:	.15	.25
124 Chandra, the Firebrand M :R:	3.00	3.50
125 Chandra's Outrage C :R:	.15	.25
126 Chandra's Phoenix R :R:	.30	.50
127 Circle of Flame U :R:	.20	.35
128 Combust U :R:	.20	.35
129 Crimson Mage U :R:	.20	.35
130 Fiery Hellhound C :R:	.15	.25
131 Fireball U :R:	.20	.35
132 Firebreathing C :R:	.15	.25
133 Flameblast Dragon R :R:	.40	.60
134 Fling C :R:	.15	.25
135 Furyborn Hellkite M :R:	1.75	2.25
136 Goblin Arsonist C :R:	.15	.25
137 Goblin Bangchuckers U :R:	.20	.35
138 Goblin Chieftain R :R:	4.00	5.50
139 Goblin Fireslinger C :R:	.15	.25
140 Goblin Grenade U :R:	.20	.35
141 Goblin Piker C :R:	.15	.25
142 Goblin Tunneler C :R:	.15	.25
143 Goblin War Paint C :R:	.15	.25
144 Gorehorn Minotaurs C :R:	.15	.25
145 Grim Lavamancer R :R:	5.00	6.00
146 Incinerate C :R:	.15	.25
147 Inferno Titan M :R:	.75	1.25
148 Lava Axe C :R:	.15	.25
149 Lightning Elemental C :R:	.15	.25
150 Manabarbs R :R:	.25	.40
151 Manic Vandal C :R:	.15	.25
152 Reverberate R :R:	.40	.60
153 Scrambleverse R :R:	.25	.40
154 Shock C :R:	.15	.25
155 Slaughter Cry C :R:	.15	.25
156 Stormblood Berserker U :R:	.20	.35
157 Tectonic Rift U :R:	.20	.35
158 Volcanic Dragon U :R:	.20	.35
159 Wall of Torches C :R:	.15	.25
160 Warstorm Surge R :R:	.25	.40
161 Acidic Slime U :G:	.20	.35
162 Arachnus Spinner R :G:	.25	.40
163 Arachnus Web C :G:	.15	.25
164 Autumn's Veil U :G:	.20	.35
165 Birds of Paradise R :G:	5.00	7.00
166 Bountiful Harvest C :G:	.15	.25
167 Brindle Boar C :G:	.15	.25
168 Carnage Wurm U :G:	.20	.35
169 Cudgel Troll U :G:	.20	.35
170 Doubling Chant R :G:	.25	.40
171 Dungrove Elder R :G:	3.00	4.50
172 Elvish Archdruid R :G:	2.00	2.50
173 Fog C :G:	.15	.25
174 Garruk, Primal Hunter M :G:	4.00	6.00
175 Garruk's Companion C :G:	.15	.25
176 Garruk's Horde R :G:	.25	.40
177 Giant Spider C :G:	.15	.25
178 Gladecover Scout C :G:	.15	.25
179 Greater Basilisk C :G:	.15	.25
180 Hunter's Insight U :G:	.20	.35
181 Jade Mage U :G:	.20	.35
182 Llanowar Elves C :G:	.15	.25
183 Lure U :G:	.20	.35
184 Lurking Crocodile C :G:	.15	.25
185 Naturalize C :G:	.15	.25
186 Overrun U :G:	.20	.35
187 Plummet C :G:	.15	.25
188 Primeval Titan M :G:	7.00	9.00
189 Primordial Hydra M :G:	5.00	7.00
190 Rampant Growth C :G:	.15	.25
191 Reclaim C :G:	.15	.25
192 Rites of Flourishing R :G:	1.00	1.50
193 Runeclaw Bear C :G:	.15	.25
194 Sacred Wolf C :G:	.15	.25
195 Skinshifter R :G:	.40	.60
196 Stampeding Rhino C :G:	.15	.25
197 Stingerfling Spider U :G:	.20	.35
198 Titanic Growth C :G:	.15	.25
199 Trollhide C :G:	.15	.25
200 Vastwood Gorger C :G:	.15	.25
201 Adaptive Automaton R	3.00	4.50
202 Angel's Feather U	.20	.35
203 Crown of Empires U	.20	.35
204 Crumbling Colossus U	.20	.35
205 Demon's Horn U	.20	.35
206 Dragon's Claw U	.20	.35
207 Druidic Satchel R	.25	.40
208 Elixir of Immortality U	.20	.35
209 Greatsword U	.20	.35
210 Kite Shield U	.20	.35
211 Kraken's Eye U	.20	.35
212 Manalith C	.15	.25
213 Pentavus R	.25	.40
214 Quicksilver Amulet R	7.00	9.00
215 Rusted Sentinel U	.20	.35
216 Scepter of Empires U	.20	.35
217 Solemn Simulacrum R	3.00	4.00
218 Sundial of the Infinite R	.40	.60
219 Swiftfoot Boots U	.20	.35
220 Thran Golem U	.20	.35
221 Throne of Empires R	.25	.40
222 Worldslayer R	.30	.50
223 Wurm's Tooth U	.20	.35
224 Buried Ruin U	.20	.35
225 Dragonskull Summit R	2.00	2.50
226 Drowned Catacomb R	2.25	2.75
227 Glacial Fortress R	1.75	2.15
228 Rootbound Crag R	1.25	1.75
229 Sunpetal Grove R	1.75	2.25
230 Plains L	.15	.25
231 Plains L	.15	.25
232 Plains L	.15	.25
233 Plains L	.15	.25
234 Island L	.15	.25
235 Island L	.15	.25
236 Island L	.15	.25
237 Island L	.15	.25
238 Swamp L	.15	.25
239 Swamp L	.15	.25
240 Swamp L	.15	.25
241 Swamp L	.15	.25
242 Mountain L	.15	.25
243 Mountain L	.15	.25
244 Mountain L	.15	.25
245 Mountain L	.15	.25
246 Forest L	.15	.25
247 Forest L	.15	.25
248 Forest L	.15	.25
249 Forest L	.15	.25

2011 Magic The Gathering Magic 2012 Tokens

1 Bird	.10	.15
2 Soldier	.10	.15
3 Zombie	.12	.20
4 Beast	.10	.15
5 Saproling	.10	.15
6 Wurm	1.00	1.50
7 Pentavite	.10	.15

2012 Magic The Gathering Magic 2013

COMPLETE SET (260)	150.00	225.00
BOOSTER BOX (36 PACKS)	80.00	120.00
BOOSTER PACK (15 CARDS)	3.00	4.50
RELEASED ON JULY 26, 2012		
1 Ajani, Caller of the Pride M :W:	4.00	6.00
2 Ajani's Sunstriker C :W:	.15	.25
3 Angel's Mercy C :W:	.15	.25
4 Angelic Benediction U :W:	.20	.35
5 Attended Knight C :W:	.15	.25
6 Aven Squire C :W:	.15	.25
7 Battleflight Eagle C :W:	.15	.25
8 Captain of the Watch R :W:	.50	.75
9 Captain's Call C :W:	.15	.25
10 Crusader of Odric U :W:	.20	.35
11 Divine Favor C :W:	.15	.25
12 Divine Verdict C :W:	.15	.25
13 Erase C :W:	.15	.25
14 Faith's Reward R :W:	.75	1.00
15 Glorious Charge C :W:	.15	.25
16 Griffin Protector C :W:	.15	.25
17 Guardian Lions C :W:	.15	.25
18 Guardians of Akrasa C :W:	.15	.25
19 Healer of the Pride U :W:	.20	.35
20 Intrepid Hero R :W:	.75	1.00
21 Knight of Glory U :W:	.20	.35
22 Oblivion Ring U :W:	.20	.35
23 Odric, Master Tactician R :W:	1.25	1.75
24 Pacifism C :W:	.15	.25
25 Pillarfield Ox C :W:	.15	.25
26 Planar Cleansing R :W:	.25	.40
27 Prized Elephant U :W:	.20	.35
28 Rain of Blades U :W:	.20	.35
29 Rhox Faithmender R :W:	3.00	5.00
30 Safe Passage C :W:	.15	.25
31 Serra Angel U :W:	.20	.35
32 Serra Avatar M :W:	.75	1.25
33 Serra Avenger R :W:	1.75	2.00
34 Show of Valor C :W:	.15	.25
35 Silvercoat Lion C :W:	.15	.25
36 Sublime Archangel M :W:	6.00	8.00
37 Touch of the Eternal R :W:	.25	.40
38 War Falcon C :W:	.15	.25
39 War Priest of Thune U :W:	.20	.35
40 Warclamp Mastiff C :W:	.15	.25
41 Archaeomancer C :B:	.15	.25
42 Arctic Aven U :B:	.20	.35
43 Augur of Bolas U :B:	.20	.35
44 Battle of Wits R :B:	.25	.40
45 Clone R :B:	.25	.40
46 Courtly Provocateur U :B:	.20	.35
47 Divination C :B:	.15	.25
48 Downpour C :B:	.15	.25
49 Encrust C :B:	.15	.25
50 Essence Scatter C :B:	.15	.25
51 Faerie Invaders C :B:	.15	.25
52 Fog Bank U :B:	.20	.35
53 Harbor Serpent C :B:	.15	.25
54 Hydrosurge C :B:	.15	.25
55 Index C :B:	.15	.25
56 Jace, Memory Adept M :B:	4.00	6.00
57 Jace's Phantasm U :B:	.20	.35
58 Kraken Hatchling C :B:	.15	.25
59 Master of the Pearl Trident R :B:	5.00	7.00
60 Merfolk of the Pearl Trident C :B:	.15	.25
61 Mind Sculpt C :B:	.15	.25
62 Negate C :B:	.15	.25
63 Omniscience M :B:	13.00	16.00
64 Redirect R :B:	.25	.40
65 Rewind U :B:	.20	.35
66 Scroll Thief C :B:	.15	.25
67 Sleep U :B:	.20	.35
68 Spelltwine R :B:	.25	.40
69 Sphinx of Uthuun R :B:	.25	.40
70 Stormtide Leviathan R :B:	.25	.40
71 Switcheroo U :B:	.20	.35
72 Talrand, Sky Summoner R :B:	.75	1.15
73 Talrand's Invocation U :B:	.20	.35
74 Tricks of the Trade C :B:	.15	.25
75 Unsummon C :B:	.15	.25
76 Vedalken Entrancer C :B:	.15	.25
77 Void Stalker R :B:	.25	.40
78 Watercourser C :B:	.15	.25
79 Welkin Tern C :B:	.15	.25
80 Wind Drake C :B:	.15	.25
81 Blood Reckoning U :K:	.20	.35
82 Bloodhunter Bat C :K:	.15	.25
83 Bloodthrone Vampire C :K:	.15	.25
84 Cower in Fear U :K:	.20	.35
85 Crippling Blight C :K:	.15	.25
86 Dark Favor C :K:	.15	.25
87 Diabolic Revelation R :K:	1.00	1.50
88 Disciple of Bolas R :K:	.40	.60
89 Disentomb C :K:	.15	.25
90 Duress C :K:	.15	.25
91 Duskmantle Prowler U :K:	.20	.35
92 Duty-Bound Dead C :K:	.15	.25
93 Essence Drain C :K:	.15	.25
94 Giant Scorpion C :K:	.15	.25
95 Harbor Bandit U :K:	.20	.35
96 Knight of Infamy U :K:	.20	.35
97 Liliana of the Dark Realms M :K:	6.00	8.00
98 Liliana's Shade C :K:	.15	.25
99 Mark of the Vampire C :K:	.15	.25
100 Mind Rot C :K:	.15	.25
101 Murder C :K:	.15	.25
102 Mutilate R :K:	.30	.50
103 Nefarox, Overlord of Grixis R :K:	.40	.60
104 Phylactery Lich R :K:	.25	.40
105 Public Execution U :K:	.20	.35
106 Ravenous Rats C :K:	.15	.25
107 Rise from the Grave U :K:	.20	.35
108 Servant of Nefarox C :K:	.15	.25
109 Shimian Specter R :K:	.25	.40
110 Sign in Blood C :K:	.15	.25
111 Tormented Soul C :K:	.15	.25
112 Vampire Nighthawk U :K:	.20	.35
113 Vampire Nocturnus M :K:	4.00	6.00
114 Veilborn Ghoul U :K:	.20	.35
115 Vile Rebirth C :K:	.15	.25
116 Walking Corpse C :K:	.15	.25
117 Wit's End R :K:	.25	.40
118 Xathrid Gorgon R :K:	.25	.40
119 Zombie Goliath C :K:	.15	.25
120 Arms Dealer U :R:	.20	.35
121 Bladetusk Boar C :R:	.15	.25
122 Canyon Minotaur C :R:	.15	.25
123 Chandra, the Firebrand M :R:	2.50	4.00
124 Chandra's Fury C :R:	.15	.25
125 Cleaver Riot U :R:	.20	.35
126 Craterize C :R:	.15	.25
127 Crimson Muckwader U :R:	.20	.35
128 Dragon Hatchling C :R:	.15	.25
129 Fervor R :R:	.25	.40
130 Fire Elemental C :R:	.15	.25
131 Firewing Phoenix R :R:	.25	.40
132 Flames of the Firebrand U :R:	.20	.35
133 Furnace Whelp U :R:	.20	.35
134 Goblin Arsonist C :R:	.15	.25
135 Goblin Battle Jester C :R:	.15	.25
136 Hamletback Goliath R :R:	.25	.40
137 Kindled Fury C :R:	.15	.25
138 Krenko, Mob Boss R :R:	3.00	5.00
139 Krenko's Command C :R:	.15	.25
140 Magmaquake R :R:	.25	.40
141 Mark of Mutiny U :R:	.20	.35
142 Mindclaw Shaman U :R:	.20	.35
143 Mogg Flunkies C :R:	.15	.25
144 Reckless Brute C :R:	.15	.25
145 Reverberate R :R:	.50	.75
146 Rummaging Goblin C :R:	.15	.25
147 Searing Spear C :R:	.15	.25
148 Slumbering Dragon R :R:	1.50	2.00
149 Smelt C :R:	.15	.25
150 Thundermaw Hellkite M :R:	6.00	8.00
151 Torch Fiend U :R:	.20	.35
152 Trumpet Blast C :R:	.15	.25
153 Turn to Slag C :R:	.15	.25
154 Volcanic Geyser U :R:	.20	.35
155 Volcanic Strength C :R:	.15	.25
156 Wall of Fire C :R:	.15	.25
157 Wild Guess C :R:	.15	.25
158 Worldfire M :R:	1.25	1.75
159 Acidic Slime U :G:	.20	.35
160 Arbor Elf C :G:	.15	.25
161 Bond Beetle C :G:	.15	.25
162 Boundless Realms R :G:	2.50	3.25
163 Bountiful Harvest C :G:	.15	.25
164 Centaur Courser C :G:	.15	.25
165 Deadly Recluse C :G:	.15	.25
166 Duskdale Wurm U :G:	.20	.35

167 Elderscale Wurm M :G: 1.75 2.50
168 Elvish Archdruid R :G: 2.00 2.75
169 Elvish Visionary C :G: .15 .25
170 Farseek C :G: .15 .25
171 Flinthoof Boar U :G: .20 .35
172 Fog C :G: .15 .25
173 Fungal Sprouting U :G: .20 .35
174 Garruk, Primal Hunter M :G: 5.00 7.00
175 Garruk's Packleader U :G: .20 .35
176 Ground Seal R :G: .25 .40
177 Mwonvuli Beast Tracker U :G: .20 .35
178 Naturalize C :G: .15 .25
179 Plummet C :G: .15 .25
180 Predatory Rampage R :G: .25 .40
181 Prey Upon C :G: .15 .25
182 Primal Huntbeast C :G: .15 .25
183 Primordial Hydra M :G: 5.00 7.00
184 Quirion Dryad R :G: .25 .40
185 Rancor U :G: 1.50 2.50
186 Ranger's Path C :G: .15 .25
187 Revive U :G: .20 .35
188 Roaring Primadox U :G: .20 .35
189 Sentinel Spider C :G: .15 .25
190 Serpent's Gift C :G: .15 .25
191 Silklash Spider R :G: .25 .40
192 Spiked Baloth C :G: .15 .25
193 Thragtusk R :G: 3.00 5.00
194 Timberpack Wolf C :G: .15 .25
195 Titanic Growth C :G: .15 .25
196 Vastwood Gorger C :G: .15 .25
197 Yeva, Nature's Herald R :G: .50 .75
198 Yeva's Forcemage C :G: .15 .25
199 Nicol Bolas, Planeswalker M :B/K/R: 7.00 10.00
200 Akroma's Memorial M 12.00 15.00
201 Chronomaton U .20 .35
202 Clock of Omens U .20 .35
203 Door to Nothingness R 1.00 1.50
204 Elixir of Immortality U .20 .35
205 Gem of Becoming U .20 .35
206 Gilded Lotus R 8.00 10.00
207 Jayemdae Tome U .20 .35
208 Kitesail U .20 .35
209 Phyrexian Hulk U .20 .35
210 Primal Clay U .20 .35
211 Ring of Evos Isle U .20 .35
212 Ring of Kalonia U .20 .35
213 Ring of Thune U .20 .35
214 Ring of Valkas U .20 .35
215 Ring of Xathrid U .20 .35
216 Sands of Delirium R .50 .75
217 Staff of Nin R .75 1.15
218 Stuffy Doll R 2.00 2.50
219 Tormod's Crypt U .20 .35
220 Trading Post R .25 .40
221 Cathedral of War R 1.25 1.75
222 Dragonskull Summit R 2.00 2.75
223 Drowned Catacomb R 2.50 3.00
224 Evolving Wilds C .15 .25
225 Glacial Fortress R 2.00 2.50
226 Hellion Crucible R .25 .40
227 Reliquary Tower U .20 .35
228 Rootbound Crag R 1.50 2.00
229 Sunpetal Grove R 2.00 2.50
230 Plains L .15 .25
231 Plains L .15 .25
232 Plains L .15 .25
233 Plains L .15 .25
234 Island L .15 .25
235 Island L .15 .25
236 Island L .15 .25
237 Island L .15 .25
238 Swamp L .15 .25
239 Swamp L .15 .25
240 Swamp L .15 .25
241 Swamp L .15 .25
242 Mountain L .15 .25
243 Mountain L .15 .25
244 Mountain L .15 .25
245 Mountain L .15 .25
246 Forest L .15 .25
247 Forest L .15 .25
248 Forest L .15 .25
249 Forest L .15 .25

2012 Magic The Gathering Magic 2013 Foil

1 Ajani, Caller of the Pride M :W: 10.00 13.00
2 Ajani's Sunstriker C :W: .50 .75
3 Angel's Mercy C :W: .25 .40
4 Angelic Benediction U :W: .25 .40
5 Attended Knight C :W: .50 .75
6 Aven Squire C :W: .25 .40
7 Battleflight Eagle C :W: .25 .40
8 Captain of the Watch R :W: 2.00 3.50
9 Captain's Call C :W: .25 .40
10 Crusader of Odric U :W: 1.00 1.50
11 Divine Favor C :W: .25 .40
12 Divine Verdict C :W: .25 .40
13 Erase C :W: .40 .60
14 Faith's Reward R :W: 3.00 5.00
15 Glorious Charge C :W: .25 .40
16 Griffin Protector C :W: .25 .40
17 Guardian Lions C :W: .25 .40
18 Guardians of Akrasa C :W: .25 .40
19 Healer of the Pride U :W: .50 .75
20 Intrepid Hero R :W: 1.50 2.50
21 Knight of Glory U :W: 1.50 2.50
22 Oblivion Ring U :W: .75 1.25
23 Odric, Master Tactician R :W: 2.00 3.50
24 Pacifism C :W: .25 .40
25 Pillarfield Ox C :W: .25 .40
26 Planar Cleansing R :W: 1.00 1.50
27 Prized Elephant U :W: .25 .40
28 Rain of Blades U :W: .25 .40
29 Rhox Faithmender R :W: 5.00 7.00
30 Safe Passage C :W: .25 .40
31 Serra Angel U :W: .40 .60
32 Serra Avatar M :W: 3.00 5.00
33 Serra Avenger R :W: 6.00 8.00
34 Show of Valor C :W: .25 .40
35 Silvercoat Lion C :W: .25 .40
36 Sublime Archangel M :W: 18.00 22.00
37 Touch of the Eternal R :W: .40 .60
38 War Falcon C :W: .25 .40
39 War Priest of Thune U :W: .40 .60
40 Warclamp Mastiff C :W: .25 .40
41 Archaeomancer C :B: 1.50 2.50
42 Arctic Aven U :B: .25 .40
43 Augur of Bolas U :B: 2.00 3.00
44 Battle of Wits R :B: .60 1.00
45 Clone R :B: .75 1.25
46 Courtly Provocateur U :B: .25 .40
47 Divination C :B: .25 .40
48 Downpour C :B: .25 .40
49 Encrust C :B: .25 .40
50 Essence Scatter C :B: .60 1.00
51 Faerie Invaders C :B: .25 .40
52 Fog Bank U :B: 2.00 3.00
53 Harbor Serpent C :B: .25 .40
54 Hydrosurge C :B: .25 .40
55 Index C :B: .25 .40
56 Jace, Memory Adept M :B: 9.00 12.00
57 Jace's Phantasm U :B: 4.00 6.00
58 Kraken Hatchling C :B: .25 .40
59 Master of the Pearl Trident R :B: 12.00 15.00
60 Merfolk of the Pearl Trident C :B: .25 .40
61 Mind Sculpt C :B: 1.00 1.50
62 Negate C :B: 1.00 1.50
63 Omniscience M :B: 45.00 55.00
64 Redirect R :B: 1.00 1.50
65 Rewind U :B: 1.50 2.50
66 Scroll Thief C :B: .25 .40
67 Sleep U :B: .25 .40
68 Spelltwine R :B: 3.00 5.00
69 Sphinx of Uthuun R :B: .75 1.25
70 Stormtide Leviathan R :B: 1.25 2.00
71 Switcheroo U :B: .25 .40
72 Talrand, Sky Summoner R :B: 1.50 2.50
73 Talrand's Invocation U :B: .60 1.00
74 Tricks of the Trade C :B: .25 .40
75 Unsummon C :B: .25 .40
76 Vedalken Entrancer C :B: .25 .40
77 Void Stalker R :B: .75 1.25
78 Watercourser C :B: .25 .40
79 Welkin Tern C :B: .25 .40
80 Wind Drake C :B: .25 .40
81 Blood Reckoning U :K: .25 .40
82 Bloodhunter Bat C :K: .25 .40
83 Bloodthrone Vampire C :K: .25 .40
84 Cower in Fear U :K: .25 .40
85 Crippling Blight C :K: .25 .40
86 Dark Favor C :K: .25 .40
87 Diabolic Revelation R :K: 5.00 7.00
88 Disciple of Bolas R :K: 5.00 7.00
89 Disentomb C :K: .25 .40
90 Duress C :K: .75 1.25
91 Duskmantle Prowler U :K: .25 .40
92 Duty-Bound Dead C :K: .40 .60
93 Essence Drain C :K: .25 .40
94 Giant Scorpion C :K: .25 .40
95 Harbor Bandit U :K: .25 .40
96 Knight of Infamy U :K: 1.25 2.00
97 Liliana of the Dark Realms M :K: 18.00 22.00
98 Liliana's Shade C :K: .25 .40
99 Mark of the Vampire C :K: .25 .40
100 Mind Rot C :K: .25 .40
101 Murder C :K: 2.00 3.50
102 Mutilate R :K: 2.00 3.50
103 Nefarox, Overlord of Grixis R :K: .75 1.25
104 Phylactery Lich R :K: 1.25 2.00
105 Public Execution U :K: .25 .40
106 Ravenous Rats C :K: .40 .60
107 Rise from the Grave U :K: .25 .40
108 Servant of Nefarox C :K: .25 .40
109 Shimian Specter R :K: .75 1.25
110 Sign in Blood C :K: .75 1.25
111 Tormented Soul C :K: .25 .40
112 Vampire Nighthawk U :K: 2.50 4.00
113 Vampire Nocturnus M :K: 6.00 10.00
114 Veilborn Ghoul U :K: .25 .40
115 Vile Rebirth C :K: .25 .40
116 Walking Corpse C :K: .25 .40
117 Wit's End R :K: .50 .75
118 Xathrid Gorgon R :K: .60 1.00
119 Zombie Goliath C :K: .25 .40
120 Arms Dealer U :R: .25 .40
121 Bladetusk Boar C :R: .25 .40
122 Canyon Minotaur C :R: .25 .40
123 Chandra, the Firebrand M :R: 8.00 11.00
124 Chandra's Fury C :R: .25 .40
125 Cleaver Riot U :R: .25 .40
126 Craterize C :R: .25 .40
127 Crimson Muckwader U :R: .25 .40
128 Dragon Hatchling C :R: .25 .40
129 Fervor R :R: 1.50 2.50
130 Fire Elemental C :R: .25 .40
131 Firewing Phoenix R :R: .75 1.25
132 Flames of the Firebrand U :R: .25 .40
133 Furnace Whelp U :R: .25 .40
134 Goblin Arsonist C :R: .75 1.25
135 Goblin Battle Jester C :R: .25 .40
136 Hamletback Goliath R :R: .50 .75
137 Kindled Fury C :R: .25 .40
138 Krenko, Mob Boss R :R: 5.00 7.00
139 Krenko's Command C :R: .25 .40
140 Magmaquake R :R: .50 .75
141 Mark of Mutiny U :R: .25 .40
142 Mindclaw Shaman U :R: 2.50 4.00
143 Mogg Flunkies C :R: .25 .40
144 Reckless Brute C :R: .25 .40
145 Reverberate R :R: 1.50 2.50
146 Rummaging Goblin C :R: .25 .40
147 Searing Spear C :R: .75 1.25
148 Slumbering Dragon R :R: 3.00 5.00
149 Smelt C :R: .25 .40
150 Thundermaw Hellkite M :R: 25.00 35.00
151 Torch Fiend U :R: .25 .40
152 Trumpet Blast C :R: .25 .40
153 Turn to Slag C :R: .25 .40
154 Volcanic Geyser U :R: .25 .40
155 Volcanic Strength C :R: .25 .40
156 Wall of Fire C :R: .25 .40
157 Wild Guess C :R: .40 .60
158 Worldfire M :R: 4.00 6.00
159 Acidic Slime U :G: 1.50 2.50
160 Arbor Elf C :G: 3.00 5.00
161 Bond Beetle C :G: .25 .40
162 Boundless Realms R :G: 7.00 9.00
163 Bountiful Harvest C :G: .40 .60
164 Centaur Courser C :G: .25 .40
165 Deadly Recluse C :G: .25 .40
166 Duskdale Wurm U :G: .25 .40
167 Elderscale Wurm M :G: 4.00 6.00
168 Elvish Archdruid R :G: 6.00 8.00
169 Elvish Visionary C :G: 1.25 2.00
170 Farseek C :G: 1.00 1.50
171 Flinthoof Boar U :G: 2.00 3.50
172 Fog C :G: .50 .75
173 Fungal Sprouting U :G: .40 .60
174 Garruk, Primal Hunter M :G: 13.00 16.00
175 Garruk's Packleader U :G: 1.00 1.50
176 Ground Seal R :G: 1.00 1.50
177 Mwonvuli Beast Tracker U :G: .40 .60
178 Naturalize C :G: .25 .40
179 Plummet C :G: .25 .40
180 Predatory Rampage R :G: .50 .75
181 Prey Upon C :G: .25 .40
182 Primal Huntbeast C :G: .25 .40
183 Primordial Hydra M :G: 9.00 11.00
184 Quirion Dryad R :G: .75 1.25
185 Rancor U :G: 5.00 7.00
186 Ranger's Path C :G: 2.00 3.50
187 Revive U :G: .25 .40
188 Roaring Primadox U :G: .25 .40
189 Sentinel Spider C :G: .25 .40
190 Serpent's Gift C :G: .25 .40
191 Silklash Spider R :G: 1.25 2.00
192 Spiked Baloth C :G: .25 .40
193 Thragtusk R :G: 14.00 17.00
194 Timberpack Wolf C :G: .25 .40
195 Titanic Growth C :G: .25 .40
196 Vastwood Gorger C :G: .25 .40
197 Yeva, Nature's Herald R :G: 1.50 2.50
198 Yeva's Forcemage C :G: .25 .40
199 Nicol Bolas, Planeswalker M :B/K/R: 25.00 30.00
200 Akroma's Memorial M 25.00 30.00
201 Chronomaton U .25 .40
202 Clock of Omens U 3.00 5.00
203 Door to Nothingness R 3.00 5.00
204 Elixir of Immortality U 2.50 4.00
205 Gem of Becoming U .60 1.00
206 Gilded Lotus R 15.00 18.00
207 Jayemdae Tome U .25 .40
208 Kitesail U .25 .40
209 Phyrexian Hulk U .25 .40
210 Primal Clay U .25 .40
211 Ring of Evos Isle U .60 1.00
212 Ring of Kalonia U 1.25 2.00
213 Ring of Thune U 1.25 2.00
214 Ring of Valkas U .60 1.00
215 Ring of Xathrid U .75 1.25
216 Sands of Delirium R 1.25 2.00
217 Staff of Nin R 2.50 4.00
218 Stuffy Doll R 6.00 8.00
219 Tormod's Crypt U 1.50 2.50
220 Trading Post R 3.00 5.00
221 Cathedral of War R 2.50 4.00
222 Dragonskull Summit R 4.00 6.00
223 Drowned Catacomb R 4.00 6.00
224 Evolving Wilds C .75 1.25
225 Glacial Fortress R 4.00 6.00
226 Hellion Crucible R .75 1.25
227 Reliquary Tower U 5.00 7.00
228 Rootbound Crag R 2.50 4.00
229 Sunpetal Grove R 4.00 6.00
230 Plains L .25 .40
231 Plains L .25 .40
232 Plains L .25 .40
233 Plains L .25 .40
234 Island L .25 .40
235 Island L .25 .40
236 Island L .25 .40
237 Island L .25 .40
238 Swamp L .25 .40
239 Swamp L .25 .40
240 Swamp L .25 .40
241 Swamp L .25 .40
242 Mountain L .25 .40
243 Mountain L .25 .40
244 Mountain L .25 .40
245 Mountain L .25 .40
246 Forest L .25 .40
247 Forest L .25 .40
248 Forest L .25 .40
249 Forest L .25 .40

2012 Magic The Gathering Magic 2013 Tokens

1 Cat .35 .50
2 Goat .35 .25
3 Soldier .10 .15
4 Drake .35 .50
5 Zombie .10 .15
6 Goblin .12 .20
7 Hellion .10 .15
8 Beast .10 .15
9 Saproling .10 .15
10 Wurm .30 .40
11 Liliana of the Dark Realms Emblem .30 .40

2013 Magic The Gathering Magic 2014

COMPLETE SET (249) 130.00 180.00
BOOSTER BOX (36 PACKS) 80.00 100.00
BOOSTER PACK (15 CARDS) 3.00 4.00
FAT PACK 35.00 45.00
1 Ajani, Caller of the Pride M :W: 4.00 6.00
2 Ajani's Chosen R :W: .25 .40
3 Angelic Accord U :W: .20 .35
4 Angelic Wall C :W: .15 .25
5 Archangel of Thune M :W: 20.00 25.00
6 Auramancer C :W: .15 .25
7 Banisher Priest U :W: .20 .35
8 Blessing U :W: .20 .35
9 Bonescythe Sliver R :W: .25 .40
10 Brave the Elements U :W: .20 .35
11 Capashen Knight C :W: .15 .25
12 Celestial Flare C :W: .15 .25
13 Charging Griffin C :W: .15 .25
14 Congregate U :W: .20 .35
15 Dawnstrike Paladin C :W: .15 .25
16 Devout Invocation M :W: 1.00 1.50
17 Divine Favor C :W: .15 .25
18 Fiendslayer Paladin R :W: .25 .40
19 Fortify C :W: .15 .25
20 Griffin Sentinel C :W: .15 .25
21 Hive Stirrings C :W: .15 .25
22 Imposing Sovereign R :W: .25 .40
23 Indestructibility R :W: .25 .40
24 Master of Diversion C :W: .15 .25
25 Pacifism C :W: .15 .25
26 Path of Bravery R :W: .25 .40
27 Pay No Heed C :W: .15 .25
28 Pillarfield Ox C :W: .15 .25
29 Planar Cleansing R :W: .25 .40
30 Sentinel Sliver C :W: .15 .25
31 Seraph of the Sword R :W: .25 .40
32 Serra Angel U :W: .20 .35
33 Show of Valor C :W: .15 .25
34 Siege Mastodon C :W: .15 .25
35 Silence R :W: .25 .40
36 Solemn Offering C :W: .15 .25
37 Soulmender C :W: .15 .25
38 Steelform Sliver U :W: .20 .35
39 Stonehorn Chanter U :W: .20 .35
40 Suntail Hawk C :W: .15 .25
41 Wall of Swords U :W: .20 .35
42 Air Servant U :B: .20 .35
43 Archaeomancer C :B: .15 .25
44 Armored Cancrix C :B: .15 .25
45 Cancel C :B: .15 .25
46 Claustrophobia C :B: .15 .25
47 Clone R :B: .25 .40
48 Colossal Whale R :B: .25 .40
49 Coral Merfolk C :B: .15 .25
50 Dismiss into Dream R :B: .25 .40
51 Disperse C :B: .15 .25
52 Divination C :B: .15 .25
53 Domestication R :B: .25 .40
54 Elite Arcanist R :B: .25 .40
55 Essence Scatter C :B: .15 .25
56 Frost Breath C :B: .15 .25
57 Galerider Sliver R :B: .25 .40
58 Glimpse the Future U :B: .20 .35
59 Illusionary Armor U :B: .20 .35
60 Jace, Memory Adept M :B: 4.00 6.00
61 Jace's Mindseeker R :B: .25 .40
62 Merfolk Spy C :B: .15 .25
63 Messenger Drake C :B: .15 .25
64 Negate C :B: .15 .25
65 Nephalia Seakite C :B: .15 .25
66 Opportunity U :B: .20 .35
67 Phantom Warrior U :B: .20 .35
68 Quicken R :B: .25 .40
69 Scroll Thief C :B: .15 .25
70 Seacoast Drake C :B: .15 .25
71 Sensory Deprivation C :B: .15 .25
72 Spell Blast U :B: .20 .35
73 Tidebinder Mage R :B: .25 .40
74 Time Ebb C :B: .15 .25
75 Tome Scour C :B: .15 .25
76 Trained Condor C :B: .15 .25
77 Traumatize R :B: .25 .40
78 Wall of Frost U :B: .20 .35
79 Warden of Evos Isle U :B: .20 .35
80 Water Servant U :B: .20 .35
81 Windreader Sphinx M :B: .50 .75
82 Zephyr Charge C :B: .15 .25
83 Accursed Spirit C :K: .15 .25
84 Altar's Reap C :K: .15 .25
85 Artificer's Hex U :K: .20 .35
86 Blightcaster U :K: .20 .35
87 Blood Bairn C :K: .15 .25
88 Bogbrew Witch R :K: .25 .40
89 Child of Night C :K: .15 .25
90 Corpse Hauler C :K: .15 .25
91 Corrupt U :K: .20 .35
92 Dark Favor C :K: .15 .25
93 Dark Prophecy R :K: .25 .40
94 Deathgaze Cockatrice C :K: .15 .25
95 Diabolic Tutor U :K: .20 .35
96 Doom Blade U :K: .20 .35
97 Duress C :K: .15 .25
98 Festering Newt C :K: .15 .25
99 Gnawing Zombie U :K: .20 .35
100 Grim Return R :K: .25 .40
101 Lifebane Zombie R :K: .40 .60
102 Liliana of the Dark Realms M :K: 6.00 8.00
103 Liliana's Reaver R :K: .30 .50
104 Liturgy of Blood C :K: .15 .25
105 Mark of the Vampire C :K: .15 .25
106 Mind Rot C :K: .15 .25
107 Minotaur Abomination C :K: .15 .25
108 Nightmare R :K: .25 .40
109 Nightwing Shade C :K: .15 .25
110 Quag Sickness C :K: .15 .25
111 Rise of the Dark Realms M :K: 6.00 8.00
112 Sanguine Bond R :K: .25 .40
113 Sengir Vampire U :K: .20 .35
114 Shadowborn Apostle C :K: .15 .25
115 Shadowborn Demon M :K: .75 1.00
116 Shrivel C :K: .15 .25
117 Syphon Sliver R :K: .25 .40
118 Tenacious Dead U :K: .20 .35
119 Undead Minotaur C :K: .15 .25
120 Vampire Warlord U :K: .20 .35
121 Vile Rebirth C :K: .15 .25
122 Wring Flesh C :K: .15 .25
123 Xathrid Necromancer R :K: .25 .40
124 Academy Raider C :R: .15 .25

Card	Low	High
125 Act of Treason C :R:	.15	.25
126 Awaken the Ancient R :R:	.25	.40
127 Barrage of Expendables U :R:	.20	.35
128 Battle Sliver U :R:	.20	.35
129 Blur Sliver C :R:	.15	.25
130 Burning Earth R :R:	.25	.40
131 Canyon Minotaur C :R:	.15	.25
132 Chandra, Pyromaster M :R:	2.00	2.75
133 Chandra's Outrage C :R:	.15	.25
134 Chandra's Phoenix R :R:	.25	.40
135 Cyclops Tyrant C :R:	.15	.25
136 Demolish C :R:	.15	.25
137 Dragon Egg U :R:	.20	.35
138 Dragon Hatchling C :R:	.15	.25
139 Flames of the Firebrand U :R:	.20	.35
140 Fleshpulper Giant U :R:	.20	.35
141 Goblin Diplomats R :R:	.25	.40
142 Goblin Shortcutter C :R:	.15	.25
143 Lava Axe C :R:	.15	.25
144 Lightning Talons C :R:	.15	.25
145 Marauding Maulhorn C :R:	.15	.25
146 Mindsparker R :R:	.25	.40
147 Molten Birth U :R:	.20	.35
148 Ogre Battledriver R :R:	.25	.40
149 Pitchburn Devils C :R:	.15	.25
150 Regathan Firecat C :R:	.15	.25
151 Scourge of Valkas M :R:	3.00	3.50
152 Seismic Stomp C :R:	.15	.25
153 Shiv's Embrace U :R:	.20	.35
154 Shivan Dragon R :R:	.25	.40
155 Shock C :R:	.15	.25
156 Smelt C :R:	.15	.25
157 Striking Sliver C :R:	.15	.25
158 Thorncaster Sliver R :R:	.25	.40
159 Thunder Strike C :R:	.15	.25
160 Volcanic Geyser U :R:	.20	.35
161 Wild Guess C :R:	.15	.25
162 Wild Ricochet R :R:	.25	.40
163 Young Pyromancer U :R:	.20	.35
164 Advocate of the Beast C :G:	.15	.25
165 Bramblecrush U :G:	.20	.35
166 Briarpack Alpha U :G:	.20	.35
167 Brindle Boar C :G:	.15	.25
168 Deadly Recluse C :G:	.15	.25
169 Elvish Mystic C :G:	.15	.25
170 Enlarge U :G:	.20	.35
171 Fog C :G:	.15	.25
172 Garruk, Caller of Beasts M :G:	4.00	6.00
173 Garruk's Horde R :G:	.25	.40
174 Giant Growth C :G:	.15	.25
175 Giant Spider C :G:	.15	.25
176 Gladecover Scout C :G:	.15	.25
177 Groundshaker Sliver C :G:	.15	.25
178 Howl of the Night Pack U :G:	.20	.35
179 Hunt the Weak C :G:	.15	.25
180 Into the Wilds R :G:	.25	.40
181 Kalonian Hydra M :G:	9.00	11.00
182 Kalonian Tusker U :G:	.20	.35
183 Lay of the Land C :G:	.15	.25
184 Manaweft Sliver U :G:	.20	.35
185 Megantic Sliver R :G:	.40	.60
186 Naturalize C :G:	.15	.25
187 Oath of the Ancient Wood R :G:	.25	.40
188 Plummet C :G:	.15	.25
189 Predatory Sliver C :G:	.15	.25
190 Primeval Bounty M :G:	3.50	4.50
191 Ranger's Guile C :G:	.15	.25
192 Rootwalla C :G:	.15	.25
193 Rumbling Baloth C :G:	.15	.25
194 Savage Summoning R :G:	.25	.40
195 Scavenging Ooze R :G:	6.00	7.00
196 Sporemound C :G:	.15	.25
197 Trollhide C :G:	.15	.25
198 Vastwood Hydra R :G:	.25	.40
199 Verdant Haven C :G:	.15	.25
200 Voracious Wurm U :G:	.20	.35
201 Windstorm U :G:	.20	.35
202 Witchstalker R :G:	.30	.50
203 Woodborn Behemoth U :G:	.20	.35
204 Accorder's Shield U	.20	.35
205 Bubbling Cauldron U	.20	.35
206 Darksteel Forge M	4.50	6.00
207 Darksteel Ingot U	.20	.35
208 Door of Destinies R	.25	.40
209 Elixir of Immortality U	.20	.35
210 Fireshrieker U	.20	.35
211 Guardian of the Ages R	.25	.40
212 Haunted Plate Mail R	.25	.40
213 Millstone U	.20	.35
214 Pyromancer's Gauntlet R	.25	.40
215 Ratchet Bomb R	.25	.40
216 Ring of Three Wishes M	4.00	6.00
217 Rod of Ruin U	.20	.35
218 Sliver Construct C	.15	.25
219 Staff of the Death Magus U	.20	.35
220 Staff of the Flame Magus U	.20	.35
221 Staff of the Mind Magus U	.20	.35
222 Staff of the Sun Magus U	.20	.35
223 Staff of the Wild Magus U	.20	.35
224 Strionic Resonator R	.25	.40
225 Trading Post R	.25	.40
226 Vial of Poison U	.20	.35
227 Encroaching Wastes U	.20	.35
228 Mutavault R	10.00	12.00
229 Shimmering Grotto U	.20	.35
230 Plains L	.15	.25
231 Plains L	.15	.25
232 Plains L	.15	.25
233 Plains L	.15	.25
234 Island L	.15	.25
235 Island L	.15	.25
236 Island L	.15	.25
237 Island L	.15	.25
238 Swamp L	.15	.25
239 Swamp L	.15	.25
240 Swamp L	.15	.25
241 Swamp L	.15	.25
242 Mountain L	.15	.25
243 Mountain L	.15	.25
244 Mountain L	.15	.25
245 Mountain L	.15	.25
246 Forest L	.15	.25
247 Forest L	.15	.25
248 Forest L	.15	.25
249 Forest L	.15	.25

2013 Magic The Gathering Magic 2014 Foil

Card	Low	High
1 Ajani, Caller of the Pride M :W:	10.00	13.00
2 Ajani's Chosen R :W:	.50	.75
3 Angelic Accord U :W:	1.50	2.50
4 Angelic Wall C :W:	.20	.35
5 Archangel of Thune M :W:	45.00	55.00
6 Auramancer C :W:	.20	.35
7 Banisher Priest U :W:	1.00	1.50
8 Blessing U :W:	.20	.35
9 Bonescythe Sliver R :W:	2.00	3.50
10 Brave the Elements U :W:	1.00	1.50
11 Capashen Knight C :W:	.20	.35
12 Celestial Flare C :W:	1.00	1.50
13 Charging Griffin C :W:	.20	.35
14 Congregate U :W:	.40	.60
15 Dawnstrike Paladin C :W:	.20	.35
16 Devout Invocation M :W:	2.00	3.50
17 Divine Favor C :W:	.20	.35
18 Fiendslayer Paladin R :W:	4.00	6.00
19 Fortify C :W:	.20	.35
20 Griffin Sentinel C :W:	.20	.35
21 Hive Stirrings C :W:	.50	.75
22 Imposing Sovereign R :W:	2.00	3.50
23 Indestructibility R :W:	1.25	2.00
24 Master of Diversion C :W:	.20	.35
25 Pacifism C :W:	.20	.35
26 Path of Bravery R :W:	1.25	2.00
27 Pay No Heed C :W:	.20	.35
28 Pillarfield Ox C :W:	.20	.35
29 Planar Cleansing R :W:	1.00	1.50
30 Sentinel Sliver C :W:	1.50	2.50
31 Seraph of the Sword R :W:	1.50	2.50
32 Serra Angel U :W:	.20	.35
33 Show of Valor C :W:	.20	.35
34 Siege Mastodon C :W:	.20	.35
35 Silence R :W:	2.00	3.50
36 Solemn Offering C :W:	.20	.35
37 Soulmender C :W:	.20	.35
38 Steelform Sliver U :W:	.40	.60
39 Stonehorn Chanter U :W:	.20	.35
40 Suntail Hawk C :W:	.20	.35
41 Wall of Swords U :W:	.20	.35
42 Air Servant U :B:	.20	.35
43 Archaeomancer C :B:	.20	.35
44 Armored Cancrix C :B:	.20	.35
45 Cancel C :B:	.20	.35
46 Claustrophobia C :B:	.20	.35
47 Clone R :B:	1.00	1.50
48 Colossal Whale R :B:	.50	.75
49 Coral Merfolk C :B:	.20	.35
50 Dismiss into Dream R :B:	.60	1.00
51 Disperse C :B:	.20	.35
52 Divination C :B:	.20	.35
53 Domestication R :B:	.60	1.00
54 Elite Arcanist R :B:	1.25	2.00
55 Essence Scatter C :B:	.40	.60
56 Frost Breath C :B:	.20	.35
57 Galerider Sliver R :B:	6.00	8.00
58 Glimpse the Future U :B:	.20	.35
59 Illusionary Armor U :B:	.20	.35
60 Jace, Memory Adept M :B:	10.00	13.00
61 Jace's Mindseeker R :B:	.60	1.00
62 Merfolk Spy C :B:	.20	.35
63 Messenger Drake C :B:	.20	.35
64 Negate C :B:	1.00	1.50
65 Nephalia Seakite C :B:	.20	.35
66 Opportunity U :B:	.60	1.00
67 Phantom Warrior U :B:	.20	.35
68 Quicken R :B:	4.00	6.00
69 Scroll Thief C :B:	.20	.35
70 Seacoast Drake C :B:	.20	.35
71 Sensory Deprivation C :B:	.20	.35
72 Spell Blast U :B:	.20	.35
73 Tidebinder Mage R :B:	3.00	5.00
74 Time Ebb C :B:	.20	.35
75 Tome Scour C :B:	.75	1.25
76 Trained Condor C :B:	.20	.35
77 Traumatize R :B:	2.00	3.50
78 Wall of Frost U :B:	.75	1.25
79 Warden of Evos Isle U :B:	.60	1.00
80 Water Servant U :B:	.20	.35
81 Windreader Sphinx M :B:	1.50	2.50
82 Zephyr Charge C :B:	.20	.35
83 Accursed Spirit C :K:	.20	.35
84 Altar's Reap C :K:	.20	.35
85 Artificer's Hex U :K:	.20	.35
86 Blightcaster U :K:	.20	.35
87 Blood Bairn C :K:	.20	.35
88 Bogbrew Witch R :K:	1.00	1.50
89 Child of Night C :K:	.20	.35
90 Corpse Hauler C :K:	.20	.35
91 Corrupt U :K:	.30	.50
92 Dark Favor C :K:	.20	.35
93 Dark Prophecy R :K:	1.25	2.00
94 Deathgaze Cockatrice C :K:	.20	.35
95 Diabolic Tutor U :K:	1.50	2.50
96 Doom Blade U :K:	2.00	3.50
97 Duress C :K:	.60	1.00
98 Festering Newt C :K:	.30	.50
99 Gnawing Zombie U :K:	.30	.50
100 Grim Return R :K:	1.00	1.50
101 Lifebane Zombie R :K:	1.50	2.50
102 Liliana of the Dark Realms M :K:	17.00	20.00
103 Liliana's Reaver R :K:	1.00	1.50
104 Liturgy of Blood C :K:	.20	.35
105 Mark of the Vampire C :K:	.20	.35
106 Mind Rot C :K:	.20	.35
107 Minotaur Abomination C :K:	.20	.35
108 Nightmare R :K:	.50	.75
109 Nightwing Shade C :K:	.20	.35
110 Quag Sickness C :K:	.20	.35
111 Rise of the Dark Realms M :K:	16.00	20.00
112 Sanguine Bond R :K:	4.00	6.00
113 Sengir Vampire U :K:	.20	.35
114 Shadowborn Apostle C :K:	4.00	6.00
115 Shadowborn Demon M :K:	3.00	5.00
116 Shrivel C :K:	.20	.35
117 Syphon Sliver R :K:	3.00	5.00
118 Tenacious Dead U :K:	.30	.50
119 Undead Minotaur C :K:	.20	.35
120 Vampire Warlord U :K:	.20	.35
121 Vile Rebirth C :K:	.20	.35
122 Wring Flesh C :K:	.20	.35
123 Xathrid Necromancer R :K:	1.00	1.50
124 Academy Raider C :R:	.20	.35
125 Act of Treason C :R:	.20	.35
126 Awaken the Ancient R :R:	.60	1.00
127 Barrage of Expendables U :R:	.30	.50
128 Battle Sliver U :R:	.50	.75
129 Blur Sliver C :R:	1.25	2.00
130 Burning Earth R :R:	.75	1.25
131 Canyon Minotaur C :R:	.20	.35
132 Chandra, Pyromaster M :R:	8.00	10.00
133 Chandra's Outrage C :R:	.20	.35
134 Chandra's Phoenix R :R:	.75	1.25
135 Cyclops Tyrant C :R:	.20	.35
136 Demolish C :R:	.20	.35
137 Dragon Egg U :R:	.75	1.25
138 Dragon Hatchling C :R:	.20	.35
139 Flames of the Firebrand U :R:	.50	.75
140 Fleshpulper Giant U :R:	.20	.35
141 Goblin Diplomats R :R:	.60	1.00
142 Goblin Shortcutter C :R:	.20	.35
143 Lava Axe C :R:	.20	.35
144 Lightning Talons C :R:	.20	.35
145 Marauding Maulhorn C :R:	.20	.35
146 Mindsparker R :R:	.50	.75
147 Molten Birth U :R:	.40	.60
148 Ogre Battledriver R :R:	1.25	2.00
149 Pitchburn Devils C :R:	.20	.35
150 Regathan Firecat C :R:	.20	.35
151 Scourge of Valkas M :R:	9.00	11.00
152 Seismic Stomp C :R:	.20	.35
153 Shiv's Embrace U :R:	.20	.35
154 Shivan Dragon R :R:	.75	1.25
155 Shock C :R:	.75	1.25
156 Smelt C :R:	.20	.35
157 Striking Sliver C :R:	2.00	3.50
158 Thorncaster Sliver R :R:	1.50	2.50
159 Thunder Strike C :R:	.20	.35
160 Volcanic Geyser U :R:	.20	.35
161 Wild Guess C :R:	.20	.35
162 Wild Ricochet R :R:	.75	1.25
163 Young Pyromancer U :R:	9.00	12.00
164 Advocate of the Beast C :G:	.20	.35
165 Bramblecrush U :G:	.20	.35
166 Briarpack Alpha U :G:	.20	.35
167 Brindle Boar C :G:	.20	.35
168 Deadly Recluse C :G:	.60	1.00
169 Elvish Mystic C :G:	2.50	4.00
170 Enlarge U :G:	.40	.60
171 Fog C :G:	.30	.50
172 Garruk, Caller of Beasts M :G:	10.00	13.00
173 Garruk's Horde R :G:	.50	.75
174 Giant Growth C :G:	.20	.35
175 Giant Spider C :G:	.20	.35
176 Gladecover Scout C :G:	1.25	2.00
177 Groundshaker Sliver C :G:	.40	.60
178 Howl of the Night Pack U :G:	.40	.60
179 Hunt the Weak C :G:	.20	.35
180 Into the Wilds R :G:	1.25	2.00
181 Kalonian Hydra M :G:	12.00	16.00
182 Kalonian Tusker U :G:	2.00	3.50
183 Lay of the Land C :G:	.20	.35
184 Manaweft Sliver U :G:	4.00	6.00
185 Megantic Sliver R :G:	1.00	1.50
186 Naturalize C :G:	.20	.35
187 Oath of the Ancient Wood R :G:	.40	.60
188 Plummet C :G:	.20	.35
189 Predatory Sliver C :G:	2.00	3.50
190 Primeval Bounty M :G:	7.00	10.00
191 Ranger's Guile C :G:	.20	.35
192 Rootwalla C :G:	.20	.35
193 Rumbling Baloth C :G:	.20	.35
194 Savage Summoning R :G:	1.00	1.50
195 Scavenging Ooze R :G:	11.00	14.00
196 Sporemound C :G:	.20	.35
197 Trollhide C :G:	.20	.35
198 Vastwood Hydra R :G:	1.50	2.50
199 Verdant Haven C :G:	.20	.35
200 Voracious Wurm U :G:	.20	.35
201 Windstorm U :G:	.20	.35
202 Witchstalker R :G:	1.25	2.00
203 Woodborn Behemoth U :G:	.20	.35
204 Accorder's Shield U	.50	.75
205 Bubbling Cauldron U	.60	1.00
206 Darksteel Forge M	16.00	20.00
207 Darksteel Ingot U	2.50	4.00
208 Door of Destinies R	6.00	8.00
209 Elixir of Immortality U	2.50	4.00
210 Fireshrieker U	.60	1.00
211 Guardian of the Ages R	.60	1.00
212 Haunted Plate Mail R	.60	1.00
213 Millstone U	.20	.35
214 Pyromancer's Gauntlet R	.75	1.25
215 Ratchet Bomb R	2.00	3.50
216 Ring of Three Wishes M	7.00	10.00
217 Rod of Ruin U	.20	.35
218 Sliver Construct C	.20	.35
219 Staff of the Death Magus U	.20	.35
220 Staff of the Flame Magus U	.20	.35
221 Staff of the Mind Magus U	.20	.35
222 Staff of the Sun Magus U	.20	.35
223 Staff of the Wild Magus U	.20	.35
224 Strionic Resonator R	13.00	16.00
225 Trading Post R	2.00	3.00
226 Vial of Poison U	.20	.35
227 Encroaching Wastes U	.40	.60
228 Mutavault R	25.00	30.00
229 Shimmering Grotto U	.20	.35
230 Plains L	.20	.35
231 Plains L	.20	.35
232 Plains L	.20	.35
233 Plains L	.20	.35
234 Island L	.20	.35
235 Island L	.20	.35
236 Island L	.20	.35
237 Island L	.20	.35
238 Swamp L	.20	.35
239 Swamp L	.20	.35
240 Swamp L	.20	.35
241 Swamp L	.20	.35
242 Mountain L	.20	.35
243 Mountain L	.20	.35
244 Mountain L	.20	.35
245 Mountain L	.20	.35
246 Forest L	.20	.35
247 Forest L	.20	.35
248 Forest L	.20	.35
249 Forest L	.20	.35

2013 Magic The Gathering Magic 2014 Tokens

Card	Low	High
1 Sliver	.50	.75
2 Angel	.30	.40
3 Cat	.30	.40
4 Goat	.15	.25
5 Zombie	.10	.15
6 Dragon	.12	.20
7 Elemental	.40	.60
8 Elemental	.60	1.00
9 Beast	.12	.20
10 Saproling	.10	.15
11 Wolf	.12	.20
12 Liliana of the Dark Realms Emblem	.35	.50
13 Garruk, Caller of Beasts Emblem	.15	.25

2013 Magic The Gathering Magic 2014 SDCC Black Variant

Card	Low	High
COMPLETE SET (5)	400.00	600.00
1 Ajani, Caller of the Pride M :W:	75.00	150.00
60 Jace, Memory Adept M :B:	75.00	150.00
102 Liliana of the Dark Realms M :K:	75.00	150.00
132 Chandra, Pyromaster M :R:	75.00	150.00
172 Garruk, Caller of Beasts M :G:	75.00	125.00

2014 Magic The Gathering Magic 2015

Card	Low	High
COMPLETE SET (301)	140.00	200.00
BOOSTER BOX (36 PACKS)	80.00	90.00
BOOSTER PACK (15 CARDS)	3.00	4.00
RELEASED ON JULY 28, 2014		
1 Ajani Steadfast M :W:	6.00	8.00
2 Ajani's Pridemate U :W:	.20	.35
3 Avacyn, Guardian Angel R :W:	.50	.75
4 Battle Mastery U :W:	.20	.35
5 Boonweaver Giant U :W:	.20	.35
6 Congregate U :W:	.20	.35
7 Constricting Sliver U :W:	.20	.35
8 Dauntless River Marshal U :W:	.20	.35
9 Devouring Light U :W:	.20	.35
10 Divine Favor C :W:	.15	.25
11 Ephemeral Shields C :W:	.15	.25
12 First Response U :W:	.20	.35
13 Geist of the Moors U :W:	.20	.35
14 Heliod's Pilgrim C :W:	.15	.25
15 Hushwing Gryff R :W:	.40	.60
16 Kinsbaile Skirmisher C :W:	.15	.25
17 Marked by Honor C :W:	.15	.25
18 Mass Calcify R :W:	.25	.40
19 Meditation Puzzle C :W:	.15	.25
20 Midnight Guard C :W:	.15	.25
21 Oppressive Rays C :W:	.15	.25
22 Oreskos Swiftclaw C :W:	.15	.25
23 Paragon of New Dawns U :W:	.20	.35
24 Pillar of Light C :W:	.15	.25
25 Preeminent Captain R :W:	.50	.75
26 Raise the Alarm C :W:	.15	.25
27 Razorfoot Griffin C :W:	.15	.25
28 Resolute Archangel R :W:	.40	.60
29 Return to the Ranks R :W:	1.00	1.25
30 Sanctified Charge C :W:	.15	.25
31 Selfless Cathar C :W:	.15	.25
32 Seraph of the Masses U :W:	.20	.35
33 Solemn Offering C :W:	.15	.25
34 Soul of Theros M :W:	.75	1.00
35 Soulmender C :W:	.15	.25
36 Spectra Ward R :W:	.50	.75
37 Spirit Bonds R :W:	.25	.40
38 Sungrace Pegasus C :W:	.15	.25
39 Tireless Missionaries C :W:	.15	.25
40 Triplicate Spirits C :W:	.15	.25
41 Wall of Essence U :W:	.20	.35
42 Warden of the Beyond U :W:	.20	.35
43 Aeronaut Tinkerer C :B:	.15	.25
44 AEtherspouts R :B:	.40	.60
45 Amphin Pathmage C :B:	.15	.25
46 Chasm Skulker R :B:	3.25	4.00
47 Chief Engineer R :B:	.40	.60
48 Chronostutter C :B:	.15	.25
49 Coral Barrier C :B:	.15	.25
50 Diffusion Sliver U :B:	.20	.35
51 Dissipate U :B:	.20	.35
52 Divination C :B:	.15	.25
53 Encrust C :B:	.15	.25
54 Ensoul Artifact U :B:	.20	.35
55 Frost Lynx C :B:	.15	.25
56 Fugitive Wizard C :B:	.15	.25
57 Glacial Crasher C :B:	.15	.25
58 Hydrosurge C :B:	.15	.25
59 Illusory Angel U :B:	.20	.35
60 Into the Void U :B:	.20	.35
61 Invisibility C :B:	.15	.25
62 Jace, the Living Guildpact M :B:	2.25	3.00
63 Jace's Ingenuity U :B:	.20	.35
64 Jalira, Master Polymorphist R :B:	.25	.40
65 Jorubai Murk Lurker U :B:	.20	.35
66 Kapsho Kitefins U :B:	.20	.35
67 Master of Predicaments R :B:	.25	.40
68 Mercurial Pretender R :B:	.25	.40
69 Military Intelligence U :B:	.20	.35
70 Mind Sculpt C :B:	.15	.25
71 Negate C :B:	.15	.25

72 Nimbus of the Isles C :B: .15 .25
73 Paragon of Gathering Mists U :B: .20 .35
74 Peel from Reality C :B: .15 .25
75 Polymorphist's Jest R :B: 1.00 1.50
76 Quickling U :B: .20 .35
77 Research Assistant C :B: .15 .25
78 Soul of Ravnica M :B: .40 .60
79 Statute of Denial C :B: .15 .25
80 Stormtide Leviathan R :B: .25 .40
81 Turn to Frog U :B: .20 .35
82 Void Snare C :B: .15 .25
83 Wall of Frost U :B: .20 .35
84 Welkin Tern C :B: .15 .25
85 Accursed Spirit C :K: .15 .25
86 Black Cat C :K: .15 .25
87 Blood Host U :K: .20 .35
88 Carrion Crow C :K: .15 .25
89 Caustic Tar U :K: .20 .35
90 Child of Night C :K: .15 .25
91 Covenant of Blood C :K: .15 .25
92 Crippling Blight C :K: .15 .25
93 Cruel Sadist R :K: .25 .40
94 Endless Obedience U :K: .20 .35
95 Eternal Thirst C :K: .15 .25
96 Feast on the Fallen U :K: .20 .35
97 Festergloom C :K: .15 .25
98 Flesh to Dust C :K: .15 .25
99 Gravedigger C :K: .15 .25
100 In Garruk's Wake R :K: .50 .75
101 Indulgent Tormentor R :K: .50 .75
102 Leeching Sliver U :K: .20 .35
103 Liliana Vess M :K: 6.50 8.00
104 Mind Rot C :K: .15 .25
105 Necrobite C :K: .15 .25
106 Necrogen Scudder U :K: .20 .35
107 Necromancer's Assistant C :K: .15 .25
108 Necromancer's Stockpile R :K: .25 .40
109 Nightfire Giant U :K: .20 .35
110 Ob Nixilis, Unshackled R :K: .25 .40
111 Paragon of Open Graves U :K: .20 .35
112 Rotfeaster Maggot C :K: .15 .25
113 Shadowcloak Vampire C :K: .15 .25
114 Sign in Blood C :K: .15 .25
115 Soul of Innistrad M :K: .75 1.25
116 Stab Wound C :K: .15 .25
117 Stain the Mind R :K: .25 .40
118 Typhoid Rats C :K: .15 .25
119 Ulcerate U :K: .20 .35
120 Unmake the Graves C :K: .15 .25
121 Wall of Limbs U :K: .20 .35
122 Waste Not R :K: 3.75 4.25
123 Witch's Familiar C :K: .15 .25
124 Xathrid Slyblade U :K: .20 .35
125 Zof Shade C :K: .15 .25
126 Act on Impulse U :R: .20 .35
127 Aggressive Mining R :R: .25 .40
128 Altac Bloodseeker U :R: .20 .35
129 Belligerent Sliver U :R: .20 .35
130 Blastfire Bolt C :R: .15 .25
131 Borderland Marauder C :R: .15 .25
132 Brood Keeper U :R: .20 .35
133 Burning Anger R :R: .25 .40
134 Chandra, Pyromaster M :R: 2.50 3.00
135 Circle of Flame U :R: .20 .35
136 Clear a Path C :R: .15 .25
137 Cone of Flame U :R: .20 .35
138 Crowd's Favor C :R: .15 .25
139 Crucible of Fire R :R: .75 1.00
140 Forge Devil C :R: .15 .25
141 Foundry Street Denizen C :R: .15 .25
142 Frenzied Goblin U :R: .20 .35
143 Generator Servant C :R: .15 .25
144 Goblin Kaboomist R :R: .25 .40
145 Goblin Rabblemaster R :R: 2.75 3.75
146 Goblin Roughrider C :R: .15 .25
147 Hammerhand C :R: .15 .25
148 Heat Ray C :R: .15 .25
149 Hoarding Dragon R :R: .25 .40
150 Inferno Fist C :R: .15 .25
151 Kird Chieftain U :R: .20 .35
152 Krenko's Enforcer C :R: .15 .25
153 Kurkesh, Onakke Ancient R :R: .25 .40
154 Lava Axe C :R: .15 .25
155 Lightning Strike C :R: .15 .25
156 Might Makes Right U :R: .20 .35
157 Miner's Bane C :R: .15 .25
158 Paragon of Fierce Defiance U :R: .20 .35
159 Rummaging Goblin C :R: .15 .25
160 Scrapyard Mongrel C :R: .15 .25
161 Shrapnel Blast U :R: .20 .35
162 Siege Dragon R :R: .25 .40
163 Soul of Shandalar M :R: .50 .75
164 Stoke the Flames U :R: .20 .35
165 Thundering Giant C :R: .15 .25
166 Torch Fiend C :R: .15 .25
167 Wall of Fire C :R: .15 .25
168 Ancient Silverback U :G: .20 .35
169 Back to Nature U :G: .20 .35
170 Carnivorous Moss-Beast C :G: .15 .25
171 Charging Rhino C :G: .15 .25
172 Chord of Calling R :G: 7.00 9.00
173 Elvish Mystic C :G: .15 .25
174 Feral Incarnation U :G: .20 .35
175 Gather Courage U :G: .20 .35
176 Genesis Hydra R :G: .75 1.00
177 Hornet Nest R :G: .75 1.15
178 Hornet Queen R :G: .75 1.15
179 Hunt the Weak C :G: .15 .25
180 Hunter's Ambush C :G: .15 .25
181 Invasive Species C :G: .15 .25
182 Kalonian Twingrove R :G: .25 .40
183 Life's Legacy R :G: .25 .40
184 Living Totem U :G: .20 .35
185 Naturalize C :G: .15 .25
186 Netcaster Spider C :G: .15 .25
187 Nissa's Expedition U :G: .20 .35
188 Nissa, Worldwaker M :G: 9.00 11.00
189 Overwhelm U :G: .20 .35
190 Paragon of Eternal Wilds U :G: .20 .35
191 Phytotitan R :G: .25 .40
192 Plummet C :G: .15 .25
193 Ranger's Guile C :G: .15 .25
194 Reclamation Sage U :G: .20 .35
195 Restock R :G: .25 .40
196 Roaring Primadox U :G: .20 .35
197 Runeclaw Bear C :G: .15 .25
198 Satyr Wayfinder C :G: .15 .25
199 Shaman of Spring C :G: .15 .25
200 Siege Wurm C :G: .15 .25
201 Soul of Zendikar M :G: .50 .75
202 Sunblade Elf U :G: .20 .35
203 Titanic Growth C :G: .15 .25
204 Undergrowth Scavenger C :G: .15 .25
205 Venom Sliver U :G: .20 .35
206 Verdant Haven C :G: .15 .25
207 Vineweft C :G: .15 .25
208 Wall of Mulch U :G: .20 .35
209 Yisan, the Wanderer Bard R :G: .30 .50
210 Garruk, Apex Predator M :K: :G: 8.00 10.00
211 Sliver Hivelord M :D: 8.00 10.00
212 Avarice Amulet R .25 .40
213 Brawler's Plate U .20 .35
214 Bronze Sable C .15 .25
215 The Chain Veil M 1.50 2.00
216 Gargoyle Sentinel U .20 .35
217 Grindclock R .25 .40
218 Haunted Plate Mail R .25 .40
219 Hot Soup U .20 .35
220 Juggernaut U .20 .35
221 Meteorite U .20 .35
222 Obelisk of Urd R 2.00 2.50
223 Ornithopter U .20 .35
224 Perilous Vault M 1.50 2.00
225 Phyrexian Revoker R .75 1.15
226 Profane Memento U .20 .35
227 Rogue's Gloves U .20 .35
228 Sacred Armory U .20 .35
229 Scuttling Doom Engine R .30 .50
230 Shield of the Avatar R .25 .40
231 Soul of New Phyrexia M 2.25 3.00
232 Staff of the Death Magus U .20 .35
233 Staff of the Flame Magus U .20 .35
234 Staff of the Mind Magus U .20 .35
235 Staff of the Sun Magus U .20 .35
236 Staff of the Wild Magus U .20 .35
237 Tormod's Crypt U .20 .35
238 Tyrant's Machine C .15 .25
239 Will-Forged Golem C .15 .25
240 Battlefield Forge R 1.00 1.50
241 Caves of Koilos R 1.00 1.50
242 Darksteel Citadel U .20 .35
243 Evolving Wilds C .15 .25
244 Llanowar Wastes R 1.25 1.75
245 Radiant Fountain C .15 .25
246 Shivan Reef R 2.25 2.75
247 Sliver Hive R 4.00 5.00
248 Urborg, Tomb of Yawgmoth R 8.00 10.00
249 Yavimaya Coast R 1.50 2.00
250 Plains L .15 .25
251 Plains L .15 .25
252 Plains L .15 .25
253 Plains L .15 .25
254 Island L .15 .25
255 Island L .15 .25
256 Island L .15 .25
257 Island L .15 .25
258 Swamp L .15 .25
259 Swamp L .15 .25
260 Swamp L .15 .25
261 Swamp L .15 .25
262 Mountain L .15 .25
263 Mountain L .15 .25
264 Mountain L .15 .25
265 Mountain L .15 .25
266 Forest L .15 .25
267 Forest L .15 .25
268 Forest L .15 .25
269 Forest L .15 .25
270 Aegis Angel R :W: .30 .50
271 Divine Verdict C :W: .15 .25
272 Inspired Charge C :W: .15 .25
273 Serra Angel U :W: .20 .35
274 Cancel C :B: .15 .25
275 Mahamoti Djinn R :B: .25 .40
276 Nightmare R :K: .25 .40
277 Sengir Vampire U :K: .20 .35
278 Walking Corpse C :K: .15 .25
279 Furnace Whelp U :R: .20 .35
280 Seismic Strike C :R: .15 .25
281 Shivan Dragon R :R: .25 .40
282 Centaur Courser C :G: .15 .25
283 Garruk's Packleader U :G: .20 .35
284 Terra Stomper R :G: .40 .60

2014 Magic The Gathering Magic 2015 Tokens

1 Sliver .40 .60
2 Soldier .10 .15
3 Spirit .10 .15
4 Squid .40 .60
5 Beast .60 1.00
6 Zombie .10 .15
7 Dragon .15 .25
8 Goblin .20 .30
9 Beast .40 .60
10 Insect 3.50 5.00
11 Treefolk Warrior .10 .15
12 Land Mine .10 .15
13 Ajani Steadfast Emblem 1.00 1.50
14 Garruk, Apex Predator Emblem .60 1.00

2014 Magic The Gathering Magic 2015 SDCC Black Variant

1 Ajani Steadfast 25.00 60.00
62 Jace, The Living Guildpact 20.00 50.00
103 Liliana Vess 25.00 60.00
134 Chandra Pyromaster 30.00 80.00
187 Nissa, Worldwaker 50.00 100.00
210 Garruk, Apex Predator 30.00 80.00
NNO Garruk's Axe NERF prop 15.00 40.00

2015 Magic The Gathering Origins

COMPLETE SET (293) 180.00 250.00
BOOSTER BOX (36 PACKS) 100.00 120.00
BOOSTER PACK (15 CARDS) 3.00 5.00
RELEASED ON JULY 17, 2015
1 Akroan Jailer C :W: .10 .20
2 Ampryn Tactician C :W: .10 .20
3 Anointer of Champions U :W: .20 .35
4 Archangel of Tithes M :W: 3.00 3.50
5 Auramancer C :W: .10 .20
6 Aven Battle Priest C :W: .10 .20
7 Blessed Spirits U :W: .20 .35
8 Celestial Flare C :W: .10 .20
9 Charging Griffin C :W: .10 .20
10 Cleric of the Forward Order C :W: .10 .20
11 Consul's Lieutenant U :W: .20 .35
12 Enlightened Ascetic C :W: .10 .20
13 Enshrouding Mist C :W: .10 .20
15 Grasp of the Hieromancer C :W: .10 .20
16 Hallowed Moonlight R :W: .75 1.00
17 Healing Hands C :W: .10 .20
18 Heavy Infantry C :W: .10 .20
19 Hixus, Prison Warden R :W: .20 .35
20 Knight of the Pilgrim's Road C :W: .10 .20
21 Knight of the White Orchid R :W: .75 1.25
22 Knightly Valor U :W: .20 .35
23 Kytheon, Hero of Akros M :W: 4.00 5.00
23 Gideon, Battle-Forged M 4.00 5.00
23a Kytheon's Tactics C :W: .10 .20
23b Gideon's Phalanx R :W: .20 .35
25 Kytheon's Irregulars R :W: .20 .35
26 Mighty Leap C :W: .10 .20
27 Murder Investigation U :W: .20 .35
28 Patron of the Valiant U :W: .20 .35
29 Relic Seeker R :W: .20 .35
30 Sentinel of the Eternal Watch U :W: .20 .35
31 Sigil of the Empty Throne R :W: .20 .35
32 Stalwart Aven C :W: .10 .20
33 Starfield of Nyx M :W: 2.00 2.50
34 Suppression Bonds C :W: .10 .20
35 Swift Reckoning U :W: .20 .35
36 Topan Freeblade C :W: .10 .20
37 Totem-Guide Hartebeest U :W: .20 .35
38 Tragic Arrogance R :W: .40 .60
39 Valor in Akros U :W: .20 .35
40 Vryn Wingmare R :W: .30 .50
41 War Oracle U :W: .20 .35
42 Yoked Ox C :W: .10 .20
43 Alhammarret's Archive M 3.00 4.50
44 Anchor to the Æther U :B: .20 .35
45 Artificer's Epiphany C :B: .10 .20
46 Aspiring Aeronaut C :B: .10 .20
47 Bone to Ash C :B: .10 .20
48 Calculated Dismissal C :B: .10 .20
49 Clash of Wills U :B: .20 .35
50 Claustrophobia C :B: .10 .20
51 Day's Undoing M :B: 3.00 3.50
52 Deep-Sea Terror C :B: .10 .20
53 Disciple of the Ring M :B: .50 .75
54 Disperse C :B: .10 .20
55 Displacement Wave R :B: .20 .35
56 Dreadwaters C :B: .10 .20
57 Faerie Miscreant C :B: .10 .20
58 Harbinger of the Tides R :B: .50 .75
59 Hydrolash U :B: .20 .35
60a Jace, Vryn's Prodigy M :B: 35.00 40.00
60b Jace, Telepath Unbound M :B: 35.00 40.00
61 Jace's Sanctum R :B: .40 .60
62 Jhessian Thief U :B: .20 .35
63 Maritime Guard C :B: .10 .20
64 Mizzium Meddler R :B: .20 .35
65 Negate C :B: .10 .20
66 Nivix Barrier C :B: .10 .20
67 Psychic Rebuttal U :B: .20 .35
68 Ringwarden Owl C :B: .10 .20
69 Scrapskin Drake C :B: .10 .20
70 Screeching Skaab C :B: .10 .20
71 Send to Sleep C :B: .10 .20
72 Separatist Voidmage C :B: .10 .20
73 Sigiled Starfish U :B: .20 .35
74 Skaab Goliath U :B: .20 .35
75 Soulblade Djinn R :B: .20 .35
76 Sphinx's Tutelage U :B: .20 .35
77 Stratus Walk C :B: .10 .20
78 Talent of the Telepath R :B: .30 .50
79 Thopter Spy Network R :B: .50 .75
80 Tower Geist U :B: .20 .35
81 Turn to Frog U :B: .20 .35
82 Watercourser C :B: .10 .20
83 Whirler Rogue U :B: .20 .35
84 Willbreaker R :B: .20 .35
85 Blightcaster U :K: .20 .35
86 Catacomb Slug C :K: .10 .20
87 Consecrated by Blood U :K: .20 .35
88 Cruel Revival U :K: .20 .35
89 Dark Dabbling C :K: .10 .20
90 Dark Petition R :K: 1.00 1.50
91 Deadbridge Shaman C :K: .10 .20
92 Demonic Pact M :K: 1.50 2.00
93 Despoiler of Souls R :K: .20 .35
94 Erebos's Titan M :K: .75 1.00
95 Eyeblight Assassin C :K: .10 .20
96 Eyeblight Massacre U :K: .20 .35
97 Fetid Imp C :K: .10 .20
98 Fleshbag Marauder U :K: .20 .35
99 Gilt-Leaf Winnower R :K: .20 .35
100 Gnarlroot Trapper U :K: .20 .35
101 Graveblade Marauder R :K: .20 .35
102 Infernal Scarring C :K: .10 .20
103 Infinite Obliteration R :K: .50 .75
104 Kothophed, Soul Hoarder R :K: .20 .35
105 Languish R :K: 1.00 1.50
106a Liliana, Heretical Healer M :K: 6.00 8.00
106b Liliana, Defiant Necromancer M 6.00 8.00
107 Macabre Waltz C :K: .10 .20
108 Malakir Cullblade U :K: .20 .35
109 Nantuko Husk C :K: .10 .20
110 Necromantic Summons U :K: .20 .35
111 Nightsnare C :K: .10 .20
112 Priest of the Blood Rite R :K: .20 .35
113 Rabid Bloodsucker C :K: .10 .20
114 Read the Bones C :K: .10 .20
115 Reave Soul C :K: .10 .20
116 Returned Centaur C :K: .10 .20
117 Revenant U :K: .20 .35
118 Shadows of the Past U :K: .20 .35
119 Shambling Ghoul C :K: .10 .20
120 Tainted Remedy R :K: .40 .60
121 Thornbow Archer C :K: .10 .20
122 Tormented Thoughts U :K: .20 .35
123 Touch of Moonglove C :K: .10 .20
124 Undead Servant C :K: .10 .20
125 Unholy Hunger C :K: .10 .20
126 Weight of the Underworld C :K: .10 .20
127 Abbot of Keral Keep R :R: 1.00 1.50
128 Acolyte of the Inferno U :R: .20 .35
129 Act of Treason C :R: .10 .20
130 Akroan Sergeant C :R: .10 .20
131 Avaricious Dragon M :R: .75 1.00
132 Bellows Lizard C :R: .10 .20
133 Boggart Brute C :R: .10 .20
134 Call of the Full Moon U :R: .20 .35
135a Chandra, Fire of Kaladesh M :R: 3.00 3.50
135b Chandra, Roaring Flame M 2.50 3.00
136 Chandra's Fury C :R: .10 .20
137 Chandra's Ignition R :R: .20 .35
138 Cobblebrute C :R: .10 .20
139 Demolish C :R: .10 .20
140 Dragon Fodder C :R: .10 .20
141 Embermaw Hellion R :R: .20 .35
142 Enthralling Victor U :R: .20 .35
143 Exquisite Firecraft R :R: 1.00 1.50
144 Fiery Conclusion U :R: .20 .35
145 Fiery Impulse C :R: .10 .20
146 Firefiend Elemental C :R: .10 .20
147 Flameshadow Conjuring R :R: .20 .35
148 Ghirapur Æther Grid U :R: .20 .35
149 Ghirapur Gearcrafter C :R: .10 .20
150 Goblin Glory Chaser U :R: .20 .35
151 Goblin Piledriver R :R: 1.00 1.50
152 Infectious Bloodlust C :R: .10 .20
153 Lightning Javelin C :R: .10 .20
154 Mage-Ring Bully C :R: .10 .20
155 Magmatic Insight U :R: .20 .35
156 Molten Vortex R :R: .20 .35
157 Pia and Kiran Nalaar R :R: .75 1.25
158 Prickleboar C :R: .10 .20
159 Ravaging Blaze U :R: .20 .35
160 Scab-Clan Berserker R :R: .20 .35
161 Seismic Elemental U :R: .20 .35
162 Skyraker Giant U :R: .20 .35
163 Smash to Smithereens C :R: .10 .20
164 Subterranean Scout C :R: .10 .20
165 Thopter Engineer U :R: .20 .35
166 Titanic Growth C :G: .10 .20
167 Volcanic Rambler C :R: .10 .20
168 Aerial Volley C :G: .10 .20
169 Animist's Awakening R :G: .40 .60
170 Caustic Caterpillar C :G: .10 .20
171 Conclave Naturalists U :G: .20 .35
172 Dwynen's Elite U :G: .20 .35
173 Dwynen, Gilt-Leaf Daen R :G: .40 .60
174 Elemental Bond U :G: .20 .35
175 Elvish Visionary C :G: .10 .20
176 Evolutionary Leap R :G: .50 .75
177 Gaea's Revenge R :G: .20 .35
178 Gather the Pack U :G: .20 .35
179 The Great Aurora M :G: .75 1.00
180 Herald of the Pantheon R :G: .30 .50
181 Hitchclaw Recluse C :G: .10 .20
182 Honored Hierarch R :G: .20 .35
183 Joraga Invocation U :G: .20 .35
184 Leaf Gilder C :G: .10 .20
185 Llanowar Empath C :G: .10 .20
186 Managorger Hydra R :G: .75 1.00
187 Mantle of Webs C :G: .10 .20
188 Might of the Masses C :G: .10 .20
189a Nissa's Revelation R :G: .20 .35
189b Nissa's Pilgrimage C :G: .10 .20
190 Nissa, Sage Animist M :G: 6.00 8.00
191 Nissa, Vastwood Seer M :G: 6.00 8.00
192 Orchard Spirit C :G: .10 .20
193 Outland Colossus R :G: .20 .35
194 Pharika's Disciple C :G: .10 .20
195 Reclaim C :G: .10 .20
196 Rhox Maulers C :G: .10 .20
197 Skysnare Spider U :G: .20 .35
198 Somberwald Alpha U :G: .20 .35
199 Sylvan Messenger U :G: .20 .35
200 Timberpack Wolf C :G: .10 .20
201 Titan's Strength C :R: .10 .20
202 Undercity Troll U :G: .20 .35
203 Valeron Wardens U :G: .20 .35
204 Vastwood Gorger C :G: .10 .20
205 Vine Snare C :G: .10 .20
206 Wild Instincts C :G: .10 .20
207 Woodland Bellower M :G: .75 1.25
208 Yeva's Forcemage C :G: .10 .20
209 Zendikar's Roil U :G: .20 .35
210 Blazing Hellhound U :M: .20 .35
211 Blood-Cursed Knight U :M: .20 .35
212 Bounding Krasis U :M: .20 .35
213 Citadel Castellan U :M: .20 .35
214 Iroas's Champion U :M: .20 .35
215 Possessed Skaab U :M: .20 .35
216 Reclusive Artificer U :M: .20 .35
217 Shaman of the Pack U :M: .20 .35
218 Thunderclap Wyvern U :M: .20 .35
219 Zendikar Incarnate U :M: .20 .35
220 Alchemist's Vial C .10 .20
221 Alhammarret, High Arbiter M :B: .20 .35
222 Angel's Tomb U .20 .35
223 Bonded Construct C .10 .20
224 Brawler's Plate U .20 .35
225 Chief of the Foundry U .20 .35
226 Gold-Forged Sentinel U .20 .35
227 Guardian Automaton C .10 .20

2015 Magic The Gathering Origins

228 Guardians of Meletis C .10 .20
229 Hangarback Walker R 4.50 6.00
230 Helm of the Gods R .20 .35
231 Jayemdae Tome U .20 .35
232 Mage-Ring Responder R .20 .35
233 Meteorite U .20 .35
234 Orbs of Warding R .30 .50
235 Prism Ring U .20 .35
236 Pyromancer's Goggles M 1.75 2.25
237 Ramroller U .20 .35
238 Runed Servitor U .20 .35
239 Sigil of Valor U .20 .35
240 Sword of the Animist R 1.50 2.25
241 Throwing Knife U .20 .35
242 Veteran's Sidearm C .10 .20
243 War Horn U .20 .35
244 Battlefield Forge R .75 1.00
245 Caves of Koilos R .75 1.00
246 Evolving Wilds C .10 .20
247 Foundry of the Consuls U .20 .35
248 Llanowar Wastes R .75 1.25
249 Mage-Ring Network U .20 .35
250 Rogue's Passage U .20 .35
251 Shivan Reef R 1.50 2.00
252 Yavimaya Coast R 1.00 1.50
253 Plains L :L: .10 .20
254 Plains L :L: .10 .20
255 Plains L :L: .10 .20
256 Plains L :L: .10 .20
257 Island L :L: .10 .20
258 Island L :L: .10 .20
259 Island L :L: .10 .20
260 Island L :L: .10 .20
261 Swamp L :L: .10 .20
262 Swamp L :L: .10 .20
263 Swamp L :L: .10 .20
264 Swamp L :L: .10 .20
265 Mountain L :L: .10 .20
266 Mountain L :L: .10 .20
267 Mountain L :L: .10 .20
268 Mountain L :L: .10 .20
269 Forest L :L: .10 .20
270 Forest L :L: .10 .20
271 Forest L :L: .10 .20
272 Forest L :L: .10 .20
273 Aegis Angel R :W: .20 .35
274 Divine Verdict C :W: .10 .20
275 Eagle of the Watch C :W: .10 .20
276 Serra Angel U :W: .10 .20
277 Into the Void U :B: .20 .35
278 Mahamoti Djinn R :B: .30 .50
279 Weave Fate C :B: .10 .20
280 Flesh to Dust C :K: .10 .20
281 Mind Rot C :K: .10 .20
282 Nightmare R :K: .20 .35
283 Sengir Vampire U :K: .20 .35
284 Fiery Hellhound C :R: .10 .20
285 Shivan Dragon R :R: .20 .35
286 Plummet C :G: .10 .20
287 Prized Unicorn U :G: .20 .35
288 Terra Stomper R :G: .20 .35

2015 Magic The Gathering Origins Foil

1 Akroan Jailer C :W: .15 .25
2 Ampryn Tactician C :W: .15 .25
3 Anointer of Champions U :W: .20 .35
4 Archangel of Tithes M :W: 7.00 10.00
5 Auramancer C :W: .15 .25
6 Aven Battle Priest C :W: .15 .25
7 Blessed Spirits U :W: .75 1.00
8 Celestial Flare C :W: .15 .25
9 Charging Griffin C :W: .15 .25
10 Cleric of the Forward Order C :W: .15 .25
11 Consul's Lieutenant U :W: 1.00 1.25
12 Enlightened Ascetic C :W: .15 .25
13 Enshrouding Mist C :W: .15 .25
15 Grasp of the Hieromancer C :W: .15 .25
16 Hallowed Moonlight R :W: 3.50 5.00
17 Healing Hands C :W: .15 .25
18 Heavy Infantry C :W: .15 .25
19 Hixus, Prison Warden R :W: .50 .75
20 Knight of the Pilgrim's Road C :W: .15 .25
21 Knight of the White Orchid R :W: 2.00 3.50
22 Knightly Valor U :W: .20 .35
14 Gideon, Battle-Forged M 10.00 18.00
24 Kytheon, Hero of Akros M :W: 9.00 11.00
25 Kytheon's Irregulars R :W: .50 1.50
26 Mighty Leap C :W: .15 .25
27 Murder Investigation U :W: .20 .35
28 Patron of the Valiant U :W: .20 .35
29 Relic Seeker R :W: .40 .60
30 Sentinel of the Eternal Watch U :W: .20 .35
31 Sigil of the Empty Throne R :W: 1.00 1.50
32 Stalwart Aven C :W: .15 .25
33 Starfield of Nyx M :W: 6.00 8.00
34 Suppression Bonds C :W: .15 .25
35 Swift Reckoning U :W: .20 .35
36 Topan Freeblade C :W: .15 .25
37 Totem-Guide Hartebeest U :W: .20 .35
38 Tragic Arrogance R :W: 2.00 3.00
39 Valor in Akros U :W: .20 .35
40 Vryn Wingmare R :W: 2.50 4.00
41 War Oracle U :W: .20 .35
42 Yoked Ox C :W: .15 .25
43 Alhammarret's Archive M 8.00 10.00
44 Anchor to the Æther U :B: .20 .35
45 Artificer's Epiphany C :B: .15 .25
46 Aspiring Aeronaut C :B: .15 .25
47 Bone to Ash C :B: .15 .25
48 Calculated Dismissal C :B: .15 .25
49 Clash of Wills U :B: 1.00 1.50
50 Claustrophobia C :B: .15 .25
51 Day's Undoing M :B: 10.00 13.00
52 Deep-Sea Terror C :B: .15 .25
53 Disciple of the Ring M :B: 2.50 4.00
54 Disperse C :B: .15 .25
55 Displacement Wave R :B: .75 1.25
56 Dreadwaters C :B: .15 .25
57 Faerie Miscreant C :B: .40 .60
58 Harbinger of the Tides R :B: 4.00 6.00
59 Hydrolash U :B: .20 .35
60b Jace, Telepath Unbound M 60.00 80.00
61 Jace's Sanctum R :B: 2.00 3.00
62 Jhessian Thief U :B: .50 .75
63 Maritime Guard C :B: .15 .25
64 Mizzium Meddler R :B: .30 .50
65 Negate C :B: .40 .60
66 Nivix Barrier C :B: .15 .25
67 Psychic Rebuttal U :B: .50 .75
68 Ringwarden Owl C :B: .15 .25
69 Scrapskin Drake C :B: .15 .25
70 Screeching Skaab C :B: .15 .25
71 Send to Sleep C :B: .15 .25
72 Separatist Voidmage C :B: .15 .25
73 Sigiled Starfish U :B: .20 .35
74 Skaab Goliath U :B: .20 .35
75 Soulblade Djinn R :B: .30 .50
76 Sphinx's Tutelage U :B: 4.00 6.00
77 Stratus Walk C :B: .15 .25
78 Talent of the Telepath R :B: 1.00 1.50
79 Thopter Spy Network R :B: 2.00 3.50
80 Tower Geist U :B: .20 .35
81 Turn to Frog U :B: .20 .35
82 Watercourser C :B: .15 .25
83 Whirler Rogue U :B: 2.00 3.00
84 Willbreaker R :B: 1.25 2.00
85 Blightcaster U :K: .20 .35
86 Catacomb Slug C :K: .15 .25
87 Consecrated by Blood U :K: .20 .35
88 Cruel Revival U :K: .20 .35
89 Dark Dabbling C :K: .15 .25
90 Dark Petition R :K: 4.00 7.00
91 Deadbridge Shaman C :K: .15 .25
92 Demonic Pact M :K: 5.00 7.00
93 Despoiler of Souls R :K: .50 .75
94 Erebos's Titan M :K: 1.25 2.00
95 Eyeblight Assassin C :K: .15 .25
96 Eyeblight Massacre U :K: .20 .35
97 Fetid Imp C :K: .15 .25
98 Fleshbag Marauder U :K: 1.50 2.50
99 Gilt-Leaf Winnower R :K: 1.00 1.50
100 Gnarlroot Trapper U :K: .50 .75
101 Graveblade Marauder R :K: .50 .75
102 Infernal Scarring C :K: .15 .25
103 Infinite Obliteration R :K: 1.50 2.50
104 Kothophed, Soul Hoarder R :K: .60 1.00
105 Languish R :K: 2.50 4.00
106b Liliana, Defiant Necromancer M 20.00 25.00
107 Macabre Waltz C :K: .15 .25
108 Malakir Cullblade U :K: .40 .60
109 Nantuko Husk C :K: .50 .75
110 Necromantic Summons U :K: .40 .60
111 Nightsnare C :K: .15 .25
112 Priest of the Blood Rite R :K: .40 .60
113 Rabid Bloodsucker C :K: .15 .25
114 Read the Bones C :K: 1.00 1.50
115 Reave Soul C :K: .15 .25
116 Returned Centaur C :K: .15 .25
117 Revenant U :K: .20 .35
118 Shadows of the Past U :K: .40 .60
119 Shambling Ghoul C :K: .15 .25
120 Tainted Remedy R :K: 1.25 2.00
121 Thornbow Archer C :K: .15 .25
122 Tormented Thoughts U :K: .20 .35
123 Touch of Moonglove C :K: .15 .25
124 Undead Servant C :K: .15 .25
125 Unholy Hunger C :K: .15 .25
126 Weight of the Underworld C :K: .15 .25
127 Abbot of Keral Keep R :R: 3.00 5.00
128 Acolyte of the Inferno U :R: .20 .35
129 Act of Treason C :R: .15 .25
130 Akroan Sergeant C :R: .15 .25
131 Avaricious Dragon M :R: 3.00 5.00
132 Bellows Lizard C :R: .15 .25
133 Boggart Brute C :R: .15 .25
134 Call of the Full Moon U :R: .20 .35
135b Chandra, Roaring Flame M 5.00 10.00
136 Chandra's Fury C :R: .15 .25
137 Chandra's Ignition R :R: 1.00 1.50
138 Cobblebrute C :R: .15 .25
139 Demolish C :R: .15 .25
140 Dragon Fodder C :R: .50 .75
141 Embermaw Hellion R :R: .50 .75
142 Enthralling Victor U :R: .20 .35
143 Exquisite Firecraft R :R: 3.00 5.00
144 Fiery Conclusion U :R: .20 .35
145 Fiery Impulse C :R: .15 .25
146 Firefiend Elemental C :R: 1.50 2.00
147 Flameshadow Conjuring R :R: 1.00 1.50
148 Ghirapur Æther Grid U :R: 3.50 5.00
149 Ghirapur Gearcrafter C :R: .15 .25
150 Goblin Glory Chaser U :R: .75 1.00
151 Goblin Piledriver R :R: 4.00 6.00
152 Infectious Bloodlust C :R: .15 .25
153 Lightning Javelin C :R: .15 .25
154 Mage-Ring Bully C :R: .15 .25
155 Magmatic Insight U :R: 1.50 2.50
156 Molten Vortex R :R: 2.00 3.00
157 Pia and Kiran Nalaar R :R: 4.00 6.00
158 Prickleboar C :R: .15 .25
159 Ravaging Blaze U :R: .20 .35
160 Scab-Clan Berserker R :R: 1.50 2.50
161 Seismic Elemental U :R: .20 .35
162 Skyraker Giant U :R: .20 .35
163 Smash to Smithereens C :R: .40 .60
164 Subterranean Scout C :R: .15 .25
165 Thopter Engineer U :R: 1.50 2.50
166 Titanic Growth C :G: .15 .25
167 Volcanic Rambler C :R: .15 .25
168 Aerial Volley C :G: .15 .25
169 Animist's Awakening R :G: 2.00 3.00
170 Caustic Caterpillar C :G: .15 .25
171 Conclave Naturalists U :G: .20 .35
172 Dwynen's Elite U :G: .20 .35
173 Dwynen, Gilt-Leaf Daen R :G: 1.00 1.50
174 Elemental Bond U :G: 1.25 2.00
175 Elvish Visionary C :G: .75 1.25
176 Evolutionary Leap R :G: 3.00 5.00
177 Gaea's Revenge R :G: .60 1.00
178 Gather the Pack U :G: 1.00 1.50
179 The Great Aurora M :G: 3.00 5.00
180 Herald of the Pantheon R :G: 1.50 2.00
181 Hitchclaw Recluse C :G: .15 .25
182 Honored Hierarch R :G: .60 1.00
183 Joraga Invocation U :G: .20 .35
184 Leaf Gilder C :G: .15 .25
185 Llanowar Empath C :G: .15 .25
186 Managorger Hydra R :G: 3.00 4.00
187 Mantle of Webs C :G: .15 .25
188 Might of the Masses C :G: .15 .25
190 Nissa, Sage Animist M 16.00 20.00
191 Nissa, Vastwood Seer M :G: 16.00 20.00
192 Orchard Spirit C :G: .15 .25
193 Outland Colossus R :G: .50 .75
194 Pharika's Disciple C :G: .15 .25
195 Reclaim C :G: .15 .25
196 Rhox Maulers C :G: .15 .25
197 Skysnare Spider U :G: .20 .35
198 Somberwald Alpha U :G: .20 .35
199 Sylvan Messenger U :G: .75 1.25
200 Timberpack Wolf C :G: .15 .25
201 Titan's Strength C :R: .15 .25
202 Undercity Troll U :G: .20 .35
203 Valeron Wardens U :G: .20 .35
204 Vastwood Gorger C :G: .15 .25
205 Vine Snare C :G: .15 .25
206 Wild Instincts C :G: .15 .25
207 Woodland Bellower M :G: 4.00 6.00
208 Yeva's Forcemage C :G: .15 .25
209 Zendikar's Roil U :G: 1.00 1.50
210 Blazing Hellhound U :M: .20 .35
211 Blood-Cursed Knight U :M: .50 .75
212 Bounding Krasis U :M: 1.50 2.00
213 Citadel Castellan U :M: .20 .35
214 Iroas's Champion U :M: .20 .35
215 Possessed Skaab U :M: .20 .35
216 Reclusive Artificer U :M: .20 .35
217 Shaman of the Pack U :M: 2.00 3.00
218 Thunderclap Wyvern U :M: .50 .75
219 Zendikar Incarnate U :M: .40 .60
220 Alchemist's Vial C .15 .25
221 Alhammarret, High Arbiter M :B: 8.00 10.00
222 Angel's Tomb U .20 .35
223 Bonded Construct C .15 .25
224 Brawler's Plate U .20 .35
225 Chief of the Foundry U .75 1.25
226 Gold-Forged Sentinel U .20 .35
227 Guardian Automaton C .15 .25
228 Guardians of Meletis C .15 .25
229 Hangarback Walker R 12.00 16.00
230 Helm of the Gods R 1.00 1.50
231 Jayemdae Tome U .20 .35
232 Mage-Ring Responder R .40 .60
233 Meteorite U .20 .35
234 Orbs of Warding R 1.50 2.50
235 Prism Ring U .50 .75
236 Pyromancer's Goggles M 6.00 8.00
237 Ramroller U .20 .35
238 Runed Servitor U .20 .35
239 Sigil of Valor U .20 .35
23a Kytheon's Tactics C :W: .15 .25
23b Gideon's Phalanx R :W: .50 1.50
240 Sword of the Animist R 5.00 8.00
241 Throwing Knife U .20 .35
242 Veteran's Sidearm C .15 .25
243 War Horn U .20 .35
244 Battlefield Forge R 2.00 3.50
245 Caves of Koilos R 3.00 5.00
246 Evolving Wilds C .75 1.25
247 Foundry of the Consuls U 1.25 2.00
248 Llanowar Wastes R 3.00 4.00
249 Mage-Ring Network U 2.50 3.50
250 Rogue's Passage U 2.00 3.00
251 Shivan Reef R 3.00 5.00
252 Yavimaya Coast R 3.00 5.00
253 Plains L :L: .15 .25
254 Plains L :L: .15 .25
255 Plains L :L: .15 .25
256 Plains L :L: .15 .25
257 Island L :L: .15 .25
258 Island L :L: .15 .25
259 Island L :L: .15 .25
260 Island L :L: .15 .25
261 Swamp L :L: .15 .25
262 Swamp L :L: .15 .25
263 Swamp L :L: .15 .25
264 Swamp L :L: .15 .25
265 Mountain L :L: .15 .25
266 Mountain L :L: .15 .25
267 Mountain L :L: .15 .25
268 Mountain L :L: .15 .25
269 Forest L :L: .15 .25
270 Forest L :L: .15 .25
271 Forest L :L: .15 .25
272 Forest L :L: .15 .25
273 Aegis Angel R :W: .50 1.50
274 Divine Verdict C :W: .15 .25
275 Eagle of the Watch C :W: .15 .25
276 Serra Angel U :W: .20 .35
277 Into the Void U :B: .20 .35
278 Mahamoti Djinn R :B: .50 1.50
279 Weave Fate C :B: .15 .25
280 Flesh to Dust C :K: .15 .25
281 Mind Rot C :K: .15 .25
282 Nightmare R :K: .50 1.50
283 Sengir Vampire U :K: .20 .35
284 Fiery Hellhound C :R: .15 .25
285 Shivan Dragon R :R: .50 1.50
286 Plummet C :G: .15 .25
287 Prized Unicorn U :G: .20 .35
288 Terra Stomper R :G: .50 1.50
60a Jace, Vryn's Prodigy M :B: 75.00 90.00
106a Liliana, Heretical Healer M :K: 20.00 25.00
135a Chandra, Fire of Kaladesh M :R: 8.00 10.00
189a Nissa's Revelation R :G: .50 1.50
189b Nissa's Pilgrimage C :G: .15 .25

2015 Magic The Gathering Origins Tokens

0 Magic Origins CL .20 .30
1 Angel .25 .35
2 Knight .10 .15
3 Soldier .10 .15
4 Demon .12 .20
5 Zombie .10 .15
6 Goblin .15 .25
7 Ashaya, the Awoken World .15 .25
8 Elemental .15 .25
9 Elf Warrior .30 .40
10 Thopter .10 .15
11 Thopter .10 .15
12 Jace, Telepath Unbound Emblem .30 .40
13 Liliana, Defiant Necromancer Emblem .50 .75
14 Chandra, Roaring Flame Emblem .35 .50

2018 Magic The Gathering Core Set 2019

COMPLETE SET (280) 200.00 300.00
BOOSTER BOX (36 PACKS)
BOOSTER PACK (15 CARDS)
RELEASED ON JULY 13, 2018
1 Aegis of the Heavens U .20 .35
2 Aethershield Artificer U .20 .35
3 Ajani, Adversary of Tyrants M 10.00 13.00
4 Ajani's Last Stand R .30 .50
5 Ajani's Pridemate U .20 .35
6 Ajani's Welcome U .20 .35
7 Angel of the Dawn C .10 .20
8 Cavalry Drillmaster C .10 .20
9 Cleansing Nova R 1.50 2.00
10 Daybreak Chaplain C .10 .20
11 Dwarven Priest C .10 .20
12 Ilant Cavalry C .10 .20
13 Herald of Faith U .20 .35
14 Hieromancer's Cage U .20 .35
15 Inspired Charge C .10 .20
16 Invoke the Divine C .10 .20
17 Isolate R .30 .50
18 Knight of the Tusk C .10 .20
19 Knight's Pledge C .10 .20
20 Knightly Valor U .20 .35
21 Lena, Selfless Champion R .30 .50
22 Leonin Vanguard U .20 .35
23 Leonin Warleader R 1.00 1.50
24 Loxodon Line Breaker C .10 .20
25 Luminous Bonds C .10 .20
26 Make a Stand U .20 .35
27 Mentor of the Meek R .30 .50
28 Mighty Leap C .10 .20
29 Militia Bugler U .20 .35
30 Novice Knight U .20 .35
31 Oreskos Swiftclaw C .10 .20
32 Pegasus Courser C .10 .20
33 Remorseful Cleric R 1.50 2.00
34 Resplendent Angel M 14.00 17.00
35 Revitalize C .10 .20
36 Rustwing Falcon C .10 .20
37 Shield Mare U .20 .35
38 Star-Crowned Stag C .10 .20
39 Suncleanser R .30 .50
40 Take Vengeance C .10 .20
41 Trusty Packbeast C .10 .20
42 Valiant Knight R .30 .50
43 Aether Tunnel U .20 .35
44 Anticipate C .10 .20
45 Aven Wind Mage C .10 .20
46 Aviation Pioneer C .10 .20
47 Bone to Ash U .20 .35
48 Cancel C .10 .20
49 Departed Deckhand U .20 .35
50 Disperse C .10 .20
51 Divination C .10 .20
52 Djinn of Wishes R .30 .50
53 Dwindle C .10 .20
54 Essence Scatter C .10 .20
55 Exclusion Mage U .20 .35
56 Frilled Sea Serpent C .10 .20
57 Gearsmith Prodigy C .10 .20
58 Ghostform C .10 .20
59 Horizon Scholar U .20 .35
60 Metamorphic Alteration R .30 .50
61 Mirror Image U .20 .35
62 Mistcaller R .30 .50
63 Mystic Archaeologist R .30 .50
64 Omenspeaker C .10 .20
65 Omniscience M 5.00 7.00
66 One with the Machine R .30 .50
67 Patient Rebuilding R .30 .50
68 Psychic Corrosion U .20 .35
69 Sai, Master Thopterist R .30 .50
70 Salvager of Secrets C .10 .20
71 Scholar of Stars C .10 .20
72 Sift U .20 .35
73 Skilled Animator U .20 .35
74 Sleep U .20 .35
75 Snapping Drake C .10 .20
76 Supreme Phantom R .30 .50
77 Surge Mare U .20 .35
78 Switcheroo U .20 .35
79 Tezzeret, Artifice Master M 15.00 20.00
80 Tolarian Scholar C .10 .20
81 Totally Lost C .10 .20
82 Uncomfortable Chill C .10 .20
83 Wall of Mist C .10 .20
84 Windreader Sphinx R .30 .50
85 Abnormal Endurance C .10 .20
86 Blood Divination U .20 .35
87 Bogstomper C .10 .20
88 Bone Dragon M 1.00 1.50
89 Child of Night C .10 .20
90 Death Baron R 3.00 5.00
91 Demon of Catastrophes R .30 .50
92 Diregraf Ghoul U .20 .35
93 Doomed Dissenter C .10 .20
94 Duress C .10 .20
95 Epicure of Blood C .10 .20
96 Fell Specter U .20 .35
97 Fraying Omnipotence R .30 .50

98 Gravedigger U .20 .35
99 Graveyard Marshal R 2.00 3.00
100 Hired Blade C .10 .20
101 Infectious Horror C .10 .20
102 Infernal Reckoning R .30 .50
103 Infernal Scarring C .10 .20
104 Isareth the Awakener R .30 .50
105 Lich's Caress C .10 .20
106 Liliana, Untouched by Death M 8.00 10.00
107 Liliana's Contract R .30 .50
108 Macabre Waltz C .10 .20
109 Mind Rot C .10 .20
110 Murder U .20 .35
111 Nightmare's Thirst U .20 .35
112 Open the Graves R .30 .50
113 Phylactery Lich R .30 .50
114 Plage Mare U .20 .35
115 Ravenous Harpy U .20 .35
116 Reassembling Skeleton U .20 .35
117 Rise from the Grave U .20 .35
118 Skeleton Archer C .10 .20
119 Skymarch Bloodletter C .10 .20
120 Sovereign's Bite C .10 .20
121 Stitcher's Supplier U .20 .35
122 Strangling Spores C .10 .20
123 Two-Headed Zombie C .10 .20
124 Vampire Neonate C .10 .20
125 Vampire Sovereign U .20 .35
126 Walking Corpse C .10 .20
127 Act of Treason C .10 .20
128 Alpine Moon R 1.50 2.50
129 Apex of Power M .60 1.00
130 Banefire R .30 .50
131 Boggart Brute C .10 .20
132 Catalyst Elemental C .10 .20
133 Crash Through C .10 .20
134 Dark-Dweller Oracle R .30 .50
135 Demanding Dragon R .30 .50
136 Dismissive Pyromancer R .30 .50
137 Doublecast U .20 .35
138 Dragon Egg U .20 .35
139 Electrify C .10 .20
140 Fiery Finish U .20 .35
141 Fire Elemental C .10 .20
142 Goblin Instigator C 1.00 1.50
143 Goblin Motivator C .10 .20
144 Goblin Trashmaster R .30 .50
145 Guttersnipe U .20 .35
146 Havoc Devils C .10 .20
147 Hostile Minotaur C .10 .20
148 Inferno Hellion U .20 .35
149 Lathliss, Dragon Queen R .30 .50
150 Lava Axe C .10 .20
151 Lightning Mare U .20 .35
152 Lightning Strike U .20 .35
153 Onakke Ogre C .10 .20
154 Sarkhan, Fireblood M 8.00 11.00
155 Sarkhan's Unsealing R .30 .50
156 Shock C .10 .20
157 Siegebreaker Giant U .20 .35
158 Smelt C .10 .20
159 Sparktongue Dragon C .10 .20
160 Spit Flame R .30 .50
161 Sure Strike C .10 .20
162 Tectonic Rift U .20 .35
163 Thud U .20 .35
164 Tormenting Voice C .10 .20
165 Trumpet Blast C .10 .20
166 Viashino Pyromancer C .10 .20
167 Volcanic Dragon U .20 .35
168 Volley Veteran U .20 .35
169 Blanchwood Armor U .20 .35
170 Bristling Boar C .10 .20
171 Centaur Courser C .10 .20
172 Colossal Dreadmaw C .10 .20
173 Colossal Majesty U .20 .35
174 Daggerback Basilisk C .10 .20
175 Declare Dominance U .20 .35
176 Druid of Horns U .20 .35
177 Druid of the Cowl C .10 .20
178 Dryad Greenseeker U .20 .35
179 Elvish Clancaller R 1.00 1.50
180 Elvish Rejuvenator C .10 .20
181 Ghastbark Twins U .20 .35
182 Ghirapur Guide U .20 .35
183 Giant Spider C .10 .20
184 Gift of Paradise U .20 .35
185 Gigantosaurus R 1.00 1.50
186 Goreclaw, Terror of Qal Sisma R 1.50 2.00
187 Greenwood Sentinel C .10 .20
188 Highland Game C .10 .20
189 Hungering Hydra R .30 .50
190 Naturalize C .10 .20
191 Oakenform C .10 .20
192 Pelakka Wurm R .30 .50
193 Plummet C .10 .20
194 Prodigious Growth R .30 .50
195 Rabid Bite C .10 .20
196 Reclamation Sage U .20 .35
197 Recollect U .20 .35
198 Rhox Oracle C .10 .20
199 Root Snare C .10 .20
200 Runic Armasaur R .30 .50
201 Scapeshift M .15 1.00
202 Talons of Wildwood C .10 .20
203 Thorn Lieutenant R .30 .50
204 Thornhide Wolves C .10 .20
205 Titanic Growth C .10 .20
206 Vigilant Baloth U .20 .35
207 Vine Mare U .20 .35
208 Vivien Reid M 6.00 8.00
209 Vivien's Invocation R .30 .50
210 Wall of Vines C .10 .20
211 Aerial Engineer U .20 .35
212 Arcades, the Strategist M 4.00 6.00
213 Brawl-Bash Ogre U .20 .35
214 Chromium, the Mutable M 6.00 8.00
215 Draconic Disciple U .20 .35
216 Enigma Drake U .20 .35
217 Heroic Reinforcements U .20 .35
218A Nicol Bolas, the Ravager M 25.00 30.00
218B Nicol Bolas, the Arisen M 25.00 30.00
219 Palladia-Mors, the Ruiner M 2.00 3.00
220 Poison-Tip Archer U .20 .35
221 Psychic Symbiont U .20 .35
222 Regal Bloodlord U .20 .35
223 Satyr Enchanter U .20 .35
224 Skyrider Patrol U .20 .35
225 Vaevictis Asmadi, the Dire M 1.50 2.00
226 Amulet of Safekeeping R .30 .50
227 Arcane Encyclopedia U .20 .35
228 Chaos Wand R .30 .50
229 Crucible of Worlds M 15.00 20.00
230 Desecrated Tomb R .30 .50
231 Diamond Mare U .20 .35
232 Dragon's Hoard R .30 .50
233 Explosive Apparatus C .10 .20
234 Field Creeper C .10 .20
235 Fountain of Renewal U .20 .35
236 Gargoyle Sentinel U .20 .35
237 Gearsmith Guardian C .10 .20
238 Magistrate's Scepter R .30 .50
239 Manalith C .10 .20
240 Marauder's Axe C .10 .20
241 Meteor Golem U .20 .35
242 Millstone U .20 .35
243 Rogue's Gloves U .20 .35
244 Sigiled Sword of Valeron R .30 .50
245 Skyscanner C .10 .20
246 Suspicious Bookcase U .20 .35
247 Transmogrifying Wand R .30 .50
248 Cinder Barrens C .10 .20
249 Detection Tower R .30 .50
250 Forsaken Sanctuary C .10 .20
251 Foul Orchard C .10 .20
252 Highland Lake C .10 .20
253 Meandering River C .10 .20
254 Reliquary Tower U .60 1.00
255 Rupture Spire U .20 .35
256 Stone Quarry C .10 .20
257 Submerged Boneyard C .10 .20
258 Timber Gorge C .10 .20
259 Tranquil Expanse C .10 .20
260 Woodland Stream C .10 .20
261 Plains C .10 .20
262 Plains C .10 .20
263 Plains C .10 .20
264 Plains C .10 .20
265 Island C .10 .20
266 Island C .10 .20
267 Island C .10 .20
268 Island C .10 .20
269 Swamp C .10 .20
270 Swamp C .10 .20
271 Swamp C .10 .20
272 Swamp C .10 .20
273 Mountain C .10 .20
274 Mountain C .10 .20
275 Mountain C .10 .20
276 Mountain C .10 .20
277 Forest C .10 .20
278 Forest C .10 .20
279 Forest C .10 .20
280 Forest C .10 .20

2018 Magic The Gathering Core Set 2019 Foil

COMPLETE SET (280) 600.00 900.00
1 Aegis of the Heavens U .40 .60
2 Aethershield Artificer U .40 .60
3 Ajani, Adversary of Tyrants M 20.00 25.00
4 Ajani's Last Stand R 3.00 5.00
5 Ajani's Pridemate U .40 .60
6 Ajani's Welcome U .40 .60
7 Angel of the Dawn C .20 .35
8 Cavalry Drillmaster C .20 .35
9 Cleansing Nova R 3.00 5.00
10 Daybreak Chaplain C .20 .35
11 Dwarven Priest C .20 .35
12 Ilant Cavalry C .20 .35
13 Herald of Faith U .40 .60
14 Hieromancer's Cage U .40 .60
15 Inspired Charge C .20 .35
16 Invoke the Divine C .20 .35
17 Isolate R 3.00 5.00
18 Knight of the Tusk C .20 .35
19 Knight's Pledge C .20 .35
20 Knightly Valor U .40 .60
21 Lena, Selfless Champion R 3.00 5.00
22 Leonin Vanguard U .40 .60
23 Leonin Warleader R 3.00 5.00
24 Loxodon Line Breaker C .20 .35
25 Luminous Bonds C .20 .35
26 Make a Stand U .40 .60
27 Mentor of the Meek R 3.00 5.00
28 Mighty Leap C .20 .35
29 Militia Bugler U .40 .60
30 Novice Knight U .40 .60
31 Oreskos Swiftclaw C .20 .35
32 Pegasus Courser C .20 .35
33 Remorseful Cleric R 3.00 5.00
34 Resplendent Angel M 25.00 30.00
35 Revitalize C .20 .35
36 Rustwing Falcon C .20 .35
37 Shield Mare U .40 .60
38 Star-Crowned Stag C .20 .35
39 Suncleanser R 3.00 5.00
40 Take Vengeance C .20 .35
41 Trusty Packbeast C .20 .35
42 Valiant Knight R 3.00 5.00
43 Aether Tunnel U .40 .60
44 Anticipate C .20 .35
45 Aven Wind Mage C .20 .35
46 Aviation Pioneer C .20 .35
47 Bone to Ash U .40 .60
48 Cancel C .20 .35
49 Departed Deckhand U .40 .60
50 Disperse C .20 .35
51 Divination C .20 .35
52 Djinn of Wishes R 3.00 5.00
53 Dwindle C .20 .35
54 Essence Scatter C .20 .35
55 Exclusion Mage U .40 .60
56 Frilled Sea Serpent C .20 .35
57 Gearsmith Prodigy C .20 .35
58 Ghostform C .20 .35
59 Horizon Scholar U .40 .60
60 Metamorphic Alteration R 3.00 5.00
61 Mirror Image U .40 .60
62 Mistcaller R 3.00 5.00
63 Mystic Archaeologist R 3.00 5.00
64 Omenspeaker C .20 .35
65 Omniscience M 20.00 25.00
66 One with the Machine R 3.00 5.00
67 Patient Rebuilding R 3.00 5.00
68 Psychic Corrosion U .40 .60
69 Sai, Master Thopterist R 3.00 5.00
70 Salvager of Secrets C .20 .35
71 Scholar of Stars C .20 .35
72 Sift U .40 .60
73 Skilled Animator U .40 .60
74 Sleep U .40 .60
75 Snapping Drake C .20 .35
76 Supreme Phantom R 7.00 9.00
77 Surge Mare U .40 .60
78 Switcheroo U .40 .60
79 Tezzeret, Artifice Master M 40.00 45.00
80 Tolarian Scholar C .20 .35
81 Totally Lost C .20 .35
82 Uncomfortable Chill C .20 .35
83 Wall of Mist C .20 .35
84 Windreader Sphinx R 3.00 5.00
85 Abnormal Endurance C .20 .35
86 Blood Divination U .40 .60
87 Bogstomper C .20 .35
88 Bone Dragon M 4.00 6.00
89 Child of Night C .20 .35
90 Death Baron R 8.00 10.00
91 Demon of Catastrophes R 3.00 5.00
92 Diregraf Ghoul U .40 .60
93 Doomed Dissenter C .20 .35
94 Duress C .20 .35
95 Epicure of Blood C .20 .35
96 Fell Specter U .40 .60
97 Fraying Omnipotence R 3.00 5.00
98 Gravedigger U .40 .60
99 Graveyard Marshal R 3.00 5.00
100 Hired Blade C .20 .35
101 Infectious Horror C .20 .35
102 Infernal Reckoning R 3.00 5.00
103 Infernal Scarring C .20 .35
104 Isareth the Awakener R 3.00 5.00
105 Lich's Caress C .20 .35
106 Liliana, Untouched by Death M 20.00 25.00
107 Liliana's Contract R 3.00 5.00
108 Macabre Waltz C .20 .35
109 Mind Rot C .20 .35
110 Murder U .40 .60
111 Nightmare's Thirst U .40 .60
112 Open the Graves R 3.00 5.00
113 Phylactery Lich R 3.00 5.00
114 Plage Mare U .40 .60
115 Ravenous Harpy U .40 .60
116 Reassembling Skeleton U .40 .60
117 Rise from the Grave U .40 .60
118 Skeleton Archer C .20 .35
119 Skymarch Bloodletter C .20 .35
120 Sovereign's Bite C .20 .35
121 Stitcher's Supplier U .40 .60
122 Strangling Spores C .20 .35
123 Two-Headed Zombie C .20 .35
124 Vampire Neonate C .20 .35
125 Vampire Sovereign U .40 .60
126 Walking Corpse C .20 .35
127 Act of Treason C .20 .35
128 Alpine Moon R 3.00 5.00
129 Apex of Power M 4.00 6.00
130 Banefire R 3.00 5.00
131 Boggart Brute C .20 .35
132 Catalyst Elemental C .20 .35
133 Crash Through C .20 .35
134 Dark-Dweller Oracle R 3.00 5.00
135 Demanding Dragon R 3.00 5.00
136 Dismissive Pyromancer R 3.00 5.00
137 Doublecast U .40 .60
138 Dragon Egg U .40 .60
139 Electrify C .20 .35
140 Fiery Finish U .40 .60
141 Fire Elemental C .20 .35
142 Goblin Instigator C .20 .35
143 Goblin Motivator C .20 .35
144 Goblin Trashmaster R 3.00 5.00
145 Guttersnipe U .40 .60
146 Havoc Devils C .20 .35
147 Hostile Minotaur C .20 .35
148 Inferno Hellion U .40 .60
149 Lathliss, Dragon Queen R 3.00 5.00
150 Lava Axe C .20 .35
151 Lightning Mare U .40 .60
152 Lightning Strike U .40 .60
153 Onakke Ogre C .20 .35
154 Sarkhan, Fireblood M 20.00 25.00
155 Sarkhan's Unsealing R 3.00 5.00
156 Shock C .20 .35
157 Siegebreaker Giant U .40 .60
158 Smelt C .20 .35
159 Sparktongue Dragon C .20 .35
160 Spit Flame R 3.00 5.00
161 Sure Strike C .20 .35
162 Tectonic Rift U .40 .60
163 Thud U .40 .60
164 Tormenting Voice C .20 .35
165 Trumpet Blast C .20 .35
166 Viashino Pyromancer C .20 .35
167 Volcanic Dragon U .40 .60
168 Volley Veteran U .40 .60
169 Blanchwood Armor U .40 .60
170 Bristling Boar C .20 .35
171 Centaur Courser C .20 .35
172 Colossal Dreadmaw C .20 .35
173 Colossal Majesty U .40 .60
174 Daggerback Basilisk C .20 .35
175 Declare Dominance U .40 .60
176 Druid of Horns U .40 .60
177 Druid of the Cowl C .20 .35
178 Dryad Greenseeker U .40 .60
179 Elvish Clancaller R 3.00 5.00
180 Elvish Rejuvenator C .20 .35
181 Ghastbark Twins U .40 .60
182 Ghirapur Guide U .40 .60
183 Giant Spider C .20 .35
184 Gift of Paradise U .40 .60
185 Gigantosaurus R 3.00 5.00
186 Goreclaw, Terror of Qal Sisma R 3.00 5.00
187 Greenwood Sentinel C .20 .35
188 Highland Game C .20 .35
189 Hungering Hydra R 3.00 5.00
190 Naturalize C .20 .35
191 Oakenform C .20 .35
192 Pelakka Wurm R 3.00 5.00
193 Plummet C .20 .35
194 Prodigious Growth R 3.00 5.00
195 Rabid Bite C .20 .35
196 Reclamation Sage U .40 .60
197 Recollect U .40 .60
198 Rhox Oracle C .20 .35
199 Root Snare C .20 .35
200 Runic Armasaur R 3.00 5.00
201 Scapeshift M 30.00 35.00
202 Talons of Wildwood C .20 .35
203 Thorn Lieutenant R 3.00 5.00
204 Thornhide Wolves C .20 .35
205 Titanic Growth C .20 .35
206 Vigilant Baloth U .40 .60
207 Vine Mare U .40 .60
208 Vivien Reid M 15.00 20.00
209 Vivien's Invocation R 3.00 5.00
210 Wall of Vines C .20 .35
211 Aerial Engineer U .40 .60
212 Arcades, the Strategist M 30.00 35.00
213 Brawl-Bash Ogre U .40 .60
214 Chromium, the Mutable M 20.00 25.00
215 Draconic Disciple U .40 .60
216 Enigma Drake U .40 .60
217 Heroic Reinforcements U .40 .60
219 Palladia-Mors, the Ruiner M 10.00 15.00
220 Poison-Tip Archer U .40 .60
221 Psychic Symbiont U .40 .60
222 Regal Bloodlord U .40 .60
223 Satyr Enchanter U .40 .60
224 Skyrider Patrol U .40 .60
225 Vaevictis Asmadi, the Dire M 15.00 20.00
226 Amulet of Safekeeping R 3.00 5.00
227 Arcane Encyclopedia U .40 .60
228 Chaos Wand R 3.00 5.00
229 Crucible of Worlds M 35.00 40.00
230 Desecrated Tomb R 3.00 5.00
231 Diamond Mare U .40 .60
232 Dragon's Hoard R 3.00 5.00
233 Explosive Apparatus C .20 .35
234 Field Creeper C .20 .35
235 Fountain of Renewal U .40 .60
236 Gargoyle Sentinel U .40 .60
237 Gearsmith Guardian C .20 .35
238 Magistrate's Scepter R 3.00 5.00
239 Manalith C .20 .35
240 Marauder's Axe C .20 .35
241 Meteor Golem U .40 .60
242 Millstone U .40 .60
243 Rogue's Gloves U .40 .60
244 Sigiled Sword of Valeron R 3.00 5.00
245 Skyscanner C .20 .35
246 Suspicious Bookcase U .40 .60
247 Transmogrifying Wand R 3.00 5.00
248 Cinder Barrens C .20 .35
249 Detection Tower R 3.00 5.00
250 Forsaken Sanctuary C .20 .35
251 Foul Orchard C .20 .35
252 Highland Lake C .20 .35
253 Meandering River C .20 .35
254 Reliquary Tower U .40 .60
255 Rupture Spire U .40 .60
256 Stone Quarry C .20 .35
257 Submerged Boneyard C .20 .35
258 Timber Gorge C .20 .35
259 Tranquil Expanse C .20 .35
260 Woodland Stream C .20 .35
261 Plains C .20 .35
262 Plains C .20 .35
263 Plains C .20 .35
264 Plains C .20 .35
265 Island C .20 .35
266 Island C .20 .35
267 Island C .20 .35
268 Island C .20 .35
269 Swamp C .20 .35
270 Swamp C .20 .35
271 Swamp C .20 .35
272 Swamp C .20 .35
273 Mountain C .20 .35
274 Mountain C .20 .35
275 Mountain C .20 .35
276 Mountain C .20 .35
277 Forest C .20 .35
278 Forest C .20 .35
279 Forest C .20 .35
280 Forest C .20 .35
218A Nicol Bolas, the Ravager M 70.00 80.00
218B Nicol Bolas, the Arisen M 70.00 80.00

2018 Magic The Gathering Core Set 2019 Tokens

1 Angel .30 .40
2 Avatar .06 .10
3 Cat .35 .50
4 Knight .12 .20
5 Ox .06 .10
6 Soldier .15 .25

7 Bat .12 .20
8 Zombie .10 .15
9 Dragon .06 .10
10 Dragon .15 .25
11 Goblin .10 .15
12 Beast .12 .20
13 Elf Warrior .25 .35
14 Thopter .12 .20
15 Ajani, Adversary of Tyrants Emblem .12 .20
16 Tezzeret, Artifice Master Emblem .20 .30
17 Vivien Reid Emblem .15 .25
CH1 Core Set 2019 CL .10 .15

2019 Magic The Gathering Magic Core Set 2020

COMPLETE SET (344) 300.00 400.00
BOOSTER BOX (36 PACKS)
BOOSTER PACK (15 CARDS)
RELEASED ON JULY 12, 2019
1 Aerial Assault C .15 .25
2 Ajani, Strength of the Pride M 4.00 6.00
3 Ancestral Blade U .20 .30
4 Angel of Vitality U .20 .30
5 Angelic Gift C .15 .25
6 Apostle of Purifying Light U .20 .30
7 Battalion Foot Soldier C .15 .25
8 Bishop of Wings R .50 .75
9 Brought Back R 1.25 2.00
10 Cavalier of Dawn M 2.00 3.50
11 Dawning Angel C .15 .25
12 Daybreak Chaplain C .15 .25
13 Devout Decree U .20 .30
14 Disenchant C .15 .25
15 Eternal Isolation U .20 .30
16 Fencing Ace U .20 .30
17 Gauntlets of Light U .20 .30
18 Glaring Aegis C .15 .25
19 Gods Willing U .20 .30
20 Griffin Protector C .15 .25
21 Griffin Sentinel C .15 .25
22 Hanged Executioner R .30 .50
23 Herald of the Sun U .20 .30
24 Inspired Charge C .15 .25
25 Inspiring Captain C .15 .25
26 Leyline of Sanctity R 4.00 6.00
27 Loxodon Lifechanter R .30 .50
28 Loyal Pegasus U .20 .30
29 Master Splicer U .20 .30
30 Moment of Heroism C .15 .25
31 Moorland Inquisitor C .15 .25
32 Pacifism C .15 .25
33 Planar Cleansing R .30 .50
34 Raise the Alarm C .15 .25
35 Rule of Law U .20 .30
36 Sephara, Sky's Blade R 1.25 2.00
37 Soulmender C .15 .25
38 Squad Captain C .15 .25
39 Starfield Mystic R .30 .50
40 Steadfast Sentry C .15 .25
41 Yoked Ox C .15 .25
42 Aether Gust U .20 .30
43 Agent of Treachery R .35 .60
44 Air Elemental U .20 .30
45 Anticipate C .15 .25
46 Atemsis, All-Seeing R .30 .50
47 Befuddle C .15 .25
48 Bone to Ash C .15 .25
49 Boreal Elemental C .15 .25
50 Brineborn Cutthroat U .20 .30
51 Captivating Gyre U .20 .30
52 Cavalier of Gales M 2.50 4.00
53 Cerulean Drake U .20 .30
54 Cloudkin Seer C .15 .25
55 Convolute C .15 .25
56 Drawn from Dreams R .60 1.00
57 Dungeon Geists R .30 .50
58 Faerie Miscreant C .15 .25
59 Flood of Tears R .75 1.25
60 Fortress Crab C .15 .25
61 Frilled Sea Serpent C .15 .25
62 Frost Lynx C .15 .25
63 Hard Cover U .20 .30
64 Leyline of Anticipation R 2.50 4.00
65 Masterful Replication R .30 .50
66 Metropolis Sprite C .15 .25
67 Moat Piranhas C .15 .25
68 Mu Yanling, Sky Dancer M 8.00 12.00
69 Negate C .15 .25
70 Octoprophet C .15 .25
71 Portal of Sanctuary U .20 .30
72 Renowned Weaponsmith U .20 .30
73 Sage's Row Denizen C .15 .25
74 Scholar of the Ages U .20 .30
75 Sleep Paralysis C .15 .25
76 Spectral Sailor U .60 1.00
77 Tale's End R .60 1.00
78 Unsummon C .15 .25
79 Warden of Evos Isle U .20 .30
80 Winged Words C .15 .25
81 Yarok's Wavecrasher U .20 .30
82 Zephyr Charge C .15 .25
83 Agonizing Syphon C .15 .25
84 Audacious Thief C .15 .25
85 Barony Vampire C .15 .25
86 Bladebrand C .15 .25
87 Blightbeetle U .20 .30
88 Blood Burglar C .15 .25
89 Blood for Bones U .20 .30
90 Bloodsoaked Altar U .20 .30
91 Bloodthirsty Aerialist U .20 .30
92 Bone Splinters C .15 .25
93 Boneclad Necromancer C .15 .25
94 Cavalier of Night M 2.50 4.00
95 Disfigure U .20 .30
96 Dread Presence R .60 1.00
97 Duress C .15 .25
98 Embodiment of Agonies R .60 1.00
99 Epicure of Blood C .15 .25
100 Fathom Fleet Cutthroat C .15 .25
101 Feral Abomination C .15 .25
102 Gorging Vulture C .15 .25
103 Gravedigger U .20 .30
104 Gruesome Scourger U .20 .30
105 Knight of the Ebon Legion R 2.00 3.50
106 Legion's End R .50 .75
107 Leyline of the Void R 10.00 15.00
108 Mind Rot C .15 .25
109 Murder C .15 .25
110 Noxious Grasp U .20 .30
111 Rotting Regisaur R 2.50 4.00
112 Sanitarium Skeleton C .15 .25
113 Scheming Symmetry R 2.50 4.00
114 Sorcerer of the Fang C .15 .25
115 Sorin, Imperious Bloodlord M 15.00 20.00
116 Soul Salvage C .15 .25
117 Thought Distortion U .20 .30
118 Undead Servant C .15 .25
119 Unholy Indenture C .15 .25
120 Vampire of the Dire Moon U .20 .30
121 Vengeful Warchief U .20 .30
122 Vilis, Broker of Blood R .75 1.25
123 Yarok's Fenlurker U .20 .30
124 Act of Treason C .15 .25
125 Cavalier of Flame M 2.00 3.50
126 Chandra, Acolyte of Flame R 3.00 8.00
127 Chandra, Awakened Inferno M 20.00 25.00
128 Chandra, Novice Pyromancer U .20 .30
129 Chandra's Embercat C .15 .25
130 Chandra's Outrage C .15 .25
131 Chandra's Regulator R .35 .60
132 Chandra's Spitfire U .20 .30
133 Daggersail Aeronaut C .15 .25
134 Destructive Digger C .15 .25
135 Dragon Mage U .20 .30
136 Drakuseth, Maw of Flames R .60 1.00
137 Ember Hauler U .20 .30
138 Fire Elemental C .15 .25
139 Flame Sweep U .20 .30
140 Fry U .30 .50
141 Glint-Horn Buccaneer R .30 .50
142 Goblin Bird-Grabber C .15 .25
143 Goblin Ringleader U .20 .30
144 Goblin Smuggler C .15 .25
145 Infuriate C .15 .25
146 Keldon Raider C .15 .25
147 Lavakin Brawler C .15 .25
148 Leyline of Combustion R .60 1.00
149 Maniacal Rage C .15 .25
150 Marauding Raptor R 1.00 1.50
151 Mask of Immolation U .20 .30
152 Pack Mastiff C .15 .25
153 Rapacious Dragon U .20 .30
154 Reckless Air Strike C .15 .25
155 Reduce to Ashes C .15 .25
156 Repeated Reverberation R .30 .50
157 Ripscale Predator C .15 .25
158 Scampering Scorcher U .20 .30
159 Scorch Spitter C .15 .25
160 Shock C .15 .25
161 Tectonic Rift C .15 .25
162 Thunderkin Awakener R 1.00 1.50
163 Uncaged Fury U .20 .30
164 Unchained Berserker U .20 .30
165 Barkhide Troll U .20 .30
166 Brightwood Tracker C .15 .25
167 Cavalier of Thorns M 8.00 12.00
168 Centaur Courser C .15 .25
169 Elvish Reclaimer R 1.25 2.00
170 Feral Invocation C .15 .25
171 Ferocious Pup C .15 .25
172 Gargos, Vicious Watcher R .60 1.00
173 Gift of Paradise C .15 .25
174 Greenwood Sentinel C .15 .25
175 Growth Cycle C .15 .25
176 Healer of the Glade C .15 .25
177 Howling Giant U .20 .30
178 Leafkin Druid C .15 .25
179 Leyline of Abundance R 2.00 3.50
180 Loaming Shaman U .20 .30
181 Mammoth Spider C .15 .25
182 Might of the Masses U .20 .30
183 Natural End C .15 .25
184 Netcaster Spider C .15 .25
185 Nightpack Ambusher R 3.00 5.00
186 Overcome U .20 .30
187 Overgrowth Elemental U .20 .30
188 Plummet C .15 .25
189 Pulse of Murasa U .20 .30
190 Rabid Bite C .15 .25
191 Season of Growth U .20 .30
192 Sedge Scorpion C .15 .25
193 Shared Summons R .30 .50
194 Shifting Ceratops R 2.50 4.00
195 Silverback Shaman C .15 .25
196 Thicket Crasher C .15 .25
197 Thrashing Brontodon U .20 .30
198 Veil of Summer U 1.25 2.00
199 Vivien, Arkbow Ranger M 3.00 5.00
200 Voracious Hydra R .30 .50
201 Vorstclaw C .15 .25
202 Wakeroot Elemental R .30 .50
203 Wolfkin Bond C .15 .25
204 Wolfrider's Saddle U .20 .30
205 Woodland Champion U .20 .30
206 Corpse Knight U .20 .30
207 Creeping Trailblazer U .20 .30
208 Empyrean Eagle U .20 .30
209 Ironroot Warlord U .20 .30
210 Kaalia, Zenith Seeker M 2.50 4.00
211 Kethis, the Hidden Hand M 2.00 3.50
212 Kykar, Wind's Fury M 2.50 4.00
213 Lightning Stormkin U .20 .30
214 Moldervine Reclamation U .20 .30
215 Ogre Siegebreaker U .20 .30
216 Omnath, Locus of the Roil M 15.00 20.00
217 Risen Reef U 1.25 2.00
218 Skyknight Vanguard U .20 .30
219 Tomebound Lich U .20 .30
220 Yarok, the Desecrated M 10.00 15.00
221 Anvilwrought Raptor C .15 .25
222 Bag of Holding R .60 1.00
223 Colossus Hammer U .35 .60
224 Diamond Knight U .20 .30
225 Diviner's Lockbox U .20 .30
226 Golos, Tireless Pilgrim R 1.25 2.00
227 Grafdigger's Cage R 1.25 2.00
228 Heart-Piercer Bow C .15 .25
229 Icon of Ancestry R 1.75 3.00
230 Manifold Key U .20 .30
231 Marauder's Axe C .15 .25
232 Meteor Golem U .20 .30
233 Mystic Forge R 1.25 2.00
234 Pattern Matcher U .20 .30
235 Prismite C .15 .25
236 Retributive Wand U .20 .30
237 Salvager of Ruin U .20 .30
238 Scuttlemutt U .20 .30
239 Steel Overseer R 1.75 3.00
240 Stone Golem C .15 .25
241 Vial of Dragonfire C .15 .25
242 Bloodfell Caves C .15 .25
243 Blossoming Sands C .15 .25
244 Cryptic Caves U .20 .30
245 Dismal Backwater C .15 .25
246 Evolving Winds C .15 .25
247 Field of the Dead R 1.50 2.50
248 Jungle Hollow C .15 .25
249 Lotus Field R 5.00 8.00
250 Rugged Highlands C .15 .25
251 Scoured Barrens C .15 .25
252 Swiftwater Cliffs C .15 .25
253 Temple of Epiphany R 1.25 2.00
254 Temple of Malady R 1.25 2.00
255 Temple of Mystery R 1.75 3.00
256 Temple of Silence R 1.25 2.00
257 Temple of Triumph R 1.25 2.00
258 Thornwood Falls C .15 .25
259 Tranquil Cove C .15 .25
260 Wind-Scarred Crag C .15 .25
261 Plains C .15 .25
262 Plains C .15 .25
263 Plains C .15 .25
264 Plains C .15 .25
265 Island C .15 .25
266 Island C .15 .25
267 Island C .15 .25
268 Island C .15 .25
269 Swamp C .15 .25
270 Swamp C .15 .25
271 Swamp C .15 .25
272 Swamp C .15 .25
273 Mountain C .15 .25
274 Mountain C .15 .25
275 Mountain C .15 .25
276 Mountain C .15 .25
277 Forest C .15 .25
278 Forest C .15 .25
279 Forest C .15 .25
280 Forest C .15 .25
281 Rienne, Angel of Rebirth M 3.00 5.00
(Buy-A-Box Exclusive)
282 Ajani, Inspiring Leader M 4.00 6.00
283 Goldmane Griffin R .60 1.00
284 Savannah Sage C .15 .25
285 Twinblade Paladin U .60 1.00
286 Mu Yanling, Celestial Wind M 4.00 6.00
287 Celestial Messenger C .15 .25
288 Waterkin Shaman U .20 .30
289 Yanling's Harbinger R .60 1.00
290 Sorin, Vampire Lord M 4.00 6.00
291 Savage Gorger C .15 .25
292 Sorin's Guide R 1.25 1.00
293 Thirsting Bloodlord U 1.25 2.00
294 Chandra, Flame's Fury M 3.00 5.00
295 Chandra's Flame Wave R .60 1.00
296 Pyroclastic Elemental U .20 .30
297 Wildfire Elemental C .15 .25
298 Viven, Nature's Avenger M 5.00 8.00
299 Ethereal Elk R .60 1.00
300 Gnarlback Rhino U .30 .50
301 Viven's Crocodile C .15 .25
302 Angelic Guardian R 8.00 12.00
303 Bastion Enforcer C .15 .25
304 Concordia Pegasus C .15 .25
305 Haazda Officer C .15 .25
306 Impassioned Orator C .15 .25
307 Imperial Outrider C 3.00 5.00
308 Ironclad Krovod C 1.25 2.00
309 Prowling Caracal C .15 .25
310 Serra's Guardian R .60 1.00
311 Show of Valor C .15 .25
312 Siege Mastodon C 1.25 2.00
313 Take Vengeance C 1.25 2.00
314 Trusted Pegasus C 1.25 2.00
315 Coral Merfolk C 1.25 2.00
316 Phantom Warrior U 2.50 4.00
317 Riddlemaster Sphinx R .60 1.00
318 Snapping Drake C 1.25 2.00
319 Bartizan Bats C 1.25 2.00
320 Bogstomper C 1.50 2.50
321 Dark Remedy C .15 .25
322 Disentomb C 1.50 2.50
323 Gravewalker R .60 1.00
324 Skeleton Archer C 1.25 2.00
325 Sorin's Thrust C .15 .25
326 Vampire Opportunist C .15 .25
327 Walking Corpse C .15 .25
328 Engulfing Eruption C .15 .25
329 Fearless Halberdier C .15 .25
330 Goblin Assailant C .15 .25
331 Hostile Minotaur C 1.25 2.00
332 Immortal Phoenix R 6.00 10.00
333 Nimble Birdsticker C 1.00 1.50
334 Rubblebelt Recluse C 1.25 2.00
335 Shivan Dragon R .60 1.00
336 Volcanic Dragon U .20 .30
337 Aggressive Mammoth R .60 1.00
338 Bristling Boar C .75 1.25
339 Canopy Spider C 1.25 2.00
340 Frilled Sandwalla C 1.25 2.00
341 Oakenform C 1.25 2.00
342 Prized Unicorn U 1.25 2.00
343 Titanic Growth C .15 .25
344 Woodland Mystic C 2.50 4.00

2019 Magic The Gathering Magic Core Set 2020 Foil

1 Aerial Assault C .25 .40
2 Ajani, Strength of the Pride M
3 Ancestral Blade U .30 .50
4 Angel of Vitality U .30 .50
5 Angelic Gift C .25 .40
6 Apostle of Purifying Light U .30 .50
7 Battalion Foot Soldier C .25 .40
8 Bishop of Wings R 1.25 2.00
9 Brought Back R 1.25 2.00
10 Cavalier of Dawn M
11 Dawning Angel C .25 .40
12 Daybreak Chaplain C .25 .40
13 Devout Decree U .30 .50
14 Disenchant C .25 .40
15 Eternal Isolation U .30 .50
16 Fencing Ace U .30 .50
17 Gauntlets of Light U .30 .50
18 Glaring Aegis C .25 .40
19 Gods Willing U .30 .50
20 Griffin Protector C .25 .40
21 Griffin Sentinel C .25 .40
22 Hanged Executioner R 1.25 2.00
23 Herald of the Sun U .30 .50
24 Inspired Charge C .25 .40
25 Inspiring Captain C .25 .40
26 Leyline of Sanctity R 1.25 2.00
27 Loxodon Lifechanter R 1.25 2.00
28 Loyal Pegasus U .30 .50
29 Master Splicer U .30 .50
30 Moment of Heroism C .25 .40
31 Moorland Inquisitor C .25 .40
32 Pacifism C .25 .40
33 Planar Cleansing R 1.25 2.00
34 Raise the Alarm C .25 .40
35 Rule of Law U .30 .50
36 Sephara, Sky's Blade R 1.25 2.00
37 Soulmender C .25 .40
38 Squad Captain C .25 .40
39 Starfield Mystic R 1.25 2.00
40 Steadfast Sentry C .25 .40
41 Yoked Ox C .25 .40
42 Aether Gust U .30 .50
43 Agent of Treachery R 1.25 2.00
44 Air Elemental U .30 .50
45 Anticipate C .25 .40
46 Atemsis, All-Seeing R 1.25 2.00
47 Befuddle C .25 .40
48 Bone to Ash C .25 .40
49 Boreal Elemental C .25 .40
50 Brineborn Cutthroat U .30 .50
51 Captivating Gyre U .30 .50
52 Cavalier of Gales M
53 Cerulean Drake U .30 .50
54 Cloudkin Seer C .25 .40
55 Convolute C .25 .40
56 Drawn from Dreams R 1.25 2.00
57 Dungeon Geists R 1.25 2.00
58 Faerie Miscreant C .25 .40
59 Flood of Tears R 1.25 2.00
60 Fortress Crab C .25 .40
61 Frilled Sea Serpent C .25 .40
62 Frost Lynx C .25 .40
63 Hard Cover U .30 .50
64 Leyline of Anticipation R 1.25 2.00
65 Masterful Replication R 1.25 2.00
66 Metropolis Sprite C .25 .40
67 Moat Piranhas C .25 .40
68 Mu Yanling, Sky Dancer M
69 Negate C .25 .40
70 Octoprophet C .25 .40
71 Portal of Sanctuary U .30 .50
72 Renowned Weaponsmith U .30 .50
73 Sage's Row Denizen C .25 .40
74 Scholar of the Ages U .30 .50
75 Sleep Paralysis C .25 .40
76 Spectral Sailor U .30 .50
77 Tale's End R 1.25 2.00
78 Unsummon C .25 .40
79 Warden of Evos Isle U .30 .50
80 Winged Words C .25 .40
81 Yarok's Wavecrasher U .30 .50
82 Zephyr Charge C .25 .40
83 Agonizing Syphon C .25 .40
84 Audacious Thief C .25 .40
85 Barony Vampire C .25 .40
86 Bladebrand C .25 .40
87 Blightbeetle U .30 .50
88 Blood Burglar C .25 .40
89 Blood for Bones U .30 .50
90 Bloodsoaked Altar U .30 .50
91 Bloodthirsty Aerialist U .30 .50
92 Bone Splinters C .25 .40
93 Boneclad Necromancer C .25 .40
94 Cavalier of Night M
95 Disfigure U .30 .50
96 Dread Presence R 1.25 2.00
97 Duress C .25 .40
98 Embodiment of Agonies R 1.25 2.00
99 Epicure of Blood C .25 .40
100 Fathom Fleet Cutthroat C .25 .40
101 Feral Abomination C .25 .40
102 Gorging Vulture C .25 .40
103 Gravedigger U .30 .50
104 Gruesome Scourger U .30 .50
105 Knight of the Ebon Legion R 1.25 2.00
106 Legion's End R 1.25 2.00
107 Leyline of the Void R 1.25 2.00
108 Mind Rot C .25 .40
109 Murder C .25 .40
110 Noxious Grasp U .30 .50

111 Rotting Regisaur R	1.25	2.00
112 Sanitarium Skeleton C	.25	.40
113 Scheming Symmetry R	1.25	2.00
114 Sorcerer of the Fang C	.25	.40
115 Sorin, Imperious Bloodlord M		
116 Soul Salvage C	.25	.40
117 Thought Distortion U	.30	.50
118 Undead Servant C	.25	.40
119 Unholy Indenture C	.25	.40
120 Vampire of the Dire Moon U	.30	.50
121 Vengeful Warchief U	.30	.50
122 Vilis, Broker of Blood R	1.25	2.00
123 Yarok's Fenlurker U	.30	.50
124 Act of Tension C	.25	.40
125 Cavalier of Flame M		
126 Chandra, Acolyte of Flame R	1.25	2.00
127 Chandra, Awakened Inferno M		
128 Chandra, Novice Pyromancer U	.30	.50
129 Chandra's Embercat C	.25	.40
130 Chandra's Outrage C	.25	.40
131 Chandra's Regulator R	1.25	2.00
132 Chandra's Spitfire U	.30	.50
133 Daggersail Aeronaut C	.25	.40
134 Destructive Digger C	.25	.40
135 Dragon Mage U	.30	.50
136 Drakuseth, Maw of Flames R	1.25	2.00
137 Ember Hauler U	.30	.50
138 Fire Elemental C	.25	.40
139 Flame Sweep U	.30	.50
140 Fry U	.30	.50
141 Glint-Horn Buccaneer R	1.25	2.00
142 Goblin Bird-Grabber C	.25	.40
143 Goblin Ringleader U	.30	.50
144 Goblin Smuggler C	.25	.40
145 Infuriate C	.25	.40
146 Keldon Raider C	.25	.40
147 Lavakin Brawler C	.25	.40
148 Leyline of Combustion R	1.25	2.00
149 Maniacal Rage C	.25	.40
150 Marauding Raptor R	1.25	2.00
151 Mask of Immolation U	.30	.50
152 Pack Mastiff C	.25	.40
153 Rapacious Dragon U	.30	.50
154 Reckless Air Strike C	.25	.40
155 Reduce to Ashes C	.25	.40
156 Repeated Reverberation R	1.25	2.00
157 Ripscale Predator C	.25	.40
158 Scampering Scorcher U	.30	.50
159 Scorch Spitter C	.25	.40
160 Shock C	.25	.40
161 Tectonic Rift C	.25	.40
162 Thunderkin Awakener R	1.25	2.00
163 Uncaged Fury U	.30	.50
164 Unchained Berserker U	.30	.50
165 Barkhide Troll U	.30	.50
166 Brightwood Tracker C	.25	.40
167 Cavalier of Thorns M		
168 Centaur Courser C	.25	.40
169 Elvish Reclaimer R	1.25	2.00
170 Feral Invocation C	.25	.40
171 Ferocious Pup C	.25	.40
172 Gargos, Vicious Watcher R	1.25	2.00
173 Gift of Paradise C	.25	.40
174 Greenwood Sentinel C	.25	.40
175 Growth Cycle C	.25	.40
176 Healer of the Glade C	.25	.40
177 Howling Giant U	.30	.50
178 Leafkin Druid C	.25	.40
179 Leyline of Abundance R	1.25	2.00
180 Loaming Shaman U	.30	.50
181 Mammoth Spider C	.25	.40
182 Might of the Masses U	.30	.50
183 Natural End C	.25	.40
184 Netcaster Spider C	.25	.40
185 Nightpack Ambusher R	1.25	2.00
186 Overcome U	.30	.50
187 Overgrowth Elemental U	.30	.50
188 Plummet C	.25	.40
189 Pulse of Murasa U	.30	.50
190 Rabid Bite C	.25	.40
191 Season of Growth U	.30	.50
192 Sedge Scorpion C	.25	.40
193 Shared Summons R	1.25	2.00
194 Shifting Ceratops R	1.25	2.00
195 Silverback Shaman C	.25	.40
196 Thicket Crasher C	.25	.40
197 Thrashing Brontodon U	.30	.50
198 Veil of Summer U	.30	.50
199 Vivien, Arkbow Ranger M		
200 Voracious Hydra R	1.25	2.00
201 Vorstclaw C	.25	.40
202 Wakeroot Elemental R	1.25	2.00
203 Wolfkin Bond C	.25	.40
204 Wolfrider's Saddle U	.30	.50
205 Woodland Champion U	.30	.50
206 Corpse Knight U	.30	.50
207 Creeping Trailblazer U	.30	.50
208 Empyrean Eagle U	.30	.50
209 Ironroot Warlord U	.30	.50
210 Kaalia, Zenith Seeker M		
211 Kethis, the Hidden Hand M		
212 Kykar, Wind's Fury M		
213 Lightning Stormkin U	.30	.50
214 Moldervine Reclamation U	.30	.50
215 Ogre Siegebreaker U	.30	.50
216 Omnath, Locus of the Roil M		
217 Risen Reef U	.30	.50
218 Skyknight Vanguard U	.30	.50
219 Tomebound Lich U	.30	.50
220 Yarok, the Desecrated M		
221 Anvilwrought Raptor C	.25	.40
222 Bag of Holding R	1.25	2.00
223 Colossus Hammer U	.30	.50
224 Diamond Knight U	.30	.50
225 Diviner's Lockbox U	.30	.50
226 Golos, Tireless Pilgrim R	1.25	2.00
227 Grafdigger's Cage R	1.25	2.00
228 Heart-Piercer Bow C	.25	.40
229 Icon of Ancestry R	1.25	2.00
230 Manifold Key U	.30	.50
231 Marauder's Axe C	.25	.40
232 Meteor Golem U	.30	.50
233 Mystic Forge R	1.25	2.00
234 Pattern Matcher U	.30	.50
235 Prismite C	.25	.40
236 Retributive Wand U	.30	.50
237 Salvager of Ruin U	.30	.50
238 Scuttlemutt U	.30	.50
239 Steel Overseer R	1.25	2.00
240 Stone Golem C	.25	.40
241 Vial of Dragonfire C	.25	.40
242 Bloodfell Caves C	.25	.40
243 Blossoming Sands C	.25	.40
244 Cryptic Caves U	.30	.50
245 Dismal Backwater C	.25	.40
246 Evolving Winds C	.25	.40
247 Field of the Dead R	1.25	2.00
248 Jungle Hollow C	.25	.40
249 Lotus Field R	1.25	2.00
250 Rugged Highlands C	.25	.40
251 Scoured Barrens C	.25	.40
252 Swiftwater Cliffs C	.25	.40
253 Temple of Epiphany R	1.25	2.00
254 Temple of Malady R	1.25	2.00
255 Temple of Mystery R	1.25	2.00
256 Temple of Silence R	1.25	2.00
257 Temple of Triumph R	1.25	2.00
258 Thornwood Falls C	.25	.40
259 Tranquil Cove C	.25	.40
260 Wind-Scarred Crag C	.25	.40
261 Plains C	.25	.40
262 Plains C	.25	.40
263 Plains C	.25	.40
264 Plains C	.25	.40
265 Island C	.25	.40
266 Island C	.25	.40
267 Island C	.25	.40
268 Island C	.25	.40
269 Swamp C	.25	.40
270 Swamp C	.25	.40
271 Swamp C	.25	.40
272 Swamp C	.25	.40
273 Mountain C	.25	.40
274 Mountain C	.25	.40
275 Mountain C	.25	.40
276 Mountain C	.25	.40
277 Forest C	.25	.40
278 Forest C	.25	.40
279 Forest C	.25	.40
280 Forest C	.25	.40
281 Rienne, Angel of Rebirth M		
282 Ajani, Inspiring Leader M		
283 Goldmane Griffin R	1.25	2.00
284 Savannah Sage C	.25	.40
285 Twinblade Paladin U	.30	.50
286 Mu Yanling, Celestial Wind M		
287 Celestial Messenger C	.25	.40
288 Waterkin Shaman U	.30	.50
289 Yanling's Harbinger R	1.25	2.00
290 Sorin, Vampire Lord M		
291 Savage Gorger C	.25	.40
292 Sorin's Guide R	1.25	2.00
293 Thirsting Bloodlord U	.30	.50
294 Chandra, Flame's Fury M		
295 Chandra's Flame Wave R	1.25	2.00
296 Pyroclastic Elemental U	.30	.50
297 Wildfire Elemental C	.25	.40
298 Viven, Nature's Avenger M		
299 Ethereal Elk R	1.25	2.00
300 Gnarlback Rhino U	.30	.50
301 Viven's Crocodile C	.25	.40
302 Angelic Guardian R	1.25	2.00
303 Bastion Enforcer C	.25	.40
304 Concordia Pegasus C	.25	.40
305 Haazda Officer C	.25	.40
306 Impassioned Orator C	.25	.40
307 Imperial Outrider C	.25	.40
308 Ironclad Krovod C	.25	.40
309 Prowling Caracal C	.25	.40
310 Serra's Guardian R	1.25	2.00
311 Show of Valor C	.25	.40
312 Siege Mastodon C	.25	.40
313 Take Vengeance C	.25	.40
314 Trusted Pegasus C	.25	.40
315 Coral Merfolk C	.25	.40
316 Phantom Warrior U	.30	.50
317 Riddlemaster Sphinx R	1.25	2.00
318 Snapping Drake C	.25	.40
319 Bartizan Bats C	.25	.40
320 Bogstomper C	.25	.40
321 Dark Remedy C	.25	.40
322 Disentomb C	.25	.40
323 Gravewalker R	1.25	2.00
324 Skeleton Archer C	.25	.40
325 Sorin's Thrust C	.25	.40
326 Vampire Opportunist C	.25	.40
327 Walking Corpse C	.25	.40
328 Engulfing Eruption C	.25	.40
329 Fearless Halberdier C	.25	.40
330 Goblin Assailant C	.25	.40
331 Hostile Minotaur C	.25	.40
332 Immortal Phoenix R	1.25	2.00
333 Nimble Birdsticker C	.25	.40
334 Rubblebelt Recluse C	.25	.40
335 Shivan Dragon R	1.25	2.00
336 Volcanic Dragon U	.30	.50
337 Aggressive Mammoth R	1.25	2.00
338 Bristling Boar C	.25	.40
339 Canopy Spider C	.25	.40
340 Frilled Sandwalla C	.25	.40
341 Oakenform C	.25	.40
342 Prized Unicorn U	.30	.50
343 Titanic Growth C	.25	.40
344 Woodland Mystic C	.25	.40

2019 Magic The Gathering Magic Core Set 2020 Tokens

1 Ajani's Pridemate	.15	.25
2 Soldier	.15	.25
3 Spirit	.15	.25
4 Elemental Bird	.15	.25
5 Demon	.15	.25
6 Zombie	.15	.25
7 Elemental	.15	.25
8 Wolf	.15	.25
9 Golem	.15	.25
10 Treasure	.15	.25
11 Chandra, Awakened Inferno Emblem	.15	.25
12 Mu Yanling, Sky Dancer Emblem	.15	.25

Expansion Sets

1993 Magic The Gathering Arabian Nights

COMPLETE SET (92)	2500.00	3500.00
BOOSTER BOX (60 PACKS)	8000.00	10000.00
BOOSTER PACK (8 CARDS)	140.00	235.00
RELEASED ON DECEMBER 15, 1993		
WITH VARIATIONS THERE ARE 92 CARDS		
1 Abu Jafar U3 :W:	3.00	5.00
2 Aladdin U2 :R:	5.00	8.00
3 Aladdin's Lamp U2 :A:	8.00	12.00
4 Aladdin's Ring U2 :A:	5.00	8.00
5 Ali Baba U3 :R:	8.00	12.00
6 Ali from Cairo U2 :R:	50.00	70.00
7 Army of Allah (dark 1) C3 :W:	2.50	4.00
8 Army of Allah (light 1) C1 :W:	2.50	4.00
9 Bazaar of Baghdad U3 :L:	400.00	600.00
10 Bird Maiden (dark 1) C2 :R:	.40	1.00
11 Bird Maiden (light 1) C2 :R:	.40	1.00
12 Bottle of Suleiman U2 :A:	3.00	5.00
13 Brass Man U3 :A:	2.50	3.50
14 Camel C5 :W:	.40	1.00
15 City in a Bottle U2 :A:	60.00	12.00
16 City of Brass U3 :L:	80.00	120.00
17 Cuombajj Witches C4 :K:	4.00	6.00
18 Cyclone U3 :G:	1.50	2.50
19 Dancing Scimitar U2 :A:	4.00	6.00
20 Dandan C4 :B:	.40	1.00
21A Desert C11 :L:	.40	1.00
21B Desert (mirage variant) C11 :L:	.40	1.00
22 Desert Nomads C4 :R:	.40	1.00
23 Desert Twister U3 :G:	8.00	10.00
24 Diamond Valley U2 :L:	150.00	200.00
25 Drop of Honey U2 :G:	50.00	80.00
26 Ebony Horse U2 :A:	2.00	3.00
27 Elephant Graveyard U2 :L:	35.00	50.00
28 El-Hajjaj U2 :K:	4.00	6.00
29 Erg Raiders (dark 1) C3 :K:	.40	1.00
30 Erg Raiders (light 1) C2 :K:	.40	1.00
31 Erhnam Djinn U2 :G:	60.00	80.00
32 Eye for an Eye U3 :W:	2.50	4.00
33 Fishliver Oil (dark 1) C3 :B:	.40	1.00
34 Fishliver Oil (light 1) C1 :B:	.40	1.00
35 Flying Carpet U3 :A:	1.75	3.00
36 Flying Men C5 :B:	1.25	2.00
37 Ghazban Ogre C4 :G:	.40	1.00
38 Giant Tortoise (dark 1) C3 :B:	.40	1.00
39 Giant Tortoise (light 1) C1 :B:	.40	1.00
40 Guardian Beast U2 :K:	125.00	175.00
41 Hasran Ogress (dark mana) C3 :K:	.40	1.00
42 Hasran Ogress (light mana) C2 :K:	.40	1.00
43 Hurr Jackal C4 :R:	.40	1.00
44 Ifh-Biff Efreet U2 :G:	15.00	20.00
45 Island Fish Jasconius U2 :B:	4.00	6.00
46 Island of Wak-Wak U2 :L:	50.00	80.00
47 Jandor's Ring U2 :A:	3.00	5.00
48 Jandor's Saddlebags U2 :A:	3.00	5.00
49 Jeweled Bird U3 :A:	1.50	2.50
50 Jihad U2 :W:	35.00	50.00
51 Junun Efreet U2 :K:	8.00	10.00
52 Juzam Djinn U2 :K:	400.00	500.00
53 Khabal Ghoul U3 :K:	12.00	20.00
54 King Suleiman U2 :W:	30.00	40.00
55 Kird Ape C5 :R:	5.00	7.00
56 Library of Alexandria U3 :L:	500.00	800.00
57 Magnetic Mountain U3 :R:	1.25	2.00
58 Merchant Ship U3 :B:	2.50	4.00
59 Metamorphosis C4 :G:	.40	1.00
60 Mijae Djinn U2 :R:	5.00	7.00
61 Moorish Cavalry (dark 2) C4 :W:	.40	1.00
62 Moorish Cavalry (light 2) C1 :W:	.40	1.00
63 Mountain C1 :L:	40.00	60.00
64 Naf's Asp (dark 1) C3 :G:	.40	1.00
65 Naf's Asp (light 1) C2 :G:	.40	1.00
66 Oasis U4 :L:	2.50	3.50
67 Old Man of the Sea U2 :B:	50.00	80.00
68 Oubliette (dark 1) C2 :K:	20.00	30.00
69 Oubliette (light 1) C2 :K:	20.00	30.00
70 Piety (dark 1) C3 :W:	.40	1.00
71 Piety (light 1) C1 :W:	.40	1.00
72 Pyramids U2 :A:	8.00	12.00
73 Repentant Blacksmith U2 :W:	2.00	3.50
74 Ring of Maruf U2 :A:	20.00	30.00
75 Rukh Egg (dark 3) C3 :R:	2.00	3.00
76 Rukh Egg (light 3) C1 :R:	2.00	3.00
77 Sandals of Abdallah U3 :A:	4.00	6.00
78 Sandstorm C4 :G:	.40	1.00
79 Serendib Djinn U2 :B:	40.00	60.00
80 Serendib Efreet U2 :B:	35.00	50.00
81 Shahrazad U2 :W:	60.00	80.00
82 Sindbad U3 :B:	3.00	5.00
83 Singing Tree U2 :G:	40.00	50.00
84 Sorceress Queen U3 :K:	8.00	12.00
85 Stone-Throwing Devils (dark mana) C3 :K:	2.50	3.50
86 Stone-Throwing Devils (light mana) C1 :K:	2.50	3.50
87 Unstable Mutation C5 :B:	.40	1.00
88 War Elephant (dark 3) C3 :W:	.40	1.00
89 War Elephant (light 3) C1 :W:	.40	1.00
90 Wyluli Wolf (dark 1) C4 :G:	.40	1.00
91 Wyluli Wolf (light 1) C1 :G:	1.00	1.50
92 Ydwen Efreet U2 :R:	8.00	12.00

1994 Magic The Gathering Antiquities

COMPLETE SET (100)	1900.00	2200.00
BOOSTER BOX (60 PACKS)	8000.00	12000.00
BOOSTER PACK (8 CARDS)	125.00	175.00
RELEASED ON MARCH 15, 1994		
1 Amulet of Kroog C4 :A:	.15	.25
2 Argivian Archaeologist U1 :W:	35.00	45.00
3 Argivian Blacksmith C4 :W:	.15	.25
4 Argothian Pixies C4 :G:	.15	.25
5 Argothian Treefolk C4 :G:	.15	.25
6 Armageddon Clock U2 :A:	.50	.75
7 Artifact Blast C4:R:	.15	.25
8 Artifact Possession C4:K:	.15	.25
9 Artifact Ward C4:W:	.15	.25
10 Ashnod's Altar U2 :A:	8.00	12.00
11 Ashnod's Battle Gear U2 :A:	.30	.50
12 Ashnod's Transmogrant U3 :A:	.30	.50
13 Atog C4 :R:	.40	.60
14 Battering Ram C4 :A:	.15	.25
15 Bronze Tablet U1 :A:	1.00	1.50
16 Candelabra of Tawnos U1 :A:	450.00	500.00
17 Circle of Protection: Artifacts U3 :W:	3.00	4.00
18 Citanul Druid U3 :G:	.50	.75
19 Clay Statue C4 :A:	.15	.25
20 Clockwork Avian U1 :A:	1.50	2.00
21 Colossus of Sardia U1 :A:	5.00	7.00
22 Coral Helm U1 :A:	.75	1.00
23 Crumble C4 :G:	.15	.25
24 Cursed Rack C1 :A:	.30	.50
25 Damping Field U3 :W:	.30	.50
26 Detonate U3 :R:	.30	.50
27 Drafna's Restoration C4 :B:	.15	.25
28 Dragon Engine C4 :A:	.15	.25
29 Dwarven Weaponsmith U3 :R:	.30	.50
30 Energy Flux U3 :B:	1.50	2.00
31 Feldon's Cane C1 :A:	1.75	2.00
32 Gaea's Avenger U1 :G:	15.00	18.00
33 Gate to Phyrexia U3 :K:	10.00	13.00
34 Goblin Artisans U3 :R:	.30	.50
35 Golgothian Sylex U1 :A:	2.75	3.25
36 Grapeshot Catapult C4 :A:	.15	.25
37 Haunting Wind U3 :K:	.50	.75
38 Hurkyl's Recall U1 :B:	25.00	35.00
39 Ivory Tower U3 :A:	4.00	6.00
40 Jalum Tome U2 :A:	.50	.75
41 Martyrs of Korlis U3 :W:	.30	.50
42 Mightstone U3 :A:	.30	.50
43 Millstone U3 :A:	1.75	2.25
44 Mishra's Factory, autumn U1 :L:	20.00	25.00
45 Mishra's Factory, spring C1 :L:	10.00	15.00
46 Mishra's Factory, summer U1 :L:	25.00	35.00
47 Mishra's Factory, winter U1 :L:	75.00	100.00
48 Mishra's War Machine U1 :A:	.75	1.25
49 Mishra's Workshop U1 :L:	900.00	1000.00
50 Obelisk of Undoing U1 :A:	1.00	1.50
51 Onulet U3 :A:	.30	.50
52 Orcish Mechanics C4 :R:	.15	.25
53 Ornithopter C4 :A:	1.75	2.25
54 Phyrexian Gremlins C4 :K:	.15	.25
55 Power Artifact U3 :B:	35.00	45.00
56 Powerleech U3 :G:	.30	.50
57 Priest of Yawgmoth C 4:K:	.15	.25
58 Primal Clay U3 :A:	.30	.50
59 Rack, The U3 :A:	5.00	7.00
60 Rakalite U3 :A:	.30	.50
61 Reconstruction C4 :B:	.15	.25
62 Reverse Polarity C4 :W:	.15	.25
63 Rocket Launcher U3 :A:	.30	.50
64 Sage of Lat-Nam C4 :B:	.15	.25
65 Shapeshifter U1 :A:	1.25	1.75
66 Shatterstorm U1 :R:	15.00	18.00
67 Staff of Zegon C4 :A:	.15	.25
68 Strip Mine, horizon, even stripe U1 :L:	18.00	22.00
69 Strip Mine, horizon, uneven stripe U1 :L:	25.00	30.00
70 Strip Mine, no horizon C1 :L:	10.00	13.00
71 Strip Mine, small tower in forest U1 :L:	20.00	25.00
72 Su-Chi U3 :A:	15.00	18.00
73 Tablet of Epityr C4 :A:	.15	.25
74 Tawnos's Coffin U1 :A:	35.00	45.00
75 Tawnos's Wand U3 :A:	.30	.50
76 Tawnos's Weaponry U3 :A:	.30	.50
77 Tetravus U1 :A:	18.00	22.00
78 Titania's Song U3 :G:	.30	.50
79 Transmute Artifact U3 :B:	45.00	55.00
80 Triskelion U1 :A:	35.00	45.00
81 Urza's Avenger U1 :A:	2.00	3.00
82 Urza's Chalice C4 :A:	.15	.25
83 Urza's Mine, clawed sphere C2 :L:	4.00	5.00
84 Urza's Mine, mouth C1 :L:	4.00	6.00
85 Urza's Mine, pulley C1 :L:	4.00	5.00
86 Urza's Mine, tower C2 :L:	2.50	3.25
87 Urza's Miter U1 :A:	14.00	16.00
88 Urza's Power Plant, bug C2 :L:	3.50	4.50
89 Urza's Power Plant, columns C1 :L:	5.50	6.50
90 Urza's Power Plant, rock in pot C1 :L:	3.50	4.50
91 Urza's Power Plant, sphere C2 :L:	3.00	4.00
92 Urza's Tower, forest C2 :L:	4.00	5.00
93 Urza's Tower, mountains C1 :L:	4.50	5.50
94 Urza's Tower, plains C1 :L:	.15	.25
95 Urza's Tower, shore C1 :L:	6.00	8.00
96 Wall of Spears U3 :A:	.30	.50
97 Weakstone U3 :A:	.30	.50
98 Xenic Poltergeist U3 :K:	.30	.50
99 Yawgmoth Demon U3 :K:	2.25	2.75
100 Yotian Soldier C4 :A:	.15	.25

1994 Magic The Gathering Legends

COMPLETE SET (310)	4000.00	5000.00
BOOSTER BOX (36 PACKS)	5500.00	7000.00
BOOSTER PACK (15 CARDS)	175.00	225.00
ITALIAN BOOSTER BOX	600.00	700.00
RELEASED ON JUNE 15, 1994		
1 Abomination U :K:	.20	.60
2 Abyss, The R :K:	380.00	400.00
3 Acid Rain R :B:	45.00	55.00
4 Active Volcano C :R:	.20	.60
5 Adun Oakenshield R :D:	90.00	100.00
6 Adventurers' Guildhouse U :L:	1.25	2.00
7 Ærathi Berserker U :R:	.20	.60

8 Aisling Leprechaun C :G:	.20	.60
9 Akron Legionnaire R :W:	1.50	2.00
10 Al-abara's Carpet R :A:	20.00	25.00
11 Alabaster Potion C :W:	.20	.60
12 Alchor's Tomb R :A:	10.00	15.00
13 All Hallow's Eve R :K:	190.00	200.00
14 Amrou Kithkin C :W:	.20	.60
15 Angelic Voices R :W:	3.00	4.00
16 Angus Mackenzie R :D:	110.00	120.00
17 Anti-Magic Aura C :B:	.20	.60
18 Arboria U :G:	6.00	8.00
19 Arcades Sabboth R :D:	6.00	8.00
20 Arena of the Ancients R :A:	5.00	7.00
21 Avoid Fate C :G:	1.00	1.50
22 Axelrod Gunnarson R :D:	2.00	3.00
23 Ayesha Tanaka R :D:	1.50	2.50
24 Azure Drake U :B:	.20	.60
25 Backdraft U :R:	.20	.60
26 Backfire U :B:	.20	.60
27 Barbary Apes C :G:	.20	.60
28 Barktooth Warbeard U :D:	.20	.60
29 Bartel Runeaxe R :D:	35.00	40.00
30 Beasts of Bogardan U :R:	.20	.60
31 Black Mana Battery U :A:	.60	1.00
32 Blazing Effigy C :R:	.20	.60
33 Blight U :K:	1.50	2.00
34 Blood Lust U :R:	5.00	7.00
35 Blue Mana Battery U :A:	.60	1.00
36 Boomerang C :B:	.20	.60
37 Boris Devilboon R :D:	15.00	20.00
38 Brine Hag U :B:	.20	.60
39 Bronze Horse R :A:	1.50	2.00
40 Brute, The C :R:	.20	.60
41 Carrion Ants R :K:	4.00	6.00
42 Cat Warriors C :G:	.20	.60
43 Cathedral of Serra U :L:	1.50	2.00
44 Caverns of Despair R :R:	45.00	50.00
45 Chain Lightning C :R:	5.00	8.00
46 Chains of Mephistopheles R :K:	350.00	400.00
47 Chromium R :D:	10.00	15.00
48 Cleanse R :W:	35.00	40.00
49 Clergy of the Holy Nimbus C :W:	.20	.60
50 Cocoon U :G:	.20	.60
51 Concordant Crossroads R :G:	55.00	60.00
52 Cosmic Horror R :K:	1.50	2.50
53 Craw Giant U :G:	.20	.60
54 Crevasse U :R:	.20	.60
55 Crimson Kobolds C :R:	.20	.60
56 Crimson Manticore R :R:	1.00	1.50
57 Crookshank Kobolds C :R:	.20	.60
58 Cyclopean Mummy C :K:	.20	.60
59 Dakkon Blackblade R :D:	10.00	15.00
60 Darkness C :K:	6.00	8.00
61 D'Avenant Archer C :W:	.20	.60
62 Deadfall U :G:	.20	.60
63 Demonic Torment U :K:	.20	.60
64 Devouring Deep C :B:	.20	.60
65 Disharmony R :R:	13.00	16.00
66 Divine Intervention R :W:	40.00	50.00
67 Divine Offering C :W:	.20	.60
68 Divine Transformation R :W:	4.00	6.00
69 Dream Coat U :B:	.20	.60
70 Durkwood Boars C :G:	.20	.60
71 Dwarven Song U :R:	.20	.60
72 Elder Land Wurm R :W:	3.00	5.00
73 Elder Spawn R :B:	15.00	20.00
74 Elven Riders R :G:	.20	.60
75 Emerald Dragonfly C :G:	.20	.60
76 Enchanted Being C :W:	.20	.60
77 Enchantment Alteration C :B:	.20	.60
78 Energy Tap C :B:	.20	.60
79 Equinox C :W:	.20	.60
80 Eternal Warrior U :R:	.20	.60
81 Eureka R :G:	300.00	350.00
82 Evil Eye of Orms-By-Gore U :K:	.20	.60
83 Fallen Angel U :K:	1.50	2.50
84 Falling Star R :R:	40.00	45.00
85 Feint C :R:	.20	.60
86 Field of Dreams R :B:	55.00	60.00
87 Fire Sprites C :G:	.20	.60
88 Firestorm Phoenix R :R:	15.00	20.00
89 Flash Counter C :B:	.20	.60
90 Flash Flood C :B:	.20	.60
91 Floral Spuzzem U :G:	.20	.60
92 Force Spike C :B:	.20	.60
93 Forethought Amulet R :A:	10.00	15.00
94 Fortified Area U :W:	.20	.60
95 Frost Giant U :R:	.20	.60
96 Gabriel Angelfire R :D:	3.00	5.00
97 Gaseous Form C :B:	.20	.60
98 Gauntlets of Chaos R :A:	.20	.60
99 Ghosts of the Damned C :K:	.20	.60
100 Giant Slug C :K:	.20	.60
101 Giant Strength C :R:	.20	.60
102 Giant Turtle C :G:	.20	.60
103 Glyph of Delusion C :B:	.20	.60
104 Glyph of Destruction C :R:	.20	.60
105 Glyph of Doom C :K:	.20	.60
106 Glyph of Life C :W:	.20	.60
107 Glyph of Reincarnation C :G:	.20	.60
108 Gosta Dirk R :D:	6.00	8.00
109 Gravity Sphere R :R:	40.00	45.00
110 Great Defender U :W:	.20	.60
111 Great Wall U :W:	.20	.60
112 Greater Realm of Preservation U :W:	1.00	1.50
113 Greed R :K:	20.00	25.00
114 Green Mana Battery U :A:	.20	.60
115 Gwendlyn Di Corci R :D:	60.00	65.00
116 Halfdane R :D:	20.00	25.00
117 Hammerheim U :L:	2.00	3.00
118 Hazezon Tamar R :D:	75.00	85.00
119 Headless Horseman C :K:	.20	.60
120 Heaven's Gate U :W:	.20	.60
121 Hell Swarm C :K:	.20	.60
122 Hellfire R :K:	50.00	55.00
123 Hell's Caretaker R :K:	10.00	15.00
124 Holy Day C :W:	.20	.60
125 Horn of Deafening R :A:	3.00	5.00
126 Hornet Cobra C :G:	.20	.60
127 Horror of Horrors U :K:	.20	.60
128 Hunding Gjornersen U :D:	.20	.60
129 Hyperion Blacksmith U :R:	.20	.60
130 Ichneumon Druid U :G:	.20	.60
131 Immolation C :R:	.20	.60
132 Imprison R :K:	15.00	20.00
133 In the Eye of Chaos R :B:	85.00	95.00
134 Indestructible Aura C :W:	.20	.60
135 Infernal Medusa U :K:	1.00	1.50
136 Infinite Authority R :W:	15.00	20.00
137 Invoke Prejudice R :B:	180.00	200.00
138 Ivory Guardians U :W:	.20	.60
139 Jacques le Vert R :D:	15.00	20.00
140 Jasmine Boreal U :D:	.20	.60
141 Jedit Ojanen U :D:	.20	.60
142 Jerrard of the Closed Fist U :D:	.20	.60
143 Johan R :D:	3.00	5.00
144 Jovial Evil R :K:	15.00	20.00
145 Juxtapose R :B:	.20	.60
146 Karakas U :L:	60.00	70.00
147 Kasimir the Lone Wolf U :D:	.20	.60
148 Keepers of the Faith C :W:	.20	.60
149 Kei Takahashi R :D:	1.50	2.00
150 Killer Bees R :G:	15.00	20.00
151 Kismet U :W:	4.00	6.00
152 Knowledge Vault R :A:	15.00	20.00
153 Kobold Drill Sergeant U :R:	2.00	3.00
154 Kobold Overlord R :R:	25.00	30.00
155 Kobold Taskmaster U :R:	1.25	2.00
156 Kobolds of Kher Keep C :R:	1.50	2.00
157 Kry Shield U :A:	.20	.60
158 Lady Caleria R :D:	10.00	15.00
159 Lady Evangela R :D:	25.00	30.00
160 Lady of the Mountain, The U :D:	.20	.60
161 Lady Orca U :D:	.20	.60
162 Land Equilibrium R :B:	90.00	100.00
163 Land Tax U :W:	30.00	35.00
164 Land's Edge R :R:	15.00	20.00
165 Lesser Werewolf U :K:	.20	.60
166 Life Chisel U :A:	.20	.60
167 Life Matrix R :A:	25.00	30.00
168 Lifeblood R :W:	25.00	30.00
169 Living Plane R :G:	180.00	190.00
170 Livonya Silone R :D:	15.00	20.00
171 Lord Magnus U :D:	.20	.60
172 Lost Soul C :K:	.20	.60
173 Mana Drain U :B:	180.00	190.00
174 Mana Matrix R :A:	45.00	50.00
175 Marble Priest U :A:	.20	.60
176 Marhault Elsdragon U :D:	.20	.60
177 Master of the Hunt R :G:	10.00	15.00
178 Mirror Universe R :A:	260.00	280.00
179 Moat R :W:	500.00	550.00
180 Mold Demon R :K:	10.00	15.00
181 Moss Monster C :G:	.20	.60
182 Mountain Stronghold U :L:	.20	.60
183 Mountain Yeti U :R:	.20	.60
184 Nebuchadnezzar R :D:	4.00	6.00
185 Nether Void R :K:	420.00	440.00
186 Nicol Bolas R :D:	40.00	45.00
187 North Star R :A:	15.00	20.00
188 Nova Pentacle R :A:	15.00	20.00
189 Osai Vultures C :W:	.20	.60
190 Palladia-Mors R :D:	8.00	10.00
191 Part Water U :B:	.20	.60
192 Pavel Maliki U :D:	.20	.60
193 Pendelhaven U :L:	10.00	15.00
194 Petra Sphinx R :W:	2.00	3.00
195 Pit Scorpion C :K:	.20	.60
196 Pixie Queen R :G:	15.00	20.00
197 Planar Gate R :A:	60.00	70.00
198 Pradesh Gypsies U :G:	.20	.60
199 Presence of the Master U :W:	2.00	3.00
200 Primordial Ooze U :R:	.20	.60
201 Princess Lucrezia U :D:	.20	.60
202 Psionic Entity R :B:	1.50	2.00
203 Psychic Purge C :B:	.20	.60
204 Puppet Master U :B:	.20	.60
205 Pyrotechnics C :R:	.20	.60
206 Quagmire U :K:	.20	.60
207 Quarum Trench Gnomes R :R:	10.00	15.00
208 Rabid Wombat U :G:	.20	.60
209 Radjan Spirit U :G:	.20	.60
210 Raging Bull C :R:	.20	.60
211 Ragnar R :D:	25.00	30.00
212 Ramirez DePietro U :D:	8.00	10.00
213 Ramses Overdark R :D:	25.00	30.00
214 Rapid Fire R :W:	8.00	10.00
215 Rasputin Dreamweaver R :D:	60.00	70.00
216 Rebirth R :G:	1.00	1.50
217 Recall R :B:	25.00	30.00
218 Red Mana Battery U :A:	.20	.60
219 Reincarnation U :G:	1.50	2.00
220 Relic Barrier U :A:	2.50	3.00
221 Relic Bind U :B:	.20	.60
222 Remove Enchantments C :W:	.20	.60
223 Remove Soul C :B:	.20	.60
224 Reset U :B:	15.00	20.00
225 Revelation R :G:	8.00	10.00
226 Reverberation R :R:	4.00	6.00
227 Righteous Avengers U :W:	.20	.60
228 Ring of Immortals R :A:	25.00	30.00
229 Riven Turnbull U :D:	.20	.60
230 Rohgahh of Kher Keep R :D:	8.00	10.00
231 Rubinia Soulsinger R :D:	4.00	6.00
232 Rust C :G:	.20	.60
233 Sea Kings' Blessing U :B:	.20	.60
234 Seafarer's Quay U :L:	.20	.60
235 Seeker U :W:	.20	.60
236 Segovian Leviathan U :B:	.20	.60
237 Sentinel R :A:	2.50	4.00
238 Serpent Generator R :A:	3.00	5.00
239 Shelkin Brownie C :G:	.20	.60
240 Shield Wall U :W:	.20	.60
241 Shimian Night Stalker U :K:	.20	.60
242 Silhouette U :B:	.20	.60
243 Sir Shandlar of Eberyn U :D:	.20	.60
244 Sivitri Scarzam U :D:	.20	.60
245 Sol'kanar the Swamp King R :D:	15.00	20.00
246 Spectral Cloak U :B:	.20	.60
247 Spinal Villain R :R:	35.00	40.00
248 Spirit Link U :W:	10.00	15.00
249 Spirit Shackle C :K:	.20	.60
250 Spiritual Sanctuary R :W:	15.00	20.00
251 Stangg R :D:	25.00	30.00
252 Storm Seeker U :G:	2.00	3.00
253 Storm World R :R:	20.00	25.00
254 Subdue C :G:	.20	.60
255 Sunastian Falconer U :D:	.20	.60
256 Sword of the Ages R :A:	80.00	90.00
257 Sylvan Library U :G:	35.00	45.00
258 Sylvan Paradise U :G:	.20	.60
259 Syphon Soul C :K:	.20	.60
260 Tabernacle at Pendrell Vale R :L:	1200.00	1400.00
261 Takklemaggot U :K:	.20	.60
262 Telekinesis R :B:	30.00	35.00
263 Teleport R :B:	1.50	2.00
264 Tempest Efreet R :R:	1.50	2.00
265 Tetsuo Umezawa R :D:	80.00	90.00
266 Thunder Spirit R :W:	80.00	85.00
267 Time Elemental R :B:	15.00	20.00
268 Tobias Andrion U :D:	.20	.60
269 Tolaria U :L:	.20	.60
270 Tor Wauki U :D:	.20	.60
271 Torsten Von Ursus U :D:	.20	.60
272 Touch of Darkness U :K:	.20	.60
273 Transmutation C :K:	.20	.60
274 Triassic Egg R :A:	3.00	5.00
275 Tuknir Deathlock R :D:	20.00	25.00
276 Tundra Wolves C :W:	.20	.60
277 Typhoon R :G:	15.00	20.00
278 Undertow U :B:	.20	.60
279 Underworld Dreams U :K:	25.00	30.00
280 Unholy Citadel U :L:	.20	.60
281 Untamed Wilds U :G:	.20	.60
282 Urborg U :L:	3.00	5.00
283 Ur-Drago R :D:	15.00	20.00
284 Vaevictis Asmadi R :D:	.20	.60
285 Vampire Bats C :K:	.20	.60
286 Venarian Gold C :B:	.20	.60
287 Visions U :W:	.20	.60
288 Voodoo Doll R :A:	1.50	2.00
289 Walking Dead C :K:	.20	.60
290 Wall of Caltrops C :W:	.20	.60
291 Wall of Dust U :R:	.20	.60
292 Wall of Earth C :R:	.20	.60
293 Wall of Heat C :R:	.20	.60
294 Wall of Light U :W:	.60	1.00
295 Wall of Opposition R :R:	1.50	2.00
296 Wall of Putrid Flesh U :K:	.20	.60
297 Wall of Shadows C :K:	.20	.60
298 Wall of Tombstones U :K:	.20	.60
299 Wall of Vapor C :B:	.20	.60
300 Wall of Wonder U :B:	.20	.60
301 Whirling Dervish U :G:	6.00	8.00
302 White Mana Battery U :A:	.20	.60
303 Willow Satyr R :G:	60.00	65.00
304 Winds of Change U :R:	10.00	15.00
305 Winter Blast R :G:	3.00	5.00
306 Wolverine Pack C :G:	.20	.60
307 Wood Elemental R :G:	8.00	10.00
308 Wretched, The R :K:	4.00	6.00
309 Xira Arien R :D:	8.00	10.00
310 Zephyr Falcon C :B:	.20	.60

1994 Magic The Gathering The Dark

COMPLETE SET (119)	130.00	170.00
BOOSTER BOX (60 PACKS)	600.00	650.00
BOOSTER PACK (8 CARDS)	10.00	15.00
RELEASED ON AUGUST 15, 1994		
1 Amnesia U2 :B:	.50	.80
2 Angry Mob U2 :W:	.15	.25
3 Apprentice Wizard U1 :B:	1.00	1.50
4 Ashes to Ashes C3 :K:	.15	.25
5 Ball Lightning U1 :R:	4.00	6.00
6 Banshee U2 :K:	.15	.25
7 Barl's Cage U1 :A:	.25	.40
8 Blood Moon U1 :R:	50.00	60.00
9 Blood of the Martyr U2 :W:	.15	.25
10 Bog Imp C3 :K:	.15	.25
11 Bog Rats C3 :K:	.15	.25
12 Bone Flute U2 :A:	.15	.25
13 Book of Rass U2 :A:	.15	.25
14 Brainwash C3 :W:	.15	.25
15 Brothers of Fire U2 :R:	.15	.25
16 Carnivorous Plant C3 :G:	.15	.25
17 Cave People U2 :R:	.15	.25
18 City of Shadows U1 :L:	10.00	15.00
19 Cleansing U1 :W:	5.00	7.00
20 Coal Golem U2 :A:	.15	.25
21 Curse Artifact U2 :K:	.15	.25
22 Dance of Many U1 :B:	.75	1.25
23 Dark Heart of the Wood C3 :D:	.15	.25
24 Dark Sphere U2 :A:	1.00	1.50
25 Deep Water C3 :B:	.15	.25
26 Diabolic Machine U2 :A:	.15	.25
27 Drowned C3 :B:	.15	.25
28 Dust to Dust C3 :W:	.15	.25
29 Eater of the Dead U2 :K:	4.00	6.00
30 Electric Eel U2 :B:	.15	.25
31 Elves of Deep Shadow U2 :G:	1.50	2.50
32 Erosion C3 :B:	.15	.25
33 Eternal Flame U1 :R:	.60	1.00
34 Exorcist U1 :W:	5.00	7.00
35 Fallen, The U2 :K:	.15	.25
36 Fasting U2 :W:	.15	.25
37 Fellwar Stone U2 :A:	3.00	5.00
38 Festival C3 :W:	.15	.25
39 Fire and Brimstone U2 :W:	.15	.25
40 Fire Drake U2 :R:	.15	.25
41 Fissure C3 :R:	.15	.25
42 Flood U2 :B:	.15	.25
43 Fountain of Youth U2 :A:	.15	.25
44 Frankenstein's Monster U1 :K:	4.00	6.00
45 Gaea's Touch C3 :G:	.30	.50
46 Ghost Ship C3 :B:	.15	.25
47 Giant Shark C3 :B:	.15	.25
48 Goblin Caves C3 :R:	.25	.40
49 Goblin Digging Team C3 :R:	.15	.25
50 Goblin Hero C3 :R:	.15	.25
51 Goblin Rock Sled C3 :R:	.15	.25
52 Goblin Shrine C3 :R:	.15	.25
53 Goblin Wizard U1 :R:	10.00	15.00
54 Goblins of the Flarg C3 :R:	.15	.25
55 Grave Robbers U1 :K:	1.00	1.50
56 Hidden Path U1 :G:	1.00	1.50
57 Holy Light C3 :W:	.15	.25
58 Inferno U1 :R:	.60	1.00
59 Inquisition C3 :K:	.15	.25
60 Knights of Thorn U1 :W:	.75	1.25
61 Land Leeches C3 :G:	.15	.25
62 Leviathan U1 :B:	.60	1.00
63 Living Armor U2 :A:	.15	.25
64 Lurker U1 :G:	3.00	5.00
65 Mana Clash U1 :R:	.30	.50
66 Mana Vortex U1 :B:	10.00	15.00
67 Marsh Gas C3 :K:	.15	.25
68 Marsh Goblins C3 :D:	.15	.25
69 Marsh Viper C3 :G:	.15	.25
70 Martyr's Cry U1 :W:	2.50	4.00
71 Maze of Ith C1 :L:	15.00	20.00
72 Merfolk Assassin U2 :B:	.30	.50
73 Mind Bomb U1 :B:	.60	1.00
74 Miracle Worker C3 :W:	.15	.25
75 Morale C3 :W:	.15	.25
76 Murk Dwellers C3 :K:	.15	.25
77 Nameless Race U1 :K:	.60	1.00
78 Necropolis U2 :A:	.15	.25
79 Niall Silvain U1 :G:	1.00	1.50
80 Orc General U2 :R:	.15	.25
81 People of the Woods U2 :G:	.15	.25
82 Pikemen C3 :W:	.15	.25
83 Preacher U1 :W:	15.00	20.00
84 Psychic Allergy U1 :B:	.60	1.00
85 Rag Man U1 :K:	.25	.40
86 Reflecting Mirror U2 :A:	.15	.25
87 Riptide C3 :B:	.15	.25
88 Runesword U2 :A:	.15	.25
89 Safe Haven U1 :L:	.60	1.00
90 Savaen Elves C3 :G:	.15	.25
91 Scarecrow U2 :A:	.15	.25
92 Scarwood Bandits U1 :G:	3.00	5.00
93 Scarwood Goblins C3 :D:	.15	.25
94 Scarwood Hag U2 :G:	.15	.25
95 Scavenger Folk C3 :G:	.15	.25
96 Season of the Witch U1 :K:	6.00	8.00
97 Sisters of the Flame U2 :R:	.15	.25
98 Skull of Orm U2 :A:	.40	.60
99 Sorrow's Path U1 :L:	2.50	4.00
100 Spitting Slug U2 :G:	.15	.25
101 Squire C3 :W:	.15	.25
102 Standing Stones U2 :A:	.15	.25
103 Stone Calendar U1 :A:	8.00	11.00
104 Sunken City C3 :B:	.15	.25
105 Tangle Kelp U2 :B:	.15	.25
106 Tivadar's Crusade U2 :W:	.40	.60
107 Tormod's Crypt U2 :A:	1.50	2.50
108 Tower of Coireall U2 :A:	.15	.25
109 Tracker U1 :G:	1.00	1.50
110 Uncle Istvan U2 :K:	.15	.25
111 Venom C3 :G:	.15	.25
112 Wand of Ith U2 :A:	.15	.25
113 War Barge U2 :A:	.15	.25
114 Water Wurm C3 :B:	.15	.25
115 Whippoorwill U2 :G:	.15	.25
116 Witch Hunter U1 :W:	.50	.80
117 Word of Binding C3 :K:	.15	.25
118 Worms of the Earth U1 :K:	1.50	2.50
119 Wormwood Treefolk U1 :G:	.50	.80

1994 Magic The Gathering Fallen Empires

COMPLETE SET (187)	40.00	60.00
BOOSTER BOX (60 PACKS)	85.00	125.00
BOOSTER PACK (8 CARDS)	2.50	4.00
RELEASED ON NOVEMBER 15, 1994		
1 Aeolipile U :A:	.30	.50
2 Armor Thrull v1 C :K:	.15	.25
3 Armor Thrull v2 C :K:	.15	.25
4 Armor Thrull v3 C :K:	.15	.25
5 Armor Thrull v4 C :K:	.15	.25
6 Balm of Restoration U :A:	.25	.40
7 Basal Thrull v1 C :K:	.15	.25
8 Basal Thrull v2 C :K:	.15	.25
9 Basal Thrull v3 C :K:	.15	.25
10 Basal Thrull v4 C :K:	.15	.25
11 Bottomless Vault U :L:	.50	.75
12 Brassclaw Orcs v1 C :R:	.15	.25
13 Brassclaw Orcs v2 C :R:	.15	.25
14 Brassclaw Orcs v3 C :R:	.15	.25
15 Brassclaw Orcs v4 C :R:	.15	.25
16 Breeding Pit U :K:	.15	.25
17 Combat Medic v1 C :W:	.15	.25
18 Combat Medic v2 C :W:	.15	.25
19 Combat Medic v3 C :W:	.15	.25
20 Combat Medic v4 C :W:	.15	.25
21 Conch Horn U :A:	.25	.40
22 Deep Spawn U :B:	.15	.25
23 Delif's Cone C :A:	.15	.25
24 Delif's Cube U :A:	.25	.40
25 Derelor U :K:	.15	.25
26 Draconian Cylix U :A:	.25	.40
27 Dwarven Armorer U :R:	.30	.50
28 Dwarven Catapult U :R:	.15	.25
29 Dwarven Hold U :L:	.50	.75
30 Dwarven Lieutenant U :R:	.15	.25
31 Dwarven Ruins U :L:	.15	.25
32 Dwarven Soldier v1 C :R:	.15	.25
33 Dwarven Soldier v2 C :R:	.15	.25
34 Dwarven Soldier v3 C :R:	.15	.25
35 Ebon Praetor U :K:	.25	.40
36 Ebon Stronghold U :L:	.15	.25
37 Elven Fortress v1 C :G:	.15	.25
38 Elven Fortress v2 C :G:	.15	.25
39 Elven Fortress v3 C :G:	.15	.25
40 Elven Fortress v4 C :G:	.15	.25
41 Elven Lyre U :A:	.25	.40
42 Elvish Farmer U :G:	.75	1.00

Card	Low	High
43 Elvish Hunter v1 C :G:	.15	.25
44 Elvish Hunter v2 C :G:	.15	.25
45 Elvish Hunter v3 C :G:	.15	.25
46 Elvish Scout v1 C :G:	.15	.25
47 Elvish Scout v2 C :G:	.15	.25
48 Elvish Scout v3 C :G:	.15	.25
49 Farrelite Priest U :W:	.15	.25
50 Farrel's Mantle U :W:	.15	.25
51 Farrel's Zealot v1 C :W:	.15	.25
52 Farrel's Zealot v2 C :W:	.15	.25
53 Farrel's Zealot v3 C :W:	.15	.25
54 Feral Thallid U :G:	.15	.25
55 Fungal Bloom U :G:	.75	1.00
56 Goblin Chirurgeon v1 C :R:	.15	.25
57 Goblin Chirurgeon v2 C :R:	.15	.25
58 Goblin Chirurgeon v3 C :R:	.15	.25
59 Goblin Flotilla U :R:	.30	.50
60 Goblin Grenade v1 C :R:	.50	.75
61 Goblin Grenade v2 C :R:	.50	.75
62 Goblin Grenade v3 C :R:	.50	.75
63 Goblin Kites U :R:	.15	.25
64 Goblin War Drums v1 C :R:	.15	.25
65 Goblin War Drums v2 C :R:	.15	.25
66 Goblin War Drums v3 C :R:	.15	.25
67 Goblin War Drums v4 C :R:	.15	.25
68 Goblin Warrens U :R:	.75	1.00
69 Hand of Justice U :W:	.25	.40
70 Havenwood Battleground U :L:	.15	.25
71 Heroism U :W:	.15	.25
72 High Tide v1 C :B:	.50	.75
73 High Tide v2 C :B:	.50	.75
74 High Tide v3 C :B:	.50	.75
75 Hollow Trees U :L:	.15	.25
76 Homarid v1 C :B:	.15	.25
77 Homarid v2 C :B:	.15	.25
78 Homarid v3 C :B:	.15	.25
79 Homarid v4 C :B:	.15	.25
80 Homarid Shaman U :B:	.25	.40
81 Homarid Spawning Bed U :B:	.15	.25
82 Homarid Warrior v1 C :B:	.15	.25
83 Homarid Warrior v2 C :B:	.15	.25
84 Homarid Warrior v3 C :B:	.15	.25
85 Hymn to Tourach v1 C :K:	1.25	1.75
86 Hymn to Tourach v2 C :K:	.75	1.25
87 Hymn to Tourach v3 C :K:	.75	1.25
88 Hymn to Tourach v4 C :K:	.75	1.25
89 Icatian Infantry v1 C :W:	.15	.25
90 Icatian Infantry v2 C :W:	.15	.25
91 Icatian Infantry v3 C :W:	.15	.25
92 Icatian Infantry v4 C :W:	.15	.25
93 Icatian Javelineers v1 C :W:	.15	.25
94 Icatian Javelineers v2 C :W:	.15	.25
95 Icatian Javelineers v3 C :W:	.15	.25
96 Icatian Lieutenant U :W:	.25	.40
97 Icatian Moneychanger v1 C :W:	.15	.25
98 Icatian Moneychanger v2 C :W:	.15	.25
99 Icatian Moneychanger v3 C :W:	.15	.25
100 Icatian Phalanx U :W:	.15	.25
101 Icatian Priest U :W:	.15	.25
102 Icatian Scout v1 C :W:	.15	.25
103 Icatian Scout v2 C :W:	.15	.25
104 Icatian Scout v3 C :W:	.15	.25
105 Icatian Scout v4 C :W:	.15	.25
106 Icatian Skirmishers U :W:	.25	.40
107 Icatian Store U :L:	.30	.50
108 Icatian Town U :W:	.15	.25
109 Implements of Sacrifice U :A:	.25	.40
110 Initiates of the Ebon Hand v1 C :K:	.15	.25
111 Initiates of the Ebon Hand v2 C :K:	.15	.25
112 Initiates of the Ebon Hand v3 C :K:	.15	.25
113 Merseine v1 C :B:	.15	.25
114 Merseine v2 C :B:	.15	.25
115 Merseine v3 C :B:	.15	.25
116 Merseine v4 C :B:	.15	.25
117 Mindstab Thrull v1 C :K:	.15	.25
118 Mindstab Thrull v2 C :K:	.15	.25
119 Mindstab Thrull v3 C :K:	.15	.25
120 Necrite v1 C :K:	.15	.25
121 Necrite v2 C :K:	.15	.25
122 Necrite v3 C :K:	.15	.25
123 Night Soil v1 C :G:	.15	.25
124 Night Soil v2 C :G:	.15	.25
125 Night Soil v3 C :G:	.15	.25
126 Orcish Captain U :R:	.15	.25
127 Orcish Spy v1 C :R:	.15	.25
128 Orcish Spy v2 C :R:	.15	.25
129 Orcish Spy v3 C :R:	.15	.25
130 Orcish Veteran v1 C :R:	.15	.25
131 Orcish Veteran v2 C :R:	.15	.25
132 Orcish Veteran v3 C :R:	.15	.25
133 Orcish Veteran v4 C :R:	.15	.25
134 Order of Leitbur v1 C :W:	.15	.25
135 Order of Leitbur v2 C :W:	.15	.25
136 Order of Leitbur v3 C :W:	.15	.25
137 Order of the Ebon Hand v1 C :K:	.15	.25
138 Order of the Ebon Hand v2 C :K:	.15	.25
139 Order of the Ebon Hand v3 C :K:	.15	.25
140 Orgg U :R:	.15	.25
141 Raiding Party U :R:	.15	.25
142 Rainbow Vale U :L:	.15	.25
143 Ring of Renewal U :A:	.25	.40
144 River Merfolk U :B:	.25	.40
145 Ruins of Trokair U :L:	.15	.25
146 Sand Silos U :L:	.40	.60
147 Seasinger U :B:	.15	.25
148 Soul Exchange U :K:	.15	.25
149 Spirit Shield U :A:	.25	.40
150 Spore Cloud v1 C :G:	.15	.25
151 Spore Cloud v2 C :G:	.15	.25
152 Spore Cloud v3 C :G:	.15	.25
153 Spore Flower U :G:	.25	.40
154 Svyelunite Priest U :B:	.15	.25
155 Svyelunite Temple U :L:	.15	.25
156 Thallid v1 C :G:	.15	.25
157 Thallid v2 C :G:	.15	.25
158 Thallid v3 C :G:	.15	.25
159 Thallid v4 C :G:	.15	.25
160 Thallid Devourer U :G:	.15	.25
161 Thelonite Druid U :G:	.25	.40
162 Thelonite Monk U :G:	.25	.40
163 Thelon's Chant U :G:	.15	.25
164 Thelon's Curse U :G:	.25	.40
165 Thorn Thallid v1 C :G:	.15	.25
166 Thorn Thallid v2 C :G:	.15	.25
167 Thorn Thallid v3 C :G:	.15	.25
168 Thorn Thallid v4 C :G:	.15	.25
169 Thrull Champion U :K:	.25	.40
170 Thrull Retainer U :K:	.15	.25
171 Thrull Wizard U :K:	.15	.25
172 Tidal Flats v1 C :B:	.15	.25
173 Tidal Flats v2 C :B:	.15	.25
174 Tidal Flats v3 C :B:	.15	.25
175 Tidal Influence U :B:	.15	.25
176 Tourach's Chant U :K:	.15	.25
177 Tourach's Gate U :K:	.25	.40
178 Vodalian Knights U :B:	.30	.50
179 Vodalian Mage v1 C :B:	.15	.25
180 Vodalian Mage v2 C :B:	.15	.25
181 Vodalian Mage v3 C :B:	.15	.25
182 Vodalian Soldiers v1 C :B:	.15	.25
183 Vodalian Soldiers v2 C :B:	.15	.25
184 Vodalian Soldiers v3 C :B:	.15	.25
185 Vodalian Soldiers v4 C :B:	.15	.25
186 Vodalian War Machine U :B:	.25	.40
187 Zelyon Sword U :A:	.25	.40

1994 Magic The Gathering Summer Edition

RELEASED IN APRIL 1994
ALSO KNOWN AS EDGAR OR SUMMER REVISED.
WHITE BORDERS WITH 1994 COPYRIGHT DATE BEFORE ARTIST'S NAME.
PALE COLORS AND NAME OF ILLUSTRATOR AT THE BOTTOM.
NO BEVELED EDGES INSIDE THE COLORED BORDERS.

Card	Low	High
1 Air Elemental U :B:	250.00	400.00
2 Aladdin's Lamp R :A:	800.00	1000.00
3 Aladdin's Ring R :A:	800.00	1000.00
4 Animate Artifact U :B:	150.00	300.00
5 Animate Dead U :K:	400.00	600.00
6 Animate Wall R :W:	800.00	1000.00
7 Ankh of Mishra R :A:	950.00	1200.00
8 Armageddon Clock R :A:	550.00	800.00
9 Armageddon R :W:	1750.00	2000.00
10 Aspect of Wolf R :G:	550.00	800.00
11 Atog C :R:	100.00	200.00
12 Bad Moon R :K:	850.00	1100.00
13 Badlands R :L:	2500.00	3000.00
14 Balance R :W:	2000.00	2500.00
15 Basalt Monolith U :A:	500.00	750.00
16 Bayou R :L:	2350.00	2800.00
17 Benalish Hero C :W:	120.00	250.00
18 Birds of Paradise R :G:	3300.00	3800.00
19 Black Knight U :K:	400.00	600.00
20 Black Vise U :A:	1450.00	1700.00
21 Black Ward U :W:	100.00	200.00
22 Blessing R :W:	750.00	950.00
23 Blue Elemental Blast C :B:	100.00	200.00
24 Blue Ward U :W:	150.00	300.00
25 Bog Wraith U :K:	120.00	250.00
26 Bottle of Suleiman R :A:	800.00	1000.00
27 Braingeyser R :B:	1750.00	2000.00
28 Brass Man U :A:	150.00	300.00
29 Burrowing U :R:	100.00	200.00
30 Castle U :W:	120.00	250.00
31 Celestial Prism U :A:	120.00	250.00
32 Channel U :G:	550.00	800.00
33 Chaoslace R :R:	550.00	800.00
34 Circle of Protection Black C :W:	150.00	300.00
35 Circle of Protection Blue C :W:	100.00	200.00
36 Circle of Protection Green C :W:	100.00	200.00
37 Circle of Protection Red C :W:	300.00	450.00
38 Circle of Protection White C :W:	100.00	200.00
39 Clockwork Beast R :A:	850.00	1100.00
40 Clone U :B:	550.00	800.00
41 Cockatrice R :G:	800.00	1000.00
42 Conservator U :A:	100.00	200.00
43 Contract from Below R :K:	1400.00	1600.00
44 Control Magic U :B:	550.00	800.00
45 Conversion U :W:	150.00	300.00
46 Copy Artifact R :B:	950.00	1200.00
47 Counterspell U :B:	1850.00	2200.00
48 Craw Wurm C :G:	120.00	250.00
49 Creature Bond C :B:	80.00	150.00
50 Crumble U :G:	200.00	350.00
51 Crusade R :W:	1000.00	1250.00
52 Crystal Rod U :A:	200.00	350.00
53 Cursed Land U :K:	150.00	300.00
54 Dancing Scimitar R :A:	800.00	1000.00
55 Dark Ritual C :K:	800.00	1000.00
56 Darkpact R :K:	550.00	800.00
57 Death Ward C :W:	120.00	250.00
58 Deathgrip U :K:	150.00	300.00
59 Deathlace R :K:	800.00	1000.00
60 Demonic Attorney R :K:	750.00	950.00
61 Demonic Hordes R :K:	1400.00	1600.00
62 Demonic Tutor U :K:	2700.00	3400.00
63 Desert Twister U :G:	150.00	300.00
64 Dingus Egg R :A:	700.00	900.00
65 Disenchant C :W:	400.00	600.00
66 Disintegrate C :R:	250.00	400.00
67 Disrupting Scepter R :A:	800.00	1000.00
68 Dragon Engine R :A:	950.00	1200.00
69 Dragon Whelp U :R:	250.00	400.00
70 Drain Life C :K:	350.00	500.00
71 Drain Power R :B:	550.00	800.00
72 Drudge Skeletons C :K:	100.00	200.00
73 Dwarven Warriors C :R:	100.00	200.00
74 Dwarven Weaponsmith U :R:	100.00	200.00
75 Earth Elemental U :R:	120.00	250.00
76 Earthbind C :R:	80.00	150.00
77 Earthquake R :R:	850.00	1100.00
78 Ebony Horse R :A:	800.00	1000.00
79 El-Hajjaj R :K:	550.00	800.00
80 Elvish Archers R :G:	800.00	1000.00
81 Energy Flux U :B:	150.00	300.00
82 Erg Raiders C :K:	100.00	200.00
83 Evil Presence U :K:	150.00	300.00
84 Eye for an Eye R :W:	850.00	1100.00
85 Farmstead R :W:	800.00	1000.00
86 Fastbond R :G:	1900.00	2300.00
87 Fear C :K:	100.00	200.00
88 Feedback U :B:	150.00	300.00
89 Fire Elemental U :R:	120.00	250.00
90 Fireball C :R:	250.00	400.00
91 Firebreathing C :R:	80.00	150.00
92 Flashfires U :R:	120.00	250.00
93 Flight C :B:	80.00	150.00
94 Flying Carpet R :A:	550.00	800.00
95 Fog C :G:	80.00	150.00
96 Force of Nature R :G:	950.00	1200.00
97 Forest v1 C :L:	250.00	400.00
98 Forest v2 C :L:	250.00	400.00
99 Forest v3 C :L:	250.00	400.00
100 Fork R :R:	2000.00	2500.00
101 Frozen Shade C :K:	100.00	200.00
102 Fungusaur R :G:	450.00	700.00
103 Gaea's Liege R :G:	450.00	700.00
104 Giant Growth C :G:	250.00	400.00
105 Giant Spider C :G:	80.00	150.00
106 Glasses of Urza U :A:	120.00	250.00
107 Gloom U :K:	250.00	400.00
108 Goblin Balloon Brigade U :R:	150.00	300.00
109 Goblin King R :R:	950.00	1200.00
110 Granite Gargoyle R :R:	700.00	900.00
111 Gray Ogre C :R:	100.00	200.00
112 Green Ward U :W:	120.00	250.00
113 Grizzly Bears C :G:	100.00	200.00
114 Guardian Angel C :W:	100.00	200.00
115 Healing Salve C :W:	100.00	200.00
116 Helm of Chatzuk R :A:	550.00	800.00
117 Hill Giant C :R:	80.00	150.00
118 Hive, The R :A:	300.00	450.00
119 Holy Armor C :W:	100.00	200.00
120 Holy Strength C :W:	100.00	200.00
121 Howl from Beyond C :K:	100.00	200.00
122 Howling Mine R :A:	1200.00	1400.00
123 Hurkyl's Recall R :B:	1750.00	2000.00
124 Hurloon Minotaur C :R:	100.00	200.00
125 Hurricane U :G:	6500.00	8000.00
126 Hypnotic Specter U :K:	1100.00	1300.00
127 Instill Energy U :G:	150.00	300.00
128 Iron Star U :A:	150.00	300.00
129 Ironroot Treefolk C :G:	80.00	150.00
130 Island Fish Jasconius R :B:	800.00	1000.00
131 Island Sanctuary R :W:	700.00	900.00
132 Island v1 C :L:	400.00	600.00
133 Island v2 C :L:	400.00	600.00
134 Island v3 C :L:	400.00	600.00
135 Ivory Cup U :A:	150.00	300.00
136 Ivory Tower R :A:	950.00	1200.00
137 Jade Monolith R :A:	950.00	1200.00
138 Jandor's Ring R :A:	950.00	1200.00
139 Jandor's Saddlebags R :A:	950.00	1200.00
140 Jayemdae Tome R :A:	950.00	1200.00
141 Juggernaut U :A:	250.00	400.00
142 Jump C :B:	80.00	150.00
143 Karma U :W:	150.00	300.00
144 Keldon Warlord U :R:	150.00	300.00
145 Kird Ape C :R:	450.00	700.00
146 Kormus Bell R :A:	550.00	800.00
147 Kudzu R :G:	350.00	500.00
148 Lance U :W:	120.00	250.00
149 Ley Druid U :G:	150.00	300.00
150 Library of Leng U :A:	120.00	250.00
151 Lifeforce U :G:	120.00	250.00
152 Lifelace R :G:	800.00	1000.00
153 Lifetap U :B:	150.00	300.00
154 Lightning Bolt C :R:	800.00	1000.00
155 Living Artifact R :G:	800.00	1000.00
156 Living Lands R :G:	800.00	1000.00
157 Living Wall U :A:	120.00	250.00
158 Llanowar Elves C :G:	550.00	800.00
159 Lord of Atlantis R :B:	1400.00	1600.00
160 Lord of the Pit R :K:	1400.00	1600.00
161 Lure U :G:	150.00	300.00
162 Magical Hack R :B:	800.00	1000.00
163 Magnetic Mountain R :R:	800.00	1000.00
164 Mahamoti Djinn R :B:	1300.00	1500.00
165 Mana Flare R :R:	1300.00	1500.00
166 Mana Short R :B:	1300.00	1500.00
167 Mana Vault R :A:	4600.00	5000.00
168 Manabarbs R :R:	550.00	800.00
169 Meekstone R :A:	550.00	800.00
170 Merfolk of the Pearl Trident C :B:	100.00	200.00
171 Mesa Pegasus C :W:	100.00	200.00
172 Mijae Djinn R :R:	550.00	800.00
173 Millstone R :A:	1200.00	1400.00
174 Mind Twist R :K:	4100.00	4500.00
175 Mishra's War Machine R :A:	800.00	1000.00
176 Mons's Goblin Raiders C :R:	100.00	200.00
177 Mountain v1 C :L:	200.00	350.00
178 Mountain v2 C :L:	200.00	350.00
179 Mountain v3 C :L:	200.00	350.00
180 Nether Shadow R :K:	950.00	1200.00
181 Nettling Imp U :K:	120.00	250.00
182 Nevinyrral's Disk R :A:	1500.00	1800.00
183 Nightmare R :K:	1450.00	1750.00
184 Northern Paladin R :W:	550.00	800.00
185 Obsianus Golem U :A:	150.00	300.00
186 Onulet R :A:	850.00	1100.00
187 Orcish Artillery U :R:	150.00	300.00
188 Orcish Oriflamme U :R:	200.00	350.00
189 Ornithopter U :A:	350.00	500.00
190 Paralyze C :K:	100.00	200.00
191 Pearled Unicorn C :W:	100.00	200.00
192 Personal Incarnation R :W:	800.00	1000.00
193 Pestilence C :K:	100.00	200.00
194 Phantasmal Forces U :B:	150.00	300.00
195 Phantasmal Terrain C :B:	80.00	150.00
196 Phantom Monster U :B:	120.00	250.00
197 Pirate Ship R :B:	800.00	1000.00
198 Plague Rats C :K:	100.00	200.00
199 Plains v1 C :L:	250.00	400.00
200 Plains v2 C :L:	250.00	400.00
201 Plains v3 C :L:	250.00	400.00
202 Plateau R :L:	2600.00	3200.00
203 Power Leak C :B:	80.00	150.00
204 Power Sink C :B:	80.00	150.00
205 Power Surge R :R:	550.00	800.00
206 Primal Clay R :A:	800.00	1000.00
207 Prodigal Sorcerer C :B:	100.00	200.00
208 Psychic Venom C :B:	100.00	200.00
209 Purelace R :W:	950.00	1200.00
210 Rack, The U :A:	80.00	1000.00
211 Raise Dead C :K:	100.00	200.00
212 Reconstruction C :B:	100.00	200.00
213 Red Elemental Blast C :R:	350.00	500.00
214 Red Ward U :W:	150.00	300.00
215 Regeneration C :G:	100.00	200.00
216 Regrowth U :G:	1450.00	1750.00
217 Resurrection U :W:	350.00	500.00
218 Reverse Damage R :W:	800.00	1000.00
219 Reverse Polarity U :W:	150.00	300.00
220 Righteousness R :W:	800.00	1000.00
221 Roc of Kher Ridges R :R:	800.00	1000.00
222 Rock Hydra R :R:	800.00	1000.00
223 Rocket Launcher R :A:	550.00	800.00
224 Rod of Ruin U :A:	120.00	250.00
225 Royal Assassin R :K:	1800.00	2100.00
226 Sacrifice U :K:	150.00	300.00
227 Samite Healer C :W:	100.00	200.00
228 Savannah Lions R :W:	1550.00	1900.00
229 Savannah R :L:	2600.00	3200.00
230 Scathe Zombies C :K:	100.00	200.00
231 Scavenging Ghoul U :K:	150.00	300.00
232 Scrubland R :L:	2500.00	3000.00
233 Scryb Sprites C :G:	80.00	150.00
234 Sea Serpent C :B:	80.00	150.00
235 Sedge Troll R :R:	550.00	800.00
236 Sengir Vampire U :K:	700.00	900.00
237 Serendib Efreet R :B:	9000.00	12000.00
238 Serra Angel U :W:	2000.00	2500.00
239 Shanodin Dryads C :G:	100.00	200.00
240 Shatter C :R:	100.00	200.00
241 Shatterstorm U :R:	350.00	500.00
242 Shivan Dragon R :R:	5400.00	6000.00
243 Simulacrum U :K:	150.00	300.00
244 Siren's Call U :B:	150.00	300.00
245 Sleight of Mind R :B:	550.00	800.00
246 Smoke R :R:	550.00	800.00
247 Sol Ring U :A:	2350.00	2800.00
248 Sorceress Queen R :K:	550.00	800.00
249 Soul Net U :A:	150.00	300.00
250 Spell Blast C :B:	100.00	200.00
251 Stasis R :B:	1450.00	1700.00
252 Steal Artifact U :B:	150.00	300.00
253 Stone Giant U :R:	150.00	300.00
254 Stone Rain C :R:	350.00	500.00
255 Stream of Life C :G:	100.00	200.00
256 Sunglasses of Urza R :A:	550.00	800.00
257 Swamp v1 C :L:	300.00	450.00
258 Swamp v2 C :L:	300.00	450.00
259 Swamp v3 C :L:	300.00	450.00
260 Swords to Plowshares U :W:	1750.00	2000.00
261 Taiga R :L:	2350.00	2800.00
262 Terror C :K:	350.00	500.00
263 Thicket Basilisk U :G:	150.00	300.00
264 Thoughtlace R :B:	800.00	1000.00
265 Throne of Bone U :A:	150.00	300.00
266 Timber Wolves R :G:	800.00	1000.00
267 Titania's Song R :G:	800.00	1000.00
268 Tranquility C :G:	100.00	200.00
269 Tropical Island R :L:	3600.00	4000.00
270 Tsunami U :G:	150.00	300.00
271 Tundra R :L:	4100.00	4500.00
272 Tunnel U :R:	150.00	300.00
273 Underground Sea R :L:	7500.00	10000.00
274 Unholy Strength C :K:	150.00	300.00
275 Unstable Mutation C :B:	100.00	200.00
276 Unsummon C :B:	150.00	300.00
277 Uthden Troll U :R:	150.00	300.00
278 Verduran Enchantress R :G:	800.00	1000.00
279 Vesuvan Doppelganger R :B:	2500.00	3000.00
280 Veteran Bodyguard R :W:	800.00	1000.00
281 Volcanic Eruption R :B:	800.00	1000.00
282 Volcanic Island R :L:	6000.00	6500.00
283 Wall of Air U :B:	150.00	300.00
284 Wall of Bone U :K:	150.00	300.00
285 Wall of Brambles U :G:	150.00	300.00
286 Wall of Fire U :R:	150.00	300.00
287 Wall of Ice U :G:	150.00	300.00
288 Wall of Stone U :R:	150.00	300.00
289 Wall of Swords U :W:	150.00	300.00
290 Wall of Water U :B:	150.00	300.00
291 Wall of Wood C :G:	100.00	200.00
292 Wanderlust U :G:	150.00	300.00
293 War Mammoth C :G:	100.00	200.00
294 Warp Artifact R :K:	550.00	800.00
295 Water Elemental U :B:	150.00	300.00
296 Weakness C :K:	100.00	200.00
297 Web R :G:	350.00	500.00
298 Wheel of Fortune R :R:	2500.00	3000.00
299 White Knight U :W:	350.00	500.00
300 White Ward U :W:	150.00	300.00
301 Wild Growth C :G:	150.00	300.00
302 Will-O'-The-Wisp R :K:	1300.00	1500.00
303 Winter Orb R :A:	1300.00	1500.00
304 Wooden Sphere U :A:	150.00	300.00
305 Wrath of God R :W:	2500.00	3000.00
306 Zombie Master R :K:	800.00	1000.00

1995 Magic The Gathering Ice Age

Card	Low	High
COMPLETE SET (383)	110.00	170.00
BOOSTER BOX (36 PACKS)	175.00	190.00
BOOSTER PACK (15 CARDS)	6.00	8.00
STARTER BOX (10 DECKS)	150.00	165.00
STARTER DECK	15.00	20.00

RELEASED ON JUNE 15, 1995

Card	Low	High
1 Abyssal Specter U :K:	.15	.25
2 Adarkar Sentinel U :A:	.15	.25
3 Adarkar Unicorn C :W:	.15	.25
4 Adarkar Wastes R :L:	5.00	6.00
5 Aegis of the Meek R :A:	.15	.25
6 Aggression U :R:	.15	.25
7 Altar of Bone R :D:	.15	.25
8 Amulet of Quoz R :A:	.15	.25
9 Anarchy U :R:	.15	.25

10 Arctic Foxes C :W: .15 .25
11 Arcum's Sleigh U :A: .15 .25
12 Arcum's Weathervane U :A: .15 .25
13 Arcum's Whistle U :A: .15 .25
14 Arenson's Aura C :W: .15 .25
15 Armor of Faith C :W: .15 .25
16 Arnjlot's Ascent C :B: .15 .25
17 Ashen Ghoul U :K: .15 .25
18 Aurochs C :G: .15 .25
19 Avalanche U :R: .15 .25
20 Balduvian Barbarians C :R: .15 .25
21 Balduvian Bears C :G: .15 .25
22 Balduvian Conjurer U :B: .15 .25
23 Balduvian Hydra R :R: .15 .25
24 Balduvian Shaman C :B: .15 .25
25 Barbarian Guides C :R: .15 .25
26 Barbed Sextant C :A: .15 .25
27 Baton of Morale U :A: .15 .25
28 Battle Cry U :W: .15 .25
29 Battle Frenzy C :R: .15 .25
30 Binding Grasp U :B: .15 .25
31 Black Scarab U :W: .15 .25
32 Blessed Wine C :W: .15 .25
33 Blinking Spirit R :W: .15 .25
34 Blizzard R :G: .15 .25
35 Blue Scarab U :W: .15 .25
36 Bone Shaman C :R: .15 .25
37 Brainstorm C :B: .60 1.00
38 Brand of Ill Omen R :R: .15 .25
39 Breath of Dreams U :B: .15 .25
40 Brine Shaman C :K: .15 .25
41 Brown Ouphe C :G: .15 .25
42 Brushland R :L: 7.00 10.00
43 Burnt Offering C :K: .15 .25
44 Call to Arms R :W: .15 .25
45 Caribou Range R :W: .15 .25
46 Celestial Sword R :A: .15 .25
47 Centaur Archer U :D: .15 .25
48 Chaos Lord R :R: .15 .25
49 Chaos Moon R :R: .15 .25
50 Chromatic Armor R :D: .15 .25
51 Chub Toad C :G: .15 .25
52 Circle of Protection Black C :W: .15 .25
53 Circle of Protection Blue C :W: .15 .25
54 Circle of Protection Green C :W: .15 .25
55 Circle of Protection Red C :W: .15 .25
56 Circle of Protection White C :W: .15 .25
57 Clairvoyance C :B: .15 .25
58 Cloak of Confusion C :K: .15 .25
59 Cold Snap U :W: .15 .25
60 Conquer U :R: .15 .25
61 Cooperation C :W: .15 .25
62 Counterspell C :B: .60 1.00
63 Crown of the Ages R :A: .15 .25
64 Curse of Marit Lage R :R: .15 .25
65 Dance of the Dead U :K: 1.50 2.00
66 Dark Banishing C :K: .15 .25
67 Dark Ritual C :K: .15 .25
68 Death Ward C :W: .15 .25
69 Deflection R :B: .15 .25
70 Demonic Consultation U :K: .15 .25
71 Despotic Scepter R :A: .15 .25
72 Diabolic Vision U :D: .15 .25
73 Dire Wolves C :G: .15 .25
74 Disenchant C :W: .15 .25
75 Dread Wight R :K: .15 .25
76 Dreams of the Dead U :B: .15 .25
77 Drift of the Dead U :K: .15 .25
78 Drought U :W: .15 .25
79 Dwarven Armory R :R: .15 .25
80 Earthlink R :D: .15 .25
81 Earthlore C :G: .15 .25
82 Elder Druid R :G: .15 .25
83 Elemental Augury R :D: .15 .25
84 Elkin Bottle R :A: .15 .25
85 Elvish Healer C :W: .15 .25
86 Enduring Renewal R :W: .60 1.00
87 Energy Storm R :W: .60 1.00
88 Enervate C :B: .15 .25
89 Errant Minion C :B: .15 .25
90 Errantry C :R: .15 .25
91 Essence Filter C :G: .15 .25
92 Essence Flare C :B: .15 .25
93 Essence Vortex U :D: .15 .25
94 Fanatical Fever U :G: .15 .25
95 Fear C :K: .15 .25
96 Fiery Justice R :D: .15 .25
97 Fire Covenant U :D: .60 1.00
98 Flame Spirit U :R: .15 .25
99 Flare C :R: .15 .25
100 Flooded Woodlands R :D: .15 .25
101 Flow of Maggots R :K: .15 .25
102 Folk of the Pines C :G: .15 .25
103 Forbidden Lore R :G: .15 .25
104 Force Void U :B: .15 .25
105 Forest v1 L :L: .15 .25
106 Forest v2 L :L: .15 .25
107 Forest v3 L :L: .15 .25
108 Forgotten Lore U :G: .15 .25
109 Formation R :W: .15 .25
110 Foul Familiar C :K: .15 .25
111 Foxfire C :G: .15 .25
112 Freyalise Supplicant U :G: .15 .25
113 Freyalise's Charm U :G: .15 .25
114 Freyalise's Winds R :G: .15 .25
115 Fumarole U :D: .15 .25
116 Fylgja C :W: .15 .25
117 Fyndhorn Bow U :A: .15 .25
118 Fyndhorn Brownie C :G: .15 .25
119 Fyndhorn Elder U :G: .15 .25
120 Fyndhorn Elves C :G: .60 1.00
121 Fyndhorn Pollen R :G: .15 .25
122 Game of Chaos R :R: 1.00 1.50
123 Gangrenous Zombies C :K: .15 .25
124 Gaze of Pain C :K: .15 .25
125 General Jarkeld R :W: .15 .25
126 Ghostly Flame R :D: .15 .25
127 Giant Growth C :G: .15 .25
128 Giant Trap Door Spider U :D: .15 .25
129 Glacial Chasm U :L: 3.00 4.00
130 Glacial Crevasses R :R: 1.50 2.00
131 Glacial Wall U :B: .15 .25
132 Glaciers R :D: .15 .25
133 Goblin Lyre R :A: .15 .25
134 Goblin Mutant U :R: .15 .25
135 Goblin Sappers C :R: .15 .25
136 Goblin Ski Patrol C :R: .15 .25
137 Goblin Snowman U :R: .15 .25
138 Gorilla Pack C :G: .15 .25
139 Gravebind R :K: .15 .25
140 Green Scarab U :W: .15 .25
141 Grizzled Wolverine C :R: .15 .25
142 Hallowed Ground U :W: .15 .25
143 Halls of Mist R :L: .40 .60
144 Heal C :W: .15 .25
145 Hecatomb R :K: .30 .50
146 Hematite Talisman U :A: .15 .25
147 Hipparion U :W: .15 .25
148 Hoar Shade C :K: .15 .25
149 Hot Springs R :G: .15 .25
150 Howl from Beyond C :K: .15 .25
151 Hurricane U :G: .15 .25
152 Hyalopterous Lemure U :K: .15 .25
153 Hydroblast C :B: .30 .50
154 Hymn of Rebirth U :D: .15 .25
155 Ice Cauldron R :A: .30 .50
156 Ice Floe U :L: .15 .25
157 Iceberg U :B: .15 .25
158 Icequake U :K: .15 .25
159 Icy Manipulator U :A: .15 .25
160 Icy Prison R :B: .15 .25
161 Illusionary Forces C :B: .15 .25
162 Illusionary Presence R :B: .15 .25
163 Illusionary Terrain U :B: .15 .25
164 Illusionary Wall C :B: .15 .25
165 Illusions of Grandeur R :B: 4.00 6.00
166 Imposing Visage C :R: .15 .25
167 Incinerate C :R: .15 .25
168 Infernal Darkness R :K: 1.50 2.00
169 Infernal Denizen R :K: .15 .25
170 Infinite Hourglass R :A: .15 .25
171 Infuse C :B: .15 .25
172 Island v1 L :L: .15 .25
173 Island v2 L :L: .15 .25
174 Island v3 L :L: .15 .25
175 Jester's Cap R :A: 1.50 2.50
176 Jester's Mask R :A: .60 1.00
177 Jeweled Amulet U :A: .15 .25
178 Johtull Wurm U :G: .15 .25
179 Jokulhaups R :R: 2.50 3.00
180 Juniper Order Druid C :G: .15 .25
181 Justice U :W: .15 .25
182 Karplusan Forest R :L: 3.00 4.00
183 Karplusan Giant U :R: .15 .25
184 Karplusan Yeti R :R: .15 .25
185 Kelsinko Ranger C :W: .15 .25
186 Kjeldoran Dead C :K: .15 .25
187 Kjeldoran Elite Guard U :W: .15 .25
188 Kjeldoran Frostbeast U :D: .15 .25
189 Kjeldoran Guard C :W: .15 .25
190 Kjeldoran Knight R :W: .15 .25
191 Kjeldoran Phalanx R :W: .15 .25
192 Kjeldoran Royal Guard R :W: .15 .25
193 Kjeldoran Skycaptain U :W: .15 .25
194 Kjeldoran Skyknight C :W: .15 .25
195 Kjeldoran Warrior C :W: .15 .25
196 Knight of Stromgald U :K: .15 .25
197 Krovikan Elementalist U :K: .15 .25
198 Krovikan Fetish C :K: .15 .25
199 Krovikan Sorcerer C :B: .15 .25
200 Krovikan Vampire U :K: .15 .25
201 Land Cap R :L: .15 .25
202 Lapis Lazuli Talisman U :A: .15 .25
203 Lava Burst C :R: .15 .25
204 Lava Tubes R :L: .15 .25
205 Legions of Lim-Dûl C :K: .15 .25
206 Leshrac's Rite U :K: .15 .25
207 Leshrac's Sigil U :K: .15 .25
208 Lhurgoyf R :G: .15 .25
209 Lightning Blow R :W: .15 .25
210 Lim-Dûl's Cohort C :K: .15 .25
211 Lim-Dûl's Hex U :K: .15 .25
212 Lost Order of Jarkeld R :W: .15 .25
213 Lure U :G: .15 .25
214 Maddening Wind U :G: .15 .25
215 Magus of the Unseen R :B: .15 .25
216 Malachite Talisman U :A: .15 .25
217 Márton Stromgald R :R: 2.00 3.00
218 Melee U :R: .15 .25
219 Melting U :R: .15 .25
220 Mercenaries R :W: .15 .25
221 Merieke Ri Berit R :D: .60 1.00
222 Mesmeric Trance R :B: .15 .25
223 Meteor Shower C :R: .15 .25
224 Mind Ravel C :K: .15 .25
225 Mind Warp U :K: .15 .25
226 Mind Whip R :K: .15 .25
227 Minion of Leshrac R :K: .40 .60
228 Minion of Tevesh Szat R :K: .15 .25
229 Mistfolk C :B: .15 .25
230 Mole Worms U :K: .15 .25
231 Monsoon R :D: .15 .25
232 Moor Fiend C :K: .15 .25
233 Mountain v1 L :L: .15 .25
234 Mountain v2 L :L: .15 .25
235 Mountain v3 L :L: .15 .25
236 Mountain Goat C :R: .15 .25
237 Mountain Titan R :D: .15 .25
238 Mudslide R :R: .15 .25
239 Musician R :B: .15 .25
240 Mystic Might R :B: .15 .25
241 Mystic Remora C :B: 1.50 2.00
242 Nacre Talisman U :A: .15 .25
243 Naked Singularity R :A: .15 .25
244 Nature's Lore U :G: .60 1.00
245 Necropotence R :K: 6.00 8.00
246 Norritt C :K: .15 .25
247 Oath of Lim-Dûl R :K: .15 .25
248 Onyx Talisman U :A: .15 .25
249 Orcish Cannoneers U :R: .15 .25
250 Orcish Conscripts C :R: .15 .25
251 Orcish Farmer C :R: .15 .25
252 Orcish Healer U :R: .15 .25
253 Orcish Librarian R :R: .15 .25
254 Orcish Lumberjack C :R: .15 .25
255 Orcish Squatters R :R: .15 .25
256 Order of the Sacred Torch R :W: .15 .25
257 Order of the White Shield U :W: .15 .25
258 Pale Bears R :G: .15 .25
259 Panic C :R: .15 .25
260 Pentagram of the Ages R :A: .15 .25
261 Pestilence Rats C :K: .15 .25
262 Phantasmal Mount U :B: .15 .25
263 Pit Trap U :A: .15 .25
264 Plains v1 L :L: .15 .25
265 Plains v2 L :L: .15 .25
266 Plains v3 L7 :L: .15 .25
267 Polar Kraken R :B: 1.00 1.50
268 Portent C :B: .60 1.00
269 Power Sink C :B: .15 .25
270 Pox R :K: 2.00 2.50
271 Prismatic Ward C :W: .15 .25
272 Pygmy Allosaurus R :G: .15 .25
273 Pyknite C :G: .15 .25
274 Pyroblast C :R: .15 .25
275 Pyroclasm U :R: .50 .80
276 Rally C :W: .15 .25
277 Ray of Command C :B: .15 .25
278 Ray of Erasure C :B: .15 .25
279 Reality Twist R :B: .40 .60
280 Reclamation R :D: .15 .25
281 Red Scarab U :W: .15 .25
282 Regeneration C :G: .15 .25
283 Rime Dryad C :G: .15 .25
284 Ritual of Subdual R :G: .15 .25
285 River Delta R :L: .15 .25
286 Runed Arch R :A: .15 .25
287 Sabretooth Tiger C :R: .15 .25
288 Sacred Boon U :W: .15 .25
289 Scaled Wurm C :G: .15 .25
290 Sea Spirit U :B: .15 .25
291 Seizures C :K: .15 .25
292 Seraph R :W: .15 .25
293 Shambling Strider C :G: .15 .25
294 Shatter C :R: .15 .25
295 Shield Bearer C :W: .15 .25
296 Shield of the Ages U :A: .15 .25
297 Shyft R :B: .15 .25
298 Sibilant Spirit R :B: .15 .25
299 Silver Erne U :B: .15 .25
300 Skeleton Ship R :D: .60 1.00
301 Skull Catapult U :A: .15 .25
302 Sleight of Mind U :B: .15 .25
303 Snow Devil C :B: .15 .25
304 Snow Fortress R :A: .15 .25
305 Snow Hound U :W: .15 .25
306 Snowblind R :G: .15 .25
307 Snow-Covered Forest L :L: .15 .25
308 Snow-Covered Island L :L: .15 .25
309 Snow-Covered Mountain L :L: .15 .25
310 Snow-Covered Plains L :L: .15 .25
311 Snow-Covered Swamp L :L: .15 .25
312 Snowfall C :B: .15 .25
313 Soldevi Golem R :A: .15 .25
314 Soldevi Machinist U :B: .15 .25
315 Soldevi Simulacrum U :A: .15 .25
316 Songs of the Damned C :K: .15 .25
317 Soul Barrier U :B: .15 .25
318 Soul Burn C :K: .15 .25
319 Soul Kiss C :K: .15 .25
320 Spectral Shield U :D: .15 .25
321 Spoils of Evil R :K: .60 1.00
322 Spoils of War R :K: .15 .25
323 Staff of the Ages R :A: .15 .25
324 Stampede R :G: .15 .25
325 Stench of Evil U :K: .15 .25
326 Stone Rain C :R: .15 .25
327 Stone Spirit U :R: .15 .25
328 Stonehands C :R: .15 .25
329 Storm Spirit R :D: .15 .25
330 Stormbind R :D: .15 .25
331 Stromgald Cabal R :K: .15 .25
332 Stunted Growth R :G: .15 .25
333 Sulfurous Springs R :L: 4.00 5.00
334 Sunstone U :A: .15 .25
335 Swamp v1 L :L: .15 .25
336 Swamp v2 L :L: .15 .25
337 Swamp v3 L :L: .15 .25
338 Swords to Plowshares U :W: 2.00 2.50
339 Tarpan C :G: .15 .25
340 Thermokarst U :G: .15 .25
341 Thoughtleech U :G: .15 .25
342 Thunder Wall U :B: .15 .25
343 Timberline Ridge R :L: .15 .25
344 Time Bomb R :A: .15 .25
345 Tinder Wall C :G: .15 .25
346 Tor Giant C :R: .15 .25
347 Total War R :R: .15 .25
348 Touch of Death C :K: .15 .25
349 Touch of Vitae U :G: .15 .25
350 Trailblazer R :G: .15 .25
351 Underground River R :L: 3.00 3.50
352 Updraft U :B: .15 .25
353 Urza's Bauble U :A: 1.50 2.00
354 Veldt R :L: .15 .25
355 Venomous Breath U :G: .15 .25
356 Vertigo U :R: .15 .25
357 Vexing Arcanix R :A: .15 .25
358 Vibrating Sphere R :A: .15 .25
359 Walking Wall U :A: .15 .25
360 Wall of Lava U :R: .15 .25
361 Wall of Pine Needles U :G: .15 .25
362 Wall of Shields U :A: .15 .25
363 War Chariot U :A: .15 .25
364 Warning C :W: .15 .25
365 Whalebone Glider U :A: .15 .25
366 White Scarab U :W: .15 .25
367 Whiteout U :G: .15 .25
368 Wiitigo R :G: .15 .25
369 Wild Growth C :G: .15 .25
370 Wind Spirit U :B: .15 .25
371 Wings of Aesthir U :D: .15 .25
372 Winter's Chill R :B: .15 .25
373 Withering Wisps U :K: .15 .25
374 Woolly Mammoths C :G: .15 .25
375 Woolly Spider C :G: .15 .25
376 Word of Blasting U :R: .15 .25
377 Word of Undoing C :B: .15 .25
378 Wrath of Marit Lage R :B: .15 .25
379 Yavimaya Gnats U :G: .15 .25
380 Zuran Enchanter C :B: .15 .25
381 Zuran Orb U :A: .60 1.00
382 Zuran Spellcaster C :B: .15 .25
383 Zur's Weirding R :B: .15 .25

1995 Magic The Gathering Homelands

COMPLETE SET (140) 40.00 65.00
BOOSTER BOX (60 PACKS) 150.00 175.00
BOOSTER PACK (8 CARDS) 4.00 5.00
RELEASED IN OCTOBER 15, 1995
1 Abbey Gargoyles U :W: .15 .25
2 Abbey Matron v1 C :W: .15 .25
3 Abbey Matron v2 C :W: .15 .25
4 AEther Storm U :B: .15 .25
5 Aliban's Tower v1 C :R: .15 .25
6 Aliban's Tower v2 C :R: .15 .25
7 Ambush C :R: .15 .25
8 Ambush Party v1 C :R: .15 .25
9 Ambush Party v2 C :R: .15 .25
10 Anaba Ancestor U :R: .50 .80
11 Anaba Bodyguard v1 C :R: .15 .25
12 Anaba Bodyguard v2 C :R: .15 .25
13 Anaba Shaman v1 C :R: .15 .25
14 Anaba Shaman v2 C :R: .15 .25
15 Anaba Spirit Crafter U :R: 2.50 3.00
16 An-Havva Constable U :G: .15 .25
17 An-Havva Inn U :G: .15 .25
18 An-Havva Township U :L: .15 .25
19 An-Zerrin Ruins U :R: .15 .25
20 Apocalypse Chime U :A: .15 .25
21 Autumn Willow U :G: .50 .80
22 Aysen Abbey U :L: .15 .25
23 Aysen Bureaucrats v1 C :W: .15 .25
24 Aysen Bureaucrats v2 C :W: .15 .25
25 Aysen Crusader U :W: .50 .80
26 Aysen Highway U :W: .15 .25
27 Baki's Curse U :B: .15 .25
28 Baron Sengir U :K: 1.50 2.00
29 Beast Walkers U :W: .15 .25
30 Black Carriage U :K: .15 .25
31 Broken Visage U :K: .15 .25
32 Carapace v1 C :G: .15 .25
33 Carapace v2 C :G: .15 .25
34 Castle Sengir U :L: .15 .25
35 Cemetery Gate v1 C :K: .50 .80
36 Cemetery Gate v2 C :K: .50 .80
37 Chain Stasis U :B: .15 .25
38 Chandler U :R: .15 .25
39 Clockwork Gnomes C :A: .15 .25
40 Clockwork Steed C :A: .15 .25
41 Clockwork Swarm C :A: .15 .25
42 Coral Reef C :B: .15 .25
43 Dark Maze v1 C :B: .50 .80
44 Dark Maze v2 C :B: .50 .80
45 Daughter of Autumn U :G: .15 .25
46 Death Speakers U :W: .15 .25
47 Didgeridoo U :A: 2.50 3.00
48 Drudge Spell U :K: .15 .25
49 Dry Spell v1 C :K: .50 .80
50 Dry Spell v2 C :K: .50 .80
51 Dwarven Pony U :R: .15 .25
52 Dwarven Sea Clan U :R: .15 .25
53 Dwarven Trader v1 C :R: .15 .25
54 Dwarven Trader v2 C :R: .15 .25
55 Ebony Rhino C :A: .15 .25
56 Eron the Relentless U :R: .15 .25
57 Evaporate U :R: .15 .25
58 Faerie Noble U :G: .15 .25
59 Feast of the Unicorn v1 C :K: .50 .80
60 Feast of the Unicorn v2 C :K: .50 .80
61 Feroz's Ban U :A: .15 .25
62 Folk of An-Havva v1 C :G: .15 .25
63 Folk of An-Havva v2 C :G: .15 .25
64 Forget U :B: .15 .25
65 Funeral March C :K: .15 .25
66 Ghost Hounds U :K: .15 .25
67 Giant Albatross v1 C :B: .15 .25
68 Giant Albatross v2 C :B: .15 .25
69 Giant Oyster U :B: .15 .25
70 Grandmother Sengir U :K: .15 .25
71 Greater Werewolf U :K: .15 .25
72 Hazduhr the Abbot U :W: .15 .25
73 Headstone C :K: .15 .25
74 Heart Wolf U :R: .15 .25
75 Hungry Mist v1 C :G: .50 .80
76 Hungry Mist v2 C :G: .50 .80
77 Ihsan's Shade U :K: .15 .25
78 Irini Sengir U :K: .15 .25
79 Ironclaw Curse U :R: .15 .25
80 Jinx C :B: .15 .25
81 Joven U :R: .15 .25
82 Joven's Ferrets C :G: .15 .25
83 Joven's Tools U :A: .15 .25
84 Koskun Falls U :K: 3.00 3.50
85 Koskun Keep U :L: .15 .25
86 Labyrinth Minotaur v1 C :B: .15 .25
87 Labyrinth Minotaur v2 C :B: .15 .25
88 Leaping Lizard C :G: .15 .25
89 Leeches U :W: .60 1.00
90 Mammoth Harness U :G: .15 .25
91 Marjhan U :B: .15 .25
92 Memory Lapse v1 C :B: .15 .25
93 Memory Lapse v2 C :B: .15 .25
94 Merchant Scroll C :B: 3.50 4.50
95 Mesa Falcon v1 C :W: .15 .25
96 Mesa Falcon v2 C :W: .15 .25

97 Mystic Decree U :B: .50 .80
98 Narwhal U :B: 1.00 1.50
99 Orcish Mine U :R: .15 .25
100 Primal Order U :G: .15 .25
101 Prophecy U :W: .15 .25
102 Rashka the Slayer U :W: .15 .25
103 Reef Pirates v1 C :B: .15 .25
104 Reef Pirates v2 C :B: .15 .25
105 Renewal C :G: .15 .25
106 Retribution U :R: .15 .25
107 Reveka, Wizard Savant U :B: .15 .25
108 Root Spider U :G: .15 .25
109 Roots U :G: .15 .25
110 Roterothopter C :A: .15 .25
111 Rysorian Badger U :G: .15 .25
112 Samite Alchemist v1 C :W: .15 .25
113 Samite Alchemist v2 C :W: .15 .25
114 Sea Sprite U :B: .15 .25
115 Sea Troll U :B: .15 .25
116 Sengir Autocrat U :K: .15 .25
117 Sengir Bats v1 C :K: .15 .25
118 Sengir Bats v2 C :K: .15 .25
119 Serra Aviary U :W: .15 .25
120 Serra Bestiary U :W: .15 .25
121 Serra Inquisitors U :W: .15 .25
122 Serra Paladin C :W: .15 .25
123 Serrated Arrows C :A: .15 .25
124 Shrink v1 C :G: .15 .25
125 Shrink v2 C :G: .15 .25
126 Soraya the Falconer U :W: .15 .25
127 Spectral Bears U :G: .15 .25
128 Timmerian Fiends U :K: .60 1.00
129 Torture v1 C :K: .50 .80
130 Torture v2 C :K: .50 .80
131 Trade Caravan v1 C :W: .15 .25
132 Trade Caravan v2 C :W: .15 .25
133 Truce U :W: .15 .25
134 Veldrane of Sengir U :K: .15 .25
135 Wall of Kelp U :B: 1.00 1.50
136 Willow Faerie v1 C :G: .60 1.00
137 Willow Faerie v2 C :G: .60 1.00
138 Willow Priestess U :G: .40 .60
139 Winter Sky U :R: .15 .25
140 Wizards' School U :L: .15 .25

1996 Magic The Gathering Alliances

COMPLETE SET (199) 160.00 215.00
BOOSTER BOX (45 PACKS) 600.00 800.00
BOOSTER PACK (12 CARDS) 15.00 20.00
RELEASED ON JUNE 10, 1996
1 Aesthir Glider v1 C :A: .20 .35
2 Aesthir Glider v2 C :A: .20 .35
3 Agent of Stromgald v1 C :R: .20 .35
4 Agent of Stromgald v2 C :R: .20 .35
5 Arcane Denial v1 C :B: .50 .80
6 Arcane Denial v2 C :B: .50 .80
7 Ashnod's Cylix R :A: .20 .35
8 Astrolabe v1 C :A: .20 .35
9 Astrolabe v2 C :A: .20 .35
10 Awesome Presence v1 C :B: .20 .35
11 Awesome Presence v2 C :B: .20 .35
12 Balduvian Dead U :K: .20 .35
13 Balduvian Horde R :R: .20 .35
14 Balduvian Trading Post R :L: .75 1.25
15 Balduvian War-Makers v1 C :R: .20 .35
16 Balduvian War-Makers v2 C :R: .20 .35
17 Benthic Explorers v1 C :B: .20 .35
18 Benthic Explorers v2 C :B: .20 .35
19 Bestial Fury v1 C :R: .20 .35
20 Bestial Fury v2 C :R: .20 .35
21 Bounty of the Hunt U :G: .20 .35
22 Browse U :B: .20 .35
23 Burnout U :R: .20 .35
24 Carrier Pigeons v1 C :W: .20 .35
25 Carrier Pigeons v2 C :W: .20 .35
26 Casting of Bones v1 C :K: .20 .35
27 Casting of Bones v2 C :K: .20 .35
28 Chaos Harlequin R :R: .20 .35
29 Contagion U :K: .20 .35
30 Deadly Insect v1 U :G: .20 .35
31 Deadly Insect v2 U :G: .20 .35
32 Death Spark U :R: .20 .35
33 Diminishing Returns R :B: .20 .35
34 Diseased Vermin U :K: .20 .35
35 Dystopia R :K: .50 .80
36 Elvish Bard U :G: .20 .35
37 Elvish Ranger v1 C :G: .20 .35
38 Elvish Ranger v2 C :G: .20 .35
39 Elvish Spirit Guide U :G: 4.00 6.00
40 Energy Arc U :D: .20 .35
41 Enslaved Scout v1 C :R: .20 .35
42 Enslaved Scout v2 C :R: .20 .35
43 Errand of Duty v1 C :W: .20 .35
44 Errand of Duty v2 C :W: .20 .35
45 Exile R :W: .75 1.25
46 False Demise v1 U :B: .20 .35
47 False Demise v2 U :B: .20 .35
48 Fatal Lore R :K: .20 .35
49 Feast or Famine v1 U :K: .20 .35
50 Feast or Famine v2 U :K: .20 .35
51 Fevered Strength v1 C :K: .20 .35
52 Fevered Strength v2 C :K: .20 .35
53 Floodwater Dam R :A: .20 .35
54 Force of Will U :B: 65.00 75.00
55 Foresight v1 C :B: .20 .35
56 Foresight v2 C :B: .20 .35
57 Fyndhorn Druid v1 C :G: .20 .35
58 Fyndhorn Druid v2 C :G: .20 .35
59 Gargantuan Gorilla R :G: .20 .35
60 Gift of the Woods v1 C :G: .20 .35
61 Gift of the Woods v2 C :G: .20 .35
62 Gorilla Berserkers v1 C :G: .20 .35
63 Gorilla Berserkers v2 C :G: .20 .35
64 Gorilla Chieftain v1 C :G: .20 .35
65 Gorilla Chieftain v2 C :G: .20 .35
66 Gorilla Shaman v1 U :R: 1.50 2.50
67 Gorilla Shaman v2 U :R: 1.50 2.50
68 Gorilla War Cry v1 C :R: .20 .35
69 Gorilla War Cry v2 C :R: .20 .35
70 Guerrilla Tactics v1 C :R: .20 .35
71 Guerrilla Tactics v2 C :R: .20 .35
72 Gustha's Scepter R :A: .20 .35
73 Hail Storm U :G: .20 .35
74 Heart of Yavimaya R :L: 1.50 2.50
75 Helm of Obedience R :A: 14.00 16.00
76 Inheritance U :W: .20 .35
77 Insidious Bookworms v1 C :K: .20 .35
78 Insidious Bookworms v2 C :K: .20 .35
79 Ivory Gargoyle R :W: .20 .35
80 Juniper Order Advocate U :W: .20 .35
81 Kaysa R :G: 1.50 2.00
82 Keeper of Tresserhorn R :K: .20 .35
83 Kjeldoran Escort v1 C :W: .20 .35
84 Kjeldoran Escort v2 C :W: .20 .35
85 Kjeldoran Home Guard U :W: .20 .35
86 Kjeldoran Outpost R :L: 4.00 5.00
87 Kjeldoran Pride v1 C :W: .20 .35
88 Kjeldoran Pride v2 C :W: .20 .35
89 Krovikan Horror R :K: .20 .35
90 Krovikan Plague U :K: .20 .35
91 Lake of the Dead R :L: 20.00 25.00
92 Lat-Nam's Legacy v1 C :B: .20 .35
93 Lat-Nam's Legacy v2 C :B: .20 .35
94 Library of Lat-Nam R :B: .20 .35
95 Lim-Dûl's High Guard v1 C :K: .20 .35
96 Lim-Dûl's High Guard v2 C :K: .20 .35
97 Lim-Dûl's Paladin U :D: .20 .35
98 Lim-Dûl's Vault U :D: 1.00 1.50
99 Lodestone Bauble R :A: 1.25 2.00
100 Lord of Tresserhorn R :D: 1.25 2.00
101 Martyrdom v1 C :W: .20 .35
102 Martyrdom v2 C :W: .20 .35
103 Misfortune R :D: .20 .35
104 Mishra's Groundbreaker U :A: .20 .35
105 Misinformation U :K: .20 .35
106 Mystic Compass U :A: .20 .35
107 Nature's Blessing U :D: .20 .35
108 Nature's Chosen U :G: .20 .35
109 Nature's Wrath R :G: .20 .35
110 Noble Steeds v1 C :W: .20 .35
111 Noble Steeds v2 C :W: .20 .35
112 Omen of Fire R :R: .20 .35
113 Phantasmal Fiend v1 C :K: .20 .35
114 Phantasmal Fiend v2 C :K: .20 .35
115 Phantasmal Sphere R :B: .20 .35
116 Phelddagrif R :D: 3.00 5.00
117 Phyrexian Boon v1 C :K: .20 .35
118 Phyrexian Boon v2 C :K: .20 .35
119 Phyrexian Devourer R :A: 6.00 8.00
120 Phyrexian Portal R :A: .20 .35
121 Phyrexian War Beast v1 C :A: .20 .35
122 Phyrexian War Beast v2 C :A: .20 .35
123 Pillage U :R: .20 .35
124 Primitive Justice U :R: .20 .35
125 Pyrokinesis U :R: .20 .35
126 Reinforcements v1 C :W: .20 .35
127 Reinforcements v2 C :W: .20 .35
128 Reprisal v1 U :W: .20 .35
129 Reprisal v2 U :W: .20 .35
130 Ritual of the Machine R :K: 1.00 1.50
131 Rogue Skycaptain R :R: .20 .35
132 Royal Decree R :W: .20 .35
133 Royal Herbalist v1 C :W: .20 .35
134 Royal Herbalist v2 C :W: .20 .35
135 Scarab of the Unseen U :A: .20 .35
136 Scars of the Veteran U :W: .20 .35
137 School of the Unseen U :L: .20 .35
138 Seasoned Tactician U :W: .20 .35
139 Sheltered Valley R :L: .20 .35
140 Shield Sphere U :A: 1.00 1.50
141 Sol Grail R :A: .20 .35
142 Soldevi Adnate v1 C :K: .20 .35
143 Soldevi Adnate v2 C :K: .20 .35
144 Soldevi Digger R :A: .20 .35
145 Soldevi Excavations R :L: 2.50 3.50
146 Soldevi Heretic v1 C :B: .20 .35
147 Soldevi Heretic v2 C :B: .20 .35
148 Soldevi Sage v1 C :B: .20 .35
149 Soldevi Sage v2 C :B: .20 .35
150 Soldevi Sentry v1 C :A: .20 .35
151 Soldevi Sentry v2 C :A: .20 .35
152 Soldevi Steam Beast v1 C :A: .20 .35
153 Soldevi Steam Beast v2 C :A: .20 .35
154 Soldier of Fortune U :R: .20 .35
155 Spiny Starfish U :B: .20 .35
156 Splintering Wind R :G: .20 .35
157 Stench of Decay v1 C :K: .20 .35
158 Stench of Decay v2 C :K: .20 .35
159 Storm Cauldron R :A: .60 1.00
160 Storm Crow v1 C :B: .20 .35
161 Storm Crow v2 C :B: .20 .35
162 Storm Elemental U :B: .20 .35
163 Storm Shaman v1 C :R: .20 .35
164 Storm Shaman v2 C :R: .20 .35
165 Stromgald Spy U :K: .20 .35
166 Suffocation U :B: .20 .35
167 Surge of Strength U :D: .20 .35
168 Sustaining Spirit R :W: 1.50 2.00
169 Swamp Mosquito v1 C :K: .20 .35
170 Swamp Mosquito v2 C :K: .20 .35
171 Sworn Defender R :W: .20 .35
172 Taste of Paradise v1 C :G: .20 .35
173 Taste of Paradise v2 C :G: .20 .35
174 Thawing Glaciers R :L: 8.00 10.00
175 Thought Lash R :B: 2.00 3.00
176 Tidal Control R :B: .20 .35
177 Tornado R :G: .20 .35
178 Undergrowth v1 C :G: .20 .35
179 Undergrowth v2 C :G: .20 .35
180 Unlikely Alliance U :W: .20 .35
181 Urza's Engine R :A: .20 .35
182 Varchild's Crusader v1 C :R: .20 .35
183 Varchild's Crusader v2 C :R: .20 .35
184 Varchild's War-Riders R :R: 1.50 2.50
185 Veteran's Voice v1 C :R: .20 .35
186 Veteran's Voice v2 C :R: .20 .35
187 Viscerid Armor v1 C :B: .20 .35
188 Viscerid Armor v2 C :B: .20 .35
189 Viscerid Drone U :B: .20 .35
190 Wandering Mage R :D: .20 .35
191 Whip Vine v1 C :G: .20 .35
192 Whip Vine v2 C :G: .20 .35
193 Whirling Catapult R :A: .20 .35
194 Wild Aesthir v1 C :W: .20 .35
195 Wild Aesthir v2 C :W: .20 .35
196 Winter's Night R :D: .20 .35
197 Yavimaya Ancients v1 C :G: .20 .35
198 Yavimaya Ancients v2 C :G: .20 .35
199 Yavimaya Ants U :G: .20 .35

1996 Magic The Gathering Mirage

COMPLETE SET (350) 235.00 325.00
BOOSTER BOX (36 PACKS) 400.00 600.00
BOOSTER PACK (15 CARDS) 15.00 20.00
STARTER BOX 350.00 500.00
STARTER DECK 35.00 50.00
RELEASED ON OCTOBER 7, 1996
1 Abyssal Hunter R :K: .20 .35
2 Acidic Dagger R :A: .20 .35
3 Afiya Grove R :G: .20 .35
4 Afterlife U :W: .20 .35
5 Agility C :R: .20 .35
6 Alarum C :W: .20 .35
7 Aleatory U :R: .20 .35
8 Amber Prison R :A: .20 .35
9 Amulet of Unmaking R :A: .20 .35
10 Ancestral Memories R :B: .20 .35
11 Armor of Thorns C :G: .20 .35
12 Armorer Guildmage C :R: .20 .35
13 Ashen Powder R :K: .50 .80
14 Asmira, Holy Avenger R :D: .20 .35
15 Auspicious Ancestor R :W: .20 .35
16 Azimaet Drake C :B: .20 .35
17 Bad River U :L: 2.00 2.50
18 Barbed Foliage U :G: .20 .35
19 Barbed-Back Wurm U :K: .20 .35
20 Barreling Attack R :R: .20 .35
21 Basalt Golem U :A: .20 .35
22 Bay Falcon C :B: .20 .35
23 Bazaar of Wonders R :B: .20 .35
24 Benevolent Unicorn C :W: .20 .35
25 Benthic Djinn R :D: .20 .35
26 Binding Agony C :K: .20 .35
27 Blighted Shaman U :K: .20 .35
28 Blind Fury U :R: .20 .35
29 Blinding Light U :W: .20 .35
30 Blistering Barrier C :R: .20 .35
31 Bone Harvest C :K: .20 .35
32 Bone Mask R :A: .20 .35
33 Boomerang C :B: .20 .35
34 Breathstealer C :K: .20 .35
35 Brushwagg R :G: .20 .35
36 Builder's Bane C :R: .20 .35
37 Burning Palm Efreet U :R: .20 .35
38 Burning Shield Askari C :R: .20 .35
39 Cadaverous Bloom R :D: .60 1.00
40 Cadaverous Knight C :K: .20 .35
41 Canopy Dragon R :G: .20 .35
42 Carrion R :K: .20 .35
43 Catacomb Dragon R :K: .60 1.00
44 Celestial Dawn R :W: .60 1.00
45 Cerulean Wyvern U :B: .20 .35
46 Chaos Charm C :R: .20 .35
47 Chaosphere R :R: 4.00 6.00
48 Charcoal Diamond U :A: .20 .35
49 Chariot of the Sun U :A: .20 .35
50 Choking Sands C :K: .20 .35
51 Cinder Cloud U :R: .20 .35
52 Circle of Despair R :D: .20 .35
53 Civic Guildmage C :W: .20 .35
54 Cloak of Invisibility C :B: .20 .35
55 Consuming Ferocity U :R: .20 .35
56 Coral Fighters U :B: .20 .35
57 Crash of Rhinos C :G: .20 .35
58 Crimson Hellkite R :R: .20 .35
59 Crimson Roc U :R: .20 .35
60 Crypt Cobra U :K: .20 .35
61 Crystal Golem U :A: .20 .35
62 Crystal Vein U :L: .20 .35
63 Cursed Totem R :A: 1.50 2.50
64 Cycle of Life R :G: .20 .35
65 Daring Apprentice R :B: .20 .35
66 Dark Banishing C :K: .20 .35
67 Dark Ritual C :K: .20 .35
68 Dazzling Beauty C :W: .20 .35
69 Decomposition U :G: .20 .35
70 Delirium U :D: .20 .35
71 Dirtwater Wraith C :K: .20 .35
72 Discordant Spirit R :D: .20 .35
73 Disempower C :W: .20 .35
74 Disenchant C :W: .20 .35
75 Dissipate U :B: .20 .35
76 Divine Offering C :W: .20 .35
77 Divine Retribution R :W: .20 .35
78 Drain Life C :K: .20 .35
79 Dread Specter U :K: .20 .35
80 Dream Cache C :B: .20 .35
81 Dream Fighter C :B: .20 .35
82 Dwarven Miner U :R: .20 .35
83 Dwarven Nomad C :R: .20 .35
84 Early Harvest R :G: .20 .35
85 Ebony Charm C :K: .20 .35
86 Ekundu Cyclops C :R: .20 .35
87 Ekundu Griffin C :W: .20 .35
88 Elixir of Vitality U :A: .20 .35
89 Emberwilde Caliph R :D: .20 .35
90 Emberwilde Djinn R :R: .20 .35
91 Energy Bolt R :D: .20 .35
92 Energy Vortex R :B: .20 .35
93 Enfeeblement C :K: .20 .35
94 Enlightened Tutor U :W: 8.00 11.00
95 Ersatz Gnomes U :A: .20 .35
96 Ether Well U :B: .20 .35
97 Ethereal Champion R :W: .20 .35
98 Fallow Earth U :G: .20 .35
99 Favorable Destiny U :W: .20 .35
100 Femeref Archers U :G: .20 .35
101 Femeref Healer C :W: .20 .35
102 Femeref Knight C :W: .20 .35
103 Femeref Scouts C :W: .20 .35
104 Feral Shadow C :K: .20 .35
105 Fetid Horror C :K: .20 .35
106 Final Fortune R :R: .60 1.00
107 Fire Diamond U :A: .20 .35
108 Firebreathing C :R: .20 .35
109 Flame Elemental U :R: .20 .35
110 Flare C :R: .20 .35
111 Flash R :B: 2.50 4.00
112 Flood Plain U :L: .60 1.00
113 Floodgate U :B: .20 .35
114 Fog C :G: .20 .35
115 Foratog U :G: .20 .35
116 Forbidden Crypt R :K: .20 .35
117 Forest A L :L: .20 .35
118 Forest B L :L: .20 .35
119 Forest C L :L: .20 .35
120 Forest D L :L: .20 .35
121 Forsaken Wastes R :K: .20 .35
122 Frenetic Efreet R :D: .20 .35
123 Giant Mantis C :G: .20 .35
124 Gibbering Hyenas C :G: .20 .35
125 Goblin Elite Infantry C :R: .20 .35
126 Goblin Scouts U :R: .20 .35
127 Goblin Soothsayer U :R: .20 .35
128 Goblin Tinkerer C :R: .20 .35
129 Granger Guildmage C :G: .20 .35
130 GrassLands U :L: .20 .35
131 Grave Servitude C :K: .20 .35
132 Gravebane Zombie C :K: .20 .35
133 Grim Feast R :D: .50 .80
134 Grinning Totem R :A: .20 .35
135 Hakim, Loreweaver R :B: .20 .35
136 Hall of Gemstone R :G: 3.00 4.00
137 Hammer of Bogardan R :R: .20 .35
138 Harbinger of Night R :K: 4.00 6.00
139 Harbor Guardian U :D: .20 .35
140 Harmattan Efreet U :B: .20 .35
141 Haunting Apparition U :D: .20 .35
142 Hazerider Drake U :D: .20 .35
143 Healing Salve C :W: .20 .35
144 Hivis of the Scale R :R: .20 .35
145 Horrible Hordes U :A: .20 .35
146 Igneous Golem U :A: .20 .35
147 Illicit Auction R :R: .60 1.00
148 Illumination U :W: .20 .35
149 Incinerate C :R: .20 .35
150 Infernal Contract R :K: .20 .35
151 Iron Tusk Elephant U :W: .20 .35
152 Island A L :L: .20 .35
153 Island B L :L: .20 .35
154 Island C L :L: .20 .35
155 Island D L :L: .20 .35
156 Ivory Charm C :W: .20 .35
157 Jabari's Influence R :W: .20 .35
158 Jolrael's Centaur C :G: .20 .35
159 Jolt C :B: .20 .35
160 Jungle Patrol R :G: .20 .35
161 Jungle Troll U :D: .20 .35
162 Jungle Wurm C :G: .20 .35
163 Kaervek's Hex U :K: .20 .35
164 Kaervek's Purge U :D: .20 .35
165 Kaervek's Torch C :R: .20 .35
166 Karoo Meerkat U :G: .20 .35
167 Kukemssa Pirates R :B: 3.00 5.00
168 Kukemssa Serpent C :B: .20 .35
169 Lead Golem U :A: .20 .35
170 Leering Gargoyle R :D: .20 .35
171 Lightning Reflexes C :R: .20 .35
172 Lion's Eye Diamond R :A: 115.00 130.00
173 Locust Swarm U :G: .20 .35
174 Lure of Prey R :G: 2.00 3.00
175 Malignant Growth R :D: .20 .35
176 Mana Prism U :A: .20 .35
177 Mangara's Blessing U :W: .20 .35
178 Mangara's Equity U :W: .20 .35
179 Mangara's Tome R :A: .60 1.00
180 Marble Diamond U :A: .20 .35
181 Maro R :G: .20 .35
182 Meddle U :B: .20 .35
183 Melesse Spirit U :W: .20 .35
184 Memory Lapse C :B: .20 .35
185 Merfolk Raiders C :B: .20 .35
186 Merfolk Seer C :B: .20 .35
187 Mind Bend U :B: .20 .35
188 Mind Harness U :B: .20 .35
189 Mindbender Spores R :G: .20 .35
190 Mire Shade U :K: .20 .35
191 Misers' Cage R :A: .20 .35
192 Mist Dragon R :B: .20 .35
193 Moss Diamond U :A: .20 .35
194 Mountain A L :L: 1.25 2.00
195 Mountain B L :L: 1.25 2.00
196 Mountain C L :L: 1.25 2.00
197 Mountain D L :L: 1.25 2.00
198 Mountain Valley U :L: .20 .35
199 Mtenda Griffin U :W: .20 .35
200 Mtenda Herder C :W: .20 .35
201 Mtenda Lion C :G: .20 .35
202 Mystical Tutor U :B: 4.00 6.00
203 Natural Balance R :G: .75 1.25
204 Nettletooth Djinn U :G: .20 .35
205 Noble Elephant C :W: .20 .35
206 Nocturnal Raid U :K: .20 .35
207 Null Chamber R :W: .20 .35
208 Pacifism C :W: .20 .35
209 Painful Memories U :K: .20 .35
210 Patagia Golem U :A: .20 .35
211 Paupers' Cage R :A: .20 .35
212 Pearl Dragon R :W: .20 .35
213 Phyrexian Dreadnought R :A: 10.00 15.00
214 Phyrexian Purge R :D: .20 .35
215 Phyrexian Tribute R :K: .20 .35
216 Phyrexian Vault U :A: .20 .35
217 Plains A L :L: .20 .35
218 Plains B L :L: .20 .35
219 Plains C L :L: .20 .35

220 Plains D L :L: .20 .35
221 Political Trickery R :B: 1.25 2.00
222 Polymorph R :B: .75 1.25
223 Power Sink C :B: .20 .35
224 Preferred Selection R :G: .20 .35
225 Prismatic Boon U :D: .20 .35
226 Prismatic Circle C :W: .20 .35
227 Prismatic Lace R :B: .20 .35
228 Psychic Transfer R :B: .20 .35
229 Purgatory R :D: .20 .35
230 Purraj of Urborg R :K: .20 .35
231 Pyric Salamander C :R: .20 .35
232 Quirion Elves C :G: .20 .35
233 Radiant Essence U :D: .20 .35
234 Raging Spirit C :R: .20 .35
235 Rampant Growth C :G: .20 .35
236 Rashida Scalebane R :W: .20 .35
237 Ravenous Vampire U :K: .20 .35
238 Ray of Command C :B: .20 .35
239 Razor Pendulum R :A: .20 .35
240 Reality Ripple C :B: .20 .35
241 Reckless Embermage R :R: .20 .35
242 Reflect Damage R :D: .20 .35
243 Regeneration C :G: .20 .35
244 Reign of Chaos U :R: .20 .35
245 Reign of Terror U :K: .20 .35
246 Reparations R :D: .75 1.25
247 Restless Dead C :K: .20 .35
248 Ritual of Steel C :W: .20 .35
249 Rock Basilisk R :D: .20 .35
250 Rocky Tar Pit U :L: .20 .35
251 Roots of Life U :G: .20 .35
252 Sabertooth Cobra C :G: .20 .35
253 Sacred Mesa R :W: .20 .35
254 Sand Golem U :A: .20 .35
255 Sandbar Crocodile C :B: .20 .35
256 Sandstorm C :G: .20 .35
257 Sapphire Charm C :B: .20 .35
258 Savage Twister U :D: .20 .35
259 Sawback Manticore R :D: .20 .35
260 Sea Scryer C :B: .20 .35
261 Sealed Fate U :D: .20 .35
262 Searing Spear Askari C :R: .20 .35
263 Seedling Charm C :G: .20 .35
264 Seeds of Innocence R :G: 1.00 1.50
265 Serene Heart C :G: .20 .35
266 Sewer Rats C :K: .20 .35
267 Shadow Guildmage C :K: .20 .35
268 Shadowbane U :W: .20 .35
269 Shallow Grave R :K: 8.00 10.00
270 Shaper Guildmage C :B: .20 .35
271 Shauku, Endbringer R :K: 7.00 9.00
272 Shauku's Minion U :D: .20 .35
273 Shimmer R :B: 4.00 .35
274 Sidar Jabari R :W: .20 .35
275 Sirocco U :R: .20 .35
276 Skulking Ghost C :K: .20 .35
277 Sky Diamond U :A: .20 .35
278 Soar C :B: .20 .35
279 Soul Echo R :W: .20 .35
280 Soul Rend U :K: .20 .35
281 Soulshriek C :K: .20 .35
282 Spatial Binding U :D: .20 .35
283 Spectral Guardian R :W: .20 .35
284 Spirit of the Night R :K: 1.50 2.50
285 Spitting Earth C :R: .20 .35
286 Stalking Tiger C :G: .20 .35
287 Stone Rain C :R: .20 .35
288 Stupor U :K: .20 .35
289 Subterranean Spirit R :R: .20 .35
290 Sunweb R :W: .20 .35
291 Superior Numbers U :G: .20 .35
292 Suq'Ata Firewalker U :B: .20 .35
293 Swamp A L :L: .20 .35
294 Swamp B L :L: .20 .35
295 Swamp C L :L: .20 .35
296 Swamp D L :L: .20 .35
297 Tainted Specter R :K: .20 .35
298 Talruum Minotaur C :R: .20 .35
299 Taniwha R :B: .20 .35
300 Teeka's Dragon R :A: 1.50 2.00
301 Teferi's Curse C :B: .20 .35
302 Teferi's Drake C :B: .20 .35
303 Teferi's Imp R :B: .20 .35
304 Teferi's Isle R :L: 1.00 1.50
305 Telim'Tor R :R: .20 .35
306 Telim'Tor's Darts U :A: .20 .35
307 Telim'Tor's Edict R :R: .20 .35
308 Teremko Griffin C :W: .20 .35
309 Thirst C :B: .20 .35
310 Tidal Wave U :B: .20 .35
311 Tombstone Stairwell R :K: 3.00 4.00
312 Torrent of Lava R :R: .20 .35
313 Tranquil Domain C :G: .20 .35
314 Tropical Storm U :G: .20 .35
315 Uktabi Faerie C :G: .20 .35
316 Uktabi Wildcats R :G: .20 .35
317 Unerring Sling U :A: .20 .35
318 Unfulfilled Desires R :D: .20 .35
319 Unseen Walker U :G: .20 .35
320 Unyaro Bee Sting U :G: .20 .35
321 Unyaro Griffin U :W: .20 .35
322 Urborg Panther C :K: .20 .35
323 Vaporous Djinn U :B: .20 .35
324 Ventifact Bottle R :A: .20 .35
325 Viashino Warrior C :R: .20 .35
326 Vigilant Martyr U :W: .20 .35
327 Village Elder C :G: .20 .35
328 Vitalizing Cascade U :D: .20 .35
329 Volcanic Dragon R :R: .20 .35
330 Volcanic Geyser U :R: .20 .35
331 Waiting in the Weeds R :G: .20 .35
332 Wall of Corpses C :K: .20 .35
333 Wall of Resistance C :W: .20 .35
334 Wall of Roots C :G: .60 1.00
335 Ward of Lights C :W: .20 .35
336 Warping Wurm R :D: .20 .35
337 Wave Elemental U :B: .20 .35
338 Wellspring R :D: .20 .35
339 Wild Elephant C :G: .20 .35
340 Wildfire Emissary U :R: .20 .35
341 Windreaper Falcon U :D: .20 .35
342 Withering Boon U :K: .20 .35
343 Worldly Tutor U :G: 9.00 11.00
344 Yare R :W: .20 .35
345 Zebra Unicorn U :D: .20 .35
346 Zhalfirin Commander U :W: .20 .35
347 Zhalfirin Knight C :W: .20 .35
348 Zirilan of the Claw R :R: 8.00 10.00
349 Zombie Mob U :K: .20 .35
350 Zuberi, Golden Feather R :W: .20 .35

1997 Magic The Gathering Visions

COMPLETE SET (167) 130.00 175.00
BOOSTER BOX (36 PACKS) 275.00 350.00
BOOSTER PACK (15 CARDS) 8.00 12.00
RELEASED ON FEBRUARY 3, 1997
1 Aku Djinn R :K: .20 .35
2 Anvil of Bogardan R :A: 8.00 10.00
3 Archangel R :W: .30 .50
4 Army Ants U :D: .20 .35
5 Betrayal C :B: .20 .35
6 Blanket of Night U :K: .20 .35
7 Bogardan Phoenix R :R: .20 .35
8 Brass-Talon Chimera U :A: .20 .35
9 Breathstealer's Crypt R :D: 2.00 3.00
10 Breezekeeper C :B: .20 .35
11 Brood of Cockroaches U :K: .20 .35
12 Bull Elephant C :G: .20 .35
13 Chronatog R :B: 1.00 1.50
14 City of Solitude R :G: 5.00 7.00
15 Cloud Elemental C :B: .20 .35
16 Coercion C :K: .20 .35
17 Coral Atoll U :L: .20 .35
18 Corrosion R :D: .20 .35
19 Creeping Mold U :G: .20 .35
20 Crypt Rats C :K: 2.00 3.00
21 Daraja Griffin U :W: .20 .35
22 Dark Privilege C :K: .20 .35
23 Death Watch C :K: .20 .35
24 Desertion R :B: 1.50 2.50
25 Desolation U :K: .20 .35
26 Diamond Kaleidoscope R :A: .20 .35
27 Dormant Volcano U :L: .20 .35
28 Dragon Mask U :A: .20 .35
29 Dream Tides U :B: .20 .35
30 Dwarven Vigilantes C :R: .20 .35
31 Elephant Grass U :G: .50 .80
32 Elkin Lair R :R: .30 .50
33 Elven Cache C :G: .20 .35
34 Emerald Charm C :G: .20 .35
35 Equipoise R :W: .60 1.00
36 Everglades U :L: .20 .35
37 Eye of Singularity R :W: .20 .35
38 Fallen Askari C :K: .20 .35
39 Femeref Enchantress R :D: 2.50 3.50
40 Feral Instinct C :G: .20 .35
41 Fireblast C :R: 1.00 1.50
42 Firestorm Hellkite R :D: .20 .35
43 Flooded Shoreline R :B: .20 .35
44 Forbidden Ritual R :K: .20 .35
45 Foreshadow U :B: .20 .35
46 Freewind Falcon C :W: .20 .35
47 Funeral Charm C :K: .60 1.00
48 Giant Caterpillar C :G: .20 .35
49 Goblin Recruiter U :R: 1.50 2.00
50 Goblin Swine-Rider C :R: .20 .35
51 Gossamer Chains C :W: .20 .35
52 Griffin Canyon R :L: .60 1.00
53 Guiding Spirit R :D: .50 .80
54 Hearth Charm C :R: .20 .35
55 Heat Wave U :R: .20 .35
56 Helm of Awakening U :A: 2.00 3.00
57 Honorable Passage U :W: .20 .35
58 Hope Charm C :W: .20 .35
59 Hulking Cyclops U :R: .20 .35
60 Impulse C :B: .30 .50
61 Infantry Veteran C :W: .20 .35
62 Infernal Harvest C :K: .20 .35
63 Inspiration C :B: .20 .35
64 Iron-Heart Chimera U :A: .20 .35
65 Jamuraan Lion C :W: .20 .35
66 Juju Bubble U :A: .20 .35
67 Jungle Basin U :L: .20 .35
68 Kaervek's Spite R :K: .30 .50
69 Karoo U :L: .20 .35
70 Katabatic Winds R :G: .30 .50
71 Keeper of Kookus C :R: .20 .35
72 King Cheetah C :G: .20 .35
73 Knight of the Mists C :B: .20 .35
74 Knight of Valor C :W: .20 .35
75 Kookus R :R: .20 .35
76 Kyscu Drake U :G: .20 .35
77 Lead-Belly Chimera U :A: .20 .35
78 Lichenthrope R :G: .20 .35
79 Lightning Cloud R :R: .20 .35
80 Longbow Archer U :W: .20 .35
81 Magma Mine U :A: .20 .35
82 Man-o'-War C :B: .20 .35
83 Matopi Golem U :A: .20 .35
84 Miraculous Recovery U :W: .20 .35
85 Mob Mentality U :R: .20 .35
86 Mortal Wound C :G: .20 .35
87 Mundungu U :D: .20 .35
88 Mystic Veil C :B: .20 .35
89 Natural Order R :G: 10.00 15.00
90 Necromancy U :K: 3.00 5.00
91 Necrosavant R :K: .20 .35
92 Nekrataal U :K: .20 .35
93 Ogre Enforcer R :R: .20 .35
94 Ovinomancer U :B: .20 .35
95 Panther Warriors C :G: .20 .35
96 Parapet C :W: .20 .35
97 Peace Talks U :W: .20 .35
98 Phyrexian Marauder R :A: .60 1.00
99 Phyrexian Walker C :A: .20 .35
100 Pillar Tombs of Aku R :K: .20 .35
101 Prosperity U :B: .20 .35
102 Pygmy Hippo R :D: .60 1.00
103 Python C :K: .20 .35
104 Quicksand U :L: .20 .35
105 Quirion Druid R :G: .20 .35
106 Quirion Ranger C :G: 3.00 5.00
107 Raging Gorilla C :R: .20 .35
108 Rainbow Efreet R :B: .40 .60
109 Relentless Assault R :R: .40 .60
110 Relic Ward U :W: .20 .35
111 Remedy C :W: .20 .35
112 Resistance Fighter C :W: .20 .35
113 Retribution of the Meek R :W: 6.00 8.00
114 Righteous Aura C :W: .20 .35
115 Righteous War R :D: .50 .80
116 River Boa C :G: .20 .35
117 Rock Slide C :R: .20 .35
118 Rowen R :G: .20 .35
119 Sands of Time R :A: .50 .80
120 Scalebane's Elite U :D: .20 .35
121 Shimmering Efreet U :B: .20 .35
122 Shrieking Drake C :B: .20 .35
123 Simoon U :D: .20 .35
124 Sisay's Ring C :A: .20 .35
125 Snake Basket R :A: 1.00 1.50
126 Solfatara C :R: .20 .35
127 Song of Blood C :R: .20 .35
128 Spider Climb C :G: .20 .35
129 Spitting Drake U :R: .20 .35
130 Squandered Resources R :D: 3.00 5.00
131 Stampeding Wildebeests U :G: .20 .35
132 Suleiman's Legacy R :D: .20 .35
133 Summer Bloom U :G: .60 1.00
134 Sun Clasp C :W: .20 .35
135 Suq'Ata Assassin U :K: .20 .35
136 Suq'Ata Lancer C :R: .20 .35
137 Talruum Champion C :R: .20 .35
138 Talruum Piper U :R: .20 .35
139 Tar Pit Warrior C :K: .20 .35
140 Teferi's Honor Guard U :W: .20 .35
141 Teferi's Puzzle Box R :A: 4.00 6.00
142 Teferi's Realm R :B: .60 1.00
143 Tempest Drake U :D: .20 .35
144 Three Wishes R :B: 1.50 2.00
145 Time and Tide U :B: .20 .35
146 Tin-Wing Chimera U :A: .20 .35
147 Tithe R :W: 8.00 10.00
148 Tremor C :R: .20 .35
149 Triangle of War R :A: .20 .35
150 Uktabi Orangutan U :G: .20 .35
151 Undiscovered Paradise R :L: 3.00 5.00
152 Undo C :B: .20 .35
153 Urborg Mindsucker C :K: .20 .35
154 Vampiric Tutor R :K: 30.00 35.00
155 Vampirism U :K: .20 .35
156 Vanishing C :B: .20 .35
157 Viashino Sandstalker U :R: .20 .35
158 Viashivan Dragon R :D: .40 .60
159 Vision Charm C :B: .20 .35
160 Wake of Vultures C :K: .20 .35
161 Wand of Denial R :A: .20 .35
162 Warrior's Honor C :W: .20 .35
163 Warthog C :G: .20 .35
164 Waterspout Djinn U :B: .20 .35
165 Wicked Reward C :K: .20 .35
166 Wind Shear U :G: .20 .35
167 Zhalfirin Crusader R :W: .30 .50

1997 Magic The Gathering Weatherlight

COMPLETE SET (167) 120.00 165.00
BOOSTER BOX (36 PACKS) 200.00 300.00
BOOSTER PACK (15 CARDS) 7.00 10.00
RELEASED ON JUNE 9, 1997
1 Abduction U :B: .20 .35
2 Abeyance R :W: 2.00 3.50
3 Abjure C :B: .20 .35
4 Aboroth R :G: .40 .60
5 Abyssal Gatekeeper C :K: .20 .35
6 AEther Flash U :R: .20 .35
7 Agonizing Memories U :K: .20 .35
8 Alabaster Dragon R :W: .40 .60
9 Alms C :W: .20 .35
10 Ancestral Knowledge R :B: 1.50 2.00
11 Angelic Renewal C :W: .20 .35
12 Apathy C :B: .20 .35
13 Arctic Wolves U :G: .20 .35
14 Ardent Militia C :W: .20 .35
15 Argivian Find U :W: .30 .50
16 Argivian Restoration U :B: .20 .35
17 Aura of Silence U :W: 1.50 2.00
18 Avizoa R :B: .20 .35
19 Barishi U :G: .20 .35
20 Barrow Ghoul C :K: .20 .35
21 Benalish Infantry C :W: .20 .35
22 Benalish Knight C :W: .20 .35
23 Benalish Missionary C :W: .20 .35
24 Betrothed of Fire C :R: .20 .35
25 Bloodrock Cyclops C :R: .20 .35
26 Blossoming Wreath C :G: .20 .35
27 Bogardan Firefiend C :R: .20 .35
28 Boiling Blood C :R: .20 .35
29 Bone Dancer R :K: 1.25 2.00
30 Bosium Strip R :A: 1.25 2.00
31 Briar Shield C :G: .20 .35
32 Bubble Matrix R :A: 2.50 3.50
33 Buried Alive U :K: 2.50 3.50
34 Call of the Wild R :G: .20 .35
35 Chimeric Sphere U :A: .20 .35
36 Choking Vines C :G: .20 .35
37 Cinder Giant U :R: .20 .35
38 Cinder Wall C :R: .20 .35
39 Circling Vultures U :K: .20 .35
40 Cloud Djinn U :B: .20 .35
41 Coils of the Medusa C :K: .20 .35
42 Cone of Flame U :R: .20 .35
43 Debt of Loyalty R :W: 3.00 5.00
44 Dense Foliage R :G: .50 .80
45 Desperate Gambit U :R: .20 .35
46 Dingus Staff U :A: .20 .35
47 Disrupt C :B: .20 .35
48 Doomsday R :K: 3.00 5.00
49 Downdraft U :G: .20 .35
50 Duskrider Falcon C :W: .20 .35
51 Dwarven Berserker C :R: .20 .35
52 Dwarven Thaumaturgist R :R: .30 .50
53 Empyrial Armor C :W: .20 .35
54 Ertai's Familiar R :B: .20 .35
55 Fallow Wurm U :G: .20 .35
56 Familiar Ground U :G: .20 .35
57 Fatal Blow C :K: .20 .35
58 Fervor R :R: .60 1.00
59 Festering Evil U :K: .20 .35
60 Fire Whip C :R: .20 .35
61 Firestorm R :R: 6.00 8.00
62 Fit of Rage C :R: .20 .35
63 Fledgling Djinn C :K: .20 .35
64 Flux C :B: .20 .35
65 Fog Elemental C :B: .20 .35
66 Foriysian Brigade U :W: .20 .35
67 Fungus Elemental R :G: .20 .35
68 Gaea's Blessing U :G: .20 .35
69 Gallowbraid R :K: .20 .35
70 Gemstone Mine U :L: 5.00 7.00
71 Gerrard's Wisdom U :W: .20 .35
72 Goblin Bomb R :R: 2.00 3.00
73 Goblin Grenadiers U :R: .20 .35
74 Goblin Vandal C :R: .20 .35
75 Guided Strike C :W: .20 .35
76 Harvest Wurm C :G: .20 .35
77 Haunting Misery C :K: .20 .35
78 Heart of Bogardan R :R: .20 .35
79 Heat Stroke R :R: 2.00 3.00
80 Heavy Ballista C :W: .20 .35
81 Hidden Horror U :K: .20 .35
82 Hurloon Shaman U :R: .20 .35
83 Infernal Tribute R :K: 1.50 2.00
84 Inner Sanctum R :W: .40 .60
85 Jabari's Banner U :A: .20 .35
86 Jangling Automaton C :A: .20 .35
87 Kithkin Armor C :W: .20 .35
88 Lava Hounds U :R: .20 .35
89 Lava Storm C :R: .20 .35
90 Liege of the Hollows R :G: 1.00 1.50
91 Llanowar Behemoth U :G: .20 .35
92 Llanowar Druid C :G: .20 .35
93 Llanowar Sentinel C :G: .20 .35
94 Lotus Vale R :L: 20.00 25.00
95 Mana Chains C :B: .20 .35
96 Mana Web R :A: 7.00 9.00
97 Manta Ray C :B: .20 .35
98 Maraxus of Keld R :R: .20 .35
99 Master of Arms U :W: .20 .35
100 Merfolk Traders C :B: .20 .35
101 Mind Stone C :A: .50 .80
102 Mischievous Poltergeist U :K: .20 .35
103 Mistmoon Griffin U :W: .20 .35
104 Morinfen R :K: .20 .35
105 Mwonvuli Ooze R :G: .20 .35
106 Nature's Kiss C :G: .20 .35
107 Nature's Resurgence R :G: .20 .35
108 Necratog U :K: .20 .35
109 Noble Benefactor U :B: .20 .35
110 Null Rod R :A: 20.00 25.00
111 Odylic Wraith U :K: .20 .35
112 Ophidian C :B: .20 .35
113 Orcish Settlers U :R: .20 .35
114 Paradigm Shift R :B: .50 .80
115 Peacekeeper R :W: 4.00 6.00
116 Pendrell Mists R :B: 4.00 6.00
117 Phantom Warrior U :B: .20 .35
118 Phantom Wings C :B: .20 .35
119 Phyrexian Furnace U :A: .20 .35
120 Psychic Vortex R :B: .20 .35
121 Razortooth Rats C :K: .20 .35
122 Redwood Treefolk C :G: .20 .35
123 Relearn U :B: .20 .35
124 Revered Unicorn U :W: .20 .35
125 Roc Hatchling U :R: .20 .35
126 Rogue Elephant C :G: .20 .35
127 Sage Owl C :B: .20 .35
128 Sawtooth Ogre C :R: .20 .35
129 Scorched Ruins R :L: 10.00 15.00
130 Serenity R :W: .75 1.25
131 Serra's Blessing U :W: .20 .35
132 Serrated Biskelion U :A: .20 .35
133 Shadow Rider C :K: .20 .35
134 Shattered Crypt C :K: .20 .35
135 Soul Shepherd C :W: .20 .35
136 Southern Paladin R :W: .20 .35
137 Spinning Darkness C :K: .20 .35
138 Steel Golem U :A: .20 .35
139 Strands of Night U :K: .20 .35
140 Straw Golem U :A: .20 .35
141 Striped Bears C :G: .20 .35
142 Sylvan Hierophant U :G: .20 .35
143 Tariff R :W: .20 .35
144 Teferi's Veil U :B: .20 .35
145 Tendrils of Despair C :K: .20 .35
146 Thran Forge U :A: .20 .35
147 Thran Tome R :A: .20 .35
148 Thunderbolt C :R: .20 .35
149 Thundermare R :R: .20 .35
150 Timid Drake U :B: .20 .35
151 Tolarian Drake C :B: .20 .35
152 Tolarian Entrancer R :B: .60 1.00
153 Tolarian Serpent R :B: .20 .35
154 Touchstone U :A: .20 .35
155 Tranquil Grove R :G: .50 .80
156 Uktabi Efreet C :G: .20 .35
157 Urborg Justice R :K: 2.00 3.50
158 Urborg Stalker R :K: .20 .35
159 Veteran Explorer U :G: .75 1.25
160 Vitalize C :G: .20 .35
161 Vodalian Illusionist U :B: .20 .35
162 Volunteer Reserves U :W: .20 .35
163 Wave of Terror R :K: .20 .35
164 Well of Knowledge R :A: 2.00 3.50
165 Winding Canyons R :L: 8.00 10.00
166 Xanthic Statue R :A: .20 .35
167 Zombie Scavengers C :K: .20 .35

1997 Magic The Gathering Tempest

COMPLETE SET (335)	360.00	450.00
BOOSTER BOX (36 PACKS)	800.00	1000.00
BOOSTER PACK (15 CARDS)	10.00	15.00
STARTER BOX (12 DECKS)	200.00	300.00
STARTER DECK	20.00	25.00
RELEASED ON OCTOBER 13, 1997		
1 Abandon Hope U :K:	.20	.35
2 Advance Scout C :W:	.20	.35
3 Aftershock C :R:	.20	.35
4 Altar of Dementia R :A:	3.00	5.00
5 Aluren R :G:	15.00	20.00
6 Ancient Runes U :R:	.20	.35
7 Ancient Tomb U :L:	30.00	35.00
8 Angelic Protector U :W:	.20	.35
9 Anoint C :W:	.20	.35
10 Apes of Rath U :G:	.20	.35
11 Apocalypse R :R:	3.00	5.00
12 Armor Sliver U :W:	.20	.35
13 Armored Pegasus C :W:	.20	.35
14 Auratog R :W:	.40	.60
15 Avenging Angel R :W:	.40	.60
16 Barbed Sliver U :R:	.20	.35
17 Bayou Dragonfly C :G:	.20	.35
18 Bellowing Fiend R :K:	.20	.35
19 Benthic Behemoth R :B:	.20	.35
20 Blood Frenzy C :R:	.20	.35
21 Blood Pet C :K:	.20	.35
22 Boil U :R:	.50	.80
23 Booby Trap R :A:	.30	.50
24 Bottle Gnomes U :A:	.20	.35
25 Bounty Hunter R :K:	2.50	4.00
26 Broken Fall C :G:	.20	.35
27 Caldera Lake R :L:	.60	1.00
28 Canopy Spider C :G:	.20	.35
29 Canyon Drake R :R:	.20	.35
30 Canyon Wildcat C :R:	.20	.35
31 Capsize C :B:	.75	1.25
32 Carrionette R :K:	.20	.35
33 Chaotic Goo R :R:	.20	.35
34 Charging Rhino U :G:	.20	.35
35 Chill U :B:	.20	.35
36 Choke U :G:	2.00	2.50
37 Cinder Marsh U :L:	.20	.35
38 Circle of Protection Black C :W:	.20	.35
39 Circle of Protection Blue C :W:	.20	.35
40 Circle of Protection Green C :W:	.20	.35
41 Circle of Protection Red C :W:	.20	.35
42 Circle of Protection Shadow C :W:	.20	.35
43 Circle of Protection White C :W:	.20	.35
44 Clergy en-Vec C :W:	.20	.35
45 Clot Sliver C :K:	.20	.35
46 Cloudchaser Eagle C :W:	.20	.35
47 Coercion C :K:	.20	.35
48 Coffin Queen R :K:	5.00	7.00
49 Coiled Tinviper C :A:	.20	.35
50 Cold Storage R :A:	.20	.35
51 Commander Greven il-Vec R :K:	.20	.35
52 Corpse Dance R :K:	10.00	15.00
53 Counterspell C :B:	1.00	1.50
54 Crazed Armodon R :G:	.20	.35
55 Crown of Flames C :R:	.20	.35
56 Cursed Scroll R :A:	4.00	6.00
57 Dark Banishing C :K:	.20	.35
58 Dark Ritual C :K:	.40	.60
59 Darkling Stalker C :K:	.20	.35
60 Dauthi Embrace U :K:	.50	.80
61 Dauthi Ghoul U :K:	.20	.35
62 Dauthi Horror C :K:	.20	.35
63 Dauthi Marauder C :K:	.20	.35
64 Dauthi Mercenary U :K:	.20	.35
65 Dauthi Mindripper U :K:	.20	.35
66 Dauthi Slayer C :K:	.20	.35
67 Deadshot R :R:	.20	.35
68 Death Pits of Rath R :K:	.50	.80
69 Diabolic Edict C :K:	.50	.80
70 Dirtcowl Wurm R :G:	.50	.80
71 Disenchant C :W:	.20	.35
72 Dismiss U :B:	.20	.35
73 Disturbed Burial C :K:	.20	.35
74 Dracoplasm R :D:	.20	.35
75 Dread of Night U :K:	.75	1.25
76 Dream Cache C :B:	.20	.35
77 Dregs of Sorrow R :K:	.20	.35
78 Duplicity R :B:	.20	.35
79 Earthcraft R :G:	25.00	30.00
80 Echo Chamber R :A:	.20	.35
81 Eladamri, Lord of Leaves R :G:	8.00	11.00
82 Eladamri's Vineyard R :G:	.75	1.25
83 Elite Javelineer C :W:	.20	.35
84 Elven Warhounds R :G:	.20	.35
85 Elvish Fury C :G:	.20	.35
86 Emerald Medallion R :A:	1.00	1.50
87 Emmessi Tome R :A:	.20	.35
88 Endless Scream C :K:	.20	.35
89 Energizer R :A:	.20	.35
90 Enfeeblement C :K:	.20	.35
91 Enraging Licid U :R:	.20	.35
92 Ertai's Meddling R :B:	.20	.35
93 Escaped Shapeshifter R :B:	.20	.35
94 Essence Bottle U :A:	.20	.35
95 Evincar's Justice C :K:	.20	.35
96 Excavator U :A:	.20	.35
97 Extinction R :K:	.50	.80
98 Fevered Convulsions R :K:	.50	.80
99 Field of Souls R :W:	.20	.35
100 Fighting Drake U :B:	.20	.35
101 Firefly U :R:	.20	.35
102 Fireslinger C :R:	.20	.35
103 Flailing Drake U :G:	.20	.35
104 Flickering Ward U :W:	1.50	2.50
105 Flowstone Giant C :R:	.20	.35
106 Flowstone Salamander U :R:	.20	.35
107 Flowstone Sculpture R :A:	.20	.35
108 Flowstone Wyvern R :R:	.20	.35
109 Fool's Tome R :A:	.20	.35
110 Forest L :L:	.20	.35
111 Frog Tongue C :G:	.20	.35
112 Fugitive Druid R :G:	.20	.35
113 Furnace of Rath R :R:	1.50	2.00
114 Fylamarid U :B:	.20	.35
115 Gallantry U :W:	.20	.35
116 Gaseous Form C :B:	.20	.35
117 Gerrard's Battle Cry R :W:	.20	.35
118 Ghost Town U :L:	.30	.50
119 Giant Crab C :B:	.20	.35
120 Giant Strength C :R:	.20	.35
121 Goblin Bombardment U :R:	1.50	2.00
122 Gravedigger C :K:	.20	.35
123 Grindstone R :A:	7.00	9.00
124 Hand to Hand R :R:	.20	.35
125 Hanna's Custody R :W:	.60	1.00
126 Harrow U :G:	.20	.35
127 Havoc U :R:	.20	.35
128 Heart Sliver C :R:	.20	.35
129 Heartwood Dryad C :G:	.20	.35
130 Heartwood Giant R :G:	.20	.35
131 Heartwood Treefolk U :G:	.20	.35
132 Helm of Possession R :A:	2.50	4.00
133 Hero's Resolve C :W:	.20	.35
134 Horned Sliver U :G:	1.50	2.50
135 Horned Turtle C :B:	.20	.35
136 Humility R :W:	15.00	20.00
137 Imps' Taunt U :K:	.20	.35
138 Insight U :B:	.20	.35
139 Interdict U :B:	.20	.35
140 Intuition R :B:	30.00	35.00
141 Invulnerability U :W:	.20	.35
142 Island L :L:	.20	.35
143 Jackal Pup U :R:	.20	.35
144 Jet Medallion R :A:	3.00	5.00
145 Jinxed Idol R :A:	.20	.35
146 Kezzerdrix R :K:	.20	.35
147 Kindle C :R:	.20	.35
148 Knight of Dawn U :W:	.20	.35
149 Knight of Dusk U :K:	.20	.35
150 Krakilin U :G:	.20	.35
151 Leeching Licid U :K:	.20	.35
152 Legacy's Allure U :B:	.20	.35
153 Legerdemain U :B:	.20	.35
154 Light of Day U :W:	.20	.35
155 Lightning Blast C :R:	.20	.35
156 Lightning Elemental C :R:	.20	.35
157 Living Death R :K:	4.00	6.00
158 Lobotomy U :D:	.20	.35
159 Lotus Petal C :A:	5.00	7.00
160 Lowland Giant C :R:	.20	.35
161 Maddening Imp R :K:	.20	.35
162 Magmasaur R :R:	.20	.35
163 Magnetic Web R :A:	.20	.35
164 Mana Severance R :B:	.60	1.00
165 Manakin C :A:	.20	.35
166 Manta Riders C :B:	.20	.35
167 Marble Titan R :W:	.20	.35
168 Marsh Lurker C :K:	.20	.35
169 Master Decoy C :W:	.20	.35
170 Mawcor R :B:	.20	.35
171 Maze of Shadows U :L:	.20	.35
172 Meditate R :B:	3.00	4.50
173 Metallic Sliver C :A:	.20	.35
174 Mindwhip Sliver U :K:	.20	.35
175 Minion of the Wastes R :K:	.20	.35
176 Mirri's Guile R :G:	15.00	20.00
177 Mnemonic Sliver U :B:	.20	.35
178 Mogg Cannon U :A:	.20	.35
179 Mogg Conscripts C :R:	.20	.35
180 Mogg Fanatic C :R:	.20	.35
181 Mogg Hollows U :L:	.20	.35
182 Mogg Raider C :R:	.20	.35
183 Mogg Squad U :R:	.20	.35
184 Mongrel Pack R :G:	.20	.35
185 Mountain L :L:	.20	.35
186 Mounted Archers C :W:	.20	.35
187 Muscle Sliver C :G:	.50	.80
188 Natural Spring C :G:	.20	.35
189 Nature's Revolt R :G:	.30	.50
190 Needle Storm U :G:	.20	.35
191 No Quarter R :R:	.20	.35
192 Nurturing Licid U :G:	.20	.35
193 Opportunist U :R:	.20	.35
194 Oracle en-Vec R :W:	.20	.35
195 Orim, Samite Healer R :W:	.40	.60
196 Orim's Prayer U :W:	.20	.35
197 Overrun U :G:	.20	.35
198 Pacifism C :W:	.20	.35
199 Pallimud R :R:	.20	.35
200 Patchwork Gnomes U :A:	.20	.35
201 Pearl Medallion R :A:	2.50	3.50
202 Pegasus Refuge R :W:	.20	.35
203 Perish U :K:	.40	.60
204 Phyrexian Grimoire R :A:	.20	.35
205 Phyrexian Hulk U :A:	.20	.35
206 Phyrexian Splicer U :A:	.20	.35
207 Pincher Beetles C :G:	.20	.35
208 Pine Barrens R :L:	.50	.80
209 Pit Imp C :K:	.20	.35
210 Plains L :L:	.20	.35
211 Power Sink C :B:	.20	.35
212 Precognition R :B:	.20	.35
213 Propaganda U :B:	3.00	5.00
214 Puppet Strings U :A:	.20	.35
215 Quickening Licid U :W:	.20	.35
216 Rain of Tears U :K:	.20	.35
217 Rampant Growth C :G:	.20	.35
218 Ranger en-Vec U :D:	.20	.35
219 Rathi Dragon R :R:	.40	.60
220 Rats of Rath C :K:	.20	.35
221 Reality Anchor C :G:	.20	.35
222 Reanimate U :K:	15.00	18.00
223 Reap U :G:	.20	.35
224 Reckless Spite U :K:	.20	.35
225 Recycle R :G:	1.00	1.50
226 Reflecting Pool R :L:	8.00	11.00
227 Renegade Warlord U :R:	.20	.35
228 Repentance U :W:	.20	.35
229 Respite C :G:	.20	.35
230 Rolling Thunder C :R:	.20	.35
231 Root Maze R :G:	.60	1.00
232 Rootbreaker Wurm C :G:	.20	.35
233 Rootwalla C :G:	.20	.35
234 Rootwater Depths U :L:	.20	.35
235 Rootwater Diver U :B:	.20	.35
236 Rootwater Hunter C :B:	.20	.35
237 Rootwater Matriarch R :B:	.20	.35
238 Rootwater Shaman R :B:	.20	.35
239 Ruby Medallion R :A:	7.00	9.00
240 Sacred Guide R :W:	.20	.35
241 Sadistic Glee C :K:	.20	.35
242 Safeguard R :W:	.20	.35
243 Salt Flats R :L:	.50	.80
244 Sandstone Warrior C :R:	.20	.35
245 Sapphire Medallion R :A:	5.00	7.00
246 Sarcomancy R :K:	1.25	2.00
247 Scabland R :L:	.50	.80
248 Scalding Tongs R :A:	.20	.35
249 Scorched Earth R :R:	.20	.35
250 Scragnoth U :G:	.20	.35
251 Screeching Harpy U :K:	.20	.35
252 Scroll Rack R :A:	25.00	30.00
253 Sea Monster C :B:	.20	.35
254 Searing Touch U :R:	.20	.35
255 Seeker of Skybreak C :G:	.20	.35
256 Segmented Wurm U :D:	.20	.35
257 Selenia, Dark Angel R :D:	.60	1.00
258 Serene Offering U :W:	.20	.35
259 Servant of Volrath C :K:	.20	.35
260 Shadow Rift C :B:	.40	.60
261 Shadowstorm U :R:	.20	.35
262 Shatter C :R:	.20	.35
263 Shimmering Wings C :B:	.20	.35
264 Shocker R :R:	.60	1.00
265 Sky Spirit U :D:	.20	.35
266 Skyshroud Condor U :B:	.20	.35
267 Skyshroud Elf C :G:	.20	.35
268 Skyshroud Forest R :L:	.50	.80
269 Skyshroud Ranger C :G:	.20	.35
270 Skyshroud Troll C :G:	.20	.35
271 Skyshroud Vampire U :K:	.20	.35
272 Soltari Crusader U :W:	.20	.35
273 Soltari Emissary R :W:	.20	.35
274 Soltari Foot Soldier C :W:	.20	.35
275 Soltari Guerrillas R :D:	.40	.60
276 Soltari Lancer C :W:	.20	.35
277 Soltari Monk U :W:	.20	.35
278 Soltari Priest U :W:	.20	.35
279 Soltari Trooper C :W:	.20	.35
280 Souldrinker U :K:	.20	.35
281 Spell Blast C :B:	.20	.35
282 Spike Drone C :G:	.20	.35
283 Spinal Graft C :K:	.20	.35
284 Spirit Mirror R :W:	.30	.50
285 Spontaneous Combustion U :D:	.20	.35
286 Squee's Toy C :A:	.20	.35
287 Stalking Stones U :L:	.20	.35
288 Starke of Rath R :R:	.40	.60
289 Static Orb R :A:	5.00	7.00
290 Staunch Defenders U :W:	.20	.35
291 Steal Enchantment U :B:	.20	.35
292 Stinging Licid U :B:	.20	.35
293 Stone Rain C :R:	.20	.35
294 Storm Front U :G:	.20	.35
295 Stun C :R:	.20	.35
296 Sudden Impact U :R:	.20	.35
297 Swamp (4 versions) L :L:	.20	.35
298 Tahngarth's Rage U :R:	.20	.35
299 Talon Sliver C :W:	.20	.35
300 Telethopter U :A:	.20	.35
301 Thalakos Dreamsower U :B:	.20	.35
302 Thalakos Lowlands U :L:	.20	.35
303 Thalakos Mistfolk C :B:	.20	.35
304 Thalakos Seer C :B:	.20	.35
305 Thalakos Sentry C :B:	.20	.35
306 Thumbscrews R :A:	.20	.35
307 Time Ebb C :B:	.20	.35
308 Time Warp R :B:	13.00	15.00
309 Tooth and Claw R :R:	.20	.35
310 Torture Chamber R :A:	.20	.35
311 Tradewind Rider R :B:	1.50	2.00
312 Trained Armodon C :G:	.20	.35
313 Tranquility C :G:	.20	.35
314 Trumpeting Armodon U :G:	.20	.35
315 Twitch C :B:	.20	.35
316 Unstable Shapeshifter R :B:	.20	.35
317 Vec Townships U :L:	.20	.35
318 Verdant Force R :G:	.50	.80
319 Verdigris U :G:	.20	.35
320 Vhati il-Dal R :D:	.50	.80
321 Volrath's Curse C :B:	.20	.35
322 Wall of Diffusion C :R:	.20	.35
323 Warmth U :W:	.20	.35
324 Wasteland U :L:	25.00	30.00
325 Watchdog U :A:	.20	.35
326 Whim of Volrath R :B:	.50	.80
327 Whispers of the Muse U :B:	.20	.35
328 Wild Wurm U :R:	.20	.35
329 Wind Dancer U :B:	.20	.35
330 Wind Drake C :B:	.20	.35
331 Winds of Rath R :W:	1.50	2.00
332 Winged Sliver C :B:	.20	.35
333 Winter's Grasp U :G:	.20	.35
334 Wood Sage R :D:	.20	.35
335 Worthy Cause U :W:	.20	.35

1998 Magic The Gathering Stronghold

COMPLETE SET (143)	240.00	300.00
BOOSTER BOX (36 PACKS)	250.00	400.00
BOOSTER PACK (15 CARDS)	10.00	15.00
STARTER BOX (12 DECKS)	175.00	250.00
STARTER DECK	15.00	20.00
RELEASED ON MARCH 2, 1998		
1 Acidic Sliver U :D:	.20	.35
2 Amok R :R:	.20	.35
3 Awakening R :G:	2.50	3.50
4 Bandage C :W:	.20	.35
5 Bottomless Pit U :K:	.20	.35
6 Brush With Death C :K:	.20	.35
7 Bullwhip U :A:	.20	.35
8 Burgeoning R :G:	3.00	5.00
9 Calming Licid U :W:	.20	.35
10 Cannibalize C :K:	.20	.35
11 Cardassid R :G:	.20	.35
12 Change of Heart C :W:	.20	.35
13 Cloud Spirit C :B:	.20	.35
14 Constant Mists U :G:	2.50	3.50
15 Contemplation U :W:	.20	.35
16 Contempt C :B:	.20	.35
17 Conviction C :W:	.20	.35
18 Convulsing Licid U :R:	.20	.35
19 Corrupting Licid U :K:	.20	.35
20 Craven Giant C :R:	.20	.35
21 Crossbow Ambush C :G:	.20	.35
22 Crovax, The Cursed R :K:	.20	.35
23 Crystalline Sliver U :D:	2.50	3.50
24 Dauthi Trapper U :K:	.20	.35
25 Death Stroke C :K:	.20	.35
26 Dream Halls R :B:	6.00	8.00
27 Dream Prowler C :B:	.20	.35
28 Duct Crawler C :R:	.20	.35
29 Dungeon Shade C :K:	.20	.35
30 Elven Rite U :G:	.20	.35
31 Endangered Armodon C :G:	.20	.35
32 Ensnaring Bridge R :A:	40.00	45.00
33 Evacuation R :B:	1.00	1.50
34 Fanning the Flames U :R:	.20	.35
35 Flame Wave U :R:	.20	.35
36 Fling C :R:	.20	.35
37 Flowstone Blade C :R:	.20	.35
38 Flowstone Hellion U :R:	.20	.35
39 Flowstone Mauler R :R:	.20	.35
40 Flowstone Shambler C :R:	.20	.35
41 Foul Imp C :K:	.20	.35
42 Furnace Spirit C :R:	.20	.35
43 Gliding Licid U :B:	.20	.35
44 Grave Pact R :K:	10.00	15.00
45 Hammerhead Shark C :B:	.20	.35
46 Heartstone U :A:	.20	.35
47 Heat of Battle U :R:	.20	.35
48 Hermit Druid R :G:	2.00	3.00
49 Hesitation U :B:	.20	.35
50 Hibernation Sliver U :D:	.20	.35
51 Hidden Retreat R :W:	.20	.35
52 Honor Guard C :W:	.20	.35
53 Horn of Greed R :A:	1.50	2.50
54 Hornet Cannon U :A:	.20	.35
55 Intruder Alarm R :B:	6.00	8.00
56 Invasion Plans R :R:	.20	.35
57 Jinxed Ring R :A:	.20	.35
58 Lab Rats C :K:	.20	.35
59 Lancers en-Kor U :W:	.20	.35
60 Leap C :B:	.20	.35
61 Lowland Basilisk C :G:	.20	.35
62 Mana Leak C :B:	.20	.35
63 Mask of the Mimic U :B:	.20	.35
64 Megrim U :K:	.20	.35
65 Mind Games C :B:	.20	.35
66 Mind Peel U :K:	.20	.35
67 Mindwarper R :K:	.20	.35
68 Mob Justice C :R:	.20	.35
69 Mogg Bombers C :R:	.20	.35
70 Mogg Flunkies C :R:	.20	.35
71 Mogg Infestation R :R:	5.00	7.00
72 Mogg Maniac U :R:	.20	.35
73 Morgue Thrull C :K:	.20	.35
74 Mortuary R :K:	.20	.35
75 Mox Diamond R :A:	140.00	150.00
76 Mulch C :G:	.20	.35
77 Nomads en-Kor C :W:	.20	.35
78 Overgrowth C :G:	.20	.35
79 Portcullis R :A:	.20	.35
80 Primal Rage U :G:	.75	1.25
81 Provoke C :G:	.20	.35
82 Pursuit of Knowledge R :W:	.20	.35
83 Rabid Rats C :K:	.20	.35
84 Ransack U :B:	.20	.35
85 Rebound U :B:	.20	.35
86 Reins of Power R :B:	.20	.35
87 Revenant R :K:	.20	.35
88 Rolling Stones R :W:	.20	.35
89 Ruination R :R:	2.50	3.50
90 Sacred Ground R :W:	.20	.35
91 Samite Blessing C :W:	.20	.35
92 Scapegoat U :W:	.20	.35
93 Seething Anger C :R:	.20	.35
94 Serpent Warrior C :K:	.20	.35
95 Shaman en-Kor R :W:	.50	.80
96 Shard Phoenix R :R:	.20	.35
97 Shifting Wall U :A:	.20	.35
98 Shock C :R:	.20	.35
99 Sift C :B:	.20	.35
100 Silver Wyvern R :B:	.20	.35
101 Skeleton Scavengers R :K:	.20	.35
102 Skyshroud Archer C :G:	.20	.35
103 Skyshroud Falcon C :W:	.20	.35
104 Skyshroud Troopers C :G:	.20	.35
105 Sliver Queen R :D:	35.00	40.00
106 Smite C :W:	.20	.35
107 Soltari Champion R :W:	.75	1.25
108 Spike Breeder R :G:	.20	.35
109 Spike Colony C :G:	.20	.35
110 Spike Feeder U :G:	.20	.35
111 Spike Soldier U :G:	.20	.35
112 Spike Worker C :G:	.20	.35
113 Spindrift Drake C :B:	.20	.35
114 Spined Sliver U :D:	.20	.35
115 Spined Wurm C :G:	.20	.35
116 Spirit en-Kor C :W:	.20	.35
117 Spitting Hydra R :R:	.20	.35
118 Stronghold Assassin R :K:	.20	.35
119 Stronghold Taskmaster U :K:	.20	.35
120 Sword of the Chosen R :A:	.20	.35
121 Temper U :W:	.20	.35
122 Tempting Licid U :G:	.20	.35
123 Thalakos Deceiver R :B:	4.00	6.00
124 Tidal Surge C :B:	.20	.35
125 Tidal Warrior C :B:	.20	.35

126 Torment C :K: .20 .35
127 Tortured Existence C :K: 2.00 3.50
128 Venerable Monk C :W: .20 .35
129 Verdant Touch R :G: .20 .35
130 Victual Sliver U :D: .20 .35
131 Volrath's Gardens R :G: .20 .35
132 Volrath's Laboratory R :A: .20 .35
133 Volrath's Shapeshifter R :B: 4.00 6.00
134 Volrath's Stronghold R :L: 30.00 35.00
135 Walking Dream U :B: .20 .35
136 Wall of Blossoms U :G: .20 .35
137 Wall of Essence U :W: .20 .35
138 Wall of Razors U :R: .20 .35
139 Wall of Souls U :K: .60 1.00
140 Wall of Tears U :B: .20 .35
141 Warrior Angel R :W: .20 .35
142 Warrior en-Kor U :W: .20 .35
143 Youthful Knight C :W: .20 .35

1998 Magic The Gathering Exodus

COMPLETE SET (143) 250.00 325.00
BOOSTER BOX 300.00 450.00
BOOSTER PACK 10.00 15.00
THEME DECK 15.00 20.00
RELEASED ON JUNE 15, 1998
1 Allay C :W: .20 .35
2 Angelic Blessing C :W: .20 .35
3 Cataclysm R :W: 3.00 5.00
4 Charging Paladin C :W: .20 .35
5 Convalescence R :W: .20 .35
6 Exalted Dragon R :W: .20 .35
7 High Ground U :W: .20 .35
8 Keeper of the Light U :W: .20 .35
9 Kor Chant C :W: .20 .35
10 Limited Resources R :W: .50 .80
11 Oath of Lieges R :W: 1.50 2.00
12 Paladin en-Vec R :W: .50 .80
13 Peace of Mind U :W: .20 .35
14 Pegasus Stampede U :W: .20 .35
15 Penance U :W: .20 .35
16 Reaping the Rewards C :W: .20 .35
17 Reconnaissance U :W: 2.00 3.00
18 Shackles C :W: .20 .35
19 Shield Mate C :W: .20 .35
20 Soltari Visionary C :W: .20 .35
21 Soul Warden C :W: .50 .80
22 Standing Troops C :W: .20 .35
23 Treasure Hunter U :W: .20 .35
24 Wall of Nets R :W: .50 .80
25 Welkin Hawk C :W: .20 .35
26 Zealots en-Dal U :W: .20 .35
27 AEther Tide C :B: .20 .35
28 Cunning C :B: .20 .35
29 Curiosity U :B: .20 .35
30 Dominating Licid R :B: .60 1.00
31 Ephemeron R :B: .20 .35
32 Equilibrium R :B: 1.50 2.00
33 Ertai, Wizard Adept R :B: 8.00 10.00
34 Fade Away C :B: .20 .35
35 Forbid U :B: 1.50 2.50
36 Keeper of the Mind U :B: .20 .35
37 Killer Whale U :B: .20 .35
38 Mana Breach U :B: .20 .35
39 Merfolk Looter C :B: .20 .35
40 Mind Over Matter R :B: 17.00 20.00
41 Mirozel U :B: .20 .35
42 Oath of Scholars R :B: .20 .35
43 Robe of Mirrors C :B: .20 .35
44 Rootwater Mystic C :B: .20 .35
45 School of Piranha C :B: .20 .35
46 Scrivener U :B: .20 .35
47 Thalakos Drifters R :B: .20 .35
48 Thalakos Scout C :B: .20 .35
49 Theft of Dreams C :B: .20 .35
50 Treasure Trove U :B: .20 .35
51 Wayward Soul C :B: .20 .35
52 Whiptongue Frog C :B: .20 .35
53 Carnophage C :K: .20 .35
54 Cat Burglar C :K: .20 .35
55 Culling the Weak C :K: .50 .80
56 Cursed Flesh C :K: .20 .35
57 Dauthi Cutthroat U :K: .20 .35
58 Dauthi Jackal C :K: .20 .35
59 Dauthi Warlord U :K: .20 .35
60 Death's Duet C :K: .20 .35
61 Entropic Specter R :K: .20 .35
62 Fugue U :K: .20 .35
63 Grollub C :K: .20 .35
64 Hatred R :K: 10.00 15.00
65 Keeper of the Dead U :K: .20 .35
66 Mind Maggots U :K: .20 .35
67 Nausea C :K: .20 .35
68 Necrologia U :K: .20 .35
69 Oath of Ghouls R :K: .40 .60
70 Pit Spawn R :K: .50 .80
71 Plaguebearer R :K: .50 .80
72 Recurring Nightmare R :K: 10.00 15.00
73 Scare Tactics C :K: .20 .35
74 Slaughter U :K: .20 .35
75 Spike Cannibal U :K: .20 .35
76 Thrull Surgeon C :K: .20 .35
77 Vampire Hounds C :K: .20 .35
78 Volrath's Dungeon R :K: .20 .35
79 Anarchist C :R: .20 .35
80 Cinder Crawler C :R: .20 .35
81 Dizzying Gaze C :R: .20 .35
82 Fighting Chance R :R: .20 .35
83 Flowstone Flood U :R: .20 .35
84 Furnace Brood C :R: .20 .35
85 Keeper of the Flame U :R: .20 .35
86 Mage il-Vec C :R: .20 .35
87 Maniacal Rage C :R: .20 .35
88 Mogg Assassin U :R: .20 .35
89 Monstrous Hound R :R: .20 .35
90 Oath of Mages R :R: .20 .35
91 Ogre Shaman R :R: .20 .35
92 Onslaught C :R: .20 .35
93 Pandemonium R :R: .60 1.00
94 Paroxysm U :R: .20 .35
95 Price of Progress U :R: 1.50 2.50
96 Raging Goblin C :R: .20 .35
97 Ravenous Baboons R :R: .20 .35
98 Reckless Ogre C :R: .20 .35
99 Sabertooth Wyvern U :R: .20 .35
100 Scalding Salamander U :R: .20 .35
101 Seismic Assault R :R: 3.00 5.00
102 Shattering Pulse C :R: .20 .35
103 Sonic Burst C :R: .20 .35
104 Spellshock U :R: .20 .35
105 Avenging Druid C :G: .20 .35
106 Bequeathal C :G: .20 .35
107 Cartographer U :G: .20 .35
108 Crashing Boars U :G: .20 .35
109 Elven Palisade U :G: .20 .35
110 Elvish Berserker C :G: .20 .35
111 Jackalope Herd C :G: .20 .35
112 Keeper of the Beasts U :G: .20 .35
113 Manabond R :G: 2.50 4.00
114 Mirri, Cat Warrior R :G: .60 1.00
115 Oath of Druids R :G: 3.00 4.00
116 Plated Rootwalla C :G: .20 .35
117 Predatory Hunger C :G: .20 .35
118 Pygmy Troll C :G: .20 .35
119 Rabid Wolverines C :G: .20 .35
120 Reclaim C :G: .20 .35
121 Resuscitate U :G: .20 .35
122 Rootwater Alligator C :G: .20 .35
123 Skyshroud Elite U :G: .20 .35
124 Skyshroud War Beast R :G: .20 .35
125 Song of Serenity U :G: .20 .35
126 Spike Hatcher R :G: .20 .35
127 Spike Rogue U :G: .20 .35
128 Spike Weaver R :G: 8.00 10.00
129 Survival of the Fittest R :G: 75.00 80.00
130 Wood Elves C :G: .20 .35
131 Coat of Arms R :A: 6.00 8.00
132 Erratic Portal R :A: 1.50 2.00
133 Medicine Bag U :A: .20 .35
134 Memory Crystal R :A: .20 .35
135 Mindless Automaton R :A: .20 .35
136 Null Brooch R :A: .20 .35
137 Skyshaper U :A: .20 .35
138 Spellbook U :A: .50 .80
139 Sphere of Resistance R :A: 17.00 20.00
140 Thopter Squadron R :A: .20 .35
141 Transmogrifying Licid U :A: .20 .35
142 Workhorse R :A: .50 .80
143 City of Traitors R :L: 135.00 145.00

1998 Magic The Gathering Urza's Saga

COMPLETE SET (350) 600.00 725.00
BOOSTER BOX (36 PACKS) 800.00 1200.00
BOOSTER PACK (15 CARDS) 25.00 40.00
STARTER BOX (12 DECKS) 150.00 200.00
STARTER DECK 15.00 20.00
RELEASED ON OCTOBER 12, 1998
1 Absolute Grace U :W: .20 .35
2 Absolute Law U :W: .20 .35
3 Angelic Chorus R :W: 3.00 5.00
4 Angelic Page C :W: .20 .35
5 Brilliant Halo C :W: .20 .35
6 Catastrophe R :W: 3.00 5.00
7 Clear U :W: .20 .35
8 Congregate C :W: .20 .35
9 Defensive Formation U :W: .20 .35
10 Disciple of Grace C :W: .20 .35
11 Disciple of Law C :W: .20 .35
12 Disenchant C :W: .20 .35
13 Elite Archers R :W: .20 .35
14 Faith Healer R :W: .20 .35
15 Glorious Anthem R :W: 1.00 1.50
16 Healing Salve C :W: .20 .35
17 Herald of Serra R :W: .40 .60
18 Humble U :W: .20 .35
19 Intrepid Hero R :W: .60 1.00
20 Monk Idealist U :W: .20 .35
21 Monk Realist C :W: .20 .35
22 Opal Acrolith U :W: .20 .35
23 Opal Archangel R :W: .20 .35
24 Opal Caryatid C :W: .20 .35
25 Opal Gargoyle C :W: .20 .35
26 Opal Titan R :W: .20 .35
27 Pacifism C :W: .20 .35
28 Pariah R :W: .75 1.25
29 Path of Peace C :W: .20 .35
30 Pegasus Charger C :W: .20 .35
31 Planar Birth R :W: .60 .80
32 Presence of the Master U :W: .20 .35
33 Redeem U :W: .20 .35
34 Remembrance R :W: .40 .60
35 Rune of Protection Artifacts U :W: .20 .35
36 Rune of Protection Black C :W: .20 .35
37 Rune of Protection Blue C :W: .20 .35
38 Rune of Protection Green C :W: .20 .35
39 Rune of Protection Lands R :W: .20 .35
40 Rune of Protection Red C :W: .20 .35
41 Rune of Protection White C :W: .20 .35
42 Sanctum Custodian C :W: .20 .35
43 Sanctum Guardian U :W: .20 .35
44 Seasoned Marshal U :W: .20 .35
45 Serra Avatar R :W: .75 1.25
46 Serra Zealot C :W: .20 .35
47 Serra's Embrace U :W: .20 .35
48 Serra's Hymn U :W: .20 .35
49 Serra's Liturgy R :W: .20 .35
50 Shimmering Barrier U :W: .20 .35
51 Silent Attendant C :W: .20 .35
52 Songstitcher U :W: .20 .35
53 Soul Sculptor R :W: .20 .35
54 Voice of Grace U :W: .20 .35
55 Voice of Law U :W: .20 .35
56 Waylay U :W: .20 .35
57 Worship R :W: 4.00 6.00
58 Academy Researchers U :B: .20 .35
59 Annul C :B: .20 .35
60 Arcane Laboratory U :B: .20 .35
61 Attunement R :B: .60 .80
62 Back to Basics R :B: 30.00 35.00
63 Barrin's Codex R :A: .20 .35
64 Catalog C :B: .20 .35
65 Cloak of Mists C :B: .20 .35
66 Confiscate U :B: .20 .35
67 Coral Merfolk C :B: .20 .35
68 Curfew C :B: .20 .35
69 Disruptive Student C :B: .20 .35
70 Douse U :B: .20 .35
71 Drifting Djinn R :B: .20 .35
72 Enchantment Alteration U :B: .20 .35
73 Energy Field R :B: 3.00 5.00
74 Exhaustion U :B: .20 .35
75 Fog Bank U :B: .20 .35
76 Gilded Drake R :B: 20.00 25.00
77 Great Whale R :B: 4.00 6.00
78 Hermetic Study C :B: .20 .35
79 Hibernation U :B: .20 .35
80 Horseshoe Crab C :B: .20 .35
81 Imaginary Pet R :B: .20 .35
82 Launch C :B: .20 .35
83 Lilting Refrain U :B: .20 .35
84 Lingering Mirage U :B: .20 .35
85 Morphling R :B: 8.00 10.00
86 Pendrell Drake C :B: .20 .35
87 Pendrell Flux C :B: .20 .35
88 Peregrine Drake U :B: .75 1.25
89 Power Sink C :B: .20 .35
90 Power Taint C :B: .20 .35
91 Recantation R :B: .20 .35
92 Rescind C :B: .20 .35
93 Rewind C :B: .20 .35
94 Sandbar Merfolk C :B: .20 .35
95 Sandbar Serpent U :B: .20 .35
96 Show and Tell R :B: 18.00 20.00
97 Somnophore R :B: .20 .35
98 Spire Owl C :B: .20 .35
99 Stern Proctor U :B: .20 .35
100 Stroke of Genius R :B: 1.50 2.00
101 Sunder R :B: 2.50 4.00
102 Telepathy U :B: .20 .35
103 Time Spiral R :B: 45.00 55.00
104 Tolarian Winds C :B: .20 .35
105 Turnabout U :B: 2.50 4.00
106 Veil of Birds C :B: .20 .35
107 Veiled Apparition U :B: .20 .35
108 Veiled Crocodile R :B: .20 .35
109 Veiled Sentry U :B: .20 .35
110 Veiled Serpent C :B: .20 .35
111 Windfall U :B: 1.50 2.00
112 Wizard Mentor C :B: .20 .35
113 Zephid R :B: .20 .35
114 Zephid's Embrace U :B: .20 .35
115 Abyssal Horror R :K: .20 .35
116 Befoul C :K: .20 .35
117 Bereavement U :K: .20 .35
118 Blood Vassal C :K: .20 .35
119 Bog Raiders C :K: .20 .35
120 Breach C :K: .20 .35
121 Cackling Fiend C :K: .20 .35
122 Carrion Beetles C :K: .20 .35
123 Contamination R :K: 13.00 15.00
124 Corrupt C :K: .20 .35
125 Crazed Skirge U :K: .20 .35
126 Dark Hatchling R :K: .20 .35
127 Dark Ritual C :K: .20 .35
128 Darkest Hour R :K: 1.50 2.00
129 Despondency C :K: .20 .35
130 Diabolic Servitude U :K: .20 .35
131 Discordant Dirge R :K: .20 .35
132 Duress C :K: .20 .35
133 Eastern Paladin R :K: .20 .35
134 Exhume C :K: 1.50 2.00
135 Expunge C :K: .20 .35
136 Flesh Reaver U :K: .20 .35
137 Hollow Dogs C :K: .20 .35
138 Ill-Gotten Gains R :K: .50 .80
139 Looming Shade C :K: .20 .35
140 Lurking Evil R :K: .20 .35
141 Mana Leech U :K: .20 .35
142 No Rest for the Wicked U :K: .20 .35
143 Oppression R :K: 1.50 2.50
144 Order of Yawgmoth U :K: .20 .35
145 Parasitic Bond U :K: .20 .35
146 Persecute R :K: .20 .35
147 Pestilence C :K: .20 .35
148 Phyrexian Ghoul C :K: .20 .35
149 Planar Void U :K: .20 .35
150 Priest of Gix U :K: .20 .35
151 Rain of Filth U :K: .60 .80
152 Ravenous Skirge C :K: .20 .35
153 Reclusive Wight U :K: .20 .35
154 Reprocess R :K: .30 .50
155 Sanguine Guard U :K: .20 .35
156 Sicken C :K: .20 .35
157 Skirge Familiar U :K: 1.50 2.00
158 Skittering Skirge C :K: .20 .35
159 Sleeper Agent R :K: .20 .35
160 Spined Fluke U :K: .20 .35
161 Tainted Æther R 2.50 4.00
162 Unnerve C :K: .20 .35
163 Unworthy Dead C :K: .20 .35
164 Vampiric Embrace U :K: .20 .35
165 Vebulid R :K: .20 .35
166 Victimize U :K: .30 .50
167 Vile Requiem U :K: .20 .35
168 Western Paladin R :K: .20 .35
169 Witch Engine R :K: .20 .35
170 Yawgmoth's Edict U :K: .20 .35
171 Yawgmoth's Will R :K: 45.00 50.00
172 Acidic Soil U :R: .20 .35
173 Antagonism R :R: .20 .35
174 Arc Lightning C :R: .20 .35
175 Bedlam R :R: .40 .60
176 Brand R :R: .75 1.25
177 Bravado C :R: .20 .35
178 Bulwark R :R: .20 .35
179 Crater Hellion R :R: .40 .60
180 Destructive Urge U :R: .20 .35
181 Disorder U :R: .20 .35
182 Dromosaur C :R: .20 .35
183 Electryte R :R: .20 .35
184 Falter C :R: .20 .35
185 Fault Line R :R: .60 1.00
186 Fiery Mantle C :R: .20 .35
187 Fire Ants U :R: .20 .35
188 Gamble R :R: 8.00 10.00
189 Goblin Cadets U :R: .20 .35
190 Goblin Lackey U :R: 5.00 7.00
191 Goblin Matron C :R: .20 .35
192 Goblin Offensive U :R: 1.00 1.50
193 Goblin Patrol C :R: .20 .35
194 Goblin Raider C :R: .20 .35
195 Goblin Spelunkers C :R: .20 .35
196 Goblin War Buggy C :R: .20 .35
197 Guma U :R: .20 .35
198 Headlong Rush C :R: .20 .35
199 Heat Ray C :R: .20 .35
200 Jagged Lightning U :R: .20 .35
201 Lay Waste C :R: .20 .35
202 Lightning Dragon R :R: .60 1.00
203 Meltdown U :R: .20 .35
204 Okk R :R: .20 .35
205 Outmaneuver U :R: .20 .35
206 Rain of Salt U :R: .20 .35
207 Raze C :R: .20 .35
208 Reflexes C :R: .20 .35
209 Retromancer C :R: .20 .35
210 Rumbling Crescendo R :R: .20 .35
211 Scald U :R: .20 .35
212 Scoria Wurm R :R: .20 .35
213 Scrap C :R: .20 .35
214 Shivan Raptor U :R: .20 .35
215 Shiv's Embrace U :R: .20 .35
216 Shivan Gorge R :L: .50 .80
217 Shower of Sparks C :R: .20 .35
218 Sneak Attack R :R: 25.00 30.00
219 Steam Blast U :R: .20 .35
220 Sulfuric Vapors R :R: .20 .35
221 Thundering Giant U :R: .20 .35
222 Torch Song U :R: .20 .35
223 Viashino Outrider C :R: .20 .35
224 Viashino Runner C :R: .20 .35
225 Viashino Sandswimmer R :R: .20 .35
226 Viashino Weaponsmith C :R: .20 .35
227 Vug Lizard U :R: .20 .35
228 Wildfire R :R: .20 .35
229 Abundance R :G: 1.25 2.00
230 Acridian C :G: .20 .35
231 Albino Troll U :G: .20 .35
232 Anaconda U :G: .20 .35
233 Argothian Elder U :G: 1.00 1.50
234 Argothian Enchantress R :G: 4.00 6.00
235 Argothian Swine C :G: .20 .35
236 Argothian Wurm R :G: .60 .80
237 Blanchwood Armor U :G: .20 .35
238 Blanchwood Treefolk C :G: .20 .35
239 Bull Hippo U :G: .20 .35
240 Carpet of Flowers U :G: 5.00 7.00
241 Cave Tiger C :G: .20 .35
242 Child of Gaea R :G: .30 .50
243 Citanul Centaurs R :G: .30 .50
244 Citanul Hierophants R :G: 1.00 1.50
245 Cradle Guard U :G: .20 .35
246 Crosswinds U :G: .20 .35
247 Elvish Herder C :G: .20 .35
248 Elvish Lyrist C :G: .20 .35
249 Endless Wurm R :G: .20 .35
250 Exploration R :G: 17.00 20.00
251 Fecundity U :G: .20 .35
252 Fertile Ground C :G: .20 .35
253 Fortitude C :G: .20 .35
254 Gaea's Bounty C :G: .20 .35
255 Gaea's Embrace U :G: .20 .35
256 Gorilla Warrior C :G: .20 .35
257 Greater Good R :G: 10.00 15.00
258 Greener Pastures R :G: .20 .35
259 Hawkeater Moth U :G: .20 .35
260 Hidden Ancients U :G: .20 .35
261 Hidden Guerrillas U :G: .20 .35
262 Hidden Herd R :G: .20 .35
263 Hidden Predators R :G: .20 .35
264 Hidden Spider C :G: .20 .35
265 Hidden Stag R :G: .20 .35
266 Hush C :G: .20 .35
267 Lull C :G: .20 .35
268 Midsummer Revel R :G: .20 .35
269 Pouncing Jaguar C :G: .20 .35
270 Priest of Titania C :G: 2.00 3.00
271 Rejuvenate C :G: .20 .35
272 Retaliation U :G: .20 .35
273 Sporogenesis R :G: .40 .60
274 Spreading Algae U :G: .20 .35
275 Symbiosis C :G: .20 .35
276 Titania's Boon U :G: .20 .35
277 Titania's Chosen U :G: .20 .35
278 Treefolk Seedlings U :G: .20 .35
279 Treetop Rangers C :G: .20 .35
280 Venomous Fangs C :G: .20 .35
281 Vernal Bloom R :G: 2.00 3.00
282 War Dance U :G: .20 .35
283 Whirlwind R :G: .40 .60
284 Wild Dogs C :G: .20 .35
285 Winding Wurm C :G: .20 .35
286 Barrin, Master Wizard R :B: 4.00 6.00
287 Cathodion U :A: .20 .35
288 Chimeric Staff R :A: .30 .50
289 Citanul Flute R :A: 1.50 2.00
290 Claws of Gix U :A: .20 .35
291 Copper Gnomes R :A: 1.50 2.00
292 Crystal Chimes U :A: .20 .35
293 Dragon Blood U :A: .20 .35
294 Endoskeleton U :A: .20 .35
295 Fluctuator R :A: 6.00 8.00
296 Grafted Skullcap R :A: .20 .35
297 Hopping Automaton U :A: .20 .35
298 Karn, Silver Golem R :A: 5.00 7.00
299 Lifeline R :A: 8.00 10.00
300 Lotus Blossom R :A: 1.00 1.50

301 Metrognome R :A:	.20	.35
302 Mishra's Helix R :A:	.60	1.00
303 Mobile Fort U :A:	.20	.35
304 Noetic Scales R :A:	.60	1.00
305 Phyrexian Colossus R :A:	.20	.35
306 Phyrexian Processor R :A:	1.00	1.50
307 Pit Trap U :A:	.20	.35
308 Purging Scythe R :A:	.20	.35
309 Smokestack R :A:	4.00	6.00
310 Temporal Aperture R :A:	3.00	5.00
311 Thran Turbine U :A:	.20	.35
312 Umbilicus R :A:	.20	.35
313 Urza's Armor U :A:	.20	.35
314 Voltaic Key U :A:	1.00	1.50
315 Wall of Junk U :A:	.20	.35
316 Whetstone R :A:	.20	.35
317 Wirecat U :A:	.20	.35
318 Worn Powerstone U :A:	.60	1.00
319 Blasted Landscape U :L:	.40	.60
320 Drifting Meadow C :L:	.20	.35
321 Gaea's Cradle R :L:	250.00	300.00
322 Phyrexian Tower R :L:	30.00	35.00
323 Polluted Mire C :L:	.20	.35
324 Remote Isle C :L:	.20	.35
325 Serra's Sanctum R :L:	55.00	60.00
326 Shivan Hellkite R :R:	.20	.35
327 Slippery Karst C :L:	.20	.35
328 Smoldering Crater C :L:	.20	.35
329 Thran Quarry R :L:	1.50	2.50
330 Tolarian Academy R :L:	30.00	35.00
331 Plains L :L:	.20	.35
332 Plains L :L:	.20	.35
333 Plains L :L:	.20	.35
334 Plains L :L:	.20	.35
335 Island L :L:	.20	.35
336 Island L :L:	.20	.35
337 Island L :L:	.20	.35
338 Island L :L:	.20	.35
339 Swamp L :L:	.20	.35
340 Swamp L :L:	.20	.35
341 Swamp L :L:	.20	.35
342 Swamp L :L:	.20	.35
343 Mountain L :L:	.20	.35
344 Mountain L :L:	.20	.35
345 Mountain L :L:	.20	.35
346 Mountain L :L:	.20	.35
347 Forest L :L:	.20	.35
348 Forest L :L:	.20	.35
349 Forest L :L:	.20	.35
350 Forest L :L:	.20	.35

1999 Magic The Gathering Urza's Legacy

COMPLETE SET (143)	140.00	185.00
BOOSTER BOX (36 PACKS)	600.00	700.00
BOOSTER PACK (15 CARDS)	15.00	20.00
RELEASED ON FEBRUARY 15, 1999		
1 Angelic Curator C :W:	.15	.25
2 Blessed Reversal R :W:	.25	.40
3 Burst of Energy C :W:	.15	.25
4 Cessation C :W:	.15	.25
5 Defender of Law C :W:	.15	.25
6 Devout Harpist C :W:	.15	.25
7 Erase C :W:	.15	.25
8 Expendable Troops C :W:	.15	.25
9 Hope and Glory U :W:	.15	.25
10 Iron Will C :W:	.15	.25
11 Karmic Guide R :W:	2.00	3.00
12 Knighthood U :W:	.15	.25
13 Martyr's Cause U :W:	.15	.25
14 Mother of Runes U :W:	1.75	2.25
15 Opal Avenger R :W:	.15	.25
16 Opal Champion C :W:	.15	.25
17 Peace and Quiet U :W:	.15	.25
18 Planar Collapse R :W:	.60	1.00
19 Purify R :W:	.15	.25
20 Radiant, Archangel R :W:	1.75	2.25
21 Radiant's Dragoons U :W:	.15	.25
22 Radiant's Judgment C :W:	.15	.25
23 Sustainer of the Realm U :W:	.15	.25
24 Tragic Poet C :W:	.15	.25
25 Anthroplasm R :B:	.30	.50
26 Archivist R :B:	.30	.50
27 Aura Flux C :B:	.15	.25
28 Bouncing Beebles C :B:	.15	.25
29 Cloud of Faeries C :B:	.60	1.00
30 Delusions of Mediocrity R :B:	.40	.60
31 Fleeting Image R :B:	.20	.35
32 Frantic Search C :B:	1.00	1.50
33 Intervene C :B:	.15	.25
34 King Crab U :B:	.15	.25
35 Levitation U :B:	.15	.25
36 Miscalculation C :B:	.15	.25
37 Opportunity U :B:	.15	.25
38 Palinchron R :B:	18.00	22.00
39 Raven Familiar U :B:	.15	.25
40 Rebuild U :B:	.15	.25
41 Second Chance R :B:	1.50	2.00
42 Slow Motion C :B:	.15	.25
43 Snap C :B:	.75	1.25
44 Thornwind Faeries C :B:	.15	.25
45 Tinker U :B:	2.00	3.00
46 Vigilant Drake C :B:	.15	.25
47 Walking Sponge U :B:	.15	.25
48 Weatherseed Faeries C :B:	.15	.25
49 Bone Shredder U :K:	.25	.40
50 Brink of Madness R :K:	.15	.25
51 Engineered Plague U :K:	.30	.50
52 Eviscerator R :K:	.20	.35
53 Fog of Gnats C :K:	.15	.25
54 Giant Cockroach C :K:	.15	.25
55 Lurking Skirge R :K:	.15	.25
56 No Mercy R :K:	15.00	18.00
57 Ostracize C :K:	.15	.25
58 Phyrexian Broodlings C :K:	.15	.25
59 Phyrexian Debaser C :K:	.15	.25
60 Phyrexian Defiler U :K:	.15	.25
61 Phyrexian Denouncer C :K:	.15	.25
62 Phyrexian Plaguelord R :K:	.15	.25
63 Phyrexian Reclamation U :K:	1.50	2.00
64 Plague Beetle C :K:	.15	.25
65 Rank and File U :K:	.15	.25
66 Sick and Tired C :K:	.15	.25
67 Sleeper's Guile C :K:	.15	.25
68 Subversion R :K:	.50	.80
69 Swat C :K:	.15	.25
70 Tethered Skirge U :K:	.15	.25
71 Treacherous Link U :K:	.15	.25
72 Unearth C :K:	1.00	1.50
73 About Face C :R:	.15	.25
74 Avalanche Riders U :R:	.60	1.00
75 Defender of Chaos C :R:	.15	.25
76 Ghitu Fire-Eater U :R:	.15	.25
77 Ghitu Slinger C :R:	.15	.25
78 Ghitu War Cry U :R:	.15	.25
79 Goblin Medics C :R:	.15	.25
80 Goblin Welder R :R:	3.00	5.00
81 Granite Grip C :R:	.15	.25
82 Impending Disaster R :R:	.60	1.00
83 Last-Ditch Effort U :R:	.15	.25
84 Lava Axe C :R:	.15	.25
85 Molten Hydra R :R:	.30	.50
86 Parch C :R:	.15	.25
87 Pygmy Pyrosaur C :R:	.15	.25
88 Pyromancy R :R:	.15	.25
89 Rack and Ruin U :R:	.15	.25
90 Rivalry R :R:	.15	.25
91 Shivan Phoenix R :R:	.25	.40
92 Sluggishness C :R:	.15	.25
93 Viashino Bey C :R:	.15	.25
94 Viashino Cutthroat U :R:	.15	.25
95 Viashino Heretic U :R:	.50	.80
96 Viashino Sandscout C :R:	.15	.25
97 Bloated Toad U :G:	.15	.25
98 Crop Rotation C :G:	1.25	2.00
99 Darkwatch Elves U :G:	.15	.25
100 Defense of the Heart R :G:	8.00	10.00
101 Deranged Hermit R :G:	8.00	10.00
102 Gang of Elk U :G:	.15	.25
103 Harmonic Convergence U :G:	.15	.25
104 Hidden Gibbons R :G:	.30	.50
105 Lone Wolf U :G:	.15	.25
106 Might of Oaks R :G:	.40	.60
107 Multani, Maro-Sorcerer R :G:	1.00	1.50
108 Multani's Acolyte C :G:	.15	.25
109 Multani's Presence U :G:	.15	.25
110 Rancor C :G:	1.50	2.00
111 Repopulate C :G:	.15	.25
112 Silk Net C :G:	.15	.25
113 Simian Grunts C :G:	.15	.25
114 Treefolk Mystic C :G:	.15	.25
115 Weatherseed Elf C :G:	.15	.25
116 Weatherseed Treefolk R :G:	.50	.80
117 Wing Snare U :G:	.15	.25
118 Yavimaya Granger C :G:	.15	.25
119 Yavimaya Scion C :G:	.15	.25
120 Yavimaya Wurm C :G:	.15	.25
121 Angel's Trumpet U :A:	.15	.25
122 Beast of Burden R :A:	.25	.40
123 Crawlspace R :A:	4.00	6.00
124 Damping Engine R :A:	.25	.40
125 Defense Grid R :A:	5.00	7.00
126 Grim Monolith R :A:	60.00	65.00
127 Iron Maiden R :A:	.75	1.25
128 Jhoira's Toolbox U :A:	.15	.25
129 Memory Jar R :A:	13.00	15.00
130 Quicksilver Amulet R :A:	7.00	9.00
131 Ring of Gix R :A:	.30	.50
132 Scrapheap R :A:	.15	.25
133 Thran Lens R :A:	.15	.25
134 Thran War Machine R :A:	.15	.25
135 Thran Weaponry R :A:	.15	.25
136 Ticking Gnomes U :A:	.15	.25
137 Urza's Blueprints R :A:	.15	.25
138 Wheel of Torture R :A:	.30	.50
139 Faerie Conclave U :L:	1.00	1.50
140 Forbidding Watchtower U :L:	.15	.25
141 Ghitu Encampment U :L:	.15	.25
142 Spawning Pool U :L:	.15	.25
143 Treetop Village U :L:	1.00	1.50

1999 Magic The Gathering Urza's Legacy Foil

COMPLETE SET (143)	375.00	500.00

1999 Magic The Gathering Urza's Destiny

COMPLETE SET (143)	170.00	225.00
BOOSTER BOX (36 PACKS)	600.00	800.00
BOOSTER PACK (15 CARDS)	18.00	25.00
RELEASED ON JUNE 7, 1999		
1 Academy Rector R :W:	25.00	30.00
2 Archery Training U :W:	.15	.25
3 Capashen Knight C :W:	.15	.25
4 Capashen Standard C :W:	.15	.25
5 Capashen Templar C :W:	.15	.25
6 False Prophet R :W:	.40	.60
7 Fend Off C :W:	.15	.25
8 Field Surgeon C :W:	.15	.25
9 Flicker R :W:	.50	.80
10 Jasmine Seer U :W:	.15	.25
11 Mask of Law and Grace C :W:	.15	.25
12 Master Healer R :W:	.20	.35
13 Opalescence R :W:	4.00	6.00
14 Reliquary Monk C :W:	.15	.25
15 Replenish R :W:	25.00	.25
16 Sanctimony U :W:	.15	.25
17 Scent of Jasmine C :W:	.15	.25
18 Scour U :W:	.15	.25
19 Serra Advocate U :W:	.15	.25
20 Solidarity C :W:	.15	.25
21 Tethered Griffin R :W:	.25	.40
22 Tormented Angel C :W:	.15	.25
23 Voice of Duty U :W:	.15	.25
24 Voice of Reason U :W:	.15	.25
25 Wall of Glare C :W:	.15	.25
26 Aura Thief R :B:	2.50	3.50
27 Blizzard Elemental R :B:	.30	.50
28 Brine Seer U :B:	.15	.25
29 Bubbling Beebles C :B:	.15	.25
30 Disappear U :B:	.15	.25
31 Donate R :B:	3.00	5.00
32 Fatigue C :B:	.15	.25
33 Fledgling Osprey C :B:	.15	.25
34 Illuminated Wings C :B:	.15	.25
35 Iridescent Drake U :B:	.15	.25
36 Kingfisher C :B:	.15	.25
37 Mental Discipline C :B:	.15	.25
38 Metathran Elite U :B:	.15	.25
39 Metathran Soldier C :B:	.15	.25
40 Opposition R :B:	3.00	5.00
41 Private Research U :B:	.15	.25
42 Quash U :B:	.15	.25
43 Rayne, Academy Chancellor R :B:	.50	.80
44 Rescue C :B:	.15	.25
45 Scent of Brine C :B:	.15	.25
46 Sigil of Sleep C :B:	.15	.25
47 Telepathic Spies C :B:	.15	.25
48 Temporal Adept R :B:	.40	.60
49 Thieving Magpie U :B:	.15	.25
50 Treachery R :B:	25.00	30.00
51 Apprentice Necromancer R :K:	1.25	2.00
52 Attrition R :K:	4.00	6.00
53 Body Snatcher R :K:	.30	.50
54 Bubbling Muck C :K:	.20	.35
55 Carnival of Souls R :K:	.75	1.25
56 Chime of Night C :K:	.15	.25
57 Disease Carriers C :K:	.15	.25
58 Dying Wail C :K:	.15	.25
59 Encroach U :K:	.15	.25
60 Eradicate U :K:	.15	.25
61 Festering Wound U :K:	.15	.25
62 Lurking Jackals U :K:	.15	.25
63 Nightshade Seer U :K:	.15	.25
64 Phyrexian Monitor C :K:	.15	.25
65 Phyrexian Negator R :K:	.60	1.00
66 Plague Dogs U :K:	.15	.25
67 Rapid Decay R :K:	.25	.40
68 Ravenous Rats C :K:	.15	.25
69 Scent of Nightshade C :K:	.15	.25
70 Skittering Horror C :K:	.15	.25
71 Slinking Skirge C :K:	.15	.25
72 Soul Feast U :K:	.15	.25
73 Squirming Mass C :K:	.15	.25
74 Twisted Experiment C :K:	.15	.25
75 Yawgmoth's Bargain R :K:	10.00	15.00
76 Aether Sting U :R:	.15	.25
77 Bloodshot Cyclops R :R:	.30	.50
78 Cinder Seer U :R:	.15	.25
79 Colos Yearling C :R:	.15	.25
80 Covetous Dragon R :R:	.60	1.00
81 Flame Jet C :R:	.15	.25
82 Goblin Berserker U :R:	.15	.25
83 Goblin Festival R :R:	.25	.40
84 Goblin Gardener C :R:	.15	.25
85 Goblin Marshal R :R:	.60	1.00
86 Goblin Masons C :R:	.15	.25
87 Hulking Ogre C :R:	.15	.25
88 Impatience R :R:	.25	.40
89 Incendiary U :R:	.15	.25
90 Keldon Champion U :R:	.15	.25
91 Keldon Vandals C :R:	.15	.25
92 Landslide U :R:	.15	.25
93 Mark of Fury C :R:	.15	.25
94 Reckless Abandon C :R:	.15	.25
95 Repercussion R :R:	5.00	7.00
96 Scent of Cinder C :R:	.15	.25
97 Sowing Salt U :R:	.50	.80
98 Trumpet Blast C :R:	.15	.25
99 Wake of Destruction R :R:	1.25	2.00
100 Wild Colos C :R:	.15	.25
101 Ancient Silverback R :G:	.20	.35
102 Compost U :G:	.15	.25
103 Elvish Lookout C :G:	.15	.25
104 Elvish Piper R :G:	5.00	7.00
105 Emperor Crocodile R :G:	.25	.40
106 Gamekeeper U :G:	.15	.25
107 Goliath Beetle C :G:	.15	.25
108 Heart Warden C :G:	.15	.25
109 Hunting Moa U :G:	.15	.25
110 Ivy Seer U :G:	.15	.25
111 Magnify C :G:	.15	.25
112 Marker Beetles C :G:	.15	.25
113 Momentum U :G:	.15	.25
114 Multani's Decree C :G:	.15	.25
115 Pattern of Rebirth R :G:	3.00	5.00
116 Plated Spider C :G:	.15	.25
117 Plow Under R :G:	.75	1.25
118 Rofellos's Gift C :G:	.15	.25
119 Rofellos, Llanowar Emissary R :G:	10.00	15.00
120 Scent of Ivy C :G:	.15	.25
121 Splinter U :G:	.15	.25
122 Taunting Elf C :G:	.15	.25
123 Thorn Elemental R :G:	.40	.60
124 Yavimaya Elder C :G:	.60	1.00
125 Yavimaya Enchantress U :G:	.15	.25
126 Braidwood Cup U :A:	.15	.25
127 Braidwood Sextant U :A:	.15	.25
128 Brass Secretary U :A:	.15	.25
129 Caltrops U :A:	.15	.25
130 Extruder U :A:	.15	.25
131 Fodder Cannon U :A:	.15	.25
132 Junk Diver R :A:	.50	.80
133 Mantis Engine U :A:	.15	.25
134 Masticore R :A:	1.00	1.50
135 Metalworker R :A:	25.00	30.00
136 Powder Keg R :A:	.75	1.25
137 Scrying Glass R :A:	.25	.25
138 Storage Matrix R :A:	.50	.80
139 Thran Dynamo U :A:	7.00	9.00
140 Thran Foundry U :A:	.15	.25
141 Thran Golem R :A:	.25	.40
142 Urza's Incubator R :A:	.15	.25
143 Yavimaya Hollow R :L:	25.00	30.00

1999 Magic The Gathering Mercadian Masques

COMPLETE SET (350)	275.00	375.00
BOOSTER BOX (36 PACKS)	400.00	500.00
BOOSTER PACK (15 CARDS)	10.00	15.00
THEME DECK BOX (12 DECKS)	100.00	125.00
THEME DECK	9.00	13.00
FAT PACK	60.00	100.00
RELEASED ON OCTOBER 4, 1999		
1 Afterlife U :W:	.15	.25
2 Alabaster Wall C :W:	.15	.25
3 Armistice R :W:	.15	.25
4 Arrest U :W:	.15	.25
5 Ballista Squad U :W:	.15	.25
6 Charm Peddler C :W:	.15	.25
7 Charmed Griffin U :W:	.15	.25
8 Cho-Arrim Alchemist R :W:	.15	.25
9 Cho-Arrim Bruiser R :W:	.15	.25
10 Cho-Arrim Legate U :W:	.15	.25
11 Cho-Manno's Blessing C :W:	.15	.25
12 Cho-Manno, Revolutionary R :W:	.40	.60
13 Common Cause R :W:	.15	.25
14 Cornered Market R :W:	.30	.50
15 Crackdown R :W:	3.00	5.00
16 Crossbow Infantry C :W:	.15	.25
17 Devout Witness C :W:	.15	.25
18 Disenchant C :W:	.15	.25
19 Fountain Watch R :W:	2.00	3.00
20 Fresh Volunteers C :W:	.15	.25
21 Honor the Fallen R :W:	.50	.80
22 Ignoble Soldier U :W:	.15	.25
23 Inviolability C :W:	.15	.25
24 Ivory Mask R :W:	.60	1.00
25 Jhovall Queen R :W:	.30	.50
26 Jhovall Rider U :W:	.15	.25
27 Last Breath U :W:	.15	.25
28 Moment of Silence C :W:	.15	.25
29 Moonlit Wake U :W:	.15	.25
30 Muzzle C :W:	.15	.25
31 Nightwind Glider C :W:	.15	.25
32 Noble Purpose U :W:	.25	.40
33 Orim's Cure C :W:	.15	.25
34 Pious Warrior C :W:	.15	.25
35 Ramosian Captain U :W:	.15	.25
36 Ramosian Commander U :W:	.15	.25
37 Ramosian Lieutenant C :W:	.15	.25
38 Ramosian Rally C :W:	.15	.25
39 Ramosian Sergeant C :W:	.15	.25
40 Ramosian Sky Marshal R :W:	.20	.35
41 Rappelling Scouts R :W:	.20	.35
42 Renounce U :W:	.15	.25
43 Revered Elder C :W:	.15	.25
44 Reverent Mantra R :W:	.30	.50
45 Righteous Aura U :W:	.15	.25
46 Righteous Indignation U :W:	.15	.25
47 Security Detail R :W:	.25	.40
48 Soothing Balm C :W:	.15	.25
49 Spiritual Focus R :W:	.30	.50
50 Steadfast Guard C :W:	.15	.25
51 Story Circle U :W:	.60	1.00
52 Task Force C :W:	.15	.25
53 Thermal Glider C :W:	.15	.25
54 Tonic Peddler U :W:	.15	.25
55 Trap Runner U :W:	.15	.25
56 Wave of Reckoning R :W:	.50	.80
57 Wishmonger U :W:	.15	.25
58 Aerial Caravan R :B:	.15	.25
59 Balloon Peddler C :B:	.15	.25
60 Blockade Runner C :B:	.15	.25
61 Brainstorm C :B:	.75	1.25
62 Bribery R :B:	15.00	20.00
63 Buoyancy C :B:	.15	.25
64 Chambered Nautilus U :B:	.15	.25
65 Chameleon Spirit U :B:	.15	.25
66 Charisma R :B:	2.00	3.00
67 Cloud Sprite C :B:	.15	.25
68 Coastal Piracy U :B:	3.00	5.00
69 Counterspell C :B:	1.00	1.50
70 Cowardice R :B:	.15	.25
71 Customs Depot U :B:	.15	.25
72 Darting Merfolk C :B:	.15	.25
73 Dehydration C :B:	.15	.25
74 Diplomatic Escort U :B:	.15	.25
75 Diplomatic Immunity C :B:	.40	.60
76 Drake Hatchling C :B:	.15	.25
77 Embargo R :B:	.40	.60
78 Energy Flux U :B:	.15	.25
79 Extravagant Spirit R :B:	.20	.35
80 False Demise U :B:	.15	.25
81 Glowing Anemone U :B:	.15	.25
82 Gush C :B:	1.50	2.50
83 High Seas U :B:	.15	.25
84 Hoodwink C :B:	.15	.25
85 Indentured Djinn U :B:	.30	.50
86 Karn's Touch R :B:	.20	.35
87 Misdirection R :B:	3.00	5.00
88 Misstep C :B:	.15	.25
89 Overtaker R :B:	.25	.40
90 Port Inspector C :B:	.15	.25
91 Rishadan Airship C :B:	.15	.25
92 Rishadan Brigand R :B:	7.00	9.00
93 Rishadan Cutpurse C :B:	.30	.50
94 Rishadan Footpad U :B:	6.00	8.00
95 Sailmonger U :B:	.15	.25
96 Sand Squid R :B:	.15	.25
97 Saprazzan Bailiff R :B:	.15	.25
98 Saprazzan Breaker U :B:	.15	.25
99 Saprazzan Heir R :B:	.60	.80
100 Saprazzan Legate U :B:	.15	.25
101 Saprazzan Outrigger C :B:	.15	.25
102 Saprazzan Raider C :B:	.15	.25
103 Shoving Match U :B:	.15	.25
104 Soothsaying U :B:	3.00	5.00
105 Squeeze R :B:	.25	.40
106 Statecraft R :B:	3.00	5.00
107 Stinging Barrier C :B:	.15	.25
108 Thwart U :B:	.50	.80
109 Tidal Bore C :B:	.15	.25
110 Tidal Kraken R :B:	.40	.60
111 Timid Drake U :B:	.15	.25
112 Trade Routes R :B:	.30	.50
113 War Tax U :B:	.30	.50
114 Waterfront Bouncer C :B:	.15	.25
115 Alley Grifters C :K:	.15	.25
116 Black Market R :K:	3.00	5.00

Card	Low	High
117 Bog Smugglers C :K:	.15	.25
118 Bog Witch C :K:	.15	.25
119 Cackling Witch U :K:	.15	.25
120 Cateran Brute C :K:	.15	.25
121 Cateran Enforcer U :K:	.15	.25
122 Cateran Kidnappers U :K:	.15	.25
123 Cateran Overlord R :K:	.25	.40
124 Cateran Persuader C :K:	.15	.25
125 Cateran Slaver R :K:	.15	.25
126 Cateran Summons U :K:	.15	.25
127 Conspiracy R :K:	3.00	5.00
128 Corrupt Official R :K:	.25	.40
129 Dark Ritual C :K:	.50	.80
130 Deathgazer U :K:	.15	.25
131 Deepwood Ghoul C :K:	.15	.25
132 Deepwood Legate U :K:	.15	.25
133 Delraich R :K:	.50	.80
134 Enslaved Horror U :K:	.15	.25
135 Extortion R :K:	.20	.35
136 Forced March R :K:	.50	.80
137 Ghoul's Feast U :K:	.15	.25
138 Haunted Crossroads U :K:	.40	.60
139 Highway Robber C :K:	.15	.25
140 Instigator R :K:	.25	.40
141 Insubordination C :K:	.15	.25
142 Intimidation U :K:	.15	.25
143 Larceny U :K:	.15	.25
144 Liability R :K:	.30	.50
145 Maggot Therapy C :K:	.15	.25
146 Midnight Ritual R :K:	.20	.35
147 Misshapen Fiend C :K:	.15	.25
148 Molting Harpy U :K:	.15	.25
149 Nether Spirit R :K:	1.50	2.50
150 Notorious Assassin R :K:	.25	.40
151 Pretender's Claim U :K:	.15	.25
152 Primeval Shambler U :K:	.15	.25
153 Putrefaction U :K:	.15	.25
154 Quagmire Lamprey U :K:	.15	.25
155 Rain of Tears U :K:	.15	.25
156 Rampart Crawler C :K:	.15	.25
157 Rouse C :K:	.15	.25
158 Scandalmonger U :K:	.15	.25
159 Sever Soul C :K:	.15	.25
160 Silent Assassin R :K:	.25	.40
161 Skulking Fugitive C :K:	.15	.25
162 Snuff Out C :K:	.30	.50
163 Soul Channeling C :K:	.15	.25
164 Specter's Wail C :K:	.15	.25
165 Strongarm Thug U :K:	.15	.25
166 Thrashing Wumpus R :K:	.40	.60
167 Undertaker C :K:	.15	.25
168 Unmask R :K:	8.00	11.00
169 Unnatural Hunger R :K:	.25	.40
170 Vendetta C :K:	.15	.25
171 Wall of Distortion C :K:	.15	.25
172 Arms Dealer U :R:	.15	.25
173 Battle Rampart C :R:	.15	.25
174 Battle Squadron R :R:	.15	.25
175 Blaster Mage C :R:	.15	.25
176 Blood Hound R :R:	.15	.25
177 Blood Oath R :R:	.15	.25
178 Brawl R :R:	.15	.25
179 Cave Sense C :R:	.15	.25
180 Cave-In R :R:	.50	.80
181 Cavern Crawler C :R:	.15	.25
182 Ceremonial Guard C :R:	.15	.25
183 Cinder Elemental U :R:	.15	.25
184 Close Quarters U :R:	.15	.25
185 Crag Saurian R :R:	.25	.40
186 Crash C :R:	.15	.25
187 Flailing Manticore R :R:	.15	.25
188 Flailing Ogre U :R:	.15	.25
189 Flailing Soldier C :R:	.15	.25
190 Flaming Sword C :R:	.15	.25
191 Furious Assault C :R:	.15	.25
192 Gerrard's Irregulars C :R:	.15	.25
193 Hammer Mage U :R:	.15	.25
194 Hired Giant U :R:	.15	.25
195 Kris Mage C :R:	.15	.25
196 Kyren Glider C :R:	.15	.25
197 Kyren Legate U :R:	.15	.25
198 Kyren Negotiations U :R:	.15	.25
199 Kyren Sniper C :R:	.15	.25
200 Lava Runner R :R:	.15	.25
201 Lightning Hounds C :R:	.15	.25
202 Lithophage R :R:	.15	.25
203 Lunge C :R:	.15	.25
204 Magistrate's Veto U :R:	.15	.25
205 Mercadian Atlas R :A:	.30	.50
206 Ogre Taskmaster U :R:	.15	.25
207 Pulverize R :R:	.40	.60
208 Puppet's Verdict R :R:	1.50	2.50
209 Robber Fly U :R:	.15	.25
210 Rock Badger U :R:	.15	.25
211 Seismic Mage R :R:	.25	.40
212 Shock Troops C :R:	.15	.25
213 Sizzle C :R:	.15	.25
214 Squee, Goblin Nabob R :R:	3.00	5.00
215 Stone Rain C :R:	.15	.25
216 Tectonic Break R :R:	.30	.50
217 Territorial Dispute R :R:	.30	.50
218 Thieves' Auction R :R:	1.50	2.50
219 Thunderclap C :R:	.15	.25
220 Tremor C :R:	.15	.25
221 Two-Headed Dragon R :R:	.75	1.25
222 Uphill Battle U :R:	.15	.25
223 Volcanic Wind U :R:	.15	.25
224 War Cadence U :R:	.15	.25
225 Warmonger U :R:	.15	.25
226 Warpath U :R:	.15	.25
227 Wild Jhovall C :R:	.15	.25
228 Word of Blasting U :R:	.15	.25
229 Ancestral Mask C :G:	.40	.60
230 Bifurcate R :G:	.40	.60
231 Boa Constrictor U :G:	.15	.25
232 Briar Patch U :G:	.15	.25
233 Caller of the Hunt R :G:	.30	.50
234 Caustic Wasps U :G:	.15	.25
235 Clear the Land R :G:	.30	.50
236 Collective Unconscious R :G:	.40	.60
237 Dawnstrider R :G:	.60	1.00
238 Deadly Insect C :G:	.15	.25
239 Deepwood Drummer C :G:	.15	.25
240 Deepwood Elder R :G:	.20	.35
241 Deepwood Tantiv U :G:	.15	.25
242 Deepwood Wolverine C :G:	.15	.25
243 Desert Twister U :G:	.15	.25
244 Erithizon R :G:	.20	.35
245 Ferocity C :G:	.15	.25
246 Food Chain R :G:	35.00	40.00
247 Foster R :G:	.15	.25
248 Game Preserve R :G:	.25	.40
249 Giant Caterpillar C :G:	.15	.25
250 Groundskeeper U :G:	.15	.25
251 Horned Troll C :G:	.15	.25
252 Howling Wolf C :G:	.15	.25
253 Hunted Wumpus U :G:	.15	.25
254 Invigorate C :G:	.30	.50
255 Land Grant C :G:	.15	.25
256 Ley Line U :G:	.15	.25
257 Lumbering Satyr U :G:	.15	.25
258 Lure U :G:	.15	.25
259 Megatherium R :G:	.20	.35
260 Natural Affinity R :G:	.30	.50
261 Pangosaur R :G:	.25	.40
262 Revive U :G:	.15	.25
263 Rushwood Dryad C :G:	.15	.25
264 Rushwood Elemental R :G:	.60	.80
265 Rushwood Herbalist C :G:	.15	.25
266 Rushwood Legate U :G:	.15	.25
267 Saber Ants U :G:	.15	.25
268 Sacred Prey C :G:	.15	.25
269 Silverglade Elemental C :G:	.15	.25
270 Silverglade Pathfinder U :G:	.15	.25
271 Snake Pit U :G:	.20	.35
272 Snorting Gahr C :G:	.15	.25
273 Spidersilk Armor C :G:	1.25	2.00
274 Spontaneous Generation R :G:	.30	.50
275 Squall C :G:	.15	.25
276 Squallmonger U :G:	.15	.25
277 Stamina U :G:	.15	.25
278 Sustenance U :G:	.15	.25
279 Tiger Claws C :G:	.15	.25
280 Tranquility C :G:	.15	.25
281 Venomous Breath U :G:	.15	.25
282 Venomous Dragonfly C :G:	.15	.25
283 Vernal Equinox R :G:	.30	.50
284 Vine Dryad R :G:	.30	.50
285 Vine Trellis C :G:	.15	.25
286 Assembly Hall R :A:	.15	.25
287 Barbed Wire U :A:	.15	.25
288 Bargaining Table R :A:	.30	.50
289 Credit Voucher U :A:	.15	.25
290 Crenellated Wall U :A:	.25	.40
291 Crooked Scales R :A:	.25	.40
292 Crumbling Sanctuary R :A:	.30	.50
293 Distorting Lens R :A:	.40	.60
294 Eye of Ramos R :A:	.30	.50
295 General's Regalia R :A:	.25	.40
296 Heart of Ramos R :A:	.40	.60
297 Henge Guardian U :A:	.15	.25
298 Horn of Plenty R :A:	.30	.50
299 Horn of Ramos R :A:	.30	.50
300 Iron Lance U :A:	.15	.25
301 Jeweled Torque U :A:	.15	.25
302 Kyren Archive R :A:	.20	.35
303 Kyren Toy R :A:	.15	.25
304 Magistrate's Scepter R :A:	4.00	6.00
305 Mercadian Bazaar U :L:	.25	.40
306 Mercadia's Downfall U :R:	.15	.25
307 Monkey Cage R :A:	.30	.50
308 Panacea U :A:	.15	.25
309 Power Matrix R :A:	1.25	2.00
310 Puffer Extract U :A:	.15	.25
311 Rishadan Pawnshop R :A:	.20	.35
312 Skull of Ramos R :A:	.60	1.00
313 Tooth of Ramos R :A:	.30	.50
314 Toymaker U :A:	.15	.25
315 Worry Beads R :A:	.15	.25
316 Dust Bowl R :L:	8.00	11.00
317 Fountain of Cho U :L:	.15	.25
318 Henge of Ramos U :L:	.15	.25
319 Hickory Woodlot C :L:	.15	.25
320 High Market R :L:	2.00	3.00
321 Mercadian Lift R :A:	.25	.40
322 Peat Bog C :L:	.15	.25
323 Remote Farm C :L:	.15	.25
324 Rishadan Port R :L:	90.00	100.00
325 Rushwood Grove U :L:	.15	.25
326 Sandstone Needle C :L:	.15	.25
327 Saprazzan Cove U :L:	.15	.25
328 Saprazzan Skerry C :L:	.15	.25
329 Subterranean Hangar U :L:	.15	.25
330 Tower of the Magistrate R :L:	2.00	3.00
331 Plains C :L:	.15	.25
332 Plains C :L:	.15	.25
333 Plains C :L:	.15	.25
334 Plains C :L:	.15	.25
335 Island C :L:	.15	.25
336 Island C :L:	.15	.25
337 Island C :L:	.15	.25
338 Island C :L:	.15	.25
339 Swamp C :L:	.15	.25
340 Swamp C :L:	.15	.25
341 Swamp C :L:	.15	.25
342 Swamp C :L:	.15	.25
343 Mountain C :L:	.15	.25
344 Mountain C :L:	.15	.25
345 Mountain C :L:	.15	.25
346 Mountain C :L:	.15	.25
347 Forest C :L:	.15	.25
348 Forest C :L:	.15	.25
349 Forest C :L:	.15	.25
350 Forest C :L:	.15	.25

1999 Magic The Gathering Mercadian Masques Foil

Item	Low	High
COMPLETE SET (350)	500.00	750.00

2000 Magic The Gathering Nemesis

Item	Low	High
COMPLETE SET (143)	50.00	75.00
BOOSTER BOX (36 PACKS)	150.00	200.00
BOOSTER PACK (15 CARDS)	5.00	8.00
STARTER BOX (12 DECKS)	90.00	125.00
STARTER DECK	10.00	12.50
FAT PACK	40.00	50.00

RELEASED ON FEBRUARY 14, 2000

Card	Low	High
1 Angelic Favor U :W:	.20	.35
2 Avenger en-Dal R :W:	.20	.35
3 Blinding Angel R :W:	1.50	2.00
4 Chieftain en-Dal U :W:	.20	.35
5 Defender en-Vec C :W:	.20	.35
6 Defiant Falcon C :W:	.20	.35
7 Defiant Vanguard U :W:	.20	.35
8 Fanatical Devotion C :W:	.20	.35
9 Lashknife C :W:	.20	.35
10 Lawbringer C :W:	.20	.35
11 Lightbringer C :W:	.20	.35
12 Lin Sivvi, Defiant Hero R :W:	.20	.35
13 Netter en-Dal C :W:	.20	.35
14 Noble Stand U :W:	.20	.35
15 Off Balance C :W:	.20	.35
16 Oracle's Attendants R :W:	.20	.35
17 Parallax Wave R :W:	3.00	5.00
18 Seal of Cleansing C :W:	.20	.35
19 Silkenfist Fighter C :W:	.20	.35
20 Silkenfist Order U :W:	.20	.35
21 Sivvi's Ruse U :W:	.20	.35
22 Sivvi's Valor R :W:	.20	.35
23 Spiritual Asylum R :W:	.20	.35
24 Topple C :W:	.20	.35
25 Voice of Truth U :W:	.20	.35
26 Accumulated Knowledge C :B:	.20	.35
27 Ather Barrier R :B:	.20	.35
28 Air Bladder C :B:	.20	.35
29 Cloudskate C :B:	.20	.35
30 Daze C :B:	1.00	1.50
31 Dominate U :B:	.20	.35
32 Ensnare U :B:	.20	.35
33 Infiltrate C :B:	.20	.35
34 Jolting Merfolk U :B:	.20	.35
35 Oraxid C :B:	.20	.35
36 Pale Moon R :B:	.20	.35
37 Parallax Tide R :B:	1.00	1.50
38 Rising Waters R :B:	.20	.35
39 Rootwater Commando C :B:	.20	.35
40 Rootwater Thief R :B:	1.00	1.50
41 Seahunter R :B:	3.00	5.00
42 Seal of Removal C :B:	.20	.35
43 Sliptide Serpent R :B:	.20	.35
44 Sneaky Homunculus C :B:	.20	.35
45 Stronghold Biologist U :B:	.20	.35
45 Harvest Mage C :G:	.20	.35
46 Stronghold Machinist U :B:	.20	.35
47 Stronghold Zeppelin U :B:	.20	.35
48 Submerge U :B:	1.00	1.50
49 Trickster Mage C :B:	.20	.35
50 Wandering Eye C :B:	.20	.35
51 Ascendant Evincar R :K:	.20	.35
52 Battlefield Percher U :K:	.20	.35
53 Belbe's Percher C :K:	.20	.35
54 Carrion Wall U :K:	.20	.35
55 Dark Triumph U :K:	.20	.35
56 Death Pit Offering R :K:	.20	.35
57 Divining Witch R :K:	.20	.35
58 Massacre U :K:	.20	.35
59 Mind Slash U :K:	.20	.35
60 Mind Swords C :K:	.20	.35
61 Murderous Betrayal R :K:	.20	.35
62 Parallax Dementia C :K:	.20	.35
63 Parallax Nexus R :K:	.20	.35
64 Phyrexian Driver C :K:	.20	.35
65 Phyrexian Prowler U :K:	.20	.35
66 Plague Witch C :K:	.20	.35
67 Rathi Fiend U :K:	.20	.35
68 Rathi Intimidator C :K:	.20	.35
69 Rath's Edge R :L:	.20	.35
70 Seal of Doom C :K:	.20	.35
71 Spineless Thug C :K:	.20	.35
72 Spiteful Bully C :K:	.20	.35
73 Stronghold Discipline C :K:	.20	.35
74 Vicious Hunger C :K:	.20	.35
75 Volrath the Fallen R :K:	.20	.35
76 Ancient Hydra U :R:	.20	.35
77 Arc Mage U :R:	.20	.35
78 Bola Warrior C :R:	.20	.35
79 Downhill Charge C :R:	.20	.35
80 Flame Rift C :R:	.20	.35
81 Flowstone Crusher C :R:	.20	.35
82 Flowstone Overseer R :R:	.20	.35
83 Flowstone Slide R :R:	.20	.35
84 Flowstone Strike C :R:	.20	.35
85 Flowstone Surge U :R:	.20	.35
86 Flowstone Wall C :R:	.20	.35
87 Laccolith Grunt C :R:	.20	.35
88 Laccolith Rig C :R:	.20	.35
89 Laccolith Titan R :R:	.20	.35
90 Laccolith Warrior U :R:	.20	.35
91 Laccolith Whelp C :R:	.20	.35
92 Mana Cache R :R:	.20	.35
93 Mogg Alarm U :R:	.20	.35
94 Mogg Salvage U :R:	.20	.35
95 Mogg Toady C :R:	.20	.35
96 Moggcatcher R :R:	3.00	5.00
97 Rupture U :R:	.20	.35
98 Seal of Fire C :R:	.20	.35
99 Shrieking Mogg R :R:	.20	.35
100 Stronghold Gambit R :R:	.20	.35
101 Animate Land U :G:	.20	.35
102 Blastoderm C :G:	.20	.35
103 Coiling Woodworm U :G:	.20	.35
104 Fog Patch C :G:	.20	.35
106 Mossdog C :G:	.20	.35
107 Nesting Wurm U :G:	.20	.35
108 Overlaid Terrain R :G:	.20	.35
109 Pack Hunt R :G:	.20	.35
110 Refreshing Rain U :G:	.20	.35
111 Reverent Silence C :G:	.20	.35
112 Rhox R :G:	.20	.35
113 Saproling Burst R :G:	.20	.35
114 Saproling Cluster R :G:	.20	.35
115 Seal of Strength C :G:	.20	.35
116 Skyshroud Behemoth R :G:	.20	.35
117 Skyshroud Claim C :G:	1.50	2.50
118 Skyshroud Cutter C :G:	.20	.35
119 Skyshroud Poacher R :G:	.20	.35
120 Skyshroud Ridgeback C :G:	.20	.35
121 Skyshroud Sentinel C :G:	.20	.35
122 Stampede Driver U :G:	.20	.35
123 Treetop Bracers C :G:	.20	.35
124 Wild Mammoth U :G:	.20	.35
125 Woodripper U :G:	.20	.35
126 Belbe's Armor U :A:	.20	.35
127 Belbe's Portal R :A:	4.00	6.00
128 Complex Automaton R :A:	.20	.35
129 Eye of Yawgmoth R :A:	.20	.35
130 Flint Golem U :A:	.20	.35
131 Flowstone Armor U :A:	.20	.35
132 Flowstone Thopter U :A:	.20	.35
133 Kill Switch R :A:	.20	.35
134 Parallax Inhibitor R :A:	.20	.35
135 Predator, Flagship R :A:	.20	.35
136 Rackling U :A:	.20	.35
137 Rejuvenation Chamber U :A:	.20	.35
138 Rusting Golem U :A:	.20	.35
139 Tangle Wire R :A:	3.00	5.00
140 Viseling U :A:	.20	.35
141 Kor Haven R :L:	5.00	7.00
142 Rathi Assassin R :K:	.20	.35
143 Terrain Generator U :L:	1.00	1.50

2000 Magic The Gathering Prophecy

Item	Low	High
COMPLETE SET (143)	40.00	60.00
BOOSTER BOX (36 PACKS)	150.00	250.00
BOOSTER PACK (15 CARDS)	5.00	8.00
STARTER BOX (12 DECKS)	120.00	175.00
STARTER DECK	15.00	20.00
FAT PACK	30.00	60.00

RELEASED ON JUNE 5, 2000

Card	Low	High
1 Abolish U :W:	.20	.35
2 Aura Fracture C :W:	.20	.35
3 Avatar of Hope R :W:	.20	.35
4 Blessed Wind R :W:	.20	.35
5 Celestial Convergence R :W:	.60	1.00
6 Diving Griffin C :W:	.20	.35
7 Entangler U :W:	.20	.35
8 Excise C :W:	.20	.35
9 Flowering Field U :W:	.20	.35
10 Glittering Lion U :W:	.20	.35
11 Glittering Lynx C :W:	.20	.35
12 Jeweled Spirit R :W:	.20	.35
13 Mageta the Lion R :W:	.20	.35
14 Mageta's Boon C :W:	.20	.35
15 Mercenary Informer R :W:	.20	.35
16 Mine Bearer C :W:	.20	.35
17 Mirror Strike U :W:	.20	.35
18 Reveille Squad U :W:	.20	.35
19 Rhystic Circle C :W:	.20	.35
20 Rhystic Shield C :W:	.20	.35
21 Samite Sanctuary R :W:	.20	.35
22 Sheltering Prayers R :W:	.20	.35
23 Shield Dancer U :W:	.20	.35
24 Soul Charmer C :W:	.20	.35
25 Sword Dancer U :W:	.20	.35
26 Trenching Steed C :W:	.20	.35
27 Troubled Healer C :W:	.20	.35
28 Alexi's Cloak C :B:	.20	.35
29 Alexi, Zephyr Mage R :B:	.20	.35
30 Avatar of Will R :B:	.20	.35
31 Coastal Hornclaw C :B:	.20	.35
32 Denying Wind R :B:	.20	.35
33 Excavation U :B:	.20	.35
34 Foil U :B:	.20	.35
35 Gulf Squid C :B:	.20	.35
36 Hazy Homunculus C :B:	.20	.35
37 Heightened Awareness R :B:	.20	.35
38 Mana Vapors U :B:	.20	.35
39 Overburden R :B:	2.50	4.00
40 Psychic Theft R :B:	.20	.35
41 Quicksilver Wall U :B:	.20	.35
42 Rethink C :B:	.20	.35
43 Rhystic Deluge C :B:	.20	.35
44 Rhystic Scrying U :B:	.20	.35
45 Rhystic Study C :B:	8.00	10.00
46 Ribbon Snake C :B:	.20	.35
47 Shrouded Serpent R :B:	.20	.35
48 Spiketail Drake U :B:	.20	.35
49 Spiketail Hatchling C :B:	.20	.35
50 Stormwatch Eagle C :B:	.20	.35
51 Sunken Field U :B:	.20	.35
52 Troublesome Spirit R :B:	.20	.35
53 Windscouter U :B:	.20	.35
54 Withdraw C :B:	.20	.35
55 Agent of Shauku C :K:	.20	.35
56 Avatar of Woe R :K:	.20	.35
57 Bog Elemental R :K:	.20	.35
58 Bog Glider C :K:	.20	.35
59 Chilling Apparition U :K:	.20	.35
60 Coffin Puppets R :K:	.20	.35
61 Death Charmer C :K:	.20	.35
62 Despoil C :K:	.20	.35
63 Endbringer's Revel U :K:	.20	.35
64 Fen Stalker C :K:	.20	.35
65 Flay C :K:	.20	.35
66 Greel's Caress C :K:	.20	.35
67 Greel, Mind Raker R :K:	.20	.35
68 Infernal Genesis R :K:	.20	.35
69 Nakaya Shade U :K:	.20	.35
70 Noxious Field U :K:	.20	.35
71 Outbreak U :K:	.20	.35
72 Pit Raptor U :K:	.20	.35
73 Plague Fiend C :K:	.20	.35
74 Plague Wind R :K:	1.50	2.00
75 Rebel Informer R :K:	.20	.35
76 Rhystic Syphon U :K:	.20	.35
77 Rhystic Tutor R :K:	.20	.35

Card	Low	High
78 Soul Strings C :K:	.20	.35
79 Steal Strength C :K:	.20	.35
80 Wall of Vipers U :K:	.20	.35
81 Whipstitched Zombie C :K:	.20	.35
82 Avatar of Fury R :R:	.20	.35
83 Barbed Field U :R:	.20	.35
84 Branded Brawlers C :R:	.20	.35
85 Brutal Suppression U :R:	.20	.35
86 Citadel of Pain U :R:	.20	.35
87 Devastate C :R:	.20	.35
88 Fault Riders C :R:	.20	.35
89 Fickle Efreet R :R:	.20	.35
90 Flameshot U :R:	.20	.35
91 Inflame C :R:	.20	.35
92 Keldon Arsonist U :R:	.20	.35
93 Keldon Berserker C :R:	.20	.35
94 Keldon Firebombers R :R:	.60	1.00
95 Latulla's Orders C :R:	.20	.35
96 Latulla, Keldon Overseer R :R:	.20	.35
97 Lesser Gargadon U :R:	.20	.35
98 Panic Attack C :R:	.20	.35
99 Rhystic Lightning C :R:	.20	.35
100 Ridgeline Rager C :R:	.20	.35
101 Scoria Cat U :R:	.20	.35
102 Search for Survivors R :R:	.20	.35
103 Searing Wind R :R:	.20	.35
104 Spur Grappler C :R:	.20	.35
105 Task Mage Assembly R :R:	.20	.35
106 Veteran Brawlers R :R:	.20	.35
107 Whip Sergeant U :R:	.20	.35
108 Zerapa Minotaur C :R:	.20	.35
109 Avatar of Might R :G:	.20	.35
110 Calming Verse C :G:	.20	.35
111 Darba U :G:	.20	.35
112 Dual Nature R :G:	.20	.35
113 Elephant Resurgence R :G:	.20	.35
114 Forgotten Harvest R :G:	.20	.35
115 Jolrael's Favor C :G:	.20	.35
116 Jolrael, Empress of Beasts R :G:	.20	.35
117 Living Terrain U :G:	.20	.35
118 Marsh Boa C :G:	.20	.35
119 Mungha Wurm R :G:	.20	.35
120 Pygmy Razorback C :G:	.20	.35
121 Rib Cage Spider C :G:	.20	.35
122 Root Cage U :G:	.20	.35
123 Silt Crawler C :G:	.20	.35
124 Snag U :G:	.20	.35
125 Spitting Spider U :G:	.20	.35
126 Spore Frog C :G:	1.50	2.00
127 Squirrel Wrangler R :G:	1.50	2.00
128 Thresher Beast C :G:	.20	.35
129 Thrive C :G:	.20	.35
130 Verdant Field U :G:	.20	.35
131 Vintara Elephant C :G:	.20	.35
132 Vintara Snapper U :G:	.20	.35
133 Vitalizing Wind R :G:	.20	.35
134 Wild Might C :G:	.20	.35
135 Wing Storm U :G:	.20	.35
136 Chimeric Idol U :A:	.20	.35
137 Copper-Leaf Angel R :A:	.20	.35
138 Hollow Warrior U :A:	.20	.35
139 Keldon Battlewagon R :A:	.20	.35
140 Well of Discovery R :A:	.20	.35
141 Well of Life U :A:	.20	.35
142 Rhystic Cave U :L:	.20	.35
143 Wintermoon Mesa R :L:	.20	.35

2000 Magic The Gathering Prophecy Foil

Card	Low	High
COMPLETE SET (143)	250.00	350.00

2000 Magic The Gathering Invasion

Card	Low	High
COMPLETE SET (340)	140.00	200.00
BOOSTER BOX (36 PACKS)	200.00	300.00
BOOSTER PACK (15 CARDS)	8.00	11.00
STARTER BOX (12 DECKS)	110.00	160.00
STARTER DECK	15.00	20.00
FAT PACK	35.00	40.00
RELEASED ON OCTOBER 2, 2000		
1 Alabaster Leech R :W:	.20	.35
2 Angel of Mercy U :W:	.20	.35
3 Ardent Soldier C :W:	.20	.35
4 Atalya, Samite Master R :W:	.20	.35
5 Benalish Emissary U :W:	.20	.35
6 Benalish Heralds U :W:	.20	.35
7 Benalish Lancer C :W:	.20	.35
8 Benalish Trapper C :W:	.20	.35
9 Blinding Light U :W:	.20	.35
10 Capashen Unicorn C :W:	.20	.35
11 Crimson Acolyte C :W:	.20	.35
12 Crusading Knight R :W:	.40	.60
13 Death or Glory R :W:	.20	.35
14 Dismantling Blow C :W:	.20	.35
15 Divine Presence R :W:	.20	.35
16 Fight or Flight R :W:	.20	.35
17 Glimmering Angel C :W:	.20	.35
18 Global Ruin R :W:	.20	.35
19 Harsh Judgment R :W:	.20	.35
20 Holy Day C :W:	.20	.35
21 Liberate U :W:	.20	.35
22 Obsidian Acolyte C :W:	.20	.35
23 Orim's Touch C :W:	.20	.35
24 Pledge of Loyalty U :W:	.20	.35
25 Prison Barricade C :W:	.20	.35
26 Protective Sphere C :W:	.20	.35
27 Pure Reflection R :W:	.20	.35
28 Rampant Elephant C :W:	.20	.35
29 Razorfoot Griffin C :W:	.20	.35
30 Restrain C :W:	.20	.35
31 Reviving Dose C :W:	.20	.35
32 Rewards of Diversity U :W:	.20	.35
33 Reya Dawnbringer R :W:	1.00	1.50
34 Rout R :W:	1.00	1.50
35 Ruham Djinn U :W:	.20	.35
36 Samite Ministration U :W:	.20	.35
37 Shackles C :W:	.20	.35
38 Spirit of Resistance R :W:	.60	.80
39 Spirit Weaver U :W:	.20	.35
40 Strength of Unity C :W:	.20	.35
41 Sunscape Apprentice C :W:	.20	.35
42 Sunscape Master R :W:	.20	.35
43 Teferi's Care U :W:	.20	.35
44 Wayfaring Giant U :W:	.20	.35
45 Winnow R :W:	.20	.35
46 Barrin's Unmaking C :B:	.20	.35
47 Blind Seer R :B:	.20	.35
48 Breaking Wave R :B:	.20	.35
49 Collective Restraint R :B:	5.00	7.00
50 Crystal Spray R :B:	.20	.35
51 Disrupt U :B:	.20	.35
52 Distorting Wake R :B:	.20	.35
53 Dream Thrush C :B:	.20	.35
54 Empress Galina R :B:	13.00	15.00
55 Essence Leak U :B:	.20	.35
56 Exclude C :B:	.20	.35
57 Fact or Fiction U :B:	.60	1.00
58 Faerie Squadron C :B:	.20	.35
59 Mana Maze R :B:	.20	.35
60 Manipulate Fate U :B:	.40	.60
61 Metathran Aerostat R :B:	.20	.35
62 Metathran Transport U :B:	.20	.35
63 Metathran Zombie C :B:	.20	.35
64 Opt C :B:	1.50	2.00
65 Phantasmal Terrain C :B:	.20	.35
66 Probe C :B:	.20	.35
67 Prohibit C :B:	.20	.35
68 Psychic Battle R :B:	.20	.35
69 Rainbow Crow U :B:	.20	.35
70 Repulse C :B:	.20	.35
71 Sapphire Leech R :B:	.20	.35
72 Shimmering Wings C :B:	.20	.35
73 Shoreline Raider C :B:	.20	.35
74 Sky Weaver U :B:	.20	.35
75 Stormscape Apprentice C :B:	.20	.35
76 Stormscape Master R :B:	.20	.35
77 Sway of Illusion U :B:	.20	.35
78 Teferi's Response R :B:	.60	1.00
79 Temporal Distortion R :B:	.20	.35
80 Tidal Visionary C :B:	.20	.35
81 Tolarian Emissary U :B:	.20	.35
82 Tower Drake C :B:	.20	.35
83 Traveler's Cloak C :B:	.20	.35
84 Vodalian Hypnotist U :B:	.20	.35
85 Vodalian Merchant C :B:	.20	.35
86 Vodalian Serpent C :B:	.20	.35
87 Wash Out U :B:	.50	.80
88 Well-Laid Plans R :B:	.20	.35
89 Worldly Counsel C :B:	.20	.35
90 Zanam Djinn U :B:	.20	.35
91 Addle U :K:	.20	.35
92 Agonizing Demise C :K:	.20	.35
93 Andradite Leech R :K:	.20	.35
94 Annihilate U :K:	.20	.35
95 Bog Initiate C :K:	.20	.35
96 Cremate U :K:	.20	.35
97 Crypt Angel R :K:	.50	.80
98 Cursed Flesh C :K:	.20	.35
99 Defiling Tears U :K:	.20	.35
100 Desperate Research R :K:	.20	.35
101 Devouring Strossus R :K:	.20	.35
102 Do or Die R :K:	1.50	2.00
103 Dredge U :K:	.20	.35
104 Duskwalker C :K:	.20	.35
105 Exotic Curse C :K:	.20	.35
106 Firescreamer C :K:	.20	.35
107 Goham Djinn U :K:	.20	.35
108 Hate Weaver U :K:	.20	.35
109 Hypnotic Cloud C :K:	.20	.35
110 Marauding Knight R :K:	.20	.35
111 Mourning C :K:	.20	.35
112 Nightscape Apprentice C :K:	.20	.35
113 Nightscape Master R :K:	.20	.35
114 Phyrexian Battleflies C :K:	.20	.35
115 Phyrexian Delver R :K:	.20	.35
116 Phyrexian Infiltrator R :K:	.20	.35
117 Phyrexian Reaper C :K:	.20	.35
118 Phyrexian Slayer C :K:	.20	.35
119 Plague Spitter U :K:	.20	.35
120 Ravenous Rats C :K:	.20	.35
121 Reckless Spite U :K:	.20	.35
122 Recover C :K:	.20	.35
123 Scavenged Weaponry C :K:	.20	.35
124 Soul Burn C :K:	.20	.35
125 Spreading Plague R :K:	2.50	3.50
126 Tainted Well C :K:	.20	.35
127 Trench Wurm U :K:	.20	.35
128 Tsabo's Assassin R :K:	.20	.35
129 Tsabo's Decree R :K:	.60	1.00
130 Twilight's Call R :K:	.20	.35
131 Urborg Emissary U :K:	.20	.35
132 Urborg Phantom C :K:	.20	.35
133 Urborg Shambler U :K:	.20	.35
134 Urborg Skeleton C :K:	.20	.35
135 Yawgmoth's Agenda R :K:	.20	.35
136 Ancient Kavu C :R:	.20	.35
137 Bend or Break R :R:	.20	.35
138 Breath of Darigaaz U :R:	.20	.35
139 Callous Giant R :R:	.20	.35
140 Chaotic Strike U :R:	.20	.35
141 Collapsing Borders R :R:	.20	.35
142 Crown of Flames C :R:	.20	.35
143 Firebrand Ranger U :R:	.20	.35
144 Ghitu Fire R :R:	.20	.35
145 Goblin Spy U :R:	.20	.35
146 Halam Djinn U :R:	.20	.35
147 Hooded Kavu C :R:	.20	.35
148 Kavu Aggressor C :R:	.20	.35
149 Kavu Monarch R :R:	.20	.35
150 Kavu Runner U :R:	.20	.35
151 Kavu Scout C :R:	.20	.35
152 Lightning Dart U :R:	.20	.35
153 Loafing Giant R :R:	.20	.35
154 Mages' Contest R :R:	.20	.35
155 Maniacal Rage C :R:	.20	.35
156 Obliterate R :R:	1.50	2.50
157 Overload C :R:	.20	.35
158 Pouncing Kavu C :R:	.20	.35
159 Rage Weaver U :R:	.20	.35
160 Rogue Kavu C :R:	.20	.35
161 Ruby Leech R :R:	.20	.35
162 Savage Offensive C :R:	.20	.35
163 Scarred Puma C :R:	.20	.35
164 Scorching Lava C :R:	.20	.35
165 Searing Rays U :R:	.20	.35
166 Shivan Emissary U :R:	.20	.35
167 Shivan Harvest U :R:	.20	.35
168 Skittish Kavu U :R:	.20	.35
169 Skizzik R :R:	.50	.80
170 Slimy Kavu C :R:	.20	.35
171 Stand or Fall R :R:	.20	.35
172 Stun C :R:	.20	.35
173 Tectonic Instability R :R:	.20	.35
174 Thunderscape Apprentice C :R:	.20	.35
175 Thunderscape Master R :R:	.20	.35
176 Tribal Flames C :R:	.20	.35
177 Turf Wound C :R:	.20	.35
178 Urza's Rage R :R:	.50	.80
179 Viashino Grappler C :R:	.20	.35
180 Zap C :R:	.20	.35
181 Aggressive Urge C :G:	.20	.35
182 Bind R :G:	.50	.80
183 Blurred Mongoose R :G:	.20	.35
184 Canopy Surge U :G:	.20	.35
185 Elfhame Sanctuary U :G:	.20	.35
186 Elvish Champion R :G:	4.00	6.00
187 Explosive Growth C :G:	.20	.35
188 Fertile Ground C :G:	.20	.35
189 Harrow C :G:	.20	.35
190 Jade Leech R :G:	.20	.35
191 Kavu Chameleon U :G:	.20	.35
192 Kavu Climber C :G:	.20	.35
193 Kavu Lair R :G:	.20	.35
194 Kavu Titan R :G:	.50	.80
195 Llanowar Cavalry C :G:	.20	.35
196 Llanowar Elite C :G:	.20	.35
197 Llanowar Vanguard C :G:	.20	.35
198 Might Weaver U :G:	.20	.35
199 Molimo, Maro-Sorcerer R :G:	.20	.35
200 Nomadic Elf C :G:	.20	.35
201 Pincer Spider C :G:	.20	.35
202 Pulse of Llanowar U :G:	.20	.35
203 Quirion Elves C :G:	.20	.35
204 Quirion Sentinel C :G:	.20	.35
205 Quirion Trailblazer C :G:	.20	.35
206 Restock R :G:	.20	.35
207 Rooting Kavu U :G:	.20	.35
208 Saproling Infestation R :G:	.20	.35
209 Saproling Symbiosis R :G:	2.00	3.00
210 Scouting Trek U :G:	.20	.35
211 Serpentine Kavu C :G:	.20	.35
212 Sulam Djinn U :G:	.20	.35
213 Tangle U :G:	5.00	7.00
214 Thicket Elemental R :G:	.20	.35
215 Thornscape Apprentice C :G:	.20	.35
216 Thornscape Master R :G:	.20	.35
217 Tranquility C :G:	.20	.35
218 Treefolk Healer U :G:	.20	.35
219 Utopia Tree R :G:	1.00	1.50
220 Verdeloth the Ancient R :G:	.20	.35
221 Verduran Emissary U :G:	.20	.35
222 Vigorous Charge C :G:	.20	.35
223 Wallop U :G:	.20	.35
224 Wandering Stream C :G:	.20	.35
225 Whip Silk C :G:	.20	.35
226 Absorb R :D:	2.00	3.00
227 AEther Rift R :D:	.30	.50
228 Angelic Shield U :D:	.20	.35
229 Armadillo Cloak C :D:	.20	.35
230 Armored Guardian R :D:	.20	.35
231 Artifact Mutation R :D:	1.25	2.00
232 Aura Mutation R :D:	1.00	1.50
233 Aura Shards U :D:	10.00	13.00
234 Backlash U :D:	.20	.35
235 Barrin's Spite R :D:	.20	.35
236 Blazing Specter R :D:	.30	.50
237 Captain Sisay R :D:	15.00	18.00
238 Cauldron Dance U :D:	.20	.35
239 Charging Troll U :D:	.20	.35
240 Cinder Shade U :D:	.20	.35
241 Coalition Victory R :D:	.20	.35
242 Crosis's Attendant U :A:	.20	.35
243 Darigaaz's Attendant U :A:	.20	.35
244 Dromar, the Banisher R :D:	2.00	3.50
245 Dueling Grounds R :D:	2.00	3.50
246 Fires of Yavimaya U :D:	.20	.35
247 Frenzied Tilling C :D:	.20	.35
248 Galina's Knight C :D:	.20	.35
249 Hanna, Ship's Navigator R :D:	2.00	3.00
250 Heroes' Reunion U :D:	.20	.35
251 Horned Cheetah U :D:	.20	.35
252 Hunting Kavu U :D:	.20	.35
253 Kangee, Aerie Keeper R :D:	.50	.80
254 Llanowar Knight C :D:	.20	.35
255 Lobotomy U :D:	.20	.35
256 Meteor Storm R :D:	.20	.35
257 Noble Panther R :D:	.20	.35
258 Ordered Migration U :D:	.20	.35
259 Overabundance R :D:	.20	.35
260 Plague Spores C :D:	.20	.35
261 Pyre Zombie R :D:	.20	.35
262 Raging Kavu R :D:	.20	.35
263 Reckless Assault R :D:	.20	.35
264 Recoil C :D:	.20	.35
265 Reviving Vapors U :D:	.20	.35
266 Riptide Crab U :D:	.20	.35
267 Rith's Attendant U :A:	.20	.35
268 Sabertooth Nishoba R :D:	.20	.35
269 Samite Archer U :D:	.20	.35
270 Seer's Vision U :D:	.20	.35
271 Shivan Zombie C :D:	.20	.35
272 Simoon U :D:	.20	.35
273 Sleeper's Robe U :D:	.20	.35
274 Slinking Serpent U :D:	.20	.35
275 Smoldering Tar U :D:	.20	.35
276 Spinal Embrace R :D:	.20	.35
277 Stalking Assassin R :D:	.20	.35
278 Sterling Grove U :D:	6.00	8.00
279 Teferi's Moat R :D:	.20	.35
280 Treva's Attendant U :A:	.20	.35
281 Tsabo Tavoc R :D:	.60	1.00
282 Undermine R :D:	1.50	2.00
283 Urborg Drake U :D:	.20	.35
284 Vicious Kavu U :D:	.20	.35
285 Vile Consumption R :D:	.40	.60
286 Vodalian Zombie C :D:	.20	.35
287 Void R :D:	.20	.35
288 Voracious Cobra U :D:	.20	.35
289 Wings of Hope C :D:	.20	.35
290 Yavimaya Barbarian C :D:	.20	.35
291 Yavimaya Kavu U :D:	.20	.35
292 Stand/Deliver (Deliver) U :B:	.20	.35
292 Stand/Deliver (Stand) U :W:	.20	.35
293 Spite/Malice (Malice) U :K:	.20	.35
293 Spite/Malice (Spite) U :B:	.20	.35
294 Pain/Suffering (Pain) U :K:	.20	.35
294 Pain/Suffering (Suffering) U :R:	.20	.35
295 Assault/Battery (Assault) U :R:	.20	.35
295 Assault/Battery (Battery) U :G:	.20	.35
296 Wax/Wane (Wane) U :W:	.20	.35
296 Wax/Wane (Wax) U :G:	.20	.35
297 Alloy Golem U :A:	.20	.35
298 Bloodstone Cameo U :A:	.20	.35
299 Chromatic Sphere U :A:	.50	.80
300 Crosis, the Purger R :D:	2.00	3.00
301 Darigaaz, the Igniter R :D:	.60	1.00
302 Drake-Skull Cameo U :A:	.20	.35
303 Dromar's Attendant U :A:	.20	.35
304 Juntu Stakes R :A:	.20	.35
305 Lotus Guardian R :A:	.20	.35
306 Phyrexian Altar R :A:	30.00	35.00
307 Phyrexian Lens R :A:	.20	.35
308 Planar Portal R :A:	2.50	4.00
309 Power Armor U :A:	.20	.35
310 Rith, the Awakener R :D:	1.00	1.50
311 Seashell Cameo U :A:	.20	.35
312 Sparring Golem U :A:	.20	.35
313 Tek R :A:	.20	.35
314 Tigereye Cameo U :A:	.20	.35
315 Treva, the Renewer R :D:	.60	1.00
316 Troll-Horn Cameo U :A:	.20	.35
317 Tsabo's Web R :A:	.60	1.00
318 Urza's Filter R :A:	.50	.80
319 Ancient Spring C :L:	.20	.35
320 Archaeological Dig U :L:	.20	.35
321 Coastal Tower U :L:	.20	.35
322 Elfhame Palace U :L:	.20	.35
323 Geothermal Crevice C :L:	.20	.35
324 Irrigation Ditch C :L:	.20	.35
325 Keldon Necropolis R :L:	.20	.35
326 Salt Marsh U :L:	.20	.35
327 Shivan Oasis U :L:	.20	.35
328 Sulfur Vent C :L:	.20	.35
329 Tinder Farm C :L:	.20	.35
330 Urborg Volcano U :L:	.20	.35
331 Plains C :L:	.20	.35
332 Plains C :L:	.20	.35
333 Plains C :L:	.20	.35
334 Plains C :L:	.20	.35
335 Island C :L:	.20	.35
336 Island C :L:	.20	.35
337 Island C :L:	.20	.35
338 Island C :L:	.20	.35
339 Swamp C :L:	.20	.35
340 Swamp C :L:	.20	.35
341 Swamp C :L:	.20	.35
342 Swamp C :L:	.20	.35
343 Mountain C :L:	.20	.35
344 Mountain C :L:	.20	.35
345 Mountain C :L:	.20	.35
346 Mountain C :L:	.20	.35
347 Forest C :L:	.20	.35
348 Forest C :L:	.20	.35
349 Forest C :L:	.20	.35
350 Forest C :L:	.20	.35

2000 Magic The Gathering Invasion Foil

Card	Low	High
COMPLETE SET (340)	600.00	800.00

2001 Magic The Gathering Planeshift

Card	Low	High
COMPLETE SET (143)	70.00	100.00
BOOSTER BOX (36 PACKS)	175.00	250.00
BOOSTER PACK (15 CARDS)	5.00	8.00
THEME DECK BOX	100.00	125.00
THEME DECK	10.00	13.50
FAT PACK	40.00	50.00
RELEASED ON FEBRUARY 5, 2001		
1 Aura Blast C :W:	.20	.35
2 Aurora Griffin C :W:	.20	.35
3 Disciple of Kangee C :W:	.20	.35
4 Dominaria's Judgment R :W:	.20	.35
5 Guard Dogs U :W:	.20	.35
6 Heroic Defiance C :W:	.20	.35
7 Hobble C :W:	.20	.35
8 Honorable Scout C :W:	.20	.35
9 Lashknife Barrier U :W:	.20	.35
10 March of Souls R :W:	.20	.35
11 Orim's Chant R :W:	4.00	6.00
12 Planeswalker's Mirth R :W:	.20	.35
13 Pollen Remedy C :W:	.20	.35
14 Samite Elder R :W:	.20	.35
15 Samite Pilgrim C :W:	.20	.35
16 Sunscape Battlemage U :W:	.20	.35
17 Sunscape Familiar C :W:	.20	.35
18 Surprise Deployment U :W:	.20	.35
19 Voice of All U :W:	.20	.35
20 Allied Strategies U :B:	.20	.35
21 Arctic Merfolk C :B:	.20	.35
22 Confound C :B:	.20	.35
23 Dralnu's Pet R :B:	.20	.35
24 Ertai's Trickery U :B:	.20	.35
25 Escape Routes C :B:	.20	.35
26 Gainsay U :B:	.20	.35
27 Hunting Drake C :B:	.20	.35
28 Planar Overlay R :B:	.20	.35
29 Planeswalker's Mischief R :B:	.20	.35
30 Rushing River C :B:	.20	.35
31 Sea Snidd C :B:	.20	.35
32 Shifting Sky U :B:	.20	.35
33 Sisay's Ingenuity C :B:	.20	.35

34 Sleeping Potion C :B:	.20	.35
35 Stormscape Battlemage U :B:	.20	.35
36 Stormscape Familiar C :B:	.20	.35
37 Sunken Hope R :B:	.20	.35
38 Waterspout Elemental R :B:	.20	.35
39 Bog Down C :K:	.20	.35
40 Dark Suspicions R :K:	.20	.35
41 Death Bomb C :K:	.20	.35
42 Diabolic Intent R :K:	15.00	20.00
43 Exotic Disease U :K:	.20	.35
44 Lord of the Undead R :K:	8.00	12.00
44 Maggot Carrier C :K:	.20	.35
46 Morgue Toad C :K:	.20	.35
47 Nightscape Battlemage U :K:	.20	.35
48 Nightscape Familiar C :K:	.20	.35
49 Noxious Vapors U :K:	.20	.35
50 Phyrexian Bloodstock C :K:	.20	.35
51 Phyrexian Scuta R :K:	.20	.35
52 Planeswalker's Scorn R :K:	.20	.35
53 Shriek of Dread C :K:	.20	.35
54 Sinister Strength C :K:	.20	.35
55 Slay U :K:	.20	.35
56 Volcano Imp C :K:	.20	.35
57 Warped Devotion U :K:	.20	.35
58 Caldera Kavu C :R:	.20	.35
59 Deadapult R :R:	.20	.35
60 Flametongue Kavu U :R:	.20	.35
61 Goblin Game R :R:	1.50	2.00
62 Implode U :R:	.20	.35
63 Insolence C :R:	.20	.35
64 Kavu Recluse C :R:	.20	.35
65 Keldon Mantle C :R:	.20	.35
66 Magma Burst C :R:	.20	.35
67 Mire Kavu C :R:	.20	.35
68 Mogg Jailer U :R:	.20	.35
69 Mogg Sentry R :R:	.20	.35
70 Planeswalker's Fury R :R:	.20	.35
71 Singe C :R:	.20	.35
72 Slingshot Goblin C :R:	.20	.35
73 Strafe U :R:	.20	.35
74 Tahngarth, Talruum Hero Alt. Art FOIL	90.00	95.00
74 Tahngarth, Talruum Hero R :R:	.20	.35
77 Alpha Kavu U :G:	.20	.35
78 Amphibious Kavu C :G:	.20	.35
79 Falling Timber C :G:	.20	.35
80 Gaea's Herald R :G:	.20	.35
81 Gaea's Might C :G:	.20	.35
82 Magnigoth Treefolk R :G:	.20	.35
83 Mirrorwood Treefolk U :G:	.20	.35
84 Multani's Harmony U :G:	.20	.35
85 Nemata, Grove Guardian R :G:	1.00	1.50
86 Planeswalker's Favor R :G:	.20	.35
87 Primal Growth C :G:	.20	.35
88 Pygmy Kavu C :G:	.20	.35
89 Quirion Dryad R :G:	.20	.35
90 Quirion Explorer C :G:	.20	.35
91 Root Greevil C :G:	.20	.35
92 Skyshroud Blessing U :G:	.20	.35
93 Stone Kavu C :G:	.20	.35
94 Thornscape Battlemage U :G:	.20	.35
95 Thornscape Familiar C :G:	.20	.35
96 Ancient Spider R :D:	.20	.35
97 Cavern Harpy C :D:	.20	.35
98 Cloud Cover R :D:	.20	.35
99 Crosis's Charm U :D:	.20	.35
100 Darigaaz's Charm U :D:	.20	.35
101 Daring Leap C :D:	.20	.35
102 Destructive Flow R :D:	.20	.35
103 Doomsday Specter R :D:	.20	.35
104 Dralnu's Crusade R :D:	.20	.35
105 Dromar's Charm U :D:	.20	.35
106 Eladamri's Call R :D:	8.00	10.00
107 Ertai, the Corrupted R :D:	.20	.35
108 Fleetfoot Panther U :D:	.20	.35
109 Gerrard's Command C :D:	.20	.35
110 Horned Kavu C :D:	.20	.35
111 Hull Breach C :D:	.20	.35
112 Keldon Twilight R :D:	.20	.35
113 Lava Zombie C :D:	.20	.35
114 Malicious Advice C :D:	.20	.35
115 Marsh Crocodile U :D:	.20	.35
116 Meddling Mage R :D:	15.00	20.00
117 Natural Emergence R :D:	.20	.35
118 Phyrexian Tyranny R :D:	2.00	3.00
119 Questing Phelddagrif R :D:	.75	1.25
120 Radiant Kavu R :D:	.20	.35
121 Razing Snidd U :D:	.20	.35
122 Rith's Charm U :D:	.20	.35
123 Sawtooth Loon U :D:	.20	.35
124 Shivan Wurm R :D:	.20	.35
125 Silver Drake C :D:	.20	.35
126 Sparkcaster U :D:	.20	.35
127 Steel Leaf Paladin C :D:	.20	.35
128 Terminate C :D:	.75	1.25
129 Treva's Charm U :D:	.20	.35
130 Urza's Guilt R :D:	.20	.35
131 Draco R :A:	1.00	1.50
132 Mana Cylix U :A:	.20	.35
133 Skyship Weatherlight Alt Art FOIL	50.00	55.00
133 Skyship Weatherlight R :A:	.20	.35
134 Star Compass U :A:	.20	.35
135 Stratadon U :A:	.20	.35
136 Crosis's Catacombs U :L:	.75	1.25
137 Darigaaz's Caldera U :L:	.20	.35
138 Dromar's Cavern U :L:	.20	.35
139 Forsaken City R :L:	.20	.35
140 Meteor Crater R :L:	1.00	1.50
141 Rith's Grove U :L:	.20	.35
142 Terminal Moraine U :L:	.20	.35
143 Treva's Ruins U :L:	.20	.35

2001 Magic The Gathering Planeshift Foil

COMPLETE SET (143)	300.00	500.00

2001 Magic The Gathering Apocalypse

COMPLETE SET (143)	50.00	80.00
BOOSTER BOX (36 PACKS)	200.00	300.00
BOOSTER PACK (15 CARDS)	8.00	12.00
THEME DECK BOX	110.00	150.00
THEME DECK	12.00	15.00
FAT PACK	30.00	60.00
RELEASED ON JUNE 4, 2001		
1 Angelfire Crusader C :W:	.20	.35
2 Coalition Flag U :W:	.20	.35
3 Coalition Honor Guard C :W:	.20	.35
4 Dega Disciple C :W:	.20	.35
5 Dega Sanctuary U :W:	.20	.35
6 Degavolver R :W:	.20	.35
7 Diversionary Tactics U :W:	.20	.35
8 Divine Light C :W:	.20	.35
9 Enlistment Officer U :W:	.20	.35
10 False Dawn R :W:	.20	.35
11 Gerrard Capashen R :W:	.20	.35
12 Haunted Angel U :W:	.20	.35
13 Helionaut C :W:	.20	.35
14 Manacles of Decay C :W:	.20	.35
15 Orim's Thunder C :W:	.20	.35
16 Shield of Duty and Reason C :W:	.20	.35
17 Spectral Lynx R :W:	.20	.35
18 Standard Bearer C :W:	2.50	4.00
19 Ceta Disciple C :B:	.20	.35
20 Ceta Sanctuary U :B:	.20	.35
21 Cetavolver R :B:	.20	.35
22 Coastal Drake C :B:	.20	.35
23 Evasive Action U :B:	.20	.35
24 Ice Cave R :B:	.20	.35
25 Index C :B:	.20	.35
26 Jaded Response C :B:	.20	.35
27 Jilt C :B:	.20	.35
28 Living Airship C :B:	.20	.35
29 Reef Shaman C :B:	.20	.35
30 Shimmering Mirage C :B:	.20	.35
31 Tidal Courier U :B:	.20	.35
32 Unnatural Selection R :B:	.20	.35
33 Vodalian Mystic U :B:	.20	.35
34 Whirlpool Drake U :B:	.20	.35
35 Whirlpool Rider C :B:	.20	.35
36 Whirlpool Warrior R :B:	.20	.35
37 Day/Night U :W:/:K:	.20	.35
38 Desolation Angel R :K:	.60	1.00
39 Foul Presence U :K:	.20	.35
40 Grave Defiler U :K:	.20	.35
41 Last Caress C :K:	.20	.35
42 Mind Extraction C :K:	.20	.35
43 Mournful Zombie C :K:	.20	.35
44 Necra Disciple C :K:	.20	.35
45 Necra Sanctuary U :K:	.20	.35
46 Necravolver R :K:	.20	.35
47 Phyrexian Arena R :K:	5.00	7.00
48 Phyrexian Gargantua U :K:	.20	.35
49 Phyrexian Rager C :K:	.20	.35
50 Planar Despair R :K:	.20	.35
51 Quagmire Druid C :K:	.20	.35
52 Suppress U :K:	.20	.35
53 Urborg Uprising C :K:	.20	.35
54 Zombie Boa C :K:	.20	.35
55 Bloodfire Colossus R :R:	.20	.35
56 Bloodfire Dwarf C :R:	.20	.35
57 Bloodfire Infusion C :R:	.20	.35
58 Bloodfire Kavu U :R:	.20	.35
59 Desolation Giant R :R:	.20	.35
60 Dwarven Landslide C :R:	.20	.35
61 Dwarven Patrol U :R:	.20	.35
62 Goblin Ringleader U :R:	1.00	1.50
63 Illuminate U :R:	.20	.35
64 Kavu Glider C :R:	.20	.35
65 Minotaur Tactician C :R:	.20	.35
66 Raka Disciple C :R:	.20	.35
67 Raka Sanctuary U :R:	.20	.35
68 Rakavolver R :R:	.20	.35
69 Smash C :R:	.20	.35
70 Tahngarth's Glare C :R:	.20	.35
71 Tundra Kavu C :R:	.20	.35
72 Wild Research R :R:	1.00	1.50
73 Ana Disciple C :G:	.20	.35
74 Ana Sanctuary U :G:	.20	.35
75 Anavolver R :G:	.20	.35
76 Bog Gnarr C :G:	.20	.35
77 Gaea's Balance U :G:	.20	.35
78 Glade Gnarr C :G:	.20	.35
79 Kavu Howler U :G:	.20	.35
80 Kavu Mauler R :G:	.20	.35
81 Lay of the Land C :G:	.20	.35
82 Penumbra Bobcat C :G:	.20	.35
83 Penumbra Kavu U :G:	.20	.35
84 Penumbra Wurm R :G:	.20	.35
85 Savage Gorilla C :G:	.20	.35
86 Strength of Night C :G:	.20	.35
87 Sylvan Messenger U :G:	.20	.35
88 Symbiotic Deployment R :G:	.20	.35
89 Tranquil Path C :G:	.20	.35
90 Urborg Elf C :G:	.20	.35
91 AEther Mutation U :D:	.20	.35
92 Captain's Maneuver U :D:	.20	.35
93 Consume Strength C :D:	.20	.35
94 Cromat R :D:	2.00	2.50
95 Death Grasp R :D:	.20	.35
96 Death Mutation U :D:	.20	.35
97 Ebony Treefolk U :D:	.20	.35
98 Fervent Charge R :D:	.20	.35
99 Flowstone Charger U :D:	.20	.35
100 Fungal Shambler R :D:	.20	.35
101 Gaea's Skyfolk C :D:	.20	.35
102 Gerrard's Verdict U :D:	.20	.35
103 Goblin Legionnaire C :D:	.20	.35
104 Goblin Trenches R :D:	.20	.35
105 Guided Passage R :D:	1.00	1.50
106 Jungle Barrier U :D:	.20	.35
107 Last Stand R :D:	.20	.35
108 Lightning Angel R :D:	.20	.35
109 Llanowar Dead C :D:	.20	.35
110 Martyrs' Tomb U :D:	.20	.35
111 Minotaur Illusionist U :D:	.20	.35
112 Mystic Snake R :D:	.60	1.00
113 Overgrown Estate R :D:	.20	.35
114 Pernicious Deed R :D:	3.00	5.00
115 Powerstone Minefield R :D:	.20	.35
116 Prophetic Bolt R :D:	.20	.35
117 Putrid Warrior C :D:	.20	.35
118 Quicksilver Dagger C :D:	.20	.35
119 Razorfin Hunter C :D:	.20	.35
120 Soul Link C :D:	.20	.35
121 Spiritmonger R :D:	.75	1.25
122 Squee's Embrace C :D:	.20	.35
123 Squee's Revenge U :D:	.20	.35
124 Suffocating Blast R :D:	.20	.35
125 Temporal Spring C :D:	.20	.35
126 Vindicate R :D:	5.00	7.00
127 Yavimaya's Embrace R :D:	.20	.35
128 Fire/Ice U :R:/:B:	.20	.35
129 Illusion/Reality U :B:/:G:	.20	.35
130 Death/Life U :G:/:K:	.20	.35
131 Dead Ringers C :K:	.20	.35
132 Chaos/Order U :R:/:W:	.20	.35
133 Brass Herald U :A:	.20	.35
134 Dodecapod U :A:	.20	.35
135 Dragon Arch U :A:	2.50	4.00
136 Emblazoned Golem U :A:	.20	.35
137 Legacy Weapon R :A:	1.00	1.50
138 Mask of Intolerance R :A:	.20	.35
139 Battlefield Forge R :L:	1.50	2.00
140 Caves of Koilos R :L:	2.00	3.00
141 Llanowar Wastes R :L:	2.00	3.00
142 Shivan Reef R :L:	2.50	4.00
143 Yavimaya Coast R :L:	2.00	3.00

2001 Magic The Gathering Odyssey

COMPLETE SET (350)	125.00	200.00
BOOSTER BOX (36 PACKS)	100.00	150.00
BOOSTER PACK (15 CARDS)	7.00	10.00
THEME DECK BOX	75.00	100.00
THEME DECK	9.00	12.00
FAT PACK	30.00	40.00
RELEASED ON SEPTEMBER 21, 2001		
1 Aegis of Honor R :W:	.60	1.00
2 Ancestral Tribute R :W:	.20	.35
3 Angelic Wall C :W:	.20	.35
4 Animal Boneyard U :W:	.20	.35
5 Auramancer C :W:	.20	.35
6 Aven Archer U :W:	.20	.35
7 Aven Cloudchaser C :W:	.20	.35
8 Aven Flock C :W:	.20	.35
9 Aven Shrine R :W:	.20	.35
10 Balancing Act R :W:	.20	.35
11 Beloved Chaplain U :W:	.20	.35
13 Cantivore R :W:	.20	.35
14 Cease-Fire C :W:	.20	.35
15 Confessor C :W:	.20	.35
16 Dedicated Martyr C :W:	.20	.35
17 Delaying Shield R :W:	.75	1.25
18 Devoted Caretaker R :W:	1.00	1.50
19 Divine Sacrament R :W:	.60	1.00
20 Dogged Hunter R :W:	.20	.35
21 Earnest Fellowship R :W:	.20	.35
22 Embolden C :W:	.20	.35
23 Gallantry U :W:	.20	.35
24 Graceful Antelope R :W:	.20	.35
25 Hallowed Healer C :W:	.20	.35
26 Karmic Justice R :W:	2.50	4.00
27 Kirtar's Desire C :W:	.20	.35
28 Kirtar's Wrath R :W:	.20	.35
29 Lieutenant Kirtar R :W:	.20	.35
30 Life Burst C :W:	.20	.35
31 Luminous Guardian U :W:	.20	.35
32 Master Apothecary R :W:	.20	.35
33 Mystic Crusader R :W:	.20	.35
34 Mystic Penitent U :W:	.20	.35
35 Mystic Visionary C :W:	.20	.35
36 Mystic Zealot C :W:	.20	.35
37 Nomad Decoy U :W:	.20	.35
37 Blessed Orator U :W:	.20	.35
38 Patrol Hound C :W:	.20	.35
39 Pianna, Nomad Captain R :W:	.20	.35
40 Pilgrim of Justice C :W:	.20	.35
41 Pilgrim of Virtue C :W:	.20	.35
42 Ray of Distortion C :W:	.20	.35
43 Resilient Wanderer U :W:	.20	.35
44 Sacred Rites C :W:	.20	.35
45 Second Thoughts C :W:	.20	.35
46 Shelter C :W:	.20	.35
47 Soulcatcher U :W:	.20	.35
48 Sphere of Duty U :W:	.20	.35
49 Sphere of Grace U :W:	.20	.35
50 Sphere of Law U :W:	.20	.35
51 Sphere of Reason U :W:	.20	.35
52 Sphere of Truth U :W:	.20	.35
53 Spiritualize U :W:	.20	.35
54 Tattoo Ward U :W:	.20	.35
55 Testament of Faith U :W:	.20	.35
56 Tireless Tribe C :W:	.20	.35
57 Wayward Angel R :W:	.20	.35
58 Aboshan's Desire C :B:	.20	.35
59 Aboshan, Cephalid Emperor R :B:	.20	.35
60 AEther Burst C :B:	.20	.35
61 Amugaba R :B:	.20	.35
62 Aura Graft U :B:	.20	.35
63 Aven Fisher C :B:	.20	.35
64 Aven Smokeweaver U :B:	.20	.35
65 Aven Windreader C :B:	.20	.35
66 Balshan Beguiler U :B:	.20	.35
67 Balshan Griffin U :B:	.20	.35
68 Bamboozle U :B:	.20	.35
69 Battle of Wits R :B:	.20	.35
70 Careful Study C :B:	.20	.35
71 Cephalid Broker U :B:	.20	.35
72 Cephalid Looter C :B:	.20	.35
73 Cephalid Retainer R :B:	.20	.35
74 Cephalid Scout C :B:	.20	.35
75 Cephalid Shrine R :B:	.20	.35
76 Chamber of Manipulation U :B:	.20	.35
77 Cognivore R :B:	.20	.35
78 Concentrate U :B:	.20	.35
79 Cultural Exchange R :B:	2.00	3.00
80 Deluge U :B:	.20	.35
81 Dematerialize C :B:	.20	.35
82 Divert R :B:	1.50	2.00
83 Dreamwinder C :B:	.20	.35
84 Escape Artist C :B:	.20	.35
85 Extract R :B:	1.00	1.50
86 Fervent Denial U :B:	.20	.35
87 Immobilizing Ink C :B:	.20	.35
88 Laquatus's Creativity U :B:	.20	.35
89 Patron Wizard R :B:	14.00	17.00
90 Pedantic Learning R :B:	.20	.35
91 Peek C :B:	.20	.35
92 Persuasion R :B:	.20	.35
93 Phantom Whelp C :B:	.20	.35
94 Predict U :B:	2.00	3.00
95 Psionic Gift C :B:	.20	.35
96 Pulsating Illusion U :B:	.20	.35
97 Puppeteer U :B:	.20	.35
98 Repel C :B:	.20	.35
99 Rites of Refusal C :B:	.20	.35
100 Scrivener C :B:	.20	.35
101 Shifty Doppelganger R :B:	.20	.35
102 Standstill U :B:	2.00	3.00
103 Syncopate C :B:	.20	.35
104 Think Tank U :B:	.20	.35
105 Thought Devourer R :B:	.20	.35
106 Thought Eater U :B:	.20	.35
107 Thought Nibbler C :B:	.20	.35
108 Time Stretch R :B:	8.00	10.00
109 Touch of Invisibility C :B:	.20	.35
110 Traumatize R :B:	1.50	2.00
111 Treetop Sentinel U :B:	.20	.35
112 Unifying Theory R :B:	.20	.35
113 Upheaval R :B:	1.00	1.50
114 Words of Wisdom C :B:	.20	.35
115 Afflict C :K:	.20	.35
116 Bloodcurdler R :K:	.20	.35
117 Braids, Cabal Minion R :K:	.60	1.00
118 Buried Alive U :K:	2.50	4.00
119 Cabal Inquisitor C :K:	.20	.35
120 Cabal Patriarch R :K:	.20	.35
121 Cabal Shrine R :K:	.20	.35
122 Caustic Tar U :K:	.20	.35
123 Childhood Horror U :K:	.20	.35
124 Coffin Purge C :K:	.20	.35
125 Crypt Creeper C :K:	.20	.35
126 Cursed Monstrosity R :K:	.20	.35
127 Decaying Soil R :K:	.20	.35
128 Decompose U :K:	.20	.35
129 Diabolic Tutor U :K:	.20	.35
130 Dirty Wererat C :K:	.20	.35
131 Dusk Imp C :K:	.20	.35
132 Entomb R :K:	15.00	18.00
133 Execute U :K:	.20	.35
134 Face of Fear U :K:	.20	.35
135 Famished Ghoul U :K:	.20	.35
136 Filthy Cur C :K:	.20	.35
137 Fledgling Imp C :K:	.20	.35
138 Frightcrawler C :K:	.20	.35
139 Ghastly Demise C :K:	.20	.35
140 Gravedigger C :K:	.20	.35
141 Gravestorm R :K:	.60	1.00
142 Haunting Echoes R :K:	.20	.35
143 Hint of Insanity R :K:	.20	.35
144 Infected Vermin U :K:	.20	.35
145 Innocent Blood C :K:	.20	.35
146 Last Rites C :K:	.20	.35
147 Malevolent Awakening U :K:	.20	.35
148 Mind Burst C :K:	.20	.35
149 Mindslicer R :K:	3.00	5.00
150 Morbid Hunger C :K:	.20	.35
151 Morgue Theft C :K:	.20	.35
152 Mortivore R :K:	.60	1.00
153 Nefarious Lich R :K:	.20	.35
154 Overeager Apprentice C :K:	.20	.35
155 Painbringer U :K:	.20	.35
156 Patriarch's Desire C :K:	.20	.35
157 Repentant Vampire R :K:	.20	.35
158 Rotting Giant U :K:	.20	.35
159 Sadistic Hypnotist U :K:	2.00	3.00
160 Screams of the Damned U :K:	.20	.35
161 Skeletal Scrying U :K:	.20	.35
162 Skull Fracture U :K:	.20	.35
163 Stalking Bloodsucker R :K:	.20	.35
164 Tainted Pact R :K:	3.00	5.00
165 Tombfire R :K:	.20	.35
166 Traveling Plague R :K:	.20	.35
167 Whispering Shade C :K:	.20	.35
168 Zombie Assassin C :K:	.20	.35
169 Zombie Cannibal C :K:	.20	.35
170 Zombie Infestation U :K:	.20	.35
171 Zombify U :K:	.20	.35
172 Acceptable Losses C :R:	.20	.35
173 Anarchist C :R:	.20	.35
174 Ashen Firebeast R :R:	.20	.35
175 Barbarian Lunatic C :R:	.20	.35
176 Bash to Bits U :R:	.20	.35
177 Battle Strain U :R:	.20	.35
178 Blazing Salvo C :R:	.20	.35
179 Bomb Squad R :R:	.20	.35
180 Burning Sands R :R:	.20	.35
181 Chainflinger C :R:	.20	.35
182 Chance Encounter R :R:	2.50	4.00
183 Demolish U :R:	.20	.35
184 Demoralize C :R:	.20	.35
185 Dwarven Grunt C :R:	.20	.35
186 Dwarven Recruiter U :R:	1.00	1.50
187 Dwarven Shrine R :R:	.20	.35
188 Dwarven Strike Force U :R:	.20	.35
189 Earth Rift C :R:	.20	.35
190 Ember Beast C :R:	.20	.35
191 Engulfing Flames U :R:	.20	.35
192 Epicenter R :R:	.20	.35
193 Firebolt C :R:	.20	.35
194 Flame Burst C :R:	.20	.35
195 Frenetic Ogre U :R:	.20	.35
196 Halberdier C :R:	.20	.35
197 Impulsive Maneuvers R :R:	.20	.35
198 Kamahl's Desire C :R:	.20	.35
199 Kamahl, Pit Fighter R :R:	.20	.35
200 Lava Blister U :R:	.20	.35
201 Liquid Fire U :R:	.20	.35
202 Mad Dog C :R:	.20	.35
203 Magma Vein U :R:	.20	.35

204 Magnivore R :R: .20 .35
205 Mine Layer R :R: 1.00 1.50
206 Minotaur Explorer U :R: .20 .35
207 Molten Influence R :R: 1.00 1.50
208 Mudhole R :R: .20 .35
209 Need for Speed R :R: .20 .35
210 Obstinate Familiar R :R: .20 .35
211 Pardic Firecat C :R: .20 .35
212 Pardic Miner R :R: .20 .35
213 Pardic Swordsmith C :R: .20 .35
214 Price of Glory U :R: 4.00 6.00
215 Reckless Charge C :R: .20 .35
216 Recoup U :R: .20 .35
217 Rites of Initiation C :R: .20 .35
218 Savage Firecat R :R: .20 .35
219 Scorching Missile C :R: .20 .35
220 Seize the Day R :R: 3.00 5.00
221 Shower of Coals U :R: .20 .35
222 Spark Mage U :R: .20 .35
223 Steam Vines U :R: .20 .35
224 Thermal Blast C :R: .20 .35
225 Tremble C :R: .20 .35
226 Volcanic Spray U :R: .20 .35
227 Volley of Boulders R :R: .20 .35
228 Whipkeeper U :R: .20 .35
229 Bearscape R :G: .20 .35
230 Beast Attack U :G: .20 .35
231 Call of the Herd R :G: .20 .35
232 Cartographer C :G: .20 .35
233 Chatter of the Squirrel C :G: .20 .35
234 Chlorophant R :G: .20 .35
235 Crashing Centaur U :G: .20 .35
236 Deep Reconnaissance U :G: .20 .35
237 Diligent Farmhand C :G: .20 .35
238 Druid Lyrist C :G: .20 .35
239 Druid's Call U :G: 1.00 1.50
240 Elephant Ambush C :G: .20 .35
241 Gorilla Titan U :G: .20 .35
242 Ground Seal R :G: .20 .35
243 Holistic Wisdom R :G: .20 .35
244 Howling Gale U :G: .20 .35
245 Ivy Elemental R :G: .20 .35
246 Krosan Archer C :G: .20 .35
247 Krosan Avenger C :G: .20 .35
248 Krosan Beast R :G: 1.00 1.50
249 Leaf Dancer C :G: .20 .35
250 Metamorphic Wurm U :G: .20 .35
251 Moment's Peace C :G: 2.00 3.00
252 Muscle Burst C :G: .20 .35
253 Nantuko Disciple C :G: .20 .35
254 Nantuko Elder U :G: .20 .35
255 Nantuko Mentor R :G: .20 .35
256 Nantuko Shrine R :G: .20 .35
257 New Frontiers R :G: 2.00 3.00
258 Nimble Mongoose U :G: .20 .35
259 Nut Collector R :G: 2.50 4.00
260 Overrun U :G: .20 .35
261 Piper's Melody U :G: .20 .35
262 Primal Frenzy C :G: .20 .35
263 Rabid Elephant C :G: .20 .35
264 Refresh C :G: .20 .35
265 Rites of Spring C :G: .20 .35
266 Roar of the Wurm U :G: .20 .35
267 Seton's Desire C :G: .20 .35
268 Seton, Krosan Protector R :G: .20 .35
269 Simplify C :G: .20 .35
270 Skyshooter U :G: .20 .35
271 Spellbane Centaur R :G: .20 .35
272 Springing Tiger C :G: .20 .35
273 Squirrel Mob R :G: 8.00 10.00
274 Squirrel Nest U :G: .20 .35
275 Still Life U :G: .20 .35
276 Stone-Tongue Basilisk R :G: .20 .35
277 Sylvan Might U :G: .20 .35
278 Terravore R :G: 2.00 3.00
279 Twigwalker U :G: .20 .35
280 Verdant Succession R :G: .20 .35
281 Vivify U :G: .20 .35
282 Werebear C :G: .20 .35
283 Wild Mongrel C :G: .20 .35
284 Woodland Druid C :G: .20 .35
285 Zoologist R :G: .20 .35
286 Atogatog R :D: .20 .35
287 Decimate R :D: 1.50 2.00
288 Iridescent Angel R :D: .60 1.00
289 Lithatog U :D: .20 .35
290 Mystic Enforcer R :D: .20 .35
291 Phantatog U :D: .20 .35
292 Psychatog U :D: .20 .35
293 Sarcatog U :D: .20 .35
294 Shadowmage Infiltrator R :D: .60 1.00
295 Thaumatog U :D: .20 .35
296 Vampiric Dragon R :D: 1.50 2.00
297 Catalyst Stone R :A: .20 .35
298 Charmed Pendant R :A: .20 .35
299 Darkwater Egg U :A: .20 .35
300 Junk Golem R :A: .20 .35
301 Limestone Golem U :A: .20 .35
302 Millikin U :A: .20 .35
303 Mirari R :A: .20 .35
304 Mossfire Egg U :A: .20 .35
305 Otarian Juggernaut R :A: .20 .35
306 Patchwork Gnomes U :A: .20 .35
307 Sandstone Deadfall U :A: .20 .35
308 Shadowblood Egg U :A: .20 .35
309 Skycloud Egg U :A: .20 .35
310 Steamclaw U :A: .20 .35
311 Sungrass Egg U :A: .20 .35
312 Abandoned Outpost C :L: .20 .35
313 Barbarian Ring U :L: .20 .35
314 Bog Wreckage C :L: .20 .35
315 Cabal Pit U :L: .20 .35
316 Centaur Garden U :L: .20 .35
317 Cephalid Coliseum U :L: 1.00 1.50
318 Crystal Quarry R :L: 2.50 4.00
319 Darkwater Catacombs R :L: 2.50 4.00
320 Deserted Temple R :L: 9.00 12.00
321 Mossfire Valley R :L: 2.50 4.00
322 Nomad Stadium U :L: .20 .35
323 Petrified Field R :L: 6.00 8.00
324 Ravaged Highlands C :L: .20 .35
325 Seafloor Debris C :L: .20 .35
326 Shadowblood Ridge R :L: 2.00 2.50
327 Skycloud Expanse R :L: 3.00 5.00
328 Sungrass Prairie R :L: .20 .35
329 Tarnished Citadel R :L: 2.50 4.00
330 Timberland Ruins C :L: .20 .35
331 Plains v1 C :L: .20 .35
332 Plains v2 C :L: .20 .35
333 Plains v3 C :L: .20 .35
334 Plains v4 C :L: .20 .35
335 Island v1 C :L: .20 .35
336 Island v2 C :L: .20 .35
337 Island v3 C :L: .20 .35
338 Island v4 C :L: .20 .35
339 Swamp v1 C :L: .20 .35
340 Swamp v2 C :L: .20 .35
341 Swamp v3 C :L: .20 .35
342 Swamp v4 C :L: .20 .35
343 Mountain v1 C :L: .20 .35
344 Mountain v2 C :L: .20 .35
345 Mountain v3 C :L: .20 .35
346 Mountain v4 C :L: .20 .35
347 Forest v1 C :L: .20 .35
348 Forest v2 C :L: .20 .35
349 Forest v3 C :L: .20 .35
350 Forest v4 C :L: .20 .35

2001 Magic The Gathering Odyssey Foil

COMPLETE SET (350) 500.00 800.00

2002 Magic The Gathering Torment

COMPLETE SET (143) 65.00 95.00
BOOSTER BOX (36 PACKS) 175.00 225.00
BOOSTER PACK (15 CARDS) 7.00 10.00
THEME DECK BOX 120.00 170.00
THEME DECK 12.00 17.00
RELEASED ON FEBRUARY 4, 2002
1 Angel of Retribution R :W: .20 .35
2 Aven Trooper C :W: .20 .35
3 Cleansing Meditation U :W: .20 .35
4 Equal Treatment U :W: .20 .35
5 Floating Shield C :W: .20 .35
7 Hypochondria U :W: .20 .35
8 Major Teroh R :W: .20 .35
9 Militant Monk C :W: .20 .35
10 Morningtide R :W: .20 .35
11 Mystic Familiar C :W: .20 .35
12 Pay No Heed C :W: .20 .35
13 Possessed Nomad R :W: .20 .35
14 Reborn Hero R :W: .20 .35
15 Spirit Flare C :W: .20 .35
16 Stern Judge U :W: .20 .35
17 Strength of Isolation U :W: .20 .35
18 Teroh's Faithful C :W: .20 .35
19 Teroh's Vanguard U :W: .20 .35
20 Transcendence R :W: .50 .75
21 Vengeful Dreams R :W: .20 .35
22 Alter Reality R :B: .20 .35
23 Ambassador Laquatus R :B: .60 1.00
24 Aquamoeba C :B: .20 .35
25 Balshan Collaborator U :B: .20 .35
26 Breakthrough U :B: .20 .35
27 Cephalid Aristocrat C :B: .20 .35
28 Cephalid Illusionist U :B: .20 .35
29 Cephalid Sage U :B: .20 .35
30 Cephalid Snitch C :B: .20 .35
31 Cephalid Vandal R :B: .20 .35
32 Churning Eddy C :B: .20 .35
33 Circular Logic U :B: 4.00 6.00
34 Compulsion U :B: .20 .35
35 Coral Net C :B: .20 .35
36 Deep Analysis C :B: .20 .35
37 False Memories R :B: .20 .35
38 Ghostly Wings C :B: .20 .35
39 Hydromorph Guardian C :B: .20 .35
40 Hydromorph Gull U :B: .20 .35
41 Liquify C :B: .20 .35
42 Llawan, Cephalid Empress R :B: .60 1.00
43 Obsessive Search C :B: .20 .35
44 Plagiarize R :B: .20 .35
45 Possessed Aven R :B: .20 .35
46 Retraced Image R :B: .20 .35
47 Skywing Aven C :B: .20 .35
48 Stupefying Touch U :B: .20 .35
49 Turbulent Dreams R :B: .20 .35
50 Boneshard Slasher U :K: .20 .35
51 Cabal Ritual C :K: 1.00 1.50
52 Cabal Surgeon C :K: .20 .35
52 Frantic Purification C :W: .20 .35
53 Cabal Torturer C :K: .20 .35
54 Carrion Rats C :K: .20 .35
55 Carrion Wurm U :K: .20 .35
56 Chainer's Edict U :K: 7.00 10.00
57 Chainer, Dementia Master R :K: 2.00 3.00
58 Crippling Fatigue C :K: .20 .35
59 Dawn of the Dead R :K: .20 .35
60 Faceless Butcher C :K: .20 .35
61 Gloomdrifter U :K: .20 .35
62 Gravegouger C :K: .20 .35
63 Grotesque Hybrid U :K: .20 .35
64 Hypnox R :K: .20 .35
65 Ichorid R :K: 1.50 2.00
66 Insidious Dreams R :K: 2.00 3.00
67 Laquatus's Champion R :K: .20 .35
68 Last Laugh R :K: .20 .35
69 Mesmeric Fiend C :K: .20 .35
70 Mind Sludge U :K: .20 .35
71 Mortal Combat R :K: .40 .60
72 Mortiphobia U :K: .20 .35
73 Mutilate R :K: .60 1.00
74 Nantuko Shade R :K: .40 .60
75 Organ Grinder C :K: .20 .35
76 Psychotic Haze C :K: .20 .35
77 Putrid Imp C :K: .20 .35
78 Rancid Earth C :K: .20 .35
79 Restless Dreams C :K: .20 .35
80 Sengir Vampire R :K: .20 .35
81 Shade's Form C :K: .20 .35
82 Shambling Swarm R :K: .20 .35
83 Sickening Dreams U :K: .20 .35
84 Slithery Stalker U :K: .20 .35
85 Soul Scourge C :K: .20 .35
86 Strength of Lunacy U :K: .20 .35
87 Unhinge C :K: .20 .35
88 Waste Away C :K: .20 .35
89 Zombie Trailblazer U :K: .50 .80
90 Accelerate C :R: .20 .35
91 Balthor the Stout R :R: .20 .35
92 Barbarian Outcast C :R: .20 .35
93 Crackling Club C :R: .20 .35
94 Crazed Firecat U :R: .20 .35
95 Devastating Dreams R :R: .40 .60
96 Enslaved Dwarf C :R: .20 .35
97 Fiery Temper C :R: .20 .35
98 Flaming Gambit U :R: .20 .35
99 Flash of Defiance C :R: .20 .35
100 Grim Lavamancer R :R: 7.00 9.00
101 Hell-Bent Raider R :R: .20 .35
102 Kamahl's Sledge C :R: .20 .35
103 Longhorn Firebeast C :R: .20 .35
104 Overmaster R :R: .75 1.25
105 Pardic Arsonist U :R: .20 .35
106 Pardic Collaborator U :R: .20 .35
107 Pardic Lancer C :R: .20 .35
108 Petradon R :R: .20 .35
109 Petravark C :R: .20 .35
110 Pitchstone Wall U :R: .20 .35
111 Possessed Barbarian R :R: .20 .35
112 Pyromania U :R: .20 .35
113 Radiate R :R: 1.00 1.50
114 Skullscorch R :R: .20 .35
115 Sonic Seizure C :R: .20 .35
116 Temporary Insanity U :R: .20 .35
117 Violent Eruption U :R: .20 .35
118 Acorn Harvest C :G: .20 .35
119 Anurid Scavenger U :G: .20 .35
120 Arrogant Wurm U :G: .20 .35
121 Basking Rootwalla C :G: .20 .35
122 Centaur Chieftain U :G: .20 .35
123 Centaur Veteran C :G: .20 .35
124 Dwell on the Past U :G: .20 .35
125 Far Wanderings C :G: .20 .35
126 Gurzigost R :G: .20 .35
127 Insist R :G: .20 .35
128 Invigorating Falls C :G: .20 .35
129 Krosan Constrictor C :G: .20 .35
130 Krosan Restorer C :G: .20 .35
131 Nantuko Blightcutter R :G: .20 .35
132 Nantuko Calmer C :G: .20 .35
133 Nantuko Cultivator R :G: .20 .35
134 Narcissism U :G: .20 .35
135 Nostalgic Dreams R :G: .20 .35
136 Parallel Evolution R :G: 2.50 4.00
137 Possessed Centaur R :G: .20 .35
138 Seton's Scout U :G: .20 .35
139 Cabal Coffers U :L: 20.00 25.00
140 Tainted Field U :L: .50 .80
141 Tainted Isle U :L: 1.50 2.00
142 Tainted Peak U :L: 2.00 3.00
143 Tainted Wood U :L: .20 .35

2002 Magic The Gathering Torment Foil

COMPLETE SET (143) 275.00 350.00

2002 Magic The Gathering Judgment

COMPLETE SET (143) 85.00 125.00
BOOSTER BOX (36 PACKS) 200.00 275.00
BOOSTER PACK (15 CARDS) 7.00 9.00
THEME DECK BOX 140.00 200.00
THEME DECK 15.00 20.00
FAT PACK 40.00 50.00
RELEASED ON MAY 27, 2002
1 Ancestor's Chosen U :W: .10 .20
3 Battle Screech U :W: 6.00 8.00
4 Battlewise Aven C :W: .10 .20
5 Benevolent Bodyguard C :W: .10 .20
6 Border Patrol C :W: .10 .20
7 Cagemail C :W: .10 .20
8 Chastise U :W: .10 .20
9 Commander Eesha R :W: 1.00 1.50
10 Funeral Pyre C :W: .10 .20
11 Glory R :W: 1.25 2.00
12 Golden Wish R :W: .10 .20
13 Guided Strike C :W: .10 .20
14 Lead Astray C :W: .10 .20
15 Nomad Mythmaker R :W: 1.00 1.50
16 Phantom Flock U :W: .10 .20
17 Phantom Nomad C :W: .10 .20
18 Prismatic Strands C :W: 1.50 2.50
19 Pulsemage Advocate R :W: .40 .60
20 Ray of Revelation C :W: .10 .20
21 Selfless Exorcist R :W: .10 .20
22 Shieldmage Advocate C :W: .10 .20
23 Silver Seraph R :W: .40 .60
24 Solitary Confinement R :W: .10 .20
25 Soulcatchers' Aerie U :W: .60 1.00
26 Spirit Cairn U :W: .10 .20
27 Spurnmage Advocate U :W: .10 .20
28 Suntail Hawk C :W: .10 .20
29 Test of Endurance R :W: 7.00 9.00
30 Trained Pronghorn C :W: .10 .20
31 Unquestioned Authority U :W: .20 .35
32 Valor U :W: .10 .20
33 Vigilant Sentry C :W: .10 .20
34 Aven Fogbringer C :B: .10 .20
35 Cephalid Constable R :B: .40 .60
36 Cephalid Inkshrouder U :B: .10 .20
37 Cunning Wish R :B: 6.00 8.00
38 Defy Gravity C :B: .10 .20
39 Envelop C :B: .10 .20
40 Flash of Insight U :B: .10 .20
41 Grip of Amnesia C :B: .10 .20
42 Hapless Researcher C :B: .10 .20
43 Keep Watch C :B: .10 .20
44 Laquatus's Disdain U :B: .10 .20
45 Lost in Thought C :B: .10 .20
46 Mental Note C :B: .10 .20
47 Mirror Wall C :B: .10 .20
48 Mist of Stagnation R :B: .10 .20
49 Quiet Speculation U :B: .10 .20
50 Scalpelexis R :B: .10 .20
51 Spelljack R :B: 3.00 5.00
52 Telekinetic Bonds R :B: .10 .20
53 Web of Inertia U :B: .10 .20
54 Wonder U :B: .10 .20
55 Wormfang Behemoth R :B: .10 .20
56 Wormfang Crab U :B: .10 .20
57 Wormfang Drake C :B: .10 .20
58 Wormfang Manta R :B: .10 .20
59 Wormfang Newt C :B: .10 .20
60 Wormfang Turtle U :B: .10 .20
61 Balthor the Defiled R :K: 3.00 4.00
62 Cabal Therapy U :K: 3.00 4.00
63 Cabal Trainee C :K: .10 .20
64 Death Wish R :K: .40 .60
65 Earsplitting Rats C :K: .10 .20
66 Filth U :K: 1.00 1.50
67 Grave Consequences U :K: .10 .20
68 Guiltfeeder R :K: 1.00 1.50
69 Masked Gorgon R :K: .10 .20
70 Morality Shift R :K: .10 .20
71 Rats' Feast C :K: .10 .20
72 Stitch Together U :K: .60 1.00
73 Sutured Ghoul R :K: .10 .20
74 Toxic Stench C :K: .10 .20
75 Treacherous Vampire U :K: .10 .20
76 Treacherous Werewolf C :K: .10 .20
77 Anger U :R: 2.50 3.50
78 Arcane Teachings C :R: .10 .20
79 Barbarian Bully C :R: .10 .20
8 Aven Warcraft U :W: .10 .20
80 Book Burning C :R: .10 .20
81 Breaking Point R :R: .60 1.00
82 Browbeat U :R: 1.00 1.50
83 Burning Wish R :R: 3.00 4.00
84 Dwarven Bloodboiler R :R: .10 .20
85 Dwarven Driller U :R: .40 .60
86 Dwarven Scorcher C :R: .10 .20
87 Ember Shot C :R: .10 .20
88 Firecat Blitz U :R: .10 .20
89 Flaring Pain C :R: .10 .20
90 Fledgling Dragon R :R: .50 .80
91 Goretusk Firebeast C :R: .10 .20
92 Infectious Rage U :R: .10 .20
93 Jeska, Warrior Adept R :R: .50 .80
94 Lava Dart C :R: .10 .20
95 Liberated Dwarf C :R: .10 .20
96 Lightning Surge R :R: .10 .20
97 Planar Chaos U :R: .60 1.00
98 Shaman's Trance R :R: .10 .20
99 Soulgorger Orgg U :R: .10 .20
100 Spellgorger Barbarian C :R: .10 .20
101 Swelter U :R: .10 .20
102 Swirling Sandstorm C :R: .10 .20
103 Worldgorger Dragon R :R: .75 1.25
104 Anurid Barkripper C :G: .10 .20
105 Anurid Swarmsnapper U :G: .10 .20
106 Battlefield Scrounger C :G: .10 .20
107 Brawn U :G: .25 .40
108 Canopy Claws C :G: .10 .20
109 Centaur Rootcaster C :G: .10 .20
110 Crush of Wurms R :G: .75 1.25
111 Elephant Guide U :G: .10 .20
112 Epic Struggle R :G: 1.50 2.00
113 Erhnam Djinn R :G: .10 .20
114 Exoskeletal Armor U :G: .10 .20
115 Folk Medicine C :G: .10 .20
116 Forcemage Advocate U :G: .10 .20
117 Genesis R :G: 4.00 6.00
118 Giant Warthog C :G: .10 .20
119 Grizzly Fate U :G: .10 .20
120 Harvester Druid C :G: .10 .20
121 Ironshell Beetle C :G: .10 .20
122 Krosan Reclamation U :G: .10 .20
123 Krosan Wayfarer C :G: .10 .20
124 Living Wish R :G: 3.00 5.00
125 Nantuko Tracer C :G: .10 .20
126 Nullmage Advocate C :G: .10 .20
127 Phantom Centaur U :G: .10 .20
128 Phantom Nantuko R :G: .10 .20
129 Phantom Tiger C :G: .10 .20
130 Seedtime R :G: 1.50 2.00
131 Serene Sunset U :G: .10 .20
132 Sudden Strength C :G: .10 .20
133 Sylvan Safekeeper R :G: 1.50 2.50
134 Thriss, Nantuko Primus R :G: .10 .20
135 Tunneler Wurm U :G: .10 .20
136 Venomous Vines C :G: .10 .20
137 Anurid Brushhopper R :D: .10 .20
138 Hunting Grounds R :D: 2.50 3.50
139 Mirari's Wake R :D: 9.00 12.00
140 Phantom Nishoba R :D: .75 1.25
141 Krosan Verge U :L: .60 1.00
142 Nantuko Monastery U :L: .10 .20
143 Riftstone Portal U :L: .40 .60

2002 Magic The Gathering Judgment Foil

COMPLETE SET (143) 300.00 400.00

2002 Magic The Gathering Onslaught

COMPLETE SET (350) 265.00 365.00
BOOSTER BOX 300.00 350.00
BOOSTER PACK 7.00 9.00
THEME DECK BOX 90.00 110.00
THEME DECK 10.00 14.00
FAT PACK 40.00 50.00
RELEASED ON OCTOBER 7, 2002
1 Akroma's Blessing U :W: .20 .35
2 Akroma's Vengeance R :W: .60 1.00
3 Ancestor's Prophet R :W: .20 .35
4 Astral Slide U :W: .20 .35
5 Aura Extraction U :W: .20 .35
6 Aurification R :W: 2.00 3.00
7 Aven Brigadier R :W: .60 1.00
8 Aven Soulgazer U :W: .20 .35
9 Battlefield Medic C :W: .20 .35
10 Catapult Master R :W: .20 .35
11 Catapult Squad U :W: .20 .35

12 Chain of Silence U :W: .20 .35
13 Circle of Solace R :W: .20 .35
14 Convalescent Care R :W: .20 .35
15 Crowd Favorites U :W: .20 .35
16 Crown of Awe C :W: .20 .35
17 Crude Rampart U :W: .20 .35
18 Daru Cavalier C :W: .20 .35
19 Daru Healer C :W: .20 .35
20 Daru Lancer C :W: .20 .35
21 Daunting Defender C :W: .20 .35
22 Dawning Purist U :W: .20 .35
23 Defensive Maneuvers C :W: .20 .35
24 Demystify C :W: .20 .35
25 Disciple of Grace C :W: .20 .35
26 Dive Bomber C :W: .20 .35
27 Doubtless One U :W: .20 .35
28 Exalted Angel R :W: 1.50 2.00
29 Foothill Guide C :W: .20 .35
30 Glarecaster R :W: .20 .35
31 Glory Seeker C :W: .20 .35
32 Grassland Crusader C :W: .20 .35
33 Gravel Slinger C :W: .20 .35
34 Gustcloak Harrier C :W: .20 .35
35 Gustcloak Runner C :W: .20 .35
36 Gustcloak Savior R :W: .20 .35
37 Gustcloak Sentinel U :W: .20 .35
38 Gustcloak Skirmisher U :W: .20 .35
39 Harsh Mercy R :W: 3.00 5.00
40 Improvised Armor U :W: .20 .35
41 Inspirit U :W: .20 .35
42 Ironfist Crusher U :W: .20 .35
43 Jareth, Leonine Titan R :W: 1.00 1.50
43 Cabal Archon U :K: .20 .35
44 Mobilization R :W: .20 .35
45 Nova Cleric U :W: .20 .35
46 Oblation R :W: .20 .35
47 Pacifism C :W: .20 .35
48 Pearlspear Courier U :W: .20 .35
49 Piety Charm C :W: .20 .35
50 Renewed Faith C :W: .20 .35
51 Righteous Cause U :W: .20 .35
52 Sandskin C :W: .20 .35
53 Shared Triumph R :W: 1.50 2.00
54 Shieldmage Elder U :W: .20 .35
55 Sigil of the New Dawn R :W: .20 .35
56 Sunfire Balm U :W: .20 .35
57 True Believer R :W: .60 1.00
58 Unified Strike C :W: .20 .35
59 Weathered Wayfarer R :W: 10.00 12.00
60 Whipcorder U :W: .20 .35
61 Words of Worship R :W: .60 1.00
62 Airborne Aid C :B: .20 .35
63 Annex U :B: .20 .35
64 Aphetto Alchemist U :B: 1.50 2.50
65 Aphetto Grifter U :B: .20 .35
66 Arcanis the Omnipotent R :B: 1.50 2.00
67 Artificial Evolution R :B: .20 .35
68 Ascending Aven C :B: .20 .35
69 Aven Fateshaper U :B: .20 .35
70 Backslide C :B: .20 .35
71 Blatant Thievery R :B: 1.50 2.00
72 Callous Oppressor R :B: .20 .35
73 Chain of Vapor U :B: .60 1.00
74 Choking Tethers C :B: .20 .35
75 Clone R :B: .20 .35
76 Complicate U :B: .20 .35
77 Crafty Pathmage C :B: .20 .35
78 Crown of Ascension C :B: .20 .35
79 Discombobulate U :B: .20 .35
80 Dispersing Orb U :B: .20 .35
81 Disruptive Pitmage C :B: .20 .35
82 Essence Fracture U :B: .20 .35
83 Fleeting Aven U :B: .20 .35
84 Future Sight R :B: .60 1.00
85 Ghosthelm Courier U :B: .20 .35
86 Graxiplon U :B: .20 .35
87 Imagecrafter C :B: .20 .35
88 Information Dealer C :B: .20 .35
89 Ixidor's Will C :B: .20 .35
90 Ixidor, Reality Sculptor R :B: .20 .35
91 Mage's Guile C :B: .20 .35
92 Meddle U :B: .20 .35
93 Mistform Dreamer C :B: .20 .35
94 Mistform Mask C :B: .20 .35
95 Mistform Mutant U :B: .20 .35
96 Mistform Shrieker U :B: .20 .35
97 Mistform Skyreaver R :B: .20 .35
98 Mistform Stalker U :B: .20 .35
99 Mistform Wall C :B: .20 .35
100 Nameless One U :B: .20 .35
101 Peer Pressure R :B: .20 .35
102 Psychic Trance R :B: .20 .35
103 Quicksilver Dragon R :B: .20 .35
104 Read the Runes R :B: .20 .35
105 Reminisce U :B: .20 .35
106 Riptide Biologist C :B: .20 .35
107 Riptide Chronologist U :B: .20 .35
108 Riptide Entrancer R :B: .20 .35
109 Riptide Shapeshifter U :B: .20 .35
110 Rummaging Wizard U :B: .20 .35
111 Sage Aven C :B: .20 .35
112 Screaming Seahawk C :B: .20 .35
113 Sea's Claim C :B: .20 .35
114 Slipstream Eel C :B: .20 .35
115 Spy Network C :B: .20 .35
116 Standardize R :B: .20 .35
117 Supreme Inquisitor R :B: 2.00 3.00
118 Trade Secrets R :B: .20 .35
119 Trickery Charm C :B: .20 .35
120 Voidmage Prodigy R :B: 2.50 4.00
121 Wheel and Deal R :B: 3.00 5.00
122 Words of Wind R :B: .20 .35
123 Accursed Centaur C :K: .20 .35
124 Anurid Murkdiver C :K: .20 .35
125 Aphetto Dredging C :K: .20 .35
126 Aphetto Vulture U :K: .20 .35
127 Blackmail U :K: 2.00 2.50
128 Boneknitter U :K: .20 .35
130 Cabal Executioner U :K: .20 .35
131 Cabal Slaver U :K: .20 .35
132 Chain of Smog U :K: .20 .35
133 Cover of Darkness R :K: 6.00 8.00
134 Crown of Suspicion C :K: .20 .35
135 Cruel Revival C :K: .20 .35
136 Death Match R :K: .20 .35
137 Death Pulse U :K: .20 .35
138 Dirge of Dread C :K: .20 .35
139 Disciple of Malice C :K: .20 .35
140 Doomed Necromancer R :K: 2.00 2.50
141 Ebonblade Reaper R :K: .20 .35
142 Endemic Plague R :K: .20 .35
143 Entrails Feaster R :K: .20 .35
144 Fade from Memory U :K: .20 .35
145 Fallen Cleric C :K: .20 .35
146 False Cure R :K: 1.50 2.00
147 Feeding Frenzy U :K: .20 .35
148 Festering Goblin C :K: .20 .35
149 Frightshroud Courier U :K: .20 .35
150 Gangrenous Goliath R :K: .20 .35
151 Gluttonous Zombie U :K: .20 .35
152 Gravespawn Sovereign R :K: 2.00 3.00
153 Grinning Demon R :K: .20 .35
154 Haunted Cadaver C :K: .20 .35
155 Head Games R :K: .20 .35
156 Headhunter U :K: .20 .35
157 Infest U :K: .20 .35
158 Misery Charm C :K: .20 .35
159 Nantuko Husk C :K: .20 .35
160 Oversold Cemetery R :K: 4.00 6.00
161 Patriarch's Bidding R :K: 15.00 18.00
162 Profane Prayers C :K: .20 .35
163 Prowling Pangolin U :K: .20 .35
164 Rotlung Reanimator R :K: 2.00 2.50
165 Screeching Buzzard C :K: .20 .35
166 Severed Legion C :K: .20 .35
167 Shade's Breath U :K: .20 .35
168 Shepherd of Rot C :K: .20 .35
169 Silent Specter R :K: .20 .35
170 Smother U :K: .20 .35
171 Soulless One U :K: 1.00 1.50
172 Spined Basher C :K: .20 .35
173 Strongarm Tactics R :K: .20 .35
174 Swat C :K: .20 .35
175 Syphon Mind C :K: .20 .35
176 Syphon Soul C :K: .20 .35
177 Thrashing Mudspawn U :K: .20 .35
178 Undead Gladiator R :K: .60 1.00
179 Visara the Dreadful R :K: 1.50 2.00
180 Walking Desecration U :K: .20 .35
181 Withering Hex U :K: .20 .35
182 Words of Waste R :K: 1.00 1.50
183 Wretched Anurid C :K: .20 .35
184 AEther Charge U :R: .20 .35
185 Aggravated Assault R :R: 10.00 13.00
186 Airdrop Condor U :R: .20 .35
187 Avarax U :R: .20 .35
188 Battering Craghorn C :R: .20 .35
189 Blistering Firecat R :R: 1.00 1.50
190 Break Open C :R: .20 .35
191 Brightstone Ritual C :R: .20 .35
192 Butcher Orgg R :R: .20 .35
193 Chain of Plasma U :R: .20 .35
194 Charging Slateback C :R: .20 .35
195 Commando Raid U :R: .20 .35
196 Crown of Fury C :R: .20 .35
197 Custody Battle U :R: .20 .35
198 Dragon Roost R :R: .20 .35
199 Dwarven Blastminer U :R: .20 .35
200 Embermage Goblin U :R: .20 .35
201 Erratic Explosion C :R: .20 .35
202 Fever Charm C :R: .20 .35
203 Flamestick Courier U :R: .20 .35
204 Goblin Machinist U :R: .20 .35
205 Goblin Piledriver R :R: 3.00 5.00
206 Goblin Pyromancer R :R: .20 .35
207 Goblin Sharpshooter R :R: 2.00 2.50
208 Goblin Sky Raider C :R: .20 .35
209 Goblin Sledder C :R: .20 .35
210 Goblin Taskmaster C :R: .20 .35
211 Grand Melee R :R: .20 .35
212 Gratuitous Violence R :R: 1.50 2.00
213 Insurrection R :R: 4.00 6.00
214 Kaboom! R :R: .20 .35
215 Lavamancer's Skill C :R: .20 .35
216 Lay Waste C :R: .20 .35
217 Lightning Rift U :R: .20 .35
218 Mana Echoes R :R: 18.00 22.00
219 Menacing Ogre R :R: .20 .35
220 Nosy Goblin C :R: .20 .35
221 Pinpoint Avalanche C :R: .20 .35
222 Reckless One U :R: .20 .35
223 Risky Move R :R: .20 .35
224 Rorix Bladewing R :R: .20 .35
225 Searing Flesh U :R: .20 .35
226 Shaleskin Bruiser U :R: .20 .35
227 Shock C :R: .20 .35
228 Skirk Commando C :R: .20 .35
229 Skirk Fire Marshal R :R: .20 .35
230 Skirk Prospector C :R: .60 1.00
231 Skittish Valesk U :R: .20 .35
232 Slice and Dice U :R: .20 .35
233 Snapping Thragg U :R: .20 .35
234 Solar Blast C :R: .20 .35
235 Sparksmith C :R: .20 .35
236 Spitfire Handler U :R: .20 .35
237 Spurred Wolverine C :R: .20 .35
238 Starstorm R :R: .20 .35
239 Tephraderm R :R: .20 .35
240 Thoughtbound Primoc U :R: .20 .35
241 Threaten U :R: .20 .35
242 Thunder of Hooves U :R: .20 .35
243 Wave of Indifference C :R: .20 .35
244 Words of War R :R: .20 .35
245 Animal Magnetism R :G: .20 .35
246 Barkhide Mauler C :G: .20 .35
247 Biorhythm R :G: .20 .35
248 Birchlore Rangers C :G: .20 .35
249 Bloodline Shaman U :G: .20 .35
250 Broodhatch Nantuko U :G: .20 .35
251 Centaur Glade U :G: .20 .35
252 Chain of Acid U :G: .20 .35
253 Crown of Vigor C :G: .20 .35
254 Elven Riders U :G: .20 .35
255 Elvish Guidance C :G: .20 .35
256 Elvish Pathcutter C :G: .20 .35
257 Elvish Pioneer C :G: .20 .35
258 Elvish Scrapper U :G: .20 .35
259 Elvish Vanguard R :G: 1.50 2.00
260 Elvish Warrior C :G: .20 .35
261 Enchantress's Presence R :G: 8.00 10.00
262 Everglove Courier U :G: .20 .35
263 Explosive Vegetation U :G: .60 1.00
264 Gigapede R :G: .20 .35
265 Heedless One U :G: .60 1.00
266 Hystrodon R :G: .20 .35
267 Invigorating Boon U :G: .20 .35
268 Kamahl's Summons U :G: .20 .35
269 Kamahl, Fist of Krosa R :G: 3.00 5.00
270 Krosan Colossus R :G: .20 .35
271 Krosan Groundshaker U :G: .20 .35
272 Krosan Tusker C :G: .20 .35
273 Leery Fogbeast C :G: .20 .35
274 Mythic Proportions R :G: .20 .35
275 Naturalize C :G: .20 .35
276 Overwhelming Instinct U :G: .20 .35
277 Primal Boost U :G: .20 .35
278 Ravenous Baloth R :G: .20 .35
279 Run Wild U :G: .20 .35
280 Serpentine Basilisk U :G: .20 .35
281 Silklash Spider R :G: .20 .35
282 Silvos, Rogue Elemental R :G: 1.00 1.50
283 Snarling Undorak C :G: .20 .35
284 Spitting Gourna C :G: .20 .35
285 Stag Beetle R :G: .20 .35
286 Steely Resolve R :G: 6.00 8.00
287 Symbiotic Beast U :G: .20 .35
288 Symbiotic Elf C :G: .20 .35
289 Symbiotic Wurm R :G: .20 .35
290 Taunting Elf C :G: .20 .35
291 Tempting Wurm R :G: .20 .35
292 Towering Baloth U :G: .20 .35
293 Treespring Lorian C :G: .20 .35
294 Tribal Unity U :G: .20 .35
295 Venomspout Brackus U :G: .20 .35
296 Vitality Charm C :G: .20 .35
297 Voice of the Woods R :G: .20 .35
298 Wall of Mulch U :G: .20 .35
299 Weird Harvest R :G: .20 .35
300 Wellwisher C :G: .60 1.00
301 Wirewood Elf C :G: .20 .35
302 Wirewood Herald C :G: .20 .35
303 Wirewood Pride C :G: .20 .35
304 Wirewood Savage C :G: .20 .35
305 Words of Wilding R :G: .20 .35
306 Cryptic Gateway R :A: 4.00 6.00
307 Doom Cannon R :A: .20 .35
308 Dream Chisel R :A: .20 .35
309 Riptide Replicator R :A: .60 1.00
310 Slate of Ancestry R :A: 2.00 2.50
311 Tribal Golem R :A: .20 .35
312 Barren Moor C :L: .20 .35
313 Bloodstained Mire R :L: 30.00 35.00
314 Contested Cliffs R :L: .20 .35
315 Daru Encampment U :L: .20 .35
316 Flooded Strand R :L: 25.00 30.00
317 Forgotten Cave C :L: .20 .35
318 Goblin Burrows U :L: .20 .35
319 Grand Coliseum R :L: 1.50 2.00
320 Lonely Sandbar C :L: .20 .35
321 Polluted Delta R :L: 30.00 35.00
322 Riptide Laboratory R :L: 12.00 15.00
323 Seaside Haven U :L: .20 .35
324 Secluded Steppe C :L: .20 .35
325 Starlit Sanctum U :L: .20 .35
326 Tranquil Thicket C :L: .20 .35
327 Unholy Grotto R :L: 4.00 6.00
328 Windswept Heath R :L: 18.00 22.00
329 Wirewood Lodge U :L: 1.50 2.50
330 Wooded Foothills R :L: 25.00 30.00
331 Plains C :L: .20 .35
332 Plains C :L: .20 .35
333 Plains C :L: .20 .35
334 Plains C :L: .20 .35
335 Island C :L: .20 .35
336 Island C :L: .20 .35
337 Island C :L: .20 .35
338 Island C :L: .20 .35
339 Swamp C :L: .20 .35
340 Swamp C :L: .20 .35
341 Swamp C :L: .20 .35
342 Swamp C :L: .20 .35
343 Mountain C :L: .20 .35
344 Mountain C :L: .20 .35
345 Mountain C :L: .20 .35
346 Mountain C :L: .20 .35
347 Forest C :L: .20 .35
348 Forest C :L: .20 .35
349 Forest C :L: .20 .35
350 Forest C :L: .20 .35

2002 Magic The Gathering Onslaught Foil

COMPLETE SET (350) 500.00 700.00

2003 Magic The Gathering Legions

COMPLETE SET (145) 70.00 100.00
BOOSTER BOX (36 PACKS) 200.00 250.00
BOOSTER PACK (12 CARDS) 6.00 8.00
THEME DECK BOX 125.00 150.00
THEME DECK 7.00 14.00
FAT PACK 38.00 45.00
RELEASED ON FEBRUARY 3, 2003
1 Akroma, Angel of Wrath R :W: 2.50 4.00
2 Akroma's Devoted U :W: .20 .35
3 Aven Redeemer C :W: .20 .35
4 Aven Warhawk U :W: .20 .35
5 Beacon of Destiny R :W: .20 .35
6 Celestial Gatekeeper R :W: .20 .35
7 Cloudreach Cavalry U :W: .20 .35
8 Daru Mender U :W: .20 .35
9 Daru Sanctifier C :W: .20 .35
10 Daru Stinger C :W: .20 .35
11 Defender of the Order R :W: .20 .35
12 Deftblade Elite C :W: 1.00 1.50
13 Essence Sliver R :W: 1.50 2.00
14 Gempalm Avenger C :W: .20 .35
15 Glowrider R :W: .20 .35
16 Liege of the Axe U :W: .20 .35
17 Lowland Tracker C :W: .20 .35
18 Planar Guide R :W: .20 .35
19 Plated Sliver C :W: .20 .35
20 Starlight Invoker C :W: .20 .35
21 Stoic Champion U :W: .20 .35
22 Sunstrike Legionnaire R :W: .20 .35
23 Swooping Talon U :W: .20 .35
24 Wall of Hope C :W: .20 .35
25 Ward Sliver U :W: .50 .80
26 Whipgrass Entangler C :W: .20 .35
27 White Knight U :W: .20 .35
28 Windborn Muse R :W: 1.50 2.50
29 Wingbeat Warrior C :W: .20 .35
30 Aven Envoy C :B: .20 .35
31 Cephalid Pathmage C :B: .20 .35
32 Chromeshell Crab R :B: .20 .35
33 Covert Operative C :B: .20 .35
34 Crookclaw Elder U :B: .20 .35
35 Dermoplasm R :B: .20 .35
36 Dreamborn Muse R :B: .30 .50
37 Echo Tracer C :B: .20 .35
38 Fugitive Wizard C :B: .20 .35
39 Gempalm Sorcerer U :B: .20 .35
40 Glintwing Invoker C :B: .20 .35
41 Keeneye Aven C :B: .20 .35
42 Keeper of the Nine Gales R :B: .20 .35
43 Embalmed Brawler C :K: .20 .35
43 Master of the Veil U :B: .20 .35
44 Merchant of Secrets C :B: .20 .35
45 Mistform Seaswift C :B: .20 .35
46 Mistform Sliver C :B: .20 .35
47 Mistform Ultimus R :B: .20 .35
48 Mistform Wakecaster U :B: .20 .35
49 Primoc Escapee U :B: .20 .35
50 Riptide Director R :B: 2.00 3.50
51 Riptide Mangler R :B: .20 .35
52 Shifting Sliver U :B: 1.00 1.50
53 Synapse Sliver R :B: 2.50 4.00
54 Voidmage Apprentice C :B: .20 .35
55 Wall of Deceit U :B: .20 .35
56 Warped Researcher U :B: .20 .35
57 Weaver of Lies R :B: .20 .35
58 Willbender U :B: .20 .35
59 Aphetto Exterminator U :K: .20 .35
60 Bane of the Living R :K: .20 .35
61 Blood Celebrant C :K: .20 .35
62 Corpse Harvester U :K: .50 .80
63 Crypt Sliver C :K: .20 .35
64 Dark Supplicant U :K: .20 .35
65 Deathmark Prelate U :K: .20 .35
66 Drinker of Sorrow R :K: .20 .35
67 Dripping Dead C :K: .20 .35
68 Earthblighter U :K: .20 .35
70 Gempalm Polluter C :K: .20 .35
71 Ghastly Remains R :K: .20 .35
72 Goblin Turncoat C :K: .20 .35
73 Graveborn Muse R :K: 1.00 1.50
74 Havoc Demon R :K: .20 .35
75 Hollow Specter R :K: .20 .35
76 Infernal Caretaker C :K: .20 .35
77 Noxious Ghoul U :K: .75 1.25
78 Phage the Untouchable R :K: 1.50 2.00
79 Scion of Darkness R :K: 1.00 1.50
80 Skinthinner C :K: .20 .35
81 Smokespew Invoker C :K: .20 .35
82 Sootfeather Flock C :K: .20 .35
83 Spectral Sliver U :K: .20 .35
84 Toxin Sliver R :K: 3.00 5.00
85 Vile Deacon C :K: .20 .35
86 Withered Wretch U :K: .20 .35
87 Zombie Brute U :K: .20 .35
88 Blade Sliver U :R: .20 .35
89 Bloodstoke Howler C :R: .20 .35
90 Clickslither R :R: .20 .35
91 Crested Craghorn C :R: .20 .35
92 Flamewave Invoker C :R: .20 .35
93 Frenetic Raptor U :R: .20 .35
94 Gempalm Incinerator U :R: .50 .80
95 Goblin Assassin U :R: .20 .35
96 Goblin Clearcutter U :R: .20 .35
97 Goblin Dynamo U :R: .20 .35
98 Goblin Firebug C :R: .20 .35
99 Goblin Goon R :R: .20 .35
100 Goblin Grappler C :R: .20 .35
101 Goblin Lookout C :R: .20 .35
102 Hunter Sliver C :R: .20 .35
103 Imperial Hellkite R :R: .40 .60
104 Kilnmouth Dragon R :R: .60 1.00
105 Lavaborn Muse R :R: .20 .35
106 Macetail Hystrodon C :R: .20 .35
107 Magma Sliver R :R: 2.50 4.00
108 Ridgetop Raptor U :R: .20 .35
109 Rockshard Elemental R :R: .20 .35
110 Shaleskin Plower C :R: .20 .35
111 Skirk Alarmist R :R: .20 .35
112 Skirk Drill Sergeant U :R: .20 .35
113 Skirk Marauder C :R: .20 .35
114 Skirk Outrider C :R: .20 .35
115 Unstable Hulk R :R: .20 .35
116 Warbreak Trumpeter U :R: .20 .35
117 Berserk Murlodont C :G: .20 .35
118 Branchsnap Lorian U :G: .20 .35
119 Brontotherium U :G: .20 .35
120 Brood Sliver R :G: 2.00 3.50
121 Caller of the Claw R :G: .60 1.00
122 Canopy Crawler U :G: .20 .35
123 Defiant Elf C :G: .20 .35
124 Elvish Soultiller R :G: .20 .35
125 Enormous Baloth U :G: .20 .35
126 Feral Throwback R :G: .20 .35

127 Gempalm Strider U :G: .20 .35
128 Glowering Rogon C :G: .20 .35
129 Hundroog C :G: .20 .35
130 Krosan Cloudscraper R :G: .20 .35
131 Krosan Vorine C :G: .20 .35
132 Nantuko Vigilante C :G: .20 .35
133 Needleshot Gourna C :G: .20 .35
134 Patron of the Wild C :G: .20 .35
135 Primal Whisperer R :G: .20 .35
136 Quick Sliver C :G: .20 .35
137 Root Sliver U :G: 1.00 1.50
138 Seedborn Muse R :G: 20.00 25.00
139 Stonewood Invoker C :G: .20 .35
140 Timberwatch Elf C :G: .20 .35
141 Totem Speaker U :G: .20 .35
142 Tribal Forcemage R :G: .20 .35
143 Vexing Beetle R :G: .20 .35
144 Wirewood Channeler U :G: .60 1.00
145 Wirewood Hivemaster U :G: .20 .35

2003 Magic The Gathering Legions Foil

COMPLETE SET (145) 250.00 375.00

2003 Magic The Gathering Scourge

COMPLETE SET (143) 70.00 100.00
BOOSTER BOX (36 PACKS) 175.00 225.00
BOOSTER PACK (15 CARDS) 7.00 9.00
THEME DECK BOX 90.00 110.00
THEME DECK 10.00 12.00
FAT PACK 25.00 30.00
RELEASED ON MAY 26, 2003
1 Ageless Sentinels R :W: .20 .35
2 Astral Steel C :W: .20 .35
3 Aven Farseer C :W: .20 .35
4 Aven Liberator C :W: .20 .35
5 Daru Spiritualist C :W: .20 .35
6 Daru Warchief U :W: 1.00 1.50
7 Dawn Elemental R :W: .20 .35
8 Decree of Justice R :W: .20 .35
9 Dimensional Breach R :W: .20 .35
10 Dragon Scales C :W: .20 .35
11 Dragonstalker U :W: .20 .35
12 Eternal Dragon R :W: .20 .35
13 Exiled Doomsayer R :W: .20 .35
14 Force Bubble R :W: .20 .35
15 Frontline Strategist C :W: .20 .35
16 Gilded Light U :W: .20 .35
17 Guilty Conscience C :W: .20 .35
18 Karona, False God R :D: .20 .35
19 Noble Templar C :W: .20 .35
20 Rain of Blades U :W: .20 .35
21 Recuperate C :W: .20 .35
22 Reward the Faithful U :W: .20 .35
23 Silver Knight U :W: .20 .35
24 Trap Digger R :W: .20 .35
25 Wing Shards U :W: .20 .35
26 Wipe Clean C :W: .20 .35
27 Zealous Inquisitor C :W: .20 .35
28 Aphetto Runecaster U :B: .20 .35
29 Brain Freeze U :B: .20 .35
30 Coast Watcher C :B: .20 .35
31 Day of the Dragons R :B: .20 .35
32 Decree of Silence R :B: 2.00 3.50
33 Dispersal Shield C :B: .20 .35
34 Dragon Wings C :B: .20 .35
35 Faces of the Past R :B: .20 .35
36 Frozen Solid C :B: .20 .35
37 Hindering Touch C :B: .20 .35
38 Long-Term Plans U :B: 1.50 2.00
39 Mercurial Kite C :B: .20 .35
40 Metamorphose U :B: .20 .35
41 Mind's Desire R :B: .20 .35
42 Mischievous Quanar R :B: .20 .35
43 Mistform Warchief U :B: .20 .35
44 Parallel Thoughts R :B: .20 .35
45 Pemmin's Aura U :B: .20 .35
46 Raven Guild Initiate C :B: .20 .35
47 Raven Guild Master R :B: .20 .35
48 Riptide Survivor U :B: .20 .35
49 Rush of Knowledge C :B: .20 .35
50 Scornful Egotist C :B: .20 .35
51 Shoreline Ranger C :B: .20 .35
51 Elvish Aberration U :G: .20 .35
52 Stifle R :B: 3.00 5.00
53 Temporal Fissure C :B: .20 .35
54 Thundercloud Elemental U :B: .20 .35
55 Bladewing's Thrall U :K: .20 .35
56 Cabal Conditioning R :K: .20 .35
57 Cabal Interrogator U :K: .20 .35
58 Call to the Grave R :K: .20 .35
59 Carrion Feeder C :K: .20 .35
60 Chill Haunting U :K: .20 .35
61 Clutch of Undeath C :K: .20 .35
62 Consumptive Goo R :K: .20 .35
63 Death's-Head Buzzard C :K: .20 .35
64 Decree of Pain R :K: 2.00 3.50
65 Dragon Shadow C :K: .20 .35
66 Fatal Mutation U :K: .20 .35
67 Final Punishment R :K: .20 .35
68 Lethal Vapors R :K: .20 .35
69 Lingering Death C :K: .20 .35
70 Nefashu R :K: .20 .35
71 Putrid Raptor U :K: .20 .35
72 Reaping the Graves C :K: .20 .35
73 Skulltap C :K: .20 .35
74 Soul Collector R :K: .20 .35
75 Tendrils of Agony U :K: 1.50 2.00
76 Twisted Abomination C :K: .20 .35
77 Unburden C :K: .20 .35
78 Undead Warchief U :K: 4.00 6.00
79 Unspeakable Symbol U :K: .20 .35
80 Vengeful Dead C :K: .20 .35
81 Zombie Cutthroat C :K: .20 .35
82 Bonethorn Valesk C :R: .20 .35
83 Carbonize U :R: .20 .35
84 Chartooth Cougar C :R: .20 .35
85 Decree of Annihilation R :R: 1.00 1.50
86 Dragon Breath C :R: .20 .35
87 Dragon Mage R :R: 1.50 2.00
88 Dragon Tyrant R :R: 1.50 2.50
89 Dragonspeaker Shaman U :R: 1.50 2.50
90 Dragonstorm R :R: .20 .35
91 Enrage U :R: .20 .35
92 Extra Arms U :R: .20 .35
93 Form of the Dragon R :R: .20 .35
94 Goblin Brigand C :R: .20 .35
95 Goblin Psychopath U :R: .20 .35
96 Goblin War Strike C :R: .20 .35
97 Goblin Warchief U :R: .20 .35
98 Grip of Chaos R :R: 1.00 1.50
99 Misguided Rage C :R: .20 .35
100 Pyrostatic Pillar U :R: .20 .35
101 Rock Jockey C :R: .20 .35
102 Scattershot C :R: .20 .35
103 Siege-Gang Commander R :R: 1.50 2.00
104 Skirk Volcanist U :R: .20 .35
105 Spark Spray C :R: .20 .35
106 Sulfuric Vortex R :R: .20 .35
107 Torrent of Fire C :R: .20 .35
108 Uncontrolled Infestation C :R: .20 .35
109 Accelerated Mutation C :G: .20 .35
110 Alpha Status U :G: .20 .35
111 Ambush Commander R :G: 1.00 1.50
112 Ancient Ooze R :G: .20 .35
113 Break Asunder C :G: .20 .35
114 Claws of Wirewood U :G: .20 .35
115 Decree of Savagery R :G: .20 .35
116 Divergent Growth C :G: .20 .35
117 Dragon Fangs C :G: .20 .35
119 Fierce Empath C :G: .20 .35
120 Forgotten Ancient R :G: 1.50 2.00
121 Hunting Pack U :G: .20 .35
122 Krosan Drover C :G: .20 .35
123 Krosan Warchief U :G: .20 .35
124 Kurgadon U :G: .20 .35
125 One with Nature U :G: .20 .35
126 Primitive Etchings R :G: .20 .35
127 Root Elemental R :G: .20 .35
128 Sprouting Vines C :G: .20 .35
129 Titanic Bulvox C :G: .20 .35
130 Treetop Scout C :G: .20 .35
131 Upwelling R :G: .20 .35
132 Wirewood Guardian C :G: .20 .35
133 Wirewood Symbiote U :G: .20 .35
134 Woodcloaker C :G: .20 .35
135 Xantid Swarm R :G: 1.50 2.00
136 Bladewing the Risen R :D: 1.50 2.00
137 Edgewalker U :D: .20 .35
138 Karona's Zealot U :W: .20 .35
139 Sliver Overlord R :D: 8.00 11.00
140 Ark of Blight U :A: .20 .35
141 Proteus Machine U :A: .20 .35
142 Stabilizer R :A: .20 .35
143 Temple of the False God U :L: .20 .35

2003 Magic The Gathering Mirrodin

COMPLETE SET (306) 260.00 350.00
BOOSTER BOX (36 PACKS) 275.00 325.00
BOOSTER PACK (15 CARDS) 8.00 11.00
STARTER BOX (12 DECKS) 80.00 125.00
STARTER DECK 10.00 13.00
FAT PACK 30.00 38.00
RELEASED ON OCTOBER 3, 2003
1 Altar's Light U :W: .20 .35
2 Arrest C :W: .20 .35
3 Auriok Bladewarden U :W: .20 .35
4 Auriok Steelshaper R :W: .20 .35
5 Auriok Transfixer C :W: .20 .35
6 Awe Strike C :W: .20 .35
7 Blinding Beam C :W: .20 .35
8 Leonin Abunas R :W: .20 .35
9 Leonin Den-Guard C :W: .20 .35
10 Leonin Elder C :W: .20 .35
11 Leonin Skyhunter U :W: .20 .35
12 Loxodon Mender C :W: .20 .35
13 Loxodon Peacekeeper R :W: .20 .35
14 Loxodon Punisher R :W: .20 .35
15 Luminous Angel R :W: .20 .35
16 Raise the Alarm C :W: .20 .35
17 Razor Barrier C :W: .20 .35
18 Roar of the Kha U :W: .20 .35
19 Rule of Law R :W: .20 .35
20 Second Sunrise R :W: .20 .35
21 Skyhunter Cub C :W: .20 .35
22 Skyhunter Patrol C :W: .20 .35
23 Slith Ascendant U :W: .20 .35
24 Solar Tide R :W: .20 .35
25 Soul Nova U :W: .20 .35
26 Sphere of Purity C :W: .20 .35
27 Taj-Nar Swordsmith U :W: .20 .35
28 Tempest of Light U :W: .20 .35
29 Annul C :B: .20 .35
30 Assert Authority U :B: .20 .35
31 Broodstar R :B: .20 .35
32 Disarm C :B: .20 .35
33 Domineer U :B: .20 .35
34 Dream's Grip C :B: .20 .35
35 Fabricate U :B: .20 .35
36 Fatespinner R :B: 4.00 6.00
37 Inertia Bubble C :B: .20 .35
38 Looming Hoverguard U :B: .20 .35
39 Lumengrid Augur R :B: .20 .35
40 Lumengrid Sentinel U :B: .20 .35
41 Lumengrid Warden C :B: .20 .35
42 March of the Machines R :B: .20 .35
43 Neurok Familiar C :B: .20 .35
44 Neurok Spy C :B: .20 .35
45 Override C :B: .20 .35
46 Psychic Membrane U :B: .20 .35
47 Quicksilver Elemental R :B: .20 .35
48 Regress C :B: .20 .35
49 Shared Fate R :B: .20 .35
50 Slith Strider U :B: .20 .35
51 Somber Hoverguard C :B: .20 .35
52 Temporal Cascade R :B: .20 .35
53 Thirst for Knowledge U :B: .20 .35
54 Thoughtcast C :B: .20 .35
55 Vedalken Archmage R :B: .20 .35
56 Wanderguard Sentry C :B: .20 .35
57 Barter in Blood U :K: .20 .35
58 Betrayal of Flesh U :K: .20 .35
59 Chimney Imp C :K: .20 .35
60 Consume Spirit C :K: .20 .35
61 Contaminated Bond C :K: .20 .35
62 Disciple of the Vault C :K: .20 .35
63 Dross Harvester R :K: .20 .35
64 Dross Prowler C :K: .20 .35
65 Flayed Nim U :K: .20 .35
66 Grim Reminder R :K: .20 .35
67 Irradiate C :K: .20 .35
68 Moriok Scavenger C :K: .20 .35
69 Necrogen Mists R :K: .20 .35
70 Nim Devourer R :K: .20 .35
71 Nim Lasher C :K: .20 .35
72 Nim Shambler U :K: .20 .35
73 Nim Shrieker C :K: .20 .35
74 Promise of Power R :K: .20 .35
75 Reiver Demon R :K: .20 .35
76 Relic Bane U :K: .20 .35
77 Slith Bloodletter U :K: .20 .35
78 Spoils of the Vault R :K: .20 .35
79 Terror C :K: .20 .35
80 Vermiculos R :K: .20 .35
81 Wail of the Nim C :K: .20 .35
82 Wall of Blood U :K: .20 .35
83 Woebearer U :K: .20 .35
84 Wrench Mind C :K: .20 .35
85 Arc-Slogger R :R: .20 .35
86 Atog U :R: .20 .35
87 Confusion in the Ranks R :R: .20 .35
88 Detonate U :R: .20 .35
89 Electrostatic Bolt C :R: .20 .35
90 Fiery Gambit R :R: .20 .35
91 Fists of the Anvil C :R: .20 .35
92 Forge Armor U :R: .20 .35
93 Fractured Loyalty U :R: .20 .35
94 Goblin Striker C :R: .20 .35
95 Grab the Reins U :R: .20 .35
96 Incite War C :R: .20 .35
97 Krark-Clan Shaman C :R: .20 .35
98 Krark's Thumb R :A: .20 .35
99 Mass Hysteria R :R: .20 .35
100 Megatog R :R: .20 .35
101 Molten Rain C :R: .20 .35
102 Ogre Leadfoot C :R: .20 .35
103 Rustmouth Ogre U :R: .20 .35
104 Seething Song C :R: .20 .35
105 Shatter C :R: .20 .35
106 Shrapnel Blast U :R: .20 .35
107 Slith Firewalker U :R: .20 .35
108 Spikeshot Goblin C :R: .20 .35
109 Trash for Treasure R :R: .20 .35
110 Vulshok Battlemaster R :R: .20 .35
111 Vulshok Berserker C :R: .20 .35
112 War Elemental R :R: .20 .35
113 Battlegrowth C :G: .20 .35
114 Bloodscent U :G: .20 .35
115 Brown Ouphe U :G: .20 .35
116 Copperhoof Vorrac R :G: .20 .35
117 Creeping Mold U :G: .20 .35
118 Deconstruct C :G: .20 .35
119 Fangren Hunter C :G: .20 .35
120 Glissa Sunseeker R :G: .20 .35
121 Groffskithur C :G: .20 .35
122 Hum of the Radix R :G: .20 .35
123 Journey of Discovery C :G: .20 .35
124 Living Hive R :G: .20 .35
125 Molder Slug R :G: .20 .35
126 One Dozen Eyes U :G: .20 .35
127 Plated Slagwurm R :G: .20 .35
128 Predator's Strike C :G: .20 .35
129 Slith Predator U :G: .20 .35
130 Sylvan Scrying U :G: .20 .35
131 Tel-Jilad Archers C :G: .20 .35
132 Tel-Jilad Chosen C :G: .20 .35
133 Tel-Jilad Exile C :G: .20 .35
134 Tooth and Nail R :G: 15.00 20.00
135 Troll Ascetic R :G: .20 .35
136 Trolls of Tel-Jilad U :G: .20 .35
137 Turn to Dust C :G: .20 .35
138 Viridian Joiner C :G: .20 .35
139 Viridian Shaman U :G: .20 .35
140 Wurmskin Forger C :G: .20 .35
141 AEther Spellbomb C :A: .20 .35
142 Alpha Myr C :A: .20 .35
143 Altar of Shadows R :A: .20 .35
144 Banshee's Blade U :A: .20 .35
145 Blinkmoth Urn R :A: .20 .35
146 Bonesplitter C :A: .20 .35
147 Bosh, Iron Golem R :A: .20 .35
148 Bottle Gnomes U :A: .20 .35
149 Cathodion U :A: .20 .35
150 Chalice of the Void R :A: 65.00 70.00
151 Chromatic Sphere C :A: .20 .35
152 Chrome Mox R :A: 25.00 .35
153 Clockwork Beetle C :A: .20 .35
154 Clockwork Condor C :A: .20 .35
155 Clockwork Dragon R :A: .20 .35
156 Clockwork Vorrac U :A: .20 .35
157 Cobalt Golem C :A: .20 .35
158 Copper Myr C :A: .20 .35
159 Crystal Shard U :A: .20 .35
160 Culling Scales R :A: .20 .35
161 Damping Matrix R :A: .20 .35
162 Dead-Iron Sledge U :A: .20 .35
163 Dragon Blood U :A: .20 .35
164 Dross Scorpion C :A: .20 .35
165 Duplicant R :A: .20 .35
166 Duskworker U :A: .20 .35
167 Elf Replica C :A: .20 .35
168 Empyrial Plate R :A: .20 .35
169 Extraplanar Lens R :A: 15.00 20.00
170 Farsight Mask U :A: .20 .35
171 Fireshrieker U :A: .20 .35
172 Frogmite C :A: .20 .35
173 Galvanic Key C :A: .20 .35
174 Gate to the Æther R :A: .20 .35
175 Gilded Lotus R :A: 10.00 15.00
176 Goblin Charbelcher R :A: .20 .35
177 Goblin Dirigible U :A: .20 .35
178 Goblin Replica C :A: .20 .35
179 Goblin War Wagon C :A: .20 .35
180 Gold Myr C :A: .20 .35
181 Golem-Skin Gauntlets U :A: .20 .35
182 Granite Shard U :A: .20 .35
183 Grid Monitor R :A: .20 .35
184 Heartwood Shard U :A: .20 .35
185 Hematite Golem C :A: .20 .35
186 Icy Manipulator U :A: .20 .35
187 Iron Myr C :A: .20 .35
188 Isochron Scepter U :A: .20 .35
189 Jinxed Choker R :A: .20 .35
190 Krark-Clan Grunt C :R: .20 .35
191 Leaden Myr C :A: .20 .35
192 Leonin Bladetrap U :A: .20 .35
193 Leonin Scimitar C :A: .20 .35
194 Leonin Sun Standard R :A: .20 .35
195 Leveler R :A: .20 .35
196 Liar's Pendulum R :A: .20 .35
197 Lifespark Spellbomb C :A: .20 .35
198 Lightning Coils R :A: .20 .35
199 Lightning Greaves U :A: .20 .35
200 Lodestone Myr R :A: .20 .35
201 Loxodon Warhammer U :A: .20 .35
202 Malachite Golem C :A: .20 .35
203 Mask of Memory U :A: .20 .35
204 Mesmeric Orb R :A: 20.00 25.00
205 Mind's Eye R :A: 7.00 10.00
206 Mindslaver R :A: .20 .35
207 Mindstorm Crown U :A: .20 .35
208 Mirror Golem U :A: .20 .35
209 Mourner's Shield U :A: .20 .35
210 Myr Adapter C :A: .20 .35
211 Myr Enforcer C :A: .20 .35
212 Myr Incubator R :A: .20 .35
213 Myr Mindservant U :A: .20 .35
214 Myr Prototype U :A: .20 .35
215 Myr Retriever U :A: .20 .35
216 Necrogen Spellbomb C :A: .20 .35
217 Needlebug U :A: .20 .35
218 Neurok Hoversail C :A: .20 .35
219 Nightmare Lash R :A: .20 .35
220 Nim Replica C :A: .20 .35
221 Nuisance Engine U :A: .20 .35
222 Oblivion Stone R :A: 8.00 11.00
223 Omega Myr C :A: .20 .35
224 Ornithopter U :A: .20 .35
225 Pearl Shard U :A: .20 .35
226 Pentavus R :A: .20 .35
227 Pewter Golem C :A: .20 .35
228 Platinum Angel R :A: .20 .35
229 Power Conduit U :A: .20 .35
230 Proteus Staff R :A: .20 .35
231 Psychogenic Probe R :A: .20 .35
232 Pyrite Spellbomb C :A: .20 .35
233 Quicksilver Fountain R :A: .20 .35
234 Rust Elemental U :A: .20 .35
235 Rustspore Ram U :A: .20 .35
236 Scale of Chiss-Goria C :A: .20 .35
237 Scrabbling Claws U :A: .20 .35
238 Sculpting Steel R :A: 6.00 8.00
239 Scythe of the Wretched R :A: .20 .35
240 Serum Tank U :A: .20 .35
241 Silver Myr C :A: .20 .35
242 Skeleton Shard U :A: .20 .35
243 Slagwurm Armor C :A: .20 .35
244 Soldier Replica C :A: .20 .35
245 Solemn Simulacrum R :A: .20 .35
246 Soul Foundry R :A: .20 .35
247 Spellweaver Helix R :A: .20 .35
248 Steel Wall C :A: .20 .35
249 Sun Droplet U :A: .20 .35
250 Sunbeam Spellbomb C :A: .20 .35
251 Sword of Kaldra R :A: 5.00 7.00
252 Synod Sanctum U :A: .20 .35
253 Talisman of Dominance U :A: .20 .35
254 Talisman of Impulse U :A: .20 .35
255 Talisman of Indulgence U :A: .20 .35
256 Talisman of Progress U :A: .20 .35
257 Talisman of Unity U :A: .20 .35
258 Tanglebloom C :A: .20 .35
259 Tangleroot R :A: .20 .35
260 Tel-Jilad Stylus U :A: .20 .35
261 Thought Prison U :A: .20 .35
262 Timesifter R :A: .20 .35
263 Titanium Golem C :A: .20 .35
264 Tooth of Chiss-Goria C :A: .20 .35
265 Tower of Champions R :A: .20 .35
266 Tower of Eons R :A: .20 .35
267 Tower of Fortunes R :A: .20 .35
268 Tower of Murmurs R :A: .20 .35
269 Triskelion R :A: .20 .35
270 Viridian Longbow C :A: .20 .35
271 Vorrac Battlehorns C :A: .20 .35
272 Vulshok Battlegear U :A: .20 .35
273 Vulshok Gauntlets C :A: .20 .35
274 Welding Jar C :A: .20 .35
275 Wizard Replica C :A: .20 .35
276 Worldslayer R :A: .20 .35
277 Yotian Soldier C :A: .20 .35
278 Ancient Den C :L: .20 .35
279 Blinkmoth Well U :L: .20 .35
280 Cloudpost C :L: .20 .35
281 Glimmervoid R :L: 15.00 20.00
282 Great Furnace C :L: .20 .35
283 Seat of the Synod C :L: .20 .35
284 Stalking Stones U :L: .20 .35
285 Tree of Tales C :L: .20 .35
286 Vault of Whispers C :L: .20 .35
287 Plains L :L: .20 .35
288 Plains L :L: .20 .35
289 Plains L :L: .20 .35
290 Plains L :L: .20 .35
291 Island L :L: .20 .35
292 Island L :L: .20 .35
293 Island L :L: .20 .35
294 Island L :L: .20 .35

295 Swamp L :L: .20 .35
296 Swamp L :L: .20 .35
297 Swamp L :L: .20 .35
298 Swamp L :L: .20 .35
299 Mountain L :L: .20 .35
300 Mountain L :L: .20 .35
301 Mountain L :L: .20 .35
302 Mountain L :L: .20 .35
303 Forest L :L: .20 .35
304 Forest L :L: .20 .35
305 Forest L :L: .20 .35
306 Forest L :L: .20 .35

2004 Magic The Gathering Darksteel

COMPLETE SET (165) 230.00 300.00
BOOSTER BOX (36 PACKS) 450.00 600.00
BOOSTER PACK (15 CARDS) 13.00 16.00
FAT PACK 30.00 60.00
RELEASED ON FEBRUARY 6, 2004
1 Auriok Glaivemaster C :W: .20 .35
2 Echoing Calm C :W: .20 .35
3 Emissary of Hope U :W: .20 .35
5 Leonin Battlemage U :W: .20 .35
6 Leonin Shikari R :W: 2.50 4.00
7 Loxodon Mystic C :W: .20 .35
8 Metal Fatigue C :W: .20 .35
9 Pristine Angel R :W: .75 1.25
10 Pteron Ghost C :W: .20 .35
11 Pulse of the Fields R :W: .20 .35
12 Purge U :W: .20 .35
13 Ritual of Restoration C :W: .20 .35
14 Soulscour R :W: .20 .35
15 Steelshaper Apprentice R :W: .20 .35
16 Stir the Pride U :W: .20 .35
17 Test of Faith U :W: .20 .35
18 Turn the Tables R :W: .20 .35
19 Carry Away U :B: .20 .35
20 Chromescale Drake R :B: .20 .35
21 Echoing Truth C :B: .20 .35
22 Hoverguard Observer U :B: .20 .35
23 Last Word R :B: .75 1.25
24 Machinate C :B: .20 .35
25 Magnetic Flux C :B: .20 .35
26 Neurok Prodigy C :B: .20 .35
27 Neurok Transmuter U :B: .20 .35
28 Psychic Overload U :B: .20 .35
29 Pulse of the Grid R :B: .20 .35
30 Quicksilver Behemoth C :B: .20 .35
31 Reshape R :B: 3.00 5.00
32 Retract R :B: 3.00 5.00
33 Second Sight U :B: .20 .35
34 Synod Artificer R :B: .20 .35
35 Vedalken Engineer C :B: .20 .35
36 Vex C :B: .20 .35
37 AEther Snap R :K: .20 .35
38 Burden of Greed C :K: .20 .35
39 Chittering Rats C :K: .60 1.00
40 Death Cloud R :K: 1.50 2.50
41 Echoing Decay C :K: .20 .35
42 Emissary of Despair U :K: .20 .35
43 Essence Drain C :K: .20 .35
44 Greater Harvester R :K: .20 .35
45 Grimclaw Bats C :K: .20 .35
46 Hunger of the Nim C :K: .20 .35
47 Mephitic Ooze R :K: .20 .35
48 Murderous Spoils U :K: .20 .35
49 Nim Abomination U :K: .20 .35
50 Pulse of the Dross R :K: .20 .35
51 Scavenging Scarab C :K: .20 .35
52 Screams from Within U :K: .20 .35
53 Scrounge U :K: .20 .35
54 Shriveling Rot R :K: .20 .35
55 Barbed Lightning C :R: .20 .35
56 Crazed Goblin C :R: .20 .35
57 Dismantle U :R: .20 .35
58 Drooling Ogre C :R: .20 .35
59 Echoing Ruin C :R: .20 .35
60 Fireball U :R: .20 .35
61 Flamebreak R :R: .60 1.00
62 Furnace Dragon R :R: .20 .35
63 Hallow C :W: .20 .35
63 Goblin Archaeologist U :R: .20 .35
64 Inflame C :R: .20 .35
65 Krark-Clan Stoker C :R: .20 .35
66 Pulse of the Forge R :R: .20 .35
67 Savage Beating R :R: 5.00 7.00
68 Shunt R :R: .20 .35
69 Slobad, Goblin Tinkerer R :R: .50 .80
70 Tears of Rage U :R: .20 .35
71 Unforge C :R: .20 .35
72 Vulshok War Boar U :R: .20 .35
73 Ageless Entity R :G: .20 .35
74 Echoing Courage C :G: .20 .35
75 Fangren Firstborn R :G: .50 .80
76 Infested Roothold U :G: .20 .35
77 Karstoderm U :G: .20 .35
78 Nourish C :G: .20 .35
79 Oxidize U :G: .20 .35
80 Pulse of the Tangle R :G: .20 .35
81 Reap and Sow C :G: .20 .35
82 Rebuking Ceremony R :G: .20 .35
83 Roaring Slagwurm R :G: .20 .35
84 Stand Together U :G: .20 .35
85 Tangle Spider C :G: .20 .35
86 Tanglewalker U :G: .20 .35
87 Tel-Jilad Outrider C :G: .20 .35
88 Tel-Jilad Wolf C :G: .20 .35
89 Viridian Acolyte C :G: .50 .80
90 Viridian Zealot R :G: .20 .35
91 AEther Vial U :A: 35.00 40.00
92 Angel's Feather U :A: .20 .35
93 Arcane Spyglass C :A: .20 .35
94 Arcbound Bruiser C :A: .20 .35
95 Arcbound Crusher U :A: .20 .35
96 Arcbound Fiend U :A: .20 .35
97 Arcbound Hybrid C :A: .20 .35
98 Arcbound Lancer U :A: .20 .35
99 Arcbound Overseer R :A: 1.00 1.50
100 Arcbound Ravager R :A: 40.00 45.00
101 Arcbound Reclaimer R :A: .60 1.00
102 Arcbound Slith U :A: .20 .35
103 Arcbound Stinger C :A: .20 .35
104 Arcbound Worker C :A: .20 .35
105 Auriok Siege Sled U :A: .20 .35
106 Chimeric Egg U :A: .20 .35
107 Coretapper U :A: 1.00 1.50
108 Darksteel Brute U :A: .20 .35
109 Darksteel Colossus R :A: 4.00 6.00
110 Darksteel Forge R :A: 7.00 10.00
111 Darksteel Gargoyle U :A: .20 .35
112 Darksteel Ingot C :A: .20 .35
113 Darksteel Pendant C :A: .20 .35
114 Darksteel Reactor R :A: 3.00 5.00
115 Death-Mask Duplicant U :A: .20 .35
116 Demon's Horn U :A: .20 .35
117 Dragon's Claw U :A: .20 .35
118 Drill-Skimmer C :A: .20 .35
119 Dross Golem C :A: .20 .35
120 Eater of Days R :A: 1.50 2.00
121 Gemini Engine R :A: .20 .35
122 Genesis Chamber U :A: 1.50 2.50
123 Geth's Grimoire U :A: .60 1.00
124 Heartseeker R :A: .50 .80
125 Juggernaut U :A: .20 .35
126 Kraken's Eye U :A: .20 .35
127 Leonin Bola C :A: .20 .35
128 Lich's Tomb R :A: .20 .35
129 Memnarch R :A: 3.00 5.00
130 Mycosynth Lattice R :A: .20 .35
131 Myr Landshaper C :A: .20 .35
132 Myr Matrix R :A: 1.50 2.50
133 Myr Moonvessel C :A: .20 .35
134 Nemesis Mask U :A: .20 .35
135 Oxidda Golem C :A: .20 .35
136 Panoptic Mirror R :A: 2.00 3.00
137 Razor Golem C :A: .20 .35
138 Serum Powder R :A: 1.50 2.50
139 Shield of Kaldra R :A: 3.00 5.00
140 Skullclamp U :A: 1.50 2.00
141 Spawning Pit U :A: .60 1.00
142 Specter's Shroud U :A: .20 .35
143 Spellbinder R :A: .20 .35
144 Spincrusher U :A: .20 .35
145 Spire Golem C :A: .50 .80
146 Sundering Titan R :A: 2.50 4.00
147 Surestrike Trident U :A: .20 .35
148 Sword of Fire and Ice R :A: 40.00 45.00
149 Sword of Light and Shadow R :A: 20.00 25.00
150 Talon of Pain U :A: .20 .35
151 Tangle Golem C :A: .20 .35
152 Thought Dissector R :A: .20 .35
153 Thunderstaff U :A: .20 .35
154 Trinisphere R :A: 35.00 40.00
155 Ur-Golem's Eye C :A: .20 .35
156 Voltaic Construct U :A: .20 .35
157 Vulshok Morningstar C :A: .20 .35
158 Wand of the Elements R :A: .20 .35
159 Well of Lost Dreams R :A: 1.50 2.50
160 Whispersilk Cloak C :A: .20 .35
161 Wirefly Hive U :A: .20 .35
162 Wurm's Tooth U :A: .20 .35
163 Blinkmoth Nexus R :L: 5.00 7.00
164 Darksteel Citadel C :L: .20 .35
165 Mirrodin's Core U :L: .20 .35

2004 Magic The Gathering Darksteel Foil

COMPLETE SET (165) 250.00 400.00

2004 Magic The Gathering Fifth Dawn

COMPLETE SET (165) 250.00 320.00
BOOSTER BOX (36 PACKS) 300.00 350.00
BOOSTER PACK (15 CARDS) 10.00 12.00
THEME DECK 10.00 15.00
FAT PACK 30.00 50.00
RELEASED ON JUNE 4, 2004
1 Abuna's Chant C :W: .20 .35
2 Armed Response C :W: .20 .35
3 Auriok Champion R :W: 8.00 12.00
4 Auriok Salvagers U :W: .20 .35
5 Auriok Windwalker R :W: .20 .35
6 Beacon of Immortality R :W: 4.00 6.00
7 Bringer of the White Dawn R :W: .75 1.25
8 Circle of Protection: Artifacts U :W: .20 .35
9 Leonin Squire C :W: .20 .35
10 Loxodon Anchorite C :W: .20 .35
11 Loxodon Stalwart U :W: .20 .35
12 Raksha Golden Cub R :W: 1.50 2.50
13 Retaliate R :W: .20 .35
14 Roar of Reclamation R :W: .20 .35
15 Skyhunter Prowler C :W: .20 .35
16 Skyhunter Skirmisher U :W: .20 .35
17 Stand Firm C :W: .20 .35
18 Stasis Cocoon C :W: .20 .35
19 Steelshaper's Gift U :W: 3.00 5.00
20 Vanquish U :W: .20 .35
21 Acquire R :B: 1.50 2.00
22 Advanced Hoverguard C :B: .20 .35
23 Artificer's Intuition R :B: .75 1.25
24 Beacon of Tomorrows R :B: 3.00 5.00
25 Blinkmoth Infusion R :B: .20 .35
26 Bringer of the Blue Dawn R :B: 1.50 2.50
27 Condescend C :B: .20 .35
28 Disruption Aura U :B: .20 .35
30 Eyes of the Watcher U :B: .20 .35
31 Fold into Æther U :B: .20 .35
32 Hoverguard Sweepers R :B: .20 .35
33 Into Thin Air C :B: .20 .35
34 Plasma Elemental U :B: .20 .35
35 Qumulox U :B: .20 .35
36 Serum Visions C :B: 2.00 3.00
37 Spectral Shift R :B: .20 .35
38 Thought Courier C :B: .20 .35
39 Trinket Mage C :B: .20 .35
40 Vedalken Mastermind U :B: .20 .35
41 Beacon of Unrest R :K: 2.00 3.00
42 Blind Creeper C :K: .20 .35
43 Bringer of the Black Dawn R :K: 1.50 2.50
44 Cackling Imp C :K: .20 .35
45 Desecration Elemental R :K: .20 .35
46 Devour in Shadow U :K: .20 .35
47 Dross Crocodile C :K: .20 .35
48 Early Frost C :B: .20 .35
48 Ebon Drake U :K: .20 .35
49 Endless Whispers R :K: .60 1.00
50 Fill with Fright C :K: .20 .35
51 Fleshgrafter C :K: .20 .35
52 Lose Hope C :K: .20 .35
53 Mephidross Vampire R :K: 4.00 6.00
54 Moriok Rigger R :K: .20 .35
55 Night's Whisper U :K: .75 1.25
56 Nim Grotesque U :K: .20 .35
57 Plunge into Darkness R :K: 2.00 3.00
58 Relentless Rats U :K: 1.50 2.50
59 Shattered Dreams U :K: .20 .35
60 Vicious Betrayal C :K: .20 .35
61 Beacon of Destruction R :R: .20 .35
62 Bringer of the Red Dawn R :R: .60 1.00
63 Cosmic Larva R :R: .20 .35
64 Feedback Bolt U :R: .20 .35
65 Furnace Whelp U :R: .20 .35
66 Goblin Brawler C :R: .20 .35
67 Granulate R :R: .20 .35
68 Ion Storm R :R: .20 .35
69 Iron-Barb Hellion U :R: .20 .35
70 Krark-Clan Engineers U :R: .20 .35
71 Krark-Clan Ogre C :R: .20 .35
72 Magma Giant R :R: .20 .35
73 Magma Jet U :R: .20 .35
74 Magnetic Theft U :R: .20 .35
75 Mana Geyser C :R: .20 .35
76 Rain of Rust C :R: .20 .35
77 Reversal of Fortune R :R: .20 .35
78 Screaming Fury C :R: .20 .35
79 Spark Elemental C :R: .20 .35
80 Vulshok Sorcerer C :R: .20 .35
81 All Suns' Dawn R :G: .20 .35
82 Beacon of Creation R :G: 2.00 3.00
83 Bringer of the Green Dawn R :G: .60 1.00
84 Channel the Suns U :G: .20 .35
85 Dawn's Reflection C :G: .20 .35
86 Eternal Witness U :G: 5.00 8.00
87 Fangren Pathcutter U :G: .20 .35
88 Ferocious Charge C :G: .20 .35
89 Joiner Adept R :G: 1.50 2.50
90 Ouphe Vandals U :G: .20 .35
91 Rite of Passage R :G: 2.00 3.00
92 Rude Awakening R :G: .20 .35
93 Sylvok Explorer C :G: .20 .35
94 Tangle Asp C :G: .20 .35
95 Tel-Jilad Justice U :G: .20 .35
96 Tel-Jilad Lifebreather C :G: .20 .35
97 Tornado Elemental R :G: .20 .35
98 Tyrranax C :G: .20 .35
99 Viridian Lorebearers U :G: .20 .35
100 Viridian Scout C :G: .20 .35
101 Anodet Lurker C :A: .20 .35
102 Arachnoid U :A: .20 .35
103 Arcbound Wanderer U :A: .20 .35
104 Avarice Totem U :A: .20 .35
105 Baton of Courage C :A: .20 .35
106 Battered Golem C :A: .20 .35
107 Blasting Station U :A: 2.50 4.00
108 Chimeric Coils U :A: .20 .35
109 Clearwater Goblet R :A: .20 .35
110 Clock of Omens U :A: .20 .35
111 Composite Golem U :A: .20 .35
112 Conjurer's Bauble C :A: .20 .35
113 Cranial Plating C :A: .20 .35
114 Crucible of Worlds R :A: 65.00 70.00
115 Door to Nothingness R :A: .75 1.25
116 Doubling Cube R :A: 10.00 15.00
117 Energy Chamber U :A: .20 .35
118 Engineered Explosives R :A: 80.00 85.00
119 Ensouled Scimitar U :A: .20 .35
120 Eon Hub R :A: .20 .35
121 Etched Oracle U :A: .20 .35
122 Ferropede U :A: .20 .35
123 Fist of Suns R :A: 2.00 3.00
124 Gemstone Array U :A: .75 1.25
125 Goblin Cannon U :A: .20 .35
126 Grafted Wargear U :A: 1.00 1.50
127 Grinding Station U :A: 1.00 1.50
128 Guardian Idol U :A: .20 .35
129 Healer's Headdress C :A: .20 .35
130 Heliophial C :A: .20 .35
131 Helm of Kaldra R :A: 3.00 5.00
132 Horned Helm C :A: .20 .35
133 Infused Arrows U :A: .20 .35
134 Krark-Clan Ironworks U :A: 7.00 10.00
135 Lantern of Insight U :A: 3.00 5.00
136 Lunar Avenger U :A: .20 .35
137 Mycosynth Golem R :A: 10.00 15.00
138 Myr Quadropod C :A: .20 .35
139 Myr Servitor C :A: .20 .35
140 Neurok Stealthsuit C :A: .20 .35
141 Opaline Bracers C :A: .20 .35
142 Paradise Mantle U :A: 1.50 2.00
143 Pentad Prism C :A: .20 .35
144 Possessed Portal R :A: .20 .35
145 Razorgrass Screen C :A: .20 .35
146 Razormane Masticore R :A: .20 .35
147 Relic Barrier U :A: .20 .35
148 Salvaging Station R :A: .20 .35
149 Sawtooth Thresher C :A: .20 .35
150 Silent Arbiter R :A: 2.00 3.00
151 Skullcage U :A: .20 .35
152 Skyreach Manta C :A: .20 .35
153 Solarion R :A: .20 .35
154 Sparring Collar C :A: .20 .35
155 Spinal Parasite U :A: .20 .35
156 Staff of Domination R :A: 20.00 25.00
157 Summoner's Egg R :A: .75 1.25
158 Summoning Station R :A: .60 1.00
159 Suncrusher R :A: .20 .35
160 Suntouched Myr C :A: .20 .35
161 Synod Centurion U :A: .20 .35
162 Thermal Navigator C :A: .20 .35
163 Vedalken Orrery R :A: 18.00 22.00
164 Vedalken Shackles R :A: 7.00 10.00
165 Wayfarer's Bauble C :A: .20 .35

2004 Magic The Gathering Fifth Dawn Foil

COMPLETE SET (165) 200.00 350.00

2004 Magic The Gathering Champions of Kamigawa

COMPLETE SET (307) 320.00 420.00
BOOSTER BOX (36 PACKS) 460.00 525.00
BOOSTER PACK (15 CARDS) 13.00 15.00
THEME DECK 9.00 12.00
RELEASED ON OCTOBER 1, 2004
1 Blessed Breath C :W: .20 .35
2 Bushi Tenderfoot U :W: .20 .35
3 Cage of Hands C :W: .20 .35
4 Call to Glory C :W: .20 .35
5 Candles' Glow U :W: .20 .35
6 Cleanfall U :W: .20 .35
7 Devoted Retainer C :W: .20 .35
8 Eight-and-a-Half-Tails R :W: .20 .35
9 Ethereal Haze C :W: .20 .35
10 Ghostly Prison U :W: 2.50 4.00
11 Harsh Deceiver C :W: .20 .35
12 Hikari, Twilight Guardian R :W: .20 .35
13 Hold the Line R :W: .20 .35
14 Honden of Cleansing Fire U :W: .20 .35
15 Horizon Seed U :W: .20 .35
16 Hundred-Talon Kami C :W: .20 .35
17 Indomitable Will C :W: .20 .35
18 Innocence Kami U :W: .20 .35
19 Isamaru, Hound of Konda R :W: 7.00 10.00
20 Kabuto Moth C :W: .20 .35
21 Kami of Ancient Law C :W: .20 .35
22 Kami of Old Stone U :W: .20 .35
23 Kami of the Painted Road C :W: .20 .35
24 Kami of the Palace Fields U :W: .20 .35
25 Kitsune Blademaster C :W: .20 .35
26 Kitsune Diviner C :W: .20 .35
27 Kitsune Healer C :W: .20 .35
28 Kitsune Mystic R :W: .20 .35
29 Kitsune Riftwalker C :W: .20 .35
30 Konda's Hatamoto U :W: .20 .35
31 Konda's Banner R :A: 5.00 7.00
32 Lantern Kami C :W: .20 .35
33 Masako the Humorless R :W: .20 .35
34 Mothrider Samurai C :W: .20 .35
35 Myojin of Cleansing Fire R :W: 3.00 5.00
36 Nagao, Bound by Honor U :W: .20 .35
37 Otherworldly Journey U :W: .20 .35
38 Pious Kitsune C :W: .20 .35
39 Quiet Purity C :W: .20 .35
40 Reciprocate U :W: .20 .35
41 Reverse the Sands R :W: .20 .35
42 Samurai Enforcers U :W: .20 .35
43 Samurai of the Pale Curtain U :W: .20 .35
44 Sensei Golden-Tail R :W: .20 .35
45 Silent-Chant Zubera C :W: .20 .35
46 Takeno, Samurai General R :W: .20 .35
47 Terashi's Cry C :W: .20 .35
48 Vassal's Duty R :W: .20 .35
49 Vigilance C :W: .20 .35
50 Yosei, the Morning Star R :W: 3.00 5.00
51 Aura of Dominion U :B: .20 .35
53 Callous Deceiver C :B: .20 .35
54 Consuming Vortex C :B: .20 .35
55 Counsel of the Soratami C :B: .20 .35
56 Cut the Tethers U :B: .20 .35
57 Dampen Thought U :B: .20 .35
58 Eerie Procession U :B: .20 .35
59 Eye of Nowhere C :B: .20 .35
60 Field of Reality C :B: .20 .35
61 Floating-Dream Zubera C :B: .20 .35
62 Gifts Ungiven R :B: 7.00 10.00
63 Graceful Adept U :B: .20 .35
64 Guardian of Solitude U :B: .20 .35
65 Hinder U :B: .20 .35
66 Hisoka's Guard C :B: .20 .35
67 Hisoka, Minamo Sensei R :B: .20 .35
68 Hisoka's Defiance C :B: .20 .35
69 Honden of Seeing Winds U :B: .20 .35
70 Jushi Apprentice R :B: .20 .35
71 Kami of Twisted Reflection C :B: .20 .35
72 Keiga, the Tide Star R :B: 2.50 4.00
73 Lifted by Clouds C :B: .20 .35
74 Meloku the Clouded Mirror R :B: .20 .35
75 Myojin of Seeing Winds R :B: 3.00 5.00
76 Mystic Restraints C :B: .20 .35
77 Part the Veil R :B: .20 .35
78 Peer Through Depths C :B: .20 .35
79 Petals of Insight U :B: .20 .35
8 Azami, Lady of Scrolls R :B: .20 .35
80 Psychic Puppetry C :B: .20 .35
81 Reach Through Mists C :B: .20 .35
82 Reweave R :B: .20 .35
83 River Kaijin C :B: .20 .35
84 Sift Through Sands C :B: .20 .35
85 Sire of the Storm U :B: .20 .35
86 Soratami Cloudskater C :B: .20 .35
87 Soratami Mirror-Guard C :B: .20 .35
88 Soratami Mirror-Mage U :B: .20 .35
89 Soratami Rainshaper C :B: .20 .35
90 Soratami Savant U :B: .20 .35
91 Soratami Seer U :B: .20 .35
92 Squelch U :B: .20 .35
93 Student of Elements U :B: .20 .35
94 Swirl the Mists R :B: .20 .35
95 Teller of Tales C :B: .20 .35
96 Thoughtbind C :B: .20 .35
97 Time Stop R :B: .20 .35
98 The Unspeakable R :B: .20 .35
99 Uyo, Silent Prophet R :B: .20 .35
100 Wandering Ones C :B: .20 .35
101 Ashen-Skin Zubera C :K: .20 .35
102 Befoul C :K: .20 .35
103 Blood Speaker U :K: .20 .35
104 Bloodthirsty Ogre U :K: .20 .35
105 Cranial Extraction R :K: .20 .35
106 Cruel Deceiver C :K: .20 .35

107 Cursed Ronin C :K:	.20	.35
108 Dance of Shadows U :K:	.20	.35
109 Deathcurse Ogre C :K:	.20	.35
110 Devouring Greed C :K:	.20	.35
111 Distress C :K:	.20	.35
112 Gibbering Kami C :K:	.20	.35
113 Gutwrencher Oni U :K:	.20	.35
114 He Who Hungers R :K:	.20	.35
115 Hideous Laughter U :K:	.20	.35
116 Honden of Night's Reach U :K:	.20	.35
117 Horobi, Death's Wail R :K:	.20	.35
118 Iname, Death Aspect R :K:	.20	.35
119 Kami of Lunacy U :K:	.20	.35
120 Kami of the Waning Moon C :K:	.20	.35
121 Kiku, Night's Flower R :K:	.20	.35
122 Kokusho, the Evening Star R :K:	8.00	11.00
123 Kuro, Pitlord R :K:	.20	.35
124 Marrow-Gnawer R :K:	8.00	11.00
125 Midnight Covenant C :K:	.20	.35
126 Myojin of Night's Reach R :K:	3.00	5.00
127 Nezumi Bone-Reader U :K:	.20	.35
128 Nezumi Cutthroat C :K:	.20	.35
129 Nezumi Graverobber U :K:	.20	.35
130 Nezumi Ronin C :K:	.20	.35
131 Nezumi Shortfang R :K:	3.00	5.00
132 Night Dealings R :K:	.20	.35
133 Night of Souls' Betrayal R :K:	2.50	4.00
134 Numai Outcast U :K:	.20	.35
135 Oni Possession U :K:	.20	.35
136 Painwracker Oni U :K:	.20	.35
137 Pull Under C :K:	.20	.35
138 Rag Dealer C :K:	.20	.35
139 Ragged Veins C :K:	.20	.35
140 Rend Flesh C :K:	.20	.35
141 Rend Spirit C :K:	.20	.35
142 Scuttling Death C :K:	.20	.35
143 Seizan, Perverter of Truth R :K:	2.00	3.50
144 Soulless Revival C :K:	.20	.35
145 Struggle for Sanity U :K:	.20	.35
146 Swallowing Plague U :K:	.20	.35
147 Thief of Hope U :K:	.20	.35
148 Villainous Ogre C :K:	.20	.35
149 Waking Nightmare C :K:	.20	.35
150 Wicked Akuba C :K:	.20	.35
151 Akki Avalanchers C :R:	.20	.35
152 Akki Coalflinger U :R:	.20	.35
153 Akki Lavarunner R :R:	.20	.35
154 Akki Rockspeaker C :R:	.20	.35
155 Akki Underminer U :R:	.20	.35
156 Battle-Mad Ronin C :R:	.20	.35
157 Ben-Ben, Akki Hermit R :R:	.20	.35
158 Blind with Anger U :R:	.20	.35
159 Blood Rites U :R:	.20	.35
160a Brothers Yamazaki U :R:	.20	.35
160b Brothers Yamazaki U :R:	.20	.35
161 Brutal Deceiver C :R:	.20	.35
162 Crushing Pain C :R:	.20	.35
163 Desperate Ritual C :R:	.20	.35
164 Devouring Rage C :R:	.20	.35
165 Earthshaker U :R:	.20	.35
166 Ember-Fist Zubera C :R:	.20	.35
167 Frostwielder C :R:	.20	.35
168 Glacial Ray C :R:	.20	.35
169 Godo, Bandit Warlord R :R:	.20	.35
170 Hanabi Blast U :R:	.20	.35
171 Hearth Kami C :R:	.20	.35
172 Honden of Infinite Rage U :R:	.20	.35
173 Initiate of Blood U :R:	.20	.35
174 Kami of Fire's Roar C :R:	.20	.35
175 Kiki-Jiki, Mirror Breaker R :R:	10.00	15.00
176 Kumano's Pupils U :R:	.20	.35
177 Kumano, Master Yamabushi R :R:	.20	.35
178 Lava Spike C :R:	3.00	5.00
179 Mana Seism U :R:	.20	.35
180 Mindblaze R :R:	.20	.35
181 Myojin of Infinite Rage R :R:	3.00	5.00
182 Ore Gorger U :R:	.20	.35
183 Pain Kami U :R:	.20	.35
184 Ronin Houndmaster C :R:	.20	.35
185 Ryusei, the Falling Star R :R:	.20	.35
186 Shimatsu the Bloodcloaked R :R:	.20	.35
187 Sideswipe U :R:	.20	.35
188 Sokenzan Bruiser C :R:	.20	.35
189 Soul of Magma C :R:	.20	.35
190 Soulblast R :R:	.20	.35
191 Stone Rain C :R:	.20	.35
192 Strange Inversion U :R:	.20	.35
193 Through the Breach R :R:	50.00	60.00
194 Tide of War R :R:	.20	.35
195 Uncontrollable Anger C :R:	.20	.35
196 Unearthly Blizzard C :R:	.20	.35
197 Unnatural Speed C :R:	.20	.35
198 Yamabushi's Flame C :R:	.20	.35
199 Yamabushi's Storm C :R:	.20	.35
200 Zo-Zu the Punisher R :R:	.20	.35
201 Azusa, Lost but Seeking R :G:	25.00	30.00
202 Budoka Gardener R :G:	2.00	3.50
203 Burr Grafter C :G:	.20	.35
204 Commune with Nature C :G:	.20	.35
205 Dosan the Falling Leaf R :G:	2.50	4.00
206 Dripping-Tongue Zubera C :G:	.20	.35
207 Feast of Worms U :G:	.20	.35
208 Feral Deceiver C :G:	.20	.35
209 Gale Force U :G:	.20	.35
210 Glimpse of Nature R :G:	15.00	20.00
211 Hana Kami U :G:	.20	.35
212 Heartbeat of Spring R :G:	10.00	15.00
213 Honden of Life's Web U :G:	.20	.35
214 Humble Budoka C :G:	.20	.35
215 Iname, Life Aspect R :G:	.20	.35
216 Joyous Respite C :G:	.20	.35
217 Jugan, the Rising Star R :G:	.20	.35
218 Jukai Messenger C :G:	.20	.35
219 Kami of the Hunt C :G:	.20	.35
220 Kashi-Tribe Reaver U :G:	.20	.35
221 Kashi-Tribe Warriors C :G:	.20	.35
222 Kodama of the North Tree R :G:	.20	.35
223 Kodama of the South Tree R :G:	.20	.35
224 Kodama's Might C :G:	.20	.35
225 Kodama's Reach C :G:	.20	.35
226 Lure U :G:	.20	.35
227 Matsu-Tribe Decoy C :G:	.20	.35
228 Moss Kami C :G:	.20	.35
229 Myojin of Life's Web R :G:	3.00	5.00
230 Nature's Will R :G:	5.00	7.00
231 Orbweaver Kumo U :G:	.20	.35
232 Order of the Sacred Bell C :G:	.20	.35
233 Orochi Eggwatcher U :G:	.20	.35
234 Orochi Leafcaller C :G:	.20	.35
235 Orochi Ranger C :G:	.20	.35
236 Orochi Sustainer C :G:	.20	.35
237 Rootrunner U :G:	.20	.35
238 Sachi, Daughter of Seshiro U :G:	.20	.35
239 Sakura-Tribe Elder C :G:	.20	.35
240 Serpent Skin C :G:	.20	.35
241 Seshiro the Anointed R :G:	6.00	8.00
242 Shisato, Whispering Hunter R :G:	.20	.35
243 Soilshaper U :G:	.20	.35
244 Sosuke, Son of Seshiro U :G:	.20	.35
245 Strength of Cedars U :G:	.20	.35
246 Thousand-legged Kami U :G:	.20	.35
247 Time of Need U :G:	.20	.35
248 Venerable Kumo C :G:	.20	.35
249 Vine Kami C :G:	.20	.35
250 Wear Away C :G:	.20	.35
251 General's Kabuto R :A:	.20	.35
252 Hair-Strung Koto R :A:	.20	.35
253 Hankyu U :A:	.20	.35
254 Honor-Worn Shaku U :A:	.20	.35
255 Imi Statue R :A:	.20	.35
256 Jade Idol U :A:	.20	.35
257 Journeyer's Kite R :A:	.20	.35
258 Junkyo Bell R :A:	.20	.35
259 Konda, Lord of Eiganjo R :W:	.20	.35
260 Kusari-Gama R :A:	.20	.35
261 Long-Forgotten Gohei R :A:	.20	.35
262 Moonring Mirror R :A:	.20	.35
263 Nine-Ringed Bo U :A:	.20	.35
264 No-Dachi U :A:	.20	.35
265 Oathkeeper, Takeno's Daisho R :A:	.20	.35
266 Orochi Hatchery R :A:	.20	.35
267 Reito Lantern U :A:	.20	.35
268 Sensei's Divining Top U :A:	10.00	15.00
269 Shell of the Last Kappa R :A:	.20	.35
270 Tatsumasa, the Dragon's Fang R :A:	.20	.35
271 Tenza, Godo's Maul U :A:	.20	.35
272 Uba Mask R :A:	.20	.35
273 Boseiju, Who Shelters All R :L:	15.00	20.00
274 Cloudcrest Lake U :L:	.20	.35
275 Eiganjo Castle R :L:	7.00	10.00
276 Forbidden Orchard R :L:	5.00	7.00
277 Hall of the Bandit Lord R :L:	8.00	12.00
278 Lantern-Lit Graveyard U :L:	.20	.35
279 Minamo, School at Water's Edge R :L:	20.00	25.00
280 Okina, Temple to the Grandfathers R :L:	2.00	3.00
281 Pinecrest Ridge U :L:	.20	.35
282 Shinka, the Bloodsoaked Keep R :L:	.20	.35
283 Shizo, Death's Storehouse R :L:	7.00	10.00
284 Tranquil Garden U :L:	.20	.35
285 Untaidake, the Cloud Keeper R :L:	3.00	5.00
286 Waterveil Cavern U :L:	.20	.35
287 Plains L :L:	.20	.35
288 Plains L :L:	.20	.35
289 Plains L :L:	.20	.35
290 Plains L :L:	.20	.35
291 Island L :L:	.20	.35
292 Island L :L:	.20	.35
293 Island L :L:	.20	.35
294 Island L :L:	.20	.35
295 Swamp L :L:	.20	.35
296 Swamp L :L:	.20	.35
297 Swamp L :L:	.20	.35
298 Swamp L :L:	.20	.35
299 Mountain L :L:	.20	.35
300 Mountain L :L:	.20	.35
301 Mountain L :L:	.20	.35
302 Mountain L :L:	.20	.35
303 Forest L :L:	.20	.35
304 Forest L :L:	.20	.35
305 Forest L :L:	.20	.35
306 Forest L :L:	.20	.35

2004 Magic The Gathering Champions of Kamigawa Foil

COMPLETE SET (307)	250.00	400.00

2005 Magic The Gathering Betrayers of Kamigawa

COMPLETE SET (165)	130.00	180.00
BOOSTER BOX (36 PACKS)	225.00	300.00
BOOSTER PACK (15 CARDS)	8.00	10.00
THEME DECK	10.00	25.00
FAT PACK	40.00	80.00
RELEASED ON FEBRUARY 4, 2005		
1 Day of Destiny R :W:	6.00	8.00
2 Empty-Shrine Kannushi U :W:	.20	.35
3 Faithful Squire U :W:	.20	.35
4 Final Judgment R :W:	2.50	3.50
5 Genju of the Fields U :W:	.20	.35
6 Heart of Light C :W:	.20	.35
7 Hokori, Dust Drinker R :W:	4.00	6.00
8 Hundred-Talon Strike C :W:	.20	.35
9 Indebted Samurai U :W:	.20	.35
10 Kami of False Hope C :W:	.20	.35
11 Kami of Tattered Shoji C :W:	.20	.35
12 Kami of the Honored Dead U :W:	.20	.35
13 Kentaro, the Smiling Cat R :W:	.20	.35
14 Kitsune Palliator U :W:	.20	.35
15 Mending Hands C :W:	.20	.35
16 Moonlit Strider C :W:	.20	.35
17 Opal-Eye, Konda's Yojimbo R :W:	.20	.35
18 Oyobi, Who Split the Heavens R :W:	.20	.35
19 Patron of the Kitsune R :W:	.20	.35
20 Scour U :W:	.20	.35
21 Shining Shoal R :W:	.20	.35
22 Silverstorm Samurai C :W:	.20	.35
23 Split-Tail Miko C :W:	.20	.35
24 Takeno's Cavalry C :W:	.20	.35
25 Tallowisp U :W:	.20	.35
26 Terashi's Grasp C :W:	.20	.35
27 Terashi's Verdict U :W:	.20	.35
28 Ward of Piety U :W:	.20	.35
29 Waxmane Baku C :W:	.20	.35
30 Yomiji, Who Bars the Way R :W:	2.00	3.00
31 Callow Jushi U :B:	.20	.35
32 Chisei, Heart of Oceans R :B:	.20	.35
33 Disrupting Shoal R :B:	15.00	20.00
34 Floodbringer C :B:	.20	.35
35 Genju of the Falls U :B:	.20	.35
36 Heed the Mists U :B:	.20	.35
37 Higure, the Still Wind R :B:	.20	.35
38 Jetting Glasskite U :B:	.20	.35
39 Kaijin of the Vanishing Touch U :B:	.20	.35
40 Kira, Great Glass-Spinner R :B:	10.00	15.00
41 Minamo Sightbender U :B:	.20	.35
42 Minamo's Meddling C :B:	.20	.35
43 Mistblade Shinobi C :B:	.20	.35
44 Ninja of the Deep Hours C :B:	.20	.35
45 Patron of the Moon R :B:	.20	.35
46 Phantom Wings C :B:	.20	.35
47 Quash U :B:	.20	.35
48 Quillmane Baku C :B:	.20	.35
49 Reduce to Dreams R :B:	.20	.35
50 Ribbons of the Reikai C :B:	.20	.35
51 Shimmering Glasskite C :B:	.20	.35
52 Soratami Mindsweeper U :B:	.20	.35
53 Stream of Consciousness U :B:	.20	.35
54 Sway of the Stars R :B:	.20	.35
55 Teardrop Kami C :B:	.20	.35
56 Threads of Disloyalty R :B:	3.00	4.50
57 Toils of Night and Day C :B:	.20	.35
58 Tomorrow, Azami's Familiar R :B:	.20	.35
59 Veil of Secrecy C :B:	.20	.35
60 Walker of Secret Ways U :B:	.20	.35
61 Iwamori of the Open Fist R :G:	.20	.35
61 Bile Urchin C :K:	.20	.35
62 Blessing of Leeches C :K:	.20	.35
63 Call for Blood C :K:	.20	.35
64 Crawling Filth C :K:	.20	.35
65 Eradicate U :K:	.20	.35
66 Genju of the Fens U :K:	.20	.35
67 Goryo's Vengeance R :K:	45.00	50.00
68 Hero's Demise R :K:	.20	.35
69 Hired Muscle U :K:	.20	.35
70 Horobi's Whisper C :K:	.20	.35
71 Ink-Eyes, Servant of Oni R :K:	3.00	4.00
72 Kyoki, Sanity's Eclipse R :K:	.20	.35
73 Mark of the Oni U :K:	.20	.35
74 Nezumi Shadow-Watcher U :K:	.20	.35
75 Ogre Marauder U :K:	.20	.35
76 Okiba-Gang Shinobi C :K:	.20	.35
77 Patron of the Nezumi R :K:	.20	.35
78 Psychic Spear C :K:	.20	.35
79 Pus Kami U :K:	.20	.35
80 Scourge of Numai U :K:	.20	.35
81 Shirei, Shizo's Caretaker R :K:	.20	.35
82 Sickening Shoal R :K:	.20	.35
83 Skullmane Baku C :K:	.20	.35
84 Skullsnatcher C :K:	.20	.35
85 Stir the Grave C :K:	.20	.35
86 Takenuma Bleeder C :K:	.20	.35
87 Three Tragedies U :K:	.20	.35
88 Throat Slitter U :K:	.20	.35
89 Toshiro Umezawa R :K:	.20	.35
90 Yukora, the Prisoner R :K:	.20	.35
91 Akki Blizzard-Herder C :R:	.20	.35
92 Akki Raider U :R:	.20	.35
93 Ashen Monstrosity U :R:	.20	.35
94 Aura Barbs U :R:	.20	.35
95 Blademane Baku C :R:	.20	.35
96 Blazing Shoal R :R:	.20	.35
97 Clash of Realities R :R:	.20	.35
98 Crack the Earth C :R:	.20	.35
99 Cunning Bandit U :R:	.20	.35
100 First Volley C :R:	.20	.35
101 Flames of the Blood Hand U :R:	.20	.35
102 Frost Ogre C :R:	.20	.35
103 Frostling C :R:	.20	.35
104 Fumiko the Lowblood R :R:	.20	.35
105 Genju of the Spires U :R:	.20	.35
106 Goblin Cohort C :R:	.20	.35
107 Heartless Hidetsugu R :R:	.20	.35
108 In the Web of War R :R:	.20	.35
109 Ire of Kaminari C :R:	.20	.35
110 Ishi-Ishi, Akki Crackshot R :R:	.20	.35
111 Kumano's Blessing C :R:	.20	.35
112 Mannichi, the Fevered Dream R :R:	.20	.35
113 Ogre Recluse U :R:	.20	.35
114 Overblaze U :R:	.20	.35
115 Patron of the Akki R :R:	.20	.35
116 Ronin Cliffrider U :R:	.20	.35
117 Shinka Gatekeeper C :R:	.20	.35
118 Sowing Salt U :R:	.20	.35
119 Torrent of Stone C :R:	.20	.35
120 Twist Allegiance R :R:	.20	.35
121 Body of Jukai U :G:	.20	.35
122 Budoka Pupil U :G:	.20	.35
123 Child of Thorns C :G:	.20	.35
124 Enshrined Memories R :G:	.20	.35
125 Forked-Branch Garami U :G:	.20	.35
126 Genju of the Cedars U :G:	.20	.35
127 Gnarled Mass C :G:	.20	.35
128 Harbinger of Spring C :G:	.20	.35
129 Isao, Enlightened Bushi R :G:	.20	.35
131 Kodama of the Center Tree R :G:	.20	.35
132 Lifegift R :G:	.20	.35
133 Lifespinner U :G:	.20	.35
134 Loam Dweller U :G:	.20	.35
135 Mark of Sakiko U :G:	.20	.35
136 Matsu-Tribe Sniper C :G:	.20	.35
137 Nourishing Shoal R :G:	5.00	7.00
138 Patron of the Orochi R :G:	4.00	6.00
139 Petalmane Baku C :G:	.20	.35
140 Roar of Jukai C :G:	.20	.35
141 Sakiko, Mother of Summer R :G:	.20	.35
142 Sakura-Tribe Springcaller C :G:	.20	.35
143 Scaled Hulk C :G:	.20	.35
144 Shizuko, Caller of Autumn R :G:	.20	.35
145 Sosuke's Summons U :G:	.20	.35
146 Splinter U :G:	.20	.35
147 Traproot Kami C :G:	.20	.35
148 Unchecked Growth U :G:	.20	.35
149 Uproot C :G:	.20	.35
150 Vital Surge C :G:	.20	.35
151 Genju of the Realm R :D:	2.50	3.50
152 Baku Altar R :A:	.20	.35
153 Blinding Powder U :A:	.20	.35
154 Mirror Gallery R :A:	10.00	15.00
155 Neko-Te R :A:	.20	.35
156 Orb of Dreams R :A:	.20	.35
157 Ornate Kanzashi R :A:	.20	.35
158 Ronin Warclub U :A:	.20	.35
159 Shuko U :A:	.20	.35
160 Shuriken U :A:	.20	.35
161 Slumbering Tora R :A:	.20	.35
162 That Which Was Taken R :A:	3.00	.35
163 Umezawa's Jitte R :A:	20.00	25.00
164 Gods' Eye, Gate to the Reikai U :L:	.20	.35
165 Tendo Ice Bridge R :L:	2.50	3.50

2005 Magic The Gathering Betrayers of Kamigawa Foil

COMPLETE SET (165)	2.00	3.00

2005 Magic The Gathering Saviors of Kamigawa

COMPLETE SET (165)	125.00	165.00
BOOSTER BOX (36 PACKS)	180.00	250.00
BOOSTER PACK (15 CARDS)	6.00	8.00
THEME DECK	5.00	10.00
FAT PACK	25.00	50.00
RELEASED ON JUNE 3, 2005		
1 AEther Shockwave U :W:	.15	.25
2 Araba Mothrider C :W:	.15	.25
3 Celestial Kirin R :W:	.30	.50
4 Charge Across the Araba U :W:	.15	.25
5 Cowed by Wisdom C :W:	.15	.25
6 Curtain of Light C :W:	.15	.25
7 Descendant of Kiyomaro U :W:	.15	.25
8 Eiganjo Free-Riders U :W:	.15	.25
9 Enduring Ideal R :W:	3.50	4.00
10 Ghost-Lit Redeemer U :W:	.15	.25
11 Hail of Arrows U :W:	.15	.25
12 Hand of Honor U :W:	.50	.75
13 Inner-Chamber Guard U :W:	.15	.25
14 Kataki, War's Wage R :W:	2.00	2.50
15 Kitsune Bonesetter C :W:	.15	.25
16 Kitsune Dawnblade C :W:	.15	.25
17 Kitsune Loreweaver C :W:	.15	.25
18 Kiyomaro, First to Stand R :W:	.30	.50
19 Michiko Konda, Truth Seeker R :W:	4.00	6.00
20 Moonwing Moth C :W:	.15	.25
21 Nikko-Onna U :W:	.15	.25
22 Plow Through Reito C :W:	.15	.25
23 Presence of the Wise U :W:	.15	.25
24 Promise of Bunrei R :W:	4.00	5.00
25 Pure Intentions R :W:	.30	.50
26 Reverence R :W:	.30	.50
27 Rune-Tail, Kitsune Ascendant R :W:	3.50	5.00
28 Shinen of Stars' Light C :W:	.15	.25
29 Spiritual Visit C :W:	.15	.25
30 Torii Watchward C :W:	.15	.25
31 Cloudhoof Kirin R :B:	.30	.50
32 Cut the Earthly Bond C :B:	.15	.25
33 Descendant of Soramaro C :B:	.15	.25
34 Dreamcatcher C :B:	.15	.25
35 Erayo, Soratami Ascendant R :B:	5.00	7.00
36 Eternal Dominion R :B:	2.00	2.50
37 Evermind U :B:	.15	.25
38 Freed from the Real C :B:	.40	.60
39 Ghost-Lit Warder U :B:	.15	.25
40 Ideas Unbound C :B:	.30	.50
41 Kaho, Minamo Historian R :B:	1.00	1.50
42 Kami of the Crescent Moon R :B:	2.75	3.25
43 Kiri-Onna U :B:	.15	.25
44 Meishin, the Mind Cage R :B:	.75	1.25
45 Minamo Scrollkeeper C :B:	.15	.25
46 Moonbow Illusionist C :B:	.15	.25
47 Murmurs from Beyond C :B:	.15	.25
48 Oboro Envoy U :B:	.15	.25
49 Oboro, Palace in the Clouds R :L:	18.00	20.00
50 Oppressive Will C :B:	.15	.25
51 Overwhelming Intellect U :B:	.15	.25
52 Rushing-Tide Zubera U :B:	.15	.25
53 Sakashima the Impostor R :B:	9.00	11.00
54 Secretkeeper U :B:	.15	.25
55 Shape Stealer U :B:	.15	.25
56 Shifting Borders U :B:	.15	.25
57 Shinen of Flight's Wings C :B:	.15	.25
58 Soramaro, First to Dream R :B:	.30	.50
58 Haru-Onna U :G:	.15	.25
59 Trusted Advisor U :B:	.15	.25
60 Twincast R :B:	2.50	3.00
61 Akuta, Born of Ash R :K:	.30	.50
62 Choice of Damnations R :K:	3.00	3.50
63 Death Denied C :K:	.15	.25
64 Death of a Thousand Stings C :K:	.15	.25
65 Deathknell Kami C :K:	.15	.25
66 Deathmask Nezumi C :K:	.15	.25
67 Exile into Darkness U :K:	.15	.25
68 Footsteps of the Goryo U :K:	1.75	2.25
69 Ghost-Lit Stalker U :K:	.15	.25
70 Gnat Miser C :K:	.15	.25
71 Hand of Cruelty U :K:	.15	.25
72 Infernal Kirin R :K:	.30	.50
73 Kagemaro, First to Suffer R :K:	1.00	1.50
74 Kagemaro's Clutch C :K:	.15	.25
75 Kami of Empty Graves C :K:	.15	.25
76 Kemuri-Onna U :K:	.15	.25
77 Kiku's Shadow U :K:	.15	.25
78 Kuon, Ogre Ascendant R :K:	.30	.50
79 Kuro's Taken C :K:	.15	.25
80 Locust Miser U :K:	.40	.60
81 Maga, Traitor to Mortals R :K:	3.00	3.50
82 Measure of Wickedness U :K:	.15	.25
83 Neverending Torment R :K:	.30	.50
84 One with Nothing R :K:	2.00	2.50
85 Pain's Reward R :K:	.50	.75
86 Raving Oni-Slave C :K:	.15	.25

87 Razorjaw Oni U :K:	.15	.25
88 Shinen of Fear's Chill C :K:	.15	.25
89 Sink into Takenuma C :K:	.15	.25
90 Skull Collector U :K:	.15	.25
91 Adamaro, First to Desire R :R:	.40	.60
92 Akki Drillmaster C :R:	.15	.25
93 Akki Underling C :R:	.15	.25
94 Barrel Down Sokenzan C :R:	.15	.25
95 Burning-Eye Zubera U :R:	.15	.25
96 Captive Flame U :R:	.15	.25
97 Feral Lightning U :R:	.15	.25
98 Gaze of Adamaro U :R:	.15	.25
99 Ghost-Lit Raider U :R:	.15	.25
100 Glitterfang C :R:	.15	.25
101 Godo's Irregulars U :R:	.15	.25
102 Hidetsugu's Second Rite R :R:	.50	.75
103 Homura, Human Ascendant R :R:	1.50	2.00
104 Iizuka the Ruthless R :R:	.30	.50
105 Inner Fire C :R:	.15	.25
106 Into the Fray C :R:	.15	.25
107 Jiwari, the Earth Aflame R :R:	.30	.50
108 Oni of Wild Places U :R:	.15	.25
109 Path of Anger's Flame C :R:	.15	.25
110 Rally the Horde R :R:	.30	.50
111 Ronin Cavekeeper C :R:	.15	.25
112 Shinen of Fury's Fire C :R:	.15	.25
113 Skyfire Kirin R :R:	.30	.50
114 Sokenzan Renegade U :R:	.15	.25
115 Sokenzan Spellblade C :R:	.15	.25
116 Spiraling Embers C :R:	.15	.25
117 Sunder from Within U :R:	.15	.25
118 Thoughts of Ruin R :R:	.30	.50
119 Undying Flames R :R:	.30	.50
120 Yuki-Onna U :R:	.15	.25
121 Arashi, the Sky Asunder R :G:	.50	.75
122 Ayumi, the Last Visitor R :G:	.30	.50
123 Bounteous Kirin R :G:	.30	.50
124 Briarknit Kami U :G:	.15	.25
125 Dense Canopy U :G:	.15	.25
126 Descendant of Masumaro U :G:	.15	.25
127 Dosan's Oldest Chant C :G:	.15	.25
128 Elder Pine of Jukai C :G:	.15	.25
129 Endless Swarm R :G:	.30	.50
130 Fiddlehead Kami C :G:	.15	.25
131 Ghost-Lit Nourisher U :G:	.15	.25
133 Inner Calm, Outer Strength C :G:	.15	.25
134 Kami of the Tended Garden U :G:	.15	.25
135 Kashi-Tribe Elite U :G:	.30	.50
136 Masumaro, First to Live R :G:	.30	.50
137 Matsu-Tribe Birdstalker C :G:	.15	.25
138 Molting Skin U :G:	.15	.25
139 Nightsoil Kami C :G:	.15	.25
140 O-Naginata U :A:	.50	.75
141 Promised Kannushi C :G:	.15	.25
142 Reki, the History of Kamigawa R :G:	.75	1.25
143 Rending Vines C :G:	.15	.25
144 Sakura-Tribe Scout C :G:	1.50	2.00
145 Sasaya, Orochi Ascendant R :G:	.50	.75
146 Seed the Land R :G:	.50	.75
147 Seek the Horizon U :G:	.15	.25
148 Sekki, Seasons' Guide R :G:	.75	1.00
149 Shinen of Life's Roar C :G:	.15	.25
150 Stampeding Serow U :G:	.15	.25
151 Iname as One R :D:	.30	.50
152 Ashes of the Fallen R :A:	.30	.50
153 Blood Clock R :A:	.30	.50
154 Ebony Owl Netsuke U :A:	.40	.60
155 Ivory Crane Netsuke U :A:	.15	.25
156 Manriki-Gusari U :A:	.50	.75
157 Oboro Breezecaller C :B:	.15	.25
158 Pithing Needle R :A:	3.50	4.25
159 Scroll of Origins R :A:	.30	.50
160 Soratami Cloud Chariot U :A:	.15	.25
161 Wine of Blood and Iron R :A:	.30	.50
162 Mikokoro, Center of the Sea R :L:	10.00	12.00
163 Miren, the Moaning Well R :L:	8.00	10.00
164 Okina Nightwatch C :G:	.15	.25
165 Tomb of Urami R :L:	.30	.50

2005 Magic The Gathering Saviors of Kamigawa Foil

COMPLETE SET (165)	150.00	300.00

2005 Magic The Gathering Ravnica City of Guilds

COMPLETE SET (306)	325.00	415.00
BOOSTER BOX (36 PACKS)	400.00	550.00
BOOSTER PACK (15 CARDS)	15.00	17.00
THEME DECK	20.00	30.00
FAT PACK	175.00	250.00
RELEASED ON OCTOBER 7, 2005		
1 Auratouched Mage U :W:	.15	.25
2 Bathe in Light U :W:	.15	.25
3 Benevolent Ancestor C :W:	.15	.25
4 Blazing Archon R :W:	1.50	2.00
5 Boros Fury-Shield C :W:	.15	.25
6 Caregiver C :W:	.15	.25
7 Chant of Vitu-Ghazi U :W:	.15	.25
8 Concerted Effort R :W:	2.50	3.00
9 Conclave Equenaut C :W:	.15	.25
10 Conclave Phalanx U :W:	.15	.25
11 Conclave's Blessing C :W:	.15	.25
12 Courier Hawk C :W:	.15	.25
13 Devouring Light U :W:	.15	.25
14 Divebomber Griffin U :W:	.15	.25
15 Dromad Purebred C :W:	.15	.25
16 Faith's Fetters C :W:	.15	.25
17 Festival of the Guildpact U :W:	.15	.25
18 Flickerform R :W:	.30	.50
19 Gate Hound C :W:	.15	.25
20 Ghosts of the Innocent R :W:	.30	.50
21 Hour of Reckoning R :W:	1.50	2.00
22 Hunted Lammasu R :W:	.30	.50
23 Leave No Trace C :W:	.15	.25
24 Light of Sanction R :W:	.30	.50
25 Loxodon Gatekeeper R :W:	1.00	1.50
26 Nightguard Patrol C :W:	.15	.25
27 Oathsworn Giant U :W:	.15	.25
28 Sandsower U :W:	.15	.25
29 Screeching Griffin C :W:	.15	.25
30 Seed Spark U :W:	.15	.25
31 Suppression Field U :W:	1.75	2.25
32 Three Dreams R :W:	.75	1.25
33 Twilight Drover R :W:	.75	1.25
34 Veteran Armorer C :W:	.15	.25
35 Votary of the Conclave C :W:	.15	.25
36 Wojek Apothecary U :W:	.15	.25
37 Wojek Siren C :W:	.15	.25
38 Belltower Sphinx U :B:	.15	.25
39 Cerulean Sphinx R :B:	.30	.50
40 Compulsive Research C :B:	.15	.25
41 Convolute C :B:	.15	.25
42 Copy Enchantment R :B:	4.00	5.00
43 Dizzy Spell C :B:	.15	.25
44 Drake Familiar C :B:	.15	.25
45 Dream Leash R :B:	.30	.50
46 Drift of Phantasms C :B:	.25	.40
47 Ethereal Usher U :B:	.15	.25
48 Eye of the Storm R :B:	.50	.75
49 Flight of Fancy C :B:	.15	.25
50 Flow of Ideas U :B:	.15	.25
51 Followed Footsteps R :B:	2.75	3.25
52 Grayscaled Gharial C :B:	.15	.25
53 Grozoth R :B:	1.25	1.75
54 Halcyon Glaze U :B:	.15	.25
55 Hunted Phantasm R :B:	.75	1.25
56 Induce Paranoia C :B:	.15	.25
57 Lore Broker U :B:	.15	.25
58 Mark of Eviction U :B:	.15	.25
59 Mnemonic Nexus U :B:	.15	.25
60 Muddle the Mixture C :B:	1.50	2.00
61 Peel from Reality C :B:	.15	.25
62 Quickchange C :B:	.15	.25
63 Remand U :B:	4.00	4.50
64 Snapping Drake C :B:	.15	.25
65 Spawnbroker R :B:	.30	.50
66 Stasis Cell C :B:	.15	.25
67 Surveilling Sprite C :B:	.15	.25
68 Tattered Drake C :B:	.15	.25
69 Telling Time U :B:	.30	.50
70 Terraformer C :B:	.15	.25
71 Tidewater Minion C :B:	.15	.25
72 Tunnel Vision R :B:	1.75	2.25
73 Vedalken Dismisser C :B:	.15	.25
74 Vedalken Entrancer C :B:	.15	.25
75 Wizened Snitches U :B:	.15	.25
76 Zephyr Spirit C :B:	.15	.25
77 Blood Funnel R :K:	.30	.50
78 Brainspoil C :K:	.15	.25
79 Carrion Howler U :K:	.15	.25
80 Clinging Darkness C :K:	.15	.25
81 Dark Confidant R :K:	35.00	40.00
82 Darkblast U :K:	1.75	2.25
83 Dimir House Guard C :K:	.15	.25
84 Dimir Machinations U :K:	.40	.60
85 Disembowel C :K:	.15	.25
86 Empty the Catacombs R :K:	.30	.50
87 Golgari Thug U :K:	2.00	2.50
88 Helldozer R :K:	1.00	1.50
89 Hex R :K:	.40	.60
90 Hunted Horror R :K:	4.00	4.50
91 Infectious Host C :K:	.15	.25
92 Keening Banshee U :K:	.15	.25
93 Last Gasp C :K:	.15	.25
94 Mausoleum Turnkey U :K:	.15	.25
95 Moonlight Bargain R :K:	.30	.50
96 Mortipede C :K:	.15	.25
97 Necromantic Thirst C :K:	.15	.25
98 Necroplasm R :K:	.30	.50
99 Netherborn Phalanx U :K:	.15	.25
100 Nightmare Void U :K:	.15	.25
101 Ribbons of Night U :K:	.15	.25
102 Roofstalker Wight C :K:	.15	.25
103 Sadistic Augermage C :K:	.15	.25
104 Sewerdreg C :K:	.15	.25
105 Shred Memory C :K:	.15	.25
106 Sins of the Past R :K:	.30	.50
107 Stinkweed Imp C :K:	.30	.50
108 Strands of Undeath C :K:	.15	.25
109 Thoughtpicker Witch C :K:	.15	.25
110 Undercity Shade U :K:	.15	.25
111 Vigor Mortis U :K:	.15	.25
112 Vindictive Mob U :K:	.15	.25
113 Woebringer Demon R :K:	.30	.50
114 Barbarian Riftcutter C :R:	.15	.25
115 Blockbuster U :R:	.15	.25
116 Breath of Fury R :R:	.50	.75
117 Char R :R:	.30	.50
118 Cleansing Beam U :R:	.15	.25
119 Coalhauler Swine C :R:	.15	.25
12 Bloodbond March R :D:	.30	.50
120 Dogpile C :R:	.15	.25
121 Excruciator R :R:	.30	.50
122 Fiery Conclusion C :R:	.15	.25
123 Flame Fusillade R :R:	.30	.50
124 Flash Conscription U :R:	.15	.25
125 Frenzied Goblin U :R:	.15	.25
126 Galvanic Arc C :R:	.15	.25
127 Goblin Fire Fiend C :R:	.15	.25
128 Goblin Spelunkers C :R:	.15	.25
129 Greater Forgeling U :R:	.15	.25
130 Hammerfist Giant R :R:	.30	.50
131 Hunted Dragon R :R:	.50	.75
132 Incite Hysteria C :R:	.15	.25
133 Indentured Oaf U :R:	.15	.25
134 Instill Furor U :R:	.15	.25
135 Mindmoil R :R:	.30	.50
136 Molten Sentry R :R:	.30	.50
137 Ordruun Commando C :R:	.15	.25
138 Rain of Embers C :R:	.15	.25
139 Reroute U :R:	.15	.25
140 Sabertooth Alley Cat C :R:	.15	.25
141 Seismic Spike C :R:	.15	.25
142 Sell-Sword Brute C :R:	.15	.25
143 Smash C :R:	.15	.25
144 Sparkmage Apprentice C :R:	.15	.25
145 Stoneshaker Shaman U :R:	.15	.25
146 Surge of Zeal C :R:	.15	.25
147 Torpid Moloch C :R:	.15	.25
148 Viashino Fangtail C :R:	.15	.25
149 Viashino Slasher C :R:	.15	.25
150 Warp World R :R:	.30	.50
151 War-Torch Goblin C :R:	.15	.25
152 Wojek Embermage U :R:	.15	.25
153 Birds of Paradise R :G:	5.00	7.00
154 Bramble Elemental C :G:	.15	.25
155 Carven Caryatid U :G:	.25	.40
156 Chord of Calling R :G:	9.00	11.00
157 Civic Wayfinder C :G:	.15	.25
158 Doubling Season R :G:	50.00	60.00
159 Dowsing Shaman U :G:	.15	.25
160 Dryad's Caress C :G:	.15	.25
161 Elves of Deep Shadow C :G:	.15	.25
162 Elvish Skysweeper C :G:	.15	.25
163 Farseek C :G:	.15	.25
164 Fists of Ironwood C :G:	.15	.25
165 Gather Courage C :G:	.15	.25
166 Golgari Brownscale C :G:	.15	.25
167 Golgari Grave-Troll R :G:	9.00	12.00
168 Goliath Spider U :G:	.15	.25
169 Greater Mossdog C :G:	.15	.25
170 Hunted Troll R :G:	.30	.50
171 Ivy Dancer U :G:	.15	.25
172 Life from the Loam R :G:	12.00	14.00
173 Moldervine Cloak U :G:	.15	.25
174 Nullmage Shepherd U :G:	.20	.35
175 Overwhelm U :G:	.15	.25
176 Perilous Forays U :G:	1.25	1.75
177 Primordial Sage R :G:	.40	.60
178 Recollect U :G:	.15	.25
179 Rolling Spoil U :R:	.15	.25
180 Root-Kin Ally U :G:	.15	.25
181 Scatter the Seeds C :G:	.15	.25
182 Scion of the Wild R :G:	.30	.50
183 Siege Wurm C :G:	.15	.25
184 Stone-Seeder Hierophant C :G:	.15	.25
185 Sundering Vitae C :G:	.15	.25
186 Transluminant C :G:	.15	.25
187 Trophy Hunter U :G:	.15	.25
188 Ursapine R :G:	.30	.50
189 Vinelasher Kudzu R :G:	.50	.75
190 Agrus Kos, WojekVeteran R :D:	.30	.50
191 Autochthon Wurm R :D:	.50	.75
193 Boros Swiftblade U :D:	.15	.25
194 Brightflame R :D:	.30	.50
195 Chorus of the Conclave R :D:	.30	.50
196 Circu, Dimir Lobotomist R :D:	2.50	3.00
197 Clutch of the Undercity U :D:	.15	.25
198 Congregation at Dawn U :D:	.75	1.25
199 Consult the Necrosages C :D:	.15	.25
200 Dark Heart of the Wood U :D:	.15	.25
201 Dimir Cutpurse R :D:	.50	.75
202 Dimir Doppelganger R :D:	.75	1.00
203 Dimir Infiltrator C :D:	.15	.25
204 Drooling Groodion U :D:	.15	.25
205 Firemane Angel R :D:	.50	.75
206 Flame-Kin Zealot U :D:	.15	.25
207 Glare of Subdual R :D:	.75	1.00
208 Glimpse the Unthinkable R :D:	25.00	30.00
209 Golgari Germination U :D:	.15	.25
210 Golgari Rotwurm C :D:	.15	.25
211 Grave-Shell Scarab R :D:	.30	.50
212 Guardian of Vitu-Ghazi C :D:	.15	.25
213 Lightning Helix U :D:	3.50	5.00
214 Loxodon Hierarch R :D:	.50	.75
215 Mindleech Mass R :D:	.50	.75
216 Moroii U :D:	.15	.25
217 Perplex C :D:	.15	.25
218 Phytohydra R :D:	2.00	2.50
219 Pollenbright Wings U :D:	.15	.25
220 Psychic Drain U :D:	.30	.50
221 Putrefy U :D:	.25	.40
222 Rally the Righteous C :D:	.15	.25
223 Razia's Purification R :D:	.40	.60
224 Razia, Boros Archangel R :D:	1.00	1.50
225 Savra,Queen of the Golgari R :D:	2.00	2.50
226 Searing Meditation R :D:	.30	.50
227 Seeds of Strength C :D:	.15	.25
228 Selesnya Evangel C :D:	.15	.25
229 Selesnya Sagittars U :D:	.15	.25
230 Shambling Shell C :D:	.15	.25
231 Sisters of Stone Death R :D:	2.50	3.00
232 Skyknight Legionnaire C :D:	.15	.25
233 Sunhome Enforcer U :D:	.15	.25
234 Szadek, Lord of Secrets R :D:	.50	.75
235 Thundersong Trumpeter C :D:	.15	.25
236 Tolsimir Wolfblood R :D:	1.75	2.25
237 Twisted Justice U :D:	.15	.25
238 Vulturous Zombie R :D:	.75	1.00
239 Watchwolf U :D:	.25	.40
240 Woodwraith Corrupter R :D:	.30	.50
241 Woodwraith Strangler C :D:	.15	.25
242 Boros Guildmage U :R::W:	.15	.25
243 Boros Recruit C :R::W:	.15	.25
244 Centaur Safeguard C :G::W:	.15	.25
245 Dimir Guildmage U :B::K:	.15	.25
246 Gaze of the Gorgon C :K::G:	.15	.25
247 Gleancrawler R :K::G:	.30	.50
248 Golgari Guildmage U :K::G:	.15	.25
249 Lurking Informant C :B::K:	.15	.25
250 Master Warcraft R :R::W:	.50	.75
251 Privileged Position R :G::W:	12.00	14.00
252 Selesnya Guildmage U :G::W:	.15	.25
253 Shadow of Doubt R :B::K:	4.00	4.50
254 Bloodletter Quill R :A:	.30	.50
255 Boros Signet C :A:	.15	.25
256 Bottled Cloister R :A:	.30	.50
257 Cloudstone Curio R :A:	8.00	10.00
258 Crown of Convergence R :A:	.30	.50
259 Cyclopean Snare U :A:	.15	.25
260 Dimir Signet C :A:	.75	1.25
261 Glass Golem U :A:	.15	.25
262 Golgari Signet C :A:	.15	.25
263 Grifter's Blade U :A:	.15	.25
264 Junktroller U :A:	.15	.25
265 Leashling U :A:	.15	.25
266 Nullstone Gargoyle R :A:	.30	.50
267 Pariah's Shield R :A:	2.75	3.25
268 Peregrine Mask U :A:	.15	.25
269 Plague Boiler R :A:	.30	.50
270 Selesnya Signet C :A:	.15	.25
271 Spectral Searchlight U :A:	.15	.25
272 Sunforger R :A:	.75	1.00
273 Terrarion C :A:	.15	.25
274 Voyager Staff U :A:	.15	.25
275 Boros Garrison C :L:	.15	.25
276 Dimir Aqueduct C :L:	.50	.75
277 Duskmantle,HouseofShadow U :L:	.15	.25
278 Golgari Rot Farm C :L:	.15	.25
279 Overgrown Tomb R :L:	10.00	12.00
280 Sacred Foundry R :L:	14.00	16.00
281 Selesnya Sanctuary C :L:	.15	.25
282 Sunhome,Fortress U :L:	.50	.75
283 Svogthos,Restless Tomb U :L:	.15	.25
284 Temple Garden R :L:	11.00	13.00
285 Vitu-Ghazi, City-Tree U :L:	.15	.25
286 Watery Grave R :L:	11.00	13.00
287 Plains C :L:	.15	.25
288 Plains C :L:	.15	.25
289 Plains C :L:	.15	.25
290 Plains C :L:	.15	.25
291 Island C :L:	.15	.25
292 Island C :L:	.15	.25
293 Island C :L:	.15	.25
294 Island C :L:	.15	.25
295 Swamp C :L:	.15	.25
296 Swamp C :L:	.15	.25
297 Swamp C :L:	.15	.25
298 Swamp C :L:	.15	.25
299 Mountain C :L:	.15	.25
300 Mountain C :L:	.15	.25
301 Mountain C :L:	.15	.25
302 Mountain C :L:	.15	.25
303 Forest C :L:	.15	.25
304 Forest C :L:	.15	.25
305 Forest C :L:	.15	.25
306 Forest C :L:	.15	.25

2006 Magic The Gathering Guildpact

COMPLETE SET (165)	130.00	170.00
BOOSTER BOX (36 PACKS)	225.00	300.00
BOOSTER PACK (15 CARDS)	10.00	13.00
THEME DECK	10.00	20.00
FAT PACK	40.00	80.00
RELEASED ON FEBRUARY 3, 2006		
1 Absolver Thrull C :W:	.10	.20
2 Belfry Spirit U :W:	.10	.20
3 Benediction of Moons C :W:	.10	.20
4 Droning Bureaucrats U :W:	.10	.20
5 Ghost Warden C :W:	.10	.20
6 Ghostway R :W:	4.00	6.00
7 Graven Dominator R :W:	.25	.40
8 Guardian's Magemark C :W:	.10	.20
9 Harrier Griffin U :W:	.10	.20
10 Leyline of the Meek R :W:	1.00	1.50
11 Lionheart Maverick C :W:	.10	.20
12 Martyred Rusalka U :W:	.10	.20
13 Order of the Stars U :W:	.20	.30
14 Shadow Lance U :W:	.10	.20
15 Shrieking Grotesque C :W:	.10	.20
16 Sinstriker's Will U :W:	.10	.20
17 Skyrider Trainee C :W:	.10	.20
18 Spelltithe Enforcer R :W:	.60	1.00
19 Storm Herd R :W:	2.00	2.50
20 To Arms! U :W:	.30	.40
21 Withstand C :W:	.10	.20
22 AEtherplasm U :B:	.20	.30
23 Crystal Seer C :B:	.10	.20
24 Drowned Rusalka U :B:	.10	.20
25 Frazzle U :B:	.10	.20
26 Gigadrowse C :B:	.40	.60
27 Hatching Plans R :B:	.30	.50
28 Infiltrator's Magemark C :B:	.10	.20
29 Leyline of Singularity R :B:	3.00	5.00
30 Mimeofacture R :B:	.25	.40
31 Quicken R :B:	.60	1.00
32 Repeal C :B:	.10	.20
33 Runeboggle C :B:	.10	.20
34 Sky Swallower R :B:	.25	.40
35 Steamcore Weird C :B:	.10	.20
36 Stratozeppelid U :B:	.10	.20
37 Thunderheads U :B:	.10	.20
38 Torch Drake C :B:	.10	.20
39 Train of Thought C :B:	.10	.20
40 Vacuumelt U :B:	.10	.20
41 Vedalken Plotter U :B:	.10	.20
42 Vertigo Spawn U :B:	.10	.20
43 Abyssal Nocturnus R :K:	1.00	1.50
44 Caustic Rain U :K:	.10	.20
45 Cremate C :K:	.10	.20
46 Cry of Contrition C :K:	.10	.20
47 Cryptwailing U :K:	.10	.20
48 Daggerclaw Imp U :K:	.10	.20
49 Douse in Gloom C :K:	.10	.20
50 Exhumer Thrull U :K:	.10	.20
51 Hissing Miasma U :K:	.20	.30
52 Leyline of the Void R :K:	25.00	30.00
53 Necromancer's Magemark C :K:	.10	.20
54 Orzhov Euthanist C :K:	.10	.20
55 Ostiary Thrull C :K:	.10	.20
56 Plagued Rusalka U :K:	.10	.20
57 Poisonbelly Ogre C :K:	.10	.20
58 Restless Bones C :K:	.10	.20
59 Revenant Patriarch U :K:	.10	.20
60 Sanguine Praetor R :K:	.25	.40
61 Seize the Soul R :K:	.25	.40
62 Skeletal Vampire R :K:	.25	.40
63 Smogsteed Rider U :K:	.10	.20
64 Bloodscale Prowler C :R:	.10	.20
65 Fencer's Magemark C :R:	.10	.20
66 Ghor-Clan Bloodscale U :R:	.10	.20
67 Hypervolt Grasp U :R:	.10	.20
68 Leyline of Lightning R :R:	.25	.40
69 Living Inferno R :R:	.25	.40
70 Ogre Savant C :R:	.10	.20
71 Parallectric Feedback R :R:	.25	.40
72 Pyromatics C :R:	.10	.20

Card	Low	High
73 Rabble-Rouser U :R:	.10	.20
74 Scorched Rusalka U :R:	.10	.20
75 Shattering Spree U :R:	10.00	15.00
76 Siege of Towers R :R:	.25	.40
77 Skarrgan Firebird R :R:	.25	.40
78 Tin Street Hooligan C :R:	.10	.20
79 Battering Wurm U :G:	.10	.20
80 Beastmaster's Magemark C :G:	.10	.20
81 Bioplasm R :G:	.30	.40
82 Crash Landing U :G:	.10	.20
83 Dryad Sophisticate U :G:	.10	.20
84 Earth Surge R :G:	.30	.50
85 Gatherer of Graces U :G:	.10	.20
86 Ghor-Clan Savage C :G:	.10	.20
87 Gristleback U :G:	.10	.20
88 Gruul Nodorog C :G:	.10	.20
89 Gruul Scrapper C :G:	.10	.20
90 Leyline of Lifeforce R :G:	2.00	2.50
91 Petrified Wood-Kin R :G:	.25	.40
92 Predatory Focus U :G:	.10	.20
93 Primeval Light U :G:	.10	.20
94 Silhana Ledgewalker C :G:	.60	1.00
95 Silhana Starfletcher C :G:	.10	.20
96 Skarrgan Pit-Skulk C :G:	.10	.20
97 Starved Rusalka U :G:	.10	.20
98 Wildsize C :G:	.10	.20
99 Wurmweaver Coil R :G:	.25	.40
100 Agent of Masks U :D:	.20	.30
101 Angel of Despair R :D:	2.50	3.00
102 Blind Hunter C :D:	.10	.20
103 Borborygmos R :D:	.40	.60
104 Burning-Tree Bloodscale C :D:	.10	.20
105 Burning-Tree Shaman R :D:	1.00	1.50
106 Castigate C :D:	.10	.20
107 Cerebral Vortex R :D:	.60	1.00
108 Conjurer's Ban U :D:	.10	.20
109 Culling Sun R :D:	.30	.50
110 Dune-Brood Nephilim R :D:	.60	1.00
111 Electrolyze U :D:	.40	.60
112 Feral Animist U :D:	.10	.20
113 Gelectrode U :D:	.50	.80
114 Ghost Council of Orzhova R :D:	.50	.80
115 Glint-Eye Nephilim R :D:	.40	.60
116 Goblin Flectomancer U :D:	.10	.20
117 Ink-Treader Nephilim R :D:	.60	1.00
118 Invoke the Firemind R :D:	.30	.50
119 Izzet Chronarch C :D:	.10	.20
120 Killer Instinct R :D:	.25	.40
121 Leap of Flame C :D:	.10	.20
122 Mortify U :D:	.10	.20
123 Nivix, Aerie of the Firemind U :L:	.10	.20
124 Orzhov Pontiff R :D:	5.00	7.00
125 Pillory of the Sleepless C :D:	.10	.20
126 Rumbling Slum R :D:	.30	.50
127 Savage Twister U :D:	.10	.20
128 Scab-Clan Mauler C :D:	.10	.20
129 Schismotivate U :D:	.10	.20
130 Skarrgan Skybreaker U :D:	.10	.20
131 Souls of the Faultless U :D:	1.00	1.50
132 Stitch in Time R :D:	4.00	6.00
133 Streetbreaker Wurm C :D:	.10	.20
134 Teysa, Orzhov Scion R :D:	2.50	3.50
135 Tibor and Lumia R :D:	.30	.40
136 Ulasht, the Hate Seed R :D:	1.50	2.00
137 Wee Dragonauts C :D:	.10	.20
138 Witch-Maw Nephilim R :D:	.60	1.00
139 Wreak Havoc U :D:	.10	.20
140 Yore-Tiller Nephilim R :D:	1.50	2.00
141 Debtors' Knell R :D:	7.00	9.00
142 Djinn Illuminatus R :D:	.30	.50
143 Giant Solifuge R :D:	.40	.60
144 Gruul Guildmage U :D:	.10	.20
145 Izzet Guildmage U :D:	.25	.40
146 Mourning Thrull C :D:	.10	.20
147 Orzhov Guildmage U :D:	.10	.20
148 Petrahydrox C :D:	.10	.20
149 Wild Cantor C :D:	.10	.20
150 Gruul Signet C :A:	.10	.20
151 Gruul War Plow R :A:	.30	.50
152 Izzet Signet C :A:	.25	.40
153 Mizzium Transreliquat R :A:	.30	.50
154 Moratorium Stone R :A:	.20	.30
155 Orzhov Signet C :A:	.10	.20
156 Sword of the Paruns R :A:	.40	.60
157 Godless Shrine R :L:	14.00	16.00
158 Gruul Turf C :L:	.20	.30
159 Izzet Boilerworks C :L:	.10	.20
160 Niv-Mizzet, the Firemind R :D:	2.00	2.50
161 Orzhov Basilica C :L:	.20	.30
162 Orzhova, the Church of Deals U :L:	.10	.20
163 Skarrg, the Rage Pits U :L:	.25	.40
164 Steam Vents R :L:	25.00	30.00
165 Stomping Ground R :L:	20.00	25.00

2006 Magic The Gathering Dissension

Card	Low	High
COMPLETE SET (180)	160.00	215.00
BOOSTER BOX (36 PACKS)	250.00	300.00
BOOSTER PACK (15 CARDS)	10.00	13.00
THEME DECK	10.00	20.00
FAT PACK	50.00	80.00
RELEASED ON MAY 5, 2006		
1 Aurora Eidolon C :W:	.10	.20
2 Azorius Herald U :W:	.20	.30
3 Beacon Hawk C :W:	.10	.20
4 Blessing of the Nephilim U :W:	.25	.40
5 Brace for Impact U :W:	.20	.30
6 Carom C :W:	.10	.20
7 Celestial Ancient R :W:	.50	.80
8 Condemn U :W:	.25	.40
9 Freewind Equenaut C :W:	.10	.20
10 Guardian of the Guildpact C :W:	.20	.30
11 Haazda Exonerator C :W:	.10	.20
12 Haazda Shield Mate R :W:	.10	.20
13 Mistral Charger U :W:	.20	.30
14 Paladin of Prahv U :W:	.20	.30
15 Proclamation of Rebirth R :W:	5.00	7.00
16 Proper Burial R :W:	.60	1.00
17 Soulsworn Jury C :W:	.10	.20
18 Steeling Stance C :W:	.10	.20
19 Stoic Ephemera U :W:	.20	.30
20 Valor Made Real C :W:	.10	.20
21 Wakestone Gargoyle R :W:	.25	.40
22 Court Hussar U :B:	.25	.40
23 Cytoplast Manipulator R :B:	3.00	5.00
24 Enigma Eidolon C :B:	.10	.20
25 Govern the Guildless R :B:	.30	.50
26 Helium Squirter C :B:	.10	.20
27 Novijen Sages R :B:	.25	.40
28 Ocular Halo C :B:	.10	.20
29 Plaxmanta U :B:	.20	.30
30 Psychic Possession R :B:	.25	.40
31 Silkwing Scout C :B:	.10	.20
32 Skyscribing U :B:	.20	.30
33 Spell Snare U :B:	3.00	5.00
34 Tidespout Tyrant R :B:	8.00	10.00
35 Vigean Graftmage U :B:	.20	.30
36 Vision Skeins C :B:	.10	.20
37 Writ of Passage C :B:	.10	.20
38 Bond of Agony U :K:	.40	.60
39 Brain Pry U :K:	.20	.30
40 Crypt Champion U :K:	.20	.30
41 Delirium Skeins C :K:	.10	.20
42 Demon's Jester C :K:	.10	.20
43 Drekavac U :K:	.20	.30
44 Enemy of the Guildpact C :K:	.10	.20
45 Entropic Eidolon C :K:	.10	.20
46 Infernal Tutor R :K:	18.00	22.00
47 Macabre Waltz C :K:	.10	.20
48 Nettling Curse C :K:	.10	.20
49 Nightcreep U :K:	.20	.30
50 Nihilistic Glee R :K:	.25	.40
51 Ragamuffyn U :K:	.20	.30
52 Ratcatcher R :K:	2.00	3.00
53 Seal of Doom C :K:	.10	.20
54 Slaughterhouse Bouncer C :K:	.10	.20
55 Slithering Shade U :K:	.20	.30
56 Unliving Psychopath R :K:	.25	.40
57 Vesper Ghoul C :K:	.10	.20
58 Wit's End R :K:	.25	.40
59 Cackling Flames C :R:	.10	.20
60 Demonfire R :R:	.50	.80
61 Flame-Kin War Scout U :R:	.20	.30
62 Flaring Flame-Kin U :R:	.20	.30
63 Gnat Alley Creeper U :R:	.20	.30
64 Ignorant Bliss U :R:	.20	.30
65 Kill-Suit Cultist C :R:	.10	.20
66 Kindle the Carnage U :R:	.20	.30
67 Ogre Gatecrasher C :R:	.10	.20
68 Psychotic Fury C :R:	.10	.20
69 Rakdos Pit Dragon R :R:	.50	.80
70 Sandstorm Eidolon C :R:	.10	.20
71 Seal of Fire C :R:	.10	.20
72 Squealing Devil U :R:	.20	.30
73 Stalking Vengeance R :R:	.50	.80
74 Stormscale Anarch R :R:	.30	.50
75 Taste for Mayhem C :R:	.10	.20
76 Utvara Scalper C :R:	.10	.20
77 War's Toll R :R:	4.00	6.00
78 Weight of Spires U :R:	.20	.30
79 Whiptail Moloch C :R:	.10	.20
80 Aquastrand Spider C :G:	.10	.20
81 Cytoplast Root-Kin R :G:	.60	1.00
82 Cytospawn Shambler C :G:	.10	.20
83 Elemental Resonance R :G:	.40	.60
84 Fertile Imagination U :G:	.20	.30
85 Flash Foliage U :G:	.20	.30
86 Indrik Stomphowler U :G:	.20	.30
87 Loaming Shaman R :G:	.60	1.00
88 Might of the Nephilim U :G:	.20	.30
89 Patagia Viper U :G:	.20	.30
90 Protean Hulk R :G:	6.00	8.00
91 Simic Basilisk U :G:	.20	.30
92 Simic Initiate C :G:	.10	.20
93 Simic Ragworm C :G:	.10	.20
94 Sporeback Troll C :G:	.10	.20
95 Sprouting Phytohydra R :G:	1.50	2.00
96 Stomp and Howl U :G:	.20	.30
97 Street Savvy C :G:	.10	.20
98 Thrive C :G:	.10	.20
99 Utopia Sprawl C :G:	3.00	4.00
100 Verdant Eidolon C :G:	.10	.20
101 AEthermage's Touch R :W: :B:	.30	.50
102 Anthem of Rakdos R :K: :R:	.40	.60
103 Assault Zeppelid C :G: :B:	.10	.20
104 Azorius AEthermage U :W: :B:	.20	.30
105 Azorius First-Wing C :W: :B:	.10	.20
106 Azorius Ploy U :W: :B:	.20	.30
107 Coiling Oracle C :G: :B:	.20	.30
108 Cytoshape R :G: :B:	.30	.50
109 Dread Slag R :K: :R:	.25	.40
110 Experiment Kraj R :G: :B:	2.50	3.50
111 Gobhobbler Rats C :K: :R:	.10	.20
112 Grand Arbiter Augustin IV R :W: :B:	8.00	10.00
113 Hellhole Rats U :K: :R:	.20	.30
114 Isperia the Inscrutable R :W: :B:	.30	.50
115 Jagged Poppet U :K: :R:	.20	.30
116 Leafdrake Roost U :G: :B:	.20	.30
117 Lyzolda, the Blood Witch R :K: :R:	.40	.60
118 Momir Vig, Simic Visionary R :G: :B:	2.50	4.00
119 Omnibian R :G: :B:	.40	.60
120 Overrule C :W: :B:	.10	.20
121 Pain Magnification U :K: :R:	.30	.50
122 Palliation Accord U :W: :B:	.20	.30
123 Plaxcaster Frogling U :G: :B:	.40	.60
124 Plumes of Peace C :W: :B:	.10	.20
125 Pride of the Clouds R :W: :B:	5.00	7.00
126 Rain of Gore R :K: :R:	3.00	5.00
127 Rakdos Augermage R :K: :R:	.30	.50
128 Rakdos Ickspitter C :K: :R:	.10	.20
129 Rakdos the Defiler R :K: :R:	2.50	4.00
130 Simic Sky Swallower R :G: :B:	.60	1.00
131 Sky Hussar U :W: :B:	.30	.50
132 Swift Silence R :W: :B:	.30	.50
133 Trygon Predator U :G: :B:	.30	.50
134 Twinstrike U :K: :R:	.10	.20
135 Vigean Hydropon C :G: :B:	.10	.20
136 Vigean Intuition U :G: :B:	.20	.30
137 Voidslime R :G: :B:	6.00	8.00
138 Windreaver R :W: :B:	.20	.35
139 Wrecking Ball C :K: :R:	.10	.20
140 Avatar of Discord R :K: :R:	1.00	1.50
141 Azorius Guildmage U :W: :B:	.40	.60
142 Biomantic Mastery R :G: :B:	.30	.50
143 Dovescape R :K: :B:	3.00	5.00
144 Minister of Impediments C :W: :B:	.10	.20
145 Rakdos Guildmage U :K: :R:	.20	.30
146 Riot Spikes C :K: :R:	.10	.20
147 Shielding Plax C :G: :B:	.10	.20
148 Simic Guildmage U :G: :B:	.40	.60
149 Bound // Determined R :K: :G:	.40	.60
150 Crime // Punishment R :W: :K:	.60	1.00
151 Hide // Seek R :R: :W:	2.00	3.00
152 Hit // Run U :K: :R:	.20	.30
153 Odds // Ends R :B: :R:	.60	1.00
154 Pure // Simple U :R: :G:	.20	.30
155 Research // Development R :G: :B:	.50	.80
156 Rise // Fall U :B: :K:	.60	1.00
157 Supply // Demand U :G: :W:	.20	.30
158 Trial // Error U :W: :B:	.20	.30
159 Azorius Signet C :A:	1.00	1.50
160 Bronze Bombshell R :A:	1.00	1.50
161 Evolution Vat R :A:	.50	.80
162 Magewright's Stone U :A:	1.50	2.00
163 Muse Vessel R :A:	.30	.50
164 Rakdos Riteknife R :A:	.25	.40
165 Rakdos Signet C :A:	.25	.40
166 Simic Signet C :A:	.20	.30
167 Skullmead Cauldron U :A:	.20	.30
168 Transguild Courier U :A:	.20	.30
169 Walking Archive R :A:	1.00	1.50
170 Azorius Chancery C :L:	.20	.30
171 Blood Crypt R :L:	20.00	25.00
172 Breeding Pool R :L:	20.00	25.00
173 Ghost Quarter U :L:	3.00	5.00
174 Hallowed Fountain R :L:	15.00	20.00
175 Novijen, Heart of Progress U :L:	.25	.40
176 Pillar of the Paruns R :L:	3.00	5.00
177 Prahv, Spires of Order U :L:	.20	.30
178 Rakdos Carnarium C :L:	.20	.30
179 Rix Maadi, Dungeon Palace U :L:	.20	.30
180 Simic Growth Chamber C :L:	.30	.50

2006 Magic The Gathering Dissension Foil

Card	Low	High
COMPLETE SET (180)	250.00	400.00

2006 Magic The Gathering Coldsnap

Card	Low	High
COMPLETE SET (155)	185.00	245.00
BOOSTER BOX (36 PACKS)	300.00	350.00
BOOSTER PACK (15 CARDS)	11.00	13.00
FAT PACK	40.00	80.00
RELEASED ON JULY 21, 2006		
1 Adarkar Valkyrie R :W:	.75	1.25
2 Boreal Griffin C :W:	.10	.20
3 Cover of Winter R :W:	.25	.40
4 Darien, King of Kjeldor R :W:	4.00	6.00
5 Field Marshal R :W:	4.00	6.00
6 Gelid Shackles C :W:	.10	.20
7 Glacial Plating U :W:	.15	.25
8 Jotun Grunt U :W:	.30	.50
9 Jotun Owl Keeper U :W:	.15	.25
10 Kjeldoran Gargoyle U :W:	.20	.30
11 Kjeldoran Javelineer C :W:	.10	.20
12 Kjeldoran Outrider C :W:	.10	.20
13 Kjeldoran War Cry C :W:	.10	.20
14 Luminesce U :W:	.20	.30
15 Martyr of Sands C :W:	1.50	2.00
16 Ronom Unicorn C :W:	.10	.20
17 Squall Drifter C :W:	.10	.20
18 Sun's Bounty C :W:	.10	.20
19 Sunscour R :W:	.60	1.00
20 Surging Sentinels C :W:	.10	.20
21 Swift Maneuver C :W:	.10	.20
22 Ursine Fylgja U :W:	.20	.30
23 Wall of Shards U :W:	2.00	3.00
24 White Shield Crusader U :W:	.20	.30
25 Woolly Razorback R :W:	.40	.60
26 Adarkar Windform U :B:	.20	.35
27 Arcum Dagsson R :B:	10.00	15.00
28 Balduvian Frostwaker U :B:	.15	.25
29 Commandeer R :B:	6.00	8.00
30 Controvert U :B:	.20	.30
31 Counterbalance U :B:	5.00	7.00
32 Drelnoch C :B:	.10	.20
33 Flashfreeze U :B:	.20	.30
34 Frost Raptor C :B:	.10	.20
35 Frozen Solid C :B:	.10	.20
36 Heidar, Rimewind Master R :B:	.25	.40
37 Jokulmorder R :B:	.30	.50
38 Krovikan Mist C :B:	.20	.30
39 Krovikan Whispers U :B:	.20	.30
40 Martyr of Frost C :B:	.20	.30
41 Perilous Research U :B:	.30	.40
42 Rimefeather Owl R :B:	.25	.40
43 Rimewind Cryomancer U :B:	.20	.30
44 Rimewind Taskmage C :B:	.10	.20
45 Ronom Serpent C :B:	.10	.20
46 Rune Snag C :B:	.50	.80
47 Surging AEther C :B:	.20	.30
48 Survivor of the Unseen C :B:	.10	.20
49 Thermal Flux C :B:	.10	.20
50 Vexing Sphinx R :B:	.40	.60
51 Balduvian Fallen U :K:	.15	.25
52 Chill to the Bone C :K:	.10	.20
53 Chilling Shade C :K:	.10	.20
54 Deathmark U :K:	.20	.30
55 Disciple of Tevesh Szat C :K:	.10	.20
56 Feast of Flesh C :K:	.10	.20
57 Garza's Assassin R :K:	.40	.60
58 Grim Harvest C :K:	.15	.25
59 Gristle Grinner U :K:	.15	.25
60 Gutless Ghoul C :K:	.10	.20
61 Haakon, Stromgald Scourge R :K:	2.50	4.00
62 Herald of Leshrac R :K:	3.00	4.00
63 Krovikan Rot U :K:	.20	.30
64 Krovikan Scoundrel C :K:	.10	.20
65 Martyr of Bones C :K:	.10	.20
66 Phobian Phantasm U :K:	.20	.30
67 Phyrexian Etchings R :K:	.30	.50
68 Rime Transfusion U :K:	.20	.30
69 Rimebound Dead C :K:	.10	.20
70 Soul Spike R :K:	.75	1.25
71 Stromgald Crusader U :K:	1.50	2.00
72 Surging Dementia C :K:	.10	.20
73 Tresserhorn Skyknight U :K:	.20	.30
74 Void Maw R :K:	.30	.50
75 Zombie Musher C :K:	.10	.20
76 Balduvian Rage U :R:	.30	.50
77 Balduvian Warlord U :R:	.20	.30
78 Braid of Fire R :R:	15.00	20.00
79 Cryoclasm U :R:	.15	.25
80 Earthen Goo U :R:	.10	.20
81 Fury of the Horde R :R:	.75	1.25
82 Goblin Furrier C :R:	.10	.20
83 Goblin Rimerunner C :R:	.10	.20
84 Greater Stone Spirit U :R:	.15	.25
85 Icefall C :R:	.10	.20
86 Karplusan Minotaur R :R:	1.50	2.00
87 Karplusan Wolverine C :R:	.10	.20
88 Lightning Serpent R :R:	1.50	2.00
89 Lightning Storm U :R:	1.00	1.50
90 Lovisa Coldeyes R :R:	.60	1.00
91 Magmatic Core U :R:	.20	.30
92 Martyr of Ashes C :R:	.20	.30
93 Ohran Yeti C :R:	.10	.20
94 Orcish Bloodpainter C :R:	.10	.20
95 Rimescale Dragon R :R:	1.00	1.50
96 Rite of Flame C :R:	1.00	1.50
97 Skred C :R:	1.00	1.50
98 Stalking Yeti U :R:	.20	.30
99 Surging Flame C :R:	.10	.20
100 Thermopod C :R:	.10	.20
101 Allosaurus Rider R :G:	2.00	3.00
102 Arctic Nishoba U :G:	.15	.25
103 Aurochs Herd C :G:	.10	.20
104 Boreal Centaur C :G:	.10	.20
105 Boreal Druid C :G:	.60	1.00
106 Brooding Saurian R :G:	.30	.50
107 Bull Aurochs C :G:	.10	.20
108 Freyalise's Radiance U :G:	.20	.30
109 Frostweb Spider C :G:	.10	.20
110 Hibernation's End R :G:	.40	.60
111 Into the North C :G:	.10	.20
112 Karplusan Strider U :G:	.20	.30
113 Martyr of Spores C :G:	.10	.20
114 Mystic Melting U :G:	.20	.30
115 Ohran Viper R :G:	.60	1.00
116 Panglacial Wurm R :G:	2.00	3.00
117 Resize U :G:	.20	.30
118 Rimehorn Aurochs U :G:	.20	.30
119 Ronom Hulk C :G:	.10	.20
120 Shape of the Wiitigo R :G:	.25	.40
121 Sheltering Ancient U :G:	1.00	1.50
122 Simian Brawler C :G:	.10	.20
123 Sound the Call C :G:	.10	.20
124 Steam Spitter U :G:	.20	.30
125 Surging Might C :G:	.10	.20
126 Blizzard Specter U :D:	.50	.80
127 Deepfire Elemental U :D:	.20	.30
128 Diamond Faerie R :D:	.30	.50
129 Garza Zol, Plague Queen R :D:	.50	.80
130 Juniper Order Ranger U :D:	.50	.80
131 Sek'Kuar, Deathkeeper R :D:	.25	.40
132 Tamanoa R :D:	.50	.80
133 Vanish into Memory U :D:	.20	.30
134 Wilderness Elemental U :D:	.20	.30
135 Zur the Enchanter R :D:	2.00	3.00
136 Coldsteel Heart U :A:	1.50	2.00
137 Jester's Scepter R :A:	.40	.60
138 Mishra's Bauble U :A:	7.00	9.00
139 Phyrexian Ironfoot U :A:	.20	.30
140 Phyrexian Snowcrusher U :A:	.20	.30
141 Phyrexian Soulgorger R :A:	3.00	4.00
142 Thrumming Stone R :A:	25.00	30.00
143 Arctic Flats U :L:	.60	1.00
144 Boreal Shelf U :L:	.50	.80
145 Dark Depths R :L:	55.00	60.00
146 Frost Marsh U :L:	.60	1.00
147 Highland Weald U :L:	.25	.40
148 Mouth of Ronom U :L:	.30	.50
149 Scrying Sheets R :L:	9.00	11.00
150 Tresserhorn Sinks U :L:	.40	.60
151 Snow-Covered Plains C :L:	.60	1.00
152 Snow-Covered Island C :L:	3.00	4.00
153 Snow-Covered Swamp C :L:	.60	1.00
154 Snow-Covered Mountain C :L:	2.00	3.00
155 Snow-Covered Forest C :L:	.50	.80

2006 Magic The Gathering Coldsnap Foil

Card	Low	High
COMPLETE SET (155)	125.00	250.00

2006 Magic The Gathering Coldsnap Token

Card	Low	High
1 Marit Lage	8.00	12.00

2006 Magic The Gathering Time Spiral

Card	Low	High
COMPLETE SET (301)	300.00	385.00
BOOSTER BOX (36 PACKS)	375.00	425.00
BOOSTER PACK (15 CARDS)	10.00	15.00
THEME DECK	8.00	15.00
FAT PACK	40.00	60.00
RELEASED ON OCTOBER 6, 2006		
1 Amrou Scout C :W:	.15	.25
2 Amrou Seekers C :W:	.15	.25
3 Angel's Grace R :W:	5.00	7.00
4 Benalish Cavalry C :W:	.15	.25
5 Castle Raptors C :W:	.15	.25
6 Cavalry Master U :W:	.15	.25
7 Celestial Crusader U :W:	.15	.25
8 Children of Korlis C :W:	.15	.25
9 Chronosavant R :W:	.30	.50
10 Cloudchaser Kestrel C :W:	.15	.25
11 D'Avenant Healer C :W:	.15	.25
12 Detainment Spell C :W:	.15	.25
13 Divine Congregation C :W:	.15	.25
14 Duskrider Peregrine U :W:	.15	.25
15 Errant Doomsayers C :W:	.15	.25
16 Evangelize R :W:	.30	.50
17 Flickering Spirit C :W:	.15	.25
18 Foriysian Interceptor C :W:	.15	.25

19 Fortify C :W: .15 .25
20 Gaze of Justice C :W: .15 .25
21 Griffin Guide U :W: .15 .25
22 Gustcloak Cavalier U :W: .15 .25
23 Icatian Crier C :W: .15 .25
24 Ivory Giant C :W: .15 .25
25 Jedit's Dragoons C :W: .15 .25
26 Knight of the Holy Nimbus U :W: .15 .25
27 Magus of the Disk R :W: 1.00 1.50
28 Mangara of Corondor R :W: 3.25 3.75
29 Momentary Blink C :W: .15 .25
30 Opal Guardian R :W: .30 .50
31 Outrider en-Kor U :W: .15 .25
32 Pentarch Paladin R :W: .75 1.00
33 Pentarch Ward C :W: .15 .25
34 Plated Pegasus U :W: .15 .25
35 Pull from Eternity U :W: .15 .25
36 Pulmonic Sliver R :W: 3.00 3.50
37 Quilled Sliver U :W: .15 .25
38 Restore Balance R :W: 3.75 4.50
39 Return to Dust U :W: 1.00 1.50
40 Serra Avenger R :W: 1.75 2.25
41 Sidewinder Sliver C :W: .50 .75
42 Spirit Loop U :W: .15 .25
43 Temporal Isolation C :W: .15 .25
44 Tivadar of Thorn R :W: .30 .50
45 Watcher Sliver C :W: .15 .25
46 Weathered Bodyguards R :W: .30 .50
47 Zealot il-Vec C :W: .15 .25
48 Ancestral Vision R :B: 45.00 50.00
49 Bewilder C :B: .15 .25
50 Brine Elemental U :B: .15 .25
51 Cancel C :B: .15 .25
52 Careful Consideration U :B: .15 .25
53 Clockspinning C :B: .15 .25
54 Coral Trickster C :B: .15 .25
55 Crookclaw Transmuter C :B: .15 .25
56 Deep-Sea Kraken R :B: .50 .75
57 Draining Whelk R :B: 2.50 3.00
58 Dream Stalker C :B: .15 .25
59 Drifter il-Dal C :B: .15 .25
60 Errant Ephemeron C :B: .15 .25
61 Eternity Snare C :B: .15 .25
62 Fathom Seer C :B: .15 .25
63 Fledgling Mawcor U :B: .15 .25
64 Fool's Demise U :B: .15 .25
65 Ixidron R :B: .50 .75
66 Looter il-Kor C :B: .15 .25
67 Magus of the Jar R :B: .30 .50
68 Moonlace R :B: .30 .50
69 Mystical Teachings C :B: .25 .40
70 Ophidian Eye C :B: .15 .25
71 Paradox Haze U :B: 1.25 1.75
72 Psionic Sliver R :B: .75 1.00
73 Riftwing Cloudskate U :B: .15 .25
74 Sage of Epityr C :B: .25 .40
75 Screeching Sliver C :B: .15 .25
76 Shadow Sliver C :B: .15 .25
77 Slipstream Serpent C :B: .15 .25
78 Snapback C :B: .15 .25
79 Spell Burst U :B: .75 1.00
80 Spiketail Drakeling C :B: .15 .25
81 Sprite Noble R :B: .30 .50
82 Stormcloud Djinn U :B: .15 .25
83 Teferi, Mage of Zhalfir R :B: 11.00 13.00
84 Telekinetic Sliver U :B: .50 .75
85 Temporal Eddy C :B: .15 .25
86 Think Twice C :B: .15 .25
87 Tolarian Sentinel C :B: .15 .25
88 Trickbind R :B: 3.75 4.50
89 Truth or Tale U :B: .15 .25
90 Vesuvan Shapeshifter R :B: 2.00 2.50
91 Viscerid Deepwalker C :B: .15 .25
92 Voidmage Husher U :B: .15 .25
93 Walk the Aeons R :B: 4.00 6.00
94 Wipe Away U :B: .15 .25
95 Assassinate C :K: .15 .25
96 Basal Sliver C :K: .15 .25
97 Call to the Netherworld C :K: .15 .25
98 Corpulent Corpse C :K: .15 .25
99 Curse of the Cabal R :K: .75 1.25
100 Cyclopean Giant C :K: .15 .25
101 Dark Withering C :K: .15 .25
102 Deathspore Thallid C :K: .15 .25
103 Demonic Collusion R :K: .30 .50
104 Dread Return U :K: .50 .75
105 Drudge Reavers C :K: .15 .25
106 Endrek Sahr, Master Breeder R :K: .30 .50
107 Evil Eye of Urborg U :K: .15 .25
108 Faceless Devourer U :K: .15 .25
109 Fallen Ideal U :K: .15 .25
110 Feebleness C :K: .15 .25
111 Gorgon Recluse C :K: .15 .25
112 Haunting Hymn U :K: .15 .25
113 Liege of the Pit R :K: .30 .50
114 Lim-Dûl the Necromancer R :K: 1.25 1.75
115 Living End R :K: 8.00 10.00
116 Magus of the Mirror R :K: .30 .50
117 Mana Skimmer C :K: .15 .25
118 Mindlash Sliver C :K: .15 .25
119 Mindstab C :K: .15 .25
120 Nether Traitor R :K: 3.75 4.50
121 Nightshade Assassin U :K: .15 .25
122 Phthisis U :K: .15 .25
123 Pit Keeper C :K: .15 .25
124 Plague Sliver R :K: .30 .50
125 Premature Burial U :K: .15 .25
126 Psychotic Episode C :K: .15 .25
127 Sangrophage C :K: .15 .25
128 Sengir Nosferatu R :K: .30 .50
129 Skittering Monstrosity U :K: .15 .25
130 Skulking Knight C :K: .15 .25
131 Smallpox U :K: .30 .50
132 Strangling Soot C :K: .15 .25
133 Stronghold Overseer R :K: .30 .50
134 Sudden Death U :K: .15 .25
135 Sudden Spoiling R :K: .75 1.00
136 Tendrils of Corruption C :K: .15 .25
137 Traitor's Clutch C :K: .15 .25
138 Trespasser il-Vec C :K: .15 .25
139 Urborg Syphon-Mage C :K: .15 .25
140 Vampiric Sliver U :K: .15 .25
141 Viscid Lemures C :K: .15 .25
142 AEtherflame Wall C :R: .15 .25
143 Ancient Grudge C :R: .30 .50
144 Barbed Shocker U :R: .15 .25
145 Basalt Gargoyle U :R: .15 .25
146 Blazing Blade Askari C :R: .15 .25
147 Bogardan Hellkite R :R: .75 1.25
148 Bogardan Rager C :R: .15 .25
149 Bonesplitter Sliver C :R: .15 .25
150 Coal Stoker C :R: .15 .25
151 Conflagrate U :R: 4.00 5.00
152 Empty the Warrens C :R: .20 .35
153 Firemaw Kavu U :R: .15 .25
154 Flamecore Elemental C :R: .15 .25
155 Flowstone Channeler C :R: .15 .25
156 Fortune Thief R :R: 2.00 2.50
157 Fury Sliver U :R: .15 .25
158 Ghitu Firebreathing C :R: .15 .25
159 Goblin Skycutter C :R: .15 .25
160 Grapeshot C :R: .15 .25
161 Greater Gargadon R :R: 7.00 9.00
162 Ground Rift C :R: .15 .25
163 Ib Halfheart, Goblin Tactician R :R: 1.00 1.50
164 Ignite Memories U :R: .15 .25
165 Ironclaw Buzzardiers C :R: .15 .25
166 Jaya Ballard, Task Mage R :R: .50 .75
167 Keldon Halberdier C :R: .15 .25
168 Lightning Axe C :R: .75 1.00
169 Magus of the Scroll R :R: .30 .50
170 Mogg War Marshal C :R: .50 .75
171 Norin the Wary R :R: 4.00 6.00
172 Orcish Cannonade C :R: .15 .25
173 Pardic Dragon R :R: .30 .50
174 Plunder C :R: .15 .25
175 Reiterate R :R: 5.00 7.00
176 Rift Bolt C :R: 1.75 2.25
177 Sedge Sliver R :R: 7.00 9.00
178 Subterranean Shambler C :R: .15 .25
179 Sudden Shock U :R: 1.50 2.00
180 Sulfurous Blast U :R: .15 .25
181 Tectonic Fiend U :R: .15 .25
182 Thick-Skinned Goblin U :R: .15 .25
183 Two-Headed Sliver C :R: .15 .25
184 Undying Rage U :R: .15 .25
185 Viashino Bladescout C :R: .15 .25
186 Volcanic Awakening U :R: .15 .25
187 Wheel of Fate R :R: 2.50 3.00
188 Word of Seizing R :R: .30 .50
189 AEther Web C :G: .15 .25
190 Ashcoat Bear C :G: .15 .25
191 Aspect of Mongoose U :G: .15 .25
192 Chameleon Blur C :G: .15 .25
193 Durkwood Baloth C :G: .15 .25
194 Durkwood Tracker U :G: .15 .25
195 Fungus Sliver R :G: .75 1.00
196 Gemhide Sliver C :G: .75 1.00
197 Glass Asp C :G: .15 .25
198 Greenseeker C :G: .15 .25
199 Havenwood Wurm C :G: .15 .25
200 Herd Gnarr C :G: .15 .25
201 Hypergenesis R :G: 1.25 1.75
202 Krosan Grip U :G: .75 1.00
203 Magus of the Candelabra R :G: .75 1.00
204 Might of Old Krosa U :G: 8.00 10.00
205 Might Sliver U :G: .50 .75
206 Molder C :G: .15 .25
207 Mwonvuli Acid-Moss C :G: 1.50 2.00
208 Nantuko Shaman C :G: .15 .25
209 Pendelhaven Elder U :G: .15 .25
210 Penumbra Spider C :G: .15 .25
211 Phantom Wurm U :G: .15 .25
212 Primal Forcemage U :G: .15 .25
213 Savage Thallid C :G: .15 .25
214 Scarwood Treefolk C :G: .15 .25
215 Scryb Ranger U :G: .15 .25
216 Search for Tomorrow C :G: .30 .50
217 Spectral Force R :G: .30 .50
218 Spike Tiller R :G: .30 .50
219 Spinneret Sliver C :G: .40 .60
220 Sporesower Thallid U :G: .15 .25
221 Sprout C :G: .15 .25
222 Squall Line R :G: .30 .50
223 Stonewood Invocation R :G: .30 .50
224 Strength in Numbers C :G: .15 .25
225 Thallid Germinator C :G: .15 .25
226 Thallid Shell-Dweller C :G: .15 .25
227 Thelon of Havenwood R :G: .30 .50
228 Thelonite Hermit R :G: .40 .60
229 Thrill of the Hunt C :G: .15 .25
230 Tromp the Domains U :G: .15 .25
231 Unyaro Bees R :G: .30 .50
232 Verdant Embrace R :G: .40 .60
233 Wormwood Dryad C :G: .15 .25
234 Wurmcalling R :G: .30 .50
235 Yavimaya Dryad U :G: .15 .25
236 Dementia Sliver U :D: .15 .25
237 Dralnu, Lich Lord R :D: .75 1.00
238 Firewake Sliver U :D: .15 .25
239 Ghostflame Sliver U :D: .15 .25
240 Harmonic Sliver U :D: 2.00 2.50
241 Ith, High Arcanist R :D: .30 .50
242 Kaervek the Merciless R :D: 1.50 2.00
243 Mishra, Artificer Prodigy R :D: .50 .75
244 Opaline Sliver U :D: .15 .25
245 Saffi Eriksdotter R :D: 2.75 3.25
246 Scion of the Ur-Dragon R :D: 4.00 6.00
247 Stonebrow, Krosan Hero R :D: .30 .50
248 Assembly-Worker U :A: .15 .25
249 Brass Gnat C :A: .15 .25
250 Candles of Leng R :A: .30 .50
251 Chromatic Star C :A: 2.50 3.00
252 Chronatog Totem U :A: .15 .25
253 Clockwork Hydra U :A: .15 .25
254 Foriysian Totem U :A: .15 .25
255 Gauntlet of Power R :A: 13.00 14.00
256 Hivestone R :A: .75 1.25
257 Jhoira's Timebug C :A: .15 .25
258 Locket of Yesterdays U :A: .15 .25
259 Lotus Bloom R :A: 6.00 8.00
260 Paradise Plume U :A: .15 .25
261 Phyrexian Totem U :A: .15 .25
262 Prismatic Lens C :A: .15 .25
263 Sarpadian Empires, Vol. VII R :A: .30 .50
264 Stuffy Doll R :A: 2.00 2.50
265 Thunder Totem U :A: .15 .25
266 Triskelavus R :A: .30 .50
267 Venser's Sliver C :A: .15 .25
268 Weatherseed Totem U :A: .15 .25
269 Academy Ruins R :L: 18.00 21.00
270 Calciform Pools U :L: .15 .25
271 Dreadship Reef U :L: .15 .25
272 Flagstones of Trokair R :L: 16.00 18.00
273 Fungal Reaches U :L: .15 .25
274 Gemstone Caverns R :L: 4.00 6.00
275 Kher Keep R :L: .50 .75
276 Molten Slagheap U :L: .15 .25
277 Saltcrusted Steppe U :L: .15 .25
278 Swarmyard R :L: 7.00 9.00
279 Terramorphic Expanse C :L: .15 .25
280 Urza's Factory U :L: .15 .25
281 Vesuva R :L: 14.00 16.00
282 Plains L :L: .15 .25
283 Plains L :L: .15 .25
284 Plains L :L: .15 .25
285 Plains L :L: .15 .25
286 Island L :L: .15 .25
287 Island L :L: .15 .25
288 Island L :L: .15 .25
289 Island L :L: .15 .25
290 Swamp L :L: .15 .25
291 Swamp L :L: .15 .25
292 Swamp L :L: .15 .25
293 Swamp L :L: .15 .25
294 Mountain L :L: .15 .25
295 Mountain L :L: .15 .25
296 Mountain L :L: .15 .25
297 Mountain L :L: .15 .25
298 Forest L :L: .15 .25
299 Forest L :L: .15 .25
300 Forest L :L: .15 .25
301 Forest L :L: .15 .25

2006 Magic The Gathering Time Spiral Timeshifted

COMPLETE SET (121) 50.00 100.00
TR = TIMESHIFTED RARE
ACCORDING TO WOTC, THE TR ARE 50% RARER THAN
THE TIME SPIRAL RARES WITHIN THE BOOSTERS.
1 Akroma, Angel of Wrath TR :W: 4.00 10.00
2 Auratog TR :W: .25 .60
3 Celestial Dawn TR :W: .25 .60
4 Consecrate Land TR :W: .10 .25
5 Defiant Vanguard TR :W: .10 .25
6 Disenchant TR :W: .25 .60
7 Enduring Renewal TR :W: .40 1.00
8 Essence Sliver TR :W: 1.50 4.00
9 Honorable Passage TR :W: .10 .25
10 Icatian Javelineers TR :W: .10 .25
11 Moorish Cavalry TR :W: .10 .25
12 Resurrection TR :W: .20 .50
13 Sacred Mesa TR :W: .30 .75
14 Soltari Priest TR :W: .50 1.25
15 Squire TR :W: .10 .25
16 Valor TR :W: .10 .25
17 Witch Hunter TR :W: .15 .40
18 Zhalfirin Commander TR :W: .10 .25
19 Dandan TR :B: .10 .25
20 Flying Men TR :B: .30 .75
21 Ghost Ship TR :B: .10 .25
22 Giant Oyster TR :B: .10 .25
23 Leviathan TR :B: .15 .40
24 Lord of Atlantis TR :B: 3.00 8.00
25 Merfolk Assassin TR :B: .10 .25
26 Mistform Ultimus TR :B: .20 .50
27 Ovinomancer TR :B: .10 .25
28 Pirate Ship TR :B: .15 .40
29 Prodigal Sorcerer TR :B: .10 .25
30 Psionic Blast TR :B: 1.00 2.50
31 Sindbad TR :B: .10 .25
32 Stormscape Familiar TR :B: .15 .40
33 Unstable Mutation TR :B: .10 .25
34 Voidmage Prodigy TR :B: .50 1.25
35 Whispers of the Muse TR :B: .10 .25
36 Willbender TR :B: .20 .50
37 Avatar of Woe TR :K: 2.00 5.00
38 Bad Moon TR :K: 1.25 3.00
39 Conspiracy TR :K: .40 1.00
40 Darkness TR :K: 1.25 3.00
41 Dauthi Slayer TR :K: .20 .50
42 Evil Eye of Orms-by-Gore TR :K: .10 .25
43 Faceless Butcher TR :K: .10 .25
44 Funeral Charm TR :K: .30 .75
45 Sengir Autocrat TR :K: .15 .40
46 Shadow Guildmage TR :K: .10 .25
47 Soul Collector TR :K: .50 1.25
48 Stupor TR :K: .30 .75
49 Swamp Mosquito TR :K: .10 .25
50 Twisted Abomination TR :K: .10 .25
51 Uncle Istvan TR :K: .10 .25
52 Undead Warchief TR :K: 2.50 6.00
53 Undertaker TR :K: .10 .25
54 Withered Wretch TR :R: :K: .30 .75
55 Avalanche Riders TR :R: .50 1.25
56 Browbeat TR :R: 1.25 3.00
57 Desolation Giant TR :R: .20 .50
58 Disintegrate TR :R: .20 .50
59 Dragon Whelp TR :R: .15 .40
60 Dragonstorm TR :R: 2.00 5.00
61 Eron the Relentless TR :R: .10 .25
62 Fiery Temper TR :R: .20 .50
63 Fire Whip TR :R: .10 .25
64 Goblin Snowman TR :R: .10 .25
65 Kobold Taskmaster TR :R: .15 .40
66 Orcish Librarian TR :R: .15 .40
67 Orgg TR :R: .15 .40
68 Pandemonium TR :R: .60 1.50
69 Suq'Ata Lancer TR :R: .10 .25
70 Tribal Flames TR :R: .15 .40
71 Uthden Troll TR :R: .10 .25
72 Wildfire Emissary TR :R: .10 .25
73 Avoid Fate TR :G: .40 1.00
74 Call of the Herd TR :G: .50 1.25
75 Cockatrice TR :G: .15 .40
76 Craw Giant TR :G: .10 .25
77 Gaea's Blessing TR :G: .75 2.00
78 Gaea's Liege TR :G: .20 .50
79 Hail Storm TR :G: .10 .25
80 Hunting Moa TR :G: .10 .25
81 Jolrael, Empress of Beasts TR :G: .15 .40
82 Krosan Cloudscraper TR :G: .40 1.00
83 Scragnoth TR :G: .10 .25
84 Spike Feeder TR :G: .10 .25
85 Spitting Slug TR :G: .10 .25
86 Thallid TR :G: .10 .25
87 Thornscape Battlemage TR :G: .10 .25
88 Verdeloth the Ancient TR :G: .40 1.00
89 Wall of Roots TR :G: .40 1.00
90 Whirling Dervish TR :G: .10 .25
91 Coalition Victory TR :D: .25 .60
92 Fiery Justice TR :D: .20 .50
93 Jasmine Boreal TR :D: .10 .25
94 Lightning Angel TR :D: .50 1.25
95 Merieke Ri Berit TR :D: .25 .60
96 Mystic Enforcer TR :D: .40 1.00
97 Mystic Snake TR :D: 1.00 2.50
98 Nicol Bolas TR :D: .60 1.50
99 Shadowmage Infiltrator TR :D: 1.00 2.50
100 Sol'kanar the Swamp King TR :D: .20 .50
101 Spined Sliver TR :D: .15 .40
102 Stormbind TR :D: .20 .50
103 Teferi's Moat TR :D: .40 1.00
104 Vhati il-Dal TR :D: .20 .50
105 Void TR :D: .20 .50
106 Assault // Battery TR :R: :G: .10 .25
107 Claws of Gix TR :A: .15 .40
108 Dodecapod TR :A: .10 .25
109 Feldon's Cane TR :A: .40 1.00
110 Grinning Totem TR :A: .20 .50
111 Mindless Automaton TR :A: .15 .40
112 Mirari TR :A: .75 2.00
113 The Rack TR :A: .75 2.00
114 Serrated Arrows TR :A: .15 .40
115 Tormod's Crypt TR :A: 1.25 3.00
116 War Barge TR :A: .10 .25
117 Arena TR :L: .20 .50
118 Desert TR :L: .30 .75
119 Gemstone Mine TR :L: 2.00 5.00
120 Pendelhaven TR :L: .60 1.50
121 Safe Haven TR :L: .20 .50

2006 Magic The Gathering Time Spiral Timeshifted Foil

TR = TIMESHIFTED RARE
ACCORDING TO WOTC, THE TR ARE 50% RARER THAN
THE TIME SPIRAL RARES WITHIN THE BOOSTERS.

2007 Magic The Gathering Planar Chaos

COMPLETE SET (165) 150.00 195.00
BOOSTER BOX (36 PACKS) 375.00 500.00
BOOSTER PACK (15 CARDS) 13.00 16.00
THEME DECK 8.00 15.00
FAT PACK 30.00 60.00
RELEASED ON FEBRUARY 2, 2007
1 Aven Riftwatcher C :W: .15 .25
2 Benalish Commander R :W: 1.00 1.50
3 Crovax, Ascendant Hero R :W: .75 1.00
4 Dawn Charm C :W: .75 1.00
5 Dust Elemental R :W: .30 .50
6 Ghost Tactician C :W: .15 .25
7 Heroes Remembered R :W: .50 .75
8 Magus of the Tabernacle R :W: 1.50 2.00
9 Mantle of Leadership U :W: .15 .25
10 Pallid Mycoderm C :W: .15 .25
11 Poultice Sliver C :W: .15 .25
12 Rebuff the Wicked U :W: 1.75 2.25
13 Retether R :W: 1.25 1.75
14 Riftmarked Knight U :W: .15 .25
15 Saltblast U :W: .15 .25
16 Saltfield Recluse C :W: .15 .25
17 Serra's Boon U :W: .15 .25
18 Shade of Trokair C :W: .15 .25
19 Stonecloaker U :W: .15 .25
20 Stormfront Riders U :W: .15 .25
21 Voidstone Gargoyle R :W: .30 .50
22 Whitemane Lion C :W: .15 .25
23 Calciderm U :W: .15 .25
24 Malach of the Dawn U :W: .15 .25
25 Mana Tithe C :W: .75 1.00
26 Mesa Enchantress R :W: .30 .50
27 Mycologist U :W: .15 .25
28 Porphyry Nodes R :W: 1.75 2.25
29 Revered Dead C :W: .15 .25
30 Sinew Sliver C :W: 1.50 2.00
31 Sunlance C :W: .15 .25
32 Aeon Chronicler R :B: .30 .50
33 Aquamorph Entity C :B: .15 .25
34 Auramancer's Guise U :B: .25 .40
35 Body Double R :B: .75 1.25
36 Braids, Conjurer Adept R :B: 1.75 2.25
37 Chronozoa R :B: 1.25 1.75
38 Dichotomancy R :B: .30 .50
39 Dismal Failure U :B: .15 .25
40 Dreamscape Artist C :B: .15 .25
41 Erratic Mutation C :B: .15 .25
42 Jodah's Avenger U :B: .15 .25
43 Magus of the Bazaar R :B: .75 1.25
44 Pongify U :B: .75 1.00
45 Reality Acid C :B: .15 .25
46 Shaper Parasite C :B: .15 .25
47 Spellshift R :B: .30 .50
48 Synchronous Sliver C :B: .15 .25
49 Tidewalker U :B: .15 .25
50 Timebender U :B: .15 .25
51 Veiling Oddity C :B: .15 .25
52 Venarian Glimmer U :B: .15 .25

Card	Low	High
53 Wistful Thinking C :B:	.15	.25
54 Frozen AEther U :B:	.75	1.00
55 Gossamer Phantasm C :B:	.15	.25
56 Merfolk Thaumaturgist C :B:	.15	.25
57 Ovinize U :B:	.15	.25
58 Piracy Charm C :B:	.15	.25
59 Primal Plasma C :B:	.15	.25
60 Riptide Pilferer U :B:	.15	.25
61 Serendib Sorcerer R :B:	.30	.50
62 Serra Sphinx R :B:	.30	.50
63 Big Game Hunter U :K:	1.75	2.25
64 Blightspeaker C :K:	.15	.25
65 Brain Gorgers C :K:	.15	.25
66 Circle of Affliction U :K:	.15	.25
67 Cradle to Grave C :K:	.15	.25
68 Dash Hopes C :K:	.75	1.00
69 Deadly Grub C :K:	.15	.25
70 Enslave U :K:	.15	.25
71 Extirpate R :K:	3.25	3.75
72 Imp's Mischief R :K:	1.75	2.25
73 Magus of the Coffers R :K:	.50	.75
74 Midnight Charm C :K:	.15	.25
75 Mirri the Cursed R :K:	1.75	2.25
76 Muck Drubb U :K:	.15	.25
77 Phantasmagorian U :K:	.40	.60
78 Ridged Kusite C :K:	.15	.25
79 Roiling Horror R :K:	.30	.50
80 Spitting Sliver C :K:	.15	.25
81 Temporal Extortion R :K:	3.00	4.00
82 Treacherous Urge U :K:	.15	.25
83 Waning Wurm U :K:	.15	.25
84 Bog Serpent C :K:	.15	.25
85 Damnation R :K:	55.00	60.00
86 Dunerider Outlaw U :K:	.15	.25
87 Kor Dirge U :K:	.15	.25
88 Melancholy C :K:	.15	.25
89 Null Profusion R :K:	.30	.50
90 Rathi Trapper C :K:	.15	.25
91 Shrouded Lore U :K:	.15	.25
92 Vampiric Link C :K:	.75	1.00
93 AEther Membrane U :R:	.50	.75
94 Akroma, Angel of Fury R :R:	2.50	3.00
95 Battering Sliver C :R:	.15	.25
96 Detritivore R :R:	.30	.50
97 Dust Corona C :R:	.15	.25
98 Fatal Frenzy R :R:	.30	.50
99 Firefright Mage C :R:	.15	.25
100 Fury Charm C :R:	.15	.25
101 Hammerheim Deadeye U :R:	.15	.25
102 Keldon Marauders C :R:	.15	.25
103 Lavacore Elemental U :R:	.15	.25
104 Magus of the Arena R :R:	.30	.50
105 Needlepeak Spider C :R:	.15	.25
106 Shivan Meteor U :R:	.25	.40
107 Stingscourger C :R:	.15	.25
108 Sulfur Elemental U :R:	.30	.50
109 Timecrafting U :R:	.15	.25
110 Torchling R :R:	.30	.50
111 Volcano Hellion R :R:	.30	.50
112 Boom // Bust R :R:	7.00	9.00
113 Dead // Gone C :R:	.15	.25
114 Rough // Tumble U :R:	.15	.25
115 Blood Knight U :R:	.15	.25
116 Brute Force C :R:	.15	.25
117 Molten Firebird R :R:	.30	.50
118 Prodigal Pyromancer C :R:	.15	.25
119 Pyrohemia U :R:	.25	.40
120 Reckless Wurm U :R:	.15	.25
121 Shivan Wumpus R :R:	.50	.75
122 Simian Spirit Guide C :R:	4.00	5.00
123 Skirk Shaman C :R:	.15	.25
124 Ana Battlemage U :G:	.15	.25
125 Citanul Woodreaders C :G:	.15	.25
126 Deadwood Treefolk U :G:	.15	.25
127 Evolution Charm C :G:	.15	.25
128 Fungal Behemoth R :G:	.50	.75
129 Giant Dustwasp C :G:	.15	.25
130 Hunting Wilds U :G:	.30	.50
131 Jedit Ojanen of Efrava R :G:	.40	.60
132 Kavu Predator U :G:	.30	.50
133 Life and Limb R :G:	.75	1.25
134 Magus of the Library R :G:	.30	.50
135 Mire Boa C :G:	.15	.25
136 Pouncing Wurm U :G:	.15	.25
137 Psychotrope Thallid U :G:	.75	1.25
138 Reflex Sliver C :G:	.15	.25
139 Sophic Centaur U :G:	.15	.25
140 Timbermare R :G:	.30	.50
141 Uktabi Drake C :G:	.15	.25
142 Utopia Vow C :G:	.15	.25
143 Vitaspore Thallid C :G:	.15	.25
144 Wild Pair R :G:	1.25	1.75
145 Essence Warden C :G:	.75	1.00
146 Fa'adiyah Seer C :G:	.15	.25
147 Gaea's Anthem R :G:	1.00	1.50
148 Groundbreaker R :G:	1.25	1.75
149 Harmonize U :G:	1.25	1.75
150 Healing Leaves C :G:	.15	.25
151 Hedge Troll U :G:	.15	.25
152 Keen Sense U :G:	2.00	2.50
153 Seal of Primordium C :G:	.15	.25
154 Cautery Sliver U :D:	.15	.25
155 Darkheart Sliver U :D:	.75	1.25
156 Dormant Sliver U :D:	.75	1.00
157 Frenetic Sliver U :D:	.15	.25
158 Intet, the Dreamer R :D:	1.75	2.25
159 Necrotic Sliver U :D:	3.00	3.50
160 Numot, the Devastator R :D:	.75	1.00
161 Oros, the Avenger R :D:	.30	.50
162 Radha, Heir to Keld R :D:	1.50	2.00
163 Teneb, the Harvester R :D:	1.00	1.50
164 Vorosh, the Hunter R :D:	.75	1.25
165 Urborg, Tomb of Yawgmoth R :L:	10.00	12.00

2007 Magic The Gathering Planar Chaos Foil

COMPLETE SET (165)

2007 Magic The Gathering Future Sight

Card	Low	High
COMPLETE SET (180)	500.00	625.00
BOOSTER BOX (36 PACKS)	700.00	850.00
BOOSTER PACK (15 CARDS)	25.00	35.00
THEME DECK	8.00	15.00
FAT PACK	40.00	80.00
RELEASED ON MAY 4, 2007		
1 Angel of Salvation R :W:	.40	.60
2 Augur il-Vec C :W:	.15	.25
3 Barren Glory R :W:	.30	.50
3 Marshaling Cry C :W:	.15	.25
4 Chronomantic Escape U :W:	.15	.25
5 Dust of Moments U :W:	.15	.25
6 Even the Odds U :W:	.15	.25
7 Gift of Granite C :W:	.15	.25
8 Intervention Pact R :W:	3.00	4.00
9 Judge Unworthy C :W:	.15	.25
10 Knight of Sursi C :W:	.15	.25
11 Lost Auramancers U :W:	.25	.40
12 Magus of the Moat R :W:	4.00	6.00
13 Magus of the Vineyard R :G:	.30	.50
14 Saltskitter C :W:	.15	.25
15 Samite Censer-Bearer C :W:	.15	.25
16 Scout's Warning R :W:	1.50	2.00
17 Spirit en-Dal U :W:	.15	.25
18 Aven Mindcensor U :W:	6.00	8.00
19 Blade of the Sixth Pride C :W:	.15	.25
20 Bound in Silence U :W:	.15	.25
21 Daybreak Coronet R :W:	5.00	7.00
22 Goldmeadow Lookout U :W:	.15	.25
23 Imperial Mask R :W:	.30	.50
24 Lucent Liminid C :W:	.15	.25
25 Lumithread Field C :W:	.15	.25
26 Lymph Sliver C :W:	.15	.25
27 Mistmeadow Skulk U :W:	.15	.25
28 Oriss, Samite Guardian R :W:	.50	.75
29 Patrician's Scorn C :W:	.15	.25
30 Ramosian Revivalist U :W:	.15	.25
31 Seht's Tiger R :W:	.50	.75
32 Aven Augur C :B:	.15	.25
33 Cloudseeder U :B:	.15	.25
34 Cryptic Annelid U :B:	.15	.25
35 Delay U :B:	1.25	1.75
36 Foresee C :B:	.15	.25
37 Infiltrator il-Kor C :B:	.15	.25
38 Leaden Fists C :B:	.15	.25
39 Maelstrom Djinn R :B:	.30	.50
40 Magus of the Future R :B:	1.25	1.75
41 Mystic Speculation U :B:	1.25	1.75
42 Pact of Negation R :B:	20.00	25.00
43 Reality Strobe U :B:	.25	.40
44 Take Possession R :B:	.30	.50
45 Unblinking Bleb C :B:	.15	.25
46 Venser's Diffusion C :B:	.15	5.00
47 Venser, Shaper Savant R :B:	15.00	18.00
48 Arcanum Wings U :B:	.25	.40
49 Blind Phantasm C :B:	.15	.25
50 Bonded Fetch U :B:	.15	.25
51 Linessa, Zephyr Mage R :B:	.30	.50
52 Logic Knot C :B:	.15	.25
54 Narcomoeba U :B:	3.00	3.50
55 Nix R :B:	.30	.50
56 Sarcomite Myr C :B:	.15	.25
57 Second Wind U :B:	.15	.25
58 Shapeshifter's Marrow R :B:	.30	.50
59 Spellweaver Volute R :B:	.50	.75
60 Spin into Myth U :B:	.25	.40
61 Vedalken AEthermage C :B:	.15	.25
62 Whip-Spine Drake C :B:	.15	.25
63 Augur of Skulls C :K:	.15	.25
64 Cutthroat il-Dal C :K:	.15	.25
65 Festering March U :K:	.15	.25
66 Gibbering Descent R :K:	.30	.50
67 Grave Peril C :K:	.15	.25
68 Ichor Slick C :K:	.15	.25
69 Lost Hours C :K:	.15	.25
70 Magus of the Abyss R :K:	.30	.50
72 Nihilith R :K:	.75	1.00
73 Oblivion Crown C :K:	.15	.25
74 Pooling Venom U :K:	.25	.40
75 Putrid Cyclops C :K:	.15	.25
76 Shimian Specter R :K:	.30	.50
77 Skirk Ridge Exhumer U :K:	.15	.25
78 Slaughter Pact R :K:	6.00	8.00
79 Stronghold Rats U :K:	.25	.40
80 Bitter Ordeal R :K:	4.00	6.00
81 Bridge from Below R :K:	13.00	15.00
82 Death Rattle C :K:	.15	.25
83 Deepcavern Imp C :K:	.15	.25
84 Fleshwrither U :K:	.15	.25
85 Frenzy Sliver C :K:	.15	.25
86 Grave Scrabbler C :K:	.15	.25
87 Korlash, Heir to Blackblade R :K:	3.00	5.00
88 Mass of Ghouls C :K:	.15	.25
89 Snake Cult Initiation U :K:	.15	.25
90 Street Wraith U :K:	2.00	2.50
91 Tombstalker R :K:	1.50	2.00
92 Witch's Mist U :K:	.15	.25
93 Yixlid Jailer U :K:	.15	.25
94 Arc Blade U :R:	.15	.25
95 Bogardan Lancer C :R:	.15	.25
96 Char-Rumbler U :R:	.15	.25
97 Emberwilde Augur C :R:	.15	.25
98 Fatal Attraction C :R:	.15	.25
99 Gathan Raiders C :R:	.15	.25
100 Haze of Rage U :R:	.15	.25
101 Magus of the Moon R :R:	20.00	25.00
103 Pact of the Titan R :R:	4.00	6.00
104 Pyromancer's Swath R :R:	.40	.60
105 Riddle of Lightning C :R:	.15	.25
106 Rift Elemental C :R:	.15	.25
107 Scourge of Kher Ridges R :R:	2.00	3.00
108 Shivan Sand-Mage U :R:	.15	.25
109 Sparkspitter U :R:	.15	.25
110 Bloodshot Trainee U :R:	.15	.25
111 Boldwyr Intimidator U :R:	.15	.25
112 Emblem of the Warmind U :R:	.15	.25
113 Flowstone Embrace C :R:	.15	.25
114 Fomori Nomad C :R:	.15	.25
115 Ghostfire C :R:	.15	.25
116 Grinning Ignus C :R:	.15	.25
117 Henchfiend of Ukor C :R:	.15	.25
118 Homing Sliver C :R:	.15	.25
119 Shah of Naar Isle R :R:	.30	.50
120 Skizzik Surger U :R:	.15	.25
121 Steamflogger Boss R :R:	2.00	2.50
122 Storm Entity U :R:	.15	.25
123 Tarox Bladewing R :R:	.30	.50
124 Thunderblade Charge R :R:	.30	.50
125 Cyclical Evolution U :G:	.15	.25
126 Force of Savagery R :G:	1.00	1.50
127 Heartwood Storyteller R :G:	3.50	4.50
128 Kavu Primarch C :G:	.15	.25
129 Llanowar Augur C :G:	.15	.25
130 Llanowar Empath C :G:	.15	.25
131 Llanowar Mentor U :G:	.25	.40
133 Petrified Plating C :G:	.15	.25
134 Quiet Disrepair C :G:	.15	.25
135 Ravaging Riftwurm U :G:	.15	.25
136 Riftsweeper U :G:	.15	.25
137 Rites of Flourishing R :G:	1.00	1.50
138 Sprout Swarm C :G:	.15	.25
139 Summoner's Pact R :G:	10.00	13.00
140 Utopia Mycon U :G:	1.25	1.75
141 Wrap in Vigor C :G:	.15	.25
142 Baru, Fist of Krosa R :G:	.50	.75
143 Centaur Omenreader U :G:	.15	.25
144 Edge of Autumn C :G:	.15	.25
145 Imperiosaur U :G:	.15	.25
147 Nacatl War-Pride U :G:	.25	.40
148 Nessian Courser C :G:	.15	.25
149 Phosphorescent Feast U :G:	.15	.25
150 Quagnoth R :G:	.30	.50
151 Spellwild Ouphe U :G:	.15	.25
152 Sporoloth Ancient C :G:	.15	.25
153 Tarmogoyf R :G:	125.00	145.00
154 Thornweald Archer C :G:	.15	.40
155 Virulent Sliver C :G:	.30	.50
156 Glittering Wish R :D:	5.00	7.00
157 Jhoira of the Ghitu R :D:	1.75	2.25
158 Sliver Legion R :D:	30.00	35.00
159 Akroma's Memorial R :A:	11.00	14.00
160 Cloud Key R :A:	5.00	7.00
161 Coalition Relic R :A:	12.00	15.00
162 Epochrasite R :A:	.30	.50
163 Sliversmith U :A:	.15	.25
164 Soultether Golem U :A:	.15	.25
165 Sword of the Meek U :A:	8.00	10.00
166 Veilstone Amulet R :A:	.30	.50
167 Darksteel Garrison R :A:	.40	.60
168 Whetwheel R :A:	.30	.50
169 Dakmor Salvage U :L:	2.50	3.00
170 Keldon Megaliths U :L:	.15	.25
171 Llanowar Reborn U :L:	.25	.40
172 New Benalia U :L:	.15	.25
173 Tolaria West U :L:	3.00	4.00
174 Dryad Arbor U :L:	8.00	10.00
175 Graven Cairns R :L:	6.00	8.00
176 Grove of the Burnwillows R :L:	48.00	55.00
177 Horizon Canopy R :L:	55.00	65.00
178 Nimbus Maze R :L:	13.00	15.00
179 River of Tears R :L:	7.00	9.00
180 Zoetic Cavern U :L:	.15	.25
97 Mesmeric Sliver C :B:	.15	.25
98 Minions' Murmurs U :K:	.15	.25
100 Molten Disaster R :R:	.30	.50
101 Muraganda Petroglyphs R :G:	1.00	1.50

2007 Magic The Gathering Future Sight Foil

Card	Low	High
COMPLETE SET (180)	300.00	450.00

2007 Magic The Gathering Lorwyn

Card	Low	High
COMPLETE SET (301)	325.00	425.00
BOOSTER BOX (36 PACKS)	500.00	600.00
BOOSTER PACK (15 CARDS)	15.00	20.00
RELEASED ON OCTOBER 12, 2007		
1 Ajani Goldmane R :W:	7.00	9.00
2 Arbiter of Knollridge R :W:	.30	.50
3 Austere Command R :W:	8.00	10.00
4 Avian Changeling C :W:	.15	.25
5 Battle Mastery U :W:	.15	.25
6 Brigid, Hero of Kinsbaile R :W:	.50	.75
7 Burrenton Forge-Tender U :W:	.75	1.00
8 Cenn's Heir C :W:	.15	.25
9 Changeling Hero U :W:	.15	.25
10 Cloudgoat Ranger U :W:	.15	.25
11 Crib Swap U :W:	.30	.50
12 Dawnfluke C :W:	.15	.25
13 Entangling Trap U :W:	.15	.25
14 Favor of the Mighty R :W:	.30	.50
15 Galepowder Mage R :W:	.30	.50
16 Goldmeadow Dodger C :W:	.15	.25
17 Goldmeadow Harrier C :W:	.15	.25
18 Goldmeadow Stalwart U :W:	.15	.25
19 Harpoon Sniper U :W:	.15	.25
20 Hillcomber Giant C :W:	.15	.25
21 Hoofprints of the Stag R :W:	.30	.50
22 Judge of Currents C :W:	.15	.25
23 Kinsbaile Balloonist C :W:	.15	.25
24 Kinsbaile Skirmisher C :W:	.15	.25
25 Kithkin Greatheart C :W:	.15	.25
26 Kithkin Harbinger U :W:	.15	.25
27 Kithkin Healer C :W:	.15	.25
28 Knight of Meadowgrain U :W:	1.25	1.75
29 Lairwatch Giant C :W:	.15	.25
30 Militia's Pride R :W:	1.75	2.25
31 Mirror Entity R :W:	1.00	1.50
32 Neck Snap C :W:	.15	.25
33 Oaken Brawler C :W:	.15	.25
34 Oblivion Ring C :W:	.15	.25
35 Plover Knights C :W:	.15	.25
36 Pollen Lullaby U :W:	.15	.25
37 Purity R :W:	1.50	2.00
38 Sentry Oak U :W:	.15	.25
39 Shields of Velis Vel C :W:	.15	.25
40 Soaring Hope C :W:	.15	.25
41 Springjack Knight C :W:	.15	.25
42 Summon the School U :W:	.15	.25
43 Surge of Thoughtweft C :W:	.15	.25
44 Thoughtweft Trio R :W:	.30	.50
45 Triclopean Sight C :W:	.15	.25
46 Veteran of the Depths U :W:	.15	.25
47 Wellgabber Apothecary C :W:	.15	.25
48 Wispmare C :W:	.15	.25
49 Wizened Cenn U :W:	.15	.25
50 Aethersnipe C :B:	.15	.25
51 Amoeboid Changeling C :B:	.15	.25
52 Aquitect's Will C :B:	.15	.25
53 Benthicore U :B:	.15	.25
54 Broken Ambitions C :B:	.15	.25
55 Captivating Glance U :B:	.15	.25
56 Cryptic Command R :B:	20.00	25.00
57 Deeptread Merrow C :B:	.15	.25
58 Drowner of Secrets U :B:	.15	.25
59 Ego Erasure U :B:	.15	.25
60 Ethereal Whiskergill U :B:	.15	.25
61 Faerie Harbinger U :B:	.15	.25
62 Faerie Trickery C :B:	.15	.25
63 Fallowsage U :B:	.15	.25
64 Familiar's Ruse U :B:	.50	.75
65 Fathom Trawl R :B:	.30	.50
66 Forced Fruition R :B:	4.00	6.00
67 Glen Elendra Pranksters U :B:	.15	.25
68 Glimmerdust Nap C :B:	.15	.25
69 Guile R :B:	.75	1.00
70 Inkfathom Divers C :B:	.15	.25
71 Jace Beleren R :B:	7.00	9.00
72 Merrow Commerce U :B:	.75	1.25
73 Merrow Harbinger U :B:	.15	.25
74 Merrow Reejerey U :B:	3.50	4.25
75 Mistbind Clique R :B:	6.00	8.00
76 Mulldrifter C :B:	.40	.60
77 Paperfin Rascal C :B:	.15	.25
78 Pestermite C :B:	.40	.60
79 Ponder C :B:	1.00	1.50
80 Protective Bubble C :B:	.15	.25
81 Ringskipper C :B:	.15	.25
82 Scattering Stroke U :B:	.15	.25
83 Scion of Oona R :B:	2.25	2.75
84 Sentinels of Glen Elendra C :B:	.15	.25
85 Shapesharer R :B:	1.50	2.00
86 Silvergill Adept U :B:	2.50	3.00
87 Silvergill Douser C :B:	.15	.25
88 Sower of Temptation R :B:	10.00	13.00
89 Spellstutter Sprite C :B:	.50	.75
90 Stonybrook Angler C :B:	.15	.25
91 Streambed Aquitects C :B:	.15	.25
92 Surgespanner R :B:	.75	1.00
93 Tideshaper Mystic C :B:	.15	.25
94 Turtleshell Changeling U :B:	.15	.25
95 Wanderwine Prophets R :B:	.75	1.00
96 Whirlpool Whelm C :B:	.15	.25
97 Wings of Velis Vel C :B:	.15	.25
98 Zephyr Net C :B:	.15	.25
99 Black Poplar Shaman C :K:	.15	.25
100 Bog Hoodlums C :K:	.15	.25
101 Boggart Birth Rite C :K:	.15	.25
102 Boggart Harbinger U :K:	.15	.25
103 Boggart Loggers C :K:	.15	.25
104 Boggart Mob R :K:	.30	.50
105 Cairn Wanderer R :K:	1.50	2.00
106 Colfenor's Plans R :K:	.30	.50
107 Dread R :K:	2.50	3.25
108 Dreamspoiler Witches R :K:	.30	.50
109 Exiled Boggart C :K:	.15	.25
110 Eyeblight's Ending C :K:	.15	.25
111 Facevaulter C :K:	.15	.25
112 Faerie Tauntings C :K:	.15	.25
113 Final Revels U :K:	.15	.25
114 Fodder Launch U :K:	.15	.25
115 Footbottom Feast U :K:	.15	.25
116 Ghostly Changeling C :K:	.15	.25
117 Hoarder's Greed U :K:	.15	.25
118 Hornet Harasser R :K:	.30	.50
119 Hunter of Eyeblights C :K:	.15	.25
120 Knucklebone Witch R :K:	.50	.75
121 Liliana Vess R :K:	5.00	7.00
122 Lys Alana Scarblade R :K:	.30	.50
123 Mad Auntie R :K:	.40	.60
124 Makeshift Mannequin U :K:	.15	.25
125 Marsh Flitter R :K:	.30	.50
126 Moonglove Winnower U :K:	.15	.25
127 Mournwhelk U :K:	.15	.25
128 Nameless Inversion C :K:	.15	.25
129 Nath's Buffoon C :K:	.15	.25
130 Nectar Faerie R :K:	.30	.50
131 Nettlevine Blight C :K:	.15	.25
132 Nightshade Stinger U :K:	.15	.25
133 Oona's Prowler R :K:	2.50	3.25
134 Peppersmoke C :K:	.15	.25
135 Profane Command R :K:	.75	1.00
136 Prowess of the Fair C :K:	.15	.25
137 Quill-Slinger Boggart R :K:	.30	.50
138 Scarred Vinebreeder U :K:	.15	.25
139 Shriekmaw U :K:	.75	1.25
140 Skeletal Changeling C :K:	.15	.25
141 Spiderwig Boggart U :K:	.15	.25
142 Squeaking Pie Sneak C :K:	.15	.25
143 Thieving Sprite C :K:	.15	.25
144 Thorntooth Witch U :K:	.15	.25
145 Thoughtseize R :K:	25.00	30.00
146 Warren Pilferers C :K:	.15	.25
147 Weed Strangle C :K:	.15	.25
148 Adder-Staff Boggart C :R:	.15	.25
149 Ashling the Pilgrim R :R:	1.25	1.75
150 Ashling's Prerogative R :R:	.30	.50
151 Axegrinder Giant C :R:	.15	.25
152 Blades of Velis Vel C :R:	.15	.25
153 Blind-Spot Giant C :R:	.15	.25
154 Boggart Forager C :R:	.15	.25
155 Boggart Shenanigans U :R:	.15	.25
156 Boggart Sprite-Chaser C :R:	.15	.25
157 Caterwauling Boggart C :R:	.15	.25
158 Ceaseless Searblades U :R:	.15	.25
159 Chandra Nalaar R :R:	3.00	4.00
160 Changeling Berserker U :R:	.15	.25
161 Consuming Bonfire C :R:	.15	.25

162 Crush Underfoot U :R: .15 .25
163 Faultgrinder C :R: .15 .25
164 Fire-Belly Changeling C :R: .15 .25
165 Flamekin Bladewhirl U :R: .15 .25
166 Flamekin Brawler C :R: .15 .25
167 Flamekin Harbinger U :R: 2.00 2.50
168 Flamekin Spitfire U :R: .15 .25
169 Giant Harbinger U :R: .15 .25
170 Giant's Ire C :R: .15 .25
171 Glarewielder U :R: .15 .25
172 Goatnapper U :R: .15 .25
173 Hamletback Goliath R :R: .30 .50
174 Hearthcage Giant U :R: .15 .25
175 Heat Shimmer R :R: .30 .50
176 Hostility R :R: .30 .50
177 Hurly-Burly C :R: .15 .25
178 Incandescent Soulstoke R :R: 1.25 1.75
179 Incendiary Command R :R: .30 .50
180 Ingot Chewer C :R: .25 .40
181 Inner-Flame Acolyte C :R: .15 .25
182 Inner-Flame Igniter U :R: .15 .25
183 Lash Out C :R: .15 .25
184 Lowland Oaf C :R: .15 .25
185 Mudbutton Torchrunner C :R: .15 .25
186 Needle Drop C :R: .15 .25
187 Nova Chaser R :R: 3.00 5.00
188 Rebellion of the Flamekin U :R: .15 .25
189 Smokebraider C :R: .15 .25
190 Soulbright Flamekin C :R: .15 .25
191 Stinkdrinker Daredevil C :R: .15 .25
192 Sunrise Sovereign R :R: .30 .50
193 Tar Pitcher U :R: .15 .25
194 Tarfire C :R: .15 .25
195 Thundercloud Shaman U :R: .15 .25
196 Wild Ricochet R :R: .30 .50
197 Battlewand Oak C :G: .15 .25
198 Bog-Strider Ash C :G: .15 .25
199 Briarhorn U :G: .15 .25
200 Changeling Titan U :G: .15 .25
201 Cloudcrown Oak C :G: .15 .25
202 Cloudthresher R :G: .50 .75
203 Dauntless Dourbark R :G: 3.00 4.00
204 Elvish Branchbender C :G: .15 .25
205 Elvish Eulogist C :G: .15 .25
206 Elvish Handservant C :G: .15 .25
207 Elvish Harbinger U :G: 1.75 2.25
208 Elvish Promenade U :G: 2.50 3.00
209 Epic Proportions R :G: .30 .50
210 Eyes of the Wisent R :G: .30 .50
211 Fertile Ground C :G: .15 .25
212 Fistful of Force C :G: .15 .25
213 Garruk Wildspeaker R :G: 7.00 9.00
214 Gilt-Leaf Ambush C :G: .15 .25
215 Gilt-Leaf Seer C :G: .15 .25
216 Guardian of Cloverdell U :G: .15 .25
217 Heal the Scars C :G: .15 .25
218 Hunt Down C :G: .15 .25
219 Immaculate Magistrate R :G: 2.25 2.75
220 Imperious Perfect U :G: 1.75 2.25
221 Incremental Growth U :G: .15 .25
222 Jagged-Scar Archers U :G: 1.50 2.00
223 Kithkin Daggerdare C :G: .15 .25
224 Kithkin Mourncaller U :G: .15 .25
225 Lace with Moonglove C :G: .15 .25
226 Lammastide Weave U :G: .15 .25
227 Leaf Gilder C :G: .15 .25
228 Lignify C :G: .15 .25
229 Lys Alana Huntmaster C :G: .25 .40
230 Masked Admirers R :G: .30 .50
231 Nath's Elite C :G: .15 .25
232 Oakgnarl Warrior C :G: .15 .25
233 Primal Command R :G: 3.00 4.00
234 Rootgrapple C :G: .15 .25
235 Seedguide Ash U :G: .30 .50
236 Spring Cleaning C :G: .15 .25
237 Sylvan Echoes U :G: .15 .25
238 Timber Protector R :G: 6.00 8.00
239 Treefolk Harbinger U :G: 1.75 2.25
240 Vigor R :G: 13.00 16.00
241 Warren-Scourge Elf C :G: .15 .25
242 Woodland Changeling C :G: .15 .25
243 Woodland Guidance U :G: .15 .25
244 Wren's Run Packmaster R :G: .75 1.00
245 Wren's Run Vanquisher U :G: .40 .60
246 Brion Stoutarm R :W: :R: .50 .75
247 Doran, the Siege Tower R :W: :K: :G: 7.00 9.00
248 Gaddock Teeg R :W: :G: 17.00 20.00
249 Horde of Notions R :W: :B: :K: :R: :G: .50 .75
250 Nath of the Gilt-Leaf R :K: :G: 2.25 2.75
251 Sygg, River Guide R :W: :B: .50 .75
252 Wort, Boggart Auntie R :K: :R: 1.00 1.50
253 Wydwen, the Biting Gale R :B: :K: .30 .50
254 Colfenor's Urn R :A: .30 .50
255 Deathrender R :A: 2.25 2.75
256 Dolmen Gate R :A: 3.00 4.00
257 Herbal Poultice C :A: .15 .25
258 Moonglove Extract C :A: .15 .25
259 Rings of Brighthearth R :A: 18.00 22.00
260 Runed Stalactite C :A: .15 .25
261 Springleaf Drum C :A: .75 1.00
262 Thorn of Amethyst R :A: 14.00 17.00
263 Thousand-Year Elixir R :A: 3.50 5.00
264 Twinning Glass R :A: .30 .50
265 Wanderer's Twig C :A: .15 .25
266 Ancient Amphitheater R :L: .50 .75
267 Auntie's Hovel R :L: 2.50 3.00
268 Gilt-Leaf Palace R :L: 12.00 15.00
269 Howltooth Hollow R :L: .30 .50
270 Mosswort Bridge R :L: 1.00 1.50
271 Secluded Glen R :L: 4.25 5.00
272 Shelldock Isle R :L: 4.00 6.00
273 Shimmering Grotto C :L: .15 .25
274 Spinerock Knoll R :L: 1.25 1.75
275 Vivid Crag U :L: .25 .40
276 Vivid Creek U :L: .25 .40
277 Vivid Grove U :L: .15 .25
278 Vivid Marsh U :L: .25 .40
279 Vivid Meadow U :L: .15 .25
280 Wanderwine Hub R :L: 6.00 8.00
281 Windbrisk Heights R :L: 1.75 2.25
282 Plains C :L: .15 .25
283 Plains C :L: .15 .25
284 Plains C :L: .15 .25
285 Plains C :L: .15 .25
286 Island C :L: .15 .25
287 Island C :L: .75 1.00
288 Island C :L: .15 .25
289 Island C :L: .15 .25
290 Swamp C :L: .15 .25
291 Swamp C :L: .75 1.00
292 Swamp C :L: .15 .25
293 Swamp C :L: .15 .25
294 Mountain C :L: .15 .25
295 Mountain C :L: .15 .25
296 Mountain C :L: .15 .25
297 Mountain C :L: .15 .25
298 Forest C :L: .15 .25
299 Forest C :L: .15 .25
300 Forest C :L: .15 .25
301 Forest C :L: .15 .25

2007 Magic The Gathering Lorwyn Tokens

1 Avatar .60 1.00
2 Elemental .15 .25
3 Kithkin Soldier .10 .15
4 Merfolk Wizard .15 .25
5 Goblin Rogue .10 .15
6 Elemental Shaman .10 .15
7 Beast .12 .20
8 Elemental .10 .15
9 Elf Warrior .10 .15
10 Wolf .15 .25
11 Shapeshifter .12 .20

2008 Magic The Gathering Morningtide

COMPLETE SET (150) 190.00 250.00
BOOSTER BOX (36 PACKS) 350.00 400.00
BOOSTER PACK (15 CARDS) 12.00 15.00
THEME DECK 10.00 20.00
FAT PACK 40.00 80.00
RELEASED ON FEBRUARY 1, 2008
1 Ballyrush Banneret C :W: .15 .25
2 Battletide Alchemist R :W: .40 .60
3 Burrenton Bombardier C :W: .15 .25
4 Burrenton Shield-Bearers C :W: .15 .25
5 Cenn's Tactician U :W: .15 .25
6 Changeling Sentinel C :W: .15 .25
7 Coordinated Barrage C :W: .15 .25
8 Daily Regimen U :W: .15 .25
9 Feudkiller's Verdict R :W: .30 .50
10 Forfend C :W: .15 .25
11 Graceful Reprieve U :W: .15 .25
12 Idyllic Tutor R :W: 16.00 19.00
13 Indomitable Ancients R :W: 2.50 3.00
14 Kinsbaile Borderguard R :W: .75 1.25
15 Kinsbaile Cavalier R :W: 1.25 1.75
16 Kithkin Zephyrnaut C :W: .15 .25
17 Meadowboon U :W: .15 .25
18 Mosquito Guard C :W: .15 .25
19 Order of the Golden Cricket C :W: .15 .25
20 Preeminent Captain R :W: 1.00 1.50
21 Redeem the Lost U :W: .15 .25
22 Reveillark R :W: 5.00 7.00
23 Shinewend C :W: .15 .25
24 Stonehewer Giant R :W: 4.00 5.50
25 Stonybrook Schoolmaster C :W: .15 .25
26 Swell of Courage U :W: .15 .25
27 Wandering Graybeard U :W: .15 .25
28 Weight of Conscience C :W: .15 .25
29 Declaration of Naught R :B: .75 1.25
30 Dewdrop Spy C :B: .15 .25
31 Disperse C :B: .15 .25
32 Distant Melody C :B: .50 .75
33 Fencer Clique C :B: .15 .25
34 Floodchaser C :B: .15 .25
35 Grimoire Thief R :B: 1.25 1.75
36 Ink Dissolver C :B: .15 .25
37 Inspired Sprite U :B: .15 .25
38 Knowledge Exploitation R :B: 2.50 3.00
39 Latchkey Faerie C :B: .15 .25
40 Merrow Witsniper C :B: .15 .25
41 Mind Spring R :B: .30 .50
42 Mothdust Changeling C :B: .15 .25
43 Negate C :B: .15 .25
44 Nevermaker U :B: .15 .25
45 Notorious Throng R :B: 1.25 1.75
46 Research the Deep U :B: .15 .25
47 Sage of Fables U :B: .75 1.00
48 Sage's Dousing U :B: .15 .25
49 Sigil Tracer R :B: 2.00 2.50
50 Slithermuse R :B: .30 .50
51 Stonybrook Banneret C :B: .15 .25
52 Stream of Unconsciousness C :B: .15 .25
53 Supreme Exemplar R :B: .30 .50
54 Thieves' Fortune U :B: .15 .25
55 Vendilion Clique R :B: 25.00 30.00
56 Waterspout Weavers U :B: .15 .25
57 Auntie's Snitch R :K: .30 .50
58 Bitterblossom R :K: 20.00 25.00
59 Blightsoil Druid C :K: .15 .25
60 Earwig Squad R :K: .40 .60
61 Fendeep Summoner R :K: .30 .50
62 Festercreep C :K: .15 .25
63 Final-Sting Faerie C :K: .15 .25
64 Frogtosser Banneret C :K: .15 .25
65 Maralen of the Mornsong R :K: 3.00 4.00
66 Mind Shatter R :K: .30 .50
67 Moonglove Changeling C :K: .15 .25
68 Morsel Theft C :K: .15 .25
69 Nightshade Schemers U :K: .15 .25
70 Noggin Whack U :K: .15 .25
71 Offalsnout U :K: .15 .25
72 Oona's Blackguard U :K: 1.00 1.50
73 Pack's Disdain C :K: .15 .25
74 Prickly Boggart C :K: .15 .25
75 Pulling Teeth C :K: .15 .25
76 Revive the Fallen U :K: .15 .25
77 Scarblade Elite R :K: .30 .50
78 Squeaking Pie Grubfellows C :K: .15 .25
79 Stenchskipper R :K: .30 .50
80 Stinkdrinker Bandit U :K: .15 .25
81 Violet Pall C :K: .15 .25
82 Warren Weirding U :K: .15 .25
83 Weed-Pruner Poplar C :K: .15 .25
84 Weirding Shaman R :K: .30 .50
85 Boldwyr Heavyweights R :R: .30 .50
86 Boldwyr Intimidator U :R: .15 .25
87 Borderland Behemoth R :R: .30 .50
88 Brighthearth Banneret C :R: .15 .25
89 Countryside Crusher R :R: .50 .75
90 Fire Juggler C :R: .15 .25
91 Hostile Realm C :R: .15 .25
92 Kindled Fury C :R: .15 .25
93 Lightning Crafter R :R: 2.00 2.50
94 Lunk Errant C :R: .15 .25
95 Mudbutton Clanger C :R: .15 .25
96 Pyroclast Consul U :R: .15 .25
97 Rage Forger U :R: .15 .25
98 Release the Ants U :R: .15 .25
99 Rivals' Duel U :R: .15 .25
100 Roar of the Crowd C :R: .15 .25
101 Seething Pathblazer C :R: .15 .25
102 Sensation Gorger R :R: .75 1.25
103 Shard Volley C :R: .75 1.25
104 Shared Animosity R :R: 7.00 9.00
105 Spitebellows U :R: .15 .25
106 Stingmoggie C :R: .15 .25
107 Stomping Slabs U :R: .15 .25
108 Sunflare Shaman C :R: .15 .25
109 Taurean Mauler R :R: 2.00 2.50
110 Titan's Revenge R :R: .30 .50
111 Vengeful Firebrand R :R: .30 .50
112 War-Spike Changeling C :R: .15 .25
113 Ambassador Oak C :G: .15 .25
114 Bosk Banneret C :G: .15 .25
115 Bramblewood Paragon U :G: 1.25 1.75
116 Chameleon Colossus R :G: 1.25 1.75
117 Cream of the Crop R :G: 1.75 2.25
118 Deglamer C :G: .15 .25
119 Earthbrawn C :G: .15 .25
120 Elvish Warrior C :G: .15 .25
121 Everbark Shaman C :G: .15 .25
122 Fertilid C :G: .15 .25
123 Game-Trail Changeling C :G: .15 .25
124 Gilt-Leaf Archdruid R :G: 3.25 3.75
125 Greatbow Doyen R :G: .50 .75
126 Heritage Druid U :G: 4.00 5.00
127 Hunting Triad U :G: .15 .25
128 Leaf-Crowned Elder R :G: 3.00 4.00
129 Luminescent Rain C :G: .15 .25
130 Lys Alana Bowmaster C :G: .15 .25
131 Orchard Warden U :G: .15 .25
132 Reach of Branches R :G: .30 .50
133 Recross the Paths U :G: .15 .25
134 Reins of the Vinesteed C :G: .15 .25
135 Rhys the Exiled R :G: 2.00 2.50
136 Scapeshift R :G: 30.00 35.00
137 Unstoppable Ash R :G: .75 1.25
138 Walker of the Grove U :G: .15 .25
139 Winnower Patrol C :G: .15 .25
140 Wolf-Skull Shaman U :G: .15 .25
141 Cloak and Dagger U :A: .25 .40
142 Diviner's Wand U :A: .15 .25
143 Door of Destinies R :A: 4.00 5.50
144 Obsidian Battle-Axe U :A: .15 .25
145 Thornbite Staff U :A: .75 1.25
146 Veteran's Armaments U :A: .15 .25
147 Murmuring Bosk R :L: 2.00 3.00
148 Mutavault R :L: 11.00 14.00
149 Primal Beyond R :L: 2.75 3.25
150 Rustic Clachan R :L: .30 .50

2008 Magic The Gathering Morningtide Foil

COMPLETE SET (150) 200.00 300.00

2008 Magic The Gathering Morningtide Tokens

1 Giant Warrior .15 .25
2 Faerie Rogue 1.50 2.00
3 Treefolk Shaman .25 .35

2008 Magic The Gathering Shadowmoor

COMPLETE SET (301) 380.00 480.00
BOOSTER BOX (36 PACKS) 350.00 500.00
BOOSTER PACK (15 CARDS) 13.00 20.00
THEME DECK 20.00 40.00
FAT PACK 50.00 100.00
RELEASED ON MAY 2, 2008
1 Apothecary Initiate C :W: .15 .25
2 Armored Ascension U :W: .15 .25
3 Ballynock Cohort C :W: .15 .25
4 Barrenton Medic C :W: .15 .25
5 Boon Reflection R :W: 4.50 6.00
6 Goldenglow Moth C :W: .15 .25
7 Greater Auramancy R :W: 18.00 22.00
8 Inquisitor's Snare C :W: .15 .25
9 Kithkin Rabble U :W: .15 .25
10 Kithkin Shielddare C :W: .15 .25
11 Last Breath C :W: .15 .25
12 Mass Calcify R :W: .75 1.00
13 Mine Excavation C :W: .15 .25
14 Mistmeadow Skulk U :W: .15 .25
15 Niveous Wisps C :W: .15 .25
16 Order of Whiteclay R :W: 1.75 2.25
17 Pale Wayfarer U :W: .15 .25
18 Prison Term U :W: .75 1.00
19 Resplendent Mentor U :W: .15 .25
20 Rune-Cervin Rider C :W: .15 .25
21 Runed Halo R :W: 7.00 9.00
22 Safehold Sentry C :W: .15 .25
23 Spectral Procession U :W: .50 .75
24 Strip Bare C :W: .15 .25
25 Twilight Shepherd R :W: .75 1.25
26 Windbrisk Raptor R :W: .75 1.00
27 Woeleecher C :W: .15 .25
28 Advice from the Fae U :B: .15 .25
29 Biting Tether U :B: .15 .25
30 Briarberry Cohort C :B: .15 .25
31 Cerulean Wisps C :B: .50 .75
32 Consign to Dream C :B: .15 .25
33 Counterbore R :B: .30 .50
34 Cursecatcher U :B: 7.00 9.00
35 Deepchannel Mentor U :B: .30 .50
36 Drowner Initiate C :B: .15 .25
37 Faerie Swarm U :B: .25 .40
38 Flow of Ideas U :B: .15 .25
39 Ghastly Discovery C :B: .15 .25
40 Isleback Spawn R :B: .30 .50
41 Kinscaer Harpoonist C :B: .15 .25
42 Knacksaw Clique R :B: .75 1.25
43 Leech Bonder U :B: .15 .25
44 Merrow Wavebreakers C :B: .15 .25
45 Parapet Watchers C :B: .15 .25
46 Prismwake Merrow C :B: .15 .25
47 Puca's Mischief R :B: 3.00 3.50
48 Put Away C :B: .15 .25
49 River Kelpie R :B: 1.00 1.50
50 Savor the Moment R :B: 3.25 3.75
51 Sinking Feeling C :B: .15 .25
52 Spell Syphon C :B: .15 .25
53 Thought Reflection R :B: .75 1.00
54 Whimwader C :B: .15 .25
55 Aphotic Wisps C :K: .15 .25
56 Ashenmoor Cohort C :K: .15 .25
57 Beseech the Queen U :K: 2.50 3.00
58 Blowfly Infestation U :K: .15 .25
59 Cinderbones C :K: .15 .25
60 Cinderhaze Wretch C :K: .15 .25
61 Corrosive Mentor U :K: .30 .50
62 Corrupt U :K: .15 .25
63 Crowd of Cinders U :K: .15 .25
64 Disturbing Plot C :K: .15 .25
65 Dusk Urchins R :K: .50 .75
66 Faerie Macabre C :K: .15 .25
67 Gloomlance C :K: .15 .25
68 Hollowborn Barghest R :K: .30 .50
69 Hollowsage U :K: .15 .25
70 Incremental Blight U :K: .15 .25
71 Loch Korrigan C :K: .15 .25
72 Midnight Banshee R :K: .75 1.25
73 Plague of Vermin R :K: .30 .50
74 Polluted Bonds R :K: 3.50 4.00
75 Puppeteer Clique R :K: 1.25 1.75
76 Rite of Consumption C :K: .25 .40
77 Sickle Ripper C :K: .15 .25
78 Smolder Initiate C :K: .15 .25
79 Splitting Headache C :K: .15 .25
80 Torture C :K: .15 .25
81 Wound Reflection R :K: 4.50 5.50
82 Blistering Dieflyn C :R: .15 .25
83 Bloodmark Mentor U :R: .75 1.25
84 Bloodshed Fever C :R: .15 .25
85 Boggart Arsonists C :R: .15 .25
86 Burn Trail C :R: .15 .25
87 Cragganwick Cremator R :R: .30 .50
88 Crimson Wisps C :R: .30 .50
89 Deep-Slumber Titan R :R: .30 .50
90 Elemental Mastery R :R: 4.00 4.50
91 Ember Gale C :R: .15 .25
92 Flame Javelin U :R: .15 .25
93 Furystoke Giant R :R: .75 1.00
94 Horde of Boggarts U :R: .25 .40
95 Inescapable Brute C :R: .15 .25
96 Intimidator Initiate C :R: .15 .25
97 Jaws of Stone U :R: .15 .25
98 Knollspine Dragon R :R: 4.00 4.50
99 Knollspine Invocation R :R: .30 .50
100 Mudbrawler Cohort C :R: .15 .25
101 Power of Fire C :R: .15 .25
102 Puncture Bolt C :R: .15 .25
103 Pyre Charger U :R: .15 .25
104 Rage Reflection R :R: 1.25 1.75
105 Rustrazor Butcher C :R: .15 .25
106 Slinking Giant U :R: .15 .25
107 Smash to Smithereens C :R: .30 .50
108 Wild Swing U :R: .15 .25
109 Crabapple Cohort C :G: .15 .25
110 Devoted Druid C :G: .75 1.00
111 Dramatic Entrance R :G: 1.25 1.75
112 Drove of Elves U :G: .50 .75
113 Farhaven Elf C :G: .25 .40
114 Flourishing Defenses U :G: .15 .25
115 Foxfire Oak C :G: .15 .25
116 Gleeful Sabotage C :G: 1.50 2.00
117 Gloomwidow U :G: .15 .25
118 Gloomwidow's Feast C :G: .15 .25
119 Howl of the Night Pack U :G: .15 .25
120 Hungry Spriggan C :G: .15 .25
121 Juvenile Gloomwidow C :G: .15 .25
122 Mana Reflection R :G: 18.00 20.00
123 Mossbridge Troll R :G: .75 1.25
124 Nurturer Initiate C :G: .15 .25
125 Presence of Gond C :G: 1.00 1.50
126 Prismatic Omen R :G: 12.00 14.00
127 Raking Canopy U :G: .25 .40
128 Roughshod Mentor U :G: .15 .25
129 Spawnwrithe R :G: .30 .50
130 Toil to Renown C :G: .15 .25
131 Tower Above U :G: .15 .25
132 Viridescent Wisps C :G: .15 .25
133 Wildslayer Elves C :G: .15 .25
134 Witherscale Wurm R :G: .30 .50
135 Woodfall Primus R :G: 5.00 7.00
136 AEthertow C :W: :B: .15 .25
137 Ashenmoor Gouger U :K: :R: .25 .40
138 Ashenmoor Liege R :K: :R: 4.00 4.50
139 Augury Adept R :W: :B: .50 .75
140 Barkshell Blessing C :G: :W: .15 .25
141 Barrenton Cragtreads C :W: :B: .15 .25
142 Boartusk Liege R :R: :G: 4.00 4.50
143 Boggart Ram-Gang U :R: :G: .50 .75
144 Cemetery Puca R :B: :K: 1.25 1.75
145 Cultbrand Cinder C :K: :R: .15 .25
146 Curse of Chains C :W: :B: .20 .35
147 Dawnglow Infusion U :G: :W: .15 .25
148 Demigod of Revenge R :K: :R: 2.75 3.25
149 Deus of Calamity R :R: :G: 1.00 1.50
150 Din of the Fireherd R :K: :R: .40 .60
151 Dire Undercurrents R :B: :K: 2.00 2.50

152 Dream Salvage U :B: :K: .75 1.00
153 Elvish Hexhunter C :G: :W: .15 .25
154 Emberstrike Duo C :K: :R: .15 .25
155 Enchanted Evening R :W: :B: 4.00 4.50
156 Everlasting Torment R :K: :R: 2.75 3.25
157 Fate Transfer C :B: :K: .15 .25
158 Firespout U :R: :G: 1.00 1.50
159 Fists of the Demigod C :K: :R: .15 .25
160 Fossil Find U :R: :G: .15 .25
161 Fracturing Gust R :G: :W: 5.00 7.00
162 Fulminator Mage R :K: :R: 18.00 20.00
163 Ghastlord of Fugue R :B: :K: 4.00 5.00
164 Giantbaiting C :R: :G: .15 .25
165 Glamer Spinners U :W: :B: .15 .25
166 Glen Elendra Liege R :B: :K: 1.75 2.75
167 Godhead of Awe R :W: :B: 2.75 3.25
168 Gravelgill Axeshark C :B: :K: .15 .25
169 Gravelgill Duo C :B: :K: .15 .25
170 Grief Tyrant U :K: :R: .15 .25
171 Guttural Response U :R: :G: 1.50 2.00
172 Heartmender R :G: :W: .50 .75
173 Helm of the Ghastlord C :B: :K: .15 .25
174 Impromptu Raid R :R: :G: .30 .50
175 Inkfathom Infiltrator U :B: :K: .75 1.00
176 Inkfathom Witch U :B: :K: .15 .25
177 Kitchen Finks U :G: :W: 11.00 13.00
178 Kulrath Knight U :K: :R: 1.00 1.50
179 Loamdragger Giant C :R: :G: .15 .25
180 Manaforge Cinder C :K: :R: .15 .25
181 Manamorphose C :R: :G: 3.75 4.25
182 Medicine Runner C :G: :W: .15 .25
183 Memory Plunder R :B: :K: 3.25 3.75
184 Memory Sluice C :B: :K: .25 .40
185 Mercy Killing U :G: :W: .30 .50
186 Merrow Grimeblotter U :B: :K: .15 .25
187 Mirrorweave R :W: :B: 1.75 2.25
188 Mistmeadow Witch U :W: :B: .15 .25
189 Morselhoarder C :R: :G: .15 .25
190 Mudbrawler Raiders C :R: :G: .15 .25
191 Murderous Redcap U :K: :R: .50 .75
192 Old Ghastbark C :G: :W: .15 .25
193 Oona, Queen of the Fae R :B: :K: 2.75 3.25
194 Oona's Gatewarden C :B: :K: .15 .25
195 Oracle of Nectars R :G: :W: 2.00 2.50
196 Oversoul of Dusk R :G: :W: 2.00 2.50
197 Plumeveil U :W: :B: .15 .25
198 Poison the Well C :K: :R: .15 .25
199 Puresight Merrow U :W: :B: .15 .25
200 Raven's Run Dragoon C :G: :W: .15 .25
201 Reknit U :G: :W: .15 .25
202 Repel Intruders U :W: :B: .15 .25
203 Rhys the Redeemed R :G: :W: 15.00 17.00
204 River's Grasp U :B: :K: .15 .25
205 Rosheen Meanderer R :R: :G: .75 1.00
206 Runes of the Deus C :R: :G: .15 .25
207 Safehold Duo C :G: :W: .15 .25
208 Safehold Elite C :G: :W: .30 .50
209 Safewright Quest C :G: :W: .15 .25
210 Scar C :K: :R: .15 .25
211 Scarscale Ritual C :B: :K: .15 .25
212 Scuzzback Marauders C :R: :G: .15 .25
213 Scuzzback Scrapper C :R: :G: .15 .25
214 Seedcradle Witch U :G: :W: .15 .25
215 Shield of the Oversoul C :G: :W: 1.00 1.50
216 Silkbind Faerie C :W: :B: .15 .25
217 Somnomancer C :W: :B: .15 .25
218 Sootstoke Kindler C :K: :R: .15 .25
219 Sootwalkers C :K: :R: .15 .25
220 Spiteflame Witch U :K: :R: .15 .25
221 Spiteful Visions R :K: :R: .40 .60
222 Steel of the Godhead C :W: :B: 1.25 1.75
223 Swans of Bryn Argoll R :W: :B: 1.00 1.50
224 Sygg, River Cutthroat R :B: :K: 4.00 5.00
225 Tattermunge Duo C :R: :G: .15 .25
226 Tattermunge Maniac U :R: :G: .25 .40
227 Tattermunge Witch U :R: :G: .15 .25
228 Thistledown Duo C :W: :B: .15 .25
229 Thistledown Liege R :W: :B: 1.25 1.75
230 Thoughtweft Gambit U :W: :B: .15 .25
231 Torpor Dust C :B: :K: .15 .25
232 Torrent of Souls U :K: :R: .15 .25
233 Traitor's Roar C :K: :R: .15 .25
234 Turn to Mist C :W: :B: .15 .25
235 Tyrannize R :K: :R: .30 .50
236 Valleymaker R :R: :G: .30 .50
237 Vexing Shusher R :R: :G: 5.00 7.00
238 Wanderbrine Rootcutters C :B: :K: .15 .25
239 Wasp Lancer U :B: :K: .15 .25
240 Wheel of Sun and Moon R :G: :W: 8.00 10.00
241 Wilt-Leaf Cavaliers U :G: :W: .40 .60
242 Wilt-Leaf Liege R :G: :W: 4.00 4.50
243 Worldpurge R :W: :B: .30 .50
244 Wort, the Raidmother R :R: :G: 1.00 1.50
245 Zealous Guardian C :W: :B: .15 .25
246 Blazethorn Scarecrow C :A: .15 .25
247 Blight Sickle C :A: .15 .25
248 Cauldron of Souls R :A: 4.00 5.00
249 Chainbreaker C :A: .15 .25
250 Elsewhere Flask C :A: .15 .25
251 Gnarled Effigy U :A: .15 .25
252 Grim Poppet R :A: .50 .75
253 Heap Doll U :A: .15 .25
254 Illuminated Folio U :A: .15 .25
255 Lockjaw Snapper U :A: .15 .25
256 Lurebound Scarecrow U :A: .15 .25
257 Painter's Servant R :A: 14.00 16.00
258 Pili-Pala C :A: .75 1.25
259 Rattleblaze Scarecrow C :A: .15 .25
260 Reaper King R :A: 4.00 5.00
261 Revelsong Horn U :A: .15 .25
262 Scrapbasket C :A: .15 .25
263 Scuttlemutt C :A: .15 .25
264 Tatterkite U :A: .25 .40
265 Thornwatch Scarecrow C :A: .15 .25
266 Trip Noose U :A: .15 .25
267 Umbral Mantle U :A: 2.50 3.00
268 Watchwing Scarecrow C :A: .15 .25
269 Wicker Warcrawler U :A: .15 .25
270 Wingrattle Scarecrow C :A: .15 .25
271 Fire-Lit Thicket R 15.00 18.00
272 Forest L .15 .25
273 Forest L .15 .25
274 Forest L .15 .25
275 Forest L .15 .25
276 Graven Cairns R 6.00 8.00
277 Island L .15 .25
278 Island L .15 .25
279 Island L .15 .25
280 Island L .15 .25
281 Leechridden Swamp U .75 1.25
282 Madblind Mountain U .15 .25
283 Mistveil Plains U 3.00 3.50
284 Moonring Island U .15 .25
285 Mountain L .15 .25
286 Mountain L .15 .25
287 Mountain L .15 .25
288 Mountain L .15 .25
289 Mystic Gate R 18.00 22.00
290 Plains L .15 .25
291 Plains L .15 .25
292 Plains L .15 .25
293 Plains L .15 .25
294 Reflecting Pool R 8.00 10.00
295 Sapseep Forest U .15 .25
296 Sunken Ruins R 14.00 16.00
297 Swamp L .15 .25
298 Swamp L .15 .25
299 Swamp L .15 .25
300 Swamp L .15 .25
301 Wooded Bastion R 10.00 12.00

2008 Magic The Gathering Shadowmoor Foil

COMPLETE SET (301) 250.00 350.00

2008 Magic The Gathering Shadowmoor Tokens

1 Kithkin Soldier .10 .15
2 Spirit .30 .40
3 Rat 1.50 2.00
4 Elemental .75 1.25
5 Elf Warrior .35 .50
6 Spider .20 .30
7 Wolf .10 .15
8 Faerie Rogue 1.50 2.00
9 Elemental .60 1.00
10 Giant Warrior .10 .15
11 Goblin Warrior .40 .55
12 Elf Warrior 1.00 1.50

2008 Magic The Gathering Eventide

COMPLETE SET (180) 285.00 365.00
BOOSTER BOX (36 PACKS) 300.00 400.00
BOOSTER PACK (15 CARDS) 13.00 15.00
THEME DECK 10.00 20.00
FAT PACK 40.00 80.00
RELEASED ON JULY 25, 2008
1 Archon of Justice R :W: .30 .50
2 Ballynock Trapper C :W: .15 .25
3 Cenn's Enlistment C :W: .15 .25
4 Endless Horizons R :W: 4.00 5.00
5 Endure U :W: .30 .50
6 Flickerwisp U :W: .30 .50
7 Hallowed Burial R :W: 3.00 3.50
8 Kithkin Spellduster C :W: .15 .25
9 Kithkin Zealot C :W: .15 .25
10 Light from Within R :W: 1.50 2.00
11 Loyal Gyrfalcon U :W: .30 .50
12 Patrol Signaler U :W: .30 .50
13 Recumbent Bliss C :W: .15 .25
14 Spirit of the Hearth R :W: 1.00 1.50
15 Springjack Shepherd U :W: .30 .50
16 Suture Spirit U :W: .30 .50
17 Banishing Knack C :B: .15 .25
18 Cache Raiders U :B: .30 .50
19 Dream Fracture U :B: .30 .50
20 Dream Thief C :B: .15 .25
21 Glamerdye R :B: .30 .50
22 Glen Elendra Archmage R :B: 13.00 15.00
23 Idle Thoughts U :B: .30 .50
24 Indigo Faerie U :B: .30 .50
25 Inundate R :B: 1.00 1.50
26 Merrow Levitator C :B: .15 .25
27 Oona's Grace C :B: .15 .25
28 Razorfin Abolisher U :B: .30 .50
29 Sanity Grinding R :B: 1.25 1.75
30 Talonrend U :B: .30 .50
31 Wake Thrasher R :B: 2.50 3.00
32 Wilderness Hypnotist C :B: .15 .25
33 Ashling, the Extinguisher R :K: 3.50 4.25
34 Creakwood Ghoul U :K: .30 .50
35 Crumbling Ashes U :K: .30 .50
36 Lingering Tormentor U :K: .30 .50
37 Merrow Bonegnawer C :K: .15 .25
38 Necroskitter R :K: 1.75 2.25
39 Needle Specter R :K: .50 .75
40 Nightmare Incursion R :K: .50 .75
41 Raven's Crime C :K: .75 1.00
42 Smoldering Butcher C :K: .15 .25
43 Soot Imp U :K: .30 .50
44 Soul Reap C :K: .15 .25
45 Soul Snuffers U :K: .30 .50
46 Syphon Life U :K: .30 .50
47 Talara's Bane C :K: .15 .25
48 Umbra Stalker R :K: .30 .50
49 Chaotic Backlash U :R: .30 .50
50 Cinder Pyromancer C :R: .15 .25
51 Duergar Cave-Guard U :R: .30 .50
52 Fiery Bombardment R :R: .30 .50
53 Flame Jab C :R: .15 .25
54 Hatchet Bully U :R: .30 .50
55 Hateflayer R :R: .50 .75
56 Heartlash Cinder C :R: .15 .25
57 Hotheaded Giant C :R: .15 .25
58 Impelled Giant U :R: .30 .50
59 Outrage Shaman U :R: .30 .50
60 Puncture Blast C :R: .15 .25
61 Rekindled Flame R :R: .30 .50
62 Stigma Lasher R :R: 4.00 5.00
63 Thunderblust R :R: .50 .75
64 Unwilling Recruit U :R: .30 .50
65 Aerie Ouphes C :G: .15 .25
66 Bloom Tender R :G: 20.00 25.00
67 Duskdale Wurm U :G: .30 .50
68 Helix Pinnacle R :G: 6.00 8.00
69 Marshdrinker Giant U :G: .30 .50
70 Monstrify C :G: .15 .25
71 Nettle Sentinel C :G: 1.75 2.00
72 Phosphorescent Feast U :G: .30 .50
73 Primalcrux R :G: 5.00 7.00
74 Regal Force R :G: 7.00 9.00
75 Savage Conception U :G: .30 .50
76 Swirling Spriggan U :G: .30 .50
77 Talara's Battalion R :G: 3.00 3.50
78 Tilling Treefolk C :G: .15 .25
79 Twinblade Slasher U :G: .30 .50
80 Wickerbough Elder C :G: .15 .25
81 Balefire Liege R :R: :W: 5.00 7.00
82 Battlegate Mimic C :R: :W: .15 .25
83 Batwing Brume U :W: :K: .30 .50
84 Beckon Apparition C :W: :K: .15 .25
85 Belligerent Hatchling U :R: :W: .30 .50
86 Bloodied Ghost U :W: :K: .30 .50
87 Call the Skybreaker R :B: :R: .30 .50
88 Canker Abomination U :K: :G: .30 .50
89 Cankerous Thirst U :K: :G: .30 .50
90 Cauldron Haze U :W: :K: .30 .50
91 Clout of the Dominus C :B: :R: .15 .25
92 Cold-Eyed Selkie R :G: :B: .75 1.25
93 Crackleburr R :B: :R: 1.25 1.75
94 Crag Puca U :B: :R: .30 .50
95 Creakwood Liege R :K: :G: 3.00 3.50
96 Deathbringer Liege R :W: :K: 10.00 12.00
97 Deity of Scars R :K: :G: 1.75 2.25
98 Desecrator Hag C :K: :G: .15 .25
99 Divinity of Pride R :W: :K: 1.75 2.25
100 Dominus of Fealty R :B: :R: 2.50 3.00
101 Doomgape R :K: :G: .50 .75
102 Double Cleave C :R: :W: .15 .25
103 Drain the Well C :K: :G: .15 .25
104 Duergar Assailant C :R: :W: .15 .25
105 Duergar Hedge-Mage U :R: :W: .30 .50
106 Duergar Mine-Captain U :R: :W: .30 .50
107 Edge of the Divinity C :W: :K: .50 .75
108 Evershrike R :W: :K: .75 1.00
109 Fable of Wolf and Owl R :G: :B: 3.50 4.50
110 Favor of the Overbeing C :G: :B: .15 .25
111 Figure of Destiny R :R: :W: 1.25 1.75
112 Fire at Will C :R: :W: .15 .25
113 Gift of the Deity C :K: :G: .15 .25
114 Gilder Bairn U :G: :B: .30 .50
115 Grazing Kelpie C :G: :B: .15 .25
116 Groundling Pouncer U :G: :B: .30 .50
117 Gwyllion Hedge-Mage U :W: :K: .30 .50
118 Hag Hedge-Mage U :K: :G: .30 .50
119 Harvest Gwyllion C :W: :K: .15 .25
120 Hearthfire Hobgoblin U :R: :W: .30 .50
121 Hobgoblin Dragoon C :R: :W: .15 .25
122 Inside Out C :B: :R: .15 .25
123 Invert the Skies U :G: :B: .30 .50
124 Mindwrack Liege R :B: :R: 1.50 2.00
125 Mirror Sheen R :B: :R: .50 .75
126 Moonhold U :R: :W: .30 .50
127 Murkfiend Liege R :G: :B: 2.00 2.50
128 Nightsky Mimic C :W: :K: .15 .25
129 Nip Gwyllion C :W: :K: .15 .25
130 Nobilis of War R :R: :W: .50 .75
131 Noggle Bandit C :B: :R: .15 .25
132 Noggle Bridgebreaker C :B: :R: .15 .25
133 Noggle Hedge-Mage U :B: :R: .30 .50
134 Noggle Ransacker U :B: :R: .30 .50
135 Noxious Hatchling U :K: :G: .30 .50
136 Nucklavee U :B: :R: .30 .50
137 Odious Trow C :K: :G: .15 .25
138 Overbeing of Myth R :G: :B: 3.00 3.50
139 Pyrrhic Revival R :W: :K: .30 .50
140 Quillspike U :K: :G: .30 .50
141 Rendclaw Trow C :K: :G: .15 .25
142 Restless Apparition U :W: :K: .30 .50
143 Rise of the Hobgoblins R :R: :W: 3.00 3.50
144 Riverfall Mimic C :B: :R: .15 .25
145 Sapling of Colfenor R :K: :G: 4.00 5.50
146 Scourge of the Nobilis C :R: :W: .15 .25
147 Selkie Hedge-Mage U :G: :B: .30 .50
148 Shorecrasher Mimic C :G: :B: .15 .25
149 Shrewd Hatchling U :B: :R: .30 .50
150 Slippery Bogle C :G: :B: 1.75 2.00
151 Snakeform C :G: :B: .15 .25
152 Spitemare U :R: :W: .30 .50
153 Spitting Image R :G: :B: 1.00 1.50
154 Stalker Hag U :K: :G: .30 .50
155 Stillmoon Cavalier R :W: :K: 3.50 4.25
156 Stream Hopper C :B: :R: .15 .25
157 Sturdy Hatchling U :G: :B: .30 .50
158 Trapjaw Kelpie C :G: :B: .15 .25
159 Unmake C :W: :K: .75 1.00
160 Unnerving Assault U :B: :R: .30 .50
161 Voracious Hatchling U :W: :K: .30 .50
162 Waves of Aggression R :R: :W: 4.00 6.00
163 Wistful Selkie U :G: :B: .30 .50
164 Woodlurker Mimic C :K: :G: .15 .25
165 Worm Harvest R :K: :G: .40 .60
166 Altar Golem R :A: .30 .50
167 Antler Skulkin C :A: .15 .25
168 Fang Skulkin C :A: .15 .25
169 Hoof Skulkin C :A: .15 .25
170 Jawbone Skulkin C :A: .15 .25
171 Leering Emblem R :A: .30 .50
172 Scarecrone R :A: 8.00 11.00
173 Shell Skulkin C :A: .15 .25
174 Ward of Bones R :A: 4.25 4.75
175 Cascade Bluffs R :L: 18.00 22.00
176 Fetid Heath R :L: 20.00 25.00
177 Flooded Grove R :L: 17.00 20.00
178 Rugged Prairie R :L: 17.00 20.00
179 Springjack Pasture R :L: .75 1.25
180 Twilight Mire R :L: 30.00 35.00

2008 Magic The Gathering Eventide Foil

COMPLETE SET (180) 250.00 400.00

2008 Magic The Gathering Eventide Tokens

1 Goat .25 .35
2 Bird .20 .30
3 Beast .15 .25
4 Spirit .20 .30
5 Elemental .20 .30
6 Worm .30 .40
7 Goblin Soldier .15 .25

2008 Magic The Gathering Shards of Alara

COMPLETE SET (249) 180.00 240.00
BOOSTER BOX (36 PACKS) 200.00 300.00
BOOSTER PACK (15 CARDS) 8.00 10.00
THEME DECK 10.00 15.00
FAT PACK 30.00 60.00
RELEASED ON OCTOBER 3, 2008
1 Akrasan Squire C :W: .15 .25
2 Angel's Herald U :W: .15 .25
3 Angelic Benediction U :W: .15 .25
4 Angelsong C :W: .15 .25
5 Bant Battlemage U :W: .15 .25
6 Battlegrace Angel R :W: .75 1.00
7 Cradle of Vitality R :W: .40 .60
8 Dispeller's Capsule C :W: .15 .25
9 Elspeth, Knight-Errant M :W: 11.00 13.00
10 Ethersworn Canonist R :W: 4.00 5.00
11 Excommunicate C :W: .15 .25
12 Guardians of Akrasa C :W: .15 .25
13 Gustrider Exuberant C :W: .15 .25
14 Invincible Hymn R :W: .30 .50
15 Knight of the Skyward Eye C :W: .15 .25
16 Knight of the White Orchid R :W: 2.25 2.75
17 Knight-Captain of Eos R :W: .75 1.25
18 Marble Chalice C :W: .15 .25
19 Metallurgeon U :W: .15 .25
20 Oblivion Ring C :W: .15 .25
21 Ranger of Eos R :W: 7.00 9.00
22 Resounding Silence C :W: .15 .25
22 Crumbling Necropolis U :L: .75 1.00
23 Rockcaster Platoon U :W: .15 .25
24 Sanctum Gargoyle C :W: .15 .25
25 Scourglass R :W: 5.00 6.00
26 Sighted-Caste Sorcerer C :W: .15 .25
27 Sigiled Paladin U :W: .50 .75
28 Soul's Grace C :W: .15 .25
29 Sunseed Nurturer U :W: .15 .25
30 Welkin Guide C :W: .15 .25
31 Yoked Plowbeast C :W: .15 .25
32 Call to Heel C :B: .15 .25
33 Cancel C :B: .15 .25
34 Cathartic Adept C :B: .15 .25
35 Cloudheath Drake C :B: .15 .25
36 Coma Veil C :B: .15 .25
37 Courier's Capsule C :B: .15 .25
38 Covenant of Minds R :B: .30 .50
39 Dawnray Archer U :B: .15 .25
40 Esper Battlemage U :B: .15 .25
41 Etherium Astrolabe U :B: .15 .25
42 Etherium Sculptor C :B: .30 .50
43 Fatestitcher U :B: .75 1.25
44 Filigree Sages U :B: .15 .25
45 Gather Specimens R :B: .40 .60
46 Jhessian Lookout C :B: .15 .25
47 Kathari Screecher C :B: .15 .25
48 Kederekt Leviathan R :B: .75 1.00
49 Master of Etherium R :B: 5.00 7.00
50 Memory Erosion R :B: 1.75 2.25
51 Mindlock Orb R :B: .30 .50
52 Outrider of Jhess C :B: .15 .25
53 Protomatter Powder U :B: .15 .25
54 Resounding Wave C :B: .15 .25
55 Sharding Sphinx R :B: .30 .50
56 Skill Borrower R :B: .30 .50
57 Spell Snip C :B: .15 .25
58 Sphinx's Herald U :B: .15 .25
59 Steelclad Serpent C :B: .15 .25
60 Tezzeret the Seeker M :B: 8.00 10.00
61 Tortoise Formation C :B: .15 .25
62 Vectis Silencers C :B: .15 .25
63 Ad Nauseam R :K: 5.00 6.00
64 Archdemon of Unx R :K: .30 .50
65 Banewasp Affliction C :K: .15 .25
66 Blister Beetle C :K: .15 .25
67 Bone Splinters C :K: .15 .25
68 Corpse Connoisseur U :K: .15 .25
69 Cunning Lethemancer R :K: .30 .50
70 Death Baron R :K: 17.00 20.00
71 Deathgreeter C :K: .15 .25
72 Demon's Herald U :K: .15 .25
73 Dreg Reaver C :K: .15 .25
74 Dregscape Zombie C :K: .15 .25
75 Executioner's Capsule C :K: .15 .25
76 Fleshbag Marauder U :K: .35
77 Glaze Fiend C :K: .15 .25
78 Grixis Battlemage U :K: .15 .25
79 Immortal Coil R :K: .30 .50
80 Infest U :K: .15 .25
81 Onyx Goblet C :K: .15 .25
82 Puppet Conjurer U :K: .15 .25
83 Resounding Scream C :K: .15 .25
84 Salvage Titan R :K: .30 .50
85 Scavenger Drake U :K: .15 .25
86 Shadowfeed C :K: .15 .25
87 Shore Snapper C :K: .15 .25
88 Skeletal Kathari C :K: .15 .25
89 Tar Fiend R :K: .30 .50
90 Undead Leotau C :K: .15 .25
91 Vein Drinker R :K: .30 .50
92 Viscera Dragger C :K: .15 .25
93 Bloodpyre Elemental C :R: .15 .25
94 Bloodthorn Taunter C :R: .15 .25
95 Caldera Hellion R :R: .30 .50
96 Crucible of Fire R :R: .75 1.25
97 Dragon Fodder C :R: .15 .25
98 Dragon's Herald U :R: .15 .25
99 Exuberant Firestoker U :R: .15 .25
100 Flameblast Dragon R :R: .40 .60

101 Goblin Assault R :R: 1.25 1.75
102 Goblin Mountaineer C :R: .15 .25
103 Hell's Thunder R :R: .30 .50
104 Hissing Iguanar C :R: .15 .25
105 Incurable Ogre C :R: .15 .25
106 Jund Battlemage U :R: .15 .25
107 Lightning Talons C :R: .15 .25
108 Magma Spray C :R: .15 .25
109 Predator Dragon R :R: .75 1.00
110 Resounding Thunder C :R: .15 .25
111 Ridge Rannet C :R: .15 .25
112 Rockslide Elemental U :R: .15 .25
113 Scourge Devil U :R: .15 .25
114 Skeletonize U :R: .15 .25
115 Soul's Fire C :R: .15 .25
116 Thorn-Thrash Viashino C :R: .15 .25
117 Thunder-Thrash Elder U :R: .15 .25
118 Viashino Skeleton C :R: .15 .25
119 Vicious Shadows R :R: .75 1.00
120 Vithian Stinger C :R: .15 .25
121 Volcanic Submersion C :R: .15 .25
122 Where Ancients Tread R :R: .30 .50
123 Algae Gharial U :G: .15 .25
124 Behemoth's Herald U :G: .15 .25
125 Cavern Thoctar C :G: .15 .25
126 Court Archers C :G: .15 .25
127 Cylian Elf C :G: .15 .25
128 Druid of the Anima C :G: .15 .25
129 Drumhunter U :G: .15 .25
130 Elvish Visionary C :G: .15 .25
131 Feral Hydra R :G: 1.00 1.50
132 Gift of the Gargantuan C :G: .15 .25
133 Godtoucher C :G: .15 .25
134 Jungle Weaver C :G: .15 .25
135 Keeper of Progenitus R :G: .30 .50
136 Lush Growth C :G: .15 .25
137 Mighty Emergence U :G: .15 .25
138 Manaplasm R :G: .30 .50
139 Mosstodon C :G: .15 .25
140 Mycoloth R :G: 2.50 3.00
141 Naturalize C :G: .15 .25
142 Naya Battlemage U :G: .15 .25
143 Ooze Garden R :G: .30 .50
144 Resounding Roar C :G: .15 .25
145 Rhox Charger U :G: .15 .25
146 Sacellum Godspeaker R :G: .30 .50
147 Savage Hunger C :G: .15 .25
148 Skullmulcher R :G: .30 .50
149 Soul's Might C :G: .15 .25
150 Spearbreaker Behemoth R :G: 1.50 2.00
151 Topan Ascetic U :G: .15 .25
152 Wild Nacatl C :G: 1.50 2.00
153 Agony Warp C :D: .15 .25
154 Ajani Vengeant M :D: 9.00 11.00
155 Bant Charm U :D: .50 .75
156 Blightning C :D: .50 .75
157 Blood Cultist U :D: .15 .25
158 Branching Bolt C :D: .15 .25
159 Brilliant Ultimatum R :D: .30 .50
160 Broodmate Dragon R :D: .75 1.25
161 Bull Cerodon U :D: .15 .25
162 Carrion Thrash C :D: .15 .25
163 Clarion Ultimatum R :D: .30 .50
164 Cruel Ultimatum R :D: .30 .50
165 Deft Duelist C :D: .15 .25
166 Empyrial Archangel M :D: 2.50 3.00
167 Esper Charm U :D: 1.25 1.75
168 Fire-Field Ogre U :D: .15 .25
169 Goblin Deathraiders C :D: .15 .25
170 Godsire M :D: 4.50 5.50
171 Grixis Charm U :D: .15 .25
172 Hellkite Overlord M :D: 5.00 6.00
173 Hindering Light C :D: .30 .50
174 Jhessian Infiltrator U :D: .15 .25
175 Jund Charm U :D: .15 .25
176 Kederekt Creeper C :D: .15 .25
177 Kiss of the Amesha U :D: .15 .25
178 Kresh the Bloodbraided M :D: 2.00 2.50
179 Mayael the Anima M :D: .75 1.25
180 Naya Charm U :D: .15 .25
181 Necrogenesis U :D: .15 .25
182 Prince of Thralls M :D: 2.75 3.25
183 Punish Ignorance R :D: .30 .50
184 Qasali Ambusher U :D: .25 .40
185 Rafiq of the Many M :D: 6.00 7.00
186 Rakeclaw Gargantuan C :D: .15 .25
187 Realm Razer R :D: .30 .50
188 Rhox War Monk U :D: .15 .25
189 Rip-Clan Crasher C :D: .15 .25
190 Sangrite Surge U :D: .15 .25
191 Sarkhan Vol M :D: 9.00 11.00
192 Sedraxis Specter R :D: .30 .50
193 Sedris, the Traitor King M :D: 2.50 3.00
194 Sharuum the Hegemon M :D: .75 1.00
195 Sigil Blessing C :D: .15 .25
196 Sphinx Sovereign M :D: 2.00 2.75
197 Sprouting Thrinax U :D: .15 .25
198 Steward of Valeron C :D: .15 .25
199 Stoic Angel R :D: 1.25 1.75
200 Swerve U :D: .25 .40
201 Thoughtcutter Agent U :D: .15 .25
202 Tidehollow Sculler U :D: .25 .40
203 Tidehollow Strix C :D: .15 .25
204 Titanic Ultimatum R :D: .30 .50
205 Tower Gargoyle U :D: .15 .25
206 Violent Ultimatum R :D: .30 .50
207 Waveskimmer Aven C :D: .15 .25
208 Windwright Mage C :D: .15 .25
209 Woolly Thoctar U :D: .15 .25
210 Lich's Mirror M :A: 4.50 5.50
211 Minion Reflector R :A: .30 .50
212 Obelisk of Bant C :A: .15 .25
213 Obelisk of Esper C :A: .15 .25
214 Obelisk of Grixis C :A: .15 .25
215 Obelisk of Jund C :A: .15 .25
216 Obelisk of Naya C :A: .15 .25
217 Quietus Spike R :A: 3.00 3.50
218 Relic of Progenitus C :A: 1.50 2.00
219 Sigil of Distinction R :A: .30 .50
220 Arcane Sanctum U :L: 1.25 1.75
221 Bant Panorama C :L: .15 .25
223 Esper Panorama C :L: .15 .25
224 Grixis Panorama C :L: .15 .25
225 Jund Panorama C :L: .15 .25
226 Jungle Shrine U :L: .75 1.00
227 Naya Panorama C :L: .15 .25
228 Savage Lands U :L: .75 1.00
229 Seaside Citadel U :L: 1.25 1.75
230 Plains L :L: .15 .25
231 Plains L :L: .15 .25
232 Plains L :L: .15 .25
233 Plains L :L: .15 .25
234 Island L :L: .15 .25
235 Island L :L: .15 .25
236 Island L :L: .15 .25
237 Island L :L: .15 .25
238 Swamp L :L: .15 .25
239 Swamp L :L: .15 .25
240 Swamp L :L: .15 .25
241 Swamp L :L: .15 .25
242 Mountain L :L: .15 .25
243 Mountain L :L: .15 .25
244 Mountain L :L: .15 .25
245 Mountain L :L: .15 .25
246 Forest L :L: .15 .25
247 Forest L :L: .15 .25
248 Forest L :L: .15 .25
249 Forest L :L: .15 .25

2008 Magic The Gathering Shards of Alara Foil

COMPLETE SET (249) 250.00 350.00

2008 Magic The Gathering Shards of Alara Tokens

1 Soldier .15 .25
2 Homunculus .10 .15
3 Thopter .50 .75
4 Skeleton .10 .15
5 Zombie .15 .25
6 Dragon .45 .60
7 Goblin .15 .25
8 Ooze .10 .15
9 Saproling .10 .25
10 Beast 3.50 5.00

2009 Magic The Gathering Conflux

COMPLETE SET (145) 175.00 225.00
BOOSTER BOX (36 PACKS) 375.00 450.00
BOOSTER PACK (15 CARDS) 10.00 15.00
THEME DECK 15.00 30.00
FAT PACK 75.00 125.00
RELEASED ON FEBRUARY 6, 2009
1 Aerie Mystics U :W: .20 .35
2 Asha's Favor C :W: .15 .25
3 Aven Squire C :W: .15 .25
4 Aven Trailblazer C :W: .15 .25
5 Celestial Purge U :W: .20 .35
6 Court Homunculus C :W: .15 .25
7 Darklit Gargoyle C :W: .15 .25
8 Gleam of Resistance C :W: .15 .25
9 Lapse of Certainty C :W: .15 .25
10 Mark of Asylum R :W: 1.50 2.00
11 Martial Coup R :W: 1.25 1.75
12 Mirror-Sigil Sergeant M :W: 1.50 2.00
13 Nacatl Hunt-Pride U :W: .20 .35
14 Paragon of the Amesha U :W: .20 .35
15 Path to Exile U :W: 8.00 11.00
16 Rhox Meditant C :W: .15 .25
17 Scepter of Dominance R :W: .25 .40
18 Sigil of the Empty Throne R :W: 1.00 1.50
19 Valiant Guard C :W: .15 .25
20 Wall of Reverence R :W: 1.75 2.25
21 Brackwater Elemental C :B: .15 .25
22 Constricting Tendrils C :B: .15 .25
23 Controlled Instincts U :B: .20 .35
24 Cumber Stone U :B: .20 .35
25 Esperzoa U :B: .20 .35
26 Ethersworn Adjudicator M :B: 4.50 5.00
27 Faerie Mechanist C :B: .15 .25
28 Frontline Sage C :B: .15 .25
29 Grixis Illusionist C :B: .15 .25
30 Inkwell Leviathan R :B: .75 1.25
31 Master Transmuter R :B: 18.00 22.00
32 Parasitic Strix C :B: .15 .25
33 Scepter of Insight R :B: .25 .40
34 Scornful AEther-Lich U :B: .20 .35
35 Telemin Performance R :B: .75 1.25
36 Traumatic Visions C :B: .15 .25
37 Unsummon C :B: .15 .25
38 View from Above U :B: .20 .35
39 Worldly Counsel C :B: .15 .25
40 Absorb Vis C :K: .15 .25
41 Corrupted Roots U :K: .20 .35
42 Drag Down C :K: .15 .25
43 Dreadwing U :K: .20 .35
44 Extractor Demon R :K: .25 .40
45 Fleshformer U :K: .20 .35
46 Grixis Slavedriver U :K: .20 .35
47 Infectious Horror C :K: .15 .25
48 Kederekt Parasite R :K: 1.50 2.00
49 Nyxathid R :K: 4.00 4.50
50 Pestilent Kathari C :K: .15 .25
51 Rotting Rats C :K: .15 .25
52 Salvage Slasher C :K: .15 .25
53 Scepter of Fugue R :K: .25 .40
54 Sedraxis Alchemist C :K: .15 .25
55 Voices from the Void U :K: .20 .35
56 Wretched Banquet C :K: .15 .25
57 Yoke of the Damned C :K: .15 .25
58 Banefire R :R: .75 1.25
59 Bloodhall Ooze R :R: .50 .75
60 Canyon Minotaur C :R: .15 .25
61 Dark Temper C :R: .15 .25
62 Dragonsoul Knight U :R: .20 .35
63 Fiery Fall C :R: .15 .25
64 Goblin Razerunners R :R: .25 .40
65 Hellspark Elemental U :R: 1.00 1.50
66 Ignite Disorder U :R: .20 .35
67 Kranioceros C :R: .15 .25
68 Maniacal Rage C :R: .15 .25
69 Molten Frame C :R: .15 .25
70 Quenchable Fire C :R: .15 .25
71 Rakka Mar R :R: 1.25 1.75
72 Toxic Iguanar C :R: .15 .25
73 Viashino Slaughtermaster U :R: .20 .35
74 Volcanic Fallout U :R: .20 .35
75 Voracious Dragon R :R: .50 .75
76 Wandering Goblins C :R: .15 .25
77 Worldheart Phoenix R :R: .25 .40
78 Beacon Behemoth C :G: .15 .25
79 Cliffrunner Behemoth R :G: .25 .40
80 Cylian Sunsinger R :G: .25 .40
81 Ember Weaver C :G: .15 .25
82 Filigree Fracture U :G: .20 .35
83 Gluttonous Slime U :G: .20 .35
84 Matca Rioters C :G: .15 .25
85 Might of Alara C :G: .15 .25
86 Nacatl Savage C :G: .15 .25
87 Noble Hierarch R :G: 60.00 65.00
88 Paleoloth R :G: .25 .40
89 Sacellum Archers U :G: .20 .35
90 Scattershot Archer C :G: .15 .25
91 Shard Convergence U :G: .20 .35
92 Soul's Majesty R :G: .50 .75
93 Spore Burst U :G: .20 .35
94 Sylvan Bounty C :G: .15 .25
95 Thornling M :G: 1.50 2.00
96 Tukatongue Thallid C :G: .15 .25
97 Wild Leotau C :G: .15 .25
98 Apocalypse Hydra M :D: 2.50 3.00
99 Blood Tyrant R :D: .40 .60
100 Charnelhoard Wurm R :D: .25 .40
101 Child of Alara M :D: 3.00 3.50
102 Conflux M :D: 3.00 3.50
103 Countersquall U :D: 2.00 3.50
104 Elder Mastery U :D: .20 .35
105 Esper Cormorants C :D: .15 .25
106 Exploding Borders C :D: .15 .25
107 Fusion Elemental U :D: .20 .35
108 Giltspire Avenger R :D: .75 1.00
109 Goblin Outlander C :D: .15 .25
110 Gwafa Hazid, Profiteer R :D: 1.00 1.50
111 Hellkite Hatchling U :D: .20 .35
112 Jhessian Balmgiver U :D: .20 .35
113 Knight of the Reliquary R :D: 8.00 10.00
114 Knotvine Mystic U :D: .20 .35
115 Maelstrom Archangel M :D: 8.00 10.00
116 Magister Sphinx R :D: 1.00 1.50
117 Malfegor M :D: 1.25 1.75
118 Meglonoth R :D: .50 .75
119 Nacatl Outlander C :D: .15 .25
120 Nicol Bolas, Planeswalker M :D: 7.00 9.00
121 Progenitus M :D: 10.00 12.00
122 Rhox Bodyguard C :D: .15 .25
123 Scarland Thrinax U :D: .20 .35
124 Shambling Remains U :D: .20 .35
125 Skyward Eye Prophets U :D: .20 .35
126 Sludge Strider U :D: .20 .35
127 Sphinx Summoner R :D: 1.25 1.75
128 Suicidal Charge C :D: .15 .25
129 Vagrant Plowbeasts U :D: .20 .35
130 Valeron Outlander C :D: .15 .25
131 Vectis Agents C :D: .15 .25
132 Vedalken Outlander C :D: .15 .25
133 Zombie Outlander C :D: .15 .25
134 Armillary Sphere C :A: .15 .25
135 Bone Saw C :A: .15 .25
136 Font of Mythos R :A: 5.00 6.00
137 Kaleidostone C :A: .15 .25
138 Mana Cylix C :A: .15 .25
139 Manaforce Mace U :A: .20 .35
140 Obelisk of Alara R :A: .75 1.00
141 Ancient Ziggurat U :L: 2.00 3.50
142 Exotic Orchard R :L: 2.50 3.00
143 Reliquary Tower U :L: 2.00 3.50
144 Rupture Spire C :L: .15 .25
145 Unstable Frontier U :L: .20 .35

2009 Magic The Gathering Conflux Foil

COMPLETE SET (145) 150.00 200.00

2009 Magic The Gathering Conflux Tokens

1 Angel .35 .50
2 Elemental .15 .25

2009 Magic The Gathering Alara Reborn

COMPLETE SET (145) 150.00 200.00
BOOSTER BOX (36 PACKS) 200.00 300.00
BOOSTER PACK (15 CARDS) 8.00 10.00
THEME DECK 10.00 20.00
FAT PACK 120.00 150.00
RELEASED ON APRIL 30, 2009
1 Ardent Plea U :W: :B: 1.25 2.00
2 Aven Mimeomancer R :W: :B: .25 .40
3 Ethercaste Knight C :W: :B: .20 .35
4 Ethersworn Shieldmage C :W: :B: .20 .35
5 Fieldmist Borderpost C :W: :B: .20 .35
6 Filigree Angel R :W: :B: .30 .50
7 Glassdust Hulk C :W: :B: .20 .35
8 Meddling Mage R :W: :B: 5.00 7.00
9 Offering to Asha C :W: :B: .20 .35
10 Sanctum Plowbeast C :W: :B: .20 .35
11 Shield of the Righteous U :W: :B: .30 .50
12 Sovereigns of Lost Alara R :W: :B: 2.00 3.00
13 Stormcaller's Boon C :W: :B: .20 .35
14 Talon Trooper C :W: :B: .20 .35
15 Unbender Tine U :W: :B: .30 .50
16 Wall of Denial U :W: :B: 1.25 2.00
17 Architects of Will C :B: :K: .20 .35
18 Brainbite C :B: :K: .20 .35
19 Deny Reality C :B: :K: .20 .35
20 Etherium Abomination C :B: :K: .20 .35
21 Illusory Demon U :B: :K: .30 .50
22 Jhessian Zombies C :B: :K: .20 .35
23 Kathari Remnant U :B: :K: .30 .50
24 Lich Lord of Unx R :B: :K: 3.00 5.00
25 Mask of Riddles U :B: :K: .30 .50
26 Mind Funeral U :B: :K: 3.00 5.00
27 Mistvein Borderpost C :B: :K: .20 .35
28 Nemesis of Reason R :B: :K: 5.00 7.00
29 Soul Manipulation C :B: :K: .20 .35
30 Soulquake R :B: :K: .25 .40
31 Time Sieve R :B: :K: 5.00 7.00
32 Vedalken Ghoul C :B: :K: .20 .35
33 Anathemancer U :D: .30 .50
34 Bituminous Blast U :K: :R: .30 .50
35 Breath of Malfegor C :K: :R: .20 .35
36 Deathbringer Thoctar R :K: :R: .25 .40
37 Defiler of Souls M :K: :R: 1.75 2.25
38 Demonic Dread C :K: :R: .20 .35
39 Demonspine Whip U :K: :R: .30 .50
40 Igneous Pouncer C :K: :R: .20 .35
41 Kathari Bomber C :K: :R: .20 .35
42 Lightning Reaver R :K: :R: .50 .75
43 Monstrous Carabid C :K: :R: .20 .35
44 Sanity Gnawers U :K: :R: .30 .50
45 Singe-Mind Ogre C :K: :R: .20 .35
46 Terminate C :K: :R: 1.50 2.50
47 Thought Hemorrhage R :K: :R: .25 .40
48 Veinfire Borderpost C :K: :R: .20 .35
49 Blitz Hellion R :R: :G: .25 .40
50 Bloodbraid Elf U :R: :G: 2.00 3.50
51 Colossal Might C :R: :G: .20 .35
52 Deadshot Minotaur C :R: :G: .20 .35
53 Dragon Broodmother M :R: :B: 11.00 13.00
54 Firewild Borderpost C :R: :G: .20 .35
55 Godtracker of Jund C :R: :G: .20 .35
56 Gorger Wurm C :R: :G: .20 .35
57 Mage Slayer U :R: :G: .30 .50
58 Predatory Advantage R :R: :G: .25 .40
59 Rhox Brute C :R: :G: .20 .35
60 Spellbreaker Behemoth R :R: :G: .50 .75
61 Valley Rannet C :R: :G: .20 .35
62 Vengeful Rebirth U :R: :G: .30 .50
63 Violent Outburst C :R: :G: .60 1.00
64 Vithian Renegades U :R: :G: .30 .50
65 Behemoth Sledge U :G: :W: .30 .50
66 Captured Sunlight C :G: :W: .20 .35
67 Dauntless Escort R :G: :W: 1.75 2.00
68 Enlisted Wurm U :G: :W: .30 .50
69 Grizzled Leotau C :G: :W: .20 .35
70 Knight of New Alara R :G: :W: .50 .75
71 Knotvine Paladin R :G: :W: .30 .50
72 Leonin Armorguard C :G: :W: .20 .35
73 Mycoid Shepherd R :G: :W: .25 .40
74 Pale Recluse C :G: :W: .20 .35
75 Qasali Pridemage C :G: :W: 1.50 2.50
76 Reborn Hope U :G: :W: .30 .50
77 Sigil Captain U :G: :W: .30 .50
78 Sigil of the Nayan Gods C :G: :W: .20 .35
79 Sigiled Behemoth C :G: :W: .20 .35
80 Wildfield Borderpost C :G: :W: .20 .35
81 Identity Crisis R :W: :B: .25 .40
82 Necromancer's Covenant R :W: :K: .40 .60
83 Tainted Sigil U :W: :B: .30 .50
84 Vectis Dominator C :W: :K: .20 .35
85 Zealous Persecution U :W: :K: .30 .50
86 Cloven Casting R :B: :R: .25 .40
87 Double Negative U :B: :R: .30 .50
88 Magefire Wings C :B: :R: .20 .35
89 Skyclaw Thrash U :B: :R: .30 .50
90 Spellbound Dragon R :B: :R: .50 .75
91 Lord of Extinction M :K: :G: 14.00 16.00
92 Maelstrom Pulse R :K: :G: 13.00 15.00
93 Marrow Chomper U :K: :G: .30 .50
94 Morbid Bloom U :B: :G: .30 .50
95 Putrid Leech C :K: :G: .20 .35
96 Cerodon Yearling C :R: :W: .20 .35
97 Fight to the Death R :R: :W: .30 .50
98 Glory of Warfare R :R: :W: .75 1.25
99 Intimidation Bolt U :R: :W: .30 .50
101 Lorescale Coatl U :G: :B: .30 .50
102 Nulltread Gargantuan U :G: :B: .30 .50
103 Sages of the Anima R :G: :B: .25 .40
104 Vedalken Heretic R :G: :B: .25 .40
105 Winged Coatl C :G: :B: .20 .35
106 Enigma Sphinx R :D: .30 .50
107 Esper Sojourners C :D: .20 .35
108 Etherwrought Page U :D: .30 .50
109 Sen Triplets M :D: 18.00 20.00
110 Sphinx of the Steel Wind M :D: 1.00 1.50
111 Drastic Revelation U :D: .30 .50
112 Grixis Sojourners C :D: .20 .35
113 Thraximundar M :D: 1.50 2.00
114 Unscythe, Killer of Kings R :D: 1.00 1.50
115 Dragon Appeasement U :D: .30 .50
116 Jund Sojourners C :D: .20 .35
117 Karrthus, Tyrant of Jund M :D: 12.00 14.00
118 Lavalanche R :D: .40 .60
119 Madrush Cyclops R :D: .25 .40
120 Gloryscale Viashino U :D: .30 .50
100 Stun Sniper U :R: :W: .30 .50
121 Mayael's Aria R :D: 2.50 4.00
122 Naya Sojourners C :D: .20 .35
123 Retaliator Griffin R :D: .25 .40
124 Uril, the Miststalker M :D: 3.50 5.00
125 Bant Sojourners C :D: .20 .35
126 Finest Hour R :D: 1.75 2.25
127 Flurry of Wings U :D: .30 .50
128 Jenara, Asura of War M :D: 4.00 5.00
129 Wargate R :D: 2.00 3.00
130 Maelstrom Nexus M :D: 6.00 8.00
131 Arsenal Thresher C :W: :K: :B: .20 .35
132 Esper Stormblade C :W: :K: :B: .20 .35
133 Thopter Foundry U :W: :K: :B: 1.50 2.50
134 Grixis Grimblade C :B: :R: :K: .20 .35
135 Sewn-Eye Drake C :B: :R: :K: .20 .35
136 Slave of Bolas U :B: :R: :K: .30 .50
137 Giant Ambush Beetle U :K: :G: :R: .30 .50
138 Jund Hackblade C :K: :G: :R: .20 .35
139 Sangrite Backlash C :K: :G: :R: .20 .35
140 Marisi's Twinclaws U :R: :W: :G: .30 .50
141 Naya Hushblade C :R: :W: :G: .20 .35
142 Trace of Abundance C :R: :W: :G: .20 .35
143 Bant Sureblade C :G: :B: :W: .20 .35
144 Crystallization C :G: :B: :W: .20 .35
145 Messenger Falcons U :G: :B: :W: .30 .50

2009 Magic The Gathering Alara Reborn Tokens

1 Bird Soldier .10 .15
2 Lizard .10 .15
3 Dragon .60 1.00
4 Zombie Wizard .45 .60

2009 Magic The Gathering Zendikar

COMPLETE SET (234) 500.00 625.00
BOOSTER BOX (36 PACKS) 475.00 525.00
BOOSTER PACK (15 CARDS) 20.00 25.00
THEME DECK 15.00 30.00
FAT PACK 200.00 300.00
RELEASED ON OCTOBER 2, 2009
1 Armament Master R :W: .25 .40
2 Arrow Volley Trap U :W: .15 .25
3 Bold Defense C :W: .15 .25
4 Brave the Elements U :W: .15 .25
5 Caravan Hurda C :W: .15 .25
6 Celestial Mantle R :W: 3.00 4.00
7 Cliff Threader C :W: .15 .25
8 Conqueror's Pledge R :W: .25 .40
9 Day of Judgment R :W: 2.00 2.50
10 Devout Lightcaster R :W: .25 .40
11 Emeria Angel R :W: 1.00 1.50
12 Felidar Sovereign M :W: 1.75 2.25
13 Iona, Shield of Emeria M :W: 5.00 7.00
14 Journey to Nowhere C :W: .75 1.25
15 Kabira Evangel R :W: 2.00 2.50
16 Kazandu Blademaster U :W: 1.00 1.50
17 Kor Aeronaut U :W: .15 .25
18 Kor Cartographer C :W: .15 .25
19 Kor Duelist U :W: .15 .25
20 Kor Hookmaster C :W: .15 .25
21 Kor Outfitter C :W: .15 .25
22 Kor Sanctifiers C :W: .15 .25
23 Kor Skyfisher C :W: .15 .25
24 Landbind Ritual U :W: .15 .25
25 Luminarch Ascension R :W: 4.00 6.00
26 Makindi Shieldmate C :W: .15 .25
27 Narrow Escape C :W: .15 .25
28 Nimbus Wings C :W: .15 .25
29 Noble Vestige C :W: .15 .25
30 Ondu Cleric C :W: .15 .25
31 Pillarfield Ox C :W: .15 .25
32 Pitfall Trap U :W: .15 .25
33 Quest for the Holy Relic U :W: .15 .25
34 Shepherd of the Lost U :W: .15 .25
35 Shieldmate's Blessing C :W: .15 .25
36 Steppe Lynx C :W: .15 .25
37 Sunspring Expedition C :W: .15 .25
38 Windborne Charge U :W: .15 .25
39 World Queller R :W: .25 .40
40 Aether Figment U :B: .15 .25
41 Archive Trap R :B: 5.00 7.00
42 Archmage Ascension R :B: .75 1.25
43 Caller of Gales C :B: .15 .25
44 Cancel C :B: .15 .25
45 Cosi's Trickster R :B: .50 .75
46 Gomazoa U :B: .15 .25
47 Hedron Crab U :B: 2.50 3.00
48 Into the Roil C :B: .15 .25
49 Ior Ruin Expedition C :B: .15 .25
50 Kraken Hatchling C :B: .15 .25
51 Lethargy Trap C :B: .15 .25
52 Living Tsunami U :B: .15 .25
53 Lorthos, the Tidemaker M :B: .75 1.25
54 Lullmage Mentor R :B: .25 .40
55 Merfolk Seastalkers U :B: .15 .25
56 Merfolk Wayfinder U :B: .15 .25
57 Mindbreak Trap M :B: 4.50 5.50
58 Paralyzing Grasp C :B: .15 .25
59 Quest for Ancient Secrets U :B: .15 .25
60 Reckless Scholar C :B: .15 .25
61 Rite of Replication R :B: 1.25 1.75
62 Roil Elemental R :B: .50 .75
63 Sea Gate Loremaster R :B: .25 .40
64 Seascape Aerialist U :B: .15 .25
65 Shoal Serpent C :B: .15 .25
66 Sky Ruin Drake C :B: .15 .25
67 Spell Pierce C :B: 1.50 2.00
68 Sphinx of Jwar Isle R :B: .25 .40
69 Sphinx of Lost Truths R :B: .25 .40
70 Spreading Seas C :B: .75 1.25
71 Summoner's Bane U :B: .15 .25
72 Tempest Owl C :B: .15 .25
73 Trapfinder's Trick C :B: .15 .25
74 Trapmaker's Snare U :B: .15 .25
75 Umara Raptor C :B: .15 .25
76 Welkin Tern C :B: .15 .25
77 Whiplash Trap C :B: .15 .25
78 Windrider Eel C :B: .15 .25
79 Bala Ged Thief R :K: .25 .40
80 Blood Seeker C :K: .15 .25
81 Blood Tribute R :K: .50 .75
82 Bloodchief Ascension R :K: 4.50 5.50
83 Bloodghast R :K: 20.00 25.00
84 Bog Tatters C :K: .15 .25
85 Crypt Ripper C :K: .15 .25
86 Desecrated Earth C :K: .15 .25
87 Disfigure C :K: .30 .50
88 Feast of Blood U :K: .40 .60
89 Gatekeeper of Malakir U :K: .75 1.25
90 Giant Scorpion C :K: .15 .25
91 Grim Discovery C :K: .15 .25
92 Guul Draz Specter R :K: .25 .40
93 Guul Draz Vampire C :K: .15 .25
94 Hagra Crocodile C :K: .15 .25
95 Hagra Diabolist U :K: .15 .25
96 Halo Hunter R :K: .25 .40
97 Heartstabber Mosquito C :K: .15 .25
98 Hideous End C :K: .15 .25
99 Kalitas, Bloodchief of Ghet M :K: 5.00 7.00
100 Malakir Bloodwitch R :K: .75 1.25
101 Marsh Casualties U :K: .15 .25
102 Mind Sludge U :K: .15 .25
103 Mindless Null C :K: .15 .25
104 Mire Blight C :K: .15 .25
105 Needlebite Trap U :K: .15 .25
106 Nimana Sell-Sword C :K: .15 .25
107 Ob Nixilis, the Fallen M :K: 5.00 7.00
108 Quest for the Gravelord U :K: .15 .25
109 Ravenous Trap U :K: 2.00 3.00
110 Sadistic Sacrament R :K: 1.00 1.50
111 Sorin Markov M :K: 14.00 17.00
112 Soul Stair Expedition C :K: .15 .25
113 Surrakar Marauder C :K: .15 .25
114 Vampire Hexmage U :K: .15 .25
115 Vampire Lacerator C :K: .15 .25
116 Vampire Nighthawk U :K: .50 .75
117 Vampire's Bite C :K: .15 .25
118 Bladetusk Boar C :R: .15 .25
119 Burst Lightning C :R: .15 .25
120 Chandra Ablaze M :R: 6.00 8.00
121 Demolish C :R: .15 .25
122 Electropotence R :R: .25 .40
123 Elemental Appeal R :R: .25 .40
124 Geyser Glider U :R: .15 .25
125 Goblin Bushwhacker C :R: .75 1.25
126 Goblin Guide R :R: 30.00 35.00
127 Goblin Ruinblaster U :R: .15 .25
128 Goblin Shortcutter C :R: .15 .25
129 Goblin War Paint C :R: .15 .25
130 Hellfire Mongrel U :R: .15 .25
131 Hellkite Charger R :R: .50 .75
132 Highland Berserker C :R: .15 .25
133 Inferno Trap U :R: .15 .25
134 Kazuul Warlord R :R: .25 .40
135 Lavaball Trap R :R: .25 .40
136 Magma Rift C :R: .15 .25
137 Mark of Mutiny U :R: .15 .25
138 Molten Ravager C :R: .15 .25
139 Murasa Pyromancer U :R: .15 .25
140 Obsidian Fireheart M :R: 1.00 1.50
141 Plated Geopede C :R: .15 .25
142 Punishing Fire U :R: .25 .40
143 Pyromancer Ascension R :R: 7.00 9.00
144 Quest for Pure Flame U :R: .15 .25
145 Ruinous Minotaur C :R: .15 .25
146 Runeflare Trap U :R: .15 .25
147 Seismic Shudder C :R: .15 .25
148 Shatterskull Giant C :R: .15 .25
149 Slaughter Cry C :R: .15 .25
150 Spire Barrage C :R: .15 .25
151 Torch Slinger C :R: .15 .25
152 Tuktuk Grunts C :R: .15 .25
153 Unstable Footing U :R: .15 .25
154 Warren Instigator M :R: 8.00 10.00
155 Zektar Shrine Expedition C :R: .15 .25
156 Baloth Cage Trap U :G: .15 .25
157 Baloth Woodcrasher U :G: .15 .25
158 Beast Hunt C :G: .15 .25
159 Beastmaster Ascension R :G: .75 1.25
160 Cobra Trap U :G: .15 .25
161 Frontier Guide U :G: .15 .25
162 Gigantiform R :G: .25 .40
163 Grazing Gladehart C :G: .15 .25
164 Greenweaver Druid U :G: .15 .25
165 Harrow C :G: .15 .25
166 Joraga Bard C :G: .15 .25
167 Khalni Heart Expedition C :G: .15 .25
168 Lotus Cobra M :G: 11.00 13.00
169 Mold Shambler C :G: .15 .25
170 Nissa Revane M :G: 10.00 12.00
171 Nissa's Chosen C :G: .15 .25
172 Oracle of Mul Daya R :G: 17.00 20.00
173 Oran-Rief Recluse C :G: .15 .25
174 Oran-Rief Survivalist C :G: .15 .25
175 Predatory Urge R :G: .25 .40
176 Primal Bellow U :G: .15 .25
177 Quest for the Gemblades U :G: .15 .25
178 Rampaging Baloths M :G: .75 1.25
179 Relic Crush C :G: .15 .25
180 River Boa U :G: .15 .25
181 Savage Silhouette C :G: .15 .25
182 Scute Mob R :G: .75 1.00
183 Scythe Tiger C :G: .15 .25
184 Summoning Trap R :G: 1.00 1.50
185 Tajuru Archer U :G: .15 .25
186 Tanglesap C :G: .15 .25
187 Terra Stomper R :G: .50 .75
188 Territorial Baloth C :G: .15 .25
189 Timbermaw Larva C :G: .15 .25
190 Turntimber Basilisk U :G: .15 .25
191 Turntimber Ranger R :G: .40 .60
192 Vastwood Gorger C :G: .15 .25
193 Vines of Vastwood C :G: .75 1.00
194 Zendikar Farguide C :G: .15 .25
195 Adventuring Gear C :A: .15 .25
196 Blade of the Bloodchief R :A: 3.00 3.50
197 Blazing Torch U :A: .15 .25
198 Carnage Altar U :A: .15 .25
199 Eldrazi Monument M :A: 4.00 4.50
200 Eternity Vessel M :A: 1.50 2.00
201 Expedition Map C :A: 1.25 1.75
202 Explorer's Scope C :A: .15 .25
203 Grappling Hook R :A: .25 .40
204 Hedron Scrabbler C :A: .15 .25
205 Khalni Gem U :A: .15 .25
206 Spidersilk Net C :A: .15 .25
207 Stonework Puma C :A: .15 .25
208 Trailblazer's Boots U :A: .15 .25
209 Trusty Machete U :A: .15 .25
210 Akoum Refuge U :L: .15 .25
211 Arid Mesa R :L: 45.00 50.00
212 Crypt of Agadeem R :L: .50 .75
213 Emeria, the Sky Ruin R :L: 3.00 4.00
214 Graypelt Refuge U :L: .20 .35
215 Jwar Isle Refuge U :L: .20 .35
216 Kabira Crossroads C :L: .15 .25
217 Kazandu Refuge U :L: .15 .25
218 Magosi, the Waterveil R :L: .25 .40
219 Marsh Flats R :L: 35.00 40.00
220 Misty Rainforest R :L: 50.00 55.00
221 Oran-Rief, the Vastwood R :L: .75 1.25
222 Piranha Marsh C :L: .15 .25
223 Scalding Tarn R :L: 70.00 80.00
224 Sejiri Refuge U :L: .20 .35
225 Soaring Seacliff C :L: .15 .25
226 Teetering Peaks C :L: .15 .25
227 Turntimber Grove C :L: .15 .25
228 Valakut, the Molten Pinnacle R :L: 6.00 8.00
229 Verdant Catacombs R :L: 65.00 70.00
230 Plains C :L: .40 .60
231 Plains C :L: .40 .60
232 Plains C :L: .15 .25
233 Plains C :L: .30 .50
234 Island C :L: .50 .75
235 Island C :L: .40 .60
236 Island C :L: 1.00 1.50
237 Island C :L: .40 .60
238 Swamp C :L: .50 .75
239 Swamp C :L: .40 .60
240 Swamp C :L: .50 .75
241 Swamp C :L: .15 .25
242 Mountain C :L: .50 .75
243 Mountain C :L: .40 .60
244 Mountain C :L: .50 .75
245 Mountain C :L: .15 .25
246 Forest C :L: .50 .75
247 Forest C :L: .40 .60
248 Forest C :L: .75 1.00
249 Forest C :L: .40 .60
250 Plains C :L: .15 .25
251 Plains C :L: .15 .25
252 Plains C :L: .15 .25
253 Plains C :L: .15 .25
254 Island C :L: .15 .25
255 Island C :L: .15 .25
256 Island C :L: .15 .25
257 Island C :L: .15 .25
258 Swamp C :L: .15 .25
259 Swamp C :L: .15 .25
260 Swamp C :L: .15 .25
261 Swamp C :L: .15 .25
262 Mountain C :L: .15 .25
263 Mountain C :L: .15 .25
264 Mountain C :L: .15 .25
265 Mountain C :L: .15 .25
266 Forest C :L: .15 .25
267 Forest C :L: .15 .25
268 Forest C :L: .15 .25
269 Forest C :L: .15 .25

2009 Magic The Gathering Zendikar Foil

1 Armament Master R :W: .60 1.50
2 Arrow Volley Trap U :W: .30 .75
3 Bold Defense C :W: .30 .75
4 Brave the Elements U :W: .60 1.50
5 Caravan Hurda C :W: .30 .75
6 Celestial Mantle R :W: .60 1.50
7 Cliff Threader C :W: .30 .75
8 Conqueror's Pledge R :W: 2.00 5.00
9 Day of Judgment R :W: 8.00 20.00
10 Devout Lightcaster R :W: 2.50 5.00
11 Emeria Angel R :W: 3.00 8.00
12 Felidar Sovereign M :W: 6.00 15.00
13 Iona, Shield of Emeria M :W: 20.00 50.00
14 Journey to Nowhere C :W: .40 1.00
15 Kabira Evangel R :W: 1.25 3.00
16 Kazandu Blademaster U :W: .75 2.00
17 Kor Aeronaut U :W: .50 1.25
18 Kor Cartographer C :W: .30 .75
19 Kor Duelist U :W: .40 1.00
20 Kor Hookmaster C :W: .30 .75
21 Kor Outfitter C :W: .30 .75
22 Kor Sanctifiers C :W: .30 .75
23 Kor Skyfisher C :W: .30 .75
24 Landbind Ritual U :W: .30 .75
25 Luminarch Ascension R :W: 3.00 8.00
26 Makindi Shieldmate C :W: .30 .75
27 Narrow Escape C :W: .30 .75
28 Nimbus Wings C :W: .30 .75
29 Noble Vestige C :W: .30 .75
30 Ondu Cleric C :W: .30 .75
31 Pillarfield Ox C :W: .30 .75
32 Pitfall Trap U :W: .50 1.25
33 Quest for the Holy Relic U :W: .40 1.00
34 Shepherd of the Lost U :W: .40 1.00
35 Shieldmate's Blessing C :W: .30 .75
36 Steppe Lynx C :W: .75 2.00
37 Sunspring Expedition C :W: .30 .75
38 Windborne Charge U :W: .30 .75
39 World Queller R :W: 1.50 4.00
40 Aether Figment U :B: .30 .75
41 Archive Trap R :B: 3.00 8.00
42 Archmage Ascension R :B: .60 1.50
43 Caller of Gales C :B: .30 .75
44 Cancel C :B: .60 1.50
45 Cosi's Trickster R :B: 1.50 4.00
46 Gomazoa U :B: .30 .75
47 Hedron Crab U :B: 1.00 2.50
48 Into the Roil C :B: .30 .75
49 Ior Ruin Expedition C :B: .30 .75
50 Kraken Hatchling C :B: .30 .75
51 Lethargy Trap C :B: .30 .75
52 Living Tsunami U :B: .30 .75
53 Lorthos, the Tidemaker M :B: 2.00 5.00
54 Lullmage Mentor R :B: 1.25 3.00
55 Merfolk Seastalkers U :B: .30 .75
56 Merfolk Wayfinder U :B: .30 .75
57 Mindbreak Trap M :B: 2.00 5.00
58 Paralyzing Grasp C :B: .30 .75
59 Quest for Ancient Secrets U :B: .40 1.00
60 Reckless Scholar C :B: .30 .75
61 Rite of Replication R :B: 4.00 10.00
62 Roil Elemental R :B: 1.25 3.00
63 Sea Gate Loremaster R :B: 1.00 2.50
64 Seascape Aerialist U :B: .30 .75
65 Shoal Serpent C :B: .30 .75
66 Sky Ruin Drake C :B: .30 .75
67 Spell Pierce C :B: 2.00 5.00
68 Sphinx of Jwar Isle R :B: 2.00 5.00
69 Sphinx of Lost Truths R :B: 2.00 5.00
70 Spreading Seas C :B: .40 1.00
71 Summoner's Bane U :B: .50 1.25
72 Tempest Owl C :B: .30 .75
73 Trapfinder's Trick C :B: .30 .75
74 Trapmaker's Snare U :B: .30 .75
75 Umara Raptor C :B: .30 .75
76 Welkin Tern C :B: .30 .75
77 Whiplash Trap C :B: .30 .75
78 Windrider Eel C :B: .30 .75
79 Bala Ged Thief R :K: .60 1.50
80 Blood Seeker C :K: .30 .75
81 Blood Tribute R :K: 1.00 2.50
82 Bloodchief Ascension R :K: 2.50 6.00
83 Bloodghast R :K: 10.00 25.00
84 Bog Tatters C :K: .30 .75
85 Crypt Ripper C :K: .30 .75
86 Desecrated Earth C :K: .30 .75
87 Disfigure C :K: .50 1.25
88 Feast of Blood U :K: .40 1.00
89 Gatekeeper of Malakir U :K: 2.00 5.00
90 Giant Scorpion C :K: .30 .75
91 Grim Discovery C :K: .30 .75
92 Guul Draz Specter R :K: 1.00 2.50
93 Guul Draz Vampire C :K: .40 1.00
94 Hagra Crocodile C :K: .30 .75
95 Hagra Diabolist U :K: .30 .75
96 Halo Hunter R :K: 1.00 2.50
97 Heartstabber Mosquito C :K: .30 .75
98 Hideous End C :K: .40 1.00
99 Kalitas, Bloodchief of Ghet M :K: 6.00 15.00
100 Malakir Bloodwitch R :K: 3.00 8.00
101 Marsh Casualties U :K: .40 1.00
102 Mind Sludge U :K: .60 1.50
103 Mindless Null C :K: .30 .75
104 Mire Blight C :K: .30 .75
105 Needlebite Trap U :K: .30 .75
106 Nimana Sell-Sword C :K: .30 .75
107 Ob Nixilis, the Fallen M :K: 5.00 12.00
108 Quest for the Gravelord U :K: .60 1.50
109 Ravenous Trap U :K: 1.50 4.00
110 Sadistic Sacrament R :K: 1.50 4.00
111 Sorin Markov M :K: 15.00 40.00
112 Soul Stair Expedition C :K: .30 .75
113 Surrakar Marauder C :K: .30 .75
114 Vampire Hexmage U :K: 2.50 6.00
115 Vampire Lacerator C :K: .60 1.50
116 Vampire Nighthawk U :K: 2.00 5.00
117 Vampire's Bite C :K: .30 .75
118 Bladetusk Boar C :R: .30 .75
119 Burst Lightning C :R: .60 1.50
120 Chandra Ablaze M :R: 8.00 20.00
121 Demolish C :R: .30 .75
122 Electropotence R :R: .60 1.50
123 Elemental Appeal R :R: 2.00 5.00
124 Geyser Glider U :R: .30 .75
125 Goblin Bushwhacker C :R: .40 1.00
126 Goblin Guide R :R: 8.00 20.00
127 Goblin Ruinblaster U :R: 1.25 3.00
128 Goblin Shortcutter C :R: .30 .75
129 Goblin War Paint C :R: .30 .75
130 Hellfire Mongrel U :R: .40 1.00
131 Hellkite Charger R :R: 1.00 2.50
132 Highland Berserker C :R: .30 .75
133 Inferno Trap U :R: .30 .75
134 Kazuul Warlord R :R: .60 1.50
135 Lavaball Trap R :R: 1.00 2.50
136 Magma Rift C :R: .30 .75
137 Mark of Mutiny U :R: .50 1.25
138 Molten Ravager C :R: .30 .75
139 Murasa Pyromancer U :R: .30 .75
140 Obsidian Fireheart M :R: 2.00 5.00
141 Plated Geopede C :R: .40 1.00
142 Punishing Fire U :R: .60 1.50
143 Pyromancer Ascension R :R: 2.00 5.00
144 Quest for Pure Flame U :R: .30 .75
145 Ruinous Minotaur C :R: .30 .75
146 Runeflare Trap U :R: .50 1.25
147 Seismic Shudder C :R: .30 .75
148 Shatterskull Giant C :R: .30 .75
149 Slaughter Cry C :R: .30 .75
150 Spire Barrage C :R: .30 .75
151 Torch Slinger C :R: .30 .75
152 Tuktuk Grunts C :R: .30 .75
153 Unstable Footing U :R: .60 1.50
154 Warren Instigator M :R: 6.00 15.00
155 Zektar Shrine Expedition C :R: .60 1.50
156 Baloth Cage Trap U :G: .40 1.00
157 Baloth Woodcrasher U :G: .40 1.00
158 Beast Hunt C :G: .30 .75
159 Beastmaster Ascension R :G: 1.25 3.00
160 Cobra Trap U :G: .50 1.25
161 Frontier Guide U :G: .30 .75
162 Gigantiform R :G: .60 1.50
163 Grazing Gladehart C :G: .30 .75
164 Greenweaver Druid U :G: .30 .75
165 Harrow C :G: .50 1.25
166 Joraga Bard C :G: .30 .75
167 Khalni Heart Expedition C :G: .40 1.00
168 Lotus Cobra M :G: 10.00 25.00
169 Mold Shambler C :G: .40 1.00
170 Nissa Revane M :G: 12.00 30.00
171 Nissa's Chosen C :G: .40 1.00
172 Oracle of Mul Daya R :G: 6.00 15.00
173 Oran-Rief Recluse C :G: .30 .75
174 Oran-Rief Survivalist C :G: .30 .75
175 Predatory Urge R :G: .60 1.50
176 Primal Bellow U :G: .30 .75
177 Quest for the Gemblades U :G: .30 .75
178 Rampaging Baloths M :G: 2.50 6.00
179 Relic Crush C :G: .30 .75
180 River Boa U :G: .50 1.25
181 Savage Silhouette C :G: .30 .75
182 Scute Mob R :G: 2.50 6.00
183 Scythe Tiger C :G: .30 .75
184 Summoning Trap R :G: 2.00 5.00
185 Tajuru Archer U :G: .30 .75
186 Tanglesap C :G: .30 .75
187 Terra Stomper R :G: 1.25 3.00
188 Territorial Baloth C :G: .30 .75
189 Timbermaw Larva C :G: .30 .75
190 Turntimber Basilisk U :G: .30 .75
191 Turntimber Ranger R :G: 1.50 4.00
192 Vastwood Gorger C :G: .30 .75

Card	Low	High
193 Vines of Vastwood C :G:	.60	1.50
194 Zendikar Farguide C :G:	.30	.75
195 Adventuring Gear C :A:	.30	.75
196 Blade of the Bloodchief R :A:	1.25	3.00
197 Blazing Torch U :A:	.30	.75
198 Carnage Altar U :A:	.30	.75
199 Eldrazi Monument M :A:	6.00	15.00
200 Eternity Vessel M :A:	2.00	5.00
201 Expedition Map C :A:	.40	1.00
202 Explorer's Scope C :A:	.30	.75
203 Grappling Hook R :A:	1.00	2.50
204 Hedron Scrabbler C :A:	.30	.75
205 Khalni Gem U :A:	.40	1.00
206 Spidersilk Net C :A:	.30	.75
207 Stonework Puma C :A:	.30	.75
208 Trailblazer's Boots U :A:	.30	.75
209 Trusty Machete U :A:	.50	1.25
210 Akoum Refuge U :L:	.60	1.50
211 Arid Mesa R :L:	50.00	100.00
212 Crypt of Agadeem R :L:	1.50	4.00
213 Emeria, the Sky Ruin R :L:	5.00	12.00
214 Graypelt Refuge U :L:	.60	1.50
215 Jwar Isle Refuge U :L:	.60	1.50
216 Kabira Crossroads C :L:	.30	.75
217 Kazandu Refuge U :L:	.60	1.50
218 Magosi, the Waterveil R :L:	1.50	4.00
219 Marsh Flats R :L:	40.00	80.00
220 Misty Rainforest R :L:	75.00	150.00
221 Oran-Rief, the Vastwood R :L:	3.00	8.00
222 Piranha Marsh C :L:	.30	.75
223 Scalding Tarn R :L:	75.00	150.00
224 Sejiri Refuge U :L:	.60	1.50
225 Soaring Seacliff C :L:	.30	.75
226 Teetering Peaks C :L:	.40	1.00
227 Turntimber Grove C :L:	.30	.75
228 Valakut, the Molten Pinnacle R :L:	2.00	5.00
229 Verdant Catacombs R :L:	50.00	100.00
230 Plains C L		
231 Plains C L		
232 Plains C L		
233 Plains C L		
234 Island C L		
235 Island C L		
236 Island C L		
237 Island C L		
238 Swamp C L		
239 Swamp C L		
240 Swamp C L		
241 Swamp C L		
242 Mountain C L		
243 Mountain C L		
244 Mountain C L		
245 Mountain C L		
246 Forest C L		
247 Forest C L		
248 Forest C L		
249 Forest C L		
250 Plains Full Art C L	.30	.75
251 Plains Full Art C L		
252 Plains Full Art C L		
253 Plains Full Art C L		
254 Island Full Art C L	.30	.75
255 Island Full Art C L		
256 Island Full Art C L		
257 Island Full Art C L		
258 Swamp Full Art C L	.30	.75
259 Swamp Full Art C L		
260 Swamp Full Art C L		
261 Swamp Full Art C L		
262 Mountain Full Art C L	.30	.75
263 Mountain Full Art C L		
264 Mountain Full Art C L		
265 Mountain Full Art C L		
266 Forest Full Art C L	.30	.75
267 Forest Full Art C L		
268 Forest Full Art C L		
269 Forest Full Art C L		

2009 Magic The Gathering Zendikar Tokens

Card	Low	High
1 Angel	.45	.60
2 Bird	.15	.25
3 Kor Soldier	.15	.25
4 Illusion	.10	.15
5 Merfolk	.35	.50
6 Vampire	1.00	1.50
7 Zombie Giant	.10	.15
8 Elemental	.10	.15
9 Beast	.20	.30
10 Snake	.12	.20
11 Wolf	.15	.25

2010 Magic The Gathering Worldwake

Card	Low	High
COMPLETE SET (145)	200.00	275.00
BOOSTER BOX (36 PACKS)	550.00	650.00
BOOSTER PACK (15 CARDS)	20.00	25.00
THEME DECK	15.00	30.00
FAT PACK	200.00	300.00
RELEASED ON FEBRUARY 2, 2010		
1 Admonition Angel M :W:	4.50	5.25
2 Apex Hawks C :W:	.15	.25
3 Archon of Redemption R :W:	.25	.40
4 Battle Hurda C :W:	.15	.25
5 Fledgling Griffin C :W:	.15	.25
6 Guardian Zendikon C :W:	.15	.25
7 Hada Freeblade U :W:	1.00	1.50
8 Iona's Judgment C :W:	.15	.25
9 Join the Ranks C :W:	.15	.25
10 Kitesail Apprentice C :W:	.15	.25
11 Kor Firewalker U :W:	.75	1.25
12 Lightkeeper of Emeria U :W:	.20	.35
13 Loam Lion U :W:	.20	.35
14 Marsh Threader C :W:	.15	.25
15 Marshal's Anthem R :W:	.25	.40
16 Perimeter Captain U :W:	.20	.35
17 Refraction Trap U :W:	.20	.35
18 Rest for the Weary C :W:	.15	.25
19 Ruin Ghost U :W:	.20	.35
20 Stoneforge Mystic R :W:	15.00	17.00
21 Talus Paladin R :W:	1.00	1.50
22 Terra Eternal R :W:	.25	.40
23 Veteran's Reflexes C :W:	.15	.25
24 Aether Tradewinds C :L:	.15	.25
25 Calcite Snapper C :B:	.15	.25
26 Dispel C :B:	.15	.25
27 Enclave Elite C :B:	.15	.25
28 Goliath Sphinx R :B:	.25	.40
29 Halimar Excavator C :B:	.15	.25
30 Horizon Drake U :B:	.20	.35
31 Jace, Mind Sculptor M :L:	50.00	60.00
32 Jwari Shapeshifter R :B:	1.75	2.25
33 Mysteries of the Deep C :B:	.15	.25
34 Permafrost Trap U :B:	.20	.35
35 Quest for Ula's Temple R :B:	1.25	1.75
36 Sejiri Merfolk U :B:	.20	.35
37 Selective Memory R :B:	.25	.40
38 Spell Contortion U :B:	.20	.35
39 Surrakar Banisher C :B:	.15	.25
40 Thada Adel, Acquisitor R :B:	.75	1.25
41 Tideforce Elemental U :B:	.20	.35
42 Treasure Hunt C :B:	.15	.25
43 Twitch C :B:	.15	.25
44 Vapor Snare U :B:	.20	.35
45 Voyager Drake U :B:	.20	.35
46 Wind Zendikon C :B:	.15	.25
47 Abyssal Persecutor M :K:	1.75	2.15
48 Agadeem Occultist R :K:	.40	.60
49 Anowon, the Ruin Sage R :K:	2.50	3.00
50 Bloodhusk Ritualist U :K:	.20	.35
51 Bojuka Brigand C :K:	.15	.25
52 Brink of Disaster C :K:	.15	.25
53 Butcher of Malakir R :K:	.40	.60
54 Caustic Crawler U :K:	.20	.35
55 Corrupted Zendikon C :K:	.15	.25
56 Dead Reckoning C :K:	.15	.25
57 Death's Shadow R :K:	13.00	16.00
58 Jagwasp Swarm C :K:	.15	.25
59 Kalastria Highborn R :K:	3.00	5.00
60 Mire's Toll C :K:	.15	.25
61 Nemesis Trap U :K:	.20	.35
62 Pulse Tracker C :K:	.15	.25
63 Quag Vampires C :K:	.15	.25
64 Quest for the Nihil Stone R :K:	.75	1.00
65 Ruthless Cullblade C :K:	.15	.25
66 Scrib Nibblers U :K:	.20	.35
67 Shoreline Salvager U :K:	.20	.35
68 Smother U :K:	.20	.35
69 Tomb Hex C :K:	.15	.25
70 Urge to Feed U :K:	.20	.35
71 Akoum Battlesinger C :R:	.15	.25
72 Bazaar Trader R :R:	.25	.40
73 Bull Rush C :R:	.15	.25
74 Chain Reaction R :R:	.25	.40
75 Claws of Valakut C :R:	.15	.25
76 Comet Storm M :R:	.75	1.00
77 Cosi's Ravager C :R:	.15	.25
78 Crusher Zendikon C :R:	.15	.25
79 Cunning Sparkmage U :R:	.20	.35
80 Deathforge Shaman U :R:	.20	.35
81 Dragonmaster Outcast M :R:	3.00	4.00
82 Goblin Roughrider C :R:	.15	.25
83 Grotag Thrasher C :R:	.15	.25
84 Kazuul, Tyrant R :R:	.75	1.00
85 Mordant Dragon R :R:	.25	.40
86 Quest for the Goblin Lord U :R:	.20	.35
87 Ricochet Trap U :R:	.60	1.00
88 Roiling Terrain C :R:	.15	.25
89 Rumbling Aftershocks U :R:	.20	.35
90 Searing Blaze C :R:	.15	.25
91 Skitter of Lizards C :R:	.15	.25
92 Slavering Nulls U :R:	.20	.35
93 Stone Idol Trap R :R:	.25	.40
94 Tuktuk Scrapper U :R:	.20	.35
95 Arbor Elf C :G:	.15	.25
96 Avenger of Zendikar M :G:	3.75	4.25
97 Bestial Menace U :G:	.20	.35
98 Canopy Cover U :G:	.20	.35
99 Explore C :G:	.15	.25
100 Feral Contest C :G:	.15	.25
101 Gnarlid Pack C :G:	.15	.25
102 Grappler Spider C :G:	.15	.25
103 Graypelt Hunter C :G:	.15	.25
104 Groundswell C :G:	.15	.25
105 Harabaz Druid R :G:	3.25	3.75
106 Joraga Warcaller R :G:	2.75	3.15
107 Leatherback Baloth U :G:	1.25	2.00
108 Nature's Claim C :G:	.15	.25
109 Omnath, Locus M :G:	8.00	10.00
110 Quest for Renewal U :G:	.20	.35
111 Slingbow Trap U :G:	.20	.35
112 Snapping Creeper C :G:	.15	.25
113 Strength of the Tajuru R :G:	.25	.40
114 Summit Apes U :G:	.20	.35
115 Terastodon R :G:	.30	.50
116 Vastwood Animist U :G:	.20	.35
117 Vastwood Zendikon C :G:	.15	.25
118 Wolfbriar Elemental R :G:	.30	.50
119 Novablast Wurm M :W: :G:	1.75	2.25
120 Wrexial, Risen Deep M :B: :K:	3.00	3.50
121 Amulet of Vigor R	5.50	7.50
122 Basilisk Collar R	15.00	20.00
123 Everflowing Chalice U	.20	.35
124 Hammer of Ruin U	.20	.35
125 Hedron Rover C	.15	.25
126 Kitesail C	.15	.25
127 Lodestone Golem R	.50	.75
128 Pilgrim's Eye C	.15	.25
129 Razor Boomerang U	.20	.35
130 Seer's Sundial R	.25	.40
131 Walking Atlas C	.15	.25
132 Bojuka Bog C	.15	.25
133 Celestial Colonnade R	25.00	30.00
134 Creeping Tar Pit R	15.00	17.00
135 Dread Statuary U	.20	.35
136 Eye of Ugin M	8.00	10.00
137 Halimar Depths C	.15	.25
138 Khalni Garden C	.15	.25
139 Lavaclaw Reaches R	1.75	2.00
140 Quicksand C	.15	.25
141 Raging Ravine R	13.00	15.00
142 Sejiri Steppe C	.15	.25
143 Smoldering Spires C	.15	.25
144 Stirring Wildwood R	1.75	2.00
145 Tectonic Edge U	1.25	2.00
R1 Rules Tip: Allies and Quests	.15	.25
R2 Rules Tip: Landfall	.15	.25
R3 Rules Tip: Lands Alive	.15	.25
R4 Rules Tip: Multikicker	.15	.25
R5 Rules Tip: Traps	.15	.25

2010 Magic The Gathering Worldwake Tokens

Card	Low	High
1 Soldier Ally	.10	.15
2 Dragon	.20	.30
3 Ogre	.60	1.00
4 Elephant	.10	.15
5 Plant	.30	.40
6 Construct	.10	.15

2010 Magic The Gathering Rise of the Eldrazi

Card	Low	High
COMPLETE SET (248)	300.00	400.00
BOOSTER BOX (36 PACKS)	450.00	550.00
BOOSTER PACK (15 CARDS)	10.00	15.00
THEME DECK	20.00	40.00
FAT PACK	75.00	125.00
RELEASED ON APRIL 23, 2010		
1 All Is Dust M	8.00	10.00
2 Artisan of Kozilek U	.40	.60
3 Eldrazi Conscription R	9.00	11.00
4 Emrakul, Aeons Torn M :A:	30.00	35.00
5 Evolving Wilds C	.15	.25
6 Keening Stone R	2.75	3.25
7 Hedron Matrix R	.75	1.00
8 Kozilek, Butcher M :A:	18.00	20.00
9 Ogre's Cleaver U	.20	.35
10 Runed Servitor U	.20	.35
11 Skittering Invasion U	.20	.35
12 Ulamog, the Infinite M	15.00	17.00
13 Sphinx-Bone Wand R	.25	.40
14 Affa Guard Hound U :W:	.20	.35
15 Caravan Escort C :W:	.15	.25
16 Dawnglare Invoker C :W:	.15	.25
17 Deathless Angel R :W:	1.75	2.15
18 Demystify C :W:	.15	.25
19 Eland Umbra C :W:	.15	.25
20 Emerge Unscathed U :W:	.20	.35
21 Gideon Jura M :W:	4.50	5.50
22 Glory Seeker C :W:	.15	.25
23 Guard Duty C :W:	.15	.25
24 Harmless Assault C :W:	.15	.25
25 Hedron-Field Purists R :W:	.25	.40
26 Hyena Umbra C :W:	.75	.25
27 Ikiral Outrider C :W:	.15	.25
28 Kabira Vindicator U :W:	.20	.35
29 Knight of Cliffhaven C :W:	.15	.25
30 Kor Line-Slinger C :W:	.15	.25
31 Kor Spiritdancer R :W:	7.00	9.00
32 Lightmine Field R :W:	.50	.75
33 Linvala, Keeper M :W:	40.00	45.00
34 Lone Missionary C :W:	.15	.25
35 Luminous Wake U :W:	.20	.35
36 Makindi Griffin C :W:	.15	.25
37 Mammoth Umbra U :W:	.20	.35
38 Near-Death Exp R :W:	.30	.50
39 Nomads' Assembly R :W:	.25	.40
40 Oust U :W:	.20	.35
41 Puncturing Light C :W:	.15	.25
42 Repel the Darkness C :W:	.15	.25
43 Smite C :W:	.15	.25
44 Soulbound Guardians U :W:	.20	.35
45 Soul's Attendant C :W:	1.25	2.00
46 Stalwart Shield-Bearers C :W:	.15	.25
47 Student of Warfare R :W:	3.00	4.00
48 Survival Cache U :W:	.20	.35
49 Time of Heroes U :W:	.20	.35
50 Totem-Guide Hartebeest C :W:	.15	.25
51 Transcendent Master M :W:	4.50	5.50
52 Umbra Mystic R :W:	.75	1.00
53 Wall of Omens U :W:	2.00	3.50
54 Aura Finesse C :B:	.15	.25
55 Cast Through Time M :B:	1.75	2.25
56 Champion's Drake C :B:	.15	.25
57 Coralhelm Commander R :B:	1.75	2.25
58 Crab Umbra U :B:	.20	.35
59 Deprive C :B:	.60	1.00
60 Distortion Strike C :B:	1.50	2.50
61 Domestication U :B:	.20	.35
62 Dormant Gomazoa R :B:	.25	.40
63 Drake Umbra U :B:	.20	.35
64 Echo Mage R :B:	.40	.60
65 Eel Umbra C :B:	.15	.25
66 Enclave Cryptologist U :B:	.20	.35
67 Fleeting Distraction C :B:	.15	.25
68 Frostwind Invoker C :B:	.15	.25
69 Gloomhunter C :B:	.15	.25
70 Gravitational Shift R :B:	.25	.40
71 Guard Gomazoa U :B:	.20	.35
72 Hada Spy Patrol U :B:	.20	.35
73 Halimar Wavewatch C :B:	.15	.25
74 Induce Despair C :B:	.15	.25
75 Inquisition of Kozilek U :B:	6.00	10.00
76 Jwari Scuttler C :B:	.15	.25
77 Lay Bare C :B:	.15	.25
78 Lighthouse Chrono M :B:	7.00	9.00
79 Merfolk Observer C :B:	.15	.25
80 Merfolk Skyscout U :B:	.20	.35
81 Mnemonic Wall C :B:	.15	.25
82 Narcolepsy C :B:	.15	.25
83 Null Champion C :B:	.15	.25
84 Phantasmal Abomination U :B:	.20	.35
85 Reality Spasm U :B:	.20	.35
86 Recurring Insight R :B:	.75	1.25
87 Regress C :B:	.15	.25
88 Renegade Doppelganger R :B:	.25	.40
89 Sea Gate Oracle C :B:	.15	.25
90 See Beyond C :B:	.15	.25
91 Shared Discovery C :B:	.15	.25
92 Skywatcher Adept C :B:	.15	.25
93 Sphinx of Magosi R :B:	.40	.60
94 Surrakar Spellblade R :B:	.25	.40
95 Training Grounds R :B:	4.00	6.00
96 Unified Will U :B:	.20	.35
97 Venerated Teacher C :B:	.15	.25
98 Arrogant Bloodlord U :K:	.20	.35
99 Baneful Omen R :K:	.25	.40
100 Bloodrite Invoker C :K:	.15	.25
101 Bloodthrone Vampire C :K:	.15	.25
102 Cadaver Imp C :K:	.15	.25
103 Consume the Meek R :K:	.30	.50
104 Consuming Vapors R :K:	.75	1.00
105 Contaminated Ground C :K:	.15	.25
106 Corpsehatch U :K:	.20	.35
107 Curse of Wizardry U :K:	.20	.35
108 Death Cultist C :K:	.15	.25
109 Demonic Appetite C :K:	.15	.25
110 Drana, Klstria Bldchf R :K:	.75	1.15
111 Dread Drone C :K:	.15	.25
112 Escaped Null U :K:	.20	.35
113 Essence Feed C :K:	.15	.25
114 Guul Draz Assassin R :K:	3.00	4.00
115 Hellcarver Demon M :K:	.75	1.00
116 Last Kiss C :K:	.15	.25
117 Mortician Beetle R :K:	.75	1.00
118 Nighthaze C :K:	.15	.25
119 Nirkana Cutthroat U :K:	.20	.35
120 Nirkana Revenant M :K:	17.00	19.00
121 Pawn of Ulamog U :K:	.20	.35
122 Perish the Thought C :K:	.15	.25
123 Pestilence Demon R :K:	.50	.75
124 Repay In Kind R :K:	.25	.40
125 Shrivel C :K:	.15	.25
126 Skeletal Wurm U :K:	.20	.35
127 Suffer the Past U :K:	.20	.35
128 Thought Gorger R :K:	.25	.40
129 Vendetta C :K:	.15	.25
130 Virulent Swipe U :K:	.20	.35
131 Zof Shade C :K:	.15	.25
132 Zulaport Enforcer C :K:	.15	.25
133 Akoum Boulderfoot U :R:	.20	.35
134 Battle Rampart C :R:	.15	.25
135 Battle-Rattle Shaman C :R:	.15	.25
136 Brimstone Mage U :R:	.20	.35
137 Brood Birthing C :R:	.15	.25
138 Conquering Manticore R :R:	.25	.40
139 Devastating Summons R :R:	.75	1.00
140 Disaster Radius R :R:	.25	.40
141 Emrakul's Hatcher C :R:	.15	.25
142 Explosive Revelation U :R:	.20	.35
143 Fissure Vent C :R:	.15	.25
144 Flame Slash C :R:	.15	.25
145 Forked Bolt U :R:	.50	.35
146 Goblin Arsonist C :R:	.15	.25
147 Goblin Tunneler C :R:	.15	.25
148 Grotag Siege-Runner C :R:	.15	.25
149 Heat Ray C :R:	.15	.25
150 Hellion Eruption R :R:	.25	.40
151 Kargan Dragonlord M :R:	4.00	6.00
152 Kiln Fiend C :R:	.75	1.25
153 Lagac Lizard C :R:	.15	.25
154 Lavafume Invoker C :R:	.15	.25
155 Lord of Shatter Pass R :R:	.75	1.00
156 Lust for War U :R:	.20	.35
157 Magmaw R :R:	.25	.40
158 Ogre Sentry C :R:	.15	.25
159 Rage Nimbus R :R:	.25	.40
160 Raid Bombardment C :R:	.15	.25
161 Rapacious One U :R:	.20	.35
162 Soulsurge Elemental U :R:	.20	.35
163 Spawning Breath C :R:	.15	.25
164 Splinter Twin R :R:	3.00	3.50
165 Staggershock C :R:	.15	.25
166 Surreal Memoir U :R:	.20	.35
167 Traitorous Instinct U :R:	.20	.35
168 Tuktuk the Explorer R :R:	.50	.75
169 Valakut Fireboar U :R:	.20	.35
170 Vent Sentinel C :R:	.15	.25
171 World at War R :R:	1.25	1.75
172 Wrap in Flames C :R:	.15	.25
173 Ancient Stirrings C :G:	2.50	3.50
174 Aura Gnarlid C :G:	.15	.25
175 Awakening Zone R :G:	3.00	4.50
176 Bala Ged Scorpion C :G:	.15	.25
177 Bear Umbra R :G:	3.00	4.50
178 Beastbreaker of Bala Ged U :G:	.20	.35
179 Boar Umbra U :G:	.20	.35
180 Bramblesnap U :G:	.20	.35
181 Broodwarden U :G:	.20	.35
182 Daggerback Basilisk C :G:	.15	.25
183 Gelatinous Genesis R :G:	.50	.75
184 Gigantomancer R :G:	.25	.40
185 Gravity Well U :G:	.20	.35
186 Growth Spasm C :G:	.15	.25
187 Haze Frog C :G:	.15	.25
188 Irresistible Prey U :G:	.20	.35
189 Jaddi Lifestrider U :G:	.20	.35
190 Joraga Treespeaker U :G:	1.25	2.00
191 Kazandu Tuskcaller R :G:	.30	.50
192 Khalni Hydra M :G:	9.00	11.00
193 Kozilek's Predator C :G:	.15	.25
194 Leaf Arrow C :G:	.15	.25
195 Living Destiny C :G:	.15	.25
196 Might of the Masses C :G:	.15	.25
197 Momentous Fall R :G:	1.25	1.75
198 Mul Daya Channelers R :G:	1.25	1.75
199 Naturalize C :G:	.15	.25
200 Nema Siltlurker C :G:	.15	.25
201 Nest Invader C :G:	.15	.25
202 Ondu Giant C :G:	.15	.25
203 Overgrown Battlement C :G:	.15	.25
204 Pelakka Wurm U :G:	.20	.35
205 Prey's Vengeance U :G:	.20	.35
206 Realms Uncharted R :G:	2.25	2.75
207 Snake Umbra C :G:	.15	.25
208 Spider Umbra C :G:	.50	.75
209 Sporecap Spider C :G:	.15	.25
210 Stomper Cub C :G:	.15	.25
211 Tajuru Preserver R :G:	1.25	1.75
212 Vengevine M :G:	16.00	18.00

213 Wildheart Invoker C :G:	.15	.25
214 Sarkhan the Mad M :K: :R:	5.00	7.00
215 Angelheart Vial R	.25	.40
216 Dreamstone Hedron U	.20	.35
217 Enatu Golem U	.20	.35
218 Hand of Emrakul C	.15	.25
219 It That Betrays R	3.00	3.50
220 Not Of This World U	1.00	1.50
221 Pathrazer of Ulamog U	1.25	2.00
222 Pennon Blade U	.20	.35
223 Prophetic Prism C	.15	.25
224 Reinforced Bulwark C	.15	.25
225 Spawnsire of Ulamog R	3.50	5.00
226 Ulamog's Crusher C	.15	.25
227 Warmonger's Chariot U	.20	.35
228 Eldrazi Temple R :L:	5.50	7.00
229 Plains (a) L	.15	.25
230 Plains (b) L	.15	.25
231 Plains (c) L	.15	.25
232 Plains (d) L	.15	.25
233 Island (a) L	.15	.25
234 Island (b) L	.15	.25
235 Island (c) L	.15	.25
236 Island (d) L	.15	.25
237 Swamp (a) L	.15	.25
238 Swamp (b) L	.15	.25
239 Swamp (c) L	.15	.25
240 Swamp (d) L	.15	.25
241 Mountain (a) L	.15	.25
242 Mountain (b) L	.15	.25
243 Mountain (c) L	.15	.25
244 Mountain (d) L	.15	.25
245 Forest (a) L	.15	.25
246 Forest (b) L	.15	.25
247 Forest (c) L	.15	.25
248 Forest (d) L	.15	.25
R2 Rules Tip: Eldrazi Abilities	.15	.25
R3 Rules Tip: Levelers	.15	.25
R4 Rules Tip: Rebound	.15	.25
R5 Rules Tip: Totem Armor	.15	.25
R1 Rules Tip: Eldrazi	.15	.25

2010 Magic The Gathering Rise of the Eldrazi Tokens

1a Eldrazi Spawn	.15	.25
1b Eldrazi Spawn	.12	.20
1c Eldrazi Spawn	.12	.20
2 Elemental	.15	.25
3 Hellion	.10	.15
4 Ooze	.10	.15
5 Tuktuk the Returned	.60	1.00

2010 Magic The Gathering Scars of Mirrodin

COMPLETE SET (249)	250.00	325.00
BOOSTER BOX (36 PACKS)	175.00	250.00
BOOSTER PACK (15 CARDS)	5.00	8.00
FAT PACK	60.00	80.00
RELEASED ON OCTOBER 1, 2010		
1 Abuna Acolyte U :W:	.20	.35
2 Arrest C :W:	.15	.25
3 Auriok Edgewright U :W:	.20	.35
4 Auriok Sunchaser C :W:	.15	.25
5 Dispense Justice U :W:	.20	.35
6 Elspeth Tirel M :W:	8.00	10.00
7 Fulgent Distraction C :W:	.15	.25
8 Ghalma's Warden C :W:	.15	.25
9 Glimmerpoint Stag U :W:	.20	.35
10 Glint Hawk C :W:	.15	.25
11 Indomitable Archangel M :W:	.75	1.25
12 Kemba, Kha Regent R :W:	.25	.40
13 Kemba's Skyguard C :W:	.15	.25
14 Leonin Arbiter R :W:	3.00	4.50
15 Loxodon Wayfarer C :W:	.15	.25
16 Myrsmith U :W:	.20	.35
17 Razor Hippogriff U :W:	.20	.35
18 Revoke Existence C :W:	.15	.25
19 Salvage Scout C :W:	.15	.25
20 Seize the Initiative C :W:	.15	.25
21 Soul Parry C :W:	.15	.25
22 Sunblast Angel R :W:	.50	.75
23 Sunspear Shikari C :W:	.15	.25
24 Tempered Steel R :W:	1.00	1.50
25 True Conviction R :W:	1.25	1.75
26 Vigil for the Lost U :W:	.20	.35
27 Whitesun's Passage C :W:	.15	.25
28 Argent Sphinx R :B:	.25	.40
29 Bonds of Quicksilver C :B:	.15	.25
30 Darkslick Drake U :B:	.20	.35
31 Disperse C :B:	.15	.25
32 Dissipation Field R :B:	.50	.75
33 Grand Architect R :B:	2.00	2.50
34 Halt Order U :B:	.20	.35
35 Inexorable Tide R :B:	.50	.75
36 Lumengrid Drake C :B:	.15	.25
37 Neurok Invisimancer C :B:	.15	.25
38 Plated Seastrider C :B:	.15	.25
39 Quicksilver Gargantuan M :B:	.75	1.00
40 Riddlesmith U :B:	.20	.35
41 Scrapdiver Serpent C :B:	.15	.25
42 Screeching Silcaw C :B:	.15	.25
43 Shape Anew R :B:	.50	.75
44 Sky-Eel School C :B:	.15	.25
45 Steady Progress C :B:	.15	.25
46 Stoic Rebuttal C :B:	.15	.25
47 Thrummingbird U :B:	.20	.35
48 Trinket Mage U :B:	.20	.35
49 Turn Aside C :B:	.15	.25
50 Twisted Image U :B:	1.25	2.00
51 Vault Skyward C :B:	.15	.25
52 Vedalken Certarch C :B:	.15	.25
53 Volition Reins U :B:	.20	.35
54 Blackcleave Goblin C :K:	.15	.25
55 Bleak Coven Vampires C :K:	.15	.25
56 Blistergrub C :K:	.15	.25
57 Carnifex Demon R :K:	.25	.40
58 Contagious Nim C :K:	.15	.25
59 Corrupted Harvester U :K:	.20	.35
60 Dross Hopper C :K:	.15	.25
61 Exsanguinate U :K:	1.25	2.00
62 Flesh Allergy U :K:	.20	.35
63 Fume Spitter C :K:	.15	.25
64 Geth, Lord of the Vault M :K:	5.00	7.00
65 Grasp of Darkness C :K:	.15	.25
66 Hand of the Praetors R :K:	.75	1.25
67 Ichor Rats U :K:	.20	.35
68 Instill Infection C :K:	.15	.25
69 Memoricide R :K:	.25	.40
70 Moriok Reaver C :K:	.15	.25
71 Necrogen Scudder U :K:	.20	.35
72 Necrotic Ooze R :K:	1.00	1.50
73 Painful Quandary R :K:	2.50	3.00
74 Painsmith U :K:	.20	.35
75 Plague Stinger C :K:	.15	.25
76 Psychic Miasma C :K:	.15	.25
77 Relic Putrescence C :K:	.15	.25
78 Skinrender U :K:	.20	.35
79 Skithiryx, the Blight M :K:	9.00	11.00
80 Tainted Strike C :K:	.15	.25
81 Arc Trail U :R:	.20	.35
82 Assault Strobe C :R:	.15	.25
83 Barrage Ogre U :R:	.20	.35
84 Blade-Tribe Berserkers C :R:	.15	.25
85 Bloodshot Trainee U :R:	.20	.35
86 Cerebral Eruption R :R:	.25	.40
87 Embersmith U :R:	.20	.35
88 Ferrovore C :R:	.15	.25
89 Flameborn Hellion C :R:	.15	.25
90 Furnace Celebration U :R:	.20	.35
91 Galvanic Blast C :R:	.15	.25
92 Goblin Gaveleer C :R:	.15	.25
93 Hoard-Smelter Dragon R :R:	.25	.40
94 Koth of the Hammer M :R:	8.00	10.00
95 Kuldotha Phoenix R :R:	.25	.40
96 Kuldotha Rebirth C :R:	.15	.25
97 Melt Terrain C :R:	.15	.25
98 Molten Psyche R :R:	.25	.40
99 Ogre Geargrabber U :R:	.20	.35
100 Oxidda Daredevil C :R:	.15	.25
101 Oxidda Scrapmelter U :R:	.20	.35
102 Scoria Elemental C :R:	.15	.25
103 Shatter C :R:	.15	.25
104 Spikeshot Elder R :R:	.25	.40
105 Tunnel Ignus R :R:	.25	.40
106 Turn to Slag C :R:	.15	.25
107 Vulshok Heartstoker C :R:	.15	.25
108 Acid Web Spider U :G:	.20	.35
109 Alpha Tyrranax C :G:	.15	.25
110 Asceticism R :G:	7.00	9.00
111 Bellowing Tanglewurm U :G:	.20	.35
112 Blight Mamba C :G:	.15	.25
113 Blunt the Assault C :G:	.15	.25
114 Carapace Forger C :G:	.15	.25
115 Carrion Call U :G:	.20	.35
116 Copperhorn Scout C :G:	.15	.25
117 Cystbearer C :G:	.15	.25
118 Engulfing Slagwurm R :G:	.75	1.00
119 Ezuri, Renegade Leader R :G:	3.00	4.50
120 Ezuri's Archers C :G:	.15	.25
121 Ezuri's Brigade R :G:	.25	.40
122 Genesis Wave R :G:	5.00	7.00
123 Liege of the Tangle M :G:	3.00	3.50
124 Lifesmith U :G:	.20	.35
125 Molder Beast C :G:	.15	.25
126 Putrefax R :G:	.25	.40
127 Slice in Twain U :G:	.20	.35
128 Tangle Angler U :G:	.20	.35
129 Tel-Jilad Defiance C :G:	.15	.25
130 Tel-Jilad Fallen C :G:	.15	.25
131 Untamed Might C :G:	.15	.25
132 Viridian Revel U :G:	.20	.35
133 Wing Puncture C :G:	.15	.25
134 Withstand Death C :G:	.15	.25
135 Venser, the Sojourner M :G:	8.00	10.00
136 Accorder's Shield C	.15	.25
137 Argentum Armor R	.50	.75
138 Auriok Replica C	.15	.25
139 Barbed Battlegear U	.20	.35
140 Bladed Pinions C	.15	.25
141 Chimeric Mass R	.25	.40
142 Chrome Steed C	.15	.25
143 Clone Shell U	.20	.35
144 Contagion Clasp U	.20	.35
145 Contagion Engine R	3.00	4.00
146 Copper Myr C	.15	.25
147 Corpse Cur C	.15	.25
148 Culling Dais U	.20	.35
149 Darksteel Axe U	.20	.35
150 Darksteel Juggernaut R	.75	1.25
151 Darksteel Myr U	.20	.35
152 Darksteel Sentinel U	.20	.35
153 Echo Circlet C	.15	.25
154 Etched Champion R	2.75	3.25
155 Flight Spellbomb C	.15	.25
156 Glint Hawk Idol C	.15	.25
157 Gold Myr C	.15	.25
158 Golden Urn C	.15	.25
159 Golem Artisan U	.20	.35
160 Golem Foundry C	.15	.25
161 Golem's Heart U	.20	.35
162 Grafted Exoskeleton U	.20	.35
163 Grindclock R	.25	.40
164 Heavy Arbalest U	.20	.35
165 Horizon Spellbomb C	.15	.25
166 Ichorclaw Myr C	.15	.25
167 Infiltration Lens U	.20	.35
168 Iron Myr C	.15	.25
169 Kuldotha Forgemaster R	1.75	2.25
170 Leaden Myr C	.15	.25
171 Liquimetal Coating U	.20	.35
172 Livewire Lash R	.25	.40
173 Lux Cannon M	2.50	3.00
174 Memnite U	1.25	2.00
175 Mimic Vat R	2.25	2.75
176 Mindslaver M	4.00	4.50
177 Molten-Tail Mast M	.40	.60
178 Moriok Replica C	.15	.25
179 Mox Opal M	30.00	35.00
180 Myr Battlesphere R	.25	.40
181 Myr Galvanizer U	.50	.80
182 Myr Propagator R	.25	.40
183 Myr Reservoir R	.30	.50
184 Necrogen Censer C	.15	.25
185 Necropede U	.50	.80
186 Neurok Replica C	.15	.25
187 Nihil Spellbomb C	.15	.25
188 Nim Deathmantle R	1.75	2.25
189 Origin Spellbomb C	.15	.25
190 Palladium Myr U	.50	.80
191 Panic Spellbomb C	.15	.25
192 Perilous Myr C	.15	.25
193 Platinum Emperion M	18.00	21.00
194 Precursor Golem R	.25	.40
195 Prototype Portal R	.75	1.25
196 Ratchet Bomb R	.75	1.00
197 Razorfield Thresher C	.15	.25
198 Rust Tick U	.20	.35
199 Rusted Relic U	.20	.35
200 Saberclaw Golem C	.15	.25
201 Semblance Anvil R	.75	1.25
202 Silver Myr C	.15	.25
203 Snapsail Glider C	.15	.25
204 Soliton C	.15	.25
205 Steel Hellkite R	.75	1.00
206 Strata Scythe R	.25	.40
207 Strider Harness C	.15	.25
208 Sword of Body M	9.00	11.00
209 Sylvok Lifestaff C	.15	.25
210 Sylvok Replica C	.15	.25
211 Throne of Geth U	.20	.35
212 Tower of Calamities R	.25	.40
213 Trigon of Corruption U	.20	.35
214 Trigon of Infestation U	.20	.35
215 Trigon of Mending U	.20	.35
216 Trigon of Rage U	.20	.35
217 Trigon of Thought U	.20	.35
218 Tumble Magnet C	.15	.25
219 Vector Asp C	.15	.25
220 Venser's Journal R	3.50	5.00
221 Vulshok Replica C	.15	.25
222 Wall of Tanglecord C	.15	.25
223 Wurmcoil Engine M	13.00	15.00
224 Blackcleave Cliffs R	17.00	19.00
225 Copperline Gorge R	9.00	11.00
226 Darkslick Shores R	6.50	8.00
227 Glimmerpost C	.15	.25
228 Razorverge Thicket R	7.00	8.00
229 Seachrome Coast R	4.00	5.50
230 Plains L	.15	.25
231 Plains L	.15	.25
232 Plains L	.15	.25
233 Plains L	.15	.25
234 Island L	.15	.25
235 Island L	.15	.25
236 Island L	.15	.25
237 Island L	.15	.25
238 Swamp L	.15	.25
239 Swamp L	.15	.25
240 Swamp L	.15	.25
241 Swamp L	.15	.25
242 Mountain L	.15	.25
243 Mountain L	.15	.25
244 Mountain L	.15	.25
245 Mountain L	.15	.25
246 Forest L	.15	.25
247 Forest L	.15	.25
248 Forest L	.15	.25
249 Forest L	.15	.25
R1 Rules Tip: Infect	.15	.25
R2 Rules Tip: Metalcraft	.15	.25
R3 Rules Tip: Proliferate	.15	.25
R4 Rules Tip: Imprint	.15	.25
R5 Rules Tip: Poison and Emblems	.15	.25

2010 Magic The Gathering Scars of Mirrodin Tokens

1 Cat	.35	.50
2 Soldier	.30	.40
3 Goblin	.35	.50
4 Insect	.15	.25
5 Wolf	.60	1.00
6 Golem	.12	.20
7 Myr	.12	.20
8 Wurm	5.00	7.00
9 Wurm	3.50	5.00
10 Poison Counter	.10	.15

2011 Magic The Gathering Mirrodin Besieged

COMPLETE SET (155)	150.00	200.00
BOOSTER BOX (36 PACKS)	175.00	200.00
BOOSTER PACK (16 CARDS)	5.00	7.00
RELEASED ON FEBRUARY 4, 2011		
1 Accorder Paladin U :W:	.20	.35
2 Ardent Recruit C :W:	.15	.25
3 Banishment Decree C :W:	.15	.25
4 Choking Fumes U :W:	.20	.35
5 Divine Offering C :W:	.15	.25
6 Frantic Salvage C :W:	.15	.25
7 Gore Vassal U :W:	.20	.35
8 Hero of Bladehold M :W:	5.00	7.00
9 Kemba's Legion U :W:	.20	.35
10 Leonin Relic-Warder U :W:	.20	.35
11 Leonin Skyhunter C :W:	.15	.25
12 Loxodon Partisan C :W:	.15	.25
13 Master's Call C :W:	.15	.25
14 Mirran Crusader R :W:	1.00	1.50
15 Phyrexian Rebirth R :W:	.50	.75
16 Priests of Norn C :W:	.15	.25
17 Tine Shrike C :W:	.15	.25
18 Victory's Herald R :W:	.25	.40
19 White Sun's Zenith R :W:	.25	.40
20 Blue Sun's Zenith R :B:	.75	1.00
21 Consecrated Sphinx M :B:	18.00	20.00
22 Corrupted Conscience U :B:	.20	.35
23 Cryptoplasm R :B:	.50	.75
24 Distant Memories R :B:	.25	.40
25 Fuel for the Cause C :B:	.15	.25
26 Mirran Spy C :B:	.15	.25
27 Mitotic Manipulation R :B:	.25	.40
28 Neurok Commando U :B:	.20	.35
29 Oculus C :B:	.15	.25
30 Quicksilver Geyser C :B:	.15	.25
31 Serum Raker C :B:	.15	.25
32 Spire Serpent C :B:	.15	.25
33 Steel Sabotage C :B:	.15	.25
34 Treasure Mage U :B:	.20	.35
35 Turn the Tide C :B:	.15	.25
36 Vedalken Anatomist U :B:	.20	.35
37 Vedalken Infuser U :B:	.20	.35
38 Vivisection C :B:	.15	.25
39 Black Sun's Zenith R :K:	1.25	1.75
40 Caustic Hound C :K:	.15	.25
41 Flensermite C :K:	.15	.25
42 Flesh-Eater Imp U :K:	.20	.35
43 Go for the Throat U :K:	.20	.35
44 Gruesome Encore U :K:	.20	.35
45 Horrifying Revelation C :K:	.15	.25
46 Massacre Wurm M :K:	6.00	8.00
47 Morbid Plunder C :K:	.15	.25
48 Nested Ghoul U :K:	.20	.35
49 Phyresis C :K:	.15	.25
50 Phyrexian Crusader R :K:	3.00	4.00
51 Phyrexian Rager C :K:	.15	.25
52 Phyrexian Vatmother R :K:	.25	.40
53 Sangromancer R :K:	1.25	1.75
54 Scourge Servant C :K:	.15	.25
55 Septic Rats U :K:	.20	.35
56 Spread the Sickness C :K:	.15	.25
57 Virulent Wound C :K:	.15	.25
58 Blisterstick Shaman C :R:	.15	.25
59 Burn the Impure C :R:	.15	.25
60 Concussive Bolt C :R:	.15	.25
61 Crush C :R:	.15	.25
62 Galvanoth R :R:	.25	.40
63 Gnathosaur C :R:	.15	.25
64 Goblin Wardriver U :R:	.20	.35
65 Hellkite Igniter R :R:	.25	.40
66 Hero of Oxid Ridge M :R:	.75	1.00
67 Into the Core U :R:	.20	.35
68 Koth's Courier C :R:	.15	.25
69 Kuldotha Flamefiend U :R:	.20	.35
70 Kuldotha Ringleader C :R:	.15	.25
71 Metallic Mastery U :R:	.20	.35
72 Ogre Resister C :R:	.15	.25
73 Rally the Forces C :R:	.15	.25
74 Red Sun's Zenith R :R:	.40	.60
75 Slagstorm R :R:	.25	.40
76 Spiraling Duelist U :R:	.20	.35
77 Blightwidow C :G:	.15	.25
78 Creeping Corrosion R :G:	1.25	1.75
79 Fangren Marauder C :G:	.15	.25
80 Glissa's Courier C :G:	.15	.25
81 Green Sun's Zenith R :G:	4.00	5.00
82 Lead the Stampede U :G:	.20	.35
83 Melira's Keepers U :G:	.20	.35
84 Mirran Mettle C :G:	.15	.25
85 Phyrexian Hydra R :G:	.30	.50
86 Pistus Strike C :G:	.15	.25
87 Plaguemaw Beast U :G:	.20	.35
88 Praetor's Counsel M :G:	1.00	1.50
89 Quilled Slagwurm U :G:	.20	.35
90 Rot Wolf C :G:	.15	.25
91 Tangle Mantis C :G:	.15	.25
92 Thrun, the Last Troll M :G:	8.00	10.00
93 Unnatural Predation C :G:	.15	.25
94 Viridian Corrupter U :G:	.20	.35
95 Viridian Emissary C :G:	.15	.25
96 Glissa, the Traitor M :K: :G:	2.00	2.50
97 Tezzeret, Agent of Bolas M :B: :K:	18.00	20.00
98 Bladed Sentinel C	.15	.25
99 Blightsteel Colossus M	20.00	24.00
100 Bonehoard R	.25	.40
101 Brass Squire U	.20	.35
102 Copper Carapace C	.15	.25
103 Core Prowler U	.20	.35
104 Darksteel Plate R	5.00	7.00
105 Decimator Web R	.25	.40
106 Dross Ripper C	.15	.25
107 Flayer Husk C	.15	.25
108 Gust-Skimmer C	.15	.25
109 Hexplate Golem C	.15	.25
110 Ichor Wellspring C	.15	.25
111 Knowledge Pool R	.25	.40
112 Lumengrid Gargoyle U	.20	.35
113 Magnetic Mine R	.25	.40
114 Mirrorworks R	1.25	1.75
115 Mortarpod U	.20	.35
116 Myr Sire C	.15	.25
117 Myr Turbine R	1.00	1.50
118 Myr Welder R	.25	.40
119 Peace Strider U	.20	.35
120 Phyrexian Digester C	.15	.25
121 Phyrexian Juggernaut U	.20	.35
122 Phyrexian Revoker R	.75	1.25
123 Pierce Strider U	.20	.35
124 Piston Sledge U	.20	.35
125 Plague Myr U	.20	.35
126 Psychosis Crawler R	.50	.75
127 Razorfield Rhino C	.15	.25
128 Rusted Slasher C	.15	.25
129 Shimmer Myr R	.75	1.25
130 Shriekhorn C	.15	.25
131 Signal Pest U	.20	.35
132 Silverskin Armor U	.20	.35
133 Skinwing U	.20	.35
134 Sphere of the Suns U	.20	.35
135 Spin Engine C	.15	.25
136 Spine of Ish Sah R	.25	.40
137 Strandwalker U	.20	.35
138 Sword of Feast and Famine M	14.00	16.00
139 Tangle Hulk C	.15	.25
140 Thopter Assembly R	.30	.50
141 Titan Forge R	.40	.60
142 Training Drone C	.15	.25
143 Viridian Claw U	.20	.35
144 Contested War Zone R	.25	.40
145 Inkmoth Nexus R	20.00	25.00
146 Plains L	.15	.25
147 Plains L	.15	.25

148 Island L .15 .25
149 Island L .15 .25
150 Swamp L .15 .25
151 Swamp L .15 .25
152 Mountain L .15 .25
153 Mountain L .15 .25
154 Forest L .15 .25
155 Forest L .15 .25
R1 Rules Tip: Battle Cry .15 .25
R2 Rules Tip: Metalcraft Imprint .15 .25
R3 Rules Tip: Living Weapon .15 .25
R4 Rules Tip: Infect .15 .25
R5 Rules Tip: Proliferate .15 .25

2011 Magic The Gathering Mirrodin Besieged Foil

1 Accorder Paladin U :W: 3.00 5.00
2 Ardent Recruit C :W: .20 .35
3 Banishment Decree C :W: .20 .35
4 Choking Fumes U :W: .20 .35
5 Divine Offering C :W: .40 .60
6 Frantic Salvage C :W: .20 .35
7 Gore Vassal U :W: .20 .35
8 Hero of Bladehold M :W: 10.00 15.00
9 Kemba's Legion U :W: .20 .35
10 Leonin Relic-Warder U :W: 3.00 5.00
11 Leonin Skyhunter C :W: .20 .35
12 Loxodon Partisan C :W: .20 .35
13 Master's Call C :W: .20 .35
14 Mirran Crusader R :W: 5.00 8.00
15 Phyrexian Rebirth R :W: 2.00 3.00
16 Priests of Norn C :W: .20 .35
17 Tine Shrike C :W: .20 .35
18 Victory's Herald R :W: .60 1.00
19 White Sun's Zenith R :W: 2.50 4.00
20 Blue Sun's Zenith R :B: 6.00 8.00
21 Consecrated Sphinx M :B: 45.00 55.00
22 Corrupted Conscience U :B: 4.00 6.00
23 Cryptoplasm R :B: 2.00 3.50
24 Distant Memories R :B: .60 1.00
25 Fuel for the Cause C :B: 5.00 8.00
26 Mirran Spy C :B: .20 .35
27 Mitotic Manipulation R :B: .40 .60
28 Neurok Commando U :B: .20 .35
29 Oculus C :B: .20 .35
30 Quicksilver Geyser C :B: .20 .35
31 Serum Raker C :B: .20 .35
32 Spire Serpent C :B: .20 .35
33 Steel Sabotage C :B: .40 .60
34 Treasure Mage U :B: 3.00 5.00
35 Turn the Tide C :B: .20 .35
36 Vedalken Anatomist U :B: .20 .35
37 Vedalken Infuser U :B: .20 .35
38 Vivisection C :B: .20 .35
39 Black Sun's Zenith R :K: 4.00 6.00
40 Caustic Hound C :K: .20 .35
41 Flensermite C :K: .30 .50
42 Flesh-Eater Imp U :K: .75 1.25
43 Go for the Throat U :K: 4.00 6.00
44 Gruesome Encore U :K: .20 .35
45 Horrifying Revelation C :K: .20 .35
46 Massacre Wurm M :K: 18.00 22.00
47 Morbid Plunder C :K: .20 .35
48 Nested Ghoul U :K: .20 .35
49 Phyresis C :K: 3.00 5.00
50 Phyrexian Crusader R :K: 6.00 10.00
51 Phyrexian Rager C :K: .60 1.00
52 Phyrexian Vatmother R :K: 1.00 1.50
53 Sangromancer R :K: 3.00 5.00
54 Scourge Servant C :K: .20 .35
55 Septic Rats U :K: .50 .75
56 Spread the Sickness C :K: .20 .35
57 Virulent Wound C :K: .30 .50
58 Blisterstick Shaman C :R: .20 .35
59 Burn the Impure C :R: .20 .35
60 Concussive Bolt C :R: .20 .35
61 Crush C :R: .20 .35
62 Galvanoth R :R: .75 2.00
63 Gnathosaur C :R: .20 .35
64 Goblin Wardriver U :R: 2.00 3.50
65 Hellkite Igniter R :R: 1.25 2.00
66 Hero of Oxid Ridge M :R: 3.00 5.00
67 Into the Core U :R: .50 .75
68 Koth's Courier C :R: .20 .35
69 Kuldotha Flamefiend U :R: .20 .35
70 Kuldotha Ringleader C :R: .20 .35
71 Metallic Mastery U :R: .20 .35
72 Ogre Resister C :R: .20 .35
73 Rally the Forces C :R: .20 .35
74 Red Sun's Zenith R :R: 2.00 3.50
75 Slagstorm R :R: 1.50 2.00
76 Spiraling Duelist U :R: .20 .35
77 Blightwidow C :G: .75 1.25
78 Creeping Corrosion R :G: 4.00 6.00
79 Fangren Marauder C :G: .20 .35
80 Glissa's Courier C :G: .20 .35
81 Green Sun's Zenith R :G: 14.00 17.00
82 Lead the Stampede U :G: 3.00 5.00
83 Melira's Keepers U :G: .20 .35
84 Mirran Mettle C :G: .20 .35
85 Phyrexian Hydra R :G: .60 1.00
86 Pistus Strike C :G: .20 .35
87 Plaguemaw Beast U :G: .40 .60
88 Praetor's Counsel M :G: 10.00 15.00
89 Quilled Slagwurm U :G: .20 .35
90 Rot Wolf C :G: .75 1.25
91 Tangle Mantis C :G: .20 .35
92 Thrun, the Last Troll M :G: 30.00 35.00
93 Unnatural Predation C :G: .20 .35
94 Viridian Corrupter U :G: 8.00 10.00
95 Viridian Emissary C :G: .75 1.25
96 Glissa, the Traitor M :K: :G: 7.00 10.00
97 Tezzeret, Agent of Bolas M :B: :K: 60.00 70.00
98 Bladed Sentinel C .20 .35
99 Blightsteel Colossus M 50.00 65.00
100 Bonehoard R 1.00 1.50
101 Brass Squire U 1.25 2.00
102 Copper Carapace C .20 .35
103 Core Prowler U 1.50 2.50
104 Darksteel Plate R 13.00 16.00
105 Decimator Web R 1.00 1.50
106 Dross Ripper C .20 .35
107 Flayer Husk C .40 .60
108 Gust-Skimmer C .20 .35
109 Hexplate Golem C .20 .35
110 Ichor Wellspring C 4.00 6.00
111 Knowledge Pool R 2.00 3.50
112 Lumengrid Gargoyle U .20 .35
113 Magnetic Mine R .50 .75
114 Mirrorworks R 6.00 8.00
115 Mortarpod U .60 1.00
116 Myr Sire C .20 .35
117 Myr Turbine R 3.00 5.00
118 Myr Welder R 1.00 1.50
119 Peace Strider U .20 .35
120 Phyrexian Digester C .20 .35
121 Phyrexian Juggernaut U .40 .60
122 Phyrexian Revoker R 10.00 13.00
123 Pierce Strider U .20 .35
124 Piston Sledge U .20 .35
125 Plague Myr U 1.50 2.50
126 Psychosis Crawler R 1.25 2.00
127 Razorfield Rhino C .20 .35
128 Rusted Slasher C .20 .35
129 Shimmer Myr R 6.00 8.00
130 Shriekhorn C 1.50 2.50
131 Signal Pest U 6.00 8.00
132 Silverskin Armor U .20 .35
133 Skinwing U .20 .35
134 Sphere of the Suns U .75 1.25
135 Spin Engine C .20 .35
136 Spine of Ish Sah R 6.00 8.00
137 Strandwalker U .20 .35
138 Sword of Feast and Famine M 35.00 45.00
139 Tangle Hulk C .20 .35
140 Thopter Assembly R 4.00 6.00
141 Titan Forge R 1.00 1.50
142 Training Drone C .20 .35
143 Viridian Claw U .20 .35
144 Contested War Zone R 2.50 4.00
145 Inkmoth Nexus R 100.00 115.00
146 Plains L .20 .35
147 Plains L .20 .35
148 Island L .20 .35
149 Island L .20 .35
150 Swamp L .20 .35
151 Swamp L .20 .35
152 Mountain L .20 .35
153 Mountain L .20 .35
154 Forest L .20 .35
155 Forest L .20 .35

2011 Magic The Gathering Mirrodin Besieged Tokens

1 Germ .10 .15
2 Zombie .30 .40
3 Golem .30 .40
4 Horror 1.50 2.00
5 Thopter .50 .75
6 Poison Counter .10 .15

2011 Magic The Gathering New Phyrexia

COMPLETE SET (175) 245.00 325.00
BOOSTER BOX (36 PACKS) 300.00 350.00
BOOSTER PACK (15 CARDS) 5.00 8.00
RELEASED ON MAY 13, 2011
1 Karn Liberated M 35.00 40.00
2 Apostle's Blessing C :W: .15 .25
3 Auriok Survivors U :W: .20 .35
4 Blade Splicer R :W: 1.00 2.50
5 Cathedral Membrane U :W: .20 .35
6 Chancellor of the Annex R :W: 1.00 1.50
7 Dispatch U :W: .20 .35
8 Due Respect U :W: .20 .35
9 Elesh Norn, Grand Cenobite M :W: 15.00 18.00
10 Exclusion Ritual U :W: .20 .35
11 Forced Worship C :W: .15 .25
12 Inquisitor Exarch U :W: .20 .35
13 Lost Leonin C :W: .15 .25
14 Loxodon Convert C :W: .15 .25
15 Marrow Shards U :W: .20 .35
16 Master Splicer U :W: .20 .35
17 Norn's Annex R :W: .75 2.00
18 Phyrexian Unlife R :W: .25 .40
19 Porcelain Legionnaire C :W: .15 .25
20 Puresteel Paladin R :W: 1.50 4.00
21 Remember the Fallen C :W: .15 .25
22 Sensor Splicer C :W: .15 .25
23 Shattered Angel U :W: .20 .35
24 Shriek Raptor C :W: .15 .25
25 Suture Priest C :W: .15 .25
26 War Report C :W: .15 .25
27 Argent Mutation U :B: .20 .35
28 Arm with AEther U :B: .20 .35
29 Blighted Agent C :B: .15 .25
30 Chained Throatseeker C :B: .15 .25
31 Chancellor of the Spires R :B: .25 .40
32 Corrupted Resolve U :B: .20 .35
33 Deceiver Exarch U :B: .60 1.00
34 Defensive Stance C :B: .15 .25
35 Gitaxian Probe C :B: .15 .25
36 Impaler Shrike C :B: .15 .25
37 Jin-Gitaxias, Core Augur M :B: 10.00 13.00
38 Mental Misstep U :B: .50 .75
39 Mindculling U :B: .20 .35
40 Numbing Dose C :B: .15 .25
41 Phyrexian Ingester R :B: .25 .40
42 Phyrexian Metamorph R :B: 5.00 7.00
43 Psychic Barrier C :B: .15 .25
44 Psychic Surgery R :B: .25 .40
45 Spined Thopter C :B: .15 .25
46 Spire Monitor C :B: .15 .25
47 Tezzeret's Gambit U :B: .20 .35
48 Vapor Snag C :B: .15 .25
49 Viral Drake U :B: .20 .35
50 Wing Splicer U :B: .20 .35
51 Xenograft R :B: .25 .40
52 Blind Zealot C :K: .15 .25
53 Caress of Phyrexia U :K: .20 .35
54 Chancellor of the Dross R :K: .25 .40
55 Dementia Bat C :K: .15 .25
56 Despise U :K: .20 .35
57 Dismember U :K: 1.25 2.00
58 Enslave U :K: .20 .35
59 Entomber Exarch U :K: .20 .35
60 Evil Presence C :K: .15 .25
61 Geth's Verdict C :K: .15 .25
62 Glistening Oil R :K: .60 1.50
63 Grim Affliction C :K: .15 .25
64 Ichor Explosion U :K: .20 .35
65 Life's Finale R :K: 1.25 1.75
66 Mortis Dogs C :K: .15 .25
67 Parasitic Implant C :K: .15 .25
68 Phyrexian Obliterator M :K: 25.00 30.00
69 Pith Driller C :K: .15 .25
70 Postmortem Lunge U :K: .20 .35
71 Praetor's Grasp R :K: .50 .75
72 Reaper of Sheoldred U :K: .20 .35
73 Sheoldred, Whispering One M :K: 15.00 18.00
74 Surgical Extraction R :K: 17.00 20.00
75 Toxic Nim C :K: .15 .25
76 Vault Skirge C :K: .15 .25
77 Whispering Specter U :K: .20 .35
78 Act of Aggression U :R: .20 .35
79 Artillerize C :R: .15 .25
80 Bludgeon Brawl R :R: .25 .40
81 Chancellor of the Forge R :R: .40 .60
82 Fallen Ferromancer U :R: .20 .35
83 Flameborn Viron C :R: .15 .25
84 Furnace Scamp C :R: .15 .25
85 Geosurge U :R: .20 .35
86 Gut Shot U :R: .20 .35
87 Invader Parasite R :R: .25 .40
88 Moltensteel Dragon R :R: .30 .50
89 Ogre Menial C :R: .15 .25
90 Priest of Urabrask U :R: .20 .35
91 Rage Extractor U :R: .20 .35
92 Razor Swine C :R: .15 .25
93 Ruthless Invasion C :R: .15 .25
94 Scrapyard Salvo C :R: .15 .25
95 Slag Fiend R :R: .40 1.00
96 Slash Panther C :R: .15 .25
97 Tormentor Exarch U :R: .20 .35
98 Urabrask the Hidden M :R: 7.00 9.00
99 Victorious Destruction C :R: .15 .25
100 Volt Charge C :R: .15 .25
101 Vulshok Refugee U :R: .20 .35
102 Whipflare U :R: .20 .35
103 Beast Within U :G: 2.00 3.50
104 Birthing Pod R :G: 5.00 12.00
105 Brutalizer Exarch U :G: .20 .35
106 Chancellor of the Tangle R :G: .25 .40
107 Corrosive Gale U :G: .20 .35
108 Death-Hood Cobra C :G: .15 .25
109 Fresh Meat R :G: .25 .40
110 Glissa's Scorn C :G: .15 .25
111 Glistener Elf C :G: .15 .25
112 Greenhilt Trainee U :G: .20 .35
113 Leeching Bite C :G: .15 .25
114 Maul Splicer C :G: .15 .25
115 Melira, Sylvok Outcast R :G: 4.50 6.00
116 Mutagenic Growth C :G: .15 .25
117 Mycosynth Fiend U :G: .20 .35
118 Noxious Revival U :G: .20 .35
119 Phyrexian Swarmlord R :G: .30 .50
120 Rotted Hystrix C :G: .15 .25
121 Spinebiter U :G: .20 .35
122 Thundering Tanadon C :G: .15 .25
123 Triumph of the Hordes U :G: .20 .35
124 Viridian Betrayers C :G: .15 .25
125 Viridian Harvest C :G: .15 .25
126 Vital Splicer U :G: .20 .35
127 Vorinclex, Voice of Hunger M :G: 18.00 20.00
128 Jor Kadeen, the Prevailer R :W/R: .25 .40
129 Alloy Myr U .20 .35
130 Batterskull M 13.00 15.00
131 Blinding Souleater C .15 .25
132 Caged Sun R 4.00 4.50
133 Conversion Chamber U .20 .35
134 Darksteel Relic U .20 .35
135 Etched Monstrosity M .50 .75
136 Gremlin Mine C .15 .25
137 Hex Parasite R .30 .50
138 Hovermyr C .15 .25
139 Immolating Souleater C .15 .25
140 Insatiable Souleater C .15 .25
141 Isolation Cell U .20 .35
142 Kiln Walker U .20 .35
143 Lashwrithe R .25 .40
144 Mindcrank U .20 .35
145 Mycosynth Wellspring C .15 .25
146 Myr Superion R 1.25 1.75
147 Necropouncer U .20 .35
148 Omen Machine R .25 .40
149 Pestilent Souleater C .15 .25
150 Phyrexian Hulk C .15 .25
151 Pristine Talisman C .15 .25
152 Shrine of Boundless Growth U .20 .35
153 Shrine of Burning Rage U .20 .35
154 Shrine of Limitless Power U .20 .35
155 Shrine of Loyal Legions U .20 .35
156 Shrine of Piercing Vision U .20 .35
157 Sickleslicer U .20 .35
158 Soul Conduit R .25 .40
159 Spellskite R 20.00 23.00
160 Surge Node U .20 .35
161 Sword of War and Peace M 12.00 14.00
162 Torpor Orb R 1.25 3.00
163 Trespassing Souleater C .15 .25
164 Unwinding Clock R 5.25 5.75
165 Phyrexia's Core U .20 .35
166 Plains L .15 .25
167 Plains L .15 .25
168 Island L .15 .25
169 Island L .15 .25
170 Swamp L .15 .25
171 Swamp L .15 .25
172 Mountain L .15 .25
173 Mountain L .15 .25
174 Forest L .15 .25
175 Forest L .15 .25
R1 Rules Tip: Phyrexian Mana .15 .25
R2 Rules Tip: Living Weapon .15 .25
R3 Rules Tip: Infect .15 .25
R4 Rules Tip: Proliferate .15 .25

2011 Magic The Gathering New Phyrexia Tokens

1 Beast .35 .50
2 Goblin 3.50 5.00
3 Golem .10 .15
4 Myr .25 .35
5 Poison Counter .10 .15

2011 Magic The Gathering Innistrad

COMPLETE SET (277) 250.00 350.00
BOOSTER BOX (36 PACKS) 275.00 300.00
BOOSTER PACK (15 CARDS) 10.00 15.00
RELEASED ON SEPTEMBER 30, 2011
1 Abbey Griffin C :W: .15 .25
2 Angel of Flight Alabaster R :W: .25 .40
3 Angelic Overseer M :W: 1.75 2.25
4 Avacynian Priest C :W: .15 .25
5 Bonds of Faith C :W: .15 .25
6 Champion of the Parish R :W: 1.75 2.25
7 Chapel Geist C :W: .15 .25
8 Cloistered Youth/Unholy Fiend U :W: :K: .20 .35
9 Dearly Departed R :W: .25 .40
10 Divine Reckoning R :W: .25 .40
11 Doomed Traveler C :W: .15 .25
12 Elder Cathar C :W: .15 .25
13 Elite Inquisitor R :W: .25 .40
14 Feeling of Dread C :W: .15 .25
15 Fiend Hunter U :W: .20 .35
16 Gallows Warden U :W: .20 .35
17 Geist-Honored Monk R :W: .25 .40
18 Ghostly Possession C :W: .15 .25
19 Intangible Virtue U :W: .20 .35
20 Mausoleum Guard U :W: .20 .35
21 Mentor of the Meek R :W: .75 1.00
22 Midnight Haunting U :W: .20 .35
23 Mikaeus, the Lunarch M :W: 2.50 4.00
24 Moment of Heroism C :W: .15 .25
25 Nevermore R :W: .50 .75
26 Paraselene U :W: .20 .35
27 Purify the Grave U :W: .20 .35
28 Rally the Peasants U :W: .20 .35
29 Rebuke C :W: .15 .25
30 Selfless Cathar C :W: .15 .25
31 Silverchase Fox C :W: .15 .25
32 Slayer of the Wicked U :W: .20 .35
33 Smite the Monstrous C :W: .15 .25
34 Spare from Evil C :W: .15 .25
35 Spectral Rider U :W: .20 .35
36 Stony Silence R :W: 8.00 10.00
37 Thraben Purebloods C :W: .15 .25
38 Thraben Sentry/Thraben Militia C :W: .15 .25
39 Unruly Mob C :W: .15 .25
40 Urgent Exorcism C :W: .15 .25
41 Village Bell-Ringer C :W: .15 .25
42 Voiceless Spirit C :W: .15 .25
43 Armored Skaab C :B: .15 .25
44 Back from the Brink R :B: .25 .40
45 Battleground Geist U :B: .20 .35
46 Cackling Counterpart R :B: .30 .50
47 Civilized Scholar/Homicidal Brute U :B: :R: .20 .35
48 Claustrophobia C :B: .15 .25
49 Curiosity U :B: .20 .35
50 Curse of the Bloody Tome C :B: .15 .25
51 Delver of Secrets/Insectile Aberration C :B: .15 .25
52 Deranged Assistant C :B: .15 .25
53 Dissipate U :B: .20 .35
54 Dream Twist C :B: .15 .25
55 Forbidden Alchemy C :B: .15 .25
56 Fortress Crab C :B: .15 .25
57 Frightful Delusion C :B: .15 .25
58 Grasp of Phantoms U :B: .20 .35
59 Hysterical Blindness C :B: .15 .25
60 Invisible Stalker U :B: .20 .35
61 Laboratory Maniac R :B: 2.00 3.00
62 Lantern Spirit U :B: .20 .35
63 Lost in the Mist C :B: .15 .25
64 Ludevic's Test Subject/Ludevic's Abomination R :B: .25 .40
65 Makeshift Mauler C :B: .15 .25
66 Memory's Journey U :B: .20 .35
67 Mindshrieker R :B: .25 .40
68 Mirror-Mad Phantasm M :B: .40 .60
69 Moon Heron C :B: .15 .25
70 Murder of Crows U :B: .20 .35
71 Rooftop Storm R :B: .75 1.25
72 Runic Repetition U :B: .20 .35
73 Selhoff Occultist C :B: .15 .25
74 Sensory Deprivation C :B: .15 .25
75 Silent Departure C :B: .15 .25
76 Skaab Goliath U :B: .20 .35
77 Skaab Ruinator M :B: .75 1.25
78 Snapcaster Mage R :B: 38.00 45.00
79 Spectral Flight C :B: .15 .25
80 Stitched Drake C :B: .15 .25
81 Stitcher's Apprentice C :B: .15 .25
82 Sturmgeist R :B: .25 .40
83 Think Twice C :B: .15 .25
84 Undead Alchemist R :B: .75 1.00
85 Abattoir Ghoul U :K: .20 .35
86 Altar's Reap C :K: .15 .25
87 Army of the Damned M :K: 2.25 2.75
88 Bitterheart Witch U :K: .20 .35
89 Bloodgift Demon R :K: .40 .60
90 Bloodline Keeper/Lord of Lineage R :K: 4.00 6.00
91 Brain Weevil C :K: .15 .25
92 Bump in the Night C :K: .15 .25
93 Corpse Lunge C :K: .15 .25
94 Curse of Death's Hold R :K: .30 .50
95 Curse of Oblivion C :K: .15 .25
96 Dead Weight C :K: .15 .25
97 Diregraf Ghoul U :K: .20 .35
98 Disciple of Griselbrand U :K: .20 .35
99 Endless Ranks of the Dead R :K: 3.00 5.00
100 Falkenrath Noble U :K: .20 .35
101 Ghoulcaller's Chant C :K: .15 .25
102 Ghoulraiser C :K: .15 .25

103 Gruesome Deformity C :K: .15 .25
104 Heartless Summoning R :K: .75 1.25
105 Liliana of the Veil M :K: 80.00 90.00
106 Manor Skeleton C :K: .15 .25
107 Markov Patrician C :K: .15 .25
108 Maw of the Mire C :K: .15 .25
109 Moan of the Unhallowed U :K: .20 .35
110 Morkrut Banshee U :K: .20 .35
111 Night Terrors C :K: .15 .25
112 Reaper from the Abyss M :K: 1.00 1.50
113 Rotting Fensnake C :K: .15 .25
114 Screeching Bat/Stalking Vampire U :K: .20 .35
115 Sever the Bloodline R :K: .25 .40
116 Skeletal Grimace C :K: .15 .25
117 Skirsdag High Priest R :K: .25 .40
118 Stromkirk Patrol C :K: .15 .25
119 Tribute to Hunger U :K: .20 .35
120 Typhoid Rats C :K: .15 .25
121 Unbreathing Horde R :K: .75 1.00
122 Unburial Rites U :K: .20 .35
123 Vampire Interloper C :K: .15 .25
124 Victim of Night C :K: .15 .25
125 Village Cannibals U :K: .20 .35
126 Walking Corpse C :K: .15 .25
127 Ancient Grudge C :R: .15 .25
128 Ashmouth Hound C :R: .15 .25
129 Balefire Dragon M :R: 6.00 8.00
130 Blasphemous Act R :R: 2.00 2.50
131 Bloodcrazed Neonate C :R: .15 .25
132 Brimstone Volley C :R: .15 .25
133 Burning Vengeance U :R: .20 .35
134 Charmbreaker Devils R :R: .25 .40
135 Crossway Vampire C :R: .15 .25
136 Curse of Stalked Prey R :R: .25 .40
137 Curse of the Nightly Hunt U :R: .20 .35
138 Curse of the Pierced Heart C :R: .15 .25
139 Desperate Ravings U :R: .20 .35
140 Devil's Play R :R: .25 .40
141 Falkenrath Marauders R :R: .25 .40
142 Feral Ridgewolf C :R: .15 .25
143 Furor of the Bitten C :R: .15 .25
144 Geistflame C :R: .15 .25
145 Hanweir Watchkeep/Bane of Hanweir U :R: .20 .35
146 Harvest Pyre C :R: .15 .25
147 Heretic's Punishment R :R: .25 .40
148 Infernal Plunge C :R: .15 .25
149 Instigator Gang/Wildblood Pack R :R: .60 .80
150 Into the Maw of Hell U :R: .20 .35
151 Kessig Wolf C :R: .15 .25
152 Kruin Outlaw/Terror of Kruin Pass R :R: 1.50 2.00
153 Night Revelers C :R: .15 .25
154 Nightbird's Clutches C :R: .15 .25
155 Past in Flames M :R: 5.00 7.00
156 Pitchburn Devils C :R: .15 .25
157 Rage Thrower U :R: .20 .35
158 Rakish Heir U :R: .20 .35
159 Reckless Waif/Merciless Predator U :R: .20 .35
160 Riot Devils C :R: .15 .25
161 Rolling Temblor U :R: .20 .35
162 Scourge of Geier Reach U :R: .20 .35
163 Skirsdag Cultist U :R: .20 .35
164 Stromkirk Noble R :R: .50 .75
165 Tormented Pariah/Rampaging Werewolf C :R: .15 .25
166 Traitorous Blood C :R: .15 .25
167 Vampiric Fury C :R: .15 .25
168 Village Ironsmith/Ironfang C :R: .15 .25
169 Ambush Viper C :G: .15 .25
170 Avacyn's Pilgrim C :G: .15 .25
171 Boneyard Wurm U :G: .20 .35
172 Bramblecrush U :G: .20 .35
173 Caravan Vigil C :G: .15 .25
174 Creeping Renaissance R :G: .25 .40
175 Darkthicket Wolf C :G: .15 .25
176 Daybreak Ranger/Nightfall Predator R :G: .40 .60
177 Elder of Laurels R :G: .25 .40
178 Essence of the Wild M :G: .50 .75
179 Festerhide Boar C :G: .15 .25
180 Full Moon's Rise U :G: .20 .35
181 Garruk Relentless/Garruk, the Veil-Cursed M :K: :G: 4.00 6.00
182 Gatstaf Shepherd/Gatstaf Howler U :G: .20 .35
183 Gnaw to the Bone C :G: .15 .25
184 Grave Bramble C :G: .15 .25
185 Grizzled Outcasts/Krallenhorde Wantons C :G: .15 .25
186 Gutter Grime R :G: .25 .40
187 Hamlet Captain U :G: .20 .35
188 Hollowhenge Scavenger U :G: .20 .35
189 Kessig Cagebreakers R :G: .25 .40
190 Kindercatch C :G: .15 .25
191 Lumberknot U :G: .20 .35
192 Make a Wish U :G: .20 .35
193 Mayor of Avabruck/Howlpack Alpha R :G: 2.50 4.00
194 Moldgraf Monstrosity R :G: .25 .40
195 Moonmist C :G: .15 .25
196 Mulch C :G: .15 .25
197 Naturalize C :G: .15 .25
198 Orchard Spirit C :G: .15 .25
199 Parallel Lives R :G: 5.00 7.00
200 Prey Upon C :G: .15 .25
201 Ranger's Guile C :G: .15 .25
202 Somberwald Spider C :G: .15 .25
203 Spider Spawning U :G: .20 .35
204 Spidery Grasp C :G: .15 .25
205 Splinterfright R :G: .25 .40
206 Travel Preparations C :G: .15 .25
207 Tree of Redemption M :G: 2.00 2.50
208 Ulvenwald Mystics/Ulvenwald Primordials U :G: .20 .35
209 Villagers of Estwald/Howlpack of Estwald C :G: .15 .25
210 Woodland Sleuth C :G: .15 .25
211 Wreath of Geists U :G: .20 .35
212 Evil Twin R :B: :K: .40 .60
213 Geist of Saint Traft M :W: :B: 6.00 8.00
214 Grimgrin, Corpse-Born M :B: :K: 3.00 4.00
215 Olivia Voldaren M :K: :R: 6.00 8.00
216 Blazing Torch C .15 .25
217 Butcher's Cleaver U .20 .35
218 Cellar Door U .20 .35
219 Cobbled Wings C .15 .25
220 Creepy Doll R .25 .40
221 Demonmail Hauberk U .20 .35
222 Galvanic Juggernaut U .20 .35
223 Geistcatcher's Rig U .20 .35
224 Ghoulcaller's Bell C .15 .25
225 Graveyard Shovel U .20 .35
226 Grimoire of the Dead M 3.00 3.50
227 Inquisitor's Flail U .20 .35
228 Manor Gargoyle R .25 .40
229 Mask of Avacyn U .20 .35
230 One-Eyed Scarecrow C .15 .25
231 Runechanter's Pike R .25 .40
232 Sharpened Pitchfork U .20 .35
233 Silver-Inlaid Dagger U .20 .35
234 Traveler's Amulet C .15 .25
235 Trepanation Blade U .20 .35
236 Witchbane Orb R .40 .60
237 Wooden Stake C .15 .25
238 Clifftop Retreat R 3.00 5.00
239 Gavony Township R 4.00 6.00
240 Ghost Quarter U .20 .35
241 Hinterland Harbor R 3.00 5.00
242 Isolated Chapel R 2.50 3.50
243 Kessig Wolf Run R 1.75 2.25
244 Moorland Haunt R .25 .40
245 Nephalia Drownyard R .25 .40
246 Shimmering Grotto C .15 .25
247 Stensia Bloodhall R .25 .40
248 Sulfur Falls R 6.00 8.00
249 Woodland Cemetery R 3.00 5.00
250 Plains L .15 .25
251 Plains L .15 .25
252 Plains L .15 .25
253 Island L .15 .25
254 Island L .15 .25
255 Island L .15 .25
256 Swamp L .15 .25
257 Swamp L .15 .25
258 Swamp L .15 .25
259 Mountain L .15 .25
260 Mountain L .15 .25
261 Mountain L .15 .25
262 Forest L .15 .25
263 Forest L .15 .25
264 Forest L .15 .25

2011 Magic The Gathering Innistrad Tokens

1 Angel 1.00 1.25
2 Spirit .10 .15
3 Homunculus .10 .15
4 Demon .15 .25
5 Vampire 1.25 1.75
6 Wolf 1.50 2.00
7 Zombie .10 .15
8 Zombie .15 .25
9 Zombie .15 .25
10 Ooze .10 .15
11 Spider .30 .40
12 Wolf .15 .25
13 Innistrad CL .10 .15

2012 Magic The Gathering Dark Ascension

COMPLETE SET (158) 110.00 150.00
BOOSTER BOX (36 PACKS) 100.00 110.00
BOOSTER PACK (15 CARDS) 3.00 5.00
RELEASED ON FEBRUARY 3, 2012
1 Archangel's Light M :W: .75 1.00
2 Bar the Door C :W: .15 .25
3 Break of Day C :W: .15 .25
4 Burden of Guilt C :W: .15 .25
5 Curse of Exhaustion U :W: .20 .35
6 Elgaud Inquisitor C :W: .15 .25
7 Faith's Shield U :W: .20 .35
8 Gather the Townsfolk C :W: .15 .25
9 Gavony Ironwright U :W: .20 .35
10 Hollowhenge Spirit U :W: .20 .35
11 Increasing Devotion R :W: .25 .40
12 Lingering Souls U :W: .20 .35
13 Loyal Cathar/Unhallowed Cathar C :W: :K: .15 .25
14 Midnight Guard C :W: .15 .25
15 Niblis of the Mist C :W: .15 .25
16 Niblis of the Urn U :W: .20 .35
17 Ray of Revelation C :W: .15 .25
18 Requiem Angel R :W: .25 .40
19 Sanctuary Cat C :W: .15 .25
20 Seance R :W: .40 .60
21 Silverclaw Griffin C :W: .15 .25
22 Skillful Lunge C :W: .15 .25
23 Sudden Disappearance R :W: .25 .40
24 Thalia, Guardian of Thraben R :W: 8.00 10.00
25 Thraben Doomsayer R :W: .75 1.00
26 Thraben Heretic U :W: .20 .35
27 Artful Dodge C :L: .15 .25
28 Beguiler of Wills M :L: .75 1.00
29 Bone to Ash C :L: .15 .25
30 Call to the Kind:R: R :L: .25 .40
31 Chant of the Skifsang C :L: .15 .25
32 Chill of Foreboding U :L: .20 .35
33 Counterlash R :L: .25 .40
34 Curse of Echoes R :L: .25 .40
35 Divination C :L: .15 .25
36 Dungeon Geists R :B: .25 .40
37 Geralf's Mindcrusher R :L: .25 .40
38 Griptide C :L: .15 .25
39 Havengul Runebinder R :L: .25 .40
40 Headless Skaab C :L: .15 .25
41 Increasing Confusion R :L: 1.00 1.50
42 Mystic Retrieval U :L: .20 .35
43 Nephalia Seakite C :L: .15 .25
44 Niblis of the Breath U :L: .20 .35
45 Relentless Skaabs U :L: .20 .35
46 Saving Grasp C :L: .15 .25
47 Screeching Skaab C :L: .15 .25
48 Secrets of the Dead U :L: .20 .35
49 Shriekgeist C :L: .15 .25
50 Soul Seizer/Ghastly Haunting U :L: .20 .35
51 Stormbound Geist C :L: .15 .25
52 Thought Scour C :L: .15 .25
53 Tower Geist U :L: .20 .35
54 Black Cat C :K: .15 .25
55 Chosen of Markov/Markov's Servant C :K: .15 .25
56 Curse of Misfortunes R :K: .25 .40
57 Curse of Thirst U :K: .20 .35
58 Deadly Allure U :K: .20 .35
59 Death's Caress C :K: .15 .25
60 Falkenrath Torturer C :K: .15 .25
61 Farbog Boneflinger U :K: .20 .35
62 Fiend of the Shadows R :K: .25 .40
63 Geralf's Messenger R :K: 4.00 4.50
64 Gravecrawler R :K: 4.00 5.00
65 Gravepurge C :K: .15 .25
66 Gruesome Discovery C :K: .15 .25
67 Harrowing Journey U :K: .20 .35
68 Highborn Ghoul C :K: .15 .25
69 Increasing Ambition R :K: .75 1.00
70 Mikaeus, the Unhallowed M :K: 18.00 20.00
71 Ravenous Demon/Archdemon of Greed R :K: .25 .40
72 Reap the Seagraf C :K: .15 .25
73 Sightless Ghoul C :K: .15 .25
74 Skirsdag Flayer U :K: .20 .35
75 Spiteful Shadows C :K: .15 .25
76 Tragic Slip C :K: .15 .25
77 Undying Evil C :K: .15 .25
78 Vengeful Vampire U :K: .20 .35
79 Wakedancer U :K: .20 .35
80 Zombie Apocalypse R :K: 1.00 1.25
81 Afflicted Deserter/Werewolf Ransacker U :R: .20 .35
82 Alpha Brawl R :R: .25 .40
83 Blood Feud U :R: .20 .35
84 Burning Oil U :R: .20 .35
85 Curse of Bloodletting R :R: .40 .60
86 Erdwal Ripper C :R: .15 .25
87 Faithless Looting C :R: .15 .25
88 Fires of Undeath C :R: .15 .25
89 Flayer of the Hatebound R :R: .25 .40
90 Fling C :R: .15 .25
91 Forge Devil C :R: .15 .25
92 Heckling Fiends U :R: .20 .35
93 Hellrider R :R: .40 .60
94 Hinterland Hermit/Hinterland Scourge C :R: .15 .25
95 Increasing Vengeance R :R: 1.00 1.50
96 Markov Blademaster R :R: .50 .75
97 Markov Warlord U :R: .20 .35
98 Mondronen Shaman/Tovolar's Magehunter R :R: .25 .40
99 Moonveil Dragon M :R: 1.75 2.00
100 Nearheath Stalker C :R: .15 .25
101 Pyreheart Wolf U :R: .20 .35
102 Russet Wolves C :R: .15 .25
103 Scorch the Fields C :R: .15 .25
104 Shatte:R: Perception U :R: .20 .35
105 Talons of Falkenrath C :R: .15 .25
106 Torch Fiend C :R: .15 .25
107 Wrack with Madness C :R: .15 .25
108 Briarpack Alpha U :G: .20 .35
109 Clinging Mists C :G: .15 .25
110 Crushing Vines C :G: .15 .25
111 Dawntreader Elk C :G: .15 .25
112 Deranged Outcast R :G: .25 .40
113 Favor of the Woods C :G: .15 .25
114 Feed the Pack R :G: .25 .40
115 Ghoultree R :G: .75 1.00
116 Gravetiller Wurm U :G: .20 .35
117 Grim Flowering U :G: .20 .35
118 Hollowhenge Beast C :G: .15 .25
119 Hunger of the Howlpack C :G: .15 .25
120 Increasing Savagery R :G: .75 1.00
121 Kessig Recluse C :G: .15 .25
122 Lambholt Elder/Silverpelt Werewolf U :G: .20 .35
123 Lost in the Woods R :G: .25 .40
124 Predator Ooze R :G: 2.00 2.50
125 Scorned Villager/Moonscarred Werewolf C :G: .15 .25
126 Somberwald Dryad C :G: .15 .25
127 Strangleroot Geist U :G: .20 .35
128 Tracker's Instincts U :G: .20 .35
129 Ulvenwald Bear C :G: .15 .25
130 Village Survivors U :G: .20 .35
131 Vorapede M :G: 1.00 1.50
132 Wild Hunger C :G: .15 .25
133 Wolfbitten Captive/Krallenhorde Killer R :G: .75 1.00
134 Young Wolf C :G: .15 .25
135 Diregraf Captain U :L: :K: .20 .35
136 Drogskol Captain U :W: :L: .20 .35
137 Drogskol Reaver M :W: :L: 1.50 2.00
138 Falkenrath Aristocrat M :K: :R: 2.50 3.00
139 Havengul Lich M :L: :K: 4.00 4.50
140 Huntmaster of the Fells: :Ravager of the Fells M :R: :G: 9.00 11.00
141 Immerwolf U :R: :G: .20 .35
142 Sorin, Lord of Innistrad M :W: :K: 5.00 6.50
143 Stromkirk Captain U :K: :R: .20 .35
144 Altar of the Lost U .20 .35
145 Avacyn's Collar U .20 .35
146 Chalice of Life/Chalice of Death U .20 .35
147 Elbrus, the Binding Blade/Withengar Unbound M :K: 3.00 4.00
148 Executioner's Hood C .15 .25
149 Grafdigger's Cage R 10.00 12.00
150 Heavy Mattock C .15 .25
151 Helvault M .40 .60
152 Jar of Eyeballs R .25 .40
153 Warden of the Wall U .20 .35
154 Wolfhunter's Quiver U .20 .35
155 Evolving Wilds C .15 .25
156 Grim Backwoods R .25 .40
157 Haunted Fengraf C .15 .25
158 Vault of the Archangel R 2.00 2.50

2012 Magic The Gathering Dark Ascension Foil

1 Archangel's Light M :W: 2.00 3.50
2 Bar the Door C :W: .20 .35
3 Break of Day C :W: .20 .35
4 Burden of Guilt C :W: .20 .35
5 Curse of Exhaustion U :W: .75 1.25
6 Elgaud Inquisitor C :W: .20 .35
7 Faith's Shield U :W: 1.25 2.00
8 Gather the Townsfolk C :W: .75 1.25
9 Gavony Ironwright U :W: .25 .40
10 Hollowhenge Spirit U :W: .25 .40
11 Increasing Devotion R :W: 2.00 3.50
12 Lingering Souls U :W: 8.00 11.00
13 Loyal Cathar/Unhallowed Cathar C :W: :K: .20 .35
14 Midnight Guard C :W: .30 .50
15 Niblis of the Mist C :W: .20 .35
16 Niblis of the Urn U :W: .25 .40
17 Ray of Revelation C :W: .50 .75
18 Requiem Angel R :W: .50 .75
19 Sanctuary Cat C :W: .20 .35
20 Seance R :W: 2.00 3.50
21 Silverclaw Griffin C :W: .20 .35
22 Skillful Lunge C :W: .20 .35
23 Sudden Disappearance R :W: .40 .60
24 Thalia, Guardian of Thraben R :W: 23.00 26.00
25 Thraben Doomsayer R :W: 1.50 2.50
26 Thraben Heretic U :W: .25 .40
27 Artful Dodge C :L: 1.00 1.50
28 Beguiler of Wills M :L: 6.00 8.00
29 Bone to Ash C :L: .20 .35
30 Call to the Kind:R: R :L: 1.25 2.00
31 Chant of the Skifsang C :L: .20 .35
32 Chill of Foreboding U :L: .25 .40
33 Counterlash R :L: .60 1.00
34 Curse of Echoes R :L: .75 1.25
35 Divination C :L: .20 .35
36 Dungeon Geists R :L: 1.00 1.50
37 Geralf's Mindcrusher R :L: 1.00 1.50
38 Griptide C :L: .20 .35
39 Havengul Runebinder R :L: .50 .75
40 Headless Skaab C :L: .20 .35
41 Increasing Confusion R :L: 2.50 4.00
42 Mystic Retrieval U :L: 3.00 5.00
43 Nephalia Seakite C :L: .20 .35
44 Niblis of the Breath U :L: .25 .40
45 Relentless Skaabs U :L: .25 .40
46 Saving Grasp C :L: .20 .35
47 Screeching Skaab C :L: .20 .35
48 Secrets of the Dead U :L: .25 .40
49 Shriekgeist C :L: .20 .35
50 Soul Seizer/Ghastly Haunting U :L: .25 .40
51 Stormbound Geist C :L: 3.00 5.00
52 Thought Scour C :L: 7.00 10.00
53 Tower Geist U :L: .25 .40
54 Black Cat C :K: 1.00 1.50
55 Chosen of Markov/Markov's Servant C :K: .20 .35
56 Curse of Misfortunes R :K: .60 1.00
57 Curse of Thirst U :K: .25 .40
58 Deadly Allure U :K: .60 1.00
59 Death's Caress C :K: .20 .35
60 Falkenrath Torturer C :K: .20 .35
61 Farbog Boneflinger U :K: .25 .40
62 Fiend of the Shadows R :K: .50 .75
63 Geralf's Messenger R :K: 7.00 10.00
64 Gravecrawler R :K: 6.00 8.00
65 Gravepurge C :K: .20 .35
66 Gruesome Discovery C :K: .20 .35
67 Harrowing Journey U :K: .25 .40
68 Highborn Ghoul C :K: .20 .35
69 Increasing Ambition R :K: 3.00 5.00
70 Mikaeus, the Unhallowed M :K: 50.00 60.00
71 Ravenous Demon/Archdemon of Greed R :K: .60 1.00
72 Reap the Seagraf C :K: .20 .35
73 Sightless Ghoul C :K: .20 .35
74 Skirsdag Flayer U :K: .25 .40
75 Spiteful Shadows C :K: .20 .35
76 Tragic Slip C :K: 1.25 2.00
77 Undying Evil C :K: 1.00 1.50
78 Vengeful Vampire U :K: .25 .40
79 Wakedancer U :K: .25 .40
80 Zombie Apocalypse R :K: 2.00 3.50
81 Afflicted Deserter/Werewolf Ransacker U :R: .60 1.00
82 Alpha Brawl R :R: .60 1.00
83 Blood Feud U :R: .25 .40
84 Burning Oil U :R: .25 1.00
85 Curse of Bloodletting R :R: 1.50 2.50
86 Erdwal Ripper C :R: .20 .35
87 Faithless Looting C :R: 7.00 10.00
88 Fires of Undeath C :R: .20 .35
89 Flayer of the Hatebound R :R: .75 1.25
90 Fling C :R: .30 .50
91 Forge Devil C :R: .20 .35
92 Heckling Fiends U :R: .25 .40
93 Hellrider R :R: 2.50 4.00
94 Hinterland Hermit/Hinterland Scourge C :R: .20 .35
95 Increasing Vengeance R :R: 3.00 5.00
96 Markov Blademaster R :R: 1.50 2.50
97 Markov Warlord U :R: .25 .40
98 Mondronen Shaman/Tovolar's Magehunter R :R: 1.25 2.00
99 Moonveil Dragon M :R: 8.00 10.00
100 Nearheath Stalker C :R: .20 .35
101 Pyreheart Wolf U :R: 1.25 2.00
102 Russet Wolves C :R: .20 .35
103 Scorch the Fields C :R: .20 .35
104 Shatte:R: Perception U :R: .25 .40
105 Talons of Falkenrath C :R: .20 .35
106 Torch Fiend C :R: .20 .35
107 Wrack with Madness C :R: .20 .35
108 Briarpack Alpha U :G: .25 .40
109 Clinging Mists C :G: .20 .35
110 Crushing Vines C :G: .20 .35
111 Dawntreader Elk C :G: .20 .35
112 Deranged Outcast R :G: .50 .75
113 Favor of the Woods C :G: .20 .35
114 Feed the Pack R :G: .60 1.00
115 Ghoultree R :G: .75 1.25
116 Gravetiller Wurm U :G: .25 .40
117 Grim Flowering U :G: .25 .40
118 Hollowhenge Beast C :G: .20 .35
119 Hunger of the Howlpack C :G: .30 .50
120 Increasing Savagery R :G: 1.50 2.50
121 Kessig Recluse C :G: .20 .35
122 Lambholt Elder/Silverpelt Werewolf U :G: .40 .60
123 Lost in the Woods R :G: .60 1.00
124 Predator Ooze R :G: 4.00 6.00
125 Scorned Villager/Moonscarred Werewolf C :G: .50 .75
126 Somberwald Dryad C :G: .20 .35
127 Strangleroot Geist U :G: 2.50 4.00
128 Tracker's Instincts U :G: .50 .75
129 Ulvenwald Bear C :G: .20 .35
130 Village Survivors U :G: .25 .40
131 Vorapede M :G: 4.00 6.00
132 Wild Hunger C :G: .20 .35
133 Wolfbitten Captive/Krallenhorde Killer R :G: 1.50 2.50
134 Young Wolf C :G: 3.00 5.00

135 Diregral Captain U :L: :K: 2.50 4.00
136 Drogskol Captain U :W: :L: 9.00 11.00
137 Drogskol Reaver M :W: :L: 6.00 8.00
138 Falkenrath Aristocrat M :K: :R: 11.00 14.00
139 Havengul Lich M :L: :K: 12.00 16.00
140 Huntmaster of the Fells :Ravager of the Fells M :R: :G: 40.00 45.00
141 Immerwolf U :R: :G: 5.00 7.00
142 Sorin, Lord of Innistrad M :W: :K: 18.00 22.00
143 Stromkirk Captain U :K: :R: 2.50 4.00
144 Altar of the Lost U .25 .40
145 Avacyn's Collar U .25 .40
146 Chalice of Life/Chalice of Death U 2.00 3.50
147 Elbrus, the Binding Blade/Withengar Unbound M :K: 13.00 16.00
148 Executioner's Hood C .20 .35
149 Gravdigger's Cage R 30.00 40.00
150 Heavy Mattock C .20 .35
151 Helvault M 2.50 4.00
152 Jar of Eyeballs R .50 .75
153 Warden of the Wall U .25 .40
154 Wolfhunter's Quiver U .25 .40
155 Evolving Wilds C 2.50 3.50
156 Grim Backwoods R 1.25 2.00
157 Haunted Fengraf C 1.00 1.50
158 Vault of the Archangel R 8.00 10.00

2012 Magic The Gathering Dark Ascension Tokens

1 Human .15
2 Vampire 2.50 4.00
3 Sorin, Lord of Innistrad Emblem 3.50 5.00
4 Dark Ascension CL .15

2012 Magic The Gathering Avacyn Restored

COMPLETE SET (244) 225.00 300.00
BOOSTER BOX (36 PACKS) 150.00 180.00
BOOSTER PACK (15 CARDS) 3.00 4.00
RELEASED ON MAY 4, 2012
1 Angel of Glory's Rise R :W: .25 .40
2 Angel of Jubilation R :W: 2.00 3.00
3 Angel's Mercy C :W: .15 .25
4 Angelic Wall C :W: .15 .25
5 Archangel U :W: .20 .35
6 Avacyn, Angel of Hope M :W: 20.00 25.00
7 Banishing Stroke U :W: .20 .35
8 Builder's Blessing U :W: .20 .35
9 Call to Serve C :W: .15 .25
10 Cathars' Crusade R :W: 1.25 1.75
11 Cathedral Sanctifier C :W: .15 .25
12 Cloudshift C :W: .15 .25
13 Commander's Authority U :W: .20 .35
14 Cursebreak C :W: .15 .25
15 Defang C :W: .15 .25
16 Defy Death U :W: .20 .35
17 Devout Chaplain U :W: .20 .35
18 Divine Deflection R :W: .25 .40
19 Emancipation Angel U :W: .20 .35
20 Entreat the Angels M :W: 4.75 5.50
21 Farbog Explorer C :W: .15 .25
22 Goldnight Commander U :W: .20 .35
23 Goldnight Redeemer U :W: .20 .35
24 Herald of War R :W: 1.00 1.50
25 Holy Justiciar U :W: .20 .35
26 Leap of Faith C :W: .15 .25
27 Midnight Duelist C :W: .15 .25
28 Midvast Protector C :W: .15 .25
29 Moonlight Geist C :W: .15 .25
30 Moorland Inquisitor C :W: .15 .25
31 Nearheath Pilgrim U :W: .20 .35
32 Restoration Angel R :W: 7.00 9.00
33 Riders of Gavony R :W: .25 .40
34 Righteous Blow C :W: .15 .25
35 Seraph of Dawn C :W: .15 .25
36 Silverblade Paladin R :W: .40 .60
37 Spectral Gateguards C :W: .15 .25
38 Terminus R :W: 2.00 3.00
39 Thraben Valiant C :W: .15 .25
40 Voice of the Provinces C :W: .15 .25
41 Zealous Strike C :W: .15 .25
42 Alchemist's Apprentice C :B: .15 .25
43 Amass the Components C :B: .15 .25
44 Arcane Melee R :B: .25 .40
45 Captain of the Mists R :B: .25 .40
46 Crippling Chill C :B: .15 .25
47 Deadeye Navigator R :B: 1.75 2.00
48 Devastation Tide R :B: .40 .60
49 Dreadwaters C :B: .15 .25
50 Elgaud Shieldmate C :B: .15 .25
51 Favorable Winds U :B: .20 .35
52 Fettergeist U :B: .20 .35
53 Fleeting Distraction C :B: .15 .25
54 Galvanic Alchemist C :B: .15 .25
55 Geist Snatch C :B: .15 .25
56 Ghostform C :B: .15 .25
57 Ghostly Flicker C :B: .15 .25
58 Ghostly Touch U :B: .20 .35
59 Gryff Vanguard C :B: .15 .25
60 Havengul Skaab C :B: .15 .25
61 Infinite Reflection R :B: .25 .40
62 Into the Void U :B: .20 .35
63A Latch Seeker U :B: .20 .35
63B Latch Seeker U :B: FULL ART .20 .35
64 Lone Revenant R :B: .25 .40
65 Lunar Mystic R :B: .25 .40
66 Mass Appeal U :B: .20 .35
67 Mist Raven C :B: .15 .25
68 Misthollow Griffin M :B: .75 1.00
69 Nephalia Smuggler U :B: .20 .35
70 Outwit C :B: .15 .25
71 Peel from Reality C :B: .15 .25
72 Rotcrown Ghoul C :B: .15 .25
73 Scrapskin Drake C :B: .15 .25
74 Second Guess U :B: .20 .35
75 Spectral Prison C :B: .15 .25
76 Spirit Away R :B: .25 .40
77 Stern Mentor U :B: .20 .35
78 Stolen Goods R :B: .25 .40
79 Tamiyo, the Moon Sage M :B: 18.00 20.00
80 Tandem Lookout U :B: .20 .35
81 Temporal Mastery M :B: 8.00 10.00
82 Vanishment U :B: .20 .35
83 Wingcrafter C :B: .15 .25
84 Appetite for Brains U :K: .20 .35
85 Barter in Blood U :K: .20 .35
86 Blood Artist U :K: 1.25 .35
87 Bloodflow Connoisseur C :K: .15 .25
88 Bone Splinters C :K: .15 .25
89 Butcher Ghoul C :K: .15 .25
90 Corpse Traders U :K: .20 .35
91 Crypt Creeper C :K: .15 .25
92 Dark Impostor R :K: .75 1.00
93 Death Wind C :K: .15 .25
94 Demonic Rising R :K: .25 .40
95 Demonic Taskmaster U :K: .20 .35
96 Demonlord of Ashmouth R :K: .25 .40
97 Descent into Madness M :K: .50 .75
98 Dread Slaver R :K: .25 .40
99 Driver of the Dead C :K: .15 .25
100 Essence Harvest C :K: .15 .25
101 Evernight Shade U :K: .20 .35
102 Exquisite Blood R :K: 8.00 10.00
103 Ghoulflesh C :K: .15 .25
104 Gloom Surgeon R :K: .25 .40
105 Grave Exchange C :K: .15 .25
106 Griselbrand M :K: 10.00 12.00
107 Harvester of Souls R :K: .75 1.00
108 Homicidal Seclusion U :K: .20 .35
109 Human Frailty U :K: .20 .35
110 Hunted Ghoul C :K: .15 .25
111A Killing Wave R :K: .75 1.00
111B Killing Wave R :K: FULL ART .25 .40
112 Maalfeld Twins U :K: .20 .35
113 Marrow Bats U :K: .20 .35
114 Mental Agony C :K: .15 .25
115 Necrobite C :K: .15 .25
116 Polluted Dead C :K: .15 .25
117 Predator's Gambit C :K: .15 .25
118 Renegade Demon C :K: .15 .25
119 Searchlight Geist C :K: .15 .25
120 Soulcage Fiend C :K: .15 .25
121 Treacherous Pit-Dweller R :K: .25 .40
122 Triumph of Cruelty U :K: .20 .35
123 Undead Executioner C :K: .15 .25
124 Unhallowed Pact C :K: .15 .25
125 Aggravate U :R: .20 .35
126 Archwing Dragon R :R: .25 .40
127 Banners Raised C :R: .15 .25
128 Battle Hymn C :R: .15 .25
129 Bonfire of the Damned M :R: 4.00 6.00
130 Burn at the Stake R :R: .25 .40
131 Dangerous Wager C :R: .15 .25
132 Demolish C :R: .15 .25
133 Dual Casting R :R: .25 .40
134 Falkenrath Exterminator U :R: .20 .35
135 Fervent Cathar C :R: .15 .25
136 Gang of Devils U :R: .20 .35
137 Guise of Fire C :R: .15 .25
138 Hanweir Lancer C :R: .15 .25
139 Havengul Vampire U :R: .20 .35
140 Heirs of Stromkirk C :R: .15 .25
141 Hound of Griselbrand R :R: .25 .40
142 Kessig Malcontents U :R: .20 .35
143 Kruin Striker C :R: .15 .25
144 Lightning Mauler U :R: .20 .35
145 Lightning Prowess U :R: .20 .35
146 Mad Prophet C :R: .15 .25
147 Malicious Intent C :R: .15 .25
148 Malignus M :R: 1.75 2.25
149 Pillar of Flame C :R: .15 .25
150 Raging Poltergeist C :R: .15 .25
151 Reforge the Soul R :R: 2.00 2.50
152 Riot Ringleader C :R: .15 .25
153 Rite of Ruin R :R: .25 .40
154 Rush of Blood U :R: .20 .35
155 Scalding Devil C :R: .15 .25
156 Somberwald Vigilante C :R: .15 .25
157 Stonewright U :R: .20 .35
158 Thatcher Revolt C :R: .15 .25
159 Thunderbolt C :R: .15 .25
160 Thunderous Wrath U :R: .20 .35
161 Tibalt, the Fiend-Blooded M :R: 2.75 3.25
162 Tyrant of Discord R :R: .25 .40
163 Uncanny Speed C :R: .15 .25
164 Vexing Devil R :R: 8.00 10.00
165 Vigilante Justice U :R: .20 .35
166 Zealous Conscripts R :R: .50 .75
167 Abundant Growth C :G: .15 .25
168 Blessings of Nature U :G: .20 .35
169 Borderland Ranger C :G: .15 .25
170 Bower Passage U :G: .20 .35
171 Champion of Lambholt R :G: 1.75 2.00
172 Craterhoof Behemoth M :G: 20.00 25.00
173 Descendants' Path R :G: 2.00 3.00
174 Diregraf Escort C :G: .15 .25
175 Druid's Familiar U :G: .20 .35
176 Druids' Repository R :G: .25 .40
177 Eaten by Spiders U :G: .20 .35
178 Flowering Lumberknot C :G: .15 .25
179 Geist Trappers C :G: .15 .25
180 Gloomwidow U :G: .20 .35
181 Grounded C :G: .15 .25
182 Howlgeist U :G: .20 .35
183 Joint Assault C :G: .15 .25
184 Lair Delve C :G: .15 .25
185 Natural End C :G: .15 .25
186 Nettle Swine C :G: .15 .25
187 Nightshade Peddler C :G: .15 .25
188 Pathbreaker Wurm C :G: .15 .25
189 Primal Surge M :G: 1.25 1.75
190 Rain of Thorns U :G: .20 .35
191 Revenge of the Hunted R :G: .25 .40
192 Sheltering Word C :G: .15 .25
193 Snare the Skies C :G: .15 .25
194 Somberwald Sage R :G: 1.00 1.50
195 Soul of the Harvest R :G: .30 .50
196 Terrifying Presence C :G: .15 .25
197 Timberland Guide C :G: .15 .25
198 Triumph of Ferocity U :G: .20 .35
199 Trusted Forcemage C :G: .15 .25
200 Ulvenwald Tracker R :G: .40 .60
201 Vorstclaw U :G: .20 .35
202 Wandering Wolf C :G: .15 .25
203 Wild Defiance R :G: 2.00 2.50
204 Wildwood Geist C :G: .15 .25
205 Wolfir Avenger U :G: .20 .35
206 Wolfir Silverheart R :G: .50 .75
207 Yew Spirit U :G: .20 .35
208 Bruna, Alabaster M :W/B: 1.75 2.25
209 Gisela, Goldnight M :W/R: 4.50 5.50
210 Sigarda, Herons M :W/G: 10.00 12.00
211 Angel's Tomb U .20 .35
212 Angelic Armaments U .20 .35
213 Bladed Bracers C .15 .25
214 Conjurer's Closet R .75 1.00
215 Gallows at Willow Hill R .25 .40
216 Haunted Guardian U .20 .35
217 Moonsilver Spear R .25 .40
218 Narstad Scrapper C .15 .25
219 Otherworld Atlas R .25 .40
220 Scroll of Avacyn C .15 .25
221 Scroll of Griselbrand C .15 .25
222 Tormentor's Trident U .20 .35
223 Vanguard's Shield C .15 .25
224 Vessel of Endless Rest U .20 .35
225 Alchemist's Refuge R .75 1.00
226 Cavern of Souls R 45.00 50.00
227 Desolate Lighthouse R .75 1.00
228 Seraph Sanctuary C .15 .25
229 Slayers' Stronghold R .25 .40
230 Plains L .15 .25
231 Plains L .15 .25
232 Plains L .15 .25
233 Island L .15 .25
234 Island L .15 .25
235 Island L .15 .25
236 Swamp L .15 .25
237 Swamp L .15 .25
238 Swamp L .15 .25
239 Mountain L .15 .25
240 Mountain L .15 .25
241 Mountain L .15 .25
242 Forest L .15 .25
243 Forest L .15 .25
244 Forest L .15 .25

2012 Magic The Gathering Avacyn Restored Foil

1 Angel of Glory's Rise R :W: 1.25 2.00
2 Angel of Jubilation R :W: 6.00 8.00
3 Angel's Mercy C :W: .15 .25
4 Angelic Wall C :W: .15 .25
5 Archangel U :W: .40 .60
6 Avacyn, Angel of Hope M :W: 45.00 55.00
7 Banishing Stroke U :W: .60 1.00
8 Builder's Blessing U :W: .20 .35
9 Call to Serve C :W: .15 .25
10 Cathars' Crusade R :W: 6.00 8.00
11 Cathedral Sanctifier C :W: .40 .60
12 Cloudshift C :W: 2.50 4.00
13 Commander's Authority U :W: .40 .60
14 Cursebreak C :W: .15 .25
15 Defang C :W: .15 .25
16 Defy Death U :W: 1.50 2.50
17 Devout Chaplain U :W: .20 .35
18 Divine Deflection R :W: .75 1.25
19 Emancipation Angel U :W: 4.00 6.00
20 Entreat the Angels M :W: 10.00 15.00
21 Farbog Explorer C :W: .15 .25
22 Goldnight Commander U :W: .20 .35
23 Goldnight Redeemer U :W: .50 .75
24 Herald of War R :W: 2.00 3.50
25 Holy Justiciar U :W: .20 .35
26 Leap of Faith C :W: .15 .25
27 Midnight Duelist C :W: .15 .25
28 Midvast Protector C :W: .15 .25
29 Moonlight Geist C :W: .15 .25
30 Moorland Inquisitor C :W: .15 .25
31 Nearheath Pilgrim U :W: .60 1.00
32 Restoration Angel R :W: 18.00 22.00
33 Riders of Gavony R :W: .75 1.25
34 Righteous Blow C :W: .15 .25
35 Seraph of Dawn C :W: 1.50 2.50
36 Silverblade Paladin R :W: 2.50 3.50
37 Spectral Gateguards C :W: .15 .25
38 Terminus R :W: 9.00 11.00
39 Thraben Valiant C :W: .15 .25
40 Voice of the Provinces C :W: .15 .25
41 Zealous Strike C :W: .15 .25
42 Alchemist's Apprentice C :L: .15 .25
43 Amass the Components C :L: .15 .25
44 Arcane Melee R :L: .60 1.00
45 Captain of the Mists R :L: .40 .60
46 Crippling Chill C :L: .15 .25
47 Deadeye Navigator R :L: 8.00 10.00
48 Devastation Tide R :L: 3.00 5.00
49 Dreadwaters C :L: .15 .25
50 Elgaud Shieldmate C :L: .30 .50
51 Favorable Winds U :L: .60 1.00
52 Fettergeist U :L: .20 .35
53 Fleeting Distraction C :L: .15 .25
54 Galvanic Alchemist C :L: .15 .25
55 Geist Snatch C :L: .15 .25
56 Ghostform C :L: .15 .25
57 Ghostly Flicker C :L: 2.00 3.50
58 Ghostly Touch U :L: .20 .35
59 Gryff Vanguard C :L: .15 .25
60 Havengul Skaab C :L: .15 .25
61 Infinite Reflection R :L: .75 1.25
62 Into the Void U :L: .20 .35
63 Latch Seeker U :L: .20 .35
64 Lone Revenant R :L: .30 .50
65 Lunar Mystic R :L: .60 1.00
66 Mass Appeal U :L: .20 .35
67 Mist Raven C :L: .15 .25
68 Misthollow Griffin M :L: 5.00 8.00
69 Nephalia Smuggler U :L: .20 .35
70 Outwit C :L: .15 .25
71 Peel from Reality C :L: .15 .25
72 Rotcrown Ghoul C :L: .15 .25
73 Scrapskin Drake C :L: .15 .25
74 Second Guess U :L: .20 .35
75 Spectral Prison C :L: .15 .25
76 Spirit Away R :L: .60 1.00
77 Stern Mentor U :L: .20 .35
78 Stolen Goods R :L: .75 1.25
79 Tamiyo, the Moon Sage M :L: 55.00 65.00
80 Tandem Lookout U :L: .20 .35
81 Temporal Mastery M :L: 20.00 30.00
82 Vanishment U :L: .20 .35
83 Wingcrafter C :L: .15 .25
84 Appetite for Brains U :K: 1.00 1.50
85 Barter in Blood U :K: .40 .60
86 Blood Artist U :K: 4.60 .35
87 Bloodflow Connoisseur C :K: .40 .60
88 Bone Splinters C :K: .25 .40
89 Butcher Ghoul C :K: .40 .60
90 Corpse Traders U :K: .20 .35
91 Crypt Creeper C :K: .15 .25
92 Dark Impostor R :K: 3.00 5.00
93 Death Wind C :K: .15 .25
94 Demonic Rising R :K: .40 .60
95 Demonic Taskmaster U :K: .40 .60
96 Demonlord of Ashmouth R :K: 1.00 1.50
97 Descent into Madness M :K: 1.50 2.00
98 Dread Slaver R :K: .75 1.25
99 Driver of the Dead C :K: .15 .25
100 Essence Harvest C :K: .40 .60
101 Evernight Shade U :K: .20 .35
102 Exquisite Blood R :K: 15.00 18.00
103 Ghoulflesh C :K: .15 .25
104 Gloom Surgeon R :K: .50 .75
105 Grave Exchange C :K: .15 .25
106 Griselbrand M :K: 35.00 40.00
107 Harvester of Souls R :K: 1.25 2.00
108 Homicidal Seclusion U :K: .20 .35
109 Human Frailty U :K: .20 .35
110 Hunted Ghoul C :K: .15 .25
111 Killing Wave R :K: 2.00 3.00
112 Maalfeld Twins U :K: .20 .35
113 Marrow Bats U :K: .20 .35
114 Mental Agony C :K: .15 .25
115 Necrobite C :K: .15 .25
116 Polluted Dead C :K: .15 .25
117 Predator's Gambit C :K: .15 .25
118 Renegade Demon C :K: .15 .25
119 Searchlight Geist C :K: .15 .25
120 Soulcage Fiend C :K: .15 .25
121 Treacherous Pit-Dweller R :K: .75 1.25
122 Triumph of Cruelty U :K: .20 .35
123 Undead Executioner C :K: .15 .25
124 Unhallowed Pact C :K: .15 .25
125 Aggravate U :R: .20 .35
126 Archwing Dragon R :R: 1.00 1.50
127 Banners Raised C :R: .15 .25
128 Battle Hymn C :R: 2.00 3.50
129 Bonfire of the Damned M :R: 15.00 20.00
130 Burn at the Stake R :R: 1.50 2.50
131 Dangerous Wager C :R: .75 1.25
132 Demolish C :R: .15 .25
133 Dual Casting R :R: 1.00 1.50
134 Falkenrath Exterminator U :R: .40 .60
135 Fervent Cathar C :R: .15 .25
136 Gang of Devils U :R: .20 .35
137 Guise of Fire C :R: .15 .25
138 Hanweir Lancer C :R: .15 .25
139 Havengul Vampire U :R: .20 .35
140 Heirs of Stromkirk C :R: .15 .25
141 Hound of Griselbrand R :R: .75 1.25
142 Kessig Malcontents U :R: .20 .35
143 Kruin Striker C :R: .15 .25
144 Lightning Mauler U :R: 1.50 2.50
145 Lightning Prowess U :R: .20 .35
146 Mad Prophet C :R: .15 .25
147 Malicious Intent C :R: .15 .25
148 Malignus M :R: 5.00 8.00
149 Pillar of Flame C :R: .75 1.25
150 Raging Poltergeist C :R: .15 .25
151 Reforge the Soul R :R: 8.00 10.00
152 Riot Ringleader C :R: .15 .25
153 Rite of Ruin R :R: .50 .75
154 Rush of Blood U :R: .20 .35
155 Scalding Devil C :R: .15 .25
156 Somberwald Vigilante C :R: .15 .25
157 Stonewright U :R: .20 .35
158 Thatcher Revolt C :R: .15 .25
159 Thunderbolt C :R: .15 .25
160 Thunderous Wrath U :R: 1.50 2.50
161 Tibalt, the Fiend-Blooded M :R: 10.00 15.00
162 Tyrant of Discord R :R: 1.00 1.50
163 Uncanny Speed C :R: .15 .25
164 Vexing Devil R :R: 15.00 18.00
165 Vigilante Justice U :R: .20 .35
166 Zealous Conscripts R :R: 2.00 3.50
167 Abundant Growth C :G: 2.00 3.00
168 Blessings of Nature U :G: .75 1.25
169 Borderland Ranger C :G: .15 .25
170 Bower Passage U :G: .20 .35
171 Champion of Lambholt R :G: 7.00 10.00
172 Craterhoof Behemoth M :G: 55.00 65.00
173 Descendants' Path R :G: 6.00 8.00
174 Diregraf Escort C :G: .15 .25
175 Druid's Familiar U :G: .20 .35
176 Druids' Repository R :G: .75 1.25
177 Eaten by Spiders U :G: .20 .35
178 Flowering Lumberknot C :G: .15 .25
179 Geist Trappers C :G: .15 .25
180 Gloomwidow U :G: .20 .35
181 Grounded C :G: .15 .25
182 Howlgeist U :G: .20 .35
183 Joint Assault C :G: .15 .25
184 Lair Delve C :G: .15 .25
185 Natural End C :G: .15 .25
186 Nettle Swine C :G: .15 .25
187 Nightshade Peddler C :G: .15 .25
188 Pathbreaker Wurm C :G: .15 .25
189 Primal Surge M :G: 8.00 11.00
190 Rain of Thorns U :G: .20 .35
191 Revenge of the Hunted R :G: 1.00 1.50

192 Sheltering Word C :G: .15 .25
193 Snare the Skies C :G: .15 .25
194 Somberwald Sage R :G: 6.00 8.00
195 Soul of the Harvest R :G: 5.00 7.00
196 Terrifying Presence C :G: .15 .25
197 Timberland Guide C :G: .15 .25
198 Triumph of Ferocity U :G: .40 .60
199 Trusted Forcemage C :G: .15 .25
200 Ulvenwald Tracker R :G: 5.00 7.00
201 Vorstclaw U :G: .20 .35
202 Wandering Wolf C :G: .15 .25
203 Wild Defiance R :G: 5.00 7.00
204 Wildwood Geist C :G: .15 .25
205 Wolfir Avenger U :G: 1.25 2.00
206 Wolfir Silverheart R :G: 1.00 1.50
207 Yew Spirit U :G: .20 .35
208 Bruna, Light of Alabaster M :W/L: 15.00 20.00
209 Gisela, Blade of Goldnight M :W/R: 40.00 50.00
210 Sigarda, Host of Herons M :W/G: 40.00 50.00
211 Angel's Tomb U .60 1.00
212 Angelic Armaments U .20 .35
213 Bladed Bracers C .15 .25
214 Conjurer's Closet R 6.00 8.00
215 Gallows at Willow Hill R .60 1.00
216 Haunted Guardian U .20 .35
217 Moonsilver Spear R 1.00 1.50
218 Narstad Scrapper C .15 .25
219 Otherworld Atlas R 1.25 2.00
220 Scroll of Avacyn C .15 .25
221 Scroll of Griselbrand C .15 .25
222 Tormentor's Trident U .20 .35
223 Vanguard's Shield C .15 .25
224 Vessel of Endless Rest U .60 1.00
225 Alchemist's Refuge R 7.00 10.00
226 Cavern of Souls R 110.00 120.00
227 Desolate Lighthouse R 8.00 11.00
228 Seraph Sanctuary C 1.00 1.50
229 Slayers' Stronghold R 4.00 6.00
230 Plains L .15 .25
231 Plains L .15 .25
232 Plains L .15 .25
233 Island L .15 .25
234 Island L .15 .25
235 Island L .15 .25
236 Swamp L .15 .25
237 Swamp L .15 .25
238 Swamp L .15 .25
239 Mountain L .15 .25
240 Mountain L .15 .25
241 Mountain L .15 .25
242 Forest L .15 .25
243 Forest L .15 .25
244 Forest L .15 .25

2012 Magic The Gathering Avacyn Restored Tokens

1 Angel .15 .25
2 Human .15 .25
3 Spirit .15 .25
4 Spirit .10 .15
5 Demon .15 .25
6 Zombie .10 .15
7 Human .10 .15
8 Tamiyo, the Moon Sage Emblem 1.75 2.50

2012 Magic The Gathering Return to Ravnica

COMPLETE SET (287) 150.00 200.00
BOOSTER BOX (36 PACKS) 80.00 120.00
BOOSTER PACK (15 CARDS) 3.00 4.00
RELEASED ON OCTOBER 5, 2012
1 Angel of Serenity M :W: .75 1.15
2 Armory Guard C :W: .15 .25
3 Arrest U :W: .20 .35
4 Avenging Arrow C :W: .15 .25
5 Azorius Arrester C :W: .15 .25
6 Azorius Justiciar U :W: .20 .35
7 Bazaar Krovod U :W: .20 .35
8 Concordia Pegasus C :W: .15 .25
9 Ethereal Armor C :W: .15 .25
10 Eyes in the Skies C :W: .15 .25
11 Fencing Ace U :W: .20 .35
12 Keening Apparition C :W: .15 .25
13 Knightly Valor C :W: .15 .25
14 Martial Law R :W: .25 .40
15 Palisade Giant R :W: .25 .40
16 Phantom General U :W: .20 .35
17 Precinct Captain R :W: .30 .50
18 Rest in Peace R :W: 4.00 5.00
19 Rootborn Defenses C :W: .15 .25
20 Security Blockade U :W: .20 .35
21 Selesnya Sentry C :W: .15 .25
22 Seller of Songbirds C :W: .15 .25
23 Soul Tithe U :W: .20 .35
24 Sphere of Safety U :W: .20 .35
25 Sunspire Griffin C :W: .15 .25
26 Swift Justice C :W: .15 .25
27 Trained Caracal C :W: .15 .25
28 Trostani's Judgment C :W: .15 .25
29 Aquus Steed U :B: .20 .35
30 Blustersquall U :B: .20 .35
31 Cancel C :B: .15 .25
32 Chronic Flooding C :B: .15 .25
33 Conjured Currency R :B: .25 .40
34 Crosstown Courier C :B: .15 .25
35 Cyclonic Rift R :B: 5.00 6.00
36 Dispel C :B: .15 .25
37 Doorkeeper C :B: .15 .25
38 Downsize C :B: .15 .25
39 Faerie Impostor U :B: .20 .35
40 Hover Barrier U :B: .20 .35
41 Inaction Injunction C :B: .15 .25
42 Inspiration C :B: .15 .25
43 Isperia's Skywatch C :B: .15 .25
44 Jace, Architect M :B: 2.50 3.00
45 Mizzium Skin C :B: .15 .25
46 Paralyzing Grasp C :B: .15 .25
47 Psychic Spiral U :B: .20 .35
48 Runewing C :B: .15 .25
49 Search the City R :B: .25 .40
50 Skyline Predator U :B: .20 .35
51 Soulsworn Spirit U :B: .20 .35
52 Sphinx of the Chimes R :B: .25 .40
53 Stealer of Secrets C :B: .15 .25
54 Syncopate U :B: .20 .35
55 Tower Drake C :B: .15 .25
56 Voidwielder C :B: .15 .25
57 Assassin's Strike U :K: .20 .35
58 Catacomb Slug C :K: .15 .25
59 Cremate C :K: .15 .25
60 Daggerdrome Imp C :K: .15 .25
61 Dark Revenant U :K: .20 .35
62 Dead Reveler C :K: .15 .25
63 Desecration Demon R :K: 1.00 1.50
64 Destroy the Evidence C :K: .15 .25
65 Deviant Glee C :K: .15 .25
66 Drainpipe Vermin C :K: .15 .25
67 Grave Betrayal R :K: 1.00 1.25
68 Grim Roustabout C :K: .15 .25
69 Launch Party C :K: .15 .25
70 Mind Rot C :K: .15 .25
71 Necropolis Regent M :K: 1.75 2.25
72 Ogre Jailbreaker C :K: .15 .25
73 Pack Rat R :K: 1.25 1.75
74 Perilous Shadow C :K: .15 .25
75 Sewer Shambler C :K: .15 .25
76 Shrieking Affliction U :K: .20 .35
77 Slum Reaper U :K: .20 .35
78 Stab Wound C :K: .15 .25
79 Tavern Swindler U :K: .20 .35
80 Terrus Wurm C :K: .15 .25
81 Thrill-Kill Assassin U :K: .20 .35
82 Ultimate Price U :K: .20 .35
83 Underworld Connections R :K: .30 .50
84 Zanikev Locust U :K: .20 .35
85 Annihilating Fire C :R: .15 .25
86 Ash Zealot R :R: .30 .50
87 Batterhorn C :R: .15 .25
88 Bellows Lizard C :R: .15 .25
89 Bloodfray Giant U :R: .20 .35
90 Chaos Imps R :R: .25 .40
91 Cobblebrute C :R: .15 .25
92 Dynacharge C :R: .15 .25
93 Electrickery C :R: .15 .25
94 Explosive Impact C :R: .15 .25
95 Goblin Rally U :R: .20 .35
96 Gore-House Chainwalker C :R: .15 .25
97 Guild Feud R :R: .25 .40
98 Guttersnipe U :R: .20 .35
99 Lobber Crew C :R: .15 .25
100 Minotaur Aggressor U :R: .20 .35
101 Mizzium Mortars R :R: .25 .40
102 Pursuit of Flight C :R: .15 .25
103 Pyroconvergence U :R: .20 .35
104 Racecourse Fury U :R: .20 .35
105 Splatter Thug C :R: .15 .25
106 Street Spasm U :R: .20 .35
107 Survey the Wreckage C :R: .15 .25
108 Tenement Crasher C :R: .15 .25
109 Traitorous Instinct C :R: .15 .25
110 Utvara Hellkite M :R: 4.00 4.50
111 Vandalblast U :R: .20 .35
112 Viashino Racketeer C :R: .15 .25
113 Aerial Predation C :G: .15 .25
114 Archweaver U :G: .20 .35
115 Axebane Guardian C :G: .15 .25
116 Axebane Stag C :G: .15 .25
117 Brushstrider U :G: .20 .35
118 Centaur's Herald C :G: .15 .25
119 Chorus of Might C :G: .15 .25
120 Deadbridge Goliath R :G: .25 .40
121 Death's Presence R :G: .25 .40
122 Drudge Beetle C :G: .15 .25
123 Druid's Deliverance C :G: .15 .25
124 Gatecreeper Vine C :G: .15 .25
125 Giant Growth C :G: .15 .25
126 Gobbling Ooze U :G: .20 .35
127 Golgari Decoy U :G: .20 .35
128 Horncaller's Chant C :G: .15 .25
129 Korozda Monitor C :G: .15 .25
130 Mana Bloom R :G: .25 .40
131 Oak Street Innkeeper U :G: .20 .35
132 Rubbleback Rhino C :G: .15 .25
133 Savage Surge U :G: .20 .35
134 Seek the Horizon U :G: .20 .35
135 Slime Molding U :G: .20 .35
136 Stonefare Crocodile C :G: .15 .25
137 Towering Indrik C :G: .15 .25
138 Urban Burgeoning C :G: .15 .25
139 Wild Beastmaster R :G: .25 .40
140 Worldspine Wurm M :G: 4.00 5.00
141 Abrupt Decay R :K/G: 6.00 8.00
142 Archon of the Triumvirate R :W: :B: .25 .40
143 Armada Wurm M :W: :G: .75 1.00
144 Auger Spree C :K: :R: .15 .25
145 Azorius Charm U :W: :B: .20 .35
146 Call of the Conclave U :W: :G: .20 .35
147 Carnival Hellsteed R :K: :R: .25 .40
148 Centaur Healer C :W: :G: .15 .25
149 Chemister's Trick C :B: :R: .15 .25
150 Collective Blessing R :W: :G: .25 .40
151 Common Bond C :W: :G: .15 .25
152 Corpsejack Menace R :K: :G: .40 .60
153 Counterflux R :B: :R: .40 .60
154 Coursers' Accord C :W: :G: .15 .25
155 Detention Sphere R :W: :B: 1.00 1.50
156 Dramatic Rescue C :W: :B: .15 .25
157 Dreadbore R :K: :R: 2.75 3.00
158a Dreg Mangler U :K: :G: .20 .35
158b Dreg Mangler ALT ART .20 .35
159 Epic Experiment M :B: :R: .50 .75
160 Essence Backlash C :B: :R: .15 .25
161 Fall of the Gavel U :W: :B: .20 .35
162 Firemind's Foresight R :B: :R: .25 .40
163 Goblin Electromancer C :B: :R: .15 .25
164 Golgari Charm U :K: :G: .20 .35
165 Grisly Salvage C :K: :G: .15 .25
166 Havoc Festival R :K: :R: .25 .40
167 Hellhole Flailer U :K: :R: .20 .35
168 Heroes' Reunion U :W: :G: .20 .35
169 Hussar Patrol C :W: :B: .15 .25
170 Hypersonic Dragon R :B: :R: .25 .40
171 Isperia, Supreme M :W/B: .50 .75
172 Izzet Charm U :B: :R: .20 .35
173 Izzet Staticaster U :B: :R: .20 .35
174 Jarad, Golgari M :K/G: .75 1.00
175 Jarad's Orders R :K: :G: .25 .40
176 Korozda Guildmage U :K: :G: .20 .35
177 Lotleth Troll R :K: :G: .50 .75
178 Loxodon Smiter R :W: :G: 1.25 1.75
179 Lyev Skyknight U :W: :B: .20 .35
180 Mercurial Chemister R :B: :R: .25 .40
181 New Prahv Guildmage U :W: :B: .20 .35
182 Nivix Guildmage U :B: :R: .20 .35
183 Niv-Mizzet M :B/R: 1.25 1.75
184 Rakdos Charm U :K: :R: .20 .35
185 Rakdos Ragemutt U :K: :R: .20 .35
186 Rakdos Ringleader U :K: :R: .20 .35
187 Rakdos, Lord of Riots M :K: :R: 2.00 2.25
188 Rakdos's Return M :K: :R: .75 1.15
189 Righteous Authority R :W: :B: .25 .40
190 Risen Sanctuary U :W: :G: .20 .35
191 Rites of Reaping U :K: :G: .20 .35
192 Rix Maadi Guildmage U :K: :R: .20 .35
193 Search Warrant C :W: :B: .15 .25
194 Selesnya Charm U :W: :G: .20 .35
195 Skull Rend C :K: :R: .15 .25
196 Skymark Roc U :W: :B: .20 .35
197 Slaughter Games R :K: :R: .40 .60
198 Sluiceway Scorpion C :K: :G: .15 .25
199 Spawn of Rix Maadi C :K: :R: .15 .25
200 Sphinx's Revelation M :W: :B: 4.50 5.50
201 Supreme Verdict R :W: :B: 4.00 5.00
202 Teleportal U :B: :R: .20 .35
203 Thoughtflare U :B: :R: .20 .35
204 Treasured Find U :K: :G: .20 .35
205 Trestle Troll C :K: :G: .15 .25
206 Trostani, Selesnya's M :W/G: 3.00 3.25
207 Vitu-Ghazi Guildmage U :W: :G: .20 .35
208 Vraska the Unseen M :K: :G: 3.50 4.00
209 Wayfaring Temple R :W: :G: .25 .40
210 Azor's Elocutors R :W: :B: .25 .40
211 Blistercoil Weird U :B: :R: .20 .35
212 Cryptborn Horror R :K: :R: .25 .40
213 Deathrite Shaman R :K: :G: 3.50 4.00
214 Dryad Militant U :W: :G: .20 .35
215 Frostburn Weird C :B: :R: .15 .25
216 Golgari Longlegs C :K: :G: .15 .25
217 Growing Ranks R :W: :G: .40 .60
218 Judge's Familiar U :W: :B: .20 .35
219 Nivmagus Elemental R :B: :R: .25 .40
220 Rakdos Cackler U :K: :R: .20 .35
221 Rakdos Shred-Freak C :K: :R: .15 .25
222 Slitherhead U :K: :G: .20 .35
223 Sundering Growth C :W: :G: .15 .25
224 Vassal Soul C :W: :B: .15 .25
225 Azorius Keyrune U .20 .35
226 Chromatic Lantern R 6.00 8.00
227 Civic Saber U .20 .35
228 Codex Shredder U .20 .35
229 Golgari Keyrune U .20 .35
230 Izzet Keyrune U .20 .35
231 Pithing Needle R 2.00 2.50
232 Rakdos Keyrune U .20 .35
233 Selesnya Keyrune U .20 .35
234 Street Sweeper U .20 .35
235 Tablet of the Guilds U .20 .35
236 Volatile Rig R .25 .40
237 Azorius Guildgate C .15 .25
238 Blood Crypt R 6.00 8.00
239 Golgari Guildgate C .15 .25
240 Grove of the Guardian R .25 .40
241 Hallowed Fountain R 5.00 7.00
242 Izzet Guildgate C .15 .25
243 Overgrown Tomb R 6.00 8.00
244 Rakdos Guildgate C .15 .25
245 Rogue's Passage U .20 .35
246 Selesnya Guildgate C .15 .25
247 Steam Vents R 8.00 10.00
248 Temple Garden R 7.00 9.00
249 Transguild Promenade C .15 .25
250 Plains L .15 .25
251 Plains L .15 .25
252 Plains L .15 .25
253 Plains L .15 .25
254 Plains L .15 .25
255 Island L .15 .25
256 Island L .15 .25
257 Island L .15 .25
258 Island L .15 .25
259 Island L .15 .25
260 Swamp L .15 .25
261 Swamp L .15 .25
262 Swamp L .15 .25
263 Swamp L .15 .25
264 Swamp L .15 .25
265 Mountain L .15 .25
266 Mountain L .15 .25
267 Mountain L .15 .25
268 Mountain L .15 .25
269 Mountain L .15 .25
270 Forest L .15 .25
271 Forest L .15 .25
272 Forest L .15 .25
273 Forest L .15 .25
274 Forest L .15 .25

2012 Magic The Gathering Return to Ravnica Tokens

1 Bird .10 .15
2 Knight .10 .15
3 Soldier .10 .15
4 Assassin .60 1.00
5 Dragon 2.00 3.00
6 Goblin .15 .25
7 Centaur .10 .15
8 Ooze .10 .15
9 Rhino .10 .15
10 Saproling .15 .25
11 Wurm .60 1.00
12 Elemental .15 .25

2013 Magic The Gathering Gatecrash

COMPLETE SET (249) 140.00 200.00
BOOSTER BOX (36 PACKS) 60.00 80.00
BOOSTER PACK (15 CARDS) 2.00 3.00
RELEASED ON FEBRUARY 1, 2013
1 Aerial Maneuver C :W: .15 .25
2 Angelic Edict C :W: .15 .25
3 Angelic Skirmisher R :W: .50 .75
4 Assault Griffin C :W: .15 .25
5 Basilica Guards C :W: .15 .25
6 Blind Obedience R :W: 1.75 2.00
7 Boros Elite U :W: .20 .35
8 Court Street Denizen C :W: .15 .25
9 Daring Skyjek C :W: .15 .25
10 Debtor's Pulpit U :W: .20 .35
11 Dutiful Thrull C :W: .15 .25
12 Frontline Medic R :W: .25 .40
13 Gideon, Champion of Justice M :W: 4.00 4.50
14 Guardian of the Gateless U :W: .20 .35
15 Guildscorn Ward C :W: .15 .25
16 Hold the Gates U :W: .20 .35
17 Holy Mantle U :W: .20 .35
18 Knight of Obligation U :W: .20 .35
19 Knight Watch C :W: .15 .25
20 Luminate Primordial R :W: .25 .40
21 Murder Investigation U :W: .20 .35
22 Nav Squad Commandos C :W: .15 .25
23 Righteous Charge U :W: .20 .35
24 Shielded Passage C :W: .15 .25
25 Smite C :W: .15 .25
26 Syndic of Tithes C :W: .15 .25
27 Urbis Protector U :W: .20 .35
28 Zarichi Tiger C :W: .15 .25
29 AEtherize U :B: .20 .35
30 Agoraphobia U :B: .20 .35
31 Clinging Anemones C :B: .15 .25
32 Cloudfin Raptor C :B: .15 .25
33 Diluvian Primordial R :B: .25 .40
34 Enter the Infinite M :B: 1.00 1.25
35 Frilled Oculus C :B: .15 .25
36 Gridlock U :B: .20 .35
37 Hands of Binding C :B: .15 .25
38 Incursion Specialist U :B: .20 .35
39 Keymaster Rogue C :B: .15 .25
40 Last Thoughts C :B: .15 .25
41 Leyline Phantom C :B: .15 .25
42 Metropolis Sprite C :B: .15 .25
43 Mindeye Drake U :B: .20 .35
44 Rapid Hybridization U :B: .20 .35
45 Realmwright R :B: .25 .40
46 Sage's Row Denizen C :B: .15 .25
47 Sapphire Drake U :B: .20 .35
48 Scatter Arc C :B: .15 .25
49 Simic Fluxmage U :B: .20 .35
50 Simic Manipulator R :B: .25 .40
51 Skygames C :B: .15 .25
52 Spell Rupture C :B: .15 .25
53 Stolen Identity R :B: .25 .40
54 Totally Lost C :B: .15 .25
55 Voidwalk U :B: .20 .35
56 Way of the Thief C :B: .15 .25
57 Balustrade Spy C :K: .15 .25
58 Basilica Screecher C :K: .15 .25
59 Contaminated Ground C :K: .15 .25
60 Corpse Blockade C :K: .15 .25
61 Crypt Ghast R :K: 2.00 2.25
62 Death's Approach C :K: .15 .25
63 Devour Flesh C :K: .15 .25
64 Dying Wish U :K: .20 .35
65 Gateway Shade U :K: .20 .35
66 Grisly Spectacle C :K: .15 .25
67 Gutter Skulk C :K: .15 .25
68 Horror of the Dim C :K: .15 .25
69 Illness in the Ranks U :K: .20 .35
70 Killing Glare U :K: .20 .35
71 Lord of the Void M :K: 3.50 4.00
72 Mental Vapors U :K: .20 .35
73 Midnight Recovery C :K: .15 .25
74 Ogre Slumlord R :K: .25 .40
75 Sepulchral Primordial R :K: .30 .50
76 Shadow Alley Denizen C :K: .15 .25
77 Shadow Slice C :K: .15 .25
78 Slate Street Ruffian C :K: .15 .25
79 Smog Elemental U :K: .20 .35
80 Syndicate Enforcer C :K: .15 .25
81 Thrull Parasite U :K: .20 .35
82 Undercity Informer U :K: .20 .35
83 Undercity Plague R :K: .25 .40
84 Wight of Precinct Six U :K: .20 .35
85 Act of Treason C :R: .15 .25
86 Bomber Corps C :R: .15 .25
87 Cinder Elemental U :R: .20 .35
88 Crackling Perimeter U :R: .20 .35
89 Ember Beast C :R: .15 .25
90 Firefist Striker U :R: .20 .35
91 Five-Alarm Fire R :R: .25 .40
92 Foundry Street Denizen C :R: .15 .25
93 Furious Resistance C :R: .15 .25
94 Hellkite Tyrant M :R: 3.00 3.25
95 Hellraiser Goblin U :R: .20 .35
96 Homing Lightning U :R: .20 .35
97 Legion Loyalist R :R: 4.75 5.25
98 Madcap Skills C :R: .15 .25
99 Mark for Death U :R: .20 .35
100 Massive Raid C :R: .15 .25
101 Molten Primordial R :R: .25 .40
102 Mugging C :R: .15 .25
103 Ripscale Predator U :R: .20 .35
104 Scorchwalker C :R: .15 .25
105 Skinbrand Goblin C :R: .15 .25
106 Skullcrack U :R: .20 .35
107 Structural Collapse C :R: .15 .25
108 Tin Street Market C :R: .15 .25
109 Towering Thunderfist C :R: .15 .25
110 Viashino Shanktail U :R: .20 .35
111 Warmind Infantry C :R: .15 .25
112 Wrecking Ogre R :R: .25 .40
113 Adaptive Snapjaw C :G: .15 .25

Card	Low	High
114 Alpha Authority U :G:	.20	.35
115 Burst of Strength C :G:	.15	.25
116 Crocanura C :G:	.15	.25
117 Crowned Ceratok U :G:	.20	.35
118 Disciple of the Old Ways C :G:	.15	.25
119 Experiment One U :G:	.20	.35
120 Forced Adaptation C :G:	.15	.25
121 Giant Adephage M :G:	1.00	1.50
122 Greenside Watcher C :G:	.15	.25
123 Gyre Sage R :G:	1.25	1.50
124 Hindervines U :G:	.20	.35
125 Ivy Lane Denizen C :G:	.15	.25
126 Miming Slime U :G:	.20	.35
127 Naturalize C :G:	.15	.25
128 Ooze Flux R :G:	.25	.40
129 Predator's Rapport C :G:	.15	.25
130 Rust Scarab U :G:	.20	.35
131 Scab-Clan Charger C :G:	.15	.25
132 Serene Remembrance U :G:	.20	.35
133 Skarrg Goliath R :G:	.25	.40
134 Slaughterhorn C :G:	.15	.25
135 Spire Tracer C :G:	.15	.25
136 Sylvan Primordial R :G:	.25	.40
137 Tower Defense U :G:	.20	.35
138 Verdant Haven C :G:	.15	.25
139 Wasteland Viper U :G:	.20	.35
140 Wildwood Rebirth C :G:	.15	.25
141 Alms Beast R :W: :K:	.25	.40
142 Assemble the Legion R :W: :R:	1.25	1.50
143 Aurelia, the Warleader M :W: :R:	4.00	4.25
144 Aurelia's Fury M :W: :R:	.75	1.00
145 Bane Alley Broker U :B: :K:	.20	.35
146 Biovisionary R :B: :G:	.25	.40
147 Borborygmos Enraged M :R: :G:	.75	1.00
148 Boros Charm U :W: :R:	.20	.35
149 Call of the Nightwing U :B: :K:	.20	.35
150 Cartel Aristocrat U :W: :K:	.20	.35
151 Clan Defiance R :R: :G:	.25	.40
152 Consuming Aberration R :B: :K:	2.50	3.00
153 Deathpact Angel M :W: :K:	.75	1.00
154 Dimir Charm U :B: :K:	.20	.35
155 Dinrova Horror U :B: :K:	.20	.35
156 Domri Rade M :R: :G:	6.00	8.00
157 Drakewing Krasis C :B: :G:	.15	.25
158 Duskmantle Guildmage U :B: :K:	.20	.35
159 Duskmantle Seer M :B: :K:	.50	.75
160 Elusive Krasis U :B: :G:	.20	.35
161 Executioner's Swing C :W: :K:	.15	.25
162 Fathom Mage R :B: :G:	.25	.40
163 Firemane Avenger R :W: :R:	.30	.50
164 Fortress Cyclops U :W: :R:	.20	.35
165 Foundry Champion R :W: :R:	.25	.40
166 Frenzied Tilling U :R: :G:	.20	.35
167 Ghor-Clan Rampager U :R: :G:	.20	.35
168 Ground Assault U :R: :G:	.20	.35
169 Gruul Charm U :R: :G:	.20	.35
170 Gruul Ragebeast R :R: :G:	.25	.40
171 High Priest of Penance R :W: :K:	.30	.50
172 Hydroform C :B: :G:	.15	.25
173 Kingpin's Pet C :W: :K:	.15	.25
174 Lazav, Dimir Mastermind M :B: :K:	2.00	2.25
175 Martial Glory C :W: :R:	.15	.25
176 Master Biomancer M :B: :G:	4.00	4.25
177 Merciless Eviction R :W: :K:	1.00	1.25
178 Mind Grind R :B: :K:	1.75	2.00
179 Mortus Strider C :B: :K:	.15	.25
180 Mystic Genesis R :B: :G:	.25	.40
181 Nimbus Swimmer U :B: :G:	.20	.35
182 Obzedat, Ghost Council M :W: :K:	2.75	3.00
183 One Thousand Lashes U :W: :K:	.20	.35
184 Ordruun Veteran U :W: :R:	.20	.35
185 Orzhov Charm U :W: :K:	.20	.35
186 Paranoid Delusions C :B: :K:	.15	.25
187 Primal Visitation C :R: :G:	.15	.25
188 Prime Speaker Zegana M :B: :G:	1.00	1.25
189 Psychic Strike C :B: :K:	.15	.25
190 Purge the Profane C :W: :K:	.15	.25
191 Rubblehulk R :R: :G:	.25	.40
192 Ruination Wurm C :R: :G:	.15	.25
193 Shambleshark C :B: :G:	.15	.25
194 Signal the Clans R :R: :G:	.25	.40
195 Simic Charm U :B: :G:	.20	.35
196 Skarrg Guildmage U :R: :G:	.20	.35
197 Skyknight Legionnaire C :W: :R:	.15	.25
198 Soul Ransom R :B: :K:	.25	.40
199 Spark Trooper R :W: :R:	.25	.40
200 Sunhome Guildmage U :W: :R:	.20	.35
201 Treasury Thrull R :W: :K:	.25	.40
202 Truefire Paladin U :W: :R:	.20	.35
203 Unexpected Results R :B: :G:	.25	.40
204 Urban Evolution U :B: :G:	.20	.35
205 Vizkopa Confessor U :W: :K:	.20	.35
206 Vizkopa Guildmage U :W: :K:	.20	.35
207 Whispering Madness R :B: :K:	.25	.40
208 Wojek Halberdiers C :W: :R:	.15	.25
209 Zameck Guildmage U :B: :G:	.20	.35
210 Zhur-Taa Swine C :R: :G:	.15	.25
211 Arrows of Justice U :W: :R:	.20	.35
212 Beckon Apparition C :W: :K:	.15	.25
213 Biomass Mutation R :B: :G:	.25	.40
214 Bioshift C :B: :G:	.15	.25
215 Boros Reckoner R :W: :R:	2.25	2.75
216 Burning-Tree Emissary U :R: :G:	.20	.35
217 Coerced Confession U :B: :K:	.20	.35
218 Deathcult Rogue C :B: :K:	.15	.25
219 Gift of Orzhova U :W: :K:	.20	.35
220 Immortal Servitude R :W: :K:	.30	.50
221 Merfolk of the Depths U :B: :G:	.20	.35
222 Nightveil Specter R :B: :K:	.75	1.00
223 Pit Fight C :R: :G:	.15	.25
224 Rubblebelt Raiders R :R: :G:	.25	.40
225 Shattering Blow C :W: :R:	.15	.25
226 Armored Transport C	.15	.25
227 Boros Keyrune U	.20	.35
228 Dimir Keyrune U	.20	.35
229 Glaring Spotlight R	.25	.40
230 Gruul Keyrune U	.20	.35
231 Illusionist's Bracers R	1.75	2.00
232 Millennial Gargoyle C	.15	.25
233 Orzhov Keyrune U	.20	.35
234 Prophetic Prism C	.15	.25
235 Razortip Whip C	.15	.25
236 Riot Gear C	.15	.25
237 Simic Keyrune U	.20	.35
238 Skyblinder Staff C	.15	.25
239 Boros Guildgate C	.15	.25
240 Breeding Pool R	10.00	14.00
241 Dimir Guildgate C	.15	.25
242 Godless Shrine R	8.00	10.00
243 Gruul Guildgate C	.15	.25
244 Orzhov Guildgate C	.15	.25
245 Sacred Foundry R	10.00	15.00
246 Simic Guildgate C	.15	.25
247 Stomping Ground R	10.00	14.00
248 Thespian's Stage R	2.50	3.00
249 Watery Grave R	8.00	10.00

2013 Magic The Gathering Gatecrash Foil

Card	Low	High
1 Aerial Maneuver C :W:	.15	.25
2 Angelic Edict C :W:	.15	.25
3 Angelic Skirmisher R :W:	1.50	2.50
4 Assault Griffin C :W:	.15	.25
5 Basilica Guards C :W:	.15	.25
6 Blind Obedience R :W:	4.00	6.00
7 Boros Elite U :W:	1.50	2.50
8 Court Street Denizen C :W:	.15	.25
9 Daring Skyjek C :W:	.15	.25
10 Debtor's Pulpit U :W:	.25	.40
11 Dutiful Thrull C :W:	.15	.25
12 Frontline Medic R :W:	1.00	1.50
13 Gideon, Champion of Justice M :W:	9.00	11.00
14 Guardian of the Gateless U :W:	1.50	2.50
15 Guildscorn Ward C :W:	.15	.25
16 Hold the Gates U :W:	.25	.40
17 Holy Mantle U :W:	.60	1.00
18 Knight of Obligation U :W:	.25	.40
19 Knight Watch C :W:	.15	.25
20 Luminate Primordial R :W:	.75	1.25
21 Murder Investigation U :W:	.25	.40
22 Nav Squad Commandos C :W:	.15	.25
23 Righteous Charge U :W:	.25	.40
24 Shielded Passage C :W:	.15	.25
25 Smite C :W:	.15	.25
26 Syndic of Tithes C :W:	.15	.25
27 Urbis Protector U :W:	.25	.40
28 Zarichi Tiger C :W:	.15	.25
29 AEtherize U :B:	2.50	4.00
30 Agoraphobia U :B:	.25	.40
31 Clinging Anemones C :B:	.15	.25
32 Cloudfin Raptor C :B:	.75	1.25
33 Diluvian Primordial R :B:	3.00	5.00
34 Enter the Infinite M :B:	8.00	10.00
35 Frilled Oculus C :B:	.15	.25
36 Gridlock U :B:	.25	.40
37 Hands of Binding C :B:	.30	.50
38 Incursion Specialist U :B:	.25	.40
39 Keymaster Rogue C :B:	.15	.25
40 Last Thoughts C :B:	.15	.25
41 Leyline Phantom C :B:	.15	.25
42 Metropolis Sprite C :B:	.15	.25
43 Mindeye Drake U :B:	.25	.40
44 Rapid Hybridization U :B:	2.00	3.50
45 Realmwright R :B:	.60	1.00
46 Sage's Row Denizen C :B:	.15	.25
47 Sapphire Drake U :B:	.25	.40
48 Scatter Arc C :B:	.15	.25
49 Simic Fluxmage U :B:	.25	.40
50 Simic Manipulator R :B:	1.00	1.50
51 Skygames C :B:	.15	.25
52 Spell Rupture C :B:	.15	.25
53 Stolen Identity R :B:	1.50	2.50
54 Totally Lost C :B:	.15	.25
55 Voidwalk U :B:	.25	.40
56 Way of the Thief C :B:	.15	.25
57 Balustrade Spy C :K:	1.00	1.50
58 Basilica Screecher C :K:	.15	.25
59 Contaminated Ground C :K:	.15	.25
60 Corpse Blockade C :K:	.15	.25
61 Crypt Ghast R :K:	6.00	8.00
62 Death's Approach C :K:	.15	.25
63 Devour Flesh C :K:	.75	1.25
64 Dying Wish U :K:	.25	.40
65 Gateway Shade U :K:	.25	.40
66 Grisly Spectacle C :K:	.15	.25
67 Gutter Skulk C :K:	.15	.25
68 Horror of the Dim C :K:	.15	.25
69 Illness in the Ranks U :K:	2.00	3.50
70 Killing Glare U :K:	.25	.40
71 Lord of the Void M :K:	9.00	11.00
72 Mental Vapors U :K:	.25	.40
73 Midnight Recovery C :K:	.15	.25
74 Ogre Slumlord R :K:	.75	1.25
75 Sepulchral Primordial R :K:	2.50	3.50
76 Shadow Alley Denizen C :K:	.15	.25
77 Shadow Slice C :K:	.15	.25
78 Slate Street Ruffian C :K:	.15	.25
79 Smog Elemental U :K:	.25	.40
80 Syndicate Enforcer C :K:	.15	.25
81 Thrull Parasite U :K:	.75	1.25
82 Undercity Informer U :K:	.75	1.25
83 Undercity Plague R :K:	.50	.75
84 Wight of Precinct Six U :K:	1.25	2.00
85 Act of Treason C :R:	.15	.25
86 Bomber Corps C :R:	.15	.25
87 Cinder Elemental U :R:	.25	.40
88 Crackling Perimeter U :R:	.30	.50
89 Ember Beast C :R:	.15	.25
90 Firefist Striker U :R:	.75	1.25
91 Five-Alarm Fire R :R:	.50	.75
92 Foundry Street Denizen C :R:	2.00	3.50
93 Furious Resistance C :R:	.15	.25
94 Hellkite Tyrant M :R:	8.00	10.00
95 Hellraiser Goblin U :R:	.25	.40
96 Homing Lightning U :R:	.25	.40
97 Legion Loyalist R :R:	7.00	10.00
98 Madcap Skills C :R:	1.00	1.50
99 Mark for Death U :R:	.25	.40
100 Massive Raid C :R:	.15	.25
101 Molten Primordial R :R:	1.00	1.50
102 Mugging C :R:	.15	.25
103 Ripscale Predator U :R:	.25	.40
104 Scorchwalker C :R:	.15	.25
105 Skinbrand Goblin C :R:	.15	.25
106 Skullcrack U :R:	6.50	8.00
107 Structural Collapse C :R:	.15	.25
108 Tin Street Market C :R:	.15	.25
109 Towering Thunderfist C :R:	.15	.25
110 Viashino Shanktail U :R:	.25	.40
111 Warmind Infantry C :R:	.15	.25
112 Wrecking Ogre R :R:	.40	.60
113 Adaptive Snapjaw C :G:	.15	.25
114 Alpha Authority U :G:	.60	1.00
115 Burst of Strength C :G:	.15	.25
116 Crocanura C :G:	.15	.25
117 Crowned Ceratok U :G:	.25	.40
118 Disciple of the Old Ways C :G:	.15	.25
119 Experiment One U :G:	2.50	3.50
120 Forced Adaptation C :G:	.40	.60
121 Giant Adephage M :G:	3.00	5.00
122 Greenside Watcher C :G:	.15	.25
123 Gyre Sage R :G:	4.00	6.00
124 Hindervines U :G:	.25	.40
125 Ivy Lane Denizen C :G:	.15	.25
126 Miming Slime U :G:	.25	.40
127 Naturalize C :G:	.15	.25
128 Ooze Flux R :G:	.60	1.00
129 Predator's Rapport C :G:	.15	.25
130 Rust Scarab U :G:	.25	.40
131 Scab-Clan Charger C :G:	.15	.25
132 Serene Remembrance U :G:	.25	.40
133 Skarrg Goliath R :G:	.50	.75
134 Slaughterhorn C :G:	.15	.25
135 Spire Tracer C :G:	.15	.25
136 Sylvan Primordial R :G:	1.25	2.00
137 Tower Defense U :G:	2.00	3.50
138 Verdant Haven C :G:	.15	.25
139 Wasteland Viper U :G:	.60	1.00
140 Wildwood Rebirth C :G:	.15	.25
141 Alms Beast R :W: :K:	.60	1.00
142 Assemble the Legion R :W: :R:	4.00	6.00
143 Aurelia, the Warleader M :W: :R:	10.00	12.00
144 Aurelia's Fury M :W: :R:	3.00	5.00
145 Bane Alley Broker U :B: :K:	.50	.75
146 Biovisionary R :B: :G:	1.25	2.00
147 Borborygmos Enraged M :R: :G:	6.00	8.00
148 Boros Charm U :W: :R:	16.00	20.00
149 Call of the Nightwing U :B: :K:	.25	.40
150 Cartel Aristocrat U :W: :K:	2.50	4.00
151 Clan Defiance R :R: :G:	.75	1.25
152 Consuming Aberration R :B: :K:	2.50	4.00
153 Deathpact Angel M :W: :K:	6.00	8.00
154 Dimir Charm U :B: :K:	.75	1.25
155 Dinrova Horror U :B: :K:	.25	.40
156 Domri Rade M :R: :G:	15.00	18.00
157 Drakewing Krasis C :B: :G:	.15	.25
158 Duskmantle Guildmage U :B: :K:	3.00	5.00
159 Duskmantle Seer M :B: :K:	1.50	2.50
160 Elusive Krasis U :B: :G:	1.00	1.50
161 Executioner's Swing C :W: :K:	.15	.25
162 Fathom Mage R :B: :G:	.60	1.00
163 Firemane Avenger R :W: :R:	1.25	2.00
164 Fortress Cyclops U :W: :R:	.25	.40
165 Foundry Champion R :W: :R:	.75	2.00
166 Frenzied Tilling U :R: :G:	.25	.40
167 Ghor-Clan Rampager U :R: :G:	2.00	3.50
168 Ground Assault U :R: :G:	.25	.40
169 Gruul Charm U :R: :G:	.60	1.00
170 Gruul Ragebeast R :R: :G:	.60	1.00
171 High Priest of Penance R :W: :K:	1.50	2.50
172 Hydroform C :B: :G:	.15	.25
173 Kingpin's Pet C :W: :K:	.15	.25
174 Lazav, Dimir Mastermind M :B: :K:	8.00	10.00
175 Martial Glory C :W: :R:	.15	.25
176 Master Biomancer M :B: :G:	7.00	10.00
177 Merciless Eviction R :W: :K:	7.00	10.00
178 Mind Grind R :B: :K:	3.00	5.00
179 Mortus Strider C :B: :K:	.15	.25
180 Mystic Genesis R :B: :G:	.60	1.00
181 Nimbus Swimmer U :B: :G:	.25	.40
182 Obzedat, Ghost Council M :W: :K:	8.00	10.00
183 One Thousand Lashes U :W: :K:	.40	.60
184 Ordruun Veteran U :W: :R:	.25	.40
185 Orzhov Charm U :W: :K:	1.25	2.00
186 Paranoid Delusions C :B: :K:	.15	.25
187 Primal Visitation C :R: :G:	.15	.25
188 Prime Speaker Zegana M :B: :G:	11.00	13.00
189 Psychic Strike C :B: :K:	1.00	1.50
190 Purge the Profane C :W: :K:	.15	.25
191 Rubblehulk R :R: :G:	.30	.50
192 Ruination Wurm C :R: :G:	.15	.25
193 Shambleshark C :B: :G:	.15	.25
194 Signal the Clans R :R: :G:	.75	1.25
195 Simic Charm U :B: :G:	3.00	5.00
196 Skarrg Guildmage U :R: :G:	.40	.60
197 Skyknight Legionnaire C :W: :R:	.15	.25
198 Soul Ransom R :B: :K:	.60	1.00
199 Spark Trooper R :W: :R:	1.00	1.50
200 Sunhome Guildmage U :W: :R:	.50	.75
201 Treasury Thrull R :W: :K:	.40	.60
202 Truefire Paladin U :W: :R:	.40	.60
203 Unexpected Results R :B: :G:	1.25	2.00
204 Urban Evolution U :B: :G:	3.00	5.00
205 Vizkopa Confessor U :W: :K:	.25	.40
206 Vizkopa Guildmage U :W: :K:	2.00	3.50
207 Whispering Madness R :B: :K:	3.00	5.00
208 Wojek Halberdiers C :W: :R:	.30	.50
209 Zameck Guildmage U :B: :G:	.75	1.25
210 Zhur-Taa Swine C :R: :G:	.15	.25
211 Arrows of Justice U :W: :R:	.25	.40
212 Beckon Apparition C :W: :K:	.15	.25
213 Biomass Mutation R :B: :G:	.60	1.00
214 Bioshift C :B: :G:	1.00	1.50
215 Boros Reckoner R :W: :R:	5.00	7.00
216 Burning-Tree Emissary U :R: :G:	6.00	8.00
217 Coerced Confession U :B: :K:	.25	.40
218 Deathcult Rogue C :B: :K:	.15	.25
219 Gift of Orzhova U :W: :K:	7.00	9.00
220 Immortal Servitude R :W: :K:	1.00	1.50
221 Merfolk of the Depths U :B: :G:	.25	.40
222 Nightveil Specter R :B: :K:	1.50	2.50
223 Pit Fight C :R: :G:	.15	.25
224 Rubblebelt Raiders R :R: :G:	.75	1.25
225 Shattering Blow C :W: :R:	.15	.25
226 Armored Transport C	.15	.25
227 Boros Keyrune U	.40	.60
228 Dimir Keyrune U	.60	1.00
229 Glaring Spotlight R	1.25	2.00
230 Gruul Keyrune U	.25	.40
231 Illusionist's Bracers R	4.00	6.00
232 Millennial Gargoyle C	.15	.25
233 Orzhov Keyrune U	.50	.75
234 Prophetic Prism C	1.00	1.50
235 Razortip Whip C	.15	.25
236 Riot Gear C	.15	.25
237 Simic Keyrune U	.25	.40
238 Skyblinder Staff C	.15	.25
239 Boros Guildgate C	.60	1.00
240 Breeding Pool R	19.00	22.00
241 Dimir Guildgate C	1.00	1.50
242 Godless Shrine R	19.00	22.00
243 Gruul Guildgate C	.60	1.00
244 Orzhov Guildgate C	.75	1.25
245 Sacred Foundry R	25.00	30.00
246 Simic Guildgate C	.75	1.25
247 Stomping Ground R	25.00	30.00
248 Thespian's Stage R	17.00	20.00
249 Watery Grave R	20.00	25.00

2013 Magic The Gathering Gatecrash Tokens

Card	Low	High
1 Angel	.20	.30
2 Rat	1.00	1.50
3 Frog Lizard	.12	.20
4 Cleric	.20	.30
5 Horror	.10	.15
6 Soldier	.10	.15
7 Spirit	.10	.15
8 Domri Rade Emblem	.35	.50

2013 Magic The Gathering Dragon's Maze

Card	Low	High
COMPLETE SET (158)	80.00	110.00
UNLISTED C	.10	.25
UNLISTED U	.15	.40
UNLISTED R	.30	.75
RELEASED ON MAY 3, 2013		
1 Boros Mastiff C :W:	.15	.25
2 Haazda Snare Squad C :W:	.15	.25
3 Lyev Decree C :W:	.15	.25
4 Maze Sentinel C :W:	.15	.25
5 Renounce the Guilds R :W:	.25	.40
6 Riot Control C :W:	.15	.25
7 Scion of Vitu-Ghazi R :W:	.25	.40
8 Steeple Roc C :W:	.15	.25
9 Sunspire Gatekeepers C :W:	.15	.25
10 Wake the Reflections C :W:	.15	.25
11 AEtherling R :B:	.25	.40
12 Hidden Strings C :B:	.15	.25
13 Maze Glider C :B:	.15	.25
14 Mindstatic C :B:	.15	.25
15 Murmuring Phantasm C :B:	.15	.25
16 Opal Lake Gatekeepers C :B:	.15	.25
17 Runner's Bane C :B:	.15	.25
18 Trait Doctoring R :B:	.25	.40
19 Uncovered Clues C :B:	.15	.25
20 Wind Drake C :B:	.15	.25
21 Bane Alley Blackguard C :K:	.15	.25
22 Blood Scrivener R :K:	.25	.40
23 Crypt Incursion C :K:	.15	.25
24 Fatal Fumes C :K:	.15	.25
25 Hired Torturer C :K:	.15	.25
26 Maze Abomination C :K:	.15	.25
27 Pontiff of Blight R :K:	.25	.40
28 Rakdos Drake C :K:	.15	.25
29 Sinister Possession C :K:	.15	.25
30 Ubul Sar Gatekeepers C :K:	.15	.25
31 Awe for the Guilds C :R:	.15	.25
32 Clear a Path C :R:	.15	.25
33 Maze Rusher C :R:	.15	.25
34 Possibility Storm R :R:	.25	.40
35 Punish the Enemy C :R:	.15	.25
36 Pyrewild Shaman R :R:	.25	.40
37 Riot Piker C :R:	.15	.25
38 Rubblebelt Maaka C :R:	.15	.25
39 Smelt-Ward Gatekeepers C :R:	.15	.25
40 Weapon Surge C :R:	.15	.25
41 Battering Krasis C :G:	.15	.25
42 Kraul Warrior C :G:	.15	.25
43 Maze Behemoth C :G:	.15	.25
44 Mending Touch C :G:	.15	.25
45 Mutant's Prey C :G:	.15	.25
46 Phytoburst C :G:	.15	.25
47 Renegade Krasis R :G:	.30	.50
48 Saruli Gatekeepers C :G:	.15	.25
49 Skylasher R :G:	.25	.40
50 Thrashing Mossdog C :G:	.15	.25
51 Advent of the Wurm R :W/G:	.40	.60
52 Armored Wolf-Rider C :W/G:	.15	.25
53 Ascended Lawmage U :W/B:	.20	.35
54 Beetleform Mage C :B/G:	.15	.25
55 Blast of Genius U :B/R:	.20	.35
56 Blaze Commando U :W/R:	.20	.35
57 Blood Baron of Vizkopa M :W/K:	2.00	2.50
58 Boros Battleshaper R :W/R:	.25	.40
59 Bred for the Hunt U :B/G:	.20	.35
60 Bronzebeak Moa U :W/G:	.20	.35
61 Carnage Gladiator U :K/R:	.20	.35
62 Council of the Absolute M :W/B:	.50	.75
63 Deadbridge Chant M :K/G:	2.25	2.75
64 Debt to the Deathless U :W/K:	.20	.35
65 Deputy of Acquittals C :W/B:	.15	.25
66 Dragonshift R :B/R:	.25	.40
67 Drown in Filth C :K/G:	.15	.25
68 Emmara Tandris R :W/G:	.30	.50
69 Exava, Rakdos Blood Witch R :K/R:	.25	.40
70 Feral Animist U :R/G:	.20	.35
71 Fluxcharger U :B/R:	.20	.35
72 Gaze of Granite R :K/G:	.25	.40
73 Gleam of Battle U :W/R:	.20	.35

Card	Low	High
74 Goblin Test Pilot U :B/R:	.20	.35
75 Gruul War Chant U :R/G:	.20	.35
76 Haunter of Nightveil U :B/K:	.20	.35
77 Jelenn Sphinx U :W/B:	.20	.35
78 Korozda Gorgon U :K/G:	.20	.35
79 Krasis Incubation U :B/G:	.20	.35
80 Lavinia of the Tenth R :W/B:	.25	.40
81 Legion's Initiative M :W/R:	1.25	1.75
82 Master of Cruelties M :K/R:	4.00	5.00
83 Maw of the Obzedat U :W/K:	.20	.35
84 Melek, Izzet Paragon R :B/R:	.25	.40
85 Mirko Vosk, Mind Drinker R :B/K:	.75	1.00
86 Morgue Burst C :K/R:	.15	.25
87 Nivix Cyclops C :B/R:	.15	.25
88 Notion Thief R :B/K:	.50	.75
89 Obzedat's Aid R :W/K:	.25	.40
90 Pilfered Plans C :B/K:	.15	.25
91 Plasm Capture R :B/G:	.25	.40
92 Progenitor Mimic M :B/G:	4.00	4.50
93 Putrefy U :K/G:	.20	.35
94 Ral Zarek M :B/R:	7.00	9.00
95 Reap Intellect M :B/K:	.50	.75
96 Render Silent R :W/B:	.75	1.00
97 Restore the Peace U :W/B:	.20	.35
98 Rot Farm Skeleton U :K/G:	.20	.35
99 Ruric Thar, the Unbowed R :R/G:	.30	.50
100 Savageborn Hydra M :R/G:	2.00	2.50
101 Scab-Clan Giant U :R/G:	.20	.35
102 Showstopper U :K/R:	.20	.35
103 Sin Collector U :W/K:	.20	.35
104 Sire of Insanity R :K/R:	.25	.40
105 Species Gorger U :B/G:	.20	.35
106 Spike Jester U :K/R:	.20	.35
107 Tajic, Blade of the Legion R :W/R:	.50	.75
108 Teysa, Envoy of Ghosts R :W/K:	.25	.40
109 Tithe Drinker C :W/K:	.15	.25
110 Trostani's Summoner U :W/G:	.20	.35
111 Unflinching Courage U :W/G:	.20	.35
112 Varolz, the Scar-Striped R :K/G:	.50	.75
113 Viashino Firstblade C :W/R:	.15	.25
114 Voice of Resurgence M :W/G:	25.00	28.00
115 Vorel of the Hull Clade R :B/G:	.50	.75
116 Warleader's Helix U :W/R:	.20	.35
117 Warped Physique U :B/K:	.20	.35
118 Woodlot Crawler U :B/K:	.20	.35
119 Zhur-Taa Ancient R :R/G:	.25	.40
120 Zhur-Taa Druid C :R/G:	.15	.25
121 Alive/Well U :G/W:	.20	.35
122 Armed/Dangerous U :R/G:	.20	.35
123 Beck/Call R :B/G/W:	2.00	3.00
124 Breaking/Entering R :B/K:	.50	.75
125 Catch/Release R :B/R/W:	.25	.40
126 Down/Dirty U :K/G:	.20	.35
127 Far/Away U :B/K:	.20	.35
128 Flesh/Blood R :K/G/R:	.25	.40
129 Give/Take U :G/B:	.20	.35
130 Profit/Loss U :W/K:	.20	.35
131 Protect/Serve U :W/B:	.20	.35
132 Ready/Willing R :W/G/K:	.25	.40
133 Toil/Trouble U :K/R:	.20	.35
134 Turn/Burn U :B/R:	.20	.35
135 Wear/Tear U :R/W:	.20	.35
136 Azorius Cluestone C	.15	.25
137 Boros Cluestone C	.15	.25
138 Dimir Cluestone C	.15	.25
139 Golgari Cluestone C	.15	.25
140 Gruul Cluestone C	.15	.25
141 Izzet Cluestone C	.15	.25
142 Orzhov Cluestone C	.15	.25
143 Rakdos Cluestone C	.15	.25
144 Selesnya Cluestone C	.15	.25
145 Simic Cluestone C	.15	.25
146 Azorius Guildgate C	.15	.25
147 Boros Guildgate C	.15	.25
148 Dimir Guildgate C	.15	.25
149 Golgari Guildgate C	.15	.25
150 Gruul Guildgate C	.15	.25
151 Izzet Guildgate C	.15	.25
152 Maze's End M	.75	1.00
153 Orzhov Guildgate C	.15	.25
154 Rakdos Guildgate C	.15	.25
155 Selesnya Guildgate C	.15	.25
156 Simic Guildgate C	.15	.25

2013 Magic The Gathering Dragon's Maze Foil

Card	Low	High
1 Boros Mastiff C :W:	.15	.25
2 Haazda Snare Squad C :W:	.15	.25
3 Lyev Decree C :W:	.15	.25
4 Maze Sentinel C :W:	.15	.25
5 Renounce the Guilds R :W:	.50	.75
6 Riot Control C :W:	.40	.60
7 Scion of Vitu-Ghazi R :W:	.60	1.00
8 Steeple Roc C :W:	.15	.25
9 Sunspire Gatekeepers C :W:	.15	.25
10 Wake the Reflections C :W:	.15	.25
11 AEtherling R :B:	2.00	3.00
12 Hidden Strings C :B:	.60	1.00
13 Maze Glider C :B:	.15	.25
14 Mindstatic C :B:	.15	.25
15 Murmuring Phantasm C :B:	.15	.25
16 Opal Lake Gatekeepers C :B:	.15	.25
17 Runner's Bane C :B:	.15	.25
18 Trait Doctoring R :B:	.30	.50
19 Uncovered Clues C :B:	.15	.25
20 Wind Drake C :B:	.15	.25
21 Bane Alley Blackguard C :K:	.15	.25
22 Blood Scrivener R :K:	.75	1.25
23 Crypt Incursion C :K:	3.00	5.00
24 Fatal Fumes C :K:	.15	.25
25 Hired Torturer C :K:	.15	.25
26 Maze Abomination C :K:	.15	.25
27 Pontiff of Blight R :K:	1.50	2.50
28 Rakdos Drake C :K:	.15	.25
29 Sinister Possession C :K:	.15	.25
30 Ubul Sar Gatekeepers C :K:	.15	.25
31 Awe for the Guilds C :R:	.15	.25
32 Clear a Path C :R:	.15	.25
33 Maze Rusher C :R:	.15	.25
34 Possibility Storm R :R:	4.00	6.00
35 Punish the Enemy C :R:	.15	.25
36 Pyrewild Shaman R :R:	.60	1.00
37 Riot Piker C :R:	.15	.25
38 Rubblebelt Maaka C :R:	.15	.25
39 Smelt-Ward Gatekeepers C :R:	.15	.25
40 Weapon Surge C :R:	.15	.25
41 Battering Krasis C :G:	.15	.25
42 Kraul Warrior C :G:	.15	.25
43 Maze Behemoth C :G:	.15	.25
44 Mending Touch C :G:	.15	.25
45 Mutant's Prey C :G:	.15	.25
46 Phytoburst C :G:	.15	.25
47 Renegade Krasis R :G:	1.00	1.50
48 Saruli Gatekeepers C :G:	.15	.25
49 Skylasher R :G:	1.00	1.50
50 Thrashing Mossdog C :G:	.15	.25
51 Advent of the Wurm R :W/G:	1.50	2.50
52 Armored Wolf-Rider C :W/G:	.15	.25
53 Ascended Lawmage U :W/B:	.40	.60
54 Beetleform Mage C :B/G:	.15	.25
55 Blast of Genius U :B/R:	.30	.50
56 Blaze Commando U :W/R:	.20	.35
57 Blood Baron of Vizkopa M :W/K:	7.00	10.00
58 Boros Battleshaper R :W/R:	.60	1.00
59 Bred for the Hunt U :B/G:	.20	.35
60 Bronzebeak Moa U :W/G:	.20	.35
61 Carnage Gladiator U :K/R:	.20	.35
62 Council of the Absolute M :W/B:	1.50	2.50
63 Deadbridge Chant M :K/G:	7.00	10.00
64 Debt to the Deathless U :W/K:	2.00	3.50
65 Deputy of Acquittals C :W/B:	.40	.60
66 Dragonshift R :B/R:	.75	1.25
67 Drown in Filth C :K/G:	.15	.25
68 Emmara Tandris R :W/G:	1.50	2.50
69 Exava, Rakdos Blood Witch R :K/R:	.60	1.00
70 Feral Animist U :R/G:	.20	.35
71 Fluxcharger U :B/R:	.20	.35
72 Gaze of Granite R :K/G:	1.00	1.50
73 Gleam of Battle U :W/R:	.30	.50
74 Goblin Test Pilot U :B/R:	.20	.35
75 Gruul War Chant U :R/G:	.20	.35
76 Haunter of Nightveil U :B/K:	.20	.35
77 Jelenn Sphinx U :W/B:	.20	.35
78 Korozda Gorgon U :K/G:	.20	.35
79 Krasis Incubation U :B/G:	.20	.35
80 Lavinia of the Tenth R :W/B:	.60	1.00
81 Legion's Initiative M :W/R:	3.00	5.00
82 Master of Cruelties M :K/R:	13.00	16.00
83 Maw of the Obzedat U :W/K:	.20	.35
84 Melek, Izzet Paragon R :B/R:	2.00	3.00
85 Mirko Vosk, Mind Drinker R :B/K:	3.00	5.00
86 Morgue Burst C :K/R:	.15	.25
87 Nivix Cyclops C :B/R:	.75	1.25
88 Notion Thief R :B/K:	5.00	7.00
89 Obzedat's Aid R :W/K:	1.00	1.50
90 Pilfered Plans C :B/K:	.15	.25
91 Plasm Capture R :B/G:	2.50	4.00
92 Progenitor Mimic M :B/G:	9.00	12.00
93 Putrefy U :K/G:	1.50	2.50
94 Ral Zarek M :B/R:	28.00	32.00
95 Reap Intellect M :B/K:	1.25	2.00
96 Render Silent R :W/B:	1.50	2.50
97 Restore the Peace U :W/B:	.20	.35
98 Rot Farm Skeleton U :K/G:	.20	.35
99 Ruric Thar, the Unbowed R :R/G:	1.25	2.00
100 Savageborn Hydra M :R/G:	5.00	8.00
101 Scab-Clan Giant U :R/G:	.20	.35
102 Showstopper U :K/R:	.20	.35
103 Sin Collector U :W/K:	1.25	2.00
104 Sire of Insanity R :K/R:	10.00	13.00
105 Species Gorger U :B/G:	.20	.35
106 Spike Jester U :K/R:	1.00	1.50
107 Tajic, Blade of the Legion R :W/R:	2.00	3.00
108 Teysa, Envoy of Ghosts R :W/K:	1.25	2.00
109 Tithe Drinker C :W/K:	.60	1.00
110 Trostani's Summoner U :W/G:	.40	.60
111 Unflinching Courage U :W/G:	1.50	2.50
112 Varolz, the Scar-Striped R :K/G:	3.50	5.00
113 Viashino Firstblade C :W/R:	.15	.25
114 Voice of Resurgence M :W/G:	65.00	80.00
115 Vorel of the Hull Clade R :B/G:	1.50	2.50
116 Warleader's Helix U :W/R:	.75	1.25
117 Warped Physique U :B/K:	.20	.35
118 Woodlot Crawler U :B/K:	.20	.35
119 Zhur-Taa Ancient R :R/G:	.50	1.25
120 Zhur-Taa Druid C :R/G:	.50	.75
121 Alive/Well U :G/W:	.20	.35
122 Armed/Dangerous U :R/G:	.40	.60
123 Beck/Call R :B/G/W:	8.00	10.00
124 Breaking/Entering R :B/K:	3.00	5.00
125 Catch/Release R :B/R/W:	.75	1.25
126 Down/Dirty U :K/G:	.20	.35
127 Far/Away U :B/K:	1.50	2.50
128 Flesh/Blood R :K/G/R:	.75	1.25
129 Give/Take U :G/B:	.50	.75
130 Profit/Loss U :W/K:	.20	.35
131 Protect/Serve U :W/B:	.20	.35
132 Ready/Willing R :W/G/K:	.75	1.25
133 Toil/Trouble U :K/R:	.40	.60
134 Turn/Burn U :B/R:	1.00	1.50
135 Wear/Tear U :R/W:	8.00	10.00
136 Azorius Cluestone C	.15	.25
137 Boros Cluestone C	.15	.25
138 Dimir Cluestone C	.15	.25
139 Golgari Cluestone C	.15	.25
140 Gruul Cluestone C	.15	.25
141 Izzet Cluestone C	.15	.25
142 Orzhov Cluestone C	.15	.25
143 Rakdos Cluestone C	.15	.25
144 Selesnya Cluestone C	.15	.25
145 Simic Cluestone C	.15	.25
146 Azorius Guildgate C	.75	1.25
147 Boros Guildgate C	.75	1.00
148 Dimir Guildgate C	1.00	1.50
149 Golgari Guildgate C	.50	.75
150 Gruul Guildgate C	.60	1.00
151 Izzet Guildgate C	.75	1.25
152 Maze's End M	2.40	6.00
153 Orzhov Guildgate C	.75	1.25
154 Rakdos Guildgate C	.75	1.25
155 Selesnya Guildgate C	.75	1.25
156 Simic Guildgate C	.75	1.25

2013 Magic The Gathering Dragon's Maze Token

Card	Low	High
1 Elemental	1.00	1.50

2013 Magic The Gathering Theros

Card	Low	High
COMPLETE SET (262)	110.00	160.00
BOOSTER BOX (36 PACKS)	85.00	100.00
BOOSTER PACK (15 CARDS)	3.00	4.00
RELEASED ON SEPTEMBER 27, 2013		
1 Battlewise Valor C :W:	.15	.25
2 Cavalry Pegasus C :W:	.15	.25
3 Celestial Archon R :W:	.20	.35
4 Chained to the Rocks R :W:	.20	.35
5 Chosen by Heliod C :W:	.15	.25
6 Dauntless Onslaught U :W:	.20	.35
7 Decorated Griffin U :W:	.20	.35
8 Divine Verdict C :W:	.15	.25
9 Elspeth, Sun's Champion M :W:	6.50	7.50
10 Ephara's Warden C :W:	.15	.25
11 Evangel of Heliod U :W:	.20	.35
12 Fabled Hero R :W:	.30	.50
13 Favored Hoplite U :W:	.20	.35
14 Gift of Immortality R :W:	.50	.75
15 Glare of Heresy U :W:	.20	.35
16 Gods Willing C :W:	.15	.25
17 Heliod, God of the Sun M :W:	3.00	4.00
18 Heliod's Emissary U :W:	.20	.35
19 Hopeful Eidolon C :W:	.15	.25
20 Hundred-Handed One R :W:	.20	.35
21 Lagonna-Band Elder C :W:	.15	.25
22 Last Breath C :W:	.15	.25
23 Leonin Snarecaster C :W:	.15	.25
24 Observant Alseid C :W:	.15	.25
25 Ordeal of Heliod U :W:	.20	.35
26 Phalanx Leader U :W:	.20	.35
27 Ray of Dissolution C :W:	.15	.25
28 Scholar of Athreos C :W:	.15	.25
29 Setessan Battle Priest C :W:	.15	.25
30 Setessan Griffin C :W:	.15	.25
31 Silent Artisan C :W:	.15	.25
32 Soldier of the Pantheon R :W:	.30	.50
33 Spear of Heliod R :W:	.40	.60
34 Traveling Philosopher C :W:	.15	.25
35 Vanquish the Foul U :W:	.20	.35
36 Wingsteed Rider C :W:	.15	.25
37 Yoked Ox C :W:	.15	.25
38 Annul C :B:	.15	.25
39 Aqueous Form C :B:	.15	.25
40 Artisan of Forms R :B:	.20	.35
41 Benthic Giant C :B:	.15	.25
42 Bident of Thassa R :B:	.20	.35
43 Breaching Hippocamp C :B:	.15	.25
44 Coastline Chimera C :B:	.15	.25
45 Crackling Triton C :B:	.15	.25
46 Curse of the Swine R :B:	.20	.35
47 Dissolve U :B:	.20	.35
48 Fate Foretold C :B:	.15	.25
49 Gainsay U :B:	.20	.35
50 Griptide C :B:	.15	.25
51 Horizon Scholar U :B:	.20	.35
52 Lost in a Labyrinth C :B:	.15	.25
53 Master of Waves M :B:	3.00	4.00
54 Meletis Charlatan R :B:	.20	.35
55 Mnemonic Wall C :B:	.15	.25
56 Nimbus Naiad C :B:	.15	.25
57 Omenspeaker C :B:	.15	.25
58 Ordeal of Thassa U :B:	.20	.35
59 Prescient Chimera C :B:	.15	.25
60 Prognostic Sphinx R :B:	.20	.35
61 Sea God's Revenge U :B:	.20	.35
62 Sealock Monster U :B:	.20	.35
63 Shipbreaker Kraken R :B:	.20	.35
64 Stymied Hopes C :B:	.15	.25
65 Swan Song R :B:	1.00	1.25
66 Thassa, God of the Sea M :B:	4.50	5.50
67 Thassa's Bounty C :B:	.15	.25
68 Thassa's Emissary U :B:	.20	.35
69 Triton Fortune Hunter U :B:	.20	.35
70 Triton Shorethief C :B:	.15	.25
71 Triton Tactics U :B:	.20	.35
72 Vaporkin C :B:	.15	.25
73 Voyage's End C :B:	.15	.25
74 Wavecrash Triton C :B:	.15	.25
75 Abhorrent Overlord R :K:	.20	.35
76 Agent of the Fates R :K:	.20	.35
77 Asphodel Wanderer C :K:	.15	.25
78 Baleful Eidolon C :K:	.15	.25
79 Blood-Toll Harpy C :K:	.15	.25
80 Boon of Erebos C :K:	.15	.25
81 Cavern Lampad C :K:	.15	.25
82 Cutthroat Maneuver U :K:	.20	.35
83 Dark Betrayal U :K:	.20	.35
84 Disciple of Phenax C :K:	.15	.25
85 Erebos, God of the Dead M :K:	5.00	7.00
86 Erebos's Emissary U :K:	.20	.35
87 Felhide Minotaur C :K:	.15	.25
88 Fleshmad Steed C :K:	.15	.25
89 Gray Merchant of Asphodel C :K:	.15	.25
90 Hero's Downfall R :K:	1.75	2.00
91 Hythonia the Cruel M :K:	.50	.75
92 Insatiable Harpy U :K:	.20	.35
93 Keepsake Gorgon U :K:	.20	.35
94 Lash of the Whip C :K:	.15	.25
95 Loathsome Catoblepas C :K:	.15	.25
96 March of the Returned C :K:	.15	.25
97 Mogis's Marauder U :K:	.20	.35
98 Nighthowler R :K:	.20	.35
99 Ordeal of Erebos U :K:	.20	.35
100 Pharika's Cure C :K:	.15	.25
101 Read the Bones C :K:	.15	.25
102 Rescue from the Underworld U :K:	.20	.35
103 Returned Centaur C :K:	.15	.25
104 Returned Phalanx C :K:	.15	.25
105 Scourgemark C :K:	.15	.25
106 Sip of Hemlock C :K:	.15	.25
107 Thoughtseize R :K:	12.00	14.00
108 Tormented Hero U :K:	.20	.35
109 Viper's Kiss C :K:	.15	.25
110 Whip of Erebos R :K:	1.25	1.75
111 Akroan Crusader C :R:	.15	.25
112 Anger of the Gods R :R:	2.00	3.00
113 Arena Athlete U :R:	.20	.35
114 Borderland Minotaur C :R:	.15	.25
115 Boulderfall C :R:	.15	.25
116 Coordinated Assault U :R:	.20	.35
117 Deathbellow Raider C :R:	.15	.25
118 Demolish C :R:	.15	.25
119 Dragon Mantle C :R:	.15	.25
120 Ember Swallower R :R:	.20	.35
121 Fanatic of Mogis U :R:	.20	.35
122 Firedrinker Satyr R :R:	.20	.35
123 Flamespeaker Adept U :R:	.20	.35
124 Hammer of Purphoros R :R:	.20	.35
125 Ill-Tempered Cyclops C :R:	.15	.25
126 Labyrinth Champion R :R:	.20	.35
127 Lightning Strike C :R:	.15	.25
128 Magma Jet U :R:	.20	.35
129 Messenger's Speed C :R:	.15	.25
130 Minotaur Skullcleaver C :R:	.15	.25
131 Ordeal of Purphoros U :R:	.20	.35
132 Peak Eruption U :R:	.20	.35
133 Portent of Betrayal C :R:	.15	.25
134 Priest of Iroas C :R:	.15	.25
135 Purphoros, God of the Forge M :R:	8.00	9.00
136 Purphoros's Emissary U :R:	.20	.35
137 Rage of Purphoros C :R:	.15	.25
138 Rageblood Shaman R :R:	.20	.35
139 Satyr Rambler C :R:	.15	.25
140 Spark Jolt C :R:	.15	.25
141 Spearpoint Oread C :R:	.15	.25
142 Stoneshock Giant U :R:	.20	.35
143 Stormbreath Dragon M :R:	1.75	2.25
144 Titan of Eternal Fire R :R:	.20	.35
145 Titan's Strength C :R:	.15	.25
146 Two-Headed Cerberus C :R:	.15	.25
147 Wild Celebrants C :R:	.15	.25
148 Agent of Horizons C :G:	.15	.25
149 Anthousa, Setessan Hero R :G:	.20	.35
150 Arbor Colossus R :G:	.20	.35
151 Artisan's Sorrow U :G:	.20	.35
152 Boon Satyr R :G:	.20	.35
153 Bow of Nylea R :G:	1.75	2.00
154 Centaur Battlemaster U :G:	.20	.35
155 Commune with the Gods C :G:	.15	.25
156 Defend the Hearth C :G:	.15	.25
157 Fade into Antiquity C :G:	.15	.25
158 Feral Invocation C :G:	.15	.25
159 Hunt the Hunter U :G:	.20	.35
160a Karametra's Acolyte U :G:	.20	.35
160b Karametra's Alcolyte ALT ART	.20	.35
161 Leafcrown Dryad C :G:	.15	.25
162 Mistcutter Hydra R :G:	.40	.60
163 Nemesis of Mortals U :G:	.20	.35
164 Nessian Asp C :G:	.15	.25
165 Nessian Courser C :G:	.15	.25
166 Nylea, God of the Hunt M :G:	4.50	5.25
167 Nylea's Disciple C :G:	.15	.25
168 Nylea's Emissary U :G:	.20	.35
169 Nylea's Presence C :G:	.15	.25
170 Ordeal of Nylea U :G:	.20	.35
171 Pheres-Band Centaurs C :G:	.15	.25
172 Polukranos, World Eater M :G:	.75	1.25
173 Reverent Hunter R :G:	.20	.35
174 Satyr Hedonist C :G:	.15	.25
175 Satyr Piper U :G:	.20	.35
176 Savage Surge C :G:	.15	.25
177 Sedge Scorpion C :G:	.15	.25
178 Shredding Winds C :G:	.15	.25
179 Staunch-Hearted Warrior C :G:	.15	.25
180 Sylvan Caryatid R :G:	1.75	2.25
181 Time to Feed C :G:	.15	.25
182 Voyaging Satyr C :G:	.15	.25
183 Vulpine Goliath C :G:	.15	.25
184 Warriors' Lesson U :G:	.20	.35
185 Akroan Hoplite U :W: :R:	.20	.35
186 Anax and Cymede R :W: :R:	.20	.35
187 Ashen Rider M :W: :K:	.75	1.25
188 Ashiok, Nightmare Weaver M :B: :K:	5.50	6.50
189 Battlewise Hoplite U :W: :B:	.20	.35
190 Chronicler of Heroes U :W: :G:	.20	.35
191 Daxos of Meletis R :W: :B:	.20	.35
192 Destructive Revelry U :R: :G:	.20	.35
193 Fleecemane Lion R :W: :G:	.75	1.00
194 Horizon Chimera U :B: :G:	.20	.35
195 Kragma Warcaller U :K: :R:	.20	.35
196 Medomai the Ageless M :W: :B:	.75	1.00
197 Pharika's Mender U :K: :G:	.20	.35
198 Polis Crusher R :R: :G:	.20	.35
199 Prophet of Kruphix R :B: :G:	1.00	1.50
200 Psychic Intrusion R :B: :K:	.20	.35
201 Reaper of the Wilds R :K: :G:	.20	.35
202 Sentry of the Underworld U :W: :K:	.20	.35
203 Shipwreck Singer U :B: :K:	.20	.35
204 Spellheart Chimera U :B: :R:	.20	.35
205 Steam Augury R :B: :R:	.20	.35
206 Triad of Fates R :W: :K:	.20	.35
207 Tymaret, the Murder King R :K: :R:	.20	.35
208 Underworld Cerberus M :K: :R:	.50	.75
209 Xenagos, the Reveler M :R: :G:	4.00	5.00
210 Akroan Horse R	.20	.35
211 Anvilwrought Raptor U	.20	.35
212 Bronze Sable C	.15	.25
213 Burnished Hart U	.20	.35
214 Colossus of Akros R	1.00	1.50
215 Flamecast Wheel U	.20	.35
216 Fleetfeather Sandals C	.15	.25
217 Guardians of Meletis C	.15	.25
218 Opaline Unicorn C	.15	.25
219 Prowler's Helm U	.20	.35
220 Pyxis of Pandemonium R	.20	.35
221 Traveler's Amulet C	.15	.25
222 Witches' Eye U	.20	.35
223 Nykthos, Shrine to Nyx R	5.00	6.00
224 Temple of Abandon R	.50	.75
225 Temple of Deceit R	1.75	2.00
226 Temple of Mystery R	.75	1.15

227 Temple of Silence R 1.25 1.75
228 Temple of Triumph R .20 .35
229 Unknown Shores C .15 .25
230 Plains L .15 .25
231 Plains L .15 .25
232 Plains L .15 .25
233 Plains L .15 .25
234 Island L .15 .25
235 Island L .15 .25
236 Island L .15 .25
237 Island L .15 .25
238 Swamp L .15 .25
239 Swamp L .15 .25
240 Swamp L .15 .25
241 Swamp L .15 .25
242 Mountain L .15 .25
243 Mountain L .15 .25
244 Mountain L .15 .25
245 Mountain L .15 .25
246 Forest L .15 .25
247 Forest L .15 .25
248 Forest L .15 .25
249 Forest L .15 .25

2013 Magic The Gathering Theros Foil

1 Battlewise Valor C :W: .15 .25
2 Cavalry Pegasus C :W: .15 .25
3 Celestial Archon R :W: .40 .60
4 Chained to the Rocks R :W: 1.25 2.00
5 Chosen by Heliod C :W: .15 .25
6 Dauntless Onslaught U :W: .20 .35
7 Decorated Griffin U :W: .20 .35
8 Divine Verdict C :W: .15 .25
9 Elspeth, Sun's Champion M :W: 18.00 22.00
10 Ephara's Warden C :W: .15 .25
11 Evangel of Heliod U :W: .20 .35
12 Fabled Hero R :W: .75 1.25
13 Favored Hoplite U :W: .75 1.25
14 Gift of Immortality R :W: 2.00 3.50
15 Glare of Heresy U :W: .20 .35
16 Gods Willing C :W: 1.25 2.00
17 Heliod, God of the Sun M :W: 9.00 12.00
18 Heliod's Emissary U :W: .20 .35
19 Hopeful Eidolon C :W: .15 .25
20 Hundred-Handed One R :W: .75 1.25
21 Lagonna-Band Elder C :W: .15 .25
22 Last Breath C :W: .15 .25
23 Leonin Snarecaster C :W: .15 .25
24 Observant Alseid C :W: .15 .25
25 Ordeal of Heliod U :W: .50 .75
26 Phalanx Leader U :W: .50 .75
27 Ray of Dissolution C :W: .15 .25
28 Scholar of Athreos C :W: .15 .25
29 Setessan Battle Priest C :W: .15 .25
30 Setessan Griffin C :W: .15 .25
31 Silent Artisan C :W: .15 .25
32 Soldier of the Pantheon R :W: 1.00 1.50
33 Spear of Heliod R :W: 2.00 3.50
34 Traveling Philosopher C :W: .15 .25
35 Vanquish the Foul U :W: .20 .35
36 Wingsteed Rider C :W: .15 .25
37 Yoked Ox C :W: .15 .25
38 Annul C :B: .30 .50
39 Aqueous Form C :B: 1.50 2.50
40 Artisan of Forms R :B: .50 .75
41 Benthic Giant C :B: .15 .25
42 Bident of Thassa R :B: .75 1.25
43 Breaching Hippocamp C :B: .15 .25
44 Coastline Chimera C :B: .15 .25
45 Crackling Triton C :B: .15 .25
46 Curse of the Swine R :B: 1.25 2.00
47 Dissolve U :B: 1.25 2.00
48 Fate Foretold C :B: .15 .25
49 Gainsay U :B: .20 .35
50 Griptide C :B: .15 .25
51 Horizon Scholar U :B: .20 .35
52 Lost in a Labyrinth C :B: .15 .25
53 Master of Waves M :B: 10.00 12.00
54 Meletis Charlatan R :B: .40 .60
55 Mnemonic Wall C :B: .15 .25
56 Nimbus Naiad C :B: .15 .25
57 Omenspeaker C :B: .30 .50
58 Ordeal of Thassa U :B: .50 .75
59 Prescient Chimera C :B: .15 .25
60 Prognostic Sphinx R :B: .75 1.00
61 Sea God's Revenge U :B: .20 .35
62 Sealock Monster U :B: .20 .35
63 Shipbreaker Kraken R :B: .25 .40
64 Stymied Hopes C :B: .15 .25
65 Swan Song R :B: 5.00 8.00
66 Thassa, God of the Sea M :B: 18.00 22.00
67 Thassa's Bounty C :B: .15 .25
68 Thassa's Emissary U :B: .20 .35
69 Triton Fortune Hunter U :B: .20 .35
70 Triton Shorethief C :B: .15 .25
71 Triton Tactics U :B: .20 .35
72 Vaporkin C :B: .15 .25
73 Voyage's End C :B: .15 .25
74 Wavecrash Triton C :B: .15 .25
75 Abhorrent Overlord R :K: .50 .75
76 Agent of the Fates R :K: .75 1.25
77 Asphodel Wanderer C :K: .15 .25
78 Baleful Eidolon C :K: .15 .25
79 Blood-Toll Harpy C :K: .15 .25
80 Boon of Erebos C :K: .15 .25
81 Cavern Lampad C :K: .15 .25
82 Cutthroat Maneuver U :K: .20 .35
83 Dark Betrayal U :K: .20 .35
84 Disciple of Phenax C :K: .15 .25
85 Erebos, God of the Dead M :K: 15.00 18.00
86 Erebos's Emissary U :K: .20 .35
87 Felhide Minotaur C :K: .15 .25
88 Fleshmad Steed C :K: .15 .25
89 Gray Merchant of Asphodel C :K: 4.50 7.00
90 Hero's Downfall R :K: 3.50 5.00
91 Hythonia the Cruel M :K: 1.50 2.50
92 Insatiable Harpy U :K: .20 .35
93 Keepsake Gorgon U :K: .20 .35
94 Lash of the Whip C :K: .15 .25
95 Loathsome Catoblepas C :K: .15 .25
96 March of the Returned C :K: .15 .25
97 Mogis's Marauder U :K: .40 .60
98 Nighthowler R :K: 1.00 1.50
99 Ordeal of Erebos U :K: .20 .35
100 Pharika's Cure C :K: .15 .25
101 Read the Bones C :K: 1.50 2.50
102 Rescue from the Underworld U :K: .20 .35
103 Returned Centaur C :K: .15 .25
104 Returned Phalanx C :K: .15 .25
105 Scourgemark C :K: .15 .25
106 Sip of Hemlock C :K: .15 .25
107 Thoughtseize R :K: 30.00 35.00
108 Tormented Hero U :K: .20 .35
109 Viper's Kiss C :K: .15 .25
110 Whip of Erebos R :K: 3.00 5.00
111 Akroan Crusader C :R: .75 1.25
112 Anger of the Gods R :R: 18.00 20.00
113 Arena Athlete U :R: .20 .35
114 Borderland Minotaur C :R: .15 .25
115 Boulderfall C :R: .15 .25
116 Coordinated Assault U :R: .40 .60
117 Deathbellow Raider C :R: .15 .25
118 Demolish C :R: .15 .25
119 Dragon Mantle C :R: .60 1.00
120 Ember Swallower R :R: .25 .40
121 Fanatic of Mogis U :R: .50 .75
122 Firedrinker Satyr R :R: .60 1.00
123 Flamespeaker Adept U :R: .20 .35
124 Hammer of Purphoros R :R: 2.00 3.00
125 Ill-Tempered Cyclops C :R: .15 .25
126 Labyrinth Champion R :R: .30 .50
127 Lightning Strike C :R: 1.50 2.50
128 Magma Jet U :R: .75 1.25
129 Messenger's Speed C :R: .15 .25
130 Minotaur Skullcleaver C :R: .15 .25
131 Ordeal of Purphoros U :R: .20 .35
132 Peak Eruption U :R: .20 .35
133 Portent of Betrayal C :R: .15 .25
134 Priest of Iroas C :R: .15 .25
135 Purphoros, God of the Forge M :R: 20.00 25.00
136 Purphoros's Emissary U :R: .20 .35
137 Rage of Purphoros C :R: .15 .25
138 Rageblood Shaman R :R: .60 1.00
139 Satyr Rambler C :R: .15 .25
140 Spark Jolt C :R: .15 .25
141 Spearpoint Oread C :R: .15 .25
142 Stoneshock Giant U :R: .20 .35
143 Stormbreath Dragon M :R: 10.00 12.00
144 Titan of Eternal Fire R :R: .30 .50
145 Titan's Strength C :R: 1.00 1.50
146 Two-Headed Cerberus C :R: .15 .25
147 Wild Celebrants C :R: .15 .25
148 Agent of Horizons C :G: .15 .25
149 Anthousa, Setessan Hero R :G: .20 .35
150 Arbor Colossus R :G: .60 1.00
151 Artisan's Sorrow U :G: .20 .35
152 Boon Satyr R :G: 1.00 1.50
153 Bow of Nylea R :G: 3.50 5.00
154 Centaur Battlemaster U :G: .20 .35
155 Commune with the Gods C :G: 1.00 1.50
156 Defend the Hearth C :G: .15 .25
157 Fade into Antiquity C :G: .15 .25
158 Feral Invocation C :G: .15 .25
159 Hunt the Hunter U :G: .20 .35
160 Karametra's Acolyte U :G: .40 .60
161 Leafcrown Dryad C :G: .15 .25
162 Mistcutter Hydra R :G: 1.50 2.50
163 Nemesis of Mortals U :G: .40 .60
164 Nessian Asp C :G: .15 .25
165 Nessian Courser C :G: .15 .25
166 Nylea, God of the Hunt M :G: 9.00 12.00
167 Nylea's Disciple C :G: .15 .25
168 Nylea's Emissary U :G: .20 .35
169 Nylea's Presence C :G: .15 .25
170 Ordeal of Nylea U :G: .20 .35
171 Pheres-Band Centaurs C :G: .15 .25
172 Polukranos, World Eater M :G: 2.50 3.50
173 Reverent Hunter R :G: .30 .50
174 Satyr Hedonist C :G: .15 .25
175 Satyr Piper U :G: .20 .35
176 Savage Surge C :G: .15 .25
177 Sedge Scorpion C :G: .15 .25
178 Shredding Winds C :G: .15 .25
179 Staunch-Hearted Warrior C :G: .15 .25
180 Sylvan Caryatid R :G: 3.00 5.00
181 Time to Feed C :G: .15 .25
182 Voyaging Satyr C :G: 1.00 1.50
183 Vulpine Goliath C :G: .15 .25
184 Warriors' Lesson U :G: .20 .35
185 Akroan Hoplite U :W: :R: .20 .35
186 Anax and Cymede R :W: :R: 1.00 1.50
187 Ashen Rider M :W: :K: 6.00 8.00
188 Ashiok, Nightmare Weaver M :B: :K: 18.00 22.00
189 Battlewise Hoplite U :W: :B: .50 .75
190 Chronicler of Heroes U :W: :G: .20 .35
191 Daxos of Meletis R :W: :B: 1.75 2.50
192 Destructive Revelry U :R: :G: 4.00 6.00
193 Fleecemane Lion R :W: :G: 2.00 3.50
194 Horizon Chimera U :B: :G: .60 1.00
195 Kragma Warcaller U :K: :R: .20 .35
196 Medomai the Ageless M :W: :B: 3.00 5.00
197 Pharika's Mender U :K: :G: .20 .35
198 Polis Crusher R :R: :G: .50 .75
199 Prophet of Kruphix R :B: :G: 2.00 3.00
200 Psychic Intrusion R :B: :K: .50 .75
201 Reaper of the Wilds R :K: :G: .60 1.00
202 Sentry of the Underworld U :W: :K: .20 .35
203 Shipwreck Singer U :B: :K: .20 .35
204 Spellheart Chimera U :B: :R: .50 .75
205 Steam Augury R :B: :R: .50 .75
206 Triad of Fates R :W: :K: .60 1.00
207 Tymaret, the Murder King R :K: :R: .75 1.25
208 Underworld Cerberus M :K: :R: 1.00 1.50
209 Xenagos, the Reveler M :R: :G: 10.00 12.00
210 Akroan Horse R .50 .75
211 Anvilwrought Raptor U .20 .35
212 Bronze Sable C .15 .25
213 Burnished Hart U 4.00 6.00
214 Colossus of Akros R 3.00 5.00
215 Flamecast Wheel U .20 .35
216 Fleetfeather Sandals C .15 .25
217 Guardians of Meletis C .15 .25
218 Opaline Unicorn C .15 .25
219 Prowler's Helm U .20 .35
220 Pyxis of Pandemonium R 1.00 1.50
221 Traveler's Amulet C .15 .25
222 Witches' Eye U .20 .35
223 Nykthos, Shrine to Nyx R 15.00 18.00
224 Temple of Abandon R 2.50 4.00
225 Temple of Deceit R 5.00 7.00
226 Temple of Mystery R 2.00 3.50
227 Temple of Silence R 3.50 5.00
228 Temple of Triumph R 3.00 5.00
229 Unknown Shores C .15 .25
230 Plains L .15 .25
231 Plains L .15 .25
232 Plains L .15 .25
233 Plains L .15 .25
234 Island L .15 .25
235 Island L .15 .25
236 Island L .15 .25
237 Island L .15 .25
238 Swamp L .15 .25
239 Swamp L .15 .25
240 Swamp L .15 .25
241 Swamp L .15 .25
242 Mountain L .15 .25
243 Mountain L .15 .25
244 Mountain L .15 .25
245 Mountain L .15 .25
246 Forest L .15 .25
247 Forest L .15 .25
248 Forest L .15 .25
249 Forest L .15 .25

2013 Magic The Gathering Theros Tokens

1 Cleric 2.00 3.00
2 Soldier .10 .15
3 Soldier .10 .15
4 Bird .30 .40
5 Elemental .35 .50
6 Harpy .10 .15
7 Soldier .10 .15
8 Boar .30 .40
9 Satyr .15 .25
10 Golem .10 .15
11 Elspeth, Sun's Champion Emblem 2.00 3.00

2014 Magic The Gathering Born of the Gods

COMPLETE SET (176) 60.00 90.00
BOOSTER BOX (36 PACKS) 60.00 90.00
BOOSTER PACK (15 CARDS) 3.00 4.00
RELEASED ON FEBRUARY 7, 2014
1 Acolyte's Reward U :W: .20 .35
2 Akroan Phalanx U :W: .20 .35
3 Akroan Skyguard C :W: .15 .25
4 Archetype of Courage U :W: .20 .35
5 Brimaz, King of Oreskos M :W: 5.00 7.00
6 Dawn to Dusk U :W: .20 .35
7 Eidolon of Countless Battles R :W: .50 .75
8 Elite Skirmisher C :W: .15 .25
9 Ephara's Radiance C :W: .15 .25
10 Excoriate C :W: .15 .25
11 Fated Retribution R :W: .20 .35
12 Ghostblade Eidolon U :W: .20 .35
13 Glimpse the Sun God U :W: .20 .35
14 God-Favored General U :W: .20 .35
15 Great Hart C :W: .15 .25
16 Griffin Dreamfinder C :W: .15 .25
17 Hero of Iroas R :W: .60 1.00
18 Hold at Bay C :W: .15 .25
19 Loyal Pegasus C :W: .15 .25
20 Mortal's Ardor C :W: .15 .25
21 Nyxborn Shieldmate C :W: .15 .25
22 Oreskos Sun Guide C :W: .15 .25
23 Ornitharch U :W: .20 .35
24 Plea for Guidance R :W: .20 .35
25 Revoke Existence C :W: .15 .25
26 Silent Sentinel R :W: .20 .35
27 Spirit of the Labyrinth R :W: .75 1.00
28 Sunbond U :W: .20 .35
29 Vanguard of Brimaz U :W: .20 .35
30 Aerie Worshippers U :B: .20 .35
31 Arbiter of the Ideal R :B: .20 .35
32 Archetype of Imagination U :B: .20 .35
33 Chorus of the Tides C :B: .15 .25
34 Crypsis C :B: .15 .25
35 Deepwater Hypnotist C :B: .15 .25
36 Divination C :B: .15 .25
37 Eternity Snare U :B: .20 .35
38 Evanescent Intellect C :B: .15 .25
39 Fated Infatuation R :B: .20 .35
40 Flitterstep Eidolon U :B: .20 .35
41 Floodtide Serpent C :B: .15 .25
42 Kraken of the Straits U :B: .20 .35
43 Meletis Astronomer U :B: .20 .35
44 Mindreaver R :B: .20 .35
45 Nullify C :B: .15 .25
46 Nyxborn Triton C :B: .15 .25
47 Oracle's Insight U :B: .20 .35
48 Perplexing Chimera R :B: .20 .35
49 Retraction Helix C :B: .15 .25
50 Siren of the Fanged Coast U :B: .20 .35
51 Sphinx's Disciple C :B: .15 .25
52 Stratus Walk C :B: .15 .25
53 Sudden Storm C :B: .15 .25
54 Thassa's Rebuff U :B: .20 .35
55 Tromokratis R :B: .20 .35
56 Vortex Elemental U :B: .20 .35
57 Whelming Wave R :B: .30 .50
58 Archetype of Finality U :K: .20 .35
59 Ashiok's Adept U :K: .20 .35
60 Asphyxiate C :K: .15 .25
61 Bile Blight U :K: .20 .35
62 Black Oak of Odunos U :K: .20 .35
63 Champion of Stray Souls M :K: .50 .75
64 Claim of Erebos C :K: .15 .25
65 Drown in Sorrow U :K: .20 .35
66 Eater of Hope R :K: .20 .35
67 Eye Gouge C :K: .15 .25
68 Fate Unraveler R :K: .20 .35
69 Fated Return R :K: .20 .35
70 Felhide Brawler C :K: .15 .25
71 Forlorn Pseudamma U :K: .20 .35
72 Forsaken Drifters C :K: .15 .25
73 Gild R :K: .20 .35
74 Grisly Transformation C :K: .15 .25
75 Herald of Torment R :K: .20 .35
76 Marshmist Titan C :K: .15 .25
77 Necrobite C :K: .15 .25
78 Nyxborn Eidolon C :K: .15 .25
79 Odunos River Trawler U :K: .20 .35
80 Pain Seer R :K: .20 .35
81 Sanguimancy U :K: .20 .35
82 Servant of Tymaret C :K: .15 .25
83 Shrike Harpy U :K: .20 .35
84 Spiteful Returned U :K: .20 .35
85 Warchanter of Mogis C :K: .15 .25
86 Weight of the Underworld C :K: .15 .25
87 Akroan Conscriptor U :R: .20 .35
88 Archetype of Aggression U :R: .20 .35
89 Bolt of Keranos C :R: .15 .25
90 Cyclops of One-Eyed Pass C :R: .15 .25
91 Epiphany Storm C :R: .15 .25
92 Everflame Eidolon U :R: .20 .35
93 Fall of the Hammer C :R: .15 .25
94 Fated Conflagration R :R: .20 .35
95 Fearsome Temper C :R: .15 .25
96 Felhide Spiritbinder R :R: .20 .35
97 Flame-Wreathed Phoenix M :R: .50 .75
98 Forgestoker Dragon R :R: .20 .35
99 Impetuous Sunchaser C :R: .15 .25
100 Kragma Butcher C :R: .15 .25
101 Lightning Volley U :R: .20 .35
102 Nyxborn Rollicker C :R: .15 .25
103 Oracle of Bones R :R: .20 .35
104 Pharagax Giant C :R: .15 .25
105 Pinnacle of Rage U :R: .20 .35
106 Reckless Reveler C :R: .15 .25
107 Rise to the Challenge C :R: .15 .25
108 Satyr Firedancer R :R: .50 .75
109 Satyr Nyx-Smith U :R: .20 .35
110 Scouring Sands C :R: .15 .25
111 Searing Blood U :R: .20 .35
112 Stormcaller of Keranos U :R: .20 .35
113 Thunder Brute U :R: .20 .35
114 Thunderous Might U :R: .20 .35
115 Whims of the Fates R :R: .20 .35
116 Archetype of Endurance U :G: .20 .35
117 Aspect of Hydra C :G: .15 .25
118 Charging Badger C :G: .15 .25
119 Courser of Kruphix R :G: 2.00 3.00
120 Culling Mark C :G: .15 .25
121 Fated Intervention R :G: .20 .35
122 Graverobber Spider U :G: .20 .35
123 Hero of Leina Tower R :G: .20 .35
124 Hunter's Prowess R :G: .20 .35
125 Karametra's Favor C :G: .15 .25
126 Mischief and Mayhem U :G: .20 .35
127 Mortal's Resolve C :G: .15 .25
128 Nessian Demolok U :G: .20 .35
129 Nessian Wilds Ravager R :G: .20 .35
130 Noble Quarry U :G: .20 .35
131 Nyxborn Wolf C :G: .15 .25
132 Peregrination U :G: .20 .35
133 Pheres-Band Raiders U :G: .20 .35
134 Pheres-Band Tromper C :G: .15 .25
135 Raised by Wolves U :G: .20 .35
136 Satyr Wayfinder C :G: .15 .25
137 Scourge of Skola Vale R :G: .20 .35
138 Setessan Oathsworn C :G: .15 .25
139 Setessan Starbreaker C :G: .15 .25
140 Skyreaping U :G: .20 .35
141 Snake of the Golden Grove C :G: .15 .25
142 Swordwise Centaur C :G: .15 .25
143 Unravel the AEther U :G: .20 .35
144 Chromanticore M :W: :B: :K: :R: :G: .75 1.00
145 Ephara, God of the Polis M :W: :B: 1.25 2.00
146 Ephara's Enlightenment U :W: :B: .20 .35
147 Fanatic of Xenagos U :R: :G: .20 .35
148 Karametra, God of Harvests M :W: :G: 3.00 4.00
149 Kiora, the Crashing Wave M :B: :G: 2.00 2.50
150 Kiora's Follower U :B: :G: .20 .35
151 Mogis, God of Slaughter M :K: :R: 3.50 5.00
152 Phenax, God of Deception M :B: :K: 3.50 5.00
153 Ragemonger U :K: :R: .20 .35
154 Reap What Is Sown U :W: :G: .20 .35
155 Siren of the Silent Song U :B: :K: .20 .35
156 Xenagos, God of Revels M :R: :G: 5.00 7.00
157 Astral Cornucopia R .30 .50
158 Gorgon's Head U .20 .35
159 Heroes' Podium R .20 .35
160 Pillar of War U .20 .35
161 Siren Song Lyre U .20 .35
162 Springleaf Drum U .20 .35
163 Temple of Enlightenment R 2.00 2.50
164 Temple of Malice R 1.00 1.50
165 Temple of Plenty R 1.00 1.50

2014 Magic The Gathering Born of the Gods Foil

1 Acolyte's Reward U :W: .40 .60
2 Akroan Phalanx U :W: .20 .35
3 Akroan Skyguard C :W: .15 .25
4 Archetype of Courage U :W: 2.00 3.50
5 Brimaz, King of Oreskos M :W: 25.00 30.00
6 Dawn to Dusk U :W: .20 .35
7 Eidolon of Countless Battles R :W: 1.50 2.50
8 Elite Skirmisher C :W: .15 .25
9 Ephara's Radiance C :W: .15 .25
10 Excoriate C :W: .15 .25
11 Fated Retribution R :W: .60 1.00
12 Ghostblade Eidolon U :W: .40 .60
13 Glimpse the Sun God U :W: .40 .60
14 God-Favored General U :W: .20 .35
15 Great Hart C :W: .15 .25

16 Griffin Dreamfinder C :W: .15 .25
17 Hero of Iroas R :W: 1.50 2.50
18 Hold at Bay C :W: .15 .25
19 Loyal Pegasus C :W: .15 .25
20 Mortal's Ardor C :W: .15 .25
21 Nyxborn Shieldmate C :W: .15 .25
22 Oreskos Sun Guide C :W: .15 .25
23 Ornitharch U :W: .20 .35
24 Plea for Guidance R :W: 1.50 2.00
25 Revoke Existence C :W: .15 .25
26 Silent Sentinel R :W: .40 .60
27 Spirit of the Labyrinth R :W: 5.00 7.00
28 Sunbond U :W: 2.00 3.50
29 Vanguard of Brimaz U :W: .60 1.00
30 Aerie Worshippers U :B: .15 .25
31 Arbiter of the Ideal R :B: .40 .60
32 Archetype of Imagination U :B: 3.50 5.00
33 Chorus of the Tides C :B: .15 .25
34 Crypsis C :B: .15 .25
35 Deepwater Hypnotist C :B: .15 .25
36 Divination C :B: .15 .25
37 Eternity Snare U :B: .20 .35
38 Evanescent Intellect C :B: .15 .25
39 Fated Infatuation R :B: .60 1.00
40 Flitterstep Eidolon U :B: .20 .35
41 Floodtide Serpent C :B: .15 .25
42 Kraken of the Straits U :B: .20 .35
43 Meletis Astronomer U :B: .20 .35
44 Mindreaver R :B: .40 .60
45 Nullify C :B: .15 .25
46 Nyxborn Triton C :B: .15 .25
47 Oracle's Insight U :B: .20 .35
48 Perplexing Chimera R :B: 1.00 1.50
49 Retraction Helix C :B: .15 .25
50 Siren of the Fanged Coast U :B: .20 .35
51 Sphinx's Disciple C :B: .15 .25
52 Stratus Walk C :B: .15 .25
53 Sudden Storm C :B: .15 .25
54 Thassa's Rebuff U :B: .40 .60
55 Tromokratis R :B: .50 .75
56 Vortex Elemental U :B: .20 .35
57 Whelming Wave R :B: 1.00 1.50
58 Archetype of Finality U :K: 3.00 5.00
59 Ashiok's Adept U :K: .20 .35
60 Asphyxiate C :K: .15 .25
61 Bile Blight U :K: 1.50 2.50
62 Black Oak of Odunos U :K: .20 .35
63 Champion of Stray Souls M :K: 2.50 3.50
64 Claim of Erebos C :K: .15 .25
65 Drown in Sorrow U :K: 2.00 3.50
66 Eater of Hope R :K: .40 .60
67 Eye Gouge C :K: .15 .25
68 Fate Unraveler R :K: 1.00 1.50
69 Fated Return R :K: 1.00 1.50
70 Felhide Brawler C :K: .15 .25
71 Forlorn Pseudamma U :K: .20 .35
72 Forsaken Drifters C :K: .15 .25
73 Gild R :K: .60 1.00
74 Grisly Transformation C :K: .15 .25
75 Herald of Torment R :K: .40 .60
76 Marshmist Titan C :K: .15 .25
77 Necrobite C :K: .15 .25
78 Nyxborn Eidolon C :K: .15 .25
79 Odunos River Trawler U :K: .20 .35
80 Pain Seer R :K: .50 .75
81 Sanguimancy U :K: .20 .35
82 Servant of Tymaret C :K: .15 .25
83 Shrike Harpy U :K: .20 .35
84 Spiteful Returned U :K: 1.00 1.50
85 Warchanter of Mogis C :K: .15 .25
86 Weight of the Underworld C :K: .15 .25
87 Akroan Conscriptor U :R: .20 .35
88 Archetype of Aggression U :R: 2.50 3.50
89 Bolt of Keranos C :R: .15 .25
90 Cyclops of One-Eyed Pass C :R: .15 .25
91 Epiphany Storm C :R: .15 .25
92 Everflame Eidolon U :R: .20 .35
93 Fall of the Hammer C :R: .15 .25
94 Fated Conflagration R :R: .75 1.00
95 Fearsome Temper C :R: .15 .25
96 Felhide Spiritbinder R :R: .50 .75
97 Flame-Wreathed Phoenix M :R: 1.50 2.50
98 Forgestoker Dragon R :R: .40 .60
99 Impetuous Sunchaser C :R: .15 .25
100 Kragma Butcher C :R: .15 .25
101 Lightning Volley U :R: .20 .35
102 Nyxborn Rollicker C :R: .15 .25
103 Oracle of Bones R :R: .50 .75
104 Pharagax Giant C :R: .15 .25
105 Pinnacle of Rage U :R: .20 .35
106 Reckless Reveler C :R: .15 .25
107 Rise to the Challenge C :R: .15 .25
108 Satyr Firedancer R :R: 1.50 2.00
109 Satyr Nyx-Smith U :R: .20 .35
110 Scouring Sands C :R: .15 .25
111 Searing Blood U :R: 3.00 4.00
112 Stormcaller of Keranos U :R: .20 .35
113 Thunder Brute U :R: .20 .35
114 Thunderous Might U :R: .20 .35
115 Whims of the Fates R :R: .40 .60
116 Archetype of Endurance U :G: 6.00 8.00
117 Aspect of Hydra C :G: 1.00 1.50
118 Charging Badger C :G: .15 .25
119 Courser of Kruphix R :G: 8.00 10.00
120 Culling Mark C :G: .15 .25
121 Fated Intervention R :G: .40 .60
122 Graverobber Spider U :G: .20 .35
123 Hero of Leina Tower R :G: .75 1.00
124 Hunter's Prowess R :G: .75 1.00
125 Karametra's Favor C :G: .15 .25
126 Mischief and Mayhem U :G: .20 .35
127 Mortal's Resolve C :G: .15 .25
128 Nessian Demolok U :G: .20 .35
129 Nessian Wilds Ravager R :G: .40 .60
130 Noble Quarry U :G: .20 .35
131 Nyxborn Wolf C :G: .15 .25
132 Peregrination U :G: .50 .75
133 Pheres-Band Raiders U :G: .20 .35
134 Pheres-Band Tromper C :G: .15 .25
135 Raised by Wolves U :G: .20 .35
136 Satyr Wayfinder C :G: .15 .25
137 Scourge of Skola Vale R :G: .75 1.00
138 Setessan Oathsworn C :G: .15 .25
139 Setessan Starbreaker C :G: .15 .25
140 Skyreaping U :G: .20 .35
141 Snake of the Golden Grove C :G: .15 .25
142 Swordwise Centaur C :G: .15 .25
143 Unravel the AEther U :G: 2.00 3.00
144 Chromanticore M :W: :B: :K: :R: :G: 4.00 6.00
145 Ephara, God of the Polis M :W: :B: 10.00 13.00
146 Ephara's Enlightenment U :W: :B: .50 .75
147 Fanatic of Xenagos U :R: :G: .60 1.00
148 Karametra, God of Harvests M :W: :G: 20.00 25.00
149 Kiora, the Crashing Wave M :B: :G: 15.00 18.00
150 Kiora's Follower U :B: :G: 1.00 1.50
151 Mogis, God of Slaughter M :K: :R: 16.00 20.00
152 Phenax, God of Deception M :B: :K: 23.00 26.00
153 Ragemonger U :K: :R: .75 1.25
154 Reap What Is Sown U :W: :G: .20 .35
155 Siren of the Silent Song U :B: :K: 1.00 1.50
156 Xenagos, God of Revels M :R: :G: 30.00 35.00
157 Astral Cornucopia R 1.50 2.50
158 Gorgon's Head U .40 .60
159 Heroes' Podium R .75 1.00
160 Pillar of War U .20 .35
161 Siren Song Lyre U .20 .35
162 Springleaf Drum U 5.00 7.00
163 Temple of Enlightenment R 6.00 8.00
164 Temple of Malice R 3.00 4.50
165 Temple of Plenty R 3.00 4.50

2014 Magic The Gathering Born of the Gods Tokens

1 Bird .10 .15
2 Cat Soldier 1.00 1.50
3 Soldier .10 .15
4 Bird .10 .15
5 Kraken 1.00 1.50
6 Zombie .12 .20
7 Elemental .10 .15
8 Centaur .10 .15
9 Wolf .12 .20
10 Gold .20 .30
11 Kiora, the Crashing Wave Emblem 6.00 8.00

2014 Magic The Gathering Journey into Nyx

COMPLETE SET (165) 80.00 120.00
BOOSTER BOX (36 PACKS) 80.00 120.00
BOOSTER PACK (15 CARDS) 4.00 5.00
RELEASED ON MAY 2, 2014
1 Aegis of the Gods R :W: .75 1.25
2 Ajani's Presence C :W: .15 .25
3 Akroan Mastiff C :W: .15 .25
4 Armament of Nyx C :W: .15 .25
5 Banishing Light U :W: .20 .35
6 Dawnbringer Charioteers R :W: .20 .35
7 Deicide R :W: .20 .35
8 Dictate of Heliod R :W: .20 .35
9 Eagle of the Watch C :W: .15 .25
10 Eidolon of Rhetoric U :W: .20 .35
11 Font of Vigor C :W: .15 .25
12 Godsend M :W: 4.50 6.00
13 Harvestguard Alseids C :W: .15 .25
14 Lagonna-Band Trailblazer C :W: .15 .25
15 Launch the Fleet R :W: .50 .75
16 Leonin Iconoclast U :W: .20 .35
17 Mortal Obstinacy C :W: .15 .25
18 Nyx-Fleece Ram U :W: .20 .35
19 Oppressive Rays C :W: .15 .25
20 Oreskos Swiftclaw C :W: .15 .25
21 Phalanx Formation U :W: .20 .35
22 Quarry Colossus U :W: .20 .35
23 Reprisal U :W: .20 .35
24 Sightless Brawler U :W: .20 .35
25 Skybind R :W: .20 .35
26 Skyspear Cavalry U :W: .20 .35
27 Stonewise Fortifier C :W: .15 .25
28 Supply-Line Cranes C :W: .15 .25
29 Tethmos High Priest U :W: .20 .35
30 Aerial Formation C :B: .15 .25
31 Battlefield Thaumaturge R :B: .20 .35
32 Cloaked Siren C :B: .15 .25
33 Countermand C :B: .15 .25
34 Crystalline Nautilus U :B: .20 .35
35 Dakra Mystic U :B: .20 .35
36 Daring Thief R :B: .20 .35
37 Dictate of Kruphix R :B: .75 1.25
38 Font of Fortunes C :B: .15 .25
39 Godhunter Octopus C :B: .15 .25
40 Hour of Need U :B: .20 .35
41 Hubris C :B: .15 .25
42 Hypnotic Siren R :B: .20 .35
43 Interpret the Signs U :B: .20 .35
44 Kiora's Dismissal U :B: .20 .35
45 Pin to the Earth C :B: .15 .25
46 Polymorphous Rush R :B: .20 .35
47 Pull from the Deep U :B: .20 .35
48 Riptide Chimera U :B: .20 .35
49 Rise of Eagles U :B: .20 .35
50 Sage of Hours M :B: 2.00 2.50
51 Scourge of Fleets R :B: .20 .35
52 Sigiled Starfish C :B: .15 .25
53 Thassa's Devourer C :B: .15 .25
54 Thassa's Ire U :B: .20 .35
55 Triton Cavalry U :B: .20 .35
56 Triton Shorestalker C :B: .15 .25
57 War-Wing Siren C :B: .15 .25
58 Whitewater Naiads U :B: .20 .35
59 Agent of Erebos U :K: .20 .35
60 Aspect of Gorgon C :K: .15 .25
61 Bloodcrazed Hoplite C :K: .15 .25
62 Brain Maggot U :K: .20 .35
63 Cast into Darkness C :K: .15 .25
64 Cruel Feeding C :K: .15 .25
65 Dictate of Erebos R :K: 2.50 3.50
66 Doomwake Giant R :K: .20 .35
67 Dreadbringer Lampads C :K: .15 .25
68 Extinguish All Hope R :K: .20 .35
69 Feast of Dreams C :K: .15 .25
70 Felhide Petrifier U :K: .20 .35
71 Font of Return C :K: .15 .25
72 Gnarled Scarhide U :K: .20 .35
73 Grim Guardian C :K: .15 .25
74 King Macar, the Gold-Cursed R :K: .20 .35
75 Master of the Feast R :K: .75 1.00
76 Nightmarish End U :K: .20 .35
77 Nyx Infusion C :K: .15 .25
78 Pharika's Chosen C :K: .15 .25
79 Returned Reveler C :K: .15 .25
80 Ritual of the Returned U :K: .20 .35
81 Rotted Hulk U :K: .20 .35
82 Silence the Believers R :K: .30 .50
83 Spiteful Blow U :K: .20 .35
84 Squelching Leeches U :K: .20 .35
85 Thoughtrender Lamia U :K: .20 .35
86 Tormented Thoughts U :K: .20 .35
87 Worst Fears M :K: .50 .75
88 Akroan Line Breaker U :R: .20 .35
89 Bearer of the Heavens R :R: .30 .50
90 Bladetusk Boar C :R: .15 .25
91 Blinding Flare U :R: .20 .35
92 Cyclops of Eternal Fury U :R: .20 .35
93 Dictate of the Twin Gods R :R: .20 .35
94 Eidolon of the Great Revel R :R: 4.00 6.00
95 Flamespeaker's Will C :R: .15 .25
96 Flurry of Horns C :R: .15 .25
97 Font of Ire C :R: .15 .25
98 Forgeborn Oreads U :R: .20 .35
99 Gluttonous Cyclops C :R: .15 .25
100 Harness by Force R :R: .20 .35
101 Knowledge and Power U :R: .20 .35
102 Lightning Diadem C :R: .15 .25
103 Magma Spray C :R: .15 .25
104 Mogis's Warhound U :R: .20 .35
105 Pensive Minotaur C :R: .15 .25
106 Prophetic Flamespeaker M :R: .75 1.00
107 Riddle of Lightning U :R: .20 .35
108 Rollick of Abandon U :R: .20 .35
109 Rouse the Mob C :R: .15 .25
110 Satyr Hoplite C :R: .15 .25
111 Sigiled Skink C :R: .15 .25
112 Spawn of Thraxes R :R: .20 .35
113 Spite of Mogis U :R: .20 .35
114 Starfall C :R: .15 .25
115 Twinflame R :R: .20 .35
116 Wildfire Cerberus U :R: .20 .35
117 Bassara Tower Archer U :G: .20 .35
118 Colossal Heroics U :G: .20 .35
119 Consign to Dust U :G: .20 .35
120 Desecration Plague C :G: .15 .25
121 Dictate of Karametra R :G: .25 .40
122 Eidolon of Blossoms R :G: .30 .50
123 Font of Fertility C :G: .15 .25
124 Golden Hind C :G: .15 .25
125 Goldenhide Ox U :G: .20 .35
126 Heroes' Bane R :G: .50 .75
127 Humbler of Mortals C :G: .15 .25
128 Hydra Broodmaster R :G: .50 .75
129 Kruphix's Insight C :G: .15 .25
130 Market Festival C :G: .15 .25
131 Nature's Panoply C :G: .15 .25
132 Nessian Game Warden U :G: .20 .35
133 Oakheart Dryads C :G: .15 .25
134 Pheres-Band Thunderhoof C :G: .15 .25
135 Pheres-Band Warchief R :G: .25 .40
136 Ravenous Leucrocota C :G: .15 .25
137 Renowned Weaver C :G: .15 .25
138 Reviving Melody U :G: .20 .35
139 Satyr Grovedancer C :G: .15 .25
140 Setessan Tactics R :G: .30 .50
141 Solidarity of Heroes U :G: .20 .35
142 Spirespine U :G: .20 .35
143 Strength from the Fallen U :G: .20 .35
144 Swarmborn Giant U :G: .20 .35
145 Ajani, Mentor of Heroes M :M: 13.00 16.00
146 Athreos, God of Passage M :M: 8.00 11.00
147 Desperate Stand U :M: .20 .35
148 Disciple of Deceit U :M: .20 .35
149 Fleetfeather Cockatrice U :M: .20 .35
150 Iroas, God of Victory M :M: 4.00 6.00
151 Keranos, God of Storms M :M: 5.00 7.00
152 Kruphix, God of Horizons M :M: 4.00 6.00
153 Nyx Weaver U :M: .20 .35
154 Pharika, God of Affliction M :M: 1.25 2.00
155 Revel of the Fallen God R :M: .20 .35
156 Stormchaser Chimera U :M: .20 .35
157 Underworld Coinsmith U :M: .20 .35
158 Armory of Iroas U .20 .35
159 Chariot of Victory U .20 .35
160 Deserter's Quarters U .20 .35
161 Gold-Forged Sentinel U .20 .35
162 Hall of Triumph R .40 .60
163 Mana Confluence R 4.00 6.00
164 Temple of Epiphany R 2.00 2.50
165 Temple of Malady R 1.50 2.00

2014 Magic The Gathering Journey into Nyx Foil

1 Aegis of the Gods R :W: 3.00 5.00
2 Ajani's Presence C :W: .60 1.00
3 Akroan Mastiff C :W: .15 .25
4 Armament of Nyx C :W: .15 .25
5 Banishing Light U :W: 2.00 3.00
6 Dawnbringer Charioteers R :W: .40 .60
7 Deicide R :W: .75 1.25
8 Dictate of Heliod R :W: 1.00 1.50
9 Eagle of the Watch C :W: .15 .25
10 Eidolon of Rhetoric U :W: 4.00 5.00
11 Font of Vigor C :W: .15 .25
12 Godsend M :W: 13.00 16.00
13 Harvestguard Alseids C :W: .15 .25
14 Lagonna-Band Trailblazer C :W: .50 .75
15 Launch the Fleet R :W: 1.50 2.00
16 Leonin Iconoclast U :W: .20 .35
17 Mortal Obstinacy C :W: .15 .25
18 Nyx-Fleece Ram U :W: 4.00 5.00
19 Oppressive Rays C :W: .15 .25
20 Oreskos Swiftclaw C :W: .15 .25
21 Phalanx Formation U :W: .20 .35
22 Quarry Colossus U :W: .20 .35
23 Reprisal U :W: .30 .50
24 Sightless Brawler U :W: .20 .35
25 Skybind R :W: .50 .75
26 Skyspear Cavalry U :W: .20 .35
27 Stonewise Fortifier C :W: .15 .25
28 Supply-Line Cranes C :W: .15 .25
29 Tethmos High Priest U :W: .20 .35
30 Aerial Formation C :B: .15 .25
31 Battlefield Thaumaturge R :B: 1.00 1.50
32 Cloaked Siren C :B: .15 .25
33 Countermand C :B: .15 .25
34 Crystalline Nautilus U :B: .20 .35
35 Dakra Mystic U :B: 1.50 2.50
36 Daring Thief R :B: .50 .75
37 Dictate of Kruphix R :B: 2.00 3.00
38 Font of Fortunes C :B: .15 .25
39 Godhunter Octopus C :B: .15 .25
40 Hour of Need U :B: .60 1.00
41 Hubris C :B: .15 .25
42 Hypnotic Siren R :B: .75 1.25
43 Interpret the Signs U :B: .25 .40
44 Kiora's Dismissal U :B: .20 .35
45 Pin to the Earth C :B: .15 .25
46 Polymorphous Rush R :B: .50 .75
47 Pull from the Deep U :B: 1.00 1.50
48 Riptide Chimera U :B: .30 .50
49 Rise of Eagles U :B: .20 .35
50 Sage of Hours M :B: 7.00 10.00
51 Scourge of Fleets R :B: .50 .75
52 Sigiled Starfish C :B: .15 .25
53 Thassa's Devourer C :B: .15 .25
54 Thassa's Ire U :B: .20 .35
55 Triton Cavalry U :B: .20 .35
56 Triton Shorestalker C :B: .50 .75
57 War-Wing Siren C :B: .15 .25
58 Whitewater Naiads U :B: .20 .35
59 Agent of Erebos U :K: 4.00 6.00
60 Aspect of Gorgon C :K: .15 .25
61 Bloodcrazed Hoplite C :K: .15 .25
62 Brain Maggot U :K: .75 1.25
63 Cast into Darkness C :K: .15 .25
64 Cruel Feeding C :K: .15 .25
65 Dictate of Erebos R :K: 7.00 10.00
66 Doomwake Giant R :K: .60 1.00
67 Dreadbringer Lampads C :K: .15 .25
68 Extinguish All Hope R :K: .75 1.25
69 Feast of Dreams C :K: .15 .25
70 Felhide Petrifier U :K: .60 1.00
71 Font of Return C :K: .15 .25
72 Gnarled Scarhide U :K: 1.50 2.50
73 Grim Guardian C :K: .15 .25
74 King Macar, the Gold-Cursed R :K: 1.00 1.50
75 Master of the Feast R :K: 2.00 3.50
76 Nightmarish End U :K: .20 .35
77 Nyx Infusion C :K: .15 .25
78 Pharika's Chosen C :K: .30 .50
79 Returned Reveler C :K: .15 .25
80 Ritual of the Returned U :K: .20 .35
81 Rotted Hulk U :K: .20 .35
82 Silence the Believers R :K: 1.25 2.00
83 Spiteful Blow U :K: .20 .35
84 Squelching Leeches U :K: .20 .35
85 Thoughtrender Lamia U :K: .20 .35
86 Tormented Thoughts U :K: .20 .35
87 Worst Fears M :K: 3.00 5.00
88 Akroan Line Breaker U :R: .20 .35
89 Bearer of the Heavens R :R: 1.00 1.50
90 Bladetusk Boar C :R: .15 .25
91 Blinding Flare U :R: .20 .35
92 Cyclops of Eternal Fury U :R: .20 .35
93 Dictate of the Twin Gods R :R: .75 1.25
94 Eidolon of the Great Revel R :R: 20.00 25.00
95 Flamespeaker's Will C :R: .15 .25
96 Flurry of Horns C :R: .15 .25
97 Font of Ire C :R: .15 .25
98 Forgeborn Oreads U :R: .20 .35
99 Gluttonous Cyclops C :R: .15 .25
100 Harness by Force R :R: .40 .60
101 Knowledge and Power U :R: .20 .35
102 Lightning Diadem C :R: .15 .25
103 Magma Spray C :R: .60 1.00
104 Mogis's Warhound U :R: .20 .35
105 Pensive Minotaur C :R: .15 .25
106 Prophetic Flamespeaker M :R: 3.00 5.00
107 Riddle of Lightning U :R: .20 .35
108 Rollick of Abandon U :R: .20 .35
109 Rouse the Mob C :R: .15 .25
110 Satyr Hoplite C :R: .15 .25
111 Sigiled Skink C :R: .15 .25
112 Spawn of Thraxes R :R: .50 .75
113 Spite of Mogis U :R: .50 .75
114 Starfall C :R: .15 .25
115 Twinflame R :R: .75 1.25
116 Wildfire Cerberus U :R: .20 .35
117 Bassara Tower Archer U :G: .75 1.25
118 Colossal Heroics U :G: .20 .35
119 Consign to Dust U :G: .20 .35
120 Desecration Plague C :G: .15 .25
121 Dictate of Karametra R :G: 1.00 1.50
122 Eidolon of Blossoms R :G: .75 1.25
123 Font of Fertility C :G: .15 .25
124 Golden Hind C :G: .15 .25
125 Goldenhide Ox U :G: .20 .35
126 Heroes' Bane R :G: .75 1.25
127 Humbler of Mortals C :G: .15 .25
128 Hydra Broodmaster R :G: 1.00 1.50
129 Kruphix's Insight C :G: .15 .25
130 Market Festival C :G: .15 .25
131 Nature's Panoply C :G: .15 .25
132 Nessian Game Warden U :G: .20 .35
133 Oakheart Dryads C :G: .15 .25
134 Pheres-Band Thunderhoof C :G: .15 .25
135 Pheres-Band Warchief R :G: .40 .60
136 Ravenous Leucrocota C :G: .15 .25
137 Renowned Weaver C :G: .15 .25
138 Reviving Melody U :G: .20 .35
139 Satyr Grovedancer C :G: .15 .25
140 Setessan Tactics R :G: 1.00 1.50

141 Solidarity of Heroes U :G: 1.25 2.00
142 Spirespine U :G: .20 .35
143 Strength from the Fallen U :G: .50 .75
144 Swarmborn Giant U :G: .20 .35
145 Ajani, Mentor of Heroes M :M: 30.00 35.00
146 Athreos, God of Passage M :M: 25.00 30.00
147 Desperate Stand U :M: .20 .35
148 Disciple of Deceit U :M: 1.00 1.50
149 Fleetfeather Cockatrice U :M: .20 .35
150 Iroas, God of Victory M :M: 15.00 20.00
151 Keranos, God of Storms M :M: 45.00 60.00
152 Kruphix, God of Horizons M :M: 25.00 30.00
153 Nyx Weaver U :M: 2.50 3.50
154 Pharika, God of Affliction M :M: 11.00 13.00
155 Revel of the Fallen God R :M: .40 .60
156 Stormchaser Chimera U :M: .20 .35
157 Underworld Coinsmith U :M: 1.25 2.00
158 Armory of Iroas U .30 .50
159 Chariot of Victory U .75 1.25
160 Deserter's Quarters U .20 .35
161 Gold-Forged Sentinel U .20 .35
162 Hall of Triumph R .75 1.25
163 Mana Confluence R 11.00 13.00
164 Temple of Epiphany R 6.00 8.00
165 Temple of Malady R 4.00 6.00

2014 Magic The Gathering Journey into Nyx Tokens

1 Sphinx .10 .15
2 Zombie .15 .25
3 Minotaur .10 .15
4 Hydra 1.00 1.50
5 Spider .10 .15
6 Snake .50 .75

2014 Magic The Gathering Khans of Tarkir

COMPLETE SET (282) 130.00 180.00
BOOSTER BOX (36 PACKS) 80.00 100.00
BOOSTER PACK (15 CARDS) 3.00 5.00
RELEASED ON SEPTEMBER 26, 2014
1 Abzan Battle Priest U :W: .20 .35
2 Abzan Falconer U :W: .20 .35
3 Ainok Bond-Kin C :W: .15 .25
4 Alabaster Kirin C :W: .15 .25
5 Brave the Sands U :W: .20 .35
6 Dazzling Ramparts U :W: .20 .35
7 Defiant Strike C :W: .15 .25
8 End Hostilities R :W: .25 .40
9 Erase C :W: .15 .25
10 Feat of Resistance C :W: .15 .25
11 Firehoof Cavalry C :W: .15 .25
12 Herald of Anafenza R :W: .25 .40
13 High Sentinels of Arashin R :W: .25 .40
14 Jeskai Student C :W: .15 .25
15 Kill Shot C :W: .15 .25
16 Mardu Hateblade C :W: .15 .25
17 Mardu Hordechief C :W: .15 .25
18 Master of Pearls R :W: .25 .40
19 Rush of Battle C :W: .15 .25
20 Sage-Eye Harrier C :W: .15 .25
21 Salt Road Patrol C :W: .15 .25
22 Seeker of the Way U :W: .20 .35
23 Siegecraft C :W: .15 .25
24 Smite the Monstrous C :W: .15 .25
25 Suspension Field U :W: .20 .35
26 Take Up Arms U :W: .20 .35
27 Timely Hordemate U :W: .20 .35
28 Venerable Lammasu U :W: .20 .35
29 War Behemoth U :W: .20 .35
30 Watcher of the Roost U :W: .20 .35
31 Wingmate Roc M :W: .75 1.00
32 Blinding Spray U :B: .20 .35
33 Cancel C :B: .15 .25
34 Clever Impersonator M :B: 3.00 4.00
35 Crippling Chill C :B: .15 .25
36 Dig Through Time R :B: 3.00 4.00
37 Disdainful Stroke C :B: .15 .25
38 Dragon's Eye Savants U :B: .20 .35
39 Embodiment of Spring C :B: .15 .25
40 Force Away C :B: .15 .25
41 Glacial Stalker C :B: .15 .25
42 Icy Blast R :B: .25 .40
43 Jeskai Elder U :B: .20 .35
44 Jeskai Windscout C :B: .15 .25
45 Kheru Spellsnatcher R :B: .25 .40
46 Mistfire Weaver U :B: .20 .35
47 Monastery Flock C :B: .15 .25
48 Mystic of the Hidden Way C :B: .15 .25
49 Pearl Lake Ancient M :B: .50 .75
50 Quiet Contemplation U :B: .20 .35
51 Riverwheel Aerialists U :B: .20 .35
52 Scaldkin C :B: .15 .25
53 Scion of Glaciers U :B: .20 .35
54 Set Adrift U :B: .20 .35
55 Singing Bell Strike C :B: .15 .25
56 Stubborn Denial U :B: .20 .35
57 Taigam's Scheming C :B: .15 .25
58 Thousand Winds R :B: .25 .40
59 Treasure Cruise C :B: .15 .25
60 Waterwhirl U :B: .20 .35
61 Weave Fate C :B: .15 .25
62 Wetland Sambar C :B: .15 .25
63 Whirlwind Adept C :B: .15 .25
64 Bellowing Saddlebrute U :K: .20 .35
65 Bitter Revelation C :K: .15 .25
66 Bloodsoaked Champion R :K: .40 .60
67 Dead Drop U :K: .20 .35
68 Debilitating Injury C :K: .15 .25
69 Despise U :K: .20 .35
70 Disowned Ancestor C :K: .15 .25
71 Dutiful Return C :K: .15 .25
72 Empty the Pits M :K: .50 .75
73 Grim Haruspex R :K: .25 .40
74 Gurmag Swiftwing U :K: .20 .35
75 Kheru Bloodsucker U :K: .20 .35
75 Shambling Attendants C :K: .15 .25
76 Kheru Dreadmaw C :K: .15 .25
77 Krumar Bond-Kin C :K: .15 .25
78 Mardu Skullhunter C :K: .15 .25
79 Mer-Ek Nightblade U :K: .20 .35
80 Molting Snakeskin C :K: .15 .25
81 Murderous Cut U :K: .20 .35
82 Necropolis Fiend R :K: .25 .40
83 Raiders' Spoils U :K: .20 .35
84 Rakshasa's Secret C :K: .15 .25
85 Retribution of the Ancients R :K: .25 .40
86 Rite of the Serpent C :K: .15 .25
87 Rotting Mastodon C :K: .15 .25
88 Ruthless Ripper U :K: .20 .35
90 Sidisi's Pet C :K: .15 .25
91 Sultai Scavenger C :K: .15 .25
92 Swarm of Bloodflies U :K: .20 .35
93 Throttle C :K: .15 .25
94 Unyielding Krumar C :K: .15 .25
95 Act of Treason C :R: .15 .25
96 Ainok Tracker C :R: .15 .25
97 Arc Lightning U :R: .20 .35
98 Arrow Storm C :R: .15 .25
99 Ashcloud Phoenix M :R: .50 .75
100 Barrage of Boulders C :R: .15 .25
101 Bloodfire Expert C :R: .15 .25
102 Bloodfire Mentor C :R: .15 .25
103 Bring Low C :R: .15 .25
104 Burn Away U :R: .20 .35
105 Canyon Lurkers C :R: .15 .25
106 Crater's Claws R :R: .25 .40
107 Dragon Grip U :R: .20 .35
108 Dragon-Style Twins R :R: .25 .40
109 Goblinslide U :R: .20 .35
110 Horde Ambusher U :R: .20 .35
111 Hordeling Outburst U :R: .20 .35
112 Howl of the Horde R :R: .25 .40
113 Jeering Instigator R :R: .25 .40
114 Leaping Master C :R: .15 .25
115 Mardu Blazebringer U :R: .20 .35
116 Mardu Heart-Piercer U :R: .20 .35
117 Mardu Warshrieker C :R: .15 .25
118 Monastery Swiftspear U :R: .20 .35
119 Sarkhan, the Dragonspeaker M :R: 2.25 2.75
120 Shatter C :R: .15 .25
121 Summit Prowler C :R: .15 .25
122 Swift Kick C :R: .15 .25
123 Tormenting Voice C :R: .15 .25
124 Trumpet Blast C :R: .15 .25
125 Valley Dasher C :R: .15 .25
126 War-Name Aspirant U :R: .20 .35
127 Alpine Grizzly C :G: .15 .25
128 Archers' Parapet C :G: .15 .25
129 Awaken the Bear C :G: .15 .25
130 Become Immense U :G: .20 .35
131 Dragonscale Boon C :G: .15 .25
132 Feed the Clan C :G: .15 .25
133 Hardened Scales R :G: 1.50 2.00
134 Heir of the Wilds U :G: .20 .35
135 Highland Game C :G: .15 .25
136 Hooded Hydra M :G: .75 1.15
137 Hooting Mandrills C :G: .15 .25
138 Incremental Growth U :G: .20 .35
139 Kin-Tree Warden C :G: .15 .25
140 Longshot Squad C :G: .15 .25
141 Meandering Towershell R :G: .25 .40
142 Naturalize C :G: .15 .25
143 Pine Walker U :G: .20 .35
144 Rattleclaw Mystic R :G: .50 .75
145 Roar of Challenge U :G: .20 .35
146 Sagu Archer C :G: .15 .25
147 Savage Punch C :G: .15 .25
148 Scout the Borders C :G: .15 .25
149 See the Unwritten M :G: .75 1.00
150 Seek the Horizon U :G: .20 .35
151 Smoke Teller C :G: .15 .25
152 Sultai Flayer U :G: .20 .35
153 Temur Charger U :G: .20 .35
154 Trail of Mystery R :G: .25 .40
155 Tusked Colossodon C :G: .15 .25
156 Tuskguard Captain U :G: .20 .35
157 Windstorm U :G: .20 .35
158 Woolly Loxodon C :G: .15 .25
159 Abomination of Gudul C :D: .15 .25
160 Abzan Ascendancy R :D: .25 .40
161 Abzan Charm U :D: .20 .35
162 Abzan Guide C :D: .15 .25
163 Anafenza, the Foremost M :D: 4.00 6.00
164 Ankle Shanker R :D: .25 .40
165 Armament Corps U :D: .20 .35
166 Avalanche Tusker R :D: .25 .40
167 Bear's Companion U :D: .20 .35
168 Butcher of the Horde R :D: .25 .40
169 Chief of the Edge U :W: :K: .20 .35
170 Chief of the Scale U :W: :K: .20 .35
171 Crackling Doom R :D: .40 .60
172 Death Frenzy U :K: :G: .20 .35
173 Deflecting Palm R :R: :W: .75 1.00
174 Duneblast R :D: .25 .40
175 Efreet Weaponmaster C :D: .15 .25
176 Flying Crane Technique R :D: .25 .40
177 Highspire Mantis U :R: :W: .20 .35
178 Icefeather Aven U :G: :B: .20 .35
179 Ivorytusk Fortress R :D: .25 .40
180 Jeskai Ascendancy R :D: .50 .75
181 Jeskai Charm U :D: .20 .35
182 Kheru Lich Lord R :D: .25 .40
183 Kin-Tree Invocation U :K: :G: .20 .35
184 Mantis Rider R :D: .30 .50
185 Mardu Ascendancy R :D: .25 .40
186 Mardu Charm U :D: .20 .35
187 Mardu Roughrider U :D: .20 .35
188 Master the Way U :B: :R: .20 .35
189 Mindswipe R :B: :R: .25 .40
190 Narset, Enlightened Master M :D: .75 1.00
191 Ponyback Brigade C :D: .15 .25
192 Rakshasa Deathdealer R :K: :G: .25 .40
193 Rakshasa Vizier R :D: .25 .40
194 Ride Down U :R: :W: .20 .35
195 Sage of the Inward Eye R :D: .25 .40
196 Sagu Mauler R :G: :B: .25 .40
197 Savage Knuckleblade R :D: .25 .40
198 Secret Plans U :G: :B: .20 .35
199 Sidisi, Brood Tyrant M :D: .75 1.00
200 Siege Rhino R :D: 1.25 1.50
201 Snowhorn Rider C :D: .15 .25
202 Sorin, Solemn Visitor M :D: 3.00 4.50
203 Sultai Ascendancy R :D: .25 .40
204 Sultai Charm U :D: .20 .35
205 Sultai Soothsayer U :D: .20 .35
206 Surrak Dragonclaw M :D: .75 1.00
207 Temur Ascendancy R :D: .25 .40
208 Temur Charm U :D: .20 .35
209 Trap Essence R :D: .25 .40
210 Utter End R :D: .50 .75
211 Villainous Wealth R :D: .25 .40
212 Warden of the Eye U :D: .20 .35
213 Winterflame U :B: :R: .20 .35
214 Zurgo Helmsmasher M :D: .50 .75
215 Abzan Banner C .15 .25
216 Altar of the Brood R .40 .60
217 Briber's Purse U .20 .35
218 Cranial Archive U .20 .35
219 Dragon Throne of Tarkir R .25 .40
220 Ghostfire Blade R .50 .75
221 Heart-Piercer Bow U .20 .35
222 Jeskai Banner C .15 .25
223 Lens of Clarity C .15 .25
224 Mardu Banner C .15 .25
225 Sultai Banner C .15 .25
226 Temur Banner C .15 .25
227 Ugin's Nexus M .50 .75
228 Witness of the Ages U .20 .35
229 Bloodfell Caves C .15 .25
230 Bloodstained Mire R 12.00 14.00
231 Blossoming Sands C .15 .25
232 Dismal Backwater C .15 .25
233 Flooded Strand R 14.00 16.00
234 Frontier Bivouac U :L: .20 .35
235 Jungle Hollow C .15 .25
236 Mystic Monastery U .20 .35
237 Nomad Outpost U .20 .35
238 Opulent Palace U :L: .20 .35
239 Polluted Delta R 15.00 17.00
240 Rugged Highlands C .15 .25
241 Sandsteppe Citadel U :L: .20 .35
242 Scoured Barrens C .15 .25
243 Swiftwater Cliffs C .15 .25
244 Thornwood Falls C .15 .25
245 Tomb of the Spirit Dragon U .20 .35
246 Tranquil Cove C .15 .25
247 Wind-Scarred Crag C .15 .25
248 Windswept Heath R 11.00 13.00
249 Wooded Foothills R 15.00 17.00
250 Plains (251) L .15 .25
251 Plains (252) L .15 .25
252 Plains (253) L .15 .25
253 Plains L .15 .25
254 Island (255) L .15 .25
255 Island (256) L .15 .25
256 Island (257) L .15 .25
257 Island L .15 .25
258 Swamp (259) L .15 .25
259 Swamp (260) L .15 .25
260 Swamp (261) L .15 .25
261 Swamp L .15 .25
262 Mountain (263) L .15 .25
263 Mountain (264) L .15 .25
264 Mountain (265) L .15 .25
265 Mountain L .15 .25
266 Forest (267) L .15 .25
267 Forest (268) L .15 .25
268 Forest (269) L .15 .25
269 Forest L .15 .25

2014 Magic The Gathering Khans of Tarkir Foil

1 Abzan Battle Priest U :W: .40 .60
2 Abzan Falconer U :W: .75 1.25
3 Ainok Bond-Kin C :W: .15 .25
4 Alabaster Kirin C :W: .15 .25
5 Brave the Sands U :W: 1.25 2.00
6 Dazzling Ramparts U :W: .20 .35
7 Defiant Strike C :W: .50 .75
8 End Hostilities R :W: 1.00 1.50
9 Erase C :W: .15 .25
10 Feat of Resistance C :W: .40 .60
11 Firehoof Cavalry C :W: .15 .25
12 Herald of Anafenza R :W: .50 .75
13 High Sentinels of Arashin R :W: .50 .75
14 Jeskai Student C :W: .15 .25
15 Kill Shot C :W: .15 .25
16 Mardu Hateblade C :W: .15 .25
17 Mardu Hordechief C :W: .15 .25
18 Master of Pearls R :W: .40 .60
19 Rush of Battle C :W: .15 .25
20 Sage-Eye Harrier C :W: .15 .25
21 Salt Road Patrol C :W: .15 .25
22 Seeker of the Way U :W: .40 .60
23 Siegecraft C :W: .15 .25
24 Smite the Monstrous C :W: .15 .25
25 Suspension Field U :W: .20 .35
26 Take Up Arms U :W: .20 .35
27 Timely Hordemate U :W: .20 .35
28 Venerable Lammasu U :W: .20 .35
29 War Behemoth U :W: .20 .35
30 Watcher of the Roost U :W: .20 .35
31 Wingmate Roc M :W: 2.00 3.50
32 Blinding Spray U :B: .20 .35
33 Cancel C :B: .15 .25
34 Clever Impersonator M :B: 13.00 16.00
35 Crippling Chill C :B: .15 .25
36 Dig Through Time R :B: 12.00 15.00
37 Disdainful Stroke C :B: .60 1.00
38 Dragon's Eye Savants U :B: .20 .35
39 Embodiment of Spring C :B: .15 .25
40 Force Away C :B: .15 .25
41 Glacial Stalker C :B: .15 .25
42 Icy Blast R :B: .50 .75
43 Jeskai Elder U :B: .20 .35
44 Jeskai Windscout C :B: .15 .25
45 Kheru Spellsnatcher R :B: .40 .60
46 Mistfire Weaver U :B: .20 .35
47 Monastery Flock C :B: .15 .25
48 Mystic of the Hidden Way C :B: .15 .25
49 Pearl Lake Ancient M :B: 1.00 1.50
50 Quiet Contemplation U :B: .20 .35
51 Riverwheel Aerialists U :B: .20 .35
52 Scaldkin C :B: .15 .25
53 Scion of Glaciers U :B: .20 .35
54 Set Adrift U :B: .20 .35
55 Singing Bell Strike C :B: .15 .25
56 Stubborn Denial U :B: 4.00 6.00
57 Taigam's Scheming C :B: .40 .60
58 Thousand Winds R :B: .25 .40
59 Treasure Cruise C :B: 4.00 6.00
60 Waterwhirl U :B: .20 .35
61 Weave Fate C :B: .15 .25
62 Wetland Sambar C :B: .15 .25
63 Whirlwind Adept C :B: .15 .25
64 Bellowing Saddlebrute U :K: .20 .35
65 Bitter Revelation C :K: .15 .25
66 Bloodsoaked Champion R :K: 1.75 2.50
67 Dead Drop U :K: .20 .35
68 Debilitating Injury C :K: .15 .25
69 Despise U :K: .60 1.00
70 Disowned Ancestor C :K: .15 .25
71 Dutiful Return C :K: .15 .25
72 Empty the Pits M :K: 1.00 1.50
73 Grim Haruspex R :K: 1.00 1.50
74 Gurmag Swiftwing U :K: .20 .35
75 Kheru Bloodsucker U :K: .20 .35
76 Kheru Dreadmaw C :K: .15 .25
77 Krumar Bond-Kin C :K: .15 .25
78 Mardu Skullhunter C :K: .15 .25
79 Mer-Ek Nightblade U :K: .20 .35
80 Molting Snakeskin C :K: .15 .25
81 Murderous Cut U :K: 3.50 5.00
82 Necropolis Fiend R :K: .30 .50
83 Raiders' Spoils U :K: .20 .35
84 Rakshasa's Secret C :K: .15 .25
85 Retribution of the Ancients R :K: .50 .75
86 Rite of the Serpent C :K: .15 .25
87 Rotting Mastodon C :K: .15 .25
88 Ruthless Ripper U :K: .50 .75
89 Shambling Attendants C :K: .15 .25
90 Sidisi's Pet C :K: .15 .25
91 Sultai Scavenger C :K: .15 .25
92 Swarm of Bloodflies U :K: .20 .35
93 Throttle C :K: .15 .25
94 Unyielding Krumar C :K: .15 .25
95 Act of Treason C :R: .15 .25
96 Ainok Tracker C :R: .15 .25
97 Arc Lightning U :R: .50 .75
98 Arrow Storm C :R: .15 .25
99 Ashcloud Phoenix M :R: 1.25 2.00
100 Barrage of Boulders C :R: .15 .25
101 Bloodfire Expert C :R: .15 .25
102 Bloodfire Mentor C :R: .15 .25
103 Bring Low C :R: .15 .25
104 Burn Away U :R: .20 .35
105 Canyon Lurkers C :R: .15 .25
106 Crater's Claws R :R: .75 1.25
107 Dragon Grip U :R: .20 .35
108 Dragon-Style Twins R :R: .50 .75
109 Goblinslide U :R: .30 .50
110 Horde Ambusher U :R: .20 .35
111 Hordeling Outburst U :R: 1.00 1.50
112 Howl of the Horde R :R: .75 1.00
113 Jeering Instigator R :R: .40 .60
114 Leaping Master C :R: .15 .25
115 Mardu Blazebringer U :R: .20 .35
116 Mardu Heart-Piercer U :R: .20 .35
117 Mardu Warshrieker C :R: .15 .25
118 Monastery Swiftspear U :R: 15.00 18.00
119 Sarkhan, the Dragonspeaker M :R: 6.00 8.00
120 Shatter C :R: .15 .25
121 Summit Prowler C :R: .15 .25
122 Swift Kick C :R: .15 .25
123 Tormenting Voice C :R: 1.00 1.50
124 Trumpet Blast C :R: .15 .25
125 Valley Dasher C :R: .15 .25
126 War-Name Aspirant U :R: .20 .35
127 Alpine Grizzly C :G: .15 .25
128 Archers' Parapet C :G: .15 .25
129 Awaken the Bear C :G: .15 .25
130 Become Immense U :G: 5.00 7.00
131 Dragonscale Boon C :G: .15 .25
132 Feed the Clan C :G: 2.00 3.00
133 Hardened Scales R :G: 5.00 7.00
134 Heir of the Wilds U :G: .20 .35
135 Highland Game C :G: .15 .25
136 Hooded Hydra M :G: 2.50 4.00
137 Hooting Mandrills C :G: 2.00 3.00
138 Incremental Growth U :G: .20 .35
139 Kin-Tree Warden C :G: .15 .25
140 Longshot Squad C :G: .15 .25
141 Meandering Towershell R :G: .50 .75
142 Naturalize C :G: .15 .25
143 Pine Walker U :G: .20 .35
144 Rattleclaw Mystic R :G: 1.00 1.50
145 Roar of Challenge U :G: .20 .35
146 Sagu Archer C :G: .15 .25
147 Savage Punch C :G: .15 .25
148 Scout the Borders C :G: .15 .25
149 See the Unwritten M :G: 3.50 5.00
150 Seek the Horizon U :G: .20 .35
151 Smoke Teller C :G: .15 .25
152 Sultai Flayer U :G: .20 .35
153 Temur Charger U :G: .20 .35
154 Trail of Mystery R :G: .40 .60
155 Tusked Colossodon C :G: .15 .25
156 Tuskguard Captain U :G: .20 .35
157 Windstorm U :G: .20 .35
158 Woolly Loxodon C :G: .15 .25
159 Abomination of Gudul C :D: .15 .25
160 Abzan Ascendancy R :D: 1.00 1.50
161 Abzan Charm U :D: 2.00 3.00
162 Abzan Guide C :D: .15 .25
163 Anafenza, the Foremost M :D: 18.00 22.00
164 Ankle Shanker R :D: .40 .60
165 Armament Corps U :D: .20 .35
166 Avalanche Tusker R :D: .25 .40
167 Bear's Companion U :D: .20 .35

Card	Low	High
168 Butcher of the Horde R :D:	1.00	1.50
169 Chief of the Edge U :W: :K:	.50	.75
170 Chief of the Scale U :W: :K:	.20	.35
171 Crackling Doom R :D:	1.50	2.50
172 Death Frenzy U :K: :G:	.20	.35
173 Deflecting Palm R :R: :W:	3.00	5.00
174 Duneblast R :D:	.60	1.00
175 Efreet Weaponmaster C :D:	.15	.25
176 Flying Crane Technique R :D:	.40	.60
177 Highspire Mantis U :R: :W:	.20	.35
178 Icefeather Aven U :G: :B:	.20	.35
179 Ivorytusk Fortress R :D:	.40	.60
180 Jeskai Ascendancy R :D:	2.50	3.50
181 Jeskai Charm U :D:	.40	.60
182 Kheru Lich Lord R :D:	.40	.60
183 Kin-Tree Invocation U :K: :G:	.20	.35
184 Mantis Rider R :D:	7.00	10.00
185 Mardu Ascendancy R :D:	.75	1.25
186 Mardu Charm U :D:	.50	.75
187 Mardu Roughrider U :D:	.20	.35
188 Master the Way U :B: :R:	.20	.35
189 Mindswipe R :B: :R:	.60	1.00
190 Narset, Enlightened Master M :D:	6.00	8.00
191 Ponyback Brigade C :D:	.15	.25
192 Rakshasa Deathdealer R :K: :G:	1.00	1.50
193 Rakshasa Vizier R :D:	.30	.50
194 Ride Down U :R: :W:	.20	.35
195 Sage of the Inward Eye R :D:	.40	.60
196 Sagu Mauler R :G: :B:	.75	1.25
197 Savage Knuckleblade R :D:	1.00	1.50
198 Secret Plans U :G: :B:	.20	.35
199 Sidisi, Brood Tyrant M :D:	3.50	5.00
200 Siege Rhino R :D:	6.00	8.00
201 Snowhorn Rider C :D:	.15	.25
202 Sorin, Solemn Visitor M :D:	11.00	13.00
203 Sultai Ascendancy R :D:	.40	.60
204 Sultai Charm U :D:	.60	1.00
205 Sultai Soothsayer U :D:	.20	.35
206 Surrak Dragonclaw M :D:	3.50	5.00
207 Temur Ascendancy R :D:	1.25	2.00
208 Temur Charm U :D:	.50	.75
209 Trap Essence R :D:	.30	.50
210 Utter End R :D:	1.50	2.00
211 Villainous Wealth R :D:	1.00	1.50
212 Warden of the Eye U :D:	.20	.35
213 Winterflame U :B: :R:	.20	.35
214 Zurgo Helmsmasher M :D:	1.50	2.50
215 Abzan Banner C	.15	.25
216 Altar of the Brood R	3.00	4.50
217 Briber's Purse U	.20	.35
218 Cranial Archive U	.20	.35
219 Dragon Throne of Tarkir R	.30	.50
220 Ghostfire Blade R	1.50	2.50
221 Heart-Piercer Bow U	.20	.35
222 Jeskai Banner C	.15	.25
223 Lens of Clarity C	.15	.25
224 Mardu Banner C	.15	.25
225 Sultai Banner C	.15	.25
226 Temur Banner C	.15	.25
227 Ugin's Nexus M	2.50	4.00
228 Witness of the Ages U	.20	.35
229 Bloodfell Caves C	.40	.60
230 Bloodstained Mire R	30.00	35.00
231 Blossoming Sands C	.40	.60
232 Dismal Backwater C	.60	1.00
233 Flooded Strand R	35.00	45.00
234 Frontier Bivouac U :L:	2.00	3.00
235 Jungle Hollow C	.50	.75
236 Mystic Monastery U	2.00	3.50
237 Nomad Outpost U	2.50	3.50
238 Opulent Palace U :L:	2.50	3.50
239 Polluted Delta R	45.00	55.00
240 Rugged Highlands C	.40	.60
241 Sandsteppe Citadel U :L:	1.25	2.00
242 Scoured Barrens C	.60	1.00
243 Swiftwater Cliffs C	.60	1.00
244 Thornwood Falls C	.40	.60
245 Tomb of the Spirit Dragon U	2.00	3.00
246 Tranquil Cove C	.50	.75
247 Wind-Scarred Crag C	.40	.60
248 Windswept Heath R	30.00	35.00
249 Wooded Foothills R	35.00	40.00
250 Plains (251) L	.15	.25
251 Plains (252) L	.15	.25
252 Plains (253) L	.15	.25
253 Plains L	.15	.25
254 Island (255) L	.15	.25
255 Island (256) L	.15	.25
256 Island (257) L	.15	.25
257 Island L	.15	.25
258 Swamp (259) L	.15	.25
259 Swamp (260) L	.15	.25
260 Swamp (261) L	.15	.25
261 Swamp L	.15	.25
262 Mountain (263) L	.15	.25
263 Mountain (264) L	.15	.25
264 Mountain (265) L	.15	.25
265 Mountain L	.15	.25
266 Forest (267) L	.15	.25
267 Forest (268) L	.15	.25
268 Forest (269) L	.15	.25
269 Forest L	.15	.25

2014 Magic The Gathering Khans of Tarkir Promos

Card	Low	High
160P Abzan Ascendancy		
163P Anafenza, the Foremost	4.00	10.00
164P Ankle Shanker	1.25	3.00
166P Avalanche Tusker	1.50	4.00
66P Bloodsoaked Champion	3.00	8.00
168P Butcher of the Horde	5.00	12.00
171P Crackling Doom	3.00	8.00
106P Crater's Claws	1.50	4.00
173P Deflecting Palm	2.50	6.00
36P Dig Through Time	12.00	30.00
108P Dragon-Style Twins	2.00	5.00
174P Duneblast	2.50	6.00
176P Flying Crane Technique	2.50	6.00
73P Grim Haruspex	1.50	4.00
133P Hardened Scales	1.50	4.00
12P Herald of Anafenza		
13P High Sentinels of Arashin		
42P Icy Blast		
179P Ivorytusk Fortress		
113P Jeering Instigator		
180P Jeskai Ascendancy	6.00	15.00
182P Kheru Lich Lord	1.50	4.00
185P Mardu Ascendancy	2.00	5.00
18P Master of Pearls		
190P Narset, Enlightened Master	5.00	12.00
82P Necropolis Fiend	2.00	5.00
193P Rakshasa Vizier		
144P Rattleclaw Mystic	2.50	6.00
195P Sage of the Inward Eye	1.25	3.00
199P Sidisi, Brood Tyrant	5.00	12.00
200P Siege Rhino	6.00	15.00
203P Sultai Ascendancy	1.25	3.00
206P Surrak Dragonclaw	5.00	12.00
207P Temur Ascendancy	2.50	6.00
58P Thousand Winds	2.50	6.00
154P Trail of Mystery	1.50	4.00
209P Trap Essence	2.50	6.00
210P Utter End	6.00	15.00
211P Villainous Wealth	3.00	8.00
214P Zurgo Helmsmasher	3.00	8.00

2014 Magic The Gathering Khans of Tarkir Tokens

Card	Low	High
1 Bird	.50	.75
2 Spirit	.10	.15
3 Warrior	.10	.15
4 Warrior	.10	.15
5 Vampire	1.50	2.00
6 Zombie	.40	.60
7 Goblin	.10	.15
8 Bear	.12	.20
9 Snake	.15	.25
10 Spirit Warrior	.10	.15
11 Morph	.10	.15
12 Sarkhan, the Dragonspeaker Emblem	.15	.25
13 Sorin, Solemn Visitor Emblem	.35	.50

2015 Magic The Gathering Fate Reforged

Card	Low	High
COMPLETE SET (189)	80.00	115.00
BOOSTER BOX (36 PACKS)	90.00	110.00
BOOSTER PACK (15 CARDS)	4.00	5.00
FAT PACK	35.00	50.00
RELEASED ON JANUARY 23, 2015		
1 Ugin, the Spirit Dragon M	30.00	35.00
2 Abzan Advantage C :W:	.10	.20
3 Abzan Runemark C :W:	.10	.20
4 Abzan Skycaptain C :W:	.10	.20
5 Arashin Cleric C :W:	.10	.20
6 Aven Skirmisher C :W:	.10	.20
7 Channel Harm U :W:	.15	.25
8 Citadel Siege R :W:	.30	.50
9 Daghatar the Adamant R :W:	.30	.50
10 Dragon Bell Monk C :W:	.10	.20
11 Dragonscale General R :W:	.30	.50
12 Elite Scaleguard U :W:	.15	.25
13 Great-Horn Krushok C :W:	.10	.20
14 Honor's Reward U :W:	.15	.25
15 Jeskai Barricade U :W:	.15	.25
16 Lightform U :W:	.15	.25
17 Lotus-Eye Mystics U :W:	.15	.25
18 Mardu Woe-Reaper U :W:	.15	.25
19 Mastery of the Unseen R :W:	.30	.50
20 Monastery Mentor M :W:	7.00	10.00
21 Pressure Point C :W:	.10	.20
22 Rally the Ancestors R :W:	.30	.50
23 Sage's Reverie U :W:	.15	.25
24 Sandblast C :W:	.10	.20
25 Sandsteppe Outcast C :W:	.10	.20
26 Soul Summons C :W:	.10	.20
27 Soulfire Grand Master M :W:	2.00	3.00
28 Valorous Stance U :W:	.15	.25
29 Wandering Champion U :W:	.15	.25
30 Wardscale Dragon U :W:	.15	.25
31 Aven Surveyor C :B:	.10	.20
32 Cloudform U :B:	.15	.25
33 Enhanced Awareness C :B:	.10	.20
34 Fascination U :B:	.15	.25
35 Frost Walker U :B:	.15	.25
36 Jeskai Infiltrator R :B:	.30	.50
37 Jeskai Runemark C :B:	.10	.20
38 Jeskai Sage C :B:	.10	.20
39 Lotus Path Djinn C :B:	.10	.20
40 Marang River Prowler U :B:	.15	.25
41 Mindscour Dragon U :B:	.15	.25
42 Mistfire Adept U :B:	.15	.25
43 Monastery Siege R :B:	.30	.50
44 Neutralizing Blast U :B:	.15	.25
45 Rakshasa's Disdain C :B:	.10	.20
46 Reality Shift U :B:	.15	.25
47 Refocus C :B:	.10	.20
48 Renowned Weaponsmith U :B:	.15	.25
49 Rite of Undoing U :B:	.15	.25
50 Sage-Eye Avengers R :B:	.30	.50
51 Shifting Loyalties U :B:	.15	.25
52 Shu Yun, the Silent Tempest R :B:	.30	.50
53 Sultai Skullkeeper C :B:	.10	.20
54 Supplant Form R :B:	.30	.50
55 Temporal Trespass M :B:	1.50	2.50
56 Torrent Elemental M :B:	.30	.50
57 Whisk Away C :B:	.10	.20
58 Will of the Naga C :B:	.10	.20
59 Write into Being C :B:	.10	.20
60 Alesha's Vanguard C :K:	.10	.20
61 Ancestral Vengeance C :K:	.10	.20
62 Archfiend of Depravity R :K:	.60	1.00
63 Battle Brawler U :K:	.15	.25
64 Brutal Hordechief M :K:	.50	.80
65 Crux of Fate R :K:	.50	.80
66 Dark Deal U :K:	.15	.25
67 Diplomacy of the Wastes U :K:	.15	.25
68 Douse in Gloom C :K:	.10	.20
69 Fearsome Awakening U :K:	.15	.25
70 Ghastly Conscription M :K:	.25	.40
71 Grave Strength U :K:	.15	.25
72 Gurmag Angler C :K:	.10	.20
73 Hooded Assassin C :K:	.10	.20
74 Mardu Shadowspear U :K:	.15	.25
75 Mardu Strike Leader R :K:	.30	.50
76 Merciless Executioner U :K:	.15	.25
77 Noxious Dragon U :K:	.15	.25
78 Orc Sureshot U :K:	.15	.25
79 Palace Siege R :K:	.40	.60
80 Qarsi High Priest U :K:	.15	.25
81 Reach of Shadows C :K:	.10	.20
82 Sibsig Host C :K:	.10	.20
83 Sibsig Muckdraggers U :K:	.15	.25
84 Soulflayer R :K:	.30	.50
85 Sultai Emissary C :K:	.10	.20
86 Sultai Runemark C :K:	.10	.20
87 Tasigur, the Golden Fang R :K:	1.50	2.50
88 Tasigur's Cruelty C :K:	.10	.20
89 Typhoid Rats C :K:	.10	.20
90 Alesha, Who Smiles at Death R :R:	.30	.50
91 Arcbond R :R:	.30	.50
92 Bathe in Dragonfire C :R:	.10	.20
93 Bloodfire Enforcers U :R:	.15	.25
94 Break Through the Line U :R:	.15	.25
95 Collateral Damage C :R:	.10	.20
96 Defiant Ogre C :R:	.10	.20
97 Dragonrage U :R:	.15	.25
98 Fierce Invocation C :R:	.10	.20
99 Flamerush Rider R :R:	.30	.50
100 Flamewake Phoenix R :R:	.30	.50
101 Friendly Fire U :R:	.15	.25
102 Goblin Heelcutter C :R:	.10	.20
103 Gore Swine C :R:	.10	.20
104 Humble Defector U :R:	.15	.25
105 Hungering Yeti U :R:	.15	.25
106 Lightning Shrieker C :R:	.10	.20
107 Mardu Runemark C :R:	.10	.20
108 Mardu Scout C :R:	.10	.20
109 Mob Rule R :R:	.30	.50
110 Outpost Siege R :R:	.30	.50
111 Pyrotechnics U :R:	.15	.25
112 Rageform U :R:	.15	.25
113 Shaman of the Great Hunt M :R:	.40	.60
114 Shockmaw Dragon U :R:	.15	.25
115 Smoldering Efreet C :R:	.10	.20
116 Temur Battle Rage C :R:	.10	.20
117 Vaultbreaker U :R:	.15	.25
118 Wild Slash U :R:	.15	.25
119 Abzan Beastmaster U :G:	.15	.25
120 Abzan Kin-Guard U :G:	.15	.25
121 Ainok Guide C :G:	.10	.20
122 Ambush Krotiq C :G:	.10	.20
123 Arashin War Beast U :G:	.15	.25
124 Archers of Qarsi C :G:	.10	.20
125 Battlefront Krushok U :G:	.15	.25
126 Cached Defenses U :G:	.15	.25
127 Destructor Dragon U :G:	.15	.25
128 Feral Krushok C :G:	.10	.20
129 Formless Nurturing C :G:	.10	.20
130 Frontier Mastodon C :G:	.10	.20
131 Frontier Siege R :G:	.30	.50
132 Fruit of the First Tree U :G:	.15	.25
133 Hunt the Weak C :G:	.10	.20
134 Map the Wastes C :G:	.10	.20
135 Return to the Earth C :G:	.10	.20
136 Ruthless Instincts U :G:	.15	.25
137 Sandsteppe Mastodon R :G:	.30	.50
138 Shamanic Revelation R :G:	.30	.50
139 Sudden Reclamation U :G:	.15	.25
140 Temur Runemark C :G:	.10	.20
141 Temur Sabertooth U :G:	.15	.25
142 Temur War Shaman R :G:	.30	.50
143 Warden of the First Tree M :G:	.50	.80
144 Whisperer of the Wilds C :G:	.10	.20
145 Whisperwood Elemental M :G:	.40	.60
146 Wildcall R :G:	.30	.50
147 Winds of Qal Sisma U :G:	.15	.25
148 Yasova Dragonclaw R :G:	.30	.50
149 Atarka, World Render R :M:	.30	.50
150 Cunning Strike C :M:	.10	.20
151 Dromoka, the Eternal R :M:	.30	.50
152 Ethereal Ambush C :M:	.10	.20
153 Grim Contest C :M:	.10	.20
154 Harsh Sustenance C :M:	.10	.20
155 Kolaghan, the Storm's Fury R :M:	.30	.50
156 Ojutai, Soul of Winter R :M:	.30	.50
157 Silumgar, the Drifting Death R :M:	.30	.50
158 War Flare C :M:	.10	.20
159 Goblin Boom Keg U	.15	.25
160 Hero's Blade U	.15	.25
161 Hewed Stone Retainers U	.15	.25
162 Pilgrim of the Fires U	.15	.25
163 Scroll of the Masters R	.30	.50
164 Ugin's Construct U	.15	.25
165 Bloodfell Caves C	.10	.20
166 Blossoming Sands C	.10	.20
167 Crucible of the Spirit Dragon R	.30	.50
168 Dismal Backwater C	.10	.20
169 Jungle Hollow C	.10	.20
170 Rugged Highlands C	.10	.20
171 Scoured Barrens C	.10	.20
172 Swiftwater Cliffs C	.10	.20
173 Thornwood Falls C	.10	.20
174 Tranquil Cove C	.10	.20
175 Wind-Scarred Crag C	.10	.20
176 Plains L	.10	.20
177 Plains L	.10	.20
178 Island L	.10	.20
179 Island L	.10	.20
180 Swamp L	.10	.20
181 Swamp L	.10	.20
182 Mountain L	.10	.20
183 Mountain L	.10	.20
184 Forest L	.10	.20
185 Forest L	.10	.20

2015 Magic The Gathering Fate Reforged Foil

Card	Low	High
1 Ugin, the Spirit Dragon M	90.00	100.00
2 Abzan Advantage C :W:	.20	.35
3 Abzan Runemark C :W:	.20	.35
4 Abzan Skycaptain C :W:	.20	.35
5 Arashin Cleric C :W:	.20	.35
6 Aven Skirmisher C :W:	.20	.35
7 Channel Harm U :W:	.30	.50
8 Citadel Siege R :W:	1.00	1.50
9 Daghatar the Adamant R :W:	.50	.80
10 Dragon Bell Monk C :W:	.20	.35
11 Dragonscale General R :W:	.50	.80
12 Elite Scaleguard U :W:	.30	.50
13 Great-Horn Krushok C :W:	.20	.35
14 Honor's Reward U :W:	.30	.50
15 Jeskai Barricade U :W:	.30	.50
16 Lightform U :W:	.30	.50
17 Lotus-Eye Mystics U :W:	.30	.50
18 Mardu Woe-Reaper U :W:	.30	.50
19 Mastery of the Unseen R :W:	.50	.80
20 Monastery Mentor M :W:	35.00	40.00
21 Pressure Point C :W:	.20	.35
22 Rally the Ancestors R :W:	1.00	1.50
23 Sage's Reverie U :W:	.30	.50
24 Sandblast C :W:	.20	.35
25 Sandsteppe Outcast C :W:	.20	.35
26 Soul Summons C :W:	.20	.35
27 Soulfire Grand Master M :W:	7.00	10.00
28 Valorous Stance U :W:	.30	.50
29 Wandering Champion U :W:	.30	.50
30 Wardscale Dragon U :W:	.30	.50
31 Aven Surveyor C :B:	.20	.35
32 Cloudform U :B:	.30	.50
33 Enhanced Awareness C :B:	.20	.35
34 Fascination U :B:	.30	.50
35 Frost Walker U :B:	.30	.50
36 Jeskai Infiltrator R :B:	.30	.50
37 Jeskai Runemark C :B:	.20	.35
38 Jeskai Sage C :B:	.20	.35
39 Lotus Path Djinn C :B:	.20	.35
40 Marang River Prowler U :B:	.30	.50
41 Mindscour Dragon U :B:	.30	.50
42 Mistfire Adept U :B:	.30	.50
43 Monastery Siege R :B:	1.50	2.50
44 Neutralizing Blast U :B:	.30	.50
45 Rakshasa's Disdain C :B:	.20	.35
46 Reality Shift U :B:	.30	.50
47 Refocus C :B:	.20	.35
48 Renowned Weaponsmith U :B:	.30	.50
49 Rite of Undoing U :B:	.30	.50
50 Sage-Eye Avengers R :B:	.30	.50
51 Shifting Loyalties U :B:	.30	.50
52 Shu Yun, the Silent Tempest R :B:	1.50	2.00
53 Sultai Skullkeeper C :B:	.20	.35
54 Supplant Form R :B:	.40	.60
55 Temporal Trespass M :B:	5.00	7.00
56 Torrent Elemental M :B:	1.50	2.50
57 Whisk Away C :B:	.20	.35
58 Will of the Naga C :B:	.20	.35
59 Write into Being C :B:	.20	.35
60 Alesha's Vanguard C :K:	.20	.35
61 Ancestral Vengeance C :K:	.20	.35
62 Archfiend of Depravity R :K:	1.50	2.00
63 Battle Brawler U :K:	.30	.50
64 Brutal Hordechief M :K:	2.00	3.00
65 Crux of Fate R :K:	5.00	8.00
66 Dark Deal U :K:	.30	.50
67 Diplomacy of the Wastes U :K:	.30	.50
68 Douse in Gloom C :K:	.20	.35
69 Fearsome Awakening U :K:	.30	.50
70 Ghastly Conscription M :K:	1.00	1.50
71 Grave Strength U :K:	.30	.50
72 Gurmag Angler C :K:	.20	.35
73 Hooded Assassin C :K:	.20	.35
74 Mardu Shadowspear U :K:	.30	.50
75 Mardu Strike Leader R :K:	.75	1.25
76 Merciless Executioner U :K:	.30	.50
77 Noxious Dragon U :K:	.30	.50
78 Orc Sureshot U :K:	.30	.50
79 Palace Siege R :K:	1.50	2.50
80 Qarsi High Priest U :K:	.30	.50
81 Reach of Shadows C :K:	.20	.35
82 Sibsig Host C :K:	.20	.35
83 Sibsig Muckdraggers U :K:	.30	.50
84 Soulflayer R :K:	.60	1.00
85 Sultai Emissary C :K:	.20	.35
86 Sultai Runemark C :K:	.20	.35
87 Tasigur, the Golden Fang R :K:	15.00	20.00
88 Tasigur's Cruelty C :K:	.20	.35
89 Typhoid Rats C :K:	.20	.35
90 Alesha, Who Smiles at Death R :R:	3.00	5.00
91 Arcbond R :R:	.50	.80
92 Bathe in Dragonfire C :R:	.20	.35
93 Bloodfire Enforcers U :R:	.30	.50
94 Break Through the Line U :R:	.30	.50
95 Collateral Damage C :R:	.20	.35
96 Defiant Ogre C :R:	.20	.35
97 Dragonrage U :R:	.30	.50
98 Fierce Invocation C :R:	.20	.35
99 Flamerush Rider R :R:	.40	.60
100 Flamewake Phoenix R :R:	.40	1.00
101 Friendly Fire U :R:	.30	.50
102 Goblin Heelcutter C :R:	.20	.35
103 Gore Swine C :R:	.20	.35
104 Humble Defector U :R:	.30	.50
105 Hungering Yeti U :R:	.30	.50
106 Lightning Shrieker C :R:	.20	.35
107 Mardu Runemark C :R:	.20	.35
108 Mardu Scout C :R:	.20	.35
109 Mob Rule R :R:	.60	1.00
110 Outpost Siege R :R:	2.50	4.00
111 Pyrotechnics U :R:	.30	.50
112 Rageform U :R:	.30	.50
113 Shaman of the Great Hunt M :R:	1.50	2.50
114 Shockmaw Dragon U :R:	.30	.50
115 Smoldering Efreet C :R:	.20	.35
116 Temur Battle Rage C :R:	.20	.35
117 Vaultbreaker U :R:	.30	.50
118 Wild Slash U :R:	.30	.50
119 Abzan Beastmaster U :G:	.30	.50
120 Abzan Kin-Guard U :G:	.30	.50
121 Ainok Guide C :G:	.20	.35
122 Ambush Krotiq C :G:	.20	.35
123 Arashin War Beast U :G:	.30	.50

124 Archers of Qarsi C :G: .20 .35
125 Battlefront Krushok U :G: .30 .50
126 Cached Defenses U :G: .30 .50
127 Destructor Dragon U :G: .30 .50
128 Feral Krushok C :G: .20 .35
129 Formless Nurturing C :G: .20 .35
130 Frontier Mastodon C :G: .20 .35
131 Frontier Siege R :G: 1.50 2.00
132 Fruit of the First Tree U :G: .30 .50
133 Hunt the Weak C :G: .20 .35
134 Map the Wastes C :G: .20 .35
135 Return to the Earth C :G: .20 .35
136 Ruthless Instincts U :G: .30 .50
137 Sandsteppe Mastodon R :G: .30 .50
138 Shamanic Revelation R :G: .60 1.00
139 Sudden Reclamation U :G: .30 .50
140 Temur Runemark C :G: .20 .35
141 Temur Sabertooth U :G: .30 .50
142 Temur War Shaman R :G: .25 .40
143 Warden of the First Tree M :G: 2.00 3.00
144 Whisperer of the Wilds C :G: .20 .35
145 Whisperwood Elemental M :G: 3.00 4.00
146 Wildcall R :G: .40 .60
147 Winds of Qal Sisma U :G: .30 .50
148 Yasova Dragonclaw R :G: 1.50 2.00
149 Atarka, World Render R :M: 1.50 2.50
150 Cunning Strike C :M: .20 .35
151 Dromoka, the Eternal R :M: .50 .80
152 Ethereal Ambush C :M: .20 .35
153 Grim Contest C :M: .20 .35
154 Harsh Sustenance C :M: .20 .35
155 Kolaghan, the Storm's Fury R :M: 2.00 3.00
156 Ojutai, Soul of Winter R :M: 1.00 1.50
157 Silumgar, the Drifting Death R :M: 1.50 2.00
158 War Flare C :M: .20 .35
159 Goblin Boom Keg U .30 .50
160 Hero's Blade U .30 .50
161 Hewed Stone Retainers U .30 .50
162 Pilgrim of the Fires U .30 .50
163 Scroll of the Masters R .30 .50
164 Ugin's Construct U .30 .50
165 Bloodfell Caves C .20 .35
166 Blossoming Sands C .20 .35
167 Crucible of the Spirit Dragon R 1.25 2.00
168 Dismal Backwater C .20 .35
169 Jungle Hollow C .20 .35
170 Rugged Highlands C .20 .35
171 Scoured Barrens C .20 .35
172 Swiftwater Cliffs C .20 .35
173 Thornwood Falls C .20 .35
174 Tranquil Cove C .20 .35
175 Wind-Scarred Crag C .20 .35
176 Plains L .20 .35
177 Plains L .20 .35
178 Island L .20 .35
179 Island L .20 .35
180 Swamp L .20 .35
181 Swamp L .20 .35
182 Mountain L .20 .35
183 Mountain L .20 .35
184 Forest L .20 .35
185 Forest L .20 .35

2015 Magic The Gathering Fate Reforged Promos

90P Alesha, Who Smiles at Death 6.00 15.00
91P Arcbond 4.00 10.00
62P Archfiend of Depravity 2.00 5.00
149P Atarka, World Render 6.00 15.00
64P Brutal Hordechief 8.00 20.00
9P Daghatar the Adamant 2.50 6.00
11P Dragonscale General 3.00 8.00
151P Dromoka, the Eternal 5.00 12.00
99P Flamerush Rider 1.50 4.00
100P Flamewake Phoenix 4.00 10.00
36P Jeskai Infiltrator 1.50 4.00
155P Kolaghan, the Storm's Fury 3.00 8.00
75P Mardu Strike Leader 4.00 10.00
19P Mastery of the Unseen 4.00 10.00
156P Ojutai, Soul of Winter 4.00 10.00
22P Rally the Ancestors 1.50 4.00
50P Sage-Eye Avengers
137P Sandsteppe Mastodon 1.50 4.00
113P Shaman of the Great Hunt 5.00 12.00
138P Shamanic Revelation 2.00 5.00
52P Shu Yun, the Silent Tempest 3.00 8.00
157P Silumgar, the Drifting Death 4.00 10.00
27P Soulfire Grand Master 15.00 40.00
84P Soulflayer 1.50 4.00
54P Supplant Form 2.50 6.00
87P Tasigur, the Golden Fang 8.00 20.00
56P Torrent Elemental 4.00 10.00
143P Warden of the First Tree 6.00 15.00
146P Wildcall 2.00 5.00
148P Yasova Dragonclaw

2015 Magic The Gathering Fate Reforged Tokens

1 Monk .75 1.25
2 Spirit .10 .15
3 Warrior .10 .15
4 Manifest .10 .15

2015 Magic The Gathering Dragons of Tarkir

COMPLETE SET (264) 125.00 180.00
BOOSTER BOX (36 PACKS) 80.00 110.00
BOOSTER PACK (15 CARDS) 4.00 5.00
FAT PACK 15.00 25.00
RELEASED ON MARCH 27, 2015
2 Anafenza, Kin-Tree Spirit R :W: .75 1.25
3 Arashin Foremost R :W: .30 .50
4 Artful Maneuver C :W: .10 .20
5 Aven Sunstriker U :W: .15 .25
6 Aven Tactician C :W: .10 .20
7 Battle Mastery U :W: .15 .25
8 Center Soul C :W: .10 .20
9 Champion of Arashin C :W: .10 .20
10 Dragon Hunter U :W: .15 .25
11 Dragon's Eye Sentry C :W: .10 .20
12 Dromoka Captain U :W: .15 .25
13 Dromoka Dunecaster C :W: .10 .20
14 Dromoka Warrior C :W: .10 .20
15 Echoes of the Kin Tree U :W: .15 .25
16 Enduring Victory C :W: .10 .20
17 Fate Forgotten C :W: .10 .20
18 Glaring Aegis C :W: .10 .20
19 Gleam of Authority R :W: .30 .50
20 Graceblade Artisan U :W: .15 .25
21 Great Teacher's Decree U :W: .15 .25
22 Herald of Dromoka C :W: .10 .20
23 Hidden Dragonslayer R :W: .50 .75
24 Lightwalker C :W: .10 .20
25 Misthoof Kirin C :W: .10 .20
26 Myth Realized R :W: .30 .50
27 Ojutai Exemplars M :W: .75 1.00
28 Orator of Ojutai U :W: .15 .25
29 Pacifism C :W: .10 .20
30 Profound Journey R :W: .30 .50
31 Radiant Purge R :W: .30 .50
32 Resupply C :W: .10 .20
33 Sandcrafter Mage C :W: .10 .20
34 Sandstorm Charger C :W: .10 .20
35 Scale Blessing U :W: .15 .25
36 Secure the Wastes R :W: 1.25 1.75
37 Shieldhide Dragon U :W: .15 .25
38 Silkwrap U :W: .15 .25
39 Strongarm Monk U :W: .15 .25
40 Student of Ojutai C :W: .10 .20
41 Sunscorch Regent R :W: .50 .75
42 Surge of Righteousness U :W: .15 .25
43 Territorial Roc C :W: .10 .20
44 Ancient Carp C :B: .10 .20
45 Anticipate C :B: .10 .20
46 Belltoll Dragon R :B: .30 .50
47 Blessed Reincarnation R :B: .30 .50
48 Clone Legion M :B: .75 1.15
49 Contradict C :B: .10 .20
50 Dance of the Skywise U :B: .15 .25
51 Dirgur Nemesis C :B: .10 .20
52 Dragonlord's Prerogative R :B: .30 .50
53 Elusive Spellfist C :B: .10 .20
54 Encase in Ice U :B: .15 .25
55 Glint C :B: .10 .20
56 Gudul Lurker U :B: .15 .25
57 Gurmag Drowner C :B: .10 .20
58 Icefall Regent R :B: .50 .75
59 Illusory Gains R :B: .30 .50
60 Learn from the Past U :B: .15 .25
61 Living Lore R :B: .30 .50
62 Mirror Mockery R :B: .30 .50
63 Monastery Loremaster C :B: .10 .20
64 Mystic Meditation C :B: .10 .20
65 Negate C :B: .10 .20
66 Ojutai Interceptor C :B: .10 .20
67 Ojutai's Breath C :B: .10 .20
68 Ojutai's Summons C :B: .10 .20
69 Palace Familiar C :B: .10 .20
70 Profaner of the Dead R :B: .30 .50
71 Qarsi Deceiver U :B: .15 .25
72 Reduce in Stature C :B: .10 .20
73 Shorecrasher Elemental M :B: .50 .75
74 Sidisi's Faithful C :B: .10 .20
75 Sight Beyond Sight U :B: .15 .25
76 Silumgar Sorcerer U :B: .15 .25
77 Silumgar Spell-Eater U :B: .15 .25
78 Silumgar's Scorn U :B: .15 .25
79 Skywise Teachings U :B: .15 .25
80 Stratus Dancer R :B: .60 1.00
81 Taigam's Strike C :B: .10 .20
82 Updraft Elemental C :B: .10 .20
83 Void Squall U :B: .15 .25
84 Youthful Scholar U :B: .15 .25
85 Zephyr Scribe C :B: .10 .20
86 Acid-Spewer Dragon U :K: .15 .25
87 Ambuscade Shaman U :K: .15 .25
88 Blood-Chin Fanatic R :K: .30 .50
89 Blood-Chin Rager U :K: .15 .25
90 Butcher's Glee C :K: .10 .20
91 Coat with Venom C :K: .10 .20
92 Corpseweft R :K: .30 .50
93 Damnable Pact R :K: .30 .50
94 Deadly Wanderings U :K: .15 .25
95 Death Wind U :K: .15 .25
96 Deathbringer Regent R :K: .30 .50
97 Defeat C :K: .10 .20
98 Duress C :K: .10 .20
99 Dutiful Attendant C :K: .10 .20
100 Flatten C :K: .10 .20
101 Foul Renewal R :K: .30 .50
102 Foul-Tongue Invocation U :K: .15 .25
103 Foul-Tongue Shriek C :K: .10 .20
104 Gravepurge C :K: .10 .20
105 Hand of Silumgar C :K: .10 .20
106 Hedonist's Trove R :K: .30 .50
107 Kolaghan Skirmisher C :K: .10 .20
108 Marang River Skeleton U :K: .15 .25
109 Marsh Hulk C :K: .10 .20
110 Mind Rot C :K: .10 .20
111 Minister of Pain U :K: .15 .25
112 Pitiless Horde R :K: .30 .50
113 Qarsi Sadist C :K: .10 .20
114 Rakshasa Gravecaller U :K: .15 .25
115 Reckless Imp C :K: .10 .20
116 Risen Executioner M :K: 1.50 2.00
117 Self-Inflicted Wound U :K: .15 .25
118 Shambling Goblin C :K: .10 .20
119 Sibsig Icebreakers C :K: .10 .20
120 Sidisi, Undead Vizier R :K: 2.00 3.00
121 Silumgar Assassin R :K: .30 .50
122 Silumgar Butcher C :K: .10 .20
123 Ukud Cobra U :K: .15 .25
124 Ultimate Price U :K: .15 .25
125 Virulent Plague U :K: .15 .25
126 Vulturous Aven C :K: .10 .20
127 Wandering Tombshell C :K: .10 .20
128 Atarka Efreet C :R: .10 .20
129 Atarka Pummeler U :R: .15 .25
130 Berserkers' Onslaught R :R: .30 .50
131 Commune with Lava R :R: .30 .50
132 Crater Elemental R :R: .30 .50
133 Descent of the Dragons M :R: 1.50 2.00
134 Draconic Roar U :R: .15 .25
135 Dragon Fodder C :R: .10 .20
136 Dragon Tempest R :R: .75 1.25
137 Dragon Whisperer M :R: .75 1.25
138 Dragonlord's Servant U :R: .15 .25
139 Hardened Berserker C :R: .10 .20
140 Impact Tremors C :R: .10 .20
141 Ire Shaman R :R: .30 .50
142 Kindled Fury C :R: .10 .20
143 Kolaghan Aspirant C :R: .10 .20
144 Kolaghan Forerunners U :R: .15 .25
145 Kolaghan Stormsinger C :R: .10 .20
146 Lightning Berserker U :R: .15 .25
147 Lose Calm C :R: .10 .20
148 Magmatic Chasm C :R: .10 .20
149 Qal Sisma Behemoth U :R: .15 .25
150 Rending Volley U :R: .15 .25
151 Roast U :R: .15 .25
152 Sabertooth Outrider C :R: .10 .20
153 Sarkhan's Rage C :R: .10 .20
154 Sarkhan's Triumph U :R: .15 .25
155 Screamreach Brawler C :R: .10 .20
156 Seismic Rupture U :R: .15 .25
157 Sprinting Warbrute C :R: .10 .20
158 Stormcrag Elemental U :R: .15 .25
159 Stormwing Dragon U :R: .15 .25
160 Summit Prowler C :R: .10 .20
161 Tail Slash C :R: .10 .20
162 Thunderbreak Regent R :R: 1.50 2.00
163 Tormenting Voice C :R: .10 .20
164 Twin Bolt C :R: .10 .20
165 Vandalize C :R: .10 .20
166 Volcanic Rush C :R: .10 .20
167 Volcanic Vision R :R: .30 .50
168 Warbringer U :R: .15 .25
169 Zurgo Bellstriker R :R: .50 .75
170 Aerie Bowmasters C :G: .10 .20
171 Ainok Artillerist C :G: .10 .20
172 Ainok Survivalist U :G: .15 .25
173 Assault Formation R :G: 1.00 1.25
174 Atarka Beastbreaker C :G: .10 .20
175 Avatar of the Resolute R :G: .75 1.00
176 Circle of Elders U :G: .15 .25
177 Collected Company R :G: 12.00 15.00
178 Colossodon Yearling C :G: .10 .20
179 Conifer Strider C :G: .10 .20
180 Deathmist Raptor M :G: 1.50 2.00
181 Den Protector R :G: .75 1.25
182 Display of Dominance U :G: .15 .25
183 Dragon-Scarred Bear C :G: .10 .20
184 Dromoka's Gift U :G: .15 .25
185 Epic Confrontation C :G: .10 .20
186 Explosive Vegetation U :G: .15 .25
187 Foe-Razer Regent R :G: .30 .50
188 Glade Watcher C :G: .10 .20
189 Guardian Shield-Bearer C :G: .10 .20
190 Herdchaser Dragon U :G: .15 .25
191 Inspiring Call U :G: .15 .25
192 Lurking Arynx U :G: .15 .25
193 Naturalize C :G: .10 .20
194 Obscuring Aether R :G: .30 .50
195 Pinion Feast C :G: .10 .20
196 Press the Advantage U :G: .15 .25
197 Revealing Wind C :G: .10 .20
198 Salt Road Ambushers U :G: .15 .25
199 Salt Road Quartermasters U :G: .15 .25
200 Sandsteppe Scavenger C :G: .10 .20
201 Scaleguard Sentinels U :G: .15 .25
202 Segmented Krotiq C :G: .10 .20
203 Servant of the Scale C :G: .10 .20
204 Shaman of Forgotten Ways M :G: 2.00 2.50
205 Shape the Sands C :G: .10 .20
206 Sheltered Aerie C :G: .10 .20
207 Sight of the Scalelords U :G: .15 .25
208 Stampeding Elk Herd C :G: .10 .20
209 Sunbringer's Touch R :G: .30 .50
210 Surrak, the Hunt Caller R :G: .30 .50
211 Tread Upon C :G: .10 .20
212 Arashin Sovereign R :M: .30 .50
213 Atarka's Command R :M: 6.00 8.00
214 Boltwing Marauder R :M: .30 .50
215 Cunning Breezedancer U :M: .15 .25
216 Dragonlord Atarka M :M: 4.00 5.00
217 Dragonlord Dromoka M :M: 4.00 5.00
218 Dragonlord Kolaghan M :M: 2.00 2.75
219 Dragonlord Ojutai M :M: 4.00 5.00
220 Dragonlord Silumgar M :M: 3.50 4.00
221 Dromoka's Command R :M: 2.00 2.50
222 Enduring Scalelord U :M: .15 .25
223 Harbinger of the Hunt R :M: .30 .50
224 Kolaghan's Command R :M: 8.00 10.00
225 Narset Transcendent M :M: 12.00 15.00
226 Necromaster Dragon R :M: .30 .50
227 Ojutai's Command R :M: 1.25 1.75
228 Pristine Skywise R :M: .30 .50
229 Ruthless Deathfang U :M: .15 .25
230 Sarkhan Unbroken M :M: 3.50 4.25
231 Savage Ventmaw U :M: .15 .25
232 Silumgar's Command R :M: .30 .50
233 Swift Warkite U :M: .15 .25
263 Forest (263) L :L: .10 .20
264 Forest (264) L :L: .10 .20
262 Forest L :L: .10 .20
254 Island (254) L :L: .10 .20
255 Island (255) L :L: .10 .20
253 Island L :L: .10 .20
260 Mountain (260) L :L: .10 .20
261 Mountain (261) L :L: .10 .20
259 Mountain L :L: .10 .20
251 Plains (251) L :L: .10 .20
252 Plains (252) L :L: .10 .20
250 Plains L :L: .10 .20
257 Swamp (257) L :L: .10 .20
258 Swamp (258) L :L: .10 .20
256 Swamp L :L: .10 .20
234 Ancestral Statue C .10 .20
235 Atarka Monument U .15 .25
236 Custodian of the Trove C .10 .20
237 Dragonloft Idol U .15 .25
238 Dromoka Monument U .15 .25
248 Evolving Wilds C .10 .20
239 Gate Smasher U .15 .25
249 Haven of the Spirit Dragon R 1.00 1.25
240 Keeper of the Lens C .10 .20
241 Kolaghan Monument U .15 .25
242 Ojutai Monument U .15 .25
1 Scion of Ugin U .15 .25
243 Silumgar Monument U .15 .25
244 Spidersilk Net C .10 .20
245 Stormrider Rig U .15 .25
246 Tapestry of the Ages U .15 .25
247 Vial of Dragonfire C .10 .20

2015 Magic The Gathering Dragons of Tarkir Foil

1 Scion of Ugin U .30 .50
2 Anafenza, Kin-Tree Spirit R :W: 3.00 5.00
3 Arashin Foremost R :W: .75 1.25
4 Artful Maneuver C :W: .25 .40
5 Aven Sunstriker U :W: .30 .50
6 Aven Tactician C :W: .25 .40
7 Battle Mastery U :W: .30 .50
8 Center Soul C :W: .25 .40
9 Champion of Arashin C :W: .25 .40
10 Dragon Hunter U :W: 1.50 2.00
11 Dragon's Eye Sentry C :W: .25 .40
12 Dromoka Captain U :W: .30 .50
13 Dromoka Dunecaster C :W: .25 .40
14 Dromoka Warrior C :W: .25 .40
15 Echoes of the Kin Tree U :W: .30 .50
16 Enduring Victory C :W: .25 .40
17 Fate Forgotten C :W: .25 .40
18 Glaring Aegis C :W: .25 .40
19 Gleam of Authority R.:W: .60 1.00
20 Graceblade Artisan U :W: .30 .50
21 Great Teacher's Decree U :W: .30 .50
22 Herald of Dromoka C :W: .25 .40
23 Hidden Dragonslayer R :W: .40 .60
24 Lightwalker C :W: .25 .40
25 Misthoof Kirin C :W: .25 .40
26 Myth Realized R :W: 1.50 2.00
27 Ojutai Exemplars M :W: 1.25 2.00
28 Orator of Ojutai U :W: .30 .50
29 Pacifism C :W: .25 .40
30 Profound Journey R :W: .50 .75
31 Radiant Purge R :W: .40 .60
32 Resupply C :W: .25 .40
33 Sandcrafter Mage C :W: .25 .40
34 Sandstorm Charger C :W: .25 .40
35 Scale Blessing U :W: .30 .50
36 Secure the Wastes R :W: 5.00 7.00
37 Shieldhide Dragon U :W: .30 .50
38 Silkwrap U :W: 1.00 1.50
39 Strongarm Monk U :W: .30 .50
40 Student of Ojutai C :W: .25 .40
41 Sunscorch Regent R :W: 2.00 3.00
42 Surge of Righteousness U :W: .30 .50
43 Territorial Roc C :W: .25 .40
44 Ancient Carp C :B: .25 .40
45 Anticipate C :B: 1.00 1.50
46 Belltoll Dragon R :B: .30 .50
47 Blessed Reincarnation R :B: .30 .50
48 Clone Legion M :B: 2.00 3.50
49 Contradict C :B: .25 .40
50 Dance of the Skywise U :B: .30 .50
51 Dirgur Nemesis C :B: .25 .40
52 Dragonlord's Prerogative R :B: 1.00 1.50
53 Elusive Spellfist C :B: .40 .60
54 Encase in Ice U :B: .30 .50
55 Glint C :B: .25 .40
56 Gudul Lurker U :B: .30 .50
57 Gurmag Drowner C :B: .25 .40
58 Icefall Regent R :B: 1.25 2.00
59 Illusory Gains R :B: .30 .50
60 Learn from the Past U :B: .30 .50
61 Living Lore R :B: .75 1.00
62 Mirror Mockery R :B: 1.00 1.50
63 Monastery Loremaster C :B: .25 .40
64 Mystic Meditation C :B: .25 .40
65 Negate C :B: 1.25 2.00
66 Ojutai Interceptor C :B: .25 .40
67 Ojutai's Breath C :B: .25 .40
68 Ojutai's Summons C :B: .25 .40
69 Palace Familiar C :B: .25 .40
70 Profaner of the Dead R :B: .75 1.25
71 Qarsi Deceiver U :B: .30 .50
72 Reduce in Stature C :B: .25 .40
73 Shorecrasher Elemental M :B: 1.00 1.50
74 Sidisi's Faithful C :B: .25 .40
75 Sight Beyond Sight U :B: .30 .50
76 Silumgar Sorcerer U :B: .30 .50
77 Silumgar Spell-Eater U :B: .30 .50
78 Silumgar's Scorn U :B: 1.00 1.50
79 Skywise Teachings U :B: .30 .50
80 Stratus Dancer R :B: 1.00 1.50
81 Taigam's Strike C :B: .25 .40
82 Updraft Elemental C :B: .25 .40
83 Void Squall U :B: .30 .50
84 Youthful Scholar U :B: .30 .50
85 Zephyr Scribe C :B: .25 .40
86 Acid-Spewer Dragon U :K: .30 .50
87 Ambuscade Shaman U :K: .30 .50
88 Blood-Chin Fanatic R :K: .25 .40
89 Blood-Chin Rager U :K: .50 .80
90 Butcher's Glee C :K: .25 .40
91 Coat with Venom C :K: .25 .40
92 Corpseweft R :K: .50 .80
93 Damnable Pact R :K: .60 1.00
94 Deadly Wanderings U :K: .30 .50
95 Death Wind U :K: .30 .50
96 Deathbringer Regent R :K: .75 1.00
97 Defeat C :K: .25 .40
98 Duress C :K: 1.50 2.00
99 Dutiful Attendant C :K: .25 .40
100 Flatten C :K: .25 .40
101 Foul Renewal R :K: .30 .50
102 Foul-Tongue Invocation U :K: .75 1.25

103 Foul-Tongue Shriek C :K: .25 .40
104 Gravepurge C :K: .25 .40
105 Hand of Silumgar C :K: .25 .40
106 Hedonist's Trove R :K: .75 1.25
107 Kolaghan Skirmisher C :K: .25 .40
108 Marang River Skeleton U :K: .30 .50
109 Marsh Hulk C :K: .25 .40
110 Mind Rot C :K: .25 .40
111 Minister of Pain U :K: .30 .50
112 Pitiless Horde R :K: .30 .50
113 Qarsi Sadist C :K: .25 .40
114 Rakshasa Gravecaller U :K: .30 .50
115 Reckless Imp C :K: .25 .40
116 Risen Executioner M :K: 4.00 6.00
117 Self-Inflicted Wound U :K: .30 .50
118 Shambling Goblin C :K: .25 .40
119 Sibsig Icebreakers C :K: .25 .40
120 Sidisi, Undead Vizier R :K: 13.00 16.00
121 Silumgar Assassin R :K: .50 .80
122 Silumgar Butcher C :K: .25 .40
123 Ukud Cobra U :K: .30 .50
124 Ultimate Price U :K: .30 .50
125 Virulent Plague U :K: .30 .50
126 Vulturous Aven C :K: .25 .40
127 Wandering Tombshell C :K: .25 .40
128 Atarka Efreet C :R: .25 .40
129 Atarka Pummeler U :R: .30 .50
130 Berserkers' Onslaught R :R: 1.00 1.50
131 Commune with Lava R :R: 1.00 1.50
132 Crater Elemental R :R: .50 .80
133 Descent of the Dragons M :R: 3.00 5.00
134 Draconic Roar U :R: 1.50 2.00
135 Dragon Fodder C :R: .50 .80
136 Dragon Tempest R :R: 10.00 15.00
137 Dragon Whisperer M :R: 2.00 3.00
138 Dragonlord's Servant U :R: 1.50 2.00
139 Hardened Berserker C :R: .25 .40
140 Impact Tremors C :R: 6.00 8.00
141 Ire Shaman R :R: .25 .40
142 Kindled Fury C :R: .25 .40
143 Kolaghan Aspirant C :R: .25 .40
144 Kolaghan Forerunners U :R: .30 .50
145 Kolaghan Stormsinger C :R: .25 .40
146 Lightning Berserker U :R: 1.00 1.50
147 Lose Calm C :R: .25 .40
148 Magmatic Chasm C :R: .25 .40
149 Qal Sisma Behemoth U :R: .30 .50
150 Rending Volley U :R: 1.00 1.50
151 Roast U :R: .75 1.25
152 Sabertooth Outrider C :R: .25 .40
153 Sarkhan's Rage C :R: .25 .40
154 Sarkhan's Triumph U :R: 3.00 5.00
155 Screamreach Brawler C :R: .25 .40
156 Seismic Rupture U :R: .30 .50
157 Sprinting Warbrute C :R: .25 .40
158 Stormcrag Elemental U :R: .30 .50
159 Stormwing Dragon U :R: .30 .50
160 Summit Prowler C :R: .25 .40
161 Tail Slash C :R: .25 .40
162 Thunderbreak Regent R :R: 3.00 5.00
163 Tormenting Voice C :R: .25 .40
164 Twin Bolt C :R: .25 .40
165 Vandalize C :R: .25 .40
166 Volcanic Rush C :R: .25 .40
167 Volcanic Vision R :R: .60 1.00
168 Warbringer U :R: .30 .50
169 Zurgo Bellstriker R :R: 1.50 2.50
170 Aerie Bowmasters C :G: .25 .40
171 Ainok Artillerist C :G: .25 .40
172 Ainok Survivalist U :G: .60 1.00
173 Assault Formation R :G: 3.00 3.50
174 Atarka Beastbreaker C :G: .25 .40
175 Avatar of the Resolute R :G: 3.00 4.00
176 Circle of Elders U :G: .30 .50
177 Collected Company R :G: 30.00 35.00
178 Colossodon Yearling C :G: .25 .40
179 Conifer Strider C :G: .25 .40
180 Deathmist Raptor M :G: 3.00 5.00
181 Den Protector R :G: 3.00 5.00
182 Display of Dominance U :G: .30 .50
183 Dragon-Scarred Bear C :G: .25 .40
184 Dromoka's Gift U :G: .30 .50
185 Epic Confrontation C :G: .25 .40
186 Explosive Vegetation U :G: 2.50 3.50
187 Foe-Razer Regent R :G: .50 .80
188 Glade Watcher C :G: .25 .40
189 Guardian Shield-Bearer C :G: .25 .40
190 Herdchaser Dragon U :G: .30 .50
191 Inspiring Call U :G: 4.00 5.00
192 Lurking Arynx U :G: .30 .50
193 Naturalize C :G: .25 .40
194 Obscuring Aether R :G: .40 .60
195 Pinion Feast C :G: .25 .40
196 Press the Advantage U :G: .30 .50
197 Revealing Wind C :G: .25 .40
198 Salt Road Ambushers U :G: .30 .50
199 Salt Road Quartermasters U :G: .30 .50
200 Sandsteppe Scavenger C :G: .25 .40
201 Scaleguard Sentinels U :G: .30 .50
202 Segmented Krotiq C :G: .25 .40
203 Servant of the Scale C :G: .75 1.25
204 Shaman of Forgotten Ways M :G: 12.00 16.00
205 Shape the Sands C :G: .25 .40
206 Sheltered Aerie C :G: .25 .40
207 Sight of the Scalelords U :G: .30 .50
208 Stampeding Elk Herd C :G: .25 .40
209 Sunbringer's Touch R :G: .30 .50
210 Surrak, the Hunt Caller R :G: 1.00 1.50
211 Tread Upon C :G: .25 .40
212 Arashin Sovereign R :M: .40 .60
213 Atarka's Command R :M: 10.00 13.00
214 Boltwing Marauder R :M: .50 .80
215 Cunning Breezedancer U :M: .30 .50
216 Dragonlord Atarka M :M: 10.00 15.00
217 Dragonlord Dromoka M :M: 20.00 25.00
218 Dragonlord Kolaghan M :M: 6.00 8.00
219 Dragonlord Ojutai M :M: 12.00 15.00
220 Dragonlord Silumgar M :M: 12.00 15.00
221 Dromoka's Command R :M: 4.00 6.00
222 Enduring Scalelord U :M: .75 1.25
223 Harbinger of the Hunt R :M: .60 1.00
224 Kolaghan's Command R :M: 28.00 35.00
225 Narset Transcendent M :M: 25.00 30.00
226 Necromaster Dragon R :M: .40 .60
227 Ojutai's Command R :M: 1.50 2.00
228 Pristine Skywise R :M: .30 .50
229 Ruthless Deathfang U :M: .30 .50
230 Sarkhan Unbroken M :M: 25.00 30.00
231 Savage Ventmaw U :M: 3.00 5.00
232 Silumgar's Command R :M: 1.00 1.50
233 Swift Warkite U :M: .30 .50
234 Ancestral Statue C .25 .40
235 Atarka Monument U .30 .50
236 Custodian of the Trove C .25 .40
237 Dragonloft Idol U .30 .50
238 Dromoka Monument U .30 .50
239 Gate Smasher U .30 .50
240 Keeper of the Lens C .25 .40
241 Kolaghan Monument U .30 .50
242 Ojutai Monument U .30 .50
244 Spidersilk Net C .25 .40
246 Tapestry of the Ages U .30 .50
247 Vial of Dragonfire C .25 .40
248 Evolving Wilds C 4.00 6.00
249 Haven of the Spirit Dragon R 5.00 8.00
250 Plains L :L: .25 .40
251 Plains (251) L :L: .25 .40
252 Plains (252) L :L: .25 .40
253 Island L :L: .25 .40
254 Island (254) L :L: .25 .40
255 Island (255) L :L: .25 .40
256 Swamp L :L: .25 .40
257 Swamp (257) L :L: .25 .40
258 Swamp (258) L :L: .25 .40
259 Mountain L :L: .25 .40
260 Mountain (260) L :L: .25 .40
243 Silumgar Monument U .30 .50
261 Mountain (261) L :L: .25 .40
262 Forest L :L: .25 .40
245 Stormrider Rig U .30 .50
263 Forest (263) L :L: .25 .40
264 Forest (264) L :L: .25 .40

2015 Magic The Gathering Dragons of Tarkir Tokens

1 Warrior .50 .75
2 Djinn Monk .10 .15
3 Zombie .15 .25
4 Zombie Horror .10 .15
5 Dragon .30 .40
6 Goblin .15 .25
7 Morph .10 .15
8 Narset Transcendent Emblem .60 1.00

2015 Magic The Gathering Battle for Zendikar

COMPLETE SET (299) 120.00 180.00
BOOSTER BOX (36 PACKS) 90.00 100.00
BOOSTER PACK (15 CARDS) 2.50 6.00
RELEASED ON OCTOBER 2, 2015
1 Bane of Bala Ged U .20 .35
2 Blight Herder R .25 .40
3 Breaker of Armies U .20 .35
4 Conduit of Ruin R .50 .75
5 Deathless Behemoth U .20 .35
6 Desolation Twin R .25 .40
7 Eldrazi Devastator C .10 .20
8 Endless One R .25 .40
9 Gruesome Slaughter R .25 .40
10 Kozilek's Channeler C .10 .20
11 Oblivion Sower M .75 1.25
12 Ruin Processor C .10 .20
13 Scour from Existence C .10 .20
14 Titan's Presence U .20 .35
15 Ulamog, the Ceaseless Hunger M 18.00 22.00
16 Ulamog's Despoiler U .20 .35
17 Void Winnower M 1.50 2.00
18 Angel of Renewal U :W: .20 .35
19 Angelic Gift C :W: .10 .20
20 Cliffside Lookout C :W: .10 .20
21 Courier Griffin C :W: .10 .20
22 Emeria Shepherd R :W: .25 .40
23 Encircling Fissure U :W: .20 .35
24 Expedition Envoy U :W: .20 .35
25 Felidar Cub C :W: .10 .20
26 Felidar Sovereign R :W: .25 .40
27 Fortified Rampart C :W: .10 .20
28 Ghostly Sentinel C :W: .10 .20
29 Gideon, Ally of Zendikar M :W: 20.00 25.00
30 Gideon's Reproach C :W: .10 .20
31 Hero of Goma Fada R :W: .25 .40
32 Inspired Charge C :W: .10 .20
33 Kitesail Scout C :W: .10 .25
34 Kor Bladewhirl U :W: .20 .35
35 Kor Castigator C :W: .10 .20
36 Kor Entanglers U :W: .20 .35
37 Lantern Scout R :W: .25 .40
38 Lithomancer's Focus C :W: .10 .20
39 Makindi Patrol C :W: .10 .20
40 Onduu Greathorn C :W: .10 .20
41 Ondu Rising U :W: .20 .35
42 Planar Outburst R :W: .25 .40
43 Quarantine Field M :W: .75 1.25
44 Retreat to Emeria U :W: .20 .35
45 Roil's Retribution U :W: .20 .35
46 Serene Steward U :W: .20 .35
47 Shadow Glider C :W: .10 .20
48 Sheer Drop C :W: .10 .20
49 Smite the Monstrous C :W: .10 .20
50 Stasis Snare U :W: .20 .35
51 Stone Haven Medic C :W: .10 .20
52 Tandem Tactics C :W: .10 .20
53 Unified Front U :W: .20 .35
54 Adverse Conditions U :B: .20 .35
55 Benthic Infiltrator C :B: .10 .20
56 Cryptic Cruiser U :B: .20 .35
57 Drowner of Hope R :B: .25 .40
58 Eldrazi Skyspawner C :B: .10 .20
59 Horribly Awry U :B: .20 .35
60 Incubator Drone C :B: .10 .20
61 Mist Intruder C :B: .10 .20
62 Murk Strider C :B: .10 .20
63 Oracle of Dust C :B: .10 .20
64 Ruination Guide U :B: .20 .35
65 Salvage Drone C :B: .10 .20
66 Spell Shrivel C :B: .10 .20
67 Tide Drifter U :B: .20 .35
68 Ulamog's Reclaimer U :B: .20 .35
69 Anticipate C :B: .10 .20
70 Brilliant Spectrum C :B: .10 .20
71 Cloud Manta C :B: .10 .20
72 Clutch of Currents C :B: .10 .20
73 Coastal Discovery U :B: .20 .35
74 Coralhelm Guide C :B: .10 .20
75 Dampening Pulse U :B: .20 .35
76 Dispel C :B: .10 .20
77 Exert Influence R :B: .25 .40
78 Guardian of Tazeem R :B: .25 .40
79 Halimar Tidecaller U :B: .20 .35
80 Part the Waterveil M :B: 3.00 3.50
81 Prism Array R :B: .25 .40
82 Retreat to Coralhelm U :B: .20 .35
83 Roilmage's Trick C :B: .10 .20
84 Rush of Ice C :B: .10 .20
85 Scatter to the Winds R :B: .25 .40
86 Tightening Coils C :B: .10 .20
87 Ugin's Insight R :B: .25 .40
88 Wave-Wing Elemental C :B: .10 .20
89 Windrider Patrol U :B: .20 .35
90 Complete Disregard C :K: .10 .20
91 Culling Drone C :K: .10 .20
92 Dominator Drone C :K: .10 .20
93 Grave Birthing C :K: .10 .20
94 Grip of Desolation U :K: .20 .35
95 Mind Raker C :K: .10 .20
96 Silent Skimmer C :K: .10 .20
97 Skitterskin U :K: .20 .35
98 Sludge Crawler C :K: .10 .20
99 Smothering Abomination R :K: .25 .40
100 Swarm Surge C :K: .10 .20
101 Transgress the Mind U :K: .20 .35
102 Wasteland Strangler R :K: .25 .40
103 Altar's Reap C :K: .10 .20
104 Bloodbond Vampire U :K: .20 .35
105 Bone Splinters C :K: .10 .20
106 Carrier Thrall U :K: .20 .35
107 Defiant Bloodlord R :K: .25 .40
108 Demon's Grasp C :K: .10 .20
109 Drana, Liberator of Malakir M :K: 3.50 4.50
110 Dutiful Return C :K: .10 .20
111 Geyserfield Stalker C :K: .10 .20
112 Guul Draz Overseer R :K: .25 .40
113 Hagra Sharpshooter U :K: .20 .35
114 Kalastria Healer C :K: .10 .20
115 Kalastria Nightwatch C :K: .10 .20
116 Malakir Familiar U :K: .20 .35
117 Mire's Malice C :K: .10 .20
118 Nirkana Assassin C :K: .10 .20
119 Ob Nixilis Reignited M :K: 3.50 4.00
120 Painful Truths R :K: .25 .40
121 Retreat to Hagra U :K: .20 .35
122 Rising Miasma U :K: .20 .35
123 Ruinous Path R :K: 1.50 2.00
124 Vampiric Rites U :K: .20 .35
125 Voracious Null C :K: .10 .20
126 Zulaport Cutthroat U :K: .20 .35
127 Barrage Tyrant R :R: .25 .40
128 Crumble to Dust U :R: .20 .35
129 Kozilek's Sentinel C :R: .10 .20
130 Molten Nursery U :R: .20 .35
131 Nettle Drone C :R: .10 .20
132 Processor Assault U :R: .20 .35
133 Serpentine Spike R :R: .25 .40
134 Touch of the Void C :R: .10 .20
135 Turn Against U :R: .20 .35
136 Vestige of Emrakul C :R: .10 .20
137 Vile Aggregate U :R: .20 .35
138 Akoum Firebird M :R: .40 .60
139 Akoum Hellkite R :R: .25 .40
140 Akoum Stonewaker U :R: .20 .35
141 Belligerent Whiptail C :R: .10 .20
142 Boiling Earth C :R: .10 .20
143 Chasm Guide U :R: .20 .35
144 Dragonmaster Outcast M :R: 2.00 2.50
145 Firemantle Mage U :R: .20 .35
146 Goblin War Paint C :R: .10 .20
147 Lavastep Raider C :R: .10 .20
148 Makindi Sliderunner C :R: .10 .20
149 Ondu Champion C :R: .10 .20
150 Outnumber C :R: .10 .20
151 Radiant Flames R :R: 1.00 1.50
152 Reckless Cohort C :R: .10 .20
153 Retreat to Valakut U :R: .20 .35
154 Rolling Thunder U :R: .20 .35
155 Shatterskull Recruit C :R: .10 .20
156 Stonefury C :R: .10 .20
157 Sure Strike C :R: .10 .20
158 Tunneling Geopede U :R: .20 .35
159 Valakut Invoker C :R: .10 .20
160 Valakut Predator C :R: .10 .20
161 Volcanic Upheaval C :R: .10 .20
162 Zada, Hedron Grinder R :R: .25 .40
163 Blisterpod C :G: .10 .20
164 Brood Monitor U :G: .20 .35
165 Call the Scions C :G: .10 .20
166 Eyeless Watcher C :G: .10 .20
167 From Beyond R :G: .25 .40
168 Unnatural Aggression C :G: .10 .20
169 Void Attendant U :G: .20 .35
170 Beastcaller Savant R :G: .25 .40
171 Broodhunter Wurm C :G: .10 .20
172 Earthen Arms C :G: .10 .20
173 Giant Mantis C :G: .10 .20
174 Greenwarden of Murasa M :G: .75 1.00
175 Infuse with the Elements U :G: .20 .35
176 Jaddi Offshoot U :G: .20 .35
177 Lifespring Druid C :G: .10 .20
178 Murasa Ranger U :G: .20 .35
179 Natural Connection C :G: .10 .20
180 Nissa's Renewal R :G: .25 .40
181 Oran-Rief Hydra R :G: .25 .40
182 Oran-Rief Invoker C :G: .10 .20
183 Plated Crusher U :G: .20 .35
184 Plummet C :G: .10 .20
185 Reclaiming Vines C :G: .10 .20
186 Retreat to Kazandu U :G: .20 .35
187 Rot Shambler U :G: .20 .35
188 Scythe Leopard U :G: .20 .35
189 Seek the Wilds C :G: .10 .20
190 Snapping Gnarlid C :G: .10 .20
191 Swell of Growth C :G: .10 .20
192 Sylvan Scrying U :G: .20 .35
193 Tajuru Beastmaster C :G: .10 .20
194 Tajuru Stalwart C :G: .10 .20
195 Tajuru Warcaller U :G: .20 .35
196 Territorial Baloth C :G: .10 .20
197 Undergrowth Champion M :G: .75 1.25
198 Woodland Wanderer R :G: .25 .40
199 Brood Butcher R :M: .25 .40
200 Brutal Expulsion R :M: .25 .40
201 Catacomb Sifter U :M: .20 .35
202 Dust Stalker R :M: .25 .40
203 Fathom Feeder R :M: .25 .40
204 Forerunner of Slaughter U :M: .20 .35
205 Herald of Kozilek U :M: .20 .35
206 Sire of Stagnation M :M: .75 1.00
207 Ulamog's Nullifier U :M: .20 .35
208 Angelic Captain R :M: .25 .40
209 Bring to Light R :M: .25 .40
210 Drana's Emissary U :M: .20 .35
211 Grove Rumbler U :M: .20 .35
212 Grovetender Druids U :M: .20 .35
213 Kiora, Master of the Depths M :M: 2.25 2.75
214 March from the Tomb R :M: .25 .40
215 Munda, Ambush Leader R :M: .25 .40
216 Noyan Dar, Roil Shaper R :M: .25 .40
217 Omnath, Locus of Rage M :M: .75 1.25
218 Resolute Blademaster U :M: .20 .35
219 Roil Spout U :M: .20 .35
220 Skyrider Elf U :M: .20 .35
221 Veteran Warleader R :M: .25 .40
222 Aligned Hedron Network R :A: .25 .40
223 Hedron Archive U :A: .20 .35
224 Hedron Blade C :A: .10 .20
225 Pathway Arrows U :A: .20 .35
226 Pilgrim's Eye U :A: .20 .35
227 Slab Hammer U :A: .20 .35
228 Ally Encampment R :L: .25 .40
229 Blighted Cataract U :L: .20 .35
230 Blighted Fen U :L: .20 .35
231 Blighted Gorge U :L: .20 .35
232 Blighted Steppe U :L: .20 .35
233 Blighted Woodland U :L: .20 .35
234 Canopy Vista R :L: 2.00 3.00
235 Cinder Glade R :L: 3.00 4.00
236 Evolving Wilds C :L: .10 .20
237 Fertile Thicket C :L: .10 .20
238 Looming Spires C :L: .10 .20
239 Lumbering Falls R :L: .75 1.25
240 Mortuary Mire C :L: .10 .20
241 Prairie Stream R :L: 3.50 5.00
242 Sanctum of Ugin R :L: 1.00 1.50
243 Sandstone Bridge C :L: .10 .20
244 Shambling Vent R :L: 3.00 4.00
245 Shrine of the Forsaken Gods R :L: .25 .40
246 Skyline Cascade C :L: .10 .20
247 Smoldering Marsh R :L: 3.00 4.00
248 Spawning Bed U :L: .20 .35
249 Sunken Hollow R :L: 3.50 5.00
250a Plains L :L: .10 .20
250b Plains Full Art L :L: .10 .20
251a Plains L :L: .10 .20
251b Plains Full Art L :L: .10 .20
252a Plains L :L: .10 .20
252b Plains Full Art L :L: .10 .20
253a Plains L :L: .10 .20
253b Plains Full Art L :L: .10 .20
254a Plains L :L: .10 .20
254b Plains Full Art L :L: .10 .20
255a Island L :L: .10 .20
255b Island Full Art L :L: .10 .20
256a Island L :L: .10 .20
256b Island Full Art L :L: .10 .20
257a Island L :L: .10 .20
257b Island Full Art L :L: .10 .20
258a Island L :L: .10 .20
258b Island Full Art L :L: .10 .20
259a Island L :L: .10 .20
259b Island Full Art L :L: .10 .20
260a Swamp L :L: .10 .20
260b Swamp Full Art L :L: .10 .20
261a Swamp L :L: .10 .20
261b Swamp Full Art L :L: .10 .20
262a Swamp L :L: .10 .20
262b Swamp Full Art L :L: .10 .20
263a Swamp L :L: .10 .20
263b Swamp Full Art L :L: .10 .20
264a Swamp L :L: .10 .20
264b Swamp Full Art L :L: .10 .20
265a Mountain L :L: .10 .20
265b Mountain Full Art L :L: .10 .20
266a Mountain L :L: .10 .20
266b Mountain Full Art L :L: .10 .20
267a Mountain L :L: .10 .20
267b Mountain Full Art L :L: .10 .20
268a Mountain L :L: .10 .20
268b Mountain Full Art L :L: .10 .20
269a Mountain L :L: .10 .20
269b Mountain Full Art L :L: .10 .20
270a Forest L :L: .10 .20
270b Forest Full Art L :L: .10 .20
271a Forest L :L: .10 .20
271b Forest Full Art L :L: .10 .20
272a Forest L :L: .10 .20
272b Forest Full Art L :L: .10 .20
273a Forest L :L: .10 .20
273b Forest Full Art L :L: .10 .20
274a Forest L :L: .10 .20
274b Forest Full Art L :L: .10 .20

2015 Magic The Gathering Battle for Zendikar Foil

Card	Low	High
COMPLETE SET (299)	425.00	630.00
1 Bane of Bala Ged U	1.50	2.50
2 Blight Herder R	.40	.60
3 Breaker of Armies U	.50	.75
4 Conduit of Ruin R	2.50	3.50
5 Deathless Behemoth U	.20	.35
6 Desolation Twin R	1.25	2.00
7 Eldrazi Devastator C	.15	.25
8 Endless One R	3.00	4.50
9 Gruesome Slaughter R	.50	.75
10 Kozilek's Channeler C	.15	.25
11 Oblivion Sower M	2.00	3.50
12 Ruin Processor C	.15	.25
13 Scour from Existence C	1.25	2.00
14 Titan's Presence U	1.00	1.50
15 Ulamog, the Ceaseless Hunger M	30.00	35.00
16 Ulamog's Despoiler U	.20	.35
17 Void Winnower M	4.00	6.00
18 Angel of Renewal U :W:	.20	.35
19 Angelic Gift C :W:	.15	.25
20 Cliffside Lookout C :W:	.15	.25
21 Courier Griffin C :W:	.15	.25
22 Emeria Shepherd R :W:	1.50	2.50
23 Encircling Fissure U :W:	.20	.35
24 Expedition Envoy U :W:	.75	1.25
25 Felidar Cub C :W:	.15	.25
26 Felidar Sovereign R :W:	1.50	2.50
27 Fortified Rampart C :W:	.15	.25
28 Ghostly Sentinel C :W:	.15	.25
29 Gideon, Ally of Zendikar M :W:	30.00	35.00
30 Gideon's Reproach C :W:	.15	.25
31 Hero of Goma Fada R :W:	.50	.75
32 Inspired Charge C :W:	.15	.25
33 Kitesail Scout C :W:	.15	.25
34 Kor Bladewhirl U :W:	.30	.50
35 Kor Castigator C :W:	.15	.25
36 Kor Entanglers U :W:	.20	.35
37 Lantern Scout R :W:	.75	1.25
38 Lithomancer's Focus C :W:	.15	.25
39 Makindi Patrol C :W:	.15	.25
40 Ondu Greathorn C :W:	.15	.25
41 Ondu Rising U :W:	.20	.35
42 Planar Outburst R :W:	1.00	1.50
43 Quarantine Field M :W:	2.00	3.00
44 Retreat to Emeria U :W:	.60	1.00
45 Roil's Retribution U :W:	.20	.35
46 Serene Steward U :W:	.60	1.00
47 Shadow Glider C :W:	.15	.25
48 Sheer Drop C :W:	.15	.25
49 Smite the Monstrous C :W:	.15	.25
50 Stasis Snare U :W:	1.50	2.50
51 Stone Haven Medic C :W:	.15	.25
52 Tandem Tactics C :W:	.15	.25
53 Unified Front U :W:	.20	.35
54 Adverse Conditions U :B:	.20	.35
55 Benthic Infiltrator C :B:	.15	.25
56 Cryptic Cruiser U :B:	.20	.35
57 Drowner of Hope R :B:	3.00	4.00
58 Eldrazi Skyspawner C :B:	2.00	3.00
59 Horribly Awry U :B:	.75	1.25
60 Incubator Drone C :B:	.15	.25
61 Mist Intruder C :B:	.15	.25
62 Murk Strider C :B:	.15	.25
63 Oracle of Dust C :B:	.15	.25
64 Ruination Guide U :B:	.75	1.25
65 Salvage Drone C :B:	.15	.25
66 Spell Shrivel C :B:	.75	1.25
67 Tide Drifter U :B:	.50	.75
68 Ulamog's Reclaimer U :B:	.20	.35
69 Anticipate C :B:	.75	1.25
70 Brilliant Spectrum C :B:	.15	.25
71 Cloud Manta C :B:	.15	.25
72 Clutch of Currents C :B:	.15	.25
73 Coastal Discovery U :B:	.20	.35
74 Coralhelm Guide C :B:	.15	.25
75 Dampening Pulse U :B:	.20	.35
76 Dispel C :B:	2.50	4.00
77 Exert Influence R :B:	.40	.60
78 Guardian of Tazeem R :B:	.30	.50
79 Halimar Tidecaller U :B:	.20	.35
80 Part the Waterveil M :B:	5.00	7.00
81 Prism Array R :B:	.25	.40
82 Retreat to Coralhelm U :B:	1.75	2.50
83 Roilmage's Trick C :B:	.15	.25
84 Rush of Ice C :B:	.15	.25
85 Scatter to the Winds R :B:	1.50	2.00
86 Tightening Coils C :B:	.15	.25
87 Ugin's Insight R :B:	.40	.60
88 Wave-Wing Elemental C :B:	.15	.25
89 Windrider Patrol U :B:	.20	.35
90 Complete Disregard C :K:	.15	.25
91 Culling Drone C :K:	.15	.25
92 Dominator Drone C :K:	.15	.25
93 Grave Birthing C :K:	.15	.25
94 Grip of Desolation U :K:	.20	.35
95 Mind Raker C :K:	.15	.25
96 Silent Skimmer C :K:	.15	.25
97 Skitterskin U :K:	.20	.35
98 Sludge Crawler C :K:	.15	.25
99 Smothering Abomination R :K:	.60	1.00
100 Swarm Surge C :K:	.15	.25
101 Transgress the Mind U :K:	3.00	4.00
102 Wasteland Strangler R :K:	2.00	3.00
103 Altar's Reap C :K:	.15	.25
104 Bloodbond Vampire U :K:	.50	.75
105 Bone Splinters C :K:	.15	.25
106 Carrier Thrall U :K:	.30	.50
107 Defiant Bloodlord R :K:	.50	.75
108 Demon's Grasp C :K:	.15	.25
109 Drana, Liberator of Malakir M :K:	7.00	10.00
110 Dutiful Return C :K:	.15	.25
111 Geyserfield Stalker C :K:	.15	.25
112 Guul Draz Overseer R :K:	.40	.60
113 Hagra Sharpshooter U :K:	.20	.35
114 Kalastria Healer C :K:	.50	.75
115 Kalastria Nightwatch C :K:	.15	.25
116 Malakir Familiar U :K:	.20	.35
117 Mire's Malice C :K:	.15	.25
118 Nirkana Assassin C :K:	.15	.25
119 Ob Nixilis Reignited M :K:	7.00	10.00
120 Painful Truths R :K:	3.00	5.00
121 Retreat to Hagra U :K:	.60	1.00
122 Rising Miasma U :K:	.20	.35
123 Ruinous Path R :K:	1.50	2.00
124 Vampiric Rites U :K:	.60	1.00
125 Voracious Null C :K:	.15	.25
126 Zulaport Cutthroat U :K:	2.50	4.00
127 Barrage Tyrant R :R:	.25	.40
128 Crumble to Dust U :R:	4.00	6.00
129 Kozilek's Sentinel C :R:	.15	.25
130 Molten Nursery U :R:	.40	.60
131 Nettle Drone C :R:	.15	.25
132 Processor Assault U :R:	.20	.35
133 Serpentine Spike R :R:	.30	.50
134 Touch of the Void C :R:	.15	.25
135 Turn Against U :R:	.20	.35
136 Vestige of Emrakul C :R:	.15	.25
137 Vile Aggregate U :R:	1.50	2.50
138 Akoum Firebird M :R:	1.00	1.50
139 Akoum Hellkite R :R:	.50	.75
140 Akoum Stonewaker U :R:	.20	.35
141 Belligerent Whiptail C :R:	.15	.25
142 Boiling Earth C :R:	.15	.25
143 Chasm Guide U :R:	.20	.35
144 Dragonmaster Outcast M :R:	3.50	5.00
145 Firemantle Mage U :R:	.20	.35
146 Goblin War Paint C :R:	.15	.25
147 Lavastep Raider C :R:	.15	.25
148 Makindi Sliderunner C :R:	.15	.25
149 Ondu Champion C :R:	.15	.25
150 Outnumber C :R:	.15	.25
151 Radiant Flames R :R:	2.00	3.00
152 Reckless Cohort C :R:	.15	.25
153 Retreat to Valakut U :R:	.20	.35
154 Rolling Thunder U :R:	.40	.60
155 Shatterskull Recruit C :R:	.15	.25
156 Stonefury C :R:	.15	.25
157 Sure Strike C :R:	.15	.25
158 Tunneling Geopede U :R:	.20	.35
159 Valakut Invoker C :R:	.15	.25
160 Valakut Predator C :R:	.15	.25
161 Volcanic Upheaval C :R:	.15	.25
162 Zada, Hedron Grinder R :R:	1.50	2.50
163 Blisterpod C :G:	.50	.75
164 Brood Monitor U :G:	.60	1.00
165 Call the Scions C :G:	.15	.25
166 Eyeless Watcher C :G:	.15	.25
167 From Beyond R :G:	2.00	3.00
168 Unnatural Aggression C :G:	.15	.25
169 Void Attendant U :G:	.20	.35
170 Beastcaller Savant R :G:	.60	1.00
171 Broodhunter Wurm C :G:	.15	.25
172 Earthen Arms C :G:	.15	.25
173 Giant Mantis C :G:	.15	.25
174 Greenwarden of Murasa M :G:	4.00	6.00
175 Infuse with the Elements U :G:	.20	.35
176 Jaddi Offshoot U :G:	1.00	1.50
177 Lifespring Druid C :G:	.15	.25
178 Murasa Ranger U :G:	.20	.35
179 Natural Connection C :G:	.15	.25
180 Nissa's Renewal R :G:	.75	1.25
181 Oran-Rief Hydra R :G:	.40	.60
182 Oran-Rief Invoker C :G:	.15	.25
183 Plated Crusher U :G:	.20	.35
184 Plummet C :G:	.15	.25
185 Reclaiming Vines C :G:	.15	.25
186 Retreat to Kazandu U :G:	.50	.75
187 Rot Shambler U :G:	.20	.35
188 Scythe Leopard U :G:	.20	.35
189 Seek the Wilds C :G:	.15	.25
190 Snapping Gnarlid C :G:	.15	.25
191 Swell of Growth C :G:	.15	.25
192 Sylvan Scrying U :G:	1.50	2.50
193 Tajiru Beastmaster C :G:	.15	.25
194 Tajuru Stalwart C :G:	.15	.25
195 Tajuru Warcaller U :G:	.20	.35
196 Territorial Baloth C :G:	.15	.25
197 Undergrowth Champion M :G:	2.00	3.00
198 Woodland Wanderer R :G:	.40	.75
199 Brood Butcher R :M:	.30	.50
200 Brutal Expulsion R :M:	.75	1.25
201 Catacomb Sifter U :M:	1.00	1.50
202 Dust Stalker R :M:	.60	1.00
203 Fathom Feeder R :M:	.50	.75
204 Forerunner of Slaughter U :M:	.50	.75
205 Herald of Kozilek U :M:	1.25	2.00
206 Sire of Stagnation M :M:	3.00	4.00
207 Ulamog's Nullifier U :M:	.20	.35
208 Angelic Captain R :M:	.25	.40
209 Bring to Light R :M:	3.00	4.00
210 Drana's Emissary U :M:	1.50	2.50
211 Grove Rumbler U :M:	.20	.35
212 Grovetender Druids U :M:	.20	.35
213 Kiora, Master of the Depths M :M:	6.00	8.00
214 March from the Tomb R :M:	.75	2.00
215 Munda, Ambush Leader R :M:	.40	.60
216 Noyan Dar, Roil Shaper R :M:	.75	1.25
217 Omnath, Locus of Rage M :M:	5.00	7.00
218 Resolute Blademaster U :M:	.20	.35
219 Roil Spout U :M:	.20	.35
220 Skyrider Elf U :M:	.20	.35
221 Veteran Warleader R :M:	.50	.75
222 Aligned Hedron Network R :A:	.50	.75
223 Hedron Archive U :A:	3.00	5.00
224 Hedron Blade C :A:	.15	.25
225 Pathway Arrows U :A:	.20	.35
226 Pilgrim's Eye U :A:	.30	.50
227 Slab Hammer U :A:	.20	.35
228 Ally Encampment R :L:	1.50	2.00
229 Blighted Cataract U :L:	.75	1.25
230 Blighted Fen U :L:	.75	1.25
231 Blighted Gorge U :L:	.20	.35
232 Blighted Steppe U :L:	.40	.60
233 Blighted Woodland U :L:	1.00	1.50
234 Canopy Vista R :L:	4.00	6.00
235 Cinder Glade R :L:	6.00	8.00
236 Evolving Wilds C :L:	1.25	2.00
237 Fertile Thicket C :L:	.15	.25
238 Looming Spires C :L:	.15	.25
239 Lumbering Falls R :L:	3.50	5.00
240 Mortuary Mire C :L:	.20	.35
241 Prairie Stream R :L:	6.00	8.00
242 Sanctum of Ugin R :L:	4.00	6.00
243 Sandstone Bridge C :L:	.15	.25
244 Shambling Vent R :L:	8.00	10.00
245 Shrine of the Forsaken Gods R :L:	1.50	2.50
246 Skyline Cascade C :L:	.15	.25
247 Smoldering Marsh R :L:	5.00	7.00
248 Spawning Bed U :L:	.40	.75
249 Sunken Hollow R :L:	5.00	7.00
250a Plains L :L:	3.00	5.00
250b Plains Full Art L :L:	3.00	5.00
251a Plains L :L:	3.00	5.00
251b Plains Full Art L :L:	3.00	5.00
252a Plains L :L:	3.00	5.00
252b Plains Full Art L :L:	3.00	5.00
253a Plains L :L:	3.00	5.00
253b Plains Full Art L :L:	3.00	5.00
254a Plains L :L:	3.00	5.00
254b Plains Full Art L :L:	3.00	5.00
255a Island L :L:	3.00	5.00
255b Island Full Art L :L:	4.00	6.00
256a Island L :L:	3.00	5.00
256b Island Full Art L :L:	4.00	6.00
257a Island L :L:	3.00	5.00
257b Island Full Art L :L:	4.00	6.00
258a Island L :L:	3.00	5.00
258b Island Full Art L :L:	4.00	6.00
259a Island L :L:	3.00	5.00
259b Island Full Art L :L:	4.00	6.00
260a Swamp L :L:	3.00	5.00
260b Swamp Full Art L :L:	3.00	5.00
261a Swamp L :L:	3.00	5.00
261b Swamp Full Art L :L:	3.00	5.00
262a Swamp L :L:	3.00	5.00
262b Swamp Full Art L :L:	3.00	5.00
263a Swamp L :L:	3.00	5.00
263b Swamp Full Art L :L:	3.00	5.00
264a Swamp L :L:	3.00	5.00
264b Swamp Full Art L :L:	3.00	5.00
265a Mountain L :L:	3.00	5.00
265b Mountain Full Art L :L:	3.00	5.00
266a Mountain L :L:	3.00	5.00
266b Mountain Full Art L :L:	3.00	5.00
267a Mountain L :L:	3.00	5.00
267b Mountain Full Art L :L:	3.00	5.00
268a Mountain L :L:	3.00	5.00
268b Mountain Full Art L :L:	3.00	5.00
269a Mountain L :L:	3.00	5.00
269b Mountain Full Art L :L:	3.00	5.00
270a Forest L :L:	3.00	5.00
270b Forest Full Art L :L:	3.00	5.00
271a Forest L :L:	3.00	5.00
271b Forest Full Art L :L:	3.00	5.00
272a Forest L :L:	3.00	5.00
272b Forest Full Art L :L:	3.00	5.00
273a Forest L :L:	3.00	5.00
273b Forest Full Art L :L:	3.00	5.00
274a Forest L :L:	3.00	5.00
274b Forest Full Art L :L:	3.00	5.00

2015 Magic The Gathering Battle for Zendikar Tokens

Card	Low	High
1 Eldrazi	.50	.75
2 Eldrazi Scion	.10	.15
3 Eldrazi Scion	.10	.15
4 Eldrazi Scion	.10	.15
5 Knight Ally	.10	.15
6 Kor Ally	.10	.15
7 Octopus	.10	.15
8 Dragon	.20	.30
9 Elemental	.10	.15
10 Plant	.10	.15
11 Elemental	.75	1.25
12 Gideon, Ally of Zendikar Emblem	.25	.35
13 Ob Nixilis Reignited Emblem	.12	.20
14 Kiora, Master of the Depths Emblem	.10	.15

2015-16 Magic The Gathering Zendikar Expeditions

Card	Low	High
COMPLETE SET (25)	1100.00	2500.00
24 Arid Mesa M :L:	90.00	120.00
8 Blood Crypt M :L:	50.00	100.00
18 Bloodstained Mire M :L:	80.00	120.00
39 Forbidden Orchard M :L:		
15 Breeding Pool M :L:	50.00	80.00
5 Canopy Vista M :L:	20.00	40.00
4 Cinder Glade M :L:	20.00	40.00
16 Flooded Strand M :L:	150.00	180.00
11 Godless Shrine M :L:	60.00	90.00
6 Hallowed Fountain M :L:	50.00	80.00
21 Marsh Flats M :L:	80.00	110.00
25 Misty Rainforest M :L:	180.00	220.00
13 Overgrown Tomb M :L:	50.00	80.00
17 Polluted Delta M :L:	180.00	240.00
1 Prairie Stream M :L:	25.00	50.00
14 Sacred Foundry M :L:	50.00	80.00
22 Scalding Tarn M :L:	200.00	250.00
3 Smoldering Marsh M :L:	20.00	40.00
12 Steam Vents M :L:	80.00	110.00
9 Stomping Ground M :L:	60.00	90.00
2 Sunken Hollow M :L:	25.00	50.00
10 Temple Garden M :L:	50.00	80.00
23 Verdant Catacombs M :L:	130.00	180.00
7 Watery Grave M :L:	50.00	80.00
20 Windswept Heath M :L:	80.00	110.00
19 Wooded Foothills M :L:	100.00	140.00
26 Mystic Gate M :L:	25.00	50.00
27 Sunken Ruins M :L:	25.00	50.00
28 Graven Cairns M :L:	25.00	50.00
29 Fire-Lit Thicket M :L:	25.00	50.00
30 Wooded Bastion M :L:	25.00	50.00
31 Fetid Heath M :L:	25.00	50.00
32 Cascade Bluffs M :L:	30.00	60.00
33 Twilight Mire M :L:	40.00	70.00
34 Rugged Prairie M :L:	20.00	45.00
35 Flooded Grove M :L:	30.00	60.00
36 Ancient Tomb M :L:	50.00	80.00
37 Dust Bowl M :L:	20.00	45.00
38 Eye of Ugin M :L:	50.00	80.00
40 Horizon Canopy M :L:	80.00	110.00
41 Kor Haven M :L:	25.00	40.00
42 Mana Confluence M :L:	30.00	50.00
43 Strip Mine M :L:	50.00	70.00
44 Tectonic Edge M :L:	20.00	45.00
45 Wasteland M :L:	110.00	150.00

2016 Magic The Gathering Oath of the Gatewatch

Card	Low	High
COMPLETE SET (184)	100.00	150.00
BOOSTER BOX	90.00	110.00
BOOSTER PACK	3.00	5.00
*FOIL: .75X TO 2X BASIC CARDS		
RELEASED ON JANUARY 22, 2016		
1 Deceiver of Form R	.20	.35
2 Eldrazi Mimic R	.30	.50
3 Endbringer R	.30	.50
4 Kozilek, the Great Distortion M	3.00	5.00
5 Kozilek's Pathfinder C	.10	.20
6 Matter Reshaper R	2.00	3.00
7 Reality Smasher R	3.00	5.00
8 Spatial Contortion U	.15	.25
9 Thought-Knot Seer R	6.00	8.00
10 Walker of the Wastes U	.15	.25
11 Warden of Geometries C	.10	.20
12 Warping Wail U	.25	.40
13 Eldrazi Displacer R :W:	2.00	3.50
14 Affa Protector C :W:	.10	.20
15 Allied Reinforcements U :W:	.15	.25
16 Call the Gatewatch R :W:	.25	.40
17 Dazzling Reflection C :W:	.10	.20
18 Expedition Raptor C :W:	.10	.20
19 General Tazri M :W:	.40	.60
20 Immolating Glare U :W:	.15	.25
21 Iona's Blessing U :W:	.15	.25
22 Isolation Zone C :W:	.10	.20
23 Kor Scythemaster C :W:	.10	.20
24 Kor Sky Climber C :W:	.10	.20
25 Linvala, the Preserver M :W:	1.00	1.50
26 Make a Stand U :W:	.15	.25
27 Makindi Aeronaut C :W:	.10	.20
28 Mighty Leap C :W:	.10	.20
29 Munda's Vanguard R :W:	.20	.35
30 Oath of Gideon R :W:	.30	.50
31 Ondu War Cleric C :W:	.10	.20
32 Relief Captain U :W:	.15	.25
33 Searing Light C :W:	.10	.20
34 Shoulder to Shoulder C :W:	.10	.20
35 Spawnbinder Mage C :W:	.10	.20
36 Steppe Glider U :W:	.15	.25
37 Stone Haven Outfitter R :W:	.30	.50
38 Stoneforge Acolyte U :W:	.15	.25
39 Wall of Resurgence U :W:	.15	.25
40 Abstruse Interference C	.10	.20
41 Blinding Drone C :B:	.10	.20
42 Cultivator Drone C :B:	.10	.20
43 Deepfathom Skulker R :B:	.20	.35
44 Dimensional Infiltrator R :B:	.20	.35
45 Gravity Negator C :B:	.10	.20
46 Prophet of Distortion U :B:	.15	.25
47 Slip Through Space C :B:	.10	.20
48 Thought Harvester U :B:	.15	.25
49 Void Shatter U :B:	.50	.80
50 Ancient Crab C :B:	.10	.20
51 Comparative Analysis C :B:	.10	.20
52 Containment Membrane C :B:	.10	.20
53 Crush of Tentacles M :B:	1.00	1.50
54 Cyclone Sire U :B:	.15	.25
55 Gift of Tusks U :B:	.15	.25
56 Grip of the Roil U :B:	.15	.25
57 Hedron Alignment R :B:	.20	.35
58 Jwar Isle Avenger C :B:	.10	.20
59 Negate C :B:	.10	.20
60 Oath of Jace R :B:	.30	.50
61 Overwhelming Denial R :B:	.20	.35
62 Roiling Waters U :B:	.15	.25
63 Sphinx of the Final Word M :B:	1.25	2.00
64 Sweep Away C :B:	.10	.20
65 Umara Entangler C :B:	.10	.20
66 Unity of Purpose U :B:	.15	.25
67 Bearer of Silence R :K:	.25	.40
68 Dread Defiler R :K:	.20	.35
69 Essence Depleter U :K:	.15	.25
70 Flaying Tendrils U :K:	.15	.25
71 Havoc Sower U :K:	.15	.25
72 Inverter of Truth M :K:	.40	.60
73 Kozilek's Shrieker C :K:	.10	.20
74 Kozilek's Translator C :K:	.10	.20
75 Oblivion Strike C :K:	.10	.20
76 Reaver Drone U :K:	.15	.25
77 Sifter of Skulls R :K:	.20	.35
78 Sky Scourer C :K:	.10	.20
79 Slaughter Drone C :K:	.10	.20
80 Unnatural Endurance C :K:	.10	.20
81 Visions of Brutality U :K:	.15	.25
82 Witness the End C :K:	.10	.20
83 Corpse Churn C :K:	.10	.20
84 Drana's Chosen R :K:	.20	.35
85 Grasp of Darkness U :K:	.60	1.00
86 Kalitas, Traitor of Ghet M :K:	10.00	13.00
87 Malakir Soothsayer U :K:	.15	.35
88 Null Caller U :K:	.15	.25
89 Remorseless Punishment R :K:	.20	.35
90 Tar Snare C :K:	.10	.20
91 Untamed Hunger C :K:	.10	.20
92 Vampire Envoy C :K:	.10	.20
93 Zulaport Chainmage C :K:	.10	.20
94 Consuming Sinkhole C :R:	.10	.20
95 Eldrazi Aggressor C :R:	.10	.20
96 Eldrazi Obligator R :R:	.30	.50
97 Immobilizer Eldrazi U :R:	.15	.25
98 Kozilek's Return M :R:	3.00	5.00
99 Maw of Kozilek C :R:	.10	.20
100 Reality Hemorrhage C :R:	.10	.20
101 Akoum Flameseeker C :R:	.10	.20

102 Boulder Salvo C :R: .10 .20
103 Brute Strength C :R: .10 .20
104 Chandra, Flamecaller M :R: 2.50 4.00
105 Cinder Hellion C :R: .10 .20
106 Devour in Flames U :R: .15 .25
107 Embodiment of Fury U :R: .15 .25
108 Expedite C :R: .10 .20
109 Fall of the Titans R :R: .20 .35
110 Goblin Dark-Dwellers R :R: .40 .60
111 Goblin Freerunner C :R: .10 .20
112 Kazuul's Toll Collector U :R: .15 .25
113 Oath of Chandra R :R: .30 .50
114 Press into Service U :R: .15 .25
115 Pyromancer's Assault U :R: .15 .25
116 Reckless Bushwhacker U :R: .50 .80
117 Sparkmage's Gambit C :R: .10 .20
118 Tears of Valakut U :R: .15 .25
119 Tyrant of Valakut R :R: .20 .35
120 Zada's Commando C :R: .10 .20
121 Birthing Hulk U :G: .15 .25
122 Ruin in Their Wake U :G: .15 .25
123 Scion Summoner C :G: .10 .20
124 Stalking Drone C :G: .10 .20
125 Vile Redeemer R :G: .20 .35
126 World Breaker M :G: 2.00 3.50
127 Baloth Pup U :G: .15 .25
128 Bonds of Mortality U :G: .15 .25
129 Canopy Gorger C :G: .10 .20
130 Elemental Uprising C :G: .10 .20
131 Embodiment of Insight U :G: .15 .25
132 Gladehart Cavalry R :G: .20 .35
133 Harvester Troll U :G: .15 .25
134 Lead by Example C :G: .10 .20
135 Loam Larva C :G: .10 .20
136 Natural State C :G: .10 .20
137 Netcaster Spider C :G: .10 .20
138 Nissa, Voice of Zendikar M :G: 3.00 5.00
139 Nissa's Judgment U :G: .15 .25
140 Oath of Nissa R :G: .75 1.25
141 Pulse of Murasa C :G: .10 .20
142 Saddleback Lagac C :G: .10 .20
143 Seed Guardian U :G: .15 .25
144 Sylvan Advocate R :G: .50 .80
145 Tajuru Pathwarden C :G: .10 .20
146 Vines of the Recluse C :G: .10 .20
147 Zendikar Resurgent R :G: .60 1.00
148 Flayer Drone U :M: .15 .25
149 Mindmelter U :M: .15 .25
150 Void Grafter U :M: .15 .25
151 Ayli, Eternal Pilgrim R :M: .50 .80
152 Baloth Null U :M: .15 .25
153 Cliffhaven Vampire U :M: .15 .25
154 Joraga Auxiliary U :M: .15 .25
155 Jori En, Ruin Diver R :M: .20 .35
156 Mina and Denn, Wildborn R :M: .30 .50
157 Reflector Mage U :M: .50 .80
158 Relentless Hunter U :M: .15 .25
159 Stormchaser Mage U :M: .15 .25
160 Weapons Trainer U :M: .15 .25
161 Bone Saw C :A: .10 .20
162 Captain's Claws R :A: .30 .50
163 Chitinous Cloak U :A: .15 .25
164 Hedron Crawler C :A: .10 .20
165 Seer's Lantern C :A: .10 .20
166 Stoneforge Masterwork R :A: .50 .80
167 Strider Harness U :A: .15 .25
168 Cinder Barrens U :L: .15 .25
169 Corrupted Crossroads R :L: .25 .40
170 Crumbling Vestige C :L: .10 .20
171 Hissing Quagmire R :L: 1.50 2.50
172 Holdout Settlement C :L: .10 .20
173 Meandering River U :L: .15 .25
174 Mirrorpool M :L: 1.25 2.00
175 Needle Spires R :L: .60 1.00
176 Ruins of Oran-Rief R :L: .20 .35
177 Sea Gate Wreckage R :L: .30 .50
178 Submerged Boneyard U :L: .15 .25
179 Timber Gorge U :L: .15 .25
180 Tranquil Expanse U :L: .15 .25
181 Unknown Shores C :L: .10 .20
182 Wandering Fumarole R :L: 2.00 3.00
183 Wastes C :L: .10 .20
183b Wastes C :L: .10 .20
184 Wastes C :L: .10 .20
184b Wastes C :L: .10 .20

2016 Magic The Gathering Oath of the Gatewatch Foil

1 Deceiver of Form R .40 .60
2 Eldrazi Mimic R 2.00 3.50
3 Endbringer R .75 1.25
4 Kozilek, the Great Distortion M 10.00 15.00
5 Kozilek's Pathfinder C .10 .20
6 Matter Reshaper R 7.00 10.00
7 Reality Smasher R 15.00 20.00
8 Spatial Contortion U .60 1.00
9 Thought-Knot Seer R 25.00 30.00
10 Walker of the Wastes U .30 .50
11 Warden of Geometries C .10 .20
12 Warping Wail U 5.00 7.00
13 Eldrazi Displacer R :W: 10.00 15.00
14 Affa Protector C :W: .10 .20
15 Allied Reinforcements U :W: .10 .20
16 Call the Gatewatch R :W: 1.00 1.50
17 Dazzling Reflection C :W: .10 .20
18 Expedition Raptor C :W: .10 .20
19 General Tazri M :W: 2.50 4.00
20 Immolating Glare U :W: .10 .20
21 Iona's Blessing U :W: .15 .25
22 Isolation Zone C :W: .15 .25
23 Kor Scythemaster C :W: .10 .20
24 Kor Sky Climber C :W: .10 .20
25 Linvala, the Preserver M :W: 3.00 5.00
26 Make a Stand U :W: .25 .40
27 Makindi Aeronaut C :W: .10 .20
28 Mighty Leap C :W: .10 .20
29 Munda's Vanguard R :W: .30 .50
30 Oath of Gideon R :W: .75 1.25
31 Ondu War Cleric C :W: .10 .20
32 Relief Captain U :W: .15 .25
33 Searing Light C :W: .10 .20
34 Shoulder to Shoulder C :W: .10 .20
35 Spawnbinder Mage C :W: .10 .20
36 Steppe Glider U :W: .10 .20
37 Stone Haven Outfitter R :W: .50 .80
38 Stoneforge Acolyte U :W: .10 .20
39 Wall of Resurgence U :W: .15 .25
40 Abstruse Interference C .15 .25
41 Blinding Drone C :B: .10 .20
42 Cultivator Drone C :B: .10 .20
43 Deepfathom Skulker R :B: .40 .60
44 Dimensional Infiltrator R :B: .20 .35
45 Gravity Negator C :B: .10 .20
46 Prophet of Distortion U :B: .15 .25
47 Slip Through Space C :B: .60 1.00
48 Thought Harvester U :B: .10 .20
49 Void Shatter U :B: 2.00 3.00
50 Ancient Crab C :B: .20 .35
51 Comparative Analysis C :B: .10 .20
52 Containment Membrane C :B: .10 .20
53 Crush of Tentacles M :B: 2.50 4.00
54 Cyclone Sire U :B: .10 .20
55 Gift of Tusks U :B: .15 .25
56 Grip of the Roil U :B: .10 .20
57 Hedron Alignment R :B: .25 .40
58 Jwar Isle Avenger C :B: .10 .20
59 Negate C :B: 1.25 2.00
60 Oath of Jace R :B: 1.00 1.50
61 Overwhelming Denial R :B: .75 1.25
62 Roiling Waters U :B: .10 .20
63 Sphinx of the Final Word M :B: 4.00 6.00
64 Sweep Away C :B: .10 .20
65 Umara Entangler C :B: .20 .35
66 Unity of Purpose U :B: .30 .50
67 Bearer of Silence R :K: .40 .60
68 Dread Defiler R :K: .20 .35
69 Essence Depleter U :K: .15 .25
70 Flaying Tendrils U :K: .30 .50
71 Havoc Sower U :K: .10 .20
72 Inverter of Truth M :K: .75 1.25
73 Kozilek's Shrieker C :K: .10 .20
74 Kozilek's Translator C :K: .10 .20
75 Oblivion Strike C :K: .10 .20
76 Reaver Drone U :K: .20 .35
77 Sifter of Skulls R :K: .40 .60
78 Sky Scourer C :K: .10 .20
79 Slaughter Drone C :K: .10 .20
80 Unnatural Endurance C :K: .10 .20
81 Visions of Brutality U :K: .10 .20
82 Witness the End C :K: .10 .20
83 Corpse Churn C :K: .10 .20
84 Drana's Chosen R :K: .20 .35
85 Grasp of Darkness U :K: 1.50 2.50
86 Kalitas, Traitor of Ghet M :K: 20.00 25.00
87 Malakir Soothsayer U :K: .10 .20
88 Null Caller U :K: .10 .20
89 Remorseless Punishment R :K: .30 .50
90 Tar Snare C :K: .10 .20
91 Untamed Hunger C :K: .10 .20
92 Vampire Envoy C :K: .10 .20
93 Zulaport Chainmage C :K: .10 .20
94 Consuming Sinkhole C :R: .10 .20
95 Eldrazi Aggressor C :R: .10 .20
96 Eldrazi Obligator R :R: .40 .60
97 Immobilizer Eldrazi U :R: .30 .50
98 Kozilek's Return M :R: 6.00 8.00
99 Maw of Kozilek C :R: .10 .20
100 Reality Hemorrhage C :R: .10 .20
101 Akoum Flameseeker C :R: .10 .20
102 Boulder Salvo C :R: .10 .20
103 Brute Strength C :R: .15 .25
104 Chandra, Flamecaller M :R: 9.00 11.00
105 Cinder Hellion C :R: .10 .20
106 Devour in Flames U :R: .10 .20
107 Embodiment of Fury U :R: .10 .20
108 Expedite C :R: .30 .50
109 Fall of the Titans R :R: .50 .80
110 Goblin Dark-Dwellers R :R: .75 1.25
111 Goblin Freerunner C :R: .10 .20
112 Kazuul's Toll Collector U :R: .15 .25
113 Oath of Chandra R :R: .30 .50
114 Press into Service U :R: .15 .25
115 Pyromancer's Assault U :R: .15 .25
116 Reckless Bushwhacker U :R: 3.00 5.00
117 Sparkmage's Gambit C :R: .10 .20
118 Tears of Valakut U :R: .20 .35
119 Tyrant of Valakut R :R: .20 .35
120 Zada's Commando C :R: .10 .20
121 Birthing Hulk U :G: .10 .20
122 Ruin in Their Wake U :G: .30 .50
123 Scion Summoner C :G: .10 .20
124 Stalking Drone C :G: .10 .20
125 Vile Redeemer R :G: .10 .20
126 World Breaker M :G: 6.00 10.00
127 Baloth Pup U :G: .15 .25
128 Bonds of Mortality U :G: .50 .80
129 Canopy Gorger C :G: .10 .20
130 Elemental Uprising C :G: .10 .20
131 Embodiment of Insight U :G: .15 .25
132 Gladehart Cavalry R :G: .40 .60
133 Harvester Troll U :G: .10 .20
134 Lead by Example C :G: .10 .20
135 Loam Larva C :G: .10 .20
136 Natural State C :G: 1.25 2.00
137 Netcaster Spider C :G: .10 .20
138 Nissa, Voice of Zendikar M :G: 6.00 8.00
139 Nissa's Judgment U :G: .10 .20
140 Oath of Nissa R :G: 4.00 6.00
141 Pulse of Murasa C :G: 1.75 2.50
142 Saddleback Lagac C :G: .10 .20
143 Seed Guardian U :G: .10 .20
144 Sylvan Advocate R :G: 2.00 3.50
145 Tajuru Pathwarden C :G: .10 .20
146 Vines of the Recluse C :G: .10 .20
147 Zendikar Resurgent R :G: 4.00 6.00
148 Flayer Drone U :M: .20 .35
149 Mindmelter U :M: .10 .20
150 Void Grafter U :M: .30 .50
151 Ayli, Eternal Pilgrim R :M: 2.00 3.50
152 Baloth Null U :M: .15 .25
153 Cliffhaven Vampire U :M: .75 1.25
154 Joraga Auxiliary U :M: .10 .20
155 Jori En, Ruin Diver R :M: .75 1.25
156 Mina and Denn, Wildborn R :M: 1.25 2.00
157 Reflector Mage U :M: 3.00 5.00
158 Relentless Hunter U :M: .20 .35
159 Stormchaser Mage U :M: 2.00 3.50
160 Weapons Trainer U :M: .30 .50
161 Bone Saw C :A: .20 .35
162 Captain's Claws R :A: .60 1.00
163 Chitinous Cloak U :A: .15 .25
164 Hedron Crawler C :A: .30 .50
165 Seer's Lantern C :A: .10 .20
166 Stoneforge Masterwork R :A: 1.25 2.00
167 Strider Harness U :A: .10 .20
168 Cinder Barrens U :L: .30 .50
169 Corrupted Crossroads R :L: .60 1.00
170 Crumbling Vestige C :L: .20 .35
171 Hissing Quagmire R :L: 5.00 8.00
172 Holdout Settlement C :L: .20 .35
173 Meandering River U :L: .40 .60
174 Mirrorpool M :L: 3.00 5.00
175 Needle Spires R :L: 2.50 4.00
176 Ruins of Oran-Rief R :L: .50 .80
177 Sea Gate Wreckage R :L: 2.00 3.50
178 Submerged Boneyard U :L: .30 .50
179 Timber Gorge U :L: .20 .35
180 Tranquil Expanse U :L: .20 .35
181 Unknown Shores C :L: .10 .20
182 Wandering Fumarole R :L: 5.00 8.00
183 Wastes C :L: 4.00 6.00
184 Wastes C :L: 4.00 6.00
183b Wastes C :L: 4.00 6.00
184b Wastes C :L: 4.00 6.00

2016 Magic The Gathering Oath of the Gatewatch Tokens

1 Eldrazi Scion .10 .15
2 Eldrazi Scion .10 .15
3 Eldrazi Scion .10 .15
4 Eldrazi Scion .10 .15
5 Eldrazi Scion .10 .15
6 Eldrazi Scion .10 .15
7 Angel .10 .15
8 Zombie .10 .15
9 Elemental .10 .15
10 Elemental .10 .15
11 Plant .25 .35

2016 Magic The Gathering Shadows over Innistrad

COMPLETE SET (297) 160.00 230.00
BOOSTER BOX (36 PACKS) 90.00 120.00
BOOSTER PACK (15 PACKS) 4.00 5.00
*FOIL: .75X TO 2X BASIC CARDS
RELEASED ON APRIL 8, 2016
1 Always Watching R :W: 1.25 1.75
2 Angel of Deliverance R :W: .25 .40
3 Angelic Purge C :W: .10 .20
4 Apothecary Geist C :W: .10 .20
5 Archangel Avacyn 3.00 5.00
6 Avacynian Missionaries .20 .35
7 Bound by Moonsilver U :W: .20 .35
8 Bygone Bishop R :W: .50 .75
9 Cathar's Companion C :W: .10 .20
10 Chaplain's Blessing C :W: .10 .20
11 Dauntless Cathar C :W: .10 .20
12 Declaration in Stone R :W: 4.00 5.00
13 Descend upon the Sinful M :W: .75 1.25
14 Devilthorn Fox C :W: .10 .20
15 Drogskol Cavalry R :W: .25 .40
16 Eerie Interlude R :W: .40 .60
17 Emissary of the Sleepless C :W: .10 .20
18 Ethereal Guidance C :W: .10 .20
19 Expose Evil C :W: .10 .20
20 Gryff's Boon U :W: .20 .35
21 Hanweir Militia Captain .40 .60
22 Hope Against Hope U :W: .20 .35
23 Humble the Brute U :W: .20 .35
24 Inquisitor's Ox C :W: .10 .20
25 Inspiring Captain C :W: .10 .20
26 Militant Inquisitor C :W: .10 .20
27 Moorland Drifter C :W: .10 .20
28 Nahiri's Machinations U :W: .20 .35
29 Nearheath Chaplain U :W: .20 .35
30 Not Forgotten U :W: .20 .35
31 Odric, Lunarch Marshal R :W: .40 .60
32 Open the Armory U :W: .20 .35
33 Paranoid Parish-Blade U :W: .20 .35
34 Pious Evangel .20 .35
35 Puncturing Light C :W: .10 .20
36 Reaper of Flight Moonsilver U :W: .20 .35
37 Silverstrike U :W: .20 .35
38 Spectral Shepherd U :W: .20 .35
39 Stern Constable C :W: .10 .20
40 Strength of Arms C :W: .10 .20
41 Survive the Night C :W: .10 .20
42 Tenacity U :W: .20 .35
43 Thalia's Lieutenant R :W: 1.50 2.00
44 Thraben Inspector C :W: .10 .20
45 Topplegeist U :W: .20 .35
46 Town Gossipmonger .20 .35
47 Unruly Mob C :W: .10 .20
48 Vessel of Ephemera C :W: .10 .20
49 Aberrant Researcher .20 .35
50 Broken Concentration U :B: .20 .35
51 Catalog C :B: .10 .20
52 Compelling Deterrence U :B: .20 .35
53 Confirm Suspicions R :B: .25 .40
54 Daring Sleuth .20 .35
55 Deny Existence C :B: .10 .20
56 Drownyard Explorers C :B: .10 .20
57 Drunau Corpse Trawler U :B: .20 .35
58 Engulf the Shore R :B: .50 .75
59 Epiphany at the Drownyard R :B: .25 .40
60 Erdwal Illuminator U :B: .20 .35
61 Essence Flux U :B: .20 .35
62 Fleeting Memories U :B: .20 .35
63 Forgotten Creation R :B: .25 .40
64 Furtive Homunculus C :B: .10 .20
65 Geralf's Masterpiece M :B: .20 .35
66 Ghostly Wings C :B: .10 .20
67 Gone Missing C :B: .10 .20
68 Invasive Surgery U :B: .20 .35
69 Jace, Unraveler of Secrets M :B: 2.50 4.00
70 Jace's Scrutiny C :B: .10 .20
71 Just the Wind C :B: .10 .20
72 Lamplighter of Selhoff C :B: .10 .20
73 Manic Scribe U :B: .20 .35
74 Nagging Thoughts C :B: .10 .20
75 Nephalia Moondrakes R :B: .25 .40
76 Niblis of Dusk C :B: .10 .20
77 Ongoing Investigation U :B: .20 .35
78 Pieces of the Puzzle C :B: .10 .20
79 Pore Over the Pages U :B: .20 .35
80 Press for Answers C :B: .10 .20
81 Rattlechains R :B: .75 1.00
82 Reckless Scholar U :B: .20 .35
83 Rise from the Tides U :B: .20 .35
84 Seagraf Skaab C :B: .10 .20
85 Silburlind Snapper C :B: .10 .20
86 Silent Observer C :B: .10 .20
87 Sleep Paralysis C :B: .10 .20
88 Startled Awake 3.00 5.00
89 Stitched Mangler C :B: .10 .20
90 Stitchwing Skaab U :B: .20 .35
91 Stormrider Spirit C :B: .10 .20
92 Thing in the Ice 6.00 8.00
93 Trail of Evidence U :B: .20 .35
94 Uninvited Geist .20 .35
95 Vessel of Paramnesia C :B: .10 .20
96 Welcome to the Fold R :B: .25 .40
97 Accursed Witch .20 .35
98 Alms of the Vein C :K: .10 .20
99 Asylum Visitor R :K: .50 .75
100 Behind the Scenes U :K: .20 .35
101 Behold the Beyond M :K: .30 .50
102 Biting Rain U :K: .20 .35
103 Call the Bloodline U :K: .20 .35
104 Creeping Dread U :K: .20 .35
105 Crow of Dark Tidings C :K: .10 .20
106 Dead Weight C :K: .10 .20
107 Diregraf Colossus R :K: .75 1.25
108 Elusive Tormentor .25 .40
109 Ever After R :K: .25 .40
110 Farbog Revenant C :K: .10 .20
111 From Under the Floorboards R :K: .25 .40
112 Ghoulcaller's Accomplice C :K: .10 .20
113 Ghoulsteed U :K: .20 .35
114 Gisa's Bidding U :K: .20 .35
115 Grotesque Mutation C :K: .10 .20
116 Heir of Falkenrath .20 .35
117 Hound of the Farbogs C :K: .10 .20
118 Indulgent Aristocrat U :K: .20 .35
119 Kindly Stranger .20 .35
120 Liliana's Indignation U :K: .20 .35
121 Macabre Waltz C :K: .10 .20
122 Markov Dreadknight R :K: .25 .40
123 Merciless Resolve C :K: .10 .20
124 Mindwrack Demon M :K: .30 .50
125 Morkrut Necropod U :K: .20 .35
126 Murderous Compulsion C :K: .10 .20
127 Olivia's Bloodsworn U :K: .20 .35
128 Pale Rider of Trostad U :K: .20 .35
129 Pick the Brain U :K: .20 .35
130 Rancid Rats C :K: .10 .20
131 Relentless Dead M :K: 7.00 9.00
132 Rottenheart Ghoul C :K: .10 .20
133 Sanitarium Skeleton C :K: .10 .20
134 Shamble Back C :K: .10 .20
135 Sinister Concoction U :K: .20 .35
136 Stallion of Ashmouth C :K: .10 .20
137 Stromkirk Mentor C :K: .10 .20
138 Throttle C :K: .10 .20
139 To the Slaughter R :K: .40 .60
140 Tooth Collector U :K: .20 .35
141 Triskaidekaphobia R :K: .25 .40
142 Twins of Maurer Estate C :K: .10 .20
143 Vampire Noble C :K: .10 .20
144 Vessel of Malignity C :K: .10 .20
145 Avacyn's Judgment R :R: .30 .50
146 Bloodmad Vampire C :R: .10 .20
147 Breakneck Rider .20 .35
148 Burn from Within R :R: .25 .40
149 Convicted Killer .10 .20
150 Dance with Devils U :R: .20 .35
151 Devils' Playground R :R: .25 .40
152 Dissension in the Ranks U :R: .20 .35
153 Dual Shot C :R: .10 .20
154 Ember-Eye Wolf C :R: .10 .20
155 Falkenrath Gorger R :R: .75 1.00
156 Fiery Temper C :R: .10 .20
157 Flameblade Angel R :R: .25 .40
158 Gatstaf Arsonists .10 .20
159 Geier Reach Bandit .50 .75
160 Geistblast U :R: .20 .35
161 Gibbering Fiend U :R: .20 .35
162 Goldnight Castigator M :R: .20 .35
163 Harness the Storm R :R: .25 .40
164 Howlpack Wolf C :R: .10 .20
165 Hulking Devil C :R: .10 .20
166 Incorrigible Youths U :R: .20 .35
167 Inner Struggle U :R: .20 .35
168 Insolent Neonate C :R: .10 .20
169 Kessig Forgemaster .20 .35
170 Lightning Axe U :R: .20 .35
171 Mad Prophet U :R: .20 .35
172 Magmatic Chasm C :R: .10 .20
173 Malevolent Whispers U :R: .20 .35
174 Pyre Hound C :R: .10 .20
175 Ravenous Bloodseeker U :R: .20 .35
176 Reduce to Ashes C :R: .10 .20
177 Rush of Adrenaline C :R: .10 .20
178 Sanguinary Mage C :R: .10 .20
179 Scourge Wolf R :R: .25 .40
180 Senseless Rage C :R: .10 .20
181 Sin Prodder R :R: .25 .40
182 Skin Invasion .20 .35

183 Spiteful Motives U :R:	.20	.35
184 Stensia Masquerade U :R:	.20	.35
185 Structural Distortion C :R:	.10	.20
186 Tormenting Voice C :R:	.10	.20
187 Ulrich's Kindred U :R:	.20	.35
188 Uncaged Fury C :R:	.10	.20
189 Vessel of Volatility C :R:	.10	.20
190 Village Messenger	.20	.35
191 Voldaren Duelist C :R:	.10	.20
192 Wolf of Devil's Breach M :R:	.20	.35
193 Aim High C :G:	.10	.20
194 Autumnal Gloom	.20	.35
195 Briarbridge Patrol U :G:	.20	.35
196 Byway Courier C :G:	.10	.20
197 Clip Wings C :G:	.10	.20
198 Confront the Unknown C :G:	.10	.20
199 Crawling Sensation U :G:	.20	.35
200 Cryptolith Rite R :G:	1.50	2.00
201 Cult of the Waxing Moon U :G:	.20	.35
202 Deathcap Cultivator R :G:	.40	.60
203 Duskwatch Recruiter	.20	.35
204 Equestrian Skill C :G:	.10	.20
205 Fork in the Road C :G:	.10	.20
206 Gloomwidow U :G:	.20	.35
207 Graf Mole U :G:	.20	.35
208 Groundskeeper U :G:	.20	.35
209 Hermit of the Natterknolls	.20	.35
210 Hinterland Logger	.10	.20
211 Howlpack Resurgence U :G:	.20	.35
212 Inexorable Blob R :G:	.25	.40
213 Intrepid Provisioner C :G:	.10	.20
214 Kessig Dire Swine C :G:	.10	.20
215 Lambholt Pacifist	.20	.35
216 Loam Dryad C :G:	.10	.20
217 Might Beyond Reason C :G:	.10	.20
218 Moldgraf Scavenger C :G:	.10	.20
219 Moonlight Hunt U :G:	.20	.35
220 Obsessive Skinner U :G:	.20	.35
221 Pack Guardian U :G:	.20	.35
222 Quilled Wolf C :G:	.10	.20
223 Rabid Bite C :G:	.10	.20
224 Root Out C :G:	.10	.20
225 Sage of Ancient Lore	.25	.40
226 Seasons Past M :G:	.60	1.00
227 Second Harvest R :G:	.25	.40
228 Silverfur Partisan R :G:	.40	.60
229 Solitary Hunter	.10	.20
230 Soul Swallower R :G:	.25	.40
231 Stoic Builder C :G:	.10	.20
232 Thornhide Wolves C :G:	.10	.20
233 Tireless Tracker R :G:	5.00	7.00
234 Traverse the Ulvenwald R :G:	2.00	2.50
235 Ulvenwald Hydra M :G:	.40	.60
236 Ulvenwald Mysteries U :G:	.20	.35
237 Vessel of Nascency C :G:	.10	.20
238 Veteran Cathar U :G:	.20	.35
239 Watcher in the Web C :G:	.10	.20
240 Weirding Wood U :G:	.20	.35
241 Altered Ego R :G::B:	.25	.40
242 Anguished Unmaking R :W::K:	1.50	2.00
243 Arlinn Kord	3.00	5.00
244 Fevered Visions R :B::R:	1.50	2.00
245 The Gitrog Monster M :K::G:	1.00	1.50
246 Invocation of Saint Traft R :W::B:	.25	.40
247 Nahiri, the Harbinger M :R::W:	8.00	11.00
248 Olivia, Mobilized for War M :K::R:	1.00	1.50
249 Prized Amalgam R :B::K:	2.50	3.00
250 Sigarda, Heron's Grace M :G::W:	.60	1.00
251 Sorin, Grim Nemesis M :W::K:	3.00	5.00
252 Brain in a Jar R :A:	.25	.40
253 Corrupted Grafstone R :A:	.25	.40
254 Epitaph Golem U :A:	.20	.35
255 Explosive Apparatus C :A:	.10	.20
256 Harvest Hand	.20	.35
257 Haunted Cloak U :A:	.20	.35
258 Magnifying Glass U :A:	.20	.35
259 Murderer's Axe U :A:	.20	.35
260 Neglected Heirloom	.20	.35
261 Runaway Carriage U :A:	.20	.35
262 Shard of Broken Glass C :A:	.10	.20
263 Skeleton Key U :A:	.20	.35
264 Slayer's Plate R :A:	.25	.40
265 Tamiyo's Journal R :A:	.25	.40
266 Thraben Gargoyle	.20	.35
267 True-Faith Censer C :A:	.10	.20
268 Wicker Witch C :A:	.10	.20
269 Wild-Field Scarecrow U :A:	.20	.35
270 Choked Estuary R :L:	1.50	2.00
271 Drownyard Temple R :L:	.25	.40
272 Foreboding Ruins R :L:	2.75	3.25
273 Forsaken Sanctuary U :L:	.20	.35
274 Fortified Village R :L:	1.00	1.50
275 Foul Orchard U :L:	.20	.35
276 Game Trail R :L:	4.00	5.00
277 Highland Lake U :L:	.20	.35
278 Port Town R :L:	3.00	3.50
279 Stone Quarry U :L:	.20	.35
280 Warped Landscape C :L:	.10	.20
281 Westvale Abbey	3.00	3.50
282 Woodland Stream U :L:	.20	.35
283 Plains L :L:	.10	.20
284 Plains L :L:	.10	.20
285 Plains L :L:	.10	.20
286 Island L :L:	.10	.20
287 Island L :L:	.10	.20
288 Island L :L:	.10	.20
289 Swamp L :L:	.10	.20
290 Swamp L :L:	.10	.20
291 Swamp L :L:	.10	.20
292 Mountain L :L:	.10	.20
293 Mountain L :L:	.10	.20
294 Mountain L :L:	.10	.20
295 Forest L :L:	.10	.20
296 Forest L :L:	.10	.20
297 Forest L :L:	.10	.20

2016 Magic The Gathering Shadows over Innistrad Foil

COMPLETE SET (297)	360.00	500.00
1 Always Watching R :W:	2.00	3.00
2 Angel of Deliverance R :W:	.50	.75
3 Angelic Purge C :W:	.75	1.00
4 Apothecary Geist C :W:	.20	.35
5 Archangel Avacyn	25.00	30.00
6 Avacynian Missionaries	.20	.35
7 Bound by Moonsilver U :W:	.20	.35
8 Bygone Bishop R :W:	1.50	2.00
9 Cathar's Companion C :W:	.20	.35
10 Chaplain's Blessing C :W:	.20	.35
11 Dauntless Cathar C :W:	.20	.35
12 Declaration in Stone R :W:	5.00	6.00
13 Descend upon the Sinful M :W:	3.00	5.00
14 Devilthorn Fox C :W:	.20	.35
15 Drogskol Cavalry R :W:	.40	.60
16 Eerie Interlude R :W:	1.50	2.25
17 Emissary of the Sleepless C :W:	.20	.35
18 Ethereal Guidance C :W:	.20	.35
19 Expose Evil C :W:	.20	.35
20 Gryff's Boon U :W:	1.00	1.50
21 Hanweir Militia Captain	1.00	1.50
22 Hope Against Hope U :W:	.20	.35
23 Humble the Brute U :W:	.20	.35
24 Inquisitor's Ox C :W:	.20	.35
25 Inspiring Captain C :W:	.20	.35
26 Militant Inquisitor C :W:	.20	.35
27 Moorland Drifter C :W:	.20	.35
28 Nahiri's Machinations U :W:	.20	.35
29 Nearheath Chaplain U :W:	.20	.35
30 Not Forgotten U :W:	.20	.35
31 Odric, Lunarch Marshal R :W:	2.00	3.00
32 Open the Armory U :W:	2.50	3.50
33 Paranoid Parish-Blade U :W:	.20	.35
34 Pious Evangel	.20	.35
35 Puncturing Light C :W:	.20	.35
36 Reaper of Flight Moonsilver U :W:	.20	.35
37 Silverstrike U :W:	.20	.35
38 Spectral Shepherd U :W:	.20	.35
39 Stern Constable C :W:	.20	.35
40 Strength of Arms C :W:	.20	.35
41 Survive the Night C :W:	.20	.35
42 Tenacity U :W:	.20	.35
43 Thalia's Lieutenant R :W:	3.00	4.00
44 Thraben Inspector C :W:	3.50	4.50
45 Topplegeist U :W:	1.25	1.75
46 Town Gossipmonger	.75	1.00
Incited Rabble U		
47 Unruly Mob C :W:	.20	.35
48 Vessel of Ephemera C :W:	.20	.35
49 Aberrant Researcher	.20	.35
50 Broken Concentration U :B:	.20	.35
51 Catalog C :B:	.20	.35
52 Compelling Deterrence U :B:	.20	.35
53 Confirm Suspicions R :B:	1.00	1.50
54 Daring Sleuth	.20	.35
55 Deny Existence C :B:	.20	.35
56 Drownyard Explorers C :B:	.20	.35
57 Drunau Corpse Trawler U :B:	.20	.35
58 Engulf the Shore R :B:	.75	1.25
59 Epiphany at the Drownyard R :B:	.60	1.00
60 Erdwal Illuminator U :B:	.20	.35
61 Essence Flux U :B:	1.00	1.50
62 Fleeting Memories U :B:	.20	.35
63 Forgotten Creation R :B:	1.00	1.25
64 Furtive Homunculus C :B:	.20	.35
65 Geralf's Masterpiece M :B:	1.50	2.00
66 Ghostly Wings C :B:	.20	.35
67 Gone Missing C :B:	.20	.35
68 Invasive Surgery U :B:	2.00	3.00
69 Jace, Unraveler of Secrets M :B:	13.00	16.00
70 Jace's Scrutiny C :B:	.20	.35
71 Just the Wind C :B:	.20	.35
72 Lamplighter of Selhoff C :B:	.20	.35
73 Manic Scribe U :B:	1.50	2.00
74 Nagging Thoughts C :B:	.20	.35
75 Nephalia Moondrakes R :B:	.30	.50
76 Niblis of Dusk C :B:	.20	.35
77 Ongoing Investigation U :B:	.50	.75
78 Pieces of the Puzzle C :B:	.20	.35
79 Pore Over the Pages U :B:	.20	.35
80 Press for Answers C :B:	.20	.35
81 Rattlechains R :B:	3.00	4.00
82 Reckless Scholar U :B:	.20	.35
83 Rise from the Tides U :B:	.20	.35
84 Seagraf Skaab C :B:	.20	.35
85 Silburlind Snapper C :B:	.20	.35
86 Silent Observer C :B:	.20	.35
87 Sleep Paralysis C :B:	.20	.35
88 Startled Awake	3.00	4.00
89 Stitched Mangler C :B:	.20	.35
90 Stitchwing Skaab U :B:	.50	.75
91 Stormrider Spirit C :B:	.20	.35
92 Thing in the Ice	13.00	16.00
93 Trail of Evidence U :B:	.50	.75
94 Uninvited Geist	.20	.35
95 Vessel of Paramnesia C :B:	.20	.35
96 Welcome to the Fold R :B:	.40	.60
97 Accursed Witch	.20	.35
98 Alms of the Vein C :K:	.60	1.00
99 Asylum Visitor R :K:	1.25	2.00
100 Behind the Scenes U :K:	.20	.35
101 Behold the Beyond M :K:	2.00	2.50
102 Biting Rain U :K:	.20	.35
103 Call the Bloodline U :K:	1.00	1.50
104 Creeping Dread U :K:	.20	.35
105 Crow of Dark Tidings C :K:	.20	.35
106 Dead Weight C :K:	.20	.35
107 Diregraf Colossus R :K:	2.00	3.00
108 Elusive Tormentor	.50	.75
109 Ever After R :K:	1.50	2.00
110 Farbog Revenant C :K:	.20	.35
111 From Under the Floorboards R :K:	.50	.75
112 Ghoulcaller's Accomplice C :K:	.20	.35
113 Ghoulsteed U :K:	.20	.35
114 Gisa's Bidding U :K:	.20	.35
115 Grotesque Mutation C :K:	.20	.35
116 Heir of Falkenrath	2.50	3.00
117 Hound of the Farbogs C :K:	.20	.35
118 Indulgent Aristocrat U :K:	1.00	1.50
119 Kindly Stranger	.20	.35
120 Liliana's Indignation U :K:	.20	.35
121 Macabre Waltz C :K:	.20	.35
122 Markov Dreadknight R :K:	.40	.60
123 Merciless Resolve C :K:	.20	.35
124 Mindwrack Demon M :K:	3.50	4.50
125 Morkrut Necropod U :K:	.20	.35
126 Murderous Compulsion C :K:	.20	.35
127 Olivia's Bloodsworn U :K:	.50	.75
128 Pale Rider of Trostad U :K:	.20	.35
129 Pick the Brain U :K:	.75	1.00
130 Rancid Rats C :K:	.20	.35
131 Relentless Dead M :K:	7.00	9.00
132 Rottenheart Ghoul C :K:	.20	.35
133 Sanitarium Skeleton C :K:	.20	.35
134 Shamble Back C :K:	.20	.35
135 Sinister Concoction U :K:	.75	1.00
136 Stallion of Ashmouth C :K:	.20	.35
137 Stromkirk Mentor C :K:	.20	.35
138 Throttle C :K:	.20	.35
139 To the Slaughter R :K:	2.00	3.00
140 Tooth Collector U :K:	.20	.35
141 Triskaidekaphobia R :K:	1.50	2.00
142 Twins of Maurer Estate C :K:	.20	.35
143 Vampire Noble C :K:	.20	.35
144 Vessel of Malignity C :K:	.20	.35
145 Avacyn's Judgment R :R:	.60	1.00
146 Bloodmad Vampire C :R:	.20	.35
147 Breakneck Rider	.75	1.00
Neck Breaker U		
148 Burn from Within R :R:	.50	.75
149 Convicted Killer	.20	.35
150 Dance with Devils U :R:	.20	.35
151 Devils' Playground R :R:	.50	.75
152 Dissension in the Ranks U :R:	.20	.35
153 Dual Shot C :R:	.20	.35
154 Ember-Eye Wolf C :R:	.20	.35
155 Falkenrath Gorger R :R:	1.50	2.00
156 Fiery Temper C :R:	1.50	2.00
157 Flameblade Angel R :R:	.40	.60
158 Gatstaf Arsonists	.20	.35
159 Geier Reach Bandit	1.75	2.50
160 Geistblast U :R:	.20	.35
161 Gibbering Fiend U :R:	.20	.35
162 Goldnight Castigator M :R:	1.50	2.00
163 Harness the Storm R :R:	.75	1.00
164 Howlpack Wolf C :R:	.20	.35
165 Hulking Devil C :R:	.20	.35
166 Incorrigible Youths U :R:	.60	1.00
167 Inner Struggle U :R:	.20	.35
168 Insolent Neonate C :R:	3.00	4.00
169 Kessig Forgemaster	.75	1.25
170 Lightning Axe U :R:	2.50	3.00
171 Mad Prophet U :R:	.20	.35
172 Magmatic Chasm C :R:	.20	.35
173 Malevolent Whispers U :R:	.20	.35
174 Pyre Hound C :R:	.20	.35
175 Ravenous Bloodseeker U :R:	.20	.35
176 Reduce to Ashes C :R:	.20	.35
177 Rush of Adrenaline C :R:	.40	.60
178 Sanguinary Mage C :R:	.20	.35
179 Scourge Wolf R :R:	.50	.75
180 Senseless Rage C :R:	.20	.35
181 Sin Prodder R :R:	1.50	2.00
182 Skin Invasion	1.00	1.50
183 Spiteful Motives U :R:	.20	.35
184 Stensia Masquerade U :R:	.50	.75
185 Structural Distortion C :R:	.20	.35
186 Tormenting Voice C :R:	.75	1.00
187 Ulrich's Kindred U :R:	.20	.35
188 Uncaged Fury C :R:	.40	.60
189 Vessel of Volatility C :R:	.20	.35
190 Village Messenger	2.00	3.00
191 Voldaren Duelist C :R:	.20	.35
192 Wolf of Devil's Breach M :R:	1.00	1.50
193 Aim High C :G:	.20	.35
194 Autumnal Gloom	.20	.35
195 Briarbridge Patrol U :G:	.20	.35
196 Byway Courier C :G:	.20	.35
197 Clip Wings C :G:	.20	.35
198 Confront the Unknown C :G:	.20	.35
199 Crawling Sensation U :G:	.20	.35
200 Cryptolith Rite R :G:	3.00	3.50
201 Cult of the Waxing Moon U :G:	.20	.35
202 Deathcap Cultivator R :G:	1.00	1.50
203 Duskwatch Recruiter	4.00	5.00
204 Equestrian Skill C :G:	.20	.35
205 Fork in the Road C :G:	.20	.35
206 Gloomwidow U :G:	.20	.35
207 Graf Mole U :G:	.20	.35
208 Groundskeeper U :G:	.20	.35
209 Hermit of the Natterknolls	1.00	1.25
210 Hinterland Logger	.20	.35
211 Howlpack Resurgence U :G:	1.50	2.00
212 Inexorable Blob R :G:	.40	.60
213 Intrepid Provisioner C :G:	.20	.35
214 Kessig Dire Swine C :G:	.20	.35
215 Lambholt Pacifist	1.50	2.00
216 Loam Dryad C :G:	.20	.35
217 Might Beyond Reason C :G:	.20	.35
218 Moldgraf Scavenger C :G:	.20	.35
219 Moonlight Hunt U :G:	.50	.75
220 Obsessive Skinner U :G:	.20	.35
221 Pack Guardian U :G:	.20	.35
222 Quilled Wolf C :G:	.20	.35
223 Rabid Bite C :G:	.20	.35
224 Root Out C :G:	.20	.35
225 Sage of Ancient Lore	.75	1.00
226 Seasons Past M :G:	5.00	6.00
227 Second Harvest R :G:	1.25	2.00
228 Silverfur Partisan R :G:	1.00	2.50
229 Solitary Hunter	.20	.35
230 Soul Swallower R :G:	.50	.75
231 Stoic Builder C :G:	.20	.35
232 Thornhide Wolves C :G:	.20	.35
233 Tireless Tracker R :G:	9.00	11.00
234 Traverse the Ulvenwald R :G:	6.00	7.00
235 Ulvenwald Hydra M :G:	4.00	5.00
236 Ulvenwald Mysteries U :G:	.50	.75
237 Vessel of Nascency C :G:	1.50	2.50
238 Veteran Cathar U :G:	.20	.35
239 Watcher in the Web C :G:	.20	.35
240 Weirding Wood U :G:	.20	.35
241 Altered Ego R :G::B:	1.25	2.00
242 Anguished Unmaking R :W::K:	3.00	3.50
243 Arlinn Kord	13.00	16.00
244 Fevered Visions R :B::R:	3.00	4.00
245 The Gitrog Monster M :K::G:	8.00	10.00
246 Invocation of Saint Traft R :W::B:	.60	1.00
247 Nahiri, the Harbinger M :R::W:	40.00	45.00
248 Olivia, Mobilized for War M :K::R:	4.00	5.00
249 Prized Amalgam R :B::K:	5.00	6.50
250 Sigarda, Heron's Grace M :G::W:	5.00	6.00
251 Sorin, Grim Nemesis M :W::K:	12.00	15.00
252 Brain in a Jar R :A:	2.00	3.00
253 Corrupted Grafstone R :A:	.75	1.00
254 Epitaph Golem U :A:	.20	.35
255 Explosive Apparatus C :A:	.20	.35
256 Harvest Hand	.20	.35
257 Haunted Cloak U :A:	.50	.75
258 Magnifying Glass U :A:	.20	.35
259 Murderer's Axe U :A:	.20	.35
260 Neglected Heirloom	1.00	1.25
261 Runaway Carriage U :A:	.20	.35
262 Shard of Broken Glass C :A:	.20	.35
263 Skeleton Key U :A:	.20	.35
264 Slayer's Plate R :A:	.40	.60
265 Tamiyo's Journal R :A:	2.00	3.00
266 Thraben Gargoyle	.20	.35
267 True-Faith Censer C :A:	.20	.35
268 Wicker Witch C :A:	.20	.35
269 Wild-Field Scarecrow U :A:	.20	.35
270 Choked Estuary R :L:	3.00	4.00
271 Drownyard Temple R :L:	1.50	2.00
272 Foreboding Ruins R :L:	3.00	4.00
273 Forsaken Sanctuary U :L:	1.25	1.75
274 Fortified Village R :L:	2.50	3.50
275 Foul Orchard U :L:	.50	.75
276 Game Trail R :L:	5.00	7.00
277 Highland Lake U :L:	1.00	1.50
278 Port Town R :L:	3.00	4.00
279 Stone Quarry U :L:	.20	.35
280 Warped Landscape C :L:	.20	.35
281 Westvale Abbey	6.00	8.00
282 Woodland Stream U :L:	.50	.75
283 Plains L :L:	.20	.35
284 Plains L :L:	.20	.35
285 Plains L :L:	.20	.35
286 Island L :L:	.20	.35
287 Island L :L:	.20	.35
288 Island L :L:	.20	.35
289 Swamp L :L:	.20	.35
290 Swamp L :L:	.20	.35
291 Swamp L :L:	.20	.35
292 Mountain L :L:	.20	.35
293 Mountain L :L:	.20	.35
294 Mountain L :L:	.20	.35
295 Forest L :L:	.20	.35
296 Forest L :L:	.20	.35
297 Forest L :L:	.20	.35

2016 Magic The Gathering Shadows over Innistrad Tokens

1 Angel	.40	.60
2 Human Soldier	.10	.15
3 Spirit	.10	.15
4 Vampire Knight	.60	1.00
5 Zombie	.10	.15
6 Devil	.30	.40
7 Insect	.15	.25
8 Ooze	.10	.15
9 Wolf	.25	.35
10 Human Cleric	2.50	4.00
11 Clue	.10	.15
12 Clue	.10	.15
13 Clue	.10	.15
14 Clue	.10	.15
15 Clue	.10	.15
16 Clue	.10	.15
17 Jace, Unraveler of Secrets Emblem	1.75	3.00
18 Arlinn Kord Emblem	.40	.60
CH1 Shadows over Innistrad CL 1	.10	.15
CH2 Shadows over Innistrad CL 2	.15	.25

2016 Magic The Gathering Eldritch Moon

COMPLETE SET (205)	160.00	220.00
BOOSTER BOX (36 PACKS)	90.00	120.00
BOOSTER PACK (15 CARDS)	4.00	5.00
*FOIL: .75X TO 2X BASIC CARDS		
RELEASED ON JULY 22, 2016		
1 Abundant Maw U	.20	.35
2 Decimator of the Provinces MR	1.25	2.00
3 Distended Mindbender R	.50	.75
4 Drownyard Behemoth U	.20	.35
5 Elder Deep Fiend R	1.50	2.00
6 Emrakul the Promised End MR	10.00	15.00
7 Eternal Scourge R	.30	.50
8 It of the Horrid Swarm C	.15	.25
9 Lashweed Lurker U	.20	.35
10 Mockery of Nature U	.20	.35
11 Vexing Scuttler U	.20	.35
12 Wretched Gryff C	.15	.25
13 Blessed Alliance U	.20	.35
14 Borrowed Grace C	.15	.25
15 Bruna, The Fading Light R	.75	1.25
16 Choking Restraints C	.15	.25
17 Collective Effort R	.30	.50
18 Courageous Outrider U	.20	.35
19 Dawn Gryff C	.15	.25
20 Deploy the Gatewatch MR	1.00	1.25
21 Desperate Sentry C	.15	.25
22 Drogskol Shieldmate U	.20	.35
23 Extricator of Sin, Extricator of Flesh U	.20	.35
24 Faith Unbroken U	.20	.35
25 Faith Bearer Paladin C	.15	.25
26 Fiend Binder C	.15	.25

27 Geist of the Lonely Vigil U .20 .35
28 Gisela, the Broken Blade MR 9.00 12.00
29 Give No Ground U .20 .35
30 Guardian of Pilgrims C .15 .25
31 Ironclad Slayer C .15 .25
32 Ironwrights Cleansing C .15 .25
33 Lone Rider, It That Rides as One U .20 .35
34 Long Road Home U .20 .35
35 Lunarch Mantle C .15 .25
36 Peace of Mind U .20 .35
37 Providence R .20 .35
38 Repel the Abominable U .20 .35
39 Sanctifier of Souls R .20 .35
40 Selfless Spirit R 7.00 9.00
41 Sigardas Aid R .75 1.00
42 Sigardian Priest C .15 .25
43 Spectral Reserves C .15 .25
44 Steadfast Cathar C .15 .25
45 Subjugator Angel U .20 .15
46 Thalia Heretic Cathar R 2.75 3.25
47 Thalias Lancers R .30 .50
48 Thraben Standard Bearer C .15 .25
49 Advanced Stitchwing U .20 .35
50 Chilling Grasp U .20 .35
51 Coax from the Blind Eternities R .20 .35
52 Contingency Plan C .15 .25
53 Convolute C .15 .25
54 Curious Homunculus, Voracious Reader U .20 .35
55 Displace C .15 .25
56 Docent of Perfection, Final Iteration R .20 .35
57 Drag Under C .15 .25
58 Enlightened Maniac C .15 .25
59 Exultant Cultist C .15 .25
60 Fogwalker C .15 .25
61 Fortunes Favor U .20 .35
62 Geist of the Archives U .20 .35
63 Grizzled Angler, Grisly Anglerfish U .20 .35
64 Identity Thief R .20 .35
65 Imprisoned in the Moon R .30 .50
66 Ingenious Skaab C .15 .25
67 Laboratory Brute C .15 .25
68 Lunar Force U .20 .35
69 Mausoleum Wanderer R .75 1.25
70 Mind's Dilation MR .75 1.25
71 Nebelgast Herald U .20 .35
72 Niblis of Frost R .30 .50
73 Scour the Laboratory U .20 .35
74 Spontaneous Mutation C .15 .25
75 Summary Dismissal R 1.50 2.00
76 Take Inventory C .15 .25
77 Tattered Haunter C .15 .25
78 Turn Aside C .15 .25
79 Unsubstantiate U .20 .35
80 Wharf Infiltrator R .20 .35
81 Boon of Emrakul C .15 .25
82 Borrowed Malevolence C .15 .25
83 Cemetery Recruitment C .15 .25
84 Certain Death C .15 .25
85 Collective Brutality R 6.00 8.00
86 Cryptbreaker R 1.25 1.75
87 Dark Salvation R .30 .50
88 Dusk Feaster U .20 .35
89 Gavony Unhallowed C .15 .25
90 Graf Harvest U .20 .35
91 Graf Rats C .15 .25
92 Haunted Dead U .20 .35
93 Liliana, the Last Hope MR 35.00 40.00
94 Lilianas Elite U .20 .35
95 Markov Crusader U .20 .35
96 Midnight Scavengers C .15 .25
97 Murder U .20 .35
98 Noosegraf Mob R .20 .35
99 Oath of Liliana R .20 .35
100 Olivias Dragoon C .15 .25
101 Prying Questions C .15 .25
102 Rise from the Grave U .20 .35
103 Ruthless Disposal U .20 .35
104 Skirsdag Supplicant C .15 .25
105 Strange Augmentation C .15 .25
106 Stromkirk Condemned R .30 .50
107 Succumb to Temptation C .15 .25
108 Thraben Foulbloods C .15 .25
109 Tree of Perdition MR 2.50 3.00
110 Vampire Cutthroat U .20 .35
111 Voldaren Pariah, Abolisher of Bloodlines R 1.00 1.50
112 Wailing Ghoul C .15 .25
113 Weirded Vampire C .15 .25
114 Whispers of Emrakul U .20 .35
115 Aandon Reason U .20 .35
116 Alchemists Greeting C .15 .25
117 Assembled Alphas R .20 .35
118 Bedlam Reveler R 1.50 2.00
119 Blood Mist U .20 .35
120 Bold Impaler C .15 .25
121 Borrowed Hostility C .15 .25
122 Brazen Wolves C .15 .25
123 Collective Defiance R 1.50 2.00
124 Conduit of Storms, Conduit of Emrakul U .20 .35
125 Deranged Whelp U .20 .35
126 Distmper of the Blood C .15 .25
127 Falkenrath Reaver C .15 .25
128 Furyblade Vampire U .20 .35
129 Galvanic Bombardment C .15 .25
130 Hanweir Garrison R 1.00 1.50
131 Harmless Offering R .20 .35
132 Impetuous Devils R .20 .35
133 Incendiary Flow U .20 .35
134 Insatiable Gorgers U .20 .35
135 Make Mischief C .15 .25
136 Mirrorwing Dragon MR .75 1.25
137 Nahiris Wrath MR 1.25 1.75
138 Otherworldly Outburst C .15 .25
139 Prophetic Ravings C .15 .25
140 Savage Alliance U .20 .35
141 Shreds of Sanity U .20 .35
142 Smoldering Werewolf, Erupting Dreadwolf U .20 .35
143 Spreading Flames U .20 .35
144 Stensia Banquet C .15 .25
145 Stensia Innkeeper C .15 .25
146 Stromkirk Occultist R .20 .35
147 Thermo Alchemist C .15 .25
148 Vildin Pack Outcast, Dronepack kindred C .15 .25
149 Weaver of Lightning U .20 .35
150 Backwoods Survivalists C .15 .25
151 Bloodbriar C .15 .25
152 Clear Shot U .20 .35
153 Crop Sigil U .20 .35
154 Crossroads Consecrator C .15 .25
155 Eldritch Evolution R 1.75 2.25
156 Emrakuls Evangel R .20 .35
157 Emrakuls Influence U .20 .35
158 Foul Emissary U .20 .35
159 Gnarlwood Dryad U .20 .35
160 Grapple with the Past C .15 .25
161 Hamlet Captain U .20 .35
162 Ishkanah, Grafwidow MR 8.00 10.00
163 Kessig Prowler, Sinuous Predator U .20 .35
164 Noose Constrictor U .20 .35
165 Permeating Mass R .20 .35
166 Prey Upon C .15 .25
167 Primal Druid C .15 .25
168 Shrill Howler, Howling Chorus U .20 .35
169 Somberwald Stag U .20 .35
170 Spirit of the Hunt R .20 .35
171 Splendid Reclamation R .40 .60
172 Springsage Ritual C .15 .25
173 Swift Spinner C .15 .25
174 Tangleclaw Werewolf, Fibrous Entangler U .20 .35
175 Ulvenwald Captive, Ulvenwald Abomination C .15 .25
176 Ulvenwald Observer R .20 .35
177 Waxing Moon C .15 .25
178 Wolfkin Bond C .15 .25
179 Woodcutters Grit C .15 .25
180 Woodland Patrol C .15 .25
181 Bloodhall Priest R .25 .40
182 Campaign of Vengeance U .20 .35
183 Gisa and Geralf MR 1.25 1.75
184 Grim Flayer MR 18.00 22.00
185 Herons Grace Champion R .20 .35
186 Mercurial Geists U .20 .35
187 Mournwillow U .20 .35
188 Ride Down U .20 .35
189 Spell Queller R 5.00 7.00
190 Tamiyo Field Researcher MR 9.00 11.00
191 Ulrich of the Krallenhorde, Ulrich, Uncontested Alpha MR .75 1.25
192 Cathars Shield U .20 .35
193 Cryptolith Fragment, Aurora of Emrakul U .20 .35
194 Cultists Staff C .15 .25
195 Field Creeper C .15 .25
196 Geist Fueled Scarecrow U .20 .35
197 Lupine Prototype R .40 .60
198 Slayers Cleaver U .20 .35
199 Soul Separator R .20 .35
200 Stitchers Graft R .20 .35
201 Terrarion C .15 .25
202 Thirsting Axe U .20 .35
203 Geier Reach Sanitarium R .50 .75
204 Hanweir Battlements R .50 .75
205 Nephalia Academy U .20 .35

2016 Magic The Gathering Eldritch Moon Foil

COMPLETE SET (205) 370.00 500.00
1 Abundant Maw U .40 .60
2 Decimator of the Provinces MR 3.00 4.00
3 Distended Mindbender R 1.75 2.50
4 Drownyard Behemoth U .40 .60
5 Elder Deep Fiend R 4.50 6.00
6 Emrakul the Promised End MR 25.00 30.00
7 Eternal Scourge R 2.00 2.50
8 It of the Horrid Swarm C .30 .50
9 Lashweed Lurker U .40 .60
10 Mockery of Nature U .40 .60
11 Vexing Scuttler U .40 .60
12 Wretched Gryff C .30 .50
13 Blessed Alliance U .40 .60
14 Borrowed Grace C .30 .50
15 Bruna, The Fading Light R 5.50 6.50
16 Choking Restraints C .30 .50
17 Collective Effort R 1.00 1.50
18 Courageous Outrider U .40 .60
19 Dawn Gryff C .30 .50
20 Deploy the Gatewatch MR 5.00 6.00
21 Desperate Sentry C .30 .50
22 Drogskol Shieldmate U .40 .60
23 Extricator of Sin, Extricator of Flesh U .40 .60
24 Faith Unbroken U .40 .60
25 Faith Bearer Paladin C .30 .50
26 Fiend Binder C .30 .50
27 Geist of the Lonely Vigil U .40 .60
28 Gisela, the Broken Blade MR 15.00 20.00
29 Give No Ground U .40 .60
30 Guardian of Pilgrims C .30 .50
31 Ironclad Slayer C .30 .50
32 Ironwrights Cleansing C .30 .50
33 Lone Rider, It That Rides as One U .40 .60
34 Long Road Home U .40 .60
35 Lunarch Mantle C .30 .50
36 Peace of Mind U .40 .60
37 Providence R .40 .60
38 Repel the Abominable U .40 .60
39 Sanctifier of Souls R .30 .50
40 Selfless Spirit R 6.00 10.00
41 Sigardas Aid R 3.00 4.00
42 Sigardian Priest C .30 .50
43 Spectral Reserves C .30 .50
44 Steadfast Cathar C .30 .50
45 Subjugator Angel U .30 .50
46 Thalia Heretic Cathar R 5.00 7.00
47 Thalias Lancers R 1.50 2.00
48 Thraben Standard Bearer C .30 .50
49 Advanced Stitchwing U .40 .60
50 Chilling Grasp U .40 .60
51 Coax from the Blind Eternities R .50 .75
52 Contingency Plan C .30 .50
53 Convolute C .30 .50
54 Curious Homunculus, Voracious Reader U .40 .60
55 Displace C .30 .50
56 Docent of Perfection, Final Iteration R 1.50 2.00
57 Drag Under C .30 .50
58 Enlightened Maniac C .30 .50
59 Exultant Cultist C .30 .50
60 Fogwalker C .30 .50
61 Fortunes Favor U .40 .60
62 Geist of the Archives U .40 .60
63 Grizzled Angler, Grisly Anglerfish U .40 .60
64 Identity Thief R .30 .50
65 Imprisoned in the Moon R 1.50 2.00
66 Ingenious Skaab C .30 .50
67 Laboratory Brute C .30 .50
68 Lunar Force U .40 .60
69 Mausoleum Wanderer R 2.50 3.50
70 Mind's Dilation MR 4.00 5.50
71 Nebelgast Herald U .40 .60
72 Niblis of Frost R .75 1.25
73 Scour the Laboratory U .40 .60
74 Spontaneous Mutation C .30 .50
75 Summary Dismissal R 3.00 4.00
76 Take Inventory C .30 .50
77 Tattered Haunter C .30 .50
78 Turn Aside C .30 .50
79 Unsubstantiate U .40 .60
80 Wharf Infiltrator R .50 .75
81 Boon of Emrakul C .30 .50
82 Borrowed Malevolence C .30 .50
83 Cemetery Recruitment C .30 .50
84 Certain Death C .30 .50
85 Collective Brutality R 15.00 20.00
86 Cryptbreaker R 5.00 8.00
87 Dark Salvation R .75 1.25
88 Dusk Feaster U .40 .60
89 Gavony Unhallowed C .30 .50
90 Graf Harvest U .40 .60
91 Graf Rats C .30 .50
92 Haunted Dead U .40 .60
93 Liliana, the Last Hope MR 55.00 65.00
94 Lilianas Elite U .40 .60
95 Markov Crusader U .40 .60
96 Midnight Scavengers C .30 .50
97 Murder U .40 .60
98 Noosegraf Mob R .50 .75
99 Oath of Liliana R 2.00 2.50
100 Olivias Dragoon C .30 .50
101 Prying Questions C .30 .50
102 Rise from the Grave U .40 .60
103 Ruthless Disposal U .40 .60
104 Skirsdag Supplicant C .30 .50
105 Strange Augmentation C .30 .50
106 Stromkirk Condemned R .75 1.25
107 Succumb to Temptation C .30 .50
108 Thraben Foulbloods C .30 .50
109 Tree of Perdition MR 4.00 6.00
110 Vampire Cutthroat U .40 .60
111 Voldaren Pariah, Abolisher of Bloodlines R 2.50 3.50
112 Wailing Ghoul C .30 .50
113 Weirded Vampire C .30 .50
114 Whispers of Emrakul U .40 .60
115 Aandon Reason U .40 .60
116 Alchemists Greeting C .30 .50
117 Assembled Alphas R .40 .60
118 Bedlam Reveler R 3.00 5.00
119 Blood Mist U .40 .60
120 Bold Impaler C .30 .50
121 Borrowed Hostility C .30 .50
122 Brazen Wolves C .30 .50
123 Collective Defiance R 2.50 3.50
124 Conduit of Storms, Conduit of Emrakul U .40 .60
125 Deranged Whelp U .40 .60
126 Distmper of the Blood C .30 .50
127 Falkenrath Reaver C .30 .50
128 Furyblade Vampire U .40 .60
129 Galvanic Bombardment C .30 .50
130 Hanweir Garrison R 3.00 4.00
131 Harmless Offering R 2.25 3.00
132 Impetuous Devils R .50 .75
133 Incendiary Flow U .40 .60
134 Insatiable Gorgers U .40 .60
135 Make Mischief C .30 .50
136 Mirrorwing Dragon MR 2.00 3.00
137 Nahiris Wrath MR 2.00 3.00
138 Otherworldly Outburst C .30 .50
139 Prophetic Ravings C .30 .50
140 Savage Alliance U .40 .60
141 Shreds of Sanity U .40 .60
142 Smoldering Werewolf, Erupting Dreadwolf U .40 .60
143 Spreading Flames U .40 .60
144 Stensia Banquet C .30 .50
145 Stensia Innkeeper C .30 .50
146 Stromkirk Occultist R .50 .75
147 Thermo Alchemist C .30 .50
148 Vildin Pack Outcast, Dronepack kindred C .30 .50
149 Weaver of Lightning U .40 .60
150 Backwoods Survivalists C .30 .50
151 Bloodbriar C .30 .50
152 Clear Shot U .40 .60
153 Crop Sigil U .40 .60
154 Crossroads Consecrator C .30 .50
155 Eldritch Evolution R 5.00 7.00
156 Emrakuls Evangel R .50 .75
157 Emrakuls Influence U .40 .60
158 Foul Emissary U .40 .60
159 Gnarlwood Dryad U .40 .60
160 Grapple with the Past C .30 .50
161 Hamlet Captain U .40 .60
162 Ishkanah, Grafwidow MR 8.00 11.00
163 Kessig Prowler, Sinuous Predator U .40 .60
164 Noose Constrictor U .40 .60
165 Permeating Mass R .75 1.00
166 Prey Upon C .30 .50
167 Primal Druid C .30 .50
168 Shrill Howler, Howling Chorus U .40 .60
169 Somberwald Stag U .40 .60
170 Spirit of the Hunt R .50 .75
171 Splendid Reclamation R 3.00 4.00
172 Springsage Ritual C .30 .50
173 Swift Spinner C .30 .50
174 Tangleclaw Werewolf, Fibrous Entangler U .40 .60
175 Ulvenwald Captive, Ulvenwald Abomination C .30 .50
176 Ulvenwald Observer R .30 .50
177 Waxing Moon C .30 .50
178 Wolfkin Bond C .30 .50
179 Woodcutters Grit C .30 .50
180 Woodland Patrol C .30 .50
181 Bloodhall Priest R 1.00 1.50
182 Campaign of Vengeance U .40 .60
183 Gisa and Geralf MR 4.00 5.00
184 Grim Flayer MR 20.00 30.00
185 Herons Grace Champion R .75 1.00
186 Mercurial Geists U .40 .60
187 Mournwillow U .40 .60
188 Ride Down U .40 .60
189 Spell Queller R 10.00 13.00
190 Tamiyo Field Researcher MR 15.00 20.00
191 Ulrich of the Krallenhorde, Ulrich, Uncontested Alpha MR 3.00 4.50
192 Cathars Shield U .40 .60
193 Cryptolith Fragment, Aurora of Emrakul U .40 .60
194 Cultists Staff C .30 .50
195 Field Creeper C .30 .50
196 Geist Fueled Scarecrow U .40 .60
197 Lupine Prototype R 1.25 1.75
198 Slayers Cleaver U .40 .60
199 Soul Separator R .50 .75
200 Stitchers Graft R .50 .75
201 Terrarion C .30 .50
202 Thirsting Axe U .40 .60
203 Geier Reach Sanitarium R 2.75 3.50
204 Hanweir Battlements R 2.00 2.50
205 Nephalia Academy U .40 .60

2016 Magic The Gathering Eldritch Moon Tokens

1 Eldrazi Horror .10 .15
2 Human Wizard .75 1.25
3 Zombie .10 .15
4 Zombie .25 .35
5 Zombie .10 .15
6 Zombie .10 .15
7 Human Wizard .10 .15
8 Spider .20 .30
9 Liliana, the Last Hope Emblem .30 .40
10 Tamiyo, Field Researcher Emblem .10 .15
CH1 Eldritch Moon CL .10 .15

2016 Magic The Gathering Kaladesh

COMPLETE SET (286) 200.00 300.00
BOOSTER BOX (36 PACKS) 90.00 120.00
BOOSTER PACK (15 CARDS) 3.00 5.00
*FOIL: .75X TO 2X BASIC CARDS
RELEASED ON SEPTEMBER 30, 2016
1 Acrobatic Maneuver C .10 .20
2 Aerial Responder U .15 .25
3 Aetherstorm Roc R .10 .20
4 Angel of Invention M 2.00 3.00
5 Authority of the Consuls R 1.00 1.50
6 Aviary Mechanic C .10 .20
7 Built to Last C .10 .20
8 Captured by the Consulate R .10 .20
9 Cataclysmic Gearhulk M .60 1.00
10 Consulate Surveillance U .15 .25
11 Consuls Shieldguard U .15 .25
12 Eddytrail Hawk C .10 .20
13 Fairgrounds Warden U .15 .25
14 Fragmentize C .10 .20
15 Fumigate R 1.25 2.00
16 Gearshift Ace U .15 .25
17 Glint Sleeve Artisan C .10 .20
18 Herald of the Fair C .10 .20
19 Impeccable Timing C .10 .20
20 Inspired Charge C .10 .20
21 Master Trinketeer R .20 .35
22 Ninth Bridge Patrol C .10 .20
23 Pressure Point C .10 .20
24 Propeller Pioneer C .10 .20
25 Refurbish U .15 .25
26 Revoke Privileges C .10 .20
27 Servo Exhibition U .15 .25
28 Skywhirl Harrier C .10 .20
29 Skywhalers Shot U .15 .25
30 Tasseled Dromedary C .15 .20
31 Thriving Ibex C .10 .20
32 Toolcraft Exemplar R .40 .60
33 Trusty Companion U .15 .25
34 Visionary Augmenter U .15 .25
35 Wispweaver Angel U .15 .25
36 Aether Meltdown U .15 .25
37 Aether Theorist C .15 .20
38 Aether Tradewinds C .10 .20
39 Aethersquall Ancient R .10 .20
40 Ceremonious Rejection U .15 .25
41 Confiscation Coup R .15 .25
42 Curio Vendor C .15 .20
43 Disappearing Trick U .15 .25
44 Dramatic Reversal C .10 .20
45 Era of Innovation U .15 .25
46 Experimental Aviator U .15 .25
47 Failed Inspection C .10 .20
48 Gearseeker Serpent C .10 .20
49 Glimmer of Genius U .75 1.25
50 Glint Nest Crane U .15 .25
51 Hightide Hermit C .15 .20
52 Insidious Will R .20 .35
53 Janjeet Sentry U .15 .25
54 Long Finned Skywhale U .15 .25
55 Malfunction C .10 .20
56 Metallurgic Summonings M 1.00 1.50
57 Minister of Inquiries U .15 .25
58 Nimble Innovator C .10 .20
59 Padeem Consul of Innovation R .20 .35
60 Paradoxical Outcome R .30 .50
61 Revolutionary Rebuff C .10 .20
62 Saheelis Artistry R .10 .20
63 Select for Inspection C .10 .20
64 Shrewd Negotiation U .15 .25
65 Tezzerets Ambition C .10 .20
66 Thrivign Turtle C .10 .20
67 Torrential Gearhulk M 20.00 25.00
68 Vedalken Blademaster C .10 .20
69 Weldfast Wingsmith C .10 .20
70 Wind Drake C .10 .20

Card	Low	High
71 Aetherborn Marauder U	.15	.25
72 Ambitious Aetherborn C	.10	.20
73 Demon of Dark Schemes M	.60	1.00
74 Dhund Operative C	.10	.20
75 Diabolic Tutor U	.15	.25
76 Die Young C	.10	.20
77 Dukhara Scavenger C	.10	.20
78 Eliminate the Competition R	.10	.20
79 Embraal Bruiser U	.15	.25
80 Essence Extraction U	.15	.25
81 Fortuitous Find C	.10	.20
82 Foundry Screecher C	.10	.20
83 Fretwork Colony U	.15	.25
84 Gonti Lord of Luxury R	.60	1.00
85 Harsh Scrutiny U	.15	.25
86 Lawless Broker C	.10	.20
87 Live Fast C	.10	.20
88 Lost Legacy R	.40	.60
89 Make Obsolete U	.15	.25
90 Marionette Master R	.10	.20
91 Maulfist Squad C	.10	.20
92 Midnight Oil R	.10	.20
93 Mind Rot C	.10	.20
94 Morbid Curiosity U	.15	.25
95 Night Market Lookout C	.10	.20
96 Noxious Gearhulk M	2.00	3.50
97 Ovalchase Daredevil U	.15	.25
98 Prakhata Club Security C	.10	.20
99 Rush of Vitality C	.10	.20
100 Subtle Strike C	.10	.20
101 Syndicate Trafficker R	.15	.25
102 Thriving Rats C	.10	.20
103 Tidy Conclusion C	.10	.20
104 Underhanded Designs U	.15	.25
105 Weaponcraft Enthusiast U	.15	.25
106 Aethertorch Renegade U	.15	.25
107 Brazen Scourge U	.15	.25
108 Built to Smash C	.10	.20
109 Cathartic Reunion C	.10	.20
110 Chandra Torch of Defiance M	17.00	21.00
111 Chandras Pyrohelix C	.10	.20
112 Combustible Gearhulk M	1.50	2.25
113 Demolish C	.10	.20
114 Fateful Showdown R	.10	.20
115 Furious Reprisal U	.15	.25
116 Giant Spectacle C	.10	.20
117 Harnessed Lightning U	1.25	2.00
118 Hijack C	.10	.20
119 Incendiary Sabotage U	.15	.25
120 Invetors Apprentice U	.15	.25
121 Lathnu Hellion R	.20	.35
122 Madcap Experiment R	.20	.35
123 Maulfist Doorbuster U	.15	.25
124 Pia Nalaar R	.20	.35
125 Quicksmith Genius U	.15	.25
126 Reckless Firewaever C	.10	.20
127 Renegade Tactics C	.10	.20
128 Ruinous Gremlin C	.10	.20
129 Salivating Gremlins C	.10	.20
130 Skyship Stalker R	.10	.20
131 Spark of Creativity U	.15	.25
132 Speedway Fanatic U	.15	.25
133 Spireside Infiltrator C	.10	.20
134 Spontaneous Artist C	.10	.20
135 Start Your Engines U	.15	.25
136 Territorial Gorger R	.10	.20
137 Terror of the Fairgrounds C	.10	.20
138 Thriving Grubs C	.10	.20
139 Wayward Giant C	.10	.20
140 Welding Sparks C	.10	.20
141 Appetite for the Unnatural C	.10	.20
142 Arborback Stomper U	.15	.25
143 Architect of the Untamed R	.15	.25
144 Armorcraft Judge U	.15	.25
145 Attune with Aether C	.10	.20
146 Blossoming Defense U	.75	1.25
147 Bristling Hydra R	.60	1.00
148 Commencement of Festivities C	.10	.20
149 Cowl Prowler C	.10	.20
150 Creeping Mold U	.15	.25
151 Cultivator of Blades R	.10	.20
152 Dubious Challenge R	.10	.20
153 Durable Handicraft U	.15	.25
154 Elegant Edgecrafters U	.15	.25
155 Fairgrounds Trumpeter U	.15	.25
156 Ghirapur Guide U	.15	.25
157 Highspire Artisan C	.10	.20
158 Hunt the Weak C	.10	.20
159 Kurjar Seedsculptor C	.10	.20
160 Larger than Life C	.10	.20
161 Longtusk Cub U	.15	.25
162 Natures Way U	.15	.25
163 Nissa Vital Force M	3.00	5.00
164 Ornamental Courage C	.10	.20
165 Ovyla Pashiri Sage Lifecrafter R	.15	.25
166 Peema Outrider C	.10	.20
167 Riparian Tiger C	.10	.20
168 Sage of Shailas Claim C	.10	.20
169 Servant of the Conduit U	.50	.80
170 Take Down C	.10	.20
171 Thriving Rhino C	.10	.20
172 Verdurous Gearhulk M	6.00	8.00
173 Wild Wanderer C	.10	.20
174 Wildest Dreams R	.10	.20
175 Wily Bandar C	.10	.20
176 Cloudblazer U	.15	.25
177 Contraband Kingpin U	.15	.25
178 Depala Pilot Exemplar R	.15	.25
179 Dovin Baan M	2.00	3.50
180 Empyreal Voyager U	.15	.25
181 Engineered Might U	.15	.25
182 Hazardous Conditions U	.15	.25
183 Kâmbal Consul of Allocation R	.25	.40
184 Rashmi Eternities Crafter M	1.00	1.50
185 Restoration Gearsmith U	.15	.25
186 Saheeli Rai M	4.00	6.00
187 Unlicensed Disintegration U	.15	.25
188 Veteran Motorist U	.15	.25
189 Voltaic Brawler U	.15	.25
190 Whirler Virtuoso U	.15	.25
191 Accomplished Automation C	.10	.20
192 Aetherflux Reservoir R	.75	1.25
193 Aetherworks Marvel M	7.00	9.00
194 Animation Module R	.50	.75
195 Aradara Express C	.10	.20
196 Ballista Charger U	.15	.25
197 Bastion Mastodon C	.10	.20
198 Bomat Bazaar Barge U	.15	.25
199 Bomat Courier R	.50	.80
200 Chief of the Foundry U	.15	.25
201 Cogworkers Puzzleknot C	.10	.20
202 Consulate Skygate C	.10	.20
203 Cultivators Caravan R	.50	.80
204 Deadlock Trap R	.10	.20
205 Decoction Module U	.15	.25
206 Demolition Stomper U	.15	.25
207 Dukhara Peafowl C	.10	.20
208 Dynavolt Tower R	.60	1.00
209 Eager Construct C	.10	.20
210 Electrostatic Pummeler R	.50	.80
211 Fabrication Module U	.15	.25
212 Filigree Familiar U	.15	.25
213 Fireforgers Puzzleknot C	.10	.20
214 Fleetwheel Cruiser R	.15	.25
215 Foundry Inspector U	.15	.25
216 Ghirapur Orrery R	.10	.20
217 Glassblowers Puzzleknot C	.10	.20
218 Inventors Goggles C	.10	.20
219 Iron League Steed U	.15	.25
220 Key to the City R	.50	.80
221 Metalspinners Puzzleknot C	.10	.20
222 Metalwork Colossus R	.30	.50
223 Multiform Wonder R	.10	.20
224 Narnam Cobra C	.10	.20
225 Ovalchase Dragster U	.15	.25
226 Panharmonicon R	2.00	3.50
227 Perpetual Timepiece U	.15	.25
228 Prakhata Pillar Bug C	.10	.20
229 Prophetic Prisim C	.10	.20
230 Renegade Freighter C	.10	.20
231 Scrapheap Scrougner R	1.75	2.50
232 Self Assembler C	.10	.20
233 Sky Skiff C	.10	.20
234 Skysovereign Consul Flagship M	1.50	2.50
235 Smugglers Copter R	1.50	2.00
236 Snare Thopter U	.15	.25
237 Torch Gauntlet C	.10	.20
238 Weldfast Monitor C	.10	.20
239 Whirlermaker U	.15	.25
240 Woodweavers Puzzleknot C	.10	.20
241 Workshop Assistant C	.10	.20
242 Aether Hub U	2.00	3.00
243 Blooming Marsh R	6.00	8.00
244 Botanical Sanctum R	4.00	6.00
245 Concealed Courtyard R	5.00	7.00
246 Inspiring Vantage R	4.00	6.00
247 Inventors Fair R	.75	1.25
248 Sequestered Stash U	.15	.25
249 Spirebluff Canal R	7.00	9.00
250 Plains C	.10	.20
251 Plains C	.10	.20
252 Plains C	.10	.20
253 Island C	.10	.20
254 Island C	.10	.20
255 Island C	.10	.20
256 Swamp C	.10	.20
257 Swamp C	.10	.20
258 Swamp C	.10	.20
259 Mountain C	.10	.20
260 Mountain C	.10	.20
261 Mountain C	.10	.20
262 Forest C	.10	.20
263 Forest C	.10	.20
264 Forest C	.10	.20
265 Chandra Pyrogenius M	2.50	4.00
266 Flame Lash C	.10	.20
267 Liberating Combustion R	.10	.20
268 Renegade Firebrand U	.15	.25
269 Stone Quarry C	.10	.20
270 Nissa Natures Artisan M	4.00	6.00
271 Guardian of the Great Conduit U	.15	.25
272 Terrain Elemental C	.10	.20
273 Verdant Crescendo R	.15	.25
274 Woodland Stream C	.10	.20

2016 Magic The Gathering Kaladesh Foil

Card	Low	High
COMPLETE SET (266)	500.00	700.00
RELEASED ON SEPTEMBER 30, 2016		
1 Acrobatic Maneuver C	.20	.35
2 Aerial Responder U	.30	.50
3 Aetherstorm Roc R	.75	1.25
4 Angel of Invention M	7.00	9.00
5 Authority of the Consuls R	5.00	6.00
6 Aviary Mechanic C	.20	.35
7 Built to Last C	.20	.35
8 Captured by the Consulate R	.75	1.00
9 Cataclysmic Gearhulk M	4.00	6.00
10 Consulate Surveillance U	.30	.50
11 Consuls Shieldguard U	.30	.50
12 Eddytrail Hawk C	.20	.35
13 Fairgrounds Warden U	.30	.50
14 Fragmentize C	.20	.35
15 Fumigate R	4.50	5.00
16 Gearshift Ace U	.30	.50
17 Glint Sleeve Artisan C	.20	.35
18 Herald of the Fair C	.20	.35
19 Impeccable Timing C	.20	.35
20 Inspired Charge C	.20	.35
21 Master Trinketeer R	1.50	2.00
22 Ninth Bridge Patrol C	.20	.35
23 Pressure Point C	.20	.35
24 Propeller Pioneer C	.20	.35
25 Refurbish U	.30	.50
26 Revoke Privileges C	.20	.35
27 Servo Exhibition U	.30	.50
28 Skyswirl Harrier C	.20	.35
29 Skywhalers Shot U	.30	.50
30 Tasseled Dromedary C	.20	.35
31 Thriving Ibex C	.20	.35
32 Toolcraft Exemplar R	3.75	4.25
33 Trusty Companion U	.30	.50
34 Visionary Augmenter U	.30	.50
35 Wispweaver Angel U	.30	.50
36 Aether Meltdown U	.30	.50
37 Aether Theorist C	.20	.35
38 Aether Tradewinds C	.20	.35
39 Aethersquall Ancient R	.75	1.00
40 Ceremonious Rejection U	.30	.50
41 Confiscation Coup R	1.50	2.00
42 Curio Vendor C	.20	.35
43 Disappearing Trick U	.30	.50
44 Dramatic Reversal C	.20	.35
45 Era of Innovation U	.30	.50
46 Experimental Aviator U	.30	.50
47 Failed Inspection C	.20	.35
48 Gearseeker Serpent C	.20	.35
49 Glimmer of Genius U	.30	.50
50 Glint Nest Crane U	.30	.50
51 Hightide Hermit C	.20	.35
52 Insidious Will R	3.00	4.00
53 Janjeet Sentry U	.30	.50
54 Long Finned Skywhale U	.30	.50
55 Malfunction C	.20	.35
56 Metallurgic Summonings M	6.00	8.00
57 Minister of Inquiries U	.30	.50
58 Nimble Innovator C	.20	.35
59 Padeem Consul of Innovation R	2.75	3.25
60 Paradoxical Outcome R	2.00	3.00
61 Revolutionary Rebuff C	.20	.35
62 Saheelis Artsitry R	.75	1.00
63 Select for Inspection C	.20	.35
64 Shrewd Negotiation U	.30	.50
65 Tezzerets Ambition C	.20	.35
66 Thrivign Turtle C	.20	.35
67 Torrentail Gearhulk M	30.00	40.00
68 Vedlaken Blademaster C	.20	.35
69 Weldfast Wingsmith C	.20	.35
70 Wind Drake C	.20	.35
71 Aetherborn Marauder U	.30	.50
72 Ambitious Aetherborn C	.20	.35
73 Demon of Dark Schemes M	3.00	5.00
74 Dhund Operative C	.20	.35
75 Diabolic Tutor U	.30	.50
76 Die Young C	.20	.35
77 Dukhara Scavenger C	.20	.35
78 Eliminate the Competition R	.75	1.00
79 Embraal Bruiser U	.30	.50
80 Essence Extraction U	.30	.50
81 Fortuitous Find C	.20	.35
82 Foundry Screecher C	.20	.35
83 Fretwork Colony U	.30	.50
84 Gonti Lord of Luxury R	3.00	4.00
85 Harsh Scrutiny U	.30	.50
86 Lawless Broker C	.20	.35
87 Live Fast C	.20	.35
88 Lost Legacy R	2.25	3.00
89 Make Obsolete U	.30	.50
90 Marionette Master R	1.00	1.50
91 Maulfist Squad C	.20	.35
92 Midnight Oil R	.50	.75
93 Mind Rot C	.20	.35
94 Morbid Curiosity U	.60	1.00
95 Night Market Lookout C	.20	.35
96 Noxious Gearhulk M	10.00	15.00
97 Ovalchase Daredevil U	.30	.50
98 Prakhata Club Security C	.20	.35
99 Rush of Vitality C	.20	.35
100 Subtle Strike C	.20	.35
101 Syndicate Trafficker R	.75	1.00
102 Thriving Rats C	.20	.35
103 Tidy Conclusion C	.20	.35
104 Underhanded Designs U	.30	.50
105 Weaponcraft Enthusiast U	.30	.50
106 Aethertorch Renegade U	.30	.50
107 Brazen Scourge U	.30	.50
108 Built to Smash C	.20	.35
109 Cathartic Reunion C	.20	.35
110 Chandra Torch of Defiance M	35.00	40.00
111 Chandras Pyrohelix C	.20	.35
112 Combustible Gearhulk M	4.00	6.00
113 Demolish C	.20	.35
114 Fateful Showdown R	1.25	1.75
115 Furious Reprisal U	.30	.50
116 Giant Spectacle C	.20	.35
117 Harnessed Lightning U	.30	.50
118 Hijack C	.20	.35
119 Incendiary Sabotage U	.30	.50
120 Invetors Apprentice U	.30	.50
121 Lathnu Hellion R	3.00	4.00
122 Madcap Experiment R	2.75	4.00
123 Maulfist Doorbuster U	.30	.50
124 Pia Nalaar R	3.50	4.00
125 Quicksmith Genius U	.30	.50
126 Reckless Firewaever C	.20	.35
127 Renegade Tactics C	.20	.35
128 Ruinous Gremlin C	.20	.35
129 Salivating Gremlins C	.20	.35
130 Skyship Stalker R	.75	1.00
131 Spark of Creativity U	.30	.50
132 Speedway Fanatic U	.30	.50
133 Spireside Infiltrator C	.20	.35
134 Spontaneous Artist C	.20	.35
135 Start Your Engines U	.30	.50
136 Territorial Gorger R	.60	1.00
137 Terror of the Fairgrounds C	.20	.35
138 Thriving Grubs C	.20	.35
139 Wayward Giant C	.20	.35
140 Welding Sparks C	.20	.35
141 Appetite for the Unnatural C	.20	.35
142 Arborback Stomper U	.30	.50
143 Architect of the Untamed R	.75	1.25
144 Armorcraft Judge U	.30	.50
145 Attune with Aether C	.20	.35
146 Blossoming Defense U	.30	.50
147 Bristling Hydra R	1.50	2.00
148 Commencement of Festivities C	.20	.35
149 Cowl Prowler C	.20	.35
150 Creeping Mold U	.30	.50
151 Cultivator of Blades R	.75	1.00
152 Dubious Challenge R	1.00	1.50
153 Durable Handicraft U	.30	.50
154 Elegant Edgecrafters U	.30	.50
155 Fairgrounds Trumpeter U	.30	.50
156 Ghirapur Guide U	.30	.50
157 Highspire Artisan C	.20	.35
158 Hunt the Weak C	.20	.35
159 Kurjar Seedsculptor C	.20	.35
160 Larger than Life C	.20	.35
161 Longtusk Cub U	.30	.50
162 Natures Way U	.30	.50
163 Nissa Vital Force M	12.00	15.00
164 Ornamental Courage C	.20	.35
165 Ovyla Pashiri Sage Lifecrafter R	1.75	2.25
166 Peema Outrider C	.20	.35
167 Riparian Tiger C	.20	.35
168 Sage of Shailas Claim C	.20	.35
169 Servant of the Conduit U	.30	.50
170 Take Down C	.20	.35
171 Thriving Rhino C	.20	.35
172 Verdurous Gearhulk M	20.00	25.00
173 Wild Wanderer C	.20	.35
174 Wildest Dreams R	.75	1.25
175 Wily Bandar C	.20	.35
176 Cloudblazer U	.30	.50
177 Contraband Kingpin U	.30	.50
178 Depala Pilot Exemplar R	4.75	5.25
179 Dovin Baan M	25.00	28.00
180 Empyreal Voyager U	.30	.50
181 Engineered Might U	.30	.50
182 Hazardous Conditions U	.30	.50
183 Kambal Consul of Allocation R	4.50	5.00
184 Rashmi Eternities Crafter M	8.00	10.00
185 Restoration Gearsmith U	.30	.50
186 Saheeli Rai M	30.00	35.00
187 Unlicensed Disintegration U	.30	.50
188 Veteran Motorist U	.30	.50
189 Voltaic Brawler U	.30	.50
190 Whirler Virtuoso U	.30	.50
191 Accomplished Automation C	.20	.35
192 Aetherflux Reservoir R	4.00	5.00
193 Aetherworks Marvel M	8.00	12.00
194 Animation Module R	2.00	2.50
195 Aradara Express C	.20	.35
196 Ballista Charger U	.30	.50
197 Bastion Mastodon C	.20	.35
198 Bomat Bazaar Barge U	.30	.50
199 Bomat Courier R	1.75	2.25
200 Chief of the Foundry U	.30	.50
201 Cogworkers Puzzleknot C	.20	.35
202 Consulate Skygate C	.20	.35
203 Cultivators Caravan R	3.00	4.00
204 Deadlock Trap R	1.00	1.50
205 Decoction Module U	.30	.50
206 Demolition Stomper U	.30	.50
207 Dukhara Peafowl C	.20	.35
208 Dynavolt Tower R	1.25	2.00
209 Eager Construct C	.20	.35
210 Electrostatic Pummeler R	2.00	2.50
211 Fabrication Module U	.30	.50
212 Filigree Familiar U	.30	.50
213 Fireforgers Puzzleknot C	.20	.35
214 Fleetwheel Cruiser R	5.00	7.00
215 Foundry Inspector U	.30	.50
216 Ghirapur Orrery R	2.00	3.00
217 Glassblowers Puzzleknot C	.20	.35
218 Inventors Goggles C	.20	.35
219 Iron League Steed U	.30	.50
220 Key to the City R	1.25	2.00
221 Metalspinners Puzzleknot C	.20	.35
222 Metalwork Colossus R	5.00	8.00
223 Multiform Wonder R	.75	1.00
224 Narnam Cobra C	.20	.35
225 Ovalchase Dragster U	.30	.50
226 Panharmonicon R	8.00	11.00
227 Perpetual Timepiece U	.30	.50
228 Prakhata Pillar Bug C	.20	.35
229 Prophetic Prisim C	.20	.35
230 Renegade Freighter C	.20	.35
231 Scrapheap Scrougner R	4.50	5.00
232 Self Assembler C	.20	.35
233 Sky Skiff C	.20	.35
234 Skysovereign Consul Flagship M	15.00	17.00
235 Smugglers Copter R	10.00	12.00
236 Snare Thopter U	.30	.50
237 Torch Gauntlet C	.20	.35
238 Weldfast Monitor C	.20	.35
239 Whirlermaker U	.30	.50
240 Woodweavers Puzzleknot C	.20	.35
241 Workshop Assistant C	.20	.35
242 Aether Hub U	.30	.50
243 Blooming Marsh R	10.00	12.00
244 Botanical Sanctum R	9.00	11.00
245 Concealed Courtyard R	12.00	14.00
246 Inspiring Vantage R	6.00	9.00
247 Inventors Fair R	.40	.60
248 Sequestered Stash U	.30	.50
249 Spirebluff Canal R	12.00	15.00
250 Plains C	.20	.35
251 Plains C	.20	.35
252 Plains C	.20	.35
253 Island C	.20	.35
254 Island C	.20	.35
255 Island C	.20	.35
256 Swamp C	.20	.35
257 Swamp C	.20	.35
258 Swamp C	.20	.35
259 Mountain C	.20	.35
260 Mountain C	.20	.35
261 Mountain C	.20	.35
262 Forest C	.20	.35
263 Forest C	.20	.35
264 Forest C	.20	.35
265 Chandra Pyrogenius M	5.00	7.00
270 Nissa Natures Artisan M	5.00	7.00

2016 Magic The Gathering Kaladesh Tokens

1 Beast .10 .15
2 Construct .10 .15
3 Construct .12 .20
4 Servo .10 .15
5 Servo .10 .15
6 Servo .10 .15
7 Thopter .10 .15
8 Thopter .10 .15
9 Thopter .10 .15
10 Chandra, Torch of Defiance Emblem .25 .35
11 Nissa, Vital Force Emblem .15 .25
12 Dovin Baan Emblem .10 .15
13 Energy Reserve .10 .15

2016 Magic The Gathering Kaladesh Inventions

COMPLETE SET (30) 1800.00 2100.00
RELEASED ON SEPTEMBER 30 , 2016
1 Cataclysmic Gearhulk M 30.00 40.00
2 Torrential Gearhulk M 30.00 40.00
3 Noxious Gearhulk M 30.00 40.00
4 Combustible Gearhulk M 30.00 40.00
5 Verdurous Gearhulk M 50.00 60.00
6 Aether Vial M 110.00 120.00
7 Champions Helm M 25.00 35.00
8 Chromatic Lantern M 50.00 60.00
9 Chrome Mox M 50.00 60.00
10 Cloudstone Curio M 30.00 40.00
11 Crucible of Worlds M 115.00 125.00
12 Gauntlet of Power M 35.00 45.00
13 Hangarback Walker M 30.00 40.00
14 Lightning Greaves M 40.00 50.00
15 Lotus Petal M 90.00 100.00
16 Mana Crypt M 145.00 155.00
17 Mana Vault M 140.00 150.00
18 Minds Eye M 20.00 30.00
19 Mox Opal M 100.00 110.00
20 Painters Servant M 40.00 50.00
21 Rings of Brighthearth M 40.00 50.00
22 Scroll Rack M 50.00 60.00
23 Sculpting Steel M 30.00 40.00
24 Sol Ring M 130.00 140.00
25 Solemn Simulacrum M 50.00 60.00
26 Static Orb M 30.00 40.00
27 Steel Overseer M 50.00 60.00
28 Sword of Feast and Famine M 80.00 90.00
29 Sword of Fire and Ice M 100.00 110.00
30 Sword of Light and Shadow M 80.00 90.00

2017 Magic The Gathering Aether Revolt

COMPLETE SET (194) 175.00 250.00
BOOSTER BOX (36 PACKS) 90.00 115.00
BOOSTER PACK (15 CARDS) 3.00 4.00
*FOIL: .75X TO 2X BASIC CARDS
RELEASED ON JANUARY 20, 2017
1 Aerial Modification U .10 .20
2 Aeronaut Admiral U .10 .20
3 Aether Inspector C .10 .20
4 Aethergeode Miner R .10 .20
5 Airdrop Aeronauts U .10 .20
6 Alley Evasion C .10 .20
7 Audacious Infiltrator C .10 .20
8 Bastion Enforcer C .10 .20
9 Call for Unity R .10 .20
10 Caught in the Brights C .10 .20
11 Consulate Crackdown R .10 .20
12 Conviction C .10 .20
13 Countless Gears Renegade C .10 .20
14 Dawnfeather Eagle C .10 .20
15 Deadeye Harpooner U .10 .20
16 Decommission C .10 .20
17 Deft Dismissal U .10 .20
18 Exquisite Archangel M 1.00 1.50
19 Felidar Guardian U .10 .20
20 Ghirapur Osprey C .10 .20
21 Restoration Specialist U .10 .20
22 Solemn Recruit R .10 .20
23 Sram, Senior Edificer R 1.50 2.00
24 Sram's Expertise R .50 .20
25 Thopter Arrest U .10 .20
26 Aether Swooper C .10 .20
27 Aethertide Whale R .10 .20
28 Baral, Chief of Compliance R 4.00 6.00
29 Baral's Expertise R .30 .50
30 Bastion Inventor C .10 .20
31 Disallow R 4.00 6.00
32 Dispersal Technician C .10 .20
33 Efficient Construction U .10 .20
34 Hinterland Drake C .10 .20
35 Ice Over C .10 .20
36 Illusionist's Stratagem U .10 .20
37 Leave in the Dust C .10 .20
38 Mechanized Production M 2.00 3.50
39 Metallic Rebuke C .10 .20
40 Negate C .10 .20
41 Quicksmith Spy R .10 .20
42 Reverse Engineer U .10 .20
43 Salvage Scuttler U .10 .20
44 Shielded Aether Thief U .10 .20
45 Shipwreck Moray C .10 .20
46 Skyship Plunderer U .10 .20
47 Take Into Custody C .10 .20
48 Trophy Mage U .10 .20
49 Whir of Invention R 1.50 2.00
50 Wind-Kin Raiders U .10 .20
51 Aether Poisoner C .10 .20
52 Alley Strangler C .10 .20
53 Battle at the Bridge R .10 .20
54 Cruel Finality C .10 .20
55 Daring Demolition C .10 .20
56 Defiant Salvager C .10 .20
57 Fatal Push U 3.00 5.00
58 Fen Hauler C .10 .20
59 Foundry Hornet U .10 .20
60 Fourth Bridge Prowler C .10 .20
61 Gifted Aetherborn U 1.50 2.00
62 Glint-Sleeve Siphoner R .30 .50
63 Gonti's Machinations U .10 .20
64 Herald of Anguish M 1.50 2.00
65 Ironclad Revolutionary U .10 .20
66 Midnight Entourage R .10 .20
67 Night Market Aeronaut C .10 .20
68 Perilous Predicament U .10 .20
69 Renegade's Getaway C .10 .20
70 Resourceful Return C .10 .20
71 Secret Salvage R .10 .20
72 Sly Requisitoner U .10 .20
73 Vengeful Rebel U .10 .20
74 Yahenni, Undying Partisan R 1.50 2.00
75 Yahenni's Expertise R .40 .60
76 Aether Chaser C .10 .20
77 Chandra's Revolution C .10 .20
78 Destructive Tampering C .10 .20
79 Embraal Gear-Smasher C .10 .20
80 Enraged Giant U .10 .20
81 Freejam Regent R .10 .20
82 Frontline Rebel C .10 .20
83 Gremlin Infestation U .10 .20
84 Hungry Flames U .10 .20
85 Indomitable Creativity M .50 .80
86 Invigorated Rampage U .10 .20
87 Kari Zev, Skyship Raider R .30 .50
88 Kari Zev's Expertise R .10 .20
89 Lathnu Sailback C .10 .20
90 Lightning Runner M .40 .60
91 Pia's Revolution R .10 .20
92 Precise Strike C .10 .20
93 Quicksmith Rebel R .10 .20
94 Ravenous Intruder U .10 .20
95 Reckless Racer U .10 .20
96 Release the Gremlins R .10 .20
97 Scrapper Champion U .10 .20
98 Shock C .10 .20
99 Siege Modification U .10 .20
100 Sweatworks Brawler C .10 .20
101 Wrangle C .10 .20
102 Aether Herder C .10 .20
103 Aetherstream Leopard C .10 .20
104 Aetherwind Basker M .40 .60
105 Aid from the Cowl R .10 .20
106 Druid of the Cowl C .10 .20
107 Greenbelt Rampager R .50 .80
108 Greenwheel Liberator R .10 .20
109 Heroic Intervention R 4.00 6.00
110 Hidden Herbalists U .10 .20
111 Highspire Infusion C .10 .20
112 Lifecraft Awakening U .10 .20
113 Lifecraft Cavalry C .10 .20
114 Lifecrafter's Gift U .10 .20
115 Maulfist Revolutionary U .10 .20
116 Monstrous Onslaught U .10 .20
117 Narnam Renegade U .10 .20
118 Natuari Obsolescence C .10 .20
119 Peema Aether-Seer U .10 .20
120 Prey Upon C .10 .20
121 Ridgescale Tusker U .10 .20
122 Rishkar, Peema Renegade R .40 .60
123 Rishkar's Expertise R 2.00 3.00
124 Scrounging Bandar C .10 .20
125 Silkweaver Elite C .10 .20
126 Unbridled Grwoth C .10 .20
127 Ajani Unyielding M 2.00 3.00
128 Dark Intimations R .10 .20
129 Hidden Stockpile U .10 .20
130 Maverick Thopterist U .10 .20
131 Oath of Ajani R .10 .20
132 Outland Boar U .10 .20
133 Renegade Rallier U .10 .20
134 Renegade Wheelsmith U .10 .20
135 Rogue Refiner U .10 .20
136 Spire Patrol U .10 .20
137 Tezzeret the Schemer M 2.00 3.00
138 Tezzert's Touch U .10 .20
139 Weldfast Engineer U .10 .20
140 Winding Constrictor U .10 .20
141 Aegis Automaton C .10 .20
142 Aethersphere Harvester R .50 .80
143 Augmenting Automaton C .10 .20
144 Barricade Breaker U .10 .20
145 Cogwork Assembler U .10 .20
146 Consulate Dreadnought U .10 .20
147 Consulate Turret C .10 .20
148 Crackdown Construct U .10 .20
149 Daredevil Dragster U .10 .20
150 Filligree Crawler C .10 .20
151 Foundry Assembler C .10 .20
152 Gonti's Aether Heart M .50 .80
153 Heart of Kiran M 1.00 1.50
154 Hope of Ghirapur R .40 .60
155 Implement of Combustion C .10 .20
156 Implement of Examination C .10 .20
157 Implement of Ferocity C .10 .20
158 Implement of Improvement C .10 .20
159 Implement of Malice C .10 .20
160 Inspiring Statuary R .40 .60
161 Irontread Crusher C .10 .20
162 Lifecrafter's Bestiary R .60 1.00
163 Merchant's Dockhand R .10 .20
164 Metallic Mimic R 5.00 8.00
165 Mobile Garrison C .10 .20
166 Night Market Guard C .10 .20
167 Ornithopter U .10 .20
168 Pacification Array U .10 .20
169 Paradox Engine M 13.00 16.00
170 Peacewalker Colossus R .10 .20
171 Planar Bridge M 2.00 3.00
172 Prizefighter Construct C .10 .20
173 Renegade Map C .10 .20
174 Reservoir Walker C .10 .20
175 Scrap Trawler R 1.00 1.50
176 Servo Schematic U .10 .20
177 Treasure Keeper U .10 .20
178 Universal Solvent C .10 .20
179 Untethered Express U .10 .20
180 Verdant Automation C .10 .20
181 Walking Ballista R 8.00 12.00
182 Watchful Automaton C .10 .20
183 Welder Automaton C .10 .20
184 Spire of Industry R .75 1.25
185 Ajani, Valiant Protector M 4.00 6.00
186 Inspiring Roar C .10 .20
187 Ajani's Comrade U .10 .20
188 Ajani's Aid R .10 .20
189 Tranquil Expanse C .10 .20
190 Tezzeret, Master of Metal M 2.00 3.50
191 Tezzeret's Betrayal R .10 .20
192 Pendulum of Patterns C .10 .20
193 Tezzeret's Simulacrum U .10 .20
194 Submerged Boneyard C .10 .20

2017 Magic The Gathering Aether Revolt Foil

COMPLETE SET (184) 400.00 550.00
RELEASED ON JANUARY 20, 2017
1 Aerial Modification U .50 .80
2 Aeronaut Admiral U .50 .80
3 Aether Inspector C .20 .35
4 Aethergeode Miner R 2.00 3.50
5 Airdrop Aeronauts U .50 .80
6 Alley Evasion C .20 .35
7 Audacious Infiltrator C .20 .35
8 Bastion Enforcer C .20 .35
9 Call for Unity R .75 1.25
10 Caught in the Brights C .20 .35
11 Consulate Crackdown R 1.50 2.00
12 Conviction C .20 .35
13 Countless Gears Renegade C .20 .35
14 Dawnfeather Eagle C .20 .35
15 Deadeye Harpooner U .50 .80
16 Decommission C .20 .35
17 Deft Dismissal U .50 .80
18 Exquisite Archangel M 6.00 8.00
19 Felidar Guardian U 6.00 7.00
20 Ghirapur Osprey C .20 .35
21 Restoration Specialist U .50 .80
22 Solemn Recruit R 2.00 2.50
23 Sram, Senior Edificer R 5.00 6.00
24 Sram's Expertise R 5.00 6.00
25 Thopter Arrest U 1.00 1.50
26 Aether Swooper C .20 .35
27 Aethertide Whale R .75 1.25
28 Baral, Chief of Compliance R 8.00 12.00
29 Baral's Expertise R 4.00 5.00
30 Bastion Inventor C .20 .35
31 Disallow R 10.00 12.00
32 Dispersal Technician C .20 .35
33 Efficient Construction U .50 .80
34 Hinterland Drake C .20 .35
35 Ice Over C .20 .35
36 Illuionist's Stratagem U .50 .80
37 Leave in the Dust C .20 .35
38 Mechanized Production M 7.00 10.00
39 Metallic Rebuke C .75 1.25
40 Negate C .20 .35
41 Quicksmith Spy R .50 .75
42 Reverse Engineer U 2.25 3.00
43 Salvage Scuttler U .50 .80
44 Shielded Aether Thief U .50 .80
45 Shipwreck Moray C .20 .35
46 Skyship Plunderer U .50 .80
47 Take Into Custody C .20 .35
48 Trophy Mage U 3.00 4.00
49 Whir of Invention R 6.00 8.00
50 Wind Kin-Raiders U .50 .80
51 Aether Poisoner C .20 .35
52 Alley Strangler C .20 .35
53 Battle at the Bridge R 1.25 1.75
54 Cruel Finality C .20 .35
55 Daring Demolition C .20 .35
56 Defiant Salvager C .20 .35
57 Fatal Push U 20.00 25.00
58 Fen Hauler C .20 .35
59 Foundry Hornet U .50 .80
60 Fourth Bridge Prowler C .20 .35
61 Gifted Aetherborn U 2.50 3.50
62 Glint-Sleeve Siphoner R 3.00 3.50
63 Gonti's Machinations U .50 .80
64 Herald of Anguish M 15.00 20.00
65 Ironclad Revolutionary U .50 .80
66 Midnight Entourage R 1.50 2.00
67 Night Market Aeronaut C .20 .35
68 Perilous Predicament U .50 .80
69 Renegade's Getaway C .20 .35
70 Resourceful Return C .20 .35
71 Secret Salvage R 1.25 1.75
72 Sly Requisitoner U .50 .80
73 Vengeful Rebel U .50 .80
74 Yahenni, Undying Partisan R 4.00 5.00
75 Yahenni's Expertise R 7.00 9.00
76 Aether Chaser C .20 .35
77 Chandra's Revolution C .20 .35
78 Destructive Tampering C .20 .35
79 Embraal Gear-Smasher C .20 .35
80 Enraged Giant U .50 .80
81 Freejam Regent R .75 1.25
82 Frontline Rebel C .20 .35
83 Gremlin Infestation U .50 .80
84 Hungry Flames U .50 .80
85 Indomitable Creativity M 4.00 6.00
86 Invigorated Rampage U .50 .80
87 Kari Zev, Skyship Raider R 5.00 6.00
88 Kari Zev's Expertise R 2.50 3.50
89 Lathnu Sailback C .20 .35
90 Lightning Runner M 4.00 6.00
91 Pia's Revolution R 1.50 2.00
92 Precise Strike C .20 .35
93 Quicksmith Rebel R .50 .80
94 Ravenous Intruder U .50 .80
95 Reckless Racer U .50 .80
96 Release the Gremlins R 1.00 1.50
97 Scrapper Champion U .50 .80
98 Shock C .75 1.25
99 Siege Modification U .50 .80
100 Sweatworks Brawler C .20 .35
101 Wrangle C .20 .35
102 Aether Herder C .20 .35
103 Aetherstream Leopard C .20 .35
104 Aetherwind Basker M 4.00 6.00
105 Aid from the Cowl R 1.25 1.75
106 Druid of the Cowl C .20 .35
107 Greenbelt Rampager R 4.00 5.00
108 Greenwheel Liberator R 1.75 2.25
109 Heroic Intervention R 2.00 3.00
110 Hidden Herbalists U 1.25 1.75
111 Highspire Infusion C .20 .35
112 Lifecraft Awakening U .50 .80
113 Lifecraft Cavalry C .20 .35
114 Lifecrafter's Gift U .50 .80
115 Maulfist Revolutionary U 1.50 2.00
116 Monstrous Onslaught U .50 .80
117 Narnam Renegade U 2.00 3.00
118 Natuari Obsolescence C .20 .35
119 Peema Aether-Seer U .50 .80
120 Prey Upon C .20 .35
121 Ridgescale Tusker U .50 .80
122 Rishkar, Peema Renegade R 7.00 10.00
123 Rishkar's Expertise R 3.50 4.50
124 Scrounging Bandar C .20 .35
125 Silkweaver Elite C .20 .35
126 Unbridled Grwoth C .20 .35
127 Ajani Unyielding M 20.00 25.00
128 Dark Intimations R 1.50 2.50
129 Hidden Stockpile U 1.00 1.50
130 Maverick Thopterist U .50 .80
131 Oath of Ajani R 4.50 5.50
132 Outland Boar U .50 .80
133 Renegade Rallier U 5.00 7.00
134 Renegade Wheelsmith U .50 .80
135 Rogue Refiner U .75 1.25
136 Spire Patrol U .50 .80
137 Tezzeret the Schemer M 20.00 25.00
138 Tezzert's Touch U 1.25 2.00
139 Weldfast Engineer U .50 .80
140 Winding Constrictor U 4.50 6.00
141 Aegis Automaton C .20 .35
142 Aethersphere Harvester R 7.00 9.00
143 Augmenting Automaton C .20 .35
144 Barricade Breaker U .50 .80
145 Cogwork Assembler U .50 .80
146 Consulate Dreadnought U 1.50 2.00
147 Consulate Turret C .20 .35
148 Crackdown Construct U 2.00 3.00
149 Daredevil Dragster U .50 .80
150 Filligree Crawler C .20 .35
151 Foundry Assembler C .20 .35
152 Gontis Aether Heart M 5.00 8.00
153 Heart of Kiran M 20.00 25.00
154 Hope of Ghirapur R 5.00 6.00
155 Implement of Combustion C .20 .35
156 Implement of Examination C .20 .35
157 Implement of Ferocity C .20 .35
158 Implement of Improvement C .20 .35
159 Implement of Malice C .20 .35
160 Inspiring Statuary R 4.00 5.00
161 Irontread Crusher C .20 .35
162 Lifecrafter's Bestiary R 3.00 5.00
163 Merchants Dockhand R 1.00 1.50
164 Metallic Mimic R 7.00 10.00
165 Mobile Garrison C .20 .35
166 Night Market Guard C .20 .35
167 Ornithopter U 2.00 2.50
168 Pacification Array U .50 .80
169 Paradox Engine M 15.00 20.00
170 Peacewalker Colossus R 2.00 2.50
171 Planar Bridge M 8.00 12.00
172 Prizefighter Construct C .20 .35
173 Renegade Map C .20 .35
174 Reservoir Walker C .20 .35
175 Scrap Trawler R 2.50 3.00
176 Servo Schematic U .50 .80
177 Treasure Keeper U 1.75 2.25
178 Universal Solvent C .20 .35
179 Untethered Express U .50 .80
180 Verdant Automation C .20 .35
181 Walking Ballista R 40.00 50.00
182 Watchful Automaton C .20 .35
183 Welder Automaton C .20 .35
184 Spire of Industry R 7.00 10.00

2017 Magic The Gathering Aether Revolt Tokens

1 Gremlin .06 .10
2 Ragavan .25 .35
3 Etherium Cell .10 .15
4 Tezzeret the Schemer Emblem .06 .10

2017 Magic The Gathering Aether Revolt Masterpiece Series

COMPLETE SET (24) 1500.00 1800.00
RELEASED ON JANUARY 20, 2017
31 Arcbound Ravager M 100.00 125.00
32 Black Vise M 30.00 40.00
33 Chalice of the Void M 135.00 150.00
34 Defense Grid M 35.00 45.00
35 Duplicant M 30.00 40.00
36 Engineered Explosives M 100.00 125.00
37 Ensnaring Bridge M 125.00 140.00
38 Extraplanar Lens M 35.00 45.00
39 Grindstone M 70.00 80.00
40 Meekstone M 30.00 40.00
41 Oblivion Stone M 90.00 100.00
42 Ornithopter M 45.00 54.00
43 Paradox Engine M 65.00 75.00
44 Pithing Needle M 55.00 65.00
45 Planar Bridge M 65.00 75.00
46 Platinum Angel M 50.00 60.00
47 Sphere of Resistance M 40.00 50.00
48 Staff od Domination M 75.00 85.00
49 Sundering Titan M 45.00 55.00
50 Sword of Body and Mind M 55.00 65.00
51 Sword of War and Peace M 80.00 90.00
52 Trinisphere M 50.00 60.00
53 Vedalken Shackles M 50.00 60.00
54 Wurmcoil Engine M 80.00 90.00

2017 Magic The Gathering Amonkhet

Card	Low	High
COMPLETE SET (278)	225.00	325.00
BOOSTER BOX (36 PACKS)	90.00	120.00
BOOSTER PACK (15 CARDS)	3.00	5.00
*FOIL: .75X TO 2X BASIC CARDS		
RELEASED ON APRIL 28, 2016		
1 Angel of Sanctions M	5.00	8.00
2 Anointed Procession R	1.25	2.00
3 Anointer Priest C	.20	.35
4 Approach of the Second Sun R	.40	.60
5 Aven Mindcensor R	1.00	1.50
6 Binding Mummy C	.20	.35
7 Cartouche of Solidarity C	.20	.35
8 Cast Out U	.30	.50
9 Compulsory Rest C	.20	.35
10 Devoted Crop Mate U	.30	.50
11 Djerus Resolve C	.20	.35
12 Fan Bearer C	.20	.35
13 Forsake the Worldly C	.20	.35
14 Gideon of the Trials M	20.00	25.00
15 Gideons Intervention R	.75	1.25
16 Glory Bound Initiate R	1.25	2.00
17 Gust Walker C	.20	.35
18 Impeccable Timing C	.20	.35
19 In Oketras Name C	.20	.35
20 Mighty Leap U	.30	.50
21 Oketra the True M	3.00	5.00
22 Oketras Attendant U	.30	.50
23 Protection of the Hekma U	.30	.50
24 Regal Caracal R	.50	.80
25 Renewed Faith U	.30	.50
26 Rhet Crop Spearmaster C	.20	.35
27 Sacred Cat C	.20	.35
28 Seraph of the Suns U	.30	.50
29 Sparring Mummy C	.20	.35
30 Supply Caravan C	.20	.35
31 Tah Crop Elite C	.20	.35
32 Those Who Serve C	.20	.35
33 Time to Reflect U	.30	.50
34 Trial of Solidarity U	.30	.50
35 Trueheart Duelist U	.30	.50
36 Unwavering Initiate C	.20	.35
37 Vizier of Deferment U	.30	.50
38 Vizier of Remedies U	.30	.50
39 Winged Shepherd U	.30	.50
40 Ancient Crab C	.20	.35
41 Angler Drake U	.30	.50
42 As Foretold M	10.00	13.00
43 Aven Initiate C	.20	.35
44 Cancel C	.20	.35
45 Cartouche of Knowledge C	.20	.35
46 Censor U	.30	.50
47 Compelling Argument C	.20	.35
48 Cryptic Serpent U	.30	.50
49 Curator of Mysteries R	.75	1.25
50 Decision Paralysis C	.20	.35
51 Drake Haven R	2.00	3.50
52 Essence Scatter C	.20	.35
53 Floodwaters C	.20	.35
54 Galestrike U	.30	.50
55 Glyph Keeper R	.60	1.00
56 Hekma Sentinels C	.20	.35
57 Hieroglyphic Illumination C	.20	.35
58 Illusory Wrappings C	.20	.35
59 Kefnet the Mindful M	4.00	6.00
60 Labyrinth Guardian U	.30	.50
61 Lay Claim U	.30	.50
62 Naga Oracle C	.20	.35
63 New Perspectives R	.30	.50
64 Open into Wonder U	.30	.50
65 Pull from Tomorrow R	3.00	5.00
66 River Serpent C	.20	.35
67 Sacred Excavation U	.30	.50
68 Scribe of the Mindful C	.20	.35
69 Seeker of Insight C	.20	.35
70 Shimmerscale Drake C	.20	.35
71 Slither Blade C	.20	.35
72 Tah Crop Skirmisher C	.20	.35
73 Trial of Knowledge U	.30	.50
74 Vizier of Many Faces R	.30	.50
75 Vizier of Tumbling Sands U	.30	.50
76 Winds of Rebuke C	.20	.35
77 Zenith Seeker U	.30	.50
78 Archfiend of Ifnir R	.75	1.25
79 Baleful Ammit U	.30	.50
80 Blighted Bat C	.20	.35
81 Bone Picker U	.30	.50
82 Bontu the Glorified M	3.00	5.00
83 Cartouche of Ambition C	.20	.35
84 Cruel Reality M	.60	1.00
85 Cursed Minotaur C	.20	.35
86 Dispossess R	.40	.60
87 Doomed Dissenter C	.20	.35
88 Dread Wanderer R	2.00	3.50
89 Dune Beetle C	.20	.35
90 Faith of the Devoted U	.30	.50
91 Festering Mummy C	.20	.35
92 Final Reward C	.20	.35
93 Gravedigger U	.30	.50
94 Grim Strider U	.30	.50
95 Horror of the Broken Lands C	.20	.35
96 Lay Bare the Heart U	.30	.50
97 Liliana Deaths Majesty M	14.00	17.00
98 Lilianas Mastery R	.50	.80
99 Lord of the Accursed U	.30	.50
100 Miasmic Mummy C	.20	.35
101 Nest of Scarabs U	.30	.50
102 Painful Lesson C	.20	.35
103 Pitiless Vizier C	.20	.35
104 Plague Belcher R	2.50	4.00
105 Ruthless Sniper U	.30	.50
106 Scarab Feast C	.20	.35
107 Shadow of the Grave R	1.25	2.50
108 Soulstinger C	.20	.35
109 Splendid Agony C	.20	.35
110 Stir the Sands U	.30	.50
111 Supernatuarl Stamina C	.20	.35
112 Trespassers Curse C	.20	.35
113 Trial of Ambition U	.30	.50
114 Unburden C	.20	.35
115 Wander in Death C	.20	.35
116 Wasteland Scorpion C	.20	.35
117 Ahn Crop Chrasher U	.30	.50
118 Battlefield Scavenger U	.30	.50
119 Blazing Volley C	.20	.35
120 Bloodlust Inciter C	.20	.35
121 Bloodrage Brawler U	.30	.50
122 Brute Strength C	.20	.35
123 By Force U	.30	.50
124 Cartouche of Zeal C	.20	.35
125 Combat Celebrant M	2.50	4.00
126 Consuming Fervor U	.30	.50
127 Deem Worthy U	.30	.50
128 Desert Cerodon C	.20	.35
129 Electrify C	.20	.35
130 Emberhorn Minotaur C	.20	.35
131 Flameblade Adept U	.30	.50
132 Fling C	.20	.35
133 Glorious End M	3.00	5.00
134 Glorybringer R	7.00	10.00
135 Harsh Mentor R	5.00	8.00
136 Hazoret the Fervent M	5.00	8.00
137 Hazorets Favor R	.20	.35
138 Heart Piercer Manticore R	1.25	2.00
139 Hyena Pack C	.20	.35
140 Limits of Solidarity U	.30	.50
141 Magma Spray C	.20	.35
142 Manticore of the Gauntlet C	.20	.35
143 Minotaur Sureshot C	.20	.35
144 Nef Crop Entangler C	.20	.35
145 Nimble Blade Khenra C	.20	.35
146 Pathmaker Initiate C	.20	.35
147 Purseue Glory C	.20	.35
148 Soul Scar Mage R	2.00	3.50
149 Sweltering Suns R	1.00	1.50
150 Thresher Lizard C	.20	.35
151 Tormenting Voice C	.20	.35
152 Trail of Zeal U	.30	.50
153 Trueheart Twins U	.30	.50
154 Violent Impact C	.20	.35
155 Warfire Javelineer U	.30	.50
156 Benefaction of Rhonas C	.20	.35
157 Bitterblade Warrior C	.20	.35
158 Cartouche of Strength C	.20	.35
159 Champion of Rhonas R	1.25	2.00
160 Channeler Initiate R	2.00	3.50
161 Colossapede C	.20	.35
162 Crocodile of the Crossing U	.30	.50
163 Defiant Greatmaw U	.30	.50
164 Dissenters Deliverance C	.20	.35
165 Exemplar of Strength U	.30	.50
166 Giant Spider C	.20	.35
167 Gift of Paradise C	.20	.35
168 Greater Sandwurm C	.20	.35
169 Hapatras Mark U	.30	.50
170 Harvest Season R	1.00	1.50
171 Haze of Pollen C	.20	.35
172 Honored Hydra R	.60	1.00
173 Hooded Brawler C	.20	.35
174 Initiates Companion C	.20	.35
175 Manglehorn U	.30	.50
176 Naga Vitalist C	.20	.35
177 Oashra Cultivator C	.20	.35
178 Ornery Kudu C	.20	.35
179 Pouncing Cheetah C	.20	.35
180 Prowling Serpopard R	1.00	1.50
181 Quarry Hauler C	.20	.35
182 Rhonas the Indomitable M	14.00	18.00
183 Sandwurm Convergence R	.30	.50
184 Scaled Behemoth U	.30	.50
185 Shed Weakness C	.20	.35
186 Shefet Monitor U	.30	.50
187 Sixth Sense U	.30	.50
188 Spidery Grasp C	.20	.35
189 Stinging Shot C	.20	.35
190 Synchronized Strike U	.30	.50
191 Trial of Strength U	.30	.50
192 Vizier of the Menagerie M	6.00	8.00
193 Watchful Naga U	.30	.50
194 Ahn Crop Champion U	.30	.50
195 Aven Wind Guide U	.30	.50
196 Bounty of the Luxa R	.40	.60
197 Decimator Beetle U	.30	.50
198 Enigma Drake U	.30	.50
199 Hapatra Vizier of Poisons R	1.00	1.50
200 Honored Crop Captain U	.30	.50
201 Khenra Charioteer U	.30	.50
202 Merciless Javelineer U	.30	.50
203 Neheb The Worthy R	.40	.60
204 Nissa Steward of Elements M	13.00	17.00
205 Samut Voice of Dissent M	3.00	5.00
206 Shadowstorm Vizier U	.30	.50
207 Temmet Vizier of Naktamun R	.30	.50
208 Wayward Servant U	.30	.50
209 Weaver of Currents U	.30	.50
210 Dusk Dawn R	.75	1.25
211 Commit Memory R	.50	.75
212 Never Return R	2.00	3.50
213 Insult Injury R	1.50	2.50
214 Mouth Feed R	.30	.50
215 Start Finish U	.30	.50
216 Reduce Rubble U	.30	.50
217 Destined Lead U	.30	.50
218 Onward Victory U	.30	.50
219 Spring Mind U	.30	.50
220 Prepare Fight R	.40	.60
221 Failure Comply R	.60	1.00
222 Rags Riches R	.15	.25
223 Cut Ribbons R	.60	1.00
224 Heaven Earth R	.40	.60
225 Bontus Monument U	.30	.50
226 Edifice of Authority U	.30	.50
227 Embalmers Tools U	.30	.50
228 Gate to the Afterlife U	.30	.50
229 Hazorets Monument U	.30	.50
230 Honed Khopesh C	.20	.35
231 Kefnets Monument U	.30	.50
232 Luxa River Shrine C	.20	.35
233 Oketras Monument U	.30	.50
234 Oracles Vault R	.40	.60
235 Pyramid of the Pantheon R	.50	.80
236 Rhonass Monument R	10.00	13.00
237 Throne of the God Pharaoh R	1.00	1.50
238 Watchers of the Dead U	.30	.50
239 Canyon Slough R	2.50	4.00
240 Cascading Cataracts R	1.00	1.50
241 Cradle of the Accursed C	.20	.35
242 Evolving Wilds C	.20	.35
243 Fetid Pools R	3.00	5.00
244 Grasping Dunes U	.30	.50
245 Irrigated Farmland R	3.00	5.00
246 Painted Bluffs C	.20	.35
247 Scattered Groves R	3.00	5.00
248 Sheltered Thicket R	2.00	3.50
249 Sunscorched Desert C	.20	.35
250 Plains Full Art C	.20	.35
251 Island Full Art C	.20	.35
252 Swamp Full Art C	.20	.35
253 Mountain Full Art C	.20	.35
254 Forest Full Art C	.20	.35
255 Plians C	.20	.35
256 Plains C	.20	.35
257 Plains C	.20	.35
258 Island C	.20	.35
259 Island C	.20	.35
260 Island C	.20	.35
261 Swamp C	.20	.35
262 Swamp C	.20	.35
263 Swamp C	.20	.35
264 Mountain C	.20	.35
265 Mountain C	.20	.35
266 Mountain C	.20	.35
267 Forest C	.20	.35
268 Forest C	.20	.35
269 Forest C	.20	.35
270 Gideon Martial Paragon M	5.00	8.00
271 Companion of the Trials U	.30	.50
272 Gideons Resolve R	.75	1.25
273 Graceful Cat C	.20	.35
274 Stone Quarry C	.20	.35
275 Liliana Death Wielder M	6.00	8.00
276 Desiccated Naga U	.30	.50
277 Lilianas Influence R	.50	.80
278 Tattered Mummy C	.20	.35

2017 Magic The Gathering Amonkhet Foil

Card	Low	High
COMPLETE SET	550.00	825.00
RELEASED ON		
1 Angel of Sanctions M	10.00	15.00
2 Anointed Procession R	4.00	7.00
3 Anointer Priest C	.25	.40
4 Approach of the Second Sun R	1.25	2.50
5 Aven Mindcensor R	5.00	8.00
6 Binding Mummy C	.25	.40
7 Cartouche of Solidarity C	.25	.40
8 Cast Out U	3.00	5.00
9 Compulsory Rest C	.25	.40
10 Devoted Crop Mate U	.40	.60
11 Djerus Resolve C	.25	.40
12 Fan Bearer C	.25	.40
13 Forsake the Worldly C	.25	.40
14 Gideon of the Trials M	40.00	50.00
15 Gideons Intervention R	1.25	2.50
16 Glory Bound Initiate R	2.00	3.50
17 Gust Walker C	.25	.40
18 Impeccable Timing C	.25	.40
19 In Oketras Name C	.25	.40
20 Mighty Leap U	.40	.60
21 Oketra the True M	10.00	15.00
22 Oketras Attendant U	.40	.60
23 Protection of the Hekma U	.40	.60
24 Regal Caracal R	1.25	2.50
25 Renewed Faith U	.40	.60
26 Rhet Crop Spearmaster C	.25	.40
27 Sacred Cat C	.25	.40
28 Seraph of the Suns U	.40	.60
29 Sparring Mummy C	.25	.40
30 Supply Caravan C	.25	.40
31 Tah Crop Elite C	.25	.40
32 Those Who Serve C	.25	.40
33 Time to Reflect U	.40	.60
34 Trial of Solidarity U	.40	.60
35 Trueheart Duelist U	.40	.60
36 Unwavering Initiate C	.25	.40
37 Vizier of Deferment U	.40	.60
38 Vizier of Remedies U	3.00	5.00
39 Winged Shepherd U	.40	.60
40 Ancient Crab C	.25	.40
41 Angler Drake U	.40	.60
42 As Foretold M	30.00	35.00
43 Aven Initiate C	.25	.40
44 Cancel C	.25	.40
45 Cartouche of Knowledge C	.25	.40
46 Censor U	3.00	5.00
47 Compelling Argument C	.25	.40
48 Cryptic Serpent U	.40	.60
49 Curator of Mysteries R	3.00	5.00
50 Decision Paralysis C	.25	.40
51 Drake Haven R	4.00	7.00
52 Essence Scatter C	.25	.40
53 Floodwaters C	.25	.40
54 Galestrike U	.40	.60
55 Glyph Keeper R	1.25	2.50
56 Hekma Sentinels C	.25	.40
57 Hieroglyphic Illumination C	.25	.40
58 Illusory Wrappings C	.25	.40
59 Kefnet the Mindful M	8.00	12.00
60 Labyrinth Guardian U	.40	.60
61 Lay Claim U	.40	.60
62 Naga Oracle C	.25	.40
63 New Perspectives R	1.25	2.50
64 Open into Wonder U	.40	.60
65 Pull from Tomorrow R	6.00	8.00
66 River Serpent C	.25	.40
67 Sacred Excavation U	.40	.60
68 Scribe of the Mindful C	.25	.40
69 Seeker of Insight C	.25	.40
70 Shimmerscale Drake C	.25	.40
71 Slither Blade C	.25	.40
72 Tah Crop Skirmisher C	.25	.40
73 Trial of Knowledge U	.40	.60
74 Vizier of Many Faces R	1.25	2.50
75 Vizier of Tumbling Sands U	.40	.60
76 Winds of Rebuke C	.25	.40
77 Zenith Seeker U	.40	.60
78 Archfiend of Ifnir R	1.25	2.50
79 Baleful Ammit U	.40	.60
80 Blighted Bat C	.25	.40
81 Bone Picker U	8.00	10.00
82 Bontu the Glorified M	8.00	12.00
83 Cartouche of Ambition C	.25	.40
84 Cruel Reality M	1.50	2.50
85 Cursed Minotaur C	.25	.40
86 Dispossess R	1.25	2.50
87 Doomed Dissenter C	.25	.40
88 Dread Wanderer R	3.00	5.00
89 Dune Beetle C	.25	.40
90 Faith of the Devoted U	.40	.60
91 Festering Mummy C	.25	.40
92 Final Reward C	.25	.40
93 Gravedigger U	.40	.60
94 Grim Strider U	.40	.60
95 Horror of the Broken Lands C	.25	.40
96 Lay Bare the Heart U	.40	.60
97 Liliana Deaths Majesty M	30.00	35.00
98 Lilianas Mastery R	1.25	2.50
99 Lord of the Accursed U	4.00	6.00
100 Miasmic Mummy C	.25	.40
101 Nest of Scarabs U	.40	.60
102 Painful Lesson C	.25	.40
103 Pitiless Vizier C	.25	.40
104 Plague Belcher R	2.50	4.00
105 Ruthless Sniper U	.40	.60
106 Scarab Feast C	.25	.40
107 Shadow of the Grave R	5.00	8.00
108 Soulstinger C	.25	.40
109 Splendid Agony C	.25	.40
110 Stir the Sands U	.40	.60
111 Supernatuarl Stamina C	.25	.40
112 Trespassers Curse C	.25	.40
113 Trial of Ambition U	.40	.60
114 Unburden C	.25	.40
115 Wander in Death C	.25	.40
116 Wasteland Scorpion C	.25	.40
117 Ahn Crop Chrasher U	.40	.60
118 Battlefield Scavenger U	.40	.60
119 Blazing Volley C	.25	.40
120 Bloodlust Inciter C	.25	.40
121 Bloodrage Brawler U	1.50	2.50
122 Brute Strength C	.25	.40
123 By Force U	3.00	5.00
124 Cartouche of Zeal C	.25	.40
125 Combat Celebrant M	7.00	10.00
126 Consuming Fervor U	.40	.60
127 Deem Worthy U	.40	.60
128 Desert Cerodon C	.25	.40
129 Electrify C	.25	.40
130 Emberhorn Minotaur C	.25	.40
131 Flameblade Adept U	.40	.60
132 Fling C	.25	.40
133 Glorious End M	7.00	10.00
134 Glorybringer R	10.00	15.00
135 Harsh Mentor R	12.00	16.00
136 Hazoret the Fervent M	13.00	17.00
137 Hazorets Favor R	1.25	2.50
138 Heart Piercer Manticore R	1.25	2.50
139 Hyena Pack C	.25	.40
140 Limits of Solidarity U	.40	.60
141 Magma Spray C	.25	.40
142 Manticore of the Gauntlet C	.25	.40
143 Minotaur Sureshot C	.25	.40
144 Nef Crop Entangler C	.25	.40
145 Nimble Blade Khenra C	.25	.40
146 Pathmaker Initiate C	.25	.40
147 Purseue Glory C	.25	.40
148 Soul Scar Mage R	7.00	10.00
149 Sweltering Suns R	3.00	5.00
150 Thresher Lizard C	.25	.40
151 Tormenting Voice C	.25	.40
152 Trail of Zeal U	.40	.60
153 Trueheart Twins U	.40	.60
154 Violent Impact C	.25	.40
155 Warfire Javelineer U	.40	.60
156 Benefaction of Rhonas C	.25	.40
157 Bitterblade Warrior C	.25	.40
158 Cartouche of Strength C	.25	.40
159 Champion of Rhonas R	5.00	8.00
160 Channeler Initiate R	4.00	6.00
161 Colossapede C	.25	.40
162 Crocodile of the Crossing U	.40	.60
163 Defiant Greatmaw U	.40	.60
164 Dissenters Deliverance C	.25	.40
165 Exemplar of Strength U	.40	.60
166 Giant Spider C	.25	.40
167 Gift of Paradise C	.25	.40
168 Greater Sandwurm C	.25	.40
169 Hapatras Mark U	.40	.60
170 Harvest Season R	2.00	3.50
171 Haze of Pollen C	.25	.40
172 Honored Hydra R	1.25	2.50
173 Hooded Brawler C	.25	.40
174 Initiates Companion C	.25	.40
175 Manglehorn U	2.50	4.00
176 Naga Vitalist C	.25	.40
177 Oashra Cultivator C	.25	.40
178 Ornery Kudu C	.25	.40
179 Pouncing Cheetah C	.25	.40
180 Prowling Serpopard R	3.00	5.00
181 Quarry Hauler C	.25	.40
182 Rhonas the Indomitable M	20.00	25.00
183 Sandwurm Convergence R	1.25	2.50
184 Scaled Behemoth U	.40	.60
185 Shed Weakness C	.25	.40
186 Shefet Monitor U	.40	.60
187 Sixth Sense U	.40	.60

188 Spidery Grasp C	.25	.40
189 Stinging Shot C	.25	.40
190 Synchronized Strike U	.40	.60
191 Trial of Strength U	.40	.60
192 Vizier of the Menagerie M	15.00	20.00
193 Watchful Naga U	.40	.60
194 Ahn Crop Champion U	.40	.60
195 Aven Wind Guide U	.40	.60
196 Bounty of the Luxa R	1.25	2.50
197 Decimator Beetle U	.40	.60
198 Enigma Drake U	.40	.60
199 Hapatra Vizier of Poisons R	4.00	6.00
200 Honored Crop Captain U	.40	.60
201 Khenra Charioteer U	.40	.60
202 Merciless Javelineer U	.40	.60
203 Neheb The Worthy R	1.25	2.50
204 Nissa Steward of Elements M	30.00	40.00
205 Samut Voice of Dissent M	10.00	15.00
206 Shadowstorm Vizier U	.40	.60
207 Temmet Vizier of Naktamun R	1.25	2.50
208 Wayward Servant U	2.00	3.50
209 Weaver of Currents U	.40	.60
210 Dusk Dawn R	3.00	5.00
211 Commit Memory R	1.25	2.50
212 Never Return R	3.00	5.00
213 Insult Injury R	3.00	5.00
214 Mouth Feed R	1.25	2.50
215 Start Finish U	.40	.60
216 Reduce Rubble U	.40	.60
217 Destined Lead U	.40	.60
218 Onward Victory U	.40	.60
219 Spring Mind U	.40	.60
220 Prepare Fight R	1.25	2.50
221 Failure Comply R	1.25	2.50
222 Rags Riches R	1.25	2.50
223 Cut Ribbons R	1.25	2.50
224 Heaven Earth R	1.25	2.50
225 Bontus Monument U	.40	.60
226 Edifice of Authority U	.40	.60
227 Embalmers Tools U	.40	.60
228 Gate to the Afterlife U	.40	.60
229 Hazorets Monument U	.40	.60
230 Honed Khopesh C	.25	.40
231 Kefnets Monument U	.40	.60
232 Luxa River Shrine C	.25	.40
233 Oketras Monument U	.40	.60
234 Oracles Vault R	1.25	2.50
235 Pyramid of the Pantheon R	3.00	5.00
236 Rhonass Monument R	3.00	5.00
237 Throne of the God Pharaoh R	3.00	5.00
238 Watchers of the Dead U	.40	.60
239 Canyon Slough R	7.00	10.00
240 Cascading Cataracts R	5.00	8.00
241 Cradle of the Accursed C	.25	.40
242 Evolving Wilds C	.25	.40
243 Fetid Pools R	7.00	10.00
244 Grasping Dunes U	.40	.60
245 Irrigated Farmland R	7.00	10.00
246 Painted Bluffs C	.25	.40
247 Scattered Groves R	7.00	10.00
248 Sheltered Thicket R	7.00	10.00
249 Sunscorched Desert C	.25	.40
250 Plains Full Art C	10.00	15.00
251 Island Full Art C	10.00	15.00
252 Swamp Full Art C	10.00	15.00
253 Mountain Full Art C	10.00	15.00
254 Forest Full Art C	10.00	15.00
255 Plians C	.25	.40
256 Plains C	.25	.40
257 Plains C	.25	.40
258 Island C	.25	.40
259 Island C	.25	.40
260 Island C	.25	.40
261 Swamp C	.25	.40
262 Swamp C	.25	.40
263 Swamp C	.25	.40
264 Mountain C	.25	.40
265 Mountain C	.25	.40
266 Mountain C	.25	.40
267 Forest C	.25	.40
268 Forest C	.25	.40
269 Forest C	.25	.40
270 Gideon Martial Paragon M	6.00	8.00
271 Companion of the Trials U	.40	.60
272 Gideons Resolve R	1.25	2.50
273 Graceful Cat C	.25	.40
274 Stone QuarryC	.25	.40
275 Liliana Death Wielder M	6.00	8.00
276 Desiccated Naga U	.40	.60
277 Lilianas Influence R	1.25	2.50
278 Tattered Mummy C	.25	.40

2017 Magic The Gathering Amonkhet Tokens

1 Angel of Sanctions	.60	1.00
2 Anointer Priest	.06	.10
3 Aven Initiate	.06	.10
4 Aven Wind Guide	.06	.10
5 Glyph Keeper	.20	.30
6 Heart-Piercer Manticore	.06	.10
7 Honored Hydra	.15	.25
8 Labyrinth Guardian	.06	.10
9 Oketra's Attendant	.06	.10
10 Sacred Cat	.15	.25
11 Tah-Crop Skirmisher	.06	.10
12 Temmet, Vizier of Naktamun	.12	.20
13 Trueheart Duelist	.06	.10
14 Unwavering Initiate	.06	.10
15 Vizier of Many Faces	.35	.50
16 Cat	.25	.35
17 Warrior	.06	.10
18 Drake	.06	.10
19 Insect	.60	1.00
20 Zombie	.06	.10
21 Beast	.06	.10
22 Hippo	.30	.40
23 Snake	.60	1.00
24 Wurm	1.00	1.50
25 Gideon of the Trials Emblem	1.50	2.00
26 Punchcard	.06	.10
27 Punchcard	.06	.10

2017 Magic The Gathering Amonkhet Invocations

COMPLETE SET (54)	2000.00	2300.00
RELEASED ON APRIL 28, 2016		
1 Austere Command M	25.00	30.00
2 Aven Mindcensor M	15.00	20.00
3 Containment Priest M	30.00	35.00
4 Loyal Retainers M	25.00	30.00
5 Oketra the True M	25.00	30.00
6 Worship M	20.00	25.00
7 Wrath of God M	40.00	45.00
8 Consecrated Sphinx M	90.00	100.00
9 Counterbalance M	15.00	20.00
10 Counterspell M	90.00	100.00
11 Cryptic Command M	60.00	70.00
12 Daze M	50.00	60.00
13 Divert M	15.00	20.00
14 Force of Will M	150.00	160.00
15 Kefnet the Mindful M	25.00	30.00
16 Pact of Negation M	45.00	55.00
17 Spell Pierce M	30.00	35.00
18 Stifle M	20.00	25.00
19 Attrition M	20.00	25.00
20 Bontu the Glorified M	25.00	30.00
21 Dark Ritual M	35.00	40.00
22 Diabolic Intent M	25.00	30.00
23 Entomb M	30.00	35.00
24 Mind Twist M	25.00	30.00
25 Aggravated Assault M	30.00	50.00
26 Chain Lightning M	20.00	25.00
27 Hazoret the Fervent M	50.00	60.00
28 Rhonas the Indomitable M	45.00	50.00
29 Maelstrom Pulse M	35.00	40.00
30 Vindicate M	25.00	30.00
31 Armageddon M	25.00	30.00
32 Capsize M	25.00	30.00
33 Forbid M	15.00	20.00
34 Omniscience M	50.00	60.00
35 Opposition M	20.00	25.00
36 Sunder M	15.00	20.00
37 Threads of Disloyalty M	15.00	20.00
38 Avatar of Woe M	15.00	20.00
39 Damnation M	90.00	100.00
40 Desolation Angel M	15.00	20.00
41 Diabolic Edict M	15.00	20.00
42 Doomsday M	25.00	30.00
43 No Mercy M	25.00	30.00
44 Slaughter Pact M	20.00	25.00
45 Thoughtseize M	100.00	110.00
46 Blood Moon M	80.00	90.00
47 Boil M	15.00	20.00
48 Shatterstorm M	15.00	20.00
49 Through the Breach M	45.00	50.00
50 Choke M	15.00	20.00
51 The Locust God M	50.00	55.00
52 Lord of Extinction M	25.00	30.00
53 The Scarab God M	80.00	90.00
54 The Scorpion God M	30.00	35.00

2017 Magic The Gathering Hour of Devastation

COMPLETE SET	140.00	220.00
BOOSTER BOX (36 PACKS)	85.00	120.00
BOOSTER PACK (15 CARDS)	3.00	5.00
*FOIL: .75X TO 2X BASIC CARDS		
RELEASED ON JULY 14 2017		
1 Act of Heroism C	.15	.25
2 Adorned Pouncer R	.60	1.00
3 Angel of Condemnation R	.25	.40
4 Angel of the God Pharaoh U	.15	.25
5 Aven of Enduring Hope C	.15	.25
6 Crested Sunmare M	5.00	8.00
7 Dauntless Aven C	.15	.25
8 Deserts Hold U	.15	.25
9 Disposal Mummy C	.15	.25
10 Djeru With Eyes Open R	.15	.25
11 Djerus Renunciation C	.15	.25
12 Dutiful Servants C	.15	.25
13 Gideons Defeat U	.15	.25
14 God Pharaohs Faithful C	.15	.25
15 Hour of Revelation R	.75	1.25
16 Mummy Paramount C	.15	.25
17 Oketras Avenger C	.15	.25
18 Oketras Last Mercy R	.30	.50
19 Overwhelming Splendor M	1.25	2.00
20 Sandblast C	.15	.25
21 Saving Grace U	.15	.25
22 Solemnity R	3.00	5.00
23 Solitary Camel C	.15	.25
24 Steadfast Sentinel C	.15	.25
25 Steward of Solidarity U	.15	.25
26 Sunscourge Champion U	.15	.25
27 Unconventional Tactics U	.15	.25
28 Vizier of the True U	.15	.25
29 Aerial Guide C	.15	.25
30 Aven Reedstalker C	.15	.25
31 Champion of Wits R	4.00	6.00
32 Countervailing Winds C	.15	.25
33 Cunning Survivor C	.15	.25
34 Eternal of Harsh Truths U	.15	.25
35 Fraying Sanity R	2.00	3.50
36 Hour of Eternity R	.15	.25
37 Imaginary Threats U	.15	.25
38 Jaces Defeat U	.15	.25
39 Kefnets Last Word R	.15	.25
40 Nimble Obstructionist R	2.00	3.00
41 Ominous Sphinx U	.15	.25
42 Proven Combatant C	.15	.25
43 Riddleform U	.15	.25
44 Seer of the Last Tomorrow C	.15	.25
45 Sinuous Striker U	.15	.25
46 Spellweaver Eternal C	.15	.25
47 Strategic Planning C	.15	.25
48 Striped Riverwinder C	.15	.25
49 Supreme Will U	1.00	1.50
50 Swarm Intelligence R	.15	.25
51 Tragic Lesson C	.15	.25
52 Unesh Criosphinx Sovereign M	.60	1.00
53 Unquenchable Thirst C	.15	.25
54 Unsummon C	.15	.25
55 Vizier of the Anointed U	.15	.25
56 Accursed Horde U	.15	.25
57 Ammit Eternal R	1.50	2.50
58 Apocalypse Demon R	.15	.25
59 Banewhip Punisher U	.15	.25
60 Bontus Last Reckoning R	2.50	3.50
61 Carrion Screecher C	.15	.25
62 Doomfall U	.15	.25
63 Dreamstealer R	.50	.80
64 Grisly Survivor C	.15	.25
65 Hour of Glory R	.15	.25
66 Khenra Eternal C	.15	.25
67 Lethal Sting C	.15	.25
68 Lilianas Defeat U	.15	.25
69 Lurching Rotbeast C	.15	.25
70 Marauding Boneslasher C	.15	.25
71 Merciless Eternal U	.15	.25
72 Moaning Wall C	.15	.25
73 Razaketh the Foulblooded M	4.00	6.00
74 Razakeths Rite U	.15	.25
75 Ruin Rat C	.15	.25
76 Scrounger of Souls C	.15	.25
77 Torment of Hailfire R	2.00	3.00
78 Torment of Scarabs U	.15	.25
79 Torment of Venom C	.15	.25
80 Vile Manifestation U	.15	.25
81 Without Weakness C	.15	.25
82 Wretched Camel C	.15	.25
83 Abrade U	2.00	3.50
84 Blur of Blades C	.15	.25
85 Burning Fist Minotaur U	.15	.25
86 Chandras Defeat U	.15	.25
87 Chaos Maw R	.60	1.00
88 Crash Through C	.15	.25
89 Defiant Khenra C	.15	.25
90 Earthshaker Khenra R	3.00	5.00
91 Fervent Paincaster U	.15	.25
92 Firebrand Archer C	.15	.25
93 Frontline Devastator C	.15	.25
94 Gilded Cerodon C	.15	.25
95 Granitic Titan C	.15	.25
96 Hazorets Undying Fury R	.10	.20
97 Hour of Devastation R	3.00	5.00
98 Imminent Doom R	.15	.25
99 Inferno Jet U	.15	.25
100 Khenra Scrapper C	.15	.25
101 Kindled Fury C	.15	.25
102 Magmaroth U	.15	.25
103 Manticore Eternal U	.15	.25
104 Neheb the Eternal M	3.00	5.00
105 Open Fire C	.15	.25
106 Puncturing Blow C	.15	.25
107 Sand Strangler U	.15	.25
108 Thorned Moloch C	.15	.25
109 Wildfire Eternal R	.30	.50
110 Ambuscade C	.15	.25
111 Beneath the Sands C	.15	.25
112 Bitterbow Sharpshooters C	.15	.25
113 Devotee of Strength U	.15	.25
114 Dune Diviner U	.15	.25
115 Feral Prowler C	.15	.25
116 Frilled Sandwalla C	.15	.25
117 Gift of Strength C	.15	.25
118 Harrier Naga C	.15	.25
119 Hope Tender U	.15	.25
120 Hour of Promise R	1.50	2.50
121 Life Goes On C	.15	.25
122 Majestic Myriarch M	1.25	2.00
123 Nissas Defeat U	.15	.25
124 Oasis Ritualist C	.15	.25
125 Overcome U	.15	.25
126 Pride Sovereign R	1.25	2.00
127 Quarry Beetle U	.15	.25
128 Rampaging Hippo C	.15	.25
129 Ramunap Excavator R	3.00	5.00
130 Ramunap Hydra R	.15	.25
131 Resilient Khenra R	.15	.25
132 Rhonass Last Stand R	.40	.60
133 Rhonass Stalwart C	.15	.25
134 Sidewinder Naga C	.15	.25
135 Sifter Wurm U	.15	.25
136 Tenacious Hunter U	.15	.25
137 Uncage the Menagerie M	1.00	1.50
138 Bloodwater Entity U	.15	.25
139 The Locust God M	8.00	12.00
140 Nicol Bolas God Pharaoh M	15.00	20.00
141 Obelisk Spider U	.15	.25
142 Resolute Survivors U	.15	.25
143 River Hoopoe U	.15	.25
144 Samut the Tested M	3.00	5.00
145 The Scarab God M	10.00	15.00
146 The Scorpion God M	4.00	6.00
147 Unraveling Mummy U	.15	.25
148 Farm Market U	.15	.25
149 Consign Oblivion U	.15	.25
150 Claim Fame U	.15	.25
151 Struggle Survive U	.15	.25
152 Appeal Authority U	.15	.25
153 Leave Chance R	.15	.25
154 Reason Believe R	.20	.35
155 Grind Dust R	.20	.35
156 Refuse Cooperate R	.15	.25
157 Driven Despair R	.30	.50
158 Abandoned Sarcophagus R	.20	.35
159 Crook of Condemnation U	.15	.25
160 Dagger of the Worthy U	.15	.25
161 God Pharaohs Gift R	1.50	2.50
162 Graven Abomination C	.15	.25
163 Hollow One R	.75	1.25
164 Manalith C	.15	.25
165 Mirage Mirror R	2.00	3.50
166 Sunset Pyramid U	.15	.25
167 Traveler s Amulet C	.15	.25
168 Wall of Forgotten Pharaohs C	.15	.25
169 Crypt of the Eternals U	.15	.25
170 Desert of the Fervent C	.15	.25
171 Desert of the Glorified C	.15	.25
172 Desert of the Indomitable C	.15	.25
173 Desert of the Mindful C	.15	.25
174 Desert of the True C	.15	.25
175 Dunes of the Dead U	.15	.25
176 Endless Sands R	.15	.25
177 Hashep Oasis U	.15	.25
178 Hostile Desert R	.30	.50
179 Ifnir Deadlands U	.15	.25
180 Ipnu Rivulet U	.15	.25
181 Ramunap Ruins U	.75	1.25
182 Scavenger Grounds R	.60	1.00
183 Shefet Dunes U	.15	.25
184 Survivors Encampment C	.15	.25
185 Plains Full Art L	.15	.25
186 Island Full Art L	.15	.25
187 Swamp Full Art L	.15	.25
188 Mountain Full Art L	.15	.25
189 Forest Full Art L	.15	.25
190 Plains L	.15	.25
191 Plains L	.15	.25
192 Island L	.15	.25
193 Island L	.15	.25
194 Swamp L	.15	.25
195 Swamp L	.15	.25
196 Mountain L	.15	.25
197 Mountain L	.15	.25
198 Forest L	.15	.25
199 Forest L	.15	.25
200 Nissa Genesis Mage M	4.00	6.00
201 Avid Reclaimer U	.15	.25
202 Bramblewelt Behemoth C	.15	.25
203 Nissas Encouragement R	.60	1.00
204 Woodland Stream C	.15	.25
205 Nicol Bolas the Deceiver M	5.00	8.00
206 Wasp of the Bitter End U	.15	.25
207 Zealot of the God Pharaoh C	.15	.25
208 Visage of Bolas R	.40	.60
209 Cinder Barrens C	.15	.25

2017 Magic The Gathering Hour of Devastation Foil

COMPLETE SET (209)	480.00	660.00
RELEASED ON JULY 14, 2017		
1 Act of Heroism C	.25	.40
2 Adorned Pouncer R	2.00	3.50
3 Angel of Condemnation R	2.00	3.50
4 Angel of the God Pharaoh U	.40	.60
5 Aven of Enduring Hope C	.25	.40
6 Crested Sunmare M	10.00	15.00
7 Dauntless Aven C	.25	.40
8 Deserts Hold U	.40	.60
9 Disposal Mummy C	.25	.40
10 Djeru With Eyes Open R	2.00	3.50
11 Djerus Renunciation C	.25	.40
12 Dutiful Servants C	.25	.40
13 Gideons Defeat U	.40	.60
14 God Pharaohs Faithful C	.25	.40
15 Hour of Revelation R	5.00	7.00
16 Mummy Paramount C	.25	.40
17 Oketras Avenger C	.25	.40
18 Oketras Last Mercy R	2.00	3.50
19 Overwhelming Splendor M	7.00	10.00
20 Sandblast C	.25	.40
21 Saving Grace U	.40	.60
22 Solemnity R	20.00	25.00
23 Solitary Camel C	.25	.40
24 Steadfast Sentinel C	.25	.40
25 Steward of Solidarity U	.40	.60
26 Sunscourge Champion U	.40	.60
27 Unconventional Tactics U	.40	.60
28 Vizier of the True U	.40	.60
29 Aerial Guide C	.25	.40
30 Aven Reedstalker C	.25	.40
31 Champion of Wits R	2.00	3.50
32 Countervailing Winds C	.25	.40
33 Cunning Survivor C	.25	.40
34 Eternal of Harsh Truths U	.40	.60
35 Fraying Sanity R	2.00	3.50
36 Hour of Eternity R	2.00	3.50
37 Imaginary Threats U	.40	.60
38 Jaces Defeat U	.40	.60
39 Kefnets Last Word R	2.00	3.50
40 Nimble Obstructionist R	15.00	20.00
41 Ominous Sphinx U	.40	.60
42 Proven Combatant C	.25	.40
43 Riddleform U	.40	.60
44 Seer of the Last Tomorrow C	.25	.40
45 Sinuous Striker U	.40	.60
46 Spellweaver Eternal C	.25	.40
47 Strategic Planning C	.25	.40
48 Striped Riverwinder C	.25	.40
49 Supreme Will U	.40	.60
50 Swarm Intelligence R	2.00	3.50
51 Tragic Lesson C	.25	.40
52 Unesh Criosphinx Sovereign M	6.00	8.00
53 Unquenchable Thirst C	.25	.40
54 Unsummon C	.25	.40
55 Vizier of the Anointed U	.40	.60
56 Accursed Horde U	.40	.60
57 Ammit Eternal R	6.00	8.00
58 Apocalypse Demon R	2.00	3.50
59 Banewhip Punisher U	.40	.60
60 Bontus Last Reckoning R	2.00	3.50
61 Carrion Screecher C	.25	.40
62 Doomfall U	.40	.60
63 Dreamstealer R	2.00	3.50
64 Grisly Survivor C	.25	.40
65 Hour of Glory R	2.00	3.50
66 Khenra Eternal C	.25	.40
67 Lethal Sting C	.25	.40
68 Lilianas Defeat U	.40	.60
69 Lurching Rotbeast C	.25	.40
70 Marauding Boneslasher C	.25	.40
71 Merciless Eternal U	.40	.60
72 Moaning Wall C	.25	.40
73 Razaketh the Foulblooded M	25.00	30.00
74 Razakeths Rite U	.40	.60
75 Ruin Rat C	.25	.40
76 Scrounger of Souls C	.25	.40
77 Torment of Hailfire R	6.00	8.00

78 Torment of Scarabs U .40 .60
79 Torment of Venom C .25 .40
80 Vile Manifestation U .40 .60
81 Without Weakness C .25 .40
82 Wretched Camel C .25 .40
83 Abrade U .40 .60
84 Blur of Blades C .25 .40
85 Burning Fist Minotaur U .40 .60
86 Chandras Defeat U .40 .60
87 Chaos Maw R 2.00 3.50
88 Crash Through C .25 .40
89 Defiant Khenra C .25 .40
90 Earthshaker Khenra R 2.00 3.50
91 Fervent Paincaster U .40 .60
92 Firebrand Archer C .25 .40
93 Frontline Devastator C .25 .40
94 Gilded Cerodon C .25 .40
95 Granitic Titan C .25 .40
96 Hazorets Undying Fury R 2.00 3.50
97 Hour of Devastation R 20.00 25.00
98 Imminent Doom R 2.00 3.50
99 Inferno Jet U .40 .60
100 Khenra Scrapper C .25 .40
101 Kindled Fury C .25 .40
102 Magmaroth U .40 .60
103 Manticore Eternal U .40 .60
104 Neheb the Eternal M 10.00 15.00
105 Open Fire C .25 .40
106 Puncturing Blow C .25 .40
107 Sand Strangler U .40 .60
108 Thorned Moloch C .25 .40
109 Wildfire Eternal R 2.00 3.50
110 Ambuscade C .25 .40
111 Beneath the Sands C .25 .40
112 Bitterbow Sharpshooters C .25 .40
113 Devotee of Strength U .40 .60
114 Dune Diviner U .40 .60
115 Feral Prowler C .25 .40
116 Frilled Sandwalla C .25 .40
117 Gift of Strength C .25 .40
118 Harrier Naga C .25 .40
119 Hope Tender U .40 .60
120 Hour of Promise R 6.00 8.00
121 Life Goes On C .25 .40
122 Majestic Myriarch M 7.00 10.00
123 Nissas Defeat U .40 .60
124 Oasis Ritualist C .25 .40
125 Overcome U .40 .60
126 Pride Sovereign R 6.00 8.00
127 Quarry Beetle U .40 .60
128 Rampaging Hippo C .25 .40
129 Ramunap Excavator R 2.00 3.50
130 Ramunap Hydra R 25.00 30.00
131 Resilient Khenra R 2.00 3.50
132 Rhonass Last Stand R 6.00 8.00
133 Rhonass Stalwart C .25 .40
134 Sidewinder Naga C .25 .40
135 Sifter Wurm U .40 .60
136 Tenacious Hunter U .40 .60
137 Uncage the Menagerie M 10.00 15.00
138 Bloodwater Entity U .40 .60
139 The Locust God M 30.00 40.00
140 Nicol Bolas God Pharaoh M 45.00 55.00
141 Obelisk Spider U .40 .60
142 Resolute Survivors U .40 .60
143 River Hoopoe U .40 .60
144 Samut the Tested M 20.00 25.00
145 The Scarab God M 30.00 40.00
146 The Scorpion God M 15.00 20.00
147 Unraveling Mummy U .40 .60
148 Farm Market U .40 .60
149 Consign Oblivion U .40 .60
150 Claim Fame U .40 .60
151 Struggle Survive U .40 .60
152 Appeal Authority U .40 .60
153 Leave Chance R 2.00 3.50
154 Reason Believe R 2.00 3.50
155 Grind Dust R 2.00 3.50
156 Refuse Cooperate R 2.00 3.50
157 Driven Despair R 2.00 3.50
158 Abandoned Sarcophagus R 2.00 3.50
159 Crook of Condemnation U .40 .60
160 Dagger of the Worthy U .40 .60
161 God Pharaohs Gift R 2.00 3.50
162 Graven Abomination C .25 .40
163 Hollow One R 8.00 12.00
164 Manalith C .25 .40
165 Mirage Mirror R 13.00 16.00
166 Sunset Pyramid U .40 .60
167 Traveler s Amulet C .25 .40
168 Wall of Forgotten Pharaohs C .25 .40
169 Crypt of the Eternals U .40 .60
170 Desert of the Fervent C .25 .40
171 Desert of the Glorified C .25 .40
172 Desert of the Indomitable C .25 .40
173 Desert of the Mindful C .25 .40
174 Desert of the True C .25 .40
175 Dunes of the Dead U .40 .60
176 Endless Sands R 2.00 3.50
177 Hashep Oasis U .40 .60
178 Hostile Desert R 5.00 7.00
179 Ifnir Deadlands U .40 .60
180 Ipnu Rivulet U .40 .60
181 Ramunap Ruins U .40 .60
182 Scavenger Grounds R 4.00 6.00
183 Shefet Dunes U .40 .60
184 Survivors Encampment C .25 .40
185 Plains Full Art L .25 .40
186 Island Full Art L .25 .40
187 Swamp Full Art L .25 .40
188 Mountain Full Art L .25 .40
189 Forest Full Art L .25 .40
190 Plains L .25 .40
191 Plains L .25 .40
192 Island L .25 .40
193 Island L .25 .40
194 Swamp L .25 .40
195 Swamp L .25 .40
196 Mountain L .25 .40
197 Mountain L .25 .40
198 Forest L .25 .40
199 Forest L .25 .40
200 Nissa Genesis Mage M 6.00 8.00
201 Avid Reclaimer U .40 .60
202 Brambleweft Behemoth C .25 .40
203 Nissas Encouragement R 2.00 3.50
204 Woodland Stream C .25 .40
205 Nicol Bolas the Deceiver M 6.00 8.00
206 Wasp of the Bitter End U .40 .60
207 Zealot of the God Pharaoh C .25 .40
208 Visage of Bolas R 2.00 3.50
209 Cinder Barrens C .25 .40

2017 Magic The Gathering Hour of Devastation Tokens

1 Adorned Pouncer .30 .40
2 Champion of Wits .10 .15
3 Dreamstealer .06 .10
4 Earthshaker Khenra .10 .15
5 Proven Combatant .06 .10
6 Resilient Khenra .06 .10
7 Sinuous Striker .06 .10
8 Steadfast Sentinel .06 .10
9 Sunscourge Champion .06 .10
10 Horse .30 .75
11 Snake .12 .20
12 Insect 1.25 1.75
13 Punchcard .06 .10
14 Punchcard .06 .10

2017 Magic The Gathering Ixalan

COMPLETE SET (299) 275.00 415.00
BOOSTER BOX (36 PACKS) 85.00 120.00
BOOSTER PACK (15 CARDS) 4.00 6.00
UNLISTED C .10 .20
UNLISTED U .20 .35
UNLISTED R .60 1.00
RELEASED ON SEPTEMBER 29, 2016
1 Adanto Vanguard U .20 .35
2 Ashes of the Abhorrent R .20 .35
3 Axis of Mortality M .50 .80
4 Bellowing Aegisaur U .20 .35
5 Bishop of Rebirth R .20 .35
6 Bishops Soldier C .10 .20
7 Bright Reprisal U .20 .35
8 Demystify C .10 .20
9 Duskborne Skymarcher U .20 .35
10 Emissary of Sunrise U .20 .35
11 Encampment Keeper C .10 .20
12 Glorifier of Dusk U .20 .35
13 Goring Ceratops R .15 .25
14 Imperial Aerosaur U .20 .35
15 Imperial Lancer U .20 .35
16 Inspiring Cleric U .20 .35
17 Ixalans Binding U .20 .35
18 Kinjallis Caller C .10 .20
19 Kinjallis Sunwing R 1.00 1.50
20 Legion Conquistador C .10 .20
21 Legions Judgment C .10 .20
22 Legions Landing R 4.00 6.00
22 Adanto The First Fort R 4.00 6.00
23 Looming Altisaur C .10 .20
24 Mavren Fein Dusk Apostle R .75 1.25
25 Paladin of the Bloodstained C .10 .20
26 Pious Interdiction C .10 .20
27 Priest of the Wakening Sun R .20 .35
28 Pterodon Knight C .10 .20
29 Queens Commission C .10 .20
30 Rallying Roar U .20 .35
31 Raptor Companion C .10 .20
32 Ritual of Rejuvenation C .10 .20
33 Sanguine Sacrament R .15 .25
34 Settle the Wreckage R 3.00 5.00
35 Sheltering Light U .20 .35
36 Shining Aerosaur C .10 .20
37 Skyblade of the Legion C .10 .20
38 Slash of Talons C .10 .20
39 Steadfast Armasaur U .20 .35
40 Sunrise Seeker C .10 .20
41 Territorial Hammerskull C .10 .20
42 Vampires Zeal C .10 .20
43 Tocatli Honor Guard R .20 .35
44 Wakening Suns Avatar M 1.00 1.50
45 Air Elemental U .20 .35
46 Arcane Adaptation R .20 .35
47 Cancel C .10 .20
48 Chart a Course U .40 .60
49 Daring Saboteur R .20 .35
50 Deadeye Quartermaster U .20 .35
51 Deeproot Waters U .20 .35
52 Depths of Desire C .10 .20
53 Dive Down C .10 .20
54 Dreamcaller Siren R .20 .35
55 Entrancing Melody R .20 .35
56 Favorable Winds U .20 .35
57 Fleet Swallower R .20 .35
58 Headwater Sentries C .10 .20
59 Herald of Secret Streams R .40 .60
60 Jace Cunning Castaway M 5.00 7.00
61 Kopala Warden of Waves R .75 1.25
62 Lookouts Dispersal U .20 .35
63 Navigators Ruin U .20 .35
64 One With the Wind C .10 .20
65 Overflowing Insight M .60 1.00
66 Opt C .10 .20
67 Perilous Voyage U .20 .35
68 Pirates Prize C .10 .20
69 Prosperous Pirates C .10 .20
70 River Sneak U .20 .35
71 Rivers Rebuke R .20 .35
72 Run Aground C .10 .20
73 Sailor of Means C .10 .20
74 Search for Azcanta R 8.00 12.00
74 Azcanta The Sunken Ruin R 8.00 12.00
75 Shaper Apprentice C .10 .20
76 Shipwreck Looter C .10 .20
77 Shore Keeper C .10 .20
78 Siren Lookout C .10 .20
79 Siren Stormtamer U .20 .35
80 Sirens Ruse C .10 .20
81 Spell Pierce C .10 .20
82 Spell Swindle R 1.00 1.50
83 Storm Fleet Aerialist U .20 .35
84 Storm Fleet Spy U .20 .35
85 Storm Sculptor C .10 .20
86 Tempest Caller U .20 .35
87 Watertrap Weaver C .10 .20
88 Wind Strider C .10 .20
89 Anointed Deacon C .10 .20
90 Arguels Blood Fast R .60 1.00
90 Temple of Aclazotz R .60 1.00
91 Bishop of the Bloodstined U .20 .35
92 Blight Keeper C .10 .20
93 Bloodcrazed Paladin R .30 .50
94 Boneyard Parley M .30 .50
95 Contract Killing C .10 .20
96 Costly Plunder C .10 .20
97 Dark Nourishment U .20 .35
98 Deadeye Tormentor C .10 .20
99 Deadeye Tracker R .75 1.25
100 Deathless Ancient U .20 .35
101 Desperate Castaways C .10 .20
102 Dire Fleet Hoarder C .10 .20
103 Dire Fleet Interloper C .10 .20
104 Dire Fleet Ravager M .75 1.25
105 Duress C .10 .20
106 Fathom Fleet Captain R .60 1.00
107 Fathom Fleet Cutthroat C .10 .20
108 Grim Captains Call U .20 .35
109 Heartless Pillage U .20 .35
110 Kitesail Freebooter U .40 .60
111 Lurking Chupacabra U .20 .35
112 March of the Drowned C .10 .20
113 Mark of the Vampire C .10 .20
114 Queens Agent C .10 .20
115 Queens Bay Soldier C .10 .20
116 Raiders Wake U .20 .35
117 Revel in Riches R .60 1.00
118 Ruin Raider R .75 1.25
119 Ruthless Knave U .20 .35
120 Sanctum Seeker R .60 1.00
121 Seekers Squire U .20 .35
122 Skittering Heartstopper C .10 .20
123 Skulduggery C .10 .20
124 Skymarch Bloodletter C .10 .20
125 Spreading Rot C .10 .20
126 Sword Point Diplomacy R 1.00 1.50
127 Vanquish the Weak C .10 .20
128 Vicious Conquistador U .20 .35
129 Vraskas Contempt R 8.00 12.00
130 Walk the Plank U .30 .50
131 Wanted Scoundrels U .20 .35
132 Angraths Marauders R .15 .25
133 Bonded Horncrest U .20 .35
134 Brazen Buccaneers C .10 .20
135 Burning Suns Avatar R .20 .35
136 Captain Lannery Storm R .60 1.00
137 Captivating Crew R .20 .35
138 Charging Monstrosaur U .20 .35
139 Demolish C .10 .20
140 Dinosaur Stampede U .20 .35
141 Dual Shot C .10 .20
142 Fathom Fleet Firebrand C .10 .20
143 Fiery Cannonade U .20 .35
144 Fire Shrine Keeper C .10 .20
145 Firecannon Blast C .10 .20
146 Frenzied Raptor C .10 .20
147 Headstrong Brute C .10 .20
148 Hijack C .10 .20
149 Lightning Strike U .20 .35
150 Lightning Rig Crew U .20 .35
151 Makeshift Munitions U .20 .35
152 Nest Robber C .10 .20
153 Otepec Huntmaster U .20 .35
154 Rampaging Ferocidon R 3.00 5.00
155 Raptor Hatchling U .20 .35
156 Repeating Barrage R .15 .25
157 Rigging Runner U .20 .35
158 Rile C .10 .20
159 Rowdy Crew M .50 .80
160 Rummaging Goblin C .10 .20
161 Star of Extinction M .75 1.25
162 Storm Fleet Arsonist U .20 .35
163 Storm Fleet Pyyromancer C .10 .20
164 Sun Crowned Hunters C .10 .20
165 Sunbirds Invocation R .60 1.00
166 Sure Strike C .10 .20
167 Swashbuckling C .10 .20
168 Thrash of Raptors C .10 .20
169 Tilonallis Knight C .10 .20
170 Tilonallis Skinshifter R .15 .25
171 Trove of Temptation U .20 .35
172 Unfriendly Fire C .10 .20
173 Vances Blasting Cannons R .40 .60
173 Spitfire Bastion R .40 .60
174 Wily Goblin U .20 .35
175 Ancient Brontodon C .10 .20
176 Atzocan Archer U .20 .35
177 Blinding Fog C .10 .20
178 Blossom Dryad C .10 .20
179 Carnage Tyrant M 14.00 16.00
180 Colossal Dreadmaw C .10 .20
181 Commune with Dinosaurs C .10 .20
182 Crash the Ramparts C .10 .20
183 Crushing Canopy C .10 .20
184 Deathgorge Scavenger R 4.00 6.00
185 Deeproot Champion R .60 1.00
186 Deeproot Warrior C .10 .20
187 Drover of the Mighty U .20 .35
188 Emergent Growth U .20 .35
189 Emperors Vanguard R .15 .25
190 Gazing Whiptail C .10 .20
191 Growing Rites of Itlimoc R 4.00 6.00
191 Itlimoc Cradle of the Sun R 4.00 6.00
192 Ixallis Diviner C .10 .20
193 Ixallis Keeper C .10 .20
194 Jade Guardian C .10 .20
195 Jungle Delver C .10 .20
196 Kumenas Speaker U .20 .35
197 Merfolk Branchwalker U .20 .35
198 New Horizons C .10 .20
199 Old Growth Dryads R .20 .35
200 Pounce C .10 .20
201 Ranging Raptors U .20 .35
202 Ravenous Daggertooth C .10 .20
203 Ripjaw Raptor R 4.00 6.00
204 River Heralds Boon C .10 .20
205 Savage Stomp U .20 .35
206 Shapers Sanctuary R .75 1.25
207 Slice in Twain U .20 .35
208 Snapping Sailback U .20 .35
209 Spike Tailed Ceratops C .10 .20
210 Thundering Spineback U .20 .35
211 Tishanas Wayfinder C .10 .20
212 Verdant Rebirth U .20 .35
213 Verdant Suns Avatar R .20 .35
214 Vineshaper Mystic U .20 .35
215 Waker of the Wilds R .15 .25
216 Wildgrowth Walker U .20 .35
217 Admiral Beckett Brass M 1.50 2.00
218 Belligerent Brontodon U .20 .35
219 Call to the Feast U .20 .35
220 Deadeye Plunderers U .20 .35
221 Dire Fleet Captain U .20 .35
222 Gishath Suns Avatar M 5.00 7.00
223 Hostage Taker R 7.00 10.00
224 Huatli Warrior Poet M 4.00 6.00
225 Marauding Looter U .20 .35
226 Raging Swordtooth U .20 .35
227 Regisaur Alpha R 2.00 3.50
228 Shapers of Nature U .20 .35
229 Sky Terror U .20 .35
230 Tishana Voice of Thunder M 1.50 2.00
231 Vona Butcher of Magan M 3.00 5.00
232 Vraska Relic Seeker M 15.00 20.00
233 Cobbled Wings C .10 .20
234 Conquerors Galleon R .20 .35
234 Conquerors Foothold R .20 .35
235 Dowsing Dagger R 1.00 1.50
235 Lost Vale R 1.00 1.50
236 Dusk Legion Dreadnought U .20 .35
237 Elaborate Firecannon U .20 .35
238 Fell Flagship R .20 .35
239 Gilded Sentinel C .10 .20
240 Hierophants Chalice C .10 .20
241 Pillar of Origins U .20 .35
242 Pirates Cutlass C .10 .20
243 Primal Amulet R 1.50 2.00
243 Primal Wellspring R 1.50 2.00
244 Prying Blade C .10 .20
245 Sentinel Totem U .20 .35
246 Shadowed Caravel R .15 .25
247 Sleek Schooner U .20 .35
248 Sorcerous Spyglass R .75 1.25
249 Thaumatic Compass R .75 1.25
249 Spires of Orazca R .75 1.25
250 Treasure Map R 3.00 5.00
250 Treasure Cove R 3.00 5.00
251 Vanquishers Banner R 1.50 2.50
252 Dragonskull Summit R 2.00 3.50
253 Drowned Catacomb R 5.00 7.00
254 Field of Ruin U .20 .35
255 Glacial Fortress R 3.00 5.00
256 Rootbound Crag R 3.00 5.00
257 Sunpetal Grove R 1.50 2.00
258 Unclaimed Territory U 1.50 2.00
259 Unknown Shores C .10 .20
260 Plains L .10 .20
261 Plains L .10 .20
262 Plains L .10 .20
263 Plains L .10 .20
264 Island L .10 .20
265 Island L .10 .20
266 Island L .10 .20
267 Island L .10 .20
268 Swamp L .10 .20
269 Swamp L .10 .20
270 Swamp L .10 .20
271 Swamp L .10 .20
272 Mountain L .10 .20
273 Mountain L .10 .20
274 Mountain L .10 .20
275 Mountain L .10 .20
276 Forest L .10 .20
277 Forest L .10 .20
278 Forest L .10 .20
279 Forest L .10 .20
280 Jace Ingenious Mind Mage M 5.00 7.00
281 Castaways Despair C .10 .20
282 Grasping Current R .20 .35
283 Jaces Sentinel U .20 .35
284 Woodland Stream C .10 .20
285 Huatli Dinosaur Knight M 6.00 8.00
286 Huatlis Snubhorn C .10 .20
287 Huatlis Spurring U .10 .20
288 Sun Blessed Mount R .60 1.00
289 Stone Quarry C .10 .20

2017 Magic The Gathering Ixalan Foil

COMPLETE SET (289) 800.00 1100.00
RELEASED ON SEPTEMBER 29, 2017
1 Adanto Vanguard U 1.50 2.00
2 Ashes of the Abhorrent R 6.00 10.00
3 Axis of Mortality M 6.00 10.00
4 Bellowing Aegisaur U .60 1.00
5 Bishop of Rebirth R 6.00 10.00
6 Bishops Soldier C .20 .35
7 Bright Reprisal U .60 1.00
8 Demystify C .20 .35
9 Duskborne Skymarcher U .60 1.00
10 Emissary of Sunrise U .75 1.25
11 Encampment Keeper C .20 .35
12 Glorifier of Dusk U .60 1.00
13 Goring Ceratops R 6.00 10.00
14 Imperial Aerosaur U .60 1.00
15 Imperial Lancer U .60 1.00
16 Inspiring Cleric U 1.50 2.50
17 Ixalans Binding U 3.00 5.00

Card	Low	High
18 Kinjallis Caller C	.20	.35
19 Kinjallis Sunwing R	6.00	10.00
20 Legion Conquistador C	.20	.35
21 Legions Judgment C	.20	.35
22 Legions Landing R	6.00	10.00
22 Adanto The First Fort R	6.00	10.00
23 Looming Altisaur C	.20	.35
24 Mavren Fein Dusk Apostle R	6.00	10.00
25 Paladin of the Bloodstained C	.20	.35
26 Pious Interdiction C	.20	.35
27 Priest of the Wakening Sun R	6.00	10.00
28 Pterodon Knight C	.20	.35
29 Queens Commission C	.20	.35
30 Rallying Roar U	.60	1.00
31 Raptor Companion C	.20	.35
32 Ritual of Rejuvenation C	.20	.35
33 Sanguine Sacrament R	6.00	10.00
34 Settle the Wreckage R	6.00	10.00
35 Sheltering Light U	.60	1.00
36 Shining Aerosaur C	.20	.35
37 Skyblade of the Legion C	.20	.35
38 Slash of Talons C	.20	.35
39 Steadfast Armasaur U	.60	1.00
40 Sunrise Seeker C	.20	.35
41 Territorial Hammerskull C	.20	.35
42 Vampires Zeal C	.20	.35
43 Tocatli Honor Guard R	6.00	10.00
44 Wakening Suns Avatar M	10.00	15.00
45 Air Elemental U	.60	1.00
46 Arcane Adaptation R	6.00	10.00
47 Cancel C	.20	.35
48 Chart a Course U	7.00	10.00
49 Daring Saboteur R	6.00	10.00
50 Deadeye Quartermaster U	2.00	3.00
51 Deeproot Waters U	3.00	5.00
52 Depths of Desire C	.20	.35
53 Dive Down C	.20	.35
54 Dreamcaller Siren R	6.00	10.00
55 Entrancing Melody R	6.00	10.00
56 Favorable Winds U	.60	1.00
57 Fleet Swallower R	6.00	10.00
58 Headwater Sentries C	.20	.35
59 Herald of Secret Streams R	6.00	10.00
60 Jace Cunning Castaway M	30.00	40.00
61 Kopala Warden of Waves R	6.00	10.00
62 Lookouts Dispersal U	2.00	3.00
63 Navigators Ruin U	.60	1.00
64 One With the Wind C	.20	.35
65 Overflowing Insight M	10.00	15.00
66 Opt C	10.00	15.00
67 Perilous Voyage U	2.00	3.00
68 Pirates Prize C	.20	.35
69 Prosperous Pirates C	.20	.35
70 River Sneak U	1.50	2.00
71 Rivers Rebuke R	6.00	10.00
72 Run Aground C	.20	.35
73 Sailor of Means C	.20	.35
74 Search for Azcanta R	15.00	20.00
74 Azcanta The Sunken Ruin R	15.00	20.00
75 Shaper Apprentice C	.20	.35
76 Shipwreck Looter C	.20	.35
77 Shore Keeper C	.20	.35
78 Siren Lookout C	.20	.35
79 Siren Stormtamer U	6.00	10.00
80 Sirens Ruse C	.20	.35
81 Spell Pierce C	3.00	5.00
82 Spell Swindle R	6.00	10.00
83 Storm Fleet Aerialist U	.60	1.00
84 Storm Fleet Spy U	.60	1.00
85 Storm Sculptor C	.20	.35
86 Tempest Caller U	.60	1.00
87 Watertrap Weaver C	.20	.35
88 Wind Strider C	.20	.35
89 Anointed Deacon C	.20	.35
90 Arguels Blood Fast R	6.00	10.00
90 Temple of Aclazotz R	6.00	10.00
91 Bishop of the Bloodstined U	.60	1.00
92 Blight Keeper C	.20	.35
93 Bloodcrazed Paladin R	6.00	10.00
94 Boneyard Parley M	6.00	10.00
95 Contract Killing C	.20	.35
96 Costly Plunder C	.20	.35
97 Dark Nourishment U	.60	1.00
98 Deadeye Tormentor C	.20	.35
99 Deadeye Tracker R	6.00	10.00
100 Deathless Ancient U	.60	1.00
101 Desperate Castaways C	.20	.35
102 Dire Fleet Hoarder C	.20	.35
103 Dire Fleet Interloper C	.20	.35
104 Dire Fleet Ravager M	10.00	15.00
105 Duress C	3.00	5.00
106 Fathom Fleet Captain R	6.00	10.00
107 Fathom Fleet Cutthroat C	.20	.35
108 Grim Captains Call U	.60	1.00
109 Heartless Pillage U	.60	1.00
110 Kitesail Freebooter U	2.00	3.00
111 Lurking Chupacabra U	.60	1.00
112 March of the Drowned C	.20	.35
113 Mark of the Vampire C	.20	.35
114 Queens Agent C	.20	.35
115 Queens Bay Soldier C	.20	.35
116 Raiders Wake U	2.00	3.00
117 Revel in Riches R	6.00	10.00
118 Ruin Raider R	6.00	10.00
119 Ruthless Knave U	1.50	2.50
120 Sanctum Seeker R	6.00	10.00
121 Seekers Squire U	.60	1.00
122 Skittering Heartstopper C	.20	.35
123 Skulduggery C	.20	.35
124 Skymarch Bloodletter C	.20	.35
125 Spreading Rot C	.20	.35
126 Sword Point Diplomacy R	6.00	10.00
127 Vanquish the Weak C	.20	.35
128 Vicious Conquistador U	1.25	2.00
129 Vraskas Contempt R	6.00	10.00
130 Walk the Plank U	4.00	6.00
131 Wanted Scoundrels U	2.00	3.00
132 Angraths Marauders R	6.00	10.00
133 Bonded Horncrest U	.60	1.00
134 Brazen Buccaneers C	.20	.35
135 Burning Suns Avatar R	6.00	10.00
136 Captain Lannery Storm R	6.00	10.00
137 Captivating Crew R	6.00	10.00
138 Charging Monstrosaur U	1.50	2.50
139 Demolish C	.20	.35
140 Dinosaur Stampede U	.60	1.00
141 Dual Shot C	.20	.35
142 Fathom Fleet Firebrand C	.20	.35
143 Fiery Cannonade U	.60	1.00
144 Fire Shrine Keeper C	.20	.35
145 Firecannon Blast C	.20	.35
146 Frenzied Raptor C	.20	.35
147 Headstrong Brute C	.20	.35
148 Hijack C	.20	.35
149 Lightning Strike U	3.00	5.00
150 Lightning Rig Crew U	.30	.50
151 Makeshift Munitions U	1.50	2.00
152 Nest Robber C	.20	.35
153 Otepec Huntmaster U	2.50	4.00
154 Rampaging Ferocidon R	6.00	10.00
155 Raptor Hatchling U	.60	1.00
156 Repeating Barrage R	6.00	10.00
157 Rigging Runner U	1.50	2.50
158 Rile C	.20	.35
159 Rowdy Crew M	6.00	10.00
160 Rummaging Goblin C	.20	.35
161 Star of Extinction M	7.00	10.00
162 Storm Fleet Arsonist U	.60	1.00
163 Storm Fleet pyromancer C	.20	.35
164 Sun Crowned Hunters C	.20	.35
165 Sunbirds Invocation R	6.00	10.00
166 Sure Strike C	.20	.35
167 Swashbuckling C	.20	.35
168 Thrash of Raptors C	.20	.35
169 Tilonallis Knight C	.20	.35
170 Tilonallis Skinshifter R	6.00	10.00
171 Trove of Temptation U	.60	1.00
172 Unfriendly Fire C	.20	.35
173 Vances Blasting Cannons R	6.00	10.00
173 Spitfire Bastion R	6.00	10.00
174 Wily Goblin U	.60	1.00
175 Ancient Brontodon C	.20	.35
176 Atzocan Archer U	.60	1.00
177 Blinding Fog C	1.00	1.50
178 Blossom Dryad C	.20	.35
179 Carnage Tyrant M	40.00	55.00
180 Colossal Dreadmaw C	.20	.35
181 Commune with Dinosaurs C	.20	.35
182 Crash the Ramparts C	.20	.35
183 Crushing Canopy C	.20	.35
184 Deathgorge Scavenger R	6.00	10.00
185 Deeproot Champion R	6.00	10.00
186 Deeproot Warrior C	.20	.35
187 Drover of the Mighty U	2.50	4.00
188 Emergent Growth U	.60	1.00
189 Emperors Vanguard R	6.00	10.00
190 Gazing Whiptail C	.20	.35
191 Growing Rites of Itlimoc R	40.00	50.00
191 Itlimoc Cradle of the Sun R	40.00	50.00
192 Ixallis Diviner C	.20	.35
193 Ixallis Keeper C	.20	.35
194 Jade Guardian C	.20	.35
195 Jungle Delver C	.20	.35
196 Kumenas Speaker U	2.50	4.00
197 Merfolk Branchwalker U	3.00	5.00
198 New Horizons C	.20	.35
199 Old Growth Dryads R	6.00	10.00
200 Pounce C	.20	.35
201 Ranging Raptors U	4.00	6.00
202 Ravenous Daggertooth C	.20	.35
203 Ripjaw Raptor R	15.00	20.00
204 River Heralds Boon C	.20	.35
205 Savage Stomp U	.60	1.00
206 Shapers Sanctuary R	6.00	10.00
207 Slice in Twain U	.60	1.00
208 Snapping Sailback U	.60	1.00
209 Spike Tailed Ceratops C	.20	.35
210 Thundering Spineback U	1.50	2.00
211 Tishanas Wayfinder C	.20	.35
212 Verdant Rebirth U	.60	1.00
213 Verdant Suns Avatar R	6.00	10.00
214 Vineshaper Mystic U	1.50	2.00
215 Waker of the Wilds R	6.00	10.00
216 Wildgrowth Walker U	.60	1.00
217 Admiral Beckett Brass M	15.00	20.00
218 Belligerent Brontodon U	.60	1.00
219 Call to the Feast U	.60	1.00
220 Deadeye Plunderers U	.60	1.00
221 Dire Fleet Captain U	1.25	2.00
222 Gishath Suns Avatar M	20.00	25.00
223 Hostage Taker R	6.00	10.00
224 Huatli Warrior Poet M	30.00	40.00
225 Marauding Looter U	1.25	2.00
226 Raging Swordtooth U	.60	1.00
227 Regisaur Alpha R	15.00	20.00
228 Shapers of Nature U	.60	1.00
229 Sky Terror U	2.50	4.00
230 Tishana Voice of Thunder M	10.00	15.00
231 Vona Butcher of Magan M	20.00	25.00
232 Vraska Relic Seeker M	35.00	45.00
233 Cobbled Wings C	.20	.35
234 Conquerors Galleon R	6.00	10.00
234 Conquerors Foothold R	6.00	10.00
235 Dowsing Dagger R	15.00	20.00
235 Lost Vale R	15.00	20.00
236 Dusk Legion Dreadnought U	.60	1.00
237 Elaborate Firecannon U	.60	1.00
238 Fell Flagship R	6.00	10.00
239 Gilded Sentinel C	.20	.35
240 Hierophants Chalice C	.20	.35
241 Pillar of Origins U	2.50	4.00
242 Pirates Cutlass C	.20	.35
243 Primal Amulet R	6.00	10.00
243 Primal Wellspring R	6.00	10.00
244 Prying Blade C	.20	.35
245 Sentinel Totem U	2.50	4.00
246 Shadowed Caravel R	6.00	10.00
247 Sleek Schooner U	.60	1.00
248 Sorcerous Spyglass R	6.00	10.00
249 Thaumatic Compass R	6.00	10.00
249 Spires of Orazca R	6.00	10.00
250 Treasure Map R	6.00	10.00
250 Treasure Cove R	6.00	10.00
251 Vanquishers Banner R	6.00	10.00
252 Dragonskull Summit R	6.00	10.00
253 Drowned Catacomb R	6.00	10.00
254 Field of Ruin U	8.00	10.00
255 Glacial Fortress R	6.00	10.00
256 Rootbound Crag R	6.00	10.00
257 Sunpetal Grove R	6.00	10.00
258 Unclaimed Territory U	10.00	15.00
259 Unknown Shores C	.20	.35
260 Plains L	.20	.35
261 Plains L	.20	.35
262 Plains L	.20	.35
263 Plains L	.20	.35
264 Island L	.20	.35
265 Island L	.20	.35
266 Island L	.20	.35
267 Island L	.20	.35
268 Swamp L	.20	.35
269 Swamp L	.20	.35
270 Swamp L	.20	.35
271 Swamp L	.20	.35
272 Mountain L	.20	.35
273 Mountain L	.20	.35
274 Mountain L	.20	.35
275 Mountain L	.20	.35
276 Forest L	.20	.35
277 Forest L	.20	.35
278 Forest L	.20	.35
279 Forest L	.20	.35
280 Jace Ingenious Mind Mage M	7.00	10.00
281 Castaways Despair C	.20	.35
282 Grasping Current R	6.00	10.00
283 Jaces Sentinel U	.60	1.00
284 Woodland Stream C	.20	.35
285 Huatli Dinosaur Knight M	7.00	10.00
286 Huatlis Snubhorn C	.20	.35
287 Huatlis Spurring U	.60	1.00
288 Sun Blessed Mount R	6.00	10.00
289 Stone Quarry C	.20	.35

2017 Magic The Gathering Ixalan Tokens

Card	Low	High
1 Vampire	.20	.30
2 Illusion	.10	.15
3 Merfolk	.06	.10
4 Pirate	.10	.15
5 Dinosaur	.06	.10
6 Plant	.06	.10
7 Treasure	.06	.10
8 Treasure	.06	.10
9 Treasure	.06	.10
10 Treasure	.06	.10
CH1 Ixalan CL	.06	.10

2018 Magic The Gathering Rivals of Ixalan

Card	Low	High
COMPLETE SET (203)	200.00	350.00
BOOSTER BOX (36 PACKS)	80.00	120.00
BOOSTER PACK (15 CARDS)	3.00	5.00
RELEASED ON JANUARY 19, 2018		
1 Baffling End U	.20	.30
2 Bishop of Binding R	.30	.50
3 Blazing Hope U	.20	.30
4 Cleansing Ray C	.10	.20
5 Divine Verdict C	.10	.20
6 Everdawn Champion U	.20	.30
7 Exultant Skymarcher C	.10	.20
8 Famished Paladin U	.20	.30
9 Forerunner of the Legion U	.20	.30
10 Imperial Ceratops U	.20	.30
11 Legion Conquistador C	.10	.20
12 Luminous Bonds C	.10	.20
13 Majestic Heliopterus U	.20	.30
14 Martyr of Dusk C	.10	.20
15 Moment of Triumph C	.10	.20
16 Paladin of Atonement R	.30	.50
17 Pride of Conquerors U	.20	.30
18 Radiant Destiny R	2.00	3.00
19 Raptor Companion C	.10	.20
20 Sanguine Glorifier C	.10	.20
21 Skymarcher Aspirant U	.20	.30
22 Slaughter the Strong R	.30	.50
23 Snubhorn Sentry C	.10	.20
24 Sphinx's Decree R	.30	.50
25 Squire's Devotion C	.10	.20
26 Sun Sentinel C	.10	.20
27 Sun-Crested Pterodon C	.10	.20
28 Temple Altisaur R	.30	.50
29 Trapjaw Tyrant M	1.50	2.00
30 Zetalpa, Primal Dawn R	1.00	1.50
31 Admiral's Order R	.30	.50
32 Aquatic Incursion U	.20	.30
33 Crafty Cutpurse R	.30	.50
34 Crashing Tide C	.10	.20
35 Curious Obsession U	.20	.30
36 Deadeye Rig-Hauler C	.10	.20
37 Expel from Orazca U	.20	.30
38 Flood of Recollection U	.20	.30
39 Hornswoggle U	.20	.30
40 Induced Amnesia R	.30	.50
41 Kitesail Corsair C	.10	.20
42 Kumena's Awakening R	.30	.50
43 Mist-Cloaked Herald C	.10	.20
44 Negate C	.10	.20
45 Nezahal, Primal Tide R	1.50	2.00
46 Release to the Wind R	.30	.50
47 River Darter C	.10	.20
48 Riverwise Augur U	.20	.30
49 Sailor of Means C	.10	.20
50 Sea Legs C	.10	.20
51 Seafloor Oracle R	.30	.50
52 Secrets of the Golden City C	.10	.20
53 Silvergill Adept U	.20	.30
54 Siren Reaver U	.20	.30
55 Slippery Scoundrel U	.20	.30
56 Soul of the Rapids C	.10	.20
57 Spire Winder C	.10	.20
58 Sworn Guardian C	.10	.20
59 Timestream Navigator M	2.00	3.00
60 Warkite Marauder R	1.50	2.00
61 Waterknot C	.10	.20
62 Arterial Flow U	.20	.30
63 Canal Monitor C	.10	.20
64 Champion of Dusk R	.30	.50
65 Dark Inquiry C	.10	.20
66 Dead Man's Chest R	.30	.50
67 Dinosaur Hunter C	.10	.20
68 Dire Fleet Poisoner R	.60	1.00
69 Dusk Charger C	.10	.20
70 Dusk Legion Zealot C	.10	.20
71 Fathom Fleet Boarder C	.10	.20
72 Forerunner of the Coalition U	.20	.30
73 Golden Demise U	.20	.30
74 Grasping Scoundrel C	.10	.20
75 Gruesome Fate C	.10	.20
76 Impale C	.10	.20
77 Mastermind's Acquisition R	1.00	1.50
78 Mausoleum Harpy U	.20	.30
79 Moment of Craving C	.10	.20
80 Oathsworn Vampire U	.20	.30
81 Pitiless Plunderer U	.20	.30
82 Ravenous Chupacabra U	.20	.30
83 Reaver Ambush U	.20	.30
84 Recover C	.10	.20
85 Sadistic Skymarcher U	.20	.30
86 Tetzimoc, Primal Death R	.30	.50
87 Tomb Robber R	.30	.50
88 Twilight Prophet M	6.00	8.00
89 Vampire Revenant C	.10	.20
90 Vona's Hunger R	.30	.50
91 Voracious Vampire C	.10	.20
92 Blood Sun R	1.00	1.50
93 Bombard C	.10	.20
94 Brass's Bounty R	.30	.50
95 Brazen Freebooter C	.10	.20
96 Buccaneer's Bravado C	.10	.20
97 Charging Tuskodon U	.20	.30
98 Daring Buccaneer U	.20	.30
99 Dire Fleet Daredevil R	2.00	3.50
100 Etali, Primal Storm R	2.50	4.00
101 Fanatical Firebrand C	.10	.20
102 Forerunner of the Empire U	.20	.30
103 Form of the Dinosaur R	.30	.50
104 Frilled Deathspitter C	.10	.20
105 Goblin Trailblazer C	.10	.20
106 Mutiny C	.10	.20
107 Needletooth Raptor U	.20	.30
108 Orazca Raptor C	.10	.20
109 Pirate's Pillage U	.20	.30
110 Reckless Rage U	.20	.30
111 Rekindling Phoenix M	20.00	25.00
112 See Red U	.20	.30
113 Shake the Foundations U	.20	.30
114 Shatter C	.10	.20
115 Silverclad Ferocidons R	.30	.50
116 Stampeding Horncrest C	.10	.20
117 Storm Fleet Swashbuckler U	.20	.30
118 Sun-Collared Raptor C	.10	.20
119 Swaggering Corsair C	.10	.20
120 Tilonalli's Crown C	.10	.20
121 Tilonalli's Summoner R	.30	.50
122 Aggressive Urge C	.10	.20
123 Cacophodon U	.20	.30
124 Cherished Hatchling U	.20	.30
125 Colossal Dreadmaw C	.10	.20
126 Crested Herdcaller U	.20	.30
127 Deeproot Elite R	1.00	1.50
128 Enter the Unknown U	.20	.30
129 Forerunner of the Heralds U	.20	.30
130 Ghalta, Primal Hunger R	8.00	11.00
131 Giltgrove Stalker C	.10	.20
132 Hardy Veteran C	.10	.20
133 Hunt the Weak C	.10	.20
134 Jade Bearer C	.10	.20
135 Jade craft Artisan C	.10	.20
136 Jadelight Ranger R	6.00	8.00
137 Jungleborn Pioneer C	.10	.20
138 Knight of the Stampede C	.10	.20
139 Naturalize C	.10	.20
140 Orazca Frillback C	.10	.20
141 Overgrown Armasaur C	.10	.20
142 Path of Discovery R	.30	.50
143 Plummet C	.10	.20
144 Polyraptor M	2.00	3.50
145 Strength of the Pack U	.20	.30
146 Swift Warden U	.20	.30
147 Tendershoot Dryad R	3.00	5.00
148 Thrashing Brontodon U	2.00	3.00
149 Thunderherd Migration U	.20	.30
150 Wayward Swordtooth R	3.00	5.00
151 World Shaper R	.30	.50
152 Angrath, the Flame-Chained M	4.00	6.00
153 Atzocan Seer U	.20	.30
154 Azor, the Lawbringer M	1.50	2.00
155 Deadeye Brawler U	.20	.30
156 Dire Fleet Neckbreaker U	.20	.30
157 Elenda, the Dusk Rose M	5.00	7.00
158A Hadana's Climb R	1.50	2.00
158B Winged Temple of Orazca R	.30	.50
159 Huatli, Radiant Champion M	4.00	6.00
160A Journey to Eternity R	1.50	2.00
160B Atzal, Cave of Eternity R	.30	.50
161 Jungle Creeper U	.20	.30
162 Kumena, Tyrant of Orazca M	5.00	7.00
163 Legion Lieutenant U	.20	.30
164 Merfolk Mistbinder U	.20	.30
165A Path of Mettle R	.30	.50
165B Metzali, Tower of Triumph R	.30	.50
166A Profane Procession R	.30	.50
166B Tomb of the Dusk Rose R	.30	.50
167 Protean Raider R	.30	.50
168 Raging Regisaur U	.20	.30
169 Relentless Raptor U	.20	.30
170 Resplendent Griffin U	.20	.30
171 Siegehorn Ceratops R	.30	.50
172 Storm Fleet Sprinter U	.20	.30

173A Storm the Vault R .30 .50
173B Vault of Catlacan R .30 .50
174 Zacama, Primal Calamity M 7.00 10.00
175 Awakened Amalgam R .30 .50
176A Azor's Gateway M 3.00 5.00
176B Sanctum of the Sun M .10 .20
177 Captain's Hook R .30 .50
178 Gleaming Barrier C .10 .20
179A Golden Guardian R .30 .50
179B Gold-Forge Garrison R .30 .50
180 The Immortal Sun M 10.00 15.00
181 Orazca Relic C .10 .20
182 Silent Gravestone R .30 .50
183 Strider Harness C .10 .20
184 Travel's Amulet C .10 .20
185 Arch of Orazca R 1.50 2.00
186 Evolving Wilds C .10 .20
187 Forsaken Sanctuary U .20 .30
188 Foul Orchard U .20 .30
189 Highland Lake U .20 .30
190 Stone Quarry U .20 .30
191 Woodland Stream U .20 .30
192 Plains L .10 .20
193 Island L .10 .20
194 Swamp L .10 .20
195 Mountain L .10 .20
196 Forest L .10 .20

2018 Magic The Gathering Rivals of Ixalan Foil

COMPLETE SET (203) 400.00 600.00
RELEASED ON
1 Baffling End U .30 .50
2 Bishop of Binding R 3.00 5.00
3 Blazing Hope U .30 .50
4 Cleansing Ray C .20 .35
5 Divine Verdict C .20 .35
6 Everdawn Champion U .30 .50
7 Exultant Skymarcher C .20 .35
8 Famished Paladin U .30 .50
9 Forerunner of the Legion U .30 .50
10 Imperial Ceratops U .30 .50
11 Legion Conquistador C .20 .35
12 Luminous Bonds C .20 .35
13 Majestic Heliopterus U .30 .50
14 Martyr of Dusk C .20 .35
15 Moment of Triumph C .20 .35
16 Paladin of Atonement R 3.00 5.00
17 Pride of Conquerors U .30 .50
18 Radiant Destiny R 3.00 5.00
19 Raptor Companion C .20 .35
20 Sanguine Glorifier C .20 .35
21 Skymarcher Aspirant U .30 .50
22 Slaughter the Strong R 3.00 5.00
23 Snubhorn Sentry C .20 .35
24 Sphinx's Decree R 3.00 5.00
25 Squire's Devotion C .20 .35
26 Sun Sentinel C .20 .35
27 Sun-Crested Pterodon C .20 .35
28 Temple Altisaur R 3.00 5.00
29 Trapjaw Tyrant M 6.00 8.00
30 Zetalpa, Primal Dawn R 3.00 5.00
31 Admiral's Order R 3.00 5.00
32 Aquatic Incursion U .30 .50
33 Crafty Cutpurse R 3.00 5.00
34 Crashing Tide C .20 .35
35 Curious Obsession U .30 .50
36 Deadeye Rig-Hauler C .20 .35
37 Expel from Orazca U .30 .50
38 Flood of Recollection U .30 .50
39 Hornswoggle U .30 .50
40 Induced Amnesia R 3.00 5.00
41 Kitesail Corsair C .20 .35
42 Kumena's Awakening R 3.00 5.00
43 Mist-Cloaked Herald C .20 .35
44 Negate C .20 .35
45 Nezahal, Primal Tide R 3.00 5.00
46 Release to the Wind R 3.00 5.00
47 River Darter C .20 .35
48 Riverwise Augur U .30 .50
49 Sailor of Means C .20 .35
50 Sea Legs C .20 .35
51 Seafloor Oracle R 3.00 5.00
52 Secrets of the Golden City C .20 .35
53 Silvergill Adept U .30 .50
54 Siren Reaver U .30 .50
55 Slippery Scoundrel U .30 .50
56 Soul of the Rapids C .20 .35
57 Spire Winder C .20 .35
58 Sworn Guardian C .20 .35
59 Timestream Navigator M 8.00 12.00
60 Warkite Marauder R 3.00 5.00
61 Waterknot C .20 .35
62 Arterial Flow U .30 .50
63 Canal Monitor C .20 .35
64 Champion of Dusk R 3.00 5.00
65 Dark Inquiry C .20 .35
66 Dead Man's Chest R 3.00 5.00
67 Dinosaur Hunter C .20 .35
68 Dire Fleet Poisoner R 3.00 5.00
69 Dusk Charger C .20 .35
70 Dusk Legion Zealot C .20 .35
71 Fathom Fleet Boarder C .20 .35
72 Forerunner of the Coalition U .30 .50
73 Golden Demise U .30 .50
74 Grasping Scoundrel C .20 .35
75 Gruesome Fate C .20 .35
76 Impale C .20 .35
77 Mastermind's Acquisition R 3.00 5.00
78 Mausoleum Harpy U .30 .50
79 Moment of Craving C .20 .35
80 Oathsworn Vampire U .30 .50
81 Pitiless Plunderer U .30 .50
82 Ravenous Chupacabra U .30 .50
83 Reaver Ambush U .30 .50
84 Recover C .20 .35
85 Sadistic Skymarcher U .30 .50
86 Tetzimoc, Primal Death R 3.00 5.00
87 Tomb Robber R 3.00 5.00
88 Twilight Prophet M 15.00 20.00
89 Vampire Revenant C .20 .35
90 Vona's Hunger R 3.00 5.00
91 Voracious Vampire C .20 .35
92 Blood Sun R 15.00 20.00
93 Bombard C .20 .35
94 Brass's Bounty R 3.00 5.00
95 Brazen Freebooter C .20 .35
96 Buccaneer's Bravado C .20 .35
97 Charging Tuskodon U .30 .50
98 Daring Buccaneer U .30 .50
99 Dire Fleet Daredevil R 3.00 5.00
100 Etali, Primal Storm R 3.00 5.00
101 Fanatical Firebrand C .20 .35
102 Forerunner of the Empire U .30 .50
103 Form of the Dinosaur R 3.00 5.00
104 Frilled Deathspitter C .20 .35
105 Goblin Trailblazer C .20 .35
106 Mutiny C .20 .35
107 Needletooth Raptor U .30 .50
108 Orazca Raptor C .20 .35
109 Pirate's Pillage U .30 .50
110 Reckless Rage U .30 .50
111 Rekindling Phoenix M 30.00 35.00
112 See Red U .30 .50
113 Shake the Foundations U .30 .50
114 Shatter C .20 .35
115 Silverclad Ferocidons R 3.00 5.00
116 Stampeding Horncrest C .20 .35
117 Storm Fleet Swashbuckler U .30 .50
118 Sun-Collared Raptor C .20 .35
119 Swaggering Corsair C .20 .35
120 Tilonalli's Crown C .20 .35
121 Tilonalli's Summoner R 3.00 5.00
122 Aggressive Urge C .20 .35
123 Cacophodon U .30 .50
124 Cherished Hatchling U .30 .50
125 Colossal Dreadmaw C .20 .35
126 Crested Herdcaller U .30 .50
127 Deeproot Elite R 3.00 5.00
128 Enter the Unknown U .30 .50
129 Forerunner of the Heralds U .30 .50
130 Ghalta, Primal Hunger R 3.00 5.00
131 Giltgrove Stalker C .20 .35
132 Hardy Veteran C .20 .35
133 Hunt the Weak C .20 .35
134 Jade Bearer C .20 .35
135 Jade craft Artisan C .20 .35
136 Jadelight Ranger R 10.00 15.00
137 Jungleborn Pioneer C .20 .35
138 Knight of the Stampede C .20 .35
139 Naturalize C .20 .35
140 Orazca Frillback C .20 .35
141 Overgrown Armasaur C .20 .35
142 Path of Discovery R 3.00 5.00
143 Plummet C .20 .35
144 Polyraptor M 8.00 12.00
145 Strength of the Pack U .30 .50
146 Swift Warden U .30 .50
147 Tendershoot Dryad R 3.00 5.00
148 Thrashing Brontodon U .30 .50
149 Thunderherd Migration U .30 .50
150 Wayward Swordtooth R 3.00 5.00
151 World Shaper R 3.00 5.00
152 Angrath, the Flame-Chained M 14.00 18.00
153 Atzocan Seer U .30 .50
154 Azor, the Lawbringer M 10.00 15.00
155 Deadeye Brawler U .30 .50
156 Dire Fleet Neckbreaker U .30 .50
157 Elenda, the Dusk Rose M 10.00 15.00
159 Huatli, Radiant Champion M 10.00 15.00
161 Jungle Creeper U .30 .50
162 Kumena, Tyrant of Orazca M 30.00 35.00
163 Legion Lieutenant U .30 .50
164 Merfolk Mistbinder U .30 .50
167 Protean Raider R 3.00 5.00
168 Raging Regisaur U .30 .50
169 Relentless Raptor U .30 .50
170 Resplendent Griffin U .30 .50
171 Siegehorn Ceratops R 3.00 5.00
172 Storm Fleet Sprinter U .30 .50
174 Zacama, Primal Calamity M 25.00 30.00
175 Awakened Amalgam R 3.00 5.00
177 Captain's Hook R 3.00 5.00
178 Gleaming Barrier C .20 .35
180 The Immortal Sun M 18.00 22.00
181 Orazca Relic C .20 .35
182 Silent Gravestone R 3.00 5.00
183 Strider Harness C .20 .35
184 Travel's Amulet C .20 .35
185 Arch of Orazca R 3.00 5.00
186 Evolving Wilds C .20 .35
187 Forsaken Sanctuary U .30 .50
188 Foul Orchard U .30 .50
189 Highland Lake U .30 .50
190 Stone Quarry U .30 .50
191 Woodland Stream U .30 .50
192 Plains L .20 .35
193 Island L .20 .35
194 Swamp L .20 .35
195 Mountain L .20 .35
196 Forest L .20 .35
158A Hadana's Climb R 3.00 5.00
158B Winged Temple of Orazca R 3.00 5.00
160A Journey to Eternity R 3.00 5.00
160B Atzal, Cave of Eternity R 3.00 5.00
165A Path of Mettle R 3.00 5.00
165B Metzali, Tower of Triumph R 3.00 5.00
166A Profane Procession R 3.00 5.00
166B Tomb of the Dusk Rose R 3.00 5.00
173A Storm the Vault R 3.00 5.00
173B Vault of Catlacan R 3.00 5.00
176A Azor's Gateway M 14.00 16.00
176B Sanctum of the Sun M 15.00 20.00
179A Golden Guardian R 3.00 5.00
179B Gold-Forge Garrison R 3.00 5.00

2018 Magic The Gathering Rivals of Ixalan Tokens

1 Elemental .12 .20
2 Elemental .12 .20
3 Saproling .10 .15
4 Golem .10 .15
5 Huatli, Radiant Champion Emblem .10 .15
6 City's Blessing .10 .15
CH1 Rivals of Ixalan CL .10 .15

2018 Magic The Gathering Dominaria

COMPLETE SET (279) 250.00 400.00
BOOSTER BOX (36 PACKS) 85.00 100.00
RELEASED ON APRIL 27, 2018
1 Karn, Scion of Urza M 30.00 35.00
2 Adamant Will C .10 .20
3 Aven Sentry C .10 .20
4 Baird, Steward of Argive U .20 .30
5 Benalish Honor Guard C .10 .20
6 Benalish Marshal R 1.00 1.50
7 Blessed Light C .10 .20
8 Board the Weatherlight U .20 .30
9 Call the Cavalry C .10 .20
10 Charge C .10 .20
11 D'Avenant Trapper C .10 .20
12 Danitha Capashen, Paragon U .20 .30
13 Daring Archaeologist R .30 .50
14 Dauntless Bodyguard U .20 .30
15 Dub C .10 .20
16 Evra, Halcyon Witness R .30 .50
17 Evxcavation Elephant C .10 .20
18 Fall of the Thran R .30 .50
19 Gideon's Reproach C .10 .20
20 Healing Grace C .10 .20
21 History of Benalia M 8.00 12.00
22 Invoke the Divine C .10 .20
23 Knight of Grace U .20 .30
24 Knight of New Benalia C .10 .20
25 Kwende, Pride of Femeref U .20 .30
26 Lyra Dawnbringer M 10.00 15.00
27 Mesa Unicorn C .10 .20
28 On Serra's Wings U .20 .30
29 Pegasus Courser C .10 .20
30 Sanctum Spirit U .20 .30
31 Seal Away U .75 1.25
32 Sergeant-at-Arms C .10 .20
33 Serra Angel U .20 .30
34 Serra Disciple C .10 .20
35 Shalai, Voice of Plenty R 2.00 3.00
36 Teshar, Ancestor's Apostle R .50 .80
37 Tragic Poet C .10 .20
38 Triumph of Gerrard U .20 .30
39 Urza's Ruinous Blast R .40 .60
40 Academy Drake C .10 .20
41 Academy Journeymage C .10 .20
42 The Antiquities War R .50 .80
43 Arcane Flight C .10 .20
44 Artificer's Assistant C .10 .20
45 Befuddle C .10 .20
46 Blink of an Eye C .10 .20
47 Cloudreader Sphinx C .10 .20
48 Cold-Water Snapper C .10 .20
49 Curator's Ward U .20 .30
50 Deep Freeze C .10 .20
51 Diligent Excavator U .20 .30
52 Divination C .10 .20
53 Homarid Explorer C .10 .20
54 In Bolas's Clutches U .20 .30
55 Karn's Temporal Sundering R .40 .60
56 Merfolk Trickster U .20 .30
57 The Mirari Conjecture R .30 .50
58 Naban, Dean of Iteration R .40 .60
59 Naru Meha, Master Wizard M 1.00 1.50
60 Opt C .10 .20
61 Precognition Field R .30 .50
62 Relic Runner C .10 .20
63 Rescue C .10 .20
64 Sage of Lat-Nam U .20 .30
65 Sentinel of the Pearl Trident U .20 .30
66 Slinn Voda, the Rising Deep U .20 .30
67 Syncopate C .10 .20
68 Tempest Djinn R .30 .50
69 Tetsuko Umezawa, Fugitive U .20 .30
70 Time of Ice U .20 .30
71 Tolarian Scholar C .10 .20
72 Unwind C .10 .20
73 Vodalian Arcanist C .10 .20
74 Weight of Memory U .20 .30
75 Wizard's Retort U .20 .30
76 Zahid, Djinn of the Lamp R .30 .50
77 Blessing of Belzenlok C .10 .20
78 Cabal Evangel C .10 .20
79 Cabal Paladin C .10 .20
80 Caligo Skin-Witch C .10 .20
81 Cast Down U .60 1.00
82 Chainer's Torment U .20 .30
83 Dark Bargain C .10 .20
84 Deathbloom Thallid C .10 .20
85 Demonic Vigor C .10 .20
86 Demonlord Belzenlok M 1.00 1.50
87 Divest C .10 .20
88 Dread Shade R .40 .60
89 Drudge Sentinel C .10 .20
90 The Eldest Reborn U .20 .30
91 Eviscerate C .10 .20
92 Feral Abomination C .10 .20
93 Final Parting U .20 .30
94 Fungal Infection C .10 .20
95 Josu Vess, Lich Knight R .50 .80
96 Kazarov, Sengir Pureblood R .30 .50
97 Knight of Malice U .20 .30
98 Lich's Mastery R .30 .50
99 Lingering Phantom U .20 .30
100 Phyrexian Scriptures M 1.50 2.00
101 Rat Colony C .60 1.00
102 Rite of Belzenlok R .30 .50
103 Settle the Score U .20 .30
104 Soul Salvage C .10 .20
105 Stronghold Confessor C .10 .20
106 Thallid Omnivore C .10 .20
107 Thallid Soothsayer U .20 .30
108 Torgaar, Famine Incarnate R .30 .50
109 Urgoros, the Empty One U .20 .30
110 Vicious Offering C .10 .20
111 whisper, Blood Liturgist U .20 .30
112 Windgrace Acolyte C .10 .20
113 Yargle, Glutton of Urborg U .20 .30
114 Yawgmoth's Vile Offering R .40 .60
115 Bloodstone Goblin C .10 .20
116 Champion of the Flame U .20 .30
117 Fervent Strike C .10 .20
118 Fiery Intervention C .10 .20
119 Fight with Fire U .20 .30
120 Fire Elemental C .10 .20
121 Firefist Adept U .20 .30
122 The First Eruption R .30 .50
123 The Flame of Keld U .20 .30
124 Frenzied Rage C .10 .20
125 Ghitu Chronicler C .10 .20
126 Ghitu Journeymage C .10 .20
127 Ghitu Lavarunner C .10 .20
128 Goblin Barrage U .20 .30
129 Goblin Chainwhirler R 3.00 5.00
130 Goblin Warchief U .20 .30
131 Haphazard Bombardment R .30 .50
132 Jaya Ballard M 3.00 5.00
133 Jaya's Immolating Inferno R .30 .50
134 Keldon Overseer C .10 .20
135 Keldon Raider C .10 .20
136 Keldon Warcaller C .10 .20
137 Orcish Vandal U .20 .30
138 Radiating Lightning C .10 .20
139 Rampaging Cyclops C .10 .20
140 Run Amok C .10 .20
141 Seismic Shift C .10 .20
142 Shivan Fire C .10 .20
143 Siege-Gang Commander R .40 .60
144 Skirk Prospector C .10 .20
145 Skizzik U .20 .30
146 Squee, the Immortal R .50 .80
147 Two-Headed Giant R .30 .50
148 Valduk, Keeper of the Flame U .20 .30
149 Verix Bladewing M 2.00 3.00
150 Warcry Phoenix U .20 .30
151 Warlord's Fury C .10 .20
152 Wizard's Lightning U .60 1.00
153 Adventurous Impulse C .10 .20
154 Ancient Animus C .10 .20
155 Arbor Armament C .10 .20
156 Baloth Gorger C .10 .20
157 Broken Bond C .10 .20
158 Corrosive Ooze C .10 .20
159 Elfhame Druid U .20 .30
160 Fungal Plots U .20 .30
161 Gaea's Blessing U .20 .30
162 Gaea's Protector C .10 .20
163 Gift of Growth C .10 .20
164 Grow from the Ashes C .10 .20
165 Grunn, the Lonely King U .20 .30
166 Kamahl's Druidic Vow R .30 .50
167 Krosan Druid C .10 .20
168 Llanowar Elves C .10 .20
169 Llanowar Envoy C .10 .20
170 Llanowar Scout C .10 .20
171 Mammoth Spider U .20 .30
172 Marwyn, the Nurturer R .40 .60
173 The Mending of Dominaria R .30 .50
174 Multani, Yavimaya's Avatar M 1.50 2.00
175 Nature's Spiral U .20 .30
176 Pierce the Sky C .10 .20
177 Primordial Wurm C .10 .20
178 Saproling Migration C .10 .20
179 Song of Freyalise U .50 .80
180 Spore Swarm U .20 .30
181 Sporecrown Thallid U .20 .30
182 Steel Leaf Champion R 2.00 3.50
183 Sylvan Awakening R .30 .50
184 Territorial Allosaurus R .30 .50
185 Thorn Elemental U .20 .30
186 Untamed Kavu U .20 .30
187 Verdant Force R .30 .50
188 Wild Onslaught U .20 .30
189 Yavimaya Sapherd C .10 .20
190 Adeliz, the Cinder Wind U .20 .30
191 Arvad the Cursed U .20 .30
192 Aryel, Knight of Windgrace R .30 .50
193 Darigaaz Reincarnated M 1.00 1.50
194 Garna, the Bloodflame U .20 .30
195 Grand Warlord Radha R .30 .50
196 Hallar, the Firefletcher U .20 .30
197 Jhoira, Weatherlight Captain M 1.50 2.00
198 Jodah, Archmage Eternal R .30 .50
199 Muldrotha, the Gravetide M 2.50 4.00
200 Oath of Teferi R .30 .50
201 Primevals' Glorious Rebirth R .30 .50
202 Raff Capashen, Ship's Mage U .20 .30
203 Rona, Disciple of Gix U .20 .30
204 Shanna, Sisay's Legacy U .20 .30
205 Slimefoot, the Stowaway U .20 .30
206 Tatyova, Benthic Druid U .20 .30
207 Teferi, Hero of Dominaria M 30.00 35.00
208 Tiana, Ship's Caretaker U .20 .30
209 Aesthir Glider C .10 .20
210 Amaranthine Wall U .20 .30
211 Blackblade Reforged R .60 1.00
212 Bloodtallow Candle C .10 .20
213 Damping Sphere U 1.00 1.50
214 Forebear's Blade R .50 .80
215 Gilded Lotus R 2.00 3.00
216 Guardians of Koilos C .10 .20
217 Helm of the Host R 2.00 3.00
218 Howling Golem U .20 .30
219 Icy Manipulator U .20 .30
220 Jhoira's Familiar U .20 .30
221 Jousting Lance C .10 .20
222 Juggernaut U .20 .30
223 Mishra's Self-Replicator R .30 .50
224 Mox Amber M 8.00 12.00
225 Navigator's Compass C .10 .20

Card	Low	High
226 Pardic Wanderer C	.10	.20
227 Powerstone Shard C	.10	.20
228 Shield of the Realm U	.20	.30
229 Short Sword C	.10	.20
230 Skittering Surveyor C	.10	.20
231 Sorcerer's Wand U	.20	.30
232 Sparring Construct C	.10	.20
233 Thran Temporal Gateway R	.50	.80
234 Traxos, Scourge of Kroog R	.50	.80
235 Urza's Tome U	.20	.30
236 Voltaic Servant C	.10	.20
237 Weatherlight M	.60	1.00
238 Cabal Stronghold R	.75	1.25
239 Clifftop Retreat R	1.50	2.00
240 Hinterland Harbor R	1.50	2.50
241 Isolated Chapel R	2.00	3.00
242 Memorial to Folly U	.20	.30
243 Memorial to Genius U	.20	.30
244 Memorial to Glory U	.20	.30
245 Memorial to Unity U	.20	.30
246 Memorial to War U	.20	.30
247 Sulfur Falls R	3.00	5.00
248 Woodland Cemetery R	2.50	4.00
249 Zhalfirin Void U	.20	.30
250 Plains L	.10	.20
251 Plains L	.10	.20
252 Plains L	.10	.20
253 Plains L	.10	.20
254 Island L	.10	.20
255 Island L	.10	.20
256 Island L	.10	.20
257 Island L	.10	.20
258 Swamp L	.10	.20
259 Swamp L	.10	.20
260 Swamp L	.10	.20
261 Swamp L	.10	.20
262 Mountain L	.10	.20
263 Mountain L	.10	.20
264 Mountain L	.10	.20
265 Mountain L	.10	.20
266 Forest L	.10	.20
267 Forest L	.10	.20
268 Forest L	.10	.20
269 Forest L	.10	.20
270 Teferi, Timebender M	3.00	5.00
271 Temporal Machinations C	.10	.20
272 Niambi, Faithful Healer R	.30	.50
273 Teferi's Sentinel U	.20	.30
274 Meandering River C	.10	.20
275 Chandra, Bold Pyromancer M	3.00	5.00
276 Chandra's Outburst R	.30	.50
277 Karplusan Hound U	.20	.30
278 Pyromantic Pilgrim C	.10	.20
279 Timber Gorge C	.10	.20

2018 Magic The Gathering Dominaria Foil

Card	Low	High
COMPLETE SET (269)	500.00	800.00
1 Karn, Scion of Urza M	110.00	115.00
2 Adamant Will C	.20	.35
3 Aven Sentry C	.20	.35
4 Baird, Steward of Argive U	.40	.60
5 Benalish Honor Guard C	.20	.35
6 Benalish Marshal R	3.00	5.00
7 Blessed Light C	.20	.35
8 Board the Weatherlight U	.40	.60
9 Call the Cavalry C	.20	.35
10 Charge C	.20	.35
11 D'Avenant Trapper C	.20	.35
12 Danitha Capashen, Paragon U	1.50	2.50
13 Daring Archaeologist R	.60	1.00
14 Dauntless Bodyguard U	2.00	3.00
15 Dub C	.20	.35
16 Evra, Halcyon Witness R	.60	1.00
17 Exvcavation Elephant C	.20	.35
18 Fall of the Thran R	2.00	3.50
19 Gideon's Reproach C	.20	.35
20 Healing Grace C	.20	.35
21 History of Benalia M	30.00	35.00
22 Invoke the Divine C	.20	.35
23 Knight of Grace U	1.00	1.50
24 Knight of New Benalia C	.20	.35
25 Kwende, Pride of Femeref U	.40	.60
26 Lyra Dawnbringer M	35.00	40.00
27 Mesa Unicorn C	.20	.35
28 On Serra's Wings U	.40	.60
29 Pegasus Courser C	.20	.35
30 Sanctum Spirit U	.40	.60
31 Seal Away U	3.00	5.00
32 Sergeant-at-Arms C	.20	.35
33 Serra Angel U	.40	.60
34 Serra Disciple C	.20	.35
35 Shalai, Voice of Plenty R	10.00	15.00
36 Teshar, Ancestor's Apostle R	4.00	6.00
37 Tragic Poet C	.20	.35
38 Triumph of Gerrard U	.40	.60
39 Urza's Ruinous Blast R	3.00	5.00
40 Academy Drake C	.20	.35
41 Academy Journeymage C	.20	.35
42 The Antiquities War R	4.00	6.00
43 Arcane Flight C	.20	.35
44 Artificer's Assistant C	.20	.35
45 Befuddle C	.20	.35
46 Blink of an Eye C	.20	.35
47 Cloudreader Sphinx C	.20	.35
48 Cold-Water Snapper C	.20	.35
49 Curator's Ward U	.40	.60
50 Deep Freeze C	.20	.35
51 Diligent Excavator U	.40	.60
52 Divination C	.20	.35
53 Homarid Explorer C	.20	.35
54 In Bolas's Clutches U	.40	.60
55 Karn's Temporal Sundering R	4.00	6.00
56 Merfolk Trickster U	7.00	9.00
57 The Mirari Conjecture R	1.50	2.50
58 Naban, Dean of Iteration R	2.00	3.50
59 Naru Meha, Master Wizard M	5.00	8.00
60 Opt C	.20	.35
61 Precognition Field R	1.00	1.50
62 Relic Runner C	.20	.35
63 Rescue C	.20	.35
64 Sage of Lat-Nam U	.40	.60
65 Sentinel of the Pearl Trident U	.40	.60
66 Slinn Voda, the Rising Deep U	.40	.60
67 Syncopate C	.20	.35
68 Tempest Djinn R	1.25	1.75
69 Tetsuko Umezawa, Fugitive U	.40	.60
70 Time of Ice U	.40	.60
71 Tolarian Scholar C	.20	.35
72 Unwind C	.20	.35
73 Vodalian Arcanist C	.20	.35
74 Weight of Memory U	.40	.60
75 Wizard's Retort U	3.00	5.00
76 Zahid, Djinn of the Lamp R	1.00	1.50
77 Blessing of Belzenlok C	.20	.35
78 Cabal Evangel C	.20	.35
79 Cabal Paladin C	.20	.35
80 Caligo Skin-Witch C	.20	.35
81 Cast Down U	1.25	2.00
82 Chainer's Torment U	.40	.60
83 Dark Bargain C	.20	.35
84 Deathbloom Thallid C	.20	.35
85 Demonic Vigor C	.20	.35
86 Demonlord Belzenlok M	7.00	10.00
87 Divest C	.20	.35
88 Dread Shade R	1.50	2.50
89 Drudge Sentinel C	.20	.35
90 The Eldest Reborn U	2.00	3.50
91 Eviscerate C	.20	.35
92 Feral Abomination C	.20	.35
93 Final Parting U	.40	.60
94 Fungal Infection C	.20	.35
95 Josu Vess, Lich Knight R	3.00	5.00
96 Kazarov, Sengir Pureblod R	.60	1.00
97 Knight of Malice U	1.00	1.50
98 Lich's Mastery R	3.00	5.00
99 Lingering Phantom U	.40	.60
100 Phyrexian Scriptures M	8.00	12.00
101 Rat Colony C	.20	.35
102 Rite of Belzenlok R	1.50	2.00
103 Settle the Score U	.40	.60
104 Soul Salvage C	.20	.35
105 Stronghold Confessor C	.20	.35
106 Thallid Omnivore C	.20	.35
107 Thallid Soothsayer U	.40	.60
108 Torgaar, Famine Incarnate R	1.50	2.50
109 Urgoros, the Empty One U	.40	.60
110 Vicious Offering C	.20	.35
111 whisper, Blood Liturgist U	.40	.60
112 Windgrace Acolyte C	.20	.35
113 Yargle, Glutton of Urborg U	.40	.60
114 Yawgmoth's Vile Offering R	2.00	3.00
115 Bloodstone Goblin C	.20	.35
116 Champion of the Flame U	.40	.60
117 Fervent Strike C	.20	.35
118 Fiery Intervention C	.20	.35
119 Fight with Fire U	.60	1.00
120 Fire Elemental C	.20	.35
121 Firefist Adept U	.40	.60
122 The First Eruption R	1.00	1.50
123 The Flame of Keld U	1.50	2.50
124 Frenzied Rage C	.20	.35
125 Ghitu Chronicler C	.20	.35
126 Ghitu Journeymage C	.20	.35
127 Ghitu Lavarunner C	.20	.35
128 Goblin Barrage U	.40	.60
129 Goblin Chainwhirler R	5.00	7.00
130 Goblin Warchief U	.75	1.25
131 Haphazard Bombardment R	.60	1.00
132 Jaya Ballard M	10.00	15.00
133 Jaya's Immolating Inferno R	1.50	2.50
134 Keldon Overseer C	.20	.35
135 Keldon Raider C	.20	.35
136 Keldon Warcaller C	.20	.35
137 Orcish Vandal U	.40	.60
138 Radiating Lightning C	.20	.35
139 Rampaging Cyclops C	.20	.35
140 Run Amok C	.20	.35
141 Seismic Shift C	.20	.35
142 Shivan Fire C	.20	.35
143 Siege-Gang Commander R	1.00	1.50
144 Skirk Prospector C	.20	.35
145 Skizzik U	.40	.60
146 Squee, the Immortal R	3.00	5.00
147 Two-Headed Giant R	.40	1.00
148 Valduk, Keeper of the Flame U	.40	.60
149 Verix Bladewing M	4.00	6.00
150 Warcry Phoenix U	.40	.60
151 Warlord's Fury C	.20	.35
152 Wizard's Lightning U	1.50	2.50
153 Adventurous Impulse C	.20	.35
154 Ancient Animus C	.20	.35
155 Arbor Armament C	.20	.35
156 Baloth Gorger C	.20	.35
157 Broken Bond C	.20	.35
158 Corrosive Ooze C	.20	.35
159 Elfhame Druid C	.40	.60
160 Fungal Plots U	1.00	1.50
161 Gaea's Blessing U	.40	.60
162 Gaea's Protector C	.20	.35
163 Gift of Growth C	.20	.35
164 Grow from the Ashes C	.20	.35
165 Grunn, the Lonely King U	.40	.60
166 Kamahl's Druidic Vow R	1.50	2.00
167 Krosan Druid C	.20	.35
168 Llanowar Elves C	.20	.35
169 Llanowar Envoy C	.20	.35
170 Llanowar Scout C	.20	.35
171 Mammoth Spider U	.40	.60
172 Marwyn, the Nurturer R	3.00	5.00
173 The Mending of Dominaria R	1.00	1.50
174 Multani, Yavimaya's Avatar M	5.00	8.00
175 Nature's Spiral U	.40	.60
176 Pierce the Sky C	.20	.35
177 Primordial Wurm C	.20	.35
178 Saproling Migration C	.20	.35
179 Song of Freyalise U	4.00	6.00
180 Spore Swarm U	.40	.60
181 Sporecrown Thallid U	.75	1.25
182 Steel Leaf Champion R	4.00	6.00
183 Sylvan Awakening R	1.25	1.75
184 Territorial Allosaurus R	.60	1.00
185 Thorn Elemental U	.40	.60
186 Untamed Kavu U	.40	.60
187 Verdant Force R	.60	1.00
188 Wild Onslaught U	.40	.60
189 Yavimaya Sapherd C	.20	.35
190 Adeliz, the Cinder Wind U	1.50	2.00
191 Arvad the Cursed U	.40	.60
192 Aryel, Knight of Windgrace R	2.00	3.50
193 Darigaaz Reincarnated M	7.00	10.00
194 Garna, the Bloodflame U	.40	.60
195 Grand Warlord Radha R	2.00	3.50
196 Hallar, the Firefletcher U	.40	.60
197 Jhoira, Weatherlight Captain M	15.00	20.00
198 Jodah, Archmage Eternal R	6.00	8.00
199 Muldrotha, the Gravetide M	30.00	35.00
200 Oath of Teferi R	3.00	5.00
201 Primevals' Glorious Rebirth R	2.00	3.00
202 Raff Capashen, Ship's Mage U	.40	.60
203 Rona, Disciple of Gix U	.40	.60
204 Shanna, Sisay's Legacy U	1.50	2.00
205 Slimefoot, the Stowaway U	4.00	6.00
206 Tatyova, Benthic Druid U	3.00	5.00
207 Teferi, Hero of Dominaria M	60.00	70.00
208 Tiana, Ship's Caretaker U	.40	.60
209 Aesthir Glider C	.20	.35
210 Amaranthine Wall U	.40	.60
211 Blackblade Reforged R	3.00	5.00
212 Bloodtallow Candle C	.20	.35
213 Damping Sphere U	18.00	22.00
214 Forebear's Blade R	.60	1.00
215 Gilded Lotus R	8.00	10.00
216 Guardians of Koilos C	.20	.35
217 Helm of the Host R	8.00	10.00
218 Howling Golem U	.40	.60
219 Icy Manipulator U	.40	.60
220 Jhoira's Familiar U	.40	.60
221 Jousting Lance C	.20	.35
222 Juggernaut U	.40	.60
223 Mishra's Self-Replicator R	.60	.50
224 Mox Amber M	40.00	50.00
225 Navigator's Compass C	.20	.35
226 Pardic Wanderer C	.20	.35
227 Powerstone Shard C	.20	.35
228 Shield of the Realm U	.40	.60
229 Short Sword C	.20	.35
230 Skittering Surveyor C	.20	.35
231 Sorcerer's Wand U	.40	.60
232 Sparring Construct C	.20	.35
233 Thran Temporal Gateway R	3.00	5.00
234 Traxos, Scourge of Kroog R	3.00	5.00
235 Urza's Tome U	.40	.60
236 Voltaic Servant C	.20	.35
237 Weatherlight M	8.00	12.00
238 Cabal Stronghold R	4.00	6.00
239 Clifftop Retreat R	4.00	6.00
240 Hinterland Harbor R	5.00	7.00
241 Isolated Chapel R	4.00	6.00
242 Memorial to Folly U	.40	.60
243 Memorial to Genius U	.40	.60
244 Memorial to Glory U	.40	.60
245 Memorial to Unity U	.40	.60
246 Memorial to War U	.40	.60
247 Sulfur Falls R	8.00	10.00
248 Woodland Cemetery R	5.00	7.00
249 Zhalfirin Void U	2.50	3.50
250 Plains L	.20	.35
251 Plains L	.20	.35
252 Plains L	.20	.35
253 Plains L	.20	.35
254 Island L	.20	.35
255 Island L	.20	.35
256 Island L	.20	.35
257 Island L	.20	.35
258 Swamp L	.20	.35
259 Swamp L	.20	.35
260 Swamp L	.20	.35
261 Swamp L	.20	.35
262 Mountain L	.20	.35
263 Mountain L	.20	.35
264 Mountain L	.20	.35
265 Mountain L	.20	.35
266 Forest L	.20	.35
267 Forest L	.20	.35
268 Forest L	.20	.35
269 Forest L	.20	.35

2018 Magic The Gathering Dominaria Tokens

Card	Low	High
1 Knight	.06	.10
2 Knight	.75	1.25
3 Soldier	.10	.15
4 Cleric	.10	.15
5 Zombie Knight	.75	1.25
6 Nightmare Horror	.06	.10
7 Demon	.20	.30
8 Elemental	.10	.15
9 Goblin	.12	.20
10 Karox Bladewing	.40	.60
11 Saproling	.06	.10
12 Saproling	.06	.10
13 Saproling	.06	.10
14 Construct	2.00	3.50
15 Jaya Ballard Emblem	.30	.40
16 Teferi, Hero of Dominaria Emblem	.60	1.00

2018 Magic The Gathering Guilds of Ravnica

Card	Low	High
COMPLETE SET (273)	350.00	500.00
RELEASED ON OCTOBER 5, 2018		
1 Blade Instructor C	.10	.20
2 Bounty Agent R	.30	.50
3 Candlelight Vigil C	.10	.20
4 Citywide Bust R	.30	.50
5 Collar the Culprit C	.10	.20
6 Conclave Tribunal U	.20	.30
7 Crush Contraband U	.20	.30
8 Dawn of Hope R	.30	.50
9 Demotion U	.20	.30
10 Divine Visitation M	4.50	6.00
11 Flight of Equenauts U	.20	.30
12 Gird for Battle U	.20	.30
13 Haazda Marshal U	.20	.30
14 Healer's Hawk C	.10	.20
15 Hunted Witness C	.10	.20
16 Inspiring Unicorn U	.20	.30
17 Intrusive Packbeast C	.10	.20
18 Ledev Guardian C	.10	.20
19 Light of the Legion R	.30	.50
20 Loxodon Restorer C	.10	.20
21 Luminous Bonds C	.10	.20
22 Parhelion Patrol C	.10	.20
23 Righteous Blow C	.10	.20
24 Roc Charger U	.20	.30
25 Skyline Scout C	.10	.20
26 Sunhome Stalwart U	.20	.30
27 Sworn Companions C	.10	.20
28 Take Heart C	.10	.20
29 Tenth District Guard C	.10	.20
30 Venerated Loxodon R	1.25	2.00
31 Capture Sphere C	.10	.20
32 Chemister's Insight U	.20	.30
33 Citywatch Sphinx U	.20	.30
34 Dazzling Lights C	.10	.20
35 Devious Cover-up C	.10	.20
36 Dimir Informant C	.10	.20
37 Disdainful Stroke C	.10	.20
38 Dream Eater M	5.00	8.00
39 Drowned Secrets R	.30	.50
40 Enhanced Surveillance U	.20	.30
41 Guild Summit U	.20	.30
42 Leapfrog C	.10	.20
43 Maximize Altitude C	.10	.20
44 Mission Briefing R	4.50	6.00
45 Murmuring Mystic U	.20	.30
46 Muse Drake C	.10	.20
47 Narcomoeba R	.30	.50
48 Nightveil Sprite U	.20	.30
49 Omnispell Adept R	.30	.50
50 Passwall Adept C	.10	.20
51 Quasiduplicate R	.30	.50
52 Radical Idea C	.10	.20
53 Selective Snare U	.20	.30
54 Sinister Sabotage U	.20	.30
55 Thoughtbound Phantasm U	.20	.30
56 Unexplained Disappearance C	.10	.20
57 Vedalken Mesmerist C	.10	.20
58 Wall of Mist C	.10	.20
59 Watcher in the Mist C	.10	.20
60 Wishcoin Crab C	.10	.20
61 Barrier of Bones C	.10	.20
62 Bartizan Bats C	.10	.20
63 Blood Operative R	.30	.50
64 Burglar Rat C	.10	.20
65 Child of Night C	.10	.20
66 Creeping Chill U	.20	.30
67 Dead Weight C	.10	.20
68 Deadly Visit C	.10	.20
69 Doom Whisperer M	20.00	25.00
70 Douser of Lights C	.10	.20
71 Gruesome Menagerie R	.30	.50
72 Hired Poisoner C	.10	.20
73 Kraul Swarm U	.20	.30
74 Lotleth Giant U	.20	.30
75 Mausoleum Secrets R	1.25	2.00
76 Mephitic Vapors C	.10	.20
77 Midnight Reaper R	.30	.50
78 Moodmark Painter C	.10	.20
79 Necrotic Wound U	.20	.30
80 Never Happened C	.10	.20
81 Pilfering Imp U	.20	.30
82 Plaguecrafter U	.20	.30
83 Price of Fame U	.20	.30
84 Ritual of Soot R	.30	.50
85 Severed Strands C	.10	.20
86 Spinal Centipede C	.10	.20
87 Undercity Necrolisk U	.20	.30
88 Veiled Shade C	.10	.20
89 Vicious Rumors C	.10	.20
90 Whispering Snitch U	.20	.30
91 Arclight Phoenix M	2.50	4.00
92 Barging Sergeant C	.10	.20
93 Book Devourer U	.20	.30
94 Command the Storm C	.10	.20
95 Cosmotronic Wave C	.10	.20
96 Direct Current C	.10	.20
97 Electrostatic Field U	.20	.30
98 Erratic Cyclops R	.30	.50
99 Experimental Frenzy R	3.50	5.00
100 Fearless Halberdier C	.10	.20
101 Fire Urchin C	.10	.20
102 Goblin Banneret U	.20	.30
103 Goblin Cratermaker U	.20	.30
104 Goblin Locksmith C	.10	.20
105 Gravitic Punch C	.10	.20
106 Hellkite Whelp U	.20	.30
107 Inescapable Blaze U	.20	.30
108 Lava Coil U	.20	.30
109 Legion Warboss R	3.50	5.00
110 Maniacal Rage C	.10	.20
111 Maximize Velocity C	.10	.20
112 Ornery Goblin C	.10	.20
113 Risk Factor R	7.00	10.00
114 Rubblebelt Boar C	.10	.20
115 Runaway Steam-Kin R	4.50	6.00
116 Smelt-Ward Minotaur U	.20	.30
117 Street Riot U	.20	.30
118 Sure Strike C	.10	.20
119 Torch Courier C	.10	.20
120 Wojek Bodyguard C	.10	.20
121 Affectionate Indrik U	.20	.30
122 Arboretum Elemental U	.20	.30
123 Beast Whisperer R	.60	1.00
124 Bounty of Might R	.30	.50
125 Circuitous Route U	.20	.30
126 Crushing Canopy C	.10	.20
127 Devkarin Dissident C	.10	.20
128 District Guide U	.20	.30

129 Generous Stray C	.10	.20
130 Golgari Raiders U	.20	.30
131 Grappling Sundew U	.20	.30
132 Hatchery Spider R	.30	.50
133 Hitchclaw Recluse C	.10	.20
134 Ironshell Beetle C	.10	.20
135 Kraul Foragers C	.10	.20
136 Kraul Harpooner U	.20	.30
137 Might of the Masses U	.20	.30
138 Nullhide Ferox M	5.00	8.00
139 Pack's Favor C	.10	.20
140 Pause for Reflection C	.10	.20
141 Pelt Collector R	5.00	8.00
142 Portcullis Vine C	.10	.20
143 Prey Upon C	.10	.20
144 Siege Wurm C	.10	.20
145 Sprouting Renewal U	.20	.30
146 Urban Utopia C	.10	.20
147 Vigorspore Wurm C	.10	.20
148 Vivid Revival R	.30	.50
149 Wary Okapi C	.10	.20
150 Wild Ceratok C	.10	.20
151 Artful Takedown C	.10	.20
152 Assassin's Trophy R	13.00	20.00
153 Aurelia, Exemplar of Justice M	12.00	15.00
154 Beacon Bolt U	.20	.30
155 Beamsplitter Mage U	.20	.30
156 Boros Challenger U	.20	.30
157 Camaraderie R	.30	.50
158 Centaur Peacemaker C	.10	.20
159 Chance for Glory M	1.50	2.50
160 Charnel Troll R	.30	.50
161 Conclave Cavalier U	.20	.30
162 Conclave Guildmage U	.20	.30
163 Crackling Drake U	.20	.30
164 Darkblade Agent C	.10	.20
165 Deafening Clarion R	.75	1.25
166 Dimir Spybug U	.20	.30
167 Disinformation Campaign U	.20	.30
168 Emmara, Soul of the Accord R	.30	.50
169 Erstwhile Trooper C	.10	.20
170 Etrata, the Silencer R	.30	.50
171 Firemind's Research R	.30	.50
172 Garrison Sergeant C	.10	.20
173 Glowspore Shaman U	.20	.30
174 Goblin Electromancer C	.10	.20
175 Golgari Findbroker U	.20	.30
176 Hammer Dropper C	.10	.20
177 House Guildmage U	.20	.30
178 Hypothesizzle C	.10	.20
179 Ionize R	2.50	4.00
180 Izoni, Thousand-Eyed R	.30	.50
181 Join Shields U	.20	.30
182 Justice Strike U	.20	.30
183 Knight of Autumn R	3.50	5.00
184 Lazav, the Multifarious M	3.50	5.00
185 League Guildmage U	.20	.30
186 Ledev Champion U	.20	.30
187 Legion Guildmage U	.20	.30
188 March of the Multitudes M	12.00	15.00
189 Mnemonic Betrayal M	1.50	2.50
190 Molderhulk U	.20	.30
191 Nightveil Predator U	.20	.30
192 Niv-Mizzet, Parun R	1.00	1.75
193 Notion Rain C	.10	.20
194 Ochran Assassin U	.20	.30
195 Ral, Izzet Viceroy M	12.00	10.00
196 Rhizome Lurcher C	.10	.20
197 Rosemane Centaur C	.10	.20
198 Skyknight Legionnaire C	.10	.20
199 Sonic Assault C	.10	.20
200 Sumala Woodshaper C	.10	.20
201 Swarm Guildmage U	.20	.30
202 Swathcutter Giant U	.20	.30
203 Swiftblade Vindicator R	1.00	1.75
204 Tajic, Legion's Edge R	1.75	3.00
205 Thief of Sanity R	1.75	3.00
206 Thought Erasure U	.20	.30
207 Thousand-Year Storm M	1.75	3.00
208 Trostani Discordant M	2.50	4.00
209 Truefire Captain U	.20	.30
210 Undercity Uprising C	.10	.20
211 Underrealm Lich M	3.50	5.00
212 Unmoored Ego R	1.25	2.00
213 Vraska, Golgari Queen M	8.00	12.00
214 Wee Dragonauts U	.20	.30
215 Worldsoul Colossus U	.20	.30
216 Fresh-Faced Recruit C	.10	.20
217 Piston-Fist Cyclops C	.10	.20
218 Pitiless Gorgon C	.10	.20
219 Vernadi Shieldmate C	.10	.20
220 Whisper Agent C	.10	.20
221 Assure // Assemble R	.30	.50
222 Connive // Concoct R	.30	.50
223 Discovery // Dispersal U	.20	.30
224 Expansion // Explosion R	.30	.50
225 Find // Finality R	1.25	2.00
226 Flower // Flourish U	.20	.30
227 Integrity // Intervention U	.20	.30
228 Invert // Invent U	.20	.30
229 Response // Resurgence R	.30	.50
230 Status // Statue U	.20	.30
231 Boros Locket C	.10	.20
232 Chamber Sentry R	.30	.50
233 Chromatic Lantern R	2.50	4.00
234 Dimir Locket C	.10	.20
235 Gatekeeper Gargoyle U	.20	.30
236 Glaive of the Guildpact U	.20	.30
237 Golgari Locket C	.10	.20
238 Izzet Locket C	.10	.20
239 Rampaging Monument U	.20	.30
240 Selesnya Locket C	.10	.20
241 Silent Dart U	.20	.30
242 Wand of Vertebrae U	.20	.30
243 Boros Guildgate C	.10	.20
244 Boros Guildgate C	.10	.20
245 Dimir Guildgate C	.10	.20
246 Dimir Guildgate C	.10	.20
247 Gateway Plaza C	.10	.20
248 Golgari Guildgate C	.10	.20
249 Golgari Guildgate C	.10	.20
250 Guildmages' Forum R	.30	.50
251 Izzet Guildgate C	.10	.20
252 Izzet Guildgate C	.10	.20
253 Overgrown Tomb R	5.00	8.00
254 Sacred Foundry R	5.00	8.00
255 Selesnya Guildgate C	.10	.20
256 Selesnya Guildgate C	.10	.20
257 Steam Vents R	7.00	10.00
258 Temple Garden R	.30	6.00
259 Watery Grave R	7.00	10.00
260 Plains C	.10	.20
261 Island C	.10	.20
262 Swamp C	.10	.20
263 Mountain C	.10	.20
264 Forest C	.10	.20
265 Ral, Caller of Storms M	4.50	6.00
266 Ral's Dispersal R	.30	.50
267 Precision Bolt C	.10	.20
268 Ral's Staticaster U	.20	.30
269 Vraska, Regal Gorgon M	4.50	6.00
270 Kraul Raider C	.10	.20
271 Attendant of Vraska U	.20	.30
272 Vraska's Stoneglare R	.30	.50
273 Impervious Greatwurm M	3.50	5.00

2018 Magic The Gathering Guilds of Ravnica Foil

COMPLETE SET (273)	700.00	1000.00
1 Blade Instructor C	.25	.40
2 Bounty Agent R	1.25	2.00
3 Candlelight Vigil C	.25	.40
4 Citywide Bust R	1.25	2.00
5 Collar the Culprit C	.25	.40
6 Conclave Tribunal U	.30	.50
7 Crush Contraband U	.30	.50
8 Dawn of Hope R	1.25	2.00
9 Demotion U	.30	.50
10 Divine Visitation M	20.00	25.00
11 Flight of Equenauts U	.30	.50
12 Gird for Battle U	.30	.50
13 Haazda Marshal U	.30	.50
14 Healer's Hawk C	.25	.40
15 Hunted Witness C	.25	.40
16 Inspiring Unicorn U	.30	.50
17 Intrusive Packbeast C	.25	.40
18 Ledev Guardian C	.25	.40
19 Light of the Legion R	1.25	2.00
20 Loxodon Restorer C	.25	.40
21 Luminous Bonds C	.25	.40
22 Parhelion Patrol C	.25	.40
23 Righteous Blow C	.25	.40
24 Roc Charger U	.30	.50
25 Skyline Scout C	.25	.40
26 Sunhome Stalwart U	.30	.50
27 Sworn Companions C	.25	.40
28 Take Heart C	.25	.40
29 Tenth District Guard C	.25	.40
30 Venerated Loxodon R	5.00	8.00
31 Capture Sphere C	.25	.40
32 Chemister's Insight U	.30	.50
33 Citywatch Sphinx U	.30	.50
34 Dazzling Lights C	.25	.40
35 Devious Cover-up C	.25	.40
36 Dimir Informant C	.25	.40
37 Disdainful Stroke C	.25	.40
38 Dream Eater M	13.00	20.00
39 Drowned Secrets R	1.25	2.00
40 Enhanced Surveillance U	.30	.50
41 Guild Summit U	.30	.50
42 Leapfrog C	.25	.40
43 Maximize Altitude C	.25	.40
44 Mission Briefing R	20.00	25.00
45 Murmuring Mystic U	.30	.50
46 Muse Drake C	.25	.40
47 Narcomoeba R	1.25	2.00
48 Nightveil Sprite U	.30	.50
49 Omnispell Adept R	1.25	2.00
50 Passwall Adept C	.25	.40
51 Quasiduplicate R	1.25	2.00
52 Radical Idea C	.25	.40
53 Selective Snare U	.30	.50
54 Sinister Sabotage U	.30	.50
55 Thoughtbound Phantasm U	.30	.50
56 Unexplained Disappearance C	.25	.40
57 Vedalken Mesmerist C	.25	.40
58 Wall of Mist C	.25	.40
59 Watcher in the Mist C	.25	.40
60 Wishcoin Crab C	.25	.40
61 Barrier of Bones C	.25	.40
62 Bartizan Bats C	.25	.40
63 Blood Operative R	1.25	2.00
64 Burglar Rat C	.25	.40
65 Child of Night C	.25	.40
66 Creeping Chill U	.30	.50
67 Dead Weight C	.25	.40
68 Deadly Visit C	.25	.40
69 Doom Whisperer M	35.00	50.00
70 Douser of Lights C	.25	.40
71 Gruesome Menagerie R	1.25	2.00
72 Hired Poisoner C	.25	.40
73 Kraul Swarm U	.30	.50
74 Lotleth Giant U	.30	.50
75 Mausoleum Secrets R	5.00	8.00
76 Mephitic Vapors C	.25	.40
77 Midnight Reaper R	1.25	2.00
78 Moodmark Painter C	.25	.40
79 Necrotic Wound U	.30	.50
80 Never Happened C	.25	.40
81 Pilfering Imp U	.30	.50
82 Plaguecrafter U	.30	.50
83 Price of Fame U	.30	.50
84 Ritual of Soot R	1.25	2.00
85 Severed Strands C	.25	.40
86 Spinal Centipede C	.25	.40
87 Undercity Necrolisk U	.30	.50
88 Veiled Shade C	.25	.40
89 Vicious Rumors C	.25	.40
90 Whispering Snitch U	.30	.50
91 Arclight Phoenix M	8.00	12.00
92 Barging Sergeant C	.25	.40
93 Book Devourer U	.30	.50
94 Command the Storm C	.25	.40
95 Cosmotronic Wave C	.25	.40
96 Direct Current C	.25	.40
97 Electrostatic Field U	.30	.50
98 Erratic Cyclops R	1.25	2.00
99 Experimental Frenzy R	15.00	20.00
100 Fearless Halberdier C	.25	.40
101 Fire Urchin C	.25	.40
102 Goblin Banneret U	.30	.50
103 Goblin Cratermaker U	.30	.50
104 Goblin Locksmith C	.25	.40
105 Gravitic Punch C	.25	.40
106 Hellkite Whelp U	.30	.50
107 Inescapable Blaze U	.30	.50
108 Lava Coil U	.30	.50
109 Legion Warboss R	15.00	20.00
110 Maniacal Rage C	.25	.40
111 Maximize Velocity C	.25	.40
112 Ornery Goblin C	.25	.40
113 Risk Factor R	30.00	40.00
114 Rubblebelt Boar C	.25	.40
115 Runaway Steam-Kin R	20.00	25.00
116 Smelt-Ward Minotaur U	.30	.50
117 Street Riot U	.30	.50
118 Sure Strike C	.25	.40
119 Torch Courier C	.25	.40
120 Wojek Bodyguard C	.25	.40
121 Affectionate Indrik U	.30	.50
122 Arboretum Elemental U	.30	.50
123 Beast Whisperer R	2.50	4.00
124 Bounty of Might R	1.25	2.00
125 Circuitous Route U	.30	.50
126 Crushing Canopy C	.25	.40
127 Devkarin Dissident C	.25	.40
128 District Guide U	.30	.50
129 Generous Stray C	.25	.40
130 Golgari Raiders U	.30	.50
131 Grappling Sundew U	.30	.50
132 Hatchery Spider R	1.25	2.00
133 Hitchclaw Recluse C	.25	.40
134 Ironshell Beetle C	.25	.40
135 Kraul Foragers C	.25	.40
136 Kraul Harpooner U	.30	.50
137 Might of the Masses U	.30	.50
138 Nullhide Ferox M	20.00	25.00
139 Pack's Favor C	.25	.40
140 Pause for Reflection C	.25	.40
141 Pelt Collector R	20.00	30.00
142 Portcullis Vine C	.25	.40
143 Prey Upon C	.25	.40
144 Siege Wurm C	.25	.40
145 Sprouting Renewal U	.30	.50
146 Urban Utopia C	.25	.40
147 Vigorspore Wurm C	.25	.40
148 Vivid Revival R	1.25	2.00
149 Wary Okapi C	.25	.40
150 Wild Ceratok C	.25	.40
151 Artful Takedown C	.25	.40
152 Assassin's Trophy R	50.00	80.00
153 Aurelia, Exemplar of Justice M	22.00	30.00
154 Beacon Bolt U	.30	.50
155 Beamsplitter Mage U	.30	.50
156 Boros Challenger U	.30	.50
157 Camaraderie R	1.25	2.00
158 Centaur Peacemaker C	.25	.40
159 Chance for Glory M	7.00	10.00
160 Charnel Troll R	1.25	2.00
161 Conclave Cavalier U	.30	.50
162 Conclave Guildmage U	.30	.50
163 Crackling Drake U	.30	.50
164 Darkblade Agent C	.25	.40
165 Deafening Clarion R	3.00	5.00
166 Dimir Spybug U	.30	.50
167 Disinformation Campaign U	.30	.50
168 Emmara, Soul of the Accord R	1.25	2.00
169 Erstwhile Trooper C	.25	.40
170 Etrata, the Silencer R	1.25	2.00
171 Firemind's Research R	1.25	2.00
172 Garrison Sergeant C	.25	.40
173 Glowspore Shaman U	.30	.50
174 Goblin Electromancer C	.25	.40
175 Golgari Findbroker U	.30	.50
176 Hammer Dropper C	.25	.40
177 House Guildmage U	.30	.50
178 Hypothesizzle C	.25	.40
179 Ionize R	10.00	15.00
180 Izoni, Thousand-Eyed R	1.25	2.00
181 Join Shields U	.30	.50
182 Justice Strike U	.30	.50
183 Knight of Autumn R	15.00	20.00
184 Lazav, the Multifarious M	30.00	40.00
185 League Guildmage U	.30	.50
186 Ledev Champion U	.30	.50
187 Legion Guildmage U	.30	.50
188 March of the Multitudes M	22.00	30.00
189 Mnemonic Betrayal M	10.00	15.00
190 Molderhulk U	.30	.50
191 Nightveil Predator U	.30	.50
192 Niv-Mizzet, Parun R	4.00	8.00
193 Notion Rain C	.25	.40
194 Ochran Assassin U	.30	.50
195 Ral, Izzet Viceroy M	35.00	50.00
196 Rhizome Lurcher C	.25	.40
197 Rosemane Centaur C	.25	.40
198 Skyknight Legionnaire C	.25	.40
199 Sonic Assault C	.25	.40
200 Sumala Woodshaper C	.25	.40
201 Swarm Guildmage U	.30	.50
202 Swathcutter Giant U	.30	.50
203 Swiftblade Vindicator R	4.00	8.00
204 Tajic, Legion's Edge R	8.00	12.00
205 Thief of Sanity R	8.00	12.00
206 Thought Erasure U	.30	.50
207 Thousand-Year Storm M	17.00	20.00
208 Trostani Discordant M	8.00	12.00
209 Truefire Captain U	.30	.50
210 Undercity Uprising C	.25	.40
211 Underrealm Lich M	8.00	12.00
212 Unmoored Ego R	5.00	8.00
213 Vraska, Golgari Queen M	75.00	90.00
214 Wee Dragonauts U	.30	.50
215 Worldsoul Colossus U	.30	.50
216 Fresh-Faced Recruit C	.25	.40
217 Piston-Fist Cyclops C	.25	.40
218 Pitiless Gorgon C	.25	.40
219 Vernadi Shieldmate C	.25	.40
220 Whisper Agent C	.25	.40
221 Assure // Assemble R	1.25	2.00
222 Connive // Concoct R	1.25	2.00
223 Discovery // Dispersal U	.30	.50
224 Expansion // Explosion R	1.25	2.00
225 Find // Finality R	5.00	8.00
226 Flower // Flourish U	.30	.50
227 Integrity // Intervention U	.30	.50
228 Invert // Invent U	.30	.50
229 Response // Resurgence R	1.25	2.00
230 Status // Statue U	.30	.50
231 Boros Locket C	.25	.40
232 Chamber Sentry R	1.25	2.00
233 Chromatic Lantern R	10.00	15.00
234 Dimir Locket C	.25	.40
235 Gatekeeper Gargoyle U	.30	.50
236 Glaive of the Guildpact U	.30	.50
237 Golgari Locket C	.25	.40
238 Izzet Locket C	.25	.40
239 Rampaging Monument U	.30	.50
240 Selesnya Locket C	.25	.40
241 Silent Dart U	.30	.50
242 Wand of Vertebrae U	.30	.50
243 Boros Guildgate C	.25	.40
244 Boros Guildgate C	.25	.40
245 Dimir Guildgate C	.25	.40
246 Dimir Guildgate C	.25	.40
247 Gateway Plaza C	.25	.40
248 Golgari Guildgate C	.25	.40
249 Golgari Guildgate C	.25	.40
250 Guildmages' Forum R	1.25	2.00
251 Izzet Guildgate C	.25	.40
252 Izzet Guildgate C	.25	.40
253 Overgrown Tomb R	20.00	30.00
254 Sacred Foundry R	20.00	30.00
255 Selesnya Guildgate C	.25	.40
256 Selesnya Guildgate C	.25	.40
257 Steam Vents R	30.00	40.00
258 Temple Garden R	20.00	25.00
259 Watery Grave R	30.00	40.00
260 Plains C	.25	.40
261 Island C	.25	.40
262 Swamp C	.25	.40
263 Mountain C	.25	.40
264 Forest C	.25	.40
265 Ral, Caller of Storms M	7.00	10.00
266 Ral's Dispersal R	1.25	2.00
267 Precision Bolt C	.25	.40
268 Ral's Staticaster U	.30	.50
269 Vraska, Regal Gorgon M	8.00	12.00
270 Kraul Raider C	.25	.40
271 Attendant of Vraska U	.30	.50
272 Vraska's Stoneglare R	1.25	2.00
273 Impervious Greatwurm M	22.00	30.00

2018 Magic The Gathering Guilds of Ravnica Tokens

1 Angel	.35	.50
2 Soldier	.10	.15
3 Bird Illusion	.10	.15
4 Goblin	.10	.15
5 Insect	.10	.15
6 Elf Knight	.10	.15
7 Ral, Izzet Viceroy Emblem	.10	.15
8 Vraska, Golgari Queen Emblem	.10	.15

2019 Magic The Gathering Ravnica Allegiance

COMPLETE SET (273)		
BOOSTER BOX (36 PACKS)		
BOOSTER PACK (15 CARDS)		
RELEASED ON JANUARY 25, 2019		
1 Angel of Grace M	5.00	8.00
2 Angelic Exaltation U	.20	.30
3 Archway Angel U	.20	.30
4 Arrester's Zeal C	.15	.25
5 Bring to Trial C	.15	.25
6 Civic Stalwart C	.15	.25
7 Concordia Pegasus C	.15	.25
8 Expose to Daylight C	.15	.25
9 Forbidding Spirit U	.20	.30
10 Haazda Officer C	.15	.25
11 Hero of Percinct One R	2.50	4.00
12 Impassioned Orator C	.15	.25
13 Justiciar's Portal C	.15	.25
14 Knight of Sorrows C	.15	.25
15 Lumbering Battlement R	.30	.50
16 Ministrant of Obligation U	.20	.30
17 Prowling Caracal C	.15	.25
18 Rally to Battle U	.20	.30
19 Resolute Watchdog U	.20	.30
20 Sentinel's Mark U	.20	.30
21 Sky Tether U	.20	.30
22 Smothering Tithe R	4.00	6.00
23 Spirit of the Spires U	.20	.30
24 Summary Judgment C	.15	.25
25 Syndicate Messenger C	.15	.25
26 Tenth District Veteran C	.15	.25
27 Tithe Taker R	1.50	2.50
28 Twilight Panther C	.15	.25
29 Unbreakable Formation R	.30	.50
30 Watchful Giant C	.15	.25
31 Arrester's Admonition C	.15	.25
32 Benthic Biomancer R	.30	.50
33 Chillbringer C	.15	.25
34 Clear the Mind C	.15	.25
35 Code of Constraint U	.20	.30
36 Coral Commando C	.15	.25
37 Essence Capture U	.20	.30
38 Eyes Everywhere U	.20	.30

39 Faerie Duelist C .15 .25
40 Gateway Sneak U .20 .30
41 Humongulus C .15 .25
42 Mass Manipulation R .30 .50
43 Mesmerizing Benthid M 2.00 3.00
44 Persistent Petitioners C 1.00 1.50
45 Precognitive Perception R .30 .50
46 Prying Eyes C .15 .25
47 Pteramander U 2.00 3.00
48 Quench C .15 .25
49 Sage's Row Savant C .15 .25
50 Senate Courier C .15 .25
51 Shimmer of Possibility C .15 .25
52 Skatewing Spy U .20 .30
53 Skitter Eel C .15 .25
54 Slimebind C .15 .25
55 Sphinx of Foresight R .30 .50
56 Swirling Torrent U .20 .30
57 Thought Collapse C .15 .25
58 Verity Circle R .30 .50
59 Wall of Lost Thoughts U .20 .30
60 Windstorm Drake U .20 .30
61 Awaken the Erstwhile R .30 .50
62 Bankrupt in Blood U .20 .30
63 Blade Juggler C .15 .25
64 Bladebrand C .15 .25
65 Bloodmist Infiltrator U .20 .30
66 Carrion Imp C .15 .25
67 Catacomb Crocodile C .15 .25
68 Clear the Stage U .20 .30
69 Consign to the Pit C .15 .25
70 Cry of the Carnarium U .20 .30
71 Dead Revels C .15 .25
72 Debtors' Transport C .15 .25
73 Drill Bit U .20 .30
74 Font of Agonies R .30 .50
75 Grotesque Demise C .15 .25
76 Gutterbones R .30 .50
77 Ill-Gotten Inheritance C .15 .25
78 Noxious Groodion C .15 .25
79 Orzhov Enforcer U .20 .30
80 Orzhov Racketeers U .20 .30
81 Pestilent Spirit R .30 .50
82 Plague Wight C .15 .25
83 Priest of Forgotten Gods R 1.50 2.50
84 Rakdos Trumpeter C .15 .25
85 Spawn of Mayhem M 8.00 12.00
86 Spire Mangler U .20 .30
87 Thirsting Shade C .15 .25
88 Undercity Scavenger C .15 .25
89 Undercity's Embrace C .15 .25
90 Vindictive Vampire U .20 .30
91 Act of Treason C .15 .25
92 Amplifire R .30 .50
93 Burn Bright C .15 .25
94 Burning-Tree Vandal C .15 .25
95 Cavalcade of Calamity U .20 .30
96 Clamor Shaman U .20 .30
97 Dagger Caster U .20 .30
98 Deface C .15 .25
99 Electrodominance R 3.50 5.00
100 Feral Maaka C .15 .25
101 Flames of the Raze-Boar U .20 .30
102 Gates Ablaze U .20 .30
103 Ghor-Clan Wrecker C .15 .25
104 Goblin Gathering C .15 .25
105 Gravel-Hide Goblin C .15 .25
106 Immolation Shaman R .30 .50
107 Light Up the Stage U 2.00 3.00
108 Mirror March R .30 .50
109 Rix Maadi Reveler R 1.00 1.50
110 Rubble Reading C .15 .25
111 Rubblebelt Recluse C .15 .25
112 Rumbling Ruin U .20 .30
113 Scorchmark C .15 .25
114 Skarrgan Hellkite M 6.00 10.00
115 Skewer the Critics C .60 1.00
116 Smelt-Ward Ignus U .20 .30
117 Spear Spewer C .15 .25
118 Spikewheel Acrobat C .15 .25
119 Storm Strike C .15 .25
120 Tin Street Dodger U .20 .30
121 Axebane Beast C .15 .25
122 Biogenic Ooze M 8.00 12.00
123 Biogenic Upgrade U .20 .30
124 End-Raze Forerunners R .30 .50
125 Enraged Ceratok U .20 .30
126 Gatebreaker Ram U .20 .30
127 Gift of Strength C .15 .25
128 Growth-Chamber Guardian R 4.00 6.00
129 Gruul Beastmaster U .20 .30
130 Guardian Project R .30 .50
131 Incubation Druid R 4.00 6.00
132 Mammoth Spider C .15 .25
133 Open the Gates C .15 .25
134 Rampage of the Clans R .30 .50
135 Rampaging Rendhorn C .15 .25
136 Regenesis U .20 .30
137 Root Snare C .15 .25
138 Sagittars' Volley C .15 .25
139 Saruli Caretaker C .15 .25
140 Sauroform Hybrid C .15 .25
141 Silhana Wayfinder U .20 .30
142 Steeple Creeper C .15 .25
143 Stony Strength C .15 .25
144 Sylvan Brushstrider C .15 .25
145 Territorial Boar C .15 .25
146 Titanic Brawl C .15 .25
147 Tower Defense U .20 .30
148 Trollbred Guardian U .20 .30
149 Wilderness Reclamation U 1.00 1.50
150 Wrecking Beast C .15 .25
151 Absorb R 1.25 2.00
152 Aeromunculus C .15 .25
153 Applied Biomancy C .15 .25
154 Azorius Knight-Arbiter C .15 .25
155 Azorius Skyguard U .20 .30
156 Basilica Bell-Haunt U .20 .30
157 Bedevil R 3.50 5.00
158 Biomancer's Familiar R .75 1.25
159 Bolrac-Clan Crusher U .20 .30
160 Captive Audience M 2.00 3.00
161 Cindervines R 1.00 1.50
162 Clan Guildmage U .20 .30
163 Combine Guildmage U .20 .30
164 Cult Guildmage U .20 .30
165 Deputy of Detention R 2.50 4.00
166 Domri, Chaos Bringer M 6.00 10.00
167 Dovin, Grand Arbiter M 5.00 8.00
168 Dovin's Acuity U .20 .30
169 Emergency Powers M 2.00 3.00
170 Ethereal Absolution R .30 .50
171 Final Payment C .15 .25
172 Fireblade Artist U .20 .30
173 Frenzied Arynx C .15 .25
174 Frilled Mystic U .20 .30
175 Galloping Lizrog U .20 .30
176 Get the Point C .15 .25
177 Grasping Thrull C .15 .25
178 Growth Spiral C .15 .25
179 Gruul Spellbreaker R 2.50 3.50
180 Gyre Engineer U .20 .30
181 Hackrobat U .20 .30
182 High Alert U .20 .30
183 Hydroid Krasis M 35.00 45.00
184 Imperious Oligarch C .15 .25
185 Judith, the Scourge Diva R 3.50 5.00
186 Kaya, Orzhov Usurper M 5.00 8.00
187 Kaya's Wrath R 2.50 4.00
188 Knight of the Last Breath U .20 .30
189 Lavinia, Azorius Renegade R .30 .50
190 Lawmage's Binding C .15 .25
191 Macabre Mockery U .20 .30
192 Mortify U .20 .30
193 Nikya of the Old Ways R .30 .50
194 Pitiless Pontiff U .20 .30
195 Prime Speaker Vannifar M 10.00 15.00
196 Rafter Demon C .15 .25
197 Rakdos Firewheeler U .20 .30
198 Rakdos Roustabout C .15 .25
199 Rakdos, the Showstopper M 2.00 3.00
200 Ravager Wurm M 2.50 4.00
201 Rhythm of the Wild U 1.00 1.50
202 Rubblebelt Runner C .15 .25
203 Savage Smash C .15 .25
204 Senate Guildmage U .20 .30
205 Seraph of the Scales M 10.00 15.00
206 Sharktocrab U .20 .30
207 Simic Ascendancy R .30 .50
208 Sphinx of New Prahv U .20 .30
209 Sphinx's Insight C .15 .25
210 Sunder Shaman U .20 .30
211 Syndicate Guildmage U .20 .30
212 Teysa Karlov R 1.50 2.50
213 Theater of Horrors R 1.25 2.00
214 Zegana, Utopian Speaker R .30 .50
215 Zhur-Taa Goblin U .20 .30
216 Footlight Fiend C .15 .25
217 Rubble Slinger C .15 .25
218 Scuttlegator C .15 .25
219 Senate Griffin C .15 .25
220 Vizkopa Vampire C .15 .25
221 Bedeck//Bedazzle R .30 .50
222 Carnival//Carnage U .20 .30
223 Collision//Colossus U .20 .30
224 Consecrate//Consume U .20 .30
225 Depose//Deploy U .20 .30
226 Incubation//Incongruity U .20 .30
227 Repudiate//Replicate R .30 .50
228 Revival//Revenge R .30 .50
229 Thrash//Threat R .30 .50
230 Warrant//Warden R .30 .50
231 Azorius Locket C .15 .25
232 Gate Colossus U .20 .30
233 Glass of the Guildpact R .30 .50
234 Gruul Locket C .15 .25
235 Junktroller U .20 .30
236 Orzhov Locket C .15 .25
237 Rakdos Locket C .15 .25
238 Scrabbling Claws U .20 .30
239 Screaming Shield U .20 .30
240 Simic Locket C .15 .25
241 Sphinx of the Guildpact U .20 .30
242 Tome of the Guildpact R .30 .50
243 Azorius Guildgate C .15 .25
244 Azorius Guildgate C .15 .25
245 Blood Crypt R 8.00 12.00
246 Breeding Pool R .30 .50
247 Gateway Plaza C .15 .25
248 Godless Shrine R 8.00 12.00
249 Gruul Guildgate C .15 .25
250 Gruul Guildgate C .15 .25
251 Hallowed Fountain R 6.00 10.00
252 Orzhov Guildgate C .15 .25
253 Orzhov Guildgate C .15 .25
254 Plaza of Harmony R 2.00 3.00
255 Rakdos Guildgate C .15 .25
256 Rakdos Guildgate C .15 .25
257 Simic Guildgate C .15 .25
258 Simic Guildgate C .15 .25
259 Stomping Ground R 8.00 12.00
260 Plains C .15 .25
261 Island C .15 .25
262 Swamp C .15 .25
263 Mountain C .15 .25
264 Forest C .15 .25
265 Dovin, Architect of Law M 5.00 8.00
266 Elite Arrester C .15 .25
267 Dovin's Dismissal R .30 .50
268 Dovin's Automaton U .20 .30
269 Domri, City Smasher M 6.00 10.00
270 Ragefire C .15 .25
271 Charging War Boar U .20 .30
272 Domri's Nodorog R .30 .50
273 The Haunt of Hightower M 5.00 8.00

2019 Magic The Gathering Ravnica Allegiance Foil

1 Angel of Grace M 12.00 20.00
2 Angelic Exaltation U .30 .50
3 Archway Angel U .30 .50
4 Arrester's Zeal C .25 .40
5 Bring to Trial C .25 .40
6 Civic Stalwart C .25 .40
7 Concordia Pegasus C .25 .40
8 Expose to Daylight C .25 .40
9 Forbidding Spirit U .30 .50
10 Haazda Officer C .25 .40
11 Hero of Precinct One R 3.00 5.00
12 Impassioned Orator C .25 .40
13 Justiciar's Portal C .25 .40
14 Knight of Sorrows C .25 .40
15 Lumbering Battlement R 1.25 2.00
16 Ministrant of Obligation U .30 .50
17 Prowling Caracal C .25 .40
18 Rally to Battle U .30 .50
19 Resolute Watchdog U .30 .50
20 Sentinel's Mark U .30 .50
21 Sky Tether U .30 .50
22 Smothering Tithe R 12.00 20.00
23 Spirit of the Spires U .30 .50
24 Summary Judgment C .25 .40
25 Syndicate Messenger C .25 .40
26 Tenth District Veteran C .25 .40
27 Tithe Taker R 2.50 4.00
28 Twilight Panther C .25 .40
29 Unbreakable Formation R 1.25 2.00
30 Watchful Giant C .25 .40
31 Arrester's Admonition C .25 .40
32 Benthic Biomancer R 3.00 5.00
33 Chillbringer C .25 .40
34 Clear the Mind C .25 .40
35 Code of Constraint U .30 .50
36 Coral Commando C .25 .40
37 Essence Capture U .30 .50
38 Eyes Everywhere U .30 .50
39 Faerie Duelist C .25 .40
40 Gateway Sneak U .30 .50
41 Humongulus C .25 .40
42 Mass Manipulation R 1.25 2.00
43 Mesmerizing Benthid M 3.00 5.00
44 Persistent Petitioners C 3.00 5.00
45 Precognitive Perception R 1.25 2.00
46 Prying Eyes C .25 .40
47 Pteramander U 15.00 25.00
48 Quench C .25 .40
49 Sage's Row Savant C .25 .40
50 Senate Courier C .25 .40
51 Shimmer of Possibility C .25 .40
52 Skatewing Spy U .30 .50
53 Skitter Eel C .25 .40
54 Slimebind C .25 .40
55 Sphinx of Foresight R 1.25 2.00
56 Swirling Torrent U .30 .50
57 Thought Collapse C .25 .40
58 Verity Circle R 1.25 2.00
59 Wall of Lost Thoughts U .30 .50
60 Windstorm Drake U .30 .50
61 Awaken the Erstwhile R 1.25 2.00
62 Bankrupt in Blood U .30 .50
63 Blade Juggler C .25 .40
64 Bladebrand C .25 .40
65 Bloodmist Infiltrator U .30 .50
66 Carrion Imp C .25 .40
67 Catacomb Crocodile C .25 .40
68 Clear the Stage U .30 .50
69 Consign to the Pit C .25 .40
70 Cry of the Carnarium U .30 .50
71 Dead Revels C .25 .40
72 Debtors' Transport C .25 .40
73 Drill Bit U .30 .50
74 Font of Agonies R 1.25 2.00
75 Grotesque Demise C .25 .40
76 Gutterbones R 1.25 2.00
77 Ill-Gotten Inheritance C .25 .40
78 Noxious Groodion C .25 .40
79 Orzhov Enforcer U .30 .50
80 Orzhov Racketeers U .30 .50
81 Pestilent Spirit R 1.50 2.50
82 Plague Wight C .25 .40
83 Priest of Forgotten Gods R 3.00 5.00
84 Rakdos Trumpeter C .25 .40
85 Spawn of Mayhem M 12.00 20.00
86 Spire Mangler U .30 .50
87 Thirsting Shade C .25 .40
88 Undercity Scavenger C .25 .40
89 Undercity's Embrace C .25 .40
90 Vindictive Vampire U .30 .50
91 Act of Treason C .25 .40
92 Amplifire R 1.25 2.00
93 Burn Bright C .25 .40
94 Burning-Tree Vandal C .25 .40
95 Cavalcade of Calamity U .30 .50
96 Clamor Shaman U .30 .50
97 Dagger Caster U .30 .50
98 Deface C .25 .40
99 Electrodominance R 10.00 15.00
100 Feral Maaka C .25 .40
101 Flames of the Raze-Boar U .30 .50
102 Gates Ablaze U 3.00 5.00
103 Ghor-Clan Wrecker C .25 .40
104 Goblin Gathering C .25 .40
105 Gravel-Hide Goblin C .25 .40
106 Immolation Shaman R 1.25 2.00
107 Light Up the Stage U 8.00 12.00
108 Mirror March R 1.25 2.00
109 Rix Maadi Reveler R 1.50 2.50
110 Rubble Reading C .25 .40
111 Rubblebelt Recluse C .25 .40
112 Rumbling Ruin U .30 .50
113 Scorchmark C .25 .40
114 Skarrgan Hellkite M 8.00 12.00
115 Skewer the Critics C 10.00 15.00
116 Smelt-Ward Ignus U .30 .50
117 Spear Spewer C .25 .40
118 Spikewheel Acrobat C .25 .40
119 Storm Strike C .25 .40
120 Tin Street Dodger U .30 .50
121 Axebane Beast C .25 .40
122 Biogenic Ooze M 12.00 20.00
123 Biogenic Upgrade U .30 .50
124 End-Raze Forerunners R 1.25 2.00
125 Enraged Ceratok U .30 .50
126 Gatebreaker Ram U 3.00 5.00
127 Gift of Strength C .25 .40
128 Growth-Chamber Guardian R 4.00 6.00
129 Gruul Beastmaster U .30 .50
130 Guardian Project R 3.00 5.00
131 Incubation Druid R 4.00 6.00
132 Mammoth Spider C .25 .40
133 Open the Gates C .25 .40
134 Rampage of the Clans R 1.25 2.00
135 Rampaging Rendhorn C .25 .40
136 Regenesis U .30 .50
137 Root Snare C .25 .40
138 Sagittars' Volley C .25 .40
139 Saruli Caretaker C .25 .40
140 Sauroform Hybrid C .25 .40
141 Silhana Wayfinder U .30 .50
142 Steeple Creeper C .25 .40
143 Stony Strength C .25 .40
144 Sylvan Brushstrider C .25 .40
145 Territorial Boar C .25 .40
146 Titanic Brawl C .25 .40
147 Tower Defense U .30 .50
148 Trollbred Guardian U .30 .50
149 Wilderness Reclamation U 8.00 12.00
150 Wrecking Beast C .25 .40
151 Absorb R 3.00 5.00
152 Aeromunculus C .25 .40
153 Applied Biomancy C .25 .40
154 Azorius Knight-Arbiter C .25 .40
155 Azorius Skyguard U .30 .50
156 Basilica Bell-Haunt U 6.00 10.00
157 Bedevil R 6.00 10.00
158 Biomancer's Familiar R 1.25 2.00
159 Bolrac-Clan Crusher U .30 .50
160 Captive Audience M 5.00 8.00
161 Cindervines R 4.00 6.00
162 Clan Guildmage U .30 .50
163 Combine Guildmage U .30 .50
164 Cult Guildmage U .30 .50
165 Deputy of Detention R 5.00 8.00
166 Domri, Chaos Bringer M 12.00 20.00
167 Dovin, Grand Arbiter M 12.00 20.00
168 Dovin's Acuity U .30 .50
169 Emergency Powers M 3.00 5.00
170 Ethereal Absolution R 1.50 2.50
171 Final Payment C .25 .40
172 Fireblade Artist U .30 .50
173 Frenzied Arynx C .25 .40
174 Frilled Mystic U 2.50 4.00
175 Galloping Lizrog U .30 .50
176 Get the Point C .25 .40
177 Grasping Thrull C .25 .40
178 Growth Spiral C 4.00 6.00
179 Gruul Spellbreaker R 3.00 5.00
180 Gyre Engineer U .30 .50
181 Hackrobat U .30 .50
182 High Alert U 1.00 1.50
183 Hydroid Krasis M 45.00 55.00
184 Imperious Oligarch C .25 .40
185 Judith, the Scourge Diva R 8.00 12.00
186 Kaya, Orzhov Usurper M 12.00 20.00
187 Kaya's Wrath R 5.00 8.00
188 Knight of the Last Breath U .30 .50
189 Lavinia, Azorius Renegade R 3.00 5.00
190 Lawmage's Binding C .25 .40
191 Macabre Mockery U .30 .50
192 Mortify U 1.25 2.00
193 Nikya of the Old Ways R 2.50 4.00
194 Pitiless Pontiff U .30 .50
195 Prime Speaker Vannifar M 35.00 50.00
196 Rafter Demon C .25 .40
197 Rakdos Firewheeler U .30 .50
198 Rakdos Roustabout C .25 .40
199 Rakdos, the Showstopper M 8.00 12.00
200 Ravager Wurm M 2.50 4.00
201 Rhythm of the Wild U 8.00 12.00
202 Rubblebelt Runner C .25 .40
203 Savage Smash C .25 .40
204 Senate Guildmage U .30 .50
205 Seraph of the Scales M 10.00 15.00
206 Sharktocrab U .30 .50
207 Simic Ascendancy R 1.25 2.00
208 Sphinx of New Prahv U .30 .50
209 Sphinx's Insight C .25 .40
210 Sunder Shaman U .30 .50
211 Syndicate Guildmage U .30 .50
212 Teysa Karlov R 10.00 15.00
213 Theater of Horrors R 1.25 2.00
214 Zegana, Utopian Speaker R 1.25 2.00
215 Zhur-Taa Goblin U .30 .50
216 Footlight Fiend C .25 .40
217 Rubble Slinger C .25 .40
218 Scuttlegator C .25 .40
219 Senate Griffin C .25 .40
220 Vizkopa Vampire C .25 .40
221 Bedeck//Bedazzle R 1.25 2.00
222 Carnival//Carnage U .30 .50
223 Collision//Colossus U .30 .50
224 Consecrate//Consume U .30 .50
225 Depose//Deploy U .30 .50
226 Incubation//Incongruity U 1.50 2.50
227 Repudiate//Replicate R 1.25 2.00
228 Revival//Revenge R 2.50 4.00
229 Thrash//Threat R 1.25 2.00
230 Warrant//Warden R 1.25 2.00
231 Azorius Locket C .25 .40
232 Gate Colossus U .30 .50
233 Glass of the Guildpact R 1.25 2.00
234 Gruul Locket C .25 .40
235 Junktroller U .30 .40
236 Orzhov Locket C .25 .40

237 Rakdos Locket C .25 .40
238 Scrabbling Claws U .30 .50
239 Screaming Shield U .30 .50
240 Simic Locket C .25 .40
241 Sphinx of the Guildpact U .30 .50
242 Tome of the Guildpact R 1.25 2.00
243 Azorius Guildgate C .25 .40
244 Azorius Guildgate C .25 .40
245 Blood Crypt R 15.00 25.00
246 Breeding Pool R 15.00 25.00
247 Gateway Plaza C .25 .40
248 Godless Shrine R 15.00 25.00
249 Gruul Guildgate C .25 .40
250 Gruul Guildgate C .25 .40
251 Hallowed Fountain R 15.00 25.00
252 Orzhov Guildgate C .25 .40
253 Orzhov Guildgate C .25 .40
254 Plaza of Harmony R 4.00 6.00
255 Rakdos Guildgate C .25 .40
256 Rakdos Guildgate C .25 .40
257 Simic Guildgate C .25 .40
258 Simic Guildgate C .25 .40
259 Stomping Ground R 15.00 25.00
260 Plains C .25 .40
261 Island C .25 .40
262 Swamp C .25 .40
263 Mountain C .25 .40
264 Forest C .25 .40
265 Dovin, Architect of Law M 4.00 6.00
266 Elite Arrester C .25 .40
267 Dovin's Dismissal R 2.50 4.00
268 Dovin's Automaton U .30 .50
269 Domri, City Smasher M 4.00 6.00
270 Ragefire C .25 .40
271 Charging War Boar U .30 .50
272 Domri's Nodorog R 2.50 4.00
273 The Haunt of Hightower M

2019 Magic The Gathering Ravnica Allegiance Mythic Edition

RA1 Karn, Scion of Urza 50.00 70.00
RA2 Tamiyo, the Moon Sage 60.00 80.00
RA3 Sorin Markov 35.00 50.00
RA4 Jaya Ballard 12.00 20.00
RA5 Ajani, Mentor of Heroes 25.00 35.00
RA6 Dack Fayden 40.00 50.00
RA7 Domri, Chaos Bringer 30.00 40.00
RA8 Kaya, Orzhov Usurper 25.00 35.00

2019 Magic The Gathering Ravnica Allegiance Tokens

1 Human .06 .10
2 Illusion .06 .10
3 Zombie .06 .10
4 Goblin .10 .15
5 Centaur .06 .10
6 Frog Lizard .06 .10
7 Ooze .06 .10
8 Beast .06 .10
9 Sphinx .06 .10
10 Spirit .06 .10
11 Thopter .10 .15
12 Treasure .15 .25
13 Domri, Chaos Bringer Emblem .06 .10

2019 Magic The Gathering War of the Spark

COMPLETE SET (294) 200.00 300.00
BOOSTER BOX
BOOSTER PACK (16 CARDS)
RELEASED ON MAY 3, 2019
1 Karn, the Great Creator R 10.00 15.00
2 Ugin, the Ineffable R 4.00 6.00
3 Ugin's Conjurant U .20 .30
4 Ajani's Pridemate U .20 .30
5 Battlefield Promotion C .15 .25
6 Bond of Discipline U .20 .30
7 Bulwark Giant C .15 .25
8 Charmed Stray C .15 .25
9 Defiant Strike C .15 .25
10 Divine Arrow C .15 .25
11 Enforcer Griffin C .15 .25
12 Finale of Glory M 2.50
13 Gideon Blackblade M 10.00 15.00
14 Gideon's Sacrifice C .15 .25
15 Gideon's Triumph U .20 .30
16 God-Eternal Oketra M 10.00 15.00
17 Grateful Apparition U .20 .30
18 Ignite the Beacon R .30 .50
19 Ironclad Krovod C .15 .25
20 Law-Rune Enforcer C .15 .25
21 Loxodon Sergeant C .15 .25
22 Makeshift Battalion C .15 .25
23 Martyr for the Cause C .15 .25
24 Parhelion II R .30 .50
25 Pouncing Lynx C .15 .25
26 Prison Realm U .20 .30
27 Rally of Wings U .20 .30
28 Ravnica at War R .30 .50
29 Rising Populace C .15 .25
30 Single Combat R .30 .50
31 Sunblade Angel U .20 .30
32 Teyo, the Shieldmage U .20 .30
33 Teyo's Lightshield C .15 .25
34 Tomik, Distinguished Advokist R .30 .50
35 Topple the Statue C .15 .25
36 Trusted Pegasus C .15 .25
37 The Wanderer U .25 .40
38 Wanderer's Strike C .15 .25
39 War Screecher C .15 .25
40 Ashiok's Skulker C .15 .25
41 Augur of Bolas U .20 .30
42 Aven Eternal C .15 .25
43 Bond of Insight U .20 .30
44 Callous Dismissal C .15 .25
45 Commence the Endgame R .30 .50
46 Contentious Plan C .15 .25
47 Crush Dissent C .15 .25
48 Erratic Visionary C .15 .25
49 Eternal Skylord U .20 .30
50 Fblthp, the Lost R .50 .75
51 Finale of Revelation M 2.50 4.00
52 Flux Channeler U .20 .30
53 God-Eternal Kefnet M 10.00 15.00
54 Jace, Wielder of Mysteries R 1.25 2.00
55 Jace's Triumph U .20 .30
56 Kasmina, Enigmatic Mentor U .20 .30
57 Kasmina's Transmutation C .15 .25
58 Kiora's Dambreaker C .15 .25
59 Lazotep Plating U .20 .30
60 Naga Eternal C .15 .25
61 Narset, Parter of Veils U 3.00 5.00
62 Narset's Reversal R 2.00 3.00
63 No Escape C .15 .25
64 Relentless Advance C .15 .25
65 Rescuer Sphinx U .20 .30
66 Silent Submersible R .30 .50
67 Sky Theater Strix C .15 .25
68 Spark Double R 1.25 2.00
69 Spellkeeper Weird C .15 .25
70 Stealth Mission C .15 .25
71 Tamiyo's Epiphany C .15 .25
72 Teferi's Time Twist C .15 .25
73 Thunder Drake C .15 .25
74 Totally Lost C .15 .25
75 Wall of Runes C .15 .25
76 Aid the Fallen C .15 .25
77 Banehound C .15 .25
78 Bleeding Edge U .20 .30
79 Bolas's Citadel R 1.50 1.75
80 Bond of Revival U .20 .30
81 Charity Extractor C .15 .25
82 Command the Dreadhorde R 1.00 1.50
83 Davriel, Rogue Shadowmage U .25 .40
84 Davriel's Shadowfugue C .15 .25
85 Deliver Unto Evil R .30 .50
86 Dreadhorde Invasion R 2.50 4.00
87 Dreadmalkin U .20 .30
88 Duskmantle Operative C .15 .25
89 The Elderspell R 2.50 4.00
90 Eternal Taskmaster U .20 .30
91 Finale of Eternity M 1.50 2.50
92 God-Eternal Bontu M 4.00 6.00
93 Herald of the Dreadhorde C .15 .25
94 Kaya's Ghostform C .15 .25
95 Lazotep Behemoth C .15 .25
96 Lazotep Reaver C .15 .25
97 Liliana, Dreadhorde General M 15.00 25.00
98 Liliana's Triumph U .20 .30
99 Massacre Girl R .50 .75
100 Ob Nixilis, the Hate-Twisted U .20 .30
101 Ob Nixilis's Cruelty C .15 .25
102 Price of Betrayal U .20 .30
103 Shriekdiver C .15 .25
104 Sorin's Thirst C .15 .25
105 Spark Harvest C .15 .25
106 Spark Reaper C .15 .25
107 Tithebearer Giant C .15 .25
108 Toll of the Invasion C .15 .25
109 Unlikely Aid C .15 .25
110 Vampire Opportunist C .15 .25
111 Vizier of the Scorpion U .20 .30
112 Vraska's Finisher C .15 .25
113 Ahn-Crop Invader C .15 .25
114 Blindblast C .15 .25
115 Bolt Bend U .20 .30
116 Bond of Passion U .20 .30
117 Burning Prophet C .15 .25
118 Chainwhip Cyclops C .15 .25
119 Chandra, Fire Artisan R 4.00 6.00
120 Chandra's Pyrohelix C .15 .25
121 Chandra's Triumph U .20 .30
122 Cyclops Electromancer U .20 .30
123 Demolish C .15 .25
124 Devouring Hellion U .20 .30
125 Dreadhorde Arcanist R 2.50 4.00
126 Dreadhorde Twins U .20 .30
127 Finale of Promise M 5.00 8.00
128 Goblin Assailant C .15 .25
129 Goblin Assault Team C .15 .25
130 Grim Initiate C .15 .25
131 Heartfire C .15 .25
132 Honor the God-Pharaoh C .15 .25
133 Ilharg, the Raze-Boar M 5.00 8.00
134 Invading Manticore C .15 .25
135 Jaya, Venerated Firemage U .20 .30
136 Jaya's Greeting C .15 .25
137 Krenko, Tin Street Kingpin R 1.00 1.50
138 Mizzium Tank R .30 .50
139 Nahiri's Stoneblades C .15 .25
140 Neheb, Dreadhorde Champion R .30 .50
141 Raging Kronch C .15 .25
142 Samut's Sprint C .15 .25
143 Sarkhan the Masterless R 2.50 4.00
144 Sarkhan's Catharsis C .15 .25
145 Spellgorger Weird C .15 .25
146 Tibalt, Rakish Instigator U .20 .30
147 Tibalt's Rager U .20 .30
148 Turret Ogre C .15 .25
149 Arboreal Grazer C .15 .25
150 Arlinn, Voice of the Pack U .20 .30
151 Arlinn's Wolf C .15 .25
152 Awakening of Vitu-Ghazi R .30 .50
153 Band Together C .15 .25
154 Bloom Hulk C .15 .25
155 Bond of Flourishing U .20 .30
156 Centaur Nurturer C .15 .25
157 Challenger Troll U .20 .30
158 Courage in Crisis C .15 .25
159 Evolution Sage U .50 .75
160 Finale of Devastation M 6.00 10.00
161 Forced Landing C .15 .25
162 Giant Growth C .15 .25
163 God-Eternal Rhonas M 4.00 6.00
164 Jiang Yanggu, Wildcrafter U .20 .30
165 Kraul Stinger C .15 .25
166 Kronch Wrangler C .15 .25
167 Mowu, Loyal Companion U .20 .30
168 New Horizons C .15 .25
169 Nissa, Who Shakes the World R 3.00 5.00
170 Nissa's Triumph U .20 .30
171 Paradise Druid U .20 .30
172 Planewide Celebration R .30 .50
173 Pollenbright Druid C .15 .25
174 Primordial Wurm C .15 .25
175 Return of Nature C .15 .25
176 Snarespinner C .15 .25
177 Steady Aim C .15 .25
178 Storm the Citadel U .20 .30
179 Thundering Ceratok C .15 .25
180 Vivien, Champion of the Wilds R 2.00 3.00
181 Vivien's Arkbow R .90 1.25
182 Vivien's Grizzly C .15 .25
183 Wardscale Crocodile C .15 .25
184 Ajani, the Greathearted R 1.00 1.50
185 Angrath's Rampage U .20 .30
186 Bioessence Hydra R .50 .75
187 Casualties of War R .40 .60
188 Cruel Celebrant U .20 .30
189 Deathsprout U .20 .30
190 Despark U .30 .50
191 Domri, Anarch of Bolas R 1.00 1.50
192 Domri's Ambush U .20 .30
193 Dovin's Veto U .90 1.25
194 Dreadhorde Butcher R .90 1.25
195 Elite Guardmage U .20 .30
196 Enter the God-Eternals R 1.25 2.00
197 Feather, the Redeemed R 1.25 2.00
198 Gleaming Overseer U .20 .30
199 Heartwarming Redemption U .20 .30
200 Huatli's Raptor U .20 .30
201 Invade the City U .20 .30
202 Leyline Prowler U .20 .30
203 Living Twister R .30 .50
204 Mayhem Devil U .20 .30
205 Merfolk Skydiver U .20 .30
206 Neoform U .30 .50
207 Nicol Bolas, Dragon-God M 15.00 25.00
208 Niv-Mizzet Reborn M 2.50 4.00
209 Oath of Kaya R .30 .50
210 Pledge of Unity U .20 .30
211 Ral, Storm Conduit R .30 .50
212 Ral's Outburst U 1.25 2.00
213 Roalesk, Apex Hybrid M 2.00 3.00
214 Role Reversal R .30 .50
215 Rubblebelt Rioters U .20 .30
216 Solar Blaze R .30 .50
217 Sorin, Vengeful Bloodlord R 2.00 3.00
218 Soul Diviner R .30 .50
219 Storrev, Devkarin Lich R .30 .50
220 Tamiyo, Collector of Tales R 2.00 3.00
221 Teferi, Time Raveler R 12.00 20.00
222 Tenth District Legionnaire U .20 .30
223 Time Wipe R .50 .75
224 Tolsimir, Friend to Wolves R .30 .50
225 Tyrant's Scorn U .20 .30
226 Widespread Brutality R .30 .50
227 Angrath, Captain of Chaos U .20 .30
228 Ashiok, Dream Render U .75 1.00
229 Dovin, Hand of Control U .20 .30
230 Huatli, the Sun's Heart U .20 .30
231 Kaya, Bane of the Dead U .20 .30
232 Kiora, Behemoth Beckoner U .20 .30
233 Nahiri, Storm of Stone U .20 .30
234 Saheeli, Sublime Artificer U .90 1.25
235 Samut, Tyrant Smasher U .20 .30
236 Vraska, Swarm's Eminence U .20 .30
237 Firemind Vessel U .20 .30
238 God-Pharaoh's Statue U .20 .30
239 Guild Globe C .15 .25
240 Iron Bully C .15 .25
241 Mana Geode C .15 .25
242 Prismite C .15 .25
243 Saheeli's Silverwing C .15 .25
244 Blast Zone L R 4.00 6.00
245 Emergence Zone L U .20 .30
246 Gateway Plaza L C .15 .25
247 Interplanar Beacon L U .20 .30
248 Karn's Bastion L R 2.50 4.00
249 Mobilized District L R .50 .75
250 Plains L .15 .25
251 Plains L .15 .25
252 Plains L .15 .25
253 Island L .15 .25
254 Island L .15 .25
255 Island L .15 .25
256 Swamp L .15 .25
257 Swamp L .15 .25
258 Swamp L .15 .25
259 Mountain L .15 .25
260 Mountain L .15 .25
261 Mountain L .15 .25
262 Forest L .15 .25
263 Forest L .15 .25
264 Forest L .15 .25
265 Gideon, the Oathsworn M 3.00 5.00
266 Desperate Lunge C .15 .25
267 Gideon's Battle Cry R .30 .50
268 Gideon's Company U .35 .60
269 Orzhov Guildgate C .15 .25
270 Jane, Arcane Strategist M 3.00 5.00
271 Guildpact Informant C .25 .40
272 Jace's Projection U .20 .30
273 Jace's Ruse R .30 .50
274 Simic Guildgate C .15 .25
275 Tezzeret, Master of the Bridge M 8.00 12.00

2019 Magic The Gathering War of the Spark Foil

1 Karn, the Great Creator R 8.00 12.00
2 Ugin, the Ineffable R 3.00 5.00
3 Ugin's Conjurant U .30 .50
4 Ajani's Pridemate U .30 .50
5 Battlefield Promotion C .25 .40
6 Bond of Discipline U .30 .50
7 Bulwark Giant C .25 .40
8 Charmed Stray C .25 .40
9 Defiant Strike C .25 .40
10 Divine Arrow C .25 .40
11 Enforcer Griffin C .25 .40
12 Finale of Glory M 4.00 6.00
13 Gideon Blackblade M 15.00 20.00
14 Gideon's Sacrifice C .25 .40
15 Gideon's Triumph U .30 .50
16 God-Eternal Oketra M 4.00 6.00
17 Grateful Apparition U .30 .50
18 Ignite the Beacon R 1.25 2.00
19 Ironclad Krovod C .25 .40
20 Law-Rune Enforcer C .25 .40
21 Loxodon Sergeant C .25 .40
22 Makeshift Battalion C .25 .40
23 Martyr for the Cause C .25 .40
24 Parhelion II R 1.25 2.00
25 Pouncing Lynx C .25 .40
26 Prison Realm U .30 .50
27 Rally of Wings U .30 .50
28 Ravnica at War R 1.25 2.00
29 Rising Populace C .25 .40
30 Single Combat R 1.25 2.00
31 Sunblade Angel U .30 .50
32 Teyo, the Shieldmage U .30 .50
33 Teyo's Lightshield C .25 .40
34 Tomik, Distinguished Advokist R 1.25 2.00
35 Topple the Statue C .25 .40
36 Trusted Pegasus C .25 .40
37 The Wanderer U .30 .50
38 Wanderer's Strike C .25 .40
39 War Screecher C .25 .40
40 Ashiok's Skulker C .25 .40
41 Augur of Bolas U .30 .50
42 Aven Eternal C .25 .40
43 Bond of Insight U .30 .50
44 Callous Dismissal C .25 .40
45 Commence the Endgame R 1.25 2.00
46 Contentious Plan C .25 .40
47 Crush Dissent C .25 .40
48 Erratic Visionary C .25 .40
49 Eternal Skylord U .30 .50
50 Fblthp, the Lost R 1.25 2.00
51 Finale of Revelation M 5.00 8.00
52 Flux Channeler U .30 .50
53 God-Eternal Kefnet M 6.00 10.00
54 Jace, Wielder of Mysteries R 1.25 2.00
55 Jace's Triumph U .30 .50
56 Kasmina, Enigmatic Mentor U .30 .50
57 Kasmina's Transmutation C .25 .40
58 Kiora's Dambreaker C .25 .40
59 Lazotep Plating U .30 .50
60 Naga Eternal C .25 .40
61 Narset, Parter of Veils U .30 .50
62 Narset's Reversal R 1.25 2.00
63 No Escape C .25 .40
64 Relentless Advance C .25 .40
65 Rescuer Sphinx U .30 .50
66 Silent Submersible R 1.25 2.00
67 Sky Theater Strix C .25 .40
68 Spark Double R 1.25 2.00
69 Spellkeeper Weird C .25 .40
70 Stealth Mission C .25 .40
71 Tamiyo's Epiphany C .25 .40
72 Teferi's Time Twist C .25 .40
73 Thunder Drake C .25 .40
74 Totally Lost C .25 .40
75 Wall of Runes C .25 .40
76 Aid the Fallen C .25 .40
77 Banehound C .25 .40
78 Bleeding Edge U .30 .50
79 Bolas's Citadel R 1.50 2.50
80 Bond of Revival U .30 .50
81 Charity Extractor C .25 .40
82 Command the Dreadhorde R 1.25 2.00
83 Davriel, Rogue Shadowmage U .30 .50
84 Davriel's Shadowfugue C .25 .40
85 Deliver Unto Evil R 1.25 2.00
86 Dreadhorde Invasion R 1.25 2.00
87 Dreadmalkin U .30 .50
88 Duskmantle Operative C .25 .40
89 The Elderspell R 2.50 4.00
90 Eternal Taskmaster U .30 .50
91 Finale of Eternity M 4.00 6.00
92 God-Eternal Bontu M 4.00 6.00
93 Herald of the Dreadhorde C .25 .40
94 Kaya's Ghostform C .25 .40
95 Lazotep Behemoth C .25 .40
96 Lazotep Reaver C .25 .40
97 Liliana, Dreadhorde General M 10.00 15.00
98 Liliana's Triumph U .30 .50
99 Massacre Girl R 1.25 2.00
100 Ob Nixilis, the Hate-Twisted U .30 .50
101 Ob Nixilis's Cruelty C .25 .40
102 Price of Betrayal U .30 .50
103 Shriekdiver C .25 .40
104 Sorin's Thirst C .25 .40
105 Spark Harvest C .25 .40
106 Spark Reaper C .25 .40
107 Tithebearer Giant C .25 .40
108 Toll of the Invasion C .25 .40
109 Unlikely Aid C .25 .40
110 Vampire Opportunist C .25 .40
111 Vizier of the Scorpion U .30 .50
112 Vraska's Finisher C .25 .40
113 Ahn-Crop Invader C .25 .40
114 Blindblast C .25 .40
115 Bolt Bend U .30 .50
116 Bond of Passion U .30 .50
117 Burning Prophet C .25 .40
118 Chainwhip Cyclops C .25 .40
119 Chandra, Fire Artisan R 1.25 2.00
120 Chandra's Pyrohelix C .25 .40
121 Chandra's Triumph U .30 .50
122 Cyclops Electromancer U .30 .50
123 Demolish C .25 .40
124 Devouring Hellion U .30 .50
125 Dreadhorde Arcanist R 8.00 12.00
126 Dreadhorde Twins U .30 .50
127 Finale of Promise M 15.00 20.00
128 Goblin Assailant C .25 .40
129 Goblin Assault Team C .25 .40
130 Grim Initiate C .25 .40

131 Heartfire C .25 .40
132 Honor the God-Pharaoh C .25 .40
133 Ilharg, the Raze-Boar M 4.00 6.00
134 Invading Manticore C .25 .40
135 Jaya, Venerated Firemage U .30 .50
136 Jaya's Greeting C .25 .40
137 Krenko, Tin Street Kingpin R 1.25 2.00
138 Mizzium Tank R 1.25 2.00
139 Nahiri's Stoneblades C .25 .40
140 Neheb, Dreadhorde Champion R 1.25 2.00
141 Raging Kronch C .25 .40
142 Samut's Sprint C .25 .40
143 Sarkhan the Masterless R 1.25 2.00
144 Sarkhan's Catharsis C .25 .40
145 Spellgorger Weird C .25 .40
146 Tibalt, Rakish Instigator U .30 .50
147 Tibalt's Rager U .30 .50
148 Turret Ogre C .25 .40
149 Arboreal Grazer C .25 .40
150 Arlinn, Voice of the Pack U .30 .50
151 Arlinn's Wolf C .25 .40
152 Awakening of Vitu-Ghazi R 1.25 2.00
153 Band Together C .25 .40
154 Bloom Hulk C .25 .40
155 Bond of Flourishing U .30 .50
156 Centaur Nurturer C .25 .40
157 Challenger Troll U .30 .50
158 Courage in Crisis C .25 .40
159 Evolution Sage U .30 .50
160 Finale of Devastation M 20.00 25.00
161 Forced Landing C .25 .40
162 Giant Growth C .25 .40
163 God-Eternal Rhonas M 3.00 5.00
164 Jiang Yanggu, Wildcrafter U .30 .50
165 Kraul Stinger C .25 .40
166 Kronch Wrangler C .25 .40
167 Mowu, Loyal Companion U .30 .50
168 New Horizons C .25 .40
169 Nissa, Who Shakes the World R 3.00 8.00
170 Nissa's Triump U .30 .50
171 Paradise Druid U .30 .50
172 Planewide Celebration R 1.25 2.00
173 Pollenbright Druid C .25 .40
174 Primordial Wurm C .25 .40
175 Return of Nature C .25 .40
176 Snarespinner C .25 .40
177 Steady Aim C .25 .40
178 Storm the Citadel U .30 .50
179 Thundering Ceratok C .25 .40
180 Vivien, Champion of the Wilds R 1.25 2.00
181 Vivien's Arkbow R 1.25 2.00
182 Vivien's Grizzly C .25 .40
183 Wardscale Crocodile C .25 .40
184 Ajani, the Greathearted R 1.25 2.00
185 Angrath's Rampage U .30 .50
186 Bioessence Hydra R 1.25 2.00
187 Casualties of War R 1.25 2.00
188 Cruel Celebrant U .30 .50
189 Deathsprout U .30 .50
190 Despark U .30 .50
191 Domri, Anarch of Bolas R 1.25 2.00
192 Domri's Ambush U .30 .50
193 Dovin's Veto U .30 .50
194 Dreadhorde Butcher R 1.25 2.00
195 Elite Guardmage U .30 .50
196 Enter the God-Eternals R 1.25 2.00
197 Feather, the Redeemed R 1.25 2.00
198 Gleaming Overseer U .30 .50
199 Heartwarming Redemption U .30 .50
200 Huatli's Raptor U .30 .50
201 Invade the City U .30 .50
202 Leyline Prowler U .30 .50
203 Living Twister R 1.25 2.00
204 Mayhem Devil U .30 .50
205 Merfolk Skydiver U .30 .50
206 Neoform U .30 .50
207 Nicol Bolas, Dragon-God M 8.00 12.00
208 Niv-Mizzet Reborn M 2.50 4.00
209 Oath of Kaya R 1.25 2.00
210 Pledge of Unity U .30 .50
211 Ral, Storm Conduit R 1.25 2.00
212 Ral's Outburst U .30 .50
213 Roalesk, Apex Hybrid M 2.50 4.00
214 Role Reversal R 1.25 2.00
215 Rubblebelt Rioters U .30 .50
216 Solar Blaze R 1.25 2.00
217 Sorin, Vengeful Bloodlord R 1.25 2.00
218 Soul Diviner R 1.25 2.00
219 Storrev, Devkarin Lich R 1.25 2.00
220 Tamiyo, Collector of Tales R 1.25 2.00
221 Teferi, Time Raveler R 10.00 15.00
222 Tenth District Legionnaire U .30 .50
223 Time Wipe R 1.25 2.00
224 Tolsimir, Friend to Wolves R 1.25 2.00
225 Tyrant's Scorn U .30 .50
226 Widespread Brutality R 1.25 2.00
227 Angrath, Captain of Chaos U .30 .50
228 Ashiok, Dream Render U .30 .50
229 Dovin, Hand of Control U .30 .50
230 Huatli, the Sun's Heart U .30 .50
231 Kaya, Bane of the Dead U .30 .50
232 Kiora, Behemoth Beckoner U .30 .50
233 Nahiri, Storm of Stone U .30 .50
234 Saheeli, Sublime Artificer U .30 .50
235 Samut, Tyrant Smasher U .30 .50
236 Vraska, Swarm's Eminence U .30 .50
237 Firemind Vessel U .30 .50
238 God-Pharaoh's Statue U .30 .50
239 Guild Globe C .25 .40
240 Iron Bully C .25 .40
241 Mana Geode C .25 .40
242 Prismite C .25 .40
243 Saheeli's Silverwing C .25 .40
244 Blast Zone L R 2.50 4.00
245 Emergence Zone L U .30 .50
246 Gateway Plaza L C .25 .40
247 Interplanar Beacon L U .30 .50
248 Karn's Bastion L R 1.25 2.00
249 Mobilized District L R 1.25 2.00
250 Plains L .25 .40
251 Plains L .25 .40
252 Plains L .25 .40
253 Island L .25 .40
254 Island L .25 .40
255 Island L .25 .40
256 Swamp L .25 .40
257 Swamp L .25 .40
258 Swamp L .25 .40
259 Mountain L .25 .40
260 Mountain L .25 .40
261 Mountain L .25 .40
262 Forest L .25 .40
263 Forest L .25 .40
264 Forest L .25 .40
265 Gideon, the Oathsworn M 4.00 6.00
266 Desperate Lunge C .25 .40
267 Gideon's Battle Cry R 1.25 2.00
268 Gideon's Company U .30 .50
269 Orzhov Guildgate C .25 .40
270 Jane, Arcane Strategist M 4.00 6.00
271 Guildpact Informant C .25 .40
272 Jace's Projection U .30 .50
273 Jace's Ruse R 1.25 2.00
274 Simic Guildgate C .25 .40
275 Tezzeret, Master of the Bridge M

2019 Magic The Gathering War of the Spark Mythic Edition

COMPLETE SET (8)
WS1 Ugin, the Spirit Dragon 175.00 225.00
WS2 Gideon Blackblade 40.00 60.00
WS3 Jace, the Mind Sculptor 275.00 350.00
WS4 Tezzeret the Seeker 50.00 75.00
WS5 Garruk, Apex Predator 30.00 50.00
WS6 Nicol Bolas, Dragon-God 90.00 120.00
WS7 Nahiri, the Harbinger 35.00 50.00
WS8 Sarkhan Unbroken 20.00 30.00

2019 Magic The Gathering War of the Spark Tokens

1 Spirit .10 .15
2 Angel .15 .25
3 Soldier .10 .15
4 Wall .06 .10
5 Wizard .06 .10
6 Assassin .06 .10
7 Zombie .15 .25
8 Zombie Army .06 .10
9 Zombie Army .06 .10
10 Zombie Army .06 .10
11 Zombie Warrior .60 1.00
12 Devil .06 .10
13 Dragon .10 .15
14 Goblin .10 .15
15 Wolf .06 .10
16 Citizen .06 .10
17 Voja, Friend to Elves .10 .15
18 Servo .10 .15
19 Nissa, Who Shakes the World Emblem .15 .25

Starter Sets

1997 Magic The Gathering Portal

COMPLETE SET (222) 215.00 285.00
BOOSTER BOX (36 PACKS) 400.00 550.00
BOOSTER PACK (15 CARDS) 15.00 20.00
RELEASED ON JUNE 1, 1997
1 Alabaster Dragon R :W: 1.50 2.00
2 Alluring Scent R :G: .50 .80
3 Anaconda v1 C :G: .20 .35
4 Anaconda v2 U :G: .20 .35
5 Ancestral Memories R :B: .30 .50
6 Angelic Blessing C :W: .20 .35
7 Archangel R :W: 1.00 1.50
8 Ardent Militia U :W: .20 .35
9 Armageddon R :W: 3.00 5.00
10 Armored Pegasus C :W: .20 .35
11 Arrogant Vampire U :K: .20 .35
12 Assassin's Blade U :K: .20 .35
13 Balance of Power R :B: .20 .35
14 Baleful Stare U :B: .50 .80
15 Bee Sting U :G: .20 .35
16 Blaze v1 C :R: .20 .35
17 Blaze v2 U :R: .20 .35
18 Blessed Reversal R :W: .40 .60
19 Blinding Light R :W: .40 .60
20 Bog Imp C :K: .20 .35
21 Bog Raiders C :K: .20 .35
22 Bog Wraith U :K: .20 .35
23 Boiling Seas U :K: .20 .35
24 Border Guard C :W: .20 .35
25 Breath of Life C :W: .20 .35
26 Bull Hippo U :G: .20 .35
27 Burning Cloak C :R: .20 .35
28 Capricious Sorcerer R :B: .50 .80
29 Charging Bandits U :K: .20 .35
30 Charging Paladin U :W: .20 .35
31 Charging Rhino R :G: .20 .35
32 Cloak of Feathers C :B: .20 .35
33 Cloud Dragon R :B: 2.00 3.00
34 Cloud Pirates C :B: 2.00 3.00
35 Cloud Spirit U :B: .20 .35
36 Command of Unsummoning U :B: .20 .35
37 Coral Eel C :B: .20 .35
38 Craven Giant C :R: .20 .35
39 Craven Knight C :K: .20 .35
40 Cruel Bargain R :K: 6.00 8.00
41 Cruel Fate R :B: .20 .35
42 Cruel Tutor R :K: 25.00 30.00
43 Deep Wood U :G: .20 .35
44 Deep-Sea Serpent U :B: .20 .35
45 Defiant Stand U :W: .20 .35
46 Deja Vu C :B: .20 .35
47 Desert Drake U :R: .20 .35
48 Devastation R :R: 15.00 18.00
49 Devoted Hero C :W: .20 .35
50 Djinn of the Lamp R :B: .40 .60
51 Dread Charge R :K: .40 .60
52 Dread Reaper R :K: .40 .60
53 Dry Spell U :K: .20 .35
54 Earthquake R :R: .75 1.25
55 Ebon Dragon R :K: 2.50 3.50
56 Elite Cat Warrior v1 C :G: .20 .35
57 Elite Cat Warrior v2 C :G: .20 .35
58 Elven Cache C :G: .20 .35
59 Elvish Ranger C :G: .20 .35
60 Endless Cockroaches R :K: 1.50 2.00
61 Exhaustion R :B: .75 1.25
62 False Peace C :W: .20 .35
63 Feral Shadow C :K: .20 .35
64 Final Strike R :K: .50 .80
65 Fire Dragon R :R: 3.00 4.00
66 Fire Imp U :R: .20 .35
67 Fire Snake C :R: .20 .35
68 Fire Tempest R :R: .50 .80
69 Flashfires U :R: .20 .35
70 Fleet-Footed Monk C :W: .20 .35
71 Flux U :B: .20 .35
72 Foot Soldiers C :W: .20 .35
73 Forest A C :L: .20 .35
74 Forest B C :L: .20 .35
75 Forest C C :L: .20 .35
76 Forest D C :L: .20 .35
77 Forked Lightning R :R: .50 .80
78 Fruition C :G: .20 .35
79 Giant Octopus C :B: .20 .35
80 Giant Spider C :G: .20 .35
81 Gift of Estates R :W: 2.00 3.00
82 Goblin Bully C :R: .20 .35
83 Gorilla Warrior C :G: .20 .35
84 Gravedigger U :K: .20 .35
85 Grizzly Bears C :G: .20 .35
86 Hand of Death v1 C :K: .20 .35
87 Hand of Death v2 C :K: .20 .35
88 Harsh Justice R :W: 1.00 2.00
89 Highland Giant C :R: .20 .35
90 Hill Giant C :R: .20 .35
91 Horned Turtle C :B: .20 .35
92 Howling Fury C :K: .20 .35
93 Hulking Cyclops U :R: .20 .35
94 Hulking Goblin C :R: .20 .35
95 Hurricane R :G: .40 .60
96 Ingenious Thief U :B: .20 .35
97 Island A C :L: .40 .60
98 Island B C :L: .40 .60
99 Island C C :L: .40 .60
100 Island D C :L: .40 .60
101 Jungle Lion C :G: .50 .80
102 Keen-Eyed Archers C :W: .20 .35
103 King's Assassin R :K: 2.00 3.00
104 Knight Errant C :W: .20 .35
105 Last Chance R :R: 2.50 3.50
106 Lava Axe C :R: .20 .35
107 Lava Flow U :R: .20 .35
108 Lizard Warrior C :R: .20 .35
109 Man-o'-War U :B: .20 .35
110 Mercenary Knight R :K: 2.50 3.50
111 Merfolk of the Pearl Trident C :B: .20 .35
112 Mind Knives C :K: .20 .35
113 Mind Rot C :K: .20 .35
114 Minotaur Warrior C :R: .20 .35
115 Mobilize C :G: 2.00 3.00
116 Monstrous Growth v1 C :G: .20 .35
117 Monstrous Growth v2 C :G: .20 .35
118 Moon Sprite U :G: .20 .35
119 Mountain A C :L: .20 .35
120 Mountain B C :L: .20 .35
121 Mountain C C :L: .20 .35
122 Mountain D C :L: .20 .35
123 Mountain Goat U :R: .20 .35
124 Muck Rats C :K: .20 .35
125 Mystic Denial U :B: .20 .35
126 Natural Order R :G: 14.00 16.00
127 Natural Spring U :G: .20 .35
128 Nature's Cloak R :G: .50 .80
129 Nature's Lore C :G: 1.00 1.50
130 Nature's Ruin U :K: 1.00 1.50
131 Needle Storm U :G: .20 .35
132 Noxious Toad U :K: .20 .35
133 Omen C :B: .20 .35
134 Owl Familiar C :B: .20 .35
135 Panther Warriors C :G: .20 .35
136 Path of Peace C :W: .20 .35
137 Personal Tutor U :B: 14.00 16.00
138 Phantom Warrior R :B: .50 .80
139 Pillaging Horde R :R: .50 .80
140 Plains A C :L: .20 .35
141 Plains B C :L: .20 .35
142 Plains C C :L: .20 .35
143 Plains D C :L: .20 .35
144 Plant Elemental U :G: .20 .35
145 Primeval Force R :G: .20 .35
146 Prosperity R :B: .75 1.25
147 Pyroclasm R :R: 2.50 3.50
148 Python C :K: .20 .35
149 Raging Cougar C :R: .20 .35
150 Raging Goblin v1 C :R: .20 .35
151 Raging Goblin v2 C :R: .20 .35
152 Raging Minotaur C :R: .20 .35
153 Rain of Salt U :R: .20 .35
154 Rain of Tears U :K: .20 .35
155 Raise Dead C :K: .20 .35
156 Redwood Treefolk C :G: .20 .35
157 Regal Unicorn C :W: .20 .35
158 Renewing Dawn U :W: .20 .35
159 Rowan Treefolk C :G: .20 .35
160 Sacred Knight C :W: .20 .35
161 Sacred Nectar C :W: .20 .35
162 Scorching Spear C :R: .20 .35
163 Scorching Winds U :R: .20 .35
164 Seasoned Marshal U :W: .20 .35
165 Serpent Assassin R :K: 1.00 1.50
166 Serpent Warrior C :K: .20 .35
167 Skeletal Crocodile C :K: .20 .35
168 Skeletal Snake C :K: .20 .35
169 Snapping Drake C :B: .20 .35
170 Sorcerous Sight C :B: .20 .35
171 Soul Shred C :K: .20 .35
172 Spined Wurm C :G: .20 .35
173 Spiritual Guardian R :W: .50 .80
174 Spitting Earth C :R: .20 .35
175 Spotted Griffin C :W: .20 .35
176 Stalking Tiger C :G: .20 .35
177 Starlight U :W: .20 .35
178 Starlit Angel U :W: .60 1.00
179 Steadfastness C :W: .20 .35
180 Stern Marshal R :W: .20 .35
181 Stone Rain C :R: .20 .35
182 Storm Crow C :B: .20 .35
183 Summer Bloom R :G: 2.00 3.00
184 Swamp A C :L: .20 .35
185 Swamp B C :L: .20 .35
186 Swamp C C :L: .20 .35
187 Swamp D C :L: .20 .35
188 Sylvan Tutor R :G: 40.00 45.00
189 Symbol of Unsummoning C :B: .20 .35
190 Taunt R :B: .20 .35
191 Temporary Truce R :W: 2.00 3.00
192 Theft of Dreams U :B: .20 .35
193 Thing from the Deep R :B: .60 1.00
194 Thundering Wurm R :G: .60 1.00
195 Thundermare R :R: .20 .35
196 Tidal Surge C :B: .20 .35
197 Time Ebb C :B: .20 .35
198 Touch of Brilliance C :G: .20 .35
199 Treetop Defense R :K: .50 .80
200 Undying Beast C :G: .20 .35
201 Untamed Wilds U :G: .20 .35
202 Valorous Charge U :W: .20 .35
203 Vampiric Feast U :K: .20 .35
204 Vampiric Touch C :K: .20 .35
205 Venerable Monk U :W: .20 .35
206 Vengeance U :W: .20 .35
207 Virtue's Ruin U :K: 1.00 1.50
208 Volcanic Dragon R :R: 1.00 1.50
209 Volcanic Hammer C :R: .20 .35
210 Wall of Granite U :R: .20 .35
211 Wall of Swords U :W: .20 .35
212 Warrior's Charge v1 C :W: .20 .35
213 Warrior's Charge v2 C :W: .20 .35
214 Whiptail Wurm U :G: .20 .35
215 Wicked Pact R :K: .50 .80
216 Willow Dryad C :G: .20 .35
217 Wind Drake C :B: .20 .35
218 Winds of Change R :R: 10.00 13.00
219 Winter's Grasp U :G: .20 .35
220 Withering Gaze U :B: .20 .35
221 Wood Elves R :G: 2.00 3.00
222 Wrath of God R :W: 6.00 8.00

1998 Magic The Gathering Portal Second Age

COMPLETE SET (165) 225.00 300.00
BOOSTER BOX (36 PACKS) 500.00 600.00
BOOSTER PACK (15 CARDS) 10.00 15.00
STARTER BOX 70.00 110.00
STARTER DECK 8.00 11.00
RELEASED ON JUNE 1, 1998
1 Abyssal Nightstalker U :K: .20 .35
2 Air Elemental U :B: .20 .35
3 Alaborn Cavalier U :W: .20 .35
4 Alaborn Grenadier C :W: .20 .35
5 Alaborn Musketeer C :W: .20 .35
6 Alaborn Trooper C :W: .20 .35
7 Alaborn Veteran R :W: .50 .80
8 Alaborn Zealot U :W: 1.50 2.00
9 Alluring Scent R :G: .50 .80
10 Ancient Craving R :K: 1.50 2.50
11 Angel of Fury R :W: 1.50 2.50
12 Angel of Mercy U :W: .20 .35
13 Angelic Blessing C :W: .20 .35
14 Angelic Wall C :W: .20 .35
15 Apprentice Sorcerer U :B: .20 .35
16 Archangel R :W: 3.00 5.00
17 Armageddon R :W: 3.00 5.00
18 Armored Galleon U :B: .60 1.00
19 Armored Griffin U :W: .20 .35
20 Barbtooth Wurm C :G: .20 .35
21 Bargain U :W: .50 .80
22 Bear Cub C :G: 1.00 1.50
23 Bee Sting U :G: .20 .35
24 Blaze U :R: .20 .35
25 Bloodcurdling Scream U :K: .20 .35
26 Breath of Life C :K: .20 .35
27 Brimstone Dragon R :R: 8.00 10.00
28 Brutal Nightstalker U :K: .20 .35
29 Chorus of Woe C :K: .20 .35
30 Coastal Wizard R :B: 4.00 6.00
31 Coercion U :K: .20 .35
32 Cruel Edict C :K: .20 .35
33 Cunning Giant R :R: .75 1.25
34 Dakmor Bat C :K: .20 .35
35 Dakmor Plague U :K: .20 .35
36 Dakmor Scorpion C :K: .20 .35
37 Dakmor Sorceress R :K: 2.50 4.00
38 Dark Offering U :K: .20 .35
39 Deathcoil Wurm R :G: 3.00 5.00
40 Deep Wood U :G: .20 .35
41 Deja Vu C :B: .50 .80
42 Denizen of the Deep R :B: 1.50 2.00
43 Earthquake R :R: 1.50 2.00
44 Exhaustion R :B: .60 1.00
45 Extinguish C :B: .20 .35
46 Eye Spy U :B: .20 .35
47 False Summoning C :B: .20 .35
48 Festival of Trokin C :W: .20 .35
49 Forest C :L: .50 .80
50 Forest B C :L: .50 .80
51 Forest C C :L: .50 .80
52 Foul Spirit U :K: .60 1.00
53 Goblin Cavaliers C :R: .20 .35
54 Goblin Firestarter U :R: .50 .80
55 Goblin General R :R: 3.00 5.00
56 Goblin Glider C :R: .20 .35
57 Goblin Lore U :R: 15.00 20.00
58 Goblin Matron U :R: .60 1.00

Card	Low	High
59 Goblin Mountaineer C :R:	.20	.35
60 Goblin Piker C :R:	.20	.35
61 Goblin Raider C :R:	.20	.35
62 Goblin War Cry U :R:	1.50	2.50
63 Goblin War Strike C :R:	1.50	2.50
64 Golden Bear C :G:	.50	.80
65 Hand of Death C :K:	.20	.35
66 Harmony of Nature U :G:	1.50	2.50
67 Hidden Horror R :K:	.75	1.25
68 Hurricane R :G:	.50	.80
69 Ironhoof Ox U :G:	.20	.35
70 Island C :L:	.60	1.00
71 Island B C :L:	.60	1.00
72 Island C C :L:	.60	1.00
73 Jagged Lightning U :R:	.20	.35
74 Just Fate R :W:	.60	1.00
75 Kiss of Death U :K:	.20	.35
76 Lava Axe C :R:	.20	.35
77 Lone Wolf U :G:	.20	.35
78 Lurking Nightstalker C :K:	.20	.35
79 Lynx C :G:	.20	.35
80 Magma Giant R :R:	.40	.60
81 Mind Rot C :K:	.20	.35
82 Moaning Spirit C :K:	.20	.35
83 Monstrous Growth C :G:	.20	.35
84 Mountain C :L:	.75	1.25
85 Mountain B C :L:	.75	1.25
86 Mountain C C :L:	.75	1.25
87 Muck Rats C :K:	.20	.35
88 Mystic Denial U :B:	.20	.35
89 Natural Spring C :G:	.20	.35
90 Nature's Lore C :G:	1.00	1.50
91 Nightstalker Engine R :K:	.50	.80
92 Norwood Archers C :G:	.20	.35
93 Norwood Priestess R :G:	30.00	35.00
94 Norwood Ranger C :G:	.20	.35
95 Norwood Riders C :G:	.20	.35
96 Norwood Warrior C :G:	.20	.35
97 Obsidian Giant U :R:	.20	.35
98 Ogre Arsonist U :R:	1.50	2.00
99 Ogre Berserker C :R:	.20	.35
100 Ogre Taskmaster U :R:	.20	.35
101 Ogre Warrior C :R:	.20	.35
102 Path of Peace C :W:	.20	.35
103 Piracy R :B:	8.00	12.00
104 Plains C :L:	.60	1.00
105 Plains B C :L:	.60	1.00
106 Plains C C :L:	.60	1.00
107 Plated Wurm C :G:	.20	.35
108 Predatory Nightstalker U :K:	4.00	6.00
109 Prowling Nightstalker C :K:	.20	.35
110 Raging Goblin C :R:	.20	.35
111 Raiding Nightstalker C :K:	.20	.35
112 Rain of Daggers R :K:	2.50	4.00
113 Raise Dead C :K:	.20	.35
114 Rally the Troops U :W:	.20	.35
115 Ravenous Rats C :K:	.20	.35
116 Razorclaw Bear R :G:	8.00	12.00
117 Relentless Assault R :R:	.50	.80
118 Remove U :B:	.20	.35
119 Renewing Touch U :G:	.40	.60
120 Return of the Nightstalkers R :K:	.40	.60
121 Righteous Charge C :W:	.20	.35
122 Righteous Fury R :W:	3.00	5.00
123 River Bear U :G:	.20	.35
124 Salvage C :G:	.20	.35
125 Screeching Drake C :B:	.20	.35
126 Sea Drake U :B:	3.00	5.00
127 Sleight of Hand C :B:	6.00	8.00
128 Spitting Earth C :R:	.20	.35
129 Steam Catapult R :W:	4.00	6.00
130 Steam Frigate C :B:	.20	.35
131 Stone Rain C :R:	.20	.35
132 Swamp C :L:	.75	1.25
133 Swamp B C :K:	.75	1.25
134 Swamp C C :G:	.75	1.25
135 Swarm of Rats C :G:	.75	1.25
136 Sylvan Basilisk R :B:	.75	1.25
137 Sylvan Yeti R :B:	.75	1.25
138 Talas Air Ship C :B:	.20	.35
139 Talas Explorer C :B:	.20	.35
140 Talas Merchant C :B:	.20	.35
141 Talas Researcher R :B:	.60	1.00
142 Talas Scout C :B:	.20	.35
143 Talas Warrior R :B:	10.00	15.00
144 Temple Acolyte C :W:	.20	.35
145 Temple Elder U :W:	.20	.35
146 Temporal Manipulation R :B:	45.00	55.00
147 Theft of Dreams U :B:	.20	.35
148 Tidal Surge C :B:	.20	.35
149 Time Ebb C :B:	.20	.35
150 Touch of Brilliance C :B:	.20	.35
151 Town Sentry C :W:	.20	.35
152 Tree Monkey C :G:	.20	.35
153 Tremor C :R:	.20	.35
154 Trokin High Guard C :W:	.20	.35
155 Undo U :B:	.20	.35
156 Untamed Wilds U :G:	.20	.35
157 Vampiric Spirit R :K:	.60	1.00
158 Vengeance U :W:	.20	.35
159 Volcanic Hammer C :R:	.20	.35
160 Volunteer Militia C :W:	.20	.35
161 Warrior's Stand U :W:	.20	.35
162 Wild Griffin C :W:	.20	.35
163 Wild Ox U :G:	.20	.35
164 Wildfire R :R:	1.00	1.50
165 Wind Sail C :B:	.20	.35

1999 Magic The Gathering Portal Three Kingdoms

Card	Low	High
COMPLETE SET (180)	3000.00	3500.00
BOOSTER BOX (36 PACKS)	8000.00	1000.00
BOOSTER PACK (15 CARDS)	80.00	100.00
STARTER DECK	10.00	30.00
RELEASED ON MAY 1, 1999		
1 Alert Shu Infantry U :W:	1.50	2.00
67 Ambition's Cost R :K:	5.00	7.00
40 Council of Advisors U :B:	1.00	1.50
34 Balance of Power R :B:	4.00	5.00
4 Barbarian General U :R:	2.00	2.50
101 Barbarian Horde C :R:	.40	.60
102 Blaze U :R:	2.00	2.50
35 Borrowing 100,000 Arrows U :B:	2.00	2.50
133 Borrowing the East Wind R :G:	10.00	12.00
36 Brilliant Plan U :B:	.75	1.25
37 Broken Dam C :B:	.75	1.00
103 Burning Fields C :R:	.40	.60
104 Burning of Xinye R :R:	55.00	65.00
68 Cao Cao, Lord of Wei R :K:	8.00	10.00
69 Cao Ren, Wei Commander R :K:	15.00	18.00
38 Capture of Jingzhou R :B:	425.00	475.00
39 Champion's Victory U :B:	2.00	2.50
70 Coercion U :K:	.75	1.25
105 Control of the Court U :R:	5.00	7.00
71 Corrupt Court Official U :K:	6.00	8.00
106 Corrupt Eunuchs U :R:	1.00	1.50
2 Counterintelligence U :B:	1.50	2.00
73 Deception C :K:	.40	.60
107 Desert Sandstorm C :R:	.40	.60
2 Desperate Charge U :K:	1.50	2.00
108 Diaochan, Artful Beauty R :R:	35.00	40.00
109 Dong Zhou, the Tyrant R :R:	125.00	140.00
2 Eightfold Maze R :W:	4.00	6.00
3 Empty City Ruse U :W:	4.00	6.00
110 Eunuchs' Intrigues U :R:	.75	1.25
42 Exhaustion R :B:	2.25	2.75
43 Extinguish C :B:	.40	.60
4 False Defeat C :W:	8.00	10.00
134 False Mourning U :G:	4.00	5.00
75 Famine U :K:	1.50	2.00
111 Fire Ambush C :R:	6.00	8.00
112 Fire Bowman U :R:	2.00	2.50
5 Flanking Troops U :W:	.75	1.25
44 Forced Retreat C :B:	.40	.60
135 Forest Bear C :G:	6.00	8.00
178 Forest C :L:	1.00	1.50
179 Forest C :L:	6.00	8.00
180 Forest C :L:	3.00	4.50
76 Ghostly Visit C :K:	.40	.60
6 Guan Yu, Sainted Warrior R :W:	17.00	20.00
7 Guan Yu's 1,000-Li March R :W:	12.00	15.00
136 Heavy Fog U :G:	25.00	30.00
137 Hua Tuo, Honored Physician R :G:	25.00	30.00
8 Huang Zhong, Shu General R :W:	15.00	18.00
138 Hunting Cheetah U :G:	12.00	15.00
77 Imperial Edict C :K:	2.00	2.50
113 Imperial Recruiter U :R:	275.00	300.00
78 Imperial Seal R :K:	475.00	550.00
114 Independent Troops C :R:	.40	.60
169 Island (with beach) C :L:	2.50	3.00
170 Island (with river) C :L:	1.50	2.00
171 Island (no sky) C :L:	2.50	3.00
9 Kongming, Sleeping Dragon R :W:	10.00	13.00
10 Kongming's Contraptions R :W:	4.00	6.00
45 Lady Sun R :B:	20.00	25.00
139 Lady Zhurong, Warrior Queen R :G:	25.00	30.00
11 Liu Bei, Lord of Shu R :W:	6.00	8.00
140 Lone Wolf U :G:	2.50	3.00
12 Loyal Retainers U :W:	40.00	45.00
115 Lu Bu, Master-at-Arms R :R:	18.00	22.00
46 Lu Meng, Wu General R :B:	20.00	25.00
47 Lu Su, Wu Advisor R :B:	8.00	10.00
48 Lu Xun, Scholar General R :B:	7.00	10.00
116 Ma Chao, Western Warrior R :R:	25.00	30.00
141 Marshaling the Troops R :G:	20.00	25.00
142 Meng Huo, Barbarian King R :G:	30.00	35.00
72 Cunning Advisor U :K:	.75	1.25
143 Meng Huo's Horde C :G:	.40	.60
13 Misfortune's Gain C :W:	.40	.60
117 Mountain Bandit C :R:	.50	.75
175 Mountain C :L:	2.00	2.50
176 Mountain C :L:	4.00	6.00
177 Mountain C :L:	.40	.60
49 Mystic Denial U :B:	1.00	1.50
79 Overwhelming Forces R :K:	50.00	60.00
14 Pang Tong, Young Phoenix R :W:	15.00	18.00
15 Peach Garden Oath U :W:	2.50	3.50
166 Plains C :L:	.40	.60
167 Plains C :L:	3.00	5.00
168 Plains C :L:	.75	1.00
80 Poison Arrow U :K:	2.25	2.75
50 Preemptive Strike C :B:	.40	.60
16 Rally the Troops U :W:	1.50	2.00
17 Ravages of War R :W:	200.00	230.00
118 Ravaging Horde U :R:	12.00	13.00
51 Red Cliffs Armada U :B:	1.50	2.00
119 Relentless Assault R :R:	4.00	6.00
120 Renegade Troops U :R:	.75	1.25
81 Return to Battle C :K:	.40	.60
18 Riding Red Hare C :W:	2.00	2.50
144 Riding the Dilu Horse R :G:	75.00	85.00
121 Rockslide Ambush U :R:	1.50	2.00
122 Rolling Earthquake R :R:	60.00	70.00
52 Sage's Knowledge C :B:	1.00	1.50
19 Shu Cavalry C :W:	1.25	1.75
20 Shu Defender C :W:	.40	.60
21 Shu Elite Companions U :W:	1.50	2.00
22 Shu Elite Infantry C :W:	.40	.60
23 Shu Farmer C :W:	.40	.60
24 Shu Foot Soldiers C :W:	.40	.60
25 Shu General U :W:	1.50	2.00
26 Shu Grain Caravan C :W:	.40	.60
27 Shu Soldier-Farmers U :W:	2.00	2.50
82 Sima Yi, Wei Field Marshal R :K:	3.00	4.50
145 Slashing Tiger R :G:	8.00	10.00
146 Southern Elephant C :G:	.40	.60
147 Spoils of Victory U :G:	8.00	10.00
148 Spring of Eternal Peace C :G:	.40	.60
149 Stalking Tiger C :G:	.40	.60
83 Stolen Grain U :K:	1.50	2.00
84 Stone Catapult R :K:	6.00	8.00
123 Stone Rain C :R:	1.00	1.50
53 Strategic Planning U :B:	8.00	10.00
54 Straw Soldiers C :B:	.40	.60
55 Sun Ce, Young Conqueror R :B:	30.00	35.00
56 Sun Quan, Lord of Wu R :B:	15.00	18.00
172 Swamp (gray) C :L:	.75	1.00
173 Swamp (green) C :L:	3.00	4.00
174 Swamp (orange) C :L:	3.00	4.00
150 Taoist Hermit U :G:	3.00	4.00
151 Taoist Mystic R :G:	3.00	4.50
152 Taunting Challenge R :G:	4.00	6.00
153 Three Visits C :G:	35.00	40.00
154 Trained Cheetah U :G:	2.00	2.50
155 Trained Jackal C :G:	.40	.60
156 Trip Wire U :G:	.75	1.25
28 Vengeance U :W:	.75	1.25
29 Virtuous Charge C :W:	.40	.60
30 Volunteer Militia C :W:	.40	.60
124 Warrior's Oath R :R:	30.00	35.00
31 Warrior's Stand U :W:	1.00	1.50
85 Wei Ambush Force C :K:	.40	.60
86 Wei Assassins U :K:	1.50	2.00
87 Wei Elite Companions U :K:	.75	1.25
88 Wei Infantry C :K:	.40	.60
89 Wei Night Raiders U :K:	8.00	10.00
90 Wei Scout C :K:	.40	.60
91 Wei Strike Force C :K:	.40	.60
157 Wielding the Green Dragon C :G:	.75	1.00
158 Wolf Pack R :G:	38.00	45.00
57 Wu Admiral U :B:	.75	1.25
58 Wu Elite Cavalry C :B:	.40	.60
59 Wu Infantry C :B:	.40	.60
60 Wu Light Cavalry C :B:	.40	.60
61 Wu Longbowman U :B:	.75	1.25
62 Wu Scout C :B:	1.00	1.50
63 Wu Spy U :B:	6.00	8.00
64 Wu Warship C :B:	.40	.60
92 Xiahou Dun, the One-Eyed R :K:	80.00	90.00
93 Xun Yu, Wei Advisor R :K:	9.00	11.00
125 Yellow Scarves Cavalry C :R:	.40	.60
126 Yellow Scarves General R :R:	5.00	7.00
127 Yellow Scarves Troops C :R:	.40	.60
94 Young Wei Recruit C :K:	.40	.60
129 Yuan Shao, the Indecisive R :R:	40.00	50.00
128 Yuan Shao's Infantry U :R:	1.00	1.50
32 Zhang Fei, Fierce Warrior R :W:	38.00	45.00
95 Zhang He, Wei General R :K:	25.00	30.00
96 Zhang Liao, Hero of Hefei R :K:	10.00	15.00
33 Zhao Zilong, Tiger General R :W:	15.00	18.00
65 Zhou Yu, Chief Commander R :B:	12.00	15.00
66 Zhuge Jin, Wu Strategist R :B:	20.00	25.00
130 Zodiac Dog C :R:	.50	.75
131 Zodiac Dragon R :R:	200.00	230.00
132 Zodiac Goat C :R:	1.00	1.50
159 Zodiac Horse U :G:	3.00	5.00
160 Zodiac Monkey C :G:	.50	.75
161 Zodiac Ox U :G:	2.50	3.50
97 Zodiac Pig U :K:	2.50	3.50
162 Zodiac Rabbit C :G:	2.00	2.50
98 Zodiac Rat C :K:	3.00	5.00
163 Zodiac Rooster C :G:	2.00	2.50
99 Zodiac Snake C :K:	.75	1.00
164 Zodiac Tiger U :G:	5.00	7.00
165 Zuo Ci, the Mocking Sage R :G:	30.00	35.00

1999 Magic The Gathering Starter

Card	Low	High
COMPLETE SET (173)	250.00	300.00
BOOSTER BOX (36 PACKS)	175.00	250.00
BOOSTER PACK (15 CARDS)	5.00	8.00
STARTER BOX (12 DECKS)	150.00	250.00
STARTER DECK	18.00	30.00
RELEASED ON APRIL 20, 1999		
63 Abyssal Horror R :K:	1.00	2.00
32 Air Elemental U :B:	.25	.50
124 Alluring Scent R :G:	1.00	2.00
64 Ancient Craving R :K:	1.50	3.00
1 Angel of Light U :W:	.25	.50
2 Angel of Mercy U :W:	.25	.50
3 Angelic Blessing C :W:	.15	.30
4 Archangel R :W:	4.00	8.00
5 Ardent Militia U :W:	.25	.50
6 Armageddon R :W:	2.50	5.00
125 Barbtooth Wurm C :G:	.15	.30
7 Bargain U :W:	.25	.50
8 Blinding Light R :W:	1.50	3.00
65 Bog Imp C :K:	.15	.30
66 Bog Raiders C :K:	.15	.30
67 Bog Wraith U :K:	.50	1.00
9 Border Guard C :W:	.15	.30
10 Breath of Life U :W:	.25	.50
126 Bull Hippo U :G:	.30	.75
11 Champion Lancer R :W:	2.00	4.00
12 Charging Paladin U :W:	.25	.50
68 Chorus of Woe C :K:	.15	.30
93 Cinder Storm U :R:	.25	.50
69 Coercion U :K:	.25	.50
33 Coral Eel C :B:	.15	.30
34 Counterspell U :B:	.25	.50
70 Dakmor Ghoul U :K:	.25	.50
71 Dakmor Lancer R :K:	1.50	3.00
72 Dakmor Plague U :K:	.25	.50
73 Dakmor Scorpion C :K:	.15	.30
74 Dakmor Sorceress R :K:	5.00	10.00
75 Dark Offering U :K:	.25	.50
35 Denizen of the Deep R :B:	2.50	5.00
94 Devastation R :R:	1.50	3.00
13 Devoted Hero C :W:	.15	.30
14 Devout Monk C :W:	.15	.30
76 Dread Reaper R :K:	1.50	3.00
127 Durkwood Boars C :G:	.15	.30
15 Eager Cadet C* :W:	.15	.30
95 Earth Elemental U :R:	.25	.50
36 Exhaustion U :B:	.25	.50
37 Extinguish C :B:	.15	.30
38 Eye Spy U :B:	.25	.50
16 False Peace U :W:	.25	.50
77 Feral Shadow C :K:	.15	.30
96 Fire Elemental U :R:	.25	.50
97 Fire Tempest R :R:	1.00	2.00
17 Foot Soldiers C :W:	.15	.30
172 Forest L :L:	.15	.30
171 Forest L :L:	.15	.30
170 Forest L :L:	.15	.30
173 Forest L :L:	.15	.30
18 Gerrard's Wisdom R :W:	1.50	3.00
39 Giant Octopus C :B:	.15	.30
98 Goblin Cavaliers C :R:	.15	.30
99 Goblin Chariot C :R:	.15	.30
100 Goblin Commando U :R:	.25	.50
101 Goblin General U :R:	.25	.50
102 Goblin Glider U :R:	.25	.50
103 Goblin Hero R* :R:	2.00	4.00
104 Goblin Lore U :R:	.25	.50
105 Goblin Mountaineer C :R:	.15	.30
106 Goblin Settler U :R:	.25	.50
128 Gorilla Warrior C :G:	.15	.30
78 Gravedigger U :K:	.25	.50
79 Grim Tutor R :K:	125.00	200.00
129 Grizzly Bears C :G:	.15	.30
80 Hand of Death C :K:	.15	.30
81 Hollow Dogs C :K:	.15	.30
82 Howling Fury U :K:	.25	.50
107 Hulking Goblin C :R:	.15	.30
108 Hulking Ogre U :R:	.25	.50
40 Ingenious Thief C :B:	.15	.30
160 Island L :L:	.15	.30
159 Island L :L:	.15	.30
158 Island L :L:	.15	.30
161 Island L :L:	.15	.30
109 Jagged Lightning U :R:	.50	1.00
19 Knight Errant C :W:	.15	.30
110 Last Chance R :R:	1.50	3.00
111 Lava Axe C :R:	.15	.30
130 Lone Wolf C :G:	.15	.30
20 Loyal Sentry R :W:	1.00	2.00
131 Lynx U :G:	.25	.50
41 Man-o-War U :B:	.25	.50
42 Merfolk of the Pearl Trident C* :B:	.25	.50
83 Mind Rot C :K:	.15	.30
112 Mons's Goblin Raiders R* :R:	1.00	2.00
132 Monstrous Growth C :G:	.15	.30
133 Moon Sprite U :G:	.25	.50
166 Mountain L :L:	.15	.30
167 Mountain L :L:	.15	.30
168 Mountain L :L:	.15	.30
169 Mountain L :L:	.15	.30
84 Muck Rats C :K:	.15	.30
134 Natural Spring U :G:	.25	.50
135 Nature's Cloak R :G:	1.00	2.00
136 Nature's Lore C :G:	.15	.30
137 Norwood Archers C :G:	.15	.30
138 Norwood Ranger C :G:	.15	.30
113 Ogre Warrior C :R:	.15	.30
43 Owl Familiar U :B:	.25	.50
21 Path of Peace C :W:	.15	.30
44 Phantom Warrior R :B:	1.00	2.00
45 Piracy R :B:	5.00	10.00
154 Plains L :L:	.15	.30
155 Plains L :L:	.15	.30
156 Plains L :L:	.15	.30
157 Plains L :L:	.15	.30
139 Pride of Lions U :G:	.25	.50
46 Psychic Transfer R :B:	1.50	3.00
114 Raging Goblin C :R:	.15	.30
85 Raise Dead C :K:	.15	.30
47 Ransack R :B:	1.00	2.00
86 Ravenous Rats U :K:	.50	1.00
48 Relearn U :B:	.25	.50
115 Relentless Assault R :R:	2.00	4.00
49 Remove Soul C :B:	.15	.30
140 Renewing Touch U :G:	.25	.50
22 Righteous Charge U :W:	2.50	5.00
23 Righteous Fury R :W:	1.00	2.00
24 Royal Falcon C* :W:	.15	.30
25 Royal Trooper U :W:	.25	.50
26 Sacred Nectar C :W:	.15	.30
87 Scathe Zombies C* :K:	.15	.30
116 Scorching Spear C :R:	.15	.30
50 Sea Eagle C* :B:	.15	.30
88 Serpent Warrior C :K:	.15	.30
89 Shrieking Specter U :K:	.25	.50
141 Silverback Ape U :G:	.25	.50
51 Sleight of Hand C :B:	.15	.30
52 Snapping Drake C :B:	.15	.30
90 Soul Feast U :K:	.25	.50
142 Southern Elephant C :G:	.15	.30
117 Spitting Earth U :R:	.25	.50
143 Squall C :G:	.15	.30
27 Steadfastness C :W:	.15	.30
118 Stone Rain C :R:	.15	.30
53 Storm Crow C :B:	.15	.30
91 Stream of Acid U :K:	.25	.50
144 Summer Bloom R :G:	1.00	2.00
162 Swamp L :L:	.15	.30
163 Swamp L :L:	.15	.30
164 Swamp L :L:	.15	.30
165 Swamp L :L:	.15	.30
145 Sylvan Basilisk R :G:	1.50	3.00
146 Sylvan Yeti R :G:	1.00	2.00
147 Thorn Elemental R :G:	1.00	2.00
119 Thunder Dragon R :R:	20.00	35.00
54 Tidings U :B:	.25	.50
55 Time Ebb C :B:	.15	.30
56 Time Warp R :B:	3.00	6.00
57 Touch of Brilliance C :B:	.15	.30
120 Trained Orgg R :R:	1.00	2.00
121 Tremor C :R:	.15	.30
58 Undo U :B:	.25	.50
148 Untamed Wilds U :G:	.25	.50
28 Venerable Monk C :W:	.15	.30
29 Vengeance U :W:	.25	.50
30 Veteran Cavalier U :W:	.25	.50
59 Vizzerdrix R :B:	1.00	2.00
122 Volcanic Dragon R :R:	2.00	4.00
123 Volcanic Hammer C :R:	.15	.30
60 Water Elemental U :B:	.25	.50
149 Whiptail Wurm U :G:	.25	.50
150 Whirlwind R :G:	.60	1.50
92 Wicked Pact R :K:	1.50	3.00

31 Wild Griffin C :W: .15 .30
151 Wild Ox U :G: .25 .50
152 Willow Elf C* :G: .15 .30
61 Wind Drake C :B: .15 .30
62 Wind Sail U :B: .25 .50
153 Wood Elves U :G: .25 .50

2000 Magic The Gathering Starter

COMPLETE SET (57) 15.00 40.00
RELEASED ON APRIL 24, 2000
1 Angelic Blessing C :W: .75 .75
2 Armored Pegasus C :W: .10 .25
3 Bog Imp C :K: .10 .25
4 Breath of Life U :W: .60 .60
5 Coercion C :K: .50 .50
6 Counterspell C :L: .75 .75
7 Disenchant C :W: 1.00 1.00
8 Drudge Skeletons C :K: .10 .25
9 Durkwood Boars C :G: .75 .75
10 Eager Cadet C :W: .60 .60
11 Flame Spirit C :R: .10 .25
12 Flight C :L: .10 .25
13 Forest L .10 .25
14 Forest L .10 .25
15 Giant Growth C :G: .10 .25
16 Giant Octopus C :L: .75 .75
17 Goblin Hero C :R: .10 .25
18 Hand of Death C :K: .75 .75
19 Hero's Resolve C :W: .10 .25
20 Inspiration C :L: .10 .25
21 Island L .10 .25
22 Island L .10 .25
23 Knight Errant C :W: .10 .25
24 Lava Axe C :R: .10 .25
25 Llanowar Elves C :G: 1.00 1.00
26 Merfolk of the Pearl Trident C :L: 20.00 20.00
27 Mons's Goblin Raiders C :R: .60 .60
28 Monstrous Growth C :G: .75 .75
29 Moon Sprite U :G: .60 .60
30 Mountain L .10 .25
31 Mountain L .10 .25
32 Obsianus Golem U 30.00 30.00
33 Ogre Warrior C :R: .50 .50
34 Orcish Oriflamme U :R: .50 .50
35 Plains L .10 .25
36 Plains L .10 .25
37 Prodigal Sorcerer C :L: .10 .25
38 Python C :K: .75 .75
39 Rod of Ruin U .50 .50
40 Royal Falcon C :W: .75 .75
41 Samite Healer C :W: .10 .25
42 Scathe Zombies C :K: .10 .25
43 Sea Eagle C :L: .10 .25
44 Shock C :R: .10 .25
45 Soul Net U .50 .50
46 Spined Wurm C :G: 3.00 3.00
47 Stone Rain C :R: .10 .25
48 Swamp L .10 .25
49 Swamp L .10 .25
50 Terror C :K: .10 .25
51 Time Ebb C :L: .10 .25
52 Trained Orgg R :R: 1.00 1.00
53 Venerable Monk C :W: .10 .25
54 Vizzerdrix R :L: 1.00 1.00
55 Wild Griffin C :W: .10 .25
56 Willow Elf C :G: .10 .25
57 Wind Drake C :L: .10 .25

Compilation Sets

1995 Magic The Gathering Chronicles

COMPLETE SET (125) 70.00 100.00
BOOSTER BOX (45 PACKS) 250.00 300.00
BOOSTER PACK (12 CARDS) 5.00 8.00
RELEASED ON JULY 1, 1995
1 Abu Ja'far U .15 .25
2 Active Volcano C .15 .25
3 Akron Legionnaire U .15 .25
4 Aladdin U .15 .25
5 Angelic Voices U .30 .50
6 Arcades Sabboth U .30 .50
7 Arena of the Ancients U .40 .60
8 Argothian Pixies C .15 .25
9 Ashnod's Altar C 1.00 1.50
10 Ashnod's Transmogrant C .15 .25
11 Axelrod Gunnarson U .15 .25
12 Ayesha Tanaka U .15 .25
13 Azure Drake U .15 .25
14 Banshee U .15 .25
15 Barl's Cage U .15 .25
16 Beasts of Bogardan U .15 .25
17 Blood Moon U 30.00 35.00
18 Blood of the Martyr U .15 .25
19 Bog Rats C .15 .25
20 Book of Rass U .15 .25
21 Boomerang C .15 .25
22 Bronze Horse U .15 .25
23 Cat Warriors C .15 .25
24 Chromium U .40 .60
25 City of Brass U 2.50 3.50
26 Cocoon U .15 .25
27 Concordant Crossroads U 5.00 7.00
28 Craw Giant U .15 .25
29 Cuombajj Witches C .30 .50
30 Cyclone U .15 .25
31 Dakkon Blackblade U .40 .60
32 Dance of Many U .15 .25
33 Dandân C .15 .25
34 D'Avenant Archer C .15 .25
35 Divine Offering C .15 .25
36 Emerald Dragonfly C .15 .25
37 Enchantment Alteration U .15 .25
38 Erhnam Djinn U .15 .25
39 Fallen Angel U .15 .25
40 Fallen, The U .15 .25
41 Feldon's Cane C .15 .25
42 Fire Drake U .15 .25
43 Fishliver Oil C .15 .25
44 Flash Flood C .15 .25
45 Fountain of Youth C .15 .25
46 Gabriel Angelfire U .25 .40
47 Gauntlets of Chaos U .15 .25
48 Ghazbán Ogre C .15 .25
49 Giant Slug C .15 .25
50 Goblin Artisans U .15 .25
51 Goblin Digging Team C .15 .25
52 Goblin Shrine C .15 .25
53 Goblins of the Flarg C .15 .25
54 Hasran Ogress C .15 .25
55 Hell's Caretaker U 2.00 2.50
56 Horn of Deafening U .15 .25
57 Indestructible Aura C .15 .25
58 Ivory Guardians U .15 .25
59 Jalum Tome U .15 .25
60 Jeweled Bird U .15 .25
61 Johan U .25 .40
62 Juxtapose U .15 .25
63 Keepers of the Faith C .15 .25
64 Kei Takahashi C .15 .25
65 Land's Edge U .15 .25
66 Living Armor C .15 .25
67 Marhault Elsdragon C .15 .25
68 Metamorphosis C .15 .25
69 Mountain Yeti C .15 .25
70 Nebuchadnezzar U .15 .25
71 Nicol Bolas U 1.00 1.50
72 Obelisk of Undoing U .15 .25
73 Palladia-Mors U .30 .50
74 Petra Sphinx U .15 .25
75 Primordial Ooze U .15 .25
76 Puppet Master U .15 .25
77 Rabid Wombat U .15 .25
78 Rakalite U .15 .25
79 Recall U .15 .25
80 Remove Soul C .15 .25
81 Repentant Blacksmith C .15 .25
82 Revelation U .15 .25
83 Rubinia Soulsinger U .15 .25
84 Runesword C .15 .25
85 Safe Haven U .15 .25
86 Scavenger Folk C .15 .25
87 Sentinel U .25 .40
88 Serpent Generator U .30 .50
89 Shield Wall U .15 .25
90 Shimian Night Stalker U .15 .25
91 Sivitri Scarzam C .15 .25
92 Sol'kanar the Swamp King U .15 .25
93 Stangg U .15 .25
94 Storm Seeker U .15 .25
95 Takklemaggot U .15 .25
96 Teleport U .15 .25
97 Tobias Andrion C .15 .25
98 Tor Wauki C .15 .25
99 Tormod's Crypt C .15 .25
100 Transmutation C .15 .25
101 Triassic Egg U .15 .25
102 Urza's Mine C 1.00 1.50
103 Urza's Mine C 1.00 1.50
104 Urza's Mine C 1.00 1.50
105 Urza's Mine C 1.00 1.50
106 Urza's Power Plant C 1.00 1.50
107 Urza's Power Plant C 1.00 1.50
108 Urza's Power Plant C 1.00 1.50
109 Urza's Power Plant C 1.00 1.50
110 Urza's Tower C 1.00 1.50
111 Urza's Tower C 1.00 1.50
112 Urza's Tower C 1.00 1.50
113 Urza's Tower C 1.00 1.50
114 Vaevictis Asmadi U .40 .60
115 Voodoo Doll U .15 .25
116 Wall of Heat C .15 .25
117 Wall of Opposition U .15 .25
118 Wall of Shadows C .15 .25
119 Wall of Vapor C .15 .25
120 Wall of Wonder U .15 .25
121 War Elephant C .15 .25
122 Witch Hunter U .15 .25
123 Wretched, The U .25 .40
124 Xira Arien U .30 .50
125 Yawgmoth Demon U .15 .25

1997 Magic The Gathering Vanguard

COMPLETE SET (32) 150.00 200.00
BOOSTER PACK 40.00 60.00
RELEASED IN SUMMER 1997
1 Ashnod R 3.00 5.00
2 Barrin R 3.00 5.00
3 Crovax R 3.00 5.00
4 Eladamri R 3.00 5.00
5 Ertai R 3.00 5.00
6 Gerrard R 3.00 5.00
7 Gix R 3.00 5.00
8 Greven il-Vec R 3.00 5.00
9 Hanna R 3.00 6.00
10 Karn R 3.00 5.00
11 Lyna R 3.00 5.00
12 Maraxus R 3.00 5.00
13 Mirri R 4.00 7.00
14 Mishra R 3.00 5.00
15 Multani R 4.00 7.00
16 Oracle R 3.00 5.00
17 Orim R 3.00 5.00
18 Rofellos R 3.00 5.00
19 Selenia R 3.00 5.00
20 Serra R 3.00 5.00
21 Sidar Kondo R 3.00 5.00
22 Sisay R 3.00 6.00
23 Sliver Queen, Brood Mother R 7.00 12.00
24 Squee R 3.00 5.00
25 Starke R 3.00 5.00
26 Tahngarth R 3.00 5.00
27 Takara R 3.00 6.00
28 Tawnos R 4.00 6.00
29 Titania R 3.00 6.00
30 Urza R 3.00 6.00
31 Volrath R 3.00 5.00
32 Xantcha R 3.00 5.00

Duel Decks

2007 Magic The Gathering Duel Decks Elves vs. Goblins

DUEL DECK 100.00 200.00
RELEASED ON NOVEMBER 16, 2007
1 Akki Coalflinger U :R: .20 .50
2 Boggart Shenanigans U :R: .30 .50
3 Clickslither R :R: .40 .75
4 Emberwilde Augur C :R: .10 .25
5 Flamewave Invoker U :R: .20 .50
6 Gempalm Incinerator U :R: .60 1.50
7 Goblin Cohort C :R: .10 .25
8 Goblin Matron U :R: .75 2.00
9 Goblin Ringleader U :R: 1.25 3.00
10 Goblin Sledder C :R: .10 .25
11 Goblin Warchief U :R: 1.50 4.00
12 Ib Halfheart, Goblin Tactician R :R: .30 .75
13 Mogg Fanatic U :R: .60 1.50
14 Mogg War Marshal C :R: .40 1.00
15 Mudbutton Torchrunner C :R: .10 .25
16 Raging Goblin C :R: .10 .25
17 Reckless One U :R: .30 .75
18 Siege-Gang Commander R :R: 1.25 3.00
19 Skirk Drill Sergeant U :R: .20 .50
20 Skirk Fire Marshal R :R: .40 1.00
21 Skirk Prospector C :R: .20 .50
22 Skirk Shaman C :R: .10 .25
23 Spitting Earth C :R: .10 .25
24 Tar Pitcher U :R: .20 .50
25 Tarfire C :R: .10 .25
26 Allosaurus Rider R :G: .40 1.00
27 Ambush Commander R :G: 1.50 4.00
28 Elvish Eulogist C :G: .10 .25
29 Elvish Harbinger U :G: 1.25 3.00
30 Elvish Promenade U :G: 1.50 4.00
31 Elvish Warrior C :G: .10 .25
32 Gempalm Strider U :G: .20 .50
33 Giant Growth C :G: .10 .25
34 Harmonize U :G: .75 2.00
35 Heedless One U :G: 1.50 4.00
36 Imperious Perfect U :G: 2.50 6.00
37 Llanowar Elves C :G: .30 .50
38 Lys Alana Huntmaster C :G: .30 .75
39 Stonewood Invoker C :G: .10 .25
40 Sylvan Messenger U :G: .75 2.00
41 Timberwatch Elf C :G: .60 1.50
42 Voice of the Woods R :G: .60 1.50
43 Wellwisher C :G: .75 2.00
44 Wildsize C :G: .10 .25
45 Wirewood Herald C :G: .20 .75
46 Wirewood Symbiote U :G: 1.25 3.00
47 Wood Elves C :G: .10 .25
48 Wren's Run Vanquisher U :G: .75 2.00
49 Forest L .10 .40
50 Forest L .10 .40
51 Forest L .10 .40
52 Forest L .10 .40
53 Mountain L .10 .40
54 Mountain L .10 .40
55 Mountain L .10 .40
56 Mountain L .10 .40
57 Forgotten Cave C .10 .25
58 Goblin Burrows U .20 .50
59 Moonglove Extract C .10 .25
60 Slate of Ancestry R .50 1.00
61 Tranquil Thicket C .10 .25
62 Wirewood Lodge U 1.25 3.00

2007 Magic The Gathering Duel Decks Elves vs. Goblins Tokens

1 Elemental .50 .75
2 Elf Warrior .60 1.00
3 Goblin .60 1.00

2008 Magic The Gathering Duel Decks Jace vs. Chandra

COMPLETE SET (63) 15.00 40.00
DUEL DECK 50.00 100.00
RELEASED ON NOVEMBER 7, 2008
1 AEthersnipe C :B: .10 .25
2 Air Elemental U :B: .20 .50
3 Ancestral Vision R :B: 2.00 5.00
4 Brine Elemental U :B: .20 .50
5 Condescend C :B: .20 .50
6 Counterspell C :B: 4.00 10.00
7 Daze C :B: 1.50 4.00
8 Errant Ephemeron C :B: .20 .50
9 Fact or Fiction U :B: 1.50 4.00
10 Fathom Seer C :B: .10 .25
11 Fledgling Mawcor U :B: .20 .50
12 Guile R :B: .50 1.25
13 Gush C :B: .40 1.00
14 Jace Beleren M :B: 6.00 15.00
15 Man-o'-War C :B: .30 .75
16 Martyr of Frost C :B: .10 .25
17 Mulldrifter C :B: .40 1.00
18 Ophidian C :B: .10 .25
19 Quicksilver Dragon R :B: .50 1.25
20 Repulse C :B: .10 .25
21 Riftwing Cloudskate U :B: .20 .50
22 Voidmage Apprentice C :B: .10 .25
23 Wall of Deceit U :B: .20 .50
24 Waterspout Djinn U :B: .20 .50
25 Willbender U :B: .25 .60
26 Chandra Nalaar M :R: 3.00 8.00
27 Chartooth Cougar C :R: .10 .25
28 Cone of Flame U :R: .20 .50
29 Demonfire R :R: .50 1.25
30 Fireball U :R: .20 .50
31 Fireblast C :R: .75 2.00
32 Firebolt C :R: .10 .25
33 Fireslinger C :R: .10 .25
34 Flame Javelin U :R: .60 1.50
35 Flamekin Brawler C :R: .10 .25
36 Flametongue Kavu U :R: .60 1.50
37 Flamewave Invoker U :R: .20 .50
38 Furnace Whelp U :R: .20 .50
39 Hostility R :R: .40 1.00
40 Incinerate C :R: .60 1.50
41 Ingot Chewer C :R: .20 .50
42 Inner-Flame Acolyte C :R: .10 .25
43 Magma Jet U :R: 2.00 5.00
44 Pyre Charger U :R: .20 .50
45 Rakdos Pit Dragon R :R: .75 2.00
46 Seal of Fire C :R: .20 .50
47 Slith Firewalker U :R: .20 .50
48 Soulbright Flamekin C :R: .20 .50
49 Bottle Gnomes U .20 .50
50 Elemental Shaman C .20 .50
51 Keldon Megaliths U .25 .60
52 Mind Stone U .50 1.25
53 Oxidda Golem C .10 .25
54 Spire Golem C .10 .25
55 Terrain Generator U .60 1.50
56 Island L .10 .25
57 Island L .10 .25
58 Island L .10 .25
59 Island L .10 .25
60 Mountain L .10 .25
61 Mountain L .10 .25
62 Mountain L .10 .25
63 Mountain L .10 .25

2008 Magic The Gathering Duel Decks Jace vs. Chandra Token

1 Elemental Shaman .12 .20

2009 Magic The Gathering Duel Decks Divine vs. Demonic

COMPLETE SET (62) 50.00 120.00
DUEL DECK 60.00 120.00
RELEASED ON APRIL 10, 2009
1 Akroma, Angel of Wrath M :W: 12.00 30.00
2 Angel of Mercy U :W: .20 .50
3 Angelic Benediction U :W: .20 .50
4 Angelic Page C :W: .20 .50
5 Angelic Protector U :W: .20 .50
6 Angelsong C :W: .10 .25
7 Charging Paladin C :W: .10 .25
8 Faith's Fetters C :W: .30 .75
9 Healing Salve C :W: .10 .25
10 Icatian Priest U :W: .20 .50
11 Luminous Angel R :W: 3.00 8.00
12 Otherworldly Journey U :W: .20 .50
13 Pacifism C :W: .10 .25
14 Reya Dawnbringer R :W: 3.00 8.00
15 Righteous Cause U :W: .20 .50
16 Serra Advocate U :W: .20 .50
17 Serra Angel R :W: .30 .75
18 Serra's Boon U :W: .20 .50
19 Serra's Embrace U :W: .30 .75
20 Sustainer of the Realm U :W: .20 .50
21 Twilight Shepherd R :W: 1.25 3.00
22 Venerable Monk C :W: .10 .25
23 Abyssal Gatekeeper C :K: .10 .25
24 Abyssal Specter U :K: .20 .50
25 Barter in Blood U :K: .40 1.00
26 Breeding Pit U :K: .30 .75
27 Cackling Imp C :K: .10 .25
28 Consume Spirit U :K: .20 .50
29 Corrupt U :K: .20 .50
30 Cruel Edict U :K: .40 1.00
31 Daggerclaw Imp U :K: .20 .50
32 Dark Banishing C :K: .10 .25
33 Dark Ritual C :K: 1.25 3.00
34 Demonic Tutor U :K: 12.00 30.00
35 Demon's Jester C :K: .10 .25
36 Duress C :K: .40 1.00
37 Dusk Imp C :K: .10 .25
38 Fallen Angel R :K: .30 .75
39 Foul Imp C :K: .10 .25
40 Kuro, Pitlord R :K: .30 .75
41 Lord of the Pit M :K: 1.50 4.00
42 Oni Possession U :K: .20 .50
43 Overeager Apprentice C :K: .10 .25
44 Promise of Power R :K: .40 1.00
45 Reiver Demon R :K: .75 2.00
46 Soot Imp U :K: .20 .50
47 Souldrinker U :K: .20 .50
48 Stinkweed Imp C :K: 2.00 5.00
49 Unholy Strength C :K: .10 .25
50 Angel's Feather U .20 .50
51 Barren Moor C .20 .50
52 Demon's Horn U .20 .50
53 Marble Diamond U .20 .50
54 Secluded Steppe C .10 .25
55 Plains L .20 .50
56 Plains L .20 .50
57 Plains L .20 .50
58 Plains L .20 .50
59 Swamp L .20 .50
60 Swamp L .20 .50
61 Swamp L .20 .50
62 Swamp L .20 .50

2009 Magic The Gathering Duel Decks Divine vs. Demonic Tokens

1 Spirit .75 1.25
2 Demon .35 .45
3 Thrull .60 1.00

2009 Magic The Gathering Duel Decks Garruk vs. Liliana

COMPLETE SET (66) 25.00 60.00
DUEL DECK 30.00 50.00
RELEASED ON OCTOBER 30, 2009
1 Bad Moon R :K: 2.50 6.00
2 Corrupt U :K: .20 .50
3 Deathgreeter C :K: .10 .25
4 Drudge Skeletons C :K: .10 .25
5 Enslave U :K: .20 .50
6 Faerie Macabre C :K: .10 .25
7 Fleshbag Marauder U :K: .20 .50
8 Genju of the Fens U :K: .20 .50
9 Ghost-Lit Stalker U :K: .20 .50
10 Hideous End C :K: .10 .25

11 Howling Banshee U :K: .20 .50
12 Ichor Slick C :K: .10 .25
13 Keening Banshee U :K: .20 .50
14 Liliana Vess M :K: 6.00 15.00
15 Mutilate R :K: 2.50 6.00
16 Phyrexian Rager C :K: .10 .25
17 Ravenous Rats C :K: .10 .25
18 Rise from the Grave U :K: .20 .50
19 Sign in Blood C :K: .10 .25
20 Skeletal Vampire R :K: 1.25 3.00
21 Snuff Out C :K: .10 .25
22 Tendrils of Corruption C :K: .10 .25
23 Twisted Abomination C :K: .10 .25
24 Urborg Syphon-Mage C :K: .10 .25
25 Vampire Bats C :K: .10 .25
26 Vicious Hunger C :K: .10 .25
27 Wall of Bone U :K: .20 .50
28 Albino Troll U :G: .30 .75
29 Basking Rootwalla C :G: .30 .75
30 Beast Attack U :G: .20 .50
31 Blastoderm C :G: .10 .25
32 Elephant Guide U :G: .20 .50
33 Garruk Wildspeaker M :G: 6.00 15.00
34 Genju of the Cedars U :G: .20 .50
35 Giant Growth C :G: .10 .25
36 Harmonize U :G: .20 .50
37 Indrik Stomphowler U :G: .20 .50
38 Invigorate C :G: .10 .25
39 Krosan Tusker C :G: .10 .25
40 Lignify C :G: .10 .25
41 Nature's Lore C :G: .10 .25
42 Overrun U :G: .20 .50
43 Plated Slagwurm R :G: 1.25 3.00
44 Rancor C :G: .10 .25
45 Ravenous Baloth R :G: 1.50 4.00
46 Rude Awakening R :G: .60 1.50
47 Stampeding Wildebeests U :G: .20 .50
48 Vine Trellis C :G: .10 .25
49 Wild Mongrel C :G: .10 .25
50 Windstorm U :G: .20 .50
51 Wirewood Savage C :G: .10 .25
52 Polluted Mire C .10 .25
53 Serrated Arrows C .10 .25
54 Slippery Karst C .10 .25
55 Treetop Village U .20 .50
56 Forest L .10 .25
57 Forest L .10 .25
58 Forest L .10 .25
59 Forest L .10 .25
60 Swamp L .10 .25
61 Swamp L .10 .25
62 Swamp L .10 .25
63 Swamp L .10 .25

2009 Magic The Gathering Duel Decks Garruk vs. Liliana Tokens

1 Beast .60 1.00
2 Beast .20 .30
3 Elephant .50 .75

2010 Magic The Gathering Duel Decks Phyrexia vs. The Coalition

COMPLETE SET (73) 15.00 40.00
DUEL DECK 15.00 40.00
RELEASED ON MARCH 19, 2012
1 Gerrard Capashen R :W: .30 .75
2 Narrow Escape C :W: .10 .25
3 Sunscape Battlemage U :W: .20 .50
4 Allied Strategies U :B: .20 .50
5 Evasive Action U :B: .20 .50
6 Bone Shredder U :K: .20 .50
7 Carrion Feeder C :K: .20 .50
9 Dark Ritual C :K: .75 2.00
10 Exotic Curse C :K: .10 .25
11 Hideous End C :K: .10 .25
12 Living Death R :K: 1.00 2.50
13 Order of Yawgmoth U :K: .20 .50
14 Phyrexian Arena R :K: 1.25 3.00
15 Phyrexian Battleflies C :K: .10 .25
16 Phyrexian Broodlings C :K: .10 .25
17 Phyrexian Debaser C :K: .10 .25
18 Phyrexian Defiler U :K: .20 .50
19 Phyrexian Denouncer C :K: .10 .25
20 Phyrexian Gargantua U :K: .20 .50
21 Phyrexian Ghoul C :K: .10 .25
22 Phyrexian Negator M :K: 1.25 3.00
23 Phyrexian Plaguelord R :K: .30 .75
24 Priest of Gix U :K: .20 .50
25 Sanguine Guard U :K: .20 .50
26 Slay U :K: .20 .50
27 Tendrils of Corruption C :K: .10 .25
28 Thunderscape Battlemage U :R: .20 .50
29 Tribal Flames C :R: .20 .50
30 Urza's Rage M :R: .60 1.50
31 Fertile Ground C :G: .10 .25
32 Harrow C :G: .20 .50
33 Nomadic Elf C :G: .10 .25
34 Quirion Elves C :G: .10 .25
35 Thornscape Apprentice C :G: .10 .25
36 Thornscape Battlemage U :G: .20 .50
37 Verduran Emissary U :G: .20 .50
38 Yavimaya Elder C :G: .40 1.00
39 Armadillo Cloak C :W: :G: .40 1.00
40 Charging Troll U :W: :G: .20 .50
41 Darigaaz, the Igniter R :K: :R: :G: .60 1.50
42 Darigaaz's Charm U :K: :R: :G: .20 .50
43 Gerrard's Command C :W: :G: .10 .25
44 Rith, the Awakener R :W: :R: :G: .75 2.00
45 Rith's Charm U :W: :R: :G: .20 .50
46 Treva, the Renewer R :W: :L: :G: .75 2.00
47 Treva's Charm U :W: :L: :G: .20 .50
48 Coalition Relic R 1.50 4.00
49 Elfhame Palace U .20 .50
50 Hornet Cannon U .20 .50
51 Lightning Greaves U 1.00 2.50
52 Phyrexian Colossus R .30 .75
53 Phyrexian Hulk U .20 .50
54 Phyrexian Processor R .75 2.00
55 Phyrexian Totem U .20 .50
56 Phyrexian Vault U .20 .50
57 Power Armor U .20 .50
58 Puppet Strings U .20 .50
59 Shivan Oasis U .20 .50
60 Terramorphic Expanse C .20 .50
61 Voltaic Key U .40 1.00
62 Whispersilk Cloak U .30 .75
63 Worn Powerstone U .40 1.00
64 Forest L .10 .25
65 Forest L .10 .25
66 Island L .10 .25
67 Mountain L .10 .25
68 Plains L .10 .25
69 Swamp L .10 .25
70 Swamp L .10 .25
71 Swamp L .10 .25
72 Swamp L .10 .25

2010 Magic The Gathering Duel Decks Phyrexia vs. The Coalition Tokens

1 Hornet 1.75 2.25
2 Minion 4.50 6.00
3 Saproling .15 .25

2010 Magic The Gathering Duel Decks Elspeth vs. Tezzeret

COMPLETE SET (79) 50.00 75.00
DUEL DECK 30.00 50.00
RELEASED ON SEPTEMBER 9, 2010
1 Elspeth, Knight-Errant M :W: 10.00 13.00
2 Elite Vanguard U :W: .15 .25
3 Goldmeadow Harrier C :W: .10 .20
4 Infantry Veteran C :W: .10 .20
5 Loyal Sentry R :W: .25 .40
6 Mosquito Guard C :W: .10 .20
7 Glory Seeker C :W: .10 .20
8 Kor Skyfisher C :W: .10 .20
9 Temple Acolyte C :W: .10 .20
10 Kor Aeronaut U :W: .15 .25
11 Burrenton Bombardier C :W: .10 .20
12 Kor Hookmaster C :W: .10 .20
13 Kemba's Skyguard C :W: .10 .20
14 Celestial Crusader U :W: .15 .25
15 Seasoned Marshal U :W: .15 .25
16 Conclave Phalanx U :W: .15 .25
17 Stormfront Riders U :W: .15 .25
18 Catapult Master R :W: .25 .40
19 Conclave Equenaut C :W: .10 .20
20 Angel of Salvation R :W: .25 .40
21 Sunlance C :W: .10 .20
22 Swords to Plowshares U :W: 2.00 2.50
23 Journey to Nowhere C :W: 1.50 2.00
24 Mighty Leap C :W: .10 .20
25 Raise the Alarm C :W: .10 .20
26 Razor Barrier C :W: .10 .20
27 Crusade R :W: .50 .75
28 Blinding Beam C :W: .10 .20
29 Abolish U :W: .15 .25
30 Saltblast U :W: .15 .25
31 Swell of Courage U :W: .15 .25
32 Daru Encampment U .15 .25
33 Kabira Crossroads C .20 .30
34 Rustic Clachan R .25 .40
35 Plains L .10 .20
36 Plains L .10 .20
37 Plains L .10 .20
38 Plains L .10 .20
39 Tezzeret the Seeker M :B: 6.00 8.00
40 Arcbound Worker C .10 .20
41 Steel Wall C .10 .20
42 Runed Servitor U .15 .25
43 Silver Myr C .10 .20
44 Steel Overseer R 10.00 12.00
45 Assembly-Worker U .15 .25
46 Serrated Biskelion U .15 .25
47 Esperzoa U :B: .15 .25
48 Master of Etherium R :B: 7.00 9.00
49 Trinket Mage C :B: .20 .30
50 Clockwork Condor C .10 .20
51 Frogmite C .20 .30
52 Juggernaut U .15 .25
53 Synod Centurion U .15 .25
54 Faerie Mechanist C :B: .10 .20
55 Clockwork Hydra U .15 .25
56 Razormane Masticore R .25 .40
57 Triskelion R .25 .40
58 Pentavus R .25 .40
59 Qumulox U :B: .15 .25
60 Everflowing Chalice U .40 .60
61 AEther Spellbomb C .10 .20
62 Elixir of Immortality U .40 .60
63 Contagion Clasp U .25 .40
64 Energy Chamber U .75 1.00
65 Trip Noose U .15 .25
66 Echoing Truth C :B: .30 .50
67 Moonglove Extract C .10 .20
68 Thirst for Knowledge U :B: 1.75 2.00
69 Argivian Restoration U :B: .15 .25
70 Foil U :B: .30 .50
71 Thoughtcast C :B: .75 1.00
72 Darksteel Citadel C .75 1.00
73 Mishra's Factory U 1.75 2.25
74 Seat of the Synod C 1.25 1.75
75 Stalking Stones U .15 .25
76 Island L .10 .20
77 Island L .10 .20
78 Island L .10 .20
79 Island L .10 .20

2010 Magic The Gathering Duel Decks Elspeth vs. Tezzeret Token

1 Soldier .10 .15

2011 Magic The Gathering Duel Decks Knights vs. Dragons

DUEL DECK 20.00 40.00
RELEASED ON APRIL 1, 2011
1 Knight of the Reliquary M :W: :G: 4.00 10.00
2 Caravan Escort C :W: .10 .25
3 Lionheart Maverick C :W: .10 .25
4 Knight of Cliffhaven C :W: .10 .25
5 Knight of Meadowgrain U :W: 1.25 3.00
6 Knight of the White Orchid R :W: 1.25 3.00
7 Leonin Skyhunter U :W: .20 .50
8 Silver Knight U :W: .75 2.00
9 White Knight U :W: .30 .75
10 Knotvine Paladin R :W: :G: .40 1.00
11 Steward of Valeron C :W: :G: .10 .25
12 Benalish Lancer C :W: .10 .25
13 Zhalfirin Commander U :W: .20 .50
14 Knight Exemplar R :W: 1.50 4.00
15 Wilt-Leaf Cavaliers U :W: :G: .75 2.00
16 Kabira Vindicator U :W: .20 .50
17 Kinsbaile Cavalier R :W: 1.50 4.00
18 Alaborn Cavalier U :W: .20 .50
19 Skyhunter Patrol C :W: .10 .25
20 Plover Knights C :W: .20 .50
21 Juniper Order Ranger U :W: :G: .75 2.00
22 Paladin of Prahv U :W: .20 .50
23 Harm's Way U :W: .20 .50
24 Reciprocate U :W: .30 .75
25 Edge of Autumn C :G: .10 .25
26 Mighty Leap C :W: .10 .25
27 Reprisal U :W: .20 .50
28 Test of Faith U :W: .20 .50
29 Heroes' Reunion U :W: :G: .30 .75
30 Sigil Blessing C :W: :G: .10 .25
31 Loxodon Warhammer R 1.00 2.50
32 Spidersilk Armor C :G: .20 .50
33 Griffin Guide U :W: .20 .50
34 Oblivion Ring C :W: 1.25 3.00
35 Grasslands U .20 .50
36 Sejiri Steppe C .10 .25
37 Selesnya Sanctuary C .20 .50
38 Treetop Village U 1.25 3.00
39 Plains L .10 .25
40 Plains L .10 .25
41 Plains L .10 .25
42 Plains L .10 .25
43 Forest L .10 .25
44 Forest L .10 .25
45 Forest L .10 .25
46 Forest L .10 .25
47 Bogardan Hellkite M :R: 2.00 5.00
48 Cinder Wall C :R: .10 .25
49 Skirk Prospector C :R: .20 .50
50 Bloodmark Mentor U :R: .40 1.00
51 Fire-Belly Changeling C :R: .10 .25
52 Mudbutton Torchrunner C :R: .20 .50
53 Dragonspeaker Shaman U :R: 1.25 3.00
54 Dragon Whelp U :R: .20 .50
55 Henge Guardian U .20 .50
56 Voracious Dragon R :R: .40 1.00
57 Bogardan Rager C :R: .10 .25
58 Mordant Dragon R :R: .40 1.00
59 Kilnmouth Dragon R :R: 1.25 3.00
60 Shivan Hellkite R :R: .40 1.00
61 Thunder Dragon R :R: .75 2.00
62 Armillary Sphere C .10 .25
63 Dragon's Claw U .20 .50
64 Breath of Darigaaz U :R: .20 .50
65 Dragon Fodder C :R: .20 .50
66 Punishing Fire U :R: .40 1.00
67 Spitting Earth C :R: .10 .25
68 Captive Flame U :R: .20 .50
69 Ghostfire C .10 .25
70 Seething Song C :R: 1.25 3.00
71 Seismic Strike C :R: .20 .50
72 Claws of Valakut C :R: .10 .25
73 Temporary Insanity U :R: .20 .50
74 Shiv's Embrace U :R: .40 1.00
75 Cone of Flame U :R: .20 .50
76 Fiery Fall C :R: .10 .25
77 Jaws of Stone U :R: .20 .50
78 Mountain L .10 .25
79 Mountain L .10 .25
80 Mountain L .10 .25
81 Mountain L .10 .25

2011 Magic The Gathering Duel Decks Knights vs. Dragons Token

1 Goblin .25 .40

2011 Magic The Gathering Duel Decks Ajani vs. Nicol Bolas

DUEL DECK 15.00 30.00
RELEASED ON SEPTEMBER 2, 2011
1 Ajani Vengeant M :W/R: 2.50 6.00
2 Kird Ape U :R: .50 1.25
3 Essence Warden C :G: .20 .50
4 Wild Nacatl C :G: .20 .50
5 Loam Lion U :W: .20 .50
6 Canyon Wildcat C :R: .10 .25
7 Jade Mage U :G: .20 .50
8 Sylvan Ranger C :G: .10 .25
9 Ajani's Pridemate U :W: .40 1.00
10 Qasali Pridemage C :W: :G: .40 1.00
11 Grazing Gladehart C :G: .10 .25
12 Fleetfoot Panther U :W: :G: .20 .50
13 Woolly Thoctar U :W: :R: :G: .30 .75
14 Briarhorn U :G: .20 .50
15 Loxodon Hierarch R :W: :G: .60 1.50
16 Spitemare U :W: :R: .20 .50
17 Marisi's Twinclaws U :W: :R: :G: .20 .50
18 Ageless Entity R :G: .50 1.25
19 Pride of Lions U :G: .20 .50
20 Nacatl Hunt-Pride U :W: .20 .50
21 Firemane Angel R :W: :R: .75 2.00
22 Ajani's Mantra C :W: .10 .25
23 Lightning Helix U :W: :R: 2.00 4.00
24 Lead the Stampede U :G: .20 .50
25 Griffin Guide U :W: .20 .50
26 Recumbent Bliss C :W: .10 .25
27 Searing Meditation R :W: :R: .40 1.00
28 Behemoth Sledge U :W: :G: .60 1.50
29 Naya Charm U :W: :R: :G: .20 .50
30 Sylvan Bounty C :G: .10 .25
31 Titanic Ultimatum R :W: :R: :G: .40 1.00
32 Evolving Wilds C .30 .75
33 Graypelt Refuge U .30 .75
34 Jungle Shrine U .75 2.00
35 Kazandu Refuge U .30 .75
36 Sapseep Forest U .20 .50
37 Vitu-Ghazi, the City-Tree U .20 .50
38 Forest L .10 .25
39 Forest L .10 .25
40 Plains L .10 .25
41 Mountain L .10 .25
42 Nicol Bolas, Planeswalker M :B: :K: :R: 5.00 12.00
43 Surveilling Sprite C :B: .10 .25
44 Nightscape Familiar C :K: .20 .50
45 Slavering Nulls U :R: .20 .50
46 Brackwater Elemental C :B: .10 .25
47 Morgue Toad C :K: .10 .25
48 Hellfire Mongrel U :R: .20 .50
49 Dimir Cutpurse R :B: :K: .60 1.50
50 Steamcore Weird C :B: .10 .25
51 Moroii U :B: :K: .20 .50
52 Blazing Specter R :K: :R: .60 1.50
53 Fire-Field Ogre U :B: :K: :R: .20 .50
54 Shriekmaw U :K: .60 1.50
55 Ogre Savant C :R: .10 .25
56 Jhessian Zombies C :B: :K: .10 .25
57 Igneous Pouncer C :K: :R: .10 .25
58 Vapor Snag C :B: .50 1.25
59 Countersquall U :B: :K: .60 1.50
60 Obelisk of Grixis C .10 .25
61 Recoil C :B: :K: .20 .50
62 Undermine R :B: :K: 1.25 3.00
63 Grixis Charm U :B: :K: :R: .20 .50
64 Icy Manipulator U .20 .50
65 Deep Analysis U :B: .50 1.25
66 Agonizing Demise C :K: .10 .25
67 Slave of Bolas U :B: :K: :R: .20 .50
68 Elder Mastery U :B: :K: :R: .20 .50
69 Cruel Ultimatum R :B: :K: :R: .75 2.00
70 Profane Command R :K: .75 2.00
71 Spite: :Malice U :B: :K: .20 .50
72 Pain: :Suffering U :K: :R: .20 .50
73 Rise: :Fall U :B: :K: :R: .20 .50
74 Crumbling Necropolis U .75 2.00
75 Rupture Spire C .20 .50
76 Terramorphic Expanse C .20 .50
77 Swamp L .10 .25
78 Swamp L .10 .25
79 Island L .10 .25
80 Mountain L .10 .25

2011 Magic The Gathering Duel Decks Ajani vs. Nicol Bolas Tokens

1 Griffin .15 .25
2 Saproling .15 .25

2012 Magic The Gathering Duel Decks Venser vs. Koth

DUEL DECK 15.00 40.00
RELEASED ON MARCH 30, 2012
1 Venser, the Sojourner M :W/B: 4.00 10.00
2 Whitemane Lion C :W: .20 .50
3 Augury Owl C :B: .10 .25
4 Coral Fighters U :B: .20 .50
5 Minamo Sightbender U :B: .20 .50
6 Mistmeadow Witch U :W/B: .20 .50
7 Scroll Thief C :B: .10 .25
8 Neurok Invisimancer C :B: .10 .25
9 Slith Strider U :B: .20 .50
10 Sky Spirit U :W/B: .20 .50
11 Wall of Denial U :W/B: .60 1.50
12 Galepowder Mage R :W: .40 1.00
13 Kor Cartographer C :W: .10 .25
14 Clone R :B: .40 1.00
15 Cryptic Annelid U :B: .20 .50
16 Primal Plasma C :B: .10 .25
17 Sawtooth Loon U :W/B: .20 .50
18 Cache Raiders U :B: .20 .50
19 Windreaver R :W/B: .40 1.00
20 Jedit's Dragoons C :W: .10 .25
21 Sunblast Angel R :W: .40 1.00
22 Sphinx of Uthuun R :B: .40 1.00
23 Path to Exile U :W: 3.00 8.00
24 Preordain C :B: .60 1.50
25 Sigil of Sleep C :B: .20 .50
26 Revoke Existence C :W: .10 .25
27 Angelic Shield U :W/B: .20 .50
28 Oblivion Ring U :W: .60 1.50
29 Safe Passage C :W: .10 .25
30 Steel of the Godhead C :W/B: .30 .75
31 Vanish into Memory U :W/B: .20 .50
32 Overrule C :W/B: .20 .50
33 Azorius Chancery C .20 .50
34 Flood Plain U .30 .75
35 New Benalia U .20 .50
36 Sejiri Refuge U .30 .75
37 Soaring Seacliff C .10 .25
38 Plains L .10 .25
39 Plains L .10 .25
40 Plains L .10 .25
41 Island L .10 .25
42 Island L .10 .25
43 Island L .10 .25
44 Koth of the Hammer M :R: 4.00 10.00
45 Plated Geopede C :R: .30 .75
46 Pygmy Pyrosaur C :R: .10 .25
47 Pilgrim's Eye C .20 .50
48 AEther Membrane U :R: .20 .50
49 Fiery Hellhound C :R: .10 .25
50 Vulshok Sorcerer C :R: .10 .25
51 Anger U :R: .60 1.50
52 Cosi's Ravager C :R: .10 .25
53 Vulshok Berserker C :R: .10 .25
54 Bloodfire Kavu U :R: .20 .50
55 Stone Giant U :R: .20 .50
56 Geyser Glider U :R: .20 .50
57 Lithophage R :R: .40 1.00
58 Torchling R :R: .40 1.00
59 Chartooth Cougar C :R: .30 .75
60 Earth Servant U :R: .20 .50
61 Greater Stone Spirit U :R: .20 .50

Card	Low	High
62 Bloodfire Colossus R :R:	.40	1.00
63 Wayfarer's Bauble C	.20	.50
64 Armillary Sphere C	.10	.25
65 Journeyer's Kite R	.75	2.00
66 Vulshok Morningstar U	.20	.50
67 Searing Blaze C :R:	.10	.25
68 Vulshok Battlegear U	.20	.50
69 Downhill Charge C :R:	.10	.25
70 Seismic Strike C :R:	.10	.25
71 Spire Barrage C :R:	.10	.25
72 Jaws of Stone U :R:	.20	.50
73 Volley of Boulders R :R:	.40	1.00
74 Mountain L	.10	.25
75 Mountain L	.10	.25
76 Mountain L	.10	.25
77 Mountain L	.10	.25

2012 Magic The Gathering Duel Decks Venser vs. Koth Tokens

Card	Low	High
1 Venser, the Sojourner Emblem	4.00	6.00
2 Koth of the Hammer Emblem	1.50	2.00

2012 Magic The Gathering Duel Decks Izzet vs. Golgari

Card	Low	High
DUAL DECK	8.00	20.00
RELEASED ON SEPTEMBER 9, 2012		
1 Brainstorm C :B:	2.00	5.00
2 Call to Heel C :B:	.10	.25
3 Dissipate U :B:	.30	.75
4 Force Spike C :B:	.20	.50
5 Overwhelming Intellect :B:	.20	.50
6 Reminisce U :B:	.20	.50
7 Steamcore Weird C :B:	.10	.25
8 Thunderheads U :B:	.20	.50
9 Train of Thought C :B:	.10	.25
10 Vacuumelt U :B:	.20	.50
11 Brain Weevil C :K:	.10	.25
12 Feast or Famine C :K:	.10	.25
13 Ghoul's Feast U :K:	.20	.50
14 Golgari Thug U :K:	.10	1.00
15 Nightmare Void U :K:	.20	.50
16 Plagued Rusalka U :K:	.20	.50
17 Ravenous Rats C :K:	.10	.25
18 Reassembling Skeleton U :K:	.20	.50
19 Sadistic Hypnotist U :K:	.20	.50
20 Stinkweed Imp C :K:	.10	.25
21 Twilight's Call R :K:	.30	.75
22 Vigor Mortis U :K:	.20	.50
23 Yoke of the Damned C :K:	.10	.25
24 Galvanoth R :R:	.30	.75
25 Kiln Fiend C :R:	.40	1.00
26 Magma Spray C :R:	.10	.25
27 Ogre Savant C :R:	.10	.25
28 Pyromatics C :R:	.10	.25
29 Street Spasm U :R:	.20	.50
30 Boneyard Wurm U :G:	.20	.50
31 Elves of Deep Shadow C :G:	.10	.25
32 Eternal Witness U :G:	1.25	3.00
33 Golgari Grave-Troll R :G:	.75	2.00
34 Greater Mossdog C :G:	.10	.25
35 Grim Flowering U :G:	.20	.50
36 Life from the Loam R :G:	1.25	3.00
37 Stingerfling Spider U :G:	.20	.50
38 Djinn Illuminatus R :B: :R:	.30	.75
39 Doomgape R :K: :G:	.30	.75
40 Dreg Mangler U :K: :G:	.20	.50
41 Fire/Ice U :R: :B:	.20	.50
42 Gelectrode U :B: :R:	.30	.75
43 Gleancrawler R :K: :G:	.30	.75
44 Goblin Electromancer C :B: :R:	.20	.50
45 Golgari Germination U :K: :G:	.20	.50
46 Golgari Rotwurm C :K: :G:	.10	.25
47 Invoke the Firemind R :B: :R:	.30	.75
48 Izzet Charm U :B: :R:	.30	.75
49 Izzet Chronarch C :B: :R:	.10	.25
50 Izzet Guildmage U :B: :R:	.20	.50
51 Jarad, Golgari Lich Lord M :K: :G:	.75	2.00
52 Korozda Guildmage U :K: :G:	.20	.50
53 Life/Death U :G: :K:	.20	.50
54 Niv-Mizzet, the Firemind :B: :R: M	1.50	4.00
55 Prophetic Bolt R :B: :R:	.30	.75
56 Putrefy U :K: :G:	.30	.75
57 Putrid Leech C :K: :G:	.10	.25
58 Quicksilver Dagger C :B: :R:	.10	.25
59 Shambling Shell C :K: :G:	.10	.25
60 Shrewd Hatchling U :B: :R:	.20	.50
61 Wee Dragonauts C :B: :R:	.10	.25
62 Barren Moor C	.10	.25
63 Dakmor Salvage U	.20	.50
64 Forgotten Cave C	.10	.25
65 Golgari Rot Farm C	.30	.75
66 Golgari Signet C	.10	.25
67 Isochron Scepter U	2.50	6.00
68 Izzet Boilerworks C	.10	.25
69 Izzet Signet C	.10	.25
70 Lonely Sandbar C	.10	.25
71 Nivix, Aerie of the Firemind U	.20	.50
72 Sphinx-Bone Wand R	.30	.75
73 Svogthos, the Restless Tomb U	.20	.50
74 Tranquil Thicket C	.10	.25
75 Forest L	.10	.25
76 Forest L	.10	.25
77 Forest L	.10	.25
78 Forest L	.10	.25
79 Island L	.10	.25
80 Island L	.10	.25
81 Island L	.10	.25
82 Island L	.10	.25
83 Mountain L	.10	.25
84 Mountain L	.10	.25
85 Mountain L	.10	.25
86 Mountain L	.10	.25
87 Swamp L	.10	.25
88 Swamp L	.10	.25
89 Swamp L	.10	.25
90 Swamp L	.10	.25

2012 Magic The Gathering Duel Decks Izzet vs. Golgari Tokens

Card	Low	High
1 Saproling	.12	.20

2013 Magic The Gathering Duel Decks Heroes vs. Monsters

Card	Low	High
COMPLETE SET		
RELEASED ON		
1 Sun Titan M	2.00	2.50
2 Somberwald Vigilante C	.15	.25
3 Figure of Destiny R	1.00	1.50
4 Cavalry Pegasus C	.15	.25
5 Fencing Ace U	.15	.25
6 Thraben Valiant C	.15	.25
7 Stun Sniper U	.15	.25
8 Truefire Paladin U	.15	.25
9 Auramancer C	.15	.25
10 Freewind Equenaut C	.15	.25
11 Anax and Cymede R	.25	.40
12 Armory Guard C	.15	.25
13 Gustcloak Sentinel U	.15	.25
14 Dawnstrike Paladin C	.15	.25
15 Nobilis of War R	.25	.40
16 Kamahl, Pit Fighter R	.15	.25
17 Condemn U	.15	.25
18 Daily Regimen U	.15	.25
19 Pay No Heed C	.15	.25
20 Righteousness U	.15	.25
21 Stand Firm C	.15	.25
22 Magma Jet U	.50	.75
23 Ordeal of Purphoros U	.15	.25
24 Bonds of Faith C	.15	.25
25 Moment of Heroism C	.15	.25
26 Undying Rage U	.15	.25
27 Battle Mastery U	.15	.25
28 Griffin Guide U	.15	.25
29 Smite the Monstrous C	.15	.25
30 Miraculous Recovery U	.15	.25
31 Winds of Rath R	.75	1.00
32 Pyrokinesis U	.25	.40
33 Boros Guildgate C	.15	.25
34 New Benalia U	.15	.25
35 Mountain L	.15	.25
36 Mountain L	.15	.25
37 Mountain L	.15	.25
38 Mountain L	.15	.25
39 Plains L	.15	.25
40 Plains L	.15	.25
41 Plains L	.15	.25
42 Plains L	.15	.25
43 Polukranos, World Eater M	1.00	1.50
44 Orcish Lumberjack C	.15	.25
45 Deadly Recluse C	.15	.25
46 Kavu Predator U	.30	.50
47 Satyr Hedonist C	.15	.25
48 Zhur-Taa Druid C	.15	.25
49 Blood Ogre C	.15	.25
50 Troll Ascetic R	.40	.60
51 Crowned Ceratok U	.15	.25
52 Gorehorn Minotaurs C	.15	.25
53 Ghor-Clan Savage C	.15	.25
54 Deus of Calamity R	1.00	1.25
55 Conquering Manticore R	.15	.25
56 Crater Hellion R	.15	.25
57 Skarrgan Firebird R	.15	.25
58 Valley Rannet C	.15	.25
59 Krosan Tusker C	.15	.25
60 Skarrgan Skybreaker U	.15	.25
61 Shower of Sparks C	.15	.25
62 Prey Upon C	.15	.25
63 Pyroclasm U	.40	.60
64 Regrowth U	2.75	3.00
65 Terrifying Presence C	.15	.25
66 Destructive Revelry U	.30	.50
67 Dragon Blood U	.15	.25
68 Volt Charge C	.15	.25
69 Beast Within U	3.50	4.00
70 Fires of Yavimaya U	.15	.25
71 Kazandu Refuge U	.15	.25
72 Llanowar Reborn U	.30	.50
73 Skarrg, the Rage Pits U	.15	.25
74 Mountain L	.15	.25
75 Mountain L	.15	.25
76 Mountain L	.15	.25
77 Mountain L	.15	.25
78 Forest L	.15	.25
79 Forest L	.15	.25
80 Forest L	.15	.25
81 Forest L	.15	.25

2013 Magic The Gathering Duel Decks Heroes vs. Monsters Tokens

Card	Low	High
1 Griffin	.12	.20
2 Beast	.15	.25

2013 Magic The Gathering Duel Decks Sorin vs. Tibalt

Card	Low	High
COMPLETE SET (81)	25.00	40.00
RELEASED IN MARCH 2013		
1 Doomed Traveler C :W:	.10	.20
2 Field of Souls R :W:	.10	.20
3 Twilight Drover R :W:	.75	1.00
4 Fiend Hunter U :W:	.10	.20
5 Mausoleum Guard U :W:	.10	.20
6 Phantom General U :W:	.10	.20
7 Spectral Procession U :W:	.25	.40
8 Wall of Omens U :W:	3.00	3.50
9 Absorb Vis C :K:	.10	.20
10 Bloodrage Vampire C :K:	.10	.20
11 Bump in the Night C :K:	.10	.20
12 Child of Night C :K:	.10	.20
13 Duskhunter Bat C :K:	.10	.20
14 Mark of the Vampire C :K:	.10	.20
15 Mesmeric Fiend C :K:	.10	.20
16 Sorin's Thirst C :K:	.10	.20
17 Strangling Soot C :K:	.10	.20
18 Vampire Lacerator C :K:	.10	.20
19 Vampire's Bite C :K:	.10	.20
20 Ancient Craving R :K:	.25	.40
21 Butcher of Malakir R :K:	.25	.40
22 Corpse Connoisseur U :K:	.10	.20
23 Decompose U :K:	.10	.20
24 Gatekeeper of Malakir U :K:	1.25	1.75
25 Lingering Souls U :K:	.75	1.00
26 Reassembling Skeleton U :K:	.10	.20
27 Revenant Patriarch U :K:	.10	.20
28 Sengir Vampire U :K:	.10	.20
29 Urge to Feed U :K:	.10	.20
30 Vampire Nighthawk U :K:	.75	1.00
31 Vampire Outcasts U :K:	.10	.20
32 Ashmouth Hound C :R:	.10	.20
33 Blazing Salvo C :R:	.10	.20
34 Coal Stoker C :R:	.10	.20
35 Faithless Looting C :R:	.30	.50
36 Flame Slash C :R:	.30	.50
37 Geistflame C :R:	.10	.20
38 Goblin Arsonist C :R:	.10	.20
39 Mad Prophet C :R:	.10	.20
40 Vithian Stinger C :R:	.10	.20
41 Tibalt, the Fiend-Blooded M :R:	2.50	4.00
42 Breaking Point R :R:	.40	.60
43 Devil's Play R :R:	.10	.20
44 Hellrider R :R:	.40	.60
45 Lavaborn Muse R :R:	.10	.20
46 Sulfuric Vortex R :R:	.50	.75
47 Browbeat U :R:	1.00	1.25
48 Flame Javelin U :R:	.10	.20
49 Gang of Devils U :R:	.10	.20
50 Hellspark Elemental U :R:	.75	1.25
51 Pyroclasm U :R:	.30	.50
52 Recoup U :R:	.10	.20
53 Scorched Rusalka U :R:	.10	.20
54 Scourge Devil U :R:	.10	.20
55 Skirsdag Cultist U :R:	.10	.20
56 Blightning C :D:	.50	.75
57 Terminate C :D:	2.00	2.75
58 Unmake C :D:	.75	1.00
59 Sorin, Lord of Innistrad M :D:	5.00	8.00
60 Death Grasp R :D:	.10	.20
61 Mortify U :D:	.50	.75
62 Shambling Remains U :D:	.10	.20
63 Torrent of Souls U :D:	.10	.20
64 Zealous Persecution U :D:	.30	.50
66 Evolving Wilds C	.10	.20
67 Rakdos Carnarium C	.10	.20
68 Mountain L	.10	.20
69 Mountain L	.10	.20
70 Mountain L	.10	.20
71 Plains L	.10	.20
72 Plains L	.10	.20
73 Plains L	.10	.20
74 Swamp (35) L	.10	.20
75 Swamp (36) L	.10	.20
76 Swamp (37) L	.10	.20
77 Swamp (78) L	.10	.20
78 Swamp (79) L	.10	.20
79 Swamp (80) L	.10	.20
80 Akoum Refuge U	.10	.20
81 Tainted Field U	.30	.50

2013 Magic The Gathering Duel Decks Sorin vs. Tibalt Token

Card	Low	High
1 Spirit	.10	.15

2014 Magic The Gathering Duel Decks Jace vs. Vraska

Card	Low	High
DUEL DECK	20.00	30.00
RELEASED ON MARCH 14, 2014		
1 Acidic Slime U :G:	.10	.20
2 Aeon Chronicler R :B:	.20	.35
3 AEther Adept C :B:	.10	.20
4 AEther Figment U :B:	.10	.20
5 Agoraphobia U :B:	.10	.20
6 Archaeomancer C :B:	.10	.20
7 Body Double R :B:	.50	.75
8 Chronomaton U	.10	.20
9 Claustrophobia C :B:	.10	.20
10 Consume Strength C :K/G:	.10	.20
11 Control Magic U :B:	.40	.60
12 Corpse Traders U :K:	.10	.20
13 Crosstown Courier C :B:	.10	.20
14 Death-Hood Cobra C :G:	.10	.20
15 Dread Statuary U	.10	.20
16 Dream Stalker C :B:	.10	.20
17 Drooling Groodion U :K/G:	.10	.20
18 Errant Ephemeron C :B:	.10	.20
19 Festerhide Boar C :G:	.10	.20
20 Forest L	.10	.20
21 Forest L	.10	.20
22 Forest L	.10	.20
23 Forest L	.10	.20
24 Forest L	.10	.20
25 Future Sight R :B:	.40	.60
26 Gatecreeper Vine C :G:	.10	.20
27 Golgari Guildgate C	.10	.20
28 Griptide C :B:	.10	.20
29 Grisly Spectacle C :K:	.10	.20
30 Halimar Depths C	.50	.75
31 Highway Robber C :K:	.10	.20
32 Hypnotic Cloud C :K:	.10	.20
33 Into the Roil C :B:	.10	.20
34 Island L	.10	.20
35 Island L	.10	.20
36 Island L	.10	.20
37 Island L	.10	.20
38 Island L	.10	.20
39 Jace, Architect of Thought M :B:	2.00	3.50
40 Jace's Ingenuity U :B:	.10	.20
41 Jace's Mindseeker R :B:	.20	.30
42 Jace's Phantasm U :B:	1.00	1.50
43 Krovikan Mist C :B:	.10	.20
44 Last Kiss C :K:	.10	.20
45 Leyline Phantom C :B:	.10	.20
46 Marsh Casualties U :K:	.10	.20
47 Memory Lapse C :B:	.10	.20
48 Merfolk Wayfinder U :B:	.10	.20
49 Mold Shambler C :G:	.10	.20
50 Nekrataal U :K:	.10	.20
51 Night's Whisper U :K:	1.25	1.75
52 Ohran Viper R :G:	.20	.35
53 Oran-Rief Recluse C :G:	.10	.20
54 Phantasmal Bear C :B:	.10	.20
55 Phantasmal Dragon U :B:	.10	.20
56 Prohibit C :B:	.10	.20
57 Pulse Tracker C :K:	.10	.20
58 Putrid Leech C :K/G:	.10	.20
59 Ray of Command C :B:	.10	.20
60 Reaper of the Wilds R :K/G:	.20	.35
61 Remand U :B:	3.00	4.50
62 Riftwing Cloudskate U :B:	.10	.20
63 River Boa U :G:	.10	.20
64 Rogue's Passage U	.10	.20
65 Sadistic Augermage C :K:	.10	.20
66 Sea Gate Oracle C :B:	.10	.20
67 Shadow Alley Denizen C :K:	.10	.20
68 Slate Street Ruffian C :K:	.10	.20
69 Spawnwrithe R :G:	.20	.35
70 Spelltwine R :B:	.20	.35
71 Stab Wound C :K:	.10	.20
72 Stealer of Secrets C :B:	.10	.20
73 Stonefare Crocodile C :G:	.10	.20
74 Summoner's Bane U :B:	.10	.20
75 Swamp L	.10	.20
76 Swamp L	.10	.20
77 Swamp L	.10	.20
78 Swamp L	.10	.20
79 Swamp L	.10	.20
80 Tainted Wood U	.20	.35
81 Tavern Swindler U :K:	.10	.20
82 Thought Scour C :B:	.75	1.00
83 Tragic Slip C :K:	.10	.20
84 Treasured Find U :K/G:	.10	.20
85 Underworld Connections R :K:	.25	.40
86 Vinelasher Kudzu R :G:	.20	.35
87 Vraska the Unseen M :K/G:	3.00	4.50
88 Wight of Precinct Six U :K:	.25	.40

2014 Magic The Gathering Duel Decks Jace vs. Vraska Tokens

Card	Low	High
1 Assassin	.50	.75

2014 Magic The Gathering Duel Decks Speed vs. Cunning

Card	Low	High
DUEL DECK	12.00	30.00
RELEASED ON SEPTEMBER 5, 2014		
1 Arrow Volley Trap U :W:	.20	.50
2 Dauntless Onslaught U :W:	.20	.50
3 Hold the Line R :W:	.40	1.00
4 Infantry Veteran C :W:	.10	.25
5 Kor Hookmaster C :W:	.10	.25
6 Leonin Snarecaster C :W:	.10	.25
7 Lone Missionary C :W:	.10	.25
8 Master Decoy C :W:	.10	.25
9 Stave Off C :W:	.10	.25
10 Stonecloaker U :W:	.20	.50
11 Swift Justice C :W:	.10	.25
12 Aquamorph Entity C :B:	.10	.25
13 Arcanis the Omnipotent M :B:	2.50	6.00
14 Coral Trickster C :B:	.10	.25
15 Dregscape Zombie C :B:	.10	.25
16 Echo Tracer C :B:	.10	.25
17 Faerie Impostor U :B:	.20	.50
18 Faerie Invaders C :B:	.10	.25
19 Fathom Seer C :B:	.10	.25
20 Fleeting Distraction C :B:	.10	.25
21 Impulse C :B:	.10	.25
22 Jeskai Elder U :B:	.20	.50
23 Mana Leak C :B:	.20	.50
24 Repeal C :B:	.10	.25
25 Sphinx of Uthuun R :B:	.40	1.00
26 Thousand Winds R :B:	.40	1.00
27 Traumatic Visions C :B:	.10	.25
28 Whiplash Trap C :B:	.10	.25
29 Willbender U :B:	.20	.50
30 Bone Splinters C :K:	.10	.25
31 Fleshbag Marauder U :K:	.20	.50
32 Act of Treason C :R:	.10	.25
33 Arc Trail U :R:	.20	.50
34 Banefire R :R:	.40	1.00
35 Beetleback Chief U :R:	.20	.50
36 Fiery Fall C :R:	.10	.25
37 Frenzied Goblin U :R:	.20	.50
38 Fury of the Horde R :R:	.60	1.50
39 Ghitu Encampment U :R:	.20	.50
40 Goblin Bombardment U :R:	.20	.50
41 Goblin Warchief U :R:	.75	2.00
42 Hell's Thunder R :R:	.40	1.00
43 Hellraiser Goblin U :R:	.20	.50
44 Inferno Trap U :R:	.20	.50
45 Krenko's Command C :R:	.10	.25
46 Krenko, Mob Boss R :R:	1.50	4.00
47 Mardu Heart-Piercer U :R:	.20	.50
48 Ogre Battledriver R :R:	.40	1.00
49 Oni of Wild Places U :R:	.20	.50
50 Orcish Cannonade C :R:	.10	.25
51 Reckless Abandon C :R:	.10	.25
52 Scourge Devil U :R:	.20	.50
53 Shock C :R:	.10	.25
54 Sparkmage Apprentice C :R:	.10	.25
55 Lightning Angel R :R:	.40	1.00
56 Zurgo Helmsmasher M :D:	2.50	6.00
57 Flame-Kin Zealot U :R :W:	.20	.50
58 Goblin Deathraiders C :K: :R:	.10	.25
59 Hussar Patrol C :W: :B:	.10	.25
60 Kathari Bomber C :K: :R:	.10	.25
61 Lightning Helix U :R: :W:	1.25	3.00
62 Shambling Remains U :K: :R:	.20	.50
63 Steam Augury R :G: :R:	.40	1.00
64 Evolving Wilds C :L:	.10	.25
65 Island L	.10	.25
66 Island L	.10	.25
67 Island L	.10	.25
68 Mountain L	.10	.25
69 Mountain L	.10	.25
70 Mountain L	.10	.25
71 Mountain L	.10	.25
72 Mystic Monastery U :L:	.30	.75
73 Nomad Outpost U :L:	.25	.60
74 Plains L	.10	.25
75 Plains L	.10	.25

76 Plains L .10 .25
77 Plains L .10 .25
78 Swamp L .10 .25
79 Swamp L .10 .25
80 Swamp L .10 .25
81 Terramorphic Expanse C :L: .10 .25
T1 Goblin Token .20 .50

2014 Magic The Gathering Duel Decks Anthology Divine vs. Demonic Tokens

1 Spirit
2 Demon
3 Thrull

2014 Magic The Gathering Duel Decks Anthology Elves vs. Goblins Tokens

1 Elemental
2 Elf Warrior
3 Goblin

2014 Magic The Gathering Duel Decks Anthology Garruk vs. Liliana Tokens

1 Beast
2 Beast
3 Elephant
4 Bat

2015 Magic The Gathering Duel Decks Elspeth vs. Kiora

COMPLETE SET (65) 20.00 35.00
DUEL DECK 10.00 25.00
RELEASED ON FEBRUARY 27, 2015
1 Banisher Priest U :W: .10 .20
2 Captain of the Watch R :W: .50 .75
3 Celestial Flare C :W: .10 .20
4 Court Street Denizen C :W: .10 .20
5 Dauntless Onslaught U :W: .10 .20
6 Decree of Justice R :W: .20 .35
7 Dictate of Heliod R :W: .20 .35
8 Elspeth, Sun's Champion M :W: 8.00 10.00
9 Gempalm Avenger C :W: .10 .20
10 Gustcloak Harrier C :W: .10 .20
11 Gustcloak Savior R :W: .20 .35
12 Gustcloak Sentinel U :W: .10 .20
13 Gustcloak Skirmisher U :W: .10 .20
14 Icatian Javelineers C :W: .10 .20
15 Kinsbaile Skirmisher C :W: .10 .20
16 Kor Skyfisher C :W: .10 .20
17 Loxodon Partisan C :W: .10 .20
18 Mighty Leap C :W: .10 .20
19 Mortal's Ardor C :W: .10 .20
20 Mother of Runes U :W: 1.75 2.25
21 Noble Templar C :W: .10 .20
22 Precinct Captain R :W: .30 .50
23 Raise the Alarm C :W: .10 .20
24 Soul Parry C :W: .10 .20
25 Standing Troops C :W: .10 .20
26 Sunlance C :W: .10 .20
27 Veteran Armorsmith C :W: .10 .20
28 Veteran Swordsmith C :W: .10 .20
29 Accumulated Knowledge C :B: .10 .20
30 AEtherize U :B: .10 .20
31 Man-o'-War C :B: .10 .20
32 Omenspeaker C :B: .10 .20
33 Scourge of Fleets R :B: .20 .35
34 Sealock Monster U :B: .10 .20
35 Surrakar Banisher C :B: .10 .20
36 Whelming Wave R :B: .25 .40
37 Explore C :G: .30 .50
38 Explosive Vegetation U :G: .75 1.25
39 Nessian Asp C :G: .10 .20
40 Netcaster Spider C :G: .10 .20
41 Time to Feed C :G: .10 .20
42 Coiling Oracle C :M: .10 .20
43 Kiora's Follower U :M: .10 .20
44 Kiora, the Crashing Wave M :M: 2.50 4.00
45 Lorescale Coatl U :M: .10 .20
46 Nimbus Swimmer U :M: .10 .20
47 Peel from Reality C :M: .10 .20
48 Plasm Capture R :M: .20 .35
49 Simic Sky Swallower R :M: .20 .35
50 Urban Evolution U :M: .10 .20
51 Evolving Wilds C .10 .20
52 Grazing Gladehart C .10 .20
53 Inkwell Leviathan R .40 .60
54 Secluded Steppe C .10 .20
55 Temple of the False God U .50 .75
56 Forest (63) L .10 .20
57 Forest (64) L .10 .20
58 Forest (65) L .10 .20
59 Island (60) L .10 .20
60 Island (61) L .10 .20
61 Island (62) L .10 .20
62 Plains (30) L .10 .20
63 Plains (31) L .10 .20
64 Plains (32) L .10 .20
65 Plains (33) L .10 .20
T1 Kraken Token T .10 .20
T2 Soldier Token T .10 .20

2015 Magic The Gathering Duel Decks Anthology

COMPLETE SET (249) 60.00 120.00
RELEASED ON DECEMBER 5, 2014
DD-1 Akroma, Angel of Wrath M :W: 6.00 15.00
DD-9 Angel of Mercy U :W: .20 .50
DD-19 Angelic Benediction U :W: .20 .50
DD-3 Angelic Page C :W: .20 .50
DD-6 Angelic Protector U :W: .20 .50
DD-15 Angelsong C :W: .10 .25
DD-4 Charging Paladin C :W: .10 .25
DD-20 Faith's Fetters C :W: .10 .25
DD-14 Healing Salve C :W: .10 .25
10 Icatian Priest U :W: .20 .50
DD-12 Luminous Angel R :W: 1.50 4.00
DD-16 Otherworldly Journey U :W: .20 .50
DD-17 Pacifism C :W: .10 .25
DD-13 Reya Dawnbringer R :W: .75 2.00
DD-22 Righteous Cause U :W: .20 .50
DD-7 Serra Advocate U :W: .20 .50
DD-10 Serra Angel U :W: .20 .50
DD-18 Serra's Boon U :W: .20 .50
DD-21 Serra's Embrace U :W: .20 .50
DD-8 Sustainer of the Realm U :W: .20 .50
DD-11 Twilight Shepherd R :W: .40 1.00
DD-5 Venerable Monk C :W: .10 .25
JC-17 Aethersnipe C :B: .10 .25
JC-13 Air Elemental U :B: .20 .50
JC-21 Ancestral Vision R :B: 3.00 8.00
JC-18 Brine Elemental U :B: .20 .50
JC-28 Condescend C :B: .10 .25
JC-24 Counterspell C :B: 1.50 4.00
JC-23 Daze C :B: 2.00 5.00
JC-20 Errant Ephemeron C :B: .10 .25
JC-26 Fact or Fiction U :B: .20 .50
JC-3 Fathom Seer C :B: .10 .25
JC-10 Fledgling Mawcor U :B: .20 .50
JC-14 Guile R :B: .40 1.00
JC-27 Gush C :B: .10 .25
JC-1 Jace Beleren M :B: 4.00 10.00
JC-8 Man-o'-War C :B: .10 .25
JC-2 Martyr of Frost C :B: .10 .25
JC-12 Mulldrifter C :B: .10 .25
JC-9 Ophidian C :B: .10 .25
JC-19 Quicksilver Dragon R :B: .40 1.00
JC-25 Repulse C :B: .10 .25
JC-15 Riftwing Cloudskate U :B: .20 .50
JC-4 Voidmage Apprentice C :B: .10 .25
JC-5 Wall of Deceit U :B: .20 .50
JC-11 Waterspout Djinn U :B: .20 .50
JC-6 Willbender U :B: .20 .50
DD-31 Abyssal Gatekeeper C :K: .10 .25
DD-40 Abyssal Specter U :K: .20 .50
GL-48 Bad Moon R :K: .75 2.00
DD-52 Barter in Blood U :K: .20 .50
DD-53 Breeding Pit U :K: .20 .50
DD-41 Cackling Imp C :K: .10 .25
DD-56 Consume Spirit U :K: .20 .50
DD-55 Corrupt U :K: .20 .50
GL-57 Corrupt U :K: .20 .50
DD-48 Cruel Edict U :K: .20 .50
DD-33 Daggerclaw Imp U :K: .20 .50
DD-50 Dark Banishing C :K: .10 .25
DD-45 Dark Ritual C :K: 1.50 4.00
GL-33 Deathgreeter C :K: .10 .25
DD-49 Demonic Tutor U :K: 8.00 20.00
DD-38 Demon's Jester C :K: .10 .25
GL-36 Drudge Skeletons C :K: .10 .25
DD-46 Duress C :K: .10 .25
DD-34 Dusk Imp C :K: .10 .25
GL-58 Enslave U :K: .20 .50
GL-42 Faerie Macabre C :K: .10 .25
DD-42 Fallen Angel U :K: .20 .50
GL-38 Fleshbag Marauder U :K: .20 .50
DD-32 Foul Imp C :K: .10 .25
GL-47 Genju of the Fens U :K: .20 .50
GL-34 Ghost-Lit Stalker U :K: .20 .50
GL-52 Hideous End C :K: .10 .25
GL-43 Howling Banshee U :K: .20 .50
GL-51 Ichor Slick C :K: .10 .25
GL-44 Keening Banshee U :K: .20 .50
DD-44 Kuro, Pitlord R :K: .40 1.00
GL-32 Liliana Vess M :K: 5.00 12.00
DD-30 Lord of the Pit M :K: 1.25 3.00
GL-55 Mutilate R :K: .50 1.25
DD-51 Oni Possession U :K: .20 .50
DD-35 Overeager Apprentice C :K: .10 .25
GL-39 Phyrexian Rager C :K: .10 .25
DD-54 Promise of Power R :K: .40 1.00
GL-37 Ravenous Rats C :K: .20 .50
DD-43 Reiver Demon R :K: 1.00 2.50
GL-56 Rise from the Grave U :K: .20 .50
GL-49 Sign in Blood C :K: .10 .25
GL-46 Skeletal Vampire R :K: .40 1.00
GL-53 Snuff Out C :K: 1.00 2.50
DD-37 Soot Imp U :K: .20 .50
DD-39 Souldrinker U :K: .20 .50
DD-36 Stinkweed Imp C :K: .10 .25
GL-54 Tendrils of Corruption C :K: .10 .25
GL-45 Twisted Abomination C :K: .10 .25
DD-47 Unholy Strength C :K: .10 .25
GL-40 Urborg Syphon-Mage C :K: .10 .25
GL-35 Vampire Bats C :K: .10 .25
GL-50 Vicious Hunger C :K: .10 .25
GL-41 Wall of Bone U :K: .20 .50
EG-33 Akki Coalflinger U :R: .20 .50
EG-54 Boggart Shenanigans U :R: .20 .50
JC-34 Chandra Nalaar M :R: 2.00 5.00
JC-47 Chartooth Cougar C :R: .10 .25
EG-34 Clickslither R :R: .40 1.00
JC-54 Cone of Flame U :R: .20 .50
JC-57 Demonfire R :R: 1.50 4.00
EG-35 Emberwilde Augur C :R: .10 .25
JC-56 Fireball U :R: .20 .50
JC-55 Fireblast C :R: .50 1.25
JC-49 Firebolt C :R: .10 .25
JC-36 Fireslinger C :R: .10 .25
JC-53 Flame Javelin U :R: .20 .50
JC-35 Flamekin Brawler C :R: .10 .25
JC-42 Flametongue Kavu U :R: .20 .50
EG-36 Flamewave Invoker U :R: .20 .50
JC-40 Flamewave Invoker U :R: .20 .50
JC-43 Furnace Whelp U :R: .20 .50
EG-37 Gempalm Incinerator U :R: .20 .50
EG-38 Goblin Cohort C :R: .10 .25
EG-39 Goblin Matron U :R: 1.50 4.00
EG-40 Goblin Ringleader U :R: 3.00 8.00
EG-41 Goblin Sledder C :R: .10 .25
EG-42 Goblin Warchief U :R: 1.50 4.00
JC-48 Hostility R :R: .40 1.00
EG-43 Ib Halfheart, Goblin Tactician R :R: .75 2.00
JC-51 Incinerate C :R: .20 .50
JC-45 Ingot Chewer C :R: .10 .25
JC-41 Inner-Flame Acolyte C :R: .10 .25
JC-52 Magma Jet U :R: .20 .50
EG-44 Mogg Fanatic U :R: .40 1.00
EG-45 Mogg War Marshal C :R: .10 .25
EG-46 Mudbutton Torchrunner C :R: .10 .25
JC-38 Pyre Charger U :R: .20 .50
EG-47 Raging Goblin C :R: .10 .25
JC-44 Rakdos Pit Dragon R :R: .40 1.00
EG-48 Reckless One U :R: .20 .50
JC-50 Seal of Fire C :R: .10 .25
EG-32 Siege-Gang Commander R :R: .40 1.00
EG-49 Skirk Drill Sergeant U :R: .20 .50
EG-50 Skirk Fire Marshal R :R: .75 2.00
EG-51 Skirk Prospector C :R: .10 .25
EG-52 Skirk Shaman C :R: .10 .25
JC-39 Slith Firewalker U :R: .20 .50
JC-37 Soulbright Flamekin C :R: .10 .25
EG-55 Spitting Earth C :R: .10 .25
EG-53 Tar Pitcher U :R: .20 .50
EG-56 Tarfire C :R: .10 .25
GL-3 Albino Troll U :G: .20 .50
EG-2 Allosaurus Rider R :G: .40 1.00
EG-1 Ambush Commander R :G: .40 1.00
GL-2 Basking Rootwalla C :G: .10 .25
GL-23 Beast Attack U :G: .20 .50
GL-7 Blastoderm C :G: .10 .25
GL-18 Elephant Guide U :G: .20 .50
EG-3 Elvish Eulogist C :G: .10 .25
EG-4 Elvish Harbinger U :G: 1.00 2.50
EG-20 Elvish Promenade U :G: 1.00 2.50
EG-5 Elvish Warrior C :G: .10 .25
GL-1 Garruk Wildspeaker M :G: 4.00 10.00
EG-6 Gempalm Strider U :G: .20 .50
GL-13 Genju of the Cedars U :G: .20 .50
EG-21 Giant Growth C :G: .10 .25
GL-14 Giant Growth C :G: .10 .25
EG-22 Harmonize U :G: .20 .50
GL-21 Harmonize U :G: .60 1.50
EG-7 Heedless One U :G: .75 2.00
EG-8 Imperious Perfect U :G: 1.00 2.50
GL-10 Indrik Stomphowler U :G: .20 .50
GL-19 Invigorate C :G: .75 2.00
GL-11 Krosan Tusker C :G: .10 .25
GL-16 Lignify C :G: .20 .50
EG-9 Llanowar Elves C :G: .10 .25
EG-10 Lys Alana Huntmaster C :G: .10 .25
GL-17 Nature's Lore C :G: 1.50 4.00
GL-24 Overrun U :G: .20 .50
GL-12 Plated Slagwurm R :G: .40 1.00
GL-15 Rancor C :G: 1.00 2.50
GL-8 Ravenous Baloth R :G: .40 1.00
GL-22 Rude Awakening R :G: .40 1.00
GL-9 Stampeding Wildebeests U :G: .20 .50
EG-11 Stonewood Invoker C :G: .10 .25
EG-12 Sylvan Messenger U :G: .20 .50
EG-13 Timberwatch Elf C :G: .10 .25
GL-4 Vine Trellis C :G: .10 .25
EG-14 Voice of the Woods R :G: .40 1.00
EG-15 Wellwisher C :G: .60 1.50
GL-5 Wild Mongrel C :G: .10 .25
EG-23 Wildsize C :G: .10 .25
GL-25 Windstorm U :G: .20 .50
EG-16 Wirewood Herald C :G: .10 .25
GL-6 Wirewood Savage C :G: .12 .30
EG-17 Wirewood Symbiote U :G: .75 2.00
EG-18 Wood Elves C :G: .12 .30
EG-19 Wren's Run Vanquisher U :G: .40 1.00
DD-58 Barren Moor C :L: .10 .25
EG-28 Forest L :L: .10 .25
EG-29 Forest L :L: .10 .25
EG-30 Forest L :L: .10 .25
EG-31 Forest L :L: .10 .25
GL-28 Forest L :L: .10 .25
GL-29 Forest L :L: .10 .25
GL-30 Forest L :L: .10 .25
GL-31 Forest L :L: .10 .25
EG-57 Forgotten Cave C :L: .10 .25
EG-58 Goblin Burrows U :L: .20 .50
JC-30 Island L :L: .10 .25
JC-31 Island L :L: .10 .25
JC-32 Island L :L: .10 .25
JC-33 Island L :L: .10 .25
JC-58 Keldon Megaliths U :L: .20 .50
EG-59 Mountain L :L: .10 .25
EG-60 Mountain L :L: .10 .25
EG-61 Mountain L :L: .10 .25
EG-62 Mountain L :L: .10 .25
JC-59 Mountain L :L: .10 .25
JC-60 Mountain L :L: .10 .25
JC-61 Mountain L :L: .10 .25
JC-62 Mountain L :L: .10 .25
DD-26 Plains L :L: .10 .25
DD-27 Plains L :L: .10 .25
DD-28 Plains L :L: .10 .25
DD-29 Plains L :L: .10 .25
GL-59 Polluted Mire C :L: .10 .25
DD-25 Secluded Steppe C :L: .10 .25
GL-26 Slippery Karst C :L: .10 .25
DD-59 Swamp L :L: .10 .25
DD-60 Swamp L :L: .10 .25
DD-61 Swamp L :L: .10 .25
DD-62 Swamp L :L: .25 .60
GL-60 Swamp L :L: .10 .25
GL-61 Swamp L :L: .10 .25
GL-62 Swamp L :L: .10 .25
GL-63 Swamp L :L: .10 .25
JC-29 Terrain Generator U :L: 1.25 3.00
EG-26 Tranquil Thicket C :L: .10 .25
GL-27 Treetop Village U :L: .20 .50
EG-27 Wirewood Lodge U :L: 1.00 2.50
DD-23 Angel's Feather U :A: .20 .50
JC-7 Bottle Gnomes U :A: .20 .50
DD-57 Demon's Horn U :A: .20 .50
DD-24 Marble Diamond U :A: .20 .50
JC-22 Mind Stone U :A: .20 .50
EG-24 Moonglove Extract C :A: .10 .25
JC-46 Oxidda Golem C :A: .10 .25
GL-20 Serrated Arrows C :A: .10 .25
EG-25 Slate of Ancestry R :A: .75 2.00
JC-16 Spire Golem C :A: .10 .25

2015 Magic The Gathering Duel Decks Zendikar vs. Eldrazi

COMPLETE SET (80) 20.00 35.00
RELEASED ON AUGUST 28, 2015
1 Avenger of Zendikar M :G: 4.00 6.00
2 Affa Guard Hound U :W: .10 .20
3 Caravan Escort C :W: .10 .20
4 Kabira Vindicator U :W: .10 .20
5 Knight of Cliffhaven C :W: .10 .20
6 Makindi Griffin C :W: .10 .20
7 Oust U :W: .10 .20
8 Repel the Darkness C :W: .10 .20
9 Sheer Drop C :W: .10 .20
10 Beastbreaker of Bala Ged U :G: .10 .20
11 Daggerback Basilisk C :G: .10 .20
12 Frontier Guide U :G: .10 .20
13 Graypelt Hunter C :G: .10 .20
14 Grazing Gladehart C :G: .10 .20
15 Groundswell C :G: .75 1.00
16 Harrow C :G: .10 .20
17 Joraga Bard C :G: .10 .20
18 Khalni Heart Expedition C :G: .10 .20
19 Ondu Giant C :G: .10 .20
20 Primal Command R :G: .75 1.25
21 Retreat to Kazandu U :G: .10 .20
22 Scute Mob R :G: .40 .60
23 Tajuru Archer U :G: .10 .20
24 Territorial Baloth C :G: .10 .20
25 Turntimber Basilisk U :G: .10 .20
26 Wildheart Invoker C :G: .10 .20
27 Veteran Warleader R :M: .30 .50
28 Explorer's Scope C :A: .10 .20
29 Seer's Sundial R :A: .20 .35
30 Stonework Puma C :A: .10 .20
31 Evolving Wilds C :L: .10 .20
32 Graypelt Refuge U :L: .10 .20
33 Stirring Wildwood R :L: .75 1.25
34 Turntimber Grove C :L: .10 .20
35 Plains L :L: .10 .20
36 Plains L :L: .10 .20
37 Plains L :L: .10 .20
38 Forest L :L: .10 .20
39 Forest L :L: .10 .20
40 Forest L :L: .10 .20
41 Oblivion Sower M 1.00 1.50
42 Artisan of Kozilek U .25 .40
43 It That Betrays R 1.75 2.25
44 Ulamog's Crusher C .10 .20
45 Bloodrite Invoker C :K: .10 .20
46 Bloodthrone Vampire C :K: .10 .20
47 Butcher of Malakir R :K: .25 .40
48 Cadaver Imp C :K: .10 .20
49 Consume the Meek R :K: .25 .40
50 Corpsehatch U :K: .10 .20
51 Dominator Drone C :K: .10 .20
52 Heartstabber Mosquito C :K: .10 .20
53 Induce Despair C :K: .10 .20
54 Marsh Casualties U :K: .10 .20
55 Pawn of Ulamog U :K: .10 .20
56 Read the Bones C :K: .10 .20
57 Smother U :K: .10 .20
58 Vampire Nighthawk U :K: .75 1.00
59 Emrakul's Hatcher C :R: .10 .20
60 Forked Bolt C :R: .25 .40
61 Hellion Eruption R :R: .25 .40
62 Magmaw R :R: .25 .40
63 Torch Slinger C :R: .10 .20
64 Forerunner of Slaughter U :M: .10 .20
65 Mind Stone U :A: .10 .20
66 Runed Servitor U :A: .10 .20
67 Akoum Refuge U :L: .10 .20
68 Eldrazi Temple U :L: 5.00 7.00
69 Rocky Tar Pit U :L: .10 .20
70 Swamp L :L: .10 .20
71 Swamp L :L: .10 .20
72 Swamp L :L: .10 .20
73 Mountain L :L: .10 .20
74 Mountain L :L: .10 .20
75 Mountain L :L: .10 .20
76 Eldrazi Spawn C :T: .10 .20
77 Eldrazi Spawn C :T: .10 .20
78 Eldrazi Spawn C :T: .10 .20
79 Hellion C :T: .10 .20
80 Plant C .10 .20

2016 Magic The Gathering Duel Decks Blessed vs. Cursed

COMPLETE SET (80) 20.00 30.00
RELEASED ON FEBRUARY 26, 2016
1 Geist of Saint Traft M :M: 5.00 6.00
2 Bonds of Faith C :W: .10 .20
3 Cathedral Sanctifier C :W: .10 .20
4 Champion of the Parish R :W: 2.00 2.50
5 Chapel Geist C :W: .10 .20
6 Dearly Departed R :W: .10 .20
7 Doomed Traveler C :W: .10 .20
8 Eerie Interlude R :W: .40 .60
9 Elder Cathar C :W: .10 .20
10 Emancipation Angel U :W: .10 .20
11 Fiend Hunter U :W: .10 .20
12 Gather the Townsfolk C :W: .10 .20
13 Goldnight Redeemer U :W: .10 .20
14 Increasing Devotion R :W: .25 .40
15 Momentary Blink C :W: .25 .40
16 Moorland Inquisitor C :W: .10 .20
17 Rebuke C :W: .10 .20
18 Slayer of the Wicked U :W: .10 .20
19 Spectral Gateguards C :W: .10 .20
20 Thraben Heretic U :W: .10 .20
21 Topplegeist U :W: .10 .20
22 Village Bell-Ringer C :W: .10 .20
23 Voice of the Provinces C :W: .10 .20
24 Captain of the Mists R :B: .10 .20
25 Gryff Vanguard C :B: .10 .20
26 Mist Raven C :B: .10 .20
27 Nephalia Smuggler U :B: .10 .20
28 Pore Over the Pages U :B: .10 .20
29 Tandem Lookout U :B: .10 .20
30 Tower Geist U :B: .10 .20
31 Butcher's Cleaver U :A: .10 .20
32 Sharpened Pitchfork U :A: .10 .20

33 Seraph Sanctuary C :L:	.10	.20
34 Tranquil Cove C :L:	.10	.20
35 Island L :L:	.10	.20
36 Island L :L:	.10	.20
37 Island L :L:	.10	.20
38 Plains L :L:	.10	.20
39 Plains L :L:	.10	.20
40 Plains L :L:	.10	.20
41 Mindwrack Demon M :K:	2.00	3.00
42 Compelling Deterrence U :B:	.10	.20
43 Forbidden Alchemy C :B:	.10	.20
44 Havengul Runebinder R :B:	.10	.20
45 Makeshift Mauler C :B:	.10	.20
46 Relentless Skaabs U :B:	.10	.20
47 Scrapskin Drake C :B:	.10	.20
48 Screeching Skaab C :B:	.10	.20
49 Stitched Drake C :B:	.10	.20
50 Abattoir Ghoul U :K:	.10	.20
51 Appetite for Brains U :K:	.10	.20
52 Barter in Blood U :K:	.10	.20
53 Butcher Ghoul C :K:	.10	.20
54 Diregraf Ghoul U :K:	.10	.20
55 Dread Return U :K:	.75	1.00
56 Driver of the Dead C :K:	.10	.20
57 Falkenrath Noble U :K:	.10	.20
58 Ghoulraiser C :K:	.10	.20
59 Gravecrawler R :K:	3.50	4.50
60 Harvester of Souls R :K:	.20	.35
61 Human Frailty U :K:	.10	.20
62 Moan of the Unhallowed U :K:	.10	.20
63 Sever the Bloodline R :K:	.10	.20
64 Tooth Collector U :K:	.10	.20
65 Tribute to Hunger U :K:	.10	.20
66 Unbreathing Horde R :K:	.60	1.00
67 Victim of Night C :K:	.10	.20
68 Diregraf Captain U :M:	.50	.75
69 Cobbled Wings C :A:	.10	.20
70 Dismal Backwater C :L:	.10	.20
71 Island L :L:	.10	.20
72 Island L :L:	.10	.20
73 Island L :L:	.10	.20
74 Swamp L :L:	.10	.20
75 Swamp L :L:	.10	.20
76 Swamp L :L:	.10	.20
77 Angel C :T:	.05	.15
78 Human C :T:	.05	.15
79 Spirit T :T:	.05	.15
80 Zombie C :T:	.05	.15

2016 Magic The Gathering Duel Decks Nissa vs. Ob Nixilis

COMPLETE SET (75)	20.00	30.00
DUEL DECK	14.00	18.00
RELEASED ON SEPTEMBER, 2 2016		
1 Nissa Voice of Zendikar MR	10.00	12.00
2 Abundance R	.75	1.00
3 Briarhorn U	.10	.20
4 Citanul Woodreaders C	.10	.20
5 Civic Wayfinder C	.10	.20
6 Cloudthresher R	.10	.20
7 Crop Rotation C	1.00	1.50
8 Elvish Visionary C	.10	.20
9 Fertilid C	.20	.30
10 Gaeas Blessing U	.10	.20
11 GiltLeaf Seer C	.10	.20
12 Jaddi Lifestrider U	.10	.20
13 Natural Connection C	.10	.20
14 Nissas Chosen C	.10	.20
15 Oakgnarl Warrior C	.10	.20
16 OranRief Hydra R	.10	.20
17 OranRief Invoker C	.10	.20
18 Saddleback Lagac C	.10	.20
19 Scythe Leopard U	.10	.20
20 Seek the Horizon U	.10	.20
21 Thicket Elemental R	.10	.20
22 Thornweald Archer C	.10	.20
23 Vines of the Recluse C	.10	.20
24 Walker of the Grove U	.10	.20
25 Wood Elves C	.10	.20
26 Woodborn Behemoth U	.10	.20
27 Fertile Thicket C	.10	.20
28 Khalni Garden C	.10	.20
29 Mosswort Bridge R	.30	.50
30 Treetop Village U	.75	1.25
31 Forest L	.10	.20
32 Forest L	.10	.20
33 Forest L	.10	.20
34 Forest L	.10	.20
35 Forest L	.10	.20
36 Ob Nixilis Reignited MR	3.00	4.50
37 Altars Reap C	.10	.20
38 Ambitions Cost U	.10	.20
39 Bala Ged Scorpion C	.10	.20
40 Blistergrub C	.10	.20
41 Cadaver Imp C	.10	.20
42 Carrier Thrall U	.10	.20
43 Demons Grasp C	.10	.20
44 Desecration Demon R	.50	.75
45 Despoiler of Souls R	.10	.20
46 Disfigure C	.25	.40
47 Doom Blade U	.25	.40
48 Fetid Imp C	.10	.20
49 Foul Imp C	.10	.20
50 Giant Scorpion C	.10	.20
51 Grim Discovery C	.10	.20
52 Hideous End C	.10	.20
53 Indulgent Tormentor R	.25	.40
54 Innocent Blood C	.10	.20
55 Mires Toll C	.10	.20
56 Pestilence Demon R	.20	.30
57 Priest of the Blood Rite R	.20	.30
58 Quest for the Gravelord U	.10	.20
59 Renegade Demon C	.10	.20
60 Shadows of the Past U	.10	.20
61 Smallpox U	.10	.20
62 Squelching Leeches U	.10	.20
63 Tendrils of Corruption C	.10	.20
64 Unhallowed Pact C	.10	.20
65 Leechridden Swamp U	.10	.20
66 Swamp L	.10	.20
67 Swamp L	.10	.20
68 Swamp L	.10	.20
69 Swamp L	.10	.20
70 Swamp L	.10	.20
71 Eldrazi Scion C	.10	.20
72 Demon C	.10	.20
73 Zombie Giant C	.10	.20
74 Elemental C	.10	.20
75 Plant C	.10	.20

2017 Magic The Gathering Duel Decks Mind vs. Might

COMPLETE SET (65)	25.00	40.00
RELEASED ON MARCH 31, 2017		
1 Jhoira of the Ghitu M	1.00	1.50
2 Beacon of Tomorrows R	1.50	2.00
3 Deep Sea Kraken R	.20	.35
4 Minds Desire R	.20	.35
5 Peer Through Depths C	.20	.35
6 Quicken R	.20	.35
7 Reach Through Mists C	.20	.35
8 Sage Eye Avengers R	.20	.35
9 Sift Through Sands C	.20	.35
10 Snap C	.50	.80
11 Talrand Sky Summoner R	.50	.80
12 Temporal Fissure C	.20	.35
13 The Unspeakable R	.20	.35
14 Desperate Ritual U	1.50	2.00
15 Empty the Warrens C	.20	.35
16 Grapeshot C	.20	.35
17 Rift Bolt C	1.25	2.00
18 Shivan Meteor U	.20	.35
19 Volcanic Vision R	.20	.35
20 Young Pyromancer U	.75	1.00
21 Fireminds Foresight R	.20	.35
22 Goblin Electromancer C	.20	.35
23 Jori En Ruin Diver R	.20	.35
24 Nivix Cyclops C	.20	.35
25 Spellheart Chimera U	.20	.35
26 Nucklavee U	.20	.35
27 Swiftwater Cliffs C	.20	.35
28 Island L	.20	.35
29 Island L	.20	.35
30 Island L	.20	.35
31 Mountain L	.20	.35
32 Mountain L	.20	.35
33 Mountain L	.20	.35
34 Lovisa Coldeyes M	.75	1.25
35 Beacon of Destruction R	.20	.35
36 Boldwyr Intimidator U	.20	.35
37 Firebolt C	.20	.35
38 Gorehorn Minotaurs C	.20	.35
39 Kamahl Pit Fighter R	.20	.35
40 Kruin Striker C	.20	.35
41 Zo Zu the Punisher R	.20	.35
42 Ambassador Oak C	.20	.35
43 Beast Attack U	.20	.35
44 Call of the Herd R	.20	.35
45 Cloudcrown Oak C	.20	.35
46 Harmonize U	.40	.60
47 Increasing Savagery R	.20	.35
48 Rampant Growth C	.20	.35
49 Roar of the Wurm U	.20	.35
50 Skarrgan Pit Skulk C	.20	.35
51 Sylvan Might C	.20	.35
52 Talaras Battalion R	.50	.80
53 Radha Heir to Keld R	.20	.35
54 Relentless Hunter U	.20	.35
55 Burning Tree Emissary U	.20	.35
56 Guttural Response U	.60	1.00
57 Rubblebelt Raiders R	.20	.35
58 Coat of Arms R	6.00	8.00
59 Rugged Highlands C	.20	.35
60 Mountain L	.20	.35
61 Mountain L	.20	.35
62 Mountain L	.20	.35
63 Forest L	.20	.35
64 Forest L	.20	.35
65 Forest L	.20	.35

2017 Magic The Gathering Duel Decks Mind vs. Might Tokens

1 Drake	.30	.40
2 Elemental	.50	.75
3 Goblin	.12	.20
4 Beast	.10	.15
5 Elephant	.10	.15
6 Elf Warrior	.30	.40
7 Wurm	.35	.50

2017 Magic The Gathering Duel Decks Merfolk vs. Goblins Tokens

1 Elemental
2 Wall
3 Goblin

2018 Magic The Gathering Duel Decks Elves vs. Inventors Tokens

1 Elf Warrior
2 Myr
3 Thopter
4 Thopter

From the Vault

2008 Magic The Gathering From the Vault Dragons

COMPLETE SET (15)	75.00	150.00
RELEASED ON AUGUST 28, 2008		
1 Ebon Dragon R :K:	3.00	8.00
2 Kokusho, the Evening Star R :K:	8.00	20.00
3 Bogardan Hellkite R :R:	2.50	6.00
4 Dragon Whelp R :R:	.75	2.00
5 Dragonstorm R :R:	5.00	12.00
6 Form of the Dragon R :R:	3.00	8.00
7 Shivan Dragon R :R:	1.50	4.00
8 Thunder Dragon R :R:	4.00	10.00
9 Two-Headed Dragon R :R:	2.00	5.00
10 Bladewing the Risen R :D:	3.00	8.00
11 Hellkite Overlord R :D:	3.00	8.00
12 Nicol Bolas R :D:	25.00	50.00
13 Niv-Mizzet, the Firemind R :D:	8.00	20.00
14 Rith, the Awakener R :D:	3.00	8.00
15 Draco R :A:	2.00	5.00

2009 Magic The Gathering From the Vault Exiled

COMPLETE SET (15)	75.00	125.00
RELEASED ON AUGUST 28, 2009		
1 Balance R :W:	2.50	6.00
2 Gifts Ungiven R :B:	3.00	8.00
3 Mystical Tutor R :B:	4.00	10.00
4 Serendib Efreet R :B:	2.50	6.00
5 Tinker R :B:	4.00	10.00
6 Necropotence R :K:	3.00	8.00
7 Goblin Lackey R :R:	6.00	15.00
8 Kird Ape R :R:	1.50	4.00
9 Berserk R :G:	20.00	50.00
10 Channel R :G:	2.00	5.00
11 Lotus Petal R :A:	4.00	10.00
12 Sensei's Divining Top R :A:	12.00	30.00
13 Skullclamp R :A:	2.50	6.00
14 Trinisphere R :A:	1.50	4.00
15 Strip Mine R :L:	6.00	15.00

2010 Magic The Gathering From the Vault Relics

COMPLETE SET (15)	75.00	125.00
RELEASED ON AUGUST 27, 2010		
1 Aether Vial M	10.00	25.00
2 Black Vise M	1.25	3.00
3 Isochron Scepter M	4.00	10.00
4 Ivory Tower M	1.50	4.00
5 Jester's Cap M	1.25	3.00
6 Karn, Silver Golem M	2.50	6.00
7 Masticore M	1.25	3.00
8 Memory Jar M	2.00	5.00
9 Mirari M	1.50	4.00
10 Mox Diamond M	12.00	30.00
11 Nevinyrral's Disk M	6.00	15.00
12 Sol Ring M	12.00	30.00
13 Sundering Titan M	1.50	4.00
14 Sword of Body and Mind M	5.00	12.00
15 Zuran Orb M	1.25	3.00

2011 Magic The Gathering From the Vault Legends

COMPLETE SET (15)	60.00	100.00
RELEASED ON AUGUST 8, 2011		
1 Mikaeus, the Lunarch M :W:	1.25	3.00
2 Sun Quan, Lord of Wu M :B:	1.50	4.00
3 Teferi, Mage of Zhalfir M :B:	4.00	10.00
4 Cao Cao, Lord of Wei M :K:	1.25	3.00
5 Visara the Dreadful M :K:	3.00	8.00
6 Kiki-Jiki, Mirror Breaker M :R:	10.00	25.00
7 Omnath, Locus of Mana M :G:	3.00	8.00
8 Captain Sisay M :W/G:	1.50	4.00
9 Doran, the Siege Tower M :W/B/G:	2.50	6.00
10 Kresh the Bloodbraided M :K/R/G:	1.50	4.00
11 Oona, Queen of the Fae M :B/K:	2.00	5.00
12 Progenitus M :W/B/K/R/G:	6.00	15.00
13 Rafiq of the Many M :W/B/G:	4.00	10.00
14 Sharuum the Hegemon M :W/B/K:	2.00	5.00
15 Ulamog, the Infinite Gyre M	20.00	40.00

2012 Magic The Gathering From the Vault Realms

COMPLETE SET (15)	75.00	150.00
RELEASED ON AUGUST 31, 2012		
1 Ancient Tomb M	10.00	25.00
2 Boseiju, Who Shelters All M	3.00	8.00
3 Cephalid Coliseum M	4.00	10.00
4 Desert M	1.50	4.00
5 Dryad Arbor M :G:	6.00	15.00
6 Forbidden Orchard M	3.00	8.00
7 Glacial Chasm M	2.50	6.00
8 Grove of the Burnwillows M	6.00	15.00
9 High Market M	2.50	6.00
10 Maze of Ith M	25.00	50.00
11 Murmuring Bosk M	2.50	6.00
12 Shivan Gorge M	2.00	5.00
13 Urborg, Tomb of Yawgmoth M	8.00	20.00
14 Vesuva M	6.00	15.00
15 Windbrisk Heights M	3.00	8.00

2013 Magic The Gathering From the Vault Twenty

COMPLETE SET (20)	150.00	175.00
RELEASED ON AUGUST 23, 2013		
1 Dark Ritual :K: M	4.00	4.50
2 Swords to Plowshares :W: M	5.00	6.00
3 Hymn to Tourach :K: M	4.00	5.00
4 Fyndhorn Elves :G: M	4.50	5.50
5 Impulse :B: M	1.50	2.00
6 Wall of Blossoms :G: M	1.50	2.00
7 Thran Dynamo M	8.00	10.00
8 Tangle Wire M	4.50	5.50
9 Fact or Fiction :B: M	1.75	2.00
10 Chainer's Edict :K: M	7.00	8.00
11 Akroma's Vengeance :W: M	1.75	2.00
12 Gilded Lotus M	13.00	15.00
13 Ink-Eyes, Servant of Oni :K: M	3.50	4.50
14 Char :R: M	.50	.75
15 Venser, Shaper Savant :B: M	16.00	18.00
16 Chameleon Colossus :G: M	1.50	2.00
17 Cruel Ultimatum :B::K::R: M	1.00	1.50
18 Jace, the Mind Sculptor :B: M	65.00	70.00
19 Green Sun's Zenith :G: M	7.00	9.00
20 Kessig Wolf Run M	3.00	3.50

2014 Magic The Gathering From the Vault Annihilation

COMPLETE SET (15)	12.00	30.00
RELEASED ON AUGUST 22, 2014		
1 Armageddon M :W:	2.00	5.00
2 Cataclysm M :W:	2.50	6.00
3 Martial Coup M :W:	1.00	2.50
4 Terminus M :W:	2.00	5.00
5 Wrath of God M :W:	2.50	6.00
6 Upheaval M :B:	.60	1.50
7 Fracturing Gust M :K:	1.25	3.00
8 Living Death M :K:	2.00	5.00
9 Virtue's Ruin M :K:	.50	1.25
10 Burning of Xinye M :R:	1.50	4.00
11 Decree of Annihilation M :R:	.40	1.00
12 Rolling Earthquake M :R:	3.00	8.00
13 Child of Alara M :D:	1.00	2.50
14 Firespout M :R: :G:	.60	1.50
15 Smokestack M :A:	2.00	5.00

2015 Magic The Gathering From the Vault Angels

COMPLETE SET (15)
RELEASED ON AUGUST 21, 2015
1 Akroma, Angel of Fury
2 Akroma, Angel of Wrath
3 Archangel of Strife
4 Aurelia, the Warleader
5 Avacyn, Angel of Hope
6 Baneslayer Angel
7 Entreat the Angels
8 Exalted Angel
9 Iona, Shield of Emeria
10 Iridescent Angel
11 Jenara, Asura of War
12 Lightning Angel
13 Platinum Angel
14 Serra Angel
15 Tariel, Reckoner of Souls

2016 Magic The Gathering From the Vault Lore

COMPLETE SET (16)	70.00	585.00
FROM THE VAULT BOX	40.00	50.00
RELEASED ON AUGUST 19, 2016		
1 Beseech the Queen M	2.00	2.50
2 Cabal Ritual M	3.25	3.75
3 Conflux M	1.00	1.25
4 Dark Depths M	25.00	30.00
5 Glissa the Traitor M	1.00	1.50
6 Helvault M	.60	1.00
7 Memnarch M	4.00	4.75
8 Minds Desire M	1.25	1.75
9 Momir Vig Simic Visionary M	3.00	3.50
10 Near Dath Experience M	.60	1.00
11 Obliterate M	1.00	1.25
12 Phyrexian Processor M	1.00	1.25
13 Tolaria West M	3.75	4.25
14 Umezawas Jitte M	16.00	18.00
15 Unmask M	2.00	2.75
16 Marit Lage Token M	3.75	4.50

Premium Series

2009 Magic The Gathering Premium Deck Series Slivers

1 Acidic Sliver U :D:	.40	1.00
2 Amoeboid Changeline C :B:	.20	.50
3 Ancient Ziggurat U :L:	1.25	3.00
4 Aphetto Dredging C :K:	.20	.50
5 Armor Sliver U :W:	.30	.75
6 Barbed Sliver U :R:	.30	.75
7 Brood Sliver R :G:	1.50	4.00
8 Clot Sliver C :K:	.20	.50
9 Coat of Arms R :A:	2.00	5.00
10 Crystalline Sliver U :D:	2.00	5.00
11 Distant Melody C :B:	.20	.50
12 Forest C :L:	.20	.50
13 Frenzy Sliver C :K:	.20	.50
14 Fungus Sliver R :G:	.75	2.00
15 Fury Sliver U :R:	.40	1.00
16 Gemhide Sliver C :G:	.75	2.00
17 Heart Sliver C :R:	.75	2.00
18 Heartstone U :A:	.60	1.50
19 Hibernation Sliver U :D:	.30	.75
20 Homing Sliver C :R:	.30	.75
21 Island C :L:	.30	.75
22 Metallic Sliver C :A:	.30	.75
23 Might Sliver U :G:	.60	1.50
24 Mountain C :L:	.30	.75
25 Muscle Sliver C :G:	.75	2.00
26 Necrotic Sliver U :D:	1.25	3.00
27 Plains C :L:	.30	.75
28 Quick Sliver C :G:	.20	.50
29 Rootbound Crag R :L:	2.00	5.00
30 Rupture Spire C :L:	.30	.75
31 Sliver Overlord M :D:	2.00	5.00
32 Spectral Sliver U :K:	.30	.75
33 Spined Sliver U :D:	.30	.75
34 Swamp C :L:	.30	.75
35 Terramorphic Expanse C :L:	.30	.75
36 Victual Sliver U :D:	.30	.75
37 Virulent Sliver C :G:	.30	.75
38 Vivid Creek U :L:	.60	1.50
39 Vivid Grove U :L:	.60	1.50
40 Wild Pair R :G:	1.00	2.50
41 Winged Sliver C :B:	1.25	3.00

2010 Magic The Gathering Premium Deck Series Fire and Lightning

COMPLETE SET (34)	12.00	30.00
RELEASED ON NOVEMBER 19, 2010		
1 Ball Lightning R :R:	1.50	4.00

2 Browbeat U :R:	.60	1.50
3 Chain Lightning C :R:	6.00	15.00
4 Cinder Pyromancer C :R:	.10	.25
5 Fire Servant U :R:	.20	.50
6 Fireball U :R:	.20	.50
7 Fireblast C :R:	1.00	2.50
8 Flames of the Blood Hand U :R:	1.50	4.00
9 Grim Lavamancer R :R:	2.50	6.00
10 Hammer of Bogardan R :R:	.40	1.00
11 Hellspark Elemental U :R:	.75	2.00
12 Jackal Pup U :R:	.20	.50
13 Jaya Ballard, Task Mage R :R:	.20	.50
14 Keldon Champion U :R:	.20	.50
15 Keldon Marauders C :R:	.20	.50
16 Lightning Bolt C :R:	1.25	3.00
17 Mogg Fanatic U :R:	.20	.50
18 Mogg Flunkies C :R:	.10	.25
19 Pillage U :R:	.30	.75
20 Price of Progress U :R:	3.00	8.00
21 Reverberate R :R:	.40	1.00
22 Spark Elemental U :R:	.20	.50
23 Sudden Impact U :R:	.20	.50
24 Thunderbolt C :R:	.10	.25
25 Vulshok Sorcerer C :R:	.20	.50
26 Boggart Ram-Gang U :D:	.30	.75
27 Figure of Destiny R :D:	.75	2.00
28 Barbarian Ring U :L:	.20	.50
29 Ghitu Encampment U :L:	.20	.50
30 Mountain (31) L	.10	.25
31 Mountain (32) L	.10	.25
32 Mountain (33) L	.10	.25
33 Mountain (34) L	.10	.25
34 Teetering Peaks C :L:	.10	.25

2011 Magic The Gathering Premium Deck Series Graveborn

COMPLETE SET (30)	15.00	40.00
RELEASED ON NOVEMBER 18, 2011		
1 Blazing Archon R :W:	1.50	4.00
2 Animate Dead U :K:	1.25	3.00
3 Avatar of Woe R :K:	.40	1.00
4 Buried Alive U :K:	1.00	2.50
5 Cabal Therapy U :K:	5.00	12.00
6 Diabolic Servitude U :K:	.20	.50
7 Dread Return U :K:	1.00	2.50
8 Duress C :K:	.20	.50
9 Entomb R :K:	10.00	25.00
10 Exhume C :K:	.30	.75
11 Faceless Butcher C :K:	.20	.50
12 Hidden Horror U :K:	.20	.50
13 Last Rites C :K:	.20	.50
14 Putrid Imp C :K:	.30	.75
15 Reanimate U :K:	3.00	8.00
16 Sickening Dreams U :K:	.20	.50
17 Twisted Abomination C :K:	.20	.50
18 Zombie Infestation U :K:	.20	.50
19 Crosis, the Purger R :G:	2.00	5.00
20 Terastodon R :G:	.60	1.50
21 Verdant Force R :G:	.40	1.00
22 Inkwell Leviathan R	2.00	5.00
23 Sphinx of the Steel Wind M	.40	1.00
24 Crystal Vein L	.20	.50
25 Ebon Stronghold L	.20	.50
26 Polluted Mire L	.20	.50
27 Swamp (27) L	.10	.25
28 Swamp (28) L	.10	.25
29 Swamp (29) L	.10	.25
30 Swamp (30) L	.10	.25

Masters Series

2013 Magic The Gathering Modern Masters

COMPLETE SET (245)	800.00	1000.00
RELEASED ON JUNE 7, 2013		
1 Adarkar Valkyrie R :W:	.75	1.00
2 Amrou Scout C :W:	.10	.20
3 Amrou Seekers C :W:	.10	.20
4 Angel's Grace R :W:	6.00	8.00
5 Auriok Salvagers R :W:	.30	.20
6 Avian Changeling C :W:	.10	.20
7 Blinding Beam C :W:	.10	.20
8 Bound in Silence C :W:	.10	.20
9 Cenn's Enlistment C :W:	.10	.20
10 Cloudgoat Ranger U :W:	.15	.25
11 Court Homunculus C :W:	.10	.20
12 Dispeller's Capsule C :W:	.10	.20
13 Elspeth, Knight-Errant M :W:	12.00	15.00
14 Ethersworn Canonist R :W:	3.50	5.00
15 Feudkiller's Verdict U :W:	.15	.25
16 Flickerwisp U :W:	3.00	3.50
17 Gleam of Resistance C :W:	.10	.20
18 Hillcomber Giant C :W:	.10	.20
19 Ivory Giant C :W:	.10	.20
20 Kataki, War's Wage R :W:	1.25	1.75
21 Kithkin Greatheart C :W:	.10	.20
22 Meadowboon U :W:	.15	.25
23 Otherworldly Journey C :W:	.10	.20
24 Pallid Mycoderm C :W:	.10	.20
25 Path to Exile U :W:	10.00	12.00
26 Reveillark R :W:	7.00	9.00
27 Saltfield Recluse C :W:	.10	.20
28 Sanctum Gargoyle C :W:	.10	.20
29 Sandsower U :W:	.15	.25
30 Stir the Pride U :W:	.15	.25
31 Stonehewer Giant R :W:	4.00	6.00
32 Terashi's Grasp U :W:	.15	.25
33 Test of Faith C :W:	.10	.20
34 Veteran Armorer C :W:	.10	.20
35 Yosei, the Morning Star M :W:	4.00	6.00
36 AEthersnipe C :B:	.10	.20
37 Careful Consideration U :B:	.15	.25
38 Cryptic Command R :B:	20.00	25.00
39 Dampen Thought C :B:	.10	.20
40 Echoing Truth C :B:	.25	.40
41 Errant Ephemeron C :B:	.10	.20
42 Erratic Mutation C :B:	.10	.20
43 Esperzoa U :B:	.15	.25
44 Etherium Sculptor C :B:	.30	.50
45 Faerie Mechanist C :B:	.10	.20
46 Gifts Ungiven R :B:	10.00	12.00
47 Glen Elendra Archmage R :B:	14.00	16.00
48 Keiga, the Tide Star M :B:	3.00	5.00
49 Kira, Great Glass-Spinner R :B:	14.00	16.00
50 Latchkey Faerie C :B:	.10	.20
51 Logic Knot C :B:	.10	.20
52 Meloku the Clouded Mirror R :B:	.30	.20
53 Mothdust Changeling C :B:	.10	.20
54 Mulldrifter U :B:	.40	.60
55 Narcomoeba U :B:	3.00	3.50
56 Pact of Negation R :B:	20.00	25.00
57 Peer Through Depths C :B:	.10	.20
58 Perilous Research C :B:	.10	.20
59 Pestermite C :B:	.50	.75
60 Petals of Insight C :B:	.10	.20
61 Reach Through Mists C :B:	.10	.20
62 Riftwing Cloudskate U :B:	.15	.25
63 Scion of Oona R :B:	2.50	3.00
64 Spell Snare U :B:	6.00	8.00
65 Spellstutter Sprite C :B:	.50	.75
66 Take Possession U :B:	.15	.25
67 Thirst for Knowledge U :B:	1.75	2.00
68 Traumatic Visions C :B:	.10	.20
69 Vedalken Dismisser C :B:	.10	.20
70 Vendilion Clique M :B:	25.00	30.00
71 Absorb Vis C :K:	.10	.20
72 Auntie's Snitch U :K:	.15	.25
73 Blightspeaker C :K:	.10	.20
74 Bridge from Below R :K:	14.00	16.00
75 Dark Confidant M :K:	30.00	35.00
76 Death Cloud R :K:	1.00	1.50
77 Death Denied C :K:	.10	.20
78 Death Rattle U :K:	.15	.25
79 Deepcavern Imp C :K:	.10	.20
80 Drag Down C :K:	.10	.20
81 Dreamspoiler Witches C :K:	.10	.20
82 Earwig Squad R :K:	.30	.20
83 Executioner's Capsule U :K:	.15	.25
84 Extirpate R :K:	2.50	4.00
85 Facevaulter C :K:	.10	.20
86 Faerie Macabre C :K:	.10	.20
87 Festering Goblin C :K:	.10	.20
88 Horobi's Whisper U :K:	.15	.25
89 Kokusho, the Evening Star M :K:	14.00	17.00
90 Mad Auntie U :K:	.25	.40
91 Marsh Flitter U :K:	.15	.25
92 Peppersmoke C :K:	.10	.20
93 Phthisis U :K:	.15	.25
94 Rathi Trapper C :K:	.10	.20
95 Raven's Crime C :K:	.75	1.15
96 Skeletal Vampire R :K:	.30	.20
97 Slaughter Pact R :K:	7.00	9.00
98 Stinkweed Imp C :K:	.25	.40
99 Street Wraith C :K:	2.00	2.50
100 Syphon Life C :K:	.10	.20
101 Thieving Sprite C :K:	.10	.20
102 Tombstalker R :K:	1.25	1.75
103 Warren Pilferers C :K:	.10	.20
104 Warren Weirding C :K:	.10	.20
105 Blind-Spot Giant C :R:	.10	.20
106 Blood Moon R :R:	38.00	42.00
107 Brute Force C :R:	.10	.20
108 Countryside Crusher R :R:	.50	.75
109 Crush Underfoot C :R:	.10	.20
110 Desperate Ritual U :R:	1.75	2.00
111 Dragonstorm R :R:	.75	1.00
112 Empty the Warrens C :R:	.25	.40
113 Fiery Fall C :R:	.10	.20
114 Fury Charm C :R:	.10	.20
115 Glacial Ray C :R:	.10	.20
116 Grapeshot C :R:	.30	.50
117 Greater Gargadon R :R:	8.00	10.00
118 Grinning Ignus U :R:	.15	.25
119 Hammerheim Deadeye C :R:	.10	.20
120 Kiki-Jiki, Mirror Breaker M :R:	12.00	15.00
121 Lava Spike C :R:	3.25	3.75
122 Mogg War Marshal C :R:	.75	1.00
123 Molten Disaster R :R:	.30	.20
124 Pardic Dragon U :R:	.15	.25
125 Pyromancer's Swath R :R:	.30	.20
126 Rift Bolt C :R:	2.25	2.75
127 Rift Elemental C :R:	.10	.20
128 Ryusei, the Falling Star M :R:	1.50	2.00
129 Shrapnel Blast U :R:	.25	.40
130 Squee, Goblin Nabob R :R:	2.50	4.00
131 Stingscourger C :R:	.10	.20
132 Stinkdrinker Daredevil C :R:	.10	.20
133 Sudden Shock U :R:	.25	.40
134 Tar Pitcher U :R:	.15	.25
135 Thundercloud Shaman U :R:	.15	.25
136 Thundering Giant C :R:	.10	.20
137 Torrent of Stone C :R:	.10	.20
138 Tribal Flames U :R:	.15	.25
139 War-Spike Changeling C :R:	.10	.20
140 Citanul Woodreaders C :G:	.10	.20
141 Doubling Season R :G:	50.00	60.00
142 Durkwood Baloth C :G:	.10	.20
143 Echoing Courage C :G:	.10	.20
144 Eternal Witness U :G:	3.50	5.00
145 Giant Dustwasp C :G:	.10	.20
146 Greater Mossdog C :G:	.10	.20
147 Hana Kami C :G:	.10	.20
148 Imperiosaur C :G:	.10	.20
149 Incremental Growth U :G:	.15	.25
150 Jugan, the Rising Star M :G:	1.75	2.25
151 Kodama's Reach C :G:	1.00	1.25
152 Krosan Grip U :G:	.50	.75
153 Life from the Loam R :G:	12.00	14.00
154 Masked Admirers U :G:	.15	.25
155 Moldervine Cloak C :G:	.10	.20
156 Nantuko Shaman C :G:	.10	.20
157 Penumbra Spider C :G:	.10	.20
158 Reach of Branches U :G:	.15	.25
159 Riftsweeper U :G:	.15	.25
160 Rude Awakening R :G:	.30	.20
161 Search for Tomorrow C :G:	.30	.50
162 Sporesower Thallid U :G:	.15	.25
163 Sporoloth Ancient C :G:	.10	.20
164 Summoner's Pact R :G:	10.00	12.00
165 Sylvan Bounty C :G:	.10	.20
166 Tarmogoyf M :G:	110.00	130.00
167 Thallid C :G:	.10	.20
168 Thallid Germinator C :G:	.10	.20
169 Thallid Shell-Dweller C :G:	.10	.20
170 Tooth and Nail R :G:	18.00	20.00
171 Tromp the Domains U :G:	.15	.25
172 Verdeloth the Ancient R :G:	.30	.20
173 Walker of the Grove C :G:	.10	.20
174 Woodfall Primus R :G:	6.00	8.00
175 Electrolyze U :B/R:	.75	1.00
176 Grand Arbiter Augustin IV R :W/B:	5.00	7.00
177 Jhoira of the Ghitu R :B/R:	1.75	2.25
178 Knight of the Reliquary R :W/G:	8.00	10.00
179 Lightning Helix U :W/R:	4.00	6.00
180 Maelstrom Pulse R :K/G:	14.00	16.00
181 Mind Funeral U :B/K:	3.50	4.00
182 Progenitus M :W/B/K/R/G:	12.00	15.00
183 Sarkhan Vol M :R/G:	10.00	12.00
184 Tidehollow Sculler U :W/K:	.30	.50
185 Trygon Predator U :B/G:	.40	.60
186 Cold-Eyed Selkie R :B/G:	.75	1.00
187 Demigod of Revenge R :K/R:	2.50	3.50
188 Divinity of Pride R :W/K:	1.75	2.25
189 Figure of Destiny R :W/R:	1.25	1.75
190 Kitchen Finks U :W/G:	12.00	15.00
191 Manamorphose U :R/G:	3.00	4.50
192 Murderous Redcap U :K/R:	.50	.75
193 Oona, Queen of the Fae R :B/K:	2.50	3.00
194 Plumeveil U :W/B:	.15	.25
195 Worm Harvest U :K/G:	.25	.40
196 AEther Spellbomb C	.10	.20
197 AEther Vial R	35.00	40.00
198 Arcbound Ravager R	30.00	35.00
199 Arcbound Stinger C	.10	.20
200 Arcbound Wanderer C	.10	.20
201 Arcbound Worker C	.10	.20
202 Bonesplitter C	.25	.40
203 Chalice of the Void R	40.00	50.00
204 Engineered Explosives R	40.00	45.00
205 Epochrasite U	.25	.40
206 Etched Oracle U	.15	.25
207 Frogmite C	.10	.20
208 Lotus Bloom R	6.00	8.00
209 Myr Enforcer C	.10	.20
210 Myr Retriever U	.25	.40
211 Paradise Mantle U	1.00	1.50
212 Pyrite Spellbomb C	.10	.20
213 Relic of Progenitus U	2.00	2.50
214 Runed Stalactite C	.10	.20
215 Skyreach Manta C	.10	.20
216 Sword of Fire and Ice M	40.00	50.00
217 Sword of Light and Shadow M	28.00	32.00
218 Vedalken Shackles M	12.00	15.00
219 Academy Ruins R	18.00	22.00
220 Blinkmoth Nexus R	4.00	6.00
221 City of Brass R	2.50	4.00
222 Dakmor Salvage U	2.75	3.25
223 Glimmervoid R	25.00	30.00
224 Terramorphic Expanse C	.10	.20
225 Vivid Crag U	.25	.40
226 Vivid Creek U	.25	.40
227 Vivid Grove U	.25	.40
228 Vivid Marsh U	.25	.40
229 Vivid Meadow U	.30	.50

2013 Magic The Gathering Modern Masters Foil

1 Adarkar Valkyrie R :W:	4.00	6.00
2 Amrou Scout C :W:	.20	.35
3 Amrou Seekers C :W:	.20	.35
4 Angel's Grace R :W:	15.00	18.00
5 Auriok Salvagers R :W:	1.50	2.50
6 Avian Changeling C :W:	.20	.35
7 Blinding Beam C :W:	.20	.35
8 Bound in Silence C :W:	.20	.35
9 Cenn's Enlistment C :W:	.20	.35
10 Cloudgoat Ranger U :W:	.75	1.25
11 Court Homunculus C :W:	.20	.35
12 Dispeller's Capsule C :W:	.20	.35
13 Elspeth, Knight-Errant M :W:	30.00	35.00
14 Ethersworn Canonist R :W:	8.00	11.00
15 Feudkiller's Verdict U :W:	.40	.60
16 Flickerwisp U :W:	11.00	14.00
17 Gleam of Resistance C :W:	.20	.35
18 Hillcomber Giant C :W:	.20	.35
19 Ivory Giant C :W:	.20	.35
20 Kataki, War's Wage R :W:	10.00	13.00
21 Kithkin Greatheart C :W:	.20	.35
22 Meadowboon U :W:	.25	.40
23 Otherworldly Journey C :W:	.20	.35
24 Pallid Mycoderm C :W:	.20	.35
25 Path to Exile U :W:	13.00	16.00
26 Reveillark R :W:	15.00	18.00
27 Saltfield Recluse C :W:	.20	.35
28 Sanctum Gargoyle C :W:	.20	.35
29 Sandsower U :W:	.25	.40
30 Stir the Pride U :W:	.25	.40
31 Stonehewer Giant R :W:	7.00	10.00
32 Terashi's Grasp U :W:	.25	.40
33 Test of Faith C :W:	.20	.35
34 Veteran Armorer C :W:	.20	.35
35 Yosei, the Morning Star M :W:	15.00	18.00
36 AEthersnipe C :B:	.20	.35
37 Careful Consideration U :B:	.50	.75
38 Cryptic Command R :B:	30.00	35.00
39 Dampen Thought C :B:	.20	.35
40 Echoing Truth C :B:	1.00	1.50
41 Errant Ephemeron C :B:	.20	.35
42 Erratic Mutation C :B:	.20	.35
43 Esperzoa U :B:	.25	.40
44 Etherium Sculptor C :B:	.60	1.00
45 Faerie Mechanist C :B:	.20	.35
46 Gifts Ungiven R :B:	11.00	14.00
47 Glen Elendra Archmage R :B:	20.00	25.00
48 Keiga, the Tide Star M :B:	9.00	12.00
49 Kira, Great Glass-Spinner R :B:	25.00	30.00
50 Latchkey Faerie C :B:	.20	.35
51 Logic Knot C :B:	1.50	2.50
52 Meloku the Clouded Mirror R :B:	3.00	5.00
53 Mothdust Changeling C :B:	.20	.35
54 Mulldrifter U :B:	1.25	2.00
55 Narcomoeba U :B:	4.00	6.00
56 Pact of Negation R :B:	35.00	45.00
57 Peer Through Depths C :B:	.75	1.25
58 Perilous Research C :B:	.20	.35
59 Pestermite C :B:	2.00	3.50
60 Petals of Insight C :B:	.20	.35
61 Reach Through Mists C :B:	.20	.35
62 Riftwing Cloudskate U :B:	.25	.40
63 Scion of Oona R :B:	4.00	6.00
64 Spell Snare U :B:	12.00	15.00
65 Spellstutter Sprite C :B:	1.50	2.50
66 Take Possession U :B:	.40	.60
67 Thirst for Knowledge U :B:	3.50	5.00
68 Traumatic Visions C :B:	.20	.35
69 Vedalken Dismisser C :B:	.20	.35
70 Vendilion Clique M :B:	60.00	70.00
71 Absorb Vis C :K:	.20	.35
72 Auntie's Snitch U :K:	.25	.40
73 Blightspeaker C :K:	.20	.35
74 Bridge from Below R :K:	18.00	24.00
75 Dark Confidant M :K:	60.00	75.00
76 Death Cloud R :K:	5.00	8.00
77 Death Denied C :K:	.20	.35
78 Death Rattle U :K:	.25	.40
79 Deepcavern Imp C :K:	.20	.35
80 Drag Down C :K:	.20	.35
81 Dreamspoiler Witches C :K:	.20	.35
82 Earwig Squad R :K:	.75	1.25
83 Executioner's Capsule U :K:	.40	.60
84 Extirpate R :K:	5.00	8.00
85 Facevaulter C :K:	.20	.35
86 Faerie Macabre C :K:	1.00	1.50
87 Festering Goblin C :K:	.20	.35
88 Horobi's Whisper U :K:	.25	.40
89 Kokusho, the Evening Star M :K:	23.00	26.00
90 Mad Auntie U :K:	.60	1.00
91 Marsh Flitter U :K:	.25	.40
92 Peppersmoke C :K:	.20	.35
93 Phthisis U :K:	.25	.40
94 Rathi Trapper C :K:	.20	.35
95 Raven's Crime C :K:	1.50	2.50
96 Skeletal Vampire R :K:	1.50	2.50
97 Slaughter Pact R :K:	15.00	18.00
98 Stinkweed Imp C :K:	2.00	3.50
99 Street Wraith C :K:	2.50	4.00
100 Syphon Life C :K:	.20	.35
101 Thieving Sprite C :K:	.20	.35
102 Tombstalker R :K:	2.50	4.00
103 Warren Pilferers C :K:	.20	.35
104 Warren Weirding C :K:	.20	.35
105 Blind-Spot Giant C :R:	.20	.35
106 Blood Moon R :R:	100.00	110.00
107 Brute Force C :R:	.20	.35
108 Countryside Crusher R :R:	2.00	3.50
109 Crush Underfoot C :R:	.20	.35
110 Desperate Ritual U :R:	2.50	4.00
111 Dragonstorm R :R:	2.00	3.50
112 Empty the Warrens C :R:	1.00	1.50
113 Fiery Fall C :R:	.20	.35
114 Fury Charm C :R:	.20	.35
115 Glacial Ray C :R:	.20	.35
116 Grapeshot C :R:	2.00	3.50
117 Greater Gargadon R :R:	13.00	16.00
118 Grinning Ignus U :R:	.30	.50
119 Hammerheim Deadeye C :R:	.20	.35
120 Kiki-Jiki, Mirror Breaker M :R:	18.00	22.00
121 Lava Spike C :R:	5.00	7.00
122 Mogg War Marshal C :R:	1.00	1.50
123 Molten Disaster R :R:	.75	1.25
124 Pardic Dragon U :R:	.25	.40
125 Pyromancer's Swath R :R:	1.25	2.00
126 Rift Bolt C :R:	3.00	5.00
127 Rift Elemental C :R:	.20	.35
128 Ryusei, the Falling Star M :R:	5.00	7.00
129 Shrapnel Blast U :R:	.50	.75
130 Squee, Goblin Nabob R :R:	6.00	8.00
131 Stingscourger C :R:	.20	.35
132 Stinkdrinker Daredevil C :R:	.20	.35
133 Sudden Shock U :R:	8.00	11.00
134 Tar Pitcher U :R:	.25	.40
135 Thundercloud Shaman U :R:	.25	.40
136 Thundering Giant C :R:	.20	.35
137 Torrent of Stone C :R:	.20	.35
138 Tribal Flames U :R:	.75	1.00
139 War-Spike Changeling C :R:	.20	.35
140 Citanul Woodreaders C :G:	.20	.35
141 Doubling Season R :G:	78.00	85.00
142 Durkwood Baloth C :G:	.20	.35
143 Echoing Courage C :G:	.20	.35
144 Eternal Witness U :G:	13.00	16.00
145 Giant Dustwasp C :G:	.20	.35
146 Greater Mossdog C :G:	.20	.35
147 Hana Kami C :G:	.20	.35
148 Imperiosaur C :G:	.20	.35
149 Incremental Growth U :G:	.25	.40
150 Jugan, the Rising Star M :G:	6.00	8.00
151 Kodama's Reach C :G:	3.00	5.00
152 Krosan Grip U :G:	3.00	5.00
153 Life from the Loam R :G:	48.00	55.00
154 Masked Admirers U :G:	.50	.75

Card	Low	High
155 Moldervine Cloak C :G:	.20	.35
156 Nantuko Shaman C :G:	.20	.35
157 Penumbra Spider C :G:	.20	.35
158 Reach of Branches U :G:	.40	.60
159 Riftsweeper U :G:	1.00	1.50
160 Rude Awakening R :G:	1.50	2.50
161 Search for Tomorrow C :G:	3.00	5.00
162 Sporesower Thallid U :G:	.40	.60
163 Sporoloth Ancient C :G:	.20	.35
164 Summoner's Pact R :G:	19.00	22.00
165 Sylvan Bounty C :G:	.20	.35
166 Tarmogoyf M :G:	240.00	300.00
167 Thallid C :G:	.20	.35
168 Thallid Germinator C :G:	.20	.35
169 Thallid Shell-Dweller C :G:	.20	.35
170 Tooth and Nail R :G:	28.00	32.00
171 Tromp the Domains U :G:	.25	.40
172 Verdeloth the Ancient R :G:	1.25	2.00
173 Walker of the Grove C :G:	.20	.35
174 Woodfall Primus R :G:	13.00	16.00
175 Electrolyze U :B/R:	2.50	4.00
176 Grand Arbiter Augustin IV R :W/B:	12.00	15.00
177 Jhoira of the Ghitu R :B/R:	9.00	11.00
178 Knight of the Reliquary R :W/G:	15.00	18.00
179 Lightning Helix U :W/R:	13.00	16.00
180 Maelstrom Pulse R :K/G:	19.00	23.00
181 Mind Funeral U :B/K:	4.00	6.00
182 Progenitus M :W/B/K/R/G:	20.00	25.00
183 Sarkhan Vol M :R/G:	15.00	18.00
184 Tidehollow Sculler U :W/K:	2.00	3.00
185 Trygon Predator U :B/G:	1.50	2.50
186 Cold-Eyed Selkie R :B/G:	2.00	3.50
187 Demigod of Revenge R :K/R:	4.00	6.00
188 Divinity of Pride R :W/K:	4.00	6.00
189 Figure of Destiny R :W/R:	1.75	2.50
190 Kitchen Finks U :W/G:	13.00	16.00
191 Manamorphose U :R/G:	8.00	10.00
192 Murderous Redcap U :K/R:	1.50	2.00
193 Oona, Queen of the Fae R :B/K:	5.00	8.00
194 Plumeveil U :W/B:	.25	.40
195 Worm Harvest U :K/G:	.60	1.00
196 AEther Spellbomb C	.20	.35
197 AEther Vial R	50.00	60.00
198 Arcbound Ravager R	50.00	60.00
199 Arcbound Stinger C	.20	.35
200 Arcbound Wanderer C	.20	.35
201 Arcbound Worker C	.20	.35
202 Bonesplitter C	1.00	1.50
203 Chalice of the Void R	70.00	80.00
204 Engineered Explosives R	70.00	85.00
205 Epochrasite U	1.00	1.50
206 Etched Oracle U	.50	.75
207 Frogmite C	.40	.60
208 Lotus Bloom R	10.00	12.00
209 Myr Enforcer C	.40	.60
210 Myr Retriever U	1.50	2.00
211 Paradise Mantle U	4.00	6.00
212 Pyrite Spellbomb C	.30	.50
213 Relic of Progenitus U	3.50	5.00
214 Runed Stalactite C	.20	.35
215 Skyreach Manta C	.20	.35
216 Sword of Fire and Ice M	110.00	130.00
217 Sword of Light and Shadow M	50.00	60.00
218 Vedalken Shackles M	25.00	30.00
219 Academy Ruins R	35.00	40.00
220 Blinkmoth Nexus R	13.00	16.00
221 City of Brass R	17.00	20.00
222 Dakmor Salvage U	5.00	8.00
223 Glimmervoid R	45.00	55.00
224 Terramorphic Expanse C	.75	1.25
225 Vivid Crag U	1.00	1.50
226 Vivid Creek U	.75	1.25
227 Vivid Grove U	1.00	1.50
228 Vivid Marsh U	1.50	2.50
229 Vivid Meadow U	1.50	2.50

2013 Magic The Gathering Modern Masters Tokens

Card	Low	High
1 Giant Warrior	.12	.20
2 Kithkin Soldier	.10	.15
3 Soldier	.60	1.00
4 Illusion	1.50	2.00
5 Bat	.30	.40
6 Goblin Rogue	.10	.15
7 Spider	.20	.30
8 Zombie	.50	.75
9 Dragon	.60	1.00
10 Goblin	.12	.20
11 Elemental	.12	.20
12 Saproling	.10	.15
13 Treefolk Shaman	.35	.50
14 Faerie Rogue	1.00	1.50
15 Worm	.35	.50
16 Elspeth, Knight-Errant Emblem	6.00	8.00

2015 Magic The Gathering Modern Masters 2015

Card	Low	High
COMPLETE SET (264)	600.00	725.00
BOOSTER BOX	240.00	260.00
BOOSTER PACK	13.00	16.00
RELEASED ON MAY 22, 2015		
1 All Is Dust R	7.00	10.00
2 Artisan of Kozilek U	.30	.50
3 Emrakul, the Aeons Torn M	30.00	35.00
4 Karn Liberated M	45.00	50.00
5 Kozilek, Butcher of Truth M	15.00	20.00
6 Ulamog, the Infinite Gyre M	12.00	15.00
7 Ulamog's Crusher C	.15	.25
8 Apostle's Blessing C :W:	.15	.25
9 Arrest C :W:	.15	.25
10 Battlegrace Angel R :W:	.40	.60
11 Celestial Purge U :W:	.20	.35
12 Conclave Phalanx C :W:	.15	.25
13 Court Homunculus C :W:	.15	.25
14 Daybreak Coronet R :W:	5.00	6.00
15 Dispatch U :W:	.50	.75
16 Elesh Norn, Grand Cenobite M :W:	18.00	22.00
17 Fortify C :W:	.15	.25
18 Hikari, Twilight Guardian U :W:	.20	.35
19 Indomitable Archangel R :W:	.40	.60
20 Iona, Shield of Emeria M :W:	6.00	7.50
21 Kami of Ancient Law C :W:	.15	.25
22 Kor Duelist U :W:	.20	.35
23 Leyline of Sanctity R :W:	10.00	13.00
24 Mighty Leap C :W:	.15	.25
25 Mirran Crusader R :W:	1.25	1.75
26 Mirror Entity R :W:	.60	1.00
27 Moonlit Strider C :W:	.15	.25
28 Myrsmith U :W:	.20	.35
29 Oblivion Ring U :W:	.20	.35
30 Otherworldly Journey C :W:	.15	.25
31 Raise the Alarm C :W:	.15	.25
32 Skyhunter Skirmisher C :W:	.15	.25
33 Spectral Procession U :W:	.20	.35
34 Sunlance C :W:	.15	.25
35 Sunspear Shikari C :W:	.15	.25
36 Taj-Nar Swordsmith U :W:	.20	.35
37 Terashi's Grasp C :W:	.15	.25
38 Waxmane Baku C :W:	.15	.25
39 Aethersnipe C :B:	.15	.25
40 Air Servant U :B:	.20	.35
41 Argent Sphinx R :B:	.15	.25
42 Cloud Elemental C :B:	.15	.25
43 Cryptic Command R :B:	18.00	21.00
44 Faerie Mechanist C :B:	.15	.25
45 Flashfreeze U :B:	.20	.35
46 Guile R :B:	.25	.40
47 Helium Squirter C :B:	.15	.25
48 Hurkyl's Recall R :B:	4.00	5.00
49 Inexorable Tide R :B:	3.00	4.00
50 Mana Leak C :B:	.15	.25
51 Mulldrifter U :B:	.40	.60
52 Narcolepsy C :B:	.15	.25
53 Novijen Sages U :B:	.20	.35
54 Qumulox U :B:	.20	.35
55 Remand U :B:	3.00	4.00
56 Repeal C :B:	.15	.25
57 Somber Hoverguard C :B:	.15	.25
58 Steady Progress C :B:	.15	.25
59 Stoic Rebuttal C :B:	.15	.25
60 Surrakar Spellblade R :B:	.15	.25
61 Telling Time C :B:	.15	.25
62 Tezzeret the Seeker M :B:	10.00	12.00
63 Tezzeret's Gambit U :B:	.30	.50
64 Thoughtcast C :B:	.15	.25
65 Thrummingbird C :B:	.15	.25
66 Vapor Snag C :B:	.15	.25
67 Vendilion Clique M :B:	25.00	30.00
68 Vigean Graftmage C :B:	.15	.25
69 Water Servant U :B:	.20	.35
70 Wings of Velis Vel C :B:	.15	.25
71 Bitterblossom M :K:	20.00	25.00
72 Bloodthrone Vampire C :K:	.15	.25
73 Bone Splinters C :K:	.15	.25
74 Daggerclaw Imp U :K:	.20	.35
75 Dark Confidant M :K:	30.00	35.00
76 Death Denied C :K:	.15	.25
77 Deathmark U :K:	.20	.35
78 Devouring Greed U :K:	.20	.35
79 Dismember U :K:	1.75	2.25
80 Dread Drone C :K:	.15	.25
81 Duskhunter Bat C :K:	.15	.25
82 Endrek Sahr, Master Breeder R :K:	.15	.25
83 Ghostly Changeling C :K:	.15	.25
84 Grim Affliction C :K:	.15	.25
85 Instill Infection C :K:	.15	.25
86 Midnight Banshee R :K:	.15	.25
87 Nameless Inversion C :K:	.15	.25
88 Necroskitter R :K:	.30	.50
89 Plagued Rusalka C :K:	.15	.25
90 Profane Command R :K:	.30	.50
91 Puppeteer Clique R :K:	.75	1.00
92 Reassembling Skeleton U :K:	.20	.35
93 Scavenger Drake U :K:	.20	.35
94 Scuttling Death C :K:	.15	.25
95 Shrivel C :K:	.15	.25
96 Sickle Ripper C :K:	.15	.25
97 Sign in Blood C :K:	.15	.25
98 Spread the Sickness U :K:	.20	.35
99 Surgical Extraction R :K:	12.00	15.00
100 Thief of Hope C :K:	.15	.25
101 Vampire Lacerator C :K:	.15	.25
102 Vampire Outcasts U :K:	.20	.35
103 Waking Nightmare C :K:	.15	.25
104 Banefire R :R:	.50	.75
105 Blades of Velis Vel C :R:	.15	.25
106 Blood Ogre C :R:	.15	.25
107 Bloodshot Trainee U :R:	.20	.35
108 Brute Force C :R:	.15	.25
109 Burst Lightning C :R:	.15	.25
110 Combust U :R:	.20	.35
111 Comet Storm M :R:	.75	1.00
112 Dragonsoul Knight C :R:	.15	.25
113 Goblin Fireslinger C :R:	.15	.25
114 Goblin War Paint C :R:	.15	.25
115 Gorehorn Minotaurs C :R:	.15	.25
117 Gut Shot C :R:	.15	.25
118 Hellkite Charger R :R:	.40	.60
119 Incandescent Soulstoke U :R:	.30	.50
120 Inner-Flame Igniter C :R:	.15	.25
121 Kiki-Jiki, Mirror Breaker M :R:	10.00	12.00
122 Lightning Bolt U :R:	3.00	3.50
123 Skarrgan Firebird U :R:	.20	.35
124 Smash to Smithereens C :R:	.15	.25
125 Smokebraider C :R:	.15	.25
126 Soulbright Flamekin C :R:	.15	.25
127 Spikeshot Elder R :R:	.15	.25
128 Spitebellows U :R:	.20	.35
129 Splinter Twin R :R:	3.00	5.00
130 Stormblood Berserker U :R:	.20	.35
131 Thunderblust R :R:	.30	.75
132 Tribal Flames C :R:	.15	.25
133 Viashino Slaughtermaster C :R:	.15	.25
134 Wildfire R :R:	.20	.30
135 Worldheart Phoenix U :R:	.20	.35
136 Wrap in Flames C :R:	.15	.25
137 Algae Gharial U :G:	.20	.35
138 All Suns' Dawn R :G:	.15	.25
139 Ant Queen R :G:	.30	.50
140 Aquastrand Spider C :G:	.15	.25
141 Bestial Menace U :G:	.20	.35
142 Commune with Nature C :G:	.15	.25
143 Cytoplast Root-Kin U :G:	.20	.35
144 Gnarlid Pack C :G:	.15	.25
145 Karplusan Strider U :G:	.20	.35
146 Kavu Primarch C :G:	.15	.25
147 Kozilek's Predator C :G:	.15	.25
148 Matca Rioters C :G:	.15	.25
149 Mutagenic Growth U :G:	.75	1.25
150 Nest Invader C :G:	.15	.25
151 Noble Hierarch R :G:	40.00	45.00
152 Overwhelm U :G:	.20	.35
153 Overwhelming Stampede R :G:	.25	.40
154 Pelakka Wurm U :G:	.20	.35
155 Plummet C :G:	.15	.25
156 Primeval Titan M :G:	8.00	10.00
157 Rampant Growth C :G:	.15	.25
158 Root-Kin Ally U :G:	.20	.35
159 Scatter the Seeds C :G:	.15	.25
160 Scion of the Wild C :G:	.15	.25
161 Scute Mob R :G:	.40	.60
162 Simic Initiate C :G:	.15	.25
163 Sundering Vitae C :G:	.15	.25
164 Sylvan Bounty C :G:	.15	.25
165 Tarmogoyf M :G:	100.00	120.00
166 Thrive C :G:	.15	.25
167 Tukatongue Thallid C :G:	.15	.25
168 Vines of Vastwood C :G:	.15	.25
169 Wolfbriar Elemental R :G:	4.00	10.00
170 Agony Warp U :M:	.20	.35
171 Apocalypse Hydra R :M:	.50	.75
172 Boros Swiftblade U :M:	.20	.35
173 Drooling Groodion U :M:	.20	.35
174 Electrolyze U :M:	.50	.75
175 Ethercaste Knight U :M:	.20	.35
176 Ghost Council of Orzhova R :M:	.25	.40
177 Glassdust Hulk U :M:	.20	.35
178 Horde of Notions R :M:	.25	.40
179 Lorescale Coatl U :M:	.20	.35
180 Mystic Snake R :M:	.40	.60
181 Necrogenesis U :M:	.20	.35
182 Niv-Mizzet, the Firemind R :M:	1.50	2.00
183 Pillory of the Sleepless U :M:	.20	.35
184 Plaxcaster Frogling U :M:	.20	.35
185 Savage Twister U :M:	.20	.35
186 Shadowmage Infiltrator R :M:	.50	.75
187 Sigil Blessing U :M:	.20	.35
188 Vengeful Rebirth U :M:	.20	.35
189 Wrecking Ball U :M:	.20	.35
190 Ashenmoor Gouger U :M:	.20	.35
191 Creakwood Liege R :M:	2.00	2.50
192 Dimir Guildmage U :M:	.20	.35
193 Fulminator Mage R :M:	15.00	18.00
194 Hearthfire Hobgoblin U :M:	.20	.35
195 Nobilis of War R :M:	.15	.25
196 Restless Apparition U :M:	.20	.35
197 Selesnya Guildmage U :M:	.20	.35
198 Shrewd Hatchling U :M:	.20	.35
199 Swans of Bryn Argoll R :M:	.40	.60
200 Wilt-Leaf Liege R :M:	2.00	3.00
201 Alloy Myr C	.15	.25
202 Blinding Souleater C	.15	.25
203 Cathodion C	.15	.25
204 Chimeric Mass R	.15	.25
205 Copper Carapace C	.15	.25
206 Cranial Plating U	.75	1.00
207 Culling Dais U	.20	.35
208 Darksteel Axe U	.20	.35
209 Etched Champion R	2.75	3.25
210 Etched Monstrosity R	.15	.25
211 Etched Oracle U	.20	.35
212 Everflowing Chalice U	.20	.35
213 Expedition Map U	1.50	2.00
214 Flayer Husk C	.15	.25
215 Frogmite C	.15	.25
216 Glint Hawk Idol C	.15	.25
217 Gust-Skimmer C	.15	.25
218 Kitesail C	.15	.25
219 Lodestone Golem R	.40	.60
220 Lodestone Myr R	.15	.25
221 Long-Forgotten Gohei R	.15	.25
222 Mortarpod U	.20	.35
223 Mox Opal M.	45.00	50.00
224 Myr Enforcer C	.15	.25
225 Precursor Golem R	.15	.25
226 Runed Servitor C	.15	.25
227 Rusted Relic C	.15	.25
228 Sickleslicer C	.15	.25
229 Skyreach Manta C	.15	.25
230 Spellskite R	17.00	20.00
231 Sphere of the Suns C	.15	.25
232 Sunforger R	.60	1.00
233 Tumble Magnet U	.20	.35
234 Wayfarer's Bauble C	.15	.25
235 Azorius Chancery U	.20	.35
236 Blinkmoth Nexus R	3.50	5.00
237 Boros Garrison U	.20	.35
238 Darksteel Citadel C	.15	.25
239 Dimir Aqueduct U	.50	.75
240 Eldrazi Temple U	5.00	7.00
241 Evolving Wilds C	.15	.25
242 Eye of Ugin R	8.00	10.00
243 Golgari Rot Farm U	.20	.35
244 Gruul Turf U	.20	.35
245 Izzet Boilerworks U	.20	.35
246 Orzhov Basilica U	.20	.35
247 Rakdos Carnarium U	.20	.35
248 Selesnya Sanctuary U	.20	.35
249 Simic Growth Chamber U	.50	.75

2015 Magic The Gathering Modern Masters 2015 Tokens

Card	Low	High
1 Eldrazi Spawn	.12	.20
2 Eldrazi Spawn	.12	.20
3 Eldrazi Spawn	.12	.20
4 Soldier	.10	.15
5 Spirit	.10	.15
6 Faerie Rogue	.75	1.25
7 Germ	.10	.15
8 Thrull	.50	.75
9 Elephant	.10	.15
10 Insect	.15	.25
11 Saproling	.12	.20
12 Snake	.12	.20
13 Wolf	.15	.25
14 Worm	.25	.35
15 Golem	.25	.35
16 Myr	.20	.30

2016 Magic The Gathering Eternal Masters

Card	Low	High
COMPLETE SET (249)	475.00	580.00
BOOSTER BOX (24 PACKS)	175.00	200.00
BOOSTER PACK (15 CARDS)	10.00	12.00
RELEASED ON JUNE 10, 2016		
1 Aven Riftwatcher C	.10	.20
2 Balance MR	1.25	2.00
3 Ballynock Cohort C	.10	.20
4 Benevolent Bodyguard C	.10	.20
5 Calciderm U	.20	.35
6 Coalition Honor Guard C	.10	.20
7 Eight and a Half Tails R	.75	1.25
8 Elite Vanguard C	.10	.20
9 Enlightened Tutor R	8.00	11.00
10 Faiths Fetters U	.20	.35
11 Field of Souls U	.20	.35
12 Glimmerpoint Stag U	.20	.35
13 Honden of Cleansing Fire U	.20	.35
14 Humble C	.10	.20
15 Intangible Virtue U	.20	.35
16 Jareth, Leonine Titan R	.20	.35
17 Karmic Guide R	2.00	3.00
18 Kor Hookmaster C	.10	.20
19 Mesa Enchantress U	.20	.35
20 Mistral Charger C	.10	.20
21 Monk Idealist C	.10	.20
22 Mother of Runes R	2.00	3.00
23 Pacifism C	.10	.20
24 Raise the Alarm C	.10	.20
25 Rally the Peasants C	.10	.20
26 Seal of Cleansing C	.10	.20
27 Second Thoughts C	.10	.20
28 Serra Angel U	.20	.35
29 Shelter C	.10	.20
30 Soulcatcher U	.20	.35
31 Squadron Hawk C	.10	.20
32 Swords to Plowshares U	1.50	2.50
33 Unexpectedly Absent R	.30	.50
34 Wall of Omens U	1.25	2.00
35 War Priest of Thune U	.20	.35
36 Welkin Guide C	.10	.20
37 Whitemane Lion C	.10	.20
38 Wrath of God R	4.00	6.00
39 Arcanis the Omnipotent R	.75	1.25
40 Brainstorm U	.75	1.25
41 Cephalid Sage C	.10	.20
42 Control Magic R	.30	.50
43 Counterspell C	1.25	2.00
44 Daze U	1.00	1.50
45 Deep Analysis C	.10	.20
46 Diminishing Returns R	.15	.25
47 Dream Twist C	.10	.20
48 Fact or Fiction U	.20	.35
49 Force of Will MR	70.00	80.00
50 Future Sight R	.40	.60
51 Gaseous Form C	.10	.20
52 Giant Tortoise C	.10	.20
53 Glacial Wall C	.10	.20
54 Honden of Seeing Winds U	.20	.35
55 Hydroblast U	.50	.80
56 Inkwell Leviathan R	.40	.60
57 Jace, the Mind Sculptor MR	55.00	60.00
58 Jetting Glasskite U	.20	.35
59 Man O' War C	.10	.20
60 Memory Lapse C	.10	.20
61 Merfolk Looter U	.20	.35
62 Mystical Tutor R	4.00	7.00
63 Oonas Grace C	.10	.20
64 Peregrine Drake C	.30	.50
65 Phantom Master C	.10	.20
66 Phyrexian Ingester U	.20	.35
67 Prodigal Sorcerer U	.20	.35
68 Quiet Speculation U	.20	.35
69 Screeching Skaab C	.10	.20
70 Serendib Efreet R	.15	.25
71 Shoreline Ranger C	.10	.20
72 Silent Departure C	.10	.20
73 Sprite Noble U	.20	.35
74 Stupefying Touch C	.10	.20
75 Tidal Wave C	.10	.20
76 Warden of Evos Isle C	.10	.20
77 Wonder U	.20	.35
78 Animate Dead U	1.25	2.00
79 Annihilate U	.20	.35
80 Blightsoil Druid C	.10	.20
81 Blood Artist U	1.00	1.50
82 Braids, Cabal Minion R	.30	.50
83 Cabal Therapy U	1.25	2.00
84 Carrion Feeder C	.10	.20
85 Deadbridge Shaman C	.10	.20
86 Duress C	.10	.20
87 Entomb R	9.00	12.00
88 Eyeblights Ending C	.10	.20
89 Gravedigger C	.10	.20
90 Havoc Demon U	.20	.35
91 Honden of Nights Reach U	.20	.35

92 Hymn to Tourach U .60 1.00
93 Ichorid R .50 .80
94 Innocent Blood C .10 .20
95 Lys Alana Scarblade U .20 .35
96 Malicious Affliction R .50 .80
97 Nausea C .10 .20
98 Necropotence MR 5.00 7.00
99 Nekrataal U .20 .35
100 Nights Whisper C .30 .50
101 Phyrexian Gargantua U .20 .35
102 Phyrexian Rager C .10 .20
103 Plague Witch C .10 .20
104 Prowling Pangolin C .10 .20
105 Sengir Autocrat U .20 .35
106 Sinkhole R 2.50 4.00
107 Skulking Ghost C .10 .20
108 Toxic Deluge R 5.00 7.00
109 Tragic Slip C .10 .20
110 Twisted Abomination C .10 .20
111 Urborg Uprising C .10 .20
112 Vampiric Tutor MR 25.00 30.00
113 Victimize U .20 .35
114 Visara the Dreadful R .60 1.00
115 Wake of Vultures C .10 .20
116 Wakedancer C .10 .20
117 Avarax C .10 .20
118 Battle Squadron U .20 .35
119 Beetleback Chief U .20 .35
120 Borderland Marauder C .10 .20
121 Burning Vengeance U .20 .35
122 Carbonize C .10 .20
123 Chain Lightning U 2.50 4.00
124 Crater Hellion R .10 .20
125 Desperate Ravings C .10 .20
126 Dragon Egg C .10 .20
127 Dualcaster Mage R .50 .75
128 Faithless Looting C .30 .50
129 Fervent Cathar C .10 .20
130 Firebolt C .10 .20
131 Flame Jab U .20 .35
132 Gamble R 4.00 6.00
133 Ghitu Slinger U .20 .35
134 Honden of Infinite Rage U .20 .35
135 Keldon Champion U .20 .35
136 Keldon Marauders C .10 .20
137 Kird Ape C .10 .20
138 Mogg Fanatic C .10 .20
139 Mogg War Marshal C .40 .60
140 Orcish Oriflamme C .10 .20
141 Price of Progress U 1.25 2.00
142 Pyroblast U 1.00 1.50
143 Pyrokinesis R .10 .20
144 Reckless Charge C .10 .20
145 Rorix Bladewing R .15 .25
146 Seismic Stomp C .10 .20
147 Siege Gang Commander R 1.25 2.00
148 Sneak Attack MR 15.00 20.00
149 Stingscourger C .10 .20
150 Sulfuric Vortex R .40 .60
151 Tooth and Claw U .20 .35
152 Undying Rage C .10 .20
153 Wildfire Emissary C .10 .20
154 Worldgorger Dragon MR .75 1.25
155 Young Pyromancer U .75 1.25
156 Abundant Growth C .10 .20
157 Ancestral Mask U .40 .60
158 Argothian Enchantress MR 4.00 6.00
159 Brawn U .20 .35
160 Centaur Chieftain U .20 .35
161 Civic Wayfinder C .10 .20
162 Commune with the Gods C .10 .20
163 Elephant Guide C .10 .20
164 Elvish Vanguard C .10 .20
165 Emperor Crocodile C .10 .20
166 Flinthoof Boar U .20 .35
167 Fog C .10 .20
168 Gaes Blessing U .20 .35
169 Green Suns Zenith R 4.00 6.00
170 Harmonize U .50 .80
171 Heritage Druid R 3.00 5.00
172 Honden of Lifes Web U .20 .35
173 Imperious Perfect R 1.25 2.00
174 Invigorate U .20 .35
175 Llanowar Elves C .10 .20
176 Lys Alana Huntmaster C .10 .20
177 Natuarl Order MR 12.00 16.00
178 Natures Claim C .30 .50
179 Nimble Mongoose C .10 .20
180 Rancor U 1.25 2.00
181 Regal Force R 1.25 2.00
182 Roar of the Wurm U .20 .35
183 Roots C .10 .20
184 Seal of Strenght C .10 .20
185 Sentinel Spider C .10 .20
186 Silvos, Rogue Elemental R .20 .35
187 Sylvan Library R 13.00 16.00
188 Sylvan Might C .10 .20
189 Thornweald Archer C .10 .20
190 Timberwatch Elf U .20 .35
191 Werebear C .10 .20
192 Wirewood Symbiote U .40 .60
193 Xantid Swarm R .30 .50
194 Yavimaya Enchantress C .10 .20
195 Armadillo Cloak U .20 .35
196 Baleful Strix R 2.50 4.00
197 Bloodbraid Elf U .50 .80
198 Brago, King Eternal R .75 1.25
199 Dack Fayden MR 10.00 13.00
200 Extract from Darkness U .20 .35
201 Flame Kin Zealot U .20 .35
202 Glare of Subdual R .20 .35
203 Goblin Trenches R .15 .25
204 Maelstrom Wanderer MR 6.00 10.00
205 Shaman of the Pack U .20 .35
206 Shardless Agent R 2.00 3.50
207 Sphinx of the Steel Wind MR .75 1.25
208 Thunderclap Wyvern U .20 .35
209 Trygon Predator U .20 .35
210 Vindicate R 4.00 5.00
211 Void R .15 .25
212 Wee Dragonauts U .20 .35
213 Zealous Persecution U .20 .35
214 Call the Skybreaker R .10 .15
215 Deathrite Shaman R 3.50 5.00
216 Giant Solifuge R .15 .25
217 Torrent of Souls U .20 .35
218 Ashnods Altar U 2.00 3.50
219 Chrome Mox MR 13.00 16.00
220 Duplicant R 3.00 4.00
221 Emmessi Tome U .20 .35
222 Goblin Charbelcher R .60 1.00
223 Isochron Scepter R 2.50 4.00
224 Juggernaut U .20 .35
225 Mana Crypt MR 50.00 55.00
226 Millikin U .20 .35
227 Mindless Automaton U .20 .35
228 Nevinyrrals Disk R .75 1.25
229 Pilgrims Eye C .10 .20
230 Prismatic Lens U .20 .35
231 Relic of Progenitus U 1.50 2.50
232 Senseis Divining Top R 13.00 17.00
233 Ticking Gnomes U .20 .35
234 Winter Orb R 3.00 4.00
235 Worn Powerstone U .50 .80
236 Bloodfell Caves C .10 .20
237 Blossoming Sands C .10 .20
238 Dismal Backwater C .10 .20
239 Jungle Hollow C .10 .20
240 Karakas MR 30.00 40.00
241 Maze of Ith R 7.00 10.00
242 Mishras Factory U .50 .80
243 Rugged Highlands C .10 .20
244 Scoured Barrens C .10 .20
245 Swiftwater Cliffs C .10 .20
246 Thornwood Falls C .10 .20
247 Tranquil Cove C .10 .20
248 Wasteland R 20.00 25.00
249 Wind Scarred Crag C .10 .20

2016 Magic The Gathering Eternal Masters Foil

COMPLETE SET (249) 1500.00 1800.00
BOOSTER BOX (24 PACKS) 175.00 200.00
BOOSTER PACK (15 CARDS) 10.00 12.00
RELEASED ON JUNE 10, 2016
1 Aven Riftwatcher C .20 .35
2 Balance MR 5.00 8.00
3 Ballynock Cohort C .20 .35
4 Benevolent Bodyguard C .20 .35
5 Calciderm U .40 .60
6 Coalition Honor Guard C .20 .35
7 Eight and a Half Tails R 3.00 5.00
8 Elite Vanguard C .20 .35
9 Enlightened Tutor R 20.00 25.00
10 Faiths Fetters U .40 .60
11 Field of Souls U .40 .60
12 Glimmerpoint Stag U .40 .60
13 Honden of Cleansing Fire U .40 .60
14 Humble C .20 .35
15 Intangible Virtue U .75 1.25
16 Jareth, Leonine Titan R 1.00 1.50
17 Karmic Guide R 6.00 8.00
18 Kor Hookmaster C .20 .35
19 Mesa Enchantress U .40 .60
20 Mistral Charger C .20 .35
21 Monk Idealist C .20 .35
22 Mother of Runes R 10.00 15.00
23 Pacifism C .20 .35
24 Raise the Alarm C .20 .35
25 Rally the Peasants C .20 .35
26 Seal of Cleansing C .20 .35
27 Second Thoughts C .20 .35
28 Serra Angel U .40 .60
29 Shelter C .20 .35
30 Soulcatcher U .40 .60
31 Squadron Hawk C .20 .35
32 Swords to Plowshares U 4.00 6.00
33 Unexpectedly Absent R 5.00 7.00
34 Wall of Omens U 2.00 3.50
35 War Priest of Thune U .40 .60
36 Welkin Guide C .20 .35
37 Whitemane Lion C .20 .35
38 Wrath of God R 7.00 10.00
39 Arcanis the Omnipotent R 1.50 2.50
40 Brainstorm U 10.00 15.00
41 Cephalid Sage C .20 .35
42 Control Magic R 4.00 6.00
43 Counterspell C 2.50 4.00
44 Daze U 7.00 10.00
45 Deep Analysis C .20 .35
46 Diminishing Returns R 1.25 2.00
47 Dream Twist C .20 .35
48 Fact or Fiction U 1.25 2.00
49 Force of Will MR 300.00 400.00
50 Future Sight R 3.00 5.00
51 Gaseous Form C .20 .35
52 Giant Tortoise C .20 .35
53 Glacial Wall C .20 .35
54 Honden of Seeing Winds U .40 .60
55 Hydroblast U 2.50 3.50
56 Inkwell Leviathan R 1.50 2.00
57 Jace, the Mind Sculptor MR 100.00 120.00
58 Jetting Glasskite U .40 .60
59 Man O War C .20 .35
60 Memory Lapse C .20 .35
61 Merfolk Looter U .40 .60
62 Mystical Tutor R 12.00 16.00
63 Oonas Grace C .20 .35
64 Peregrine Drake C .75 1.25
65 Phantom Monster C .20 .35
66 Phyrexian Ingester U .40 .60
67 Prodigal Sorcerer U .40 .60
68 Quiet Speculation U .40 .60
69 Screeching Skaab C .20 .35
70 Serendib Efreet R .60 1.00
71 Shoreline Ranger C .20 .35
72 Silent Departure C .20 .35
73 Sprite Noble U .40 .60
74 Stupefying Touch C .20 .35
75 Tidal Wave C .20 .35
76 Warden of Evos Isle C .20 .35
77 Wonder U .60 1.00
78 Animate Dead U 4.00 6.00
79 Annihilate U .40 .60
80 Blightsoil Druid C .20 .35
81 Blood Artist U 2.50 4.00
82 Braids, Cabal Minion R 2.00 3.50
83 Cabal Therapy U 2.50 4.00
84 Carrion Feeder C .50 .80
85 Deadbridge Shaman C .20 .35
86 Duress C .20 .35
87 Entomb R 13.00 16.00
88 Eyeblights Ending C .20 .35
89 Gravedigger C .20 .35
90 Havoc Demon U .40 .60
91 Honden of Nights Reach U .40 .60
92 Hymn to Tourach U 2.00 3.00
93 Ichorid R 2.50 4.00
94 Innocent Blood C .20 .35
95 Lys Alana Scarblade U .40 .60
96 Malicious Affliction R 2.50 4.00
97 Nausea C .20 .35
98 Necropotence MR 10.00 15.00
99 Nekrataal U .40 .60
100 Nights Whisper C .20 .35
101 Phyrexian Gargantua U .40 .60
102 Phyrexian Rager C .20 .35
103 Plague Witch C .20 .35
104 Prowling Pangolin C .20 .35
105 Sengir Autocrat U .40 .60
106 Sinkhole R 6.00 8.00
107 Skulking Ghost C .20 .35
108 Toxic Deluge R 35.00 40.00
109 Tragic Slip C .30 .50
110 Twisted Abomination C .20 .35
111 Urborg Uprising C .20 .35
112 Vampiric Tutor MR 65.00 70.00
113 Victimize U 2.00 3.00
114 Visara the Dreadful R 1.50 2.50
115 Wake of Vultures C .20 .35
116 Wakedancer C .20 .35
117 Avarax C .20 .35
118 Battle Squadron U .40 .60
119 Beetleback Chief U 2.00 3.50
120 Borderland Marauder C .20 .35
121 Burning Vengeance U .40 .60
122 Carbonize C .20 .35
123 Chain Lightning U 3.00 5.00
124 Crater Hellion R .75 1.25
125 Desperate Ravings C .20 .35
126 Dragon Egg C .20 .35
127 Dualcaster Mage R 2.50 3.50
128 Faithless Looting C 2.00 3.50
129 Fervent Cathar C .20 .35
130 Firebolt C .20 .35
131 Flame Jab U .40 .60
132 Gamble R 15.00 20.00
133 Ghitu Slinger U .40 .60
134 Honden of Infinite Rage U .40 .60
135 Keldon Champion U .40 .60
136 Keldon Marauders C .20 .35
137 Kird Ape C .30 .50
138 Mogg Fanatic C .20 .35
139 Mogg War Marshal C .75 1.25
140 Orcish Oriflamme C .20 .35
141 Price of Progress U 2.00 3.00
142 Pyroblast U 10.00 15.00
143 Pyrokinesis R 1.50 2.50
144 Reckless Charge C .20 .35
145 Rorix Bladewing R 1.50 2.00
146 Seismic Stomp C .20 .35
147 Siege Gang Commander R 2.00 2.50
148 Sneak Attack MR 25.00 35.00
149 Stingscourger C .20 .35
150 Sulfuric Vortex R 3.00 5.00
151 Tooth and Claw U .40 .60
152 Undying Rage C .20 .35
153 Wildfire Emissary C .20 .35
154 Worldgorger Dragon MR 3.00 5.00
155 Young Pyromancer U 4.00 6.00
156 Abundant Growth C .20 .35
157 Ancestral Mask U 1.00 1.50
158 Argothian Enchantress MR 8.00 12.00
159 Brawn U .60 1.00
160 Centaur Chieftain U .40 .60
161 Civic Wayfinder C .20 .35
162 Commune with the Gods C .20 .35
163 Elephant Guide C .20 .35
164 Elvish Vanguard C .40 .60
165 Emperor Crocodile C .20 .35
166 Flinthoof Boar U .40 .60
167 Fog C .20 .35
168 Gaes Blessing U .40 .60
169 Green Suns Zenith R 7.00 10.00
170 Harmonize U .60 1.00
171 Heritage Druid R 8.00 11.00
172 Honden of Lifes Web U .40 .60
173 Imperious Perfect R 3.00 5.00
174 Invigorate U 1.50 2.50
175 Llanowar Elves C 1.00 1.50
176 Lys Alana Huntmaster C .20 .35
177 Natuarl Order MR 30.00 35.00
178 Natures Claim C 1.00 1.50
179 Nimble Mongoose C .20 .35
180 Rancor U 2.50 3.50
181 Regal Force R 2.50 3.50
182 Roar of the Wurm U .40 .60
183 Roots C .20 .35
184 Seal of Strenght C .20 .35
185 Sentinel Spider C .20 .35
186 Silvos, Rogue Elemental R 1.00 1.50
187 Sylvan Library R 25.00 30.00
188 Sylvan Might C .20 .35
189 Thornweald Archer C .20 .35
190 Timberwatch Elf U .75 1.25
191 Werebear C .20 .35
192 Wirewood Symbiote U 1.50 2.50
193 Xantid Swarm R 1.50 2.50
194 Yavimaya Enchantress C .20 .35
195 Armadillo Cloak U .60 1.00
196 Baleful Strix R 35.00 40.00
197 Bloodbraid Elf U 3.00 5.00
198 Brago, King Eternal R 6.00 8.00
199 Dack Fayden MR 50.00 60.00
200 Extract from Darkness U .40 .60
201 Flame Kin Zealot U .40 .60
202 Glare of Subdual R 1.00 1.50
203 Goblin Trenches R .40 .60
204 Maelstrom Wanderer MR 20.00 25.00
205 Shaman of the Pack U 1.50 2.00
206 Shardless Agent R 10.00 15.00
207 Sphinx of the Steel Wind MR 2.50 4.00
208 Thunderclap Wyvern U .40 .60
209 Trygon Predator U .75 1.00
210 Vindicate R 8.00 10.00
211 Void R .60 1.00
212 Wee Dragonauts U .40 .60
213 Zealous Persecution U 1.25 2.00
214 Call the Skybreaker R .40 .60
215 Deathrite Shaman R 20.00 25.00
216 Giant Solifuge R .50 .80
217 Torrent of Souls U .40 .60
218 Ashnods Altar U 6.00 8.00
219 Chrome Mox MR 20.00 26.00
220 Duplicant R 5.00 7.00
221 Emmessi Tome U .40 .60
222 Goblin Charbelcher R 2.00 3.50
223 Isochron Scepter R 4.00 6.00
224 Juggernaut U .40 .60
225 Mana Crypt MR 75.00 85.00
226 Millikin U .40 .60
227 Mindless Automaton U .40 .60
228 Nevinyrrals Disk R 3.50 4.50
229 Pilgrims Eye C .20 .35
230 Prismatic Lens U .40 .60
231 Relic of Progenitus U 3.00 5.00
232 Senseis Divining Top R 30.00 35.00
233 Ticking Gnomes U .40 .60
234 Winter Orb R 15.00 20.00
235 Worn Powerstone U 4.00 5.00
236 Bloodfell Caves C .20 .35
237 Blossoming Sands C .20 .35
238 Dismal Backwater C .20 .35
239 Jungle Hollow C .20 .35
240 Karakas MR 55.00 65.00
241 Maze of Ith R 10.00 15.00
242 Mishras Factory U 2.50 4.00
243 Rugged Highlands C .20 .35
244 Scoured Barrens C .20 .35
245 Swiftwater Cliffs C .20 .35
246 Thornwood Falls C .20 .35
247 Tranquil Cove C .20 .35
248 Wasteland R 45.00 55.00
249 Wind Scarred Crag C .20 .35

2016 Magic The Gathering Eternal Masters Tokens

1 Spirit .50 .75
2 Soldier .10 .15
3 Spirit .10 .15
4 Wall .10 .15
5 Serf .20 .30
6 Zombie .10 .15
7 Carnivore .10 .15
8 Dragon .10 .15
9 Elemental .40 .60
10 Goblin .10 .15
11 Elephant .10 .15
12 Elf Warrior .25 .35
13 Wurm .35 .50
14 Elemental .10 .15
15 Goblin Soldier .10 .15
16 Dack Fayden Emblem 1.00 1.50

2017 Magic The Gathering Modern Masters 2017

COMPLETE SET (249) 550.00 750.00
BOOSTER BOX (24 PACKS) 200.00 240.00
BOOSTER PACK (15 CARDS) 8.00 12.00
RELEASED ON MARCH 17, 2016
1 Attended Knight C .10 .20
2 Banishing Stroke U .25 .40
3 Blade Splicer R .60 1.00
4 Entreat the Angels M 2.00 3.50
5 Eyes in the Skies C .10 .20
6 Flickerwisp U 1.50 2.00
7 Gideons Lawkeeper C .10 .20
8 Graceful Reprieve C .10 .20
9 Intangible Virtue U .25 .40
10 Kor Hookmaster C .10 .20
11 Kor Skyfisher C .10 .20
12 Lingering Souls U .60 1.00
13 Linvala Keeper of Silence M 8.00 12.00
14 Lone Missionary C .10 .20
15 Master Splicer U .25 .40
16 Momentary Blink C .10 .20
17 Path to Exile U 5.00 7.00
18 Pitfall Trap C .10 .20
19 Ranger of Eos R 1.00 1.50
20 Restoration Angel R 1.50 2.50
21 Rootborn Defenses C .10 .20
22 Séance R .10 .20
23 Sensor Splicer C .10 .20

24 Soul Warden C	.10	.20
25 Stony Silence R	4.00	6.00
26 Terminus R	.40	.60
27 Urbis Protector U	.40	.60
28 Wake the Reflections C	.10	.20
29 Youthful Knight C	.10	.20
30 Augur of Bolas C	.10	.20
31 Azure Mage U	.25	.40
32 Cackling Counterpart R	.15	.25
33 Compulsive Research U	.25	.40
34 Crippling Chill C	.10	.20
35 Cyclonic Rift R	5.00	7.00
36 Deadeye Navigator R	.75	1.25
37 Familiars Ruse U	.50	.80
38 Forbidden Alchemy C	.10	.20
39 Ghostly Flicker C	.10	.20
40 Gifts Ungiven R	5.00	7.00
41 Grasp of Phantoms C	.10	.20
42 Kraken Hatchling C	.10	.20
43 Mist Raven C	.10	.20
44 Mystical Teachings C	.10	.20
45 Opportunity U	.25	.40
46 Phantasmal Image R	1.50	2.00
47 Rewind C	.10	.20
48 Sea Gate Oracle C	.10	.20
49 Serum Visions U	1.50	2.50
50 Snapcaster Mage M	45.00	50.00
51 Spell Pierce C	.10	.20
52 Spire Monitor C	.10	.20
53 Tandem Lookout C	.10	.20
54 Temporal Mastery M	3.00	5.00
55 Venser Shaper Savant R	2.00	3.00
56 Wall of Frost U	.25	.40
57 Wing Splicer U	.25	.40
58 Wingcrafter C	.10	.20
59 Abyssal Specter U	.25	.40
60 Bone Splinters C	.10	.20
61 Corpse Connoisseur U	.25	.40
62 Cower in Fear C	.10	.20
63 Damnation R	15.00	20.00
64 Deaths Shadow R	5.00	8.00
65 Delirium Skeins C	.10	.20
66 Desecration Demon R	.30	.50
67 Dregscape Zombie C	.10	.20
68 Entomber Exarch U	.25	.40
69 Extractor Demon R	.10	.20
70 Falkenrath Noble C	.10	.20
71 Gnawing Zombie C	.10	.20
72 Griselbrand M	4.00	6.00
73 Grisly Spectacle C	.10	.20
74 Grixis Slavedriver C	.10	.20
75 Inquisition of Kozilek U	2.50	4.00
76 Liliana of the Veil M	70.00	80.00
77 Mind Shatter R	.10	.20
78 Mortician Beetle C	.10	.20
79 Night Terrors C	.10	.20
80 Ogre Jailbreaker C	.10	.20
81 Pit Keeper C	.10	.20
82 Recover C	.10	.20
83 Seal of Doom U	.25	.40
84 Sever the Bloodline R	.60	1.00
85 Unburial Rites U	.25	.40
86 Vampire Aristocrat C	.10	.20
87 Vampire Nighthawk U	.75	1.25
88 Ancient Grudge U	.60	1.00
89 Battle Rattle Shaman C	.10	.20
90 Blood Moon R	15.00	20.00
91 Bonfire of the Damned M	1.50	2.00
92 Chandras Outrage C	.10	.20
93 Dragon Fodder C	.10	.20
94 Dynacharge C	.10	.20
95 Goblin Assault U	1.00	1.50
96 Goblin Guide R	10.00	15.00
97 Hanweir Lancer C	.10	.20
98 Hellrider R	.15	.25
99 Madcap Skills C	.10	.20
100 Magma Jet C	.10	.20
101 Mizzium Mortars R	.10	.20
102 Mogg Flunkies C	.10	.20
103 Molten Rain U	.60	1.00
104 Mudbutton Torchrunner C	.10	.20
105 Past in Flames M	2.00	3.50
106 Pyrewild Shaman U	.25	.40
107 Pyroclasm U	.60	1.00
108 Pyromancer Ascension R	.20	.35
109 Rubblebelt Maaka C	.10	.20
110 Scorched Rusalka C	.10	.20
111 Scourge Devil C	.10	.20
112 Skirsdag Cultist U	.25	.40
113 Thunderous Wrath C	.10	.20
114 Traitorous Instinct C	.10	.20
115 Vithian Stinger U	.25	.40
116 Zealous Conscripts R	.20	.35
117 Arachnus Spinner U	.25	.40
118 Archnus Web C	.10	.20
119 Avacyns Pilgrim C	.10	.20
120 Baloth Cage Trap U	.25	.40
121 Call of the Herd R	.60	1.00
122 Craterhoof Behemoth M	10.00	15.00
123 Death Hood Cobra C	.10	.20
124 Druids Deliverance C	.10	.20
125 Explore C	.10	.20
126 Fists of Ironwood C	.10	.20
127 Gaeas Anthem U	.75	.40
128 Harmonize U	.75	1.25
129 Hungry Spriggan C	.10	.20
130 Might of Old Krosa U	.50	.80
131 Penumbra Spider C	.10	.20
132 Primal Command R	.50	.80
133 Revive C	.10	.20
134 Scavenging Ooze R	1.50	2.50
135 Seal of Primordium C	.10	.20
136 Slaughterhorn C	.10	.20
137 Slime Molding C	.10	.20
138 Strenght in Numbers C	.10	.20
139 Summoning Trap R	.10	.20
140 Sylvan Ranger C	.10	.20
141 Tarmogoyf M	50.00	55.00
142 Thronscape Battlemage U	.25	.40
143 Thragtusk R	.75	1.25
144 Ulvenwald Tracker R	.15	.25
145 Vital Splicer U	.25	.40
146 Abrupt Decay R	2.50	4.00
147 Advent of the Wurm R	.15	.25
148 Aethermages Touch R	.15	.25
149 Agent of Masks U	.25	.40
150 Agony Warp C	.10	.20
151 Auger Spree C	.10	.20
152 Bronzebeak Moa U	.25	.40
153 Broodmate Dragon R	.15	.25
154 Call of the Conclave C	.10	.20
155 Carnage Gladiator U	.25	.40
156 Centaur Healer C	.10	.20
157 Coiling Oracle C	.10	.20
158 Cruel Ultimatum R	.15	.25
159 Deputy of Acquittals C	.10	.20
160 Dinrova Horror C	.10	.20
161 Domri Rade M	1.50	2.50
162 Evil Twin R	.15	.25
163 Falkenrath Aristocrat R	.20	.35
164 Fiery Justice R	.50	.75
165 Ghor Clan Rampager U	.25	.40
166 Goblin Electromancer C	.10	.20
167 Golgari Germination U	.25	.40
168 Golgari Rotwurm C	.10	.20
169 Ground Assault C	.10	.20
170 Gruul War Chant U	.25	.40
171 Izzet Charm U	.40	.60
172 Kathari Bomber C	.10	.20
173 Moroii U	.25	.40
174 Mystic Genesis U	.25	.40
175 Niv Mizzet Dracogenius R	.15	.25
176 Obzedat Ghost Council R	.40	.60
177 Olivia Voldaren M	4.00	6.00
178 Pilfered Plans C	.10	.20
179 Putrefy U	.25	.40
180 Rhox War Monk U	.25	.40
181 Sedraxis Specter U	.25	.40
182 Simic Sky Swallower R	.60	1.00
183 Sin Collector U	.25	.40
184 Skyknight Legionnaire C	.10	.20
185 Soul Manipulation U	.25	.40
186 Soul Ransom U	.25	.40
187 Sphinx's Revelation M	2.00	3.50
188 Spike Jester C	.10	.20
189 Sprouting Thrinax U	.25	.40
190 Stoic Angel R	.15	.25
191 Sunhome Guildmage U	.25	.40
192 Talon Trooper C	.10	.20
193 Teleportal U	.25	.40
194 Terminate U	.60	1.00
195 Thundersong Trumpeter U	.25	.40
196 Tower Gargoyle U	.25	.40
197 Unflinching Courage U	.25	.40
198 Urban Evolution U	.25	.40
199 Vanish into Memory U	.25	.40
200 Voice of Resurgence M	6.00	8.00
201 Wall of Denial U	.60	1.00
202 Wayfaring Temple U	.50	.75
203 Woolly Thoctar U	.25	.40
204 Zur the Enchanter R	.40	.60
205 Aethertow U	.25	.40
206 Boros Reckoner R	.40	.60
207 Burning Tree Emissary C	.10	.20
208 Giantbaiting C	.10	.20
209 Gift of Orzhova C	.10	.20
210 Mistmeadow Witch U	.25	.40
211 Sundering Growth C	.10	.20
212 Tattermunge Witch U	.25	.40
213 Torrent of Souls U	.25	.40
214 Wort the Raidmother R	.75	1.25
215 Azorius Signet U	.50	.80
216 Basilisk Collar R	2.50	4.00
217 Boros Signet U	.25	.40
218 Damping Matrix R	.10	.20
219 Dimir Signet U	.60	1.00
220 Golgari Signet U	.25	.40
221 Grafdiggers Cage R	3.00	5.00
222 Gruul Signet U	.25	.40
223 Izzet Signet U	.25	.40
224 Orzhov Signet U	.25	.40
225 Rakdos Signet U	.25	.40
226 Selesnya Signet U	.25	.40
227 Simic Signet U	.25	.40
228 Arcane Sanctum U	.60	1.00
229 Arid Mesa R	25.00	30.00
230 Azorius Guildgate C	.10	.20
231 Boros Guildgate C	.10	.20
232 Cavern of Souls M	45.00	50.00
233 Crumbling Necropolis U	.25	.40
234 Dimir Guildgate C	.10	.20
235 Golgari Guildgate C	.10	.20
236 Gruul Guildgate C	.10	.20
237 Izzet Guildgate C	.10	.20
238 Jungle Shrine U	.25	.40
239 Marsh Flats R	25.00	30.00
240 Misty Rainforest R	25.00	30.00
241 Orzhov Guildgate C	.10	.20
242 Rakdos Guildgate C	.10	.20
243 Savage Lands U	.25	.40
244 Scalding Tarn R	50.00	55.00
245 Seaside Citadel U	.75	1.25
246 Selesnya Guildgate C	.10	.20
247 Shimmering Grotto C	.10	.20
248 Simic Guildgate C	.10	.20
249 Verdant Catacombs R	35.00	40.00

2017 Magic The Gathering Modern Masters 2017 Foil

COMPLETE SET (249)	1100.00	1400.00
RELEASED ON MARCH 17, 2017		
1 Attended Knight C	.25	.40
2 Banishing Stroke U	.30	.50
3 Blade Splicer R	1.00	2.50
4 Entreat the Angels M	6.00	8.00
5 Eyes in the Skies C	.25	.40
6 Flickerwisp U	3.00	5.00
7 Gideons Lawkeeper C	.25	.40
8 Graceful Reprieve C	.25	.40
9 Intangible Virtue U	.30	.50
10 Kor Hookmaster C	.25	.40
11 Kor Skyfisher C	.25	.40
12 Lingering Souls U	2.00	3.50
13 Linvala Keeper of Silence M	40.00	50.00
14 Lone Missionary C	.25	.40
15 Master Splicer U	.30	.50
16 Momentary Blink C	.25	.40
17 Path to Exile U	6.00	8.00
18 Pitfall Trap C	.25	.40
19 Ranger of Eos R	4.00	6.00
20 Restoration Angel R	6.00	8.00
21 Rootborn Defenses C	.25	.40
22 Séance R	1.00	2.50
23 Sensor Splicer C	.25	.40
24 Soul Warden C	.25	.40
25 Stony Silence R	8.00	11.00
26 Terminus R	2.00	3.50
27 Urbis Protector U	.30	.50
28 Wake the Reflections C	.25	.40
29 Youthful Knight C	.25	.40
30 Augur of Bolas C	.25	.40
31 Azure Mage U	.30	.50
32 Cackling Counterpart R	1.00	2.50
33 Compulsive Research U	.30	.50
34 Crippling Chill C	.25	.40
35 Cyclonic Rift R	9.00	12.00
36 Deadeye Navigator R	1.00	2.50
37 Familiars Ruse U	.30	.50
38 Forbidden Alchemy C	.25	.40
39 Ghostly Flicker C	.25	.40
40 Gifts Ungiven R	6.00	8.00
41 Grasp of Phantoms C	.25	.40
42 Kraken Hatchling C	.25	.40
43 Mist Raven C	.25	.40
44 Mystical Teachings C	.25	.40
45 Opportunity U	.30	.50
46 Phantasmal Image R	5.00	7.00
47 Rewind C	.25	.40
48 Sea Gate Oracle C	.25	.40
49 Serum Visions U	6.00	8.00
50 Snapcaster Mage M	70.00	90.00
51 Spell Pierce C	.25	.40
52 Spire Monitor C	.25	.40
53 Tandem Lookout C	.25	.40
54 Temporal Mastery M	8.00	12.00
55 Venser Shaper Savant R	8.00	11.00
56 Wall of Frost U	.30	.50
57 Wing Splicer U	.30	.50
58 Wingcrafter C	.25	.40
59 Abyssal Specter U	.30	.50
60 Bone Splinters C	.25	.40
61 Corpse Connoisseur U	.30	.50
62 Cower in Fear C	.25	.40
63 Damnation R	35.00	45.00
64 Deaths Shadow R	15.00	20.00
65 Delirium Skeins C	.25	.40
66 Desecration Demon R	1.00	2.50
67 Dregscape Zombie C	.25	.40
68 Entomber Exarch U	.30	.50
69 Extractor Demon R	1.00	2.50
70 Falkenrath Noble C	.25	.40
71 Gnawing Zombie C	.25	.40
72 Griselbrand M	12.00	16.00
73 Grisly Spectacle C	.25	.40
74 Grixis Slavedriver C	.25	.40
75 Inquisition of Kozilek U	12.00	15.00
76 Liliana of the Veil M	120.00	140.00
77 Mind Shatter R	1.00	2.50
78 Mortician Beetle C	.25	.40
79 Night Terrors C	.25	.40
80 Ogre Jailbreaker C	.25	.40
81 Pit Keeper C	.25	.40
82 Recover C	.25	.40
83 Seal of Doom U	.30	.50
84 Sever the Bloodline R	1.00	2.50
85 Unburial Rites U	.30	.50
86 Vampire Aristocrat C	.25	.40
87 Vampire Nighthawk U	1.00	1.50
88 Ancient Grudge U	.30	.50
89 Battle Rattle Shaman C	.25	.40
90 Blood Moon R	35.00	40.00
91 Bonfire of the Damned M	6.00	8.00
92 Chandras Outrage C	.25	.40
93 Dragon Fodder	.25	.40
94 Dynacharge C	.25	.40
95 Goblin Assault U	.30	.50
96 Goblin Guide R	20.00	25.00
97 Hanweir Lancer C	.25	.40
98 Hellrider R	1.00	2.50
99 Madcap Skills C	.25	.40
100 Magma Jet C	.25	.40
101 Mizzium Mortars R	1.00	2.50
102 Mogg Flunkies C	.25	.40
103 Molten Rain U	1.50	2.50
104 Mudbutton Torchrunner C	.25	.40
105 Past in Flames M	7.00	10.00
106 Pyrewild Shaman U	.30	.50
107 Pyroclasm U	.30	.50
108 Pyromancer Ascension R	1.00	2.50
109 Rubblebelt Maaka C	.25	.40
110 Scorched Rusalka C	.25	.40
111 Scourge Devil C	.25	.40
112 Skirsdag Cultist U	.30	.50
113 Thunderous Wrath C	.25	.40
114 Traitorous Instinct C	.25	.40
115 Vithian Stinger U	.30	.50
116 Zealous Conscripts R	2.00	3.50
117 Arachnus Spinner U	.30	.50
118 Archnus Web C	.25	.40
119 Avacyns Pilgrim C	.25	.40
120 Baloth Cage Trap U	.30	.50
121 Call of the Herd R	1.00	2.50
122 Craterhoof Behemoth M	20.00	25.00
123 Death Hood Cobra C	.25	.40
124 Druids Deliverance C	.25	.40
125 Explore C	.25	.40
126 Fists of Ironwood C	.25	.40
127 Gaeas Anthem U	1.00	1.50
128 Harmonize U	1.00	1.50
129 Hungry Spriggan C	.25	.40
130 Might of Old Krosa U	3.00	5.00
131 Penumbra Spider C	.25	.40
132 Primal Command R	1.00	2.50
133 Revive C	.25	.40
134 Scavenging Ooze R	4.00	6.00
135 Seal of Primordium C	.25	.40
136 Slaughterhorn C	.25	.40
137 Slime Molding C	.25	.40
138 Strenght in Numbers C	.25	.40
139 Summoning Trap R	1.00	2.50
140 Sylvan Ranger C	.25	.40
141 Tarmogoyf M	130.00	150.00
142 Thronscape Battlemage U	.30	.50
143 Thragtusk R	4.00	6.00
144 Ulvenwald Tracker R	1.00	2.50
145 Vital Splicer U	.30	.50
146 Abrupt Decay R	13.00	16.00
147 Advent of the Wurm R	1.00	2.50
148 Aethermages Touch R	1.00	2.50
149 Agent of Masks U	.30	.50
150 Agony Warp	.25	.40
151 Auger Spree C	.25	.40
152 Bronzebeak Moa U	.30	.50
153 Broodmate Dragon R	1.00	2.50
154 Call of the Conclave C	.25	.40
155 Carnage Gladiator U	.30	.50
156 Centaur Healer C	.25	.40
157 Coiling Oracle C	.25	.40
158 Cruel Ultimatum R	1.00	2.50
159 Deputy of Acquittals C	.25	.40
160 Dinrova Horror C	.25	.40
161 Domri Rade M	7.00	10.00
162 Evil Twin R	1.00	2.50
163 Falkenrath Aristocrat R	1.00	2.50
164 Fiery Justice R	1.00	2.50
165 Ghor Clan Rampager U	.30	.50
166 Goblin Electromancer C	.25	.40
167 Golgari Germination U	.30	.50
168 Golgari Rotwurm C	.25	.40
169 Ground Assault C	.25	.40
170 Gruul War Chant U	.30	.50
171 Izzet Charm U	.30	.50
172 Kathari Bomber C	.25	.40
173 Moroii U	.30	.50
174 Mystic Genesis U	.30	.50
175 Niv Mizzet Dracogenius R	1.00	2.50
176 Obzedat Ghost Council R	1.00	2.50
177 Olivia Voldaren M	9.00	12.00
178 Pilfered Plans C	.25	.40
179 Putrefy U	.30	.50
180 Rhox War Monk U	.30	.50
181 Sedraxis Specter U	.30	.50
182 Simic Sky Swallower R	1.00	2.50
183 Sin Collector U	.30	.50
184 Skyknight Legionnaire C	.25	.40
185 Soul Manipulation U	.30	.50
186 Soul Ransom U	.30	.50
187 Sphinx's Revelation M	7.00	10.00
188 Spike Jester C	.25	.40
189 Sprouting Thrinax U	.30	.50
190 Stoic Angel R	1.00	2.50
191 Sunhome Guildmage U	.30	.50
192 Talon Trooper C	.25	.40
193 Teleportal U	.30	.50
194 Terminate U	2.50	4.00
195 Thundersong Trumpeter U	.30	.50
196 Tower Gargoyle U	.30	.50
197 Unflinching Courage U	.30	.50
198 Urban Evolution U	.30	.50
199 Vanish into Memory U	.30	.50
200 Voice of Resurgence M	30.00	40.00
201 Wall of Denial U	.30	.50
202 Wayfaring Temple U	.30	.50
203 Woolly Thoctar U	.30	.50
204 Zur the Enchanter R	7.00	10.00
205 Aethertow U	.30	.50
206 Boros Reckoner R	1.00	2.50
207 Burning Tree Emissary C	.25	.40
208 Giantbaiting C	.25	.40
209 Gift of Orzhova C	.25	.40
210 Mistmeadow Witch U	.30	.50
211 Sundering Growth C	.25	.40
212 Tattermunge Witch U	.30	.50
213 Torrent of Souls U	.30	.50
214 Wort the Raidmother R	1.00	2.50
215 Azorius Signet U	3.00	5.00
216 Basilisk Collar R	6.00	8.00
217 Boros Signet U	.30	.50
218 Damping Matrix R	1.00	2.50
219 Dimir Signet U	3.00	5.00
220 Golgari Signet U	.30	.50
221 Grafdiggers Cage R	7.00	10.00
222 Gruul Signet U	.30	.50
223 Izzet Signet U	.30	.50
224 Orzhov Signet U	.30	.50
225 Rakdos Signet U	.30	.50
226 Selesnya Signet U	.30	.50
227 Simic Signet U	.30	.50
228 Arcane Sanctum U	1.25	2.00
229 Arid Mesa R	40.00	50.00
230 Azorius Guildgate C	.25	.40

231 Boros Guildgate C .25 .40
232 Cavern of Souls M 80.00 100.00
233 Crumbling Necropolis U 1.00 1.50
234 Dimir Guildgate C .25 .40
235 Golgari Guildgate C .25 .40
236 Gruul Guildgate C .25 .40
237 Izzet Guildgate C .25 .40
238 Jungle Shrine U 1.00 1.50
239 Marsh Flats M 35.00 45.00
240 Misty Rainforest R 55.00 65.00
241 Orzhov Guildgate C .25 .40
242 Rakdos Guildgate C .25 .40
243 Savage Lands U .30 .50
244 Scalding Tarn R 75.00 90.00
245 Seaside Citadel U 1.25 2.00
246 Selesnya Guildgate C .25 .40
247 Shimmering Grotto C .25 .40
248 Simic Guildgate C .25 .40
249 Verdant Catacombs R 60.00 70.00

2017 Magic The Gathering Modern Masters 2017 Tokens

1 Angel .25 .35
2 Bird .10 .15
3 Soldier .20 .30
4 Spirit .10 .15
5 Spider .12 .20
6 Zombie .10 .15
7 Dragon .15 .25
8 Goblin .15 .25
9 Beast .15 .25
10 Beast .20 .30
11 Centaur .10 .15
12 Elephant .12 .20
13 Ooze .10 .15
14 Saproling .10 .15
15 Wurm .35 .50
16 Elemental .25 .35
17 Giant Warrior .10 .15
18 Goblin Warrior .10 .15
19 Soldier .10 .15
20 Golem .10 .15
21 Domri Rade Emblem .50 .75

2017 Magic The Gathering Iconic Masters

COMPLETE SET (249) 350.00 500.00
BOOSTER BOX (24 PACKS) 145.00 240.00
BOOSTER PACK (15 CARDS) 6.00 10.00
RELEASED ON NOVEMBER 17, 2017
1 Scion of Ugin C .10 .20
2 Abzan Battle Priest U .10 .20
3 Abzan Falconer U .10 .20
4 Ainok Bond Kin C .10 .20
5 Ajanis Pridemate U .10 .20
6 Angel of Mercy C .10 .20
7 Angelic Accord U .10 .20
8 Archangel of Thune M 10.00 15.00
9 Auriok Champion R 3.00 5.00
10 Austere Command R 3.00 5.00
11 Avacyn Angel of Hope M 10.00 15.00
12 Benevolent Ancestor C .10 .20
13 Blinding Mage C .10 .20
14 Burrenton Forge Tender U .10 .20
15 Disenchant C .10 .20
16 Doomed Traveler C .10 .20
17 Dragon Bell Monk C .10 .20
18 Elesh Norn Grand Cenobite M 10.00 15.00
19 Emerge Unscathed C .10 .20
20 Emeria Angel R .25 .40
21 Great Teachers Decree U .10 .20
22 Guard Duty C .10 .20
23 Guided Strike C .10 .20
24 Infantry Veteran C .10 .20
25 Ionas Judgment C .10 .20
26 Path of Bravery R .25 .40
27 Pentarch Ward C .10 .20
28 Restoratoin Angel R 1.25 2.00
29 Seeker of the Way C .10 .20
30 Serra Angel U .10 .20
31 Serra Ascendant R 6.00 8.00
32 Stalwart Aven C .10 .20
33 Student of Ojutai C .10 .20
34 Survival Cache C .10 .20
35 Sustainer of the Realm C .10 .20
36 Swords to Plowshares U .60 1.00
37 Topan Freeblade U .10 .20
38 Wing Shards U .10 .20
39 Yosei the Morning Star R 1.00 1.50
40 Aetherize U .10 .20
41 Amass the Components C .10 .20
42 Ancestral Vision R 13.00 16.00
43 Bewilder C .10 .20
44 Cephalid Broker U .10 .20
45 Claustrophobia C .10 .20
46 Condescend U .10 .20
47 Consecrated Sphinx M 10.00 15.00
48 Cryptic Command R 18.00 22.00
49 Day of the Dragons R .25 .40
50 Diminish C .10 .20
51 Dissolve C .10 .20
52 Distortion Strike U .10 .20
53 Doorkeeper C .10 .20
54 Elusive Spellfist C .10 .20
55 Flusterstorm R 15.00 20.00
56 Fog Bank U .10 .20
57 Frost Lynx C .10 .20
58 Illusory Ambusher U .10 .20
59 Illusory Angel U .10 .20
60 Jaces Phantasm C .10 .20
61 Jhessian Thief C .10 .20
62 Jin Gitaxias Core Augur M 5.00 8.00
63 Keiga the Tide Star R 1.00 1.50
64 Mahamoti Djinn U .10 .20
65 Mana Drain M 55.00 65.00
66 Mana Leak C .10 .20
67 Mnemonic Wall C .10 .20
68 Ojutais Breath C .10 .20
69 Phantom Monster C .10 .20
70 Repeal C .10 .20
71 Riverwheel Aerialists C .10 .20
72 Shriekgeist C .10 .20
73 Skywise Teachings U .10 .20
74 Sphinx of Uthuun R .25 .40
75 Teferi Mage of Zhalfir R 2.00 3.50
76 Thought Scour C .10 .20
77 Windfall U .10 .20
78 Abyssal Persecutor R .25 .40
79 Bala Ged Scorpion C .10 .20
80 Balustrade Spy C .10 .20
81 Bladewings Thrall U .10 .20
82 Bloodghast R 7.00 9.00
83 Bogbrew Witch U .10 .20
84 Butchers Glee C .10 .20
85 Child of Night C .10 .20
86 Dead Reveler C .10 .20
87 Doom Blade U .10 .20
88 Duress C .10 .20
89 Eternal Thirst C .10 .20
90 Festering Newt C .10 .20
91 Foul Tongue Invocation C .10 .20
92 Grisly Spectacle C .10 .20
93 Haunting Hymn U .10 .20
94 Indulgent Tormentor U .10 .20
95 Kokusho the Evening Star R 4.00 6.00
96 Lord of the Pit R .25 .40
97 Mer Ek Nightblade U .10 .20
98 Necropotence M 4.00 6.00
99 Night of Souls Betrayal R .30 .50
100 Noxious Dragon U .10 .20
101 Ob Nixilis the Fallen M 1.50 2.00
102 Phyrexian Rager C .10 .20
103 Rakdos Drake C .10 .20
104 Reave Soul C .10 .20
105 Rotfeaster Maggot C .10 .20
106 Rune Scarred Demon R 1.00 1.50
107 Sanguine Bond U .10 .20
108 Sheoldred Whispering One M 8.00 12.00
109 Tavern Swindler U .10 .20
110 Thoughtseize R 10.00 15.00
111 Thrill Kill Assassin C .10 .20
112 Ulcerate U .10 .20
113 Virulent Swipe C .10 .20
114 Wight of Precinct Six C .10 .20
115 Wrench Mind C .10 .20
116 Anger of the Gods R .75 1.25
117 Battle Rattle Shaman C .10 .20
118 Bogardan Hellkite R .25 .40
119 Borderland Marauder C .10 .20
120 Charmbreaker Devils R .25 .40
121 Coordinated Assault U .10 .20
122 Crucible of Fire R .25 .40
123 Draconic Roar C .10 .20
124 Dragon Egg C .10 .20
125 Dragon Tempest U .10 .20
126 Dragonlords Servant C .10 .20
127 Earth Elemental C .10 .20
128 Fireball U .10 .20
129 Furnace Whelp C .10 .20
130 Fury Charm C .10 .20
131 Guttersnipe U .10 .20
132 Hammerhand C .10 .20
133 Heat Ray C .10 .20
134 Hoarding Dragon U .10 .20
135 Keldon Halberdier C .10 .20
136 Kiki Jiki Mirror Breaker M 5.00 8.00
137 Kiln Fiend C .10 .20
138 Magus of the Moon R 6.00 8.00
139 Mark of Mutiny C .10 .20
140 Monastery Swiftspear U .30 .50
141 Pillar of Flame C .10 .20
142 Prodigal Pyromancer U .10 .20
143 Rift Bolt U .30 .50
144 Ryusei the Falling Star R .40 .60
145 Scourge of Valkas R .25 .40
146 Splatter Thug C .10 .20
147 Staggershock U .10 .20
148 Surreal Memoir U .10 .20
149 Thundermaw Hellkite M 2.50 4.00
150 Tormenting Voice C .10 .20
151 Trumpet Blast C .10 .20
152 Urabrask the Hidden M 3.00 5.00
153 Vent Sentinel C .10 .20
154 Aerial Predation C .10 .20
155 Assault Formation U .10 .20
156 Carven Caryatid U .10 .20
157 Channel M .60 1.00
158 Crowned Ceratok C .10 .20
159 Curse of Predation R .25 .40
160 Durkwood Baloth C .10 .20
161 Duskdale Wurm C .10 .20
162 Enlarge U .10 .20
163 Genesis Hydra R .25 .40
164 Genesis Wave R 1.25 2.00
165 Greater Basilisk C .10 .20
166 Heroes Bane U .10 .20
167 Hunt the Weak C .10 .20
168 Hunting Pack U .10 .20
169 Inspiring Call U .10 .20
170 Ivy Elemental C .10 .20
171 Jaddi Offshoot C .10 .20
172 Jugan the Rising Star R .50 .80
173 Lead the Stampede C .10 .20
174 Lotus Cobra R 3.00 5.00
175 Lure U .10 .20
176 Nantuko Shaman C .10 .20
177 Natures Claim C .10 .20
178 Netcaster Spider C .10 .20
179 Obstinate Baloth R .40 .60
180 Overgrown Battlement U .10 .20
181 Phantom Tiger C .10 .20
182 Preys Vengeance C .10 .20
183 Primeval Titan M 5.00 8.00
184 Rampaging Baloths R .25 .40
185 Search for Tomorrow C .10 .20
186 Sultai Flayer U .10 .20
187 Timberland Guide C .10 .20
188 Undercity Troll U .10 .20
189 Vorinclex Voice of Hunger M 8.00 12.00
190 Wall of Roots C .10 .20
191 Wildsize C .10 .20
192 Azorius Charm U .10 .20
193 Bladewing the Risen U .10 .20
194 Blizzard Specter U .10 .20
195 Blood Baron of Vizkopa R .25 .40
196 Chronicler of Heroes U .10 .20
197 Corpsejack Menace U .10 .20
198 Electrolyze U .10 .20
199 Firemane Angel R .25 .40
200 Glimpse the Unthinkable R 6.00 8.00
201 Hypersonic Dragon R .25 .40
202 Jungle Barrier U .10 .20
203 Knight of the Reliquary R 2.50 4.00
204 Lightning Helix U 1.50 2.00
205 Malfegor R .25 .40
206 Rosheen Meanderer U .10 .20
207 Savageborn Hydra R .25 .40
208 Simic Sky Swallower R .25 .40
209 Spiritmonger R .25 .40
210 Supreme Verdict R 2.50 4.00
211 Vizkopa Guildmage U .10 .20
212 Aether Vial R 25.00 30.00
213 Bubbling Cauldron U .10 .20
214 Darksteel Axe C .10 .20
215 Dragonloft Idol U .10 .20
216 Guardian Idol C .10 .20
217 Kolaghan Monument U .10 .20
218 Manakin C .10 .20
219 Mind Stone C .10 .20
220 Mindcrank U .40 .60
221 Mishras Bauble U 3.00 5.00
222 Moonglove Extract C .10 .20
223 Oblivion Stone R 3.00 5.00
224 Palladium Myr U .10 .20
225 Pristine Talisman U .10 .20
226 Runed Servitor C .10 .20
227 Sandstone Oracle U .10 .20
228 Serum Powder R .25 .40
229 Star Compass C .10 .20
230 Thran Dynamo U 2.50 4.00
231 Trepanation Blade U .10 .20
232 Azorius Chancery U .10 .20
233 Boros Garrison U .10 .20
234 Dimir Aqueduct U .10 .20
235 Evolving Wilds C .10 .20
236 Golgari Rot Farm U .10 .20
237 Graven Cairns R 1.50 2.50
238 Grove of the Burnwillows R 8.00 12.00
239 Gruul Turf U .10 .20
240 Horizon Canopy R 25.00 30.00
241 Izzet Boilerworks U .10 .20
242 Nimbus Maze R 1.50 2.00
243 Orzhov Basilica U .10 .20
244 Radiant Fountain C .10 .20
245 Rakdos Carnarium U .10 .20
246 River of Tears R .75 1.25
247 Selesnya Sanctuary U .10 .20
248 Shimmering Grotto C .10 .20
249 Simic Growth Chamber U .10 .20

2017 Magic The Gathering Iconic Masters Foil

1 Scion of Ugin C .60 1.00
2 Abzan Battle Priest U 2.00 3.50
3 Abzan Falconer U 2.00 3.50
4 Ainok Bond Kin C .60 1.00
5 Ajanis Pridemate U 2.00 3.50
6 Angel of Mercy C .60 1.00
7 Angelic Accord U 2.00 3.50
8 Archangel of Thune M 25.00 40.00
9 Auriok Champion R 6.00 10.00
10 Austere Command R 6.00 10.00
11 Avacyn Angel of Hope M 25.00 40.00
12 Benevolent Ancestor C .60 1.00
13 Blinding Mage C .60 1.00
14 Burrenton Forge Tender U 2.00 3.50
15 Disenchant C .60 1.00
16 Doomed Traveler C .60 1.00
17 Dragon Bell Monk C .60 1.00
18 Elesh Norn Grand Cenobite M 25.00 40.00
19 Emerge Unscathed C .60 1.00
20 Emeria Angel R 6.00 10.00
21 Great Teachers Decree U 2.00 3.50
22 Guard Duty C .60 1.00
23 Guided Strike C .60 1.00
24 Infantry Veteran C .60 1.00
25 Ionas Judgment C .60 1.00
26 Path of Bravery R 6.00 10.00
27 Pentarch Ward C .60 1.00
28 Restoratoin Angel R 6.00 10.00
29 Seeker of the Way C .60 1.00
30 Serra Angel U 2.00 3.50
31 Serra Ascendant R 6.00 10.00
32 Stalwart Aven C .60 1.00
33 Student of Ojutai C .60 1.00
34 Survival Cache C .60 1.00
35 Sustainer of the Realm C .60 1.00
36 Swords to Plowshares U 2.00 3.50
37 Topan Freeblade U 2.00 3.50
38 Wing Shards U 2.00 3.50
39 Yosei the Morning Star R 6.00 10.00
40 Aetherize U 2.00 3.50
41 Amass the Components C .60 1.00
42 Ancestral Vision R 6.00 10.00
43 Bewilder C .60 1.00
44 Cephalid Broker U 2.00 3.50
45 Claustrophobia C .60 1.00
46 Condescend U 2.00 3.50
47 Consecrated Sphinx M 25.00 40.00
48 Cryptic Command R 6.00 10.00
49 Day of the Dragons R 6.00 10.00
50 Diminish C .60 1.00
51 Dissolve C .60 1.00
52 Distortion Strike U 2.00 3.50
53 Doorkeeper C .60 1.00
54 Elusive Spellfist C .60 1.00
55 Flusterstorm R 6.00 10.00
56 Fog Bank U 2.00 3.50
57 Frost Lynx C .60 1.00
58 Illusory Ambusher U 2.00 3.50
59 Illusory Angel U 2.00 3.50
60 Jaces Phantasm C .60 1.00
61 Jhessian Thief C .60 1.00
62 Jin Gitaxias Core Augur M 25.00 40.00
63 Keiga the Tide Star R 6.00 10.00
64 Mahamoti Djinn U 2.00 3.50
65 Mana Drain M 25.00 40.00
66 Mana Leak C .60 1.00
67 Mnemonic Wall C .60 1.00
68 Ojutais Breath C .60 1.00
69 Phantom Monster C .60 1.00
70 Repeal C .60 1.00
71 Riverwheel Aerialists C .60 1.00
72 Shriekgeist C .60 1.00
73 Skywise Teachings U 2.00 3.50
74 Sphinx of Uthuun R 6.00 10.00
75 Teferi Mage of Zhalfir R 6.00 10.00
76 Thought Scour C .60 1.00
77 Windfall U 2.00 3.50
78 Abyssal Persecutor R 6.00 10.00
79 Bala Ged Scorpion C .60 1.00
80 Balustrade Spy C .60 1.00
81 Bladewings Thrall U 2.00 3.50
82 Bloodghast R 6.00 10.00
83 Bogbrew Witch U 2.00 3.50
84 Butchers Glee C .60 1.00
85 Child of Night C .60 1.00
86 Dead Reveler C .60 1.00
87 Doom Blade U 2.00 3.50
88 Duress C .60 1.00
89 Eternal Thirst C .60 1.00
90 Festering Newt C .60 1.00
91 Foul Tongue Invocation C .60 1.00
92 Grisly Spectacle C .60 1.00
93 Haunting Hymn U 2.00 3.50
94 Indulgent Tormentor U 2.00 3.50
95 Kokusho the Evening Star R 6.00 10.00
96 Lord of the Pit R 6.00 10.00
97 Mer Ek Nightblade U 2.00 3.50
98 Necropotence M 25.00 40.00
99 Night of Souls Betrayal R 6.00 10.00
100 Noxious Dragon U 2.00 3.50
101 Ob Nixilis the Fallen M 25.00 40.00
102 Phyrexian Rager C .60 1.00
103 Rakdos Drake C .60 1.00
104 Reave Soul C .60 1.00
105 Rotfeaster Maggot C .60 1.00
106 Rune Scarred Demon R 6.00 10.00
107 Sanguine Bond U 2.00 3.50
108 Sheoldred Whispering One M 25.00 40.00
109 Tavern Swindler U 2.00 3.50
110 Thoughtseize R 6.00 10.00
111 Thrill Kill Assassin C .60 1.00
112 Ulcerate U 2.00 3.50
113 Virulent Swipe C .60 1.00
114 Wight of Precinct Six C .60 1.00
115 Wrench Mind C .60 1.00
116 Anger of the Gods R 6.00 10.00
117 Battle Rattle Shaman C .60 1.00
118 Bogardan Hellkite R 6.00 10.00
119 Borderland Marauder C .60 1.00
120 Charmbreaker Devils R 6.00 10.00
121 Coordinated Assault U 2.00 3.50
122 Crucible of Fire R 6.00 10.00
123 Draconic Roar C .60 1.00
124 Dragon Egg C .60 1.00
125 Dragon Tempest U 2.00 3.50
126 Dragonlords Servant C .60 1.00
127 Earth Elemental C .60 1.00
128 Fireball U 2.00 3.50
129 Furnace Whelp C .60 1.00
130 Fury Charm C .60 1.00
131 Guttersnipe U 2.00 3.50
132 Hammerhand C .60 1.00
133 Heat Ray C .60 1.00
134 Hoarding Dragon U 2.00 3.50
135 Keldon Halberdier C .60 1.00
136 Kiki Jiki Mirror Breaker M 25.00 40.00
137 Kiln Fiend C .60 1.00
138 Magus of the Moon R 6.00 10.00
139 Mark of Mutiny C .60 1.00
140 Monastery Swiftspear U 2.00 3.50
141 Pillar of Flame C .60 1.00
142 Prodigal Pyromancer U 2.00 3.50
143 Rift Bolt U 2.00 3.50
144 Ryusei the Falling Star R 6.00 10.00
145 Scourge of Valkas R 6.00 10.00
146 Splatter Thug C .60 1.00
147 Staggershock U 2.00 3.50
148 Surreal Memoir U 2.00 3.50
149 Thundermaw Hellkite M 25.00 40.00
150 Tormenting Voice C .60 1.00
151 Trumpet Blast C .60 1.00
152 Urabrask the Hidden M 25.00 40.00
153 Vent Sentinel C .60 1.00
154 Aerial Predation C .60 1.00
155 Assault Formation U 2.00 3.50
156 Carven Caryatid U 2.00 3.50
157 Channel M 25.00 40.00
158 Crowned Ceratok C .60 1.00
159 Curse of Predation R 6.00 10.00
160 Durkwood Baloth C .60 1.00
161 Duskdale Wurm C .60 1.00

162 Enlarge U 2.00 3.50
163 Genesis Hydra R 6.00 10.00
164 Genesis Wave R 6.00 10.00
165 Greater Basilisk C .60 1.00
166 Heroes Bane U 2.00 3.50
167 Hunt the Weak C .60 1.00
168 Hunting Pack U 2.00 3.50
169 Inspiring Call U 2.00 3.50
170 Ivy Elemental C .60 1.00
171 Jaddi Offshoot C .60 1.00
172 Jugan the Rising Star R 6.00 10.00
173 Lead the Stampede C .60 1.00
174 Lotus Cobra R 6.00 10.00
175 Lure U 2.00 3.50
176 Nantuko Shaman C .60 1.00
177 Natures Claim C .60 1.00
178 Netcaster Spider C .60 1.00
179 Obstinate Baloth R 6.00 10.00
180 Overgrown Battlement U 2.00 3.50
181 Phantom Tiger C .60 1.00
182 Preys Vengeance C .60 1.00
183 Primeval Titan M 25.00 40.00
184 Rampaging Baloths R 6.00 10.00
185 Search for Tomorrow C .60 1.00
186 Sultai Flayer U 2.00 3.50
187 Timberland Guide C .60 1.00
188 Undercity Troll U 2.00 3.50
189 Vorinclex Voice of Hunger M 25.00 40.00
190 Wall of Roots C .60 1.00
191 Wildsize C .60 1.00
192 Azorius Charm U 2.00 3.50
193 Bladewing the Risen U 2.00 3.50
194 Blizzard Specter U 2.00 3.50
195 Blood Baron of Vizkopa R 6.00 10.00
196 Chronicler of Heroes U 2.00 3.50
197 Corpsejack Menace U 2.00 3.50
198 Electrolyze U 2.00 3.50
199 Firemane Angel R 6.00 10.00
200 Glimpse the Unthinkable R 6.00 10.00
201 Hypersonic Dragon R 6.00 10.00
202 Jungle Barrier U 2.00 3.50
203 Knight of the Reliquary R 6.00 10.00
204 Lightning Helix U 2.00 3.50
205 Maelstrom R 6.00 10.00
206 Rosheen Meanderer U 2.00 3.50
207 Savageborn Hydra R 6.00 10.00
208 Simic Sky Swallower R 6.00 10.00
209 Spiritmonger R 6.00 10.00
210 Supreme Verdict R 6.00 10.00
211 Vizkopa Guildmage U 2.00 3.50
212 Aether Vial R 6.00 10.00
213 Bubbling Cauldron U 2.00 3.50
214 Darksteel Axe C .60 1.00
215 Dragonloft Idol U 2.00 3.50
216 Guardian Idol C .60 1.00
217 Kolaghan Monument U 2.00 3.50
218 Manakin C .60 1.00
219 Mind Stone C .60 1.00
220 Mindcrank U 2.00 3.50
221 Mishras Bauble U 2.00 3.50
222 Moonglove Extract C .60 1.00
223 Oblivion Stone R 6.00 10.00
224 Palladium Myr U 2.00 3.50
225 Pristine Talisman U 2.00 3.50
226 Runed Servitor C .60 1.00
227 Sandstone Oracle U 2.00 3.50
228 Serum Powder R 6.00 10.00
229 Star Compass C .60 1.00
230 Thran Dynamo U 2.00 3.50
231 Trepanation Blade U 2.00 3.50
232 Azorius Chancery U 2.00 3.50
233 Boros Garrison U 2.00 3.50
234 Dimir Aqueduct U 2.00 3.50
235 Evolving Wilds C .60 1.00
236 Golgari Rot Farm U 2.00 3.50
237 Graven Cairns R 6.00 10.00
238 Grove of the Burnwillows R 6.00 10.00
239 Gruul Turf U 2.00 3.50
240 Horizon Canopy R 6.00 10.00
241 Izzet Boilerworks U 2.00 3.50
242 Nimbus Maze R 6.00 10.00
243 Orzhov Basilica U 2.00 3.50
244 Radiant Fountain C .60 1.00
245 Rakdos Carnarium U 2.00 3.50
246 River of Tears R 6.00 10.00
247 Selesnya Sanctuary U 2.00 3.50
248 Shimmering Grotto C .60 1.00
249 Simic Growth Chamber U 2.00 3.50

2017 Magic The Gathering Iconic Masters Tokens

1 Angel .12 .20
2 Bird .06 .10
3 Spirit .06 .10
4 Djinn Monk .06 .10
5 Dragon .10 .15
6 Dragon .10 .15
7 Beast .10 .15

2018 Magic The Gathering Masters 25

COMPLETE SET (249) 600.00 800.00
BOOSTER BOX
BOOSTER PACK (15 CARDS)
RELEASED ON MARCH 16, 2018
1 Act of Heroism U .40 .60
2 Akroma, Angel of Wrath M 3.00 5.00
3 Akroma's Vengeance R 3.00 5.00
4 Angelic Page U .40 .60
5 Armageddon M 3.00 5.00
6 Auramancer U .40 .60
7 Cloudshift C .20 .35
8 Congregate U .40 .60
9 Darien, King of Kjeldor R 3.00 5.00
10 Dauntless Cathar C .20 .35
11 Decree of Justice R 3.00 5.00
12 Disenchant C .20 .35
13 Fencing Ace C .20 .35
14 Fiend Hunter U .40 .60
15 Geist of the Moors C .20 .35
16 Gods Willing C .20 .35
17 Griffin Protector C .20 .35
18 Karona's Zealot U .40 .60
19 Knight of the Skyward Eye C .20 .35
20 Kongming, "Sleeping Dragon" U .40 .60
21 Kor Firewalker U .40 .60
22 Loyal Sentry C .20 .35
23 Luminarch Ascension R 3.00 5.00
24 Lunarch Mantle C .20 .35
25 Noble Templar C .20 .35
26 Nyx-Fleece Ram U .40 .60
27 Ordeal of Heliod U .40 .60
28 Pacifism C .20 .35
29 Path of Peace C .20 .35
30 Promise of Bunrei U .40 .60
31 Renewed Faith C .20 .35
32 Rest in Peace R 3.00 5.00
33 Savannah Lions C .20 .35
34 Squadron Hawk C .20 .35
35 Swords to Plowshares U .40 .60
36 Thalia, Guardian of Thraben R 3.00 5.00
37 Urbis Protector U .40 .60
38 Valor in Akros U .40 .60
39 Whitemane Lion C .20 .35
40 Accumulated Knowledge C .20 .35
41 Arcane Denial C .20 .35
42 Bident of Thassa R 3.00 5.00
43 Blue Elemental Blast U .40 .60
44 Blue Sun's Zenith R 3.00 5.00
45 Borrowing 100,000 Arrows C .20 .35
46 Brainstorm C .20 .35
47 Brine Elemental U .40 .60
48 Choking Tethers C .20 .35
49 Coralhelm Guide C .20 .35
50 Counterspell C .20 .35
51 Court Hussar C .20 .35
52 Curiosity U .40 .60
53 Cursecatcher U .40 .60
54 Dragon's Eye Savants C .20 .35
55 Exclude U .40 .60
56 Fathom Seer C .20 .35
57 Flash R 3.00 5.00
58 Freed from the Real U .40 .60
59 Genju of the Falls U .40 .60
60 Ghost Ship C .20 .35
61 Horseshoe Crab C .20 .35
62 Jace, the Mind Sculptor M 100.00 110.00
63 Jalira, Master Polymorphist U .40 .60
64 Man-o'-War C .20 .35
65 Merfolk Looter U .40 .60
66 Murder of Crows U .40 .60
67 Mystic of the Hidden Way C .20 .35
68 Pact of Negation R 3.00 5.00
69 Phantasmal Bear C .20 .35
70 Reef Worm R 3.00 5.00
71 Retraction Helix C .20 .35
72 Shoreline Ranger C .20 .35
73 Sift C .20 .35
74 Totally Lost C .20 .35
75 Twisted Image U .40 .60
76 Vendilion Clique M 20.00 25.00
77 Vesuvan Shapeshifter R 3.00 5.00
78 Willbender U .40 .60
79 Ancient Craving U .40 .60
80 Bloodhunter Bat C .20 .35
81 Caustic Tar U .40 .60
82 Dark Ritual C .20 .35
83 Deadly Designs U .40 .60
84 Death's-Head Buzzard C .20 .35
85 Diabolic Edict C .20 .35
86 Dirge of Dread C .20 .35
87 Disfigure C .20 .35
88 Doomsday M 3.00 5.00
89 Dusk Legion Zealot C .20 .35
90 Erg Raiders C .20 .35
91 Fallen Angel U .40 .60
92 Hell's Caretaker R 3.00 5.00
93 Horror of the Broken Lands U .40 .60
94 Ihsan's Shade U .40 .60
95 Laquatus's Champion R 3.00 5.00
96 Living Death R 3.00 5.00
97 Mesmeric Fiend U .40 .60
98 Murder C .20 .35
99 Nezumi Cutthroat C .20 .35
100 Phyrexian Ghoul C .20 .35
101 Phyrexian Obliterator M 15.00 18.00
102 Plague Wind R 3.00 5.00
103 Ratcatcher R 3.00 5.00
104 Ravenous Chupacabra U .40 .60
105 Relentless Rats C .20 .35
106 Returned Phalanx C .20 .35
107 Ruthless Ripper C .20 .35
108 Street Wraith U .40 .60
109 Supernatural Stamina C .20 .35
110 Triskaidekaphobia R 3.00 5.00
111 Twisted Abomination C .20 .35
112 Undead Gladiator U .40 .60
113 Unearth C .20 .35
114 Vampire Lacerator C .20 .35
115 Will-o'-the-Wisp U .40 .60
116 Zombify U .40 .60
117 Zulaport Cutthroat U .40 .60
118 Act of Treason C .20 .35
119 Akroma, Angel of Fury M 3.00 5.00
120 Balduvian Horde C .20 .35
121 Ball Lightning R 3.00 5.00
122 Blood Moon R 3.00 5.00
123 Browbeat U .40 .60
124 Chandra's Outrage C .20 .35
125 Chartooth Cougar C .20 .35
126 Cinder Storm C .20 .35
127 Crimson Mage C .20 .35
128 Eidolon of the Great Revel R 3.00 5.00
129 Enthralling Victor U .40 .60
130 Fortune Thief R 3.00 5.00
131 Frenzied Goblin C .20 .35
132 Genju of the Spires U .40 .60
133 Goblin War Drums U .40 .60
134 Hordeling Outburst C .20 .35
135 Humble Defector U .40 .60
136 Imperial Recruiter M 65.00 70.00
137 Ire Shaman U .40 .60
138 Izzet Chemister R 3.00 5.00
139 Jackal Pup C .20 .35
140 Kindle C .20 .35
141 Lightning Bolt U .40 .60
142 Magus of the Wheel R 3.00 5.00
143 Mogg Flunkies C .20 .35
144 Pillage C .20 .35
145 Pyre Hound C .20 .35
146 Pyroclasm U .40 .60
147 Red Elemental Blast U .40 .60
148 Simian Spirit Guide U .40 .60
149 Skeletonize C .20 .35
150 Skirk Commando C .20 .35
151 Soulbright Flamekin C .20 .35
152 Spikeshot Goblin U .40 .60
153 Thresher Lizard C .20 .35
154 Trumpet Blast C .20 .35
155 Uncaged Fury C .20 .35
156 Zada, Hedron Grinder U .40 .60
157 Ainok Survivalist C .20 .35
158 Ambassador Oak C .20 .35
159 Ancient Stirrings U .40 .60
160 Arbor Elf C .20 .35
161 Azusa, Lost but Seeking R 3.00 5.00
162 Broodhatch Nantuko U .40 .60
163 Colossal Dreadmaw C .20 .35
164 Courser of Kruphix R 3.00 5.00
165 Cultivate C .20 .35
166 Echoing Courage C .20 .35
167 Elvish Aberration C .20 .35
168 Elvish Piper R 3.00 5.00
169 Ember Weaver C .20 .35
170 Epic Confrontation C .20 .35
171 Fierce Empath U .40 .60
172 Giant Growth C .20 .35
173 Invigorate U .40 .60
174 Iwamori of the Open Fist U .40 .60
175 Kavu Climber C .20 .35
176 Kavu Predator U .40 .60
177 Krosan Colossus U .40 .60
178 Krosan Tusker U .40 .60
179 Living Wish R 3.00 5.00
180 Lull C .20 .35
181 Master of the Wild Hunt M 3.00 5.00
182 Nettle Sentinel C .20 .35
183 Plummet C .20 .35
184 Presence of Gond C .20 .35
185 Protean Hulk R 3.00 5.00
186 Rancor U .40 .60
187 Regrowth U .40 .60
188 Stampede Driver U .40 .60
189 Summoner's Pact R 3.00 5.00
190 Timberpack Wolf C .20 .35
191 Tree of Redemption M 3.00 5.00
192 Utopia Sprawl U .40 .60
193 Vessel of Nascency C .20 .35
194 Wildheart Invoker C .20 .35
195 Woolly Loxodon C .20 .35
196 Animar, Soul of Elements M 14.00 16.00
197 Baloth Null U .40 .60
198 Blightning U .40 .60
199 Boros Charm U .40 .60
200 Brion Stoutarm R 3.00 5.00
201 Cloudblazer U .40 .60
202 Conflux R 3.00 5.00
203 Eladamri's Call R 3.00 5.00
204 Gisela, Blade of Goldnight M 3.00 5.00
205 Grenzo, Dungeon Warden R 3.00 5.00
206 Hanna, Ship's Navigator R 3.00 5.00
207 Lorescale Coatl U .40 .60
208 Mystic Snake R 3.00 5.00
209 Nicol Bolas R 3.00 5.00
210 Niv-Mizzet, the Firemind R 3.00 5.00
211 Notion Thief R 3.00 5.00
212 Pernicious Deed R 3.00 5.00
213 Pillory of the Sleepless U .40 .60
214 Prossh, Skyraider of Kher M .20 .35
215 Quicksilver Dagger U .40 .60
216 Ruric Thar, the Unbowed R 3.00 5.00
217 Shadowmage Infiltrator U .40 .60
218 Stangg U .40 .60
219 Vindicate R 3.00 5.00
220 Watchwolf U .40 .60
221 Assembly-Worker C .20 .35
222 Chalice of the Void M 50.00 55.00
223 Coalition Relic R 3.00 5.00
224 Ensnaring Bridge M 30.00 35.00
225 Heavy Arbalest U .40 .60
226 Nihil Spellbomb U .40 .60
227 Perilous Myr U .40 .60
228 Primal Clay C .20 .35
229 Prophetic Prism C .20 .35
230 Sai of the Shinobi U .40 .60
231 Self-Assembler C .20 .35
232 Strionic Resonator R 3.00 5.00
233 Sundering Titan R 3.00 5.00
234 Swiftfoot Boots U .40 .60
235 Treasure Keeper U .40 .60
236 Ash Barrens U .40 .60
237 Cascade Bluffs R 3.00 5.00
238 Fetid Heath R 20.00 25.00
239 Flooded Grove R 3.00 5.00
240 Haunted Fengraf R 3.00 5.00
241 Mikokoro, Center of the Sea R 3.00 5.00
242 Mishra's Factory U .40 .60
243 Myriad Landscape U .40 .60
244 Pendelhaven R 3.00 5.00
245 Quicksand U .40 .60
246 Rishadan Port R 45.00 50.00
247 Rugged Prairie R 3.00 5.00
248 Twilight Mire R 15.00 20.00
249 Zoetic Cavern U .40 .60

2018 Magic The Gathering Masters 25 Foil

COMPLETE SET (249) 1400.00 1800.00
1 Act of Heroism U .75 1.25
2 Akroma, Angel of Wrath M 3.00 5.00
3 Akroma's Vengeance R 4.00 7.00
4 Angelic Page U .75 1.25
5 Armageddon M 15.00 20.00
6 Auramancer U .75 1.25
7 Cloudshift C .40 .60
8 Congregate U .75 1.25
9 Darien, King of Kjeldor R 6.00 8.00
10 Dauntless Cathar C .40 .60
11 Decree of Justice R 4.00 7.00
12 Disenchant C .40 .60
13 Fencing Ace C .40 .60
14 Fiend Hunter U .75 1.25
15 Geist of the Moors C .40 .60
16 Gods Willing C .40 .60
17 Griffin Protector C .40 .60
18 Karona's Zealot U .75 1.25
19 Knight of the Skyward Eye C .40 .60
20 Kongming, "Sleeping Dragon" U .75 1.25
21 Kor Firewalker U .75 1.25
22 Loyal Sentry C .40 .60
23 Luminarch Ascension R 4.00 7.00
24 Lunarch Mantle C .40 .60
25 Noble Templar C .40 .60
26 Nyx-Fleece Ram U .75 1.25
27 Ordeal of Heliod U .75 1.25
28 Pacifism C .40 .60
29 Path of Peace C .40 .60
30 Promise of Bunrei U .75 1.25
31 Renewed Faith C .40 .60
32 Rest in Peace R 8.00 11.00
33 Savannah Lions C .40 .60
34 Squadron Hawk C .40 .60
35 Swords to Plowshares U 2.00 3.00
36 Thalia, Guardian of Thraben R 15.00 20.00
37 Urbis Protector U .75 1.25
38 Valor in Akros U .75 1.25
39 Whitemane Lion C .40 .60
40 Accumulated Knowledge C .40 .60
41 Arcane Denial C 3.00 4.00
42 Bident of Thassa R 4.00 7.00
43 Blue Elemental Blast U 3.00 5.00
44 Blue Sun's Zenith R 4.00 7.00
45 Borrowing 100,000 Arrows C .40 .60
46 Brainstorm C 8.00 10.00
47 Brine Elemental U .75 1.25
48 Choking Tethers C .40 .60
49 Coralhelm Guide C .40 .60
50 Counterspell C 2.00 3.00
51 Court Hussar C .40 .60
52 Curiosity U .75 1.25
53 Cursecatcher U 8.00 11.00
54 Dragon's Eye Savants C .40 .60
55 Exclude U .75 1.25
56 Fathom Seer C .40 .60
57 Flash R 8.00 11.00
58 Freed from the Real U .75 1.25
59 Genju of the Falls U .75 1.25
60 Ghost Ship C .40 .60
61 Horseshoe Crab C .40 .60
62 Jace, the Mind Sculptor M 170.00 200.00
63 Jalira, Master Polymorphist U .75 1.25
64 Man-o'-War C .40 .60
65 Merfolk Looter U .75 1.25
66 Murder of Crows U .75 1.25
67 Mystic of the Hidden Way C .40 .60
68 Pact of Negation R 20.00 25.00
69 Phantasmal Bear C .40 .60
70 Reef Worm R 4.00 7.00
71 Retraction Helix C .40 .60
72 Shoreline Ranger C .40 .60
73 Sift C .40 .60
74 Totally Lost C .40 .60
75 Twisted Image U .75 1.25
76 Vendilion Clique M 45.00 55.00
77 Vesuvan Shapeshifter R 4.00 7.00
78 Willbender U .75 1.25
79 Ancient Craving U .75 1.25
80 Bloodhunter Bat C .40 .60
81 Caustic Tar U .75 1.25
82 Dark Ritual C 2.00 3.00
83 Deadly Designs U .75 1.25
84 Death's-Head Buzzard C .40 .60
85 Diabolic Edict C 4.00 6.00
86 Dirge of Dread C .40 .60
87 Disfigure C .40 .60
88 Doomsday M 25.00 30.00
89 Dusk Legion Zealot C .40 .60
90 Erg Raiders C .40 .60
91 Fallen Angel U .75 1.25
92 Hell's Caretaker R 4.00 7.00
93 Horror of the Broken Lands U .75 1.25
94 Ihsan's Shade U .75 1.25
95 Laquatus's Champion R 4.00 7.00
96 Living Death R 4.00 7.00
97 Mesmeric Fiend U .75 1.25
98 Murder C .40 .60
99 Nezumi Cutthroat C .40 .60
100 Phyrexian Ghoul C .40 .60
101 Phyrexian Obliterator M 25.00 30.00
102 Plague Wind R 4.00 7.00
103 Ratcatcher R 4.00 7.00
104 Ravenous Chupacabra U 2.00 3.00
105 Relentless Rats C 2.00 3.00
106 Returned Phalanx C .40 .60
107 Ruthless Ripper C .40 .60

108 Street Wraith U 10.00 13.00
109 Supernatural Stamina C .40 .60
110 Triskaidekaphobia R 4.00 7.00
111 Twisted Abomination C .40 .60
112 Undead Gladiator U .75 1.25
113 Unearth C 1.50 2.50
114 Vampire Lacerator C .40 .60
115 Will-o'-the-Wisp U 2.00 3.00
116 Zombify U .75 1.25
117 Zulaport Cutthroat U .75 1.25
118 Act of Treason C .40 .60
119 Akroma, Angel of Fury M 3.00 5.00
120 Balduvian Horde C .40 .60
121 Ball Lightning R 4.00 7.00
122 Blood Moon R 35.00 40.00
123 Browbeat U .75 1.25
124 Chandra's Outrage C .40 .60
125 Chartooth Cougar C .40 .60
126 Cinder Storm C .40 .60
127 Crimson Mage C .40 .60
128 Eidolon of the Great Revel R 10.00 15.00
129 Enthralling Victor U .75 1.25
130 Fortune Thief R 4.00 7.00
131 Frenzied Goblin C .40 .60
132 Genju of the Spires U .75 1.25
133 Goblin War Drums U .75 1.25
134 Hordeling Outburst C .40 .60
135 Humble Defector U .75 1.25
136 Imperial Recruiter M 100.00 110.00
137 Ire Shaman U .75 1.25
138 Izzet Chemister R 4.00 7.00
139 Jackal Pup C .40 .60
140 Kindle C .40 .60
141 Lightning Bolt U 5.00 7.00
142 Magus of the Wheel R 8.00 11.00
143 Mogg Flunkies C .40 .60
144 Pillage C .40 .60
145 Pyre Hound C .40 .60
146 Pyroclasm U .75 1.25
147 Red Elemental Blast U 6.00 8.00
148 Simian Spirit Guide U 20.00 25.00
149 Skeletonize C .40 .60
150 Skirk Commando C .40 .60
151 Soulbright Flamekin C .40 .60
152 Spikeshot Goblin U .75 1.25
153 Thresher Lizard C .40 .60
154 Trumpet Blast C .40 .60
155 Uncaged Fury C .40 .60
156 Zada, Hedron Grinder U .75 1.25
157 Ainok Survivalist C .40 .60
158 Ambassador Oak C .40 .60
159 Ancient Stirrings U 10.00 15.00
160 Arbor Elf C .40 .60
161 Azusa, Lost but Seeking R 25.00 30.00
162 Broodhatch Nantuko U .75 1.25
163 Colossal Dreadmaw C .40 .60
164 Courser of Kruphix R 4.00 7.00
165 Cultivate C 2.00 3.00
166 Echoing Courage C .40 .60
167 Elvish Aberration C .40 .60
168 Elvish Piper R 4.00 7.00
169 Ember Weaver C .40 .60
170 Epic Confrontation C .40 .60
171 Fierce Empath U 3.00 4.00
172 Giant Growth C .40 .60
173 Invigorate U .75 1.25
174 Iwamori of the Open Fist U .75 1.25
175 Kavu Climber C .40 .60
176 Kavu Predator U .75 1.25
177 Krosan Colossus U .75 1.25
178 Krosan Tusker U .75 1.25
179 Living Wish R 7.00 10.00
180 Lull C .40 .60
181 Master of the Wild Hunt M 10.00 15.00
182 Nettle Sentinel C 3.00 5.00
183 Plummet C .40 .60
184 Presence of Gond C .40 .60
185 Protean Hulk R 15.00 20.00
186 Rancor U 2.00 3.00
187 Regrowth U 6.00 8.00
188 Stampede Driver U .75 1.25
189 Summoner's Pact R 20.00 25.00
190 Timberpack Wolf C .40 .60
191 Tree of Redemption M 2.50 4.00
192 Utopia Sprawl U 10.00 13.00
193 Vessel of Nascency C .40 .60
194 Wildheart Invoker C .40 .60
195 Woolly Loxodon C .40 .60
196 Animar, Soul of Elements M 90.00 100.00
197 Baloth Null U .75 1.25
198 Blightning U .75 1.25
199 Boros Charm U 7.00 10.00
200 Brion Stoutarm R 4.00 7.00
201 Cloudblazer U .75 1.25
202 Conflux R 4.00 7.00
203 Eladamri's Call R 15.00 20.00
204 Gisela, Blade of Goldnight M 15.00 20.00
205 Grenzo, Dungeon Warden R 4.00 7.00
206 Hanna, Ship's Navigator R 4.00 7.00
207 Lorescale Coatl U .75 1.25
208 Mystic Snake R 4.00 7.00
209 Nicol Bolas R 14.00 16.00
210 Niv-Mizzet, the Firemind R 4.00 7.00
211 Notion Thief R 4.00 7.00
212 Pernicious Deed R 4.00 7.00
213 Pillory of the Sleepless U .75 1.25
214 Prossh, Skyraider of Kher M 40.00 45.00
215 Quicksilver Dagger U .75 1.25
216 Ruric Thar, the Unbowed R 4.00 7.00
217 Shadowmage Infiltrator U .75 1.25
218 Stangg U .75 1.25
219 Vindicate R 8.00 11.00
220 Watchwolf U .75 1.25
221 Assembly-Worker C .40 .60
222 Chalice of the Void M 75.00 85.00
223 Coalition Relic R 35.00 40.00
224 Ensnaring Bridge M 80.00 90.00
225 Heavy Arbalest U .75 1.25
226 Nihil Spellbomb U 4.00 6.00
227 Perilous Myr U .75 1.25
228 Primal Clay C .40 .60
229 Prophetic Prism C .40 .60
230 Sai of the Shinobi U .75 1.25
231 Self-Assembler C .40 .60
232 Strionic Resonator R 4.00 7.00
233 Sundering Titan R 4.00 7.00
234 Swiftfoot Boots U 5.00 7.00
235 Treasure Keeper U .75 1.25
236 Ash Barrens U 10.00 13.00
237 Cascade Bluffs R 15.00 20.00
238 Fetid Heath R 10.00 15.00
239 Flooded Grove R 10.00 15.00
240 Haunted Fengraf R 4.00 7.00
241 Mikokoro, Center of the Sea R 8.00 11.00
242 Mishra's Factory U .75 1.25
243 Myriad Landscape U 6.00 8.00
244 Pendelhaven R 8.00 11.00
245 Quicksand U .75 1.25
246 Rishadan Port R 70.00 80.00
247 Rugged Prairie R 10.00 15.00
248 Twilight Mire R 15.00 20.00
249 Zoetic Cavern U .75 1.25

2018 Magic The Gathering Masters 25 Tokens

1 Spirit .15 .25
2 Angel .06 .10
3 Soldier .06 .10
4 Spirit .06 .10
5 Fish .20 .30
6 Kraken 1.00 1.50
7 Whale .20 .30
8 Skeleton .06 .10
9 Goblin .12 .20
10 Kobolds of Kher Keep 1.25 1.75
11 Elf Warrior .12 .20
12 Insect .10 .15
13 Wolf .10 .15
14 Stangg Twin .06 .10
15 Morph .06 .10

2018 Magic The Gathering Ultimate Masters

RELEASED ON DECEMBER 7, 2018
1 All Is Dust R 3.50 6.00
2 Artisan of Kozilek U .20 .30
3 Eldrazi Conscription R 2.50 4.00
4 Emrakul, the Aeons Torn M 15.00 25.00
5 Karn Liberated M 60.00 75.00
6 Kozilek, Butcher of Truth M 15.00 25.00
7 Ulamog, the Infinite Gyre M 15.00 25.00
8 Ulamog's Crusher C .15 .25
9 Ancestor's Chosen U .20 .30
10 Angelic Renewal C .15 .25
11 Containment Priest R 3.50 6.00
12 Conviction C .15 .25
13 Dawn Charm U .20 .30
14 Daybreak Coronet R 2.50 4.00
15 Emancipation Angel U .20 .30
16 Faith's Fetters C .15 .25
17 Fiend Hunter U .20 .30
18 Gods Willing C .15 .25
19 Heliod's Pilgrim C .15 .25
20 Hero of Iroas U .20 .30
21 Hyena Umbra C .15 .25
22 Icatian Crier C .15 .25
23 Lotus-Eye Mystics C .15 .25
24 Mammoth Umbra C .15 .25
25 Martyr of Sands C .15 .25
26 Miraculous Recovery U .20 .30
27 Phalanx Leader U .20 .30
28 Rally the Peasants U .20 .30
29 Repel the Darkness C .15 .25
30 Resurrection C .15 .25
31 Reveillark R .60 1.00
32 Reya Dawnbringer R .60 1.00
33 Ronom Unicorn C .15 .25
34 Runed Halo R 3.50 6.00
35 Sigil of the New Dawn U .20 .30
36 Skyspear Cavalry C .15 .25
37 Spirit Cairn U .20 .30
38 Sublime Archangel R 1.50 2.50
39 Swift Reckoning U .20 .30
40 Tethmos High Priest C .15 .25
41 Wall of Reverence R .60 1.00
42 Wandering Champion C .15 .25
43 Wingsteed Rider C .15 .25
44 Aethersnipe C .15 .25
45 Archaeomancer C .15 .25
46 Back to Basics R 10.00 15.00
47 Circular Logic U .20 .30
48 Defy Gravity C .15 .25
49 Deranged Assistant C .15 .25
50 Dig Through Time R .60 1.00
51 Disrupting Shoal R 1.00 1.75
52 Dreamscape Artist U .20 .30
53 Eel Umbra C .15 .25
54 Flight of Fancy C .15 .25
55 Foil C .15 .25
56 Forbidden Alchemy U .20 .30
57 Frantic Search C .15 .25
58 Glen Elendra Archmage R 4.00 7.50
59 Iridescent Drake U .20 .30
60 Just the Wind C .15 .25
61 Laboratory Maniac U 1.25 2.00
62 Living Lore U .20 .30
63 Magus of the Bazaar R .60 1.00
64 Mahamoti Djinn U .20 .30
65 Marang River Prowler U .20 .30
66 Mystic Retrieval U .20 .30
67 Rise from the Tides U .20 .30
68 Rune Snag C .15 .25
69 Skywing Aven C .15 .25
70 Sleight of Hand U 1.25 2.00
71 Snapcaster Mage M 50.00 65.00
72 Stitched Drake C .15 .25
73 Stitcher's Apprentice C .15 .25
74 Stream of Consciousness U .20 .30
75 Sultai Skullkeeper C .15 .25
76 Talrand, Sky Summoner R .60 1.00
77 Temporal Manipulation M 15.00 25.00
78 Think Twice C .15 .25
79 Treasure Cruise C .15 .25
80 Unstable Mutation U .20 .30
81 Visions of Beyond R 1.25 2.00
82 Whirlwind Adept C .15 .25
83 Appetite for Brains U .20 .30
84 Apprentice Necromancer U .20 .30
85 Bitterblossom M 25.00 35.00
86 Bloodflow Connoisseur C .15 .25
87 Bridge from Below R 3.50 6.00
88 Buried Alive U .60 1.00
89 Chainer's Edict U 1.25 2.00
90 Crow of Dark Tidings C .15 .25
91 Dark Dabbling C .15 .25
92 Death Denied C .15 .25
93 Demonic Tutor R 20.00 25.00
94 Entomb R 5.00 8.00
95 Fume Spitter C .15 .25
96 Ghoulcaller's Accomplice C .15 .25
97 Ghoulsteed U .20 .30
98 Golgari Thug U .20 .30
99 Goryo's Vengeance R 10.00 15.00
100 Grave Scrabbler C .15 .25
101 Grave Strength U .20 .30
102 Gurmag Angler C .15 .25
103 Last Gasp C .15 .25
104 Liliana of the Veil M 65.00 80.00
105 Mark of the Vampire C .15 .25
106 Mikaeus, the Unhallowed M 12.00 20.00
107 Moan of the Unhallowed C .15 .25
108 Offalsnout C .15 .25
109 Olivia's Dragoon C .15 .25
110 Reanimate R 8.00 12.00
111 Sanitarium Skeleton C .15 .25
112 Shirei, Shizo's Caretaker U .20 .30
113 Shriekmaw U .20 .30
114 Slum Reaper C .15 .25
115 Songs of the Damned U .20 .30
116 Spoils of the Vault R .60 1.00
117 Tasigur, the Golden Fang R .75 1.25
118 Twins of Maurer Estate C .15 .25
119 Unburial Rites U .20 .30
120 Unholy Hunger C .15 .25
121 Akroan Crusader C .15 .25
122 Anger U .20 .30
123 Arena Athlete C .15 .25
124 Balefire Dragon M 5.00 7.50
125 Brazen Scourge U .20 .30
126 Conflagrate U .20 .30
127 Desperate Ritual U .20 .30
128 Faithless Looting C .15 .25
129 Fiery Temper C .15 .25
130 Firewing Phoenix U .20 .30
131 Furnace Celebration U .20 .30
132 Gamble R 2.00 3.50
133 Generator Servant C .15 .25
134 Hissing Iguanar C .15 .25
135 Ingot Chewer C .15 .25
136 Lava Spike U 1.50 2.50
137 Mad Prophet C .15 .25
138 Magmaw U .20 .30
139 Malevolent Whispers U .20 .30
140 Molten Birth C .15 .25
141 Nightbird's Clutches C .15 .25
142 Raid Bombardment C .15 .25
143 Reckless Charge C .15 .25
144 Reckless Wurm C .15 .25
145 Rolling Temblor U .20 .30
146 Seismic Assault R .75 1.25
147 Seize the Day R .60 1.00
148 Soul's Fire C .15 .25
149 Sparkspitter C .15 .25
150 Squee, Goblin Nabob R .75 1.25
151 Thermo-Alchemist C .15 .25
152 Through the Breach R 10.00 15.00
153 Undying Rage C .15 .25
154 Vexing Devil R 2.50 4.00
155 Young Pyromancer U .20 .30
156 Basking Rootwalla C .15 .25
157 Become Immense U .20 .30
158 Boar Umbra U .20 .30
159 Boneyard Wurm U .20 .30
160 Brawn U .20 .30
161 Crushing Canopy C .15 .25
162 Devoted Druid U 1.00 1.50
163 Eternal Witness U 2.50 4.00
164 Fauna Shaman R 2.50 4.00
165 Fecundity U .20 .30
166 Golgari Brownscale C .15 .25
167 Golgari Grave-Troll R 1.00 1.50
168 Groundskeeper C .15 .25
169 Hero of Leina Tower U .20 .30
170 Hooting Mandrills C .15 .25
171 Kodama's Reach C .15 .25
172 Life from the Loam R 10.00 15.00
173 Miming Slime C .15 .25
174 Noble Hierarch R 40.00 50.00
175 Nourishing Shoal R 1.00 1.75
176 Pattern of Rebirth R 1.50 2.50
177 Penumbra Wurm U .20 .30
178 Prey Upon C .15 .25
179 Pulse of Murasa C .15 .25
180 Satyr Wayfinder C .15 .25
181 Shed Weakness C .15 .25
182 Snake Umbra U .20 .30
183 Spider Spawning U .20 .30
184 Spider Umbra C .15 .25
185 Staunch-Hearted Warrior C .15 .25
186 Stingerfling Spider U .20 .30
187 Tarmogoyf M 50.00 65.00
188 Travel Preparations U .20 .30
189 Vengevine M 12.00 20.00
190 Verdant Eidolon C .15 .25
191 Walker of the Grove C .15 .25
192 Wickerbough Elder C .15 .25
193 Wild Hunger U .20 .30
194 Wild Mongrel C .15 .25
195 Woodfall Primus R 1.50 2.50
196 Angle of Despair U .20 .30
197 Blast of Genius U .20 .30
198 Countersqaull U .20 .30
199 Gaddock Teeg R 8.00 12.00
200 Garna, the Bloodflame U .20 .30
201 Golgari Charm U .20 .30
202 Leovold, Emissary of Trest M 10.00 15.00
203 Lord of Extinction M 5.00 7.50
204 Maelstrom Pulse R 5.00 8.00
205 Reviving Vapors U .20 .30
206 Sigarda, Hose of Herons M 7.00 10.00
207 Sovereigns of Lost Alara R .60 1.00
208 Urban Evolution U .20 .30
209 Vengeful Rebirth U .20 .30
210 Warleader's Helix U .20 .30
211 Beckon Apparition C .15 .25
212 Canker Abomination C .15 .25
213 Dimir Guildmage C .15 .25
214 Double Cleave C .15 .25
215 Fulminator Mage R 8.00 12.00
216 Kitchen Finks U 2.00 3.50
217 Murderous Redcap U .20 .30
218 Plumeveil U .20 .30
219 Rakdos Shred-Freak C .15 .25
220 Safehold Elite C .15 .25
221 Scuzzback Marauders C .15 .25
222 Shielding Plax C .15 .25
223 Slippery Bogle U .20 .30
224 Turn to Mist C .15 .25
225 Fire//Ice C .15 .25
226 Cathodion C .15 .25
227 Engineered Explosives R 25.00 35.00
228 Heap Doll U .20 .30
229 Mana Vault M 20.00 30.00
230 Myr Servitor C .15 .25
231 Patchwork Gnomes C .15 .25
232 Phyrexian Altar R 12.00 20.00
233 Platinum Emperion M 7.00 10.00
234 Prismatic Lens U .20 .30
235 Vessel of Endless Rest C .15 .25
236 Ancient Tomb R 20.00 25.00
237 Cavern of Souls M 60.00 75.00
238 Celestial Colonnade R 20.00 25.00
239 Creeping Tar Pit R 3.50 6.00
240 Dakmor Salvage U .20 .30
241 Dark Depths M 20.00 30.00
242 Desolate Lighthouse R .60 1.00
243 Flagstones of Trokair R 3.50 6.00
244 Karakas M 20.00 30.00
245 Lavaclaw Reachers R .60 1.00
246 Mage-Ring Network U .20 .30
247 Mistveil Plains U .20 .30
248 Phyrexian Tower R 10.00 15.00
249 Raging Ravine R 3.00 5.00
250 Rogue's Passage U .20 .30
251 Stirring Wildwood R .60 1.00
252 Terramorphic Expanse C .15 .25
253 Thespian's Stage R 1.25 2.00
254 Urborg, Tomb of Yawgmoth R 8.00 12.00

2018 Magic The Gathering Ultimate Masters Foil

1 All Is Dust R 5.00 8.00
2 Artisan of Kozilek U .35 .50
3 Eldrazi Conscription R 3.50 6.00
4 Emrakul, the Aeons Torn M 20.00 35.00
5 Karn Liberated M 60.00 80.00
6 Kozilek, Butcher of Truth M 20.00 30.00
7 Ulamog, the Infinite Gyre M 15.00 25.00
8 Ulamog's Crusher C .25 .40
9 Ancestor's Chosen U .35 .50
10 Angelic Renewal C .25 .40
11 Containment Priest R 20.00 25.00
12 Conviction C .25 .40
13 Dawn Charm U .35 .50
14 Daybreak Coronet R 3.50 6.00
15 Emancipation Angel U .35 .50
16 Faith's Fetters C .25 .40
17 Fiend Hunter U .35 .50
18 Gods Willing C .25 .40
19 Heliod's Pilgrim C .25 .40
20 Hero of Iroas U .35 .50
21 Hyena Umbra C .25 .40
22 Icathian Crier C .25 .40
23 Lotus-Eye Mystics C .25 .40
24 Mammoth Umbra C .25 .40
25 Martyr of Sands C .25 .40
26 Miraculous Recovery U .35 .50
27 Phalanx Leader U .35 .50
28 Rally the Peasants U .35 .50
29 Repel the Darkness C .25 .40
30 Resurrection C .25 .40
31 Reveillark R 3.00 5.00
32 Reya Dawnbringer R 1.25 2.00
33 Ronom Unicorn C .25 .40
34 Runed Halo R 8.00 12.00
35 Sigil of the New Dawn U .35 .50
36 Skyspear Cavalry C .25 .40
37 Spirit Cairn U .35 .50
38 Sublime Archangel R 2.50 4.00
39 Swift Reckoning U .35 .50
40 Tethmos High Priest C .25 .40
41 Wall of Reverence R 1.50 2.50
42 Wandering Champion C .25 .40
43 Wingsteed Rider C .25 .40
44 Aethersnipe C .25 .40
45 Archaeomancer C .25 .40

Card	Low	High
46 Back to Basics R	50.00	75.00
47 Circular Logic U	.35	.50
48 Defy Gravity C	.25	.40
49 Deranged Assistant C	.25	.40
50 Dig Through Time R	1.75	3.00
51 Disrupting Shoal R	1.75	3.00
52 Dreamscape Artist U	.35	.50
53 Eel Umbra C	.25	.40
54 Flight of Fancy C	.25	.40
55 Foil C	.25	.40
56 Forbidden Alchemy U	.35	.50
57 Frantic Search C	.25	.40
58 Glen Elendra Archmage R	10.00	15.00
59 Iridescent Drake U	.35	.50
60 Just the Wind C	.25	.40
61 Laboratory Maniac U	.35	.50
62 Living Lore U	.35	.50
63 Magus of the Bazaar R	1.25	2.00
64 Mahamoti Dhinn U	.35	.50
65 Marang River Prowler U	.35	.50
66 Mystic Retrieval U	.35	.50
67 Rise from the Tides U	.35	.50
68 Rune Snag C	.25	.40
69 Skywing Aven C	.25	.40
70 Sleight of Hand U	.35	.50
71 Snapcaster Mage M	80.00	110.00
72 Stitched Drake C	.25	.40
73 Stitcher's Apprentice C	.25	.40
74 Stream of Consciousness U	.35	.50
75 Sultai Skullkeeper C	.25	.40
76 Talrand, Sky Summoner R	1.25	2.00
77 Temporal Manipulation M	20.00	30.00
78 Think Twice C	.25	.40
79 Treasure Cruise C	.25	.40
80 Unstable Mutation U	.35	.50
81 Visions of Beyond R	1.75	3.00
82 Whirlwind Adept C	.25	.40
83 Appetite for Brains U	.35	.50
84 Apprentice Necromancer U	.35	.50
85 Bitterblossom M	35.00	50.00
86 Bloodflow Connoisseur C	.25	.40
87 Bridge from Below R	5.00	8.00
88 Buried Alive U	.35	.50
89 Chainer's Edict U	.35	.50
90 Crow of Dark Tidings C	.25	.40
91 Dark Dabbling C	.25	.40
92 Death Denied C	.25	.40
93 Demonic Tutor R	35.00	50.00
94 Entomb R	6.00	10.00
95 Fume Spitter C	.25	.40
96 Ghoulcaller's Accomplice C	.25	.40
97 Ghoulsteed U	.35	.50
98 Golgari Thug U	.35	.50
99 Goryo's Vengeance R	10.00	15.00
100 Grave Scrabbler C	.25	.40
101 Grave Strength U	.35	.50
102 Gurmag Angler C	.25	.40
103 Last Gasp C	.25	.40
104 Liliana of the Veil M	75.00	125.00
105 Mark of the Vampire C	.25	.40
106 Mikaeus, the Unhallowed M	20.00	30.00
107 Moan of the Unhallowed C	.25	.40
108 Offalsnout C	.25	.40
109 Olivia's Dragoon C	.25	.40
110 Reanimate R	10.00	15.00
111 Sanitarium Skeleton C	.25	.40
112 Shirei, Shizo's Caretaker U	.35	.50
113 Shriekmaw U	.35	.50
114 Slum Reaper C	.25	.40
115 Songs of the Damned U	.35	.50
116 Spoils of the Vault R	1.25	2.00
117 Tasigur, the Golden Fang R	1.75	3.00
118 Twins of Maurer Estate C	.25	.40
119 Unburial Rites U	.35	.50
120 Unholy Hunger C	.25	.40
121 Akroan Crusader C	.25	.40
122 Anger U	.35	.50
123 Arena Athlete C	.25	.40
124 Balefire Dragon M	8.00	12.00
125 Brazen Scourge U	.35	.50
126 Conflagrate U	.35	.50
127 Desperate Ritual U	.35	.50
128 Faithless Looting C	.25	.40
129 Fiery Temper C	.25	.40
130 Firewing Phoenix U	.35	.50
131 Furnace Celebration U	.35	.50
132 Gamble R	5.00	8.00
133 Generator Servant C	.25	.40
134 Hissing Iguanar C	.25	.40
135 Ingot Chewer C	.25	.40
136 Lava Spike U	.35	.50
137 Mad Prophet C	.25	.40
138 Magmaw U	.35	.50
139 Malevolent Whispers U	.35	.50
140 Molten Birth C	.25	.40
141 Nightbird's Clutches C	.25	.40
142 Raid Bombardment C	.25	.40
143 Reckless Charge C	.25	.40
144 Reckless Wurm C	.25	.40
145 Rolling Temblor U	.35	.50
146 Seismic Assault R	1.75	3.00
147 Seize the Day R	1.75	3.00
148 Soul's Fire C	.25	.40
149 Sparkspitter C	.25	.40
150 Squee, Goblin Nabob R	1.75	3.00
151 Thermo-Alchemist C	.25	.40
152 Through the Breach R	20.00	30.00
153 Undying Rage C	.25	.40
154 Vexing Devil R	5.00	8.00
155 Young Pyromancer U	.35	.50
156 Basking Rootwalla C	.25	.40
157 Become Immense U	.35	.50
158 Boar Umbra U	.35	.50
159 Boneyard Wurm U	.35	.50
160 Brawn U	.35	.50
161 Crushing Canopy C	.25	.40
162 Devoted Droid U	.35	.50
163 Eternal Witness U	.35	.50
164 Fauna Shaman R	5.00	8.00
165 Fecundity U	.35	.50
166 Golgari Brownscale C	.25	.40
167 Golgari Grave-Troll R	2.50	4.00
168 Groundskeeper C	.25	.40
169 Hero of Leina Tower U	.35	.50
170 Hooting Mandrills C	.25	.40
171 Kodama's Reach C	.25	.40
172 Life from the Loam R	12.00	20.00
173 Miming Slime C	.25	.40
174 Noble Hierarch R	40.00	60.00
175 Nourishing Shoal R	1.75	3.00
176 Pattern of Rebirth R	8.00	12.00
177 Penumbra Wurm U	.35	.50
178 Prey Upon C	.25	.40
179 Pulse of Murasa C	.25	.40
180 Satyr Wayfinder C	.25	.40
181 Shed Weakness C	.25	.40
182 Snake Umbra U	.35	.50
183 Spider Spawning U	.35	.50
184 Spider Umbra C	.25	.40
185 Staunch-Hearted Warrior C	.25	.40
186 Stingerfling Spider U	.35	.50
187 Tarmogoyf M	60.00	80.00
188 Travel Preparations U	.35	.50
189 Vengevine M	15.00	25.00
190 Verdant Eidolon C	.25	.40
191 Walker of the Grove C	.25	.40
192 Wickerbough Elder C	.25	.40
193 Wild Hunger U	.35	.50
194 Wild Mongrel C	.25	.40
195 Woodfall Primus R	2.50	4.00
196 Angle of Despair U	.35	.50
197 Blast of Genius U	.35	.50
198 Countersqaull U	.35	.50
199 Gaddock Teeg R	10.00	15.00
200 Garna, the Bloodflame U	.35	.50
201 Golgari Charm U	.35	.50
202 Leovold, Emissary of Trest M	20.00	30.00
203 Lord of Extinction M	5.00	8.00
204 Maelstrom Pulse R	8.00	12.00
205 Reviving Vapors U	.35	.50
206 Sigarda, Hose of Herons M	12.00	20.00
207 Sovereigns of Lost Alara R	1.25	2.00
208 Urban Evolution U	.35	.50
209 Vengeful Rebirth U	.35	.50
210 Warleader's Helix U	.35	.50
211 Beckon Apparition C	.25	.40
212 Canker Abomination C	.25	.40
213 Dimir Guildmage C	.25	.40
214 Double Cleave C	.25	.40
215 Fulminator Mage R	10.00	15.00
216 Kitchen Finks U	.35	.50
217 Murderous Redcap U	.35	.50
218 Plumeveil U	.35	.50
219 Rakdos Shred-Freak C	.25	.40
220 Safehold Elite C	.25	.40
221 Scuzzback Marauders C	.25	.40
222 Shielding Plax C	.25	.40
223 Slippery Bogle U	.35	.50
224 Turn to Mist C	.25	.40
225 Fire//Ice C	.25	.40
226 Cathodion C	.25	.40
227 Engineered Explosives R	30.00	40.00
228 Heap Doll U	.35	.50
229 Mana Vault M	75.00	100.00
230 Myr Servitor C	.25	.40
231 Patchwork Gnomes C	.25	.40
232 Phyrexian Altar R	35.00	50.00
233 Platinum Emperion M	10.00	15.00
234 Prismatic Lens U	.35	.50
235 Vessel of Endless Rest C	.25	.40
236 Ancient Tomb R	15.00	25.00
237 Cavern of Souls M	75.00	100.00
238 Celestial Colonnade R	20.00	25.00
239 Creeping Tar Pit R	8.00	12.00
240 Dakmor Salvage U	.35	.50
241 Dark Depths M	35.00	50.00
242 Desolate Lighthouse R	1.25	2.00
243 Flagstones of Trokair R	6.00	10.00
244 Karakas M	20.00	35.00
245 Lavaclaw Reachers R	1.25	2.00
246 Mage-Ring Network U	.35	.50
247 Mistveil Plains U	.35	.50
248 Phyrexian Tower R	35.00	50.00
249 Raging Ravine R	8.00	12.00
250 Rogue's Passage U	.35	.50
251 Stirring Wildwood R	1.25	2.00
252 Terramorphic Expanse C	.25	.40
253 Thespian's Stage R	5.00	7.50
254 Urborg, Tomb of Yawgmoth R	12.00	20.00

2018 Magic The Gathering Ultimate Masters Box-Toppers

Card	Low	High
U1 Emrakul, the Aeons Torn	65.00	90.00
U2 Karn Liberated	175.00	250.00
U3 Kozilek, Butcher of Truth	65.00	90.00
U4 Ulamog, the Infinite Gyre	50.00	75.00
U5 Snapcaster Mage	20.00	30.00
U6 Temporal Manipulation	50.00	75.00
U7 Bitterblossom	75.00	100.00
U8 Demonic Tutor	150.00	200.00
U9 Goryo's Vengeance	50.00	75.00
U10 Liliana of the Veil	225.00	300.00
U11 Mikaeus, the Unhallowed	45.00	60.00
U12 Reanimate	65.00	90.00
U13 Tasigur, the Golden Fang	35.00	50.00
U14 Balefire Dragon	35.00	50.00
U15 Through the Breach	65.00	90.00
U16 Eternal Witness	65.00	90.00
U17 Life from the Loam	65.00	90.00
U18 Noble Hierarch	100.00	125.00
U19 Tarmogoyf	175.00	250.00
U20 Vengevine	50.00	75.00
U21 Gaddock Teeg	45.00	60.00
U22 Leovold, Emissary of Trest	65.00	90.00
U23 Lord of Extinction	25.00	35.00
U24 Maelstrom Pulse	30.00	40.00
U25 Sigarda, Hose of Herons	45.00	60.00
U26 Fulminator Mage	45.00	60.00
U27 Kitchen Finks	35.00	50.00
U28 Engineered Explosives	65.00	90.00
U29 Mana Vault	125.00	150.00
U30 Platinum Emperion	35.00	50.00
U31 Ancient Tomb	125.00	150.00
U32 Cavern of Souls	175.00	250.00
U33 Celestial Colonnade	75.00	100.00
U34 Creeping Tar Pit	45.00	60.00
U35 Dark Depths	105.00	130.00
U36 Karakas	65.00	90.00
U37 Lavaclaw Reaches	20.00	30.00
U38 Raging Ravine	35.00	50.00
U39 Stirring Wildwood	20.00	30.00
U40 Urborg, Tomb of Yawgmoth	65.00	90.00

2018 Magic The Gathering Ultimate Masters Tokens

Card	Low	High
1 Citizen	.10	.15
2 Spirit	.06	.10
3 Drake	.40	.60
4 Homunculus	.06	.10
5 Faerie Rogue	.75	1.25
6 Marit Lage	.60	1.00
7 Wurm	.10	.15
8 Zombie	.12	.20
9 Elemental	.15	.25
10 Elemental	.20	.30
11 Soldier	.10	.15
12 Spark Elemental	.06	.10
13 Elemental	.06	.10
14 Ooze	.06	.10
15 Spider	.12	.20
16 Spirit	.06	.10

2019 Magic The Gathering Modern Horizons

COMPLETE SET (255)
BOOSTER BOX (36 PACKS)
BOOSTER PACK
RELEASED ON JUNE 14, 2019

Card	Low	High
1 Morophon, the Boundless M	7.00	10.00
2 Answered Prayers C	.15	.25
3 Astral Drift R	.30	.50
4 Battle Screech U	.12	.30
5 Dismantling Blow U	.12	.30
6 Enduring Silver C	.15	.25
7 Ephemerate C	.15	.25
8 Face of Divinity U	.12	.30
9 First Silver's Chosen U	.12	.30
10 Force of Virtue R	.60	1.00
11 Generous Gift U	.75	1.25
12 Gilded Light C	.15	.25
13 Giver of Runes R	8.00	12.00
14 Imposter of the Sixth Pride C	.15	.25
15 Irregular Cohort C	.15	.25
16 King of the Pride U	.12	.30
17 Knight of Old Benalia C	.15	.25
18 Lancer Silver C	.15	.25
19 Martyr's Soul C	.15	.25
20 On Thin Ice R	.35	.60
21 Ranger-Captain of Eos M	15.00	20.00
22 Recruit the Worthy C	.15	.25
23 Reprobation C	.15	.25
24 Rhox Veteran C	.15	.25
25 Segovian Angel C	.15	.25
26 Serra the Benevolent M	10.00	15.00
27 Settle Beyond Reality C	.15	.25
28 Shelter C	.15	.25
29 Sisay, Weatherlight Captain R	.30	.50
30 Soul-Strike Technique C	.15	.25
31 Splicer's Skill U	.12	.30
32 Stirring Address C	.15	.25
33 Trustworthy Scout C	.15	.25
34 Valiant Changeling U	.12	.30
35 Vesperlark U	.12	.30
36 Wall of One Thousand Cuts C	.15	.25
37 Winds of Abandon R	1.50	2.50
38 Wing Shards U	.12	.30
39 Zhalfirin Decoy U	.12	.30
40 Archmage's Charm R	2.00	3.50
41 Bazaar Trademage R	.50	.75
42 Blizzard Strix U	.12	.30
43 Chillerpillar C	.15	.25
44 Choking Tethers C	.15	.25
45 Cunning Evasion U	.12	.30
46 Echo of Eons M	8.00	12.00
47 Everdream U	.12	.30
48 Exclude U	.12	.30
49 Eyekite C	.15	.25
50 Fact or Fiction U	.12	.30
51 Faerie Seer C	.15	.25
52 Force of Negation R	35.00	50.00
53 Future Sight R	.30	.50
54 Iceberg Cancrix C	.15	.25
55 Man-o-War C	.15	.25
56 Marit Lage's Slumber R	.50	.75
57 Mirrodin Besieged R	.60	1.00
58 Mist-Syndicate Naga R	.50	.75
59 Moonblade Shinobi C	.15	.25
60 Oneirophage U	.12	.30
61 Phantasmal Form C	.15	.25
62 Phantom Ninja C	.15	.25
63 Pondering Mage C	.15	.25
64 Prohibit C	.15	.25
65 Rain of Revelation C	.15	.25
66 Rebuild U	.12	.30
67 Scour All Possibilities C	.15	.25
68 Scuttling Sliver U	.12	.30
69 Smoke Shroud C	.15	.25
70 Spell Snuff C	.15	.25
71 Stream of Thought C	.15	.25
72 String of Disappearances C	.15	.25
73 Tribute Mage U	.35	.60
74 Twisted Reflection U	.12	.30
75 Urza, Lord High Artificer M	35.00	45.00
76 Watcher for Tomorrow U	.12	.30
77 Windcaller Aven C	.15	.25
78 Winter's Rest C	.15	.25
79 Azra Smokeshaper C	.15	.25
80 Cabal Therapist R	.75	1.25
81 Carrion Feeder U	.30	.50
82 Changeling Outcast C	.15	.25
83 Cordial Vampire R	.75	1.25
84 Crypt Rats U	.12	.30
85 Dead of Winter R	1.25	2.00
86 Defile C	.15	.25
87 Diabolic Edict C	.15	.25
88 Dregscape Sliver U	.12	.30
89 Endling R	.35	.60
90 Feaster of Fools U	.12	.30
91 First-Sphere Gargantua C	.15	.25
92 Force of Despair R	1.75	3.00
93 Gluttonous Slug C	.15	.25
94 Graveshifter U	.12	.30
95 Headless Specter C	.15	.25
96 Mind Rake C	.15	.25
97 Mob C	.15	.25
98 Nether Spirit R	.30	.50
99 Ninja of the New Moon C	.15	.25
100 Plague Engineer R	5.00	8.00
101 Putrid Goblin C	.15	.25
102 Rank Officer C	.15	.25
103 Ransack the Lab C	.15	.25
104 Return from Extinction C	.15	.25
105 Sadistic Obsession U	.12	.30
106 Shatter Assumptions U	.12	.30
107 Silumgar Scavenger C	.15	.25
108 Sling-Gang Lieutenant U	.12	.30
109 Smiting Helix U	.12	.30
110 Throatseeker U	.12	.30
111 Umezawa's Charm C	.15	.25
112 Undead Augur U	.30	.50
113 Unearth C	.15	.25
114 Venomous Changeling C	.15	.25
115 Warteye Witch C	.15	.25
116 Yawgmoth, Thran Physician M	15.00	20.00
117 Alpine Guide U	.12	.30
118 Aria of Flame R	4.00	6.00
119 Bladeback Sliver C	.15	.25
120 Bogardan Dragonheart C	.75	1.25
121 Cleaving Sliver C	.15	.25
122 Firebolt U	.12	.30
123 Fists of Flame C	.15	.25
124 Force of Rage R	.35	.60
125 Geomancer's Gambit C	.15	.25
126 Goatnap C	.15	.25
127 Goblin Champion C	.15	.25
128 Goblin Engineer R	3.00	5.00
129 Goblin Matron U	.25	.40
130 Goblin Oriflamme U	.12	.30
131 Goblin War Party C	.15	.25
132 Hollowhead Sliver U	.12	.30
133 Igneous Elemental C	.15	.25
134 Lava Dart C	.15	.25
135 Magmatic Sinkhole C	.15	.25
136 Orcish Hellraiser C	.15	.25
137 Ore-Scale Guardian U	.12	.30
138 Pashalik Mons R	.60	1.00
139 Pillage U	.12	.30
140 Planebound Accomplice R	.60	1.00
141 Pyrophobia C	.15	.25
142 Quakefoot Cyclops C	.15	.25
143 Ravenous Giant U	.12	.30
144 Reckless Charge C	.15	.25
145 Seasoned Pyromancer M	25.00	30.00
146 Shenanigans C	.15	.25
147 Spinehorn Minotaur C	.15	.25
148 Spiteful Sliver R	.60	1.00
149 Tectonic Reformation R	.35	1.25
150 Throes of Chaos U	.12	.30
151 Urza's Rage U	.12	.30
152 Vengeful Devil U	.12	.30
153 Viashino Sandsprinter C	.15	.25
154 Volatile Claws C	.15	.25
155 Ayula, Queen Among Bears R	.30	1.00
156 Ayula's Influence R	.35	.60
157 Bellowing Elk C	.15	.25
158 Collector Ouphe R	3.00	5.00
159 Conifer Wurm U	.12	.30
160 Crashing Footfalls R	1.75	3.00
161 Deep Forest Hermit R	.35	.60
162 Elvish Fury C	.15	.25
163 Excavating Anurid C	.15	.25
164 Force of Vigor R	5.00	8.00
165 Frostwalla C	.15	.25
166 Genesis R	.60	1.00
167 Glacial Revelation U	.12	.30
168 Hexdrinker M	20.00	25.00
169 Krosan Tusker C	.15	.25
170 Llanowar Tribe U	.35	.60
171 Mother Bear C	.15	.25
172 Murasa Behemoth C	.15	.25
173 Nantuko Cultivator U	.12	.30
174 Nimble Mongoose C	.15	.25
175 Regrowth U	.12	.30
176 Rime Tender C	.15	.25
177 Saddled Rimestag U	.12	.30
178 Savage Swipe C	.15	.25
179 Scale Up U	1.00	1.50
180 Spore Frog C	.15	.25
181 Springbloom Druid C	.15	.25
182 Squirrel Nest U	.12	.30
183 Tempered Sliver U	.12	.30
184 Thornado C	.15	.25
185 Treefolk Umbra C	.15	.25
186 Treetop Ambusher C	.15	.25

187 Trumpeting Herd C .15 .25
188 Twin-Silk Spider C .15 .25
189 Unbound Flourishing M 8.00 12.00
190 Wall of Blossoms U .12 .30
191 Weather the Storm C .15 .25
192 Webweaver Changeling U .12 .30
193 Winding Way C .15 .25
194 Abominable Treefolk U .12 .30
195 Cloudshredder Sliver R 1.50 2.50
196 Collected Conjuring R .50 .75
197 Eladamri's Call R 1.75 3.00
198 Etchings of the Chosen U .12 .30
199 Fallen Shinobi R .75 1.25
200 The First Sliver M 15.00 20.00
201 Good-Fortune Unicorn U .12 .30
202 Hogaak, Arisen Necropolis R 4.00 6.00
203 Ice-Fang Coatl R 2.50 4.00
204 Ingenious Infiltrator U .12 .30
205 Kaya's Guile R 1.75 3.00
206 Kess, Dissident Mage M 1.75 3.00
207 Lavabelly Sliver U .12 .30
208 Lightning Skelemental R 2.50 4.00
209 Munitions Expert U .30 .50
210 Nature's Chant C .15 .25
211 Reap the Past R .30 .50
212 Rotwidow Pack U .12 .30
213 Ruination Rioter U .12 .30
214 Soulherder U .35 .60
215 Thundering Djinn U .12 .30
216 Unsettled Mariner R 2.00 3.50
217 Wrenn and Six M 75.00 90.00
218 Altar of Dementia A R 2.00 3.50
219 Amorphous Axe A C .15 .25
220 Arcum's Astrolabe A C .15 .25
221 Birthing Boughs A U .12 .30
222 Farmstead Gleaner A U .12 .30
223 Fountain of Ichor A C .15 .25
224 Icehide Golem A U .12 .30
225 Lesser Masticore A U .12 .30
226 Mox Tantalite A M 5.00 8.00
227 Scrapyard Recombiner A R .50 .75
228 Sword of Sinew and Steel A M 8.00 12.00
229 Sword of Truth and Justice A M 10.00 15.00
230 Talisman of Conviction A U .50 .75
231 Talisman of Creativity A U .60 1.00
232 Talisman of Curiosity A U .35 .60
233 Talisman of Hierarchy A U .50 .75
234 Talisman of Resilience A U .35 .60
235 Universal Automaton A C .15 .25
236 Barren Moor L U .12 .30
237 Cave of Temptation L C .15 .25
238 Fiery Islet L R 15.00 25.00
239 Forgotten Cave L U .12 .30
240 Frostwalk Bastion L U .12 .30
241 Hall of Heliod's Generosity L R 3.00 5.00
242 Lonely Sandbar L U .12 .30
243 Nurturing Peatland L R 15.00 20.00
244 Prismatic Vista L R 20.00 25.00
245 Secluded Steppe L U .12 .30
246 Silent Clearing L R 10.00 15.00
247 Sunbaked Canyon L R 15.00 20.00
248 Tranquil Thicket L U .12 .30
249 Waterlogged Grove L R 10.00 15.00
250 Snow-Covered Plains L C .30 .50
251 Snow-Covered Island L C .60 1.00
252 Snow-Covered Swamp L C .60 1.00
253 Snow-Covered Mountain L C .60 1.00
254 Snow-Covered Forest L C .50 .75
255 Flusterstorm R .30 .50

2019 Magic The Gathering Modern Horizons Foil

1 Morophon, the Boundless M 50.00 60.00
2 Answered Prayers C .25 .40
3 Astral Drift R 1.25 2.00
4 Battle Screech U .30 .50
5 Dismantling Blow U .30 .50
6 Enduring Sliver C .25 .40
7 Ephemerate C .25 .40
8 Face of Divinity U .30 .50
9 First Sliver's Chosen U .30 .50
10 Force of Virtue R 2.50 4.00
11 Generous Gift U .30 .50
12 Gilded Light C .25 .40
13 Giver of Runes R 25.00 35.00
14 Imposter of the Sixth Pride C .25 .40
15 Irregular Cohort C .25 .40
16 King of the Pride U .30 .50
17 Knight of Old Benalia C .25 .40
18 Lancer Sliver C .25 .40
19 Martyr's Soul C .25 .40
20 On Thin Ice R 1.25 2.00
21 Ranger-Captain of Eos M 40.00 50.00
22 Recruit the Worthy C .25 .40
23 Reprobation C .25 .40
24 Rhox Veteran C .25 .40
25 Segovian Angel C .25 .40
26 Serra the Benevolent M 50.00 60.00
27 Settle Beyond Reality C .25 .40
28 Shelter C .25 .40
29 Sisay, Weatherlight Captain R 8.00 12.00
30 Soul-Strike Technique C .25 .40
31 Splicer's Skill U .30 .50
32 Stirring Address C .25 .40
33 Trustworthy Scout C .25 .40
34 Valiant Changeling U .30 .50
35 Vesperlark U .30 .50
36 Wall of One Thousand Cuts C .25 .40
37 Winds of Abandon R 10.00 15.00
38 Wing Shards U .30 .50
39 Zhalfirin Decoy U .30 .50
40 Archmage's Charm R 8.00 12.00
41 Bazaar Trademage R 4.00 6.00
42 Blizzard Strix U .30 .50
43 Chillerpillar C .25 .40
44 Choking Tethers C .25 .40
45 Cunning Evasion U .30 .50
46 Echo of Eons M 8.00 50.00
47 Everdream U .30 .50
48 Exclude U .30 .50
49 Eyekite C .25 .40
50 Fact or Fiction U .30 .50
51 Faerie Seer C .25 .40
52 Force of Negation R 150.00 200.00
53 Future Sight R 1.25 2.00
54 Iceberg Cancrix C .25 .40
55 Man-o-War C .25 .40
56 Marit Lage's Slumber R 2.50 4.00
57 Mirrodin Besieged R 4.00 6.00
58 Mist-Syndicate Naga R 1.75 3.00
59 Moonblade Shinobi C .25 .40
60 Oneirophage U .30 .50
61 Phantasmal Form C .25 .40
62 Phantom Ninja C .25 .40
63 Pondering Mage C .25 .40
64 Prohibit C .25 .40
65 Rain of Revelation C .25 .40
66 Rebuild U .30 .50
67 Scour All Possibilities C .25 .40
68 Scuttling Sliver U .30 .50
69 Smoke Shroud C .25 .40
70 Spell Snuff C .25 .40
71 Stream of Thought C .25 .40
72 String of Disappearances C .25 .40
73 Tribute Mage U .30 .50
74 Twisted Reflection U .30 .50
75 Urza, Lord High Artificer M 125.00 150.00
76 Watcher for Tomorrow U .30 .50
77 Windcaller Aven C .25 .40
78 Winter's Rest C .25 .40
79 Azra Smokeshaper C .25 .40
80 Cabal Therapist R 5.00 8.00
81 Carrion Feeder U .30 .50
82 Changeling Outcast C .25 .40
83 Cordial Vampire R 2.50 4.00
84 Crypt Rats U .30 .50
85 Dead of Winter R 25.00 30.00
86 Defile C .25 .40
87 Diabolic Edict C .25 .40
88 Dregscape Sliver U .30 .50
89 Endling R 1.25 2.00
90 Feaster of Fools U .30 .50
91 First-Sphere Gargantua C .25 .40
92 Force of Despair R 8.00 12.00
93 Gluttonous Slug C .25 .40
94 Graveshifter U .30 .50
95 Headless Specter C .25 .40
96 Mind Rake C .25 .40
97 Mob C .25 .40
98 Nether Spirit R 1.25 2.00
99 Ninja of the New Moon C .25 .40
100 Plague Engineer R 30.00 40.00
101 Putrid Goblin C .25 .40
102 Rank Officer C .25 .40
103 Ransack the Lab C .25 .40
104 Return from Extinction C .25 .40
105 Sadistic Obsession U .30 .50
106 Shatter Assumptions U .30 .50
107 Silumgar Scavenger C .25 .40
108 Sling-Gang Lieutenant U .30 .50
109 Smiting Helix U .30 .50
110 Throatseeker U .30 .50
111 Umezawa's Charm C .25 .40
112 Undead Augur U .30 .50
113 Unearth C .25 .40
114 Venomous Changeling C .25 .40
115 Warteye Witch C .25 .40
116 Yawgmoth, Thran Physician M 100.00 120.00
117 Alpine Guide U .30 .50
118 Aria of Flame R 15.00 20.00
119 Bladeback Sliver C .25 .40
120 Bogardan Dragonheart C .25 .40
121 Cleaving Sliver C .25 .40
122 Firebolt U .30 .50
123 Fists of Flame C .25 .40
124 Force of Rage R 1.25 2.00
125 Geomancer's Gambit C .25 .40
126 Goatnap C .25 .40
127 Goblin Champion C .25 .40
128 Goblin Engineer R 20.00 25.00
129 Goblin Matron U .30 .50
130 Goblin Oriflamme U .30 .50
131 Goblin War Party C .25 .40
132 Hollowhead Sliver U .30 .50
133 Igneous Elemental C .25 .40
134 Lava Dart C .25 .40
135 Magmatic Sinkhole C .25 .40
136 Orcish Hellraiser C .25 .40
137 Ore-Scale Guardian U .30 .50
138 Pashalik Mons R 5.00 8.00
139 Pillage U .30 .50
140 Planebound Accomplice R 2.50 4.00
141 Pyrophobia C .25 .40
142 Quakefoot Cyclops C .25 .40
143 Ravenous Giant U .30 .50
144 Reckless Charge C .25 .40
145 Seasoned Pyromancer M 70.00 80.00
146 Shenanigans C .25 .40
147 Spinehorn Minotaur C .25 .40
148 Spiteful Sliver R 3.00 5.00
149 Tectonic Reformation R 2.50 4.00
150 Throes of Chaos U .30 .50
151 Urza's Rage U .30 .50
152 Vengeful Devil U .30 .50
153 Viashino Sandsprinter C .25 .40
154 Volatile Claws C .25 .40
155 Ayula, Queen Among Bears R 5.00 8.00
156 Ayula's Influence R 1.25 2.00
157 Bellowing Elk C .25 .40
158 Collector Ouphe R 25.00 30.00
159 Conifer Wurm U .30 .50
160 Crashing Footfalls R 8.00 12.00
161 Deep Forest Hermit R 2.50 4.00
162 Elvish Fury C .25 .40
163 Excavating Anurid C .25 .40
164 Force of Vigor R 25.00 30.00
165 Frostwalla C .25 .40
166 Genesis R 1.25 2.00
167 Glacial Revelation U .30 .50
168 Hexdrinker M 60.00 70.00
169 Krosan Tusker C .25 .40
170 Llanowar Tribe U .30 .50
171 Mother Bear C .25 .40
172 Murasa Behemoth C .25 .40
173 Nantuko Cultivator U .30 .50
174 Nimble Mongoose C .25 .40
175 Regrowth U .30 .50
176 Rime Tender C .25 .40
177 Saddled Rimestag U .30 .50
178 Savage Swipe C .25 .40
179 Scale Up U .30 .50
180 Spore Frog C .25 .40
181 Springbloom Druid C .25 .40
182 Squirrel Nest U .30 .50
183 Tempered Sliver U .30 .50
184 Thornado C .25 .40
185 Treefolk Umbra C .25 .40
186 Treetop Ambusher C .25 .40
187 Trumpeting Herd C .25 .40
188 Twin-Silk Spider C .25 .40
189 Unbound Flourishing M 25.00 35.00
190 Wall of Blossoms U .30 .50
191 Weather the Storm C .25 .40
192 Webweaver Changeling U .30 .50
193 Winding Way C .25 .40
194 Abominable Treefolk U .30 .50
195 Cloudshredder Sliver R 5.00 8.00
196 Collected Conjuring R 1.25 2.00
197 Eladamri's Call R 4.00 6.00
198 Etchings of the Chosen U .30 .50
199 Fallen Shinobi R 4.00 6.00
200 The First Sliver M 70.00 80.00
201 Good-Fortune Unicorn U .30 .50
202 Hogaak, Arisen Necropolis R 20.00 25.00
203 Ice-Fang Coatl R 10.00 15.00
204 Ingenious Infiltrator U .30 .50
205 Kaya's Guile R 8.00 12.00
206 Kess, Dissident Mage M 6.00 10.00
207 Lavabelly Sliver U .30 .50
208 Lightning Skelemental R 20.00 25.00
209 Munitions Expert U .30 .50
210 Nature's Chant C .25 .40
211 Reap the Past R 1.25 2.00
212 Rotwidow Pack U .30 .50
213 Ruination Rioter U .30 .50
214 Soulherder U .30 .50
215 Thundering Djinn U .30 .50
216 Unsettled Mariner R 10.00 15.00
217 Wrenn and Six M 250.00 350.00
218 Altar of Dementia A R 5.00 8.00
219 Amorphous Axe A C .25 .40
220 Arcum's Astrolabe A C .25 .40
221 Birthing Boughs A U .30 .50
222 Farmstead Gleaner A U .30 .50
223 Fountain of Ichor A C .25 .40
224 Icehide Golem A U .30 .50
225 Lesser Masticore A U .30 .50
226 Mox Tantalite A M 25.00 30.00
227 Scrapyard Recombiner A R 2.50 4.00
228 Sword of Sinew and Steel A M 35.00 45.00
229 Sword of Truth and Justice A M 40.00 50.00
230 Talisman of Conviction A U .30 .50
231 Talisman of Creativity A U .30 .50
232 Talisman of Curiosity A U .30 .50
233 Talisman of Hierarchy A U .30 .50
234 Talisman of Resilience A U .30 .50
235 Universal Automaton A C .25 .40
236 Barren Moor L U .30 .50
237 Cave of Temptation L C .25 .40
238 Fiery Islet L R 50.00 60.00
239 Forgotten Cave L U .30 .50
240 Frostwalk Bastion L U .30 .50
241 Hall of Heliod's Generosity L R 20.00 25.00
242 Lonely Sandbar L U .30 .50
243 Nurturing Peatland L R 50.00 60.00
244 Prismatic Vista L R 90.00 110.00
245 Secluded Steppe L U .30 .50
246 Silent Clearing L R 35.00 45.00
247 Sunbaked Canyon L R 50.00 60.00
248 Tranquil Thicket L U .30 .50
249 Waterlogged Grove L R 40.00 50.00
250 Snow-Covered Plains L C .25 .40
251 Snow-Covered Island L C .25 .40
252 Snow-Covered Swamp L C .25 .40
253 Snow-Covered Mountain L C .25 .40
254 Snow-Covered Forest L C .25 .40
255 Flusterstorm R 1.25 2.00

2019 Magic The Gathering Modern Horizons Tokens

1 Shapeshifter .15 .25
2 Angel .15 .25
3 Bird .15 .25
4 Soldier .15 .25
5 Illusion .15 .25
6 Marit Lage .15 .25
7 Zombie .15 .25
8 Elemental .15 .25
9 Elemental .15 .25
10 Goblin .15 .25
11 Bear .15 .25
12 Elephant .15 .25
13 Rhino .15 .25
14 Spider .15 .25
15 Squirrel .15 .25
16 Spirit .15 .25
17 Construct .15 .25
18 Golem .15 .25
19 Myr .15 .25
20 Serra the Benevolent Emblem .15 .25
21 Wrenn and Six Emblem .15 .25

Multiplayer Sets

Planechase

2009 Magic The Gathering Planechase

COMPLETE SET (211) 60.00 150.00
RELEASED ON SEPTEMBER 4, 2009
1 Akroma's Vengeance R :W: .40 1.00
2 Congregate C :W: .10 .25
3 Kor Sanctifiers C :W: .10 .25
4 Oblivion Ring C :W: .10 .25
5 Order U :W: .20 .50
6 Orim's Thunder C :W: .10 .25
7 Prison Term U :W: .20 .50
8 Soul Warden C :W: .10 .25
9 Ascendant Evincar R :K: .40 1.00
10 Beacon of Unrest R :K: 2.00 5.00
11 Beseech the Queen U :K: 1.50 4.00
12 Cadaverous Knight C :K: .10 .25
13 Consume Spirit U :K: .20 .50
14 Corpse Harvester U :K: .20 .50
15 Cruel Revival C :K: .10 .25
16 Dark Ritual C :K: .75 2.00
17 Death Baron R :K: 6.00 15.00
18 Dregscape Zombie C :K: .10 .25
19 Festering Goblin C :K: .10 .25
20 Grave Pact R :K: 4.00 10.00
21 Gravedigger C :K: .10 .25
22 Helldozer R :K: .40 1.00
23 Hideous End C :K: .10 .25
24 Incremental Blight U :K: .20 .50
25 Innocent Blood C :K: .10 .25
26 Nefashu R :K: .40 1.00
27 Noxious Ghoul U :K: .20 .50
28 Phyrexian Arena R :K: 4.00 10.00
29 Phyrexian Ghoul C :K: .10 .25
30 Profane Command R :K: .40 1.00
31 Rotting Rats C :K: .10 .25
32 Shepherd of Rot C :K: .10 .25
33 Soulless One U :K: .20 .50
34 Syphon Mind C :K: .10 .25
35 Syphon Soul C :K: .10 .25
36 Undead Warchief U :K: 2.00 5.00
37 Withered Wretch U :K: .20 .50
38 Arc Lightning C :R: .10 .25
39 Assault U :R: .20 .50
40 Blaze U :R: .20 .50
41 Bogardan Firefiend C :R: .10 .25
42 Bogardan Rager C :R: .10 .25
43 Browbeat U :R: .50 1.25
44 Chaos U :R: .20 .50
45 Cinder Elemental U :R: .20 .50
46 Cone of Flame U :R: .20 .50
47 Flamekin Harbinger U :R: .40 1.00
48 Flametongue Kavu U :R: .20 .50
49 Furnace of Rath R :R: .40 1.00
50 Goblin Offensive U :R: .40 1.00
51 Insurrection R :R: 1.50 4.00
52 Keldon Champion U :R: .20 .50
53 Menacing Ogre R :R: .40 1.00
54 Pyrotechnics U :R: .20 .50
55 Reckless Charge C :R: .10 .25
56 Relentless Assault R :R: .40 1.00
57 Rockslide Elemental U :R: .20 .50
58 Rolling Thunder C :R: .10 .25
59 Rorix Bladewing R :R: .40 1.00
60 Smokebraider C :R: .10 .25
61 Taurean Mauler R :R: .40 1.00
62 Battery U :G: .20 .50
63 Beast Hunt C :G: .10 .25
64 Briarhorn U :G: .20 .50
65 Explosive Vegetation U :G: .75 2.00
66 Fertile Ground C :G: .10 .25
67 Fertilid C :G: .10 .25
68 Forgotten Ancient R :G: 1.25 3.00
69 Ivy Elemental R :G: .40 1.00
70 Living Hive R :G: .40 1.00
71 Rampant Growth C :G: .10 .25
72 Search for Tomorrow C :G: .10 .25
73 Silverglade Elemental C :G: .10 .25
74 Tornado Elemental R :G: .40 1.00
75 Tribal Unity U :G: .20 .50
76 Verdant Force R :G: .40 1.00
77 Arsenal Thresher C :W/L/K: .10 .25
78 Balefire Liege R :W/R: 3.00 8.00
79 Battlegate Mimic C :W/R: .10 .25
80 Boros Guildmage U :W/R: .20 .50
81 Boros Swiftblade U :W/R: .20 .50
82 Branching Bolt C :R/G: .10 .25
83 Bull Cerodon U :W/R: .20 .50
84 Captain's Maneuver U :W/R: .20 .50
85 Cerodon Yearling C :W/R: .10 .25
86 Double Cleave C :W/R: .10 .25
87 Duergar Hedge-Mage U :W/R: .20 .50
88 Fires of Yavimaya U :R/G: .20 .50
89 Glory of Warfare R :W/R: .40 1.00
90 Hearthfire Hobgoblin U :W/R: .20 .50
91 Hull Breach C :R/G: .75 2.00
92 Lightning Helix U :W/R: 1.25 3.00
93 Mage Slayer U :R/G: .20 .50
94 Razia, Boros Archangel R :W/R: .75 2.00
95 Rumbling Slum R :R/G: .40 1.00
96 Savage Twister U :R/G: .20 .50
97 Sludge Strider U :W/L/K: .20 .50
98 Academy at Tolaria West C 1.25 3.00
99 Agyrem C 1.25 3.00
100 Ancient Den C .75 2.00
101 Arcbound Crusher U .40 1.00
102 Arcbound Slith U .20 .50
103 Bant C 1.25 3.00
104 Boros Garrison C .30 .75
105 Boros Signet C .10 .25
106 Bosh, Iron Golem R .40 1.00
107 Cabal Coffers U 5.00 12.00
108 Cliffside Market C 1.25 3.00

109 Copper Myr C .10 .25
110 Cranial Plating C 1.25 3.00
111 Darksteel Forge R 1.50 4.00
112 Door to Nothingness R .40 1.00
113 Eloren Wilds C .10 .25
114 Etched Oracle U .20 .50
115 Feeding Grounds C 1.25 3.00
116 Fields of Summer C 1.50 4.00
117 Glimmervoid Basin C .75 2.00
118 Gold Myr C .10 .25
119 Goldmeadow C .10 .25
120 Great Furnace C .40 1.00
121 Grixis C 1.25 3.00
122 Gruul Turf C .10 .25
123 Immersturm C .10 .25
124 Iron Myr C .10 .25
125 Isle of Vesuva C .10 .25
126 Izzet Steam Maze C .10 .25
127 Krosa C .10 .25
128 Leaden Myr C .10 .25
129 Leechridden Swamp U .50 1.25
130 Lethe Lake C 1.25 3.00
131 Llanowar C .10 .25
132 Lodestone Myr R .40 1.00
133 Loxodon Warhammer R .60 1.50
134 Mask of Memory U .20 .50
135 Minamo C .10 .25
136 Murasa C .10 .25
137 Myr Enforcer C .10 .25
138 Naar Isle C .10 .25
139 Naya C .10 .25
140 Nuisance Engine U .20 .50
141 Otaria C 1.50 4.00
142 Panopticon C .10 .25
143 Pentad Prism C .10 .25
144 Pentavus R .40 1.00
145 Pools of Becoming C .10 .25
146 Raven's Run C 1.25 3.00
147 Relic of Progenitus C .40 1.00
148 Sanctum of Serra C .10 .25
149 Sea of Sand C .10 .25
150 Seat of the Synod C .10 .25
151 Serum Tank U .20 .50
152 Shiv C .10 .25
153 Shivan Oasis U .20 .50
154 Silver Myr C .10 .25
155 Skeleton Shard U .20 .50
156 Skybreen C .10 .25
157 Sokenzan C .10 .25
158 Stronghold Furnace C .10 .25
159 Sunhome, Fortress of the Legion U .20 .50
160 Suntouched Myr C .10 .25
161 Tazeem C 10.00 25.00
162 Terramorphic Expanse C .10 .25
163 The Aether Flues C 1.50 4.00
164 The Dark Barony C 1.25 3.00
165 The Eon Fog C 1.25 3.00
166 The Fourth Sphere C 1.25 3.00
167 The Great Forest C 1.25 3.00
168 The Hippodrome C 1.25 3.00
169 The Maelstrom C 1.25 3.00
170 Tree of Tales C .10 .25
171 Turri Island C .10 .25
172 Undercity Reaches C .10 .25
173 Vault of Whispers C .10 .25
174 Velis Vel C .10 .25
175 Wizard Replica C .10 .25
176 Broodstar R :L: .40 1.00
177 Fabricate U :L: .75 2.00
178 Forest L .10 .25
179 Forest L .10 .25
180 Forest L .10 .25
181 Forest L .10 .25
182 Forest L .10 .25
183 Island L .10 .25
184 Island L .10 .25
185 Island L .10 .25
186 Island L .10 .25
187 Keep Watch C :L: .10 .25
188 Master of Etherium R :L: 2.50 6.00
189 Mountain L .10 .25
190 Mountain L .10 .25
191 Mountain L .10 .25
192 Mountain L .10 .25
193 Mountain L .10 .25
194 Mountain L .10 .25
195 Mountain L .10 .25
196 Mountain L .10 .25
197 Mountain L .10 .25
198 Plains L .10 .25
199 Plains L .10 .25
200 Plains L .10 .25
201 Plains L .10 .25
202 Plains L .10 .25
203 Qumulox U :L: .20 .50
204 Sarcomite Myr C :L: .10 .25
205 Swamp L .10 .25
206 Swamp L .10 .25
207 Swamp L .10 .25
208 Swamp L .10 .25
209 Swamp L .10 .25
210 Thirst for Knowledge U :L: .20 .50
211 Vedalken Engineer C :L: .10 .25
212 Whiplash Trap C :L: .10 .25

2012 Magic The Gathering Planechase

COMPLETE SET (156) 50.00 120.00
CHAOS REIGNS DECK 25.00 50.00
NIGHT OF THE NINJA DECK 30.00 60.00
PRIMORDIAL HUNGER DECK 20.00 40.00
SAVAGE AURAS DECK 20.00 40.00
RELEASED ON SEPTEMBER 4, 2009
1 Armored Griffin U :W: .15 .40
2 Auramancer C :W: .10 .25
3 Auratouched Mage U :W: .15 .40
4 Cage of Hands C :W: .10 .25
5 Celestial Ancient R :W: .30 .75
6 Felidar Umbra U :W: 1.50 4.00
7 Ghostly Prison U :W: 2.50 6.00
8 Hyena Umbra C :W: .30 .75
9 Kor Spiritdancer R :W: 4.00 10.00
10 Mammoth Umbra U :W: .15 .40
11 Sigil of the Empty Throne R :W: .75 2.00
12 Spirit Mantle U :W: 1.00 2.50
13 Three Dreams R :W: .30 .75
14 Augury Owl C :B: .10 .25
15 Cancel C :B: .10 .25
16 Concentrate U :B: .15 .40
17 Guard Gomazoa U :B: .40 1.00
18 Higure, the Still Wind R :B: .40 1.00
19 Illusory Angel U :B: 1.25 3.00
20 Mistblade Shinobi C :B: .15 .40
21 Ninja of the Deep Hours C :B: .30 .75
22 Peregrine Drake U :B: .15 .40
23 Primal Plasma C :B: .10 .25
24 Sakashima's Student R :B: 4.00 10.00
25 See Beyond C :B: .10 .25
26 Sunken Hope R :B: .30 .75
27 Walker of Secret Ways U :B: .15 .40
28 Wall of Frost U :B: .15 .40
29 Whirlpool Warrior R :B: .30 .75
30 Assassinate C :K: .10 .25
31 Cadaver Imp C :K: .10 .25
32 Dark Hatchling R :K: .30 .75
33 Ink-Eyes, Servant of Oni R :K: 2.50 6.00
34 Liliana's Specter C :K: .10 .25
35 Okiba-Gang Shinobi C :K: .30 .75
36 Skullsnatcher C :K: .10 .25
37 Throat Slitter U :K: .40 1.00
38 Tormented Soul C :K: .10 .25
39 Arc Trail U :R: .15 .40
40 Beetleback Chief U :R: .75 2.00
41 Erratic Explosion C :R: .10 .25
42 Fiery Conclusion C :R: .10 .25
43 Fiery Fall C :R: .10 .25
44 Fling C :R: .10 .25
45 Hellion Eruption R :R: .30 .75
46 Hissing Iguanar C :R: .10 .25
47 Mark of Mutiny U :R: .15 .40
48 Mass Mutiny R :R: .40 1.00
49 Mudbutton Torchrunner C :R: .10 .25
50 Preyseizer Dragon R :R: 2.00 5.00
51 Rivals' Duel U :R: .15 .40
52 Thorn-Thrash Viashino C :R: .10 .25
53 Thunder-Thrash Elder U :R: .15 .40
54 Warstorm Surge R :R: .30 .75
55 Aura Gnarlid C :G: .10 .25
56 Awakening Zone R :G: .75 2.00
57 Beast Within U :G: .75 2.00
58 Boar Umbra U :G: .15 .40
59 Bramble Elemental C :G: .10 .25
60 Brindle Shoat U :G: .15 .40
61 Brutalizer Exarch U :G: .15 .40
62 Cultivate C :G: .75 2.00
63 Dowsing Shaman U :G: .15 .40
64 Dreampod Druid U :G: .15 .40
65 Gluttonous Slime U :G: .15 .40
66 Lumberknot U :G: .15 .40
67 Mitotic Slime R :G: .30 .75
68 Mycoloth R :G: 2.50 6.00
69 Nest Invader C :G: .10 .25
70 Nullmage Advocate C :G: .10 .25
71 Ondu Giant C :G: .10 .25
72 Overrun U :G: .15 .40
73 Penumbra Spider C :G: .10 .25
74 Predatory Urge R :G: .30 .75
75 Quiet Disrepair C :G: .10 .25
76 Rancor C :G: .75 2.00
77 Silhana Ledgewalker C :G: .75 2.00
78 Snake Umbra C :G: .10 .25
79 Tukatongue Thallid C :G: .10 .25
80 Viridian Emissary C :G: .10 .25
81 Wall of Blossoms U :G: 1.00 2.50
82 Baleful Strix U :B/K: 6.00 15.00
83 Bituminous Blast U :K/R: .15 .40
84 Bloodbraid Elf U :R/G: .75 2.00
85 Deny Reality C :B/K: .10 .25
86 Dimir Infiltrator C :B/K: .10 .25
87 Dragonlair Spider R :R/G: 2.00 5.00
88 Elderwood Scion R :W/G: .75 2.00
89 Enigma Sphinx R :W/B/K: .30 .75
90 Enlisted Wurm U :W/G: .15 .40
91 Etherium-Horn Sorcerer R :B/R: .75 2.00
92 Fires of Yavimaya U :R/G: .40 1.00
93 Fusion Elemental U :W/B/K/R/G: .15 .40
94 Glen Elendra Liege R :B/K: .75 2.00
95 Hellkite Hatchling U :R/G: .15 .40
96 Indrik Umbra R :W/G: .75 2.00
97 Inkfathom Witch U :B/K: .15 .40
98 Kathari Remnant U :B/K: .15 .40
99 Krond the Dawn-Clad M :W/G: 2.50 6.00
100 Last Stand R :W/B/K/R/G: .30 .75
101 Maelstrom Wanderer M :B/R/G: 4.00 10.00
102 Noggle Ransacker U :B/R: .15 .40
103 Pollenbright Wings U :W/G: .15 .40
104 Shardless Agent U :B/G: 8.00 20.00
105 Silent-Blade Oni R :B/K: 3.00 8.00
106 Thromok the Insatiable M :R/G: 3.00 8.00
107 Vela the Night-Clad M :B/K: 2.00 5.00
108 Armillary Sphere C .10 .25
109 Farsight Mask U .15 .40
110 Flayer Husk C .10 .25
111 Fractured Powerstone C .10 .25
112 Quietus Spike R .75 2.00
113 Sai of the Shinobi U .15 .40
114 Thran Golem U .15 .40
115 Whispersilk Cloak U .40 1.00
116 Dimir Aqueduct C .60 1.50
117 Exotic Orchard R .60 1.50
118 Graypelt Refuge U .15 .40
119 Gruul Turf C .10 .25
120 Jwar Isle Refuge U .30 .75
121 Kazandu Refuge U .15 .40
122 Khalni Garden C .10 .25
123 Krosan Verge U .15 .40
124 Rupture Spire C .10 .25
125 Selesnya Sanctuary C .30 .75
126 Shimmering Grotto C .10 .25
127 Skarrg, the Rage Pits U .15 .40
128 Tainted Isle U .75 2.00
129 Terramorphic Expanse C .10 .25
130 Vitu-Ghazi, the City-Tree U .15 .40
131 Vivid Creek U .30 .75
132 Plains L .10 .25
133 Plains L .10 .25
134 Plains L .10 .25
135 Plains L .10 .25
136 Plains L .10 .25
137 Island L .10 .25
138 Island L .10 .25
139 Island L .10 .25
140 Island L .10 .25
141 Island L .10 .25
142 Swamp L .10 .25
143 Swamp L .10 .25
144 Swamp L .10 .25
145 Swamp L .10 .25
146 Swamp L .10 .25
147 Mountain L .10 .25
148 Mountain L .10 .25
149 Mountain L .10 .25
150 Mountain L .10 .25
151 Forest L .10 .25
152 Forest L .10 .25
153 Forest L .10 .25
154 Forest L .10 .25
155 Forest L .10 .25
156 Forest L .10 .25

2016 Magic The Gathering Planechase Anthology

COMPLETE SET (156) 80.00 115.00
PLANECHASE ANTHOLOGY SEALED 90.00 115.00
RELEASED ON NOVEMBER 25, 2016
1 Armored Griffin U .15 .25
2 Auramancer C .10 .20
3 Auratouched Mage U .15 .25
4 Cage of Hands C .10 .20
5 Celestial Ancient R .40 .60
6 Felidar Umbra U .75 1.25
7 Ghostly Prison U 1.50 2.00
8 Hyena Umbra C .75 1.00
9 Kor Spiritdancer R 5.00 7.00
10 Mammoth Umbra U .15 .25
11 Sigil of the Empty Throne R .75 1.00
12 Spirit Mantle U 1.25 1.75
13 Three Dreams R .75 1.00
14 Augury Owl C .10 .20
15 Cancel C .10 .20
16 Concentrate U .15 .25
17 Guard Gomazoa U .20 .35
18 Higure the Still Wind R .50 .75
19 Illusory Angel U .20 .35
20 Mistblade Shinobi C .15 .25
21 Ninja of the Deep Hours C .30 .50
22 Peregrine Drake U .50 .75
23 Primal Plasma C .10 .20
24 Sakashimas Student R 6.00 8.00
25 See Beyond C .10 .20
26 Sunken Hope R .40 .60
27 Walker of Secret Ways U .20 .35
28 Wall of Frost U .15 .25
29 Whirlpool Warrior R .30 .50
30 Assassinate C .10 .20
31 Cadaver Imp C .10 .20
32 Dark Hatchling R .25 .40
33 InkEyes Servant of Oni R 2.75 3.25
34 Lilianas Specter C .10 .20
35 OkibaGang Shinobi C .15 .25
36 Skullsnatcher C .10 .20
37 Throat Slitter U .50 .75
38 Tormented Soul C .10 .20
39 Arc Trail U .15 .25
40 Beetleback Chief U .10 .20
41 Erratic Explosion C .10 .20
42 Fiery Conclusion C .10 .20
43 Fiery Fall C .10 .20
44 Fling C .10 .20
45 Hellion Eruption R .30 .50
46 Hissing Iguanar C .10 .20
47 Mark of Mutiny U .15 .25
48 Mass Mutiny R .40 .60
49 Mudbutton Torchrunner C .10 .20
50 Preyseizer Dragon R 2.00 2.50
51 Rivals Duel U .15 .25
52 ThornThrash Viashino C .10 .20
53 ThunderThrash Elder U .15 .25
54 Warstorm Surge R .30 .50
55 Aura Gnarlid C .10 .20
56 Awakening Zone R 2.00 2.50
57 Beast Within U 1.25 1.75
58 Boar Umbra U .15 .25
59 Bramble Elemental C .10 .20
60 Brindle Shoat U .75 1.00
61 Brutalizer Exarch U .15 .25
62 Cultivate C 1.00 1.50
63 Dowsing Shaman U .15 .25
64 Dreampod Druid U .15 .25
65 Gluttonous Slime U .15 .25
66 Lumberknot U .15 .25
67 Mitotic Slime R .30 .50
68 Mycoloth R 1.00 1.50
69 Nest Invader C .10 .20
70 Nullmage Advocate C .10 .20
71 Ondu Giant C .10 .20
72 Overrun U .15 .25
73 Penumbra Spider C .10 .20
74 Predatory Urge R .40 .60
75 Quiet Disrepair C .10 .20
76 Rancor C 1.50 2.00
77 Silhana Ledgewalker C .50 .75
78 Snake Umbra C .15 .25
79 Tukatongue Thallid C .10 .20
80 Viridian Emissary C .10 .20
81 Wall of Blossoms U .50 .75
82 Baleful Strix U 2.00 2.50
83 Bituminous Blast U .15 .25
84 Bloodbraid Elf U 1.50 2.00
85 Deny Reality C .10 .20
86 Dimir Infiltrator C .10 .20
87 Dragonlair Spider R .75 1.00
88 Elderwood Scion R .75 1.00
89 Enigma Sphinx R .40 .60
90 Enlisted Wurm U .15 .25
91 EtheriumHorn Sorcerer R .50 .75
92 Fires of Yavimaya U .15 .25
93 Fusion Elemental U .15 .25
94 Glen Elendra Liege R 1.50 2.00
95 Hellkite Hatchling U .15 .25
96 Indrik Umbra R .75 1.00
97 Inkfathom Witch U .15 .25
98 Kathari Remnant U .15 .25
99 Krond the DawnClad MR 2.00 2.50
100 Last Stand R .40 .60
101 Maelstrom Wanderer MR 8.00 10.00
102 Noggle Ransacker U .15 .25
103 Pollenbright Wings U .15 .25
104 Shardless Agent U 3.00 4.00
105 SilentBlade Oni R 4.00 4.50
106 Thromok the Insatiable MR 2.75 3.25
107 Vela the NightClad MR 2.00 3.00
108 Armillary Sphere C .10 .20
109 Farsight Mask U .15 .25
110 Flayer Husk C .10 .20
111 Fractured Powerstone C .10 .20
112 Quietus Spike R 2.00 2.50
113 Sai of the Shinobi U .40 .60
114 Thran Golem U .15 .25
115 Whispersilk Cloak U .40 .60
116 Dimir Aqueduct C .25 .40
117 Exotic Orchard R .75 1.25
118 Graypelt Refuge U .15 .25
119 Gruul Turf C .10 .20
120 Jwar Isle Refuge U .15 .25
121 Kazandu Refuge U .15 .25
122 Khalni Garden C .10 .20
123 Krosan Verge U .75 1.25
124 Rupture Spire C .10 .20
125 Selesnya Sanctuary C .20 .30
126 Shimmering Grotto C .10 .20
127 Skarrg the Rage Pits U .15 .25
128 Tainted Isle U .75 1.00
129 Terramorphic Expanse C .10 .20
130 VituGhazi the CityTree U .15 .25
131 Vivid Creek U .20 .35
132 Plains L .10 .20
133 Plains L .10 .20
134 Plains L .10 .20
135 Plains L .10 .20
136 Plains L .10 .20
137 IsL L .10 .20
138 IsL L .10 .20
139 IsL L .10 .20
140 IsL L .10 .20
141 IsL L .10 .20
142 Swamp L .10 .20
143 Swamp L .10 .20
144 Swamp L .10 .20
145 Swamp L .10 .20
146 Swamp L .10 .20
147 Mountain L .10 .20
148 Mountain L .10 .20
149 Mountain L .10 .20
150 Mountain L .10 .20
151 Forest L .10 .20
152 Forest L .10 .20
153 Forest L .10 .20
154 Forest L .10 .20
155 Forest L .10 .20
156 Forest L .10 .20

2016 Magic The Gathering Planechase Anthology Tokens

1 Eldrazi .10 .15
2 Eldrazi Spawn .10 .15
3 Eldrazi Spawn .10 .15
4 Eldrazi Spawn .10 .15
5 Angel .10 .15
6 Goat .10 .15
7 Germ .10 .15
8 Spider .10 .15
9 Zombie .10 .15
10 Dragon .10 .15
11 Goblin .10 .15
12 Hellion .10 .15
13 Beast .10 .15
14 Boar .10 .15
15 Insect .10 .15
16 Ooze .10 .15
17 Ooze .10 .15
18 Plant .10 .15
19 Saproling .10 .15

Archenemy

2010 Magic The Gathering Archenemy

COMPLETE SET (150) 130.00 185.00
THEME DECK 25.00 40.00
RELEASED ON JUNE 18, 2010
1 Leonin Abunas R :W: 1.50 2.00
2 Metallurgeon U :W: .15 .25
3 Oblivion Ring C :W: .50 .75
4 Path to Exile U :W: 10.00 12.00
5 Sanctum Gargoyle C :W: .15 .25
6 March of the Machines R :B: .30 .50
7 Master Transmuter R :B: 30.00 35.00
8 Spin into Myth U :B: .50 .75
9 Avatar of Woe R :K: 2.00 2.50
10 Beacon of Unrest R :K: 3.00 4.00
11 Bog Witch C :K: .15 .25
12 Cemetery Reaper R :K: 2.00 2.50
13 Corpse Connoisseur U :K: .20 .30

14 Dregscape Zombie C :K:	.15	.25
15 Extractor Demon R :K:	.30	.50
16 Festering Goblin C :K:	.15	.25
17 Incremental Blight U :K:	.15	.25
18 Infectious Horror C :K:	.15	.25
19 Infest U :K:	.15	.25
20 Makeshift Mannequin U :K:	.20	.35
21 Reanimate U :K:	9.00	11.00
22 Reassembling Skeleton U :K:	.30	.50
23 Scion of Darkness R :K:	1.25	1.75
24 Shriekmaw U :K:	1.00	1.25
25 Sign in Blood C :K:	.15	.25
26 Twisted Abomination C :K:	.15	.25
27 Urborg Syphon-Mage C :K:	.15	.25
28 Zombie Infestation U :K:	.75	1.00
29 Zombify U :K:	.50	.75
30 Battering Craghorn C :R:	.15	.25
31 Breath of Darigaaz U :R:	.15	.25
32 Chandra's Outrage C :R:	.15	.25
33 Dragon Breath C :R:	.15	.25
34 Dragon Fodder C :R:	.30	.50
35 Dragon Whelp U :R:	.15	.25
36 Dragonspeaker Shaman U :R:	4.00	4.50
37 Fireball U :R:	.20	.30
38 Flameblast Dragon R :R:	.50	.75
39 Furnace Whelp U :R:	.15	.25
40 Gathan Raiders C :R:	.15	.25
41 Hellkite Charger R :R:	.75	1.25
42 Imperial Hellkite R :R:	.45	.60
43 Inferno Trap U :R:	.15	.25
44 Kilnmouth Dragon R :R:	1.00	1.50
45 Ryusei, the Falling Star R :R:	1.00	1.50
46 Seething Song C :R:	1.00	1.25
47 Skirk Commando C :R:	.15	.25
48 Skirk Marauder C :R:	.15	.25
49 Taurean Mauler R :R:	1.75	2.00
50 Two-Headed Dragon R :R:	1.00	1.50
51 Volcanic Fallout U :R:	.75	1.00
52 Chameleon Colossus R :G:	1.50	2.00
53 Feral Hydra R :G:	1.75	2.00
54 Fertilid C :G:	.15	.25
55 Fierce Empath C :G:	2.50	3.00
56 Fog C :G:	.15	.25
57 Forgotten Ancient R :G:	2.50	3.00
58 Gleeful Sabotage C :G:	.15	.25
59 Harmonize U :G:	1.00	1.50
60 Hunting Moa U :G:	.30	.50
61 Kamahl, Fist of Krosa R :G:	4.00	6.00
62 Krosan Tusker C :G:	.15	.25
63 Leaf Gilder C :G:	.15	.25
64 Molimo, Maro-Sorcerer R :G:	.30	.50
65 Plummet C :G:	.15	.25
66 Primal Command R :G:	3.50	4.25
67 Rancor C :G:	2.50	3.00
68 Sakura-Tribe Elder C :G:	.50	.75
69 Shinen of Life's Roar C :G:	.15	.25
70 Spider Umbra C :G:	.75	1.25
71 Thelonite Hermit R :G:	.50	.75
72 Verdeloth the Ancient R :G:	.50	.75
73 Wall of Roots C :G:	2.50	3.00
74 Wickerbough Elder C :G:	.15	.25
75 Yavimaya Dryad U :G:	.15	.25
76 Agony Warp C :B/:K:	.15	.25
77 Architects of Will C :B/:K:	.25	.40
78 Armadillo Cloak C :W/:G:	.75	1.25
79 Avatar of Discord R :K/:R:	.75	1.25
80 Batwing Brume U :W/:K:	1.25	1.75
81 Bituminous Blast U :K/:R:	.30	.50
82 Branching Bolt C :R/:G:	.15	.25
83 Colossal Might C :R/:G:	.15	.25
84 Etherswom Shieldmage C :W/:B:	.15	.25
85 Fieldmist Borderpost C :W/:B:	.15	.25
86 Fires of Yavimaya U :R/:G:	.40	.60
87 Heroes' Reunion U :W/:G:	.30	.50
88 Kaervek the Merciless R :K/:R:	1.75	2.15
89 Magister Sphinx R :W/:B/:K:	1.00	1.50
90 Mistvein Borderpost C :B/:K:	.15	.25
91 Pale Recluse C :W/:G:	.15	.25
92 Rakdos Guildmage U :K/:R:	.30	.50
93 Savage Twister U :R/:G:	.15	.25
94 Selesnya Guildmage U :W/:G:	.15	.25
95 Terminate C :K/:R:	2.50	3.00
96 Torrent of Souls U :K/:R:	.20	.30
97 Unbender Tine U :W/:B:	.15	.25
98 Unmake C :W/:K:	.75	1.25
99 Vampiric Dragon R :K/:R:	2.00	2.50
100 Watchwolf U :W/:G:	.50	.75
101 Wax/Wane U :G/:W:	.15	.25
102 AEther Spellbomb C	.15	.25
103 Azorius Signet C	.15	.25
104 Dimir Signet C	2.50	3.00
105 Dreamstone Hedron U	.20	.30
106 Duplicant R	5.00	7.00
107 Everflowing Chalice U	.50	.75
108 Gruul Signet C	.15	.25
109 Juggernaut U	.15	.25
110 Lightning Greaves U	4.00	5.00
111 Lodestone Golem R	.75	1.00
112 Memnarch R	5.00	7.00
113 Obelisk of Esper C	.15	.25
114 Rakdos Signet C	.20	.35
115 Skullcage U	.15	.25
116 Sorcerer's Strongbox U	.15	.25
117 Sun Droplet U	1.00	1.50
118 Sundering Titan R	4.00	6.00
119 Synod Centurion U	.15	.25
120 Synod Sanctum U	.15	.25
121 Thran Dynamo U	7.00	8.50
122 Thunderstaff U	.15	.25
123 Artisan of Kozilek U	1.00	1.25
124 Barren Moor C	.15	.25
125 Graypelt Refuge U	.30	.50
126 Kazandu Refuge U	.20	.30
127 Khalni Garden C	.20	.30
128 Krosan Verge U	2.75	3.25
129 Llanowar Reborn U	.30	.50
130 Mosswort Bridge R	1.25	1.75
131 Nantuko Monastery U	.30	.50
132 Rakdos Carnarium C	.25	.40
133 Secluded Steppe C	.15	.25
134 Terramorphic Expanse C	.15	.25
135 Tranquil Thicket C	.15	.25
136 Vitu-Ghazi, the City-Tree U	.20	.30
137 Plains L	.15	.20
138 Plains L	.15	.25
139 Island L	.15	.25
140 Island L	.15	.25
141 Island L	.15	.25
142 Swamp L	.15	.25
143 Swamp L	.15	.25
144 Swamp L	.15	.25
145 Mountain L	.15	.25
146 Mountain L	.15	.25
147 Mountain L	.15	.25
148 Forest L	.15	.25
149 Forest L	.15	.25
150 Forest L	.15	.25

2010 Magic The Gathering Archenemy Oversized Schemes

COMPLETE SET (45)	25.00	60.00
RELEASED ON JUNE 18, 2010		
1 All in Good Time	3.00	8.00
2 All Shall Smolder in My Wake	.20	.50
3 Approach My Molten Realm	.60	1.50
4 Behold the Power of Destruction	3.00	8.00
5 Choose Your Champion	.20	.50
6 Dance, Pathetic Marionette	2.50	6.00
7 The Dead Shall Serve	.20	.50
8 A Display of My Dark Power	.60	1.50
9 Embrace My Diabolical Vision	1.25	3.00
10 Every Hope Shall Vanish	.20	.50
11 Every Last Vestige Shall Rot	.20	.50
12 Evil Comes to Fruition	.60	1.50
13 The Fate of the Flammable	.60	1.50
14 Feed the Machine	.20	.50
15 I Bask in Your Silent Awe	.20	.50
16 I Call on the Ancient Magics	1.25	3.00
17 I Delight in Your Convulsions	.20	.50
18 I Know All, I See All	.20	.50
19 Ignite the Cloneforge!	.20	.50
20 Into the Earthen Maw	1.25	3.00
21 Introductions Are in Order	.20	.50
22 The Iron Guardian Stirs	.20	.50
23 Know Naught but Fire	1.25	3.00
24 Look Skyward and Despair	.20	.50
25 May Civilization Collapse	1.00	2.50
26 Mortal Flesh Is Weak	2.00	5.00
27 My Crushing Masterstroke	3.00	8.00
28 My Genius Knows No Bounds	1.00	2.50
29 My Undead Horde Awakens	2.50	6.00
30 My Wish Is Your Command	.20	.50
31 Nature Demands an Offering	.20	.50
32 Nature Shields Its Own	.20	.50
33 Nothing Can Stop Me Now	.60	1.50
34 Only Blood Ends Your Nightmares	.20	.50
35 The Pieces Are Coming Together	.20	.50
36 Realms Befitting My Majesty	.20	.50
37 Roots of All Evil	.20	.50
38 Rotted Ones, Lay Siege	.20	.50
39 Surrender Your Thoughts	1.25	3.00
40 Tooth, Claw, and Tail	3.00	8.00
41 The Very Soil Shall Shake	1.25	3.00
42 Which of You Burns Brightest	.20	.50
43 Your Fate Is Thrice Sealed	.20	.50
44 Your Puny Minds Cannot Fathom	.20	.50
45 Your Will Is Not Your Own	.20	.50

2017 Magic The Gathering Archenemy Nicol Bolas

COMPLETE SET (106)	60.00	90.00
RELEASED ON JUNE 16, 2016		
1 Aegis Angel R	.10	.20
2 Aerial Responder U	.10	.20
3 Anointer of Champions U	.10	.20
4 Doomed Traveler C	.10	.20
5 Excoriate C	.10	.20
6 Expedition Raptor C	.10	.20
7 Fencing Ace U	.10	.20
8 Fiendslayer Paladin R	1.25	2.00
9 Flickerwisp U	.60	1.00
10 Gideon Jura M	6.00	8.00
11 Gideons Lawkeeper C	.10	.20
12 Grand Abolisher R	4.00	6.00
13 Grasp of the Hieromancer C	.10	.20
14 Lightwielder Paladin R	.10	.20
15 Mentor of the Meek R	.50	.80
16 Moment of Heroism C	.10	.20
17 Odric Master Tactician R	.75	1.25
18 Precinct Captain R	.10	.20
19 Relief Captain U	.10	.20
20 Shoulder to Shoulder C	.10	.25
21 Sun Titan M	3.00	5.00
22 Youthful Knight C	.10	.20
23 Compulsive Research C	.10	.20
24 Icefall Regent R	.10	.20
25 Ior Ruin Expedition C	.10	.20
26 Prognostic Sphinx R	.10	.20
27 Reckless Scholar U	.10	.20
28 Sphinx of Jwar Isle R	.10	.20
29 Vision Skeins C	.10	.20
30 Windrider Eel C	.10	.20
31 Archfiend of Depravity R	.10	.20
32 Deathbringer Regent R	.20	.35
33 Doom Blade U	.10	.20
34 Harvester of Souls R	.10	.20
35 Nightscape Familiar C	.10	.20
36 Overseer of the Damned R	1.50	2.50
37 Reckless Spite U	.10	.20
38 Vampire Nighthawk U	.40	.60
39 Avatar of Fury R	.30	.50
40 Battle-Rattle Shaman C	.10	.20
41 Blood Ogre C	.10	.20
42 Chandra Pyromaster M	1.50	2.50
43 Chandras Outrage C	.10	.20
44 Chandras Phoenix R	.25	.40
45 Coordinated Assault U	.10	.20
46 Dualcaster Mage R	.30	.50
47 Fiery Fall C	.10	.20
48 Flametongue Kavu U	.10	.20
49 Gorehorn Minotaurs C	.10	.20
50 Grim Lavamancer R	3.00	5.00
51 Guttersnipe U	.10	.20
52 Hammerhand C	.10	.20
53 Inferno Titan M	.75	1.25
54 Lightning Bolt U	1.50	2.00
55 Obsidian Fireheart M	.60	1.00
56 Searing Spear C	.10	.20
57 Skarrgan Firebird U	.10	.20
58 Stormblood Berserker U	.10	.20
59 Sudden Demise R	.50	.80
60 Torchling R	.10	.20
61 Volcanic Geyser U	.10	.20
62 Cultivate C	1.00	1.50
63 Explore C	.10	.20
64 Fertilid C	.10	.20
65 Forgotten Ancient R	.10	.20
66 Hunters Prowess R	.10	.20
67 Khalni Heart Expedition C	.10	.20
68 Nissa Worldwaker M	6.00	8.00
69 Oran-Rief Hydra R	.10	.20
70 Press the Advantage U	.10	.20
71 Rampaging Baloths M	.75	1.25
72 Retreat to Kazandu U	.10	.20
73 Scute Mob R	.30	.50
74 Sylvan Bounty C	.10	.20
75 Thragtusk R	1.00	1.50
76 Turntimber Basilisk U	.10	.20
77 Vastwood Zendikon C	.10	.20
78 Vines of the Recluse C	.10	.20
79 Woodborn Behemoth U	.10	.20
80 Baleful Strix U	1.50	2.50
81 Blood Tyrant R	.10	.20
82 Cruel Ultimatum R	.10	.20
83 Dreadbore R	1.50	2.50
84 Extract from Darkness U	.10	.20
85 Nicol Bolas Planeswalker M	6.00	8.00
86 Slave of Bolas U	.10	.20
87 Soul Ransom U	.10	.20
88 Obelisk of Grixis C	.10	.20
89 Sword of the Animist R	2.00	3.50
90 Talisman of Dominance U	1.00	1.50
91 Talisman of Indulgence U	.30	.50
92 Crumbling Necropolis U	.10	.20
93 Dragonskull Summit R	1.50	2.50
94 Drowned Catacomb R	2.00	3.50
95 Grixis Panorama C	.10	.20
96 Smoldering Spires C	.10	.20
97 Plains L	.10	.20
98 Island L	.10	.20
99 Swamp L	.10	.20
100 Mountain L	.10	.20
101 Forest L	.10	.20
102 Plains L	.10	.20
103 Island L	.10	.20
104 Swamp L	.10	.20
105 Mountain L	.10	.20
106 Forest L	.10	.20

2017 Magic The Gathering Archenemy Nicol Bolas Tokens

1 Soldier	.10	.15
2 Spirit	.10	.15
3 Horror	.06	.10
4 Beast	.06	.10
5 Beast	.15	.25

Commander

2011 Magic The Gathering Commander

COMPLETE SET (318)	75.00	200.00
BOOSTER BOX (36 PACKS)		
BOOSTER PACK (15 CARDS)		
RELEASED ON JUNE 17, 2011		
1 Acidic Slime U :G:	.20	.50
2 Acorn Catapult R	.40	1.00
3 Aethersnipe C :B:	.10	.25
4 Afterlife U :W:	.20	.50
5 Akoum Refuge U	.40	1.00
6 Akroma's Vengeance R :W:	.60	1.50
7 Akroma, Angel of Fury R :R:	2.50	6.00
8 Alliance of Arms R :W:	.40	1.00
9 Angel of Despair R	1.50	4.00
10 Angelic Arbiter R :W:	.60	1.50
11 Anger U :R:	.75	2.00
12 Animar, Soul of Elements M	6.00	15.00
13 Aquastrand Spider C :G:	.10	.25
14 Arbiter of Knollridge R :W:	.40	1.00
15 Archangel of Strife R :W:	.75	2.00
16 Armillary Sphere C	.10	.25
17 Artisan of Kozilek U	.75	2.00
18 Attrition R :K:	.60	1.50
19 Aura Shards U	2.50	6.00
20 Austere Command R :W:	3.00	8.00
21 Avatar of Fury R :R:	.40	1.00
22 Avatar of Slaughter R :R:	.40	1.00
23 Avatar of Woe R :K:	1.50	4.00
24 Awakening Zone R :G:	1.00	2.50
25 Azorius Chancery C	.40	1.00
26 Azorius Guildmage U	.20	.50
27 Baloth Woodcrasher U :G:	.20	.50
28 Barren Moor C	.10	.25
29 Basandra, Battle Seraph R	1.50	4.00
30 Bathe in Light U :W:	.20	.50
31 Bestial Menace U :G:	.20	.50
32 Bladewing the Risen R	.75	2.00
33 Bojuka Bog C	.40	1.00
34 Boros Garrison C	.40	1.00
35 Boros Guildmage U	.20	.50
36 Boros Signet C	.10	.25
37 Brainstorm C :B:	1.50	4.00
38 Brawn U :G:	.40	1.00
39 Breath of Darigaaz U :R:	.20	.50
40 Brion Stoutarm R	.40	1.00
41 Buried Alive U :K:	.75	2.00
42 Butcher of Malakir R :K:	.40	1.00
43 Call the Skybreaker R	.40	1.00
44 Celestial Force R :W:	.40	1.00
45 Chain Reaction R :R:	.40	1.00
46 Champion's Helm R	2.00	5.00
47 Chaos Warp R :R:	5.00	12.00
48 Chartooth Cougar C :R:	.10	.25
49 Chorus of the Conclave R	.40	1.00
50 Chromeshell Crab R :B:	.40	1.00
51 Cleansing Beam U :R:	.20	.50
52 Cobra Trap U :G:	.20	.50
53 Collective Voyage R :G:	1.50	4.00
54 Colossal Might C	.10	.25
55 Comet Storm M :R:	.60	1.50
56 Command Tower C	1.25	3.00
57 Congregate C :W:	.20	.50
58 Conundrum Sphinx R :B:	.40	1.00
59 Court Hussar U :B:	.20	.50
60 Crescendo of War R :W:	.40	1.00
61 Cultivate C :G:	.60	1.50
62 Damia, Sage of Stone M	4.00	10.00
63 Dark Hatchling R :K:	.40	1.00
64 Darksteel Ingot C	.20	.50
65 Deadly Recluse C :G:	.10	.25
66 Deadwood Treefolk U :G:	.30	.75
67 Death by Dragons U :R:	.20	.50
68 Death Mutation U	.20	.50
69 Desecrator Hag C	.10	.25
70 Diabolic Tutor U :K:	.20	.50
71 Dimir Aqueduct C	.40	1.00
72 Dimir Signet C	.40	1.00
73 Disaster Radius R :R:	.40	1.00
74 Dominus of Fealty R	1.25	3.00
75 Doom Blade C :K:	.20	.50
76 Dragon Whelp U :R:	.20	.50
77 Dread Cacodemon R :K:	1.00	2.50
78 Dreadship Reef U	.40	1.00
79 Dreamborn Muse R :B:	.40	1.00
80 Dreamstone Hedron U	.20	.50
81 Duergar Hedge-Mage U	.20	.50
82 Earthquake R :R:	.40	1.00
83 Edric, Spymaster of Trest R	2.00	5.00
84 Electrolyze U	1.00	2.50
85 Elvish Aberration U :G:	.20	.50
86 Eternal Witness U :G:	1.50	4.00
87 Evincar's Justice C :K:	.20	.50
88 Evolving Wilds C	.20	.50
89 Explosive Vegetation U :G:	1.25	3.00
90 Extractor Demon R :K:	.40	1.00
91 Fact or Fiction U :B:	1.25	3.00
92 Fallen Angel R :K:	.40	1.00
93 False Prophet R :W:	.40	1.00
94 Faultgrinder C :R:	.10	.25
95 Fellwar Stone U	.40	1.00
96 Fertilid C :G:	.10	.25
97 Fierce Empath C :G:	.40	1.00
98 Fire // Ice U	.40	1.00
99 Firespout U	.60	1.50
100 Fists of Ironwood C :G:	.20	.50
101 Flametongue Kavu U :R:	.60	1.50
102 Fleshbag Marauder U :K:	.40	1.00
103 Flusterstorm R :B:	12.00	30.00
104 Fog Bank U :B:	.75	2.00
105 Footbottom Feast C :K:	.10	.25
106 Forest (315) L	.10	.25
107 Forest (316) L	.10	.25
108 Forest (317) L	.10	.25
109 Forest (318) L	.10	.25
110 Forgotten Cave C	.10	.25
111 Fungal Reaches U	.30	.75
112 Furnace Whelp U :R:	.20	.50
113 Garruk Wildspeaker M :G:	4.00	10.00
114 Ghave, Guru of Spores M	3.00	8.00
115 Ghostly Prison U :W:	3.00	8.00
116 Goblin Cadets U :R:	.20	.50
117 Golgari Guildmage U	.20	.50
118 Golgari Rot Farm C	.10	.25
119 Golgari Signet C	.10	.25
120 Gomazoa U :B:		.50
121 Grave Pact R :K:	4.00	10.00
122 Gravedigger C :K:	.10	.25
123 Gruul Signet C	.10	.25
124 Gruul Turf C		.25
125 Guard Gomazoa U :B:	.20	.50
126 Gwyllion Hedge-Mage U		.50
127 Harmonize U :G:	1.25	3.00
128 Hex R :K:	.40	1.00
129 Homeward Path R	2.00	5.00
130 Hornet Queen R :G:		2.00
131 Hour of Reckoning R :W:	.40	1.00
132 Howling Mine R		1.50
133 Hull Breach C	.60	1.50
134 Hunting Pack U :G:	.20	.50
135 Hydra Omnivore R :G:	1.50	4.00
136 Insurrection R :R:	.75	2.00
137 Intet, the Dreamer R	.40	1.00
138 Invigorate C :G:	1.25	3.00
139 Island (303) C	.10	.25
140 Island (304) C	.10	.25
141 Island (305) C	.10	.25
142 Island (306) C	.10	.25
143 Izzet Boilerworks C	.40	1.00
144 Izzet Chronarch C	.20	.50
145 Izzet Signet C	.20	.50
146 Jotun Grunt U :W:	.20	.50
147 Journey to Nowhere C :W:	.30	.75
148 Jwar Isle Refuge U	.40	1.00
149 Kaalia of the Vast M	12.00	30.00
150 Karador, Ghost Chieftain M	3.00	8.00
151 Kazandu Refuge U	.20	.50
152 Kodama's Reach C :G:	.40	1.00
153 Krosan Tusker C :G:	.10	.25
154 Lash Out C :R:	.10	.25
155 Lhurgoyf R :G:	.40	1.00
156 Lightkeeper of Emeria U :W:	.20	.50
157 Lightning Greaves U	2.50	6.00
158 Living Death R :K:	1.25	3.00
159 Lonely Sandbar C	.20	.50
160 Magmatic Force R :R:	.75	2.00
161 Magus of the Vineyard R :G:	.40	1.00

162 Malfegor M .60 1.50
163 Mana-Charged Dragon R :R: 1.50 4.00
164 Martyr's Bond R :W: 1.00 2.50
165 Master Warcraft R .40 1.00
166 Memory Erosion R :B: .60 1.50
167 Minds Aglow R :B: 1.00 2.50
168 Molten Slagheap U .20 .50
169 Monk Realist C :W: .10 .25
170 Mortify U .60 1.50
171 Mortivore R :K: .40 1.00
172 Mother of Runes U :W: 3.00 8.00
173 Mountain (311) C .10 .25
174 Mountain (312) C .10 .25
175 Mountain (313) C .10 .25
176 Mountain (314) C .10 .25
177 Mulldrifter C :B: .40 1.00
178 Murmurs from Beyond C :B: .10 .25
179 Nantuko Husk C :K: .10 .25
180 Necrogenesis U .20 .50
181 Nemesis Trap U :K: .20 .50
182 Nezumi Graverobber U :K: .40 1.00
183 Nin, the Pain Artist R 1.50 4.00
184 Nucklavee U .20 .50
185 Numot, the Devastator R .40 1.00
186 Oblation R :W: .60 1.50
187 Oblivion Ring C :W: .20 .50
188 Oblivion Stone R 5.00 12.00
189 Oni of Wild Places U :R: .20 .50
190 Orim's Thunder C :W: .10 .25
191 Oros, the Avenger R .40 1.00
192 Orzhov Basilica C .40 1.00
193 Orzhov Guildmage U .40 1.00
194 Orzhov Signet C .20 .50
195 Path to Exile U :W: 3.00 8.00
196 Patron of the Nezumi R :K: .40 1.00
197 Penumbra Spider C :G: .10 .25
198 Perilous Research U :B: .20 .50
199 Plains (299) C .10 .25
200 Plains (300) C .10 .25
201 Plains (301) C .10 .25
202 Plains (302) C .10 .25
203 Plumeveil U .20 .50
204 Pollen Lullaby U :W: .20 .50
205 Prison Term U :W: .60 1.50
206 Propaganda U :B: 1.50 4.00
207 Prophetic Bolt R .40 1.00
208 Prophetic Prism C .10 .25
209 Punishing Fire U :R: .60 1.50
210 Pyrohemia U :R: .30 .75
211 Rakdos Carnarium C .40 1.00
212 Rakdos Signet C .20 .50
213 Rapacious One U :R: .20 .50
214 Ray of Command C :B: .10 .25
215 Razorjaw Oni U :K: .20 .50
216 Reins of Power R :B: .40 1.00
217 Reiver Demon R :K: .60 1.50
218 Relic Crush C :G: .10 .25
219 Repulse C :B: .10 .25
220 Return to Dust U :W: .75 2.00
221 Riddlekeeper R :B: .60 1.50
222 Righteous Cause U :W: .20 .50
223 Riku of Two Reflections M 4.00 10.00
224 Rise from the Grave U :K: .20 .50
225 Ruhan of the Fomori M .60 1.50
226 Ruination R :R: .40 1.00
227 Rupture Spire C .20 .50
228 Sakura-Tribe Elder C :G: .75 2.00
229 Savage Twister U .20 .50
230 Scattering Stroke U :B: .20 .50
231 Scavenging Ooze R :G: 3.00 8.00
232 Scythe Specter R :K: .40 1.00
233 Secluded Steppe C .20 .50
234 Selesnya Evangel C .10 .25
235 Selesnya Guildmage U .20 .50
236 Selesnya Sanctuary C .40 1.00
237 Selesnya Signet C .20 .50
238 Serra Angel U :W: .20 .50
239 Sewer Nemesis R :K: 2.00 5.00
240 Shared Trauma R :K: .40 1.00
241 Shattered Angel U :W: .20 .50
242 Shriekmaw U :K: .60 1.50
243 Sigil Captain U .20 .50
244 Sign in Blood C :K: .20 .50
245 Simic Growth Chamber C .60 1.50
246 Simic Signet C .20 .50
247 Simic Sky Swallower R .75 2.00
248 Skullbriar, the Walking Grave R 2.50 6.00
249 Skullclamp U 3.00 8.00
250 Skyscribing U :B: .20 .50
251 Slipstream Eel C :B: .10 .25
252 Sol Ring U 2.00 5.00
253 Solemn Simulacrum R 2.50 6.00
254 Soul Snare U :W: .20 .50
255 Spawnwrithe R :G: .40 1.00
256 Spell Crumple U :B: 3.00 8.00
257 Spike Feeder U :G: .30 .75
258 Spitebellows U :R: .20 .50
259 Spurnmage Advocate U :W: .20 .50
260 Squallmonger U :G: .20 .50
261 Stitch Together U :K: .60 1.50
262 Storm Herd R :W: .40 1.00
263 Stranglehold R :R: 5.00 12.00
264 Sulfurous Blast U :R: .20 .50
265 Svogthos, the Restless Tomb U .50
266 Swamp (307) C .10 .25
267 Swamp (308) C .10 .25
268 Swamp (309) C .10 .25
269 Swamp (310) C .10 .25
270 Symbiotic Wurm R :G: .40 1.00
271 Syphon Flesh U :K: .30 .75
272 Syphon Mind C :K: .20 .50
273 Szadek, Lord of Secrets R .40 1.00
274 Tariel, Reckoner of Souls M 4.00 10.00
275 Temple of the False God U .30 .75
276 Teneb, the Harvester R .40 1.00
277 Terminate C .60 1.50
278 Terramorphic Expanse C .10 .25
279 The Mimeoplasm M 3.00 8.00
280 Trade Secrets R :B: .40 1.00
281 Tranquil Thicket C .20 .50
282 Trench Gorger R :B: .40 1.00
283 Tribute to the Wild U :G: .20 .50
284 Triskelavus R .40 1.00
285 Troll Ascetic R :G: .40 1.00
286 Unnerve C :K: .10 .25
287 Valley Rannet C .10 .25
288 Vampire Nighthawk U :K: .60 1.50
289 Vedalken Plotter U :B: .20 .50
290 Vengeful Rebirth U .20 .50
291 Veteran Explorer U :G: 1.50 4.00
292 Vish Kal, Blood Arbiter R .40 1.00
293 Vision Skeins C :B: .10 .25
294 Vivid Crag U .40 1.00
295 Vivid Creek U .40 1.00
296 Vivid Grove U .40 1.00
297 Vivid Marsh U .40 1.00
298 Vivid Meadow U .40 1.00
299 Voice of All U :W: .30 .75
300 Vorosh, the Hunter R .40 1.00
301 Vow of Duty U :W: .20 .50
302 Vow of Flight U :B: .20 .50
303 Vow of Lightning U :R: .20 .50
304 Vow of Malice U :K: .20 .50
305 Vow of Wildness U :G: .20 .50
306 Vulturous Zombie R .60 1.50
307 Wall of Denial U .60 1.50
308 Wall of Omens U :W: 1.00 2.50
309 Whirlpool Whelm C :B: .10 .25
310 Wild Ricochet R :R: .40 1.00
311 Windborn Muse R :W: .60 1.50
312 Windfall U :B: .40 1.00
313 Wonder U :B: .40 1.00
314 Wrecking Ball C .20 .50
315 Wrexial, the Risen Deep M .75 2.00
316 Yavimaya Elder C :G: .60 1.50
317 Zedruu the Greathearted M .75 2.00
318 Zoetic Cavern U .20 .50

2012 Magic The Gathering Commander's Arsenal

COMPLETE SET (18) 60.00 150.00
RELEASED ON NOVEMBER 2, 2012
1 Loyal Retainers U :W: 12.00 30.00
2 Desertion R :B: 4.00 10.00
3 Rhystic Study C :B: 5.00 12.00
4 Decree of Pain R :K: 5.00 12.00
5 Chaos Warp R :R: 8.00 20.00
6 Diaochan, Artful Beauty R :R: 2.00 5.00
7 Sylvan Library R :G: 20.00 50.00
8 Dragonlair Spider R :D: 3.00 8.00
9 Edric, Spymaster of Trest R :D: 2.50 6.00
10 Kaalia of the Vast M :D: 15.00 40.00
11 Maelstrom Wanderer M :D: 10.00 25.00
12 Mirari's Wake R :D: 8.00 20.00
13 The Mimeoplasm M :D: 5.00 12.00
14 Vela the Night-Clad M :D: 2.50 6.00
15 Command Tower C 6.00 15.00
16 Duplicant R 6.00 15.00
17 Mind's Eye R 4.00 10.00
18 Scroll Rack R 12.00 30.00

2013 Magic The Gathering Commander 2013

COMPLETE SET (356) 100.00 200.00
RELEASED ON DECEMBER 20, 2013
1 Act of Authority R :W: .30 .50
2 Aerie Mystics U :W: .15 .25
3 Ajani's Pridemate U :W: .50 .75
4 Angel of Finality R :W: 2.75 3.00
5 Archangel U :W: .15 .25
6 Azorius Herald U :W: .15 .25
7 Cradle of Vitality R :W: .40 .60
8 Curse of the Forsaken U :W: .15 .25
9 Darksteel Mutation U :W: .15 .25
10 Eternal Dragon R :W: .40 .60
11 Fiend Hunter U :W: .10 .25
12 Flickerform R :W: .30 .50
13 Flickerwisp U :W: 3.25 3.75
14 Karmic Guide R :W: 2.75 3.00
15 Kirtar's Wrath R :W: .30 .50
16 Kongming, "Sleeping Dragon" R :W: .30 .50
17 Mirror Entity R :W: 1.00 1.25
18 Mystic Barrier R :W: .30 .50
19 Razor Hippogriff U :W: .15 .25
20 Serene Master R :W: .30 .50
21 Serra Avatar M :W: .75 1.00
22 Stonecloaker U :W: .15 .25
23 Survival Cache U :W: .15 .25
24 Tempt with Glory R :W: .30 .50
25 Unexpectedly Absent R :W: .75 1.15
26 Wall of Reverence R :W: 2.25 2.75
27 Wrath of God R :W: 5.00 6.00
28 Arcane Denial C :B: 5.00 7.00
29 Arcane Melee R :B: .30 .50
30 Augur of Bolas U :B: .20 .30
31 Azami, Lady of Scrolls R :B: .40 .60
32 Blue Sun's Zenith R :B: .75 1.00
33 Borrowing 100,000 Arrows U :B: .15 .25
34 Brilliant Plan U :B: .15 .25
35 Control Magic U :B: .50 .75
36 Curse of Inertia U :B: .15 .25
37 Deceiver Exarch U :B: 1.25 1.75
38 Deep Analysis C :B: .15 .25
39 Dismiss U :B: .15 .25
40 Diviner Spirit U :B: .15 .25
41 Djinn of Infinite Deceits R :B: .30 .50
42 Dungeon Geists R :B: .30 .50
43 Echo Mage R :B: .30 .50
44 Fog Bank U :B: .50 .75
45 Guard Gomazoa U :B: .15 .25
46 Hada Spy Patrol U :B: .15 .25
47 Illusionist's Gambit R :B: .30 .50
48 Jace's Archivist R :B: .30 .50
49 Lu Xun, Scholar General R :B: .30 .50
50 Mnemonic Wall C :B: .15 .25
51 Opportunity U :B: .15 .25
52 Order of Succession R :B: .30 .50
53 Propaganda U :B: 4.00 5.00
54 Prosperity U :B: .15 .25
55 Raven Familiar U :B: .15 .25
56 Sharding Sphinx R :B: .30 .50
57 Skyscribing U :B: .15 .25
58 Stormscape Battlemage U :B: .15 .25
59 Strategic Planning U :B: .25 .40
60 Tempt with Reflections R :B: .30 .50
61 Thornwind Faeries C :B: .15 .25
62 Tidal Force R :B: .30 .50
63 True-Name Nemesis R :B: 10.00 12.00
64 Uyo, Silent Prophet R :B: .30 .50
65 Vision Skeins C :B: .15 .25
66 Wash Out U :B: .50 .75
67 Wonder U :B: .25 .40
68 Annihilate U :K: .15 .25
69 Army of the Damned M :K: 2.00 3.00
70 Baleful Force R :K: .30 .50
71 Curse of Shallow Graves U :K: .15 .25
72 Decree of Pain R :K: 2.00 2.50
73 Dirge of Dread C :K: .15 .25
74 Disciple of Griselbrand U :K: .15 .25
75 Endless Cockroaches R :K: .30 .50
76 Endrek Sahr, Master Breeder R :K: .30 .50
77 Famine U :K: .15 .25
78 Fell Shepherd R :K: .30 .50
79 Greed R :K: .30 .50
80 Hooded Horror U :K: .15 .25
81 Infest U :K: .15 .25
82 Marrow Bats U :K: .15 .25
83 Nightscape Familiar C :K: .15 .25
84 Ophiomancer R :K: 2.25 2.75
85 Phthisis U :K: .15 .25
86 Phyrexian Delver R :K: .30 .50
87 Phyrexian Gargantua U :K: .15 .25
88 Phyrexian Reclamation U :K: .40 .60
89 Price of Knowledge R :K: .30 .50
90 Quagmire Druid C :K: .15 .25
91 Reckless Spite U :K: .15 .25
92 Sanguine Bond R :K: 2.25 2.75
93 Stronghold Assassin R :K: .30 .50
94 Sudden Spoiling R :K: .30 .50
95 Tempt with Immortality R :K: .30 .50
96 Toxic Deluge R :K: 8.00 10.00
97 Vampire Nighthawk U :K: .75 1.00
98 Vile Requiem U :K: .15 .25
99 Viscera Seer C :K: 1.75 2.00
100 Wight of Precinct Six U :K: .30 .50
101 Blood Rites U :R: .15 .25
102 Capricious Efreet R :R: .30 .50
103 Charmbreaker Devils R :R: .30 .50
104 Crater Hellion R :R: .30 .50
105 Curse of Chaos U :R: .15 .25
106 Fireball U :R: .15 .25
107 Fissure Vent C :R: .15 .25
108 From the Ashes R :R: .30 .50
109 Furnace Celebration U :R: .15 .25
110 Goblin Bombardment U :R: .75 1.00
111 Goblin Sharpshooter R :R: 1.50 2.00
112 Guttersnipe U :R: .30 .50
113 Incendiary Command R :R: .30 .50
114 Inferno Titan M :R: .75 1.15
115 Magus of the Arena R :R: .30 .50
116 Mass Mutiny R :R: .30 .50
117 Molten Disaster R :R: .30 .50
118 Rough/Tumble U :R: .15 .25
119 Slice and Dice U :R: .15 .25
120 Spitebellows U :R: .15 .25
121 Stalking Vengeance R :R: .30 .50
122 Starstorm R :R: .30 .50
123 Street Spasm U :R: .15 .25
124 Sudden Demise R :R: .75 1.00
125 Tempt with Vengeance R :R: 4.00 5.00
126 Terra Ravager U :R: .15 .25
127 Tooth and Claw R :R: .30 .50
128 War Cadence U :R: .15 .25
129 Warstorm Surge R :R: .30 .50
130 Where Ancients Tread R :R: .30 .50
131 Widespread Panic R :R: .30 .50
132 Wild Ricochet R :R: .30 .50
133 Witch Hunt R :R: .30 .50
134 Acidic Slime U :G: .15 .25
135 Avenger of Zendikar M :G: 3.00 5.00
136 Baloth Woodcrasher U :G: .15 .25
137 Bane of Progress R :G: 1.25 1.75
138 Brooding Saurian R :G: .30 .50
139 Cultivate C :G: 1.75 2.00
140 Curse of Predation U :G: .15 .25
141 Deadwood Treefolk U :G: .15 .25
142 Drumhunter U :G: .15 .25
143 Elvish Skysweeper C :G: .15 .25
144 Farhaven Elf C :G: .30 .50
145 Fecundity U :G: .30 .50
146 Foster R :G: .30 .50
147 Grazing Gladehart C :G: .15 .25
148 Harmonize U :G: 1.50 1.75
149 Hua Tuo, Honored Physician R :G: .30 .50
150 Hunted Troll R :G: .30 .50
151 Jade Mage U :G: .15 .25
152 Kazandu Tuskcaller R :G: .30 .50
153 Krosan Grip U :G: .75 1.00
154 Krosan Tusker C :G: .15 .25
155 Krosan Warchief U :G: .15 .25
156 Mold Shambler C :G: .15 .25
157 Naya Soulbeast R :G: .30 .50
158 Night Soil C :G: .15 .25
159 One Dozen Eyes U :G: .15 .25
160 Phantom Nantuko R :G: .30 .50
161 Presence of Gond C :G: 1.75 2.25
162 Primal Vigor R :G: 9.00 11.00
163 Rain of Thorns U :G: .15 .25
164 Rampaging Baloths M :G: 1.00 1.25
165 Ravenous Baloth R :G: .30 .50
166 Reincarnation U :G: .15 .25
167 Restore U :G: .15 .25
168 Sakura-Tribe Elder C :G: .40 .60
169 Silklash Spider R :G: .30 .50
170 Slice in Twain U :G: .15 .25
171 Spawning Grounds R :G: .30 .50
172 Spoils of Victory U :G: .15 .25
173 Sprouting Vines C :G: .15 .25
174 Tempt with Discovery R :G: 5.00 7.00
175 Walker of the Grove U :G: .15 .25
176 AEthermage's Touch R :W:/:B: .30 .50
177 Baleful Strix U :B:/:K: 4.00 5.00
178 Behemoth Sledge U :W:/:G: .25 .40
179 Boros Charm U :W:/:R: 2.75 3.25
180 Charnelhoard Wurm R :K:/:R:/:G: .30 .50
181 Crosis's Charm U :B:/:K:/:R: .15 .25
182 Cruel Ultimatum R :B:/:K:/:R: .30 .50
183 Death Grasp R :W:/:K: .30 .50
184 Deathbringer Thoctar R :K:/:R: .30 .50
185 Deepfire Elemental U :K:/:R: .15 .25
186 Derevi, Empyrial Tactician M :W:/:B:/:G: .75 1.00
187 Dromar's Charm U :W:/:B:/:K: .15 .25
188 Fiery Justice R :W:/:R:/:G: .30 .50
189 Filigree Angel R :W:/:B: .30 .50
190 Fires of Yavimaya U :R:/:G: .15 .25
191 Gahiji, Honored One M :W:/:R:/:G: .15 .25
192 Grixis Charm U :B:/:K:/:R: .15 .25
193 Hull Breach C :R:/:G: .15 .25
194 Jeleva, Nephalia's Scourge M :B:/:K:/:R: .15 .25
195 Jund Charm U :K:/:R:/:G: .15 .25
196 Leafdrake Roost U :B:/:G: .15 .25
197 Lim-Dûl's Vault U :B:/:K: .75 1.00
198 Marath, Will of the Wild M :W:/:R:/:G: .15 .25
199 Mayael the Anima M :W:/:R:/:G: .15 .25
200 Naya Charm U :W:/:R:/:G: .15 .25
201 Nekusar, the Mindrazer M :B:/:K:/:R: .15 .25
202 Nivix Guildmage U :B:/:R: .15 .25
203 Oloro, Ageless Ascetic M :W:/:B:/:K: 1.00* 1.50
204 Prossh, Skyraider of Kher M :K:/:R:/:G: .15 .25
205 Rakeclaw Gargantuan C :W:/:R:/:G: .15 .25
206 Roon of the Hidden Realm M :W:/:B:/:G: .15 .25
207 Rubinia Soulsinger R :W:/:B:/:G: .30 .50
208 Savage Twister U :R:/:G: .15 .25
209 Scarland Thrinax U :K:/:R:/:G: .15 .25
210 Sek'Kuar, Deathkeeper R :K:/:R:/:G: .30 .50
211 Selesnya Charm U :W:/:G: .25 .40
212 Sharuum the Hegemon M :W:/:B:/:K: .15 .25
213 Shattergang Brothers M :K:/:R:/:G: .15 .25
214 Skyward Eye Prophets U :W:/:B:/:G: .15 .25
215 Soul Manipulation C :B:/:K: .15 .25
216 Spellbreaker Behemoth R :R:/:G: .40 .60
217 Sphinx of the Steel Wind M :W:/:B:/:K: .75 1.00
218 Spinal Embrace R :B:/:K: .30 .50
219 Sprouting Thrinax U :K:/:R:/:G: .15 .25
220 Sydri, Galvanic Genius M :W:/:B:/:K: .15 .25
221 Thraximundar M :B:/:K:/:R: .15 .25
222 Tidehollow Strix C :B:/:K: .15 .25
223 Tower Gargoyle U :W:/:B:/:K: .15 .25
224 Valley Rannet C :R:/:G: .15 .25
225 Vizkopa Guildmage U :W:/:K: .15 .25
226 Winged Coatl C :B:/:G: .15 .25
227 Augury Adept R :W:/:B: .30 .50
228 Divinity of Pride R :W:/:K: 2.00 2.50
229 Golgari Guildmage U :K:/:G: .15 .25
230 Mistmeadow Witch U :W:/:B: .15 .25
231 Murkfiend Liege R :B:/:G: 1.75 2.00
232 Selesnya Guildmage U :W:/:G: .15 .25
233 Spiteful Visions R :K:/:R: .30 .50
234 Thopter Foundry U :W:/:B:/:K: 2.75 3.00
235 Armillary Sphere C .15 .25
236 Azorius Keyrune U .15 .25
237 Basalt Monolith U 1.25 1.75
238 Carnage Altar U .15 .25
239 Conjurer's Closet R .75 1.15
240 Crawlspace R 3.25 3.75
241 Darksteel Ingot U .25 .40
242 Druidic Satchel R .30 .50
243 Eye of Doom R .30 .50
244 Jar of Eyeballs R .30 .50
245 Leonin Bladetrap U .15 .25
246 Mirari R .30 .50
247 Myr Battlesphere R .30 .50
248 Nevinyrral's Disk R 1.25 1.75
249 Nihil Spellbomb C .25 .40
250 Obelisk of Esper C .15 .25
251 Obelisk of Grixis C .15 .25
252 Obelisk of Jund C .15 .25
253 Pilgrim's Eye C .15 .25
254 Plague Boiler R .30 .50
255 Pristine Talisman C .15 .25
256 Seer's Sundial R .30 .50
257 Selesnya Signet C .15 .25
258 Simic Signet C .15 .25
259 Sol Ring U 2.75 3.00
260 Spine of Ish Sah R .30 .50
261 Sun Droplet U 1.25 1.75
262 Surveyor's Scope R .30 .50
263 Swiftfoot Boots U .40 .60
264 Sword of the Paruns R .30 .50
265 Temple Bell R .30 .50
266 Thousand-Year Elixir R 4.00 5.00
267 Thunderstaff U .15 .25
268 Tower of Fortunes R .30 .50
269 Viseling U .15 .25
270 Wayfarer's Bauble C .15 .25
271 Well of Lost Dreams R 2.00 2.50
272 Akoum Refuge U .15 .25
273 Arcane Sanctum U 2.25 2.75
274 Azorius Chancery C .25 .40
275 Azorius Guildgate C .15 .25
276 Bant Panorama C .15 .25
277 Barren Moor C .15 .25
278 Bojuka Bog C 1.00 1.50
279 Boros Garrison C .30 .50
280 Boros Guildgate C .15 .25
281 Command Tower C 1.50 1.75
282 Contested Cliffs R .30 .50
283 Crumbling Necropolis U .75 1.15
284 Dimir Guildgate C .15 .25
285 Drifting Meadow C .15 .25
286 Esper Panorama C .15 .25
287 Evolving Wilds C .15 .25
288 Faerie Conclave U 1.25 1.75
289 Forgotten Cave C .15 .25
290 Golgari Guildgate C .15 .25
291 Golgari Rot Farm C .25 .40

292 Grim Backwoods R .30 .50
293 Grixis Panorama C .15 .25
294 Gruul Guildgate C .15 .25
295 Homeward Path R 6.00 8.00
296 Izzet Boilerworks C .15 .25
297 Izzet Guildgate C .15 .25
298 Jund Panorama C .15 .25
299 Jungle Shrine U 1.00 1.25
300 Jwar Isle Refuge U .30 .50
301 Kazandu Refuge U .15 .25
302 Khalni Garden C .15 .25
303 Kher Keep R .75 1.00
304 Llanowar Reborn U .25 .40
305 Lonely Sandbar C .15 .25
306 Molten Slagheap U .15 .25
307 Mosswort Bridge R .75 1.15
308 Naya Panorama C .15 .25
309 New Benalia U .15 .25
310 Opal Palace C .15 .25
311 Orzhov Basilica C .30 .50
312 Orzhov Guildgate C .15 .25
313 Rakdos Carnarium C .20 .35
314 Rakdos Guildgate C .15 .25
315 Rupture Spire C .15 .25
316 Saltcrusted Steppe U .15 .25
317 Savage Lands U 1.00 1.50
318 Seaside Citadel U 1.75 2.25
319 Secluded Steppe C .15 .25
320 Sejiri Refuge U .15 .25
321 Selesnya Guildgate C .15 .25
322 Selesnya Sanctuary C .20 .35
323 Simic Guildgate C .15 .25
324 Slippery Karst C .15 .25
325 Smoldering Crater C .15 .25
326 Springjack Pasture R .75 1.00
327 Temple of the False God U .25 .40
328 Terramorphic Expanse C .15 .25
329 Tranquil Thicket C .15 .25
330 Transguild Promenade C .15 .25
331 Urza's Factory U .15 .25
332 Vitu-Ghazi, the City-Tree U .15 .25
333 Vivid Crag U .25 .40
334 Vivid Creek U .25 .40
335 Vivid Grove U .25 .40
336 Vivid Marsh U .25 .40
337 Plains L .15 .25
338 Plains L .15 .25
339 Plains L .15 .25
340 Plains L .15 .25
341 Island L .15 .25
342 Island L .15 .25
343 Island L .15 .25
344 Island L .15 .25
345 Swamp L .15 .25
346 Swamp L .15 .25
347 Swamp L .15 .25
348 Swamp L .15 .25
349 Mountain L .15 .25
350 Mountain L .15 .25
351 Mountain L .15 .25
352 Mountain L .15 .25
353 Forest L .15 .25
354 Forest L .15 .25
355 Forest L .15 .25
356 Forest L .15 .25

2014 Magic The Gathering Commander 2014

COMPLETE SET (366) 290.00 380.00
RELEASED ON NOVEMBER 7, 2014
63 Adarkar Valkyrie R :W: .40 .60
64 Afterlife U :W: .15 .25
1 Angel of the Dire Hour R :W: 3.50 4.00
2 Angelic Field Marshal R :W: .25 .40
65 Armistice R :W: .25 .40
3 Benevolent Offering R :W: .25 .40
66 Brave the Elements U :W: .25 .40
67 Cathars' Crusade R :W: 1.50 1.75
68 Celestial Crusader U :W: .15 .25
4 Comeuppance R :W: .50 .75
69 Condemn U :W: .15 .25
5 Containment Priest R :W: 8.00 12.00
70 Decree of Justice R :W: .25 .40
6 Deploy to the Front R :W: .25 .40
7 Fell the Mighty R :W: .25 .40
71 Flickerwisp U :W: .15 .25
72 Geist-Honored Monk R :W: .25 .40
73 Gift of Estates U :W: .40 .60
74 Grand Abolisher R :W: 4.00 5.00
8 Hallowed Spiritkeeper R :W: .30 .50
9 Jazal Goldmane M :W: .75 1.00
75 Kemba, Kha Regent R :W: .25 .40
76 Kor Sanctifiers C :W: .10 .20
77 Marshal's Anthem R :W: .25 .40
78 Martial Coup R :W: 1.50 1.75
79 Mentor of the Meek R :W: 1.00 1.50
80 Midnight Haunting U :W: .15 .25
81 Mobilization R :W: .25 .40
10A Nahiri, the Lithomancer M :W: 4.00 6.00
10B Nahiri, the Lithomancer (Oversized) M :W: 4.00 6.00
82 Nomads' Assembly R :W: .25 .40
83 Oblation R :W: .25 .40
84 Requiem Angel R :W: .25 .40
85 Return to Dust U :W: 1.75 2.00
86 Sacred Mesa R :W: .25 .40
87 Serra Avatar M :W: .75 1.00
88 Silverblade Paladin R :W: .40 .60
89 Skyhunter Skirmisher U :W: .15 .25
90 Spectral Procession U :W: .25 .40
91 Sun Titan M :W: 2.00 2.50
92 Sunblast Angel R :W: .40 .60
93 True Conviction R :W: 1.50 1.75
94 Twilight Shepherd R :W: .25 .40
95 White Sun's Zenith R :W: .25 .40
96 Whitemane Lion C :W: .10 .20
97 Wing Shards U :W: .15 .25
11 AEther Gale R :B: .25 .40
98 Azure Mage U :B: .15 .25
12 Breaching Leviathan R :B: .25 .40
99 Brine Elemental U :B: .15 .25
100 Cackling Counterpart R :B: .25 .40
101 Call to Mind U :B: .15 .25
102 Compulsive Research C :B: .10 .20
103 Concentrate U :B: .15 .25
104 Cyclonic Rift R :B: 5.00 7.00
105 Deep-Sea Kraken R :B: .40 .60
106 Dismiss U :B: .15 .25
107 Distorting Wake R :B: .25 .40
13 Domineering Will R :B: .25 .40
14 Dulcet Sirens R :B: .25 .40
108 Exclude C :B: .20 .30
109 Fathom Seer C :B: .10 .20
110 Fog Bank U :B: .75 .25
111 Fool's Demise U :B: .15 .25
112 Frost Titan M :B: .75 1.00
113 Hoverguard Sweepers R :B: .25 .40
114 Infinite Reflection R :B: .25 .40
15 Intellectual Offering R :B: .25 .40
115 Into the Roil C :B: .10 .20
116 Ixidron R :B: .25 .40
117 Lorthos, the Tidemaker M :B: .75 1.00
118 Mulldrifter C :B: .40 .60
119 Phyrexian Ingester R :B: .25 .40
120 Pongify U :B: 1.00 1.25
16 Reef Worm R :B: 1.00 1.25
121 Riptide Survivor U :B: .15 .25
122 Rite of Replication R :B: 1.25 1.75
123 Rush of Knowledge C :B: .10 .20
124 Sea Gate Oracle C :B: .20 .30
125 Shaper Parasite C :B: .10 .20
126 Sphinx of Jwar Isle R :B: .25 .40
127 Sphinx of Magosi R :B: .25 .40
128 Sphinx of Uthuun R :B: .25 .40
17 Stitcher Geralf M :B: 1.00 1.25
18 Stormsurge Kraken R :B: .25 .40
129 Stroke of Genius R :B: .25 .40
19A Teferi, Temporal Archmage M :B: 12.00 15.00
19B Teferi, Temporal Archmage (Oversized) M :B: 7.00 9.00
130 Turn to Frog U :B: .15 .25
20 Well of Ideas R :B: .40 .60
131 Willbender U :B: .15 .25
132 Abyssal Persecutor M :K: 1.25 1.75
133 AEther Snap R :K: .25 .40
134 Annihilate U :K: .15 .25
135 Bad Moon R :K: .50 .75
136 Black Sun's Zenith R :K: 1.50 2.00
137 Bloodgift Demon R :K: .50 .75
138 Butcher of Malakir R :K: .25 .40
139 Crypt Ghast R :K: 2.25 2.75
21 Demon of Wailing Agonies R :K: .25 .40
140 Disciple of Bolas R :K: .50 .75
141 Drana, Kalastria Bloodchief R :K: .75 1.00
142 Dread Return U :K: .75 1.00
143 Dregs of Sorrow R :K: .25 .40
144 Evernight Shade U :K: .15 .25
22 Flesh Carver R :K: .25 .40
23 Ghoulcaller Gisa M :K: 7.00 9.00
145 Grave Titan M :K: 5.00 7.00
146 Gray Merchant of Asphodel C :K: .20 .30
24 Infernal Offering R :K: .25 .40
147 Liliana's Reaver R :K: .40 .60
148 Magus of the Coffers R :K: .50 .75
25 Malicious Affliction R :K: 1.00 1.25
149 Morkrut Banshee U :K: .15 .25
150 Mutilate R :K: .40 .60
151 Nantuko Shade R :K: .25 .40
26 Necromantic Selection R :K: .25 .40
152 Nekrataal U :K: .15 .25
27A Ob Nixilis of the Black Oath M :K: 6.00 7.50
27B Ob Nixilis of the Black Oath (Oversized) M :K: 6.00 7.50
28 Overseer of the Damned R :K: 1.75 2.15
153 Pestilence Demon R :K: .25 .40
154 Phyrexian Gargantua U :K: .15 .25
155 Pontiff of Blight R :K: .25 .40
156 Profane Command R :K: .30 .50
157 Promise of Power R :K: .25 .40
29 Raving Dead R :K: .50 .75
158 Read the Bones C :K: .10 .20
159 Reaper from the Abyss M :K: .75 1.00
160 Shriekmaw U :K: .75 1.00
161 Sign in Blood C :K: .10 .20
162 Skeletal Scrying U :K: .15 .25
163 Skirsdag High Priest R :K: .30 .50
30 Spoils of Blood R :K: .25 .40
164 Sudden Spoiling R :K: .40 .60
165 Syphon Mind C :K: .10 .20
166 Tendrils of Corruption C :K: .10 .20
167 Tragic Slip C :K: .20 .30
168 Vampire Hexmage U :K: .15 .25
169 Victimize U :K: .15 .25
31 Wake the Dead R :K: .30 .50
170 Xathrid Demon M :K: .50 .75
171 Beetleback Chief U :R: .15 .25
32 Bitter Feud R :R: .25 .40
172 Blasphemous Act R :R: 2.75 3.00
173 Bogardan Hellkite M :R: .75 1.00
174 Chaos Warp R :R: 3.00 3.50
33A Daretti, Scrap Savant M :R: 2.50 3.00
33B Daretti, Scrap Savant (Oversized) M :R: 2.50 3.00
34 Dualcaster Mage R :R: 1.00 1.25
175 Faithless Looting C :R: .40 .60
35 Feldon of the Third Path M :R: 1.00 1.25
176 Flametongue Kavu U :R: .15 .25
177 Goblin Welder R :R: 1.00 1.50
178 Hoard-Smelter Dragon R :R: .25 .40
36 Impact Resonance R :R: .25 .40
37 Incite Rebellion R :R: .25 .40
179 Ingot Chewer C :R: .30 .50
180 Magmaquake R :R: .25 .40
38 Scrap Mastery R :R: .25 .40
181 Spitebellows U :R: .15 .25
182 Starstorm R :R: .25 .40
183 Tuktuk the Explorer R :R: .25 .40
39 Tyrant's Familiar R :R: .50 .75
40 Volcanic Offering R :R: .25 .40
41 Warmonger Hellkite R :R: .25 .40
184 Whipflare U :R: .25 .40
185 Word of Seizing R :R: .25 .40
186 Beastmaster Ascension R :G: 1.00 1.50
187 Collective Unconscious R :G: .25 .40
42 Creeperhulk R :G: .25 .40
188 Desert Twister U :G: .15 .25
189 Drove of Elves U :G: .30 .50
190 Elvish Archdruid R :G: 2.75 3.00
191 Elvish Mystic C :G: .60 1.00
192 Elvish Skysweeper C :G: .10 .20
193 Elvish Visionary C :G: .10 .20
194 Essence Warden C :G: 1.25 1.75
195 Ezuri, Renegade Leader R :G: 4.00 5.00
196 Farhaven Elf C :G: .30 .50
197 Fresh Meat R :G: .25 .40
43A Freyalise, Llanowar's Fury M :G: 10.00 12.00
43B Freyalise, Llanowar's Fury (Oversized) M :G: 10.00 12.00
44 Grave Sifter R :G: .25 .40
198 Grim Flowering U :G: .15 .25
199 Harrow C :G: .10 .20
200 Hunting Triad U :G: .15 .25
201 Immaculate Magistrate R :G: 2.25 2.75
202 Imperious Perfect U :G: 2.00 2.50
203 Joraga Warcaller R :G: 2.75 3.15
45 Lifeblood Hydra C :G: 2.00 2.50
204 Llanowar Elves C :G: .30 .50
205 Lys Alana Huntmaster C :G: .30 .50
206 Masked Admirers R :G: .25 .40
207 Overrun U :G: .15 .25
208 Overwhelming Stampede R :G: .25 .40
209 Praetor's Counsel M :G: 1.50 2.00
210 Priest of Titania C :G: 3.00 4.00
211 Primordial Sage R :G: .25 .40
212 Rampaging Baloths M :G: 1.00 1.15
213 Reclamation Sage U :G: .15 .25
46 Siege Behemoth R :G: .50 .75
214 Silklash Spider R :G: .25 .40
47 Song of the Dryads R :G: 4.00 5.00
215 Soul of the Harvest R :G: .40 .60
48 Sylvan Offering R :G: .25 .40
216 Sylvan Ranger C :G: .10 .20
217 Sylvan Safekeeper R :G: .40 .60
218 Terastodon R :G: .25 .40
219 Thornweald Archer C :G: .10 .20
49 Thunderfoot Baloth R :G: 2.00 2.25
220 Timberwatch Elf C :G: .25 .40
50 Titania, Protector of Argoth M :G: 5.00 7.00
221 Titania's Chosen U :G: .15 .25
222 Tornado Elemental R :G: .25 .40
51 Wave of Vitriol R :G: .25 .40
223 Wellwisher C :G: 1.25 1.75
224 Whirlwind R :G: .25 .40
225 Wolfbriar Elemental R :G: .25 .40
52 Wolfcaller's Howl C :G: .10 .20
226 Wood Elves C :G: .10 .20
227 Wren's Run Packmaster R :G: .25 .40
59 Arcane Lighthouse U :L: 2.50 3.00
284 Barren Moor C :L: .10 .20
286 Buried Ruin U :L: .50 .25
287 Coral Atoll U :L: .15 .25
288 Crypt of Agadeem R :L: .40 .60
289 Crystal Vein U :L: .25 .40
290 Darksteel Citadel U :L: .50 .25
60 Flamekin Village R :L: .50 .75
296 Forgotten Cave C :L: .10 .20
297 Gargoyle Castle R :L: .25 .40
298 Ghost Quarter U :L: 1.00 .25
299 Great Furnace C :L: .50 .75
61 Myriad Landscape U :L: 3.00 3.25
305 Oran-Rief, the Vastwood R :L: 1.00 1.25
307 Polluted Mire C :L: .10 .20
310 Secluded Steppe C :L: .10 .20
314 Temple of the False God U :L: .25 .40
315 Terramorphic Expanse C :L: .10 .20
316 Tranquil Thicket C :L: .10 .20
317 Zoetic Cavern U :L: .15 .25
228 Argentum Armor R :A: .75 1.00
229 Bonehoard R :A: .25 .40
231 Bottle Gnomes U :A: .15 .25
232 Burnished Hart U :A: .30 .50
233 Caged Sun R :A: 4.00 5.00
234 Cathodion U :A: .15 .25
235 Charcoal Diamond U :A: .15 .25
236 Dreamstone Hedron U :A: .15 .25
237 Emerald Medallion R :A: .75 1.00
239 Everflowing Chalice U :A: .25 .40
240 Fire Diamond U :A: .15 .25
241 Ichor Wellspring C :A: .20 .30
242 Jalum Tome R :A: .25 .40
244 Junk Diver R :A: .25 .40
245 Lashwrithe R :A: .30 .50
246 Liquimetal Coating U :A: .15 .25
248 Marble Diamond U :A: .15 .25
250 Mind Stone U :A: .15 .25
252 Moss Diamond U :A: .15 .25
256 Myr Sire C :A: .10 .20
258 Palladium Myr U :A: .75 1.00
259 Panic Spellbomb C :A: .10 .20
260 Pearl Medallion R :A: 2.00 2.25
261 Pentavus R :A: .25 .40
263 Predator, Flagship R :A: .25 .40
265 Ruby Medallion R :A: 2.00 2.50
266 Sapphire Medallion R :A: 2.75 3.00
268 Skullclamp U :A: 2.00 2.25
269 Sky Diamond U :A: .15 .25
271 Solemn Simulacrum R :A: 4.00 4.50
273 Steel Hellkite R :A: .75 1.00
276 Sword of Vengeance R :A: .40 .60
277 Thran Dynamo U :A: 6.00 .25
280 Ur-Golem's Eye C :A: .10 .20
282 Worn Powerstone U :A: .40 .60
62 Artisan of Kozilek U .30 .25
53 Assault Suit U .15 .25
285 Bojuka Bog C 1.25 1.75
230 Bosh, Iron Golem R .25 .40
54 Commander's Sphere C 1.50 2.00
55 Crown of Doom R .25 .40
291 Dormant Volcano U .15 .25
292 Drifting Meadow C .10 .20
293 Emeria, the Sky Ruin R 3.50 4.00
238 Epochrasite U .15 .25
294 Everglades U .15 .25
295 Evolving Wilds C .10 .20
334 Forest (334) C .10 .20
335 Forest (335) C .10 .20
336 Forest (336) C .10 .20
337 Forest (337) C .10 .20
300 Haunted Fengraf C .10 .20
301 Havenwood Battleground U .15 .25
322 Island (322) C .10 .20
323 Island (323) C .10 .20
324 Island (324) C .10 .20
325 Island (325) C .10 .20
243 Jet Medallion R 2.50 2.75
302 Jungle Basin U .15 .25
303 Karoo U .15 .25
304 Lonely Sandbar C .10 .20
56 Loreseeker's Stone U .15 .25
247 Loxodon Warhammer R .50 .75
249 Mask of Memory U .15 .25
57 Masterwork of Ingenuity R 1.00 1.50
251 Moonsilver Spear R .25 .40
330 Mountain (330) C .10 .20
331 Mountain (331) C .10 .20
332 Mountain (332) C .10 .20
333 Mountain (333) C .10 .20
253 Mycosynth Wellspring C .10 .20
254 Myr Battlesphere R .40 .60
255 Myr Retriever U .15 .25
257 Nevinyrral's Disk R 1.50 1.75
306 Phyrexia's Core U .15 .25
262 Pilgrim's Eye C .10 .20
318 Plains (318) C .10 .20
319 Plains (319) C .10 .20
320 Plains (320) C .10 .20
321 Plains (321) C .10 .20
264 Pristine Talisman C .10 .20
308 Reliquary Tower U 2.75 3.00
309 Remote Isle C .10 .20
267 Seer's Sundial R .25 .40
311 Slippery Karst C .10 .20
312 Smoldering Crater C .10 .20
270 Sol Ring U 2.75 3.00
272 Spine of Ish Sah R .25 .40
274 Strata Scythe R .25 .40
326 Swamp (326) C .10 .20
327 Swamp (327) C .10 .20
328 Swamp (328) C .10 .20
329 Swamp (329) C .10 .20
275 Swiftfoot Boots U .30 .50
313 Tectonic Edge U 1.75 2.00
278 Tormod's Crypt U .15 .25
279 Trading Post R .25 .40
58 Unstable Obelisk U .15 .25
281 Wayfarer's Bauble C .10 .20
283 Wurmcoil Engine M 12.00 15.00

2014 Magic The Gathering Commander 2014 Tokens

1 Angel
2 Cat
3 Goat
4 Kor Soldier
5 Pegasus
6 Soldier
7 Spirit
8 Fish
9 Kraken
10 Whale
11 Zombie
12 Demon
13 Demon
14 Germ
15 Horror
16 Zombie
17 Goblin
18 Ape
19 Beast
20 Beast
21 Elemental
22 Elephant
23 Elf Druid
24 Elf Warrior
25 Treefolk
26 Wolf
27 Gargoyle
28 Myr
29 Pentavite
30 Stoneforged Blade
31 Tuktuk the Returned
32 Wurm
33 Wurm
34 Teferi, Temporal Archmage Emblem
35 Ob Nixilis of the Black Oath Emblem
36 Daretti, Scrap Savant Emblem

2015 Magic The Gathering Commander 2015

COMPLETE SET (368) 200.00 300.00
RELEASED ON NOVEMBER 13, 2015
1 Bastion Protector R :W: 4.00 6.00
2 Dawnbreak Reclaimer R :W: .25 .40
3 Grasp of Fate R :W: 3.00 4.00
4 Herald of the Host U :W: .15 .25
5 Kalemne's Captain R :W: .25 .40
6 Oreskos Explorer U :W: .25 .40
7 Righteous Confluence R :W: .75 1.00
8 Shielded by Faith R :W: 2.00 2.50
9 Aethersnatch R :B: .50 .75
10 Broodbirth Viper U :B: .15 .25

11 Gigantoplasm R :B: .25 .40
12 Illusory Ambusher U :B: .20 .30
13 Mirror Match U :B: .15 .25
14 Mystic Confluence R :B: 8.00 10.00
15 Synthetic Destiny R :B: .25 .40
16 Banshee of the Dread Choir U :K: .15 .25
17 Corpse Augur U :K: .20 .30
18 Daxos's Torment R :K: .25 .40
19 Deadly Tempest R :K: .50 .75
20 Dread Summons R :K: .75 1.00
21 Scourge of Nel Toth R :K: 1.25 1.75
22 Elephant .15 .25
Saproling
23 Elemental Shaman .15 .25
Shapeshifter
24 Seal of Doom C :K: .10 .20
25 Breath of Darigaaz U :R: .15 .25
26 Curse of the Nightly Hunt U :R: .15 .25
27 Fiery Confluence R :R: 7.00 9.00
28 Fumiko the Lowblood R :R: .25 .40
29 Hammerfist Giant R :R: .25 .40
30 Hostility R :R: .25 .40
31 Mizzix's Mastery R :R: 2.50 4.00
32 Sunrise Sovereign R :R: .25 .40
33 Vandalblast U :R: .50 .75
34 Warstorm Surge R :R: .25 .40
35 Word of Seizing R :R: .25 .40
36 Caller of the Pack U :G: .15 .25
37 Chameleon Colossus R :G: .25 .40
38 Krosan Grip U :G: .75 1.00
39 Ohran Viper R :G: .25 .40
40 Rampant Growth C :G: .10 .20
41 Thelonite Hermit R :G: .25 .40
42 Tribute to the Wild U :G: .15 .25
43 Wall of Blossoms U :G: .75 1.00
44 Biomantic Mastery R :M: .25 .40
45 Epic Experiment M :M: .50 .75
46 Etherium-Horn Sorcerer R :M: .25 .40
47 Ezuri, Claw of Progress M :M: 4.00 4.50
48 Golgari Charm U :M: .25 .40
49 Jarad, Golgari Lich Lord M :M: .75 1.00
50 Kalemne, Disciple of Iroas M :M: .75 1.00
51 Snakeform C :M: .10 .20
52 Golgari Signet C :A: .10 .20
53 Izzet Signet C :A: .10 .20
54 Lightning Greaves U :A: 3.00 4.00
55 Seer's Sundial R :A: .25 .40
56 Thought Vessel C :A: 2.50 3.50
57 Ajani's Chosen R :W: .25 .40
58 Angel of Serenity M :W: 1.00 1.25
59 Arbiter of Knollridge R :W: .25 .40
60 Aura of Silence U :W: 1.00 1.25
61 Banishing Light U :W: .15 .25
62 Cage of Hands C :W: .10 .20
63 Celestial Ancient R :W: .25 .40
64 Celestial Archon R :W: .25 .40
65 Crib Swap U :W: .15 .25
66 Dawn to Dusk U :W: .15 .25
67 Dawnglare Invoker C :W: .10 .20
68 Dictate of Heliod R :W: .25 .40
69 Faith's Fetters C :W: .10 .20
70 Ghostblade Eidolon U :W: .15 .25
71 Jareth, Leonine Titan R :W: .25 .40
72 Karmic Justice R :W: 1.00 1.50
73 Kor Sanctifiers C :W: .10 .20
74 Marshal's Anthem R :W: .25 .40
75 Mesa Enchantress R :W: .25 .40
76 Monk Idealist U :W: .15 .25
77 Open the Vaults R :W: .75 1.00
78 Orim's Thunder C :W: .10 .20
79 Seal of Cleansing C :W: .10 .20
80 Sigil of the Empty Throne R :W: .25 .40
81 Silent Sentinel R :W: .25 .40
82 Sun Titan M :W: 2.50 3.25
83 Victory's Herald R :W: .25 .40
84 Vow of Duty U :W: .15 .25
85 Aetherize U :B: .15 .25
86 Bident of Thassa R :B: .25 .40
87 Blatant Thievery R :B: 1.00 1.25
88 Blue Sun's Zenith R :B: .75 1.00
89 Blustersquall U :B: .15 .25
90 Brainstorm C :B: 1.00 1.25
91 Day of the Dragons R :B: .25 .40
92 Dominate U :B: .15 .25
93 Echoing Truth C :B: .10 .20
94 Fact or Fiction U :B: .30 .50
95 Jace's Archivist R :B: .25 .40
96 Lone Revenant R :B: .25 .40
97 Mulldrifter U :B: .40 .60
98 Mystic Retrieval U :B: .15 .25
99 Ninja of the Deep Hours C :B: .75 1.25
100 Plaxmanta U :B: .15 .25
101 Preordain C :B: 1.75 2.00
102 Rapid Hybridization U :B: .30 .50
103 Reins of Power R :B: .25 .40
104 Repeal C :B: .10 .20
105 Rite of Replication R :B: 1.50 2.00
106 Sleep U :B: .15 .25
107 Stolen Goods R :B: .25 .40
108 Stroke of Genius R :B: .25 .40
109 Talrand, Sky Summoner R :B: .75 1.00
110 Thought Reflection R :B: .25 .40
111 Windfall U :B: 1.50 2.00
112 Altar's Reap C :K: .10 .20
113 Ambition's Cost U :K: .15 .25
114 Ancient Craving R :K: .25 .40
115 Barter in Blood U :K: .15 .25
116 Black Market R :K: 4.00 6.00
117 Blood Bairn C :K: .10 .20
118 Butcher of Malakir R :K: .25 .40
119 Champion of Stray Souls M :K: .50 .75
120 Diabolic Servitude U :K: .15 .25
121 Doomwake Giant R :K: .25 .40
122 Dreadbringer Lampads C :K: .10 .20
123 Eater of Hope R :K: .25 .40
124 Extractor Demon R :K: .25 .40
125 Fallen Ideal U :K: .15 .25
126 Fate Unraveler R :K: .25 .40
127 Gild R :K: .25 .40
128 Grave Peril C :K: .10 .20
129 Nighthowler R :K: .25 .40
130 Phyrexian Arena R :K: 3.00 5.00
131 Phyrexian Plaguelord R :K: .25 .40
132 Phyrexian Rager C :K: .10 .20
133 Phyrexian Reclamation U :K: .30 .50
134 Rise from the Grave U :K: .15 .25
135 Angel .15 .25
Knight
136 Bear .15 .25
Spider
137 Beast .15 .25
Snake
138 Cat .15 .25
Zombie
139 Dragon .15 .25
Dragon
140 Drake .15 .25
Elemental
141 Experience .15 .25
142 Sever the Bloodline R :K: .25 .40
143 Shriekmaw U :K: .75 1.00
144 Underworld Connections R :K: .25 .40
145 Victimize U :K: .15 .25
146 Vow of Malice U :K: .15 .25
147 Wretched Confluence R :K: .75 1.00
148 Thief of Blood U :K: .15 .25
149 Act of Aggression U :R: .15 .25
150 Awaken the Sky Tyrant R :R: .25 .40
151 Borderland Behemoth R :R: .25 .40
152 Chain Reaction R :R: .25 .40
153 Charmbreaker Devils R :R: .25 .40
154 Comet Storm M :R: .75 1.00
155 Desolation Giant R :R: .25 .40
156 Desperate Ravings U :R: .15 .25
157 Disaster Radius R :R: .25 .40
158 Dragon Mage R :R: .50 .75
159 Dream Pillager R :R: .25 .40
160 Earthquake R :R: .25 .40
161 Faithless Looting C :R: .40 .60
162 Fall of the Hammer C :R: .10 .20
163 Hamletback Goliath R :R: .25 .40
164 Hunted Dragon R :R: .25 .40
165 Inferno Titan M :R: 1.00 1.25
166 Magma Giant R :R: .25 .40
167 Magmaquake R :R: .25 .40
168 Magus of the Wheel R :R: 3.00 4.00
169 Meteor Blast U :R: .15 .25
170 Mizzium Mortars R :R: .25 .40
171 Rite of the Raging Storm U :R: .15 .25
172 Stinkdrinker Daredevil C :R: .10 .20
173 Stoneshock Giant U :R: .15 .25
174 Taurean Mauler R :R: .50 .75
175 Thundercloud Shaman U :R: .15 .25
176 Urza's Rage R :R: .25 .40
177 Warchief Giant U :R: .15 .25
178 Acidic Slime U :G: .15 .25
179 Arachnogenesis R :G: 4.00 6.00
180 Arbor Colossus R :G: .25 .40
181 Bane of Progress R :G: 1.50 2.00
182 Beastmaster Ascension R :G: 1.00 1.50
183 Bloodspore Thrinax R :G: 4.00 6.00
184 Caller of the Claw R :G: .25 .40
185 Centaur Vinecrasher R :G: .50 .75
186 Cloudthresher R :G: .25 .40
187 Cobra Trap U :G: .15 .25
188 Desert Twister U :G: .15 .25
189 Elvish Visionary C :G: .10 .20
190 Eternal Witness U :G: 3.50 5.00
191 Experiment One U :G: 1.25 1.75
192 Ezuri's Predation R :G: .25 .40
193 Forgotten Ancient R :G: .75 1.00
194 Great Oak Guardian U :G: .15 .25
195 Indrik Stomphowler U :G: .15 .25
196 Kessig Cagebreakers R :G: .25 .40
197 Kodama's Reach C :G: 1.25 1.75
198 Loaming Shaman R :G: .25 .40
199 Mulch C :G: .10 .20
200 Mycoloth R :G: 1.50 2.00
201 Noble Quarry U :G: .15 .25
202 Overrun U :G: .15 .25
203 Overwhelming Stampede R :G: .25 .40
204 Patagia Viper U :G: .15 .25
205 Pathbreaker Ibex R :G: 4.00 6.00
206 Primal Growth C :G: .10 .20
207 Sakura-Tribe Elder C :G: .30 .50
208 Satyr Wayfinder C :G: .10 .20
209 Skullwinder U :G: .25 .40
210 Spider Spawning U :G: .15 .25
211 Stingerfling Spider U :G: .15 .25
212 Terastodon R :G: .25 .40
213 Viridian Emissary C :G: .10 .20
214 Viridian Zealot R :G: .25 .40
215 Wood Elves C :G: .10 .20
216 Anya, Merciless Angel M :M: 1.50 2.00
217 Arjun, the Shifting Flame M :M: .75 1.00
218 Call the Skybreaker R :M: .25 .40
219 Coiling Oracle C :M: .25 .40
220 Cold-Eyed Selkie R :M: .25 .40
221 Counterflux R :M: .50 1.25
222 Daxos the Returned M :M: .75 1.00
223 Death Grasp R :M: .25 .40
224 Firemind's Foresight R :M: .25 .40
225 Gisela, Blade of Goldnight M :M: 4.50 5.50
226 Goblin Electromancer C :M: .10 .20
227 Grisly Salvage C :M: .10 .20
228 Karlov of the Ghost Council M :M: 4.00 5.00
229 Kaseto, Orochi Archmage M :M: .75 1.00
230 Korozda Guildmage U :M: .15 .25
231 Lorescale Coatl U :M: .15 .25
232 Lotleth Troll R :M: .50 .75
233 Melek, Izzet Paragon R :M: .25 .40
234 Meren of Clan Nel Toth M :M: 6.00 8.00
235 Mizzix of the Izmagnus M :M: 1.00 1.25
236 Mystic Snake R :M: .40 .60
237 Necromancer's Covenant R :M: .25 .40
238 Prime Speaker Zegana M :M: .75 1.00
239 Verdant Confluence R :G: 1.50 2.00
240 Verdant Force R :G: .25 .40
241 Viridian Shaman U :G: .15 .25
242 Mazirek, Kraul Death Priest M :M: 2.25 2.75
243 Prophetic Bolt R :M: .25 .40
244 Putrefy U :M: .20 .30
245 Steam Augury R :M: .25 .40
246 Teysa, Envoy of Ghosts R :M: .25 .40
247 Treasury Thrull R :M: .25 .40
248 Trygon Predator U :M: .25 .40
249 Underworld Coinsmith U :M: .15 .25
250 Vulturous Zombie R :M: .25 .40
251 Wistful Selkie U :M: .15 .25
252 Basalt Monolith U :A: 1.00 1.25
253 Blade of Selves R :A: 5.00 7.00
254 Bonehoard R :A: .25 .40
255 Boros Cluestone C :A: .10 .20
256 Boros Signet C :A: .10 .20
257 Burnished Hart U :A: .30 .50
258 Coldsteel Heart U :A: 1.00 1.25
259 Crystal Chimes U :A: .15 .25
260 Darksteel Ingot U :A: .25 .40
261 Dreamstone Hedron U :A: .15 .25
262 Eldrazi Monument M :A: 4.00 4.50
263 Fellwar Stone U :A: .50 .75
264 Loxodon Warhammer R :A: .50 .75
265 Mind Stone U :A: .15 .25
266 Orochi Hatchery R :A: .25 .40
267 Orzhov Cluestone C :A: .10 .20
268 Orzhov Signet C :A: .10 .20
269 Psychosis Crawler R :A: .50 .75
270 Sandstone Oracle U :A: .15 .25
271 Scytheclaw R :A: .25 .40
272 Seal of the Guildpact R :A: .60 1.00
273 Simic Keyrune U :A: .15 .25
274 Simic Signet C :A: .10 .20
275 Skullclamp U :A: 1.75 2.15
276 Sol Ring U :A: 2.75 3.25
277 Solemn Simulacrum R :A: 3.00 5.00
278 Staff of Nin R :A: .75 1.15
279 Swiftfoot Boots U :A: .75 1.00
280 Sword of Vengeance R :A: .25 .40
281 Urza's Incubator R :A: 4.00 6.00
282 Wayfarer's Bauble C :A: .10 .20
283 Worn Powerstone U :A: .40 .60
284 Boros Guildgate C :L: .10 .20
285 Command Beacon R :L: 6.00 8.00
286 Command Tower C :L: 1.00 1.50
287 Drifting Meadow C :L: .10 .20
288 Evolving Wilds C :L: .10 .20
289 Forest L :L: .10 .20
290 Ghost Quarter U :L: 1.00 1.50
291 Golgari Guildgate C :L: .10 .20
292 Golgari Rot Farm C :L: .20 .30
293 Grim Backwoods R :L: .25 .40
294 High Market R :L: .75 1.00
295 Izzet Boilerworks C :L: .10 .20
296 Izzet Guildgate C :L: .10 .20
297 Jungle Hollow C :L: .10 .20
298 Llanowar Reborn U :L: .15 .25
299 Mosswort Bridge R :L: .75 1.00
300 New Benalia U :L: .15 .25
301 Novijen, Heart of Progress U :L: .15 .25
302 Oran-Rief, the Vastwood R :L: 1.00 1.25
303 Orzhov Basilica C :L: .20 .30
304 Orzhov Guildgate C :L: .10 .20
305 Plains L :L: .10 .20
306 Plains L :L: .10 .20
307 Plains L :L: .10 .20
308 Plains L :L: .10 .20
309 Polluted Mire C :L: .10 .20
310 Simic Growth Chamber C :L: .50 .75
311 Simic Guildgate C :L: .10 .20
312 Slippery Karst C :L: .10 .20
313 Smoldering Crater C :L: .10 .20
314 Spinerock Knoll R :L: .25 .40
315 Swamp L :L: .10 .20
316 Swamp L :L: .10 .20
317 Swamp L :L: .10 .20
318 Swamp L :L: .10 .20
319 Swiftwater Cliffs C :L: .10 .20
320 Tainted Field U :L: .30 .50
321 Tainted Wood U :L: .15 .25
322 Temple of the False God U :L: .30 .50
323 Mountain L :L: .10 .20
324 Mountain L :L: .10 .20
325 Mountain L :L: .10 .20
326 Mountain L :L: .10 .20
327 Forest L :L: .10 .20
328 Forest L :L: .10 .20
329 Forest L :L: .10 .20
330 Forgotten Cave C :L: .10 .20
331 Reliquary Tower U :L: 2.50 3.00
332 Rogue's Passage U :L: .15 .25
333 Scoured Barrens C :L: .10 .20
334 Secluded Steppe C :L: .10 .20
334 Terramorphic Expanse C :L: .10 .20
335 Thornwood Falls C :L: .10 .20
335 Island L :L: .10 .20
336 Island L :L: .10 .20
336 Vivid Crag U :L: .15 .25
337 Vivid Creek U :L: .15 .25
337 Island L :L: .10 .20
338 Island L :L: .10 .20
338 Vivid Grove U :L: .15 .25
339 Vivid Marsh U :L: .15 .25
339 Ancient Amphitheater R :L: .25 .40
340 Barren Moor C :L: .10 .20
340 Vivid Meadow U :L: .15 .25
341 Wind-Scarred Crag C :L: .10 .20
341 Blasted Landscape U :L: .15 .25
342 Boros Garrison C :L: .10 .20
342 Zoetic Cavern U :L: .15 .25

2015 Magic The Gathering Commander 2015 Tokens

0 Experience Coutner .10 .15
1 Shapeshifter .10 .15
2 Angel .10 .15
3 Cat .10 .15
4 Knight .10 .15
5 Knight .25 .35
6 Drake .10 .15
7 Germ .10 .15
8 Zombie .10 .15
9 Dragon .10 .15
10 Elemental Shaman .10 .15
11 Lightning Rager .10 .15
12 Bear 1.00 1.50
13 Beast .10 .15
14 Elephant .10 .15
15 Frog Lizard .10 .15
16 Saproling .10 .15
17 Snake .10 .15
18 Spider .10 .15
19 Wolf .10 .15
20 Elemental .10 .15
21 Snake .10 .15
22 Spirit .10 .15
23 Spirit .50 .75
24 Gold .10 .15

2016 Magic The Gathering Commander 2016

COMPLETE SET (351) 300.00 400.00
RELEASED ON NOVEMBER 14, 2016
1 Duelists Heritage R .75 1.00
2 Entrapment Maneuver R .50 .75
3 Orzhov Advokist U .25 .40
4 Selfless Squire R 2.00 2.50
5 Sublime Exhalation R .75 1.00
6 Coastal Breach R .40 .60
7 Deepglow Skate R 7.00 9.00
8 Faerie Artisans R 2.00 2.50
9 Grip of Phyresis U .75 1.00
10 Manifold Insights R .75 1.00
11 Cruel Entertainment R .75 1.00
12 Curse of Vengeance R .50 .75
13 Curtains Call R 3.00 3.50
14 Magus of the Will R 4.00 5.00
15 Parting Thoughts U .50 .75
16 Charging Cinderhorn R .50 .75
17 Divergent Transformations R .50 .75
18 Frenzied Fugue U .25 .40
19 Gobline Spymaster R .75 1.00
20 Runehorn Hellkite R 2.00 2.50
21 Benefactors Draught R 1.50 1.75
22 Evolutionary Escalation U .30 .50
23 Primeval Protector R 1.25 1.75
24 Seeds of Renewal R .40 .60
25 Stonehoof Chieftain R 5.00 7.00
26 Akiri Line Slinger R 2.00 2.50
27 Ancient Excavation U .25 .40
28 Atraxa Praetors Voice M 20.00 25.00
29 Breya Etherium Shaper M 3.00 4.00
30 Bruse Tarl Boorish Herder M 1.00 1.50
31 Grave Upheaval U .30 .50
32 Ikra Shidiqi the Usurper M 1.50 2.00
33 Ishai Ojutai Dragonspeaker M .75 1.25
34 Kraum Ludevics Opus R .75 1.25
35 Kydele Chosen of Kruphix M 2.50 3.00
36 Kynaios and Tiro of Meletis M 1.00 1.50
37 Ludevic Necro Alchemist M .75 1.00
38 Migratory Route U .15 .25
39 Ravos Soultender M 3.50 4.00
40 Reyhan Last of the Abzan R 2.50 3.25
41 Saskia the Unyielding M 1.75 2.25
42 Sidar Kondo of Jamuraa M 1.00 1.50
43 Silas Renn Seeker Adept M 2.00 2.50
44 Sylvan Reclamation U .50 .75
45 Tana the Bloodsower M .75 1.25
46 Thrasios Triton Hero R 1.75 2.25
47 Treacherous Terrain U .15 .25
48 Tymna the Weaver R 1.50 2.00
49 Vial Smasher the Fierce M 8.00 12.00
50 Vidris Maelstrom Wielder M 3.00 3.50
51 Armory Automation R 1.00 1.50
52 Boompile R 1.50 2.00
53 Conqueror's Flail R 2.75 3.50
54 Crystalline Crawler R 2.25 3.00
55 Prismatic Geoscope R 1.75 2.25
56 Ash Barrens C 2.50 4.00
57 Abzan Falconer U .15 .25
58 Blazing Archon R .75 1.00
59 Blind Obedience R .75 1.25
60 Brave the Sands U .15 .25
61 Cathars Crusade R .75 1.00
62 Citadel Siege R .25 .40
63 Custodi Soulbinders R .25 .40
64 Dispellers Capsule C .10 .20
65 Elite Scaleguard U .15 .25
66 Ghostly Prison U 1.75 2.25
67 Hoffprints of the Stag R .25 .40
68 Hushwing Gryff R .25 .40
69 Mentor of the Meek R .40 .60
70 Mirror Entity R .50 .75
71 Oblation R .25 .40
72 Open the Vaults R .25 .40
73 Phyrexian Rebirth R .25 .40
74 Reveillark R 2.50 3.00
75 Reverse the Sands R .25 .40
76 Sanctum Gargoyle C .10 .20
77 Sphere of Safety U .50 .75
78 Swords to Plowshares U 2.00 2.50
79 Wave of Reckoning R .25 .40
80 Windborn Muse R 1.00 1.50
81 Academy Elite R .25 .40
82 Aeon Chronicler R .25 .40
83 Arcane Denial C 4.00 6.00
84 Chain of Vapor U .50 .75
85 Chasm Skulker R 2.50 3.50

86 Chief Engineer R .25 .40
87 Devastation Tide R .25 .40
88 Disdainful Stroke C .10 .20
89 Etherium Sculptor C .40 .75
90 Etersworn Adjudicator M .75 1.00
91 Evacuation R .75 1.00
92 Master of Etherium R 4.50 5.50
93 Minds Aglow R .75 1.25
94 Propaganda U 2.00 2.50
95 Read the Runes R .25 .40
96 Reins of Power R .25 .40
97 Spelltwine R .25 .40
98 Swan Song R .40 .60
99 Tezzerets Gambit U .15 .25
100 Thrummingbird U .15 .25
101 Treasure Cruise C .10 .20
102 Trinket Mage C .10 .20
103 Vedalken Engineer C .10 .20
104 Windfall U .50 .75
105 Army of the Damned M .75 1.25
106 Bane of the Living R .25 .40
107 Beacon of Unrest R 1.75 2.00
108 Brutal Hordechief M .30 .50
109 Executioneers Capsule U .15 .25
110 Festercreep C .10 .20
111 Ghastly Conscription M .30 .50
112 Guiltfeeder R .40 .60
113 In Garruks Wake R .25 .40
114 Languish R .40 .60
115 Necroplasm R .25 .40
116 Sangromancer R .25 .40
117 Waste Not R 2.00 2.50
118 Wight of Precinct Six U .15 .25
119 Alesha Who Smiles at Death R .25 .40
120 Blasphemous Act R 1.00 1.50
121 Breath of Fury R .25 .40
122 Chaos Warp R 1.50 2.00
123 Daretti Scrap Savant M 1.50 2.00
124 Dragon Mage R .50 .75
125 Godo Bandit Warlord R .75 1.25
126 Grab the Reins U .15 .25
127 Hellkite Igniter R .25 .40
128 Hellkite Tyrant M .75 1.25
129 Humble Defector U .15 .25
130 Kazuul Tyrant of the Cliffs R .25 .40
131 Past in Flames M 1.50 2.00
132 Reforge the Soul R .75 1.00
133 Slobad Goblin Tinkerer R .25 .40
134 Stalking Vengeance R .25 .40
135 Taurean Mauler R .40 .60
136 Trash for Treasure R .40 .60
137 Volcanic Vision R .25 .40
138 Wheel of Fate R 1.00 1.50
139 Whims of the Fates R .25 .40
140 Whipflare U .15 .25
141 Beast Within U .75 1.00
142 Beastmaster Ascension R .75 1.00
143 Burgeoning R 3.00 3.50
144 Champion of Lambholt R .50 .75
145 Collective Voyage R 1.50 2.00
146 Cultivate C 1.50 2.50
147 Den Protector R .50 .75
148 Far Wanderings C .10 .20
149 Farseek C .10 .20
150 Forgotten Ancient R .25 .40
151 Gamekeeper U .15 .25
152 Hardened Scales R 3.00 3.50
153 Inspiring Call U .15 .25
154 Kalonian Hydra M 3.50 5.00
155 Kodamas Reach C 1.50 2.50
156 Lurking Predators R 1.75 2.25
157 Managorger Hydra R 1.50 2.25
158 Mycoloth R 1.00 1.50
159 Oath of Druids R 2.25 2.75
160 Quirion Explorer C .10 .20
161 Rampant Growth C .10 .20
162 Realm Seekers R .25 .40
163 Rites of Flourishing R .40 .60
164 Sakura Tribe Elder C .60 1.00
165 Satyr Wayfinder C .10 .20
166 Scavenging Ooze R 3.50 4.25
167 Shamanic Revelation R .25 .40
168 Solidarity of Heroes U .15 .25
169 Sylvok Explorer C .10 .20
170 Tempt with Discovery R 1.25 1.75
171 Thelonite Hermit R .25 .40
172 Thunderfoot Baloth R .75 1.00
173 Tuskguard Captain U .15 .25
174 Veteran Explorer U .75 1.25
175 Wall of Blossoms U .50 .75
176 Wild Beastmaster R .25 .40
177 Abzan Charm U .15 .25
178 Ankle Shanker R .25 .40
179 Artifact Mutation R .50 .75
180 Aura Mutation R .50 .75
181 Baleful Strix U 2.50 3.00
182 Bituminous Blast U .15 .25
183 Blood Tyrant R .25 .40
184 Bloodbraid Elf U .75 1.25
185 Boros Charm U 1.50 2.00
186 Bred for the Hunt U .15 .25
187 Clan Defiance R .25 .40
188 Coiling Oracle C .10 .20
189 Consuming Aberration R .75 1.00
190 Corpsejack Menace R .25 .40
191 Crackling Doom R .25 .40
192 Dauntless Escort R .75 1.15
193 Decimate R .40 .60
194 Duneblast R .25 .40
195 Edric Spymaster of Trest R .25 .40
196 Enduring Scalelord U .15 .25
197 Etherium Horn Sorcerer R .30 .50
198 Fathom Mage R .25 .40
199 Filigree Angel R .25 .40
200 Ghave Guru of Spores M 1.00 1.50
201 Glint Eye Nephilim R .25 .40
202 Gwafa Hazid Profiteer R .40 .60
203 Hanna Ships Navigator R 1.50 2.00
204 Horizon Chimera U .15 .25
205 Iroas God of Victory M 2.00 2.50
206 Jor Kadeen the Prevailer R .25 .40
207 Juniper Order Ranger U .15 .25
208 Korozda Guildmage U .15 .25
209 Lavalanche R .25 .40
210 Master Biomancer M 1.00 1.50
211 Merciless Eviction R .40 .60
212 Mortify U .75 1.00
213 Nath of the Gilt Leaf R .75 1.25
214 Naya Charm U .15 .25
215 Necrogenesis U .15 .25
216 Progenitor Mimic M 1.25 1.75
217 Putrefy U .15 .25
218 Rakdos Charm U .15 .25
219 Rubblehulk R .25 .40
220 Selvala Explorer Returned R .30 .50
221 Sharuum the Hegemon M .50 .75
222 Spellheart Chimera U .15 .25
223 Sphinx Summoner R .50 .75
224 Sydri Galvanic Genius M .50 .75
225 Terminate C 1.50 2.50
226 Utter End R .25 .40
227 Vorel of the Hull Clade R .25 .40
228 Vulturous Zombie R .25 .40
229 Whispering Madness R .25 .40
230 Wilderness Elemental U .15 .25
231 Zedruu the Greathearted M .60 1.00
232 Zhur Taa Druid C .10 .20
233 Everlasting Torment R .75 1.25
234 Mirrorweave R .50 .75
235 Selesnya Guildmage U .15 .25
236 Spitting Image R .40 .60
237 Thopter Foundry U .50 .75
238 Worm Harvest R .25 .40
239 Trial Error U .15 .25
240 Order Chaos U .15 .25
241 Akroan Horse R .25 .40
242 Assault Suit U .15 .25
243 Astral Cornucopia R .25 .40
244 Blinkmoth Urn R .75 1.25
245 Bonehoard R .25 .40
246 Cauldron of Souls R 1.50 2.00
247 Chromatic Lantern R 9.00 11.00
248 Commanders Sphere C .50 .80
249 Cranial Plating U .75 1.00
250 Darksteel Ingot U .40 .60
251 Empyrial Plate R .25 .40
252 Etched Oracle U .15 .25
253 Everflowing Chalice U .15 .25
254 Fellwar Stone U .30 .50
255 Golgari Signet C .10 .20
256 Gruul Signet C .10 .20
257 Howling Mine R 1.00 1.50
258 Ichor Wellspring C .10 .20
259 Keening Stone R .75 1.25
260 Lightning Greaves U 4.00 5.50
261 Loxodon Warhammer U .40 .60
262 Mycosynth Wellspring C .10 .20
263 Myr Battlesphere R .25 .40
264 Myr Retriever U .15 .25
265 Nevinyrrals Disk R .75 1.00
266 Orzhov Signet C .60 1.00
267 Psychosis Crawler R .25 .40
268 Rakdos Signet C .40 .75
269 Shimmer Myr R .25 .40
270 Simic Signet C .10 .20
271 Skullclamp U 1.25 1.75
272 Sol Ring U 2.00 3.00
273 Solemn Simulacrum R 3.50 4.50
274 Soul of New Phyrexia M .75 1.00
275 Sunforger R .25 .40
276 Swiftfoot Boots U .50 .75
277 Temple Bell R .25 .40
278 Trading Post R .25 .40
279 Vensers Journal R 1.00 1.50
280 Whispersilk Cloak U .25 .40
281 Arcane Sanctum U .50 .75
282 Azorius Chancery U .15 .25
283 Boros Garrison U .15 .25
284 Buried Ruin U .25 .40
285 Caves of Koilos R .75 1.15
286 Command Tower C 1.00 1.50
287 Crumbling Necropolis U .50 .75
288 Darksteel Citadel U 1.00 1.25
289 Darkwater Catacombs R 1.75 2.25
290 Dimir Aqueduct U .30 .50
291 Dismal Backwater C .10 .20
292 Dragonskull Summit R 1.50 2.00
293 Dreadship Reef U .15 .25
294 Evolving Wilds C .10 .20
295 Exotic Orchard R .50 .75
296 Forbidden Orchard R 2.25 3.00
297 Frontier Bivouac U .15 .25
298 Golgari Rot Farm C .10 .20
299 Grand Coliseum R .50 .75
300 Gruul Turf U .15 .25
301 Homeward Path R 2.50 3.00
302 Izzet Boilerworks C .10 .20
303 Jungle Hollow C .10 .20
304 Jungle Shrine U .50 .75
305 Karplusan Forest R 2.00 2.50
306 Krosan Verge U .50 .75
307 Mosswort Bridge R .40 .60
308 Murmuring Bosk R 1.00 1.50
309 Myriad Landscape U 1.50 2.00
310 Mystic Monastery U .15 .25
311 Nomad Outpost U .15 .25
312 Opal Palace C .10 .20
313 Opulent Palace U .15 .25
314 Orzhov Basilica U .15 .25
315 Rakdos Carnarium U .15 .25
316 Reliquary Tower U 3.50 4.50
317 Rootbound Crag R .75 1.25
318 Rugged Highlands C .10 .20
319 Rupture Spire C .10 .20
320 Sandsteppe Citadel U .30 .50
321 Savage Lands U .50 .75
322 Seaside Citadel U .50 .75
323 Seat of the Synod C 1.25 2.00
324 Selesnya Sanctuary U .15 .25
325 Shadowblood Ridge R 1.00 1.50
326 Simic Growth Chamber U .30 .50
327 Spinerock Knoll R .40 .60
328 Sungrass Prairie R 1.00 1.50
329 Sunpetal Grove R 2.25 3.00
330 Swiftwater Cliffs C .10 .20
331 Temple of the False God U .25 .40
332 Terramorphic Expanse C .10 .20
333 Thornwood Falls C .10 .20
334 Transguild Promenade C .10 .20
335 Underground River R 1.50 2.00
336 Windbrisk Heights R .75 1.00
337 Plains L .10 .20
338 Plains L .10 .20
339 Plains L .10 .20
340 Island L .10 .20
341 Island L .10 .20
342 Island L .10 .20
343 Swamp L .10 .20
344 Swamp L .10 .20
345 Swamp L .10 .20
346 Mountain L .10 .20
347 Mountain L .10 .20
348 Mountain L .10 .20
349 Forest L .10 .20
350 Forest L .10 .20
351 Forest L .10 .20

2016 Magic The Gathering Commander 2016 Tokens

1 Spirit .10 .15
2 Bird .10 .15
3 Elemental .10 .15
4 Goat .15 .25
5 Soldier .10 .15
6 Spirit .10 .15
7 Bird .10 .15
8 Squid .10 .15
9 Thopter .25 .35
10 Germ .10 .15
11 Zombie .10 .15
12 Goblin .25 .35
13 Ogre .25 .35
14 Beast .20 .30
15 Elf Warrior .25 .35
16 Saproling .10 .15
17 Saproling .10 .15
18 Worm .10 .15
19 Horror .10 .15
20 Myr .10 .15
21 Daretti, Scrap Savant Emblem .12 .20

2017 Magic The Gathering Commander Anthology Tokens

1 Kithkin Soldier
2 Knight
3 Spirit
4 Germ
5 Zombie
6 Dragon
7 Beast
8 Beast
9 Elemental
10 Elephant
11 Elf Druid
12 Elf Warrior
13 Saproling
14 Spider
15 Treefolk
16 Wolf
17 Wolf
18 Drake
19 Gargoyle
20 Experience Counter

2017 Magic The Gathering Commander 2017

COMPLETE SET (309) 250.00 400.00
RELEASED ON AUGUST 25, 2017
1 Alms Collector R 2.00 3.50
2 Balan Wandering Knight R 1.00 1.50
3 Curse of Vitality U .25 .40
4 Fortunate Few R .60 1.00
5 Kindred Boon R 1.50 2.00
6 Sacalelord Reckoner R 1.50 2.00
7 Stalking Leonin R .75 1.25
8 Teferis Protection R 20.00 25.00
9 Curse of Verbosity U .30 .50
10 Galecaster Colossus R .60 1.00
11 Kindred Discovery R 10.00 15.00
12 Magus of the Mind R 1.00 1.50
13 Portal Mage R .75 1.25
14 Bloodline Necromancer U .25 .40
15 Boneyard Scourge R 1.50 2.00
16 Curse of Disturbance U .25 .40
17 Kheru Mind Eater R 1.00 1.50
18 Kindred Dominance R 1.25 2.00
19 New Blood R 1.00 1.50
20 Patron of the Vein R 1.00 1.50
21 Vindictive Lich R 2.00 3.00
22 Bloodsworn Steward R 1.00 1.50
23 Crimson Honor Guard R .40 .60
24 Curse of Opulence U 1.50 2.00
25 Disrupt Decorum R 2.00 3.50
26 Izzet Chemister R 1.00 1.50
27 Kindred Charge R 1.00 1.50
28 Shifting Shadow R 1.50 2.00
29 Territorial Hellkite R .75 1.25
30 Curse of Bounty U .25 .40
31 Hungry Lynx R .60 1.00
32 Kindred Summons R 2.00 3.00
33 Qasali Slingers R .60 1.00
34 Traverse the Outlands R 5.00 7.00
35 Arahbo Roar of the World M 2.00 3.50
36 Edgar Markov M 3.00 5.00
37 Fractured Identity R 2.00 3.00
38 Inalla Archmage Ritualist M 2.00 3.50
39 Kess Dissident Mage M 10.00 15.00
40 Licia Sanguine Tribune M 2.00 3.00
41 Mairsil the Pretender M 3.00 4.00
42 Mathas Fiend Seeker M 3.00 5.00
43 Mirri Weatherlight Duelist M 3.00 5.00
44 Nazahn Revered Bladesmith M 1.00 1.50
45 O Kagachi Vengeful Kami M 3.00 4.00
46 Taigam Ojutai Master R 2.00 3.50
47 Taigam Sidisis Hand R 1.00 1.50
48 The Ur Dragon M 7.00 10.00
49 Wasitora Nekoru Queen R 1.50 2.50
50 Bloodforged Battle Axe R 2.00 3.50
51 Hammer of Nazahn R 5.00 7.00
52 Heirloom Blade U .60 1.00
53 Heralds Horn U 4.00 6.00
54 Mirror of the Forebears U 1.50 2.00
55 Ramos Dragon Engine M 10.00 15.00
56 Path of Ancestry C 3.00 4.00
57 Blind Obedience R .40 .60
58 Condemn U .25 .40
59 Divine Reckoning R .40 .60
60 Fell the Mighty R .40 .60
61 Jareth Leonine Titan R .40 .60
62 Jazal Goldmane M .50 .80
63 Kemba Kha Regent R .40 .60
64 Leonin Arbiter R 2.00 3.00
65 Leonin Relic Warder U .25 .40
66 Leonin Shikari R 1.50 2.00
67 Orator of Ojutai U .25 .40
68 Oreskos Explorer U .25 .40
69 Raksha Golden Cub R .60 1.00
70 Return to Dust U .75 1.25
71 Rout R .15 .25
72 Sehts Tiger R .40 .60
73 Spirit of the Hearth R .40 .60
74 Sunscorch Regent R .40 .60
75 Sunspear Shikari C .15 .25
76 Swords to Plowshares U 1.50 2.00
77 Taj Nar Swordsmith U .25 .40
78 White Suns Zenith R .40 .60
79 Wing Shards U .25 .40
80 Arcanis the Omnipotent R .40 .60
81 Archaeomancer C .15 .25
82 Azami Lady of Scrolls R .40 .60
83 Body Double R .40 .60
84 Clone Legion M .50 .80
85 Harbinger of the Tides R .40 .60
86 Into the Roil C .15 .25
87 Merchant of Secrets C .15 .25
88 Monastery Siege R .40 .60
89 Opportunity U .25 .40
90 Polymorphists Jest R .40 .60
91 Reality Shift U .25 .40
92 Sea Gate Oracle C .15 .25
93 Serendib Sorcerer R .40 .60
94 Spelltwine R .40 .60
95 Ambitions Cost U .25 .40
96 Anowon the Ruin Sage R .40 .60
97 Apprentice Necromancer R .60 1.00
98 Black Market R 2.00 3.00
99 Blood Artist U .75 1.25
100 Blood Tribute R .40 .60
101 Bloodhusk Ritualist U .25 .40
102 Bloodlord of Vaasgoth M .50 .80
103 Butcher of Malakir R .40 .60
104 Captivating Vampire R 2.50 3.50
105 Consuming Vapors R .40 .60
106 Corpse Augur U .25 .40
107 Crux of Fate R .40 .60
108 Damnable Pact R .40 .60
109 Dark Imposter R .40 .60
110 Deathbringer Regent R .40 .60
111 Decree of Pain R 1.50 2.00
112 Drana Kalastria Bloodchief R .40 .60
113 Falkenrath Noble C .15 .25
114 Go for the Throat U .75 1.25
115 Magus of the Abyss R .40 .60
116 Malakir Bloodwitch R .40 .60
117 Necromantic Selection R .40 .60
118 Painful Truths R .40 .60
119 Palace Siege R .40 .60
120 Pawn of Ulamog U .25 .40
121 Puppeteer Clique R .40 .60
122 Read the Bones C .15 .25
123 Sangromancer R .40 .60
124 Sanguine Bond R 1.25 2.00
125 Skeletal Scrying U .25 .40
126 Skeletal Vampire R .40 .60
127 Syphon Mind C .15 .25
128 Underworld Connections R .40 .60
129 Vampire Nighthawk U .30 .50
130 Vein Drinker R .40 .60
131 Chaos Warp R 1.50 2.00
132 Comet Storm M .40 .60
133 Crucible of Fire R .40 .60
134 Dragon Tempest R .40 .60
135 Dragonlords Servant U .25 .40
136 Dragonspeaker Shaman U 1.50 2.00
137 Earthquake R .40 .60
138 Hellkite Charger R .40 .60
139 Outpost Siege R .40 .60
140 Rakish Heir U .25 .40
141 Ryusei the Falling Star M .50 .80
142 Scourge of Valkas M .75 1.25
143 Tyrants Familiar R .40 .60
144 Utvara Hellkite M 1.50 2.50
145 Abundance R .40 .60
146 Crushing Vines C .15 .25
147 Cultivate C .75 1.25

148 Elemental Bond U .25 .40
149 Farseek C .15 .25
150 Frontier Siege R .40 .60
151 Harmonize U .25 .40
152 Hunters Prowess R .40 .60
153 Jedit Ojanen of Efrava R .40 .60
154 Kodamas Reach C 1.00 1.50
155 Nissas Pilgrimage C .15 .25
156 Rain of Thorns U .25 .40
157 Relic Crush U .25 .40
158 Souls Majesty R .40 .60
159 Temur Sabertooth U .25 .40
160 Zendikar Resurgent R .40 .60
161 Atarka World Render R .40 .60
162 Behemoth Sledge U .25 .40
163 Bladewing the Risen R .40 .60
164 Blood Baron of Vizkopa M .50 .80
165 Broodmate Dragon R .40 .60
166 Cauldron Dance U .25 .40
167 Crackling Doom R .40 .60
168 Crosis the Purger R .60 1.00
169 Crosis Charm U .25 .40
170 Dromoka the Eternal R .40 .60
171 Etherium Horn Sorcerer R .40 .60
172 Fleecemane Lion R .40 .60
173 Havengul Lich M 1.50 2.00
174 Intet the Dreamer R .60 1.00
175 Izzet Chronarch C .15 .25
176 Kolaghan the Storms Fury R .40 .60
177 Marchesa the Black Rose M .75 1.25
178 Memory Plunder R 1.00 1.50
179 Merciless Eviction R .75 1.25
180 Mercurial Chemister R .40 .60
181 Miraris Wake M 7.00 10.00
182 Mortify U .25 .40
183 Nin the Pain Artist R .40 .60
184 Niv Mizzet Dracogenius R .40 .60
185 Niv Mizzet the Firemind R .75 1.25
186 Nivix Guildmage U .25 .40
187 Ojutai Soul of Winter R .40 .60
188 Phantom Nishoba R .40 .60
189 Qasali Pridemage C 1.00 1.50
190 Rakdos Charm U .25 .40
191 Savage Ventmaw U .25 .40
192 Scion of the Ur Dragon R 1.00 1.50
193 Shadowmage Infiltrator R .40 .60
194 Silumgar the Drifting Death R .40 .60
195 Silumgars Command R .40 .60
196 Spellbound Dragon R .40 .60
197 Stromkirk Captain U .25 .40
198 Teneb the Harvester R .60 1.00
199 Terminate U .75 1.25
200 Tithe Drinker C .15 .25
201 Vela the Night Clad M .75 1.25
202 Argentum Armor R .40 .60
203 Armillary Sphere C .15 .25
204 Blade of the Bloodchief R 1.00 1.50
205 Boros Signet U .25 .40
206 Commanders Sphere C .30 .50
207 Darksteel Ingot U .25 .40
208 Door of Destinies R 3.00 4.00
209 Dreamstone Hedron U .25 .40
210 Fellwar Stone U .25 .40
211 Fist of Suns R 1.00 1.50
212 Grappling Hook R .40 .60
213 Hedron Archive U .25 .40
214 Heros Blade U .25 .40
215 Lightning Greaves U 2.50 4.00
216 Loxodon Warhammer U .25 .40
217 Nevinyrrals Disk R .75 1.25
218 Nighil Spellbomb C .30 .50
219 Orzhov Signet U .25 .40
220 Quietus Spike R .75 1.25
221 Rakdos Signet U .25 .40
222 Skullclamp U .75 1.25
223 Sol Ring U 2.00 3.00
224 Staff of Nin R .40 .60
225 Steel Hellkite R .40 .60
226 Swiftfoot Boots U .60 1.00
227 Sword of the Animist R 1.00 1.50
228 Sword of Vengeance R .40 .60
229 Unstable Obelisk U .25 .40
230 Wayfarers Bauble C .15 .25
231 Well of Lost Dreams R 1.00 1.50
232 Worn Powerstone U .25 .40
233 Akoum Refuge U .25 .40
234 Arcane Sanctum U .25 .40
235 Blighted Woodland U .25 .40
236 Bloodfell Caves C .15 .25
237 Blossoming Sands C .15 .25
238 Bojuka Bog C .75 1.25
239 Boros Garrison C .15 .25
240 Boros Guildgate C .15 .25
241 Cinder Barrens C .15 .25
242 Command Tower C .75 1.25
243 Crucible of the Spirit Dragon R .40 .60
244 Crumbling Necropolis U .25 .40
245 Dimir Aqueduct U .40 .60
246 Dismal Backwater C .15 .25
247 Elfhame Palace U .25 .40
248 Evolving Wilds C .15 .25
249 Exotic Orchard R .40 .60
250 Forsaken Sanctuary U .25 .40
251 Frontier Bivouac U .25 .40
252 Grasslands U .25 .40
253 Graypelt Refuge U .25 .40
254 Grixis Panorama C .15 .25
255 Haven of the Spirit Dragon R .40 .60
256 Izzet Boilerworks U .25 .40
257 Jungle Shrine U .25 .40
258 Jwar Isel Refuge U .25 .40
259 Kabira Crossroads C .15 .25
260 Krosan Verge U .25 .40
261 Mosswort Bridge R .40 .60
262 Myriad Landscape U 1.00 1.50
263 Mystic Monastery U .25 .40
264 Mystifying Maze R .40 .60
265 Nomad Outpost U .25 .40
266 Opal Palace C .15 .25
267 Opulent Palace U .25 .40
268 Orzhov Basilica C .15 .25
269 Orzhov Guildgate C .15 .25
270 Rakdos Carnarium C .15 .25
271 Rakdos Guildgate C .15 .25
272 Rogues Passage U .25 .40
273 Saltcrusted Steppe U .25 .40
274 Sandsteppe Citadel U .25 .40
275 Savage Lands U .25 .40
276 Scoured Barrens C .15 .25
277 Seaside Citadel U .25 .40
278 Secluded Steppe C .15 .25
279 Selesnya Guildgate C .15 .25
280 Selesnya Sanctuary C .15 .25
281 Stirring Wildwood R .75 1.25
282 Stone Quarry U .25 .40
283 Swiftwater Cliffs C .15 .25
284 Temple of the False God U .25 .40
285 Terramorphic Expanse C .15 .25
286 Tranquil Expanse U .25 .40
287 Tranquil Thicket C .15 .25
288 Urborg Volcano U .25 .40
289 Vivid Crag U .25 .40
290 Vivid Creek U .25 .40
291 Vivid Grove U .25 .40
292 Vivid Marsh U .25 .40
293 Vivid Meadow U .25 .40
294 Wind Scarred Crag C .15 .25
295 Plains L .15 .25
296 Plains L .15 .25
297 Plains L .15 .25
298 Island L .15 .25
299 Island L .15 .25
300 Island L .15 .25
301 Swamp L .15 .25
302 Swamp L .15 .25
303 Swamp L .15 .25
304 Mountain L .15 .25
305 Mountain L .15 .25
306 Mountain L .15 .25
307 Forest L .15 .25
308 Forest L .15 .25
309 Forest L .15 .25

2017 Magic The Gathering Commander 2017 Tokens

1 Cat .06 .10
2 Bat .15 .25
3 Rat .10 .15
4 Vampire .35 .50
5 Zombie .06 .10
6 Dragon .10 .15
7 Dragon .15 .25
8 Cat Warrior .10 .15
9 Cat Dragon .25 .35
10 Gold .10 .15
11 Eldrazi Spawn .25 .35

2018 Magic The Gathering Commander Anthology Volume II Tokens

1 Shapeshifter .15 .25
2 Bird .15 .25
3 Goat .15 .25
4 Knight .15 .25
5 Spirit .15 .25
6 Germ .15 .25
7 Zombie .15 .25
8 Elemental Shaman .15 .25
9 Goblin .15 .25
10 Lightning Rager .15 .25
11 Saproling .15 .25
12 Myr .15 .25
13 Pentavite .15 .25
14 Triskelavite .15 .25
15 Tuktuk the Returned .15 .25
16 Wurm (Deathtouch) 2.00 3.50
17 Wurm (Lifelink) 2.00 3.50
18 Daretti, Scrap Savant .15 .25
19 Experience Counter .15 .25

2018 Magic The Gathering Commander 2018

COMPLETE SET (307) 180.00 260.00
RELEASED ON AUGUST 10, 2018
1 Boreas Charger R 1.50 2.00
2 Empyrial Storm R .15 .25
3 Heavenly Blademaster R 1.50 2.00
4 Loyal Unicorn U .15 .25
5 Magus of the Balance R 1.50 2.50
6 Aminatou's Augury R .60 1.00
7 Echo Storm R 1.00 1.50
8 Estrid's Invocation R 3.00 5.00
9 Ever-Watching Threshold R 1.00 1.50
10 Loyal Drake U .15 .25
11 Octopus Umbra R .15 .25
12 Primordial Mist R .15 .25
13 Vedalken Humiliator R 1.00 1.50
14 Bloodtracker R 1.00 1.50
15 Entreat the Dead R 3.00 4.00
16 Loyal Subordinate U .15 .25
17 Night Incarnate R .15 .25
18 Skull Storm R .15 .25
19 Sower of Discord R 1.00 1.50
20 Emissary of Grudges R .15 .25
21 Enchanter's Bane R 1.00 1.50
22 Fury Storm R 1.50 2.00
23 Loyal Apprentice U .15 .25
24 Nesting Dragon R 3.00 5.00
25 Reality Scramble R 1.00 1.50
26 Saheeli's Directive R 1.50 2.00
27 Treasure Nabber R 8.00 10.00
28 Varchild, Betrayer of Kjeldor R 1.50 2.00
29 Crash of Rhino Beetles R .15 .25
30 Genesis Storm R .75 1.25
31 Loyal Guardian U .15 .25
32 Myth Unbound R 3.00 4.00
33 Nylea's Colossus R .15 .25
34 Ravenous Slime R 2.00 2.50
35 Turntimber Sower R 1.50 2.00
36 Whiptongue Hydra R 1.00 1.50
37 Aminatou, the Fateshifter M 8.00 10.00
38 Arixmethes, Slumbering Isle R 4.00 6.00
39 Brudiclad, Telchor Engineer M 2.00 3.00
40 Estrid, the Masked M 4.00 6.00
41 Gyrus, Waker of Corpses M 1.50 2.50
42 Kestia, the Cultivator M 2.00 3.00
43 Lord Windgrace M 6.00 8.00
44 Saheeli, the Gifted M 5.00 7.00
45 Tawnos, Urza's Apprentice M 2.00 3.00
46 Thantis, the Warweaver M 1.00 1.50
47 Tuvasa the Sunlit M 3.00 5.00
48 Varina, Lich Queen M 2.00 3.00
49 Windgrace's Judgment R 4.00 6.00
50 Xantcha, Sleeper Agent R 4.00 6.00
51 Yennett, Cryptic Sovereign M 2.00 3.00
52 Yuriko, the Tiger's Shadow R 15.00 20.00
53 Ancient Stone Idol R 1.00 1.50
54 Coveted Jewel R 2.00 2.50
55 Endless Atlas R 3.00 4.00
56 Geode Golem U 1.50 2.00
57 Retrofitter Foundry R 1.00 1.50
58 Forge of Heroes C .15 .25
59 Isolated Watchtower R 2.00 2.50
60 Adarkar Valkyrie R .15 .25
61 Ajani's Chosen R .15 .25
62 Akroma's Vengeance R .15 .25
63 Banishing Stroke U .15 .25
64 Celestial Archon R .15 .25
65 Crib Swap U .15 .25
66 Dismantling Blow C .15 .25
67 Entreat the Angels M 1.50 2.50
68 Lightform U .15 .25
69 Martial Coup R .15 .25
70 Phyrexian Rebirth R .15 .25
71 Return to Dust U .15 .25
72 Sage's Reverie U .15 .25
73 Serra Avatar M .15 .25
74 Sigil of the Empty Throne R .15 .25
75 Silent Sentinel R .15 .25
76 Soul Snare U .15 .25
77 Terminus R 1.50 2.00
78 Unquestioned Authority U .15 .25
79 Winds of Rath R .15 .25
80 Aether Gale R .15 .25
81 Archetype of Imagination U .15 .25
82 Brainstorm U .15 .25
83 Cloudform U .15 .25
84 Conundrum Sphinx R .15 .25
85 Devastation Tide R .15 .25
86 Dictate of Kruphix R .15 .25
87 Djinn of Wishes R .15 .25
88 Dream Cache C .15 .25
89 Eel Umbra C .15 .25
90 Etherium Sculptor C .15 .25
91 Inkwell Leviathan R .15 .25
92 Into the Roil C .15 .25
93 Jeskai Infiltrator R .15 .25
94 Mulldrifter U .15 .25
95 Ninja of the Deep Hours C .15 .25
96 Ponder C 1.50 2.50
97 Portent C .15 .25
98 Predict U .15 .25
99 Reverse Engineer U .15 .25
100 Saheeli's Artistry R .15 .25
101 Sharding Sphinx R .15 .25
102 Sigiled Starfish U .15 .25
103 Sphinx of Jwar Isle R .15 .25
104 Sphinx of Uthuun R .15 .25
105 Telling Time C .15 .25
106 Thirst for Knowledge U .15 .25
107 Thopter Spy Network R .15 .25
108 Tidings U .15 .25
109 Treasure Hunt C .15 .25
110 Vow of Flight U .15 .25
111 Whirler Rogue U .15 .25
112 Whitewater Naiads U .15 .25
113 Army of the Damned M .15 .25
114 Moonlight Bargain R .15 .25
115 Phyrexian Delver R .15 .25
116 Retreat to Hagra U .15 .25
117 Ruinous Path R .15 .25
118 Soul of Innistrad M .15 .25
119 Stitch Together U .15 .25
120 Blasphemous Act R 1.50 2.50
121 Chain Reaction R .15 .25
122 Chaos Warp R 1.00 1.50
123 Flameblast Dragon R .15 .25
124 Hellkite Igniter R .15 .25
125 Magmaquake R .15 .25
126 Thopter Engineer U .15 .25
127 Acidic Slime U .15 .25
128 Aura Gnarlid C .15 .25
129 Avenger of Zendikar M 2.50 3.50
130 Baloth Woodcrasher U .15 .25
131 Bear Umbra R 2.50 3.50
132 Boon Satyr R .15 .25
133 Borderland Explorer C .15 .25
134 Budoka Gardener // Dokai, Weaver of Life R .15 .25
135 Centaur Vinecrasher R .15 .25
136 Consign to Dust U .15 .25
137 Creeping Renaissance R .15 .25
138 Cultivate C .15 .25
139 Dawn's Reflection C .15 .25
140 Eidolon of Blossoms R .15 .25
141 Enchantress's Presence R 3.00 4.00
142 Epic Proportions R .15 .25
143 Explore C .15 .25
144 Explosive Vegetation U .15 .25
145 Far Wanderings C .15 .25
146 Farhaven Elf C .15 .25
147 Fertile Ground C .15 .25
148 Grapple with the Past C .15 .25
149 Ground Seal R .15 .25
150 Harrow C .15 .25
151 Herald of the Pantheon R .15 .25
152 Hunting Wilds U .15 .25
153 Hydra Omnivore M .75 1.25
154 Khalni Heart Expedition C .15 .25
155 Kruphix's Insight C .15 .25
156 Moldgraf Monstrosity R .15 .25
157 Overgrowth C .15 .25
158 Rampaging Baloths R .15 .25
159 Reclamation Sage U .15 .25
160 Sakura-Tribe Elder C .15 .25
161 Scute Mob R .15 .25
162 Snake Umbra C .15 .25
163 Spawning Grounds R .15 .25
164 Vow of Wildness U .15 .25
165 Wild Growth C .15 .25
166 Yavimaya Elder C .15 .25
167 Yavimaya Enchantress C .15 .25
168 Aethermage's Touch R .15 .25
169 Bant Charm U .15 .25
170 Bruna, Light of Alabaster M .15 .25
171 Charnelhoard Wurm R .15 .25
172 Cold-Eyed Selkie R .15 .25
173 Daxos of Meletis R .15 .25
174 Deathreap Ritual U .15 .25
175 Decimate R .15 .25
176 Duskmantle Seer R .15 .25
177 Elderwood Scion R .15 .25
178 Enigma Sphinx R .15 .25
179 Esper Charm U .15 .25
180 Finest Hour R .15 .25
181 Gaze of Granite R .15 .25
182 Grisly Salvage C .15 .25
183 High Priest of Penance R .15 .25
184 Lavalanche R .15 .25
185 Maverick Thopterist U .15 .25
186 Mortify U .15 .25
187 Putrefy U .15 .25
188 Righteous Authority R .15 .25
189 Rubblehulk R .15 .25
190 Savage Twister U .15 .25
191 Silent-Blade Oni R 1.50 2.00
192 Unflinching Courage U .15 .25
193 Utter End R .15 .25
194 Worm Harvest R .15 .25
195 Zendikar Incarnate U .15 .25
196 Azorius Signet U .15 .25
197 Blinkmoth Urn R .15 .25
198 Bosh, Iron Golem R .15 .25
199 Chief of the Foundry U .15 .25
200 Commander's Sphere C .15 .25
201 Crystal Ball U .15 .25
202 Darksteel Juggernaut R .15 .25
203 Dimir Signet U .75 1.25
204 Dreamstone Hedron U .15 .25
205 Duplicant R .75 1.25
206 Hedron Archive U .15 .25
207 Izzet Signet U .15 .25
208 Magnifying Glass U .15 .25
209 Mimic Vat R 1.00 1.50
210 Mind Stone C .15 .25
211 Mirrorworks R .15 .25
212 Myr Battlesphere R .15 .25
213 Orzhov Signet C .15 .25
214 Pilgrim's Eye C .15 .25
215 Prismatic Lens U .15 .25
216 Prototype Portal R .15 .25
217 Psychosis Crawler R .15 .25
218 Scrabbling Claws U .15 .25
219 Scuttling Doom Engine R .15 .25
220 Seer's Lantern C .15 .25
221 Seer's Sundial R .15 .25
222 Sol Ring U 2.00 3.00
223 Soul of New Phyrexia M .15 .25
224 Steel Hellkite R .15 .25
225 Swiftfoot Boots U .60 1.00
226 Thopter Assembly R .15 .25
227 Unstable Obelisk U .15 .25
228 Unwinding Clock R 2.50 3.50
229 Vessel of Endless Rest U .15 .25
230 Worn Powerstone U .15 .25
231 Akoum Refuge U .15 .25
232 Arcane Sanctum U .15 .25
233 Azorius Chancery U .15 .25
234 Azorius Guildgate C .15 .25
235 Barren Moor C .15 .25
236 Blighted Woodland U .15 .25
237 Blossoming Sands C .15 .25
238 Bojuka Bog C 1.00 1.50
239 Buried Ruin U .15 .25
240 Command Tower C 1.00 1.50
241 Darksteel Citadel U .15 .25
242 Dimir Aqueduct U .15 .25
243 Dimir Guildgate C .15 .25
244 Dismal Backwater C .15 .25
245 Evolving Wilds C .15 .25
246 Forgotten Cave C .15 .25
247 Forsaken Sanctuary U .15 .25
248 Foundry of the Consuls U .15 .25
249 Golgari Rot Farm U .15 .25
250 Great Furnace C .15 .25
251 Grim Backwoods R .15 .25
252 Gruul Turf U .15 .25
253 Halimar Depths C .15 .25
254 Haunted Fengraf C .15 .25
255 Highland Lake U .15 .25
256 Izzet Boilerworks U .15 .25
257 Izzet Guildgate C .15 .25
258 Jund Panorama C .15 .25
259 Jungle Hollow C .15 .25
260 Jwar Isle Refuge U .15 .25
261 Kazandu Refuge U .15 .25

262 Khalni Garden C .15 .25
263 Krosan Verge U .15 .25
264 Lonely Sandbar C .15 .25
265 Meandering River U .15 .25
266 Mortuary Mire C .15 .25
267 Mosswort Bridge R .15 .25
268 Mountain Valley U .15 .25
269 Myriad Landscape U 1.00 1.50
270 New Benalia U .15 .25
271 Orzhov Basilica U .15 .25
272 Orzhov Guildgate C .15 .25
273 Rakdos Carnarium C .15 .25
274 Rocky Tar Pit U .15 .25
275 Savage Lands U .15 .25
276 Scoured Barrens C .15 .25
277 Seaside Citadel U .15 .25
278 Seat of the Synod C .15 .25
279 Secluded Steppe C .15 .25
280 Sejiri Refuge U .15 .25
281 Selesnya Sanctuary C .15 .25
282 Simic Growth Chamber U .15 .25
283 Submerged Boneyard U .15 .25
284 Swiftwater Cliffs C .15 .25
285 Temple of the False God U .15 .25
286 Terramorphic Expanse C .15 .25
287 Thornwood Falls C .15 .25
288 Tranquil Cove C .15 .25
289 Tranquil Expanse U .15 .25
290 Tranquil Thicket C .15 .25
291 Warped Landscape C .15 .25
292 Woodland Stream C .15 .25
293 Plains C .15 .25
294 Plains C .15 .25
295 Plains C .15 .25
296 Island C .15 .25
297 Island C .15 .25
298 Island C .15 .25
299 Swamp C .15 .25
300 Swamp C .15 .25
301 Swamp C .15 .25
302 Mountain C .15 .25
303 Mountain C .15 .25
304 Mountain C .15 .25
305 Forest C .15 .25
306 Forest C .15 .25
307 Forest C .15 .25

2018 Magic The Gathering Commander 2018 Tokens

1 Manifest .06 .10
2 Shapeshifter .06 .10
3 Angel .10 .15
4 Mask .10 .15
5 Cat .06 .10
6 Soldier .06 .10
7 Myr .10 .15
8 Thopter .06 .10
9 Zombie .06 .10
10 Dragon Egg .75 1.25
11 Dragon .06 .10
12 Survivor .20 .30
13 Beast .06 .10
14 Beast .06 .10
15 Cat Warrior .06 .10
16 Elemental .06 .10
17 Plant .06 .10
18 Worm .06 .10
19 Clue .06 .10
20 Construct .06 .10
21 Construct .06 .10
22 Horror .06 .10
23 Myr .20 .30
24 Servo .06 .10
25 Thopter .06 .10
26 Thopter .06 .10

2019 Magic The Gathering Commander 2019

COMPLETE SET (302)
BOOSTER BOX (PACKS)
BOOSTER PACK (CARDS)
RELEASED ON AUGUST 23, 2019
1 Cliffside Rescuer U .15 .25
2 Commander's Insignia R .20 .30
3 Doomed Artisan R .20 .30
4 Mandate of Peace R .20 .30
5 Sevinne's Reclamation R .20 .30
6 Song of the Worldsoul R .20 .30
7 Thalia's Geistcaller R .20 .30
8 Kadena's Silencer R .20 .30
9 Leadership Vacuum U .15 .25
10 Mass Diminish R .20 .30
11 Sudden Substitution R .20 .30
12 Thought Sponge R .20 .30
13 Wall of Stolen Identity R .20 .30
14 Archfiend of Spite R .20 .30
15 Bone Miser R .20 .30
16 Curse of Fool's Wisdom R .20 .30
17 Gift of Doom R .20 .30
18 K'rrik, Son of Yawgmoth R .20 .30
19 Mire in Misery U .15 .25
20 Nightmare Unmaking R .20 .30
21 Thieving Amalgam R .20 .30
22 Anje's Ravager R .20 .30
23 Backdraft Hellkite R .20 .30
24 Dockside Extortionist R .20 .30
25 Ghired's Belligerence R .20 .30
26 Hate Mirage U .15 .25
27 Ignite the Future R .20 .30
28 Skyfire Phoenix R .20 .30
29 Tectonic Hellion R .20 .30
30 Wildfire Devils R .20 .30
31 Apex Altisaur R .20 .30
32 Full Flowering R .20 .30
33 Ohran Frostfang R .20 .30
34 Road of Return R .20 .30
35 Selesnya Eulogist R .20 .30
36 Voice of Many U .15 .25
37 Anje Falkenreath M 3.00 5.00
38 Atla Palani, Nest Tender M 5.00 8.00
39 Chainer, Nightmare Adept M 3.00 5.00
40 Elsha of the Infinite M 4.00 6.00
41 Gerrard, Weatherlight Hero R .20 .30
42 Ghired, Conclave Exile M 3.00 5.00
43 Greven, Predator Captain M 1.50 2.50
44 Grismold, the Dreadsower R .20 .30
45 Kadena, Slinking Sorcerer M 2.50 4.00
46 Marisi, Breaker of the Coil M 2.50 4.00
47 Pramikon Sky Rampant M 2.00 3.00
48 Rayami, First of the Fallen M 1.25 2.00
49 Sevinne, the Chronoclasm M 1.50 2.50
50 Tahngarth, First Mate R .20 .30
51 Volrath, the Shapestealer M 2.50 4.00
52 Aeon Engine R .20 .30
53 Bloodthirsty Blade U .15 .25
54 Empowered Autogenerator R .20 .30
55 Idol of Oblivion R .20 .30
56 Pendant of Prosperity R .20 .30
57 Scareteller C .10 .15
58 Scroll of Fate R .20 .30
59 Sanctum of Eternity R .20 .30
60 Desolation Twin R .20 .30
61 Angel of Sanctions M .30 .50
62 Divine Reckoning R .20 .30
63 Dusk // Dawn R .20 .30
64 Ghostly Prison U .15 .25
65 Hour of Reckoning R .20 .30
66 Increasing Devotion R .20 .30
67 Intangible Virtue U .15 .25
68 Phyrexian Rebirth R .20 .30
69 Prismatic Strands C .10 .15
70 Pristine Angel M .30 .50
71 Purify the Grave U .15 .25
72 Ray of Distortion C .10 .15
73 Roc Egg U .15 .25
74 Rootborn Defenses C .10 .15
75 Storm Herd R .20 .30
76 Sun Titan M 1.25 2.50
77 Trostani's Judgment C .10 .15
78 Wingmate Roc M .30 .50
79 Zetalpa, Primal Dawn R .20 .30
80 Chemister's Insight U .15 .25
81 Chromeshell Crab R .20 .30
82 Clever Impersonator M 2.00 3.00
83 Deep Analysis C .10 .15
84 Echoing Truth C .10 .15
85 Fact or Fiction U .15 .25
86 Fervent Denial U .15 .25
87 Ixidron R .20 .30
88 Jace's Sanctum R .20 .30
89 Kheru Spellsnatcher R .20 .30
90 Mystic Retrieval U .15 .25
91 Oona's Grace C .10 .15
92 Reality Shift U .15 .25
93 River Kelpie R .20 .30
94 Runi Repetition U .15 .25
95 Secrets of the Dead U .15 .25
96 Stratus Dancer R .20 .30
97 Talrand, Sky Summoner R .20 .30
98 Tezzeret's Gambit U .15 .25
99 Think Twice C .10 .15
100 Thousand Winds R .20 .30
101 Vesuvan Shapeshifter R .20 .30
102 Willbender U .15 .25
103 Asylum Visitor R .20 .30
104 Bane of the Living R .20 .30
105 Beacon of Unrest R .20 .30
106 Big Game Hunter U .15 .25
107 Boneyard Parley M .30 .50
108 Call to the Netherworld C .10 .15
109 Champion of Stray Souls M .30 .50
110 Dark Withering C .10 .15
111 Doomed Necromancer R .20 .30
112 Faith of the Devoted U .15 .25
113 From Under the Floorboards R .20 .30
114 Geth, Lord of the Vault M 2.50 4.00
115 Ghastly Conscription M .30 .50
116 Gorgon Recluse C .10 .15
117 Grave Scrabbler C .10 .15
118 Grim Haruspex R .20 .30
119 Hedonist's Trove R .20 .30
120 Hex R .20 .30
121 In Garruk's Wake R .20 .30
122 Murderous Compulsion C .10 .15
123 Nightshade Assassin U .15 .25
124 Ob Nixilis Reignited M .75 1.25
125 Overseer of the Damned R .20 .30
126 Plaguecrafter U .15 .25
127 Sanitarium Skeleton C .10 .15
128 Silumgar Assassin R .20 .30
129 Skinthinner C .10 .15
130 Soul of Innistrad M .30 .50
131 The Eldest Reborn U .15 .25
132 Zombie Infestation U .15 .25
133 Alchemist's Greeting C .10 .15
134 Avacyn's Judgment R .20 .30
135 Burning Vengeance U .15 .25
136 Chaos Warp R .20 .30
137 Desperate Ravings U .15 .25
138 Devil's Play R .20 .30
139 Dragonmaster Outcast M .75 1.25
140 Faithless Looting C .10 .15
141 Feldon of the Third Path M .50 .75
142 Fiery Temper C .10 .15
143 Flamerush Rider R .20 .30
144 Flayer of the Hatebound R .20 .30
145 Guttersnipe U .15 .25
146 Heart-Piercer Manticore R .20 .30
147 Increasing Vengeance R .20 .30
148 Magmaquake R .20 .30
149 Magus of the Wheel R .20 .30
150 Malevolent Whispers U .15 .25
151 Rolling Temblor U .15 .25
152 Squee, Goblin Nabob R .20 .30
153 Stromkirk Occultist R .20 .30
154 Violent Eruption U .15 .25
155 Warstorm Surge R .20 .30
156 Ainok Survivalist C .10 .15
157 Beast Within U .15 .25
158 Colossal Majesty U .15 .25
159 Cultivate C .10 .15
160 Deathmist Raptor M .40 .60
161 Den Protector R .20 .30
162 Druid's Deliverance C .10 .15
163 Elemental Bond U .15 .25
164 Explore C .10 .15
165 Farseek C .10 .15
166 Fresh Meat R .20 .30
167 Garruk, Primal Hunter M 2.00 3.00
168 Garruk's Packleader U .15 .25
169 Giant Adephage M .40 .60
170 Great Oak Guardian U .15 .25
171 Harmonize U .15 .25
172 Hooded Hydra M .50 .75
173 Momentous Fall R .20 .30
174 Nanfuko Vigilante C .10 .15
175 Overwhelming Stampede R .20 .30
176 Rampaging Baloths R .20 .30
177 Sakura-Tribe Elder C .10 .15
178 Second Harvest R .20 .30
179 Seedborn Muse R .20 .30
180 Shamanic Revelation R .20 .30
181 Slice in Twain U .15 .25
182 Soul of Zendikar M .30 .50
183 Tempt with Discovery R .20 .30
184 Thelonite Hermit R .20 .30
185 Thragtusk R .20 .30
186 Trail of Mystery R .20 .30
187 Biomass Mutation R .20 .30
188 Bloodhall Priest R .20 .30
189 Bounty of the Luxa R .20 .30
190 Crackling Drake U .15 .25
191 Emmara Tandris R .20 .30
192 Farm // Market U .15 .25
193 Growing Ranks R .20 .30
194 Icefeather Aven U .15 .25
195 Naya Charm U .15 .25
196 Pristine Skywise R .20 .30
197 Putrefy U .15 .25
198 Ral Zarek M 1.25 2.00
199 Refuse // Cooperate R .20 .30
200 Sagu Mauler R .20 .30
201 Secret Plans U .15 .25
202 Sultai Charm U .15 .25
203 Sundering Growth C .10 .15
204 Trostani, Selesnya's Voice M .40 .60
205 Urban Evolution U .15 .25
206 Vitu-Ghazi Guildmage U .15 .25
207 Vraska the Unseen M 1.00 1.50
208 Wayfaring Temple R .20 .30
209 Armillary Sphere C .10 .15
210 Azorius Locket C .10 .15
211 Burnished Hart U .15 .25
212 Commander's Sphere C .10 .15
213 Grimoire of the Dead M .60 1.00
214 Hedron Archive U .15 .25
215 Izzet Locket C .10 .15
216 Key to the City R .20 .30
217 Lightning Greaves U .15 .25
218 Meteor Golem U .15 .25
219 Mimic Vat R .20 .30
220 Rakdos Locket C .10 .15
221 Sol Ring U .15 .25
222 Solemn Simulacrum R .20 .30
223 Soul Foundry R .20 .30
224 Strionic Resonator R .20 .30
225 Thran Dynamo U .15 .25
226 Akoum Refuge U .15 .25
227 Ash Barrens C .10 .15
228 Azorius Chancery U .15 .25
229 Barren Moor U .15 .25
230 Bloodfell Caves C .10 .15
231 Blossoming Sands C .10 .15
232 Bojuka Bog C .10 .15
233 Boros Garrison C .10 .15
234 Boros Guildgate C .10 .15
235 Cinder Barrens R .20 .30
236 Cinder Glade R .20 .30
237 Command Tower C .10 .15
238 Darkwater Catacombs R .20 .30
239 Dimir Aqueduct U .15 .25
240 Drownyard Temple R .20 .30
241 Evolving Wilds C .10 .15
242 Exotic Orchard R .20 .30
243 Forgotten Cave C .10 .15
244 Foul Orchard U .15 .25
245 Gargoyle Castle R .20 .30
246 Geier Reach Sanitarium R .20 .30
247 Golgari Guildgate C .10 .15
248 Golgari Rot Farm U .15 .25
249 Graypelt Refuge U .15 .25
250 Gruul Turf U .15 .25
251 Highland Lake U .15 .25
252 Izzet Boilerworks U .15 .25
253 Izzet Guildgate C .10 .15
254 Jungle Hollow C .10 .15
255 Jungle Shrine U .15 .25
256 Kazandu Refuge U .15 .25
257 Krosan Verge U .15 .25
258 Llanowar Wastes R .20 .30
259 Memorial to Folly U .15 .25
260 Mortuary Mire C .10 .15
261 Myriad Landscape U .15 .25
262 Mystic Monastery U .15 .25
263 Naya Panorama C .10 .15
264 Opulent Palace U .15 .25
265 Prairie Stream R .20 .30
266 Rakdos Carnarium C .10 .15
267 Rakdos Guildgate C .10 .15
268 Reliquary Tower U .15 .25
269 Rix Maadi, Dungeon Palace U .15 .25
270 Rogue's Passage U .15 .25
271 Rugged Highlands C .10 .15
272 Selesnya Sanctuary C .10 .15
273 Shrine of the Forsaken Gods R .20 .30
274 Simic Growth Chamber U .15 .25
275 Simic Guildgate C .10 .15
276 Stone Quarry U .15 .25
277 Sungrass Prairie R .20 .30
278 Sunken Hollow R .20 .30
279 Swiftwater Cliffs C .10 .15
280 Temple of the False God U .15 .25
281 Terramorphic Expanse C .10 .15
282 Thespian's Stage R .20 .30
283 Thornwood Falls C .10 .15
284 Tranquil Cove C .10 .15
285 Wind-Scarred Crag C .10 .15
286 Woodland Stream C .10 .15
287 Yavimaya Coast R .20 .30
288 Plains L C .10 .15
289 Plains L C .10 .15
290 Plains L C .10 .15
291 Island L C .10 .15
292 Island L C .10 .15
293 Island L C .10 .15
294 Swamp L C .10 .15
295 Swamp L C .10 .15
296 Swamp L C .10 .15
297 Mountain L C .10 .15
298 Mountain L C .10 .15
299 Mountain L C .10 .15
300 Forest L C .10 .15
301 Forest L C .10 .15
302 Forest L C .10 .15

2019 Magic The Gathering Commander 2019 Tokens

COMPLETE SET (29) 4.00 6.00
1 Bird .40
2 Bird .40
3 Human .25 .40
4 Pegasus .25 .40
5 Spirit .25 .40
6 Angel of Sanctions .25 .40
7 Heart-Piercer Manticore .25 .40
8 Drake .25 .40
9 Assassin .25 .40
10 Zombie .25 .40
11 Zombie .25 .40
12 Dragon .25 .40
13 Beast .25 .40
14 Beast .25 .40
15 Centaur .25 .40
16 Egg .25 .40
17 Plant .25 .40
18 Rhino .25 .40
19 Saproling .25 .40
20 Snake .25 .40
21 Wurm .25 .40
22 Gargoyle .25 .40
23 Horror .25 .40
24 Sculpture .25 .40
25 Treasure .25 .40
26 Eldrazi .25 .40
27 Morph .25 .40
28 Manifest .25 .40
29 Ob Nixilis Reignited Emblem .25 .40

Conspiracy

2014 Magic The Gathering Conspiracy

COMPLETE SET (219) 120.00 175.00
RELEASED ON JUNE 6, 2014
1 Advantageous Proclamation U .20 .35
2 Backup Plan R .30 .50
3 Brago's Favor C .15 .25
4 Double Stroke U .20 .35
5 Immediate Action C .15 .25
6 Iterative Analysis U .20 .35
7 Muzzio's Preparations C .15 .25
8 Power Play U .20 .35
9 Secret Summoning U .20 .35
10 Secrets of Paradise C .15 .25
11 Sentinel Dispatch C .15 .25
12 Unexpected Potential U .20 .35
14 Brago's Representative C :W: .15 .25
15 Council Guardian U :W: .20 .35
16 Council's Judgment R :W: 4.00 5.50
17 Custodi Soulbinders R :W: .30 .50
18 Custodi Squire C :W: .15 .25
19 Rousing of Souls C :W: .15 .25
20 Academy Elite R :B: .30 .50
21 Marchesa's Emissary C :B: .15 .25
22 Marchesa's Infiltrator U :B: .20 .35
23 Muzzio, Visionary Architect M :B: 1.75 2.25
24 Plea for Power R :B: .40 .60
25 Split Decision U :B: .20 .35
26 Bite of the Black Rose U :K: .20 .35
27 Drakestown Forgotten R :K: .30 .50
28 Grudge Keeper C :K: .15 .25
29 Reign of the Pit R :K: .30 .50
30 Tyrant's Choice C :K: .15 .25
31 Enraged Revolutionary C :R: .15 .25
32 Grenzo's Cutthroat C :R: .15 .25
33 Grenzo's Rebuttal R :R: .30 .50
34 Ignition Team R :R: .30 .50
35 Scourge of the Throne M :R: 6.00 8.00
36 Treasonous Ogre U :R: .20 .35
37 Predator's Howl U :G: .20 .35
38 Realm Seekers R :G: .30 .50
39 Selvala's Charge U :G: .20 .35
40 Selvala's Enforcer C .15 .25
41 Brago, King Eternal M :W: :B: 1.00 1.50
42 Dack Fayden M :B: :R: 10.00 15.00

43 Dack's Duplicate R :B: :R:	1.00	1.25
44 Deathreap Ritual U :K: :G:	.20	.35
45 Extract from Darkness U :G: :K:	.20	.35
46 Flamewright U :R: :W:	.20	.35
47 Grenzo, Dungeon Warden R :K: :R:	1.25	1.75
48 Magister of Worth R :W: :K:	.30	.50
49 Marchesa, the Black Rose M :D:	4.00	6.00
50 Marchesa's Smuggler U :B: :R:	.20	.35
51 Selvala, Explorer Returned R :G: :W:	.75	1.00
52 Woodvine Elemental U :G: :W:	.20	.35
53 Aether Searcher R	.30	.50
54 Agent of Acquisitions U	.20	.35
55 Canal Dredger R	.30	.50
56 Coercive Portal M	2.50	3.50
57 Cogwork Grinder R	.30	.50
58 Cogwork Librarian C	.15	.25
59 Cogwork Spy C	.15	.25
60 Cogwork Tracker U	.20	.35
61 Deal Broker R	.30	.50
62 Lore Seeker R	.30	.50
63 Lurking Automaton C	.15	.25
64 Whispergear Sneak C	.15	.25
65 Paliano, the High City R	.30	.50
66 Ajani's Sunstriker C :W:	.15	.25
67 Apex Hawks C :W:	.15	.25
68 Courier Hawk C :W:	.15	.25
69 Doomed Traveler C :W:	.15	.25
70 Glimmerpoint Stag U :W:	.20	.35
71 Guardian Zendikon C :W:	.15	.25
72 Intangible Virtue U :W:	.20	.35
73 Kor Chant C :W:	.15	.25
74 Moment of Heroism C :W:	.15	.25
75 Noble Templar C :W:	.15	.25
76 Pillarfield Ox C :W:	.15	.25
77 Pride Guardian C :W:	.15	.25
78 Pristine Angel M :W:	1.00	1.50
79 Reya Dawnbringer R :W:	.75	1.15
80 Rout R :W:	1.00	1.50
81 Silverchase Fox C :W:	.15	.25
82 Soulcatcher U :W:	.20	.35
83 Stave Off C :W:	.15	.25
84 Swords to Plowshares U :W:	.20	.35
85 Unquestioned Authority U :W:	.20	.35
86 Valor Made Real C :W:	.15	.25
87 Vow of Duty U :W:	.20	.35
88 Wakestone Gargoyle U :W:	.20	.35
89 AEther Tradewinds C :B:	.15	.25
90 Air Servant U :B:	.20	.35
91 Brainstorm C :B:	.15	.25
92 Breakthrough U :B:	.20	.35
93 Compulsive Research C :B:	.15	.25
94 Crookclaw Transmuter C :B:	.15	.25
95 Dream Fracture C :B:	.15	.25
96 Enclave Elite C :B:	.15	.25
97 Fact or Fiction U :B:	.20	.35
98 Favorable Winds U :B:	.20	.35
99 Grixis Illusionist C :B:	.15	.25
100 Jetting Glasskite U :B:	.20	.35
101 Minamo Scrollkeeper C :B:	.15	.25
102 Misdirection R :B:	1.50	2.00
103 Plated Seastrider C :B:	.15	.25
104 Reckless Scholar C :B:	.15	.25
105 Screaming Seahawk C :B:	.15	.25
106 Shoreline Ranger C :B:	.15	.25
107 Stasis Cell C :B:	.15	.25
108 Stifle R :B:	3.00	4.00
109 Traveler's Cloak C :B:	.15	.25
110 Turn the Tide C :B:	.15	.25
111 Wind Dancer U :B:	.20	.35
112 Altar's Reap C :K:	.15	.25
113 Assassinate C :K:	.15	.25
114 Ill-Gotten Gains R :K:	.30	.50
115 Infectious Horror C :K:	.15	.25
116 Liliana's Specter C :K:	.15	.25
117 Magus of the Mirror R :K:	.30	.50
118 Morkrut Banshee U :K:	.20	.35
119 Necromantic Thirst C :K:	.15	.25
120 Phage the Untouchable M :K:	1.25	1.75
121 Plagued Rusalka U :K:	.20	.35
122 Quag Vampires C :K:	.15	.25
123 Reckless Spite U :K:	.20	.35
124 Skeletal Scrying U :K:	.20	.35
125 Smallpox U :K:	.20	.35
126 Stronghold Discipline C :K:	.15	.25
127 Syphon Soul C :K:	.15	.25
128 Tragic Slip C :K:	.15	.25
129 Twisted Abomination C :K:	.15	.25
130 Typhoid Rats C :K:	.15	.25
131 Unhallowed Pact C :K:	.15	.25
132 Vampire Hexmage U :K:	.20	.35
133 Victimize U :K:	.20	.35
134 Wakedancer C :K:	.15	.25
135 Zombie Goliath C :K:	.15	.25
136 Barbed Shocker U :R:	.20	.35
137 Boldwyr Intimidator U :R:	.20	.35
138 Brimstone Volley C :R:	.15	.25
139 Chartooth Cougar C :R:	.15	.25
140 Cinder Wall C :R:	.15	.25
141 Deathforge Shaman U :R:	.20	.35
142 Flaring Flame-Kin U :R:	.20	.35
143 Flowstone Blade C :R:	.15	.25
144 Heartless Hidetsugu R :R:	.40	.60
145 Heckling Fiends U :R:	.20	.35
146 Lizard Warrior C :R:	.15	.25
147 Mana Geyser C :R:	.15	.25
148 Orcish Cannonade C :R:	.15	.25
149 Pitchburn Devils C :R:	.15	.25
150 Power of Fire C :R:	.15	.25
151 Skitter of Lizards C :R:	.15	.25
152 Sulfuric Vortex R :R:	.60	1.00
153 Torch Fiend C :R:	.15	.25
154 Trumpet Blast C :R:	.15	.25
155 Uncontrollable Anger U :R:	.20	.35
156 Vent Sentinel C :R:	.15	.25
157 Volcanic Fallout U :R:	.20	.35
158 Wrap in Flames C :R:	.15	.25
159 Charging Rhino C :G:	.15	.25
160 Copperhorn Scout C :G:	.15	.25
161 Echoing Courage C :G:	.15	.25
162 Elephant Guide U :G:	.20	.35
163 Elvish Aberration C :G:	.15	.25
164 Exploration R :G:	10.00	13.00
165 Gamekeeper U :G:	.20	.35
166 Gnarlid Pack C :G:	.15	.25
167 Howling Wolf C :G:	.15	.25
168 Hunger of the Howlpack C :G:	.15	.25
169 Hydra Omnivore M :G:	2.25	3.00
170 Lead the Stampede U :G:	.20	.35
171 Nature's Claim C :G:	.15	.25
172 Pelakka Wurm U :G:	.20	.35
173 Plummet C :G:	.15	.25
174 Provoke C :G:	.15	.25
175 Relic Crush U :G:	.20	.35
176 Respite C :G:	.15	.25
177 Sakura-Tribe Elder C :G:	.15	.25
178 Scaled Wurm C :G:	.15	.25
179 Sporecap Spider C :G:	.15	.25
180 Squirrel Nest U :G:	.20	.35
181 Terastodon R :G:	.30	.50
182 Wolfbriar Elemental R :G:	.30	.50
183 Wrap in Vigor C :G:	.15	.25
184 Basandra, Battle Seraph R :R: :W:	.50	.75
185 Decimate R	1.25	1.75
186 Dimir Doppelganger R :B: :K:	.60	1.00
187 Edric, Spymaster of Trest R :G: :B:	1.25	1.75
188 Fires of Yavimaya U :R: :G:	.20	.35
189 Mirari's Wake M :G: :W:	9.00	11.00
190 Mortify U :W: :K:	.20	.35
191 Pernicious Deed M :K: :G:	4.00	5.00
192 Sky Spirit U :W: :B:	.20	.35
193 Spiritmonger R :K: :G:	.40	.60
194 Spontaneous Combustion U :K: :R:	.20	.35
195 Wood Sage U :G: :B:	.20	.35
196 Altar Of Dementia R	2.00	3.00
197 Deathrender R	2.00	3.00
198 Explorer's Scope U	.20	.35
199 Fireshrieker U	.20	.35
200 Galvanic Juggernaut U	.20	.35
201 Peace Strider U	.20	.35
202 Reito Lantern U	.20	.35
203 Runed Servitor U	.20	.35
204 Silent Arbiter R	1.25	1.75
205 Spectral Searchlight U	.20	.35
206 Vedalken Orrery R	4.00	5.00
207 Warmonger's Chariot U	.20	.35
208 Mirrodin's Core U	.20	.35
209 Quicksand U :L:	.20	.35
210 Worldknit R	.30	.50
210 Reflecting Pool R :L:	6.00	8.00

2014 Magic The Gathering Conspiracy Tokens

1 Spirit	.10	.15
2 Demon	.15	.25
3 Zombie	.10	.15
4 Ogre	.30	.40
5 Elephant	.15	.25
6 Squirrel	.60	1.00
7 Wolf	.15	.25
8 Construct	.10	.15
9 Dack Fayden Emblem	1.50	2.00

2016 Magic The Gathering Conspiracy Take the Crown

COMPLETE SET (221)	325.00	425.00
BOOSTER BOX (36 PACKS)	90.00	100.00
BOOSTER PACK (15 CARDS)	4.00	5.00
RELEASED ON AUGUST 26, 2016		
1 Adrianas Valor C	.10	.25
2 Assemble the Rank and Vile C	.10	.25
3 Echoing Boon U	.10	.20
4 Emissarys Ploy R	.20	.35
5 Hired Heist C	.10	.25
6 Hold the Perimeter R	.20	.35
7 Hymn of the Wilds M	.50	.75
8 Incendiary Dissent C	.10	.25
9 Natuarl Unity C	.10	.25
10 Sovereigns Realm M	.50	.75
11 Summoners Bond U	.10	.20
12 Weight Advantage R	.20	.35
13 Ballot Broker C	.10	.25
14 Custodi Peacekeeper C	.10	.25
15 Custodi Soulcaller U	.10	.20
16 Lieutenants of the Guard C	.10	.25
17 Noble Banneret U	.10	.20
18 Palace Jailer U	.10	.20
19 Palace Sentinels C	.10	.25
20 Paliano Vanguard R	.20	.35
21 Protector of the Crown R	.20	.35
22 Recruiter of the Guard R	11.00	14.00
23 Sanctum Prelate M	14.00	16.00
24 Spectral Grasp U	.10	.20
25 Throne Warden C	.10	.25
26 Wings of the Guard C	.10	.25
27 Arcane Savant R	.20	.35
28 Canal Courier C	.10	.25
29 Coveted Peacock U	.10	.20
30 Expropriate M	15.00	18.00
31 Illusion of Choice U	.10	.20
32 Illusionary Informant C	.10	.25
33 Jeering Homunculus C	.10	.25
34 Keeper of Keys R	.20	.35
35 Messenger Jays C	.10	.25
36 Skittering Crustacean C	.10	.25
37 Spire Phantasm U	.10	.20
38 Stunt Double R	1.50	2.00
39 Archdemon of Paliano R	.20	.35
40 Capital Punishment R	.20	.35
41 Custodi Lich R	.20	.35
42 Deadly Designs U	.10	.20
43 Garrulous Sycophant C	.10	.25
44 Marchesas Decree U	.10	.20
45 Regicide C	.10	.25
46 Sinuous Vermin C	.10	.25
47 Smuggler Captain U	.10	.20
48 Thorn of the Black Rose C	.10	.25
49 Besmirch U	.10	.20
50 Crown Hunter Hireling C	.10	.25
51 Deputized Protester C	.10	.25
52 Garbage Fire C	.10	.25
53 Goblin Racketeer C	.10	.25
54 Grenzo Havoc Raiser R	1.25	1.75
55 Grenzos Ruffians U	.10	.20
56 Pyretic Hunter U	.10	.20
57 Skyline Despot R	.30	.50
58 Subterranean Tremors M	2.00	2.50
59 Volatile Chimera R	.20	.35
60 Animus of Predation U	.10	.20
61 Borderland Explorer C	.10	.25
62 Caller of the Untamed R	.20	.35
63 Domesticated Hydra U	.10	.20
64 Entourage of Trest C	.10	.25
65 Fang of the Pack U	.10	.20
66 Leovolds Operative C	.10	.25
67 Menagerie Liberator C	.10	.25
68 Orchard Elemental C	.10	.25
69 Regal Behemoth R	.30	.50
70 Selvala Heart of the Wilds M	10.00	12.00
71 Selvalas Stampede R	1.25	1.75
72 Splitting Slime R	.20	.35
73 Adriana Captain of the Guard R	.20	.35
74 Daretti Ingenious Iconoclast M	10.00	12.00
75 Kaya Ghost Assassin M	10.00	12.00
76 Knights of the Black Rose U	.10	.20
77 Leovold Emissary of Trest M	45.00	50.00
78 Queen Marchesa M	3.50	4.50
79 Spy Kit U	.10	.20
80 Throne of the High City R	.40	.60
81 Affa Guard Hound U	.10	.20
82 Disenchant C	.10	.25
83 Doomed Traveler C	.10	.25
84 Faiths Reward R	.20	.35
85 Ghostly Possession C	.10	.25
86 Ghostly Prison U	1.50	2.00
87 Gleam of Resistance C	.10	.25
88 Gods Willing C	.10	.25
89 Guardian of the Gateless U	.10	.20
90 Hall of Arrows U	.10	.20
91 Hallowed Burial R	.40	.60
92 Hollowhenge Spirit U	.10	.20
93 Hundred Handed One R	.20	.35
94 Kill Shot C	.10	.25
95 Pariah R	.30	.50
96 Raise the Alarm C	.10	.25
97 Reviving Dose C	.10	.25
98 Spirit of the Hearth R	.20	.35
99 Wild Griffin C	.10	.25
100 Windborne Charge U	.10	.20
101 Zealous Strike C	.10	.25
102 Bonds of Quicksilver C	.10	.25
103 Caller of Gales C	.10	.25
104 Cloaked Siren C	.10	.25
105 Covenant of Minds R	.20	.35
106 Deceiver Exarch U	.10	.20
107 Desertion R	.75	1.00
108 Dismiss U	.10	.20
109 Divination C	.10	.25
110 Fleeting Distraction C	.10	.25
111 Followed Footsteps R	.30	.50
112 Into the Void U	.10	.20
113 Kami of the Crescent Moon R	.50	.75
114 Merfolk Looter U	.10	.20
115 Merfolk Skyscout U	.10	.20
116 Mnemonic Wall C	.10	.25
117 Negate C	.10	.25
118 Omenspeaker C	.10	.25
119 Repulse C	.10	.25
120 Serum Visions U	2.00	2.75
121 Show and Tell M	15.00	17.00
122 Sphinx of Magosi R	.20	.35
123 Traumatic Visions C	.10	.25
124 Vaporkin C	.10	.25
125 Vertigo Spawn U	.10	.20
126 Absorb Vis C	.10	.25
127 Altars Reap C	.10	.25
128 Avatar of Woe M	.75	1.25
129 Blood Toll Harpy C	.10	.25
130 Child of Night C	.10	.25
131 Death Wind C	.10	.25
132 Diabolic Tutor U	.10	.20
133 Festergloom C	.10	.25
134 Driver of the Dead C	.10	.25
135 Farbog Boneflinger U	.10	.20
136 Fleshbag Marauder U	.10	.20
137 Guul Draz Specter R	.20	.35
138 Harvester of Souls R	.20	.35
139 Infest U	.10	.20
140 Inquisition of Kozilek R	7.00	9.00
141 Keepsake Gorgon U	.10	.20
142 Mausoleum Turnkey U	.10	.20
143 Murder C	.10	.25
144 Phyrexian Arena R	2.50	3.25
145 Public Execution U	.10	.20
146 Raise Dead C	.10	.25
147 Sangromancer R	.20	.35
148 Shambling Goblin C	.10	.25
149 Stormkirk Patrol C	.10	.25
150 Unnerve C	.10	.25
151 Burn Away U	.10	.20
152 Burning Wish R	.75	1.25
153 Charmbreaker Devils R	.20	.35
154 Coordinated Assault U	.10	.20
155 Ember Beast C	.10	.25
156 Fiery Fall C	.10	.25
157 Flame Slash C	.10	.25
158 Gang of Devils U	.10	.20
159 Goblin Balloon Brigade C	.10	.25
160 Goblin Tunneler C	.10	.25
161 Gratuitous Violence R	.50	.75
162 Guttersnipe U	.10	.20
163 Hamletback Goliath R	.20	.35
164 Havengul Vampire U	.10	.20
165 Hurly Burly C	.10	.25
166 Ill Tempered Cyclops C	.10	.25
167 Kilin Fiend C	.10	.25
168 Ogre Sentry C	.10	.25
169 Stoneshock Giant U	.10	.20
170 Sulfurous Blast U	.10	.20
171 Tormenting Voice C	.10	.25
172 Trumpet Blast C	.10	.25
173 Twing Bolt C	.10	.25
174 Beast Within U	.75	1.00
175 Berserk M	13.00	16.00
176 Birds of Paradise R	4.00	5.50
177 Bushstrider U	.10	.20
178 Burgeoning R	2.50	3.50
179 Copperhorn Scout C	.10	.25
180 Explosive Vegetation U	.40	.60
181 Fade into Antiquity C	.10	.25
182 Forgotten Ancient R	.20	.35
183 Irresistible Prey U	.10	.20
184 Lace with Moonglove C	.10	.25
185 Lay of the Land C	.10	.25
186 Manaplasm U	.10	.20
187 Nessian Asp U	.10	.20
188 Netcaster Spider C	.10	.25
189 Overrun U	.10	.20
190 Plummet C	.10	.25
191 Prey Upon C	.10	.25
192 Ravenous Leucrocota C	.10	.25
193 Stength in Numbers C	.10	.25
194 Sylvan Bounty C	.10	.25
195 Voyaging Satyr C	.10	.25
196 Wild Pair R	.20	.35
197 Akroan Hoplite U	.10	.20
198 Ascended Lawmage U	.10	.20
199 Carnage Gladiator U	.10	.20
200 Coiling Oracle U	.10	.20
201 Dragonlair Spider R	.20	.35
202 Duskmantle Seer R	.20	.35
203 Gruul War Chant U	.10	.20
204 Juniper Order Ranger U	.20	.35
205 Pharikas Mender U	.10	.20
206 Shipwreck Singer U	.10	.20
207 Stormchaser Chimera U	.10	.20
208 Bronze Sable C	.10	.25
209 Hedron Matrix R	.20	.35
210 Hexplate Golem C	.10	.25
211 Horn of Greed R	.75	1.25
212 Kitesail C	.10	.25
213 Opaline Unicorn C	.10	.25
214 Platinum Angel M	3.00	4.00
215 Psychosis Crawler R	.20	.35
216 Runed Servitor U	.10	.20
217 Dread Statuary U	.10	.20
218 Evolving Wilds C	.10	.25
219 Exotic Orchard R	.75	1.00
220 Rogues Passage U	.10	.20
221 Shimmering Grotto U	.10	.20
222 Kaya Ghost Assassin Alt Foil	120.00	150.00

2016 Magic The Gathering Conspiracy Take the Crown Foil

COMPLETE SET (223)	1100.00	1400.00
BOOSTER BOX (36 PACKS)	90.00	120.00
BOOSTER PACK (15 CARDS)	4.00	5.00
RELEASED ON AUGUST 26, 2016		
1 Adrianas Valor C	.20	.35
2 Assemble the Rank and Vile C	.20	.35
3 Echoing Boon U	.60	1.00
4 Emissarys Ploy R	1.50	2.25
5 Hired Heist C	.20	.35
6 Hold the Perimeter R	1.00	1.50
7 Hymn of the Wilds M	6.00	8.00
8 Incendiary Dissent C	.20	.35
9 Natuarl Unity C	.20	.35
10 Sovereigns Realm M	6.00	8.00
11 Summoners Bond U	1.00	1.50
12 Weight Advantage R	1.00	1.50
13 Ballot Broker C	.20	.35
14 Custodi Peacekeeper C	.20	.35
15 Custodi Soulcaller U	1.00	1.50
16 Lieutenants of the Guard C	.20	.35
17 Noble Banneret U	.40	.60
18 Palace Jailer U	25.00	30.00
19 Palace Sentinels C	.20	.35
20 Paliano Vanguard R	1.25	2.00
21 Protector of the Crown R	2.00	3.00
22 Recruiter of the Guard R	65.00	70.00
23 Sanctum Prelate M	75.00	85.00
24 Spectral Grasp U	.50	.75
25 Throne Warden C	.20	.35
26 Wings of the Guard C	.20	.35
27 Arcane Savant R	2.00	3.00
28 Canal Courier C	.20	.35
29 Coveted Peacock U	.40	.60
30 Expropriate M	55.00	65.00
31 Illusion of Choice U	1.50	2.50
32 Illusionary Informant C	.20	.35
33 Jeering Homunculus C	.20	.35
34 Keeper of Keys R	1.25	2.00
35 Messenger Jays C	.20	.35
36 Skittering Crustacean C	.20	.35
37 Spire Phantasm U	.20	.35
38 Stunt Double R	13.00	16.00
39 Archdemon of Paliano R	1.00	1.50
40 Capital Punishment R	2.00	3.50
41 Custodi Lich R	4.00	6.00
42 Deadly Designs U	.40	.60
43 Garrulous Sycophant C	.20	.35
44 Marchesas Decree U	1.00	1.50
45 Regicide C	.20	.35
46 Sinuous Vermin C	.20	.35
47 Smuggler Captain U	.40	.60

48 Thorn of the Black Rose C	.20	.35
49 Besmirch U	.20	.35
50 Crown Hunter Hireling C	.20	.35
51 Deputized Protester C	.20	.35
52 Garbage Fire C	.20	.35
53 Goblin Racketeer C	.20	.35
54 Grenzo Havoc Raiser R	13.00	16.00
55 Grenzos Ruffians U	1.00	1.25
56 Pyretic Hunter U	.20	.35
57 Skyline Despot R	3.00	5.00
58 Subterranean Tremors M	13.00	16.00
59 Volatile Chimera R	2.00	3.00
60 Animus of Predation U	.20	.35
61 Borderland Explorer C	.20	.35
62 Caller of the Untamed R	1.50	2.50
63 Domesticated Hydra U	.40	.60
64 Entourage of Trest C	.20	.35
65 Fang of the Pack U	.20	.35
66 Leovolds Operative C	.20	.35
67 Menagerie Liberator C	.20	.35
68 Orchard Elemental C	.20	.35
69 Regal Behemoth R	6.00	8.00
70 Selvala Heart of the Wilds M	50.00	60.00
71 Selvalas Stampede R	10.00	12.00
72 Splitting Slime R	1.50	2.00
73 Adriana Captain of the Guard R	4.00	6.00
74 Daretti Ingenious Iconoclast M	60.00	70.00
75 Kaya Ghost Assassin M	65.00	85.00
76 Knights of the Black Rose U	.60	1.00
77 Leovold Emissary of Trest M	225.00	300.00
78 Queen Marchesa M	40.00	45.00
79 Spy Kit U	1.50	2.50
80 Throne of the High City R	5.00	6.50
81 Affa Guard Hound U	.20	.35
82 Disenchant C	.20	.35
83 Doomed Traveler C	.40	.60
84 Faiths Reward R	1.50	2.50
85 Ghostly Possession C	.20	.35
86 Ghostly Prison U	6.00	8.00
87 Gleam of Resistance C	.20	.35
88 Gods Willing C	.40	.60
89 Guardian of the Gateless U	.50	.75
90 Hall of Arrows U	.20	.35
91 Hallowed Burial R	2.00	3.00
92 Hollowhenge Spirit U	.20	.35
93 Hundred Handed One R	.40	.60
94 Kill Shot C	.20	.35
95 Pariah R	1.50	2.50
96 Raise the Alarm C	.20	.35
97 Reviving Dose C	.20	.35
98 Spirit of the Hearth R	1.00	1.50
99 Wild Griffin C	.20	.35
100 Windborne Charge U	.20	.35
101 Zealous Strike C	.20	.35
102 Bonds of Quicksilver C	.20	.35
103 Caller of Gales C	.20	.35
104 Cloaked Siren C	.20	.35
105 Covenant of Minds R	.50	.75
106 Deceiver Exarch U	3.50	4.50
107 Desertion R	4.00	6.00
108 Dismiss U	1.00	1.50
109 Divination C	.20	.35
110 Fleeting Distraction C	.20	.35
111 Followed Footsteps R	1.00	1.50
112 Into the Void U	.20	.35
113 Kami of the Crescent Moon R	5.00	7.00
114 Merfolk Looter U	.20	.35
115 Merfolk Skyscout U	.20	.35
116 Mnemonic Wall C	.20	.35
117 Negate C	.20	.35
118 Omenspeaker C	.20	.35
119 Repulse C	.20	.35
120 Serum Visions U	6.00	8.00
121 Show and Tell M	35.00	45.00
122 Sphinx of Magosi R	.50	.75
123 Traumatic Visions C	.20	.35
124 Vaporkin C	.20	.35
125 Vertigo Spawn U	.20	.35
126 Absorb Vis C	.20	.35
127 Altars Reap C	.20	.35
128 Avatar of Woe M	3.50	4.50
129 Blood Toll Harpy C	.20	.35
130 Child of Night C	.20	.35
131 Death Wind C	.20	.35
132 Diabolic Tutor U	1.00	1.50
133 Festergloom C	.20	.35
134 Driver of the Dead C	.20	.35
135 Farbog Boneflinger U	.20	.35
136 Fleshbag Marauder U	1.00	1.50
137 Guul Draz Specter R	.50	.75
138 Harvester of Souls R	.75	1.25
139 Infest U	.20	.35
140 Inquisition of Kozilek R	40.00	45.00
141 Keepsake Gorgon U	.20	.35
142 Mausoleum Turnkey U	.20	.35
143 Murder C	.75	1.25
144 Phyrexian Arena R	13.00	16.00
145 Public Execution U	.20	.35
146 Raise Dead C	.20	.35
147 Sangromancer R	1.50	2.50
148 Shambling Goblin C	.20	.35
149 Stormkirk Patrol C	.20	.35
150 Unnerve C	.20	.35
151 Burn Away U	.20	.35
152 Burning Wish R	5.00	8.00
153 Charmbreaker Devils R	.75	1.25
154 Coordinated Assault U	.20	.35
155 Ember Beast C	.20	.35
156 Fiery Fall C	.20	.35
157 Flame Slash C	1.00	1.50
158 Gang of Devils U	.20	.35
159 Goblin Balloon Brigade C	.20	.35
160 Goblin Tunneler C	.20	.35
161 Gratuitous Violence R	2.50	4.00
162 Guttersnipe U	1.00	1.50
163 Hamletback Goliath R	.30	.50
164 Havengul Vampire U	.20	.35
165 Hurly Burly C	.20	.35
166 Ill Tempered Cyclops C	.20	.35
167 Kiln Fiend C	2.00	3.50
168 Ogre Sentry C	.20	.35
169 Stoneshock Giant U	.20	.35
170 Sulfurous Blast U	.20	.35
171 Tormenting Voice C	.40	.60
172 Trumpet Blast C	.20	.35
173 Twing Bolt C	.20	.35
174 Beast Within U	6.00	8.00
175 Berserk M	25.00	35.00
176 Birds of Paradise R	9.00	11.00
177 Bushstrider U	.20	.35
178 Burgeoning R	16.00	20.00
179 Copperhorn Scout C	.20	.35
180 Explosive Vegetation U	2.50	3.50
181 Fade into Antiquity C	.20	.35
182 Forgotten Ancient R	2.50	4.00
183 Irresistible Prey U	.20	.35
184 Lace with Moonglove C	.20	.35
185 Lay of the Land C	.20	.35
186 Manaplasm U	.30	.50
187 Nessian Asp U	.20	.35
188 Netcaster Spider C	.20	.35
189 Overrun U	.20	.35
190 Plummet C	.20	.35
191 Prey Upon C	.20	.35
192 Ravenous Leucrocota C	.20	.35
193 Stength in Numbers C	.20	.35
194 Sylvan Bounty C	.20	.35
195 Voyaging Satyr C	.40	.60
196 Wild Pair R	1.50	2.50
197 Akroan Hoplite U	.20	.35
198 Ascended Lawmage U	.20	.35
199 Carnage Gladiator U	.20	.35
200 Coiling Oracle U	3.00	3.50
201 Dragonlair Spider R	1.50	2.50
202 Duskmantle Seer R	1.00	1.50
203 Gruul War Chant U	.20	.35
204 Juniper Order Ranger U	1.25	2.00
205 Pharikas Mender U	.20	.35
206 Shipwreck Singer U	.20	.35
207 Stormchaser Chimera U	.20	.35
208 Bronze Sable C	.20	.35
209 Hedron Matrix R	.75	1.25
210 Hexplate Golem C	.20	.35
211 Horn of Greed R	6.00	8.00
212 Kitesail C	.20	.35
213 Opaline Unicorn C	.20	.35
214 Platinum Angel M	7.00	10.00
215 Psychosis Crawler R	1.00	1.50
216 Runed Servitor U	.20	.35
217 Dread Statuary U	.30	.50
218 Evolving Wilds C	.60	1.00
219 Exotic Orchard R	4.00	6.00
220 Rogues Passage U	1.50	2.50
221 Shimmering Grotto U	.20	.35
T1 The Monarch Token T	.10	.25
222 Kaya Ghost Assassin Alt Foil M	110.00	125.00

2016 Magic The Gathering Conspiracy Take the Crown Tokens

1 The Monarch	.10	.15
2 Soldier	.10	.15
3 Soldier	.10	.15
4 Spirit	.10	.15
5 Assassin	.50	.75
6 Zombie	.10	.15
7 Dragon	.15	.25
8 Goblin	.10	.15
9 Lizard	.10	.15
10 Beast	.10	.15
11 Insect	.10	.15
12 Construct	.10	.15

2018 Magic The Gathering Battlebond

COMPLETE SET (254)	175.00	225.00
RELEASED ON JUNE 8, 2018		
1 Will Kenrith M	8.00	10.00
2 Rowan Kenrith M	6.00	8.00
3 Regna, the Redeemer R	.30	.50
4 Krav, the Unredeemed R	.30	.50
5 Zndrsplt, Eye of Wisdom R	.30	.50
6 Okaun, Eye of Chaos R	.30	.50
7 Virtus the Veiled R	.30	.50
8 Gorm the Great R	.30	.50
9 Khorvath Brightflame R	.30	.50
10 Sylvia Brightspear R	.30	.50
11 Pir, Imaginative Rascal R	.30	.50
12 Toothy, Imaginary Friend R	.30	.50
13 Blaring Recruiter U	.20	.30
14 Blaring Captain U	.20	.30
15 Chakram Retriever U	.20	.30
16 Chakram Slinger U	.20	.30
17 Soulblade Corrupter U	.20	.30
18 Soulblade Renewer U	.20	.30
19 Impetuous Protégé U	.20	.30
20 Proud Mentor U	.20	.30
21 Ley Weaver U	.20	.30
22 Lore Weaver U	.20	.30
23 Arena Rector M	18.00	20.00
24 Aurora Champion C	.10	.20
25 Brightling M	4.00	6.00
26 Bring Down U	.20	.30
27 Dwarven Lightsmith C	.10	.20
28 Jubilant Mascot U	.20	.30
29 Play the Game R	.30	.50
30 Regna's Sanction R	.30	.50
31 Skystreamer C	.10	.20
32 Together Forever R	.30	.50
33 Arcane Artisan M	2.00	2.50
34 Fumble U	.20	.30
35 Game Plan R	.30	.50
36 Huddle Up C	.10	.20
37 Nimbus Champion U	.20	.30
38 Out of Bounds U	.20	.30
39 Saltwater Stalwart C	.10	.20
40 Soaring Show-Off C	.10	.20
41 Spellseeker R	.30	.50
42 Spellweaver Duo C	.10	.20
43 Zndrsplt's Judgment R	.30	.50
44 Archfiend of Despair M	2.50	4.00
45 Bloodborn Scoundrels C	.10	.20
46 Fan Favorite C	.10	.20
47 Gang Up U	.20	.30
48 Inner Demon U	.20	.30
49 Mindblade Render R	.30	.50
50 Sickle Dancer C	.10	.20
51 Stunning Reversal M	2.50	4.00
52 Thrasher Brute U	.20	.30
53 Thrilling Encore R	.30	.50
54 Virtus's Maneuver R	.30	.50
55 Azra Bladeseeker C	.10	.20
56 Bonus Round R	.30	.50
57 Bull-Rush Bruiser C	.10	.20
58 Cheering Fanatic U	.20	.30
59 Khorvath's Fury R	.30	.50
60 Lava-Field Overlord U	.20	.30
61 Magma Hellion C	.10	.20
62 Najeela, the Blade-Blossom M	10.00	13.00
63 Stadium Vendors C	.10	.20
64 Stolen Strategy R	.30	.50
65 Bramble Sovereign M	7.00	10.00
66 Charging Binox C	.10	.20
67 Combo Attack C	.10	.20
68 The Crowd Goes Wild U	.20	.30
69 Decorated Champion U	.20	.30
70 Generous Patron R	.30	.50
71 Grothama, All-Devouring M	1.25	2.00
72 Jungle Wayfinder C	.10	.20
73 Pir's Whim R	.30	.50
74 Archon of Valor's Reach R	.30	.50
75 Azra Oddsmaker U	.20	.30
76 Last One Standing R	.30	.50
77 Rushblade Commander U	.20	.30
78 Vampire Charmseeker U	.20	.30
79 Sentinel Tower R	.30	.50
80 Victory Chimes R	.30	.50
81 Bountiful Promenade R	.30	.50
82 Luxury Suite R	.30	.50
83 Morphic Pool R	.30	.50
84 Sea of Clouds R	.30	.50
85 Spire Garden R	.30	.50
86 Angel of Retribution U	.20	.30
87 Angelic Chorus R	.30	.50
88 Angelic Gift C	.10	.20
89 Battle Mastery U	.20	.30
90 Champion of Arashin C	.10	.20
91 Doomed Traveler C	.10	.20
92 Expedition Raptor C	.10	.20
93 Kor Spiritdancer R	.30	.50
94 Land Tax M	15.00	20.00
95 Lightwalker C	.10	.20
96 Long Road Home U	.20	.30
97 Loyal Pegasus U	.20	.30
98 Mangara of Corondor R	.30	.50
99 Midnight Guard C	.10	.20
100 Oreskos Explorer U	.20	.30
101 Pacifism C	.10	.20
102 Raptor Companion C	.10	.20
103 Rebuke C	.10	.20
104 Royal Trooper C	.10	.20
105 Shoulder to Shoulder C	.10	.20
106 Silverchase Fox C	.10	.20
107 Solemn Offering U	.20	.30
108 Sparring Mummy C	.10	.20
109 Steppe Glider U	.20	.30
110 Swords to Plowshares U	.20	.30
111 Take Up Arms U	.20	.30
112 Tandem Tactics C	.10	.20
113 Benthic Giant C	.10	.20
114 Call to Heel C	.10	.20
115 Claustrophobia C	.10	.20
116 Coralhelm Guide C	.10	.20
117 Fog Bank U	.20	.30
118 Frost Lynx C	.10	.20
119 Impulse C	.10	.20
120 Kitesail Corsair C	.10	.20
121 Kraken Hatchling C	.10	.20
122 Mystic Confluence R	.30	.50
123 Negate C	.10	.20
124 Nimbus of the Isles C	.10	.20
125 Omenspeaker C	.10	.20
126 Opportunity U	.20	.30
127 Oracle's Insight U	.20	.30
128 Peregrine Drake U	.20	.30
129 Phantom Warrior U	.20	.30
130 Reckless Scholar U	.20	.30
131 Sower of Temptation R	.30	.50
132 Spell Snare U	.20	.30
133 Switcheroo U	.20	.30
134 Tidespout Tyrant R	.30	.50
135 Totally Lost C	.10	.20
136 True-Name Nemesis M	10.00	13.00
137 Watercourser C	.10	.20
138 Assassin's Strike U	.20	.30
139 Assassinate C	.10	.20
140 Daggerdrome Imp C	.10	.20
141 Diabolic Intent R	.30	.50
142 Doomed Dissenter C	.10	.20
143 Eyeblight Assassin C	.10	.20
144 Fill with Fright C	.10	.20
145 Grotesque Mutation C	.10	.20
146 Hand of Silumgar C	.10	.20
147 Last Gasp C	.10	.20
148 Liturgy of Blood C	.10	.20
149 Morbid Curiosity U	.20	.30
150 Nirkana Revenant M	5.00	7.00
151 Noosegraf Mob R	.30	.50
152 Noxious Dragon U	.20	.30
153 Nyxathid R	.30	.50
154 Painful Lesson C	.10	.20
155 Prakhata Club Security C	.10	.20
156 Quest for the Gravelord U	.20	.30
157 Rotfeaster Maggot C	.10	.20
158 Screeching Buzzard C	.10	.20
159 Shambling Ghoul C	.10	.20
160 Slum Reaper U	.20	.30
161 Swarm of Bloodflies U	.20	.30
162 Tavern Swindler U	.20	.30
163 Tenacious Dead U	.20	.30
164 Bathe in Dragonfire C	.10	.20
165 Battle Rampart C	.10	.20
166 Battle-Rattle Shaman U	.20	.30
167 Blaze U	.20	.30
168 Blood Feud U	.20	.30
169 Boldwyr Intimidator U	.20	.30
170 Borderland Marauder C	.10	.20
171 Chain Lightning U	.20	.30
172 Dragon Breath U	.20	.30
173 Dragon Hatchling C	.10	.20
174 Earth Elemental C	.10	.20
175 Ember Beast C	.10	.20
176 Enthralling Victor U	.20	.30
177 Expedite C	.10	.20
178 Flamewave Invoker U	.20	.30
179 Goblin Razerunners R	.30	.50
180 Lightning Talons C	.10	.20
181 Magmatic Force R	.30	.50
182 Pathmaker Initiate C	.10	.20
183 Reckless Reveler C	.10	.20
184 Shock C	.10	.20
185 Thunder Strike C	.10	.20
186 Trumpet Blast U	.20	.30
187 War's Toll R	.30	.50
188 Wrap in Flames C	.10	.20
189 Aim High U	.20	.30
190 Beast Within U	.20	.30
191 Canopy Spider C	.10	.20
192 Charging Rhino C	.10	.20
193 Cowl Prowler C	.10	.20
194 Daggerback Basilisk C	.10	.20
195 Doubling Season M	35.00	40.00
196 Elvish Visionary C	.10	.20
197 Feral Hydra U	.20	.30
198 Fertile Ground C	.10	.20
199 Fertilid U	.20	.30
200 Giant Growth C	.10	.20
201 Greater Good R	.30	.50
202 Hunted Wumpus U	.20	.30
203 Karametra's Favor U	.20	.30
204 Kraul Warrior C	.10	.20
205 Lead by Example C	.10	.20
206 Magus of the Candelabra R	.30	.50
207 Plated Crusher U	.20	.30
208 Primal Huntbeast C	.10	.20
209 Pulse of Murasa U	.20	.30
210 Return to the Earth C	.10	.20
211 Saddleback Lagac C	.10	.20
212 Seedborn Muse R	.30	.50
213 Skyshroud Claim C	.10	.20
214 Veteran Explorer U	.20	.30
215 Vigor R	.30	.50
216 Wandering Wolf C	.10	.20
217 Apocalypse Hydra R	.30	.50
218 Auger Spree C	.10	.20
219 Centaur Healer C	.10	.20
220 Dinrova Horror U	.20	.30
221 Enduring Scalelord U	.20	.30
222 Evil Twin R	.30	.50
223 Gwafa Hazid, Profiteer R	.30	.50
224 Jelenn Sphinx U	.20	.30
225 Kiss of the Amesha U	.20	.30
226 Relentless Hunter U	.20	.30
227 Rhox Brute C	.10	.20
228 Riptide Crab C	.10	.20
229 Savage Ventmaw U	.20	.30
230 Unflinching Courage U	.20	.30
231 Urborg Drake C	.10	.20
232 Consulate Skygate C	.10	.20
233 Culling Dais U	.20	.30
234 Eager Construct C	.10	.20
235 Genesis Chamber U	.20	.30
236 Gold-Forged Sentinel U	.20	.30
237 Hexplate Golem C	.10	.20
238 Juggernaut U	.20	.30
239 Millennial Gargoyle C	.10	.20
240 Mind's Eye R	.30	.50
241 Mycosynth Lattice M	4.00	6.00
242 Night Market Guard C	.10	.20
243 Peace Strider C	.10	.20
244 Pierce Strider C	.10	.20
245 Seer's Lantern C	.10	.20
246 Spectral Searchlight U	.20	.30
247 Stone Golem C	.10	.20
248 Tyrant's Machine C	.10	.20
249 Yotian Soldier C	.10	.20
250 Plains L	.10	.20
251 Island L	.10	.20
252 Swamp L	.10	.20
253 Mountain L	.10	.20
254 Forest L	.10	.20

2018 Magic The Gathering Battlebond Foil

COMPLETE SET (254)	1300.00	1600.00
1 Will Kenrith M	35.00	45.00
2 Rowan Kenrith M	35.00	45.00
3 Regna, the Redeemer R	3.00	5.00
4 Krav, the Unredeemed R	8.00	10.00
5 Zndrsplt, Eye of Wisdom R	3.00	5.00
6 Okaun, Eye of Chaos R	3.00	5.00
7 Virtus the Veiled R	3.00	5.00
8 Gorm the Great R	3.00	5.00
9 Khorvath Brightflame R	3.00	5.00

10 Sylvia Brightspear R 3.00 5.00
11 Pir, Imaginative Rascal R 8.00 10.00
12 Toothy, Imaginary Friend R 7.00 9.00
13 Blaring Recruiter U .20 .35
14 Blaring Captain U .20 .35
15 Chakram Retriever U .20 .35
16 Chakram Slinger U .20 .35
17 Soulblade Corrupter U .20 .35
18 Soulblade Renewer U .20 .35
19 Impetuous Protégé U .20 .35
20 Proud Mentor U .20 .35
21 Ley Weaver U 1.00 1.50
22 Lore Weaver U .20 .35
23 Arena Rector M 70.00 75.00
24 Aurora Champion C .15 .25
25 Brightling M 90.00 100.00
26 Bring Down U .20 .35
27 Dwarven Lightsmith C .15 .25
28 Jubilant Mascot U .20 .35
29 Play the Game R 3.00 5.00
30 Regna's Sanction R 3.00 5.00
31 Skystreamer C .15 .25
32 Together Forever R 3.00 5.00
33 Arcane Artisan M 75.00 80.00
34 Fumble U 4.00 .35
35 Game Plan R 3.00 5.00
36 Huddle Up C .15 .25
37 Nimbus Champion U .20 .35
38 Out of Bounds U .20 .35
39 Saltwater Stalwart C .15 .25
40 Soaring Show-Off C .15 .25
41 Spellseeker R 40.00 45.00
42 Spellweaver Duo C .15 .25
43 Zndrsplt's Judgment R 3.00 5.00
44 Archfiend of Despair M 28.00 32.00
45 Bloodborn Scoundrels C .15 .25
46 Fan Favorite C .15 .25
47 Gang Up U .20 .35
48 Inner Demon U .20 .35
49 Mindblade Render R 3.00 5.00
50 Sickle Dancer C .15 .25
51 Stunning Reversal M 20.00 25.00
52 Thrasher Brute U .20 .35
53 Thrilling Encore R 15.00 20.00
54 Virtus's Maneuver R 3.00 5.00
55 Azra Bladeseeker C .15 .25
56 Bonus Round R 3.00 5.00
57 Bull-Rush Bruiser C .15 .25
58 Cheering Fanatic U .20 .35
59 Khorvath's Fury R 3.00 5.00
60 Lava-Field Overlord U .20 .35
61 Magma Hellion C .15 .25
62 Najeela, the Blade-Blossom M 80.00 90.00
63 Stadium Vendors C .15 .25
64 Stolen Strategy R 14.00 16.00
65 Bramble Sovereign M 40.00 45.00
66 Charging Binox C .15 .25
67 Combo Attack C .15 .25
68 The Crowd Goes Wild U .20 .35
69 Decorated Champion U .75 1.00
70 Generous Patron R 3.00 5.00
71 Grothama, All-Devouring M 10.00 15.00
72 Jungle Wayfinder C .30 .50
73 Pir's Whim R 3.00 5.00
74 Archon of Valor's Reach R 10.00 13.00
75 Azra Oddsmaker U 1.25 1.75
76 Last One Standing R 3.00 5.00
77 Rushblade Commander U 1.50 2.00
78 Vampire Charmseeker U .20 .35
79 Sentinel Tower R 3.00 5.00
80 Victory Chimes R 3.00 5.00
81 Bountiful Promenade R 35.00 40.00
82 Luxury Suite R 35.00 40.00
83 Morphic Pool R 40.00 45.00
84 Sea of Clouds R 40.00 45.00
85 Spire Garden R 35.00 40.00
86 Angel of Retribution U .20 .35
87 Angelic Chorus R 3.00 5.00
88 Angelic Gift C .15 .25
89 Battle Mastery U .20 .35
90 Champion of Arashin C .15 .25
91 Doomed Traveler C .15 .25
92 Expedition Raptor C .15 .25
93 Kor Spiritdancer R 3.00 5.00
94 Land Tax M 50.00 55.00
95 Lightwalker C .15 .25
96 Long Road Home U .20 .35
97 Loyal Pegasus U .20 .35
98 Mangara of Corondor R 3.00 5.00
99 Midnight Guard C .15 .25
100 Oreskos Explorer U .20 .35
101 Pacifism C .15 .25
102 Raptor Companion C .15 .25
103 Rebuke C .15 .25
104 Royal Trooper C .15 .25
105 Shoulder to Shoulder C .15 .25
106 Silverchase Fox C .15 .25
107 Solemn Offering U .20 .35
108 Sparring Mummy C .15 .25
109 Sleppe Glider U .20 .35
110 Swords to Plowshares U 2.00 3.50
111 Take Up Arms U .20 .35
112 Tandem Tactics C .15 .25
113 Benthic Giant C .15 .25
114 Call to Heel C .15 .25
115 Claustrophobia C .15 .25
116 Coralhelm Guide C .15 .25
117 Fog Bank U .20 .35
118 Frost Lynx C .15 .25
119 Impulse C .40 .60
120 Kitesail Corsair C .15 .25
121 Kraken Hatchling C .15 .25
122 Mystic Confluence R 10.00 13.00
123 Negate C .30 .50
124 Nimbus of the Isles C .15 .25
125 Omenspeaker C .15 .25
126 Opportunity U .20 .35
127 Oracle's Insight U .20 .35
128 Peregrine Drake U .20 .35
129 Phantom Warrior U .20 .35
130 Reckless Scholar U .20 .35
131 Sower of Temptation R 3.00 5.00
132 Spell Snare U 5.00 7.00
133 Switcheroo U .20 .35
134 Tidespout Tyrant R 3.00 5.00
135 Totally Lost C .15 .25
136 True-Name Nemesis M 200.00 210.00
137 Watercourser C .15 .25
138 Assassin's Strike U .20 .35
139 Assassinate C .15 .25
140 Daggerdrome Imp C .15 .25
141 Diabolic Intent R 15.00 18.00
142 Doomed Dissenter C .15 .25
143 Eyeblight Assassin C .15 .25
144 Fill with Fright C .15 .25
145 Grotesque Mutation C .15 .25
146 Hand of Silumgar C .15 .25
147 Last Gasp C .15 .25
148 Liturgy of Blood C .15 .25
149 Morbid Curiosity U .20 .35
150 Nirkana Revenant M 15.00 20.00
151 Noosegraf Mob R 3.00 5.00
152 Noxious Dragon U .20 .35
153 Nyxathid R 3.00 5.00
154 Painful Lesson C .15 .25
155 Prakhata Club Security C .15 .25
156 Quest for the Gravelord U .20 .35
157 Rotfeaster Maggot C .15 .25
158 Screeching Buzzard C .15 .25
159 Shambling Ghoul C .15 .25
160 Slum Reaper U .20 .35
161 Swarm of Bloodflies U .20 .35
162 Tavern Swindler U .20 .35
163 Tenacious Dead U .20 .35
164 Bathe in Dragonfire C .15 .25
165 Battle Rampart C .15 .25
166 Battle-Rattle Shaman U .20 .35
167 Blaze U .20 .35
168 Blood Feud U .20 .35
169 Boldwyr Intimidator U .20 .35
170 Borderland Marauder C .15 .25
171 Chain Lightning U 3.00 5.00
172 Dragon Breath U .20 .35
173 Dragon Hatchling C .15 .25
174 Earth Elemental C .15 .25
175 Ember Beast C .15 .25
176 Enthralling Victor U .20 .35
177 Expedite C .15 .25
178 Flamewave Invoker U .20 .35
179 Goblin Razerunners R 3.00 5.00
180 Lightning Talons C .15 .25
181 Magmatic Force R 3.00 5.00
182 Pathmaker Initiate C .15 .25
183 Reckless Reveler C .15 .25
184 Shock C .15 .25
185 Thunder Strike C .15 .25
186 Trumpet Blast U .20 .35
187 War's Toll R 3.00 5.00
188 Wrap in Flames C .15 .25
189 Aim High U .20 .35
190 Beast Within U 6.00 8.00
191 Canopy Spider C .15 .25
192 Charging Rhino C .15 .25
193 Cowl Prowler C .15 .25
194 Daggerback Basilisk C .15 .25
195 Doubling Season M 60.00 65.00
196 Elvish Visionary C .15 .25
197 Feral Hydra U .20 .35
198 Fertile Ground C .15 .25
199 Fertilid U .20 .35
200 Giant Growth C .15 .25
201 Greater Good R 10.00 15.00
202 Hunted Wumpus U .20 .35
203 Karametra's Favor U .20 .35
204 Kraul Warrior C .15 .25
205 Lead by Example C .15 .25
206 Magus of the Candelabra R 3.00 5.00
207 Plated Crusher U .20 .35
208 Primal Huntbeast C .15 .25
209 Pulse of Murasa U .40 .60
210 Return to the Earth C .15 .25
211 Saddleback Lagac C .15 .25
212 Seedborn Muse R 18.00 22.00
213 Skyshroud Claim C 7.00 9.00
214 Veteran Explorer U 9.00 11.00
215 Vigor R 3.00 5.00
216 Wandering Wolf C .15 .25
217 Apocalypse Hydra R 3.00 5.00
218 Auger Spree C .15 .25
219 Centaur Healer C .15 .25
220 Dinrova Horror U .20 .35
221 Enduring Scalelord U .20 .35
222 Evil Twin R 3.00 5.00
223 Gwafa Hazid, Profiteer R 3.00 5.00
224 Jelenn Sphinx U .20 .35
225 Kiss of the Amesha U .20 .35
226 Relentless Hunter U .20 .35
227 Rhox Brute C .15 .25
228 Riptide Crab C .15 .25
229 Savage Ventmaw U .40 .60
230 Unflinching Courage U .20 .35
231 Urborg Drake C .15 .25
232 Consulate Skygate C .15 .25
233 Culling Dais U .20 .35
234 Eager Construct C .15 .25
235 Genesis Chamber U 1.00 1.50
236 Gold-Forged Sentinel U .20 .35
237 Hexplate Golem C .15 .25
238 Juggernaut U .20 .35
239 Millennial Gargoyle C .15 .25
240 Mind's Eye R 3.00 5.00
241 Mycosynth Lattice M 18.00 21.00
242 Night Market Guard C .15 .25
243 Peace Strider C .15 .25
244 Pierce Strider C .15 .25
245 Seer's Lantern C .15 .25
246 Spectral Searchlight U .20 .35
247 Stone Golem C .15 .25
248 Tyrant's Machine C .15 .25
249 Yotian Soldier C .15 .25
250 Plains L .15 .25
251 Island L .15 .25
252 Swamp L .15 .25
253 Mountain L .15 .25
254 Forest L .15 .25

2018 Magic The Gathering Battlebond Tokens

1 Spirit .10 .15
2 Warrior .15 .25
3 Zombie .10 .15
4 Zombie Giant .10 .15
5 Beast .10 .15
6 Myr .10 .15
7 Will Kenrith Emblem .10 .15
8 Rowan Kenrith Emblem .12 .20

1993 Magic The Gathering Collector's Edition

COMPLETE SET (302) 1200.00 2000.00
BOOSTER BOX
BOOSTER PACK
*INTERNATIONAL: SAME VALUE
RELEASED IN DECEMBER 1993
1 Air Elemental U :B: .20 .50
2 Ancestral Recall R :B: 60.00 120.00
3 Animate Artifact U :B: .15 .40
4 Animate Dead U :K: 2.00 5.00
5 Animate Wall R :W: .40 1.00
6 Ankh of Mishra R :A: 1.50 4.00
7 Armageddon R :W: 1.50 4.00
8 Aspect of Wolf R :G: .50 1.25
9 Bad Moon R :K: 1.00 2.50
10 Badlands R :L: 25.00 60.00
11 Balance R :W: 2.00 5.00
12 Basalt Monolith U :A: .75 2.00
13 Bayou R :L: 25.00 60.00
14 Benalish Hero C :W: .30 .75
15 Berserk U :G: 20.00 50.00
16 Birds of Paradise R :G: 8.00 20.00
17 Black Knight U :K: 1.00 2.50
18 Black Lotus R :A: 500.00 750.00
19 Black Vise U :A: 1.00 2.50
20 Black Ward U :W: .20 .50
21 Blaze of Glory R :W: 1.00 2.50
22 Blessing R :W: .40 1.00
23 Blue Elemental Blast C :B: .30 .75
24 Blue Ward U :W: .20 .50
25 Bog Wraith U :K: .25 .60
26 Braingeyser R :B: 1.50 4.00
27 Burrowing U :R: .25 .60
28 Camouflage U :G: .20 .50
29 Castle U :W: .25 .60
30 Celestial Prism U :A: .20 .50
31 Channel U :G: .75 2.00
32 Chaos Orb R :A: 6.00 15.00
33 Chaoslace R :R: .40 1.00
34 Circle of Protection Black C :W: .12 .30
35 Circle of Protection Blue C :W: .12 .30
36 Circle of Protection Green C :W: .12 .30
37 Circle of Protection Red C :W: .12 .30
38 Circle of Protection White C :W: .12 .30
39 Clockwork Beast R :A: .50 1.25
40 Clone U :B: 1.50 4.00
41 Cockatrice R :G: .40 1.00
42 Consecrate Land U :W: .20 .50
43 Conservator U :A: .20 .50
44 Contract from Below R :K: .40 1.00
45 Control Magic U :B: 1.25 3.00
46 Conversion U :W: .20 .50
47 Copper Tablet U :A: .25 .60
48 Copy Artifact R :B: 3.00 8.00
49 Counterspell U :B: 2.00 5.00
50 Craw Wurm C :G: .12 .30
51 Creature Bond C :B: .12 .30
52 Crusade R :W: 1.00 2.50
53 Crystal Rod U :A: .25 .60
54 Cursed Land U :K: .25 .60
55 Cyclopean Tomb R :A: 3.00 8.00
56 Dark Ritual C :K: 2.50 6.00
57 Darkpact R :K: .60 1.50
58 Death Ward C :W: .12 .30
59 Deathgrip U :K: .20 .50
60 Deathlace R :K: .40 1.00
61 Demonic Attorney R :K: .30 .75
62 Demonic Hordes R :K: .75 2.00
63 Demonic Tutor U :K: 10.00 25.00
64 Dingus Egg R :A: .40 1.00
65 Disenchant C :W: .50 1.25
66 Disintegrate C :R: .20 .50
67 Disrupting Scepter R :A: .40 1.00
68 Dragon Whelp U :R: .75 2.00
69 Drain Life C :K: .20 .50
70 Drain Power R :B: .40 1.00
71 Drudge Skeletons C :K: .12 .30
72 Dwarven Demolition Team U :R: .25 .60
73 Dwarven Warriors C :R: .12 .30
74 Earth Elemental U :R: .20 .50
75 Earthbind C :R: .20 .50
76 Earthquake R :R: 1.00 2.50
77 Elvish Archers R :G: .40 1.00
78 Evil Presence U :K: .25 .60
79 False Orders C :R: .25 .60
80 Farmstead R :W: .40 1.00
81 Fastbond R :G: 2.50 6.00
82 Fear C :K: .12 .30
83 Feedback U :B: .20 .50
84 Fire Elemental U :R: .25 .60
85 Fireball C :R: .50 1.25
86 Firebreathing C :R: .12 .30
87 Flashfires U :R: .25 .60
88 Flight C :B: .12 .30
89 Fog C :G: .15 .40
90 Force of Nature R :G: .60 1.50
91 Forcefield R :A: 12.00 30.00
92 Forest (blue) C :L: .50 1.25
93 Forest (black) C :L: .50 1.25
94 Forest (with trail) v3 C :L: .50 1.25
95 Fork R :R: 3.00 8.00
96 Frozen Shade C :K: .12 .30
97 Fungusaur R :G: .40 1.00
98 Gaea's Liege R :G: .60 1.50
99 Gauntlet of Might R :A: 20.00 50.00
100 Giant Growth C :G: .25 .60
101 Giant Spider C :G: .25 .60
102 Glasses of Urza U :A: .20 .50
103 Gloom U :K: .20 .50
104 Goblin Balloon Brigade U :R: .20 .50
105 Goblin King R :R: 1.00 2.50
106 Granite Gargoyle R :R: .40 1.00
107 Gray Ogre C :R: .12 .30
108 Green Ward U :W: .20 .50
109 Grizzly Bears C :G: .25 .60
110 Guardian Angel C :W: .12 .30
111 Healing Salve C :W: .12 .30
112 Helm of Chatzuk R :A: .50 1.25
113 Hill Giant C :R: .12 .30
114 Hive, The R :A: .40 1.00
115 Holy Armor C :W: .12 .30
116 Holy Strength C :W: .12 .30
117 Howl from Beyond C :K: .12 .30
118 Howling Mine R :A: 2.00 5.00
119 Hurloon Minotaur C :R: .15 .40
120 Hurricane U :G: .25 .60
121 Hypnotic Specter U :K: 3.00 8.00
122 Ice Storm U :G: 2.50 6.00
123 Icy Manipulator U :A: 1.50 4.00
124 Illusionary Mask R :A: 8.00 20.00
125 Instill Energy U :G: .30 .75
126 Invisibility C :B: .12 .30
127 Iron Star U :A: .15 .40
128 Ironclaw Orcs C :R: .12 .30
129 Ironroot Treefolk C :G: .12 .30
130 Island Sanctuary R :W: .40 1.00
131 Island v1 C :L: .50 1.25
132 Island v2 C :L: .50 1.25
133 Island v3 C :L: .50 1.25
134 Ivory Cup U :A: .25 .60
135 Jade Monolith R :A: .60 1.50
136 Jade Statue U :A: 1.50 4.00
137 Jayemdae Tome R :A: .40 1.00
138 Juggernaut U :A: .50 1.25
139 Jump C :B: .15 .40
140 Karma U :W: .20 .50
141 Keldon Warlord U :R: .20 .50
142 Kormus Bell R :A: .50 1.25
143 Kudzu R :G: .40 1.00
144 Lance U :W: .30 .75
145 Ley Druid U :G: .20 .50
146 Library of Leng U :A: .40 1.00
147 Lich R :K: 3.00 8.00
148 Lifeforce U :G: .25 .60
149 Lifelace R :G: .40 1.00
150 Lifetap U :B: .20 .50
151 Lightning Bolt C :R: 4.00 10.00
152 Living Artifact R :G: .40 1.00
153 Living Lands R :G: .40 1.00
154 Living Wall U :A: .20 .50
155 Llanowar Elves C :G: 1.00 2.50
156 Lord of Atlantis R :B: 1.50 4.00
157 Lord of the Pit R :K: 1.00 2.50
158 Lure U :G: .30 .75
159 Magical Hack R :B: .40 1.00
160 Mahamoti Djinn R :B: .40 1.00
161 Mana Flare R :R: 1.25 3.00
162 Mana Short R :B: .75 2.00
163 Mana Vault R :A: 5.00 12.00
164 Manabarbs R :R: .50 1.25
165 Meekstone R :A: .75 2.00
166 Merfolk of the Pearl Trident C :B: .15 .40
167 Mesa Pegasus C :W: .12 .30
168 Mind Twist R :K: 3.00 8.00
169 Mons's Goblin Raiders C :R: .12 .30
170 Mountain v1 C :L: .40 1.00
171 Mountain v2 C :L: .40 1.00
172 Mountain v3 C :L: .40 1.00
173 Mox Emerald R :A: 80.00 150.00
174 Mox Jet R :A: 80.00 150.00
175 Mox Pearl R :A: 60.00 120.00
176 Mox Ruby R :A: 80.00 150.00
177 Mox Sapphire R :A: 80.00 150.00
178 Natural Selection R :G: 1.25 3.00
179 Nether Shadow R :K: 1.50 4.00
180 Nettling Imp U :K: .30 .75
181 Nevinyrral's Disk R :A: 2.50 6.00
182 Nightmare R :K: 1.00 2.50
183 Northern Paladin R :W: .40 1.00
184 Obsianus Golem U :A: .25 .60
185 Orcish Artillery U :R: .20 .50
186 Orcish Oriflamme U :R: .20 .50
187 Paralyze C :K: .12 .30
188 Pearled Unicorn C :W: .12 .30
189 Personal Incarnation R :W: .50 1.25
190 Pestilence C :K: .12 .30
191 Phantasmal Forces U :B: .25 .60
192 Phantasmal Terrain C :B: .12 .30
193 Phantom Monster U :B: .20 .50
194 Pirate Ship R :B: .40 1.00
195 Plague Rats C :K: .12 .30
196 Plains v1 C :L: .40 1.00
197 Plains v2 C :L: .40 1.00
198 Plains v3 C :L: .40 1.00
199 Plateau R :L: 25.00 60.00
200 Power Leak C :B: .12 .30
201 Power Sink C :B: .12 .30
202 Power Surge R :R: .50 1.25
203 Prodigal Sorcerer C :B: .25 .60
204 Psionic Blast U :B: 1.50 4.00
205 Psychic Venom C :B: .12 .30
206 Purelace R :W: .40 1.00

Card	Low	High
207 Raging River R :R:	1.00	2.50
208 Raise Dead C :K:	.12	.30
209 Red Elemental Blast C :R:	.75	2.00
210 Red Ward U :W:	.25	.60
211 Regeneration C :G:	.12	.30
212 Regrowth U :G:	3.00	8.00
213 Resurrection U :W:	.20	.50
214 Reverse Damage R :W:	.40	1.00
215 Righteousness R :W:	.40	1.00
216 Roc of Kher Ridges R :R:	.40	1.00
217 Rock Hydra R :R:	.40	1.00
218 Rod of Ruin U :A:	.20	.50
219 Royal Assassin R :K:	1.50	4.00
220 Sacrifice U :K:	.25	.60
221 Samite Healer C :W:	.12	.30
222 Savannah Lions R :W:	2.00	5.00
223 Savannah R :L:	30.00	80.00
224 Scathe Zombies C :K:	.25	.60
225 Scavenging Ghoul U :K:	.20	.50
226 Scrubland R :L:	25.00	60.00
227 Scryb Sprites C :G:	.12	.30
228 Sea Serpent C :B:	.12	.30
229 Sedge Troll R :R:	.40	1.00
230 Sengir Vampire U :K:	1.00	2.50
231 Serra Angel U :W:	4.00	10.00
232 Shanodin Dryads C :G:	.12	.30
233 Shatter C :R:	.12	.30
234 Shivan Dragon R :R:	3.00	8.00
235 Simulacrum U :K:	.20	.50
236 Sinkhole C :K:	12.00	30.00
237 Siren's Call U :B:	.20	.50
238 Sleight of Mind R :B:	.40	1.00
239 Smoke R :R:	.40	1.00
240 Sol Ring U :A:	10.00	25.00
241 Soul Net U :A:	.20	.50
242 Spell Blast C :B:	.12	.30
243 Stasis R :B:	1.50	4.00
244 Steal Artifact U :B:	.20	.50
245 Stone Giant U :R:	.20	.50
246 Stone Rain C :R:	.20	.50
247 Stream of Life C :G:	.12	.30
248 Sunglasses of Urza R :A:	.40	1.00
249 Swamp v1 C :L:	.50	1.25
250 Swamp v2 C :L:	.50	1.25
251 Swamp v3 C :L:	.50	1.25
252 Swords to Plowshares U :W:	2.50	6.00
253 Taiga R :L:	30.00	80.00
254 Terror C :K:	.75	2.00
255 Thicket Basilisk U :G:	.20	.50
256 Thoughtlace R :B:	.40	1.00
257 Throne of Bone U :A:	.20	.50
258 Timber Wolves R :G:	.40	1.00
259 Time Vault R :A:	20.00	50.00
260 Time Walk R :B:	100.00	200.00
261 Timetwister R :B:	50.00	100.00
262 Tranquility C :G:	.25	.60
263 Tropical Island R :L:	30.00	80.00
264 Tsunami U :G:	.20	.50
265 Tundra R :L:	50.00	100.00
266 Tunnel U :R:	.25	.60
267 Twiddle C :B:	.12	.30
268 Two-Headed Giant of Foriys R :R:	.75	2.00
269 Underground Sea R :L:	100.00	200.00
270 Unholy Strength C :K:	.20	.50
271 Unsummon C :B:	.12	.30
272 Uthden Troll U :R:	.20	.50
273 Verduran Enchantress R :G:	.40	1.00
274 Vesuvan Doppelganger R :B:	2.00	5.00
275 Veteran Bodyguard R :W:	.40	1.00
276 Volcanic Eruption R :B:	.40	1.00
277 Volcanic Island R :L:	60.00	120.00
278 Wall of Air U :B:	.20	.50
279 Wall of Bone U :K:	.25	.60
280 Wall of Brambles U :G:	.25	.60
281 Wall of Fire U :R:	.20	.50
282 Wall of Ice U :G:	.20	.50
283 Wall of Stone U :R:	.20	.50
284 Wall of Swords U :W:	.25	.60
285 Wall of Water U :B:	.30	.75
286 Wall of Wood C :G:	.12	.30
287 Wanderlust U :G:	.25	.60
288 War Mammoth C :G:	.12	.30
289 Warp Artifact R :K:	.40	1.00
290 Water Elemental U :B:	.20	.50
291 Weakness C :K:	.12	.30
292 Web R :G:	.40	1.00
293 Wheel of Fortune R :R:	10.00	25.00
294 White Knight U :W:	1.25	3.00
295 White Ward U :W:	.20	.50
296 Wild Growth C :G:	.40	1.00
297 Will-O'-The-Wisp R :K:	1.00	2.50
298 Winter Orb R :A:	3.00	8.00
299 Wooden Sphere U :A:	.20	.50
300 Word of Command R :K:	5.00	12.00
301 Wrath of God R :W:	6.00	15.00
302 Zombie Master R :K:	1.50	4.00

1998 Magic The Gathering Unglued

Card	Low	High
COMPLETE SET (93)	60.00	90.00
BOOSTER BOX (48 PACKS)	800.00	900.00
BOOSTER PACK (15 CARDS)	15.00	18.00
RELEASED ON AUGUST 11, 1998		
69 Ashnod's Coupon R :A:	3.00	5.00
28 Big Furry Monster-L R :K:	3.00	5.00
29 Big Furry Monster-R R :K:	3.00	5.00
70 Blacker Lotus R :A:	4.00	6.00
71 Bronze Calendar U :A:	.20	.35
14 Bureaucracy R :B:	.30	.60
40 Burning Cinder Fury of Crimson Chaos Fire R :R:	.50	.75
54 Cardboard Carapace R :G:	1.50	2.00
15 Censorship U :B:	.75	1.25
72 Chaos Confetti C :A:	.25	.40
1 Charm School U :W:	.20	.35
16 Checks and Balances U :B:	.20	.35
17 Chicken a la King R :B:	.60	1.00
41 Chicken Egg C :R:	.15	.25
18 Clam Session C :B:	.15	.25
19 Clambassadors C :B:	.15	.25
20 Clam-I-Am C :B:	.15	.25
73 Clay Pigeon U :A:	.20	.35
21 Common Courtesy U :B:	.40	.60
30 Deadhead C :K:	.15	.25
22 Denied! C :B:	.15	.25
31 Double Cross C :K:	.15	.25
42 Double Deal C :R:	.15	.25
2 Double Dip C :W:	.15	.25
55 Double Play C :G:	.15	.25
23 Double Take C :B:	.15	.25
56 Elvish Impersonators C :G:	.15	.25
57 Flock of Rabid Sheep U :G:	.20	.35
88 Forest C :G:	3.00	5.00
24 Fowl Play C :B:	.15	.25
25 Free-for-All R :B:	.15	.25
58 Free-Range Chicken C :G:	.15	.25
59 Gerrymandering U :G:	.20	.35
3 Get a Life U :W:	.20	.35
60 Ghazban Ogress C :G:	.15	.25
74 Giant Fan R :A:	.40	.60
43 Goblin Bookie C :R:	.15	.25
44 Goblin Bowling Team C :R:	.15	.25
45 Goblin Tutor U :R:	.50	.75
92 Goblin U :R:	.20	.35
61 Growth Spurt C :G:	.15	.25
62 Gus C :G:	.15	.25
32 Handcuffs U :K:	.20	.35
63 Hungry Hungry Heifer U :G:	.20	.35
46 Hurloon Wrangler C :R:	.15	.25
4 I'm Rubber, You're Glue R :W:	.40	.60
64 Incoming! R :G:	.50	.75
33 Infernal Spawn of Evil R :K:	1.50	2.00
85 Island C :B:	4.00	6.00
75 Jack-in-the-Mox R :A:	.75	1.25
47 Jalum Grifter R :R:	.40	.60
76 Jester's Sombrero R :A:	.40	.60
34 Jumbo Imp U :K:	.20	.35
5 Knight of the Hokey Pokey C :W:	.15	.25
48 Krazy Kow C :R:	.40	.60
49 Landfill R :R:	.40	.60
6 Lexivore U :W:	.20	.35
7 Look at Me, I'm the DCI R :W:	.50	.75
8 Mesa Chicken C :W:	.15	.25
65 Mine, Mine, Mine! R :G:	.50	.75
77 Mirror Mirror R :A:	.50	.75
9 Miss Demeanor U :W:	.20	.35
87 Mountain C :R:	3.00	5.00
10 Once More with Feeling R :W:	.40	.60
35 Organ Harvest C :K:	.15	.25
36 Ow R :K:	.40	.60
78 Paper Tiger C :A:	1.00	1.50
89 Pegasus U :W:	.20	.35
84 Plains C :W:	3.00	4.00
37 Poultrygeist C :K:	.15	.25
11 Prismatic Wardrobe C :W:	.15	.25
26 Psychic Network R :B:	.40	.60
50 Ricochet U :R:	.20	.35
79 Rock Lobster C :A:	1.25	1.75
80 Scissors Lizard C :A:	.75	1.25
12 Sex Appeal C :W:	.15	.25
93 Sheep U :G:	.20	.35
90 Soldier U :W:	.20	.35
27 Sorry U :B:	.20	.35
51 Spark Fiend R :R:	.40	.60
81 Spatula of the Ages U :A:	.20	.35
66 Squirrel Farm R :G:	1.00	1.50
94 Squirrel U :G:	.20	.35
52 Strategy, Schmategy R :R:	1.50	2.00
86 Swamp C :K:	3.00	5.00
67 Team Spirit C :G:	.15	.25
38 Temp of the Damned C :K:	.15	.25
13 The Cheese Stands Alone R :W:	1.00	1.50
53 The Ultimate Nightmare U :B:	1.25	1.75
68 Timmy, Power Gamer R :G:	.75	1.25
82 Urza's Contact Lenses U :A:	.20	.35
83 Urza's Science Fair Project U :A:	.20	.35
39 Volrath's Motion Sensor U :K:	.20	.35
91 Zombie U :K:	.20	.35

1998 Magic The Gathering Unglued Tokens

Card	Low	High
1 Pegasus	.35	.50
2 Soldier	2.00	3.00
3 Zombie	3.50	5.00
4 Goblin	2.00	3.00
5 Sheep	1.25	1.75
6 Squirrel	3.50	5.00

2004 Magic The Gathering Unhinged

Card	Low	High
COMPLETE SET (141)	100.00	140.00
BOOSTER BOX (36 PACKS)	500.00	600.00
BOOSTER PACK (15 CARDS)	15.00	20.00
RELEASED ON NOVEMBER 19, 2004		
1 ____ U :B:	.40	.60
2 Ach! Hans, Run! R :D:	.75	1.00
3 Aesthetic Consultation R :K:	.40	.60
4 Ambiguity R :B:	.40	.60
5 Artful Looter C :B:	.15	.25
6 Ass Whuppin' R :D:	.50	.75
7 Assquatch R :R:	.75	1.00
8 Atinlay Igpay U :W:	.20	.35
9 Avatar of Me R :B:	.40	.60
10 AWOL C :W:	.30	.50
11 Bad Ass C :K:	.15	.25
12 B-I-N-G-O R :G:	.50	.75
13 Blast from the Past R :R:	.75	1.00
14 Bloodletter C :K:	.15	.25
15 Booster Tutor U :K:	.50	.75
16 Bosom Buddy U :W:	.20	.35
17 Brushstroke Paintermage C :B:	.15	.25
18 Bursting Beebles C :B:	.15	.25
19 Cardpecker C :W:	.15	.25
20 Carnivorous Death-Parrot C :B:	.15	.25
21 Cheap Ass C :W:	.15	.25
22 Cheatyface U :B:	3.00	3.50
23 Circle of Protection: Art C :W:	.15	.25
24 City of Ass R :L:	4.00	6.00
25 Collector Protector R :W:	.40	.60
26 Creature Guy U :G:	.20	.35
27 Curse of the Fire Penguin R :R:	.50	.75
28 Deal Damage U :R:	.20	.35
29 Double Header C :B:	.15	.25
30 Drawn Together R :W:	.40	.60
31 Duh C :K:	.15	.25
32 Dumb Ass C :R:	.15	.25
33 Elvish House Party U :G:	.20	.35
34 Emcee U :W:	.20	.35
35 Enter the Dungeon R :K:	1.50	2.00
36 Erase C :W:	.15	.25
37 Eye to Eye U :K:	.20	.35
38 Face to Face U :R:	.20	.35
39 Farewell to Arms C :K:	.15	.25
40 Fascist Art Director C :W:	.15	.25
41 Fat Ass C :G:	.15	.25
42 First Come, First Served U :W:	.20	.35
43 Flaccify C :B:	.15	.25
44 Forest L :L:	7.00	10.00
45 Form of the Squirrel R :G:	2.00	3.00
46 Fraction Jackson R :G:	.40	.60
47 Framed! C :B:	.15	.25
48 Frankie Peanuts R :W:	.75	1.25
49 Frazzled Editor C :R:	1.50	2.00
50 Gleemax R :A:	2.50	3.25
51 Gluetius Maximus U :G:	.20	.35
52 Goblin Mime C :R:	.15	.25
53 Goblin S.W.A.T. Team C :R:	.15	.25
54 Goblin Secret Agent C :R:	.15	.25
55 Granny's Payback U :G:	.20	.35
56 Graphic Violence C :G:	.15	.25
57 Greater Morphling R :B:	.75	1.00
58 Head to Head U :W:	.20	.35
59 Infernal Spawn of Infernal Spawn of Evil R :K:	1.00	1.50
60 Island L :L:	7.00	10.00
61 Johnny, Combo Player R :B:	2.00	3.00
62 Keeper of the Sacred Word C :G:	.15	.25
63 Kill! Destroy! U :K:	.75	1.00
64 Ladies' Knight U :W:	.20	.35
65 Land Aid '04 C :G:	.15	.25
66 Laughing Hyena C :G:	.15	.25
67 Letter Bomb R :A:	2.00	2.50
68 Little Girl C :W:	.15	.25
69 Look at Me, I'm R&D R :W:	.40	.60
70 Loose Lips C :B:	.15	.25
71 Magical Hacker U :B:	.20	.35
72 Man of Measure C :W:	.15	.25
73 Mana Flair C :R:	.15	.25
74 Mana Screw U :A:	.20	.35
75 Market Research Long Card Name C :G:	.15	.25
76 Meddling Kids R :D:	.50	.75
77 Mise U :B:	.20	.35
78 Moniker Mage C :B:	.15	.25
79 Monkey Monkey Monkey C :G:	.15	.25
80 Mons's Goblin Waiters C :R:	.15	.25
81 Mother of Goons C :K:	.15	.25
82 Mountain L :L:	6.00	8.00
83 Mouth to Mouth U :B:	.20	.35
84 Mox Lotus R :A:	7.00	9.00
85 My First Tome U :A:	.20	.35
86 Name Dropping U :G:	.20	.35
87 Necro-Impotence R :K:	.40	.60
88 Now I Know My ABC's R :B:	.50	.75
89 Number Crunch C :B:	.15	.25
90 Old Fogey R :G:	.75	1.00
91 Orcish Paratroopers C :R:	.15	.25
92 Persecute Artist U :K:	.20	.35
93 Phyrexian Librarian U :K:	.20	.35
94 Plains L :L:	5.00	7.00
95 Pointy Finger of Doom R :A:	1.50	2.00
96 Punctuate C :R:	.15	.25
97 Pygmy Giant U :R:	.20	.35
98 Question Elemental? U :B:	.20	.35
99 R&D's Secret Lair R :L:	.40	.60
100 Rare-B-Gone R :D:	.40	.60
101 Red-Hot Hottie C :R:	.15	.25
102 Remodel C :G:	.15	.25
103 Richard Garfield, Ph.D. R :B:	3.00	4.00
104 Rocket-Powered Turbo Slug U :R:	.50	.75
105 Rod of Spanking U :A:	.75	1.00
106 S.N.O.T. C :G:	.15	.25
107 Sauté C :R:	.15	.25
108 Save Life U :W:	.20	.35
109 Shoe Tree C :G:	.15	.25
110 Side to Side U :G:	.20	.35
111 Six-y Beast U :R:	.20	.35
112 Smart Ass C :B:	.15	.25
113 Spell Counter U :B:	.20	.35
114 Standing Army C :W:	.15	.25
115 Staying Power R :W:	.75	1.25
116 Stone-Cold Basilisk U :G:	.20	.35
117 Stop That C :K:	.15	.25
118 Supersize C :G:	.15	.25
119 Swamp L :L:	7.00	9.00
120 Symbol Status U :G:	.20	.35
121 Tainted Monkey C :K:	.15	.25
122 The Fallen Apart C :K:	.15	.25
123 Time Machine R :A:	.40	.60
124 Togglodyte U :A:	.20	.35
125 Topsy Turvy R :B:	.50	.75
126 Touch and Go C :R:	.15	.25
127 Toy Boat U :A:	.20	.35
128 Uktabi Kong R :G:	.40	.60
129 Urza's Hot Tub U :A:	.20	.35
130 Vile Bile C :K:	.15	.25
131 Water Gun Balloon Game R :A:	.50	.75
132 Wet Willie of the Damned C :K:	.15	.25
133 When Fluffy Bunnies Attack C :K:	.15	.25
134 Who/What/When/Where/Why R :D:	2.25	2.75
135 Wordmail C :W:	.15	.25
136 Working Stiff U :K:	.20	.35
137 World-Bottling Kit R :A:	.40	.60
138 Yet Another Æther Vortex R :R:	.40	.60
139 Zombie Fanboy U :K:	.20	.35
140 Zzzyxas's Abyss R :K:	.40	.60
141 Super Secret Tech R :A:	.40	.60

2004 Magic The Gathering Unhinged Foil

Card	Low	High
COMPLETE SET (141)	150.00	250.00

2017 Magic The Gathering Unstable

Card	Low	High
COMPLETE SET (216)	125.00	200.00
BOOSTER BOX (36 PACKS)	95.00	120.00
BOOSTER PACK (15 CARDS)	4.00	6.00
RELEASED ON DECEMBER 9, 2017		
1 Adorable Kitten C	.05	.15
2 Aerial Toastmaster U	.10	.20
3 Amateur Auteur "Innistrad" C	.05	.15
3 Amateur Auteur "Theros" C	.05	.15
3 Amateur Auteur "Zendikar" C	.05	.15
3 Amateur Auteur "Ravnica" C	.05	.15
4 By Gnome Means R	.30	.50
5 Chivalrous Chevalier C	.05	.15
6 Do-It-Yourself Seraph M	.75	1.25
7 Gimme Five U	.10	.20
8 GO TO JAIL C	.05	.15
9 Half-Kitten, Half- U	.10	.20
10 Humming- C	.05	.15
11 Jackknight R	.30	.50
12 Knight of the Kitchen Sink "pro two-word names" U	.10	.20
12 Knight of the Kitchen Sink "pro odd collector numbers" U	.10	.20
12 Knight of the Kitchen Sink "pro loose lips" U	.10	.20
12 Knight of the Kitchen Sink "pro even collector numbers" U	.10	.20
12 Knight of the Kitchen Sink "pro black borders" U	.10	.20
12 Knight of the Kitchen Sink "pro watermarks" U	.10	.20
13 Knight of the Widget U	.10	.20
14 Midlife Upgrade U	.10	.20
15 Oddly Uneven R	.30	.50
16 Old Guard C	.05	.15
17 Ordinary Pony C	.05	.15
18 Rhino- U	.10	.20
19 Riveting Rigger C	.05	.15
20 Rules Lawyer R	.30	.50
21 Sacrifice Play C	.05	.15
22 Shaggy Camel C	.05	.15
23 Side Quest U	.10	.20
24 Success! C	.05	.15
25 Teacher's Pet U	.10	.20
26 Animate Library R	.30	.50
27 Blurry Beeble C	.05	.15
28 Chipper Chopper C	.05	.15
29 Clocknapper R	.30	.50
30 Crafty Octopus C	.05	.15
31 Crow Storm U	.10	.20
32 Defective Detective C	.05	.15
33 Fiver-Finger Discount R	.30	.50
34 Graveyard Busybody R	.30	.50
35 Half-Shark, Half U	.10	.20
36 Incite Insight R	.30	.50
37 Kindly Cognician U	.10	.20
38 Magic Word C	.05	.15
39 Mer Man C	.05	.15
40 More or Less U	.10	.20
41 Novellamental "chain" C	.05	.15
41 Novellamental "pendant" C	.05	.15
41 Novellamental "grandmother" C	.05	.15
41 Novellamental "heart" C	.05	.15
42 Numbing Jellyfish C	.05	.15
43 S.N.E.A.K. Dispatcher U	.10	.20
44 Socketed Sprocketer U	.10	.20
45 Spell Suck C	.05	.15
46 Spye Eye U	.10	.20
47 Suspicious Nanny U	.10	.20
48 Time Out C	.05	.15
49 Very Cryptic Command "Scry 3" R	10.00	15.00
49 Very Cryptic Command "Counter black-bordered" R	10.00	15.00
49 Very Cryptic Command "Return target permanent" R	6.00	8.00
49 Very Cryptic Command "Draw a card" R	10.00	15.00
49 Very Cryptic Command "Untap two target permanents" R	10.00	15.00
49 Very Cryptic Command "Alternate Art" R	15.00	20.00
50 Wall of Fortune C	.05	.15
51 Big Boa Constrictor C	.05	.15
52 capital offense C	.05	.15
53 Dirty Rat C	.05	.15
54 Extremely Slow Zombie "Winter" C	.05	.15
54 Extremely Slow Zombie "Fall" C	.05	.15
54 Extremely Slow Zombie "Summer" C	.05	.15
54 Extremely Slow Zombie "Spring" C	.05	.15
55 Finders, Keepers C	.05	.15
56 Hangman R	.30	.50
57 Hazmat Suit (Used) C	.05	.15
58 Hoisted Hireling C	.05	.15
59 Inhumaniac U	.10	.20
60 Masterful Ninja R	.30	.50
61 Ninja U	.10	.20
62 Old-Fashioned Vampire U	.10	.20
63 Over My Daed Bodies R	.30	.50
64 Overt Operative U	.10	.20
65 Rumors of My Death… U	.10	.20
66 Skull Saucer U	.10	.20
67 Sly Spy Subpar Notoriously Evil Agent Killers U	.10	.20
67 Sly Spy Spies Nimbly Eluding Adversaries' Knives U	.10	.20
67 Sly Spy Skilled, Notably Efficient Assassin-Kickers. U	.10	.20
67 Sly Spy Sinister Nerds Eliminating All Knowledge. U	.10	.20
67 Sly Spy Silent Ninjas Evading Any Kapture. U	.10	.20
67 Sly Spy Serious, Nonstop Espionage and Kidnapping U	.10	.20
68 Snickering Squirrel C	.05	.15
69 Spike, Tournament Grinder R	.30	.50
70 Squirrel-Powered Scheme U	.10	.20
71 Steady-Handed Mook C	.05	.15
72 Stinging Scorpion C	.05	.15
73 Subcontract C	.05	.15
74 Summon the Pack M	.75	1.25
75 Zombified U	.10	.20
76 The Big Idea R	.30	.50
77 Box of Free-Range Goblins C	.05	.15
78 Bumbling Pangolin C	.05	.15
79 Common Iguana C	.05	.15
80 The Countdown Is at One R	.30	.50
81 Feisty Stegosaurus C	.05	.15
82 Garbage Elemental "Unleash" U	.05	.15
82 Garbage Elemental "Cascade" U	.05	.15
82 Garbage Elemental "Battle cry" U	.05	.15
82 Garbage Elemental "Undying" U	.05	.15
82 Garbage Elemental "Frenzy 2" U	.05	.15
82 Garbage Elemental "Last strike" U	.05	.15
83 Goblin Haberdasher U	.10	.20
84 Half-Orc, Half- U	.10	.20

85 Hammer Helper C .05 .15
86 Hammer Jammer U .10 .20
87 Hammerfest Boomtacular U .10 .20
88 Infinity Elemental M .75 1.25
89 It That Gets Left Hanging C .05 .15
90 Just Desserts C .05 .15
91 Painiac C .05 .15
92 Party Crasher U .10 .20
93 Steamflogger Boss R .30 .50
94 Steamflogger of the Month R .30 .50
95 Steamflogger Temp U .10 .20
96 Steamfloggery U .10 .20
97 Super-Duper Death Ray U .10 .20
98 Target Minotaur "Fireballs" C .05 .15
98 Target Minotaur "Blood Rain" C .05 .15
98 Target Minotaur "Frozen" C .05 .15
98 Target Minotaur "Vines" C .05 .15
99 Three-Headed Goblin R .30 .50
100 Work a Double C .05 .15
101 Wrench-Rigger C .05 .15
102 As Luck Would Have It R .30 .50
103 Beast in Show "Dragon" C .05 .15
103 Beast in Show "Goat" C .05 .15
103 Beast in Show "Dinosaur" C .05 .15
103 Beast in Show "Ox" C .05 .15
104 Chittering Doom U .10 .20
105 Clever Combo U .10 .20
106 Druid of the Sacred Beaker U .10 .20
107 Eager Beaver C .05 .15
108 Earl of the Squirrel R .75 1.25
109 First Pick U .10 .20
110 Ground Pounder C .05 .15
111 Half-Squirrel, Half- U .10 .20
112 Hydradoodle R .30 .50
113 Ineffable Blessing "choose odd or even" R .30 .50
113 Ineffable Blessing "choose a rarity" R .30 .50
113 Ineffable Blessing "choose white or silver-bordered" R .30 .50
113 Ineffable Blessing "choose an artist" R .30 .50
113 Ineffable Blessing "choose Flavorful or Bland" R .30 .50
113 Ineffable Blessing "choose a number" R .30 .50
114 Joyride Rigger C .05 .15
115 Monkey- U .10 .20
116 Mother Kangaroo C .05 .15
117 Multi-Headed C .05 .15
118 Really Epic Punch C .05 .15
119 Selfie Preservation C .05 .15
120 Serpentine R .30 .50
121 Shellephant U .10 .20
122 Slaying Mantis U .10 .20
123 Squirrel Dealer C .05 .15
124 Steamflogger Service Rep U .10 .20
125 Wild Crocodile C .05 .15
126 Willing Test Subject C .05 .15
127 Baron Von Count M .75 1.25
128 Better Than One R .30 .50
129 Cramped Bunker R .30 .50
130 Dr. Julius Jumblemorph M .75 1.25
131 The Grand Calcutron M .75 1.25
132 Grusilda, Monster Masher R .30 .50
133 Hot Fix R .30 .50
134 Ol'Buzzbark M .75 1.25
135 Phoebe, Head of S.N.E.A.K. M 1.50 2.50
136 Urza, Academy Headmaster M 6.00 8.00
137 X R .30 .50
138 Mary O'Kill R .30 .50
139 Angelic Rocket R .30 .50
140 Border Guardian U .10 .20
141 Buzzing Whack-a-Doodle U .10 .20
142 Clock of DOOOOOOOOOOOOM! U .10 .20
143 Cogmentor U .10 .20
144 Contraption Cannon U .10 .20
145 Enraged Killbot C .05 .15
145 Despondent Killbot C .05 .15
145 Delighted Killbot C .05 .15
145 Curious Killbot C .05 .15
146 Entirely Normal Armchair U .10 .20
147 Everythingamajig "Sacrifice a land" R .75 1.25
147 Everythingamajig "Add one mana" R .75 1.25
147 Everythingamajig "Flip a coin" R .75 1.25
147 Everythingamajig "Draw a card" R .75 1.25
147 Everythingamajig "Move a counter" R .75 1.25
147 Everythingamajig "Scry 2" R .75 1.25
148 Gnome-Made Engine C .05 .15
149 Handy Dandy Clone Machine R .30 .50
150 Kindslaver R .30 .50
151 Krark's Other Thumb U .10 .20
152 Labro Bot U .10 .20
153 Lobe Lobber U .10 .20
154 Mad Science Fair Project C .05 .15
155 Modular Monstrosity R .30 .50
156 Proper Laboratory Attire U .05 .15
157 Robo- U .10 .20
158 Split Screen R .30 .50
159 Staff of the Letter Magus U .10 .20
160 Stamp of Approval U .10 .20
161 Steam-Powered U .10 .20
162 Steel Squirrel U .10 .20
163 Sword of Dungeons & Dragons M 3.00 5.00
164 Voracious Vacuum C .05 .15
165 Secret Base "Agents of S.N.E.A.K." C .05 .15
165 Secret Base "League of Dastardly Doom" C .05 .15
165 Secret Base "Goblin Explosioneers" C .05 .15
165 Secret Base "Crossbreed Labs" C .05 .15
165 Secret Base "Order of the Widget" C .05 .15
166 Watermarket R .30 .50
167 Accessories to Murder U .10 .20
168 Applied Aeronautics C .05 .15
169 Arms Depot U .10 .20
170 Auto-Key C .05 .15
171 Bee-Bee Gun M .75 1.25
172 Boomflinger C .05 .15
173 Buzz Buggy C .05 .15
174 Deadly Poison Sampler R .30 .50
175 Dictation Quillograph C .05 .15
176 Dispatch Dispensary U .10 .20
177 Division Table C .05 .15
178 Dogsnail Engine U .10 .20
179 Dual Doomsuits R .30 .50
180 Duplication Device R .30 .50
181 Faerie Aerie M .75 1.25
182 Genetic Recombinator U .10 .20
183 Gift Horse R .30 .50
184 Gnomeball Machine U .10 .20
185 Goblin Slingshot R .30 .50
186 Guest List R .30 .50
187 Hard Hat Area M .75 1.25
188 Head Banger C .05 .15
189 Hypnotic Swirly Disc R .30 .50
190 Inflation Station C .05 .15
191 Insufferable Syphon U .10 .20
192 Jamming Device U .10 .20
193 Lackey Recycler C .05 .15
194 Mandatory Friendship Shackles C .05 .15
195 Neural Network U .10 .20
196 Oaken Power Suit R .30 .50
197 Optical Optimizer U .10 .20
198 Pet Project M .75 1.25
199 Quick-Stick Lick Trick C .05 .15
200 Rapid Prototyper M .75 1.25
201 Record Store R .30 .50
202 Refibrillator R .30 .50
203 Sap Sucker C .05 .15
204 Sundering Fork U .10 .20
205 Targeting Rocket U .10 .20
206 Thud-for-Duds U .10 .20
207 Top-Secret Tunnel C .05 .15
208 Tread Mill C .05 .15
209 Turbo-Thwacking Auto-Hammer U .10 .20
210 Twiddlestick Charger C .05 .15
211 Widget Contraption U .10 .20
212 Plains L 2.00 3.00
213 Island L 3.00 4.00
214 Swamp L 2.00 3.00
215 Mountain L 2.00 3.00
216 Forest L 2.00 3.00

2017 Magic The Gathering Unstable Foil

1 Adorable Kitten C .40 .60
2 Aerial Toastmaster U .75 1.25
3 Amateur Auteur "Theros" C .40 .60
3 Amateur Auteur "Innistrad" C .40 .60
3 Amateur Auteur "Ravnica" C .40 .60
3 Amateur Auteur "Zendikar" C .40 .60
4 By Gnome Means R 4.00 6.00
5 Chivalrous Chevalier C .40 .60
6 Do-It-Yourself Seraph M 10.00 15.00
7 Gimme Five U .75 1.25
8 GO TO JAIL C .40 .60
9 Half-Kitten, Half- U .75 1.25
10 Humming- C .40 .60
11 Jackknight R 4.00 6.00
12 Knight of the Kitchen Sink "pro two-word names" U .75 1.25
12 Knight of the Kitchen Sink "pro odd collector numbers" U .75 1.25
12 Knight of the Kitchen Sink "pro loose lips" U .75 1.25
12 Knight of the Kitchen Sink "pro even collector numbers" U .75 1.25
12 Knight of the Kitchen Sink "pro black borders" U .75 1.25
12 Knight of the Kitchen Sink "pro watermarks" U .75 1.25
13 Knight of the Widget U .75 1.25
14 Midlife Upgrade U .75 1.25
15 Oddly Uneven R 4.00 6.00
16 Old Guard C .40 .60
17 Ordinary Pony C .40 .60
18 Rhino- U .75 1.25
19 Riveting Rigger C .40 .60
20 Rules Lawyer R 4.00 6.00
21 Sacrifice Play C .40 .60
22 Shaggy Camel C .40 .60
23 Side Quest U .75 1.25
24 Success! C .40 .60
25 Teacher's Pet U .75 1.25
26 Animate Library R 4.00 6.00
27 Blurry Beeble C .40 .60
28 Chipper Chopper C .40 .60
29 Clocknapper R 4.00 6.00
30 Crafty Octopus C .40 .60
31 Crow Storm U .75 1.25
32 Defective Detective C .40 .60
33 Fiver-Finger Discount R 4.00 6.00
34 Graveyard Busybody R 4.00 6.00
35 Half-Shark, Half U .75 1.25
36 Incite Insight R 4.00 6.00
37 Kindly Cognician U .75 1.25
38 Magic Word C .40 .60
39 Mer Man C .40 .60
40 More or Less U .75 1.25
41 Novellamental "chain" C .40 .60
41 Novellamental "pendant" C .40 .60
41 Novellamental "grandmother" C .40 .60
41 Novellamental "heart" C .40 .60
42 Numbing Jellyfish C .40 .60
43 S.N.E.A.K. Dispatcher U .75 1.25
44 Socketed Sprocketer U .75 1.25
45 Spell Suck C .40 .60
46 Spye Eye U .75 1.25
47 Suspicious Nanny U .75 1.25
48 Time Out C .40 .60
49 Very Cryptic Command "Counter black-bordered" R 30.00 50.00
49 Very Cryptic Command "Return target permanent" R 30.00 50.00
49 Very Cryptic Command "Draw a card" R 30.00 50.00
49 Very Cryptic Command "Untap two target permanent" R 30.00 50.00
49 Very Cryptic Command "Alternate Art" R 60.00 80.00
49 Very Cryptic Command "Scry 3" R 30.00 50.00
50 Wall of Fortune C .40 .60
51 Big Boa Constrictor C .40 .60
52 capital offense C .40 .60
53 Dirty Rat C .40 .60
54 Extremely Slow Zombie "Winter" C .40 .60
54 Extremely Slow Zombie "Fall" C .40 .60
54 Extremely Slow Zombie "Summer" C .40 .60
54 Extremely Slow Zombie "Spring" C .40 .60
55 Finders, Keepers C .40 .60
56 Hangman R 4.00 6.00
57 Hazmat Suit (Used) C .40 .60
58 Hoisted Hireling C .40 .60
59 Inhumaniac U .75 1.25
60 Masterful Ninja R 4.00 6.00
61 Ninja U .75 1.25
62 Old-Fashioned Vampire U .75 1.25
63 Over My Daed Bodies R 4.00 6.00
64 Overt Operative U .75 1.25
65 Rumors of My Death... U .75 1.25
66 Skull Saucer U .75 1.25
67 Sly Spy "Spies Nimbly Eluding Adversaries' Knives." U .75 1.25
67 Sly Spy "Skilled, Notably Effiecint Assassin-Kickers." U .75 1.25
67 Sly Spy "Sinister Nerds Eliminating All Knowledge." U .75 1.25
67 Sly Spy "Silent Ninjas Evading Any Kapture." U .75 1.25
67 Sly Spy "Serious, Nonstop Espionage and Kidnapping." U .75 1.25
67 Sly Spy "Subpar, Notoriously Evil Agent Killers." U .75 1.25
68 Snickering Squirrel C .40 .60
69 Spike, Tournament Grinder R 15.00 20.00
70 Squirrel-Powered Scheme U .75 1.25
71 Steady-Handed Mook C .40 .60
72 Stinging Scorpion C .40 .60
73 Subcontract C .40 .60
74 Summon the Pack M 10.00 15.00
75 Zombified U .75 1.25
76 The Big Idea R 4.00 6.00
77 Box of Free-Range Goblins C .40 .60
78 Bumbling Pangolin C .40 .60
79 Common Iguana C .40 .60
80 The Countdown Is at One R 4.00 6.00
81 Feisty Stegosaurus C .40 .60
82 Garbage Elemental "Unleash" U .75 1.25
82 Garbage Elemental "Cascade" U .75 1.25
82 Garbage Elemental "Battle cry" U .75 1.25
82 Garbage Elemental "Undying" U .75 1.25
82 Garbage Elemental "Frenzy 2" U .75 1.25
82 Garbage Elemental "Last strike" U .75 1.25
83 Goblin Haberdasher U .75 1.25
84 Half-Orc, Half- U .75 1.25
85 Hammer Helper C .40 .60
86 Hammer Jammer U .75 1.25
87 Hammerfest Boomtacular U .75 1.25
88 Infinity Elemental M 10.00 15.00
89 It That Gets Left Hanging C .40 .60
90 Just Desserts C .40 .60
91 Painiac C .40 .60
92 Party Crasher U .75 1.25
93 Steamflogger Boss R 4.00 6.00
94 Steamflogger of the Month R 4.00 6.00
95 Steamflogger Temp U .75 1.25
96 Steamfloggery U .75 1.25
97 Super-Duper Death Ray U .75 1.25
98 Target Minotaur "Fireballs" C .40 .60
98 Target Minotaur "Blood Rain" C .40 .60
98 Target Minotaur "Frozen" C .40 .60
98 Target Minotaur "Vines" C .40 .60
99 Three-Headed Goblin R 4.00 6.00
100 Work a Double C .40 .60
101 Wrench-Rigger C .40 .60
102 As Luck Would Have It R 4.00 6.00
103 Beast in Show "Dragon" C .40 .60
103 Beast in Show "Goat" C .40 .60
103 Beast in Show "Dinosaur" C .40 .60
103 Beast in Show "Ox" C .40 .60
104 Chittering Doom U .75 1.25
105 Clever Combo U .75 1.25
106 Druid of the Sacred Beaker U .75 1.25
107 Eager Beaver C .40 .60
108 Earl of the Squirrel R 4.00 6.00
109 First Pick U .75 1.25
110 Ground Pounder C .40 .60
111 Half-Squirrel, Half- U .75 1.25
112 Hydradoodle R 4.00 6.00
113 Ineffable Blessing "choose odd or even" R 4.00 6.00
113 Ineffable Blessing "choose a rarity" R 4.00 6.00
113 Ineffable Blessing "choose white or silver-bordered" R 4.00 6.00
113 Ineffable Blessing "choose an artist" R 4.00 6.00
113 Ineffable Blessing "choose Flavorful or Bland" R 4.00 6.00
113 Ineffable Blessing "choose a number" R 4.00 6.00
114 Joyride Rigger C .40 .60
115 Monkey- U .75 1.25
116 Mother Kangaroo C .40 .60
117 Multi-Headed C .40 .60
118 Really Epic Punch C .40 .60
119 Selfie Preservation C .40 .60
120 Serpentine R 4.00 6.00
121 Shellephant U .75 1.25
122 Slaying Mantis U .75 1.25
123 Squirrel Dealer C .40 .60
124 Steamflogger Service Rep U .75 1.25
125 Wild Crocodile C .40 .60
126 Willing Test Subject C .40 .60
127 Baron Von Count M 15.00 20.00
128 Better Than One R 4.00 6.00
129 Cramped Bunker R 4.00 6.00
130 Dr. Julius Jumblemorph M 10.00 15.00
131 The Grand Calcutron M 10.00 15.00
132 Grusilda, Monster Masher R 4.00 6.00
133 Hot Fix R 4.00 6.00
134 Ol'Buzzbark M 10.00 15.00
135 Phoebe, Head of S.N.E.A.K. M 15.00 20.00
136 Urza, Academy Headmaster M 60.00 65.00
137 X R 4.00 6.00
138 Mary O'Kill R 4.00 6.00
139 Angelic Rocket R 4.00 6.00
140 Border Guardian U .75 1.25
141 Buzzing Whack-a-Doodle U .75 1.25
142 Clock of DOOOOOOOOOOOOM! U .75 1.25
143 Cogmentor U .75 1.25
144 Contraption Cannon U .75 1.25
145 Enraged Killbot C .40 .60
145 Despondent Killbot C .40 .60
145 Delighted Killbot C .40 .60
145 Curious Killbot C .40 .60
146 Entirely Normal Armchair U .75 1.25
147 Everythingamajig "Sacrifice a land" R 4.00 6.00
147 Everythingamajig "Add one mana" R 4.00 6.00
147 Everythingamajig "Flip a coin" R 4.00 6.00
147 Everythingamajig "Draw a card" R 4.00 6.00
147 Everythingamajig "Move a counter" R 4.00 6.00
147 Everythingamajig "Scry 2" R 4.00 6.00
148 Gnome-Made Engine C .40 .60
149 Handy Dandy Clone Machine R 4.00 6.00
150 Kindslaver R 4.00 6.00
151 Krark's Other Thumb U .75 1.25
152 Labro Bot U .75 1.25
153 Lobe Lobber U .75 1.25
154 Mad Science Fair Project C .40 .60
155 Modular Monstrosity R 4.00 6.00
156 Proper Laboratory Attire U .75 1.25
157 Robo- U .75 1.25
158 Split Screen R 4.00 6.00
159 Staff of the Letter Magus U .75 1.25
160 Stamp of Approval U .75 1.25
161 Steam-Powered U .75 1.25
162 Steel Squirrel U .75 1.25
163 Sword of Dungeons & Dragons M 15.00 20.00
164 Voracious Vacuum C .40 .60
165 Secret Base "Agents of S.N.E.A.K." C .40 .60
165 Secret Base "League of Dastardly Doom" C .40 .60
165 Secret Base "Goblin Explosioneers" C .40 .60
165 Secret Base "Crossbreed Labs" C .40 .60
165 Secret Base "Order of the Widget" C .40 .60
166 Watermarket R 4.00 6.00
167 Accessories to Murder U .75 1.25
168 Applied Aeronautics C .40 .60
169 Arms Depot U .75 1.25
170 Auto-Key C .40 .60
171 Bee-Bee Gun M 10.00 15.00
172 Boomflinger C .40 .60
173 Buzz Buggy C .40 .60
174 Deadly Poison Sampler R 4.00 6.00
175 Dictation Quillograph C .40 .60
176 Dispatch Dispensary U .75 1.25
177 Division Table C .40 .60
178 Dogsnail Engine U .75 1.25
179 Dual Doomsuits R 4.00 6.00
180 Duplication Device R 4.00 6.00
181 Faerie Aerie M 10.00 15.00
182 Genetic Recombinator U .75 1.25
183 Gift Horse R 4.00 6.00
184 Gnomeball Machine U .75 1.25
185 Goblin Slingshot R 4.00 6.00
186 Guest List R 4.00 6.00
187 Hard Hat Area M 10.00 15.00
188 Head Banger C .40 .60
189 Hypnotic Swirly Disc R 4.00 6.00
190 Inflation Station C .40 .60
191 Insufferable Syphon U .75 1.25
192 Jamming Device U .75 1.25
193 Lackey Recycler C .40 .60
194 Mandatory Friendship Shackles C .40 .60
195 Neural Network U .75 1.25
196 Oaken Power Suit R 4.00 6.00
197 Optical Optimizer U .75 1.25
198 Pet Project M 10.00 15.00
199 Quick-Stick Lick Trick C .40 .60
200 Rapid Prototyper M 10.00 15.00
201 Record Store R 4.00 6.00
202 Refibrillator R 4.00 6.00
203 Sap Sucker C .40 .60
204 Sundering Fork U .75 1.25
205 Targeting Rocket U .75 1.25
206 Thud-for-Duds U .75 1.25
207 Top-Secret Tunnel C .40 .60
208 Tread Mill C .40 .60
209 Turbo-Thwacking Auto-Hammer U .75 1.25
210 Twiddlestick Charger C .40 .60
211 Widget Contraption U .75 1.25
212 Plains L 45.00 55.00
213 Island L 75.00 85.00
214 Swamp L 45.00 55.00
215 Mountain L 45.00 55.00
216 Forest L 45.00 55.00

2017 Magic The Gathering Unstable Tokens

1 Angel 1.00 1.50
2 Goat .20 .30
3 Spirit .60 1.00
4 Faerie Spy .10 .15
5 Storm Crow .12 .20
6 Thopter .60 1.00
7 Rogue .10 .15
8 Vampire .60 1.00
9 Zombie .50 .75
10 Brainiac .10 .15
11 Elemental .60 1.00
12 Goblin .60 1.00
13 Beast .15 .25
14 Saproling .35 .50
15 Squirrel .50 .75
16 Dragon .25 .35
17 Elemental .20 .30
18 Clue .35 .50
19 Construct .20 .30
20 Gnome .10 .15

2012 Magic The Gathering League Tokens

1 Goblin T
2 Knight T

2013 Magic The Gathering League Tokens

1 Soldier T
2 Bird T
3 Sliver T
4 Soldier T

2014 Magic The Gathering League Tokens

1 Soldier T
2 Minotaur T
3 Squid T
4 Warrior T

2017 Magic The Gathering League Token

1 Gremlin // Energy Reserve C

2014 Magic The Gathering Modern Event Deck 2014 Tokens

1 Soldier .10 .15
2 Spirit .10 .15
3 Myr .10 .15
4 Elspeth, Knight-Errant Emblem 4.50 6.00

1993-15 Magic The Gathering Richard Garfield Promos

RG93 Proposal/9*
RG97 Splendid Genesis/110* 8000.00 10000.00
RG99 Fraternal Exaltation/220* 5000.00 6000.00
RG2015 Phoenix Heart

GAMING

Brought to you by Hills Wholesale Gaming www.wholesalegaming.com

2016 Afterworld Atlantean Starter Set

COMPLETE SET (35)	15.00	25.00
RELEASED ON OCTOBER 14, 2016		
GENS1 Ivantra Inquisitive Daughter Vertical S	.60	1.00
GENS1 Ivantra Inquisitive Daughter Horizontal S	.60	1.00
GENS2 Satrus Atlantean Crier Vertical S	.60	1.00
GENS2 Satrus Atlantean Crier Horizontal S	.60	1.00
GENS3 Varyn Ardent Leader Vertical S	.60	1.00
GENS3 Varyn Ardent Leader Horizontal S	.60	1.00
GENS4 Coral Reef S	.60	1.00
GENS5 Crystal Mine S	.60	1.00
GENS6 Crystal Pool S	.60	1.00
GENS7 Fountain of Life S	.60	1.00
GENS8 Great Library Fortress S	.60	1.00
GENS9 Royal Farm S	.60	1.00
GENS10 Varyns Treasure Trove S	.60	1.00
GENS11 Underwater Forest S	.60	1.00
GENS12 Underwater Hatchery S	.60	1.00
GENS13 Ambush S	.30	.50
GENS14 Poseidons Aid S	.30	.50
GENS15 Torrential Rain S	.30	.50
GENS16 Undertow S	.30	.50
GENS17 Coral Sword S	.30	.50
GENS18 Crystal Double Blade S	.30	.50
GENS19 Crystal Staff S	.30	.50
GENS20 Laser Trident S	.30	.50
GENS21 Leviathans Tooth S	.30	.50
GENS22 Spear Gun S	.30	.50
GENS23 Caiman S	.30	.50
GENS24 Cenna Atlantean Outfitter S	.30	.50
GENS25 Giant Frog S	.30	.50
GENS26 Komodo Dragon S	.30	.50
GENS27 Manta Ray S	.30	.50
GENS28 Merfolk Infiltrator S	.30	.50
GENS29 Merfolk Spearman S	.30	.50
GENS30 Sea Dragon S	.30	.50
GENS31 Water Elementalist S	.30	.50
GENS32 Water Moccasin S	.30	.50

2016 Afterworld Atlantean Starter Set Foil

COMPLETE SET (35)	80.00	125.00
RELEASED ON OCTOBER 14, 2016		
GENS1 Ivantra Inquisitive Daughter Vertical S	7.00	10.00
GENS1 Ivantra Inquisitive Daughter Horizontal S	5.00	8.00
GENS2 Satrus Atlantean Crier Vertical S	7.00	10.00
GENS2 Satrus Atlantean Crier Horizontal S	5.00	8.00
GENS3 Varyn Ardent Leader Vertical S	7.00	10.00
GENS3 Varyn Ardent Leader Horizontal S	5.00	8.00
GENS4 Coral Reef S	3.00	5.00
GENS5 Crystal Mine S	3.00	5.00
GENS6 Crystal Pool S	3.00	5.00
GENS7 Fountain of Life S	3.00	5.00
GENS8 Great Library Fortress S	5.00	8.00
GENS9 Royal Farm S	3.00	5.00
GENS10 Varyns Treasure Trove S	3.00	5.00
GENS11 Underwater Forest S	3.00	5.00
GENS12 Underwater Hatchery S	3.00	5.00
GENS13 Ambush S	1.00	1.50
GENS14 Poseidons Aid S	1.00	1.50
GENS15 Torrential Rain S	1.00	1.50
GENS16 Undertow S	1.00	1.50
GENS17 Coral Sword S	1.00	1.50
GENS18 Crystal Double Blade S	1.00	1.50
GENS19 Crystal Staff S	1.00	1.50
GENS20 Laser Trident S	1.00	1.50
GENS21 Leviathans Tooth S	1.00	1.50
GENS22 Spear Gun S	1.00	1.50
GENS23 Caiman S	1.00	1.50
GENS24 Cenna Atlantean Outfitter S	1.00	1.50
GENS25 Giant Frog S	1.00	1.50
GENS26 Komodo Dragon S	1.00	1.50
GENS27 Manta Ray S	1.00	1.50
GENS28 Merfolk Infiltrator S	1.00	1.50
GENS29 Merfolk Spearman S	1.00	1.50
GENS30 Sea Dragon S	1.00	1.50
GENS31 Water Elementalist S	1.00	1.50
GENS32 Water Moccasin S	1.00	1.50

2016 Afterworld Egyptian Starter Set

COMPLETE SET (31)	15.00	25.00
RELEASED ON OCTOBER 14, 2016		
GENS33 Kaba Akh Lead General Vertical S	.60	1.00
GENS33 Kaba Akh Lead General Horizontal S	.60	1.00
GENS34 Rehema Resourceful Djinn Vertical S	.60	1.00
GENS34 Rehema Resourceful Djinn Horizontal S	.60	1.00
GENS35 Sara First Servant Vertical S	.60	1.00
GENS35 Sara First Servant Horizontal S	.60	1.00
GENS36 Excavation Site S	.60	1.00
GENS37 Fertile Shore S	.60	1.00
GENS38 Great Pyramid Fortress S	.60	1.00
GENS39 Kitchen of the Pharaoh S	.60	1.00
GENS40 Mineral Deposists S	.60	1.00
GENS41 Freshwater Fishery S	.60	1.00
GENS42 Palace Market S	.60	1.00
GENS43 Pharaohs Treasury S	.60	1.00
GENS44 Acid Spray S	.30	.50
GENS45 Call of the Dead S	.30	.50
GENS46 Resupply S	.30	.50
GENS47 Devastating Winds S	.30	.50
GENS48 Search For the Lost City S	.30	.50
GENS49 Shower of Scarabs S	.30	.50
GENS50 Ankh of Osiris S	.30	.50
GENS51 Cursed Dagger S	.30	.50
GENS52 Greaves of the Pharaoh S	.30	.50
GENS53 Elite Slinger S	.30	.50
GENS54 Follower of Ra S	.30	.50
GENS55 Harbinger of Death S	.30	.50
GENS56 Onyx Scarab S	.30	.50
GENS57 Palace Guard S	.30	.50
GENS58 Prophet of the Gods S	.30	.50
GENS59 Sapphire Scarab S	.30	.50
GENS60 Vindictive Hurler S	.30	.50

2016 Afterworld Egyptian Starter Set Foil

COMPLETE SET (31)	80.00	125.00
RELEASED ON OCTOBER 14, 2016		
GENS33 Kaba Akh Lead General Vertical S	7.00	10.00
GENS33 Kaba Akh Lead General Horizontal S	5.00	8.00
GENS34 Rehema Resourceful Djinn Vertical S	7.00	10.00
GENS34 Rehema Resourceful Djinn Horizontal S	5.00	8.00
GENS35 Sara First Servant Vertical S	7.00	10.00
GENS35 Sara First Servant Horizontal S	5.00	8.00
GENS36 Excavation Site S	3.00	5.00
GENS37 Fertile Shore S	3.00	5.00
GENS38 Great Pyramid Fortress S	5.00	8.00
GENS39 Kitchen of the Pharaoh S	3.00	5.00
GENS40 Mineral Deposists S	3.00	5.00
GENS41 Freshwater Fishery S	3.00	5.00
GENS42 Palace Market S	3.00	5.00
GENS43 Pharaohs Treasury S	3.00	5.00
GENS44 Acid Spray S	1.00	1.50
GENS45 Call of the Dead S	1.00	1.50
GENS46 Resupply S	1.00	1.50
GENS47 Devastating Winds S	1.00	1.50
GENS48 Search For the Lost City S	1.00	1.50
GENS49 Shower of Scarabs S	1.00	1.50
GENS50 Ankh of Osiris S	1.00	1.50
GENS51 Cursed Dagger S	1.00	1.50
GENS52 Greaves of the Pharaoh S	1.00	1.50
GENS53 Elite Slinger S	1.00	1.50
GENS54 Follower of Ra S	1.00	1.50
GENS55 Harbinger of Death S	1.00	1.50
GENS56 Onyx Scarab S	1.00	1.50
GENS57 Palace Guard S	1.00	1.50
GENS58 Prophet of the Gods S	1.00	1.50
GENS59 Sapphire Scarab S	1.00	1.50
GENS60 Vindictive Hrler S	1.00	1.50

2016 Afterworld Japanese Starter Set

COMPLETE SET (32)	15.00	25.00
RELEASED ON OCTOBER 14, 2016		
GENS61 Amaterasu Sun Goddess Vertical S	.60	1.00
GENS61 Amaterasu Sun Goddess Horizontal S	.60	1.00
GENS62 Takezo Master Swordsman Vertical S	.60	1.00
GENS62 Takezo Master Swordsman Horizontal S	.60	1.00
GENS63 Yagyu Revered Teacher Vertical S	.60	1.00
GENS63 Yagyu Revered Teacher Horizontal S	.60	1.00
GENS64 Geisha House S	.60	1.00
GENS65 Izanagis Fields S	.60	1.00
GENS66 Jade Mine S	.60	1.00
GENS67 Mineral Vein S	.60	1.00
GENS68 Peach Orhard S	.60	1.00
GENS69 Rice Paddy S	.60	1.00
GENS70 Shoguns Tower Fortress S	.60	1.00
GENS71 Yomi Land of the Dead S	.60	1.00
GENS72 Die by the Sword S	.30	.50
GENS73 Honorable Seppuku S	.30	.50
GENS74 Live by the Sword S	.30	.50
GENS75 Visiting the Kabuki S	.30	.50
GENS76 Youre Not Worthy S	.30	.50
GENS77 Kabuto S	.30	.50
GENS78 Katana S	.30	.50
GENS79 Sakabatou S	.30	.50
GENS80 Wakizashi S	.30	.50
GENS81 Archers S	.30	.50
GENS82 Dojo Sensei S	.30	.50
GENS83 Feudal Samurai S	.30	.50
GENS84 Friendly Kami S	.30	.50
GENS85 Loyal Yojimbo S	.30	.50
GENS86 Yamabushi of Yang S	.30	.50
GENS87 Spiritual Yamabushi S	.30	.50
GENS88 Wandering Ronin S	.30	.50
GENS89 Weaponsmith of Fire S	.30	.50

2016 Afterworld Japanese Starter Set Foil

COMPLETE SET (32)	80.00	125.00
RELEASED ON OCTOBER 14, 2016		
GENS61 Amaterasu Sun Goddess Vertical S	7.00	10.00
GENS61 Amaterasu Sun Goddess Horizontal S	5.00	8.00
GENS62 Takezo Master Swordsman Vertical S	7.00	10.00
GENS62 Takezo Master Swordsman Horizontal S	5.00	8.00
GENS63 Yagyu Revered Teacher Vertical S	7.00	10.00
GENS63 Yagyu Revered Teacher Horizontal S	5.00	8.00
GENS64 Geisha House S	3.00	5.00
GENS65 Izanagis Fields S	3.00	5.00
GENS66 Jade Mine S	3.00	5.00
GENS67 Mineral Vein S	3.00	5.00
GENS68 Peach Orhard S	3.00	5.00
GENS69 Rice Paddy S	3.00	5.00
GENS70 Shoguns Tower Fortress S	5.00	8.00
GENS71 Yomi Land of the Dead S	3.00	5.00
GENS72 Die by the Sword S	1.00	1.50
GENS73 Honorable Seppuku S	1.00	1.50
GENS74 Live by the Sword S	1.00	1.50
GENS75 Visiting the Kabuki S	1.00	1.50
GENS76 Youre Not Worthy S	1.00	1.50
GENS77 Kabuto S	1.00	1.50
GENS78 Katana S	1.00	1.50
GENS79 Sakabatou S	1.00	1.50
GENS80 Wakizashi S	1.00	1.50
GENS81 Archers S	1.00	1.50
GENS82 Dojo Sensei S	1.00	1.50
GENS83 Feudal Samurai S	1.00	1.50
GENS84 Friendly Kami S	1.00	1.50
GENS85 Loyal Yojimbo S	1.00	1.50
GENS86 Yamabushi of Yang S	1.00	1.50
GENS87 Spiritual Yamabushi S	1.00	1.50
GENS88 Wandering Ronin S	1.00	1.50
GENS89 Weaponsmith of Fire S	1.00	1.50

2016 Afterworld Norse Starter Set

COMPLETE SET (29)	15.00	25.00
RELEASED ON OCTOBER 14, 2016		
GENS90 Fenris Uncontrollable Wolf Vertical S	.60	1.00
GENS90 Fenris Uncontrollable Wolf Horizontal S	.60	1.00
GENS91 Freya Goddess of Love Vertical S	.60	1.00
GENS91 Freya Goddess of Love Horizontal S	.60	1.00
GENS92 Rorik Translation of One Vertical S	.60	1.00
GENS92 Rorik Translation of One Horizontal S	.60	1.00
GENS93 Aesirs Landing S	.60	1.00
GENS94 Asgard Fishery S	.60	1.00
GENS95 Idunns Orchard S	.60	1.00
GENS96 Mead Brewery S	.60	1.00
GENS97 Midgard Mining Outpost S	.60	1.00
GENS98 Plains of Valhall S	.60	1.00
GENS99 Svartalfheim Mining Center S	.60	1.00
GENS100 Valhalla Fortress S	.60	1.00
GENS101 Waters of Elivagar S	.60	1.00
GENS102 Drunken Apathy S	.30	.50
GENS103 Falcon Shape Change S	.30	.50
GENS104 Kick Into the Fire S	.30	.50
GENS105 Lightning Strike S	.30	.50
GENS106 Axe of the Berserker S	.30	.50
GENS107 Claws of the Savage S	.30	.50
GENS108 Potion of Rage S	.30	.50
GENS109 Dwarven Infantry S	.30	.50
GENS110 Jotun Elementalist S	.30	.50
GENS111 Jotun Shaman S	.30	.50
GENS112 Muspelheim Sky Raider S	.30	.50
GENS113 Niflheim Battler S	.30	.50
GENS114 Skald of Aesir S	.30	.50
GENS115 Warriors of Asgard S	.30	.50

2016 Afterworld Norse Starter Set Foil

COMPLETE SET (29)	80.00	125.00
RELEASED ON OCTOBER 14, 2016		
GENS90 Fenris Uncontrollable Wolf Vertical S	7.00	10.00
GENS90 Fenris Uncontrollable Wolf Horizontal S	5.00	8.00
GENS91 Freya Goddess of Love Vertical S	7.00	10.00
GENS91 Freya Goddess of Love Horizontal S	5.00	8.00
GENS92 Rorik Translation of One Vertical S	7.00	10.00
GENS92 Rorik Translation of One Horizontal S	5.00	8.00
GENS93 Aesirs Landing S	3.00	5.00
GENS94 Asgard Fishery S	3.00	5.00
GENS95 Idunns Orchard S	3.00	5.00
GENS96 Mead Brewery S	3.00	5.00
GENS97 Midgard Mining Outpost S	3.00	5.00
GENS98 Plains of Valhall S	3.00	5.00
GENS99 Svartalfheim Mining Center S	3.00	5.00
GENS100 Valhalla Fortress S	5.00	8.00
GENS101 Waters of Elivagar S	3.00	5.00
GENS102 Drunken Apathy S	1.00	1.50
GENS103 Falcon Shape Change S	1.00	1.50
GENS104 Kick Into the Fire S	1.00	1.50
GENS105 Lightning Strike S	1.00	1.50
GENS106 Axe of the Berserker S	1.00	1.50
GENS107 Claws of the Savage S	1.00	1.50
GENS108 Potion of Rage S	1.00	1.50
GENS109 Dwarven Infantry S	1.00	1.50
GENS110 Jotun Elementalist S	1.00	1.50
GENS111 Jotun Shaman S	1.00	1.50
GENS112 Muspelheim Sky Raider S	1.00	1.50
GENS113 Niflheim Battler S	1.00	1.50
GENS114 Skald of Aesir S	1.00	1.50
GENS115 Warriors of Asgard S	1.00	1.50

2016 Afterworld Genesis

COMPLETE SET (149)	100.00	150.00
BOOSTER BOX (20 PACKS)	50.00	65.00
BOOSTER PACK (10 CARDS)	3.00	4.00

Card	Low	High
RELEASED ON OCTOBER 14, 2016		
GENC1 Merfolk Salvaging C	.15	.25
GENC2 Tidal Wave C	.15	.25
GENC3 Undersea Eruption C	.15	.25
GENC4 Wall of the Deep C	.15	.25
GENC5 Charge Prod C	.15	.25
GENC6 Circlet of Protection C	.15	.25
GENC7 Crystal Javelin C	.15	.25
GENC8 Dagger of Atlantis C	.15	.25
GENC9 Fishing Net C	.15	.25
GENC10 Plato's Myth C	.15	.25
GENC11 Lagoon Serpent C	.15	.25
GENC12 Merfolk Innocent C	.15	.25
GENC13 Merfolk Saboteur C	.15	.25
GENC14 Water Salamander C	.15	.25
GENC15 Water Sprite C	.15	.25
GENC16 Dispel C	.15	.25
GENC17 Eunuch's Luck C	.15	.25
GENC18 Reversal of Fortune C	.15	.25
GENC19 Book of the Dead C	.15	.25
GENC20 Golden Ticket C	.15	.25
GENC21 Pouch of Sand C	.15	.25
GENC22 Atlantean Servant C	.15	.25
GENC23 Demonic Mummy C	.15	.25
GENC24 Diamond Scarab C	.15	.25
GENC25 Experienced Servant C	.15	.25
GENC26 Japanese Servant C	.15	.25
GENC27 Minion of Isis C	.15	.25
GENC28 Norse Servant C	.15	.25
GENC29 Scarab Wall C	.15	.25
GENC30 Taskmaster C	.15	.25
GENC31 Worshipper of Osiris C	.15	.25
GENC32 For My Lord C	.15	.25
GENC33 Spy's Eyes C	.15	.25
GENC34 Under Cover of Darkness C	.15	.25
GENC35 Amenonuhoko C	.15	.25
GENC36 Kikou C	.15	.25
GENC37 Yata No Kagami C	.15	.25
GENC38 Daimyo Ninjas C	.15	.25
GENC39 Fancy Geisha C	.15	.25
GENC40 Geisha Mistress C	.15	.25
GENC41 Ninja Apprentice C	.15	.25
GENC42 Peasants C	.15	.25
GENC43 Yamabushi of Yin C	.15	.25
GENC44 Gathering of the Aesir C	.15	.25
GENC45 Serpent Shape Change C	.15	.25
GENC46 Brisingamen C	.15	.25
GENC47 Falcon Feather Cloak C	.15	.25
GENC48 Mjollnir C	.15	.25
GENC49 Alfheim Protector C	.15	.25
GENC50 Devout Thegn C	.15	.25
GENC51 Midgard Foot Soldier C	.15	.25
GENC52 Muspelheim Archer C	.15	.25
GENC53 Muspelheim Rider C	.15	.25
GENC54 Niflheim Assistant C	.15	.25
GENC55 Niflheim Champion C	.15	.25
GENC56 Relentless Einherjar C	.15	.25
GENC57 Svartalf Provider C	.15	.25
GENC58 Dwarven Thrower C	.15	.25
GENC59 Svartalf Tinkerer C	.15	.25
GENC60 Tenacious Savage C	.15	.25
GENU61 Poseidon, God of the Sea U	.25	.40
GENU62 Qisk, Right-hand Man U	.25	.40
GENU63 Squiddy, Deep Sea Kraken U	.25	.40
GENU64 Depth Charge U	.25	.40
GENU65 Dome of Technology U	.25	.40
GENU66 Poison Vial U	.25	.40
GENU67 Poseidon's Trident U	.25	.40
GENU68 Aquatic Siren U	.25	.40
GENU69 Giant Lobster U	.25	.40
GENU70 Great White Shark U	.25	.40
GENU71 Isis, Goddess of Fertility U	.25	.40
GENU72 Osiris, God of the Dead U	.25	.40
GENU73 Ra, Sun God U	.25	.40
GENU74 Hymn to Osiris U	.25	.40
GENU75 Shifting Sands U	.25	.40
GENU76 Unnatural Sandstorm U	.25	.40
GENU77 Bracers of Ra U	.25	.40
GENU78 Hounds of Anubis U	.25	.40
GENU79 Priest of Ra U	.25	.40
GENU80 Sphinx U	.25	.40
GENU81 Tahirah, Pristine Warrior U	.25	.40
GENU82 Vengeful Dead U	.25	.40
GENU83 Izanagi, The First Male U	.25	.40
GENU84 Izanami, The First Female U	.25	.40
GENU85 Koji, Enlightened One U	.25	.40
GENU86 Following the Way U	.25	.40
GENU87 Imperial Court U	.25	.40
GENU88 Samurai Fury U	.25	.40
GENU89 Kusanagi U	.25	.40
GENU90 Shoguns Banner U	.25	.40
GENU91 Shuriken U	.25	.40
GENU92 Bushi U	.25	.40
GENU93 Daimyo Courtier U	.25	.40
GENU94 Jonin U	.25	.40
GENU95 Kazuo, Royal Magistrate U	.25	.40
GENU96 Ninja of the Full Moon U	.25	.40
GENU97 Fafnir, Zealous Dragon U	.25	.40
GENU98 Loki, Mischievous God U	.25	.40
GENU99 Odin, Head of Aesir U	.25	.40
GENU100 Ring of Fire U	.25	.40
GENU101 Thor's Intervention U	.25	.40
GENU102 Traversing Bifrost U	.25	.40
GENU103 Gjallarhorn U	.25	.40
GENU104 Idunn's Apples U	.25	.40
GENU105 Dwarven Commander U	.25	.40
GENU106 Dwarven Ranger U	.25	.40
GENU107 Jotun Charioteer U	.25	.40
GENU108 Jotun Warcaller U	.25	.40
GENU109 Midgard Rune Caster U	.25	.40
GENR110 Abyss R	2.00	3.00
GENR111 Feeding Frenzy R	1.00	1.50
GENR112 Restraints R	2.00	3.00
GENR113 Transformation R	1.00	1.50
GENR114 Underwater Traps R	2.00	3.00
GENR115 Charge Crystal R	2.00	3.00
GENR116 Defiant Orca R	2.00	3.00
GENR117 Hammerhead Shark R	3.00	5.00
GENR118 Melandria, Decisive Leader R	1.00	1.50
GENR119 Talmara, Master Salvager R	4.00	6.00
GENR120 Compel R	2.00	3.00
GENR121 Forceful Encouragement R	3.00	5.00
GENR122 Power of the Pharaoh R	4.00	6.00
GENR123 Scales of Judgment R	1.00	1.50
GENR124 Fanatical Judgment R	3.00	5.00
GENR125 Golden Scarab R	3.00	5.00
GENR126 Sand Elemental R	1.00	1.50
GENR127 Shapeshifter R	2.00	3.00
GENR128 Sudi, Practiced Transmuter R	2.00	3.00
GENR129 Teremun, Devoted Fighter R	1.00	1.50
GENR130 Bushido R	1.00	1.50
GENR131 Duel of the Samurai R	2.00	3.00
GENR132 Peaceful Meditation R	2.00	3.00
GENR133 Swiftly, Silently, Deadly R	1.00	1.50
GENR134 Imperial Regalia R	3.00	5.00
GENR135 Akiko, Faithful Servant R	1.00	1.50
GENR136 Ninjutsu Masters R	4.00	6.00
GENR137 Orochi, Eight-Pronged Dragon R	1.00	1.50
GENR138 Susanowo, Storm God R	1.00	1.50
GENR139 Veteran Samurai R	5.00	8.00
GENR140 Odin's Wrath R	1.00	1.50
GENR141 Ragnarok R	1.00	1.50
GENR142 To the Gates of Hell R	2.00	3.00
GENR143 Draupnir R	1.00	1.50
GENR144 Alfheim Vanguard R	3.00	5.00
GENR145 Brynhild, Shieldmaiden R	1.00	1.50
GENR146 Raging Berserker R	4.00	6.00
GENR147 Rorik, Norse Savior R	4.00	6.00
GENR148 Tyr, God of Duty R	1.00	1.50
GENR149 Valkyrie R	4.00	6.00

2016 Afterworld Genesis Foil

Card	Low	High
COMPLETE SET (149)	225.00	350.00
BOOSTER BOX (20 PACKS)	50.00	65.00
BOOSTER PACK (10 CARDS)	3.00	4.00
RELEASED ON OCTOBER 14, 2016		
GENC1 Merfolk Salvaging C	.30	.50
GENC2 Tidal Wave C	.30	.50
GENC3 Undersea Eruption C	.30	.50
GENC4 Wall of the Deep C	.30	.50
GENC5 Charge Prod C	.30	.50
GENC6 Circlet of Protection C	.30	.50
GENC7 Crystal Javelin C	.30	.50
GENC8 Dagger of Atlantis C	.30	.50
GENC9 Fishing Net C	.30	.50
GENC10 Platos Myth C	.30	.50
GENC11 Lagoon Serpent C	.30	.50
GENC12 Merfolk Innocent C	.30	.50
GENC13 Merfolk Saboteur C	.30	.50
GENC14 Water Salamander C	.30	.50
GENC15 Water Sprite C	.30	.50
GENC16 Dispel C	.30	.50
GENC17 Eunuchs Luck C	.30	.50
GENC18 Reversal of Fortune C	.30	.50
GENC19 Book of the Dead C	.30	.50
GENC20 Golden Ticket C	.30	.50
GENC21 Pouch of Sand C	.30	.50
GENC22 Atlantean Servant C	.30	.50
GENC23 Demonic Mummy C	.30	.50
GENC24 Diamond Scarab C	.30	.50
GENC25 Experienced Servant C	.30	.50
GENC26 Japanese Servant C	.30	.50
GENC27 Minion of Isis C	.30	.50
GENC28 Norse Servant C	.30	.50
GENC29 Scarab Wall C	.30	.50
GENC30 Taskmaster C	.30	.50
GENC31 Worshipper of Osiris C	.30	.50
GENC32 For My Lord C	.30	.50
GENC33 Spys Eyes C	.30	.50
GENC34 Under Cover of Darkness C	.30	.50
GENC35 Amenonuhoko C	.30	.50
GENC36 Kikou C	.30	.50
GENC37 Yata No Kagami C	.30	.50
GENC38 Daimyo Ninjas C	.30	.50
GENC39 Fancy Geisha C	.30	.50
GENC40 Geisha Mistress C	.30	.50
GENC41 Ninja Apprentice C	.30	.50
GENC42 Peasants C	.30	.50
GENC43 Yamabushi of Yin C	.30	.50
GENC44 Gathering of the Aesir C	.30	.50
GENC45 Serpent Shape Change C	.30	.50
GENC46 Brisingamen C	.30	.50
GENC47 Falcon Feather Cloak C	.30	.50
GENC48 Mjollnir C	.30	.50
GENC49 Alfheim Protector C	.30	.50
GENC50 Devout Thegn C	.30	.50
GENC51 Midgard Foot Soldier C	.30	.50
GENC52 Muspelheim Archer C	.30	.50
GENC53 Muspelheim Rider C	.30	.50
GENC54 Niflheim Assistant C	.30	.50
GENC55 Niflheim Champion C	.30	.50
GENC56 Relentless Einherjar C	.30	.50
GENC57 Svartalf Provider C	.30	.50
GENC58 Dwarven Thrower C	.30	.50
GENC59 Svartalf Tinkerer C	.30	.50
GENC60 Tenacious Savage C	.30	.50
GENU61 Poseidon God of the Sea U	3.00	5.00
GENU62 Qisk Right Hand Man U	3.00	5.00
GENU63 Squiddy Deep Sea Kraken U	3.00	5.00
GENU64 Depth Charge U	.60	1.00
GENU65 Dome of Technology U	.60	1.00
GENU66 Poison Vial U	.60	1.00
GENU67 Poseidons Trident U	.60	1.00
GENU68 Aquatic Siren U	.60	1.00
GENU69 Giant Lobster U	.60	1.00
GENU70 Great White Shark U	.60	1.00
GENU71 Isis Goddess of Fertility U	3.00	5.00
GENU72 Osiris God of the Dead U	3.00	5.00
GENU73 Ra Sun God U	3.00	5.00
GENU74 Hymn to Osiris U	.60	1.00
GENU75 Shifting Sands U	.60	1.00
GENU76 Unnatural Sandstorm U	.60	1.00
GENU77 Bracers of Ra U	.60	1.00
GENU78 Hounds of Anubis U	.60	1.00
GENU79 Priest of Ra U	.60	1.00
GENU80 Sphinx U	.60	1.00
GENU81 Tahirah Pristine Warrior U	.60	1.00
GENU82 Vengeful Dead U	.60	1.00
GENU83 Izanagi The First Male U	3.00	5.00
GENU84 Izanami The First Female U	3.00	5.00
GENU85 Koji Enlightened One U	3.00	5.00
GENU86 Following the Way U	.60	1.00
GENU87 Imperial Court U	.60	1.00
GENU88 Samurai Fury U	.60	1.00
GENU89 Kusanagi U	.60	1.00
GENU90 Shoguns Banner U	.60	1.00
GENU91 Shuriken U	.60	1.00
GENU92 Bushi U	.60	1.00
GENU93 Daimyo Courtier U	.60	1.00
GENU94 Jonin U	.60	1.00
GENU95 Kazuo Royal Magistrate U	.60	1.00
GENU96 Ninja of the Full Moon U	.60	1.00
GENU97 Fafnir Zealous Dragon U	3.00	5.00
GENU98 Loki Mischievous God U	3.00	5.00
GENU99 Odin Head of Aesir U	3.00	5.00
GENU100 Ring of Fire U	.60	1.00
GENU101 Thors Intervention U	.60	1.00
GENU102 Traversing Bifrost U	.60	1.00
GENU103 Gjallarhorn U	.60	1.00
GENU104 Idunns Apples U	.60	1.00
GENU105 Dwarven Commander U	.60	1.00
GENU106 Dwarven Ranger U	.60	1.00
GENU107 Jotun Charioteer U	.60	1.00
GENU108 Jotun Warcaller U	.60	1.00
GENU109 Midgard Rune Caster U	.60	1.00
GENR110 Abyss R	3.00	5.00
GENR111 Feeding Frenzy R	2.00	3.00
GENR112 Restraints R	3.00	5.00
GENR113 Transformation R	2.00	3.00
GENR114 Underwater Traps R	3.00	5.00
GENR115 Charge Crystal R	3.00	5.00
GENR116 Defiant Orca R	3.00	5.00
GENR117 Hammerhead Shark R	5.00	8.00
GENR118 Melandria Decisive Leader R	2.00	3.00
GENR119 Talmara Master Salvager R	7.00	10.00
GENR120 Compel R	3.00	5.00
GENR121 Forceful Encouragement R	5.00	8.00
GENR122 Power of the Pharaoh R	7.00	10.00
GENR123 Scales of Judgment R	2.00	3.00
GENR124 Fanatical Judgment R	5.00	8.00
GENR125 Golden Scarab R	5.00	8.00
GENR126 Sand Elemental R	2.00	3.00
GENR127 Shapeshifter R	3.00	5.00
GENR128 Sudi Practiced Transmuter R	2.00	3.00
GENR129 Teremun Devoted Fighter R	2.00	3.00
GENR130 Bushido R	2.00	3.00
GENR131 Duel of the Samurai R	3.00	5.00
GENR132 Peaceful Meditation R	3.00	5.00
GENR133 Swiftly Silently Deadly R	2.00	3.00
GENR134 Imperial Regalia R	2.00	3.00
GENR135 Akiko Faithful Servant R	2.00	3.00
GENR136 Ninjutsu Masters R	7.00	10.00
GENR137 Orochi Eight Pronged Dragon R	2.00	3.00
GENR138 Susanowo Storm God R	2.00	3.00
GENR139 Veteran Samurai R	7.00	10.00
GENR140 Odins Wrath R	2.00	3.00
GENR141 Ragnarok R	2.00	3.00
GENR142 To the Gates of Hell R	3.00	5.00
GENR143 Draupnir R	2.00	3.00
GENR144 Alfheim Vanguard R	5.00	8.00
GENR145 Brynhild Shieldmaiden R	7.00	10.00
GENR146 Raging Berserker R	7.00	10.00
GENR147 Rorik Norse Savior R	7.00	10.00
GENR148 Tyr God of Duty R	2.00	3.00
GENR149 Valkyrie R	7.00	10.00

2019 Bakugan Battle Brawlers

Card	Low	High
BOOSTER BOXES DON'T EXIST		
BOOSTER PACK (5 CARDS)		
RELEASED ON		
1 Absorb AR	4.00	6.00
2 Aquos Shield C	.20	.30
3 Aquos Slam SR	1.25	2.50
4 Bubble Net R	.75	1.25
5 Cycling Thoughts C	.20	.30
6 Deep Illusion R	.60	1.00
7 Ebb C	.20	.30
8 Fixation C	.20	.30
9 Flooding Waters R	1.00	1.50
10 Greater Water Boost C	.20	.30
11 Hurricane Slash R	1.00	1.50
12 Hydro Blast C	.20	.30
13 Ice Barrier C	.20	.30
14 Ice Elation C	.20	.30
15 Ice Sickle C	.20	.30
16 Ice Wall C	.20	.30
17 Inspire C	.20	.30
18 Liquid Strike C	.20	.30
19 Mind Flood SR	2.00	3.00
20 Shuryuken R	.75	1.25
21 Solitude R	.60	1.00
22 Think Again C	.20	.30
23 Tidal Wave C	.20	.30
24 Tides C	.20	.30
25 Triple Blast Cannon C	.20	.30
26 Water Slash C	.20	.30
27 Wave Slash C	.20	.30
28 Whirlpool R	.60	1.00
29 Chaotic Darkness C	.20	.30
30 Cloak in Shadow C	.20	.30
31 Corrupting Mist R	1.25	2.00
32 Curse of Darkus C	.20	.30
33 Cycling Madness C	.20	.30
34 Dark Boost C	.20	.30
35 Dark Fire C	.20	.30
36 Darkus Strike C	.20	.30
37 Garganoid's Gaze R	1.25	2.00
38 Gravity Shift SR	1.00	1.50
39 Hero's Demise R	1.25	2.00
40 Might of Night R	.60	1.00
41 Night Lightning AR	2.00	3.00
42 Prismatic Bolt C	.20	.30
43 Prismatic Shield C	.20	.30
44 Rite of Darkus R	.75	1.25
45 Shade Blade C	.20	.30
46 Shadow Coil R	1.50	2.50
47 Shadow Hue C	.20	.30
48 Shadow Trap R	.60	1.00
49 Smoke Armor C	.20	.30
50 Stoneskin C	.20	.30
51 Storm Generator R	1.25	2.00
52 Tainted Touch C	.20	.30
53 Terrify C	.20	.30

54 Thought Decay C .20 .30
55 Umbral Slash R 1.00 1.50
56 Unrivaled Jump C .20 .30
57 Wither C .20 .30
58 Beaming Blaster C .20 .30
59 Blinding Glam C .20 .30
60 Body Guard SR 1.25 2.00
61 Bone Defense C .20 .30
62 Consort R .60 1.00
63 Cutepocalypse SR 1.25 2.00
64 Cycling Light C .20 .30
65 Dream Illusion C .20 .30
66 Fragile to Light C .20 .30
67 Heroic Strength C .20 .30
68 Light Break C .20 .30
69 Light's Courage C .20 .30
70 Luminous Armor C .20 .30
71 Pandoxx Punch C .20 .30
72 Reflection Rays R .60 1.00
73 Revitalize SR 1.00 1.50
74 Shine C .20 .30
75 Stoic Shot C .20 .30
76 Super Shot C .20 .30
77 Surge of Light C .20 .30
78 The Sky's Hymn SR 3.00 5.00
79 Thunder Sword C .20 .30
80 Wane R 1.50 2.50
81 Wax AR 1.25 2.00
82 Whiteout C .20 .30
83 Wing Cutter R .60 1.00
84 Cinder Coil SR 1.25 2.00
85 Cycling Warmth C .20 .30
86 Cyndeus Stand SR 1.25 2.00
87 Drago's Fury R .60 1.00
88 Engulfing Embers R .60 1.00
89 Fierce Boost C .20 .30
90 Fiery Rage C .20 .30
91 Fire Boost C .20 .30
92 Fire Vortex C .20 .30
93 Fireball C .20 .30
94 Furious Blast R 1.25 2.00
95 Hot Potato R .60 1.00
96 Impact Lazer C .20 .30
97 Implosion R .60 1.00
98 Inferno R .60 1.00
99 Inferno Wings SR 2.50 4.00
100 Lava Boost C .20 .30
101 Magma Boost R .60 1.00
102 Meltdown C .20 .30
103 Meteoric Lance C .20 .30
104 Might of Cyndeus R 2.00 3.00
105 Molten Helix C .20 .30
106 Power Ritual R .60 1.00
107 Pyrus Strike C .20 .30
108 Sifting Ashes C .20 .30
109 Song of Fire C .20 .30
110 Talon Slash C .20 .30
111 Cocoon Shield R .60 1.00
112 Crushing Grasp C .20 .30
113 Cycling Ichor C .20 .30
114 Deafening Roar C .20 .30
115 Endless Growth AR 2.50 4.00
116 Envenom R 1.25 2.00
117 Invigoration Blast R .60 1.00
118 Lazer Claw C .20 .30
119 Mulch SR 1.50 2.50
120 Nature's Power R 2.50 4.00
121 Oaken Shield C .20 .30
122 One with Nature SR 2.50 4.00
123 Paralyzing Potion C .20 .30
124 Piercing Scream C .20 .30
125 Razor Claws C .20 .30
126 Recycling Boost R .60 1.00
127 Shell Shield R .60 1.00
128 Shock and Awe C .20 .30
129 Smash C .20 .30
130 Sonic Howl C .20 .30
131 Stomping Quake SR 1.25 2.00
132 Strength of Maxotaur C .20 .30
133 Toxify C .20 .30
134 Turn to Energy C .20 .30
135 Venom Blast C .20 .30
136 Ventus Moonbeam C .20 .30
137 Wild Strike R .60 1.00
138 Brain Geyser SR 1.50 2.50
139 Counter Aggression C .20 .30
140 Counter Aquos C .20 .30
141 Counter Haos C .20 .30
142 Counter Outsiders C .20 .30
143 Counter Pyrus C .20 .30
144 Exhilarate C .20 .30
145 Fading Dash R .60 1.00
146 Blackhole AR 3.00 5.00
147 Cease Darkus C .20 .30
148 Cease Haos C .20 .30
149 Cease Outsiders C .20 .30
150 Cease Serenity R .60 1.00
151 Cease Ventus C .20 .30
152 Pact of Darkness SR 25.00 40.00
153 Punish C .20 .30
154 Shadow Breath SR 1.50 2.50
155 Halt Aquos C .20 .30
156 Halt Darkus C .20 .30
157 Halt Haos C .20 .30
158 Halt Outsiders C .20 .30
159 Halt Unknown C .20 .30
160 Haos Ascendancy C .20 .30
161 Heroic Inspiration R .60 1.00
162 Light as a Feather R .60 1.00
163 Luck Aura AR 1.00 1.50
164 Razor Wings C .20 .30
165 Stand Together SR 5.00 8.00
166 Block Aquos C .20 .30
167 Block Growth C .20 .30
168 Block Outsiders C .20 .30
169 Block Pyrus C .20 .30
170 Block Ventus C .20 .30
171 Fierce Termination SR 1.50 2.50
172 Lava Flow C .20 .30
173 Pyrus Dominance C .20 .30
174 Spark C .20 .30
175 Hyperdrive SR 1.50 2.50
176 Nature Assimilation SR 4.00 6.00
177 Photosynthesis C .20 .30
178 Repel Darkus C .20 .30
179 Repel Destruction C .20 .30
180 Repel Outsiders C .20 .30
181 Repel Pyrus C .20 .30
182 Repel Ventus C .20 .30
183 Sowing Seeds R .60 1.00
184 Tiger Reflex SR 15.00 25.00
185 Trox's Moxy R 1.25 2.00
186 Ventus Power C .20 .30
187 BEE SR .60 1.00
188 Everett Ray SR 5.00 8.00
189 Maggie SR 1.25 2.00
190 Masato Kazami R 1.50 2.50
191 Shun Kazami AR 3.00 5.00
192 Strata SR 3.00 5.00
193 Toshi BE 2.50 4.00
194 Benton Dusk SR 1.50 2.50
195 CEE SR 1.25 2.00
196 China Riot R 2.00 3.00
197 Kurin SR .60 1.00
198 Lightning R 1.25 2.00
199 Magnus BE 2.00 3.00
200 Col. Armstrong Tripp R .60 1.00
201 DEE R .60 1.00
202 Lia Venegas BE 2.50 4.00
203 Philomena Dusk SR .60 1.00
204 Veronica Venegas R .60 1.00
205 Barbara Kouzo R 1.00 1.50
206 Bill Kouzo R .60 1.00
207 Dan Kouzo BE 20.00 30.00
208 Duran Dane AR .75 1.25
209 E AR 2.00 3.00
210 Mac SR 2.50 4.00
211 Marco SR .60 1.00
212 AAY R .60 1.00
213 Max AR .60 1.00
214 Olivia Styles R 1.00 1.50
215 Wynton Styles BE 6.00 10.00
216 Hydorous (Diamond Card) R 1.00 1.50
217 Hydorous Ultra (Diamond Card) R 1.00 1.50
218 Serpenteze (Diamond Card) R 1.00 1.50
219 Hyper Pegatrix (Aquos Card) R 1.00 1.50
220 Hyper Fangzor (Aquos Card) AR 5.00 8.00
221 Hyper Hydorous (Aquos Card) R 1.00 1.50
222 Hyper Hydorous Ultra (Aquos Card) AR 3.00 5.00
223 Hyper Mantonoid Ultra (Aquos Card) R 1.00 1.50
224 Hyper Serpenteze Ultra (Aquos Card) R 1.00 1.50
225 Hyper Trox (Aquos Card) R 1.00 1.50
226 Maximus Hydorous Ultra (Aquos Card) BE 3.00 5.00
227 Titan Dragonoid (Aquos Card) R 1.00 1.50
228 Titan Garganoid Ultra (Aquos Card) SR .60 1.00
229 Hyper Dragonoid (Aurelus Card) R 2.00 3.00
230 Hyper Howlkor Ultra (Aurelus Card) SR 1.25 2.50
231 Hyper Maxotaur Ultra (Aurelus Card) AR .75 1.25
232 Hyper Nillious (Aurelus Card) R 1.25 2.00
233 Hyper Pegatrix (Aurelus Card) R 1.00 1.50
234 Hyper Garganoid Ultra (Aurelus Card) SR 2.00 3.00
235 Titan Fangzor (Aurelus Card) R 1.25 2.00
236 Titan Hydorous (Aurelus Card) BE 2.50 4.00
237 Garganoid Ultra (Diamond Card) R .60 1.00
238 Nillious (Diamond Card) R .60 1.00
239 Hyper Dragonoid (Darkus Card) R 1.00 1.50
240 Hyper Fangzor (Darkus Card) R 1.25 2.00
241 Hyper Hydorous (Darkus Card) R .60 1.00
242 Hyper Hydorous Ultra (Darkus Card) AR 2.00 3.00
243 Hyper Trox (Darkus Card) SR 1.25 2.00
244 Hyper Nillious (Darkus Card) SR 2.00 3.00
245 Titan Howlkor Ultra (Darkus Card) AR .75 1.25
246 Titan Mantonoid Ultra (Darkus Card) SR 3.00 5.00
247 Titan Nillious (Darkus Card) BE 8.00 12.00
248 Gorthion Ultra (Diamond Card) R .60 1.00
249 Pegatrix (Diamond Card) R .60 1.00
250 Hyper Fangzor (Haos Card) R .60 1.00
251 Hyper Garganoid Ultra (Haos Card) AR 1.50 2.50
252 Hyper Nillious (Haos Card) SR 1.25 2.00
253 Hyper Hydorous Ultra (Haos Card) R .60 1.00
254 Hyper Serpenteze Ultra (Haos Card) R 1.25 2.00
255 Maximus Hydorous Ultra (Haos Card) BE 2.00 3.00
256 Titan Howlkor Ultra (Haos Card) R .60 1.00
257 Titan Nillious (Haos Card) AR 6.00 10.00
258 Titan Pegatrix (Haos Card) SR .60 1.00
259 Dragonoid (Diamond Card) SR 1.25 2.00
260 Fangzor (Diamond Card) R .60 1.00
261 Hyper Hydorous (Pyrus Card) SR 1.25 2.00
262 Hyper Hydorous Ultra (Pyrus Card) R .60 1.00
263 Hyper Maxotaur Ultra (Pyrus Card) SR .60 1.00
264 Hyper Trox (Pyrus Card) R .60 1.00
265 Hyper Dragonoid (Pyrus Card) R .60 1.00
266 Hyper Mantonoid Ultra (Pyrus Card) R .60 1.00
267 Hyper Serpenteze Ultra (Pyrus Card) AR 2.50 4.00
268 Titan Fangzor (Pyrus Card) R .60 1.00
269 Titan Hydorous Ultra (Pyrus Card) AR 1.50 2.50
270 Titan Dragonoid (Pyrus Card) BE 10.00 15.00
271 Maxotaur Ultra (Diamond Card) AR 1.00 1.50
272 Trox (Diamond Card) R 1.25 2.00
273 Trox Ultra (Diamond Card) R 1.25 2.00
274 Hyper Dragonoid (Ventus Card) SR 1.25 2.00
275 Hyper Fangzor (Ventus Card) R .60 1.00
276 Hyper Nillious (Ventus Card) R .60 1.00
277 Hyper Pegatrix (Ventus Card) SR 1.25 2.00
278 Hyper Mantonoid Ultra (Ventus Card) BE 5.00 8.00
279 Titan Howlkor Ultra (Ventus Card) R 1.00 1.50
280 Titan Maxotaur Ultra (Ventus Card) R 1.00 1.50
281 Titan Trox (Ventus Card) AR 2.00 3.00
282 Cyndeous Ultra (Aquos Card) F
283 Dragonoid (Aquos Card) F
284 Fangzor (Aquos Card) F
285 Garganoid Ultra (Aquos Card) F
286 Krakelios Ultra (Haos Card) F
287 Hydorous (Aquos Card) F
288 Hydorous Ultra (Aquos Card) F
289 Krakelios Ultra (Aquos Card) F
290 Mantonoid Ultra (Aquos Card) F
291 Nillious (Aquos Card) F
292 Pegatrix (Aquos Card) F
293 Serpenteze (Aquos Card) F
294 Serpenteze Ultra (Aquos Card) F
295 Trox (Aquos Card) F
296 Turtonium (Aquos Card) F
297 Trox Ultra (Aquos Card) F
298 Dragonoid (Aurelus Card) F
299 Fangzor (Aurelus Card) F
300 Fangzor Ultra (Aurelus Card) F
301 Garganoid Ultra (Aurelus Card) F
302 Howlkor Ultra (Aurelus Card) F
303 Hydorous (Aurelus Card) F
304 Hydorous Ultra (Aurelus Card) F
305 Mantonoid (Aurelus Card) F
306 Maxotaur Ultra (Aurelus Card) F
307 Nillious (Aurelus Card) F
308 Pegatrix (Aurelus Card) F
309 Trox Ultra (Aurelus Card) F
310 Turtonium (Aurelus Card) F
311 Cyndeous Ultra (Darkus Card) F
312 Dragonoid (Darkus Card) F
313 Fangzor (Darkus Card) F
314 Fangzor Ultra (Darkus Card) F
315 Garganoid Ultra (Darkus Card) F
316 Krakelios Ultra (Ventus Card) F
317 Howlkor Ultra (Darkus Card) F
318 Hydorous (Darkus Card) F
319 Hydorous Ultra (Darkus Card) F
320 Mantonoid Ultra (Darkus Card) F
321 Nillious (Darkus Card) F
322 Nillious Ultra (Darkus Card) F
323 Pegatrix (Darkus Card) F
324 Serpenteze (Darkus Card) F
325 Trox (Darkus Card) F
326 Turtonium Ultra (Darkus Card) F
327 Dragonoid (Haos Card) F
328 Fangzor (Haos Card) F
329 Garganoid Ultra (Haos Card) F
330 Gorthion Ultra (Haos Card) F
331 Howlkor Ultra (Haos Card) F
332 Hydorous (Haos Card) F
333 Hydorous Ultra (Haos Card) F
334 Mantonoid (Haos Card) F
335 Mantonoid Ultra (Haos Card) F
336 Maxotaur Ultra (Haos Card) F
337 Nillious (Haos Card) F
338 Nillious Ultra (Haos Card) F
339 Pegatrix (Haos Card) F
340 Serpenteze (Haos Card) F
341 Serpenteze Ultra (Haos Card) F
342 Trox (Haos Card) F
343 Dragonoid (Pyrus Card) F
344 Fangzor (Pyrus Card) F
345 Fangzor Ultra (Pyrus Card) F
346 Garganoid Ultra (Pyrus Card) F
347 Gorthion (Pyrus Card) F
348 Gorthion Ultra (Pyrus Card) F
349 Howlkor Ultra (Pyrus Card) F
350 Hydorous (Pyrus Card) F
351 Hydorous Ultra (Pyrus Card) F
352 Cyndeous Ultra (Pyrus Card) F
353 Mantonoid Ultra (Pyrus Card) F
354 Maxotaur Ultra (Pyrus Card) F
355 Serpenteze Ultra (Pyrus Card) F
356 Trox (Pyrus Card) F
357 Dragonoid Ultra (Pyrus Card) F
358 Gorthion Ultra (Ventus Card) F
359 Dragonoid (Ventus Card) F
360 Fangzor (Ventus Card) F
361 Fangzor Ultra (Ventus Card) F
362 Garganoid Ultra (Ventus Card) F
363 Gorthion (Ventus Card) F
364 Howlkor Ultra (Ventus Card) F
365 Mantonoid (Ventus Card) F
366 Mantonoid Ultra (Ventus Card) F
367 Maxotaur Ultra (Ventus Card) F
368 Nillious (Ventus Card) F
369 Pegatrix (Ventus Card) F
370 Serpenteze (Ventus Card) F
371 Serpenteze Ultra (Ventus Card) F
372 Trox (Ventus Card) F
373 Trox Ultra (Ventus Card) F
374 Serpenteze (Aurelus Card) F

2019 Bakugan Resurgence

COMPLETE SET (249)
BOOSTER BOX (24 PACKS)
BOOSTER PACK (10 CARDS)
RELEASED IN MAY 2019
1 Aquify R
2 Aquos Splash C
3 Blinding Ink R
4 Claw Cutter C
5 Dark Waters C
6 Deep Dive C
7 Hurricane Winds SR
8 Mud Pit R
9 Rip Tide SR
10 Sneak Attack BE
11 Unstoppable C
12 Water to Ice C
13 Dark Fortune SR
14 Dark Path C
15 Darkus Howl C
16 Darkus Petrify C
17 Darkus Slicer C
18 Dust to Dust C
19 Mind Control AR
20 Mind Slip C
21 Second Strike C
22 Shadow Cloak C
23 Shadow Dogs SR
24 Thunder Bolt C
25 Blinding Light C
26 Divine Inspiration C
27 Divine Intervention AR
28 Energy Draw C
29 Haos Blessing C
30 Spirit Guide C
31 Holy Flame C
32 Karmic Balance R
33 Mega Punch C
34 Pegatrix Drill SR

2019 Bakugan Resurgence

35 Shield of the Faithful C
36 Air Zero SR
37 Anger R
38 Blaze C
39 Boom AR
40 Dual Strike C
41 Flame Wave C
42 Magma Shield C
43 Pyrus Heat Shield C
44 Quickfire C
45 Superfuel SR
46 Sword Barrage C
47 Twisting Inferno R
48 Crystal Quake SR
49 Etropic Blast C
50 Huge Knowledge AR
51 Nature's Blessing SR
52 Rabid Attack SR
53 Shatterfist C
54 Solar Powered C
55 Stoneblade C
56 Tanglevines C
57 Tremor C
58 Ventus Shield C
59 Ventus Mirage R
60 Deep Freeze C
61 Freeze C
62 Lost at Sea R
63 Flash Flood C
64 Darkus Snare C
65 Darkus Blitz R
66 Sonic Shield C
67 Confuse C
68 Dazzle C
69 Haos Curse C
70 Trick Trap R
71 Ash Cloud C
72 Constrictor C
73 Spontaneous Combustion R
74 Rock Riser R
75 Ruin C
76 Web Snare C
77 Shun Kazami SR
78 Lightning SR
79 Shargo Ronin R
80 Strata SR
81 Dan Kouzo SR
82 Emily R
83 Jenkins R
84 China Riot R
85 Hydranoid (Diamond Card) R
86 Hydranoid Ultra (Diamond Card) R
87 Serpenteze Ultra (Diamond Card) R
88 Hyper Gorthion (Aquos Card) R
89 Hyper Krakelios Ultra (Aquos Card) SR
90 Hyper Mantonoid (Aquos Card) SR
91 Hyper Serpenteze (Aquos Card) C
92 Hyper Trox Ultra (Aquos Card) R
93 Hyper Turtonium (Aquos Card) C
94 Hyper Turtonium Ultra (Aquos Card) R
95 Titan Cyndeous Ultra (Aquos Card) AR
96 Titan Nillious (Aquos Card) R
97 Titan Pegatrix Ultra (Aquos Card) AR
98 Hyper Hydorous Ultra (Aurelus Card) R
99 Hyper Mantonoid (Aurelus Card) R
100 Hyper Serpenteze (Aurelus Card) R
101 Hyper Trox (Aurelus Card) SR
102 Maximus Fangzor Ultra (Aurelus Card) BE
103 Maximus Trox Ultra (Aurelus Card) R
104 Titan Dragonoid Ultra (Aurelus Card) AR
105 Titan Gorthion (Aurelus Card) SR
106 Titan Krakelios Ultra (Aurelus Card) AR
107 Titan Turtonium (Aurelus Card) SR
108 Phaedrus (Diamond Card) R
109 Hyper Cyndeous Ultra (Darkus Card) SR
110 Hyper Dragonoid Ultra (Darkus Card) C
111 Hyper Fangzor Ultra (Darkus Card) R
112 Hyper Gorthion Ultra (Darkus Card) SR
113 Hyper Nillious Ultra (Darkus Card) R
114 Hyper Pegatrix (Darkus Card) R
115 Hyper Serpenteze Ultra (Darkus Card) SR
116 Maximus Garganoid Ultra (Darkus Card) AR
117 Titan Cyndeous (Darkus Card) C
118 Titan Mantonoid (Darkus Card) R
119 Titan Serpenteze (Darkus Card) R
120 Titan Turtonium Ultra (Darkus Card) BE
121 Cubbo (Diamond Card) R
122 Gorthion (Diamond Card) R
123 Pegatrix Ultra (Diamond Card) R
124 Hyper Dragonoid (Haos Card) R
125 Hyper Hydorous (Haos Card) C
126 Hyper Pegatrix Ultra (Haos Card) R
127 Hyper Serpenteze (Haos Card) AR
128 Maximus Mantonoid Ultra (Haos Card) SR
129 Maximus Maxotaur Ultra (Haos Card) AR
130 Titan Gorthion Ultra (Haos Card) BE
131 Titan Krakelios Ultra (Haos Card) C
132 Titan Mantonoid (Haos Card) C
133 Titan Nillious Ultra (Haos Card) SR
134 Titan Trox (Haos Card) SR
135 Cyndeous (Diamond Card) C
136 Cyndeous Ultra (Diamond Card) R
137 Dragonoid Ultra (Diamond Card) R
138 Hyper Dragonoid Ultra (Pyrus Card) C
139 Hyper Fangzor Ultra (Pyrus Card) C
140 Hyper Garganoid Ultra (Pyrus Card) AR
141 Hyper Gorthion (Pyrus Card) C
142 Hyper Mantonoid (Pyrus Card) C
143 Hyper Pegatrix (Pyrus Card) C
144 Hyper Serpenteze (Pyrus Card) SR
145 Hyper Trox Ultra (Pyrus Card) R
146 Maximus Turtonium Ultra (Pyrus Card) AR
147 Titan Gorthion Ultra (Pyrus Card) R
148 Titan Trox Ultra (Pyrus Card) SR
149 Hyper Howlkor Ultra (Pyrus Card) BE
150 Mantonoid (Diamond Card) C
151 Turtonium (Diamond Card) R
152 Webam Ultra (Diamond Card) C
153 Hyper Garganoid Ultra (Ventus Card) R
154 Hyper Krakelios Ultra (Ventus Card) R
155 Hyper Serpenteze (Ventus Card) C
156 Hyper Serpenteze Ultra (Ventus Card) R
157 Hyper Trox Ultra (Ventus Card) SR
158 Maximus Gorthion (Ventus Card) C
159 Maximus Gorthion Ultra (Ventus Card) SR
160 Maximus Webam Ultra (Ventus Card) AR
161 Titan Fangzor Ultra (Ventus Card) R
162 Titan Garganoid Ultra (Ventus Card) AR
163 Titan Serpenteze Ultra (Ventus Card) AR
164 Titan Trox Ultra (Ventus Card) BE
165 Hyper Turtonium Ultra (Ventus Card) SR
166 Cloptor Ultra (Aquos Card) F
167 Cubbo (Aquos Card) F
168 Fangzor Ultra (Aquos Card) F
169 Gorthion (Aquos Card) F
170 Gorthion Ultra (Aquos Card) F
171 Hydranoid (Aquos Card) F
172 Hydranoid Ultra (Aquos Card) F
173 Mantonoid (Aquos Card) F
174 Nobilious Ultra (Aquos Card) F
175 Pegatrix Ultra (Aquos Card) F
176 Pyravian Ultra (Aquos Card) F
177 Trhyno (Aquos Card) F
178 Turtonium Ultra (Aquos Card) F
179 Vicerox (Aquos Card) F
180 Webam Ultra (Aquos Card) F
181 Cubbo (Aurelus Card) F
182 Dragonoid Ultra (Aurelus Card) F
183 Gorthion (Aurelus Card) F
184 Hydranoid Ultra (Aurelus Card) F
185 Krakelios Ultra (Aurelus Card) F
186 Lupitheon Ultra (Aurelus Card) F
187 Nobilious Ultra (Aurelus Card) F
188 Phaedrus Ultra (Aurelus Card) F
189 Trhyno (Aurelus Card) F
190 Trox (Aurelus Card) F
191 Vicerox (Aurelus Card) F
192 Vicerox Ultra (Aurelus Card) F
193 Zentaur (Aurelus Card) F
194 Cubbo (Darkus Card) F
195 Cyndeous (Darkus Card) F
196 Dragonoid Ultra (Darkus Card) F
197 Gorthion (Darkus Card) F
198 Gorthion Ultra (Darkus Card) F
199 Hydranoid Ultra (Darkus Card) F
200 Krakelios Ultra (Darkus Card) F
201 Lupitheon Ultra (Darkus Card) F
202 Mantonoid (Darkus Card) F
203 Phaedrus (Darkus Card) F
204 Serpenteze Ultra (Darkus Card) F
205 Skorporos (Darkus Card) F
206 Skorporos Ultra (Darkus Card) F
207 Trhyno (Darkus Card) F
208 Webam Ultra (Darkus Card) F
209 Zentaur (Darkus Card) F
210 Cubbo (Haos Card) F
211 Gorthion (Haos Card) F
212 Lupitheon Ultra (Haos Card) F
213 Nobilious Ultra (Haos Card) F
214 Pandoxx Ultra (Haos Card) F
215 Pegatrix Ultra (Haos Card) F
216 Phaedrus (Haos Card) F
217 Trhyno (Haos Card) F
218 Turtonium (Haos Card) F
219 Vicerox (Haos Card) F
220 Vicerox Ultra (Haos Card) F
221 Pyravian Ultra (Aurelus Card) F
221 Artulean Ultra (Pyrus Card) F
222 Cyndeous (Pyrus Card) F
223 Hydranoid Ultra (Pyrus Card) F
224 Mantonoid (Pyrus Card) F
225 Nillious (Pyrus Card) F
226 Nillious Ultra (Pyrus Card) F
227 Nobilious Ultra (Pyrus Card) F
228 Pegatrix (Pyrus Card) F
229 Phaedrus (Pyrus Card) F
230 Serpenteze (Pyrus Card) F
231 Trhyno (Pyrus Card) F
232 Trox Ultra (Pyrus Card) F
233 Turtonium Ultra (Pyrus Card) F
234 Vicerox (Pyrus Card) F
235 Vicerox Ultra (Pyrus Card) F
236 Cubbo (Ventus Card) F
237 Cyndeous (Ventus Card) F
238 Hydranoid Ultra (Ventus Card) F
239 Lupitheon Ultra (Ventus Card) F
240 Phaedrus (Ventus Card) F
241 Phaedrus Ultra (Ventus Card) F
242 Skorporos Ultra (Ventus Card) F
243 Turtonium (Ventus Card) F
244 Turtonium Ultra (Ventus Card) F
245 Vicerox Ultra (Ventus Card) F
246 Webam Ultra (Ventus Card) F
247 Vicerox (Ventus Card) F
248 Phaedrus (Aquos Card) F

CardFight Vanguard

2011 Cardfight Vanguard Booster Set 1 Descent of the King of Knights

COMPLETE SET (92)	150.00	300.00
RELEASED ON DECEMBER 10, 2011		
BT01001 King of Knights, Alfred RRR	10.00	15.00
BT01002 Blaster Blade RRR	10.00	15.00
BT01003 Barcgal RRR	3.00	5.00
BT01004 Dragonic Overlord RRR	6.00	10.00
BT01005 Embodiment of Victory, Aleph RRR	2.50	4.00
BT01006 CEO Amaterasu RRR	6.00	10.00
BT01007 Battle Sister, Cocoa RRR	3.00	5.00
BT01008 Asura Kaiser RRR	6.00	10.00
BT01009 Demon Slaying Knight, Lohengrin RR	1.25	2.00
BT01010 Solitary Knight, Gancelot RR	1.25	2.00
BT01011 Flash Shield, Iseult RR	12.00	20.00
BT01012 Future Knight, Llew RR	3.00	5.00
BT01013 Vortex Dragon RR	1.25	2.00
BT01014 Dragon Knight, Aleph RR	1.25	2.00
BT01015 Wyvern Guard, Barri RR	12.00	20.00
BT01016 Lizard Soldier, Conroe RR	4.00	6.00
BT01017 Maiden of Libra RR	1.25	2.00
BT01018 Battle Sister, Mocha RR	3.00	5.00
BT01019 Battle Sister, Chocolat RR	10.00	15.00
BT01020 Juggernaut Maximum RR	5.00	8.00
BT01021 Knight of Silence, Gallatin R	.30	.50
BT01022 Dragon Knight, Nehalem R	.30	.50
BT01023 Wyvern Strike, Tejas R	.30	.50
BT01024 Embodiment of Spear, Tahr R	1.25	2.00
BT01025 Oracle Guardian, Apollon R	1.25	2.00
BT01026 Oracle Guardian, Wiseman R	1.25	2.00
BT01027 Lozenge Magus R	1.25	2.00
BT01028 Mr. Invincible R	.60	1.00
BT01029 Brutal Jack R	1.25	2.00
BT01030 King of Sword R	.60	1.00
BT01031 Queen of Heart R	.60	1.00
BT01032 Battleraizer R	1.00	1.50
BT01033 Tyrant, Deathrex R	.30	.50
BT01034 Assault Dragon, Blightops R	.30	.50
BT01035 Stealth Dragon, Voidmaster R	.30	.50
BT01036 Demon Eater R	.30	.50
BT01037 Monster Frank R	.30	.50
BT01038 Commodore Blueblood R	1.00	1.50
BT01039 Hell Spider R	.30	.50
BT01040 Bloody Hercules R	.30	.50
BT01041 Covenant Knight, Randolf C	.15	.25
BT01042 Little Sage, Marron C	.15	.25
BT01043 Lake Maiden, Lien C	.15	.25
BT01044 Wingal C	.15	.25
BT01045 Weapons Dealer, Govannon C	.15	.25
BT01046 Flogal C	.15	.25
BT01047 Yggdrasil Maiden, Elaine C	.15	.25
BT01048 Embodiment of Armor, Bahr C	.15	.25
BT01049 Dragon Monk, Gojo C	.15	.25
BT01050 Wyvern Strike, Jarran C	.15	.25
BT01051 Dragon Dancer, Monica C	.15	.25
BT01052 Lizard Soldier, Ganlu C	.15	.25
BT01053 Dragon Monk, Genjo C	.15	.25
BT01054 Oracle Guardian, Gemini C	.15	.25
BT01055 Weather Girl, Milk C	.15	.25
BT01056 Oracle Guardian, Nike C	.15	.25
BT01057 Dream Eater C	.15	.25
BT01058 Miracle Kid C	.15	.25
BT01059 Hungry Dumpty C	.15	.25
BT01060 Tough Boy C	.15	.25
BT01061 Screamin' and Dancin' Announcer, Shout C	.15	.25
BT01062 Clay-doll Mechanic C	.15	.25
BT01063 Shining Lady C	.15	.25
BT01064 Lucky Girl C	.15	.25
BT01065 Ring Girl, Clara C	.15	.25
BT01066 Sonic Noa C	.15	.25
BT01067 Ironclad Dragon, Shieldon C	.15	.25
BT01068 Stealth Beast, Chigasumi C	.15	.25
BT01069 Stealth Dragon, Dreadmaster C	.15	.25
BT01070 Stealth Beast, Hagakure C	.15	.25
BT01071 Blue Dust C	.15	.25
BT01072 Nightmare Baby C	.15	.25
BT01073 Rock the Wall C	.15	.25
BT01074 Highspeed, Brakki C	.15	.25
BT01075 Wonder Boy	.15	.25
BT01076 Redshoe, Milly C	.15	.25
BT01077 Dandy Guy, Romario C	.15	.25
BT01078 Guiding Zombie C	.15	.25
BT01079 Karma Queen C	.15	.25
BT01080 Madame Mirage C	.15	.25
BT01S01 King of Knights, Alfred SP	25.00	40.00
BT01S02 Blaster Blade SP	30.00	50.00
BT01S03 Barcgal SP	10.00	15.00
BT01S04 Dragonic Overlord SP	20.00	30.00
BT01S05 CEO Amaterasu SP	25.00	40.00
BT01S06 Battle Sister, Cocoa SP	20.00	30.00
BT01S07 Asura Kaiser SP	20.00	30.00
BT01S08 Solitary Knight, Gancelot SP	10.00	15.00
BT01S09 Vortex Dragon SP	6.00	10.00
BT01S10 Maiden of Libra SP	6.00	10.00
BT01S11 Lozenge Magus SP	30.00	50.00
BT01S12 Battleraizer SP	15.00	25.00

2012 Cardfight Vanguard Booster Set 2 Onslaught of Dragon Souls

COMPLETE SET (92)	250.00	400.00
RELEASE DATE MARCH 10, 2012		
BT02001 Sky Diver RRR	10.00	15.00
BT02002 Spirit Exceed RRR	4.00	6.00
BT02003 Ruin Shade RRR	12.00	20.00
BT02004 Soul Savior Dragon RRR	20.00	30.00
BT02005 Blazing Flare Dragon RRR	10.00	15.00
BT02006 Seal Dragon, Blockade RRR	6.00	10.00
BT02007 Scarlet Witch, Coco RRR	3.00	5.00
BT02008 Lion Heat RRR	5.00	8.00
BT02009 General Seifried RR	3.00	5.00
BT02010 Cheer Girl, Marilyn RR	10.00	15.00
BT02011 King of Demonic Seas, Basskirk RR	5.00	8.00
BT02012 Witch Doctor of the Abyss, Negromarl RR	1.75	3.00
BT02013 Captain Nightmist RR	5.00	8.00
BT02014 Gust Jinn RR	10.00	15.00
BT02015 Young Pegasus Knight RR	4.00	6.00
BT02016 Chain-attack Sutherland RR	1.50	2.50
BT02017 Silent Tom RR	12.00	20.00
BT02018 Magician Girl Kirara RR	2.50	4.00
BT02019 Twin Blader RR	12.00	20.00
BT02020 Top Idol, Flores RR	1.50	2.50
BT02021 Unite Attacker R	.30	.50
BT02022 Treasured, Black Panther R	.30	.50
BT02023 Dudley Dan R	.50	.75
BT02024 Mecha Trainer R	.30	.50
BT02025 Dancing Cutlass R	.30	.50
BT02026 Chappie the Ghostie R	.50	.75
BT02027 Gigantech Charger R	.50	.75
BT02028 Great Sage, Barron R	.30	.50
BT02029 High Dog Breeder, Akane R	.60	1.00
BT02030 Pongal R	1.50	2.50
BT02031 Blazing Core Dragon R	1.75	3.00
BT02032 Demonic Dragon Mage, Kimnara R	1.75	3.00
BT02033 Luck Bird R	.30	.50
BT02034 Winged Dragon, Skyptero R	.30	.50
BT02035 Dragon Egg R	.30	.50
BT02036 Top Idol, Aqua R	.30	.50
BT02037 Bermuda Triangle Cadet, Caravel R	.30	.50
BT02038 Master Fraude R	.30	.50
BT02039 Scientist Monkey Rue R	.30	.50
BT02040 Geograph Giant R	.30	.50

BT02041 Panzer Gale C .15 .25
BT02042 Devil Summoner C .15 .25
BT02043 Cyclone Blitz C .15 .25
BT02044 Spike Brothers Assault Squad C .15 .25
BT02045 Sonic Breaker C .15 .25
BT02046 Cheerful Lynx C .15 .25
BT02047 Cheer Girl, Tiara C .15 .25
BT02048 Silence Joker C .15 .25
BT02049 Skeleton Swordsman C .15 .25
BT02050 Samurai Spirit C .15 .25
BT02051 Evil Shade C .15 .25
BT02052 Knight Spirit C .15 .25
BT02053 Skeleton Lookout C .15 .25
BT02054 Rick the Ghostie C .15 .25
BT02055 Rough Seas Banshee C .15 .25
BT02056 Knight of Truth, Gordon C .60 1.00
BT02057 Soul Guiding Elf C .15 .25
BT02058 Pixy Fife and Drum C .15 .25
BT02059 Margal C .15 .25
BT02060 Dragon Knight, Berger C .15 .25
BT02061 Iron Tail Dragon C .15 .25
BT02062 Follower, Reas C .15 .25
BT02063 Lizard Runner, Nafd C .15 .25
BT02064 Gatling Claw Dragon C .50 .75
BT02065 Security Guardian C .15 .25
BT02066 One Who Gazes at the Truth C .15 .25
BT02067 Emergency Alarmer C .15 .25
BT02068 Psychic Bird C .15 .25
BT02069 Chaos Dragon, Dinochaos C .15 .25
BT02070 Cannon Fire Dragon, Cannon Gear C .15 .25
BT02071 NGM Prototype C .15 .25
BT02072 Cray Soldier C .15 .25
BT02073 Three Minutes C .15 .25
BT02074 Red Lightning C .15 .25
BT02075 Blazer Idols C .15 .25
BT02076 Lady Bomb C .15 .25
BT02077 Phantom Black C .15 .25
BT02078 Megacolony Battler A C .15 .25
BT02079 Silver Wolf C .15 .25
BT02080 Intelli-Mouse C .15 .25
BT02S01 Sky Diver SP 15.00 25.00
BT02S02 Spirit Exceed SP 12.00 20.00
BT02S03 Ruin Shade SP 20.00 30.00
BT02S04 Soul Savior Dragon SP 40.00 60.00
BT02S05 Blazing Flare Dragon SP 20.00 30.00
BT02S06 Seal Dragon, Blockade SP 12.00 20.00
BT02S07 Scarlet Witch, Coco SP 15.00 25.00
BT02S08 Lion Heat SP 20.00 30.00
BT02S09 General Seifried SP 12.00 20.00
BT02S10 Witch Doctor of the Abyss, Negromarl SP 6.00 10.00
BT02S11 Top Idol, Flores SP 25.00 40.00
BT02S12 Top Idol, Aqua SP 20.00 30.00

2012 Cardfight Vanguard Booster Set 3 Demonic Lord Invasion

COMPLETE SET (94) 300.00 450.00
RELEASED ON AUGUST 11, 2012
BT03001 Stil Vampir RRR 3.00 5.00
BT03002 Demon World Marquis, Amon RRR 12.00 20.00
BT03003 Nightmare Doll, Alice RRR 12.00 20.00
BT03004 Ravenous Dragon, Gigarex RRR 3.00 5.00
BT03005 Swordsman of the Explosive Flames, Palamedes RRR 20.00 30.00
BT03006 Goddess of the Full Moon, Tsukuyomi RRR 15.00 25.00
BT03007 Goddess of the Half Moon, Tsukuyomi RRR 20.00 30.00
BT03008 Ultimate Lifeform, Cosmo Lord RRR 1.50 2.50
BT03009 Edel Rose RR 2.50 4.00
BT03010 Gwynn the Ripper RR 1.75 3.00
BT03011 March Rabbit of Nightmareland RR 10.00 15.00
BT03012 Doreen the Thruster RR 4.00 6.00
BT03013 Dusk Illusionist, Robert RR 1.75 3.00
BT03014 Crimson Beast Tamer RR 10.00 15.00
BT03015 Mirror Demon RR 1.75 3.00
BT03016 Hades Hypnotist RR 12.00 20.00
BT03017 Archbird RR 8.00 12.00
BT03018 Knight of Godly Speed, Galahad RR 5.00 8.00
BT03019 Dual Axe Archdragon RR 4.00 6.00
BT03020 Super Dimensional Robo, Daiyusha RR 6.00 10.00
BT03021 Imprisoned Fallen Angel, Saraqael R .60 1.00
BT03022 Werwolf Sieger R .75 1.25
BT03023 Demon of Aspiration, Amon R .60 1.00
BT03024 Alluring Succubus R 1.75 3.00
BT03025 Vermillion Gatekeeper R .60 1.00
BT03026 Bloody Calf R .60 1.00
BT03027 Barking Manticore R .75 1.25
BT03028 Barking Cerberus R .60 1.00
BT03029 Skull Juggler R .60 1.00
BT03030 Midnight Bunny R 1.50 2.50
BT03031 Turquoise Beast Tamer R .75 1.25
BT03032 Hades Ringmaster R .60 1.00
BT03033 Raging Dragon, Blastsaurus R 1.00 1.50
BT03034 Ravenous Dragon, Megarex R 1.50 2.50
BT03035 Savage Warrior R .60 1.00
BT03036 Toypugal R 1.25 2.00
BT03037 Drangal R .75 1.25
BT03038 Oracle Guardian, Blue Eye R .60 1.00
BT03039 Godhawk, Ichibyoshi R .60 1.00
BT03040 Circle Magus R .75 1.25
BT03041 Death Army Lady R 1.25 2.00
BT03042 Death Army Guy R 1.50 2.50
BT03043 Decadent Succubus C .15 .25
BT03044 Prisoner Beast C .15 .25
BT03045 Poet of Darkness, Amon C .15 .25
BT03046 Blitzritter C .15 .25
BT03047 Hades Puppet Master C .15 .25
BT03048 Cursed Doctor C .15 .25
BT03049 Dark Queen of Nightmareland C .15 .25
BT03050 Elephant Juggler C .15 .25
BT03051 Hungry Clown C .15 .25
BT03052 Dark Metal Bicorn C .15 .25
BT03053 Dynamite Juggler C .15 .25
BT03054 Spiral Master C .15 .25
BT03055 Candy Clown C .15 .25
BT03056 Rainbow Magician C .15 .25
BT03057 Vacuum Mammoth C .15 .25
BT03058 Savage Destroyer C .15 .25
BT03059 Raging Dragon, Sparksaurus C .15 .25
BT03060 Herbivorous Dragon, Brutosaurus C .15 .25
BT03061 Pack Dragon, Tinyrex C .15 .25
BT03062 Savage Shaman C .15 .25
BT03063 Black Cannon Tiger C .15 .25
BT03064 Knight of Tribulations, Galahad C .15 .25
BT03065 Gigantech Dozer C .15 .25
BT03066 Swordsman of the Blaze, Palamedes C .15 .25
BT03067 Knight of Quests, Galahad C .15 .25
BT03068 Borgal C .15 .25
BT03069 Alabaster Owl C .15 .25
BT03070 Secretary Angel C .15 .25
BT03071 Oracle Guardian, Red Eye C .15 .25
BT03072 Faithful Angel C .15 .25
BT03073 Goddess of the Crescent Moon, Tsukuyomi C .15 .25
BT03074 Battle Sister, Vanilla C .15 .25
BT03075 Victory Maker C .15 .25
BT03076 Flame Edge Dragon C .15 .25
BT03077 Dragon Dancer, Lourdes C .15 .25
BT03078 Blue Ray Dracokid C .15 .25
BT03079 Cannon Ball C .15 .25
BT03080 Masked Police, Grander C .15 .25
BT03081 Karenroid, Daisy C .15 .25
BT03082 Workerpod, Saturday C .15 .25
BT03S02 Demon World Marquis, Amon SP 20.00 30.00
BT03S03 Nightmare Doll, Alice SP 20.00 30.00
BT03S04 Ravenous Dragon, Gigarex SP 10.00 15.00
BT03S05 Swordsman of the Explosive Flames, Palamedes SP 30.00 50.00
BT03S06 Goddess of the Full Moon, Tsukuyomi SP 40.00 60.00
BT03S08 Ultimate Lifeform, Cosmo Lord SP 10.00 15.00
BT03S10 Gwynn the Ripper SP 12.00 20.00
BT03S14 Crimson Beast Tamer SP 25.00 40.00
BT03S18 Knight of Godly Speed, Galahad SP 10.00 15.00
BT03S19 Dual Axe Archdragon SP 12.00 20.00
BT03S20 Super Dimensional Robo, Daiyusha SP 25.00 40.00
BT03S30 Turquoise Beast Tamer SP 30.00 50.00

2012 Cardfight Vanguard Booster Set 4 Eclipse of Illusionary Shadows

COMPLETE SET (94) 400.00 550.00
RELEASED ON DECEMBER 14, 2012
BT04001 Phantom Blaster Dragon RRR 25.00 40.00
BT04002 Darkness Maiden, Macha RRR 10.00 15.00
BT04003 Skull Witch, Nemain RRR 12.00 20.00
BT04004 Enigman Storm RRR 5.00 8.00
BT04005 Evil Armor General, Giraffa RRR 8.00 12.00
BT04006 Amber Dragon, Eclipse RRR 8.00 12.00
BT04007 Heatnail Salamander RRR 6.00 10.00
BT04008 Stern Blaukluger RRR 10.00 15.00
BT04009 Dark Metal Dragon RR 5.00 8.00
BT04010 Gururubau RR 5.00 8.00
BT04011 Dark Shield, Mac Lir RR 15.00 25.00
BT04012 Enigman Wave RR 4.00 6.00
BT04013 Cosmo Break RR 5.00 8.00
BT04014 Diamond Ace RR 8.00 12.00
BT04015 Commander Laurel RR 4.00 6.00
BT04016 Elite Mutant, Giraffa RR 5.00 8.00
BT04017 Paralize Madonna RR 6.00 10.00
BT04018 Amber Dragon, Dusk RR 5.00 8.00
BT04019 Blaukluger RR 8.00 12.00
BT04020 Fang of Light, Garmore RR 6.00 10.00
BT04021 Silver Spear Demon, Gusion R .60 1.00
BT04022 Dark Mage, Badhabh Caar R 1.25 2.00
BT04023 Knight of Darkness, Rugos R 1.25 2.00
BT04024 Blaster Dark R 8.00 12.00
BT04025 Cursed Lancer R 1.25 2.00
BT04026 Fullbau R .60 1.00
BT04027 Enigman Rain R .60 1.00
BT04028 Twin Order R .60 1.00
BT04029 Platinum Ace R .60 1.00
BT04030 Cosmo Roar R 1.25 2.00
BT04031 Enigman Flow R .60 1.00
BT04032 Death Warden Ant Lion R 1.25 2.00
BT04033 Violent Vesper R .60 1.00
BT04034 Water Gang R .60 1.00
BT04035 Gloom Flyman R .60 1.00
BT04036 Megacolony Battler B R 1.25 2.00
BT04037 Larva Mutant, Giraffa R .60 1.00
BT04038 Lizard Soldier, Raopia R .60 1.00
BT04039 Amber Dragon, Dawn R 1.25 2.00
BT04040 Armored Fairy, Shubiela R .60 1.00
BT04041 Blaujunger R .60 1.00
BT04042 Beast Knight, Garmore R .60 1.00
BT04043 Demon World Castle, Donnerschlag C .15 .25
BT04044 Demon World Castle, Fatalita C .15 .25
BT04045 Black Sage, Charon C .15 .25
BT04046 Witch of Nostrum, Arianrhod C .15 .25
BT04047 Doranbau C .15 .25
BT04048 Blaster Javelin C .15 .25
BT04049 Zappbau C .15 .25
BT04050 Grim Reaper C .15 .25
BT04051 Abyss Freezer C .15 .25
BT04052 Darkside Trumpeter C .15 .25
BT04053 Abyss Healer C .15 .25
BT04054 Enigman Shine C .15 .25
BT04055 Enigroid Comrade C .15 .25
BT04056 Enigman Ripple C .15 .25
BT04057 Glory Maker C .15 .25
BT04058 Justice Cobalt C .15 .25
BT04059 Army Penguin C .15 .25
BT04060 Cosmo Fang C .15 .25
BT04061 Justice Rose C .15 .25
BT04062 Ironcutter Beetle C .15 .25
BT04063 Tail Joe C .15 .25
BT04064 Pupa Mutant, Giraffa C .15 .25
BT04065 Stealth Millepede C .15 .25
BT04066 Sharp Nail Scorpio C .15 .25
BT04067 Raider Mantis C .15 .25
BT04068 Sonic Cicada C .15 .25
BT04069 Medical Battler, Ranpli C .15 .25
BT04070 Garnet Dragon, Flash C .15 .25
BT04071 Lava Arm Dragon C .15 .25
BT04072 Amber Dragon, Daylight C .15 .25
BT04073 Red Gem Carbuncle C .15 .25
BT04074 Flame Seed Salamander C .15 .25
BT04075 Eisenkugel C .15 .25
BT04076 Dancing Wolf C .15 .25
BT04077 Blaupanzer C .15 .25
BT04078 Toolkit Boy C .15 .25
BT04079 Fighting Battleship, Prometheus C .15 .25
BT04080 Grapple Mania C .15 .25
BT04081 Snogal C .15 .25
BT04082 Brugal C .15 .25
BT04S01 Phantom Blaster Dragon SP 75.00 125.00
BT04S02 Darkness Maiden, Macha SP 30.00 50.00
BT04S03 Skull Witch, Nemain SP 25.00 40.00
BT04S04 Enigman Storm SP 15.00 25.00
BT04S05 Evil Armor General, Giraffa SP 15.00 25.00
BT04S06 Amber Dragon, Eclipse SP 20.00 30.00
BT04S07 Stern Blaukluger SP 25.00 40.00
BT04S08 Dark Metal Dragon SP 15.00 25.00
BT04S09 Amber Dragon, Dusk SP 20.00 30.00
BT04S10 Blaukluger SP 15.00 25.00
BT04S11 Fang of Light, Garmore SP 15.00 25.00
BT04S12 Blaster Dark SP 25.00 40.00

2012 Cardfight Vanguard Booster Set 6 Breaker of Limits

COMPLETE SET (125) 200.00 350.00
RELEASED ON MAY 19, 2012
BT06001 Circular Saw, Kiriel RRR 4.00 6.00
BT06002 Battle Cupid, Nociel RRR 6.00 10.00
BT06003 Ice Prison Necromancer, Cocytus RRR 6.00 10.00
BT06004 Incandescent Lion, Blond Ezel RRR 20.00 30.00
BT06005 Player of the Holy Bow, Viviane RRR 5.00 8.00
BT06006 Dragonic Kaiser, Vermillion RRR 20.00 30.00
BT06007 Desert Gunner, Shiden RRR 2.50 4.00
BT06008 Beast Deity, Azure Dragon RRR 5.00 8.00
BT06009 Cosmo Healer, Ergodiel RR 2.50 4.00
BT06010 Core Memory, Armaros RR 1.50 2.50
BT06011 Love Machine Gun, Nociel RR 4.00 6.00
BT06012 Pure Keeper, Requiel RR 8.00 12.00
BT06013 Deadly Swordmaster RR 1.25 2.00
BT06014 Death Seeker, Thanatos RR 1.25 2.00
BT06015 Knight of Fury, Agravain RR 1.25 2.00
BT06016 Sleygal Dagger RR 3.00 5.00
BT06017 Halo Shield, Mark RR 12.00 20.00
BT06018 Vajra Emperor, Indra RR 3.00 5.00
BT06019 Dragonic Deathscythe RR 5.00 8.00
BT06020 Wyvern Guard, Guld RR 8.00 12.00
BT06021 Mobile Hospital, Feather Palace R 1.00 1.50
BT06022 Drill Bullet, Geniel R 1.00 1.50
BT06023 The Phoenix, Calamity Flame R 1.00 1.50
BT06024 Gatling Shot, Barbiel R 1.25 2.00
BT06025 Fate Healer, Ergodiel R 1.00 1.50
BT06026 Miracle Feather Nurse R 1.00 1.50
BT06027 Master Swordsman, Nightstorm R .60 1.00
BT06028 Skeleton Demon World Knight R .60 1.00
BT06029 Deadly Spirit R 1.00 1.50
BT06030 Three Star Chef, Pietro R 1.00 1.50
BT06031 Deadly Nightmare R 1.00 1.50
BT06032 Knight of Superior Skills, Beaumains R 1.00 1.50
BT06033 Mage of Calamity, Tripp R 1.00 1.50
BT06034 Player of the Holy Axe, Nimue R 1.25 2.00
BT06035 Crimson Lion Cub, Kyrph R 1.00 1.50
BT06036 Riot General, Gyras R 1.00 1.50
BT06037 Thunderstorm Dragoon R .60 1.00
BT06038 Demonic Dragon Berserker, Garuda R 1.00 1.50
BT06039 Desert Gunner, Raien R 1.00 1.50
BT06040 Photon Bomber Wyvern R 1.00 1.50
BT06041 Lizard Soldier, Saishin R 1.00 1.50
BT06042 Beast Deity, White Tiger R 1.00 1.50
BT06043 Pulse Wave, Adriel C .15 .25
BT06044 Million Ray Pegasus C .15 .25
BT06045 Ironheart, Mastima C .15 .25
BT06046 Sacred Barrier, Penem C .15 .25
BT06047 Burst Shot, Besnel C .15 .25
BT06048 Thousand Ray Pegasus C .15 .25
BT06049 Heavenly Injector C .15 .25
BT06050 Lancet Shooter C .15 .25
BT06051 Bringer of the Water of Life C .15 .25
BT06052 Clutch Rifle Angel C .15 .25
BT06053 Lightning Charger C .15 .25
BT06054 Thermometer Angel C .15 .25
BT06055 Rocket Dash Unicorn C .15 .25
BT06056 Bouquet Toss Messenger C .15 .25
BT06057 Aurora Ribbon Pidgeon C .15 .25
BT06058 Critical Hit Angel C .15 .25
BT06059 Happy Bell, Nociel C .15 .25
BT06060 Sunny Smile Angel C .15 .25
BT06061 Divine Eater, Zombie Shark C .15 .25
BT06062 Storm Ride, Ghost Ship C .15 .25
BT06063 Ghost Pirate of the Freezing Night C .15 .25
BT06064 Sea Navigator, Silver C .15 .25
BT06065 Skeleton Gargoyle C .15 .25
BT06066 Child Frank C .15 .25
BT06067 John the Ghost C .15 .25
BT06068 Ripple's Banshee C .15 .25
BT06069 Dragon Spirit C .15 .25
BT06070 Ghost Pirate of the Cursed Gun C .15 .25
BT06071 Captain Night Kid C .15 .25
BT06072 Skeleton Captain Cut C .15 .25
BT06073 Demon Cannonball C .15 .25
BT06074 Hook Arm Zombie C .15 .25
BT06075 Doctor Rouge C .15 .25
BT06076 Underworld's Helmsman C .15 .25
BT06077 Greed Shade C .15 .25
BT06078 Gigantech Crusher C .15 .25
BT06079 Sacred Mage, Manaidan C .15 .25
BT06080 Gigantech Commander C .15 .25
BT06081 Sacred Guardian Beast, Elephas C .15 .25
BT06082 Providence Strategist C .15 .25
BT06083 Knight of Fine Skill, Gareth C .15 .25
BT06084 Waving Owl C .15 .25
BT06085 Little Battler, Tron C .15 .25
BT06086 Little Fighter, Cron C .15 .25
BT06087 Greeting Drummer C .15 .25
BT06088 Flames of Victory C .15 .25
BT06089 Coongal C .15 .25
BT06090 Battle Flag Knight, Laudine C .15 .25
BT06091 Satellitefall Dragon C .15 .25
BT06092 Breakthrough Dragon C .15 .25
BT06093 Curse Gun Wyvern C .15 .25
BT06094 Dragon Monk, Ensei C .15 .25
BT06095 Red River Dragoon C .15 .25
BT06096 Stealth Fighter C .15 .25
BT06097 Lizard Soldier, Youtsu C .15 .25
BT06098 Spark Kid Dragoon C .15 .25
BT06099 Dragon Dancer, Katarina C .15 .25
BT06100 Malevolent Djinn C .15 .25
BT06101 DreadCharge Dragon C .15 .25
BT06102 Brightlance Dragon C .15 .25
BT06103 Rising Phoenix C .15 .25
BT06104 Moai the Great C .15 .25
BT06105 Beast Deity, Black Tortoise C .15 .25
BT06106 Marvelous Honey C .15 .25
BT06107 Almighty Reporter C .15 .25

BT06108 Beast Deity, Scarlet Bird C	.15	.25
BT06109 Red Card Dealer C	.15	.25
BT06110 Turboraizer C	.15	.25
BT06111 Muscle Hercules C	.15	.25
BT06112 Kungfu Kid, Bolta C	.15	.25
BT06113 Cup Bowler C	.15	.25
BT06S01 Circular Saw, Kiriel SP	15.00	25.00
BT06S02 Battle Cupid, Nociel SP	10.00	15.00
BT06S03 Ice Prison Necromancer, Cocytus SP	12.00	20.00
BT06S04 Incandescent Lion, Blond Ezel SP	40.00	60.00
BT06S05 Player of the Holy Bow, Viviane SP	20.00	30.00
BT06S06 Dragonic Kaiser, Vermillion SP	30.00	50.00
BT06S07 Desert Gunner, Shiden SP	10.00	15.00
BT06S08 Beast Deity, Azure Dragon SP	12.00	20.00
BT06S09 Cosmo Healer, Ergodiel SP	10.00	15.00
BT06S10 Death Seeker, Thanatos SP	10.00	15.00
BT06S11 Knight of Fury, Agravain SP	6.00	10.00
BT06S12 Vajra Emperor, Indra SP	6.00	10.00

2013 Cardfight Vanguard Booster Set 5 Awakening of Twin Blades

COMPLETE SET (92)	250.00	400.00
RELEASED ON FEBRUARY 22, 2013		
BT05001 Covert Demonic Dragon, Mandala Lord RRR	8.00	12.00
BT05002 Majesty Lord Blaster RRR	20.00	30.00
BT05003 Star Call Trumpeter RRR	10.00	15.00
BT05004 Phantom Blaster Overlord RRR	20.00	30.00
BT05005 Dragonic Overlord The End RRR	30.00	50.00
BT05006 Miracle Beauty RRR	6.00	10.00
BT05007 King of Diptera, Beelzebub RRR	3.00	5.00
BT05008 Mistress Hurricane RRR	2.50	4.00
BT05009 Maiden of Trailing Rose RR	6.00	10.00
BT05010 Glass Beads Dragon RR	3.00	5.00
BT05011 Maiden of Blossom Rain RR	8.00	12.00
BT05012 Stealth Fiend, Midnight Crow RR	1.75	3.00
BT05013 Stealth Beast, Leaves Mirage RR	8.00	12.00
BT05014 Knight of Loyalty, Bedivere RR	6.00	10.00
BT05015 Knight of Friendship, Kay RR	5.00	8.00
BT05016 Wingal Brave RR	5.00	8.00
BT05017 Moonlight Witch, Vaha RR	2.50	4.00
BT05018 Knight of Nullity, Masquerade RR	8.00	12.00
BT05019 Evil-eye Princess, Euryale RR	2.50	4.00
BT05020 Street Bouncer RR	1.75	3.00
BT05021 Frontline Valkyrie, Laurel R	1.50	2.50
BT05022 Knight of Harvest, Gene R	.30	.50
BT05023 Avatar of the Plains, Behemoth R	.30	.50
BT05024 Iris Knight R	.30	.50
BT05025 Hey Yo Pineapple R	.30	.50
BT05026 Shield Seed Squire R	.30	.50
BT05027 Stealth Fiend, Kurama Lord R	.30	.50
BT05028 Stealth Dragon, Voidgelga R	1.25	2.00
BT05029 Stealth Beast, Bloody Mist R	.30	.50
BT05030 Caped Stealth Rogue, Shanaou R	.30	.50
BT05031 Stealth Dragon, Cursed Breath R	1.25	2.00
BT05032 Stealth Dragon, Turbulent Edge R	1.25	2.00
BT05033 Stealth Beast, Million Rat R	1.25	2.00
BT05034 Stealth Beast, Evil Ferret R	.30	.50
BT05035 Conjurer of Mithril R	1.25	2.00
BT05036 Knight of Purgatory, Skull Face R	1.25	2.00
BT05037 Apocalypse Bat R	1.25	2.00
BT05038 Burning Horn Dragon R	1.75	3.00
BT05039 Flame of Promise, Aermo R	1.25	2.00
BT05040 Demonic Dragon Mage, Mahoraga R	.30	.50
BT05041 Magical Police Quilt R	1.25	2.00
BT05042 Devil Child R	1.25	2.00
BT05043 Knight of Verdure, Gene C	.15	.25
BT05044 Colossal Wings, Simurgh C	.15	.25
BT05045 Spiritual Tree Sage, Irminsul C	.15	.25
BT05046 Corolla Dragon C	.15	.25
BT05047 Caramel Popcorn C	.15	.25
BT05048 Lady of the Sunlight Forest C	.15	.25
BT05049 Blade Seed Squire C	.15	.25
BT05050 Lily Knight of the Valley C	.15	.25
BT05051 Pea Knight C	.15	.25
BT05052 Chestnut Bullet C	.15	.25
BT05053 Dancing Sunflower C	.15	.25
BT05054 Sweet Honey C	.15	.25
BT05055 Watering Elf C	.15	.25
BT05056 Stealth Beast, White Mane C	.15	.25
BT05057 Stealth Rogue of Silence, Shijimamaru C	.15	.25
BT05058 Stealth Beast, Leaf Raccoon C	.15	.25
BT05059 Stealth Beast, Moon Edge C	.15	.25
BT05060 Stealth Beast, Cat Rouge C	.15	.25
BT05061 Stealth Fiend, Yukihime C	.15	.25
BT05062 Stealth Fiend, Dart Spider C	.15	.25
BT05063 Powerful Sage, Bairon C	.15	.25
BT05064 Dream Painter C	.15	.25
BT05065 Silent Sage, Sharon C	.15	.25
BT05066 Nightmare Painter C	.15	.25
BT05067 Phantom Bringer Demon C	.15	.25
BT05068 Death Feather Eagle C	.15	.25
BT05069 Battle Maiden, Tagitsuhime C	.15	.25
BT05070 White Rabbit of Inaba C	.15	.25
BT05071 Battle Sister, Ginger C	.15	.25
BT05072 Doom Bringer Griffin C	.15	.25
BT05073 Top Gun C	.15	.25
BT05074 Anthrodroid C	.15	.25
BT05075 The Gong C	.15	.25
BT05076 Super Dimensional Robo, Dailady C	.15	.25
BT05077 Guide Dolphin C	.15	.25
BT05078 Dark Soul Conductor C	.15	.25
BT05079 Hysteric Shirley C	.15	.25
BT05080 Big League Bear C	.15	.25
BT05081 Madcap Marionette C	.15	.25
BT05082 Sky High Walker C	.15	.25
BT05S01 Covert Demonic Dragon, Mandala Lord SP	25.00	40.00
BT05S02 Majesty Lord Blaster SP	40.00	60.00
BT05S03 Star Call Trumpeter SP	12.00	20.00
BT05S04 Phantom Blaster Overlord SP	30.00	50.00
BT05S05 Dragonic Overlord the End SP	40.00	60.00
BT05S06 Miracle Beauty SP	12.00	20.00
BT05S07 King of Diptera, Beelzebub SP	12.00	20.00
BT05S08 Mistress Hurricane SP	10.00	15.00
BT05S09 Maiden of Trailing Rose SP	12.00	20.00
BT05S10 Stealth Fiend, Midnight Crow SP	10.00	15.00

2013 Cardfight Vanguard Booster Set 7 Rampage of the Beast King

COMPLETE SET (114)	200.00	350.00
RELEASED ON SEPTEMBER 29, 2012		
BT07001 School Hunter, Leo-paid RRR	8.00	12.00
BT07002 Guardian of Truth, Lox RRR	3.00	5.00
BT07003 Binoculus Tiger RRR	10.00	15.00
BT07004 Silver Thorn Dragon Tamer, Luquier RRR	15.00	25.00
BT07005 Dark Lord of Abyss RRR	4.00	6.00
BT07006 Emerald Witch, LaLa RRR	3.00	5.00
BT07007 White Hare in the Moon's Shadow, Pellinore RRR	8.00	12.00
BT07008 Chief Nurse, Shamsiel RRR	12.00	20.00
BT07009 School Dominator, Apt RR	1.50	2.50
BT07010 Lamp Camel RR	1.50	2.50
BT07011 Monoculus Tiger RR	2.00	3.00
BT07012 Cable Sheep RR	8.00	12.00
BT07013 Sword Magician, Sarah RR	4.00	6.00
BT07014 Fire Breeze, Carrie RR	1.50	2.50
BT07015 Peek-a-boo RR	1.50	2.50
BT07016 Magician of Quantum Mechanics RR	1.50	2.50
BT07017 Blade Wing Reijy RR	8.00	12.00
BT07018 Emblem Master RR	5.00	8.00
BT07019 Yellow Bolt RR	5.00	8.00
BT07020 Listener of Truth, Dindrane RR	8.00	12.00
BT07021 Pencil Hero, Hammsuke R	.40	.60
BT07022 Dumbbell Kangaroo R	.40	.60
BT07023 Magnet Crocodile R	.60	1.00
BT07024 Law Official, Lox R	.40	.60
BT07025 Pencil Squire, Hammsuke R	1.25	2.00
BT07026 Thermometer Giraffe R	.40	.60
BT07027 Tank Mouse R	.40	.60
BT07028 Flask Marmoset R	.40	.60
BT07029 Midnight Invader R	.60	1.00
BT07030 Dancing Princess of the Night Sky R	.60	1.00
BT07031 Bull's Eye, Mia R	.40	.60
BT07032 Purple Trapezist R	2.50	4.00
BT07033 Evil Eye Basilisk R	.40	.60
BT07034 Hades Carriage of the Witching Hour R	.40	.60
BT07035 Free Traveler R	.40	.60
BT07036 Courting Succubus R	2.00	3.00
BT07037 Sky Witch, NaNa R	.40	.60
BT07038 Battle Sister, Glace R	1.25	2.00
BT07039 Little Witch, LuLu R	.40	.60
BT07040 Photon Archer, Griflet R	.60	1.00
BT07041 Lop Ear Shooter R	3.00	5.00
BT07042 Spring Breeze Messenger R	.40	.60
BT07043 Calculator Hippo C	.15	.25
BT07044 Schoolbag Sea Lion C	.15	.25
BT07045 Red Pencil Rhino C	.15	.25
BT07046 Pencil Knight, Hammsuke C	.15	.25
BT07047 Globe Armadillo C	.15	.25
BT07048 Explosion Scientist, Bunta C	.15	.25
BT07049 Multimeter Giraffe C	.15	.25
BT07050 Canvas Koala C	.15	.25
BT07051 Thumbtack Fighter, Resanori C	.15	.25
BT07052 Tick Tock Flamingo C	.15	.25
BT07053 Bringer of Knowledge, Lox C	.15	.25
BT07054 Element Glider C	.15	.25
BT07055 Failure Scientist, Ponkichi C	.15	.25
BT07056 Feather Penguin C	.15	.25
BT07057 Hula Hoop Capybara C	.15	.25
BT07058 Acorn Master C	.15	.25
BT07059 Schoolyard Prodigy, Lox C	.15	.25
BT07060 Triangle Cobra C	.30	.50
BT07061 Fortune-bringing Cat C	.30	.50
BT07062 Alarm Chicken C	.15	.25
BT07063 Eraser Alpaca C	.15	.25
BT07064 Dictionary Goat C	.60	1.00
BT07065 Ruler Chameleon C	.30	.50
BT07066 Nightmare Doll, Amy C	.15	.25
BT07067 Dreamy Fortress C	.15	.25
BT07068 See-saw Game Loser C	.15	.25
BT07069 Drawing Dread C	.15	.25
BT07070 Jumping Glenn C	.15	.25
BT07071 Dreamy Ammonite C	.15	.25
BT07072 See-saw Game Winner C	.15	.25
BT07073 Pinky Piggy C	.15	.25
BT07074 Girl Who Crossed the Gap C	.15	.25
BT07075 Innocent Magician C	.15	.25
BT07076 Flyer Flyer C	.15	.25
BT07077 Cracker Musician C	.15	.25
BT07078 Popcorn Boy C	.30	.50
BT07079 Poison Juggler C	.60	1.00
BT07080 Demon Chariot of the Witching Hour C	.15	.25
BT07081 Beast in Hand C	.15	.25
BT07082 Cyber Beast C	.15	.25
BT07083 Demon Bike of the Witching Hour C	.30	.50
BT07084 Beautiful Harpuia C	.15	.25
BT07085 Mirage Maker C	.15	.25
BT07086 Rune Weaver C	.15	.25
BT07087 Greedy Hand C	.15	.25
BT07088 Devil in Shadow C	.15	.25
BT07089 Mad Hatter of Nightmareland C	.15	.25
BT07090 Hungry Egg of Nightmareland C	.15	.25
BT07091 Cheshire Cat of Nightmareland C	.30	.50
BT07092 Dark Knight of Nightmareland C	.60	1.00
BT07093 Battle Sister, Souffle C	.15	.25
BT07094 Oracle Guardian, Shisa C	.15	.25
BT07095 Moonsault Swallow C	.15	.25
BT07096 Battle Sister, Eclair C	.15	.25
BT07097 Master of Pain C	.15	.25
BT07098 Disciple of Pain C	.30	.50
BT07099 Speeder Hound C	.30	.50
BT07100 Doctroid Megalos C	.15	.25
BT07101 Doctroid Micros C	.15	.25
BT07102 Hope Child, Turiel C	.15	.25
BT07S01 School Hunter, Leo-paid SP	12.00	20.00
BT07S02 Guardian of Truth, Lox SP	6.00	10.00
BT07S03 Binoculus Tiger SP	10.00	15.00
BT07S04 Silver Thorn Dragon Tamer, Luquier SP	25.00	40.00
BT07S05 Dark Lord of Abyss SP	10.00	15.00
BT07S06 Emerald Witch, LaLa SP	8.00	12.00
BT07S07 White Hare in the Moon's Shadow, Pellinore SP	15.00	25.00
BT07S08 Chief Nurse, Shamsiel SP	25.00	40.00
BT07S09 School Dominator, Apt SP	6.00	10.00
BT07S10 Monoculus Tiger SP	6.00	10.00
BT07S11 Sword Magician, Sarah SP	15.00	25.00
BT07S12 Blade Wing Reijy SP	20.00	30.00

2013 Cardfight Vanguard Booster Set 8 Blue Storm Armada

COMPLETE SET (114)	200.00	350.00
RELEASED ON SEPTEMBER 22, 2013		
BT08001 Ultimate Dimensional Robo, Great Daiyusha RRR	10.00	15.00
BT08002 Galactic Beast, Zeal RRR	5.00	8.00
BT08003 Arboros Dragon, Sephirot RRR	6.00	10.00
BT08004 White Lily Musketeer, Cecilia RRR	8.00	12.00
BT08005 Blue Storm Dragon, Maelstrom RRR	15.00	25.00
BT08006 Hydro Hurricane Dragon RRR	3.00	5.00
BT08007 Storm Rider, Basil RRR	12.00	20.00
BT08008 Sealed Demon Dragon, Dungaree RRR	3.00	5.00
BT08009 Operator Girl, Mika RR	1.00	1.50
BT08010 Dimensional Robo, Daidragon RR	4.00	6.00
BT08011 Cherry Blossom Musketeer, Augusto RR	2.50	4.00
BT08012 Lily of the Valley Musketeer, Kaivant RR	1.25	2.00
BT08013 Maiden of Rainbow Wood RR	1.25	2.00
BT08014 Water Lily Musketeer, Ruth RR	1.75	3.00
BT08015 Lily of the Valley Musketeer, Rebecca RR	2.50	4.00
BT08016 Military Dragon, Raptor Colonel RR	8.00	12.00
BT08017 Destruction Dragon, Dark Rex RR	3.00	5.00
BT08018 Tear Knight, Valeria RR	3.00	5.00
BT08019 Emerald Shield, Paschal RR	15.00	25.00
BT08020 Armed Instructor, Bison RR	1.00	1.50
BT08021 Enigman Cyclone R	.40	.60
BT08022 Lady Justice R	.40	.60
BT08023 Subterranean Beast, Magma Lord R	.40	.60
BT08024 Devourer of Planets, Zeal R	.40	.60
BT08025 Dimensional Robo, Dailander R	.60	1.00
BT08026 Dimensional Robo, Goyusha R	.40	.60
BT08027 Larva Beast, Zeal R	.40	.60
BT08028 Arboros Dragon, Timber R	.60	1.00
BT08029 Arboros Dragon, Ratoon R	.40	.60
BT08030 Military Dragon, Raptor Captain R	.60	1.00
BT08031 Winged Dragon, Slashptero R	.40	.60
BT08032 Assault Dragon, Pachyphalos R	.40	.60
BT08033 Winged Dragon, Beamptero R	.40	.60
BT08034 Military Dragon, Raptor Soldier R	.40	.60
BT08035 Storm Rider, Diamantes R	.60	1.00
BT08036 Tear Knight, Lazarus R	.40	.60
BT08037 Storm Rider, Eugen R	.40	.60
BT08038 Torpedo Rush Dragon R	.40	.60
BT08039 Aqua Breath Dracokid R	.40	.60
BT08040 Thunder Spear Wielding Exorcist Knight R	.40	.60
BT08041 Compass Lion R	.40	.60
BT08042 Coiling Duckbill R	.40	.60
BT08043 Interdimensional Ninja, Tsukikage C	.15	.25
BT08044 Cosmic Mothership C	.15	.25
BT08045 Cosmic Rider C	.15	.25
BT08046 Assault Monster, Gunrock C	.15	.25
BT08047 Eye of Destruction, Zeal C	.15	.25
BT08048 Dimensional Robo, Daimariner C	.15	.25
BT08049 Mysterious Navy Admiral, Gogoth C	.15	.25
BT08050 Psychic Grey C	.15	.25
BT08051 Speedster C	.15	.25
BT08052 Fighting Saucer C	.15	.25
BT08053 Warrior of Destiny, Dai C	.15	.25
BT08054 Gem Monster, Jewelmine C	.15	.25
BT08055 Noise Monster, Decibelon C	.15	.25
BT08056 Dissection Monster, Kaizon C	.15	.25
BT08057 Dimensional Robo, Daibattles C	.15	.25
BT08058 Black Lily Musketeer, Hermann C	.15	.25
BT08059 World Snake, Ouroboros C	.15	.25
BT08060 Exploding Tomato C	.15	.50
BT08061 World Bearing Turtle, Ahkbara C	.15	.25
BT08062 Tulip Musketeer, Almira C	.15	.25
BT08063 Poison Mushroom C	.15	.25
BT08064 Arboros Dragon, Branch C	.15	.25
BT08065 Tulip Musketeer, Mina C	.15	.25
BT08066 Boon Bana-na C	.15	.25
BT08067 Fruits Basket Elf C	.15	.25
BT08068 Broccolini Musketeer, Kirah C	.15	.25
BT08069 Night Queen Musketeer, Daniel C	.15	.25
BT08070 Four Leaf Fairy C	.15	.25
BT08071 Maiden of Morning Glory C	.15	.25
BT08072 Hibiscus Musketeer, Hanah C	.15	.25
BT08073 Savage War Chief C	.15	.25
BT08074 Citadel Dragon, Brachiocastle C	.15	.25
BT08075 Savage Warlock C	.15	.25
BT08076 Carrier Dragon, Brachiocarrier C	.15	.25
BT08077 Military Dragon, Raptor Sergeant C	.15	.25
BT08078 Savage Magus C	.15	.25
BT08079 Fortress Ammonite C	.15	.25
BT08080 Transport Dragon, Brachioporter C	.15	.25
BT08081 Baby Ptero C	.15	.25
BT08082 Dragon Bird, Firepteryx C	.15	.25
BT08083 Carry Trilobite C	.15	.25
BT08084 Matriarch's Bombardment Beast C	.15	.25
BT08085 Ironclad Dragon, Steelsaurus C	.15	.25
BT08086 Titan of the Pyroxene Mine C	.15	.25
BT08087 Distant Sea Advisor, Vassilis C	.15	.25
BT08088 Veteran Strategic Commander C	.15	.25
BT08089 Whale Supply Fleet, Kairin Maru C	.15	.25
BT08090 Tear Knight, Theo C	.15	.25
BT08091 Stream Trooper C	.15	.25
BT08092 Reliable Strategic Commander C	.15	.25
BT08093 Officer Cadet, Erikk C	.15	.25
BT08094 Mothership Intelligence C	.15	.25
BT08095 Enemy Seeking Seagull Soldier C	.15	.25
BT08096 Black Celestial Maiden, Kali C	.15	.25
BT08097 Dragon Monk, Kinkaku C	.15	.25
BT08098 Lightning Sword Wielding Exorcist Knight C	.15	.25
BT08099 Dragon Monk, Ginkaku C	.15	.25
BT08100 Exorcist Mage, Koh Koh C	.15	.25
BT08101 Mischievous Girl, Kyon-she C	.15	.25
BT08102 Blackboard Parrot C	.15	.25
BT08S01 Ultimate Dimensional Robo, Great Daiyusha SP	15.00	25.00
BT08S02 Galactic Beast, Zeal SP	12.00	20.00
BT08S03 Arboros Dragon, Sephirot SP	12.00	20.00
BT08S04 White Lily Musketeer, Cecilia SP	15.00	25.00
BT08S05 Blue Storm Dragon, Maelstrom SP	40.00	60.00
BT08S06 Hydro Hurricane Dragon SP	8.00	12.00
BT08S07 Storm Rider, Basil SP	25.00	40.00
BT08S08 Sealed Demon Dragon, Dungaree SP	12.00	20.00
BT08S09 Operator Girl, Mika SP	20.00	30.00
BT08S10 Maiden of Rainbow Wood SP	20.00	30.00
BT08S11 Military Dragon, Raptor Colonel SP	10.00	15.00
BT08S12 Destruction Dragon, Dark Rex SP	12.00	20.00

2013 Cardfight Vanguard Booster Set 9 Clash of the Knights and Dragons

COMPLETE SET (114)	350.00	500.00
RELEASED ON JUNE 28, 2013		
BT09001 Covert Demonic Dragon, Magatsu Storm RRR	5.00	8.00
BT09002 Blue Storm Supreme Dragon, Glory Maelstrom RRR	12.00	20.00
BT09003 Goddess of the Sun, Amaterasu RRR	6.00	10.00
BT09004 Ultra Beast Deity, Illuminal Dragon RRR	6.00	10.00
BT09005 Crimson Impact, Metatron RRR	8.00	12.00
BT09006 Blazing Lion, Platina Ezel RRR	20.00	30.00
BT09007 Conviction Dragon, Chromejailer Dragon RRR	10.00	15.00
BT09008 Dragonic Kaiser Vermillion THE BLOOD RRR	25.00	40.00
BT09009 Fantasy Petal Storm, Shirayuki RR	4.00	6.00
BT09010 Platinum Blond Fox Spirit, Tamamo RR	3.00	5.00
BT09011 Tri-Stinger Dragon RR	.60	1.00
BT09012 Battle Sister, Cookie RR	3.00	5.00
BT09013 Battler of the Twin Brush, Polaris RR	1.75	3.00
BT09014 Halo Shield, Mark RR	8.00	12.00
BT09015 Lord of the Demonic Winds, Vayu RR	.60	1.00
BT09016 Wyvern Guard, Guld RR	5.00	8.00
BT09017 Starlight Melody Tamer, Farah RR	1.75	3.00
BT09018 Nightmare Summoner, Raqiel RR	1.50	2.50
BT09019 Blaster Blade Spirit RR	4.00	6.00
BT09020 Blaster Dark Spirit RR	2.50	4.00
BT09021 Stealth Dragon, Magatsu Gale R	.60	1.00
BT09022 Stealth Fiend, Oboro Cart R	.40	.60
BT09023 Stealth Dragon, Magatsu Wind R	.40	.60
BT09024 Storm Rider, Lysander R	.40	.60
BT09025 Storm Rider, Damon R	.40	.60
BT09026 Battle Siren, Theresa R	.40	.60
BT09027 Storm Rider, Nicolas R	.40	.60
BT09028 Tri-holl DracokidR	.40	.60
BT09029 Battle Deity, Susanoo R	.40	.60
BT09030 Battle Maiden, Sayorihime R	.40	.60
BT09031 Beast Deity, Yamatano Drake R	.40	.60
BT09032 Hollow Nomad R	.40	.60
BT09033 Beast Deity, Golden Anglet R	.60	1.00
BT09034 Beast Deity, Blank Marsh R	.50	.75
BT09035 Mobile Hospital, Elysium R	.40	.60
BT09036 Knight of Passion, Bagdemagus R	.60	1.00
BT09037 Advance of the Black Chains, Kahedin R	.40	.60
BT09038 Dreaming Sage, Corron R	.40	.60
BT09039 Dusty Plasma Dragon R	1.50	2.50
BT09040 Exorcist Demonic Dragon, Indigo R	.40	.60
BT09041 Barking Wyvern R	.40	.60
BT09042 Fire Juggler R	.40	.60
BT09043 Spiked Club Stealth Rogue, Arahabaki C	.15	.25
BT09044 Stealth Beast, Gigantoad C	.15	.25
BT09045 Stealth Dragon, Royale Nova C	.15	.25
BT09046 Stealth Beast, Spell Hound C	.15	.25
BT09047 Stealth Rogue of Summoning, Jiraiya C	.15	.25
BT09048 Stealth Dragon, Magatsu Breath C	.15	.25
BT09049 Stealth Beast, Night Panther C	.15	.25
BT09050 Stealth Beast, Flame Fox C	.15	.25
BT09051 Stealth Rogue of Body Replacement, Kokuenmaru C	.15	.25
BT09052 Fox Tamer, Izuna C	.30	.50
BT09053 Stealth Fiend, Monster Lantern C	.15	.25
BT09054 Stealth Fiend, Rokuro Lady C	.15	.25
BT09055 Stealth Fiend, Karakasa Spirit C	.15	.25
BT09056 Stealth Fiend, River Child C	.15	.25
BT09057 Stealth Beast, Cat Devil C	.15	.25
BT09058 Deck Sweeper C	.15	.25
BT09059 Light Signals Penguin Soldier C	.15	.25
BT09060 Officer Cadet, Astraea C	.15	.25
BT09061 Pyroxene Beam Blue Dragon Soldier C	.15	.25
BT09062 Supersonic Sailor C	.15	.25
BT09063 Gentle Jimm C	.15	.25
BT09064 Oracle Guardian, Sphinx C	.15	.25
BT09065 Rock Witch, GaGa C	.15	.25
BT09066 Battle Sister, Cream C	.15	.25
BT09067 Machine-gun Talk RyanC	.15	.25
BT09068 Solar Maiden, Uzume C	.15	.25
BT09069 Supple Bamboo Princess, Kaguya C	.15	.25
BT09070 Heroic Hani C	.15	.25
BT09071 Transraizer C	.15	.25
BT09072 Burstraizer C	.15	.25
BT09073 Stoic Hani C	.15	.25
BT09074 Transmigrating Evolution, Miraioh C	.15	.25
BT09075 Lionet Heat C	.15	.25
BT09076 Crimson Drive, Aphrodite C	.30	.50
BT09077 Examine Angel C	.15	.25
BT09078 Crimson Mind, Baruch C	.30	.50
BT09079 Emergency Vehicle C	.15	.25
BT09080 Candlelight Angel C	.15	.25
BT09081 Crimson Heart, Nahas C	.15	.25
BT09082 Rampage Cart Angel C	.15	.25
BT09083 Fever Therapy Nurse C	.30	.50
BT09084 Vocal Chicken C	.15	.25
BT09085 Melodica Cat C	.15	.25
BT09086 Parabolic Moose C	.15	.25
BT09087 Barcode Zebra C	.15	.25
BT09088 Recorder Dog C	.15	.25
BT09089 Sharpener Beaver C	.15	.25
BT09090 Protractor Peacock C	.15	.25
BT09091 Gardening Mole C	.15	.25
BT09092 Castanet Donkey C	.15	.25
BT09093 Holy Mage of the Gale C	.15	.25
BT09094 Stronghold of the Black Chains, Hoel C	.15	.25
BT09095 Dantegal C	.15	.25
BT09096 Runebau C	.15	.25
BT09097 Exorcist Mage, Roh Roh C	.15	.25
BT09098 Deity Sealing Kid, Soh Koh C	.15	.25
BT09099 Spark Edge Dracokid C	.30	.50
BT09100 Exorcist Mage, Lin Lin C	.15	.25
BT09101 Magical Partner C	.15	.25
BT09102 Smiling Presenter C	.15	.25
BT09S01 Covert Demonic Dragon, Magatsu Storm SP	12.00	20.00
BT09S02 Blue Storm Supreme Dragon, Glory Maelstrom SP	25.00	40.00
BT09S03 Goddess of the Sun, Amaterasu SP	25.00	40.00
BT09S04 Ultra Beast Deity, Illuminal Dragon SP	15.00	25.00
BT09S05 Crimson Impact, Metatron SP	20.00	30.00
BT09S06 Blazing Lion, Platina Ezel SP	40.00	60.00
BT09S07 Conviction Dragon, Chromejailer Dragon SP	20.00	30.00
BT09S08 Dragonic Kaiser Vermillion THE BLOOD SP	40.00	60.00
BT09S09 Battle Sister, Cookie SP	20.00	30.00
BT09S10 Starlight Melody Tamer, Farah SP	12.00	20.00
BT09S11 Blaster Blade Spirit SP	15.00	25.00
BT09S12 Blaster Dark Spirit SP	20.00	30.00

2013 Cardfight Vanguard Booster Set 10 Triumphant Return of the King of Knights

COMPLETE SET (114)	250.00	400.00
RELEASED ON DECEMBER 14, 2013		
BT10001 Pure Heart Jewel Knight, Ashlei RRR	12.00	20.00
BT10002 Leading Jewel Knight, Salome RRR	5.00	8.00
BT10003 Liberator of the Round Table, Alfred RRR	15.00	25.00
BT10004 Oracle Queen, Himiko RRR	12.00	20.00
BT10005 Eternal Goddess, Iwanagahime RRR	4.00	6.00
BT10006 Eradicator, Dragonic Descendant RRR	12.00	20.00
BT10007 Eradicator, Gauntlet Buster Dragon RRR	10.00	15.00
BT10008 Beast Deity, Ethics Buster RRR	10.00	15.00
BT10009 Dogmatize Jewel Knight, Sybill RR	2.00	3.00
BT10010 Flashing Jewel Knight, Iseult RR	10.00	15.00
BT10011 Halo Liberator, Mark RR	12.00	20.00
BT10012 Liberator of the Flute, Escrad RR	6.00	10.00
BT10013 Battle Deity of the Night, Artemis RR	2.00	3.00
BT10014 Broom Witch, Callaway RR	.60	1.00
BT10015 Goddess of Self-sacrifice, Kushinada RR	12.00	20.00
BT10016 Supreme Army Eradicator, Zuitan RR	4.00	6.00
BT10017 Eradicator Wyvern Guard, Guld RR	12.00	20.00
BT10018 Grateful Catapult RR	.60	1.00
BT10019 Bad End Dragger RR	2.50	4.00
BT10020 Cheer Girl, Marilyn RR	2.50	4.00
BT10021 Dignified Silver Dragon R	.30	.50
BT10022 Fellowship Jewel Knight, Tracie R	.60	1.00
BT10023 Jewel Knight, Prizmy R	.30	.50
BT10024 Dreaming Jewel Knight, Tiffany R	.30	.50
BT10025 Fast Chase Liberator, Josephus R	.60	1.00
BT10026 Wingal Liberator R	.30	.50
BT10027 Witch of Wolves, Saffron R	.30	.50
BT10028 Battle Maiden, Izunahime R	.30	.50
BT10029 Battle Maiden, Sahohime R	1.25	2.00
BT10030 Twilight Hunter, Artemis R	.60	1.00
BT10031 Battle Maiden, Tatsutahime R	.30	.50
BT10032 Battle Maiden, Tamayorihime R	.30	.50
BT10033 Aiming for the Stars, Artemis R	.30	.50
BT10034 Martial Arts General, Daimu R	.30	.50
BT10035 Double Gun Eradicator, Hakusho R	.30	.50
BT10036 Eradicator, Saucer Cannon Wyvern R	.30	.50
BT10037 Ceremonial Bonfire Eradicator, Castor R	.30	.50
BT10038 Ambush Dragon Eradicator, Linchu R	.30	.50
BT10039 Armored Heavy Gunner R	.30	.50
BT10040 Beast Deity, Hatred Chaos R	1.25	2.00
BT10041 Rabbit House R	.30	.50
BT10042 Dudley Mason R	.60	1.00
BT10043 Knight of the Explosive Axe, Gornement C	.15	.25
BT10044 Uncompromising Knight, Ideale C	.15	.25
BT10045 Knight of Details, Claudin C	.15	.25
BT10046 Stinging Jewel Knight, Shellie C	.15	.25
BT10047 Rushhgal C	.15	.25
BT10048 Jewel Knight, Glitmy C	.15	.25
BT10049 Blazing Jewel Knight, Rachelle C	.30	.50
BT10050 Primgal C	.15	.25
BT10051 Devoting Jewel Knight, Tabitha C	.15	.25
BT10052 Ardent Jewel Knight, Polli C	.15	.25
BT10053 Muungal C	.15	.25
BT10054 Knight of Far Arrows, Saphir C	.30	.50
BT10055 Boulder Smashing Knight, Segwarides C	.15	.25
BT10056 Guiding Falcony C	.15	.25
BT10057 Liberator, Flare Mane Stallion C	.15	.25
BT10058 Holy Squire, Enide C	.15	.25
BT10059 Liberator of Hope, Epona C	.30	.50
BT10060 Flogal Liberator C	.30	.50
BT10061 Scheduler Angel C	.15	.25
BT10062 Myth Guard, Antares C	.15	.25
BT10063 Clever Jake C	.15	.25
BT10064 Witch of Owls, Paprika C	.15	.25
BT10065 Myth Guard, Orion C	.15	.25
BT10066 Battle Maiden, Mihikarihime C	.15	.25
BT10067 Bowstring of Heaven and Earth, Artemis C	.15	.25
BT10068 Witch of Cats, Cumin C	.15	.25
BT10069 Snipe Snake C	.30	.50
BT10070 Myth Guard, Sirius C	.15	.25
BT10071 Cluster Hamster C	.30	.50
BT10072 Cyber Tiger C	.15	.25
BT10073 Battle Maiden, Kukurihime C	.30	.50
BT10074 Bandit Danny C	.15	.25
BT10075 Fancy Monkey C	.15	.25
BT10076 Spark Cockerel C	.15	.25
BT10077 Patrol Guardian C	.15	.25
BT10078 Witch of Big Pots, Laurier C	.15	.25
BT10079 Demonic Dragon Berserker, Sandila C	.30	.50
BT10080 Blood Axe Dragoon C	.15	.25
BT10081 Demonic Dragon Mage, Majila C	.15	.25
BT10082 Sword Dance Eradicator, Hisen C	.30	.50
BT10083 Dragon Dancer, Agnes C	.15	.25
BT10084 Lightning Fist Eradicator, Dui C	.15	.25
BT10085 Eradicator, Strike-dagger Dragon C	.15	.25
BT10086 Djinn of the Thunder Break C	.15	.25
BT10087 Sacred Spear Eradicator, Pollux C	.30	.50
BT10088 Eradicator, Spy-eye Wyvern C	.15	.25
BT10089 Bloody Reign C	.15	.25
BT10090 Beast Deity, Hilarity Destroyer C	.15	.25
BT10091 Machinery Angel C	.30	.50
BT10092 Beast Deity, Riot Horn C	.15	.25
BT10093 Battle Arm Leprechaun C	.30	.50
BT10094 Anti-battleroid Gunner C	.15	.25
BT10095 Blow Kiss Olivia C	.15	.25
BT10096 Go For Broke C	.15	.25
BT10097 Charging Bill Collector C	.15	.25
BT10098 UFO (Unlucky Flying Object) C	.15	.25
BT10099 Tyrant Receiver C	.30	.50
BT10100 Dudley Phantom C	.30	.50
BT10101 Reign of Terror, Thermidor C	.15	.25
BT10102 Baby Face Izaac C	.30	.50
BT10S01 Pure Heart Jewel Knight, Ashlei SP	25.00	40.00
BT10S02 Leading Jewel Knight, Salome SP	20.00	30.00
BT10S03 Liberator of the Round Table, Alfred SP	20.00	30.00
BT10S04 Oracle Queen, Himiko SP	15.00	25.00
BT10S05 Eternal Goddess, Iwanagahime SP	10.00	15.00
BT10S06 Eradicator, Dragonic Descendant SP	30.00	50.00
BT10S07 Eradicator, Gauntlet Buster Dragon SP	20.00	30.00
BT10S08 Beast Deity, Ethics Buster SP	20.00	30.00
BT10S09 Dogmatize Jewel Knight, Sybill SP	12.00	20.00
BT10S10 Battle Deity of the Night, Artemis SP	12.00	20.00
BT10S11 Wingal Liberator SP	10.00	15.00
BT10S12 Blaster Blade Liberator SP	40.00	60.00

2013 Cardfight Vanguard Booster Set 11 Seal Dragons Unleashed

COMPLETE SET (114)	250.00	400.00
RELEASED ON OCTOBER 25, 2013		
BT11001 Prophecy Celestial, Ramiel RRR	12.00	20.00
BT11002 Solidify Celestial, Zerachiel RRR	10.00	15.00
BT11003 Goddess of Good Luck, Fortuna RRR	6.00	10.00
BT11004 Hellfire Seal Dragon, Blockade Inferno RRR	6.00	10.00
BT11005 Dauntless Drive Dragon RRR	25.00	40.00
BT11006 Eradicator, Sweep Command Dragon RRR	5.00	8.00
BT11007 Blue Flight Dragon, Trans-core Dragon RRR	20.00	30.00
BT11008 Last Card, Revonn RRR	5.00	8.00
BT11009 Adamantine Celestial, Aniel RR	6.00	10.00
BT11010 Seal Dragon, Blockade RR	1.00	1.50
BT11011 Seal Dragon, Rinocross RR	8.00	12.00
BT11012 Ancient Dragon, Spinodriver RR	8.00	12.00
BT11013 Ancient Dragon, Tyrannolegend RR	2.50	4.00
BT11014 Ravenous Dragon, Battlerex RR	.30	.50
BT11015 Ancient Dragon, Paraswall RR	4.00	6.00
BT11016 Armor Break Dragon RR	1.00	1.50
BT11017 Fiendish Sword Eradicator, Cho-Ou RR	8.00	12.00
BT11018 Thundering Ripple, Genovious RR	2.50	4.00
BT11019 Tear Knight, Lucas RR	1.00	1.50
BT11020 Emerald Shield, Paschal RR	6.00	10.00
BT11021 Mobile Hospital, Assault Hospice R	.30	.50
BT11022 Reverse Aura Phoenix R	.30	.50
BT11023 Essence Celestial, Becca R	.30	.50
BT11024 Wild Shot Celestial, Raguel R	.60	1.00
BT11025 Candle Celestial, Sariel R	1.00	1.50
BT11026 Underlay Celestial, Hesediel R	.60	1.00
BT11027 Myth Guard, La Superba R	.30	.50
BT11028 Witch of Ravens, Chamomile R	1.25	2.00
BT11029 Witch of Frogs, Melissa R	1.25	2.00
BT11030 Demonic Dragon Berserker, Gandharva R	.30	.50
BT11031 Seal Dragon, Hunger Hell Dragon R	1.00	1.50
BT11032 Seal Dragon, Jacquard R	.60	1.00
BT11033 Seal Dragon, Chambray R	.30	.50
BT11034 Savage Hunter R	.30	.50
BT11035 Ancient Dragon, Criollofall R	.60	1.00
BT11036 Ancient Dragon, Beamankylo R	.60	1.00
BT11037 Ancient Dragon, Iguanogorg R	.60	1.00
BT11038 Demonic Sword Eradicator, Raioh R	.30	.50
BT11039 Steel-blooded Eradicator, Shuki R	2.00	3.00
BT11040 Titan of the Beam Cannon Tower R	.30	.50
BT11041 Rising Ripple, Pavroth R	.60	1.00
BT11042 Starting Ripple, Alecs R	.30	.50
BT11043 Booting Celestial, Sandalphon C	.15	.25
BT11044 Capsule Gift Nurse C	.15	.25
BT11045 Doctroid Argus C	.15	.25
BT11046 Marking Celestial, Arabhaki C	.30	.50
BT11047 Order Celestial, Yeqon C	.15	.25
BT11048 Drugstore Nurse C	.30	.50
BT11049 First Aid Celestial, Peniel C	.30	.50
BT11050 Cure Drop Angel C	.15	.25
BT11051 Hot Shot Celestial, Samyaza C	.30	.50
BT11052 Celestial, Landing Pegasus C	.15	.25
BT11053 Encourage Celestial, Tamiel C	.15	.25
BT11054 Recovery Celestial, Ramuel C	.30	.50
BT11055 Crimson Witch, Radish C	.15	.25
BT11056 Pineapple Law C	.15	.25
BT11057 Witch of Prohibited Books, Cinnamon C	.15	.25
BT11058 Vivid Rabbit C	.15	.25
BT11059 Seal Dragon, Spike Hell Dragon C	.15	.25
BT11060 Seal Dragon, Corduroy C	.30	.50
BT11061 Breath of Demise, Vulcanis C	.15	.25
BT11062 Dragon Knight, Lotf C	.15	.25
BT11063 Demonic Dragon Berserker, Kubanda C	.30	.50
BT11064 Seal Dragon, Flannel C	.30	.50
BT11065 Seal Dragon, Kersey C	.30	.50
BT11066 Breath of Origin, Rolamandri C	.15	.25
BT11067 Demonic Dragon Mage, Shagara C	.15	.25
BT11068 Seal Dragon, Terrycloth C	.15	.25
BT11069 Demonic Dragon Mage, Diva C	.15	.25
BT11070 Red Pulse Dracokid C	.15	.25
BT11071 Seal Dragon, Biella C	.30	.50
BT11072 Seal Dragon, Dobby C	.15	.25
BT11073 Seal Dragon, Shirting C	.30	.50
BT11074 Seal Dragon, Artpique C	.60	1.00
BT11075 Ancient Dragon, Stegobuster C	.15	.25
BT11076 Ancient Dragon, Dinocrowd C	.15	.25
BT11077 Launcher Mammoth C	.15	.25
BT11078 Savage Archer C	.15	.25
BT11079 Ancient Dragon, Triplasma C	.15	.25
BT11080 Ancient Dragon, Gattlingaro C	.15	.25
BT11081 Savage Illuminator C	.15	.25
BT11082 Ancient Dragon, Baby Rex C	.15	.25
BT11083 Savage Patriarch C	.15	.25
BT11084 Ancient Dragon, Dinodile C	.15	.25
BT11085 Ancient Dragon, Titanocargo C	.15	.25
BT11086 Ancient Dragon, Caudinoise C	.15	.25
BT11087 Ancient Dragon, Ornithhealer C	.15	.25
BT11088 Dragon Dancer, Julia C	.15	.25
BT11089 Lizard Soldier, Ryoshin C	.15	.25
BT11090 Eradicator, First Thunder Dracokid C	.15	.25
BT11091 Flag of Raijin, Corposant C	.15	.25
BT11092 Mobile Battleship, Archelon C	.15	.25
BT11093 Twin Strike Brave Shooter C	.30	.50
BT11094 Titan of the Beam Rifle C	.15	.25
BT11095 Silent Ripple, Sotirio C	.15	.25
BT11096 Mercenary Brave Shooter C	.30	.50
BT11097 Battle Siren, Euphenia C	.15	.25
BT11098 Advance Party Brave Shooter C	.15	.25
BT11099 Battle Siren, Cagli C	.15	.25
BT11100 Jet-ski Rider C	.15	.25
BT11101 Ice Floe Angel C	.15	.25
BT11102 Mass Production Sailor C	.30	.50
BT11S01 Prophecy Celestial, Ramiel SP	20.00	30.00
BT11S02 Solidify Celestial, Zerachiel SP	20.00	30.00
BT11S03 Goddess of Good Luck, Fortuna SP	20.00	30.00
BT11S04 Hellfire Seal Dragon, Blockade Inferno SP	10.00	15.00
BT11S05 Dauntless Drive Dragon SP	40.00	60.00
BT11S06 Eradicator, Sweep Command Dragon SP	12.00	20.00
BT11S07 Blue Flight Dragon, Trans-core Dragon SP	25.00	40.00
BT11S08 Last Card, Revonn SP	12.00	20.00
BT11S09 Ancient Dragon, Spinodriver SP	15.00	25.00
BT11S10 Ancient Dragon, Tyrannolegend SP	10.00	15.00
BT11S11 Armor Break Dragon SP	3.00	5.00
BT11S12 Thundering Ripple, Genovious SP	12.00	20.00

2014 Cardfight Vanguard Booster Set 12 Binding Force of the Black Rings

COMPLETE SET (114)	400.00	550.00
RELEASED ON FEBRUARY 21, 2014		
BT12001 Revenger, Raging Form Dragon RRR	20.00	50.00
BT12002 Wolf Fang Liberator, Garmore RRR	5.00	12.00
BT12003 Eradicator, Vowing Saber Dragon Reverse RRR	4.00	10.00
BT12004 Demon Conquering Dragon, Dungaree Unlimited RRR	1.25	3.00
BT12005 Star-vader, Nebula Lord Dragon RRR	10.00	25.00
BT12006 Schwarzschild Dragon RRR	3.00	8.00
BT12007 Demon Marquis, Amon Reverse RRR	6.00	15.00
BT12008 Silver Thorn Dragon Queen, Luquier Reverse RRR	10.00	25.00
BT12009 Witch of Cursed Talisman, Etain RR	1.25	3.00
BT12010 Dark Cloak Revenger, Tartu RR	6.00	15.00
BT12011 Dark Revenger, Mac Lir RR	10.00	25.00
BT12012 Barcgal Liberator RR	1.25	3.00
BT12013 Iron Fan Eradicator, Nirrti RR	.60	1.50
BT12014 Barrier Star-vader, Promethium RR	10.00	25.00
BT12015 King of Masks, Dantarian RR	2.00	5.00
BT12016 Master of Fifth Element RR	1.25	3.00
BT12017 Amon's Follower, Vlad Specula RR	2.50	6.00
BT12018 Miracle Pop, Eva RR	4.00	10.00
BT12019 Nightmare Doll, Chelsea RR	1.50	4.00
BT12020 Silver Thorn Hypnos, Lydia RR	5.00	12.00
BT12021 Barrier Troop Revenger, Dorint R	1.00	2.50
BT12022 Revenger, Dark Bond Trumpeter R	.40	1.00
BT12023 Frontline Revenger, Claudas R	.40	1.00
BT12024 Liberator, Bagpipe Angel R	.60	1.50
BT12025 Whirlwind Axe Wielding Exorcist Knight R	.40	1.00
BT12026 Homing Eradicator, Rochishin R	.40	1.00
BT12027 Rising Phoenix R	.40	1.00
BT12028 Resonance Hammer Wielding Exorcist Knight R	.40	1.00
BT12029 Exorcist Mage, Dan Dan R	.40	1.00
BT12030 Schrodinger's Lion R	.40	1.00
BT12031 Gravity Collapse Dragon R	.60	1.50
BT12032 Opener of Dark Gates R	.40	1.00
BT12033 Star-vader, Dust Tail Unicorn R	.40	1.00
BT12034 Micro-hole Dracokid R	.20	.50
BT12035 Werbear Soldner R	.20	.50
BT12036 Amon's Follower, Psycho Grave R	.40	1.00
BT12037 Amon's Follower, Ron Geenlin R	.40	1.00
BT12038 Amon's Follower, Fool's Palm R	.40	1.00
BT12039 Fire Ring Griffin R	.20	.50
BT12040 Silver Thorn Marionette, Lillian R	1.25	3.00
BT12041 Silver Thorn Beast Tamer, Maricica R	1.00	2.50
BT12042 Silver Thorn, Rising Dragon R	1.00	2.50
BT12043 Demon World Castle, Zerschlagen C	.20	.50
BT12044 Jacbau Revenger C	.20	.50
BT12045 Demon World Castle, Zweispeer C	.10	.25
BT12046 Malice Revenger, Dylan C	.20	.50
BT12047 Sonbau C	.10	.25
BT12048 Spinbau Revenger C	.10	.25
BT12049 Revenger, Air Raid Dragon C	.40	1.00
BT12050 Revenger, Waking Angel C	.20	.50
BT12051 Gigantech Pillar Fighter C	.10	.25
BT12052 Overcast Liberator, Geraint C	.10	.25
BT12053 Pikgal C	.10	.25
BT12054 May Rain Liberator, Bruno C	.10	.25
BT12055 Sunrise Unicorn C	.10	.25
BT12056 Liberator, Cheer Up Trumpeter C	.10	.25
BT12057 Daybreak Liberator, Muron C	.10	.25
BT12058 Conquering Eradicator, Dokkasei C	.20	.50
BT12059 Eradicator, Blade Hang Dracokid C	.20	.50
BT12060 Eradicator, Blue Gem Carbuncle C	.40	1.00
BT12061 Catastrophstinger C	.10	.25
BT12062 Innocent Blade, Heartless C	.10	.25
BT12063 Furious Claw Star-vader, Niobium C	.10	.25
BT12064 Gamma Burst, Fenrir C	.10	.25
BT12065 Singularity Sniper C	.20	.50
BT12066 Le Maul C	.20	.50
BT12067 Gravity Ball Dragon C	.20	.50
BT12068 Demon Claw Star-vader, Lanthanum C	.40	1.00
BT12069 Strafing Star-vader, Ruthenium C	.20	.50
BT12070 Paradox Nail, Fenrir C	.20	.50
BT12071 White Night, Fenrir C	.20	.50
BT12072 Star-vader, Weiss Soldat C	.40	1.00
BT12073 Star-vader, Scounting Ferris C	.10	.25
BT12074 Star-vader, Moon Commander C	.20	.50
BT12075 Number of Terror C	.10	.25
BT12076 Amon's Follower, Hell's Draw C	.20	.50
BT12077 Werleopard Soldat C	.20	.50
BT12078 Frog Knight C	.20	.50
BT12079 Amon's Follower, Hell's Deal C	.10	.25
BT12080 Amon's Follower, Phu Geenlin C	.10	.25
BT12081 Dimension Creeper C	.10	.25
BT12082 Werhase Bandito C	.20	.50
BT12083 Amon's Follower, Fate Collector C	.20	.50
BT12084 Werfuchs Hexa C	.10	.25
BT12085 Amon's Follower, Cruel Hand C	.20	.50
BT12086 Amon's Follower, Psychic Waitress C	.20	.50
BT12087 Amon's Follower, Meteor Cracker C	.10	.25
BT12088 Amon's Follower, Hell's Trick C	.20	.50
BT12089 Master of Giant Flying Knives C	.20	.50
BT12090 Tightrope Holder C	.10	.25
BT12091 Flying Hippogriff C	.10	.25
BT12092 Silver Thorn Assistant, Irina C	.20	.50
BT12093 Silver Thorn Beast Tamer, Ana C	.20	.50
BT12094 Silver Thorn, Breathing Dragon C	.40	1.00
BT12095 Tightrope Tumbler C	.20	.50
BT12096 Elegant Elephant C	.10	.25
BT12097 Silver Thorn Assistant, Ionela C	.20	.50
BT12098 Tone of a Journey, Willi C	.10	.25
BT12099 Silver Thorn Barking, Dragon C	.40	1.00
BT12100 Silver Thorn Marionette, Natasha C	.20	.50
BT12101 Silver Thorn Beast Tamer, Serge C	.20	.50
BT12102 Silver Thorn Juggler, Nadia C	.10	.25
BT12S01 Revenger, Raging Form Dragon SP	30.00	80.00
BT12S02 Wolf Fang Liberator, Garmore SP	15.00	40.00
BT12S03 Eradicator, Vowing Saber Dragon Reverse SP	12.00	30.00
BT12S04 Demon Conquering Dragon, Dungaree Unlimited SP	6.00	15.00
BT12S05 Star-vader, Nebula Lord Dragon SP	20.00	50.00
BT12S06 Schwarzschild Dragon SP	8.00	20.00
BT12S07 Demon Marquis, Amon Reverse SP	12.00	30.00
BT12S08 Silver Thorn Dragon Queen, Luquier Reverse SP	30.00	80.00
BT12S09 King of Masks, Dantarian SP	8.00	20.00
BT12S10 Miracle Pop, Eva SP	10.00	25.00
BT12S11 Demon World Marquis, Amon SP	12.00	30.00
BT12S12 Blaster Dark Revenger SP	30.00	80.00

2014 Cardfight Vanguard Booster Set 13 Catastrophic Outbreak

COMPLETE SET (114)	500.00	650.00
RELEASED ON MAY 2, 2014		
BT13001 Cleanup Celestial, Ramiel Reverse RRR	12.00	30.00
BT13002 Shura Stealth Dragon, Kujikiricongo RRR	10.00	25.00
BT13003 Strongest Beast Deity, Ethics Buster Extreme RRR	15.00	40.00
BT13004 Deadliest Beast Deity, Ethics Buster Reverse RRR	12.00	30.00
BT13005 Dark Dimensional Robo, Reverse Daiyusha RRR	12.00	30.00
BT13006 Original Saver, Zero RRR	6.00	15.00
BT13007 Star-vader, Chaos Breaker Dragon RRR	30.00	80.00
BT13008 Blue Wave Dragon, Tetra-drive Dragon RRR	15.00	40.00
BT13009 Emergency Celestial, Danielle RR	.10	.25
BT13010 Shura Stealth Dragon, Kabukicongo RR	5.00	12.00
BT13011 Stealth Beast, Mijingakure RR	4.00	10.00
BT13012 Beast Deity, Brainy Papio RR	2.50	6.00
BT13013 Beast Deity, Solar Falcon RR	4.00	10.00
BT13014 Dimensional Robo, Daishield RR	6.00	15.00
BT13015 Star-vader, Colony Maker RR	6.00	15.00
BT13016 Lord of the Seven Seas, Nightmist RR	8.00	20.00
BT13017 Ice Prison Hades Emperor, Cocytus Reverse RR	10.00	25.00
BT13018 Cobalt Wave Dragon RR	12.00	30.00
BT13019 School Punisher, Leo-pald Reverse RR	6.00	15.00
BT13020 Honorary Professor, Chatnoir RR	8.00	20.00
BT13020 Honorary Professor, Chatnoir SP		
BT13021 Operation Celestial, Armen R	1.25	3.00
BT13022 Nursing Celestial, Narelle R	1.25	3.00
BT13023 Stealth Fiend, Daidarahoushi R	1.25	3.00
BT13024 Stealth Beast, Tamahagane R	.75	2.00
BT13025 Stealth Beast, Kuroko R	1.25	3.00
BT13026 Beast Deity, Max Beat R	1.25	3.00
BT13027 Energy Charger R	1.25	3.00
BT13028 Space Leviathan, Dogrumadra R	.40	1.00
BT13029 Dimensional Robo, Daiheart R	.30	.75
BT13030 Dimensional Robo, Daidriller R	1.25	3.00
BT13031 Dimensional Robo, Gocannon R	1.50	4.00
BT13032 Dimensional Robo, Daimagnum R	1.50	4.00
BT13033 Knight of Entropy R	8.00	20.00
BT13034 Paradise Elk R	1.25	3.00
BT13035 Earnest Star-vader, Selenium R	1.25	3.00
BT13036 Rotten Sea Necromancer, Barbaros R	.30	.75
BT13037 Sea Strolling Banshee R	1.25	3.00
BT13038 Tidal Assault R	.75	2.00
BT13039 Wheel Assault R	2.00	5.00
BT13040 Bubble Edge Dracokid R	1.25	3.00
BT13041 Abacus Bear R	2.00	5.00
BT13042 Wash Up Racoon R	.30	.75
BT13043 Dressing Barrage, Sathariel C	.10	.25
BT13044 Surgical Celestial, Batariel C	.10	.25
BT13045 Twinkle Knife Angel C	.10	.25
BT13046 Anesthesia Celestial, Rumael C	.10	.25
BT13047 Tender Pigeon C	.10	.25
BT13048 Puncture Celestial, Gadriel C	.10	.25
BT13049 Stealth Rogue of a Thousand Blades, Oborozakura C	.20	.50
BT13050 Stealth Dragon, Kokujyo C	.10	.25
BT13051 Stealth Fiend, Gozuou C	.10	.25
BT13052 Stealth Rogue of the Night, Sakurafubuki C	.20	.50
BT13053 Tempest Stealth Rogue, Fuuki C	.10	.25
BT13054 Stealth Dragon, Kodachi Fubuki C	.10	.25
BT13055 Stealth Fiend, Mezuou C	.10	.25
BT13056 Banquet Stealth Rogue, Shutenmaru C	.10	.25
BT13057 Stealth Dragon, Kurogane C	.30	.75
BT13058 Stealth Fiend, Ohtsuzura C	.10	.25
BT13059 Stealth Fiend, Zashikihime C	.10	.25
BT13060 Stealth Fiend, Mashiromomen C	.10	.25
BT13061 Death Army Commander C	.10	.25
BT13062 Beast Deity, Damned Leo C	.40	1.00
BT13063 Gattlingraizer C	.10	.25
BT13064 Beast Deity, Desert Gator C	.10	.25
BT13065 Beast Deity, Night Jackal C	.10	.25
BT13066 Beast Deity, Death Stinger C	.10	.25
BT13067 Beast Deity, Van Paurus C	.10	.25
BT13068 Beast Deity, Bright Cobra C	.40	1.00
BT13069 Beast Deity, Rescue Bunny C	.10	.25
BT13070 Fusion Monster, Bugreed C	.10	.25
BT13071 Shock Monster, Vipple C	.30	.75
BT13072 Heat Ray Monster, Gigabolt C	.10	.25
BT13073 Beam Monster, Raidrum C	.10	.25
BT13074 Hypnotism Monster, Nechoroly C	.10	.25
BT13075 Demon-eye Monster, Gorgon C	.10	.25
BT13076 Dimensional Robo, Daicrane C	.10	.25
BT13077 Dimensional Robo, Goflight C	.10	.25
BT13078 Dimensional Robo, Gorescue C	.10	.25
BT13079 Supergiant Lady Gunner C	.10	.25
BT13080 Devastation Star-vader, Tungsten C	.10	.25
BT13081 Prison Gate Star-vader, Palladium C	.10	.25
BT13082 Asteroid Belt Lady Gunner C	.10	.25
BT13083 Star-vader, Chaos Beat Dragon C	.10	.25
BT13084 Black Ring Chain, Pleiades C	.10	.25
BT13085 Dragon Corrode, Corrupt Dragon C	.10	.25
BT13086 Peter the Ghostie C	.10	.25
BT13087 Gunshot of Sorrow, Nightflare C	.10	.25
BT13088 Keen Eye Sky Trooper C	.10	.25
BT13089 Marine General of the Furious Tides, Myrtus C	.10	.25
BT13090 Battle Siren, Calista C	.10	.25
BT13091 Abyssal Sniper C		.25
BT13092 Deuterium Gun Dragon C	.10	.25
BT13093 Tidal Rescue Sea Turtle Soldier C	.10	.25
BT13094 Shallows Sweeper C	.10	.25
BT13095 Heavy Rush Dragon C	.10	.25
BT13096 Swimming Patrol Seal Soldier C	.10	.25
BT13097 Apprentice Gunner, Solon C	.10	.25
BT13098 Battle Siren, Mallika C	.30	.75
BT13099 Cosmic Cheetah C	.10	.25
BT13100 Whistle Hyena C	.10	.25
BT13101 Telescope Rabbit C	.10	.25
BT13102 Holder Hedgehog C	.10	.25
BT13S001 Cleanup Celestial, Ramiel Reverse SP	12.00	30.00
BT13S002 Shura Stealth Dragon, Kujikiricongo SP	10.00	25.00
BT13S003 Strongest Beast Deity, Ethics Buster Extreme SP	15.00	40.00
BT13S004 Deadliest Beast Deity, Ethics Buster Reverse SP	12.00	30.00
BT13S005 Dark Dimensional Robo, Reverse Daiyusha SP	12.00	30.00
BT13S006 Original Saver, Zero SP	6.00	15.00
BT13S007 Star-vader, Chaos Breaker Dragon SP	30.00	80.00
BT13S008 Blue Wave Dragon, Tetra-drive Dragon SP	15.00	40.00
BT13S016 Lord of the Seven Seas, Nightmist SP	8.00	20.00
BT13S017 Ice Prison Hades Emperor, Cocytus Reverse SP	6.00	15.00
BT13S019 School Punisher, Leo-pald Reverse SP	8.00	20.00

2014 Cardfight Vanguard Booster Set 14 Brilliant Strike

COMPLETE SET (114)	150.00	300.00
RELEASED ON JULY 18, 2014		
BT14001 Broken Heart Jewel Knight, Ashlei Reverse RRR	8.00	20.00
BT14002 Liberator of Bonds, Gancelot Zenith RRR	12.00	30.00
BT14003 Salvation Lion, Grand Ezel Scissors RRR	10.00	25.00
BT14004 Sunlight Goddess, Yatagarasu RRR	5.00	12.00
BT14005 Omniscience Regalia, Minerva RRR	10.00	25.00
BT14006 Dauntless Dominate Dragon "Reverse" RRR	6.00	15.00
BT14007 Eradicator, Ignition Dragon RRR	8.00	20.00
BT14008 Eradicator, Tempest Bolt Dragon RRR	2.50	6.00
BT14009 Sanctuary of Light, Planetal Dragon RR	2.00	5.00
BT14010 Banding Jewel Knight, Miranda RR	2.00	5.00
BT14011 Summoning Jewel Knight, Gloria RR	3.00	8.00
BT14012 Sword Formation Liberator, Igraine RR	2.50	6.00
BT14013 Goddess of the Shield, Aegis RR	2.50	6.00
BT14014 Covert Demonic Dragon, Kagurabloom RR	3.00	8.00
BT14015 Covert Demonic Dragon, Hyakki Vogue "Reverse" RR	2.50	6.00
BT14016 Silver Collar Snowstorm, Sasame RR	1.50	4.00
BT14017 Eradicator, Lorentz Force Dragon RR	1.25	3.00
BT14018 Maiden of Venus Trap "Reverse" RR	1.50	4.00
BT14019 Lord of the Deep Forests, Master Wisteria RR	2.00	5.00
BT14020 Red Rose Musketeer, Antonio RR	3.00	8.00
BT14021 Sanctuary of Light, Determinator R	.40	1.00
BT14022 Linking Jewel Knight, Tilda R	.40	1.00
BT14023 Sanctuary of Light, Planet Lancer R	.40	1.00
BT14024 Treasure Liberator, Calogrenant R	.40	1.00
BT14025 Blue Sky Liberator, Hengist R	.40	1.00
BT14026 Knight of Scorching Scales, Eliwood R	.40	1.00
BT14027 Battle Maiden, Mizuha R	.40	1.00
BT14028 Goddess of Trees, Jupiter R	.40	1.00
BT14029 Battle Maiden, Amenohoakari R	.40	1.00
BT14030 Vorpal Cannon Dragon R	.40	1.00
BT14031 Fire God, Agni R	.40	1.00
BT14032 Dominate Drive Dragon R	.40	1.00
BT14033 Dragon Knight, Akram R	.40	1.00
BT14034 Dragon Knight, Sadig R	.40	1.00
BT14035 Investigating Stealth Rogue, Amakusa R	.40	1.00
BT14036 Stealth Rogue of DemoniCHair, Gurenjishi R	.40	1.00
BT14037 Stealth Rogue of Umbrella, Sukerokku R	.40	1.00
BT14038 Certain Kill Eradicator, Ouei R	.40	1.00
BT14039 Spiritual Sphere Eradicator, Nata R	.40	1.00
BT14040 White Rose Musketeer, Alberto R	.40	1.00
BT14041 Maiden of Cherry Bloom R	.40	1.00
BT14042 Maiden of Cherry Stone R	.40	1.00
BT14043 Knight of Courage, Ector C	.10	.25
BT14044 Mystical Hermit C	.10	.25
BT14045 Jewel Knight, Treanme C	.10	.25
BT14046 Sanctuary of Light, Little Storm C	.10	.25
BT14047 Jewel Knight, Melme C	.10	.25
BT14048 Security Jewel Knight, Arwen C	.10	.25
BT14049 Desire Jewel Knight, Heloise C	.10	.25
BT14050 Jewel Knight, Noble Stinger C	.10	.25
BT14051 Jewel Knight, Sacred Unicorn C	.10	.25
BT14052 Jewel Knight, Opt Harpist C	.10	.25
BT14053 Jewel Knight, Hilmy C	.10	.25
BT14054 Sacred Guardian Beast, Ceryneian C	.10	.25
BT14055 Liberator, Burning Blow C	.10	.25
BT14056 Dorgal Liberator C	.10	.25
BT14057 Twin Holy Beast, Black Lion C	.10	.25
BT14058 Green Axe Knight, Taliesyn C	.10	.25
BT14059 Knight of Passion, Tor C	.10	.25
BT14060 Twin Holy Beast, White Lion C	.10	.25
BT14061 Flying Sword Liberator, Gorlois C	.10	.25
BT14062 Throw Blade Knight, Maleagant C	.10	.25
BT14063 Scarlet Lion Cub, Caria C	.10	.25
BT14064 Liberator, Grand Crack C	.10	.25
BT14065 Nappgal Liberator C	.10	.25
BT14066 Angelic Wiseman C	.10	.25
BT14067 Myth Guard, Fomalhaut C	.10	.25
BT14068 Grape Witch, Grappa C	.10	.25
BT14069 Myth Guard, Denebola C	.10	.25
BT14070 Battle Maiden, Kayanarumi C	.10	.25
BT14071 Orange Witch, Valencia C	.10	.25
BT14072 Myth Guard, Achernar C	.10	.25
BT14073 Goddess of Union, Juno C	.10	.25
BT14074 Ordain Owl C	.10	.25
BT14075 Spectral Sheep C	.10	.25
BT14076 Dragon Knight, Jalal C	.10	.25
BT14077 Flame Star Seal Dragon Knight C	.10	.25
BT14078 Dragon Knight, Lezar C	.10	.25
BT14079 Demonic Dragon Mage, Taksaka C	.10	.25
BT14080 Diable Drive Dragon C	.10	.25
BT14081 Explosive Claw Seal Dragon Knight C	.10	.25
BT14082 Calamity Tower Wyvern C	.10	.25
BT14083 Prison Egg Seal Dragon Knight C	.10	.25
BT14084 Lizard Soldier, Goraha C	.10	.25
BT14085 Fire of Repose, Gira C	.10	.25
BT14086 Wyvern Strike, Free C	.10	.25
BT14087 Dragon Dancer, Barbara C	.10	.25
BT14088 Stealth Beast, Chain Geek C	.10	.25
BT14089 Stealth Beast, Deathly Dagger C	.10	.25
BT14090 Stealth Rogue of Kite, Goemon C	.10	.25
BT14091 Stealth Rogue of Dagger, Yaiba C	.10	.25
BT14092 Stealth Rogue of Dark Night, Krog C	.10	.25
BT14093 Roaring Thunder Bow, Zafura C	.10	.25
BT14094 Plasma Scimitar Dragoon C	.10	.25
BT14095 Dragon Dancer, Agatha C	.10	.25
BT14096 Wyvern Strike, Zaroos C	.10	.25
BT14097 Wishing Djinn C	.10	.25
BT14098 Jackin' Pumpkin C	.10	.25
BT14099 Lotus Druid C	.10	.25
BT14100 Maiden of Physalis C	.10	.25
BT14101 Maiden of Egg Plant C	.10	.25
BT14102 Blue Rose Musketeer, Ernest C	.10	.25
BT14S01 Broken Heart Jewel Knight, Ashlei "Reverse" SP	8.00	20.00
BT14S02 Liberator of Bonds, Gancelot Zenith SP	12.00	30.00
BT14S03 Salvation Lion, Grand Ezel Scissors SP	10.00	25.00
BT14S04 Sunlight Goddess, Yatagarasu SP	6.00	15.00
BT14S05 Omniscience Regalia, Minerva SP	25.00	60.00
BT14S06 Dauntless Dominate Dragon "Reverse" SP	8.00	20.00
BT14S07 Eradicator, Ignition Dragon SP	15.00	40.00
BT14S08 Eradicator, Tempest Bolt Dragon SP	6.00	15.00
BT14S09 Sanctuary of Light, Planetal Dragon SP	8.00	20.00
BT14S10 Banding Jewel Knight, Miranda SP	12.00	30.00
BT14S15 Covert DemoniCDragon, Hyakki Vogue "Reverse" SP	5.00	12.00
BT14S18 Maiden of Venus Trap "Reverse" SP	6.00	15.00

2014 Cardfight Vanguard Booster Set 15 Infinite Rebirth

COMPLETE SET (115)	150.00	300.00
RELEASED ON SEPTEMBER 19, 2014		
BT15000 Star-vader, "Omega" Glendios RRR	5.00	8.00
BT15001 Revenger, Desperate Dragon RRR	3.00	5.00
BT15002 Revenger, Dragruler Phantom RRR	6.00	10.00
BT15003 Liberator, Monarch Sanctuary Alfred RRR	5.00	8.00
BT15004 Dragonic Overlord RRR	12.00	20.00
BT15005 Dragonic Overlord "The Re-birth" RRR	6.00	10.00
BT15006 Star-vader, "Reverse" Cradle RRR	3.00	5.00
BT15007 Silver Thorn Dragon Empress, Venus Luquier RRR	10.00	15.00
BT15008 Blue Storm Karma Dragon, Maelstrom "Reverse" RRR	5.00	8.00
BT15009 Revenger, Bloodmaster RR	1.75	3.00
BT15010 Hellrage Revenger, Quesal RR	3.00	5.00
BT15011 Black-winged Swordbreaker RR	1.75	3.00
BT15013 Liberator, Star Rain Trumpeter RR	3.00	5.00
BT15014 Dragonic Burnout RR	10.00	15.00
BT15015 Dragon Knight, Gimel RR	4.00	6.00
BT15016 Star-vader, Freezeray Dragon RR	3.00	5.00
BT15017 Blue Storm Guardian Dragon, Icefall Dragon RR	3.00	5.00
BT15018 Machining Spark Hercules RR	5.00	8.00
BT15019 Unrivaled Blade Rogue, Cyclomatooth RR	8.00	12.00
BT15020 Machining Ladybug RR	3.00	5.00
BT15021 Sharp Fang Witch, Fodla R	.20	.30
BT15022 Cursed Lancer R	.20	.30
BT15023 Wily Revenger, Mana R	.20	.30
BT15024 Judgebau Revenger R	.20	.30
BT15025 Red Rainbow Liberator, Balin R	.20	.30
BT15026 White Rainbow Liberator, Balan R	.20	.30
BT15027 Starry Skies Liberator, Guinevere R	.20	.30
BT15028 Yearning Liberator, Arum R	.20	.30
BT15029 Lizard Soldier, Fargo R	.20	.30
BT15030 Star-vader, Magnet Hollow R	.20	.30
BT15031 Star-vader, Cold Death Dragon R	.20	.30
BT15032 Taboo Star-vader, Rubidium R	.20	.30
BT15033 Star-vader, Ruin Magician R	.20	.30
BT15034 Star-vader, Worldline Dragon R	.20	.30
BT15035 Nightmare Doll, Carroll R	.20	.30
BT15036 Silver Thorn Assistant, Zelma R	.20	.30
BT15037 Marinefall Dragon R	.20	.30
BT15038 Blue Storm Marine General, Gregorios R	.20	.30
BT15039 Blue Storm Battle Princess, Crysta Elizabeth R	.20	.30
BT15040 Blue Storm Cadet, Marios R	.20	.30
BT15041 Machining Red Soldier R	.20	.30
BT15042 Machining Locust R	.20	.30
BT15043 Gigantech Keeper C	.10	.15
BT15044 Overcoming Revenger, Rukea C	.10	.15
BT15045 Demon World Castle, Sturmangriff C	.10	.15
BT15046 Sharp Point Revenger, Shadow Lancer C	.10	.15
BT15047 Self-control Revenger, Rakia C	.10	.15
BT15048 Eloquence Revenger, Glonn C	.10	.15
BT15049 Wing Edge Panther C	.10	.15
BT15050 Guutgal C	.10	.15
BT15051 History Liberator, Merron C	.10	.15
BT15052 Mastigal C	.10	.15
BT15053 Sharp Point Liberator, Gold Lancer C	.10	.15
BT15054 Physical Force Liberator, Zorron C	.10	.15
BT15055 Lucky Sign Rabbit C	.10	.15
BT15056 Flower Gardener C	.10	.15
BT15057 Demonic Dragon Berserker, Houkenyasha C	.10	.15
BT15058 Dragon Knight, Dalette C	.10	.15
BT15059 Wyvern Strike, Jiet C	.10	.15
BT15060 Eternal Bringer Griffin C	.10	.15
BT15061 Violence Horn Dragon C	.10	.15
BT15062 Dragon Knight, Razer C	.10	.15
BT15063 Lizard Soldier, Grom C	.10	.15
BT15064 Demonic Dragon Mage, Apalala C	.10	.15
BT15065 Treasure Hunt Dracokid C	.10	.15
BT15066 Fire of Determination, Puralis C	.10	.15
BT15067 Dragon Dancer, Therese C	.10	.15
BT15068 Soundless Archer, Conductance C	.10	.15
BT15069 Negligible Hydra C	.10	.15
BT15070 Planet Collapse Star-vader, Erbium C	.10	.15
BT15071 Imaginary Orthos C	.10	.15
BT15072 Engraving Star-vader, Praseodymium C	.10	.15
BT15073 Origin Fist, Big Bang C	.10	.15
BT15074 Star-vader, Sparkdoll C	.10	.15
BT15075 Star-vader, Jeiratail C	.10	.15
BT15076 Star-vader, Brushcloud C	.10	.15
BT15077 Recollection Star-vader, Tellurium C	.10	.15
BT15078 Silver Thorn, Upright Lion C	.10	.15
BT15079 Miss Direction C	.10	.15
BT15080 Brassie Bunny C	.10	.15
BT15081 Silver Thorn Beast Tamer, Emile C	.10	.15
BT15082 Titan of the Capturing Arm C	.10	.15
BT15083 Blue Storm Marine General, Lysandros C	.10	.15
BT15084 Blue Storm Soldier, Tempest Assault C	.10	.15
BT15085 Blue Storm Marine General, Spyros C	.10	.15
BT15086 Mobile Battleship, Cetus C	.10	.15
BT15087 Blue Storm Marine General, Hermes C	.10	.15
BT15088 Blue Storm Soldier, Tempest Blader C	.10	.15
BT15089 Swim Patrol Jellyfish Soldier C	.10	.15
BT15090 Battle Siren, Ketty C	3.00	.15
BT15091 Blue Storm Soldier, Missile Trooper C	.10	.15
BT15092 Blue Storm Battle Princess, Doria C	.10	.15
BT15093 Angler Soldier of the Blue Storm Fleet C	.10	.15
BT15094 Blue Storm Soldier, Kitchen Sailor C	.10	.15
BT15095 Machining Tarantula C	.10	.15
BT15096 Machining Papilio C	.10	.15
BT15097 Machining Black Soldier C	.10	.15
BT15098 Machining Caucasus C	.10	.15
BT15099 Machining Little Bee C	.10	.15
BT15100 Machining Scorpion C	.10	.15
BT15101 Machining Bombyx C	.10	.15
BT15102 Machining Cicada C	.10	.15
BT15S01 Revenger, Desperate Dragon SP	3.00	5.00
BT15S02 Revenger, Dragruler Phantom SP	15.00	25.00
BT15S03 Liberator, Monarch Sanctuary Alfred SP	15.00	25.00
BT15S04 Dragonic Overlord SP	25.00	40.00
BT15S05 Dragonic Overlord "The Re-birth" SP	12.00	20.00
BT15S06 Star-vader, "Reverse" Cradle SP	10.00	15.00
BT15S07 Silver Thorn Dragon Empress, Venus Luquier SP	20.00	30.00
BT15S08 Blue Storm Karma Dragon, Maelstrom "Reverse" SP	10.00	15.00
BT15S09 Liberator, Star Rain Trumpeter SP	3.00	5.00
BT15S10 Dragonic Burnout SP	12.00	20.00
BT15S11 Machiningark Hercules SP	6.00	10.00
BT15S12 Unrivaled Blade Rogue, Cyclomatooth SP	6.00	10.00
BT15012 Liberator, Holy Shine Dragon RR	6.00	10.00

2014 Cardfight Vanguard Booster Set 16 Legion of Dragons and Blades Version E

COMPLETE SET (116)	300.00	450.00
RELEASED ON DECEMBER 19, 2014		
BT16001 Seeker, Sing Saver Dragon RRR	10.00	15.00
BT16002 Honest Seeker, Egbert RRR	3.00	5.00
BT16003 Brawler, Bigbang Knuckle Dragon RRR	10.00	15.00
BT16004 Brawler, Wild Rush Dragon RRR	6.00	10.00
BT16005 Ultimate Raizer Mega Flare RRR	12.00	20.00
BT16006 Metalborg, Sin Buster RRR	8.00	12.00
BT16007 Emerald Blaze RRR	3.00	5.00
BT16008 Peony Musketeer, Martina RRR	8.00	12.00
BT16009 Blaster Blade Seeker RR	8.00	12.00
BT16010 Guardian Law Seeker, Shiron RR	6.00	10.00
BT16011 Brawler, Bigbang Slash Dragon RR	3.00	5.00
BT16012 Hardship Brawler, Toshu RR	3.00	5.00
BT16013 Phoenix Raizer Drill Wing RR	3.00	5.00
BT16014 Shieldraizer RR	3.00	5.00
BT16015 Metalborg, Dryon RR	8.00	12.00
BT16016 Metalborg, Bri Knuckle RR	3.00	5.00
BT16017 Bloody Ogre RR	3.00	5.00
BT16018 Baron Amadeus RR	3.00	5.00
BT16019 Licorice Musketeer, Vera RR	20.00	30.00
BT16020 Moth Orchid Musketeer, Christie RR	4.00	6.00
BT16021 Crossbow Seeker, Gildas R	.20	.30
BT16022 Flail Seeker, Hasbasado R	.20	.30
BT16023 Glynngal Seeker R	.20	.30
BT16025 Brawler Youjin R	.20	.30
BT16026 Threatening Brawler, Koumei R	.20	.30
BT16027 Tonfa Wielding Brawler, Aak R	.20	.30
BT16028 Brawler, Fighting Dracokid R	.20	.30
BT16029 Ultimate Raizer Dual Flare R	.20	.30
BT16030 Phoenix Raizer Flame Wing R	.20	.30
BT16031 Tankraizer R	.20	.30
BT16032 Energyraizer R	.20	.30
BT16033 Metalborg, Ur Buster R	.20	.30
BT16034 Metalborg, Lionetter R	.20	.30
BT16035 Metalborg, Iunbot R	.20	.30
BT16036 Metalborg, Black Boy R	.20	.30
BT16037 Silver Blaze R	.20	.30
BT16038 Frozen Ogre R	.20	.30
BT16039 Machine Gun Gloria R	.20	.30
BT16040 Peony Musketeer, Thule R	.20	.30
BT16041 Licorice Musketeer, Saul R	.20	.30
BT16042 Camellia Musketeer, Tamara R	.20	.30
BT16043 Seeker, Gigantech Driver C	.15	.25
BT16044 Sky Bow Seeker, Morvi C	.15	.25
BT16045 Shibelgal Seeker C	.15	.25
BT16046 Sky Arrow Seeker, Lunete C	.15	.25
BT16047 Seeker, Tranquil Unicorn C	.15	.25
BT16048 Seeker, Hartmy C	.15	.25
BT16049 Seeker, Harold Breath Dragon C	.15	.25
BT16050 Seeker, Bucephalus C	.15	.25
BT16051 Brawler, Headband of Grid C	.15	.25
BT16052 Wild Brawler, Shugi C	.15	.25
BT16053 Demonic Dragon Brawler, Kadloo C	.15	.25
BT16054 Brawler, Igo C	.15	.25
BT16055 Brawler, Dropkick Wyvern C	.15	.25
BT16056 Fledging Phoenix Brawler, Koutenshou C	.15	.25
BT16057 Brawler of Heavens, Youzen C	.15	.25
BT16058 Brawler of Battles, Haoka C	.15	.25
BT16059 Nobody From Orimecha C	.15	.25
BT16060 Marine Raizer Anchor Arm C	.15	.25
BT16061 Marine Raizer High Torpedo C	.15	.25
BT16062 Wingraizer C	.15	.25
BT16063 Rapidraizer C	.15	.25
BT16064 Cannonraizer C	.15	.25
BT16065 Carvingraizer C	.15	.25
BT16066 Reserveraizer C	.15	.25
BT16067 Space Pit C	.15	.25
BT16068 Raizer Pilot, Huey C	.15	.25
BT16069 Meteoraizer C	.15	.25
BT16070 Raizer Crew C	.15	.25
BT16071 Raizer Girl, Kate C	.15	.25
BT16072 Subliminal Gray C	.15	.25
BT16073 Metalborg, Sandstorm C	.15	.25
BT16074 Metalborg, Cezalion C	.15	.25
BT16075 Metalborg, Digarion C	.15	.25
BT16076 Metalborg, Russell Blizzard C	.15	.25
BT16077 Metalborg, Bull Dump C	.15	.25
BT16078 Metalborg, Express C	.15	.25
BT16079 Metalborg, Mist Ghost C	.15	.25
BT16080 Metalborg, Black Doctor C	.15	.25
BT16081 Metalborg, Death Blade C	.15	.25
BT16082 Metalborg, Mech Rogue C	.15	.25
BT16083 Metalborg, Battle Roller C	.15	.25
BT16084 Metalborg, Black Nurse C	.15	.25
BT16085 Metalborg, Devil Loader C	.15	.25
BT16086 Metalborg, Operator Kirika C	.15	.25
BT16087 Dudley Moses C	.15	.25
BT16088 Dudley Monti C	.15	.25
BT16089 Jumbo the Stungun C	.15	.25
BT16090 Treasured, Mirage Panther C	.15	.25
BT16091 Oasis Boy C	.15	.25
BT16092 Cyclone Johnny C	.15	.25
BT16093 Cheer Girl, Pauline C	.15	.25
BT16094 Cheer Girl, Adared C	.15	.25
BT16095 Carnation Musketeer, Richard C	.15	.25
BT16096 Carnation Musketeer, Berutti C	.15	.25
BT16097 Bellflower Musketeer, Ewelina C	.15	.25
BT16098 Narcissus Musketeer, Joachim C	.15	.25
BT16099 Hydrangea Musketeer, Ivar C	.15	.25
BT16100 Anemone Musketeer, Susanna C	.15	.25
BT16101 Baby's Breath Musketeer, Laisa C	.15	.25
BT16102 Lotus Musketeer, Liana C	.15	.25
BT16L01 Seeker, Sing Saver Dragon LR	20.00	30.00
BT16L02 Blaster Blade Seeker LR	20.00	30.00
BT16S01 Seeker, Sing Saver Dragon SP	50.00	75.00
BT16S02 Brawler, Bigbang Knuckle Dragon SP	15.00	25.00
BT16S03 Ultimate Raizer Mega Flare SP	40.00	60.00
BT16S04 Metalborg, Sin Buster SP	12.00	20.00
BT16S05 Emerald Blaze SP	8.00	12.00
BT16S06 Peony Musketeer, Martina SP	20.00	30.00
BT16S07 Blaster Blade Seeker SP	10.00	15.00
BT16S08 Brawler, Bigbang Slash Dragon SP	30.00	50.00
BT16S09 Ultimate Raizer Dual Flare SP	20.00	30.00
BT16S10 Metalborg, Ur Buster SP	12.00	20.00
BT16S11 Silver Blaze SP	25.00	40.00
BT16S12 Peony Musketeer, Thule SP	20.00	30.00
BT16-024 Advance Party Seeker, File R	.20	.30

2015 Cardfight Vanguard Booster Set 17 Blazing Perdition Version E

COMPLETE SET (164)	150.00	300.00
RELEASED ON JANUARY 23, 2015		
BT17001 Bluish Flame Liberator, Prominence Core RRR	6.00	15.00
BT17002 Murasame Liberator, Coil RRR	.75	2.00
BT17003 Perdition Dragon, Pain Laser Dragon RRR	3.00	8.00
BT17004 Perdition Dragon, Vortex Dragonewt RRR	6.00	15.00
BT17005 Brawler, Big Bang Knuckle Buster RRR	8.00	20.00
BT17006 Star-vader, Imaginary Plane Dragon RRR	1.25	3.00
BT17007 Star-vader, Dark Zodiac RRR	1.50	4.00
BT17008 Blue Storm Wave Dragon, Tetra-burst Dragon RRR	5.00	12.00
BT17009 Seeker, Purgation Breath Dragon RR	3.00	8.00
BT17010 Locus Liberator, Asclepius RR	6.00	15.00
BT17011 Light Formation Liberator, Erdre RR	5.00	12.00
BT17012 Perdition Dragon, Menace Laser Dragon RR	1.25	3.00
BT17013 Perdition Dragon, Rampart Dragon RR	.40	1.00
BT17014 Ancient Dragon, Tyrannoquake RR	1.50	4.00
BT17015 Ancient Dragon, Rockmine RR	2.50	6.00
BT17016 Ionization Star-vader, Hafnium RR	.40	1.00
BT17017 Star-vader, Rejection Dragon RR	.75	2.00
BT17018 Young Pirate Noble, Pinot Noir RR	.40	1.00
BT17019 Reef Banshee RR	.40	1.00
BT17020 Blue Storm Battle Princess, Electra RR	.75	2.00
BT17021 Brave Stride Seeker, Cherin R	.40	1.00
BT17022 Shower Liberator, Trahern R	.40	1.00
BT17023 Liberator, Lawful Trumpeter R	1.00	2.50
BT17024 Twin Axe Liberator, Bassia R	.40	1.00
BT17025 Koronagal Liberator R	1.25	3.00
BT17026 Perdition Dragon, Heat Wing Dragon R	.40	1.00
BT17027 Perdition Dragon, Whirlwind Dragon R	.40	1.00
BT17028 Perdition Dragon, Tinder Spear Dracokid R	.40	1.00
BT17029 Ancient Dragon, Magmaarmor R	.40	1.00
BT17030 Ancient Dragon, Tyrannobite R	1.25	3.00
BT17031 Ancient Dragon, Night Armor R	.40	1.00
BT17032 Brawler, Big Bang Slash Buster R	.40	1.00
BT17033 Star-vader, Astro Reaper R	.40	1.00
BT17034 Flash Gun Star-vader, Osmium R	.75	2.00
BT17035 Star-vader, Volt Line R	.40	1.00
BT17036 Star-vader, Robin Knight R	.40	1.00
BT17037 Witch Doctor of the Dead Sea, Negrobolt R	.40	1.00
BT17038 Pirate Belle, Pinot Blanc R	.40	1.00
BT17039 Dragon Undead, Ghoul Dragon R	.40	1.00
BT17040 Blue Storm Marine General, Zaharias R	.40	1.00
BT17041 Blue Storm Marine General, Ianis R	.40	1.00
BT17042 Blue Storm Marine General, Starless R	.40	1.00
BT17043 Seeker, Sebrumy C	.10	.25
BT17044 Jewel Knight, Sabremy C	2.00	5.00
BT17045 Lake Maiden, Lien C	.25	.60
BT17046 Composed Seeker, Lucius C	.75	2.00
BT17047 Seeker, Platina Rider C	.10	.25
BT17048 Spear-line Liberator, Marius C	.10	.25
BT17049 Liberator, Feather Lion C	.10	.25
BT17050 Liberator, Holy Wizard C	.10	.25
BT17051 Nalegal Liberator C	.15	.40
BT17052 Liberator, Bright Bicorn C		.60
BT17053 Liberator, Holy Acolyte C	.20	.50
BT17054 Liberator, Blessing Arrow Angel C	.20	.50
BT17055 Steel Blade Liberator, Alwilla C	.20	.50
BT17056 Ketchgal Liberator C	.10	.25
BT17057 Perdition Berserker, Jaratkaru C	.10	.25
BT17058 Perdition Dragon Knight, Jamileh C	.10	.25
BT17059 Perdition Mage, Asticah C	.10	.25
BT17060 Perdition Dragon Knight, Sabha C	.10	.25
BT17061 Perdition Wyvern, Boom C	.10	.25
BT17062 Perdition Battler, Maleikoh C	.10	.25
BT17063 Perdition Battler, Maleisei C	.10	.25
BT17064 Seal Dragon Sprite, Mulciber C	.10	.25
BT17065 Perdition Dragon Knight, Gia C	.10	.25
BT17066 Perdition Wyvern, Grue C	.10	.25
BT17067 Perdition Dragon Knight, Sahar C	.10	.25
BT17068 Perdition Dragon, Buster Rain Dragon C	.10	.25
BT17069 Perdition Sprite, Flarelooper C	.10	.25
BT17070 Perdition Dancer, Agafia C	.10	.25
BT17071 Perdition Cleric, Hakkai C	.10	.25
BT17072 Ancient Dragon Twin Axe Warrior C	.10	.25
BT17073 Ancient Dragon, Tyrannoblaze C	.10	.25
BT17074 Ancient Dragon, Crestrunner C	.10	.25
BT17075 Ancient Dragon, Babysaurus C	.10	.25
BT17076 Ancient Dragon Flame Maiden C	.10	.25
BT17077 Ancient Dragon, Chaoticbird C	.10	.25
BT17078 Spirited Brawler, Kohkin C	.10	.25
BT17079 Eradicator, Egghelm Dracokid C	.10	.25
BT17080 Sturdy Feet Brawler, Tohkon C	.10	.25
BT17081 Brawler, Volt Knuckle Dracokid C	.10	.25
BT17082 Brawler, Heavy Trailer Dragon C	.10	.25
BT17083 Star-vader, Metal Griffin C	.10	.25
BT17084 Emission Line Star-vader, Antimony C	.10	.25
BT17085 Ray Star-vader, Samarium C	.10	.25
BT17086 Eclipse Star-vader, Charcoal C	.10	.25
BT17087 Deception Star-vader, Nickel C	.10	.25
BT17088 Star-vader, Atom Router C	.10	.25
BT17089 Star-vader, Butterfly Effect C	.10	.25
BT17090 Star-vader, Null Chameleon C	.10	.25
BT17091 Shockwave Star-vader, Dysprosium C	.10	.25
BT17092 Boatswain, Arman C	.10	.25
BT17093 Brutal Shade C	.10	.25
BT17094 Cleaving Shade C	.10	.25
BT17095 Fledgling Pirate, Pinot Gris C	.10	.25
BT17096 Jimmy the Ghostie C	.10	.25
BT17097 Hungry Mimick C	.10	.25
BT17098 Performing Zombie C	.10	.25
BT17099 Mako Shark Soldier of the Blue Storm Fleet C	.10	.25
BT17100 Blue Storm Soldier, Tempest Boarder C	.10	.25
BT17101 Mola Mola Soldier of the Blue Storm Fleet C	.10	.25
BT17102 Blue Storm Cadet, Anos C	.10	.25
BT17L01 Bluish Flame Liberator, Prominence Core LR	10.00	25.00
BT17L02 Oath Liberator, Aglovale LR	12.00	30.00
BT17L03 Perdition Dragon, Vortex Dragonewt LR	5.00	12.00
BT17L13 Perdition Dragon, Whirlwind Dragon LR	12.00	30.00
BT17S01 Bluish Flame Liberator, Prominence Core SP	12.00	30.00
BT17S02 Murasame Liberator, Coil SP	3.00	8.00
BT17S03 Perdition Dragon, Pain Laser Dragon SP	6.00	15.00
BT17S04 Perdition Dragon, Vortex Dragonewt SP	2.50	6.00
BT17S05 Brawler, Big Bang Knuckle Buster SP	6.00	15.00
BT17S06 Star-vader, Imaginary Plane Dragon SP	10.00	25.00
BT17S07 Star-vader, Dark Zodiac SP	8.00	20.00
BT17S08 Blue Storm Wave Dragon, Tetra-burst Dragon SP	15.00	40.00
BT17S09 Seeker, Purgation Breath Dragon SP	4.00	10.00
BT17S10 Perdition Dragon, Menace Laser Dragon SP	4.00	10.00

BT17S11 Ancient Dragon, Tyrannoquake SP 12.00 30.00
BT17S12 Young Pirate Noble, Pinot Noir SP 6.00 15.00

2015 Cardfight Vanguard G Booster Set 1 Generation Stride

RELEASED ON MARCH 13, 2015
GBT01001 Interdimensional Dragon, Chronoscommand Dragon GR 2.00 3.00
GBT01002 Holy Dragon, Saint Blow Dragon RRR 1.50 2.50
GBT01003 Sword Deity of the Thunder Break, Takemikazuchi RRR 1.25 2.00
GBT01004 Supreme Heavenly Battle Deity, Susanoo RRR .60 1.00
GBT01005 Flame Emperor Dragon King, Root Flare Dragon RRR 1.25 2.00
GBT01006 Dragonic Overlord The X RRR 15.00 25.00
GBT01007 Meteorkaiser, Viktoplasma RRR 2.50 4.00
GBT01008 Exxtreme Battler, Victor RRR 1.50 2.50
GBT01009 Interdimensional Dragon, Ragnaclock Dragon RRR 2.00 3.00
GBT01010 Knight of Fragment RR .30 .50
GBT01011 Holy Knight Guardian RR .30 .50
GBT01012 Diviner, Kuroikazuchi RR .50 .75
GBT01013 Arbitrator, Amenosagiri RR 2.50 4.00
GBT01014 Dragonic Blademaster RR .50 .75
GBT01015 Twilight Arrow Dragon RR .50 .75
GBT01016 Protect Orb Dragon RR 3.00 5.00
GBT01017 Cool Hank RR 1.00 1.50
GBT01018 Lady Cyclone RR .30 .50
GBT01019 Fatewheel Dragon RR .30 .50
GBT01020 Relic Master Dragon RR .30 .50
GBT01021 Steam Maiden, Arlim RR 2.00 3.00
GBT01022 Knight of Great Spear R .15 .25
GBT01023 Starlight Violinist R .15 .25
GBT01024 Laurel Knight, Sicilus R .15 .25
GBT01025 Soaring Auspicious Beast, Qilin R .15 .25
GBT01026 Obligate Robin R .15 .25
GBT01027 Tankman Mode Morning Star R .15 .25
GBT01028 Divine Sword, Ame-no-Murakumo R .60 1.00
GBT01029 Imperial Shrine Guard, Hahiki R .15 .25
GBT01030 Divine Dragon Knight, Mahmud R .15 .25
GBT01031 Flame of Strength, Aetniki R .75 1.25
GBT01032 Lava Flow Dragon R 1.00 1.50
GBT01033 Dragon Monk Gyokuryu R .15 .25
GBT01034 Wyvernkid Ragla R .15 .25
GBT01035 Meteorkaiser, Vikt Ten R .40 .60
GBT01036 Muscle Shriek R .15 .25
GBT01037 Masuraraizer R .15 .25
GBT01038 Extreme Battler, Arashid R .15 .25
GBT01039 Ruin Disposal Dragon R .15 .25
GBT01040 Steam Knight, Puzur Ili R .15 .25
GBT01041 Steam Breath Dragon R .15 .25
GBT01042 Steam Scalar, Gigi R .15 .25
GBT01043 Miracle Element, Atmos R .15 .25
GBT01044 Knight of Militarism, Marianus C .10 .15
GBT01045 Seeker, Proud Roar Lion C .10 .15
GBT01046 Gigantech Shot-Putter C .20 .30
GBT01047 Knight of Shield Bash C .10 .15
GBT01048 Bravogal Seeker C .10 .15
GBT01049 Knight of Drawn Sword C .10 .15
GBT01050 Knight of Flash C .10 .15
GBT01051 Encourage Angel C .10 .15
GBT01052 Battle Sister, Mille-feuille C .10 .15
GBT01053 Imperial Shrine Guard, Asuha C .10 .15
GBT01054 Diviner, Shinatsuhiko C .10 .15
GBT01055 Tankman Mode Beam Cannon C .10 .15
GBT01056 Battle Sister, Marshmallow C .10 .15
GBT01057 Imperial Shrine Guard, Tsunagai C .10 .15
GBT01058 Diviner, Kuebiko C .10 .15
GBT01059 Battle Sister, Lollipop C .10 .15
GBT01060 Able Neil C .10 .15
GBT01061 Assault Dive Eagle C .10 .15
GBT01062 Huge Harvest Daikokuten C .10 .15
GBT01063 Diviner, Sukunahikona C .10 .15
GBT01064 Paisley Magus C .10 .15
GBT01065 Nebula Witch, NoNo C .30 .50
GBT01066 Double Perish Dragon C .10 .15
GBT01067 Wyvern Strike, Doha C .10 .15
GBT01068 Dragon Knight, Jabad C .10 .15
GBT01069 Hulk Roar Dragon C .10 .15
GBT01070 Perdition Berserker, Heileita C .10 .15
GBT01071 Dragon Knight, Tanaz C .10 .15
GBT01072 Wyvern Strike, Garan C .10 .15
GBT01073 Dragon Knight, Monireh C .10 .15
GBT01074 Perdition Dancer, Anna C .10 .15
GBT01075 Dragon Knight, Rashid C .10 .15
GBT01076 Magnum Shot Dracokid C .10 .15
GBT01077 Dragon Dancer, Ekaterina C .10 .15
GBT01078 Mother Orb Dragon C .10 .15
GBT01079 Lizard Soldier, Beira C 1.00 1.50
GBT01080 Super Extreme Leader, Mu Sashi C .10 .15
GBT01081 Extreme Battler, Kenbeam C .10 .15
GBT01082 Extreme Battler, Gunzork C .10 .15
GBT01083 Extreme Battler, Sazanda C .30 .50
GBT01084 Starlight Hedgehog C .10 .15
GBT01085 Extreme Battler, Kendhol C .10 .15
GBT01086 Aura Baller C .10 .15
GBT01087 Katanaraizer C .10 .15
GBT01088 Beast Deity, Frog Master C .10 .15
GBT01089 Final Wrench C .10 .15
GBT01090 Extreme Battler, Runbhol C .10 .15
GBT01091 Extreme Battler, Hajimaru C .10 .15
GBT01092 Extreme Battler, Zanbara C .10 .15
GBT01093 Drone Baron C .10 .15
GBT01094 Shadow Clone, Gesoraz C .10 .15
GBT01095 Ring Girl, Ai C .10 .15
GBT01096 Energy Girl C 2.50 4.00
GBT01097 Steam Maiden, Elul C .10 .15
GBT01098 Mechanized Gear Tiger C .10 .15
GBT01099 Summit Crest Gear Wolf C .10 .15
GBT01100 Steam Rider, Dizcal C .10 .15
GBT01101 Timepiece Dracokid C .10 .15
GBT01102 Steam Battler, Meshda C .10 .15
GBT01103 Wakey Wakey Worker C .10 .15

2015 Cardfight Vanguard G Booster Set 2 Soaring Ascent of Gale and Blossom

COMPLETE SET (115) 150.00 300.00
RELEASED ON MAY 22, 2015
GBT02001 Flower Princess of Spring's Beginning, Primavera GR 3.00 5.00
GBT02002 Divine Knight of Flashing Flame, Samuel RRR 5.00 8.00
GBT02003 Conquering Supreme Dragon, Conquest Dragon RRR 15.00 25.00
GBT02004 Dragonic Vanquisher RRR 1.75 3.00
GBT02005 Interdimensional Dragon, Fateride Dragon RRR 5.00 8.00
GBT02006 Marine General of Heavenly Silk, Lambros RRR 25.00 40.00
GBT02007 Omniscience Dragon, Managarmr RRR 6.00 10.00
GBT02008 Famous Professor, Bigbelly RRR 4.00 6.00
GBT02009 Sacred Tree Dragon, Jingle Flower Dragon RRR 12.00 20.00
GBT02010 Knight of Refinement, Benizel RR 5.00 8.00
GBT02011 Bringer of Dreams, Belenus RR 4.00 6.00
GBT02012 Dragonic Kaiser Crimson RR 1.75 3.00
GBT02013 Voltage Horn Dragon RR 3.00 5.00
GBT02014 Dragon Dancer, Anastasia RR 8.00 12.00
GBT02015 Glimmer Breath Dragon RR 8.00 12.00
GBT02016 Heart Thump Worker RR 10.00 15.00
GBT02017 Blue Storm Marine General, Michael RR .75 1.25
GBT02018 Ocean Keeper, Plato RR 1.75 3.00
GBT02019 Crayon Tiger RR 4.00 6.00
GBT02020 Contradictory Instructor, Shell Master RR 3.00 5.00
GBT02021 Maiden of Passionflower RR 2.50 4.00
GBT02022 Hidden Sage, Miron R .60 1.00
GBT02023 Lightning Dragon Knight, Zorras R 1.25 2.00
GBT02024 Mighty Bolt Dragoon R .60 1.00
GBT02025 Harbringer Dracokid R .60 1.00
GBT02026 Nixie Number Dragon R .60 1.00
GBT02027 Steam Knight, Xang R .60 1.00
GBT02028 Steam Mage, En-narda R .60 1.00
GBT02029 Marine General of the Wave Sword Slash, Max R .60 1.00
GBT02030 Blue Storm Marine General, Milos R .60 1.00
GBT02031 Kelpie Rider, Nikki R 1.25 2.00
GBT02032 Battle Siren, Orthia R .60 1.00
GBT02033 Immortality fessor, Phoeniciax R .60 1.00
GBT02034 Hot-blooded Professor, Guru Tiger R .60 1.00
GBT02035 Capable Assistant, Guru Wolf R .60 1.00
GBT02036 Set Square Penguin R .60 1.00
GBT02037 Diligent Assistant, Minibelly R .60 1.00
GBT02038 Balloon Raccoon R .60 1.00
GBT02039 Maiden of Frilldrod R .60 1.00
GBT02040 Knight of Transience, Maredream R .60 1.00
GBT02041 Valkyrie of Reclamation, Padmini R .60 1.00
GBT02042 Knight of Transience, Marehope R .60 1.00
GBT02043 Snow Element, Blizza R 1.75 3.00
GBT02044 Pure Wind Jewel Knight, Kymbelinus C .15 .25
GBT02045 Heat Wind Jewel Knight, Cymbeline C .15 .25
GBT02046 Jaggy Shot Dragoon C .15 .25
GBT02047 Roar of Chaos Deity, Rudra C .15 .25
GBT02048 Wyvern Strike, Bargs C .15 .25
GBT02049 Heat Blade Dragoon C .15 .25
GBT02050 Two-sword Eradicator, Koenshak C .15 .25
GBT02051 Undying Eradicator, Schub C .15 .25
GBT02052 Demonic Dragon Berserker, Chatura C .15 .25
GBT02053 Thunder Shout Dragoon C .15 .25
GBT02054 Assault Eradicator, Saikei C .15 .25
GBT02055 Wyvern Strike, Pyglma C .15 .25
GBT02056 Plasma Dance Dragoon C .15 .25
GBT02057 Djinn of Paranoia C .15 .25
GBT02058 Deity of Love, Kama C .15 .25
GBT02059 Ionization Eradicator, Capnis C .15 .25
GBT02060 Dragon Dancer, Vianne C .15 .25
GBT02061 Dimension Expulsion Colossus C .15 .25
GBT02062 Steam Maiden, Ishin C .15 .25
GBT02063 Distance-running Gear Horse C .15 .25
GBT02064 Iron-fanged Gear Hound C .15 .25
GBT02065 Steam Maiden, Ul-nin C .15 .25
GBT02066 Mist Geyser Dragon C .15 .25
GBT02067 Brass-winged Gear Hawk C .15 .25
GBT02068 Steam Maiden, Jushil C .15 .25
GBT02069 Vainglory-dream Gear Cat C .15 .25
GBT02070 Strikehead Dragon C .15 .25
GBT02071 Blue Storm Soldier, Rascal Sweeper C .15 .25
GBT02072 High Tide Sniper C .15 .25
GBT02073 Sabre Flow Sailor C .15 .25
GBT02074 Assassinate Sailor C .15 .25
GBT02075 Tactics Sailor C .15 .25
GBT02076 Whirlwind Brave Shooter C .15 .25
GBT02077 Battle Siren, Stacia C .15 .25
GBT02078 Officer Cadet, Cyril C .15 .25
GBT02079 Surge Breath Dragon C .15 .25
GBT02080 Blue Storm Marine General, Despina C .15 .25
GBT02081 Contradiction Instructor, Tusk Master C .15 .25
GBT02082 Hardworking Scientist, Nyanshiro C .15 .25
GBT02083 Sleepy Tapir C .15 .25
GBT02084 Malicious Sabre C .15 .25
GBT02085 Deposition Scientist, Nyankuro C .15 .25
GBT02086 Paint Otter C .15 .25
GBT02087 Mohawk Hyena C .15 .25
GBT02088 Pencil Koala C .15 .25
GBT02089 Cutter Falcon C .15 .25
GBT02090 Cafeteria Sea Otter C .15 .25
GBT02091 Broadcast Rabbit C .15 .25
GBT02092 Protractor Ulan C .15 .25
GBT02093 Vegetable Avatar Dragon C .15 .25
GBT02094 Barrage Warrior, Watermelon C .15 .25
GBT02095 Wheel Wind Dragon C .15 .25
GBT02096 Maiden of Lost Memory C .15 .25
GBT02097 Snowdrop Musketeer, Pirkko C .15 .25
GBT02098 Maiden of Canna C .15 .25
GBT02099 Melancholy Warrior, Onion C .15 .25
GBT02100 Maiden of Sprouts, Ho C .15 .25
GBT02101 Magnolia Knight C .15 .25
GBT02102 Gardenia Musketeer, Alan C .15 .25
GBT02103 Rain Elemental, Tear C .15 .25
GBT02S01 Flash Flame Divine Knight, Samuil SP 12.00 20.00
GBT02S02 Supreme Conquering Dragon, Conquest Dragon SP 15.00 25.00
GBT02S03 Dragonic Vanquisher SP 5.00 8.00
GBT02S04 Interdimensional Dragon, Fate Rider Dragon SP 8.00 12.00
GBT02S05 Marine General of the Sky and Earth, Lambros SP 30.00 50.00
GBT02S06 Omniscience Dragon, Managarmr SP 12.00 20.00
GBT02S07 Famous Professor, Bigbelly SP 10.00 15.00
GBT02S08 Sacred Tree Dragon, Jingle Flower Dragon SP 15.00 25.00
GBT02S09 Dream Bringer, Belenus SP 12.00 20.00
GBT02S10 Dragonic Kaiser Crimson SP 10.00 15.00
GBT02S11 Voltage Horn Dragon SP 8.00 12.00
GBT02S12 Heart Thump Worker SP 12.00 20.00

2015 Cardfight Vanguard G Booster Set 3 Sovereign Star Dragon

COMPLETE SET (116) 200.00 350.00
RELEASED ON JULY 10, 2015
GBT03001 Phantom Blaster Dragon GR 25.00 40.00
GBT03002 Genesis Dragon, Amnesty Messiah GR 30.00 50.00
GBT03003 Supremacy Black Dragon, Aurageyser Dragon RRR 15.00 25.00
GBT03004 Supremacy Dragon, Claret Sword Dragon RRR 6.00 10.00
GBT03005 Golden Dragon, Spearcross Dragon RRR 8.00 12.00
GBT03006 Sunrise Ray Knight, Gurguit RRR 5.00 8.00
GBT03007 Divine Dragon Knight, Mustafa RRR 4.00 6.00
GBT03008 Ambush Demon Stealth Dragon, Homura Raider RRR 3.00 5.00
GBT03009 Nebula Dragon, Big Crunch Dragon RRR 12.00 20.00
GBT03010 Abominable One, Gilles de Rais RRR 10.00 15.00
GBT03011 Karma Collector RR 5.00 8.00
GBT03012 Holy Mage, Pwyll RR 2.50 4.00
GBT03013 Holy Mage, Bryderi RR 2.50 4.00
GBT03014 Dragon Knight, Jannat RR .60 1.00
GBT03015 Covert Demonic Dragon, Magatsu Typhoon RR .60 1.00
GBT03016 Stealth Rogue of Revelation, Yasuie RR 1.75 3.00
GBT03017 Stealth Beast, White Heron RR 1.75 3.00
GBT03018 Mixed Deletor, Keios RR .60 1.00
GBT03019 Flowers in Vacuum, Cosmo Wreath RR 12.00 20.00
GBT03020 Scharhrot Vampir RR 2.50 4.00
GBT03021 Squallmaker Vampir RR .75 1.25
GBT03022 Flag Breaker RR 1.25 2.00
GBT03023 Adroit Revenger, Teyrnon R .60 1.00
GBT03024 Scornful Knight, Gyva R .60 1.00
GBT03025 Cherishing Knight, Branwen R .60 1.00
GBT03026 Fast Chase Golden Knight, Cambell R 1.50 2.50
GBT03027 Taciturn Liberator, Brennius R .60 1.00
GBT03028 Dawning Knight, Gorboduc R .60 1.00
GBT03029 Ascendant Liberator, Barbtruc R .60 1.00
GBT03030 Heroic Saga Dragon R .60 1.00
GBT03031 Dragon Knight, Imahd R .60 1.00
GBT03032 Ambush Demon Stealth Fiend, Ushimitsu Train R .60 1.00
GBT03033 Stealth Dragon, Runestar R .60 1.00
GBT03034 Stealth Rogue of the Flowered Hat, Fujino R .60 1.00
GBT03035 Gateway Stealth Rogue, Alaka R .60 1.00
GBT03036 Cradle of the Stars, Stellar Maker R 1.50 2.50
GBT03037 Lady Battler of the Gravity Well R .60 1.00
GBT03038 Destiny Dealer R .60 1.00
GBT03039 Love Tempest, Kisskill Lira R .60 1.00
GBT03040 Psychic of Storm, Rigil R .60 1.00
GBT03041 Sweet Predator R .60 1.00
GBT03042 Flirtatious Succubus R .60 1.00
GBT03043 Succubus of Pure Love R .60 1.00
GBT03044 Earth Elemental, Pokkur R .60 1.00
GBT03045 Demon World Castle, Totwachter C .15 .25
GBT03046 Fair Knight, Gwawl C .15 .25
GBT03047 Knight of Diligence, Mazorlf C .15 .25
GBT03048 Tempting Revenger, Finegas C .15 .25
GBT03049 Night Sky Eagle C .15 .25
GBT03050 Blitz Knight, Bolfri C .15 .25
GBT03051 Demon World Castle, Streitenturm C .15 .25
GBT03052 Promising Knight, David C .15 .25
GBT03053 Witch of Black Doves, Goewin C .15 .25
GBT03054 Cursed Eye Raven C .15 .25
GBT03055 Veteran Knight, Danvallo C .15 .25
GBT03056 Lofty Head Lion C .15 .25
GBT03057 Knight of Dawnlight, Jago C .15 .25
GBT03058 Law-abiding Knight, Cloten C .15 .25
GBT03059 Braygal C .15 .25
GBT03060 Knight of Morning Shadow, Kimarcus C .15 .25
GBT03061 Butterfly Liberator, Korderia C .15 .25
GBT03062 After-glow Liberator, Belinus C .15 .25
GBT03063 Sleimy C .15 .25
GBT03064 Rising Lionet C .15 .25
GBT03065 Air Raid Lion C .15 .25
GBT03066 Peeping Rabbit C .15 .25
GBT03067 Pharmacy Witch C .15 .25
GBT03068 Gigantech Ringer C .15 .25
GBT03069 Dragon Knight, Soheil C .15 .25
GBT03070 Demonic Dragon Berserker, Putana C .15 .25
GBT03071 Dragon Knight, Mahmit C .15 .25
GBT03072 Seal Dragon, Gariserge C .15 .25
GBT03073 Dragon Knight, Mafdi C .15 .25
GBT03074 Volcano Gale Dragon C .15 .25
GBT03075 Seal Dragon, Tarpaulin Dracokid C .15 .25
GBT03076 Tenjiku Stealth Rogue, Dokube C .15 .25
GBT03077 Stealth Beast, Emissary Crow C .15 .25
GBT03078 Stealth Fiend, Yunayuki C .15 .25
GBT03079 Stealth Beast, Charcoal Fox C .15 .25
GBT03080 Chain Sickle Stealth Rogue, Onifundo C .15 .25
GBT03081 Stealth Dragon, Hiden Scroll C .15 .25
GBT03082 Lady Gunner of the Neutron Star C .15 .25
GBT03083 Heavymaterial Dragon C .15 .25
GBT03084 Chain-battle Star-vader, Technetium C .15 .25
GBT03085 Deriding Deletor, Aieda C .15 .25
GBT03086 Sword Draw Star-vader, Vorium C .15 .25
GBT03087 Spawn of the Spiral Nebula C .15 .25
GBT03088 Asteroid Wolf C .15 .25
GBT03089 Cramping Deletor, Edy C .15 .25
GBT03090 Werwolf Jaeger C .15 .25
GBT03091 Amon's Follower, Hell's Nail C .15 .25
GBT03092 Knife Conductor C .15 .25
GBT03093 Krise Vampir C .15 .25
GBT03094 Amon's Follower, Mad Eye C .15 .25
GBT03095 Killing Dollmaster C .15 .25
GBT03096 Lunatic Masquerade C .15 .25
GBT03097 Amon's Follower, Barmaid Grace C .15 .25
GBT03098 Werfleder Ordonnaz C .15 .25
GBT03099 Amon's Follower, Grausam C .15 .25
GBT03100 Wertigre Fanatica C .15 .25
GBT03101 Endless Boozer C .15 .25
GBT03102 Monochrome of Nightmareland C .15 .25
GBT03103 Alice of Nightmareland C .15 .25
GBT03104 Air Elemental, Fwarlun C .15 .25
GBT03S01 Sovereign Black Dragon, Aurageyser Dragon SP 30.00 50.00
GBT03S02 Sovereign Dragon, Claret Sword Dragon SP 20.00 30.00
GBT03S03 Golden Dragon, Spear Cross Dragon SP 12.00 20.00
GBT03S04 Knight of Rising Sunshine, Gurguit SP 5.00 8.00
GBT03S05 Divine Dragon Knight, Mustafa SP 3.00 5.00
GBT03S06 Ambush Demonic Stealth Dragon, Homura Raider SP 10.00 15.00
GBT03S07 Nebula Dragon, Big Crunch Dragon SP 20.00 30.00
GBT03S08 One Who is Abhorrent, Gilles de Rais SP 15.00 25.00
GBT03S09 Karma Collector SP 25.00 40.00
GBT03S10 Covert Demonic Dragon, Magatsu Typhoon SP 6.00 10.00
GBT03S11 Stealth Fiend, White Heron SP 6.00 10.00
GBT03S12 Flower Blooming in the Vacuum, Cosmolis SP 15.00 25.00

2015 Cardfight Vanguard G Booster Set 4 Soul Strike Against the Supreme

RELEASED ON OCTOBER 2, 2015
GBT04SR01 Interdimensional Dragon, Chronoscommand Dragon SCR 15.00 25.00
GBT04SR05 Supremacy Black Dragon, Aurageyser Doomed SCR 20.00 30.00
GBT04001 Supremacy Black Dragon, Aurageyser Doomed GR 6.00 10.00
GBT04002 Chronodragon Nextage GR 5.00 8.00
GBT04003 Soaring Divine Knight, Altmile RRR 6.00 10.00
GBT04004 Holy Seraph, Raphael RRR 6.00 10.00

GBT04005 Black Shiver, Gabriel RRR	1.25	2.00
GBT04006 Mythical Destroyer Beast, Vanargandr RRR	2.00	3.00
GBT04007 Mythic Beast, Fenrir RRR	8.00	12.00
GBT04008 Raging Spear Mutant Deity, Stun Beetle RRR	1.25	2.00
GBT04009 Intimidating Mutant, Darkface RRR	4.00	6.00
GBT04010 Dream-spinning Ranunculus, Ahsha RRR	10.00	15.00
GBT04011 Knight of Reform, Pir RR	.40	.60
GBT04012 Crimson Lore, Metatron RR	.30	.50
GBT04013 Black Slice, Harut RR	1.00	1.50
GBT04014 Black Record, Israfil RR	1.00	1.50
GBT04015 Taboo Demonic Mage, Kafir RR	.75	1.25
GBT04016 Unappeasable Biter, Gleipnir RR	.60	1.00
GBT04017 Goddess of Decline, Hel RR	.60	1.00
GBT04018 Upstream Dragon RR	.60	1.00
GBT04019 Rebel Mutant, Starshield RR	.60	1.00
GBT04020 Maiden of Rambling Rose RR	.75	1.25
GBT04021 Flower Cluster Maiden, Salianna RR	.40	.60
GBT04022 Flower Garden Maiden, Mailis RR	.60	1.00
GBT04023 Techgal R	.15	.25
GBT04024 Holy Seraph, Raziel R	.15	.25
GBT04025 Accident Celestial, Batarel R	.15	.25
GBT04026 Control Celestial, He-el R	.15	.25
GBT04027 Black Call, Nakir R	.15	.25
GBT04028 Solid Celestial, Adnarel R	.15	.25
GBT04029 Knight of Inflation, Gilvers R	.40	.60
GBT04030 Darkpride Dragon R	.15	.25
GBT04031 Dark Quartz Dragon R	.15	.25
GBT04032 Goddess of the Skies, Dione R	.15	.25
GBT04033 Mythic Serpent, Jormungand R	.15	.25
GBT04034 Mythic Beast, Skoll R	1.00	1.50
GBT04035 Steam Fighter, Balif R	.15	.25
GBT04036 Steam Fighter, Ul-nigin R	.15	.25
GBT04037 Poisonous Spear Mutant Deity, Paraspear R	.15	.25
GBT04038 Machining Scorpion mk II R	.15	.25
GBT04039 Machining Mosquito mk II R	.40	.60
GBT04040 Fascinated Mutant, Sweet Cocktail R	.25	.40
GBT04041 Nova Mutant, Little Dorcas R	.15	.25
GBT04042 Maiden of Flower Screen R	.15	.25
GBT04043 Early Flowering Maiden, Pia R	.15	.25
GBT04044 Heat Elemental, Bwah R	.30	.50
GBT04045 Archer of Sanctuary C	.10	.15
GBT04046 Knight of Dexterity, Jed C	.10	.15
GBT04047 Battle Song Angel C	.10	.15
GBT04048 Jumpgal C	.10	.15
GBT04049 Straight Jewel Knight, Bartram C	.10	.15
GBT04050 Mobile Hospital, Healing Palace C	.10	.15
GBT04051 Nurse of Broken Heart C	1.00	1.50
GBT04052 Dream Light Unicorn C	.10	.15
GBT04053 Black Pain, Marut C	.10	.15
GBT04054 Confidence Celestial, Lumiel C	.10	.15
GBT04055 Doctoroid Premas C	.10	.15
GBT04056 Nurse Cap Dalmatian C	.10	.15
GBT04057 Black Candle, Azrael C	.10	.15
GBT04058 Nurse of Danger Heart C	.10	.15
GBT04059 MRI Angel C	.10	.15
GBT04060 Nurse of Sweet Heart C	.10	.15
GBT04061 Invert Celestial, Asbeel C	.10	.15
GBT04062 Doctoroid Lifros C	.40	.60
GBT04063 Sturdy Knight, Grosne C	.10	.15
GBT04064 Witch of Treasured Books, Adra C	.10	.15
GBT04065 Cleverness Knight, Convalle C	.10	.15
GBT04066 Witch's Familiar, Kuroma C	.10	.15
GBT04067 Meditation Knight, Mac Nessa C	.10	.15
GBT04068 Goddess of Hearths, Hestia C	.10	.15
GBT04069 God of Dreams, Oneiroi C	.10	.15
GBT04070 Witch of White Hares, Cardamom C	.10	.15
GBT04071 Flying Kelly C	.10	.15
GBT04072 String Warning, Dromi C	.10	.15
GBT04073 Reflecting Regalia, Mirror Angel C	.10	.15
GBT04074 Mythic Beast, Hati C	.10	.15
GBT04075 Witch of Melons, Thyme C	.10	.15
GBT04076 Cramer Harry C	.10	.15
GBT04077 Feter of Leather, Leyding C	.10	.15
GBT04078 Bumping Buffalo C	.10	.15
GBT04079 Witch of Cherries, Poppy C	.10	.15
GBT04080 Goddess of Youth, Hebe C	.10	.15
GBT04081 Witch's Familiar, Shiroma C	.30	.50
GBT04082 Dreaming Dragon C	1.00	1.50
GBT04083 Steam Knight, Kalium C	.10	.15
GBT04084 Forethought Gear Fox C	.10	.15
GBT04085 Steam Worker, Kuda C	.10	.15
GBT04086 Steam Fighter, Rugal-Banda C	.10	.15
GBT04087 Long Horn Hunter C	.10	.15
GBT04088 Buster Mantis C	.10	.15
GBT04089 Abyss Diver C	.10	.15
GBT04090 Megacolony Battler D C	.10	.15
GBT04091 Scissor Finger C	.10	.15
GBT04092 Machining Yellow Jacket C	.10	.15
GBT04093 Machining Slater C	.10	.15
GBT04094 Young Executive, Crimebug C	.10	.15
GBT04095 Bad Trip C	.10	.15
GBT04096 Machining Scarab C	.10	.15
GBT04097 Cocoon Healer C	.10	.15
GBT04098 Machining Firefly C	.10	.15
GBT04099 Earth Dreamer C	.10	.15
GBT04100 Crystalwing Dragon C	.10	.15
GBT04101 Wisteria Knight C	.10	.15
GBT04102 Hollyhock Knight C	.10	.15
GBT04103 3 Apple Sisters C	.10	.15
GBT04104 Dark Elemental, Dokuzurk C	.10	.15
GBT04S01 Soaring Divine Knight, Altmile SP	10.00	15.00
GBT04S02 Holy Seraph, Raphael SP	20.00	30.00
GBT04S03 Black Shiver, Gabriel SP	12.00	20.00
GBT04S04 Mythical Destroyer Beast, Vanargandr SP	15.00	25.00
GBT04S05 Mythic Beast, Fenrir SP	12.00	20.00
GBT04S06 Raging Spear Mutant Deity, Stun Beetle SP	2.00	3.00
GBT04S07 Intimidating Mutant, Darkface SP	20.00	30.00
GBT04S08 Dream-spinning Ranunculus, Ahsha SP	60.00	100.00
GBT04S09 Black Record, Israfil SP	3.00	5.00
GBT04S10 Goddess of Decline, Hel SP	2.50	4.00
GBT04S11 Rebellion Mutant, Star Shield SP	3.00	5.00
GBT04S12 Maiden of Rambling Rose SP	4.00	6.00
GBT04SR02 Flower Princess of Spring's Beginning, Primavera SCR	15.00	25.00
GBT04SR03 Phantom Blaster Dragon SCR	50.00	75.00
GBT04SR04 Genesis Dragon, Amnesty Messiah SCR	25.00	40.00
GBT04SR06 Chronodragon Nextage SCR	25.00	40.00

2016 Cardfight Vanguard G Booster Set 5 Moonlit Dragonfang

COMPLETE SET (121)	300.00	500.00
UNLISTED C	.15	.25
UNLISTED R	.20	.30
RELEASED ON JANUARY 29, 2016		
GBT05001 Genesis Dragon Excelics Messiah GR	20.00	30.00
GBT05002 Dragon Masquerade Harri GR	20.00	30.00
GBT05003 Dragon Destroyer Battle Deity Kamususanoo RRR	5.00	8.00
GBT05003 Dragon Destroyer Battle Deity Kamususanoo SP	15.00	25.00
GBT05004 One Who Views the Planet Globe Magus RRR	3.00	5.00
GBT05004 One Who Views the Planet Globe Magus SP	12.00	20.00
GBT05005 Conquering Supreme Dragon Dragonic Vanquisher VOLTAGE RRR	5.00	8.00
GBT05005 Conquering Supreme Dragon Dragonic Vanquisher VOLTAGE SP	12.00	20.00
GBT05006 True Eradicator Finish Blow Dragon RRR	1.75	3.00
GBT05006 True Eradicator Finish Blow Dragon SP	5.00	8.00
GBT05007 Death Starvader Chaos Universe RRR	8.00	12.00
GBT05007 Death Starvader Chaos Universe SP	30.00	50.00
GBT05008 Jester Demonic Dragon Lunatec Dragon RRR	8.00	12.00
GBT05008 Jester Demonic Dragon Lunatec Dragon SP	20.00	30.00
GBT05009 Nightmare Doll Catherine RRR	1.50	2.50
GBT05009 Nightmare Doll Catherine SP	12.00	20.00
GBT05010 Clockfencer Dragon RRR	2.50	4.00
GBT05010 Clockfencer Dragon SP	8.00	12.00
GBT05011 Imperial Shrine Guard Akagi RR	.40	.60
GBT05011 Imperial Shrine Guard Akagi SP	5.00	8.00
GBT05012 Divine Sword Kusanagi RR	1.50	2.50
GBT05013 Eradicator Angercharge Dragon RR	.40	.60
GBT05014 Rockclimb Dragoon RR	.40	.60
GBT05014 Rockclimb Dragoon SP	6.00	10.00
GBT05015 Lightning of Triumphant Return Reseph RR	.75	1.25
GBT05016 Arrester Messiah RR	6.00	10.00
GBT05016 Arrester Messiah SP	20.00	30.00
GBT05017 Lady Battler of the White Dwarf RR	.40	.60
GBT05018 Blink Messiah RR	5.00	8.00
GBT05019 Darkside Princess RR	6.00	10.00
GBT05020 Darkside Mirror Master RR	6.00	10.00
GBT05020 Darkside Mirror Master SP	20.00	30.00
GBT05021 Darkside Sword Master RR	5.00	8.00
GBT05022 Steam Maiden Melem RR	12.00	20.00
GBT05023 Rigid Crane R	.20	.30
GBT05024 Imperial Shrine Guard Sumiyoshi R	.20	.30
GBT05025 Virtuoso Housekeeper R	.20	.30
GBT05026 Battle Sister Taffy R	.20	.30
GBT05027 Great Composure Dragon R	.20	.30
GBT05028 Detonix Stinger Dragon R	.20	.30
GBT05029 One Strike Two Hits Djinn R	.20	.30
GBT05030 Cloudmaster Dragon R	.20	.30
GBT05031 Recklessness Dragon R	.20	.30
GBT05032 Chainbolt Dragoon R	.20	.30
GBT05033 Starvader Chaosbringer R	.40	.60
GBT05034 Meteor Monk of the Force Foot R	.20	.30
GBT05035 Sacrifice Messiah R	.60	1.00
GBT05036 Burstlaugh Dragon R	.20	.30
GBT05037 Flying Peryton R	.75	1.25
GBT05038 Masquerade Bunny R	2.50	4.00
GBT05039 Silver Thorn Matador Maddock R	.20	.30
GBT05040 Fiery March Colossus R	.60	1.00
GBT05041 Steam Battler KugBau R	.20	.30
GBT05042 Twicetalented Gear Hound R	.20	.30
GBT05043 Cornerstone Gear Turtle R	.20	.30
GBT05044 Earth Elemental Dogetts R	.20	.30
GBT05045 Flip Croony C	.15	.25
GBT05046 Ring Magus C	.15	.25
GBT05047 Shrewd Concierge C	.15	.25
GBT05048 Rhombus Magus C	.15	.25
GBT05049 Tankman Mode Interrupt C	.15	.25
GBT05050 Octagon Magus C	.15	.25
GBT05051 Cone Magus C	.15	.25
GBT05052 Beamshower Turtle C	.15	.25
GBT05053 Semilunar Magus C	.15	.25
GBT05054 Magical Calico C	.15	.25
GBT05055 Triangle Magus C	.15	.25
GBT05056 Battle Sister Muffin C	.15	.25
GBT05057 Blitzspear Dragoon C	.15	.25
GBT05058 Foot Brawler Teiroc C	.15	.25
GBT05059 Hammerknuckle Dragon C	.15	.25
GBT05060 Fiendish Sword Eradicator Chojun C	.15	.25
GBT05061 Desert Gunner Kojin C	.15	.25
GBT05062 Machinegun Eradicator Kantou C	.15	.25
GBT05063 Secret Fist Brawler Kokon C	.15	.25
GBT05064 Dragon Dancer Bernadette C	.15	.25
GBT05065 Eradicator Raretalent Dracokid C	.15	.25
GBT05066 Wildrun Dragoon C	.15	.25
GBT05067 Brawler Streetfight Dragon C	.15	.25
GBT05068 Lady Battler of the Accretion Disc C	.15	.25
GBT05069 Mirrorworld Lion C	.15	.25
GBT05070 Disorder Starvader Iron C	.15	.25
GBT05071 Starholder Dragon C	.15	.25
GBT05072 Turmoil Starvader Zinc C	.15	.25
GBT05073 Divide Monk of the Shattering Fist C	.15	.25
GBT05074 Providential Child of Gravitational Collapse C	.15	.25
GBT05075 Involution Starvader Carbon C	.15	.25
GBT05076 Starvader Paradigm Shift Dragon C	.15	.25
GBT05077 Beauteous Beast Tamer Alexis C	.15	.25
GBT05078 Fullsmile Wyvern C	.15	.25
GBT05079 Intensely Spicy Clown C	.15	.25
GBT05080 Silver Thorn Magician Clemens C	.15	.25
GBT05081 Nightmare Doll Ginny C	.15	.25
GBT05082 Hellsgate Magician C	.15	.25
GBT05083 Intensely Sweet Clown C	.15	.25
GBT05084 Silver Thorn Puppet Master Euphemia C	.15	.25
GBT05085 Silver Thorn Magician Colette C	.15	.25
GBT05086 Nightmare Doll Leslie C	.15	.25
GBT05087 Fire Ring Wyvern C	.15	.25
GBT05088 Dreaming Bicorn C	.15	.25
GBT05089 Nightmare Doll Mirabel C	.15	.25
GBT05090 Prankster Girl of Mirrorland C	.15	.25
GBT05091 Breastflare Dragon C	.15	.25
GBT05092 Metalglider Dragon C	.15	.25
GBT05093 Heavy Ironhammer Colossus C	.15	.25
GBT05094 Steam Knight Lugal C	.15	.25
GBT05095 Lost City Dragon C	.15	.25
GBT05096 Steam Maiden Balulu C	.15	.25
GBT05097 Steam Fighter UrZaba C	.15	.25
GBT05098 Steam Worker Etana C	.15	.25
GBT05099 Gear Bat of Recasting C	.15	.25
GBT05100 Steam Scara Merkar C	.15	.25
GBT05101 Tick Tock Worker C	.15	.25
GBT05102 Paradoxcannon Dracokid C	.15	.25
GBT05103 Steam Battler UrWatar C	.15	.25
GBT05104 Heat Elemental Juge C	.15	.25
GBT05SR01EN Supreme Heavenly Battle Deity Susanoo SCR	20.00	30.00
GBT05SR02EN Pentagonal Magus SCR	12.00	20.00
GBT05SR03EN Eradicator Gauntlet Buster Dragon SCR	15.00	25.00
GBT05SR04EN Starvader Chaos Breaker Dragon SCR	60.00	100.00
GBT05SR05EN Nightmare Doll Alice SCR	50.00	80.00

2016 Cardfight Vanguard G Booster Set 6 Transcension of Blade and Blossom

COMPLETE SET (121)	500.00	800.00
UNLISTED C	.15	.25
UNLISTED R	.10	.30
RELEASED ON MARCH 25, 2016		
GBT06001 Transcending the Heavens Altmile GR	12.00	20.00
GBT06002 Ranunculus in Glorious Bloom Ahsha GR	20.00	30.00
GBT06003 Counteroffensive Knight Suleiman RRR	1.75	3.00
GBT06003 Counteroffensive Knight Suleiman SP	10.00	15.00
GBT06004 Dark Dragon Spectral Blaster Diablo RRR	12.00	20.00
GBT06004 Dark Dragon Spectral Blaster Diablo SP	25.00	40.00
GBT06005 Whirlwind of Darkness Vortimer Diablo RRR	5.00	8.00
GBT06005 Whirlwind of Darkness Vortimer Diablo SP	20.00	30.00
GBT06006 Meteokaiser Victor RRR	5.00	8.00
GBT06006 Meteokaiser Victor SP	20.00	30.00
GBT06007 Exxtreme Battler Danshark RRR	.75	1.25
GBT06007 Exxtreme Battler Danshark SP	5.00	8.00
GBT06008 Mist Phantasm Pirate King Nightrose RRR	20.00	30.00
GBT06008 Mist Phantasm Pirate King Nightrose SP	50.00	75.00
GBT06009 Ghoul Dragon Gast Dragon RRR	1.75	3.00
GBT06009 Ghoul Dragon Gast Dragon SP	8.00	12.00
GBT06010 Cornflower Flower Maiden Ines RRR	3.00	5.00
GBT06010 Cornflower Flower Maiden Ines SP	10.00	15.00
GBT06011 Model Knight Orhan RR	.40	.60
GBT06012 Hope Keeper RR	1.25	2.00
GBT06012 Hope Keeper SP	8.00	12.00
GBT06013 Black Chain Flame Dance Formation Hoel RR	5.00	8.00
GBT06014 Extreme Battler Headstrongbattle RR	.60	1.00
GBT06015 Extreme Battler Breakpass RR	1.25	2.00
GBT06016 Curtain Call Announcer Mephisto RR	3.00	5.00
GBT06017 Crescent Moon Juggler RR	1.25	2.00
GBT06018 Hoop Master RR	1.75	3.00
GBT06018 Hoop Master SP	8.00	12.00
GBT06019 Witch Doctor of Languor Negrolazy RR	5.00	8.00
GBT06020 Waterspout Djinn RR	8.00	12.00
GBT06020 Waterspout Djinn SP	20.00	30.00
GBT06021 Ideal Maiden Thuria RR	1.50	2.50
GBT06022 Cherry Blossom Blizzard Maiden Lilga RR	1.25	2.00
GBT06022 Cherry Blossom Blizzard Maiden Lilga SP	10.00	15.00
GBT06023 Knight of Light Order R	.20	.30
GBT06024 Favored Pupil of Light and Dark Llew R	.60	1.00
GBT06025 Headwind Knight Selim R	.20	.30
GBT06026 Resurgent Knight Stius R	.20	.30
GBT06027 Black Chain Spirit Dance Formation Kahedin R	.60	1.00
GBT06028 Bassinet Knight Oscar R	.20	.30
GBT06029 Ultimate Raizer Gloryhand R	.20	.30
GBT06030 Ultimate Raizer Speedstar R	.20	.30
GBT06031 Extreme Battler Arbarail R	.20	.30
GBT06032 Extreme Battler Malyaki R	.20	.30
GBT06033 Extreme Battler Kabutron R	.20	.30
GBT06034 Flying Manticore R	.20	.30
GBT06035 Cutie Paratrooper R	.40	.60
GBT06036 Cat Knight in High Boots R	.20	.30
GBT06037 Ghostie Great King Obadiah R	.40	.60
GBT06038 Ruin Shade R	.20	.30
GBT06039 Tommy the Ghostie Brothers R	1.75	3.00
GBT06040 Witch Doctor of the Powdered Bone Negrobone R	.60	1.00
GBT06041 Forbidden Space Banshee R	.20	.30
GBT06042 Redleaf Dragon R	.20	.30
GBT06043 Pure Maiden Katrina R	.20	.30
GBT06044 Peach Orchard Maiden Elmy R	.20	.30
GBT06045 Shyngal C	.15	.25
GBT06046 Hopesong Angel C	.15	.25
GBT06047 Scouting Owl C	.15	.25
GBT06048 Blasterfriend Barcgal C	.15	.25
GBT06049 Knight of Powercharge C	.15	.25
GBT06050 Sarugal C	.15	.25
GBT06051 Floral Paladin Flogal C	.15	.25
GBT06052 Deathspray Dragon C	.15	.25
GBT06053 Blaster Axe C	.15	.25
GBT06054 Greymyu C	.15	.25
GBT06055 Dark Saga Painter C	.15	.25
GBT06056 Blaster Rapier C	.15	.25
GBT06057 Revenger Darkbless Angel C	.15	.25
GBT06058 Abyss Summoner C	.15	.25
GBT06059 Revenger of Vigor Maur C	.15	.25
GBT06060 Blaster Dagger C	.15	.25
GBT06061 Fullbau Diablo C	.15	.25
GBT06062 Grave Horn Unicorn C	.15	.25
GBT06063 Tactician of Godlycalculations Orphe C	.15	.25
GBT06064 Illegal Alchemist C	.15	.25
GBT06065 Mage of the Rogue Eye Arsur C	.15	.25
GBT06066 Envoy of Righteousness Crystaldevil C	.15	.25
GBT06067 Beast Deity Jackalord C	.15	.25
GBT06068 Babyface Narcissus C	.15	.25
GBT06069 Master Kungfu C	.15	.25
GBT06070 Kumar the Destroyer C	.15	.25
GBT06071 Shinobiraizer C	.15	.25
GBT06072 Beast Deity Horned Hulk C	.15	.25
GBT06073 Rajadamnern Kid C	.15	.25
GBT06074 Turboraizer Custom C	.15	.25
GBT06075 Totem Brothers C	.15	.25
GBT06076 Training Therapist C	.15	.25
GBT06077 Beast Deity Great Eater C	.15	.25
GBT06078 Perfect Referee 299 C	.15	.25
GBT06079 Artilleryman C	.15	.25
GBT06080 Dreaming Pegasus C	.15	.25
GBT06081 Signal Snake Tamer C	.15	.25
GBT06082 Silver Thorn Assistant Dixie C	.15	.25
GBT06083 Mighty Rogue Nightstorm C	.15	.25
GBT06084 Seven Seas Dragon Undead Prisoner Dragon C	.15	.25
GBT06085 Sleepless Skipper Blackgick C	.15	.25
GBT06086 Seven Seas Master Swordsman Slash Shade C	.15	.25
GBT06087 Skeleton Cannoneer C	.15	.25
GBT06088 Witch Doctor of the Seven Seas Raisruler C	.15	.25
GBT06089 Seven Seas Helmsman Nightcrow C	.15	.25
GBT06090 Headstart Zombie C	.15	.25
GBT06091 Seven Seas Apprentice Nightrunner C	.15	.25
GBT06092 Assault Command Carignan C	.15	.25
GBT06093 Looting Cutlass C	.15	.25
GBT06094 Mick the Ghostie and Family C	.15	.25

GBT06095 Greenshot Elf C	.15	.25
GBT06096 Maiden of Damask Rose C	.15	.25
GBT06097 Cropmaker Dragon C	.15	.25
GBT06098 Af Roccoli C	.15	.25
GBT06099 Tomboy Elf C	.15	.25
GBT06100 Maiden of Rambler C	.15	.25
GBT06101 Maiden of Noisette C	.15	.25
GBT06102 Tsukken Don C	.15	.25
GBT06103 Cosmos Pixy Lizbeth C	.15	.25
GBT06104 Air Elemental Twitterun C	.15	.25
GBT06SCR01 Blue Sky Knight Altmile SCR	50.00	75.00
GBT06SCR02 Ranunculus Flower Maiden Ahsha SCR	75.00	125.00
GBT06SCR03 Exxtreme Battler Victor SCR	50.00	75.00
GBT06SCR04 Revenger Phantom Blaster Abyss SCR	20.00	30.00
GBT06SCR05 Blaster Dark Revenger Abyss SCR	20.00	30.00

2016 Cardfight Vanguard G Booster Set 7 Glorious Bravery of Radiant Sword

COMPLETE SET (141)	600.00	1000.00
UNLISTED C	.15	.25
UNLISTED R	.10	.30
RELEASED ON JUNE 17, 2016		
GBT07001 Sunrise Ray Radiant Sword Gurguit GR	25.00	40.00
GBT07001 Sunrise Ray Radiant Sword Gurguit SGR	30.00	50.00
GBT07002 Supreme Heavenly Emperor Dragon Defeat Flare Dragon GR	12.00	20.00
GBT07002 Supreme Heavenly Emperor Dragon Defeat Flare Dragon SGR	12.00	20.00
GBT07003 Black Seraph Gavrail RRR	10.00	15.00
GBT07003 Black Seraph Gavrail SP	25.00	40.00
GBT07004 Knight of Springs Light Perimore RRR	5.00	8.00
GBT07004 Knight of Springs Light Perimore SP	12.00	20.00
GBT07005 Supreme Heavenly Emperor Dragon Dragonic Blademaster Taiten RRR	12.00	20.00
GBT07005 Supreme Heavenly Emperor Dragon Dragonic Blademaster Taiten SP	25.00	40.00
GBT07006 Super Cosmic Hero Xgallop RRR	3.00	5.00
GBT07006 Super Cosmic Hero Xgallop SP	8.00	12.00
GBT07007 Cosmic Hero Grandvolver RRR	1.50	2.50
GBT07007 Cosmic Hero Grandvolver SP	20.00	30.00
GBT07008 Wings of Recurrence Blade Wing Reijy RRR	1.00	1.50
GBT07008 Wings of Recurrence Blade Wing Reijy SP	10.00	15.00
GBT07009 Interdimensional Dragon Bind Time Dragon RRR	6.00	10.00
GBT07009 Interdimensional Dragon Bind Time Dragon SP	12.00	20.00
GBT07010 Chronofang Tiger RRR	5.00	8.00
GBT07010 Chronofang Tiger SP	20.00	30.00
GBT07011 Holy Seraph Suriel RR	1.00	1.50
GBT07012 Doctroid Remnon RR	1.75	3.00
GBT07012 Doctroid Remnon SP	12.00	20.00
GBT07013 Black Spark Munkar RR	1.75	3.00
GBT07014 Golden Beast Sleimy Flare RR	1.25	2.00
GBT07015 Scarface Lion RR	3.00	5.00
GBT07016 Flame Wing Steel Beast Denial Griffin RR	3.00	5.00
GBT07017 Escort Dragon Attendant Reas RR	.75	1.25
GBT07017 Escort Dragon Attendant Reas SP	8.00	12.00
GBT07018 Super Cosmic Hero Xcarivou RR	.60	1.00
GBT07019 Cosmic Hero Grandleaf RR	.40	.60
GBT07019 Cosmic Hero Grandleaf SP	10.00	15.00
GBT07020 Nighttime Gentleman SaintGermain RR	.75	1.25
GBT07021 Oneeyed Succubus RR	.75	1.25
GBT07022 Highbrow Steam Raphanna RR	1.00	1.50
GBT07022 Highbrow Steam Raphanna SP	5.00	8.00
GBT07023 Retractor Sarakiel R	.20	.30
GBT07024 Black Dream Zabaniya R	.20	.30
GBT07025 Black Bomber Maalik R	.20	.30
GBT07026 Nurse of Smash Heart R	.20	.30
GBT07027 Dawnngal R	.20	.30
GBT07028 Flame Wind Lion Wonder Ezel R	.20	.30
GBT07029 Sunshine Knight Jeffrey R	.60	1.00
GBT07030 Holy Mage Irena R	.20	.30
GBT07031 Spherical Lord Dragon R	.20	.30
GBT07032 Dragon Fang Chainshots Sutherland R	.20	.30
GBT07033 Radiant Dragon R	.40	.60
GBT07034 Dragon Knight Roia R	.20	.30
GBT07035 Super Giant of Light Enigman Crossray R	.20	.30
GBT07036 Great Cosmic Hero Grandmantle R	.20	.30
GBT07037 Cosmic Hero Grandrifter R	.20	.30
GBT07038 Mask of Demonic Frenzy Ericrius R	.40	.60
GBT07039 Ninebreak Hustler R	.20	.30
GBT07040 Doppel Vampir R	.60	1.00
GBT07041 Doreen the Thruster R	.60	1.00
GBT07042 Blade Wing Tynwhitt R	.20	.30
GBT07043 Interdimensional Beast Floatgear Hippogriff R	.20	.30
GBT07044 Steam Scalar Emellanna R	.20	.30
GBT07045 Requiem Pegasus C	.15	.25
GBT07046 Treatment Nurse C	.15	.25
GBT07047 Frontal Celestial Melejal C	.15	.25
GBT07048 Laser Clutcher Keel C	.15	.25
GBT07049 Rear Impetus Celestial Armaiti C	.15	.25
GBT07050 Celestial Emergency Pegasus C	.15	.25
GBT07051 Drill Motor Nurse C	.15	.25
GBT07052 Black Report Ridwan C	.15	.25
GBT07053 Surgery Angel C	.15	.25
GBT07054 Knight of Compassionate Light Bradott C	.15	.25
GBT07055 Bullrgal C	.15	.25
GBT07056 Knight of the Faint Sun Marcia C	.15	.25
GBT07057 Crimson Lion Beast Howell C	.15	.25
GBT07058 Holy Mage Connor C	.15	.25
GBT07059 Aquamarine Lion Shyle C	.15	.25
GBT07060 Bashhgal C	.15	.25
GBT07061 Player of the Holy Pipe Gerrie C	.15	.25
GBT07062 Dragon Knight Basuit C	.15	.25
GBT07063 Wyvern Strike Galgi C	.15	.25
GBT07064 Dragon Knight Nadim C	.15	.25
GBT07065 Seal Dragon Barathea C	.15	.25
GBT07066 Apex Dragon Mage Kinnara C	.15	.25
GBT07067 Dragon Dancer Marcel C	.15	.25
GBT07068 Dragon Knight Nadel C	.15	.25
GBT07069 Seal Dragon Doskin C	.15	.25
GBT07070 Serrated Dracokid C	.15	.25
GBT07071 Spiritburn Dragon C	.15	.25
GBT07072 Inspire Yell Dragon C	.15	.25
GBT07073 Cosmic Hero Grandgardy C	.15	.25
GBT07074 Elegance Feather C	.15	.25
GBT07075 Enigman Crescent C	.15	.25
GBT07076 Menacing Monster Golmenas C	.15	.25
GBT07077 Enigman Squall C	.15	.25
GBT07078 Cosmic Hero Grandvicle C	.15	.25
GBT07079 Foxy Charmy C	.15	.25
GBT07080 Magical Inspector Tolbe C	.15	.25
GBT07081 Cosmic Hero Grandhop C	.15	.25
GBT07082 Justice Gold C	.15	.25
GBT07083 Enigman Warm C	.15	.25
GBT07084 Operator Girl Erika C	.15	.25
GBT07085 Cosmic Hero Grandscold C	.15	.25
GBT07086 Frosty Steeple C	.15	.25
GBT07087 Tragic Claw C	.15	.25
GBT07088 Blade Wing Sykes C	.15	.25
GBT07089 Threein the Dark C	.15	.25
GBT07090 Combust Vampir C	.15	.25
GBT07091 Serpent Charmer C	.15	.25
GBT07092 Blade Wing Rodbiss C	.15	.25
GBT07093 Enigmatic Assassin C	.15	.25
GBT07094 Werbrummbar Soldat C	.15	.25
GBT07095 Squareone Dragon C	.15	.25
GBT07096 Steam Knight Mudar C	.15	.25
GBT07097 Drainvalve Dragon C	.15	.25
GBT07098 Quiet Sleepcalling Gear Tapir C	.15	.25
GBT07099 Steam Fighter Attab C	.15	.25
GBT07100 Parallel Barrel Dragon C	.15	.25
GBT07101 Steam Fighter Nanneya C	.15	.25
GBT07102 Toothedge Dracokid C	.15	.25
GBT07103 Steam Scalar Lange C	.15	.25
GBT07104 Snow Elemental Hyakko C	.15	.25
GBT07S13 Golden Beast Sleimy Flare SP	6.00	10.00
GBT07S14 Sunrise Ray Knight Gurguit SP	20.00	30.00
GBT07S15 Dawning Knight Gorboduc SP	12.00	20.00
GBT07S16 Scarface Lion SP	10.00	15.00
GBT07S17 Holy Seraph Suriel SP	15.00	25.00
GBT07S18 Black Shiver Gavrail SP	25.00	40.00
GBT07S19 Black Call Nakir SP	20.00	30.00
GBT07S20 Black Spark Munkar SP	15.00	25.00
GBT07S21 Flame Wing Steel Beast Denial Griffin SP	20.00	30.00
GBT07S22 Dragonic Blademaster SP	15.00	25.00
GBT07S23 Lava Flow Dragon SP	40.00	60.00
GBT07S24 Dragon Knight Jannat SP	20.00	30.00
GBT07S25 Super Cosmic Hero Xcarivou SP	8.00	12.00
GBT07S26 Great Cosmic Hero Grandgallop SP	30.00	50.00
GBT07S27 Cosmic Hero Grandrope SP	12.00	20.00
GBT07S28 Cosmic Hero Grandbeat SP	12.00	20.00
GBT07S29 Abominable One Gilles de Rais SP	20.00	30.00
GBT07S30 Nighttime Gentleman SaintGermain SP	6.00	10.00
GBT07S31 Scharhrot Vampir SP	20.00	30.00
GBT07S32 Succubus of Pure Love SP	25.00	40.00
GBT07S33 Oneeyed Succubus SP	20.00	30.00
GBT07S34 Steam Scalar Emellanna SP	10.00	15.00
GBT07S35 Steam Maiden Arlim SP	40.00	60.00

2016 Cardfight Vanguard G Booster Set 8 Absolute Judgment

RELEASED ON OCTOBER 7, 2016		
GBT08001 Mythical Hellsky Beast Fenrir GR	4.00	6.00
GBT08001 Mythical Hellsky Beast Fenrir SGR	10.00	15.00
GBT08002 One Steeped in Sin Scharhrot GR	5.00	8.00
GBT08002 One Steeped in Sin Scharhrot SGR	8.00	12.00
GBT08003 Blazing Sword Fides RRR	4.00	6.00
GBT08003 Blazing Sword Fides SP	10.00	15.00
GBT08004 Golden Dragon Glorious Reigning Dragon RRR	8.00	12.00
GBT08004 Golden Dragon Glorious Reigning Dragon SP	20.00	30.00
GBT08005 Prehistoric Regalia Urth RRR	5.00	8.00
GBT08005 Prehistoric Regalia Urth SP	15.00	25.00
GBT08006 Genesis Dragon Flageolet Messiah RRR	4.00	6.00
GBT08006 Genesis Dragon Flageolet Messiah SP	10.00	15.00
GBT08007 Glanzend Vampir RRR	1.00	1.50
GBT08007 Glanzend Vampir SP	5.00	8.00
GBT08008 Carnivorous Megatrick Prana RRR	1.00	1.50
GBT08008 Carnivorous Megatrick Prana SP	4.00	6.00
GBT08009 Tempestcalling Pirate King Goauche RRR	6.00	10.00
GBT08009 Tempestcalling Pirate King Goauche SP	10.00	15.00
GBT08010 Flower Princess of Balmy Breeze Ilmatar RRR	1.00	1.50
GBT08010 Flower Princess of Balmy Breeze Ilmatar SP	2.50	4.00
GBT08011 Vivid Sacred Staff Andragius RR	.20	.30
GBT08011 Vivid Sacred Staff Andragius SP	2.50	4.00
GBT08012 Holy Mage Lavinia RR	.20	.30
GBT08013 Skydome Battle Maiden Hanasatsuki RR	.20	.30
GBT08014 Regalia of the Present Age Verthandi RR	.20	.30
GBT08015 Stake Fetter Thviti RR	.20	.30
GBT08016 Genesis Beast Destiny Guardian RR	2.00	3.00
GBT08017 Succubus of Avarice RR	.75	1.25
GBT08018 Doting Harlequin Maja RR	.75	1.25
GBT08018 Doting Harlequin Maja SP	20.00	30.00
GBT08019 Great Witch Doctor of Banquets Negrolily RR	.40	.60
GBT08019 Great Witch Doctor of Banquets Negrolily SP	12.00	20.00
GBT08020 Rampage Shade RR	.60	1.00
GBT08021 Flower Princess of Autumn Scenery Verna RR	.50	.75
GBT08021 Flower Princess of Autumn Scenery Verna SP	5.00	8.00
GBT08022 Arboros Dragon Ain Soph Aur RR	.20	.30
GBT08023 Knight of Persistence Fulgenius R	.15	.25
GBT08024 Knight of Flight Danius R	.15	.25
GBT08025 Stilling Jewel Knight Estelle R	.15	.25
GBT08026 Knight of the Remaining Sun Henrinus R	.75	1.25
GBT08027 Knight of Morning Light Horsa R	.40	.60
GBT08028 Ice Crest Goddess Svava R	.40	.60
GBT08029 Boulder Fetter Gjoll R	.15	.25
GBT08030 Secret Elsie R	.15	.25
GBT08031 Starvader Infinite Distarv R	.15	.25
GBT08032 Punishment Deletor Gieron R	.15	.25
GBT08033 Reversal Starvader Nobelium R	.15	.25
GBT08034 Demonted Executioner R	1.25	2.00
GBT08035 Edge in the Darkness R	.15	.25
GBT08036 Barking Dragon Tamer R	.15	.25
GBT08037 Praised Evil Tamer Mireille R	.15	.25
GBT08038 Nightmare Doll Claris R	.15	.25
GBT08039 Great Skipper Supreme Solger R	.15	.25
GBT08040 Rambling Shade R	.15	.25
GBT08041 Summers Height Flower Maiden Marjukka R	.15	.25
GBT08042 Warden of Arboros Airi R	.15	.25
GBT08043 Sunwheel Maiden Rauni R	.15	.25
GBT08044 Bulwark of Arboros Sanelma R	.15	.25
GBT08045 Knight of Mastery Glenus C	.10	.15
GBT08046 Escort Eagle C	.10	.15
GBT08047 Knight of Influence Ornas C	.10	.15
GBT08048 Knight of Ceremonies Pil C	.10	.15
GBT08049 Mariningal C	.10	.15
GBT08050 Sanctuary of Light Shooting Ray C	.40	.60
GBT08051 Silent Sage Sharon C	.10	.15
GBT08052 Knight of the Scorching Sun Arvirarkus C	.10	.15
GBT08053 Knight of Autumn Light Regan C	.10	.15
GBT08054 Dexxgal C	.10	.15
GBT08055 Riding Rookie C	.10	.15
GBT08056 Battle Maiden Azusa C	.10	.15
GBT08057 Battle Maiden Kotonoha C	.60	1.00
GBT08058 Battle Maiden Touka C	.10	.15
GBT08059 Shackle Fetter Gelgja C	.50	.75
GBT08060 Nextera Regalia Skuld C	.10	.15
GBT08061 Fetter Creator Van C	.10	.15
GBT08062 Goddess of Extension Auxesia C	.10	.15
GBT08063 Goddess of Fruition Carpo C	.10	.15
GBT08064 Ringing Rabbit C	.10	.15
GBT08065 Goddess of Sound Sleep Tahro C	.50	.75
GBT08066 Drill Monk of the Fierce Foot C	.10	.15
GBT08067 Lady Battler of the Black Dwarf C	.40	.60
GBT08068 Starvader Gemingar Dragon C	.10	.15
GBT08069 Overeat Deletor Onagil C	.10	.15
GBT08070 Starvader Heliopause Dragon C	.10	.15
GBT08071 Proton Kicker Protonstriker C	.10	.15
GBT08072 Queen of Nightmareland Hartrud C	.10	.15
GBT08073 Dum of Nightmareland C	.10	.15
GBT08074 Blood Sacrifice Ruthven C	.10	.15
GBT08075 Succubus of Desire C	.10	.15
GBT08076 Dormouse of Nightmareland C	.10	.15
GBT08077 Vroukalakas C	.10	.15
GBT08078 Spade Jack of Nightmareland C	.10	.15
GBT08079 Dee of Nightmareland C	.10	.15
GBT08080 Redstar Dualhorn C	.10	.15
GBT08081 Magical Boxtreamer C	.10	.15
GBT08082 Unicycle Tumbler C	.10	.15
GBT08083 Novelty Introductor C	.10	.15
GBT08084 Entertain Messenger C	.10	.15
GBT08085 Nightmare Doll Pamela C	.10	.15
GBT08086 Nightmare Doll Dory C	.10	.15
GBT08087 Seven Seas Pillager Nightspinel C	.10	.15
GBT08088 Handsomeness Gianmario C	.10	.15
GBT08089 Carl the Ghostie C	.10	.15
GBT08090 Bale the Ghostie C	.10	.15
GBT08091 Witch Doctor of the Seven Seas Raistutor C	.10	.15
GBT08092 Skeleton Assault Soldier C	.10	.15
GBT08093 Rookie Pirate Gina C	.10	.15
GBT08094 Cody the Ghostie C	.10	.15
GBT08095 Arboros Compost Dragon C	.10	.15
GBT08096 Battle Maiden of the Southern Wind Plume C	.10	.15
GBT08097 Hydrangea Knight C	.10	.15
GBT08098 Screen of Arboros Aila C	.10	.15
GBT08099 Pleasantsound Maiden Imarlute C	.10	.15
GBT08100 Bittergourd in Chanpuru C	.10	.15
GBT08101 Saladada Familia C	.10	.15
GBT08102 Maiden of Evolvulus C	.10	.15
GBT08103 Maiden of Zephyranthes C	.10	.15
GBT08104 Rain Elemental Pichan C	.10	.15
GBT08Re01 Genesis Dragon Amnesty Messiah R	3.00	5.00
GBT08S13 Transcending the Heavens Altmile SP	5.00	8.00
GBT08S14 Aerial Divine Knight Altmile SP	15.00	25.00
GBT08S15 Blue Sky Knight Altmile SP	2.50	4.00
GBT08S16 Laurel Knight Sicilus SP	20.00	30.00
GBT08S17 Skydome Battle Maiden Hanasatsuki SP	5.00	8.00
GBT08S18 Mythic Beast Fenrir SP	20.00	30.00
GBT08S19 Mythic Beast Skoll SP	12.00	20.00
GBT08S20 Stake Fetter Thviti SP	4.00	6.00
GBT08S21 Genesis Beast Destiny Guardian SP	20.00	30.00
GBT08S22 Alter Ego Messiah SP	6.00	10.00
GBT08S23 Destiny Dealer SP	15.00	25.00
GBT08S24 Blink Messiah SP	12.00	20.00
GBT08S25 Dragon Masquerade Harri SP	12.00	20.00
GBT08S26 Masked Magician Harri SP	10.00	15.00
GBT08S27 Masquerade Bunny SP	8.00	12.00
GBT08S28 Darkside Sword Master SP	6.00	10.00
GBT08S29 Mist Phantasm Pirate King Nightrose SP	8.00	12.00
GBT08S30 Vampire Princess of Night Fog Nightrose SP	15.00	25.00
GBT08S31 Tommy the Ghostie Brothers SP	8.00	12.00
GBT08S32 Rampage Shade SP	15.00	25.00
GBT08S33 Ranunculus in Glorious Bloom Ahsha SP	6.00	10.00
GBT08S34 Dreamspinning Ranunculus Ahsha SP	25.00	40.00
GBT08S35 Ranunculus Flower Maiden Ahsha SP	5.00	8.00
GBT08S36 Valkyrie of Reclamation Padmini SP	6.00	10.00

2016 Cardfight Vanguard G Booster Set 9 Divine Dragon Caper

RELEASED ON DECEMBER 16, 2016		
GBT09001 Conquering Supreme Dragon Dragonic Vanquisher VMAX GR	4.00	6.00
GBT09001 Conquering Supreme Dragon Dragonic Vanquisher VMAX SGR	10.00	15.00
GBT09002 Storm of Lament Wailing Thavas GR	4.00	6.00
GBT09002 Storm of Lament Wailing Thavas SGR	6.00	10.00
GBT09003 Holy Seraph Altiel RRR	4.00	6.00
GBT09003 Holy Seraph Altiel SP	10.00	15.00
GBT09004 True Revenger Raging Rapt Dragon RRR	4.00	6.00
GBT09004 True Revenger Raging Rapt Dragon SP	15.00	25.00
GBT09005 Dragdriver Luard RRR	2.50	4.00
GBT09005 Dragdriver Luard SP	8.00	12.00
GBT09006 Dragwizard Morfessa RRR	2.00	3.00
GBT09006 Dragwizard Morfessa SP	10.00	15.00
GBT09007 True Eradicator Dragonic Descendant Zillion RRR	4.00	6.00
GBT09007 True Eradicator Dragonic Descendant Zillion SP	12.00	20.00
GBT09008 Great Hero Rising Supernova RRR	2.00	3.00
GBT09008 Great Hero Rising Supernova SP	4.00	6.00
GBT09009 Metapulsar Split Pegasus RRR	2.50	4.00
GBT09009 Metapulsar Split Pegasus SP	15.00	25.00
GBT09010 Blue Storm Helical Dragon Disaster Maelstrom RRR	4.00	6.00
GBT09010 Blue Storm Helical Dragon Disaster Maelstrom SP	20.00	30.00
GBT09011 Holy Celestial Anafiel RR	.20	.30
GBT09012 Black Devote Phaleg RR	.50	.75
GBT09013 Dark Dragon Plotmaker Dragon RR	2.50	4.00
GBT09013 Dark Dragon Plotmaker Dragon SP	15.00	25.00
GBT09014 Dragsaver Esras RR	20.00	30.00
GBT09015 Sky Guardian Supreme Dragon Bulwark Dragon RR	3.00	5.00
GBT09015 Sky Guardian Supreme Dragon Bulwark Dragon SP	15.00	25.00
GBT09016 Wyvern Defender Guld RR	.60	1.00
GBT09017 King of Sadism Dudley Caligula RR	.50	.75
GBT09018 Juggernaut Maximum Maximum RR	.40	.60
GBT09018 Juggernaut Maximum Maximum SP	2.00	3.00
GBT09019 Pulsar Tamer LugalUre RR	.60	1.00
GBT09020 Blue Wave Brave General Artiom RR	.30	.50
GBT09021 Blue Storm Deterrence Dragon Ice Barrier Dragon RR	2.00	3.00
GBT09021 Blue Storm Deterrence Dragon Ice Barrier Dragon SP	10.00	15.00
GBT09022 Battle Siren Janka RR	.30	.50
GBT09023 Excellence Celestial Yophiel R	.15	.25
GBT09024 Absorb Celestial Bahariya R	.15	.25
GBT09025 Black Mirage Hageete R	.15	.25
GBT09026 Mage of Enticement Ildona R	.15	.25
GBT09027 Revenger Slay Hex Dragon R	.15	.25
GBT09028 Revenger Detonate Heat Dragon R	.15	.25
GBT09029 Abyssal Owl R	1.25	2.00
GBT09030 Pole Star Eradicator Zuitan R	.15	.25
GBT09031 Roaring Thunder Spear Jalil R	.15	.25
GBT09032 Eradicator Dragonic Deathscythe R	.50	.75

GBT09033 Trainee Monk Dragon R	.15	.25
GBT09034 Ascetic Dracokid R	.15	.25
GBT09035 Dudley Turborappler R	.15	.25
GBT09036 Lethal Forward R	.15	.25
GBT09037 Dudley Jetter R	.15	.25
GBT09038 Dudley Cheers Linda R	.15	.25
GBT09039 Pulsar Flarescent Dragon R	.15	.25
GBT09040 Pulsar Stratos Falcon R	.15	.25
GBT09041 Marine General of Twin Bullets Cretas R	.15	.25
GBT09042 Blue Wave Marine General Iason R	.15	.25
GBT09043 Kelpie Rider Nikitas R	.15	.25
GBT09044 Kelpie Rider Vallas R	.15	.25
GBT09045 Elastic Bipolar Rahtiel C	.10	.15
GBT09046 Artistic Celestial Machariel C	.10	.15
GBT09047 Black Relief Aratoron C	.10	.15
GBT09048 Million Ray Pegasus C	.10	.15
GBT09049 Thousand Ray Pegasus C	.10	.15
GBT09050 First Aid Corgi C	.10	.15
GBT09051 Black Omen Phul C	.10	.15
GBT09052 Doctoroid Felias C	.10	.15
GBT09053 Teardrop Phoenix C	.30	.50
GBT09054 High Treble Angel C	.10	.15
GBT09055 Knight of Serial Blade Diarmud C	.10	.15
GBT09056 Ferocious Attack Revenger Dylan C	.10	.15
GBT09057 Assist Owlner Maighneis C	.10	.15
GBT09058 Revenger Weitgore Dragon C	.10	.15
GBT09059 Detecting Revenger Aife C	.10	.15
GBT09060 Leadbau C	.10	.15
GBT09061 Commanding Knight Gnesa C	.10	.15
GBT09062 Lingering Night Revenger Conrad C	.10	.15
GBT09063 Rabidmyu C	.10	.15
GBT09064 Knight of Ironcluster Craiftine C	1.25	2.00
GBT09065 Groundbreaking General Bisham C	.10	.15
GBT09066 Eradicator Lightning Phoenix C	.10	.15
GBT09067 Martial Arts Dragon C	.10	.15
GBT09068 Zoomdive Dragoon C	.10	.15
GBT09069 Eradicator Strike Slasher Dragon C	.10	.15
GBT09070 Grudge Toxin Eradicator Seiobo C	.10	.15
GBT09071 Dragon Dancer Fatine C	.25	.40
GBT09072 Eradicator Ambitious Dragoon C	.10	.15
GBT09073 Honorable Monk Dragon C	.10	.15
GBT09074 Demonic Dragon Nymph Cordo C	.10	.15
GBT09075 Djinn of Rainy Duststorm C	.10	.15
GBT09076 Serial Bomber C	.10	.15
GBT09077 Outrage Lineback C	.10	.15
GBT09078 Dudley Ingram C	.10	.15
GBT09079 Mayhem Tiger C	.10	.15
GBT09080 Airforce Eliza C	.10	.15
GBT09081 Fullspeed Specter C	.10	.15
GBT09082 Dudley Littleroad C	.10	.15
GBT09083 Mecha Coach C	.10	.15
GBT09084 Dandy Regista C	.10	.15
GBT09085 Cheer Girl Sundra C	.10	.15
GBT09086 Silence Joker C	.10	.15
GBT09087 Pulsar Speedy Bunny C	.10	.15
GBT09088 Pulsar Tamer Nepada C	.10	.15
GBT09089 Heavy Wrench Dracokid C	.10	.15
GBT09090 Pulsar Rush Boar C	.10	.15
GBT09091 Pulsar Hypnosis Sheep C	.10	.15
GBT09092 Stragglefin Dragon C	.10	.15
GBT09093 Blue Wave Marine General Damia C	.10	.15
GBT09094 Blue Wave Marine General Lucianos C	.25	.40
GBT09095 Kelpie Rider Paul C	.10	.15
GBT09096 Blue Wave Soldier Cimon C	.10	.15
GBT09097 Blue Wave Dragon Submerge Dragon C	.10	.15
GBT09098 Battle Siren Cressida C	.10	.15
GBT09099 Blue Wave Recruit Yiotis C	.10	.15
GBT09100 Harpoon Dracokid C	.10	.15
GBT09101 Flambe Sailor C	.10	.15
GBT09102 Battle Siren Mallika C	.10	.15
GBT09103 Dolphin Soldier of Leaping Windy Seas C	.10	.15
GBT09104 Light Elemental Honoly C	1.00	1.50
GBT09Re01 Storm Dominator Commander Thavas R	2.00	3.00
GBT09Re02 Conquering Supreme Dragon Dragonic Vanquisher VOLTAGE R	2.00	3.00
GBT09Re03 Revenger Raging Form Dragon R	2.00	3.00
GBT09Re04 Eradicator Dragonic Descendant R	2.00	3.00
GBT09Re05 Blue Storm Supreme Dragon Glory Maelstrom R	2.00	3.00
GBT09S13 Dragheart Luard SP	50.00	75.00
GBT09S14 Abyssal Owl SP	15.00	25.00
GBT09S15 Karma Collector SP	8.00	12.00
GBT09S16 Conquering Supreme Dragon Dragonic Vanquisher VOLTAGE SP	10.00	15.00
GBT09S17 Dragonic Vanquisher SP	4.00	6.00
GBT09S18 Mighty Bolt Dragoon SP	10.00	15.00
GBT09S19 Lightning of Triumphant Return Reseph SP	5.00	8.00
GBT09S20 Exceptional Expertise Rising Nova SP	12.00	20.00
GBT09S21 Acrobat Verdi SP	10.00	15.00
GBT09S22 Liar Lips SP	2.50	4.00
GBT09S23 Storm Dominator Commander Thavas SP	8.00	12.00
GBT09S24 One Who Surpasses the Storm Thavas SP	4.00	6.00
GBT09S25 Kelpie Rider Nikki SP	15.00	25.00
GBT09S26 Kelpie Rider Petros SP	8.00	12.00

2017 Cardfight Vanguard G Booster Set 10 Raging Clash of the Blade Fangs

RELEASED ON APRIL 14, 2017

GBT10001 Draganger Ogma GR	10.00	15.00
GBT10001 Draganger Ogma SGR	20.00	30.00
GBT10002 Favorite Champ Victor GR	10.00	15.00
GBT10002 Favorite Champ Victor SGR	12.00	20.00
GBT10003 Holy Dragon Luminous Hope Dragon RRR	1.25	2.00
GBT10003 Holy Dragon Luminous Hope Dragon SP	4.00	6.00
GBT10004 Golden Knight of Gleaming Fang Garmore RRR	2.50	4.00
GBT10004 Golden Knight of Gleaming Fang Garmore SP	10.00	15.00
GBT10005 Holy Sword of Heavenly Law Gurguit RRR	5.00	8.00
GBT10005 Holy Sword of Heavenly Law Gurguit SP	15.00	25.00
GBT10006 Golden Holy Sword Gurguit RRR	2.50	4.00
GBT10006 Golden Holy Sword Gurguit SP	25.00	40.00
GBT10007 Great Emperor Dragon Gaia Dynast RRR	4.00	6.00
GBT10007 Great Emperor Dragon Gaia Dynast SP	5.00	8.00
GBT10008 Rogue Deity of the Third Realm Yasuie Gouma RRR	4.00	6.00
GBT10008 Rogue Deity of the Third Realm Yasuie Gouma SP	15.00	25.00
GBT10009 Exxcessive Battler Victor RRR	1.25	2.00
GBT10009 Exxcessive Battler Victor SP	2.00	3.00
GBT10010 Governing Flower Princess Selfina RRR	1.00	1.50
GBT10010 Governing Flower Princess Selfina SP	2.50	4.00
GBT10011 Belial Owl RR	8.00	12.00
GBT10012 Knight of Daylight Kinarius RR	.60	1.00
GBT10013 Holy Mage Alessia RR	.60	1.00
GBT10013 Holy Mage Alessia SP	6.00	10.00
GBT10014 Absolute Authority Giant Wall Blockade Ganga RR	.60	1.00
GBT10015 Frenzy Emperor Dragon Gaia Death Parade RR	.50	.75
GBT10015 Frenzy Emperor Dragon Gaia Death Parade SP	1.50	2.50
GBT10016 Baking Flame Dragon Gigant Flame RR	.40	.60
GBT10017 Ambush Demon Stealth Dragon Hyakki Zora Asogi RR	.20	.30
GBT10018 Stealth Rogue of the Trial Yasuie RR	.50	.75
GBT10018 Stealth Rogue of the Trial Yasuie SP	1.25	2.00
GBT10019 Stealth Rogue of Envy Ikyuu RR	.50	.75
GBT10020 Sonne Blaukluger RR	.50	.75
GBT10021 Meteokaiser Unior RR	.40	.60
GBT10021 Meteokaiser Unior SP	2.00	3.00
GBT10022 Vollmond Blaukluger RR	.25	.40
GBT10023 Holy Dragon Attract Rune Dragon R	.15	.25
GBT10024 Knight of Encouragement Harbon R	.15	.25
GBT10025 Dark Dragon Animus Pile Dragon R	.15	.25
GBT10026 Evil Refuser Dragon R	.15	.25
GBT10027 Golden Dragon Build Peak Dragon R	.15	.25
GBT10028 Knight of Teaching Judon R	.15	.25
GBT10029 Super Ancient Dragon Burn Geryon R	.15	.25
GBT10030 Destruction Tyrant Full Bladerex R	.15	.25
GBT10031 Savage Sorcerer R	.15	.25
GBT10032 Savage Mystique R	.15	.25
GBT10033 Covert Demonic Dragon Hyakki Zora R	.15	.25
GBT10034 Stealth Dragon Fudoublast R	.30	.50
GBT10035 Stealth Rogue of Compression Sarashinahime R	.15	.25
GBT10036 Loveholic Stealth Rogue Tamanoi R	.15	.25
GBT10037 Giant Star of Zenith Moai the Supreme R	.15	.25
GBT10038 Uranus Blaukluger R	.30	.50
GBT10039 Bare Knuckle Ernest R	.15	.25
GBT10040 Extreme Battler Banget R	.15	.25
GBT10041 Defending Goddess R	.15	.25
GBT10042 Sacred Tree Dragon Resonate Dragon R	.15	.25
GBT10043 Charm Maiden Nicola R	.15	.25
GBT10044 Heat Elemental Bobo R	3.00	5.00
GBT10045 Knight of Crescent Moon Gratia C	.10	.15
GBT10046 Knight of Backwater Remis C	.10	.15
GBT10047 Plusgal C	.10	.15
GBT10048 Knight of Contest Edern C	.10	.15
GBT10049 Knight of Selection Fergus C	.10	.15
GBT10050 Dragwizard Midir C	.10	.15
GBT10051 Knight of Rebellious Spirit Aldan C	.10	.15
GBT10052 Dragwizard Siarl C	.10	.15
GBT10053 Holy Mage Rossa C	.10	.15
GBT10054 Liberator Stiletto Hawk C	.10	.15
GBT10055 Holy Mage Maraine C	.10	.15
GBT10056 Chasegal Liberator C	.10	.15
GBT10057 Banagal Liberator C	.10	.15
GBT10058 Sparkling Flash Glint Knight C	.10	.15
GBT10059 Explorer of Good News C	.10	.15
GBT10060 Sword Horned Dragon Scatherex C	.10	.15
GBT10061 Savage Head C	.10	.15
GBT10062 Steel Bullet Dragon Barragerex C	.10	.15
GBT10063 Ancient Dragon Hilaeonpike C	.10	.15
GBT10064 Rusher Erasmo C	.10	.15
GBT10065 Evil Bullet Dragon Raptrex C	.10	.15
GBT10066 Fullfire Elk C	.10	.15
GBT10067 Savage Lancer C	.10	.15
GBT10068 Ancient Dragon Pterakid C	.10	.15
GBT10069 Rupture Dragon Minirex C	.10	.15
GBT10070 Young Dragon Dinobaby C	.10	.15
GBT10071 Savage Notice C	.10	.15
GBT10072 Aid Styraco C	.10	.15
GBT10073 Ancient Dragon Dinodile C	.10	.15
GBT10074 Louder Ammonite C	.10	.15
GBT10075 Stealth Rogue of Tricks Taemahime C	.10	.15
GBT10076 Stealth Fiend Murder Lantern C	.10	.15
GBT10077 Stealth Dragon Katon Slayer C	.10	.15
GBT10078 Stealth Rogue of Nirvana Yaegaki C	.10	.15
GBT10079 Stealth Dragon Senryou Raid C	.10	.15
GBT10080 Stealth Fiend Watayuki C	.10	.15
GBT10081 Stealth Fiend Umbredanuki C	.10	.15
GBT10082 Stealth Dragon Hitodama Handler C	.10	.15
GBT10083 Stealth Rogue of Sturdiness Terukage C	.10	.15
GBT10084 Stealth Beast Sting Wolf C	.10	.15
GBT10085 Stealth Rogue of Beauty Agemaki C	.10	.15
GBT10086 Stealth Beast Oyama Cat C	.10	.15
GBT10087 Stealth Fiend Dart Spider C	.10	.15
GBT10088 Quad Gigas C	.10	.15
GBT10089 Saturn Blaukluger C	.10	.15
GBT10090 Spart Centaur C	.10	.15
GBT10091 Magical Spinner C	.10	.15
GBT10092 Venus Blaukluger C	.10	.15
GBT10093 Neptune Blaukluger C	.10	.15
GBT10094 Furious Puncher C	.10	.15
GBT10095 Clay doll Chariots C	.10	.15
GBT10096 Petit Ace C	.10	.15
GBT10097 Mega Hammer Lady C	.10	.15
GBT10098 Toughness Jane C	.10	.15
GBT10099 Red Lightning C	.10	.15
GBT10100 Extreme Battler Winning break C	2.00	3.00
GBT10101 Lily Narcissus Flower Maiden Eliana C	.10	.15
GBT10102 Assistant Maiden Lucie C	.10	.15
GBT10103 Maiden of Cucumber C	.10	.15
GBT10104 Ringer Paprika C	.10	.15
GBT10Re01 Supremacy Black Dragon Aurageyser Dragon RRR	2.50	4.00
GBT10Re02 Wolf Fang Liberator Garmore RRR	1.00	1.50
GBT10Re03 Galaxy Blaukluger RRR	1.25	2.00
GBT10Re04 Blau Dunkelheit RRR	.40	.60
GBT10S13 Emperor Dragon Gaia Emperor SP	4.00	6.00
GBT10S14 Prism Bird SP	3.00	5.00
GBT10S15 Cannon Fire Dragon Parasaulauncher SP	1.25	2.00
GBT10S16 Ambush Demon Stealth Rogue Yasuie Tenma SP	4.00	6.00
GBT10S17 Stealth Rogue of Revelation Yasuie SP	2.50	4.00
GBT10S18 Gateway Stealth Rogue Ataka SP	4.00	6.00
GBT10S19 Meteokaiser Victor SP	2.00	3.00
GBT10S20 Exxtreme Battler Victor SP	4.00	6.00
GBT10S21 Extreme Battler Arashid SP	4.00	6.00

2017 Cardfight Vanguard G Booster Set 11 Demonic Advent

RELEASED ON SEPTEMBER 1, 2017

GBT11001 Holy Divine Knight Gancelot Peace Saver GR	10.00	15.00
GBT11001 Holy Divine Knight Gancelot Peace Saver SGR	25.00	40.00
GBT11002 Metapulsar Mystery freeze Dragon GR	1.25	2.00
GBT11002 Metapulsar Mystery freeze Dragon SGR	8.00	12.00
GBT11003 Divine Knight of Valor Halbwachs RRR	.50	.75
GBT11003 Divine Knight of Valor Halbwachs SP	2.50	4.00
GBT11004 Goddess of Investigation Ishtar RRR	2.00	3.00
GBT11004 Goddess of Investigation Ishtar SP	10.00	15.00
GBT11005 Prime Beauty Amaruda RRR	.50	.75
GBT11005 Prime Beauty Amaruda SP	3.00	5.00
GBT11006 Flare Arms Ziegenburg RRR	6.00	10.00
GBT11006 Flare Arms Ziegenburg SP	25.00	40.00
GBT11007 Dragonic Blademaster Kouen RRR	.60	1.00
GBT11007 Dragonic Blademaster Kouen SP	3.00	5.00
GBT11008 Enma Stealth Rogue Mujinlord RRR	3.00	5.00
GBT11008 Enma Stealth Rogue Mujinlord SP	6.00	10.00
GBT11009 One who Splits Darkness Bledermaus RRR	2.00	3.00
GBT11009 One who Splits Darkness Bledermaus SP	5.00	8.00
GBT11010 One who Scatters Sin Scharhrot RRR	3.00	5.00
GBT11010 One who Scatters Sin Scharhrot SP	6.00	10.00
GBT11011 Metapulsar Avenir Phoenix RRR	2.00	3.00
GBT11011 Metapulsar Avenir Phoenix SP	10.00	15.00
GBT11012 Maiden of Divine Spring Lien RR	.75	1.25
GBT11013 Witch Queen of Congratulation Nasturtium RR	.20	.30
GBT11014 Dark Wolf that Hunts Deities Fenrir RR	.20	.30
GBT11015 Goddess of Fort Kibitsuhime RR	.60	1.00
GBT11015 Goddess of Fort Kibitsuhime SP	3.00	5.00
GBT11016 ?Flare Trooper Dumjid RR	.20	.30
GBT11016 ?Flare Trooper Dumjid SP	2.00	3.00
GBT11017 Enma Stealth Dragon Maguntenbu RR	2.50	4.00
GBT11018 Rikudo Stealth Dragon Gehourakan RR	.20	.30
GBT11019 Stealth Dragon Fuurai RR	.60	1.00
GBT11020 Stealth Dragon Utsuroi RR	1.00	1.50
GBT11020 Stealth Dragon Utsuroi SP	2.50	4.00
GBT11021 Amons Red Eye Forneus RR	.20	.30
GBT11022 Closet Balloon RR	.20	.30
GBT11023 Pulsar Drastic Colossus RR	.20	.30
GBT11024 Pulsar Cruising Dragon RR	3.00	5.00
GBT11025 Little Great Sage Marron R	.40	.60
GBT11026 New Style Blaster Llew R	.40	.60
GBT11027 Goddess of Twill Tagwoot R	.15	.25
GBT11028 Witch of Pure Star Anis R	.15	.25
GBT11029 Goddess of Favorable Wind Ninnil R	.15	.25
GBT11030 Witch of Aster Star R	.15	.25
GBT11031 Witch of Fruit of Knowledge Rooibos R	.15	.25
GBT11032 Helldeity Seal Dragon Granitcross R	.15	.25
GBT11033 Divine Dragon Knight Abd Salam R	.40	.60
GBT11034 Dragon Knight Mbudi R	.15	.25
GBT11035 Seal Dragon Prison Guard Atar R	.15	.25
GBT11036 Rikudo Stealth Rogue Kurehalord R	.15	.25
GBT11037 Stealth Dragon Tenrei R	.50	.75
GBT11038 Sorrowful Slice Lujairus R	.15	.25
GBT11039 Cryptid Gnaw Liege Sabnac R	.15	.25
GBT11040 Amons Eye Agares R	.15	.25
GBT11041 Covetous Succubus R	.15	.25
GBT11042 Brennen Vampir R	.15	.25
GBT11043 Wertiger Jaeger R	1.00	1.50
GBT11044 Amons Vallation Bufstare R	.15	.25
GBT11045 Pulsar Tamer Manish R	.15	.25
GBT11046 Pulsar Transit Dragon R	.75	1.25
GBT11047 Pulsar Revolver Dracokid R	.15	.25
GBT11048 Pulsar Tamer Dagan R	.15	.25
GBT11049 Aspire Painter C	.10	.15
GBT11050 Knight of Pulsation Starius C	.10	.15
GBT11051 Arongal C	.20	.30
GBT11052 Battle Maiden Senri C	.10	.15
GBT11053 Multitask Angel C	.10	.15
GBT11054 Goddess of Transitory Awanami C	.10	.15
GBT11055 Detect Angel C	.10	.15
GBT11056 Myth Guard Markab C	.10	.15
GBT11057 Black feathered Witch Stevia C	.10	.15
GBT11058 Goddess of Headwater Nakisawame C	.10	.15
GBT11059 Wraith Witch Sorel C	.10	.15
GBT11060 Teabreak Angel C	.10	.15
GBT11061 Transport Harpy C	.10	.15
GBT11062 Drip Witch Rosemary C	.10	.15
GBT11063 Seal Dragon Seersucker C	.10	.15
GBT11064 Wyvern Strike Jaugo C	.10	.15
GBT11065 Dragon Knight Shakur C	.10	.15
GBT11066 Seal Dragon Grograin C	.10	.15
GBT11067 Wyvern Strike Heineger C	.10	.15
GBT11068 Dragon Knight Tahir C	.10	.15
GBT11069 Dragon Monk Shinsen C	.10	.15
GBT11070 Seal Dragon Birdseye C	.10	.15
GBT11071 Wyvernkid Deidda C	.10	.15
GBT11072 Muzzle Flash Dragon C	.10	.15
GBT11073 Dragon Monk Kikira C	.10	.15
GBT11074 Seal Dragon Artpique C	.10	.15
GBT11075 Dragon Dancer Nilda C	.10	.15
GBT11076 Remarkable Stealth Rogue Morishige C	.10	.15
GBT11077 Demon Stealth Dragon Kassen Myouou C	.10	.15
GBT11078 Stealth Beast Uzuitachi C	.10	.15
GBT11079 Tempest Stealth Rogue Fuuki C	.10	.15
GBT11080 Stealth Dragon Tengai C	.10	.15
GBT11081 Aggressive Stealth Rogue Cheenah C	.10	.15
GBT11082 Hardworking Stealth Rogue Torasada C	.50	.75
GBT11083 Stealth Fiend Daruma Collapse C	.10	.15
GBT11084 Spread Arson C	.10	.15
GBT11085 Amons Follower Audios Thunder C	.10	.15
GBT11086 Big Shaker C	.10	.15
GBT11087 Amons Follower Hateful Cyclone C	.10	.15
GBT11088 Listig Vampir C	.10	.15
GBT11089 Deranged Singular C	.10	.15
GBT11090 Emotional Succubus C	.10	.15
GBT11091 Dark Knight of Nightmareland C,	.10	.15
GBT11092 Hysteric Shirley C	.10	.15
GBT11093 Werkatze Rekrut C	.10	.15
GBT11094 Pulsar Replenish Coatl C	.10	.15
GBT11095 Pulsar Valve Laser Dragon C	.10	.15
GBT11096 Pulsar Rewind Tiger C	.20	.30
GBT11097 Pulsar Nibble Rat C	.10	.15
GBT11098 Pulsar Bling Hawk C	.10	.15
GBT11099 Pulsar Sentry Dracokid C	.10	.15
GBT11100 Pulsar Slash Dog C	.10	.15
GBT11101 Pulsar Fickle Monkey C	.10	.15
GBT11102 Pulsar Tamer Annem C	.10	.15
GBT11103 Pulsar Tamer Mara C	.10	.15
GBT11104 Earth Elemental Connell C	.10	.15
GBT11Re01 Witch Queen of Holy Water Clove RRR	.40	.60
GBT11Re02 Stealth Dragon Shiranui RRR	.40	.60
GBT11Re03 Stealth Dragon Noroi RRR	1.25	2.00
GBT11S13 Maiden of Divine Spring Lien SP	6.00	10.00
GBT11S14 Little Great Sage Marron SP	10.00	15.00
GBT11S15 New Style Blaster Llew SP	5.00	8.00
GBT11S16 Divine Knight King Alfred Holy Saver SP	15.00	25.00
GBT11S17 Blaster Blade Exceed SP	10.00	15.00
GBT11S18 Wingal Youth SP	4.00	6.00
GBT11S19 Enma Stealth Dragon Maguntenbu SP	15.00	25.00
GBT11S20 Stealth Dragon Shiranui SP	2.00	3.00
GBT11S21 Stealth Dragon Noroi SP	10.00	15.00

GBT11S22 Demon Stealth Dragon Shiranui Oboro SP	3.00	5.00
GBT11S23 Rikudo Stealth Dragon Tsukumorakan SP	5.00	8.00
GBT11S24 Closet Balloon SP	2.50	4.00
GBT11S25 Covetous Succubus SP	8.00	12.00
GBT11S26 Wertiger Jaeger SP	12.00	20.00
GBT11S27 One Steeped in Sin Scharhrot SP	6.00	10.00
GBT11S28 Scharhrot Vampir SP	2.50	4.00
GBT11S29 Divine Dragon Knight Abd Salam SP	10.00	15.00
GBT11S30 Dragon Knight Mbudi SP	3.00	5.00
GBT11S31 Supreme Heavenly Emperor Dragon Dragonic Blademaster Taiten SP	4.00	6.00
GBT11S32 Dragonic Blademaster SP	1.50	2.50
GBT11S33 Dark Wolf that Hunts Deities Fenrir SP	2.50	4.00
GBT11S34 Goddess of Twill Tagwoot SP	2.00	3.00
GBT11S35 Goddess of Favorable Wind Ninnil SP	6.00	10.00
GBT11S36 Mythical Hellsky Beast Fenrir SP	4.00	6.00

2017 Cardfight Vanguard G Booster Set 12 Dragon King's Awakening

RELEASED ON OCTOBER 13, 2017

GBT12001 Dragstrider Luard GR	4.00	6.00
GBT12001 Dragstrider Luard SGR	8.00	12.00
GBT12002 Evil eye Hades Emperor Shiranui Mukuro GR	2.50	4.00
GBT12002 Evil eye Hades Emperor Shiranui Mukuro SGR	6.00	10.00
GBT12003 Excite Battle Sister Stollen RRR	1.00	1.50
GBT12003 Excite Battle Sister Stollen SP	8.00	12.00
GBT12004 Still Water Festival Deity Ichikishima RRR	10.00	15.00
GBT12004 Still Water Festival Deity Ichikishima SP	40.00	60.00
GBT12005 Supremacy True Dragon Claret Sword Helheim RRR	4.00	6.00
GBT12005 Supremacy True Dragon Claret Sword Helheim SP	10.00	15.00
GBT12006 Conquering Supreme Dragon Dragonic Vanquisher VBUSTER RRR	2.00	3.00
GBT12006 Conquering Supreme Dragon Dragonic Vanquisher VBUSTER SP	30.00	50.00
GBT12007 Eradicator Dragonic Descendant Sigma RRR	3.00	5.00
GBT12007 Eradicator Dragonic Descendant Sigma SP	12.00	20.00
GBT12008 Dragonic Vanquisher SPARKING RRR	2.50	4.00
GBT12008 Dragonic Vanquisher SPARKING SP	10.00	15.00
GBT12009 Chronodragon Gearnext RRR	4.00	6.00
GBT12009 Chronodragon Gearnext SP	25.00	40.00
GBT12010 Midsummer Flower Princess Lieta RRR	1.00	1.50
GBT12010 Midsummer Flower Princess Lieta SP	4.00	6.00
GBT12011 Plumeria Flower Maiden Sharl RRR	.60	1.00
GBT12011 Plumeria Flower Maiden Sharl SP	5.00	8.00
GBT12012 Battle Sister Florentine RR	.20	.30
GBT12013 Battle Sister Marmalade RR	.50	.75
GBT12014 Supremacy Dragon Claret Sword Dragon Revolt RR	.40	.60
GBT12014 Supremacy Dragon Claret Sword Dragon Revolt SP	12.00	20.00
GBT12015 Dragwizard Naoise RR	2.00	3.00
GBT12016 Stealth Beast Tamahagane Metsu RR	.50	.75
GBT12017 True Eradicator Bravesky Linchu RR	.25	.60
GBT12018 Strong Lightning Circular Blade Gliselle RR	.50	.75
GBT12019 Summon Lightning Dancing Princess Anastasia RR	.75	1.25
GBT12019 Summon Lightning Dancing Princess Anastasia SP	12.00	20.00
GBT12020 Chronotiger Gear Glare RR	.25	.40
GBT12020 Chronotiger Gear Glare SP	6.00	10.00
GBT12021 Pulsar Spearhead Unicorn RR	.40	.60
GBT12022 Pulsar Duplex Dragon RR	.20	.30
GBT12023 Governor Lily Maiden of Fertility RR	.20	.30
GBT12024 Prosperity Maiden Diane RR	.20	.30
GBT12025 Excite Battle Sister Bavarois R	.60	1.00
GBT12026 One Advantage Miko Nanase R	1.25	2.00
GBT12027 Battle Sister Sable R	.15	.25
GBT12028 Rapport Miko Nazuna R	.15	.25
GBT12029 Battle Sister Baumkuchen R	.15	.25
GBT12030 Dragwiser Bronach R	.15	.25
GBT12031 Morion Spear Dragon R	.15	.25
GBT12032 Sweep Owlner Cethlenn R	.15	.25
GBT12033 Cherishing Knight Branwen R	.25	.40
GBT12034 Dragwizard Semias R	.15	.25
GBT12035 Stealth Dragon Ungai R	1.25	2.00
GBT12036 Stealth Beast Meimoudanuki R	.15	.25
GBT12037 Stealth Beast Gekisouookami R	.15	.25
GBT12038 Spiritual Wisdom Creator Brahma R	.15	.25
GBT12039 Lightning Strike of Aspiration Helena R	.15	.25
GBT12040 Smash Boxer Dragon R	.15	.25
GBT12041 Fire Pillar Eradicator Castor R	.15	.25
GBT12042 Mighty Bolt Dragoon R	.15	.25
GBT12043 Steam Lynx Adad apra R	.15	.25
GBT12044 Pushing Advance Gear Tiger R	.15	.25
GBT12045 Protector Lotus Maiden of Yggdrasil R	.15	.25
GBT12046 Sacred Tree Dragon Rainbow Cycle Dragon R	.15	.25
GBT12047 Maiden of Profuse R	.15	.25
GBT12048 Resistant Lemone R	.15	.25
GBT12049 Goddess of Regimentation? Tagirihime C	.10	.15
GBT12050 Remaining Moon Miko Haruzuki C	.10	.15
GBT12051 Dawning Moon Miko Akizuki C	.10	.15
GBT12052 Elite Heath C	.10	.15
GBT12053 Weather Girl Shake C	.10	.15
GBT12054 Weather Girl Lassi C	.10	.15
GBT12055 Protective Cat C	.10	.15
GBT12056 Battle Sister Kipferl C	.10	.15
GBT12057 Wonder Child of Elegance Asahiko C	.10	.15
GBT12058 Hauser Dario C	.10	.15
GBT12059 Battle Sister Churros C	.10	.15
GBT12060 Battle Sister Ganache C	.10	.15
GBT12061 Efficient Carp C	.10	.15
GBT12062 Gigantech Shutter C	.10	.15
GBT12063 Demon World Castle Fangenbose C	.10	.15
GBT12064 Swift Owl C	.10	.15
GBT12065 Dragwizard Enid C	.10	.15
GBT12066 Blue Espada Dragon C	.10	.15
GBT12067 Dilarbau C	.10	.15
GBT12068 Pedigree Knight Tigresse C	.10	.15
GBT12069 Dragwizard Babd C	.10	.15
GBT12070 Stealth Rogue of Rejection Yorihira C	.10	.15
GBT12071 Stealth Dragon Houjin C	.10	.15
GBT12072 Blasting Stealth Rogue Teruyoshi C	.10	.15
GBT12073 Dashing Stealth Rogue Genzou C	.10	.15
GBT12074 Stealth Dragon Dreadmaster C	.10	.15
GBT12075 Stealth Beast Kazemomo C	.10	.15
GBT12076 Electrobutcher Dragon C	.10	.15
GBT12077 Shutdown Eradicator Dokukakuji C	.10	.15
GBT12078 Plasmatron Dragon C	.10	.15
GBT12079 Demonic Dragon Berserker Chatura C	.10	.15
GBT12080 Wyvern Strike Timlarsh C	.10	.15
GBT12081 Ambush Eradicator Kosangyou C	.10	.15
GBT12082 Hardrod Dracokid C	.10	.15
GBT12083 Eradicator Drag Phoenix C	.10	.15
GBT12084 Soothing Eradicator Gyokumen C	.10	.15
GBT12085 Storm Eradicator Shiva C	.10	.15
GBT12086 Eradicator Sharp Impact Dragon C	.10	.15
GBT12087 Pulsar Overrush Ox C	.10	.15
GBT12088 Steam Knight Shulgi C	.10	.15
GBT12089 Steam Lynx Nadin C	.10	.15
GBT12090 Steam Lynx Enme C	.10	.15
GBT12091 Pulsar Tamer Hegardo C	.10	.15
GBT12092 Steam Gunner Shusin C	.10	.15
GBT12093 Pulsar Thruster Bison C	.10	.15
GBT12094 Integrity Flower Maiden Ritaleena C	.10	.15
GBT12095 Knight of Consideration Memorim C	.10	.15
GBT12096 Maiden of Grow Shine C	.10	.15
GBT12097 Little Benefit Dragon C	.10	.15
GBT12098 Loving Maiden Valilla C	.10	.15
GBT12099 Knight of Discretion Memorid C	.10	.15
GBT12100 Maiden of Breed Rain C	.10	.15
GBT12101 Maiden of Collantes C	.10	.15
GBT12102 Flowerpot Elf C	.10	.15
GBT12103 Lupinus Knight C	.10	.15
GBT12104 Air Elemental Broorun C	.10	.15
GBT12Re01 Dragonic Vanquisher RRR	.30	.50
GBT12Re02 Steam Tamer Arka RRR	5.00	8.00

2017 Cardfight Vanguard G Booster Set 13 Ultimate Stride

RELEASED ON DECEMBER 17, 2017

GBT13001 Zeroth Dragon of Inferno, Drachma ZR	50.00	75.00
GBT13002 Zeroth Dragon of Distant Sea, Megiddo ZR	30.00	50.00
GBT13003 Supreme Heavenly Emperor Dragon, Dragonic Overlord "The Purge" GR	8.00	12.00
GBT13004 Marshal General of Surging Seas, Alexandros GR	8.00	12.00
GBT13005 Fanatic Seraph, Gavrail Eden RRR	2.50	4.00
GBT13005 Fanatic Seraph, Gavrail Eden SP	15.00	25.00
GBT13006 Black Shock, Gavrail Prim RRR	5.00	8.00
GBT13006 Black Shock, Gavrail Prim SP	50.00	75.00
GBT13007 Master Swordsman of First Light, Gurguit Helios RRR	10.00	15.00
GBT13007 Master Swordsman of First Light, Gurguit Helios SP	40.00	60.00
GBT13008 Dragonic Overlord "The Destiny" RRR	4.00	6.00
GBT13008 Dragonic Overlord "The Destiny" SP	30.00	50.00
GBT13009 New Destruction Emperor, Gaia Devastate RRR	.60	1.00
GBT13009 New Destruction Emperor, Gaia Devastate SP	5.00	8.00
GBT13010 Dharma Deity of the Five Precepts, Yasuie Genma RRR	2.00	3.00
GBT13010 Dharma Deity of the Five Precepts, Yasuie Genma SP	15.00	25.00
GBT13011 Blue Wave Marshal Dragon, Flood Hazard Dragon RRR	1.00	1.50
GBT13011 Blue Wave Marshal Dragon, Flood Hazard Dragon SP	12.00	20.00
GBT13012 Supreme Ruler of the Storm, Thavas RRR	2.00	3.00
GBT13012 Supreme Ruler of the Storm, Thavas SP	25.00	40.00
GBT13013 Blue Wave Marshal, Valeos RRR	6.00	10.00
GBT13013 Blue Wave Marshal, Valeos SP	8.00	12.00
GBT13014 Black Prepare, Arakiba RR	.60	1.00
GBT13015 Eradicate Celestial, Raviel RR	.50	.75
GBT13016 Flash Fang Liberator, Garmore Excel RR	.20	.30
GBT13016 Flash Fang Liberator, Garmore Excel SP	3.00	5.00
GBT13017 Liberator, Shaggy Rabbit RR	1.25	2.00
GBT13018 Dragon Dancer, Tara RR	2.00	3.00
GBT13019 Convalesce Aunis RR	.40	.60
GBT13020 Stealth Fiend, Tamayuki RR	.30	.50
GBT13021 Black Horn King, Bullpower Agrias RR	2.50	4.00
GBT13021 Black Horn King, Bullpower Agrias SP	25.00	40.00
GBT13022 Giant, Rising Great Star RR	.20	.30
GBT13023 Dudley Cheers, Linsey RR	.75	1.25
GBT13024 Blue Storm Breaking Dragon, Engulf Maelstrom RR	.75	1.25
GBT13024 Blue Storm Breaking Dragon, Engulf Maelstrom SP	12.00	20.00
GBT13025 Blue Storm Supreme Dragon, Lordly Maelstrom RR	.75	1.25
GBT13026 Blue Wave Shield General, Yorgos RR	.20	.30
GBT13027 Blue Wave Engineer, Refit Sailor RR	2.50	4.00
GBT13028 Holy Celestial, Raguel R	.15	.25
GBT13029 Holy Seraph, Parashel R	.15	.25
GBT13030 Grafting Celestial, Jhudiel R	.15	.25
GBT13031 Black Carve, Ezezel R	.15	.25
GBT13032 Black Call, Nakir R	.15	.25
GBT13033 Shining True Liberator, Solemn Glitter R	.15	.25
GBT13034 Knight of Sunny Day, Salonius R	.15	.25
GBT13035 Liberator, Improve Falcon R	.40	.60
GBT13036 Supreme Heavenly Emperor Dragon, Accend Grave Dragon R	.15	.25
GBT13037 Glow Heater Dragon R	.50	.75
GBT13038 Light Wave Dragon, Chasmolukes R	.15	.25
GBT13039 Heavy Bullet Dragon, Diablocannon R	.15	.25
GBT13040 Prism Bird R	.15	.25
GBT13041 Sweetly Smiling Ice Petal, Shirayuki R	.15	.25
GBT13042 Six Flowers of Phantasms, Shirayuki R	.15	.25
GBT13043 Stealth Rogue of Revenge, Ooboshi R	.30	.50
GBT13044 Gateway Stealth Rogue, Ataka R	.15	.25
GBT13045 Durable Barrier, Hecaton Gyace R	.15	.25
GBT13046 Cold-blooded Advisor, Cunning Brain R	.15	.25
GBT13047 Blue Wave Armor General, Galfilia R	.15	.25
GBT13048 Blue Storm Soldier, Eldermoss R	.25	.40
GBT13049 Blue Wave Marine General, Galleass R	.40	.60
GBT13050 Blue Wave Marine General, Foivos R	.15	.25
GBT13051 Kelpie Rider, Nikki R	.15	.25
GBT13052 Mixed Element, Colburn R	.15	.25
GBT13053 Black Wisdom, Sraosha C	.10	.15
GBT13054 Antibody Pegasus C	.10	.15
GBT13055 Thermic Shot Nurse C	.10	.15
GBT13056 Kind Care, Sartael C	.25	.40
GBT13057 Black Talent, Lyla C	.10	.15
GBT13058 Doctoroid Doritas C	.10	.15
GBT13059 Initial Celestial, Ruhiel C	.10	.15
GBT13060 Black Curse, Muriel C	.10	.15
GBT13061 Hospital Diet Angel C	.10	.15
GBT13062 Nutrient Angel C	.10	.15
GBT13063 Doctoroid Radlas C	.10	.15
GBT13064 Militant Act Dragon C	.10	.15
GBT13065 Ajargal Liberator C	.10	.15
GBT13066 Easgal Liberator C	.10	.15
GBT13067 Knight of Insolation, Carinus C	.10	.15
GBT13068 Liberator, Board Andalusian C	.10	.15
GBT13069 Young Lion Liberator, Romanus C	.10	.15
GBT13070 Plodmy Liberator C	.10	.15
GBT13071 Dragon Knight, Ysaar C	.10	.15
GBT13072 Burning Horn Evolute C	.60	1.00
GBT13073 Doom Bringer High Flame C	.75	1.25
GBT13074 Dragon Knight, Naim C	.10	.15
GBT13075 Recuperate Dracokid C	.10	.15
GBT13076 Lizard Attacker, Conroe C	.10	.15
GBT13077 Fire Chase Dragon C	.30	.50
GBT13078 Great Cannon Dragon, Heavy Arzene C	.10	.15
GBT13079 Savage Ranger C	.10	.15
GBT13080 Gliding Dragon, Dimorglide C	.10	.15
GBT13081 Buckshot Dragon, Spread Amarga C	.10	.15
GBT13082 Black Wing Dragon, Raven Ptera C	.10	.15
GBT13083 Savage Conjurer C	.10	.15
GBT13084 Child Dragon, Little Tyranno C	.10	.15
GBT13085 Furious Hair Stealth Rogue, Ikkaku C	.10	.15
GBT13086 Stealth Rogue of Enmity, Sodehagi C	.10	.15
GBT13087 Stealth Beast, Instant Swapper C	.10	.15
GBT13088 Stealth Rogue of Entertainment, Senbei C	.10	.15
GBT13089 Stealth Beast, Siren Fox C	.10	.15
GBT13090 Disciple Stealth Rogue, Minosuke C	.10	.15
GBT13091 Stealth Rogue of Unhappiness, Shirasagi C	.10	.15
GBT13092 Power Flicker C	.10	.15
GBT13093 Prompt Cheetah C	.10	.15
GBT13094 Laser Blackguard C	.10	.15
GBT13095 Jet Power Dusty C	.10	.15
GBT13096 Fake Bomber C	.10	.15
GBT13097 Jet Motor Dosty C	.10	.15
GBT13098 Prospective Starkie C	.10	.15
GBT13099 Dudley Striker C	.10	.15
GBT13100 Dudley Schemer C	.10	.15
GBT13101 Mecha Instructor C	.10	.15
GBT13102 Blue Wave Dragon, Arsenal Fleet Dragon C	.10	.15
GBT13103 Battle Siren, Cipla C	.10	.15
GBT13104 Blue Wave Marine General, Media C	.10	.15
GBT13105 Blue Wave Soldier Senior, Beragios C	.10	.15
GBT13106 Dragon Rider, Dinos C	.10	.15
GBT13107 Blue Wave Recruit, Kosty C	.10	.15
GBT13108 Blue Wave Soldier, Brutal Trooper C	.10	.15
GBT13109 Blue Wave Soldier, Bluegill Trooper C	.10	.15
GBT13110 Blue Wave Soldier, Twinhead Shark C	.10	.15
GBT13Re01 Black Shiver, Gavrail RRR	1.25	2.00
GBT13Re02 Emperor Dragon, Gaia Emperor RRR	2.50	4.00
GBT13Re03 Blue Wave Marshal Dragon, Tetra-boil Dragon RRR	1.00	1.50
GBT13Re04 One Who Surpasses the Storm, Thavas RRR	.30	.50
GBT13Re05 Great Warrior, Dudley Geronimo RRR	.50	.75

2018 Cardfight Vanguard G Booster Set 14 Divine Dragon Apocrypha

RELEASED ON MARCH 9, 2018

GBT14001 Dragon Deity of Destruction, Gyze // Neon Gyze ZR	15.00	25.00
GBT14002 Zeroth Dragon of Zenith Peak, Ultima ZR	60.00	100.00
GBT14003 Zeroth Dragon of End of the World, Dust ZR	20.00	30.00
GBT14004 Immortal Holy Sword, Fides GR	2.00	3.00
GBT14005 Chronovisor Heritage GR	1.25	2.00
GBT14006 Higher Deity Knight, Altmile RRR	.75	1.25
GBT14006 Higher Deity Knight, Altmile SP	10.00	15.00
GBT14007 Dragabyss, Luard RRR	1.00	1.50
GBT14007 Dragabyss, Luard SP	20.00	30.00
GBT14008 Dragfall, Luard RRR	2.00	3.00
GBT14008 Dragfall, Luard SP	50.00	75.00
GBT14009 Ultimate Regalia of Almighty, Minerva RRR	3.00	5.00
GBT14009 Ultimate Regalia of Almighty, Minerva SP	40.00	60.00
GBT14010 Evil-eye Vidya Emperor, Shiranui "Rinne" RRR	5.00	8.00
GBT14010 Evil-eye Vidya Emperor, Shiranui "Rinne" SP	25.00	40.00
GBT14011 Blazing Demonic Stealth Dragon, Shiranui "Zanki" RRR	2.00	3.00
GBT14011 Blazing Demonic Stealth Dragon, Shiranui "Zanki" SP	15.00	25.00
GBT14012 One who Hunts Souls, Balaam RRR	3.00	5.00
GBT14012 One who Hunts Souls, Balaam SP	12.00	20.00
GBT14013 One who Proceeds Towards Daybreak, Scharhrot RRR	1.00	1.50
GBT14013 One who Proceeds Towards Daybreak, Scharhrot SP	10.00	15.00
GBT14014 Chronojet Dragon Z RRR	4.00	6.00
GBT14014 Chronojet Dragon Z SP	25.00	40.00
GBT14015 Peerless Knight, Livarot RR	.20	.30
GBT14016 Remedy Angel RR	.60	1.00
GBT14017 Slaptail Dragon RR	.60	1.00
GBT14018 Emancipating Revenger, Allyl RR	1.00	1.50
GBT14019 Goddess of Mercy, Inanna RR	.20	.30
GBT14020 Regalia of Wisdom, Angelica RR	.60	1.00
GBT14020 Regalia of Wisdom, Angelica SP	20.00	30.00
GBT14021 Regalia of Frost, Jotun RR	.40	.60
GBT14021 Regalia of Frost, Jotun SP	10.00	15.00
GBT14022 Regalia of Service, Eir RR	1.00	1.50
GBT14023 Stealth Fiend, Quesera Basara RR	.50	.75
GBT14024 Evil God Bishop, Gastille RR	.20	.30
GBT14024 Evil God Bishop, Gastille SP	8.00	12.00
GBT14025 Fallen Angel of Disconnection, Akrasiel RR	.20	.30
GBT14026 Amon's Follower, Abysm Lust RR	.60	1.00
GBT14027 Chronomedical Hamster RR	.75	1.25
GBT14028 Holy Dragon, Defendhold Dragon R	.15	.25
GBT14029 Septgal R	.15	.25
GBT14030 Lunarfang Knight, Felax R	.15	.25
GBT14031 Knight of Favorable Odds, Ascanius R	.15	.25
GBT14032 Dark Dragon, Darkveil Dragon R	.15	.25
GBT14033 Dragfencer, Dagda R	.15	.25
GBT14034 Draglancer, Daellad R	.15	.25
GBT14035 Ultimate Regalia of Crimson, Muspell R	.15	.25
GBT14036 Ultimate Regalia of Affection, Eir R	.15	.25
GBT14037 Goddess of Karmic Wind, Ningal R	.15	.25
GBT14038 Regalia of Abundance, Freyja R	.15	.25
GBT14039 Regalia of Benevolent Wind, Flap Angel R	.15	.25
GBT14040 Regalia of Hypocenter, Kukurihime R	.15	.25
GBT14041 Rikudo Stealth Dragon, Gandokurakan R	.15	.25
GBT14042 Stealth Rogue of Liquidation, Sadatsugu R	.15	.25
GBT14043 Darkness Unleashed, Freiheit R	.15	.25
GBT14044 Accumulated Attachment, Druj Nasu R	.15	.25
GBT14045 Succubus of Jealousy R	.15	.25
GBT14046 Succubus of Pure Love R	.15	.25
GBT14047 Pulsar Saver, Ilishu R	.15	.25
GBT14048 Pulsar, Metal Party Dragon R	.15	.25
GBT14049 Pulsar, Merry Block Dragon R	.15	.25
GBT14050 Pulsar, Revolver Dracokid R	.15	.25
GBT14051 Pulsar, Bombard Hog R	.15	.25
GBT14052 Knight of Connection, Pictus C	.10	.15
GBT14053 Big Sword Angel C	.10	.15
GBT14054 Gyoonmy C	.10	.15
GBT14055 ?Blinking Knight, Millius C	.10	.15
GBT14056 Knight of Vibrancy, Lyrrdis C	.10	.15
GBT14057 Subjugate Dragon C	.10	.15
GBT14058 Dragwizard, Gaunan C	.10	.15
GBT14059 Dragwizard, Iucharba C	.10	.15
GBT14060 Dragwizard, Fuamnach C	.10	.15
GBT14061 Dragraptor, Mauthe C	.10	.15
GBT14062 Dragwizard, Vicreau C	.10	.15
GBT14063 Zagghau C	.10	.15
GBT14064 Regalia of Activity, Iouun C	.10	.15
GBT14065 Goddess of the Abyss, Ereshkigal C	.10	.15
GBT14066 Regalia of Poem, Bragi C	.10	.15
GBT14067 Regalia of Ideas, Genil C	.10	.15
GBT14068 Deemed Angel C	.10	.15
GBT14069 Regalia of Amulets, Expel Angel C	.10	.15
GBT14070 Regalia of Brewing, Bennu C	.10	.15
GBT14071 Regalia of Dawn, Daylight Angel C	.10	.15
GBT14072 Tinkling Angel C	.10	.15
GBT14073 Regalia of Offering, Offer Angel C	.10	.15
GBT14074 Regalia of Thoughts, Feeling Angel C	.10	.15

GBT14075 Spirit-calling Stealth Master, Suzu C	.10	.15
GBT14076 Stealth Dragon, Enbai C	.10	.15
GBT14077 Stealth Dragon, Bakuren C	.10	.15
GBT14078 Stealth Rogue of Vista, Ayagiri C	.10	.15
GBT14079 Stealth Dragon, Ouzai C	.10	.15
GBT14080 Stealth Beast, Mistfrog C	.10	.15
GBT14081 Stealth Dragon, Burai C	.10	.15
GBT14082 Stealth Fiend, Kageusa C	.10	.15
GBT14083 Forschung Vampir C	.10	.15
GBT14084 Baleful Repressor C	.10	.15
GBT14085 Gamboling Psychokiller C	.10	.15
GBT14086 Wertiger Plunderer C	.10	.15
GBT14087 Revolting Bolt C	.10	.15
GBT14088 Whitefang Wielder C	.10	.15
GBT14089 Wackstum Vampir C	.10	.15
GBT14090 Werwolf Angreifer C	.10	.15
GBT14091 Spirit Inviter C	.10	.15
GBT14092 Werfrede Informant C	.10	.15
GBT14093 Pulsar, Proceed Sheep C	.10	.15
GBT14094 Pulsar Tamer, Igigi C	.10	.15
GBT14095 Pulsar, Crash Monkey C	.10	.15
GBT14096 Pulsar Tamer, Zanbiia C	.10	.15
GBT14097 Pulsar, Spring Rabbit C	.10	.15
GBT14098 Chrono Dran Z C	.10	.15
GBT14099 Pulsar, Hypnosis Sheep C	.10	.15
GBT14100 Shadow Elemental, Bikkun C	.10	.15
GBT14Re01 Knight of Heavenly Decree, Altmile RRR	.60	1.00
GBT14Re02 Dragwizard, Morfessa RRR	.60	1.00
GBT14Re03 Rikudo Stealth Dragon, Tsukumorakan RRR	.50	.75
GBT14SR01 Zeroth Dragon of Zenith Peak, Ultima SCR	60.00	100.00
GBT14SR02 Zeroth Dragon of Inferno, Drachma SCR	40.00	60.00
GBT14SR03 Zeroth Dragon of Destroy Star, Stark SCR	30.00	50.00
GBT14SR04 Zeroth Dragon of End of the World, Dust SCR	25.00	40.00
GBT14SR05 Zeroth Dragon of Distant Sea, Megiddo SCR	25.00	40.00
GBT14SR06 Zeroth Dragon of Death Garden, Zoa SCR	25.00	40.00

2018 Cardfight Vanguard V Booster Set 1 Unite Team Q4

COMPLETE SET (93)	350.00	450.00
RELEASED ON JUNE 22, 2018		
VBT01001 King of Knights, Alfred VR	12.00	20.00
VBT01001 King of Knights, Alfred SVR	20.00	30.00
VBT01002 Imperial Daughter VR	15.00	25.00
VBT01002 Imperial Daughter SVR	20.00	30.00
VBT01003 Dragonic Waterfall VR	15.00	25.00
VBT01003 Dragonic Waterfall SVR	20.00	30.00
VBT01004 Perfect Raizer VR	12.00	20.00
VBT01004 Perfect Raizer SVR	15.00	25.00
VBT01005 Soul Saver Dragon RRR	4.00	6.00
VBT01006 High Dog Breeder, Akane RRR	3.00	5.00
VBT01007 CEO Amaterasu RRR	3.00	4.00
VBT01007 CEO Amaterasu OR	25.00	40.00
VBT01008 Silent Tom RRR	2.00	3.00
VBT01009 Circle Magus RRR	2.00	3.00
VBT01010 Berserk Dragon RRR	6.00	10.00
VBT01011 Flame of Hope, Aermo RRR	3.00	5.00
VBT01012 Asura Kaiser RRR	.60	1.00
VBT01012 Asura Kaiser OR	6.00	10.00
VBT01013 Conjurer of Mithril RR	.20	.30
VBT01014 Little Sage, Marron RR	.50	.75
VBT01015 Flash Shield, Iseult RR	4.00	5.00
VBT01016 Victorious Deer RR	.20	.30
VBT01017 Promise Daughter RR	.40	.60
VBT01018 Weather Forecaster, Miss Mist RR	.75	1.25
VBT01019 Cruel Dragon RR	.20	.30
VBT01020 Dragonic Gaias RR	.20	.30
VBT01021 Wyvern Guard, Barri RR	2.00	3.00
VBT01022 Hi-powered Raizer Custom RR	.30	.50
VBT01023 Raizer Custom RR	.30	.50
VBT01024 Twin Blader RR	1.00	1.50
VBT01025 Funelgal R	.15	.25
VBT01026 Knight of Rose, Morgana R	.15	.25
VBT01027 Pongal R	.15	.25
VBT01028 Yellow Witch, MeMe R	.15	.25
VBT01029 Goddess of Insight, Sotoorihime R	.15	.25
VBT01030 Oracle Guardian, Gemini R	.15	.25
VBT01031 Farfalle Magus R	.15	.25
VBT01032 Ruote Magus R	.15	.25
VBT01033 Vortex Dragon R	.15	.25
VBT01034 Prowling Dragon, Striken R	.15	.25
VBT01035 Bellicosity Dragon R	.15	.25
VBT01036 Lizard Soldier, Raopia R	.15	.25
VBT01037 Battledore Fighter R	.15	.25
VBT01038 Miss Splendor R	.15	.25
VBT01039 Burstraizer R	.15	.25
VBT01040 Boomerang Thrower R	.15	.25
VBT01041 Hate Reflector R	.15	.25
VBT01042 Gigantech Charger C	.10	.15
VBT01043 Knight of Devotion, Bergius C	.10	.15
VBT01044 Herculean Knight, Allobrox C	.10	.15
VBT01045 Radical Knight, Anil C	.10	.15
VBT01046 Miru Biru C	.10	.15
VBT01047 Lion Mane Stallion C	.10	.15
VBT01048 Giro C	.10	.15
VBT01049 Battle Maiden, Sarasa C	.10	.15
VBT01050 Resolute Maiden, Chitose C	.10	.15
VBT01051 Weather Girl, Saft C	.10	.15
VBT01052 Solid Turtle C	.10	.15
VBT01053 Goddess of Tide of Times, Mizunohame C	.10	.15
VBT01054 Petal Fairy C	.10	.15
VBT01055 Shooting Hobby C	.10	.15
VBT01056 Luck Bird C	.10	.15
VBT01057 Whiteness Rabbit C	.10	.15
VBT01058 Lozenge Magus C	.10	.15
VBT01059 Oracle Guardian, Nike C	.10	.15
VBT01060 Psychic Bird C	.10	.15
VBT01061 Miracle Kid C	.10	.15
VBT01062 Sphere Magus C	.10	.15
VBT01063 Spillover Dragon C	.10	.15
VBT01064 Flame of Destruction, Verbti C	.10	.15
VBT01065 Dominance Dragon C	.10	.15
VBT01066 Instigate Griffon C	.10	.15
VBT01067 Great Bombing of Hellfire, Gabija C	.10	.15
VBT01068 Fright Lock C	.10	.15
VBT01069 Maximum Raizer C	.10	.15
VBT01070 Iron Killer C	.10	.15
VBT01071 Cup Bowler C	.10	.15
VBT01072 Death Army Guy C	.10	.15
VBT01073 Transraizer C	.10	.15
VBT01074 Rocket Hammer Man C	.10	.15
VBT01075 Jetraizer C	.10	.15
VBT01076 Tap the Hyper C	.10	.15
VBT01077 Battleraizer C	.10	.15
VBT01078 Cat Butler C	.10	.15
VBT01079 Shining Lady C	.10	.15
VBT01080 Red Lightning C	.10	.15
VBT01081 Three Minutes C	.10	.15
VBT01082 Cannon Ball C	.10	.15
VBT01083 Turboraizer C	.10	.15
VBT01084 Wall Boy C	.10	.15
VBT01I01 Blaster Blade IMR	20.00	30.00
VBT01I01 Blaster Blade OR	20.00	30.00
VBT01OR03 Dragonic Overlord OR	20.00	30.00

2018 Cardfight Vanguard V Booster Set 2 Strongest Team AL4

RELEASED ON OCTOBER 19, 2018		
VBT02001 Phantom Blaster Dragon VR	10.00	15.00
VBT02001 Phantom Blaster Dragon SVR	20.00	30.00
VBT02002 Dueling Dragon, ZANBAKU VR	5.00	8.00
VBT02002 Dueling Dragon, ZANBAKU SVR		
VBT02003 No Life King, Death Anchor VR	10.00	15.00
VBT02003 No Life King, Death Anchor SVR	20.00	30.00
VBT02004 Golden Beast Tamer VR	8.00	12.00
VBT02004 Golden Beast Tamer SVR	15.00	25.00
VBT02005 Darkness Maiden, Macha RRR	4.00	6.00
VBT02005 Darkness Maiden, Macha OR	40.00	60.00
VBT02006 Black Sage, Charon RRR	4.00	6.00
VBT02007 Skull Witch, Nemain RRR	10.00	15.00
VBT02008 Swift Archer, FUSHIMI RRR	.50	.75
VBT02008 Swift Archer, FUSHIMI OR	4.00	6.00
VBT02009 Gwynn the Ripper RRR	.50	.75
VBT02009 Gwynn the Ripper OR	4.00	6.00
VBT02010 Vroukalakas RRR	.75	1.25
VBT02011 Nightmare Doll, Alice RRR	2.50	4.00
VBT02011 Nightmare Doll, Alice OR	15.00	25.00
VBT02012 Purple Trapezist RRR	3.00	5.00
VBT02013 Blaster Rapier RR	.20	.30
VBT02014 Blaster Dagger RR	.20	.30
VBT02015 Dark Shield, Mac Lir RR	3.00	5.00
VBT02016 Covert Demonic Dragon, Mandala Lord RR	.20	.30
VBT02017 Twin Swordsman, MUSASHI RR	.20	.30
VBT02018 Stealth Beast, Leaves Mirage RR	.20	.30
VBT02019 Demon Eater RR	.20	.30
VBT02020 Doreen the Thruster RR	1.25	2.00
VBT02021 March Rabbit of Nightmareland RR	2.00	3.00
VBT02022 Artilleryman RR	.20	.30
VBT02023 Jumping Jill RR	.20	.30
VBT02024 Hades Hypnotist RR	2.50	4.00
VBT02025 Dark Mage, Badhabh Caar R	.15	.25
VBT02026 Cursed Lancer R	.15	.25
VBT02027 Stealth Beast, Bloody Mist R	.15	.25
VBT02028 Right Arrester R	.15	.25
VBT02029 Left Arrester R	.15	.25
VBT02030 Stealth Beast, Million Rat R	.15	.25
VBT02031 Stealth Fiend, Hamper Gapper R	.15	.25
VBT02032 Ghoulish Despoiler R	.15	.25
VBT02033 Werwolf Sieger R	.15	.25
VBT02034 Blood Sacrifice, Ruthven R	.15	.25
VBT02035 Prisoner Beast R	.15	.25
VBT02036 Succubus of Dedicated Love R	.15	.25
VBT02037 Nitro Juggler R	.15	.25
VBT02038 Magical Boxtreamer R	.15	.25
VBT02039 Starting Presenter R	.15	.25
VBT02040 Midnight Bunny R	.15	.25
VBT02041 Entire Monkey R	.15	.25
VBT02042 Fiery Knight, Loeg C	.10	.15
VBT02043 Reclusive Knight, Aengus C	.10	.15
VBT02044 Tragic Knight, Cathbad C	.10	.15
VBT02045 Mage of Destruction, Feidlech C	.10	.15
VBT02046 Invest Falcon C	.10	.15
VBT02047 Abyss Router C	.10	.15
VBT02048 Nightmare Painter C	.10	.15
VBT02049 Stealth Fiend, Hyakume Shadow C	.10	.15
VBT02050 Stealth Dragon, Magai Mandala C	.10	.15
VBT02051 Stealth Dragon, Soukoku Zapper C	.10	.15
VBT02052 Stealth Dragon, Turbulent Edge C	.10	.15
VBT02053 Stealth Rogue of Silence, Shijimamaru C	.10	.15
VBT02054 Stealth Dragon, Amatsu Snipe C	.10	.15
VBT02055 Stealth Beast, Cat Devil C	.10	.15
VBT02056 Stealth Beast, Moon Edge C	.10	.15
VBT02057 Stealth Dragon, Zanba Rider C	.10	.15
VBT02058 Stealth Beast, Cat Rouge C	.10	.15
VBT02059 Fox Tamer, Izuna C	.10	.15
VBT02060 Stealth Beast, Ahead Panther C	.10	.15
VBT02061 Stealth Fiend, Yukihime C	.10	.15
VBT02062 Terrifying Fist C	.10	.15
VBT02063 Obstacle Offender C	.10	.15
VBT02064 Succubus of Seductive Smile C	.10	.15
VBT02065 Werbear Verfolger C	.10	.15
VBT02066 Werwolf Freiwilliger C	.10	.15
VBT02067 Anomalous Esper C	.10	.15
VBT02068 Vermillion Gatekeeper C	.10	.15
VBT02069 Werluchs Gefreiter C	.10	.15
VBT02070 Blitzritter C	.10	.15
VBT02071 Hysteric Shirley C	.10	.15
VBT02072 Cursed Doctor C	.10	.15
VBT02073 Comicality Chimera C	.10	.15
VBT02074 Amaranth Beast Tamer C	.10	.15
VBT02075 Dancing Knifedancer C	.10	.15
VBT02076 Dark Metal Bicorn C	.10	.15
VBT02077 Fluster Cadet C	.10	.15
VBT02078 Entertain Messenger C	.10	.15
VBT02079 Dynamite Juggler C	.10	.15
VBT02080 Poison Juggler C	.10	.15
VBT02081 Rainbow Magician C	.10	.15
VBT02082 Skyhigh Walker C	.10	.15
VBT02083 Hoop Magician C	.10	.15
VBT02084 Candy Clown C	.10	.15
VBT02I01 Blaster Dark IMR	30.00	50.00

2019 Cardfight Vanguard V Booster Set 3 Miyaji Academy Cardfight Club

RELEASED ON FEBRUARY 15, 2019		
VBT03001 Monarch Sanctuary Alfred VR	15.00	25.00
VBT03001 Monarch Sanctuary Alfred SVR	15.00	25.00
VBT03002 Pentagonal Magus VR	5.00	8.00
VBT03002 Pentagonal Magus SVR	12.00	20.00
VBT03003 Raven-haired Ezel VR	8.00	12.00
VBT03003 Raven-haired Ezel SVR	15.00	25.00
VBT03004 Covert Demonic Dragon, Magatsu Storm VR	4.00	6.00
VBT03004 Covert Demonic Dragon, Magatsu Storm SVR	4.00	6.00
VBT03005 Detonix Drill Dragon VR	15.00	25.00
VBT03005 Detonix Drill Dragon SVR	15.00	25.00
VBT03006 Knight of Loyalty, Bedivere RRR	4.00	6.00
VBT03006 Knight of Loyalty, Bedivere OR	25.00	40.00
VBT03007 Knight of Friendship, Kay RRR	4.00	6.00
VBT03007 Knight of Friendship, Kay OR	25.00	40.00
VBT03008 Scarlet Witch, CoCo RRR	1.00	1.50
VBT03008 Scarlet Witch, CoCo OR	15.00	25.00
VBT03009 Tetra Magus RRR	10.00	15.00
VBT03010 Great Silver Wolf, Garmore RRR	1.00	1.50
VBT03010 Great Silver Wolf, Garmore OR	12.00	20.00
VBT03011 Stealth Dragon, Magatsu Gale RRR	.30	.50
VBT03012 Detonix Stinger Dragon RRR	2.50	4.00
VBT03013 Dragonic Deathscythe RRR	4.00	6.00
VBT03013 Dragonic Deathscythe OR	20.00	30.00
VBT03014 Swordsman of the Explosive Flames, Palamedes RR	.20	.30
VBT03015 Dream Painter RR	.20	.30
VBT03016 Wisteria Witch, ZoZo RR	.20	.30
VBT03017 Rhombus Magus RR	.20	.30
VBT03018 Flame Wind Lion, Wonder Ezel RR	.25	.40
VBT03019 Crimson Lion Beast, Howell RR	.20	.30
VBT03020 Shura Stealth Dragon, Kujikiricongo RR	.50	.75
VBT03020 Shura Stealth Dragon, Kujikiricongo OR	25.00	40.00
VBT03021 Stealth Dragon, Magatsu Breath RR	.20	.30
VBT03022 Stealth Beast, Mijingakure RR	.20	.30
VBT03023 Dragonic Kaiser Vermillion RR	.20	.30
VBT03024 Rising Phoenix RR	.20	.30
VBT03025 Wyvern Guard, Guld RR	.20	.30
VBT03026 Gifted Knight, Emrys R	.15	.25
VBT03027 Knight of Exemplary Sword, Lucius R	.15	.25
VBT03028 Stellar Magus R	.15	.25
VBT03029 Topaz Witch, PiPi R	.15	.25
VBT03030 Sprout Witch, RoRo R	.15	.25
VBT03031 All-out Knight, Athels R	.15	.25
VBT03032 Knight of Vitality, Brennius R	.15	.25
VBT03033 Stealth Dragon, Voidmaster R	.15	.25
VBT03034 Stealth Rogue of a Thousand Blades, Oborozakura R	.15	.25
VBT03035 Stealth Rogue of the Night, Sakurafubuki R	.15	.25
VBT03036 Stealth Fiend, Oboro Cart R	.15	.25
VBT03037 Stealth Dragon, Dreadmaster R	.15	.25
VBT03038 Stealth Beast, Etekon R	.15	.25
VBT03039 Dusty Plasma Dragon R	.15	.25
VBT03040 Hammerknuckle Dragon R	.15	.25
VBT03041 Lightning of Hope, Helena R	.15	.25
VBT03042 Demolition Dragon R	.15	.25
VBT03043 Rendering Angel C	.10	.15
VBT03044 Knight of Dignity, Caratacus C	.10	.15
VBT03045 Espogal C	.10	.15
VBT03046 Shiftgal C	.10	.15
VBT03047 Dramatic Composer C	.10	.15
VBT03048 Ablagal C	.10	.15
VBT03049 Oracle Guardian, Bia C	.10	.15
VBT03050 Battle Sister, Chouquette C	.10	.15
VBT03051 Briolette Magus C	.10	.15
VBT03052 Phoenix-winged Miko, Chizuru C	.10	.15
VBT03053 Miko of Elegance, Fumino C	.10	.15
VBT03054 Crescent Magus C	.10	.15
VBT03055 Disregard Monkey C	.10	.15
VBT03056 Semilunar Magus C	.10	.15
VBT03057 Knight of Vigorous Strength, Belanus C	.10	.15
VBT03058 Zealous Knight, Gracianus C	.10	.15
VBT03059 Unvarnished Knight, Virargus C	.10	.15
VBT03060 Direcgal C	.10	.15
VBT03061 Bold Sparrow C	.10	.15
VBT03062 Counterattack Knight, Digueillus C	.10	.15
VBT03063 Charjgal C	.10	.15
VBT03064 Stealth Beast, Kokushigarasu C	.10	.15
VBT03065 Shura Stealth Dragon, Kabukicongo C	.10	.15
VBT03066 Stealth Dragon, Dan Breach C	.10	.15
VBT03067 Stealth Beast, Chigasumi C	.10	.15
VBT03068 Momentary Stealth Rogue, Tsunamasa C	.10	.15
VBT03069 Tempest Stealth Rogue, Fuuki C	.10	.15
VBT03070 Stealth Rogue of Intimidation, Kirihage C	.10	.15
VBT03071 Stealth Dragon, Magatsu Wind C	.10	.15
VBT03072 Stealth Beast, Hagakure C	.10	.15
VBT03073 Stealth Dragon, Kurogane C	.10	.15
VBT03074 Stealth Beast, Tobihiko C	.10	.15
VBT03075 Stealth Fiend, Ohtsuzura C	.10	.15
VBT03076 Stealth Fiend, Zashikihime C	.10	.15
VBT03077 Beathawk Dragon C	.10	.15
VBT03078 Fulgurate Foil Dragon C	.10	.15
VBT03079 Rampant Thundering Wyvern C	.10	.15
VBT03080 Scathing Electric Spear, Ramzi C	.10	.15
VBT03081 Dragon Dancer, Regina C	.10	.15
VBT03082 Electrichase Dracokid C	.10	.15
VBT03083 Malevolent Djinn C	.10	.15
VBT03084 Dragon Dancer, Catharina C	.10	.15
VBT03I01 Incandescent Lion, Blond Ezel IMR	40.00	60.00
VBT03I02 Lozenge Magus IMR	25.00	40.00
VBT03Re01 Blaster Blade SP	6.00	10.00

2019 Cardfight Vanguard V Booster Set 4 Vilest Deletor

RELEASED ON MARCH 22, 2019		
VBT04001 Gust Blaster Dragon VR	8.00	12.00
VBT04001 Gust Blaster Dragon SVR	15.00	25.00
VBT04001 Gust Blaster Dragon VDR	60.00	100.00
VBT04002 Dueling Dragon King, ZANGEKI VR	1.50	2.50
VBT04002 Dueling Dragon King, ZANGEKI SVR	5.00	8.00
VBT04002 Dueling Dragon King, ZANGEKI VDR	20.00	30.00
VBT04003 Waving Deletor, Greidhol VR	30.00	50.00
VBT04003 Waving Deletor, Greidhol SVR	10.00	15.00
VBT04003 Waving Deletor, Greidhol VDR	40.00	60.00
VBT04004 King of Masks, Dantarian VR	20.00	30.00
VBT04004 King of Masks, Dantarian SVR	10.00	15.00
VBT04004 King of Masks, Dantarian VDR	25.00	40.00
VBT04005 Gun Salute Dragon, End of Stage VR	2.50	4.00
VBT04005 Gun Salute Dragon, End of Stage SVR	5.00	8.00
VBT04005 Gun Salute Dragon, End of Stage VDR	15.00	25.00
VBT04006 Dark Bond Trumpeter RRR	1.50	2.50
VBT04006 Dark Bond Trumpeter DR	25.00	40.00
VBT04006 Dark Bond Trumpeter OR	25.00	40.00
VBT04007 Black-winged Swordbreaker RRR	5.00	8.00
VBT04007 Black-winged Swordbreaker DR	60.00	100.00
VBT04008 Fantasy Petal Storm, Shirayuki RRR	5.00	8.00
VBT04008 Fantasy Petal Storm, Shirayuki DR	40.00	60.00
VBT04008 Fantasy Petal Storm, Shirayuki OR	40.00	60.00
VBT04009 Schwarzschild Dragon RRR	2.50	4.00
VBT04010 Lie-down Deletor, Given RRR	1.50	2.50
VBT04010 Lie-down Deletor, Given OR	10.00	15.00
VBT04011 Opener of Dark Gates RRR	2.00	3.00
VBT04012 Dimension Creeper RRR	2.50	4.00

VBT04012 Dimension Creeper DR	30.00	50.00
VBT04013 Miss Direction RRR	1.50	2.50
VBT04013 Miss Direction OR	15.00	25.00
VBT04014 Dark Metal Dragon RR	.20	.30
VBT04015 Apocalypse Bat RR	.20	.30
VBT04016 Stealth Fiend, Morote Surveillant RR	.20	.30
VBT04017 Stealth Fiend, Midnight Crow RR	.20	.30
VBT04018 Demonic Hair Stealth Rogue, Grenjin RR	.20	.30
VBT04019 Hailing Deletor, Alba RR	.40	.60
VBT04020 Hailing Deletor, Elro RR	.40	.60
VBT04021 Flowers in Vacuum, Cosmo Wreath RR	10.00	15.00
VBT04022 Master of Fifth Element RR	.25	.40
VBT04023 Flirtatious Succubus RR	.30	.50
VBT04023 Flirtatious Succubus OR	12.00	20.00
VBT04024 Dancing Princess of the Night Sky RR	.20	.30
VBT04024 Dancing Princess of the Night Sky DR	15.00	25.00
VBT04025 Magician of Quantum Mechanics RR	.20	.30
VBT04026 Shadow Blaze Dragon R	.15	.25
VBT04027 Knight of Fighting Spirit, Dordona R	.15	.25
VBT04028 Stealth Fiend, Jakotsu Girl R	.15	.25
VBT04029 Stealth Fiend, Rainy Madame R	.15	.25
VBT04030 Stealth Dragon, Hitsumetsu Blazer R	.15	.25
VBT04031 Penetrate Deletor, Iggy R	.15	.25
VBT04032 Gravity Collapse Dragon R	.15	.25
VBT04033 Ill-fate Deletor, Drown R	.15	.25
VBT04034 Gravity Ball Dragon R	.15	.25
VBT04035 Looting Deletor, Gunec R	.15	.25
VBT04036 Demon Duke of Death, Baal R	.15	.25
VBT04037 Dark Soul Conductor R	.15	.25
VBT04038 Alluring Succubus R	.15	.25
VBT04039 Visible Songster R	.15	.25
VBT04040 Barking Dragon Tamer R	.15	.25
VBT04041 Nightmare Doll, Rhoda R	.15	.25
VBT04042 Nightmare Doll, Edith R	.15	.25
VBT04043 Refusal Mage, Bregis C	.10	.15
VBT04044 Solbau C	.10	.15
VBT04045 Productive Witch, Neness C	.10	.15
VBT04046 Gururubau C	.10	.15
VBT04047 Manibau C	.10	.15
VBT04048 Ensnaring Mage, Conohr C	.10	.15
VBT04049 Fullbau C	.10	.15
VBT04050 Darkside Trumpeter C	.10	.15
VBT04051 Death Feather Eagle C	.10	.15
VBT04052 Howl Owl C	.10	.15
VBT04053 Abyss Healer C	.10	.15
VBT04054 Covert Demonic Dragon, Dansetsu Anarch C	.10	.15
VBT04055 Unyielding Stealth Rogue, Houkaku C	.10	.15
VBT04056 Stealth Dragon, Midoro Pyro C	.10	.15
VBT04057 Stealth Beast, White Mane C	.10	.15
VBT04058 Jamming Impeder C	.10	.15
VBT04059 Stealth Beast, Metamorfox C	.10	.15
VBT04060 Bangasa Stealth Rogue, Sukerock C	.10	.15
VBT04061 Stealth Dragon, Reikou Slug C	.10	.15
VBT04062 Nordstrom Dragon C	.10	.15
VBT04063 Lemaitre Code Dragon C	.10	.15
VBT04064 Brazen Deletor, Gougai C	.10	.15
VBT04065 Embroil Deletor, Jaega C	.10	.15
VBT04066 Manipulator of Gravity Fields C	.10	.15
VBT04067 Micro-hole Dracokid C	.10	.15
VBT04068 Cuticle Killer, Mirche C	.10	.15
VBT04069 Succubus of Worldly Affairs C	.10	.15
VBT04070 Authority of Water C	.10	.15
VBT04071 Awful Nail C	.10	.15
VBT04072 Cuticle Assassin, Sabina C	.10	.15
VBT04073 Silhouette Tracker C	.10	.15
VBT04074 Cuticle Breaker, Pavla C	.10	.15
VBT04075 Direful Noise C	.10	.15
VBT04076 Pathfinder of Wind C	.10	.15
VBT04077 Tricky Assistant C	.10	.15
VBT04078 Diffusion Clown C	.10	.15
VBT04079 Trihex Chimera C	.10	.15
VBT04080 Humorous Chimera C	.10	.15
VBT04081 Endive Beast Tamer C	.10	.15
VBT04082 Nephrite Beast Tamer C	.10	.15
VBT04083 Brassie Bunny C	.10	.15
VBT04084 Barbarous Chimera C	.10	.15
VBT04Re01 Blaster Dark SP	25.00	40.00
VBT04Re02 Dark Shield, Mac Lir SP	25.00	40.00
VBT04SDR06 Docking Deletor, Greion VDR	30.00	50.00

2019 Cardfight Vanguard V Booster Set 5 Aerial Steed Liberation

RELEASED ON AUGUST 30, 2019

VBT05001 Solitary Knight, Gancelot VR	25.00	40.00
VBT05001 Solitary Knight, Gancelot SVR	25.00	40.00
VBT05001 Solitary Knight, Gancelot XVR	150.00	250.00
VBT05002 Goddess of the Full Moon, Tsukuyomi VR	20.00	30.00
VBT05002 Goddess of the Full Moon, Tsukuyomi SVR	25.00	40.00
VBT05003 Blazing Lion, Platina Ezel VR	10.00	15.00
VBT05003 Blazing Lion, Platina Ezel SVR	20.00	30.00
VBT05004 Shura Stealth Dragon, Jamyocongo VR	10.00	15.00
VBT05004 Shura Stealth Dragon, Jamyocongo SVR	20.00	30.00
VBT05005 Eradicator, Gauntlet Buster Dragon VR	15.00	25.00
VBT05005 Eradicator, Gauntlet Buster Dragon SVR	25.00	40.00
VBT05006 Knight of Truth, Gordon RRR	2.00	3.00
VBT05006 Knight of Truth, Gordon SP	30.00	50.00
VBT05007 Knight of the Harp, Tristan RRR	3.00	5.00
VBT05007 Knight of the Harp, Tristan SP	30.00	50.00
VBT05008 Goddess of the Half Moon, Tsukuyomi RRR	5.00	8.00
VBT05008 Goddess of the Half Moon, Tsukuyomi SP	120.00	200.00
VBT05009 Goddess of the Crescent Moon, Tsukuyomi RRR	4.00	6.00
VBT05009 Goddess of the Crescent Moon, Tsukuyomi SP	120.00	200.00
VBT05010 Advance of the Black Chains, Kahedin RRR	2.00	3.00
VBT05010 Advance of the Black Chains, Kahedin SP	25.00	40.00
VBT05011 Stronghold of the Black Chains, Hoel RRR	1.50	2.50
VBT05011 Stronghold of the Black Chains, Hoel SP	25.00	40.00
VBT05012 Stealth Beast, Tamahagane RRR	2.00	3.00
VBT05012 Stealth Beast, Tamahagane SP	30.00	50.00
VBT05013 Fiendish Sword Eradicator, Cho-Ou RRR	5.00	8.00
VBT05013 Fiendish Sword Eradicator, Cho-Ou SP	60.00	100.00
VBT05014 Powerful Sage, Bairon RR	.60	1.00
VBT05014 Powerful Sage, Bairon SP	6.00	10.00
VBT05015 Great Sage, Barron RR	.60	1.00
VBT05016 Soul Guiding Elf RR	.60	1.00
VBT05017 Evil-eye Princess, Euryale RR	.60	1.00
VBT05018 Battle Sister, Macaron RR	.75	1.25
VBT05019 Maiden of Libra RR	.60	1.00
VBT05019 Maiden of Libra SP	15.00	25.00
VBT05020 Shura Stealth Dragon, Tendocongo RR	.60	1.00
VBT05021 Stealth Rogue of Reckless Action, Suou RR	.75	1.25
VBT05021 Stealth Rogue of Reckless Action, Suou SP	15.00	25.00
VBT05022 Stealth Fiend, Tsumujibashou RR	.30	.50
VBT05023 Thunder Break Dragon RR	.75	1.25
VBT05023 Thunder Break Dragon SP	25.00	40.00
VBT05024 Supreme Army Eradicator, Zuitan RR	1.00	1.50
VBT05025 Dragon Dancer, RaiRai RR	.75	1.25
VBT05026 Knight of Severity, Hengist R	.15	.25
VBT05027 Knight of Determination, Lamorak R	.15	.25
VBT05028 Pure Bright Unicorn R	.15	.25
VBT05029 Knight of Indestructibility, Aerina R	.15	.25
VBT05030 Pluck Enchanter R	.15	.25
VBT05031 Fusilli Magus R	.15	.25
VBT05032 Convoy Angel R	.15	.25
VBT05033 White Hare of Inaba R	.15	.25
VBT05034 Diviner Angel R	.15	.25
VBT05035 Coral Witch, ZaZa R	.15	.25
VBT05036 Stealth Rogue of Proscription, Mizukaze R	.15	.25
VBT05037 Stealth Dragon, Daidoku R	.15	.25
VBT05038 Stealth Dragon, Kokujyo R	.15	.25
VBT05039 Landshocker Dragon R	.15	.25
VBT05040 Ceremonial Bonfire Eradicator, Castor R	.15	.25
VBT05041 Desert Gunner, Gaiban R	.15	.25
VBT05042 Dragon Dancer, Eluisa R	.15	.25
VBT05043 Field Feather Dragon C	.10	.15
VBT05044 Gigantech Pulverizer C	.10	.15
VBT05045 Loading Angel C	.10	.15
VBT05046 Engage Griffin C	.10	.15
VBT05047 Inspiring Knight, Cynegils C	.10	.15
VBT05048 Barcgal C	.10	.15
VBT05049 Bringer of Good Luck, Epona C	.10	.15
VBT05050 Future Knight, Llew C	.10	.15
VBT05051 Margal C	.10	.15
VBT05052 Yggdrasil Maiden, Elaine C	.10	.15
VBT05053 Blian Witch, PoPo C	.10	.15
VBT05054 Lilac Witch, BiBi C	.10	.15
VBT05055 Ravioli Magus C	.10	.15
VBT05056 Solid Condo Wizard C	.10	.15
VBT05057 Penne Magus C	.10	.15
VBT05058 Lime Witch, ReRe C	.10	.15
VBT05059 Godhawk, Ichibyoshi C	.10	.15
VBT05060 Psychic Bird C	.10	.15
VBT05061 Battle Sister, Ginger C	.10	.15
VBT05062 Miracle Kid C	.10	.15
VBT05063 Sphere Magus C	.10	.15
VBT05064 Fortune Bell C	.10	.15
VBT05065 Greeting Drummer C	.10	.15
VBT05066 Stealth Beast, Muhou Garou C	.10	.15
VBT05067 Stealth Beast, Arakuregitsune C	.10	.15
VBT05068 Brat Arrow Dragon C	.10	.15
VBT05069 Turning Bash Dragon C	.10	.15
VBT05070 Dragon Knight, Zubayr C	.10	.15
VBT05071 Desert Gunner, Doran C	.10	.15
VBT05072 Dragon Dancer, Noemi C	.10	.15
VBT05073 Dragon Monk, Egan C	.10	.15
VBT05074 Bolt Capture Dragon C	.10	.15
VBT05075 Hundred Thunder Djinn C	.10	.15
VBT05076 Varit Dracokid C	.10	.15
VBT05077 Spark Edge Dracokid C	.10	.15
VBT05078 Old Dragon Mage C	.10	.15
VBT05079 Exorcist Mage, Lin Lin C	.10	.15
VBT05080 Worm Toxin Eradicator, Seiobo C	.10	.15
VBT05XV02 Blaster Blade XVR	120.00	200.00

2012 Cardfight Vanguard Extra Booster Set 2 Diva Festival

RELEASED ON

EB02001 Top Idol, Pacifica RRR	.60	1.00
EB02002 Top Idol, Riviere RRR	8.00	12.00
EB02003 Bermuda Princess, Lena RR	.30	.50
EB02004 Pearl Sisters, Perle RR	.30	.50
EB02005 Pearl Sisters, Perla RR	.60	1.00
EB02006 Girls Rock, Rio RR	.30	.50
EB02007 Mermaid Idol, Ellie RR	1.25	2.00
EB02008 Super Idol, Salem R	.15	.25
EB02009 Top Idol, Flores R	.15	.25
EB02010 Top Idol, Aqua R	.15	.25
EB02011 Super Idol, Riviere R	2.00	3.00
EB02012 Mermaid Idol, Flute R	.15	.25
EB02013 Turquoise Blue, Tyrrhenian R	.15	.25
EB02014 Bermuda [Delta] Cadet, Weddell R	.15	.25
EB02015 Bermuda [Delta] Cadet, Riviere R	.15	.25
EB02016 Velvet Voice, Raindear C	.50	.75
EB02017 Rainbow Light, Carine C	.10	.15
EB02018 Inteli Idol, Mervill C	.10	.15
EB02019 Snow White of the Corals, Claire C	.10	.15
EB02020 Diva of the Clear Seas, Izumi C	.10	.15
EB02021 Mermaid Idol, Sedna C	.10	.15
EB02022 Prism of the Water's Surface, Miltoa C	.10	.15
EB02023 Mermaid Idol, Felucca C	.60	1.00
EB02024 Mermaid Idol, Riviere C	.15	.25
EB02025 Navy Dolphin, Ameer C	.15	.25
EB02026 Blazer Idols C	.10	.15
EB02027 Comical Rainie C	.12	.20
EB02028 Cooking Caspian C	.10	.15
EB02029 Sleeping Beauty, Mousse C	.10	.15
EB02030 Drive Quartet, Ressac C	.10	.15
EB02031 Drive Quartet, Flows C	.10	.15
EB02032 Drive Quartet, Shuplu C	.10	.15
EB02033 Drive Quartet, Bubblin C	.10	.15
EB02034 Bermuda [Delta] Cadet, Shizuku C	.25	.40
EB02035 Bermuda Triangle Cadet, Caravel C	.10	.15
EB02S01 Top Idol, Pacifica SP	5.00	8.00
EB02S06 Girls Rock, Rio SP	10.00	15.00

2012 Cardfight Vanguard Extra Booster Set 3 Cavalry of Black Steel

COMPLETE SET (53)	100.00	200.00
RELEASED ON JULY 7, 2012		
EB03001 Demonic Lord, Dudley Emperor RRR	8.00	12.00
EB03002 Spectral Duke Dragon RRR	15.00	25.00
EB03003 Reckless Express RR	4.00	6.00
EB03004 Martial Arts Mutant, Master Beetle RR	4.00	6.00
EB03005 White Dragon Knight, Pendragon RR	4.00	6.00
EB03006 Origin Mage, Ildona RR	4.00	6.00
EB03007 Dragonic Lawkeeper RR	6.00	10.00
EB03008 Jelly Beans R	1.00	1.50
EB03009 Dudley Daisy R	1.00	1.50
EB03010 Bewitching Officer, Lady Butterfly R	1.25	2.00
EB03011 Toxic Trooper R	1.00	1.50
EB03012 Toxic Soldier R	1.25	2.00
EB03013 Gigantech Destroyer R	1.50	2.50
EB03014 Black Dragon Knight, Vortimer R	1.75	3.00
EB03015 Black Dragon Whelp, Vortimer R	1.25	2.00
EB03016 Twin Shine Swordsman, Marhaus R	1.50	2.50
EB03017 Dragonic Executioner R	1.50	2.50
EB03018 Dudley Douglas C	.15	.25
EB03019 Fierce Leader, Zachary C	.15	.25
EB03020 Field Driller C	.15	.25
EB03021 Medical Manager C	.15	.25
EB03022 Smart Leader, Dark Bringer C	.15	.25
EB03023 Kungfu Kicker C	.15	.25
EB03024 Gyro Slinger C	.15	.25
EB03025 Commander, Garry Gannon C	.15	.25
EB03026 Iron Fist Mutant, Roly Poly C	.15	.25
EB03027 Transmutated Thief, Steal Spider C	.15	.25
EB03028 Machining Mosquito C	.15	.25
EB03029 Pest Professor, Mad Fly C	.15	.25
EB03030 Megacolony Battler C C	.15	.25
EB03031 Awaking Dragonfly C	.15	.25
EB03032 Flash Edge Valkyrie C	.15	.25
EB03033 Scout of Darkness, Vortimer C	.50	.75
EB03034 Blade Feather Valkyrie C	.15	.25
EB03035 War-horse, Raging Storm C	.30	.50
EB03036 Falcon Knight of the Azure C	.30	.50
EB03037 Knight of Determination, Lamorak C	.30	.50
EB03038 Eagle Knight of the Skies C	.15	.25
EB03039 Miru Biru C	.15	.25
EB03040 Knight of Fighting Spirit, Dordona C	.15	.25
EB03041 Cross Shot, Garp C	.15	.25
EB03042 Dragon Armored Knight C	.15	.25
EB03043 Grapeshot Wyvern C	.15	.25
EB03044 Omniscience Madonna C	.15	.25
EB03045 Onmyoji of the Moonlit Night C	.15	.25
EB03046 Blue Scale Deer C	.15	.25
EB03047 Petal Fairy C	.15	.25
EB03S01 Demonic Lord, Dudley Emperor SP	30.00	50.00
EB03S02 Spectral Duke Dragon SP	50.00	75.00
EB03S03 Martial Arts Mutant, Master Beetle SP	25.00	40.00
EB03S04 White Dragon Knight, Pendragon SP	15.00	25.00
EB03S05 Origin Mage, Ildona SP	15.00	25.00
EB03S06 Dragonic Lawkeeper SP	25.00	40.00

2013 Cardfight Vanguard Extra Booster Set 1 Comic Style Volume 1

RELEASED ON MARCH 29, 2013

EB01001 Perfect Raizer RRR	.60	1.00
EB01002 Dueling Dragon, ZANBAKU RRR	.75	1.25
EB01003 High-Powered Riser Custom RR	.20	.30
EB01004 Golden Beast Tamer RR	.30	.50
EB01005 Machining Stag Beetle RR	.50	.75
EB01006 Imperial Daughter RR	.30	.50
EB01007 Weather Forecaster, Miss Mist RR	.30	.50
EB01008 Miss Splendor R	.15	.25
EB01009 Rocket Hammerman R	.15	.25
EB01010 Twin Swordsman, MUSASHI R	.15	.25
EB01011 Promise Daughter R	.20	.30
EB01012 Bellicosity Dragon R	.20	.30
EB01013 Guard Gryphon R	.15	.25
EB01014 Sage of Guidance, Zenon R	.15	.25
EB01015 Savage King R	.15	.25
EB01016 Boomerang Thrower C	.10	.15
EB01017 Raizer Custom C	.10	.15
EB01018 Wall Boy C	.10	.15
EB01019 Cat Butler C	.20	.30
EB01020 Battleraizer C	.15	.25
EB01021 Jumping Jill C	.10	.15
EB01022 Nitro Juggler C	.10	.15
EB01023 Starting Presenter C	.10	.15
EB01024 Hoop Magician C	.10	.15
EB01025 Lark Pigeon C	.10	.15
EB01026 Quick Archer, FUSHIMI C	.20	.30
EB01027 Left Arrester C	.10	.15
EB01028 Right Arrester C	.10	.15
EB01029 Machining Mantis C	.10	.15
EB01030 Machining Hornet C	.25	.40
EB01031 Machining Worker Ant C	.10	.15
EB01032 Shelter Beetle C	.10	.15
EB01033 Lozenge Magus C	.10	.15
EB01034 Crouching Dragon, Striken C	.10	.15
EB01035 Spike Bouncer C	.10	.15
EB01014p Sage of Guidance, Zenon SP	4.00	6.00

2013 Cardfight Vanguard Extra Booster Set 6 Dazzling Divas

RELEASED ON JULY 26, 2013

EB06001 Eternal Idol, Pacifica RRR	.60	1.00
EB06002 PRISM-Promise, Labrador RRR	2.00	3.00
EB06003 PRISM-Image, Vert RR	2.00	3.00
EB06004 Aurora Star, Coral RR	.60	1.00
EB06005 PRISM-Promise, Celtic RR	.75	1.25
EB06006 PRISM-Image, Clear RR	.60	1.00
EB06007 Mermaid Idol, Elly RR	.20	.50
EB06008 Shining Singer, Ionia R	.15	.25
EB06009 PRISM-Smile, Ligurian R	.15	.25
EB06010 Shiny Star, Coral R	.75	1.25
EB06011 PRISM-Romance, Lumiere R	.25	.40
EB06012 Sweets Harmony, Mona R	.15	.25
EB06013 PRISM-Romance, Mercure R	.15	.25
EB06014 Mirror Diva, Biscayne R	.15	.25
EB06015 Angelic Star, Coral R	.15	.25
EB06016 Dancing Fan Princess, Minato C	.10	.15
EB06017 PRISM-Romance, Etoile C	.10	.15
EB06018 Intelli-beauty, Loire C	.10	.15
EB06019 PRISM-Image, Rosa C	.10	.15
EB06020 PRISM-Smile, Scotia C	.10	.15
EB06021 Mermaid Idol, Sedna C	.10	.15
EB06022 Fresh Star, Coral C	.25	.40
EB06023 PRISM-Promise, Leyte C	.50	.75
EB06024 Mascot Lady, Oria C	.10	.15
EB06025 Library Madonna, Rion C	.10	.15
EB06026 Dolphin Friend, Plage C	.10	.15
EB06027 PRISM-Smile, Coro C	.10	.15
EB06028 Costume Change, Alk C	.10	.15
EB06029 Gunslinger Star, Florida C	.10	.15
EB06030 PRISM-Miracle, Canary C	.60	1.00
EB06031 PRISM-Miracle, Adria C	.10	.15
EB06032 Mystery Smile, Aral C	.10	.15
EB06033 PRISM-Miracle, Timor C	.10	.15
EB06034 Heartful Ale, Fundy C	.10	.15
EB06035 PRISM-Miracle, Irish C	.10	.15

EB06S01 Eternal Idol, Pacifica SP 15.00
EB06S02 PRISM-Promise, Labrador SP 15.00
EB06S03 PRISM-Image, Vert SP 40.00
EB06S04 Aurora Star, Coral SP 12.00
EB06S05 PRISM-Promise, Celtic SP 15.00
EB06S23 PRISM-Promise, Leyte SP 12.00

2013 Cardfight Vanguard Extra Booster Set 4 Infinite Phantom Legion

RELEASED ON SEPTEMBER 6, 2013
EB04001 Perfect Raizer RRR .50 .75
EB04002 Infinite Corrosion Form, Death Army Cosmo Lord RRR 1.25 2.00
EB04003 Beast Deity, Azure Dragon RR .15 .25
EB04004 Magician Girl, Kirara RR .20 .30
EB04005 Hi-powered Raizer Custom RR .40 .60
EB04006 Death Army Bishop RR .60 1.00
EB04007 Twin Blader RR .50 .75
EB04008 Gold Rutile R .15 .25
EB04009 Brutal Joker R .15 .25
EB04010 Death Metal Droid R .15 .25
EB04011 Brutal Jack R .15 .25
EB04012 Death Army Knight R .50 .75
EB04013 Death Army Lady R .40 .60
EB04014 Street Bouncer R .20 .30
EB04015 Death Army Guy R .25 .40
EB04016 Mr. Invincible C .10 .15
EB04017 Armored Fairy, Shubiela C .10 .15
EB04018 Death Army Rook C .10 .15
EB04019 Boomerang Thrower C .10 .15
EB04020 NGM Prototype C .10 .15
EB04021 Marvelous Hani C .10 .15
EB04022 Tough Boy C .10 .15
EB04023 Oasis Girl C .10 .15
EB04024 Screamin' and Dancin' Announcer, Shout C .10 .15
EB04025 Dancing Wolf C .10 .15
EB04026 Raizer Custom C .10 .15
EB04027 Beast Deity, White Tiger C .10 .15
EB04028 Death Army Pawn C .10 .15
EB04029 Minimum Raizer C .10 .15
EB04030 Three Minutes C .10 .15
EB04031 The Gong C .10 .15
EB04032 Wall Boy C .10 .15
EB04033 Red Lightning C .10 .15
EB04034 Turboraizer C .10 .15
EB04035 Battleraizer C .10 .15
EB04S01 Perfect Raizer SP .10 .15
EB04S02 Infinite Corrosion Form, Death Army Cosmo Lord SP 2.00 3.00

2013 Cardfight Vanguard Extra Booster Set 5 Celestial Valkyries

RELEASED ON SEPTEMBER 6, 2013
EB05001 CEO Amaterasu RRR 1.00 1.50
EB05002 Battle Sister, Fromage RRR .30 .50
EB05003 Scarlet Witch, CoCo RR .60 1.00
EB05004 Goddess of Flower Divination, Sakuya RR .30 .50
EB05005 Battle Sister, Macaron RR .40 .60
EB05006 Silent Tom RR 1.25 2.00
EB05007 Battle Sister, Chocolat RR .40 .60
EB05008 Meteor Break Wizard R .15 .25
EB05009 Maiden of Libra R .15 .25
EB05010 Battle Sister, Glace R .15 .25
EB05011 Battle Sister, Mocha R .15 .25
EB05012 Circle Magus R .15 .25
EB05013 Battle Sister, Omelet R .15 .25
EB05014 Weather Forecaster, Miss Mist R .15 .25
EB05015 Battle Sister, Cocoa R 3.00 5.00
EB05016 Omniscience Madonna C .10 .15
EB05017 Oracle Guardian, Apollon C .10 .15
EB05018 Battle Sister, Souffle C .10 .15
EB05019 Battle Sister, Tarte C .10 .15
EB05020 Battle Maiden, Tagitsuhime C .10 .15
EB05021 Oracle Guardian, Red Eye C .15 .25
EB05022 Oracle Guardian, Gemini C .10 .15
EB05023 Dark Cat C .10 .15
EB05024 White Hare of Inaba C .10 .15
EB05025 Battle Sister, Vanilla C .10 .15
EB05026 One Who Gazes at the Truth C .10 .15
EB05027 Luck Bird C .10 .15
EB05028 Battle Sister, Waffle C .10 .15
EB05029 Battle Sister, Ginger C .10 .15
EB05030 Dream Eater C .10 .15
EB05031 Battle Sister, Tiramisu C .12 .20
EB05032 Battle Sister, Assam C .10 .15
EB05033 Battle Sister, Chai C .10 .15
EB05034 Psychic Bird C .20 .30
EB05035 Lozenge Magus C .10 .15
EB05S01 CEO Amaterasu SP 2.50 4.00
EB05S02 Battle Sister, Fromage SP 2.50 4.00

2014 Cardfight Vanguard Extra Booster Set 7 Mystical Magus

COMPLETE SET (39) 50.00 100.00
RELEASED ON APRIL 11, 2014
EB07001 Hexagonal Magus RRR .60 1.00
EB07002 Battle Sister, Parfait RRR .60 1.00
EB07003 Battle Sister, Monaka RR 1.75 3.00
EB07004 Stellar Magus RR 10.00 15.00
EB07005 Battle Sister, Cocotte RR 4.00 6.00
EB07006 Briolette Magus RR 1.25 2.00
EB07007 Tetra Magus RR 2.50 4.00
EB07008 Imperial Daughter R 1.00 2.50
EB07009 Evil-eye Princess, Euryale R 1.25 3.00
EB07010 Oracle Agent, Roys R .30 .75
EB07011 Cuore Magus R 1.50 4.00
EB07012 Promise Daughter R .40 1.00
EB07013 Battle Sister, Macaron R 1.50 4.00
EB07014 Crescent Magus R 2.00 5.00
EB07015 Little Witch, LuLu R .60 1.50
EB07016 Sailand Magus C .10 .15
EB07017 Battle Sister, Tart C .10 .15
EB07018 Battle Sister, Caramel C .10 .15
EB07019 Blue Scale Deer C .60 1.50
EB07020 Onmyoji of the Moonlit Night C .20 .50
EB07021 Oracle Guardian, Gemini C .10 .15
EB07022 Circle Magus C .10 .15
EB07023 Battle Sister, Omelet C .30 .75
EB07024 Ripis Magus C .10 .15
EB07025 Battle Sister, Maple C .10 .15
EB07026 Petal Fairy C .10 .15
EB07027 Battle Sister, Lemonade C .10 .15
EB07028 Luck Bird C .10 .15
EB07029 Battle Sister, Ginger C .10 .15
EB07030 Miracle Kid C .10 .15
EB07031 Battle Sister, Tiramisu C .10 .15
EB07032 Battle Sister, Assam C .10 .15
EB07033 Battle Sister, Chai C .10 .15
EB07034 Psychic Bird C .20 .50
EB07035 Lozenge Magus C .10 .15
EB07S01 Hexagonal Magus SP 10.00 15.00
EB07S02 Battle Sister, Parfait SP 8.00 12.00
EB07S03 Battle Sister, Monaka SP 6.00 10.00
EB07S04 Battle Sister, Cocotte SP 20.00 30.00

2014 Cardfight Vanguard Extra Booster Set 8 Champions of the Cosmos

COMPLETE SET (39) 80.00 120.00
RELEASED ON JUNE 6, 2014
EB08001 Immortal, Asura Kaiser RRR 1.50 4.00
EB08002 Galaxy Blaukluger RRR 6.00 15.00
EB08003 Mond Blaukluger RRR 8.00 20.00
EB08004 Asura Kaiser RR 2.00 5.00
EB08005 Stern Blaukluger RR 4.00 10.00
EB08006 Mars Blaukluger RR 2.00 5.00
EB08007 Flower Ray Leprechaun RR .40 1.00
EB08008 Blau Dunkelheit RR 1.50 4.00
EB08009 Armored Heavy Gunner R .75 2.00
EB08010 Brutal Jack R .40 1.00
EB08011 Jupiter Blaukluger R .75 2.00
EB08012 Grosse Baer R .50 1.25
EB08013 Daredevil Samurai R .40 1.00
EB08014 Blaukluger R .50 1.25
EB08015 Polar Stern R .60 1.50
EB08016 Morgenrot R .60 1.50
EB08017 Pluto Blaukluger C .30 .75
EB08018 Muscle Hercules C .30 .75
EB08019 Eisenkugel C .30 .75
EB08020 Hungry Dumpty C .30 .75
EB08021 Tough Boy C .30 .75
EB08022 Oasis Girl C .30 .75
EB08023 Clay-doll Mechanic C .30 .75
EB08024 Bear Down Samurai C 1.50 4.00
EB08025 Almighty Reporter C .30 .75
EB08026 Blaupanzer C .30 .75
EB08027 Blade Arm Leprechaun C .30 .75
EB08028 Blaujunger C .30 .75
EB08029 Schones Wetter C .50 1.25
EB08030 Shining Lady C .30 .75
EB08031 Schnee Regen C .30 .75
EB08032 The Gong C .30 .75
EB08033 Regenbogen C .40 1.00
EB08034 Starker Wind C .30 .75
EB08035 Battleraizer C .30 .75
EB08S01 Immortal, Asura Kaiser SP 6.00 15.00
EB08S02 Galaxy Blaukluger SP 15.00 40.00
EB08S03 Mond Blaukluger SP 12.00 30.00
EB08S08 Blau Dunkelheit SP 15.00 40.00

2014 Cardfight Vanguard Extra Booster Set 9 Divine Dragon Progression

COMPLETE SET (39) 50.00 100.00
RELEASED ON JUNE 6, 2014
EB09001 Transcendence Dragon, Dragonic Nouvelle Vague RRR 4.00 6.00
EB09002 Cruel Dragon RRR 6.00 10.00
EB09003 Blast Bulk Dragon RRR 3.00 5.00
EB09004 Dragonic Overlord RR 1.00 1.50
EB09005 Dragonic Lawkeeper RR .60 1.00
EB09006 Nouvellecritic Dragon RR .60 1.00
EB09007 Dragonic Gaias RR .60 1.00
EB09008 Dragon Dancer, Maria RR .75 1.25
EB09009 Dragon Monk, Goku R .30 .50
EB09010 Dragon Knight, Neshat R .15 .25
EB09011 Berserk Dragon R .15 .25
EB09012 Bellicosity Dragon R .40 .60
EB09013 Dragon Knight, Ashgar R .15 .25
EB09014 Nouvelleroman Dragon R .30 .50
EB09015 Lizard Soldier, Raopia R .20 .30
EB09016 Lizard Soldier, Conroe R .20 .30
EB09017 Dragon Knight, Morteza C .10 .15
EB09018 Beikin Grim Dragon C .10 .15
EB09019 Genie Soldat C .10 .15
EB09020 Prowling Dragon, Striken C .20 .40
EB09021 Dragon Knight, Nehalem C .20 .30
EB09022 Demonic Dragon Mage, Kongara C .10 .15
EB09023 Embodiment of Armor, Bahr C .10 .15
EB09024 Guard Griffin C .10 .15
EB09025 Flame of Hope, Aermo C .10 .15
EB09026 Demonic Dragon Madonna, Joka C .10 .15
EB09027 Scale Dragon of the Magma Cave C .10 .15
EB09028 Red Pulse Dracokid C .10 .15
EB09029 Blue Ray Dracokid C .10 .15
EB09030 Embodiment of Spear, Tahr C .10 .15
EB09031 Dragon Dancer, Monica C .10 .15
EB09032 Lizard Soldier, Ganlu C .10 .15
EB09033 Dragon Monk, Genjo C .10 .15
EB09034 Gatling Claw Dragon C .40 .60
EB09035 Flame Seed Salamander C .12 .20
EB09S01 Transcendence Dragon, Dragonic Nouvelle Vague SP 15.00 25.00
EB09S02 Cruel Dragon SP 20.00 30.00
EB09S03 Blast Bulk Dragon SP 3.00 5.00
EB09S04 Dragonic Gaias SP 5.00 8.00

2014 Cardfight Vanguard Extra Booster Set 10 Diva's Duet

COMPLETE SET (43) 250.00 400.00
RELEASED ON AUGUST 15, 2014
EB10001 Duo Stage Storm, Iori RRR 8.00 20.00
EB10002 Duo Temptation, Reit RRR 30.00 80.00
EB10003 Duo True Sister, Meer RRR 25.00 60.00
EB10004 Duo Flower Girl, Lily RR 5.00 12.00
EB10005 Duo Mini Heart, Rhone RR 2.50 6.00
EB10006 PRISM-Duo, Yarmuk C .20 .50
EB10007 Duo Promise Day, Colima RR 5.00 12.00
EB10008 PRISM-Duo, Slaney RR 6.00 15.00
EB10009 Duo Sweet Rhythm, Vilaine R 1.25 3.00
EB10010 Duo Kelpie Jockey, Syr Darya R .30 .75
EB10011 Duo Dream Idol, Sana R 1.25 3.00
EB10012 Duo Magical Mic, Sharlene R .25 .60
EB10013 Duo Far Marine Chateau, Thames R .75 2.00
EB10014 Duo Petit Etoile, Peace R .75 2.00
EB10015 Duo Pretty Horn, Ural R .40 1.00
EB10016 PRISM-Duo, Avon C .40 1.00
EB10017 Duo Lady Canotier, Salinas C .30 .75
EB10018 Duo Toybox, Menam C .30 .75
EB10019 Duo White Crystal, Ricca C .30 .75
EB10020 PRISM-Duo, Aria RR 12.00 30.00
EB10021 Duo Afternoon Tea, Parana C .30 .75
EB10022 Duo Shiny Tone, Chicora C .20 .50
EB10023 Duo Dream Idol, Myne C .30 .75
EB10024 Duo Beast Ear, Loulou C .50 1.25
EB10025 PRISM-Duo, Tisa R .40 1.00
EB10026 Duo Clear Parasol, Kura C .30 .75
EB10027 Duo Lovers' Singer, Darling C .30 .75
EB10028 Duo Treasure Hunter, Swany C .20 .50
EB10029 Duo Pride Crown, Madeira C .40 1.00
EB10030 Duo Gran Pasturn, Syanon C .20 .50
EB10031 Duo Morning Charm, Liffey C .30 .75
EB10032 Duo Lamplight Melody, Tigris C .30 .75
EB10033 Duo Soulful Melody, Selenga C .30 .75
EB10034 Duo Tropical Healer, Mejelda C .40 1.00
EB10035 Duo Night Wing, Dungrilo C .40 1.00
EB10S01 Duo Stage Storm, Iori SP 20.00 50.00
EB10S02 Duo Temptation, Reit SP 80.00 150.00
EB10S03 Duo True Sister, Meer SP 50.00 100.00
EB10S04 Duo Flower Girl, Lily SP 8.00 20.00
EB10S05 Duo Mini Heart, Rhone SP 8.00 20.00
EB10S06 PRISM-Duo, Slaney SP 8.00 20.00
EB10S07 Duo Promise Day, Colima SP 6.00 15.00
EB10S08 PRISM-Duo, Aria SP 15.00 40.00

2014 Cardfight Vanguard Extra Booster Set 11 Requiem at Dusk

COMPLETE SET (43) 150.00 300.00
EB11001 Witch of Enchantment, Fianna RRR 10.00 15.00
EB11002 Revenger, Phantom Blaster Abyss RRR 5.00 8.00
EB11003 Blaster Dark Revenger Abyss RRR 8.00 12.00
EB11004 Cultus Witch, Rias RR 1.50 2.50
EB11005 Ambitious Spirit Revenger, Cormac RR .60 1.00
EB11006 Inspection Witch, Deirdre RR 2.00 3.00
EB11007 Battle Spirit Revenger, Mackart RR .60 1.00
EB11008 Barrier Witch, Grainne RR .50 .75
EB11009 Witch of Cursed Talisman, Etain R .15 .25
EB11010 Demon World Castle, ToteZiegel R .15 .25
EB11011 Witch of Reality, Femme R .15 .25
EB11012 Moonlight Witch, Vaha R .15 .25
EB11013 Skull Witch, Nemain R .40 .60
EB11014 Witch of Precious Stones, Dana R .40 .60
EB11015 Witch of Choice, Eriu R .15 .25
EB11016 Witch of Banquets, Lir R .15 .25
EB11017 Meteor Witch, Manisa C .10 .15
EB11018 Dark Mage, Badhabh Caar C .10 .15
EB11019 Comet Witch, Serva C .10 .15
EB11020 Witch of Godly Speed, Amel C .10 .15
EB11021 Demon World Castle, Fatalita C .10 .15
EB11022 Redmew Revenger C .10 .15
EB11023 Ruin Witch, Scathach C .10 .15
EB11024 Fighting Spirit Revenger, Lyfechure C .10 .15
EB11025 Witch of Nostrum, Arianrhod C .10 .15
EB11026 Witch of Pursuit, Sekuana C .10 .15
EB11027 Howlbau Revenger C .10 .15
EB11028 Creeping Dark Goat C .10 .15
EB11029 Revenger, Air Raid Dragon C .10 .15
EB11030 Black Crow Witch, Eine C .10 .15
EB11031 Lizard Witch, Aife C .10 .15
EB11032 Freezing Revenger C .10 .15
EB11033 Revenger, Waking Angel C .10 .15
EB11034 Black Cat Witch, Milkre C .10 .15
EB11035 Witch of Goats, Medb C .10 .15
EB11L01 Revenger, Phantom Blaster Abyss LR 15.00 25.00
EB11L02 Blaster Dark Revenger Abyss LR 20.00 30.00
EB11S01 Witch of Enchantment, Fianna SP 15.00 40.00
EB11S02 Revenger, Phantom Blaster Abyss SP 12.00 20.00
EB11S03 Blaster Dark Revenger Abyss SP 15.00 25.00
EB11S04 Barrier Witch, Grainne SP 8.00 12.00
EB11S05 Witch of Reality, Femme SP 15.00 25.00
EB11S06 Illusionary Revenger, Mordred Phantom SP 30.00 50.00

2014 Cardfight Vanguard Extra Booster Set 12 Waltz of the Goddess

COMPLETE SET (43) 200.00 350.00
RELEASED ON NOVEMBER 21, 2014
EB12001 Cosmic Regalia, CEO Yggdrasill RRR 4.00 6.00
EB12002 White Snake Witch, Mint RRR 6.00 10.00
EB12003 Regalia of Wisdom and Courage, Brynhildr RRR 1.25 2.00
EB12004 Witch of Sea Eagles, Fennel RR .60 1.00
EB12005 Regalia of Midnight, Nyx RR .60 1.00
EB12006 Regalia of Midday, Hemera RR 2.00 3.00
EB12007 Witch of Strawberries, Framboise RR 2.00 3.00
EB12008 Regalia of Frozen Breath, Svalin RR .60 1.00
EB12009 Wisdom Keeper, Metis R .15 .25
EB12010 Myth Guard, Procyon R .15 .25
EB12011 Witch of Golden Eagles, Jasmine R .40 .60
EB12012 Regalia of Fate, Norn R 1.00 1.50
EB12013 Black Snake Witch, Chicory R .15 .25
EB12014 Goddess of Trees, Jupiter R .15 .25
EB12015 Regalia of Abundance, Freya R .15 .25
EB12016 Regalia of Prayer, Pray Angel R .15 .25
EB12017 Regalia of Love, Cypris C .10 .15
EB12018 Regalia of Beauty, Venus C .10 .15
EB12019 Witch of Ravens, Chamomile C .10 .15
EB12020 Myth Guard, Orion C .10 .15
EB12021 Witch of Frogs, Melissa C .10 .15
EB12022 Regalia of Purity, Pure Angel C .10 .15
EB12023 Exorcism Regalia, Shiny Angel C .60 1.00
EB12024 Goddess of Union, Juno C .10 .15
EB12025 Witch of Peaches, Bellini C .10 .15
EB12026 Regalia of Congratulations, Bleach Angel C .10 .15
EB12027 Myth Guard, Sirius C .10 .15
EB12028 Witch of House Mouse, Koroha C .10 .15
EB12029 Far Sight Regalia, Clear Angel C .10 .15
EB12030 Fancy Monkey C .10 .15
EB12031 Spark Cockerel C .10 .15
EB12032 Regalia of Benevolence, Eir C .10 .15
EB12033 Battle Maiden, Kukurihime C .10 .15
EB12034 Regalia of Foredoom, Lot Angel C .10 .15
EB12035 Mirror Regalia, Achlis C .10 .15
EB12L01 Cosmic Regalia, CEO Yggdrasill LR 15.00 25.00
EB12L02 Regalia of Fate, Norn LR 15.00 25.00
EB12S01 Cosmic Regalia, CEO Yggdrasill SP 30.00 50.00
EB12S02 White Snake Witch, Mint SP 30.00 50.00
EB12S03 Regalia of Wisdom and Courage, Brynhildr SP 10.00 15.00

EB12S04 Regalia of Fate, Norn SP 20.00 35.00
EB12S05 Black Snake Witch, Chicory SP 15.00 25.00
EB12S06 Regalia of Wisdom, Angelica SP 10.00 15.00

2018 Cardfight Vanguard G Extra Booster Set 2 The Awakening Zoo

RELEASED ON JANUARY 26, 2018
GEB02001 Zeroth Dragon of Death Garden, Zoa ZR 30.00 50.00
GEB02002 Poison Sickle Mutant Deity, Overwhelm GR 5.00 8.00
GEB02003 Omniscience Dragon, Balaurl GR 8.00 12.00
GEB02004 Flower Princess of Four Seasons, Velhemina GR 12.00 20.00
GEB02005 Intimidating Mutant King, Darkface Alicides RRR 1.50 2.50
GEB02005 Intimidating Mutant King, Darkface Alicides SP 6.00 10.00
GEB02006 Evil Governor, Darkface Gredora RRR 10.00 15.00
GEB02006 Evil Governor, Darkface Gredora SP 30.00 50.00
GEB02007 Amazing Professor, Bigbelly RRR 3.00 5.00
GEB02007 Amazing Professor, Bigbelly SP 15.00 25.00
GEB02008 Artistic Ocelot RRR 1.50 2.50
GEB02008 Artistic Ocelot SP 15.00 25.00
GEB02009 Ranunculus of Phantasmic Blue, Ahsha RRR 10.00 15.00
GEB02009 Ranunculus of Phantasmic Blue, Ahsha SP 75.00 125.00
GEB02010 Collective Blooming Maiden, Kera RRR 3.00 5.00
GEB02010 Collective Blooming Maiden, Kera SP 25.00 40.00
GEB02011 Oppression Mutant Deity, Machining Despot RR 1.00 1.50
GEB02012 Machining Beet Atlas RR .40 .60
GEB02012 Machining Beet Atlas SP 8.00 12.00
GEB02013 Adherence Mutant, Black Weevil RR .50 .75
GEB02013 Adherence Mutant, Black Weevil SP 6.00 10.00
GEB02014 Machining Snow Wing RR .75 1.25
GEB02015 Super Honorary Professor, Meilleur Chatnoir RR .20 .30
GEB02016 Honorary Professor, Chaverite RR .20 .30
GEB02016 Honorary Professor, Chaverite SP 4.00 6.00
GEB02017 Revision Scientist, Delibelly RR .30 .50
GEB02017 Revision Scientist, Delibelly SP 12.00 20.00
GEB02018 Automatism Koala RR .75 1.25
GEB02019 Maiden Lily Musketeer Captain, Virginal Cecilia RR 1.00 1.50
GEB02020 Lantana Musketeer, Rozeeta RR .50 .75
GEB02020 Lantana Musketeer, Rozeeta SP 10.00 15.00
GEB02021 Seeding Maiden, Tierney RR .40 .60
GEB02021 Seeding Maiden, Tierney SP 10.00 15.00
GEB02022 Anthurium Musketeer, Nikla RR 1.00 1.50
GEB02023 Master Swordsman Mutant Deity, Anguish Sword R .15 .25
GEB02024 Feather Wall Mutant Deity, Morphosian R .15 .25
GEB02025 Light Horn Mutant, Dangerous Horn R .15 .25
GEB02026 Black Spear Mutant, Bolg Wasp R .15 .25
GEB02027 New Face Mutant, Little Dorcas R .15 .25
GEB02028 Flowing Mutant, Twilight Madder R .15 .25
GEB02029 Machining Tardigrade R .15 .25
GEB02030 Immortality Professor, Vairagya R .15 .25
GEB02031 Immortality Professor, Sankalpa R .15 .25
GEB02032 Bicolor Baku R .15 .25
GEB02033 Bootcamp Cymric R .15 .25
GEB02034 Body Faction, Maox R .15 .25
GEB02035 Diligent Assistant, Minibelly R .15 .25
GEB02036 Sitter Bobtail R .15 .25
GEB02037 Sacred Tree Dragon, Breakweather Dragon R .15 .25
GEB02038 Bond Protector Musketeer, Antero R 2.00 3.00
GEB02039 Cumulative Maiden, Purcell R .15 .25
GEB02040 Valkyrie of Reclamation, Padmini R .15 .25
GEB02041 Repeated Cultivation Maiden, Leslie R .15 .25
GEB02042 Artemisia Musketeer, Kiara R .15 .25
GEB02043 San San Mango R .15 .25
GEB02044 Lethargy Mutant, Silk Sleeper C .10 .15
GEB02045 Machining Princess C .10 .15
GEB02046 Vulgar Blister C .10 .15
GEB02047 Machining Leafy C .10 .15
GEB02048 Bad Luck Star C .10 .15
GEB02049 Outstanding Mutant, Promularva C .10 .15
GEB02050 Machining Bagworm C .10 .15
GEB02051 Machining Killer Ant C .10 .15
GEB02052 Machining Bizarreness C .10 .15
GEB02053 Machining Treehopper C .10 .15
GEB02054 Megacolony Battler G C .10 .15
GEB02055 Talented Rhinos C .10 .15
GEB02056 Trickle British C .10 .15
GEB02057 Matrix Code Zebra C .10 .15
GEB02058 Animal Clip Lesser C .10 .15
GEB02059 Adorable Balinese C .10 .15
GEB02060 Errand Somali C .10 .15
GEB02061 Stationery Hero C .10 .15
GEB02062 Pearl Wit Chihuahua C .10 .15
GEB02063 Part-time Researcher, Iguano C .10 .15
GEB02064 Approval Frigate C .10 .15
GEB02065 Essayist, Yapoon C .10 .15
GEB02066 Poinsettia Flower Maiden, Grennel C .10 .15
GEB02067 Cyclamen Musketeer, Favila C .10 .15
GEB02068 Promotion Maiden, Lipset C .10 .15
GEB02069 Black Rose Musketeer, Verneri C .10 .15
GEB02070 Stokesia Musketeer, Daphne C .10 .15
GEB02071 Dragon Seed Spitter C .10 .15
GEB02072 Calluna Musketeer, Elma C .10 .15
GEB02073 Planting Maiden, Ozu C .10 .15
GEB02074 Cirsium Musketeer, Umbra C .10 .15
GEB02075 Red Poppy Musketeer, Marinetta C .10 .15
GEB02076 Marigold Musketeer, Rachele C .10 .15
GEB02Re01 Scissor-shot Mutant, Bombsissor RRR .75 1.25
GEB02Re02 Application Researcher, Ponbelly RRR .60 1.00
GEB02Re03 Flower Garden Maiden, Mylis RRR .60 1.00

2018 Cardfight Vanguard G Extra Booster Set 3 The Galaxy Star Gate

RELEASED ON JUNE 22, 2018
GEB03001 Zeroth Dragon of Destroy Star, Stark ZR 25.00 40.00
GEB03002 Winning Champ, Victor GR 10.00 15.00
GEB03003 Bravest Peak, X-gallop GR 6.00 10.00
GEB03004 Genesis Dragon, Integral Messiah GR 12.00 20.00
GEB03005 Zubat Battler, Victor RRR 8.00 12.00
GEB03005 Zubat Battler, Victor SP 40.00 60.00
GEB03006 Extreme Battler, Golshachi RRR 8.00 12.00
GEB03006 Extreme Battler, Golshachi SP 25.00 40.00
GEB03007 Bravest Viktor, Grandgallop RRR .60 1.00
GEB03007 Bravest Viktor, Grandgallop SP 10.00 15.00
GEB03008 Super Dimensional Robo, Dainexus RRR .75 1.25
GEB03008 Super Dimensional Robo, Dainexus SP 8.00 12.00
GEB03009 Ideal Ego Messiah RRR 2.00 3.00
GEB03009 Ideal Ego Messiah SP 15.00 25.00
GEB03010 Star-vader, Chaos Breaker Close RRR 3.00 5.00
GEB03010 Star-vader, Chaos Breaker Close SP 25.00 40.00
GEB03011 Blazar Blaukluger RR .25 .40
GEB03012 Neumond Blaukluger RR .25 .40
GEB03012 Neumond Blaukluger SP 4.00 6.00
GEB03013 Extreme Battler, Baryon RR .25 .40
GEB03013 Extreme Battler, Baryon SP 5.00 8.00
GEB03014 Arago Blauenergie RR .25 .40
GEB03015 Dimensional Robo Battle Commander, Magna Daibird RR .25 .40
GEB03015 Dimensional Robo Battle Commander, Magna Daibird SP 5.00 8.00
GEB03016 Dimensional Robo, Daibalest RR .25 .40
GEB03017 Cosmic Hero, Grandmonk RR .25 .40
GEB03017 Cosmic Hero, Grandmonk SP 4.00 6.00
GEB03018 Dimensional Robo Outfitter, Cassie RR .75 1.25
GEB03019 Original Deletor, Gaoield RR .25 .40
GEB03020 Death Star-vader, Chaos Universe Althithani RR .25 .40
GEB03020 Death Star-vader, Chaos Universe Althithani SP 8.00 12.00
GEB03021 Hack Deletor, Greigiil RR .25 .40
GEB03021 Hack Deletor, Greigiil SP 10.00 15.00
GEB03022 Star-vader, Magellanic Stream RR 1.25 2.50
GEB03023 Demolition Beast, Demolzaurus R .15 .25
GEB03024 Meteokaiser, Dogantitan R .15 .25
GEB03025 Extreme Battler, Sever-temper R .15 .25
GEB03026 Extreme Battler, Arashid R .15 .25
GEB03027 Extreme Battler, Gunzdon R .30 .50
GEB03028 Extreme Battler, Jerohawk R .30 .50
GEB03029 Varuna Blauwand R .15 .25
GEB03030 Heaven and Earth Combination, Triearth R .15 .25
GEB03031 Great Galactic Beast, Zeal R .15 .25
GEB03032 Dimensional Robo, Daiball R .15 .25
GEB03033 Cosmic Hero, Grandhogan R .15 .25
GEB03034 Cosmic Hero, Grandrope R .15 .25
GEB03035 Dimensional Robo, Daisupporter R .15 .25
GEB03036 Dimensional Robo, Daimagnel R .15 .25
GEB03037 Large Wheel of the Cosmos, Cosmo Wreath R .15 .25
GEB03038 Myga Messiah R .15 .25
GEB03039 Fierce Attack Star-vader, Dubnium R 1.00 1.50
GEB03040 Racer Deletor, Baird R .15 .25
GEB03041 Vlastos Messiah R .15 .25
GEB03042 High Pressure Star-vader, Americium R .15 .25
GEB03043 Lurk Deletor, Elinge R .15 .25
GEB03044 Dr. Angstrom C .10 .15
GEB03045 Baade Blaukanone C .10 .15
GEB03046 Magical Performer C .10 .15
GEB03047 Extreme Battler, Ninjaad C .10 .15
GEB03048 Regia Blaulanze C .10 .15
GEB03049 Oda Blauschleife C .10 .15
GEB03050 Vesta Blauklinge C .10 .15
GEB03051 Riema Blaurakete C .10 .15
GEB03052 Extreme Battler, Victhead C .10 .15
GEB03053 Young Blaufechter C .10 .15
GEB03054 Otero Blaufliegen C .10 .15
GEB03055 Saar Blauglanz C .10 .15
GEB03056 Orchis Blaukreuzer C .10 .15
GEB03057 Great Cosmic Hero, Grandabbot C .10 .15
GEB03058 Cosmic Hero, Grandwisdom C .10 .15
GEB03059 Cosmic Hero, Grandbalger C .10 .15
GEB03060 Dimensional Robo, Daicrusher C .10 .15
GEB03061 Cosmic Hero, Grandgunner C .10 .15
GEB03062 Cosmic Hero, Grandscout C .10 .15
GEB03063 Dimensional Robo, Daicutter C .10 .15
GEB03064 Dimensional Robo, Dairapter C .10 .15
GEB03065 Dimensional Robo Pilot, Matthew C .10 .15
GEB03066 Build Standard C .10 .15
GEB03067 Dimensional Robo, Daimoon C .10 .15
GEB03068 Dimensional Robo, Daibloom C .10 .15
GEB03069 Dimensional Robo, Daidraft C .10 .15
GEB03070 Lady Bomber of the Magnetic Storm C .10 .15
GEB03071 Star-vader, Vela Junior Dragon C .10 .15
GEB03072 Depose Deletor, Gelora C .10 .15
GEB03073 Resistance Star-vader, Polonium C .10 .15
GEB03074 Wild Child of the Many-worlds Interpretation C .10 .15
GEB03075 Trick Deletor, Zaog C .10 .15
GEB03076 Biting Deletor, Geeva C .10 .15
GEB03Re01 Extreme Battler, Break-pass RRR .60 1.00
GEB03Re02 Cosmic Hero, Grandbeat RRR .50 .75
GEB03Re03 Companion Star Star-vader, Photon RRR 3.00 5.00

2015 Cardfight Vanguard G Extra Booster Set 1 Cosmic Roar

COMPLETE SET (35) 20.00 50.00
RELEASED ON APRIL 17, 2015
GEB01001 99th-gen Dimensional Robo Commander, Great Daiearth RRR 10.00 15.00
GEB01002 Super Cosmic Hero, X-tiger RRR 15.00 25.00
GEB01003 Great Cosmic Hero, Grandgallop RRR 10.00 15.00
GEB01004 Dark Superhuman, Omega RR 1.25 2.00
GEB01005 Super Cosmic Hero, X-falcon RR 1.50 2.50
GEB01006 Cosmic Hero, Grandfire RR 1.50 2.50
GEB01007 Cosmic Hero, Grandguard RR 8.00 12.00
GEB01008 Cosmic Hero, Grandbeat RR 1.00 1.50
GEB01009 Enigman Tornado R .60 1.00
GEB01010 New Era Beast, Zeal R .60 1.00
GEB01011 Metalborg, Barrengrader R .60 1.00
GEB01012 Cosmic Hero, Grandsub R .60 1.00
GEB01013 Dimensional Robo, Daijet R .60 1.00
GEB01014 Cosmic Hero, Grandrope R .60 1.00
GEB01015 Cosmic Hero, Grandwagon R .60 1.00
GEB01016 Metalborg, Grasscutter R .60 1.00
GEB01017 Great Cosmic Hero, Grandbazooka C .15 .25
GEB01018 Enigman Night Sky C .15 .25
GEB01019 Cosmic Hero, Grandkungfu C .15 .25
GEB01020 Ionization Monster, Plazm C .15 .25
GEB01021 Metalborg, Magmafork C .15 .25
GEB01022 Cosmic Hero, Grandpolice C .15 .25
GEB01023 Enigman Cloud C .15 .25
GEB01024 Cosmic Hero, Grandchopper C .15 .25
GEB01025 Dimensional Robo, Dailion C .15 .25
GEB01026 Evolution Monster, Davain C .15 .25
GEB01027 Metalborg, Hammerhel C .15 .25
GEB01028 Cosmic Hero, Grandseed C .15 .25
GEB01029 Dimensional Robo, Daishoot C .15 .25
GEB01030 Metalborg, Locobattler C .15 .25
GEB01031 Dimensional Robo, Daiwolf C .15 .25
GEB01032 Masked Police, Guunjoe C .15 .25
GEB01033 Cosmic Hero, Grandrescue C .15 .25
GEB01034 Enigman Sunset C .15 .25
GEB01035 Operator Girl, Reika C .15 .25

2018 Cardfight Vanguard V Extra Booster Set 1 The Destructive Roar

RELEASED ON AUGUST 2, 2018
VEB01001 Ravenous Dragon, Gigarex VR 10.00 15.00
VEB01001 Ravenous Dragon, Gigarex SVR 25.00 40.00
VEB01002 General Seifried VR 12.00 20.00
VEB01002 General Seifried SVR 15.00 25.00
VEB01003 Machining Spark Hercules VR 6.00 10.00
VEB01003 Machining Spark Hercules SVR 6.00 10.00
VEB01004 Tyrant, Deathrex RRR 2.00 3.00
VEB01004 Tyrant, Deathrex OR 2.00 3.00
VEB01005 Ravenous Dragon, Megarex RRR 5.00 8.00
VEB01006 Juggernaut Maximum RRR 3.00 5.00
VEB01006 Juggernaut Maximum OR 3.00 5.00
VEB01007 Spike Bouncer RRR 5.00 8.00
VEB01008 Machining Stag Beetle RRR 1.25 2.00
VEB01008 Machining Stag Beetle OR 1.50 2.50
VEB01009 Machining Mantis RRR 8.00 12.00
VEB01010 Assault Dragon, Blightops RR .40 .60
VEB01011 Sonic Noa RR .60 1.00
VEB01012 Archbird RR 2.00 3.00
VEB01013 Unite Attacker RR .30 .50
VEB01014 Gyro Slinger RR .75 1.25
VEB01015 Cheer Girl, Marilyn RR 2.50 4.00
VEB01016 Death Warden Ant Lion RR .30 .50
VEB01017 Machining Hornet RR 2.50 4.00
VEB01018 Paralyze Madonna RR 2.50 4.00
VEB01019 Savage King R .15 .25
VEB01020 Attempt Mammoth R .15 .25
VEB01021 Winged Dragon, Skyptero R .15 .25
VEB01022 Vicious Claw Dragon, Laceraterex R .15 .25
VEB01023 Stronghold Dragon, Robustops R .15 .25
VEB01024 Treasured, Black Panther R .15 .25
VEB01025 Highspeed, Brakki R .15 .25
VEB01026 Commander, Garry Gannon R .15 .25
VEB01027 Wonder Boy R .15 .25
VEB01028 Cheer Girl, Jamie R .15 .25
VEB01029 Water Gang R .15 .25
VEB01030 Bloody Hercules R .15 .25
VEB01031 Spiteful Hopper R .15 .25
VEB01032 Phantom Black R .15 .25
VEB01033 Delusional Mutant, Dazzle Moth R .15 .25
VEB01034 Heavy Artillery Dragon, Sharangastego C .10 .15
VEB01035 Savage Raider C .10 .15
VEB01036 Sharp Blade Dragon, Reflistego C .10 .15
VEB01037 Assistopteryx C .10 .15
VEB01038 Dragon Egg C .10 .15
VEB01039 Savage Aggressor C .10 .15
VEB01040 Black Cannon Tiger C .10 .15
VEB01041 Cannon Fire Dragon, Sledge Ankylo C .10 .15
VEB01042 Herbivorous Dragon, Brutosaurus C .10 .15
VEB01043 Pack Dragon, Tinyrex C .10 .15
VEB01044 Savage Shaman C .10 .15
VEB01045 Front-line Command, Sigiswald C .10 .15
VEB01046 Bombing Tail-back C .10 .15
VEB01047 Diabolic Middle Guard C .10 .15
VEB01048 White Tight End C .10 .15
VEB01049 Funky Bazooka C .10 .15
VEB01050 Mecha Trainer C .10 .15
VEB01051 Cheer Girl, Franny C .10 .15
VEB01052 Silence Joker C .10 .15
VEB01053 Sonic Breaker C .10 .15
VEB01054 Cheerful Lynx C .10 .15
VEB01055 Cheer Girl, Tiara C .10 .15
VEB01056 Strong Toxin Mutant, Hell Demise C .10 .15
VEB01057 Nasty Smog C .10 .15
VEB01058 Burner Ant C .10 .15
VEB01059 Karma Queen C .10 .15
VEB01060 Small Captain, Butterfly Officer C .10 .15
VEB01061 Jocular Cicada C .10 .15
VEB01062 Machining Worker Ant C .10 .15
VEB01063 Shelter Beetle C .10 .15
VEB01064 Sharp Nail Scorpio C .10 .15
VEB01065 Larva Mutant, Larvadraf C .10 .15
VEB01066 Medical Battler, Ranpli C .10 .15

2018 Cardfight Vanguard V Extra Booster Set 2 Champions of the Asia Circuit

RELEASED ON AUGUST 31, 2018
VEB02001 Ultimate Dimensional Robo, Great Daiyusha VR 20.00 30.00
VEB02001 Ultimate Dimensional Robo, Great Daiyusha SVR 30.00 50.00
VEB02002 King of Demonic Seas, Basskirk VR 10.00 15.00
VEB02002 King of Demonic Seas, Basskirk SVR 20.00 30.00
VEB02003 Blue Storm Dragon, Maelstrom VR 15.00 25.00
VEB02003 Blue Storm Dragon, Maelstrom SVR 25.00 40.00
VEB02004 Super Dimensional Robo, Daiyusha RRR 2.00 3.00
VEB02004 Super Dimensional Robo, Daiyusha OR 12.00 20.00
VEB02005 Dimensional Robo, Daidragon RRR 6.00 10.00
VEB02006 Ruin Shade RRR 4.00 6.00
VEB02006 Ruin Shade OR 10.00 15.00
VEB02007 Dandy Guy, Romario RRR 6.00 10.00
VEB02008 Storm Rider, Diamantes RRR 1.50 2.50
VEB02009 Tidal Assault RRR 5.00 8.00
VEB02009 Tidal Assault OR 15.00 25.00
VEB02010 Dimensional Robo, Daibrave RR .40 .60
VEB02011 Commander Laurel RR .20 .30
VEB02012 Diamond Ace RR 2.00 3.00
VEB02013 Dragon Undead, Skull Dragon RR 1.00 1.50
VEB02014 Captain Nightmist RR .60 1.00
VEB02015 Gust Jinn RR 1.25 2.00
VEB02016 Battle Siren, Viviana RR .20 .30
VEB02017 Emerald Shield, Paschal RR 5.00 8.00
VEB02018 Miracle Beauty R .15 .25
VEB02019 Cosmo Beak R .15 .25
VEB02020 Masked Police, Grander R .15 .25
VEB02021 Dimensional Robo, Daimariner R .15 .25
VEB02022 Masked Police, Elvino R .15 .25
VEB02023 Witch Doctor of Treachery, Negrobreach R .15 .25
VEB02024 Commodore Blueblood R .15 .25
VEB02025 Evil Shade R .15 .25
VEB02026 Retreat Francine R .15 .25
VEB02027 Dancing Cutlass R .15 .25
VEB02028 Chappie the Ghostie R .15 .25
VEB02029 Trident Shooter R .15 .25
VEB02030 Light Signals Penguin Soldier R .60 1.00
VEB02031 Masked Police Leader, Silbard C .10 .15
VEB02032 Mad Scepter X C .10 .15
VEB02033 Miracle Cutie C .10 .15
VEB02034 Miracle Dandy C .10 .15
VEB02035 Dimensional Robo, Daitiger C .10 .15
VEB02036 Dimensional Robo, Dailander C .10 .15
VEB02037 Miracle Fairy, Larabi C .10 .15
VEB02038 Dimensional Robo, Goyusha C .10 .15
VEB02039 Dimensional Robo, Daibattles C .10 .15
VEB02040 Justice Cobalt C .10 .15
VEB02041 Army Penguin C .10 .15

VEB02042 Dimensional Robo, Gorescue C .10 .15
VEB02043 Violence Flanger C .10 .15
VEB02044 Trendy Guy, Alvaro C .10 .15
VEB02045 Skeleton Bomber C .10 .15
VEB02046 Grieving Bullet, Nightgewehr C .10 .15
VEB02047 Injury Shade C .10 .15
VEB02048 Norman the Ghostie C .10 .15
VEB02049 Guiding Zombie C .10 .15
VEB02050 Knight Spirit C .10 .15
VEB02051 Mortal Mimic C .10 .15
VEB02052 Pirate Ship Handler, Paolo C .10 .15
VEB02053 Rick the Ghostie C .10 .15
VEB02054 Riptide Dragon C .10 .15
VEB02055 Storm Rider, Basil C .10 .15
VEB02056 Influent Dagger C .10 .15
VEB02057 Supersonic Sailor C .10 .15
VEB02058 Outride Dracokid C .10 .15

2018 Cardfight Vanguard V Extra Booster Set 3 Ultrarare Miracle Collection

RELEASED ON DECEMBER 14, 2018
VEB03001 Solidify Celestial, Zerachiel VR 15.00 25.00
VEB03001 Solidify Celestial, Zerachiel SVR 25.00 40.00
VEB03002 Incandescent Lion, Blond Ezel VR 20.00 30.00
VEB03002 Incandescent Lion, Blond Ezel SVR 30.00 50.00
VEB03003 White Lily Musketeer, Cecilia VR 15.00 25.00
VEB03003 White Lily Musketeer, Cecilia SVR 25.00 40.00
VEB03004 Crimson Impact, Metatron RRR 5.00 8.00
VEB03004 Crimson Impact, Metatron OR 15.00 25.00
VEB03005 Rear Impetus Celestial, Armaiti RRR 3.00 5.00
VEB03006 Knight of Superior Skills, Beaumains RRR 10.00 15.00
VEB03007 Player of the Holy Bow, Viviane RRR 4.00 6.00
VEB03007 Player of the Holy Bow, Viviane OR 12.00 20.00
VEB03008 Pansy Musketeer, Sylvia RRR 6.00 10.00
VEB03008 Pansy Musketeer, Sylvia OR 10.00 15.00
VEB03009 Lily of the Valley Musketeer, Rebecca RRR 3.00 5.00
VEB03010 Mobile Hospital, Feather Palace RR .40 .60
VEB03011 Wild Shot Celestial, Raguel RR .75 1.25
VEB03012 Battle Cupid, Nociel RR 2.00 3.00
VEB03013 Battlefield Storm, Sagramore RR 1.50 2.50
VEB03014 White Hare in the Moon's Shadow, Pellinore RR .30 .50
VEB03015 Halo Shield, Mark RR 6.00 10.00
VEB03016 Maiden of Trailing Rose RR 2.00 3.00
VEB03017 Dandelion Musketeer, Mirkka RR 2.00 3.00
VEB03018 Maiden of Blossom Rain RR 2.00 3.00
VEB03019 Million Ray Pegasus R .15 .25
VEB03020 Underlay Celestial, Hesediel R .15 .25
VEB03021 Thousand Ray Pegasus R .15 .25
VEB03022 Marking Celestial, Arabhaki R .15 .25
VEB03023 Shadowless Angel R .15 .25
VEB03024 Sacred Guardian Beast, Nemean Lion R .15 .25
VEB03025 Lop Ear Shooter R .15 .25
VEB03026 Evil Slaying Swordsman, Haugan R .15 .25
VEB03027 Cladcrest Lion R .15 .25
VEB03028 Listener of Truth, Dindrane R 1.00 1.50
VEB03029 Exploding Tomato R .15 .25
VEB03030 Lily of the Valley Musketeer, Kaivant R .15 .25
VEB03031 Spiritual Tree Sage, Irminsul R .15 .25
VEB03032 Fruits Basket Elf R .15 .25
VEB03033 Guardian Force Fist Deity, Oni Burdoc R .15 .25
VEB03034 Perdurable Phoenix C .10 .15
VEB03035 Essence Celestial, Becca C .10 .15
VEB03036 Shocking Shot, Nuwqael C .10 .15
VEB03037 Doctroid Eiter C .10 .15
VEB03038 Syringe Lesser C .10 .15
VEB03039 Doctroid Circadian C .10 .15
VEB03040 First Aid Celestial, Peniel C .10 .15
VEB03041 Critical Hit Angel C .10 .15
VEB03042 Hot Shot Celestial, Samyaza C .10 .15
VEB03043 Bouquet Toss Messenger C .10 .15
VEB03044 Sunny Smile Angel C .10 .15
VEB03045 Mach Slash Dragon C .10 .15
VEB03046 Knight of Heroism, Tornus C .10 .15
VEB03047 Waving Owl C .10 .15
VEB03048 Knight of Elegant Skills, Gareth C .10 .15
VEB03049 Crimson Lion Cub, Kyrph C .10 .15
VEB03050 Knight of Blue Skies, Shanak C .10 .15
VEB03051 Flame of Victory C .10 .15
VEB03052 Foresight Courier C .10 .15
VEB03053 Dantegal C .10 .15
VEB03054 Knight of Forceful Fight, Nalnes C .10 .15
VEB03055 Elixir Sommelier C .10 .15
VEB03056 Maiden of Pure Splash C .10 .15
VEB03057 Iris Knight C .10 .15
VEB03058 Spinach Advisor C .10 .15
VEB03059 Maiden of Salix C .10 .15
VEB03060 Corolla Dragon C .10 .15
VEB03061 Knight of Coprosperity, Craig C .10 .15
VEB03062 Broccolini Musketeer, Kirah C .10 .15
VEB03063 Night Queen Musketeer, Daniel C .10 .15
VEB03064 Chestnut Bullet C .10 .15
VEB03065 Dancing Sunflower C .10 .15
VEB03066 Watering Elf C .10 .15
VEB03T01 Plant Token .15 .25
VEB03T02 Plant Token .15 .25

2019 Cardfight Vanguard V Extra Booster Set 4 The Answer of Truth

RELEASED ON JANUARY 18, 2019
VEB04001 Oracle Queen, Himiko VR 10.00 15.00
VEB04001 Oracle Queen, Himiko SVR 25.00 40.00
VEB04002 Interdimensional Dragon, Mystery-flare Dragon VR 8.00 12.00
VEB04002 Interdimensional Dragon, Mystery-flare Dragon SVR 15.00 25.00
VEB04003 School Hunter, Leo-pald VR 10.00 15.00
VEB04003 School Hunter, Leo-pald SVR 20.00 30.00
VEB04004 Battle Deity of the Night, Artemis RRR 2.00 3.00
VEB04005 Battle Maiden, Sahohime RRR 6.00 10.00
VEB04005 Battle Maiden, Sahohime OR 12.00 20.00
VEB04006 Interdimensional Dragon, Idealize Dragon RRR 3.00 5.00
VEB04007 Interdimensional Dragonknight, Lost Legend RRR 5.00 8.00
VEB04007 Interdimensional Dragonknight, Lost Legend OR 15.00 25.00
VEB04008 Pencil Hero, Hammsuke RRR 4.00 6.00
VEB04009 Binoculus Tiger RRR 5.00 8.00
VEB04009 Binoculus Tiger OR 12.00 20.00
VEB04010 Eternal Goddess, Iwanagahime RR .50 .75
VEB04011 Battle Maiden, Shitateruhime RR 2.50 4.00
VEB04012 Goddess of Self-sacrifice, Kushinada RR 2.50 4.00
VEB04013 Lost Break Dragon RR 2.50 4.00
VEB04014 Steam Guard, Kastilia RR 3.00 5.00
VEB04015 Armed Instructor, Bison RR .30 .50
VEB04016 Monoculus Tiger RR 1.00 1.50
VEB04017 Cable Sheep RR 2.00 3.00
VEB04018 Battle Maiden, Izunahime R .15 .25
VEB04019 Twilight Hunter, Artemis R .15 .25
VEB04020 Bowstring of Heaven and Earth, Artemis R .15 .25
VEB04021 Witch of Cats, Cumin R .15 .25
VEB04022 Administrator of Hope, Pandora R .15 .25
VEB04023 Escrude Dragon R .15 .25
VEB04024 Steam Mechanic, Nabu R .15 .25
VEB04025 Wedgemove Dragon R .15 .25
VEB04026 Steam Artist, Abi-ratta R .15 .25
VEB04027 Geograph Giant R .15 .25
VEB04028 Pencil Knight, Hammsuke R .15 .25
VEB04029 Pencil Squire, Hammsuke R .15 .25
VEB04030 Speculate Chipmunk R .15 .25
VEB04031 Tank Mouse R .15 .25
VEB04032 Goddess of the Milky Way, Pleione C .10 .15
VEB04033 Strong Bow of the Starry Night, Ulixes C .10 .15
VEB04034 Deity of Shepherds, Volos C .10 .15
VEB04035 Battle Maiden, Mihikarihime C .10 .15
VEB04036 Swift Runner of the Clear Skies, Achilles C .10 .15
VEB04037 Witch of Frogs, Melissa C .10 .15
VEB04038 Aiming for the Stars, Artemis C .10 .15
VEB04039 Battle Maiden, Kukurihime C .10 .15
VEB04040 Cyber Tiger C .10 .15
VEB04041 Talisman Angel C .10 .15
VEB04042 Witch of Big Pots, Laurier C .10 .15
VEB04043 Steam Expert, Zerix C .10 .15
VEB04044 Steam Hunter, Lippitt C .10 .15
VEB04045 Missing-clamp Dragon C .10 .15
VEB04046 Gun-bezel Dragon C .10 .15
VEB04047 Steam Fighter, Ahne C .10 .15
VEB04048 Steam Scara, Kalain C .10 .15
VEB04049 Quicky Quicky Worker C .10 .15
VEB04050 Steam Fighter, Memenne C .10 .15
VEB04051 Primordial Dracokid C .10 .15
VEB04052 Steam Bomber, Digul C .10 .15
VEB04053 Ring Ring Worker C .10 .15
VEB04054 Roly-poly Worker C .10 .15
VEB04055 Steam Doctor, Mar-tash C .10 .15
VEB04056 Heavy Brain, Mormodon C .10 .15
VEB04057 Toolbox Wallaby C .10 .15
VEB04058 Barcode Zebra C .10 .15
VEB04059 Idol Teacher, Hatsune C .10 .15
VEB04060 Triad Dog C .10 .15
VEB04061 Silver Wolf C .10 .15
VEB04062 Blackboard Parrot C .10 .15
VEB04063 Triangle Cobra C .10 .15
VEB04064 Ruler Chameleon C .10 .15
VEB04065 Slip Pangolin C .10 .15
VEB04066 Alarm Chicken C .10 .15
VEB04067 Castanet Donkey C .10 .15
VEB04068 Dictionary Goat C .10 .15

2019 Cardfight Vanguard V Extra Booster Set 5 Primary Melody

RELEASED ON MAY 17, 2019
VEB05001 Colorful Pastorale, Sonata SSP (Rainbow Signature)
VEB05001 Colorful Pastorale, Sonata SSP (Silver Signature)
VEB05001 Colorful Pastorale, Sonata VR 10.00 15.00
VEB05001 Colorful Pastorale, Sonata SVR 25.00 40.00
VEB05001 Colorful Pastorale, Sonata SP 125.00
VEB05001 Colorful Pastorale, Sonata SSP (Gold Signature)
VEB05002 Colorful Pastorale, Canon VR .75 1.25
VEB05002 Colorful Pastorale, Canon SVR 6.00 10.00
VEB05002 Colorful Pastorale, Canon SP 75.00 125.00
VEB05002 Colorful Pastorale, Canon SSP (Gold Signature)
VEB05002 Colorful Pastorale, Canon SSP (Silver Signature)
VEB05002 Colorful Pastorale, Canon SSP (Rainbow Signature)
VEB05003 Colorful Pastorale, Serena SSP (Rainbow Signature)
VEB05003 Colorful Pastorale, Serena SSP (Silver Signature)
VEB05003 Colorful Pastorale, Serena VR .75 1.25
VEB05003 Colorful Pastorale, Serena SVR 4.00 6.00
VEB05003 Colorful Pastorale, Serena SP 40.00 60.00
VEB05003 Colorful Pastorale, Serena SSP (Gold Signature)
VEB05004 Colorful Pastorale, Fina VR 2.50 4.00
VEB05004 Colorful Pastorale, Fina SVR 8.00 12.00
VEB05004 Colorful Pastorale, Fina SP 60.00 100.00
VEB05004 Colorful Pastorale, Fina SSP (Gold Signature)
VEB05004 Colorful Pastorale, Fina SSP (Silver Signature)
VEB05004 Colorful Pastorale, Fina SSP (Rainbow Signature)
VEB05005 Colorful Pastorale, Caro SSP (Rainbow Signature)
VEB05005 Colorful Pastorale, Caro SSP (Silver Signature)
VEB05005 Colorful Pastorale, Caro VR 12.00 20.00
VEB05005 Colorful Pastorale, Caro SVR 15.00 25.00
VEB05005 Colorful Pastorale, Caro SP 75.00 125.00
VEB05005 Colorful Pastorale, Caro SSP (Gold Signature)
VEB05006 Top Star, Cier VR 10.00 15.00
VEB05006 Top Star, Cier SVR 15.00 25.00
VEB05006 Top Star, Cier SP 60.00 100.00
VEB05006 Top Star, Cier SSP (Gold Signature)
VEB05006 Top Star, Cier SSP (Silver Signature)
VEB05006 Top Star, Cier SSP (Rainbow Signature)
VEB05007 Diva of Atlantea, Iryna SSP (Rainbow Signature)
VEB05007 Diva of Atlantea, Iryna SSP (Silver Signature)
VEB05007 Diva of Atlantea, Iryna LIR 5.00 8.00
VEB05007 Diva of Atlantea, Iryna SP 30.00 50.00
VEB05007 Diva of Atlantea, Iryna SSP (Gold Signature)
VEB05008 Unparalleled Ingenuity, Loura LIR 5.00 8.00
VEB05008 Unparalleled Ingenuity, Loura SP 75.00 125.00
VEB05008 Unparalleled Ingenuity, Loura SSP (Gold Signature)
VEB05008 Unparalleled Ingenuity, Loura SSP (Silver Signature)
VEB05008 Unparalleled Ingenuity, Loura SSP (Rainbow Signature)
VEB05009 Heart Monopoly, Anezka SSP (Rainbow Signature)
VEB05009 Heart Monopoly, Anezka SSP (Silver Signature)
VEB05009 Heart Monopoly, Anezka LIR 15.00 25.00
VEB05009 Heart Monopoly, Anezka SP 60.00 100.00
VEB05009 Heart Monopoly, Anezka SSP (Gold Signature)
VEB05010 Greenness Energy, Salia RR .20 .30
VEB05011 Blue-Silver Diva, Brume RR .20 .30
VEB05012 Masterly Cover, Minne RR .20 .30
VEB05013 Favored Child Idol, Eno RR .20 .30
VEB05014 Fluffy Wonder, Preenez RR .20 .30
VEB05015 Rainy Tear, Stezza RR .40 .60
VEB05016 Glittery Baby, Lene RR 4.00 6.00
VEB05017 Shapely Eyes, Ruhe R .15 .25
VEB05018 Super Hit Medley, Paterle R .15 .25
VEB05019 Devoted Time, Inasta R .15 .25
VEB05020 Friendly High-Touch, Scioltia R .15 .25
VEB05021 Reverberator, Dies R .15 .25
VEB05022 Lovable Spontaneity, Voll R .15 .25
VEB05023 Admirative Solo, Atri R .15 .25
VEB05024 Sugary Lordling, Ravoure R .15 .25
VEB05025 Equable Career, Spiana R .15 .25
VEB05026 Officious Luscious, Thoria R .15 .25
VEB05027 Crawl-up Girl, Est R .15 .25
VEB05028 Deliberate Bash, Strasica R .15 .25
VEB05029 Fixation on Cuteness, Paparia C .10 .15
VEB05030 Social Fig, Intime C .10 .15
VEB05031 Up Up Flight, Rigore C .10 .15
VEB05032 Welcome Sing, Ouvil C .10 .15
VEB05033 Class Session, Ostina C .10 .15
VEB05034 Strive Dream, Radue C .10 .15
VEB05035 Boistered Elegance, Leshar C .10 .15
VEB05036 Full of Mischievousness, Sirrah C .10 .15
VEB05037 Novice Idol, Piena C .10 .15
VEB05038 Self-Management, Ralentesse C .10 .15
VEB05039 Dance Queen, Prach C .10 .15
VEB05040 Pure Gifter, Aliche C .10 .15
VEB05041 Max Shout, Culie C .10 .15
VEB05042 Direct Sign, Pursh C .10 .15
VEB05043 Lover Hope, Rina C .10 .15
VEB05044 Joyful A la Carte, Irma C .10 .15
VEB05045 Handmade Lover, Elena C .10 .15

2019 Cardfight Vanguard V Extra Booster Set 6 Light of Salvation Logic of Destruction

RELEASED ON JUNE 7, 2019
VEB06001 Messianic Lord Blaster VR 10.00 15.00
VEB06001 Messianic Lord Blaster SVR 15.00 25.00
VEB06001 Messianic Lord Blaster IMR 100.00 150.00
VEB06002 Dragonic Overlord the Great VR 25.00 40.00
VEB06002 Dragonic Overlord the Great SVR 50.00 75.00
VEB06003 Beast Deity, Azure Dragon VR 25.00 40.00
VEB06003 Beast Deity, Azure Dragon SVR 40.00 60.00
VEB06004 Wandering Starhulk Deity, Brandt Ringer VR 4.00 6.00
VEB06004 Wandering Starhulk Deity, Brandt Ringer SVR 10.00 15.00
VEB06005 Arc Saver Dragon RRR .75 1.25
VEB06005 Arc Saver Dragon OR 3.00 5.00
VEB06006 Dragon Full-armored Buster RRR 4.00 6.00
VEB06006 Dragon Full-armored Buster OR 10.00 15.00
VEB06007 Sabel Dragonewt RRR 10.00 15.00
VEB06008 Clay-doll Mechanic RRR 2.50 4.00
VEB06009 Wandering Starhulk Ruler, Brandt RRR 3.00 5.00
VEB06009 Wandering Starhulk Ruler, Brandt OR 10.00 15.00
VEB06010 Whiteouter, Vect RRR 5.00 8.00
VEB06011 Blaster Arrow RR .60 1.00
VEB06011 Blaster Arrow IMR 60.00 100.00
VEB06012 Blaster Rapier (Royal Paladin) RR .75 1.25
VEB06012 Blaster Rapier (Royal Paladin) IMR 60.00 100.00
VEB06013 Blaster Javelin (Royal Paladin) RR .75 1.25
VEB06013 Blaster Javelin (Royal Paladin) IMR 50.00 75.00
VEB06014 Blaster Dagger (Royal Paladin) RR .50 .75
VEB06014 Blaster Dagger (Royal Paladin) IMR 30.00 50.00
VEB06015 Dragonic Neoflame RR .60 1.00
VEB06016 Incise Raizer RR .50 .75
VEB06017 Brutal Jack RR 2.00 3.00
VEB06017 Brutal Jack OR 10.00 15.00
VEB06018 Starhulk, Letaluk RR .50 .75
VEB06019 Taintless Feather Dragon R .15 .25
VEB06020 Rotary Sage, Belk R .15 .25
VEB06021 Undulatory Sage, Tarna R .15 .25
VEB06022 Fire Rage Dragon R .15 .25
VEB06023 Dragonic Burnout R .15 .25
VEB06024 Meganton Powerdon R .15 .25
VEB06025 Beast Deity, Black Tortoise R .15 .25
VEB06026 Beast Deity, Scarlet Bird R .15 .25
VEB06027 Decaydal Automata R .15 .25
VEB06028 Black Lightwhip, Flick Hitter R .15 .25
VEB06029 Starhulk, Chiral R .15 .25
VEB06030 Starhulk, Gicurs R .15 .25
VEB06031 Refreshing Knight, Gruhil C .10 .15
VEB06032 Wyvern Strike, Gajil Bird C .10 .15
VEB06033 Dragon Knight, Waleed C .10 .15
VEB06034 Demonic Dragon Mage, Kimnara C .10 .15
VEB06035 Calamity Tower Wyvern C .10 .15
VEB06036 Refilling Raizer C .10 .15
VEB06037 Screamin' and Dancin' Announcer, Shout C .10 .15
VEB06038 Beast Deity, White Tiger C .10 .15
VEB06039 Treasured Child of Nuclear Magnetic Resonance C .10 .15
VEB06040 Fatal Shockwave, Jetshaft C .10 .15
VEB06041 Sharpened Loop of Despondency, Alnilam C .10 .15
VEB06042 Starhulk, Lurli C .10 .15
VEB06043 Asteroid Wolf C .10 .15
VEB06044 Pulse Monk of the Quaking Foot C .10 .15
VEB06045 Beloved Child of Superstring Theory C .10 .15
VEB06046 Lady Healer of the Torn World C .10 .15
VEB06I03 Blaster Blade IMR 60.00 100.00
VEB06Re01 Flowers in Vacuum, Cosmo Wreath SP 25.00 40.00

2019 Cardfight Vanguard V Extra Booster Set 7 Heroic Evolution

RELEASED ON JULY 19, 2019
VEB07001 Dragonic Overlord the End VR 10.00 15.00
VEB07001 Dragonic Overlord the End SVR 25.00 40.00
VEB07001 Dragonic Overlord the End XVR 120.00 200.00
VEB07002 Spinning Valiant VR 2.50 4.00
VEB07002 Spinning Valiant SVR 8.00 12.00
VEB07002 Spinning Valiant XVR 30.00 50.00
VEB07003 Harmonics Messiah SVR 20.00 30.00
VEB07003 Harmonics Messiah XVR 75.00 125.00
VEB07003 Harmonics Messiah VR 6.00 10.00
VEB07004 Dragonic Blademaster RRR 2.50 4.00
VEB07004 Dragonic Blademaster SP 25.00 40.00
VEB07005 Wyvern Strike, Doha RRR 2.50 4.00
VEB07005 Wyvern Strike, Doha SP 3.00 5.00
VEB07006 Ultra Beast Deity, Illuminal Dragon RRR 2.50 4.00
VEB07006 Ultra Beast Deity, Illuminal Dragon SP 3.00 5.00
VEB07007 Kick Kick Typhoon RRR 2.00 3.00
VEB07007 Kick Kick Typhoon SP 2.00 3.00
VEB07008 Lady Battler of the Gravity Well RRR 2.00 3.00
VEB07008 Lady Battler of the Gravity Well SP 2.00 3.00
VEB07009 Sunset Edge, Duskblade RRR 1.00 1.50
VEB07009 Sunset Edge, Duskblade SP 1.25 2.00
VEB07010 Shine Bardiche Dragon RR .20 .30
VEB07011 Wyvern Strike, Dekat RR .25 .40
VEB07011 Wyvern Strike, Dekat SP .30 .50
VEB07012 Red Dive Griffin RR .30 .50
VEB07013 Glad Grad RR .20 .30
VEB07014 Beast Deity, Eclair Dragon RR .25 .40
VEB07015 Beast Deity, Glanz Dragon RR .25 .40
VEB07016 Claw of Occlusion, Ghastly Nail RR .20 .30
VEB07017 Blast Monk of the Thundering Foot RR 1.50 2.50
VEB07018 Destiny Dealer RR 1.25 2.00
VEB07019 Exile Dragon R .15 .25
VEB07020 Lava Blast Dragon R .15 .25
VEB07021 Wyvern Strike, Garan R .15 .25
VEB07022 Dragon Dancer, Josee R .15 .25
VEB07023 Girly Dolly R .15 .25
VEB07024 Savanna Wild R .15 .25
VEB07025 Stylish Hustler R .15 .25
VEB07026 Spin Kid R .15 .25
VEB07027 Drill the Dual R .15 .25
VEB07028 Competent Mechanic, Spechanic R .15 .25
VEB07029 Topological Dragon R .15 .25
VEB07030 Remarkable Burst Monk R .15 .25
VEB07031 Binodal Dragon R .15 .25
VEB07032 Calderon Wing R .15 .25
VEB07033 Iron Staff of Forbid Extinguish, Ilinvert R .15 .25
VEB07034 Dragon Knight, Zarina C .10 .15
VEB07035 Dragon Knight, Fahim C .10 .15
VEB07036 Dragon Knight, Mukhtar C .10 .15
VEB07037 Demonic Dragon Mage, Keiten C .10 .15
VEB07038 Flame of Varied Change, Peklenc C .10 .15
VEB07039 Dragon Knight, Nasser C .10 .15
VEB07040 Wyvern Strike, Membuas C .10 .15
VEB07041 Wyvernkid Ragla C .10 .15
VEB07042 Angry Horn Dragon C .10 .15
VEB07043 Embodiment of Spear, Tahr C .10 .15
VEB07044 Red Gem Carbuncle C .10 .15
VEB07045 Dragon Monk, Genjo C .10 .15
VEB07046 Warrior of Chakram C .10 .15
VEB07047 Vernal Cracker C .10 .15
VEB07048 Farmed Gaias C .10 .15
VEB07049 Dividing Rose C .10 .15
VEB07050 Smash Masher C .10 .15
VEB07051 Sling Burster C .10 .15
VEB07052 Ord Anchor C .10 .15
VEB07053 Three Minutes C .10 .15
VEB07054 Eight-language Announcer, Blabber C .10 .15
VEB07055 Wall Boy C .10 .15
VEB07056 Deep Scorpius C .10 .15
VEB07057 Envelope Panther C .10 .15
VEB07058 Metrial Fang C .10 .15
VEB07059 Spinodal Dragon C .10 .15
VEB07060 Blow Monk of Twin Foot C .10 .15
VEB07061 Black Star of Increase, Balerother C .10 .15
VEB07062 Neon Messiah C .10 .15
VEB07063 Axino Dragon C .10 .15
VEB07064 Asteroid Wolf C .10 .15
VEB07065 Beloved Child of Superstring Theory C .10 .15
VEB07066 Lady Healer of the Torn World C .10 .15
VEB07T01 Vision Token .15 .25

2019 Cardfight Vanguard V Extra Booster Set 8 My Glorious Justice

RELEASED ON AUGUST 9, 2019
VEB08001 Super Dimensional Robo, Dailiner VR 8.00 12.00
VEB08001 Super Dimensional Robo, Dailiner SVR 15.00 25.00
VEB08002 Ice Prison Necromancer, Cocytus VR 8.00 12.00
VEB08002 Ice Prison Necromancer, Cocytus SVR 15.00 25.00
VEB08003 Blue Storm Supreme Dragon, Glory Maelstrom VR 10.00 15.00
VEB08003 Blue Storm Supreme Dragon, Glory Maelstrom SVR 15.00 25.00
VEB08003 Blue Storm Supreme Dragon, Glory Maelstrom XVR 150.00 250.00
VEB08004 Platinum Ace RRR 2.50 4.00
VEB08004 Platinum Ace SP 15.00 25.00
VEB08005 Magical Police Quilt RRR 1.00 1.50
VEB08005 Magical Police Quilt SP 10.00 15.00
VEB08006 Greed Shade RRR 5.00 8.00
VEB08006 Greed Shade SP 20.00 30.00
VEB08007 Ripple Banshee RRR 2.00 3.00
VEB08007 Ripple Banshee SP 15.00 25.00
VEB08008 Coral Assault RRR 5.00 8.00
VEB08008 Coral Assault SP 25.00 40.00
VEB08009 Wheel Assault RRR 2.00 3.00
VEB08009 Wheel Assault SP 3.00 5.00
VEB08010 Super Dimensional Robo, Daizaurus RR .60 1.00
VEB08010 Super Dimensional Robo, Daizaurus SP 20.00 30.00
VEB08011 Roaring Beast, Audion RR .50 .75
VEB08012 Glory Maker RR .20 .30
VEB08013 Master Swordsman, Nightstorm RR .20 .30
VEB08013 Master Swordsman, Nightstorm SP 5.00 8.00
VEB08014 Stormride Ghost Ship RR .25 .40
VEB08015 Troubadour Cadaver, Alfio RR .20 .30
VEB08016 Hydro Hurricane Dragon RR .20 .30
VEB08017 Blue Wings of Great Cause, Phayllos RR .25 .40
VEB08018 Storm Rider, Nikoloz RR .40 .60
VEB08018 Storm Rider, Nikoloz SP 15.00 25.00
VEB08019 Battle Unit Commandant, Glegio R .15 .25
VEB08020 Quick Hero, Active Mask R .15 .25
VEB08021 Star King's Ambassador, Ginguard R .15 .25
VEB08022 Heat Source Monster, Genelaser R .15 .25
VEB08023 Battle Heroine, Enola R .15 .25
VEB08024 Seabed Demon Beast, Scaredick R .15 .25
VEB08025 Skeleton Sharpshooter R .15 .25
VEB08026 Dragon Spirit R .15 .25
VEB08027 Dolph the Ghostie R .15 .25
VEB08028 Pat the Ghostie R .15 .25
VEB08029 Marine General of the White Waves, Philogatos R .15 .25
VEB08030 Blue Wings of Obduracy, Simeon R .15 .25
VEB08031 Blue Wings of Resonance, Maxios R .15 .25
VEB08032 Blue Wings of Faith, Basilia R .15 .25
VEB08033 Blue Ward Command R .15 .25
VEB08034 Subterfuge Unit Commandant, Secilia C .10 .15
VEB08035 Potent Poison Monster, Dakgiri C .10 .15
VEB08036 Lightning Saucer C .10 .15
VEB08037 Excavation Monster, Mogdrilla C .10 .15
VEB08038 Operator Girl, Haruka C .10 .15
VEB08039 Little Hero Dracokid C .10 .15
VEB08040 Dimensional Robo, Daibattles C .10 .15
VEB08041 Dimensional Robo, Dairacer C .10 .15
VEB08042 Army Penguin C .10 .15
VEB08043 Dimensional Robo, Gorescue C .10 .15
VEB08044 King Tentacle C .10 .15
VEB08045 Kicking Frangal C .10 .15
VEB08046 Punching Frangul C .10 .15
VEB08047 Nightwatch Pirate, Nilde C .10 .15
VEB08048 Skeleton Drawn-Sword Soldier C .10 .15
VEB08049 Captain Nightkid C .10 .15
VEB08050 Rough Seas Banshee C .10 .15
VEB08051 Knight Spirit C .10 .15
VEB08052 Pirate Ship Handler, Paolo C .10 .15
VEB08053 Rick the Ghostie C .10 .15
VEB08054 Bleb Bomber Dragon C .10 .15
VEB08055 Metal Cut Sailor C .10 .15
VEB08056 Calm Assault C .10 .15
VEB08057 Blue Wings of Empathy, Makarios C .10 .15
VEB08058 Battle Siren, Hesper C .10 .15
VEB08059 Blow Bubble Dracokid C .10 .15
VEB08060 Blue Storm Marine General, Despina C .10 .15
VEB08061 Pyroxene Communications Sea Otter Soldier C .10 .15
VEB08062 Enemy Seeking Seagull Soldier C .10 .15
VEB08063 Medical Officer of the Rainbow Elixir C .10 .15

2017 Cardfight Vanguard G Character Booster Set 1 Try3 Next

RELEASED ON MARCH 3, 2017
GBT09Re01 Laurel Knight Sicilus RRR 5.00 8.00
GBT09Re02 Holy Knight Guardian RRR 1.00 1.50
GBT09Re03 Bringer of Dreams Belenus RRR 1.50 2.50
GBT09Re04 Steam Breath Dragon RRR .60 1.00
GBT09Re05 Steam Maiden Arlim RRR 2.50 4.00
GBT09Re06 Heart Thump Worker RRR 2.00 3.00
GBT09Re07 Valkyrie of Reclamation Padmini RRR .75 1.25
GBT09Re08 Maiden of Passionflower RRR 1.25 2.00
GBT09Re09 Flower Garden Maiden Mylis RRR .40 .60
GCHB01001 Holy Dragon Brave Lancer Dragon GR 2.50 4.00
GCHB01001 Holy Dragon Brave Lancer Dragon SGR 4.00 6.00
GCHB01002 Interdimensional Dragon Crossover Dragon GR .75 1.25
GCHB01002 Interdimensional Dragon Crossover Dragon SGR 3.00 5.00
GCHB01003 Flower Princess of Beautiful Winter Inverno GR 4.00 6.00
GCHB01003 Flower Princess of Beautiful Winter Inverno SGR 8.00 12.00
GCHB01004 Luminous Light King of Knights Alfred Oath RRR 2.50 4.00
GCHB01004 Luminous Light King of Knights Alfred Oath SP 10.00 15.00
GCHB01005 Knight of Heavenly Decree Altmile RRR 1.00 1.50
GCHB01005 Knight of Heavenly Decree Altmile SP 50.00 75.00
GCHB01006 Knight of Enlightenment Albion RRR .60 1.00
GCHB01006 Knight of Enlightenment Albion SP 4.00 6.00
GCHB01007 Pulsar Shiftbullet Dragon RRR .40 .60
GCHB01007 Pulsar Shiftbullet Dragon SP 3.00 5.00
GCHB01008 Ranunculus of Searing Heart Ahsha RRR 3.00 5.00
GCHB01008 Ranunculus of Searing Heart Ahsha SP 40.00 60.00
GCHB01009 Tenacious Maiden Noel RRR 1.25 2.00
GCHB01009 Tenacious Maiden Noel SP 5.00 8.00
GCHB01010 Holy Dragon Legit Sword Dragon RR .20 .30
GCHB01010 Holy Dragon Legit Sword Dragon SP 10.00 15.00
GCHB01011 Divine Knight of Godly Defense Igraine RR .75 1.25
GCHB01011 Divine Knight of Godly Defense Igraine SP 15.00 25.00
GCHB01012 Knight of Ambuscade Redon RR 1.50 2.50
GCHB01013 Security Knight Regius RR 2.00 3.00
GCHB01014 Highbrow Steam Arlim RR .20 .30
GCHB01014 Highbrow Steam Arlim SP 1.25 2.00
GCHB01015 Throttle Caliber Dragon RR .20 .30
GCHB01016 Linear Feed Dragon RR .20 .30
GCHB01017 Steam Tamer Arka RR 5.00 8.00
GCHB01017 Steam Tamer Arka SP 50.00 75.00
GCHB01018 Rubellum Lily Splendorous Musketeer Myra RR 4.00 6.00
GCHB01018 Rubellum Lily Splendorous Musketeer Myra SP 25.00 40.00
GCHB01019 Passiflora Flower Princess Marleena RR .20 .30
GCHB01019 Passiflora Flower Princess Marleena SP 5.00 8.00
GCHB01020 White Clover Musketeer Mia Reeta RR 1.25 2.00
GCHB01021 Flower Keeper Dragon RR .30 .50
GCHB01022 Emit Hammer Dragon R .15 .25
GCHB01023 Swordsman of Light Picos R .15 .25
GCHB01024 Mace of Pledge Iasius R .15 .25
GCHB01025 Energetic Knight Romus R .15 .25
GCHB01026 Starlight Violinist R .15 .25
GCHB01027 Acute Knight Paris R .15 .25
GCHB01028 Knight of Battle Preparation Porrex R .15 .25
GCHB01029 Interdimensional Beast Upheaval Pegasus R .15 .25
GCHB01030 Steam Maiden Ishuiil R .15 .25
GCHB01031 Grey Exhaust Dragon R .15 .25
GCHB01032 Steam Fighter Galumu R .15 .25
GCHB01033 Pulsar Farm Peacock R .15 .25
GCHB01034 Timebreak Dragon R .15 .25
GCHB01035 Maiden of Flower Pistol R .15 .25
GCHB01036 Lisianthus Musketeer Loraine R .15 .25
GCHB01037 Sunshine Maiden Paula R .15 .25
GCHB01038 Prunus Serrulata Musketeer Tessa R 1.25 2.00
GCHB01039 Pansy Musketeer Silvia R .15 .25
GCHB01040 Amaryllis Musketeer Tatiana R .15 .25
GCHB01041 Faith Maiden Odette R .40 .60
GCHB01042 Maiden of Sweet Berry R .15 .25
GCHB01043 Scramble Griffin C .10 .15
GCHB01044 Knight of Cast C .10 .15
GCHB01045 Hopesong Angel C .10 .15
GCHB01046 Sage of Innovation Libron C .10 .15
GCHB01047 Tamamy C .10 .15
GCHB01048 Rynegal C .10 .15
GCHB01049 Maru Baru C .10 .15
GCHB01050 Weapons Dealer Brutu C .10 .15
GCHB01051 Refresh Healer C .10 .15
GCHB01052 Scion Rider C .60 1.00
GCHB01053 Encourage Angel C .10 .15
GCHB01054 Steam Rider Sharrum C .10 .15
GCHB01055 Steam Fighter Nagish C .10 .15
GCHB01056 Rough Play Outrageous Gear Bear C .10 .15
GCHB01057 Steam Soldier Undalulu C .10 .15
GCHB01058 Smart Fender Dragon C .10 .15
GCHB01059 Chic Folk Dracokid C .10 .15
GCHB01060 Grind Grind Worker C .10 .15
GCHB01061 Steam Engineer Kushaana C .10 .15
GCHB01062 Steam Doctor Enja C .10 .15
GCHB01063 Vainglorydream Gear Cat C .10 .15
GCHB01064 Knight of Development Rallye C .10 .15
GCHB01065 Greenshot Elf C .10 .15
GCHB01066 Rindo Gentian Musketeer Antero C .10 .15
GCHB01067 Mixfruits Dragon C .10 .15
GCHB01068 Avoca Doze C .10 .15
GCHB01069 Maiden Dancing in the Wind Francoise C .10 .15
GCHB01070 Maiden of Delphinium C .10 .15
GCHB01071 Babyblueeyes Musketeer May Len C .10 .15
GCHB01072 Freesia Musketeer Rosalia C .10 .15
GCHB01073 Roselle Musketeer Randy C .10 .15
GCHB01074 Kamille Musketeer Nicole C .10 .15
GCHB01075 Watering Elf C .10 .15

2017 Cardfight Vanguard G Character Booster Set 2 We Are Trinity Dragon

RELEASED ON MARCH 24, 2017
GCHB02001 State Affair Subjugation Deity Kamususanoo GR 5.00 8.00
GCHB02001 State Affair Subjugation Deity Kamususanoo SGR 10.00 15.00
GCHB02002 Great Galactic Governor Commander Laurel D GR 1.25 2.00
GCHB02002 Great Galactic Governor Commander Laurel D SGR 10.00 15.00
GCHB02003 Omniscience Dragon Fernyiges GR 1.25 2.00
GCHB02003 Omniscience Dragon Fernyiges SGR 4.00 6.00
GCHB02004 Sun of Eternity Amaterasu RRR 2.50 4.00
GCHB02004 Sun of Eternity Amaterasu SP 50.00 75.00
GCHB02005 Spiritual Sword of Rough Deity Susanoo RRR 1.00 1.50
GCHB02005 Spiritual Sword of Rough Deity Susanoo SP 8.00 12.00
GCHB02006 Dimensional Robo Command Chief Final Daimax RRR 10.00 15.00
GCHB02006 Dimensional Robo Command Chief Final Daimax SP 50.00 75.00
GCHB02007 Bravest Rush Grandgallop RRR 2.00 3.00
GCHB02007 Bravest Rush Grandgallop SP 12.00 20.00
GCHB02008 Immortality Professor Brahmananda RRR 1.00 1.50
GCHB02008 Immortality Professor Brahmananda SP 10.00 15.00
GCHB02009 Teachers Cane of Affection Bigbelly RRR .40 .60
GCHB02009 Teachers Cane of Affection Bigbelly SP 2.00 3.00
GCHB02010 Excite Battle Sister Miroir RR 3.00 5.00
GCHB02010 Excite Battle Sister Miroir SP 12.00 20.00
GCHB02011 Battle Sister Madeleine RR 2.50 4.00
GCHB02012 Deity Spirit Loyalist Amenooshiho RR .20 .30
GCHB02013 Higher Deity Protecting Official Amatsuhikone RR 3.00 5.00
GCHB02013 Higher Deity Protecting Official Amatsuhikone SP 12.00 20.00
GCHB02014 Hyper Metalborg Guilt Digger RR .20 .30
GCHB02014 Hyper Metalborg Guilt Digger SP 2.50 4.00
GCHB02015 Gallant Incarnation GOFive RR 1.50 2.50
GCHB02016 Enigman Helm RR .25 .40
GCHB02017 Enigman Calm RR 6.00 10.00
GCHB02017 Enigman Calm SP 30.00 50.00
GCHB02018 Omniscience Dragon Almiraj RR .50 .75
GCHB02019 Honorary Professor Chatsauvage RR .40 .60
GCHB02019 Honorary Professor Chatsauvage SP 12.00 20.00
GCHB02020 Lesser Writer RR .60 1.00
GCHB02021 Finecoat Maltese RR .25 .40
GCHB02021 Finecoat Maltese SP 5.00 8.00
GCHB02022 Spiritual Deity of Benevolence Amenosagume R 1.25 2.00
GCHB02023 Goddess of Astrology Yasaka R .15 .25
GCHB02024 Battle Sister Crepe R .40 .60
GCHB02025 Deity Spirit Loyalist Kumanokusubi R .15 .25
GCHB02026 Precious Ophidian R .15 .25
GCHB02027 Battle Sister Compote R .15 .25
GCHB02028 Bellringing Miko Ouka R .50 .75
GCHB02029 Super Cosmic Hero Xlead R .15 .25
GCHB02030 Enigman Gigastorm R .15 .25
GCHB02031 Dimensional Robo Daireson R .30 .50
GCHB02032 Cosmic Hero Grandberet R .15 .25
GCHB02033 Enigman Blanc R .15 .25
GCHB02034 Enigman Zephyr R .15 .25
GCHB02035 Operator Girl Rinka R 3.00 5.00
GCHB02036 Omniscience Dragon Kieltimka R .15 .25
GCHB02037 Fullmark Gorilla R .15 .25
GCHB02038 Treatise Panther R .15 .25
GCHB02039 Honorary Assistant Mikesaburo R .60 1.00
GCHB02040 Traveling Momonga R .15 .25
GCHB02041 Label Pangolin R .15 .25
GCHB02042 Gifted Bear R .15 .25
GCHB02043 Fighting Strike Sword Deity Toyokuninushi C .10 .15
GCHB02044 Battle Sister Pannacotta C .10 .15
GCHB02045 Battle Sister Berrymousse C .10 .15
GCHB02046 Apprentice Weather Girl Smoothie C .10 .15
GCHB02047 Foredoom Miko Sachi C .10 .15
GCHB02048 Battle Sister Syrup C .10 .15
GCHB02049 Battle Sister Rusk C .10 .15
GCHB02050 Astrologer Miss Haze C .10 .15
GCHB02051 Deity Spirit Loyalist Ikutsuhikone C .10 .15
GCHB02052 Aqua Witch NeNe C .10 .15
GCHB02053 Medicinal Miko Yakushiji C .10 .15
GCHB02054 Enigman Megacurrent C .10 .15
GCHB02055 Cosmic Hero Grandsmasher C .10 .15
GCHB02056 Enigman Sirocco C .10 .15
GCHB02057 Metalborg Blacking Barrow C .10 .15
GCHB02058 Enigman Swirl C .10 .15
GCHB02059 Metalborg Jet Sider C .10 .15
GCHB02060 Reducing Monster Weaking C .10 .15
GCHB02061 Dimensional Robo Daihawk C .10 .15
GCHB02062 Enigman Fall C .10 .15
GCHB02063 Enigman Feign C .10 .15
GCHB02064 Enigman Mistral C .10 .15
GCHB02065 Edging Condor C .10 .15
GCHB02066 Go Home Toad C .10 .15
GCHB02067 Fullsack Squirrel C .10 .15
GCHB02068 Pastel Deer C .10 .15
GCHB02069 Reader Pig C .10 .15
GCHB02070 Magnifier Chow Chow C .10 .15
GCHB02071 Specs Chinchilla C .10 .15
GCHB02072 Polish Penguin C .10 .15
GCHB02073 Pen Case Pelican C .10 .15
GCHB02074 Brushing Kitten C .10 .15
GCHB02075 Chemical Skunk C .10 .15

GCHB02Re01 Psychic Bird RRR	3.00	5.00
GCHB02Re02 Super Dimensional Robo Daikaiser RRR	2.00	3.00
GCHB02Re03 Dimensional Robo Kaisergrader RRR	10.00	15.00
GCHB02Re04 Honorary Professor Chatnoir RRR	2.00	3.00
GCHB02S13 Dragon Destroyer Battle Deity Kamususanoo SP	6.00	10.00
GCHB02S14 Supreme Heavenly Battle Deity Susanoo SP	2.00	3.00
GCHB02S15 Divine Sword AmenoMurakumo SP	6.00	10.00
GCHB02S16 Arbitrator AmenoSagiri SP		
GCHB02S17 Divine Sword Kusanagi SP	2.50	4.00
GCHB02S18 Super Cosmic Hero Xtiger SP	5.00	8.00
GCHB02S19 Enigman Gigastorm SP	2.00	3.00
GCHB02S20 Enigman Helm SP	2.00	3.00
GCHB02S21 Enigman Blanc SP	3.00	5.00
GCHB02S22 Enigman Zephyr SP	1.25	2.00
GCHB02S23 Sagesaint Professor Bigbelly SP	6.00	10.00
GCHB02S24 Famous Professor Bigbelly SP	2.50	4.00
GCHB02S25 Diligent Assistant Minibelly SP	10.00	15.00
GCHB02S26 Contradictory Instructor Shell Master SP	4.00	6.00
GCHB02S27 Application Researcher Ponbelly SP	6.00	10.00

2017 Cardfight Vanguard G Character Booster Set 3 Rummy Labyrinth Under the Moonlight

COMPLETE SET (78)	700.00	900.00
UNLISTED C	.10	.15
UNLISTED R	.15	.25
RELEASED ON MAY 15, 2017		
GCHB03001 Parallel Megatrick Fairfield GR	10.00	15.00
GCHB03001 Parallel Megatrick Fairfield SGR	15.00	25.00
GCHB03002 Pirate King of Redemption Dragut GR	15.00	25.00
GCHB03002 Pirate King of Redemption Dragut SGR	25.00	40.00
GCHB03003 Silver Thorn Dragon Master Venus Luquier RRR	3.00	5.00
GCHB03003 Silver Thorn Dragon Master Venus Luquier SP	40.00	60.00
GCHB03004 Masked Phantom Harri RRR	4.00	6.00
GCHB03004 Masked Phantom Harri SP	10.00	15.00
GCHB03004 Masked Phantom Harri RLR	75.00	125.00
GCHB03005 Diabolist of Corpse Negrosonger RRR	8.00	12.00
GCHB03005 Diabolist of Corpse Negrosonger SP	30.00	50.00
GCHB03006 Vampire Princess of Starlight Nightrose RRR	6.00	10.00
GCHB03006 Vampire Princess of Starlight Nightrose SP	20.00	30.00
GCHB03006 Vampire Princess of Starlight Nightrose RLR	125.00	200.00
GCHB03007 Nightmare Doll of the Abyss Eleanore RR	.75	1.25
GCHB03008 Silver Thorn Dragon Tamer Luquier RR	2.00	3.00
GCHB03008 Silver Thorn Dragon Tamer Luquier SP	50.00	75.00
GCHB03009 Face Magician Lappin RR	2.00	3.00
GCHB03010 Lovely Companion RR	.75	1.25
GCHB03010 Lovely Companion SP	10.00	15.00
GCHB03011 Seven Seas Dignitary Nightzeolla RR	.75	1.25
GCHB03011 Seven Seas Dignitary Nightzeolla SP	8.00	12.00
GCHB03012 Ghostie Leader Demetria RR	.75	1.25
GCHB03013 Maltreat Shade RR	2.00	3.00
GCHB03014 Seawall Banshee RR	2.00	3.00
GCHB03014 Seawall Banshee SP	30.00	50.00
GCHB03015 Crudelis Dragon Master Janet R	.20	.35
GCHB03016 Jester Demonic Dragon Wandering Dragon R	.40	.60
GCHB03017 Gun Salute Dragon End of Stage R	.25	.40
GCHB03018 Silver Thorn Acrobat Lucamia R	.20	.35
GCHB03019 Dagger Magician Ety R	.20	.35
GCHB03020 Nightmare Doll Liza R	.30	.50
GCHB03021 Masquerade Bunny R	.60	1.00
GCHB03022 Pleasure Caster R	.20	.35
GCHB03023 Eclipse Dragonhulk Jumble Dragon R	.20	.35
GCHB03024 Diabolist of Tombs Negromode R	.40	.60
GCHB03025 Seven Seas Crack Soldier Nightjasper R	.15	.25
GCHB03026 King Serpent R	.30	.50
GCHB03027 Tommy the Ghostie Brothers R	.60	1.00
GCHB03028 Swordmaster Mimic R	.15	.25
GCHB03029 Fatal Shade R	.30	.50
GCHB03030 Guile Shade R	.20	.40
GCHB03031 Silver Thorn Masher Dragon C	.10	.15
GCHB03032 Silver Thorn Acute Dragon C	.10	.15
GCHB03033 Dancing Knifedancer C	.10	.15
GCHB03034 Nightmare Doll Gerda C	.10	.15
GCHB03035 Throwing Bear C	.10	.15
GCHB03036 Silver Thorn Clown Cernay C	.10	.15
GCHB03037 Immortal Target C	.10	.15
GCHB03038 Nightmare Doll Juliet C	.10	.15
GCHB03039 Silver Thorn Beast Tamer Lolotte C	.10	.15
GCHB03040 Nightmare Doll Natalie C	.10	.15
GCHB03041 Nightmare Doll Wendy C	.10	.15
GCHB03042 Nightmare Doll Sydney C	.10	.15
GCHB03043 Vanishment Dracokid C	.10	.15
GCHB03044 Explode Gentle C	.10	.15
GCHB03045 Skyhigh Walker C	.10	.15
GCHB03046 Fabian the Ghostie C	.10	.15
GCHB03047 Clemmie the Ghostie C	.10	.15
GCHB03048 Hesketh the Ghostie C	.10	.15
GCHB03049 Skeleton Marauder C	.10	.15
GCHB03050 Quincy the Ghostie C	.10	.15
GCHB03051 Jackie the Ghostie C	.10	.15
GCHB03052 Seven Seas Shipmate Nightalert C	.10	.15
GCHB03053 Madness Franky C	.10	.15
GCHB03054 Matt the Ghostie C	.10	.15
GCHB03055 Seven Seas Private Styx C	.10	.15
GCHB03056 Seven Seas Dragon Undead Scavenge Dragon C	.10	.15
GCHB03057 Dead of the Seven Seas Aurelio C	.10	.15
GCHB03058 Crusher Francesca C	.10	.15
GCHB03059 Howard the Ghostie C	.10	.15
GCHB03060 Screaming Banshee C	.10	.15
GCHB03Re01 Masked Magician Harri RRR	2.00	3.00
GCHB03Re02 Vampire Princess of Night Fog Nightrose RRR	4.00	6.00
GCHB03S09 Masked Magician Harri SP	12.00	20.00
GCHB03S10 Masquerade Bunny SP	15.00	25.00
GCHB03S11 Vampire Princess of Night Fog Nightrose SP	50.00	75.00
GCHB03S12 Tommy the Ghostie Brothers SP	15.00	25.00

2015 Cardfight Vanguard G Clan Booster Set 1 Academy of Divas

COMPLETE SET (53)	400.00	600.00
RELEASED ON AUGUST 25, 2015		
GCB01001 School Etoile, Olyvia GR	1.50	2.50
GCB01002 PR?ISM-Promise, Princess Labrador RRR	25.00	60.00
GCB01003 Duo Eternal Sister, Meer RRR	15.00	25.00
GCB01004 Miracle Voice, Lauris RRR	1.25	2.00
GCB01005 Ideal Walking Weather, Emilia RRR	25.00	40.00
GCB01006 Sincere Girl, Liddy RR	25.00	60.00
GCB01007 Admired Sparkle, Spica RR	3.00	5.00
GCB01008 Duo Fantasia, Lamry RR	4.00	6.00
GCB01009 Unbelievagirl, Potpourri RR	20.00	30.00
GCB01010 Superb New Student, Shizuku RR	1.50	2.50
GCB01011 Image Master, Kukuri RR	1.25	2.00
GCB01012 Cherished Phrase, Reina RR	4.00	6.00
GCB01013 Fluffy Ribbon, Somni R	.60	1.00
GCB01014 Duo Lovely Angel, Nemuel R	1.00	1.50
GCB01015 Duo Lovely Devil, Vepar R	1.25	2.00
GCB01016 Duo Beloved Child of the Sea Palace, Minamo R	3.00	5.00
GCB01017 PR?ISM-Promise, Princess Celtic R	1.25	2.00
GCB01018 Talent of Perseverance, Shandee R	2.50	4.00
GCB01019 Duo Gorgeous Lady, Kazuha R	1.25	2.00
GCB01020 PR?ISM-Promise, Princess Leyte R	1.25	2.00
GCB01021 Secret Smile, Puumo R	1.25	2.00
GCB01022 First Lesson, Akari R	.75	1.25
GCB01023A Duo Love Joker, Chulym R	.60	1.00
GCB01023B Duo Love Joker, Chulym (B) R	1.75	3.00
GCB01024 Dreamer Dreamer! Krk R	.60	1.00
GCB01025 Little Princess, Himari C	3.00	5.00
GCB01026 Afternoon Tea Party, Couver C	.15	.25
GCB01027 Top Gear Idol, Sanya C	.15	.25
GCB01028 Mystery Solving Time, Ithil C	.15	.25
GCB01029 Victory Appeal, Filier C	.15	.25
GCB01030 Reticent Diva, Isuca C	.15	.25
GCB01031 PR?ISM-Duo, Loretta (B) C	.15	.25
GCB01032 Full Throttle Idol, Lurrie C	.15	.25
GCB01033 Sweet Paradise, Manya C	.15	.25
GCB01034 Beware of Surprises, Almin C	.15	.25
GCB01035 One Blow Fight, Hinata C	.15	.25
GCB01036 Finger Magic, Mako C	.15	.25
GCB01037 Morning Impact, Lips C	.15	.25
GCB01038 Southern Harmony, Melvi C	.15	.25
GCB01039 Cold Eye, Sara C	.15	.25
GCB01040 Lover of Hearts, Penelotta C	.15	.25
GCB0131W PR?ISM-Duo, Loretta (W) C	.15	.25
GCB01S01 School Etoile, Olyvia SP	175.00	300.00
GCB01S02 Duo Eternal Sister, Meer SP		
GCB01S03 Miracle Voice, Lauris SP	100.00	150.00
GCB01S04 Strolling Weather, Emilia SP	40.00	60.00
GCB01S05 Sincere Girl, Liddy SP	20.00	30.00
GCB01S06 Admired Sparkle, Spica SP	60.00	100.00
GCB01S07 Duo Fantasia, Lamry SP		
GCB01S08 Unbelievagirl, Potpourri SP	30.00	50.00
GCB01S09 Superb New Student, Shizuku SP	175.00	300.00
GCB01S10 Image Master, Kukuri SP	75.00	125.00
GCB01S11 Important Phrase, Reina SP	15.00	25.00

2015 Cardfight Vanguard G Clan Booster Set 2 Commander of the Incessant Waves

COMPLETE SET (46)	200.00	300.00
UNLISTED C	.10	.15
UNLISTED R	.15	.25
RELEASED ON DECEMBER 11, 2015		
GCB02001 Storm Dominator Commander Thavas GR	50.00	75.00
GCB02002 Blue Wave Marshal Dragon Tetraboil Dragon RRR	6.00	10.00
GCB02002 Blue Wave Marshal Dragon Tetraboil Dragon SP	20.00	30.00
GCB02003 Blue Wave Dragon Angerboil Dragon RRR	8.00	12.00
GCB02003 Blue Wave Dragon Angerboil Dragon SP	25.00	40.00
GCB02004 Blue Storm Dragon Maelstrom RRR	4.00	6.00
GCB02004 Blue Storm Dragon Maelstrom SP	20.00	35.00
GCB02005 Jockey of the Great Sea Skyros RRR	3.00	5.00
GCB02005 Jockey of the Great Sea Skyros SP	12.00	20.00
GCB02006 Surging Ripple Prodromos RR	1.50	2.50
GCB02007 Blue Wave Marine General Foivos RR	2.50	4.00
GCB02008 Battle Siren Adelaide RR	1.75	3.00
GCB02009 Blue Wave Soldier Bright Shooter RR	.60	1.00
GCB02010 Blue Storm Battle Princess Theta RR	.40	.60
GCB02011 Blue Storm Shield Homerus RR	1.00	1.50
GCB02011 Blue Storm Shield Homerus SP	6.00	10.00
GCB02012 Kelpie Rider Petros RR	3.00	5.00
GCB02013 Rolling Ripple Miltiadis R	.15	.25
GCB02014 Titan of the Trench Patrol R	.15	.25
GCB02015 Wavehunt Sailor R	.15	.25
GCB02016 Marine General of the Sonic Speed Nektarios R	.15	.25
GCB02017 Couple Dagger Sailor R	.15	.25
GCB02018 Blue Storm Battle Princess Lynpia R	.15	.25
GCB02019 Penguin Soldier of the Blue Storm Fleet R	.15	.25
GCB02020 Battle Siren Melania R	.15	.25
GCB02021 Flash Ripple Odysseus R	.15	.25
GCB02022 Battle Siren Cloris R	.15	.25
GCB02023 Blue Wave Dragon Dagger Master Dracokid R	.15	.25
GCB02024 Blue Wave Soldier Brutal Trooper R	.15	.25
GCB02025 Cobalt Neon Dragon C	.10	.15
GCB02026 Blue Storm Marine General Sebastian C	.10	.15
GCB02027 Unruly Ripple Lapis C	.10	.15
GCB02028 Tear Knight Timos C	.10	.15
GCB02029 Battle Siren Nicoletta C	.10	.15
GCB02030 Reconinforce Orca Soldier C	.10	.15
GCB02031 Dispatch Mission Seagull Soldier C	.10	.15
GCB02032 Violent Shooter C	.10	.15
GCB02033 Mindeye Sailor C	.10	.15
GCB02034 Flashroll Commando C	.10	.15
GCB02035 Kelpie Rider Mitros C	.10	.15
GCB02036 Blue Storm Battleship Wadatsumi C	.10	.15
GCB02037 Sea Otter Soldier of the Blue Storm Fleet C	.10	.15
GCB02038 Medical Officer of the Blue Storm Fleet C	.10	.15
GCB02039 Ripple of Demise Orest C	.10	.15
GCB02040 Blue Storm Battle Princess Doris C	.10	.15
GCB02S06 One Who Surpasses the Storm Thavas SP	50.00	75.00

2016 Cardfight Vanguard G Clan Booster Set 3 Blessing of Divas

COMPLETE SET (73)	2000.00	3000.00
UNLISTED C	.15	.25
UNLISTED R	.20	.30
RELEASED ON JULY 29, 2016		
GCB03001 Celebrate Voice Lauris GR	12.00	20.00
GCB03001 Celebrate Voice Lauris SGR	20.00	30.00
GCB03001 Celebrate Voice Lauris SP	50.00	75.00
GCB03001 Celebrate Voice Lauris WSP	175.00	300.00
GCB03002 PRISMImage Sunshine Vert RRR	8.00	12.00
GCB03002 PRISMImage Sunshine Vert SP	100.00	150.00
GCB03002 PRISMImage Sunshine Vert WSP	250.00	400.00
GCB03003 Frontier Star Coral RRR	4.00	6.00
GCB03003 Frontier Star Coral SP	50.00	75.00
GCB03003 Frontier Star Coral WSP	150.00	250.00
GCB03004 Peaceful Voice Raindear RRR	4.00	6.00
GCB03004 Peaceful Voice Raindear SP	50.00	75.00
GCB03004 Peaceful Voice Raindear WSP	150.00	250.00
GCB03005 Sparkle in Her Heart Spica RRR	1.50	2.50
GCB03005 Sparkle in Her Heart Spica SP	30.00	50.00
GCB03005 Sparkle in Her Heart Spica WSP	60.00	100.00
GCB03006 Prestige Cetia RRR	1.50	2.50
GCB03006 Prestige Cetia SP	25.00	40.00
GCB03006 Prestige Cetia WSP	60.00	100.00
GCB03007 Hand in Hand Leona RR	.75	1.25
GCB03007 Hand in Hand Leona SP	40.00	60.00
GCB03007 Hand in Hand Leona WSP	100.00	150.00
GCB03008 Great Ascent Liddy RR	.60	1.00
GCB03008 Great Ascent Liddy SP	30.00	50.00
GCB03008 Great Ascent Liddy WSP	50.00	75.00
GCB03009 BrandNewPRISM Garnet RR	.60	1.00
GCB03009 BrandNewPRISM Garnet SP	30.00	50.00
GCB03009 BrandNewPRISM Garnet WSP	100.00	150.00
GCB03010 Magical Charge Vita RR	.60	1.00
GCB03010 Magical Charge Vita SP	30.00	50.00
GCB03010 Magical Charge Vita WSP	75.00	125.00
GCB03011 Brilliant Ocean Elly RR	.40	.60
GCB03011 Brilliant Ocean Elly SP	30.00	50.00
GCB03011 Brilliant Ocean Elly WSP	50.00	75.00
GCB03012 Garland Blossom Ayna RR	.40	.60
GCB03012 Garland Blossom Ayna SP	30.00	45.00
GCB03012 Garland Blossom Ayna WSP	75.00	125.00
GCB03013 Miracle Twintail Wyz RR	1.25	2.00
GCB03013 Miracle Twintail Wyz SP	25.00	40.00
GCB03013 Miracle Twintail Wyz WSP	40.00	60.00
GCB03014 Flying Mermaid Frederica R	.20	.30
GCB03015 Whitely Noble Fantine R	.20	.30
GCB03016 Active Pink Lalana R	.20	.30
GCB03017 Inspect Sisters Robel R	.20	.30
GCB03018 PRISMImage Sunshine Rosa R	.20	.30
GCB03019 Artless Charmy Wakana R	.20	.30
GCB03020 Admire Successor Lyrica R	.20	.30
GCB03021 Monotone Innocence Yuka R	.20	.30
GCB03022 Dash Sisters Rabel R	.20	.30
GCB03023 BrandNewPRISM Emeral R	.20	.30
GCB03024 Duo Create Quill Ilya R	.20	.30
GCB03025 Wholehearted Dream Meruru R	.20	.30
GCB03026 PRISMImage Sunshine Clear R	.20	.30
GCB03027 Jump to the Water Surface Amelie R	.20	.30
GCB03028 Skillful Performer Minori C	.15	.25
GCB03029 Splash Daughter Rachel C	.15	.25
GCB03030 Shyness Laguna Lapla C	.15	.25
GCB03031 Duo Creamy Caramel Cornet C	.15	.25
GCB03032 Onestroke Art Carla C	.15	.25
GCB03033 Intellect Polish Seyna C	.15	.25
GCB03034 Duo Caprice Cats Marjona C	.15	.25
GCB03035 Piping Hot Suifa C	.15	.25
GCB03036 Tidal Art Marie C	.15	.25
GCB03037 New Song Announcement Alti C	.15	.25
GCB03038 Colorful Smiling Fratte C	.15	.25
GCB03039 Duo Cotton Sleeper Ichika C	.15	.25
GCB03040 BrandNewPRISM Sapphire C	.15	.25
GCB03041 Tiny Precious May C	.15	.25
GCB03042 Impact Punch Michiru C	.15	.25
GCB03043 Voice of Fate Kasumi C	.15	.25
GCB03044 Sweet Temptation Riko C	.15	.25
GCB03045 Heartful Ale Fundy C	.15	.25
GCB03Re01 School Etoile Olyvia R	12.00	20.00

2016 Cardfight Vanguard G Clan Booster Set 4 Gear of Fate

RELEASED ON NOVEMBER 4, 2016		
GCB04001 Deus Ex Machina Demiurge GR	1.25	2.00
GCB04001 Deus Ex Machina Demiurge SGR	8.00	12.00
GCB04002 Chronotiger Rebellion RRR	3.00	5.00
GCB04002 Chronotiger Rebellion SP	15.00	25.00
GCB04003 Chronodragon Gear Groovy RRR	10.00	15.00
GCB04003 Chronodragon Gear Groovy SP	20.00	30.00
GCB04004 Ephemeral Wand Dragon RRR	.60	1.00
GCB04004 Ephemeral Wand Dragon SP	2.50	4.00
GCB04005 Prospatheia Ideadrone RRR	.40	.60
GCB04005 Prospatheia Ideadrone SP	2.00	3.00
GCB04006 Delayed Blazer Dragon RRR	4.00	6.00
GCB04006 Delayed Blazer Dragon SP	15.00	25.00
GCB04007 Interdimensional Beast Pandora Chimera RR	.40	.60
GCB04007 Interdimensional Beast Pandora Chimera SP	2.50	4.00
GCB04008 Interdimensional Dragon Heteroround Dragon RR	1.00	1.50
GCB04008 Interdimensional Dragon Heteroround Dragon SP	5.00	8.00
GCB04009 Steam Tamer Nanni RR	.75	1.25
GCB04010 Diaperno Ideadrone RR	.40	.60
GCB04011 Steam Maiden Meshkia RR	.60	1.00
GCB04012 Steam Keeper Labashim RR	.60	1.00
GCB04012 Steam Keeper Labashim SP	1.50	2.50
GCB04013 Nightbarking Gear Tabby RR	.75	1.25
GCB04014 Deus Ex Machina Ergos R	.15	.25
GCB04015 Ergasia Ideadrone R	.15	.25
GCB04016 Slow Divider Dragon R	.15	.25
GCB04017 Extend Magne Dragon R	.15	.25
GCB04018 Kaigomai Ideadrone R	.15	.25
GCB04019 Steam Knight Puzurlli R	.15	.25
GCB04020 Steam Maiden Shagkusa R	.15	.25
GCB04021 Causality Dragon R	.25	.40
GCB04022 Steam Maiden Lasinabel R	.15	.25
GCB04023 Tickaway Dragon R	.25	.40
GCB04024 Chanomai Ideadrone R	.15	.25
GCB04025 Steam Maiden Ishme R	.15	.25
GCB04026 Chrono Tigar R	.15	.25
GCB04027 Anarchia Ideadrone R	.15	.25
GCB04028 Unbounded Colossus C	.10	.15
GCB04029 Everchanging Gear Peacock C	.10	.15
GCB04030 Steam Maiden Limer C	.10	.15
GCB04031 Prompturret Dragon C	.10	.15
GCB04032 Steam Soldier Urzi C	.10	.15
GCB04033 Faceless Knight Starda C	.10	.15
GCB04034 Alithinos Ideadrone C	.10	.15
GCB04035 Steam Hunter Emenbara C	.10	.15
GCB04036 Steam Fighter Agar C	.10	.15
GCB04037 Steam Maiden Muti C	.10	.15
GCB04038 Gear Owl Perching at Nightfall C	.10	.15
GCB04039 Trumpeting Worker C	.10	.15
GCB04040 Progress Second Dragon C	.25	.40
GCB04041 Voltaro Ideadrone C	.10	.15
GCB04042 Meow Meow Worker C	.10	.15
GCB04043 Faceless Maiden Iter C	.10	.15
GCB04044 Steam Maiden Sadum C	.10	.15
GCB04045 Steam Maiden Magala C	.10	.15
GCB04Re01 Chronodragon Nextage R	4.00	6.00
GCB04S09 Chronodragon Nextage SP	15.00	25.00
GCB04S10 Chronojet Dragon SP	6.00	10.00
GCB04S11 Steam Breath Dragon SP	6.00	10.00
GCB04S12 Heart Thump Worker SP	8.00	12.00
GCB04S13 Chrono Dran SP	8.00	12.00
GCB04S14 Chronofang Tiger SP	5.00	8.00

GCB04S15 Chrono Tigar SP 3.00 5.00
GCB04S16 Nightbarking Gear Tabby SP 12.00 20.00

2017 Cardfight Vanguard G Clan Booster Set 5 Prismatic Divas

RELEASED ON JULY 21, 2017
GCB05001 Perfect Performance Ange GR 15.00 25.00
GCB05001 Perfect Performance Ange SP 60.00 100.00
GCB05002 Fantastic Passion? Pacifica GR 1.25 2.00
GCB05002 Fantastic Passion? Pacifica SP 20.00 30.00
GCB05003 Arcadia Star Coral RRR 5.00 8.00
GCB05003 Arcadia Star Coral SP 50.00 75.00
GCB05004 Orient PRISM Kaname RRR 2.50 4.00
GCB05004 Orient PRISM Kaname SP 50.00 75.00
GCB05005 Chouchou Headliner Lapria RRR 5.00 8.00
GCB05005 Chouchou Headliner Lapria SP 50.00 75.00
GCB05006 Song of Gracious Raindear RRR 4.00 6.00
GCB05006 Song of Gracious Raindear SP 125.00 200.00
GCB05007 Duo Everlasting Reit RRR .60 1.00
GCB05007 Duo Everlasting Reit SP 15.00 25.00
GCB05008 Legendary Idol Riviere RRR 10.00 15.00
GCB05008 Legendary Idol Riviere SP 75.00 125.00
GCB05009 Full Bright Wish Shizuku RRR 1.25 2.00
GCB05009 Full Bright Wish Shizuku SP 125.00 200.00
GCB05010 Chouchou Engage Lead Platy RR .40 .60
GCB05010 Chouchou Engage Lead Platy SP 10.00 15.00
GCB05011 Highest Society Citron RR 4.00 6.00
GCB05011 Highest Society Citron SP 30.00 50.00
GCB05012 Wonderful Voice Lauris RR .75 1.25
GCB05012 Wonderful Voice Lauris SP 30.00 50.00
GCB05013 Duo Sprinkle Light Priani RR .20 .30
GCB05014 Chouchou Blanche RR .60 1.00
GCB05014 Chouchou Blanche SP 10.00 15.00
GCB05015 Love Collect Eleanor RR .20 .30
GCB05015 Love Collect Eleanor SP 10.00 15.00
GCB05016 Limpid Chorus Maylene RR .20 .30
GCB05017 Image Master Kukuri RR 1.00 1.50
GCB05018 Chouchou Tino RR 1.00 1.50
GCB05018 Chouchou Tino SP 15.00 25.00
GCB05019 Chouchou Serah RR 2.50 4.00
GCB05019 Chouchou Serah SP 25.00 40.00
GCB05020 Duo Idol Emperal Kuna R .15 .25
GCB05021 Maximum Rapture Lucia R .15 .25
GCB05022 Orient PRISM Karina R .15 .25
GCB05023 Chouchou Muritz R .15 .25
GCB05024 Eager Envy Marronnier R .50 .75
GCB05025 Orient PRISM Ayari R .15 .25
GCB05026 Chouchou Suguri R .15 .25
GCB05027 Tsundere Rival Ruruka R .15 .25
GCB05028 Duo Stream Showtime Paytonia R .15 .25
GCB05029 Friend of the Moon Marina R .15 .25
GCB05030 Talent of Perseverance Shandee R .30 .50
GCB05031 Chouchou Praire R .15 .25
GCB05032 Sweet PRISM Rupina R .15 .25
GCB05033 Ambient Silence Etosha R .15 .25
GCB05034 Duo Happy Diary Sheryl R .15 .25
GCB05035 Friend of the Star Mimosa R .15 .25
GCB05036 Sweet PRISM Tytis R .15 .25
GCB05037 Sweet PRISM Nelum R .15 .25
GCB05038 Traditional Fighter Ku nyan C .10 .15
GCB05039 Chouchou Melviz C .10 .15
GCB05040 Dual Oculus Lumisia C .10 .15
GCB05041 Applause Flower Palche C .10 .15
GCB05042 Hard Stroke Linwell C .10 .15
GCB05043 Happy Ears Melovil C .10 .15
GCB05044 Inactive Pretty Yuyuka C .10 .15
GCB05045 Chouchou Selviz C .10 .15
GCB05046 Impressed Tear Subaru C .10 .15
GCB05047 Chouchou Melare C .10 .15
GCB05048 Slow Tempo Lorbia C .10 .15
GCB05049 Hearty Dancer Courage C .10 .15
GCB05050 Faithful Follower Lauroca C .10 .15
GCB05051 Lunch Maker Aika C .10 .15
GCB05052 Chouchou Malviz C .10 .15
GCB05053 Chouchou Hulala C .10 .15
GCB05054 Mystical Motion La Theta C .10 .15
GCB05055 Negative Addict Villetta C .10 .15
GCB05056 Chouchou Putilna C .10 .15
GCB05057 Togetoge Beat Arty C .10 .15
GCB05058 Punpun Bulge Mahaka C .10 .15
GCB05059 Teacup Fairy Ruhuna C .10 .15
GCB05060 Dancing Designer Lauren C .10 .15
GCB05Re01 Duo Absolute Sister Meer RRR .30 .50
GCB05Re02 Cheerfully Etoile Olyvia RRR .25 .40
GCB05Re03 Dreaming Step Shizuku RRR 1.00 1.50
GCB05S17 Chouchou Debut Stage Tirua SP 6.00 10.00
GCB05S18 Friend of the Moon Marina SP 15.00 25.00
GCB05S19 Friend of the Star Mimosa SP 10.00 15.00
GCB05S20 Twinkle Happiness? Pacifica SP 10.00 15.00
GCB05S21 Top Idol Pacifica SP 25.00 40.00
GCB05S22 Eternal Idol Pacifica SP 20.00 30.00
GCB05S23 Planet Idol Pacifica SP 20.00 30.00
GCB05S24 Frontier Star Coral SP 25.00 40.00
GCB05S25 Shangri La Star Coral SP 15.00 25.00
GCB05S26 Aurora Star Coral SP 25.00 40.00
GCB05S27 Shiny Star Coral SP 40.00 60.00
GCB05S28 Fresh Star Coral SP 60.00 100.00
GCB05S29 Angelic Star Coral SP 25.00 40.00
GCB05S30 Happy Ears Melovil SP 10.00 15.00
GCB05S31 Velvet Voice Raindear SP 8.00 12.00
GCB05S32 Peaceful Voice Raindear SP 20.00 30.00
GCB05S33 Inspect Sisters Robel SP 40.00 60.00
GCB05S34 Dash Sisters Rabel SP 30.00 50.00
GCB05S35 Colorful Smiling Fratte SP 15.00 25.00
GCB05S36 Limpid Chorus Maylene SP 10.00 15.00
GCB05S37 Hearty Dancer Courage SP 10.00 15.00
GCB05S38 Top Idol Riviere SP .15
GCB05S39 Super Idol Riviere SP 30.00 50.00
GCB05S40 Mermaid Idol Riviere SP 30.00 50.00
GCB05S41 Bermuda Triangle Cadet Riviere SP 20.00 30.00
GCB05S42 Eager Envy Marronnier SP 30.00 50.00
GCB05S43 Impressed Tear Subaru SP 20.00 30.00
GCB05S44 Celebrate Voice Lauris SP 10.00 15.00
GCB05S45 Miracle Voice Lauris SP 10.00 15.00
GCB05S46 Talent of Perseverance Shandee SP 25.00 40.00
GCB05S47 Cherished Phrase Reina SP 10.00 15.00
GCB05S48 Duo Idol Emperal Kuna SP 4.00 6.00
GCB05S49 Duo Sprinkle Light Priani SP 4.00 6.00
GCB05S50 Duo Temptation Reit SP 15.00 25.00
GCB05S51 Duo Fantasia Lamry SP 4.00 6.00
GCB05S52 PRISM Duo Loretta SP 12.00 20.00
GCB05S53 PRISM Duo Aria SP 10.00 15.00

2017 Cardfight Vanguard G Clan Booster Set 6 Rondeau of Chaos and Salvation

RELEASED ON DECEMBER 1, 2017
GCB06001 Genesis Dragon, Harmonics Neo Messiah GR 8.00 12.00
GCB06001 Genesis Dragon, Harmonics Neo Messiah SGR 10.00 15.00
GCB06002 Death Star-vader, Chaos Breaker Deluge GR 20.00 30.00
GCB06002 Death Star-vader, Chaos Breaker Deluge SGR 25.00 40.00
GCB06003 Genesis Dragon, Basaltis Messiah RRR 12.00 20.00
GCB06003 Genesis Dragon, Basaltis Messiah SP 30.00 50.00
GCB06004 Death Star-vader, "Omega Fall" Glendios RRR .60 1.00
GCB06004 Death Star-vader, "Omega Fall" Glendios SP 15.00 25.00
GCB06005 Death Star-vader, Glueball Dragon RRR 8.00 12.00
GCB06005 Death Star-vader, Glueball Dragon SP 25.00 40.00
GCB06006 Deliberate Deletor, Aodaien RRR 5.00 8.00
GCB06006 Deliberate Deletor, Aodaien SP 25.00 40.00
GCB06007 Star-vader, Chaos Breaker Crisis RRR 12.00 20.00
GCB06007 Star-vader, Chaos Breaker Crisis SP 50.00 75.00
GCB06008 Darkjet Deletor, Greiend RRR 2.00 3.00
GCB06008 Darkjet Deletor, Greiend SP 10.00 15.00
GCB06009 Lady Fencer of Matter Transmission RR 3.00 5.00
GCB06010 Star-vader, Colony Maker RR .30 .50
GCB06011 Star-vader, Strange Dragon RR .50 .75
GCB06012 Globule Dober RR .20 .30
GCB06013 Star-vader, Metonaxe Dragon RR .60 1.00
GCB06014 Prayer Child of Steady State Cosmo RR .60 1.00
GCB06014 Prayer Child of Steady State Cosmo SP 10.00 15.00
GCB06015 Iron Wall Star-vader, Thorium RR 2.00 3.00
GCB06015 Iron Wall Star-vader, Thorium SP 12.00 20.00
GCB06016 Remove Deletor, Igalga RR .40 .60
GCB06017 Nebula Dragon, Cyclic Dragon R .15 .25
GCB06018 Genesis Machine Deity, Desthergen R .15 .25
GCB06019 Blaming Deletor, Ibiores R .15 .25
GCB06020 Confront Deletor, Jagwokk R .20 .30
GCB06021 Star-vader, Boseritter R .15 .25
GCB06022 Star-vader, Crusgabel R .15 .25
GCB06023 Star-vader, Globuladia R .15 .25
GCB06024 Black Bullet of Iron Star, Photosphere R .15 .25
GCB06025 Forbid Deletor, Zakuelad R .20 .30
GCB06026 Star-vader, Spiral Arm R .25 .40
GCB06027 Star-vader, Penrose Gate R .40 .60
GCB06028 Dark Metal Chameleon R .15 .25
GCB06029 Hire Deletor, Farwon R .15 .25
GCB06030 Lady Gunner of the Neutron Star C .10 .15
GCB06031 One who Bisects the Interstellar Gap C .10 .15
GCB06032 Rapid Gunner of Degeneration C .10 .15
GCB06033 Star-vader, Red Sprite Dragon C .10 .15
GCB06034 Gravitate Turtle C .10 .15
GCB06035 Abolition Star-vader, Neodymium C .10 .15
GCB06036 Cosmosphere Cat C .10 .15
GCB06037 Star-vader, Elgibs C .10 .15
GCB06038 Flutter Deletor, Zuiije C .10 .15
GCB06039 Star-vader, Planck Dracokid C .10 .15
GCB06040 Star-vader, Magnetor Hedgehog C .10 .15
GCB06041 Star-vader, Roche Wave C .10 .15
GCB06042 Star-vader, Ether Looper C .10 .15
GCB06043 Star-vader, Paradigm Shift Dragon C .10 .15
GCB06044 Star-vader, Quark Shoebill C .10 .15
GCB06045 Rendering Deletor, Efames C .10 .15
GCB06Re01 Death Star-vader, Chaos Universe RRR 3.00 5.00
GCB06Re02 Star-vader, Chaos Breaker Dragon RRR 12.00 20.00
GCB06Re03 Flowers in Vacuum, Cosmo Wreath RRR 2.00 3.00
GCB06Re04 Blink Messiah RRR 2.00 3.00

2018 Cardfight Vanguard G Clan Booster Set 7 Divas' Festa

RELEASED ON APRIL 27, 2018
GCB07001 Zeroth Dragon of Distant Sea, Megiddo ZR 60.00 100.00
GCB07002 Chouchou Popular Favor, Tirua GR 15.00 25.00
GCB07002 Chouchou Popular Favor, Tirua SP 100.00 150.00
GCB07003 School Student Council President, Alk RRR 1.00 1.50
GCB07003 School Student Council President, Alk SP 20.00 30.00
GCB07004 Splendid Fortune, Shizuku RRR .30 .50
GCB07004 Splendid Fortune, Shizuku SP 50.00 75.00
GCB07005 Duo Amazing Sister, Meer RRR .30 .50
GCB07005 Duo Amazing Sister, Meer SP 8.00 12.00
GCB07006 Brand-New-PR?ISM, Shining Garnet RRR .40 .60
GCB07006 Brand-New-PR?ISM, Shining Garnet SP 15.00 25.00
GCB07007 Aurora Star, Coral RRR 1.00 1.50
GCB07007 Aurora Star, Coral SP 50.00 75.00
GCB07008 Spirited Star, Trois RRR 5.00 8.00
GCB07008 Spirited Star, Trois SP 75.00 125.00
GCB07009 Delight Genius, Ange RRR 3.00 5.00
GCB07009 Delight Genius, Ange SP 75.00 125.00
GCB07010 Velvet Voice, Raindear RRR .30 .50
GCB07010 Velvet Voice, Raindear SP 30.00 50.00
GCB07011 Chouchou Cradle Lullaby, Milena RR .20 .30
GCB07012 Luxury Wave, Elly RR 2.00 3.00
GCB07012 Luxury Wave, Elly SP 50.00 75.00
GCB07013 Brand-New-PR?ISM, Glister Emeral RR .20 .30
GCB07014 Magical Center, Nina RR .20 .30
GCB07015 Attractive Glow, Sandy RR 1.50 2.50
GCB07015 Attractive Glow, Sandy SP 60.00 100.00
GCB07016 Chouchou, Darina RR .20 .30
GCB07017 Duo Achievement Promise, Colima RR .20 .30
GCB07017 Duo Achievement Promise, Colima RR .20 .30
GCB07018 Transcend Idol, Aqua RR 4.00 6.00
GCB07018 Transcend Idol, Aqua SP 75.00 125.00
GCB07019 Brand-New-PRISM, Flash Sapphire RR .20 .30
GCB07020 Chouchou, Milena RR 1.00 1.50
GCB07021 Chouchou Lively Icon, Ilya R .15 .25
GCB07022 Duo Memorial Days, Sheryl R .15 .25
GCB07023 Chouchou, Ranfa R .15 .25
GCB07024 Gift of Effort, Shandee R .15 .25
GCB07025 Maturity Talent, Salena R .15 .25
GCB07026 Light Blue Heartbeat, Myrtoa R .15 .25
GCB07027 Duo Making Dream, Iori R .15 .25
GCB07028 Abundant Pink, Sedna R .15 .25
GCB07029 Immaculate Symbol, Fria R .15 .25
GCB07030 Chouchou, Irune R .15 .25
GCB07031 Chouchou, Schera R .15 .25
GCB07032 Dinky Echoes, Parra R .15 .25
GCB07033 Little Pride, Honoka R .15 .25
GCB07034 Epochal Model, Shibuki C .10 .15
GCB07035 Chouchou, Verne C .10 .15
GCB07036 Chouchou, Lucille C .10 .15
GCB07037 Interesting Hope, Shiratsuyu C .10 .15
GCB07038 Chouchou, Lirun C .10 .15
GCB07039 Trend Leader, Felucca C .10 .15
GCB07040 Chouchou, Sonia C .10 .15
GCB07041 Novel Dress, Akari C .10 .15
GCB07042 Powerful Song, Lacol C .10 .15
GCB07043 Seedling Voice, Lauris C .10 .15
GCB07044 Chouchou, Amalia C .10 .15
GCB07045 Duo Minimum Truth, Rhone C .10 .15
GCB07046 Restful Music, Lumie C .10 .15
GCB07047 Chouchou, Meret C .10 .15
GCB07048 Chouchou, Roberta C .10 .15
GCB07049 Chouchou, Merluse C .10 .15
GCB07050 Popping Melody, Layla C .10 .15
GCB07Re01 Superb New Student, Shizuku RRR .60 1.00

2018 Cardfight Vanguard V Mini Booster Set 1 Psyqualia Strife

RELEASED ON NOVEMBER 9, 2018
VMB01001 Exculpate the Blaster VR 15.00 25.00
VMB01001 Exculpate the Blaster SVR 50.00 75.00
VMB01002 Transcendence Dragon, Dragonic Nouvelle Vague VR 3.00 5.00
VMB01002 Transcendence Dragon, Dragonic Nouvelle Vague SVR 15.00 25.00
VMB01003 Sage of Salvation, Benon RRR .30 .50
VMB01004 Sage of Guidance, Zenon RRR .30 .50
VMB01005 Nouvellecritic Dragon RRR 1.00 1.50
VMB01006 Nouvelleroman Dragon RRR .75 1.25
VMB01007 Alfred Early RR .15 .25
VMB01008 Blaster Blade RR .30 .50
VMB01009 Knight Squire, Allen RR .20 .30
VMB01010 Dragonic Overlord RR .20 .30
VMB01011 Dragon Knight, Nehalem RR .25 .40
VMB01012 Embodiment of Armor, Bahr RR .15 .25
VMB01013 Aggregate Knight?, Firno R .15 .25
VMB01014 Knight of Devotion, Bergius R .15 .25
VMB01015 Sage of the Arts, Jauron R .15 .25
VMB01016 Wingal R .15 .25
VMB01017 Strong Knight, Rounoria R .15 .25
VMB01018 Wyvern Strike, Agaruda R .15 .25
VMB01019 Dragon Armored Knight R .15 .25
VMB01020 Bellicosity Dragon R .15 .25
VMB01021 Dragon Monk, Gojo R .15 .25
VMB01022 Guard Griffin R .15 .25
VMB01023 Knight of Silence, Gallatin C .10 .15
VMB01024 Miru Biru C .10 .15
VMB01025 Glyme C .10 .15
VMB01026 Bringer of Good Luck, Epona C .10 .15
VMB01027 Flogal C .10 .15
VMB01028 Margal C .10 .15
VMB01029 Yggdrasil Maiden, Elaine C .10 .15
VMB01030 Embodiment of Shield, Lahm C .10 .15
VMB01031 Dominance Dragon C .10 .15
VMB01032 Lizard Runner, Undeux C .10 .15
VMB01033 Embodiment of Spear, Tahr C .10 .15
VMB01034 Demonic Dragon Mage, Rakshasa C .10 .15
VMB01035 Red Gem Carbuncle C .10 .15
VMB01036 Dragon Monk, Genjo C .10 .15

2015 Cardfight Vanguard G Technical Booster Set 1 The Reckless Rampage

RELEASED ON FEBRUARY 19, 2016
GTCB01001 Rikudo Stealth Dragon, Tsukumorakan GR 2.00 3.00
GTCB01002 Destruction Tyrant, Twintempest GR 1.50 2.50
GTCB01003 Great Villain, Dirty Picaro GR 5.00 8.00
GTCB01004 Rikudo Stealth Rogue, Atagolord RRR 6.00 10.00
GTCB01005 Stealth Dragon, Shiranui RRR 1.00 1.50
GTCB01006 Absolute Ruler, Gluttony Dogma RRR 8.00 12.00
GTCB01007 Emperor Dragon, Gaia Emperor RRR 3.00 5.00
GTCB01008 Shootdown King, Miracle Ace RRR 2.00 3.00
GTCB01009 Exceptional Expertise, Rising Nova RRR 3.00 5.00
GTCB01010 Stealth Dragon, Nibikatabira RR 1.00 1.50
GTCB01011 Stealth Rogue of Night Fog, Miyabi RR 1.25 2.00
GTCB01012 Stealth Rogue of Veils, Kurenai RR 1.25 2.00
GTCB01013 Stealth Dragon, Noroi RR 2.50 4.00
GTCB01014 Ancient Dragon, Spinocommando RR 1.25 2.00
GTCB01015 Blade Dragon, Jigsawsaurus RR 1.25 2.00
GTCB01016 Savage Guardian RR 2.50 4.00
GTCB01017 Cannon Fire Dragon, Parasalauncher RR 2.00 3.00
GTCB01018 Axe Diver RR 1.25 2.00
GTCB01019 Wink-killer Misery RR 2.00 3.00
GTCB01020 Kiss-mark, Alma RR 1.00 1.50
GTCB01021 Liar Lips RR .30 .50
GTCB01022 Rikudo Stealth Dragon, Zaramerakan R .15 .25
GTCB01023 Shura Stealth Dragon, Hokagecongo R .15 .25
GTCB01024 Stealth Dragon, Kegareshinmyo R .15 .25
GTCB01025 Shura Stealth Dragon, Murasamecongo R .15 .25
GTCB01026 Stealth Beast, Katarigitsune R .75 1.25
GTCB01027 Stealth Beast, Aramatatabi R .60 1.00
GTCB01028 Stealth Rogue of the Wintry Wind, Kamojigusa R .15 .25
GTCB01029 Destructive Equipment, Hammer Gewalt R .15 .25
GTCB01030 Rage Dragon, Tyrannobrute R .15 .25
GTCB01031 Beam Dragon, Apatomaser R .15 .25
GTCB01032 Tank Mammoth R 1.50 2.50
GTCB01033 Prism Bird R .15 .25
GTCB01034 Barrier Dragon, Styracolord R 2.50 4.00
GTCB01035 Baby Camara R .15 .25
GTCB01036 Great Villainess, Dhampir Lily R .40 .60
GTCB01037 Dudley Jessica R .60 1.00
GTCB01038 Hive Maker R .30 .50
GTCB01039 Acrobat Verdi R 2.50 4.00
GTCB01040 Frog Raider R 1.50 2.50
GTCB01041 Untouchable, Milly R .30 .50
GTCB01042 Mecha Analyzer R .15 .25
GTCB01043 Stealth Beast, Hagurejishi C .10 .15
GTCB01044 Stealth Beast, Kibamaru C .10 .15
GTCB01045 Stealth Dragon, Hashiribi C .10 .15
GTCB01046 Stealth Beast, Kurosakazuki C .10 .15
GTCB01047 Stealth Dragon, Chigiregumo C .40 .60
GTCB01048 Stealth Rogue of the Mirrored Moon, Tsubakuro C .10 .15
GTCB01049 Stealth Beast, Karasudoji C .10 .15
GTCB01050 Killing Method Stealth Rogue, Samidare C .10 .15
GTCB01051 Stealth Fiend, Warashibehime C .10 .15
GTCB01052 Living Method Stealth Rogue, Shigure C .10 .15
GTCB01053 Stealth Dragon, Onibidoushi C .50 .75
GTCB01054 Accel Tiger C .10 .15
GTCB01055 Ancient Dragon, Hypnohang C .10 .15
GTCB01056 Assault Dragon, Assault Rex C .10 .15
GTCB01057 Explosive Dragon, Sarcoblaze C 2.00 3.00
GTCB01058 Ancient Dragon, Nodtank C .10 .15
GTCB01059 Cold Dragon, Freezernyx C .60 1.00
GTCB01060 Savage Heroine C .10 .15
GTCB01061 Ancient Dragon, Babybird C .10 .15

GTCB01062 Savage Healer C .10 .15
GTCB01063 Sheer Magnum C .50 .75
GTCB01064 Cannon Fire Dragon, Sledge Ankylo C .10 .15
GTCB01065 Bulldozer Dobe C .10 .15
GTCB01066 Heave Wheeze C .10 .15
GTCB01067 Cobalt Impulse C .10 .15
GTCB01068 Genie, Lamp Receiver C .10 .15
GTCB01069 Cheer Girl, Elza C .10 .15
GTCB01070 Moodmaker Nyanrook C .10 .15
GTCB01071 Commander, Garry Gannon C .10 .15
GTCB01072 Psychic Mel C .10 .15
GTCB01073 Mecha Advisor C .10 .15
GTCB01074 Magical Manager C .10 .15
GTCB01075 Devil Watch C .10 .15
GTCB01S01 Rikudo Stealth Rogue, Atagolord SP
GTCB01S02 Stealth Dragon, Shiranui SP
GTCB01S03 Absolute King, Gluttony Dogma SP 60.00 100.00
GTCB01S04 Emperor Dragon, Gaiaemperor SP 15.00 25.00
GTCB01S05 Shootdown King, Miracle Ace SP 15.00 25.00
GTCB01S06 Exceptional Expertise, Rising Nova SP 20.00 30.00
GTCB01S07 Stealth Rogue of Night Fog, Miyabi SP 15.00 25.00
GTCB01S08 Stealth Rogue of Veils, Kurenai SP 20.00 30.00
GTCB01S09 Ancient Dragon, Spinocommando SP 10.00 15.00
GTCB01S10 Savage Guardian SP 30.00 50.00
GTCB01S11 Wink-killer Misery SP 8.00 12.00
GTCB01S12 Kiss-mark, Alma SP 12.00 20.00

2016 Cardfight Vanguard G Technical Booster 2 The Genius Strategy

RELEASED ON AUGUST 26, 2016
GTCB02001 Ambush Demon Stealth Dragon Shibarakku Buster GR 5.00 8.00
GTCB02001 Ambush Demon Stealth Dragon Shibarakku Buster SGR 10.00 15.00
GTCB02002 Lawless Mutant Deity Obtirandus GR 15.00 25.00
GTCB02002 Lawless Mutant Deity Obtirandus SGR 25.00 40.00
GTCB02003 Omniscience Dragon Afanc GR 4.00 6.00
GTCB02003 Omniscience Dragon Afanc SGR 8.00 12.00
GTCB02004 Ambush Demon Stealth Rogue Yasuie Tenma RRR 3.00 5.00
GTCB02004 Ambush Demon Stealth Rogue Yasuie Tenma SP 20.00 30.00
GTCB02005 Covert Demonic Dragon Aragoto Spark RRR .60 1.00
GTCB02005 Covert Demonic Dragon Aragoto Spark SP 6.00 10.00
GTCB02006 Merciless Mutant Deity Darkface RRR 5.00 8.00
GTCB02006 Merciless Mutant Deity Darkface SP 15.00 25.00
GTCB02007 Skyslicing Rending General Superior Mantis RRR .60 1.00
GTCB02007 Skyslicing Rending General Superior Mantis SP 1.25 2.00
GTCB02008 Sagesaint Professor Bigbelly RRR 6.00 10.00
GTCB02008 Sagesaint Professor Bigbelly SP 12.00 20.00
GTCB02009 Special Appointment Professor Arusha RRR .50 .75
GTCB02009 Special Appointment Professor Arusha SP 4.00 6.00
GTCB02010 Ambush Demon Stealth Rogue Shishiyuzuki RR 1.00 1.50
GTCB02010 Ambush Demon Stealth Rogue Shishiyuzuki SP 20.00 30.00
GTCB02011 Dueling Dragon King ZANGEKI RR .30 .50
GTCB02012 Stealth Rogue of the Silk Umbrella Shizune RR 1.50 2.50
GTCB02012 Stealth Rogue of the Silk Umbrella Shizune SP 8.00 12.00
GTCB02013 Stealth Rogue of the Fiendish Blade Masamura RR .75 1.25
GTCB02014 Mutant Deity Fortification Grysfort RR .60 1.00
GTCB02014 Mutant Deity Fortification Grysfort SP 10.00 15.00
GTCB02015 Machining Stag Beetle RR .30 .50
GTCB02016 Hexagon Mutant Honeycomb Queen RR .30 .50
GTCB02016 Hexagon Mutant Honeycomb Queen SP 3.00 5.00
GTCB02017 Scissorshot Mutant Bombscissor RR .60 1.00
GTCB02018 Head of the Bastion Ardillo RR .75 1.25
GTCB02018 Head of the Bastion Ardillo SP 20.00 30.00
GTCB02019 Hammsukes Rival Fountain Pen Hammkichi RR .30 .50
GTCB02020 Triruler Cat RR .30 .50
GTCB02020 Triruler Cat SP 6.00 10.00
GTCB02021 Application Researcher Ponbelly RR .30 .50
GTCB02022 Ambush Demon Stealth Rogue Kiyohime R .15 .25
GTCB02023 Swordhunter Stealth Rogue Oniwaka R .15 .25
GTCB02024 Stealth Beast Slicer Wolf R .15 .25
GTCB02025 Stealth Dragon Yashabayashi R .60 1.00
GTCB02026 Stealth Beast Trickarts R .15 .25
GTCB02027 Stealth Dragon Onibayashi R .60 1.00
GTCB02028 Stealth Demon of Crow Feathers Fugen R .15 .25
GTCB02029 Dazzling Mutant Deity Waspytail R .15 .25
GTCB02030 Arank Mutant Sangiraffa R .15 .25
GTCB02031 Despot Mutant Arie Antoinette R .15 .25
GTCB02032 Punish Stag R .50 .75
GTCB02033 Machining Dive Beetle R .15 .25
GTCB02034 Vulcan Lafertei R .15 .25
GTCB02035 Childhood Command Rosenberg R .15 .25
GTCB02036 Lifelong Honorary Professor Silvest R .15 .25
GTCB02037 Stapler Penguin R .15 .25
GTCB02038 Hammsukes Rival Oilbased Pen Hammjiro R .15 .25
GTCB02039 Problem Child Greybelly R .30 .50
GTCB02040 Coiling Duckbill R .40 .60
GTCB02041 Scholarship Student Alibelly R .25 .40
GTCB02042 Scintillating Firstyear Student Littlebelly R .15 .25
GTCB02043 Inkdyed Stealth Rogue Minetsuki C .10 .15
GTCB02044 Stealth Beast Stab Fang C .10 .15
GTCB02045 Stealth Dragon Dual Weapon C 1.25 2.00
GTCB02046 Stealth Fiend Awakohime C .10 .15
GTCB02047 Stealth Beast Dron Shifter C .10 .15
GTCB02048 Stealth Fiend Lake Diver C .10 .15
GTCB02049 Stealth Dragon Mangy Shooter C .10 .15
GTCB02050 Stealth Beast Foxfire C .10 .15
GTCB02051 Stealth Rogue Hinoekomachi C .10 .15
GTCB02052 Stealth Beast Cat Devil C .10 .15
GTCB02053 Stealth Beast Drench Serpent C .10 .15
GTCB02054 Arank Mutant Gragiraffa C .10 .15
GTCB02055 Cyclic Sickle Mutant Aristscythe C .10 .15
GTCB02056 Hypnotic Mutant Hypnomoth C .10 .15
GTCB02057 Scarlet Venom C .10 .15
GTCB02058 Machining Cricket C .10 .15
GTCB02059 Megacolony Battler E C .10 .15
GTCB02060 Bullet Mutant Pillbugler C .10 .15
GTCB02061 Machining Butterfly C .10 .15
GTCB02062 Machining Honeybee C .10 .15
GTCB02063 Ingot Chafer C .10 .15
GTCB02064 Makeup Widow C .10 .15
GTCB02065 Ink Panda C .10 .15
GTCB02066 Archaeology Junior Cornegie C .10 .15
GTCB02067 Field Glass Otter C .10 .15
GTCB02068 Anchor Rabbit C .10 .15
GTCB02069 Hammsukes Classmate Mechanical Pencil Hammy C .10 .15
GTCB02070 Hammsukes Rival Crayon Hammzo C .10 .15
GTCB02071 Chalk Eraser Fennec C .10 .15
GTCB02072 Draft Unicorn C .10 .15
GTCB02073 Draw of the School Cafeteria Abysia C .10 .15
GTCB02074 Castanet Donkey C .10 .15
GTCB02075 Watering Elephant C .10 .15

2017 Cardfight Vanguard G Title Booster Set 2 Touken Ranbu Online

RELEASED ON FEBRUARY 3, 2017
GTB02001 Juzumaru Tsunetsugu GR 10.00 15.00
GTB02001 Juzumaru Tsunetsugu SP 20.00 30.00
GTB02002 Mikazuki Munechika Toku GR 5.00 8.00
GTB02003 Ishikirimaru Toku RRR 2.00 3.00
GTB02004 Ichigo Hitofuri Toku RRR 1.00 1.50
GTB02005 Tsurumaru Kuninaga Toku RRR 4.00 6.00
GTB02005 Tsurumaru Kuninaga Toku SP 30.00 50.00
GTB02006 Nihongou RRR 2.50 4.00
GTB02007 Uguisumaru Toku RRR 2.00 3.00
GTB02008 Hotarumaru Toku RRR 1.50 2.50
GTB02008 Hotarumaru Toku SP 12.00 20.00
GTB02009 Kousetsu Samonji Toku RR 1.00 1.50
GTB02010 Iwatooshi Toku RR .20 .30
GTB02011 Shokudaikiri Mitsutada Toku RR .20 .30
GTB02012 Jiroutachi Toku RR .20 .30
GTB02013 Taroutachi Toku RR .60 1.00
GTB02014 Izuminokami Kanesada Toku RR 2.00 3.00
GTB02015 Hizamaru RR .50 .75
GTB02016 Horikawa Kunihiro Toku RR .75 1.25
GTB02016 Horikawa Kunihiro Toku SP 15.00 25.00
GTB02017 Monoyoshi Sadamune RR .60 1.00
GTB02018 Tonbokiri Toku R .15 .25
GTB02019 Shishiou Toku R .15 .25
GTB02020 Ookurikara Toku R .15 .25
GTB02021 Doudanuki Masakuni Toku R .15 .25
GTB02022 Nakigitsune Toku R .15 .25
GTB02023 Kashuu Kiyomitsu Toku R .15 .25
GTB02024 Kasen Kanesada Toku R .15 .25
GTB02025 Mutsunokami Yoshiyuki Toku R .15 .25
GTB02025 Mutsunokami Yoshiyuki Toku SP 12.00 20.00
GTB02026 Yamanbagiri Kunihiro Toku R .15 .25
GTB02027 Urashima Kotetsu R .15 .25
GTB02028 Gokotai Toku R .15 .25
GTB02029 Hachisuka Kotetsu Toku R .15 .25
GTB02030 Yamabushi Kunihiro Toku C .10 .15
GTB02031 Otegine Toku C .10 .15
GTB02032 Heshikiri Hasebe Toku C .10 .15
GTB02033 Yamatonokami Yasusada Toku C .10 .15
GTB02034 Souza Samonji Toku C .10 .15
GTB02035 Namazuo Toushirou Toku C .10 .15
GTB02036 Nikkari Aoe Toku C .10 .15
GTB02037 Honebami Toushirou Toku C .10 .15
GTB02038 Akita Toushirou Toku C .10 .15
GTB02039 Sayo Samonji Toku C .10 .15
GTB02040 Midare Toushirou Toku C .10 .15
GTB02041 Yagen Toushirou Toku C .10 .15
GTB02042 Hirano Toushirou Toku C .10 .15
GTB02043 Maeda Toushirou Toku C .10 .15
GTB02044 Atsushi Toushirou Toku C .10 .15
GTB02045 Imanotsurugi Toku C .10 .15
GTB02046 Aizen Kunitoshi Toku C .10 .15

2014 Cardfight Vanguard Fighters Collection 2014

COMPLETE SET (37) 60.00 120.00
RELEASED ON NOVEMBER 7, 2014
FC02001 Splitting Seeker, Brutus RRR .60 1.00
FC02002 Brawler, Shotgun Blow Dragon RRR 1.00 1.50
FC02003 Ultimate Dimensional Robo, Great Daikaiser RRR 5.00 8.00
FC02004 Sprout Jewel Knight, Camille RRR .20 .30
FC02005 Floral Magus RRR .20 .30
FC02006 Halberd Revenger, Peredur RRR .20 .30
FC02007 Twin Blade Liberator, Margaux RRR .20 .30
FC02008 Spiral Celestial, Hellm RRR .20 .30
FC02009 Goddess of Four Seasons, Persephone RRR .20 .30
FC02010 Hellfire Seal Dragon, Weathercloth RRR .30 .50
FC02011 Ancient Dragon, Volcatops RRR .20 .30
FC02012 Shura Stealth Dragon, Yozakuracongo RRR .20 .30
FC02013 Covert Demonic Dragon, Kasumi Rouge RRR .20 .30
FC02014 Eradicator, Twin Thunder Dragon RRR .20 .30
FC02015 Merkur Blaukluger RRR .30 .50
FC02016 Super Dimensional Robo, Shadowkaiser RRR .20 .30
FC02017 Super Dimensional Robo, Daiyard RRR .20 .30
FC02018 Edicting Star-vader, Halcium RRR .20 .30
FC02019 Echo of Nemesis RRR .20 .30
FC02020 Demonic Lord, Dudley Lucifer RRR .20 .30
FC02021 Bunny Queen Beast Tamer RRR .20 .30
FC02022 Drift Ice Swordsman, Nightsnow RRR .20 .30
FC02023 Duo Delicious Girl, Chao RRR .20 .30
FC02024 Blue Storm Marine General, Demetrius RRR .20 .30
FC02025 Machining Warsickle RRR .30 .50
FC02026 Sage's Egg, Minette RRR .20 .30
FC02027 Holly Musketeer, Elvira RRR .40 .60
FC02028 Combined Strength Seeker, Locrinus RRR .20 .30
FC02029 Military Brawler, Lisei RRR .20 .30
FC02S01 Majesty Lord Blaster SP 10.00 15.00
FC02S02 Goddess of the Full Moon, Tsukuyomi SP 10.00 15.00
FC02S03 Phantom Blaster Overlord SP 5.00 8.00
FC02S04 Dragonic Overlord the End SP 4.00 6.00
FC02S05 Eradicator, Vowing Sword Dragon SP 1.25 2.00
FC02S06 Perfect Raizer SP 2.00 3.00
FC02S07 Top Idol, Pacifica SP 4.00 6.00

2015 Cardfight Vanguard Fighters Collection 2015

COMPLETE SET (50) 60.00 100.00
RELEASED ON JUNE 19, 2015
GFC01001 Holy Dragon, Religious Soul Saver GR 5.00 8.00
GFC01002 Moon Deity Who Governs Night, Tsukuyomi GR 3.00 5.00
GFC01003 Absolution Lion King, Mithril Ezel GR 5.00 8.00
GFC01004 Supreme Heavenly Emperor Dragon, Dragonic Overlord the Ace GR 12.00 20.00
GFC01005 True Brawler, Big Bang Knuckle Turbo GR 8.00 12.00
GFC01006 Death Star-vader, Omega Loop Glendios GR 4.00 6.00
GFC01007 Blue Storm Marshal Dragon, Admiral Maelstrom GR 4.00 6.00
GFC01008 Interdimensional Dragon, Epoch-maker Dragon GR 1.75 3.00
GFC01009 Holy Celestial, Mikhael RRR 1.75 3.00
GFC01010 True Revenger, Dragruler Revenant RRR 1.75 3.00
GFC01011 Sacred Flame Ultimate Regalia, Demeter RRR 2.50 4.00
GFC01012 Rikudo Stealth Dragon, Jorurirakan RRR 1.75 3.00
GFC01013 Super Ancient Dragon, Pearly Titan RRR 3.00 5.00
GFC01014 Cosmetic Snowfall, Shirayuki RRR .60 1.00
GFC01015 War Deity, Asura Kaiser RRR .75 1.25
GFC01016 Hyper Metalborg, Heavyduke RRR 1.75 3.00
GFC01017 Great Warrior, Dudley Geronimo RRR .60 1.00
GFC01018 Amon's Talon, Marchocias RRR 1.25 2.00
GFC01019 Silver Thorn Dragon Master, Mystique Luquier RRR 5.00 8.00
GFC01020 Ice Prison Hades Deity, Cocytus Negative RRR 1.25 2.00
GFC01021 Legendary PR?ISM-Duo, Nectaria RRR 5.00 8.00
GFC01022 Carapace Mutant Deity, Machining Destroyer RRR 6.00 10.00
GFC01023 School Special Investigator, Leo-pald Chaser RRR .30 .50
GFC01024 White Lily Musketeer Captain, Cecilia RRR .60 1.00
GFC01025 Holy Dragon, Sanctuary Guard Regalie RR .60 1.00
GFC01026 Raincloud-calling Nine-headed Dragon King RR .50 .75
GFC01027 Holy Seraph, Uriel RR 1.25 2.00
GFC01028 Dark Knight, Efnysien RR .75 1.25
GFC01029 Golden Dragon, Scourge Point Dragon RR 2.50 4.00
GFC01030 Great Angel, Doom Brace RR 1.75 3.00
GFC01031 Divine Dragon Knight, Zahm RR .30 .50
GFC01032 Rikudo Stealth Dragon, Gedatsurakan RR .30 .50
GFC01033 Destruction Tyrant, Archraider RR .30 .50
GFC01034 Ambush Demon Stealth Rogue, Kagamijishi RR 1.75 3.00
GFC01035 Avatar of Heroic Spirits, Vishnu RR .30 .50
GFC01036 Meteokaiser, Tribrut RR .40 .60
GFC01037 Dark Superhuman, Pretty Cat RR .30 .50
GFC01038 Nebula Dragon, Maximum Seal Dragon RR 1.25 2.00
GFC01039 Godly-speed, Flash Bruce RR .30 .50
GFC01040 Great Demon, Soulless Demagogue RR .60 1.00
GFC01041 Miracle of Luna Square, Clifford RR .40 .60
GFC01042 Interdimensional Beast, Upheaval Pegasus RR 1.50 2.50
GFC01043 Pirate King of the Abyss, Blueheart RR .60 1.00
GFC01044 Legend of the Glass Shoe, Amoris RR 1.50 2.50
GFC01045 Marine General of Heavenly Silk, Sokrates RR .40 .60
GFC01046 Deforestation Mutant Deity, Jaggydevil RR .30 .50
GFC01047 Omniscience Dragon, Wisdom Teller Dragon RR .30 .50
GFC01048 Sacred Tree Dragon, Multivitamin Dragon RR .30 .50
GFC01049 Rain Element, Madew RR 3.00 5.00
GFC01050 Light Elemental, Peaker RR .30 .50

2015 Cardfight Vanguard Fighters Collection 2015 Winter

RELEASED ON JANUARY 8, 2016
GFC02001 Climax Jewel Knight Lord, Evangeline GR 1.50 2.50
GFC02002 Bluish Flame True Liberator, Holy Flame GR 2.00 3.00
GFC02003 Helldeity Seal Dragon, Crossorigin GR 1.00 1.50
GFC02004 Conquering Supreme Dragon, Dragonic Kaiser Warning GR 3.00 5.00
GFC02005 Ultimate Beast Deity, Ethics Buster Catastrophe GR 4.00 6.00
GFC02006 Legendary Dimensional Robo, Daikaiser Leon GR 3.00 5.00
GFC02007 Interdimensional Dragon, Chronoscommand Revolution GR 3.00 5.00
GFC02008 Twinkle Happiness?, Pacifica GR 1.25 2.00
GFC02009 Floral Witch Master, MiMi RRR 1.00 1.50
GFC02010 Holy Seraph, Nociel RRR .60 1.00
GFC02011 Witch Queen of Transfiguration, Sinclair RRR .75 1.25
GFC02012 Witch Queen of Holy Water, Clove RRR .20 .30
GFC02013 Steel Blade Shura Stealth Dragon, Hayakujirakan RRR .60 1.00
GFC02014 Destruction Tyrant, Hellrex Maxima RRR 1.00 1.50
GFC02015 Ambush Demon Stealth Dragon, Hyakki Vogue Nayuta RRR .20 .30
GFC02016 Death Star-vader, Quintessence Dragon RRR .60 1.00
GFC02017 Divine Hand, Good End Dragger RRR 5.00 8.00
GFC02018 Wings of Annihilation, Blade Wing Tibold RRR 4.00 6.00
GFC02019 Nightmare Doll of the Abyss, Beatrix RRR 5.00 8.00
GFC02020 Loved by the Seven Seas, Nightmist RRR .50 .75
GFC02021 Blue Flight Marshal Dragon, Mithril-core Dragon RRR .20 .30
GFC02022 Evil Armor Mutant Deity, Goliath RRR .30 .50
GFC02023 Omniscience Dragon, Cath Palug RRR .30 .50
GFC02024 Protector Lotus Maiden of Yggdrasil RRR .20 .30
GFC02025 Calling Jewel Knight, Christine RR .15 .25
GFC02026 Rose Red Witch, CooCoo RR .15 .25
GFC02027 Love Sniper, Nociel RR .15 .25
GFC02028 Witch of Intelligence, Dehtail RR .15 .25
GFC02029 Sword Principle Liberator, Magnus RR .15 .25
GFC02030 Witch of Quill Pens, Oneon RR .15 .25
GFC02031 Hellfire Seal Dragon Knight RR .15 .25
GFC02032 Stealth Rogue of Night Fog, Agitomaru RR .15 .25
GFC02033 Destruction Dragon, Squallrex RR .40 .60
GFC02034 Stealth Dragon Oboro Keeper RR .15 .25
GFC02035 Crownholder Dragon RR .30 .50
GFC02036 Beast Deity, Dragotwist RR .15 .25
GFC02037 Dimensional Robo, Daibazooka RR .15 .25
GFC02038 Clearout Star-vader, Buromin RR .15 .25
GFC02039 Death Flag Dragger RR .15 .25
GFC02040 Blade Wing Sullivan RR 2.00 3.00
GFC02041 Nightmare Doll Master, Brenda RR .75 1.25
GFC02042 Reform-calling Gear Eagle RR .15 .25
GFC02043 Seven Seas Sage, Plegeton RR .15 .25
GFC02044 Friend of the Sun, Marlkka RR .15 .25
GFC02045 Amphibian Dragon RR .15 .25
GFC02046 Elite Mutant, Tryghul RR .15 .25
GFC02047 Honorary Assistant, Mikesaburo RR .60 1.00
GFC02048 Maiden of Waterpot RR .15 .25

2016 Cardfight Vanguard Fighters Collection 2016

RELEASED ON MAY 20, 2016
GFC03001 Divine Knight of Rainbow Brocade Clotenus GR 1.00 1.50
GFC03002 Lord of Guidance Wakahirume GR 6.00 10.00
GFC03003 Meteokaiser Bustered GR 4.00 6.00
GFC03004 Genesis Dragon Transelse Messiah GR 4.00 6.00
GFC03005 Dreamiy Axel Milward GR 4.00 6.00
GFC03006 Interdimensional Dragon Warp Drive Dragon GR 2.50 4.00
GFC03007 Demon Sea Queen Maread GR 1.50 2.50
GFC03008 Flower Princess of Perpetual Summer Verano GR 2.50 4.00
GFC03009 Holy Seraph Zachariel RRR .60 1.00
GFC03010 Dark Dragon Distress Dragon RRR 1.00 1.50
GFC03011 Golden Knight of Incandescence Ebraucus RRR .75 1.25
GFC03012 BeastSlayer Military Deity Tyr RRR 1.25 2.00
GFC03013 Flame Emperor Dragon King Irresist Dragon RRR .60 1.00
GFC03014 Rikudo Stealth Dragon Gounrakan RRR .50 .75
GFC03015 Destruction Tyrant Gradogigant RRR .30 .50
GFC03016 Ambush Demon Stealth Dragon Onibibu Radar RRR .40 .60
GFC03017 Conquering Supreme Dragon Voltechzapper Dragon RRR .75 1.25
GFC03018 Super Cosmic Hero Xphoenix RRR .40 .60
GFC03019 Super Heavy Chariot Tiger Centurion RRR .30 .50
GFC03020 Rebellious Retainer of Fresh Blood Frederick RRR .60 1.00
GFC03021 Lucky Rise Elprina RRR 1.25 2.00
GFC03022 Marine General of Heavenly Silk Christos RRR .60 1.00
GFC03023 Wildfire Mutant Deity Staggle Dipper RRR .40 .60
GFC03024 Omniscience Dragon Hrimthurs RRR .75 1.25
GFC03025 Holy Dragon Laserguard Dragon RR .50 .75
GFC03026 Sunriseonhigh Godhawk Ichibyoshi RR .20 .30
GFC03027 Holy Seraph Oriphiel RR .20 .30
GFC03028 Dark Knight Ludvik RR .20 .30
GFC03029 Sacred Heaven Prayer Master Reia RR .75 1.25
GFC03030 Goddess of Seven Colors Iris RR 2.50 4.00
GFC03031 Flame Emperor Dragon King Asyl Orb Dragon RR .20 .30
GFC03032 Jinx Stealth Hermit Abudataishi RR .20 .30
GFC03033 Ironarmored Chancellor Dymorphalanx RR .20 .30
GFC03034 Ambush Demon Stealth Fiend Hougen Wing RR .25 .40
GFC03035 Lightning King Spirit Emperor Vritra RR .20 .30
GFC03036 Righteous Superhuman Blue Prison RR .20 .30
GFC03037 Enigman Patriot RR .30 .50

GFC03038 Death Starvader Demon Maxwell RR .60 1.00
GFC03039 Excellent Cheer Leader Aery RR .20 .30
GFC03040 False Dark Wings Agrat bat Mahlat RR .75 1.25
GFC03041 Chainsaw Megatrick Furnival RR .75 1.25
GFC03042 Retroactive Time Maiden Uluru RR .40 .60
GFC03043 Eclipse Dragonhulk Deep Corpse Dragon RR .60 1.00
GFC03044 Sailors Medley Nasha RR .20 .30
GFC03045 Guard Leader of Sky and Water Flotia RR .20 .30
GFC03046 Dream Mutant Deity Scarabgas RR .30 .50
GFC03047 Immortality Professor Kundalini RR .20 .30
GFC03048 Sacred Tree Dragon Rain Breath Dragon RR 1.00 1.50
GFC03049 Air Element Sebreeze RR 1.00 1.50
GFC03050 Metal Element Scryew RR .30 .50
GFC03051 Dark Element Dizmel RR .20 .30

2017 Cardfight Vanguard Fighters Collection 2017

RELEASED ON JUNE 9, 2017
GFC04001 Divine Knight of Condensed Light Olbius Avalon GR 3.00 5.00
GFC04002 Chief Deity of the Heavens Amaterasu GR 5.00 8.00
GFC04003 Black Seraph Vellator Terminal GR 2.50 4.00
GFC04004 Dark Knight Irgahn Vert GR 1.25 2.00
GFC04005 Golden Knight of Links Celtis Winner GR 1.00 1.50
GFC04006 Goddess of Settlement Pallas Athena GR 5.00 8.00
GFC04007 Supreme Heavenly Emperor Dragon Blazing Burst Dragon GR 3.00 5.00
GFC04008 Rikudo Stealth Dragon Rokushikirakan GR 4.00 6.00
GFC04009 Destruction Tyrant Volcaine Tyranno GR .50 .75
GFC04010 Ambush Demon Stealth Dragon Mandala Ryu Ou GR .50 .75
GFC04011 Conquering Supreme Dragon Closer Dragon GR 3.00 5.00
GFC04012 Fang Dragon King Fist Driger GR 5.00 8.00
GFC04013 Dimensional Robo Overall Command Ultimate Daiking GR 8.00 12.00
GFC04014 Genesis Machine Deity Altwilder GR .60 1.00
GFC04015 Rampage Evil Rogue Hellhard Eight GR 6.00 10.00
GFC04016 Coffin of Absolute Zero Rutland Vitrei GR 1.25 2.00
GFC04017 Scream Dragon Master Dolor Kimberly GR 2.00 3.00
GFC04018 Interdimensional Dragon Beyond Order Dragon GR .75 1.25
GFC04019 Unfading Ship Immortal Galleon GR 10.00 15.00
GFC04020 Festal Finale Final Priscila GR 10.00 15.00
GFC04021 Blue Vortex Marshal Dragon Last Twister Dragon GR .30 .50
GFC04022 Seal Assassin Mutant Deity Tyrantis GR 5.00 8.00
GFC04023 Immortality Professor Sahasrara Veera GR .75 1.25
GFC04024 Flower Princess of Sincerity Lindrose Premier GR 4.00 6.00
GFC04025 Holy Beast Divine Maskgal RRR 4.00 6.00
GFC04026 Singularity Protector Lozenge Magus Apex RRR 4.00 6.00
GFC04027 Black Seraph Eleleth RRR 1.25 2.00
GFC04028 Witch Queen of Iniquity Jeliddo RRR 2.50 4.00
GFC04029 Healing True Liberator Ellise RRR 4.00 6.00
GFC04030 Witch Queen of Big Achievement Laurier RRR 2.50 4.00
GFC04031 Supreme Heavenly Emperor Dragon Advance Guard Dragon RRR 1.25 2.00
GFC04032 Jinx Stealth Fiend Zashikihime RRR 5.00 8.00
GFC04033 Barrage Gigantic Cannon Boorish Primer RRR .75 1.25
GFC04034 Ambush Demon Stealth Rogue Shirahagino RRR 2.50 4.00
GFC04035 Sky Guardian Supreme Dragon Impede Dragon RRR 4.00 6.00
GFC04036 Meteokaiser Gandread RRR 5.00 8.00
GFC04037 Oceanic Transformation Atlantis Dolphin RRR 2.00 3.00
GFC04038 Demise Lit by Darkness Lacus Carina RRR 3.00 5.00
GFC04039 Obstruction King Terrible Linus RRR 2.50 4.00
GFC04040 Medicine of Discontinuation Vincent RRR 3.00 5.00
GFC04041 Kinesis Megatrick Coulthard RRR 2.00 3.00
GFC04042 Far Away Time Maiden Uluru RRR 2.50 4.00
GFC04043 Diabolist of Invitation Negronola RRR 4.00 6.00
GFC04044 Best Sparkle Sandy RRR 3.00 5.00
GFC04045 Guard Leader of Sky and Water Ioanes RRR 1.50 2.50
GFC04046 Seven Stars Mutant Deity Relish Lady RRR 2.50 4.00
GFC04047 Boxed Daughter Spangled RRR 1.25 2.00
GFC04048 Flower Princess of Cherries Coschellina RRR 1.25 2.00
GFC04049 Maskgal RR .25 .40
GFC04050 Lozenge Magus Fine RR .15 .25
GFC04051 Black Medic Eleleth RR .15 .25
GFC04052 Witch of Heresy Jeliddo RR .15 .25
GFC04053 Elixir Liberator RR .15 .25
GFC04054 Witch of Big Bowls Laurier RR .15 .25
GFC04055 Positive Dracokid RR .15 .25
GFC04056 Lucky Smile Zashikihime RR .15 .25
GFC04057 Artillery Dragon Flintankylo RR .15 .25
GFC04058 Stealth Rogue of Secret Affair Hagino RR .15 .25
GFC04059 Meditate Dracokid RR .25 .40
GFC04060 Extreme Battler Ganseal RR .15 .25
GFC04061 Saving Dolphin RR .40 .60
GFC04062 Demise Lit by Light Carina RR .15 .25
GFC04063 Reserver Linus RR .15 .25
GFC04064 Specialist Vincent RR .15 .25
GFC04065 Psycho Magician Coulthard RR .15 .25
GFC04066 Time carving Maiden Uluru RR .15 .25
GFC04067 Bernard the Ghostie RR .15 .25
GFC04068 Happy Rune Sandy RR .15 .25
GFC04069 Officer Cadet Ioanes RR .15 .25
GFC04070 Gastronomic Battler Relish Girl RR .40 .60
GFC04071 Refugee Spangled RR .15 .25
GFC04072 Cherry and Blossom RR .15 .25
GFC04073 Snow Element Valancher RR .15 .25
GFC04074 Heat Element Melandru RR .75 1.25
GFC04075 Air Element Luctorm RR 2.00 3.00

2015 Cardfight Vanguard G Legend Deck 1 The Dark Ren Suzugamori

RELEASED ON JUNE 19, 2015
GLD01001 Dark Dragon, Phantom Blaster Diablo .75 1.25
GLD01002 Dark Great Mage, Badhabh Caar .15 .25
GLD01003 Blaster Dark Diablo .30 .50
GLD01004 Bloodstained Battle Knight, Dorint .15 .25
GLD01005 Dark Night Maiden, Macha .40 .60
GLD01006 Unorthodox Shield, Mac Lir .15 .25
GLD01007 Dark Heart Trumpeter .60 1.00
GLD01008 Pitch Black Sage, Charon .20 .30
GLD01009 Arduous Battle Knight, Claudas .20 .30
GLD01010 Little Skull Witch, Nemain .60 1.00
GLD01011 Fullbau Brave 8.00 12.00
GLD01012 Revenger, Undead Angel .15 .25
GLD01013 Leaping Knight, Ligan Lumna .15 .25
GLD01014 Flatbau .15 .25
GLD01015 Howl Owl .20 .30

2016 Cardfight Vanguard G Legend Deck 2 The Overlord Blaze Toshiki Kai

RELEASED ON APRIL 29, 2016
GLD02001 Transcendence Divine Dragon Nouvelle Vague LExpress C .10 .15
GLD02001 Transcendence Divine Dragon Nouvelle Vague LExpress RRR .15 .25
GLD02002 Supreme Heavenly Emperor Dragon Vortex Desire C .30 .50
GLD02002 Supreme Heavenly Emperor Dragon Vortex Desire RRR .40 .60
GLD02003 Amber Dragon Midnight C .10 .15
GLD02003 Amber Dragon Midnight RRR .60 1.00
GLD02004 Dragonic Overlord The Legend C .10 .15
GLD02004 Dragonic Overlord The Legend RRR .40 .60
GLD02004 Dragonic Overlord The Legend SP 4.00 6.00
GLD02005 Armor of the Flame Dragon Bahr C .10 .15
GLD02005 Armor of the Flame Dragon Bahr RRR .15 .25
GLD02006 Emperor Dragon Knight Nehalem C .10 .15
GLD02006 Emperor Dragon Knight Nehalem RRR .60 1.00
GLD02007 Berserk Lord Dragon C .10 .15
GLD02007 Berserk Lord Dragon RRR .15 .25
GLD02008 Spear of the Flame Dragon Tahr C .10 .15
GLD02008 Spear of the Flame Dragon Tahr RRR .15 .25
GLD02009 Dragon Partner Monica C .10 .15
GLD02009 Dragon Partner Monica RRR .15 .25
GLD02010 Lizard General Conroe RRR 2.00 3.00
GLD02010 Lizard General Conroe C .60 1.00
GLD02011 Flame of Tranquility Aermo C .10 .15
GLD02011 Flame of Tranquility Aermo RRR .15 .25
GLD02012 Lizard Hero Undeux RRR .15 .25
GLD02013 Seiten Master Goku C .10 .15
GLD02013 Seiten Master Goku RRR .15 .25
GLD02014 Tenpou Master Hakkai C .10 .15
GLD02014 Tenpou Master Hakkai RRR .15 .25
GLD02015 Kenren Master Gojo C .10 .15
GLD02015 Kenren Master Gojo RRR .15 .25
GLD02016 Sanzou Master Genjo C .10 .15
GLD02016 Sanzou Master Genjo RRR .15 .25

2018 Cardfight Vanguard V Start Deck 1 Free Experience Deck Royal Paladin

RELEASED ON MAY 29, 2018
VSD01001 Stardrive Dragon .50 .75
VSD01002 Aggregate Knight?, Firno .50 .75
VSD01003 Knight of Silence, Gallatin .10 .15
VSD01004 Knight of Devotion, Bergius .10 .15
VSD01005 Sage of the Arts, Jauron .20 .30
VSD01006 Knight Squire, Allen .10 .15
VSD01007 Strong Knight, Rounoria .10 .15
VSD01008 Radical Knight, Anil .15 .25
VSD01009 Wingal .50 .75
VSD01010 Glyme .50 .75
VSD01011 Bringer of Good Luck, Epona .25 .40
VSD01012 Flogal .25 .40
VSD01013 Margal .25 .40
VSD01014 Yggdrasil Maiden, Elaine .15 .25

2018 Cardfight Vanguard V Start Deck 2 Free Experience Deck Kagero

RELEASED IN JUNE 2018
VSD02001 Crested Dragon .75 1.25
VSD02002 Wyvern Strike, Agaruda .10 .15
VSD02003 Embodiment of Shield, Lahm .60 1.00
VSD02004 Dragon Armored Knight 2.00 3.00
VSD02005 Dragon Knight, Nehalem .10 .15
VSD02006 Embodiment of Armor, Bahr .50 .75
VSD02007 Guard Griffin .50 .75
VSD02008 Dragon Knight, Burj .60 1.50
VSD02009 Dragon Monk, Gojo .60 1.50
VSD02010 Lizard Runner, Undeux .60 1.00
VSD02011 Embodiment of Spear, Tahr .40 .60
VSD02012 Demonic Dragon Mage, Rakshasa .50 .75
VSD02013 Red Gem Carbuncle .40 .60
VSD02014 Dragon Monk, Genjo .50 .75

2011 Cardfight Vanguard Trial Deck 1 Blaster Blade

RELEASED ON DECEMBER 3, 2011
TD01001 Crimson Butterfly, Brigitte .12 .20
TD01002 Knight of Conviction, Bors .10 .15
TD01003 Solitary Knight, Gancelot .25 .40
TD01004 Knight of Silence, Gallatin .10 .15
TD01005 Blaster Blade .60 1.00
TD01006 Knight of the Harp, Tristan .10 .15
TD01007 Covenant Knight, Randolf .10 .15
TD01008 Little Sage, Marron .10 .15
TD01009 Wingal .15 .25
TD01010 Starlight Unicorn .10 .15
TD01011 Knight of Rose, Morgana .10 .15
TD01012 Stardust Trumpeter .12 .20
TD01013 Bringer of Good Luck, Epona .15 .25
TD01014 Yggdrasil Maiden, Elaine .20 .30
TD01015 Weapons Dealer, Govannon .10 .15
TD01016 Flogal .15 .25

2011 Cardfight Vanguard Trial Deck 2 Dragonic Overlord

RELEASED ON DECEMBER 3, 2011
TD02001 Dragonic Overlord HOLO 1.25 2.00
TD02001 Dragonic Overlord .75 1.25
TD02002 Dragon Monk, Goku .12 .20
TD02003 Demonic Dragon Berserker, Yaksha .10 .15
TD02004 Dragon Knight, Nehalem .15 .25
TD02005 Berserk Dragon HOLO .50 .75
TD02005 Berserk Dragon .10 .15
TD02006 Wyvern Strike, Tejas .20 .30
TD02007 Embodiment of Armor, Bahr .10 .15
TD02008 Dragon Monk, Gojo .30 .50
TD02009 Flame of Hope, Aermo .10 .15
TD02010 Demonic Dragon Madonna, Joka .10 .15
TD02011 Wyvern Strike, Jarran .20 .30
TD02012 Lizard Runner, Undeux .10 .15
TD02013 Dragon Dancer, Monica .10 .15
TD02014 Lizard Soldier, Ganlu .10 .15
TD02015 Dragon Monk, Genjo .10 .15
TD02016 Demonic Dragon Mage, Rakshasa .40 .60

2013 Cardfight Vanguard Trial Deck 4 Maiden Princess of the Cherry Blossoms

RELEASED ON JANUARY 25, 2013
TD04001 Oracle Guardian, Apollon .10 .15
TD04002 Goddess of Flower Divination, Sakuya .25 .40
TD04003 Meteor Break Wizard HOLO .20 .30
TD04003 Meteor Break Wizard .10 .15
TD04004 Oracle Guardian, Wiseman .10 .15
TD04005 Security Guardian .10 .15
TD04006 Sword Dancer Angel .10 .15
TD04007 Oracle Guardian, Gemini .10 .15
TD04008 Dark Cat .12 .20
TD04009 Weather Girl, Milk .10 .15
TD04010 Battle Sister, Maple .15 .25
TD04011 Luck Bird .10 .15
TD04012 Oracle Guardian, Nike .15 .25
TD04013 Dream Eater .10 .15
TD04014 Victory Maker .10 .15
TD04015 Lozenge Magus HOLO 1.50 2.50
TD04015 Lozenge Magus .10 .15

2013 Cardfight Vanguard Trial Deck 3 Golden Mechanical Soldier

RELEASED ON JANUARY 25, 2013
TD03001 Gold Rutile .60 1.00
TD03002 Death Metal Droid HOLO .75 1.25
TD03002 Death Metal Droid .10 .15
TD03003 Mr. Invincible .40 .60
TD03004 King of Sword .20 .30
TD03005 Super Electromagnetic Lifeform, Storm .60 1.00
TD03006 NGM Prototype .10 .15
TD03007 Tough Boy .10 .15
TD03008 Oasis Girl .10 .15
TD03009 Screamin' and Dancin' Announcer, Shout .10 .15
TD03010 Queen of Heart .10 .15
TD03011 Battering Minotaur .15 .25
TD03012 Shining Lady .10 .15
TD03013 Cannon Ball .10 .15
TD03014 Ring Girl, Clara .10 .15
TD03015 Battleraizer HOLO .75 1.25
TD03015 Battleraizer .30 .50

2012 Cardfight Vanguard Trial Deck 5 Slash of the Silver Wolf

RELEASED ON MAY 19, 2012
TD05001 Great Silver Wolf, Garmore .50 .75
TD05002 Sleygal Double Edge .20 .50
TD05003 Battlefield Storm, Sagramore .10 .15
TD05004 Knight of Superior Skills, Beaumains .10 .15
TD05005 Sleygal Sword .10 .15
TD05006 Sacred Guardian Beast, Nemean Lion .10 .15
TD05007 Charging Chariot Knight .10 .15
TD05008 Knight of Elegant Skills, Gareth .10 .15
TD05009 Evil Slaying Swordsman, Haugan .10 .15
TD05010 Precipice Whirlwind, Sagramore .10 .15
TD05011 Charjgal .10 .15
TD05012 Blessing Owl .10 .15
TD05013 Silver Fang Witch .10 .15
TD05014 Grassland Breeze, Sagramore .10 .15
TD05015 Silent Punisher .10 .15
TD05016 Weapons Dealer, Gwydion .10 .15
TD05017 Fortune Bell .10 .15
TD05018 Elixir Sommelier .10 .15

2012 Cardfight Vanguard Trial Deck 6 Resonance of Thunder Dragon

RELEASED ON MAY 19, 2012
TD06001 Thunder Break Dragon .10 .15
TD06002 Djinn of the Lightning Flash .10 .15
TD06003 Plasmabite Dragon .15 .25
TD06004 Thunderstorm Dragoon .10 .15
TD06005 Shieldblade Dragoon .10 .15
TD06006 Djinn of the Lightning Flare .10 .15
TD06007 Brightjet Dragon .10 .15
TD06008 Red River Dragoon .10 .15
TD06009 Lizard Soldier, Riki .10 .15
TD06010 Thunder of Hope, Helena .10 .15
TD06011 Djinn of the Lightning Spark .20 .30
TD06012 Dragon Dancer, Rai Rai .10 .15
TD06013 Wyvern Supply Unit .12 .20
TD06014 Lizard Soldier, Sishin .10 .15
TD06015 Yellow Gem Carbuncle .12 .20
TD06016 Old Dragon Mage .10 .15
TD06017 Zephyr Kid, Hayate .10 .15
TD06018 Demonic Dragon Nymph, Seiobo .15 .25

2013 Cardfight Vanguard Trial Deck 7 Descendants of the Marine Emperor

RELEASED ON APRIL 19, 2013
TD07001 Navalgazer Dragon .10 .15
TD07002 Marine General of the Full Tides, Xenophon .10 .15
TD07003 Key Anchor, Dabid .10 .15
TD07004 Tear Knight, Lazarus .10 .15
TD07005 Marine General of the Restless Tides, Algos .60 1.00
TD07006 Coral Assault .40 .60
TD07007 Titan of the Infinite Trench .10 .15
TD07008 Tear Knight, Theo .10 .15
TD07009 Tear Knight, Cyprus .40 .60
TD07010 Accelerated Command .10 .15
TD07011 Splash Assault .10 .15
TD07012 Battle Siren, Cynthia .10 .15
TD07013 Battle Siren, Dorothea HOLO .75 1.25
TD07013 Battle Siren, Dorothea .25 .40
TD07014 Officer Cadet of the First Battle .10 .15
TD07015 Battleship Intelligence .10 .15
TD07016 Pyroxene Communications Sea Otter Soldier .10 .15
TD07017 Dolphin Soldier of High Speed Raids .10 .15
TD07018 Medical Officer of the Rainbow Elixir .20 .30

2013 Cardfight Vanguard Trial Deck 8 Liberator of the Sanctuary

RELEASED ON
TD08001 Solitary Liberator, Gancelot 2.00 3.00
TD08002 Dignified Gold Dragon .10 .15
TD08003 Onslaught Liberator, Maelzion .10 .15
TD08004 Liberator of Silence, Gallatin .10 .15
TD08005 Liberator of Royalty, Phallon .30 .50
TD08006 Blaster Blade Liberator 2.50 4.00
TD08007 Zoom Down Eagle .10 .15
TD08008 Zoigal Liberator .10 .15
TD08009 Knight of Elegant Skills, Gareth .10 .15
TD08010 Little Liberator, Marron .10 .15
TD08011 Pomerugal Liberator .10 .15
TD08012 Future Liberator, Llew .15 .25
TD08013 Angelic Liberator .30 .50
TD08014 Strike Liberator .20 .30
TD08015 Armed Liberator, Gwydion .15 .25
TD08016 Fortune Liberator .30 .50
TD08017 Elixir Liberator .10 .15

2013 Cardfight Vanguard Trial Deck 9 Eradicator of the Empire

RELEASED ON OCTOBER 4, 2013
TD09001 Eradicator, Vowing Sword Dragon .10 .15
TD09002 Barrage Eradicator, Zion .10 .15
TD09003 Discharging Dragon HOLO .20 .30

TD09003 Discharging Dragon .15 .25
TD09004 Eradicator, Thunder Boom Dragon .10 .15
TD09005 Eradicator, Spark Rain Dragon 2.00 3.00
TD09006 Assassin Sword Eradicator, Susei .10 .15
TD09007 Dragon Dancer, Veronica .10 .15
TD09008 Lightning Blade Eradicator, Jeem .10 .15
TD09009 Red River Dragoon .10 .15
TD09010 Eradicator, Demolition Dragon .10 .15
TD09011 Dust Storm Eradicator, Toko .10 .15
TD09012 Eradicator of Fire, Kohkaiji .10 .15
TD09013 Stone Bullet Eradicator, Houki .10 .15
TD09014 Eradicator, Yellow Gem Carbuncle .10 .15
TD09015 Eradicator, Dragon Mage .10 .15
TD09016 Zephyr Eradicator, Hayate .10 .15
TD09017 Worm Toxin Eradicator, Seiobo .25 .40

2014 Cardfight Vanguard Trial Deck 10 Purgatory Revenger

RELEASED ON FEBRUARY 7, 2014
TD10001 Illusionary Revenger, Mordred Phantom 1.50 2.50
TD10002 Venomous Breath Dragon .10 .15
TD10003 Labyrinth Revenger, Arawn .10 .15
TD10004 Darkness Revenger, Rugos .10 .15
TD10005 Nullity Revenger, Masquerade 2.00 3.00
TD10006 Blaster Dark Revenger 2.00 3.00
TD10007 Koilbau Revenger .10 .15
TD10008 Revenger Fortress, Fatalita .10 .15
TD10009 Black Sage, Charon .10 .15
TD10010 Sacrilege Revenger, Baal-berith .10 .15
TD10011 Transient Revenger, Masquerade .20 .30
TD10012 Branbau Revenger .10 .15
TD10013 Crisis Revenger, Fritz .10 .15
TD10014 Grim Revenger .15 .25
TD10015 Freezing Revenger .10 .15
TD10016 Awaking Revenger .10 .15
TD10017 Healing Revenger .40 .60

2014 Cardfight Vanguard Trial Deck 11 Star-Vader Invasion

RELEASED ON FEBRUARY 7, 2014
TD11001 Star-vader, Infinite Zero Dragon 1.25 2.00
TD11002 Raid Star-vader, Francium .10 .15
TD11003 Twilight Baron .10 .15
TD11004 Soaring Star-vader, Krypton .10 .15
TD11005 Star-vader, Mobius Breath Dragon 1.25 2.00
TD11006 Unrivaled Star-vader, Radon 1.50 2.50
TD11007 Star-vader, Pulsar Bear .10 .15
TD11008 Swift Star-vader, Strontium .10 .15
TD11009 Hollow Twin Blades, Binary Star .10 .15
TD11010 Pursuit Star-vader, Fermium .10 .15
TD11011 Demonic Bullet Star-vader, Neon .10 .15
TD11012 Star-vader, Aurora Eagle .10 .15
TD11013 Nova Star-vader, Actinium .10 .15
TD11014 Star-vader, Meteor Liger .20 .30
TD11015 Star-vader, Nebula Captor .20 .30
TD11016 Keyboard Star-vader, Bismuth .10 .15
TD11017 Star-vader, Stellar Garage .10 .15

2014 Cardfight Vanguard Trial Deck 12 Dimensional Brave Kaiser

RELEASED ON MARCH 14, 2014
TD12001 Super Dimensional Robo, Daikaiser 5.00 12.00
TD12002 Super Dimensional Robo, Daiyusha 1.50 4.00
TD12003 Electro-star Combination, Cosmogreat .30 .75
TD12004 Dimensional Robo, Daifighter .30 .75
TD12005 Dimensional Robo, Daidragon 1.50 4.00
TD12006 Dimensional Robo, Kaizard 3.00 8.00
TD12007 Super Dimensional Robo, Dailady .30 .75
TD12008 Dimensional Robo, Daidriller .30 .75
TD12009 Karenroid, Daisy .30 .75
TD12010 Dimensional Robo, Daitiger .30 .75
TD12011 Dimensional Robo, Daimariner .30 .75
TD12012 Dimensional Robo, Daibrave 1.25 3.00
TD12013 Dimensional Robo, Goyusha .30 .75
TD12014 Dimensional Robo, Daibattles .30 .75
TD12015 Dimensional Robo, Daicrane .30 .75
TD12016 Dimensional Robo, Goflight .30 .75
TD12017 Dimensional Robo, Gorescue .30 .75

2014 Cardfight Vanguard Trial Deck 14 Seeker of Hope

RELEASED ON NOVEMBER 21, 2014
TD14001 Seeker, Sacred Wingal .50 .75
TD14002 Secret Sword Seeker, Vortigern .12 .20
TD14003 Blue Flame Seeker, Taranis .10 .15
TD14004 Natural Talent Seeker, Valrod .10 .15
TD14005 Blaster Blade Seeker 2.50 4.00
TD14006 Full Bloom Seeker, Cerdic .75 1.25
TD14007 Provocation Seeker, Blumenthal .10 .15
TD14008 Vladgal Seeker .10 .15
TD14009 Seeker, Youthful Mage .10 .15
TD14010 Good Faith Seeker, Cynric .25 .40
TD14011 Seeker of the Right Path, Gangalen .10 .15
TD14012 Seeker, Rune Eagle .10 .15
TD14013 Heroic Spirit Seeker, Mark .25 .40
TD14014 Certain Kill Seeker, Modron .25 .40
TD14015 Messegal Seeker .10 .15
TD14016 Warning Seeker, Maris .10 .15
TD14017 Seeker, Loving Healer .20 .30

2014 Cardfight Vanguard Trial Deck 13 Successor of the Sacred Regalia

RELEASED ON JUNE 27, 2014
TD13001 Regalia of Wisdom, Angelica 1.25 2.00
TD13002 Battle Maiden, Mizuha .10 .15
TD13003 Witch of Wolves, Saffron .10 .15
TD13004 Battle Maiden, Izunahime .10 .15
TD13005 Battle Maiden, Sahohime .10 .15
TD13006 Goddess of Trees, Jupiter .10 .15
TD13007 Battle Maiden, Shitateruhime .10 .15
TD13008 Battle Maiden, Mihikarihime .10 .15
TD13009 Battle Maiden, Tatsutahime .10 .15
TD13010 Existence Angel .15 .25
TD13011 Witch of Cats, Cumin .10 .15
TD13012 Apple Witch, Cider .10 .15
TD13013 Reflector Angel .10 .15
TD13014 Lemon Witch, Limonccino .10 .15
TD13015 Bandit Danny .10 .15
TD13016 Patrol Guardian .10 .15
TD13017 Witch of Big Pots, Laurier .10 .15

2014 Cardfight Vanguard Trial Deck 16 Divine Judgment of the Bluish Flames

RELEASED ON NOVEMBER 21, 2014
TD16001 Bluish Flame Liberator, Percival 1.00 1.50
TD16002 Liberator of Vigor, Kadvan .10 .15
TD16003 Liberator, Blue Flame Dragon .20 .30
TD16004 Unbending Liberator, Keredic .10 .15
TD16005 Liberator of Royalty, Phallon 1.25 2.00
TD16006 Liberator of Oath, Aglovale 5.00 8.00
TD16007 Liberator of Preparation, Caradox .10 .15
TD16008 Huntgal Liberator .12 .20
TD16009 Opposing Liberator, Polyus .10 .15
TD16010 Liberator of Quiet, Cador .10 .15
TD16011 Little Liberator, Marron .10 .15
TD16012 Boardgal Liberator .10 .15
TD16013 Genius Liberator, Woltimer .60 1.00
TD16014 Liberator of Ambition, Asus .20 .30
TD16015 Liberator, Lucky Charmy .10 .15
TD16016 Wise Liberator, Yuron .10 .15
TD16017 Liberator of Holy Tree, Elkia .12 .20

2014 Cardfight Vanguard Trial Deck 17 Will of the Locked Dragon

RELEASED ON NOVEMBER 21, 2014
TD17001 Star-vader, Garnet Star Dragon .30 .50
TD17002 Star-vader, Graviton .10 .15
TD17003 Heavy Bomber Star-vader, Berkelium .10 .15
TD17004 Bombing Star-vader, Magnesium .10 .15
TD17005 Companion Star Star-vader, Photon 1.25 2.00
TD17006 Unrivaled Star-vader, Radon .75 1.25
TD17007 Star-vader, Sinister Eagle .10 .15
TD17008 Star-vader, Stronghold .10 .15
TD17009 Star-vader, Satellite Mirage .10 .15
TD17010 Throwing Star-vader, Thorium .10 .15
TD17011 Mana Shot Star-vader, Neon .10 .15
TD17012 Star-vader, Crumble Mare .10 .15
TD17013 Vacant Space Star-vader, Quantum .10 .15
TD17014 Star-vader, Apollo Nail Dragon .10 .15
TD17015 Vortex Star-vader, Molybdenum .10 .15
TD17016 Star-vader, Gamma Dile .10 .15
TD17017 Star-vader, Pixie Powder .20 .30

2015 Cardfight Vanguard G Trial Deck 1 Awakening of the Interdimensional Dragon

RELEASED ON FEBRUARY 27, 2015
GTD01001 Interdimensional Dragon, Mystery Flare Dragon .30 .50
GTD01002 Chronojet Dragon 2.50 4.00
GTD01003 Smithereen Colossus .15 .25
GTD01004 Steam Knight, Ubaru Tutu .15 .25
GTD01005 Smokegear Dragon .15 .25
GTD01006 Steam Fighter, Amber 1.25 2.00
GTD01007 Twin Maser Dragon .15 .25
GTD01008 Great Carapace, Gear Turtle .15 .25
GTD01009 Masergear Dragon .15 .25
GTD01010 Brasswing Dragon .15 .25
GTD01011 Steam Soldier, Tauge .15 .25
GTD01012 Steam Rider, Burnham .15 .25
GTD01013 Withdrawn Gear Raven 1.25 2.00
GTD01014 Gunnergear Dracokid .15 .25
GTD01015 Steam Battler, Dadasig .15 .25
GTD01016 Steam Knight, Shu Sin .15 .25
GTD01017 Stomach Clock Gear Rabbit .15 .25
GTD01018 Steam Maiden, Uluru .15 .25
GTD01019 Lucky Pot Dracokid .75 1.25

2015 Cardfight Vanguard G Trial Deck 2 Divine Swordsman of the Shiny Star

RELEASED ON FEBRUARY 27, 2015
GTD02001 Vague Sacred Knight, Gablade FOIL RRR .60 1.00
GTD02001 Vague Sacred Knight, Gablade C .15 .25
GTD02002 Knight of Blue Heavens, Altomile FOIL RRR .75 1.25
GTD02002 Knight of Blue Heavens, Altomile FOIL RRR AU
GTD02002 Knight of Blue Heavens, Altomile C .50 .75
GTD02003 Aura Shooter Dragon .15 .25
GTD02004 Great Scholar Sage, Kunron .10 .15
GTD02005 Absolute Sword Knight, Rivarlo .10 .15
GTD02006 Knight of Twin Sword FOIL RRR 1.00 1.50
GTD02006 Knight of Twin Sword C .60 1.00
GTD02007 Knight of Vicissitude, Brede .20 .30
GTD02008 Mithril Guard Lion .10 .15
GTD02009 Knight of Crescent Moon, Phelex .10 .15
GTD02010 Archer of Aerial Tower .10 .15
GTD02011 Knight of Steel Wing .10 .15
GTD02012 Milky Way Unicorn .10 .15
GTD02013 Rainbow Guardian .60 1.00
GTD02014 Shining Knight, Millius .60 1.00
GTD02015 Burning Mane Lion .10 .15
GTD02016 Little Fairy of Assault Captain .10 .15
GTD02017 Knight of Festival .10 .15
GTD02018 Healing Pegasus .10 .15
GTD02019 Margal FOIL RRR 1.00
GTD02019 Margal C .10 .15

2015 Cardfight Vanguard G Trial Deck 3 Flower Maiden of Purity

RELEASED ON FEBRUARY 27, 2015
GTD03001 Flower Princess of Spring, Arborea 1.25 2.00
GTD03002 Ranunculus Flower Maiden, Ahsha 4.00 6.00
GTD03003 Jungle Lord Dragon .15 .25
GTD03004 Full Bloom Dragon .15 .25
GTD03005 Blossoming Maiden, Cela .15 .25
GTD03006 Grace Knight .20 .30
GTD03007 Maiden of Gladiolus 1.00 1.50
GTD03008 Qool Qute Qiwi .15 .25
GTD03009 Budding Maiden, Diane .15 .25
GTD03010 Coral Berry Squire .15 .25
GTD03011 Gardener Elf .15 .25
GTD03012 100 Orange .30 .50
GTD03013 Maiden of Safflower .15 .25
GTD03014 Spring-Heralding Maiden, Ozu .15 .25
GTD03015 Maiden of Dimorphotheca .15 .25
GTD03016 Heave-ho Turnip .15 .25
GTD03017 Lavender Knight .15 .25
GTD03018 Fairy Light Dragon .15 .25
GTD03019 Maiden of Daybreak 1.00 1.50

2015 Cardfight Vanguard G Trial Deck 5 Fateful Star Messiah

RELEASED ON JUNE 19, 2015
GTD05001 Genesis Dragon, Judgement Messiah RRR .60 1.00
GTD05001 Genesis Dragon, Judgement Messiah .30 .50
GTD05002 Alter Ego Messiah .60 1.00
GTD05002 Alter Ego Messiah RRR .30 .50
GTD05002 Alter Ego Messiah RRR HOT STAMP .60 1.00
GTD05003 Astrobreak Dragon .10 .15
GTD05004 Wings of Phenomenon, Wingmatter .10 .15
GTD05005 Awaking Messiah 1.00 1.50
GTD05006 Sunset Edge, Duskblade .15 .25
GTD05006 Sunset Edge, Duskblade RRR .25 .40
GTD05007 Gyre Flower, Dark Chakram .10 .15
GTD05008 Lightspeed Cheetah .10 .15
GTD05009 Asleep Messiah .10 .15
GTD05010 Lockbreaker, Riddle Biter .10 .15
GTD05011 Lady Keeper of Virtual Reality .10 .15
GTD05012 Grab Hand Gorilla .10 .15
GTD05013 Protosun Dracokid .10 .15
GTD05014 Neon Messiah .30 .50
GTD05015 Pulse Monk of the Quaking Foot .10 .15
GTD05016 Sprig Birdy .10 .15
GTD05017 Hollow Gazer of the Imaginary Area .15 .25
GTD05018 Lady Healer of the Torn World .10 .15
GTD05019 Beloved Child of Superstring Theory .10 .15
GTD05019 Beloved Child of Superstring Theory RRR .75 1.25

2016 Cardfight Vanguard G Trial Deck 10 Ritual of Dragon Sorcery

RELEASED ON DECEMBER 9, 2016
GTD10001 Dark Dragon Carnivore Dragon TD .60 1.00
GTD10001 Dark Dragon Carnivore Dragon RRR 1.00 1.50
GTD10002 Crestvicious Dragon TD .10 .15
GTD10003 Dragheart Luard TD 1.25 2.00
GTD10003 Dragheart Luard SP 10.00 15.00
GTD10003 Dragheart Luard RRR 6.00 10.00
GTD10004 Blue Thorn Heavyslash Valdemar TD .10 .15
GTD10005 Demon World Castle Eingang TD .10 .15
GTD10006 Direct Owlner Debihira TD .10 .15
GTD10007 Dragwizard Liafail TD .10 .15
GTD10007 Dragwizard Liafail RRR .40 .60
GTD10008 Bladeproof Knight Youghal TD .10 .15
GTD10009 Dragwizard Knies TD .10 .15
GTD10010 Killermyu TD .10 .15
GTD10011 Puzzled Owlner Clothru TD .10 .15
GTD10012 Demon World Castle Vorbeugen TD .10 .15
GTD10013 Dragprince Rute TD .10 .15
GTD10014 Deadcrash Dragon TD .10 .15
GTD10015 Dragprentice Miach TD .10 .15
GTD10016 Knight of Craving Brian TD .10 .15
GTD10017 Abyss Grail TD .10 .15
GTD10018 Howl Owl TD .20 .30
GTD10018 Howl Owl RRR .60 1.00

2017 Cardfight Vanguard G Trial Deck 11 Divine Knight of Heavenly Decree

RELEASED ON FEBRUARY 17, 2017
GTD11001 Divine Knight of Lore Selfes .30 .50
GTD11001 Divine Knight of Lore Selfes RRR .40 .60
GTD11002 Conspicuous Knight Concianus .10 .15
GTD11003 Blue Sky Knight Altmile .10 .15
GTD11003 Blue Sky Knight Altmile RRR .60 1.00
GTD11003 Blue Sky Knight Altmile SP 1.00 1.50
GTD11004 Devout Falx Dragon .10 .15
GTD11005 Ashgal .10 .15
GTD11006 Flying Swallow Knight Claus .10 .15
GTD11006 Flying Swallow Knight Claus RRR .40 .60
GTD11007 Knight of Honesty Carausius .10 .15
GTD11008 Knight of Resilience Baldus .10 .15
GTD11009 Knight of Respect Diotius .10 .15
GTD11010 Support Sorcerer of Damascus 1.00 1.50
GTD11011 Knight of Tomahawk .10 .15
GTD11012 Walgal .10 .15
GTD11013 Knight of Discipline Alectos 3.00 5.00
GTD11014 Painful Blow Knight Gurgitus .10 .15
GTD11015 Augment Sorcerer of Adamant .10 .15
GTD11016 Blast Knight Gradaucus .10 .15
GTD11017 Knight of Pretty Sword .10 .15
GTD11018 Gliding Eagle .10 .15
GTD11018 Gliding Eagle RRR .50 .75

2017 Cardfight Vanguard G Trial Deck 12 Flower Princess of Abundant Blooming

RELEASED ON FEBRUARY 17, 2017
GTD12001 Flower Princess of Faith Celine .30 .50
GTD12001 Flower Princess of Faith Celine RRR .40 .60
GTD12002 Abundant Flower Maiden Patricia .10 .15
GTD12003 Ranunculus Flower Maiden Ahsha .50 .75
GTD12003 Ranunculus Flower Maiden Ahsha RRR .60 1.00
GTD12003 Ranunculus Flower Maiden Ahsha SP 8.00 12.00
GTD12004 Floraneura Dragon .10 .15
GTD12005 Hiratake Monjirou .10 .15
GTD12006 Osmanthus Maiden Anelma .10 .15
GTD12006 Osmanthus Maiden Anelma RRR .50 .75
GTD12007 Irrigating Maiden Ramona .10 .15
GTD12008 Monstera Knight .10 .15
GTD12009 Ravishing Maiden Penelope .10 .15
GTD12010 Crested Ibis Color Valkyrie Nelly .10 .15
GTD12011 Pis Tateo .10 .15
GTD12012 Maple Leaf Squire .10 .15
GTD12013 Augury Maiden Ida 1.50 2.50
GTD12014 Agave Knight .10 .15
GTD12015 Onemorapple .10 .15
GTD12016 Pleading Maiden Elmire .10 .15
GTD12017 Color Pixy Quitterie .10 .15
GTD12018 Monkeypod Dragon 1.00 1.50
GTD12018 Monkeypod Dragon RRR .60 1.00

2017 Cardfight Vanguard G Trial Deck 13 Evil Eye Sovereign

RELEASED ON JUNE 9, 2017
GTD13001 Enma Stealth Dragon Kingoku Tenbu .10 .15
GTD13001 Enma Stealth Dragon Kingoku Tenbu RRR .30 .50
GTD13002 Secret Message Stealth Hermit Abudataishi .10 .15
GTD13003 Demon Stealth Rogue Genba .10 .15
GTD13004 Demon Stealth Dragon Jaken Myouou .10 .15
GTD13005 Demon Stealth Dragon Shiranui Oboro .10 .15
GTD13005 Demon Stealth Dragon Shiranui Oboro RRR .75 1.25

GTD13005 Demon Stealth Dragon Shiranui Oboro SP 3.00 5.00
GTD13006 Stealth Dragon Shibari Kusari .10 .15
GTD13007 Stealth Dragon Genkai .10 .15
GTD13007 Stealth Dragon Genkai RRR .30 .50
GTD13008 Stealth Rogue of Departed Soul Toranaga .10 .15
GTD13009 Stealth Beast Kabe Itachi .10 .15
GTD13010 Stealth Dragon Gouka .10 .15
GTD13011 Stealth Dragon Seizui .10 .15
GTD13012 Stealth Beast Katarigitsune .30 .50
GTD13013 Isolation Stealth Rogue Matsuba .10 .15
GTD13014 Stealth Dragon Madoi .60 1.00
GTD13015 Stealth Dragon Kokusha .10 .15
GTD13016 Stealth Fiend Kakuregama .10 .15
GTD13017 Voracious Stealth Rogue Kosode .10 .15
GTD13018 Almsgiving Stealth Rogue Jirokichi .10 .15
GTD13018 Almsgiving Stealth Rogue Jirokichi RRR .60 1.00

2017 Cardfight Vanguard G Trial Deck 14 Debut of the Divas

RELEASED ON JULY 21, 2017
GTD14001 Chouchou Lillinel RRR .60 1.00
GTD14001 Chouchou Lillinel C .10 .15
GTD14002 Chouchou Palffy C .10 .15
GTD14003 Chouchou Debut Stage Tirua C .10 .15
GTD14003 Chouchou Debut Stage Tirua RRR 1.25 2.00
GTD14004 Chouchou Pierine C .10 .15
GTD14005 Chouchou Piorina C .10 .15
GTD14006 Chouchou Torua C .10 .15
GTD14007 Chouchou Ayana C .40 .60
GTD14007 Chouchou Ayana RRR .75 1.25
GTD14008 Chouchou Listella C .50 .75
GTD14009 Chouchou Milda C .10 .15
GTD14010 Chouchou Sabrina C .40 .60
GTD14011 Chouchou Clenes C .10 .15
GTD14012 Chouchou Marl C .10 .15
GTD14013 Chouchou Corrin C .10 .15
GTD14014 Chouchou Resaca C .10 .15
GTD14015 Chouchou Sasha C .30 .50
GTD14016 Chouchou Ietta C .10 .15
GTD14017 Chouchou Namig C .10 .15
GTD14018 Chouchou Richell C .20 .30
GTD14019 Chouchou Pitte C .15 .25
GTD14019 Chouchou Pitte RRR 2.00 3.00
GTD14S01 Chouchou Debut Stage Tirua SP 12.00 20.00

2017 Cardfight Vanguard G Trial Deck 15 Messiah Dragon of Rebirth

RELEASED ON DECEMBER 1, 2017
GTD15001 Genesis Dragon, Bearing Messiah C .10 .15
GTD15001 Genesis Dragon, Bearing Messiah RRR .40 .60
GTD15002 Light that Seals the Tear, Lady Healer C .40 .60
GTD15003 Alter Ego Neo Messiah C 2.00 3.00
GTD15003 Alter Ego Neo Messiah RRR 3.00 5.00
GTD15003 Alter Ego Neo Messiah SP 12.00 20.00
GTD15004 Alter Ego Messiah RRR .30 .50
GTD15004 Alter Ego Messiah C .10 .15
GTD15005 Restrain Dragon C .10 .15
GTD15006 Albedo Condor C .10 .15
GTD15007 Arrester Messiah C .10 .15
GTD15008 Metallia Messiah C .10 .15
GTD15009 Great Wall C .10 .15
GTD15010 Destiny Dealer C .10 .15
GTD15011 Dunamis Messiah C .30 .50
GTD15012 Allbirth Pangolin C .10 .15
GTD15013 Multiple Star of Binding, Cluster Mine C .10 .15
GTD15014 Neon Messiah Aurion C .10 .15
GTD15015 Spicule Shark C .10 .15
GTD15016 Long Sword of the Protostar, Protosword C .10 .15
GTD15017 Mourning Child of Reaction C .10 .15
GTD15018 Beloved Child of Superstring Theory C .10 .15

2013 Cardfight Vanguard Mega Trial Deck 1 Rise to Royalty

RELEASED ON NOVEMBER 29, 2013
MT01001EN Sanctuary Guard Dragon 1.25 2.00
MT01002EN Dignified Silver Dragon HOLO .15 .25
MT01002EN Dignified Silver Dragon .12 .20
MT01003EN Knight of Conviction, Bors .10 .15
MT01004EN Knight of Determination, Lamorak .10 .15
MT01005EN Knight of Silence, Gallatin .15 .25
MT01006EN Battle Flag Knight, Constance .10 .15
MT01007EN Pathetic Jewel Knight, Olwen .60 1.00
MT01008EN Knight of Truth, Gordon .15 .25
MT01009EN Little Sage, Marron .30 .50
MT01010EN Regret Jewel Knight, Urien .20 .30
MT01011EN Rendgal .10 .15
MT01012EN Rainbow-calling Bard .10 .15
MT01013EN Starting Legend, Ambrosius .15 .25
MT01014EN Bringer of Good Luck, Epona .20 .30
MT01015EN Weapons Dealer, Govannon .10 .15
MT01016EN Flogal .10 .15
MT01017EN Yggdrasil Maiden, Elaine .12 .20

2018 Cardfight Vanguard V Trial Deck 1 Aichi Sendou

RELEASED ON JUNE 8, 2018
VTD01001 Alfred Early RRR 1.00 1.50
VTD01001 Alfred Early .15 .25
VTD01002 Stardrive Dragon .10 .15
VTD01003 Knight of Silence, Gallatin .10 .15
VTD01004 Blaster Blade RRR 2.50 4.00
VTD01005 Blaster Blade .25 .40
VTD01005 Blaster Blade RRR 1.00 1.50
VTD01006 Sage of the Arts, Jauron .12 .20
VTD01007 Wingal .10 .15
VTD01008 Knight Squire, Allen .10 .15
VTD01008 Knight Squire, Allen RRR .60 1.00
VTD01009 Strong Knight, Rounoria .10 .15
VTD01010 Auspice Falcon .10 .15
VTD01011 Glyme .10 .15
VTD01012 Bringer of Good Luck, Epona .10 .15
VTD01013 Flogal .10 .15
VTD01014 Margal .10 .15
VTD01015 Yggdrasil Maiden, Elaine .10 .15
VTD01S01 Blaster Blade SP 30.00 50.00

2018 Cardfight Vanguard V Trial Deck 2 Toshiki Kai

RELEASED ON JUNE 8, 2018
VTD02001 Dragonic Overlord RRR 2.50 4.00
VTD02002 Dragonic Overlord .25 .40
VTD02002 Dragonic Overlord RRR 1.25 2.00
VTD02003 Crested Dragon .10 .15
VTD02004 Dragon Armored Knight .10 .15
VTD02004 Dragon Armored Knight RRR .60 1.00
VTD02005 Dragon Knight, Nehalem .10 .15
VTD02006 Embodiment of Shield, Lahm .10 .15
VTD02006 Embodiment of Armor, Bahr RRR .75 1.25
VTD02007 Guard Griffin .10 .15
VTD02008 Dragon Monk, Gojo .10 .15
VTD02009 Embodiment of Armor, Bahr .10 .15
VTD02010 Dragon Knight, Burj .10 .15
VTD02011 Lizard Runner, Undeux .10 .15
VTD02012 Embodiment of Spear, Tahr .10 .15
VTD02013 Demonic Dragon Mage, Rakshasa .10 .15
VTD02014 Red Gem Carbuncle .10 .15
VTD02015 Dragon Monk, Genjo .10 .15
VTD02S01 Dragonic Overlord SP 40.00 60.00

2018 Cardfight Vanguard V Trial Deck 3 Leon Soryu

RELEASED ON AUGUST 31, 2018
VTD03001 Navalgazer Dragon .12 .20
VTD03001 Navalgazer Dragon FOIL RRR 1.50 2.50
VTD03002 Marine General of Raging Waves, Gondikas .12 .20
VTD03003 Marine General of the Restless Tides, Algos .50 .75
VTD03003 Marine General of the Restless Tides, Algos FOIL RRR 3.00 5.00
VTD03003 Marine General of the Restless Tides, Algos SP 50.00 75.00
VTD03004 Shotgun Assault .12 .20
VTD03005 Tear Knight, Lazarus .12 .20
VTD03006 Storm Rider, Stelios .12 .20
VTD03007 Tear Knight, Theo .12 .20
VTD03007 Tear Knight, Theo FOIL RRR 1.50 2.50
VTD03008 Battle Siren, Emelda .12 .20
VTD03009 Battle Siren, Dorothea .12 .20
VTD03010 Officer Cadet, Erikk .12 .20
VTD03011 Battleship Intelligence .25 .40
VTD03012 Pyroxene Communications Sea Otter Soldier .12 .20
VTD03013 Dolphin Soldier of High Speed Raids .12 .20
VTD03013 Dolphin Soldier of High Speed Raids FOIL RRR 1.25 2.00
VTD03014 Medical Officer of the Rainbow Elixir .30 .50

2018 Cardfight Vanguard V Trial Deck 4 Ren Suzugamori

RELEASED ON SEPTEMBER 14, 2018
VTD04001 The Dark Dictator FOIL RRR 1.00 1.50
VTD04001 The Dark Dictator .12 .20
VTD04002 Pulverize Knight, Daman .12 .20
VTD04003 Witch of Calamity, Emer .12 .20
VTD04004 Blaster Axe .12 .20
VTD04005 Blaster Dark FOIL RRR 3.00 5.00
VTD04006 Blaster Dark .12 .20
VTD04006 Blaster Dark FOIL RRR 3.00 5.00
VTD04007 Foldbau .12 .20
VTD04008 Blaster Javelin .12 .20
VTD04008 Blaster Javelin FOIL RRR 1.25 2.00
VTD04009 Knight of Resistance, Limwris .12 .20
VTD04010 Witch of Nostrum, Arianrhod .12 .20
VTD04011 Fullbau .12 .20
VTD04012 Darkside Trumpeter .25 .40
VTD04013 Death Feather Eagle .25 .40
VTD04014 Howl Owl .12 .20
VTD04015 Abyss Healer .12 .20
VTD04S01 Blaster Dark SP 30.00 50.00

2019 Cardfight Vanguard V Trial Deck 5 Misaki Tokura

VTD05001 Hexagonal Magus .15 .25
VTD05002 Miko of the Treasured Blade, Shizuki .10 .15
VTD05003 Battle Sister, Orangette .12 .20
VTD05004 Rectangle Magus 1.00 1.50
VTD05005 Miko of Spiritual Light, Kinuka .10 .15
VTD05006 Cuore Magus .10 .15
VTD05007 Ripis Magus .10 .15
VTD05008 Ruote Magus .10 .15
VTD05009 Weal Crane .10 .15
VTD05010 Lozenge Magus .15 .25
VTD05011 Oracle Guardian, Nike .10 .15
VTD05012 Psychic Bird .10 .15
VTD05013 Miracle Kid .10 .15
VTD05014 Sphere Magus .10 .15

2019 Cardfight Vanguard V Trial Deck 6 Naoki Ishida

VTD06001 Great Composure Dragon .15 .25
VTD06002 Duress Clap Dragon .10 .15
VTD06003 Thunderstorm Dragoon .10 .15
VTD06004 Recklessness Dragon .25 .40
VTD06005 Excess Streak Dragon .10 .15
VTD06006 Red River Dragoon .10 .15
VTD06007 Photon Bomber Wyvern .10 .15
VTD06008 Lizard Soldier, Riki .10 .15
VTD06009 Lizard Soldier, Ouho .10 .15
VTD06010 Spark Kid Dragoon .20 .30
VTD06011 Yellow Gem Carbuncle .12 .20
VTD06012 Old Dragon Mage .10 .15
VTD06013 Zephyr Kid, Hayate .12 .20
VTD06014 Worm Toxin Eradicator, Seiobo .25 .40

2019 Cardfight Vanguard V Trial Deck 7 Kouji Ibuki

VTD07001 Docking Deletor, Greion .10 .15
VTD07002 Aromatalber Dragon .10 .15
VTD07003 Swift Deletor, Geali .15 .25
VTD07004 Bloating Deletor, Gio .10 .15
VTD07005 Big Gunner of the Cataclysmic Variable Star .10 .15
VTD07006 Ferment Deletor, Gaen .10 .15
VTD07007 Breaking Deletor, Gatario .10 .15
VTD07008 Wheel of the Galaxy, Cosmo Chaplet .10 .15
VTD07009 Cathode of Collapse, Magnotear .10 .15
VTD07010 Sprout Deletor, Luchi .10 .15
VTD07011 Asteroid Wolf .10 .15
VTD07012 Pulse Monk of the Quaking Foot .10 .15
VTD07013 Beloved Child of Superstring Theory .10 .15
VTD07014 Lady Healer of the Torn World .10 .15

2019 Cardfight Vanguard V Trial Deck 8 Schokolade Melody

VTD08001 Full Full Appeal, Farlull
VTD08002 Graceful Prayer, Amie
VTD08003 Choco Love Heart, Liselotte
VTD08004 Feeling Hide, Rilm
VTD08005 Concealed Bitter, Enes
VTD08006 Anybody Like, Lahti
VTD08007 Special Message, Ourora
VTD08008 Suave Heart, Lilly
VTD08009 Best of Best, Isabella
VTD08010 Pure Gifter, Aliche
VTD08011 Direct Sign, Pursh
VTD08012 Lover Hope, Rina
VTD08013 Joyful A la Carte, Irma
VTD08014 Handmade Lover, Elena
VTD08PR01 Sonata
VTD08PR02 Canon
VTD08PR03 Serena
VTD08PR04 Fina
VTD08PR05 Caro

2017 The Caster Chronicles The Magic Battle Begins

COMPLETE SET (195)
BOOSTER BOX (20 PACKS)
BOOSTER PACK (8 CARDS)
RELEASED ON OCTOBER 20, 2017
BP01001 Orange Peko (level 1) R 2.00 3.00
BP01002 Orange Peko (level 2) UR 15.00 25.00
BP01003 Sunny (level 1) SR .25 .40
BP01004 Tricker Heather R 1.25 2.00
BP01005 Nebula Soleil R 2.00 3.00
BP01006 Mia Laira R 3.00 5.00
BP01007 Mona Styla R 2.50 4.00
BP01008 Lufue Yuni SR 8.00 12.00
BP01009 Crispy Cookie C .12 .20
BP01010 Bitter Chocolate C .12 .20
BP01011 Melty Ice Cream C .12 .20
BP01012 Rich Macaron C .12 .20
BP01013 Juicy Crepe C .12 .20
BP01014 Strawberry on the Shortcake C .12 .20
BP01015 Zhu Bajie R 1.00 1.50
BP01016 Toxic Turkey C .12 .20
BP01017 Hard Pancake C .12 .20
BP01018 Mixed Parfait C .12 .20
BP01019 Afternoon Tea U .20 .30
BP01020 Cerberoast U .20 .30
BP01021 Bealzeborne, Demon of Gluttony R .25 .40
BP01022 Evaporation U .20 .30
BP01023 Price of Overeating U .20 .30
BP01024 Carrion Scrounge U .20 .30
BP01025 Paper Eating Virus U .20 .30
BP01026 Total Eclipse U .20 .30
BP01027 Sunbeam Roasting U .20 .30
BP01028 Carella (level 1) R .25 .40
BP01029 Kiro Centura R .25 .40
BP01030 Shera Angellica SR 6.00 10.00
BP01031 Crimson Nicola R .25 .40
BP01032 Passion Wing (level 1) R .25 .40
BP01033 Passion Wing (level 2) UR 10.00 15.00
BP01034 Paruetta R .25 .40
BP01035 Flame Rouge SR 3.00 5.00
BP01036 Disembodied Soul C .12 .20
BP01037 Straw Effigy C .12 .20
BP01038 Explosive Bamboo C .12 .20
BP01039 Little Match Girl C .12 .20
BP01040 Tanuki of Kachi-Kachi Mountain C .12 .20
BP01041 Patience Bag C .12 .20
BP01042 Yoshitsune R .25 .40
BP01043 Wandering Flames C .12 .20
BP01044 Firewheel C .12 .20
BP01045 Salamander C .12 .20
BP01046 Asura, the Three Sided U .20 .30
BP01047 Furious Dragon U .20 .30
BP01048 Diablos the Deciever R .25 .40
BP01049 Kindle the Spirit U .20 .30
BP01050 Fire Arrow U .20 .30
BP01051 Incite Ferocity U .20 .30
BP01052 Demonic Hellfire U .20 .30
BP01053 Flame of Indignation U .20 .30
BP01054 World of Rage U .20 .30
BP01055 Kiberia Yosha (level 1) R 2.50 4.00
BP01056 Kiberia Yosha (level 2) UR 8.00 12.00
BP01057 Sweet Pea R .25 .40
BP01058 Stella R 2.00 3.00
BP01059 Chain of Hearts (level 1) R 5.00 8.00
BP01060 Forre Mellow SR 6.00 10.00
BP01061 Ran Berfield R .25 .40
BP01062 Lily Verde SR 1.25 2.00
BP01063 Holy Monk C .12 .20
BP01064 Cactusman C .12 .20
BP01065 Lively Monk C .12 .20
BP01066 Venus Flytrap C .12 .20
BP01067 Lazy Spirit C .12 .20
BP01068 Unreliable Monk C .12 .20
BP01069 Harpy C .12 .20
BP01070 Lethargic Bear C .12 .20
BP01071 Ancient Tree C .12 .20
BP01072 Primal Sloth U .20 .30
BP01073 Wooden Bear U .20 .30
BP01074 Phoenix R .25 .40
BP01075 Belfegozz, Beast of Indolence R 2.00 3.00
BP01076 Exorcism U .20 .30
BP01077 Do Your Best! U .20 .30
BP01078 Procrastination U .20 .30
BP01079 Come Back Again Sometime U .20 .30
BP01080 A Leisurely Pace U .20 .30
BP01081 Sophmore Slump U .20 .30
BP01082 Iroha Maltz R 1.25 2.00
BP01083 Eli Superior SR 4.00 6.00
BP01084 Glory Butterfly (level 1) R .25 .40
BP01085 Glory Butterfly (level 2) UR 10.00 15.00
BP01086 Princess Papillon R .25 .40
BP01087 Miu (level 1) R 4.00 6.00
BP01088 Louise Bayli R .25 .40
BP01089 Loura Harie SR 4.00 6.00
BP01090 Bombastic Lily C .12 .20
BP01091 Spiteful Clam C .12 .20
BP01092 Impudent Swallowtail C .12 .20
BP01093 Rose of Insolence C .12 .20
BP01094 Sneering Orchid C .12 .20
BP01095 Tokitada R 1.25 2.00
BP01096 Tactless Butterfly C .12 .20
BP01097 Pompous Delphinium C .12 .20
BP01098 Ferocious Mantis C .12 .20
BP01099 Prideful Peafowl C .12 .20
BP01100 Buzen Bou TENGU48 U .20 .30
BP01101 Vagrant Lion C .12 .20
BP01102 Griphon U .20 .30
BP01103 Lucifell, Flawless Beauty R 1.25 2.00

BP01104 Sudden Evacuation U .20 .30
BP01105 Proclamation of Life and Death U .20 .30
BP01106 Grudge Attack U .20 .30
BP01107 Forced Repatriation U .20 .30
BP01108 Kneel Before Me! U .20 .30
BP01109 Barrier of Arrogance U .20 .30
BP01110 Ayutaila SR 8.00 12.00
BP01111 Grace R .25 .40
BP01112 Glow Desire (level 1) R .60 1.00
BP01113 Twinkle Charm R 4.00 6.00
BP01114 Rafina Soa R 1.25 2.00
BP01115 Luna Esperansa SR 2.00 3.00
BP01116 Ruka Eremi (level 1) R 10.00 15.00
BP01117 Ruka Eremi (level 2) UR 12.00 20.00
BP01118 Pentachi C .12 .20
BP01119 Birdog C .12 .20
BP01120 White Fox C .12 .20
BP01121 Gadfly Wasp C .12 .20
BP01122 Ouroboros C .12 .20
BP01123 Infini-Coin C .12 .20
BP01124 Extravagant Necklace C .40 .60
BP01125 Double Rabbit U .20 .30
BP01126 Greedy Vase C .12 .20
BP01127 Gem Pouch C .12 .20
BP01128 Split Eagle U .20 .30
BP01129 Goblin Merchant R .25 .40
BP01130 Bamanon, Source of Greed R 1.25 2.00
BP01131 Magic Paper U .20 .30
BP01132 Expensive Jar U .20 .30
BP01133 Compensation U .20 .30
BP01134 Compulsory Journey U .20 .30
BP01135 Servant Seal U .20 .30
BP01136 Shopping Plaza U .20 .30
BP01137 Karen Urania (level 1) SR 2.00 3.00
BP01138 Canal R .25 .40
BP01139 Saira Treverse R 5.00 8.00
BP01140 Zoi Russel SR 12.00 20.00
BP01141 Chakoru Senti (level 1) R .60 1.00
BP01142 Chakoru Senti (level 2) UR 12.00 20.00
BP01143 Deshi Lion R 1.00 1.50
BP01144 Hilde Willow R 1.25 2.00
BP01145 Wise Pencil C .12 .20
BP01146 Witty Mechanical Pencil C .12 .20
BP01147 Clever Set Square C .12 .20
BP01148 Brain Eraser C .12 .20
BP01149 Jealous Hera U .20 .30
BP01150 Spirit Scissors C .12 .20
BP01151 Capable Compass C .12 .20
BP01152 Intelligent Stapler C .12 .20
BP01153 Resourceful Box Cutter C .12 .20
BP01154 Brain Sharpener U .20 .30
BP01155 Snake-Eye C .12 .20
BP01156 Mr. Maid R .25 .40
BP01157 Leviathos, Spirit of Envy R .25 .40
BP01158 Call Forth U .20 .30
BP01159 Hit the Weak Point U .20 .30
BP01160 Brain Embody U .20 .30
BP01161 Critical Hit U .20 .30
BP01162 Servant Exchange U .20 .30
BP01163 Sage Advice U .20 .30
BP01164 Almeria R 2.00 3.00
BP01165 Clara Shurei R 1.00 1.50
BP01166 Sherry R 8.00 12.00
BP01167 Citra Cayce (level 1) SR 10.00 15.00
BP01168 Chaleur Suu (level 1) SR 10.00 15.00
BP01169 Cestria R 1.50 2.50
BP01170 Maisey Queen (level 1) R .75 1.25
BP01171 Maisey Queen (level 2) UR 12.00 20.00
BP01172 Irresistible Rouge C .12 .20
BP01173 Bouncing Perfume C .12 .20
BP01174 Dirty Mascara C .12 .20
BP01175 Cloudy Powder Brush C .12 .20
BP01176 Chaos Curler C .12 .20
BP01177 Messy Compact C .12 .20
BP01178 Komachi U .20 .30
BP01179 Heartbreak Cupid C .12 .20
BP01180 Enticing Nightwear C .12 .20
BP01181 Cosmetic Doctor, Sakasu U .20 .30
BP01182 Pumpkin Chariot C .12 .20
BP01183 Succubus R .25 .40
BP01184 Ashmodae, Apparition of Seduction R .25 .40
BP01185 I'll Be Right Over U .20 .30
BP01186 Wait There, Okay? U .20 .30
BP01187 Play Nice U .20 .30
BP01188 Be Born Again As A Caster U .20 .30
BP01189 Be Mine U .20 .30
BP01190 Back to Basics U .20 .30
BP01191 Loura Harie SEC 50.00 75.00
BP01192 Ayutaila SEC 15.00 25.00
BP01193 Chaleur Suu SEC 30.00 50.00
BP01194 Faare-A-Popierre SEC 25.00 40.00
BP01195 Passion Wing (level 1) HR 60.00 100.00

2017 The Caster Chronicles Starter Deck Arrogant Swallowtail

RELEASED ON OCTOBER 20, 2017
SD02001 Iroha Maltz R .60 1.00
SD02002 Eli Superior SR 4.00 6.00
SD02003 Glory Butterfly (level 1) R .60 1.00
SD02003 Glory Butterfly (level 1) R FOIL .60 1.00
SD02004 Glory Butterfly (level 2) UR 1.25 2.50
SD02005 Princess Papillon R .60 1.00
SD02005 Princess Papillon R FOIL .60 1.00
SD02006 Miu (level 1) R FOIL .60 1.00
SD02006 Miu (level 1) R .60 1.00
SD02007 Louise Bayli R .60 1.00
SD02008 Loura Harie SR 4.00 6.00
SD02009 Bombastic Lily C .20 .30
SD02010 Spiteful Clam C .20 .30
SD02011 Impudent Swallowtail C .20 .30
SD02012 Rose of Insolence C .20 .30
SD02013 Sneering Orchid C .20 .30
SD02014 Tokitada R .60 1.00
SD02015 Tactless Butterfly C .20 .30
SD02016 Ferocious Mantis C .20 .30
SD02017 Prideful Peafowl C .20 .30
SD02018 Griphon U .30 .50
SD02019 Proclamation of Life and Death U .30 .50
SD02020 Grudge Attack U .30 .50
SD02021 Forced Repatriation U .30 .50
SD02022 Kneel Before Me! U .30 .50

2017 The Caster Chronicles Starter Deck Wings of Anger

RELEASED ON 10/20/2017
SD01001 Carella (level 1) R .60 1.00
SD01002 Kiro Centura R .60 1.00
SD01003 Shera Angellica SR 4.00 6.00
SD01004 Crimson Nicola R .60 1.00
SD01004 Crimson Nicola R FOIL 5.00 8.00
SD01005 Passion Wing (level 1) R FOIL 4.00 6.00
SD01005 Passion Wing (level 1) R .60 1.00
SD01006 Passion Wing (level 2) UR 3.00 5.00
SD01007 Paruetta R .60 1.00
SD01008 Flame Rouge SR 4.00 6.00
SD01009 Disembodied Soul C .20 .30
SD01010 Straw Effigy C .20 .30
SD01011 Explosive Bamboo C .20 .30
SD01012 Little Match Girl C .20 .30
SD01013 Tanuki of Kachi-Kachi Mountain C .20 .30
SD01014 Patience Bag C .20 .30
SD01015 Yoshitsune R .60 1.00
SD01016 Firewheel C .20 .30
SD01017 Salamander C .20 .30
SD01018 Furious Dragon U .40 .60
SD01019 Kindle the Spirit U .40 .60
SD01020 Fire Arrow U .40 .60
SD01021 Incite Ferocity U .40 .60

2018 The Caster Chronicles PIth Dimension Battle Royale

BOOSTER BOX (20 PACKS)
BOOSTER PACK (8 CARDS)
RELEASED ON FEBRUARY 9, 2018
BP02001 Aria Citrus R .25 .40
BP02002 Gentry Gold R .25 .40
BP02003 Lilia Chocolate SR 10.00 15.00
BP02004 Sunny (level 2) UR 20.00 30.00
BP02005 Tomoe C .15 .25
BP02006 Yoshinaka C .15 .25
BP02007 Pâtissier C .15 .25
BP02008 Gyoza Tiger C .15 .25
BP02009 Lapse of Memory C .15 .25
BP02010 Swallow Whole U .20 .30
BP02011 Dealing With Demons U .20 .30
BP02012 Flambe R .60 1.00
BP02013 Vega Scarlet Star SR 8.00 12.00
BP02014 Risa Tarivan R .25 .40
BP02015 Carella (level 2) UR 15.00 25.00
BP02016 Sun Wukong C .15 .25
BP02017 Yoshitomo C .15 .25
BP02018 Yoritomo C .15 .25
BP02019 High Priest TENGU48 C .15 .25
BP02020 Raging Flame Counterattack U .20 .30
BP02021 Clothing Combustion U .20 .30
BP02022 Passion of Genji U .20 .30
BP02023 Solol Baton SR 10.00 15.00
BP02024 Nadeshiko R .25 .40
BP02025 Roseria Bell R .25 .40
BP02026 Chain of Hearts (level 2) UR 15.00 25.00
BP02027 Biwa Monk C .15 .25
BP02028 Bear Boy C .15 .25
BP02029 Benkei C .15 .25
BP02030 Tale of the Heike C .15 .25
BP02031 Zero Motivation U .20 .30
BP02032 Just a Short Rest U .20 .30
BP02033 San-Tonal R .25 .40
BP02034 Shura Psyche R .25 .40
BP02035 Haru Michelle SR 6.00 10.00
BP02036 Miu (level 2) UR 20.00 30.00
BP02037 Tadamori C .15 .25
BP02038 Kiyomori C .15 .25
BP02039 Vampiress C .15 .25
BP02040 Praying to Deaf Ears U .20 .30
BP02041 Summoning Obstruction U .20 .30
BP02042 Heishi's Pride U .20 .30
BP02043 Merril Laisse R .25 .40
BP02044 Broom Schlein R .25 .40
BP02045 Lumielle SR 10.00 15.00
BP02046 Glow Desire (level 2) UR 15.00 25.00
BP02047 Tadanori C .15 .25
BP02048 Usamaru C .15 .25
BP02049 Goblin Thief C .15 .25
BP02050 Pillage U .20 .30
BP02051 Preparation U .20 .30
BP02052 Abolition U .20 .30
BP02053 Lineal SR 3.00 5.00
BP02054 Lady Lupinus R .25 .40
BP02055 Broom Spica R .25 .40
BP02056 Karen Urania (level 2) UR 20.00 30.00
BP02057 Tadamasa C .15 .25
BP02058 Rocket Pencil Hedgehog C .15 .25
BP02059 Iemori C .15 .25
BP02060 Increased Exposure U .20 .30
BP02061 Knowledge From Ancestors U .20 .30
BP02062 Ambush U .20 .30
BP02063 Rei Ranpole R .25 .40
BP02064 Oar Schlein R .25 .40
BP02065 Tenel Frula SR 2.50 4.00
BP02066 Citra Cayce (level 2) UR 20.00 30.00
BP02067 Tokiwa C .15 .25
BP02068 Masako C .15 .25
BP02069 Sagami Bou TENGU48 C .15 .25
BP02070 Soul Bond U .20 .30
BP02071 Forbidden Love U .20 .30
BP02072 Partner Change U .20 .30
BP02073 Kururu Sentline SR 6.00 10.00
BP02074 Sirius Lucin SR 5.00 8.00
BP02075 Floom Heidi SR 4.00 6.00
BP02076 Mipheel SR 3.00 5.00
BP02077 Ranniart SR 3.00 5.00
BP02078 Lily-Lulu SR 4.00 6.00
BP02079 Soul Bond SEC 60.00 100.00
BP02080 Soul Bond SEC 25.00 40.00
BP02081 Soul Bond SEC 25.00 40.00
BP02082 Soul Bond SEC 25.00 40.00
BP02083 Soul Bond SEC 40.00 60.00
BP02084 Soul Bond SEC 25.00 40.00
BP02085 Risa Tarivan HR 200.00 300.00
BP02086 Sherry HR 150.00 250.00
BP02RE01 Toxic Turkey R .25 .40
BP02RE02 Hard Pancake R .30 .50
BP02RE03 Tanuki of Kachi-Kachi Mountain R .30 .50
BP02RE04 Patience Bag R .30 .50
BP02RE05 Harpy R .25 .40
BP02RE06 Primal Sloth R .25 .40
BP02RE07 Tactless Butterfly R .30 .50
BP02RE08 Ferocious Mantis R .25 .40
BP02RE09 White Fox R .25 .40
BP02RE10 Ouroboros R .25 .40
BP02RE11 Capable Compass R .25 .40
BP02RE12 Intelligent Stapler R .25 .40
BP02RE13 Irresistible Rouge R .50 .75
BP02RE14 Cloudy Powder Brush R .25 .40

2014 Dice Masters Avengers vs. X-Men

RELEASED IN APRIL 2014
1 Beast, Big Boy Blue S .60 1.00
2 Beast, Genetic Expert S 1.00 1.50
3 Beast, Mutate #666 S .60 1.00
4 Captain America, American Hero S .30 .50
5 Captain America, Natural Leader S .75 1.25
6 Captain America, Star-Spangled Avenger S .30 .50
7 Hulk, Anger Issues S .30 .50
8 Hulk, Annihilator S .60 1.00
9 Hulk, Jade Giant S .30 .50
10 Human Torch, Flame On S .30 .50
11 Human Torch, Matchstick S .30 .50
12 Human Torch, Playing with Fire S 1.00 1.50
13 Iron Man, Inventor S .75 1.25
14 Iron Man, Philanthropist S 1.25 2.00
15 Iron Man, Playboy S .30 .50
16 Spider-Man, Tiger S 1.00 1.50
17 Spider-Man, Webhead S .50 .75
18 Spider-Man, Webslinger S .60 1.00
19 Storm, African Princess S 1.50 2.50
20 Storm, Goddess of the Plains S 1.50 2.50
21 Storm, Ro S 1.00 1.50
22 Thor, Legendary Warrior S .75 1.25
23 Thor, Lord of Asgard S 1.25 2.00
24 Thor, Odinson S 1.25 2.00
25 Distraction, Basic Action Card S .30 .50
26 Focus Power, Basic Action Card S 1.00 1.50
27 Force Beam, Basic Action Card S 1.75 3.00
28 Gearing Up, Basic Action Card S 1.25 2.00
29 Inner Rage, Basic Action Card S .75 1.25
30 Invulnerability, Basic Action Card S .60 1.00
31 Power Bolt, Basic Action Card S 1.75 3.00
32 Smash!, Basic Action Card S .30 .50
33 Take Cover, Basic Action Card S 1.50 2.50
34 Thrown Car, Basic Action Card S 1.00 1.50
35 Angel, High Ground C .15 .25
36 Black Widow, Natural C 1.25 2.00
37 Colossus, Unstoppable C .40 .60
38 Cyclops, Slim C .15 .25
39 Deadpool, Assassin C .40 .60
40 Doctor Doom, Reed Richards' Rival C .15 .25
41 Doctor Octopus, Megalomaniac C .15 .25
42 Doctor Strange, Sorcerer Supreme C .15 .25
43 Gambit, Ace in the Hole C 1.50 2.50
44 Ghost Rider, Johnny Blaze C .60 1.00
45 Green Goblin, Goblin-Lord C 2.50 4.00
46 Hawkeye, Longbow C 1.25 2.00
47 Loki, Trickster C .15 .25
48 Magneto, Former Comrade C .15 .25
49 Mr. Fantastic, Brilliant Scientist C .50 .75
50 Mystique, Unknown C .15 .25
51 Nick Fury, Mr. Anger C .15 .25
52 Nightcrawler, Fuzzy Elf C .40 .60
53 Nova, Quasar C .60 1.00
54 Phoenix, Ms. Psyche C .15 .25
55 Professor X, Principal C .15 .25
56 Punisher, McRook C .15 .25
57 Rogue, Anna Raven C .15 .25
58 Silver Surfer, Silverado C .15 .25
59 Thing, Ever-Lovin' Blue-Eyed C .15 .25
60 Venom, Eddie Brock C .40 .60
61 War Machine, Combat Comrade C 1.25 2.00
62 Wolverine, Wildboy C .30 .50
63 Mjolnir, Fist of the Righteous C .15 .25
64 Vibranium Shield, One of a Kind C .15 .25
65 Angel, Avenging Angel U 1.25 2.00
66 Beast, Kreature U 1.75 3.00
67 Captain America, Sentintel of Liberty U 1.50 2.50
68 Colossus, Russian Bear U .60 1.00
69 Cyclops, If Looks Could Kill U .30 .50
70 Deadpool, Jack U .60 1.00
71 Doctor Doom, Nemesis U .60 1.00
72 Doctor Octopus, Fully Armed U 1.50 2.50
73 Doctor Strange, Master of the Mystic Arts U 1.00 1.50
74 Gambit, Le Diable Blanc U 1.50 2.50
75 Ghost Rider, Spirit of Vengeance U .30 .50
76 Hawkeye, Br'er Hawkeye U .30 .50
77 Hulk, Green Goliath U 1.50 2.50
78 Human Torch, Johnny Storm U 1.25 2.00
79 Iron Man, Billionaire U .60 1.00
80 Loki, Illusionist U .60 1.00
81 Magneto, Holocaust Survivor U 1.25 2.00
82 Mystique, Shapeshifter U .30 .50
83 Nick Fury, WWII Veteran U 1.00 1.50
84 Nightcrawler, Abandoned U .60 1.00
85 Nova, Buckethead U .30 .50
86 Phoenix, Redd U .30 .50
87 Professor X, Powerful Telepath U .30 .50
88 Punisher, Vigilante U 1.00 1.50
89 Rogue, Anna Marie U .30 .50
90 Silver Surfer, Sentinel U .30 .50
91 Spider-Man, Wall-Crawler U .60 1.00
92 Storm, Wind-Rider U 1.50 2.50
93 Thing, Grim Ben U .60 1.00
94 Thor, God of Thunder U .60 1.00
95 Venom, Mac Gargan U .60 1.00
96 War Machine, Parnell Jacobs U .30 .50
97 Mjolnir, Forged by Odin U .30 .50
98 Vibranium Shield, Irreplaceable U .30 .50
99 Angel, Soaring R 2.50 4.00
100 Black Widow, Killer Instinct R
101 Colossus, Piotr Rasputin R 4.00 6.00
102 Cyclops, Scott Summers R 1.25 2.50
103 Deadpool, Chiyonosake R 4.00 6.00
104 Doctor Doom, Victor R 4.00 6.00

105 Doctor Octopus, Mad Scientist R	4.00	6.00
106 Doctor Strange, Probably a Charlatan R	1.75	3.00
107 Gambit, Cardsharp R	8.00	12.00
108 Ghost Rider, Brimstone Biker R	1.75	3.00
109 Green Goblin, Norman Osborn R	3.00	5.00
110 Hawkeye, Robin Hood R	2.50	4.00
111 Loki, Gem-Keeper R	2.50	4.00
112 Magneto, Sonderkommando R	3.00	5.00
113 Mr. Fantastic, The Invincible Man R	3.00	5.00
114 Mystique, Could Be Anyone R	1.75	3.00
115 Nick Fury, Patch R		
116 Nightcrawler, Circus Freak R	3.00	5.00
117 Nova, The Human Rocket R		
118 Phoenix, Jeannie R	4.00	6.00
119 Professor X, Charles Francis Xavier R	10.00	15.00
120 Punisher, Big Nothing R	1.75	3.00
121 Rogue, Can't Touch This R	1.75	3.00
122 Silver Surfer, Sky-Rider R	1.50	2.50
123 Thing, Idol of Millions R	1.50	2.50
124 Venom, Angelo Fortunado R	3.00	5.00
125 War Machine, James Rhodes R	1.50	2.50
126 Wolverine, Formerly Weapon Ten R	8.00	12.00
127 Mjolnir, Thor's Hammer R	2.50	4.00
128 Vibranium Shield, Cap's Protection R	1.50	2.50
129 Black Widow, Tsarina SR	30.00	45.00
130 Green Goblin, Gobby SR	40.00	60.00
131 Mr. Fantastic, Elastic SR	8.00	12.00
132 Wolverine, Canucklehead SR	12.00	20.00

2014 Dice Masters Avengers vs. X-Men Organized Play

COMPLETE SET (13)		
1 Teamwork LE	1.50	2.50
2 Rally! LE	1.50	2.50
3 Deflection LE	1.00	1.50
4 Teleport LE	1.50	2.50
5 Collateral Damage LE	.60	1.00
6 Takedown LE	.60	1.00
7 Thor, The Might LE	12.00	20.00
8 Spider-Man, The Amazing LE	12.00	20.00
9 Wolverine, Walking His Own Path LE	4.00	6.00
10 Colossus LE		
11 Iron Man, Phoenix Buster LE		
12 Cyclops, Phoenix Force LE	.75	1.25
13 Phoenix Force, Force of Nature LE	10.00	15.00

2014 Dice Masters Uncanny X-Men

COMPLETE STARTER SET (34)		
RELEASED IN SEPTEMBER 2014		
1 Angel, Air Transport S	.60	1.00
2 Angel, Inspiring S	.60	1.00
3 Angel, Superhero S	.60	1.00
4 Cyclops, Optic Blast S	.60	1.00
5 Cyclops, Overlook S	.60	1.00
6 Cyclops, Superhero S	.60	1.00
7 Iceman, Cryokinetic S	.60	1.00
8 Iceman, Robert Louis Drake S	.60	1.00
9 Iceman, Too Cool for Words S	1.00	1.50
10 Juggernaut, Cain Marko S	.60	1.00
11 Juggernaut, Unstoppable S	.60	1.00
12 Juggernaut, Archvillain S	.60	1.00
13 Kitty Pryde, Ariel S	1.25	2.00
14 Kitty Pryde, Sprite S	1.25	2.00
15 Kitty Pryde, Shadowcat S	1.25	2.00
16 Magneto, Field Control S	.60	1.00
17 Magneto, Will to Live S	.60	1.00
18 Magneto, Archvillain S	.60	1.00
19 Quicksilver, Pietro Maximoff S	.60	1.00
20 Quicksilver, Thanks to Isotope E S	.60	1.00
21 Quicksilver, Former Villain S	.60	1.00
22 Wolverine, The Best There Is S	.60	1.00
23 Wolverine, Not Very Nice S	.60	1.00
24 Wolverine, Superhero S	.60	1.00
25 Ambush S	.60	1.00
26 Enrage S	.60	1.00
27 Feedback S	.60	1.00
28 Imprisoned S	.60	1.00
29 Possession S	.60	1.00
30 Reckless Melee S	.60	1.00
31 Relentless S	.60	1.00
32 Selective Shield S	.60	1.00
33 Take That, Villain! S	.60	1.00
34 Transfer Power S	.60	1.00
35 Ant-Man, Biophysicist C	.30	.50
36 Apocalypse, Awakened C	.15	.25
37 Bishop, Omega Squad C	.15	.25
38 Black Panther, Wakanda Chief C	1.00	1.50
39 Cable, Man of Action C	.15	.25
40 Captain America, Special Ops C	.15	.25
41 Emma Frost, Archvillain C	.15	.25
42 Falcon, Samuel Wilson C	.15	.25
43 Iron Man, Upright C	.15	.25
44 Magik, Illyana Rasputina C	.15	.25
45 Marvel Girl, Telekinetic C	.15	.25
46 Mister Sinister, Archvillain C	.15	.25
47 Mystique, Ageless C	.15	.25
48 Namor, The Sub-Mariner C	.15	.25
49 Professor X, Recruiting Young Mutants C	1.25	2.00
50 Psylocke, Betsy Braddock C	.15	.25
51 Pyro, Saint-John Allerdyce C	1.00	1.50
52 Red Hulk, Thunderbolt Ross C	.30	.50
53 Sabretooth, Something to Prove C	.30	.50
54 Scarlet Witch, Wanda Maximoff C	.15	.25
55 Sentinel, Mutant Hunter C	.15	.25
56 She-Hulk, Jennifer Walters C	.75	1.25
57 Spider-Man, Hero for Hire C	.15	.25
58 Storm, Weather Witch C	.15	.25
59 Toad, Tongue Lashing C	.40	.60
60 Vision, Density Control C	.40	.60
61 X-23, Scent of Murder C	.15	.25
62 Cerebro, Cybernetic Intelligence C	1.25	2.00
63 Angel, Air Transport U	.60	1.00
64 Ant-Man, Pym Particles U	1.00	1.50
65 Apocalypse, Archvillain U	.30	.50
66 Bishop, Branded a Mutant U	1.00	1.50
67 Black Panther, T'Challa U	.30	.50
68 Cable, Techno-Organic U	.60	1.00
69 Captain America, "Follow Me!" U	.30	.50
70 Cyclops, Field Leader U	.60	1.00
71 Falcon, Recon U	.30	.50
72 Iceman, Mister Friese U	.60	1.00
73 Juggernaut, Kuurth U	.30	.50
74 Kitty Pryde, Just a Phase U	.30	.50
75 Magik, Lightchylde U	.30	.50
76 Magneto, Hellfire Club U	.30	.50
77 Marvel Girl, Superhero U	.30	.50
78 Mister Sinister, Nasty Boy U	2.00	3.00
79 Mystique, Raven Darkholme U	.30	.50
80 Namor, Atlantean U	.30	.50
81 Professor X, Founder U	.60	1.00
82 Psylocke, Ninjutsu U	.30	.50
83 Pyro, Pyrokinetic U	.60	1.00
84 Quicksilver, Villainous U	.60	1.00
85 Red Hulk, a.k.a. Rulk U	.30	.50
86 Sabretooth, Survivor U	1.00	1.50
87 Sentinel, Archvillain U	.30	.50
88 She-Hulk, Lady Liberator U	.60	1.00
89 Storm, Superhero U	.30	.50
90 Toad, Sniveling Servant U	.30	.50
91 Vision, Android U	.30	.50
92 Wolverine, Antihero U	1.25	2.00
93 X-23, Assassin U	.30	.50
94 Cerebro, Supercomputer U	1.25	2.00
95 Ant-Man, The Insect World R	1.50	2.50
96 Apocalypse, Time of Testing R	1.50	2.50
97 Bishop, XSE R	2.00	3.00
98 Black Panther, Diversion R	2.00	3.00
99 Cable, Time Traveller R	2.50	4.00
100 Captain America, Superhero R	1.50	2.50
101 Emma Frost, Graceful R	2.50	4.00
102 Falcon, Air Strike R	1.25	2.00
103 Iron Man, Superhero R	1.00	1.50
104 Magik, Redflag #133 R	1.50	2.50
105 Marvel Girl, Telepath R	1.25	2.00
106 Mister Sinister, Nathaniel Essex R	1.00	1.50
107 Mystique, Alias: You R	1.50	2.50
108 Namor, Imperius Rex R	1.00	1.50
109 Professor X, Trainer R	3.00	5.00
110 Psylocke, Kwannon the Assassin R	5.00	8.00
111 Pyro, Uncontrolled R	1.50	2.50
112 Red Hulk, Superhero R	1.00	1.50
113 Sabretooth, Superpowered R	2.50	4.00
114 Scarlet Witch, Unity Squad R	2.00	3.00
115 Sentinel, Robot R	2.50	4.00
116 She-Hulk, Superhero R	2.00	3.00
117 Spider-Man, Spider Sense R	1.50	2.50
118 Storm, Lady Liberator R	1.00	1.50
119 Toad, Mortimer Toynbee R	2.00	3.00
120 Vision, Victor Shade R	2.00	3.00
121 X-23, Killing Machine R	3.00	5.00
122 Cerebro, Mutant Hunter R	1.00	1.50
123 Emma Frost, Hellfire Club SR	5.00	8.00
124 Iron Man, Industrialist SR	5.00	8.00
125 Scarlet Witch, Controls Probability SR	10.00	15.00
126 Spider-Man, Superhero SR	6.00	10.00

2014 Dice Masters Uncanny X-Men Avengers Disassembled Organized Play

1 Hawkeye	1.50	2.50
2 Scarlet Witch	1.50	2.50
3 She-Hulk	1.50	2.50

2014 Dice Masters Uncanny X-Men Organized Play

1 Magneto	2.00	3.00
2 Apocalypse Earth 295	5.00	8.00
3 Beast	3.00	5.00
4 Sentinel	2.00	3.00
5 Kitty Pryde	2.00	3.00
6 Wolverine	3.00	5.00
7 Marvel Gir	1.50	2.50
8 Emma Frost	2.50	4.00
9 Phoeni	2.00	3.00

2015 Dice Masters Avengers Age of Ultron

RELEASED IN JULY 2015		
1 Black Widow, Natasha S	.60	1.00
2 Black Widow, Spy S	.60	1.00
3 Black Widow, Cold Warrior S	.60	1.00
4 Captain America, Super Soldier S	.60	1.00
5 Captain America, The First Avenger S	.60	1.00
6 Captain America, Man out of Time S	.60	1.00
7 Hawkeye, Formerly Ronin S	.60	1.00
8 Hawkeye, Clint S	.60	1.00
9 Hawkeye, Trick shot S	.60	1.00
10 Hulk, Smash! S	.60	1.00
11 Hulk, Bruce Banner S	.60	1.00
12 Hulk, Big Green Bruiser S	.60	1.00
13 Iron Man, Big Man S	.60	1.00
14 Iron Man, Genius S	.60	1.00
15 Iron Man, Invincible S	.60	1.00
16 Thor, Not Who You Expected? S	.60	1.00
17 Thor, Goddess of Thunder S	.60	1.00
18 Thor, Worthy S	.60	1.00
19 Ultron, Bringing Order S	.60	1.00
20 Ultron, Peacekeeper Gone Wrong S	.60	1.00
21 Ultron, Creation S	.60	1.00
22 Vision, Phasin S	.60	1.00
23 Vision, Ultron's Spy S	.60	1.00
24 Vision, Negotiator S	.60	1.00
25 Assemble S	.60	1.00
26 Call them Out! S	.60	1.00
27 Coordinated Strike S	.60	1.00
28 Enslavement S	.60	1.00
29 Hulk Out S	.60	1.00
30 Infiltrate S	.60	1.00
31 Nasty Plot S	.60	1.00
32 Ready to Rocket! S	.60	1.00
33 Surprise Attack S	.60	1.00
34 The Oppression Begins S	.60	1.00
35 Baron Zemo, Helmut J. Zemo C	.15	.25
36 Beast, Dr. Hank McCoy C	.50	.75
37 Black Widow, Oktober C	.15	.25
38 Bucky, James Buchanan Barnes C	.15	.25
39 Captain America, Symbol of Freedom C	.15	.25
40 Captain Marvel, Maj. Carol Danvers C	.15	.25
41 Captain Universe, Tamara Devoux C	.15	.25
42 Daredevil, Matthew Murdock, Attorney-at-Law C	.50	.75
43 Enchantress, Amora C	.15	.25
44 Gamora, Assassin C	.15	.25
45 Giant Man, Dr. Henry Pym C	.15	.25
46 Groot, Reincarnated C	.15	.25
47 Hawkeye, What Kind of Arrow? C	.15	.25
48 Hulk, Gamma Powered C	.60	1.00
49 Hyperion, Eternal C	.15	.25
50 Iron Man, Tinhead C	.15	.25
51 Jocasta, Titanium Body C	.15	.25
52 Kang, The Conqueror C	.15	.25
53 Loki, Loki Laufeyson C	.15	.25
54 Loki's Scepter, Magic C	.15	.25
55 Maria Hill, Avengers Liaison C	.15	.25
56 Moondragon, Heather Douglas C	.15	.25
57 Nick Fury, Sgt. Fury C	.15	.25
58 Odin, The All-Father C	1.25	2.00
59 Pepper Potts, Personal Secretary of Tony Stark C	.15	.25
60 Phil Coulson, Inspirational Leader C	1.50	2.50
61 Red Skull, Johann Schmidt C	.15	.25
62 Rocket Raccoon, "Blam! Murdered you!" C	1.00	1.50
63 S.H.I.E.L.D. Agent, Level 6 Access C	.15	.25
64 S.H.I.E.L.D. Helicarrier, Iliad C	.15	.25
65 Spider-Woman, Jessica Drew C	.15	.25
66 Starhawk, Stakar Ogord C	.15	.25
67 Star-Lord, Peter Jason Quill C	.30	.50
68 Thanos, Courting Death C	1.00	1.50
69 Thor, Thunderer C	.15	.25
70 Ultron, New World Order C	.15	.25
71 Ultron Drone, 01000100 01101001 01100101 C	.15	.50
72 Vision, Punisher C	.15	.25
73 Wasp, The Winsome Wasp C	.15	.25
74 Wonder Man, Simon Williams C	.15	.25
75 Baron Zemo, Master of Evil U	.30	.50
76 Beast, Bouncing Blue Beast U	.50	.75
77 Bucky, Cap's Sidekick U	.50	.75
78 Captain Marvel, Human/Kree Hybrid U	.30	.50
79 Captain Universe, Uni-Power U	.30	.50
80 Daredevil, Man Without Fear U	.30	.50
81 Enchantress, Manipulator U	.30	.50
82 Gamora, Raised by Thanos U	.30	.50
83 Giant Man, Original Avenger U	.30	.50
84 Groot, Protector U	1.50	2.50
85 Hyperion, Avenger U	.30	.50
86 Jocasta, Wife of Ultron U	.30	.50
87 Kang, Rama-Tut U	.30	.50
88 Loki, Trickster God U	.30	.50
89 Loki's Scepter, Mind Control U	.30	.50
90 Maria Hill, Trained Agent U	1.00	1.50
91 Moondragon, Dragon of the Moon U	.30	.50
92 Nick Fury, Life Model Decoy U	1.00	1.50
93 Odin, Gungnir U	2.00	3.00
94 Pepper Potts, CEO of Stark Industries U	2.50	4.00
95 Phil Coulson, Man with the Plan U	.30	.50
96 Red Skull, Embodiment of Evil U	.30	.50
97 Rocket Raccoon, Weapons Expert U	.30	.50
98 S.H.I.E.L.D. Agent, You're Not Cleared For That U	.30	.50
99 S.H.I.E.L.D. Helicarrier, Argonaut U	.30	.50
100 Spider-Woman, Playing Both Sides U	1.50	2.50
101 Starhawk, The One Who Knows U	.30	.50
102 Star-Lord, Reluctant Prince U	.30	.50
103 Thanos, The Mad Titan U	1.00	1.50
104 Ultron Drone, 1 of a Million U	.30	.50
105 Wasp, Bio-Electric Blasts U	1.50	2.50
106 Wonder Man, Ionic Energy U	.30	.50
107 Baron Zemo, Thunderbolt R	3.00	5.00
108 Beast, Not Your Average Pretty Face R	1.00	1.50
109 Bucky, Soldier R	2.00	3.00
110 Captain Marvel, Inspiration R	2.50	4.00
111 Daredevil, Guardian of Hell's Kitchen R	1.00	1.50
112 Enchantress, Hypnotic R	2.50	4.00
113 Gamora, Deadliest Woman In The Universe R	3.00	5.00
114 Giant Man, Pym Particles R	2.00	3.00
115 Hyperion, Atomic Vision R	1.50	2.50
116 Kang, Time-Ship R	1.50	2.50
117 Loki, Agent of Asgard R	2.00	3.00
118 Loki's Scepter, Piercing R	1.00	1.50
119 Maria Hill, Director of S.H.I.E.L.D. R	1.00	1.50
120 Moondragon, Daughter of the Destroyer R	1.00	1.50
121 Nick Fury, Schemes Upon Schemes R	2.00	3.00
122 Odin, Asgardian Monarch R	1.25	2.00
123 Pepper Potts, Stark International R	2.00	3.00
124 Phil Coulson, Expert Recruiter R	3.00	5.00
125 Red Skull, "Hail Hydra!" R	1.50	2.50
126 Rocket Raccoon, Smartest Mammal In The D'ast Galaxy R	2.00	3.00
127 S.H.I.E.L.D. Agent, Need to Know Basis R	2.00	3.00
128 S.H.I.E.L.D. Helicarrier, Odyssey R	2.00	3.00
129 Spider-Woman, Pheromones R	2.50	4.00
130 Starhawk, Precognitive R	1.25	2.50
131 Star-Lord, Element Gun R	3.00	5.00
132 Ultron Drone, Swarm of Destruction R	1.50	2.50
133 Wasp, Founding Avenger R	3.00	5.00
134 Wonder Man, Movie Star R	1.50	2.50
135 Captain Universe, Enigma Force SR	5.00	8.00
136 Groot, We Are Groot SR	20.00	30.00
137 Jocasta, Patterned After Janet SR	3.00	5.00
138 Thanos, Infinite SR	10.00	15.00
139 Magneto, Magnetic Monster SR	15.00	25.00
140 Red Skull, Undying Evil SR	8.00	12.00
141 Gladiator, Intergalactic Terror SR	6.00	10.00
142 Electro, Cooked Meat SR	6.00	10.00
143 Magneto - Magnetic Monster FULL ART		
144 Red Skull - Undying Evil FULL ART		
145 Gladiator - Intergalactic Terror FULL ART		
146 Electro - Cooked Meat FULL ART		

2015 Dice Masters DC Comics War of Light

1 Anti-Monitor, Enemy of the Multiverse S
2 Anti-Monitor, Symbol of Fear S
3 Anti-Monitor, Universal Destruction S
4 Batman, Bruce Wayne of Earth S
5 Batman, Cowardly and Superstitious Lot S
6 Batman, Instill Great Fear S
7 Guy Gardner, Blinding Rage S
8 Guy Gardner, Seeing Red S
9 Guy Gardner, Warrior's Spirit S
10 Hal Jordan, Green Lantern S
11 Hal Jordan, Highball S
12 Hal Jordan, Test Pilot S
13 John Stewart, Architect S
14 John Stewart, Indigo Tribe S
15 John Stewart, Compassionate S
16 Kyle Rayner, Artist S
17 Kyle Rayner, Dreamer S
18 Kyle Rayner, Look To The Stars S
19 Lex Luthor, Greed S
20 Lex Luthor, Legitimate Businessman S
21 Lex Luthor, Xenophobe S
22 Sinestro, Corps Namesake S

23 Sinestro, Greatest Lantern of them All S
24 Sinestro, Thaal Sinestro of Korugar S
25 Big Entrance BA
26 Enormous Destruction BA
27 Heroic Defense BA
28 Lethal Force BA
29 Monument to Evil BA
30 Relaxing BA
31 Stealth Ops BA
32 Vicious Struggle BA
33 Fighting BA
34 You've Been Chosen BA
35 Anti-Monitor, Warp Reality C
36 Atom, Dr. Ray Palmer C
37 Atrocitus, Atros of Ryut C
38 Batman, Fear as a Weapon C
39 Beast Boy, Gar C
40 Bleez, Victim C
41 Carol Ferris, Star Sapphire C
42 Dex-Starr, Dexter of Earth C
43 Fatality, Yrra Cynril C
44 The Flash, Barry Allen of Earth C
45 Guy Gardner, Heated C
46 Hal Jordan, Fearless C
47 Indigo-1, Iroque C
48 Jade, Jennifer-Lynn Hayden C
49 John Stewart, Marine C
50 Kilowog, Drill Instructor C
51 Kyle Rayner, Hopeful Will C
52 Lantern Battery, Speak The Oath C
53 Lantern Ring, Not Just Jewelry C
54 Larfleeze, Avarice C
55 Lex Luthor, Egomaniac C
56 Lyssa Drak, Keeper of the Book of Parallax C
57 Mera, Queen of Atlantis C
58 Miri Riam, Beacon In The Dark C
59 Mogo, Living Planet C
60 Mongul, Usurper of the Corps C
61 Munk, Empath C
62 Parallax, Source of Terror C
63 Ranx, Sentient City C
64 Raven, Rachel Roth C
65 Saint Walker, Bro'Dee Walker of Astonia C
66 Scarecrow, Dr. Jonathan Crane C
67 Sinestro, Fears Made Into Light C
68 Spectre, Divine Retribution C
69 Starfire, Princess of Tamaran C
70 Superboy Prime, Clark Kent of Earth Prime C
71 Supergirl, Angry Alien C
72 Warth, Peace Be With You C
73 Wonder Girl, Cassie Sandsmark C
74 Wonder Woman, Loved By the Gods C
75 Atom, Great Compassion U
76 Atrocitus, Raging Vengence U
77 Beast Boy, Changeling U
78 Bleez, Winged Fury U
79 Carol Ferris, Link Between Hearts U
80 Dex-Starr, Rage Kitty U
81 Fatality, Bounty Hunter U
82 The Flash, A Promise of Hope U
83 Indigo-1, Merciful Leader U
84 Jade, Daughter of the Golden Age U
85 Kilowog, Brute Force U
86 Lantern Battery, Recharge U
87 Lantern Ring, Power Ring U
88 Larfleeze, One-of-a-Kind U
89 Lyssa Drak, Future Sight U
90 Mera, Mournful Rage U
91 Miri Riam, Unextinguished Devotion U
92 Mogo, Planet-Sized Will U
93 Mongul, Black Mercy U
94 Munk, Compassionate Protector U
95 Parallax, Shattered Will U
96 Ranx, Malevolent Metropolis U
97 Raven, Trigon's Heir U
98 Saint Walker, Hopeful Hero U
99 Scarecrow, Fear Gas U
100 Spectre, Blinded By Sin U
101 Starfire, Outlaw U
102 Superboy Prime, Shattered Reality U
103 Supergirl, Enraged U
104 Warth, Brother U
105 Wonder Girl, Silent Armor U
106 Wonder Woman, Aphrodite's Emissary U
107 Atom, Professor of Physics R
108 Atrocitus, Bloody Leader R
109 Beast Boy, Animal Magnetism R
110 Bleez, Controlled Rage R
111 Carol Ferris, True Love R
112 Dex-Starr, "I good kitty" R
113 Fatality, Forgiving Heart R
114 The Flash, Believe In The Impossible R
115 Indigo-1, "Nok!" R
116 Jade, Empowered by the Starheart R
117 Kilowog, Poozer R
118 Lantern Ring, Limited Only By Imagination R
119 Larfleeze, MINE! R
120 Lyssa Drak, Fear of the Unknown R
121 Mera, Furious Fatale R
122 Miri Riam, Capable of Great Love R
123 Mogo, Doesn't Socialize R
124 Mongul, Ruler of Warworld R
125 Munk, New Guardian R
126 Ranx, Blot Out the Stars R
127 Raven, Azarath, Metrion, Zinthos! R
128 Saint Walker, "All Will Be Well." R
129 Scarecrow, Hallucinogenic Phobias R
130 Spectre, Celestial Frenzy R
131 Superboy Prime, Troublesome R
132 Supergirl, Last Daughter of Krypton R
133 Warth, Hope Burns Bright R
134 Wonder Girl, Barbed Lasso R
135 Lantern Battery, Power Source SR
136 Parallax, Fear SR
137 Starfire, Koriand'r SR
138 Wonder Woman, Princess Diana of Earth SR
139 Black Lantern Aquaman, From the Depths SR
140 Black Lantern Batman, Blackest Knight SR
141 Black Lantern Superman, Krypton's Fall SR
142 Black Lantern Wonder Woman, Undead Warrior SR
39B Beast Boy, Gar (BLANK) P
64A Raven, Rachel Roth (ALT) LE

2015 Dice Masters Dungeons and Dragons Battle for Faerun

COMPLETE SET W/O S (114)	100.00	200.00
COMPLETE STARTER SET (24)		
RELEASED IN FEBRUARY 2015		
1 Beholder, Minion Aberration S	.60	1.00
2 Beholder, Apprentice Aberration S	.60	1.00
3 Beholder, Master Aberration S	.60	1.00
4 Blue Dragon, Minion Dragon S	.60	1.00
5 Blue Dragon, Apprentice Dragon S	.60	1.00
6 Blue Dragon, Master Dragon S	.60	1.00
7 Gelatinous Cube, Minion Ooze S	.60	1.00
8 Gelatinous Cube, Apprentice Ooze S	.60	1.00
9 Gelatinous Cube, Master Ooze S	.60	1.00
10 Green Dragon, Minion Dragon S	.60	1.00
11 Green Dragon, Apprentice Dragon S	.60	1.00
12 Green Dragon, Master Dragon S	.60	1.00
13 Halfling Thief, Minion Harper S	.60	1.00
14 Halfling Thief, Apprentice Emerald Enclave S	.60	1.00
15 Halfling Thief, Master Zhentarim S	.60	1.00
16 Human Paladin, Minion Order of the Gauntlet S	.60	1.00
17 Human Paladin, Apprentice Harper S	.60	1.00
18 Human Paladin, Master Lords Apprentice S	.60	1.00
19 Troll, Minion Humanoid S	.60	1.00
20 Troll, Apprentice Humanoid S	.60	1.00
21 Troll, Master Humanoid S	.60	1.00
22 Vampire, Minion Undead S	.60	1.00
23 Vampire, Apprentice Undead S	.60	1.00
24 Vampire, Master Undead S	.60	1.00
25 Beholder, Lesser Aberration C	2.50	4.00
26 Blue Dragon, Lesser Dragon C	1.50	2.50
27 Carrion Crawler, Lesser Aberration C	.15	.25
28 Copper Dragon, Lesser Dragon C	1.00	1.50
29 Dracolich, Lesser Undead Dragon C	.15	.25
30 Drow Assassin, Lesser Humanoid C	.15	.25
31 Dwarf Cleric, Lesser Order of the Gauntlet C	.15	.25
32 Elf Wizard, Lesser Harper C	.75	1.25
33 Frost Giant, Lesser Elemental C	.15	.25
34 Gelatinous Cube, Lesser Ooze C	1.50	2.50
35 Green Dragon, Lesser Dragon C	2.00	3.00
36 Half-Dragon, Lesser Humanoid C	.15	.25
37 Half-Orc Fighter, Lesser Emerald Alliance C	1.00	1.50
38 Halfling Thief, Lesser Lords Alliance C	2.50	4.00
39 Human Paladin, Lesser Emerald Enclave C	2.00	3.00
40 Invisible Stalker, Lesser Elemtal C	.15	.25
41 Kobold, Lesser Humanoid C	1.25	2.00
42 Manticore, Lesser Beast C	.75	1.25
43 Mind Flayer, Lesser Humanoid C	.60	1.00
44 Minotaur, Lesser Humanoid C	.75	1.25
45 Mummy, Lesser Undead C	1.00	1.50
46 Orc, Lesser Humanoid C	1.00	1.50
47 Owlbear, Lesser Beast C	.15	.25
48 Pit Fiend, Lesser Fiend C	.15	.25
49 Purple Worm, Lesser Beast C	.15	.25
50 Red Dragon, Lesser Dragon C	1.00	1.50
51 Skeleton, Lesser Undead C	.15	.25
52 Stirge, Lesser Beast C	1.00	1.50
53 Tarrasque, Lesser Aberration C	1.25	2.00
54 Treant, Lesser Beast C	.15	.25
55 Troll, Lesser Humanoid C	2.50	4.00
56 Umber Hulk, Lesser Beast C	1.50	2.50
57 Unicorn, Lesser Beast C	.15	.25
58 Vampire, Lesser Undead C	2.50	4.00
59 Wererat, Lesser Lycanthrope C	.15	.25
60 Zombie, Lesser Undead C	.15	.25
61 Magic Helmet, Lesser Gear C	.15	.25
62 Magic Sword, Lesser Gear C	.15	.25
63 Limited Wish, Lesser Spell C	.15	.25
64 Prismatic Spray, Lesser Spell C	.15	.25
65 Carrion Crawler, Greater Aberration U	2.50	4.00
66 Copper Dragon, Greater Dragon U	2.50	4.00
67 Dracolich, Greater Undead Dragon U	3.00	5.00
68 Drow Assassin, Greater Humanoid U	2.50	4.00
69 Dwarf Cleric, Greater Emerald Enclave U	2.50	4.00
70 Elf Wizard, Greater Order of the Gauntlet U	2.50	4.00
71 Frost Giant, Greater Elemental U	.30	.50
72 Half-Dragon, Greater Humanoid U	2.50	4.00
73 Half-Orc Fighter, Greater Lords Alliance U	2.50	4.00
74 Invisible Stalker, Greater Elemental U	2.50	4.00
75 Kobold, Greater Humanoid U	2.00	3.00
76 Manticore, Greater Beast U	.30	.50
77 Mind Flayer, Greater Humanoid U	.30	.50
78 Minotaur, Greater Humanoid U	3.00	5.00
79 Mummy, Greater Undead U	2.00	3.00
80 Orc, Greater Humanoid U	.30	.50
81 Owlbear, Greater Beast U	2.50	4.00
82 Pit Fiend, Greater Fiend U	.30	.50
83 Purple Worm, Greater Beast U	2.50	4.00
84 Red Dragon, Greater Dragon U	3.00	5.00
85 Skeleton, Greater Undead U	.30	.50
86 Stirge, Greater Beast U	2.50	4.00
87 Tarrasque, Greater Aberration U	.30	.50
88 Treant, Greater Beast U	2.00	3.00
89 Umber Hulk, Greater Beast U	.30	.50
90 Unicorn, Greater Beast U	2.00	3.00
91 Wererat, Greater Lycanthrope U	3.00	5.00
92 Zombie, Greater Undead U	2.00	3.00
93 Magic Helmet, Greater Gear U	2.50	4.00
94 Magic Sword, Greater Gear U	2.50	4.00
95 Limited Wish, Greater Spell U	1.25	2.00
96 Prismatic Spray, Greater Spell U	2.50	4.00
97 Carrion Crawler, Paragon Aberration R	1.25	2.00
98 Copper Dragon, Paragon Dragon R	3.00	5.00
99 Dracolich, Paragon Undead Dragon R	5.00	8.00
100 Drow Assassin, Paragon Humanoid R	4.00	6.00
101 Dwarf Cleric, Paragon Lords Alliance R	5.00	8.00
102 Elf Wizard, Paragon Zhentarim R	4.00	6.00
103 Frost Giant, Paragon Elemental R	1.25	2.00
104 Half-Dragon, Paragon Humanoid R	3.00	5.00
105 Half-Orc Fighter, Paragon Zhentarim R	3.00	5.00
106 Invisible Stalker, Paragon Elemental R	3.00	5.00
107 Kobold, Paragon Humanoid R	3.00	5.00
108 Manticore, Paragon Beast R	1.25	2.00
109 Minotaur, Paragon Humanoid R	1.25	2.00
110 Mummy, Paragon Undead R	3.00	5.00
111 Orc, Paragon Humanoid R	3.00	5.00
112 Owlbear, Paragon Beast R	1.25	2.00
113 Pit Fiend, Paragon Fiend R	3.00	5.00
114 Purple Worm, Paragon Beast R	3.00	5.00
115 Skeleton, Paragon Undead R	2.50	4.00
116 Treant, Paragon Beast R	3.00	5.00
117 Umber Hulk, Paragon Beast R	3.00	5.00
118 Unicorn, Paragon Beast R	3.00	5.00
119 Wererat, Paragon Lycanthrope R	1.25	2.00
120 Zombie, Paragon Undead R	2.50	4.00
121 Magic Helmet, Paragon Gear R	5.00	8.00
122 Magic Sword, Paragon Gear R	1.25	2.00
123 Limited Wish, Paragon Spell R	4.00	6.00
124 Prismatic Spray, Paragon Spell R	1.25	2.00
125 Mind Flayer, Epic Humanoid SR	20.00	30.00
126 Red Dragon, Epic Dragon SR	15.00	25.00
127 Stirge, Epic Beast SR	15.00	25.00
128 Tarrasque, Epic Aberration SR	12.00	20.00
129 Blessing, Basic Action Card S	.60	1.00
130 Charm, Basic Action Card S	.60	1.00
131 Cone of Cold, Basic Action Card S	.60	1.00
132 Dimension Door, Basic Action Card S	.60	1.00
133 Finger of Death, Basic Action Card S	.60	1.00
134 Fireball, Basic Action Card S	.60	1.00
135 Magic Missile, Basic Action Card S	.60	1.00
136 Polymorph, Basic Action Card S	.60	1.00
137 Resurrection, Basic Action Card S	.60	1.00
138 Stinking Cloud, Basic Action Card S	.60	1.00

2015 Dice Masters Dungeons and Dragons Battle for Faerun Organized Play

1 Drow Assassin	1.50	2.50
2 Elf Wizard	1.50	2.50
3 Dwarf Cleric	1.50	2.50
4 Halfling Thief	1.50	2.50
5 Treant	1.50	2.50
6 Copper Dragon	1.50	2.50
7 Zombie	1.50	2.50
8 Owlbear	1.50	2.50
9 Green Dragon	1.50	2.50
NNO Zombie	1.50	2.50

2015 Dice Masters Justice League

RELEASED IN APRIL 2015		
1 Batman, Bruce Wayne S	.60	1.00
2 Batman, The Dark Knight S	.60	1.00
3 Batman, World's Greatest Detective S	.60	1.00
4 Darkseid, God of Apokolips S	.60	1.00
5 Darkseid, In Search of Anti-Life S	.60	1.00
6 Darkseid, Immortal S	.60	1.00
7 Deathstroke, Slade Wilson S	.60	1.00
8 Deathstroke, The Terminator S	.60	1.00
9 Deathstroke, Villain for Hire S	.60	1.00
10 Green Arrow, Oliver Queen S	.60	1.00
11 Green Arrow, The Battling Bowman S	.60	1.00
12 Green Arrow, The Emerald Archer S	.60	1.00
13 Martian Manhunter, J'onn J'onnz S	.60	1.00
14 Martian Manhunter, Founding Member S	.60	1.00
15 Martian Manhunter, John Jones S	.60	1.00
16 Superman, Man of Steel S	.60	1.00
17 Superman, Last Son of Krypton S	.60	1.00
18 Superman, Kal-El S	.60	1.00
19 Wonder Woman, Daughter of Zeus S	.60	1.00
20 Wonder Woman, Warrior Princess S	.60	1.00
21 Wonder Woman, Champion of Themyscira S	.60	1.00
22 Zatanna, Zatanna Zatara S	.60	1.00
23 Zatanna, Actual Magician S	.60	1.00
24 Zatanna, Stage Magician S	.60	1.00
25 Anger Issues S	.60	1.00
26 Casualties S	.60	1.00
27 Fist of Fury S	.60	1.00
28 Phantom Zone S	.60	1.00
29 Pick Your Battles S	.60	1.00
30 Righteous Charge S	.60	1.00
31 Save Civilians S	.60	1.00
32 Shockwave S	.60	1.00
33 Villainous Pact S	.60	1.00
34 Vulnerability S	.60	1.00
35 Aquaman, Arthur Curry C	.15	.25
36 The Atom, Ray Palmer C	.15	.25
37 Batarang, Tool of the Bat C	.15	.25
38 Batman, The Caped Crusader C	.15	.25
39 Black Manta, David C	.15	.25
40 Blue Beetle, Jaime Reyes C	.15	.25
41 Booster Gold, Michael Jon Carter C	.15	.25
42 Brainiac, Terror of Kandor C	.15	.25
43 Captain Cold, Leonard Snart C	.15	.25
44 Catwoman, Selina Kyle C	.15	.25
45 Cheetah, Cursed Archaeologist C	.15	.25
46 Constantine, Antihero C	.15	.25
47 Cyborg, Vic Stone C	.15	.25
48 Darkseid, Omega Beams C	.15	.25
49 Deadman, Boston Brand C	.15	.25
50 Deathstroke, Weapons Master C	2.50	4.00
51 Firestorm, Jason and Ronnie C	.15	.25
52 The Flash, Barry Allen C	.15	.25
53 Green Arrow, Former Mayor C	.15	.25
54 Green Lantern, Hal Jordan C	.15	.25
55 Harley Quinn, Dr. Harleen Quinzel C	2.00	3.00
56 Hawkman, Thanagarian C	.15	.25
57 The Joker, Unpredictable C	.15	.25
58 Katana, Tatsu Yamashiro C	.15	.25
59 Lantern Power Ring, Energy Projection C	.15	.25
60 Lex Luthor, Power Suit C	.15	.25
61 Martian Manhunter, Green Martian C	.15	.25
62 Red Tornado, Rannian C	.15	.25
63 Robin, Boy Wonder C	.15	.25
64 Shazam!, Billy Batson C	.15	.25
65 Sinestro, Instills Fear C	.15	.25
66 Solomon Grundy, Born on a Monday C	.15	.25
67 Stargirl, Courtney Whitmore C	.15	.25
68 Superman, Not a Bird or a Plane C	2.50	4.00
69 Swamp Thing, Dr. Alec Holland C	.15	.25
70 Vibe, Francisco Ramon C	.15	.25
71 Vixen, Mari McCabe C	.15	.25
72 Wonder Woman, Princess Diana C	.15	.25
73 Zatanna, Backwards Magic C	.15	.25
74 Aquaman, King of Atlantis U	2.50	4.00
75 The Atom, Subatomic Superhero U	2.00	3.00
76 Batarang, Instrument of Distraction U	.30	.50
77 Black Canary, Crime-Fighter U	5.00	8.00
78 Black Manta, Deep Sea Deviant U	.30	.50
79 Blue Beetle, Magically Infused U	.30	.50

80 Booster Gold, Glory-Seeking Showboat U	.30	.50
81 Brainiac, Collector of Worlds U	.30	.50
82 Captain Cold, Leonard Wynters U	.30	.50
83 Cheetah, Powered by Urkartaga U	.30	.50
84 Constantine, Con Artist U	6.00	10.00
85 Cyborg, Expectionally Gifted U	2.50	4.00
86 Deadman, Possessive Talents U	2.50	4.00
87 Firestorm, Atom Rearranger U	4.00	6.00
88 The Flash, Speedster U	5.00	8.00
89 Green Lantern, Willpower U	2.50	4.00
90 Harley Quinn, Femme Fatale U	2.50	4.00
91 Hawkman, World's Fiercest Attacker U	.30	.50
92 The Joker, Clown Prince of Crime U	.30	.50
93 Katana, Outsider U	.30	.50
94 Lantern Power Ring, Energy Constructs U	.30	.50
95 Lex Luthor, Former President U	.30	.50
96 Red Tornado, Lab Creation U	2.00	3.00
97 Robin, Circus Star U	2.00	3.00
98 Shazam!, Wisdom of Solomon U	2.50	4.00
99 Sinestro, Order Through Fear U	2.50	4.00
100 Solomon Grundy, Died on a Saturday U	2.00	3.00
101 Stargirl, Yankee Poodle Fangirl U	2.00	3.00
102 Swamp Thing, Plant Elemental U	.30	.50
103 Vibe, Paco U	2.00	3.00
104 Vixen, Healing Factor U	.30	.50
105 The Atom, Science Advisor R	4.00	6.00
106 Aquaman, Orin R	3.00	5.00
107 Batarang, From Wayne Enterprises R	3.00	5.00
108 Black Canary, Canary Cry R	5.00	8.00
109 Black Manta, Artificial Gills R	2.50	4.00
110 Blue Beetle, High School Hero R	2.50	4.00
111 Booster Gold, High Publicity Hijinks R	1.25	2.00
112 Brainiac, Twelfth-Level Intelligence R	3.00	5.00
113 Captain Cold, Master of Absolute Zero R	3.00	5.00
114 Catwoman, Femme Fatale R	3.00	5.00
115 Cheetah, Dr. Barbara Ann Minerva R	3.00	5.00
116 Cyborg, Mentor R	3.00	5.00
117 Deadman, Embracing Life R	2.50	4.00
118 Firestorm, Matter Master R	4.00	6.00
119 Green Lantern, Brightest Day R	5.00	8.00
120 Harley Quinn, Psychopathic Psychiatrist R	3.00	5.00
121 Hawkman, Carter Hall R	4.00	6.00
122 The Joker, Red Hood R	5.00	8.00
123 Katana, Soultaker Sword R	4.00	6.00
124 Lantern Power Ring, Flight R	3.00	5.00
125 Lex Luthor, Billionaire Industrialist R	4.00	6.00
126 Red Tornado, Android R	3.00	5.00
127 Robin, Acrobatic Adolescent R	2.50	4.00
128 Shazam!, Strength of Hercules R	3.00	5.00
129 Sinestro, Sinestro Corps Leader R	4.00	6.00
130 Solomon Grundy, Buried on a Sunday R	3.00	5.00
131 Stargirl, Star-Spangled Kid R	3.00	5.00
132 Swamp Thing, Part of The Green R	5.00	8.00
133 Vibe, Formerly Hardline R	4.00	6.00
134 Vixen, Animal Mimicry R	4.00	6.00
135 Black Canary, Dinah Laurel Lance SR	8.00	12.00
136 Catwoman, Nine Lives SR	4.00	6.00
137 Constantine, Hellblazer SR	12.00	20.00
138 The Flash, Connected to the Speed Force SR	10.00	15.00

2015 Dice Masters Justice League Organized Play

1 Pandora's Box	8.00	12.00
2 Superman	8.00	12.00
3 House of Mystery	6.00	10.00
4 Constantine	2.50	4.00
5 Wonder Woman	1.50	2.50
6 Shazam!	1.50	2.50
7 Martian Manhunter	1.50	2.50
8 Firestorm	1.50	2.50
9 The Outsider	1.50	2.50
10 Batman	6.00	10.00
11 Atomica	8.00	12.00

2015 Dice Masters Marvel The Amazing Spider-Man

1 Carnage, Cletus Kassidy S
2 Carnage, Sinister S
3 Carnage, Symbiote S
4 Drax, Arthur Douglas S
5 Drax, The Destroyer S
6 Drax, Pained S
7 Ghost Rider, Alejandra S
8 Ghost Rider, New Rider S
9 Ghost Rider, Penance Stare S
10 Kingpin, Empire Builder S
11 Kingpin, Payback S
12 Kingpin, Wilson Fisk S
13 Silver Sable, Wild Pack S
14 Silver Sable, Mercenary S
15 Silver Sable, Outlaw S
16 Spider-Man, Spectacular S
17 Spider-Man, Tangled Web S
18 Spider-Man, Public Menace! S
19 Spider-Woman, Secret Avenger S
20 Spider-Woman, Lady Liberator S
21 Spider-Woman, Agent S
22 White Tiger, Hero for Hire S
23 White Tiger, Mystical Amulet S
24 White Tiger, Razor Sharp S
25 Archnemesis! BA
26 Back for Seconds! BA
27 Betrayal BA
28 Exposed! BA
29 Great Responsibility BA
30 Slander BA
31 Spideys Last Stand BA
32 True Believer BA
33 Web Blast BA
34 With Great Power... BA
35 Agent Venom, Thunderbolt C
36 Aunt May, Caring Aunt C
37 Black Cat, Felicia Hardy C
38 Black Widow, Stinger C
39 Blade, Vampire Hunter C
40 Blink, Clarice C
41 Carnage, Insane C
42 Cloak, Tyrone Johnson C
43 Dagger, Tandy Bowen C
44 Daredevil, Master Acrobat C
45 Doctor Octopus, Sinister C
46 Drax, Infinity Watch C
47 Electro, Sinister C
48 Firestar, M-Day Survivor C
49 Ghost Rider, Hellfire Manipulator C
50 Gladiator, Servant of the Empress C
51 Goblin Glider, Goblin Tech C
52 Green Goblin, Evil Genius C
53 Gwen Stacy, Public Menace C
54 Hobgoblin, Amoral Billionaire C
55 Hulk, Planet Hulk C
56 Iceman, Amazing Friend C
57 Iron Spidey, Science Nerd C
58 Kingpin, We Do Not Speak His Name C
59 Kraven the Hunter, Dangerous C
60 Lizard, Dr. Curt Connors C
61 Luke Cage, Hero for Hire C
62 Mary Jane, Jackpot C
63 Mysterio, Dr. Ludwig Rinehart C
64 Rhino, Big Brute C
65 Sandman, Million Little Pieces C
66 Scarlet Spider, Ben C
67 Silver Sable, Hero for Hire C
68 Spider-Girl, Mayday C
69 Spider-Man, Great Responsibility C
70 Spider-Woman, Bio-Electric C
71 Vulture, Fear from Above C
72 Web Shooters, A Spiders Best Friend C
73 White Tiger, New Avenger C
74 Wolverine, Targeted C
75 Agent Venom, Eugene U
76 Aunt May, Independent U
77 Black Cat, Probability Control U
78 Black Widow, Stealthy U
79 Blade, Daywalker U
80 Blink, Dimension Jumper U
81 Cloak, Secret Defender U
82 Dagger, Secret Defender U
83 Daredevil, Radar Sense U
84 Doctor Octopus, 8 Dangers U
85 Electro, Supercharged U
86 Firestar, New Warrior U
87 Gladiator, Kallark U
88 Goblin Glider, High Flying U
89 Green Goblin, Goblin Grandmaster U
90 Gwen Stacy, Earth-65 U
91 Hobgoblin, Evil Legacy U
92 Hulk, Back from Outer Space U
93 Iceman, Chilling U
94 Iron Spidey, Invincible U
95 Kraven the Hunter, Sergei Kravenoff U
96 Lizard, Sewer Dweller U
97 Luke Cage, Power Man U
98 Mary Jane, First Aid U
99 Mysterio, Quentin Beck U
100 Rhino, Persistent Vengeance U
101 Sandman, Sandy U
102 Scarlet Spider, The Spectacular U
103 Spider-Girl, Webslinger U
104 Vulture, Adrian Toomes U
105 Web Shooters, Stinging Web U
106 Wolverine, Regenerative U
107 Agent Venom, Flash Thompson R
108 Aunt May, Fresh Cookies R
109 Black Widow, Professional R
110 Blade, Vengeful R
111 Blink, Exile R
112 Cloak, Darkforce Dimension R
113 Dagger, Light Daggers R
114 Daredevil, Fearless R
115 Doctor Octopus, Otto R
116 Electro, Massive Discharge R
117 Firestar, Amazing Friend R
118 Gladiator, Strontian R
119 Goblin Glider, Borrowed Transportation R
120 Green Goblin, Goblin Legacy R
121 Gwen Stacy, The Amazing Spider-Gwen R
122 Hobgoblin, Mad Fashion Designer R
123 Iceman, Cool Dude R
124 Kraven the Hunter, Proud Hunter R
125 Lizard, Scientist R
126 Luke Cage, Thick Skin R
127 Mary Jane, MJ R
128 Mysterio, Francis Klum R
129 Rhino, Uncommon Thug R
130 Sandman, Shifting R
131 Scarlet Spider, Webslinger R
132 Vulture, Genius Engineer R
133 Web Shooters, Webbing All Over R
134 Wolverine, Weapon Plus R
135 Black Cat, Party Hardy SR
136 Hulk, Warbound SR
137 Iron Spidey, Armored Arachnid SR
138 Spider-Girl, May Parker SR
139 Green Goblin, Rotting Goblin SR
140 Kingpin, Cerebral Crime Boss SR
141 Morbius, Unliving Vampire SR
142 Venom, Staggering Symbiote SR
69A Spider-Man, Great Responsibility (ALT) C

2016 Dice Masters Dungeons and Dragons Faerun Under Siege

COMPLETE SET (142)
RELEASED IN FEBRUARY 2016

1 Bronze Dragon, Minion Dragon S	.60	1.00
2 Bronze Dragon, Apprentice Dragon S	.60	1.00
3 Bronze Dragon, Master Dragon S	.60	1.00
4 Cockatrice, Minion Monstrosity S	.60	1.00
5 Cockatrice, Apprentice Monstrosity S	.60	1.00
6 Cockatrice, Master Monstrosity S	.60	1.00
7 Glabrezu, Minion Fiend S	.60	1.00
8 Glabrezu, Apprentice Fiend S	.60	1.00
9 Glabrezu, Master Fiend S	.60	1.00
10 Gnome Ranger, Minion Harper S	.60	1.00
11 Gnome Ranger, Apprentice Emerald Enclave S	.60	1.00
12 Gnome Ranger, Master Lords' Alliance S	.60	1.00
13 Half-Elf Bard, Minion Harper S	.60	1.00
14 Half-Elf Bard, Apprentice Order of the Gauntlet S	.60	1.00
15 Half-Elf Bard, Master Lords' Alliance S	.60	1.00
16 Hell Hound, Minion Fiend S	.60	1.00
17 Hell Hound, Apprentice Fiend S	.60	1.00
18 Hell Hound, Master Fiend S	.60	1.00
19 Hill Giant, Minion Giant S	.60	1.00
20 Hill Giant, Apprentice Giant S	.60	1.00
21 Hill Giant, Master Giant S	.60	1.00
22 White Dragon, Minion Dragon S	.60	1.00
23 White Dragon, Apprentice Dragon S	.60	1.00
24 White Dragon, Master Dragon S	.60	1.00
25 Banishment, Basic Action Card S	.60	1.00
26 Barkskin, Basic Action Card S	.60	1.00
27 Blink - Transmutation, Basic Action Card S	.60	1.00
28 Chainmail Armor, Basic Action Card S	.60	1.00
29 Cloudkill, Basic Action Card S	.60	1.00
30 Delayed Blast Fireball, Basic Action Card S	.60	1.00
31 Flaming Sword, Basic Action Card S	.60	1.00
32 Mordenkainen's Sword, Basic Action Card S	.60	1.00
33 Power Word Kill, Basic Action Card S	.60	1.00
34 Shocking Grasp, Basic Action Card S	.60	1.00
35 Bahamut, Dragon of Justice C	.40	.60
36 Balor, Lesser Fiend C	.15	.25
37 Beholder, Lesser Aberration C	.60	1.00
38 Black Dragon, Lesser Dragon C	.30	.50
39 Blink Dog, Lesser Fey C	.15	.25
40 Bronze Dragon, Lesser Dragon C	.40	.60
41 Bugbear Ambusher, Lesser Humanoid C	.15	.25
42 Clay Golem, Lesser Construct C	1.00	1.50
43 Cockatrice, Lesser Monstrosity C	.15	.25
44 Displacer Beast, Lesser Monstrosity C	.15	.25
45 Drizzt, The Exile C	.15	.25
46 Dwarf Wizard, Lesser Emerald Enclave C	.15	.25
47 Elf Thief, Lesser Harper C	1.25	2.00
48 Erinyes, Lesser Fiend C	.15	.25
49 Flesh Golem, Lesser Construct C	.15	.25
50 Gelatinous Cube, Lesser Ooze C	.15	.25
51 Ghost, Lesser Undead C	.15	.25
52 Giant Spider, Lesser Beast C	.15	.25
53 Glabrezu, Lesser Fiend C	.15	.25
54 Gnome Ranger, Lesser Harper C	.15	.25
55 Goblin, Lesser Humanoid C	.30	.50
56 Gorgon, Lesser Monstrosity C	.30	.50
57 Half-Orc Barbarian, Lesser Harper C	.15	.25
58 Half-Elf Bard, Lesser Emerald Enclave C	.15	.25
59 Hell Hound, Lesser Fiend C	.15	.25
60 Hill Giant, Lesser Giant C	.15	.25
61 Human Fighter, Lesser Emerald Enclave C	.15	.25
62 Intellect Devourer, Lesser Aberration C	.15	.25
63 Iron Golem, Lesser Construct C	.15	.25
64 Lich, Lesser Undead C	.15	.25
65 Lizardfolk, Lesser Humanoid C	.15	.25
66 Lolth, The Demon Dark Mother C	.15	.25
67 Oni, Lesser Giant C	.15	.25
68 Orcus, Demon Lord of Thanatos C	.15	.25
69 Potion, Lesser Spell C	.15	.25
70 Ring, Lesser Gear C	.15	.25
71 Rust Monster, Lesser Monstrosity C	.15	.25
72 Storm Giant, Lesser Giant C	.15	.25
73 White Dragon, Lesser Dragon C	.15	.25
74 Wraith, Lesser Undead C	.15	.25
75 Bahamut, The Platinum Dragon U	.30	.50
76 Balor, Greater Fiend U	.30	.50
77 Beholder, Greater Aberration U	.30	.50
78 Black Dragon, Greater Dragon U	.30	.50
79 Blink Dog, Greater Fey U	.30	.50
80 Bugbear Ambusher, Greater Humanoid U	.30	.50
81 Clay Golem, Greater Construct U	.30	.50
82 Displacer Beast, Greater Monstrosity U	.30	.50
83 Drizzt, The Hunter U	.30	.50
84 Dwarf Wizard, Greater Harper U	.30	.50
85 Elf Thief, Greater Emerald Enclave U	.30	.50
86 Erinyes, Greater Fiend U	.30	.50
87 Flesh Golem, Greater Construct U	.30	.50
88 Gelatinous Cube, Greater Ooze U	.30	.50
89 Ghost, Greater Undead U	.30	.50
90 Giant Spider, Greater Beast U	.30	.50
91 Goblin, Greater Humanoid U	.30	.50
92 Gorgon, Greater Monstrosity U	.30	.50
93 Half-Orc Barbarian, Greater Zhentarim U	.30	.50
94 Human Fighter, Greater Lords Alliance U	.30	.50
95 Intellect Devourer, Greater Aberration U	.30	.50
96 Iron Golem, Greater Construct U	.30	.50
97 Lich, Greater Undead U	.30	.50
98 Lizardfolk, Greater Humanoid U	.30	.50
99 Lolth, Demon Ruler of the Demonweb Pits U	.30	.50
100 Oni, Greater Giant U	.30	.50
101 Orcus, Demon Prince of Undeath U	.30	.50
102 Potion, Greater Spell U	.30	.50
103 Ring, Greater Gear U	.30	.50
104 Rust Monster, Greater Monstrosity U	.30	.50
105 Storm Giant, Greater Giant U	.30	.50
106 Wraith, Greater Undead U	.30	.50
107 Bahamut, Dragon God of Good R	.50	.75
108 Balor, Paragon Fiend R	.50	.75
109 Black Dragon, Paragon Dragon R	.50	.75
110 Blink Dog, Paragon Fey R	.50	.75
111 Clay Golem, Paragon Construct R	.50	.75
112 Displacer Beast, Paragon Monstrosity R	.50	.75
113 Dwarf Wizard, Paragon Zhentarim R	.50	.75
114 Elf Thief, Paragon Emerald Enclave R	.50	.75
115 Erinyes, Paragon Fiend R	.50	.75
116 Flesh Golem, Paragon Construct R	.50	.75
117 Gelatinous Cube, Paragon Ooze R	.50	.75
118 Ghost, Paragon Undead R	.50	.75
119 Giant Spider, Paragon Beast R	.50	.75
120 Goblin, Paragon Humanoid R	.50	.75
121 Gorgon, Paragon Monstrosity R	.50	.75
122 Half-Orc Barbarian, Paragon Order of the Gauntlet R	.50	.75
123 Human Fighter, Paragon Zhentarim R	.50	.75
124 Intellect Devourer, Paragon Aberration R	.50	.75
125 Iron Golem, Paragon Construct R	.50	.75
126 Lich, Paragon Undead R	.50	.75
127 Lizardfolk, Paragon Humanoid R	.50	.75
128 Lolth, Demon Queen of Spiders R	.50	.75
129 Oni, Paragon Giant R	.50	.75
130 Orcus, Demon Lord of Undeath R	.50	.75
131 Potion, Paragon Spell R	.50	.75
132 Rust Monster, Paragon Monstrosity R	.50	.75
133 Storm Giant, Paragon Giant R	.50	.75
134 Wraith, Paragon Undead R	.50	.75
135 Beholder, Epic Aberration SR	15.00	25.00
136 Bugbear Ambusher, Epic Humanoid SR	10.00	15.00
137 Drizzt, The Legendary Hero SR	25.00	40.00
138 Ring, Epic Gear SR	15.00	25.00
139 Deck of Many Things, Epic Magical Object SR	20.00	30.00
140 Hammer of Thunderbolts, Epic Magical Object SR	25.00	40.00

141 Talisman of Ultimate Evil, Epic Magical Object SR	15.00	25.00
142 Robe of the Archmagi, Epic Magical Gear SR	25.00	40.00
143 Belaphoss, The Mad Demon LE		

2016 Dice Masters Green Arrow and The Flash

COMPLETE SET (124)		
BOOSTER BOX ()		
BOOSTER PACK ()		
RELEASED ON SEPTEMBER 7, 2016		
1 Amanda Waller: White Queen C	.15	.25
2 Barry Allen: Super-Sonic Punch C	.15	.25
3 Batgirl: Commish's Daughter C	.15	.25
4 Black Adam: No Mercy C	.15	.25
5 Black Canary: Like Mother, Like Daughter C	.15	.25
6 Captain Cold: Rogue Leader C	.15	.25
7 Captain Cold's Cold Gun: Snowy Schematics C	.15	.25
8 Clayface: Malleable Menace C	.15	.25
9 Cosmic Treadmill: Antique Shop Discovery C	.15	.25
10 Cyborg: A New Man C	.15	.25
11 Deadshot: Villains United C	.15	.25
12 Deathstroke: Guerilla Warfare C	.15	.25
13 Diggle: Green Beret C	.15	.25
14 Doctor Light: Hard Light C	.15	.25
15 Felicity Smoak: Gray Hat C	.15	.25
16 Firestorm: Host of the Matrix C	.15	.25
17 Giganta: Big Ups C	.15	.25
18 Gorilla Grodd: Supplanting Solovar C	.15	.25
19 Green Arrow: Robin Hood C	.15	.25
20 Hal Jordan: Green Lantern's Light C	.15	.25
21 Huntress: The Hunt Begins C	.15	.25
22 Jay Garrick: Leadfoot C	.15	.25
23 Katana: Bladerunner C	.15	.25
24 Killer Frost: Thermodynamic Disaster C	.15	.25
25 King Shark: Underwater Aggression C	.15	.25
26 Martian Manhunter: My True Form C	.15	.25
27 Merlyn: The Magnificent C	.15	.25
28 Power Ring: Harold Jordan C	.15	.25
29 Professor Zoom: Out of Time C	.15	.25
30 Ra's Al Ghul: The Demon C	.15	.25
31 Rip Hunter's Chalkboard: "Only Zatara Can Reach The POINT" C	.15	.25
32 Roy Harper: Don't Call Me Speedy C	.15	.25
33 S.T.A.R. Labs: Advanced Research C	.15	.25
34 Speedy: Runaway C	.15	.25
35 Static: Virgil Hawkins C	.15	.25
36 Superman: Man of Tomorrow C	.15	.25
37 The Atom: Sword of The Atom C	.15	.25
38 Weather Wizard: Dark Clouds C	.15	.25
39 Wonder Girl: Supergirl's Gal Pal C	.15	.25
40 Zatanna: Main Attraction C	.15	.25
41 Amanda Waller: The Wall U	.30	.50
42 Barry Allen: Central City Streak U	.30	.50
43 Batgirl: Protecting Innocents U	.30	.50
44 Black Adam: Teth Adam U	.30	.50
45 Black Canary: Volatile U	.30	.50
46 Captain Cold: Elegant Egomaniac U	.30	.50
47 Captain Cold's Cold Gun: Beautifully Designed U	.30	.50
48 Clayface: The Clayface of Tragedy U	.30	.50
49 Cosmic Treadmill: Flash Museum Relic U	.30	.50
50 Cyborg: Half-Man, Half-Machine U	.30	.50
51 Deadshot: Pinpoint Accuracy U	.30	.50
52 Deathstroke: High Price U	.30	.50
53 Diggle: Problem Solver U	.30	.50
54 Doctor Light: Blinding Bright U	.30	.50
55 Felicity Smoak: Hacker-For-Hire U	.30	.50
56 Firestorm: The Nuclear Man U	.30	.50
57 Giganta: Tall Glass of Water U	.30	.50
58 Gorilla Grodd: Force of Mind U	.30	.50
59 Green Arrow: Ollie U	.30	.50
60 Hal Jordan: Rebuilding Coast City U	.30	.50
61 Huntress: Brutal Justice U	.30	.50
62 Jay Garrick: The Crimson Comet U	.30	.50
63 Katana: Crisis and Tragedy U	.30	.50
64 Killer Frost: Coldsnap U	.30	.50
65 King Shark: Feeding Frenzy U	.30	.50
66 Martian Manhunter: Watchtower U	.30	.50
67 Merlyn: League of His Own U	.30	.50
68 Power Ring: Curse of Volthoom U	.30	.50
69 Professor Zoom: Inescapable Fate U	.30	.50
70 Ra's Al Ghul: The Demon's Head U	.30	.50
71 Rip Hunter's Chalkboard: NEW KRYPTON? U	.30	.50
72 Roy Harper: Red Arrow U	.30	.50
73 S.T.A.R. Labs: Guided Development U	.30	.50
74 Speedy: Mia Dearden U	.30	.50
75 Static: The Big Bang U	.30	.50
76 Superman: Truth and Justice U	.30	.50
77 The Atom: Rebuilding Coast City U	.30	.50
78 Weather Wizard: Weather Wand U	.30	.50
79 Wonder Girl: Ares's Champion U	.30	.50
80 Zatanna: Hex Appeal U	.30	.50
81 Amanda Waller: Squad Leader R	.50	.75
82 Batgirl: Eidetic Memory R	.50	.75
83 Black Adam: Ruler of Khandaq R	.50	.75
84 Black Canary: Sonic Cry R	.50	.75
85 Captain Cold: Icy Revenge R	.50	.75
86 Captain Cold's Cold Gun: Frozen "Firearm" R	.50	.75
87 Clayface: The Terror R	.50	.75
88 Cosmic Treadmill: Time Travel Tech R	.50	.75
89 Cyborg: Technis Imperative R	.50	.75
90 Deadshot: Floyd Lawton R	.50	.75
91 Deathstroke: Lt. Colonel R	.50	.75
92 Diggle: Team Player R	.50	.75
93 Doctor Light: Actual Doctor R	.50	.75
94 Felicity Smoak: Manipulating Technology R	.50	.75
95 Firestorm: Elemental Fury R	.50	.75
96 Giganta: Larger Than Life R	.50	.75
97 Gorilla Grodd: Brains and Brawn R	.50	.75
98 Hal Jordan: Punching a Hole in the Sky R	.50	.75
99 Huntress: Sins of the Father R	.50	.75
100 Jay Garrick: Guardian of Keystone City R	.50	.75
101 Killer Frost: On Thin Ice R	.50	.75
102 King Shark: "I'm a Shark!" R	.50	.75
103 Martian Manhunter: In Disguise R	.50	.75
104 Merlyn: League of Assassins R	.50	.75
105 Power Ring: Weak-willed R	.50	.75
106 Professor Zoom: Dead Ringer R	.50	.75
107 Ra's Al Ghul: League of Assassins R	.50	.75
108 Rip Hunter's Chalkboard: WHEN AM I? R	.50	.75
109 Roy Harper: Arsenal R	.50	.75
110 S.T.A.R. Labs: Science and Technology R	.50	.75
111 Speedy: Accomplished Archer R	.50	.75
112 Static: Taser Punch R	.50	.75
113 Superman: Up, Up, and Away! R	.50	.75
114 The Atom: Littlest Big Man R	.50	.75
115 Weather Wizard: The Storm is Here R	.50	.75
116 Wonder Girl: Daughter of Zeus R	.50	.75
117 Barry Allen: CSI SR	10.00	15.00
118 Green Arrow: Star City Savior SR	6.00	10.00
119 Katana: Bushi SR		
120 Zatanna: Inverted Incantations SR		
121 White Lantern Batman: Light in the Darkness SR	15.00	25.00
122 White Lantern Deadman: Defender of Life Itself SR	25.00	40.00
123 White Lantern Sinestro: Destiny Awaits SR	15.00	25.00
124 White Lantern Wonder Woman: Life Endures SR	20.00	30.00

2001-02 Digimon Digi-Battle Bandai Promos

DMEX Gallantmon (CM)
DPC3 Digi-Trinity
DPR1 Impmon
DPX1 Guilmon
DPX2 Renamon
DPX3 Terriermon
DPY1 WarGrowlmon
DPY2 Taomon
DPY3 Rapidmon
DMMG1 Gallantmon
DMMG2 MegaGargomon
DMMG3 Sakuyamon
DPower D-Power

2017 Dragoborne Rally To War

COMPLETE SET (125)	500.00	800.00
BOOSTER BOX (20 PACKS)	55.00	70.00
BOOSTER PACK (8 CARDS)	4.00	6.00
RELEASED ON AUGUST 18, 2017		
DBBT01001 Sunscale Dragon RR	4.00	6.00
DBBT01002 Angelica the Light of Logres RR	10.00	15.00
DBBT01003 Kaddar Dragonmage Adept R	1.25	2.00
DBBT01004 Tariel High Prestess R	1.25	2.00
DBBT01005 Darion Brutal Enforcer R	1.25	2.00
DBBT01006 Sanctuary Enforcer R	1.25	2.00
DBBT01007 Elven Bladesmith R	1.25	2.00
DBBT01008 Centaur Ranger U	.40	.60
DBBT01009 Sunscale Swordsman U	.40	.60
DBBT01010 Azraeus Blade of the Justicar U	.40	.60
DBBT01011 Spellweaver Magus U	.40	.60
DBBT01012 Frontline Stormer C	.15	.25
DBBT01013 Veteran Knight C	.15	.25
DBBT01014 Earthen Guard Golem C	.15	.25
DBBT01015 Sunscale Sage C	.15	.25
DBBT01016 Stoneskin Charger C	.15	.25
DBBT01017 Goldleaf Hunter C	.15	.25
DBBT01018 Logres Swiftblade C	.15	.25
DBBT01019 Sunscale Ascetic C	.15	.25
DBBT01020 Rookie Knight C	.15	.25
DBBT01021 Replenish the Ranks R	1.25	2.00
DBBT01022 Allied Front U	.40	.60
DBBT01023 Dragons Presence U	.40	.60
DBBT01024 Althaines Blessing C	.15	.25
DBBT01025 Terraxx Earthshaker RR	6.00	8.00
DBBT01026 Eleanor Queen of Storm RR	10.00	15.00
DBBT01027 The Prismatic King R	1.25	2.00
DBBT01028 Tireless Hunter R	1.25	2.00
DBBT01029 Redfang Born Leader R	1.25	2.00
DBBT01030 Stormbranch Knowledge of Ages R	1.25	2.00
DBBT01031 Fal thalas the Lost Wind R	1.25	2.00
DBBT01032 Springleaf Angel U	.40	.60
DBBT01033 Elven Farstriker U	.40	.60
DBBT01034 Guardian of the Forest U	.40	.60
DBBT01035 Mischievous Sprite U	.40	.60
DBBT01036 Tanglewood Druid U	.40	.60
DBBT01037 Ancient Gnarlwood C	.15	.25
DBBT01038 Gigantor Weevil C	.15	.25
DBBT01039 Primeape Javelineer C	.15	.25
DBBT01040 Bloodscent Arachnid C	.15	.25
DBBT01041 Fleetwing Sprite C	.15	.25
DBBT01042 Tanglewood Menace C	.15	.25
DBBT01043 Timid Scout C	.15	.25
DBBT01044 Chromatic Distubrance R	1.25	2.00
DBBT01045 Natures Touch U	.40	.60
DBBT01046 Growing Touch C	.15	.25
DBBT01047 Laelanias Call C	.15	.25
DBBT01048 Power of a Conquerer C	.15	.25
DBBT01049 Zero Mecha Warrior RR	10.00	15.00
DBBT01050 Aquatic Battle Unit Hydra RR	7.00	10.00
DBBT01051 Fleur Tide of Avarice R	1.25	2.00
DBBT01052 Telios Erstwhile Guardian R	1.25	2.00
DBBT01053 Variable Assault Unit Fuuma R	1.25	2.00
DBBT01054 Vrrglsk Plunderer of the Deep R	1.25	2.00
DBBT01055 Hajime Righteous Blade R	1.25	2.00
DBBT01056 Plato Accomplished Scientist R	1.25	2.00
DBBT01057 Typhos Relentless Hunter U	.40	.60
DBBT01058 The Keeper U	.40	.60
DBBT01059 The Researcher U	.40	.60
DBBT01060 Tidechaser Captian C	.15	.25
DBBT01061 The Ripper C	.15	.25
DBBT01062 Black Market Armsdealer C	.15	.25
DBBT01063 Gillman Raider C	.15	.25
DBBT01064 Expedition Merfolk C	.15	.25
DBBT01065 Frontier Explorer C	.15	.25
DBBT01066 Hidden Arts Waters Edge Shuriken U	.40	.60
DBBT01067 Rejuvenate U	.40	.60
DBBT01068 EMP U	.40	.60
DBBT01069 All Guns Blazing C	.15	.25
DBBT01070 Shieldbreaker C	.15	.25
DBBT01071 Displacer C	.15	.25
DBBT01072 Hidden Arts Reverse Thunderstrike C	.15	.25
DBBT01073 Fafneer Volatile Fire RR	10.00	15.00
DBBT01074 Vylon Great Horned General RR	7.00	10.00
DBBT01075 Xeras the Battleforged R	1.25	2.00
DBBT01076 Doomfire Avatar R	1.25	2.00
DBBT01077 Burbo Shrewd Merchant R	1.25	2.00
DBBT01078 Glauce Will of Steel R	1.25	2.00
DBBT01079 Sahrg Renowned Bladesmith R	1.25	2.00
DBBT01080 Spleenshooter Goblin U	.40	.60
DBBT01081 Ravenwing Mistress of the Hunt U	.40	.60
DBBT01082 Harpy Embermage U	.40	.60
DBBT01083 Goblin Madcap U	.40	.60
DBBT01084 Bothered Orcwife C	.15	.25
DBBT01085 Runic Battlesmith C	.15	.25
DBBT01086 Wandering Orc C	.15	.25
DBBT01087 Boneclub Giant C	.15	.25
DBBT01088 Hidden Blade C	.15	.25
DBBT01089 Bladedance Rogue C	.15	.25
DBBT01090 Harypy Huntress C	.15	.25
DBBT01091 Goblin Toestabber C	.15	.25
DBBT01092 Goblin made Avalanche R	1.25	2.00
DBBT01093 Torch U	.40	.60
DBBT01094 Pyroblast U	.40	.60
DBBT01095 Earthcrack C	.15	.25
DBBT01096 Explosive Counter C	.15	.25
DBBT01097 Shadowcrest the Subjugator RR	7.00	10.00
DBBT01098 Albert Plague Spreader RR	10.00	15.00
DBBT01099 Ajeel of the Dark Reins R	1.25	2.00
DBBT01100 Midnight Visitor R	1.25	2.00
DBBT01101 Sinister Festering Stringman R	1.25	2.00
DBBT01102 Succubus of Deception U	.40	.60
DBBT01103 Bloodly Baroness U	.40	.60
DBBT01104 Flesh Shredder U	.40	.60
DBBT01105 Baltheos Devourer of Hope U	.40	.60
DBBT01106 Cavalier Nosferatu U	.40	.60
DBBT01107 Soul of the Lost C	.15	.25
DBBT01108 Death Metal Rotter C	.15	.25
DBBT01109 Grave Champion C	.15	.25
DBBT01110 Bass Wrecker C	.15	.25
DBBT01111 Liliths Charmer C	.15	.25
DBBT01112 Mindflayer Demon C	.15	.25
DBBT01113 Rattlebone Fighter C	.15	.25
DBBT01114 Wandering Apparition C	.15	.25
DBBT01115 Offering of Souls R	1.25	2.00
DBBT01116 Gluttony of Albert R	1.25	2.00
DBBT01117 Death and Decay R	1.25	2.00
DBBT01118 Death Trap U	.40	.60
DBBT01119 Adrastes Disdain C	.15	.25
DBBT01120 Despair C	.15	.25
DBBT01S01 Althaine Exemplar of Vashr SCR	80.00	120.00
DBBT01S02 Laelania Keeper of Vashr SCR	80.00	120.00
DBBT01S03 Linx Savant of Vashr SCR	80.00	120.00
DBBT01S04 Grousk Warmonger of Vashr SCR	80.00	120.00
DBBT01S05 Adraste Hellion of Vashr SCR	80.00	120.00

2017 Dragoborne Oath of Blood

COMPLETE SET (120)	130.00	200.00
BOOSTER BOX (20 PACKS)	65.00	80.00
BOOSTER PACK (8 CARDS)	4.00	6.00
RELEASED ON NOVEMBER 10, 2017		
DBBT02001 Yvel Lord of the Skies RR	8.00	12.00
DBBT02002 Sigrun the Holy Hand RR	8.00	12.00
DBBT02003 Vainglory Incarnate R	1.25	2.00
DBBT02004 Bacchus Patron of the Blossom R	1.25	2.00
DBBT02005 Wings of the Sunscale R	1.25	2.00
DBBT02006 Elis Aegis of Light R	1.25	2.00
DBBT02007 Intimidating Guardian R	1.25	2.00
DBBT02008 Arsenal of Justice U	.30	.50
DBBT02009 Mechanized Rubblewalker U	.30	.50
DBBT02010 Highelf Shieldmage U	.30	.50
DBBT02011 Exalted Duelist U	.30	.50
DBBT02012 Battleworn Colossus C	.15	.25
DBBT02013 Exalted Runemage C	.15	.25
DBBT02014 Highborn Sage C	.15	.25
DBBT02015 Fleetfoot Highborn C	.15	.25
DBBT02016 Highborn Exemplar C	.15	.25
DBBT02017 Chromegear Zealot C	.15	.25
DBBT02018 Dignified Brawler C	.15	.25
DBBT02019 Sunscale Warden C	.15	.25
DBBT02020 Angelicas Guard C	.15	.25
DBBT02021 United in Purpose R	1.25	2.00
DBBT02022 Shining Decree U	.30	.50
DBBT02023 Righteous End U	.30	.50
DBBT02024 Supreme Judgement C	1.25	2.00
DBBT02025 Gravos Lord of the Loam RR	8.00	12.00
DBBT02026 Amarok Lone Avenger RR	8.00	12.00
DBBT02027 Star of Divinity R	1.25	2.00
DBBT02028 Thalessa Partisan of Life R	1.25	2.00
DBBT02029 Axel Little Fang R	1.25	2.00
DBBT02030 Voice of the Living World R	1.25	2.00
DBBT02031 Shadow Hunter R	1.25	2.00
DBBT02032 Gallant Chevalier U	.30	.50
DBBT02033 Gifted Geomancer U	.30	.50
DBBT02034 Resolute Paladin U	.30	.50
DBBT02035 Elder Horn Druid U	.30	.50
DBBT02036 Holt Stalker C	.15	.25
DBBT02037 Crusher of Armies C	.15	.25
DBBT02038 Swampland Berserker C	.15	.25
DBBT02039 Brutal Grizzly C	.15	.25
DBBT02040 Devastator Boar C	.15	.25
DBBT02041 Maiden of the Grove C	.15	.25
DBBT02042 Augmented Sniper C	.15	.25
DBBT02043 Canopy Scout C	.15	.25
DBBT02044 Fairy Ally C	.15	.25
DBBT02045 Ferocity Unleashed R	1.25	2.00
DBBT02046 Supreme Foresight U	.30	.50
DBBT02047 Violent Gale U	.30	.50
DBBT02048 Sky and Earth C	1.25	2.00
DBBT02049 The End of Tides RR	8.00	12.00
DBBT02050 Ulrisc Lord of the Glacier RR	8.00	12.00
DBBT02051 Gorgoth the Devourer R	1.25	2.00
DBBT02052 The First Daughter R	1.25	2.00
DBBT02053 Amnat the Omniscient R	1.25	2.00
DBBT02054 Wavefinder Dragon R	1.25	2.00
DBBT02055 Mea Whimsical Caper R	1.25	2.00
DBBT02056 Merfolk Tinkerer R	1.25	2.00
DBBT02057 The Overseer U	.30	.50
DBBT02058 The Nightingale U	.30	.50
DBBT02059 The Quartermaster U	.30	.50
DBBT02060 Knightbane Manticore C	.15	.25
DBBT02061 Vessel of the End C	.15	.25
DBBT02062 The Healer C	.15	.25
DBBT02063 Tidechaser Rogue C	.15	.25
DBBT02064 The Gardener C	.15	.25
DBBT02065 The Potioneer C	.15	.25
DBBT02066 Tidechaser Cannoneer C	.15	.25
DBBT02067 The Experiment C	.15	.25
DBBT02068 Tidechaser Grunt C	.15	.25
DBBT02069 Supreme Ambition U	.30	.50
DBBT02070 Augment U	.30	.50
DBBT02071 Sabotage U	.30	.50
DBBT02072 Seafarers End C	.15	.25
DBBT02073 Eldrun Lord of the Blaze RR	8.00	12.00
DBBT02074 Hrist of the Infernal Blades RR	8.00	12.00
DBBT02075 Zavzas Mechanized Fury R	1.25	2.00
DBBT02076 Ancient Skylord R	1.25	2.00
DBBT02077 Halvast the Searing Horn R	1.25	2.00
DBBT02078 Darkforge Battlesmith R	1.25	2.00

DBBT02079 Master of the Harvest R	1.25	2.00
DBBT02080 Reeda Scrappers Ally R	1.25	2.00
DBBT02081 Taurissian Arsonist U	.30	.50
DBBT02082 Darkforge Wallsmasher U	.30	.50
DBBT02083 Grimblade Fighter U	.30	.50
DBBT02084 Shrouded Stalker U	.30	.50
DBBT02085 Fervent Battlesmith U	.30	.50
DBBT02086 Earthbreaker Titan C	.15	.25
DBBT02087 Castlebreaker C	.15	.25
DBBT02088 Daredevil Brat C	.15	.25
DBBT02089 Industrialized Battlesmith C	.15	.25
DBBT02090 Goblin Stalker C	.15	.25
DBBT02091 Ingenious Saboteurs C	.15	.25
DBBT02092 Skiving Troop C	.15	.25
DBBT02093 Sudden Eruption U	.30	.50
DBBT02094 Raid C	.15	.25
DBBT02095 Supreme Brutality C	.15	.25
DBBT02096 Titanic Foce C	.15	.25
DBBT02097 Sennes Lord of the Rampage RR	8.00	12.00
DBBT02098 Kaine the Bane of Humans RR	8.00	12.00
DBBT02099 Dark Diviner R	1.25	2.00
DBBT02100 Necros the Unending R	1.25	2.00
DBBT02101 Ichorback Whelp R	1.25	2.00
DBBT02102 Dark Puppeteer R	1.25	2.00
DBBT02103 Esseria the Cruel R	1.25	2.00
DBBT02104 Augmented Hellbound U	.30	.50
DBBT02105 Augmented Cragborn U	.30	.50
DBBT02106 Remorseful Succubus U	.30	.50
DBBT02107 Fender Bender U	.30	.50
DBBT02108 Vivacious Vampire C	.15	.25
DBBT02109 Dread Gravekeeper C	.15	.25
DBBT02110 Grotesque Cragborn C	.15	.25
DBBT02111 Ravenous Gargoyle C	.15	.25
DBBT02112 Augmented Stonegazer C	.15	.25
DBBT02113 Bewitching Stonegazer C	.15	.25
DBBT02114 Cragborn Proudstalker C	.15	.25
DBBT02115 Risen Crusader C	.15	.25
DBBT02116 Forgotten Acolyte C	.15	.25
DBBT02117 Drag into the Abyss R	1.25	2.00
DBBT02118 Devour U	.30	.50
DBBT02119 Supreme Power U	.30	.50
DBBT02120 Back from the Grave C	.15	.25

2017 Dragoborne Promos

DBPR0001 Izarco Tvash Born of Magma	1.50	2.50
DBPR0002 Elven Farstriker	1.25	2.00
DBPR0003 Baltheos Devourer of Hope	4.00	6.00
DBPR0004 The Keeper	3.00	5.00
DBPR0005 Alluring Temptress	2.00	3.00
DBPR0006 Merchant of Scrolls	2.00	3.00
DBPR0007 Aldienne Verdant Protector	1.00	1.50
DBPR0008 Helkion the Desolator	1.50	2.50
DBPR0009 Helkion the Desolator	4.00	6.00
DBPR0010 Deftarm Scout		
DBPR0011 Deftarm Scout		
DBPR0019 Goblin Toestabber		

2018 Dragoborne Gears of Apocalypse

BOOSTER BOX (20 PACKS)		
BOOSTER PACK (8 CARDS)		
RELEASED ON MARCH 2, 2018		
DBBT03001 Hyperion, Sovereign Avatar RR	10.00	15.00
DBBT03002 Chromegear Liberator R	3.00	5.00
DBBT03003 Giorno, Eyes of Fate R	.60	1.00
DBBT03004 Althea, Hand of Althaine R	1.50	2.50
DBBT03005 Guardian Whelp R	.60	1.00
DBBT03006 Amadeo, Cloudrunner Sneak R	.60	1.00
DBBT03007 Serene Prelate U	.30	.50
DBBT03008 Angel of Divine Balance U	.30	.50
DBBT03009 Darkbane Acolyte U	.30	.50
DBBT03010 Unstoppable Charioteer U	.30	.50
DBBT03011 Besieged Colossus C	.60	1.00
DBBT03012 Lightglobe Angel C	.15	.25
DBBT03013 Fortified Golem C	.15	.25
DBBT03014 Gearbreaker Angel C	.15	.25
DBBT03015 Solemn Dragonsblade C	.15	.25
DBBT03016 Darkbane Priest C	.15	.25
DBBT03017 Determined Neophyte C	.15	.25
DBBT03018 Mending Angel C	.15	.25
DBBT03019 Sanctuary Squire C	.15	.25
DBBT03020 Against All Odds RR	5.00	8.00
DBBT03021 Divergent Ideals R	1.00	1.50
DBBT03022 Nourish the Brood U	.30	.50
DBBT03023 Answered Prayer U	.30	.50
DBBT03024 Spur to Action C	.15	.25
DBBT03025 Lady Luthiel Feanis RR	5.00	8.00
DBBT03026 Erymanthias, Rankbreaker RR	3.00	5.00
DBBT03027 Granvel, Arboreal Protector R	1.00	1.50
DBBT03028 Amarie, Tanglewood Enchantress R	1.50	2.50
DBBT03029 Cirdin, Repurposed R	1.00	1.50
DBBT03030 Axel, Hardened Resolve R	1.00	1.50
DBBT03031 Valiant Knight-Errant R	1.00	1.50
DBBT03032 Obnoxious Liege-lord U	.30	.50
DBBT03033 Favored Scholar U	.30	.50
DBBT03034 Galewind Mage U	.30	.50
DBBT03035 Nimble Outrider U	.50	.75
DBBT03036 Spry Lookout U	.30	.50
DBBT03037 Chromegear Paladin C	.60	1.00
DBBT03038 Backline Raider C	.15	.25
DBBT03039 Bovine Sentinel C	.15	.25
DBBT03040 Grassland Skirmisher C	.15	.25
DBBT03041 Dauntless Lancer C	.15	.25
DBBT03042 Thornwood Gunner C	.15	.25
DBBT03043 Fairy Enchantress C	.15	.25
DBBT03044 Warfront Disenchanter C	.15	.25
DBBT03045 Erudite Archer C	.15	.25
DBBT03046 Rallying Call R	1.00	1.50
DBBT03047 Earthen Fury U	.30	.50
DBBT03048 Heated Confrontation C	.15	.25
DBBT03049 Kronus, Fist of the Rune Lord RR	5.00	8.00
DBBT03050 Celedros, Deepswell Champion RR	5.00	8.00
DBBT03051 Infini, Ancient Automaton R	1.00	1.50
DBBT03052 Reconstructed Sphinx R	.60	1.00
DBBT03053 Menacing Manticore R	.60	1.00
DBBT03054 Nephthyria, Solemn Jailor R	1.25	2.00
DBBT03055 Windchaser Griffin R	1.00	1.50
DBBT03056 Deepswell Merchant U	1.25	2.00
DBBT03057 The Slasher U	.30	.50
DBBT03058 Explosives Expert U	.30	.50
DBBT03059 Swordtail Griffin U	.30	.50
DBBT03060 Deepswell Cavekeeper C	.15	.25
DBBT03061 Duskreach Manticore C	.15	.25
DBBT03062 Bellicose Brinemage C	.15	.25
DBBT03063 Boarding Swashbuckler C	.15	.25
DBBT03064 Mobile Resupplier C	.15	.25
DBBT03065 Hypnotic Dreamweaver C	.15	.25
DBBT03066 The Exterminator C	.15	.25
DBBT03067 Press-ganged Sailor C	.15	.25
DBBT03068 Restrain R	1.00	1.50
DBBT03069 Manipulate U	.30	.50
DBBT03070 Battle Preparations U	.30	.50
DBBT03071 Reinforce Equipment C	.50	.75
DBBT03072 Unexpected Discovery C	.15	.25
DBBT03073 Tawosret, Ancient Ruler RR	2.50	4.00
DBBT03074 Galeras, Moltenscale Whelp RR	6.00	10.00
DBBT03075 Phoenixfire Dragon R	1.00	1.50
DBBT03076 Battlefield Looter R	.60	1.00
DBBT03077 Bugo the Craven R	1.00	1.50
DBBT03078 Devout of Darkness R	.75	1.25
DBBT03079 Commander Krict R	1.00	1.50
DBBT03080 Energetic Farmhand U	.75	1.25
DBBT03081 Smith of Resonating Steel U	.30	.50
DBBT03082 Magma Elemental U	1.25	2.00
DBBT03083 Spare Part Collector U	.30	.50
DBBT03084 Wild Gunner U	.30	.50
DBBT03085 Dragonsmiter Giant C	.15	.25
DBBT03086 Furious Battlechief C	.15	.25
DBBT03087 Bouldershot Giant C	.15	.25
DBBT03088 Dwarven Panzer C	.15	.25
DBBT03089 Elderly Gunner C	.60	1.00
DBBT03090 Outland Wanderer C	.15	.25
DBBT03091 Reckless Raider C	.15	.25
DBBT03092 Goblin Darkcaller C	.15	.25
DBBT03093 Flamefeather Shot R	1.50	2.50
DBBT03094 Furious Outburst U	.30	.50
DBBT03095 Pellet Shot C	.15	.25
DBBT03096 Fortunate Encounter C	.15	.25
DBBT03097 Erigor, Putrid Behemoth RR	5.00	8.00
DBBT03098 Amorphous Skinchanger R	.60	1.00
DBBT03099 Agres, Defiler of Minds R	1.50	2.50
DBBT03100 Gretia the Beguiling R	1.00	1.50
DBBT03101 Nabries, Putrid Headsman R	2.00	3.00
DBBT03102 Stormcharged Brawler U	.30	.50
DBBT03103 Ghatano, Ancient One U	.30	.50
DBBT03104 Adraste's Guard U	.40	.60
DBBT03105 Doombringer Goblin U	.30	.50
DBBT03106 Hollow Bowman U	.30	.50
DBBT03107 Hellhound Legionnaire C	.15	.25
DBBT03108 Steelforged Cragborn C	.50	.75
DBBT03109 Entrancing Stoneweaver C	.15	.25
DBBT03110 Junkheap Gargoyle C	.60	1.00
DBBT03111 Banetalon Temptress C	.15	.25
DBBT03112 Mooncursed Hunter C	.15	.25
DBBT03113 Noxious Rotwhale C	.15	.25
DBBT03114 Seeker of Dark Truth C	.15	.25
DBBT03115 Raving Dead C	.15	.25
DBBT03116 Unholy Alliance RR	5.00	8.00
DBBT03117 Scorn R	1.00	1.50
DBBT03118 Mortal Wound R	.60	1.00
DBBT03119 Tempting Offer U	.60	1.00
DBBT03120 Altar of Dark Machinations C	.15	.25
DBBT03S01 The Citadel of Logres SCR		
DBBT03S02 The Haven of Tir na Nog SCR	40.00	60.00
DBBT03S03 The Ruins of Olous SCR		
DBBT03S04 The March of Tauris SCR		
DBBT03S05 The Burg of Niflheim SCR		

2018 Dragoborne Reckoning of Vashr

BOOSTER BOX (20 PACKS)		
BOOSTER PACK (8 CARDS)		
RELEASED ON OCTOBER 26, 2018		
DBBT05001 Lazarus, Commander of the Guard RR	10.00	15.00
DBBT05002 Angel of Judgement RR	12.00	20.00
DBBT05003 Wandering Colossus R	1.25	2.00
DBBT05004 Dragon of Divine Penance R	1.25	2.00
DBBT05005 Cardinal Brawler R	1.25	2.00
DBBT05006 Bloodclaw Skyguard U	1.25	2.00
DBBT05007 Flagbearer of Logres U	.50	.75
DBBT05008 Refurbished Battlesmith C	.15	.25
DBBT05009 Devoted Centaur C	.15	.25
DBBT05010 Thoughtful Scholar C	.15	.25
DBBT05011 Warden of the Sanctuary C	.15	.25
DBBT05012 Fearless Dragonrider C	.15	.25
DBBT05013 Only the Worthy R	2.50	4.00
DBBT05014 Faith's Requital U	.50	.75
DBBT05015 Angelica's Ward U	2.00	3.00
DBBT05016 Virtuous Light C	.15	.25
DBBT05017 Angel of Silence RR	10.00	15.00
DBBT05018 Darius, Nature's Majesty RR	15.00	25.00
DBBT05019 Dragon of Origins R	1.25	2.00
DBBT05020 Palas, the Radiant R	1.25	2.00
DBBT05021 Voracious Eater R	1.25	2.00
DBBT05022 Jamira, Woodland Keeper R	2.00	3.00
DBBT05023 Bringer of Serenity U	.75	1.25
DBBT05024 Mystical Transmuter U	.50	.75
DBBT05025 Sureshot Elf C	.15	.25
DBBT05026 Determined Sprite C	.15	.25
DBBT05027 Lightstream Angel C	.15	.25
DBBT05028 Tanglewood Fae C	.15	.25
DBBT05029 Mistcloaked Scout C	.15	.25
DBBT05030 Vicious Blow U	.50	.75
DBBT05031 Beck and Call U	.50	.75
DBBT05032 Entangling Path C	.15	.25
DBBT05033 Dragon of Omniscience RR	15.00	25.00
DBBT05034 Angel of Mystery RR	10.00	15.00
DBBT05035 Proteus, the Ancient Deep R	1.25	2.00
DBBT05036 Ubudugu, Questionable Mage R	1.25	2.00
DBBT05037 Enthralling Songstress U	1.25	2.00
DBBT05038 The Enchantress U	1.00	1.50
DBBT05039 Seeker of Truth C	.15	.25
DBBT05040 The Provocateur C	.15	.25
DBBT05041 Wavestrider C	.15	.25
DBBT05042 Combat Unit Prototype C	.15	.25
DBBT05043 Steelsaber Adept C	.15	.25
DBBT05044 Caught Unawares R	1.25	2.00
DBBT05045 Tempest Wave R	1.25	2.00
DBBT05046 Reboot U	.50	.75
DBBT05047 Devious Ploy U	.50	.75
DBBT05048 Siren Song C	.15	.25
DBBT05049 Dragon of Aggression RR	12.00	20.00
DBBT05050 Angel of Destruction RR	10.00	15.00
DBBT05051 Grakk, Apex Hunter R	1.25	2.00
DBBT05052 Doomchaser Dragon R	1.50	2.50
DBBT05053 Stonebreaker Goretops R	1.25	2.00
DBBT05054 Avatar of Anarchy U	1.50	2.50
DBBT05055 Wild Raptor U	.50	.75
DBBT05056 Careless Orc C	.15	.25
DBBT05057 Duskcliff Bandit C	.15	.25
DBBT05058 Goblin Weedwhacker C	.15	.25
DBBT05059 Savage Horticulturist C	.15	.25
DBBT05060 The Rankbreaker C	.15	.25
DBBT05061 War Lord's Challenge R	2.50	4.00
DBBT05062 Moment of Confusion U	.50	.75
DBBT05063 Strength and Cunning U	.50	.75
DBBT05064 Molten Breath C	.15	.25
DBBT05065 Baron Elliott, the Grand Mastermind RR	10.00	15.00
DBBT05066 Angel of Denial RR	10.00	15.00
DBBT05067 Daredevil Vampire R	1.25	2.00
DBBT05068 Dragon of Calamity R	2.50	4.00
DBBT05069 Captious Vampire R	2.00	3.00
DBBT05070 Shambling Spearman U	2.00	3.00
DBBT05071 Manipulator of Reflections U	1.50	2.50
DBBT05072 Adaptive Ooze C	.15	.25
DBBT05073 Contemptuous Vampire C	.15	.25
DBBT05074 Master of Progress C	.15	.25
DBBT05075 Mausoleum Horror C	.15	.25
DBBT05076 Overburdened Porter C	.15	.25
DBBT05077 Reawaken R	1.25	2.00
DBBT05078 Deathblossom U	2.00	3.00
DBBT05079 Shredding Burst U	.50	.75
DBBT05080 Without Remorse C	.15	.25

2018 Dragoborne Surge of Titans

BOOSTER BOX (20 PACKS)		
BOOSTER PACK (8 CARDS)		
RELEASED ON JULY 6, 2018		
DBBT04001 Lothien, Sunscale Punisher RR	12.00	20.00
DBBT04002 Lyssandra, Angel of Fervor RR	10.00	15.00
DBBT04003 Baldr, Faith's Champion R	1.25	2.00
DBBT04004 Guardian of the Meek R	1.25	2.00
DBBT04005 Lord Hector of the Holy Legion R	1.25	2.00
DBBT04006 Wary Lookout R	1.25	2.00
DBBT04007 Rousing Angel R	1.25	2.00
DBBT04008 Vardys, Hope Resonant U	.40	.60
DBBT04009 Augmented Responder U	.40	.60
DBBT04010 Signal Rider U	.40	.60
DBBT04011 Justice's Toll C	.15	.25
DBBT04012 Distressed Fighter C	.15	.25
DBBT04013 Fearless Dragonmage C	.15	.25
DBBT04014 Knight of the Sanctuary C	.15	.25
DBBT04015 Tanglewood Venator C	.15	.25
DBBT04016 Enervate C	.15	.25
DBBT04017 Dirge, the Corrupted RR		
DBBT04018 Scourgelord Turannos RR	12.00	20.00
DBBT04019 Astragalus, Broodlord R	5.00	8.00
DBBT04020 Bane, Venom's Lament R	1.25	2.00
DBBT04021 Medeina, Merciful Warden R	2.50	4.00
DBBT04022 Ridgetusk, Warfront Leader U	.40	.60
DBBT04023 Arbor Ranger U	.40	.60
DBBT04024 Sword of the Forest Spirits C	.15	.25
DBBT04025 Dragonling Caretaker C	.15	.25
DBBT04026 Tanglewood Wildspeaker C	.15	.25
DBBT04027 Worldspirit Angel C	.15	.25
DBBT04028 Snarling Raptors C	.15	.25
DBBT04029 Stand As One R	1.25	2.00
DBBT04030 Gaea Lord's Invocation U	.40	.60
DBBT04031 Ferocious Rebuke U	.40	.60
DBBT04032 Galvanize C	.15	.25
DBBT04033 Deus Ex Machina RR	12.00	20.00
DBBT04034 Khione of the Blizzard RR	15.00	25.00
DBBT04035 Borrhas, Winter's Grasp R	2.00	3.00
DBBT04036 Hyperstatic Serpent R	2.00	3.00
DBBT04037 Idle Whale-shark R	2.50	4.00
DBBT04038 Oricius, the Stormwinged R	2.00	3.00
DBBT04039 Captivating Technician U	.40	.60
DBBT04040 Rancorous Tidechaser U	.40	.60
DBBT04041 Linx's Windslicer C	1.25	2.00
DBBT04042 Agent of Advancement C	.15	.25
DBBT04043 Augmented Sprite C	1.25	2.00
DBBT04044 Fay Pilferer C	.15	.25
DBBT04045 Purifier Sprite C	.15	.25
DBBT04046 Masterful Strategem U	.40	.60
DBBT04047 Reroute U	.40	.60
DBBT04048 Paralyze C	.15	.25
DBBT04049 Scorian, the Deathless Flame RR	12.00	20.00
DBBT04050 Gurzil, Avatar of Fury RR	20.00	30.00
DBBT04051 Aerial Assault Unit, Ascraeus R	2.50	4.00
DBBT04052 Bloodtalon, Aerial Assault Leader R	2.50	4.00
DBBT04053 Randgriz, Angel of Ferocity R	3.00	5.00
DBBT04054 Flamewreathed Dragon R	1.25	2.00
DBBT04055 Hailfire Gunner U	.40	.60
DBBT04056 Angel Instigator U	.40	.60
DBBT04057 Goblin Gatecrasher C	.15	.25
DBBT04058 Furious Shrieker C	.15	.25
DBBT04059 Malevolent Darkcaller C	.15	.25
DBBT04060 Steelwing Glider C	.15	.25
DBBT04061 Goblin Eviscerator C	.15	.25
DBBT04062 Focused Assault U	.40	.60
DBBT04063 Fiery Demise U	.40	.60
DBBT04064 Goblinzooka C	.15	.25
DBBT04065 Xevios, the Thundering Night RR	10.00	15.00
DBBT04066 Enarach, the Scavenger RR	12.00	20.00
DBBT04067 Daemos, Herald of Ruin R	1.25	2.00
DBBT04068 Greenskinned Basher R	1.25	2.00
DBBT04069 Lachrande Gurn, the Grotesque R	1.25	2.00
DBBT04070 Olivaria, Death's Envoy R	2.00	3.00
DBBT04071 Tub Smasher R	1.25	2.00
DBBT04072 Rock Breaker U	.40	.60
DBBT04073 Cantankerous Patrician C	.15	.25
DBBT04074 Manipulator of Souls C	.15	.25
DBBT04075 Mob Assault C	.15	.25
DBBT04076 Mortified Axeman C	.15	.25
DBBT04077 Show Stopper C	.15	.25
DBBT04078 Soulsiphon U	.40	.60
DBBT04079 Albert's Gift U	.40	.60
DBBT04080 Grave Retribution C	.15	.25
DBBT04S01 The Skies of Justice SCR	1.25	2.00
DBBT04S02 The Tree of Life SCR	1.25	2.00
DBBT04S03 The Factories of War SCR	1.25	2.00
DBBT04S04 The Gates of Fury SCR	1.25	2.00
DBBT04S05 The Castle of Revelry SCR	1.25	2.00

2017 Dragoborne Trial Deck 1 Shadow Legion

COMPLETE SET (27) 20.00 35.00
TRIAL DECK (53 CARDS) 15.00 20.00
RELEASED ON AUGUST 4, 2017
DBTD01001 Bountiful Angel R Foil 1.50 2.50
DBTD01001 Bountiful Angel R Non Foil 3.00 5.00
DBTD01002 Sunscale Sage C .15 .25
DBTD01003 Goldleaf Hunter C .15 .25
DBTD01004 Althaines Blessing C .15 .25
DBTD01005 Shield of Logres C .15 .25
DBTD01006 Ravian Battlefield Shriker R Foil 1.50 2.50
DBTD01006 Ravian Battlefield Shriker R Non Foil 3.00 5.00
DBTD01007 Goblin Madcap U .40 .60
DBTD01008 Bladedance Rogue C .15 .25
DBTD01009 Goblin Toestabber C .15 .25
DBTD01010 Pyroblast U .40 .60
DBTD01011 Standard of Tauris C .15 .25
DBTD01012 Lady Valistra Bloodlines Tormented RR Foil 3.00 5.00
DBTD01012 Lady Valistra Bloodlines Tormented RR Non Foil 2.50 4.00
DBTD01013 Undying Executioner R Foil 1.25 2.00
DBTD01013 Undying Executioner R Non Foil 2.00 3.50
DBTD01014 Cavalier Nosferatu U .40 .60
DBTD01015 Crowd Surfer U .40 .60
DBTD01015 Crowd Surfer U Non Foil .40 .60
DBTD01016 Death Metal Rotter C .15 .25
DBTD01017 Carbuncle Imp C Foil .15 .25
DBTD01017 Carbuncle Imp C Non Foil .15 .25
DBTD01018 Wandering Apparition C .15 .25
DBTD01019 Death Trap U .40 .60
DBTD01020 Adrastes Disdain C .15 .25
DBTD01021 Curse of Niflheim C .15 .25

2017 Dragoborne Trial Deck 2 Mystical Hunters

COMPLETE SET (27) 15.00 25.00
TRIAL DECK (53 CARDS) 15.00 20.00
RELEASED ON AUGUST 4, 2017
DBTD02001 Axion Herald of Armies R 1.50 2.50
DBTD02001 Axion Herald of Armies R Non Foil 2.00 3.50
DBTD02002 Elegant Fencer R 1.50 2.50
DBTD02002 Elegant Fencer R Non Foil 2.00 3.50
DBTD02003 Earthen Guard Golem C .15 .25
DBTD02004 Logres Swiftblade C .15 .25
DBTD02005 Sunscale Ascetic C .15 .25
DBTD02006 Shield of Logres C .15 .25
DBTD02007 Remus Hunter Adept RR 3.00 5.00
DBTD02007 Remus Hunter Adept RR Non Foil 2.00 3.50
DBTD02008 Guardian of the Forest U .40 .60
DBTD02009 Kingslayer Bee U .40 .60
DBTD02009 Kingslayer Bee U Non Foil .40 .60
DBTD02010 Primeape Javelineer C .15 .25
DBTD02011 Tanglewood Menace C .15 .25
DBTD02012 Runemark of Tir na Nog C .15 .25
DBTD02013 Ambushing Tidechaster R .15 .25
DBTD02013 Ambushing Tidechaster R Non Foil .15 .25
DBTD02014 The Keeper U .40 .60
DBTD02015 The Ripper C .15 .25
DBTD02016 Frontier Explorer C .15 .25
DBTD02017 Hidden Arts Waters Edge Shuriken U .40 .60
DBTD02018 EMP U .40 .60
DBTD02019 Dismantle C .15 .25
DBTD02019 Dismantle C Non Foil .15 .25
DBTD02020 Hidden Arts Reverse Thunderstrike C .15 .25
DBTD02021 Insignia of Olous C .15 .25

2017 Dragoborne Trial Deck 3 Alpha Dominance

COMPLETE SET (27) 25.00 40.00
TRIAL DECK (53 CARDS) 15.00 20.00
RELEASED ON AUGUST 4, 2017
DBTD03001 Thornbark Walker U .40 .60
DBTD03001 Thornbark Walker U Non Foil .40 .60
DBTD03002 Elven Farstriker U .40 .60
DBTD03003 Primeape Javelineer C .15 .25
DBTD03004 Fleetwing Sprite C .15 .25
DBTD03005 Natures Touch U .40 .60
DBTD03006 Laelanias Call C .15 .25
DBTD03007 Runemark of Tir na Nog C .15 .25
DBTD03008 Dramph Tommar Kingpin R 1.50 2.50
DBTD03008 Dramph Tommar Kingpin R Non Foil 2.00 3.50
DBTD03009 Gillman Raider C .15 .25
DBTD03010 Rejuvenate U .40 .60
DBTD03011 All Guns Blazing C .15 .25
DBTD03012 Insignia of Olous C .15 .25
DBTD03013 Izarco Tvash Born of Magma RR 7.00 9.00
DBTD03013 Izarco Tvash Born of Magma RR Non Foil 4.00 6.00
DBTD03014 Stormfeather Screecher R 1.50 2.50
DBTD03014 Stormfeather Screecher R Non Foil 2.00 3.50
DBTD03015 Carefree Orc R Non Foil 2.00 3.50
DBTD03015 Carefree Orc R 1.50 2.50
DBTD03016 Wandering Orc C .15 .25
DBTD03017 Boneclub Giant C .15 .25
DBTD03018 Hidden Blade C .15 .25
DBTD03019 Highlands Rogue C .15 .25
DBTD03019 Highlands Rogue C Non Foil .15 .25
DBTD03020 Torch U .40 .60
DBTD03021 Standard of Tauris C .15 .25

2017 Dragoborne Trial Deck 4 Reapers Gift

DBTD04001 Knightbane Manticore C .15 .25
DBTD04002 The Servitor U .30 .50
DBTD04003 Tidechaser Rogue C .15 .25
DBTD04004 The Gardener C .15 .25
DBTD04005 Tidechaser Grunt C .15 .25
DBTD04006 Supreme Ambition U .30 .50
DBTD04007 Sabotage U .30 .50
DBTD04008 Insignia of Olous NR .15 .25
DBTD04009 Hilda of the Gearmagnus R Foil 1.25 2.00
DBTD04009 Hilda of the Gearmagnus R Non Foil 1.25 2.00
DBTD04010 Gearmagnus Saboteur R Foil 1.25 2.00
DBTD04010 Gearmagnus Saboteur R Non Foil 1.25 2.00
DBTD04011 Fervent Battlesmith U .30 .50
DBTD04012 Skiving Troop C .15 .25
DBTD04013 Titanic Force C .15 .25
DBTD04014 Standard of Tauris NR .15 .25
DBTD04015 Kazzakh the Hellbent RR Foil 3.00 5.00
DBTD04015 Kazzakh the Hellbent RR Non Foil 2.50 4.00
DBTD04016 Cursed eye Gargoyle R Foil 1.25 2.00
DBTD04016 Cursed eye Gargoyle R Non Foil 1.25 2.00
DBTD04017 Fender Bender U .30 .50
DBTD04018 Bewitching Stonegazer C .15 .25
DBTD04019 Merciless Punisher C .15 .25
DBTD04020 Curse of Niflheim NR .15 .25

2018 Dragoborne Trial Deck 5 Nature's Wrath

COMMON CARD
RELEASED ON MARCH 2, 2018
DBTD05001 Emissary of Flourishing
DBTD05002 Escutcheon Angel
DBTD05003 Darkbane Priest
DBTD05004 Sanctuary Squire
DBTD05005 Answered Prayer
DBTD05006 Incapacitate
DBTD05007 Shield of Logres
DBTD05008 Ghis, Unending Fury
DBTD05009 Threa, Blessed by Fairies
DBTD05010 Fearful Sprite
DBTD05011 Favored Scholar
DBTD05012 Nimble Outrider
DBTD05013 Chromegear Paladin
DBTD05014 Dauntless Lancer
DBTD05015 Untested Scout
DBTD05016 Erudite Archer
DBTD05017 Cleanse
DBTD05018 Runemark of Tir na Nog

Dragon Ball Z

2003 Dragon Ball Z Babidi Saga Android Movie

INSERTED IN THE BABIDI SAGA CARD PACKS.
M1 Android 13 5.00 10.00
M2 Android 13 5.00 10.00
M3 Super Android 13 6.00 12.00
M4 Android 15 4.00 8.00
M5 Android 15 4.00 8.00
M6 Android 15 5.00 8.00
M7 Android 14 8.00 12.00
M8 Super Android 13's Destruction Bomb 5.00 10.00
M9 Super Android 13's Ridge Hand 2.00 4.00
M10 Android 13's Prepared Stance 6.00 12.00
M11 Goku's Defense Drill 3.00 6.00
M12 Blue Android 15's Energy Ball 2.00 4.00
M13 Gohan's Braced Energy Beam 3.00 6.00
M14 Android 14's Power Kick 4.00 8.00
M15 Gohan 5.00 10.00
M16 Super Saiyan Goku 5.00 10.00
M17 Saiyan Power Stance 2.00 4.00
M18 Goku's Quick Save 2.00 4.00
M19 Straining Spirit Bomb 2.00 4.00
M20 Super Android 13's Physical Resistance 2.00 4.00
M21 Red Android 13's Rapid Blast 3.00 6.00
M22 Heroic Final Strike 2.00 4.00
M23 Super Saiyan Trunks 6.00 10.00
M24 Trunks Swordplay Drill 10.00 15.00
M25 Android 18's Drop Kick 3.00 6.00
M26 Android 16's Grapple 2.00 4.00
M27 Breakfall 2.00 4.00
M28 Android 17's Left Blast 2.00 4.00
M29 Android Tag Team 3.00 6.00
M30 Android 18's Palm Blast 3.00 6.00
M31 Android 19's Dodge 2.00 4.00
M32 Android 18's Left Hook 2.00 4.00
M33 Betrayal 2.00 4.00
M34 Injured Circuits 3.00 6.00

2003 Dragon Ball Z Babidi Saga Limited

COMPLETE SET (123) 150.00 225.00
BOOSTER BOX (36 PACKS) 45.00 80.00
BOOSTER PACK (12 CARDS) 3.00 4.00
*FOIL: .75X TO 1.5X BASIC CARDS
1 Android 18's Iron Defense C .25 .50
2 Black Chained Strike C .75 1.50
3 Black Palm Reversal C .25 .50
4 Black Personal Smack C .50 1.00
5 Black Power Catch C .25 .50
6 Black Quick Kick C .25 .50
7 Blue Cape Swing C .25 .50
8 Blue Reflexes C .25 .50
9 Blue Shifting Maneuver C .25 .50
10 Blue Speediness C .25 .50
11 Combo C .50 1.00
12 Entering the Arena C .25 .50
13 Hercule's Power Stance C .25 .50
14 Heroic Shoulder Slam C .25 .50
15 Majin Death Focus C .25 .50
16 Orange Crushing Kick C .25 .50
17 Orange Dodge C .25 .50
18 Orange Elbow Smash C .25 .50
19 Orange Firebreath C .25 .50
20 Orange Right Punch C .25 .50
21 Red Forearm Block C .25 .50
22 Red Resistance C .25 .50
23 Red Slide C .25 .50
24 Red Thrusting Beam C .25 .50
25 Red Uppercut C .25 .50
26 Saiyan Duck C .25 .50
27 Saiyan Energy Rapture C .25 .50
28 Saiyan Might C .25 .50
29 Saiyan Power Block C .25 .50
30 Saiyan Prepared Smash C .25 .50
31 Straining Counter Punch U .25 .50
32 Android 18's Kneeing Drill U .25 .50
33 Android 18's Pressure Routine U .25 .50
34 Android 18's Throwing Drill U .25 .50
35 Majin Babidi's Ship U .25 .50
36 Black Backstab U .25 .50
37 Black Conservation Drill U .25 .50
38 Black Face Crush U .25 .50
39 Black Pummeling Strike U .25 .50
40 Black Reverse Kick U .25 .50
41 Black Surprise Maneuver U .25 .50
42 Blue Destruction Beam U .25 .50
43 Blue Leverage U .25 .50
44 Blue Palm Sphere U .25 .50
45 Blue Prevention Drill U .25 .50
46 Blue Torso Strike U .25 .50
47 Majin Vegeta U 3.00 6.00
48 Chi-Chi's Cheering Drill U .50 1.00
49 Majin Dabura's Offensive Leverage U .50 1.00
50 Majin Dabura's Petrifying Spit U .50 1.00
51 Energy Empowerment Drill U .50 1.00
52 Energy Storage Drill U .50 1.00
53 Goku's Berserk U .50 1.00
54 Goku's Shifted Balance Drill U .50 1.00
55 Goten's Flying Drill U .50 1.00
56 Hercule, the World Champion U .50 1.00
57 Majin Vegeta, the Evil U 2.00 4.00
58 In the Grove U .50 1.00
59 Majin Buu's Egg Drill U .50 1.00
60 Majin Defense Drill U .50 1.00
61 Majin Lightning Hit U .50 1.00
62 Majin Power Deflection U .50 1.00
63 Majin Power Drill U .50 1.00
64 Majin Power Shift U .50 1.00
65 Majin Pui Pui U .50 1.00
66 Majin Pui Pui, the Henchman U .50 1.00
67 Majin Babidi U 3.00 6.00
68 Majin Vegeta's Frantic Attack U .50 1.00
69 Majin Vegeta's Powerful Drill U .50 1.00
70 Majin Yakon U 1.00 3.00
71 Majin Yakon, the Monster U 1.00 3.00
72 Majin Babidi, the Wizard U 1.00 3.00
73 Majin Dabura U .50 1.00
74 Orange Critical Hit U .50 1.00
75 Orange High Block U .50 1.00
76 Orange Body Kick U .50 1.00
77 Orange Surprise Reaction U 1.00 2.00
78 Orange Temple Strike U .50 1.00
79 Paper, Rock, Sissors U .50 1.00
80 Red Energy Outburst U .50 1.00
81 Majin Dabura, King of Fighting U .50 1.00
82 Red Air Kick U .50 1.00
83 Red Physical Drill U .50 1.00
84 Splash Damage Drill U .50 1.00
85 Surprising Strength Drill U .50 1.00
86 Red Tilted Punch U .50 1.00
87 Saiyan Chin Kick U .50 1.00
88 Saiyan Movement U .50 1.00
89 Saiyan Aura Blast U .50 1.00
90 Saiyan Suspended Blast U .50 1.00
91 Majin Vegeta's Rage U 3.00 6.00
92 Videl, Tournament Ready U 1.00 3.00
93 Android 18, the Mom R 2.00 4.00
94 Majin Babidi's Power Extension R 2.00 4.00
95 Black Pivot Kick R 1.00 3.00
96 Blue Energy Dive R 2.00 4.00
97 Daughter's Joy R 2.00 4.00
98 Gohan, Energized R 3.00 6.00
99 Goku, the Legendary R 5.00 10.00
100 Hercule's Close Save U 2.00 4.00
101 Heroic Force R 2.00 4.00
102 Initiative R 2.00 4.00
103 M R 1.00 3.00
104 Majin Pui Pui, the Flashy R 2.00 4.00
105 Majin Yakon, the Absorber R 1.00 3.00
106 Majin Babidi, the Evil Genius R 3.00 5.00
107 Orange Backstab R 1.00 3.00
108 Red Face Slap R 1.00 3.00
109 Majin Dabura, Meditated R 3.00 6.00
110 Majin Quickness R 4.00 8.00
111 Blue Trapped Strike R 2.00 4.00
112 Heroic Sword Catch R 2.00 4.00
113 Majin Vegeta, Uncontrollable R 4.00 8.00
114 Majin Vegeta, the Malicious R 4.00 8.00
115 Orange Rapid Attack R 3.00 6.00
116 Red Energy Rings R 1.00 3.00
117 Red Meditation Drill R 2.00 4.00
118 Red Sniping Shot R 3.00 6.00
119 Risky Maneuver R 3.00 6.00
120 Saiyan Headshot R 1.00 3.00
121 Supreme Kai, the Mentor R 2.00 4.00
122 Majin Vegeta UR 30.00 60.00
123 Majin Vegeta, the Malevolent UR 50.00 80.00

2003 Dragon Ball Z Buu Saga Broly Movie

INSERTED IN THE BUU SAGA CARD PACKS
1 Broly 12.00 20.00
2 Broly, the Enraged Saiyan 12.00 20.00
3 Broly, Super Saiyan 12.00 20.00
4 Broly, the Legendary Saiyan 20.00 30.00
5 Broly, the Unstoppable 8.00 15.00
6 Broly's Energy Burst 6.00 12.00
7 Broly's Evil Drill 4.00 8.00
8 Broly's Might 4.00 8.00
9 Broly's Overwhelming Attacks 4.00 8.00
10 Broly's Supreme Power 4.00 8.00
11 Saiyan Broly Smash 5.00 8.00
12 Saiyan Charge 3.00 6.00
13 Saiyan Cliff Slam 3.00 5.00
14 Saiyan Clothesline 2.00 4.00
15 Saiyan Enraged 3.00 6.00
16 Saiyan Setup 3.00 6.00
17 Saiyan Surprise 4.00 8.00
18 Battle of the Saiyans 2.00 4.00
19 Common Techniques 1.00 3.00
20 Goku's Instant Teleportation 2.00 4.00
21 Goku's Running Defense 3.00 6.00
22 Heroic Drill 3.00 6.00
23 Power Smack 1.00 3.00
24 Pure Defense 2.00 4.00
25 Krillin's Quick Kicks 2.00 4.00
26 Efficient Medicine .50 1.00
27 Master Roshi 2.00 4.00
28 Comet Kumolre 1.00 2.00
29 Mind Control Device 2.00 4.00
30 New Vegeta 3.00 6.00
31 Paragus 1.00 2.00
32 Heroic Double Team 2.00 4.00
33 Namekian Precise Aim Drill 2.00 4.00
34 Power Transfer .50 1.00
35 Saiyan Energy Toss 1.00 2.00
36 Vegeta's Energy Blast 3.00 6.00

2003 Dragon Ball Z Buu Saga Limited

COMPLETE SET (200) 225.00 275.00
BOOSTER BOX (36 PACKS) 50.00 75.00
BOOSTER PACK (12 CARDS) 3.00 4.00
*FOIL: .75X TO 1.5X BASIC CARDS

1 Alt. Dende Dragon Ball 1 C .50 1.00
2 Alt. Dende Dragon Ball 2 C .50 1.00
3 Black Arm Stretch C .25 .50
4 Black Head Crush C .25 .50
5 Black Floating Popo Defense C .25 .50
6 Black Diving Energy Drop C .25 .50
7 Blue Healing Ray C .25 .50
8 Blue High Block C .25 .50
9 Blue Slam C .25 .50
10 Carpet Attack Technique C .25 .50
11 Energy Gathering C .25 .50
12 Focused Sword Strike C .25 .50
13 Gohan's Sword Slash C .50 1.00
14 Gohan's Sword Sweep C .50 1.00
15 Gohan's Sword Thrust C .50 1.00
16 Goku's Power Attack C .25 .50
17 Heroic Quick Kick C .25 .50
18 Horrified C .25 .50
19 Krillin's Flight C .25 .50
20 Majin Demise C .25 .50
21 Majin Hand Clap C .25 .50
22 Orange Chin Break C .25 .50
23 Orange Energy Catch C .25 .50
24 Orange Energy Guard C .25 .50
25 Orange Spy Drill C .25 .50
26 Red Ball Throw C .25 .50
27 Red Fast Ball C .25 .50
28 Red Fist Catch C .25 .50
29 Red Passive Block C .25 .50
30 Red Power Block C .25 .50
31 Red Vigor Orb C .25 .50
32 Saiyan Energy Deflection C .25 .50
33 Saiyan Hand Swipe C .25 .50
34 Saiyan Snap Kick C .25 .50
35 Saiyan Direct Strike C .25 .50
36 Underwater Kick C .25 .50
37 West City U .50 1.00
38 Alt. Dende Dragon Ball 3 U .75 1.50
39 Alt. Dende Dragon Ball 4 U .75 1.50
40 Alt. Dende Dragon Ball 5 U .75 1.50
41 Bee U .75 1.50
42 Black Face Smash U .50 1.00
43 Black Gambit U .50 1.00
44 Black Gravity Drop U .50 1.00
45 Black Heroic Side Kick U .50 1.00
46 Black Overhead Smack U .50 1.00
47 Black Secret U .50 1.00
48 Black Snap Kick U .50 1.00
49 Black Weakness Drill U .50 1.00
50 Blue Devastation U .50 1.00
51 Blue Belly Kick U .50 1.00
52 Blue Draining Blast U .50 1.00
53 Blue Energy Cannon U .50 1.00
54 Blue Eye Gouge U .50 1.00
55 Blue Friendship U .50 1.00
56 Blue Gambit U .50 1.00
57 Blue Head Kick U .50 1.00
58 Blue Protective Bubble U 1.00 2.00
59 Blue Stomach Smash U .50 1.00
60 Blue Upward Block U .50 1.00
61 City Ablaze U .50 1.00
62 Cookie! U .75 1.50
63 Energy Ricochet U .50 1.00
64 Flight Training U 1.00 2.00
65 Gohan's Swordplay Drill U .50 1.00
66 Goku Swiftly Moving U .50 1.00
67 Goku's Escape U .50 1.00
68 Healing Magic U .50 1.00
69 Hercule's Underground Training Area U .50 1.00
70 Heroic Head Kick U .50 1.00
71 Heroic Kamehameha U .50 1.00
72 Krillin, Z Warrior U .50 1.00
73 Majin Buu's House U 1.00 2.00
74 Majin Buu's Invincibility U 1.00 2.00
75 Majin Buu's Magical Ray U .50 1.00
76 Majin Buu's Stomach Throw U .50 1.00
77 Majin Head Blow U 1.00 2.00
78 Namekian Gambit U .50 1.00
79 Namekian Shield Destruction U .75 1.50
80 Namekian Shuto U .50 1.00
81 Orange Car Push U .50 1.00
82 Orange Face Breaker U .50 1.00
83 Orange Face Crunch U .50 1.00
84 Orange Flight U .50 1.00
85 Orange Gambit U .50 1.00
86 Orange Hiding Drill U .50 1.00
87 Orange Mouth Shot U .50 1.00
88 Orange Right Hook U .50 1.00
89 Orange Sneak Attack U .50 1.00
90 Orange Trick Shot U .50 1.00
91 Physical Defense Drill U .50 1.00
92 Red Arm Swioe U .50 1.00
93 Red Force Punch U .50 1.00
94 Red Front Jab U .50 1.00
95 Red Gambit U .50 1.00
96 Red Joker Drill U .50 1.00
97 Red Overhead Crush U .50 1.00
98 Red Pressure Technique U .50 1.00
99 Red Spiked Blast U .50 1.00
100 Saiyan Assault U .50 1.00
101 Saiyan Energy Bomb U .50 1.00
102 Saiyan Concentrated Blast U .50 1.00
103 Saiyan Gambit U .50 1.00
104 Saiyan Hurricane Kick U .50 1.00
105 Saiyan Ki Ball U 1.00 2.00
106 Saiyan Onslaught U .50 1.00
107 Saiyan Overwhelming Drill U .50 1.00
108 Saiyan Power Beam U .50 1.00
109 Saiyan Strength Blast U .50 1.00
110 The Other World U .50 1.00
111 Vegeta's Sacrifice U 1.00 2.00
112 Whiplash U .50 1.50
113 Z Sword Plateau U .50 1.00
114 Majin Buu U 1.00 2.00
115 Korin R 1.00 3.00
116 Goku, Super Saiyan Ascended R 2.00 4.00
117 Kid Trunks R 1.00 2.00
118 Goten R 2.00 4.00
119 Majin Dabura D.O.A. R 2.00 4.00
120 Majin Babidi R 1.00 2.00
121 Alt. Dende Dragon Ball 6 R 1.00 2.00
122 Alt. Dende Dragon Ball 7 R 1.00 2.00
123 Black Front Punch R 1.00 3.00
124 Black Right Kick R 1.00 3.00
125 Black Royal Flush Drill R 1.00 3.00
126 Black Style Mastery R 3.00 5.00
127 Blue Electrical Gunk R 1.00 3.00
128 Blue Style Mastery R 3.00 5.00
129 Deal! R 1.00 3.00
130 Dende R 1.00 3.00
131 Freestyle Mastery R 2.00 4.00
132 Gotenks' Flight R 1.00 3.00
133 Hercule R 1.00 3.00
134 Losing Battle R 1.00 2.00
135 Majin Buu's Body Slam R 1.00 2.00
136 Majin Buu's Charged Attack R 1.00 2.00
137 Majin Buu's Flight R 3.00 5.00
138 Elder Kai Sensei R 4.00 6.00
139 Namekian Style Mastery R 2.00 4.00
140 Oolong R 1.00 3.00
141 Orange Destruction Ball R 1.00 2.00
142 Orange Style Mastery R 2.00 4.00
143 Red Cross Punch R 1.00 3.00
144 Red Style Mastery R 2.00 4.00
145 Saiyan Pressure Technique R 1.00 3.00
146 Saiyan Style Mastery R 5.00 10.00
147 Supreme Kai's Help R 2.00 4.00
148 Supreme Kai's Kid Push R 2.00 4.00
149 The Fusion Dance R 3.00 6.00
150 The Eternal Dragon Quest UR 25.00 50.00
151 Majin Buu UR 30.00 60.00
152 Goku, Super Saiyan 3 UR 50.00 80.00
153 Master Roshi Sensei UR 30.00 60.00
154 Gotenks (PC) HT 15.00 20.00
155 Gotenks, Super Saiyan (PC) HT 20.00 35.00
156 Goku 3.00 5.00
157 Goku, Super Saiyan 3.00 5.00
158 Goku, Super Saiyan 2 3.00 5.00
159 Goku HT 4.00 8.00
160 Goku GF 4.00 8.00
161 Gohan 3.00 5.00
162 Gohan 3.00 5.00
163 Gohan, Mystic Training 4.00 8.00
164 Gohan HT 4.00 8.00
165 Gohan GF 4.00 8.00
166 Kid Trunks 2.00 4.00
167 Kid Trunks 2.00 4.00
168 Kid Trunks 2.00 4.00
169 Kid Trunks HT 3.00 6.00
170 Kid Trunks GF 2.00 4.00
171 Goten 2.00 4.00
172 Goten 2.00 4.00
173 Goten 2.00 4.00
174 Goten HT 3.00 5.00
175 Goten GF 3.00 5.00
176 Piccolo 2.00 4.00
177 Piccolo 2.00 4.00
178 Piccolo 2.00 4.00
179 Piccolo HT 3.00 5.00
180 Majin Dabura 1.00 3.00
181 Majin Dabura 1.00 3.00
182 Majin Dabura 1.00 3.00
183 Majin Dabura HT 2.00 4.00
184 Majin Babidi 1.00 3.00
185 Majin Babidi 1.00 3.00
186 Majin Babidi 1.00 3.00
187 Majin Babidi HT 2.00 4.00
188 Majin Babidi GF 2.00 4.00
189 Majin Vegeta 3.00 5.00
190 Majin Vegeta 3.00 5.00
191 Majin Vegeta 3.00 5.00
192 Majin Vegeta HT 4.00 8.00
193 Majin Vegeta GF 4.00 8.00
194 Majin Buu 2.00 4.00
195 Majin Buu, the Rotund 2.00 4.00
196 Majin Buu, Pink People Eater 2.00 4.00
197 Majin Buu HT 4.00 8.00
198 Majin Buu GF 4.00 8.00
199 Majin Buu HT 4.00 8.00
200 Majin Buu GF 4.00 8.00

2003 Dragon Ball Z Fusion Saga Cosmic Anthology

INSERTED IN THE FUSION SAGA CARD PACKS
CA1 Supreme West Kai (Level 1) 8.00 16.00
CA2 Supreme West Kai (Level 2) 6.00 10.00
CA3 Supreme West Kai (Level 3) 5.00 10.00
CA4 Dr. Willow (Level 1) 3.00 6.00
CA5 Dr. Willow (Level 2) 3.00 6.00
CA6 Dr. Willow (Level 3) 3.00 6.00
CA7 Zarbon (Level 1) 2.00 4.00
CA8 Zarbon, Transformed (Level 2) 2.00 4.00
CA9 Zarbon, Fanatical (Level 3) 2.00 4.00
CA10 Turles, the Mysterious (Level 1) 4.00 8.00
CA11 Turles, the Proud (level 2) 2.00 4.00
CA12 Turles, the Saiyan Warrior (level 3) 2.00 4.00
CA13 Caterpy (Level 1) 3.00 6.00
CA14 Caterpy, the Grappler (Level 2) 2.00 4.00
CA15 Caterpy, the Tenacious (Level 3) .10 .25
CA16 Gohan's Immense Power 2.00 4.00
CA17 Goku's Power Pole 4.00 8.00
CA18 Energetic Fruit 2.00 4.00
CA19 Icarus 3.00 6.00
CA20 Tree of Might 3.00 6.00
CA21 Goku's Super Saiyan Catch 4.00 8.00
CA22 Knowledge Transfer 3.00 6.00
CA23 Piccolo's Power Blast 5.00 10.00
CA24 Cooler's Surprise Attack 3.00 6.00
CA25 Returning the Favor 1.00 3.00
CA26 Ingrain in the Membrane 1.00 3.00
CA27 Alt. Earth Dragon Ball 3 3.00 6.00
CA28 Goku's Quick Dodge 5.00 10.00
CA29 Energy Pouch 4.00 6.00
CA30 Master Roshi's Back Kick 3.00 6.00
CA31 Gohan's Energy Deflection 2.00 4.00
CA32 Makyo Star 3.00 6.00
CA33 Piccolo's Destruction Attack 2.00 4.00
CA34 Blue Style Mastery 3.00 6.00
CA35 A Hero's Heart is Strong 2.00 4.00
CA36 Black Scout Maneuver 3.00 6.00

2003 Dragon Ball Z Fusion Saga

COMPLETE SET (125) 150.00 200.00
BOOSTER BOX (36 PACKS) BOOSTER PACK (12 CARDS) 55.00 75.00
BOOSTER PACK (12 CARDS) 3.00 4.00
*FOIL: .75X TO 1.5X BASIC CARDS
1 Black High Kick C .25 .50
2 Black Jaw Hammer C .25 .50
3 Black Shift Kick C .25 .50
4 Blue Knockdown C .25 .50
5 Determination Drill C .25 .50
6 Dimension Scream C .25 .50
7 Hercule's Assault Drill C .25 .50
8 Hercule's Immunity C .25 .50
9 Heroic Effort C .25 .50
10 Majin Buu, Evil Buu (Level 1) C .50 1.00
11 Majin Buu's Heel Kick C .50 1.00
12 Majin Buu's Taunt C .25 .50
13 Nooooooooooooooo! C .25 .50
14 Orange Splitting Headache C .25 .50
15 Orange Strength C .25 .50
16 Paused Pose C .25 .50
17 Red Holding Drill C .25 .50
18 Red Striking Drill C .25 .50
19 Release C .25 .50
20 Saiyan Neutralization C .25 .50
21 Saiyan Power C .25 .50
22 Saiyan Spindletop Punch C .25 .50
23 Taking Cover C .25 .50
24 Tien's Surprise Technique C .25 .50
25 Underdog Drill C .25 .50
26 Underdog Drop Kick C .25 .50
27 Up Close and Personal C .25 .50
28 Vegito's Charged Blast C .25 .50
29 Vegito's Drop Kick C .25 .50
30 Vegito's Leg Catch C .25 .50
31 Vegito's Uppercut C .25 .50
32 Advanced Basics C .25 .50
33 Apocalyptic Battle U .30 .75
34 Black Big Bang U .30 .75
35 Black Dark Energy U .30 .75
36 Black Jawbreaker U .30 .75
37 Black Karmic Strike U .30 .75
38 Black Protection Orb U .30 .75
39 Black Restraint U .30 .75
40 Black Spin Kick U .30 .75
41 Blue Beatdown U .30 .75
42 Blue Energy Guard U .30 .75
43 Blue Forceful Explosion U .30 .75
44 Blue Gut Implosion U .30 .75
45 Blue Longshot U .30 .75
46 Blue Multi-Jab U .30 .75
47 Blue Stopping Technique U .30 .75
48 Blue Weaving U .30 .75
49 Boomstick U .30 .75
50 Devious Moves U .30 .75
51 Elder Kai's Sacrifice U .30 .75
52 Gohan's Forearm Block U .30 .75
53 Gohan's Left Energy Release U .30 .75
54 Heroic Charge U .30 .75
55 Intensity Drill U .30 .75
56 Krillin's Sacrifice U .50 1.00
57 Majin Buu, Piccolo Absorbed (Level 3) U 1.00 2.00
58 Majin Buu, Super Buu (Level 2) U 1.00 2.00
59 Majin Buu's Bicycle Kick U .30 .75
60 Majin Buu's Goo U .30 .75
61 Majin Buu's Stomach U .30 .75
62 Majin Static Orb U .30 .75
63 Namekian Finger Blast U .30 .75
64 Narrow Escape U .30 .75
65 Orange Energy Break U .30 .75
66 Orange Headshot U .30 .75
67 Orange Laser Drill U .30 .75
68 Orange Protection Drill U .30 .75
69 Orange Rush U .30 .75
70 Overcharge U .30 .75
71 Ready for Action U .30 .75
72 Red Cross Slash U .30 .75
73 Red Energy Slap U .30 .75
74 Red Physical Fortification U .30 .75
75 Red Rapid Deflection U .30 .75
76 Red Rapid Energy U .30 .75
77 Red Repeated Flares U .30 .75
78 Red Static Shot U .30 .75
79 Redeemed U .30 .75
80 Saiyan Blitz U .30 .75
81 Saiyan Elusion U .30 .75
82 Saiyan Explosion U .30 .75
83 Saiyan Gut Kick U .30 .75
84 Saiyan Neckbreaker U .30 .75
85 Saiyan Perfect Defense U .30 .75
86 Saiyan Push U .30 .75
87 Saiyan Two Gun Woo U .30 .75
88 Sneaky Tricks U .30 .75
89 Unlocked Potential U .30 .75
90 Vegeta, the Celestial (Level 1) U .75 1.50
91 Vegeta's Blurred Kick U .30 .75
92 Yamcha, the Amazing (Level 1) U .30 .75
93 Black Energy Swirl R 1.00 2.00
94 Black Uppercut R 2.00 4.00
95 Blue Backhand R 1.00 3.00
96 Blue Leapfrog Drill R 1.00 3.00
97 Blue Lunge R 2.00 4.00
98 Dazed R 1.00 3.00
99 Den-Goku (Level 1) R 3.00 5.00
100 Gohan, Earth's Protector (Level 5) R 3.00 6.00
101 Gohan, Mystic Empowered (Level 4) R 2.00 4.00
102 Gotenks' Kamikaze Ghost R 3.00 6.00
103 Hercule-Goku (Level 1) R 3.00 6.00
104 Last Ditch Effort R 1.00 3.00
105 Majin Buu, Gohan Absorbed (Level 5) R 3.00 6.00
106 Majin Buu, Gotenks Absorbed (Level 4) R 3.00 6.00
107 Majin Buu's Energy Spray R 1.00 3.00
108 Majin Buu's Kamikaze Ghost (Level 1) R 2.00 4.00
109 Majin Buu's New House R 1.00 3.00
110 Majin Planet Destruction Blast R 1.00 3.00
111 Majin Thrust R 2.00 4.00
112 Namekian Door Explosion R 1.00 3.00
113 Orange Reflex R 1.00 3.00
114 Potara Earrings R 4.00 8.00
115 Red Drop R 1.00 3.00

116 Red Leverage Blast R 1.00 3.00
117 Red Mouth Cannon R 1.00 3.00
118 Red Whiplash R 2.00 4.00
119 Saiyan Overcharged Blast R 1.00 3.00
120 Straining Power Move R 1.00 3.00
121 Transformation R 2.00 4.00
122 Vegeta's Fury R 1.00 3.00
123 Vegito (Level 1) R 6.00 12.00
124 Gotenks, Super Saiyan 3 (Level 3) UR 50.00 75.00
125 Vegito, Super Saiyan (Level 2) UR 50.00 75.00

2003 Dragon Ball Z Fusion Saga Preview Limited

COMPLETE SET (6) 8.00 15.00
INSERTS IN BABIDI SAGA BOOSTER PACKS
1 Gokus Flight .50 1.00
2 Majin Buus Choke Hold 1.00 2.00
3 Majin Bibidi the Mastermind 1.00 2.00
4 Peaceful Times U 1.00 2.00
5 The Power of Porunga R 3.00 6.00
6 Devastation Drill R 5.00 10.00

2003 Dragon Ball Z Goku Season

COMPLETE SET (11) 10.00 20.00

2003 Dragon Ball Z Kid Buu Preview Limited

INSERTS IN THE FUSION SAGA PACKS
1 Trunks Aerial Kick C .25 .50
2 Pans Right Blast C .25 .50
3 Uubs Energy Drill U .30 .75
4 Goku Young Again R .30 .75
5 The Power of Porunga R 1.00 3.00
6 The Might of Shenron R 1.00 2.50

2003 Dragon Ball Z Kid Buu Saga Bojack Unbound

INSERTED IN THE KID BUU SAGA PACKS
1 Ohhhhhhhhhhh YEAH! 3.00 6.00
2 Krillin's Smoothness Drill 2.00 4.00
3 Trunks, the Weaponmaster (Level 1) 8.00 12.00
4 Kogu (Level 1) 3.00 6.00
5 Zangya (Level 1) 5.00 10.00
6 Bujin (Level 1) 4.00 8.00
7 Bido (Level 1) 5.00 10.00
8 Bojack (Level 1) 8.00 16.00
9 Bojack, the Villianous (Level 2) 4.00 10.00
10 Bojack, the Notorious (Level 3) 8.00 16.00
11 The Sword of Trunks 6.00 10.00
12 Snake Way 1.00 3.00
13 Saiyan Outburst 1.00 3.00
14 Vegeta's Elbow Slam 5.00 10.00
15 Orange Brick Breaker 1.00 3.00
16 Red Plasma Catapult 2.00 4.00
17 Black Eradication 1.00 3.00
18 Master Roshi's Gawking Drill 2.00 4.00
19 Bulma and Chi-chi's Stare Off 1.00 3.00
20 Tien's Focused Beam 2.00 4.00
21 Trunks' Back Bash 2.00 4.00
22 Zangya's Leaping Rush Down 1.00 3.00
23 Kogu's Dual Strike 2.00 4.00
24 Trunks' Deadly Impact 2.00 4.00
25 Heroic Power Shot 1.00 3.00
26 Triple Torpedo 6.00 10.00
27 Bojack's Overhead Toss 3.00 6.00
28 Bojack's Left Palm Charge 3.00 6.00
29 Bojack's Defensive Shield 3.00 6.00
30 Zangya's Entrapping Strings 1.00 3.00
31 Gohan's Obliteration 2.00 4.00
32 Power Overwhelming 1.00 3.00
33 Bojack's Extreme Assailment 3.00 6.00
34 Bido's Charge 3.00 6.00
35 Bojack's Double-Palmed Blitz .50 1.00
36 Empowered Kamehameha 2.00 4.00

2003 Dragon Ball Z Kid Buu Saga Limited

COMPLETE SET (125) 120.00 200.00
BOOSTER BOX (36 PACKS) 45.00 65.00
BOOSTER PACK (12 CARDS) 2.50 3.50
*FOIL: 1X TO 2X BASIC CARDS
1 Alt. Namek Dragon Ball 1 C .25 .50
2 Alt. Namek Dragon Ball 2 C .25 .50
3 Alt. Namek Dragon Ball 3 C .25 .50
4 Black Exertion C .25 .50
5 Black Groveling Drill C .25 .50
6 Black Magic C .25 .50
7 Black Parry C .25 .50
8 Blue Biting Drill C .25 .50
9 Blue Double Blast C .25 .50
10 Blue Ki Build Up C .25 .50
11 Blue Sledgehammer C .25 .50
12 Blue Stretch Kick C .25 .50
13 Fierce Left Kick C .25 .50
14 Hercule's Realization C .25 .50
15 Heroic Power Detonation C .25 .50
16 Ki Catalyst C .25 .50
17 Majin Hair Pull C .25 .50
18 Namekian Remedy Drill C .25 .50
19 Orange Arm Break C .25 .50
20 Orange Discharge Drill C .25 .50
21 Orange Hand-clasp Drill C .25 .50
22 Overwhelmed C .25 .50
23 Pan's High Slap C .25 .50
24 Red Bullrush Drill C .25 .50
25 Red Kaio-Ken Drill C .25 .50
26 Red Puppy Slap C .25 .50
27 Saiyan Aggression Drill C .25 .50
28 Saiyan Dashing Kick C .25 .50
29 Saiyan Stop C .25 .50
30 Stupendous Strike C .25 .50
31 The Help of Earth C .25 .50
32 Alt. Namek Dragon Ball 4 U 1.00 3.00
33 Alt. Namek Dragon Ball 5 U 1.00 3.00
34 Android 18, the Mom (Level 1) U 1.00 3.00
35 Black Bicycle Kick U .30 .75
36 Black Buffer Block U .30 .75
37 Black Impressive Slap U .30 .75
38 Black Swivel Attack U .30 .75
39 Blue Alliance U .30 .75
40 Blue Deviation Drill U .30 .75
41 Blue Dikaio Blast U .30 .75
42 Blue Face Crunch U .30 .75
43 Blue Impulse U .30 .75
44 Blue Villains Drill U .30 .75
45 Bulma, the Wife (Level 1) U 1.00 3.00
46 CHARGE! U .30 .75
47 Chi-chi, the Grandmother (Level 1) U 1.00 3.00
48 Earth's Demise U .30 .75
49 Energy Lob U .30 .75
50 Goku's Setup Strike U 1.00 3.00
51 Goku's Supreme Kamehameha U 1.00 3.00
52 Hercule, the Everlasting World Champ (Level 1) U 2.00 4.00
53 Kid Trunks, Teenager (Level 1) U 3.00 6.00
54 Krillin's Destructo Disk U 1.00 3.00
55 Majin Buu, Kid Buu (Level 2) U 2.00 5.00
56 Majin Buu, Kid Buu (Level 3) U 2.00 5.00
57 Majin Buu's Backstabbing Kick U 1.00 3.00
58 Majin Dabura, the Redeemed (Level 1) U .30 .75
59 Billions of Mini Majin Buus U 2.00 5.00
60 Masterful Moves U .30 .75
61 Orange Carnage U 2.00 5.00
62 Orange Gutter Swipe U .30 .75
63 Orange Might U .30 .75
64 Orange Obliteration U .30 .75
65 Orange Vegeta's Assault U 1.00 3.00
66 Pan, Granddaughter of Goku (Level 1) U 1.00 3.00
67 Poof! U .30 .75
68 Power Headbutt U .30 .75
69 Provoke Drill U .30 .75
70 Quick Teleportation Drill U 2.00 5.00
71 Recoome's Vogue Drill U .30 .75
72 Red Aerial Force U .30 .75
73 Red Annihilation U .30 .75
74 Red Clap U .30 .75
75 Red Elbow Drop U .30 .75
76 Red Power Slam U .30 .75
77 Red Sword Cleave U .30 .75
78 Red Thunder Clap U .30 .75
79 Saiyan Brace U .30 .75
80 Saiyan Desperation U .30 .75
81 Saiyan Energy Bullet U .30 .75
82 Saiyan Jeering Drill U .30 .75
83 Saiyan Youth Bruise U .30 .75
84 Ultimate Defense U .30 .75
85 Ultra Uppercut U 2.00 5.00
86 Uub (Level 1) U 1.00 3.00
87 Uub, the Quick Learner (Level 2) U 1.00 3.00
88 Vegeta's Ill Temper U .30 .75
89 Videl, the Heroic (Level 1) U 1.00 3.00
90 Welcome Home Drill U .30 .75
91 Yajirobe, Retired (Level 1) U 1.00 3.00
92 Yamcha, the Single (Level 2) U 1.00 3.00
93 Alt. Namek Dragon Ball 6 R 3.00 5.00
94 Alt. Namek Dragon Ball 7 R 3.00 5.00
95 Black Chaos Detonation R 1.00 3.00
96 Black Disarray Drill R 1.00 3.00
97 Black Drop Kick R 1.00 3.00
98 Black Swerve R 1.00 3.00
99 Blue Reverse R 1.00 3.00
100 Fond Memories R 1.00 3.00
101 Gohan, the Bookworm (Level 1) R 3.00 6.00
102 Goku Sensei R 4.00 8.00
103 Hercule's "Dream Sequence" R 1.00 3.00
104 King Kai, Earth's Mentor (Level 1) R 1.00 3.00
105 Majin Buu, Kid Buu (Level 4) R 3.00 6.00
106 Majin Buu, Kid Buu (Level 5) R 4.00 8.00
107 Majin Buu's Prepped Crash R 1.00 3.00
108 Orange Head Mash R 1.00 3.00
109 Orange Intense Power R 1.00 3.00
110 Orange Ki Assailment R 1.00 3.00
111 Orange Massacre R 1.00 3.00
112 Red Axe Heel Kick R 1.00 3.00
113 Red Hunger Drill R 1.00 3.00
114 Red Left Bolt R 1.00 3.00
115 Red Voltage Missle R 1.00 3.00
116 Saiyan Acute Rapid Slam R 1.00 3.00
117 Saiyan Beef R 2.00 4.00
118 Saiyan Handstand R 1.00 3.00
119 Saiyan Lurch R 1.00 3.00
120 Intense Observation Drill R 2.00 4.00
121 Uub, Enraged (Level 3) R 2.00 4.00
122 Vegeta, Settled Down (Level 2) R 2.00 4.00
123 Vile Energy R 1.00 3.00
124 Earth's Spirit Bomb UR 25.00 40.00
125 Piccolo Sensei UR 25.00 40.00

2003 Dragon Ball Z Krillin Season

COMPLETE SET (11) 10.00 20.00
THESE CARDS WERE GIVEN OUT FOR
PARTICIPATING IN TOURNAMENT PLAY.
L2 Line Up 5.00 10.00
L2-0 Krillin Season 3.00 6.00
L2-1 Krillin's Help 2.00 4.00
L2-2 Below the Belt 2.00 4.00
L2-3 Krillin's Face Slap 1.00 3.00
L2-4 Clash of the Titans 4.00 8.00
L2-5 Feeding Frenzy 3.00 6.00
L2-6 Taunt 1.00 3.00
L2-7 I Want You! 3.00 6.00
L2-8 That Tickles! 3.00 6.00
L2-9 Krillin Season (Redemption Card) 10.00 20.00

2003 Dragon Ball Z Limited Edition Collector's Tin

PICCOLO TIN 20.00 25.00
SUPER SAIYAN GOHAN TIN 20.00 25.00
SUPER SAIYAN VEGETA TIN 25.00 30.00
SUPER SAIYAN 3 GOKU TIN 25.00 30.00
EACH TIN INCLUDES THE FOLLOWING:
9 EXCLUSIVE COLLECTOR'S CLUB CARDS
2 BABIDI SAGA BOOSTERS PACKS
2 BUU SAGA BOOSTERS PACKS
2 FUSION SAGA BOOSSTER PACKS
1 Majin Buu's Loogie 1.00 3.00
2 A New Addition 1.00 3.00
3 Jawbreaker Hailstorm 2.00 4.00
4 Pan's Victory 2.00 4.00

2003 Dragon Ball Z Majin Buu Season

COMPLETE SET (11) 15.00 25.00

2003 Dragon Ball Z Promos

F1 Grand Kai's Palace (DBGT Video) 8.00 12.00
F1 Grand Kai's Palace (DBGT Video) Gold 12.00 20.00
F2 Half Nelson (DBGT Video) 8.00 12.00
F2 Half Nelson (DBGT Video) Gold 12.00 20.00
F3 Orange Conversion Drill (DBGT Video) 5.00 10.00
F4 Black Stomach Breaker 5.00 10.00
J1 Fatherly Advice 25.00 45.00
J2 Blue Backbreaker 30.00 60.00
K4 Gohan's Power Hit 20.00 30.00
X1 Frieza's Anger Blast 10.00 20.00
X2 Vegeta's Energy Focus 10.00 20.00
X3 Motherly Rage 8.00 15.00
X4 Body Slam 8.00 15.00
X5 Piccolo's Power Ball 10.00 20.00
BR1 Broly, the Calm 2.00 4.00
BR2 Broly, Super Saiyan 2.00 4.00
BR3 Broly, Empowered 3.00 6.00
CB1 Power of Cookies! 10.00 15.00
CC2 Aerial Maneuver 12.00 25.00
CC3 Homework Time... 8.00 16.00
CC4 Impressive Power 8.00 16.00
CC5 Piccolo's Multiform 8.00 16.00
CC6 Majin Funny Face 8.00 16.00
CC7 Unbelievable Strength 3.00 5.00
CC8 Namekian Sky Beam 6.00 12.00
GS1 Startled 3.00 6.00
SJ1 Goku, the Mighty 4.00 8.00
SZ7 Let the Games Begin 8.00 15.00
TR1 Krillin's Overhead Smack 3.00 6.00
TR2 Vegeta's Energy Thrust 7.00 12.00
TR3 Trunks Sword Slice 15.00 30.00
GKI1 You're Invited 110.00 185.00
UR15 Vegeta, the Revitalized
UR16 Goku, the All Powerful
UR20 Goku, the Galaxy's Hero

2003 Dragon Ball Z Score Wrapper Redemption Promos

CR1 Mr. Popo 3.00 6.00
CR2 Mr. Popo 3.00 6.00
CR3 Mr. Popo 4.00 8.00
CR4 Rescuing Drill 3.00 6.00
CR5 Feverish 3.00 6.00
CR6 Frieza's Daunting Bombardment 2.00 4.00
CR7 Interview with the Green Guy 4.00 8.00
CR8 DELETED! 4.00 8.00
CR9 Gotenks' Potential 4.00 8.00
CR10 Nagging Drill 3.00 6.00
CR11 Goku's High Kick 4.00 8.00

2003 Dragon Ball Z Yamcha Season

COMPLETE SET (12) 12.00 20.00
THESE CARDS WERE GIVEN OUT FOR
PARTICIPATING IN TOURNAMENT PLAY.
L3 Team Work Kamehameha 1.00 2.00
L3 Team Work Kamehameha (Foil) 1.00 2.00
L3-0 Yamcha Season 1.00 2.00
L3-1 Defensive Stance 1.00 2.00
L3-2 Super Arm Cannon of Super Stuff! 1.00 2.00
L3-3 Huge Strength Maneuver 1.00 2.00
L3-4 Yamcha Practice Drill 1.00 2.00
L3-5 A Pair of Goodness 1.00 2.00
L3-6 Yamcha Vigor 1.00 2.00
L3-7 Out for a Walk 1.00 2.00
L3-8 Mean Squeeze 1.00 2.00
L3-9 Yamcha season you Win 1.00 2.00

2014 Dragon Ball Z

COMPLETE SET (314) 200.00 400.00
BOOSTER BOX (24 PACKS) 60.00 80.00
BOOSTER PACK (12 CARDS) 2.50 6.00
STARTER DECK (69 CARDS) 12.00 15.00
*FOIL: 1.2X TO 3X BASIC CARDS
COMPLETE RAINBOW SET (30) 30.00 80.00
RELEASED ON OCTOBER 17, 2014
C1 Namek Dragon Ball 1 C .10 .25
C2 Namek Dragon Ball 2 C .10 .25
C3 Namek Dragon Ball 3 C .10 .25
C4 Trunks - Inquisitive C .10 .25
C5 Trunks - Resolved C .10 .25
C6 Captain Ginyu - Leader C .10 .25
C7 Captain Ginyu - Energized C .10 .25
C8 Chaozu - Resurrected C .10 .25
C9 Tenshinhan - Returned C .10 .25
C10 Guldo - Ginyu Force C .10 .25
C11 Recoome - Ginyu Force C .10 .25
C12 Nappa - Space Traveler C .10 .25
C13 Black Erasing Drill C .10 .25
C14 Black Concussive Blast C .10 .25
C15 Black Corruption C .10 .25
C16 Black Hug Maneuver C .10 .25
C17 Black Knee Catch C .10 .25
C18 Black Lunge C .10 .25
C19 Black Punishment C .10 .25
C20 Blue Battle Readiness C .10 .25
C21 Blue Trick C .10 .25
C22 Blue Battle Drill C .10 .25
C23 Blue Biting Drill C .10 .25
C24 Blue Defensive Effect C .10 .25
C25 Blue Defensive Flight C .10 .25
C26 Blue Draining Blast C .10 .25
C27 Blue Head Knock C .10 .25
C28 Blue Reverse C .10 .25
C29 Namekian Chop C .10 .25
C30 Namekian Double Strike C .10 .25
C31 Namekian Dragon Blast C .10 .25
C32 Namekian Energy Toss C .10 .25
C33 Namekian Maximum Will C .10 .25
C34 Namekian Onslaught C .10 .25
C35 Namekian Right Throw C .10 .25
C36 Orange Aura Drill C .10 .25
C37 Orange Joint Restraint Drill C .10 .25
C38 Orange Defensive Blast C .10 .25
C39 Orange Distracting Beam C .10 .25
C40 Orange Energy Absorption C .10 .25
C41 Orange Precise Shot C .10 .25
C42 Orange Refocus C .10 .25
C43 Orange Revenge C .10 .25
C44 Red Hunting Drill C .10 .25
C45 Red Back Kick C .10 .25
C46 Red Double Strike C .10 .25
C47 Red Duck C .10 .25
C48 Red Flares C .10 .25
C49 Red Shattering Leap C .10 .25
C50 Red Shoulder Grab C .10 .25
C51 Saiyan Cheap Shot C .10 .25

Card	Low	High
C52 Saiyan Energy Focus C	.10	.25
C53 Saiyan Clothesline C	.10	.25
C54 Saiyan Energy Toss C	.10	.25
C55 Saiyan Foot Stomp C	.10	.25
C56 Saiyan Pinpoint Blast C	.10	.25
C57 Saiyan Scouting C	.10	.25
C58 Saiyan Supreme Block C	.10	.25
C59 Saiyan Uppercut C	.10	.25
C60 It's Over 9,000! C	.10	.25
U61 Namek Dragon Ball 4 U	.20	.50
U62 Namek Dragon Ball 5 U	.20	.50
U63 Namek Dragon Ball 6 U	.20	.50
U64 Trunks - Energy Charged U	.20	.50
U65 Trunks - Young Super Saiyan U	.20	.50
U66 Captain Ginyu - Body Change U	.20	.50
U67 Captain Ginyu - Frog U	.20	.50
U68 Bulma - Genius U	.20	.50
U69 ChiChi - Armed and Dangerous U	.20	.50
U70 Yamcha - Action Ready U	.20	.50
U71 Burter - Ginyu Force U	.20	.50
U72 Jiece - Ginyu Force U	.20	.50
U73 Black Searching Technique U	.20	.50
U74 Black Adaptation U	.20	.50
U75 Black Barrage U	.20	.50
U76 Black Delay U	.20	.50
U77 Black Swerve U	.20	.50
U78 Black Swirl U	.20	.50
U79 Blue Blockade U	.20	.50
U80 Blue Betrayal U	.20	.50
U81 Blue Farewell U	.20	.50
U82 Blue Lunar Ray U	.20	.50
U83 Blue Shifting Maneuver U	.20	.50
U84 Namekian Wish U	.20	.50
U85 Namekian Finger Lasers U	.20	.50
U86 Namekian Flinch U	.20	.50
U87 Namekian Hybrid Defense U	.20	.50
U88 Namekian Targeted Strike U	.20	.50
U89 Namekian Zone Pressure U	.20	.50
U90 Orange Empowered Drill U	.20	.50
U91 Orange Energy Phasing Drill U	.20	.50
U92 Orange Escape U	.20	.50
U93 Orange Inspection U	.20	.50
U94 Orange Offensive Strike U	.20	.50
U95 Orange Overhead Smash U	.20	.50
U96 Red Despair Drill U	.20	.50
U97 Red Escape U	.20	.50
U98 Red Jump Kick U	.20	.50
U99 Red Lightning Slash U	.20	.50
U100 Red Power Punch U	.20	.50
U101 Red Shielded Strike U	.20	.50
U102 Saiyan Domination U	.20	.50
U103 Saiyan Gut Kick U	.20	.50
U104 Saiyan Multi-blast U	.20	.50
U105 Saiyan Surprise U	.20	.50
U106 Saiyan Wrist Block U	.20	.50
U107 Visiting The Past U	.20	.50
U108 Battle Pausing U	.20	.50
U109 Blinding Energy Move U	.20	.50
U110 Devastating Blow U	.20	.50
U111 Empowered Flying Kick U	.20	.50
U112 Enraged Blast U	.20	.50
U113 Overpowering Attack U	.20	.50
U114 Quickness Drill U	.20	.50
U115 Frieza's Captive Strike U	.20	.50
U116 Gohan's Power Punch U	.20	.50
U117 Goku's Kaio-Ken U	.20	.50
U118 Krillin's Solar Flare U	.20	.50
U119 Piccolo's Weighted Clothing U	.20	.50
U120 Vegeta's Anger U	.20	.50
R121 Namek Dragon Ball 7 R	2.00	5.00
R122 Black Devious Mastery R	.75	2.00
R123 Black Mischievous Drill R	.75	2.00
R124 Black Disorienting Blow R	.75	2.00
R125 Black Reflection R	.75	2.00
R126 Black Scout Maneuver R	.75	2.00
R127 Blue Protective Mastery R	.75	2.00
R128 Blue Lunge R	1.00	2.50
R129 Blue Terror R	.75	2.00
R130 Blue Trapped Strike R	.75	2.00
R131 Namekian Knowledge Mastery R	.75	2.00
R132 Namekian Dragon Clan R	.75	2.00
R133 Namekian Overtime R	.75	2.00
R134 Namekian Palm Shots R	.75	2.00
R135 Namekian Planned Attack R	.75	2.00
R136 Orange Adaptive Mastery R	.75	2.00
R137 Orange Focusing Drill R	.75	2.00
R138 Orange Searching Maneuver R	.75	2.00
R139 Orange Uppercut R	.75	2.00
R140 Red Enraged Mastery R	.75	2.00
R141 Red Forward Stance Drill R	1.00	2.50
R142 Red Heel Kick R	.75	2.00
R143 Red Left Bolt R	.75	2.00
R144 Red Observation R	.75	2.00
R145 Saiyan Empowered Mastery R	.75	2.00
R146 Saiyan Acute Rapid Slam R	.75	2.00
R147 Saiyan Elbow Drop R	.75	2.00
R148 Saiyan Power Up R	.75	2.00
R149 Dragon Radar R	.75	2.00
R150 Confrontation R	2.00	5.00
R151 Stare Down R	2.00	5.00
R152 Time Is A Warrior's Tool R	3.00	8.00
R153 Captain Ginyu's Body Switch R	1.50	4.00
R154 Frieza's Supernova R	1.50	4.00
R155 Gohan's Masenko R	.75	2.00
R156 Goku's Kamehameha R	1.50	4.00
R157 Krillin's Destructo Disk R	1.50	4.00
R158 Piccolo's Special Beam Cannon R	.75	2.00
R159 Trunks' Sword Slash R	.75	2.00
R160 Vegeta's Galick Gun R	.75	2.00
UR161 Heroic Plan UR	20.00	40.00
UR162 Villainous Visage UR	40.00	70.00
UR163 Heroic Energy Sphere UR	100.00	120.00
UR164 Villainous Energy Sphere UR	100.00	120.00
S1 Vegeta – Prince of Saiyans	.60	1.50
S2 Vegeta - Villainous	.60	1.50
S3 Vegeta - Empowered	.60	1.50
S4 Vegeta - Renewed	.60	1.50
S5 Goku - Protector of Earth	.60	1.50
S6 Goku - Kaio-Ken Enhanced	.60	1.50
S7 Goku - Energy Gatherer	.60	1.50
S8 Goku - Super Saiyan	.60	1.50
S9 Gohan - Resilient Child	.60	1.50
S10 Gohan - Young Warrior	.60	1.50
S11 Gohan - Determined	.60	1.50
S12 Gohan - Armored	.60	1.50
S13 Krillin - Ready	.60	1.50
S14 Krillin - Energetic	.60	1.50
S15 Krillin - Ready For Battle	.60	1.50
S16 Krillin - Enraged	.60	1.50
S17 Frieza - Tyrant	.60	1.50
S18 Frieza - Transformed	.60	1.50
S19 Frieza - Galactic Conquerer	.60	1.50
S20 Frieza - Revived	.60	1.50
S21 Piccolo - Stoic	.60	1.50
S22 Piccolo - Combat Stance	.60	1.50
S23 Piccolo - Unleashed	.60	1.50
S24 Piccolo - Fused	.60	1.50
S25 Saiyan Empowered Mastery	.75	2.00
S26 Orange Adaptive Mastery	.60	1.50
S27 Red Enraged Mastery	.60	1.50
S28 Black Devious Mastery	.60	1.50
S29 Blue Protective Mastery	.60	1.50
S30 Namekian Knowledge Mastery	.60	1.50
S31 Black Power Up	.60	1.50
S32 Blue Stretch Kick	.60	1.50
S33 Namekian Concentration	.60	1.50
S34 Orange Energy Gathering	.60	1.50
S35 Red Burning Rage	.60	1.50
S36 Saiyan Offensive Rush	.60	1.50
S37 Black Targeting Drill	.60	1.50
S38 Blue Mental Drill	.60	1.50
S39 Namekian Combat Drill	.60	1.50
S40 Orange Devouring Drill	.60	1.50
S41 Orange Energy Dan Drill	.60	1.50
S42 Orange Steady Drill	.60	1.50
S43 Red Tactical Drill	.60	1.50
S44 Saiyan Retaliation Drill	.60	1.50
S45 Black Command	.60	1.50
S46 Blue Reprimand	.60	1.50
S47 Namekian Silencing	.60	1.50
S48 Orange Excavation	.60	1.50
S49 Red Blazing Aura	.60	1.50
S50 Saiyan Prelude	.60	1.50
S51 Black Lightning Storm	.60	1.50
S52 Black Capture	.60	1.50
S53 Blue Arm Blast	.60	1.50
S54 Blue Energy Overload	.60	1.50
S55 Namekian Overhead Blast	.60	1.50
S56 Namekian Focused Beams	.60	1.50
S57 Orange Palm Blasts	.60	1.50
S58 Orange Rage	.60	1.50
S59 Red Heating Beams	.60	1.50
S60 Red Energy Blast	.60	1.50
S61 Red Energy Outburst	.60	1.50
S62 Saiyan Triangle Beams	.60	1.50
S63 Saiyan Energy Rupture	.60	1.50
S64 Black Swipe	.60	1.50
S65 Blue Guard	.60	1.50
S66 Blue Avoidance	.60	1.50
S67 Namekian Crossed Guard	.60	1.50
S68 Orange Energy Evasion	.60	1.50
S69 Red Energy Defensive Stance	.60	1.50
S70 Saiyan Focus	.60	1.50
S71 Black Defensive Burst	.60	1.50
S72 Black Entanglement	.60	1.50
S73 Black Side Thrust	.60	1.50
S74 Blue Torpedo	.60	1.50
S75 Blue Round Throw	.60	1.50
S76 Namekian Crushing Slam	.60	1.50
S77 Namekian Elbow Strike	.60	1.50
S78 Orange Truck Lift	.60	1.50
S79 Red Lifting Kick	.60	1.50
S80 Red Power Lift	.60	1.50
S81 Saiyan Direct Strike	.60	1.50
S82 Saiyan Flying Tackle	.60	1.50
S83 Saiyan Left Kick	.60	1.50
S84 Saiyan Sabotage	.60	1.50
S85 Black Finger Block	.60	1.50
S86 Blue Fist Catch	.60	1.50
S87 Blue Wrist Block	.60	1.50
S88 Namekian Knee Block	.60	1.50
S89 Namekian Narrow Escape	.60	1.50
S90 Red Catch	.60	1.50
S91 Blue Ki Build Up	.60	1.50
S92 Namekian Fusion	.60	1.50
S93 Orange Celebration	.60	1.50
S94 Red Blaze	.60	1.50
S95 Saiyan Enraged	.60	1.50
S96 Black Smoothness Drill	.60	1.50
S97 Blue Positioning Drill	.60	1.50
S98 Namekian Heritage Drill	.60	1.50
S99 Orange Burning Aura Drill	.60	1.50
S100 Orange Guardian Drill	.60	1.50
S101 Orange Hiding Drill	.60	1.50
S102 Red Intimidation Drill	.60	1.50
S103 Saiyan Analysis Drill	.60	1.50
S104 Black Taunt	.60	1.50
S105 Blue Rest	.60	1.50
S106 Namekian Regeneration	.60	1.50
S107 Orange Destruction	.60	1.50
S108 Red Burning Stance	.60	1.50
S109 Saiyan Preparation	.60	1.50
S110 Black Energy Toss	.60	1.50
S111 Black Interceptor Barrage	.60	1.50
S112 Black Energy Web	.60	1.50
S113 Blue Neck Beam	.60	1.50
S114 Namekian Double Palm Burst	.60	1.50
S115 Namekian Sudden Blast	.60	1.50
S116 Orange Power Point	.60	1.50
S117 Orange Stare Down	.60	1.50
S118 Red Frenzied Blasts	.60	1.50
S119 Red Surrounded Beams	.60	1.50
S120 Red Static Shot	.60	1.50
S121 Saiyan Diving Burst	.60	1.50
S122 Saiyan Straight Shot	.60	1.50
S123 Black Speedy Dodge	.60	1.50
S124 Blue Defensive Stance	.60	1.50
S125 Blue Narrow Escape	.60	1.50
S126 Namekian Stance	.60	1.50
S127 Namekian Energy Guard	.60	1.50
S128 Orange Energy Catch	.60	1.50
S129 Red Energy Shield	.60	1.50
S130 Saiyan Energy Deflection	.60	1.50
S131 Black Flying Kick	.60	1.50
S132 Black Left Kick	.60	1.50
S133 Black Jab	.60	1.50
S134 Black Strike	.60	1.50
S135 Blue Fist Smash	.60	1.50
S136 Namekian Pound	.60	1.50
S137 Namekian Side Kick	.60	1.50
S138 Orange Launcher	.60	1.50
S139 Red Right Cross	.60	1.50
S140 Red Power Rush	.60	1.50
S141 Saiyan Face Stomp	.60	1.50
S142 Saiyan Light Jab	.60	1.50
S143 Blue Crouch	.60	1.50
S144 Blue Swift Block	.60	1.50
S145 Namekian Forceful Block	.60	1.50
S146 Orange Cover Up	.60	1.50
S147 Orange Quick Dodge	.60	1.50
S148 Red Blocking Hand	.60	1.50
S149 Saiyan Arm Catch	.60	1.50
S150 Saiyan Lightning Dodge	.60	1.50

2014 Dragon Ball Z Rainbow

Card	Low	High
COMPLETE SET (30)	30.00	80.00
S1 Vegeta – Prince of Saiyans	1.25	3.00
S2 Vegeta - Villainous	1.25	3.00
S3 Vegeta - Empowered	4.00	10.00
S4 Vegeta - Renewed	5.00	12.00
S5 Goku - Protector of Earth	3.00	8.00
S6 Goku - Kaio-Ken Enhanced	1.25	3.00
S7 Goku - Energy Gatherer	1.25	3.00
S8 Goku - Super Saiyan	6.00	15.00
S9 Gohan - Resilient Child	2.50	6.00
S10 Gohan - Young Warrior	2.50	6.00
S11 Gohan - Determined	2.50	6.00
S12 Gohan - Armored	1.25	3.00
S13 Krillin - Ready	3.00	8.00
S14 Krillin - Energetic	1.25	3.00
S15 Krillin - Ready For Battle	1.25	3.00
S16 Krillin - Enraged	1.25	3.00
S17 Frieza - Tyrant	1.25	3.00
S18 Frieza - Transformed	1.25	3.00
S19 Frieza - Galactic Conquerer	5.00	12.00
S20 Frieza - Revived	1.25	3.00
S21 Piccolo - Stoic	4.00	10.00
S22 Piccolo - Combat Stance	2.50	6.00
S23 Piccolo - Unleashed	3.00	8.00
S24 Piccolo - Fused	4.00	10.00
S25 Saiyan Empowered Mastery	1.25	3.00
S26 Orange Adaptive Mastery	1.25	3.00
S27 Red Enraged Mastery	1.25	3.00
S28 Black Devious Mastery	1.25	3.00
S29 Blue Protective Mastery	1.25	3.00
S30 Namekian Knowledge Mastery	1.25	3.00

2014 Dragon Ball Z Promos

Card	Low	High
P6 Piccolo - Stoic	8.00	20.00
P7 Goku's Kamehameha	1.00	2.50
P8 Time Is A Warrior's Tool	6.00	15.00
P9 Vegeta's Galick Gun	1.25	3.00
P10 Confrontation	4.00	10.00
P11 Trunks' Sword Slash	1.25	3.00
P12 Stare Down	8.00	20.00
P13 Frieza - Tyrant	8.00	20.00
P14 Gohan's Masenko	2.00	5.00
P15 Frieza's Supernova	1.50	4.00
P16 Black Scout Maneuver	5.00	12.00
P17 Piccolo's Special Beam Cannon	.75	2.00
P18 Blue Terror	3.00	8.00
P19 Captain Ginyu's Body Switch	1.50	4.00
P20 Saiyan Power Up	4.00	10.00
P21 Krillin's Destructo Disk	3.00	8.00

2014 Dragon Ball Z SDCC Promos

Card	Low	High
EXCLUSIVE TO SAN DIEGO COMIC CON		
P1 Vegeta Prince Of Saiyans	2.00	5.00
P2 Goku Protector Of Earth	2.00	5.00
P3 Gohan Resilient Child	2.00	5.00
P4 Krillin Ready	8.00	20.00
P5 Goku Super Saiyan God	60.00	100.00

2015 Dragon Ball Z Heroes and Villains

Card	Low	High
COMPLETE SET (142)	60.00	120.00
BOOSTER BOX (24 PACKS)	60.00	80.00
BOOSTER PACK (12 CARDS)	2.00	3.00
*FOIL: 1.2X TO 3X BASIC CARDS		
RELEASED ON MARCH 6, 2015		
C1 Nail - Watchful C	.10	.25
C2 Nail - Protector C	.10	.25
C3 Nappa - Rested C	.10	.25
C4 Nappa - Smirking C	.10	.25
C5 Raditz - True Saiyan C	.10	.25
C6 Raditz - Confident C	.10	.25
C7 Tenshinhan - Patient C	.10	.25
C8 Tenshinhan - Stubborn C	.10	.25
C9 Captain Ginyu - Aggressive C	.10	.25
C10 Dodoria - Lackey C	.10	.25
C11 Frieza - Mastermind C	.10	.25
C12 Gohan - Trained C	.10	.25
C13 Krillin - Supportive C	.10	.25
C14 Zarbon - Loyal Servant C	.10	.25
C15 Black Radiating Drill C	.10	.25
C16 Black Barrier Destruction C	.10	.25
C17 Black Evasion C	.10	.25
C18 Black Fist Lock C	.10	.25
C19 Black Overpowering Attack C	.10	.25
C20 Black Chomp C	.10	.25
C21 Black Refusal C	.10	.25
C22 Black Hair Trap C	.10	.25
C23 Blue Lifting Drill C	.10	.25
C24 Blue Cover Up C	.10	.25
C25 Blue Fear C	.10	.25
C26 Blue Bat Attack C	.10	.25
C27 Blue Determined Attack C	.10	.25
C28 Blue Hand Blast C	.10	.25
C29 Blue Glare C	.10	.25
C30 Namekian Self-training C	.10	.25
C31 Namekian Forearm Block C	.10	.25
C32 Namekian Chin Grab C	.10	.25
C33 Namekian Lift C	.10	.25
C34 Namekian Short Kick C	.10	.25
C35 Namekian Energy Beams C	.10	.25

Card	Low	High
C36 Namekian Quick Shot C	.10	.25
C37 Orange Driving Drill C	.10	.25
C38 Orange Torching Drill C	.10	.25
C39 Orange Calming Drill C	.25	.25
C40 Orange Crashing Drill C	.25	.25
C41 Orange Energy Bubble C	.25	.25
C42 Orange Nudge C	.25	.25
C43 Orange Double Palm Beam C	.25	.25
C44 Red Destiny C	.25	.25
C45 Red Emergency C	.25	.25
C46 Red Containment C	.25	.25
C47 Red Sacrifice C	.25	.25
C48 Red Restraint C	.25	.25
C49 Red Knee Lift C	.25	.25
C50 Red Leap C	.25	.25
C51 Saiyan Protection Drill C	.25	.25
C52 Saiyan Strength Test C	.25	.25
C53 Saiyan Drive By C	.25	.25
C54 Saiyan Blocking Technique C	.25	.25
C55 Saiyan Hand Swipe C	.25	.25
C56 Saiyan Driving Punch C	.25	.25
C57 Saiyan Charged Fist C	.25	.25
C58 Captain Ginyu's Pain C	.25	.25
C59 Energetic Left Blast C	.25	.25
C60 Combination Drill C	.25	.25
U61 Nail - Unflinching U	.20	.50
U62 Nail - Combat Ready U	.20	.50
U63 Nappa - Overconfident U	.20	.50
U64 Nappa - Enraged U	.20	.50
U65 Raditz - Angered U	.20	.50
U66 Raditz - Triumphant U	.20	.50
U67 Tenshinhan - Prepared U	.20	.50
U68 Tenshinhan - Smug U	.20	.50
U69 Goku - Thoughtful U	.20	.50
U70 Piccolo - Waiting U	.20	.50
U71 Trunks - Bashful U	.20	.50
U72 Vegeta - Impatient U	.20	.50
U73 Black Viewing Drill U	.20	.50
U74 Black Foreshadowing U	.20	.50
U75 Black Upward Dodge U	.20	.50
U76 Black Overhead Burst U	.20	.50
U77 Blue Joy Ride U	.20	.50
U78 Blue Flinch U	.20	.50
U79 Blue Leverage U	.20	.50
U80 Blue Face Crunch U	.20	.50
U81 Namekian Shocking Drill U	.20	.50
U82 Namekian Hurried Quest U	.20	.50
U83 Namekian Patient Block U	.20	.50
U84 Namekian Jump Kick U	.20	.50
U85 Orange Catch U	.20	.50
U86 Orange Charged Kick U	.20	.50
U87 Orange Saving Kick U	.20	.50
U88 Orange Elbow U	.20	.50
U89 Red City Destruction U	.20	.50
U90 Red Palm Strike U	.20	.50
U91 Red Stomach Dive U	.20	.50
U92 Red Club U	.20	.50
U93 Saiyan Unleashing Drill U	.20	.50
U94 Saiyan Rescue U	.20	.50
U95 Saiyan Spin Kick U	.20	.50
U96 Saiyan Right Blast U	.20	.50
U97 Raditz's Dirty Tactics U	.20	.50
U98 Nail's Heritage U	.20	.50
U99 Nappa's Confidence U	.20	.50
U100 Tenshinhan's Preparation U	.20	.50
R101 Black Declaration R	.75	2.00
R102 Black Head Charge R	.75	2.00
R103 Black Enraged Assault R	1.00	2.50
R104 Focused Assault R	1.25	3.00
R105 Black Counter Ball R	.75	2.00
R106 Blue Taming Technique R	.75	2.00
R107 Blue Overpowering Drill R	.75	2.00
R108 Blue Leaping Kick R	.75	2.00
R109 Blue Crush R	.75	2.00
R110 Blue Back Break R	.75	2.00
R111 Namekian Cut Off R	.75	2.00
R112 Namekian Backhand R	1.25	3.00
R113 Namekian Clash R	.75	2.00
R114 Namekian High Knee R	.75	2.00
R115 Namekian Confident Burst R	1.25	3.00
R116 Orange Possession Drill R	.75	2.00
R117 Orange Chasing Drill R	.75	2.00
R118 Orange Dodge R	.75	2.00
R119 Orange Hand Cannon R	.75	2.00
R120 Orange Mini Ball R	.75	2.00
R121 Red Embarrassing Drill R	.75	2.00
R122 Red Stop R	.75	2.00
R123 Red Controlled Attack R	.75	2.00
R124 Red Overpower R	.75	2.00
R125 Red Combined Blast R	.75	2.00
R126 Saiyan Intimidation R	.75	2.00
R127 Saiyan Outrage R	.75	2.00
R128 Saiyan Grab R	.75	2.00
R129 Saiyan Body Blow R	.75	2.00
R130 Saiyan Prepped Ball R	.75	2.00
R131 Isolation R	.75	2.00
R132 Withering Fire R	1.50	4.00
R133 Crushing Beam R	4.00	10.00
R134 Face Smash R	.75	2.00
R135 Wall Breaker R	5.00	12.00
R136 Nail's Dashing Attack R	.75	2.00
R137 Nappa's Energized Charge R	.75	2.00
R138 Raditz's Offensive Guard R	.75	2.00
R139 Tenshinhan's Draining Blast R	.75	2.00
R140 Trunks' Sword Stance R	.75	2.00
UR141 Heroic Assistance UR	8.00	20.00
UR142 Villainous Empowerment UR	8.00	20.00

2015 Dragon Ball Z Heroes and Villains Promos

Card	Low	High
P1 Saiyan Intimidation	1.25	3.00
P2 Isolation	4.00	10.00
P3 Orange Dodge	2.00	5.00
P4 Wall Breaker	8.00	20.00
P5 Red Overpower	1.25	3.00
P6 Withering Fire	6.00	15.00
P7 Blue Crush	1.25	3.00
P8 Black Enraged Assault	4.00	10.00
P9 Namekian Clash	4.00	10.00
P10 Saiyan Outrage	8.00	20.00
P11 Red Controlled Attack	4.00	10.00
P12 Orange Possession Drill	3.00	8.00
P13 Black Declaration	2.00	5.00
P14 Blue Overpowering Drill	3.00	8.00
P15 Saiyan Body Blow	1.50	4.00
P16 Red Stop	6.00	15.00
P17 Orange Hand Cannon	3.00	8.00

2015 Dragon Ball Z The Movie Collection

Card	Low	High
COMPLETE SET (142)	60.00	120.00
BOOSTER BOX (24 PACKS)	60.00	80.00
BOOSTER PACK (12 CARDS)	2.00	3.00
*FOIL: 1.2X TO 3X BASIC CARDS		
RELEASED ON JUNE 26, 2015		
C1 Kami - Guardian C	.10	.25
C2 Master Roshi - Scouted C	.10	.25
C3 Oolong - Concerned C	.10	.25
C4 Yajirobe - Bundled C	.10	.25
C5 Dr. Wheelo - Intelligent C	.10	.25
C6 Garlic Jr. - Confrontational C	.10	.25
C7 Lord Slug - Amazed C	.10	.25
C8 Turles - Fighter C	.10	.25
C9 Black Amusement Drill C	.10	.25
C10 Black Chopping Drill C	.10	.25
C11 Black Blinding Burst C	.10	.25
C12 Black Dense Ball C	.10	.25
C13 Black Dismissal C	.10	.25
C14 Black Flying Knee C	.10	.25
C15 Black Resistance C	.10	.25
C16 Black Stop C	.10	.25
C17 Blue Minions C	.10	.25
C18 Blue Escaping Drill C	.10	.25
C19 Blue Barrier C	.10	.25
C20 Blue Encircled Strike C	.10	.25
C21 Blue Floating Beam C	.10	.25
C22 Blue Rejection C	.10	.25
C23 Blue Safeguard C	.10	.25
C24 Blue Slash C	.10	.25
C25 Namekian Reinforced Drill C	.10	.25
C26 Namekian Choke C	.10	.25
C27 Namekian Clench C	.10	.25
C28 Namekian Mouth Beam C	.10	.25
C29 Namekian Reinforced Block C	.10	.25
C30 Namekian Reinforced Defense C	.10	.25
C31 Namekian Reinforced Charge C	.10	.25
C32 Namekian Reinforced Jab C	.10	.25
C33 Namekian Right Burst C	.10	.25
C34 Orange Disaster Drill C	.10	.25
C35 Orange Confidence C	.10	.25
C36 Orange Desperation C	.10	.25
C37 Orange Eruption C	.10	.25
C38 Orange Extension C	.10	.25
C39 Orange Flee C	.10	.25
C40 Orange Gathering C	.10	.25
C41 Orange Reactive Strike C	.10	.25
C42 Orange Smash C	.10	.25
C43 Red Maneuvering Drill C	.10	.25
C44 Red Saving Drill C	.10	.25
C45 Red Face Break C	.10	.25
C46 Red Hop C	.10	.25
C47 Red Resourceful Block C	.10	.25
C48 Red Right Punch C	.10	.25
C49 Red Slide C	.10	.25
C50 Red Vaulted Kick C	.10	.25
C51 Saiyan Hanging Out Drill C	.10	.25
C52 Saiyan Charge C	.10	.25
C53 Saiyan Counter Kick C	.10	.25
C54 Saiyan Enjoyment C	.10	.25
C55 Saiyan Evasion C	.10	.25
C56 Saiyan Headbutt C	.10	.25
C57 Saiyan Leaping Burst C	.10	.25
C58 Saiyan Overpowering Blast C	.10	.25
C59 Saiyan Swat C	.10	.25
C60 Lookout Drill C	.10	.25
U61 Dr. Wheelo - Big Brain U	.20	.50
U62 Dr. Wheelo - Scheming U	.20	.50
U63 Dr. Wheelo - Confined U	.20	.50
U64 Dr. Wheelo - Robotic U	.20	.50
U65 Garlic Jr. - Commanding U	.20	.50
U66 Garlic Jr. - Crazed U	.20	.50
U67 Garlic Jr. - Observant U	.20	.50
U68 Garlic Jr. - Transformed U	.20	.50
U69 Lord Slug - Aged U	.20	.50
U70 Lord Slug - Successful U	.20	.50
U71 Lord Slug - Renewed U	.20	.50
U72 Lord Slug - Huge U	.20	.50
U73 Turles - Shadowy U	.20	.50
U74 Turles - Watchful U	.20	.50
U75 Turles - Triumphant U	.20	.50
U76 Turles - Conquering U	.20	.50
U77 Black Chaos U	.20	.50
U78 Black Entrance U	.20	.50
U79 Black Back Strike U	.20	.50
U80 Black Teamwork U	.20	.50
U81 Black Tracing Beam U	.20	.50
U82 Blue Dominance U	.20	.50
U83 Blue Double Blast U	.20	.50
U84 Blue Intervention U	.20	.50
U85 Blue Surround U	.20	.50
U86 Blue Upward Barrage U	.20	.50
U87 Namekian Disturbance U	.20	.50
U88 Namekian Erasing Blast U	.20	.50
U89 Namekian Gut Punch U	.20	.50
U90 Orange Captivity Drill U	.20	.50
U91 Orange Commanding Drill U	.20	.50
U92 Orange Distracting Drill U	.20	.50
U93 Red Dazing Drill U	.20	.50
U94 Red Freezing Beam U	.20	.50
U95 Red Tandem Attack U	.20	.50
U96 Red Trailing Blast U	.20	.50
U97 Saiyan Freedom U	.20	.50
U98 Saiyan Aerial Attack U	.20	.50
U99 Saiyan Lunge U	.20	.50
U100 Saiyan Upward Kick U	.20	.50
R101 Black Chin Kick R	2.00	5.00
R102 Black Combo R	1.50	4.00
R103 Black Dash R	1.50	4.00
R104 Black Daze R	1.00	2.50
R105 Blue Observation Drill R	.75	2.00
R106 Blue Precarious Defense R	1.25	3.00
R107 Blue Surprise R	.75	2.00
R108 Blue Takedown R	1.50	4.00
R109 Namekian Growth R	1.25	3.00
R110 Namekian Knockback R	1.00	2.50
R111 Namekian Overwatch R	1.50	4.00
R112 Namekian Right Kick R	.75	2.00
R113 Namekian Surprise Attack R	.75	2.00
R114 Orange Spotlight R	1.25	3.00
R115 Orange Electricity R	1.25	3.00
R116 Orange Empowered Kick R	1.25	3.00
R117 Orange Uncontrolled Blast R	1.00	2.50
R118 Red Relaxation R	2.00	5.00
R119 Red Threatening Drill R	.75	2.00
R120 Red Mule Kick R	1.50	4.00
R121 Red Restriction R	1.25	3.00
R122 Red Retreat R	1.00	2.50
R123 Saiyan Arrival R	.75	2.00
R124 Saiyan Menace R	1.00	2.50
R125 Saiyan Backbreaker R	.75	3.00
R126 Saiyan Studying R	.75	2.00
R127 Dr. Wheelo's Revival R	1.00	2.50
R128 Dr. Wheelo's History R	1.25	3.00
R129 Garlic Jr.'s Dead Zone R	1.25	3.00
R130 Garlic Jr.'s Counter Blast R	1.25	3.00
R131 Lord Slug's Fist Slam R	1.00	2.50
R132 Lord Slug's Regeneration R	1.25	3.00
R133 Turles' Fruit R	1.25	3.00
R134 Turles' Energy Ring R	1.50	4.00
R135 Information Gathering R	1.00	2.50
R136 Tree of Might R	1.50	4.00
R137 Ensnared R	.75	2.00
R138 Flip Toss R	.75	2.00
R139 Pulverize R	3.00	8.00
R140 Sagacious Strike R	2.50	6.00
UR141 I'll Dig Your Gravel UR	90.00	125.00
UR142 True Power UR	8.00	20.00

2015 Dragon Ball Z Evolution

Card	Low	High
COMPLETE SET (174)	150.00	300.00
RELEASED ON OCTOBER 30, 2015		
C1 Black Pop-up C	.10	.25
C2 Black Inactivity Drill C	.10	.25
C3 Black Remembrance Drill C	.10	.25
C4 Black Explosion C	.10	.25
C5 Black Headbutt C	.10	.25
C6 Black Impediment C	.10	.25
C7 Black Protection C	.10	.25
C8 Black Request C	.10	.25
C9 Black Travelling Punch C	.10	.25
C10 Blue Cleanse C	.10	.25
C11 Blue Counter C	.10	.25
C12 Blue Energy Focus C	.10	.25
C13 Blue Eye Lasers C	.10	.25
C14 Blue Flight C	.10	.25
C15 Blue Knee C	.10	.25
C16 Blue Shopping C	.10	.25
C17 Blue Vehicle Destruction C	.10	.25
C18 Namekian Reinforced Catch C	.10	.25
C19 Namekian Assistance Drill C	.10	.25
C20 Namekian Cleansing Drill C	.10	.25
C21 Namekian Catch C	.10	.25
C22 Namekian Deflection C	.10	.25
C23 Namekian Door Destruction C	.10	.25
C24 Namekian Elbow Drop C	.10	.25
C25 Namekian Intervention C	.10	.25
C26 Namekian Wrist Strike C	.10	.25
C27 Orange Audience C	.10	.25
C28 Orange Intense Training Drill C	.10	.25
C29 Orange Investigation Drill C	.10	.25
C30 Orange Retrieval Drill C	.10	.25
C31 Orange Concealment C	.10	.25
C32 Orange Duck C	.10	.25
C33 Orange Fracture C	.10	.25
C34 Orange Ki Blast C	.10	.25
C35 Orange Left Punch C	.10	.25
C36 Orange Outburst C	.10	.25
C37 Orange Sideswipe C	.10	.25
C38 Orange Upward Strike C	.10	.25
C39 Red Examination Drill C	.10	.25
C40 Red Chop C	.10	.25
C41 Red Cross Block C	.10	.25
C42 Red Quick Jab C	.10	.25
C43 Red Right Knee C	.10	.25
C44 Red Robotic Blast C	.10	.25
C45 Red Smash C	.10	.25
C46 Red Vault C	.10	.25
C47 Saiyan Flight C	.10	.25
C48 Saiyan Inspection Drill C	.40	1.00
C49 Saiyan Blockade C	.10	.25
C50 Saiyan Concussive Blast C	.10	.25
C51 Saiyan Discovery C	.10	.25
C52 Saiyan Empowered Smash C	.10	.25
C53 Saiyan Energy Outburst C	.60	1.50
C54 Saiyan Lifting Kick C	.10	.25
C55 Saiyan Overhead Kick C	.10	.25
C56 Saiyan Palm Block C	.10	.25
C57 Saiyan Smack C	.10	.25
C58 Acquisition Drill C	.10	.25
C59 Android Superiority C	.10	.25
C60 Shoulder Slam C	.10	.25
U61 Black Signal U	.20	.50
U62 Black Empowered Elbow U	.20	.50
U63 Black Energy Discharge U	.20	.50
U64 Black Shoulder Charge U	.20	.50
U65 Black Tunneling Ball U	.20	.50
U66 Black Wilt U	.20	.50
U67 Blue Hush U	.20	.50
U68 Blue Awakening Drill U	.20	.50
U69 Blue Face Grab U	.20	.50
U70 Blue Palm Shot U	.20	.50
U71 Namekian Aerial Knee U	.20	.50
U72 Namekian Downward Blast U	.20	.50
U73 Namekian Energy Assault U	.20	.50
U74 Namekian Leaping Kick U	1.00	2.50
U75 Orange Scorn U	.20	.50
U76 Red Premonition U	.20	.50
U77 Red Chest Beam U	.20	.50
U78 Red Collision U	1.00	2.50
U79 Red Forceful Strike U	.20	.50
U80 Red Intense Blast U	.20	.50
U81 Saiyan Empowered Slide U	1.00	2.50
U82 Saiyan Fierce Kick U	.20	.50
U83 Saiyan Interruption U	.20	.50
U84 Saiyan Sword Strike U	.20	.50

Card	Low	High
U85 Android 19 - Stoic U	.20	.50
U86 Android 19 - Pondering U	.20	.50
U87 Android 19 - Unimpressed U	.20	.50
U88 Android 19 - Patient U	.20	.50
U89 Android 20 - Focused U	.20	.50
U90 Android 20 - Unfazed U	.20	.50
U91 Android 20 - Surprised U	.20	.50
U92 Android 20 - Master Planner U	.20	.50
U93 Vegeta - Unrelenting U	.20	.50
U94 Korin - Watching From Afar U	.20	.50
U95 Maron - Popular U	.20	.50
U96 Turtle - Protective U	.20	.50
U97 Android 17 - Beckoning U	.20	.50
U98 Android 18 - Smirking U	.20	.50
U99 Android 19 - Injured U	.20	.50
U99b Android 20 - Mastermind U	.20	.50
R101 Black Learning Drill R	.75	2.00
R102 Black Empowered Sword Slash R	1.00	2.50
R103 Blue Kiss R	.75	2.00
R104 Blue Entertaining Drill R	.75	2.00
R105 Blue Transportation Drill R	.75	2.00
R106 Blue Belly Bash R	.75	2.00
R107 Blue Wash R	.75	2.00
R108 Namekian Waiting R	.75	2.00
R109 Namekian Enhancement R	.75	2.00
R110 Namekian Overcharge R	.75	2.00
R111 Orange Freezing Drill R	.75	2.00
R112 Orange Reading Drill R	.75	2.00
R113 Orange Accumulated Burst R	.75	2.00
R114 Orange Drain R	.75	2.00
R115 Red Analysis R	.75	2.00
R116 Red Antidote R	.75	2.00
R117 Red Eye Beams R	.75	2.00
R118 Red Rage R	.75	2.00
R119 Saiyan Peace R	.75	2.00
R120 Saiyan Dash R	.75	2.00
R121 Saiyan Destructive Blast R	.75	2.00
R122 Saiyan Tracking Blast R	.75	2.00
R123 Android 17's Van R	1.25	3.00
R124 Android 17's Back Smash R	1.00	2.50
R125 Android 18's Arm Breaker R	.75	2.00
R126 Android 18's Toss R	1.25	3.00
R127 Android 19's Energy Absorption R	1.25	3.00
R128 Android 19's Choke R	.75	2.00
R129 Android 20's Scouting Drill R	1.00	2.50
R130 Android 20's Domination R	2.50	6.00
R131 Vegeta's Destruction Blast R	.75	2.00
R132 Elimination R	.75	2.00
R133 Android Attack Drill R	1.50	4.00
R134 Moment of Peace R	.75	2.00
R135 Android Presence R	.75	2.00
R136 Energized Strike R	2.50	6.00
R137 Enhanced Reflexes R	3.00	8.00
R138 Optic Blast R	3.00	8.00
R139 Sinister Choke R	8.00	20.00
R140 Tug of War R	1.25	3.00
UR141 Defiant Challenge UR	40.00	80.00
UR142 Hidden Power Drill UR	25.00	50.00
UR143 Goku - Dashing UR	8.00	20.00
UR144 Vegeta - Elite UR	8.00	20.00
S1 Trunks - Returned	1.50	4.00
S2 Trunks - Swordmaster	3.00	8.00
S3 Trunks - Defiant	3.00	8.00
S4 Trunks - Overpowering	4.00	10.00
S5 Saiyan Rampaging Mastery	2.50	6.00
S6 Goku - Relaxed	2.00	5.00
S7 Goku - Motivated	6.00	15.00
S8 Goku - Calm	4.00	10.00
S9 Goku - Dashing	5.00	12.00
S10 Blue Tag Team Mastery	1.50	4.00
S11 Piccolo - Composed	1.50	4.00
S12 Piccolo - Anticipating	3.00	8.00
S13 Piccolo - Ferocious	1.50	4.00
S14 Piccolo - Revitalized	1.25	3.00
S15 Namekian Restored Mastery	1.25	3.00
S16 Vegeta - Calculating	4.00	10.00
S17 Vegeta - On The Move	2.50	6.00
S18 Vegeta - Super Saiyan	3.00	8.00
S19 Vegeta - Elite	5.00	12.00
S20 Orange Adept Mastery	2.50	6.00
S21 Android 17 - Judgmental	1.25	3.00
S22 Android 17 - Imposing	4.00	10.00
S23 Android 17 - Battle Ready	1.25	3.00
S24 Android 17 - In Action	2.50	6.00
S25 Red Ruthless Mastery	3.00	8.00
S26 Android 18 - Directing	1.25	3.00
S27 Android 18 - Threatening	1.25	3.00
S28 Android 18 - Effective	1.50	4.00
S29 Android 18 - Determined	4.00	10.00
S30 Black Perceptive Mastery	2.50	6.00

2016 Dragon Ball Z Perfection

Card	Low	High
COMPLETE SET (142)	100.00	150.00
COMPLETE SET W/DR (147)	150.00	250.00
COMPLETE SET W/DR AND HI-TECH (152)	200.00	300.00
COMPLETE SET W/DR, HI-TECH, AND RAINBOW (157)	300.00	450.00
BOOSTER BOX		
BOOSTER PACK		
RELEASED ON FEBRUARY 26, 2016		
C1 Android Headbutt C	.10	.25
C2 Debilitating Volley C	.10	.25
C3 Vicious Strike C	.10	.25
C4 Villainous Energy Beam C	.10	.25
C5 Black Analysis C	.10	.25
C6 Black Obstructing Drill C	.10	.25
C7 Black Destructive Beam C	.10	.25
C8 Black Easy Block C	.10	.25
C9 Black Energy Bubble C	.10	.25
C10 Black Enraged Outburst C	.10	.25
C11 Black Haunting C	.10	.25
C12 Black Nightmare C	.10	.25
C13 Black Sidestep C	.10	.25
C14 Black Unstable Punch C	.10	.25
C15 Blue Vision C	.10	.25
C16 Blue Guarding Drill C	.10	.25
C17 Blue Clash C	.10	.25
C18 Blue Concentrated Blast C	.10	.25
C19 Blue Energy Shield C	.10	.25
C20 Blue Head Kick C	.10	.25
C21 Blue Outbreak C	.10	.25
C22 Blue Overcharge C	.10	.25
C23 Blue Slide C	.10	.25
C24 Blue Sword Rage C	.10	.25
C25 Namekian Flight C	.10	.25
C26 Namekian Risk C	.10	.25
C27 Namekian Back Kick C	.10	.25
C28 Namekian Backflip C	.10	.25
C29 Namekian Chest Explosion C	.10	.25
C30 Namekian Counter Blast C	.10	.25
C31 Namekian Heel Kick C	.10	.25
C32 Namekian Resistance C	.10	.25
C33 Namekian Right Elbow C	.10	.25
C34 Orange Charging Drill C	.10	.25
C35 Orange Examination Drill C	.10	.25
C36 Orange Observing Drill C	.10	.25
C37 Orange Thumbs Up Drill C	.10	.25
C38 Orange Energy Deflection C	.10	.25
C39 Orange Enraged Bash C	.10	.25
C40 Orange Fixation C	.10	.25
C41 Orange Planned Block C	.10	.25
C42 Orange Tank Barrage C	.10	.25
C43 Red Bribe C	.10	.25
C44 Red Cover Drill C	.10	.25
C45 Red Cannon C	.10	.25
C46 Red Capture C	.10	.25
C47 Red Chest Pierce C	.10	.25
C48 Red Inferno C	.10	.25
C49 Red Interference C	.10	.25
C50 Red Sword Stab C	.10	.25
C51 Red Tandem Blast C	.10	.25
C52 Saiyan Demolishing Beam C	.10	.25
C53 Saiyan Emergence C	.10	.25
C54 Saiyan Energy Aura C	.10	.25
C55 Saiyan Face Strike C	.10	.25
C56 Saiyan Flip C	.10	.25
C57 Saiyan Leaping Strike C	.10	.25
C58 Saiyan Obstruction C	.10	.25
C59 Saiyan Rapid Fire C	.10	.25
C60 Saiyan Skull Jab C	.10	.25
U61 Master Roshi - Expectant U	.20	.50
U62 Master Roshi - Overwhelmed U	.20	.50
U63 Master Roshi - Catcher U	.20	.50
U64 Master Roshi - Barricade U	.20	.50
U65 Yamcha - Sleeping U	.20	.50
U66 Yamcha - On The Move U	.20	.50
U67 Yamcha - Surprised U	.20	.50
U68 Yamcha - Happy U	.20	.50
U69 Android 16 - Awoken U	.20	.50
U70 Android 16 - Distracted U	.20	.50
U71 Android 16 - Enraged U	.20	.50
U72 Android 16 - Injured U	.20	.50
U73 Dr. Brief - Analyzing U	.20	.50
U74 Mr. Popo - Guide U	.20	.50
U75 Android 16 - Unmoving U	.20	.50
U76 Cell - Larval U	.20	.50
U77 Android Defensive Blast U	.20	.50
U78 Pesky Barrage U	.20	.50
U79 Playful Punch U	.20	.50
U80 Black Confident Shot U	.20	.50
U81 Black Grounding Bash U	.20	.50
U82 Black Sharp Kick U	.20	.50
U83 Blue Eating Drill U	.20	.50
U84 Blue Challenging Strike U	.20	.50
U85 Blue Dispersing Beam U	.20	.50
U86 Namekian Searching Drill U	.20	.50
U87 Namekian Focused Ball U	.20	.50
U88 Namekian Hand Burst U	.20	.50
U89 Namekian Preparation U	.20	.50
U90 Orange Dressing Room U	.20	.50
U91 Orange Charge U	.20	.50
U92 Orange Clearing Blast U	.20	.50
U93 Orange Stab U	.20	.50
U94 Red Glare U	.20	.50
U95 Red Infuriated Attack U	.20	.50
U96 Red Right Blast U	.20	.50
U97 Saiyan Transformation Drill U	.20	.50
U98 Saiyan Back Crash U	.20	.50
U99 Saiyan Crunch U	.20	.50
U100 Saiyan Sword Skill U	.20	.50
R101 Master Roshi's Slumber R	1.50	4.00
R102 Master Roshi's Back Strike R	3.00	8.00
R103 Yamcha's Expert Assistance R	1.00	2.50
R104 Yamcha's Rescue R	2.00	5.00
R105 Android 16's Tranquility R	.75	2.00
R106 Android 16's Rocket Punch R	1.00	2.50
R107 Cell's Draining Attack R	1.25	3.00
R108 Cell's Style R	1.50	4.00
R109 Tenshinhan's Tri-Beam R	1.00	2.50
R110 Trunks' Slam R	1.50	4.00
R111 Aggressive Sword Drill R	.75	2.00
R112 Clash of Wills R	.75	2.00
R113 Dashing Sword Attack R	1.50	4.00
R114 Heroic Jab R	.75	2.00
R115 Overwhelming Power R	2.50	6.00
R116 Black Discovery R	.75	2.00
R117 Black Choke R	.75	2.00
R118 Black Double Team R	.75	2.00
R119 Black Extreme Blast R	.75	2.00
R120 Blue Training R	.75	2.00
R121 Blue Head Charge R	.75	2.00
R122 Blue Restraint R	.75	2.00
R123 Blue Toss R	.75	2.00
R124 Namekian Back Smash R	.75	2.00
R125 Namekian Energized Bash R	.75	2.00
R126 Namekian Face Crush R	.75	2.00
R127 Namekian Resilience R	.75	2.00
R128 Orange Hoping Drill R	.75	2.00
R129 Orange Ki Ball R	.75	2.00
R130 Orange Overflowing Burst R	.75	2.00
R131 Orange Right Beam R	.75	2.00
R132 Red Channel Surfing Drill R	.75	2.00
R133 Red Aerial Assault R	.75	2.00
R134 Red Back Bash R	.75	2.00
R135 Red Downward Burst R	.75	2.00
R136 Red Powerful Strike R	.75	2.00
R137 Saiyan Extreme Training R	.75	2.00
R138 Saiyan Charged Kick R	.75	2.00
R139 Saiyan Ki Burst R	.75	2.00
R140 Saiyan Overhead Flare R	.75	2.00
UR141 Power Mimic UR	15.00	30.00
UR142 Heroic Dashing Punch UR	25.00	50.00
DR1A Cell - Imperfect DR	15.00	30.00
DR1 Cell - Imperfect DR	6.00	15.00
DR2 Cell - Semi-Perfect DR	10.00	20.00
DR3 Cell - Perfect DR	15.00	30.00
DR4 Cell - Unstoppable DR	15.00	30.00
DR1AHT Cell - Imperfect DR Hi-Tech	8.00	20.00
DR1BHT Cell - Imperfect DR Hi-Tech	6.00	15.00
DR2HT Cell - Semi-Perfect DR Hi-Tech	6.00	15.00
DR3HT Cell - Perfect DR Hi-Tech	6.00	15.00
DR4HT Cell - Unstoppable DR Hi-Tech	8.00	20.00
DR1ARB Cell - Imperfect DR Rainbow	15.00	40.00
DR1BRB Cell - Imperfect DR Rainbow	10.00	25.00
DR2RB Cell - Semi-Perfect DR Rainbow	10.00	25.00
DR3RB Cell - Perfect DR Rainbow	12.00	30.00
DR4RB Cell - Unstoppable DR Rainbow	15.00	30.00

2016 Dragon Ball Z Vengeance

Card	Low	High
COMPLETE SET (143 CARDS)	170.00	260.00
BOOSTER BOX 24 PACKS	50.00	85.00
BOOSTER PACK 12 CARDS	2.50	6.00
UNLISTED C	.10	.30
UNLISTED U	.10	.30
UNLISTED R	2.00	5.00
RELEASED ON JULY 1ST, 2016		
C1 Black Android Programming C	.05	.15
C2 Black Astonishing Drill C	.05	.15
C3 Black Recollection Drill C	.05	.15
C4 Black Downward Beam C	.05	.15
C5 Black Face Kick C	.05	.15
C6 Black Fist Catch C	.05	.15
C7 Black Impact C	.05	.15
C8 Black Overload C	.05	.15
C9 Black Running Guard C	.05	.15
C10 Black Sword Attack C	.05	.15
C11 Black Vaulted Strike C	.05	.15
C12 Blue Intimidation C	.05	.15
C13 Blue Reinforcements C	.05	.15
C14 Blue Save C	.05	.15
C15 Blue Seizing Drill C	.05	.15
C16 Blue Waiting Drill C	.05	.15
C17 Blue Android Headbutt C	.05	.15
C18 Blue Brush Aside C	.05	.15
C19 Blue Flying Kick C	.05	.15
C20 Blue Rehabilitation C	.05	.15
C21 Blue Swat C	.05	.15
C22 Namekian Impending Doom C	.05	.15
C23 Namekian Vanishing Drill C	.05	.15
C24 Namekian Airborne Attack C	.05	.15
C25 Namekian Arm Shield C	.05	.15
C26 Namekian Concern C	.05	.15
C27 Namekian MultiOpponent Combat C	.05	.15
C28 Namekian Protective Posture C	.05	.15
C29 Namekian Robotic Destruction C	.05	.15
C30 Namekian Team Up C	.05	.15
C31 Orange Bravado C	.05	.15
C32 Orange Eviction C	.05	.15
C33 Orange Shopping Drill C	.05	.15
C34 Orange Welcoming Drill C	.05	.15
C35 Orange Combined Burst C	.05	.15
C36 Orange Earthquake C	.05	.15
C37 Orange Fierce Attack C	.05	.15
C38 Orange Frenzied Assault C	.05	.15
C39 Orange Interference C	.05	.15
C40 Orange Withdrawal C	.05	.15
C41 Red Reconnaissance Drill C	.05	.15
C42 Red Android Palm Blast C	.05	.15
C43 Red Body Block C	.05	.15
C44 Red Departing Shot C	.05	.15
C45 Red Disregard C	.05	.15
C46 Red Ejection C	.05	.15
C47 Red High Kick C	.05	.15
C48 Red Lasers C	.05	.15
C49 Red Training Burst C	.05	.15
C50 Red Wallop C	.05	.15
C51 Saiyan Targeting C	.05	.15
C52 Saiyan Assistance C	.05	.15
C53 Saiyan Clash C	.05	.15
C54 Saiyan Club C	.05	.15
C55 Saiyan Ferocious Blast C	.05	.15
C56 Saiyan Severing Punch C	.05	.15
C57 Saiyan Sword Dodge C	.05	.15
C58 Saiyan Tantrum C	.05	.15
C59 Android Arm Breaker C	.05	.15
C60 Quick Blast C	.05	.15
U61 Android 13 Redneck Robot U	.15	.25
U62 Android 13 Amused U	.15	.25
U63 Android 13 Dark Villain U	.15	.25
U64 Android 13 Surging Strength U	.15	.25
U65 Broly Survivor U	.15	.25
U66 Broly Determined U	.15	.25
U67 Broly Legendary U	.15	.25
U68 Broly Relentless U	.15	.25
U69 Cooler Familiar Face U	.15	.25
U70 Cooler Transformed U	.15	.25
U71 Cooler Menace U	.15	.25
U72 Cooler Overlord U	.15	.25
U73 Gohan To The Rescue U	.15	.25
U74 Krillin Quick U	.15	.25
U75 Master Roshi Restrained U	.15	.25
U76 Trunks Protective U	.15	.25
U77 Icarus Supportive U	.15	.25
U78 Android 13 Powerful U	.15	.25
U79 Android 14 Stoic U	.15	.25
U80 Android 15 Relaxed U	.15	.25
U81 Broly Undaunted U	.15	.25
U82 Cooler Angered U	.15	.25
U83 Paragus Desperate Father U	.15	.25
U84 Salza Henchman U	.15	.25
U85 Black Invitation U	.15	.25
U86 Black Liberation U	.15	.25
U87 Blue Hunt U	.15	.25
U88 Blue Skid U	.15	.25

U89 Namekian Empowered Charge U .15 .25
U90 Namekian Face Off U .15 .25
U91 Namekian Salvo U .15 .25
U92 Orange Snoozing Drill U .15 .25
U93 Orange Android Rising Punch U .15 .25
U94 Red Integration U .15 .25
U95 Red Double Blast U .15 .25
U96 Red Furious Lunge U .15 .25
U97 Saiyan Recovery U .15 .25
U98 Saiyan Terrifying Strike U .15 .25
U99 PointBlank Volley U 1.00 1.25
U100 Villainous Power Ball U 1.00 1.25
R101 Black Impatience R 1.25 2.00
R102 Black Dispersion R 1.25 2.00
R103 Black Dive R 1.25 2.00
R104 Black Drain R 1.25 2.00
R105 Blue Blanketing Blasts R 1.75 3.00
R106 Blue Decapitation R 1.75 3.00
R107 Blue Discharge R 1.25 2.00
R108 Blue Ki Ball R 1.25 2.00
R109 Blue Return Fire R 1.25 2.00
R110 Namekian Pep Talk R 1.25 2.00
R111 Namekian Harvesting Drill R 1.25 2.00
R112 Namekian Electrifying Grab R 1.25 2.00
R113 Namekian Dash R 1.25 2.00
R114 Namekian Ending R 1.25 2.00
R115 Orange Intimidating Drill R 1.25 2.00
R116 Orange Counter Ball R 1.25 2.00
R117 Orange Hug R 1.25 2.00
R118 Orange Immense Blast R 1.25 2.00
R119 Orange Sword Chop R 1.25 2.00
R120 Red Sword Slicing Drill R 1.25 2.00
R121 Red Fantasy R 1.25 2.00
R122 Red Motivational Kick R 1.25 2.00
R123 Red Stylish Entrance R 1.25 2.00
R124 Saiyan Overpowering Aura Drill R 1.25 2.00
R125 Saiyan Denial R 1.25 2.00
R126 Saiyan Extinguishing Blast R 1.00 1.50
R127 Saiyan Lob R 1.25 2.00
R128 Saiyan Thrust R 1.25 2.00
R129 Saiyan Trample R 2.00 3.00
R130 Saiyan Trap R 1.00 1.50
R131 Singing Drill R 1.00 1.50
R132 Android Insubordination R 3.00 5.00
R133 Sobering Hammer R 4.00 6.00
R134 Stomach Crusher R 3.00 5.00
R135 Android 13s SS Deadly Bomber R 3.00 5.00
R136 Android 13s Impenetrable Defense R 4.00 6.00
R137 Brolys Eraser Cannon R 5.00 7.00
R138 Brolys Face Crusher R 5.00 7.00
R139 Coolers Rebirth R 3.00 5.00
R140 Coolers Supernova R 4.00 6.00
UR141 Surprise Attack UR 20.00 30.00
UR142 Unleashed UR 45.00 60.00
DR1 Instant Transmission DR 15.00 20.00
NONUM Broly Active Player T 3.00 8.00
NONUM Goku Active Player T 3.00 8.00

2016 Dragon Ball Z Vengeance Foil

COMPLETE SET (143 CARDS) 650.00 1500.00
BOOSTER BOX 24 PACKS 50.00 85.00
BOOSTER PACK 12 CARDS 2.50 6.00
RELEASED ON JULY 1ST, 2016
C1 Black Android Programming C 1.50 4.00
C2 Black Astonishing Drill C 1.50 4.00
C3 Black Recollection Drill C 1.50 4.00
C4 Black Downward Beam C 1.50 4.00
C5 Black Face Kick C 1.50 4.00
C6 Black Fist Catch C 1.50 4.00
C7 Black Impact C 1.50 4.00
C8 Black Overload C 1.50 4.00
C9 Black Running Guard C 1.50 4.00
C10 Black Sword Attack C 1.50 4.00
C11 Black Vaulted Strike C 1.50 4.00
C12 Blue Intimidation C 1.50 4.00
C13 Blue Reinforcements C 1.50 4.00
C14 Blue Save C 1.50 4.00
C15 Blue Seizing Drill C 1.50 4.00
C16 Blue Waiting Drill C 2.50 6.00
C17 Blue Android Headbutt C 1.50 4.00
C18 Blue Brush Aside C 1.50 4.00
C19 Blue Flying Kick C 1.50 4.00
C20 Blue Rehabilitation C 1.50 4.00
C21 Blue Swat C 1.50 4.00
C22 Namekian Impending Doom C 1.50 4.00
C23 Namekian Vanishing Drill C 1.50 4.00
C24 Namekian Airborne Attack C 1.50 4.00
C25 Namekian Arm Shield C 1.50 4.00
C26 Namekian Concern C 1.50 4.00
C27 Namekian MultiOpponent Combat C 1.50 4.00
C28 Namekian Protective Posture C 1.50 4.00
C29 Namekian Robotic Destruction C 1.50 4.00
C30 Namekian Team Up C 1.50 4.00
C31 Orange Bravado C 1.50 4.00
C32 Orange Eviction C 1.50 4.00
C33 Orange Shopping Drill C 1.50 4.00
C34 Orange Welcoming Drill C 1.50 4.00
C35 Orange Combined Burst C 1.50 4.00
C36 Orange Earthquake C 1.50 4.00
C37 Orange Fierce Attack C 1.50 4.00
C38 Orange Frenzied Assault C 1.50 4.00
C39 Orange Interference C 1.50 4.00
C40 Orange Withdrawal C 1.50 4.00
C41 Red Reconnaissance Drill C 1.50 4.00
C42 Red Android Palm Blast C 1.50 4.00
C43 Red Body Block C 1.50 4.00
C44 Red Departing Shot C 1.50 4.00
C45 Red Disregard C 1.50 4.00
C46 Red Ejection C 1.50 4.00
C47 Red High Kick C 1.50 4.00
C48 Red Lasers C 1.50 4.00
C49 Red Training Burst C 1.50 4.00
C50 Red Wallop C 1.50 4.00
C51 Saiyan Targeting C 1.50 4.00
C52 Saiyan Assistance C 1.50 4.00
C53 Saiyan Clash C 1.50 4.00
C54 Saiyan Club C 1.50 4.00
C55 Saiyan Ferocious Blast C 1.50 4.00
C56 Saiyan Severing Punch C 1.50 4.00
C57 Saiyan Sword Dodge C 1.50 4.00
C58 Saiyan Tantrum C 2.50 6.00
C59 Android Arm Breaker C 8.00 20.00
C60 Quick Blast C 6.00 15.00
U61 Android 13 Redneck Robot U 6.00 15.00
U62 Android 13 Amused U 6.00 15.00
U63 Android 13 Dark Villain U 6.00 15.00
U64 Android 13 Surging Strength U 6.00 15.00
U65 Broly Survivor U 8.00 20.00
U66 Broly Determined U 8.00 20.00
U67 Broly Legendary U 8.00 20.00
U68 Broly Relentless U 8.00 20.00
U69 Cooler Familiar Face U 8.00 20.00
U70 Cooler Transformed U 8.00 20.00
U71 Cooler Menace U 8.00 20.00
U72 Cooler Overlord U 8.00 20.00
U73 Gohan To The Rescue U 5.00 12.00
U74 Krillin Quick U 3.00 8.00
U75 Master Roshi Restrained U 5.00 12.00
U76 Trunks Protective U 8.00 20.00
U77 Icarus Supportive U 5.00 12.00
U78 Android 13 Powerful U 3.00 8.00
U79 Android 14 Stoic U 3.00 8.00
U80 Android 15 Relaxed U 3.00 8.00
U81 Broly Undaunted U 3.00 8.00
U82 Cooler Angered U 3.00 8.00
U83 Paragus Desperate Father U 3.00 8.00
U84 Salza Henchman U 3.00 8.00
U85 Black Invitation U 5.00 12.00
U86 Black Liberation U 1.50 4.00
U87 Blue Hunt U 1.50 4.00
U88 Blue Skid U 1.50 4.00
U89 Namekian Empowered Charge U 1.50 4.00
U90 Namekian Face Off U 1.50 4.00
U91 Namekian Salvo U 1.50 4.00
U92 Orange Snoozing Drill U 1.50 4.00
U93 Orange Android Rising Punch U 1.50 4.00
U94 Red Integration U 1.50 4.00
U95 Red Double Blast U 1.50 4.00
U96 Red Furious Lunge U 1.50 4.00
U97 Saiyan Recovery U 1.50 4.00
U98 Saiyan Terrifying Strike U 1.50 4.00
U99 PointBlank Volley U 15.00 30.00
U100 Villainous Power Ball U 10.00 25.00
R101 Black Impatience R 5.00 12.00
R102 Black Dispersion R 5.00 12.00
R103 Black Dive R 5.00 12.00
R104 Black Drain R 5.00 12.00
R105 Blue Blanketing Blasts R 5.00 12.00
R106 Blue Decapitation R 5.00 12.00
R107 Blue Discharge R 5.00 12.00
R108 Blue Ki Ball R 5.00 12.00
R109 Blue Return Fire R 5.00 12.00
R110 Namekian Pep Talk R 5.00 12.00
R111 Namekian Harvesting Drill R 5.00 12.00
R112 Namekian Electrifying Grab R 5.00 12.00
R113 Namekian Dash R 5.00 12.00
R114 Namekian Ending R 5.00 12.00
R115 Orange Intimidating Drill R 5.00 12.00
R116 Orange Counter Ball R 5.00 12.00
R117 Orange Hug R 5.00 12.00
R118 Orange Immense Blast R 5.00 12.00
R119 Orange Sword Chop R 5.00 12.00
R120 Red Sword Slicing Drill R 5.00 12.00
R121 Red Fantasy R 5.00 12.00
R122 Red Motivational Kick R 5.00 12.00
R123 Red Stylish Entrance R 5.00 12.00
R124 Saiyan Overpowering Aura Drill R 5.00 12.00
R125 Saiyan Denial R 5.00 12.00
R126 Saiyan Extinguishing Blast R 5.00 12.00
R127 Saiyan Lob R 5.00 12.00
R128 Saiyan Thrust R 5.00 12.00
R129 Saiyan Trample R 5.00 12.00
R130 Saiyan Trap R 5.00 12.00
R131 Singing Drill R 5.00 12.00
R132 Android Insubordination R 6.00 15.00
R133 Sobering Hammer R 10.00 25.00
R134 Stomach Crusher R 25.00 50.00
R135 Android 13s SS Deadly Bomber R 8.00 20.00
R136 Android 13s Impenetrable Defense R 8.00 20.00
R137 Brolys Eraser Cannon R 10.00 25.00
R138 Brolys Face Crusher R 20.00 40.00
R139 Coolers Rebirth R 10.00 25.00
R140 Coolers Supernova R 10.00 25.00
UR141 Surprise Attack UR 20.00 30.00
NONUM Broly Active Player T 3.00 8.00
NONUM Goku Active Player T 3.00 8.00

2016 Dragon Ball Z Awakening

COMPLETE SET (176 CARDS) 550.00 800.00
BOOSTER BOX 24 PACKS 60.00 75.00
BOOSTER PACK 12 CARDS 4.00 5.00
RELEASED ON OCTOBER 28, 2016
C1 Black Protective Drill .15 .25
C2 Black Breaker .15 .25
C3 Black Dispel .15 .25
C4 Black Duck .15 .25
C5 Black Energy Beam .15 .25
C6 Black Flinch .15 .25
C7 Black Halt .15 .25
C8 Black Narrow Beam .15 .25
C9 Black Schematics .15 .25
C10 Black Heel .15 .25
C11 Blue Rebuke .15 .25
C12 Blue Introduction .15 .25
C13 Blue Brace .15 .25
C14 Blue Deterrence .15 .25
C15 Blue Feast .15 .25
C16 Blue Patience .15 .25
C17 Blue Retaliation .15 .25
C18 Blue Reckless Charge .15 .25
C19 Blue Strike .15 .25
C20 Blue Sweep .15 .25
C21 Blue Arrest .15 .25
C22 Namekian Cover .15 .25
C23 Namekian Discharge .15 .25
C24 Namekian Eviction .15 .25
C25 Namekian Head Kick .15 .25
C26 Namekian Left Block .15 .25
C27 Namekian Training Ball .15 .25
C28 Namekian Wallop .15 .25
C29 Namekian Clamp .15 .25
C30 Namekian Buffer .15 .25
C31 Orange Encouragement .15 .25
C32 Orange Checkup Drill .15 .25
C33 Orange Spying Drill .15 .25
C34 Orange Dismissal .15 .25
C35 Orange Guard .15 .25
C36 Orange Paired Blast .15 .25
C37 Orange Redirection .15 .25
C38 Orange Left Burst .15 .25
C39 Orange Aid .15 .25
C40 Orange Defense .15 .25
C41 Red Driving Knee .15 .25
C42 Red Evade .15 .25
C43 Red Explosion .15 .25
C44 Red Hurl .15 .25
C45 Red Repel .15 .25
C46 Red Sneaky Strike .15 .25
C47 Red Takeover .15 .25
C48 Red Tilt .15 .25
C49 Red Determination .15 .25
C50 Red Jab .15 .25
C51 Saiyan Vacation .15 .25
C52 Saiyan Escape .15 .25
C53 Saiyan High Kick .15 .25
C54 Saiyan Intercept .15 .25
C55 Saiyan Internal Conflict .15 .25
C56 Saiyan Ki Web .15 .25
C57 Saiyan Stomach Thrust .15 .25
C58 Saiyan Turning Kick .15 .25
C59 Saiyan Bash .15 .25
C60 Saiyan Crouch .15 .25
U61 Earth Dragon Ball 1 .15 .25
U62 Earth Dragon Ball 2 .15 .25
U63 Earth Dragon Ball 3 .15 .25
U64 Earth Dragon Ball 4 .15 .25
U65 Earth Dragon Ball 5 .15 .25
U66 Earth Dragon Ball 6 .15 .25
U67 Earth Dragon Ball 7 .15 .25
U68 Taunting .15 .25
U69 On the Move .15 .25
U70 Oppressive .15 .25
U71 Confident .15 .25
U72 Old Foe .15 .25
U73 Reckless .15 .25
U74 Armed .15 .25
U75 Shielded .15 .25
U76 Trapped .15 .25
U77 Escaping .15 .25
U78 Unrelenting .15 .25
U79 Surprise Visitor .15 .25
U80 Inquisitive .15 .25
U81 Naming Genius .15 .25
U82 Cheerful .15 .25
U83 Black Confinement .15 .25
U84 Black Construction Drill .15 .25
U85 Black Left Burst .15 .25
U86 Blue Release Drill .15 .25
U87 Blue Tracking Beam .15 .25
U88 Namekian Hunt .15 .25
U89 Namekian Hospitality Drill .15 .25
U90 Namekian Whack .15 .25
U91 Orange Crying Drill .15 .25
U92 Orange Restructuring Drill .15 .25
U93 Orange Leaping Punch .15 .25
U94 Red Flourish .15 .25
U95 Red Scanning Drill .15 .25
U96 Red Counter Kick .15 .25
U97 Red Pummel .15 .25
U98 Saiyan Clench .15 .25
U99 Saiyan Parry .15 .25
U100 Saiyan Slap .15 .25
R101 Black Memories 1.75 3.00
R102 Black Annihilation 1.75 3.00
R103 Black Flashback 1.75 3.00
R104 Black Strength Display 1.75 3.00
R105 Black Vehicle Toss 1.75 3.00
R106 Blue Doze 3.00 5.00
R107 Blue Friendliness 1.75 3.00
R108 Blue Elbow 1.75 3.00
R109 Blue Left Blast 1.75 3.00
R110 Blue Smug Punch 1.75 3.00
R111 Namekian Barricade 3.00 5.00
R112 Namekian Fierce Punch 1.75 3.00
R113 Namekian Inheritance 1.75 3.00
R114 Namekian Surge 1.75 3.00
R115 Namekian Thrust 1.75 3.00
R116 Orange Affection Drill 1.75 3.00
R117 Orange Viewing Drill 3.00 5.00
R118 Orange Aggression 1.75 3.00
R119 Orange Collision 1.75 3.00
R120 Orange Knee Strike 3.00 5.00
R121 Red Awakening 1.75 3.00
R122 Red Clock 1.75 3.00
R123 Red Mischief 1.75 3.00
R124 Red Pound 1.75 3.00
R125 Saiyan Anguish Drill 1.75 3.00
R126 Saiyan Despair 1.75 3.00
R127 Saiyan Dive 1.75 3.00
R128 Saiyan Energy Barrage 1.75 3.00
R129 Saiyan Face Off 1.75 3.00
R130 Cell Jrs Swarm 1.75 3.00
R131 Cell Jrs Surround 3.00 5.00
R132 Cells Provocation 3.00 5.00
R133 Gohans Backlash 3.00 5.00
R134 Gokus Search 3.00 5.00
R135 Hercules Dynamite Kick 3.00 5.00
R136 Hercules Grand Entrance 3.00 5.00
R137 Mercenary Taos Super Dodon Wave 3.00 5.00
R138 Mercenary Taos Puzzles 3.00 5.00
R139 Trunks Knee Bash 3.00 5.00
R140 Vegetas Final Flash 4.00 7.00
UR141 Allied Blitz 50.00 80.00
UR142 Assisted Kamehameha 125.00 175.00
UR143 Flurry of Blows 50.00 80.00

UR144 Heroic Energy Sphere	70.00	85.00
UR145 The Ultimate Sacrifice	35.00	50.00
UR146 Villainous Energy Sphere	70.00	85.00
DR1 Training	1.75	3.00
DR2 Determined	1.75	3.00
DR3 Courageous	1.75	3.00
DR4 Selfless	1.75	3.00
DR5 Blue Resolute Mastery	1.75	3.00
DR6 Experienced	1.75	3.00
DR7 Imposing	1.75	3.00
DR8 Energized	1.75	3.00
DR9 Pinnacle of Power	1.75	3.00
DR10 Orange Retribution Mastery	1.75	3.00
DR11 Prepared	1.75	3.00
DR12 Combative	1.75	3.00
DR13 Smooth	1.75	3.00
DR14 Unstoppable	1.75	3.00
DR15 Namekian Radiant Mastery	1.75	3.00
DR17 Unlocked	1.75	3.00
DR18 Unassuming	1.75	3.00
DR16 Adept	1.75	3.00
DR19 Undeniable	1.75	3.00
DR20 Saiyan Dynamic Mastery	1.75	3.00
DR21 Champion	1.75	3.00
DR22 Posing	1.75	3.00
DR23 Guarded	1.75	3.00
DR24 In Action	1.75	3.00
DR25 Black Conflict Mastery	1.75	3.00
DR26 Dashing	1.75	3.00
DR27 Frenzied	1.75	3.00
DR28 Bold	1.75	3.00
DR29 Overwhelming	1.75	3.00
DR30 Red Ascension Mastery	1.75	3.00

2016 Dragon Ball Z Awakening Starter Deck

COMPLETE SET (171 CARDS)	60.00	100.00
RELEASED ON OCTOBER 28, 2016		
S1 Goku Training	1.25	1.75
S2 Goku Determined	1.25	1.75
S3 Goku Courageous	1.25	1.75
S4 Goku Selfless	1.25	1.75
S5 Blue Resolute Mastery	1.25	1.75
S6 Vegeta Experienced	1.25	1.75
S7 Vegeta Imposing	1.25	1.75
S8 Vegeta Energized	1.25	1.75
S9 Vegeta Pinnacle of Power	1.25	1.75
S10 Orange Retribution Mastery	1.25	1.75
S11 Cell Prepared	1.25	1.75
S12 Cell Combative	1.25	1.75
S13 Cell Smooth	1.25	1.75
S14 Cell Unstoppable	1.25	1.75
S15 Namekian Radiant Mastery	1.25	1.75
S16 Gohan Adept	1.25	1.75
S17 Gohan Unlocked	1.25	1.75
S18 Gohan Unassuming	1.25	1.75
S19 Gohan Undeniable	1.25	1.75
S20 Saiyan Dynamic Mastery	1.25	1.75
S21 Hercule Champion	1.25	1.75
S22 Hercule Posing	1.25	1.75
S23 Hercule Guarded	1.25	1.75
S24 Hercule In Action	1.25	1.75
S25 Black Conflict Mastery	1.25	1.75
S26 Trunks Dashing	1.25	1.75
S27 Trunks Frenzied	1.25	1.75
S28 Trunks Bold	1.25	1.75
S29 Trunks Overwhelming	1.25	1.75
S30 Red Ascension Mastery	1.25	1.75
S31 Confrontation	4.00	7.00
S32 Blue Head Kick	.15	.25
S33 Blue Slide	.15	.25
S34 Blue Concentrated Blast	.15	.25
S35 Blue Outbreak	.15	.25
S36 Blue Overcharge	.15	.25
S37 Blue Mental Drill	.15	.25
S38 Blue Draining Blast	.15	.25
S39 Blue Energy Overload	.15	.25
S40 Blue Head Knock	.15	.25
S41 Blue Betrayal	.15	.25
S42 Blue Fear	.15	.25
S43 Blue Arm Blast	.15	.25
S44 Blue Face Crunch	.15	.25
S45 Blue Narrow Escape	.15	.25
S46 Blue Hand Blast	.15	.25
S47 Blue Crouch	.15	.25
S48 Blue Stretch Kick	.15	.25
S49 Blue Round Throw	.15	.25
S50 Blue Guard	.15	.25
S51 Blue Neck Beam	.15	.25
S52 Blue Cover Up	.15	.25
S53 Blue Energy Focus	.15	.25
S54 Vegeta's Galick Gun	.15	.25
S55 Orange Upward Strike	.15	.25
S56 Orange Enraged Bash	.15	.25
S57 Orange Excavation	.15	.25
S58 Orange Inspection	.15	.25
S59 Orange Energy Absorption	.15	.25
S60 Orange Precise Shot	.15	.25
S61 Orange Offensive Strike	.15	.25
S62 Orange Launcher	.15	.25
S63 Orange Truck Lift	.15	.25
S64 Orange Refocus	.15	.25
S65 Orange Overhead Smash	.15	.25
S66 Orange Left Punch	.15	.25
S67 Orange Possession Drill	.15	.25
S68 Orange Aura Drill	.15	.25
S69 Orange Joint Restraint Drill	.15	.25
S70 Orange Stare Down	.15	.25
S71 Orange Energy Gathering	.15	.25
S72 Orange Celebration	.15	.25
S73 Orange Burning Aura Drill	.15	.25
S74 Orange Hiding Drill	.15	.25
S75 Orange Steady Drill	.15	.25
S76 Orange Energy Dan Drill	.15	.25
S77 Stare Down	4.00	7.00
S78 Namekian Hand Burst	.15	.25
S79 Namekian Heel Kick	.15	.25
S80 Namekian Wish	.15	.25
S81 Namekian Downward Blast	.15	.25
S82 Namekian Aerial Knee	.15	.25
S83 Namekian Hybrid Defense	.15	.25
S84 Namekian Silencing	.15	.25
S85 Namekian Maximum Will	.15	.25
S86 Namekian Right Throw	.15	.25
S87 Namekian Flinch	.15	.25
S88 Namekian Elbow Drop	.15	.25
S89 Namekian Regeneration	.15	.25
S90 Namekian Dragon Clan	.15	.25
S91 Namekian Concentration	.15	.25
S92 Namekian Forceful Block	.15	.25
S93 Namekian Knee Block	.15	.25
S94 Namekian Crossed Guard	.15	.25
S95 Namekian Combat Drill	.15	.25
S96 Namekian Finger Lasers	.15	.25
S97 Namekian Focused Beams	.15	.25
S98 Namekian Zone Pressure	.15	.25
S99 Namekian Chest Explosion	.15	.25
S100 Saiyan Rapid Fire	.15	.25
S101 Saiyan Back Crash	.15	.25
S102 Saiyan Skull Jab	.15	.25
S103 Saiyan Offensive Rush	.15	.25
S104 Saiyan Cheap Shot	.15	.25
S105 Saiyan Energy Focus	.15	.25
S106 Saiyan Energy Outburst	.15	.25
S107 Saiyan Palm Block	.15	.25
S108 Saiyan Face Strike	.15	.25
S109 Saiyan Analysis Drill	.15	.25
S110 Saiyan Pinpoint Blast	.15	.25
S111 Saiyan Multi-Blast	.15	.25
S112 Saiyan Domination	.15	.25
S113 Saiyan Hand Swipe	.15	.25
S114 Saiyan Drive By	.15	.25
S115 Saiyan Rescue	.15	.25
S116 Saiyan Spin Kick	.15	.25
S117 Saiyan Intimidation	.15	.25
S118 Saiyan Energy Deflection	.15	.25
S119 Saiyan Left Kick	.15	.25
S120 Saiyan Sabotage	.15	.25
S121 Saiyan Light Jab	.15	.25
S122 Saiyan Arm Catch	.15	.25
S123 Saiyan Unleashing Drill	.15	.25
S124 Black Command	.15	.25
S125 Black Corruption	.15	.25
S126 Black Defensive Burst	.15	.25
S127 Black Finger Block	.15	.25
S128 Black Flying Kick	.15	.25
S129 Black Hug Maneuver	.15	.25
S130 Black Knee Catch	.15	.25
S131 Black Lunge	.15	.25
S132 Black Nightmare	.15	.25
S133 Black Request	.15	.25
S134 Black Side Thrust	.15	.25
S135 Black Swipe	.15	.25
S136 Black Travelling Punch	.15	.25
S137 Black Easy Block	.15	.25
S138 Black Unstable Punch	.15	.25
S139 Devastating Blow	.15	.25
S140 Black Hair Trap	.15	.25
S141 Black Fist Lock	.15	.25
S142 Black Radiating Drill	.15	.25
S143 Black Strike	.15	.25
S144 Black Overpowering Attack	.15	.25
S145 Black Speedy Dodge	.15	.25
S146 Black Declaration	.15	.25
S147 Black Entanglement	.15	.25
S148 Red Back Kick	.15	.25
S149 Red Blazing Aura	.15	.25
S150 Red Blocking Hand	.15	.25
S151 Red Catch	.15	.25
S152 Red Chop	.15	.25
S153 Red Destiny	.15	.25
S154 Red Double Strike	.15	.25
S155 Red Duck	.15	.25
S156 Red Energy Blast	.15	.25
S157 Red Energy Defensive Stance	.15	.25
S158 Red Flares	.15	.25
S159 Red Frenzied Blasts	.15	.25
S160 Red Heating Beams	.15	.25
S161 Red Intimidation Drill	.15	.25
S162 Red Power Lift	.15	.25
S163 Red Power Rush	.15	.25
S164 Red Right Cross	.15	.25
S165 Red Smash	.15	.25
S166 Red Sword Stab	.15	.25
S167 Red Tactical Drill	.15	.25
S168 Red Tandem Blast	.15	.25
S169 Red Vault	.15	.25
S170 Red Right Knee	.15	.25
S171 Red Energy Outburst	.15	.25

2016 Dragon Ball Z Awakening Starter Deck Rainbow Foil

COMPLETE SET (30 CARDS)	35.00	60.00
RELEASED ON OCTOBER 28,2016		
S1 Goku Training	1.25	2.00
S2 Goku Determined	1.25	2.00
S3 Goku Courageous	1.25	2.00
S4 Goku Selfless	1.25	2.00
S5 Blue Resolute Mastery	1.25	2.00
S6 Vegeta Experienced	1.25	2.00
S7 Vegeta Imposing	1.25	2.00
S8 Vegeta Energized	1.25	2.00
S9 Vegeta Pinnacle of Power	1.25	2.00
S10 Orange Retribution Mastery	1.25	2.00
S11 Cell Prepared	1.25	2.00
S12 Cell Combative	1.25	2.00
S13 Cell Smooth	1.25	2.00
S14 Cell Unstoppable	1.25	2.00
S15 Namekian Radiant Mastery	1.25	2.00
S16 Gohan Adept	1.25	2.00
S17 Gohan Unlocked	1.25	2.00
S18 Gohan Unassuming	1.25	2.00
S19 Gohan Undeniable	1.25	2.00
S20 Saiyan Dynamic Mastery	1.25	2.00
S21 Hercule Champion	1.25	2.00
S22 Hercule Posing	1.25	2.00
S23 Hercule Guarded	1.25	2.00
S24 Hercule In Action	1.25	2.00
S25 Black Conflict Mastery	1.25	2.00
S26 Trunks Dashing	1.25	2.00
S27 Trunks Frenzied	1.25	2.00
S28 Trunks Bold	1.25	2.00
S29 Trunks Overwhelming	1.25	2.00
S30 Red Ascension Mastery	1.25	2.00

Dragon Ball Super

2017 Dragon Ball Super Galactic Battle

COMPLETE SET (114 CARDS)	275.00	450.00
BOOSTER BOX (24 CARDS)	70.00	95.00
BOOSTER PACK (12 CARDS)	3.00	5.00
SPECIAL PACK SET (4 PACKS AND 1 PROMO)	15.00	20.00
UNLISTED C	.20	.35
UNLISTED U	.30	.50
UNLISTED R	2.50	4.00
RELEASED ON JULY 28TH, 2017		
BT1001 God of Destruction Champa R	3.00	5.00
BT1002 Aide Vados U	.30	.50
BT1003 Assassin Hit U	.30	.50
BT1004 Destructive Terror Champa SR	8.00	12.00
BT1005 Furthering Destruction Champa U	.30	.50
BT1006 Scheming Champa C	.20	.35
BT1007 Manipulating God Champa C	.20	.35
BT1008 Bewitching God Vados R	1.50	2.50
BT1009 Calm-Hearted Vados U	.30	.50
BT1010 Divine Aide Vados C	.20	.35
BT1011 Lightning-fast Hit SR	8.00	12.00
BT1011 Lightning-fast Hit SPR	30.00	50.00
BT1012 Hit U	.30	.50
BT1013 Raging Cabba R	3.00	5.00
BT1014 Saiyan Cabba C	.20	.35
BT1015 Terror Assault Frost U	.30	.50
BT1016 Unceasing Evolution Frost C	.20	.35
BT1017 Evolution Premonition Frost C	.20	.35
BT1018 Confident Botamo U	.30	.50
BT1019 Botamo of Universe 6 C	.20	.35
BT1020 Iron Wall Magetta U	.30	.50
BT1021 Magetta of Universe 6 C	.20	.35
BT1022 Universe 6 Supreme Kai C	.20	.35
BT1023 Kai Attendant of Universe 6 C	.20	.35
BT1024 Assassination Plot C	.20	.35
BT1025 Vados's Assistance C	.20	.35
BT1026 Fickle Destruction C	.20	.35
BT1027 Cabba's Awakening C	.20	.35
BT1028 Super Saiyan Blue Vegeta R	3.00	5.00
BT1029 Beerus, God of Destruction U	.30	.50
BT1030 Super Saiyan Blue Son Goku U	.30	.50
BT1031 God Break Son Goku SR	8.00	12.00
BT1031 God Break Son Goku SPR	50.00	80.00
BT1032 Overflowing Spirit SSGSS Son Goku U	.30	.50
BT1033 Kind Saiyan Son Goku C	.20	.35
BT1034 Mighty Striker Son Gohan C	.20	.35
BT1035 Son Goten C	.20	.35
BT1036 God Charge Vegeta R	1.50	2.50
BT1037 Assailant Vegeta U	.30	.50
BT1038 Vegeta C	.20	.35
BT1039 Trunks C	.20	.35
BT1040 Bulma, God Tempter C	.20	.35
BT1041 Beerus, General of Demolition SR	10.00	15.00
BT1042 Energy Boost Beerus U	.30	.50
BT1043 Whis, Judge of the Gods R	.50	.80
BT1044 Whis, The Resting Attendant U	.30	.50
BT1045 Boost Attack Piccolo C	.20	.35
BT1046 Taunting Piccolo C	.20	.35
BT1047 Energy Boosted Majin Buu C	.20	.35
BT1048 Ultimate Judgment Jaco C	.20	.35
BT1049 Mysterious Presence Monaka U	.30	.50
BT1050 Guardian North Kai C	.20	.35
BT1051 Result of Training U	.30	.50
BT1052 Objection C	.20	.35
BT1053 Senzu Bean C	.20	.35
BT1054 Encouraging Presence Monaka C	.20	.35
BT1055 Whis's Coercion C	.20	.35
BT1056 Super Saiyan God Son Goku U	.30	.50
BT1057 Broly, The Legendary Super Saiyan R	3.00	5.00
BT1058 Full Power Son Gohan U	.30	.50
BT1059 Awakening Rage Son Goku SR	8.00	12.00
BT1060 Son Goku C	.20	.35
BT1061 Friend-Summoning Son Gohan U	.30	.50
BT1062 Son Gohan, Family of Justice C	.20	.35
BT1063 Son Goten, Family of Justice C	.20	.35
BT1064 Raging Attacker Vegeta R	3.00	5.00
BT1065 Furious Yell Vegeta U	.30	.50
BT1066 Tenacious Vegeta C	.20	.35
BT1067 Implacable Trunks U	.30	.50
BT1068 Slasher Trunks C	.20	.35
BT1069 Trunks, Protector of Children C	.20	.35
BT1070 Super Saiyan Gotenks R	3.00	5.00
BT1071 Energy Power Gotenks C	.20	.35
BT1072 Human Shield Krillin C	.20	.35
BT1073 Broly, The Rampaging Horror SR	8.00	12.00
BT1073 Broly, The Rampaging Horror SPR	50.00	80.00
BT1074 Rampaging Lifeform Bio-Broly U	.30	.50
BT1075 Rampaging Super Saiyan Broly C	.20	.35
BT1076 Broly, Dawn of the Rampage C	.20	.35
BT1077 Paragus, Controller of Monsters C	.20	.35
BT1078 Overflowing Bio Warrior Army C	.20	.35
BT1079 King Vegeta's Surprise Attack U	.30	.50
BT1080 Full Power Energy C	.20	.35
BT1081 Broly's Ring C	.20	.35
BT1082 Family kamehameha C	.20	.35
BT1083 Ultimate Form Golden Frieza R	3.00	5.00
BT1084 Frieza, The Galactic Emperor U	.30	.50
BT1085 Ginyu, The Malicious Transformation U	.30	.50
BT1086 Golden Frieza, The Resurrected Terror SR	8.00	12.00
BT1086 Golden Frieza, The Resurrected Terror SPR	30.00	50.00
BT1087 Full-Power Frieza R	3.00	5.00
BT1088 Frieza, Hellish Terror C	.20	.35
BT1089 Avenging Frieza C	.20	.35
BT1090 Mecha-Frieza, The Returning Terror U	.30	.50
BT1091 King Cold, Father of the Emperor R	3.00	5.00
BT1092 Sorbet, The Loyal Commander U	.30	.50
BT1093 Tagoma, The Loyal Warrior U	.30	.50
BT1094 Shisami, The Loyal Warrior U	.30	.50
BT1095 Elite Force Captain Ginyu SR	8.00	12.00
BT1096 Ginyu Force Recoome C	.20	.35
BT1097 Ginyu Force Burter C	.20	.35
BT1098 Ginyu Force Jeice C	.20	.35
BT1099 Ginyu Force Guldo C	.20	.35
BT1100 Dodoria, The Emperors Attendant C	.20	.35
BT1101 Zarbon, The Emperors Attendant C	.20	.35
BT1102 Appule C	.20	.35
BT1103 Sui C	.20	.35

BT1104 Banan C	.20	.35
BT1105 Cui C	.20	.35
BT1106 Recoome Eraser Gun U	.30	.50
BT1107 Cold Bloodlust C	.20	.35
BT1108 Bad Ring Laser C	.20	.35
BT1109 Friezas Call C	.20	.35
BT1110 Crusher Ball C	.20	.35

2017 Dragon Ball Super Union Force

COMPLETE SET (127 CARDS)	500.00	750.00
BOOSTER BOX 24 PACKS	70.00	90.00
BOOSTER PACK 12 CARDS	4.00	6.00
UNLISTED C	.15	.25
UNLISTED U	.30	.50
UNLISTED R	.75	1.25
RELEASED ON NOVEMBER 3RD, 2017		
BT2001 Fusion Warrior Super Saiyan Vegito R	.75	1.25
BT2002 Soul Unleashed Son Goku U	.20	.35
BT2003 Babidi Creator of Evil U	.20	.35
BT2004 Relentless Super Saiyan 3 Son Goku R	.75	1.25
BT2005 Super Saiyan Son Goku C	.10	.20
BT2006 Miraculous Comeback Ultimate Gohan SR	10.00	15.00
BT2007 Fully Trained Son Gohan C	.10	.20
BT2008 Leap to The Future Son Goten C	.10	.20
BT2009 Ultimate Evil Dark Prince Vegeta R	.75	1.25
BT2010 Double Shot Super Saiyan 2 Vegeta C	.10	.20
BT2011 Leap to The Future Trunks C	.10	.20
BT2012 Repeated Force Vegito SR	10.00	15.00
BT2013 Lightning Speed Vegito R	.75	1.25
BT2014 Ghost Attack Super Saiyan 3 Gotenks R	3.00	5.00
BT2015 Prodigy Fusion Super Saiyan Gotenks U	.20	.35
BT2016 Mighty Mask The Mysterious Warrior C	.10	.20
BT2017 Hercule Buus Assistant C	.10	.20
BT2018 Videl Gohans Partner C	.10	.20
BT2019 Foreseeing East Supreme Kai C	.10	.20
BT2020 Kibito C	.10	.20
BT2021 Sensing Old Kai C	.10	.20
BT2022 Mind Controlling Babidi U	.20	.35
BT2023 Dabura The Wizards Right Hand U	.20	.35
BT2024 Attendants Spopovich and Yamu C	.10	.20
BT2025 Grand Evil Absorption Majin Buu SR	8.00	10.00
BT2026 Prodigy Absorption Majin Buu U	.20	.35
BT2027 Awakening Evil Majin Buu U	.20	.35
BT2028 Majin Buu Revived C	.10	.20
BT2029 Jiren Fist of Justice SR	10.00	15.00
BT2030 Potara The Kais Secret U	.20	.35
BT2031 Majin Buus Sealed Ball C	.10	.20
BT2032 Piccolos Help C	.10	.20
BT2033 Super Ghost Kamikaze Attack C	.10	.20
BT2034 Absolute God Fused Zamasu R	.75	1.25
BT2035 Trunks Hope for the Future U	.20	.35
BT2036 Goku Black The Bringer of Despair U	.20	.35
BT2037 Determined Striker SSB Son Goku R	.75	1.25
BT2038 Mighty Attack Son Goku U	.20	.35
BT2039 Raging Spirit Son Gohan C	.10	.20
BT2040 Restless Spirit SSB Vegeta SR	4.00	6.00
BT2041 Vegeta The Proud Father U	.20	.35
BT2042 Trunks The Constant Hope SR	4.00	6.00
BT2043 Trunks Creator of the Future R	.75	1.25
BT2044 Unyielding Spirit Trunks C	.10	.20
BT2045 Bulma Supporter of the Future C	.10	.20
BT2046 Beerus Essence of Destruction U	.20	.35
BT2047 Whis the Sacred Guard C	.10	.20
BT2048 Group Leader Pilaf C	.10	.20
BT2049 Shu C	.10	.20
BT2050 Mai Supporter of Hope C	.10	.20
BT2051 Power of Love Mai C	.10	.20
BT2052 Courageous Heart Yajirobe C	.10	.20
BT2053 Tiny Heroes Haru and Maki C	.10	.20
BT2054 Unstoppable Despair Goku Black Rose SR	6.00	8.00
BT2055 Warrior of the Gods Goku Black C	.10	.20
BT2056 Zamasu The Alert God R	.75	1.25
BT2057 Zamasu The Invincible U	.20	.35
BT2058 Infinite Force Fused Zamasu SR	3.00	5.00
BT2059 God of the Gods Great Priest U	.20	.35
BT2060 Zen Oh The Plain God U	.20	.35
BT2061 Universe 10 Supreme Kai Gowasu C	.10	.20
BT2062 Returning Evil Golden Frieza SR	6.00	8.00
BT2063 Father Son Galick Gun C	.10	.20
BT2064 Matuba C	.10	.20
BT2065 Time Ring C	.10	.20
BT2066 Trunks Time Machine C	.10	.20
BT2067 Zen Oh Button C	.10	.20
BT2068 Ultimate Lifeform Cell R	.75	1.25
BT2069 Father Son Kamehameha Goku and Gohan U	.20	.35
BT2070 Diabolical Duo Androis 17 and 18 U	.20	.35
BT2071 Inherited Will Super Saiyan Son Goku R	.75	1.25
BT2072 Bundle of Curiosity Son Goku C	.10	.20
BT2073 Piercing Super Saiyan 2 Son Gohan SR	3.00	5.00
BT2074 Fully Traine Super Saiyan Son Gohan U	.20	.35
BT2075 Supreme DNA Son Gohan C	.10	.20
BT2076 Full Power Vegeta R	.75	1.25
BT2077 Vegeta C	.10	.20
BT2078 Full Power Trunks U	.20	.35
BT2079 Aura of Rage Super Saiyan Trunks C	.10	.20
BT2080 Ready to Strike Piccolo C	.10	.20
BT2081 Destined Deed Krillin C	.10	.20
BT2082 Yamcha C	.10	.20
BT2083 Martial Expert Tien Shinhan U	.20	.35
BT2084 Perfect Force Cell SR	10.00	15.00
BT2085 Evolving Evil Lifeform Cell R	5.00	7.00
BT2086 Growing Evil Lifeform Cell U	.20	.35
BT2087 Uncountable Many Cell Jr C	.10	.20
BT2088 Expanding Energy Android 17 U	.20	.35
BT2089 Twin Brother Android 17 C	.10	.20
BT2090 Exterminating Energy Android 18 U	.20	.35
BT2091 Twin Sister Android 18 C	.10	.20
BT2092 Encroaching Terror Android 19 C	.10	.20
BT2093 Terrible Creator Android 20 C	.10	.20
BT2094 Iron Hammer of Justice Android 16 C	.10	.20
BT2095 Hidden Awakening Kale SR	10.00	15.00
BT2096 Cell Absorption C	.10	.20
BT2097 Enraged Gohan Awakening C	.10	.20
BT2098 Father Son Kamehameha C	.10	.20
BT2099 Cells Birth C	.10	.20
BT2100 Nucleus of Evil Meta Cooler Core R	.75	1.25
BT2101 Cooler Leader of Troops U	.20	.35
BT2102 Chilled Harbinger of Destruction U	.20	.35
BT2103 Heartless Strike Frieza R	.75	1.25
BT2104 Destructive Occupation Frieza U	.20	.35
BT2105 Overpowering King Cold R	.75	1.25
BT2106 Awakening Core Meta Cooler U	.20	.35
BT2107 Infinite Multiplication Meta Cooler C	.10	.20
BT2108 The Infinite Force Meta Cooler SR	1.50	2.50
BT2109 Meta Cooler Core U	.20	.35
BT2110 Cooler Blood of the Tyrant Clan SR	1.50	2.50
BT2111 Secret Evolution Cooler R	.75	1.25
BT2112 Chilled Army General R	.75	1.25
BT2113 Pivotal Defense Cyclopian Guard C	.10	.20
BT2114 Guide Robo Usher of Death C	.10	.20
BT2115 Coolers Armored Squadron Leader Salza U	.20	.35
BT2116 Coolers Armored Squadron Dore C	.10	.20
BT2117 Coolers Armored Squadron Neiz C	.10	.20
BT2118 Tobi The Obedient Soldier C	.10	.20
BT2119 Cabira The Obedient Soldier C	.10	.20
BT2120 Darkness Eye Beam C	.10	.20
BT2121 Death Razor C	.10	.20
BT2122 Big Gete Star C	.10	.20
BT2123 Ultimate Force SSB Vegito SCR	80.00	90.00
BT2012SPR Repeated Force Vegito SPR	30.00	35.00
BT2058SPR Infinite Force Fused Zamasu SPR	20.00	25.00
BT2084SPR Perfect Force Cell SPR	35.00	40.00
BT2108SPR The Infinite Force Meta Cooler SPR	15.00	20.00

2018 Dragon Ball Super Cross Worlds

COMPLETE SET (127 CARDS)	90.00	130.00
BOOSTER BOX (24 PACKS)	55.00	65.00
BOOSTER PACK (12 CARDS)	3.00	5.00
RELEASED ON MARCH 9TH, 2018		
BT3001 Pan R	.10	.20
BT3002 Dr.Myuu U	.10	.20
BT3003 Victorious Fist Super Saiyan 3 Son Goku SR	.60	1.00
BT3004 Rising Fist Super Saiyan 2 Son Goku R	.10	.20
BT3005 Determined Super Saiyan Son Goku U	.10	.20
BT3006 Pint-sized Warrior Son Goku C	.10	.20
BT3007 Shocking Future Son Goku C	.10	.20
BT3008 Fearless Pan SR	6.00	8.00
BT3009 Pan C	.10	.20
BT3010 Reliable Trunks R	.10	.20
BT3011 Quick Rush Trunks U	.10	.20
BT3012 Dependable Robot Giru C	.10	.20
BT3013 Handy Giru C	.10	.20
BT3014 Hidden Power Uub C	.10	.20
BT3015 Bodyguard Ledgic U	.10	.20
BT3016 Power-absorbing Luud U	.10	.20
BT3017 Dr. Myuu, Under Baby's Control C	.10	.20
BT3018 Meta-Rilldo, Form Perfected SR	.10	.20
BT3019 General Evolved, Hyper Meta-Rilldo R	.10	.20
BT3020 Hidden Ability, General Rilldo C	.10	.20
BT3021 Triple Union Super Sigma U	.10	.20
BT3022 Commander Nezi C	.10	.20
BT3023 Mega Cannon Sigma, Natt C	.10	.20
BT3024 Mega Cannon Sigma, Bizu C	.10	.20
BT3025 Mega Cannon Sigma Ribet C	.10	.20
BT3026 Pride and Justice Toppo U	.10	.20
BT3027 Unending Awakening C	.10	.20
BT3028 Grand Tour Spaceship C	.10	.20
BT3029 Baby's Subdual R	.10	.20
BT3030 Planet M-2 C	.10	.20
BT3031 Majin Buu R	.10	.20
BT3032 Son Goku U	.10	.20
BT3033 Ultra Instinct -Sign- Son Goku SR	1.50	2.00
BT3033 Ultra Instinct -Sign- Son Goku SPR	9.00	11.00
BT3034 Ultimate Spirit Bomb Son Goku R	.10	.20
BT3035 Furious Rush Super Saiyan 3 Son Goku U	.10	.20
BT3036 Final Explosion Prince of Destruction Vegeta R	.10	.20
BT3037 Universal Leader, Grand Supreme Kai U	.10	.20
BT3038 Unyielding Defender, East Supreme Kai C	.10	.20
BT3039 Majin Defier, West Supreme Kai C	.10	.20
BT3040 Majin Defier, South Supreme Kai C	.10	.20
BT3041 Majin Defier, North Supreme Kai C	.10	.20
BT3042 Kibito, Kai's Attendant C	.10	.20
BT3043 Powers Combined, Kibito Kai C	.10	.20
BT3044 Thinks He's the Best Hercule C	.10	.20
BT3045 Agent of Resurrection, Babidi C	.10	.20
BT3046 Magician's Father, Bibidi C	.10	.20
BT3047 The Ultimate Evil, Majin Buu SR	1.00	1.50
BT3048 Out of Control Evil, Majin Buu U	.10	.20
BT3049 Power Absorbing Majin R	.10	.20
BT3050 Majin Buu, Dawn of the Rampage C	.10	.20
BT3051 God Absorber Majin Buu C	.10	.20
BT3052 The Most Evil Absorption in History U	.10	.20
BT3053 Rebirth of Justice C	.10	.20
BT3054 Buu Make You Cookie C	.10	.20
BT3055 Vegito R	.10	.20
BT3056 Android 13 U	.10	.20
BT3057 Finishing Spirit Bomb Son Goku R	.10	.20
BT3058 Pressure Assault Super Saiyan Son Goku U	.10	.20
BT3059 Indomitable Spirit SSB Son Goku C	.10	.20
BT3060 Dauntless Spirit SSB Vegeta R	.10	.20
BT3061 Unyielding Justice SS2 Trunks U	.10	.20
BT3062 Trunks, Bridge to the Future C	.10	.20
BT3063 Hyper Rush SSB Vegito SR	.10	.20
BT3063 Hyper Rush SSB Vegito SPR	5.00	7.00
BT3064 Dreadful Duo, Android 17 C	.10	.20
BT3065 Dreadful Duo, Android 18 C	.10	.20
BT3066 Made to Destroy, Android 19 C	.10	.20
BT3067 Dr. Gero, Evil's Inventor C	.10	.20
BT3068 Stouthearted Android 16 C	.10	.20
BT3069 Unending Destruction, Android 13 SR	.10	.20
BT3070 Dawn of Terror, Android 13 U	.10	.20
BT3071 Unfeeling Destroyer Android 14 U	.10	.20
BT3072 Combination Attack Android 14 C	.10	.20
BT3073 Unfeeling Destroyer Android 15 U	.10	.20
BT3074 Android 15, Just Saying Hi C	.10	.20
BT3075 Terror Scythe Goku Black U	.10	.20
BT3076 Twisted Justice, Fused Zamasu R	.10	.20
BT3077 Evil Psyche, Zamasu C	.10	.20
BT3078 Unstoppable Ambition Super Saiyan Caulifla SR	6.00	8.00
BT3079 To Save a Hopeful Future C	.10	.20
BT3080 Create Android C	.10	.20
BT3081 Speedy Surprise Attack C	.10	.20
BT3082 Bardock R	.10	.20
BT3083 Son Goku U	.10	.20
BT3084 Desperate Warrior Super Saiyan Bardock SR	.10	.20
BT3085 Great Protector, Great Ape Bardock U	.10	.20
BT3086 Striker Bardock C	.10	.20
BT3087 Gine, Family of Justice C	.10	.20
BT3088 Explosive Spirit Son Goku SR	2.00	3.50
BT3088 Explosive Spirit Son Goku SPR	8.00	10.00
BT3089 Rampaging Great Ape Son Goku R	.10	.20
BT3090 No Openings Son Goku U	.10	.20
BT3091 Kakarot, the Child Who Got Away C	.10	.20
BT3092 Absolute Defense Great Ape King Vegeta R	.10	.20
BT3093 Lord of the Great Apes, King Vegeta C	.10	.20
BT3094 Vegeta C	.10	.20
BT3095 Youthful Bulma C	.10	.20
BT3096 Hidden Power Great Ape Tora U	.10	.20
BT3097 Unwavering Solidarity Tora C	.10	.20
BT3098 Hidden Power Great Ape Fasha U	.10	.20
BT3099 Unwavering Solidarity Fasha C	.10	.20
BT3100 Unwavering Solidarity Shugesh C	.10	.20
BT3101 Unwavering Solidarity Borgos C	.10	.20
BT3102 Nappa, Vegeta's Attendant C	.10	.20
BT3103 Burgeoning Power Bergamo U	.10	.20
BT3104 Flying Nimbus C	.10	.20
BT3105 Planet Vegeta U	.10	.20
BT3106 March of the Great Ape C	.10	.20
BT3107 Mira R	.10	.20
BT3108 Trunks U	.10	.20
BT3109 SS3 Bardock, Power Unleashed SR	.60	1.00
BT3110 Awakened Warrior Bardock U	.10	.20
BT3111 Trunks, Power Overseeing Time SR	5.00	7.00
BT3112 Unrelenting Assault Trunks U	.10	.20
BT3113 Supreme Kai of Time, World's Protector C	.10	.20
BT3114 Towa, Reprogrammed Menace R	.10	.20
BT3115 Towa, Space Time Unleashed C	.10	.20
BT3116 Dimension Breaker Mira SR	.10	.20
BT3117 Relentless Destruction Mira U	.10	.20
BT3118 Fu, Shrouded in Mystery SPR	7.00	9.00
BT3118 Fu, Shrouded in Mystery SR	1.50	2.00
BT3119 Shun Shun, Protector Majin C	.10	.20
BT3120 Haru Haru, Attacker Majin C	.10	.20
BT3121 Dark Plot C	.10	.20
BT3122 Time's Judgement C	.10	.20
BT3123 Hyper Evolution Super Saiyan 4 Son Goku SCR	30.00	35.00

2018 Dragon Ball Super The Tournament of Power

COMPLETE SET (101 CARDS)	400.00	500.00
BOOSTER BOX (24 PACKS)	85.00	95.00
BOOSTER PACK (12 CARDS)	3.00	5.00
RELEASED ON MAY 25TH, 2018		
TB1001 Vegeta U	.10	.20
TB1002 Kale C	.10	.20
TB1003 Backbone of Universe 7 Son Goku C	.10	.20
TB1004 Universe 7 Saiyan Prince Vegeta SR	.60	1.00
TB1004 Universe 7 Saiyan Prince Vegeta SPR	60.00	100.00
TB1005 Gale Strike Vegeta U	.10	.20
TB1006 Majin Buu, Full of Energy R	.10	.20
TB1007 Surprise Attack Majin Buu U	.10	.20
TB1008 Foreseeing Hit SR	5.00	8.00
TB1009 Dimension Leaper Hit C	.10	.20
TB1010 Impeccable Super Saiyan Cabba R	1.00	1.50
TB1011 Cabba, Universe Mediator C	.10	.20
TB1012 Bold Super Saiyan 2 Caulifla R	.60	1.00
TB1013 Sister Attack Saiyan Caulifla U	.10	.20
TB1014 Caulifla C	.10	.20
TB1015 Relentless Super Saiyan Kale SR	.10	.20
TB1016 Sister Attack Saiyan Kale U	.60	1.00
TB1017 Dauntless Kale C	.10	.20
TB1018 Ultimate Evolution Frost U	.10	.20
TB1019 Frost, the Tactician C	.10	.20
TB1020 Universe 6 Combination Botamo C	.10	.20
TB1021 Universe 6 Combination Magetta C	.10	.20
TB1022 Union Attack Botamo and Magetta C	.10	.20
TB1023 Strategies of Universe 7 U	.10	.20
TB1024 Time Kicker C	.10	.20
TB1025 Son Gohan U	.10	.20
TB1026 Bergamo C	.10	.20
TB1027 Ready to Fight Son Goku C	.10	.20
TB1028 Results of Training Son Gohan R	.10	.20
TB1029 Focused Mind Son Gohan C	.10	.20
TB1030 Beerus, Universe 7 Divine Vanquisher SR	5.00	8.00
TB1030 Beerus, Universe 7 Divine Vanquisher SPR	40.00	60.00
TB1031 Whis, Mentor of Beerus U	.10	.20
TB1032 Focused Mind Piccolo R	.10	.20
TB1033 Multi-Form Tien Shinhan C	.10	.20
TB1034 Universe 9 Supreme Kai Roh C	.10	.20
TB1035 Trio De Dangers Bergamo SR	4.00	6.00
TB1036 Brothers of Terror Bergamo U	.10	.20
TB1037 Trio De Dangers Lavender U	.10	.20
TB1038 Trio De Dangers Basil R	.10	.20
TB1039 Iron Skin Battler Chappil U	.10	.20
TB1040 Universe 9 Striker Comfrey C	.10	.20
TB1041 Universe 9 Striker Hop C	.10	.20
TB1042 Universe 9 Striker Oregano C	.10	.20
TB1043 Universe 9 Striker Hyssop C	.10	.20
TB1044 Sorrel, The Small Warrior C	.10	.20
TB1045 Universe 9 Striker Roselle C	.10	.20
TB1046 Spectrum Attack Obuni C	.10	.20
TB1047 Murichim C	.10	.20
TB1048 Dangers Triangle U	.10	.20
TB1049 Shining Blaster C	.10	.20
TB1050 Son Goku U	.10	.20
TB1051 Brianne De Chateau C	.10	.20
TB1052 Son Goku, Hope of Universe 7 SR	3.00	5.00
TB1052 Son Goku, Hope of Universe 7 SPR	75.00	125.00
TB1053 Destructo Disk Krillin R	.10	.20
TB1054 Energy Guard Android 17 U	.10	.20
TB1055 Infinite Energy Android 18 U	.10	.20
TB1056 Maiden Squadron Leader Ribrianne SR	1.50	2.50
TB1057 Girl Warrior Brianne De Chateau C	.10	.20
TB1058 Maiden Squadron Kakunsa R	.10	.20
TB1059 Maiden Squadron Rozie U	.10	.20
TB1060 Zarbuto, Maiden Attendant C	.10	.20
TB1061 Rabanra, Maiden Attendant C	.10	.20
TB1062 Teleporting Jimeze U	.10	.20
TB1063 Vikal, Master of the Sky C	.10	.20
TB1064 Zirloin, Maiden Attendant U	.10	.20
TB1065 Attack Reflecting Prum C	.10	.20
TB1066 Hermilla, The Sniper C	.10	.20
TB1067 True Form Ganos R	.10	.20
TB1068 Trickster Ganos U	.10	.20
TB1069 Caway, Ki Master C	.10	.20
TB1070 Dercori C	.10	.20
TB1071 Maiden Transformation U	.10	.20
TB1072 Maiden Charge C	.10	.20
TB1073 Frieza U	.10	.20
TB1074 Jiren C	.10	.20
TB1075 Full Power Spirit Bomb Son Goku R	.10	.20
TB1076 Master Roshi, Forged of Will U	2.00	3.00

Card	Low	High
TB1077 Frieza, Emperor of Universe 7 SR	1.50	2.00
TB1077 Frieza, Emperor of Universe 7 SPR	50.00	75.00
TB1078 Coldhearted Strike Frieza R	.10	.20
TB1079 Agony of Hell Frieza U	.10	.20
TB1080 Ally of Justice Toppo R	.10	.20
TB1081 Absolute Justice Jiren SR	2.50	3.00
TB1082 Secret Vitality Jiren U	.10	.20
TB1083 Swift Warrior Dyspo U	.10	.20
TB1084 Hero Combination Vuon C	.10	.20
TB1085 Hero Combination Kunshi C	.10	.20
TB1086 Hero Combination Tupper C	.10	.20
TB1087 Hero Combination Zoiray C	.10	.20
TB1088 Ki Bomb Support Cocotte C	.10	.20
TB1089 Hero Combination Kettol U	.10	.20
TB1090 Hand Strike Kahseral U	.10	.20
TB1091 Protean Being Majikayo C	.10	.20
TB1092 Super Reaction Narirama C	.10	.20
TB1093 Cyborg Warrior Nigrisshi U	.10	.20
TB1094 Katopesla C	.10	.20
TB1095 Universe 7 Representative U	.10	.20
TB1096 Cocotte Zone C	.10	.20
TB1097 Son Goku, The Awakened Power SCR	250.00	400.00

2018 Dragon Ball Super Colossal Warfare

Card	Low	High
COMPLETE SET (128 CARDS	150.00	200.00
BOOSTER BOX (24 PACKS)	55.00	65.00
BOOSTER PACK (12 CARDS)	3.00	5.00
RELEASED ON JULY 13TH, 2018		
BT4001 Son Goku U	.10	.20
BT4002 Baby R	.10	.20
BT4003 Triple Flash SS4 Son Goku SR	2.00	3.50
BT4003 Triple Flash SS4 Son Goku SPR	10.00	15.00
BT4004 Untapped Power SS3 Son Goku R	.10	.20
BT4005 Blazing Spirit Son Goku C	.10	.20
BT4006 Blaze of Glory Son Gohan C	.10	.20
BT4007 Extra Strike SS Son Goten U	.10	.20
BT4008 Charging Up Son Goten C	.10	.20
BT4009 Power of Friendship Pan C	.10	.20
BT4010 Digging Deep Vegeta U	.10	.20
BT4011 Daily Training Vegeta C	.10	.20
BT4012 Intensifying Power Trunks U	.60	1.00
BT4013 Dependable Mom Bulma C	.10	.20
BT4014 Saiyan Daughter Bulla C	.10	.20
BT4015 Mr. Buu C	.10	.20
BT4016 Epochal Grudge Great Ape Baby SR	1.00	1.50
BT4017 Saiyan Strength Baby R	.10	.20
BT4018 Baby, Vengeance Unleashed C	.10	.20
BT4019 Saiyan Onslaught Kefla SR	6.00	8.00
BT4020 Vow Revenge U	.10	.20
BT4021 Revenge Death Ball U	.10	.20
BT4022 Vengeful Onslaught C	.10	.20
BT4023 Trunks U	.10	.20
BT4024 Hirudegarn R	.10	.20
BT4025 Dragon Fist SS3 Son Goku R	.75	1.25
BT4026 Sneak Attack Son Goku C	.10	.20
BT4027 City Patrol Great Saiyaman U	.10	.20
BT4028 Son Gohan C	.10	.20
BT4029 Quick Dodge Son Goten C	.10	.20
BT4030 At All Costs Vegeta SR	5.00	7.00
BT4031 Sneak Attack Vegeta C	.10	.20
BT4032 Oath's Power Trunks R	.10	.20
BT4033 Heroic Encounter Trunks C	.10	.20
BT4034 Raging Energy Blast Gotenks C	.10	.20
BT4035 City Patrol Great Saiyaman 2 C	.10	.20
BT4036 Colossal Malice Hirudegarn SR	.10	.20
BT4037 Impenetrable Defense Hirudegarn U	.10	.20
BT4038 Hirudegarn, the Wanderer C	.10	.20
BT4039 Oath's Power, Tapion U	.10	.20
BT4040 Hidden Darkness Tapion C	.10	.20
BT4041 Hidden Darkness Minotia C	.10	.20
BT4042 Hoi, Emissary of Flame U	.10	.20
BT4043 Phantom Flame Cannon U	.10	.20
BT4044 Ectoplasm C	.10	.20
BT4045 The Legendary Flute C	.10	.20
BT4046 Piccolo U	.10	.20
BT4047 Lord Slug R	.10	.20
BT4048 Newfound Power Son Gohan U	.10	.20
BT4049 Kami's Power Piccolo SR	5.00	7.00
BT4049 Kami's Power Piccolo SPR	10.00	15.00
BT4050 Power Barrier Piccolo C	.10	.20
BT4051 Reign of Terror King Piccolo R	.10	.20
BT4052 Gift of Power Guru C	.10	.20
BT4053 Nail, the Namekian Ace R	.50	.80
BT4054 Kami, the Watcher U	.10	.20
BT4055 Kindhearted Namekian Dende C	.10	.20
BT4056 Popo, Guardian's Aide C	.10	.20
BT4057 Namekian Duo Saonel U	.10	.20
BT4058 Namekian Duo Pirina U	.10	.20
BT4059 Titanic Ambition Lord Slug SR	.10	.20
BT4060 Lord Slug, Young Again R	.10	.20
BT4061 Lord Slug, Returned to Form C	.10	.20
BT4062 Adonic Warrior Angila C	.10	.20
BT4063 Head Honcho Medamatcha C	.10	.20
BT4064 Dark Vassal Tambourine C	.10	.20
BT4065 Dark Vassal Cymbal C	.10	.20
BT4066 Dark Vassal Drum C	.10	.20
BT4067 Combo Killer Anilaza SR	4.00	6.00
BT4068 Special Beam Cannon U	.10	.20
BT4069 Planet Namek C	.10	.20
BT4070 Sacrifice C	.10	.20
BT4071 Bardock U	.10	.20
BT4072 Son Goku R	.10	.20
BT4073 Bardock, the Progenitor SR	25.00	30.00
BT4074 Gine, Here to Support C	.10	.20
BT4075 Height of Mastery Son Goku SR	3.00	5.00
BT4075 Height of Mastery Son Goku SPR	10.00	15.00
BT4076 Abrupt Breakthrough Son Goku R	.10	.20
BT4077 Indomitable Dynasty SS Son Goku U	.10	.20
BT4078 Dependable Dynasty Son Goku C	.10	.20
BT4079 Unbroken Dynasty Son Goku C	.10	.20
BT4080 Deadly Golden Great Ape Son Goku C	.10	.20
BT4081 Dynasty Deferred Son Goku U	.10	.20
BT4082 Kakarot C	.10	.20
BT4083 Discovered Dynasty Son Gohan R	.60	1.00
BT4084 Intrepid Dynasty Son Gohan C	.10	.20
BT4085 Prodigal Dynasty Son Goten C	.10	.20
BT4086 Plucky Dynasty Pan U	.10	.20
BT4087 Fledgling Talent Pan C	.10	.20
BT4088 Ox-King Dad at Heart C	.10	.20
BT4089 Dynasty's Solace Chi-Chi C	.10	.20
BT4090 Caring Mother Videl C	.10	.20
BT4091 Adoptive Father Son Gohan C	.10	.20
BT4092 Multimech Bulma U	.10	.20
BT4093 Explorer Bulma C	.10	.20
BT4094 Jiren, Universe's Strongest SR	2.00	3.00
BT4095 Successor of Hope R	1.00	1.50
BT4-096 10x Kamehameha U	.10	.20
BT4097 Instant Trnasmission C	.10	.20
BT4098 Demigra R	.10	.20
BT4099 Mira U	.10	.20
BT4100 Burst Energy SS Bardock R	.10	.20
BT4101 Absolute Space SS3 Trunks SR	.10	.20
BT4102 Dimension Support Trunks C	.10	.20
BT4103 Time's Choice, Supreme Kai of Time C	.10	.20
BT4104 Time Control Chronoa C	.10	.20
BT4105 Temporal Darkness Demigra SR	.10	.20
BT4105 Temporal Darkness Demigra SPR	3.00	5.00
BT4106 Dark Control Demon God Demigra R	.10	.20
BT4107 Heavenly Wizard Demigra C	.10	.20
BT4108 Mira, Creator Absorbed SR	2.50	4.00
BT4109 Invasive Power Mira U	.10	.20
BT4110 Dark Absorption Mira C	.10	.20
BT4111 Umbral Invitation Towa C	.10	.20
BT4112 Dark Rejuvenator Towa C	.10	.20
BT4113 Gravy, Lightning's Might U	.10	.20
BT4114 Gravy, in Demigra's Thrall C	.10	.20
BT4115 Frigid Blast Putine C	.10	.20
BT4116 Putine, in Demigra's Thrall C	.10	.20
BT4117 Time Trauma Masked Saiyan U	.10	.20
BT4118 Dimensional Banisher Fu R	1.50	2.50
BT4119 Tokitoki, Time Creator C	.10	.20
BT4120 Seasoning Arrow U	.10	.20
BT4121 Dark Kamehameha U	.10	.20
BT4122 Minus Kili Zone C	.10	.20
BT4123 Distant Descendant, Son Goku Jr. SCR	25.00	30.00
BT4124 Beyond Darkness Demigra SCR	30.00	35.00

2018 Dragon Ball Super Miraculous Revival

Card	Low	High
BT5001 Yamcha U	.25	.40
BT5002 Pilaf R	.40	.60
BT5003 Oblivious Rampage Son Goku R	.40	.60
BT5004 Son Goku C	.15	.25
BT5005 Feisty Chi-Chi U	.25	.40
BT5006 Grandpa Gohan U	.25	.40
BT5007 Grandpa Gohan, to the Rescue U	.25	.40
BT5008 Sideline Assist Bulma C	.15	.25
BT5009 Yamcha, at 100 SR	2.50	4.00
BT5010 Yamcha C	.15	.25
BT5011 Deadly Defender Krillin R	.40	.60
BT5012 Master Roshi, Martial Expert C	.15	.25
BT5013 Puar, Best Pal C	.15	.25
BT5014 Scheming Oolong U	.25	.40
BT5015 Combiner Mecha Pilaf Machine R	.40	.60
BT5016 Pilaf, Leader of the Crew C	.15	.25
BT5017 Shu, Trusted Lackey C	.15	.25
BT5018 Mai, Trusted Lackey U	.25	.40
BT5019 Bandages, to the Rescue C	.15	.25
BT5020 Spike, to the Rescue C	.15	.25
BT5021 Baba, Champions' Leader U	.25	.40
BT5022 King Piccolo, Terror Unleashed SR	.50	.75
BT5023 Afterimage Technique C	.15	.25
BT5024 Oolong's Wish U	.25	.40
BT5025 A King's Return to Youth C	.15	.25
BT5026 Son Gohan U	.25	.40
BT5027 Janemba R	.40	.60
BT5028 Ready Stance Son Goku C	.15	.25
BT5029 Super Saiyan Son Goku C	.15	.25
BT5030 Resolute Strength Son Goku R	.40	.60
BT5031 Surestrike Son Gohan U	.25	.40
BT5032 Great Saiyaman, Town Hero C	.15	.25
BT5033 Ki Barrage Son Goten C	.15	.25
BT5034 Deadly Defender Vegeta R	1.75	3.00
BT5035 Super Saiyan Vegeta C	.15	.25
BT5036 Ki Barrage Trunks C	.15	.25
BT5037 Vexing Outcome Veku U	.25	.40
BT5038 Gogeta, Hero Revived SR	10.00	15.00
BT5039 Quick Thinkin' Gotenks U	.25	.40
BT5040 Ghost Rampage SS Gotenks SR	.75	1.25
BT5041 North Kai, Keeping Watch C	.15	.25
BT5042 South Kai, Keeping Watch C	.15	.25
BT5043 West Kai, Keeping Watch C	.15	.25
BT5044 East Kai, Keeping Watch U	.25	.40
BT5045 King Yemma, Soul Supervisor C	.15	.25
BT5046 Saike Demon, Rockin' Out U	.25	.40
BT5047 Infernal Chain Janemba SR	1.00	1.50
BT5048 Phantom Strike Janemba R	.40	.60
BT5049 Childish Heart Janemba U	.25	.40
BT5050 Dimension Magic C	.15	.25
BT5051 Call of Justice C	.15	.25
BT5052 Soul Punisher U	.25	.40
BT5053 Pilaf U	.25	.40
BT5054 Super 17 R	.40	.60
BT5055 Twin Onslaught SS4 Son Goku SR	5.00	7.50
BT5056 Super Saiyan Son Goku C	.15	.25
BT5057 Spirited Search Pan U	.25	.40
BT5058 SS Vegeta, No Holding Back R	.40	.60
BT5059 Defensive Stance SS Vegeta C	.15	.25
BT5060 Spirited Search SS Trunks R	.60	1.00
BT5061 Defensive Stance Piccolo C	.15	.25
BT5062 Negotiator Krillin C	.15	.25
BT5063 Physical Mastery Uub C	.15	.25
BT5064 Endless Malice Android 17 C	.15	.25
BT5065 Deadly Defender Android 18 R	2.00	3.50
BT5066 Hell Fighter 17, Evil Revived C	.15	.25
BT5067 Super 17, Cell Absorbed SR	15.00	20.00
BT5068 Super 17, to Further Heights R	1.50	2.50
BT5069 Dr. Myuu, Evil Genius C	.15	.25
BT5070 Android 20, Vile Creator U	.25	.40
BT5071 Infernal Fighter Nappa C	.15	.25
BT5072 Infernal Emperor Frieza C	.15	.25
BT5073 Infernal Villainy Cell C	.15	.25
BT5074 General Rilldo C	.15	.25
BT5075 Shocking Death Ball C	.15	.25
BT5076 Unthinkable Fate C	.15	.25
BT5077 Hidden Feelings C	.15	.25
BT5078 Infernal Messenger U	.25	.40
BT5079 Master Roshi U	.25	.40
BT5080 Sorbet R	.40	.60
BT5081 Super Saiyan Blue Son Goku C	.15	.25
BT5082 Fired Up SS Son Gohan R	.40	.60
BT5083 SSB Vegeta, Testing His Limits SR	.60	1.00
BT5084 Kick Barrage Piccolo C	.15	.25
BT5085 Krillin, Raring to Fight C	.15	.25
BT5086 Tri-Beam Tien Shinhan C	.15	.25
BT5087 Master Roshi, All Warmed Up U	.25	.40
BT5088 Full Surveillance Jaco C	.15	.25
BT5089 Divine Cry Beerus C	.15	.25
BT5090 Quick Obstruction Whis C	.15	.25
BT5091 Frieza, Back from Hell SR	.75	1.25
BT5092 Deadly Defender Frieza R	.40	.60
BT5093 Frieza, Biding His Time C	.15	.25
BT5094 Frieza, Revenge in Motion C	.15	.25
BT5095 Military Command Frieza U	.25	.40
BT5096 Bitter Past Ginyu C	.15	.25
BT5097 Dragon Ball Seeker Sorbet U	.25	.40
BT5098 Ginyu C	.15	.25
BT5099 Vicious Lackey Tagoma U	.25	.40
BT5100 Savage Shisami U	.25	.40
BT5101 Time Magic C	.15	.25
BT5102 Revival of the Emperor U	.25	.40
BT5103 Personal Ambition C	.15	.25
BT5104 Death Ball C	.15	.25
BT5105 Black Masked Saiyan U	.25	.40
BT5106 Adventurous Son Goku C	.15	.25
BT5107 Dragon Ball Seeker Bulma C	.15	.25
BT5108 Kami, Global Unifier C	.15	.25
BT5109 Dende, New to the Job C	.15	.25
BT5110 Shenron, the Wishgranter SR	1.50	2.50
BT5111 Black Masked Saiyan, the Devastator SR	.75	1.25
BT5112 Dark Power Black Masked Saiyan U	.75	1.25
BT5113 Deadly Defender Son Goku R	.50	.75
BT5114 Temporal Rescue Trunks C	.15	.25
BT5115 Power Burst C	.15	.25
BT5116 Dragon Radar R	3.00	5.00
BT5117 Dragon Ball C	.15	.25
BT5118 A Child's Wish C	.15	.25
BT5119 World Peace U	.25	.40
BT5120 Miraculous Fighter SS3 Gogeta SCR	65.00	75.00
BT5009SPR Yamcha, at 100 SPR	8.00	12.00
BT5022SPR King Piccolo, Terror Unleashed SPR	4.50	6.00
BT5038SPR Gogeta, Hero Revived SPR	30.00	40.00
BT5040SPR Ghost Rampage SS Gotenks SPR	8.00	12.00
BT5047SPR Infernal Chain Janemba SPR	8.00	12.00
BT5053PR Pilaf PR		
BT5055SPR Twin Onslaught SS4 Son Goku SPR	5.00	8.00
BT5067SPR Super 17, Cell Absorbed SPR	10.00	15.00
BT5083SPR SSB Vegeta, Testing His Limits SPR	6.00	10.00
BT5091SPR Frieza, Back from Hell SPR	10.00	15.00
BT5110SPR Shenron, the Wishgranter SPR	10.00	15.00
BT5111SPR Black Masked Saiyan, the Devastator SPR	6.00	10.00

2019 Dragon Ball Super Clash of Fates

Card	Low	High
RELEASED ON JANUARY 18, 2019		
TB3001 Frieza // Frieza Metamorphic Threat U	.12	.20
TB3002 Final Showdown Frieza SR	3.00	5.00
TB3003 Frieza, Storm of Blows R	.60	1.00
TB3004 Evolutionary Process Frieza U	.25	.40
TB3005 Frieza, Overture to Battle C	.15	.25
TB3006 Body Change Ginyu R	.75	1.25
TB3007 Strikeforce Recoome U	.12	.20
TB3008 Strikeforce Burter C	.10	.15
TB3009 Strikeforce Jeice C	.10	.15
TB3010 Strikeforce Guldo C	.10	.15
TB3011 Dodoria, the Expendable U	.12	.20
TB3012 Super Zarbon C	.10	.15
TB3013 Zarbon, Hidden Potential C	.10	.15
TB3014 Strategic Mind Kikono FR	.40	.60
TB3015 Recoome Ultra Fighting Bomber C	.10	.15
TB3016 Frieza's Spaceship U	.12	.20
TB3017 Paralysis Technique C	.10	.15
TB3018 Bardock // Bardock, Hope of the Saiyans U	.12	.20
TB3019 Final Strike Bardock SR	.60	1.00
TB3020 Gine, Mother of Hope U	.12	.20
TB3021 Son Goku, Striving to Be the Best FR	5.00	8.00
TB3022 Kakarot, Bearer of Fate C	.10	.15
TB3023 Prince Vegeta C	.10	.15
TB3024 Burnished Bonds Tora R	.15	.25
TB3025 Planetary Invader Tora U	.12	.20
TB3026 Burnished Bonds Fasha R	.25	.40
TB3027 Planetary Invader Fasha U	.12	.20
TB3028 Burnished Bonds Shugesh C	.10	.15
TB3029 Burnished Bonds Borgos C	.40	.60
TB3030 Toolo, the Seer C	.10	.15
TB3031 Future Punch C	.10	.15
TB3032 Tora's Red Armband R	.15	.25
TB3033 Dream the Future C	.10	.15
TB3034 Son Goku // Son Goku, the Legendary Super Saiyan U	.12	.20
TB3035 Final Showdown Son Goku SR	3.00	5.00
TB3036 Hyperspeed Son Goku U	.12	.20
TB3037 Tenacious Spirit Son Gohan SR	2.00	3.00
TB3038 Fledgling Duo Son Gohan C	.10	.15
TB3039 Vegeta, Fully Recovered C	.10	.15
TB3040 Tactical Victory Vegeta C	.10	.15
TB3041 Ever-Dependable Bulma C	.10	.15
TB3042 Persistent Assault Krillin R	.50	.75
TB3043 Fledgling Duo Krillin U	.12	.20
TB3044 Dende C	.10	.15
TB3045 Cheelai, the Beautiful FR	4.00	6.00
TB3046 Plea for Salvation C	.10	.15
TB3047 Frieza Army, Healing Pod R	.60	1.00
TB3048 Preemptive Strike U	2.00	3.00
TB3049 Dende // Piccolo, Brimming with Confidence U	.12	.20
TB3050 Son Gohan C	.10	.15
TB3051 Vegeta, Striving to Be the Best FR	2.50	4.00
TB3052 Krillin, Ability Unleashed C	.10	.15
TB3053 Piccolo, Fused with Nail SR	4.00	.60
TB3054 Piccolo, Potential Unleashed R	.15	.25
TB3055 Namekian Solidarity Piccolo U	.12	.20
TB3056 Ancient Wisdom Guru C	.10	.15
TB3057 Life or Death Nail R	.25	.40
TB3058 Nail, Pride of Namek U	.12	.20
TB3059 Wishmaker Dende R	.50	.75
TB3060 Cargo, Namekian Youth C	.10	.15
TB3061 Twin Revival U	.12	.20
TB3062 Assimilate C	.10	.15
TB3063 Solar Flare C	.10	.15
TB3064 Dragon Ball // Porunga, Saviour of Namekians U	.12	.20
TB3065 No Escape Son Goku C	.10	.15
TB3066 Newfound Power Porunga SR	2.00	3.00
TB3067 Porunga's Dragon Ball C	.30	.50
TB3068 Wish to Porunga C	.10	.15
TB3069 Frieza, Army Reborn SCR	40.00	60.00
TB3002SPR Final Showdown Frieza SPR	5.00	8.00

TB3006SPR Body Change Ginyu SPR 6.00 10.00
TB3019SPR Final Strike Bardock SPR 4.00 6.00
TB3032SPR Tora's Red Armband SPR 2.50 4.00
TB3035SPR Final Showdown Son Goku SPR 10.00 15.00
TB3037SPR Tenacious Spirit Son Gohan SPR 5.00 8.00
TB3053SPR Piccolo, Fused with Nail SPR 2.50 4.00
TB3066SPR Newfound Power Porunga SPR 10.00 15.00

2019 Dragon Ball Super Destroyer Kings

RELEASED ON MARCH 15, 2019
BT6001 Son Golu and Vegeta // SSB Gogeta, Fusion Perfected U .12 .20
BT6002 Frieza // Golden Frieza, the Majestic Emperor U .12 .20
BT6003 Harmonic Energy SSB Son Goku U .12 .20
BT6004 Preemptive Strike SSG Son Goku C .10 .15
BT6005 Son Goku, Prepping for Fusion C .10 .15
BT6006 Support Attack Son Goten C .10 .15
BT6007 Harmonic Energy SSB Vegeta U .12 .20
BT6008 Preemptive Strike SSG Vegeta C .10 .15
BT6009 Vegeta, Prepping for Fusion C .10 .15
BT6010 Support Attack Trunks C .10 .15
BT6011 Bulma, from the Sidelines C .10 .15
BT6012 Veku, Contents Under Pressure R .50 .75
BT6013 Veku, the Fragile C .10 .15
BT6014 SSB Gogeta, Fusion Onslaught SR 1.25 2.00
BT6015 Gogeta, Unparalleled Fusion Warrior R 1.25 2.00
BT6016 Piccolo C .10 .15
BT6017 Golden Frieza Indomitable Emperor SR .50 .75
BT6018 Frieza, the Finisher R .15 .25
BT6019 Berryblue, the Negotiator C .10 .15
BT6020 Quickshift Berryblue U .12 .20
BT6021 Loyal Kikono C .10 .15
BT6022 Kikono, the Fledgeling U .12 .20
BT6023 Live to Fight Another Day U .12 .20
BT6024 New Model Scouter C .10 .15
BT6025 Transcendent Strike C .10 .15
BT6026 Is That All You've Got? C .10 .15
BT6027 Dende // Son Goku, Energy Restored U .12 .20
BT6028 Majin Buu // Majin Buu, Ability Absorber U .12 .20
BT6029 SS3 Son Goku, Pushing Forward U .12 .20
BT6030 Son Goku, Spirit Forger C .10 .15
BT6031 Saiyan Duo Son Goku C .10 .15
BT6032 Son Gohan, Ability Attained C .10 .15
BT6033 Vegeta, Penitent Martyr U .12 .20
BT6034 Saiyan Duo Vegeta C .10 .15
BT6035 Vegito, at Full Throttle R .50 .75
BT6036 Vegito, Powers Combined C .10 .15
BT6037 Vegito, World's Strongest Candy R .30 .50
BT6038 Gokule, the Ultimate Option C .10 .15
BT6039 Buu Buu Volleyball SS3 Gotenks C .10 .15
BT6040 Hercule, Smile and Nod C .10 .15
BT6041 Ultimate Absorption Majin Buu SR .60 1.00
BT6042 Prodigious Absorption Majin Buu SR .60 1.00
BT6043 Majin Buu, the Intensifying Evil R .30 .50
BT6044 Unadulterated Evil Majin Buu C .10 .15
BT6045 Quickshift Majin Buu U .12 .20
BT6046 Majin Buu, Prelude to Villainy C .10 .15
BT6047 Babidi, Overseer of Destruction R .15 .25
BT6048 Dabura C .10 .15
BT6049 Fount of Spirit C .10 .15
BT6050 Bring Back Buu U .12 .20
BT6051 Dawn of Evil C .10 .15
BT6052 Spirit Sword C .10 .15
BT6053 Paragus // Paragus, Father of the Demon U .12 .20
BT6054 Cheelai and Lemo // Cheelai and Lemo, the Kindhearted U .12 .20
BT6055 SS Son Goku, Exploding with Energy C .10 .15
BT6056 SS Vegeta, Exploding with Energy C .10 .15
BT6057 Godstrike Beerus C .10 .15
BT6058 Godgrace Whis C .10 .15
BT6059 Energy Barrage Frieza R .15 .25
BT6060 Broly, Limits Transcended SR .75 1.25
BT6061 Broly, Power Unleashed R 1.00 1.50
BT6062 Broly, Berserker Origins U .12 .20
BT6063 Broly, Unrealized Ambition C .10 .15
BT6064 Paragus, Rampage Trigger SR 1.25 2.00
BT6065 Paragus, Deadly Premonition U .12 .20
BT6066 Quickshift Angila U .12 .20
BT6067 Wings, the Morale Booster U .12 .20
BT6068 Zeiun, the Loyal C .10 .15
BT6069 Ties that Bind Ba C .10 .15
BT6070 Goliamite, the New Breed C .10 .15
BT6071 Speedy Entrance Cheelai R .15 .25
BT6072 Speedy Partner Lemo R .15 .25
BT6073 Beets C .10 .15
BT6074 Broly, the Supreme Berserker SR 1.50 2.50
BT6075 A Kind Wish C .10 .15
BT6076 Broly Control Mechanism U .12 .20
BT6077 Tragic Awakening C .10 .15
BT6078 Wrathful Charge C .10 .15
BT6079 Son Gohan // Untapped Power SS2 Son Gohan U .12 .20
BT6080 Boujack // Boujack, the Pirate Captain U .12 .20
BT6081 Son Goku, Guardian Angel R .15 .25
BT6082 Finishing Blow Son Gohan SR .30 .50
BT6083 Display of Power Son Gohan R .15 .25
BT6084 Son Gohan, Ready for a Match C .10 .15
BT6085 Impenetrable Defense Trunks U .12 .20
BT6086 Dependable Saiyan Trunks C .10 .15
BT6087 Hercule, the Champion C .10 .15
BT6088 Piccolo, the Resolute C .10 .15
BT6089 Fearless Assault Krillin C .10 .15
BT6090 Tien Shinhan C .10 .15
BT6091 Yamcha, Ready to Brawl C .10 .15
BT6092 X.S. Cash, the Gazillionaire C .10 .15
BT6093 Boujack, the Plunderer SR .30 .50
BT6094 Space Pirate Boujack R .15 .25
BT6095 Quickshift Gokua U .12 .20
BT6096 Space Pirate Gokua U .12 .20
BT6097 Space Pirate Zangya R .15 .25
BT6098 Merciless Strike Zangya C .10 .15
BT6099 Space Pirate Bido C .10 .15
BT6100 Space Pirate Bujin C .10 .15
BT6101 Arrival of the Space Pirates U .12 .20
BT6102 Merciless Farewell C .10 .15
BT6103 Full-Power Kamehameha C .10 .15
BT6104 Fatherly Love Saves the Day C .10 .15
BT6105 Son Goku // Bonds of Friendship Son Goku U .12 .20
BT6106 Super Dragon Balls // Super Shenron, the Almighty U .12 .20
BT6107 Son Goku, the Adventure Begins SR 2.00 3.00
BT6108 Quickshift Krillin U .12 .20
BT6109 Training Buddy Krillin R .15 .25
BT6110 Master Roshi C .10 .15
BT6111 Tien Shinhan, Returning Fire C .10 .15
BT6112 Mercenary Tao, Ruthless Trainer C .10 .15
BT6113 Commander Red, Head of the RR Army R .15 .25
BT6114 Bonds of Friendship Android 8 C .10 .15
BT6115 Super Shenron, Ultimate Wishmaster SR .30 .50
BT6116 Restore the Universes! U .12 .20
BT6117 Four-Star Ball R 4.00 6.00
BT6118 Super Dragon Balls // Super Shenron, the Almighty C .10 .15
BT6119 Eighter Aid C .10 .15
BT6120 Vegeta, Agent of Destruction DR 1.00 1.50
BT6121 Janemba, Agent of Destruction DR 3.00 5.00
BT6122 Lord Slug, Agent of Destruction DR 1.00 1.50
BT6123 Android 13, Agent of Destruction DR .60 1.00
BT6124 Boujack, Agent of Destruction DR .75 1.25
BT6125 Broly, Ultimate Agent of Destruction SCR 200.00 300.00
BT6126 Arcane Absorption Majin Buu SCR 100.00 150.00
BT6014SPR SSB Gogeta, Fusion Onslaught SPR 10.00 15.00
BT6017SPR Golden Frieza Indomitable Emperor SPR 4.00 6.00
BT6041SPR Ultimate Absorption Majin Buu SPR 3.00 5.00
BT6042SPR Prodigious Absorption Majin Buu SPR 4.00 6.00
BT6060SPR Broly, Limits Transcended SPR 8.00 12.00
BT6064SPR Paragus, Rampage Trigger SPR 5.00 8.00
BT6074SPR Broly, the Supreme Berserker SPR 10.00 15.00
BT6082SPR Finishing Blow Son Gohan SPR 4.00 6.00
BT6093SPR Boujack, the Plunderer SPR 4.00 6.00
BT6107SPR Son Goku, the Adventure Begins SPR 10.00 15.00
BT6115SPR Super Shenron, Ultimate Wishmaster SPR 2.00 3.00

2019 Dragon Ball Super Assault of the Saiyans

RELEASED ON AUGUST 2, 2019
BT7001 Son Gohan // Son Gohan & Son Goten, Brotherly Bonds C .10 .15
BT7002 Broly // Broly, Recurring Nightmare U .12 .20
BT7003 Raditz, the Oppressor U .12 .20
BT7004 Son Goku, Heavenly Salvation C .10 .15
BT7005 Machspeed Kaio-Ken Son Goku R .30 .50
BT7006 Dependable Brother Son Gohan SPR 4.00 6.00
BT7006 Dependable Brother Son Gohan SPRS 50.00 75.00
BT7006 Dependable Brother Son Gohan SR 1.50 2.50
BT7007 Helping Hand Son Gohan C .10 .15
BT7008 Wilderness Training Son Gohan C .10 .15
BT7009 Exalted Trio Son Goten C .10 .15
BT7010 Last Resort Vegeta R .15 .25
BT7011 Exalted Trio Trunks C .10 .15
BT7012 Father Figure Piccolo C .10 .15
BT7013 Krillin, Unforeseen Savior C .10 .15
BT7014 Exalted Trio Videl C .10 .15
BT7015 Coco, Village Princess C .10 .15
BT7016 Coco's Grandpa, Village Oldster C .10 .15
BT7017 Elder, Village Guardian C .10 .15
BT7018 Natade Village Monster C .10 .15
BT7019 Shaman, Ritual Master C .10 .15
BT7020 Broly, Counter Reversal SR 4.00 6.00
BT7021 Familial Bonds C .10 .15
BT7022 Dormant Legend U .12 .20
BT7023 Denial of Hope U .12 .20
BT7024 The Final Guardian R .15 .25
BT7025 Son Goku & Vegeta // SSB Vegito, Energy Eruption C .10 .15
BT7026 Goku Black & Zamasu // Fused Zamasu, Supreme Strike U .12 .20
BT7027 SSB Son Goku, the Sweeper U .12 .20
BT7028 Saiyan Bloodline Son Goku U .12 .20
BT7029 Undying Spirit Son Gohan R .30 .50
BT7030 SS2 Trunks, Memories of the Past SPR 6.00 10.00
BT7030 SS2 Trunks, Memories of the Past SPRS 50.00 75.00
BT7030 SS2 Trunks, Memories of the Past SR 1.50 2.50
BT7031 Trunks, Fighting the Darkness C .10 .15
BT7032 Trunks, the Sweeper C .10 .15
BT7033 Bulma, Saying Farewell C .10 .15
BT7034 Mai, Filled with Energy C .10 .15
BT7035 Whis, the Regulator C .10 .15
BT7036 Gowasu, Zamasu's Master C .10 .15
BT7037 Almighty Do-Over Zen-Oh U .12 .20
BT7038 Vados C .10 .15
BT7039 Kale, Sister of Annihilation C .10 .15
BT7040 Kale, the Awakened Sister SR 10.00 15.00
BT7041 Kale, Timid Sister C .10 .15
BT7042 Goku Black, the Replicator U .12 .20
BT7043 SS Rose Goku Black, Inviting the Darkness R .15 .25
BT7044 Goku Black, Evil's Accomplice C .10 .15
BT7045 Betrayal of the Master C .10 .15
BT7046 Mass Replication U .12 .20
BT7047 You're Wide Open! U .12 .20
BT7048 All Too Easy... R .15 .25
BT7049 Raditz // Raditz, Brotherly Hate U .12 .20
BT7050 Son Goku // Kaio-Ken Son Goku, Training Complete C .10 .15
BT7051 Raditz, Saiyan-in-Arms SPR 4.00 6.00
BT7051 Raditz, Saiyan-in-Arms SR .75 1.25
BT7052 Raditz, Saiyan Assailant R .15 .25
BT7053 Unlikely Duo Son Goku U .12 .20
BT7054 Son Gohan, Hope of the People C .10 .15
BT7055 Son Gohan, Momentary Awakening U .12 .20
BT7056 Son Goten, Out Adventuring C .10 .15
BT7057 Great Ape Vegeta, Energy Manipulation C .10 .15
BT7058 Vegeta the Cruel R 2.50 4.00
BT7059 Trunks, Out Adventuring C .10 .15
BT7060 Piccolo, Special Beam Cannon Unleashed SR 2.50 4.00
BT7061 Krillin C .10 .15
BT7062 Kamehameha Blast Yamcha C .10 .15
BT7063 Sorrowful Strike Tien Shinhan C .10 .15
BT7064 Chiaotzu, Desperate Measures C .10 .15
BT7065 Yajirobe, Lying in Wait C .10 .15
BT7066 Urgent Aid Kami U .12 .20
BT7067 Nappa, the Cultivator C .10 .15
BT7068 Saibaimen, Endless Explosions C .10 .15
BT7069 SS Broly, Legend Unleashed U .12 .20
BT7070 Double Sunday C .10 .15
BT7071 Power Ball C .10 .15
BT7072 Hidden Power of the Saiyans U .12 .20
BT7073 For the Greater Good R .15 .25
BT7074 Hit // Time-Skip Hit C .10 .15
BT7075 Caulifla & Kale // Kefla, Soul Overflowing U .12 .20
BT7076 Super Saiyan Blue Vegeta C .10 .15
BT7077 Saiyan Bloodline Vegeta R .15 .25
BT7078 Champa the Trickster R 2.00 3.00
BT7079 Hit, Pride of Universe 6 SPR 4.00 6.00
BT7079 Hit, Pride of Universe 6 SPRS 50.00 75.00
BT7079 Hit, Pride of Universe 6 SR 1.00 1.50
BT7080 Hit, Afterimage Master C .10 .15
BT7081 Cabba, Undisguised Rage U .12 .20
BT7082 Cabba, Brimming with Spirit U .12 .20
BT7083 Caulifla, the Awakened Sister SR 10.00 15.00
BT7084 Caulifla, the Resilient Sister C .10 .15
BT7085 Caulifla, the Bold Sister U .12 .20
BT7086 Ironclad Defense Frost C .10 .15
BT7087 Frost, the Path to Full Power C .10 .15
BT7088 Botamo, Defender of Universe 6 C .10 .15
BT7089 Magetta, Defender of Universe 6 C .10 .15
BT7090 Namekian Partner Saonel C .10 .15
BT7091 Namekian Partner Pirina C .10 .15
BT7092 Zamasu, Inviting Despair U .12 .20
BT7093 Hidden Ambition Zamasu C .10 .15
BT7094 Zamasu, the Mastermind C .10 .15
BT7095 Weak Spot Protection C .10 .15
BT7096 Zero Mortals Plan U .12 .20
BT7097 Kefla's Fury U .12 .20
BT7098 Restrain R .15 .25
BT7099 Son Goku, Dimensional Defender U .12 .20
BT7100 Son Goku, Making an Entrance U .12 .20
BT7101 Vegeta, Making an Entrance U .12 .20
BT7102 Super Saiyan Trunks C .10 .15
BT7103 Trunks, Time Regulator C .10 .15
BT7104 Supreme Kai of Time, Time Regulator R .15 .25
BT7105 Demigra, the Sorcerer U .12 .20
BT7106 Towa, Dimension Leaper R .15 .25
BT7107 Assembling the Sqaud C .10 .15
BT7108 Time Transmission G C .10 .15
BT7109 Tokitoki City C .10 .15
BT7110 An Unexpected Turn U .12 .20
BT7111 Kaio-Ken Son Goku, Defender of Earth SPR 15.00 25.00
BT7111 Kaio-Ken Son Goku, Defender of Earth SR 10.00 15.00
BT7112 Son Goku & Piccolo, Budding Friendship R .15 .25
BT7112 Son Goku & Piccolo, Budding Friendship R .30 .50
(Non-Foil Deck Exclusive)
BT7113 Son Gohan & Son Goten, Familial Bonds SPR 8.00 12.00
BT7113 Son Gohan & Son Goten, Familial Bonds SR 4.00 6.00
BT7114 Vegeta, Saiyan Elite SR 3.00 5.00
BT7115 Broly, Tragedy Foretold SPR 10.00 15.00
BT7115 Broly, Tragedy Foretold SR 2.00 3.00
BT7116 Broly, Rapid Barrage U .12 .20
BT7117 Broly, Demonic Origins R .15 .25
BT7118 Meteoric Energy SSB Vegito SPR 8.00 12.00
BT7118 Meteoric Energy SSB Vegito SPRS 100.00 150.00
BT7118 Meteoric Energy SSB Vegito SR 2.50 4.00
BT7119 Champa and Vados, Gracious Aid SR 2.50 4.00
BT7120 Beerus, Fickle God R 2.50 4.00
BT7121 Meteoric Energy Kefla SPR 12.00 20.00
BT7121 Meteoric Energy Kefla SR 1.50 2.50
BT7122 Kefla, the Peak of Perfection U .12 .20
BT7123 Fused Zamasu, Divine Providence SPR 10.00 15.00
BT7123 Fused Zamasu, Divine Providence SR 3.00 5.00
BT7124 Fused Zamasu, the Cunning R .15 .25
BT7125 SS3 Nappa, Saiyan Might ISR 1.00 1.50
BT7126 SS3 Trunks, Saiyan Harmonizer ISR .50 .75
BT7127 SS3 Brooly, Saiyan Berserker ISR .75 1.25
BT7128 SS2 Kefla, Saiyan Synthesis ISR .50 .75
BT7129 Son Goku, Saiyan Transcendence ISR .50 .75
BT7130 SS3 Scramble - Raditz, Vegeta & Broly SCR 50.00 75.00
BT7131 Power of Potara - Vegito SCR 75.00 125.00

2018 Dragon Ball Super Expansion Deck Mighty Heroes

EX0101 Comrades Combined Son Goku EX .15 .25
EX0102 Comrades Combined Vegeta EX .15 .25
EX0103 Trunks, Link to the Future EX .15 .25
EX0104 SSB Vegito, the Savior EX .15 .25
EX0105 Unified Spirit Son Goten EX .15 .25
EX0106 Unified Spirit Trunks EX .15 .25
EX0107 Psyched Up Gotenks EX .15 .25

2018 Dragon Ball Super Expansion Deck Mighty Heroes Foil

EX0101 Comrades Combined Son Goku EX .10 .20
EX0102 Comrades Combined Vegeta EX .10 .20
EX0103 Trunks, Link to the Future EX .10 .20
EX0104 SSB Vegito, the Savior EX .10 .20
EX0105 Unified Spirit Son Goten EX .10 .20
EX0106 Unified Spirit Trunks EX .10 .20
EX0107 Psyched Up Gotenks EX .10 .20

2018 Dragon Ball Super Expansion Deck Dark Demon's Villains

EX0201 Time Patrol Trunks EX .10 .20
EX0202 Masked Saiyan, the Mysterious Warrior EX .10 .20
EX0203 Supreme Kai of Time, Continuity Keeper EX .10 .20
EX0204 Time Ruler Towa EX .10 .20
EX0205 Mira, From the Darkness EX .10 .20
EX0206 Majin Twin Shun Shun EX .10 .20
EX0207 Majin Twin Haru Haru EX .10 .20

2018 Dragon Ball Super Expansion Deck Dark Demon's Villains Foil

EX0201 Time Patrol Trunks EX .10 .20
EX0202 Masked Saiyan, the Mysterious Warrior EX .10 .20
EX0203 Supreme Kai of Time, Continuity Keeper EX .10 .20
EX0204 Time Ruler Towa EX .10 .20
EX0205 Mira, From the Darkness EX .10 .20
EX0206 Majin Twin Shun Shun EX .10 .20
EX0207 Majin Twin Haru Haru EX .10 .20

2017 Dragon Ball Super Starter Deck The Awakening

SD101 SSGSS Son Goku, The Soul Striker ST 3.00 5.00
SD102 God Rush Son Goku ST 1.50 2.50
SD103 SS3 Son Goku, Maximum Energy ST 1.50 2.50
SD104 Rapid Spirit Ball Son Goku ST 1.50 2.50
SD105 Vegeta, Prince of Speed ST 1.50 2.50

2018 Dragon Ball Super Starter Deck The Dark Invasion

SD301 The Masked Saiyan ST .10 .20
SD302 Killer Sword Trunks ST .10 .20
SD303 Quick blade Trunks ST .10 .20
SD304 Encroaching Threat Masked Saiyan ST .10 .20
SD305 Power Aura Mira ST .10 .20

2018 Dragon Ball Super Starter Deck The Extreme Evolution

SD201 Son Goku ST .10 .20
SD202 Broken Limits Super Saiyan 3 Son Goku ST .10 .20
SD203 Unbreakable Super Saiyan Son Goku ST .10 .20
SD204 Rushing Warrior Pan ST .10 .20
SD205 Chain Attack Trunks ST .10 .20

2018 Dragon Ball Super Starter Deck The Crimson Saiyan

SD501 Golden Great Ape Son Goku ST .10 .20
SD502 Power Charge Bardock ST .10 .20

SD503 SSB Son Goku, at the Apex ST	.10	.20
SD504 Reborn Might SS4 Son Goku ST	.10	.20
SD505 Ultimate Potential SS2 Son Gohan ST	.10	.20

2018 Dragon Ball Super Starter Deck The Guardian of Namekians

SD401 Piccolo Jr. ST	.10	.20
SD402 Indomitable Link Son Gohan ST	.10	.20
SD403 Indomitable Link Piccolo ST	.10	.20
SD404 King Piccolo, Lord of Terror ST	.10	.20
SD405 Namekian Bond Saonel ST	.10	.20

2019 Dragon Ball Super Assault of the Saiyans Starter Deck

SD901 King Vegeta // King Vegeta, Leader of the Saiyans	.60	1.00
SD902 Raditz, Earth Invader	.20	.30
SD903 Vegeta, Royal Prince	.75	1.25
SD904 Fated Kaio-Ken Son Goku	2.00	3.00
SD905 King Vegeta's Dynasty	.60	1.00
XD101 Cabba // Vegeta & Cabba, Master & Pupil	.75	1.25
XD102 Vegeta, Saiyan of Universe 7	.15	.25
XD103 Champa, Scheming God of Destruction	.20	.30
XD104 Sisterly Bonds Kale	1.25	2.00
XD105 Hit, Ace of Universe 6	.15	.25
XD106 Cabba, Saiyan of Universe 6	.25	.40
XD107 Caulifla, Troublemaker of Universe 6	.40	.60
XD108 Vegeta & Cabba, Master-Pupil Bond	.30	.50
XD109 Planet Sadala	.40	.60
XD110 Frost's Deadly Poison	1.25	2.00

2019 Dragon Ball Super Destroyer Kings Starter Deck

SD801 Broly // Broly, Evil Unleashed	.60	1.00
SD802 Broly, the Ravager	.30	.50
SD803 Broly, Rushing Forth	.25	.40
SD804 Defending Father Paragus	6.00	10.00
SD805 Cheelai, Frieza Force Soldier	.75	1.25
SD806 Lemo, Frieza Force Soldier	.15	.25
SD807 Son Goku, Time to Fight	.15	.25
SD808 Vegeta, Time to Fight	.30	.50
SD809 Godly Destruction Whis	2.00	3.00
SD810 Godly Destruction Beerus	.15	.25

2016 Final Fantasy Opus Pre-Launch Promo

A001 Cloud P

2016 Final Fantasy Opus I

COMPLETE SET (216)	785.00	1150.00
BOOSTER BOX (36 PACKS)	250.00	400.00
BOOSTER PACK (12 CARDS)	8.00	20.00
STARTER DECK FINAL FANTASY VII	25.00	40.00
STARTER DECK FINAL FANTASY X	25.00	40.00
STARTER DECK FINAL FANTASY XII	25.00	40.00
RELEASED ON OCTOBER 28, 2016		
1-001 Auron H	5.00	8.00
1-002 Auron R	4.00	6.00
1-003 Red Mage C	.60	1.00
1-004 Ifrit C	.60	1.00
1-005 Warrior of Light R	4.00	6.00
1-006 Garland H	5.00	8.00
1-007 Gadot R	4.00	6.00
1-008 Ranger C	.60	1.00
1-009 Cloud C	.60	1.00
1-010 Black Mage C	.60	1.00
1-011 Evoker C	.60	1.00
1-012 Zack R	4.00	6.00
1-013 Sazh H	5.00	8.00
1-014 Samurai C	.60	1.00
1-015 Jecht L	10.00	15.00
1-016 Tifa C	.60	1.00
1-017 Dajh R	4.00	6.00
1-018 Bahamut L	14.00	18.00
1-019 Chocobo Chick C	.60	1.00
1-020 Fang R	4.00	6.00
1-021 Firion H	5.00	8.00
1-022 Firion R	4.00	6.00
1-023 Brynhildr R	4.00	6.00
1-024 Magus C	.60	1.00
1-025 Squire C	.60	1.00
1-026 Squire C	.60	1.00
1-027 Lann H	5.00	8.00
1-028 Reynn R	4.00	6.00
1-029 Red XIII C	.60	1.00
1-030 Lebreau R	4.00	6.00
1-031 Chemist C	.60	1.00
1-032 Chemist C	.60	1.00
1-033 Argath C	.60	1.00
1-034 Orran R	4.00	6.00
1-035 Bard C	.60	1.00
1-036 Bard C	.60	1.00
1-037 Kuja H	5.00	8.00
1-038 Shiva R	4.00	6.00
1-039 Shiva C	.60	1.00
1-040 Summoner C	.60	1.00
1-041 Squall L	20.00	25.00
1-042 Squall R	4.00	6.00
1-043 Snow H	5.00	8.00
1-044 Sephiroth R	4.00	6.00
1-045 Serah R	4.00	6.00
1-046 Terra H	5.00	8.00
1-047 Terra R	4.00	6.00
1-048 Devout C	.60	1.00
1-049 Time Mage C	.60	1.00
1-050 Knight C	.60	1.00
1-051 Nooj R	4.00	6.00
1-052 Hades R	4.00	6.00
1-053 Summoner C	.60	1.00
1-054 Dark Knight C	.60	1.00
1-055 Dark Knight C	.60	1.00
1-056 Josef H	5.00	8.00
1-057 Duke Larg R	4.00	6.00
1-058 Laguna L	15.00	20.00
1-059 Laguna R	4.00	6.00
1-060 Leon H	5.00	8.00
1-061 Alexander R	4.00	6.00
1-062 Valefor L	10.00	15.00
1-063 Vaan H	5.00	8.00
1-064 Aerith R	4.00	6.00
1-065 Aerith C	.60	1.00
1-066 Dancer C	.60	1.00
1-067 Onion Knight R	4.00	6.00
1-068 Evoker C	.60	1.00
1-069 Thief C	.60	1.00
1-070 Thief C	.60	1.00
1-071 Zidane L	20.00	25.00
1-072 Cid Highwind R	4.00	6.00
1-073 Cid Highwind C	.60	1.00
1-074 Sylph R	4.00	6.00
1-075 Chocobo C	.60	1.00
1-076 Chocobo C	.60	1.00
1-077 Devout C	.60	1.00
1-078 Ninja C	.60	1.00
1-079 Nora R	4.00	6.00
1-080 Bartz H	5.00	8.00
1-081 Bartz R	4.00	6.00
1-082 Hope R	4.00	6.00
1-083 Maria H	5.00	8.00
1-084 Y'shtola H	5.00	8.00
1-085 Yuffie R	4.00	6.00
1-086 Yuffie C	.60	1.00
1-087 Archer C	.60	1.00
1-088 Archer C	.60	1.00
1-089 Rikku H	5.00	8.00
1-090 Rikku R	4.00	6.00
1-091 Amodar R	4.00	6.00
1-092 Dark Knight C	.60	1.00
1-093 Vanille H	5.00	8.00
1-094 Vincent R	4.00	6.00
1-095 Enna Kros R	4.00	6.00
1-096 Mystic C	.60	1.00
1-097 Guy H	5.00	8.00
1-098 Gabranth R	4.00	6.00
1-099 Black Belt C	.60	1.00
1-100 Black Belt C	.60	1.00
1-101 Gippal R	4.00	6.00
1-102 Kimahri H	5.00	8.00
1-103 Kimahri C	.60	1.00
1-104 Kefka H	5.00	8.00
1-105 Evoker C	.60	1.00
1-106 Golem C	.60	1.00
1-107 Shantotto L	12.00	15.00
1-108 Cecil H	5.00	8.00
1-109 Serafie R	4.00	6.00
1-110 Titan C	.60	1.00
1-111 Tama C	.60	1.00
1-112 Delita R	4.00	6.00
1-113 Delita C	.60	1.00
1-114 Barret R	4.00	6.00
1-115 Geomancer C	.60	1.00
1-116 Prishe L	12.00	15.00
1-117 Hecatonchier R	4.00	6.00
1-118 Mustadio R	4.00	6.00
1-119 Monk C	.60	1.00
1-120 Monk C	.60	1.00
1-121 Red Mage C	.60	1.00
1-122 Exdeath H	5.00	8.00
1-123 Odin R	4.00	6.00
1-124 Odin R	4.00	6.00
1-125 Onion Knight R	4.00	6.00
1-126 Orlandeau H	5.00	8.00
1-127 Kain H	5.00	8.00
1-128 Gilgamesh R	4.00	6.00
1-129 Gilgamesh C	.60	1.00
1-130 Black Mage C	.60	1.00
1-131 Cait Sith R	4.00	6.00
1-132 Cait Sith C	.60	1.00
1-133 Sage C	.60	1.00
1-134 Duke Goltanna R	4.00	6.00
1-135 Golbez L	15.00	18.00
1-136 Zalbaag C	.60	1.00
1-137 Seymour R	4.00	6.00
1-138 Summoner C	.60	1.00
1-139 Summoner C	.60	1.00
1-140 Magus C	.60	1.00
1-141 Lightning L	20.00	30.00
1-142 Lightning R	4.00	6.00
1-143 Ramuh C	.60	1.00
1-144 Ramza R	4.00	6.00
1-145 Ramza C	.60	1.00
1-146 Ricard H	5.00	8.00
1-147 Dragoon C	.60	1.00
1-148 Dragoon C	.60	1.00
1-149 Lulu H	5.00	8.00
1-150 Lulu R	4.00	6.00
1-151 Agrias R	4.00	6.00
1-152 Ultimecia L	20.00	25.00
1-153 Alma C	.60	1.00
1-154 Vaan R	4.00	6.00
1-155 Warrior of Light R	4.00	6.00
1-156 Ovelia C	.60	1.00
1-157 Scholar C	.60	1.00
1-158 Cloud of Darkness H	10.00	15.00
1-159 Evoker C	.60	1.00
1-160 Gordon H	5.00	8.00
1-161 White Mage C	.60	1.00
1-162 Cecil R	4.00	6.00
1-163 Tidus L	30.00	35.00
1-164 Tidus R	4.00	6.00
1-165 Knight C	.60	1.00
1-166 Knight C	.60	1.00
1-167 Viking C	.60	1.00
1-168 Geomancer C	.60	1.00
1-169 Geomancer C	.60	1.00
1-170 Fairy C	.60	1.00
1-171 Minwu H	15.00	25.00
1-172 Moogle C	.60	1.00
1-173 Mime C	.60	1.00
1-174 Yaag Rosch R	4.00	6.00
1-175 Yuj R	4.00	6.00
1-176 Yuna H	5.00	8.00
1-177 Yuna R	4.00	6.00
1-178 Leviathan R	4.00	6.00
1-179 Leila H	5.00	8.00
1-180 Wakka R	4.00	6.00
1-181 Onion Knight H	5.00	8.00
1-182 Cloud L	35.00	45.00
1-183 Cosmos H	12.00	16.00
1-184 Chaos H	10.00	15.00
1-185 The Emperor H	13.00	17.00
1-186 Sephiroth L	25.00	30.00
1-187 Cloud S	1.25	2.00
1-188 Zangan S	1.25	2.00
1-189 Tifa S	1.25	2.00
1-190 Bahamut Fury S	1.25	2.00
1-191 Red XIII S	1.25	2.00
1-192 Cid Raines S	1.25	2.00
1-193 Jihl Nabaat S	1.25	2.00
1-194 Snow S	1.25	2.00
1-195 Serah S	1.25	2.00
1-196 Mog XIII2 S	1.25	2.00
1-197 Brother S	1.25	2.00
1-198 Valefor S	1.25	2.00
1-199 Paine S	1.25	2.00
1-200 Baralai S	1.25	2.00
1-201 Rikku S	1.25	2.00
1-202 Vincent S	1.25	2.00
1-203 Wedge S	1.25	2.00
1-204 Jessie S	1.25	2.00
1-205 Barrett S	1.25	2.00
1-206 Biggs S	1.25	2.00
1-207 Gilgamesh S	1.25	2.00
1-208 Noel S	1.25	2.00
1-209 Maqui S	1.25	2.00
1-210 Lightning S	1.25	2.00
1-211 Rygdea S	1.25	2.00
1-212 Shuyin S	1.25	2.00
1-213 Tidus S	1.25	2.00
1-214 Yuna S	1.25	2.00
1-215 Lenne S	1.25	2.00
1-216 Wakka S	1.25	2.00

2016 Final Fantasy Opus I Premium Foil

COMPLETE SET (216)	1500.00	2000.00
RELEASED ON OCTOBER 28, 2016		
1-001 Auron H	8.00	10.00
1-002 Auron R	10.00	12.00
1-003 Red Mage C	2.00	3.50
1-004 Ifrit C	2.00	3.50
1-005 Warrior of Light R	6.00	10.00
1-006 Garland H	6.00	10.00
1-007 Gadot R	5.00	8.00
1-008 Ranger C	2.00	3.50
1-009 Cloud C	6.00	8.00
1-010 Black Mage C	2.00	3.50
1-011 Evoker C	2.00	3.50
1-012 Zack R	8.00	10.00
1-013 Sazh H	8.00	10.00
1-014 Samurai C	2.00	3.50
1-015 Jecht L	25.00	40.00
1-016 Tifa C	4.50	5.50
1-017 Dajh R	6.00	8.00
1-018 Bahamut L	20.00	25.00
1-019 Chocobo Chick C	2.00	3.50
1-020 Fang R	6.00	8.00
1-021 Firion H	10.00	12.00
1-022 Firion R	7.00	9.00
1-023 Brynhildr R	4.00	6.00
1-024 Magus C	2.00	3.50
1-025 Squire C	2.00	3.50
1-026 Squire C	2.00	3.50
1-027 Lann H	10.00	12.00
1-028 Reynn R	8.00	10.00
1-029 Red XIII C	4.00	5.00
1-030 Lebreau R	4.00	6.00
1-031 Chemist C	2.00	3.50
1-032 Chemist C	2.00	3.50
1-033 Argath C	2.00	3.50
1-034 Orran R	4.00	6.00
1-035 Bard C	2.00	3.50
1-036 Bard C	2.00	3.50
1-037 Kuja H	10.00	15.00
1-038 Shiva R	8.00	10.00
1-039 Shiva C	2.00	3.50
1-040 Summoner C	2.00	3.50
1-041 Squall L	35.00	50.00
1-042 Squall R	8.00	10.00
1-043 Snow H	15.00	20.00
1-044 Sephiroth R	8.00	10.00
1-045 Serah R	4.00	6.00
1-046 Terra H	13.00	16.00
1-047 Terra R	8.00	12.00
1-048 Devout C	2.00	3.50
1-049 Time Mage C	2.00	3.50
1-050 Knight C	2.00	3.50
1-051 Nooj R	7.00	9.00
1-052 Hades R	7.00	9.00
1-053 Summoner C	2.00	3.50
1-054 Dark Knight C	2.00	3.50
1-055 Dark Knight C	2.00	3.50
1-056 Josef H	9.00	11.00
1-057 Duke Larg R	6.00	8.00
1-058 Laguna L	20.00	35.00
1-059 Laguna R	8.00	10.00
1-060 Leon H	8.00	10.00
1-061 Alexander R	8.00	10.00
1-062 Valefor L	20.00	25.00
1-063 Vaan H	8.00	10.00
1-064 Aerith R	10.00	12.00
1-065 Aerith C	4.50	5.50
1-066 Dancer C	2.00	3.50
1-067 Onion Knight R	4.00	6.00
1-068 Evoker C	2.00	3.50
1-069 Thief C	2.00	3.50
1-070 Thief C	2.00	3.50
1-071 Zidane L	40.00	50.00
1-072 Cid Highwind R	7.00	9.00
1-073 Cid Highwind C	2.00	3.50
1-074 Sylph R	6.00	8.00
1-075 Chocobo C	4.00	4.50
1-076 Chocobo C	2.00	3.50
1-077 Devout C	2.00	3.50
1-078 Ninja C	2.00	3.50
1-079 Nora R	6.00	8.00
1-080 Bartz H	8.00	10.00
1-081 Bartz R	6.00	8.00
1-082 Hope R	5.00	7.00
1-083 Maria H	11.00	13.00
1-084 Y'shtola H	10.00	12.00
1-085 Yuffie R	10.00	12.00
1-086 Yuffie C	2.00	3.50
1-087 Archer C	2.00	3.50

1-088 Archer C	2.00	3.50
1-089 Rikku H	10.00	12.00
1-090 Rikku R	8.00	10.00
1-091 Amodar R	6.00	8.00
1-092 Dark Knight C	2.00	3.50
1-093 Vanille H	8.00	11.00
1-094 Vincent R	8.00	10.00
1-095 Enna Kros R	7.00	9.00
1-096 Mystic C	2.00	3.50
1-097 Guy H	8.00	10.00
1-098 Gabranth R	7.00	9.00
1-099 Black Belt C	2.00	3.50
1-100 Black Belt C	2.00	3.50
1-101 Gippal R	7.00	9.00
1-102 Kimahri H	4.00	6.00
1-103 Kimahri C	2.00	3.50
1-104 Kefka H	10.00	12.00
1-105 Evoker C	2.00	3.50
1-106 Golem C	2.00	3.50
1-107 Shantotto L	20.00	30.00
1-108 Cecil H	15.00	20.00
1-109 Serafie R	8.00	10.00
1-110 Titan C	2.00	3.50
1-111 Tama C	4.00	5.00
1-112 Delita R	8.00	10.00
1-113 Delita C	2.00	3.50
1-114 Barret R	7.00	9.00
1-115 Geomancer C	2.00	3.50
1-116 Prishe L	25.00	30.00
1-117 Hecatonchier R	9.00	11.00
1-118 Mustadio R	7.00	9.00
1-119 Monk C	2.00	3.50
1-120 Monk C	2.00	3.50
1-121 Red Mage C	2.00	3.50
1-122 Exdeath H	10.00	15.00
1-123 Odin R	8.00	10.00
1-124 Odin R	8.00	10.00
1-125 Onion Knight R	4.00	6.00
1-126 Orlandeau H	11.00	13.00
1-127 Kain H	8.00	10.00
1-128 Gilgamesh R	4.00	6.00
1-129 Gilgamesh C	4.00	5.00
1-130 Black Mage C	2.00	3.50
1-131 Cait Sith R	6.00	8.00
1-132 Cait Sith C	2.00	3.50
1-133 Sage C	2.00	3.50
1-134 Duke Goltanna R	4.00	6.00
1-135 Golbez L	10.00	12.00
1-136 Zalbaag C	2.00	3.50
1-137 Seymour R	6.00	8.00
1-138 Summoner C	2.00	3.50
1-139 Summoner C	2.00	3.50
1-140 Magus C	2.00	3.50
1-141 Lightning L	45.00	55.00
1-142 Lightning R	10.00	15.00
1-143 Ramuh C	2.00	3.50
1-144 Ramza R	8.00	10.00
1-145 Ramza C	2.00	3.50
1-146 Ricard H	10.00	15.00
1-147 Dragoon C	2.00	3.50
1-148 Dragoon C	2.00	3.50
1-149 Lulu H	10.00	15.00
1-150 Lulu R	4.00	6.00
1-151 Agrias R	4.00	6.00
1-152 Ultimecia L	30.00	35.00
1-153 Alma C	2.00	3.50
1-154 Vaan R	10.00	12.00
1-155 Warrior of Light R	6.00	8.00
1-156 Ovelia C	2.00	3.50
1-157 Scholar C	2.00	3.50
1-158 Cloud of Darkness H	20.00	25.00
1-159 Evoker C	2.00	3.50
1-160 Gordon H	10.00	12.00
1-161 White Mage C	2.00	3.50
1-162 Cecil R	8.00	12.00
1-163 Tidus L	45.00	50.00
1-164 Tidus R	10.00	12.00
1-165 Knight C	2.00	3.50
1-166 Knight C	2.00	3.50
1-167 Viking C	2.00	3.50
1-168 Geomancer C	2.00	3.50
1-169 Geomancer C	2.00	3.50
1-170 Fairy C	2.00	3.50
1-171 Minwu H	25.00	40.00
1-172 Moogle C	4.50	5.50
1-173 Mime C	2.00	3.50
1-174 Yaag Rosch R	7.00	9.00
1-175 Yuj R	8.00	10.00
1-176 Yuna H	11.00	13.00
1-177 Yuna R	10.00	12.00
1-178 Leviathan R	5.00	7.00
1-179 Leila H	10.00	12.00
1-180 Wakka R	10.00	12.00
1-181 Onion Knight H	13.00	16.00
1-182 Cloud L	55.00	70.00
1-183 Cosmos H	15.00	20.00
1-184 Chaos H	20.00	25.00
1-185 The Emperor H	20.00	30.00
1-186 Sephiroth L	40.00	50.00
1-187 Cloud S	7.00	9.00
1-188 Zangan S	4.00	6.00
1-189 Tifa S	6.00	8.00
1-190 Bahamut Fury S	7.00	9.00
1-191 Red XIII S	4.00	6.00
1-192 Cid Raines S	4.00	6.00
1-193 Jihl Nabaat S	6.00	8.00
1-194 Snow S	4.00	6.00
1-195 Serah S	4.00	6.00
1-196 Mog XIII2 S	4.00	6.00
1-197 Brother S	4.00	6.00
1-198 Valefor S	4.00	6.00
1-199 Paine S	4.00	6.00
1-200 Baralai S	4.00	6.00
1-201 Rikku S	4.00	6.00
1-202 Vincent S	4.00	6.00
1-203 Wedge S	4.00	6.00
1-204 Jessie S	4.00	6.00
1-205 Barrett S	4.00	6.00
1-206 Biggs S	4.00	6.00
1-207 Gilgamesh S	4.00	6.00
1-208 Noel S	4.00	6.00
1-209 Maqui S	4.00	6.00
1-210 Lightning S	6.00	8.00
1-211 Rygdea S	4.00	6.00
1-212 Shuyin S	4.00	6.00
1-213 Tidus S	6.00	8.00
1-214 Yuna S	7.00	9.00
1-215 Lenne S	4.00	6.00
1-216 Wakka S	4.00	6.00

2017 Final Fantasy Opus II

RELEASED ON MARCH 24, 2017

1 Irvine H	1.00	2.00
2 Ifrit C	.20	.35
3 Ward C	.20	.35
4 Ephemeral Phantom C	.20	.35
5 Sage C	.20	.35
6 Sazh R	.30	.50
7 Emperor Xande L	14.00	17.00
8 Zell C	.20	.35
9 Selphie R	.30	.50
10 Warrior C	.20	.35
11 Tifa L	15.00	18.00
12 Tellah R	.30	.50
13 Ninja C	.20	.35
14 Basch H	1.00	2.00
15 Palom H	1.00	2.00
16 Palom R	.30	.50
17 Bergan R	.30	.50
18 Summoner C	.20	.35
19 Belias the Gigas R	.30	.50
20 Imitation Liegeman C	.20	.35
21 Montblanc C	.20	.35
22 Luneth H	1.00	2.00
23 Rubicante H	1.00	2.00
24 Rosso R	.30	.50
25 Weiss H	1.00	2.00
26 Vayne L	10.00	15.00
27 Scholar C	.20	.35
28 Semblance of a Lion C	.20	.35
29 Imaginary champion C	.20	.35
30 Edward H	1.00	2.00
31 Edward C	.20	.35
32 Bard C	.20	.35
33 Black Mage C	.20	.35
34 Zargabaath R	.30	.50
35 Shelke H	1.00	2.00
36 Shalua R	.30	.50
37 Jihl Nabaat R	.30	.50
38 Squall H	3.00	5.00
39 Capricious Reaper C	.20	.35
40 Time Mage C	.20	.35
41 Doctor Cid H	1.00	2.00
42 Nero R	.30	.50
43 Hurdy C	.20	.35
44 Mateus the Corrupt R	.30	.50
45 Moomba C	.20	.35
46 Laguna R	.30	.50
47 Rinoa L	20.00	25.00
48 Rinoa R	.30	.50
49 Asura H	1.00	2.00
50 Arc H	1.00	2.00
51 Vaan L	5.00	8.00
52 Vaan C	.20	.35
53 Edge H	1.00	2.00
54 Edge R	.30	.50
55 Kan E Senna H	1.00	2.00
56 Ranger C	.20	.35
57 Cid Pollendina C	.20	.35
58 White Mage C	.20	.35
59 Capricious Thief C	.20	.35
60 Chocobo C	.20	.35
61 Ninja C	.20	.35
62 Nono C	.20	.35
63 Paine R	.30	.50
64 Barbariccia H	1.00	2.00
65 Balthier L	5.00	8.00
66 Balthier R	.30	.50
67 Penelo R	.30	.50
68 Fran R	.30	.50
69 Fallacious Wanderer C	.20	.35
70 Shemhazai the Whisperer R	.30	.50
71 Rikku R	.30	.50
72 Reddas C	.20	.35
73 Dark Knight C	.20	.35
74 Warrior of Antiquity C	.20	.35
75 Ingus H	1.00	2.00
76 Vanille R	.30	.50
77 Vincent L	15.00	20.00
78 Vincent R	.30	.50
79 Ormi R	.30	.50
80 Carbuncle C	.20	.35
81 Gabranth L	3.00	5.00
82 Ranger C	.20	.35
83 Machinist C	.20	.35
84 Logos R	.30	.50
85 Scarmiglione H	1.00	2.00
86 Sorbet C	.20	.35
87 Hashmal Bringer of Order R	.30	.50
88 Ba Gamnan C	.20	.35
89 Monk C	.20	.35
90 Yang H	1.00	2.00
91 Yang C	.20	.35
92 Phantasmal Harlequine C	.20	.35
93 Raubahn H	3.00	5.00
94 Rydia H	2.50	4.00
95 Rydia R	.30	.50
96 Leblanc H	1.00	2.00
97 A1 Cid H	3.00	5.00
98 Amon L	20.00	25.00
99 Edea L	9.00	11.00
100 Edea H	1.00	2.00
101 Exdeath H	1.00	2.00
102 Gurdy C	.20	.35
103 Kain H	3.00	5.00
104 Kain R	.30	.50
105 Krios C	.20	.35
106 Gramis R	.30	.50
107 Cyclops C	.20	.35
108 Black Mage C	.20	.35
109 Golbez H	1.00	2.00
110 Seifer R	.30	.50
111 Seifer C	.20	.35
112 Fleeting Flash C	.20	.35
113 Drace R	.30	.50
114 Ninja C	.20	.35
115 Ninja C	.20	.35
116 Fusoya R	.30	.50
117 Adrammelech the Wroth R	.30	.50
118 Arborous Simulacrum C	.20	.35
119 Reeve R	.30	.50
120 Dragoon C	.20	.35
121 Ashe H	1.00	2.00
122 Agrias R	.30	.50
123 Ephemeral Vision C	.20	.35
124 Cagnazzo H	1.00	2.00
125 Semblance of a Witch C	.20	.35
126 Ghis R	.30	.50
127 Quistis R	.30	.50
128 Summoner C	.20	.35
129 Cecil L	10.00	15.00
130 Astrologian C	.20	.35
131 Knight C	.20	.35
132 Viking C	.20	.35
133 Cuchulainn the Impure R	.30	.50
134 Horne C	.20	.35
135 Porom H	1.00	2.00
136 Porom R	.30	.50
137 Merlwyb H	1.00	2.00
138 Yuna L	10.00	15.00
139 Larsa C	.20	.35
140 Leviathan C	.20	.35
141 Refia H	1.00	2.00
142 Lenne R	.30	.50
143 Rosa R	.30	.50
144 Rosa C	.20	.35
145 Warrior of Light L	10.00	15.00
146 Fusoya H	1.00	2.00
147 The Emperor L	8.00	11.00
148 Zemus H	2.50	4.00

2017 Final Fantasy Opus II Premium Foil

COMPLETE SET (148)
RELEASED ON

1 Irvine H	2.00	4.00
2 Ifrit C	.40	.75
3 Ward C	.40	.75
4 Ephemeral Phantom C	.40	.75
5 Sage C	.40	.75
6 Sazh R	.60	1.00
7 Emperor Xande L	30.00	40.00
8 Zell C	.40	.75
9 Selphie R	.60	1.00
10 Warrior C	.40	.75
11 Tifa L	30.00	40.00
12 Tellah R	.60	1.00
13 Ninja C	.40	.75
14 Basch H	2.00	4.00
15 Palom H	2.00	4.00
16 Palom R	.60	1.00
17 Bergan R	.60	1.00
18 Summoner C	.40	.75
19 Belias the Gigas R	.60	1.00
20 Imitation Liegeman C	.40	.75
21 Montblanc C	.40	.75
22 Luneth H	2.00	4.00
23 Rubicante H	2.00	4.00
24 Rosso R	.60	1.00
25 Weiss H	2.00	4.00
26 Vayne L	20.00	30.00
27 Scholar C	.40	.75
28 Semblance of a Lion C	.40	.75
29 Imaginary champion C	.40	.75
30 Edward H	2.00	4.00
31 Edward C	.40	.75
32 Bard C	.40	.75
33 Black Mage C	.40	.75
34 Zargabaath R	.60	1.00
35 Shelke H	2.00	4.00
36 Shalua R	.60	1.00
37 Jihl Nabaat R	.60	1.00
38 Squall H	6.00	10.00
39 Capricious Reaper C	.40	.75
40 Time Mage C	.40	.75
41 Doctor Cid H	2.00	4.00
42 Nero R	.60	1.00
43 Hurdy C	.40	.75
44 Mateus the Corrupt R	.60	1.00
45 Moomba C	.40	.75
46 Laguna R	.60	1.00
47 Rinoa L	40.00	50.00
48 Rinoa R	.60	1.00
49 Asura H	2.00	4.00
50 Arc H	2.00	4.00
51 Vaan L	10.00	15.00
52 Vaan C	.40	.75
53 Edge H	2.00	4.00
54 Edge R	.60	1.00
55 Kan E Senna H	2.00	4.00
56 Ranger C	.40	.75
57 Cid Pollendina C	.40	.75
58 White Mage C	.40	.75
59 Capricious Thief C	.40	.75
60 Chocobo C	.40	.75
61 Ninja C	.40	.75
62 Nono C	.40	.75
63 Paine R	.60	1.00
64 Barbariccia H	2.00	4.00
65 Balthier L	10.00	15.00
66 Balthier R	.60	1.00
67 Penelo R	.60	1.00
68 Fran R	.60	1.00
69 Fallacious Wanderer C	.40	.75
70 Shemhazai the Whisperer R	.60	1.00
71 Rikku R	.60	1.00
72 Reddas C	.40	.75
73 Dark Knight C	.40	.75
74 Warrior of Antiquity C	.40	.75
75 Ingus H	2.00	4.00
76 Vanille R	.60	1.00
77 Vincent L	30.00	40.00
78 Vincent R	.60	1.00

79 Ormi R .60 1.00
80 Carbuncle C .40 .75
81 Gabranth L 6.00 10.00
82 Ranger C .40 .75
83 Machinist C .40 .75
84 Logos R .60 1.00
85 Scarmiglione H 2.00 4.00
86 Sorbet C .40 .75
87 Hashmal Bringer of Order R .60 1.00
88 Ba Gamnan C .40 .75
89 Monk C .40 .75
90 Yang H 2.00 4.00
91 Yang C .40 .75
92 Phantasmal Harlequine C .40 .75
93 Raubahn H 6.00 10.00
94 Rydia H 5.00 8.00
95 Rydia R .60 1.00
96 Leblanc H 2.00 4.00
97 A1 Cid H 6.00 10.00
98 Amon L 40.00 50.00
99 Edea L 15.00 25.00
100 Edea H 2.00 4.00
101 Exdeath H 2.00 4.00
102 Gurdy C .40 .75
103 Kain H 6.00 10.00
104 Kain R .60 1.00
105 Krios C .40 .75
106 Gramis R .60 1.00
107 Cyclops C .40 .75
108 Black Mage C .40 .75
109 Golbez H 2.00 4.00
110 Seifer R .60 1.00
111 Seifer C .40 .75
112 Fleeting Flash C .40 .75
113 Drace R .60 1.00
114 Ninja C .40 .75
115 Ninja C .40 .75
116 Fusoya R .60 1.00
117 Adrammelech the Wroth R .60 1.00
118 Arborous Simulacrum C .40 .75
119 Reeve R .60 1.00
120 Dragoon C .40 .75
121 Ashe H 2.00 4.00
122 Agrias R .60 1.00
123 Ephemeral Vision C .40 .75
124 Cagnazzo H 2.00 4.00
125 Semblance of a Witch C .40 .75
126 Ghis R .60 1.00
127 Quistis R .60 1.00
128 Summoner C .40 .75
129 Cecil L 20.00 30.00
130 Astrologian C .40 .75
131 Knight C .40 .75
132 Viking C .40 .75
133 Cuchulainn the Impure R .60 1.00
134 Horne C .40 .75
135 Porom H 2.00 4.00
136 Porom R .60 1.00
137 Merlwyb H 2.00 4.00
138 Yuna L 20.00 30.00
139 Larsa C .40 .75
140 Leviathan C .40 .75
141 Refia H 2.00 4.00
142 Lenne R .60 1.00
143 Rosa R .60 1.00
144 Rosa C .40 .75
145 Warrior of Light L 20.00 30.00
146 Fusoya H 2.00 4.00
147 The Emperor L 15.00 25.00
148 Zemus H 5.00 8.00

2017 Final Fantasy Opus III

COMPLETE SET (154) 250.00 400.00
BOOSTER BOX (36 PACKS) 115.00 135.00
BOOSTER PACK (12 CARDS) 3.00 5.00
RELEASED ON AUGUST 4, 2017
1 Red Mage C .30 .50
2 Ifrit R .75 1.25
3 Ace R .75 1.25
4 Garland H 2.50 4.00
5 Imaginary Brawler C .30 .50
6 King R .75 1.25
7 Bard C .30 .50
8 Cloud C .30 .50
9 Cater C .30 .50
10 Gekkou R .75 1.25
11 Gladiator C .30 .50
12 Zack L 8.00 12.00
13 Amarant R .75 1.25
14 Clinque C .30 .50
15 Black Waltz 2 R .75 1.25
16 Palom H 2.50 4.00
17 Vivi L 8.00 12.00
18 Vivi C .30 .50
19 Faris H 2.50 4.00
20 Phoenix H 2.50 4.00
21 Cannoneer C .30 .50
22 Machina H 2.50 4.00
23 Luca C .30 .50
24 Rubicante R .75 1.25
25 Emina C .30 .50
26 Kazusa C .30 .50
27 Qator Bashtar R .75 1.25
28 Semblance of a Gunslinger C .30 .50
29 Edward R .75 1.25
30 Kuja L 12.00 16.00
31 Kurasame R .75 1.25
32 Shiva R .75 1.25
33 Genesis L 8.00 12.00
34 Genesis Avatar H 2.50 4.00
35 Shelke R .75 1.25
36 Cid Aulstyne H 2.50 4.00
37 Zalera, the Death Seraph H 2.50 4.00
38 Xezat H 2.50 4.00
39 Sephiroth R .75 1.25
40 DGS Trooper 1st Class C .30 .50
41 Deepground Soldier C .30 .50
42 Deepground Soldier C .30 .50
43 Time Mage C .30 .50
44 Harley C .30 .50
45 White Tiger l'Cie Qun'mi R .75 1.25
46 White Tiger L'Cie Nimbus H 2.50 4.00
47 Cannoneer C .30 .50
48 Mystic Knight C .30 .50
49 Izana C .30 .50
50 Aerith L 8.00 12.00
51 Eight R .75 1.25
52 Dancer C .30 .50
53 Ranger C .30 .50
54 Black Chocobo C .30 .50
55 Thief C .30 .50
56 Zidane H 2.50 4.00
57 Seven R .75 1.25
58 Sky Pirate Replica C .30 .50
59 King Tycoon H 2.50 4.00
60 Tsukinowa R .75 1.25
61 Diablos R .75 1.25
62 Deuce C .30 .50
63 Dorgann H 2.50 4.00
64 Trey H 2.50 4.00
65 Bartz L 8.00 12.00
66 Barbariccia R .75 1.25
67 Wind Drake R .75 1.25
68 Geomancer C .30 .50
69 Yuffie C .30 .50
70 Oracle C .30 .50
71 Chaos, Walker of the Wheel H 2.50 4.00
72 Rem R .75 1.25
73 Ursula C .30 .50
74 Atomos R .75 1.25
75 Horror of Antiquity C .30 .50
76 Masked Woman R .75 1.25
77 Galuf H 2.50 4.00
78 Krile H 2.50 4.00
79 Kefka H 2.50 4.00
80 Black Tortoise L'cie Gilgamesh R .75 1.25
81 Summoner C .30 .50
82 Scarmiglione R .75 1.25
83 Segwarides C .30 .50
84 WRO Member C .30 .50
85 WRO Member C .30 .50
86 WRO Commander C .30 .50
87 Zeromus the Condemner H 2.50 4.00
88 Delita L 18.00 22.00
89 The Girl Who Forgot Her Name R .75 1.25
90 Ninja C .30 .50
91 Berserker C .30 .50
92 Prishe L 8.00 12.00
93 Brandelis H 2.50 4.00
94 Pellinore C .30 .50
95 Yang R .75 1.25
96 Rydia R .75 1.25
97 Arecia Al-Rashia R .75 1.25
98 Angeal R .75 1.25
99 Angeal Penance R .75 1.25
100 Exdeath L 8.00 12.00
101 Enuo R .75 1.25
102 Odin R .75 1.25
103 Gilgamesh H 2.50 4.00
104 Queen C .30 .50
105 Black Waltz 2 C .30 .50
106 Black Mage C .30 .50
107 Black Mage C .30 .50
108 Kelger H 2.50 4.00
109 Sice C .30 .50
110 Zangetsu R .75 1.25
111 Jack H 2.50 4.00
112 Exodus, the Judge Sal H 2.50 4.00
113 Nine R .75 1.25
114 Freya C .30 .50
115 Cannoneer C .30 .50
116 Mystic Knight C .30 .50
117 Simulacrum of a Hero C .30 .50
118 Lightning H 2.50 4.00
119 Ramza L 8.00 12.00
120 Dragoon C .30 .50
121 Blue Mage C .30 .50
122 Artemicion C .30 .50
123 Fanfrit, the Darkening Cloud R .75 1.25
124 Izayoi R .75 1.25
125 Ephemeral Summoner C .30 .50
126 Eiko H 2.50 4.00
127 Eiko R .75 1.25
128 Dancer C .30 .50
129 Garnet L 10.00 15.00
130 Cagnazzo R .75 1.25
131 Ghido H 2.50 4.00
132 Quacho Queen R .75 1.25
133 Quina C .30 .50
134 Summoner C .30 .50
135 Syldra H 2.50 4.00
136 White Mage C .30 .50
137 Steiner R .75 1.25
138 Ceodore H 2.50 4.00
139 Knight C .30 .50
140 Prorom R .75 1.25
141 Mog C .30 .50
142 Famed Mimic Gogo H 2.50 4.00
143 Leonora C .30 .50
144 Lenna L 8.00 12.00
145 Ultima, the High Seraph L 8.00 12.00
146 Minerva H 2.50 4.00
147 Zodiark, Keeper of Precepts L 8.00 12.00
148 Feral Chaos H 2.50 4.00
149 Vivi ST .75 1.25
150 Moogle Class Zero ST .75 1.25
151 Queen ST .75 1.25
152 Garnet ST .75 1.25
153 Ace ST .75 1.25
154 Zidane ST .75 1.25

2017 Final Fantasy Opus III Premium Foil

COMPLETE SET (154) 550.00 850.00
BOOSTER BOX (36 PACKS) 115.00 135.00
BOOSTER PACK (12 CARDS) 3.00 5.00
RELEASED ON AUGUST 4, 2017
1 Red Mage C .60 1.00
2 Ifrit R 2.00 3.50
3 Ace R 2.00 3.50
4 Garland H 5.00 8.00
5 Imaginary Brawler C .60 1.00
6 King R 2.00 3.50
7 Bard C .60 1.00
8 Cloud C .60 1.00
9 Cater C .60 1.00
10 Gekkou R 2.00 3.50
11 Gladiator C .60 1.00
12 Zack L 25.00 30.00
13 Amarant R 2.00 3.50
14 Clinque C .60 1.00
15 Black Waltz 2 R 2.00 3.50
16 Palom H 5.00 8.00
17 Vivi L 20.00 25.00
18 Vivi C .60 1.00
19 Faris H 5.00 8.00
20 Phoenix H 5.00 8.00
21 Cannoneer C .60 1.00
22 Machina H 5.00 8.00
23 Luca C .60 1.00
24 Rubicante R 2.00 3.50
25 Emina C .60 1.00
26 Kazusa C .60 1.00
27 Qator Bashtar R 2.00 3.50
28 Semblance of a Gunslinger C .60 1.00
29 Edward R 2.00 3.50
30 Kuja L 25.00 30.00
31 Kurasame R 2.00 3.50
32 Shiva R 2.00 3.50
33 Genesis L 15.00 20.00
34 Genesis Avatar H 5.00 8.00
35 Shelke R 2.00 3.50
36 Cid Aulstyne H 5.00 8.00
37 Zalera, the Death Seraph H 5.00 8.00
38 Xezat H 5.00 8.00
39 Sephiroth R 2.00 3.50
40 DGS Trooper 1st Class C .60 1.00
41 Deepground Soldier C .60 1.00
42 Deepground Soldier C .60 1.00
43 Time Mage C .60 1.00
44 Harley C .60 1.00
45 White Tiger l'Cie Qun'mi R 2.00 3.50
46 White Tiger L'Cie Nimbus H 5.00 8.00
47 Cannoneer C .60 1.00
48 Mystic Knight C .60 1.00
49 Izana C .60 1.00
50 Aerith L 25.00 30.00
51 Eight R 2.00 3.50
52 Dancer C .60 1.00
53 Ranger C .60 1.00
54 Black Chocobo C .60 1.00
55 Thief C .60 1.00
56 Zidane H 5.00 8.00
57 Seven R 2.00 3.50
58 Sky Pirate Replica C .60 1.00
59 King Tycoon H 5.00 8.00
60 Tsukinowa R 2.00 3.50
61 Diablos R 2.00 3.50
62 Deuce C .60 1.00
63 Dorgann H 5.00 8.00
64 Trey H 5.00 8.00
65 Bartz L 15.00 20.00
66 Barbariccia R 2.00 3.50
67 Wind Drake R 2.00 3.50
68 Geomancer C .60 1.00
69 Yuffie C .60 1.00
70 Oracle C .60 1.00
71 Chaos, Walker of the Wheel H 5.00 8.00
72 Rem R 2.00 3.50
73 Ursula C .60 1.00
74 Atomos R 2.00 3.50
75 Horror of Antiquity C .60 1.00
76 Masked Woman R 2.00 3.50
77 Galuf H 5.00 8.00
78 Krile H 5.00 8.00
79 Kefka H 5.00 8.00
80 Black Tortoise L'cie Gilgamesh R 2.00 3.50
81 Summoner C .60 1.00
82 Scarmiglione R 2.00 3.50
83 Segwarides C .60 1.00
84 WRO Member C .60 1.00
85 WRO Member C .60 1.00
86 WRO Commander C .60 1.00
87 Zeromus the Condemner H 5.00 8.00
88 Delita L 30.00 35.00
89 The Girl Who Forgot Her Name R 2.00 3.50
90 Ninja C .60 1.00
91 Berserker C .60 1.00
92 Prishe L 15.00 20.00
93 Brandelis H 5.00 8.00
94 Pellinore C .60 1.00
95 Yang R 2.00 3.50
96 Rydia R 2.00 3.50
97 Arecia Al-Rashia R 2.00 3.50
98 Angeal R 2.00 3.50
99 Angeal Penance R 2.00 3.50
100 Exdeath L 15.00 20.00
101 Enuo R 2.00 3.50
102 Odin R 2.00 3.50
103 Gilgamesh H 5.00 8.00
104 Queen C .60 1.00
105 Black Waltz 2 C .60 1.00
106 Black Mage C .60 1.00
107 Black Mage C .60 1.00
108 Kelger H 5.00 8.00
109 Sice C .60 1.00
110 Zangetsu R 2.00 3.50
111 Jack H 5.00 8.00
112 Exodus, the Judge Sal H 5.00 8.00
113 Nine R 2.00 3.50
114 Freya C .60 1.00
115 Cannoneer C .60 1.00
116 Mystic Knight C .60 1.00
117 Simulacrum of a Hero C .60 1.00
118 Lightning H 5.00 8.00
119 Ramza L 20.00 25.00
120 Dragoon C .60 1.00
121 Blue Mage C .60 1.00
122 Artemicion C .60 1.00
123 Fanfrit, the Darkening Cloud R 2.00 3.50
124 Izayoi R 2.00 3.50
125 Ephemeral Summoner C .60 1.00
126 Eiko H 5.00 8.00
127 Eiko R 2.00 3.50

Card	Low	High
128 Dancer C	.60	1.00
129 Garnet L	25.00	30.00
130 Cagnazzo R	2.00	3.50
131 Ghido H	5.00	8.00
132 Quacho Queen R	2.00	3.50
133 Quina C	.60	1.00
134 Summoner C	.60	1.00
135 Syldra H	5.00	8.00
136 White Mage C	.60	1.00
137 Steiner R	2.00	3.50
138 Ceodore H	5.00	8.00
139 Knight C	.60	1.00
140 Prorom R	2.00	3.50
141 Mog C	.60	1.00
142 Famed Mimic Gogo H	5.00	8.00
143 Leonora C	.60	1.00
144 Lenna L	15.00	20.00
145 Ultima, the High Seraph L	15.00	20.00
146 Minerva H	5.00	8.00
147 Zodiark, Keeper of Precepts L	15.00	20.00
148 Feral Chaos H	5.00	8.00
149 Vivi ST	3.00	5.00
150 Moogle Class Zero ST	3.00	5.00
151 Queen ST	3.00	5.00
152 Garnet ST	3.00	5.00
153 Ace ST	3.00	5.00
154 Zidane ST	3.00	5.00

2017 Final Fantasy Opus IV

Card	Low	High
COMPLETE SET (148)	165.00	275.00
BOOSTER BOX (36 PACKS)	95.00	110.00
BOOSTER PACK (12 CARDS)	4.00	6.00
RELEASED ON DECEMBER 1, 2017		
4-001H Hauyn H	2.00	3.50
4-002C Red Mage C	.15	.25
4-003C Ifrit EX C	.15	.25
4-004H Edgar EX H	2.00	3.50
4-005R Garland R	.30	.50
4-006L Caius L	8.00	12.00
4-007H Cyan H	2.00	3.50
4-008C Scholar C	.15	.25
4-009C Ranger C	.15	.25
4-010C Black Mage C	.15	.25
4-011C Sage C	.15	.25
4-012C Goblin C	.15	.25
4-013C Zack EX C	.15	.25
4-014C Samurai C	.15	.25
4-015H Shadow H	2.00	3.50
4-016R Bahamut R	.30	.50
4-017R Marauder R	.30	.50
4-018R Bomb R	.30	.50
4-019C Bomb C	.15	.25
4-020R Marche R	.30	.50
4-021L Sabin L	14.00	18.00
4-022R Montblanc EX R	.30	.50
4-023H General Leo H	2.00	3.50
4-024R Llednar R	.30	.50
4-025H Umaro EX H	2.00	3.50
4-026H Gestahilian Empire Cid H	2.00	3.50
4-027C Bard C	.15	.25
4-028C Bard C	.15	.25
4-029C Ghoul C	.15	.25
4-030C Black Mage C	.15	.25
4-031C Sage C	.15	.25
4-032C Arithmetician C	.15	.25
4-033C Shiva EX C	.15	.25
4-034R Cid WOFF R	.30	.50
4-035R Cid Randell R	.30	.50
4-036H Setzer H	2.50	4.00
4-037H Serah H	3.00	5.00
4-038L Celes L	7.00	10.00
4-039R Rogue R	.30	.50
4-040C Knight C	.15	.25
4-041R Swampmonk R	.30	.50
4-042C Babus C	.15	.25
4-043C Flan C	.15	.25
4-044R Mewt EX R	.30	.50
4-045H Mecha Chocobo H	2.00	3.50
4-046R Lich R	.30	.50
4-047R Remedi R	.30	.50
4-048L Locke L	4.00	7.00
4-049C Ahriman C	.15	.25
4-050R A-Ruhn-Senna R	.30	.50
4-051H Alexander EX H	2.00	3.50
4-052C Alexander EX C	.15	.25
4-053R Ezel R	.30	.50
4-054L Onion Knight L	4.00	7.00
4-055H Kan-E-Senna H	2.00	3.50
4-056R Archer R	.30	.50
4-057R Koboldroid Yin R	.30	.50
4-058C Cactuar C	.15	.25
4-059C Thief C	.15	.25
4-060R Shara EX R	.30	.50
4-061C White Mage C	.15	.25
4-062C Chocobo C	.15	.25
4-063C Chocobo C	.15	.25
4-064L Fat Chocobo L	2.00	3.50
4-065C Doned C	.15	.25
4-066R Nono R	.30	.50
4-067C Geomancer C	.15	.25
4-068H Hope EX H	2.00	3.50
4-069H Moogle H	2.00	3.50
4-070C Archer C	.15	.25
4-071R Raya-O-Senna R	.30	.50
4-072H Ritz H	2.00	3.50
4-073C Atomos EX C	.15	.25
4-074C Dark Knight C	.15	.25
4-075H Vincent EX H	2.50	4.00
4-076R Wedge R	.30	.50
4-077R Pugilist R	.30	.50
4-078C Black Belt C	.15	.25
4-079C Black Mage C	.15	.25
4-080L Kefka L	4.00	7.00
4-081C Goblin C	.15	.25
4-082C Jessie C	.15	.25
4-083L Shantotto L	4.00	7.00
4-084C Warrior C	.15	.25
4-085H Dadaluma H	2.00	3.50
4-086H Tama H	2.00	3.50
4-087R Delita R	.30	.50
4-088C Bangaa Thief C	.15	.25
4-089R Barret R	.30	.50
4-090R Bigss R	.30	.50
4-091C Geomancer C	.15	.25
4-092H Prishe H	2.00	3.50
4-093R Hecatoncheir R	.30	.50
4-094R Magic Plot R	.30	.50
4-095C Monk C	.15	.25
4-096H Raubahn H	2.00	3.50
4-097H Ark Angel EV H	2.00	3.50
4-098H Azul H	2.00	3.50
4-099C Usher EX C	.15	.25
4-100C Esthar Soldier C	.15	.25
4-101H Orlandeau H	2.00	3.50
4-102R Black Waltz 3 R	.30	.50
4-103C Warrior C	.15	.25
4-104R Lancer R	.30	.50
4-105R Dycedarg R	.30	.50
4-106C Dragon C	.15	.25
4-107R Nashu R	.30	.50
4-108C Ninja C	.15	.25
4-109H Hildibrand H	2.00	3.50
4-110R King of Burmecia EX R	.30	.50
4-111H Behemoth H	2.00	3.50
4-112C Magus C	.15	.25
4-113C Magus C	.15	.25
4-114L Raiden L	4.00	7.00
4-115L Lightning L	4.00	7.00
4-116C Ramuh EX C	.15	.25
4-117R Ramza R	.30	.50
4-118C Yeoman C	.15	.25
4-119C Dragoon C	.15	.25
4-120R Restrictor EX R	.30	.50
4-121C Adamantoise C	.15	.25
4-122C Mystic C	.15	.25
4-123H Gau H	2.50	4.00
4-124C Green Dragon C	.15	.25
4-125C Cilone C	.15	.25
4-126R Gladiator R	.30	.50
4-127H Gogo H	2.00	3.50
4-128C PuPu EX C	.15	.25
4-129L Steiner L	4.00	7.00
4-130H Strago EX H	2.00	3.50
4-131R Tonbetty EX R	.30	.50
4-132R Tonberries R	.30	.50
4-133C Viking C	.15	.25
4-134C Brahne EX C	.15	.25
4-135R Beatrix R	.30	.50
4-136C Summoner C	.15	.25
4-137L Mira L	4.00	7.00
4-138R Merlwyb R	.30	.50
4-139C Moogle THEATRHYTHM C	.15	.25
4-140H Mog VI H	2.00	3.50
4-141C Mime C	.15	.25
4-142R Malboro R	.30	.50
4-143R Leviathan EX R	.30	.50
4-144H Relm EX H	2.00	3.50
4-145H Cloud EX H	7.00	10.00
4-146L Terra L	7.00	10.00
4-147H Kefka EX H	2.00	3.50
4-148L Shadow Lord L	4.00	7.00

2017 Final Fantasy Opus IV Premium Foil

Card	Low	High
COMPLETE SET (148)	300.00	500.00
4-001H Hauyn H	3.00	5.00
4-002C Red Mage C	.30	.50
4-003C Ifrit EX C	.30	.50
4-004H Edgar EX H	3.00	5.00
4-005R Garland R	1.00	1.50
4-006L Caius L	10.00	15.00
4-007H Cyan H	3.00	5.00
4-008C Scholar C	.30	.50
4-009C Ranger C	.30	.50
4-010C Black Mage C	.30	.50
4-011C Sage C	.30	.50
4-012C Goblin C	.30	.50
4-013C Zack EX C	.30	.50
4-014C Samurai C	.30	.50
4-015H Shadow H	3.00	5.00
4-016R Bahamut R	1.00	1.50
4-017R Marauder R	1.00	1.50
4-018R Bomb R	1.00	1.50
4-019C Bomb C	.30	.50
4-020R Marche R	1.00	1.50
4-021L Sabin L	20.00	25.00
4-022R Montblanc EX R	1.00	1.50
4-023H General Leo H	3.00	5.00
4-024R Llednar R	1.00	1.50
4-025H Umaro EX H	3.00	5.00
4-026H Gestahilian Empire Cid H	3.00	5.00
4-027C Bard C	.30	.50
4-028C Bard C	.30	.50
4-029C Ghoul C	.30	.50
4-030C Black Mage C	.30	.50
4-031C Sage C	.30	.50
4-032C Arithmetician C	.30	.50
4-033C Shiva EX C	.30	.50
4-034R Cid WOFF R	1.00	1.50
4-035R Cid Randell R	1.00	1.50
4-036H Setzer H	8.00	12.00
4-037H Serah H	8.00	12.00
4-038L Celes L	10.00	15.00
4-039R Rogue R	1.00	1.50
4-040C Knight C	.30	.50
4-041R Swampmonk R	1.00	1.50
4-042C Babus C	.30	.50
4-043C Flan C	.30	.50
4-044R Mewt EX R	1.00	1.50
4-045H Mecha Chocobo H	3.00	5.00
4-046R Lich R	1.00	1.50
4-047R Remedi R	1.00	1.50
4-048L Locke L	10.00	15.00
4-049C Ahriman C	.30	.50
4-050R A-Ruhn-Senna R	1.00	1.50
4-051H Alexander EX H	3.00	5.00
4-052C Alexander EX C	.30	.50
4-053R Ezel R	1.00	1.50
4-054L Onion Knight L	10.00	15.00
4-055H Kan-E-Senna H	3.00	5.00
4-056R Archer R	1.00	1.50
4-057R Koboldroid Yin R	1.00	1.50
4-058C Cactuar C	.30	.50
4-059C Thief C	.30	.50
4-060R Shara EX R	1.00	1.50
4-061C White Mage C	.30	.50
4-062C Chocobo C	.30	.50
4-063C Chocobo C	.30	.50
4-064L Fat Chocobo L	10.00	15.00
4-065C Doned C	.30	.50
4-066R Nono R	1.00	1.50
4-067C Geomancer C	.30	.50
4-068H Hope EX H	3.00	5.00
4-069H Moogle H	3.00	5.00
4-070C Archer C	.30	.50
4-071R Raya-O-Senna R	1.00	1.50
4-072H Ritz H	3.00	5.00
4-073C Atomos EX C	.30	.50
4-074C Dark Knight C	.30	.50
4-075H Vincent EX H	10.00	15.00
4-076R Wedge R	1.00	1.50
4-077R Pugilist R	1.00	1.50
4-078C Black Belt C	.30	.50
4-079C Black Mage C	.30	.50
4-080L Kefka L	10.00	15.00
4-081C Goblin C	.30	.50
4-082C Jessie C	.30	.50
4-083L Shantotto L	10.00	15.00
4-084C Warrior C	.30	.50
4-085H Dadaluma H	3.00	5.00
4-086H Tama H	3.00	5.00
4-087R Delita R	1.00	1.50
4-088C Bangaa Thief C	.30	.50
4-089R Barret R	1.00	1.50
4-090R Bigss R	1.00	1.50
4-091C Geomancer C	.30	.50
4-092H Prishe H	3.00	5.00
4-093R Hecatoncheir R	1.00	1.50
4-094R Magic Plot R	1.00	1.50
4-095C Monk C	.30	.50
4-096H Raubahn H	3.00	5.00
4-097H Ark Angel EV H	3.00	5.00
4-098H Azul H	3.00	5.00
4-099C Usher EX C	.30	.50
4-100C Esthar Soldier C	.30	.50
4-101H Orlandeau H	3.00	5.00
4-102R Black Waltz 3 R	1.00	1.50
4-103C Warrior C	.30	.50
4-104R Lancer R	1.00	1.50
4-105R Dycedarg R	1.00	1.50
4-106C Dragon C	.30	.50
4-107R Nashu R	1.00	1.50
4-108C Ninja C	.30	.50
4-109H Hildibrand H	3.00	5.00
4-110R King of Burmecia EX R	1.00	1.50
4-111H Behemoth H	3.00	5.00
4-112C Magus C	.30	.50
4-113C Magus C	.30	.50
4-114L Raiden L	10.00	15.00
4-115L Lightning L	10.00	15.00
4-116C Ramuh EX C	.30	.50
4-117R Ramza R	1.00	1.50
4-118C Yeoman C	.30	.50
4-119C Dragoon C	.30	.50
4-120R Restrictor EX R	1.00	1.50
4-121C Adamantoise C	.30	.50
4-122C Mystic C	.30	.50
4-123H Gau H	8.00	12.00
4-124C Green Dragon C	.30	.50
4-125C Cilone C	.30	.50
4-126R Gladiator R	1.00	1.50
4-127H Gogo H	3.00	5.00
4-128C PuPu EX C	.30	.50
4-129L Steiner L	10.00	15.00
4-130H Strago EX H	3.00	5.00
4-131R Tonbetty EX R	1.00	1.50
4-132R Tonberries R	1.00	1.50
4-133C Viking C	.30	.50
4-134C Brahne EX C	.30	.50
4-135R Beatrix R	1.00	1.50
4-136C Summoner C	.30	.50
4-137L Mira L	10.00	15.00
4-138R Merlwyb R	1.00	1.50
4-139C Moogle THEATRHYTHM C	.30	.50
4-140H Mog VI H	3.00	5.00
4-141C Mime C	.30	.50
4-142R Malboro R	1.00	1.50
4-143R Leviathan EX R	1.00	1.50
4-144H Relm EX H	3.00	5.00
4-145H Cloud EX H	10.00	15.00
4-146L Terra L	10.00	15.00
4-147H Kefka EX H	.30	.50
4-148L Shadow Lord L	10.00	15.00

2018 Final Fantasy Opus V

Card	Low	High
RELEASED ON		
5001C Red Mage C	.10	.15
5002R Ayame R	.12	.20
5003C Ifrit C	.10	.15
5004R Caius R	.12	.20
5005R Gadot R	.12	.20
5006R Carla R	.12	.20
5007H Royal Ripeness H	.20	.30
5008R Grenade R	.12	.20
5009C Black Mage C	.10	.15
5010C Manasvin Warmech C	.10	.15
5011H Vermilion Bird l'Cie Zhuyu H	.20	.30
5012H Vermilion Bird l'Cie Caetuna H	.20	.30
5013C Warrior C	.10	.15
5014C Warrior C	.10	.15
5015H Tellah H	.20	.30
5016C Fighter C	.10	.15
5017C Ninja C	.10	.15
5018L Palom L	.40	.60
5019L Phoenix L	10.00	15.00
5020R Volker R	.12	.20
5021R Mutsuki R	.12	.20
5022C Parivir C	.10	.15
5023C Ryid C	.10	.15
5024H Luneth H	.20	.30
5025H Aloeidai H	.20	.30
5026C Vayne C	.10	.15
5027R Unei R	.12	.20
5028C Arcanist C	.10	.15

5029L Orphan L 2.50 4.00
5030C Scholar C .10 .15
5031H Edward H 1.00 1.50
5032H Glasya Labolas H .20 .30
5033R Gumbah R .12 .20
5034C Gesper C .10 .15
5035C Conjurer C .10 .15
5036L The Emperor L .60 1.00
5037R Zeid R .12 .20
5038C Arithmetician C .10 .15
5039R Cid Raines R .12 .20
5040C Thaumaturge C .10 .15
5041R Snow R .12 .20
5042C Trickster C .10 .15
5043R Hurdy R .12 .20
5044C Mateus, the Corrupt C .10 .15
5045H Barnabas H .20 .30
5046R Buccaboo R .12 .20
5047C Mystic Knight C .10 .15
5048H Lugae H .20 .30
5049C Asura C .10 .15
5050H Adelle H 1.25 2.00
5051R Aria (TYPE-0) R .12 .20
5052H Arc H .20 .30
5053R Echo R .12 .20
5054C Ranger C .10 .15
5055C Thief C .10 .15
5056H Cid Pollendina H .20 .30
5057C White Mage C .10 .15
5058C Elementalist C .10 .15
5059R Semih Lafihna R .12 .20
5060C Chocobo C .10 .15
5061C Chocobo Knight C .10 .15
5062L Diabolos L 12.00 20.00
5063H Deathgaze H .20 .30
5064R Nanaa Mihgo R .12 .20
5065C Ninja C .10 .15
5066R Penelo R .12 .20
5067R Miounne R .12 .20
5068L Y'shtola L 10.00 15.00
5069H Luso H .20 .30
5070C Reks C .10 .15
5071R Leyak R .12 .20
5072C Spiceacilian C .10 .15
5073R Heretical Knight Garland R .12 .20
5074H Ingus H .60 1.00
5075L Wol L 15.00 25.00
5076C Botanist C .10 .15
5077H Carbuncle H .20 .30
5078R Gabranth R .12 .20
5079H Calbrena H .20 .30
5080R Grav'iton R .12 .20
5081C Cockatrice C .10 .15
5082C Miner C .10 .15
5083C PSICOM Enforcer C .10 .15
5084C PSICOM Warden C .10 .15
5085R Sarah (MOBIUS) R .12 .20
5086L Cecil L 10.00 15.00
5087R Doga R .12 .20
5088C Flandit C .10 .15
5089C Berserker C .10 .15
5090R Hill Gigas R .12 .20
5091H Star Sibyl H .75 1.25
5092C Master Monk C .10 .15
5093C Mog (MOBIUS) C .10 .15
5094R Momodi R .12 .20
5095H Yang H .20 .30
5096C Lanista C .10 .15
5097C Red Mage C .10 .15
5098C Assassin C .10 .15
5099H Illua H 1.50 2.50
5100H Odin H .50 .75
5101H Twilight Odin H .20 .30
5102C Scholar C .10 .15
5103R Cid of Clan Gully R .12 .20
5104R Khalia Chival R .12 .20
5105R Quon R .12 .20
5106R Black Knight R .12 .20
5107H Thancred H .60 1.00
5108L Zemus L 5.00 8.00
5109R Destin R .12 .20
5110C Bunkerbeast C .10 .15
5111R Trion R .12 .20
5112R Naghi R .12 .20
5113C Ravager C .10 .15
5114C Cannoneer C .10 .15
5115C Dark Knight C .10 .15
5116H Lightning H .20 .30
5117C Ramuh C .10 .15
5118L Ramza L 3.00 5.00
5119C Dragoon C .10 .15
5120C Louisoix C .10 .15
5121R Andoria R .12 .20
5122R Vossler R .12 .20
5123H Aria (III) H .20 .30
5124H Ozma H .20 .30
5125C Ondore C .10 .15
5126L Cloud of Darkness L 10.00 15.00
5127R Curilla R .12 .20
5128R Claidie R .12 .20
5129C Schrodinger C .10 .15
5130R Tonberry R .12 .20
5131C Arcanist C .10 .15
5132R Baderon R .12 .20
5133H Bismarck H 1.25 2.00
5134R Celestia R .12 .20
5135L Porom L 4.00 6.00
5136C Flintlock C .10 .15
5137C Green Mage C .10 .15
5138C Moogle Knight C .10 .15
5139C Leviathan C .10 .15
5140C Fisher C .10 .15
5141H Refia H 1.00 1.50
5142H Rosa H .20 .30
5143C Orator C .10 .15
5144C Orator C .10 .15
5145L Vaan L 1.00 1.50
5146H Wol H .20 .30
5147L Eald'narche L .75 1.25
5148H Kam'lanaut H .50 .75
5149S Amodar S .60 1.00
5150S Noel S .60 1.00
5151S Lebreau S .40 .60
5152S Serah S 1.00 1.50
5153S Mog (XIII-2) S .40 .60
5154S Yeul S .60 1.00
5155S Vaan S .40 .60
5156S Balthier S .75 1.25
5157S Fran S .75 1.25
5158S Yda S .40 .60
5159S Papalymo S .40 .60
5160S Minfilia S .40 .60
5161S Alisaie S .50 .75
5162S Alphinaud S .60 1.00
5163S Urianger S 1.25 2.00
5164S Ashe S .40 .60
5165S Larsa S .40 .60
5166S Rasler S 1.50 2.50

Force of Will

2014 Force of Will The Dawn of Valhalla

RELEASED ON FEBRUARY 4, 2014
1001 Siegfried, the Knight Commander R .20 .30
1002 Arthur, the King of Knights R .20 .30
1003 Commander of the Flash Knights U .15 .25
1004 Wandering Knight U .15 .25
1005 Lofty Knight C .12 .20
1006 Knight Errant U .15 .25
1007 Order of Gartar C .12 .20
1008 Suicidal Knights U .15 .25
1009 Tristan, the Lusting Knight R .20 .30
1010 Mordred, the Dueling Knight U .15 .25
1011 Garahad, the Oracle Knight R .20 .30
1012 Shield Bearer of the Kingdom C .12 .20
1013 Lanslot, the Knight of the Lake R .20 .30
1014 Hardworking Followers C .12 .20
1015 Ironwall Monk C .12 .20
1016 Kingdom Alchemist Wizards Force C .12 .20
1017 Healing Master C .12 .20
1018 Glorious Lion R .20 .30
1019 Sleeping Lion C .12 .20
1020 Snowwhite, the White Scale Dragon R .20 .30
1021 Kingdom Wyvern U .15 .25
1022 Sphinx, the Guardian of the King's Tomb R .20 .30
1023 Will-o'-the-Wisp R .20 .30
1024 Raphael, the Healing Archangel R .20 .30
1025 Benem, the Guardian Angel C .12 .20
1026 Amaterasu, the Oracle of Sacred Text SR
1027 Thor, the White Lightning SR
1028 Chivalry R .20 .30
1029 Etape C .12 .20
1030 Ward of Protection C .12 .20
1031 Power from Inside C .12 .20
1032 Will of Peace C .12 .20
1033 Iron-Tight C .12 .20
1034 Aroundight, the Holy Sword R .20 .30
1035 Restoration C .12 .20
1036 Search for the Holy Site C .12 .20
1037 Expedition U .15 .25
1038 Bless of the Holy Grail C .12 .20
1039 Besieged Battle C .12 .20
1040 Head On Attack C .12 .20
1041 Battle Cry C .12 .20
1042 Blessed Protection U .15 .25
1043 Disarm C .12 .20
1044 Light of Faith U .15 .25
1045 Duel C .12 .20
1046 Glory Light of Submission C .12 .20
1047 Oath of Round Table R .20 .30
1048 Castling U .15 .25
1049 Shuren, the King of Supremacy R .20 .30
1050 Raging Flame Kabuki R .20 .30
1051 Warlord of Exploding Flame U .15 .25
1052 Shock Troop of Asakna C .12 .20
1053 Suicidal Troop of Asakna C .12 .20
1054 Guardian of Asakna C .12 .20
1055 Cavalry of Asakna C .12 .20
1056 Charger of Asakna C .12 .20
1057 Battle Archer of Asakna U .15 .25
1058 Fantian-Huaji, the Pyre R .20 .30
1059 Beard Duke Warrior of One-Thousand R .20 .30
1060 Barrooga, the Raging Fire Beast C .12 .20
1061 The Flame R .20 .30
1062 Bammoo, the Raging Fire Beast U .15 .25
1063 Sabretooth Tiger C .12 .20
1064 Flame Djinn U .15 .25
1065 Gark, the Pyre Beast U .15 .25
1066 Parrot Dragon C .12 .20
1067 Lava Stream Drake C .12 .20
1068 Wyvern of Mount Olga U .15 .25
1069 Flare Dragon R .20 .30
1070 Berserk Dragon SR
1071 Phoenix R .20 .30
1072 Efreet, the Blazing Elemental C .12 .20
1073 Hino Kagutsuchino Mikoto, the Flaming God of Fate SR .20 .30
1074 Belial, the Crimson Lord R .20 .30
1075 Coorat, the Bond of Dead Dragon R .20 .30
1076 Spreading Anger U .15 .25
1077 Urge of Destruction C .12 .20
1078 Stampede C .12 .20
1079 Boiling Blood C .12 .20
1080 Cursed Sword of Asakna C .12 .20
1081 Inspiration of War C .12 .20
1082 Fireball C .12 .20
1083 Blazing U .15 .25
1084 Banzai Attack R .20 .30
1085 Raging Inferno C .12 .20
1086 When I die, you too R .20 .30
1087 Flaming Art -Carnage- U .15 .25
1088 Bursting Shot C .12 .20
1089 Eyes in Anger C .12 .20
1090 Flame Lance R .20 .30
1091 Prepare to Fall Together C .12 .20
1092 Black Flame R .20 .30
1093 Enlarge Body C .12 .20
1094 Flaming Art -Foxfire- C .12 .20
1095 Flaming Art -White Lotus- C .12 .20
1096 Flaming Art -Giant Scorch- R .20 .30
1097 Oathkeeper of the Sacred Sea R .20 .30
1098 Labyrinth Master, Chronos R .20 .30
1099 Twin Swords of Water's Mercy U .15 .25
1100 Mermaid Apprentice Student C .12 .20
1101 Ea, the Wisdom Mermaid C .12 .20
1102 Sweeper of Coral C .12 .20
1103 Queen of Atlantis U .15 .25
1104 Song of Tides U .15 .25
1105 High Tide Warrior R .20 .30
1106 Antorite, the Guardian of Deep Blue R .20 .30
1107 Amazon of Blue Ocean C .12 .20
1108 Guide of Chaos C .12 .20
1109 Clockwork Messenger C .12 .20
1110 Clown of Labyrinth C .12 .20
1111 Phantom Reviver C .12 .20
1112 Magic Tricker C .12 .20
1113 Mirage Golem SR
1114 Mirage Knight R .20 .30
1115 Gravephantom R .20 .30
1116 Illusionary Guardian U .15 .25
1117 Labyrinth Capturer C .12 .20
1118 Mirage Slime C .12 .20
1119 Acidic Slime U .15 .25
1120 Aspidochelone, the Giant Turtle of Wisdom R .20 .30
1121 Wall of Blizzard U .15 .25
1122 Ayakashi, the Serpent of Oil Mud R .20 .30
1123 Water Dragon U .15 .25
1124 Disappearing Drake U .15 .25
1125 Rahab, the Emperor Dragon of Riptide SR
1126 Mirage Drake R .20 .30
1127 Landing Point of Ice C .12 .20
1128 Labyrinth of Doubt R .20 .30
1129 Mutating Potion -Eclosion- C .12 .20
1130 Mirage Mail C .12 .20
1131 Forget C .12 .20
1132 Nerve Control R .20 .30
1133 New Stream R .20 .30
1134 Flow Back C .12 .20
1135 Mind Control C .12 .20
1136 Call of Illusion C .12 .20
1137 Wash Away C .12 .20
1138 Diffuse Reflection U .15 .25
1139 Turnaround C .12 .20
1140 Windfall C .12 .20
1141 Peace Negotiation C .12 .20
1142 Spiral Shift C .12 .20
1143 Forced Repatriation Machine U .15 .25
1144 Exchange Condition of Chronos R .20 .30
1145 Guardian of Outland U .15 .25
1146 Sprout of Treasure Tree SR
1147 Tree of Heaven's Blessing C .12 .20
1148 Tree of Eternity U .15 .25
1149 Cyclone Tree R .20 .30
1150 Windcalling Flower U .15 .25
1151 Babel Tree C .12 .20
1152 Solid Giant Tree U .15 .25
1153 Gottfried, Elemental Knight SR
1154 Gnome, Element of Earth U .15 .25
1155 Faun, the Player of Stub U .15 .25
1156 Tempting Alraune R .20 .30
1157 Updraft C .12 .20
1158 Parasite Seed C .12 .20
1159 Stampeding Summon R .20 .30
1160 Force Drain C .12 .20
1161 Wind Cutter C .12 .20
1162 Thousands Rain C .12 .20
1163 Throwback U .15 .25
1164 Grasp of Magic Power R .20 .30
1165 Sprout the Seeds C .12 .20
1166 Sneak Attack C .12 .20
1167 Black Wizard U .15 .25
1168 Phantom Wall C .12 .20
1169 Knight of Regret U .15 .25
1170 Spitting Imp U .15 .25
1171 Rotting Bloodsucker U .15 .25
1172 Enforcer of Conviction R .20 .30
1173 Skeleton Soldier C .12 .20
1174 Wraith, the Pained Soul C .12 .20
1175 Wondering Soul C .12 .20
1176 Jack-o-Lantern C .12 .20
1177 Amon, the Demon Prince of Conspiracy SR
1178 Grendel R .20 .30
1179 Faust, the Promising Warrior SR
1180 Black Magnetic Field R .20 .30
1181 Mark of Binding C .12 .20
1182 Oath of Dead R .20 .30
1183 Oath of Dark Night U .15 .25
1184 Shriek of the Dead U .15 .25
1185 Black Sun R .20 .30
1186 Kiss of Death U .15 .25
1187 Ghost's Beckoning C .12 .20
1188 Black Order C .12 .20
1189 Fake Wall U .15 .25
1190 Bomber Gimmick C .12 .20
1191 Blast Gimmick U .15 .25
1192 Healing Gimmick U .15 .25
1193 Gimmick Mimic U .15 .25
1194 Flying Gimmick C .12 .20
1195 Sting Gimmick U .15 .25
1196 Gimmick Golem R .20 .30
1197 Circle of Nullify U .15 .25
1198 Resolute Will U .15 .25
1199 Second Chance C .12 .20
1200 Recycle U .15 .25
1201 Bind Trap C .12 .20
1202 Light Magic Stone C .12 .20
1203 Fire Magic Stone C .12 .20
1204 Water Magic Stone C .12 .20
1205 Wind Magic Stone C .12 .20
1206 Darkness Magic Stone C .12 .20
2060 Arwyn, the Queen of Deep Green R .20 .30
2061 Green Wizard U .15 .25
2062 Artemis, the Goddess of Hunt R .20 .30
2065 Jabberwock, the Chaotic Disaster R .20 .30
2071 Guardian Warrior in Flower Garden C .12 .20
2074 Yggnitsvay, the Guardian of Green Branch C .12 .20
2076 Elvish Patrol Soldier C .12 .20
2077 Jungle Hunter C .12 .20
2078 Alberich, the King of Elemental SR
2079 Elvish Berserker C .12 .20
2081 Forest Guard C .12 .20
2082 Elven Archer C .12 .20

2084 Rambletree C .12 .20
2085 Life Dryad C .12 .20
2087 Magicsucker Beetle C .12 .20
2090 Deep Forest of Elves U .15 .25
2091 Sealed Circle of Wind U .15 .25
2092 Ward of Bramble C .12 .20
2093 Bless of Jewel Tree C .12 .20
2094 Oaken Bow C .12 .20
2095 Wrath of the Earth R .20 .30
2098 Spring of Magic Power C .12 .20
2099 Flash of Void C .12 .20
2102 Synchrojamming C .12 .20
2103 Forbidden Fruit R .20 .30
2104 Elvish Reinforcement C .12 .20
2108 Sariel, the Lord of the End R .20 .30
2109 Enforcer of Grudge U .15 .25
2111 Osiris, the Nether God of King's Tomb R .20 .30
2112 Cerberus, the Nether Watchdog U .15 .25
2113 Cu Chulainn, the Hero in a Far Land SR
2114 Marching Band of the End U .15 .25
2115 Familiar of Hades U .15 .25
2119 Lantern, the Spirit of Grave Keeper C .12 .20
2120 Ghost Swordsman C .12 .20
2121 Dark Sorcerer C .12 .20
2123 Orpheus, the Nether Player R .20 .30
2127 Bloodthirst Baron C .12 .20
2129 Dullahan, the Death Knight C .12 .20
2133 Wight, Fallen King C .12 .20
2134 Skeleton Horseman C .12 .20
2135 Dragon Zombie, the Necrodragon U .15 .25
2139 Soul Cord C .12 .20
2140 Gae Bolg, the Magic Spear R .20 .30
2142 Power of Hatred C .12 .20
2144 End of Despair C .12 .20
2146 Binding Chain C .12 .20
2147 Miasma of the Glyph C .12 .20
2149 Soul Sympathy C .12 .20
2150 Culling the Weak C .12 .20
2151 Grasp of Life C .12 .20
2152 Corpse Guard U .15 .25
2154 Laplace, the Tuner U .15 .25

2014 Force of Will The War of Valhalla

COMPLETE SET (239)
BOOSTER BOX (36 PACKS)
BOOSTER PACK (10 CARDS)
RELEASED ON JULY 25, 2014
2001 White Wizard U .15 .25
2002 Ishtar, the Great Goddess of Kindness SR
2003 Ywain, the Knight of Leo R .20 .30
2004 Angel of Wisdom U .15 .25
2005 Kingdom Protection Circle C .12 .20
2006 Trainer of Kings C .12 .20
2007 Priestess of Kindness C .12 .20
2008 Monk of Blessing C .12 .20
2009 Knight of Honor C .12 .20
2010 Heavy Horseman C .12 .20
2011 One Who Reaches to the Sky U .15 .25
2012 Pouncing Lion R .20 .30
2013 Fair and Square C .12 .20
2014 Surging Battle Cry R .20 .30
2015 Spear from God U .15 .25
2016 Queen's Prayer C .12 .20
2017 Lightning Ray C .12 .20
2018 Stab Each Other R .20 .30
2019 Allied Force C .12 .20
2020 Supply Distribution C .12 .20
2021 Red Wizard U .15 .25
2022 Kanna, the Oracle of Flames SR
2023 Gilgamesh, the Tyrant of the Hunt R .20 .30
2024 Enkidu, the Sworn Friend R .20 .30
2025 Gugalanna, the Bull of Heaven R .20 .30
2026 Firefloor Drake U .15 .25
2027 Baby Dragon of Asakna C .12 .20
2028 Exploding Rock Golem C .12 .20
2029 Blasting Beetle C .12 .20
2030 Blood Moon R .20 .30
2031 Kamikaze Battery C .12 .20
2032 Flaming Art -Purgatory- C .12 .20
2033 Pyre Shield C .12 .20
2034 Surprise Attack C .12 .20
2035 Burning Will C .12 .20
2036 Magic Flame C .12 .20
2037 Booby Trap U .15 .25
2038 Flaming Art -Ash and Smoke- C .12 .20
2039 Flaming Art -Beacon Fire- C .12 .20
2040 Blue Wizard U .15 .25
2041 Poseidon, the Great Emperor God of Oceans SR .20 .30
2042 Abzu, the Water God of Truth U .15 .25
2043 Gear Golem, the Magical Soldier R .20 .30
2044 Dagon, the Abomination of the Deep Sea R .20 .30
2045 Tsunami Spirit C .12 .20
2046 Sea Serpent in the Storm C .12 .20
2047 Indigo Siren C .12 .20
2048 Maid of Siren C .12 .20
2049 Mirage Arowana C .12 .20
2050 Predator Anemone C .12 .20
2051 Deep Sea Paradise R .20 .30
2052 Water Bubble Robe U .15 .25
2053 Mutating Potion -Regenerate- C .12 .20
2054 Aqua Magic -Tempest- R .20 .30
2055 Angelic Voice C .12 .20
2056 Coral Rain C .12 .20
2057 Magic Wave C .12 .20
2058 Mind Pollution U .15 .25
2059 Mermaid's Allure C .12 .20
2060 Arwyn, the Queen of Deep Green R .20 .30
2063 Orion, the Celestial Hegemon U .15 .25
2064 Durathror, the Herald of the End R .20 .30
2066 Hraesvelgr , the Giant Hawk of the Jewel Tree U .15 .25
2067 Heithrun, the Goat of Mead U .15 .25
2068 Dainn, the Herald of Beginning C .12 .20
2069 Dvalinn, the Herald of Continuation C .12 .20
2070 Duneyrr, the Herald of Change C .12 .20
2072 Ratatoskr, the Messenger of the Jewel Tree U .15 .25
2073 Kukunochi, the Errand of the Jewel Tree SR
2075 Alseid, the Amorous Spirit C .12 .20
2080 Elvish Warrior C .12 .20
2083 Elvish Weaver C .12 .20
2086 Woodgardner C .12 .20
2088 Sanctuary of Yggdrasil U .15 .25
2089 Sealed Vault U .15 .25
2097 Whisper of Wind U .15 .25
2100 Shortage of Magic Power U .15 .25
2101 Magic Storm U .15 .25
2105 Wind Magic Circle -Aura- C .12 .20
2107 Garmheld, the King of the Dead R .20 .30
2108 Sariel, the Lord of the End R .20 .30
2116 Demon Lady of Grudge U .15 .25
2117 Soul Eater U .15 .25
2118 Carrion Devourer C .12 .20
2122 Ancient Black Knight U .15 .25
2124 Nether Horseman C .12 .20
2125 Reanimated Knight C .12 .20
2126 Butz, the Ebony Knight U .15 .25
2128 Lifesucker C .12 .20
2130 Grudge Berserker C .12 .20
2131 Disappointing Swordsman C .12 .20
2132 Compensation Warrior C .12 .20
2136 Cemetery Rose U .15 .25
2137 Specter Circle C .12 .20
2138 Paradise of the Exiled R .20 .30
2141 Sword of Miasma C .12 .20
2143 Heavy Rain of Distress U .15 .25
2145 Curse of Garheld C .12 .20
2148 Unreasonable Choice C .12 .20
2153 Soul Slave C .12 .20
2155 Revive Gimmick U .15 .25
2156 Tone Gimmick C .12 .20
2157 Triumph Gate of Spellproof U .15 .25
2158 The Gate U .15 .25
3001 Sister of Linorsphairia U .15 .25
3002 Angrboda, the Sunset Giant SR
3003 Eletos, the Granite Giant U .15 .25
3004 Balder, Light God of the White Heaven R .20 .30
3005 Griffon C .12 .20
3006 Ancient Dragon R .20 .30
3007 Perseus, Divine Blade of the Gleaming Skies C .12 .20
3008 Merlin the Wizard of the Round Table R .20 .30
3009 Warder of Light Chain U .15 .25
3010 Brunhild, the Valkyrie U .15 .25
3011 Knight of the Barbaric Axe C .12 .20
3012 Knight of the Tough Shield U .15 .25
3013 Knight of the Twin Swords C .12 .20
3014 Aslan C .12 .20
3015 Light of Truth U .15 .25
3016 Purify Souls C .12 .20
3017 Sleipnir C .12 .20
3018 Mjolnir, the Hammer of White Lightning R .20 .30
3019 Relic Research Party C .12 .20
3020 Head of Mimir U .15 .25
3021 Kvesa Gardula C .12 .20
3022 Order of Retirement R .20 .30
3023 Fruits of Dawn U .15 .25
3024 Mumble of Summer Wind C .12 .20
3025 Flame Entertainer U .15 .25
3026 Surtr, the Incinerating Giant SR
3027 Bogallo, the Lava Giant U .15 .25
3028 Tyr, the Brave War God R .20 .30
3029 Rio, the Sword Dancer of Crimson Fire C .12 .20
3030 Cannonneer of Asakna U .15 .25
3031 Attendant of Asakna C .12 .20
3032 Guerrilla Soldier of Asakna C .12 .20
3033 Manticore R .20 .30
3034 Mad Dog of Dichroite C .12 .20
3035 Tinder Kobold Garou C .12 .20
3036 Smaug R .20 .30
3037 Barbed Volcano Scorpion U .15 .25
3038 Dwarven Craftsman U .15 .25
3039 Gauguin's Studio R .20 .30
3040 Dwarven Magical Mine U .15 .25
3041 Kosetsu, Katana of Chikuzen C .12 .20
3042 Mithril Armor C .12 .20
3043 Inferno of Muspell R .20 .30
3044 Spiral Flair U .15 .25
3045 Reckless Strength C .12 .20
3046 Dragonflame C .12 .20
3047 Flame Snake of Manipulation U .15 .25
3048 Flaming Scheme U .15 .25
3049 Lailah, the Maiden of the Fountain U .15 .25
3050 Bergelmir, the Giant of Absolute Coldness SR
3051 Sva, the Giant of the Sea Trench U .15 .25
3052 Aegir, the Sea God of the Tempest R .20 .30
3053 Princess of Dragon Palace U .15 .25
3054 Tethys, the Wise Goddess R .20 .30
3055 Kriti, the Water Element C .12 .20
3056 Hydra R .20 .30
3057 Tri, the Mermaid Fencer U .15 .25
3058 Medusa, the Evil Eye of Binding C .12 .20
3059 Orfeo C .12 .20
3060 Euridice C .12 .20
3061 Tortuga U .15 .25
3062 Tridacna C .12 .20
3063 Commedia Erudita U .15 .25
3064 Sea Monster Zone R .20 .30
3065 Mermaid Weapon U .15 .25
3066 Water Spirit Kris Knife C .12 .20
3067 Close Encounters C .12 .20
3068 Mutation Potion -Activate Body C .12 .20
3069 Crime of Wave and Abandon U .15 .25
3070 Devotion for Sound and Heat U .15 .25
3071 Mirror of Medusa C .12 .20
3072 Breath of God R .20 .30
3073 Athenia, the Wind Master R .20 .30
3074 Richesse, the Swordsman U .15 .25
3075 Trou, the Giant of the Fairie's Stronghold R .20 .30
3076 Troll, the Raging Giant U .15 .25
3077 Frey, the Noble God of Sunshine SR
3078 Unicorn U .15 .25
3079 Siren of the Stream U .15 .25
3080 Maiden of Yggdrasil R .20 .30
3081 Fairy Dragon of Beryl R .20 .30
3082 Caith Sith Roun, the Weaver of Miracles C .12 .20
3083 Caith Sith Roo, the Caller of Miracles C .12 .20
3084 Cu Sith Rey, the Carrier of Miracles C .12 .20
3085 Wise Elder of Eltheim U .15 .25
3086 Evergreen Sentinel C .12 .20
3087 Waldkobold Joyy C .12 .20
3088 Sephirothic Tree R .20 .30
3089 Caith Sith Township C .12 .20
3090 Mithril Sword C .12 .20
3091 Live Oak Helm C .12 .20
3092 Mead of Poetry C .12 .20
3093 Mumble of Spring Wind C .12 .20
3094 Spell Transcription U .15 .25
3095 Ring of Nibelungen R .20 .30
3096 Mead of Knowledge U .15 .25
3097 Morning Mist C .12 .20
3098 Laurier, the Twilight Witch U .15 .25
3099 Utgarda Loki, the Skeletal Giant R .20 .30
3100 Cyclops, the One-eyed Giant U .15 .25
3101 Hermod, Nether God of the Dark Heaven R .20 .30
3102 Freya, Goddess of the full moon U .15 .25
3103 Demon Crusader C .12 .20
3104 Shemhaza, the Fallen Angel of Alchemy SR
3105 Sahriel, the Fallen Angel of Binding C .12 .20
3106 Armaros, the Fallen Angel of Negating U .15 .25
3107 Fafnir R .20 .30
3108 Empusa, the Temptation C .12 .20
3109 Death, the Pope of Nether U .15 .25
3110 Twin Blade Skeleton C .12 .20
3111 Garm, the Ashen Black C .12 .20
3112 Nether Fleshpot U .15 .25
3113 Crypt of Strustu C .12 .20
3114 Potion of Compensation C .12 .20
3115 Draupnir, Brace of Twin Magic R .20 .30
3116 Cursed Doll of the Mourning Witch U .15 .25
3117 Sorcery of Seiz C .12 .20
3118 Muddle the Ego C .12 .20
3119 Tunnel Vision C .12 .20
3120 Parting Gift to the Dead R .20 .30
3121 Disappear Magic C .12 .20
3122 Monument of Wisdom R .20 .30
3123 Thiessen Gimmick C .12 .20
3124 Encode Gimmick U .15 .25
3125 Tribe Gimmick C .12 .20
3126 Monument of Rune U .15 .25
3127 Bind of Silence C .12 .20
3128 Time of Ragnarok R .20 .30
3129 Gungnir, the Holy Spear R .20 .30
3130 Hoenir, the Bishop God R .20 .30
3131 Light Magic Stone C .12 .20
3132 Fire Magic Stone C .12 .20
3133 Water Magic Stone C .12 .20
3134 Wind Magic Stone C .12 .20
3135 Darkness Magic Stone C .12 .20

2015 Force of Will The Castle of Heaven and the Two Towers

COMPLETE SET (105) 55.00 85.00
BOOSTER BOX (36 PACKS) 120.00 160.00
BOOSTER PACK (10 CARDS) 5.00 8.00
RELEASED ON FEBRUARY 13, 2015
TAT001 Breath of the God C .10 .20
TAT002 Caterina, the Saint of Fantasy U .10 .25
TAT003 Don Quijote, the Wandering Knight R .10 .25
TAT004 Grimm, the Avenger of Fairy Tales SR .30 .50
TAT005 Guardian of Tower C .10 .20
TAT006 Jeanne d'Arc, the Awakening Purity SR .25 .40
TAT007 Jump to the Sky C .10 .20
TAT008 Light of Lumia U .10 .25
TAT009 Longinus, the Holy Lance C .10 .20
TAT010 Lumiel, the Tower of Hope R .10 .25
TAT011 March of Saints C .10 .20
TAT012 Pure Spirit of Fantasy C .10 .20
TAT013 Realm of Pure Spirits U .25 .40
TAT014 Sacred Princess of Guidance R 1.50 2.25
TAT015 Sacred Scepter of Exorcism U .10 .25
TAT016 Seeking Sky Soldier C .10 .20
TAT017 Sleeping Beauty R .10 .25
TAT018 The Queen's Butler C .10 .20
TAT019 Beowulf, the Blazing Wolf C .15 .30
TAT020 Big-Bang Revolution C .10 .20
TAT021 Card Soldier Diamond C .10 .20
TAT022 Card Soldier Heart C .10 .20
TAT023 Dragon King's Flame R .10 .25
TAT024 Duel of Truth C .30 .50
TAT025 Endless War U .10 .25
TAT026 Falltgold, the Dragoon R 3.50 5.00
TAT027 Forced Growth C .10 .20
TAT028 Fthaggua, the Flame Spirit R .10 .25
TAT029 Gliding Dragon Knight C .10 .20
TAT030 Kusanagi Sword C .10 .20
TAT031 Little Dread, the Fake Red Moon SR .75 1.25
TAT032 Rapid Decay U .10 .25
TAT033 Realm of the Dragon King R .10 .25
TAT034 Redbird of Omen U .10 .25
TAT035 Wicked Witch of the West U .10 .25
TAT036 Yamata-no-Orochi, the Eight Disasters SR .60 1.00
TAT037 Alice in Wonderland R 2.25 3.25
TAT038 Alice's World R .10 .25
TAT039 Cheshire Cat, the Grinning Remnant SR 8.00 12.00
TAT040 Crossroad of Worlds U .10 .25
TAT041 Destructive Flow C .10 .20
TAT042 Dreams of Wonderland R .10 .25
TAT043 Humpty Dumpty SR .30 .50
TAT044 Little Mermaid of Tragic Love U .10 .25
TAT045 Mad Hatter U .10 .25
TAT046 Mad Tea-Party U .10 .25
TAT047 March Hare R .10 .25
TAT048 Riina, the Girl with Nothing C .10 .20
TAT049 Seashore Fisherman C .10 .20
TAT050 Shallows Giant Dolphin C .10 .20
TAT051 Sleeping Rat C .10 .20
TAT052 Star Money C .10 .20
TAT053 Whirlpool of Knowledge C .10 .20
TAT054 Witch's Dagger C .10 .20
TAT055 Brainless Scarecrow C .10 .20
TAT056 Cowardly Lion C .10 .20
TAT057 Crimson Girl in the Sky R 5.00 7.00
TAT058 Dorothy, the Lost Girl R .10 .25
TAT059 Dragonslayer C .10 .20
TAT060 Evolution of Limits C .10 .20
TAT061 Gardea, the Guardian Dragon of Heaven SR .10 .25
TAT062 Glinda, the Fairy SR .50 .75
TAT063 Guide of Heaven U .10 .25
TAT064 Heartless Tin Man C .10 .20
TAT065 Oz, the Great Wizard U .10 .25
TAT066 Oz's Magic U .10 .25
TAT067 Portal of Truth C .10 .20
TAT068 Realm of Evolution U .10 .25

Card	Low	High
TAT069 Refarth, the Castle in Heaven R	.40	.75
TAT070 Silver Shoes C	.10	.20
TAT071 Wolf in the Sky C	.10	.20
TAT072 Xeex the Ancient Magic R	1.25	1.50
TAT073 Al-Haber, the Tower of Despair R	.10	.25
TAT074 Card Soldier Club C	.10	.20
TAT075 Card Soldier Spade C	.10	.20
TAT076 Death Sentence from the Queen C	.10	.20
TAT077 Demon's Curse C	.10	.20
TAT078 Ebony Devil C	.10	.20
TAT079 Ebony Prophet R	1.25	1.75
TAT080 Elder Things U	.10	.25
TAT081 Joker's Suit C	.10	.20
TAT082 Laplacia, the Demon of Fate SR	.10	.25
TAT083 Mephistopheles, the Abyssal Tyrant SR	.75	1.15
TAT084 Necronomicon U	.10	.25
TAT085 Neithardt, the Demon Knight U	.10	.25
TAT086 Queen of Hearts R	.10	.25
TAT087 Spire Shadow Drake C	.10	.20
TAT088 Stoning to Death R	.60	1.00
TAT089 Summoning Art of Alhazred U	.10	.25
TAT090 Whisper from the Abyss C	.10	.20
TAT091 Almerius, the Levitating Stone SR	3.50	5.00
TAT092 Feethsing, the Holy Wind Stone SR	1.25	1.75
TAT093 Grusbalesta, the Sealing Stone SR	4.00	6.00
TAT094 Magic Stone of Blasting Waves R	2.00	3.00
TAT095 Magic Stone of Dark Depth R	1.75	2.25
TAT096 Magic Stone of Gusting Skies R	2.00	3.50
TAT097 Magic Stone of Light Vapors R	1.00	1.50
TAT098 Magic Stone of Scorched Bales R	2.00	3.00
TAT099 Milest, the Ghostly Flame Stone SR	1.25	2.00
TAT100 Moojdart, the Fantasy Stone SR	1.25	1.75
TAT101 Magic Stone of Light C	.10	.20
TAT102 Magic Stone of Flame C	.10	.20
TAT103 Magic Stone of Water C	.10	.20
TAT104 Magic Stone of Wind C	.10	.20
TAT105 Magic Stone of Darkness C	.10	.20

2015 Force of Will The Crimson Moon's Fairy Tale

Card	Low	High
COMPLETE SET (105)	40.00	70.00
BOOSTER BOX (36 PACKS)	80.00	100.00
BOOSTER PACK (10 CARDS)	2.00	3.00
RELEASED ON FEBRUARY 13, 2015		
CMF001 Aesop, the Prince's Tutor U	.10	.25
CMF002 Blinded Prince C	.10	.20
CMF003 Clothes Tailor C	.10	.20
CMF004 Dream of Juliet C	.40	.75
CMF005 Grimm, the Fairy Tale Prince R	.10	.25
CMF006 Holy Grail C	.10	.20
CMF007 Jeweled Branch of Horai U	.10	.25
CMF008 Juliet, the Hope SR	.10	.20
CMF009 King's Servant C	.10	.20
CMF010 Knight of Loyalty C	.10	.20
CMF011 Light of Hope C	.10	.20
CMF012 Light Palace, the King's Castle R	.10	.25
CMF013 Pandora, Girl of the Box / Pandora of Light R	1.00	1.50
CMF014 Rapunzel, the Long-Haired Princess SR	.10	.25
CMF015 Return to Stories U	.10	.25
CMF016 Silver Stake C	.10	.20
CMF017 Tell a Fairy Tale R	.10	.25
CMF018 The Emperor with New Clothes U	.10	.25
CMF019 Tinker Bell, the Spirit R	.10	.25
CMF020 Basket of Little Red C	.10	.20
CMF021 Bloody Moon R	.10	.25
CMF022 Clockwork Apple Bomb C	.10	.20
CMF023 Commander of Wolves R	.10	.25
CMF024 Gilles de Rais, the Golden Dragon SR	.75	1.25
CMF025 Granny by the Fireplace C	.10	.20
CMF026 Hunter in Black Forest C	.20	.35
CMF027 Little Red Riding Hood R	2.00	3.50
CMF028 Loup-Garou, the New Moon SR	.60	1.00
CMF029 Moon Night Pouncer U	.10	.25
CMF030 Murderous Snowman C	.10	.20
CMF031 Poison Apple C	.30	.50
CMF032 Purifying Fire U	.30	.50
CMF033 Red Hot Iron Shoes C	.10	.20
CMF034 Robe of Fire-Rat U	.40	.60
CMF035 Seven Dwarfs C	.10	.20
CMF036 Snow White R	2.00	3.50
CMF037 Wolf-Haunted in Black Forest U	.10	.25
CMF038 Thunder R	1.50	2.25
CMF039 Archer of the Crescent Moon C	.10	.20
CMF040 Charles VII U	.10	.25
CMF041 Deep Ones SR	.10	.25
CMF042 Five Challenges C	.10	.20
CMF043 Hamelin's Pied Piper R	.10	.25
CMF044 Heavenly Feathered Robe U	.10	.25
CMF045 Inquisition R	.10	.25
CMF046 Knight of the New Moon C	.10	.20
CMF047 Nameless Girl R	1.25	2.00
CMF048 One-Inch Boy C	.10	.20
CMF049 Pale Moon R	.10	.25
CMF050 Rabbit Kick U	.10	.25
CMF051 Rat Catcher's Pipe C	.10	.20
CMF052 Seer of the Blue Moon R	3.00	4.00
CMF053 Servant of Kaguya C	.10	.20
CMF054 Squirmer of the Dark C	.10	.20
CMF055 Stone Bowl of Buddha U	.10	.25
CMF056 Swordsman of the Full Moon SR	.75	1.25
CMF057 Voice of the False God C	.10	.20
CMF058 Absolute Cake Zone C	.40	.60
CMF059 Aramis, the Three Musketeers U	.10	.25
CMF060 Athos, the Three Musketeers SR	.50	.75
CMF061 Christie, the Wind Tracker R	1.25	2.00
CMF062 Cottage of Cakes R	.10	.25
CMF063 Cowrie of Swallows U	.10	.25
CMF064 Crucifix C	.10	.20
CMF065 Elvish Bowman C	.10	.20
CMF066 Elvish Exorcist C	.10	.20
CMF067 Elvish Priest C	.60	1.00
CMF068 Fina, the Silver Player R	.10	.25
CMF069 Gretel U	1.25	1.75
CMF070 Hansel SR	.10	.25
CMF071 Law of Silence R	.10	.25
CMF072 Musketeer's Bayonet C	.10	.20
CMF073 Porthos, the Three Musketeers C	.10	.20
CMF074 Puss in Boots R	1.00	1.50
CMF075 Siege Warfare C	.10	.20
CMF076 Silver Bullet U	.10	.25
CMF077 Alucard, the Dark Noble R	3.00	4.50
CMF078 Alvarez, the Demon Castle R	.10	.25
CMF079 Black Coffin of Vampires C	.10	.20
CMF080 Bloodsucking Impulse C	.10	.20
CMF081 Carmilla, the Queen of Vampires SR	1.50	2.50
CMF082 Cinderella, the Ashen Maiden SR	.75	1.25
CMF083 Deadman Prince C	.10	.20
CMF084 Jewels on Dragon's Neck U	.10	.25
CMF085 Lora, the Blood Speaker U	.75	1.25
CMF086 Midnight Bell C	.10	.20
CMF087 Pandora, Girl of the Box / Pandora of Dark R	1.00	1.50
CMF088 Pumpkin Witch C	.10	.20
CMF089 Resurrection of Vampire U	.10	.25
CMF090 Romeo, the Despair U	.10	.25
CMF091 Servant of Vampire C	.10	.20
CMF092 Slipper of Cinderella C	.10	.20
CMF093 Spiral of Despair R	.75	1.15
CMF094 Vampire Bat C	.10	.20
CMF095 Vampire's Staff R	.10	.25
CMF096 Magic Stone of Black Silence R	1.25	2.00
CMF097 Magic Stone of Deep Wood R	1.25	2.00
CMF098 Magic Stone of Hearth's Core R	1.25	2.00
CMF099 Magic Stone of Heat Ray R	1.25	2.00
CMF100 Magic Stone of Heaven's Rift R	1.25	2.00
CMF101 Magic Stone of Darkness C	.10	.20
CMF102 Magic Stone of Flame C	.10	.20
CMF103 Magic Stone of Light C	.10	.20
CMF104 Magic Stone of Water C	.10	.20
CMF105 Magic Stone of Wind C	.10	.20

2015 Force of Will The Moon Priestess Returns

Card	Low	High
COMPLETE SET (105)	35.00	60.00
BOOSTER BOX (36 PACKS)	70.00	90.00
BOOSTER PACK (10 CARDS)	3.00	5.00
RELEASED ON APRIL 24, 2015		
MPR001 I, the Pilot R	.10	.25
MPR002 Abel, the Avenger of Gods SR	.25	.40
MPR003 Accede the Light C	.10	.20
MPR004 Apostle of Paradise C	.10	.20
MPR005 Book of Genesis U	.10	.25
MPR006 Genesis Creation R	.10	.25
MPR007 Holy Warrior of Hope C	.10	.20
MPR008 Jekyll, the Order U	.10	.25
MPR009 Mind Reading Fox U	.10	.25
MPR010 Pandora, the Weaver of Myth R	.60	1.00
MPR011 Ragnarok, the Divine Sword of Savior R	.25	.40
MPR012 Savior of Splendor U	.10	.25
MPR013 Seal of Grimmia C	.10	.20
MPR014 Sign to the Future C	.25	.40
MPR015 Speaker of Creation C	.10	.20
MPR016 Sweet Rose C	.10	.20
MPR017 The Little Prince SR	.40	.60
MPR018 White Spirit C	.10	.20
MPR019 Akashic Records of Eternal Flame R	.10	.25
MPR020 Apostle of Cain C	.10	.20
MPR021 Apostle of Creation R	1.50	2.00
MPR022 Black Goat C	.10	.20
MPR023 Blazer, the Eater of Dimensions SR	1.00	1.50
MPR024 Bullet of Envy C	.10	.20
MPR025 Cain Complex U	.10	.25
MPR026 Crime and Punishment C	.10	.20
MPR027 Eden, the Crimson Garden U	.10	.25
MPR028 Forty Thieves C	.10	.20
MPR029 Glyph of Unkill C	.10	.20
MPR030 Jabal, the Grandsire of Nomads C	.10	.20
MPR031 Jubal, the Grandsire of Musicians U	.10	.25
MPR032 Shubb-Niggurath, the Goddess of Fertility SR	.20	.35
MPR033 Spawn of Blazer C	.10	.20
MPR034 Split Heaven and Earth R	1.25	1.75
MPR035 The First Lie U	.10	.25
MPR036 The Hound of Tindalos R	.10	.25
MPR037 Apollosphere, the Moon Lance R	.10	.25
MPR038 Campanella, the Milky Way Moon SR	.30	.50
MPR039 Dark Shining Swordsman C	.10	.20
MPR040 Elixir of Immortality C	.10	.20
MPR041 Etna, the Snow Queen SR	.50	.80
MPR042 Fallen Comet R	.10	.25
MPR043 Glimpse of Kaguya R	.40	.75
MPR044 Joyful Bird-Catcher C	.10	.20
MPR045 Kai, the Frozen Heart U	.10	.25
MPR046 Moon Princess of Stellar Wars R	.60	1.00
MPR047 Moonglow Bird C	.10	.20
MPR048 Pilot of Universe C	.10	.20
MPR049 Shooting Star U	.10	.25
MPR050 The Milky Way C	.10	.20
MPR051 Total Eclipse C	.10	.20
MPR052 Tsukuyomi, the Moon City U	.10	.25
MPR053 Yang Mage of Decrescent U	.10	.25
MPR054 Yin Mage of Increscent C	.10	.20
MPR055 Aladdin's Lamp R	.10	.25
MPR056 Ali Baba, The Earnest Worker C	.10	.20
MPR057 Art of Sinbad C	.10	.20
MPR058 Barrier Field U	.10	.25
MPR059 Djinn, the Spirit of Lamp R	.10	.25
MPR060 Exceed, the Ancient Magic U	.25	.40
MPR061 Familiar of Holy Wind C	.60	1.00
MPR062 Fiethsing, the Magus of Holy Wind SR	2.00	3.00
MPR063 Flying Carpet C	.10	.20
MPR064 Liberator of Wind R	1.50	2.00
MPR065 Morgiana, the Wise Servant U	.60	1.00
MPR066 Open Sesame C	.10	.20
MPR067 Rukh C	.10	.20
MPR068 Sinbad, the Windrider Merchant SR	.30	.50
MPR069 Stories Told in 1001 Nights R	.10	.25
MPR070 Survivor of Heaven Castle C	.10	.20
MPR071 Wind Dagger C	.10	.20
MPR072 Wiseman of Winds U	.10	.25
MPR073 Acolyte of Darkness C	.10	.20
MPR074 Awakening at the End R	.10	.25
MPR075 Bind of Gravity C	.10	.20
MPR076 Black Miasma C	.10	.20
MPR077 Black Moon U	.10	.25
MPR078 Byakhee, the Winged Lady R	.50	.75
MPR079 Call of Cthulhu C	.10	.20
MPR080 Fiend of Dark Pyre R	1.25	2.00
MPR081 Hyde, the Chaos U	.10	.25
MPR082 King in Yellow C	.20	.35
MPR083 Phantasm of Void C	.10	.20
MPR084 Shantak C	.10	.20
MPR085 Sheharyar, the Distrust King U	.10	.25
MPR086 Shining Trapezohedron R	.10	.25
MPR087 Void Blast U	.10	.25
MPR088 Yellow Sign C	.10	.20
MPR089 Yog-Sothoth, the Dark Myth SR	.60	1.00
MPR090 Zero, the Magus of Null SR	1.50	2.25
MPR091 Alice, the Guardian of Dimensions R	.60	1.00
MPR092 Apollobreak, the Moon Blast R	.10	.25
MPR093 Flame of Outer World R	2.75	3.50
MPR094 Gherta, the Tear of Passion R	.10	.25
MPR095 Giovanni, the Lonely Child R	.10	.25
MPR096 Hastur, the Unspeakable R	1.00	1.50
MPR097 Seth, the Arbiter R	.60	1.00
MPR098 Little Red, the Pure Stone SR	4.00	6.00
MPR099 Magic Stone of Moon Light R	1.50	2.00
MPR100 Magic Stone of Moon Shade R	2.50	3.00
MPR101 Magic Stone of Darkness C	.10	.20
MPR102 Magic Stone of Flame C	.10	.20
MPR103 Magic Stone of Light C	.10	.20
MPR104 Magic Stone of Water C	.10	.20
MPR105 Magic Stone of Wind C	.10	.20

2015 Force of Will The Millennia of Ages

Card	Low	High
COMPLETE SET (50)	8.00	15.00
BOOSTER BOX (36 PACKS)	40.00	50.00
BOOSTER PACK (10 CARDS)	3.00	5.00
RELEASED ON JULY 24, 2015		
MOA001 Almerius, the Magus of Light R	.10	.25
MOA002 Duet of Light C	.10	.20
MOA003 Grimm, the Heroic King of Aspiration U	.40	.75
MOA004 Kaguya, the Tale of the Bamboo Cutter SR	.10	.25
MOA005 Lumia, the Saint Lady of World Rebirth U	.10	.25
MOA006 Pandora, the Princess of History Chanter U	.10	.25
MOA007 Pandora's Box of Hope C	.10	.20
MOA008 Shining Bamboo C	.10	.20
MOA009 Temporal Spell of Millennia C	.10	.20
MOA010 Zero, the Flashing Mage-Warrior R	.10	.25
MOA011 Ame-no-Habakiri C	.30	.50
MOA012 Blazer, the Awakener R	.10	.25
MOA013 Cthugha, the Living Flame U	1.25	1.75
MOA014 Emissary of Another Dimension U	.10	.25
MOA015 Fetal Movement in Outer World C	.10	.20
MOA016 Ghostflame C	.10	.20
MOA017 Little Red, the Hope of Millennia R	.10	.25
MOA018 Milest, the Invisible Ghostly Flame SR	.10	.25
MOA019 Susanowo, the Ten-Fist Sword U	.60	1.00
MOA020 Wormhole C	.10	.20
MOA021 Alice's Pursuit C	.10	.20
MOA022 Alice's Soldier U	.10	.25
MOA023 Emperor of Millennia U	.10	.25
MOA024 House of the Old Man C	.10	.20
MOA025 Lunya, the Liar Girl R	.10	.25
MOA026 Moojdart, the Queen of Fantasy World SR	.10	.25
MOA027 Moon Incarnation C	.10	.20
MOA028 Oracle of Tsukuyomi U	.10	.25
MOA029 Purplemist, the Fantasy Dragon R	.10	.25
MOA030 Transparent Moon C	.10	.20
MOA031 Bastet, the Elder God U	.10	.25
MOA032 Christie, the Warden of Sanctuary U	.10	.25
MOA033 Fiethsing, the Elvish Oracle R	.10	.25
MOA034 Hansel and Gretel U	.10	.25
MOA035 Leaves of Yggdrasil C	.10	.20
MOA036 Liberate the World C	.10	.20
MOA037 Melfee, the Successor of Sacred Wind R	.10	.25
MOA038 Refarth, the Wind Castle C	.10	.20
MOA039 Scheherazade, the Teller of the Crimson Moon SR	.10	.25
MOA040 Wind of Gods C	.10	.20
MOA041 Aria, the Last Vampire U	.10	.25
MOA042 Book of Elbon C	.10	.20
MOA043 Dark Pulse C	.10	.20
MOA044 Elbon, the Mage R	.10	.25
MOA045 Grusbalesta, the Keeper of Magic Stones SR	.10	.25
MOA046 Hazzard, the Dark Forest Augur U	.10	.25
MOA047 Mephistopheles, the Demon Collaborator U	.10	.25
MOA048 Mount Immortal C	.10	.20
MOA049 Nyarlathotep, the Usurper R	.60	1.00
MOA050 Ritual of Millennia C	.10	.20

2015 Force of Will The Millennia of Ages Foil

Card	Low	High
MOA001 Almerius, the Magus of Light R	.10	.25
MOA002 Duet of Light C	.10	.20
MOA003 Grimm, the Heroic King of Aspiration U	.10	.25
MOA004 Kaguya, the Tale of the Bamboo Cutter SR	.10	.25
MOA005 Lumia, the Saint Lady of World Rebirth U	.40	.60
MOA006 Pandora, the Princess of History Chanter U	.75	1.00
MOA007 Pandora's Box of Hope C	.10	.20
MOA008 Shining Bamboo C	.10	.20
MOA009 Temporal Spell of Millennia C	.10	.20
MOA010 Zero, the Flashing Mage-Warrior R	.10	.25
MOA011 Ame-no-Habakiri C	1.25	1.75
MOA012 Blazer, the Awakener R	.10	.25
MOA013 Cthugha, the Living Flame U	3.00	4.00
MOA014 Emissary of Another Dimension U	.10	.25
MOA015 Fetal Movement in Outer World C	.50	.75
MOA016 Ghostflame C	.10	.20
MOA017 Little Red, the Hope of Millennia R	.10	.25
MOA018 Milest, the Invisible Ghostly Flame SR	.10	.25
MOA019 Susanowo, the Ten-Fist Sword U	1.25	1.75
MOA020 Wormhole C	.10	.20
MOA021 Alice's Pursuit C	.30	.50
MOA022 Alice's Soldier U	.30	.50
MOA023 Emperor of Millennia U	.10	.25
MOA024 House of the Old Man C	.10	.20
MOA025 Lunya, the Liar Girl R	.10	.25
MOA026 Moojdart, the Queen of Fantasy World SR	.10	.25
MOA027 Moon Incarnation C	.10	.20
MOA028 Oracle of Tsukuyomi U	.30	.50
MOA029 Purplemist, the Fantasy Dragon R	.10	.25
MOA030 Transparent Moon C	.10	.20
MOA031 Bastet, the Elder God U	.75	1.25
MOA032 Christie, the Warden of Sanctuary U	.10	.25
MOA033 Fiethsing, the Elvish Oracle R	.10	.25
MOA034 Hansel and Gretel U	.10	.25
MOA035 Leaves of Yggdrasil C	.10	.20
MOA036 Liberate the World C	.10	.20
MOA037 Melfee, the Successor of Sacred Wind R	.10	.25
MOA038 Refarth, the Wind Castle C	.10	.20
MOA039 Scheherazade, the Teller of the Crimson Moon SR	.10	.25
MOA040 Wind of Gods C	.10	.20
MOA041 Aria, the Last Vampire U	.10	.25
MOA042 Book of Elbon C	.75	1.15
MOA043 Dark Pulse C	.15	.30
MOA044 Elbon, the Mage R	.10	.25
MOA045 Grusbalesta, the Keeper of Magic Stones SR	.10	.25
MOA046 Hazzard, the Dark Forest Augur U	.10	.25

MOA047 Mephistopheles, the Demon Collaborator U .10 .25
MOA048 Mount Immortal C .10 .20
MOA049 Nyarlathotep, the Usurper R 1.25 1.75
MOA050 Ritual of Millennia C .10 .20

2015 Force of Will The Seven Kings of the Lands

COMPLETE SET (105) 50.00 100.00
BOOSTER BOX (36 PACKS) 70.00 90.00
BOOSTER PACK (10 CARDS) 2.00 5.00
RELEASED ON SEPTEMBER 15, 2015
SKL001 Arla, the Winged Lord R .40 1.00
SKL002 Bai Hu, the Sacred Beast R .40 1.00
SKL003 Bedivere, the Restorer of Souls SR .75 2.00
SKL004 Blessed Holy Wolf C .12 .30
SKL005 Celestial Wing Seraph SR .75 2.00
SKL006 Dignified Seraph U .25 .60
SKL007 Faria, the Sacred Queen R .75 2.00
SKL008 Give Wings C .12 .30
SKL009 Gwiber, the White Dragon U .25 .60
SKL010 Heavenly Garden of Armalla R .60 1.50
SKL011 Herald of the Winged Lord C .12 .30
SKL012 Invigoration of the Winged Lord R .40 1.00
SKL013 Little Angel of Armalla C .12 .30
SKL014 Order of Sacred Queen C .12 .30
SKL015 Protection of the Seraph C .12 .30
SKL016 Protective Barrier U .25 .60
SKL017 Wingman of Armalla C .12 .30
SKL018 Alice's Little Assault Force C .12 .30
SKL019 Certo, the Blazing Volcano U .60 1.50
SKL020 Dragoon of Certo C .12 .30
SKL021 Draig, the Red Dragon U .25 .60
SKL022 Familiar of Primogenitor C .12 .30
SKL023 Fear of Battle C .12 .30
SKL024 Flame Cat C .12 .30
SKL025 Flame King's Shout C .12 .30
SKL026 Gareth, the Dauntless Knight U .25 .60
SKL027 Melgis, the Flame King R .40 1.00
SKL028 Ouroboros, the Snake of Reincarnation SR .60 1.50
SKL029 Phantom of Primogenitor R .40 1.00
SKL030 Shadow Flame C .12 .30
SKL031 Snow White, the Valkyrie of Passion SR 1.00 3.00
SKL032 War Dance of the Valkyries U .25 .60
SKL033 Zhu Que, the Sacred Beast R .40 1.00
SKL034 Alice's Castling C .20 .50
SKL035 Alice's Little Scout C .12 .30
SKL036 Charm of the Princess R .40 1.00
SKL037 Cinderella, the Valkyrie of Glass SR 1.00 3.00
SKL038 Euryale, the Dark Eye of Blindness U .25 .60
SKL039 Foresee C .12 .30
SKL040 Heat Gaze C .12 .30
SKL041 Medusa, the Dead Eye of Petrification SR .75 2.00
SKL042 Petrifying Gaze U .25 .60
SKL043 Sailor of Shangri-La C .12 .30
SKL044 Shangri-La, the Paradise on the Ocean R .40 1.00
SKL045 Squire of the Ocean Lady C .12 .30
SKL046 Stheno, the Evil Eye of Temptation U .25 .60
SKL047 Trader of Shangri-La C .12 .30
SKL048 Valentina, the Princess of Love R 2.50 10.00
SKL049 Xuan Wu, the Sacred Beast R .40 1.00
SKL050 Afanc, the Phantom Beast U .25 .60
SKL051 Alice's Little Guardian C .12 .30
SKL052 Behemoth, the Earth Eater R .40 1.00
SKL053 Blessing of Yggdrasil C .12 .30
SKL054 Branch of Yggdrasil C .12 .30
SKL055 Elite Commander U .25 .60
SKL056 Guardian of the Forest C .12 .30
SKL057 Herald of the Beast Lady C .12 .30
SKL058 Keen Sense U .25 .60
SKL059 Pricia, the Beast Lady R 5.00 12.00
SKL060 Qing Long, the Sacred Beast SR 1.25 3.00
SKL061 Rapid Growth C .12 .30
SKL062 Ratatoskr, the Spirit of Yggdrasil SR 1.50 4.00
SKL063 Sissei, the Ancient Forest R .40 1.00
SKL064 Sprint of the Beast Lady R .40 1.00
SKL065 Sprinting Wolf C .12 .30
SKL066 Arthur, the Dead Lord of Vengeance SR 2.00 5.00
SKL067 Dark Purge C .12 .30
SKL068 Endless Night U .25 .60
SKL069 Forbidden Spell of the Undead Lord R .40 1.00
SKL070 Herald of the Undead Lord C .12 .30
SKL071 Hunter of Souls C .12 .30
SKL072 Merlin, the Wizard of Distress R .40 1.00
SKL073 Necromancy of the Undead Lord C .12 .30
SKL074 Niflheim, the Realm of the Dead R .40 1.00
SKL075 Persephone, the Nether Empress SR .60 1.50
SKL076 Prowler of Niflheim C .12 .30
SKL077 Rezzard, the Undead Lord R 2.50 6.00
SKL078 Scion of Ancient Lore U .25 .60
SKL079 Soulhunt C .12 .30
SKL080 Soulless Soldier C .12 .30
SKL081 Underground Dragger U .25 .60
SKL082 Charging Assaulter C .20 .50
SKL083 Clockwork Scout Plane C .12 .30
SKL084 Clockwork Soldiers C .12 .30
SKL085 Imitation Dragon U .25 .60
SKL086 Leginus, the Mechanical City U .25 .60
SKL087 Machina, the Machine Lord R 3.00 8.00
SKL088 March of the Machine Lord U .25 .60
SKL089 Power Supply Team C .12 .30
SKL090 Special Armor U .25 .60
SKL091 Winding Mender C .12 .30
SKL092 Alice, the Girl in the Looking Glass R .40 1.00
SKL093 Alice, the Girl in the Looking Glass R .40 1.00
SKL094 Blazer Gill Rabus R .40 1.00
SKL095 Artemis, the God's Bow R .40 1.00
SKL096 Deathscythe, the Life Reaper R .40 1.00
SKL097 Deep Blue, the Phantom Board R .50 1.25
SKL098 Gleipnir, the Red Binding of Fate R .40 1.00
SKL099 Horn of Sacred Beasts R .40 1.00
SKL100 Marybell, the Steel Doll R .40 1.00
SKL101 Darkness Magic Stone C .12 .30
SKL102 Fire Magic Stone C .12 .30
SKL103 Light Magic Stone C .12 .30
SKL104 Water Magic Stone C .12 .30
SKL105 Wind Magic Stone C .12 .30

2015 Force of Will The Twilight Wanderer

COMPLETE SET (104) 50.00 100.00
BOOSTER BOX (36 PACKS) 80.00 100.00
BOOSTER PACK (10 CARDS) 2.50 6.00
RELEASED ON DECEMBER 11, 2015
TTW001 Alice, Girl of the Lake/Alice, Fairy Queen R 3.00 5.00
TTW002 Alice's Little Supply Force C .12 .20
TTW003 Arthur Pendragon, King of the Round Table SR 2.00 3.00
TTW004 Elaine, the Fairy U .15 .25
TTW005 Fairy of the Lake C .12 .20
TTW006 Galahad, The Son of God .15 .25
TTW007 Gawain, the Knight of the Sun R .20 .30
TTW008 Gloria's Castle Town R .20 .30
TTW009 Grand Cross R .20 .30
TTW010 Justice of God's Sword C .12 .20
TTW011 Light Sprite C .12 .20
TTW012 Nimue, the Fairy U .15 .25
TTW013 Perceval, the Seeker of Holy Grail R 1.25 2.00
TTW014 Pride of Knights C .12 .20
TTW015 Protection of the Fairies C .12 .20
TTW016 The Final Word U .15 .25
TTW017 Viviane, Lady of the Lake SR 1.50 2.50
TTW018 Young Knight of Gloria C .12 .20
TTW019 Barrier of Flame R .20 .30
TTW020 Beat of the Phoenix Wings R .20 .30
TTW021 Burn to Cinders C .12 .20
TTW022 Caldera-Born Dragon U .15 .25
TTW023 Flame Dragon Commandant U .15 .25
TTW024 Flame Sprite C .12 .20
TTW025 Flamewing Wyvern C .12 .20
TTW026 Flash of Demon Sword C .12 .20
TTW027 Guinevere, the Jealous Queen R 2.00 3.00
TTW028 Hector de Maris, the Acolyte of Mad Demon U .15 .25
TTW029 Lancelot, the Knight of Mad Demon R 1.25 2.00
TTW030 Magic Matchstick C .12 .20
TTW031 Phoenix, the Flame of the World SR 1.25 2.00
TTW032 Sylvia Gill Palarilias / Sylvia Gill Palarilias (J) R 5.00 8.00
TTW033 Sylvia's Clanmate C .12 .20
TTW034 Sylvia's Roar U .15 .25
TTW035 The Little Match Girl SR .75 1.25
TTW036 Whelp Drake C .12 .20
TTW037 Adombrali, the Unfathomable SR 2.50 4.00
TTW038 All Consuming Suspicion C .12 .20
TTW039 Hera, Goddess of Jealousy R 1.25 2.00
TTW040 Insomniac Dormouse C .12 .20
TTW041 Invasion Ship, Golden Hind R .20 .30
TTW042 Laying the Foundation C .12 .20
TTW043 Leviathan, the First of the Sea SR .75 1.25
TTW044 Maritime Lookout C .12 .20
TTW045 Valentina, Plotting Lord of the Seas 3.00 5.00
Overlord of the Seven Lands, Valentina R
TTW046 Sane Hatter U .15 .25
TTW047 Send Back C .12 .20
TTW048 September Hare U .15 .25
TTW049 Suseri-hime, Goddess of Passion R .20 .30
TTW050 The Overlord's Baptism R .20 .30
TTW051 The Overlord's Invasion Party U .15 .25
TTW052 Valentina's Zealot C .12 .20
TTW053 Wall of Ideas U .15 .25
TTW054 Water Sprite C .12 .20
TTW055 Beastly Attack C .12 .20
TTW056 Drop of Yggdrasil C .12 .20
TTW057 Familiar of Refrain C .12 .20
TTW058 Final Forfeit U .15 .25
TTW059 Fruit of Yggdrasil C .12 .20
TTW060 Holy Ground of the Four Sacred Beasts R .20 .30
TTW061 Hraesvelgr, Drinker of Death R .20 .30
TTW062 Pricia, Beast Queen in Hiding SR .75 1.25
TTW063 Reflect, Child of Potential 6.00 10.00
Refrain, Child of Convergence R
TTW064 Rewriting Laws C .12 .20
TTW065 Servant of Reflect C .12 .20
TTW066 Spell-Weaver Elf U .15 .25
TTW067 Spirit of Yggdrasil U .15 .25
TTW068 The Beast Queen's Counterattack R .20 .30
TTW069 The Beast Queen's Guardian U .15 .25
TTW070 Vedfolnir, Eraser of Wind R .20 .30
TTW071 Wind Sprite C .12 .20
TTW072 Ziz, the Bird that Envelopes the Sky SR .75 1.25
TTW073 Barrier of Shadows R .20 .30
TTW074 Black Ribbon .12 .20
TTW075 Dance of the Shadows U .15 .25
TTW076 Girl in Twilight Garb R 6.00 10.00
TTW077 Dark Alice's Familiar C .12 .20
TTW078 Dark Alice's Shadow Warrior C .12 .20
TTW079 Dark Arla, the Shadow Wing U .15 .25
TTW080 Dark Faria, Shadow Princess of Ebony SR 2.00 3.00
TTW081 Dark Melgis, the Shadow Flame U .15 .25
TTW082 Dark Rezzard, the Dying Shadow R .20 .30
TTW083 Elisabeth, Shadow Princess of Blood SR 1.00 1.50
TTW084 Jeanne d'Arc, Shadow Princess of Purity R .20 .30
TTW085 Progenitor Demon C .12 .20
TTW086 Recollection of Dystopia R .20 .30
TTW087 Shadow Assassin C .12 .20
TTW088 Shadow Doppelganger U .15 .25
TTW089 The Scorn of Dark Alice .12 .20
TTW090 Unseen Pressure .12 .20
TTW091 Dark Machina, Gliding Shadow R .20 .30
TTW092 Deployable Defense Device U .15 .25
TTW093 Mass Produced Giant Land Mine C .12 .20
TTW094 Mechanical Knight C .12 .20
TTW095 Mechanical Sprite C .12 .20
TTW096 Change the World, Orb of Illusion R 2.50 4.00
TTW097 Excalibur, The God's Sword .20 .30
TTW098 Excalibur, the Spirit God's Sword R .20 .30
TTW099 Laevateinn, the Demon Sword R .20 .30
TTW100 Schrödinger, the Fallen Black Cat R .20 .30
TTW101 Fairy's Memoria R 2.00 3.00
TTW102 Ruler's Memoria R 4.00 6.00
TTW103 Sacred Beast's Memoria R .20 .30
TTW104 Shadow's Memoria R .20 .30
TTW105 Unyielding Flame's Memoria R .20 .30
TTW106 Darkness Magic Stone NR .12 .20
TTW107 Fire Magic Stone NR .12 .20
TTW108 Light Magic Stone NR .12 .20
TTW109 Water Magic Stone NR .12 .20
TTW110 Wind Magic Stone NR .12 .20

2016 Force of Will The Moonlit Savior

COMPLETE SET (105) 60.00 120.00
BOOSTER BOX (36 PACKS) 70.00 90.00
BOOSTER PACK (10 CARDS) 2.00 3.00
*FOIL: .75X TO 2X BASIC CARDS
RELEASED ON MARCH 11, 2016
TMS001 Angel of Wisdom, Cherudim U .25 .60
TMS002 Crescent Moon Magician R .40 1.00
TMS003 Friend from Another World, Kaguya R 2.50 10.00
TMS004 Holy Moon of Pure Nights U .25 .60
TMS005 Izanagi, Keeper of the Seal SR .60 1.50
TMS006 Kaguya's Premonition C .20 .50
TMS007 Knight of the Solstice R .40 1.00
TMS008 Luminescent Bamboo Bullet R .40 1.00
TMS009 Lunar Ibis C .20 .50
TMS010 Moonbreeze Fairy C .20 .50
TMS011 Pale Savior C .20 .50
TMS012 Seal of Shining Bamboo C .20 .50
TMS013 Shining Strike U .25 .60
TMS014 Temple Monk C .20 .50
TMS015 Tristan, the Knight of Sorrow C .20 .50
TMS016 Tsukuyomi Noble SR 1.25 3.00
TMS017 Veteran Master C .20 .50
TMS018 Athena, Titan of Revenge SR 1.50 4.00
TMS019 Blazing Metropolis, Vell-Savaria U .25 .60
TMS020 Blessing of Athena C .20 .50
TMS021 Demonflame U .25 .60
TMS022 Infernal Spirit of Vell-Savaria C .20 .50
TMS023 Keeper of the Future, Skuld SR 1.00 2.50
TMS024 Keeper of the Past, Urthr R .40 1.00
TMS025 Keeper of the Present, Verdandi R .60 1.50
TMS026 Memory of Disappearance R .40 1.00
TMS027 Memory of Flame C .20 .50
TMS028 Mordred, the Traitor U .25 .60
TMS029 Rukh Egg C .20 .50
TMS030 Spirit of Certo C .20 .50
TMS031 The Observer R 2.50 6.00
TMS032 Time Traveling Emissary C .20 .50
TMS033 Torching the Timeline C .20 .50
TMS034 Vell-Savarian Dragon U .25 .60
TMS035 Dance of Inspiration C .20 .50
TMS036 Drill Sergeant R .40 1.00
TMS037 Dying Swallow U .25 .60
TMS038 Flower Kingdom U .25 .60
TMS039 Magic Conductor's Baton C .20 .50
TMS040 Muse, Celestial of Music SR 1.00 2.50
TMS041 Musician of Shangri-La C .20 .50
TMS042 Peasant Revolt C .30 .75
TMS043 Prison in the Lunar Lake C .20 .50
TMS044 Puppet Soldier C .20 .50
TMS045 Shion's Hymn R .40 1.00
TMS046 Songstress of Shangri-La R 3.00 8.00
TMS047 The Flower Prince U .25 .60
TMS048 Thumbelina R .40 1.00
TMS049 Valentina, Puppet Monarch SR .50 1.25
TMS050 Valentina's Resistance U .25 .60
TMS051 Wererabbit of the Aqua Moon C .20 .50
TMS052 Ambush! C .20 .50
TMS053 Avatar of the Seven Lands, Alice SR 1.25 3.00
TMS054 Child of the Forest C .20 .50
TMS055 Foment of the World Tree R .40 1.00
TMS056 Heart Stirring Sage U .25 .60
TMS057 Huanglong, Leader of the Four Sacred Beasts SR .60 1.50
TMS058 Kujata, Sacred Ox R .40 1.00
TMS059 Moonbreeze Elf C .20 .50
TMS060 Pricia's Call to Action C .20 .50
TMS061 Rhythm of Life C .20 .50
TMS062 Servant to the Sacred Moon C .20 .50
TMS063 Timekeeper Elf U .25 .60
TMS064 Wall of Wind U .25 .60
TMS065 Wind-Secluded Refuge U .25 .60
TMS066 Wolf in the Moonlight C .20 .50
TMS067 World Tree Protector R .40 1.00
TMS068 Yggdrasil, the World Tree R 3.00 8.00
TMS069 Auspicious Bird of the Black Moon C .20 .50
TMS070 Black Moon Fairy C .20 .50
TMS071 Call of the Primogenitor C .20 .50
TMS072 Conqueror of the Black Moon, Gill Lapis R 4.00 10.00
TMS072 Conqueror of the Black Moon, Gill Lapis UBR 130.00 180.00
TMS073 Demon of the Black Moon, Lilith R .40 1.00
TMS074 Demonic Commander R .40 1.00
TMS075 Fallen Angelic Destroyer, Lucifer SR 1.50 4.00
TMS076 Fallen Hero U .25 .60
TMS077 Izanami, the Sealed Terror SR .60 1.50
TMS078 Izanami's Curse U .25 .60
TMS079 Knight's Shade C .20 .50
TMS080 Nighttime Raiders C .20 .50
TMS081 Pitch Black Moon U .25 .60
TMS082 Silencing Spell C .20 .50
TMS083 Space-Time Collapse R .60 1.50
TMS084 The Executioner C .20 .50
TMS085 Witch of the Night U .25 .60
TMS086 Magic Screw C .20 .50
TMS087 Marybell, Insane Self-Aware Machine R .40 1.00
TMS088 Pricia, Pursuant of Exploding Flame R .50 1.25
TMS089 Seal of Wind and Light R .40 1.00
TMS090 Space-Time Anomaly C .20 .50
TMS091 Blade of the Seven Lands, Excalibur X R .60 1.50
TMS092 Heavenly Instrument, Hydromonica R 1.00 2.50
TMS093 Illusory Demonic Globe, The Earth R .60 1.50
TMS094 Interdimensional Vessel, Apollo R 1.00 2.50
TMS095 Orb of Disaster, Ifrit Glass R .60 1.50
TMS096 Black Moon's Memoria R .40 1.00
TMS097 Disaster's Memoria R 1.00 2.50
TMS098 Hymnal's Memoria R .60 1.50
TMS099 Moonbreeze's Memoria R .40 1.00
TMS100 Yggdrasil's Memoria R .40 1.00
TMS101 Darkness Magic Stone NR .20 .50
TMS102 Fire Magic Stone NR .20 .50
TMS103 Light Magic Stone NR .20 .50
TMS104 Water Magic Stone NR .20 .50
TMS105 Wind Magic Stone NR .20 .50

2016 Force of Will Battle for Attoractia

COMPLETE SET (111) 750.00 1200.00
BOOSTER BOX (36 PACKS) 80.00 110.00
BOOSTER PACK (10 CARDS) 2.50 6.00
*FOIL: .75X TO 2X BASIC CARDS
RELEASED ON JULY 19, 2013
BFA001 Avalon Illusionary Home of Knights U .10 .30
BFA002 Bors Returned Adventurer R .20 .60
BFA003 Circle of Trust U .10 .30
BFA004 Fairy of Sacred Vision U .10 .30
BFA005 Gathering of Fairies C .10 .25
BFA006 Guardian Angel Raphael R .20 .60
BFA007 Interdimensional Escape R .50 1.25
BFA008 Kaguya Rabbit Princess of the Lunar Halo SR .75 2.00
BFA009 Last People of Gloria C .10 .25
BFA010 Life Profiteering Priest C .10 .25

Card	Low	High
BFA011 Rabbit of Moonlit Nights U	.10	.30
BFA012 Rabbit Trap C	.10	.25
BFA013 Reflective Water Shield C	.10	.25
BFA014 Sacred Knight of the North C	.10	.25
BFA015 Sacred Knight of the South C	.10	.25
BFA016 Alisaris Avatar of Destruction SR	.25	.75
BFA017 Battle for Attoractia R	.20	.60
BFA018 Blood Boil C	.10	.25
BFA019 Blood Covered War Axe C	.10	.25
BFA020 Bloodfire Dragon U	.10	.30
BFA021 Enraged Knight C	.10	.25
BFA022 Flame Soldier of Volga C	.10	.25
BFA023 Flame Trap C	.10	.25
BFA024 Lapis Beast of Flame C	.10	.25
BFA025 Napping Lion U	.10	.30
BFA026 Ring of Fate U	.10	.30
BFA027 Sanguine Arena U	.10	.30
BFA028 True Successor of Certo Volga R	.20	.60
BFA029 VellSavarian Apparition C	.10	.25
BFA030 Ywain Knight of Lions R	.20	.60
BFA031 Bulwark Architect C	.10	.25
BFA032 CrocoShark U	2.00	5.00
BFA033 CrocoShark Crossing U	.10	.30
BFA034 Disassembly Line U	.10	.30
BFA035 Down the Drain C	.10	.25
BFA036 Engineer of Leginus C	.10	.25
BFA037 Fairy Flower Extract C	.10	.25
BFA038 Machine Sympathizer R	.20	.60
BFA039 Queens Envoy C	.10	.25
BFA040 Separation of Body and Soul C	.10	.25
BFA041 Set Free R	.20	.60
BFA042 Shion Liberator of ShangriLa SR	.25	.75
BFA043 Spectating Magician C	.10	.25
BFA044 Technician of Leginus U	.10	.30
BFA045 Titania Prideful Queen R	.20	.60
BFA046 Alices Little Decoy C	.10	.25
BFA047 Earthbound Wingman C	.10	.25
BFA048 Escort of the Fairy King C	.10	.25
BFA049 Hare of Inaba SR	.25	.75
BFA050 High Speed Dash R	.20	.60
BFA051 Home of the Wingmen U	.10	.30
BFA052 Midsummers Night King Oberon R	.20	.60
BFA053 Moonbreeze Rabbit U	.10	.30
BFA054 Protection of Alice C	.10	.25
BFA055 Song of the Fairy King U	.10	.30
BFA056 Survivors of Sissei C	.10	.25
BFA057 The Last Drop C	.10	.25
BFA058 TimeGazer Elf U	.10	.30
BFA059 Wing Trap C	.10	.25
BFA060 Yggdor Beast of the World R	.20	.60
BFA061 Black Moonbeam R	.75	2.00
BFA062 Collapsing World U	.10	.30
BFA063 Corrosion C	.10	.25
BFA064 Covert Operative C	.10	.25
BFA065 Death Trap C	.10	.25
BFA066 Eyes In The Darkness C	.10	.25
BFA067 Fairy Shadow U	.10	.30
BFA068 Hades Lord of the Dead SR	.25	.75
BFA069 Lapis Dark Beast C	.10	.25
BFA070 Lapis Dark Storm C	.10	.25
BFA071 Melder Last of the Dead R	.20	.60
BFA072 Messenger Familiar C	.10	.25
BFA073 Remnants of Niflheim C	.10	.25
BFA074 Riza First of the Dead R	.20	.60
BFA075 Rotting Black Moon Dragon U	.10	.30
BFA076 Alice of Light Alice of Shadow SR	.25	.75
BFA077 Lars Inheritor of the Sacred Spirit	.25	.75
Glorian Princess of Water Charlotte SR		
BFA078 Reflect the Beginning of Time	.50	1.25
Refrain the End of Ages SR		
BFA079 Slayer of the Overlord Pricia•Possessor	1.50	4.00
Princess of Love Valentina SR		
BFA079 Slayer of the Overlord Pricia•Possessor	75.00	125.00
BFA080 Interdimensional Monarch Gill Lapis	.50	1.25
Space Time Pursuer Gill Lapis SR		
BFA081 Attoractia Dimension of the Seven Kings	.20	.60
Illusory Demonic Globe Attoractia R		
BFA082 Artificial Moon U	.10	.30
BFA083 Dummy Doll U	.10	.30
BFA084 Machine Lab of Leginus R	.20	.60
BFA085 Mariabellas Work C	.10	.25
BFA086 Remote Control Beast C	.10	.25
BFA087 Remote Control Golem R	.20	.60
BFA088 Small Assistant Mariabella SR	.75	2.00
BFA089 The RoBox C	.10	.25
BFA090 TickTock Automaton C	.10	.25
BFA093 Memoria of the Seven Lands	3.00	8.00
Machina Clever Researcher R		
BFA093 Memoria of the Seven Lands	50.00	75.00
BFA094 Memoria of the Seven Lands	2.00	5.00
Arla Guardian of the Skies R		
BFA094 Memoria of the Seven Lands	40.00	60.00
BFA095 Memoria of the Seven Lands	2.00	5.00
Razzard Dark Necromancer R		
BFA095 Memoria of the Seven Lands	50.00	75.00
BFA096 Call to Actions Memoria R	.50	1.25
BFA097 Brutal Conquerors Memoria R	.50	1.25
BFA098 Aloof Researchers Memoria R	.50	1.25
BFA099 First Flights Memoria R	.75	2.00
BFA100 Sorrowful Necromancys Memoria R	.50	1.25
BFA101 Darkness Magic Stone NR	.10	.25
BFA102 Fire Magic Stone NR	.10	.25
BFA103 Light Magic Stone NR	.10	.25
BFA104 Water Magic Stone NR	.10	.25
BFA105 Wind Magic Stone NR	.10	.25
BFA091• Memoria of the Seven Lands	3.00	8.00
Faria Chosen Girl R		
BFA091• Memoria of the Seven Lands	30.00	50.00
BFA092• Memoria of the Seven Lands	2.50	6.00
Melgis Conqueror of Flame R		
BFA092• Memoria of the Seven Lands	50.00	75.00

2016 Force of Will Curse of the Frozen Casket

Card	Low	High
COMPLETE SET (106)	150.00	200.00
BOOSTER BOX (36 PACKS)	80.00	110.00
BOOSTER PACK (10 CARDS)	3.00	5.00
RELEASED ON SEPTEMBER 9, 2016		
CFC001 Dreaming Girl Wendy R	.60	1.00
CFC002 Dreams of Flight C	.15	.25
CFC003 Escape from Crisis C	.15	.25
CFC004 Eternal Boy Peter Pan SR	1.25	2.00
CFC005 Fairy of Neverland C	.15	.25
CFC006 Glorius the Silver Knight SR	4.00	5.00
CFC007 Glorius Summoned Soldier C	.15	.25
CFC008 Neverland the Parallel World U	.15	.25
CFC009 Pandora the Hope Weaving Queen R	.20	.30
CFC010 Pandoras Mark of Hope U	.15	.25
CFC011 Pumpkin Carriage U	.15	.25
CFC012 Retelling Stories C	.15	.25
CFC013 Safeguard of the Light Palace C	.15	.25
CFC014 Storytelling Bard C	.15	.25
CFC015 Zero Six Sage of Light R	10.00	15.00
CFC015 Zero Master of the Magic Saber R	10.00	15.00
CFC016 Zeros Familiar U	.30	.50
CFC017 Zeros Magic Light R	1.00	1.50
CFC018 Ancient Heartfelt Fire U	.30	.50
CFC019 Combat Wizard of Altea C	.15	.25
CFC020 Demon of the Crest Namblot SR	1.50	2.00
CFC021 Dragon Knight of Altea C	.15	.25
CFC022 Fairy Tale Library Alexandria U	.15	.25
CFC023 Fiery Chariot Red Boy SR	1.50	2.00
CFC024 Flame Dragon of Altea R	.40	.60
CFC025 Introspective Jutsu C	.15	.25
CFC026 Invitation of Disaster R	.60	1.00
CFC027 Mars Fortuneteller of the Fire Star R	8.00	10.00
CFC027 Mars Dark Commander of Fire R	8.00	10.00
CFC028 Sacred Radiant Soul U	.15	.25
CFC029 Spirit of Fire C	.15	.25
CFC030 Stalking Tiger in the Woods C	.15	.25
CFC031 The Ox King U	.15	.25
CFC032 Tiger Charge C	.15	.25
CFC033 Tiger Lily Tribal Princess R	.30	.50
CFC034 Tiny Reconnaissance Drake C	.15	.25
CFC035 Altea Nation of Dark Magics U	.15	.25
CFC036 Ancient Automation R	.30	.50
CFC037 Captain Hook the Pirate R	1.25	1.75
CFC038 Charlotte Determined Girl R	10.00	13.00
CFC038 Charlotte The Mage of Sacred Spirit R	10.00	13.00
CFC039 Charlottes Protector C	.15	.25
CFC040 Charlottes Water Transformation Magic U	.15	.25
CFC041 Cheshire Cat Guide to the Mysterious World SR	5.00	6.00
CFC042 Guide to the Ancient Ice Wall C	.15	.25
CFC043 Lumia Sealed in the Frozen Casket SR	1.50	2.00
CFC043 Lumia Saint of World Awakening SR	1.50	2.00
CFC044 Melt to Nothing C	.15	.25
CFC045 Mermaid of Neverland C	.15	.25
CFC046 Rabbit of the Aqua Moon U	.30	.50
CFC047 Return to the Moon Wererabbit C	.15	.25
CFC048 Rising from the Depths R	.60	1.00
CFC049 Shackles of Ice U	.15	.25
CFC050 Stargazing Fortune Teller C	.15	.25
CFC051 Summon from Memoria C	.15	.25
CFC052 Bird of Paradise Dancing in the Sky R	.60	1.00
CFC053 Cloning Magic C	.15	.25
CFC054 Crea Musician of Wind R	.30	.50
CFC055 Elf of the Gusty Hills C	.15	.25
CFC056 Favorable Winds C	.15	.25
CFC057 Flying Cloud U	.15	.25
CFC058 Heavenly Gust R	1.00	1.50
CFC059 Magic Born Vegetation C	.15	.25
CFC060 Magic Stone Analysis C	.15	.25
CFC061 Protector of the Forest C	.15	.25
CFC062 Red Riding Hood SR	4.00	6.00
CFC063 Secluded Elven Village Amonsulle U	.25	.40
CFC064 Sha Wujing U	.25	.40
CFC065 Sorceress of Heavenly Wind Melfee SR	5.00	7.00
CFC066 The Monkey King Born from Stone R	8.00	10.00
CFC066 Great Sky Sage Sun Wukong R	8.00	10.00
CFC067 Wiseman of Amonsulle C	.15	.25
CFC068 Zhu Bajie U	.15	.25
CFC069 Alhazreds Zealot C	.15	.25
CFC070 An Encounter With Cthulhu C	.15	.25
CFC071 Azathoth Hunter of Reality SR	.75	1.00
CFC072 Creature from Chaos C	.15	.25
CFC073 Eternal Recurrence R	.60	1.00
CFC074 Mad Oni C	.15	.25
CFC075 Oni Governor U	.15	.25
CFC076 Priest of Darkness Abdul Alhazred R	.30	.50
CFC077 Princess of the Dragon Palace Otohime R	.30	.50
CFC078 Resonance of Madness C	.15	.25
CFC079 Rinka Second Daughter of the Mikage SR	3.75	4.15
CFC080 Servant of the Mikage C	.15	.25
CFC081 The Black Treasure Box U	.25	.40
CFC082 The Gate of the Silver Key U	.15	.25
CFC083 The Nameless Mist C	.15	.25
CFC084 Umr atTawil Master of 1000 Keys R	8.00	10.00
CFC084 YogSothoth the Chaos of 1000 Doors R	8.00	10.00
CFC085 Urashima Taro U	.15	.25
CFC086 Magic Stone of Black Silence R	2.00	3.00
CFC087 Magic Stone of Blasting Waves R	2.00	3.00
CFC088 Magic Stone of Dark Depth R	2.00	3.00
CFC089 Magic Stone of Deep Wood R	2.00	3.00
CFC090 Magic Stone of Gusting Skies R	3.00	4.00
CFC091 Magic Stone of Hearths Core R	2.00	3.00
CFC092 Magic Stone of Heat Ray R	2.00	3.00
CFC093 Magic Stone of Heavens Rift R	1.00	1.50
CFC094 Magic Stone of Light Vapors R	1.50	2.00
CFC095 Magic Stone of Scorched Bales R	2.00	3.00
CFC096 Darkness Magic Stone C	1.00	2.00
CFC097 Fire Magic Stone C	1.00	2.00
CFC098 Light Magic Stone C	1.00	2.00
CFC099 Water Magic Stone C	1.00	2.00
CFC100 Wind Magic Stone C	1.00	2.00

2016 Force of Will Curse of the Frozen Casket Foil

Card	Low	High
COMPLETE SET (106)	160.00	225.00
BOOSTER BOX (36 PACKS)	80.00	110.00
BOOSTER PACK (10 CARDS)	3.00	5.00
RELEASED ON SEPTEMBER 9, 2016		
CFC001 Dreaming Girl Wendy R	.60	1.00
CFC002 Dreams of Flight C	.30	.50
CFC003 Escape from Crisis C	.30	.50
CFC004 Eternal Boy Peter Pan SR	.60	1.00
CFC005 Fairy of Neverland C	.30	.50
CFC006 Glorius the Silver Knight SR	.60	1.00
CFC007 Glorius Summoned Soldier C	.30	.50
CFC008 Neverland the Parallel World U	.40	.75
CFC009 Pandora the Hope Weaving Queen R	.60	1.00
CFC010 Pandoras Mark of Hope U	.40	.75
CFC011 Pumpkin Carriage U	.40	.75
CFC012 Retelling Stories C	.30	.50
CFC013 Safeguard of the Light Palace C	.30	.50
CFC014 Storytelling Bard C	.30	.50
CFC015 Zero Six Sage of Light R	15.00	20.00
CFC015 Zero Master of the Magic Saber R	15.00	20.00
CFC016 Zeros Familiar U	4.50	6.00
CFC017 Zeros Magic Light R	2.00	3.00
CFC018 Ancient Heartfelt Fire U	.40	.75
CFC019 Combat Wizard of Altea C	.30	.50
CFC020 Demon of the Crest Namblot SR	.60	1.00
CFC021 Dragon Knight of Altea C	.30	.50
CFC022 Fairy Tale Library Alexandria U	.40	.75
CFC023 Fiery Chariot Red Boy SR	.60	1.00
CFC024 Flame Dragon of Altea R	.60	1.00
CFC025 Introspective Jutsu C	.30	.50
CFC026 Invitation of Disaster R	.60	1.00
CFC027 Mars Fortuneteller of the Fire Star R	8.00	10.00
CFC027 Mars Dark Commander of Fire R	8.00	10.00
CFC028 Sacred Radiant Soul U	.40	.75
CFC029 Spirit of Fire C	.30	.50
CFC030 Stalking Tiger in the Woods C	.30	.50
CFC031 The Ox King U	.40	.75
CFC032 Tiger Charge C	.30	.50
CFC033 Tiger Lily Tribal Princess R	.60	1.00
CFC034 Tiny Reconnaissance Drake C	.30	.50
CFC035 Altea Nation of Dark Magics U	.40	.75
CFC036 Ancient Automation R	.60	1.00
CFC037 Captain Hook the Pirate R	1.50	2.00
CFC038 Charlotte Determined Girl R	8.00	10.00
CFC038 Charlotte The Mage of Sacred Spirit R	8.00	10.00
CFC039 Charlottes Protector C	.30	.50
CFC040 Charlottes Water Transformation Magic U	2.75	3.25
CFC041 Cheshire Cat Guide to the Mysterious World SR	.60	1.00
CFC042 Guide to the Ancient Ice Wall C	.30	.50
CFC043 Lumia Sealed in the Frozen Casket SR	.60	1.00
CFC043 Lumia Saint of World Awakening SR	.60	1.00
CFC044 Melt to Nothing C	.30	.50
CFC045 Mermaid of Neverland C	.30	.50
CFC046 Rabbit of the Aqua Moon U	1.25	2.00
CFC047 Return to the Moon Wererabbit C	.30	.50
CFC048 Rising from the Depths R	.60	1.00
CFC049 Shackles of Ice U	.40	.75
CFC050 Stargazing Fortune Teller C	.30	.50
CFC051 Summon from Memoria C	.30	.50
CFC052 Bird of Paradise Dancing in the Sky R	.60	1.00
CFC053 Cloning Magic C	.30	.50
CFC054 Crea Musician of Wind R	.60	1.00
CFC055 Elf of the Gusty Hills C	.30	.50
CFC056 Favorable Winds C	.30	.50
CFC057 Flying Cloud U	.40	.75
CFC058 Heavenly Gust R	1.00	1.50
CFC059 Magic Born Vegetation C	.30	.50
CFC060 Magic Stone Analysis C	.30	.50
CFC061 Protector of the Forest C	.30	.50
CFC062 Red Riding Hood SR	.60	1.00
CFC063 Secluded Elven Village Amonsulle U	.40	.75
CFC064 Sha Wujing U	.40	.75
CFC065 Sorceress of Heavenly Wind Melfee SR	.60	1.00
CFC066 The Monkey King Born from Stone R	8.00	10.00
CFC066 Great Sky Sage Sun Wukong R	8.00	10.00
CFC067 Wiseman of Amonsulle C	.30	.50
CFC068 Zhu Bajie U	.40	.75
CFC069 Alhazreds Zealot C	.30	.50
CFC070 An Encounter With Cthulhu C	.30	.50
CFC071 Azathoth Hunter of Reality SR	.60	1.00
CFC072 Creature from Chaos C	.30	.50
CFC073 Eternal Recurrence R	.60	1.00
CFC074 Mad Oni C	.30	.50
CFC075 Oni Governor U	.40	.75
CFC076 Priest of Darkness Abdul Alhazred R	.60	1.00
CFC077 Princess of the Dragon Palace Otohime R	.60	1.00
CFC078 Resonance of Madness C	.30	.50
CFC079 Rinka Second Daughter of the Mikage SR	.60	1.00
CFC080 Servant of the Mikage C	.30	.50
CFC081 The Black Treasure Box U	.40	.75
CFC082 The Gate of the Silver Key U	.40	.75
CFC083 The Nameless Mist C	.30	.50
CFC084 Umr atTawil Master of 1000 Keys R	8.00	10.00
CFC084 YogSothoth the Chaos of 1000 Doors R	8.00	10.00
CFC085 Urashima Taro U	.40	.75
CFC086 Magic Stone of Black Silence R	2.00	3.00
CFC087 Magic Stone of Blasting Waves R	2.00	3.00
CFC088 Magic Stone of Dark Depth R	2.00	2.50
CFC089 Magic Stone of Deep Wood R	2.00	3.00
CFC090 Magic Stone of Gusting Skies R	3.50	4.00
CFC091 Magic Stone of Hearths Core R	2.00	3.00
CFC092 Magic Stone of Heat Ray R	2.00	3.00
CFC093 Magic Stone of Heavens Rift R	1.00	2.00
CFC094 Magic Stone of Light Vapors R	2.00	2.50
CFC095 Magic Stone of Scorched Bales R	2.00	3.00
CFC096 Darkness Magic Stone C	.30	.50
CFC097 Fire Magic Stone C	.30	.50
CFC098 Light Magic Stone C	.30	.50
CFC099 Water Magic Stone C	.30	.50
CFC100 Wind Magic Stone C	.30	.50

2016 Force of Will Curse of the Frozen Casket Textured Foil

Card	Low	High
COMPLETE SET (46)	200.00	300.00
RELEASED ON SEPTEMBER 9, 2016		
CFC001 Dreaming Girl Wendy R	2.00	2.50
CFC004 Eternal Boy Peter Pan SR	3.00	5.00
CFC006 Glorius the Silver Knight SR	8.00	10.00
CFC009 Pandora the Hope Weaving Queen R	1.00	2.00
CFC015 Zero Six Sage of Light R	20.00	25.00
CFC015 Zero Master of the Magic Saber R	20.00	25.00
CFC017 Zeros Magic Light R	5.00	8.00
CFC020 Demon of the Crest Namblot SR	2.00	3.00
CFC023 Fiery Chariot Red Boy SR	2.00	3.00
CFC024 Flame Dragon of Altea R	6.00	8.00
CFC026 Invitation of Disaster R	1.00	2.00
CFC027 Mars Fortuneteller of the Fire Star R	10.00	12.00
CFC027 Mars Dark Commander of Fire R	10.00	12.00
CFC033 Tiger Lily Tribal Princess R	1.00	2.00
CFC036 Ancient Automation R	1.00	2.00
CFC037 Captain Hook the Pirate R	8.00	10.00
CFC038 Charlotte Determined Girl R	10.00	13.00
CFC038 Charlotte The Mage of Sacred Spirit R	10.00	13.00
CFC041 Cheshire Cat Guide to the Mysterious World SR	10.00	12.00
CFC043 Lumia Sealed in the Frozen Casket SR	3.00	5.00
CFC043 Lumia Saint of World Awakening SR	3.00	5.00
CFC048 Rising from the Depths R	1.00	2.00

CFC052 Bird of Paradise Dancing in the Sky R 1.00 2.00
CFC054 Crea Musician of Wind R 1.00 2.00
CFC058 Heavenly Gust R 3.00 4.00
CFC062 Red Riding Hood SR 8.00 10.00
CFC065 Sorceress of Heavenly Wind Melfee SR 8.00 10.00
CFC066 The Monkey King Born from Stone R 10.00 13.00
CFC066 Great Sky Sage Sun Wukong R 10.00 13.00
CFC071 Azathoth Hunter of Reality SR 1.75 2.25
CFC073 Eternal Recurrence R 1.00 2.00
CFC076 Priest of Darkness Abdul Alhazred R 1.00 2.00
CFC077 Princess of the Dragon Palace Otohime R 1.00 2.00
CFC079 Rinka Second Daughter of the Mikage SR 10.00 13.00
CFC084 Umr atTawil Master of 1000 Keys R 9.00 12.00
CFC084 YogSothoth the Chaos of 1000 Doors R 9.00 12.00
CFC086 Magic Stone of Black Silence R 3.00 5.00
CFC087 Magic Stone of Blasting Waves R 3.00 5.00
CFC088 Magic Stone of Dark Depth R 3.00 5.00
CFC089 Magic Stone of Deep Wood R 3.00 5.00
CFC090 Magic Stone of Gusting Skies R 3.00 5.00
CFC091 Magic Stone of Hearths Core R 3.00 5.00
CFC092 Magic Stone of Heat Ray R 3.00 5.00
CFC093 Magic Stone of Heavens Rift R 3.00 5.00
CFC094 Magic Stone of Light Vapors R 3.00 5.00
CFC095 Magic Stone of Scorched Bales R 3.00 5.00

2016 Force of Will Curse of the Frozen Casket Uber Rare

COMPLETE SET (10) 400.00 600.00
RELEASED ON SEPTEMBER 9, 2016
CFC015 Zero Six Sage of Light 150.00 250.00
CFC027 Mars Fortuneteller of the Fire Star 50.00 75.00
CFC038 Charlotte Determined Girl 50.00 75.00
CFC066 The Monkey King Born from Stone 40.00 75.00
CFC084 Umr atTawil Master of 1000 Keys 75.00 125.00
SDL1009 Millium Prince of the Light Palace 50.00 75.00
SDL2007 Lunya the Wolf Girl 50.00 75.00
SDL3007 Mercurius Wizard of the Water Star 50.00 75.00
SDL4002 Fiethsing Six Sage of Wind 100.00 150.00
Fiethsing Master Magus of Holy Wind UBR
SDL5001 Ally of the Black Moon 50.00 75.00

2015 Force of Will Vingolf Engage Knights

COMPLETE SET (143)
COMPLETE SERIES BOX (218)
RELEASED ON JULY 30, 2015
VIN001001 Abe no Seimei NR .10 .15
VIN001001 Abe no Seimei SR 2.00 3.00
VIN001002 Achilles NR .10 .15
VIN001002 Achilles SR 1.00 1.50
VIN001003 Breath of the God NR .10 .15
VIN001004 Duel of Light NR .10 .15
VIN001005 Emperor Guangwu of Han NR .10 .15
VIN001005 Emperor Guangwu of Han SR .75 1.25
VIN001006 Hammurabi NR .10 .15
VIN001006 Hammurabi SR .75 1.25
VIN001007 Hannibal Barca R .15 .25
VIN001008 Jeanne d'Arc NR .10 .15
VIN001008 Jeanne d'Arc SR 4.00 6.00
VIN001009 Louis XIV NR .10 .15
VIN001009 Louis XIV SR .60 1.00
VIN001010 March of Saints NR .10 .15
VIN001011 Pride of Knights NR .30 .50
VIN001012 Siegfried NR .10 .15
VIN001012 Siegfried SR 4.00 6.00
VIN001013 Silver Stake NR .10 .15
VIN001014 Tutankhamun NR .10 .15
VIN001014 Tutankhamun SR 1.00 1.50
VIN001015 Xuanzang Sanzang NR .25 .40
VIN001015 Xuanzang Sanzang SR .40 .60
VIN001016 Alexander R .15 .25
VIN001017 Banzai Attack NR .10 .15
VIN001018 Calamity Jane NR .10 .15
VIN001018 Calamity Jane SR .75 1.25
VIN001019 Crime and Punishment NR .10 .15
VIN001020 King Ashoka NR .10 .15
VIN001020 King Ashoka SR .40 .60
VIN001021 Kleitos NR .10 .15
VIN001021 Kleitos SR .40 .60
VIN001022 Kusanagi Sword NR .10 .15
VIN001023 Lu Bu NR .10 .15
VIN001023 Lu Bu SR 1.00 1.50
VIN001024 Musashi Miyamoto NR .10 .15
VIN001024 Musashi Miyamoto SR 2.00 3.00
VIN001025 Pachacuti NR .10 .15
VIN001025 Pachacuti SR .40 .60
VIN001026 Rapid Decay NR .10 .15
VIN001027 Saladin NR .10 .15
VIN001027 Saladin SR 1.00 1.50
VIN001028 Sun Tzu NR .10 .15
VIN001028 Sun Tzu SR .40 .60
VIN001029 Thunder NR .60 1.00
VIN001030 William Wallace NR .10 .15
VIN001030 William Wallace SR .60 1.00
VIN001031 Aqua Magic –Tempest– NR .10 .15
VIN001032 Captain Cook NR .10 .15
VIN001032 Captain Cook SR .75 1.25
VIN001033 Colombus NR .10 .15
VIN001033 Colombus SR 3.00 5.00
VIN001034 Hanzo Hattori NR .10 .15
VIN001034 Hanzo Hattori SR 5.00 8.00
VIN001035 Julius Caesar R .15 .25
VIN001036 Marco Polo NR .10 .15
VIN001036 Marco Polo SR .60 1.00
VIN001037 Napoleon NR .10 .15
VIN001037 Napoleon SR .40 .60
VIN001038 Paracelsus NR .10 .15
VIN001038 Paracelsus SR 1.00 1.50
VIN001039 Dreams of Wonderland NR .10 .15
VIN001040 Glimpse of Kaguya NR .10 .15
VIN001041 Soji Okita NR .10 .15
VIN001041 Soji Okita SR .75 1.25
VIN001042 Tai Gong Wang NR .10 .15
VIN001042 Tai Gong Wang SR .40 .60
VIN001043 Vainamoinen NR .10 .15
VIN001043 Vainamoinen SR .75 1.25
VIN001044 Whirlpool of Knowledge NR .10 .15
VIN001045 Witch's Dagger NR .10 .15
VIN001046 Archimedes NR .10 .15
VIN001046 Archimedes SR .60 1.00
VIN001047 Art of Sinbad NR .10 .15
VIN001048 Attila NR .10 .15
VIN001048 Attila SR 1.00 1.50
VIN001049 D'Artagnan NR .10 .15
VIN001049 D'Artagnan SR .75 1.25
VIN001050 Darwin NR .10 .15
VIN001050 Darwin SR .50 .75
VIN001051 Evolution of Limits NR .10 .15
VIN001052 Genghis Khan NR .10 .15
VIN001052 Genghis Khan SR 2.00 3.00
VIN001053 Geronimo NR .10 .15
VIN001053 Geronimo SR .60 1.00
VIN001054 Law of Silence NR .25 .40
VIN001055 Minamoto no Yoshitsune R .15 .25
VIN001056 Pyotr I NR .10 .15
VIN001056 Pyotr I SR .40 .60
VIN001057 Silver Shoes NR .10 .15
VIN001058 Timur NR .10 .15
VIN001058 Timur SR .40 .60
VIN001059 William Tell NR .10 .15
VIN001059 William Tell SR .50 .75
VIN001060 Wind of Gods NR .10 .15
VIN001061 Binding Chain NR .10 .15
VIN001062 Dante NR .10 .15
VIN001062 Dante SR 1.00 1.50
VIN001063 Demon's Curse NR .10 .15
VIN001064 Edward, the Black Prince NR .10 .15
VIN001064 Edward, the Black Prince SR 1.00 1.50
VIN001065 Faust NR .10 .15
VIN001065 Faust SR .50 .75
VIN001066 Michizane Sugawara NR .10 .15
VIN001066 Michizane Sugawara SR .40 .60
VIN001067 Mozart NR .50 .75
VIN001067 Mozart SR 2.50 4.00
VIN001068 Nobunaga Oda NR .20 .30
VIN001068 Nobunaga Oda SR .75 1.25
VIN001069 Nostradamus NR .20 .30
VIN001069 Nostradamus SR .75 1.25
VIN001070 Rasputin NR .40 .60
VIN001070 Rasputin SR 4.00 6.00
VIN001071 Ritual of Millennia NR .10 .15
VIN001072 Solomon NR .10 .15
VIN001072 Solomon SR 1.50 2.50
VIN001073 Stoning to Death NR .50 .75
VIN001074 Tunnel Vision NR .10 .15
VIN001075 Vlad Tepes R .15 .25
VIN001076 Leonardo da Vinci NR .10 .15
VIN001076 Leonardo da Vinci SR .60 1.00
VIN001077 Ryoma Sakamoto NR .40 .60
VIN001077 Ryoma Sakamoto SR 3.00 5.00
VIN001078 Shakespeare NR .10 .15
VIN001078 Shakespeare SR 1.50 2.50
VIN001079 Socrates NR .10 .15
VIN001079 Socrates SR .75 1.25
VIN001080 Magic Stone of Black Silence NR .50 .75
VIN001081 Magic Stone of Blasting Waves NR .75 1.25
VIN001082 Magic Stone of Dark Depth NR .25 .40
VIN001083 Magic Stone of Deep Wood NR .60 1.00
VIN001084 Magic Stone of Gusting Skies NR .75 1.25
VIN001085 Magic Stone of Hearth's Core NR .40 .60
VIN001086 Magic Stone of Heat Ray NR .40 .60
VIN001087 Magic Stone of Heaven's Rift NR 1.00 1.50
VIN001088 Magic Stone of Light Vapors NR .40 .60
VIN001089 Magic Stone of Scorched Bales NR 1.25 2.00
VIN001090 Darkness Magic Stone NR .10 .15
VIN001091 Fire Magic Stone NR .10 .15
VIN001092 Light Magic Stone NR .10 .15
VIN001093 Water Magic Stone NR .10 .15
VIN001094 Wind Magic Stone NR .10 .15

2016 Force of Will Vingolf 2 Valkryia Chronicles

COMPLETE SET (95) 40.00 60.00
RELEASED ON JULY 29, 2016
VIN002001 Alica Melchiott•R 1.25 3.00
VIN002001 Alica Gunther J R 1.25 3.00
VIN002002 Clementia Forster NR .10 .30
VIN002003 Edy Nelson NR .10 .30
VIN002004 Elshan Flower NR .10 .30
VIN002005 FirstAid NR .10 .30
VIN002006 Flak Jacket NR .10 .30
VIN002007 Homer Peron NR .10 .30
VIN002008 Irene Ellet NR .10 .30
VIN002009 Jann Walker NR .10 .30
VIN002010 Lynn NR .10 .30
VIN002011 Marina Wulfstan NR .10 .30
VIN002012 Martha Lipponen NR .10 .30
VIN002013 Susie Evans NR .10 .30
VIN002014 Symbol of Peace NR .10 .30
VIN002015 Welvar Glenn NR .10 .30
VIN002016 Alfons Avclair NR .10 .30
VIN002017 Amy Apple NR .10 .30
VIN002018 Bombardment NR .10 .30
VIN002019 Carisa Contzen NR .10 .30
VIN002020 Clarissa Callaghan NR .10 .30
VIN002021 Courageous Stand NR .10 .30
VIN002022 Frederica Lipps NR .10 .30
VIN002023 Gusurg NR .10 .30
VIN002024 Imca NR .10 .30
VIN002025 Kurt Irving NR .10 .30
VIN002026 Large Explosion NR .10 .30
VIN002027 Leila Peron NR .10 .30
VIN002028 Margit Ravelli NR .10 .30
VIN002029 Riela Marcellis• R .75 2.00
VIN002029 Riela Marcellis J R .75 2.00
VIN002030 Rielas Lance NR .10 .30
VIN002031 Alicia Melchiott•R 1.25 3.00
VIN002031 Alicia Melchiott J R 1.25 3.00
VIN002032 Alicias Lance NR .10 .30
VIN002033 Brigette Rosie Stark NR .10 .30
VIN002034 Cordelia Gi Randgriz NR .10 .30
VIN002035 Eleanor Varrot NR .10 .30
VIN002036 Faldio Landzaat NR .10 .30
VIN002037 Isara Gunther NR .10 .30
VIN002038 Kreis Czherny NR .10 .30
VIN002039 Largo Potter NR .10 .30
VIN002040 Maurits Con Borg NR .10 .30
VIN002041 Momentary Respite NR .10 .30
VIN002042 Sniping From The Blind Spot NR .10 .30
VIN002043 The Carefree Three NR .10 .30
VIN002044 Welkin Gunther NR .10 .30
VIN002045 Zaka NR .10 .30
VIN002046 Alexis Hilden NR .10 .30
VIN002047 Aliasse•R 1.50 4.00
VIN002047 Aliasse J R 1.50 4.00
VIN002048 Aliasses Lance NR .10 .30
VIN002049 Anisette Nelson NR .10 .30
VIN002050 Avan Hardins NR .10 .30
VIN002051 Cosette Coalhearth NR .10 .30
VIN002052 Bulletproof Barrier NR .10 .30
VIN002053 Destructive Assult NR .10 .30
VIN002054 Juliana Everhart NR .10 .30
VIN002055 Lavinia Lane NR .10 .30
VIN002056 Margari NR .10 .30
VIN002057 Marion Siegbahn NR .10 .30
VIN002058 Power of Unity NR .10 .30
VIN002059 Rene Randall NR .10 .30
VIN002060 Zeri NR .10 .30
VIN002061 Audrey Gassenarl NR .10 .30
VIN002062 Baldren Gassenarl NR .10 .30
VIN002063 Berthold Gregor NR .10 .30
VIN002064 Dahav NR .10 .30
VIN002065 Dirk Gassenarl NR .10 .30
VIN002066 Gilbert Gassenarl NR .10 .30
VIN002067 Hammer of the Valkyrur NR .10 .30
VIN002068 Lydia Agthe NR .10 .30
VIN002069 Maximilian NR .10 .30
VIN002070 Radi Iaeger NR .10 .30
VIN002071 Ragnide Gas NR .10 .30
VIN002072 Schemes of the Empire NR .10 .30
VIN002073 Selvaria Bles• R 1.25 3.00
VIN002073 Selvaria Bles J R 1.25 3.00
VIN002074 Selvarias Lance NR .10 .30
VIN002075 Zig NR .10 .30
VIN002076 Class Gs Tank NR 2.00 5.00
VIN002077 Edelweiss NR 1.50 4.00
VIN002078 Imperial Tank NR 1.25 3.00
VIN002079 Nameless Tank NR 1.50 4.00
VIN002080 Ragnite NR 1.50 4.00
VIN0020xx Magic Stone of Black Silence NR .75 2.00
VIN0020xx Magic Stone of Blasting Waves NR .75 2.00
VIN0020xx Magic Stone of Dark Depth NR .75 2.00
VIN0020xx Magic Stone of Deep Wood NR .75 2.00
VIN0020xx Magic Stone of Gusting Skies NR 1.25 3.00
VIN0020xx Magic Stone of Hearths Core NR .75 2.00
VIN0020xx Magic Stone of Heat Ray NR .75 2.00
VIN0020xx Magic Stone of Heavens Rift NR .75 2.00
VIN0020xx Magic Stone of Light Vapors NR .75 2.00
VIN0020xx Magic Stone of Scorched Bales NR .75 2.00
VIN0020xx Darkness Magic Stone NR .10 .30
VIN0020xx Fire Magic Stone NR .10 .30
VIN0020xx Light Magic Stone NR .10 .30
VIN0020xx Water Magic Stone NR .10 .30
VIN0020xx Wind Magic Stone NR .10 .30

2017 Force of Will Vingolf 3 Ruler All-Stars

COMPLETE SET (100)
RELEASED ON FEBRUARY 10, 2017
VIN003001 Arla, the Light Wing 1.25 2.00
VIN003002 Arthur, Paladin King of the Round Table .15 .25
VIN003003 Dragon Knight Commander, Siegfried .60 1.00
VIN003004 Faria, Paladin of the Dawn 1.00 1.50
VIN003005 Gloria's Castle Town .15 .25
VIN003006 Grimm, the Legendary King of Fairy Tales .60 1.00
VIN003007 Guardian of Light Magic Stones .60 1.00
Avatar of Light Magic Stones
VIN003008 Knight Lord of Godspeed .15 .25
VIN003009 Light Wizard .30 .50
VIN003010 Lumia, Saint of Creation 1.50 2.50
VIN003011 Manifestation of Power .75 1.25
VIN003012 Protective Barrier .15 .25
VIN003013 Sol, Envoy of Light 1.25 2.00
VIN003014 The Final Word .15 .25
VIN003015 Zero's Magic Light .75 1.25
VIN003016 Bahamut, Phantasmal Dragon .15 .25
VIN003017 Barbatos, World's Greatest Eccentric .15 .25
VIN003018 Barust, Machine Deity of Purgatory .15 .25
VIN003019 Blood Boil .15 .25
VIN003020 Burn to Cinders 1.00 1.50
VIN003021 Cain, Teacherous Killer of the Gods .15 .25
VIN003022 Certo, the Blazing Volcano .15 .25
VIN003023 Demonflame 1.00 1.50
VIN003024 Fire Wizard .75 1.25
VIN003025 Guardian of Fire Magic Stones .75 1.25
Avatar of Fire Magic Stones
VIN003026 Introspective Jutsu .25 .40
VIN003027 Melgis, King of Conquest .15 .25
VIN003028 Salamander, Envoy of Fire .15 .25
VIN003029 Shimazu Yoshihiro, Feudal Flame Lord .20 .30
VIN003030 Sylvia Gill Palarilias, Infernal Dragon 1.25 2.00
VIN003031 Alice, Dimensional Traveler .75 1.25
VIN003032 Charlotte's Water Transformation Magic .60 1.00
VIN003033 Charm of the Princess .15 .25
VIN003034 Chronos, the God of Time .15 .25
VIN003035 Dance of Inspiration .15 .25
VIN003036 Guardian of Water Magic Stones .60 1.00
Avatar of Water Magic Stones
VIN003037 Kaguya, Guardian of the Moon .60 1.00
VIN003038 Nymph, Envoy of Water .15 .25
VIN003039 Separation of Body and Soul .40 .60
VIN003040 Shackles of Ice .15 .25
VIN003041 Shion, the Entrancing Songstress .15 .25
VIN003042 Tomoe Gozen, Merciful Aqua Twin Swords .30 .50
VIN003043 Triton, Emperor of the Seven Seas .15 .25
VIN003044 Valentina, Maiden of the Ocean .15 .25
VIN003045 Water Wizard 2.00 3.00
VIN003046 Count D'Artagnan .15 .25
VIN003047 Frigg, Goddess of Abundant Harvest 1.00 1.50
VIN003048 Guardian of Wind Magic Stones .15 .25
Avatar of Wind Magic Stones
VIN003049 Heavenly Gust .15 .25
VIN003050 Helsing, Hunter of the Undead .15 .25
VIN003051 Little Red, Fairy Tale of Air 3.00 5.00
VIN003052 Oberon, Lord of Elves .60 1.00
VIN003053 Pricia, Wild Child .75 1.25
VIN003054 Pricia's Call to Action .40 .60
VIN003055 Rapid Growth 1.00 1.50
VIN003056 Scheherazade, the Prophet .15 .25
VIN003057 Silph, Envoy of Wind .15 .25
VIN003058 The Beast Queen's Counterattack .15 .25
VIN003059 The World Tree's Guardian .15 .25
VIN003060 Wind-Secluded Refuge 1.00 1.50
VIN003061 Abdul Alhazred, Poet of Madness 2.50 4.00
VIN003062 Baleful Avatar .15 .25
VIN003063 Dark Purge .50 .75
VIN003064 Darkness Wizard .30 .50

Card	Low	High
VIN003065 Dracula, King of the Undead	.15	.25
VIN003066 Endless Night	.60	1.00
VIN003067 Gill Lapis, the Pure Youth	.75	1.25
VIN003068 Guardian of Darkness Magic Stones	.75	1.25
Avatar of Darkness Magic Stones		
VIN003069 Loki, Being of the End	.15	.25
VIN003070 Rezzard, the Vampire Lord	.30	.50
VIN003071 Sariel, Lord of the Moons	.15	.25
VIN003072 Shade, Envoy of Darkness	1.00	1.50
VIN003073 The Gate of the Silver Key	.15	.25
VIN003074 The Scorn of Dark Alice	2.00	3.00
VIN003075 Unseen Pressure	.40	.60
VIN003076 Alisaris, Scholar of Phenomena	.15	.25
VIN003077 Blazer Gill Rabus, the Pursuer	.15	.25
VIN003078 Jeanne d'Arc, the Maid of Orleans	.30	.50
VIN003079 Karmic Governor, Laplace	.25	.40
VIN003080 Machina, the Clockwork King	.15	.25
VIN003081 Odin the Omniscient	.30	.50
VIN003082 Pandora, the Goddess of Light and Dark	2.00	3.00
VIN003083 Snow White, the Avenger	.25	.40
VIN003084 Valthruthnir, Giant Wiseman	.15	.25
VIN003085 Yggdrasil, the First Tree	.15	.25
VIN003086 Burning Water Magic Stone	.75	1.25
VIN003087 Gusting Darkness Magic Stone	1.00	1.50
VIN003088 Magic Stone of Murky Waters	.60	1.00
VIN003089 Magic Stone of Nature's Beauty	1.00	1.50
VIN003090 Magic Stone of Purgatory	.60	1.00
VIN003091 Magic Stone of Radiant Waves	1.00	1.50
VIN003092 Magic Stone of Summer's Breeze	1.25	2.00
VIN003093 Mysty Wind Magic Stone	.60	1.00
VIN003094 Shadowy Light Magic Stone	2.00	3.00
VIN003095 Sparkling Fire Magic Stone	1.00	1.50
VIN003096 Darkness Magic Stone	1.00	1.50
VIN003097 Fire Magic Stone	1.00	1.50
VIN003098 Light Magic Stone	.75	1.25
VIN003099 Water Magic Stone	.60	1.00
VIN003100 Wind Magic Stone	.75	1.25

2016 Force of Will Legacy Lost

Card	Low	High
COMPLETE SET (105)	120.00	160.00
BOOSTER BOX (36 PACKS)	85.00	100.00
BOOSTER PACK (10 CARDS)	3.00	5.00
RELEASED ON DECEMBER 9, 2016		
LEL001 Amaterasu Guide of Light SR	1.50	2.00
LEL002 Amaterasus Foresight U	.20	.35
LEL003 Beast of Holy Light C	.15	.25
LEL004 Lumias Purification R	1.25	2.00
LEL005 Milliums Weapon C	.15	.25
LEL006 Snow White of the Crystal Apple R	2.50	3.00
LEL007 Spirit of Light C	.15	.25
LEL008 The Seven Dwarves U	.20	.35
LEL009 Ancient Manager C	.15	.25
LEL010 Bastet Goddess of Cats SR	2.25	2.75
LEL011 Bastets Fascination C	.15	.25
LEL012 Conjure Time Bomb U	.20	.35
LEL013 Invisible Flame C	.15	.25
LEL014 Skyscraper Giant U	.30	.50
LEL015 TimeGuide Admiral Alfred R	1.25	2.00
LEL016 World Flame Summoning R	1.25	2.00
LEL017 Alhamaat Mage Knight U	.20	.35
LEL018 Charlotte Wielder of the Sacred Spirit SR	1.50	2.00
LEL019 Fishing C	.15	.25
LEL020 Jiang Ziya the Fisherman U	.20	.35
LEL021 Moojdarts Illusionary Soldier C	.15	.25
LEL022 Rachel Alhamaats Advisor R	1.25	2.00
LEL023 Rachels Smile U	.20	.35
LEL024 Reunion of Sisters R	1.25	2.00
LEL025 Fiethsing The Fate Spinning Winds SR	2.75	3.25
LEL026 Final Breeze R	1.25	2.00
LEL027 Gale Force U	.75	1.00
LEL028 Jack Climbing the Beanstalk U	.20	.35
LEL029 Luan Auspicious Beast U	.20	.35
LEL030 Magic Stone Life Form R	2.00	2.50
LEL031 Planting Beans C	.15	.25
LEL032 Sacred Beast of Wind C	.15	.25
LEL033 Alhamaats Black Lightning U	.20	.35
LEL034 Death at Midnight C	.15	.25
LEL035 Dimension Dragon Nidhogg SR	1.25	1.75
LEL036 Fated Reunion R	1.25	2.00
LEL037 Kumomaru U	.20	.35
LEL038 Shadow of Lapis U	.20	.35
LEL039 Yashahime First Daughter of the Mikage R	1.25	2.00
LEL040 Yashamaru C	.15	.25
LEL041 A Rendezvous of Light and Wind U	.20	.35
LEL042 Alteas Elite C	.15	.25
LEL043 Ammit Beast of Gluttony U	.75	1.00
LEL044 Ancient Barrier U	.20	.35
LEL045 Barrier Seal U	.20	.35
LEL046 Blessed Knight C	.15	.25
LEL047 Catalyst Spirit C	.15	.25
LEL048 Crimson Ray C	.15	.25
LEL049 Curse of the Kyuubi R	2.00	2.50
LEL050 Deceptive Dream C	.15	.25
LEL051 Demonic Instigator C	.15	.25
LEL052 Divine Beast of Attoractia R	1.25	2.00
LEL053 Dragon of Scenic Beauty U	.20	.35
LEL054 Fairy of Recurrence C	.15	.25
LEL055 Farias Summon C	.15	.25
LEL056 Fiethsings Monocle U	.20	.35
LEL057 Ghost of Attoractia U	.20	.35
LEL058 Glorius Masked Crusader Faria	7.00	9.00
Ruler of Divine Beasts R		
LEL059 Griphon Racing Across Darkness C	.15	.25
LEL060 Grusbalesta Magic Stone Researcher SR	1.50	2.00
LEL061 Grusbalestas Secret Technique C	.15	.25
LEL062 Healing Wing Dragon U	.20	.35
LEL063 Illusion Wizard C	.15	.25
LEL064 Illusory Projection C	.15	.25
LEL065 Invading Demon of Water Valentina	5.00	7.00
Valentina Released Terror R		
LEL066 Jeanne dArc the Pious Flame R	1.25	2.00
LEL067 Kaguya Lunar Researcher SR	1.75	2.25
LEL068 Kaguyas Moonbeam Butterfly R	1.25	2.00
LEL069 Lilias Petal Agent of Salvation	10.00	12.00
The Nine Tailed Fox R		
LEL070 Lilias Petals Assistant C	.15	.25
LEL071 Lumia the Fated Rebirth Lumia	10.00	12.00
Saint of the Crimson Lotus R		
LEL072 Lumias Judgment R	3.50	4.00
LEL073 Magic Rebound C	.15	.25
LEL074 Meeting of Light and Fire U	.20	.35
LEL075 Messenger of Lilias Petal C	.15	.25
LEL076 Moojdart Lady of Illusions SR	2.50	3.00
LEL077 Muul the Town Thar Never Was C	.15	.25
LEL078 Nightmare the Ashen Dream R	1.25	2.00
LEL079 Nyarlathotep the Crimson Radiance SR	3.50	4.00
LEL080 Plot of Water and Darkness U	.20	.35
LEL081 Priest of Divine Protection C	.15	.25
LEL082 Prokaryotic Being U	.20	.35
LEL083 Rune of Sol C	.15	.25
LEL084 Runic Commander Demon Akiot SR	3.00	3.50
LEL085 Sacred Komainu C	.15	.25
LEL086 Shining Kirin C	.15	.25
LEL087 Sol Hierophant of the Helio Star Sol	8.00	10.00
Dark Commander of Steam R		
LEL088 Steam Explosion R	1.25	2.00
LEL089 Sympathy of Fire and Water U	.20	.35
LEL090 The Manticore R	1.25	2.00
LEL091 Tuning of Wind and Darkness U	.20	.35
LEL092 TwinHeaded Dragon R	1.25	2.00
LEL093 Valentinas Reach R	2.00	2.50
LEL094 Wetlands of Magical Origin U	.20	.35
LEL095 White Horn Kaichi C	.15	.25
LEL096 Awakened Magic Stone the Earth R	3.50	4.00
LEL097 Killing Stone R	4.00	4.50
LEL098 Magic Stone of Vaporization R	3.00	3.50
LEL099 Pricias Memoria R	2.00	2.50
LEL100 Remains of Attoractia R	2.50	3.00
LEL101 Darkness Magic Stone C	.15	.25
LEL102 Fire Magic Stone C	.15	.25
LEL103 Light Magic Stone C	.15	.25
LEL104 Water Magic Stone C	.15	.25
LEL105 Wind Magic Stone C	.15	.25

2016 Force of Will Legacy Lost Foil

Card	Low	High
COMPLETE SET (105)	175.00	250.00
BOOSTER BOX (36 PACKS)	85.00	100.00
BOOSTER PACK (10 CARDS)	3.00	5.00
RELEASED ON DECEMBER 9, 2016		
LEL001 Amaterasu Guide of Light SR	3.00	4.50
LEL002 Amaterasus Foresight U	1.25	2.00
LEL003 Beast of Holy Light C	.30	.50
LEL004 Lumias Purification R	2.00	3.50
LEL005 Milliums Weapon C	.30	.50
LEL006 Snow White of the Crystal Apple R	2.00	3.50
LEL007 Spirit of Light C	.30	.50
LEL008 The Seven Dwarves U	1.25	2.00
LEL009 Ancient Manager C	.30	.50
LEL010 Bastet Goddess of Cats SR	3.00	4.50
LEL011 Bastets Fascination C	.30	.50
LEL012 Conjure Time Bomb U	1.25	2.00
LEL013 Invisible Flame C	.30	.50
LEL014 Skyscraper Giant U	1.25	2.00
LEL015 TimeGuide Admiral Alfred R	2.00	3.50
LEL016 World Flame Summoning R	2.00	3.50
LEL017 Alhamaat Mage Knight U	1.25	2.00
LEL018 Charlotte Wielder of the Sacred Spirit SR	1.75	2.25
LEL019 Fishing C	.30	.50
LEL020 Jiang Ziya the Fisherman U	1.25	2.00
LEL021 Moojdarts Illusionary Soldier C	.30	.50
LEL022 Rachel Alhamaats Advisor R	2.00	3.50
LEL023 Rachels Smile U	1.25	2.00
LEL024 Reunion of Sisters R	2.00	3.50
LEL025 Fiethsing The Fate Spinning Winds SR	3.00	4.50
LEL026 Final Breeze R	2.00	3.50
LEL027 Gale Force U	4.00	5.00
LEL028 Jack Climbing the Beanstalk U	1.25	2.00
LEL029 Luan Auspicious Beast U	1.25	2.00
LEL030 Magic Stone Life Form R	2.00	3.50
LEL031 Planting Beans C	.30	.50
LEL032 Sacred Beast of Wind C	.30	.50
LEL033 Alhamaats Black Lightning U	1.25	2.00
LEL034 Death at Midnight C	.30	.50
LEL035 Dimension Dragon Nidhogg SR	2.00	2.50
LEL036 Fated Reunion R	2.00	3.50
LEL037 Kumomaru U	1.25	2.00
LEL038 Shadow of Lapis U	1.25	2.00
LEL039 Yashahime First Daughter of the Mikage R	2.00	3.50
LEL040 Yashamaru C	.30	.50
LEL041 A Rendezvous of Light and Wind U	1.25	2.00
LEL042 Alteas Elite C	.30	.50
LEL043 Ammit Beast of Gluttony U	1.25	2.00
LEL044 Ancient Barrier U	1.25	2.00
LEL045 Barrier Seal U	1.25	2.00
LEL046 Blessed Knight C	.75	1.00
LEL047 Catalyst Spirit C	.30	.50
LEL048 Crimson Ray C	.30	.50
LEL049 Curse of the Kyuubi R	2.00	3.50
LEL050 Deceptive Dream C	.30	.50
LEL051 Demonic Instigator C	.30	.50
LEL052 Divine Beast of Attoractia R	2.00	3.50
LEL053 Dragon of Scenic Beauty U	1.25	2.00
LEL054 Fairy of Recurrence C	.75	1.00
LEL055 Farias Summon C	.30	.50
LEL056 Fiethsings Monocle U	1.25	2.00
LEL057 Ghost of Attoractia U	1.25	2.00
LEL058 Glorius Masked Crusader Faria	7.00	9.00
Ruler of Divine Beasts R		
LEL059 Griphon Racing Across Darkness C	.30	.50
LEL060 Grusbalesta Magic Stone Researcher SR	1.75	2.00
LEL061 Grusbalestas Secret Technique C	.30	.50
LEL062 Healing Wing Dragon U	1.25	2.00
LEL063 Illusion Wizard C	.30	.50
LEL064 Illusory Projection C	.30	.50
LEL065 Invading Demon of Water Valentina	5.00	7.00
Valentina Released Terror R		
LEL066 Jeanne dArc the Pious Flame R	2.00	3.50
LEL067 Kaguya Lunar Researcher SR	3.00	4.50
LEL068 Kaguyas Moonbeam Butterfly R	2.00	3.50
LEL069 Lilias Petal Agent of Salvation	10.00	12.00
The Nine Tailed Fox R		
LEL070 Lilias Petals Assistant C	.30	.50
LEL071 Lumia the Fated Rebirth Lumia	10.00	12.00
Saint of the Crimson Lotus R		
LEL072 Lumias Judgment R	2.00	3.50
LEL073 Magic Rebound C	.30	.50
LEL074 Meeting of Light and Fire U	1.25	2.00
LEL075 Messenger of Lilias Petal C	.30	.50
LEL076 Moojdart Lady of Illusions SR	3.00	4.50
LEL077 Muul the Town Thar Never Was C	.30	.50
LEL078 Nightmare the Ashen Dream R	2.00	3.50
LEL079 Nyarlathotep the Crimson Radiance SR	3.00	4.50
LEL080 Plot of Water and Darkness U	1.25	2.00
LEL081 Priest of Divine Protection C	.30	.50
LEL082 Prokaryotic Being U	1.25	2.00
LEL083 Rune of Sol C	.30	.50
LEL084 Runic Commander Demon Akiot SR	1.25	2.00
LEL085 Sacred Komainu C	.30	.50
LEL086 Shining Kirin C	.30	.50
LEL087 Sol Hierophant of the Helio Star Sol	8.00	10.00
Dark Commander of Steam R		
LEL088 Steam Explosion R	2.00	3.50
LEL089 Sympathy of Fire and Water U	1.25	2.00
LEL090 The Manticore R	2.00	3.50
LEL091 Tuning of Wind and Darkness U	1.25	2.00
LEL092 TwinHeaded Dragon R	2.00	3.50
LEL093 Valentinas Reach R	2.00	3.50
LEL094 Wetlands of Magical Origin U	1.25	2.00
LEL095 White Horn Kaichi C	.30	.50
LEL096 Awakened Magic Stone the Earth R	3.00	5.00
LEL097 Killing Stone R	3.00	5.00
LEL098 Magic Stone of Vaporization R	3.00	5.00
LEL099 Pricias Memoria R	3.00	5.00
LEL100 Remains of Attoractia R	3.00	5.00
LEL101 Darkness Magic Stone C	.30	.50
LEL102 Fire Magic Stone C	.30	.50
LEL103 Light Magic Stone C	.30	.50
LEL104 Water Magic Stone C	.75	1.00
LEL105 Wind Magic Stone C	.30	.50

2016 Force of Will Legacy Lost Full Art

Card	Low	High
COMPLETE SET		
BOOSTER BOX		
BOOSTER PACK		
RELEASED ON		
LEL001 Amaterasu Guide of Light SR	4.00	6.00
LEL004 Lumias Purification R	4.00	6.00
LEL006 Snow White of the Crystal Apple R	4.00	6.00
LEL010 Bastet Goddess of Cats SR	4.00	6.00
LEL015 TimeGuide Admiral Alfred R	4.00	6.00
LEL016 World Flame Summoning R	4.00	6.00
LEL018 Charlotte Wielder of the Sacred Spirit SR	5.00	7.00
LEL022 Rachel Alhamaats Advisor R	4.00	6.00
LEL024 Reunion of Sisters R	4.00	6.00
LEL025 Fiethsing The Fate Spinning Winds SR	8.00	10.00
LEL026 Final Breeze R	4.00	6.00
LEL030 Magic Stone Life Form R	4.00	6.00
LEL035 Dimension Dragon Nidhogg SR	4.00	6.00
LEL036 Fated Reunion R	4.00	6.00
LEL039 Yashahime First Daughter of the Mikage R	4.00	6.00
LEL049 Curse of the Kyuubi R	4.00	6.00
LEL052 Divine Beast of Attoractia R	4.00	6.00
LEL058 Glorius Masked Crusader Faria	8.00	10.00
Ruler of Divine Beasts R		
LEL060 Grusbalesta Magic Stone Researcher SR	5.00	7.00
LEL065 Invading Demon of Water Valentina	10.00	12.00
Valentina Released Terror R		
LEL066 Jeanne dArc the Pious Flame R	4.00	6.00
LEL067 Kaguya Lunar Researcher SR	4.00	6.00
LEL068 Kaguyas Moonbeam Butterfly R	4.00	6.00
LEL069 Lilias Petal Agent of Salvation	18.00	20.00
The Nine Tailed Fox R		
LEL071 Lumia the Fated Rebirth Lumia	18.00	20.00
Saint of the Crimson Lotus R		
LEL072 Lumias Judgment R	4.00	6.00
LEL076 Moojdart Lady of Illusions SR	4.00	5.00
LEL078 Nightmare the Ashen Dream R	4.00	6.00
LEL079 Nyarlathotep the Crimson Radiance SR	10.00	13.00
LEL084 Runic Commander Demon Akiot SR	8.00	10.00
LEL087 Sol Hierophant of the Helio Star	13.00	15.00
Sol Dark Commander of Steam R		
LEL088 Steam Explosion R	4.00	6.00
LEL090 The Manticore R	4.00	6.00
LEL092 TwinHeaded Dragon R	4.00	6.00
LEL093 Valentinas Reach R	4.00	6.00
LEL096 Awakened Magic Stone the Earth R	10.00	13.00
LEL097 Killing Stone R	10.00	13.00
LEL098 Magic Stone of Vaporization R	10.00	13.00
LEL099 Pricias Memoria R	10.00	13.00
LEL100 Remains of Attoractia R	10.00	13.00

2016 Force of Will Legacy Lost Uber Rare

Card	Low	High
LEL065 Invading Demon of Water Valentina	50.00	75.00
LEL069 Lilias Petal Agent of Salvation	100.00	150.00
LEL071 Lumia the Fated Rebirth	75.00	125.00
LEL087 Sol Hierophant of the Helio Star	50.00	75.00

2017 Force of Will Return of the Dragon Emperor

Card	Low	High
COMPLETE SET (111)	200.00	275.00
BOOSTER BOX (36 PACKS)	90.00	120.00
BOOSTER PACK (10 CARDS)	3.00	5.00
RELEASED ON MARCH 10, 2017		
RDE001 Dragon Power R	.50	.75
RDE002 Guardian of Altean Law U	.20	.35
RDE003 Rachel Nephilim Commander R	.50	.75
RDE004 Ryula Alabaster Dragon Princess SR	1.00	1.50
RDE005 Shield of the Nephilim U	.20	.35
RDE006 Tiny Alabaster Drake C	.15	.25
RDE007 Unleashed Dragonoid C	.15	.25
RDE008 Zeros Wrath C	.15	.25
RDE009 Fiery Soldier of Milest U	.20	.35
RDE010 Memory to Memoria C	.15	.25
RDE011 Milest the First Flame SR	1.00	1.50
RDE012 Reincarnation R	.50	.75
RDE013 Rising Fire Strike U	.20	.35
RDE014 Salamander the Spirit of Fire R	.50	.75
RDE015 Sprinting Flame Horse C	.15	.25
RDE016 Vengeful Attoractian Wizard C	.15	.25
RDE017 Apprentice Wererabbit C	.15	.25
RDE018 Charlottes Water Dragon Technique U	.20	.35
RDE019 Dragonoid Jailor C	.15	.25
RDE020 Eia God of Water SR	2.00	3.50
RDE021 Kaguyas Decision R	.40	.60
RDE022 Manservant to the Water God U	.20	.35
RDE023 Undine the Spirit of Water R	.40	.60
RDE024 Water Kimono of Twelve Parts C	.15	.25
RDE025 Divine Bird of Attoractia C	.15	.25
RDE026 Gilgamesh Immortal Hunter SR	2.00	3.50
RDE027 Heavenly Ox U	.20	.35
RDE028 Miracle Millennia Medicine C	.15	.25
RDE029 Research U	.20	.35
RDE030 Silph the Spirit of Wind R	.50	.75
RDE031 Spinning Myths R	.50	.50

RDE032 Wind Clad Elf C	.15	.25
RDE033 Alhamaats Purge U	.20	.35
RDE034 Buer Great President of Hell U	.20	.35
RDE035 Demon Captain Eligos R	.30	.50
RDE036 Demon Orderly C	.15	.25
RDE037 Fury of the Obsidian Dragon R	.50	.75
RDE038 The Insane Dark Hatter C	.15	.25
RDE039 Viola Obsidian Dragon Princess SR	1.50	2.50
RDE040 Violas Machinations C	.15	.25
RDE041 Alabaster Dragon Knight C	.15	.25
RDE042 Alices World of Madness U	.20	.35
RDE043 Almerius Summoner of Spirits SR	1.50	2.50
RDE044 Black Heart Alice SR	1.50	2.50
RDE045 Black Hole of the Spirit World U	.20	.35
RDE046 Blazer Prisoner of Flame R	.30	.50
RDE047 Burning Pot U	.20	.35
RDE048 Concord of Saints and Beasts U	.20	.35
RDE049 Cryptid of Tenacious Fire C	.15	.25
RDE050 Door of Time R	.50	.75
RDE051 Dragon of Fire and Wind C	.15	.25
RDE052 Earthfallen Giant C	.15	.25
RDE053 End of Days R	.40	.60
RDE054 Erasure C	.15	.25
RDE055 Fallen Angel U	.20	.35
RDE056 Fallen Saint C	.15	.25
RDE057 Fiery Bird of Reincarnation R	.40	.60
RDE058 Fiery Fox of Reincarnation C	.15	.25
RDE059 Forest Spirit C	.15	.25
RDE060 Gill Alhamaat Ruler	18.00	22.00
RDE060 Ebon Dragon Emperor Gill Alhamaat Ruler	18.00	22.00
RDE060 Gill Alhamaat He Who Grasps All Ruler	18.00	22.00
RDE061 Gill Lapis Conqueror of Attoractia Ruler	10.00	13.00
RDE061 Gill Lapis Rebel of Darkest Fires Ruler	10.00	13.00
RDE062 Glistening Chick U	.20	.35
RDE063 Gnome the Spirit of Earth U	.20	.35
RDE064 Kaguya Tears of the Moon Ruler	8.00	11.00
RDE064 Kaguya Millennium Princess Ruler	8.00	11.00
RDE065 Kaguyas Pictorial Scroll C	.15	.25
RDE066 Kingdom of Spirits U	.20	.35
RDE067 Mariabella the Machine Hearted SR	2.00	3.50
RDE068 Mermaid of Lifegiving C	.15	.25
RDE069 Millennia Bond U	.20	.35
RDE070 Millium Successor of the Dragon Crest Ruler	10.00	13.00
RDE070 Millium the Sacred Dragon Ruler	10.00	13.00
RDE071 Milliums Roar C	.15	.25
RDE072 Moon View Rabbit R	.20	.35
RDE073 Moonlit Treasury Tree C	.15	.25
RDE074 Mystia Manager of the Treasury SR	2.00	3.50
RDE075 Nightmoon Blossom C	.15	.25
RDE076 Pricia True Beastmaster Ruler	13.00	16.00
RDE076 Reincarnated Maiden of Flame Pricia Ruler	13.00	16.00
RDE077 Pricias Leap R	.40	.60
RDE078 Rain of Light R	.50	.75
RDE079 Rapid Shot C	.15	.25
RDE080 Schrödinger the Cat in Flux R	1.25	2.00
RDE081 Schrödingers Observation R	.50	.75
RDE082 Searing Dead C	.15	.25
RDE083 Secret Messenger of the Mikage U	.20	.35
RDE084 Sissei Pricias Barrier U	.20	.35
RDE085 Spirit of Sacred Rains C	.15	.25
RDE086 Swirling Demon Dimension C	.15	.25
RDE087 The Alabaster Dragon Princess Rescue U	.20	.35
RDE088 The Dark March Hare C	.15	.25
RDE089 The Dark Sleeping Dormouse C	.15	.25
RDE090 The First Moon U	.20	.35
RDE091 The Two Dragon Princesses U	.20	.35
RDE092 Unending Hatred U	.20	.35
RDE093 Valentina the Twilight Passion SR	2.00	3.50
RDE094 WaterWind Knight C	.15	.25
RDE095 Will othe Wisp R	.75	1.25
RDE096 Ancient Magic Stone R	2.50	4.00
RDE097 Kaguyas Stone of Sorrow R	5.00	8.00
RDE098 Magic Stone of the Ebon Home R	3.00	5.00
RDE099 Memoria of Reincarnation R	8.00	10.00
RDE100 Stone of the Dragonoids R	4.00	6.00
RDE101 Darkness Magic Stone	.15	.25
RDE102 Fire Magic Stone	.15	.25
RDE103 Light Magic Stone	.15	.25
RDE104 Water Magic Stone	.15	.25
RDE105 Wind Magic Stone	.15	.25

2017 Force of Will Return of the Dragon Emperor Foil

RDE001 Dragon Power R	1.50	2.50
RDE002 Guardian of Altean Law U	.40	.60
RDE003 Rachel Nephilim Commander R	1.50	2.50
RDE004 Ryula Alabaster Dragon Princess SR	3.00	5.00
RDE005 Shield of the Nephilim U	.40	.60
RDE006 Tiny Alabaster Drake C	.20	.35
RDE007 Unleashed Dragonoid C	.20	.35
RDE008 Zeros Wrath C	.20	.35
RDE009 Fiery Soldier of Milest U	.40	.60
RDE010 Memory to Memoria C	.20	.35
RDE011 Milest the First Flame SR	3.00	5.00
RDE012 Reincarnation R	1.50	2.50
RDE013 Rising Fire Strike U	.40	.60
RDE014 Salamander the Spirit of Fire R	1.50	2.50
RDE015 Sprinting Flame Horse C	.20	.35
RDE016 Vengeful Attoractian Wizard C	.20	.35
RDE017 Apprentice Wererabbit C	.20	.35
RDE018 Charlottes Water Dragon Technique U	.40	.60
RDE019 Dragonoid Jailor C	.20	.35
RDE020 Eia God of Water SR	3.00	5.00
RDE021 Kaguyas Decision R	1.50	2.50
RDE022 Manservant to the Water God U	.40	.60
RDE023 Undine the Spirit of Water R	1.50	2.50
RDE024 Water Kimono of Twelve Parts C	.20	.35
RDE025 Divine Bird of Attoractia C	.20	.35
RDE026 Gilgamesh Immortal Hunter SR	3.00	5.00
RDE027 Heavenly Ox U	.40	.60
RDE028 Miracle Millennia Medicine C	.20	.35
RDE029 Research U	.40	.60
RDE030 Silph the Spirit of Wind R	1.50	2.50
RDE031 Spinning Myths R	1.50	2.50
RDE032 Wind Clad Elf C	.20	.35
RDE033 Alhamaats Purge U	.40	.60
RDE034 Buer Great President of Hell U	.40	.60
RDE035 Demon Captain Eligos R	1.50	2.50
RDE036 Demon Orderly C	.20	.35
RDE037 Fury of the Obsidian Dragon R	1.50	2.50
RDE038 The Insane Dark Hatter C	.20	.35
RDE039 Viola Obsidian Dragon Princess SR	3.00	5.00
RDE040 Violas Machinations C	.20	.35
RDE041 Alabaster Dragon Knight C	.20	.35
RDE042 Alices World of Madness U	.40	.60
RDE043 Almerius Summoner of Spirits SR	3.00	5.00
RDE044 Black Heart Alice SR	3.00	5.00
RDE045 Black Hole of the Spirit World U	.40	.60
RDE046 Blazer Prisoner of Flame R	1.50	2.50
RDE047 Burning Pot U	.40	.60
RDE048 Concord of Saints and Beasts U	.40	.60
RDE049 Cryptid of Tenacious Fire C	.20	.35
RDE050 Door of Time R	1.50	2.50
RDE051 Dragon of Fire and Wind C	.20	.35
RDE052 Earthfallen Giant C	.20	.35
RDE053 End of Days R	1.50	2.50
RDE054 Erasure C	.20	.35
RDE055 Fallen Angel U	.40	.60
RDE056 Fallen Saint C	.20	.35
RDE057 Fiery Bird of Reincarnation R	1.50	2.50
RDE058 Fiery Fox of Reincarnation C	.20	.35
RDE059 Forest Spirit C	.20	.35
RDE060 Gill Alhamaat Ruler	1.50	2.50
RDE060 Ebon Dragon Emperor Gill Alhamaat Ruler	10.00	15.00
RDE060 Gill Alhamaat He Who Grasps All Ruler	10.00	15.00
RDE061 Gill Lapis Conqueror of Attoractia Ruler	10.00	15.00
RDE061 Gill Lapis Rebel of Darkest Fires Ruler	10.00	15.00
RDE062 Glistening Chick U	.40	.60
RDE063 Gnome the Spirit of Earth U	.40	.60
RDE064 Kaguya Tears of the Moon Ruler	10.00	15.00
RDE064 Kaguya Millennium Princess Ruler	10.00	15.00
RDE065 Kaguyas Pictorial Scroll C	.20	.35
RDE066 Kingdom of Spirits U	.40	.60
RDE067 Mariabella the Machine Hearted SR	3.00	5.00
RDE068 Mermaid of Lifegiving C	.20	.35
RDE069 Millennia Bond U	.40	.60
RDE070 Millium Successor of the Dragon Crest Ruler	10.00	15.00
RDE070 Millium the Sacred Dragon Ruler	10.00	15.00
RDE071 Milliums Roar C	.20	.35
RDE072 Moon View Rabbit R	1.50	2.50
RDE073 Moonlit Treasury Tree C	.20	.35
RDE074 Mystia Manager of the Treasury SR	3.00	5.00
RDE075 Nightmoon Blossom C	.20	.35
RDE076 Pricia True Beastmaster Ruler	10.00	15.00
RDE076 Reincarnated Maiden of Flame Pricia Ruler	10.00	15.00
RDE077 Pricias Leap R	1.50	2.50
RDE078 Rain of Light R	1.50	2.50
RDE079 Rapid Shot C	.20	.35
RDE080 Schrödinger the Cat in Flux R	1.50	2.50
RDE081 Schrödingers Observation R	1.50	2.50
RDE082 Searing Dead C	.20	.35
RDE083 Secret Messenger of the Mikage U	.40	.60
RDE084 Sissei Pricias Barrier U	.40	.60
RDE085 Spirit of Sacred Rains C	.20	.35
RDE086 Swirling Demon Dimension C	.20	.35
RDE087 The Alabaster Dragon Princess Rescue U	.40	.60
RDE088 The Dark March Hare C	.20	.35
RDE089 The Dark Sleeping Dormouse C	.20	.35
RDE090 The First Moon U	.40	.60
RDE091 The Two Dragon Princesses U	.40	.60
RDE092 Unending Hatred U	.40	.60
RDE093 Valentina the Twilight Passion SR	3.00	5.00
RDE094 WaterWind Knight C	.20	.35
RDE095 Will othe Wisp R	1.50	2.50
RDE096 Ancient Magic Stone R	1.50	2.50
RDE097 Kaguyas Stone of Sorrow R	1.50	2.50
RDE098 Magic Stone of the Ebon Home R	1.50	2.50
RDE099 Memoria of Reincarnation R	1.50	2.50
RDE100 Stone of the Dragonoids R	1.50	2.50
RDE101 Darkness Magic Stone	.20	.35
RDE102 Fire Magic Stone	.20	.35
RDE103 Light Magic Stone	.20	.35
RDE104 Water Magic Stone	.20	.35
RDE105 Wind Magic Stone	.20	.35

2017 Force of Will Return of the Dragon Emperor Uber Rare

RDE061 Gill Lapis Conqueror of Attoractia Gill Lapis Rebel of Darkest Fires	60.00	100.00
RDE064 Kaguya Tears of the Moon Kaguya Millennium Princess	60.00	100.00
RDE070 Millium Successor of the Dragon Crest Millium the Sacred Dragon Ruler	50.00	75.00
RDE076 Pricia True Beastmaster Reincarnated Maiden of Flame Pricia	100.00	150.00

2017 Force of Will Echoes of the New World

COMPLETE SET (105)	115.00	180.00
BOOSTER BOX (36 PACKS)	85.00	100.00
BOOSTER PACK (10 CARDS)	3.00	5.00
RELEASED ON JUNE 23, 2017		
ENW001 Ancient Bauble C	.15	.25
ENW002 Arla Demonic Flying Ace U	.20	.35
ENW003 Arlas Blackwing Guard C	.15	.25
ENW004 Book of Light Ruler	10.00	15.00
ENW004 Re Earth New World Fairy Tale J Ruler	10.00	15.00
ENW005 Grimm the Rightful King R	.30	.50
ENW006 Light Dragons Egg C	.15	.25
ENW007 Lumia Praying for the Future R	.30	.50
ENW008 Millium Successor of the Future SR	.75	1.25
ENW009 Pandora Queen of Miracles U	.20	.35
ENW010 Release C	.15	.25
ENW011 Ryulas Volition U	.20	.35
ENW012 Sacred Record of Fairy Tales C	.15	.25
ENW013 Skygazing Girl C	.15	.25
ENW014 Spirit of Protection C	.15	.25
ENW015 Strange Miracle R	.30	.50
ENW016 Zero The Kings Blade R	.30	.50
ENW017 Zeros Circle of Protection U	.20	.35
ENW018 Adelberts Crossflame C	.15	.25
ENW019 Bahamut the Dragonoid R	.30	.50
ENW020 Blazing Floating Castle Refarth U	.20	.35
ENW021 Crimson Sanction SR	.75	1.25
ENW022 Fayli Genius Rip Off Artist U	.20	.35
ENW023 Flames of Nyarlathotep C	.15	.25
ENW024 Melgis King of Black Flame U	.20	.35
ENW025 Melgis War Beast C	.15	.25
ENW026 Nyarlathotep the Realized Truth SR	.75	1.25
ENW027 Rainbow Arrow C	.15	.25
ENW028 Red Hood C	.15	.25
ENW029 Red Riding Hood Rainbow to the Heavens R	.30	.50
ENW030 Refarths Wall of Flames U	.20	.35
ENW031 Swordsman of Fire Ruler	10.00	15.00
ENW031 Dimension Brigades Leader Adelbert J Ruler	10.00	15.00
ENW032 Tiny Aggressive Dragon C	.15	.25
ENW033 Transforming Scarecrow C	.15	.25
ENW034 Yamata no Orochi the Resurrected Calamity R	.30	.50
ENW035 Ahriman The Wicked Spirit Eye U	.20	.35
ENW036 Alice Girl of the Blue Planet SR	.75	1.25
ENW037 Charlotte Last Hope of Attoractia R	.30	.50
ENW038 Charlottes Water Beast Construct C	.15	.25
ENW039 Cheshire Cat Phantasmal Fighter R	.30	.50
ENW040 Detachment U	.20	.35
ENW041 Dragon Shrine Maiden Ruler	10.00	15.00
ENW041 Flute Time Altering Priestess J Ruler	10.00	15.00
ENW042 Flutes Awakening C	.15	.25
ENW043 Flutes Water Dragon C	.15	.25
ENW044 Luna Magician of the Moon Star R	.30	.50
ENW045 Lunas Attendant C	.15	.25
ENW046 Spawn of Umr C	.15	.25
ENW047 Staff of Dragonoids C	.15	.25
ENW048 The Blue Planet U	.20	.35
ENW049 The Cheshire Cats Assistance C	.15	.25
ENW050 The Truth of Time R	.30	.50
ENW051 Umr at Tawil U	.20	.35
ENW052 Confront the Unknown C	.15	.25
ENW053 Fairy of the Malefic Tree C	.15	.25
ENW054 Fox Spirit C	.15	.25
ENW055 Gale Force Pursuer Christie U	.20	.35
ENW056 Heavenly Spirit Tree C	.15	.25
ENW057 Interdimensional Space U	.20	.35
ENW058 Leaf of the Malefic Tree C	.15	.25
ENW059 Melfee Child of Refarth R	.30	.50
ENW060 Pricia Ready for the Final Battle R	.30	.50
ENW061 Resistance Forces of Amonsulle C	.15	.25
ENW062 Scheherazade Speaker of Yet Unknown Truths SR	.75	1.25
ENW063 Severing Winds SR	.75	1.25
ENW064 Soul Debt U	.20	.35
ENW065 Sun Wukong Enforcer for the Future U	.20	.35
ENW066 Words of Scheherazade C	.15	.25
ENW067 Yggdor Beast of Disaster R	.30	.50
ENW068 Yggdrasil Malefic Verdant Tree Ruler	10.00	15.00
ENW069 Abdul Alhazred Sinister Vizier R	.30	.50
ENW070 Ambition of Lapis C	.15	.25
ENW071 Book of Dark Ruler	10.00	15.00
ENW071 Lapistory Subjugation Fairy Tale J Ruler	10.00	15.00
ENW072 Corrupted One Inch Boy C	.15	.25
ENW073 Dark Alice Manifestation of Rage SR	.75	1.25
ENW074 Demonic Dead C	.15	.25
ENW075 Heteroclite Excalibur SR	.75	1.25
ENW076 Mikage Seijuro Patriarch of the Vampires R	.30	.50
ENW077 Neo Barrier of Shadows U	.20	.35
ENW078 Nightfall Bloodsucker C	.15	.25
ENW079 Reshuberos the Devilish Brute U	.20	.35
ENW080 Rezzard King of the Damned R	.30	.50
ENW081 Schrödingers Box C	.15	.25
ENW082 Shadow Stalker C	.15	.25
ENW083 Tell a Dark Fairy Tale C	.15	.25
ENW084 The Final Battle U	.20	.35
ENW085 The Mikage Sisters U	.20	.35
ENW086 Dawn of the Earth SR	.75	1.25
ENW087 Gill Lapis Usurper of Maddening Power SR	.75	1.25
ENW088 Kaguya Love of the Moon R	.30	.50
ENW089 Lars Swordsman of the Dusk R	.30	.50
ENW090 Lilias Petal Kitsune King R	.30	.50
ENW091 Shining Demon Mephistopheles R	.30	.50
ENW092 Sylvia Blade of the Supreme King R	.30	.50
ENW093 Ultimate Swordsmaster Faria R	.30	.50
ENW094 Valentina the Crumbling Illusion R	.30	.50
ENW095 Viola Vengeful Ebon Dragon R	.30	.50
ENW096 Machina King of Accursed Machines R	.30	.50
ENW097 Mariabella the True Shot R	.30	.50
ENW098 Regained Heart R	.30	.50
ENW099 Star Fragment R	.30	.50
ENW100 Time Altering Magic Stone R	.30	.50
ENW101 Darkness Magic Stone NR	.15	.25
ENW102 Fire Magic Stone NR	.15	.25
ENW103 Light Magic Stone NR	.15	.25
ENW104 Water Magic Stone NR	.15	.25
ENW105 Wind Magic Stone NR	.15	.25

2017 Force of Will Echoes of the New World Foil

COMPLETE SET (105)	130.00	200.00
BOOSTER BOX (36 PACKS)	85.00	100.00
BOOSTER PACK (10 CARDS)	3.00	5.00
RELEASED ON JUNE 23, 2017		
ENW001 Ancient Bauble C	.25	.40
ENW002 Arla Demonic Flying Ace U	.30	.50
ENW003 Arlas Blackwing Guard C	.25	.40
ENW004 Book of Light Ruler	10.00	15.00
ENW004 Re Earth New World Fairy Tale J Ruler	10.00	15.00
ENW005 Grimm the Rightful King R	.50	.80
ENW006 Light Dragons Egg C	.25	.40
ENW007 Lumia Praying for the Future R	.50	.80
ENW008 Millium Successor of the Future SR	1.25	2.00
ENW009 Pandora Queen of Miracles U	.30	.50
ENW010 Release C	.25	.40
ENW011 Ryulas Volition U	.30	.50
ENW012 Sacred Record of Fairy Tales C	.25	.40
ENW013 Skygazing Girl C	.25	.40
ENW014 Spirit of Protection C	.25	.40
ENW015 Strange Miracle R	.50	.80
ENW016 Zero The Kings Blade R	.50	.80
ENW017 Zeros Circle of Protection U	.30	.50
ENW018 Adelberts Crossflame C	.25	.40
ENW019 Bahamut the Dragonoid R	.50	.80
ENW020 Blazing Floating Castle Refarth U	.30	.50
ENW021 Crimson Sanction SR	1.25	2.00
ENW022 Fayli Genius Rip Off Artist U	.30	.50
ENW023 Flames of Nyarlathotep C	.25	.40
ENW024 Melgis King of Black Flame U	.30	.50
ENW025 Melgis War Beast C	.25	.40
ENW026 Nyarlathotep the Realized Truth SR	1.25	2.00
ENW027 Rainbow Arrow C	.25	.40
ENW028 Red Hood C	.25	.40
ENW029 Red Riding Hood Rainbow to the Heavens R	.50	.80
ENW030 Refarths Wall of Flames U	.30	.50
ENW031 Swordsman of Fire Ruler	10.00	15.00
ENW031 Dimension Brigades Leader Adelbert J Ruler	10.00	15.00
ENW032 Tiny Aggressive Dragon C	.25	.40
ENW033 Transforming Scarecrow C	.25	.40
ENW034 Yamata no Orochi the Resurrected Calamity R	.50	.80
ENW035 Ahriman The Wicked Spirit Eye U	.30	.50

Card	Low	High
ENW036 Alice Girl of the Blue Planet SR	1.25	2.00
ENW037 Charlotte Last Hope of Attoractia R	.50	.80
ENW038 Charlottes Water Beast Construct C	.25	.40
ENW039 Cheshire Cat Phantasmal Fighter R	.50	.80
ENW040 Detachment U	.30	.50
ENW041 Dragon Shrine Maiden Ruler	10.00	15.00
ENW041 Flute Time Altering Priestess J Ruler	10.00	15.00
ENW042 Flutes Awakening C	.25	.40
ENW043 Flutes Water Dragon C	.25	.40
ENW044 Luna Magician of the Moon Star R	.50	.80
ENW045 Lunas Attendant C	.25	.40
ENW046 Spawn of Umr C	.25	.40
ENW047 Staff of Dragonoids C	.25	.40
ENW048 The Blue Planet U	.30	.50
ENW049 The Cheshire Cats Assistance C	.25	.40
ENW050 The Truth of Time R	.50	.80
ENW051 Umr at Tawil U	.30	.50
ENW052 Confront the Unknown C	.25	.40
ENW053 Fairy of the Malefic Tree C	.25	.40
ENW054 Fox Spirit C	.25	.40
ENW055 Gale Force Pursuer Christie U	.30	.50
ENW056 Heavenly Spirit Tree C	.25	.40
ENW057 Interdimensional Space U	.30	.50
ENW058 Leaf of the Malefic Tree C	.25	.40
ENW059 Melfee Child of Refarth R	.50	.80
ENW060 Pricia Ready for the Final Battle R	.50	.80
ENW061 Resistance Forces of Amonsulle C	.25	.40
ENW062 Scheherazade Speaker of Yet Unknown Truths SR	1.25	2.00
ENW063 Severing Winds SR	1.25	2.00
ENW064 Soul Debt U	.30	.50
ENW065 Sun Wukong Enforcer for the Future U	.30	.50
ENW066 Words of Scheherazade C	.25	.40
ENW067 Yggdor Beast of Disaster R	.50	.80
ENW068 Yggdrasil Malefic Verdant Tree Ruler	10.00	15.00
ENW069 Abdul Alhazred Sinister Vizier R	.50	.80
ENW070 Ambition of Lapis C	.25	.40
ENW071 Book of Dark Ruler	10.00	15.00
ENW071 Lapistory Subjugation Fairy Tale J Ruler	10.00	15.00
ENW072 Corrupted One Inch Boy C	.25	.40
ENW073 Dark Alice Manifestation of Rage SR	1.25	2.00
ENW074 Demonic Dead C	.25	.40
ENW075 Heteroclite Excalibur SR	1.25	2.00
ENW076 Mikage Seijuro Patriarch of the Vampires R	.50	.80
ENW077 Neo Barrier of Shadows U	.30	.50
ENW078 Nightfall Bloodsucker C	.25	.40
ENW079 Reshuberos the Devilish Brute U	.30	.50
ENW080 Rezzard King of the Damned R	.50	.80
ENW081 Schrödingers Box C	.25	.40
ENW082 Shadow Stalker C	.25	.40
ENW083 Tell a Dark Fairy Tale C	.25	.40
ENW084 The Final Battle U	.30	.50
ENW085 The Mikage Sisters U	.30	.50
ENW086 Dawn of the Earth SR	1.25	2.00
ENW087 Gill Lapis Usurper of Maddening Power SR	1.25	2.00
ENW088 Kaguya Love of the Moon R	.50	.80
ENW089 Lars Swordsman of the Dusk R	.50	.80
ENW090 Lilias Petal Kitsune King R	.50	.80
ENW091 Shining Demon Mephistopheles R	.50	.80
ENW092 Sylvia Blade of the Supreme King R	.50	.80
ENW093 Ultimate Swordsmaster Faria R	.50	.80
ENW094 Valentina the Crumbling Illusion R	.50	.80
ENW095 Viola Vengeful Ebon Dragon R	.50	.80
ENW096 Machina King of Accursed Machines R	.50	.80
ENW097 Mariabella the True Shot R	.50	.80
ENW098 Regained Heart R	.50	.80
ENW099 Star Fragment R	.50	.80
ENW100 Time Altering Magic Stone R	.50	.80
ENW101 Darkness Magic Stone NR	.25	.40
ENW102 Fire Magic Stone NR	.25	.40
ENW103 Light Magic Stone NR	.25	.40
ENW104 Water Magic Stone NR	.25	.40
ENW105 Wind Magic Stone NR	.25	.40

2017 Force of Will Echoes of the New World Full Art

Card	Low	High
COMPLETE SET (105)	175.00	250.00
BOOSTER BOX (36 PACKS)	85.00	100.00
BOOSTER PACK (10 CARDS)	3.00	5.00
RELEASED ON JUNE 23, 2017		
ENW004 Book of Light Ruler	15.00	20.00
ENW004 Re Earth New World Fairy Tale J Ruler	15.00	20.00
ENW005 Grimm the Rightful King R	.60	1.00
ENW008 Millium Successor of the Future SR	2.00	3.50
ENW015 Strange Miracle R	.60	1.00
ENW016 Zero The Kings Blade R	.60	1.00
ENW019 Bahamut the Dragonoid R	.60	1.00
ENW021 Crimson Sanction SR	2.00	3.50
ENW026 Nyarlathotep the Realized Truth SR	2.00	3.50
ENW029 Red Riding Hood Rainbow to the Heavens R	.60	1.00
ENW031 Swordsman of Fire Ruler	15.00	20.00
ENW031 Dimension Brigades Leader Adelbert J Ruler	15.00	20.00
ENW034 Yamata no Orochi the Resurrected Calamity R	.60	1.00
ENW036 Alice Girl of the Blue Planet SR	2.00	3.50
ENW037 Charlotte Last Hope of Attoractia R	.60	1.00
ENW039 Cheshire Cat Phantasmal Fighter R	.60	1.00
ENW041 Dragon Shrine Maiden Ruler	15.00	20.00
ENW041 Flute Time Altering Priestess J Ruler	15.00	20.00
ENW044 Luna Magician of the Moon Star R	.60	1.00
ENW050 The Truth of Time R	.60	1.00
ENW059 Melfee Child of Refarth R	.60	1.00
ENW060 Pricia Ready for the Final Battle R	.60	1.00
ENW062 Scheherazade Speaker of Yet Unknown Truths SR	2.00	3.50
ENW063 Severing Winds SR	2.00	3.50
ENW067 Yggdor Beast of Disaster R	.60	1.00
ENW068 Yggdrasil Malefic Verdant Tree Ruler	15.00	20.00
ENW069 Abdul Alhazred Sinister Vizier R	.60	1.00
ENW071 Book of Dark Ruler	15.00	20.00
ENW071 Lapistory Subjugation Fairy Tale J Ruler	15.00	20.00
ENW073 Dark Alice Manifestation of Rage SR	2.00	3.50
ENW075 Heteroclite Excalibur SR	2.00	3.50
ENW076 Mikage Seijuro Patriarch of the Vampires R	.60	1.00
ENW080 Rezzard King of the Damned R	.60	1.00
ENW086 Dawn of the Earth SR	2.00	3.50
ENW087 Gill Lapis Usurper of Maddening Power SR	2.00	3.50
ENW088 Kaguya Love of the Moon R	.60	1.00
ENW089 Lars Swordsman of the Dusk R	.60	1.00
ENW090 Lilias Petal Kitsune King R	.60	1.00
ENW091 Shining Demon Mephistopheles R	.60	1.00
ENW092 Sylvia Blade of the Supreme King R	.60	1.00
ENW093 Ultimate Swordsmaster Faria R	.60	1.00
ENW094 Valentina the Crumbling Illusion R	.60	1.00
ENW095 Viola Vengeful Ebon Dragon R	.60	1.00
ENW096 Machina King of Accursed Machines R	.60	1.00
ENW097 Mariabella the True Shot R	.60	1.00
ENW098 Regained Heart R	.60	1.00
ENW099 Star Fragment R	.60	1.00
ENW100 Time Altering Magic Stone R	.60	1.00

2017 Force of Will Echoes of the New World Uber Rare

Card	Low	High
ENW004 Book of Light	25.00	40.00
ENW031 Swordsman of Fire	75.00	125.00
ENW041 Dragon Shrine Maiden	10.00	150.00
ENW068 Yggdrasil Malefic Verdant Tree	50.00	75.00
ENW071 Book of Dark	40.00	60.00

2017 Force of Will Ancient Nights

Card	Low	High
COMPLETE SET (170)	130.00	200.00
BOOSTER BOX (36 PACKS)	90.00	115.00
BOOSTER PACK (10 CARDS)	3.00	5.00
RELEASED ON SEPTEMBER 8, 2017		
ACN001 Conjure Constructs R	.75	2.00
ACN002 Crippling Light SR	2.50	4.00
ACN003 Discovery C	.10	.20
ACN004 Gem Beast U	.20	.35
ACN005 Gem Blade Emerald U	.20	.35
ACN006 Gem Minister Garnet R	.75	2.00
ACN007 Gem Trader C	.10	.20
ACN008 Heavy Arms Panda C	.10	.20
ACN009 Jewel Bullet R	.75	2.00
ACN010 Jewel Protection C	.10	.20
ACN011 Jewel Shield C	.10	.20
ACN012 Jewel Sword C	.10	.20
ACN013 Jeweler of Sasaru Palace U	.20	.35
ACN014 Light of Transmigration U	.20	.35
ACN015 Magic Light Warrior C	.10	.20
ACN016 Magic Shield Warrior C	.10	.20
ACN017 Magic Sword Warrior U	.20	.35
ACN018 Oprhica Dancer in the White Mist SR	2.50	4.00
ACN019 Panda Acrobat C	.10	.20
ACN020 Pandora Ruler	15.00	20.00
ACN020 Pandora Guardian of the Sacred Temple Ruler	15.00	20.00
ACN021 Profitable Transactions U	.20	.35
ACN022 Reduction C	.10	.20
ACN023 Sacred Temple of Light U	.20	.35
ACN024 Shin Shin&Rei Rei Acrobatic Twins R	.75	2.00
ACN025 Summon Magic Warriors U	.20	.35
ACN026 Ultimate Magic Warrior Gear Atmos R	.75	2.00
ACN027 White Cat of Sasaru Palace C	.10	.20
ACN028 White Raven C	.10	.20
ACN029 Wing Rider Panda C	.10	.20
ACN030 Apprentice Beast Tamer C	.10	.20
ACN031 Archaeopteryx U	.20	.35
ACN032 Beast Den on Mt Hoelle U	.20	.35
ACN033 Burning Awakening C	.10	.20
ACN034 Demon Watcher U	.10	.20
ACN035 Devils Advocate U	.10	.20
ACN036 Dino Rush C	.10	.20
ACN037 Dragon Call R	.75	2.00
ACN038 Dragonoid Martial Artist C	.10	.20
ACN039 Environmental Researcher Fabre R	.75	2.00
ACN040 Eruptiphant R	.75	2.00
ACN041 Explorer on Mt Hoelle C	.10	.20
ACN042 Fiend Fire SR	.10	.20
ACN043 Fire Dragons Egg C	.10	.20
ACN044 Flame Style U	.20	.35
ACN045 Flying Drill C	.10	.20
ACN046 Food Supply C	.10	.20
ACN047 Gourmet Chef Sherry Shera R	.75	2.00
ACN048 Hell Flame C	.10	.20
ACN049 High Speed U	.20	.35
ACN050 Hoelle Pig C	.10	.20
ACN051 Hoellesaurus C	.10	.20
ACN052 Kaim Demon of Vice SR	2.50	4.00
ACN053 Master of Faithful Beasts U	.20	.35
ACN054 Red Cap C	.10	.20
ACN055 Stone Tongued Basilisk C	.10	.20
ACN056 Two Horned Almiraj U	.20	.35
ACN057 Vanish in Fire R	.75	2.00
ACN058 Alternating Current Crystal R	.75	2.00
ACN059 Aqua Rifle Mermaid C	.10	.20
ACN060 Aquamarine Panda Diplomat U	.20	.35
ACN061 Bubble Golem C	.10	.20
ACN062 Cleansing Rain C	.10	.20
ACN063 Confinement U	.20	.35
ACN064 Coral Reef Mermaid C	.10	.20
ACN065 Electrical Discharge C	.10	.20
ACN066 Giant Squid C	.10	.20
ACN067 Guard at the Coral Palace U	.20	.35
ACN068 Keez the Wise Dolphin R	.75	2.00
ACN069 Keezs Call C	.10	.20
ACN070 Magic Sound Warrior U	.20	.35
ACN071 Magic Water Warrior C	.10	.20
ACN072 Magical Tidal Surge SR	2.50	4.00
ACN073 Mega Thunderfish SR	2.50	4.00
ACN074 Ocean Floor Archelon U	.20	.35
ACN075 Pandoras Order U	.20	.35
ACN076 Princess Shaelas Attendant C	.10	.20
ACN077 Seabed Investigation U	.20	.35
ACN078 Shaelas Elite R	.75	2.00
ACN079 Shaelas Foresight R	.75	2.00
ACN080 Song of Sympathy R	.75	2.00
ACN081 Spinning Aquasol C	.10	.20
ACN082 The Coral Palace U	.20	.35
ACN083 Thunderfish C	.10	.20
ACN084 Waterfowl C	.10	.20
ACN085 Weather Change: Rain C	.10	.20
ACN086 Absolute Awareness C	.10	.20
ACN087 Arrow Trap U	.20	.35
ACN088 Bullseye Bow C	.10	.20
ACN089 Commander of the Crowd U	.20	.35
ACN090 Elemental Blast R	.75	2.00
ACN091 Elf in the Trees C	.10	.20
ACN092 Elvish Hunter C	.10	.20
ACN093 Faerur Letoliel Ruler	15.00	20.00
ACN093 Faerur Letoliel King of Wind Ruler	15.00	20.00
ACN094 Faerurs Command R	.75	2.00
ACN095 Faerurs Escort C	.10	.20
ACN096 Faerurs Spell U	.20	.35
ACN097 Gentle Breeze Elemental C	.10	.20
ACN098 Great Tornado SR	.10	.20
ACN099 Leaf Archer U	.20	.35
ACN100 Leaf Fighter C	.10	.20
ACN101 Leaf Guard C	.10	.20
ACN102 Leaf Healer U	.20	.35
ACN103 Leaf Knight R	.75	2.00
ACN104 Messenger of the King U	.20	.35
ACN105 Portal in the Woods U	.20	.35
ACN106 Spirit Caller Elf C	.10	.20
ACN107 Spiritual Guidance U	.20	.35
ACN108 Tia Letoliel Archer Princess of Elves SR	2.50	4.00
ACN109 Tias White Falcon R	.75	2.00
ACN110 Trap Master Lemuria R	.75	2.00
ACN111 Tree Root Sprite C	.10	.20
ACN112 Wind Blade C	.10	.20
ACN113 Wind Ferryman C	.10	.20
ACN114 Winds of Vitality C	.10	.20
ACN115 Ahriman Malicious Eye in the Dark C	.10	.20
ACN116 Black Blood Knight U	.20	.35
ACN117 Bloodspray C	.10	.20
ACN118 Dark Elf of the Murky Grove C	.10	.20
ACN119 Dark Elf Sorcerer U	.20	.35
ACN120 Dark Elf Spy C	.10	.20
ACN121 Dark Night Butterfly C	.10	.20
ACN122 Dark Revolution R	.75	2.00
ACN123 Dark Riding Hood SR	2.50	4.00
ACN124 Demonic Rabbit C	.10	.20
ACN125 Feast on Mortals C	.10	.20
ACN126 Frayla Ruler	15.00	20.00
ACN126 Frayla the Revolutionist Ruler	15.00	20.00
ACN127 Gate to Outer World U	.20	.35
ACN128 Hilda Fraylas Left Hand R	.75	2.00
ACN129 Lethal Arrow C	.10	.20
ACN130 Moon in the Mist U	.20	.35
ACN131 Moonlight Shadow C	.10	.20
ACN132 Saffina Fraylas Right Hand R	.75	2.00
ACN133 Shade Assassin U	.20	.35
ACN134 Stealth Demon U	.20	.35
ACN135 Sword of the New Moon C	.10	.20
ACN136 Tactics of the Dark Elves U	.20	.35
ACN137 The Three Evil Little Pigs U	.20	.35
ACN138 Transforming Vampire C	.10	.20
ACN139 Treasonous Guard C	.10	.20
ACN140 Truth Amongst Darkness U	.20	.35
ACN141 Vicious Wounded Beast C	.10	.20
ACN142 Vitality Drain SR	.10	.20
ACN143 Wolfs Rain R	.75	2.00
ACN144 Idol of Magic C	.10	.20
ACN145 Idol of Vitality C	.10	.20
ACN146 Idol of Willpower C	.10	.20
ACN147 Statue in the Sacred Temple R	.75	2.00
ACN148 Demonic Soulstone R	.75	2.00
ACN149 Mysterious Magic Stone R	.75	2.00
ACN150 Saintly Elven Stone R	.75	2.00
ACN151 [Variant] Wing Rider Panda C	.10	.20
ACN152 [Variant] Stone Tongued Basilisk C	.10	.20
ACN153 [Variant] Giant Squid C	.10	.20
ACN154 [Variant] Faerurs Escort C	.10	.20
ACN155 [Variant] Vicious Wounded Beast C	.10	.20
ACN156 Darkness Magic Stone NR	.10	.20
ACN157 Fire Magic Stone NR	.10	.20
ACN158 Light Magic Stone NR	.10	.20
ACN159 Water Magic Stone NR	.10	.20
ACN160 Wind Magic Stone NR	.10	.20
ACN161 Treasure Hunter Fierica NR	.10	.20
ACN161 Treasure Hunter Fierica NR	.10	.20
ACN162 Martial Artist Pialle Eille NR	.10	.20
ACN162 Martial Artist Pialle Eille NR	.10	.20
ACN163 Mephina Mermaid Shaman NR	.10	.20
ACN163 Mephina Mermaid Shaman NR	.10	.20
ACN164 Leaf Elder NR	.10	.20
ACN164 Leaf Elder NR	.10	.20
ACN165 Bloodsucking Butler NR	.10	.20
ACN165 Bloodsucking Butler NR	.10	.20

2017 Force of Will Ancient Nights Foil

Card	Low	High
COMPLETE SET (155)	200.00	250.00
ACN001 Conjure Constructs R	2.00	3.50
ACN002 Crippling Light SR	4.00	6.00
ACN003 Discovery C	.30	.50
ACN004 Gem Beast U	.60	1.00
ACN005 Gem Blade Emerald U	.60	1.00
ACN006 Gem Minister Garnet R	2.00	3.50
ACN007 Gem Trader C	.30	.50
ACN008 Heavy Arms Panda C	.30	.50
ACN009 Jewel Bullet R	2.00	3.50
ACN010 Jewel Protection C	.30	.50
ACN011 Jewel Shield C	.30	.50
ACN012 Jewel Sword C	.30	.50
ACN013 Jeweler of Sasaru Palace U	.60	1.00
ACN014 Light of Transmigration U	.60	1.00
ACN015 Magic Light Warrior C	.30	.50
ACN016 Magic Shield Warrior C	.30	.50
ACN017 Magic Sword Warrior U	.60	1.00
ACN018 Oprhica Dancer in the White Mist SR	4.00	6.00
ACN019 Panda Acrobat C	.30	.50
ACN020 Pandora Ruler	15.00	20.00
ACN020 Pandora Guardian of the Sacred Temple Ruler	15.00	20.00
ACN021 Profitable Transactions U	.60	1.00
ACN022 Reduction C	.30	.50
ACN023 Sacred Temple of Light U	.60	1.00
ACN024 Shin Shin&Rei Rei Acrobatic Twins R	2.00	3.50
ACN025 Summon Magic Warriors U	.60	1.00
ACN026 Ultimate Magic Warrior Gear Atmos R	2.00	3.50
ACN027 White Cat of Sasaru Palace C	.30	.50
ACN028 White Raven C	.30	.50
ACN029 Wing Rider Panda C	.30	.50
ACN030 Apprentice Beast Tamer C	.30	.50
ACN031 Archaeopteryx U	.60	1.00
ACN032 Beast Den on Mt Hoelle U	.60	1.00
ACN033 Burning Awakening C	.30	.50
ACN034 Demon Watcher U	.30	.50
ACN035 Devils Advocate U	.30	.50
ACN036 Dino Rush C	.30	.50
ACN037 Dragon Call R	2.00	3.50
ACN038 Dragonoid Martial Artist C	.30	.50
ACN039 Environmental Researcher Fabre R	2.00	3.50
ACN040 Eruptiphant R	2.00	3.50
ACN041 Explorer on Mt Hoelle C	.30	.50
ACN042 Fiend Fire SR	.30	.50
ACN043 Fire Dragons Egg C	.30	.50
ACN044 Flame Style U	.60	1.00
ACN045 Flying Drill C	.30	.50
ACN046 Food Supply C	.30	.50
ACN047 Gourmet Chef Sherry Shera R	2.00	3.50

ACN048 Hell Flame C .30 .50
ACN049 High Speed U .60 1.00
ACN050 Hoelle Pig C .30 .50
ACN051 Hoellesaurus C .30 .50
ACN052 Kaim Demon of Vice SR 4.00 6.00
ACN053 Master of Faithful Beasts U .60 1.00
ACN054 Red Cap C .30 .50
ACN055 Stone Tongued Basilisk C .30 .50
ACN056 Two Horned Almiraj U .60 1.00
ACN057 Vanish in Fire R 2.00 3.50
ACN058 Alternating Current Crystal R 2.00 3.50
ACN059 Aqua Rifle Mermaid C .30 .50
ACN060 Aquamarine Panda Diplomat U .60 1.00
ACN061 Bubble Golem C .30 .50
ACN062 Cleansing Rain C .30 .50
ACN063 Confinement U .60 1.00
ACN064 Coral Reef Mermaid C .30 .50
ACN065 Electrical Discharge C .30 .50
ACN066 Giant Squid C .30 .50
ACN067 Guard at the Coral Palace U .60 1.00
ACN068 Keez the Wise Dolphin R 2.00 3.50
ACN069 Keezs Call C .30 .50
ACN070 Magic Sound Warrior U .60 1.00
ACN071 Magic Water Warrior C .30 .50
ACN072 Magical Tidal Surge SR 4.00 6.00
ACN073 Mega Thunderfish SR 4.00 6.00
ACN074 Ocean Floor Archelon U .60 1.00
ACN075 Pandoras Order U .60 1.00
ACN076 Princess Shaelas Attendant C .30 .50
ACN077 Seabed Investigation U .60 1.00
ACN078 Shaelas Elite R 2.00 3.50
ACN079 Shaelas Foresight R 2.00 3.50
ACN080 Song of Sympathy R 2.00 3.50
ACN081 Spinning Aquasol C .30 .50
ACN082 The Coral Palace U .60 1.00
ACN083 Thunderfish C .30 .50
ACN084 Waterfowl C .30 .50
ACN085 Weather Change: Rain C .30 .50
ACN086 Absolute Awareness C .30 .50
ACN087 Arrow Trap U .60 1.00
ACN088 Bullseye Bow C .30 .50
ACN089 Commander of the Crowd U .60 1.00
ACN090 Elemental Blast R 2.00 3.50
ACN091 Elf in the Trees C .30 .50
ACN092 Elvish Hunter C .30 .50
ACN093 Faerur Letoliel Ruler 15.00 20.00
ACN093 Faerur Letoliel King of Wind Ruler 15.00 20.00
ACN094 Faerurs Command R 2.00 3.50
ACN095 Faerurs Escort C .30 .50
ACN096 Faerurs Spell U .60 1.00
ACN097 Gentle Breeze Elemental C .30 .50
ACN098 Great Tornado SR .30 .50
ACN099 Leaf Archer U .60 1.00
ACN100 Leaf Fighter C .30 .50
ACN101 Leaf Guard C .30 .50
ACN102 Leaf Healer U .60 1.00
ACN103 Leaf Knight R 2.00 3.50
ACN104 Messenger of the King U .60 1.00
ACN105 Portal in the Woods U .60 1.00
ACN106 Spirit Caller Elf C .30 .50
ACN107 Spiritual Guidance U .60 1.00
ACN108 Tia Letoliel Archer Princess of Elves SR 4.00 6.00
ACN109 Tias White Falcon R 2.00 3.50
ACN110 Trap Master Lemuria R 2.00 3.50
ACN111 Tree Root Sprite C .30 .50
ACN112 Wind Blade C .30 .50
ACN113 Wind Ferryman C .30 .50
ACN114 Winds of Vitality C .30 .50
ACN115 Ahriman Malicious Eye in the Dark C .30 .50
ACN116 Black Blood Knight U .60 1.00
ACN117 Bloodspray C .30 .50
ACN118 Dark Elf of the Murky Grove C .30 .50
ACN119 Dark Elf Sorcerer U .60 1.00
ACN120 Dark Elf Spy C .30 .50
ACN121 Dark Night Butterfly C .30 .50
ACN122 Dark Revolution R 2.00 3.50
ACN123 Dark Riding Hood SR 4.00 6.00
ACN124 Demonic Rabbit C .30 .50
ACN125 Feast on Mortals C .30 .50
ACN126 Frayla Ruler 15.00 20.00
ACN126 Frayla the Revolutionist Ruler 15.00 20.00
ACN127 Gate to Outer World U .60 1.00
ACN128 Hilda Fraylas Left Hand R 2.00 3.50
ACN129 Lethal Arrow C .30 .50
ACN130 Moon in the Mist U .60 1.00
ACN131 Moonlight Shadow C .30 .50
ACN132 Saffina Fraylas Right Hand R 2.00 3.50
ACN133 Shade Assassin U .60 1.00
ACN134 Stealth Demon U .60 1.00
ACN135 Sword of the New Moon C .30 .50
ACN136 Tactics of the Dark Elves U .60 1.00
ACN137 The Three Evil Little Pigs U .60 1.00
ACN138 Transforming Vampire C .30 .50
ACN139 Treasonous Guard C .30 .50
ACN140 Truth Amongst Darkness U .60 1.00
ACN141 Vicious Wounded Beast C .30 .50
ACN142 Vitality Drain SR .30 .50
ACN143 Wolfs Rain R 2.00 3.50
ACN144 Idol of Magic C .30 .50
ACN145 Idol of Vitality C .30 .50
ACN146 Idol of Willpower C .30 .50
ACN147 Statue in the Sacred Temple R 2.00 3.50
ACN148 Demonic Soulstone R 2.00 3.50
ACN149 Mysterious Magic Stone R 2.00 3.50
ACN150 Saintly Elven Stone R 2.00 3.50
ACN151 [Variant] Wing Rider Panda C .30 .50
ACN152 [Variant] Stone Tongued Basilisk C .30 .50
ACN153 [Variant] Giant Squid C .30 .50
ACN154 [Variant] Faerurs Escort C .30 .50
ACN155 [Variant] Vicious Wounded Beast C .30 .50

2017 Force of Will Ancient Nights Full Art

COMPLETE SET (150) 350.00 600.00
ACN001 Conjure Constructs R 3.00 5.00
ACN002 Crippling Light SR 6.00 10.00
ACN003 Discovery C .75 2.00
ACN004 Gem Beast U 2.00 3.50
ACN005 Gem Blade Emerald U 2.00 3.50
ACN006 Gem Minister Garnet R 3.00 5.00
ACN007 Gem Trader C .75 2.00
ACN008 Heavy Arms Panda C .75 2.00
ACN009 Jewel Bullet R 3.00 5.00
ACN010 Jewel Protection C .75 2.00
ACN011 Jewel Shield C .75 2.00
ACN012 Jewel Sword C .75 2.00
ACN013 Jeweler of Sasaru Palace U 2.00 3.50
ACN014 Light of Transmigration U 2.00 3.50
ACN015 Magic Light Warrior C .75 2.00
ACN016 Magic Shield Warrior C .75 2.00
ACN017 Magic Sword Warrior U 2.00 3.50
ACN018 Ophica Dancer in the White Mist SR 6.00 10.00
ACN019 Panda Acrobat C .75 2.00
ACN020 Pandora Ruler 15.00 20.00
ACN020 Pandora Guardian of the Sacred Temple Ruler 15.00 20.00
ACN021 Profitable Transactions U 2.00 3.50
ACN022 Reduction C .75 2.00
ACN023 Sacred Temple of Light U 2.00 3.50
ACN024 Shin Shin&Rei Rei Acrobatic Twins R 3.00 5.00
ACN025 Summon Magic Warriors U 2.00 3.50
ACN026 Ultimate Magic Warrior Gear Atmos R 3.00 5.00
ACN027 White Cat of Sasaru Palace C .75 2.00
ACN028 White Raven C .75 2.00
ACN029 Wing Rider Panda C .75 2.00
ACN030 Apprentice Beast Tamer C .75 2.00
ACN031 Archaeopteryx U 2.00 3.50
ACN032 Beast Den on Mt Hoelle U 2.00 3.50
ACN033 Burning Awakening C .75 2.00
ACN034 Demon Watcher U .75 2.00
ACN035 Devils Advocate U .75 2.00
ACN036 Dino Rush C .75 2.00
ACN037 Dragon Call R 3.00 5.00
ACN038 Dragonoid Martial Artist C .75 2.00
ACN039 Environmental Researcher Fabre R 3.00 5.00
ACN040 Eruptiphant R 3.00 5.00
ACN041 Explorer on Mt Hoelle C .75 2.00
ACN042 Fiend Fire SR .75 2.00
ACN043 Fire Dragons Egg C .75 2.00
ACN044 Flame Style U 2.00 3.50
ACN045 Flying Drill C .75 2.00
ACN046 Food Supply C .75 2.00
ACN047 Gourmet Chef Sherry Shera R 3.00 5.00
ACN048 Hell Flame C .75 2.00
ACN049 High Speed U 2.00 3.50
ACN050 Hoelle Pig C .75 2.00
ACN051 Hoellesaurus C .75 2.00
ACN052 Kaim Demon of Vice SR 6.00 10.00
ACN053 Master of Faithful Beasts U 2.00 3.50
ACN054 Red Cap C .75 2.00
ACN055 Stone Tongued Basilisk C .75 2.00
ACN056 Two Horned Almiraj U 2.00 3.50
ACN057 Vanish in Fire R 3.00 5.00
ACN058 Alternating Current Crystal R 3.00 5.00
ACN059 Aqua Rifle Mermaid C .75 2.00
ACN060 Aquamarine Panda Diplomat U 2.00 3.50
ACN061 Bubble Golem C .75 2.00
ACN062 Cleansing Rain C .75 2.00
ACN063 Confinement U 2.00 3.50
ACN064 Coral Reef Mermaid C .75 2.00
ACN065 Electrical Discharge C .75 2.00
ACN066 Giant Squid C .75 2.00
ACN067 Guard at the Coral Palace U .75 2.00
ACN068 Keez the Wise Dolphin R 3.00 5.00
ACN069 Keezs Call C .75 2.00
ACN070 Magic Sound Warrior U 2.00 3.50
ACN071 Magic Water Warrior C .75 2.00
ACN072 Magical Tidal Surge SR 6.00 10.00
ACN073 Mega Thunderfish SR 6.00 10.00
ACN074 Ocean Floor Archelon U 2.00 3.50
ACN075 Pandoras Order U 2.00 3.50
ACN076 Princess Shaelas Attendant C .75 2.00
ACN077 Seabed Investigation U 2.00 3.50
ACN078 Shaelas Elite R 3.00 5.00
ACN079 Shaelas Foresight R 3.00 5.00
ACN080 Song of Sympathy R 3.00 5.00
ACN081 Spinning Aquasol C .75 2.00
ACN082 The Coral Palace U 2.00 3.50
ACN083 Thunderfish C .75 2.00
ACN084 Waterfowl C .75 2.00
ACN085 Weather Change: Rain C .75 2.00
ACN086 Absolute Awareness C .75 2.00
ACN087 Arrow Trap U 2.00 3.50
ACN088 Bullseye Bow C .75 2.00
ACN089 Commander of the Crowd U 2.00 3.50
ACN090 Elemental Blast R 3.00 5.00
ACN091 Elf in the Trees C .75 2.00
ACN092 Elvish Hunter C .75 2.00
ACN093 Faerur Letoliel Ruler 15.00 20.00
ACN093 Faerur Letoliel King of Wind Ruler 15.00 20.00
ACN094 Faerurs Command R 3.00 5.00
ACN095 Faerurs Escort C .75 2.00
ACN096 Faerurs Spell U 2.00 3.50
ACN097 Gentle Breeze Elemental C .75 2.00
ACN098 Great Tornado SR .75 2.00
ACN099 Leaf Archer U 2.00 3.50
ACN100 Leaf Fighter C .75 2.00
ACN101 Leaf Guard C .75 2.00
ACN102 Leaf Healer U 2.00 3.50
ACN103 Leaf Knight R 3.00 5.00
ACN104 Messenger of the King U 2.00 3.50
ACN105 Portal in the Woods U 2.00 3.50
ACN106 Spirit Caller Elf C .75 2.00
ACN107 Spiritual Guidance U 2.00 3.50
ACN108 Tia Letoliel Archer Princess of Elves SR 6.00 10.00
ACN109 Tias White Falcon R 3.00 5.00
ACN110 Trap Master Lemuria R 3.00 5.00
ACN111 Tree Root Sprite C .75 2.00
ACN112 Wind Blade C .75 2.00
ACN113 Wind Ferryman C .75 2.00
ACN114 Winds of Vitality C .75 2.00
ACN115 Ahriman Malicious Eye in the Dark C .75 2.00
ACN116 Black Blood Knight U 2.00 3.50
ACN117 Bloodspray C .75 2.00
ACN118 Dark Elf of the Murky Grove C .75 2.00
ACN119 Dark Elf Sorcerer U 2.00 3.50
ACN120 Dark Elf Spy C .75 2.00
ACN121 Dark Night Butterfly C .75 2.00
ACN122 Dark Revolution R 3.00 5.00
ACN123 Dark Riding Hood SR 6.00 10.00
ACN124 Demonic Rabbit C .75 2.00
ACN125 Feast on Mortals C .75 2.00
ACN126 Frayla Ruler 15.00 20.00
ACN126 Frayla the Revolutionist Ruler 15.00 20.00
ACN127 Gate to Outer World U 2.00 3.50
ACN128 Hilda Fraylas Left Hand R 3.00 5.00
ACN129 Lethal Arrow C .75 2.00
ACN130 Moon in the Mist U 2.00 3.50
ACN131 Moonlight Shadow C .75 2.00
ACN132 Saffina Fraylas Right Hand R 3.00 5.00
ACN133 Shade Assassin U 2.00 3.50
ACN134 Stealth Demon U 2.00 3.50
ACN135 Sword of the New Moon C .75 2.00
ACN136 Tactics of the Dark Elves U 2.00 3.50
ACN137 The Three Evil Little Pigs U 2.00 3.50
ACN138 Transforming Vampire C .75 2.00
ACN139 Treasonous Guard C .75 2.00
ACN140 Truth Amongst Darkness U 2.00 3.50
ACN141 Vicious Wounded Beast C .75 2.00
ACN142 Vitality Drain SR .75 2.00
ACN143 Wolfs Rain R 3.00 5.00
ACN144 Idol of Magic C .75 2.00
ACN145 Idol of Vitality C .75 2.00
ACN146 Idol of Willpower C .75 2.00
ACN147 Statue in the Sacred Temple R 3.00 5.00
ACN148 Demonic Soulstone R 3.00 5.00
ACN149 Mysterious Magic Stone R 3.00 5.00
ACN150 Saintly Elven Stone R 3.00 5.00
ACN151 [Variant] Wing Rider Panda C .75 2.00
ACN152 [Variant] Stone Tongued Basilisk C .75 2.00
ACN153 [Variant] Giant Squid C .75 2.00
ACN154 [Variant] Faerurs Escort C .75 2.00
ACN155 [Variant] Vicious Wounded Beast C .75 2.00

2017 Force of Will Ancient Nights Uber Rare

ACN020 Pandora 100.00 150.00
ACN093 Faerur Letoliel 40.00 60.00
ACN126 Frayla 50.00 75.00
SDR1010 Taegrus Pearlshine 125.00 200.00
Taegrus Pearlshine Lord of the Mountain
SDR2009 Kirik Rerik 125.00 200.00
Kirik Rerik the Draconic Warrior
SDR3007 Shaela 15.00 25.00
SDR4004 Gill 125.00 200.00
Gill the Gifted Conjurer
SDR5009 Reiya Fourth Daughter of the Mikage 125.00 200.00

2017 Force of Will Advent of the Demon King

ADK001 A New Radiance C .15 .25
ADK002 Gem Blade Opal U .20 .35
ADK003 Gem Boat Alexandrite R .60 1.00
ADK004 Gem Jail U .20 .35
ADK005 Golden Bird C .15 .25
ADK006 Indomitable Spirit C .15 .25
ADK007 Ivy on the Floating Isle C .15 .25
ADK008 Jewel Cutter C .15 .25
ADK009 Jewel Golem R .60 1.00
ADK010 Jewel Shell C .15 .25
ADK011 Jeweler's Children C .15 .25
ADK012 Light Majin U .20 .35
ADK013 Magic Crest of Light C .15 .25
ADK014 Magic Warrior on the Floating Isle C .15 .25
ADK015 Master of the Sky U .20 .35
ADK016 Panda Pilot C .15 .25
ADK017 Ra, the Golden Bird SR 2.00 3.50
ADK018 Rainbow Shimmers SR 2.00 3.50
ADK019 Rallying Song of the Panda U .20 .35
ADK020 Rampaging Magic Warrior U .20 .35
ADK021 Rose Quartz, the Panda Queen R .60 1.00
ADK022 Sealing the Gates of Darkness U .15 .25
ADK023 Soothsayer Panda C .15 .25
ADK024 Taegrus Pearlshine Ruler .60 1.00
ADK024 Taegrus Pearlshine, Lord of the Mountain Ruler .60 1.00
ADK025 The Floating Isle U .20 .35
ADK026 Voyage to the Floating Isle R .60 1.00
ADK027 White Dog of Sasaru Palace C .15 .25
ADK028 White Dragonoid Child C .15 .25
ADK029 Wings of Gold R .60 1.00
ADK030 Burning Pteranodon U .20 .35
ADK031 Callous Blaze C .15 .25
ADK032 Corrupted Dragonoid R .60 1.00
ADK033 Cross Counter C .15 .25
ADK034 Devoted Squadron R .60 1.00
ADK035 Dragonoid Doctor C .15 .25
ADK036 Dragonoid Rogue C .15 .25
ADK037 Elixir, the Majin SR 2.00 3.50
ADK038 Elixir's Fighting Spirit R .60 1.00
ADK039 Evil Dragon, Hellblaze R .60 1.00
ADK040 Fast Food C .15 .25
ADK041 Ferocious Triceratops C .15 .25
ADK042 Fire Majin U .20 .35
ADK043 Fire Wave U .20 .35
ADK044 Fires of the Demon King C .15 .25
ADK045 Frayla, Servant of Demon Fire SR 2.00 3.50
ADK046 Frayla's Devotee C .15 .25
ADK047 Giant Enraged Ox U .20 .35
ADK048 Hoelle Chicken C .15 .25
ADK049 Magic Crest of Fire C .15 .25
ADK050 Magic Impact U .20 .35
ADK051 Majin Dark Elf U .20 .35
ADK052 Majin Madness C .15 .25
ADK053 Majin Subjugation R .60 1.00
ADK054 Panda Pugilist C .15 .25
ADK055 Play Dead U .20 .35
ADK056 Unstable Golem U .20 .35
ADK057 Velociraptor, Mountain Hunter C .15 .25
ADK058 Welser, the Archmage Ruler .60 1.00
ADK058 Welser, King of Demons Ruler .60 1.00
ADK059 Angler Panda C .15 .25
ADK060 Ayu, Lunar Swordswoman Ruler .60 1.00
ADK060 Ayu, Shaman Swordswoman Ruler .60 1.00
ADK061 Ayu's Pictorial Scroll U .20 .35
ADK062 Ayu's Special Power Medicine C .15 .25
ADK063 Ayu's Swordstrike U .20 .35
ADK064 Crier Mermaid C .15 .25
ADK065 Dinosaur Surfacing C .15 .25
ADK066 Diver Panda U .20 .35
ADK067 Duplication Mirror SR 2.00 3.50
ADK068 Flood C .15 .25
ADK069 Lethargy R .60 1.00
ADK070 Lowly Spirit Bug C .15 .25
ADK071 Magic Crest of Water C .15 .25
ADK072 Magic Warrior on the Coast C .15 .25
ADK073 Magical Wind Chime C .15 .25

ADK074 Mermaid Visionary C .15 .25
ADK075 Misty Dragon Spirit SR 2.00 3.50
ADK076 Mosasaurus R .60 1.00
ADK077 One and Only U .20 .35
ADK078 Optional Possession R .60 1.00
ADK079 Shaela's Return C .15 .25
ADK080 Sleepy Cat Spirit C .15 .25
ADK081 Soaring Falcon Spirit U .20 .35
ADK082 Swirling Mermaid U .20 .35
ADK083 Unexpected Visitor U .20 .35
ADK084 Valorous Tiger Spirit R .60 1.00
ADK085 Watchman on the Coast C .15 .25
ADK086 Water Majin U .20 .35
ADK087 Willful Samurai Spirit R .60 1.00
ADK088 Ciel, Sorcerous Priestess R .60 1.00
ADK089 Ciel's Familiar, Mikay C .15 .25
ADK090 Ciel's Wind Blast C .15 .25
ADK091 Destruction of the Portal U .20 .35
ADK092 Dispersal C .15 .25
ADK093 Elven Exorcist U .20 .35
ADK094 End of the Revolution R .60 1.00
ADK095 Envoy of the Dragon Priestess C .15 .25
ADK096 Faerur Letoliel, Rallying King R .60 1.00
ADK097 Gill Ruler .60 1.00
ADK097 Gill, the Gifted Conjurer Ruler .60 1.00
ADK098 Grieving Elf Spirit U .20 .35
ADK099 Insight C .15 .25
ADK100 Leaf Digger C .15 .25
ADK101 Leaf Garb C .15 .25
ADK102 Leaf Golem R .60 1.00
ADK103 Leaf Punisher U .20 .35
ADK104 Leaf Wing C .15 .25
ADK105 Magic Crest of Wind C .15 .25
ADK106 Otherworld Dreams U .20 .35
ADK107 Phase Shift U .20 .35
ADK108 Portal Magus C .15 .25
ADK109 Ryula, the Dragon Priestess SR 2.00 3.50
ADK110 The Eternal Tower U .15 .25
ADK111 Tower Guardian C .20 .35
ADK112 Travelling Panda C .15 .25
ADK113 True Blade of Spirits C .15 .25
ADK114 Ultra-Awakening R .60 1.00
ADK115 Viola, the Dragon Priestess SR 2.00 3.50
ADK116 Wind Majin U .20 .35
ADK117 Advent of the Demon King U .20 .35
ADK118 Annihilation Beetle C .15 .25
ADK119 Beelzebub, Lord of the Flies SR 2.00 3.50
ADK120 Blood Ritual C .15 .25
ADK121 Bloodsucker Dragon U .20 .35
ADK122 Ceaseless Devotion C .15 .25
ADK123 Command of Life and Death C .15 .25
ADK124 Corrupted Knight C .15 .25
ADK125 Corrupted Panda C .15 .25
ADK126 Dance in the Moonlight R .60 1.00
ADK127 Dark Blade's Harvest C .15 .25
ADK128 Dark Elf Fugitive U .20 .35
ADK129 Darkness Majin U .20 .35
ADK130 Deadly Housefly C .15 .25
ADK131 Digestion U .20 .35
ADK132 Faith in the Darkness R .60 1.00
ADK133 Faithful Vampire U .20 .35
ADK134 Hilda and Saffina R .60 1.00
ADK135 Jeanne d'Arc, Mad Maiden SR 2.00 3.50
ADK136 Jet, Ambitious Panda R .60 1.00
ADK137 Magic Crest of Darkness C .15 .25
ADK138 Magic Majin Warrior C .15 .25
ADK139 Rapunzel R .60 1.00
ADK140 Reiya, Fourth Daughter of the Mikage Ruler .60 1.00
ADK140 Reiya, Fourth Daughter of the Mikage J Ruler .60 1.00
ADK141 Sonic Bat C .15 .25
ADK142 Spawn of Beelzebub U .20 .35
ADK143 Spider's Web U .20 .35
ADK144 The Welser Copy C .15 .25
ADK145 Vampire Bard C .15 .25
ADK146 Angel Statue of the Tower C .15 .25
ADK147 Crystal on the Floating Isle C .15 .25
ADK148 Shattered Golem C .15 .25
ADK149 Majin Stone R .60 1.00
ADK150 Possession Stone R .60 1.00
ADK151 Variant White Dragonoid Child C .15 .25
ADK152 Variant Ferocious Triceratops C .15 .25
ADK153 Variant Crier Mermaid C .15 .25
ADK154 Variant Tower Guardian C .15 .25
ADK155 Variant Sonic Bat C .15 .25
ADK156 Darkness Magic Stone NR .60 1.00
ADK157 Fire Magic Stone NR .60 1.00
ADK158 Light Magic Stone NR .60 1.00
ADK159 Water Magic Stone NR .60 1.00
ADK160 Wind Magic Stone NR .60 1.00
ADK161 Treasure Hunter Fierica NR .60 1.00
ADK161 Treasure Hunter Fierica J NR .60 1.00
ADK162 Martial Artist Pialle Eille NR .60 1.00
ADK162 Martial Artist Pialle Eille J NR .60 1.00
ADK163 Mephina, Mermaid Shaman NR .60 1.00
ADK163 Mephina, Mermaid Shaman J NR .60 1.00
ADK164 Leaf Elder NR .60 1.00
ADK164 Leaf Elder J NR .60 1.00
ADK165 Bloodsucking Butler NR .60 1.00
ADK165 Bloodsucking Butler J NR .60 1.00

2017 Force of Will Advent of the Demon King Foil

ADK001 A New Radiance C .30 .50
ADK002 Gem Blade Opal U .60 1.00
ADK003 Gem Boat Alexandrite R 1.25 2.00
ADK004 Gem Jail U .60 1.00
ADK005 Golden Bird C .30 .50
ADK006 Indomitable Spirit C .30 .50
ADK007 Ivy on the Floating Isle C .30 .50
ADK008 Jewel Cutter C .30 .50
ADK009 Jewel Golem R 1.25 2.00
ADK010 Jewel Shell C .30 .50
ADK011 Jeweler's Children C .30 .50
ADK012 Light Majin U .60 1.00
ADK013 Magic Crest of Light C .30 .50
ADK014 Magic Warrior on the Floating Isle C .30 .50
ADK015 Master of the Sky U .60 1.00
ADK016 Panda Pilot C .30 .50
ADK017 Ra, the Golden Bird SR 4.00 6.00
ADK018 Rainbow Shimmers SR 4.00 6.00
ADK019 Rallying Song of the Panda U .60 1.00
ADK020 Rampaging Magic Warrior U .60 1.00
ADK021 Rose Quartz, the Panda Queen R 1.25 2.00
ADK022 Sealing the Gates of Darkness U .30 .50
ADK023 Soothsayer Panda C .30 .50
ADK024 Taegrus Pearlshine Ruler 1.25 2.00
ADK024 Taegrus Pearlshine, Lord of the Mountain Ruler 1.25 2.00
ADK025 The Floating Isle U .60 1.00
ADK026 Voyage to the Floating Isle R 1.25 2.00
ADK027 White Dog of Sasaru Palace C .30 .50
ADK028 White Dragonoid Child C .30 .50
ADK029 Wings of Gold R 1.25 2.00
ADK030 Burning Pteranodon U .60 1.00
ADK031 Callous Blaze C .30 .50
ADK032 Corrupted Dragonoid R 1.25 2.00
ADK033 Cross Counter C .30 .50
ADK034 Devoted Squadron R 1.25 2.00
ADK035 Dragonoid Doctor C .30 .50
ADK036 Dragonoid Rogue C .30 .50
ADK037 Elixir, the Majin SR 4.00 6.00
ADK038 Elixir's Fighting Spirit R 1.25 2.00
ADK039 Evil Dragon, Hellblaze R 1.25 2.00
ADK040 Fast Food C .30 .50
ADK041 Ferocious Triceratops C .30 .50
ADK042 Fire Majin U .60 1.00
ADK043 Fire Wave U .60 1.00
ADK044 Fires of the Demon King C .30 .50
ADK045 Frayla, Servant of Demon Fire SR 4.00 6.00
ADK046 Frayla's Devotee C .30 .50
ADK047 Giant Enraged Ox U .60 1.00
ADK048 Hoelle Chicken C .30 .50
ADK049 Magic Crest of Fire C .30 .50
ADK050 Magic Impact U .60 1.00
ADK051 Majin Dark Elf U .60 1.00
ADK052 Majin Madness C .30 .50
ADK053 Majin Subjugation R 1.25 2.00
ADK054 Panda Pugilist C .30 .50
ADK055 Play Dead U .60 1.00
ADK056 Unstable Golem U .60 1.00
ADK057 Velociraptor, Mountain Hunter C .30 .50
ADK058 Welser, the Archmage Ruler 1.25 2.00
ADK058 Welser, King of Demons Ruler 1.25 2.00
ADK059 Angler Panda C .30 .50
ADK060 Ayu, Lunar Swordswoman Ruler 1.25 2.00
ADK060 Ayu, Shaman Swordswoman Ruler 1.25 2.00
ADK061 Ayu's Pictorial Scroll U .60 1.00
ADK062 Ayu's Special Power Medicine C .30 .50
ADK063 Ayu's Swordstrike U .60 1.00
ADK064 Crier Mermaid C .30 .50
ADK065 Dinosaur Surfacing C .30 .50
ADK066 Diver Panda U .60 1.00
ADK067 Duplication Mirror SR 4.00 6.00
ADK068 Flood C .30 .50
ADK069 Lethargy R 1.25 2.00
ADK070 Lowly Spirit Bug C .30 .50
ADK071 Magic Crest of Water C .30 .50
ADK072 Magic Warrior on the Coast C .30 .50
ADK073 Magical Wind Chime C .30 .50
ADK074 Mermaid Visionary C .30 .50
ADK075 Misty Dragon Spirit SR 4.00 6.00
ADK076 Mosasaurus R 1.25 2.00
ADK077 One and Only U .60 1.00
ADK078 Optional Possession R 1.25 2.00
ADK079 Shaela's Return C .30 .50
ADK080 Sleepy Cat Spirit C .30 .50
ADK081 Soaring Falcon Spirit U .60 1.00
ADK082 Swirling Mermaid U .60 1.00
ADK083 Unexpected Visitor U .60 1.00
ADK084 Valorous Tiger Spirit R 1.25 2.00
ADK085 Watchman on the Coast C .30 .50
ADK086 Water Majin U .60 1.00
ADK087 Willful Samurai Spirit R 1.25 2.00
ADK088 Ciel, Sorcerous Priestess R 1.25 2.00
ADK089 Ciel's Familiar, Mikay C .30 .50
ADK090 Ciel's Wind Blast C .30 .50
ADK091 Destruction of the Portal U .60 1.00
ADK092 Dispersal C .30 .50
ADK093 Elven Exorcist U .60 1.00
ADK094 End of the Revolution R 1.25 2.00
ADK095 Envoy of the Dragon Priestess C .30 .50
ADK096 Faerur Letoliel, Rallying King R 1.25 2.00
ADK097 Gill Ruler 1.25 2.00
ADK097 Gill, the Gifted Conjurer Ruler 1.25 2.00
ADK098 Grieving Elf Spirit U .60 1.00
ADK099 Insight C .30 .50
ADK100 Leaf Digger C .30 .50
ADK101 Leaf Garb C .30 .50
ADK102 Leaf Golem R 1.25 2.00
ADK103 Leaf Punisher U .60 1.00
ADK104 Leaf Wing C .30 .50
ADK105 Magic Crest of Wind C .30 .50
ADK106 Otherworld Dreams U .60 1.00
ADK107 Phase Shift U .60 1.00
ADK108 Portal Magus C .30 .50
ADK109 Ryula, the Dragon Priestess SR 4.00 6.00
ADK110 The Eternal Tower U .60 1.00
ADK111 Tower Guardian C .30 .50
ADK112 Travelling Panda C .30 .50
ADK113 True Blade of Spirits C .30 .50
ADK114 Ultra-Awakening R 1.25 2.00
ADK115 Viola, the Dragon Priestess SR 4.00 6.00
ADK116 Wind Majin U .60 1.00
ADK117 Advent of the Demon King U .60 1.00
ADK118 Annihilation Beetle C .30 .50
ADK119 Beelzebub, Lord of the Flies SR 4.00 6.00
ADK120 Blood Ritual C .30 .50
ADK121 Bloodsucker Dragon U .60 1.00
ADK122 Ceaseless Devotion C .30 .50
ADK123 Command of Life and Death C .30 .50
ADK124 Corrupted Knight C .30 .50
ADK125 Corrupted Panda C .30 .50
ADK126 Dance in the Moonlight R 1.25 2.00
ADK127 Dark Blade's Harvest C .30 .50
ADK128 Dark Elf Fugitive U .60 1.00
ADK129 Darkness Majin U .60 1.00
ADK130 Deadly Housefly C .30 .50
ADK131 Digestion U .60 1.00
ADK132 Faith in the Darkness R 1.25 2.00
ADK133 Faithful Vampire U .60 1.00
ADK134 Hilda and Saffina R 1.25 2.00
ADK135 Jeanne d'Arc, Mad Maiden SR 4.00 6.00
ADK136 Jet, Ambitious Panda R 1.25 2.00
ADK137 Magic Crest of Darkness C .30 .50
ADK138 Magic Majin Warrior C .30 .50
ADK139 Rapunzel R 1.25 2.00
ADK140 Reiya, Fourth Daughter of the Mikage Ruler 1.25 2.00
ADK140 Reiya, Fourth Daughter of the Mikage J Ruler 1.25 2.00
ADK141 Sonic Bat C .30 .50
ADK142 Spawn of Beelzebub U .60 1.00
ADK143 Spider's Web U .60 1.00
ADK144 The Welser Copy C .30 .50
ADK145 Vampire Bard C .30 .50
ADK146 Angel Statue of the Tower C .30 .50
ADK147 Crystal on the Floating Isle C .30 .50
ADK148 Shattered Golem C .30 .50
ADK149 Majin Stone R 1.25 2.00
ADK150 Possession Stone R 1.25 2.00
ADK151 Variant White Dragonoid Child C .30 .50
ADK152 Variant Ferocious Triceratops C .30 .50
ADK153 Variant Crier Mermaid C .30 .50
ADK154 Variant Tower Guardian C .30 .50
ADK155 Variant Sonic Bat C .30 .50
ADK156 Darkness Magic Stone NR 1.25 2.00
ADK157 Fire Magic Stone NR 1.25 2.00
ADK158 Light Magic Stone NR 1.25 2.00
ADK159 Water Magic Stone NR 1.25 2.00
ADK160 Wind Magic Stone NR 1.25 2.00
ADK161 Treasure Hunter Fierica NR 1.25 2.00
ADK161 Treasure Hunter Fierica J NR 1.25 2.00
ADK162 Martial Artist Pialle Eille NR 1.25 2.00
ADK162 Martial Artist Pialle Eille J NR 1.25 2.00
ADK163 Mephina, Mermaid Shaman NR 1.25 2.00
ADK163 Mephina, Mermaid Shaman J NR 1.25 2.00
ADK164 Leaf Elder NR 1.25 2.00
ADK164 Leaf Elder J NR 1.25 2.00
ADK165 Bloodsucking Butler NR 1.25 2.00
ADK165 Bloodsucking Butler J NR 1.25 2.00

2017 Force of Will Advent of the Demon King Full Art

ADK001 A New Radiance C .60 1.00
ADK002 Gem Blade Opal U .75 1.25
ADK003 Gem Boat Alexandrite R 4.00 6.00
ADK004 Gem Jail U .75 1.25
ADK005 Golden Bird C .60 1.00
ADK006 Indomitable Spirit C .60 1.00
ADK007 Ivy on the Floating Isle C .60 1.00
ADK008 Jewel Cutter C .60 1.00
ADK009 Jewel Golem R 4.00 6.00
ADK010 Jewel Shell C .60 1.00
ADK011 Jeweler's Children C .60 1.00
ADK012 Light Majin U .75 1.25
ADK013 Magic Crest of Light C .60 1.00
ADK014 Magic Warrior on the Floating Isle C .60 1.00
ADK015 Master of the Sky U .75 1.25
ADK016 Panda Pilot C .60 1.00
ADK017 Ra, the Golden Bird SR 7.00 10.00
ADK018 Rainbow Shimmers SR 7.00 10.00
ADK019 Rallying Song of the Panda U .75 1.25
ADK020 Rampaging Magic Warrior U .75 1.25
ADK021 Rose Quartz, the Panda Queen R 4.00 6.00
ADK022 Sealing the Gates of Darkness U .60 1.00
ADK023 Soothsayer Panda C .60 1.00
ADK024 Taegrus Pearlshine Ruler 4.00 6.00
ADK024 Taegrus Pearlshine, Lord of the Mountain Ruler 4.00 6.00
ADK025 The Floating Isle U .75 1.25
ADK026 Voyage to the Floating Isle R 4.00 6.00
ADK027 White Dog of Sasaru Palace C .60 1.00
ADK028 White Dragonoid Child C .60 1.00
ADK029 Wings of Gold R 4.00 6.00
ADK030 Burning Pteranodon U .75 1.25
ADK031 Callous Blaze C .60 1.00
ADK032 Corrupted Dragonoid R 4.00 6.00
ADK033 Cross Counter C .60 1.00
ADK034 Devoted Squadron R 4.00 6.00
ADK035 Dragonoid Doctor C .60 1.00
ADK036 Dragonoid Rogue C .60 1.00
ADK037 Elixir, the Majin SR 7.00 10.00
ADK038 Elixir's Fighting Spirit R 4.00 6.00
ADK039 Evil Dragon, Hellblaze R 4.00 6.00
ADK040 Fast Food C .60 1.00
ADK041 Ferocious Triceratops C .60 1.00
ADK042 Fire Majin U .75 1.25
ADK043 Fire Wave U .75 1.25
ADK044 Fires of the Demon King C .60 1.00
ADK045 Frayla, Servant of Demon Fire SR 7.00 10.00
ADK046 Frayla's Devotee C .60 1.00
ADK047 Giant Enraged Ox U .75 1.25
ADK048 Hoelle Chicken C .60 1.00
ADK049 Magic Crest of Fire C .60 1.00
ADK050 Magic Impact U .75 1.25
ADK051 Majin Dark Elf U .75 1.25
ADK052 Majin Madness C .60 1.00
ADK053 Majin Subjugation R 4.00 6.00
ADK054 Panda Pugilist C .60 1.00
ADK055 Play Dead U .75 1.25
ADK056 Unstable Golem U .75 1.25
ADK057 Velociraptor, Mountain Hunter C .60 1.00
ADK058 Welser, the Archmage Ruler 4.00 6.00
ADK058 Welser, King of Demons Ruler 4.00 6.00
ADK059 Angler Panda C .60 1.00
ADK060 Ayu, Lunar Swordswoman Ruler 4.00 6.00
ADK060 Ayu, Shaman Swordswoman Ruler 4.00 6.00
ADK061 Ayu's Pictorial Scroll U .75 1.25
ADK062 Ayu's Special Power Medicine C .60 1.00
ADK063 Ayu's Swordstrike U .75 1.25
ADK064 Crier Mermaid C .60 1.00
ADK065 Dinosaur Surfacing C .60 1.00
ADK066 Diver Panda U .75 1.25
ADK067 Duplication Mirror SR 7.00 10.00
ADK068 Flood C .60 1.00
ADK069 Lethargy R 4.00 6.00
ADK070 Lowly Spirit Bug C .60 1.00
ADK071 Magic Crest of Water C .60 1.00
ADK072 Magic Warrior on the Coast C .60 1.00
ADK073 Magical Wind Chime C .60 1.00
ADK074 Mermaid Visionary C .60 1.00
ADK075 Misty Dragon Spirit SR 7.00 10.00
ADK076 Mosasaurus R 4.00 6.00
ADK077 One and Only U .75 1.25
ADK078 Optional Possession R 4.00 6.00
ADK079 Shaela's Return C .60 1.00
ADK080 Sleepy Cat Spirit C .60 1.00
ADK081 Soaring Falcon Spirit U .75 1.25
ADK082 Swirling Mermaid U .75 1.25

ADK083 Unexpected Visitor U	.75	1.25
ADK084 Valorous Tiger Spirit R	4.00	6.00
ADK085 Watchman on the Coast C	.60	1.00
ADK086 Water Majin U	.75	1.25
ADK087 Willful Samurai Spirit R	4.00	6.00
ADK088 Ciel, Sorcerous Priestess R	4.00	6.00
ADK089 Ciel's Familiar, Mikay C	.60	1.00
ADK090 Ciel's Wind Blast C	.60	1.00
ADK091 Destruction of the Portal U	.75	1.25
ADK092 Dispersal C	.60	1.00
ADK093 Elven Exorcist U	.75	1.25
ADK094 End of the Revolution R	4.00	6.00
ADK095 Envoy of the Dragon Priestess C	.60	1.00
ADK096 Faerur Letoliel, Rallying King R	4.00	6.00
ADK097 Gill Ruler	4.00	6.00
ADK097 Gill, the Gifted Conjurer Ruler	4.00	6.00
ADK098 Grieving Elf Spirit U	.75	1.25
ADK099 Insight C	.60	1.00
ADK100 Leaf Digger C	.60	1.00
ADK101 Leaf Garb C	.60	1.00
ADK102 Leaf Golem R	4.00	6.00
ADK103 Leaf Punisher U	.75	1.25
ADK104 Leaf Wing C	.60	1.00
ADK105 Magic Crest of Wind C	.60	1.00
ADK106 Otherworld Dreams U	.75	1.25
ADK107 Phase Shift U	.75	1.25
ADK108 Portal Magus C	.60	1.00
ADK109 Ryula, the Dragon Priestess SR	7.00	10.00
ADK110 The Eternal Tower U	.75	1.25
ADK111 Tower Guardian C	.60	1.00
ADK112 Travelling Panda C	.60	1.00
ADK113 True Blade of Spirits C	.60	1.00
ADK114 Ultra-Awakening R	4.00	6.00
ADK115 Viola, the Dragon Priestess SR	7.00	10.00
ADK116 Wind Majin U	.75	1.25
ADK117 Advent of the Demon King U	.75	1.25
ADK118 Annihilation Beetle C	.60	1.00
ADK119 Beelzebub, Lord of the Flies SR	7.00	10.00
ADK120 Blood Ritual C	.60	1.00
ADK121 Bloodsucker Dragon U	.75	1.25
ADK122 Ceaseless Devotion C	.60	1.00
ADK123 Command of Life and Death C	.60	1.00
ADK124 Corrupted Knight C	.60	1.00
ADK125 Corrupted Panda C	.60	1.00
ADK126 Dance in the Moonlight R	4.00	6.00
ADK127 Dark Blade's Harvest C	.60	1.00
ADK128 Dark Elf Fugitive U	.75	1.25
ADK129 Darkness Majin U	.75	1.25
ADK130 Deadly Housefly C	.60	1.00
ADK131 Digestion U	.75	1.25
ADK132 Faith in the Darkness R	4.00	6.00
ADK133 Faithful Vampire U	.75	1.25
ADK134 Hilda and Saffina R	4.00	6.00
ADK135 Jeanne d'Arc, Mad Maiden SR	7.00	10.00
ADK136 Jet, Ambitious Panda R	4.00	6.00
ADK137 Magic Crest of Darkness C	.60	1.00
ADK138 Magic Majin Warrior C	.60	1.00
ADK139 Rapunzel R	4.00	6.00
ADK140 Reiya, Fourth Daughter of the Mikage Ruler	4.00	6.00
ADK140 Reiya, Fourth Daughter of the Mikage J Ruler	4.00	6.00
ADK141 Sonic Bat C	.60	1.00
ADK142 Spawn of Beelzebub U	.75	1.25
ADK143 Spider's Web U	.75	1.25
ADK144 The Welser Copy C	.60	1.00
ADK145 Vampire Bard C	.60	1.00
ADK146 Angel Statue of the Tower C	.60	1.00
ADK147 Crystal on the Floating Isle C	.60	1.00
ADK148 Shattered Golem C	.60	1.00
ADK149 Majin Stone R	4.00	6.00
ADK150 Possession Stone R	4.00	6.00
ADK151 Variant White Dragonoid Child C	.60	1.00
ADK152 Variant Ferocious Triceratops C	.60	1.00
ADK153 Variant Crier Mermaid C	.60	1.00
ADK154 Variant Tower Guardian C	.60	1.00
ADK155 Variant Sonic Bat C	.60	1.00
ADK156 Darkness Magic Stone NR	4.00	6.00
ADK157 Fire Magic Stone NR	4.00	6.00
ADK158 Light Magic Stone NR	4.00	6.00
ADK159 Water Magic Stone NR	4.00	6.00
ADK160 Wind Magic Stone NR	4.00	6.00
ADK161 Treasure Hunter Fierica NR	4.00	6.00
ADK161 Treasure Hunter Fierica J NR	4.00	6.00
ADK162 Martial Artist Pialle Eille NR	4.00	6.00
ADK162 Martial Artist Pialle Eille J NR	4.00	6.00
ADK163 Mephina, Mermaid Shaman NR	4.00	6.00
ADK163 Mephina, Mermaid Shaman J NR	4.00	6.00
ADK164 Leaf Elder NR	4.00	6.00
ADK164 Leaf Elder J NR	4.00	6.00
ADK165 Bloodsucking Butler NR	4.00	6.00
ADK165 Bloodsucking Butler J NR	4.00	6.00

2017 Force of Will Advent of the Demon King Uber Rare

ADK024 Teagrus Pearlshine	40.00	60.00
Taegrus Pearlshine, Lord of the Mountain		
ADK058 Welser, the Archmage	100.00	150.00
Welser, King of Demons		
ADK060 Ayu, Lunar Swordswoman	200.00	300.00
Ayu, Shaman Swordswoman		
ADK097 Gil	40.00	60.00
Gill, the Gifted Conjurer		
ADK140 Reiya, Fourth Daughter of the Mikage	50.00	75.00

2018 Force of Will The Time Spinning Witch

RELEASED ON

TSW001 Aimul's Unicorn/Aimul's Twisted Beast C	.12	.20
TSW002 Angel of Hope/Angel of Despair U	.15	.25
TSW003 Dr. Jekyll/Ms. Hyde R	.20	.30
TSW004 Escaped Jeweler C	.12	.20
TSW005 False Peace/Deadly Pox C	.12	.20
TSW006 Fierica, Honorable Thief R	.20	.30
TSW007 Fierica's Expedition U	.15	.25
TSW008 Flourishing Hope/Burgeoning Despair R	5.00	8.00
TSW009 Gem Hammer Panda C	.12	.20
TSW010 Gem Mallet Panda R	2.50	4.00
TSW011 Jewel Aura C	.12	.20
TSW012 Jewel Step U	.15	.25
TSW013 Karmic Retribution U	.15	.25
TSW014 Knight of Hope/Knight of Despair C	.12	.20
TSW015 Light Castle, Palace of Hope/Dark Castle, Palace of Despair U	.15	.25
TSW016 Life Stealing Altar/Soul Returning Altar C	.12	.20
TSW017 Magic Transforming Warrior C	.12	.20
TSW018 Mephistopheles/Mephistopheles I SR	1.25	2.00
TSW019 Miscalculation C	.12	.20
TSW020 Panda Medium/Possessed Panda U	.15	.25
TSW021 Panda Performer C	.12	.20
TSW022 Princess of Fleeting Hope/Aimul, Princess of Despair RULER R	50.00	75.00
TSW023 Relief Aid C	.12	.20
TSW024 Sacred Knight of Atonement/Dark Knight of Conviction C	.12	.20
TSW025 Separation of Fates R	1.25	2.00
TSW026 The Jewel Princess U	.15	.25
TSW027 Treasure Knight Panda U	.15	.25
TSW028 White Sacred Beast C	.12	.20
TSW029 Ancient Impact R	.20	.30
TSW030 Apprentice Martial Artist C	.12	.20
TSW031 Combat Loving Dragonoid C	.12	.20
TSW032 Dino Calling Demon U	.15	.25
TSW033 Dino-Rider R	.20	.30
TSW034 Domesticated Dragon C	.12	.20
TSW035 Dragon Aura U	.15	.25
TSW036 Ferocious Attack C	.12	.20
TSW037 Fictitious Fire C	.12	.20
TSW038 Flame Claw Saber Tooth C	.12	.20
TSW039 Flying Dragon of Mt. Hoelle C	.12	.20
TSW040 Heaven Sundering Dragon Palm R	2.00	3.00
TSW041 Hero's Bracelet U	.15	.25
TSW042 Hoelle's Martial Arts Tournament U	.15	.25
TSW043 Hollow Flame Shadow C	.12	.20
TSW044 Home of the Ultra Dragon R	.20	.30
TSW045 Kirik Rerik/Kirik Rerik, the Draconic Warrir RULER R	5.00	8.00
TSW046 Mad Scarlasodon C	.12	.20
TSW047 Martial Arts Competitor U	.15	.25
TSW048 Pialle Eille, the Flaming Fist SR	.75	1.25
TSW049 Piggy, Hoelle's Great Hero Pig R	2.00	3.00
TSW050 Piggy's Child U	.15	.25
TSW051 Red Fang Allosaurus U	.15	.25
TSW052 Scarlet's Vision C	.12	.20
TSW053 Selection C	.12	.20
TSW054 Spirit of Mt. Hoelle C	.12	.20
TSW055 Twin Dragon Claw C	.12	.20
TSW056 Ultra Dragon Flame Sphere U	.15	.25
TSW057 Ultra Dragon, Shooting Star SR	1.50	2.50
TSW058 Biri-Biri Ball C	.12	.20
TSW059 Dr. Mermaid C	.12	.20
TSW060 Giant Rabbit C	.12	.20
TSW061 Giga Thunderfish SR	.30	.50
TSW062 Keez Corkscrew R	.20	.30
TSW063 Keez, the Electric Dolphin R	.20	.30
TSW064 Lightning Cave R	5.00	8.00
TSW065 Lightning Dragon U	.15	.25
TSW066 Lightning Phantom C	.12	.20
TSW067 Lightning Shield C	.12	.20
TSW068 Lonely Moon Wererabbit C	.12	.20
TSW069 Lunar Prophet U	.15	.25
TSW070 Magic Electric Warrior U	.15	.25
TSW071 Mephina, Thunder Cloud Wizard R	.20	.30
TSW072 Mermaid Researcher C	.12	.20
TSW073 Raijuu U	.15	.25
TSW074 Rebellious Soul, Ayu SR	.30	.50
TSW075 Sea Serpent C	.12	.20
TSW076 Shaela/Shaela, the Mermaid Princess RULER R	10.00	15.00
TSW077 Shaela's Adventure C	.12	.20
TSW078 Shaela's Battle U	.15	.25
TSW079 Silent Mermaid U	.15	.25
TSW080 Small Whale C	.12	.20
TSW081 Soaked Panda C	.12	.20
TSW082 Thunder Call C	.12	.20
TSW083 Thunder Wave U	.15	.25
TSW084 Thunderstorm R	.20	.30
TSW085 Treachery U	.15	.25
TSW086 Witch's Shadow C	.12	.20
TSW087 Approaching the Truth C	.12	.20
TSW088 Cleaning Doll C	.12	.20
TSW089 Doll Audience C	.12	.20
TSW090 Enormous Effigy C	.12	.20
TSW091 Evil Djinni U	.15	.25
TSW092 Intervention of Reality C	.12	.20
TSW093 Last Days of a Powerless Dragonoid U	.15	.25
TSW094 Laurite, Seven Luminaries Astrologian SR	6.00	10.00
TSW095 Laurite's Deletion Magic U	.15	.25
TSW096 Laurite's Wind C	.12	.20
TSW097 Leaf Guardsman C	.12	.20
TSW098 Leaf Reflector C	.12	.20
TSW099 Leaf Steward U	.15	.25
TSW100 Null Page R	.30	.50
TSW101 Patrolling Guard Doll U	.15	.25
TSW102 Puppet Maker U	.15	.25
TSW103 Rachel, the Ancient Library Researcher R	1.50	2.50
TSW104 Scarlet's Agony R	3.00	5.00
TSW105 Scheherazade's Marionette C	.12	.20
TSW106 Secluded Village Elf C	.12	.20
TSW107 Shifting Minstrel C	.12	.20
TSW108 Small Flatterer C	.12	.20
TSW109 Speaker of Eternal Night/Scheherazade of the Catastrophic Nights RULER R	6.00	10.00
TSW110 Story Listener, Eva R	.20	.30
TSW111 Story Speaker, Eve R	.20	.30
TSW112 The Ancient Library U	.15	.25
TSW113 The Mighty Leaf Elder R	.20	.30
TSW114 The Puppet's Last Days C	.12	.20
TSW115 Unanswered Mermaid Prayers U	.15	.25
TSW116 Black Fang Tyrannosaurus U	.15	.25
TSW117 Black Star, Blazer Thieves Gang Leader U	.15	.25
TSW118 Black Tears C	.12	.20
TSW119 Black Wing Dinosaur C	.12	.20
TSW120 Blazer Thieves Gang Underling C	.12	.20
TSW121 Bloodsucking Butler, Reiya's Attendant R	.30	.50
TSW122 Crumbling Majin C	.12	.20
TSW123 Dark Elf Gravekeeper U	.15	.25
TSW124 Dark Impact R	.25	.40
TSW125 Dark Riding Hood, Messenger of Truth/Red Riding Hood, Recovered Hope R	.75	1.25
TSW126 Disaster at Sasaru Palace U	.15	.25
TSW127 Embrace of Darkness C	.12	.20
TSW128 Evil Elemental Uprising U	.15	.25
TSW129 Final Words U	.15	.25
TSW130 Grimm of the Crimson Moon/Grimm, Hope from the Future SR	1.25	2.00
TSW131 Heavenly Fruit R	.75	1.25
TSW132 Kurosaurus C	.12	.20
TSW133 Lily, the Last Flower R	.20	.30
TSW134 Lily's Protector C	.12	.20
TSW135 Look of Despair C	.12	.20
TSW136 Lurker in the Null R	.20	.30
TSW137 Null Illusion U	.15	.25
TSW138 Refuse Collector C	.12	.20
TSW139 Revival of the Clan C	.12	.20
TSW140 Soul Concentration C	.12	.20
TSW141 Stagehand Doll C	.12	.20
TSW142 The Dusk Girl/Scarlet, the Crimson Beast RULER R	20.00	30.00
TSW143 Thought Control U	.15	.25
TSW144 Voidosaurus C	.12	.20
TSW145 Null Darkness SR	1.00	1.50
TSW146 Ruined Story SR	2.00	3.00
TSW147 Twin Blades of Hope and Despair/Sword of Fate SR	1.25	2.00
TSW148 Magic Stone of Hope/Magic Stone of Despair R	6.00	10.00
TSW149 Null Magic Stone R	.20	.30
TSW150 Speaking Stone R	5.00	8.00
TSW151 White Sacred Beast C VAR	.12	.20
TSW152 Mad Scarlasodon C VAR	.12	.20
TSW153 Small Whale C VAR	.12	.20
TSW154 Enormous Effigy C VAR	.12	.20
TSW155 Voidosaurus C VAR	.12	.20

2018 Force of Will Winds of the Ominous Moon

RELEASED ON JUNE 8, 2018

WOM001 A Mother's Love U	.15	.25
WOM002 Alexandrite's Crash U	.15	.25
WOM003 Arrival of the Hero R	3.00	5.00
WOM004 Atom Seikhart, the Envoy of Valhalla SR	.40	.60
WOM005 Aura of Hope C	.12	.20
WOM006 Beast of Light U	.15	.25
WOM007 Gem Blade Amethyst U	.15	.25
WOM008 Grimmia's Fairy C	.12	.20
WOM009 Holy Prince's Nanny, Citrin R	.20	.30
WOM010 Honorable Thief Guild Member C	.12	.20
WOM011 Isolate C	.12	.20
WOM012 Jewel Illusion C	.12	.20
WOM013 Naughty Child's Chastising U	.15	.25
WOM014 Panda Carpenter U	.15	.25
WOM015 Power Gem Warrior C	.12	.20
WOM016 Resuscitating Will R	.20	.30
WOM017 Technique Gem Warrior C	.12	.20
WOM018 The Second Advent of Hope, Grimmia R	.20	.30
WOM019 White Leaf C	.12	.20
WOM020 Xiang Xiang, the Holy Prince SR	.30	.50
WOM021 Xiang Xiang's Bodyguard C	.12	.20
WOM022 Burnt Cooking C	.12	.20
WOM023 Dragon Hunter U	.15	.25
WOM024 Dread Touch C	.12	.20
WOM025 Earthquake Observer C	.12	.20
WOM026 Eruption U	.15	.25
WOM027 Fire Bow Elf C	.12	.20
WOM028 Firebird C	.12	.20
WOM029 Ground and Air Supremacy U	.15	.25
WOM030 Hoelle Pig Squadron R	1.25	2.00
WOM031 Kaiser Phoenix SR	.30	.50
WOM032 Lava Majin U	.15	.25
WOM033 Mt. Hoelle Bodyguard Squad C	.12	.20
WOM034 Pialle's Cook, Sylvia R	.20	.30
WOM035 Power Spike C	.12	.20
WOM036 Prismatic Flame R	.20	.30
WOM037 Red Leaf C	.12	.20
WOM038 Reunion between the Master and Pupil R	.20	.30
WOM039 Scarlet's Testament U	.15	.25
WOM040 Sprinting Time Horse C	.12	.20
WOM041 The Three Sisters of Time U	.15	.25
WOM042 Welser, the Archmage of Fire SR	1.25	2.00
WOM043 Analyst of the Ocean Floor, Alisaris R	.20	.30
WOM044 Blue Leaf C	.12	.20
WOM045 Drifting Little Moon R	.50	.75
WOM046 Lightning Speed Crash C	.12	.20
WOM047 Lightning Waterfowl U	.15	.25
WOM048 Magic Soldier of Time C	.12	.20
WOM049 Meditation U	.15	.25
WOM050 Praying Mermaid C	.12	.20
WOM051 Roar of the Soul R	.20	.30
WOM052 Spirit of Time U	.15	.25
WOM053 The Distortion of Time SR	1.25	2.00
WOM054 The Dragon Lord's Breath C	.12	.20
WOM055 The End of Possession U	.15	.25
WOM056 The Last Thunder R	.30	.50
WOM057 The Time Spinning Witch RULER R	10.00	15.00
WOM058 The Witch's Minion C	.12	.20
WOM059 Time Bound Spirit C	.12	.20
WOM060 Time Dilation U	.15	.25
WOM061 Unyielding Dragon Lord, Ragnarok SR	.30	.50
WOM062 Wererabbit of the Null Moon U	.15	.25
WOM063 Wings of Ragnarok C	.12	.20
WOM064 Witch's Lament C	.12	.20
WOM065 Cecil and Tia R	.30	.50
WOM066 Ciel, Ancestor of the Priestess RULER R	3.00	5.00
WOM067 Fairy of the Holy Tree C	.12	.20
WOM068 Fifth Element C	.12	.20
WOM069 Herbivorous Beast, Silomosaurus C	.12	.20
WOM070 Laurite's Seven Disciples R	5.00	8.00
WOM071 Leaf Assassin C	.12	.20
WOM072 Leaf Dragon U	.15	.25
WOM073 Leaf Fairy C	.12	.20
WOM074 Leaf Paladin R	3.00	5.00
WOM075 Power of the Emperor C	.12	.20
WOM076 Reincarnation of the Holy Tree, Yggdrasil SR	.30	.50
WOM077 Seed of Rebirth R	.20	.30
WOM078 Spirit Searching U	.15	.25
WOM079 The End of Dreams U	.15	.25
WOM080 The Last Audience U	.15	.25
WOM081 Time Composing Elf C	.12	.20
WOM082 Viviane, the Envoy of Rebirth U	.15	.25
WOM083 Whirling Winds C	.12	.20
WOM084 Wind Blade Elf C	.12	.20
WOM085 Winds of Guidance U	.15	.25
WOM086 Winds of Salvation R	3.00	5.00
WOM087 Bird of Demise U	.15	.25
WOM088 Black Leaf C	.12	.20
WOM089 Bloodied Winds C	.12	.20
WOM090 Dark Bokuro C	.12	.20
WOM091 Demon in the Moonlight C	.12	.20
WOM092 Essence of the Void C	.12	.20
WOM093 Every Last Ounce of Strength U	.15	.25
WOM094 Glint of Insight U	.15	.25
WOM095 Kintaro R	.20	.30
WOM096 Kintaro's Partner U	.15	.25
WOM097 Knight of the Black Moon U	.15	.25
WOM098 Life or Death Struggle R	.60	1.00
WOM099 Moonlit Canopy R	.20	.30
WOM100 Rei, the Black Owl/ Zero SR	5.00	8.00

WOM101 Rei's Gale C .12 .20
WOM102 Reiya, Fourth Daughter of the Mikage RULER R 10.00 15.00
WOM103 Requiem of the Soul C .12 .20
WOM104 Sleeping Vampire C .12 .20
WOM105 The Night Before the Decisive Battle U .15 .25
WOM106 The Resistor of Destiny C .12 .20
WOM107 Time Reversal SR 1.25 2.00
WOM108 Vice-Leader of the Chivalrous Thieves, Blazer R .20 .30
WOM109 A Heroic Epic for the Thousandth Night R .75 1.25
WOM110 Attoractia, City of Verdant Green R 1.50 2.50
WOM111 Beyond the Threshold of Time R 1.00 1.50
WOM112 Inheritor of the Stars, Gill Lapis SR 2.00 3.00
WOM113 Invitation to Valhalla U .15 .25
WOM114 Journey to the Future U .15 .25
WOM115 Reincarnation of the Soul U .15 .25
WOM116 Restoration U .15 .25
WOM117 The Kingdom of Diversity, Light Palace R 2.00 3.00
WOM118 The Path We Part U .15 .25
WOM119 Ethereal Wind Magic Stone R .20 .30
WOM120 Magic Stone of Time R 6.00 10.00
WOM121 Grimmia's Fairy C VAR .12 .20
WOM122 Dread Touch C VAR .12 .20
WOM123 Wings of Ragnarok C VAR .12 .20
WOM124 Herbivorous Beast, Silomosaurus C VAR .12 .20
WOM125 Essence of the Void C VAR .12 .20

2018 Force of Will New Dawn Rises

RELEASED ON SEPTEMBER 28, 2018
NDR001 Aratron, Angel of Knowledge U .15 .25
NDR002 Ayu, the Mysterious Wanderer R .20 .30
NDR003 Balmung R .20 .30
NDR004 Blessing of the Sun C .12 .20
NDR005 Child of the Hero C .12 .20
NDR006 Commander of Minerva C .12 .20
NDR007 Country of the Sun, Minerva U .15 .25
NDR008 Eir, Bringer of Destruction U .15 .25
NDR009 Haggith, Angel of Alchemy C .12 .20
NDR010 Light of the Moon U .15 .25
NDR011 Moonlit Paradise, Lunar Heaven U .15 .25
NDR012 Och, Angel of Clairvoyance C .12 .20
NDR013 One Who Gazes at the Soul C .12 .20
NDR014 Ophiel, Angel of Guidance SR .75 1.25
NDR015 Protection of the Angels R 2.50 4.00
NDR016 Siegfried, the Hundred Years Hero SR .60 1.00
NDR017 Skuld, Valkyrie of the Future R .40 .60
NDR018 Spear of the Valkyries U .15 .25
NDR019 Tiny Trader C .12 .20
NDR020 Whispers of an Angel C .12 .20
NDR021 Anubis, Administrator of the Hounds SR 1.25 2.00
NDR022 Bird of Fire C .12 .20
NDR023 Black Spot Tiger R .60 1.00
NDR024 Burial Rites R .20 .30
NDR025 Carrier Camel C .12 .20
NDR026 Carrier Dragon C .12 .20
NDR027 Chain Bind U .15 .25
NDR028 City of Mirage, Sandora U .15 .25
NDR029 Desert Fennec U .15 .25
NDR030 Explosion Wizard U .15 .25
NDR031 Heaven Thundering Strike R .40 .60
NDR032 Land of Fiery Ambition, Kunlun U .15 .25
NDR033 Osiris, Lord of the Afterlife R .20 .30
NDR034 Sandstorm U .15 .25
NDR035 Scalding Breath C .12 .20
NDR036 Scorching Winds C .12 .20
NDR037 Shen Gongbao, Taoist of Kunlun SR .60 1.00
NDR038 Trader of Sandora C .12 .20
NDR039 Venomous Scorpion C .12 .20
NDR040 Wooden Ox C .12 .20
NDR041 Arondight, the Nitrogen Blade R .20 .30
NDR042 Forest of the Lost, Misty Woods U .15 .25
NDR043 Giant of Mist C .12 .20
NDR044 Hamelin, the Sound of Temptation R .20 .30
NDR045 Invitation U .15 .25
NDR046 Iron Cauldron Witch C .12 .20
NDR047 Jörmungandr, Little Eater of Worlds SR 1.00 1.50
NDR048 Lancelot, the Glass Knight SR 2.50 4.00
NDR049 Mad Hatter of Misty Woods U .15 .25
NDR050 Massive Growth R .20 .30
NDR051 Mechanized Knight C .12 .20
NDR052 Merlin, the Control Unit of Sky Round R 1.00 1.50
NDR053 Messenger of Death C .12 .20
NDR054 Scrap and Build U .15 .25
NDR055 Sky Round Guardian C .12 .20
NDR056 Sky Round Technician C .12 .20
NDR057 The Knight's Castle in the Sky, Sky Round U .15 .25
NDR058 Thick Fog C .12 .20
NDR059 Torrent of Energy C .12 .20
NDR060 Viviane, the Mechanical Fairy U .15 .25
NDR061 Atlantis, the Wielder of Knowledge R .20 .30
NDR062 Cat Ninja Scout C .12 .20
NDR063 Eccentric Oni C .12 .20
NDR064 Explore the Unknown U .15 .25
NDR065 Grand Bird of the Lost Isles C .12 .20
NDR066 In a Single Stroke C .12 .20
NDR067 Ittan-Momen C .12 .20
NDR068 Jubei, the One-Eyed Swordsmaster R .20 .30
NDR069 Karura, the Crow Tengu SR .75 1.25
NDR070 Kotaro, Ninja of the Wind U .15 .25
NDR071 Lemuria of the Magic Boomerang SR .30 .50
NDR072 Magic Boomerang R .60 1.00
NDR073 Mimi Tribe Explorer U .15 .25
NDR074 River Snake C .12 .20
NDR075 Song of the Fairies C .12 .20
NDR076 Squall of the Tengu R .20 .30
NDR077 The Forgotten Sanctuary, Lost Isles U .15 .25
NDR078 The Mimi Tribe's Cook C .12 .20
NDR079 The Village of the Spirited Away, Kouga U .15 .25
NDR080 Youkai Festival U .15 .25
NDR081 Apostle of the Devil C .12 .20
NDR082 Azazel, the Fallen Angel of Gloom R .20 .30
NDR083 Belial, the Evil from the Scriptures SR 1.25 2.00
NDR084 Bottomless Chasm of Death, the Abyss U .15 .25
NDR085 Corpse Demon C .12 .20
NDR086 Corpse Sorcerer U .15 .25
NDR087 Craving U .15 .25
NDR088 Diseased Rat C .12 .20
NDR089 Disgraced Knight R .20 .30
NDR090 Fresh Blood Vampire C .12 .20
NDR091 Gatherer of Despair C .12 .20
NDR092 Life Severing Blade R 5.00 8.00
NDR093 Look of Corruption R 5.00 8.00
NDR094 Miasma of the Abyss C .12 .20
NDR095 Minister of Grief U .15 .25
NDR096 Oborozuki SR 2.00 3.00
NDR097 Rain of Tears C .12 .20
NDR098 Ruins of Neverending Rain, Rainruins U .15 .25
NDR099 Skeleton Knight C .12 .20
NDR100 Whispers of the Devil U .15 .25
NDR101 Magic Stone of Adventure U .15 .25
NDR102 Magic Stone of Chaos R 1.25 2.00
NDR103 Magic Stone of Corruption U .15 .25
NDR104 Magic Stone of Dramaturgy U .15 .25
NDR105 Magic Stone of Dueling R 1.00 1.50
NDR106 Magic Stone of Faith R 1.50 2.50
NDR107 Magic Stone of Omniscience U .15 .25
NDR108 Magic Stone of the Hermit U .15 .25
NDR109 Magic Stone of the Undead R .30 .50
NDR110 Magic Stone of Tranquility R .40 .60
NDRSEC001 Ophiel, Angel of Guidance SCR 40.00 60.00
NDRSEC002 Anubis, Administrator of the Hounds SCR 50.00 75.00
NDRSEC003 Karura, the Crow Tengu SCR 50.00 75.00

2019 Force of Will The Strangers of New Valhalla

COMPLETE SET (100)
BOOSTER BOX (36 PACKS)
BOOSTER PACK (10 CARDS)
RELEASED ON JANUARY 18, 2019
SNV001 Alice, Otherworldly Visitor SR
SNV002 Barrier of Faith U
SNV003 Blade of Faith R
SNV004 Card Conscript C
SNV005 Dark Alice Doll R
SNV006 God's Choice C
SNV007 March Hare of Valhalla U
SNV008 Messenger of the Sun C
SNV009 Misteltein, the Pious Sword Saint SR
SNV010 Monk Heroic Spirit U
SNV011 Musician of the Moon U
SNV012 Mysterious Welcome Party C
SNV013 Palace Chef C
SNV014 Reginleif, Inheritor of God's Will R
SNV015 Spirit of Moonlit Nights C
SNV016 Swordsman Heroic Spirit C
SNV017 The Battle of Sun and Moon U
SNV018 The Stranger from Re-Earth R
SNV019 Valkyrie of the Dawn C
SNV020 Wizard Heroic Spirit U
SNV021 All Under Heaven Shall Perish U
SNV022 Annihilation Dragon C
SNV023 Frontline Warrior C
SNV024 Gaze of the Fire Emperor C
SNV025 Ladies of the Three Stars U
SNV026 Lady Huang's Karakuri Soldiers C
SNV027 Ma'at, Arbiter of Judgment R
SNV028 Neo-Berserk Dragon R
SNV029 Numbing Hedgehog C
SNV030 Ruins Beneath the Sand U
SNV031 Sand Awakening R
SNV032 Sand Soldier C
SNV033 Sandora's Invasion U
SNV034 Scales of the Ascendant C
SNV035 Searing Wall of Sand U
SNV036 Sima Hui, the Crafty Tactician U
SNV037 Surtr, the Sand Giant SR
SNV038 The Three Kingdoms Partition Plan R
SNV039 Underhanded Assassin C
SNV040 Zhuge Liang SR
SNV041 Antorite, Sealed God of the Riverbed R
SNV042 Bloodberry C
SNV043 Diverse Evolution U
SNV044 Guinevere, the Mobility Queen SR
SNV045 Guinevere's Imperial Guard C
SNV046 Mermaid of the Misty Spring C
SNV047 Mordred, the Operator U
SNV048 Mutation Slime U
SNV049 Mystery Box R
SNV050 Parallel World Schrödinger C
SNV051 Percision-Guided Munition, Sky Beat U
SNV052 Ruins Submerged Beneath the Misty Spring U
SNV053 Schrödinger, the Harlequin of Phenomena SR
SNV054 Shackles of Mist C
SNV055 Sky Round Musketeer C
SNV056 Skyfall C
SNV057 Skynet R
SNV058 Super Mobile Fortress Camelot R
SNV059 Teleport U
SNV060 Wheel Drone C
SNV061 Ancient Ruins Researcher C
SNV062 Bullet Ball Thunder Clap R
SNV063 Bunbuku, the Legendary Tea Kettle R
SNV064 Chamimi's Contemplation C
SNV065 Flying Squirrel C
SNV066 Fox Shikigami C
SNV067 Friend Calling Whistle U
SNV068 Guardian Beast of Nature C
SNV069 Liz, Sealed God of the Island R
SNV070 Magellanica, the Ball Warrior SR
SNV071 Molmol, King of Rare Beasts U
SNV072 Ninja Students C
SNV073 Rikyu, Cat Tongued Tea Master SR
SNV074 Ruins Beneath the Flora U
SNV075 Seimei's Disciple C
SNV076 Storm Cat C
SNV077 Table Flip R
SNV078 The Six Jizo Statues U
SNV079 The Unsealing of God U
SNV080 Tsunade, Brawny Cat Ninja U
SNV081 Amon, Conspirer of Atrocities R
SNV082 Astema, the Returnee of Hatred SR
SNV083 Athenia, Sealed God of the Ruins SR
SNV084 Black-Eyed Angel C
SNV085 Caspiel, the Fallen Angel of Rebellion U
SNV086 Chaining Hatred U
SNV087 Contract Demon U
SNV088 Corrupt Teachings C
SNV089 Dark Soldier of the Fallen C
SNV090 Dragon Zombie U
SNV091 Graveyard Vampire C
SNV092 March of the Dead C
SNV093 Orchard of the Immortals U
SNV094 Orpheus, the Immortal Player R
SNV095 Price of Immortality U
SNV096 Ruined Earth R
SNV097 Ruins Devil C
SNV098 Sewing Zombie C
SNV099 Soul Prison R
SNV100 Specter of the Abyss C

2019 Force of Will The Strangers of New Valhalla Foil

COMPLETE SET (100)
RELEASED ON

2015 Force of Will Starter Deck Faria the Sacred Queen and Melgis the Flame King

VS01001 Blessed Holy Wolf C
VS01002 Excalibur, the God's Sword R
VS01003 Faria, the Sacred Queen/Faria, the Ruler of God Sword R
VS01004 Galahad, the Son of the God R
VS01005 Gawain, the Knight of the Sun SR
VS01006 Gloria's Castle Town U
VS01007 Gwiber, the White Dragon U
VS01008 Herald of Sacred Queen C
VS01009 Justice of God's Sword U
VS01010 Order of Sacred Queen C
VS01011 Perceval, the Seeker of Holy Grail SR
VS01012 Pride of Knights C
VS01013 Temple Monk C
VS01014 Tristan, the Knight of Sorrow U
VS01015 Veteran Master C
VS01016 Young Knight of Gloria C
VS01017 Certo, the Blazing Volcano U
VS01018 Demonflame C
VS01019 Dragoon of Certo C
VS01020 Draig, the Red Dragon U
VS01021 Flame King's Shout C
VS01022 Flamewing Wyvern C
VS01023 Flash of Demon Sword U
VS01024 Guinevere, the Jealous Queen SR
VS01025 Hector de Maris, the Acolyte of Mad Demon U
VS01026 Laevateinn, the Demon Sword R
VS01027 Lancelot, the Knight of Mad Demon SR
VS01028 Melgis, the Flame King/Melgis, the One Charmed by the Demon Sword R
VS01029 Mordred, the Traitor R
VS01030 Rukh Egg C
VS01031 Spirit of Certo C
VS01032 Whelp Drake C
VS01033 Fire Magic Stone NR
VS01034 Light Magic Stone NR

2015 Force of Will Starter Deck Jet Black Phantom

1173 Skeleton Soldier C
2115 Familiar of Hades U
2119 Lantern, the Spirit of Grave Keeper C
2120 Ghost Swordsman C
2123 Orpheus, the Nether Player R
2127 Bloodthirst Baron C
2129 Dullahan, the Death Knight C
2134 Skeleton Horseman C
2135 Dragon Zombie, the Necrodragon U
2142 Power of Hatred C
2146 Binding Chain C
2149 Soul Sympathy C
2151 Grasp of Life C
2168 Darkness Magic Stone C
S013 Zain, the Warrior of Condemnation/Anubis, the Guardian of Throne
(Starter Exclusive)
S014 Astema, the Fallen Angel of Desolation
(Starter Exclusive)
S015 Nidhogg, the Hell Dragon
(Starter Exclusive)

2015 Force of Will Starter Deck Knights of the Round Table

1005 Lofty Knight C
1007 Order of Gartar C
1011 Garahad, the Oracle Knight R
1012 Shield Bearer of the Kingdom C
1015 Ironwall Monk C
1016 Kingdom Alchemist Wizards Force C
1017 Healing Master C
1019 Sleeping Lion C
1025 Benem, the Guardian Angel C
1031 Power from Inside C
1035 Restoration C
1040 Head On Attack C
1048 Castling U
1202 Light Magic Stone C
S001 Delphinius, the Knight of the Sun/Apollon, the God of Light
(Starter Exclusive)
S002 Michael, the Archangel
(Starter Exclusive)
S003 Rukh, the Pure White Divine Hawk
(Starter Exclusive)

2015 Force of Will Starter Deck Magic Circle of the Hurricane

2071 Guardian Warrior in Flower Garden C
2074 Yggnitsvay, the Guardian of Green Branch C
2076 Elvish Patrol Soldier C
2077 Jungle Hunter C
2079 Elvish Berserker C
2081 Forest Guard C
2084 Rambletree C
2087 Magicsucker Beetle C
2090 Deep Forest of Elves U
2094 Oaken Bow C
2102 Synchrojamming C
2103 Forbidden Fruit R
2104 Elvish Reinforcement C
2167 Wind Magic Stone C
S010 Deep Green Magician/Liz Titania, the Fairy Queen
(Starter Exclusive)
S011 Amphisbaena, the Two-Headed Dragon
(Starter Exclusive)
S012 Spriggan, the Treasure Watch
(Starter Exclusive)

2015 Force of Will Starter Deck Royal Palace of the Roaring Seas

1100 Mermaid Apprentice Student C
1109 Clockwork Messenger C
1110 Clown of Labyrinth C
1111 Phantom Reviver C

1114 Mirage Knight R
1117 Labyrinth Capturer C
1118 Mirage Slime C
1129 Mutating Potion -Eclosion- C
1135 Mind Control C
1137 Wash Away C
1141 Peace Negotiation C
1142 Spiral Shift C
1195 Sting Gimmick U
1204 Water Magic Stone C
S007 Royal Palace Guardian Mage/Freya Undine, the Spirit
(Starter Exclusive)
S008 Leviathan, the Tyrant of Ocean
(Starter Exclusive)
S009 Hight Tide Dancer
(Starter Exclusive)

2015 Force of Will Starter Deck Wolves of the Raging Flames

1052 Shock Troop of Asakna C
1053 Suicidal Troop of Asakna C
1056 Charger of Asakna C
1058 Fantian-Huaji, the Pyre R
1062 Bammoo, the Raging Fire Beast U
1063 Sabretooth Tiger C
1066 Parrot Dragon C
1068 Wyvern of Mount Olga U
1072 Efreet, the Blazing Elemental C
1079 Boiling Blood C
1082 Fireball C
1091 Prepare to Fall Together C
1093 Enlarge Body C
1203 Fire Magic Stone C
S004 Ushuah, the Flame Samurai Swordman/Agni, the Pyre War God
(Starter Exclusive)
S005 Azazel, the Blazing Charger
(Starter Exclusive)
S006 Regulus, the King of Volcano
(Starter Exclusive)

2016 Force of Will Starter Deck Fairy Tale Force

COMPLETE SET (12)
RELEASED ON SEPTEMBER 9, 2016

SDL1001 Confectioner Hansel C	.10	.15
SDL1002 Fairy Tale Kingdom Light Palace U	.40	.60
SDL1003 Gourmand Gretel C	.10	.15
SDL1004 Grimm King of Fairy Tales SR	.50	.75
SDL1005 Kid Puss in Boots R	1.00	1.50
SDL1006 Light Dress Cinderella SR	.30	.50
SDL1007 Magic Sweets C	1.50	2.50
SDL1008 Manifestation of Power C	1.00	1.50
SDL1009 Millium Prince of the Light Palace / Millium Voice of a New Generation R	.60	1.00
SDL1010 Summoning from the Fairy Tale World U	.40	.60
SDL1011 Tinker Bell the Fairy R	1.25	2.00
SDL1012 Light Magic Stone C	.10	.15

2016 Force of Will Starter Deck Malefic Ice

COMPLETE SET (12)
RELEASED ON SEPTEMBER 9, 2016

SDL3001 Ancient Frozen Casket U	.12	.20
SDL3002 Ancient Knowledge R	.75	1.25
SDL3003 Astaroth Great Duke of Hell SR	.30	.50
SDL3004 Ice Dragon of Altea SR	.30	.50
SDL3005 Keeper of the Frozen Casket C	.20	.30
SDL3006 Malefic Ice Wall C	.40	.60
SDL3007 Mercurius Wizard of the Water Star / Mercurius Dark Commander of Ice R	.50	.75
SDL3008 Mercurius Icy Spear U	.12	.20
SDL3009 Messenger of Altea C	.10	.15
SDL3010 Servant of Mercurius C	.10	.15
SDL3011 Spirit of Ice R	.20	.30
SDL3012 Water Magic Stone C	.10	.15

2016 Force of Will Starter Deck Rage of Rlyeh

COMPLETE SET (12)
RELEASED ON SEPTEMBER 9, 2016

SDL2001 Charlatan's Tricks R	.30	.50
SDL2002 Emissary of Rlyeh U	.12	.20
SDL2003 Fayli the Charlatan C	.10	.15
SDL2004 Gentle Goat C	.10	.15
SDL2005 Hastur Chasing the Goats SR	.30	.50
SDL2006 Lightning Strike R	.60	1.00
SDL2007 Lunya the Wolf Girl / Nyarlathotep the True False Legend R	2.50	4.00
SDL2008 Lunyas Best Friend C	.10	.15
SDL2009 Niggurath the Shepherd SR	.30	.50
SDL2010 Nightmares of Rlyeh U	1.00	1.50
SDL2011 Rlyeh World of No Lies C	.10	.15
SDL2012 Fire Magic Stone C	.10	.15

2016 Force of Will Starter Deck Swarming Elves

COMPLETE SET (12)
RELEASED ON SEPTEMBER 9, 2016

SDL4001 Aria Friendly Vampire SR	.40	.60
SDL4002 Fiethsing Six Sage of Wind / Fiethsing Master Magus of Holy Wind R	5.00	8.00
SDL4003 Great Holy Sealing Wave R	.20	.30
SDL4004 Home of the Sages U	.12	.20
SDL4005 Sacred Elf C	1.00	1.50
SDL4006 Spirit of Wind C	.20	.30
SDL4007 Tama Familiar of Holy Wind R	1.00	1.50
SDL4008 Torrent Elf C	.20	.30
SDL4009 TwoFold Chant U	.12	.20
SDL4010 Vampire Hunter Christie SR	.30	.50
SDL4011 Whisper from the Wind C	1.00	1.50
SDL4012 Wind Magic Stone C	.10	.15

2016 Force of Will Starter Deck Vampiric Hunger

COMPLETE SET (12)
RELEASED ON SEPTEMBER 9, 2016

SDL5001 Ally of the Black Moon / Eternal Vampire Mikage Seijuro R	1.50	2.50
SDL5002 Blood of the Mikage C	.10	.15
SDL5003 Castle of Oni U	.40	.60
SDL5004 Faithful Hellhound U	.12	.20
SDL5005 Heaven Bound Pheasant C	.10	.15
SDL5006 Momotaro of the Sanzu River SR	.30	.50
SDL5007 Oni Strike C	.30	.50
SDL5008 Power Absorption C	.10	.15
SDL5009 Shara Third Daughter of the Mikage SR	.60	1.00
SDL5010 The Drunken Oni R	.40	.60
SDL5011 The Monkey Trapped in Life C	.10	.15
SDL5012 Darkness Magic Stone C	.20	.30

2017 Force of Will Starter Deck Below the Waves

COMPLETE SET (13)
RELEASED ON AUGUST 18, 2017

SDR3001 Angelic Voice Mermaid C	.10	.15
SDR3002 Aqua Rifle Mermaid R	.10	.15
SDR3003 Cleansing Rain R	.10	.15
SDR3004 Giant Sea Jelly U	.10	.15
SDR3005 Peko, the Wise Dolphin SR	.30	.50
SDR3006 Princess Shaela's Attendant C	.20	.30
SDR3007 Shaela/Shaela, the Mermaid Princess RULER R	1.25	2.00
SDR3008 Stormbolt C	.10	.15
SDR3009 The White Whale U	.10	.15
SDR3010 Wave Rider Mermaid SR	.30	.50
SDR3011 Weather Change: Rain C	.10	.15
SDR3012 Shoal Coral Stone R	.40	.60
SDR3013 Water Magic Stone C	.40	.60

2017 Force of Will Starter Deck Blood of Dragons

COMPLETE SET (13)
RELEASED ON AUGUST 18, 2017

SDR2001 Apprentice Cook C	.10	.15
SDR2002 Burning Awakening C	.10	.15
SDR2003 Dragon Breath C	.10	.15
SDR2004 Dragon of Mt. Hoelle SR	.30	.50
SDR2005 Ella Rua, the Combat Chef SR	.30	.50
SDR2006 Hell Flame R	.20	.30
SDR2007 Hoelle Pig C	.10	.15
SDR2008 Hoellesaurus U	.10	.15
SDR2009 Kirk Rerik/Kirk Rerik, the Draconic Warrior RULER R	.50	.75
SDR2010 Kirik's Partner R	.10	.15
SDR2011 Mad Boar of Mt. Hoelle U	.75	1.25
SDR2012 Dragon Ore R	.50	.75
SDR2013 Fire Magic Stone NR	.50	.75

2017 Force of Will Starter Deck Children of the Night

COMPLETE SET (13)
RELEASED ON AUGUST 18, 2017

SDR5001 Ahriman, Malicious Eye in the Dark SR	.30	.50
SDR5002 Alucard, the Vampiric Noble U	1.00	1.50
SDR5003 Ashen Snow White R	.20	.30
SDR5004 Bats from the Dark Castle C	.10	.15
SDR5005 Dark Night Butterfly C	.10	.15
SDR5006 Empress Carmilla U	.12	.20
SDR5007 Grimm, the Pitch Black Vampire SR	.30	.50
SDR5008 Moonlight Shadow C	.10	.15
SDR5009 Reiya, Fourth Daughter of the Mikage/Reiya, Fourth Daughter of the Mikage RULER R	6.00	10.00
SDR5010 Sword of the Half Moon C	.10	.15
SDR5011 Sword of the New Moon R	.20	.30
SDR5012 Stone From the Dark Castle R	2.00	3.00
SDR5013 Darkness Magic Stone NR	.10	.15

2017 Force of Will Starter Deck Elemental Surge

COMPLETE SET (13)
RELEASED ON AUGUST 18, 2017

SDR4001 Cecil Letoliel, Elven Prince SR	.30	.50
SDR4002 Elven Guide R	.20	.30
SDR4003 Gentle Breeze Elemental C	.10	.15
SDR4004 Gill/Gill, the Gifted Conjurer RULER R	.40	.60
SDR4005 Guardian of the Portal U	.12	.20
SDR4006 Leaf Fighter C	.10	.15
SDR4007 Leaf Magician U	.12	.20
SDR4008 Travelling Trader C	.10	.15
SDR4009 Tree Root Sprite SR	.30	.50
SDR4010 Vanish R	.40	.60
SDR4011 Winds of Vitality C	.10	.15
SDR4012 Spirit Stone R	1.50	2.50
SDR4013 Wind Magic Stone NR	.10	.15

2017 Force of Will Starter Deck King of the Mountain

COMPLETE SET (13)
RELEASED ON AUGUST 18, 2017

SDR1001 Diamond, the One-Eyed Treasury Magician SR	.30	.50
SDR1002 Gem Blade Onyx SR	.30	.50
SDR1003 Gem Blade Ruby U	.12	.20
SDR1004 Gem Blade Sapphire U	.12	.20
SDR1005 Gem Craftsman R	.20	.30
SDR1006 Gem Trader C	.10	.15
SDR1007 Jewel Burst R	.20	.30
SDR1008 Jewel Shield C	.10	.15
SDR1009 Jewel Sword C	.10	.15
SDR1010 Taegrus Pearlshine/Taegrus Pearlshine, Lord of the Mountain RULER R	.40	.60
SDR1011 White Raven C	.10	.15
SDR1012 Ore from the Treasure Mountain R	.75	1.25
SDR1013 Light Magic Stone NR	.10	.15

2018 Force of Will Starter Deck The Lost Tomes

COMPLETE SET (18)
RELEASED ON MARCH 9, 2018

SDR6001 Venus, Magus of the Metal Star	1.00	1.50
SDR6002 Chrono Researcher, Alisaris	.75	1.25
SDR6003 Sylvia, the Slave Girl	1.25	2.00
SDR6004 Saturneus, Enchanter of the Earth Star	1.50	2.50
SDR6005 Scant Vision	.60	1.00
SDR6006 Jupiter, Warlock of the Wood Star	.75	1.25
SDR6007 Viola, Treacherous Maiden	3.00	5.00
SDR6008 Blazer, the Legendary Thief	1.00	1.50
SDR6009 Rachel, Nephilim Contract Maker	1.00	1.50
SDR6010 Forbidden Arts	1.50	2.50
SDR6011 Gill Alhama'at, He Who Controls the Taboo Gill Alhama'at, Treasonous Emperor	2.50	4.00
SDR6012 Alhama'at's Ultra Magic Stone		
SDR6013 Historical Magic Stone	.60	1.00
SDR6014 Darkness Magic Stone	.60	1.00
SDR6015 Fire Magic Stone	.60	1.00
SDR6016 Light Magic Stone	.60	1.00
SDR6017 Water Magic Stone	.60	1.00
SDR6018 Wind Magic Stone	.60	1.00

2018 Force of Will Starter Deck New Valhalla Entry Set Darkness

COMPLETE SET (23)
RELEASED ON SEPTEMBER 21, 2018

SDV5001 Amaros, the Fallen Angel of Nullification U	.20	.30
SDV5002 Black Rosario R	4.00	6.00
SDV5003 Cycle of Death R	1.25	2.00
SDV5004 Demon Division C	.10	.15
SDV5005 Fanatic of Grief C	.10	.15
SDV5006 Fleurety C	.10	.15
SDV5007 Immortal Commander U	.12	.20
SDV5008 Jet-Black Wings U	2.50	4.00
SDV5009 Lich/Lich, the Saint of Death RULER R	2.50	4.00
SDV5010 Lower Fallen Angel C	.10	.15
SDV5011 Lucifer/Lucifer, the Fallen Angel of Sorror RULER R	10.00	15.00
SDV5012 Patchwork Frankenstein C	.10	.15
SDV5013 Putrefy C	.40	.60
SDV5014 Scythe of the Reaper C	.60	1.00
SDV5015 Shemhaza, the Fallen Angel of Sadism SR	1.25	2.00
SDV5016 Skeleton Horde C	2.00	3.00
SDV5017 Specter Rush U	.60	1.00
SDV5018 Sword of Lament C	.75	1.25
SDV5019 Tears of the Fallen C	.10	.15
SDV5020 Undeath C	.50	.75
SDV5021 Vlad, the Insatiable SR	.60	1.00
SDV5022 Wanderer of the Abyss C	.10	.15
SDV5023 Darkness Magic Stone C	.10	.15

2018 Force of Will Starter Deck New Valhalla Entry Set Fire

COMPLETE SET (23)
RELEASED ON SEPTEMBER 21, 2018

SDV2001 Chu-Ko-Nu Soldier C	.10	.15
SDV2002 Concealed Khopesh C	.10	.15
SDV2003 Dragon Dance C	.10	.15
SDV2004 Dragon of Kunlun SR	.30	.50
SDV2005 Dragon's Flight U	.12	.20
SDV2006 Explosion C	.10	.15
SDV2007 Flame Enchant C	.10	.15
SDV2008 Flame Soldier Formation R	.60	1.00
SDV2009 Fu Xi/Fu Xi, King of Kunlun RULER R	2.50	4.00
SDV2010 Giant Sandstorm U	.60	1.00
SDV2011 Isis/Isis, the Hundred Weapon Master RULER R	10.00	15.00
SDV2012 Magician of Molding C	.10	.15
SDV2013 Pang Tong U	.12	.20
SDV2014 Poison Stinger C	.10	.15
SDV2015 Reckless Flame Soldier C	.10	.15
SDV2016 Sand Dragon U	.12	.20
SDV2017 Sandora Blacksmith C	.10	.15
SDV2018 Sandworm C	.10	.15
SDV2019 Set, the Commander of Destruction SR	.30	.50
SDV2020 Soldier Ambush C	.10	.15
SDV2021 Tiger of Kunlun C	.10	.15
SDV2022 Whirlwind Conflagration R	.60	1.00
SDV2023 Fire Magic Stone C	.10	.15

2018 Force of Will Starter Deck New Valhalla Entry Set Light

COMPLETE SET (23)
RELEASED ON SEPTEMBER 21, 2018

SDV1001 Acolyte of the Sun C	.10	.15
SDV1002 Atom Seikhart/Atom Seikhart, the Shimmering Rabbit RULER R	3.00	5.00
SDV1003 Bethor, the Angel of Treasure C	.10	.15
SDV1004 Bewilder C	.10	.15
SDV1005 Brunhild/Brunhild, Caller of Spirits RULER R	12.00	20.00
SDV1006 Brunhild's Wrath C	.10	.15
SDV1007 Dispel C	.10	.15
SDV1008 Einherjar's Summons U	1.25	2.00
SDV1009 Eir, Valkyrie of Mercy U	2.50	4.00
SDV1010 Karmic Reversal C	.10	.15
SDV1011 Mini Meteor U	.60	1.00
SDV1012 Odin's Judgment R	5.00	8.00
SDV1013 Phaleg, the Angel of War U	1.25	2.00
SDV1014 Phul, the Administrator of the Moon SR	1.00	1.50
SDV1015 Ring of Legend C	.10	.15
SDV1016 Sigrun, Valkyrie of Victory SR	.30	.50
SDV1017 Sorceress of the Moon C	.10	.15
SDV1018 The Valkyrie's Chosen C	.10	.15
SDV1019 Turn Tail C	.10	.15
SDV1020 Warrior of the Sun C	.10	.15
SDV1021 Wererabbit Warrior C	.10	.15
SDV1022 Zeus' Grand Lightning R	.60	1.00
SDV1023 Light Magic Stone C	.10	.15

2018 Force of Will Starter Deck New Valhalla Entry Set Water

COMPLETE SET (23)
RELEASED ON SEPTEMBER 21, 2018

SDV3001 Anti-Matter Cannon, Excalibur R	.60	1.00
SDV3002 Arthur/Arthur, King of Machines	6.00	10.00
SDV3003 Caliburn, the Sword of Judgment U	.60	1.00
SDV3004 Charm C	.40	.60
SDV3005 Checkmate C	.20	.30
SDV3006 Consume R	2.00	3.00
SDV3007 Donut Drone C	2.00	3.00
SDV3008 Gawain, the Swift Knight U	.12	.20
SDV3009 Gretel of Misty Woods C	.15	.25
SDV3010 Hansel of Misty Woods C	.15	.25
SDV3011 Loki/Loki, the Witch of Chaos	8.00	12.00
SDV3012 Loki's Watchdog, Fenrir SR	.30	.50
SDV3013 Maintenance C	2.00	3.00
SDV3014 Mechanical Bishop C	.12	.20
SDV3015 Mechanical Soldier C	.12	.20
SDV3016 Monstrosity U	.40	.60
SDV3017 Overflowing Knowledge C	1.25	2.00
SDV3018 Perceval, the Shining Knight SR	.30	.50
SDV3019 Petrification C	2.50	4.00
SDV3020 Reconnaissance C	2.00	3.00
SDV3021 Scarecrow Guide C	1.25	2.00
SDV3022 Witch's House U	.15	.25
SDV3023 Water Magic Stone C	.10	.15

2018 Force of Will Starter Deck New Valhalla Entry Set Wind

COMPLETE SET (23)
RELEASED ON SEPTEMBER 21, 2018

SDV4001 Chamimi/Chamimi, Guardian of the Sacred Bow RULER R	2.50	4.00
SDV4002 Chiyome, the Captivating Kunoichi SR	.25	.40
SDV4003 Elephant Rush!! R	1.00	1.50
SDV4004 Fairy of the Lost Isles C	1.25	2.00
SDV4005 Forest Meditation C	6.00	10.00
SDV4006 Fuhma Shuriken C	.60	1.00
SDV4007 Grand Mallet Warrior SR	.30	.50
SDV4008 Hanzo/Hanzo, Chief of the Kouga RULER R	6.00	10.00
SDV4009 Huge Toad C	.25	.40
SDV4010 Jiraiya, the Toad User U	.15	.25
SDV4011 Mu, the Hero of the Greatshield C	.15	.25
SDV4012 Pygmy Hippo C	.60	1.00
SDV4013 Raft Downstream U	.60	1.00
SDV4014 Rapid Fire Mi-!! C	3.00	5.00
SDV4015 Sanctuary Elephant U	.15	.25

SDV4016 Sealing Scroll R	4.00	6.00
SDV4017 Shadow Step C	.60	1.00
SDV4018 Snipe Away Mi-!! C	.60	1.00
SDV4019 Soot Sprite C	.15	.25
SDV4020 Spirited Away U	.60	1.00
SDV4021 The Hundred Eyed One C	.15	.25
SDV4022 Whirlwind Technique C	.60	1.00
SDV4023 Wind Magic Stone C	.15	.25

Future Card Buddyfight

2014 Future Card Buddyfight Booster Set 1 Dragon Chief

RELEASED ON JANUARY 31, 2014

BT010001 Super Armordragon, Buster Cannon Dragon RRR	1.00	1.50
BT010001 Super Armordragon, Buster Cannon Dragon SP	8.00	12.00
BT010002 Drum Bunker Dragon, "Barrier Breaker" RRR	.75	1.25
BT010002 Drum Bunker Dragon, "Barrier Breaker" SP	10.00	15.00
BT010003 Pile Bunker Dragon RRR	2.50	4.00
BT010004 Rebel, Belial RRR	.50	.75
BT010004 Rebel, Belial SP	5.00	8.00
BT010005 Herb Magician, Soichiro Tenjiku RRR	1.00	1.50
BT010006 Demon Lord, Asmodai RRR	4.00	6.00
BT010006 Demon Lord, Asmodai SP	30.00	50.00
BT010007 Devil Advantage RRR	3.00	5.00
BT010008 Armorknight Demon RRR	.75	1.25
BT010008 Armorknight Demon SP	4.00	6.00
BT010009 Dragon Knight, Maximilian RR	.60	1.00
BT010010 Day of the Dragon RR	.30	.50
BT010011 Steel Fist, Dragoknuckle RR	1.50	2.50
BT010011 Steel Fist, Dragoknuckle SP	10.00	15.00
BT010012 Gargantua Punisher!! RR	1.50	2.50
BT010012 Gargantua Punisher!! SP	25.00	40.00
BT010013 Demon Realm Negotiator, Gusion RR	.30	.50
BT010014 Magician of Glass, Will Glassart RR	.75	1.25
BT010015 Magical Goodbye RR	4.00	6.00
BT010016 Diabolical Hardcore! RR	1.50	2.50
BT010016 Diabolical Hardcore! SP	6.00	10.00
BT010017 Armorknight Medusa RR	.75	1.25
BT010018 Fighting Dragon, Demongodol RR	.60	1.00
BT010018 Fighting Dragon, Demongodol SP	5.00	8.00
BT010019 Thunder Devastation RR	.60	1.00
BT010020 Lord Aura Meditation RR	3.00	5.00
BT010021 Drum Bunker Dragon R	2.00	3.00
BT010021 Drum Bunker Dragon SP	8.00	12.00
BT010022 Dragonic Destroy R	.15	.25
BT010023 Knightenergy R	.15	.25
BT010024 Blue Dragon Shield R	1.25	2.00
BT010025 Dragon's Seal R	.15	.25
BT010026 Demon Programmer, Marbas R	.15	.25
BT010027 Liar, Fullfool R	.15	.25
BT010028 Barriermaster, Shadowflash R	.15	.25
BT010029 Demon Doctor, Buer R	1.25	2.00
BT010030 Begone!! R	4.00	6.00
BT010031 Nice one! R	.15	.25
BT010032 The Ark R	.15	.25
BT010033 Great Spell, Saturday Night Devil Fever R	.15	.25
BT010034 Gunrod, Bechstein R	.15	.25
BT010035 Axe Dragon, Dorcas R	.15	.25
BT010036 Armorknight Golem R	.15	.25
BT010037 Armorknight Cerberus R	1.50	2.50
BT010037 Armorknight Cerberus SP	10.00	15.00
BT010038 Saberclaw Dragon, Valken R	.15	.25
BT010039 Armorknight Succubus R	.15	.25
BT010040 Double Guillotine R	.15	.25
BT010041 Hysteric Spear R	.15	.25
BT010042 Drill Bunker!! R	.15	.25
BT010042 Drill Bunker!! SP	10.00	15.00
BT010043 King the Dominator R	.15	.25
BT010044 Buddy Help R	1.25	2.00
BT010045 Dragon Knight, Masakado UC	.12	.20
BT010046 Dragon Knight, Hannibal UC	.12	.20
BT010047 Dragon Knight, Jeanne d'Arc UC	.12	.20
BT010048 Spike Shoulder Dragon UC	.12	.20
BT010049 Dragonic Heal UC	.12	.20
BT010050 The Skies in your Hand UC	2.00	3.00
BT010051 Twin Attack Tactics UC	.12	.20
BT010052 Fallen Angel of Rage, Beleth UC	.12	.20
BT010053 Fire Starter, Ganzack UC	.12	.20
BT010054 Demon Realm Death Metal, Valefar UC	.12	.20
BT010055 Mage Disciple, Rody UC	.12	.20
BT010056 Preacher of Beauty, Gremory UC	.12	.20
BT010057 Trans-flame UC	1.25	2.50
BT010058 Quick Summon UC	.12	.20
BT010059 Abra Cadabra! UC	5.00	8.00
BT010060 Noisy Danceroom UC	2.50	4.00
BT010061 Gunrod, Stradivarius UC	.12	.20
BT010062 Grassland Dragon, Grassrunner UC	.12	.20
BT010063 Clash Dragon, Gaelcorga UC	.12	.20
BT010064 Armor Reuse UC	3.00	5.00
BT010065 Battle Spirit Unite UC	4.00	6.00
BT010066 Duel Law UC	.50	.75
BT010067 Night in the Wild UC	.12	.20
BT010068 Control Unit, Suppression Queen UC	.12	.20
BT010069 Combat Unit, Guardian Rook UC	1.25	2.00
BT010070 Skewer UC	.12	.20
BT010071 Buddy Charge UC	2.00	3.00
BT010072 Chessenergy UC	.12	.20
BT010073 Battlefield Military Band UC	.12	.20
BT010074 Checkmate UC	.12	.20
BT010075 Dragon Knight, Alexander C	.10	.15
BT010076 Steel Gauntlet Dragon C	.10	.15
BT010077 Latale Shield Dragon C	.10	.15
BT010078 Dragon Knight, Leonidas C	.10	.15
BT010079 Dragonic Shoot C	.10	.15
BT010080 Dragonblade, Dragobrave C	.10	.15
BT010081 Dance Magician, Albrecht C	.10	.15
BT010082 Fallen Angel, Paimon C	.10	.15
BT010083 Kenjy of the Explosive Fists C	.10	.15
BT010084 Demon Maestro, Bathin C	.10	.15
BT010085 Demon Knight, Aibolos C	.10	.15
BT010086 Demon Realm Warrior, Zepar C	.10	.15
BT010087 Oops! C	1.50	2.50
BT010088 Solomon's Shield C	.60	1.00
BT010089 Raging Dragon, Zargus C	.10	.15
BT010090 Soaring Dragon, Sylphide C	.10	.15
BT010091 Bloodwind Dragon, Elyrseagar C	.10	.15
BT010092 Armorknight Gargoyle C	.10	.15
BT010093 Bluechase Dragon, Garg C	.10	.15
BT010094 Earth-shattering Slash C	.10	.15
BT010095 Boulder Piercing Spear C	.10	.15
BT010096 Attack Unit, Flying Bishop C	.10	.15
BT010097 Mobile Unit, Soldier Pawn C	.10	.15
BT010098 Battle Unit, Knight Fighter C	.10	.15
BT010099 Royal Fork C	.10	.15
BT010100 Destruction (card) C	.10	.15
BT010101 Neutralize C	.10	.15
BT010102 Pawn Storm C	.10	.15
BT010103 Burning Sword C	.10	.15
BT010104 Burning Dagger C	.10	.15
BT010105 Jackknife Dragon BR	15.00	25.00

2014 Future Card Buddyfight Booster Set 2 Cyber Ninja Squad

RELEASED ON APRIL 5, 2014

BT020001 Super Armordragon, Galvanic Feather Dragon RRR	1.50	2.50
BT020002 Center of the World, Mary Sue RRR	5.00	8.00
BT020003 Great Spell, My Grandfather Clock RRR	10.00	15.00
BT020004 Emperor Dragon, Gael Khan RRR	2.50	4.00
BT020005 Superior Strength Ninja, Kotaro Fuma RRR	1.25	2.00
BT020006 Nanomachine Ninja, Tsukikage RRR	3.00	5.00
BT020007 Evil in Heart, Yamigitsune RRR	4.00	6.00
BT020008 Secret Sword, Star Crusher RRR	15.00	25.00
BT020009 Dragon Knight, Vlad Dracula RR	1.00	1.50
BT020010 Emigurette Dragon RR	1.00	1.50
BT020011 Witch of Destruction, Hearty the Devastator RR	1.50	2.50
BT020012 Great Duke, Astaroth RR	1.00	1.50
BT020013 Twin Horn Dragon, Ark Giraffa RR	.30	.50
BT020014 Nightflight Dragon, Rahal RR	.30	.50
BT020015 Extermination Ninja, Slashing Asura RR	.30	.50
BT020016 Tempest, Garo-oh RR	.60	1.00
BT020017 Electron Ninja, Shiden RR	5.00	8.00
BT020018 Art of Explosive Hades Fall RR	1.50	2.50
BT020019 Demon Way, Karakurenai RR	.75	1.25
BT020020 Secret Sword, Lethal Formation RR	5.00	8.00
BT020021 Psychic Knife Dragon R	.15	.25
BT020022 Dragonic Paratrooper R	.15	.25
BT020023 Victory Slash! R	.15	.25
BT020024 Magic Knight of Darkness, Dunkelheit R	.30	.50
BT020025 Magic Knight of Light, Licht R	.15	.25
BT020026 Kosher R	1.50	2.50
BT020027 Key of Solomon, First Volume R	1.25	2.00
BT020028 Key of Solomon, Second Volume R	1.25	2.00
BT020029 Armorknight Ifrit R	.15	.25
BT020030 Armorknight Tiger R	.15	.25
BT020031 Exorcist Stomp R	.40	.60
BT020032 Armorknight Formation R	.60	1.00
BT020033 Sky Rush, Garyu-oh R	.15	.25
BT020034 Flash Strike, Yamaihebi R	.15	.25
BT020035 Cyber Onmyoji, Seimei R	.15	.25
BT020036 Phantom Ninja, Kashinkoji R	.15	.25
BT020037 Clear Serenity R	1.25	2.00
BT020038 Shinobi Scrolls R	.60	1.00
BT020039 Return to the Underworld R	1.00	1.50
BT020040 Elite Sword, Mikazuki Munechika R	.60	1.00
BT020041 Secret Sword, Moon Fang R	.50	.75
BT020042 Secret Sword, Shooting Star R	.40	.60
BT020043 Actor Knights the World R	2.00	3.00
BT020044 Ultimate Buddy! R	1.00	1.50
BT020045 Blaze Gauntlet Dragon U	.12	.20
BT020046 Dragon Knight, Ryoma U	.50	.75
BT020047 White Dragon Shield U	.75	1.25
BT020048 Dragonblade, Dragobreach U	.50	.75
BT020049 Dandy Guy, Sitri U	.12	.20
BT020050 Cloud-riding Hop Hob U	.30	.50
BT020051 Demon Realm Computer, Vassago U	.12	.20
BT020052 De Guaita Crush Knuckle! U	1.25	2.00
BT020053 Holy Moly! U	.12	.20
BT020054 Chillax! U	.30	.50
BT020055 Bastin Caps U	.12	.20
BT020056 Armorknight Trent U	.12	.20
BT020057 Strong Horn Dragon, Diatlus U	.12	.20
BT020058 Armorknight Wall Lizard U	.12	.20
BT020059 Wandering Ninja, Tobikato U	.12	.20
BT020060 Blood Knife, Kimensai U	.40	.60
BT020061 Accelerate Ninja, Hayate U	.12	.20
BT020062 Art of Item Blasting U	.40	.60
BT020063 Art of Body Replacement U	2.00	3.00
BT020064 Ninja Arts, Steel Ball U	.12	.20
BT020065 Shooting Cross Knives, Right-hand U	.12	.20
BT020066 Spinning Windmill Knives, Back-hand U	.12	.20
BT020067 Demon Way, Geppakugiri U	.12	.20
BT020068 Demon Way, Shienrekka U	.12	.20
BT020069 Actor Knights Chariot U	.50	.75
BT020070 Actor Knights High Priestess U	.12	.20
BT020071 Actor Knights the Magician U	.12	.20
BT020072 Fool Aims for the Wilderness U	.12	.20
BT020073 Fool's Journey U	.12	.20
BT020074 Burning Bow U	.12	.20
BT020075 Thousand Rapier Dragon C	.10	.15
BT020076 Raid Claw Dragon C	.10	.15
BT020077 Dragon Knight, Shingen C	.10	.15
BT020078 Force Return C	.10	.15
BT020079 Dragobond C	.10	.15
BT020080 Eastern Demon Sword Emperor, Baal C	.10	.15
BT020081 Protector of Friendship, Barbados C	.10	.15
BT020082 Black Demon Swordsman, Jace Aldis C	.10	.15
BT020083 Finisher Bow, Leraje C	.10	.15
BT020084 Gunrod, Martil C	.10	.15
BT020085 Violent Dragon, Boralios C	.10	.15
BT020086 Fire Manipulating Dragon, Volgaraid C	.10	.15
BT020087 Mantis Dragon, Drantis C	.10	.15
BT020088 Armorknight Chimera C	.10	.15
BT020089 Armorknight Polar Bear C	.10	.15
BT020090 Blade Tiger, Gurenenbu C	.10	.15
BT020091 Mobile Ninja, Jiraiya C	.10	.15
BT020092 Armed Priest Soldier, Benkei C	.10	.15
BT020093 Sea-splitting Irukamaru C	.10	.15
BT020094 Steel Wall, Beheading Crab C	.10	.15
BT020095 Stealth Ninja, Kirikakure Saizo C	.10	.15
BT020096 Steel Head, Helmet Bear C	.10	.15
BT020097 Demon Way, Sakurafubuki C	.60	1.00
BT020098 Demon Way, Noroihikagami C	.10	.15
BT020099 Ninja Blade, Kurogachi C	.10	.15
BT020100 Actor Knights Hermit C	.10	.15
BT020101 Actor Knights the Fool C	.10	.15
BT020102 Actor Knights Lovers C	.10	.15
BT020103 Gambit C	1.50	2.50
BT020104 Castling C	.10	.15
BT020105 Martial Arts Dragon Emperor, Duel Siegar BR	15.00	25.00
BTS020001 Super Armordragon, Galvanic Feather Dragon SP	15.00	25.00
BTS020002 Center of the World, Mary Sue SP	12.00	20.00
BTS020004 Emperor Dragon, Gael Khan SP	15.00	25.00
BTS020005 Superior Strength Ninja, Kotaro Fuma SP	4.00	6.00
BTS020006 Nanomachine Ninja, Tsukikage SP	20.00	30.00
BTS020007 Evil in Heart, Yamigitsune SP	12.00	20.00
BTS020009 Dragon Knight, Vlad Dracula SP	10.00	15.00
BTS020011 Witch of Destruction, Hearty the Devastator SP	20.00	30.00
BTS020012 Great Duke, Astaroth SP	12.00	20.00
BTS020016 Tempest, Garo-oh SP	6.00	10.00
BTS020017 Electron Ninja, Shiden SP	30.00	50.00
BTS020020 Secret Sword, Lethal Formation SP	10.00	15.00

2014 Future Card Buddyfight Booster Set 3 Drum's Adventures

RELEASED ON JULY 4, 2014

BT030001 Jackknife "Beistand" RRR	2.00	3.00
BT030002 Thunder Knights Leader, Kommandeur Fahne RRR	1.50	2.50
BT030002 Thunder Knights Leader, Kommandeur Fahne SP		
BT030003 Dragon Knight, Kondou RRR	3.00	6.00
BT030003 Dragon Knight, Kondou SP	1.25	3.00
BT030004 Dragowizard, Qinus Axia RRR	4.00	6.00
BT030005 Wanderer, the Gold RRR	1.25	2.00
BT030006 Demon Lord, Gagnar RRR	.60	1.00
BT030007 Legendary Brave, Tasuku RRR	3.00	5.00
BT030007 Legendary Brave, Tasuku SP	20.00	30.00
BT030008 Dragonblade Wielding Sheila Vanna RRR	2.00	3.00
BT030009 Super Armordragon, Vulverize Dragon RR	.30	.50
BT030010 Thunder Knights, Bastard-sword Dragon RR	1.25	2.00
BT030011 Dragon Knight, Soushi RR	2.00	3.00
BT030012 Barbarish Anger-! RR	.50	.75
BT030012 Barbarish Anger-! SP		
BT030013 Magical Secretary, Genjuro Saki RR	.30	.50
BT030014 Mana Booster, Melerqim RR	.60	1.00
BT030015 Undefeatable, Setsujishi RR	.30	.50
BT030016 Sky Ninja, Yamigarasu RR	.60	1.00
BT030016 Sky Ninja, Yamigarasu SP	4.00	6.00
BT030017 Bladewing Phoenix RR	1.25	2.00
BT030018 Dancing Magician, Tetsuya RR	.60	1.00
BT030019 Dungeon Explosion RR	.60	1.00
BT030020 Brave Equipment, Glory Seeker RR	1.50	2.50
BT030020 Brave Equipment, Glory Seeker SP	5.00	12.00
BT030021 Super Armordragon, Daring Armor Dragon R	.15	.25
BT030022 Million Rapier Dragon R	.15	.25
BT030023 Thunder Knights, Battle Axe Dragon R	.15	.25
BT030024 Thunder Knights, Drum Bunker Dragon SP	5.00	8.00
BT030025 Awl Pike Dragon R	.15	.25
BT030026 Thunder Knights, Dragoarcher R	.15	.25
BT030027 Dragon Barrier R	.60	1.00
BT030028 Thunder Formation! R	.15	.25
BT030029 Thunder Blade, Dragobreaker R	.15	.25
BT030030 Dragowizard, Magician Drum R	.75	1.25
BT030030 Dragowizard, Magician Drum SP	.15	.25
BT030031 Great Spell, Deus Ex Machina R	.15	.25
BT030032 Power Ray Maximum R	.15	.25
BT030033 Gotcha! R	.15	.25
BT030034 Elite Sword, Onimaru R	.15	.25
BT030035 Guardian Dragon of Ruins, Meteor Rain R	.15	.25
BT030036 Brave, Drum R	1.50	2.50
BT030036 Brave, Drum SP	8.00	12.00
BT030037 Magical Fortress, Orser Kleinz R	.15	.25
BT030038 Mimic with Surprise R	.15	.25
BT030039 Missile Wizard, Adrick R	.15	.25
BT030040 Evil-Break R	.15	.25
BT030041 Continue! R	1.00	1.50
BT030042 Mission Card "Rest at Nozaro Hot Springs!" R	.15	.25
BT030043 Brave's Sword, Sommer Sword R	.15	.25
BT030044 Actor Knights Emperor R	.15	.25
BT030045 Tail Sword Dragon U	.12	.20
BT030046 Thunder Knights, Sword Shield Dragon U	.12	.20
BT030047 Tuck Sword Dragon U	.12	.20
BT030048 Dragon Knight, Hijikata U	.12	.20
BT030049 Wolf of Mibu U	.12	.20
BT030050 Dragonblade, Dragoseele U	.12	.20
BT030052 Flame Master, Ganzack "Dva" U	.12	.20
BT030053 Dragowizard, Tempest Wing U	.12	.20
BT030054 Dragowizard, Burning Wand U	.12	.20
BT030055 You The Man! U	.12	.20
BT030056 Magic Arm, Burning Fist U	.12	.20
BT030057 Sniping Ninja, Yoichi U	.12	.20
BT030058 Secret Arts, Dance of the Guardian Swords U	.12	.20
BT030059 Ninja Arts, Serpent Glare U	.12	.20
BT030060 Dark Ninja Technique, Poisonous Swamp Formation U	.12	.20
BT030061 Blood Bath on Gojo Great Bridge U	.12	.20
BT030062 Tosa Dog, Kobold U	.12	.20
BT030063 Thunder Spaltis U	.12	.20
BT030064 One-Eyed Demon Lord, Keith One-Eyed U	.12	.20
BT030065 Big Surprise Pandora U	.12	.20
BT030066 Magic Release of Sicilia U	.12	.20
BT030067 Dangerous Fuse U	.12	.20
BT030068 Divine Protection of Shalsana U	.12	.20
BT030069 Demon Lord's Dungeon U	.12	.20
BT030070 Dragon Vanquishing Sword, Dragon Slayer U	.12	.20
BT030071 Dominion Rod U	.12	.20
BT030072 Actor Knights High Priest U	.12	.20
BT030073 Actor Knights Hanged Man U	.12	.20
BT030074 Justice Hammer U	.12	.20
BT030075 Bardiche Drake C	.20	.30
BT030076 Shadow Shamshir Dragon C	.10	.15
BT030077 Dragon Knight, Kagekiyo C	.10	.15
BT030078 Aroi Lance Dragon C	.60	1.00
BT030079 Blade Chakram Dragon C	.10	.15
BT030080 Thunder Knights, Broad Sword Dragon C	.10	.15
BT030081 Dragon Knight, Saito C	.25	.40
BT030082 Thunder Knights, Main Gauche Dragon C	.10	.15
BT030083 Thunder Knights, Iron Fist Dragon C	.10	.15
BT030084 Bucket Arm Dragon C	.10	.15
BT030085 Dragon Knight, Nagakura C	.10	.15
BT030086 Thunder Knights, Brass Shield Dragon C	.10	.15
BT030087 Leather Buckler Dragon C	.10	.15
BT030088 Dragogenius C	.10	.15
BT030089 Magical Fighter, Seijuro Mado C	.10	.15
BT030090 Dragowizard, Rainbow Horn C	.10	.15
BT030091 Toudou the Unseen Hand C	.10	.15
BT030092 Bye Bye Later! C	.30	.50
BT030093 Aftermath, Gagaku C	.75	1.25
BT030094 Flame Art Ninja, Gokuen C	.10	.15
BT030095 Jumping Ninja, Sarutobi C	.10	.15
BT030096 Skull Golem, Mazubaha C	.10	.15
BT030097 Doberman, Kobold C	.10	.15

BT030098 Gummy Slime C	.10	.15
BT030099 Scout, Kiwa the Straight Man C	.10	.15
BT030100 Fate Skeleton C	.10	.15
BT030101 Monster Master's Staff, Arelta C	.10	.15
BT030102 Actor Knights Justice C	.10	.15
BT030103 Actor Knights Empress C	.10	.15
BT030104 Emperor Shield C	.10	.15
BT030105 Armorknight Cerberus "A" BR	12.00	20.00

2014 Future Card Buddyfight Booster Set 4 Darkness Fable

RELEASED ON OCTOBER 10, 2014

BT040001 Super Armordragon, Gargantua Blade Dragon RRR	.60	1.00
BT040001 Super Armordragon, Gargantua Blade Dragon SP	10.00	15.00
BT040002 Jackknife "Gold Ritter" SP	12.00	20.00
BT040002 Jackknife "Gold Ritter" RRR	3.00	5.00
BT040003 Demon Wolf, Fenrir RRR	2.00	3.00
BT040004 Great Magician, Merlin RRR	5.00	8.00
BT040005 Sword of the King, Excalibur RRR	4.00	6.00
BT040006 Black Dragon, Maveltaker RRR	.60	1.00
BT040006 Black Dragon, Maveltaker SP	5.00	8.00
BT040007 Devil Stigma RRR	15.00	25.00
BT040008 Slow Pain Fall RRR	1.25	2.00
BT040008 Slow Pain Fall SP	8.00	12.00
BT040009 Dragon Knight, Napoleon RR	.60	1.00
BT040010 Jackknife "Berserker" RR	2.00	3.00
BT040011 Jackknife "Burn Energy" RR	4.00	6.00
BT040012 Gorgon Three Sisters, Euryale RR	.60	1.00
BT040013 Knights of the Round Table, King Arthur RR	1.00	1.50
BT040013 Knights of the Round Table, King Arthur SP	12.00	20.00
BT040014 Lord of the Forest, Zlatorog RR	6.00	10.00
BT040015 Wind Fairy, Sylph RR	1.25	2.00
BT040016 Symbel Gard RR	2.00	3.00
BT040017 Death Ruler, Curse RR	.30	.50
BT040018 Death Wizard Dragon RR	1.50	2.50
BT040019 Judgment Day RR	.75	1.25
BT040020 Nightmare Despair RR	2.50	4.00
BT040021 Jackknife "Jaeger" R	.15	.25
BT040022 Twin Horned King of Knights, Alexander R	.15	.25
BT040023 Gargantua Blade, Black Smasher R	.15	.25
BT040024 Roaring Slash!! Gargantua Punisher!! R	.15	.25
BT040024 Roaring Slash!! Gargantua Punisher!! SP	10.00	15.00
BT040025 Colossal Sea Monster, Cetus R	.15	.25
BT040026 Demonic Beast, Grendel R	.15	.25
BT040027 Armored Dragon, Cuelebre R	.15	.25
BT040028 Golden Blade, Chrysaor R	.15	.25
BT040029 Gorgon Three Sisters, Medusa R	.15	.25
BT040030 Spring Healed Jack R	.15	.25
BT040031 Ice Blade, Joker R	.15	.25
BT040031 Ice Blade, Joker SP		
BT040032 Great Spell, Ragnarok SP	8.00	12.00
BT040032 Great Spell, Ragnarok R	.15	.25
BT040033 Great Spell, Thunder of Zeus R	.15	.25
BT040034 Decree of Dullahan R	.15	.25
BT040035 Breathen Gard R	2.00	3.00
BT040036 Immortal Sword, Durandal R	.15	.25
BT040036 Immortal Sword, Durandal SP	10.00	15.00
BT040037 Divine Protection, Prydwen R	.15	.25
BT040038 Bloody Moon Dragon R	.15	.25
BT040039 Death Dragon, Deathgaze Dragon R	.15	.25
BT040039 Death Dragon, Deathgaze Dragon SP	10.00	15.00
BT040040 Death Ruler, Gallows SP	10.00	15.00
BT040040 Death Ruler, Gallows R	.15	.25
BT040041 Death Grip R	.15	.25
BT040041s Death Grip SP	10.00	15.00
BT040042 Abyss Symphony R	1.25	2.00
BT040043 Evil Death Scythe R	.15	.25
BT040044 Arcana Flash R	.15	.25
BT040045 Destroy Hammer Dragon U	.12	.20
BT040046 Spike Shoulder "Blazing" U	.12	.20
BT040047 Dragonic Counter U	.12	.20
BT040048 Jackknife Gift U	.12	.20
BT040049 Dragonic Force Field U	.12	.20
BT040050 Corpse Swallower, Hraesvelgr U	.12	.20
BT040051 Wawel Drache U	.12	.20
BT040052 Frost Giant, Hrimthurs U	.12	.20
BT040053 Knights of the Round Table, Gawain U	.12	.20
BT040054 Furious Unicorn U	.12	.20
BT040055 Knights of the Round Table, Galahad U	.12	.20
BT040056 Dragon Vanquishing Emperor, Beowulf U	.12	.20
BT040057 Knights of the Round Table, Gareth U	.12	.20
BT040058 Ainsel's Damage Rebound U	.12	.20
BT040059 Great Spell, Fimbulwinter U	.12	.20
BT040060 Elixir of Aesculapius U	.12	.20
BT040061 Shield of Achilles U	.12	.20
BT040062 Dragon Vanquishing Sword, Balmung U	.12	.20
BT040063 Rune Staff U	.12	.20
BT040064 Death Ruler, Pain U	.12	.20
BT040065 Death Ruler, Executei U	.12	.20
BT040066 Black Dragon, Fundula U	.12	.20
BT040067 Death Ruler, Cremation U	.12	.20
BT040068 Black Dragon, Cold Blade U	.12	.20
BT040069 Death Ruler, Burial U	.12	.20
BT040070 Death Shield U	.12	.20
BT040071 Guillotine Cutter U	.12	.20
BT040072 Lunatic U	.12	.20
BT040073 Dark Energy U	.12	.20
BT040074 Actor Knights Fortune U	.12	.20
BT040075 Forbidden Edge Dragon C	.10	.15
BT040076 Thunder Knights, Pallasch Sword Dragon C	.10	.15
BT040077 Dragon Knight, Musashi C	.10	.15
BT040078 Left Sword Dragon C	.10	.15
BT040079 Right Sword Dragon C	.10	.15
BT040080 Center Sword Dragon C	.10	.15
BT040081 Viking Sword Dragon C	.10	.15
BT040082 Enchant Wand Dragon C	.10	.15
BT040083 Iron Dragon, Tarasque C	.10	.15
BT040084 Knights of the Round Table, Percival C	.10	.15
BT040085 Getters Cursed Dragon C	.10	.15
BT040086 Gorgon Three Sisters, Stheno C	.10	.15
BT040087 Divine Stallion, Pegasus C	.10	.15
BT040088 Power of Mythology C	.10	.15
BT040089 Heroic Spirit C	.10	.15
BT040090 The Wydar Sarkal C	.10	.15
BT040091 Berserk Gard C	.10	.15
BT040092 Gleipnir C	.10	.15
BT040093 Holy Grail C	.10	.15
BT040094 Divine Armor, Aegis C	.10	.15
BT040095 Famous Sword, Hrunting C	.10	.15
BT040096 Death Ruler, Soulbreaker C	.10	.15
BT040097 Black Dragon, Death Hang C	.10	.15
BT040098 Death Ruler, Atihima C	.10	.15
BT040099 Dark Stalker Dragon C	.10	.15
BT040100 Black Dragon, Needle Fang C	.10	.15
BT040101 Black Dragon Shield C	.10	.15
BT040102 Demonic Talon, Vampire Claw C	.10	.15
BT040103 Actor Knights Devil C	.10	.15
BT040104 Fortune-shield C	.10	.15
BT040105 Purgatory Knights Leader, Demios Sword Dragon BR	10.00	15.00

2015 Future Card Buddyfight Booster Set 5 Break to the Future

RELEASED ON JANUARY 30, 2015

BT050001 Super Armordragon, General Boldness RRR	.30	.50
BT050001 Super Armordragon, General Boldness SP	10.00	15.00
BT050002 Super Armordragon, Drum Breaker Dragon RRR	4.00	6.00
BT050002 Super Armordragon, Drum Breaker Dragon SP	6.00	10.00
BT050003 Venom Harpe Dragon RRR	.30	.50
BT050004 Cavalry Dragon, Hyperion RRR	.75	1.25
BT050004 Cavalry Dragon, Hyperion SP	25.00	40.00
BT050005 Artificial Angel, Virginie Casta RRR	2.50	4.00
BT050005 Artificial Angel, Virginie Casta SP	12.00	20.00
BT050006 Super Lethal Formation RRR	3.00	5.00
BT050006 Super Lethal Formation SP	15.00	25.00
BT050007 Death Ruler, Thirteen RRR	2.00	3.00
BT050007 Death Ruler, Thirteen SP	6.00	10.00
BT050008 Black Dragon of Demise, Death Tallica RRR	3.00	5.00
BT050008 Black Dragon of Demise, Death Tallica SP		
BT050009 Great Evil Dragon, Samael Apocalypse RRR	.75	1.25
BT050009 Great Evil Dragon, Samael Apocalypse SP	2.50	4.00
BT050010 Purgatory Knights, Gairahm Lance Dragon RR		6.00
BT050011 Dragon Knight, Spartax RR	.30	.50
BT050012 Dragon Knight, Tomoe RR	1.25	2.00
BT050013 Gauntlet Sword Dragon RR	.75	1.25
BT050014 Tomahawk Dragon RR	.30	.50
BT050015 Street Racer, Eligos RR	.60	1.00
BT050016 Great Spell, Devil's Rock and Roll RR	1.25	2.00
BT050016 Great Spell, Devil's Rock and Roll SP	4.00	6.00
BT050017 White Dragon Hermit, Nanase RR		
BT050017 White Dragon Hermit, Nanase SP	6.00	10.00
BT050018 Cat Shadow, Aoihime RR	2.50	4.00
BT050019 Electric Speed Ninja, Inazuma RR	1.00	1.50
BT050020 Treachery, Jakikarasu RR	.75	1.25
BT050021 Death Ruler, Gruen RR	.30	.50
BT050022 Black Dragon, Spinechiller RR	.50	.75
BT050023 Purgatory Knights, Sword Breaker Dragon RR	4.00	6.00
BT050024 Purgatory Knights, Crossbow Dragon RR	5.00	8.00
BT050025 Purgatory Knights, Forever RR	6.00	10.00
BT050026 Zweihander Dragon R	.20	.30
BT050027 Dragon Knight, Motonari R	.20	.30
BT050028 Dragon Knight, Mitsuhide R	.20	.30
BT050029 Missile Bunker Dragon R	.20	.30
BT050030 Dragon Trust R	.60	1.00
BT050031 Demon Sommelier, Zagan R	.60	1.00
BT050032 Magic Artist, Andy R	.75	1.25
BT050033 No Pain No Gain R	6.00	10.00
BT050034 Overstand! R	.20	.30
BT050035 Check It Out! R	1.50	2.50
BT050036 Solomon's Great Barrier R	.75	1.25
BT050037 Magic School, Sephirot R	.20	.30
BT050038 Gunrod, Del Gesu R	.60	1.00
BT050039 Martial Arts, Oosumi R	.50	.75
BT050040 Lock Ninja, Setsui R	.40	.60
BT050041 Diversion Troublemaker, Bakemujina R	.20	.30
BT050042 Secret Sword, Comet R	.60	1.00
BT050043 Secret Sword, Morning Star R	.20	.30
BT050044 Divine Demon Slayer, Amenoohahari R	.20	.30
BT050045 Lamenting Black Steel, Balomdahl R	.20	.30
BT050046 Purgatory Knights Leader, Demios Sword Dragon R	3.00	5.00
BT050046 Purgatory Knights Leader, Demios Sword Dragon SP	12.00	20.00
BT050047 Death Ruler, Mastermind R	.20	.30
BT050048 Death Ruler, Averia R	2.50	4.00
BT050049 Purgatory Knights, Knuckleduster Dragon R	.40	.60
BT050050 Death Astray R	2.50	4.00
BT050051 Nightmare Revive R	.20	.30
BT050052 Crush that Body, and Sustain Mine R	.20	.30
BT050053 Distortion Punisher!! R	3.00	5.00
BT050053 Distortion Punisher!! SP		
BT050054 Brutal Disaster! R	.60	1.00
BT050055 Actor Knights Judgement R	.60	1.00
BT050056 Ultimate Sword Dragon U	.12	.20
BT050057 Great Labrys Dragon U	.40	.60
BT050058 Dragon Knight, Bokuden U	.12	.20
BT050059 Twin Brudes Dragon U	.12	.20
BT050060 One to One U	.12	.20
BT050061 Dragon Cavalry Arts, The Glorious Legacy U	.12	.20
BT050062 57th Generation Great Magician Merlin, Unryu Togetsu U	.12	.20
BT050063 Demon Realm Architect, Gamigin U	3.00	5.00
BT050064 Warrior, Halphas U	1.50	2.50
BT050065 Gentleman, Malphas U	.12	.20
BT050066 Epic Fail! U	.20	.30
BT050067 Disperser of Conflagration, Shiromizuchi U	.60	1.00
BT050068 Arts of Heat Haze U	.12	.20
BT050069 Water Technique, Minawagakushi U	2.50	4.00
BT050070 Elite Sword, Juzumaru U	.12	.20
BT050071 Secret Sword, Glittering Star U	1.00	1.50
BT050072 Purgatory Knights, Mad Halberd Dragon U	.12	.20
BT050073 Black Knight, Goldred U	.12	.20
BT050074 Purgatory Knights, Cruel Command U	.40	.60
BT050075 Shooter of Magic Bullets, Gaspard U	.12	.20
BT050076 Purgatory Flame that Resides Within that Body U	.50	.75
BT050077 Dead Scream U	.12	.20
BT050078 Death Game U	.12	.20
BT050079 Death Counter U	.20	.30
BT050080 Accel End U	1.00	1.50
BT050081 Redupsion Blood U	.20	.30
BT050082 Life Dwells in the Flames of Hades Too U	.12	.20
BT050083 Pain Field U	.50	.75
BT050084 Black Agenda U	1.00	1.50
BT050085 Purgatory Sword, Fatal U	.12	.20
BT050086 Actor Knights Death U	.12	.20
BT050087 Celtic Cross Spread U	.12	.20
BT050088 One Oracle U	.12	.20
BT050089 Blade of Athame U	.12	.20
BT050090 Behemoth Claymore Dragon C	.10	.15
BT050091 Dragon Knight, Hartman C	.10	.15
BT050092 Dragon Knight, Crazy Horse C	.20	.30
BT050093 Blue Sky Knights, Bonblade Dragon C	.10	.15
BT050094 Diamond Shield Dragon C	.10	.15
BT050095 Separate Whip Dragon C	.25	.40
BT050096 Knight Counter C	.10	.15
BT050097 Dragonic Survey C	.10	.15
BT050098 Golden Dragon Shield C	.60	1.00
BT050099 Dragon Arms, Dragokeeper C	.10	.15
BT050100 Sky Poet, Amon C	.10	.15
BT050101 Dragowizard, Gan Alkimia C	.10	.15
BT050102 Dragowizard, Mitschuler C	.10	.15
BT050103 Demon Realm Scientist, Purson C	.20	.30
BT050104 Bestie! C	.20	.30
BT050105 Fang Style Ninja, Kibashachi C	.20	.30
BT050106 Perfect Beauty, Hyoshi Shirasagi C	.10	.15
BT050107 Runaway Female Ninja, Yukishiro C	.10	.15
BT050108 Loud Laugh Ninja, Fugumaru C	.20	.30
BT050109 Striking with the Back of My Sword! C	.10	.15
BT050110 Demon Way, Kiribusuma C	.10	.15
BT050111 Water Technique, Shinotsukuame C	.10	.15
BT050112 Demon Swordsman, Deathstorm C	.10	.15
BT050113 Death Ruler, Skull C	.10	.15
BT050114 Demonic Dark Emperor, Grobius C	.10	.15
BT050115 Obsidian Mane, Grieva C	.10	.15
BT050116 Purgatory Knights, Blood Axe Dragon C	.10	.15
BT050117 Black Knight, Hell Rapier C	.10	.15
BT050118 Purgatory Knights, Silver Staff Dragon C	.10	.15
BT050119 Hand of Muramasa, Katsukiyo C	.10	.15
BT050120 Thirsting Creature, Zanzara C	.10	.15
BT050121 Purgatory Knights, Iron Gerd Dragon C	.10	.15
BT050122 Unfulfilled Desire, Greedy Beak C	.10	.15
BT050123 Death Ruler, Deathcusion C	.10	.15
BT050124 Hades Knight, Goldba C	.10	.15
BT050125 Death Ruler, Asphyxia C	.20	.30
BT050126 Death Ruler, Gespenst C	.60	1.00
BT050127 Bloody Dance C	.10	.15
BT050128 Black Armor C	.10	.15
BT050129 Crisis Field C	.10	.15
BT050130 Purgatory Hyme, The Cursed Being of the Faraway Homeland C	.10	.15
BT050131 Actor Knights Strength C	.10	.15
BT050132 Actor Knights Tower C	.10	.15
BT050133 Actor Knights Temperance C	.10	.15
BT050134 Burn Ship Soul C	.10	.15
BT050135 Card Burn BR	15.00	25.00

2015 Future Card Buddyfight H Booster Set 1 Neo Enforcer Ver. E

RELEASED ON MAY 1, 2015

HBT010001EN Second Crimson Chieftain Burning Fore RRR	.30	.50
HBT010002EN Fifth Omni Dragon Lord Tenbu RRR	1.50	2.50
HBT010002EN Fifth Omni Dragon Lord Tenbu SP	15.00	25.00
HBT010003EN Ultimate Neo Dragon Drum the Future RRR	1.50	2.50
HBT010004EN Ethereal Overlord Gang the King RRR	.30	.50
HBT010005EN TwinHeaded Hellhound Orthrus RRR	1.00	1.50
HBT010006EN Rigel Orion RRR	3.00	5.00
HBT010007EN Ultimate Card Burn RRR	1.00	1.50
HBT010008EN Captain Answer RRR	1.25	2.00
HBT010009EN Dragon Knight Calamity Jane RR	.50	.75
HBT010010EN Crimson Battler Guns Knuckle Dragon RR	.40	.60
HBT010011EN Wicked Dragon Emperor Billion Knuckle RR	8.00	12.00
HBT010012EN Ice Prison Emperor Cocytus Greed RR	.40	.60
HBT010013EN Dekalfar Demon Swordsman Heim RR	.30	.50
HBT010014EN Starfall Night RR	.30	.50
HBT010015EN Oswira Gard RR	15.00	25.00
HBT010016EN Infinite Robo Mathematics RR	2.50	4.00
HBT010017EN Martian UFO Takosuke RR	1.00	1.50
HBT010018EN Rescue Dragon Mach Braver RR	.75	1.25
HBT010019EN Call Super Machine RR	8.00	12.00
HBT010020EN Buddy Sword RR	.50	.75
HBT010021EN Crimson Battler Drum Bunker Dragon R	3.00	5.00
HBT010021EN Crimson Battler Drum Bunker Dragon SP	20.00	30.00
HBT010022EN Dragon Knight Shohashou R	.25	.40
HBT010023EN Dragodefense R	.25	.40
HBT010024EN Crimson Fist Dragoblaze R	.25	.40
HBT010025EN Gigantic Crusher R	.25	.40
HBT010026EN Fifth Omni Divine Arts Howling Storm R	.25	.40
HBT010027EN Bash Dragon Emperor Champion Lord R	.40	.60
HBT010028EN Demonic Fairy Dragon Sorciere R	2.00	3.00
HBT010029EN Dragon Kid Ricky R	.60	1.00
HBT010030EN Maximum Manliness Palm of the Fury Dragon R	.25	.40
HBT010031EN Stellar Deity Astraeus R	1.50	2.50
HBT010032EN Dragon Extermination Knight Siegfried R	.25	.40
HBT010033EN Great Fate Frozen Stars R	.60	1.00
HBT010034EN Buddy Police Decker Drum R	.25	1.00
HBT010034EN Buddy Police Decker Drum SP	8.00	12.00
HBT010035EN Explosive Takedown Rampage Sonic R	.60	1.00
HBT010035EN Explosive Takedown Rampage Sonic SP	8.00	12.00
HBT010036EN Cyber Police Lightning Chaser R	.50	.75
HBT010037EN Card Burn R	.60	1.00
HBT010038EN Ninth Warrior Nine R	1.50	2.50
HBT010039EN Hyper Energy R	6.00	10.00
HBT010040EN Impact Double Sword Slasher R	.40	.60
HBT010041EN Rampage Blaster R	.25	.40
HBT010042EN Damage Control R	2.00	3.00
HBT010043EN Wind Call Cavalry Voltex Arms U	.60	1.00
HBT010044EN Machaela Sword Dragon U	.60	1.00
HBT010045EN Crimson Battler Break Shoulder Dragon U	1.00	1.50
HBT010046EN Dragon Knight Bat Masterson U	.30	.50
HBT010047EN Dragonic Air Raid U	.50	.75
HBT010048EN Superior Buddy U	.60	1.00
HBT010049EN Rage Thirst Emperor Grand Wilderness U	.20	.30
HBT010050EN Burning Right Bruder U	1.00	1.50
HBT010051EN Blizzard Left Bruder U	.60	1.00
HBT010052EN Soaring Dragon Fair Skylines U	5.00	8.00
HBT010053EN Dragon Arcadia U	3.00	5.00
HBT010054EN Taurus Aldebaran U	.40	.60
HBT010055EN Bronze Giant Talos U	.20	.30
HBT010056EN Moon Celestial Selene U	1.00	1.50
HBT010057EN Star Bow Artemis Arrow U	.60	1.00
HBT010058EN Chosen Being U	1.00	1.50
HBT010059EN Type36 Armored Convoy Raigo U	.20	.30
HBT010060EN Card Rhino U	.20	.30
HBT010061EN Hero Hunter Sieben U	1.50	2.50
HBT010062EN Cyber Police Assault Leader U	.20	.30
HBT010063EN New Program 3Man Squad Quartet Five U	.50	.75
HBT010064EN Or So the Dream I had Went U	10.00	15.00
HBT010065EN Why is there a banana peel here U	.20	.30
HBT010066EN Hero Climax U	.40	.60
HBT010067EN Battle Deity Robo Genbu U	.20	.30
HBT010068EN Actor Knights the Star U	.20	.30
HBT010069EN Battle Deity Support U	.40	.60
HBT010070EN Disasquake Dragon C	1.50	2.50
HBT010071EN Crimson Battler ShieldArm Dragon C	.15	.25
HBT010072EN Crimson Battler Bay Rush Drake C	.40	.60

HBT010073EN Dragon Knight Tadakatsu C .30 .50
HBT010074EN Crimson Battler Radical Leg Dragon C .50 .75
HBT010075EN Dragonic Survive C .15 .25
HBT010076EN Dragonic Repair Weapon C .15 .25
HBT010077EN Dragonic Repair Shield C .15 .25
HBT010078EN Blazing Dragon Fist Dragoburst C .40 .60
HBT010079EN Blade Dragon Emperor Vorpal Spartar C .60 1.00
HBT010080EN Island Dragon of the Origin Little Land Mu C .15 .25
HBT010081EN Gathering of the Armed Dragons C .15 .25
HBT010082EN Dragon Prudent C .15 .25
HBT010083EN Sky Splitting Armor Masurao C .15 .25
HBT010084EN Sirius Lailaps C .60 1.00
HBT010085EN Capella Origar C .15 .25
HBT010086EN Procyon Melampus C .15 .25
HBT010087EN Sulizers Gard C .15 .25
HBT010088EN Mobile Berserker Gomaguts C .15 .25
HBT010089EN Card Serpent C .15 .25
HBT010090EN First Warrior Einder C .15 .25
HBT010091EN Second Warrior Zweider C .15 .25
HBT010092EN Heavy Trooper Metal Prisoner C .15 .25
HBT010093EN Third Warrior Dreider C .15 .25
HBT010094EN Fire All Cannons C .15 .25
HBT010095EN Reckless Bravery C .60 1.00
HBT010096EN Actor Knights the Sun C .15 .25
HBT010097EN Actor Knights the Moon C .15 .25
HBT010098EN Battle Deity Robo Sky Dragon C .15 .25
HBT010099EN Battle Deity Robo Nightmare C .15 .25
HBT010100EN Crimson Battler Drum Bunker Dragon BR 10.00 15.00
HBT010101EN Demonic Demise Dragon Azi Dahaka SCR 3.00 5.00
HBT010102EN Twin Demon Dragon Zahhak SCR 4.00 6.00
HBT010103EN Dragon Throne SCR 12.00 20.00
HBT010104EN Demonic Demise Sword Aqulta Gwaneff SCR 3.00 5.00
HBT010105EN Dragon Ein SCR 10.00 15.00
HBT010106EN Super Armordragon Vajra Blaster Dragon RR .75 1.25
HBT010107EN Loki the Ehrgeiz RR 2.50 4.00
HBT010108EN Dragon Return System R .60 1.00
HBT010109EN Dragonblade Drumsword R .60 1.00
HBT010110EN Fang Slade Drum U 1.25 2.00
HBT010111EN Moon Wolf Managarmr U 1.00 1.50
HBT010112EN Frost Wall Nevel Vans U .20 .30
HBT010113EN Red Dragon Shield C 1.50 2.50
HBT010114EN Ice Emperor Thrudgelmir C .15 .25
HBT010115EN Secret Army of the Divine King Vodan Shadow C .15 .25
HBT010116EN Horn of Demise Gjallarhorn C .15 .25

2015 Future Card Buddyfight H Booster Set 2 Galaxy Burst

RELEASED ON JULY 17, 2015
HBT020001EN Armordeity Dynamis RRR .60 1.00
HBT020002EN First Omni Beast Lord Ziun RRR 1.00 1.50
HBT020002EN First Omni Beast Lord Ziun SP 8.00 12.00
HBT020003EN Nanomachine Ninja Byakuya RRR 3.00 5.00
HBT020004EN Fairy King Oberon RRR 4.00 6.00
HBT020005EN Seventh Omni Earth Lord Count Dawn RRR 6.00 10.00
HBT020005EN Seventh Omni Earth Lord Count Dawn SP 10.00 15.00
HBT020006EN Cosmic Storm Greisen ZK RRR .40 .60
HBT020007EN Sixth Omni Storm Lord Variable Cord RRR 6.00 10.00
HBT020007EN Sixth Omni Storm Lord Variable Cord SP 10.00 15.00
HBT020008EN Star Guardian Jackknife RRR 2.50 4.00
HBT020009 Jackknife Anzestor RR 1.00 1.50
HBT020010 Ghoul Deity Gojinmaru RR 1.50 2.50
HBT020011 Yumi Ninja Suiha RR 5.00 8.00
HBT020012 Lightning Speed Tsukiusagi RR 1.00 1.50
HBT020013 Water Slash Sword Murasame RR .40 .60
HBT020014 Deity of Sun and Death Bloody King RR .75 1.25
HBT020015 Odd Bird Harpy RR .40 .60
HBT020016 Divine Spear Gungnir RR .30 .50
HBT020017 Dragonic Armored Ship Marshal Fortress RR .60 1.00
HBT020018 Dragonarms Factory RR 10.00 15.00
HBT020019EN Sudden Wormhole RR 1.50 2.50
HBT020020EN Thunder Claw Narukami RR .75 1.25
HBT020021EN Drum Bunker Dragon Spinning Lance R .60 1.00
HBT020022EN Fatal Arms Dragon R .30 .50
HBT020023 Crimson Battler Double Katar Dragon R .60 1.00
HBT020024 Crimson Battler Power Stamp Dragon R .60 1.00
HBT020025 Dragon Knight Lincoln R .25 .40
HBT020026 Trap Master Dragon R .25 .40
HBT020027 Dragon Knight Cromwell R .25 .40
HBT020028 Dragon Knight Lenus R .25 .40
HBT020029 Thunder Knights Silverchain Dragon R .25 .40
HBT020030 4000 Festival R .25 .40
HBT020031 Ring of Crimson R 1.25 2.00
HBT020032 Demonic Descend Ninja Zeon R .25 .40
HBT020033 Kalavinka Uguisukomachi R .25 .40
HBT020034 Hidden Sword Ninja Sekitetsu R .25 .40
HBT020035 Demonic Way of Hundred Demons Akishoki R .25 .40
HBT020036 Odd Ritual Skull Festival R .25 .40
HBT020037 Absolute Sword Azure Cascade Formation R .25 .40
HBT020038 Wolfman Gutz R .25 .40
HBT020039 Valkyrie Brilliant Brynhildr R .60 1.00
HBT020040 Purplish Green Dragon Peluda R .25 .40
HBT020041 Cait Sith in Boots R .25 .40
HBT020042 Vert Deus Matrix R .60 1.00
HBT020043 Dragonarms Elgar Cannon R .60 1.00
HBT020044 Barracal Barret R .25 .40
HBT020045 Earth Barrier R .25 .40
HBT020046 Radiant Punisher R .25 .40
HBT020047 Battle Deity Robo GIZAI Emperor R .25 .40
HBT020048 Cut Whip Dragon U .15 .25
HBT020049 Thunder Knights Spike Shoulder Dragon U 1.25 2.00
HBT020050 Thunder Knights Slide Wing Dragon U .15 .25
HBT020051 Fist of the Red Battler U .15 .25
HBT020052 Dragonic Loop U .15 .25
HBT020053 Thunderclap Goraiko U .15 .25
HBT020054 Outlander Bokunryu U .15 .25
HBT020055 OneEyed Ninja Refu U .15 .25
HBT020056 Demon Kid Hiunmaru U .15 .25
HBT020057 Rampage Chizomegumo U .15 .25
HBT020058 Sword Skill Sen no Sen U .15 .25
HBT020059 Reinforced Formation of Hundred Demons U .15 .25
HBT020060 Ninja Arts Mat Flipping Technique U 5.00 8.00
HBT020061 Demon Way Oborogenbu U .15 .25
HBT020062 Dashing in the Moonlight Red Cap U .15 .25
HBT020063 Fairy Knight Daoine Shee U .15 .25
HBT020064 Loyal Unicorn U .15 .25
HBT020065 Night Witch Clear U .15 .25
HBT020066 Death Summoning Tears of the Banshee U .15 .25
HBT020067 Book of Illusions Mabinogion U .15 .25
HBT020068 Annoying Ways of the Troll U .15 .25
HBT020069 The Godjenesis U .15 .25
HBT020070 Photon Crown Geocorona U .15 .25
HBT020071 Brun Deus Akision U 1.00 1.50
HBT020072 Dragonarms Artiliger U .15 .25
HBT020073 Star Saber Asteroid U .15 .25
HBT020074 Photon Saber Filament U .15 .25
HBT020075 Battle Deity Robo Azul Dragon U .15 .25
HBT020076 Battle Deity Robo Search Whale U .15 .25
HBT020077 Operation Restraint U .15 .25
HBT020078 Thunder Knights Sword Bunker Dragon C .10 .15
HBT020079 Kris Knife Dragon C .10 .15
HBT020080 Crimson Battler Burn Guts Dragon C .10 .15
HBT020081 Systemic Dagger Black Edge C .10 .15
HBT020082 Dragon Knight Ranmaru C .10 .15
HBT020083 Dragonic Teamwork C .10 .15
HBT020084 Martial Bones Fist Dragosquare C .10 .15
HBT020085 Almighty Dokakusai C .10 .15
HBT020086 Japanese Blade Ninja Hachimonji C .10 .15
HBT020087 Composed Kageitachi C .10 .15
HBT020088 Ceremony of Exorcism C .10 .15
HBT020089 Demon Way Fools Festival C .10 .15
HBT020090 Elite Sword Dojigiri C .10 .15
HBT020091 White Dragon Gwiber C .60 1.00
HBT020092 Carved Stallion of Dreams Dalahast C .10 .15
HBT020093 Red Dragon Welsh C .60 1.00
HBT020094 Demonic Beast of Gem Vouivre C .10 .15
HBT020095 Great Spell Weiterstadt C 2.00 3.00
HBT020096 Algiz Gard C .10 .15
HBT020097 Giant Star Leitning C .10 .15
HBT020098 Mother Space Oortcloud C .10 .15
HBT020099 Azul Tesslamagna C .10 .15
HBT020100 Shooting Star Balmeteor C .10 .15
HBT020101 Star Cruiser Orbital C .10 .15
HBT020102 Dragonarms Winchisker C .10 .15
HBT020103 Battle Deity Robo Spear Kart C .10 .15
HBT020104 Battle Deity Robo Missile Dog C .10 .15
HBT020105 End of War C .10 .15
HBT020106 Fall Back C .10 .15
HBT020107 Disturb C .10 .15
HBT020108 Star Guardian Jackknife BR 8.00 12.00
HBT020109 Great Fiend Yamigedo SCR 8.00 12.00
HBT020110 Great Fiend Yamigedo SCR 3.00 5.00
HBT020111 Soaring Flame Lindwurm SCR 4.00 6.00
HBT020112 Reinforced Formation of Hundred Demons SCR .60 1.00
HBT020113 Thunder Claw Narukami SCR 1.00 1.50
HBT020114 Parade of Hundred Demons SCR 1.25 2.00
HBT020115 Crimson Battler Rock Bunker Dragon R .25 .40
HBT020116 Crimson Battler Heavyimpact Dragon R .25 .40
HBT020117 Dragonic Assault U .15 .25
HBT020118 Tempest Sword Makiarashi U .15 .25
HBT020119 Fire Stone Dragon C .10 .15
HBT020120 Buddy Buddy BAAAAAN C .10 .15
HBT020121 Fire Giant Surtr C .10 .15
HBT020122 Evil Dragon Nidhogg C .10 .15

2015 Future Card Buddyfight H Booster Set 3 Assault of the Omni Lords

RELEASED ON OCTOBER 16, 2015
HBT030001EN Fifth Omni Cavalry Dragon Magical Blade Mizaru RRR 1.00 1.50
HBT030002EN Dragon Knight Pisaro RRR 2.50 4.00
HBT030003EN Second Omni Demon Lord Asmodai RRR 8.00 12.00
HBT030003EN Second Omni Demon Lord Asmodai SP 15.00 25.00
HBT030004EN Witch of Illusions Luvia the Mirage RRR .60 1.00
HBT030005EN Eliminator Glasya Labolas RRR 1.00 1.50
HBT030006EN Fourth Omni Fire Lord Burn Nova RRR 3.00 5.00
HBT030006EN Fourth Omni Fire Lord Burn Nova SP 25.00 40.00
HBT030007EN Third Omni Water Lord Miserea RRR 1.50 2.50
HBT030007EN Third Omni Water Lord Miserea SP 20.00 30.00
HBT030008EN Baptism Knight Kamil RRR 8.00 12.00
HBT030009EN Fifth Omni Cavalry Dragon Fire Sword Doble RR 1.00 1.50
HBT030010EN Double Squeek Hammer Dragon RR .60 1.00
HBT030011EN Fifth Omni Dragon Fist Ablaze RR 1.00 1.50
HBT030012EN Fallen Demon Lord Rucifiel RR .60 1.00
HBT030013EN Follower Gaap RR .75 1.25
HBT030014EN DJ of Graveyard Bune RR .30 .50
HBT030015EN Never Say Never RR 1.25 2.00
HBT030016EN Armorider Dragon Emperor Suvarious RR .40 .60
HBT030017EN Boundless Dragon Emperor Merabacshin RR .75 1.25
HBT030018EN Underling of the Fire Lord Ricky RR 1.50 2.50
HBT030019EN Flash Lance Blitz Tiger RR 1.25 2.00
HBT030020EN Unorthodox Arts Shoraiabare Kandachi RR 1.50 2.50
HBT030021EN Dragon Lightning Emperor Ivan R .60 1.00
HBT030022EN Fifth Omni Cavalry Dragon Ice Lance Merak R .60 1.00
HBT030023EN Thunder Knights Hardy Knife Dragon R .30 .50
HBT030024EN Dragonic Grimoire Backwater Inscription R .60 1.00
HBT030025EN Fifth Omni Oath Dragoundertake R .30 .50
HBT030026EN Dragon Lord Initiation Giga Howling Crusher R .30 .50
HBT030027EN Dragowizard Gorgas R .30 .50
HBT030028EN Battle Wizard The Ace R .30 .50
HBT030029EN Great Spell Auld Lang Syne R 2.50 4.00
HBT030030EN Mind of Hardcore R .30 .50
HBT030031EN Gunrod Symphonion R .30 .50
HBT030032EN Gatling Hardcore R .30 .50
HBT030033EN Honor Emperor Dragon Magic Gun Riki R .30 .50
HBT030034EN Rainbow Dragon Arcenciel R .30 .50
HBT030035EN Wicked Dragon of Fabrication Demonica R .30 .50
HBT030036EN Wrath Trigger R .30 .50
HBT030037EN A Dragon Against Thousands R .30 .50
HBT030038EN Sturdy Dragon Strike R .30 .50
HBT030039EN Demon Knight of Destruction Fold Break R .30 .50
HBT030040EN Dragon Guardian of the Sanctuary Lumiere R .30 .50
HBT030041EN Purge Knight Vlad Dracula R .30 .50
HBT030042EN Revolution Knight Rebellious R .30 .50
HBT030043EN Knight of Glory El Quixote R .30 .50
HBT030044EN Aide of the Water Lord Stein Blade Joker R .30 .50
HBT030045EN Savage Lance Eisen Tiger R .30 .50
HBT030046EN Full Strash Formation R 1.50 2.50
HBT030047EN Darkness Final Mission Card World End R .30 .50
HBT030048EN Fifth Omni Armored Dragon Soul Returner Seikirei U .25 .40
HBT030049EN Fifth Omni Armored Dragon Steel Ball Rindo U .25 .40
HBT030050EN Fly Trap Dragon U .25 .40
HBT030051EN Thunder Knights Double Flail Dragon U .25 .40
HBT030052EN Fifth Omni Cavalry Dragon Wind Bow Meglax U .25 .40
HBT030053EN Dragon Bind Attack U .25 .40
HBT030054EN Lords Dragon Shield U .25 .40
HBT030055EN Dragon Land U .25 .40
HBT030056EN Dragon Lord Sword Dragoemperor U .25 .40
HBT030057EN Great Commander Dvorak U .25 .40
HBT030058EN Battle Wizard The Straight U .25 .40
HBT030059EN Trio U .25 .40
HBT030060EN Thats How I Roll U .25 .40
HBT030061EN Happy Camper U .25 .40
HBT030062EN Ring Dragon Emperor Rust Igliha U .25 .40
HBT030063EN Guardian Dragon Emperor Amuray U .25 .40
HBT030064EN Blowout Emperor Las Volganon U .25 .40
HBT030065EN Amber Dragon Kantal U .25 .40
HBT030066EN Makings of a Great Dragon U .25 .40
HBT030067EN Manliness Spirit Shield U .25 .40
HBT030068EN Unwielding Dragon U .25 .40
HBT030069EN Scatter Armor Enma U .25 .40
HBT030070EN Dragon Demon Lord Arkdra U .25 .40
HBT030071EN Demon Lord Joker Grunwald U .25 .40
HBT030072EN Apprentice Knight Ruu U .25 .40
HBT030073EN Basilisk Slime U .25 .40
HBT030074EN Twin Tail Incubus U .25 .40
HBT030075EN Mission Card Earn Experience Points U .25 .40
HBT030076EN Great Battle Deity Robo KISIN Rakshasa U .25 .40
HBT030077EN Barbed Wire U .25 .40
HBT030078EN Buzzsaw Roar Dragon C .12 .20
HBT030079EN Fifth Omni Armored Dragon Giant Battle Axe Dokuju C .12 .20
HBT030080EN Crimson Battler The Blacksmith C .12 .20
HBT030081EN Crimson Battler Sesters Dragon C .12 .20
HBT030082EN Fifth Omni Armored Dragon Smuggler Torame C .12 .20
HBT030083EN Fifth Omni Armored Dragon Disintegrate Arale C .12 .20
HBT030084EN Dragon Knight Galileo C .12 .20
HBT030085EN Fifth Omni Cavalry Dragon Sand Staff Arkaid C .12 .20
HBT030086EN Dragon Knight Enrique C .12 .20
HBT030087EN Dragon Guard C .12 .20
HBT030088EN Dragosolid C .12 .20
HBT030089EN Dragon Change C .12 .20
HBT030090EN Dragopride Fifth Omni Dignity C .12 .20
HBT030091EN Secret Treasure of Dragons Dragopotion C .12 .20
HBT030092EN Dragon Knight Formation C .12 .20
HBT030093EN Extreme Dragon Sword Dragobraver C .12 .20
HBT030094EN Blue Flame Master Zustein C .12 .20
HBT030095EN Mediator Botis C .12 .20
HBT030096EN Magic Realm Bouncer Andless C .12 .20
HBT030097EN Magic Realm Fantasista Selle C .12 .20
HBT030098EN Hundred Demons Sorcery Go Away C .12 .20
HBT030099EN Its All Cool C .12 .20
HBT030100EN Hundred Demons Sorcery Pathetic C .12 .20
HBT030101EN Vehement Dragon Emperor Super Shine C 1.50 2.50
HBT030102EN Shimmer Energy Dragon Aurora C .12 .20
HBT030103EN Green Dragon Belmoss C .12 .20
HBT030104EN Ash Dragon Defores C .12 .20
HBT030105EN Bronze Dragon Daygala C .12 .20
HBT030106EN Dragon Kid Lesser C .12 .20
HBT030107EN Dragon Kid Ruse C .12 .20
HBT030108EN Disaster and Bliss Comes with Dragons C .12 .20
HBT030109EN Surging Dragon Waves C .12 .20
HBT030110EN No Matter Where Dragon Rules Supreme C .12 .20
HBT030111EN Ringlet Loop of Fire C .12 .20
HBT030112EN Explosive Happiness Endless Magnum C .12 .20
HBT030113EN Archdemon C .12 .20
HBT030114EN Dragon Wing Knight Dragon Gard C .12 .20
HBT030115EN Purgatory Block C .12 .20
HBT030116EN Wandering Knight Roy C .12 .20
HBT030117EN Demonic Eye General Rhodes Dylan C .12 .20
HBT030118EN Thunder Emperor Zein Blestand C .12 .20
HBT030119EN Hundred Demons Sorcery Evil Pulse C .12 .20
HBT030120EN Command of the Water Lord C .12 .20
HBT030121EN Battle Deity Robo Mass Soldier C .12 .20
HBT030122EN Buddy Remodel C .12 .20
HBT030123EN Fifth Omni Dragon Lord Drum BR 25.00 40.00
HBT030124EN Fifth Omni Dragon Lord Drum SCR 8.00 12.00
HBT030125EN Fifth Omni Dragon Lord Drum SCR ALT ART 40.00 60.00
HBT030126EN Fifth Omni Armored Dragon Leaping Zakuro SCR 5.00 8.00
HBT030127EN Lords Dragon Shield SCR 2.50 4.00
HBT030128EN Dragon Lord Initiation Giga Howling Crusher SCR 2.50 4.00
HBT030129EN Dragon World SCR 5.00 8.00
HBT030130EN Crimson Battler Catapult Knuckle R .30 .50
HBT030131EN Blue Dragon Shield R .30 .50
HBT03132EN Descend Dragon Emperor Everrock U .25 .40
HBT03133EN Brawling Dragons U .25 .40
HBT03134EN Magic Realm Seaman Forneus C .12 .20
HBT03135EN Revolution Dragon Evolution C .12 .20

2016 Future Card Buddyfight H Booster Set 4 Mikado Evolution

RELEASED ON JANUARY 22, 2016
HBT040001EN Fifth Omni Super Dragon Lord Kaizer Drum RRR .50 .75
HBT040001EN Fifth Omni Super Dragon Lord Kaizer Drum SP 15.00 25.00
HBT040002EN Dragon Knight Faust RRR .75 1.25
HBT040003EN Eighth Omni Deity Lord Grangadez RRR 2.00 3.00
HBT040003EN Eighth Omni Deity Lord Grangadez SP 10.00 15.00
HBT040004EN Armorknight Demon A RRR 4.00 6.00
HBT040005EN Messenger of Despair Metameria RRR .50 .75
HBT040006EN First Knight of the Apocalypse Gratos RRR 2.00 3.00
HBT040006EN First Knight of the Apocalypse Gratos SP 10.00 15.00
HBT040007EN The Genesic Omega Big Bang RRR .50 .75
HBT040008EN Specter of Darkness Wasteland OYamigedo RRR 2.50 4.00
HBT040008EN Specter of Darkness Wasteland OYamigedo SP 25.00 40.00
HBT040009EN Fifth Omni Armored Dragon Sound Speed Sen RR .30 .50
HBT040010EN Chieftain Fist Dragogeneral RR 2.50 4.00
HBT040011EN Armorknight Lion Drake RR 1.00 1.50
HBT040012EN Armorknight Asura RR .30 .50
HBT040013EN Demon Slay Come Forth RR 5.00 8.00
HBT040014EN Jinxed Landfill Curse Count RR .30 .50
HBT040015EN Hundred Demons Sorcery Soul Drain RR 1.00 1.50
HBT040016EN Apocalypse Death Shield RR .60 1.00
HBT040017EN Blooddrain Sword Bloody Fate RR 2.50 4.00
HBT040018EN Fourth Dimension Mobius RR 1.00 1.50
HBT040019EN V Gradation Quantum Ruler RR .60 1.00
HBT040020EN Radiant Saber Providence RR .30 .50
HBT040021EN Fifth Omni Armored Dragon Dark Arms Suu R .40 .60
HBT040022EN Fifth Omni Armored Dragon Toxin Tenki R .40 .60
HBT040023EN Dragon Knight Martell R .50 .75
HBT040024EN Dragowisdom Knowledge of the Fifth Omni R 5.00 8.00
HBT040025EN Thunder Break Stance R .20 .30
HBT040026EN Dragon Lance Stronghorn R .40 .60
HBT040027EN Armorknight Dragon Earthshaker R .30 .50
HBT040028EN Armorknight Noise Bat R .30 .50
HBT040029EN Armorknight Little Drake R .30 .50
HBT040030EN Ritual of Deity Lord Descend R .75 1.25
HBT040031EN Dangerous REIZI R .40 .60
HBT040032EN Supreme Ji Asura Demon Slay R .20 .30
HBT040033EN True Ultimate Battle Skill GIGA Demon Slay R .40 .60
HBT040034EN Final Gate Guider Giudecca R .40 .60
HBT040035EN Death Ruler Blixt R 1.00 1.50
HBT040036EN Gate Guider Gallows Gestus R .60 1.00
HBT040037EN Inferno Shield R 3.00 5.00

HBT040038EN DEATH Wave Rod Sterben R	.75	1.25
HBT040039EN Hell Gate Walter R	.75	1.25
HBT040040EN Biggest Dragonarms Sonic Blast R	.40	.60
HBT040041EN Dragonarms Transportal R	.75	1.25
HBT040042EN Sphere Cemetery Star Remnant R	.75	1.25
HBT040043EN Fate Information R	4.00	6.00
HBT040044EN Antimatter Cloud R	10.00	15.00
HBT040045EN Cosmo Saber Eternal Anthem R	.60	1.00
HBT040046EN Radiant Stream R	.40	.60
HBT040047EN Battle Deity Robo City Void Fort Mumyo R	.40	.60
HBT040048EN Heavy Canon Cavalry Dragon Big Guns U	.75	1.25
HBT040049EN Crimson Battler Spike Nail Dragon U	.12	.20
HBT040050EN Bloody Chainsaw Dragon U	.40	.60
HBT040051EN Dragonic Climax U	.12	.20
HBT040052EN Fifth Omni Great Dragon Shield U	1.00	1.50
HBT040053EN Fifth Omni Dragon Sword Emperor Fang U	.12	.20
HBT040054EN Dragon World Alliance U	1.25	2.00
HBT040055EN Reverberation Dragon Gin Gon Gan U	.12	.20
HBT040056EN Strongarmed Dragon Iron Caesar U	.12	.20
HBT040057EN Armorknight Battleborg U	.12	.20
HBT040058EN Raging Chained Strikes U	3.00	5.00
HBT040059EN Super Strength Replenishment U	2.50	4.00
HBT040060EN Demon Slay Circle U	.12	.20
HBT040061EN Hundred Demons Spear Aratogame U	.12	.20
HBT040062EN Death Ruler Vroukalakas U	.12	.20
HBT040063EN Third Knight of the Apocalypse Aberrucia U	.12	.20
HBT040064EN Second Knight of the Apocalypse Voremos U	.12	.20
HBT040065EN Fourth Knight of the Apocalypse Thanatos U	.12	.20
HBT040066EN Apparition Demon Knight Lasty U	.60	1.00
HBT040067EN Great River of Hades Archelon U	.50	.75
HBT040068EN Gap of Blood Phantom Dust U	.60	1.00
HBT040069EN Jupiter Two Eumercular U	.12	.20
HBT040070EN Ultra Violet Black Specter U	.12	.20
HBT040071EN Jupiter One Iorctos U	.12	.20
HBT040072EN Swingby Smash U	.12	.20
HBT040073EN Cosmic Evolution U	.12	.20
HBT040074EN Mars Barrier U	1.25	2.00
HBT040075EN Cosmo Saber Luna Zeele U	.12	.20
HBT040076EN Battle Deity Robo Gaolion U	.12	.20
HBT040077EN Operation Hound U	.50	.75
HBT040078EN Sword Cemetery Dragon C	.10	.15
HBT040079EN Dragon Knight Pedro C	.60	1.00
HBT040080EN Fifth Omni Cavalry Dragon Explosive Hammer Fuad C	.25	.40
HBT040081EN Crimson Battler Cheering Squad Good Luck C	.30	.50
HBT040082EN Dragonic Fiercefight C	.75	1.25
HBT040083EN Dragon Chase C	.10	.15
HBT040084EN Dragonic Maneuver C	.40	.60
HBT040085EN Carapace Dragon Algalos C	.10	.15
HBT040086EN Armorknight Fairy C	.10	.15
HBT040087EN Clash Deity Dragon Gaelcorga Ark C	.10	.15
HBT040088EN Violent Dragon Geolga C	.20	.30
HBT040089EN Hundred Demons Sorcery Manbutsu Bakusai C	.10	.15
HBT040090EN Return to Hades C	.10	.15
HBT040091EN Death Ruler Eclipse C	.10	.15
HBT040092EN Gate Guider Limbo C	.10	.15
HBT040093EN Gate Guider Andino C	.30	.50
HBT040094EN Gate Guider De Lomeer C	.10	.15
HBT040095EN Black Dragon G C	1.00	1.50
HBT040096EN Gate Guider Gainare C	.10	.15
HBT040097EN Hundred Demons Sorcery Bad Trap C	.10	.15
HBT040098EN Dark Fog C	.30	.50
HBT040099EN Execute Sword Tragedy C	.25	.40
HBT040100EN Dragonarms Reconnaissance C	.10	.15
HBT040101EN Dynamic Star Meteor Fallen C	.10	.15
HBT040102EN Energy of Universe C	.20	.30
HBT040103EN Soularms C	1.00	1.50
HBT040104EN Cosmo Base G Attractor C	.10	.15
HBT040105EN Battle Deity Robo Stone General C	.10	.15
HBT040106EN Emergency Evade C	.10	.15
HBT040107EN Battle Deity Robo Rifle Varian C	.10	.15
HBT040108EN Fifth Omni Super Dragon Lord Kaizer Drum BR	5.00	8.00
HBT040109EN Radiant Guardian Jackknife Aster SCR	2.50	4.00
HBT040110EN Radiant Guardian Jackknife Aster SCR	25.00	40.00
HBT040111EN V Gradation Quantum Ruler SCR	1.50	2.50
HBT040112EN Dragonarms Radiant Scudo SCR	10.00	15.00
HBT040113EN Radiant Saber Providence SCR	3.00	5.00
HBT040114EN Star Dragon World card SCR	3.00	5.00
HBT040115EN Drink on the Soul Empower from the Blood R	.20	.30
HBT040116EN Red Shift Spectrums R	.40	.60
HBT040117EN Undying Skull Sol Darion U	.50	.75
HBT040118EN Line Legion Safer Tear U	.12	.20
HBT040119EN Purgatory Knights Chain Sword Dragon C	.40	.60
HBT040120EN Purgatory Knights Viking Axe Dragon C	.10	.15
HBT040121EN Enshrouding All in Darkness Gafner C	.10	.15
HBT040122EN Core Recycle C	.40	.60

2016 Future Card Buddyfight D Booster Set 1 Unleash Impact Dragon

RELEASED ON APRIL 15, 2016

DBT010001 Scorching Cavalry Dragon Second Helios RRR	.30	.50
DBT010002 Bal Dragon Bal Burst Smasher RRR	3.00	5.00
DBT010003 Manipulator of Shadowform Silhouette Terry RRR	10.00	15.00
DBT010004 Fervent Demon Lord Teacher Asmodai RRR	6.00	10.00
DBT010005 Blackeye Demonic Dragon Blagg Za Bath RRR	.50	.75
DBT010006 Abygale Vanishing Death Hole RRR	5.00	8.00
DBT010007 The Over EX Dimenzion RRR	.40	.60
DBT010008 Jackknife Full Liberate Cannon RRR	.60	1.00
DBT010009 Flamewing Dragon RR	.30	.50
DBT010010 Flarefang Dragon RR	3.00	5.00
DBT010011 Fifth Omni Cavalry Dragon Cavalry Dragon Arts Seven Divine Execute RR	.50	.75
DBT010012 Illusionist of Shadowform Silhouette Joe RR	.60	1.00
DBT010013 Asmodai Diabolical Sparta Teachings RR	3.00	5.00
DBT010014 Mary Sue Eternal Ideal RR	.30	.50
DBT010015 Black Diadem Zacrown RR	3.00	5.00
DBT010016 Gale Destruction RR	6.00	10.00
DBT010017 Gallows Bloodsucker RR	1.00	1.50
DBT010018 Star Dragoner Luminous Blue RR	.30	.50
DBT010019 Star Jack Repair RR	.30	.50
DBT010020 Star Alternate RR	1.00	1.50
DBT010021 Fifth Omni Super Cavalry Dragon Hellfire Sword Doble R	.75	1.25
DBT010022 Sun Dragon Bal Dragon R	4.00	6.00
DBT010023 Blazehorn Dragon R	.20	.30
DBT010024 Stout Arm of the Sun R	.20	.30
DBT010025 Blue Dragon Shield R	1.25	2.00
DBT010026 Sun Fist Bal Knuckle R	.20	.30
DBT010027 Unparalleled Arts Omni Lord Burst R	.20	.30
DBT010028 Bal Dragon All Out Bal Aura R	.20	.30
DBT010029 Green Wind Master Rafaga R	.20	.30
DBT010030 Magic Knights of Bonds Dunkelheit and Licht R	.20	.30
DBT010031 Deceiving Shax R	.20	.30
DBT010032 Silhouette Max R	.20	.30
DBT010033 Betrayal Expert Aunas R	.20	.30
DBT010034 Trick or Trick R	.20	.30
DBT010035 Great Spell Saturday Night Devil Fever R	.20	.30
DBT010036 Magical Goodbye R	.20	.30
DBT010037 Gunrod Boesendorfer R	.20	.30
DBT010038 Gate Guider Malebolge R	.20	.30
DBT010039 Black Death Dragon Abygale R	.20	.30
DBT010039 Black Death Dragon Abygale R		
DBT010040 Black Fire Inflame R	.20	.30
DBT010041 Black Drain R	.20	.30
DBT010042 Death Dragon Sickle Gale Scythe R	.20	.30
DBT010043 Abygale Jet Black Storm R	.20	.30
DBT010044 Star Dragoner Jackknife R	.20	.30
DBT010044 Star Dragoner Jackknife R		
DBT010045 Jackarms J Thruster R	.20	.30
DBT010046 Dragonarms Onebarrett R	.20	.30
DBT010047 Dragoners Beat R	.20	.30
DBT010048 Proto Barrier R	.20	.30
DBT010049 Twin Star Jack and Fang R	.20	.30
DBT010050 Jackknife Astro Guardner R	.20	.30
DBT010051 Soularmor Dragon U	.12	.20
DBT010052 Fireclaw Dragon U	.12	.20
DBT010053 Blue Sky Knights Systemic Dagger Dragon U	.12	.20
DBT010054 Heat Dragon Jr U	.12	.20
DBT010055 Bal Support U	.30	.50
DBT010056 Bal Climax U	.60	1.00
DBT010057 Shining Smash U	.40	.60
DBT010058 Dragon Staff Dragogift U	.12	.20
DBT010059 Witch of Variance Alice the Adjuster U	.12	.20
DBT010060 Silhouette Sinbar U	.50	.75
DBT010061 Messenger of Sunlight Sol U	.12	.20
DBT010062 Messenger of Moonlight Luna U	.12	.20
DBT010063 The Shade U	1.00	1.50
DBT010064 Whazzap U	.12	.20
DBT010065 Great Spell Special Elegant Amazing Wall U	.75	1.25
DBT010066 Solomons Great Barrier U	1.25	2.00
DBT010067 Sorcery Book Goetia U	.75	1.25
DBT010068 Black Scar Stigmata U	.12	.20
DBT010069 Black Epicenter Deadlock U	.12	.20
DBT010070 Black Wolf Ulbha U	.60	1.00
DBT010071 Black Revenger U	.12	.20
DBT010072 Purgatory Loophole U	1.00	1.50
DBT010073 Biggest Dragonarms Photonlancer U	.12	.20
DBT010074 Star Dragoner Meteoroid U	.12	.20
DBT010075 Dragonarms Emergence U	.12	.20
DBT010076 Jackarms J Igniter U	1.00	1.50
DBT010077 Star Launcher Soulcanon U	.12	.20
DBT010078 Magellaclouds Magellanic Stream U	.12	.20
DBT010079 Battle Deity Robo Old Kite U	.12	.20
DBT010080 Escape U	.12	.20
DBT010081 Burstdash Dragon C	.10	.15
DBT010082 Dragon Knight Kagekatsu C	.10	.15
DBT010083 Sparkedge Dragon C	.10	.15
DBT010084 Fireball Dragon C	.10	.15
DBT010085 Dragon Knight Kanetsugu C	.10	.15
DBT010086 Sunbooster Dragon C	.60	1.00
DBT010087 Shineknuckle Dragon C	.10	.15
DBT010088 Born Bal Dragon C	.10	.15
DBT010089 Blue Sky Knights Boomerang Dragon C	.10	.15
DBT010090 Break Time C	.75	1.25
DBT010091 Shinestorm C	.10	.15
DBT010092 Mercenaries C	.10	.15
DBT010093 Cover Fire of the Solar Cannon C	.10	.15
DBT010094 Sun Blade Gurensoul C	.10	.15
DBT010095 Sun Fist Burning Sun C	.10	.15
DBT010096 Demon Realm Prosecutor Nebiros C	.10	.15
DBT010097 Hunter of the Magical Forest Leraje C	.40	.60
DBT010098 Silhouette Balun C	.30	.50
DBT010099 Transmitter Dendo C	.60	1.00
DBT010100 Tiny Professor Crocell C	.10	.15
DBT010101 Silhouette Leon C	.60	1.00
DBT010102 Malicious Selector C	.10	.15
DBT010103 Magical Glue C	.75	1.25
DBT010104 Solomons Shield C	.10	.15
DBT010105 Good to go C	.60	1.00
DBT010106 Great Spell Sacred Bless C	.10	.15
DBT010107 Emergency Ward Neverland C	.10	.15
DBT010108 Sorcery Book Theurgy C	.10	.15
DBT010109 Black Sleepless City Dimmborgil C	.10	.15
DBT010110 Death Ruler Blind C	.10	.15
DBT010111 Gate Guider Flegetonte C	.40	.60
DBT010112 Death Damage C	.75	1.25
DBT010113 Scapegoat C	.10	.15
DBT010114 Black Bargain C	.60	1.00
DBT010115 Midnight Shadow C	1.50	2.50
DBT010116 Star Dragoner Magellaclouds C	.10	.15
DBT010117 Star Dragoner Duaraizer C	.10	.15
DBT010118 Star Dragoner Zextant C	.10	.15
DBT010119 Star Dragoner Currentring C		
DBT010120 Barely Attack C	.20	.30
DBT010121 Sonic Move C	.10	.15
DBT010122 Mirage Vision C	.10	.15
DBT010123 Battle Deity Robo Dashogre C	.40	.60
DBT010124 Battle Deity Robo Cutcat C	.10	.15
DBT010125 Field Canceller C	6.00	10.00
DBT010126 Sun Dragon Bal Dragon BR	4.00	6.00
DBT010127 Hotblooded Demon King Teacher Asmodai BR	8.00	12.00
DBT010128 Black Death Dragon Abygale BR	8.00	12.00
DBT010129 Star Dragoner Jackknife BR	4.00	6.00
DBT010130 Evil Deity of Cataclysm Hyakugan Yamigedo Sky Half SCR	2.50	4.00
DBT010131 Evil Deity of Cataclysm Hyakugan Yamigedo Earth Half SCR	3.00	5.00
DBT010132 Evil Deity Sorcery Hyakuganho SCR	3.00	5.00
DBT010133 Cataclysmic Invasion SCR	8.00	12.00
DBT010134 Evil Deity Sorcery Kodamagurai SCR	3.00	5.00

2016 Future Card Buddyfight D Booster Set 2 Roar Invincible Dragon

RELEASED ON JULY 22, 2016

DBT020001 Breastcorona Dragon RRR	.30	.50
DBT020002 Bal Dragon Great Full Bal Lariat RRR	2.00	3.00
DBT020003 Blade Beast of Blinder Mikazuki Munechika RRR	10.00	15.00
DBT020004 Gojinmaru Ghoul Deity Arts Dance of Yashagami RRR	4.00	6.00
DBT020005 Tradition Chief Oriental Jo RRR	4.00	6.00
DBT020006 Underling Badguy Moto RRR	1.25	2.00
DBT020007 Death Gauge Timer RRR	2.00	3.00
DBT020008 Abygale Unlimited Death Drain RRR	5.00	8.00
DBT020009 Ragingfire Dragon Agnagras RR	.30	.50
DBT020010 Fifth Omni Cavalry Dragon Merak SD RR	.60	1.00
DBT020011 Sun Fist Balguard RR	.30	.50
DBT020012 Tsukikage Kuroyasha Mode RR	.30	.50
DBT020013 Nanomachine Ninja Tsukikage RR	3.00	5.00
DBT020014 Blade Beast of Ghostslash Tojikiri Yasutsuna RR	5.00	8.00
DBT020015 Yamigitsune White Fire Shigaisoshi RR	.75	1.25
DBT020016 Guardian Dragon of the Deity Gate Fulham Sasterader RR	1.50	2.50
DBT020017 Ocean Emperor's Anchor Wild Waves RR	.75	1.25
DBT020018 Purgatory Knights Death Sickle Calvary RR	1.25	2.00
DBT020019 Blackslash Ghost Dragon Galnibael RR	.30	.50
DBT020020 Black Demon Swordsman Vader RR	3.00	5.00
DBT020021 Blazing Forge Dragon Svarog R	.20	.30
DBT020022 Fire Dragon Shield R	.50	.75
DBT020023 Transportation Air Lane R	.20	.30
DBT020024 Edward the Black Battle of Gargantua R	2.00	3.00
DBT020025 Bal Dragon Tempest Bal Steel Sword R	.60	1.00
DBT020026 Revelation Tactician Keiganryu R	.20	.30
DBT020027 Byakuya Shiroyasha Mode R	.60	1.00
DBT020028 LowRank Ninja Mikazukimaru R	.30	.50
DBT020029 Snake Princess Setsuna R	.60	1.00
DBT020030 Elite Sword Odenta R	.50	.75
DBT020031 Great Ocean Highking Duel Jaeger R	.75	1.25
DBT020032 Duel Sieger Tempest Enforcer R	1.25	2.00
DBT020033 Chief of Steel Iron Tetsu R	.20	.30
DBT020034 Chief of Heal Healing Rin R	3.00	5.00
DBT020035 Fortune Dragon Forbolka R	1.50	2.50
DBT020036 Divine Dragon Creation R	4.00	6.00
DBT020037 Great Demonic Black Dragon Arch Enemy R	.20	.30
DBT020038 Graveyard of Demonic Swords Graybard R	.20	.30
DBT020039 Purgatory Knights Leader Demios Sword Dragon R	4.00	6.00
DBT020040 Black Crazed Warrior Bellzelgal R	.20	.30
DBT020041 Death Wizard Dragon R	1.25	2.00
DBT020042 Million Edge R	2.50	4.00
DBT020043 Great Battle Deity Robo EMPEROR Dragon R	.40	.60
DBT020044 Dragon Knight Prince Edward the Black U	.75	1.25
DBT020045 Dragon Knight Sekishusai U	.12	.20
DBT020046 Dragon Knight Bertrand U	.60	1.00
DBT020047 Dragonic Exchange U	5.00	8.00
DBT020048 Dragonic Thunder Rage of the Thunder Dragon U	1.00	1.50
DBT020049 Blade Beast of Guillotine Oden Tamitsuyo U	.12	.20
DBT020050 Blade Beast of Phantasm Onimaru Kunitsuna U	.60	1.00
DBT020051 Patrol Ninja Shokai U	.12	.20
DBT020052 Undying Benishojo U	.12	.20
DBT020053 Godlyspeed Natsubame U	.12	.20
DBT020054 Blade Beast of Exorcism Juzumaru Tsunetsugu U	1.25	2.00
DBT020055 Clear Serenity U	3.00	5.00
DBT020056 Raiton Art of Stored Electricity U	.75	1.25
DBT020057 Sword Skill Zanteisettetsu U	.12	.20
DBT020058 Five Heavenly Swords Onimaru U	.60	1.00
DBT020059 Blade Beast Formation Shape of the Elite U	.60	1.00
DBT020060 Duel Sieger Spartand U	1.00	1.50
DBT020061 Schloss Dragon Wanstein U	1.00	1.50
DBT020062 Total Devastate Chief Broken Gai U	.12	.20
DBT020063 Martial Arts Dragon Emperor Duel Sieger U	1.50	2.50
DBT020064 Underling Kicker Shun U	.12	.20
DBT020065 Apprentice Underling Helper Sei U	.12	.20
DBT020066 Wrath Trigger U	1.25	2.00
DBT020067 Dragons All Staked in U	1.25	2.00
DBT020068 Black Dreaded Motion Gataclysm U	1.00	1.50
DBT020069 Purgatory Knights Venom Spike Dragon U	.12	.20
DBT020070 Black Twin Head Skavv U	.50	.75
DBT020071 Jet Black Wind U	.12	.20
DBT020072 Sickle of Traces Revenant U	.12	.20
DBT020073 Battle Deity Robo Silver Rabbit U	.12	.20
DBT020074 Shiningboard Dragon C	.10	.15
DBT020075 Black Spotted Dragon Black Dot C	.10	.15
DBT020076 Dragon Knight Jean C	.10	.15
DBT020077 Dragon Knight Carrasco C	.10	.15
DBT020078 Geothermal Dragon C	.10	.15
DBT020079 Dragon Bow Dragonspirit C	.10	.15
DBT020080 Sun Hammer Bal Hammer C	.10	.15
DBT020081 Solemn Zogesennin C	.10	.15
DBT020082 Gale Conflagration Amakujaku C	.10	.15
DBT020083 Air Slash Ninja Ryusei C	.10	.15
DBT020084 Dodan Chaos Pebbles C	.10	.15
DBT020085 Katon Blazing Armors C	.10	.15
DBT020086 Art of Body Replacement C	1.00	1.50
DBT020087 Ninja Arts Snake Gaze C	2.00	3.00
DBT020088 Demon Way Kasumienran C	1.50	2.50
DBT020089 Water Calling Sword Suiryu C	.10	.15
DBT020090 Reglisse Dragon Notre Dame C	.40	.60
DBT020091 Chief of Steel Protect Ko C	.30	.50
DBT020092 Mount Dragon Jean Julon C	.10	.15
DBT020093 Valley Dragon Talgunt C	.60	1.00
DBT020094 River Dragon Amlia C	.10	.15
DBT020095 Lake Dragon Testaria C	.10	.15
DBT020096 Underling Tricky Baku C	.10	.15
DBT020097 Apprentice Chief Next Zero C	.10	.15
DBT020098 Apprentice Underling Cutter Sen C	.10	.15
DBT020099• Godlyspeed of Dragons C	.50	.75
DBT020100 Dragon from the Origin C	.10	.15
DBT020101 Cintamani Stone C	.10	.15
DBT020102 Soaring Dragon Spirits C	1.00	1.50
DBT020103 Dragon and Strong C	.60	1.00
DBT020104 Dragon Wall of the Distant Sea C	1.25	2.00
DBT020105 Corpse Black Skeleton Dragon Cheld Bodom C	.10	.15
DBT020106 Black Corruption Eixist C	.75	1.25
DBT020107 Purgatory Knights Paindagger Dragon C	.10	.15
DBT020108 Black Savage Dragon Zerion C	.10	.15
DBT020109 Black Swamp Fen C	.10	.15
DBT020110 We Are Immortal C	.40	.60
DBT020111 Fabricated Scar C	.10	.15
DBT020112 Black Dragon Remade C	.10	.15
DBT020113 Black Cloth Blade C	1.25	2.00
DBT020114 Black Flame Bullet C	.10	.15
DBT020115 Blade of Lament Sadgrieve C	.40	.60
DBT020116 Blood Dragon Ceremony Bloody Operate C	.50	.75
DBT020117 Battle Deity Robo Sightless Bear C	.10	.15
DBT020118 A Wise Move C	2.00	3.00
DBT020119 Bal Dragon Great Full Bal Lariat BR	2.50	4.00
DBT020120 Tsukikage Kuroyasha Mode BR	3.00	5.00
DBT020121 Byakuya Shiroyasha Mode BR	.60	1.00
DBT020122 Martial Arts Chief Duel Jaeger BR	2.50	4.00
DBT020123 Stout Wrist Unmatched Chief Duel Jaeger Revolted SCR	6.00	10.00
DBT020124 Martial Arts Chief Duel Jaeger SCR	3.00	5.00
DBT020125 Ocean Chief Spirit SCR	5.00	8.00
DBT020126 Legend of the Colossal Ocean SCR	2.50	4.00
DBT020127 Ancient World SCR	4.00	6.00

2016 Future Card Buddyfight D Booster Set 3 Annihilate Great Demonic Dragon

RELEASED ON OCTOBER 21, 2016

Card	Low	High
DBT020067 Fury of Odin U	.12	.20
DBT020074 Eliminator Dust Remnant U	.12	.20
DBT020077 Hazard Dragon Emperor Gadelgoamer U	.12	.20
DBT020078 Successor Dragon Gaia Link U	.12	.20
DBT030001 Dragon Force Dragon World RRR	.75	1.25
DBT030001 Dragon Force Dragon World SP	12.00	20.00
DBT030002 Bal Dragon Bal Saucer Over Rush RRR	.30	.50
DBT030002 Bal Dragon Bal Saucer Over Rush SP	15.00	25.00
DBT030003 Tyrant Cerberus RRR	5.00	8.00
DBT030004 Leo Starsentinel Leaon RRR	4.00	6.00
DBT030005 Dragon Force Star Dragon World RRR	5.00	8.00
DBT030005 Dragon Force Star Dragon World SP	10.00	15.00
DBT030006 Jackknife Galactical Punisher RRR	8.00	12.00
DBT030007 Star Deity Dragon Zodiac RRR	2.50	4.00
DBT030008 Darkness Rune RRR	8.00	12.00
DBT030009 Phoenix Wing Virtuous Dragon Zellhorus RR	.30	.50
DBT030010 Swordsman of the Sun Bal Dragon RR	.60	1.00
DBT030011 Thunder Knights Rising Flare Dragon RR	2.50	4.00
DBT030012 Tyrant Healer RR	5.00	8.00
DBT030013 Deep Qigong of the Hungry Wolf RR	8.00	12.00
DBT030014 Pisces Starsentinel Pisis RR	1.00	1.50
DBT030015 Capricorn Starsentinel Capricorneo RR	.60	1.00
DBT030016 All Alive Gordirocs Z RR	.30	.50
DBT030017 Future Gazer Jackknife RR	2.00	3.00
DBT030018 Number of Staff RR	.30	.50
DBT030019 Transcend Dragon Emperor Ewigkeit RR	2.00	3.00
DBT030020 Ninja Dragon Knight Hanzo RR	2.00	3.00
DBT030021 Fifth Omni Super Cavalry Dragon Magical Deity Blade Mizaru R	.20	.30
DBT030022 Dragon Knight Bartholomew R	.20	.30
DBT030023 Burning Rapier Dragon R	1.00	1.50
DBT030024 Mera Power Dragon R	.20	.30
DBT030025 Dragon Twin Sword Bal Saber R	.75	1.25
DBT030026 Zellhorus Eradicate Flame R	.20	.30
DBT030027 Destructive Sky Subjugator Tyrant Asura R	1.25	2.00
DBT030028 Tyrant Diablo R	.20	.30
DBT030029 Pyramid of the Danger Emperor R	.20	.30
DBT030030 Fang Spear Axe Ogar Demon Slay R	.20	.30
DBT030031 Cerberus Violence Gazer R	1.25	2.00
DBT030032 Demongodol Gordric Jolt R	.75	1.25
DBT030033 Valkyrie Eruroon the Divine Will R	.20	.30
DBT030034 Rigel Orion R	.20	.30
DBT030035 Aries Starsentinel Arieez R	.20	.30
DBT030036 Libra Starsentinel Leebra R	.20	.30
DBT030037 Starfall Night R	.20	.30
DBT030038 Jackarms J Galaxion R	.20	.30
DBT030039 Dragonarms Roadworker R	.20	.30
DBT030040 Eliminator Torus R	.20	.30
DBT030041 Dragoneraser Hind Lance R	1.50	2.50
DBT030042 Arms Commander R	.30	.50
DBT030043 Star Magnum Dragnapulse R	.20	.30
DBT030044 Zenislator Rain the Vertex R	.20	.30
DBT030045 High Eliminator Zodiac R	.20	.30
DBT030046 Warrior Emperor Red Arthur R	.20	.30
DBT030047 Armorknight Deathgaze R	.60	1.00
DBT030048 Divine Dragon Knight Jeanne dArc R	1.25	2.00
DBT030049 Uninvited Deity Inspector R	.20	.30
DBT030050 Dragon Spell Hiding Bomber R	1.25	2.00
DBT030051 Dragon Knight Billy the Kid U	.12	.20
DBT030052 Spiritbeat Dragon U	.12	.20
DBT030053 Skyrunner Dragon U	.30	.50
DBT030054 Burning Rapier Dragon SD U	.12	.20
DBT030055 Flame Dragon Jr U	.12	.20
DBT030056 Refract Sunbeam U	.12	.20
DBT030057 Bal Exciting U	.12	.20
DBT030058 Sun Furnace Type Solarbattery Type1 U	.12	.20
DBT030059 Tyrant Griffon U	.12	.20
DBT030060 Tyrant Ogre U	.12	.20
DBT030061 Tyrant Eagle U	.60	1.00
DBT030062 Tyrant Jinn U	.40	.60
DBT030063 Battle Aura Rampage U	2.00	3.00
DBT030064 Explosive Demolition Axe U	.12	.20
DBT030065 Dead Spirit Staff Dangeroustick U	.12	.20
DBT030066 Cancer Starsentinel Cancel U	1.00	1.50
DBT030068 Breathen Gard U	1.00	1.50
DBT030069 Light of Guidance U	1.50	2.50
DBT030070 Divine Sword Gallatin U	.30	.50
DBT030071 Meteoswarm Zenislator U	.12	.20
DBT030072 Dragonarms Debrisweeper U	.12	.20
DBT030073 Jackarms J Holder U	.12	.20
DBT030075 Jackknife Linker U	.40	.60
DBT030076 Leg Blade Expel U	.12	.20
DBT030079 On the Same Boat as a Hazardous Dragon U	2.00	3.00
DBT030080 Illusion of the Void Deity U	3.00	5.00
DBT030081 Sunbeam Dragon C	.10	.15
DBT030082 Merakunai Dragon C	.10	.15
DBT030083 Explosive Bullet Dragon Ultrabomb C	.10	.15
DBT030084 Solwise Dragon C	.60	1.00
DBT030085 Thunder Knights Katzbalger Drake C	.10	.15
DBT030086 Whiteshield Dragon C	.10	.15
DBT030087 Bomber Dragon Jr C	.10	.15
DBT030088 Shining Wall C	.10	.15
DBT030089 Sun Blade Bal Beeline C	.10	.15
DBT030090 Tyrant Minotaur C	.10	.15
DBT030091 Armorknight Big Mummy C	.10	.15
DBT030092 Armorknight Many Mummy C	.40	.60
DBT030093 Demon Slay Interment Formation C	.10	.15
DBT030094 Insanity Circle C	.10	.15
DBT030095 Violent Spear AllPiercing C	.10	.15
DBT030096 Protecting the Secret Treasure Grootslang C	.10	.15
DBT030097 Shoe Artisan of the Fairy Realm Leprechaun C	.10	.15
DBT030098 Sagittarius Starsentinel Sagitario C	.10	.15
DBT030099• Perseus Algol C	.10	.15
DBT030100 Berserk Gard C	.10	.15
DBT030101 Brilliance of the Yellow Path C	.10	.15
DBT030102 Dragonarms Talnada C	.10	.15
DBT030103 Dragoneraser Comatter C	.10	.15
DBT030104 Retainer of the Demonic Dragon Orthmatter C	.10	.15
DBT030105 Core Recycle C	.10	.15
DBT030106 Star Hand Fieldleader C	.60	1.00
DBT030107 Single Star Barrier Barret C	.10	.15
DBT030108 Jackknife History C	1.00	1.50
DBT030109 Sword of the First Generation Knights Leader Orcus Sword C	.10	.15
DBT030110 Sharpness Field C	.10	.15
DBT030111 Tyrant Cerberus BR	10.00	15.00
DBT030112 Great Demonic End Dragon Azi Dahaka BR	2.50	4.00
DBT030113 Future Gazer Jackknife BR	3.00	5.00
DBT030114 Star Deity Dragon Zodiac BR	1.50	2.50
DBT030115 Great Demonic End Dragon Azi Dahaka SCR	.30	.50
DBT030116 Retainer of the Demonic Dragon Fernyiges SCR	3.00	5.00
DBT030117 Retainer of the Demonic Dragon King Gorai SCR	4.00	6.00
DBT030118 Retainer of the Demonic Dragon Destructor SCR	5.00	8.00
DBT030119 Dragon Zwei SCR	2.00	3.00
DBT03S004 Jackknife Galactical Punisher SP	15.00	25.00

2016 Future Card Buddyfight D Booster Set 4 Shine Super Sun Dragon

RELEASED ON DECEMBER 23, 2016

Card	Low	High
DBT040001 Flarefang Dragon SD RRR	.75	1.25
DBT040002 Remote Trickster Lone Remote RRR	1.50	2.50
DBT040003 Dragon Force Darkness Dragon World RRR	5.00	8.00
DBT040003 Dragon Force Darkness Dragon World SP	30.00	50.00
DBT040004 Abygale Last Death Violence RRR	3.00	5.00
DBT040004 Abygale Last Death Violence SP	12.00	20.00
DBT040005 Party Supression Type Uniform Blazer Frill RRR	4.00	6.00
DBT040006 Gemclone Fake Healer RRR	.50	.75
DBT040007 Jet Black Grim Reaper Gaito RRR	2.00	3.00
DBT040008 Super Sun Dragon Balle Soleil RRR	1.25	2.00
DBT040009 Fifth Omni Super Cavalry Dragon Aurora Spiral Alliot RR	.50	.75
DBT040010 Lavapick Dragon RR	.40	.60
DBT040011 Mera Blade Dragon SD RR	3.00	5.00
DBT040012 Thunder Beast Spear Bestia RR	.30	.50
DBT040012 Thunder Beast Spear Bestia SP	10.00	15.00
DBT040013 El Quixote Golden Age RR	2.00	3.00
DBT040014 Black Blast Death Napalm RR	2.00	3.00
DBT040015 Black Wind Blade Devos RR	3.00	5.00
DBT040016 Gigadroid Gigantes RR	.60	1.00
DBT040017 Ride Changer Vice Captain Quick Connect mk II RR	3.00	5.00
DBT040018 Armor Talisman VOID HOLE RR	3.00	5.00
DBT040019 Judgment of the Cold blooded King Miserea RR	5.00	8.00
DBT040020 Sun in the Darkness RR	.50	.75
DBT040021 Baan Gong Dragon R	.20	.30
DBT040022 Dragon Knight Kaishuu R	.30	.50
DBT040023 Glow Dragon Jr R	.20	.30
DBT040024 Sun Mirror R	.20	.30
DBT040025 Sun Stone Bal Flame R	.50	.75
DBT040026 Ozon Z R	.20	.30
DBT040027 Triumphal Knight El Quixote R	2.50	4.00
DBT040028 Tempting Trickster Iyan R	.50	.75
DBT040029 Ozon A R	.20	.30
DBT040030 Ozon B R	.20	.30
DBT040031 Wind Scaled Spear Eskamal R	2.00	3.00
DBT040031 Wind Scaled Spear Eskamal SP	20.00	30.00
DBT040032 Engraved Stigmata Dragon Stigmata R	.20	.30
DBT040033 Knight Brigade Leader of the Apocalypse Gratos R	.20	.30
DBT040034 Gloomy Black Dragon Snake Bal zam R	4.00	6.00
DBT040035 Awakened Black Death Dragon Abygale R	5.00	8.00
DBT040036 Treacherous Subject Belzergald R	.60	1.00
DBT040037 Black Bard Ballad R	1.25	2.00
DBT040038 Cage of Nightmares R	5.00	8.00
DBT040039 Soul Sucking Blade Suctiwon R	.30	.50
DBT040040 Gigadroid Biggest R	.20	.30
DBT040041 Grand Calibur Alvarossterria R	.40	.60
DBT040042 Uniform Warrior Police Frill R	.20	.30
DBT040043 Rescue Dragon Mach Braver R	.50	.75
DBT040044 Armor Talisman ELEMENT RETURN R	.20	.30
DBT040045 Armor Talisman GAUGE and DRAW R	2.50	4.00
DBT040046 Force Element Master Zetta R	2.50	4.00
DBT040047 Gemclone Wall Replica R	.60	1.00
DBT040048 Fake Replica Weapon Gemclone R	.20	.30
DBT040049 Double Loss R	.60	1.00
DBT040050 Mission Card of Judgment Great Spell Apocalypse R	.50	.75
DBT040051 Dragon Knight Magellan U	.12	.20
DBT040052 Powered Dragon Jr U	.12	.20
DBT040053 Dragon Scale U	.12	.20
DBT040054 Dragonic Fortune U	.12	.20
DBT040055 Dragonic Loop U	.12	.20
DBT040056 Sun Fist Bal Knuckle Charge U	.60	1.00
DBT040057 Sun Sword Cloud Slasher U	.12	.20
DBT040058 Perforating Trickster Pitt U	.60	1.00
DBT040059 Dangerous Fuse U	3.00	5.00
DBT040060 Glacious Defense Wall U	4.00	6.00
DBT040061 Hidden Crossbow U	.60	1.00
DBT040062 Black Downpour Zicron U	3.00	5.00
DBT040063 Obituary U	3.00	5.00
DBT040064 Claws of Black Death Galefang U	1.00	1.50
DBT040065 Death Napalm Grind Core U	.12	.20
DBT040066 Blast Soldier Form U	.40	.60
DBT040067 Lapeledge Soldier Form U	.12	.20
DBT040068 Gaigrander 03 U	.12	.20
DBT040069 Ride Changer Blast U	.12	.20
DBT040070 Megadroid Huge U	.12	.20
DBT040071 Body of Steel U	1.25	2.00
DBT040072 Armor Talisman 10000 D U	.60	1.00
DBT040073 Wind Demon Caymon U	.40	.60
DBT040074 Wind Demon Cololoon U	1.00	1.50
DBT040075 Black Sage Bem U	.12	.20
DBT040076 Dangerous Bed of Damage U	.12	.20
DBT040077 Mission Complete Extreme Spell Apocalypse Day U	.75	1.25
DBT040078 Betrayer U	.60	1.00
DBT040079 Remove U	1.50	2.50
DBT040080 Benefit U	.75	1.25
DBT040081 Blazing Horn Dragon C	.10	.15
DBT040082 Fifth Omni Armored Dragon Psychokinetic Kai C	.10	.15
DBT040083 Bal Reviver C	.10	.15
DBT040084 Monopolize Sun C	.10	.15
DBT040085 Sun Deity's Aura C	.10	.15
DBT040086 Dragonblade Dragopendulum C	.10	.15
DBT040087 Ozon C C	.10	.15
DBT040088 Reset Button C	.60	1.00
DBT040089 Obstinacy Drink Bunny Call C	.50	.75
DBT040090 Divine Protection of Shalsana C	.50	.75
DBT040091 Quiescence of Cassiade C	1.25	2.00
DBT040092 Bind Trap C	.10	.15
DBT040093 Dig a Hole C	.25	.40
DBT040094 Rolling Punch C	.10	.15
DBT040095 Trap Maker C	.10	.15
DBT040096 Staff of the Calm King Rod of Miserea C	.10	.15
DBT040097 Black Dragon Poet Destrange C	.10	.15
DBT040098 Black Life Nord C	.30	.50
DBT040099 Soul Steal C	1.00	1.50
DBT040100 Enemy Wall C	.60	1.00
DBT040101 Caardian Mode Lethal C	.10	.15
DBT040102 Rescue Dragon Wave Slicer C	.75	1.25
DBT040103 Ride Changer Lapeledge C	.10	.15
DBT040104 Battle Poet Reporting C	.10	.15
DBT040105 Big Machine Sledgehammer C	.10	.15
DBT040106 Flame Demon Effesteo C	.10	.15
DBT040107 Water Demon Hydraules C	.10	.15
DBT040108 Mud Demon Eyetopicon C	.10	.15
DBT040109 Mud Demon Bobaross C	.10	.15
DBT040110 Steel Hammer of Justice C	.10	.15
DBT040111 Awakened Black Death Dragon Abygale BR	6.00	10.00
DBT040112 Fake Replica Weapon Gemclone BR	8.00	12.00
DBT040113 Judgment of the Cold blooded King Miserea BR	6.00	10.00
DBT040114 Super Sun Dragon Balle Soleil BR	10.00	15.00
DBT040115 Gemclone Origin Breaker SCR	2.00	3.00
DBT040116 Armored Battle Demon Zetta SCR	4.00	6.00
DBT040117 Dark Demon Aionio Meran SCR	.60	1.00
DBT040118 Light Demon Excephon Pose SCR	4.00	6.00
DBT040119 Hero World SCR	6.00	10.00

2017 Future Card Buddyfight X Booster Set 1 The Dark Lord's Rebirth

RELEASED ON APRIL 21, 2017

Card	Low	High
XBT010001 Misfiring Demon, Globes RRR	4.00	6.00
XBT010002 Batzz X Link RRR	12.00	20.00
XBT010003 Oni Boss, Kid Ibuki RRR	.30	.50
XBT010004 Searing Surging Chief, Duel Jaeger "Dynamite" RRR	.30	.50
XBT010005 Apprentice Underling, Kon Kon Kong RRR	.50	.75
XBT010006 Green Crystal Dragon, Sheldre RRR	.75	1.25
XBT010007 Prism Eye RRR	.30	.50
XBT010008 Banquet for the Unrighteous RRR	25.00	40.00
XBT010009 Espada Dragons Officer, Tyrakk RR	.30	.50
XBT010010 Thunder Knights Vice Captain, Goldion Halberd RR	.30	.50
XBT010011 Heavenz Sunshine RR	6.00	10.00
XBT010012 Hiding Oni RR	10.00	15.00
XBT010013 Dark Skill, Eerie Wailings RR	10.00	15.00
XBT010014 Chief of Seven Seas, Duel Jaeger "Ocean" RR	.30	.50
XBT010015 Stout Wrist's Headgear RR	.30	.50
XBT010016 Blue Crystal Dragon, Kalvados RR	.50	.75
XBT010017 Candy Crystal Dragon, Galette RR	.30	.50
XBT010018 Enhancement RR	3.00	5.00
XBT010019 Trilight of the Black Sword RR	.30	.50
XBT010020 Balle Soleil, "Eternal Bal-Blaster!" RR	.50	.75
XBT010021 Flame Dragon Officer, Freyhein R	.30	.50
XBT010022 Explosive Sun Dragon, Bal Dragon R	.20	.30
XBT010023 Double Circle of Shock R	.20	.30
XBT010024 Replenisher, Pentar R	.60	1.00
XBT010025 Tactician, Krone R	.20	.30
XBT010026 Arc Dragon Shield R	1.25	2.00
XBT010027 Arc Dragon Sword Cane R	.40	.60
XBT010028 Thunder Lance X Tempest Buster! R	3.00	5.00
XBT010029 Sturdy Oni, A Lad from Kibi R	.75	1.25
XBT010030 Blade Beast of Sixteenth Night, Crane Princess Ichimonji R	.75	1.25
XBT010031 Middle-class Ninja, Hangetsumaru R	.50	.75
XBT010032 Fiend of a Hundred Flogs, Rashomon R	.50	.75
XBT010033 Fiend of Ailments, Affliction Oni R	.30	.50
XBT010034 Nanomachine Ninja, Zangetsu R	1.25	2.00
XBT010035 Fiend of Gaze, Ayo R	.40	.60
XBT010036 Lesser Fiend, Amanojaku R	.40	.60
XBT010037 House of Assassins, Oni Convoy R	.30	.50
XBT010038 Dark Arms, Steel-slicing Strings R	.50	.75
XBT010039 Dark Arms, Soaring Blade R	1.00	1.50
XBT010040 Incineration Chief, Excited Homura R	.20	.30
XBT010041 Phantasmal Fox Chief, Lonely Shu R	.20	.30
XBT010042 Erudite Dragon Emperor, Philosophia R	1.50	2.50
XBT010043 Red Crystal Dragon, Campary R	.20	.30
XBT010044 White Crystal Dragon, Furmint R	.50	.75
XBT010045 Dragonarms, M4Y-D1 R	2.50	4.00
XBT010046 Radian Shell R	1.25	2.00
XBT010047 Brush Upper R	3.00	5.00
XBT010048 Cristiano Crystal Shoot! R	.50	.75
XBT010049 Fairy Dragon Emperor, Felistas R	.75	1.25
XBT010050 Metal Dragoner, Gear Drake R	.60	1.00
XBT010051 Sun Deity's Choice R	.40	.60
XBT010052 CHAOS Yamigedo R	.75	1.25
XBT010053 King the Dominator, "End Game" R	.20	.30
XBT010054 Rhombus the Bravebow U	.12	.20
XBT010055 Dragon Knight, Gilnter U	.12	.20
XBT010056 Fifth Omni Armored Dragon, Thunder Blade Kokuyo U	.12	.20
XBT010057 Mera Exhaust Dragon U	.12	.20
XBT010058 Scimitar Wielder, Krvar U	.12	.20
XBT010059 Bashful Boule U	.12	.20
XBT010060 Add X Thunder U	.40	.60
XBT010061 Irregular Attack U	.12	.20
XBT010062 Dual Spark U	.12	.20
XBT010063 Pale Yellow Fiend, Kid Hoshiguma U	.12	.20
XBT010064 Red Lady Oni, Kureha U	1.50	2.50
XBT010065 Premature Passing, Bibikawazu U	.12	.20
XBT010066 Lesser Fiend, Yama Oni U	.12	.20
XBT010067 Under The Table U	1.50	2.50
XBT010068 Optics Operation, Shrouded Strawcoat U	1.25	2.00
XBT010069 Shinobi Scrolls U	1.00	1.50
XBT010070 Blood Dragon, Sylvania U	.60	1.00
XBT010071 Tenacious Chief, Smasher Gekt U	.12	.20
XBT010072 Chief of Steel, Iron Tetsu U	.12	.20
XBT010073 Apprentice Underling, Cheery En U	.12	.20
XBT010074 Apprentice Underling, Devil Men U	.12	.20
XBT010075 Amish Dragons U	.12	.20
XBT010076 Childhood Carapace, A Man's Tears U	.60	1.00
XBT010077 Black Crystal Dragon, Shao Xin U	.12	.20
XBT010078 Stronger Lowe: 07 U	.12	.20
XBT010079 Red Crystal Dragon, Almarone U	.60	1.00
XBT010080 Red Crystal Dragon, Gamein U	.12	.20
XBT010081 Mystery Setting U	.12	.20
XBT010082 Soul Generator U	1.00	1.50
XBT010083 Gunrod, Hammerschmidt Type-CLA U	.75	1.25
XBT010084 Steel Ball Wielder, Holgan C	.10	.15
XBT010085 All-Rounder Warrior, Tetra C	.10	.15
XBT010086 Raid Officer, Delta C	.10	.15
XBT010087 Straight Sword Wielder, Rekt C	.10	.15
XBT010088 Military Tactics, "Two-Stage Plan" C	.10	.15
XBT010089 Bolting Knuckle C	.10	.15
XBT010090 Thunder Wave X Tempest Explosion! C	.10	.15
XBT010091 White Fiend, Kid Toraguma C	.10	.15
XBT010092 Dusk Fiend, Yagyo C	.10	.15
XBT010093 Red Fiend, Kid Kaneguma C	.10	.15
XBT010094 Half-Fiend, Kid Yase C	.10	.15
XBT010095 Underhanded Means, Sneak Attack C	.50	.75
XBT010096 Midnight Bodyguard C	1.25	2.00
XBT010097 Art of Item Blasting C	.10	.15
XBT010098 Demon Way, Oborogenbu C	.60	1.00
XBT010099 Scuffle Chief, Grappler Gan C	.10	.15
XBT010100 Blood Dragon, Follower C	.10	.15
XBT010101 Apprentice Underling, Value Dai C	.10	.15
XBT010102 Dragonic Determination C	.75	1.25
XBT010103 Dragonic Deluge C	.10	.15

XBT010104 Golden Dragon Iron Wall C .10 .15
XBT010105 Hot-blooded Headgear C .10 .15
XBT010106 Shiny Crystal Dragon, Vermolt C .10 .15
XBT010107 Minute Crystal Dragon, Ceicul C .10 .15
XBT010108 Pink Crystal Dragon, Rose C .10 .15
XBT010109 White Crystal Dragon, Colombal C .10 .15
XBT010110 Fragment Reload C .40 .60
XBT010111 Dead Copy C .10 .15
XBT010112 Emerald Spikes C .10 .15
XBT010113 Pawn the Promotion C .10 .15
XBT010114 Demon Lord Dragon, Batzz SCR .60 1.00
XBT010115 Chibi Panda SCR .60 1.00
XBT010116 Arc Dragon Shield SCR 2.00 3.00
XBT010117 Arc Dragon Sword SCR 3.00 5.00
XBT010118 Thunder Lance X Tempest Buster! SCR 2.50 4.00
XBT010119 Quintessence Crystal Dragon, Athora SCR 2.50 4.00
XBT010120 White Crystal Dragon, Rizzling SCR 10.00 15.00
XBT010121 Radian Shell SCR .75 1.25
XBT010122 Crystal Spikes SCR 1.00 1.50
XBT010123 Cristiano Crystal Shoot! SCR .60 1.00
XBT010124 Demonic Dragon Deity of the Black Sun, Gaen SCR .60 1.00
XBT010125 Terminus Dragon Emperor, Endervelt SCR .30 .50
XBT010126 Retainer of the Demonic Dragon, Devil Orb Dragon SCR 1.25 2.00
XBT010127 Retainer of the Demonic Dragon, Walm SCR .75 1.25
XBT010128 Dragon Drei SCR 12.00 20.00
XBT01BR01 Demon Lord Dragon, Batzz BR 15.00 25.00
XBT01BR02 Quintessence Crystal Dragon, Athora BR 8.00 12.00
XBT01BR03 Demonic Dragon Deity of the Black Sun, Gaen BR 6.00 10.00
XBT01S001 Demon Lord Dragon, Batzz SP .60 1.00
XBT01S002 Searing Surging Chief, Duel Jaeger "Dynamite" SP 40.00 60.00
XBT01S003 Oni Boss, Kid Ibuki SP 15.00 25.00
XBT01S004 Quintessence Crystal Dragon, Athora SP 20.00 30.00
XBT01S005 Star Dragon World (card) SP 25.00 40.00
XBT01S006 Dragon Drei SP 25.00 40.00

2017 Future Card Buddyfight X Booster Set 2 Chaos Control Crisis

RELEASED ON JULY 14, 2017
XBT020001 Modernized Dragon Deity Dynamis RRR .50 .75
XBT020002 Thunder X Attract RRR 3.00 5.00
XBT020003 CHAOS Tartaros RRR .30 .50
XBT020004 CHAOS Dialberg RRR 15.00 25.00
XBT020005 Black Ritual RRR 5.00 8.00
XBT020006 Life Crystal Dragon Diamaria RRR .30 .50
XBT020007 Crystallization RRR 5.00 8.00
XBT020008 CHAOS Adil Diablos RRR 1.00 1.50
XBT020009 Rage of Arc Blade Batzz RR .40 .60
XBT020010 Demon Lord Sword Dragoroyale RR .60 1.00
XBT020011 The Hanako In The Toilet RR 1.00 1.50
XBT020012 CHAOS Osiris RR 3.00 5.00
XBT020013 A Rulers Privilege RR 2.50 4.00
XBT020014 Immortal Sword of the King Durandal RR 2.50 4.00
XBT020015 Black Crest Dragon Zillowzest RR 2.50 4.00
XBT020016 Bone Master Rebel Gallows RR 1.25 2.00
XBT020017 Electrification RR 1.00 1.50
XBT020018 Purple Crystal Dragon Sangria RR .30 .50
XBT020019 R20 Bradbury RR .75 1.25
XBT020020 Jackknife World Linker RR .60 1.00
XBT020021 100 Dragon Overseer of Mercenary Band Anthem the Dual Sword R .20 .30
XBT020022 Ideal Invincible Dragon Bal Dragon R .20 .30
XBT020023 Fire Deity Cavalry Dragon Ameno Kaguzuchi R .20 .30
XBT020024 Bombardier Cylinder R .20 .30
XBT020025 Disk Master Discus R .20 .30
XBT020026 CHAOS Azrael R .20 .30
XBT020027 CHAOS Aquario R .40 .60
XBT020028 One tenth Cotton Paper R .60 1.00
XBT020029 Knights of the Round Table Lancelot R .40 .60
XBT020030 Skeletal Specimen Skull Dandy R .20 .30
XBT020031 School Building 3rd Floor 3rd Toilet From the Front R .20 .30
XBT020032 CHAOS Envana R .20 .30
XBT020033 CHAOS Delt Bolt R .20 .30
XBT020034 CHAOS Voremos R .20 .30
XBT020035 Bone Labor Sub Large R .20 .30
XBT020036 Removable Voice R .20 .30
XBT020037 DEATH Pen Shriver R .60 1.00
XBT020038 Incense Crystal Dragon Cointreau R .75 1.25
XBT020039 Glass Crystal Dragon Wishkeht R .20 .30
XBT020040 Mystical Water Envoy Water of Life R .20 .30
XBT020041 Cosmo Salute R .50 .75
XBT020042 Neodragon Protector R .40 .60
XBT020043 Turquoise Mark R .20 .30
XBT020044 Professor Benjo R 1.25 2.00
XBT020045 Chaos Wall R .75 1.25
XBT020046 Mercenary Braver of Extreme Dragon U .12 .20
XBT020047 Hunter Dogleg U .12 .20
XBT020048 Crimson Battler Greatest Dragon U .12 .20
XBT020049 Fifth Omni Cavalry Dragon Disciple Explosive Hammer Fechter U .12 .20
XBT020050 Thunder X Brave Attack U .12 .20
XBT020051 Gemini Stone Sword U .12 .20
XBT020052 Cursed Doll Sister Meri U .12 .20
XBT020053 Fortitude Warrior Rinaldo U .12 .20
XBT020054 Wisdom Warrior Olivier U .12 .20
XBT020055 Human Body Model Migi Nice Guy U .50 .75
XBT020056 Big Cleaning U .12 .20
XBT020057 Ruthless Pressure U .12 .20
XBT020058 Disparity World U .60 1.00
XBT020059 Sword of the King Carnwenhan U .75 1.25
XBT020060 Emperor Sword of the King Joyeuse U .12 .20
XBT020061 Death Attendant Dragon Belphegor U .12 .20
XBT020062 CHAOS Thanatos U .60 1.00
XBT020063 Black Crest Dragon Redzett U .12 .20
XBT020064 Purgatory Knights Necropalm Dragon U 1.50 2.50
XBT020065 Black Crest Dragon Earlbow U .12 .20
XBT020066 Bone Labor Au Darks U .12 .20
XBT020067 Soul Reset U .12 .20
XBT020068 Dead Earth Invitation U 3.00 5.00
XBT020069 Mixed Crystal Dragon Baldwin U .12 .20
XBT020070 Mixed Crystal Dragon Limoncello U .12 .20
XBT020071 Red Crystal Dragon Weigelt U .12 .20
XBT020072 White Crystal Dragon Pinot Gris U .12 .20
XBT020073 Prism Guardian U .50 .75
XBT020074 CHAOS Nine Dragon Blade U .12 .20
XBT020075 Void System U .12 .20
XBT020076 CHAOS Spiritbeat C .10 .15
XBT020077 CHAOS White Shield C .10 .15
XBT020078 Blood Suker Dragon Fangs C .10 .15
XBT020079 Little Shaman Bell C .10 .15
XBT020080 Head butt Trooper Bumpy C .10 .15
XBT020081 Batzz X Again C .10 .15
XBT020082 CHAOS Cu Chulainn C .10 .15
XBT020083 CHAOS Brute C .10 .15
XBT020084 CHAOS Kraken C .10 .15
XBT020085 Man Eating Demonic Beast Guivre C .10 .15
XBT020086 Knights of the Round Table Ywain C .10 .15
XBT020087 Heroic Tale C .40 .60
XBT020088 Selfish Purification C .25 .40
XBT020089 Locked Door C .10 .15
XBT020090 Drag into the Toilet C .10 .15
XBT020091 CHAOS Fersen C .10 .15
XBT020092 Jet Black Crest Dragon Jayblist C .10 .15
XBT020093 CHAOS Beimder C .10 .15
XBT020094 Black Crest Dragon Double Snake C .10 .15
XBT020095 Black Crest Dragon Vaneich C .10 .15
XBT020096 Lonely Jailor Zaster C .10 .15
XBT020097 Black Dragon Huev C .10 .15
XBT020098 Black Crest Dragon Beaklowes C .10 .15
XBT020099 Ruin of the Enemy C .10 .15
XBT020100 Rejection Crisis C .10 .15
XBT020101 Chain Blade Killing Chain C .10 .15
XBT020102 UK29 Le Guin C .10 .15
XBT020103 Heavenarms Zeena C .10 .15
XBT020104 Topaz Spikes C .10 .15
XBT020105 CHAOS Diragarian C .10 .15
XBT020106 Black Crest Dragon Deilpad SCR .50 .75
XBT020107 Annihilation Black Death Dragon Abygale SCR 2.50 4.00
XBT020108 Removable Voice SCR .30 .50
XBT020109 Sickle of Slaughter Gale Haken SCR 2.00 3.00
XBT020110 Death Count Requiem SCR 6.00 10.00
XBT020111 Spinel Crystal Dragon Spirytas SCR 1.25 2.00
XBT020112 Flying Crystal Dragon Athora SCR .50 .75
XBT020113 Asterism Effect SCR 3.00 5.00
XBT020114 Prism Interrupt SCR .30 .50
XBT020115 Neodragon Protector SCR .50 .75
XBT020116 Ruler of CHAOS Geargod VII SCR 5.00 8.00
XBT020117 CHAOS Hadeath SCR 1.25 2.00
XBT020118 Launch the Autodeity SCR 5.00 8.00
XBT020119 Chaos Wall Barrier of Havoc SCR .60 1.00
XBT020120 the Chaos SCR .75 1.25
XBT02BR01 Ruler of CHAOS Geargod VII BR 30.00 50.00
XBT02BR02 Annihilation Black Death Dragon Abygale BR 10.00 15.00
XBT02BR03 Immortal Sword of the King Durandal BR 25.00 40.00
XBT02S001 Immortal Sword of the King Durandal SP 50.00 75.00
XBT02S002 Annihilation Black Death Dragon Abygale SP 15.00 25.00
XBT02S003 Bone Master Rebel Gallows SP 20.00 30.00
XBT02S004 Ruler of CHAOS Geargod VII SP
XBT02S005 Darkness Dragon World card SP 20.00 30.00
XBT02S006 the Chaos SP 30.00 50.00

2017 Future Card Buddyfight X Booster Set 3 Overturn Thunder Empire

RELEASED ON OCTOBER 20, 2017
XBT030001 Execute Officer, Quadrangle RRR .50 .75
XBT030002 Edward the CHAOS RRR 3.00 5.00
XBT030003 CHAOS Basili-gollum RRR 4.00 6.00
XBT030004 Earth Cluster Demonic Rock Palm RRR .60 1.00
XBT030005 Giant Tanuki RRR 4.00 6.00
XBT030006 Overturn Ninja, Tsukikage RRR 4.00 6.00
XBT030007 CHAOS Vydallur RRR .40 .60
XBT030008 Black Arc Dragon, Riverpain RRR 1.25 2.00
XBT030009 Guardian Cavalry Dragon, Glittoneah RR .60 1.00
XBT030010 Operative, Sphere RR 10.00 15.00
XBT030011 Arc Dragon Sword, Dracross RR 1.25 2.00
XBT030012 Impartial Cane, Fabulous Rod RR 2.00 3.00
XBT030013 Double Rock Mech Trooper, Orth-gollum RR .50 .75
XBT030014 Ground Alpha RR .30 .50
XBT030015 Celestial Deity of Misty Dew Water, Nanase RR .30 .50
XBT030016 Secret Scroll RR 2.00 3.00
XBT030017 Thunder Bones, Spark Gallows RR .50 .75
XBT030018 Sealed Black Crest Dragon, Elgod RR 1.00 1.50
XBT030019 Execution Ground RR 1.25 2.00
XBT030020 CHAOS Alberion RR 1.00 1.50
XBT030021 Fifth Omni Super Cavalry Dragon, Ice Spear Merak R .20 .30
XBT030022 CHAOS Rising Flare R .40 .60
XBT030023 Envoy of Sol, Meraciel R .20 .30
XBT030024 Haven's Gift R .50 .75
XBT030025 Thunder Emperor Dragon Shield R .20 .30
XBT030026 Guardians? Executioners? Or Worse?! R .40 .60
XBT030027 Violent Thunder Evil Demon, Tyrant Demon R .20 .30
XBT030028 Thunderbolt Fighting Dragon, Demonogodol R 1.00 1.50
XBT030029 Violent Thunder, Armorknight Cerberus R .75 1.25
XBT030030 Iron-Legs Kasu-gollum R .75 1.25
XBT030031 Where The Souls Fuse R .20 .30
XBT030032 Lynx-Eyed Military Deviser, Keiganryu R .60 1.00
XBT030033 Ibuki's Right-hand Man, Kid Ibaraki R .20 .30
XBT030034 Heavenly Vengeance, Full-Equip Kannon R .20 .30
XBT030035 Thunder Sky Ninja, Byakuya R .20 .30
XBT030036 Connect Ninja, Tomonoshin R 2.00 3.00
XBT030037 Hidden Dark Arms, Yobigatana R .40 .60
XBT030038 Unclean Demonic Dragon, Jahi Baligah R .50 .75
XBT030039 Black Crest Dragon, Ladyzie R .25 .40
XBT030040 Purgatory Knights, Ringblade Dragon R .75 1.25
XBT030041 Death Tallica Servant R .40 .60
XBT030042 Apocalypse Knights Brigade, Pale Riders R .75 1.25
XBT030043 Gale Impulse R .20 .30
XBT030044 Sunken Seabed Ruins R .20 .30
XBT030045 Fifth Omni Super Cavalry Dragon, Blowout Hammer Fuad U .12 .20
XBT030046 Dragon Lord of the Far East, Blade the Emperor U .60 1.00
XBT030047 Papa Panda U .12 .20
XBT030048 Impartial Dragon, Monochrome Dragon U .30 .50
XBT030049 Dragon Knight, Georgios U .12 .20
XBT030050 Dragon Knight, Todo U .12 .20
XBT030051 Frenzy Bear-gollum U .12 .20
XBT030052 Gliding Swall-gollum U .12 .20
XBT030053 Violent Thunder, Armorknight Eagle U .60 1.00
XBT030054 Armorknight Reborn Mummy U .75 1.25
XBT030055 Raiding Fal-Gollum U .12 .20
XBT030056 Sandstorm? Calena Palm U .40 .60
XBT030057 Eradication Spear, Skypierce U .12 .20
XBT030058 Flash of Purple Arc, Hyojuro U .12 .20
XBT030059 Camouflage Ninja, Getazaemon U .12 .20
XBT030060 White Dew Blade Beast, Murasamemaru U .12 .20
XBT030061 Demon Way, Fresh Blood Nectar U .60 1.00
XBT030062 Art of Shadow Stitching U 4.00 6.00
XBT030063 Exquisite Sword, Crane Princess U .12 .20
XBT030064 Moonlight Secret Katana, Kirameki U .12 .20
XBT030065 Dark Black Arc Dragon, Zem Sevens U .50 .75
XBT030066 CHAOS Terrorizer U .12 .20
XBT030067 Black Arc Dragon, Rolldice U .75 1.25
XBT030068 Impartial Knight, Justlaw U .12 .20
XBT030069 Black Dragon, Nam U .12 .20
XBT030070 Doll Strings U .12 .20
XBT030071 Black Provoke U .12 .20
XBT030072 Collapsing Roar U .12 .20
XBT030073 Blacksand Castle U 2.00 3.00
XBT030074 Skill Binder U 4.00 6.00
XBT030075 Fervent Blacksmith, Rechthoek C .60 1.00
XBT030076 Dragon Knight, Naotora C .10 .15
XBT030077 Offerings for the Thunder Emperor C .10 .15
XBT030078 Dragonic Chaos C .10 .15
XBT030079 Impartial Beast, Garrdias C .40 .60
XBT030080 Thwackdrill C .10 .15
XBT030081 Ramming Ultra Grunt, Dogon C .10 .15
XBT030082 Explo-gollum C .20 .30
XBT030083 Arc Dragon, Bariballo C .10 .15
XBT030084 Stone Purge C .40 .60
XBT030085 Terror! The Dangerous Mummy Man C .10 .15
XBT030086 Rock Crushing Style, Highblood Quake! C .10 .15
XBT030087 Shikigami Ninja, Kunoichi Keika C .10 .15
XBT030088 Vagrant Dragon, Semimaru C .60 1.00
XBT030089 Blue Fiend, Kid Kuma C .10 .15
XBT030090 Watchful Eyes C .10 .15
XBT030091 CHAOS Deletus C .10 .15
XBT030092 Black Arc Dragon, Dartyelle C .10 .15
XBT030093 Bone Labor, Vendetta C .30 .50
XBT030094 Landmine Jailer, Izmine C .40 .60
XBT030095 Cestino C .10 .15
XBT030096 Demon Slay Battle Aura "Bind" C .75 1.25
XBT030097 Thunder Emperor Dragon, Barlbatzz SCR 12.00 20.00
XBT030098 Saint Holy Sword Dragon SCR 3.00 5.00
XBT030099 Thunder Emperor's Dragon Shield SCR 1.25 2.00
XBT030100 Turbulent Thunder Spear X Tempest Ulti-Buster! SCR 10.00 15.00
XBT030101 Thunder Emperor's Fangs SCR 2.00 3.00
XBT030102 Overturn Black Death Dragon, Abygale SCR 10.00 15.00
XBT030103 Earlbow "SD" SCR 2.50 4.00
XBT030104 Sealed Black Crest Dragon, Vidor Nove SCR .40 .60
XBT030105 Black Crest, Gale Emblem SCR 5.00 8.00
XBT030106 Gale Impulse SCR .30 .50
XBT030107 Demonic Rock Mech Trooper Dra-gollum SCR 10.00 15.00
XBT030108 Voracious Wolf-gollum SCR .30 .50
XBT030109 Shuten Demonic Deity Kid Ibuki SCR 8.00 12.00
XBT030110 Ibuki's Right-hand Man, Kid Ibaraki SCR .50 .75
XBT030111 Proto Chaos Machina, Geargod VIII SCR 2.50 4.00
XBT03BR01 Thunder Emperor Dragon, Barlbatzz BR 40.00 60.00
XBT03BR02 Overturn Black Death Dragon, Abygale BR 25.00 40.00
XBT03BR03 Shuten Demonic Deity Kid Ibuki BR 10.00 15.00
XBT03S001 Thunder Emperor Dragon, Barlbatzz SP 50.00 75.00
XBT03S002 Demonic Rock Mech Trooper Dra-gollum SP 30.00 50.00
XBT03S003 Shuten Demonic Deity Kid Ibuki SP 20.00 30.00
XBT03S004 Overturn Black Death Dragon, Abygale SP 50.00 75.00
XBT03S005 Proto Chaos Machina, Geargod VIII SP 20.00 30.00
XBT03S006 Thunder Emperor's Fangs SP 50.00 75.00

2017 Future Card Buddyfight X Booster Set 4 Rainbow Striker

RELEASED ON DECEMBER 22, 2017
XBT040001 Fifth Omni Super Cavalry Dragon, Sandstorm Staff Arkaid RRR 2.50 4.00
XBT040002 World Linking Key the First, Drago-Uno RRR 2.50 4.00
XBT040003 Seeker of Knight's Way, El Quixote RRR 2.50 4.00
XBT040004 Knight of Victory Odds, Vict RRR 10.00 15.00
XBT040005 Bloody Holy Grail RRR 10.00 15.00
XBT040006 Demonic Descent Sword of the King Laevateinn RRR 12.00 20.00
XBT040007 Rainbow Gem Crystal Dragon, Kirschgeist RRR 3.00 5.00
XBT040008 Prismatic Bless RRR 10.00 15.00
XBT040009 Battle Skills Diplomat, Diremand RR .30 .50
XBT040010 Inexhaustible Dragon, Lord of Shadow Dragons RR 3.00 5.00
XBT040011 Dragonic Heal "Plus" RR 1.00 1.50
XBT040012 Guardian Dragon of Nativity, Mother Dragon RR .60 1.00
XBT040013 Shield of Glory, Order Guard RR 4.00 6.00
XBT040014 Fable of the Sword Sage RR 1.00 1.50
XBT040015 Merlin's Advice RR 3.00 5.00
XBT040016 Sword of the King Scabbard, Surtr Cross RR 3.00 5.00
XBT040017 Jade Gem Crystal Dragon, Schartreuze RR 2.50 4.00
XBT040018 Flying Crystal Dragon, Sheldre RR 10.00 15.00
XBT040019 Aldo Ground RR 3.00 5.00
XBT040020 Mini Geargods Factory RR .75 1.25
XBT040021 Anatta Overshadow Dragon R .20 .30
XBT040022 Dragonic Shadow Gauge R .20 .30
XBT040023 Steel Dragon Fangs R .75 1.25
XBT040024 Machining Sacrifice R 2.50 4.00
XBT040025 Dragon Fangs Fist, Batzz Fang R .50 .75
XBT040026 Gold-laying Dragon, Mother Dragon R .20 .30
XBT040027 Gold Monster Egg R .20 .30
XBT040028 Thunder Emperor's Symbol R .20 .30
XBT040029 Sword of Glory, Order Edge R .25 .40
XBT040030 Reborn! The Hanako In The Toilet R .60 1.00
XBT040031 Powerful Battle Deity, Magni R .20 .30
XBT040032 CHAOS Freyja R .20 .30
XBT040033 CHAOS Carbuncle R .20 .30
XBT040034 Skilled General's Insight R 1.50 2.50
XBT040035 Fabricated Sword of the King, Dainsleif Replica R .50 .75
XBT040036 Minyas' Treasures Chamber - Room of Sword of the King - R .20 .30
XBT040037 CHAOS Campary R .20 .30
XBT040038 I20: Asimov R .75 1.25
XBT040039 Gemologist R 6.00 10.00
XBT040040 Mirrors Valley R .60 1.00
XBT040041 Crystal Greaves R 2.50 4.00
XBT040042 Direct Dynamic Diamond Overhead!! R .75 1.25
XBT040043 Thunderblade Joker R .60 1.00
XBT040044 Mini Geargod Blue R .20 .30
XBT040045 Dread Shadow Dragon U .12 .20
XBT040046 Dragotrap U 2.50 4.00
XBT040047 Second Barrier U .12 .20
XBT040048 Sorcery Barrier Device U .12 .20
XBT040049 Shadowscale Sword, Dragoshadow U .12 .20
XBT040050 Shadow Dragon Arts, Dividing Shadows U .50 .75
XBT040051 Ice-blooded Emperor, Van Glacier U .12 .20
XBT040052 CHAOS Lumiere U .12 .20
XBT040053 Silver Monster Egg U .12 .20
XBT040054 Hawkeye U 1.50 2.50
XBT040055 Razed Castle Town U 1.25 2.00
XBT040056 Mother Dragon Returns U .12 .20
XBT040057 Giant Bird, Thunderbird U .30 .50
XBT040058 Anemic Vampire, Dizzy Dracula U .12 .20
XBT040059 Virgen Unleashed U .12 .20
XBT040060 Autodeity's Favor U .12 .20
XBT040061 Mimisbrunnr U .12 .20
XBT040062 Folklore of Wydar Sarkal U .25 .40
XBT040063 Unyielding Dignity U .12 .20
XBT040064 Fabricated Sword of the King, Eckesachs Replica U .12 .20
XBT040065 Fabricated Sword of the King, Armas Replica U .60 1.00

XBT040066 Life Crystal Dragon, Yomei U .12 .20
XBT040067 Dragonarms, Return Bit U .12 .20
XBT040068 Red Crystal Dragon, Nimue U .75 1.25
XBT040069 Heavenly Crystal Awakening U 3.00 5.00
XBT040070 Full Bright Eye U .12 .20
XBT040071 Life in Space Colony U .12 .20
XBT040072 Lapis Lazuli Greaves U .12 .20
XBT040073 Mini Geargod Green U .40 .60
XBT040074 Mini Geargod Yellow U .75 1.25
XBT040075 Duskbreaker Dragon C .10 .15
XBT040076 Die Shadow Dragon C .10 .15
XBT040077 Dragon Knight, Inuchiyo C .10 .15
XBT040078 Shadow Dragon C 4.00 6.00
XBT040079 Dragon Press C .10 .15
XBT040080 CHAOS Slime C .10 .15
XBT040081 Monster Egg C .10 .15
XBT040082 Merit Awards Ceremony? C .10 .15
XBT040083 CHAOS Balor C .10 .15
XBT040084 Ground Fairy, Gnome C .10 .15
XBT040085 Fabricated Sword of the King, Gramr Replica C .10 .15
XBT040086 Fabricated Sword of the King, Mistilteinn Replica C .10 .15
XBT040087 Fabricated Sword of the King, Caladbolg Replica C .10 .15
XBT040088 Fabricated Sword of the King, Nagelring Replica C .10 .15
XBT040089 CHAOS Gamma Radius C .10 .15
XBT040090 Arc Crystal Dragon, Denki Bran C .10 .15
XBT040091 LD15: Brackett C .10 .15
XBT040092 Phase Seal Chains C 1.50 2.50
XBT040093 Star Dragon Lance, Androids Sheep C .10 .15
XBT040094 Chess Break C 4.00 6.00
XBT040095 Mini Geargod Red C .10 .15
XBT040096 Mini Geargod Purple C .10 .15
XBT040097 CHAOS Zoruaga SCR 2.00 3.00
XBT040098 CHAOS Carbuncle SCR .30 .50
XBT040099 CHAOS Transcendant, Geargod ver.099 SCR 10.00 15.00
XBT040100 Interception Barrier SCR 3.00 5.00
XBT040101 Machining Sacrifice SCR 2.00 3.00
XBT040102 Thunder Emperor Corps Leader, Barlbatzz SCR 4.00 6.00
XBT040103 Overturn Ice Emperor, Miserea SCR 25.00 40.00
XBT040104 Overturn Knight, El Quixote SCR 1.00 1.50
XBT040105 Thunderblade Joker SCR .75 1.25
XBT040106 Steel Dragon Fangs SCR .30 .50
XBT040107 Heavenly Crystal Dragon, Aldo Athora SCR 20.00 30.00
XBT040108 Spirytas "SD" SCR .50 .75
XBT040109 Prismatic Prisma SCR 8.00 12.00
XBT040110 Mirrors Valley SCR 1.25 2.00
XBT040111 Direct Dynamic Diamond Overhead!! SCR .30 .50
XBT04BR01 Thunder Emperor Corps Leader, Barlbatzz BR 10.00 15.00
XBT04BR02 Heavenly Crystal Dragon, Aldo Athora BR 30.00 50.00
XBT04BR03 CHAOS Transcendant, Geargod ver.099 BR 20.00 30.00
XBT04S001 Demonic Descent Sword of the King Laevateinn SP 60.00 100.00
XBT04S002 CHAOS Transcendant, Geargod ver.099 SP 25.00 40.00
XBT04S003 Sword of Glory, Order Edge SP 15.00 25.00
XBT04S004 Shield of Glory, Order Guard SP 25.00 40.00
XBT04S005 Overturn Ice Emperor, Miserea SP 40.00 60.00
XBT04S006 Heavenly Crystal Dragon, Aldo Athora SP 60.00 100.00

2018 Future Card Buddyfight S Booster Set 1 Gargantua Awakened

RELEASED ON AUGUST 31, 2018
SBT010001 Gargantua Dragon, "Sonic Mode" RRR 4.00 6.00
SBT010002 Lanze Gardragon RRR 1.25 2.00
SBT010003 Dragod's Shine RRR 1.00 1.50
SBT010004 Topfist Vainglory, Brawlzeus RRR 5.00 8.00
SBT010005 Bloated, Harahara RRR 4.00 6.00
SBT010006 Linkdragon Order's Hunt RRR 2.50 4.00
SBT010007 Seerfight Dragon, Argent Ore RRR .60 1.00
SBT010008 Golden Dragoner, Jackknife RRR .75 1.25
SBT010009 Gargantua Switch Mode! RR 4.00 6.00
SBT010010 Gar-Oracle RR 1.25 2.00
SBT010011 Deity Dragon Sword, Garkris RR 1.25 2.00
SBT010012 Thrasher, Diepan RR 2.50 4.00
SBT010013 Immortal Speech! RR 2.50 4.00
SBT010014 Members Only Club, Deadeity RR 2.50 4.00
SBT010015 Shredder, Takatsume RR 1.00 1.50
SBT010016 Keen Ear, Jisen RR 1.00 1.50
SBT010017 Linkdragon Order's Links RR 3.00 5.00
SBT010018 Proclaim: Steer the Stars RR 1.25 2.00
SBT010019 Proclaim: Battle Supplies RR 2.50 4.00
SBT010020 Notify: Destruction Tactics RR .40 .60
SBT010021 Garcat R 2.00 3.00
SBT010022 Gardog R .60 1.00
SBT010023 Deity Gargantua Punisher!! (Dragon World) R .50 .75
SBT010024 Fingers Myriad, Zapuranos R .60 1.00
SBT010025 All Is Mine! R .50 .75
SBT010026 Junk Wheels! R .60 1.00
SBT010027 Heavystriker, Kaina R .60 1.00
SBT010028 Linkdragon Order Gathering R 2.00 3.00
SBT010029 Thunder Dragon Tornado R .60 1.00
SBT010030 Govern Star Dragon, Fret R 2.00 3.00
SBT010031 Sentence: Battle Preparations R .60 1.00
SBT010032 Tri-Star Decision R .60 1.00
SBT010033 Gardragon Schwert III U .12 .20
SBT010034 Force Return U .12 .20
SBT010035 Gar-Parry U .50 .75
SBT010036 Bash Sage, Bashermes U .25 .40
SBT010037 Crazed Warfficer, Gutsares U .30 .50
SBT010038 Invincible Knuckle! U .50 .75
SBT010039 Skygod Jacket U .12 .20
SBT010040 Skybad Jacket U .12 .20
SBT010041 Resolute, Hirate U .30 .50
SBT010042 Sturdy Dragon Strike U .12 .20
SBT010043 Undying Linkdragon Order U 1.00 1.50
SBT010044 Order's Axe, "Wildaxe" U .50 .75
SBT010045 Govern Star Dragon, Bordure U .12 .20
SBT010046 Star Jack Boost U .50 .75
SBT010047 Notify: Immobilize Tactics U .75 1.25
SBT010048 Seertool, Rune Stones U .12 .20
SBT010049 Riese Gardragon C .10 .15
SBT010050 Wildt Gardra C .10 .15
SBT010051 Garbird C .10 .15
SBT010052 Garbat C .10 .15
SBT010053 Gar-Break C .10 .15
SBT010054 Dragonic Grimoire C .30 .50
SBT010055 Mercenaries C .10 .15
SBT010056 Dragon Barrier C .10 .15
SBT010057 Bonesplitter, Shearzelus C .10 .15
SBT010058 Dysfunctional, Gyheheleia C .10 .15
SBT010059 Crazed Girl Deity, Gothiris C .10 .15
SBT010060 Wicked Giant, Trasharges C .10 .15
SBT010061 Roaring Hydra C .10 .15
SBT010062 Topfist Punishment! Keravnos Burst Fist! C .10 .15
SBT010063 Heavyquake, Futomo C .10 .15
SBT010064 Unperturbed, Mikoshi C .10 .15
SBT010065 Assailant, Tategami C .10 .15
SBT010066 Novice, Koyubi C .10 .15
SBT010067 Throwaxe, "Tsumuji" C .10 .15
SBT010068 Guardseer Dragon, Gules Bend C .10 .15
SBT010069 Guardseer Dragon, Gyron C .10 .15
SBT010070 Notify: Defensive Tactics C .30 .50
SBT010071 Seerbow, Babylon C .20 .30
SBT010072 J. Star Saber C .10 .15
SBT010073 Gargantua Dragon SCR 2.00 3.00
SBT010074 Gargantua Dragon, "Blast Mode" SCR 4.00 6.00
SBT010075 Protector of Swords, Gar-Einer SCR 1.25 2.00
SBT010076 Deity Dragon Sword, Garblade SCR 1.00 1.50
SBT010077 Deity Gargantua Punisher!! (Dragon World) SCR 1.25 2.00
SBT010078 Skyseer Dragon, Cross Astrologia SCR 1.00 1.50
SBT010079 Seerfight Dragon, Inchevron SCR 5.00 8.00
SBT010080 Notify: Emergency Tactics SCR 8.00 12.00
SBT010081 Proclaim: Decisive Point SCR 10.00 15.00
SBT010082 Tri-Star Decision SCR 2.50 4.00
SBT010083 Thunderaxe, Agito SCR .50 .75
SBT010084 Spiral Thunderaxe, King Agito SCR 10.00 15.00
SBT010085 Quickwit, Tsumasaki SCR 15.00 25.00
SBT010086 Linkdragon Order's Oath SCR 4.00 6.00
SBT010087 Thunder Dragon Tornado SCR .50 .75
SBT010088 Gargantua Dragon AR 1.25 2.00
SBT010089 Skyseer Dragon, Cross Astrologia AR .60 1.00
SBT010090 Thunderaxe, Agito AR .60 1.00
SBT01BR01 Gargantua Dragon BR 15.00 25.00
SBT01BR02 Skyseer Dragon, Cross Astrologia BR 4.00 6.00
SBT01BR03 Thunderaxe, Agito BR 20.00 30.00
SBT01S001 Gargantua Dragon SP 15.00 25.00
SBT01S002 Skyseer Dragon, Cross Astrologia SP 8.00 12.00
SBT01S003 Spiral Thunderaxe, King Agito SP 30.00 50.00
SBT01S004 Golden Dragoner, Jackknife SP 10.00 15.00

2018 Future Card Buddyfight S Booster Set 2 Dimension Destroyer

RELEASED ON NOVEMBER 2, 2018
SBT020001 Dimension Dragon, Agonia RRR 10.00 15.00
SBT020002 Gargantua Dragon, "Double Body Mode" RRR 2.50 4.00
SBT020003 Steelframe Swordsman, KUROGANE RRR 10.00 15.00
SBT020004 Thundercry And Thunderflash, Agito RRR 10.00 15.00
SBT020005 Guidance of Stars, Cross Astrologia RRR 8.00 12.00
SBT020006 Lostknight: Nero Lance RRR 15.00 25.00
SBT020007 Iregeit Delusion RRR 20.00 30.00
SBT020008 Dimension Draw RRR 25.00 40.00
SBT020009 Dimension Dragon, Deugain RR 10.00 15.00
SBT020010 D Suction RR 6.00 10.00
SBT020011 Gargantua Koga Dragon RR 3.00 5.00
SBT020012 Art of Truancy RR 6.00 10.00
SBT020013 Excelblade, Godslash KANESADA RR 3.00 5.00
SBT020014 Pinnacle of Iai, Godspeed RR 4.00 6.00
SBT020015 Chain Select RR 5.00 8.00
SBT020016 King: Rosso Scepter RR 4.00 6.00
SBT020017 Celesphere Control RR 3.00 5.00
SBT020018 Cho-Tokyo Gambit RR 5.00 8.00
SBT020019 Oxideos Aralgeine RR 1.50 2.50
SBT020020 Dimension Absorb RR 10.00 15.00
SBT020021 Dimension Dragon, Ire R .60 1.00
SBT020022 Nadel Gardra R .20 .30
SBT020023 Deity Dragon Sword, Gardeus R .20 .30
SBT020024 Nindog R .25 .40
SBT020025 Training -Fire Crafting- R .20 .30
SBT020026 Deity Dragon Blade, Garkunai R .20 .30
SBT020027 Deity Gargantua Punisher!! (Katana World) R .20 .30
SBT020028 Linkdragon Order's Comeback R .20 .30
SBT020029 Knight: Argento Lance R .50 .75
SBT020030 Govern Star Dragon, Biletty R .40 .60
SBT020031 Agoniagill Dlhyvalam R .20 .30
SBT020032 Vanity Zero Blazer!! R 1.00 1.50
SBT020033 Dimension Dragon, Arl U .12 .20
SBT020034 Dimension Dragon, Odio U .30 .50
SBT020035 D Scapegoat U .12 .20
SBT020036 Gar-Pressure U .12 .20
SBT020037 Radiant Electrodeity, Ameno-Wakahiko U .12 .20
SBT020038 Alloy Teacher, SHAKUDO U .12 .20
SBT020039 Magnetic Swordsman, NEO U .12 .20
SBT020040 Silver Orchid Swordsman, SUZU U .12 .20
SBT020041 Art of Getting Fish U .12 .20
SBT020042 Exploring, Mazuru U .12 .20
SBT020043 Linkdragon Order Anthem U .12 .20
SBT020044 Wild Guard U .12 .20
SBT020045 Seerfight Dragon, Sable U .12 .20
SBT020046 Seiji Kido Defense U .12 .20
SBT020047 Queen Side Castling U .12 .20
SBT020048 Seercrossbow, Babylon Lupus U .30 .50
SBT020049 D Alteration C .10 .15
SBT020050 Dimension Staff, Ponirea C .10 .15
SBT020051 Iris Swordsman, TITAN C .10 .15
SBT020052 Heavyblade Swordsman, NAMARI C .10 .15
SBT020053 Ninbird C .10 .15
SBT020054 Deity Dragon Ninja, Yashiromaru C .10 .15
SBT020055 Art of Speedrun C .10 .15
SBT020056 Kouken School, Steadfast, Style One C .10 .15
SBT020057 Excelblade, Kemonokiri C .10 .15
SBT020058 Quake, Estoma C .10 .15
SBT020059 Willed, Johaku C .10 .15
SBT020060 Sturdy?, Ton C .10 .15
SBT020061 Links Chain Blade, "Wild Chain" C .10 .15
SBT020062 Seerfight Dragon, Bart Pile C .10 .15
SBT020063 Bishop: Giallo Mace C .10 .15
SBT020064 Pawn: Verde Spear C .10 .15
SBT020065 Notify: Blessed Rain Tactic C .10 .15
SBT020066 Grandmaster Cane C .10 .15
SBT020067 End Game Study C .10 .15
SBT020068 Vanity Cells C .10 .15
SBT020069 Gargantua Wind Demon Dragon AR .60 1.00
SBT020070 Lost World (card) AR 1.50 2.50
SBT020071 Gargantua Dragon, "Cyclone Mode" SCR 5.00 8.00
SBT020072 Nadel Gardra SCR .30 .50
SBT020073 Guardian of Book, Gar Zexa SCR .50 .75
SBT020074 Gar-Spirit SCR .60 1.00
SBT020075 Deity Dragon Sword, Gardeus SCR .30 .50
SBT020076 Gargantua Wind Demon Dragon SCR 1.25 2.00
SBT020077 Nincat SCR 8.00 12.00
SBT020078 Deity Dragon Blade, Garkunai SCR 1.25 2.00
SBT020079 Deity Dragon Ninja Arts, Cy-clones Sword Dance SCR 3.00 5.00
SBT020080 Deity Gargantua Punisher!! (Katana World) SCR .30 .50
SBT020081 Vile Demonic Dragon, Vanity Husk Destroyer SCR 75.00 125.00
SBT020082 Dimension Razor SCR 3.00 5.00
SBT020083 Vile Demonic Gun, Lostless Buster SCR 10.00 15.00
SBT020084 Vanity Zero Blazer!! SCR 8.00 12.00
SBT020085 Lost World (card) SCR 4.00 6.00
SBT02BR01 Gargantua Dragon, "Double Body Mode" BR 10.00 15.00
SBT02BR02 Gargantua Wind Demon Dragon BR 10.00 15.00
SBT02BR03 Vile Demonic Dragon, Vanity Husk Destroyer BR 75.00 125.00
SBT02S001 Gargantua Dragon, "Cyclone Mode" SP 30.00 50.00
SBT02S002 Steelframe Swordsman, KUROGANE SP 30.00 50.00
SBT02S003 Lostknight: Nero Lance SP 50.00 75.00
SBT02S004 Vile Demonic Dragon, Vanity Husk Destroyer SP 75.00 125.00

2019 Future Card Buddyfight S Booster Set 3 True Awakening of Deities

RELEASED ON JANUARY 11.2019
SBT030001 Dimension Dragon, Episto RRR 5.00 8.00
SBT030002 Gargantua Dragon, "Gattling Mode" RRR 3.00 5.00
SBT030003 Magic Singer, Sync RRR 15.00 25.00
SBT030004 Examinate RRR 4.00 6.00
SBT030005 Domilord, Zerberos RRR 12.00 20.00
SBT030006 Lord Dragon Charge RRR 4.00 6.00
SBT030007 Seerfight Dragon, Coupe RRR 10.00 15.00
SBT030008 Ankosred Noitdead RRR 3.00 5.00
SBT030009 Bloodstained Dark Princess Marrow Ellis RR 2.00 3.00
SBT030010 Dimension Dragon, Ankos RR 4.00 6.00
SBT030011 Gar-Down RR 1.25 2.00
SBT030012 Magicat RR 1.25 2.00
SBT030013 Flame of Memories RR 6.00 10.00
SBT030014 Telcare! RR 8.00 12.00
SBT030015 Emplord, Zerberos Lost RR 2.50 4.00
SBT030016 Seamless Dragon Lord RR 4.00 6.00
SBT030017 Combined Attack Dive! RR 1.25 2.00
SBT030018 Queen: Naranja Staff RR 2.50 4.00
SBT030019 Govern Star Dragon, Feslon RR 2.50 4.00
SBT030020 Dimension Denial RR 10.00 15.00
SBT030021 Bolt Gardra R .20 .30
SBT030022 Spirit Echo» Raison D'etre R .30 .50
SBT030023 D. Decline R .20 .30
SBT030024 Sorcery Deity Dragon, Brauhait R .20 .30
SBT030025 Magic Guitarist, Hisui R .20 .30
SBT030026 Magic Bassist, Asagi R .20 .30
SBT030027 Drop of Temptation R .40 .60
SBT030028 Viclord, Zerberos Zeed R .20 .30
SBT030029 Tyralord, Zerberos Aog R .20 .30
SBT030030 Overcrest R .20 .30
SBT030031 Champion of Heaven R .25 .40
SBT030032 Govern Star Dragon, Dexter Arbus R .20 .30
SBT030033 Garlence Shield U .12 .20
SBT030034 Deity Dragon Greatsword, Garbuster U .12 .20
SBT030035 Sorcery Deity Dragon, Goshe U .12 .20
SBT030036 Jean Tester U .12 .20
SBT030037 Abra Cadabra! U .40 .60
SBT030038 Gentle Wakarito U .12 .20
SBT030039 Lordbreak, Flame Gale U .12 .20
SBT030040 Lordbreak, Hard Win Summon U .12 .20
SBT030041 Lordbreak, Unyielding Emplord U .12 .20
SBT030042 Tesla Line Field U .12 .20
SBT030043 Episto Ira Gnitz U .12 .20
SBT030044 Vile Vortex U .25 .40
SBT030045 Darkness Roar Catastrophe Abyss C .10 .15
SBT030046 Zeele Gardra C .10 .15
SBT030047 Garmonkey C .10 .15
SBT030048 Lost Stone C .10 .15
SBT030049 Magic Violinist, Gray C .10 .15
SBT030050 Magic Keyboardist, Shion C .10 .15
SBT030051 Magibird C .10 .15
SBT030052 Magic Drummer, Byakuren C .10 .15
SBT030053 Magic Manipulator, Night C .10 .15
SBT030054 Magidog C .10 .15
SBT030055 Flame Quartet C .10 .15
SBT030056 Revolution of Red C .10 .15
SBT030057 Wings of Revolution C .10 .15
SBT030058 Deep Blaze Singularity C .10 .15
SBT030059 Magic Guitar, Kinari C .10 .15
SBT030060 Relaxed, Heribara C .10 .15
SBT030061 Armor of the Champion, Kongou C .10 .15
SBT030062 Subaru's Holiday C .10 .15
SBT030063 Astro Formation, Astellion C .10 .15
SBT030064 Suppression Advantage C .10 .15
SBT030065 Skyseer Ardent Dragon, Cross Farnese Astrologia AR .50 .75
SBT030066 Rumbling Thunderaxe, Agito AR .50 .75
SBT030067 Gargantua Blade Mage SCR 12.00 20.00
SBT030068 Godmagic, Firstry SCR 2.00 3.00
SBT030069 Godmagic, Nexent SCR 1.25 2.00
SBT030070 Deity Dragon Broom, Gar-Broom SCR 1.25 2.00
SBT030071 Deity Gargantua Punisher!! (Magic World) SCR .50 .75
SBT030072 Skyseer Ardent Dragon, Cross Farnese Astrologia SCR .75 1.25
SBT030073 Seerfight Dragon, Sultalion SCR .60 1.00
SBT030074 Skyseer Bow, Kaus Alnasl SCR 2.50 4.00
SBT030075 Notify: Convertible Tactics SCR .75 1.25
SBT030076 Victory Equation SCR 2.00 3.00
SBT030077 Rumbling Spiral Thunderaxe, Emperor Agito SCR 10.00 15.00
SBT030078 Rumbling Thunderaxe, Agito SCR 1.25 2.00
SBT030079 Swift Claws, Wings SCR 3.00 5.00
SBT030080 Linkdragon Order the Wicked Fight SCR .60 1.00
SBT030081 Links Arms "Bonds Glove" SCR 4.00 6.00
SBT03BR01 Gargantua Dragon, "Gattling Mode" BR 10.00 15.00
SBT03BR02 Skyseer Ardent Dragon, Cross Farnese Astrologia BR 5.00 8.00
SBT03BR03 Rumbling Thunderaxe, Agito BR 15.00 25.00
SBT03S001 Gargantua Blade Mage SP 30.00 50.00
SBT03S002 Skyseer Ardent Dragon, Cross Farnese Astrologia SP 30.00 50.00
SBT03S003 Rumbling Thunderaxe, Agito SP 40.00 60.00
SBT03S004 Emplord, Zerberos Lost SP 40.00 60.00

2019 Future Card Buddyfight S Booster Set 4 Drago Knight

RELEASED ON MAY 10, 2019
SBT040001 Gardragon Heiglut IV RRR 3.00 5.00
SBT040002 Dimension Dragon, Deacae RRR 4.00 6.00
SBT040003 G BOOST Over! RRR 5.00 8.00
SBT040004 Great Dragon of Genesis, Bigbang Dragon RRR 6.00 10.00
SBT040005 Swordflash, Goeh-goeh RRR 4.00 6.00
SBT040006 Genesis Pulsation RRR 5.00 8.00
SBT040007 Guardseer Dragon, Gyron Magna RRR 5.00 8.00
SBT040008 Aquinas Dogma RRR 1.00 1.50
SBT040009 Evolution Cyres, Vellute Dragon RR .60 1.00
SBT040010 Awakened Deity Dragon, Gardog RR 4.00 6.00
SBT040011 D. Aura Burst RR 1.25 2.00
SBT040012 YEAH! HIKARU? RR 2.00 3.00

SBT040013 IT'S SHOWTIME? RR	3.00	5.00
SBT040014 LDO's Lunch Time RR	2.00	3.00
SBT040015 Cross Pair Slash RR	1.00	1.50
SBT040016 Star Jack Revival RR	1.00	1.50
SBT040017 Crystallization Phenomenon RR	1.25	2.00
SBT040018 Buddy Block! RR	3.00	5.00
SBT040019 Dimension Ruin RR	1.25	2.00
SBT040020 Vile Demonic Arms, Lostless Wall RR	4.00	6.00
SBT040021 Awakened Deity Dragon, Garcat R	.20	.30
SBT040022 Gargantua Gate R	.20	.30
SBT040023 Combat Deity Dragon Shield - Base - R	.40	.60
SBT040024 Deity Creations Fangflare, Gargantua Punisher!! R	.40	.60
SBT040025 D. Zenith R	.40	.60
SBT040026 Darkshadow?, Genji R	.20	.30
SBT040027 Right Arm of Genesis, Rightes R	.20	.30
SBT040028 Left Arm of Genesis, Leftes R	.20	.30
SBT040029 Linkdragon Order's Links R	.75	1.25
SBT040030 Proclaim: Steer the Stars R	.20	.30
SBT040031 Skyseer Rising Light R	.20	.30
SBT040032 Formation Clear R	.20	.30
SBT040033 Celesphere Decision R	.20	.30
SBT040034 Fallen Fang Orcaliner Odorio R	.20	.30
SBT040035 Dimension Gain R	.20	.30
SBT040036 Awakened Deity Dragon, Kuhler Gardragon U	.12	.20
SBT040037 Awakened Deity Dragon, Wildt Gardra U	.12	.20
SBT040038 Awakened Deity Dragon, Genie Gardra U	.12	.20
SBT040039 Awakened Deity Dragon, Garbird U	.12	.20
SBT040040 Road to Champion U	.50	.75
SBT040041 Dimensional Secret Treasure, Mnesia U	.12	.20
SBT040042 Weather the Dragons U	.12	.20
SBT040043 Genesis Tenacity U	.12	.20
SBT040044 Resonance of Bonds U	.12	.20
SBT040045 Linkblast Chain, Agito Mines U	.12	.20
SBT040046 Asteros Star U	.20	.30
SBT040047 Linkdragon Order Secret Arts, Thunderbomb U	.12	.20
SBT040048 Star Jack Docking U	.12	.20
SBT040049 Ivory Barrier U	.12	.20
SBT040050 Awakened Deity Dragon, Sukhbart Gardragon C	.10	.15
SBT040051 Dimension Dragon, Dolor C	.10	.15
SBT040052 Dimension Dragon, Gelidus C	.10	.15
SBT040053 Awakened Deity Dragon, Fel Gradra C	.10	.15
SBT040054 Gar-Beaver C	.10	.15
SBT040055 Gar-Swallow C	.10	.15
SBT040056 Gar-E-Ungl C	.10	.15
SBT040057 Dragod's Breath C	.10	.15
SBT040058 Deity Dragon Beamlance, Garknight Lance C	.10	.15
SBT040059 Wicked Dragon of Fabrication, Demonica C	.10	.15
SBT040060 Jaunty, Bodolo C	.10	.15
SBT040061 Genesis Existence C	.10	.15
SBT040062 COME ON! BABY? C	.10	.15
SBT040063 HIKARU OF THE WORLD? C	.10	.15
SBT040064 Twinseer Dragon, Vee Starunner C	.10	.15
SBT040065 Twinseer Dragon, Lya Stroner C	.10	.15
SBT040066 Gargantua Knight Dragon SCR	10.00	15.00
SBT040067 Garknight Strash SCR	1.25	2.00
SBT040068 Gar-E-Burst SCR	3.00	5.00
SBT040069 Deity Dragon Duobeam, Gartwin Saber SCR	4.00	6.00
SBT040070 Deity Gargantua Crusher!! SCR	1.25	2.00
SBT040071 Skyseer Ardent Dragon, Cross Irisnese Astrologia SCR	4.00	6.00
SBT040072 Everseer Bow, Caelum Rex SCR	4.00	6.00
SBT040073 Thunderpeak Spiral Linkaxe, King Agito SCR	1.25	2.00
SBT040074 Thunderpeak Linkaxe, Agito SCR	4.00	6.00
SBT040075 Cross Intersect SCR	6.00	10.00
SBT040076 Vile Demonic Husk Deity Dragon, Vanity End Destroyer SCR	5.00	8.00
SBT040077 Gargantua Lost Dragon SCR	2.50	4.00
SBT040078 Lost Cross Astrologia SCR	2.00	3.00
SBT040079 Void Thunderaxe, Agito SCR	2.00	3.00
SBT040080 Dimension Gate SCR	4.00	6.00
SBT04BR01 Gargantua Knight Dragon BR	15.00	25.00
SBT04BR02 Vile Demonic Husk Deity Dragon, Vanity End Destroyer BR	15.00	25.00
SBT04S001 Gargantua Knight Dragon SP	40.00	60.00
SBT04S002 Skyseer Ardent Dragon, Cross Irisnese Astrologia SP	30.00	50.00
SBT04S003 Thunderpeak Spiral Linkaxe, King Agito SP	12.00	20.00
SBT04S004 Vile Demonic Husk Deity Dragon, Vanity End Destroyer SP	50.00	75.00

2019 Future Card Buddyfight S Booster Set 5 War of Dragods

RELEASED ON AUGUST 23, 2019

SBT050001 Evolution Storm, Reshoot Dragon RRR	2.00	3.00
SBT050002 Gar-E-Invitation RRR	2.00	3.00
SBT050003 Grand Sage, Ilanral RRR	4.00	6.00
SBT050004 De Ju Mau RRR	10.00	15.00
SBT050005 Retainer Shield RRR	6.00	10.00
SBT050006 Jealousy Evil Demonic Dragon, Envy RRR	10.00	15.00
SBT050007 Evil Demonic Dragon, Lupus RRR	10.00	15.00
SBT050008 Diablos Soul RRR	10.00	15.00
SBT050009 Eifer Gardra RR	2.00	3.00
SBT050010 Deity Dragon Strategist, Valheit RR	1.50	2.50
SBT050011 Fifth Omni Cavalry Dragon, Arkaid "SD" RR	2.00	3.00
SBT050012 Gar-E-C'mon RR	2.50	4.00
SBT050013 Fairy King, Alberich RR	1.25	2.00
SBT050014 Starry Night Enchanter, Duric RR	3.00	5.00
SBT050015 The King's Guidance Ara Saas RR	3.00	5.00
SBT050016 The Arcane Crown Al Coronation RR	2.50	4.00
SBT050017 Evil Demonic Dragon, Simiae RR	8.00	12.00
SBT050018 Contract Circle of Evil Calling RR	3.00	5.00
SBT050019 Melody of the Evil Moon RR	3.00	5.00
SBT050020 Purgatory Knights Reborn, Needle Claw Dragon RR	2.00	3.00
SBT050021 Melza Gardragon R	.30	.50
SBT050022 Dragowhite, Fifth Omni Holy Light R	.30	.50
SBT050023 Fortuitous Valor, Astolfo R	.50	.75
SBT050024 Serf of Decoration, Alla Al R	.30	.50
SBT050025 Junior Long-spear Warrior, Liim R	.50	.75
SBT050026 Allegiant Shield R	.50	.75
SBT050027 Lightblaze Sword of the King, Claiomh Solais R	.50	.75
SBT050028 Indolent Evil Demonic Dragon, Sloth R	.30	.50
SBT050029 Evil Demonic Dragon, Gryphus R	.60	1.00
SBT050030 Evil Demonic Dragon, Draco R	.60	1.00
SBT050031 Chaotic Pain R	2.00	3.00
SBT050032 Diablos Grave R	.60	1.00
SBT050033 Diablos Compassion R	.60	1.00
SBT050034 CHAOS Alberion R	.30	.50
SBT050035 Pride to the Sword, the Blade Never Dies R	.30	.50
SBT050036 Combat Deity Roar U	.15	.25
SBT050037 Deity Dragon Throwblade, Garlight Edge U	.15	.25
SBT050038 Reinforcing Swordsman, Sheif U	.15	.25
SBT050039 Devoted Scholar of Hermetics, Kiamya U	.15	.25
SBT050040 The Majestic Audience Pharaonic Apadana U	.15	.25
SBT050041 Pyramidal Peak U	.40	.60
SBT050042 Undying Charisma U	.15	.25
SBT050043 Bracelet of Sehel U	.15	.25
SBT050044 Evil Demonic Dragon, Capra U	.15	.25
SBT050045 Evil Demonic Dragon, Cervus U	.15	.25
SBT050046 Hundred Demons Sorcery, Death Sacrifice U	2.00	3.00
SBT050047 Diablos Disposal U	.15	.25
SBT050048 Diablos Shield U	.15	.25
SBT050049 Waltz of Blood Moon U	.15	.25
SBT050050 Awakened Deity Dragon, Garrabbit C	.10	.15
SBT050051 Dragonic Exchange C	.10	.15
SBT050052 Dragobright, Fifth Omni Light C	.10	.15
SBT050053 Battle Deity Flame Slash Wave C	.10	.15
SBT050054 Devotee of the Dead, Alamgar C	.10	.15
SBT050055 Unfettering Vassal, Ishtar C	.10	.15
SBT050056 Skilled General, Odysseus C	.10	.15
SBT050057 Bottle Dweller, Smasma C	.10	.15
SBT050058 Sector Collapse C	.10	.15
SBT050059 The Hardworking Fairies C	.10	.15
SBT050060 Great Spell, Weiterstadt C	1.00	1.50
SBT050061 Evil Demonic Dragon, Cornix C	.10	.15
SBT050062 Evil Demonic Dragon, Pavo C	.10	.15
SBT050063 Death Astray C	.10	.15
SBT050064 Diablos Storm C	.10	.15
SBT050065 Diablos Death-toll C	.10	.15
SBT050066 Gargantua Bladecentaur SCR	6.00	10.00
SBT050067 Awakened Deity Dragon, Caliburn Gardra SCR	1.25	2.00
SBT050068 Awakened Deity Dragon, Garmouse SCR	2.00	3.00
SBT050069 Gar-E-Stream SCR	2.00	3.00
SBT050070 Deity Dragon Beamsword, Garknight Rapier SCR	2.50	4.00
SBT050071 Flame Deity, Magma Horus SCR	8.00	12.00
SBT050072 Ice Deity, Freeza Horus SCR	10.00	15.00
SBT050073 Heavy Shield of Adjuvancy, Qalxan SCR	2.50	4.00
SBT050074 Seat of Absolute, Hieratic throne SCR	4.00	6.00
SBT050075 Forbidden Light of Double Deity Aktar Pheido SCR	2.50	4.00
SBT050076 Exterminating Evil Demonic Dragon, Belial SCR	10.00	15.00
SBT050077 Evil Demonic Dragon, Vespertilio SCR	3.00	5.00
SBT050078 Negative Survive SCR	10.00	15.00
SBT050079 Ever Dark Shadowing, Umbrelle SCR	6.00	10.00
SBT050080 Eradicate Avenge SCR	6.00	10.00
SBT05BR01 Gargantua Bladecentaur BR	12.00	20.00
SBT05BR02 Flame Deity, Magma Horus BR	15.00	25.00
SBT05BR03 Ice Deity, Freeza Horus BR	20.00	30.00
SBT05S001 Gargantua Bladecentaur SP	50.00	75.00
SBT05S002 Flame Deity, Magma Horus SP	40.00	60.00
SBT05S003 Ice Deity, Freeza Horus SP	30.00	50.00
SBT05S004 Exterminating Evil Demonic Dragon, Belial SP	50.00	75.00

2017 Future Card Buddyfight X Booster Set Alternative 1 Crossing Generations

RELEASED ON JUNE 16, 2017

XBT01ACP010001EN Armordeity, Energeia RRR	1.25	2.00
XBT01ACP010002EN Head of Explosive Dragon Family, Vumvorl RRR	.30	.50
XBT01ACP010003EN Unyielding Rampage Dragon, Batzz RRR	.50	.75
XBT01ACP010004EN Veteran Thunder Knights Leader, Kommandeur Fahne RRR	4.00	6.00
XBT01ACP010005EN Crimson Battler, Bal Dragon RRR	2.50	4.00
XBT01ACP010006EN Batzz "SD" RRR	.40	.60
XBT01ACP010007EN In the Name of Thunder Empire! RRR	4.00	6.00
XBT01ACP010008EN Dragosucceed RRR	1.50	2.50
XBT01ACP010009EN Bal Dragon, "Double Balverize Blade!" RRR	.30	.50
XBT01ACP010010EN Drum Bunker Dragon, "Drill Ram Buster Break!" RRR	1.50	2.50
XBT01ACP010011EN Rapid Master, Crescente RR	.75	1.25
XBT01ACP010012EN Ice Dragon Race Czar, Icicle RR	.30	.50
XBT01ACP010013EN Golden Dragon Knight Lord, Tutankhamun RR	.30	.50
XBT01ACP010014EN A Hero's Spirit, Jackknife "Spirit" RR	2.00	3.00
XBT01ACP010015EN Undying Dragon Knight Duke, Vlad Dracula RR	.30	.50
XBT01ACP010016EN Rumored Ruiner, Manicrack RR	.50	.75
XBT01ACP010017EN Sun Deity's Fragment, Bal Flamme RR	2.00	3.00
XBT01ACP010018EN Sun Deity's Fragments, Bal Glow RR	.30	.50
XBT01ACP010019EN Dragonic Charge, "Plus" RR	8.00	12.00
XBT01ACP010020EN Demon Lord's Roaring Dragon Blast RR	4.00	6.00
XBT01ACP010021EN Blade Dragon Shield RR	4.00	6.00
XBT01ACP010022EN Arc Dragon Odachi RR	2.00	3.00
XBT01ACP010023EN Super Armordragon, Galvanic Horn Dragon R	.20	.30
XBT01ACP010024EN Third Crimson Chieftain, Heedless Agni R	.60	1.00
XBT01ACP010025EN Alps Dragon Knight Lord, Geronimo R	.20	.30
XBT01ACP010026EN A Faint Memory, Batzz R	.50	.75
XBT01ACP010027EN Orsogoneon of Ten-Heads Chopper R	.20	.30
XBT01ACP010028EN Sun Deity's Fragments, Bal Burn R	.20	.30
XBT01ACP010029EN Chained Strikes Warlock, Rabukh R	.20	.30
XBT01ACP010030EN Crimson Battler, Rock Bunker Dragon R	.20	.30
XBT01ACP010031EN Famed Military Deviser, Fanning R	.60	1.00
XBT01ACP010032EN Dragon Knight Great Emperor, Maximilian R	.50	.75
XBT01ACP010033EN Cavalry Dragon, Rocinante R	.75	1.25
XBT01ACP010034EN Burning Dragon Jr. R	.30	.50
XBT01ACP010035EN Tiny Flame Dragon, Linear R	.20	.30
XBT01ACP010036EN Sand Dragon Shield R	1.00	1.50
XBT01ACP010037EN Thunder X Flash R	.20	.30
XBT01ACP010038EN Arc Dragon Pistol R	.50	.75
XBT01ACP010039EN Thunder Knights Banner R	1.25	2.00
XBT01ACP010040EN Crimson Fist, Dragoplus R	.40	.60
XBT01ACP010041EN Fist Dragon of Torrid Flames, Olganorls C	.10	.15
XBT01ACP010042EN Eliminator Warlock, Paydos C	.10	.15
XBT01ACP010043EN Cannonball Squad C	.50	.75
XBT01ACP010044EN Recovery Warlock, Tohal C	.10	.15
XBT01ACP010045EN Dragon Knight Directive, Bertrand C	.10	.15
XBT01ACP010046EN Aloof Jaggy C	.60	1.00
XBT01ACP010047EN Thunder Knights, Broadsword "with Shield" C	.10	.15
XBT01ACP010048EN Dragon Knight of Mirror, Carrasco C	.10	.15
XBT01ACP010049EN Crimson Battler, Gunzarm Dragon C	.10	.15
XBT01ACP010050EN Giant Arm Man, Bulbus C	.10	.15
XBT01ACP010051EN Lightkeeper Dragon C	.10	.15
XBT01ACP010052EN Systemic Commander Dragon C	.10	.15
XBT01ACP010053EN Tactician, Sanjao C	.10	.15
XBT01ACP010054EN Recce, Fan-Fan C	.10	.15
XBT01ACP010055EN Combat Medic, Stripe C	.10	.15
XBT01ACP010056EN Thunder Knights, Dragoarcher C	.60	1.00
XBT01ACP010057EN Support Warlock, Yaida C	.10	.15
XBT01ACP010058EN Surprise Spike C	.60	1.00
XBT01ACP010059EN Dragon Knight of Mind's Eye, Galileo C	.10	.15
XBT01ACP010060EN Winning With Wits C	.10	.15
XBT01ACP010061EN Buddy C'mon! C	.10	.15
XBT01ACP010062EN Buddy Together! C	.10	.15
XBT01ACP010063EN Fire Dragon Shield C	.10	.15
XBT01ACP010064EN Sun Dragon Shield C	.10	.15
XBT01ACP010065EN Thunder X Doll C	.10	.15
XBT01ACP010066EN Dragobond C	.10	.15
XBT01ACP010067EN Vanguard Retreat C	.10	.15
XBT01ACP010068EN Convertible Dragon Lance, Gearzlance C	.10	.15
XBT01ACP010069EN Thunder Orb C	.10	.15
XBT01ACP010070EN Dragon Cavalry Arts, Spirit Aura! C	.10	.15
XBT01ACP010071EN Bearer of Sins, Batzz SCR		
XBT01ACP010072EN Famed Military Deviser, Fanning SCR		
XBT01ACP010073EN Thunder X Flash SCR		
XBT01ACP010074EN Style of Impact, Bal Dragon SCR		
XBT01ACP010075EN Sun Deity's Fragments, Bal Burn SCR		
XBT01ACP010076EN Burning Dragon Jr. SCR		
XBT01ACP010077EN Paramount Neo Dragon, Drum the Maximum Future SCR		
XBT01ACP010078EN Sand Dragon Shield SCR		
XBT01ACP010079EN Crimson Fist, Dragoplus SCR		
XBT01ACP01BR01EN Bearer of Sins, Batzz BR	10.00	15.00
XBT01ACP01BR02EN Style of Impact, Bal Dragon BR	20.00	30.00
XBT01ACP01BR03EN Paramount Neo Dragon, Drum the Maximum Future BR	10.00	15.00
XBT01ACP020001EN Too Over-Dimensional Dragon, EXA Dimenzion RRR	5.00	8.00
XBT01ACP020002EN Suzaku Kenran Variable Cord RRR	3.00	5.00
XBT01ACP020003EN Indigo Gem Crystal Dragon, Athora RRR	.30	.50
XBT01ACP020004EN Jade Crystal Dragon, Schartreuze RRR	.60	1.00
XBT01ACP020005EN Eternal Guardian Dragon, Aettir RRR	.60	1.00
XBT01ACP020006EN SAC17: Clarke RRR	.60	1.00
XBT01ACP020007EN RA07: Heinlein RRR	4.00	6.00
XBT01ACP020008EN Athora "SD" RRR	4.00	6.00
XBT01ACP020009EN Red Crystal Dragon, Merurol RRR	1.25	2.00
XBT01ACP020010EN Transcend Star Dragon Emperor, Ewigkeit RRR	2.50	4.00
XBT01ACP020011EN Shiny Crystal Dragon, Jenova RR	.30	.50
XBT01ACP020012EN BW25: Aldiss RR	.60	1.00
XBT01ACP020013EN Big Crystal Dragon, Vulcan RR	.50	.75
XBT01ACP020014EN Iron Crystal Dragon, Evaclear RR	1.00	1.50
XBT01ACP020015EN Stronger Schlange:04 RR	.30	.50
XBT01ACP020016EN Life Envoy, Nectar RR	.75	1.25
XBT01ACP020017EN Fifth Focus RR	2.00	3.00
XBT01ACP020018EN Star Believer RR	15.00	25.00
XBT01ACP020019EN Master Domination RR	.60	1.00
XBT01ACP020020EN Extend Defender RR	1.00	1.50
XBT01ACP020021EN Delete Jewel RR	.75	1.25
XBT01ACP020022EN Lapis Lazuli Spikes RR	.50	.75
XBT01ACP020023EN GA47: Effinger R	.75	1.25
XBT01ACP020024EN Light Crystal Dragon, Graparl R	.20	.30
XBT01ACP020025EN Patient Athora R	.50	.75
XBT01ACP020026EN Biggest Dragonarms, Triple Buster R	2.50	4.00
XBT01ACP020027EN Black Crystal Dragon, Lucien Black R	1.00	1.50
XBT01ACP020028EN ER75: Burroughs R	.40	.60
XBT01ACP020029EN Dragonarms, Wieger R	1.00	1.50
XBT01ACP020030EN RF15: Young R	.60	1.00
XBT01ACP020031EN Red Crystal Dragon, Tarnat R	.75	1.25
XBT01ACP020032EN Prism Canceler R	.75	1.25
XBT01ACP020033EN Star Jack Destruction R	.20	.30
XBT01ACP020034EN Cosmo Heal Protection R	1.00	1.50
XBT01ACP020035EN Glitter Stone R	.20	.30
XBT01ACP020036EN Star Dragon Lance, Black Clock R	.60	1.00
XBT01ACP020037EN Dragoon Skill, Stardust Maneuver R	.40	.60
XBT01ACP020038EN EX Dimenzion, "Terminate 8!" R	.20	.30
XBT01ACP020039EN Meteorarms, Altoalizal R	.20	.30
XBT01ACP020040EN Mind Faker R	.50	.75
XBT01ACP020041EN Acid Crystal Dragon, Gaimlett C	.10	.15
XBT01ACP020042EN Lost Dragonarms, Giant Fragment C	.10	.15
XBT01ACP020043EN Candy Crystal Dragon, Nuts C	.10	.15
XBT01ACP020044EN Pink Crystal Dragon, Tarvel C	.10	.15
XBT01ACP020045EN AA12: Norton C	.10	.15
XBT01ACP020046EN Dragonarms, Bigger Brave C	.10	.15
XBT01ACP020047EN White Crystal Dragon, Schunerblain C	.10	.15
XBT01ACP020048EN A13: Bester C	.10	.15
XBT01ACP020049EN J15: Tiptree C	.10	.15
XBT01ACP020050EN White Crystal Dragon, Kelnar C	.10	.15
XBT01ACP020051EN White Crystal Dragon, Carinyan C	.10	.15
XBT01ACP020052EN Prism Relic C	.50	.75
XBT01ACP020053EN Colloid Armor C	.10	.15
XBT01ACP020054EN Revival Prism C	.60	1.00
XBT01ACP020055EN Space Agent C	.10	.15
XBT01ACP020056EN Crystal Shower C	.10	.15
XBT01ACP020057EN Vivid Move C	.10	.15
XBT01ACP020058EN Additional Jewel C	.10	.15
XBT01ACP020059EN Phantasm Counter C	.10	.15
XBT01ACP020060EN Star Alternative C	2.00	3.00
XBT01ACP020061EN Jewelry Chest C	.10	.15
XBT01ACP020062EN Cosmo Charge Protection C	.40	.60
XBT01ACP020063EN Proto Barrier C	1.25	2.00
XBT01ACP020064EN Earth Barrier C	1.25	2.00
XBT01ACP020065EN Star Dragon Lance, Fahrenheit C	.10	.15
XBT01ACP020066EN Red Gem Ball C	.10	.15
XBT01ACP020067EN Wild Wise Trap C	.10	.15
XBT01ACP020068EN Meteorarms, Vaishal C	.10	.15
XBT01ACP020069EN Blade of Stellar Deity, Viaraktear C	.10	.15
XBT01ACP020070EN Super Gravity Device, Graviton Generator C	.10	.15
XBT01ACP020071EN Avatar of Glass Crystal, Athora SCR		
XBT01ACP020072EN Red Crystal Dragon, Tarnat SCR		
XBT01ACP020073EN Prism Canceler SCR		
XBT01ACP020074EN Galaxy Dragoner, Jackknife SCR		
XBT01ACP020075EN Biggest Dragonarms, Triple Buster SCR		
XBT01ACP020076EN Dragonarms, Wieger SCR		
XBT01ACP020077EN Space-Time Distortion Dragon, Zodiac "if" SCR		
XBT01ACP020078EN Meteorarms, Altoalizal SCR		
XBT01ACP020079EN Mind Faker SCR		
XBT01ACP02BR01EN Avatar of Glass Crystal, Athora BR	3.00	5.00
XBT01ACP02BR02EN Galaxy Dragoner, Jackknife BR	40.00	60.00
XBT01ACP02BR03EN Space-Time Distortion Dragon, Zodiac "if" BR	15.00	25.00

2017 Future Card Buddyfight X Booster Set Alternative 2 Evolution and Mutation

RELEASED ON AUGUST 25, 2017

XBT02ACP030001EN Hellfire Executioners Dragon, Gagalgarios RRR		
XBT02ACP030002EN Evil Deity Karma Demonic Dragon, Aga Manafh RRR		
XBT02ACP030003EN Tenacious Omni Lord, Negulbalz RRR		
XBT02ACP030004EN Ruler of Battle Zone, Abygale RRR		
XBT02ACP030005EN Sealed Black Crest Dragon, Ganmarl RRR		
XBT02ACP030006EN Phantom Router, Gallows Demento RRR		
XBT02ACP030007EN Truth of Darkness RRR		
XBT02ACP030008EN Evil Sword Deity, Dark Kaizerion RRR		
XBT02ACP030009EN Dark Black Crystal Dragon, Athora RRR		
XBT02ACP030010EN Batzz, Afflicted by Darkness RRR		
XBT02ACP030011EN Despaired Skull, Thirteen RR		
XBT02ACP030012EN Provenance-gnawing Dragon, Death Tallica Zegalia RR		
XBT02ACP030013EN Alluring Sword Demon, Vioroza RR		
XBT02ACP030014EN Finale Gate Guider, Coda Giudecca RR		
XBT02ACP030015EN Daredevil, "Dark Prisoner" RR		
XBT02ACP030016EN Purgatory Knights, Grudge Arrow Dragon RR		
XBT02ACP030017EN Misbegotten Child of a Demonic Dragon, Tchimno RR		
XBT02ACP030018EN Black Dragon, Dubie RR		
XBT02ACP030019EN Demolition Bite RR		
XBT02ACP030020EN Death Gauge Timer RR		
XBT02ACP030021EN Darkness Dragoner, Jackknife RR		
XBT02ACP030022EN Evil Fake Tsukikage Type-0 & Byakuya Type-0 RR		
XBT02ACP030023EN Jet Black Crest Dragon, Yngwem R	.20	.30

XBT02ACP030024EN Demonic Deity General, Gathura R .20 .30
XBT02ACP030025EN Source of Demonic Dragon, Zahhak R .20 .30
XBT02ACP030026EN Purgatory Knights, Pendulum Dragon R .20 .30
XBT02ACP030027EN Purgatory Knights, Demios Sword Early R .20 .30
XBT02ACP030028EN A Short Repose, Abygale R .20 .30
XBT02ACP030029EN Abygale Spare R .20 .30
XBT02ACP030030EN The Beginning of Demise, Azi Dahaka R .20 .30
XBT02ACP030031EN Bone Labor, Quenatar R .20 .30
XBT02ACP030032EN Death Ruler, Iron Maiden R .20 .30
XBT02ACP030033EN Rebels' Armor R .20 .30
XBT02ACP030034EN Vendidart Disaster R .20 .30
XBT02ACP030035EN Judgment of the Evil Deity Dragon R .20 .30
XBT02ACP030036EN Black Crest Volcano R .20 .30
XBT02ACP030037EN Purgatory Hymn, "Tune of Cursed Endless Battles" R .20 .30
XBT02ACP030038EN Gale Destruction R .20 .30
XBT02ACP030039EN Black Poison Dragon, Bloodknife R .20 .30
XBT02ACP030040EN Yamigitsune Hidden in Garments R .20 .30
XBT02ACP030041EN Impure Demonic Dragon, Durzinas U .12 .20
XBT02ACP030042EN World-Breaking Demonic Dragon, Zalfar U .12 .20
XBT02ACP030043EN Purgatory Knights, Scrap-Drill Dragon U .12 .20
XBT02ACP030044EN Black Crest Dragon, Arngrei U .12 .20
XBT02ACP030045EN Black Crest Dragon, Seafrost U .12 .20
XBT02ACP030046EN Purgatory Knights, Shifturn Dragon U .12 .20
XBT02ACP030047EN Black Crest Dragon, Jeisykes U .12 .20
XBT02ACP030048EN Black Crest Dragon, Estryber U .12 .20
XBT02ACP030049EN Death Tallica Hand U .12 .20
XBT02ACP030050EN Underhanded Magus, Dseydo U .12 .20
XBT02ACP030051EN Destroy Advantage U .12 .20
XBT02ACP030052EN Endless Black U .12 .20
XBT02ACP030053EN Vengeful Slash U .12 .20
XBT02ACP030054EN Dragon Mirror Image U .12 .20
XBT02ACP030055EN Zarathustra's Armillary Sphere U .12 .20
XBT02ACP030056EN Black Crest Conversion U .12 .20
XBT02ACP030057EN Shadow Dive District, Ombre U .12 .20
XBT02ACP030058EN Phantom Getter U .12 .20
XBT02ACP030059EN Purgatory Sorcery, Blood Oath Formation U .12 .20
XBT02ACP030060EN Cornerstone of Victory U .12 .20
XBT02ACP030061EN Noble Sacrifice U .12 .20
XBT02ACP030062EN Accel End U .12 .20
XBT02ACP030063EN Dark Energy U .12 .20
XBT02ACP030064EN Death Shield U .12 .20
XBT02ACP030065EN Black Dragon Shield U .12 .20
XBT02ACP030066EN Abyss Symphony C .12 .20
XBT02ACP030067EN The Book of Good and Evil?, Avesta U .12 .20
XBT02ACP030068EN Evil Deity of Red Flash, Anti Verethragna U .12 .20
XBT02ACP030069EN Shadow Hero, Growl U .12 .20
XBT02ACP030070EN Black Knight of Clarity, El Quixote U .12 .20
XBT02ACP030071EN Purple Rag of Ruin, Abygale SCR
XBT02ACP030072EN Abygale Spare SCR
XBT02ACP030073EN Black Crest Volcano SCR
XBT02ACP030074EN Purgatory Knights Leader of Condolence, Geist Demios SCR
XBT02ACP030075EN Purgatory Knights, Demios Sword Early SCR
XBT02ACP030076EN Purgatory Hymn, "Tune of Cursed Endless Battles" SCR
XBT02ACP030077EN Demonic Dragon Deity of Demise World, Azi Dahaka "Gaen" SCR
XBT02ACP030078EN Source of Demonic Dragon, Zahhak SCR
XBT02ACP030079EN The Beginning of Demise, Azi Dahaka SCR
XBT02ACP03BR01EN Purple Rag of Ruin, Abygale BR 30.00 50.00
XBT02ACP03BR02EN Purgatory Knights Leader of Condolence, Geist Demios BR 30.00 50.00
XBT02ACP03BR03EN Demonic Dragon Deity of Demise World, Azi Dahaka "Gaen" BR15.00 25.00
XBT02ASS010001EN Fifth Omni Super Dragon Great Emperor, Kaizer Drum RRR
XBT02ASS010002EN Fifth Omni Super Dragon Lord, Kaizer Drum RRR
XBT02ASS010003EN Fifth Omni Dragon Lord, Drum RRR
XBT02ASS010004EN Hundred Demons General, Yomotsugozuryu RRR
XBT02ASS010005EN Specter of Darkness Wasteland, O-Yamigedo RRR
XBT02ASS010006EN Great Fiend, Yamigedo RRR
XBT02ASS010007EN Dragon Knight, Pisaro RR
XBT02ASS010008EN Ice Prison Emperor, Cocytus Greed RR
XBT02ASS010009EN Lord's Dragon Shield RR
XBT02ASS010010EN Dragoguts! RR
XBT02ASS010011EN Gedo Shield RR
XBT02ASS010012EN Dragon Lord Initiation, Giga Howling Crusher!! RR
XBT02ASS010013EN INV Fifth Omni Dragon Lord, Crazed Tenbu R .20 .30
XBT02ASS010014EN Fifth Omni Dragon Lord, Tenbu R .20 .30
XBT02ASS010015EN Fifth Omni Dragon Lord, Drum the Punisher R .20 .30
XBT02ASS010016EN Awakened Fifth Omni Dragon Lord, Drum R .20 .30
XBT02ASS010017EN Fifth Omni Dragon Lord, Tenbu "SD" R .20 .30
XBT02ASS010018EN Great Leader, Anson R .20 .30
XBT02ASS010019EN Fifth Omni Dragon Fist, Shiny Dragon C .10 .15
XBT02ASS010020EN Dragobright, Fifth Omni Light C .10 .15
XBT02ASS010021EN Dragodesperate C .10 .15
XBT02ASS010022EN Emblem of Omni Lords C .10 .15
XBT02ASS010023EN Fifth Omni Dragon Sword, Emperor Fang C .10 .15
XBT02ASS010024EN Unparalleled Arts, Omni Lord 8 Burst! C .10 .15
XBT02ASS010025EN Eliminator, Glasya Labolas C .10 .15
XBT02ASS010026EN Hasted Evolution, Yamigedo C .10 .15
XBT02ASS010027EN Starved Yamigedo C .10 .15
XBT02ASS010028EN Hundred Demons Sorcery, Yamitagae C .10 .15
XBT02ASS010029EN Evil Deity Sorcery, Unorthodox Miasma C .10 .15
XBT02ASS010030EN Shrine of the Corrupted Fuchigami C .10 .15
XBT02ASS010031EN Burst Claw, Raijin C .10 .15
XBT02ASS010032EN Fifth Omni Successor, Drum SCR
XBT02ASS010033EN Unruly Fifth Omni Dragon Lord, Tenbu SCR
XBT02ASS010034EN Fifth Omni Cavalry Dragon Disciple, Hagun of Sand Cane SCR
XBT02ASS010035EN INV Stern Spirit, Kokujo Yamigedo SCR
XBT02ASS010036EN A Nameless Valkyrie SCR
XBT02ASS010037EN Guiding Demon, Dyingas SCR
XBT02ASS01BR01EN Fifth Omni Successor, Drum BR 25.00 40.00
XBT02ASS01BR02EN INV Stern Spirit, Kokujo Yamigedo BR 25.00 40.00
XBT02ASS020001EN Purgatory Knights Leader, Demios Sword "Inferno" RRR
XBT02ASS020002EN Purgatory Knights Leader, Demios Sword Dragon RRR
XBT02ASS020003EN Purgatory Knights, Demons Rapier Dragon RRR
XBT02ASS020004EN Radiant Guardian, Jackknife "Aster" RRR
XBT02ASS020005EN Star Guardian, Jackknife RRR
XBT02ASS020006EN Star Dragoner, Jackknife "SD" RRR
XBT02ASS020007EN V Gradation, Quantum Ruler RR
XBT02ASS020008EN Star Dragoner, Luminous Blue RR
XBT02ASS020009EN Radiant Punisher!! RR
XBT02ASS020010EN Purgatory Knights, Forever RR
XBT02ASS020011EN Life Dwells in the Flames of Hades Too RR
XBT02ASS020012EN Purgatory Knights Leader, Demios Sword "Chaos Execution!" RR
XBT02ASS020013EN Purgatory Knights, Death Sickle "Calvary" R .20 .30
XBT02ASS020014EN Purgatory Knights, Gairahm Lance Dragon R .20 .30
XBT02ASS020015EN Distortion Punisher!! R .20 .30
XBT02ASS020016EN Great Dragonarms, The Main Force R .20 .30
XBT02ASS020017EN Dragonarms, Radiant Scudo R .20 .30
XBT02ASS020018EN Radiant Saber, Providence R .20 .30
XBT02ASS020019EN Void Omni Wicked Lord, Negulbalz C .10 .15
XBT02ASS020020EN Purgatory Knights, Venom Spike Dragon C .10 .15
XBT02ASS020021EN Purgatory Knights, Eraser Hand Dragon C .10 .15
XBT02ASS020022EN Purgatory Knights, Eval Grebe Dragon C .10 .15
XBT02ASS020023EN Purgatory Knights, Angry Hand Dragon C .10 .15
XBT02ASS020024EN Sword of Purgatory Knights Leader, Demios Sword C .10 .15
XBT02ASS020025EN Crush that Body, and Sustain Mine C .10 .15
XBT02ASS020026EN We Traverse the Blood-soaked Demonic Path C .10 .15
XBT02ASS020027EN Biggest Dragonarms, Sonic Blast C .10 .15
XBT02ASS020028EN Dragonarms, Vogel C .10 .15
XBT02ASS020029EN Dragonarms, Charger C .10 .15
XBT02ASS020030EN Dragonarms, Radiant Alma C .10 .15
XBT02ASS020031EN Dragonarms, Garbel Anchor C .10 .15
XBT02ASS020032EN Star Jack Docking C .10 .15
XBT02ASS020033EN Star Jack Boost C .10 .15
XBT02ASS020034EN Star Jack Repair C .10 .15
XBT02ASS020035EN Radiant Star, Linkage C .10 .15
XBT02ASS020036EN The Foundation of Purgatory Knights, Lord Demios SCR
XBT02ASS020037EN Purgatory Knights, Needle Claw Dragon SCR
XBT02ASS020038EN Genocide Punisher!! SCR
XBT02ASS020039EN Hero Dragon, Jackknife SCR
XBT02ASS020040EN Radiant Dragoner, Jackknife "Sol Aster" SCR
XBT02ASS020041EN Dragonarms, Radiant Fuel SCR
XBT02ASS02BR01EN The Foundation of Purgatory Knights, Lord Demios BR 40.00 60.00
XBT02ASS02BR02EN Hero Dragon, Jackknife BR 30.00 50.00

2017 Future Card Buddyfight X Booster Set Alternative 3 LVL Up Heroes and Adventures

RELEASED ON SEPTEMBER 22, 2017
XBT03AUB010001EN Great Demon Lord of Thunderstorm, Batzz RRR 3.00 5.00
XBT03AUB010002EN Interstellar Great Demon Lord, Jackknife RRR 1.50 2.50
XBT03AUB010003EN Protector of Fate, Tasuku RRR 3.00 5.00
XBT03AUB010004EN The Tempestuous Brave, Gao RRR 2.50 4.00
XBT03AUB010005EN Princess of the Azure Skies, Ku RRR 2.50 4.00
XBT03AUB010006EN Bonus Quest RRR 10.00 15.00
XBT03AUB010007EN Quintessence Crystal Demon Lord, Athora RR .75 1.25
XBT03AUB010008EN Demon Lord of the Hundred Demons, Yamigedo RR 2.00 3.00
XBT03AUB010009EN Purgatory Demon Lord, Demios RR .75 1.25
XBT03AUB010010EN Windmill Knight, Noboru RR 4.00 6.00
XBT03AUB010011EN Dark Black Knight, Gaito RR 3.00 5.00
XBT03AUB010012EN Friends of the Braves, Baku & Kuguru RR 1.00 1.50
XBT03AUB010013EN Merchant of Darkness, Jin RR 1.00 1.50
XBT03AUB010014EN Fist Fighter of Blistering Kicks, Kanata RR 1.25 2.00
XBT03AUB010015EN Dispatcher from Assassin Circle, Sakate RR .75 1.25
XBT03AUB010016EN Apprentice Sister, Hanako RR 2.00 3.00
XBT03AUB010017EN Masked Swordsman, Kiri RR 4.00 6.00
XBT03AUB010018EN Mission Card "Adventurer Guild, Aibo Academy" RR 6.00 10.00
XBT03AUB010019EN Demon Lord Castle in the Sky, Satsuki Palace RR 4.00 6.00
XBT03AUB010020EN Magic Sword, Etherstorm RR 1.25 2.00
XBT03AUB010021EN Ice Dragon Demon Lord, Miserea R .60 1.00
XBT03AUB010022EN Ghoul Deity Demon Lord, Ibuki R .75 1.25
XBT03AUB010023EN Demon Lord of the Sun, Bal Dragon R .60 1.00
XBT03AUB010024EN Demon Lord Chief, Duel Jaeger R .20 .30
XBT03AUB010025EN Vortex Demon Lord, Drum R .60 1.00
XBT03AUB010026EN Bird Demon Lord, Bladewing Phoenix R .75 1.25
XBT03AUB010027EN Demon Lord of Apocalypse, Gratos R .75 1.25
XBT03AUB010028EN Black Winged Demon Lord, Abygale R .60 1.00
XBT03AUB010029EN Tutor of the Four Deities, Suzaku R .50 .75
XBT03AUB010030EN Immortal Sword Sage, Shosetsu R 1.50 2.50
XBT03AUB010031EN Three Knights of Konoe, Nano-Guardians R .60 1.00
XBT03AUB010032EN Revenger, Ikazuchi R .75 1.25
XBT03AUB010033EN Purgatory Demonic Swordsman R .50 .75
XBT03AUB010034EN Chivalrous Thief of Justice, Mukuro R .75 1.25
XBT03AUB010035EN Armored Knights Leader, Genesis R .20 .30
XBT03AUB010036EN Brave of the Sun, Yota R .20 .30
XBT03AUB010037EN Drunkard Mentor, El Quixote R .20 .30
XBT03AUB010038EN Demon Lords' Invasion R .20 .30
XBT03AUB010039EN Abominable Ritual R 4.00 6.00
XBT03AUB010040EN Growles Wand R .75 1.25
XBT03AUB010041EN Demon Lord, Gagnar "Second Form: Iron Hand" C .10 .15
XBT03AUB010042EN Traveling Mage Duo, Tetsuya & Asmodai C .10 .15
XBT03AUB010043EN King Gummy Slime C .10 .15
XBT03AUB010044EN Martial Arts Demon Lord, Duel Sieger C .10 .15
XBT03AUB010045EN Archbishop, Genma C .10 .15
XBT03AUB010046EN Hellhound Lord, Bolzoye Cobalt Lord C .10 .15
XBT03AUB010047EN Shadow Wielder, Wataru C .10 .15
XBT03AUB010048EN Armored Demon Lord, Cerberus C .10 .15
XBT03AUB010049EN Master Monk, Suzumi C .10 .15
XBT03AUB010050EN Demon Lord of Rebellion, Rebellious C .10 .15
XBT03AUB010051EN Vagabond, Munechika C .10 .15
XBT03AUB010052EN Master Clown, Dark Fox C .10 .15
XBT03AUB010053EN Guild Guider, Tsurugi & Stella C .10 .15
XBT03AUB010054EN Princes from the East, Zanya & Akatsuki C .10 .15
XBT03AUB010055EN Death Dragon Demon Lord, Deathgaze C .10 .15
XBT03AUB010056EN Death Summoner, Kageura C .10 .15
XBT03AUB010057EN Gossip Burglar, Paruko C .10 .15
XBT03AUB010058EN Battle Master, Ban C .10 .15
XBT03AUB010059EN Former Province Baron, Shido C .10 .15
XBT03AUB010060EN Demon Lord's Pet Cat, Cait Sith C .10 .15
XBT03AUB010061EN Vampire, Shura C .10 .15
XBT03AUB010062EN Empress, Queen Ageha C .25 .40
XBT03AUB010063EN Archaic Weapon Pilot, Dash C .40 .60
XBT03AUB010064EN Suspicious Craftsman, Gara C .10 .15
XBT03AUB010065EN Summon Trap C .10 .15
XBT03AUB010066EN Pillar of Fire C .10 .15
XBT03AUB010067EN Divine Protection of Shalsana C .40 .60
XBT03AUB010068EN Mission Card "Looking for Group!" C .10 .15
XBT03AUB010069EN Mission Card "Form a Party!" C .10 .15
XBT03AUB010070EN Demon Lord's Dungeon C .10 .15
XBT03AUB010071EN The Tempestuous Brave, Gao SCR 3.00 5.00
XBT03AUB010072EN Protector of Fate, Tasuku SCR 10.00 15.00
XBT03AUB010073EN Dark Black Knight, Gaito SCR 10.00 15.00
XBT03AUB01BR01EN Great Demon Lord of Thunderstorm, Batzz BR 30.00 50.00
XBT03AUB01BR02EN The Tempestuous Brave, Gao BR 12.00 20.00
XBT03AUB01S004EN Dragon World (card) SP
XBT03AUB01S005EN Star Dragon World (card) SP
XBT03AUB01S006EN Dungeon World (card) SP
XBT03AUB01SS001EN Protector of Fate, Tasuku ER 6.00 10.00
XBT03AUB01SS002EN Dark Black Knight, Gaito ER 20.00 30.00
XBT03AUB020001EN Koyomi-class Fifth Fleet, Satsuki RRR 2.50 4.00
XBT03AUB020002EN Super Sword Deity, King Kaizerion RRR 1.50 2.50
XBT03AUB020003EN Black-White Shadow Lord, Mukuro RRR 2.50 4.00
XBT03AUB020004EN Wrath of a Maiden! Blazer Frill RRR 2.00 3.00
XBT03AUB020005EN Martian Handsome Superhero, Takosuke RRR 5.00 8.00
XBT03AUB020006EN Battle Demon of Revenge, Zetta RRR 1.25 2.00
XBT03AUB020007EN Piercing Specialist Chassis, Stregia RR 4.00 6.00
XBT03AUB020008EN Heavy Cannon Specialist Chassis, Veronica RR .75 1.25
XBT03AUB020009EN Winning Maximum, "Powered Form" RR 1.50 2.50
XBT03AUB020010EN Mukuro's Shadow, Schwarz RR 3.00 5.00
XBT03AUB020011EN Computer Warrior, Netman RR 8.00 12.00
XBT03AUB020012EN Quinq Lada, Swift Mobile Frame RR 1.25 2.00
XBT03AUB020013EN 2nd Generation!? Captain Answer RR 2.50 4.00
XBT03AUB020014EN Gaigrander 04 RR 1.25 2.00
XBT03AUB020015EN Uniform Warrior, Doctor Frill RR 3.00 5.00
XBT03AUB020016EN Computer Warrior, Protocolulu RR 8.00 12.00
XBT03AUB020017EN All Crew Pattern One Battlestations! RR 10.00 15.00
XBT03AUB020018EN Brave Machine Hangar RR 15.00 25.00
XBT03AUB020019EN Gemclone "SD" RR 2.50 4.00
XBT03AUB020020EN Jackknife, "Kaizerion" RR 6.00 10.00
XBT03AUB020021EN Aerial Battleship, Satsuki R .20 .30
XBT03AUB020022EN Mobile Specialist Chassis, Westeria R .20 .30
XBT03AUB020023EN Netman, "Red Reboot" R 1.50 2.50
XBT03AUB020024EN Beast Deity, Elphasean R .40 .60
XBT03AUB020025EN Computer Warrior, Archive R .20 .30
XBT03AUB020026EN Fifth Warrior, Funf R .20 .30
XBT03AUB020027EN Shadow Sniper, Scope R .75 1.25
XBT03AUB020028EN Quinq Lada, Probe Frame R 1.25 2.00
XBT03AUB020029EN Uniform Warrior of Darkness, Garter Frill R 1.25 2.00
XBT03AUB020030EN Uniform Professional, Assassin Frill R 1.50 2.00
XBT03AUB020031EN Uniform Hero, Valkyrie Frill R .60 1.00
XBT03AUB020032EN Be Careful of Your Surroundings! R 1.25 2.00
XBT03AUB020033EN Call, Super Machine! R 6.00 10.00
XBT03AUB020034EN Hyper Energy R 5.00 8.00
XBT03AUB020035EN Control C R .50 .75
XBT03AUB020036EN Armor Talisman: GAIN ADVANTAGE R .60 1.00
XBT03AUB020037EN Armor Talisman: ELEMENT CONTROL R .60 1.00
XBT03AUB020038EN 100,000 Years Too Early! R 3.00 5.00
XBT03AUB020039EN Main Cannon, May Blaster! R .20 .30
XBT03AUB020040EN Water-Flame Demon, Hydropyro R .20 .30
XBT03AUB020041EN Battle Poet, Shouting C .10 .15
XBT03AUB020042EN Quinq Lada, Sniping Frame C .10 .15
XBT03AUB020043EN Computer Warrior, Assemble C .10 .15
XBT03AUB020044EN Netman, "Yellow Module" C .10 .15
XBT03AUB020045EN Cyber Police, Stun Bat C .10 .15
XBT03AUB020046EN Quinq Lada, Cloaking Frame C .10 .15
XBT03AUB020047EN Computer Warrior, Hackman C .10 .15
XBT03AUB020048EN Quinq Lada, Energy Frame C .10 .15
XBT03AUB020049EN Gray Wind, Vint C .10 .15
XBT03AUB020050EN Computer Warrior, Antivirus C .10 .15
XBT03AUB020051EN Quinq Lada Operated Work Pod C .10 .15
XBT03AUB020052EN Megadroid, Larger C .10 .15
XBT03AUB020053EN Quinq Lada Recall Frame C .10 .15
XBT03AUB020054EN Shiny Mobile Uniform Warrior, Jewelry Frill C .10 .15
XBT03AUB020055EN Sorry To Keep You Waiting! C .10 .15
XBT03AUB020056EN The Ace Arrives! C .10 .15
XBT03AUB020057EN I've Seen Through Your Moves! C .40 .60
XBT03AUB020058EN Suppressive Barrage! C .10 .15
XBT03AUB020059EN F5 Attack C .10 .15
XBT03AUB020060EN Control XV C .10 .15
XBT03AUB020061EN Backspace C .10 .15
XBT03AUB020062EN Logout C .10 .15
XBT03AUB020063EN I've Waited For This Moment! C .10 .15
XBT03AUB020064EN Powered Body C .10 .15
XBT03AUB020065EN Gaigrander Communicator C .10 .15
XBT03AUB020066EN Artificial Talisman: SACRIFICE SHIELD C .10 .15
XBT03AUB020067EN Maintenance Machine, Caar Dock C .10 .15
XBT03AUB020068EN Physical Format! C .10 .15
XBT03AUB020069EN Water Demon, Darkquarion C .10 .15
XBT03AUB020070EN Mud-Wind Demon, Geanemos C .10 .15
XBT03AUB020071EN Koyomi-class Fifth Fleet, Satsuki SCR 20.00 30.00
XBT03AUB020072EN Martian Handsome Superhero, Takosuke SCR 5.00 8.00
XBT03AUB02BR01EN Koyomi-class Fifth Fleet, Satsuki BR 30.00 50.00
XBT03AUB02BR02EN Black-White Shadow Lord, Mukuro BR 15.00 25.00
XBT03AUB02S001EN Koyomi-class Fifth Fleet, Satsuki SP
XBT03AUB02S002EN Black-White Shadow Lord, Mukuro SP
XBT03AUB02S003EN Wrath of a Maiden! Blazer Frill SP
XBT03AUB02S004EN Hero World (card) SP
XBT03AUB02S005EN Hero World (card) SP
XBT03AUB02S006EN Hero World (card) SP
XBT03AUB02SS001EN Koyomi-class Fifth Fleet, Satsuki ER 50.00 75.00
XBT03AUB02SS002EN Martian Handsome Superhero, Takosuke ER 10.00 15.00

2018 Future Card Buddyfight X Booster Set Alternative 4 New World Chaos

RELEASED ON MARCH 23, 2018
XBT04ASS030001EN Demon Lord of Violent Storm, Batzz RRR .60 1.00
XBT04ASS030002EN Charismatic Demon Lord Teacher, Asmodai RRR 1.50 2.50
XBT04ASS030002EN Charismatic Demon Lord Teacher, Asmodai BR 10.00 15.00
XBT04ASS030003EN White Mask Tyrant, Kid Ibuki RRR 1.25 2.00
XBT04ASS030004EN Searing Tekko Chief, Duel Jaeger RRR .60 1.00
XBT04ASS030004EN Searing Tekko Chief, Duel Jaeger BR 15.00 25.00
XBT04ASS030005EN Resurrected Demon Wolf, Fenrir RRR 1.25 2.00
XBT04ASS030006EN Omni Lord Elder, Tenbu RR .50 .75
XBT04ASS030007EN Drum Bunker Dragon the XIV RR .50 .75
XBT04ASS030008EN Dancer of Shadowform, Silhouette Joe RR .50 .75
XBT04ASS030009EN Absolute Girl of the Convent, Mary Sue RR .30 .50
XBT04ASS030010EN Sephirot's Lectures RR 4.00 6.00
XBT04ASS030011EN Tumultuous Omni Lord, Ziun RR .75 1.25
XBT04ASS030012EN Apex of Flashstep, Tsukikage RR 1.00 1.50
XBT04ASS030013EN CHAOS Valvaros RR .30 .50
XBT04ASS030014EN Martial Arts Imperial Dragon Emperor, Duel Sieger RR .40 .60
XBT04ASS030015EN Spring Breeze Bearer, Sylph RR .30 .50
XBT04ASS030016EN Bal Dragon of Roaring Fist R .20 .30
XBT04ASS030017EN Blue Dragon Shield R .60 1.00
XBT04ASS030018EN Sky Dragon Divinity R 2.50 4.00
XBT04ASS030019EN Rockin' Demon Lord Teacher, Rucifiel R .60 1.00
XBT04ASS030020EN Licht "SD" & Dunkelheit "SD" R .20 .30
XBT04ASS030021EN Never Say Never R 1.25 2.00
XBT04ASS030022EN Evil Ocular Arts, Yamigitsune R .20 .30
XBT04ASS030023EN Fuuton, Tengu Draft R .60 1.00
XBT04ASS030024EN Hairpin Blade, Hoozuki R .50 .75
XBT04ASS030025EN Demon Way, Akeshigure R 2.00 3.00
XBT04ASS030026EN Fullblast Omni Lord, Burn Nova R .20 .30
XBT04ASS030027EN Divine Dragon Creation R 3.00 5.00
XBT04ASS030028EN Wrath Trigger R .20 .30
XBT04ASS030029EN Shineblade Joker R .40 .60
XBT04ASS030030EN Valkyrie, All-knowing Alwidol R .60 1.00
XBT04ASS030031EN Thunder Preacher, Inazumack C .10 .15
XBT04ASS030032EN Dragodeflect C .10 .15
XBT04ASS030033EN Treasure Dragon Sword, Dragotreasure C .10 .15
XBT04ASS030034EN Dragon Spell, Hiding Bomber C .10 .15
XBT04ASS030035EN Solomon's Wall C .10 .15
XBT04ASS030036EN Dance! Asmodai C .10 .15
XBT04ASS030037EN Nice one! C .10 .15
XBT04ASS030038EN Godspeed Sword Draw, Mikazuki Munechika C .10 .15
XBT04ASS030039EN Clear Serenity C .10 .15
XBT04ASS030040EN Ninja Arts, Half-kill C .10 .15
XBT04ASS030041EN Grand Dragon, Czelzarl C .10 .15
XBT04ASS030042EN Invincible Bonds, Ricky & The Raging Spirits C .10 .15
XBT04ASS030043EN A Dragon's Will C .20 .30
XBT04ASS030044EN Dragon Emperor Legend C .10 .15
XBT04ASS030045EN Conciliation Omni Lord, Count Dawn C .10 .15
XBT04ASS030046EN Great Spell, Bifrost of Haven and Earth? C .10 .15
XBT04ASS030047EN Eluned's Ring C .10 .15
XBT04ASS030048EN Sword of the King, Sequence C .10 .15

XBT04ASS030049EN Symbel Gard C .10 .15
XBT04ASS030050EN Breathen Gard C 1.25 2.00
XBT04ASS030051EN Around the World, Chibi Panda & Batzz "SD" C .10 .15
XBT04ASS030052EN Around the World, Athora "SD" C 3.00 5.00
XBT04ASS030053EN Around the World, Abygale "SD" C .20 .30
XBT04ASS030054EN Time Sale C .10 .15
XBT04ASS030055EN Loyalty C .10 .15
XBT04ASS030056EN Neo Buddy Sword C .10 .15
XBT04ASS030057EN Damage Control C .10 .15
XBT04ASS030058EN Omni Lord Elder, Tenbu SCR .30 .50
XBT04ASS030059EN Absolute Girl of the Convent, Mary Sue SCR .30 .50
XBT04ASS030060EN Apex of Flashstep, Tsukikage SCR .25 .40
XBT04ASS030061EN Martial Arts Imperial Dragon Emperor, Duel Sieger SCR .30 .50
XBT04ASS030062EN Spring Breeze Bearer, Sylph SCR .50 .75
XBT04ASS030063EN Dragodeflect SCR .25 .40
XBT04ASS030064EN Sephirot's Lectures SCR 2.50 4.00
XBT04ASS030065EN Fuuton, Tengu Draft SCR 1.25 2.00
XBT04ASS030066EN Dragon Emperor Legend SCR 3.00 5.00
XBT04ASS030067EN Eluned's Ring SCR 1.00 1.50
XBT04AUB030001EN Ultimate CHAOS, Geargod COMPLETE RRR 10.00 15.00
XBT04AUB030002EN Autodeity Conquer Dragon, CHAOS Gear Batzz RRR 2.50 4.00
XBT04AUB030003EN Witching Hour Oni, Kid Ibuki "Gedomaru" RRR 5.00 8.00
XBT04AUB030004EN Full Mechrystal Dragon, Zindo Beta RRR 3.00 5.00
XBT04AUB030005EN Chaos Millennium RRR 4.00 6.00
XBT04AUB030006EN Eroded Beast Sword of the King, Laevateinn Savage RRR 10.00 15.00
XBT04AUB030007EN Corrosion Code 315, Machining CHAOS Dragon RR 1.00 1.50
XBT04AUB030008EN CHAOS Billion Knuckle RR 2.50 4.00
XBT04AUB030009EN Demon Lords Controller, CHAOS Constructor RR .25 .40
XBT04AUB030010EN Mini Geargod Rainbow RR 2.50 4.00
XBT04AUB030011EN Autodeity Great Sorcery, CHAOS Yersinieas RR 10.00 15.00
XBT04AUB030012EN Corrosion Code 450, Dis CHAOS Prism RR .25 .40
XBT04AUB030013EN Corrosion Code 666, Zeno CHAOS Darkness RR 1.25 2.00
XBT04AUB030014EN Corrosion Code 564, Fallen CHAOS Superhero RR 1.00 1.50
XBT04AUB030015EN Lastdroid, Dra-gollum Dolmando RR .40 .60
XBT04AUB030016EN Oni Consort Style, Trigger Tatami RR 3.00 5.00
XBT04AUB030017EN Chaos Gear RR 6.00 10.00
XBT04AUB030018EN The Overkiller RR .60 1.00
XBT04AUB030019EN Infinity the Chaos R .60 1.00
XBT04AUB030020EN Remote Supervisor, Mini Geargod Black R .20 .30
XBT04AUB030021EN Hundred Mechs General, CHAOS Gishingyuki R .30 .50
XBT04AUB030022EN Hundred Mechs General, CHAOS Gokumengaiou R .30 .50
XBT04AUB030023EN Hundred Mechs General, CHAOS Braiden R .30 .50
XBT04AUB030024EN Ruinous Beast Battle Robo, CHAOS Gaidenoh R .20 .30
XBT04AUB030025EN Mechrystal Dragon, Madslide R .40 .60
XBT04AUB030026EN Fifth Omni Dragon Mech, CHAOS Dokujun R .20 .30
XBT04AUB030027EN Twin Swords Mech, CHAOS Andorochi R .20 .30
XBT04AUB030028EN Mechrystal Dragon, Saratoga R .20 .30
XBT04AUB030029EN Weapon of Destruction, Dragoon R .40 .60
XBT04AUB030030EN Death Plague Caster, Mordol R .20 .30
XBT04AUB030031EN Enigma Virus R .60 1.00
XBT04AUB030032EN Corrosion Prosthesis R 1.25 2.00
XBT04AUB030033EN Unfreezing R 10.00 15.00
XBT04AUB030034EN Taboo Contract R .20 .30
XBT04AUB030035EN Chaos Brand Dimensional Sword R .20 .30
XBT04AUB030036EN Fabricated Sword of the King, Fragarach Replica R .20 .30
XBT04AUB030037EN CHAOS Ravarager U .12 .20
XBT04AUB030038EN CHAOS Mothman U .12 .20
XBT04AUB030039EN CHAOS David U .12 .20
XBT04AUB030040EN CHAOS Unzen U .12 .20
XBT04AUB030041EN CHAOS Meraglaive U .12 .20
XBT04AUB030042EN CHAOS Radromarl U .12 .20
XBT04AUB030043EN CHAOS Vivod U .12 .20
XBT04AUB030044EN CHAOS Teo Lao U .12 .20
XBT04AUB030045EN Mini Geargod Pink U .12 .20
XBT04AUB030046EN CHAOS Garg-gollum U .12 .20
XBT04AUB030047EN CHAOS Spikey-gollum U .12 .20
XBT04AUB030048EN CHAOS Lament Oni U .12 .20
XBT04AUB030049EN CHAOS Parvo U .12 .20
XBT04AUB030050EN Chaos Absorption U .12 .20
XBT04AUB030051EN Martial Essence U .12 .20
XBT04AUB030052EN Performance Test U .12 .20
XBT04AUB030053EN Contagious Weakening Gas U .12 .20
XBT04AUB030054EN Ninja Arts, Vapor Crow U .12 .20
XBT04AUB030055EN Havoc in Dragon Land U .12 .20
XBT04AUB030056EN Secret Spikes U .12 .20
XBT04AUB030057EN Black Chaos Claw U .12 .20
XBT04AUB030058EN The Chaos Upgrade U .12 .20
XBT04AUB030059EN Mechsplosive Axe, Chaos Demon Slay U .12 .20
XBT04AUB030060EN Corrosion Code 315, Machining CHAOS Dragon SCR .60 1.00
XBT04AUB030061EN Demon Lords Controller, CHAOS Constructor SCR 1.00 1.50
XBT04AUB030062EN Lastdroid, Dra-gollum Dolmando SCR .50 .75
XBT04AUB030063EN Death Plague Caster, Mordol SCR 1.25 2.00
XBT04AUB030064EN CHAOS Valvaros SCR .50 .75
XBT04AUB038EN 8 Infinity the Chaos 8 IR 6.00 10.00
XBT04AUB03BR01EN Ultimate CHAOS, Geargod COMPLETE BR 12.00 20.00
XBT04AUB03BR02EN Autodeity Conquer Dragon, CHAOS Gear Batzz BR 10.00 15.00
XBT04AUB03S001EN Ultimate CHAOS, Geargod COMPLETE SP 50.00 75.00
XBT04AUB03S002EN Witching Hour Oni, Kid Ibuki "Gedomaru" SP 30.00 50.00
XBT04AUB03S003EN Autodeity Great Sorcery, CHAOS Yersinieas SP 40.00 60.00
XBT04AUB03S004EN Eroded Beast Sword of the King, Laevateinn Savage SP 50.00 75.00
XBT04AUB03S005EN Infinity the Chaos SP 30.00 50.00
XBT04AUB03S006EN the Chaos SP

2018 Future Card Buddyfight X2 Booster Set 1 Buddy Legends

RELEASED ON APRIL 20, 2018
X2BT010001 Batzz's Protection, "Dragonificator" Gao RRR 5.00 8.00
X2BT010002 Mark of Transgression, Azi Dahaka "SYS" RRR 6.00 10.00
X2BT010003 Mark of Atonement, Azi Dahaka Daeva "SYS" RRR 10.00 15.00
X2BT010004 Ardent Heavenly Crystal Dragon, Athora Alexand RRR 10.00 15.00
X2BT010005 Ice Dragon of Rebirth, Roi Miserea RRR 2.00 3.00
X2BT010006 Super Sun Deity Dragon, Balle Soleil Dios RRR 10.00 15.00
X2BT010007 Heavenly Specter, Yamigedo Mikazuchi RRR 10.00 15.00
X2BT010008 White Supreme Dragon Deity of Creations, Gaen RRR 6.00 10.00
X2BT010009 Jackknife, "Glanzend" RR 3.00 5.00
X2BT010010 Overturn Sun Dragon, Bal Dragon RR 5.00 8.00
X2BT010011 Armorknight Cougar "A" RR 1.00 1.50
X2BT010012 Artist of Shadowform, Silhouette Olivar RR 2.50 4.00
X2BT010013 Rampaging Evil Demon, Akuro-oh RR .40 .60
X2BT010014 Duel Sieger, "Centurion" RR 2.00 3.00
X2BT010015 Knight of Daybreak, Neoswadel RR 3.00 5.00
X2BT010016 One Who Leads RR 1.25 2.00
X2BT010017 Abygale, "Armed Howl Bringer" RR 10.00 15.00
X2BT010018 Mobile Specialist Chassis, Casablanca RR 1.25 2.00
X2BT010019 Karuna Cycle Emperor, Miserea RR 2.50 4.00
X2BT010020 Eventual Star Deity Dragon, Zodiac Nohva RR 1.25 2.00
X2BT010021 Thunderflash Swordsman, Billion Rapier R .50 .75
X2BT010022 Fifth Omni Dragon Lord, Drum "SD" R .50 .75
X2BT010023 Delusion Butterfly-gollum R .20 .30
X2BT010024 Dogged Demon Lord, Asmodai R 1.00 1.50
X2BT010025 Mikazuchi Follower, Glasya Labolas R .20 .30
X2BT010026 Arc Particles Ghoul Deity, Gojinmaru R .60 1.00
X2BT010027 Fist Emperor of Manliness, Burn Nova R .20 .30
X2BT010028 Dragon's Temper R .50 .75
X2BT010029 Bladewing Raven R .30 .50
X2BT010030 Omni Lords' Loyal Knight, El Quixote R .20 .30
X2BT010031 Golden Apples Custodian, Ydun R .20 .30
X2BT010032 Black Crest Dragon, Vidor Nove R 1.00 1.50
X2BT010033 Spawn of the Demonic Dragon, Abyssgate R 2.50 4.00
X2BT010034 Deity Sword of Creations, Aqulta Gwaneff R 1.00 1.50
X2BT010035 Second Darkhero Hideout R .20 .30
X2BT010036 Dragonarms, Swobit R 1.00 1.50
X2BT010037 Purgatory Knights Reborn, Holy Grebe Dragon R 2.00 3.00
X2BT010038 Heavenly Claws, Raikiri R .20 .30
X2BT010039 Mera Blade Inazuma U .12 .20
X2BT010040 Contrition Healing U .12 .20
X2BT010041 Voice of the Blade U .12 .20
X2BT010042 Dysautonomia U .12 .20
X2BT010043 Ricky on the Ban U .12 .20
X2BT010044 Demon Lord's Armor U .12 .20
X2BT010045 Spica Virgo U .12 .20
X2BT010046 Rules of the Depths U .12 .20
X2BT010047 Evil Spirit of Bevar-Asp U .12 .20
X2BT010048 Uniform Warrior, China Frill U .12 .20
X2BT010049 Winning Wing U .12 .20
X2BT010050 Purgatory Knights Reborn, Silver Staff Dragon U .12 .20
X2BT010051 Purgatory Knights Reborn, Crossbow Dragon U .12 .20
X2BT010052 Backfeeding Source U .12 .20
X2BT010053 From the Brink of Death C .10 .15
X2BT010054 Dragomemoria - Dragon's Reminiscence - C .10 .15
X2BT010055 Titanic Violent Dragon, Zargilragne C .10 .15
X2BT010056 Executioner's Lance, Gehenna Gretsch C .10 .15
X2BT010057 Witch of Ruination, Cathy the Devastator C .10 .15
X2BT010058 Tome of Sorcery, Almandel C .10 .15
X2BT010059 Humanoid Beast, Yaejako C .10 .15
X2BT010060 Dragon Life Inherit C .10 .15
X2BT010061 All Dragons Go To Haven C .10 .15
X2BT010062 Trap Up C .10 .15
X2BT010063 Freaky Strength Girl, Hikiko C .10 .15
X2BT010064 Black Dragon, Dies C .10 .15
X2BT010065 Bone Router, Grazia C .10 .15
X2BT010066 Special Weapon, Virus Buster C .10 .15
X2BT010067 T18: Sturgeon C .10 .15
X2BT010068 Deity Meteorarms, Azavoarl C .10 .15
X2BT010069 Overturn Armordragon, Drum Bunker Dragon SCR 4.00 6.00
X2BT010070 Bal Dragon, "Bal-Buster Granbolt!" SCR 2.00 3.00
X2BT010071 Future Fangs, Barlbatzz Future Cross SCR 1.00 1.50
X2BT010072 Buddy X Cross SCR .30 .50
X2BT010073 Future Force, "DX" SCR 1.25 2.00
X2BT010074 Future Sword, Jackknife "Granthese" SCR 4.00 6.00
X2BT010075 Jackknife, "Genesic Batterizer!" SCR .60 1.00
X2BT010076 Purgatory Knights Liberator, Orcus Sword Dragon SCR 10.00 15.00
X2BT010077 Jackknife Statue SCR .60 1.00
X2BT010078 Into the future... SCR 15.00 25.00
X2BT01BR01 Future Fangs, Barlbatzz Future Cross BR 10.00 15.00
X2BT01BR02 Future Sword, Jackknife "Granthese" BR 6.00 10.00
X2BT01BR03 Mark of Transgression, Azi Dahaka "SYS" BR 15.00 25.00
X2BT01BR04 Heavenly Specter, Yamigedo Mikazuchi BR 30.00 50.00
X2BT01S001 Future Fangs, Barlbatzz Future Cross SP 50.00 75.00
X2BT01S002 Future Sword, Jackknife "Granthese" SP 40.00 60.00
X2BT01S003 White Supreme Dragon Deity of Creations, Gaen SP 40.00 60.00

2018 Future Card Buddyfight X2 Booster Set Alternative 1 Solar Strife

RELEASED ON JUNE 15, 2018
X2BT01AD0001EN Demon Lord of Demise, Kyoya C .10 .15
X2BT01AD0002EN Black Dragon Priest, Gremlin C .10 .15
X2BT01AD0003EN Death Dragon Knight, Davide C .10 .15
X2BT01AD0004EN Demon Lord's Puppet, Terumi C .10 .15
X2BT01AD0005EN Self-proclaimed Healing Alchemist, Kabala C .10 .15
X2BT01AD0006EN Demon Lord's Fangs, Rouga C .10 .15
X2BT01AD0007EN Security Chief, Shido C .10 .15
X2BT01AD0008EN Demon Lord's Arm, Sofia C .10 .15
X2BT01AD0009EN Purgatory Demonic Swordsman's Armor C .10 .15
X2BT01ASS01S001EN Dragon World SP 40.00 60.00
X2BT01ASS01S002EN Dragon Zwei SP 20.00 30.00
X2BT01ASS01S003EN Dragon Drei SP 30.00 50.00
XBT01ASP0001EN Unwavering Shadow Lord, Mukuro RRR 3.00 5.00
XBT01ASP0002EN Fifth Omni Super Dragon Lord, Fierce Deity Tenbu RRR 2.00 3.00
XBT01ASP0003EN Freak-Wrist Beast Lord, Ziun RRR 4.00 6.00
XBT01ASP0004EN Dragosorcerer, Magician Drum RRR .75 1.25
XBT01ASP0005EN Returning Brave, Drum RRR .60 1.00
XBT01ASP0006EN Thunder Knights, Gyral Strikes Drum RRR .60 1.00
XBT01ASP0007EN Fourth Crimson Chieftain, Drum RRR 1.25 2.00
XBT01ASP0008EN Hyper Rescue Dragon, Justice Drum Fire RRR 2.00 3.00
XBT01ASP0009EN Thunder Knights, Heavenly Bow Dragoarcher RRR .60 1.00
XBT01ASP0010EN Awakened Brave's Equipment, Glory Seeker RRR 1.25 2.00
XBT01ASP0011EN Valorous Deity Lord, Grangadez R .50 .75
XBT01ASP0012EN Blue Sky Knights, Drum the Tempest R .40 .60
XBT01ASP0013EN Thunder Knights, Motivated Halberd Dragon R .50 .75
XBT01ASP0014EN Delta & Tetra of Thunder Empire! R .20 .30
XBT01ASP0015EN Morning Star Radiant Lord, Variable Cord R .20 .30
XBT01ASP0016EN Explosive Takedown, Rampage Sonic "Turbo" R .20 .30
XBT01ASP0017EN Fifth Omni Cavalry Dragon, Alliot "SD" R .40 .60
XBT01ASP0018EN Clashing Crimson Battler, Guns Knuckle Dragon R .30 .50
XBT01ASP0019EN Clashing Crimson Battler, Spin Nail Dragon R .30 .50
XBT01ASP0020EN Comrade, Systemic Dagger Dragon R .25 .40
XBT01ASP0021EN Shocking Magic, Qinus Axia R .40 .60
XBT01ASP0022EN XL Pandora R .20 .30
XBT01ASP0023EN Boomerang Dragon Returns R .50 .75
XBT01ASP0024EN Undying Wise King, Count Dawn R 2.50 4.00
XBT01ASP0025EN Home Sweet Home Cait Sith R .40 .60
XBT01ASP0026EN Omni Lords' Resonance R 2.00 3.00
XBT01ASP0027EN Gotcha! (I Catch It!) R .40 .60
XBT01ASP0028EN Crimson Iron Fist, Dragoknuckle R .50 .75
XBT01ASP0029EN Tempest Thunder Knights Formation! R .50 .75
XBT01ASP0030EN Rampage Blaster Red Heat! R .20 .30
XBT01ASP0031EN Fifth Omni Super Dragon Sky Emperor, Mugen Drum SCR 10.00 15.00
XBT01ASP0032EN Future Powers, Drum the Future Limitbreak SCR 1.00 1.50
XBT01ASP0033EN Fifth Omni Cavalry Dragon, Doble "SD" & Meglax "SD" SCR 2.00 3.00
XBT01ASP0034EN Dragon Lord Quake Slash!! SCR 2.00 3.00
XBT01ASP0035EN Fifth Omni Dragon Sword, Dragobrave SCR 2.50 4.00
XBT01ASP0036EN Sovereign War Dragon Lord, Batzz the Infinity SCR 4.00 6.00
XBT01ASP0037EN Warlord Sword Released SCR 15.00 25.00
XBT01ASP0038EN Saint Holy Sword "Thunder Edge" SCR 1.00 1.50
XBT01ASP0039EN Veteran Replenisher, Pentar SCR 1.00 1.50
XBT01ASP0040EN Delta & Tetra of Thunder Empire! SCR .30 .50
XBT01ASP0041EN Innocent Sun Deity, Bal Dragon SCR 2.00 3.00
XBT01ASP0042EN Inheritable Sun, Sunshine Impact SCR 1.00 1.50
XBT01ASP0043EN Bal Dragon, "Bal Force Regeneration!" SCR 1.00 1.50
XBT01ASP0044EN Loyal Dragon, Flarefang Dragon SCR 15.00 25.00
XBT01ASP0045EN Bestest Bal, bal! SCR 1.25 2.00
XBT01ASPBR01EN Fifth Omni Super Dragon Sky Emperor, Mugen Drum BR 25.00 40.00
XBT01ASPBR02EN Innocent Sun Deity, Bal Dragon BR 12.00 20.00
XBT01ASPBR03EN Sovereign War Dragon Lord, Batzz the Infinity BR 15.00 25.00
XBT01ASPEN Gargantua Punisher!! FR 15.00 25.00
XBT01ASPS001EN Batzz X Link SP 30.00 50.00
XBT01ASPS002EN Blue Dragon Shield SP 50.00 75.00
XBT01ASPS003EN Green Dragon Shield SP 30.00 50.00
XBT01ASPS004EN Sun Dragon Shield SP 20.00 30.00
XBT01ASPS005EN Arc Dragon Shield SP 15.00 25.00
XBT01ASS010001EN Sun Deity's Fragment, Bal Dragon RRR 8.00 12.00
XBT01ASS010001EN Sun Deity's Fragment, Bal Dragon BR 15.00 25.00
XBT01ASS010002EN Dragon Force, "Style of Super Sun" RRR 10.00 15.00
XBT01ASS010003EN Balle Soleil, "The End of Bal-Break!" RRR 6.00 10.00
XBT01ASS010004EN Sun Deity's Buddy RRR 2.50 4.00
XBT01ASS010005EN Bal Dragon, "Bal Burst Smasher!!" RRR .40 .60
XBT01ASS010006EN Super Sun Dragon Shield RR 10.00 15.00
XBT01ASS010007EN Bal-Shine Buster RR .60 1.00
XBT01ASS010008EN Super Sun Dragon, Balle Soleil RR 1.00 1.50
XBT01ASS010008EN Super Sun Dragon, Balle Soleil BR 12.00 20.00
XBT01ASS010009EN Style of Impact, Bal Dragon RR 3.00 5.00
XBT01ASS010010EN Flarefang Dragon "SD" RR 1.25 2.00
XBT01ASS010011EN Dragon Force (Dragon World) RR 2.00 3.00
XBT01ASS010012EN Dragon Force, "Style of the Straight Fist" RR .60 1.00
XBT01ASS010013EN Dragon Force, "Style of Impact" RR 1.25 2.00
XBT01ASS010014EN Bal Dragon, "Great Full Bal Lariat!!" RR .30 .50
XBT01ASS010015EN Bal Dragon, "Bal Saucer Over Rush!" RR .60 1.00
XBT01ASS010016EN Balle Soleil, "Eternal Bal-Blaster!" RR .30 .50
XBT01ASS010017EN Retainer of the Demonic Dragon, Malgheld RR 2.50 4.00
XBT01ASS010018EN Retainer of the Demonic Dragon, Reset Black Scale RR 1.25 2.00
XBT01ASS010019EN Demonic Dragon Deity of the Black Sun, Gaen RR 2.50 4.00
XBT01ASS010019EN Demonic Dragon Deity of the Black Sun, Gaen BR 15.00 25.00
XBT01ASS010020EN Black Sky Sun Dragon, Azi Dahaka "Daeva" RR 2.00 3.00
XBT01ASS010021EN Great Demonic End Dragon, Azi Dahaka RR .75 1.25
XBT01ASS010022EN Transcend Dragon Emperor, Ewigkeit RR 1.25 2.00
XBT01ASS010023EN Spawn of the Demonic Dragon, Haarid RR .30 .50
XBT01ASS010024EN Apprentice Underling, Kon Kon Kong RR 2.00 3.00
XBT01ASS010025EN Balle Soleil Imagine C .10 .15
XBT01ASS010026EN Pizza Race! C .10 .15
XBT01ASS010027EN Dragon of the Sun, Bal Dragon C .10 .15
XBT01ASS010028EN Shining Sun Dragon, Bal Dragon C .10 .15
XBT01ASS010029EN Flarefang Dragon C .25 .40
XBT01ASS010030EN Mera Blade Dragon "SD" C .10 .15
XBT01ASS010031EN Sun Dragon Shield C .10 .15
XBT01ASS010032EN Sun Fist, Bal Knuckle C .10 .15
XBT01ASS010033EN Sun Fist, Balguard C .10 .15
XBT01ASS010034EN Scrap of Malice, Angra Mainyu Element C .10 .15
XBT01ASS010035EN Retainer of the Demonic Dragon, Bloodeon C .10 .15
XBT01ASS010036EN Darkdeity Dragon, Jamjammer C .10 .15
XBT01ASS010037EN Black Crystal Dragon, Lucien Black C .10 .15
XBT01ASS010038EN Retainer of the Demonic Dragon, Fiellder C .10 .15
XBT01ASS010039EN Retainer of the Demonic Dragon, Devil Orb Dragon C .10 .15
XBT01ASS010040EN Retainer of the Demonic Dragon, King Gorai C .10 .15
XBT01ASS010041EN Retainer of the Demonic Dragon, Jovnozuk C .10 .15
XBT01ASS010042EN Spawn of the Demonic Dragon, Booze C .10 .15
XBT01ASS010043EN Retainer of the Demonic Dragon, Vong C .10 .15
XBT01ASS010044EN Retainer of the Demonic Dragon, Walm C .10 .15
XBT01ASS010045EN Retainer of the Demonic Dragon, Destructor C .10 .15
XBT01ASS010046EN Sky Carnage Sun Deity, Azi Dahaka "Zurvan" SCR 10.00 15.00
XBT01ASS010046EN Retainer of the Demonic Dragon, Phrovraga SCR 6.00 10.00
XBT01ASS010046EN Sky Carnage Sun Deity, Azi Dahaka "Zurvan" BR 20.00 30.00
XBT01ASS010048EN Retainer of the Demonic Dragon, Future-Eater SCR 6.00 10.00
XBT01ASS010049EN Retainer of the Demonic Dragon, Abyss Shield Dragon SCR 6.00 10.00
XBT01ASS010050EN Dragon Zwei SCR 1.25 2.00

2017 Future Card Buddyfight D Climax Booster Set 1 Dragon Fighters

RELEASED ON FEBRUARY 24, 2017
DCBT0001 Deity Fire Cavalry Dragon Romedius RRR .30 .50
DCBT0002 Pinnacle of Martial Arts Duel Jaeger God Vortoise RRR .30 .50
DCBT0003 Earth Tremor Black Dragon Soulvaag RRR .50 .75
DCBT0004 Star Dragoner Astrobeacon RRR 1.25 2.00
DCBT0005 Demonic Battle Demon Zetta RRR 2.00 3.00
DCBT0006 Successor of the Omni Lord Mukuro RRR 1.50 2.50
DCBT0007 Star Deity Fusion Dragon Zodiac es RRR .60 1.00
DCBT0008 Mysterious Fortune Teller Sofia RRR 8.00 12.00
DCBT0009 Flaredevice Dragon RR .30 .50
DCBT0010 Armorknight Buster Cerberus A RR 4.00 6.00
DCBT0011 Passion Trainer Asmodai RR .75 1.25
DCBT0012 Companion Katana of Magatsu Yamigitsune RR .30 .50
DCBT0013 Steel Rending Wings Bladewing Phoenix RR .40 .60
DCBT0014 Great Spell Collapse of Valhalla RR .40 .60
DCBT0015 Spawn of the Demonic Dragon Booze RR 2.50 4.00
DCBT0016 Aettir SD RR .30 .50
DCBT0017 Great Pirate Captain Kaido RR 4.00 6.00
DCBT0018 Purgatory Knights Jackknife Dragon RR 2.00 3.00
DCBT0019 Meteorarms Dragsolar RR 2.00 3.00
DCBT0020 Ghostly Spirit Yamigedo Hundred Demons Thunder Mine RR 1.25 2.00
DCBT0021 Fifth Omni Super Cavalry Dragon Phoenix Bow Meglax R .20 .30
DCBT0022 Unlocked Eye Helle Gepard R .20 .30
DCBT0023 Nice one R 1.25 2.00
DCBT0024 Rucifiel Rewind Clock R .20 .30
DCBT0025 Luck Determined Outcome Tsukikage SD R .60 1.00
DCBT0026 Art of Explosive Hades Fall R .60 1.00
DCBT0027 Mikazuki Munechika Forbidden Art Blade Deity Descends R 1.25 2.00
DCBT0028 Pinnacle of Martial Arts Duel Sieger God Eclipse R 2.00 3.00
DCBT0029 Reflection Dragon Moon R .20 .30
DCBT0030 Champion Lord Bravery of Chief R .20 .30
DCBT0031 Wind Frolicker Sylph R .20 .30
DCBT0032 Astraeus Birthday of Wind and Stars R 1.00 1.50
DCBT0033 Dead Carrier R .50 .75
DCBT0034 Lost Memory Masked Vantage Mid Knight R 1.00 1.50
DCBT0035 Captain Answer THE Another Lesson R .20 .30
DCBT0036 Water Demon Katarakutes R .20 .30
DCBT0037 Stronger Teagle01 R .20 .30
DCBT0038 Dragoneraser Octojammer R .20 .30
DCBT0039 Composite Black Dragon Bahamut Death Tallica R .20 .30
DCBT0040 Composite Black Dragon Gallows Karn R .50 .75
DCBT0041 Noble Magician Suzuha R .20 .30
DCBT0042 Chaos Blade Joker R .75 1.25
DCBT0043 Explosive Claw Raiko R .20 .30
DCBT0044 Retainer of the Demonic Dragon Badegg U .12 .20
DCBT0045 Dragon Life Spear Royal Lance U .12 .20
DCBT0046 Tyrant Virus U .12 .20
DCBT0047 Binds of a Despot U .12 .20
DCBT0048 Invoke Impetuous Deity Hibakara U .12 .20
DCBT0049 Magical Artillery Soldier Canooner U .12 .20
DCBT0050 Silhouette Elfin U 1.00 1.50
DCBT0051 Great Spell Amanosuzu Chance U .12 .20

Card	Low	High
DCBT0052 Luck Determined Outcome Byakuya SD U	.12	.20
DCBT0053 Secret Sword Dragon Vanquish Formation U	.12	.20
DCBT0054 Chief of Roar Howling Kiba U	.12	.20
DCBT0055 Chief of Adversity Revenger Sho U	.12	.20
DCBT0056 Underling Battery Den U	.12	.20
DCBT0057 Son of the Demon Lord Delis Highlow U	.12	.20
DCBT0058 Caplico Life Noboru U	.60	1.00
DCBT0059 Golden Treasurebox U	1.25	2.00
DCBT0060 Ophiuchus Starsentinel Orphiuco U	.12	.20
DCBT0061 Tevas Gard U	.40	.60
DCBT0062 Gymirs Staff U	1.25	2.00
DCBT0063 Black Mausoleum Ruins Sepultura U	.12	.20
DCBT0064 Retainer of the Demonic Dragon Agaarok U	.12	.20
DCBT0065 Retainer of the Demonic Dragon Bazolii U	.12	.20
DCBT0066 Gate Guider Dte U	.12	.20
DCBT0067 Death Grip U	.12	.20
DCBT0068 Uniform Warrior Hakuran Frill U	1.25	2.00
DCBT0069 Ride Changer Scouting Team Seekerz U	.12	.20
DCBT0070 Wind Ghost Aeril U	1.25	2.00
DCBT0071 Dragoneraser Spare U	.12	.20
DCBT0072 Synthetic Enemy Deathgaze With a Hit U	.12	.20
DCBT0073 Throwing Dragon Nagerucorga U	.12	.20
DCBT0074 Crimson Battler Splendor Needle C	.10	.15
DCBT0075 Rompire Dragon C	.50	.75
DCBT0076 Weep Dragon Jr C	.10	.15
DCBT0077 Armorknight Werewolf C	.60	1.00
DCBT0078 Tyrant Statue C	.10	.15
DCBT0079 Demon Slay Bloodwind Wall C	1.50	2.50
DCBT0080 Violent Axe Bind Cutter Slash C	.10	.15
DCBT0081 Passion Fighter Beleth C	.10	.15
DCBT0082 Strength Summoner Kotenso C	.10	.15
DCBT0083 Blue Secret Blade Zetsu C	.10	.15
DCBT0084 Underling Nocurve Sei C	.50	.75
DCBT0085 Lightning Tail Bruder C	.60	1.00
DCBT0086 Arrival of Raging Spirits C	.10	.15
DCBT0087 Ozon Bs Cat C	.10	.15
DCBT0088 Rolling Stone C	.10	.15
DCBT0089 Magical Beast Tamer Flute Gboy C	.10	.15
DCBT0090 Columba Fact C	.10	.15
DCBT0091 Taurus Starsentinel Tauro C	.10	.15
DCBT0092 Heros Base Castle Camelot C	.10	.15
DCBT0093 Spawn of the Demonic Dragon Rust C	.10	.15
DCBT0094 Scar Face C	.10	.15
DCBT0095 DEATH Favor C	.10	.15
DCBT0096 Cursed Demon Idol C	.10	.15
DCBT0097 Armor Talisman COUNTER ATTACK C	.10	.15
DCBT0098 Its Here the NEW Suit C	.10	.15
DCBT0099 Ride Changer Headquarters Maintenance Dock C	.10	.15
DCBT0100 Flame Demon Mega Ecliksys C	.10	.15
DCBT0101 Retainer of the Demonic Dragon Worldporter C	.10	.15
DCBT0102 Eliminator Shugar C	.50	.75
DCBT0103 Legblade Avenge C	.10	.15
DCBT0104 Dragon Force Style of Impact BR	20.00	30.00
DCBT0105 Dragon Force Style of Retaliation BR	20.00	30.00
DCBT0106 Dragon Force Style of Justice BR	20.00	30.00
DCBT0107 Black Sky Sun Dragon Azi Dahaka Daeva BR	15.00	25.00
DCBT0108 Dragon of the Shining Sun Bal Dragon SCR	.60	1.00
DCBT0109 Shake Hands Dragon SCR	1.50	2.50
DCBT0110 Heat Wave SCR	.50	.75
DCBT0111 Sun Dragon Shield SCR	3.00	5.00
DCBT0112 Dragon Force Style of Impact SCR	.50	.75
DCBT0113 Black Large Canyon Disgorge SCR	1.50	2.50
DCBT0114 Black Death Dragon of Retaliation Abygale SCR	10.00	15.00
DCBT0115 Abygale SD SCR	2.50	4.00
DCBT0116 Black Cloth Blade SCR	4.00	6.00
DCBT0117 Dragon Force Style of Retaliation SCR	10.00	15.00
DCBT0118 Full Liberate Jackknife SCR	.50	.75
DCBT0119 Dragonarms Silfighter SCR	5.00	8.00
DCBT0120 Proto Barrier SCR	2.00	3.00
DCBT0121 Liberate Shoot SCR	1.50	2.50
DCBT0122 Dragon Force Style of Justice SCR	10.00	15.00
DCBT0123 Black Sky Sun Dragon Azi Dahaka Daeva SCR	12.00	20.00
DCBT0124 Black Sky Sun Dragon Azi Dahaka Daeva SCR	12.00	20.00
DCBT0125 Retainer of the Demonic Dragon Fiellder SCR	4.00	6.00
DCBT0126 Spawn of the Demonic Dragon Haarid SCR	.30	.50
DCBT0127 Retainer of the Demonic Dragon Jovnozuk SCR	1.00	1.50
DCBT0128 Retainer of the Demonic Dragon Horned Serpent SCR	1.50	2.50
DCBTSTAR1 Dragon World SCR	40.00	60.00
DCBTSTAR2 Darkness Dragon World SCR	25.00	40.00
DCBTSTAR3 Star Dragon World SCR	25.00	40.00
DCBTSTAR4 Dragon Zwei SCR	10.00	15.00

2019 Future Card Buddyfight S Climax Booster Set 1 Golden Garga

RELEASED ON MARCH 1, 2019

Card	Low	High
SCBT010001 Glory of Shining Combat Deity RRR	8.00	12.00
SCBT010001 Glory of Shining Combat Deity CLR	20.00	30.00
SCBT010002 Unequaled Deity Might, Brawlzeus RRR	4.00	6.00
SCBT010003 Nirvana Deity of Affection, Amaterasu RRR	6.00	10.00
SCBT010004 Cyclonic Thunderaxe, Agito RRR	2.50	4.00
SCBT010005 Memorial Sweet, Red Riding Hood Emma RRR	6.00	10.00
SCBT010006 Curse Ritual RRR	10.00	15.00
SCBT010007 Shooting Star Galaxy Exalt, Ultra Cosmoman RRR	4.00	6.00
SCBT010008 King's Brilliance, Cross Farnese Astrologia RRR	4.00	6.00
SCBT010009 Aegir Gardra RR	2.50	4.00
SCBT010010 Getting Serious Sometime, Garbird RR	1.00	1.50
SCBT010011 Combat Deity Dragonfang Sword, Garga-Saber RR	2.50	4.00
SCBT010012 Frightening Extortion! RR	3.00	5.00
SCBT010013 Bird Magic -Trial Edition- RR	1.00	1.50
SCBT010014 Deity Dragon Ninja Arts, Shadowflash Slash RR	.75	1.25
SCBT010015 Reinforcement of Bonds RR	2.00	3.00
SCBT010016 Filling Memories! RR	2.00	3.00
SCBT010017 Black Dragon Knight, Zevens the "Stygian" RR	3.00	5.00
SCBT010018 Black Dragon Knight, Lzam RR	2.50	4.00
SCBT010019 Curse Decline RR	2.50	4.00
SCBT010020 Galaxy Braver, Gargantua Quasar RR	5.00	8.00
SCBT010021 Teets Gardra R	.30	.50
SCBT010022 Gar-Through R	.30	.50
SCBT010023 Gar-Hailen R	.30	.50
SCBT010024 Nirvana Group! R	.20	.30
SCBT010025 Acqteus R	.20	.30
SCBT010026 Sol Aurora R	.20	.30
SCBT010027 Cherry Blossom Stage R	.30	.50
SCBT010028 Deity Against All, Gargantua Dragon "Eisenwaechter" R	.30	.50
SCBT010029 Expert?, Touteki R	.20	.30
SCBT010030 Fired Up! R	.20	.30
SCBT010031 Linkdragon Spirit R	.20	.30
SCBT010032 Black Dragon Knight, Abowl R	.20	.30
SCBT010033 Underration R	.20	.30
SCBT010034 Curse Light R	.20	.30
SCBT010035 Black Dragon Sword, Geilblade R	.20	.30
SCBT010036 Cosmo Change! R	.50	.75
SCBT010037 Notify: Missing Mission R	.25	.40
SCBT010038 Cerezocitation R	.40	.60
SCBT010039 Naha Gardragon U	.12	.20
SCBT010040 Voute Gardra U	.12	.20
SCBT010041 Traum Gardra U	.12	.20
SCBT010042 Garraccoon U	.12	.20
SCBT010043 Combat Deity Stirring U	.12	.20
SCBT010044 Deity Dragon Flash U	.12	.20
SCBT010045 Evolution Spirit U	.12	.20
SCBT010046 Bullet-Eyes Claimer U	.12	.20
SCBT010047 Preeminence Wizard, Magidog U	.12	.20
SCBT010048 Sorcery Deity Dragon, Shima U	.12	.20
SCBT010049 Tidy Effect U	.12	.20
SCBT010050 Nyan Nyan Replicate, Nincat U	.12	.20
SCBT010051 Deity Dragon Ninja, Shiryumaru U	.12	.20
SCBT010052 Art of Scattered Kunai U	.12	.20
SCBT010053 Three Shots, Saisai U	.12	.20
SCBT010054 Good Arm, Cook U	.12	.20
SCBT010055 Burn, My Soul! Bawl, My Linkdragon Order! U	.12	.20
SCBT010056 Linkdragon Hammer, Agito Crush U	.12	.20
SCBT010057 Black Dragon Knight, Birth the "Demon-Eye" U	.12	.20
SCBT010058 Black Dragon Knight, Leopard U	.12	.20
SCBT010059 Black Dragon Knight, Ynllay U	.12	.20
SCBT010060 Black Dragon Knight, Eth U	.12	.20
SCBT010061 Black Dragon Knight, Namm U	.12	.20
SCBT010062 Scar Bind U	.12	.20
SCBT010063 Curse Field U	.12	.20
SCBT010064 Seerfight Dragon, Azure Chief U	.12	.20
SCBT010065 Seerfight Dragon, Bari U	.12	.20
SCBT010066 Seerfight Dragon, Paylet U	.12	.20
SCBT010067 Notify: Skyseer Pulse U	.12	.20
SCBT010068 Celesphere Force U	.12	.20
SCBT010069 Deity Gargantua Dragon SCR	25.00	40.00
SCBT010070 Gargantua Dragon, "Raging Mode" SCR	1.50	2.50
SCBT010071 Gargantua Blade Mage Neo SCR	.75	1.25
SCBT010072 Gargantua Thunder Deity Wind Demon Dragon SCR	1.50	2.50
SCBT010073 Fickle Dragon of Blackflames, Gargantua Phantom SCR	1.00	1.50
SCBT010074 Black Dragon Knight, Geil SCR	4.00	6.00
SCBT010075 Black Dragon Knight, Belze SCR	.75	1.25
SCBT010076 Black Dragon Knight, Zest SCR	.50	.75
SCBT010077 Curse Destruction SCR	.60	1.00
SCBT010078 Sentence of Curse SCR	2.50	4.00
SCBT01BR01 Deity Gargantua Dragon BR	40.00	60.00
SCBT01BR02 Black Dragon Knight, Geil BR	25.00	40.00
SCBT01S001 Deity Gargantua Dragon SP	50.00	75.00
SCBT01S002 King's Brilliance, Cross Farnese Astrologia SP	15.00	25.00
SCBT01S003 Cyclonic Thunderaxe, Agito SP	40.00	60.00
SCBT01S004 Black Dragon Knight, Geil SP	30.00	50.00

2019 Future Card Buddyfight S Climax Booster Set 2 Violence Vanity

RELEASED ON MARCH 1, 2019

Card	Low	High
SCBT020001 Deep and Invasion of Vile RRR	10.00	15.00
SCBT020001 Deep and Invasion of Vile CLR	20.00	30.00
SCBT020002 Huskblood Eyes Deadly Eyes RRR	5.00	8.00
SCBT020003 D. Endbringer RRR	2.50	4.00
SCBT020004 A Bewitching Crimson Mirage. Sync RRR	5.00	8.00
SCBT020005 Iron Gold Steelframe, KUROGANE RRR	1.25	2.00
SCBT020006 Archangel Dragon, Raphael RRR	3.00	5.00
SCBT020007 Glory of Heaven RRR	10.00	15.00
SCBT020008 Oleteius Olgenes RRR	2.00	3.00
SCBT020009 Evil Diving Frolic Deep Looker RR	1.00	1.50
SCBT020010 Dimension Dragon, Katasuri RR	1.00	1.50
SCBT020011 Almighty Overlord, Zerberos Lost RR	1.25	2.00
SCBT020012 Natural of Absolute Strongest RR	1.25	2.00
SCBT020013 Angel Troop, Esia RR	3.00	5.00
SCBT020014 Angel Brilliant RR	4.00	6.00
SCBT020015 Deathraider Orven RR	4.00	6.00
SCBT020016 Lostknight: Nero Schilltance RR	2.00	3.00
SCBT020017 Knowledge Wave RR	1.00	1.50
SCBT020018 Merren Coskegoal RR	1.25	2.00
SCBT020019 Dimension Zeggaine RR	2.50	4.00
SCBT020020 Vile Demonic Cannon, Lostless Heizer RR	4.00	6.00
SCBT020021 Despair D. Raider R	.20	.30
SCBT020022 Dragon Cruel Execute» Dragion Judge R	.30	.50
SCBT020023 King of Da-Dan R	.20	.30
SCBT020024 Origin Power, Zerberos R	.20	.30
SCBT020025 Exsteed, "Black Crown" R	.20	.30
SCBT020026 Mystic Girl, Hanako R	.20	.30
SCBT020027 Archangel Dragon, Uilitis R	.20	.30
SCBT020028 Angel Troop, Reclis R	.20	.30
SCBT020029 Authority of Heavenly Realm R	.20	.30
SCBT020030 Sacred Holy Grail R	.20	.30
SCBT020031 Holy Wish R	.20	.30
SCBT020032 Deathraider Chelicala R	.40	.60
SCBT020033 Venom Pain R	.40	.60
SCBT020034 Rook: Viore Sword R	.20	.30
SCBT020035 Declaration Check R	.40	.60
SCBT020036 Double Check Tactics R	.25	.40
SCBT020037 Kuh Phodomando R	.50	.75
SCBT020038 Distortion Wall R	.50	.75
SCBT020039 Dimension Dragon, Phobos U	.12	.20
SCBT020040 Dimension Dragon, Efsla U	.12	.20
SCBT020041 Crazy Moonlight Madness Luna U	.12	.20
SCBT020042 D. Quake U	.12	.20
SCBT020043 Deep Crimson? Wave» Scarlet Finger U	.12	.20
SCBT020044 Dragonic Forcefield U	.12	.20
SCBT020045 False Soul Fake Heart U	.12	.20
SCBT020046 Dimension Bequest, Enelodis U	.12	.20
SCBT020047 Selector of SIN U	.12	.20
SCBT020048 Twin Blade Training Field, KAZIBA U	.12	.20
SCBT020049 Peerless Ferocious? Dragon U	.12	.20
SCBT020050 Unbreakable Domilord U	.12	.20
SCBT020051 Angel Troop, Virche U	.12	.20
SCBT020052 Angel Troop, Livan U	.12	.20
SCBT020053 Angel Troop, Rintis U	.12	.20
SCBT020054 Angel Soldier, Taxh U	.12	.20
SCBT020055 Angelic Charge U	.12	.20
SCBT020056 Cleansing Judgement U	.12	.20
SCBT020057 Circle of Reflect U	.12	.20
SCBT020058 Sword of the King, Dainsleif U	.12	.20
SCBT020059 Divine Staff, Mass Fortune U	.12	.20
SCBT020060 Hell Deathraider Kalawana U	.12	.20
SCBT020061 Deathraider Dismal U	.12	.20
SCBT020062 Venom Bind U	.12	.20
SCBT020063 Venom Spell U	.12	.20
SCBT020064 Venom Swamp U	1.00	1.50
SCBT020065 Poison Mask U	.12	.20
SCBT020066 Grandmaster Crown U	.12	.20
SCBT020067 Kataslubach U	.12	.20
SCBT020068 Flourish of Nihility? and Desperation U	.12	.20
SCBT020069 Vile Demonic Deity Dragon, Vanity Epoch Destroyer SCR	5.00	8.00
SCBT020070 Inummael Katarant SCR	.60	1.00
SCBT020071 Effeslay Rallface SCR	.75	1.25
SCBT020072 Dimension Wave SCR	1.25	2.00
SCBT020073 Day of Devastation SCR	2.50	4.00
SCBT020074 Archangel Dragon, Gavriel SCR	4.00	6.00
SCBT020075 Angel Troop, Caldeen SCR	1.25	2.00
SCBT020076 Angel Troop, Zeruel SCR	1.00	1.50
SCBT020077 Angel Wings SCR	1.25	2.00
SCBT020078 Judgment Holy Rain SCR	.75	1.25
SCBT02BR01 Archangel Dragon, Gavriel BR	10.00	15.00
SCBT02BR02 Vile Demonic Deity Dragon, Vanity Epoch Destroyer BR	10.00	15.00
SCBT02S001 Huskblood Eyes Deadly Eyes SP	50.00	75.00
SCBT02S002 Archangel Dragon, Gavriel SP	60.00	100.00
SCBT02S003 A Bewitching Crimson Mirage. Sync SP	20.00	30.00
SCBT02S004 Vile Demonic Deity Dragon, Vanity Epoch Destroyer SP	50.00	75.00

2018 Future Card Buddyfight X Climax Booster Set 2 Driven to Disorder

RELEASED ON FEBRUARY 23, 2018

Card	Low	High
XCBTA0001EN Red Thunder Emperor's Awakening RRR		
XCBTA0001EN Red Thunder Emperor's Awakening CLR	30.00	50.00
XCBTA0002EN Awakened as Thunder Emperor, Batzz RRR		
XCBTA0003EN Destructive Sword of the King, Trishula RRR		
XCBTA0004EN Reverse Black Eddy, Abygale Asyl RRR		
XCBTA0005EN Overturn Battleship, Satsuki G. RRR		
XCBTA0006EN Provenance Crystal Dragon, Athora Adamant RRR		
XCBTA0007EN Divine Sword Dragon, Saint Glory Sword Dragon RR		
XCBTA0008EN Batzz the Spirit RR		
XCBTA0009EN Fallen Angel of Rebellion, Rucifiel RR		
XCBTA0010EN Top-Rank Ninja, Mangetsumaru RR		
XCBTA0011EN Unequaled Immortal Chief, Duel Jaeger "Gaia Bust" RR		
XCBTA0012EN Pulse Headgear RR		
XCBTA0013EN Twin-fanged Knight, Versellia RR		
XCBTA0014EN Black Arc Dragon, Gentlegee RR		
XCBTA0015EN Quing Lada II, Command Mech RR		
XCBTA0016EN Thunderstar, Birkeland RR		
XCBTA0017EN J. Star Ring RR		
XCBTA0018EN Crystal Crescent Greaves RR		
XCBTA0019EN Battlefield Blitz, Brokenline R	.20	.30
XCBTA0020EN Dragon Knight, Nikola Tesla R	.20	.30
XCBTA0021EN Turbulent Thunder Shock, Roaring Dragon X Tempest Wave! R	.20	.30
XCBTA0022EN Devil Reverse R	.20	.30
XCBTA0023EN Asmodai Onstage! R	.20	.30
XCBTA0024EN Magnetic Ninja, Magnetojiro R	.20	.30
XCBTA0025EN Spider Thread Art R	.20	.30
XCBTA0026EN Famous Blade, Kogane-chidori R	.20	.30
XCBTA0027EN Secret Sword, Waves-Splitting Arc Fangs R	.20	.30
XCBTA0028EN Deluge of Life R	.20	.30
XCBTA0029EN Robo of Urban Legends, Hanako WC R	.20	.30
XCBTA0030EN Illegal Counter R	.20	.30
XCBTA0031EN Quing Lada II, Broadsword Frame R	.20	.30
XCBTA0032EN Prepare For Sortie! R	.20	.30
XCBTA0033EN Star Ocean Envoy, K22: Vonnegut R	.20	.30
XCBTA0034EN Tractor Beam R	.20	.30
XCBTA0035EN Guru Bunbuku, Serious Mode! R	.20	.30
XCBTA0036EN Guru Bunbuku R	.20	.30
XCBTA0037EN Vortex Noble, Spirallel C	.10	.15
XCBTA0038EN Lifelong Service, Bone Gramps C	.10	.15
XCBTA0039EN Tiny Ice Dragon, Glacion C	.10	.15
XCBTA0040EN Thunder X Wall C	.10	.15
XCBTA0041EN Thunder Emperor's Orders C	.10	.15
XCBTA0042EN Thunder Emperor's Formation C	.10	.15
XCBTA0043EN Thunder Emperor's Fan, Leilong C	.10	.15
XCBTA0044EN Thunder Emperor's Fist, Drapunch C	.10	.15
XCBTA0045EN Demon Lord's Deputy, Vineah C	.10	.15
XCBTA0046EN Searchlight C	.10	.15
XCBTA0047EN Millionaire? Chief, Million Dollar Kin C	.10	.15
XCBTA0048EN Apprentice Underling, Robo Mecha Shin C	.10	.15
XCBTA0049EN Dragon Soul Infusion! C	.10	.15
XCBTA0050EN Unmatched in All Seas, Birth of a Chief! C	.10	.15
XCBTA0051EN Knight of Tender Love, Philia C	.10	.15
XCBTA0052EN Knight of Thunder Tale, Nils C	.10	.15
XCBTA0053EN Yellowbat C	.10	.15
XCBTA0054EN Deflection C	.25	.40
XCBTA0055EN On Throne! Go! Hanako WC! C	.10	.15
XCBTA0056EN Black Arc Dragon, Teegas C	.10	.15
XCBTA0057EN Black Reduce C	.10	.15
XCBTA0058EN Impartial Warrior, Justi Hope C	.10	.15
XCBTA0059EN Quing Lada II, Assault Frame C	.10	.15
XCBTA0060EN Quing Lada Operated Fixation Cannon C	.10	.15
XCBTA0061EN Deploy Impact Canceler! C	.10	.15
XCBTA0062EN Arc Crystal Dragon, Mimosa C	.10	.15
XCBTA0063EN Dragonarms, Diversion C	.10	.15
XCBTA0064EN Dragoner Wings C	.40	.60
XCBTA0065EN Prism Order C	.10	.15
XCBTA0066EN Jupiter Barrier C	.10	.15
XCBTA0067EN Turbulent Warlord Dragon, Barlbatzz Dragoroyale SCR		
XCBTA0068EN Thunder Emperor's Descendant, X Jr. SCR		
XCBTA0069EN Thunder Emperor's Descendant?, Cross Jr. SCR		
XCBTA0070EN Warlord Crimson Thunder Wave SCR		
XCBTA0071EN Turbulent Warlord Fist, Dragrumble SCR		
XCBTA0072EN Shining Dragoner, Jackknife SCR		
XCBTA0073EN Jackarms, J. Arsenal SCR		
XCBTA0074EN Star Dragoner, Dimenzion E SCR		
XCBTA0075EN Arms Bomber SCR		
XCBTA0076EN Shining Punisher!! SCR		
XCBTA0077EN Overturn Demon Lord, Asmodai SCR		
XCBTA0078EN Hellheaven Dragon, Hellrend Heavens SCR		
XCBTA0079EN Seeker of Superior Strength, Duel Jaeger SCR		
XCBTA0080EN Batzz the Spirit SCR		
XCBTABR01EN Turbulent Warlord Dragon, Barlbatzz Dragoroyale BR	25.00	40.00
XCBTABR02EN Shining Dragoner, Jackknife BR	15.00	25.00
XCBTAS001EN Turbulent Warlord Dragon, Barlbatzz Dragoroyale SP		
XCBTAS002EN Shining Dragoner, Jackknife SP		
XCBTAS003EN Reverse Black Eddy, Abygale Asyl SP		
XCBTB0001EN Awakening of the Black Autodeity CR		
XCBTB0001EN Awakening of the Black Autodeity RRR		
XCBTB0002EN Cavalry Dragon Mech, CHAOS Kegale Byde RRR		
XCBTB0003EN Replenish Mech, CHAOS Pentar RRR		
XCBTB0004EN Death Plague Priest, Zyebola RRR		
XCBTB0005EN Divine Demonic Sword of the King, Excalibur Replica RRR		
XCBTB0006EN Genome Upgrader, Geargod ver.1000 RRR		
XCBTB0007EN Bombard Mech, CHAOS Cylinder RR		
XCBTB0008EN Assault of Autodeity Army RR		
XCBTB0009EN Steel-Beak Vul-gollium RR		
XCBTB0010EN Immense Pressure RR		

XCBTB0011EN Death Plague Caster, Varicellur RR
XCBTB0012EN Narcolepsy RR
XCBTB0013EN Lady Oni, Uji Bridge Princess RR
XCBTB0014EN Ibuki's Encouragement RR
XCBTB0015EN Yngl Gard RR
XCBTB0016EN Fabricated Sword of the King, Unsigned Iron Sword Replica RR
XCBTB0017EN Mini Geargods Control Mech, Big Wisdom RR
XCBTB0018EN Mini Geargod Gold RR
XCBTB0019EN Forging Mech, CHAOS Rectangle? R
XCBTB0020EN Chaos Signal R
XCBTB0021EN Deity Lance CHAOS X Tempest Buster! R
XCBTB0022EN Sturdy-Horned Beetle-gollum R
XCBTB0023EN Emergency Fuel Supply R
XCBTB0024EN Death Plague Pastor, Burgmal R
XCBTB0025EN CHAOS Beleth R
XCBTB0026EN Death Plague Caster, Rubellurs R
XCBTB0027EN Great Spell, Godspeed Learning R
XCBTB0028EN Great Spell, Diagnosis R
XCBTB0029EN The Hot Zone R
XCBTB0030EN Yatsuka Fiend, Tsuchigumo R
XCBTB0031EN Grudge Fiend, Hannya R
XCBTB0032EN Underhanded Means, Piercing Pins R
XCBTB0033EN Oni Castle of Contraptions R
XCBTB0034EN CHAOS Bloody King R
XCBTB0035EN Sword of the King and Sham, Lobera & Lobera Replica R
XCBTB0036EN Mini Geargod Silver R
XCBTB0037EN Misfiring Mech, CHAOS Globes C
XCBTB0038EN Military Deviser Mech, CHAOS Fanning C
XCBTB0039EN CHAOS Chibi Panda C
XCBTB0040EN Flame Dragon Mech, CHAOS Linear C
XCBTB0041EN Autodeity Armor, Chaos Finger C
XCBTB0042EN CHAOS Uni-gollum C
XCBTB0043EN Painful Needlefish-gollum C
XCBTB0044EN Firstaid-gollum C
XCBTB0045EN Chaos Arms C
XCBTB0046EN Unknown Grit C
XCBTB0047EN Giant Cadaver Catapult C
XCBTB0048EN Cadaver Debris Palm C
XCBTB0049EN Death Plague Caster, Malariah C
XCBTB0050EN Epidemic - Outbreak - C
XCBTB0051EN Contagion Gel C
XCBTB0052EN Malignant Tumor C
XCBTB0053EN Mycotoxin C
XCBTB0054EN Great Spell Circle of Reservoir C
XCBTB0055EN CHAOS Kimensai C
XCBTB0056EN CHAOS Ox-Head Horse-Face C
XCBTB0057EN Oni Horde, Underworld Legion C
XCBTB0058EN Dark Arms, Demonic Poison Fumes Cube C
XCBTB0059EN For The Chosen Ones C
XCBTB0060EN Trismegistos' Alchemy C
XCBTB0061EN Parasite Yggdrasil C
XCBTB0062EN Fabricated Sword of the King, Zulfiqar Replica C
XCBTB0063EN Fabricated Sword of the King, Hrotti Replica C
XCBTB0064EN Fabricated Sword of the King, Hovd Replica C
XCBTB0065EN Taboo, Savage Form! C
XCBTB0066EN Mini Geargod Orange C
XCBTB0067EN Autodeity Dragon, CHAOS Batzz SCR
XCBTB0068EN Special Attack Mech, CHAOS Delta SCR
XCBTB0069EN Evil Sword Dragon, Demons Chaos Sword Dragon SCR
XCBTB0070EN All-Purpose Mech, CHAOS Tetra SCR
XCBTB0071EN Autodeity Sword, CHAOS Dragoroyale SCR
XCBTB0072EN Ashen Death Sorcery Yersinieas SCR
XCBTB0073EN Ultimate Great Spell, World Pandemic! SCR
XCBTB0074EN Great Spell, Incubation Period SCR
XCBTB0075EN Great Spell, Latent Infection SCR
XCBTB0076EN Scholarly Tome of Death, Aneotomy SCR
XCBTB0077EN Demonic Rock Dragon Mech, Dol Dra-gollum SCR
XCBTB0078EN Oni-Devouring Oni, Kid Ibuki "Arabone" SCR
XCBTB0079EN Infallible Blade Wall SCR
XCBTB0080EN Death Plague Caster, Varicellur SCR
XCBTBBR01EN Autodeity Dragon, CHAOS Batzz BR
XCBTBBR02EN Ashen Death Sorcery Yersinieas BR
XCBTBS001EN Evil Sword Dragon, Demons Chaos Sword Dragon SP
XCBTBS002EN Ashen Death Sorcery Yersinieas SP
XCBTBS003EN Genome Upgrader, Geargod ver.1000 SP

2014 Future Card Buddyfight Extra Booster Set 1 Immortal Entities

RELEASED ON JUNE 6, 2014
EB010001 Sun Fist, Sunshine Impact RRR .75 1.25
EB010001 Sun Fist, Sunshine Impact SP
EB010002 Duel Sieger "Tempest Enforcer" SP
EB010002 Duel Sieger "Tempest Enforcer" RRR 5.00 8.00
EB010003 Dragon Knight, Richard RR .30 .50
EB010003 Dragon Knight, Richard SP
EB010004 Dimensional Demonic Dragon, Ladis the Tyrant SP
EB010004 Dimensional Demonic Dragon, Ladis the Tyrant RR .30 .50
EB010005 Fortune Dragon, Forbolka RR .60 1.00
EB010006 Evil Crusher, Steel Dragon Barrage! SP
EB010006 Evil Crusher, Steel Dragon Barrage! RR 1.00 1.50
EB010007 Divine Dragon Creation RR 6.00 10.00
EB010008 Systemic Dagger "Onca" R .15 .25
EB010009 Dragobulk Stormschlag R .15 .25
EB010010 Evil Sins, Shumokuzame R .15 .25
EB010011 Bandit Ninja, Goemon R .15 .25
EB010012 Duel Sieger "Spartand" R .15 .25
EB010013 Martial Arts Dragon Emperor, Duel Sieger R .15 .25
EB010014 Space Dragon Emperor, Galiazond R .15 .25
EB010014 Space Dragon Emperor, Galiazond SP
EB010015 Flame Dragon Emperor, Magmanova R .15 .25
EB010016 Dragon Emperor Legend R .15 .25
EB010017 Dragon Flame Cascade R .15 .25
EB010018 Blow-hammer Dragon U .12 .20
EB010019 Ironchain Dragon U .12 .20
EB010020 Hundred Face Ninja, Muraku U .12 .20
EB010021 Silver Dragon, Adelaide U .12 .20
EB010022 Storm Dragon Emperor, Thundertornado U .12 .20
EB010023 Rock Dragon Emperor, Vragos U .12 .20
EB010024 Blue Dragon, Thunder Horn U .12 .20
EB010025 Dragonverse U .12 .20
EB010026 Dragonlution U .12 .20
EB010027 Rise & Fall of Dragons U .12 .20
EB010028 Dragon Knight, Gilles de Rais C .10 .15
EB010029 Dirge Drill Dragon C .10 .15
EB010030 Dragon Knight, Socrates C .10 .15
EB010031 Dragonic Dash C .10 .15
EB010032 Dragospeed C .10 .15
EB010033 Sword Skill Bare Hand Intercept C .10 .15
EB010034 Ninja Arts, Half-kill C .10 .15
EB010035 Gold Dragon, Abend C .10 .15
EB010036 Ice Dragon, Knoke-isle C .10 .15
EB010037 Vitesse, Purple Diamond Dragon C .30 .50
EB010038 Ice Dragon Emperor, Glacies C 1.00 1.50
EB010039 Flame Fairy Dragon, Tialvette C .10 .15
EB010040 Wind Fairy Dragon, Sufa C .10 .15
EB010041 Ice Fairy Dragon, Garbolette C .10 .15
EB010042 Feather Dragon, Talwar C .10 .15
EB010043 Dies, Azurite Dragon C .10 .15
EB010044 Dragon Outlaw C .10 .15
EB010045 Bold Dragon C .10 .15
EB010046 Dragon Dreams C .10 .15
EB010047 Dragon Thunder C .10 .15
EB010048 Thunder Knights, Drum Bunker Dragon BR 4.00 6.00

2015 Future Card Buddyfight H Extra Booster Set 1 Miracle Impack

RELEASED ON JUNE 12, 2015
HEB010001 Armorknight Archangel RRR .30 .50
HEB010002 Blue Knight, Noboru RRR 1.00 1.50
HEB010003 Legendary Messiah, Tasuku RRR .30 .50
HEB010003 Legendary Messiah, Tasuku SP 40.00 60.00
HEB010004 Emergency Launch! Decker Drum RRR .75 1.25
HEB010005 Super Combidragon, Brainbaltes RR .40 .60
HEB010006 Armorknight Iblis RR .30 .50
HEB010006 Armorknight Iblis SP 6.00 10.00
HEB010007 Infinite Armament, Dangerous Cradle RR 2.00 3.00
HEB010008 Death Master, Lelag Monarch RR .60 1.00
HEB010009 Province Baron, Shido RR 1.00 1.50
HEB010010 Mech Army Demon Lord, Agos Marh RR 1.25 2.00
HEB010011 King's Wave, Caliburn Grief RR 2.00 3.00
HEB010012 Red Warrior, Road Blader RR .60 1.00
HEB010013 Dragon Secret Arts, Dragonic Resurrection R .50 .75
HEB010014 Battle Aura Dragon, Extreme-Aura R .25 .40
HEB010015 Battle Dragon Slaying Crush R .25 .40
HEB010016 Unyielding Spirit R .60 1.00
HEB010017 Battle Dragon Bursting Charge! R .25 .40
HEB010018 Shredding Battle Wall R 3.00 5.00
HEB010019 Judge Asmodai's Super Impartial 3 Rounds, Rock! Paper! Scissors! R 1.50 2.50
HEB010020 New-Era Great Spell, The Creation R .50 .75
HEB010021 Ninja Arts, Art of Bursting Machine Gun R .25 .40
HEB010022 Dragon's Life and Death, Future and Past! R .50 .75
HEB010023 Hades Dragon Chief, Red Arrogant R .25 .40
HEB010024 Dragon Tooth Warrior R .75 1.25
HEB010025 Bronze Golem, Jaish R .25 .40
HEB010026 Hidden Crossbow R 3.00 5.00
HEB010027 Adventurer's Staff, Alcsbane R .75 1.25
HEB010028 Phoenix Radiation! R .25 .40
HEB010028 Phoenix Radiation! SP 10.00 15.00
HEB010029 Asgard Saga R .25 .40
HEB010030 Violence Familiar! R .25 .40
HEB010031 Unmovable Steel Mech, Ganzallar R .60 1.00
HEB010032 Prepped and OK to Launch! R .75 1.25
HEB010033 Determination of the Fist Fighter, Grapple Soul U 1.25 2.00
HEB010034 Armorknight Centaur U .15 .25
HEB010035 Armorknight Salamander U .15 .25
HEB010036 Sibling Dragon, Foonbaltes U .15 .25
HEB010037 Armorknight Ogre A U .60 1.00
HEB010038 Armorknight Jetfighter U .15 .25
HEB010039 Sibling Dragon, Kibaltes U .15 .25
HEB010040 Infinite Demon Slay Slash U .15 .25
HEB010041 Training of Skill and Life U .40 .60
HEB010042 Spear of Will, Agito U .40 .60
HEB010043 Demon Arms Door, ArMoreD Gate! U .60 1.00
HEB010044 Demon Way, Ukishizumi Ikusabune U .40 .60
HEB010045 Charge of Virtuous Blood! U .15 .25
HEB010046 Diamond Golem, Fluud U .15 .25
HEB010047 Steel Golem, Futoff U .15 .25
HEB010048 Trouble Ghost, Shuffler X U .15 .25
HEB010049 Iron Golem, Nasr U .15 .25
HEB010050 Swordsman of the East, Zanya U .40 .60
HEB010051 Apprentice Ninja, Akatsuki U .60 1.00
HEB010052 Entangle Roper U .15 .25
HEB010053 Quiescence of Cassiade U 1.00 1.50
HEB010054 Mission Card THE Teamwork U .75 1.25
HEB010055 Fortune Select! U .15 .25
HEB010056 Dark Interment, Over the Grudge U .15 .25
HEB010057 White Valor, Lord Takuto U .15 .25
HEB010058 That is an Afterimage U 1.00 1.50
HEB010059 Rock Splitter Sword, Gaia Crush! U .15 .25
HEB010060 Emergency Trans! U .15 .25
HEB010061 Emergency Launch! Decker Drum BR 6.00 10.00
NNO Dungeon World SCR
NNO Dragon World ** SCR
NNO Katana World SCR
NNO Danger World * SCR
NNO Magic World SCR

2015 Future Card Buddyfight H Extra Booster Set 2 Shadow vs. Hero

RELEASED ON AUGUST 14, 2015
HEB020001 Great Sword Deity, Kaizerion RRR 5.00 8.00
HEB020002 Captain Answer Final Mode RRR .60 1.00
HEB020003 Shadow Hero, Schwarz RRR 4.00 6.00
HEB020003 Shadow Hero, Schwarz SP 25.00 40.00
HEB020004 Rescue Dragon, Justice Drum RRR 1.25 2.00
HEB020004 Rescue Dragon, Justice Drum SP 15.00 25.00
HEB020005 Rescue Dragon Leader, Immortal Spirit RR .50 .75
HEB020005 Rescue Dragon Leader, Immortal Spirit SP 4.00 6.00
HEB020006 Rescue Dragon, Forcearms RR .60 1.00
HEB020007 Gaigrander 02 RR .60 1.00
HEB020008 Fiery Inspector, Prominence Burst RR .60 1.00
HEB020008 Fiery Inspector, Prominence Burst SP 15.00 25.00
HEB020009 Gaigrander 01 RR .60 1.00
HEB020010 Darkness Fist, Gwen RR 3.00 5.00
HEB020011 Evil Esthetics RR 3.00 5.00
HEB020012 Sneak Judgement RR 1.50 2.50
HEB020013 Combitrooper, Dziem R .25 .40
HEB020014 Grand Calibur, Zeldline R .25 .40
HEB020015 Violet Valor, Lord Crow R .25 .40
HEB020016 Rescue Dragon, Dragschoebel R .25 .40
HEB020017 Rescue Dragon, Transmission R .25 .40
HEB020018 Rescue Dragon, Northern Bird R .25 .40
HEB020019 Rescue Dragon, Projet Gunner R .25 .40
HEB020020 Cyber Police, Commander Gale R .25 .40
HEB020021 Grand RuLer, Silbarrier R .25 .40
HEB020022 Bird Deity, Sabird R .25 .40
HEB020023 Combatant, Nebatt R .25 .40
HEB020024 Momentary Flash R .25 .40
HEB020025 Body of Steel R .25 .40
HEB020026 Fighting for the Sake of Others R .25 .40
HEB020027 I'm Finished with You R .25 .40
HEB020028 First Darkhero Hideout R .25 .40
HEB020029 Super Headquarters, Brave Fort R .25 .40
HEB020030 I've Come Back to Take You Down! R .25 .40
HEB020031 But He is of the Lowest Rank R .25 .40
HEB020032 Infinity Death Crest! R .25 .40
HEB020033 Brave Energy Full Drive! R .25 .40
HEB020034 Steel Beast Battle Robo, Gaidenor U .15 .25
HEB020035 Corrupted One, Erational U .15 .25
HEB020036 Buster Bone Armor U .15 .25
HEB020037 Gaigrander, Finish Form U .15 .25
HEB020038 Gaigrander, Analyze Form U .15 .25
HEB020039 Sacrifice, Iron Moon Slash U .15 .25
HEB020040 Cyber Police, Stealth Hunter U .15 .25
HEB020041 Radio Controlled Machine, Bodhum Breaker U .15 .25
HEB020042 The Scar U .15 .25
HEB020043 Beast Deity, Tigerthrust U .15 .25
HEB020044 Cyber Police, Heroic Blader U .15 .25
HEB020045 Rescue Dragon, Erase Flare U .15 .25
HEB020046 Judgement, Hollow Strydom U .15 .25
HEB020047 Rescue Dragon, Doctor Aid U .15 .25
HEB020048 Radio Control Machine, Makishi Rider U .15 .25
HEB020049 Thief Cat U .15 .25
HEB020050 Rescue Dragon, Nightstalker U .15 .25
HEB020051 Ocean Deity, Slashark U .15 .25
HEB020052 Be Glad That You Can be of Use to Me U .15 .25
HEB020053 I Have No Business with the Likes of You! U .15 .25
HEB020054 I Leave...the Rest to You U .15 .25
HEB020055 It's Here, the NEW Suit! U .15 .25
HEB020056 Arduous Training U .15 .25
HEB020057 Long-Range Cannon U .15 .25
HEB020058 I Won`t Let that Happen! U .15 .25
HEB020059 For Such an Attack to... U .15 .25
HEB020060 It Doesn't Work!! U .15 .25
HEB020061 Shadow Requiem U .15 .25
HEB020062 Superior Justice Driver! U .15 .25
HEB020063 Dead or Alive! U .15 .25
HEB020064 Rescue Dragon, Justice Drum BR .15 .25

2015 Future Card Buddyfight H Extra Booster Set 3 Lord of Hundred Thunders

RELEASED ON SEPTEMBER 25, 2015
HEB030001 Hundred Demons General, Iyonorasetsuryu RRR 1.50 2.50
HEB030002 Hundred Demons General, Gishingyuki RRR .60 1.00
HEB030003 Hundred Demons General, Braiden RRR .60 1.00
HEB030004 Resurrected Evil Deity, Yamigedo RRR 1.50 2.50
HEB030005 Gedo Shield RR 2.50 4.00
HEB030006 Armorknight Tiger A RR 2.00 3.00
HEB030007 Dark Caster, Dunstan RR .60 1.00
HEB030008 Poison Dragon Emperor, Misty Envy RR 1.50 2.50
HEB030009 Caster of Forbidden Techniques, Velgaren RR 6.00 10.00
HEB030010 Gate of Darkness Dragon RR 2.00 3.00
HEB030011 Stranger Dilemma RR 3.00 5.00
HEB030012 There are no Places for You to Run! RR .75 1.25
HEB030013 Nightmare Scream Dragon R .60 1.00
HEB030014 Armorknight Serpent R .25 .40
HEB030015 Hundred Demons Destructive Power Raiga R .60 1.00
HEB030016 Hundred Demons Spear, Onikuzushi R 1.25 2.00
HEB030017 Demon Realm Trivia Lord, Forcas R .60 1.00
HEB030018 Fiendish Sword, Kuromuramasa R .25 .40
HEB030019 Phantom Dragon Emperor, Lux Vision R .25 .40
HEB030020 Call Dragon, Megitus R .25 .40
HEB030021 Hundred Demons Sorcery, Rinneryusho R .25 .40
HEB030022 Iron Cyclops R .25 .40
HEB030023 Battle Hyena, Dolz R .25 .40
HEB030024 Proto Golem, Jarima R .25 .40
HEB030025 Hundred Demons Mission Card AIM THE CHAIN R .25 .40
HEB030026 Demonic Beast, Afanc R .25 .40
HEB030027 Mockery of Gremlins R 5.00 8.00
HEB030028 Black Dragon, Beflyen R .25 .40
HEB030029 Great Leader, Anson R .25 .40
HEB030030 World Domination of Terror R .25 .40
HEB030031 Guillotine Axe Dragon U .12 .20
HEB030032 Hundred Demons Formation, Thunder Mine Stance U .12 .20
HEB030033 Gate of Dragon U 1.50 2.50
HEB030034 Crush Execute Dragon, Zarrtelganger U .12 .20
HEB030035 Armorknight Naga U .12 .20
HEB030036 Rock Dragon, Garagoron U .12 .20
HEB030037 Mysterious Decarabia U .12 .20
HEB030038 Hundred Demons Sorcery, Do or Die U .12 .20
HEB030039 Hundred Demons Sorcery, No Brainer U 2.00 3.00
HEB030040 Hundred Demons Sorcery, Mad Dancing U 2.50 4.00
HEB030041 Wolf Face Ninja, Benitsume U .12 .20
HEB030042 Robust, Kinoesasori U .12 .20
HEB030043 Hundred Demons Sorcery, Yamitsuito U .12 .20
HEB030044 Hundred Demons Sorcery, Hyakkaryoran U .12 .20
HEB030045 Red Dragon, Igneel U .12 .20
HEB030046 Hundred Demons Sorcery, Ryuzenshakuma U .12 .20
HEB030047 Hundred Demons Sorcery, Manryufuto U .12 .20
HEB030048 Evil Dryad U 1.50 2.50
HEB030049 Evil Deity Altar U .12 .20
HEB030050 Hundred Demons Assault, Hundred Legion! U .12 .20
HEB030051 World Snake, Jormungandr U .12 .20
HEB030052 Destruction Demon, Razorback U .12 .20
HEB030053 Water Spirit, Rusalka U .12 .20
HEB030054 Hundred Demons Sorcery, Nemesis Thunder U .12 .20
HEB030055 Demon Sword of the King, Clarent U .12 .20
HEB030056 One Winged Hatred Dragon, Leftslasher U .12 .20
HEB030057 Hundred Demons Sorcery, Death Sacrifice U 6.00 10.00
HEB030058 Hundred Demons Sorcery, Dark Target U .12 .20
HEB030059 Steel Fist, Blacknuckle U .12 .20
HEB030060 It Was My Doing! U .12 .20

2015 Future Card Buddyfight H Extra Booster Set 4 Buddy All-Stars+

RELEASED ON DECEMBER 18, 2015
HEB040012EN Hasted Evolution, Yamigedo SP 30.00 50.00
HEB040001EN Jackknife, Drum Bunker RRR .60 1.00
HEB040002EN Art of Body Duplication! Asmodai RRR 6.00 10.00
HEB040002EN Art of Body Duplication! Asmodai SP 40.00 60.00
HEB040003EN Magical Beast Tamer, Kazane RRR 1.00 1.50
HEB040004EN Star Guardian, Jackknife SD RRR 1.00 1.50
HEB040005EN Drum Bunker Dragon SD RR 1.25 2.00
HEB040005EN Drum Bunker Dragon SD SP 20.00 30.00
HEB040006EN Fifth Omni Dragon Lord, Tenbu SD RR .40 .60
HEB040007EN Nanomachine Ninja, Tsukikage SD RR .75 1.25
HEB040008EN Count Dawn of the Distant Days RR .75 1.25
HEB040009EN Emissary of Ruin, Megiddo Death Tallica RR .75 1.25
HEB040010EN Purgatory Knights Leader, Demios Sword Inferno RR 2.00 3.00
HEB040011EN Schwarz SD RR 1.50 2.50

Card	Low	High
HEB040012EN Hasted Evolution, Yamigedo RR	4.00	6.00
HEB040013EN Sorrowful Face Dragon Knight, El Quixote R	.25	.40
HEB040014EN Origin Fighting Dragon, Demongodol R	.25	.40
HEB040015EN Armorknight Cerberus SD R	2.00	3.00
HEB040016EN Burst Deity Calling Ritual R	2.50	4.00
HEB040017EN Ideal Girl, Mary Sue R	.25	.40
HEB040018EN Nothing to It! R	.25	.40
HEB040019EN Nanomachine Ninja, Byakuya SD R	.25	.40
HEB040020EN Boy Transformation, Yamigitsune R	.60	1.00
HEB040021EN Demon Way, Arakuyou R	.25	.40
HEB040022EN Duel Sieger SD R	.25	.40
HEB040023EN Gang the King SD R	.25	.40
HEB040024EN Dragon Baby, Ricky R	.25	.40
HEB040025EN Bladewing Phoenix SD R	1.25	2.00
HEB040026EN Heat Blade Joker R	.25	.40
HEB040027EN Secret Arts of the Water Lord R	.25	.40
HEB040028EN Great Wind Fairy, Sylph R	.25	.40
HEB040029EN Deathgaze Dragon SD R	.25	.40
HEB040030EN Decker Drum SD R	.60	1.00
HEB040031EN Respective Battles R	.25	.40
HEB040032EN Star Jack Boost R	.25	.40
HEB040033EN Speed of Light, Tri Elements R	.25	.40
HEB040034EN Shrine of the Corrupted Fuchigami R	.25	.40
HEB040035EN Crimson Battler, Halberd Gauntlet U	.20	.30
HEB040036EN Dragonic Endure U	.20	.30
HEB040037EN Divine Crash U	.20	.30
HEB040038EN Hades Axe, Demon Wind Slash U	.20	.30
HEB040039EN Qinus Axia SD U	.20	.30
HEB040040EN Make Some Noise! U	.20	.30
HEB040041EN One More Set! U	.20	.30
HEB040042EN Hidden Secret Sword Cloud Billow U	.20	.30
HEB040043EN Secret Sword, Starlight U	.20	.30
HEB040044EN Loyal Dragons and Courage U	.20	.30
HEB040045EN Result of Dragonwork U	.20	.30
HEB040046EN Champion of Arena, Rouga U	.20	.30
HEB040047EN A Handful of Rewards U	.40	.60
HEB040048EN Colossal Deity of Phantom Star, Astraeus U	.20	.30
HEB040049EN Shield of Knowledge, Tetra Vibrion U	.20	.30
HEB040050EN Final Battle Ground, Vigrior U	.20	.30
HEB040051EN Death Ruler, Gallows SD U	.20	.30
HEB040052EN Absolute Attack U	6.00	10.00
HEB040053EN Death Hiding U	.20	.30
HEB040054EN Nameless Assassin U	.20	.30
HEB040055EN The Man Who Answers for Justice! U	.20	.30
HEB040056EN Stop Right There! U	.20	.30
HEB040057EN All Deus, Stellmion U	.20	.30
HEB040058EN Dragonarms, Nanobreak U	.20	.30
HEB040059EN Arms Reboot U	.20	.30
HEB040060EN Hundred Demons Sorcery, Raijogeki U	.20	.30
HEB040061EN Jackknife, "Drum Bunker" BR		
HEB040062EN Fifth Omni Cavalry Dragon, Light Rim Alliot RRR	1.00	1.50
HEB040063EN Commandant of Enma Alliance, Burn Nova RRR	2.00	3.00
HEB040064EN Jackknife, Superior Plasma (blue) RRR	6.00	10.00
HEB040064EN Jackknife, Superior Plasma (red) RRR	2.00	3.00
HEB040065EN Fifth Omni Armored Dragon, Furious Iron Kongo RR	.40	.60
HEB040066EN Fifth Omni Dragon Lord, Crimson Drum RR	.50	.75
HEB040067EN An Encounter with a Dragon RR	1.50	2.50
HEB040068EN Divine Dragon Creation RR	2.50	4.00
HEB040069EN Dragonarms, Radiant Alma RR	.40	.60
HEB040070EN Cosmo Saber, Gold Ritter RR	1.50	2.50
HEB040071EN Fifth Omni Armored Dragon, Mountain Crush Gon R	.25	.40
HEB040072EN Fifth Omni Divine Arts, Giga Howling Phantom! R	.25	.40
HEB040073EN Enma Alliance, Regenthorn R	.25	.40
HEB040074EN Charging Head-first Ricky R	.60	1.00
HEB040075EN Dragon Emperor Legend R	2.50	4.00
HEB040076EN Disposition of the Chief R	1.50	2.50
HEB040077EN Our Friendship Will Never Perish! R	.25	.40
HEB040078EN Dragonarms, Garbel Anchor R	.25	.40
HEB040079EN Fifth Omni Armored Dragon, Thousand Dachis Yoko U	.20	.30
HEB040080EN Fifth Omni Armored Dragon, Thunder Blade Kokuyo U	.20	.30
HEB040081EN Fifth Omni Armored Dragon, Holy Scripture Hisui U	.20	.30
HEB040082EN Dragodesperate U	.20	.30
HEB040083EN Dragorevival U	.20	.30
HEB040084EN Fifth Omni Dragon Fist, Roaring Fire U	.20	.30
HEB040085EN Hungry Wolf Dragon Emperor, Edgeknuckle U	.20	.30
HEB040086EN Enma Alliance, Jetcowl U	.20	.30
HEB040087EN Enma Alliance, Onizorihead U	.20	.30
HEB040088EN Enma Alliance, Killmainte U	.20	.30
HEB040089EN Enma Alliance, Cutbilly U	.20	.30
HEB040090EN Dragon Kid, Giry U	.20	.30
HEB040091EN Surges and Dragons of Life U	.20	.30
HEB040092EN Radiate Burst, Gamma Radius U	.20	.30
HEB040093EN Fix Star, Athtress U	.20	.30
HEB040094EN Clustar, Magma Ocean U	.20	.30
HEB040095EN Dragonarms, Charger U	.20	.30
HEB040096EN Dustring, Mini Spiral U	.20	.30
HEB040097EN Brown Dwarf, Crewgar U	.20	.30
HEB040098EN Dragonarms, Edge Shooter U	.20	.30
HEB040099EN Space Building, Bulge U	.20	.30
HEB040100EN Space Elevator U	.20	.30
HEB040101EN Terraforming U	.20	.30
HEB040102EN Star Hand, Arms Controller U	.20	.30
HEB040103EN The Radiant Guardians! U	.20	.30
NNO Dragon World SCR		
NNO Dungeon World SCR		
NNO Darkness Dragon World SCR		
NNO Star Dragon World SCR		
NNO Dragon Ein SCR		

2018 Future Card Buddyfight S Ultimate Booster Set 1 Superhero Wars Omega Advent of Cosmoman

RELEASED ON SEPTEMBER 14, 2018

Card	Low	High
SUB010001 Satsuki Operated Convertible Outframe, Hazakura RRR	.30	.50
SUB010002 Galaxy Exalt, Cosmoman RRR	10.00	15.00
SUB010003 Friendship Combi, I-Borg RRR	6.00	10.00
SUB010004 Zeroth Style Gale, Azure Skies Mayuzumi Fubuki RRR	6.00	10.00
SUB010005 Martian UFO Transformation, Takokichi Omega RRR	5.00	8.00
SUB010006 It's Superhero Time!! RRR	40.00	60.00
SUB010007 Super T-Titan, Sky3 RR	.40	.60
SUB010008 Galaxy Exalt, Cosmonine RR	.50	.75
SUB010009 Fourth Style Whirlwind, Clear Skies Sakanagi Kaname RR	5.00	8.00
SUB010010 Heavy Spider RR	.25	.40
SUB010011 Cosmo Falcon No.2 RR	.40	.60
SUB010012 First Style Coldwind, Snow Skies Ilona Gulayev RR	1.25	2.00
SUB010013 Battle Building! Online! RR	.60	1.00
SUB010014 Infonet Operation RR	2.50	4.00
SUB010015 Cosmo Barrier! RR	.40	.60
SUB010016 Build Combination! RR	.40	.60
SUB010017 Buddy Academy Hostel RR	.50	.75
SUB010018 Mobile Armored Shield, "Asanagi" RR	2.50	4.00
SUB010019 Omen Chronicles, Big Cy-Bird R	.20	.30
SUB010020 Galaxy Exalt, Cosmoman Draco R	.20	.30
SUB010021 Simul Lock-on, G-Gold Pav & S-Silver Pav R	.25	.40
SUB010022 Imperial Fleet Operated, Quing Lada III R	.20	.30
SUB010023 Hydro Mariner R	.20	.30
SUB010024 First Style Tempest, Blue Skies Ichijo Haruka R	.50	.75
SUB010025 Seventh Style Heatwind, Fiery Skies Oba Kagari R	.60	1.00
SUB010026 Galaxy Defense Team Alpha R	.20	.30
SUB010027 This is the Key of Justice! R	.20	.30
SUB010028 Two-man Team R	.20	.30
SUB010029 Hyper Energy R	1.25	2.00
SUB010030 Galaxy Defense Team will not go down without a fight! R	.20	.30
SUB010031 Fluegel Shield R	.25	.40
SUB010032 Super T Skytower R	.25	.40
SUB010033 Super T Dynamicyte R	.20	.30
SUB010034 Feather Blade, "MAT-I" R	.30	.50
SUB010035 Astium Photon Wave! R	.40	.60
SUB010036 Turbulence Vanish R	.40	.60
SUB010037 MST, Mack Harry Messer U	.12	.20
SUB010038 Majestic Deity, Grand Hallder U	.12	.20
SUB010039 Horizon Fire U	.12	.20
SUB010040 Cosmo Falcon No.3 U	.12	.20
SUB010041 Third Style Northwind?, Dusk Clouds Mano Yukari U	.40	.60
SUB010042 Cosmo Falcon No.1 U	.12	.20
SUB010043 Shadow Hero, Zuilupin U	.12	.20
SUB010044 Drill Rhinos U	.12	.20
SUB010045 Galaxy Defense Team Resupply Vessel No.1, Tsugami U	.12	.20
SUB010046 Third Style Southwind, Thin Clouds Nanami Lisa U	.25	.40
SUB010047 Galaxy Defense Team Far East Base U	.12	.20
SUB010048 Cosmoflasher U	.12	.20
SUB010049 Life As an Aircraft Mechanic U	.12	.20
SUB010050 Azure Skies Descend U	.12	.20
SUB010051 Futile!! U	.12	.20
SUB010052 Golden Pavilion, Silver Pavilion U	.12	.20
SUB010053 Super World Grand Hall U	.12	.20
SUB010054 McOcean Messe U	.12	.20
SUB010055 White Cloth Rosen, Frill Rose U	.12	.20
SUB010056 Cardian Secret Base U	.12	.20
SUB010057 Type II Sniping Rifle, "Shooting Star" U	.12	.20
SUB010058 Feather Rifle, "Wetter" U	.12	.20
SUB010059 Power of Justice, Build Power Extension! U	.12	.20
SUB010060 Light Darkness Demon, Phobos Apeiron U	.12	.20
SUB01BR01 Galaxy Exalt, Cosmoman BR	20.00	30.00
SUB01BR02 Martian UFO Transformation, Takokichi Omega BR	20.00	30.00
SUB01S001 Satsuki Operated Convertible Outframe, Hazakura SP	75.00	125.00
SUB01S002 Zeroth Style Gale, Azure Skies Mayuzumi Fubuki SP	125.00	200.00
SUB01S003 Hero World SP	75.00	125.00
SUB01S004 Hero World SP	75.00	125.00
SUB01SS001 Galaxy Exalt, Cosmoman PR	50.00	75.00
SUB01SS002 Martian UFO Transformation, Takokichi Omega PR	60.00	100.00

2018 Future Card Buddyfight S Ultimate Booster Set 2 Miracle Fighters Miko and Mel

RELEASED ON SEPTEMBER 14, 2018

Card	Low	High
SUB020001 Unruly Electrodeity, Susanoo RRR	6.00	10.00
SUB020002 Electrodeity of Light, Amaterasu RRR	15.00	25.00
SUB020003 Guardian Electrobeast, Goryou RRR	10.00	15.00
SUB020004 Red Riding Hood, Emma RRR	15.00	25.00
SUB020005 Hexen Ceremony RRR	10.00	15.00
SUB020006 Miracle Fighters RRR	15.00	25.00
SUB020007 Electrodeity of Water, Mizuhanome RR	.60	1.00
SUB020008 Electrobeast Emissary, Shuto RR	.50	.75
SUB020009 Ritual, Harvest Prayer RR	.60	1.00
SUB020010 Electrodeity Festival RR	1.00	1.50
SUB020011 Celestial Arts, Returning Water RR	2.50	4.00
SUB020012 Kagura-bell of Worship RR	1.50	2.50
SUB020013 Illusions Dragon, Red-cape Dragon RR	.75	1.25
SUB020014 Illusions Dragon, Thorns Dragon RR	.60	1.00
SUB020015 Blood Lance Doyenne, Lady Wallachia RR	.50	.75
SUB020016 White Snow Princess, Christa RR	1.00	1.50
SUB020017 Grimm Asche RR	.50	.75
SUB020018 Illusions Folktale, Echt Biblio RR	1.25	2.00
SUB020019 Electrodeity of Wind, Amatsuhikone R	.20	.30
SUB020020 Guardian Electrobeast, Mizuchi R	.20	.30
SUB020021 Guardian Electrobeast, Komaji R	.30	.50
SUB020022 Electrobeast Emissary, Otora R	.50	.75
SUB020023 Electrodeity Return R	.20	.30
SUB020024 Kagura, Electrodeity Welcome R	.20	.30
SUB020025 Ceremonial, Fire Mirror R	.20	.30
SUB020026 Comeback Electrodeity, Bright Future R	.20	.30
SUB020027 Illusions Dragon, Snow White Dragon R	.20	.30
SUB020028 Demon Lord, Nil Genia R	.20	.30
SUB020029 Hunter, Jordan R	.20	.30
SUB020030 Sleeping Princess, Stef R	.25	.40
SUB020031 Illusions Tea Time R	.40	.60
SUB020032 Deadly Serious Teufel R	.50	.75
SUB020033 Red Cape Brulee! R	.25	.40
SUB020034 Throw Throw Swallow R	.20	.30
SUB020035 Delusions Running Amok!? R	.20	.30
SUB020036 Marchen Decoration! R	.20	.30
SUB020037 Guardian Electrobeast, Inamaro U	.12	.20
SUB020038 Clean-up Ninja, Kunoichi Saori U	.12	.20
SUB020039 Guardian Electrobeast, Kiun U	.12	.20
SUB020040 Guardian Electrobeast, Komaichi U	.12	.20
SUB020041 Shutting Out the World, Yoroinezumi U	.12	.20
SUB020042 Guardian Electrobeast, Hakuro U	.12	.20
SUB020043 Wind Arc Deity, Uzu-ikazuchi U	.12	.20
SUB020044 Ceremonial, Worded Breath U	.12	.20
SUB020045 Ceremonial, Water Mirror U	.12	.20
SUB020046 Ceremonial, Winged Arrows U	.12	.20
SUB020047 Ceremonial, Execution of Divine Punishment U	.12	.20
SUB020048 Underhanded Means, Live Another Day U	.12	.20
SUB020049 Electrodeity City Center, Takamagahara U	.12	.20
SUB020050 Ideal Prinz U	.12	.20
SUB020051 Man-eating Wolf, Wolff U	.12	.20
SUB020052 Schwarz Hexen U	.12	.20
SUB020053 The Twelfth Witch U	.12	.20
SUB020054 Sister Guiltina U	.12	.20
SUB020055 Seven Dwarves U	.12	.20
SUB020056 Magic Mirror U	.12	.20
SUB020057 Tempting Tanzer U	.12	.20
SUB020058 Insanity Chevre U	.12	.20
SUB020059 Drain Trap U	.12	.20
SUB020060 Wonder Princess! U	.12	.20
SUB02BR01 Electrodeity of Light, Amaterasu BR	40.00	60.00
SUB02BR02 Red Riding Hood, Ema BR	30.00	50.00
SUB02S001 Kagura-bell of Worship SP	125.00	200.00
SUB02S002 Illusions Folktale, Echt Biblio SP	75.00	125.00
SUB02S003 Katana World SP	150.00	250.00
SUB02S004 Dungeon World SP	100.00	150.00
SUB02SS001 Electrodeity of Light, Amaterasu PR	100.00	150.00
SUB02SS002 Red Riding Hood, Ema PR	100.00	150.00

2014 Future Card Buddyfight Character Pack 1 Burning Valor

RELEASED ON MARCH 14, 2014

Card	Low	High
CP010001 Purgatory Knights, Death Sickle Dragon RRR	1.00	1.50
CP010002 Dragon Knight, Geronimo RRR	.50	.75
CP010003 Jackknife Aggressor RRR	3.00	5.00
CP010004 Thunder Knights, Halberd Dragon RRR	4.00	6.00
CP010005 Dragon Knight, Nobunaga RRR	1.50	2.50
CP010006 Dragon Fist Mystery, Dragonic Kaiser Nova RRR	.60	1.00
CP010007 Inferno Armor Dragon RR	.60	1.00
CP010008 Super Armordragon, Aura Sword Dragon RR	1.00	1.50
CP010009 Dragon Knight, Kamitsumiyaou RR	.20	.30
CP010010 Jackknife Thunder Storm RR	.60	1.00
CP010011 Dragon Knight, Iwamoto RR	.20	.30
CP010012 Dragon Knight, El Quixote RR	1.00	1.50
CP010013 Twin Dragonblades, Dragoanthem RR	.20	.30
CP010014 Dragon Knight Mystery, Ultimate Smash RR	.60	1.00
CP010015 Dragon Knight, Hammurabi the Great R	.15	.25
CP010016 Jackknife Dragon R	.60	1.00
CP010017 Drum Bunker Dragon R	1.00	1.50
CP010018 Dragon Knight, Rudel R	.15	.25
CP010019 Dragon Knight, Wyatt Earp R	.15	.25
CP010020 Dragon Knight, Red Baron R	.50	.75
CP010021 Dragonic Formation R	.40	.60
CP010022 Dragon Crush R	.15	.25
CP010023 Green Dragon Shield R	1.00	1.50
CP010024 Cavalry Academy R	.30	.50
CP010025 Damascus Armor Dragon C	.10	.15
CP010026 Firerod Dragon C	.10	.15
CP010027 Hammer Mace Dragon C	.10	.15
CP010028 Katzvalker Drake C	.10	.15
CP010029 Double Sword Dragon C	.10	.15
CP010030 Dragon Knight, Liechtenauer C	.10	.15
CP010031 Dragon Knight, Jeanne d'Arc C	.10	.15
CP010032 Dragon Knight, Masamune C	.10	.15
CP010033 Blade Wing Dragon C	1.00	1.50
CP010034 Bronze Shield Dragon C	.10	.15
CP010035 Death Rattle Dragon C	.10	.15
CP010036 Super Slash, Dragothrasher C	.10	.15
CP010037 Dragonic Thunder C	.40	.60
CP010038 Dragon Breath C	.10	.15
CP010039 Astral Force C	.10	.15
CP010040 Wrath of Dragon C	.10	.15
CP010041 Dragoenergy C	.10	.15
CP010042 Red Dragon Knights Burning Devastation Song C	.50	.75
CP010043 Blue Dragon Knights Proud Soul Song C	.10	.15
CP010044 Dragonblade, Dragofearless C	2.50	6.00
CP010045 Jackknife Diaspash RR	5.00	8.00
CPS010001 Purgatory Knights, Death Sickle Dragon SP	8.00	12.00
CPS010002 Dragon Knight, Geronimo SP	6.00	10.00
CPS010003 Jackknife Aggressor SP	5.00	8.00
CPS010004 Thunder Knights, Halberd Dragon SP	20.00	30.00
CPS010006 Dragon Fist Mystery, Dragonic Kaiser Nova SP	6.00	10.00
CPS010012 Dragon Knight, El Quixote SP	10.00	15.00

2014 Future Card Buddyfight Introductory Set 1 Dragon World

Card	Low	High
IS010001EN Gigant Sword Dragon	.15	.25
IS010002EN Extreme Sword Dragon	.15	.25
IS010003EN Steel Gauntlet Dragon	.15	.25
IS010004EN Thousand Rapier Dragon	.15	.25
IS010005EN Bear-Trap Fang Dragon	.15	.25
IS010006EN Systemic Dagger Dragon	.15	.25
IS010007EN Latale Shield Dragon	.15	.25
IS010008EN Dragonic Heal	.15	.25
IS010009EN Dragon Breath	.15	.25
IS010010EN Dragonic Shoot	.15	.25
IS010011EN Green Dragon Shield	.15	.25
IS010012EN Dragonblade, Dragobrave	.15	.25
IS010013EN Dragonblade, Dragofearless	.15	.25
IS010014EN Reckless Angerrrr!!	.15	.25
IS010015EN Dragon World	.15	.25

2015 Future Card Buddyfight Perfect Pack 1 Golden Buddy Pack Ver. E

RELEASED ON MARCH 6, 2015

Card	Low	High
PP010001 Skyblue Dragon, Crystal Saber RR	.40	.60
PP010002 Drop Arms Dragon RR	.10	.15
PP010003 Colichemarde Dragon RR	.10	.15
PP010004 Dragon Knight, Sanosuke RR	.10	.15
PP010005 Dragon Knight, Selim RR	.10	.15
PP010006 Disturb Hand Dragon RR	5.00	8.00
PP010007 Heavy-Armor Dragon RR	.10	.15
PP010008 Dragon Knight, Slayman RR	.10	.15
PP010009 Armorknight Lethal Drake RR	.60	1.00
PP010010 Wasp Blast Dragon, Gigabeera RR	.10	.15
PP010011 Skeleton Armored Dragon, Medrogirus RR	.60	1.00
PP010012 Armorknight Eagle A RR	1.25	2.00
PP010013 Demon Realm Knights Leader, Sabnac RR	.10	.15
PP010014 Chain Magic Master, Link RR	.10	.15
PP010015 Reminiscing the Homeland Marcosius RR	.10	.15
PP010016 Magic Power Researcher, Ren Kogasaki RR	.10	.15
PP010017 Breakthrough Ninja, Rasenmaru RR	.10	.15
PP010018 Defiant, Sabifukuro RR	.10	.15
PP010019 Agent Ninja, Mamiya RR	.10	.15
PP010020 Moss Wall, Fudogame RR	.10	.15
PP010021 Ghoul Dragon Emperor, Adil Diablos RR	1.25	2.00
PP010022 Emerald Dragon Emperor, Jedaflight RR	.10	.15
PP010023 Seek Dragon Emperor, Azludea RR	.10	.15
PP010024 Sky Dragon, Japerrot RR	.10	.15
PP010025 Guardian Dragon of Demon Lord Castle, Deukruzar RR	.10	.15
PP010026 Wandering Salaryman Buddyfighter, Amigo?Takata RR	.10	.15
PP010027 Young Pope, Alex RR	.10	.15
PP010028 One Gauge Demon RR	.50	.75
PP010029 First Tribulation, Gold Lion of Nemea RR	.10	.15
PP010030 Glacier Dragon, Zilant RR	.10	.15
PP010031 Panther Robed Knight, Tariel RR	.10	.15
PP010032 Valkyrie, Omniscience Alvidol RR	1.50	2.50
PP010033 Graveyard of Demonic Swords, Graybard RR	.30	.50
PP010034 Eternal Silence, Orbit RR	.10	.15
PP010035 Extreme Prison, Zwinger RR	.30	.50
PP010036 Infectious Malevolence, Yuberium RR	.10	.15
PP010037 Death Ruler, Manifile RR	.10	.15
PP010038 Death Ruler, Galkheight RR	.10	.15
PP010039 Purgatory Knights, Eval Grebe Dragon RR	2.50	4.00
PP010040 Purgatory Knights, Lunacy Wand Dragon RR	.40	.60
PP010041 Jackknife Aggressor BR	25.00	40.00

PP010042 Drum Bunker Dragon BR 20.00 30.00
PP010043 Dragon Knight, El Quixote BR 20.00 30.00
PP010044 Armorknight Demon BR 30.00 50.00
PP010045 Fighting Dragon, Demongodol BR 15.00 25.00
PP010046 Center of the World, Mary Sue BR 25.00 40.00
PP010047 Demon Lord, Asmodai BR 25.00 40.00
PP010048 Nanomachine Ninja, Tsukikage BR 25.00 40.00
PP010049 Evil in Heart, Yamigitsune BR 25.00 40.00
PP010050 Duel Sieger Tempest Enforcer BR 25.00 40.00
PP010051 Duel Sieger Spartand BR 25.00 40.00
PP010052 Bladewing Phoenix BR 25.00 40.00
PP010053 Legendary Brave, Tasuku BR 15.00 25.00
PP010054 Immortal Sword, Durandal BR 20.00 30.00
PP010055 Wind Fairy, Sylph BR 20.00 30.00
PP010056 Demonic Demise Dragon, Azi Dahaka BR 25.00 40.00
PP010057 Death Ruler, Gallows BR 25.00 40.00
PP010058 Captain Answer BR 60.00 100.00
PP010059 Drum Bunker Dragon, Dual Wield RR .50 .75
PP010060 Boomerang Dragon RR .60 1.00
PP010061 Ice Blade Astralkus RR 2.50 4.00
PP010062 Stallion of the Divine King, Sleipnir RR .40 .60

2016 Future Card Buddyfight D Special Series 3 Golden Buddy Champion Box

RELEASED ON DECEMBER 3, 2016
DSS030001 Great Sun Dragon, Bal Dragon BR .75 1.25
DSS030001 Great Sun Dragon, Bal Dragon C 2.00 3.00
DSS030002 Champion the Sungreat C .10 .15
DSS030003 Double Knee Flare Dragon C .30 .50
DSS030004 Mera Driver Dragon C .40 .60
DSS030005 Tail Blazer Dragon C .10 .15
DSS030006 Prominence Dragon C .10 .15
DSS030007 Awaken! Bal Dragon C 1.00 1.50
DSS030008 Jet Dragon Jr. C .10 .15
DSS030009 Bal Rescue C 1.25 2.00
DSS030010 Dragon Force Cancel C 1.25 2.00
DSS030011 Sunshine Rush C .10 .15
DSS030012 Sun Dragon Shield RRR
DSS030012 Sun Dragon Shield C 1.00 1.50
DSS030013 Blue Dragon Shield C 1.00 1.50
DSS030014 Dragobond C 1.00 1.50
DSS030015 Dragon Force, "Style of the Straight Fist" RRR
DSS030015 Dragon Force, "Style of the Straight Fist" C 2.50 4.00
DSS030016 Sun Sword, Balsword C .10 .15
DSS030017 Sun Fist, Jet Knuckle C .10 .15
DSS030018 Bal Dragon, "Bal Weapon Combination!" RRR
DSS030018 Bal Dragon, "Bal Weapon Combination!" C 1.00 1.50
DSS030019 Dragon World C 1.25 2.00
DSS030020 Revolutionary Zetta BR 1.25 2.00
DSS030020 Revolutionary Zetta C .10 .15
DSS030021 Fake Lord, Riddle Phantom C .60 1.00
DSS030022 Fake Black, Abygale C 2.00 3.00
DSS030023 Fake the Sun, Bal Dragon C .10 .15
DSS030024 Fake Dragoner, Jackknife C .30 .50
DSS030025 Fake Knight, Legion C .20 .30
DSS030026 Flame Demon, Elytron C 1.25 2.00
DSS030027 Water Demon, Kynoeides C 2.00 3.00
DSS030028 Fake Replica Weapon, Gemclone RRR
DSS030028 Fake Replica Weapon, Gemclone C .60 1.00
DSS030029 Gemclone "Variable Bit" C 2.00 3.00
DSS030030 Artificial Talisman: FIND JOKER RRR
DSS030030 Artificial Talisman: FIND JOKER C .60 1.00
DSS030031 Hyper Energy C 2.00 3.00
DSS030032 It's About Time I Got Serious! C .60 1.00
DSS030033 Artificial Talisman: THREE GAUGE C 1.25 2.00
DSS030034 Artificial Talisman: TWO DRAW RRR
DSS030034 Artificial Talisman: TWO DRAW C 2.50 4.00
DSS030035 Armor Talisman: FINISH ROAD C 1.00 1.50
DSS030036 Armor Talisman: ZERO DAMAGE C 1.00 1.50
DSS030037 I've Seen Through Your Moves! C .60 1.00
DSS030038 Hero World C 2.00 3.00
DSS030039 Destruction Deity of the Old World, Azi Dahaka BR .40 .60
DSS030039 Destruction Deity of the Old World, Azi Dahaka C .60 1.00
DSS030040 Lord of Purgatory Demise, Last Emperor RRR
DSS030040 Lord of Purgatory Demise, Last Emperor C .10 .15
DSS030041 Demise Star Dragon, Big Crunch C .10 .15
DSS030042 Retainer of the Demonic Dragon, Jilnitra C .30 .50
DSS030043 Retainer of the Demonic Dragon, Sinblade Dragon C .75 1.25
DSS030044 Retainer of the Demonic Dragon, Arhat Narhat RRR
DSS030044 Retainer of the Demonic Dragon, Arhat Narhat C .10 .15
DSS030045 Retainer of the Demonic Dragon, Einst C 1.25 2.00
DSS030046 Retainer of the Demonic Dragon, Masked Dragon C .30 .50
DSS030047 Retainer of the Demonic Dragon, Fallen Wing Dragon RRR
DSS030047 Retainer of the Demonic Dragon, Fallen Wing Dragon C .10 .15
DSS030048 Ice Dragon Emperor, Glacies C 1.00 1.50
DSS030049 Retainer of the Demonic Dragon, Hadron C .75 1.25
DSS030050 Retainer of the Demonic Dragon, Girielka C 3.00 5.00
DSS030051 Retainer of the Demonic Dragon, Resurrected Dragon Bones C 6.00 10.00
DSS030052 Retainer of the Demonic Dragon, Geodol C 1.25 2.00
DSS030053 Retainer of the Demonic Dragon, Arakaze C .10 .15
DSS030054 Retainer of the Demonic Dragon, Vong C .60 1.00
DSS030055 Retainer of the Demonic Dragon, Curse Dragon Jr. C 3.00 5.00
DSS030056 Retainer of the Demonic Dragon, Varion C .10 .15
DSS030057 Dragon Zwei C 1.25 2.00

2018 Future Card Buddyfight S Special Series 1 Lost Dimension

RELEASED ON OCTOBER 5, 2018
SSS010001 Dimension Dragon, Laimargia C .10 .15
SSS010002 Dimension Dragon, Apostro C .10 .15
SSS010003 Dimension Dragon, Aplistos C .10 .15
SSS010004 Dimension Dragon, Paidia C .10 .15
SSS010005 Dimension Dragon, Chrimata C .15 .25
SSS010006 Dimension Dragon, Oleksiy C .10 .15
SSS010007 Dimension Dragon, Aschimos C .10 .15
SSS010008 Lost of D. C .50 .75
SSS010009 Dragonic Charge, "Plus" C 1.50 2.50
SSS010010 Demon Lord's Roaring Dragon Blast C .50 .75
SSS010011 D. Death Struggle C .25 .40
SSS010012 Blue Dragon Shield C .40 .60
SSS010013 Green Dragon Shield C .25 .40
SSS010014 Dragotrap C 1.50 2.50
SSS010015 Dimension Spirit Gun, Krachea C .10 .15
SSS010016 Lost World (card) C .75 1.25
SSS010017 Dragon World (card) C .10 .15
SSS010018 Whistle Fedwal Ugaine C .10 .15
SSS010019 Hannel Kant Dauf C .10 .15
SSS010020 Demonic Dragon Release, Vanity Husk Destroyer RRR 1.00 1.50
SSS010020 Demonic Dragon Release, Vanity Husk Destroyer C .10 .15
SSS010021 Zorune Zorken C .10 .15
SSS010022 Arlpow Peyduwallr C 2.50 4.00
SSS010023 Deugaine Zascyth C 1.00 1.50
SSS010024 Dimension Lifestream C 2.50 4.00
SSS010024 Dimension Lifestream RRR 50.00 75.00
SSS010025 Dimension Revive C 1.00 1.50
SSS010026 Dimension Mirror C 1.00 1.50
SSS010027 Dimension Jamming C 3.00 5.00
SSS010027 Dimension Jamming RRR 40.00 60.00
SSS010028 Dimension Revenge C .25 .40
SSS010029 Dimension Shadowgate C .25 .40
SSS010030 Vile Demonic Cannon, Lostless Maser C .20 .30
SSS010031 Carnage Destroy Blaster!! C .40 .60

2018 Future Card Buddyfight S Special Series 2 Three Garga Decks Impact Triple Punisher

RELEASED ON DECEMBER 7, 2018
SSS020001 Gargantua Dragon C .10 .15
SSS020002 Daybreak Roar, Gargantua Dragon RRR
SSS020002 Daybreak Roar, Gargantua Dragon C .10 .15
SSS020003 Gargantua Dragon, "Tempest Mode" BR
SSS020003 Gargantua Dragon, "Tempest Mode" C .10 .15
SSS020004 Gargantua Dragon, "Return Mode" RRR
SSS020004 Gargantua Dragon, "Return Mode" C .10 .15
SSS020005 Sturm Gardragon C .10 .15
SSS020006 Gale Garda C .10 .15
SSS020007 Taiyaki Is the Best! Garcat C .10 .15
SSS020008 Gardog In the Sunlight Forest C .10 .15
SSS020009 Garbird Taking It Easy C .10 .15
SSS020010 Garostrich C .10 .15
SSS020011 Gar-Run-Up C .10 .15
SSS020012 Gar-High Ring C .10 .15
SSS020013 Gar-Segen C .10 .15
SSS020014 Fighting Emperor Dragon Shield C .10 .15
SSS020015 Deity Green Dragon Shield C .10 .15
SSS020016 Deity Dragon Twin Swords, Gar-Anthem C .10 .15
SSS020017 Deity Dragon Sword, Gar-Cutlass C .10 .15
SSS020018 Deity Gargantua Punisher!! (Dragon World) SP
SSS020019 Gargablade Blast!! C .10 .15
SSS020020 Dragon World C .10 .15
SSS020021 Gargantua Jiraiya Dragon BR
SSS020021 Gargantua Jiraiya Dragon C
SSS020022 Gargantua Kirigakure Dragon C
SSS020022 Gargantua Kirigakure Dragon RRR
SSS020023 Knives Ninja Technique, Ninbird C
SSS020024 Flash of Momiji, Nincat C
SSS020025 Battle Dog Under the Moon, Nindog C
SSS020026 Deity Dragon Ninja, Musashi C
SSS020027 Deity Dragon Low-Rank Ninja, Kogarashimaru C
SSS020028 Deity Dragon Low-Rank Ninja, Karakazemaru C
SSS020029 Fuuton, Sweeping Whirlwind C
SSS020030 Ninja Arts, Hiding in Fallen Leaves C
SSS020031 Deity Dragon Fuuton, Gale Blade C
SSS020032 Combat Rations -Gar-Rice- C
SSS020033 Deity Dragon Doton, Cliff-Splitting Wall C
SSS020034 Deity Dragon Wristguard, Gar-Claw C
SSS020035 Deity Dragon Kodachi, Gar-Tsubaki C
SSS020036 Deity Gargantua Punisher!! (Katana World) SP
SSS020037 Deity Dragon Ninja Arts, Multiblade Whirlwind C
SSS020038 Katana World C
SSS020039 Gargantua Flare Mage BR
SSS020039 Gargantua Flare Mage C
SSS020040 Sorcery Deity Dragon, Beelboros C
SSS020041 Gargantua Ice Mage C
SSS020041 Gargantua Ice Mage RRR
SSS020042 Magicat, "Heat Magic" C
SSS020043 Transmitter Magic, Magidog C
SSS020044 Synthesis Failed! Magibird C
SSS020045 Sorcery Deity Dragon, Vansage C
SSS020046 Oulu Owl C
SSS020047 Nice one! C
SSS020048 Teachings of Fighting Emperor C
SSS020049 Godmagic, TioForti C
SSS020050 Warrior C
SSS020051 Protect Magic C
SSS020052 Great Spell Circle of Deity Dragon C
SSS020053 Deity Dragon Sword Cane, Gar-Courage C
SSS020054 Deity Gargantua Punisher!! (Magic World) SP
SSS020055 Spiral Ur Ignis C
SSS020056 Magic World C

2017 Future Card Buddyfight X Special Series 4 X Duel Chest

RELEASED ON DECEMBER 8, 2017
XSS040001 Barbatzz the Lightning BR
XSS040001 Barbatzz the Lightning R .20 .30
XSS040001 Barbatzz the Lightning C .10 .15
XSS040002 Overturn Chief, Duel Jaeger R .20 .30
XSS040002 Overturn Chief, Duel Jaeger C .10 .15
XSS040003 Arc Deity Dragon Lord, Duel Sieger C .10 .15
XSS040004 Black Wings of Thunder Emperor, Abygale R .20 .30
XSS040004 Black Wings of Thunder Emperor, Abygale C .10 .15
XSS040005 Arc Crystal Dragon, Athora R .20 .30
XSS040005 Arc Crystal Dragon, Athora C .10 .15
XSS040006 Lone Wing of Thunder Knights, Thunder Halberd R .20 .30
XSS040006 Lone Wing of Thunder Knights, Thunder Halberd C .10 .15
XSS040007 Thunder Emperor's Chum, Saint Holy Sword Dragon R .20 .30
XSS040007 Thunder Emperor's Chum, Saint Holy Sword Dragon C .10 .15
XSS040008 Meravolt Dragon C .10 .15
XSS040009 An Unexpected Helper, Takosuke C .10 .15
XSS040010 Clashing Arc Dragon, Gaelcorga C .10 .15
XSS040011 Zappy Ninja, Denkuro C .10 .15
XSS040012 Arc Hammer Knight, Brontes C .10 .15
XSS040013 Storm Summoning Fullfool C .10 .15
XSS040014 Thunder X Tri-Guard C .10 .15
XSS040015 Loud Voice C .10 .15
XSS040016 Secret Dragon Life Exhalation C .10 .15
XSS040017 Thunder X Goodbye! C .10 .15
XSS040018 Batzz Stone, Thunder Emperor's Augite R .20 .30
XSS040018 Batzz Stone, Thunder Emperor's Augite C .10 .15
XSS040019 Overpowering Arc Dragons R .20 .30
XSS040019 Overpowering Arc Dragons C .10 .15
XSS040020 The Fighters' Oath C .10 .15
XSS040021 Black Arc Splints C .10 .15
XSS040022 Thunder Pike, Vajra Demon Slay C .10 .15
XSS040023 Thunderstroke, Keranols C .10 .15
XSS040024 Turbulent Thunder Sword, Rupture X Tempest Slash! R .20 .30
XSS040024 Turbulent Thunder Sword, Rupture X Tempest Slash! C .10 .15
XSS040025 Thunder Emperor's Fangs C .10 .15
XSS040026 Proto Deleter, Geargod ver.088 BR
XSS040026 Proto Deleter, Geargod ver.088 R
XSS040026 Proto Deleter, Geargod ver.088 C
XSS040027 CHAOS Breastcorona C
XSS040028 CHAOS Gilquine C
XSS040028 CHAOS Gilquine R
XSS040029 Oniseer of Autodeity, CHAOS Ibuki C
XSS040029 Oniseer of Autodeity, CHAOS Ibuki R
XSS040030 CHAOS Death Tallica C
XSS040030 CHAOS Death Tallica R
XSS040031 CHAOS Jesterra C
XSS040032 CHAOS Champion Lord C
XSS040033 CHAOS Deathgaze C
XSS040034 Sentry of Autodeity, CHAOS Dra-gollum C
XSS040034 Sentry of Autodeity, CHAOS Dra-gollum R
XSS040035 CHAOS Stregia C
XSS040036 Ladis the CHAOS C
XSS040037 CHAOS Kalvados C
XSS040038 CHAOS Zodiac C
XSS040038 CHAOS Zodiac R
XSS040039 CHAOS Orser Kleinz C
XSS040040 CHAOS Mach Braver C
XSS040041 Chaos Wall, Healing Barrier C
XSS040041 Chaos Wall, Healing Barrier R
XSS040042 Externally Controlled Chaos Guided Missile C
XSS040043 Forced Summoning: Shalsana C
XSS040044 Population Reduction C
XSS040045 Chaotic Pain C
XSS040046 All According To My Volition C
XSS040047 Watchsword of Autodeity, CHAOS Laevateinn C
XSS040047 Watchsword of Autodeity, CHAOS Laevateinn R
XSS040048 Chaos Shooter C
XSS040049 Directive Code: Forced Reboot C
XSS040049 Directive Code: Forced Reboot R
XSS040050 the Chaos C

2015 Future Card Buddyfight D Start Deck 1 Scorching Sun Dragon

RELEASED ON MARCH 4, 2016
DSD010001 Scorching Sun Dragon, Blazing Sun C .50 .75
DSD010002 Giant Flare Dragon C .25 .40
DSD010003 Shine Claymore Dragon C .15 .25
DSD010004 Messer Groote Dragon C .20 .30
DSD010005 Mera Blade Dragon C .60 1.00
DSD010006 Vivid Flash Dragon C .30 .50
DSD010007 Light Shield Dragon C .15 .25
DSD010008 Bright Hammer Dragon C .15 .25
DSD010009 Hot Dragon Junior C .15 .25
DSD010010 Dragonic Grimoire C .75 1.25
DSD010011 Touch of the Sun C .75 1.25
DSD010012 Shine Energy C .15 .25
DSD010013 Green Dragon Shield C .25 .40
DSD010014 Sun Dragon Shield C .40 .60
DSD010015 Sun Fist, Rising Knuckle C .15 .25
DSD010016 Sun Sword, Daylight C .15 .25
DSD010017 Bal Dragon Bal Grand Strike! C .40 .60
DSD010018 Dragon World C .30 .50

2015 Future Card Buddyfight D Start Deck 2 Cross Dragoner

RELEASED ON MARCH 4, 2016
DTD020001 Four Quasar, Steincross C .15 .25
DTD020002 Star Dragoner, T Alpha C .30 .50
DTD020003 Star Dragoner, Protofuser C .15 .25
DTD020004 Star Dragoner, Straggler C .15 .25
DTD020005 Dragonarms, Vogel C .20 .30
DTD020006 Star Dragoner, Blazer C .15 .25
DTD020007 Dragonarms, Slowing C .15 .25
DTD020008 Dragonarms, Strength C .15 .25
DTD020009 Star Dragoner, Cross Vier C .15 .25
DTD020010 Brave Memory C .50 .75
DTD020011 Cosmo Healing C .15 .25
DTD020012 Surprise Laser C .15 .25
DTD020013 Speculight Ring C .15 .25
DTD020014 Earth Barrier C .50 .75
DTD020015 Single Star, Neometeor C .15 .25
DTD020016 Photon Saber, Oro Light C .15 .25
DTD020017 Jackknife Dragoner Wall! C .15 .25
DTD020018 Star Dragon World C 4.00 6.00

2015 Future Card Buddyfight D Start Deck 3 Hollow Black Dragon

RELEASED ON MARCH 4, 2016
DTD030001 Twin Blade Black Dragon, Zarkandilac C .50 .75
DTD030002 Black Armored Dragon, Pentagra C .20 .40
DTD030003 Black Assailant, Gors Golby C .60 1.00
DTD030004 Black Companion, Bephegol C .20 .30
DTD030005 Black Swing Cage, Clayburs C .40 .60
DTD030006 Black Shock, Knogdeath C .40 .60
DTD030007 Black Depressed Buckling, Barzam C .40 .60
DTD030008 Black Tyranny, Fanagul C .15 .25
DTD030009 Black Star, Sils C .20 .40
DTD030010 Void Slasher C 1.50 2.50
DTD030011 Abyss Symphony C 2.00 3.00
DTD030012 Death Break C .15 .25
DTD030013 Dark Spirit C .40 .60
DTD030014 Black Dragon Shield C 1.50 2.50
DTD030015 Revenge Sickle, Avenger C .60 1.00
DTD030016 Black Dragonblade, Evil Fearless C .20 .30
DTD030017 Abygale Lost Horizon! C .40 .60
DTD030018 Darkness Dragon World C 2.50 4.00

2017 Future Card Buddyfight X Start Deck 1 Demon Lord Dragon of Tempest

RELEASED ON APRIL 21, 2017
XSD010001 Resurrected Arc Dragon, Batzz RRR .60 1.00
XSD010001 Resurrected Arc Dragon, Batzz C .75 1.25
XSD010002 Captain of the Cavalry Dragons, Kegale Byde C .40 .60
XSD010003 Blusterous Brat, Roller C .40 .60
XSD010004 Frontline Blacksmith, Rectangle C .60 1.00
XSD010005 Ringblade Wielder, Ring C .20 .30
XSD010006 Spear Knight, Dikon C .60 1.00
XSD010007 Mono-horn Dragon, Kornos C .30 .50
XSD010008 Replenisher, Heptor C .20 .30
XSD010009 Destroy X Thunder C .20 .30
XSD010010 A Distinguished Replenisher! C 1.25 2.00
XSD010011 Thunder X Energy C .12 .20
XSD010012 Blue Dragon Shield C 1.50 2.50
XSD010013 Green Dragon Shield C .50 .75
XSD010014 Electric Spear C .10 .15
XSD010015 Arc Dragon Dagger C .40 .60

XSD010016 Thunder Sword X Tempest Blade! RRR	.30	.50
XSD010016 Thunder Sword X Tempest Blade! C	1.25	2.00
XSD010017 Dragon World (card) C	.20	.30

2017 Future Card Buddyfight X Start Deck 2 Dragon Fielder

RELEASED ON APRIL 21, 2017

XSD020001 Radiant Crystal Dragon, Athora C	.10	.15
XSD020001 Radiant Crystal Dragon, Athora RRR	.75	1.25
XSD020002 Yellow Crystal Dragon, Lameur C	.60	1.00
XSD020003 Green Crystal Dragon, Blante C	.60	1.00
XSD020004 Foam Crystal Dragon, Jibeel C	.20	.30
XSD020005 Red Crystal Dragon, Pinoeur C	.50	.75
XSD020006 White Crystal Dragon, Morskat C	.60	1.00
XSD020007 Red Crystal Dragon, Malbeck C	.10	.15
XSD020008 White Crystal Dragon, Vioneir C	.10	.15
XSD020009 Dispersion C	.60	1.00
XSD020010 Visible Light C	6.00	10.00
XSD020011 Prism Amulet C	2.00	.30
XSD020012 Mars Barrier C	1.00	1.50
XSD020013 Harry Glynde C	.60	1.00
XSD020014 Crystal Ball C	.60	1.00
XSD020015 Crystal Mark C	.60	1.00
XSD020016 Crystal Flawless Shoot! C	.10	.15
XSD020016 Crystal Flawless Shoot! RRR	.50	.75
XSD020017 Star Dragon World C	4.00	6.00

2018 Future Card Buddyfight S Start Deck 1 Dradeity

RELEASED ON JULY 27, 2018

SSD010001 Awakened Deity, Gargantua Dragon C	1.00	1.50
SSD010001 Awakened Deity, Gargantua Dragon RR	6.00	10.00
SSD010002 Gargantua Dragon, "Recover Mode" C	.60	1.00
SSD010003 Gargantua Dragon, "Slash Mode" C	.50	.75
SSD010004 Laufen Gardragon C	.15	.25
SSD010005 Dolch Gardra C	.15	.25
SSD010006 Mout Gardra C	.40	.60
SSD010007 Degen Gardra C	.15	.25
SSD010008 Gargazelle C	.15	.25
SSD010009 Gargantua Lexicon C	.40	.60
SSD010010 Deity Green Dragon Shield C	.40	.60
SSD010011 Gar-Energy C	.15	.25
SSD010012 Blue Dragon Shield C	.40	.60
SSD010013 Deity Dragon Sword, Garsabre C	.40	.60
SSD010014 Deity Dragon Sword, Gardagger C	.40	.60
SSD010015 Gargaraid Punisher!! C	.60	1.00
SSD010016 Dragon World RR	25.00	40.00
SSD010016 Dragon World C	.15	.25

2018 Future Card Buddyfight S Start Deck 2 Triangulum Galaxy

RELEASED ON JULY 27, 2018

SSD020001 Rainbow Wings, Cross Astrologia C	.15	.25
SSD020001 Rainbow Wings, Cross Astrologia RR	2.50	4.00
SSD020002 Seerfight Dragon, Bend C	.15	.25
SSD020003 Guardseer Dragon, Canton C	.15	.25
SSD020004 Seerfight Dragon, Pellet C	.15	.25
SSD020005 Govern Star Dragon, Fountain C	.15	.25
SSD020006 Seerfight Dragon, Sinister C	.15	.25
SSD020007 Seer Dragon, Cotise C	.15	.25
SSD020008 Seer Dragon, Barrulet C	.60	1.00
SSD020009 Edict: Divination C	.75	1.25
SSD020010 Notice: Defensive Battle C	.20	.30
SSD020011 Notice: Enhancement Tactic C	1.00	1.50
SSD020012 Mars Barrier C	1.00	1.50
SSD020013 Seertool, Star Pendulum C	.15	.25
SSD020014 Seertool, Arcana C	.60	1.00
SSD020015 Shining Tri-Star C	.15	.25
SSD020016 Star Dragon World RR	25.00	40.00
SSD020016 Star Dragon World C	10.00	15.00

2018 Future Card Buddyfight S Start Deck 3 Spiral Linkdragon Order

RELEASED ON JULY 27, 2018

SSD030001 Head of Linkdragon Order, Agito C	.40	.60
SSD030001 Head of Linkdragon Order, Agito RR	4.00	6.00
SSD030002 Resonance of Bonds, King Agito C	.40	.60
SSD030003 Vanguard, Kezume C	.15	.25
SSD030004 Firstaid, Manako C	.15	.25
SSD030005 Runner, Nakayubi C	.15	.25
SSD030006 Tempest, Shokushi C	.15	.25
SSD030007 Imperial Envoy, Kurubushi C	.15	.25
SSD030008 Linkdragon Order's Retaliation C	.15	.25
SSD030009 Linkdragon Order's Repose C	.15	.25
SSD030010 Bonds Shield C	.30	.50
SSD030011 Dragon Emperor Legend C	.75	1.25
SSD030012 Divine Dragon Creation C	4.00	6.00
SSD030013 Throwspear, "Dragojavelin" C	.15	.25
SSD030014 Throwblade, "Flyingsaucer" C	.15	.25
SSD030015 Triple Trio Attack C	.15	.25
SSD030016 Ancient World RR	20.00	30.00
SSD030016 Ancient World C	1.25	2.00

2014 Future Card Buddyfight Trial Deck 1 Dominant Dragons

RELEASED ON JANUARY 24, 2014

TD01001EN Gigant Sword Dragon C	.10	.15
TD01002EN Jamadhar Dragon C	.10	.15
TD01003EN Rising Flare Dragon C	.10	.15
TD01003EN Rising Flare Dragon RR	2.50	4.00
TD01004EN Extreme Sword Dragon C	.20	.30
TD01005EN Thousand Rapier Dragon C	.20	.30
TD01006EN Bear-Trap Fang Dragon C	.10	.15
TD01007EN Systemic Dagger Dragon C	.10	.15
TD01008EN Bronze Shield Dragon C	.10	.15
TD01009EN Dragonic Grimoire C	2.00	3.00
TD01010EN Dragon Breath C	.10	.15
TD01011EN Dragoenergy C	.75	1.25
TD01012EN Green Dragon Shield C	.60	1.00
TD01013EN Dragonblade, Dragobrave C	.10	.15
TD01014EN Dragonblade, Dragofearless C	.10	.15
TD01015EN Gargantua Punisher!! C	.75	1.25
TD01015EN Gargantua Punisher!! RR	.75	1.25
TD01016EN My Buddy! (Drum Bunker Dragon) C	.60	1.00
TD01017EN Dragon World C	.60	1.00

2014 Future Card Buddyfight Trial Deck 2 Savage Steel

RELEASED ON JANUARY 24, 2014

TD020001 Armorknight Black Drake C	.25	.40
TD020002 Armorknight Griffin C	.10	.15
TD020003 Armorknight Cerberus C	.60	1.00
TD020003 Armorknight Cerberus RR	.75	1.25
TD020004 Armorknight Minotaur C	.10	.15
TD020005 Armorknight Ogre C	.10	.15
TD020006 Armorknight Hellhound C	.10	.15
TD020007 Armorknight Wizard C	.10	.15
TD020008 Armorknight Eagle C	.10	.15
TD020009 Crimson Slash C	.75	1.25
TD020010 Survival Chance C	.75	1.25
TD020011 Battle Aura Circle C	1.00	1.50
TD020012 Invigorating Breath C	1.00	1.50
TD020013 Hysteric Spear C	.20	.30
TD020014 Boulder Piercing Spear C	.10	.15
TD020015 Drill Bunker!! C	.10	.15
TD020015 Drill Bunker!! RR	1.25	2.00
TD020016 My Buddy! (Armorknight Cerberus) C	6.00	10.00
TD020017 Danger World C	1.50	2.50

2014 Future Card Buddyfight Trial Deck 3 Dragonic Force

RELEASED ON MARCH 28, 2014

TD030001 Jackknife "Thunder Storm" C	.20	.30
TD030002 Jackknife "Dispersal" C	.10	.15
TD030002 Jackknife "Dispersal" RR	.15	.15
TD030003 Gust Charging Dragon C	.10	.15
TD030004 Jackknife Dragon C	.75	1.25
TD030004 Jackknife Dragon RR	1.00	1.50
TD030005 Hammer Mace Dragon C	.60	1.00
TD030006 Zantetsunodachi Dragon C	.10	.15
TD030007 Grave Horn Dragon C	.10	.15
TD030008 Slashknife Dragon C	.75	1.25
TD030009 Latale Shield Dragon C	.10	.15
TD030010 Bronze Shield Dragon C	.10	.15
TD030011 Jackknife Braveheart C	.10	1.50
TD030012 Dragon Flame C	.75	1.25
TD030013 Dragoenergy C	.10	.15
TD030014 Dragonic Charge C	.40	.60
TD030015 Green Dragon Shield C	.60	1.00
TD030016 Dragonblade, Dragobrave C	.10	.15
TD030017 Dragonblade, Dragofearless C	.10	.15
TD030018 Dragonic Punisher C	.40	.60
TD030018 Dragonic Punisher RR	.60	1.00
TD030019 Dragon World C	.10	.15

2014 Future Card Buddyfight Trial Deck 4 Braves Explosion

RELEASED ON JULY 4, 2014

TD040001 Silver Warrior, Quenzwei C	.10	.15
TD040002 Legendary Warrior, Gao C	.60	1.00
TD040002 Legendary Warrior, Gao RR	.75	1.25
TD040003 Monk of Bread Deity, Prios C	.10	.15
TD040004 Craftsman, Baku C	.60	1.25
TD040005 Dachs, Cobalt C	.25	.40
TD040006 Master Thief, Strohl Bird C	.10	.15
TD040007 Fledgling Warrior, Ocker Glaser C	.10	.15
TD040008 Sage, Kuguru C	.10	.15
TD040009 Mameshiba, Cobalt C	.60	1.00
TD040010 Rolling Stone C	.10	.15
TD040011 Oracle of Tuval C	.75	1.25
TD040012 Pillar of Fire C	.75	1.25
TD040013 Dungeon Pit C	.30	.50
TD040014 Divine Protection of Shalsana C	.75	1.25
TD040015 Mission Card "Form a Party!" C	.10	.15
TD040015 Mission Card "Form a Party!" RR	.75	1.25
TD040016 Mission Card "Defeat the Monsters!" C	.10	.15
TD040017 Conquering Blade, Dungeon Domination C	.25	.40
TD040018 Origin Blade, Enemy Breaker C	.10	.15
TD040019 Dead End Crush! C	.40	.60
TD040019 Dead End Crush! RR	.10	.15
TD040020 Dungeon World C	2.00	3.00

2014 Future Card Buddyfight Trial Deck 5 Ninja Onslaught

RELEASED ON JULY 4, 2014

TD050001 Noble Ninja, Momochitanba C	.40	.60
TD050001 Noble Ninja, Momochitanba RR	.75	1.25
TD050002 Lethal Sword Ninja, Zantetsu C	.20	.30
TD050003 Wandering Ninja, Tobikato C	.10	.15
TD050004 Agent Ninja, Rinzo C	.30	.50
TD050005 Tsukikage, Blademaster Mode C	.75	1.25
TD050005 Tsukikage, Blademaster Mode RR	.75	1.25
TD050006 Electro Ninja, Electric Teru C	.40	.60
TD050007 Stealth Ninja, Kirikakure Saizo C	.10	.15
TD050008 Accelerate Ninja, Hayate C	.10	.15
TD050009 Demon Way, Geppakugiri C	.25	.40
TD050010 Demon Way, Noroihikagami C	.25	.40
TD050011 Shooting Cross Knives, Right-hand C	.40	.60
TD050012 Ninja Arts, Steel Ball C	.10	.15
TD050013 Clear Serenity C	1.00	1.50
TD050014 Art of Item Blasting C	.40	.60
TD050015 Art of Body Replacement C	1.50	2.50
TD050016 Ninja Blade, Kurogachi C	.10	.15
TD050017 Secret Sword, Lethal Formation RR	3.00	5.00
TD050018 Secret Sword, Shooting Star C	.10	.15
TD050019 Secret Sword, Moon Fang C	.75	1.25
TD050020 Katana World (card) C	2.50	4.00

2014 Future Card Buddyfight Trial Deck 6 Dark Pulse

RELEASED ON OCTOBER 10, 2014

TD060001 Purgatory Knights, Satan Force Dragon C		.15
TD060001 Purgatory Knights, Satan Force Dragon RR	.75	1.25
TD060002 There is Only Death, Dalleon C		.15
TD060003 Black Dragon, Dividers C		.15
TD060004 Death Ruler, Abriel C		.15
TD060004 Death Ruler, Abriel RR		.15
TD060005 Black Dragon, Tarandus C		.15
TD060006 Purgatory Knights, Giant Scissor Dragon C		.15
TD060007 Black Dragon, Death Gracia C		.15
TD060008 Black Dragon, Decipience C		.15
TD060009 Purgatory Knights, Black Knife Dragon C		.15
TD060010 Death Ruler, Alea C		.15
TD060011 Death Damage C	.60	1.00
TD060012 Sudden DEATH! C		.15
TD060013 Vampire Fang C	1.25	2.00
TD060014 Black Revenger C	.40	.60
TD060015 Midnight Shadow C	3.00	5.00
TD060016 Death Claw, Grim Reaper C		.15
TD060017 Black Sword, Heartbreaker C		.15
TD060018 Demonic Strike Arts, Death Requiem C	.40	.60
TD060018 Demonic Strike Arts, Death Requiem RR	.75	1.25
TD060020 Darkness Dragon World C	1.50	2.50

2014 Future Card Buddyfight Trial Deck 7 Tomorrow Asmodai

RELEASED ON JANUARY 23, 2015

TD070001 Champion Wrestler Asmodai C	.20	.30
TD070001 Champion Wrestler Asmodai RR	3.00	5.00
TD070002 Dance! Asmodai C	1.00	1.50
TD070003 Fallen Angel of Rage, Beleth C	.10	.15
TD070004 Demon Realm Death Metal, Valefar C	.10	.15
TD070005 Let's Play! Asmodai C	1.50	2.50
TD070005 Let's Play! Asmodai RR	2.00	3.00
TD070006 Fallen Angel, Paimon C	.10	.15
TD070007 Demon Realm Warrior, Zepar C	.10	.15
TD070008 Event Producer Aym C	.10	.15
TD070009 Oops! C	.20	.30
TD070010 Key of Solomon, First Volume C	.75	1.25
TD070011 Speed Summon C	.20	.30
TD070012 Nice One! C	1.25	2.50
TD070013 Solomon's Shield C	.30	.50
TD070014 Chillax! C	.50	.75
TD070015 I'm Wicked! C	.20	.30
TD070016 Gunrod, Bechstein C	.10	.15
TD070017 Asmodai Eternal Rolling Back-drop! C	.75	1.25
TD070017 Asmodai Eternal Rolling Back-drop! RR	.75	1.25
TD070018 Magic World C	.20	.30

2015 Future Card Buddyfight H Trial Deck 1 Crimson Fist

RELEASED ON APRIL 24, 2015

HSD010001 First Crimson Chieftain, Greatest General C	.10	.15
HSD010001 First Crimson Chieftain, Greatest General RR	.10	.15
HSD010002 Crimson Battler, Extreme Blow Dragon C	.10	.15
HSD010003 Crimson Battler, Boosted Dragon C	.10	.15
HSD010004 Crimson Battler, Grand Kick Dragon C	.20	.30
HSD010004 Crimson Battler, Grand Kick Dragon RR	.20	.30
HSD010005 Crimson Battler, Spin Nail Dragon C	.10	.15
HSD010006 Crimson Battler, Hammer Ball Dragon C	.10	.15
HSD010007 Crimson Battler, Starting Dragon C	.10	.15
HSD010008 Crimson Battler, Maintenance Kid C	.10	.15
HSD010009 Dragonic Gate Breaker C	.10	.15
HSD010010 Dragonic Directive C	.10	.15
HSD010011 Primeval Dragon Shield C	.10	.15
HSD010012 Dragonic Aura C	.50	.75
HSD010013 Green Dragon Shield C	.10	.15
HSD010014 Assail Sword, Dragoraptor C	.10	.15
HSD010015 Battle Spirit Fist, Dragosoul C	.10	.15
HSD010016 Crimson Soul Grenade!! C	.10	.15
HSD010016 Crimson Soul Grenade!! RR	.10	.15
HSD010017 Dragon World C	.75	1.25

2015 Future Card Buddyfight H Trial Deck 2 Radiant Force

RELEASED ON APRIL 24, 2015

HSD020001 Adventure Continent, Gunvellz RR	.20	.30
HSD020001 Adventure Continent, Gunvellz C	.10	.15
HSD020002 Rescue Dragon, Crossbuster RR	.20	.30
HSD020002 Rescue Dragon, Crossbuster C	.10	.15
HSD020003 Eco-Hero Solarpanelman C	.40	.60
HSD020004 Heavy Trooper, Iron Saver C	.20	.30
HSD020005 Radio Controlled Machine, Maxstorm C	.20	.30
HSD020006 Stray Warrior, Vier C	.30	.50
HSD020007 Cyber Police Hyper Rescue C	.10	.15
HSD020008 Draw Away the Lackeys! C	.10	.15
HSD020009 There, I See It! C	.10	.15
HSD020010 Justice Will Prevail! C	.30	.50
HSD020011 It's About Time I Got Serious! C	.10	.15
HSD020012 I've Seen Through Your Moves! C	.10	.15
HSD020013 Launch! Buddy Police C	.60	1.00
HSD020014 I'm Still Alive! C	.10	.15
HSD020015 Army Rifle, Line Thunder C	.10	.15
HSD020016 Equation of Victory, Winning Formula! RR	.10	.15
HSD020016 Equation of Victory, Winning Formula! C	.10	.15
HSD020017 Hero World (card) C	.10	.15

2015 Future Card Buddyfight H Trial Deck 3 Dragonic Star

RELEASED ON JULY 10, 2015

HTD010001 Cosmo Strada, Galaxias C	.10	.15
HTD010001 Cosmo Strada, Galaxias RR		
HTD010002 Demonblaze, Maxwell C	.10	.15
HTD010003 Stardust, Globule C	.10	.15
HTD010004 Rainbow Vision, Shadowscare C	.10	.15
HTD010005 Child Star, Astrojet C	.10	.15
HTD010006 Dragonarms, Cavalier C	.10	.15
HTD010006 Dragonarms, Cavalier RR		
HTD010007 Dragonarms, Vogel C	.10	.15
HTD010008 The Crater, Basin C	.10	.15
HTD010009 Dragonarms, Divisigator C	.10	.15
HTD010010 Star Blast C	.10	.15
HTD010011 Planet Memory C	.10	.15
HTD010012 Speculight Ring C	.10	.15
HTD010013 Shining Rain C	.10	.15
HTD010014 Proto Barrier C	.10	.15
HTD010015 Star Saber, Reflection C	.10	.15
HTD010016 Photon Saber, Meteor C	.10	.15
HTD010017 Photon Edge Universe! C	.10	.15
HTD010017 Photon Edge Universe! RR		
HTD010018 Star Dragon World C	.10	.15

2015 Future Card Buddyfight H Trial Deck 4 Malicious Demons

RELEASED ON JULY 10, 2015

HTD020001 Hundred Demons General, Gokumengaiou C	.15	.25
HTD020001 Hundred Demons General, Gokumengaiou RR	.60	1.00
HTD020002 Dark Dragon, Demochill C	.15	.25
HTD020003 Evil Dragon, Gataraoroch C	.15	.25
HTD020004 Poisonous Water Dragon, Zazamera C	.60	1.00
HTD020005 Thunder Summoner, Reiki C	.15	.25
HTD020006 Corpse Spirit, Draogul C	.15	.25
HTD020007 Living Mad Gazer C	.50	.75
HTD020008 Ogre Size Dragon C	.75	1.25
HTD020009 Hundred Demons Sorcery, Tennomimakari C	1.50	2.50
HTD020010 Hundred Demons Sorcery, Ryubokushihai C	.75	1.25
HTD020011 Hundred Demons' Tome of Judgement C	2.00	3.00
HTD020012 Starved Yamigedo C	.15	.25
HTD020012 Starved Yamigedo RR	1.25	2.00
HTD020013 Hundred Demons Sorcery, Yamitagae C	.15	.25
HTD020013 Hundred Demons Sorcery, Yamitagae RR	1.25	2.00
HTD020014 Hungry Claw, Raiga C	.25	.40
HTD020015 Fiendish Blade, Urahonekui C	.15	.25
HTD020016 Beast Mode, Hungry Claw War! C	.60	1.00
HTD020017 Parade of Hundred Demons C	1.50	2.50

2016 Future Card Buddyfight D Trial Deck 1 Dragon Emperor of the Colossal Ocean

RELEASED ON JULY 15, 2016
DTD010001 Great Ocean Deity Duel Jaeger, "Seazarion" C .10 .15
DTD010001 Great Ocean Deity Duel Jaeger, "Seazarion" RRR .75 1.25
DTD010002 Colossal Ocean Chief, Duel Jaeger C .25 .40
DTD010002 Colossal Ocean Chief, Duel Jaeger RRR .25 .40
DTD010003 Iron Fist Chief, Strong Go C .75 1.25
DTD010003 Iron Fist Chief, Strong Go RRR 2.00 3.00
DTD010004 Chief of Armors, Under the Ken C .50 .75
DTD010005 Ice Dragon Emperor, Glacies C .40 .60
DTD010006 Chief of Wind, Messenger Jin C .10 .15
DTD010007 Underling, Knuckler Dan C .10 .15
DTD010008 Apprentice Underling, Rookie Ichi C .10 .15
DTD010009 Dragon Within the Ocean C .75 1.25
DTD010010 Dragon Emperor Legend C 2.00 3.00
DTD010011 Dragon Dreams C 1.00 1.50
DTD010012 Dragon Thunder C .10 .15
DTD010013 Rise & Fall of Dragons C 4.00 6.00
DTD010014 Ocean Emperor Style, Whirlpool Seal C .75 1.25
DTD010015 Strength of a Thousand Dragons C .75 1.25
DTD010016 Trying a Dragon's Best C .75 1.25
DTD010017 Ocean Boy's Anchor, Ripple C .10 .15
DTD010018 Big Catch Kigan, Ocean Cleaving Twin Dragon Wave! C .10 .15
DTD010019 Ancient World C .60 1.00

2017 Future Card Buddyfight X Trial Deck 1 Decimating Black Dragon

RELEASED ON JULY 14, 2017
XTD010001 Black Death Dragon of Sentence, Abygale RRR
XTD010001 Black Death Dragon of Sentence, Abygale C 2.00 3.00
XTD010002 Jet Black Crest Dragon, Vie Revolver C .10 .15
XTD010003 Black Crest Dragon, Oathbring C .10 .15
XTD010004 Black Crest Dragon, Zaston Owl C .10 .15
XTD010005 Black Crest Dragon, Aeroess C .10 .15
XTD010006 Black Crest Dragon, Dyurandy C .10 .15
XTD010007 Black Dragon, Luarl C .10 .15
XTD010008 Black Dragon, Elhopper C .10 .15
XTD010009 Poison Diver C 2.00 3.00
XTD010010 Venom Splash RRR
XTD010010 Venom Splash C .10 .15
XTD010011 Black Dragon Shield C 2.50 4.00
XTD010012 Midnight Shadow C .60 1.00
XTD010013 Toxic Zone C .10 .15
XTD010014 Nonfatal Sword, Pain Bringer C .10 .15
XTD010015 Human-Eating Sickle, Vital Eater C .60 1.00
XTD010016 Death Count ~Serenade~ RRR
XTD010016 Death Count ~Serenade~ C 1.25 2.00
XTD010017 Darkness Dragon World (card) C 1.50 2.50

2017 Future Card Buddyfight X Trial Deck 2 Ruler of Havoc

RELEASED ON JULY 14, 2017
XTD020001 The Manufactured Havoc, Geargod VII RRR
XTD020001 The Manufactured Havoc, Geargod VII C 1.25 2.00
XTD020002 CHAOS Highlow C .10 .15
XTD020003 CHAOS Managarmr C .10 .15
XTD020004 CHAOS Jabberwock C .10 .15
XTD020005 CHAOS Aesculapius C .10 .15
XTD020006 CHAOS Garjion C 3.00 5.00
XTD020007 CHAOS Sekitetsu C .75 1.25
XTD020008 CHAOS Gorgas C .10 .15
XTD020009 Electron Disorder C .60 1.00
XTD020010 One Who Comes From Havoc RRR
XTD020010 One Who Comes From Havoc C 1.25 2.00
XTD020011 CHAOS Corrosion C .10 .15
XTD020012 Chaos Energy C .10 .15
XTD020013 Chaos Defenser C .60 1.00
XTD020014 Chaos Ejecter C .10 .15
XTD020015 Chaos Absorber C .60 1.00
XTD020016 Forced Global Shutdown RRR
XTD020016 Forced Global Shutdown C 2.00 3.00
XTD020017 the Chaos C 1.50 2.50

2017 Future Card Buddyfight X Trial Deck 3 Thunderous Warlords Alliance

RELEASED ON OCTOBER 20, 2017
XTD030001 Overturn Arc Dragon, Barlbatzz RRR .60 1.00
XTD030001 Overturn Arc Dragon, Barlbatzz C 1.25 2.00
XTD030002 Destruction Arc Duke, Gatastol C .30 .50
XTD030003 Thunderstar, Leitning C 2.00 3.00
XTD030004 Divine Sword Dragon, Saint Holy Sword Dragon RRR 1.50 2.50
XTD030004 Divine Sword Dragon, Saint Holy Sword Dragon C .75 1.25
XTD030005 Violent Thunder, Armorknight Ogre C .30 .50
XTD030006 Rescue Dragon, Electripaddle C .30 .50
XTD030007 Thunder Warrior, Ocker Glaser C 2.50 4.00
XTD030008 Lightning Star, Thunder Procyon C .30 .50
XTD030009 Nice Thunder! C 1.25 2.00
XTD030010 Blackbolt Ring C 3.00 5.00
XTD030011 Ninja Arts, Flash Dance C .40 .60
XTD030012 Thunderbolt Marked Urn C .75 1.25
XTD030013 Bring It On! C 3.00 5.00
XTD030014 Descending Lightning Deity, Tsuchi-Ikazuchi C .50 .75
XTD030015 Thunder Emperor Sword, Draglare C .30 .50
XTD030016 Turbulent Thunder Fist, Blowout X Tempest Shatter! RRR 2.50 4.00
XTD030016 Turbulent Thunder Fist, Blowout X Tempest Shatter! C .30 .50
XTD030017 Thunder Emperor's Fangs C 1.50 2.50

2019 Future Card Buddyfight S Trial Deck 1 Draknight

RELEASED ON APRIL 26, 2019
STD010001 Awakened Deity Dragon, Gargantua Knight Dragon C .75 1.25
STD010001 Awakened Deity Dragon, Gargantua Knight Dragon RR 4.00 6.00
STD010002 Evolution Blaze, Garflamme Dragon C .60 1.00
STD010003 Awakened Deity Dragon, Laufen Gardragon C .15 .25
STD010004 Lanze Gardragon C .75 1.25
STD010005 Awakened Deity Dragon, Degen Gardragon C .15 .25
STD010006 Awakened Deity Dragon, Dolch Gardra C .15 .25
STD010007 Awakened Deity Dragon, Mout Gardra C 1.00 1.50
STD010008 Garcat C 1.50 2.50
STD010009 Awakened Deity Dragon, Gargazelle C .15 .25
STD010010 Boost On! C .60 1.00
STD010011 Gar-Lit C .75 1.25
STD010012 Dragod's Shine C .60 1.00
STD010013 Gar-Oracle C 2.50 4.00
STD010014 Deity Purple Dragon Shield C 1.50 2.50
STD010015 Deity Green Dragon Shield C .15 .25
STD010016 Loud Voice C 2.50 4.00
STD010017 Deity Dragon Beamsword, Garknight Saber C .15 .25
STD010018 Deity Dragon Sword, Garkris C .75 1.25
STD010019 Deity Dragon Beamblade, Garknight Dagger C .15 .25
STD010020 Dragod Strike! C .15 .25
STD010021 Dragon World C RR 20.00 30.00
STD010021 Dragon World C .15 .25

2019 Future Card Buddyfight S Trial Deck 2 Legend of Double Horus

RELEASED ON AUGUST 23, 2019
STD020001 Legendary Flame Deity, Magma Horus FOIL RR 2.00 3.00
STD020001 Legendary Flame Deity, Magma Horus .15 .25
STD020002 Legendary Ice Deity, Freeza Horus FOIL RR 2.00 3.00
STD020002 Legendary Ice Deity, Freeza Horus .15 .25
STD020003 High Priest of Harvest, Mosone .15 .25
STD020004 Warrior of Zeal, Terias .30 .50
STD020005 Breeze Bearer, Garaig .60 1.00
STD020006 Wandering Merchant, Otta .15 .25
STD020007 Devoting Mummy Maker, Jutha Laash .50 .75
STD020008 Valkyrie, All-knowing Alwidol 1.00 1.50
STD020009 Wyrmling of The Rocks, Risha .15 .25
STD020010 Inheritance of Honor- Taara .15 .25
STD020011 Darghner le Bark .75 1.25
STD020012 Fire and Ice .60 1.00
STD020013 Yngl Gard 1.50 2.50
STD020014 Frozen Circulation .40 .60
STD020015 Ahraamic Red Hot .60 1.00
STD020016 Eluned's Ring .60 1.00
STD020017 Staff of Mathaf .15 .25
STD020018 Sceptre of Midan .15 .25
STD020019 Judgment of Ice and Flame- Da Awa Hajuma .15 .25
STD020020 Legend World FOIL RR 15.00 25.00
STD020020 Legend World 1.50 2.50

2019 Future Card Buddyfight S Trial Deck Cross 1 Detective Conan Side White

RELEASED ON JUNE 7, 2019
STDC010001 Small Detective, Conan Edogawa FOIL 2.50 4.00
STDC010001 Small Detective, Conan Edogawa .40 .60
STDC010002 Calm and Collected, Conan Edogawa FOIL 2.00 3.00
STDC010002 Calm and Collected, Conan Edogawa .75 1.25
STDC010003 Detective of the East, Shinichi Kudo .15 .25
STDC010004 Peaceful Days, Ai Haibara .50 .75
STDC010005 High School Girl, Ran Mori .60 1.00
STDC010006 Mystery Detective, Kogoro Mori .15 .25
STDC010007 Friend or Foe, Toru Amuro .40 .60
STDC010008 Silver Bullet, Shuichi Akai .15 .25
STDC010009 Detective of the West, Heiji Hattori .50 .75
STDC010010 Heiji's Girlfriend, Kazuha Toyama .60 1.00
STDC010011 Elegant, Kid the Phantom Thief .60 1.00
STDC010012 Mori Detective Agency .30 .50
STDC010013 Painful Blow 1.25 2.00
STDC010014 KEEP OUT .15 .25
STDC010015 Stretchy Suspenders .50 .75
STDC010016 Junior Detective League .50 .75
STDC010017 Ai Haibara's Day FOIL 8.00 12.00
STDC010017 Ai Haibara's Day 5.00 8.00
STDC010018 Kicking Enhancement Shoes .15 .25
STDC010019 There is always only one truth! FOIL 2.00 3.00
STDC010019 There is always only one truth! .15 .25
STDC010020 Detective Conan (flag) .60 1.00

2019 Future Card Buddyfight S Trial Deck Cross 2 Detective Conan Side Black

RELEASED ON JUNE 7, 2019
STDC020001 Cruel Man, Gin FOIL 2.50 4.00
STDC020001 Cruel Man, Gin .15 .25
STDC020002 Member of Black Organization, Gin .30 .75
STDC020003 Member of Black Organization, Rye .30 .75
STDC020004 Gin's Subordinate, Vodka FOIL 2.50 4.00
STDC020004 Gin's Subordinate, Vodka .15 .25
STDC020005 Master of Disguise, Vermouth .60 1.00
STDC020006 Secretive, Vermouth .50 .75
STDC020007 Informant, Bourbon .75 1.25
STDC020008 Member of Black Organization, Scotch .75 1.25
STDC020009 Astonishment .75 1.25
STDC020010 Black Organization Pulling the Strings in Secret FOIL 4.00 6.00
STDC020010 Black Organization Pulling the Strings in Secret 3.00 5.00
STDC020011 Organization's Pressure .15 .25
STDC020012 Mystery Train .40 .60
STDC020013 Manhunt? .30 .50
STDC020014 Are you ready? .50 .75
STDC020015 Sherry Swallowed by the Snake .40 .60
STDC020016 Last Stop 1.00 1.50
STDC020017 Handgun .30 .50
STDC020018 Orders from the Boss .15 .25
STDC020019 Detective Conan (flag) .30 .50

2016 Future Card Buddyfight Triple D Booster Set Alternative 1 Buddy Rave

RELEASED ON JUNE 24, 2016
DBT1AEB020002EN Winning Maximum Soldier Form RRR 1.25 2.00
DBT1AEB020003EN Protection Deity of Steel Caardian RRR 3.00 5.00
DBT1AEB020004EN Masked Vantage Lavish Body Gorgeous Mask RRR 3.00 5.00
DBT1AEB020005EN Bandage Warrior Masked Vantage RR 4.00 6.00
DBT1AEB020006EN Battle Poet Talking RR 1.00 1.50
DBT1AEB020007EN Caardian Mode SPEED RR .75 1.25
DBT1AEB020008EN Uniform Warrior Formal Frill RR 3.00 5.00
DBT1AEB020009EN Eighth Warrior Acht RR 2.50 4.00
DBT1AEB02001EN Ultimate Card Burn DWing RRR 1.00 1.50
DBT1AEB020020EN RideChanger Officer Winning Maximum R .20 .30
DBT1AEB020021EN Uniform Warrior Racer Frill R .20 .30
DBT1AEB020022EN Familiar Plitz R .20 .30
DBT1AEB020023EN Energy Absorption Machinery R .20 .30
DBT1AEB020024EN I am a Rose Who Cuts Down Evil R .20 .30
DBT1AEB020025EN Hyper Energy R .20 .30
DBT1AEB020026EN Call Super Machine R 4.00 6.00
DBT1AEB020027EN Youre a Superhero From Now On R .20 .30
DBT1AEB020028EN Lend Me Your Strength R .20 .30
DBT1AEB020029EN Ill Be Troubled If You Forget R .20 .30
DBT1AEB020030EN Resupply Complete Battle Poets Launch R .20 .30
DBT1AEB020031EN Activate Barrier R 1.25 2.00
DBT1AEB020032EN Transform Belt Card Winder R .20 .30
DBT1AEB020033EN Shout Out Battle Poets Lyric Over R .20 .30
DBT1AEB020034EN Spiker Soldier Form C .10 .15
DBT1AEB020035EN Battle Poet Speaking C .10 .15
DBT1AEB020036EN Card Wyvern C .10 .15
DBT1AEB020037EN Caardian Mode ARMOR C .10 .15
DBT1AEB020038EN Cyber Police Side Watcher C .10 .15
DBT1AEB020039EN Uniform Warrior Millitary Frill C .10 .15
DBT1AEB020040EN Rescue Dragon Projet Gunner C .10 .15
DBT1AEB020041EN Sixth Warrior Sechs C .10 .15
DBT1AEB020042EN Uniform Warrior Sailor Frill C .10 .15
DBT1AEB020043EN RideChanger Silver Beak C .10 .15
DBT1AEB020044EN RideChanger Spiker C .10 .15
DBT1AEB020045EN Constructor Buildian C .10 .15
DBT1AEB020046EN Cyber Police Hold Hunter C .10 .15
DBT1AEB020047EN Military Launcher C .10 .15
DBT1AEB020048EN I Cannot Afford to Lose C .10 .15
DBT1AEB020049EN This is My Fight C .10 .15
DBT1AEB020050EN Thats a Shallow Shot C .10 .15
DBT1AEB020051EN Beaaaaaaaaam C .10 .15
DBT1AEB020052EN RideChange C .10 .15
DBT1AEB020053EN Ive Seen Through Your Moves C .10 .15
DBT1AEB020054EN Tears Dont Suit a Maiden C .10 .15
DBT1AEB020055EN Sailor Barrier C .10 .15
DBT1AEB020056EN I Wont Let You C .10 .15
DBT1AEB020057EN Defeat Them in My Place C .10 .15
DBT1AEB020058EN New Plasmamine C .10 .15
DBT1AEB020059EN Attack Power Amplification Device C .10 .15
DBT1AEB020060EN Prepped and OK to Launch C .10 .15
DBT1AEB020061EN Blazer Blaezer C .10 .15
DBT1AEB020062EN Caardian OVER HEAT C .10 .15
DBT1AEB020063EN All Members Dispatched Quartet Five C .10 .15
DBT1AEB020064EN Ultimate Card Burn DWing BR 2.50 4.00
DBT1AEB020065EN Winning Maximum Soldier Form BR 5.00 8.00
DBT1AEB02010EN Watch My Back RR .75 1.25
DBT1AEB02011EN Gaidenoh Steel Beast Explosive Battle Cry RR .60 1.00
DBT1AEB02012EN Reverse Skull Guilty Wave RR .60 1.00
DBT1AEB02013EN Silver Beak Soldier Formk R .20 .30
DBT1AEB02014EN Battle Poet Thinking R .20 .30
DBT1AEB02015EN Uniform Warrior Blazer Frill R .20 .30
DBT1AEB02016EN General Command Tausend of Thousand R .20 .30
DBT1AEB02017EN Inverted Cranium Reverse Skull R .20 .30
DBT1AEB02018EN Gravity Battlearmor GForce R .20 .30
DBT1AEB02019EN Ironing Man R .20 .30
DBT1AEB02EN Dragon World SCR 15.00 25.00
DBT1AEB02EN Star Dragon World SCR 20.00 30.00
DBT1AEB10002EN Silhouette Joe Illusion Shadow Dragons RRR 2.00 3.00
DBT1AEB10003EN Schwarz Kugel XIII RRR 1.00 1.50
DBT1AEB10004EN Star Dragon of Bonds Jackknife RRR 1.25 2.00
DBT1AEB10005EN Thunder Knights Leader Kommandeur Fahne Command of the Lightning General RRR 1.25 2.00
DBT1AEB10006EN Center of the World Mary Sue RR 3.00 5.00
DBT1AEB10007EN Tsukikage and Byakuya Chaotic Nano Art of Body Duplication RR .75 1.25
DBT1AEB10008EN Duel Sieger Sieger Turbulence RR 4.00 6.00
DBT1AEB10009EN Bladewing Immortal Phoenix RR 2.50 4.00
DBT1AEB1001EN Godlyspeed Bal Dragon RRR 2.00 3.00
DBT1AEB10020EN Dragon Emperor Legend R 1.25 2.00
DBT1AEB10021EN Billion Knuckle Spirit of the Chief R .60 1.00
DBT1AEB10022EN Dancing Magician Tetsuya R 2.00 3.00
DBT1AEB10023EN Deukruzar Second Manifestation Demonknight R .20 .30
DBT1AEB10024EN Rebellious Rebellion Rhapsody R .20 .30
DBT1AEB10025EN Valkyrie Skuld the Lamenter of the Future R .20 .30
DBT1AEB10026EN Fenrir Curse of Vanargand R .20 .30
DBT1AEB10027EN Sylph Fairies Banquet R .20 .30
DBT1AEB10028EN Gratos Destruction Blade R .20 .30
DBT1AEB10029EN Professor Menjo Instructions Cosmo Tactic R .20 .30
DBT1AEB10030EN Marshall Fortress Megalo Sanction R .20 .30
DBT1AEB10031EN Epicenter Cavalry Dragon Ground Zero C .10 .15
DBT1AEB10032EN Merabaselard Dragon C .10 .15
DBT1AEB10033EN Sun Furnace Jet Type1 C .10 .15
DBT1AEB10034EN White Dragon Shield C .10 .15
DBT1AEB10035EN Great Raging Dragon Zargilragne Crazed Claw Raging Fang C .10 .15
DBT1AEB10036EN Battle Aura Circle C .10 .15
DBT1AEB10037EN Explosive Axe Ricdeau Demon Slay C .10 .15
DBT1AEB10038EN Demon Musician Amdukias C .10 .15
DBT1AEB10039EN Chillax C .10 .15
DBT1AEB10040EN Ninja Arts Halfkill C .10 .15
DBT1AEB10041EN Unarmed Brawl Dragon Emperor Leadbangers C .10 .15
DBT1AEB10042EN Ladis the Tyrant Golden Dragon Eyes C .10 .15
DBT1AEB10043EN Tactful Knight Arron C .10 .15
DBT1AEB10044EN Loaned Possession Knight Jake C .10 .15
DBT1AEB10045EN Magical Eyes Release C .10 .15
DBT1AEB10046EN Stellar Deity Astraeus C .10 .15
DBT1AEB10047EN Redeyed Succubus C .10 .15
DBT1AEB10048EN Loki the Ehrgeiz C .10 .15
DBT1AEB10049EN Valkyrie Rota the Caller of Blizzard C .10 .15
DBT1AEB10050EN Faceless Black Dragon Laysface C .10 .15
DBT1AEB10051EN Noble Sacrifice C .10 .15
DBT1AEB10052EN Black Wilderness Golgoth C .10 .15
DBT1AEB10053EN Great Rifle Deity Tigarion Kaizeru Sword Buster C .10 .15
DBT1AEB10054EN Star Dragoner Heliopause C .10 .15
DBT1AEB10055EN Jackknife Overwrite C .10 .15
DBT1AEB10056EN Dragonarms Logisticker C .10 .15
DBT1AEB10057EN Electric Source C .10 .15
DBT1AEB10058EN Buddy Help C .10 .15
DBT1AEB10059EN Ultimate Buddy C .10 .15
DBT1AEB10060EN Damage Control C .10 .15
DBT1AEB10061EN Godlyspeed Bal Dragon BR 2.50 4.00
DBT1AEB1010EN Black Panoply Abygale RR 2.00 3.00
DBT1AEB1011EN Devil Stigma RR 15.00 25.00
DBT1AEB1012EN Purgatory Knights Leader Demios Sword Chaos Execution RR 1.50 2.50
DBT1AEB1013EN Crimson Duo Battler Double Crimson Impact R .20 .30
DBT1AEB1014EN Mysterious Sun Dragon Hidden Strength R .20 .30
DBT1AEB1015EN GIGA Armorknight Cerberus A R .20 .30
DBT1AEB1016EN Street Racer Eligos R .20 .30
DBT1AEB1017EN Hearty ABSC Annihilate Buster Staff Custom R .20 .30
DBT1AEB1018EN Electron Ninja Shiden R .20 .30
DBT1AEB1019EN Skull Warrior Bones of the Four Birds Akuten Haba R .60 1.00
DBT1AEB1EN Dragon World SCR 15.00 25.00
DBT1AEB1EN Darkness Dragon World SCR 25.00 40.00
DBT1ASS10002EN Yearner of Extinction Azi Dahaka RRR 2.00 3.00
DBT1ASS10003EN Wicked Lord Dragon Sword Aqulta Gwaneff RRR 1.00 1.50
DBT1ASS10004EN Jackknife Gewalt RR 1.25 2.00
DBT1ASS10005EN Curse Dragon Tragose RR .50 .75
DBT1ASS10006EN Bushknife Dragon R 1.25 2.00
DBT1ASS10007EN Dragon Knight Cagliostro R .20 .30
DBT1ASS10008EN Jackknife Joint R .20 .30
DBT1ASS10009EN Jackknife Charge R .20 .30
DBT1ASS1001EN Jackknife Neo Gold Ritter RRR 1.25 2.00
DBT1ASS1010EN Captive of Eternity Zamseed R .40 .60
DBT1ASS1011EN Jackknife Dragon Stragrite the X C .10 .15
DBT1ASS1012EN Jackknife Dragon Baby C .10 .15
DBT1ASS1013EN Circleknife Dragon C .10 .15
DBT1ASS1014EN Severing Dragon Scissor Gilos C .10 .15
DBT1ASS1015EN Dragon Deity Tyrant C .10 .15
DBT1ASS1016EN Abyss Aura C .10 .15
DBT1ASS1017EN Jackknife Neo Gold Ritter BR 5.00 8.00
DBT1ASS1018EN Yearner of Extinction Azi Dahaka BR 2.00 3.00
DBT1ASS1EN Dragon Ein SCR 40.00 60.00
DBT1ASS1EN Dragon World SCR 15.00 25.00

2016 Future Card Buddyfight Triple D Booster Set Alternative 2 Four Dimensions

RELEASED ON SEPTEMBER 23, 2016

Card	Low	High
DBT2A0001EN Fourth Omni Fire Lord Burn Nova RRR	1.50	2.50
DBT2A0004EN Never Say Never RR	2.00	3.00
DBT2A0005EN Ultimate Card Burn RR	.40	.60
DBT2A0006EN Heated Up Sun Bal Dragon R	.20	.30
DBT2A0007EN Silhouette Spirit R	.20	.30
DBT2A0008EN Ocean Champion Duel Jaeger R	.20	.30
DBT2A0009EN Black Superior Strength Goradori R	.20	.30
DBT2A0010EN Abygale SD R	.75	1.25
DBT2A0011EN Flash Lance Blitz Tiger R	2.00	3.00
DBT2A0012EN Full Strash Formation R	.20	.30
DBT2A0013EN ExGeneration Fifth Omni Cavalry Dragon Sand Staff Benetnasch C	.10	.15
DBT2A0014EN Eighth Omni Duel Dragon Zubanell C	.10	.15
DBT2A0015EN Sealed Master Zustein C	.10	.15
DBT2A0016EN Tsukikage Canis Mode C	.10	.15
DBT2A0017EN Knight of Glory El Quixote C	.10	.15
DBT2A0018EN Shining Up Hanako C	.10	.15
DBT2A0019EN Savage Lance Eisen Tiger C	.10	.15
DBT2A002EN Third Omni Water Lord Miserea RRR	2.00	3.00
DBT2A003EN Great Fiend Yamigedo RRR	2.00	3.00
DBT2A020EN Lua Nova C	.60	1.00
DBT2A021EN Great Fate Frozen Stars C	.10	.15
DBT2A022EN Bequeathed Despair Testament C	.10	.15
DBT2A023EN Daredevil Barrett C	.10	.15
DBT2A024EN Card Rhino C	.10	.15
DBT2A025EN Card Serpent C	.10	.15
DBT2A026EN Card Burn C	.10	.15
DBT2A027EN Rescue Dragon Metamorph Effect C	.10	.15
DBT2A028EN Uniform Warrior Sister Frill C	.10	.15
DBT2A029EN Dragonarms Schrodinger C	.10	.15
DBT2A030EN Fourth Omni Fire Lord Burn Nova BR	4.00	6.00
DBT2AEB30001EN Perpetual Envoy Elixiel RRR	.60	1.00
DBT2AEB30004EN Gagalgarios Prison Pyre Demonic Wave RRR	3.00	5.00
DBT2AEB30005EN Deity Dragon Envoy Muriel RR	1.00	1.50
DBT2AEB30006EN Justice Envoy Angel Frill RR	.40	.60
DBT2AEB30007EN Eternal Envoy Aettir RR	.75	1.25
DBT2AEB30008EN Sky Pillar Armor Doreamarti RR	5.00	8.00
DBT2AEB30009EN Tempest Jailer Helle Cougar RR	2.50	4.00
DBT2AEB30010EN Master of the Evil Shadow Executioners Silhouette Damian RR	1.25	2.00
DBT2AEB30011EN Demon Way Akeshigure RR	2.50	4.00
DBT2AEB30012EN Purgatory Sword Silver GiVSon RR	1.50	2.50
DBT2AEB30013EN Guardian Deity Dragon of Paradise Avalon R	.20	.30
DBT2AEB30014EN Unsullied Executer Dragon Judge Charuthea R	.20	.30
DBT2AEB30015EN Dragon Protector of the Celestial Gate Luminalion R	.20	.30
DBT2AEB30016EN Swoop Envoy Angelus R	.20	.30
DBT2AEB30017EN Deity Age Envoy Michaelis R	.20	.30
DBT2AEB30018EN Heavens Shield R	.20	.30
DBT2AEB30019EN Gate of Pardon Forgiven R	2.50	4.00
DBT2AEB3002EN Avalon Benedict Ray RRR	1.50	2.50
DBT2AEB3003EN Sound Speed Jailer Helle Gepard RRR	1.25	2.00
DBT2AEB30040EN Encouragement of the White Veil C	.10	.15
DBT2AEB30041EN The Shield of Justice will Never Shatter C	1.00	1.50
DBT2AEB30042EN Deity of Law C	.10	.15
DBT2AEB30043EN Dragon Blessing C	2.00	3.00
DBT2AEB30044EN Nirvana Sword Heavens Marius C	.10	.15
DBT2AEB30045EN Glee GleeBig Wave C	.10	.15
DBT2AEB30046EN Sword Edge Jailer Zagulus C	.10	.15
DBT2AEB30047EN Lethal Poison Jailer Silhouette Leroy C	.10	.15
DBT2AEB30048EN Sword Mountain Jailer Oniyamaarashi C	.10	.15
DBT2AEB30049EN Formless Jailer Izumonokami C	.10	.15
DBT2AEB30050EN Hazel Emperor Jailer Alking C	.10	.15
DBT2AEB30051EN Treasure Jailer Sonderdach C	.10	.15
DBT2AEB30052EN Glutton Jailer Glugiu C	.10	.15
DBT2AEB30053EN Headslay Jailer Brujeria C	.10	.15
DBT2AEB30054EN Thousand Limbed Jailer Cadval C	.10	.15
DBT2AEB30055EN OwnStyle Sliding Fang C	.10	.15
DBT2AEB30056EN Black Beast Battle Arts C	.10	.15
DBT2AEB30057EN Little Light C	2.00	3.00
DBT2AEB30058EN Shadow Crusader C	2.00	3.00
DBT2AEB30059EN Executioner Hammer Helles Fander C	.10	.15
DBT2AEB30060EN Blazing in my Hands is a White Light of Black C	.10	.15
DBT2AEB30061EN Guardian Deity Dragon of Paradise Avalon BR	1.50	2.50
DBT2AEB30062EN Master of the Searing Executioners Gagalgarios BR	2.00	3.00
DBT2AEB3020EN Dragon Sky Regression R	.20	.30
DBT2AEB3021EN Sky Dragon Divinity R	6.00	10.00
DBT2AEB3022EN Violent Jailer Dogaragan R	.20	.30
DBT2AEB3023EN Chaotic Hunt Jailer Soku R	1.50	2.50
DBT2AEB3024EN Master of the Searing Executioners Gagalgarios R	.20	.30
DBT2AEB3025EN Headhunt Jailer Sai R	.20	.30
DBT2AEB3026EN Damians Decision R	1.00	1.50
DBT2AEB3027EN Demon Way Jigokuezu R	.20	.30
DBT2AEB3028EN Inferno Rule R	.20	.30
DBT2AEB3029EN Helles Shield R	.20	.30
DBT2AEB3030EN Gate of Verdict Judgment R	2.00	3.00
DBT2AEB3031EN Melody Envoy Sword Flute Dragon C	.10	.15
DBT2AEB3032EN Nativity Envoy Bloom Dragon Jr C	.10	.15
DBT2AEB3033EN Regeneration Envoy Feather Dragon Mellow C	.10	.15
DBT2AEB3034EN Pure White Envoy Whitia C	.10	.15
DBT2AEB3035EN Trust Envoy Sephleed C	.10	.15
DBT2AEB3036EN Sparkling Envoy Kirarian C	.10	.15
DBT2AEB3037EN Blitz Envoy Shinybell C	1.25	2.00
DBT2AEB3038EN Aeon Envoy Soma C	.10	.15
DBT2AEB3039EN Infinitude Envoy Amrita C	.10	.15
DBT2AEB3EN Legend World SCR	20.00	30.00
DBT2AEB3EN Star Dragon World SCR	20.00	30.00
DBT2ASS20001EN Hollowed Arms Zodiac RRR	2.50	4.00
DBT2ASS20004EN Future Astrology RR	6.00	10.00
DBT2ASS20005EN Legblade Rejecter RR	.60	1.00
DBT2ASS20006EN Aquarius Starsentinel Aquario R	1.00	1.50
DBT2ASS20007EN Endeavor Star Deity Tierkreis R	.20	.30
DBT2ASS20008EN Meteorarms Nebulosa R	2.00	3.00
DBT2ASS20009EN Meteorarms Pisca Pisca R	.20	.30
DBT2ASS20010EN Espada Runar R	.20	.30
DBT2ASS20011EN The Law Gairaplus R	.20	.30
DBT2ASS20012EN Eliminator Jerkline R	.20	.30
DBT2ASS20013EN Scorpio Starsentinel Escorpia C	.10	.15
DBT2ASS20014EN Gemini Starsentinel Gemios C	.10	.15
DBT2ASS20015EN Virgo Starsentinel Virgen C	.10	.15
DBT2ASS20016EN Light Horn of the False Deity C	.10	.15
DBT2ASS20017EN Sentinels of the Stars C	.10	.15
DBT2ASS20018EN Medusa Shield C	.10	.15
DBT2ASS20019EN Divine Guidance C	.60	1.00
DBT2ASS2002EN Valkyrie Allknowing Alwidol RR	3.00	5.00
DBT2ASS2003EN Star Pole Sword Estrela RR	1.25	2.00
DBT2ASS2020EN Dragoneraser Jamming C	.10	.15
DBT2ASS2021EN Dragoneraser Defiler C	.60	1.00
DBT2ASS2022EN Eliminator Discarnea C	.10	.15
DBT2ASS2023EN Eliminator Qualia C	.10	.15
DBT2ASS2024EN Null Place C	.10	.15
DBT2ASS2025EN Speculight Ring C	.10	.15
DBT2ASS2026EN Hollowed Arms Zodiac BR	5.00	8.00
DBT2ASS2EN Legend World SCR	15.00	25.00
DBT2ASS2EN Star Dragon World SCR	10.00	15.00

2001 Harry Potter

Card	Low	High
COMPLETE SET (118)	100.00	200.00
BOOSTER BOX (36 PACKS)	60.00	100.00
BOOSTER PACK (11 CARDS)	3.00	5.00
RELEASED IN 2001		
1 Dean Thomas HPP	3.00	8.00
2 Draco Malfoy HPP	3.00	8.00
3 Draco Malfoy FP	3.00	8.00
4 Dragon's Escape FP	2.50	6.00
5 Elixir of Life FP	2.50	6.00
6 Gringotts Cart Ride FP	2.50	6.00
7 Hannah Abbott HPP	2.50	6.00
8 Harry Potter HPP	3.00	8.00
9 Hermione Granger HPP	3.00	8.00
10 Hermione Granger FP	3.00	8.00
11 Human Chess Game FP	2.50	6.00
12 Invisibility Cloak FP	2.50	6.00
13 Nearly Headless Nick HPP	2.50	6.00
14 Obliviate FP	2.50	6.00
15 Professor Filius Flitwick HPP	2.50	6.00
16 Professor Severus Snape HPP	3.00	8.00
17 Ron Weasley HPP	3.00	8.00
18 Rubeus Hagrid HPP	3.00	8.00
19 Troll in the Bathroom FP	2.50	6.00
20 Unicorn FP	5.00	12.00
21 Delivery Owl R	1.25	3.00
22 Draught of Living Death R	1.25	3.00
23 Harry Hunting R	1.25	3.00
24 History of Magic R	1.25	3.00
25 Incendio R	1.25	3.00
26 Malevolent Mixture R	1.25	3.00
27 Meet the Centaurs R	1.25	3.00
28 Mountain Troll R	1.25	3.00
29 Mrs Norris R	1.25	3.00
30 Norbert R	1.25	3.00
31 Phoenix Feather Wand R	1.25	3.00
32 Platform 9 3/4 R	1.25	3.00
33 Potion Ingredients R	1.25	3.00
34 Raven to Writing Desk R	1.25	3.00
35 Shrinking Potion R	1.25	3.00
36 Titillando R	1.25	3.00
37 Transfiguration Exam R	1.25	3.00
38 Transfiguration Test R	1.25	3.00
39 Privet Drive U	.30	.75
3b Draco Malfoy C	.30	.75
40 Alchemy U	.30	.75
41 Apothecary U	.30	.75
42 Apparate U	.30	.75
43 Baby Dragon U	.30	.75
44 Bluebell U	.30	.75
45 Burning Bitterroot Balm U	.30	.75
46 Cage U	.30	.75
47 Confundus U	.30	.75
48 Diagon Alley U	.30	.75
49 Dogbreath Potion U	.30	.75
50 Draco's Trick U	.30	.75
51 Dragon Heart Wand U	.30	.75
52 Fumos U	.30	.75
53 Guard Dog U	.30	.75
54 Hiding From Snape U	.30	.75
55 Kelpie U	.30	.75
56 Logic Puzzle U	.30	.75
57 Mysterious Egg U	.30	.75
58 Nurture U	.30	.75
59 Ollivanders U	.30	.75
60 Peeves Causes Trouble U	.30	.75
61 Pet Toad U	.30	.75
62 Pomfrey's Pick-Me-Up U	.30	.75
63 Potions Exam U	.30	.75
64 Reptile House U	.30	.75
65 Silver Cauldron U	.30	.75
66 Snuffling Potion U	.30	.75
67 Stupefy U	.30	.75
68 Take Root U	.30	.75
69 Transmogrify U	.30	.75
70 Unusual Pets U	.30	.75
71 Vanishing Glass U	.30	.75
72 Winged Keys U	.30	.75
73 Accio C	.15	.40
74 Avifors C	.15	.40
75 Baubillious C	.15	.40
76 Boa Constrictor C	.15	.40
77 Boil Cure C	.15	.40
78 Borrowed Wand C	.15	.40
79 Cauldron to Sieve C	.15	.40
80 Curious Raven C	.15	.40
81 Dungbomb C	.15	.40
82 Epoximise C	.15	.40
83 Erumpent Potion C	.15	.40
84 Fluffy Falls Asleep C	.15	.40
85 Forest Troll C	.15	.40
86 Forgetfulness Potion C	.15	.40
87 Foul Brew C	.15	.40
88 Giant Tarantula C	.15	.40
89 Hagrid and the Stranger C	.15	.40
90 Homework C	.15	.40
91 Hospital Wing C	.15	.40
92 Illegibilus C	.15	.40
93 Incarcifors C	.15	.40
94 Lost Notes C	.15	.40
95 Magical Mishap C	.15	.40
96 Noxious Poison C	.15	.40
97 Out of the Woods C	.15	.40
98 Pet Rat C	.15	.40
99 Pewter Cauldron C	.15	.40
100 Potions Mistake C	.15	.40
101 Remembrall C	.15	.40
102 Restricted Section C	.15	.40
103 Scottish Stag C	.15	.40
104 Snape's Question C	.15	.40
105 Squiggle Quill C	.15	.40
106 Steelclaw C	.15	.40
107 Surly Hound C	.15	.40
108 Toe Biter C	.15	.40
109 Vermillious C	.15	.40
10b Hermione Granger FP	.15	.40
110 Vicious Wolf C	.15	.40
111 Wingardium Leviosa! C	.15	.40
112 Wizard Crackers C	.15	.40
113 Care of Magical Creatures	.15	.40
114 Charms	.15	.40
115 Potions	.15	.40
116 Transfiguration	.15	.40

2012 Kaijudo Evo Fury

Card	Low	High
COMPLETE SET (61)	20.00	50.00
BOOSTER BOX (24 PACKS)	30.00	40.00
BOOSTER PACK (9 CARDS)	1.00	2.00
RELEASED ON NOVEMBER 3, 2012		
1 Chasm Entangler C	.30	.75
2 Cloudwalker Drone C	.10	.25
3 Cobalt, the Storm Knight VR	.40	1.00
4 Halon, Paragon of Light U	.20	.50
5 Helios Rings C	.10	.25
6 Photon Squad C	.10	.25
7 Prism-Blade Enforcer U	.30	.75
8 Recharge R	.30	.75
9 Shock Sentinel R	.30	.75
10 Starwing U	.20	.50
11 Twilight Commander R	.30	.75
12 Aquatic Expulsion R	.30	.75
13 Cyber Sprite C	.30	.75
14 Cyber Trader C	.10	.25
15 Emperor Axon U	.20	.50
16 Forklift Tank Glu-urrgle VR	.40	1.00
17 King Neptas R	.75	2.00
18 Neuron's Oracle R	.30	.75
19 Rapids Lurker Wwhhshrll C	.10	.25
20 Reef Gladiator U	.60	1.50
21 Search the Depths C	.10	.25
22 Sopan, Cyber Renegade U	.20	.50
23 Chimera Tyrant R	.30	.75
24 Gigabolver C	.10	.25
25 Gigazanda C	.10	.25
26 Hydra Medusa U	.75	2.00
27 Locomotivator U	.20	.50
28 Olgate, Knight of Shadow R	.30	.75
29 Return from Beyond R	.30	.75
30 Scavenging Chimera U	.40	1.00
31 Screeching Scaradorable VR	3.00	8.00
32 Slyth C	.10	.25
33 Swampstench Worm C	.10	.25
34 Big Hissy VR	.40	1.00
35 Blastforge Captain R	.30	.75
36 Cliffcutter C	.10	.25
37 Drakon Warchief U	.20	.50
38 Gunwing Dragon U	.20	.50
39 Heat Seekers C	.10	.25
40 Jet-Thrust Darter C	.60	1.50
41 Jetflame Bodyguard C	.30	.75
42 Laser-Arm Drakon U	.20	.50
43 Lava Leaper R	.30	.75
44 Twin-Cannon Maelstrom R	.30	.75
45 Bronze-Arm Sabertooth U	.30	.75
46 Forsett, Heroic Shaman R	.30	.75
47 Granite Avenger R	.30	.75
48 Illusory Berry C	.10	.25
49 Lepidos the Ancient VR	.40	1.00
50 Moonhowler Tribe C	.10	.25
51 Prickleback C	.40	1.00
52 Reap and Sow C	.30	.75
53 Silver Fist U	.20	.50
54 Snapclaw U	.20	.50
55 Tendril Grasp R	.40	1.00
D1 Ra-Vu the Stormbringer SR	1.00	2.50
S1 Orion, Radiant Fury SR	3.00	8.00
S2 Emperor Neuron SR	8.00	20.00
S3 Tekamora the Wretched SR	.75	2.00
S4 Evo Fury Tatsurion SR	1.25	3.00
S5 Flamespike Tatsurion SR	1.50	4.00

2012 Kaijudo Rise of the Duel Masters

Card	Low	High
COMPLETE SET (182)	30.00	80.00
BOOSTER BOX (24 PACKS)		
BOOSTER PACK (9 CARDS)		
RELEASED ON SEPTEMBER 7, 2012		
1 Argus, Vigilant Seer C	.10	.25
2 Astinos, the Cloud Knight R	.30	.75
3 Blinder Beetle C	.30	.75
4 Covering Fire C	.40	1.00
5 Current Charger R	.30	.75
6 Grand Gure, Tower Keeper VR	.40	1.00
7 Halon U	.20	.50
8 Jade Monitor C	.10	.25
9 Keeper of Clouds U	.20	.50
10 Keeper of Dawn R	.30	.75
11 Keeper of Twilight R	.30	.75
12 Logic Cube U	.40	1.00
13 Luminar C	.10	.25
14 Magris the Magnetizer C	.40	1.00
15 Nimbus Scout C	.10	.25
16 Orbital Observer U	.20	.50
17 Paladio, Patrol Leader U	.20	.50
18 Perimeter Drone U	.20	.50
19 Portal Tech R	.30	.75
20 Rally the Reserves U	.30	.75
21 Razorpine Tree R	.30	.75
22 Regroup U	.20	.50
23 Seer Serpent VR	.40	1.00
24 Shaw K'Naw R	.30	.75
25 Spyweb Scurrier U	.20	.50
26 Stalker Sphere C	.10	.25
27 Starlight Strategist R	.30	.75
28 Stormspark Blast R	2.50	6.00
29 Strobe Flash C	.10	.25
30 Sun-Stalk Seed C	.10	.25
31 Sunshock C	.10	.25
32 Thunder Cruiser C	.30	.75
33 Urth, the Overlord VR	.40	1.00
34 Aqua Commando U	.20	.50
35 Aqua Knight R	.30	.75
36 Aqua Seneschal C	.10	.25
37 Aqua Soldier C	.10	.25

38 Buoyant Blowfish C .10 .25
39 Crystal Memory R .75 2.00
40 Finbarr, Council of Logos U .20 .50
41 Fluorogill Manta C .10 .25
42 Frogzooka U .20 .50
43 Hokira, Council of Logos R .30 .75
44 Hydro Spy U .20 .50
45 Hydrobot Crab U .20 .50
46 Ice Blade C .10 .25
47 Ice Launcher C .10 .25
48 King Bullfang R .30 .75
49 King Coral R .75 2.00
50 King Nautilus VR .40 1.00
51 King Pontias U .20 .50
52 Knowledge Warden C .10 .25
53 Logos Scan C .10 .25
54 Memory Swarm C .10 .25
55 Midnight Crawler VR .40 1.00
56 Milporo, Council of Logos R .30 .75
57 Predict C .10 .25
58 Queen Orion VR .40 1.00
59 Reef Prince Glu-urrgle R .30 .75
60 Reef-Eye C .10 .25
61 Rusalka, Aqua Chaser U .60 1.50
62 Spy Mission U .20 .50
63 Steam Star Grapplog C .10 .25
64 Teleport U .20 .50
65 Thought Probe R .30 .75
66 Veil Vortex R .30 .75
67 Acid-Tongue Chimera U .20 .50
68 Black Feather of Shadow Abyss R .30 .75
69 Bone Blades C .10 .25
70 Brain Squirmer C .10 .25
71 Dark Return U .20 .50
72 Death Smoke U .60 1.50
73 Draxar, the Soul Crusher C .10 .25
74 Dream Pirate U .20 .50
75 Fumes C .10 .25
76 Gigargon R .30 .75
77 Gigastand U .50 1.25
78 Gorgeon, Shadow of Gluttony U .20 .50
79 Grave Scrounger C .10 .25
80 Grave Worm Hatchling C .10 .25
81 Horrid Stinger U .20 .50
82 Kronkos, General of Fear R .30 .75
83 Marrow Ooze C .30 .75
84 Quakes the Unclean C .10 .25
85 Razorkinder Puppet VR .40 1.00
86 Roton the Destroyer R .30 .75
87 Rupture Spider U .20 .50
88 Scaradorable of Gloom Hollow R 8.00 20.00
89 Scaradorable the Hunter VR .40 1.00
90 Skeeter Swarmer C .30 .75
91 Skull Cutter C .40 1.00
92 Skull Shatter R .30 .75
93 Specter Claw C .40 1.00
94 Terror Pit R 2.00 5.00
95 Trox, General of Destruction VR .40 1.00
96 Venom Worm C .10 .25
97 Voidwing R .30 .75
98 Writhing Bone Ghoul U .20 .50
99 Zagaan, the Bone Knight R .30 .75
100 Badlands Lizard U .20 .50
101 Barrage U .30 .75
102 Blastforge Slaver U .20 .50
103 Blaze Belcher C .50 1.25
104 Bolgash Dragon VR .40 1.00
105 Bolshack Dragon R .30 .75
106 Bolt-Tail Dragon R .30 .75
107 Comet Missile C .10 .25
108 Draglide the Swiftest C .10 .25
109 Drakon Weaponsmith C .10 .25
110 Flame Aura C .10 .25
111 Flametropus R .30 .75
112 Gatling Skyterror C .10 .25
113 Gilaflame the Assaulter VR 1.25 3.00
114 Hyperspeed Dragon R .40 1.00
115 Kenina the Igniter C .10 .25
116 Legionnaire Lizard R .30 .75
117 Little Hissy U .20 .50
118 Magma Madness R .30 .75
119 Meteosaur U .20 .50
120 Moorna, Gatling Dragon VR .40 1.00
121 Om Nom Nom U .20 .50
122 Overcharge U .20 .50
123 Pyro Trooper C .10 .25
124 Rock Bite C .10 .25
125 Simian Trooper Grash C .10 .25
126 Skycrusher's Elite R .30 .75
127 Snaptongue Lizard U .20 .50
128 Stonesaur C .20 .50
129 Super Bazooka Volcanodon U .20 .50
130 Tornado Flame R .30 .75
131 Tracer Rounds R .30 .75
132 Vorg C .10 .25
133 Ambush Scorpion C .10 .25
134 Brave Giant U .20 .50
135 Breach the Veil U .20 .50
136 Bronze-Arm Tribe C .10 .25
137 Carnivorous Dahlia U .20 .50
138 Deathblade Beetle VR .40 1.00
139 Drifting Toadstool U .20 .50
140 Essence Elf C .10 .25
141 Fear Fang C .10 .25
142 Forest Hornet C .10 .25
143 Gasbag C .10 .25
144 Gigahorn Charger R .30 .75
145 Karate Carrot U .20 .50
146 Launcher Locust R .30 .75
147 Mana Storm R 2.00 5.00
148 Manabind U .20 .50
149 Mighty Shouter VR .40 1.00
150 Power Surge U .20 .50
151 Raging Goliant U .30 .75
152 Razorhide C .10 .25
153 Red-Eye Scorpion R .30 .75
154 Return to the Soil C .10 .25
155 Roaming Bloodmane VR .40 1.00
156 Root Trap R 1.00 2.50
157 Rumbling Terrasaur C .10 .25
158 Shell Dome R .30 .75
159 Sniper Mosquito C .10 .25
160 Splinterclaw Wasp R .30 .75
161 Sprout C .40 1.00
162 Stampeding Longhorn R .30 .75
163 The Great Arena R .50 1.25
164 Thorny Creeper C .10 .25
165 Three-Eyed Dragonfly C .10 .25
D1 Dark Scaradorable SR 1.00 2.50
D2 Wrist-Rockets Tatsurion SR .40 1.00
S1 Ra-Vu, Seeker of Lightning SR 2.50 6.00
S2 Radiant, the Lawbringer SR .40 1.00
S3 Sasha, Channeler of Light SR .40 1.00
S4 Hovercraft Glu-urrgle SR 3.00 8.00
S5 King Tsunami SR .40 1.00
S6 Waterspout Gargoyle SR 1.25 3.00
S7 Death Liger, Lion of Chaos SR .40 1.00
S8 Diabrost, Shadow Marshal SR .40 1.00
S9 Megaria, the Collector SR .40 1.00
S10 Crimson Wyvern SR 1.50 4.00
S11 Meteor Dragon SR .40 1.00
S12 Tatsurion the Unchained SR 2.50 6.00
S13 Bestial Rage Tatsurion SR .75 2.00
S14 Earthstomp Giant SR .40 1.00
S15 Xeno Mantis SR .75 2.00

2012 Kaijudo Tatsurion vs. Razorkinder Battle Deck

COMPLETE SET (45) 8.00 20.00
RELEASED ON JUNE 27, 2012
1 Aqua Seneschal C .10 .25
2 Frogzooka U .20 .50
3 Hydro Spy U .20 .50
4 Hydrobot Crab U .20 .50
5 Ice Blade C .10 .25
6 King Nautilus VR .40 1.00
7 King Pontias U .20 .50
8 Reef-Eye C .10 .25
9 Spy Mission U .20 .50
10 Teleport U .20 .50
11 Bone Blades C .10 .25
12 Brain Squirmer C .10 .25
13 Death Smoke U .30 .75
14 Dream Pirate U .20 .50
15 Fumes C .10 .25
16 Gigargon R .30 .75
17 Grave Worm Hatchling C .10 .25
18 Horrid Stinger U .20 .50
19 Skeeter Swarmer C .10 .25
20 Skull Cutter C .10 .25
21 Terror Pit R 2.00 5.00
22 Zagaan, the Bone Knight R .30 .75
23 Blaze Belcher C .10 .25
24 Comet Missile C .50 1.25
25 Draglide the Swiftest C .10 .25
26 Flametropus R .30 .75
27 Gatling Skyterror C .10 .25
28 Little Hissy U .20 .50
29 Overcharge U .20 .50
30 Pyro Trooper C .10 .25
31 Rock Bite C .10 .25
32 Simian Trooper Grash C .10 .25
33 Tornado Flame R .30 .75
34 Ambush Scorpion C .10 .25
35 Brave Giant U .20 .50
36 Bronze-Arm Tribe C .40 1.00
37 Essence Elf C .10 .25
38 Raging Goliant U .20 .50
39 Return to the Soil C .10 .25
40 Roaming Bloodmane VR .40 1.00
41 Root Trap R 1.25 3.00
42 Rumbling Terrasaur C .10 .25
43 Sprout C .50 1.25
S1 Razorkinder SR .40 1.00
S2 Tatsurion SR .40 1.00

2012 Kaijudo The Dojo Edition

COMPLETE SET (61) 12.00 30.00
BOOSTER BOX (24 PACKS) 30.00 40.00
BOOSTER PACK (9 CARDS) 1.00 2.00
RELEASED ON JULY 24, 2012
1 Blinder Beetle C .10 .25
2 Grand Gure, Tower Keeper VR .30 .75
3 Keeper of Clouds C .10 .25
4 Keeper of Dawn R .25 .60
5 Keeper of Twilight R .25 .60
6 Luminar C .10 .25
7 Regroup U .20 .50
8 Shaw K'Naw R .40 1.00
9 Star Lantern U .20 .50
10 Sun-Stalk Seed C .10 .25
11 Sunshock C .10 .25
12 Aqua Commando U .20 .50
13 Aqua Soldier C .10 .25
14 Fluorogill Manta C .10 .25
15 Hydro Spy U .20 .50
16 Ice Blade C .10 .25
17 King Bullfang R .25 .60
18 Logos Scan C .10 .25
19 Potato Gun Glu-urrgle VR .30 .75
20 Reef Prince Glu-urrgle R .25 .60
21 Veil Vortex R .25 .60
22 Vikorakas U .20 .50
23 Acid-Tongue Chimera U .20 .50
24 Black Feather of Shadow Abyss R .25 .60
25 Brain Squirmer C .10 .25
26 Ghost Spy U .20 .50
27 Gigargon R .25 .60
28 Skeeter Swarmer C .10 .25
29 Skull Cutter C .10 .25
30 Specter Claw C .10 .25
31 Terror Pit R 1.25 3.00
32 Trox, General of Destruction VR .30 .75
33 Writhing Bone Ghoul U .20 .50
34 Bolt-Tail Dragon R .25 .60
35 Chain-Lash Tatsurion R .40 1.00
36 Comet Missile C .30 .75
37 Draglide the Swiftest C .10 .25
38 Drakon Weaponsmith C .10 .25
39 Gatling Skyterror C .10 .25
40 Gilaflame the Assaulter VR 1.25 3.00
41 Little Hissy U .20 .50
42 Om Nom Nom U .20 .50
43 Super Bazooka Volcanodon U .20 .50
44 Tornado Flame R .25 .60
45 Brave Giant U .20 .50
46 Chief Many-Tribes U .20 .50
47 Deathblade Beetle VR .30 .75
48 Forest Hornet C .10 .25
49 Karate Carrot U .20 .50
50 Razorhide C .40 1.00
51 Root Trap R .75 2.00
52 Rumbling Terrasaur C .10 .25
53 Splinterclaw Wasp R .25 .60
54 Sprout C .30 .75
55 Stampeding Longhorn R .25 .60
D1 Quillspike Tatsurion SR .40 1.00
S1 Alcadeus, Winged Justice SR .40 1.00
S2 King Tsunami SR .40 1.00
S3 Bat-Breath Scaradorable SR 4.00 10.00
S4 Lord Skycrusher SR 2.50 6.00
S5 Terradragon Regarion Doom SR 4.00 10.00

2013 Kaijudo Clash of the Duel Masters

COMPLETE SET (122) 40.00 100.00
BOOSTER BOX (24 PACKS) 30.00 40.00
BOOSTER PACK (9 CARDS) 1.00 2.00
RELEASED ON MAY 24, 2013
1 Azuri, the Dawnbreaker VR .40 1.00
2 Beliqua the Ascender C .10 .25
3 Citadel Magistrate R .30 .75
4 Citadel Steward U .20 .50
5 Containment Field C .10 .25
6 Halo Hawk C .10 .25
7 Keeper of Laws R 6.00 15.00
8 Lars, Virtuous Imager U .20 .50
9 Rain-Cloud Kraken C .10 .25
10 Rodi Gale, Night Guardian U .20 .50
11 Shimmerwing C .10 .25
12 Spire Zealot U .20 .50
13 Thunder Reaper C .10 .25
14 Zone Defense R .30 .75
15 Aeropica C .10 .25
16 Aqua Rider C .10 .25
17 Aqua-Ranger Commander U .20 .50
18 Cyber Cyclones U .20 .50
19 Cyber Lord Corile U .20 .50
20 Cybergrid Bandit C .10 .25
21 Glu-urrgle 2.0 R .30 .75
22 Hazard Crawler R .40 1.00
23 King Poseidon VR .40 1.00
24 Mark of Tritonus R .30 .75
25 Queen Sargasso C .10 .25
26 Reef Scout C .10 .25
27 Tenuous Trove C .10 .25
28 Time Rime U .20 .50
29 Arachnoir of Cobweb Cavern C .10 .25
30 Cave Gulper C .10 .25
31 Dreadhusk C .10 .25
32 Fanged Horror C .10 .25
33 Gregoria the Malevolent R .30 .75
34 Gregoria's Fortress R .30 .75
35 Mesmerize U .20 .50
36 Shapeshifter Scaradorable VR 1.00 2.50
37 Skeleton Soldier C .10 .25
38 Soul Schism U .20 .50
39 Spectral Mummy U .20 .50
40 Suffocate R .30 .75
41 Thunder Grub U .20 .50
42 Toxic Fog C .10 .25
43 Assault Dragon R .30 .75
44 Blade-Rush Wyvern C .10 .25
45 Blastforge Bruiser C .10 .25
46 Chaotic Skyterror C .10 .25
47 Drill Storm U .20 .50
48 Ember-Eye U .20 .50
49 Flame Spinner U .20 .50
50 Jump Jets C .10 .25
51 Kaboom! R .30 .75
52 Magma Dragon Melgars VR .40 1.00
53 Mark of Infernus R .30 .75
54 Redscale Drakon C .10 .25
55 Scaled Impaler U .20 .50
56 Toolbot C .10 .25
57 Chief Thorn-Bringer R .40 1.00
58 Deepwood Druid C .10 .25
59 Ironvine Dragon VR .40 1.00
60 Jackalax C .10 .25
61 Lumbering Elderwood U .20 .50
62 Mana Tick U .20 .50
63 Noble Rumbling Terrasaur R .30 .75
64 Reinforce C .10 .25
65 Saber Mantis C .10 .25
66 Shaman Broccoli C .10 .25
67 Shardhide Tusker C .10 .25
68 Silver Axe U .20 .50
69 Slumbering Titan R .30 .75
70 Spore Siren U .20 .50
71 Aqua Strider C .30 .75
72 Crusader Engine R .30 .75
73 Elevan the Seeker R .30 .75
74 Memory Keeper C .10 .25
75 Panopter VR .40 1.00
76 Piercing Judgment R .75 2.00
77 Sunspout Quartz U .20 .50
78 Wave Lancer U .20 .50
79 Blade Seer U .20 .50
80 Dawnflower Quartz U .20 .50
81 Fullmetal Lemon C .40 1.00
82 Humonculon the Blaster R 1.50 4.00
83 Oathsworn Call R .40 1.00
84 Starseed Squadron VR .40 1.00
85 Suncloak Protector R .30 .75
86 Sword Horned C .10 .25
87 Cryptic Worm C .10 .25
88 Featherfin Stalker R .40 1.00
89 Freakish Test Subject U .20 .50
90 Grip of Despair R .30 .75
91 Ramis the Cloaked C .10 .25
92 Seacurse Quartz U .20 .50
93 Skarvos the Assassin R .30 .75
94 Spelljacker VR .40 1.00
95 Baron Burnfingers R .30 .75

96 Chasmblaze Quartz U	.20	.50
97 Galzak of Shadow Pass VR	.40	1.00
98 Haunted Mech C	.10	.25
99 Kronax the Brutal R	.30	.75
100 Lizard-Skin Puppet U	.20	.50
101 Oozing Lavasaur C	.10	.25
102 Soul Vortex R	.30	.75
103 Cindermoss Quartz U	.20	.50
104 Fight R	.30	.75
105 Gorim the Striker R	.30	.75
106 Lotus Warrior U	.20	.50
107 Smolderhorn C	.10	.25
108 Steamtank Kryon VR	.60	1.50
109 Tatsurion the Champion R	.30	.75
110 Weaponized Razorcat C	.10	.25
D1 General Finbarr SR	3.00	8.00
D2 General Skycrusher SR	1.50	4.00
S1 Sasha the Observer SR	.75	2.00
S2 King Tritonus SR	8.00	20.00
S3 Death Liger, Apex Predator SR	.75	2.00
S4 Infernus the Immolator SR	6.00	15.00
S5 The Hive Queen SR	8.00	20.00
S6 Truthseeker Forion SR	.40	1.00
S7 Guardian Akhal-Teek SR	2.00	5.00
S8 Squillace Scourge SR	8.00	20.00
S9 Shadeblaze the Corruptor SR	4.00	10.00
S10 Tatsurion the Relentless SR	2.50	6.00

2013 Kaijudo Dragon Master Collection Kit

2-CARD SET ISSUED W/DRAGON MASTER KIT
RELEASED ON FEBRUARY 19, 2013

1 Necrodragon of Vile Ichor SR	.40	1.00
2 Hammer Dragon Foulbyrn SR	.40	1.00

2013 Kaijudo DragonStrike Infernus

COMPLETE SET (60)	30.00	80.00
BOOSTER BOX (24 PACKS)	30.00	40.00
BOOSTER PACK (9 CARDS)	1.00	2.00
RELEASED ON MARCH 15, 2013		
1 Arachnopod R	.25	.60
2 Aurora Valkyrie U	.20	.50
3 Canyon Skimmer C	.10	.25
4 Defense Mode C	.10	.25
5 Gemini Dragon R	.40	1.00
6 Lux U	.60	1.50
7 Lyra, the Blazing Sun VR	5.00	12.00
8 Reflector Cannon R	.25	.60
9 Spark Cage U	.20	.50
10 Storm Seeker C	.10	.25
11 Vectro Scout C	.10	.25
12 Bottle of Wishes R	.25	.60
13 Coral-Claw C	.10	.25
14 Dragon of Reflections R	.30	.75
15 Emperor Dendrite U	.20	.50
16 Eye of the Tides C	.10	.25
17 Kindrix the Psionic VR	.30	.75
18 Logos Lookout C	.10	.25
19 Man o' Warden U	.20	.50
20 Nix U	.30	.75
21 Queen Taniwha R	.25	.60
22 Trial and Error C	.10	.25
23 Ancient Grave Worm U	.20	.50
24 Bonerattle Dragon R	.40	1.00
25 Devouring Smog U	.20	.50
26 Dreadclaw, Dark Herald VR	.30	.75
27 Drooling Worm C	.10	.25
28 Gloom Tomb C	.20	.50
29 Grudge Weaver U	.30	.75
30 Patchwork Surgeon R	.25	.60
31 Ripper Reaper R	1.00	2.50
32 Toothed Grubling C	.10	.25
33 Umbra U	.40	1.00
34 Bagash U	.20	.50
35 Blastforge Dragon C	.10	.25
36 Branca the Treacherous C	.20	.50
37 Burnclaw the Relentless U	.30	.75
38 Dragon's Breath R	.25	.60
39 Explosive Infantry C	.20	.50
40 Hammer Fist C	.10	.25
41 Herald of Infernus R	2.50	6.00
42 Kenina U	.40	1.00
43 Ragefire Tatsurion VR	.30	.75
44 Spellbane Dragon R	.30	.75
45 Belua U	.20	.50
46 Copper Locust C	.10	.25
47 Dauntless Tusker R	.30	.75
48 Energize C	.20	.50
49 Ensnare R	.25	.60
50 Hornblade Dragon R	.25	.60
51 Manapod Beetle C	.20	.50
52 Sok'ran the Untamed VR	.30	.75
53 Steel Hammer C	.10	.25
54 The Swarmleader U	.20	.50
55 Treetop Dragon U	.20	.50
S1 Andromeda of the Citadel SR	15.00	40.00
S2 Issyl of the Frozen Wastes SR	1.00	2.50
S3 Dracothane of the Abyss SR	6.00	15.00
S4 Infernus the Awakened SR	8.00	20.00
S5 Kurragar of the Hordes SR	6.00	15.00

2013 Kaijudo Invasion Earth

COMPLETE SET (91)	50.00	120.00
BOOSTER BOX (24 PACKS)	20.00	30.00
BOOSTER PACK (9 CARDS)	.75	1.25
RELEASED ON NOVEMBER 8, 2013		
1 Arc Ward U	.20	.50
2 Detain C	.10	.25
3 Graviton Generator U	.20	.50
4 Haven's Elite VR	1.00	2.50
5 Ion Cruiser C	.10	.25
6 Sunmote Field R	.30	.75
7 Sunwhip Sentry R	.30	.75
8 Aqua Trickster C	.10	.25
9 Engulf C	.10	.25
10 Guardian Rusalka U	.20	.50
11 King Barnacle R	.30	.75
12 Morphing Pod R	.30	.75
13 Seneschal, Choten's Lieutenant VR	.40	1.00
14 Veil Slip U	.20	.50
15 Chimera Predator C	.10	.25
16 Ravenous Web-Leg R	.30	.75
17 Sickly Larva U	.20	.50
18 Snake Trap C	.10	.25
19 Spinning Terror R	.40	1.00
20 Vile Malvictus VR	.60	1.50
21 Wandering Brain-Eater U	.20	.50
22 Aerial Bombardment R	.30	.75
23 Blastforge Marauder R	.30	.75
24 Drakon Upstart C	.10	.25
25 Flame Fangs U	.20	.50
26 Galsaur VR	.60	1.50
27 Manic Mechanic U	.20	.50
28 Ricochet Shot C	.10	.25
29 Broadsword Butterfly C	.10	.25
30 Cultivate C	.10	.25
31 Defiant Shaman U	.20	.50
32 Mark of Almighty Colossus R	.30	.75
33 Nurturing Hive U	.20	.50
34 Tricky Turnip VR	3.00	8.00
35 Tusked Shouter R	.30	.75
36 Choten's Stalker Sphere C	.10	.25
37 Fallen Keeper U	.20	.50
38 Luminar Unleashed VR	.40	1.00
39 Reverberate R	1.00	2.50
40 Skyvolt Mech C	.10	.25
41 Corvus Dragon R	.30	.75
42 Lamp-Lighter C	.10	.25
43 Mad Watcher C	.10	.25
44 Panic and Disorder U	.20	.50
45 Bodyguard Vorg C	.10	.25
46 Crash and Burn U	.20	.50
47 Dawnblaze Patrol C	.10	.25
48 Volcano Dervish R	.30	.75
49 Beam Bloom U	.20	.50
50 Chief Toko R	.30	.75
51 Hunter Sphere C	.10	.25
52 Stratus Beetle C	.10	.25
53 Emergency Protocol R	.30	.75
54 Essence Shade C	.10	.25
55 Fate's Hand U	.20	.50
56 Sabotage Worm C	.10	.25
57 The Reviled VR	.60	1.50
58 Ballistic Skyterror C	.10	.25
59 Blitz Commando R	.30	.75
60 Cyber Trooper C	.10	.25
61 Frantic Blast U	.20	.50
62 Bad Apple VR	2.50	6.00
63 Bronze-Arm Renegade C	.10	.25
64 Crystal Pulse U	.20	.50
65 Tainted Quartz C	.10	.25
66 Telanar, the Stormer R	.30	.75
67 Boom Skull C	.10	.25
68 Flamespine Ravager VR	.60	1.50
69 Infernal Taskmaster R	.30	.75
70 Lava-Tube Crawler C	.10	.25
71 XT-4 Brutefist U	.20	.50
72 Cackling Fiend C	.10	.25
73 Fearfeather the Scavenger VR	.40	1.00
74 Looming Devourer R	.30	.75
75 Shadow Strike U	.20	.50
76 Skulking Cypress C	.10	.25
77 Armored Sentinel U	.20	.50
78 Corporal Pepper C	.10	.25
79 Emblazoned Giant C	.10	.25
80 Victory Gunner R	.60	1.50
D1 Vicious Squillace Scourge SR	2.00	5.00
S1 Cassiopeia Starborn SR	15.00	40.00
S2 Warbringer Poseidon SR	6.00	15.00
S3 Megaria, the Deceiver SR	8.00	20.00
S4 Napalmeon the Conquering SR	5.00	12.00
S5 Almighty Colossus SR	10.00	25.00
S6 Dark-Seer Jurlon SR	10.00	25.00
S7 Major Ao SR	8.00	20.00
S8 Elder Titan Auralia SR	2.00	5.00
S9 General Charzon SR	3.00	8.00
S10 Tatsurion the Brawler SR	1.50	4.00

2013 Kaijudo Shattered Alliances

COMPLETE SET (91)	40.00	100.00
BOOSTER BOX (24 PACKS)	20.00	30.00
BOOSTER PACK (9 CARDS)	.75	1.25
RELEASED ON SEPTEMBER 13, 2013		
1 Blade Barrier C	.10	.25
2 Blinder Beetle Prime R	1.25	3.00
3 Heliosphere C	.10	.25
4 Mark of Eternal Haven R	.30	.75
5 Ra-Vu the Indomitable VR	.40	1.00
6 Replicator Patrol C	.10	.25
7 Repulse U	.20	.50
8 Sentrus U	.20	.50
9 Angler Cluster C	.10	.25
10 Aqua-Reflector Nomulos R	.30	.75
11 Bladefish C	.10	.25
12 Cyber Scamp R	1.50	4.00
13 Deep Mind Probe C	.10	.25
14 Finbarr's Dreadnought VR	.40	1.00
15 Phase Scout U	.20	.50
16 Recon Mission U	.20	.50
17 Curse-Eye Black Feather R	.30	.75
18 Dagger Doll C	.10	.25
19 Doomblast Scaradorable VR	.40	1.00
20 Gaunt Boneweaver U	.20	.50
21 Ghost Bite C	.10	.25
22 Maddening Whispers VR	.40	1.00
23 Mark of Kalima R	.30	.75
24 Tygrif C	.10	.25
25 Blastforge Scrapper C	.10	.25
26 Blazetrail Gilaflame R	.30	.75
27 Cinder Fist C	.10	.25
28 Magma Ram U	.20	.50
29 Onslaught Trooper R	.30	.75
30 Skycrusher's Volcano-Ship VR	.40	1.00
31 Skytalon Harrier U	.20	.50
32 Sledgehammer Slammer C	.10	.25
33 Dawn Giant VR	.40	1.00
34 Headstrong Wanderer C	.10	.25
35 Jarbala Keeper C	.10	.25
36 Monstrify C	.10	.25
37 Ninja Pumpkin R	.30	.75
38 Striding Hearthwood R	.30	.75
39 Transforming Totem U	.20	.50
40 Wild Growth U	.20	.50
41 Calamity Bell R	.30	.75
42 Glimmergloom Quartz U	.20	.50
43 Lost Patrol C	.10	.25
44 Serpens, the Spirit Shifter VR	.60	1.50
45 Spire Puppet C	.10	.25
46 Stingwing C	.10	.25
47 Tar Gusher U	.20	.50
48 Zoltara the Mercenary R	.30	.75
49 Axos the Avenger R	.30	.75
50 Blitzer-Mech Falkora VR	.60	1.50
51 Flamewing Phoenix U	.20	.50
52 Metal Max C	.10	.25
53 Plasma Pincer C	.10	.25
54 Prototype Gunship C	.10	.25
55 Starforge Quartz U	.20	.50
56 Sunstrike R	.30	.75
57 Aqua Trooper XJ-3 C	.10	.25
58 Flamespitter U	.20	.50
59 Flame-Vent Diver C	.10	.25
60 Frostburn Quartz U	.20	.50
61 Krazzix the Volatile VR	.40	1.00
62 Mar-Blurpa the Weaponsmith R	.30	.75
63 Scalding Surge R	.30	.75
64 Unstable Rockhound C	.10	.25
65 Bloomwarden C	.10	.25
66 Crystalize R	.30	.75
67 Kivu, Ingenious Shaman VR	1.25	3.00
68 Lore-Strider U	.20	.50
69 Mistvine Quartz U	.20	.50
70 Oktuska the Infused R	.30	.75
71 Squall Darter C	.10	.25
72 Wavebreaker Tribe C	.10	.25
73 Cavernmold Quartz U	.20	.50
74 Foul Mana R	.30	.75
75 Goop Striker C	.10	.25
76 Haunted Harvest C	.10	.25
77 Masked Gravewing U	.20	.50
78 Obsidian Death VR	.40	1.00
79 Skaak the Stinger R	.30	.75
80 Terror Hound C	.10	.25
D1 Death Liger the Justicar SR	1.25	3.00
S1 Eternal Haven SR	15.00	40.00
S2 King Alboran SR	1.00	2.50
S3 Queen Kalima SR	10.00	25.00
S4 Forgelord Vesuvius SR	.60	1.50
S5 Wildstrider Ramnoth SR	5.00	12.00
S6 Twilight Archon SR	6.00	15.00
S7 Dragon Knight Volaron SR	4.00	10.00
S8 Heretic Prince Var-rakka SR	4.00	10.00
S9 Borran, the Reality Shaper SR	2.00	5.00
S10 Khordia, the Soul Tyrant SR	4.00	10.00

2013 Kaijudo Triple Strike

COMPLETE SET (25)	5.00	12.00
RELEASED ON JULY 12, 2013		
1 Aqua Seneschal C	.10	.25
2 Bottle of Wishes R	.30	.75
3 Crystal Memory R	1.25	3.00
4 Fluorogill Manta C	.10	.25
5 Logos Scan C	.10	.25
6 Reef-Eye C	.10	.25
7 Black Feather of Shadow Abyss R	.30	.75
8 Bone Blades C	.10	.25
9 Dream Pirate U	.20	.50
10 Razorkinder SR	.40	1.00
11 Skull Shatter R	.30	.75
12 Terror Pit R	1.50	4.00
13 Bolshack Dragon R	.30	.75
14 Comet Missile C	.30	.75
15 Dragon's Breath R	.30	.75
16 Hyperspeed Dragon R	.30	.75
17 Meteosaur U	.20	.50
18 Moorna, Gatling Dragon VR	.40	1.00
19 Rock Bite C	.10	.25
20 Tornado Flame R	.75	2.00
21 Grip of Despair R	.30	.75
22 Soul Vortex R	.30	.75
D1 Magnet Mech Glu-urrgle SR	.40	1.00
D2 Feral Scaradorable SR	.40	1.00
D3 Rampaging Tatsurion SR	.40	1.00

2014 Kaijudo The 5 Mystics

COMPLETE SET (60)	100.00	150.00
RELEASED ON MARCH 14, 2014		
1 Arcane Warden U	.30	.50
2 Beacon Drone C	.15	.25
3 Caelum Skysworn R	1.25	2.00
4 Cerulean Core C	.15	.25
5 Haven's Command U	.30	.50
6 Lightning Sniper C	.15	.25
7 Luminous Shieldwing R	.60	1.00
8 Radiant Purification VR	3.00	5.00
9 Restrain C	.15	.25
10 Solar Helix U	.30	.50
11 Captain Orwellia C	.15	.25
12 Captive Squill C	.15	.25
13 Hypergrid Hacker U	.30	.50
14 Liquid Compulsion VR	2.50	4.00
15 Neural Helix U	.30	.50
16 Octobot Infiltrator U	.30	.50
17 Queen Riptide R	1.00	1.50
18 Saucer-Head Shark U	.30	.50
19 Sawtooth Cyclone C	.15	.25
20 The Mystic of Water R	.75	1.25
21 Absolute Darkness VR	3.00	5.00
22 Eager Cleaver C	.15	.25
23 Harbringer of the Void R	1.00	1.50
24 Night Haunt U	.30	.50
25 Nightmare Helix U	.30	.50
26 Rib Collector C	.15	.25
27 Scourge Lord U	.30	.50
28 Terrorfang Clinger C	.15	.25
29 The Mystic of Darkness R	1.50	2.50
30 Vengeful Blast C	.15	.25
31 Absolute Incineration VR	5.00	8.00
32 Blaze Helix U	.30	.50
33 Bluescale Drakon C	.15	.25
34 Doomcannon Mech U	.30	.50
35 Lavanator 3000 C	.15	.25
36 Morkaz the Defiant R	1.75	3.00
37 Sparkspine Lizard U	.30	.50

Card	Low	High
38 The Disassembler C	.15	.25
39 The Mystic of Fire R	3.00	5.00
40 Waylay C	.15	.25
41 Blademane C	.15	.25
42 Broodmother R	1.00	1.50
43 Jarbala Swordbreaker C	.15	.25
44 Rampage C	.15	.25
45 Seedpod Puffer C	.15	.25
46 Sledgefoot U	.30	.50
47 Swift Regeneration VR	3.00	5.00
48 Taunting Totem U	.30	.50
49 The Mystic of Nature R	4.00	6.00
50 Verdant Helix U	.15	.25
51 Twilight Worm R	1.50	2.50
52 Fornax, the Juggernaut R	1.00	1.50
53 Deathtongue Leech R	2.50	4.00
54 Vectron Crawler R	2.50	4.00
55 Magmaclysm Rex R	3.00	5.00
S1 The Mystic of Light SR	10.00	15.00
S2 Psychic Predator Rusalka SR	25.00	40.00
S3 Soul-Devourer Black Feather SR	10.00	15.00
S4 Humonguru SR	12.00	20.00
S5 Overlord Sargon SR	10.00	15.00

2014 Kaijudo Booster Brawl

Card	Low	High
COMPLETE SET (3)	8.00	20.00
RELEASED ON FEBRUARY 21, 2014		
1 Kolani, Dragon Oracle	3.00	8.00
2 Spire Widow	4.00	10.00
3 Krakatoa the Shattered	3.00	8.00

2014 Kaijudo Quest for the Gauntlet

Card	Low	High
COMPLETE SET (171)	125.00	200.00
BOOSTER BOX (36 PACKS)		
BOOSTER PACK (14 CARDS)		
RELEASED ON MAY 30, 2014		
1 Battlesworn Seer U	.30	.50
2 Blinder Beetle C	.15	.25
3 Citadel Knight U	.30	.50
4 Cloudweave R	.60	1.00
5 Commissar Soris U	.30	.50
6 Eternity Pulse R	.60	1.00
7 Eye Spy C	.15	.25
8 Flux Drone U	.30	.50
9 Garrison Duty C	.15	.25
10 General Dorzim VR	2.50	4.00
11 Glare of Sanction U	.30	.50
12 Harmony Wing U	.30	.50
13 Hover-Talon C	.15	.25
14 Ironwill Tree R	.60	1.00
15 Laser Drone C	.15	.25
16 Magistrate Jazuri R	.60	1.00
17 Magris the Magnetizer U	.30	.50
18 Nova Cruiser C	.15	.25
19 Pentarc C	.15	.25
20 Photon Weaver C	.15	.25
21 Reactor Sphere C	.15	.25
22 Safe Passage C	.15	.25
23 Sentinel Orb C	.15	.25
24 Sky-Ring Captain C	.15	.25
25 Skybound Keeper C	.15	.25
26 Spire Keeper C	.15	.25
27 Stratus Dart C	.15	.25
28 Strobe Flash C	.15	.25
29 Sunstorm Dreadnought U	.30	.50
30 The Arbiter VR	8.00	12.00
31 Aqua Initiate C	.15	.25
32 Aqua Inquisitor U	.30	.50
33 Aqua Scout C	.15	.25
34 Citizen Tokori U	.30	.50
35 Cryo-Nucleus U	.30	.50
36 Cyber Lord Wakiki R	.60	1.00
37 Ethereal Agent VR	2.00	3.00
38 Gobblemaw U	.30	.50
39 Hydro Spy C	.15	.25
40 Hydrobot Nautilus C	.15	.25
41 Icebelly Blowfish C	.15	.25
42 Kalorth, Lord of Tides VR	1.50	2.50
43 Mind Core U	.30	.50
44 Ocean Ravager R	.60	1.00
45 Outpost Sentry U	.30	.50
46 Pincer-Fin C	.15	.25
47 Reef Kraken C	.15	.25
48 Scavenging Cenophor R	.60	1.00
49 Scrutinize C	.15	.25
50 Shore Chomper U	.30	.50
51 Snapping Eel C	.15	.25
52 Steadfast Vorwhal C	.15	.25
53 Stockade Virus C	.15	.25
54 Temporal Tinkering C	.15	.25
55 Thought Collective U	.30	.50
56 Tide Angler C	.15	.25
57 Tide Seer C	.15	.25
58 Veil Bubble C	.15	.25
59 Wave Spears R	.60	1.00
60 Whirlpool Warden C	.15	.25
61 Attic Reaper C	.15	.25
62 Baleful Drummer R	.60	1.00
63 Cavern Snapper C	.15	.25
64 Creeping Heap C	.15	.25
65 Cursed Phantom C	.15	.25
66 Den Gorger U	.30	.50
67 Dream Pirate C	.15	.25
68 Eldritch Lightning C	.15	.25
69 Forsaken Puppet U	.30	.50
70 Fumes C	.15	.25
71 Gloom-Hollow Taskmaster U	.30	.50
72 Gloomlurker Drask C•	.15	.25
73 Gorgalisk C	.15	.25
74 Grave Call C	.15	.25
75 Grievous Strike U	.30	.50
76 Horrific Tick C	.15	.25
77 Horror Box R	.60	1.00
78 Lurking Skull Cutter C	.15	.25
79 Mindwrack Moth U	.30	.50
80 Mr. Smiles C	.15	.25
81 Oblivion Knight R	.60	1.00
82 Ravenous Whiptongue U	.30	.50
83 Shadowblade Conqueror U	.30	.50
84 Shanok, the Soul Harvester VR	1.50	2.50
85 Skrap Skull C	.15	.25
86 Snakebite C	.15	.25
87 Terror Pit R	.60	1.00
88 Underworld Stalker VR	6.00	10.00
89 Venomancer C	.15	.25
90 Vile Reanimator C	.15	.25
91 Blastforge Sweeper C	.15	.25
92 Bloodbound Dragon U	.30	.50
93 Convoy Runner C	.15	.25
94 Drakon Mercenary C	.15	.25
95 Dropship Commando U	.30	.50
96 Ember Adept C	.15	.25
97 Firemane Dragon R	.60	1.00
98 Flame Auger U	.30	.50
99 Kenina the Igniter C	.15	.25
D1 Beastlord Rulchor SR	4.00	6.00
S1 Caius of Cloud Legion SR	4.00	6.00
S2 Regent Sasha SR	20.00	30.00
S3 Change-o-bot Glu-urrgle SR	4.00	6.00
S4 Exalarc, Grand Metachron SR	5.00	8.00
S5 Grand Manipulator Agaryx SR	8.00	12.00
S6 Trox the Merciless SR	6.00	10.00
S7 Supreme Dragon Bolshack SR	8.00	12.00
S8 Warmaster Tatsurion SR	10.00	15.00
S9 Boulderfist the Pulverizer SR	10.00	15.00
100 Krakus the Dominator R	.60	1.00
101 Laserize C	.15	.25
102 Megacannon Renegade C	.15	.25
103 Railgun Raptor C	.15	.25
104 Rally Bot C	.15	.25
105 Relentless Vanguard C	.15	.25
106 Restless Conflagration VR	3.00	5.00
107 Rocket Hawk C	.15	.25
108 Scrapheap Hunter U	.30	.50
109 Searing Spears U	.30	.50
110 Sergeant Maddox U	.30	.50
111 Shock Trooper C	.15	.25
112 Siege Dragon C	.15	.25
113 Slagcannon Grunt U	.30	.50
114 Technoraptor C	.15	.25
115 Thundering Clap C	.15	.25
116 Torhelm, Stomper Elite R	.60	1.00
117 Tornado Flame R	.60	1.00
118 Volcano Trooper U	.30	.50
119 Warchief Kyo VR	5.00	8.00
120 Wreck Mech C	.15	.25
121 Allure U	.30	.50
122 Amberhorn C	.15	.25
123 Anjak, the All-Kin VR	2.00	3.00
124 Ardu Ranger C	.15	.25
125 Ardu Totem C	.15	.25
126 Barbed Crusher C	.15	.25
127 Bronze-Arm Gladiator U	.30	.50
128 Bronze-Arm Tribe C	.15	.25
129 Charging Greatclaw R	.60	1.00
130 Colonel Corn C	.15	.25
131 Cumulofungus U	.30	.50
132 Grasslands Goliath U	.30	.50
133 Hunter Blossom C	.15	.25
134 Huntmaster Taegrin U	.30	.50
135 Instill Might C	.15	.25
136 Mesa Behemoth R	.60	1.00
137 Moss Giant C	.15	.25
138 Pouncing Crickant C	.15	.25
139 Predatory Snapdragon U	.30	.50
140 Rapscallion C	.15	.25
141 Root Trap R	.60	1.00
142 Shouter, Paragon of Nature VR	2.00	3.00
143 Sigil of Primacy U	.30	.50
144 Snarling Craghorn C	.15	.25
145 Sprout C	.15	.25
146 Sumo Artichoke R	.60	1.00
147 Sun-Clan Tortoise U	.30	.50
148 Vine Bind C	.15	.25
149 Violet Puffer C	.15	.25
150 Woolly Tusker C	.15	.25
151 Sky Shark R	.60	1.00
152 Eye of Inquisition R	.60	1.00
153 Solstar Commander R	.60	1.00
154 Battlebred Defender R	.60	1.00
155 Mind Censor R	.60	1.00
156 Flame Serpent R	.60	1.00
157 Hydrobot Scarab R	.60	1.00
158 Zombie Backhoe R	.60	1.00
159 Johnny Darkseed R	.60	1.00
160 Thunderaxe Shaman R	.60	1.00
S10 Voksa, Herd Matriarch SR	4.00	6.00

2014 Kaijudo Vortex

Card	Low	High
UNLISTED R	.60	1.00
RELEASED ON AUGUST 29, 2014		
1 Aerial Arcavore C	.15	.25
2 Ancient Keeper C	.15	.25
3 Ardent Observer C	.15	.25
4 Aurora Scout C	.15	.25
5 Bewildering Blast U	.30	.50
6 Bolt-Hawk U	.30	.50
7 Citadel Judge R	.60	1.00
8 Cloud Grappler C	.15	.25
9 Empyrean Overseer U	.30	.50
10 Galvanize U	.30	.50
11 Hydrus the Oathbound VR	2.00	3.00
12 Intrepid Invader C	.15	.25
13 Justice Archon C	.15	.25
14 Karstara the Warder R	.60	1.00
15 Overshields R	.60	1.00
16 Perseus Dragon R	.60	1.00
17 Phase Generator C	.15	.25
18 Prelate of Wind C	.15	.25
19 Radion Sphere C	.15	.25
20 Regent's Attendant C	.15	.25
21 Salvation Reckoner R	.60	1.00
22 Scroll Orb C	.15	.25
23 Skyforce Adjutant U	.30	.50
24 Spark Drone C	.15	.25
25 Stormstrike Enforcer C	.15	.25
26 Sunshock C	.15	.25
27 Superia-Citadel Militia C	.15	.25
28 Temple Lantern U	.30	.50
29 Virtuous Alcadeus VR	5.00	8.00
30 Zephyr Keeper U	.30	.50
31 Aeronaut Glu-urrgle VR	2.00	3.00
32 Aqua Infiltrator U	.30	.50
33 Aqua Swordsman C	.15	.25
34 Cloaked Saboteur C	.15	.25
35 Cranky Leviathan U	.30	.50
36 Cyber Savant C	.15	.25
37 Deep-Currents Drifter U	.30	.50
38 Dreamfish C	.15	.25
39 Emperor Palata U	.30	.50
40 Garglevision C	.15	.25
41 Hydrobot Elite C	.15	.25
42 Hypnobot C	.15	.25
43 Master Trader Cephelia R	.60	1.00
44 Metroplex Operative U	.30	.50
45 Metroplex Scout C	.15	.25
46 Optic Cell C	.15	.25
47 Rip Swirl C	.15	.25
48 Runemaster Zyr VR		
49 Spy Mission C	.15	.25
50 Spy Tide C	.15	.25
51 Tarvox the Voracious R	.60	1.00
52 Teleportation Equation U	.30	.50
53 Tide Gulper C	.15	.25
54 Time Tethers C	.15	.25
55 Tusked Nautiloid R	.60	1.00
56 Veil Vortex R	.60	1.00
57 Void Seer C	.15	.25
58 Wave Skimmer C	.15	.25
59 Wavecrest Crawler U	.30	.50
60 Waveforce Seer R	.60	1.00
61 Agent of Lies C	.15	.25
62 Batter-Axe C	.15	.25
63 Bloated Gatekeeper U	.30	.50
64 Chasm Gigabolver C	.15	.25
65 Darkbolt C	.15	.25
66 Decay C	.15	.25
67 Deteriorate C	.15	.25
68 Foul Cave Worm C	.15	.25
69 Gloom Wraith C	.15	.25
70 Gregoria's Guile U	.30	.50
71 Grim Specter C	.15	.25
72 Gullet Ghost C	.15	.25
73 Hollow Worm R	.60	1.00
74 Ichor Spider C	.15	.25
75 Joko, Lunatic Chimp VR	3.00	5.00
76 Legionnaire Corpse C	.15	.25
77 Lethal Lockbox U	.30	.50
78 Malphalgus the Tormenter R	.60	1.00
79 Megaria's Trapheap C	.15	.25
80 Nether Tactician R	.60	1.00
81 Prowling Chimera C	.15	.25
82 Rite of Revival U	.30	.50
83 Shredmane R	.60	1.00
84 Sinister Scheme U	.30	.50
85 Slithering Phantasm U	.30	.50
86 Soul Reflection R	.60	1.00
87 Timelost Phantom VR		
88 Vicious Coffer C	.15	.25
89 Vile Piercer U	.30	.50
90 Wraith Hound C	.15	.25
91 Ammo Train U	.30	.50
92 Artillery Dragon C	.15	.25
93 Ashen Tribute C	.15	.25
94 Battering Monolith C	.15	.25
95 Blade-Rush Wyvern C	.15	.25
96 Blaze Darter C	.15	.25
97 Cannonade Dragon R	.60	1.00
98 Flaming Arrow Volley U	.30	.50
99 Furywing Trooper U	.30	.50
D1 Dragon Engine Glu-urrgle SR	8.00	12.00
S1 Toronok the Voidshaper SR	10.00	15.00
S2 The Chronarch SR	5.00	8.00
S3 Baelgor, Accursed Dragon SR	5.00	8.00
S4 Krogon, Blazing Devastation SR	8.00	12.00
S5 Eternal Gaia Dragon SR	15.00	25.00
S6 Ulphonas, Fendish Overlord SR	5.00	8.00
S7 Drakomech Commander SR	10.00	15.00
S8 Krotork, the Mirror SR	5.00	8.00
S9 Worldwaker Omgoth SR	5.00	8.00
100 Hydragon C	.15	.25
101 Igniss U	.30	.50
102 Jack, the Hammer C	.15	.25
103 Jetpack Thug C	.15	.25
104 Kuth the Dervish R	.60	1.00
105 Lava Burst C	.15	.25
106 Lava Racer U	.30	.50
107 Meteor Rider U	.30	.50
108 Mighty Stomp U	.30	.50
109 Mischievous Fire-Chick C	.15	.25
110 Quetaro the Gladiator R	.60	1.00
111 Raging Firebrand C	.15	.25
112 Raptor-Ace Valko C	.15	.25
113 Rothos the Destroyer R	.60	1.00
114 Runes of Fortune R	.60	1.00
115 Rygar the Tank VR		
116 Sandstorm Prowler C	.15	.25
117 Sledge Bot C	.15	.25
118 Smoldering Brute C	.15	.25
119 Stormdiver C	.15	.25
120 Wildfire Valkyrie R	.60	1.00
121 Ancestor Bear U	.30	.50
122 Ardu Cloudstrider C	.15	.25
123 Bronze-Arm Fanatic U	.30	.50
124 Colossal Avenger C	.15	.25
125 Creeper Snare C	.15	.25
126 Daunting Presence U	.30	.50
127 Duke Durian C	.15	.25
128 Earthbond Giant R	.60	1.00
129 Embolden U	.30	.50
130 Field Marshal Cornucopia VR		
131 Granite Titan C	.15	.25
132 Grove Protector U	.30	.50
133 Horned Chameleon C	.15	.25
134 Jarbala Hatchery R	.60	1.00
135 Leafwing Totem C	.15	.25
136 Lumbering Coliseum C	.15	.25
137 Lunar Boar U	.30	.50
138 Lurking Orchid U	.30	.50
139 Moonhowler Hunter R	.60	1.00
140 Muk'tak, Lifespark Guide VR	10.00	15.00
141 Pesky Pineapple C	.15	.25

142 Ringleader Radish C	.15	.25
143 Ritual of Challenge R	.60	1.00
144 Ragonite the Obliterator R	.60	1.00
145 Runestone Goliath C	.15	.25
146 Savage Spawn C	.15	.25
147 Solstice Chanter C	.15	.25
148 Sprite's Gift C	.15	.25
149 Trapdoor Tunneler C	.15	.25
150 Warren Shaman C	.15	.25
151 Cetus the Augur R	.60	1.00
152 Wave Keeper U	.30	.50
153 Brave Shalloteer U	.30	.50
154 Radiant Blinderhorn R	.60	1.00
155 Abyssal Scavenger U	.30	.50
156 Magglekax R	.60	1.00
157 Bile Raptor U	.30	.50
158 Taksha, Scourge Gunner VR	4.00	6.00
159 Arachnomech R	.60	1.00
160 Riot Sprite U	.30	.50
S10 Scaradorable the Behemoth SR	20.00	30.00

2012-13 Kaijudo Promos

P1Y1 Draglide the Swiftest (issued in Bull Rush deck at WPN stores)	1.00	1.50
P2Y1 Aqua Seneschal (issued in Wal-Mart Rise of the Duel Masters packs)	2.50	4.00
P3Y1 Blinder Beetle (issued in Wal-Mart Rise of the Duel Masters packs)	2.00	3.00
P4Y1 Blaze Belcher (issued in Wal-Mart Rise of the Duel Masters packs)	2.00	3.00
P5Y1 Fumes (issued in Wal-Mart Rise of the Duel Masters packs)	1.00	1.50
P6Y1 Razorhide (issued in Wal-Mart Rise of the Duel Masters packs)	1.00	1.50
P7Y1 Mighty Shouter, the Shaman (issued at Kaijudo League 2012, 9/12-10/12)	1.25	2.00
P8Y1 Flare Inhibitor (issued at Kaijudo League 2012, 9/12-10/12)	1.00	1.50
P9Y1 Moorna the Vengeful (issued at Kaijudo League 2012, 9/12-10/12)	1.00	1.50
P10Y1 Mother Virus (issued at Kaijudo League 2012, 11/12-12/12)	1.00	1.50
P11Y1 Impalicus (issued at Kaijudo League 2012, 11/12-12/12)	1.00	1.50
P12Y1 Sparkblade Protector (issued at Kaijudo League 2012, 11/12-12/12)	2.50	4.00
P13Y1 Bronze-Arm Sabertooth (issued at Summer 2013 Kaijudo Championship)	10.00	15.00
P14Y1 Kenina the Igniter (issued in Creatures Unleashed DVD)	2.50	4.00
P15Y1 Old Man Winter (2012 Holiday)	40.00	60.00
P16Y1 Thorn Dragon (issued at DragonStrike Infernus premiere)	2.00	3.00
P17Y1 Cybersphere Dragon (issued at DragonStrike Infernus premiere)	1.50	2.50
P18Y1 Dorado, Golden Dragon (issued at Kaijudo Duel Day, 4/13)	2.00	3.00
P19Y1 Billion-Degree Dragon (issued at Kaijudo Duel Day, 4/13)	1.50	2.50
P20Y1 Herald of Infernus (issued in DragonStrike DVD)	6.00	10.00

2013-14 Kaijudo Promos

P1Y2 Memory Swarm (issued in Darkness of Heart DVD)		
P2Y2 Wild Sky Sword (issued at Clash of the Duel Masters premiere)	3.00	5.00
P3Y2 Fault-Line Dragon (issued at Clash of the Duel Masters premiere)	3.00	5.00
P4Y2 Grybolos the Gatherer (issued at May 2013 Kaijudo Duel Day)	3.00	5.00
P5Y2 Saracon, Storm Dynamo (issued at May 2013 Kaijudo Duel Day)	2.50	4.00
P6Y2 Sprout (issued at June 2013 Kaijudo Duel Day)	2.00	3.00
P7Y2 Magris the Magnetizer (issued at August 2013 Kaijudo Duel Day)	1.50	2.50
P8Y2 Veil Stalker (issued at Shattered Alliances premiere)	1.50	2.50
P9Y2 Ba'kaar Frostwing (issued at Shattered Alliances premiere)	2.00	3.00
P10Y2 Necrose, Nightmare Bloom (issued at September 2013 Kaijudo Duel Day)	1.25	2.00
P11Y2 Cyber Walker Kaylee (issued at October 2013 Kaijudo Duel Day)	1.25	2.00
P12Y2 Forgotten Chief (issued at Invasion Earth premiere)	1.25	2.00
P13Y2 Skraven, Draconic Reaper (issued at Invasion Earth premiere)	1.25	2.00
P14Y2 Enslaved Flametropus (issued at November 2013 Kaijudo Duel Day)	1.25	2.00
P15Y2 Shaman of the Vigil (issued at December 2013 Kaijudo Duel Day)	2.50	4.00
P16Y2 Ember Titan (issued at January 2014 Kaijudo Duel Day)	2.00	3.00
P17Y2 Gilded Archon (issued at February 2014 Kaijudo Duel Day)	1.25	2.00
P18Y2 Snow Fort (2013 Holiday)	10.00	15.00
P19Y2 Fullmetal Lemon (issued at Kaijudo Master Challenge 2014)	2.00	3.00
P20Y2 Reckoning (issued at The 5 Mystics premiere)	1.50	2.50
P21Y2 Wavebreaker Shaman (issued at The 5 Mystics premiere)	2.00	3.00
P22Y2 Cyber Seer (issued at March 2014 Kaijudo Duel Day)	1.50	2.50

2018 KeyForge Call of the Archons

COMPLETE SET (370)
BOOSTER BOX (12 DECKS)
BOOSTER PACK (37 CARDS)
RELEASED ON NOVEMBER 15, 2018
1 Anger C
2 Barehanded R
3 Blood Money U
4 Brothers in Battle R
5 Burn the Stockpile U
6 Champion's Challenge R
7 Coward's End C
8 Follow the Leader U
9 Lava Ball R
10 Loot the Bodies C
11 Take that, Smartypants R
12 Punch C
13 Relentless Assault U
14 Smith U
15 Sound the Horns U
16 Tremor C
17 Unguarded Camp U
18 Warsong C
19 Autocannon R
20 Banner of Battle R
21 Cannon U
22 Gauntlet of Command C
23 Iron Obelisk R
24 Mighty Javelin U
25 Pile of Skulls R
26 Screechbomb U
27 The Warchest U
28 Bilgum Avalanche R
29 Valdr C
30 Bumpsy C
31 Earthshaker U
32 Firespitter C
33 Ganger Chieftain C
34 Grenade Snib U
35 Headhunter C
36 Hebe the Huge U
37 Kelifi Dragon R
38 King of the Crag R
39 Krump C
40 Lomir Flamefist U
41 Looter Goblin R
42 Mugwump R
43 Pingle Who Annoys R
44 Rock-Hurling Giant R
45 Rogue Ogre R
46 Smaaash C
47 Tireless Crocag R
48 Troll C
49 Wardrummer C
50 Blood of Titans U
51 Phoenix Heart R
52 Yo Mama Mastery R
53 A Fair Game R
54 Arise! C
55 Control the Weak C
56 Creeping Oblivion R
57 Dance of Doom R
58 Fear C
59 Gateway to Dis C
60 Gongoozle U
61 Guilty Hearts R
62 Hand of Dis C
63 Hectacomb R
64 Tendrils of Pain U
65 Hysteria U
66 Key Hammer U
67 Mind Barb C
68 Pandemonium U
69 Poltergeist U
70 Red Hot Armor R
71 Three Fates U
72 Annihilation Ritual R
73 Dominator Bubble C
74 Key to Dis R
75 Lash of Broken Dreams C
76 Library of the Damned U
77 Lifeward U
78 Sacrificial Altar R
79 Screaming Cave R
80 Soul Snatcher R
81 Charette C
82 Drumble U
83 Dust Imp C
84 Eater of the Dead R
85 Ember Imp C
86 Gabos Longarms R
87 Overlord Greking R
88 Guardian Demon U
89 Master of 1 R
90 Master of 2 S
91 Master of 3 S
92 Pit Demon C
93 Pitlord R
94 Restringuntus R
95 Shaffles U
96 Shooler C
97 Snudge U
98 Stealer of Souls U
99 Succubus C
100 Tentacus U
101 The Terror C
102 Tocsin C
103 Tolas R
104 Truebaru R
105 Collar of Subordination R
106 Flame Wreathed U
107 Bouncing Deathquark U
108 Dimension Door U
109 Effervescent Principle C
110 Foggify C
111 Help From Future Self S
112 Interdimensional Graft U
113 Knowledge is Power R
114 Labwork C
115 Library Access C
116 Neuro Syphon U
117 Phase Shift C
118 Positron Bolt U
119 Random Access Archives R
120 Remote Access U
121 Reverse Time R
122 Scrambler Storm U
123 Sloppy Labwork U
124 Twin Bolt Emission C
125 Wild Wormhole C
126 Anomaly Exploiter U
127 Chaos Portal R
128 Crazy Killing Machine R
129 Library of Babble C
130 Mobius Scroll R
131 Pocket Universe R
132 Spangler Box R
133 Spectral Tunneler U
134 Strange Gizmo R
135 The Howling Pit R
136 Batdrone C
137 Brain Eater U
138 Dextre C
139 Doc Bookton C
140 Dr. Escotera C
141 Dysania R
142 Ganymede Archivist C
143 Harland Mindlock R
144 Quixo the "Adventurer" C
145 Mother C
146 Neutron Shark R
147 Novu Archaeologist U
148 Ozmo, Martianologist R
149 Psychic Bug R
150 Replicator R
151 Research Smoko U
152 Skippy Timehog R
153 Timetraveller R
154 Titan Mechanic C
155 Vespilon Theorist R
156 Veylan Analyst U
157 Experimental Therapy U
158 Rocket Boots U
159 Transposition Sandals R
160 Ammonia Clouds C
161 Battle Fleet U
162 Deep Probe U
163 EMP Blast U
164 Hypnotic Command R
165 Irradiated Æmber R
166 Key Abduction U
167 Martian Hounds R
168 Martians Make Bad Allies R
169 Mass Abduction R
170 Mating Season R
171 Mothership Support U
172 Orbital Bombardment U
173 Phosphorus Stars C
174 Psychic Network U
175 Sample Collection U
176 Shatter Storm R
177 Soft Landing C
178 Squawker C
179 Total Recall R
180 Combat Pheromones U
181 Commpod R
182 Crystal Hive U
183 Custom Virus R
184 Feeding Pit R
185 Invasion Portal R
186 Incubation Chamber R
187 Mothergun C
188 Sniffer R
189 Swap Widget R
190 Blypyp U
191 Chuff Ape R
192 Ether Spider U
193 Grabber Jammer C
194 Grommid R
195 John Smyth C
196 Mindwarper C
197 Phylyx the Disintegrator R
198 Qyxxlyx Plague Master R
199 Tunk C
200 Ulyq Megamouth C
201 Uxlyx the Zookeeper U
202 Vezyma Thinkdrone C
203 Yxili Maurauder C
204 Yxilo Bolter C
205 Yxilx Dominator C
206 Zorg U
207 Zyzzix the Many C
208 Biomatrix Backup C
209 Brain Stem Antenna R
210 Jammer Pack U
211 Red Planet Ray Gun U
212 Begone! R
213 Blinding Light C
214 Charge! R
215 Cleansing Wave C
216 Clear Mind R
217 Doorstep to Heaven U
218 Glorious Few U
219 Honorable Claim R
220 Inspiration C
221 Mighty Lance R
222 Oath of Poverty R
223 One Stood Against Many R
224 Radiant Truth U
225 Shield of Justice C
226 Take Hostages C
227 Terms of Redress C
228 The Harder They Come U
229 The Spirit's Way U
230 Virtuous Works U
231 Epic Quest R
232 Gorm of Omm U
233 Hallowed Blaster C
234 Potion of Invulnerability U
235 Round Table R
236 Sigil of Brotherhood U
237 Whispering Reliquary U
238 Bulwark C
239 Champion Anaphiel C
240 Champion Tabris U
241 Commander Remiel C
242 Duma the Martyr R
243 Francus U
244 Grey Monk U
245 Hayell the Merchant R
246 Horseman of Death S
247 Horseman of Famine S
248 Horseman of Pestilence R
249 Horseman of War S

250 Jehu the Bureaucrat R
251 Lady Maxena U
252 Lord Golgotha R
253 Numquid the Fair R
254 Protectrix C
255 Raiding Knight C
256 Sanctum Guardian R
257 Sequis C
258 Sergeant Zakiel C
259 Staunch Knight C
260 Gatekeeper U
261 The Vaultkeeper R
262 Veemos Lightbringer R
263 Armageddon Cloak R
264 Mantle of the Zealot R
265 Protect the Weak C
266 Shoulder Armor U
267 Bait and Switch C
268 Booby Trap U
269 Finishing Blow R
270 Ghostly Hand C
271 Hidden Stash U
272 Imperial Traitor R
273 Key of Darkness R
274 Lights Out U
275 Miasma C
276 Nerve Blast C
277 One Last Job R
278 Oubliette U
279 Pawn Sacrifice C
280 Poison Wave C
281 Relentles Whispers C
282 Routine Job R
283 Too Much to Protect U
284 Treasure Map R
285 Customs Office R
286 Evasion Sigil R
287 Longfused Mines R
288 Masterplan R
289 Safe Place R
290 Seeker Needle C
291 Skeleton Key U
292 Special Delivery U
293 Speed Sigil U
294 Subtle Maul U
295 The Sting R
296 Bad Penny C
297 Bulleteye R
298 Carlo Phantom U
299 Deipno Spymaster R
300 Faygin R
301 Macis Asp U
302 Mack the Knife R
303 Magda the Rat U
304 Mooncurser U
305 Nexus C
306 Noddy the Thief C
307 Old Bruno U
308 Dodger C
309 Selwyn the Fence R
310 Shadow Self C
311 Silvertooth C
312 Smiling Ruth R
313 Sneklifter R
314 Umbra C
315 Urchin C
316 Duskrunner U
317 Ring of Invisibility R
318 Silent Dagger U
319 Cooperative Hunting C
320 Curosity R
321 Fertility Chant R
322 Fogbank U
323 Full Moon C
324 Grasping Vines U
325 Key Charge C
326 Lifeweb U
327 Lost in the Woods C
328 Mimicry U
329 Nature's Call U
330 Nocturnal Maneuver C
331 Perilous Wild R
332 Regrowth C
333 Save the Pack C
334 Scout R
335 Stampede R
336 The Common Cold R
337 Troop Call U
338 Vigor C
339 Word of Returning R
340 Bear Flute R
341 Nepenthe Seed U
342 Ritual of Balance U
343 Ritual of the Hunt R
344 World Tree R
345 Ancient Bear C
346 Bigtwig U
347 Witch of the Wilds R
348 Briar Grubbling R
349 Chota Hazri U
350 Dew Faerie C
351 Dust Pixie C
352 Flaxia U
353 Fuzzy Gruen R
354 Giant Sloth R
355 Halacor U
356 Inka the Spider R
357 Kindrith Longshot R
358 Snufflegator C
359 Lupo the Scarred R
360 Mighty Tiger R
361 Murmook C
362 Mushroom Man U
363 Niffle Ape C
364 Niffle Queen U
365 Piranha Monkeys R
366 Teliga R
367 Hunting Witch C
368 Witch of the Eye C
369 Way of the Bear U
370 Way of the Wolf U

2017 Lightseekers Awakening

1 Anti-Gravity Field R
2 Anti-Gravity Snail C .15 .25
3 Astral Priest C .15 .25
4 Astronomer C .15 .25
5 Black Hole R
6 Blinding Beetle R
7 Cassini U .30 .50
8 Chimchu Farseer U .30 .50
9 Chimchu Infiltrator R
10 Chimchu Lookout U .30 .50
11 Chimchu Militant C .15 .25
12 Constella R
13 Dawn Stalker U .30 .50
14 Dimensional Hunter U .30 .50
15 Dusk Feeder C .15 .25
16 Eclipse U .30 .50
17 Elara U .30 .50
18 Flying Fortress R
19 Force Shield U .30 .50
20 Frostflare Axe U .30 .50
21 Full Moon C .15 .25
22 Gravity Bubble U .30 .50
23 Hollowtooth Dagger U .30 .50
24 Howling Blade U .30 .50
25 Leo C .15 .25
26 Light Lasher R
27 Lunatic R
28 Lynx C .15 .25
29 Mageship U .30 .50
30 Mirror Beast R
31 Moon Pearl Mace U .30 .50
32 Moon Song R
33 Orion R
34 Paralysis Bug U .30 .50
35 Pathfinder C .15 .25
36 Phase Shift C .15 .25
37 Planetary Alignment C .15 .25
38 Prismatic Sun Feeder U .30 .50
39 Reality Twister R
40 Rippling Flare R
41 Shapeshifter C .15 .25
42 Skyward Observatory U .30 .50
43 Solar Wind C .15 .25
44 Spectral Guide U .30 .50
45 Starflake Defender U .30 .50
46 Starsail U .30 .50
47 Stellar Fusion R
48 Subjugator R
49 Sun Beacon U .30 .50
50 Sun Blade U .30 .50
51 Sun Hugger R
52 Sun Strike C .15 .25
53 Suntop Monastery R
54 Tidal Shift C .15 .25
55 Ursa U .30 .50
56 Vela R
57 Yikona Oracle C .15 .25
58 Yikona Tactician R
59 Zeppelin Scout R
60 Abyss Tentacle U .30 .50
61 Abyss Weaver U .30 .50
62 Amplification Hex C .15 .25
63 Assassins' Guild U .30 .50
64 Bone Reaper C .15 .25
65 Breach the Veil R
66 Burst of Venom C .15 .25
67 Corrupted Spirit C .15 .25
68 Crippling Toxin R
69 Defiler U .30 .50
70 Devourer R
71 Draga Hunter C .15 .25
72 Drain Life U .30 .50
73 Dripping Dagger U .30 .50
74 Ghostly Grasp R
75 Gorged Stalker U .30 .50
76 Graveyard R
77 Grimglider U .30 .50
78 Gurgling Ooze R
79 Horrific Manifestation U .30 .50
80 Leeching Scimitar U .30 .50
81 Mantix Spitter C .15 .25
82 Mimicking Horror R
83 Necroskull Ward U .30 .50
84 Night Lurker C .15 .25
85 Nightshade R
86 Nova U .30 .50
87 Noxin Assassin R
88 Noxin Hexmaster R
89 Noxious Mantis R
90 Putrid Shaman U .30 .50
91 Rigor Mortis C .15 .25
92 Ritual of Awakening R
93 Serpent's Fang U .30 .50
94 Shade Ripper U .30 .50
95 Shadow Prison C .15 .25
96 Shadow Puppet C .15 .25
97 Shadow Supplier C .15 .25
98 Shadow Wraith R
99 Shadowy Grave R
100 Shambler C .15 .25
101 Shroud of Night C .15 .25
102 Sicario U .30 .50
103 Skull Scepter U .30 .50
104 Soul Thief C .15 .25
105 Soul Trader R
106 Spirit Gate U .30 .50
107 Swamp Creeper R
108 Tenebra R
109 Terrify U .30 .50
110 The Undying R
111 Toxic Frog R
112 Toxic Haunt R
113 Virila C .15 .25
114 Wall of Bones U .30 .50
115 Witch Doctor U .30 .50
116 Withering C .15 .25
117 Xenith C .15 .25
118 Zyrus R
119 Apocalypse R
120 Avalanche R
121 Blood Moon R
122 Chilling Curse R
123 Corrupt Wildlife R
124 Electrify R
125 Life Imbue R
126 Living Whirlpool R
127 Meteor Shower R
128 Moss Armour R
129 Night Hunt R
130 Rock Bomb R
131 Spirit Tap R
132 Star Blast R
133 Tsunami R
134 Ambush Worm U .30 .50
135 Ancient Ignu R
136 Ancient Miner C .15 .25
137 Blazing Cauldron U .30 .50
138 Boulder R
139 Boulder Feast C .15 .25
140 Clay U .30 .50
141 Colossi Ritual Site U .30 .50
142 Crushing Blow U .30 .50
143 Crystal Bat C .15 .25
144 Crystal Leech C .15 .25
145 Crystal Maze U .30 .50
146 Crystal Scepter U .30 .50
147 Crystal Skin C .15 .25
148 Crystalcore U .30 .50
149 Dolo the Mighty R
150 Earthquake C .15 .25
151 Enchanted Soil R
152 Everok Carver U .30 .50
153 Everok Racer U .30 .50
154 Everok Relic C .15 .25
155 Exteria Defender R
156 Fiery Blade U .30 .50
157 Firesparker R
158 Flame Bat C .15 .25
159 Flamechained Elder R
160 Flamechained Warrior R
161 Focus Chamber U .30 .50
162 Geode Hatchling R
163 Geoplate Defender U .30 .50
164 Granite R
165 Impenetrable Shield C .15 .25
166 Inferno C .15 .25
167 Lava Bouncer R
168 Lava Shedding U .30 .50
169 Magma Blast R
170 Magma Spitter C .15 .25
171 Magma Worm U .30 .50
172 Molten Blade U .30 .50
173 Mountain Fort U .30 .50
174 Obsidian Maul U .30 .50
175 Pegma U .30 .50
176 Prism Cannon C .15 .25
177 Prism Cannon Mk2 R
178 Quart C .15 .25
179 Rickety Mine U .30 .50
180 Rock Fists C .15 .25
181 Rock Maul U .30 .50
182 Rock Rager C .15 .25
183 Scorched Earth R
184 Scoria C .15 .25
185 Scrying Crystal R
186 Shatter Flame C .15 .25
187 Shattered Volcano U .30 .50
188 Stone Scribe R
189 Stream of Tantos C .15 .25
190 Stubborn Everok R
191 Temple of Patience R
192 Wrath of the Mountain R
193 Ambush C .15 .25
194 Beast Control C .15 .25
195 Beast Master R
196 Beast Within R
197 Cedrus C .15 .25
198 Cessilia U .30 .50
199 Coercive Spirit C .15 .25
200 Corvid Conspiracy C .15 .25
201 Den Mother U .30 .50
202 Feral Rage U .30 .50
203 Flower Garden U .30 .50
204 Forest Mender R
205 Fungal King R
206 Fungal Leecher U .30 .50
207 Fungal Medium U .30 .50
208 Fungal Spores C .15 .25
209 Great Daku U .30 .50
210 Hazel the Hermit R
211 Hungry Behemoth R
212 Infected Wasp U .30 .50
213 Insect Swarm R
214 Jadewing U .30 .50
215 Life Binding C .15 .25
216 Living Thorns R
217 Mantix Raider C .15 .25
218 Mantix Tunneler C .15 .25
219 Meyku the Young C .15 .25
220 Mossridge Defender C .15 .25
221 Oakthorn Warrior C .15 .25
222 Old Oak R
223 One With Nature R
224 Ouves U .30 .50
225 Pollen Weaver R
226 Raging Spirit R
227 Reckless Spirit C .15 .25
228 Regrowth R
229 Root Singer R
230 Sacred Aura U .30 .50
231 Sgt. Ironbark R
232 Singing Blade U .30 .50
233 Soul of War U .30 .50
234 Spectral Mantix R
235 Spectral Web R
236 Spirit Channeler U .30 .50

Card	Low	High
237 Spirit Mob C	.15	.25
238 Spiritual Turmoil C	.15	.25
239 Spore Feeder U	.30	.50
240 Stampeding Tusker R		
241 Stumpdrift Shaman C	.15	.25
242 Swarm Caller U	.30	.50
243 Symbiotic Gnarler U	.30	.50
244 Territorial Dominance U	.30	.50
245 Thornleaf Crossbow U	.30	.50
246 Timberstrike U	.30	.50
247 Treanu R		
248 Tree Sprout R		
249 Verdant Guard U	.30	.50
250 Vine Lash C	.15	.25
251 Wildroot U	.30	.50
252 Aquadart Crab U	.30	.50
253 Broken Dam R		
254 Bubble Fish C	.15	.25
255 Bubbly Relic U	.30	.50
256 Cleansing Wind C	.15	.25
257 Cloud Harvester U	.30	.50
258 Cloud King Kashi U	.30	.50
259 Cold Snap U	.30	.50
260 Confused Shaman U	.30	.50
261 Crab Rider Neida C	.15	.25
262 Crackling Beast C	.15	.25
263 Crackling Rod U	.30	.50
264 Dancing Flutterer C	.15	.25
265 Delivery Crab U	.30	.50
266 Dust Fiend U	.30	.50
267 Electrified Deluge R		
268 Electrified Moat U	.30	.50
269 Electro Eel U	.30	.50
270 Electro Stun U	.30	.50
271 Elishi U	.30	.50
272 Evaporator R		
273 Eye of the Storm U	.30	.50
274 Fish Singer Ushi R		
275 Flood R		
276 Flying Debris R		
277 Gaurd Snail R		
278 Healing Rain C	.15	.25
279 Heroic Starfish C	.15	.25
280 Hurricane Spirit C	.15	.25
281 Impressed Seahorse R		
282 Impressed Sludgefin U	.30	.50
283 Kora R		
284 Lalu the Rascal R		
285 Lightning Bringer R		
286 Lightning Storm C	.15	.25
287 Living Cloud C	.15	.25
288 Malia R		
289 Mari Bard R		
290 Meeka C	.15	.25
291 Murky Waters C	.15	.25
292 Overload C	.15	.25
293 Rolling Thunder R		
294 Skyrider U	.30	.50
295 Sleepy Crab Staff U	.30	.50
296 Soaring Scout U	.30	.50
297 Spark Wisp C	.15	.25
298 Storm Shaman U	.30	.50
299 Storm Wall C	.15	.25
300 Storm Whisperer R		
301 Stormshell U	.30	.50
302 Suspicious Squid R		
303 Swooping Corvid R		
304 Tempest Rod U	.30	.50
305 Therapeutic Eel U	.30	.50
306 Thunder Slug C	.15	.25
307 Tornado R		
308 Turkle Captain R		
309 Vitalizing Frog C	.15	.25
310 Wind Controller R		
311 Zapper Bug R		
312 Alchemy Lab U	.30	.50
313 Anzi the Mender R		
314 Automatic Avenger R		
315 Blasting Cannon U	.30	.50
316 Body Morph C	.15	.25
317 Bombling U	.30	.50
318 Bone Chewer C	.15	.25
319 Bulwark Carrier U	.30	.50
320 C-Teck Cannon U	.30	.50
321 Celerity C	.15	.25
322 Chrono Moth C	.15	.25
323 Chrono Wrangler U	.30	.50
324 Clockwork Construct R		
325 Colossi Cannon R		
326 Combat Tech Fusion R		
327 Crazed Bomber C	.15	.25
328 Dugout Sentinel R		
329 Duplication R		
330 Emergency System R		
331 Flynamo U	.30	.50
332 Force Converter R		
333 Forgewall U	.30	.50
334 Fountain of Time C	.15	.25
335 Fumbling Alchemist C	.15	.25
336 Impex the Insane U	.30	.50
337 Jax R		
338 Leaking Generator R		
339 Lexi U	.30	.50
340 Looper C	.15	.25
341 Maniacal Machine U	.30	.50
342 Maxili C	.15	.25
343 Mine Field U	.30	.50
344 Nitro Hammer U	.30	.50
345 Nitro Heal C	.15	.25
346 Nuke R		
347 Olax R		
348 Oversized Wrench U	.30	.50
349 Overwhelming Blast C	.15	.25
350 Perpetual Cannon R		
351 Ramparts C	.15	.25
352 Regen Chamber U	.30	.50
353 Shatter Blast U	.30	.50
354 Smart Bomb U	.30	.50
355 Spinblade 3000 U	.30	.50
356 Steel Fortification C	.15	.25
357 The Heap U	.30	.50
358 Time Chamber U	.30	.50
359 Time Collapse R		
360 Time Flicker C	.15	.25
361 Time Leap R		
362 Time Worm U	.30	.50
363 Tyrax Engineer R		
364 Tyrax Fixer C	.15	.25
365 Tyrax Historian U	.30	.50
366 Tyrax Mercenary C	.15	.25
367 Unstable Defender U	.30	.50
368 Warden of Time R		
369 Warp Toad R		
370 Zilia C	.15	.25
371 Zuna R		
372 Colossi Artifact U	.30	.50
373 Frenzied Kreebal C	.15	.25
374 Kreebal Infiltrator U	.30	.50
375 Kreebal Jester C	.15	.25
376 Kreebal Potion Master R		
377 Kreebal Raid Party U	.30	.50
378 Kreebal Saboteur U	.30	.50
379 Shadowy Figure C	.15	.25
380 Sneaky Kreebal C	.15	.25
381 Tantosian Blacksmith U	.30	.50
382 Umbron Informant U	.30	.50
383 Umbron Marauder C	.15	.25
384 Umbron Thief C	.15	.25
385 Unruly Mob R		
386 Weapon Master R		

Lord of the Rings

2001 Lord of the Rings The Fellowship of the Ring

Card	Low	High
COMPLETE SET (365)	50.00	100.00
BOOSTER BOX (36 PACKS)	25.00	50.00
BOOSTER PACK (11 CARDS)	1.00	2.00
RELEASED ON NOVEMBER 6, 2001		
1C2 The One Ring, The Ruling Ring	.12	.30
1C3 Axe Strike	.12	.30
1C4 Battle Fury	.12	.30
1C5 Cleaving Blow	.12	.30
1C6 Delving	.12	.30
1C7 Dwarf Guard	.12	.30
1C8 Dwarven Armor	.12	.30
1C9 Dwarven Axe	.12	.30
1R1a The One Ring, Isildur's Bane	1.25	3.00
1R1b The One Ring, Isildur's Bane TENGWAR		
1C10 Dwarven Heart	.12	.30
1C11 Farin, Dwarven Emissary	.12	.30
1C18 Halls of My Home	.12	.30
1C19 Here Lies Balin, Son of Fundin	.12	.30
1C20 Let Them Come!	.12	.30
1C21 Lord of Moria	.12	.30
1C24 Stairs of Khazad-dum	.12	.30
1C25 Still Draws Breath	.12	.30
1C26 Their Halls of Stone	.12	.30
1C32 Border Defenses	.12	.30
1C37 Defiance	.12	.30
1C39 Elf-song	.12	.30
1C41 Elven Bow	.12	.30
1C42 Elven Cloak	.12	.30
1C43 Far-seeing Eyes	.12	.30
1C52 Lightfootedness	.12	.30
1C53 Lorien Elf	.12	.30
1C58 The Seen and the Unseen	.12	.30
1C59 Shoulder to Shoulder	.12	.30
1C61 Songs of the Blessed Realm	.12	.30
1C67 Uruviel, Maid of Lorien	.12	.30
1C68 The White Arrows of Lorien	.12	.30
1C76 Intimidate	.12	.30
1C78 Mysterious Wizard	.12	.30
1C82 Risk a Little Light	.12	.30
1C84 Sleep, Caradhras	.12	.30
1C85 Strength of Spirit	.12	.30
1C86 Treachery Deeper Than You Know	.12	.30
1C92 Armor	.12	.30
1R13a Gimli, Son of Gloin	.60	1.50
1R13b Gimli, Son of Gloin TENGWAR		
1R15 Gimli's Helm	1.00	2.50
1R16 Greatest Kingdom of My People	.60	1.50
1R22 Mithril Shaft	.60	1.50
1R23 Nobody Tosses a Dwarf	.75	2.00
1R28 Wealth of Moria	.60	1.50
1R30a Arwen, Daughter of Elrond	1.50	4.00
1R30b Arwen, Daughter of Elrond TENGWAR		
1R33 Bow of the Galadhrim	1.50	4.00
1R34 Celeborn, Lord of Lorien	.60	1.50
1R35 The Council of Elrond	.60	1.50
1R36 Curse Their Foul Feet!	.60	1.50
1R38 Double Shot	6.00	12.00
1R40 Elrond, Lord of Rivendell	1.00	2.50
1R45 Galadriel, Lady of Light	.60	1.50
1R47 Gwemegil	1.00	2.50
1R49 The Last Alliance of Elves and Men	1.00	2.50
1R50a Legolas, Greenleaf	1.50	4.00
1R50b Legolas, Greenleaf TENGWAR		
1R55 The Mirror of Galadriel	.60	1.50
1R62 The Splendor of Their Banners	.60	1.50
1R66 The Tale of Gil-galad	1.00	2.50
1R69 Albert Dreary, Entertainer From Bree	.60	1.50
1R71 Durin's Secret	.60	1.50
1R72a Gandalf, Friend of the Shirefolk	1.25	3.00
1R72b Gandalf, Friend of the Shirefolk TENGWAR		
1R75 Glamdring	.60	1.50
1R79 The Nine Walkers	.60	1.50
1R80 Ottar, Man of Laketown	.60	1.50
1R81 Questions That Need Answering	.60	1.50
1R83a Servant of the Secret Fire	1.25	3.00
1R83b Servant of the Secret Fire TENGWAR		
1R87 A Wizard Is Never Late	1.50	4.00
1R88 An Able Guide	.60	1.50
1R89a Aragorn, Ranger of the North	1.25	3.00
1R89b Aragorn, Ranger of the North TENGWAR		
1R90 Aragorn's Bow	1.50	4.00
1R93 Arwen's Fate	.60	1.50
1R95 Blade of Gondor	1.00	2.50
1R96a Boromir, Lord of Gondor	1.25	3.00
1R96b Boromir, Lord of Gondor TENGWAR		
1R99 Change of Plans	.60	1.50
1U12 Gimli, Dwarf of Erebor	.30	.75
1U17 Grimir, Dwarven Elder	.30	.75
1U27 Thrarin, Dwarven Smith	.30	.75
1U29 Ancient Enmity	.30	.75
1U31 Asfaloth	.30	.75
1U44 Foul Creation	.30	.75
1U46 Gift of Boats	.30	.75
1U48 Haldir, Elf of the Golden Wood	.30	.75
1U51 Legolas, Prince of Mirkwood	.30	.75
1U54 Mallorn-trees	.30	.75
1U56 Orophin, Lorien Bowman	.30	.75
1U57 Rumil, Elven Protector	.30	.75
1U60 Silinde, Elf of Mirkwood	.30	.75
1U63 Stand Against Darkness	.30	.75
1U64 Support of the Last Homely House	.30	.75
1U65 Swan-ship of the Galadhrim	.30	.75
1U70 Barliman Butterbur	.30	.75
Prancing Pony Proprietor		
1U73 Gandalf's Cart	.30	.75
1U74 Gandalf's Pipe	.30	.75
1U77 Let Folly Be Our Cloak	.30	.75
1U91 Aragorn's Pipe	.30	.75
1U94 Athelas	.30	.75
1U97 Boromir, Son of Denethor	.30	.75
1U98 Boromir's Cloak	.30	.75
1C101 Coat of Mail	.12	.30
1C102 Dagger Strike	.12	.30
1C103 Elendil's Valor	.12	.30
1C104 Eregion's Trails	.12	.30
1C106 Gondor's Vengeance	.12	.30
1C107 Great Shield	.12	.30
1C110 Pathfinder	.12	.30
1C116 Swordarm of the White Tower	.12	.30
1C117 Swordsman of the Northern Kingdom	.12	.30
1C119 What Are They?	.12	.30
1C121 Bred for Battle	.12	.30
1C122 Breeding Pit	.12	.30
1C133 Saruman's Ambition	.12	.30
1C134 Saruman's Chill	.12	.30
1C138 Saruman's Snows	.12	.30
1C141 Their Arrows Enrage	.12	.30
1C144 Uruk Bloodlust	.12	.30
1C145 Uruk Brood	.12	.30
1C146 Uruk Fighter	.12	.30
1C149 Uruk Messenger	.12	.30
1C150 Uruk Rager	.12	.30
1C151 Uruk Savage	.12	.30
1C152 Uruk Shaman	.12	.30
1C154 Uruk Soldier	.12	.30
1C156 Uruk Warrior	.12	.30
1C157 Uruk-hai Armory	.12	.30
1C158 Uruk-hai Raiding Party	.12	.30
1C160 Uruk-hai Sword	.12	.30
1C168 Drums in the Deep	.12	.30
1C171 Frenzy	.12	.30
1C174 Goblin Backstabber	.12	.30
1C176 Goblin Marksman	.12	.30
1C177 Goblin Patrol Troop	.12	.30
1C179 Goblin Scavengers	.12	.30
1C180 Goblin Scimitar	.12	.30
1C182 Goblin Spear	.12	.30
1C184 Goblin Wallcrawler	.12	.30
1C185 Goblin Warrior	.12	.30
1C187 Host of Thousands	.12	.30
1C191 Moria Scout	.12	.30
1C192 Pinned Down	.12	.30
1C193 Plundered Armories	.12	.30
1C196 They Are Coming	.12	.30
1C197 Threat of the Unknown	.12	.30
1C201 Unfamiliar Territory	.12	.30
1C248 Forces of Mordor	.12	.30
1C255 Mordor's Strength	.12	.30
1C261 Orc Ambusher	.12	.30
1C266 Orc Chieftain	.12	.30
1C268 Orc Inquisitor	.12	.30
1C269 Orc Scimitar	.12	.30
1C271 Orc Soldier	.12	.30
1C273 The Ring's Oppression	.12	.30
1C277 Shadow's Reach	.12	.30
1C278 Strength Born of Fear	.12	.30
1C281 Under the Watching Eye	.12	.30
1C283 You Bring Great Evil	.12	.30
1C286 Bounder	.12	.30
1C287 Extraordinary Resilience	.12	.30
1C290 Frodo, Son of Drogo	.12	.30
1C294 Hobbit Appetite	.12	.30
1C295 Hobbit Farmer	.12	.30
1C296 Hobbit Intuition	.12	.30
1C297 Hobbit Party Guest	.12	.30
1C298 Hobbit Stealth	.12	.30
1C299 Hobbit Sword	.12	.30
1C300 Longbottom Leaf	.12	.30
1C303 Merry, From O'er the Brandywine	.12	.30
1C304 Noble Intentions	.12	.30
1C305 Old Toby	.12	.30
1C306 Pippin, Friend to Frodo	.12	.30
1C311 Sam, Son of Hamfast	.12	.30
1C312 Sorry About Everything	.12	.30
1C315 Stout and Sturdy	.12	.30
1C317 There and Back Again	.12	.30
1C326 Westfarthing	.12	.30
1C331 Ettenmoors	.12	.30
1C337 Council Courtyard	.12	.30
1C346 Moria Lake	.12	.30
1C349 The Bridge of Khazad-dum	.12	.30
1C351 Galadriel's Glade	.12	.30
1C354 Anduin Wilderland	.12	.30
1C356 Anduin Banks	.12	.30
1C362 Summit of Amon Hen	.12	.30
1P364 Gandalf, The Grey Wizard	.40	1.00
1P365 Aragorn, King in Exile	.40	1.00
1R100 The Choice of Luthien	.60	1.50
1R111 Pursuit Just Behind	.60	1.50
1R114a The Saga of Elendil	1.00	2.50
1R114b The Saga of Elendil TENGWAR		
1R115 Strength of Kings	.60	1.50
1R118 Valiant Man of the West	.60	1.50
1R120 Alive and Unspoiled	.60	1.50

Card	Low	High
1R123 Caradhras Has Not Forgiven Us	.60	1.50
1R124 Cruel Caradhras	.60	1.50
1R125 Greed	.60	1.50
1R127a Lurtz, Servant of Isengard	.75	2.00
1R127b Lurtz, Servant of Isengard TENGWAR		
1R128 Lurtz's Battle Cry		
1R129 The Misadventure of Mr. Underhill	.60	1.50
1R131 Orthanc Assassin	.60	1.50
1R132 Parry	.60	1.50
1R137 Saruman's Reach	.60	1.50
1R139 Savagery to Match Their Numbers	1.25	3.00
1R140 Spies of Saruman	.60	1.50
1R143 Troop of Uruk-hai	.75	2.00
1R147 Uruk Guard	.60	1.50
1R148 Uruk Lieutenant	1.25	3.00
1R14a Gimli's Battle Axe	.60	1.50
1R14b Gimli's Battle Axe TENGWAR		
1R155 Uruk Spy	.60	1.50
1R163 Ancient Chieftain	.60	1.50
1R165a Cave Troll of Moria	1.50	4.00
Scourge of the Black Pit		
1R165b Cave Troll of Moria		
Scourge of the Black Pit TENGWAR		
1R166 Cave Troll's Hammer	.60	1.50
1R167 Denizens Enraged	.60	1.50
1R169 The End Comes	.60	1.50
1R170 Fool of a Took!	.60	1.50
1R172 Goblin Archer	.75	2.00
1R173 Goblin Armory	5.00	10.00
1R175 Goblin Domain	.60	1.50
1R183 Goblin Swarms	1.50	4.00
1R186 Guard Commander	.60	1.50
1R189 Lost to the Goblins	.60	1.50
1R190 Moria Axe	.75	2.00
1R195 Relics of Moria	.60	1.50
1R199 Troll's Keyward	.75	2.00
1R200 The Underdeeps of Moria	.60	1.50
1R204 All Veils Removed	.60	1.50
1R205 Beauty Is Fading	.60	1.50
1R206 Bent on Discovery	.60	1.50
1R208 Black Steed	.60	1.50
1R210 Dark Whispers	.60	1.50
1R212 Fear	.60	1.50
1R214 In the Ringwraith's Wake	.60	1.50
1R216 Morgul Blade	.60	1.50
1R217 Morgul Gates	2.50	6.00
1R221 The Pale Blade	.60	1.50
1R224 Return to Its Master	.75	2.00
1R228 The Twilight World	.60	1.50
1R229 Ulaire Attea, Keeper of Dol Guldur	1.25	3.00
1R230 Ulaire Cantea	1.50	4.00
Lieutenant of Dol Guldur		
1R236 Ulaire Toldea, Messenger of Morgul	1.25	3.00
1R237a The Witch-king, Lord of Angmar	.75	2.00
1R237b The Witch-king		
Lord of Angmar TENGWAR		
1R240 Band of the Eye	.60	1.50
1R243 Despair	.60	1.50
1R244 Desperate Defense of the Ring	1.25	3.00
1R245 Desperate Measures	.60	1.50
1R246 Enduring Evil	.75	2.00
1R247 Enheartened Foe	.60	1.50
1R250 Hate	1.50	4.00
1R252 The Irresistible Shadow	.60	1.50
1R253 Journey Into Danger	.60	1.50
1R254 Mordor Enraged	.60	1.50
1R256a Morgul Hunter	.60	1.50
1R256b Morgul Hunter TENGWAR		
1R259 Morgul Warden	.60	1.50
1R263 Orc Banner	.60	1.50
1R264 Orc Bowmen	2.50	6.00
1R265 Orc Butchery	.60	1.50
1R272 Orc War Band	.60	1.50
1R276 Seeking Its Master	.60	1.50
1R279 Thin and Stretched	.60	1.50
1R282 The Weight of a Legacy	.60	1.50
1R284 Bilbo, Retired Adventurer	.60	1.50
1R288 Farmer Maggot, Chaser of Rascals	.60	1.50
1R289 Frodo, Old Bilbo's Heir	.75	2.00
1R291 The Gaffer, Sam's Father	.60	1.50
1R302 Merry, Friend to Sam	.60	1.50
1R307 Pippin, Hobbit of Some Intelligence	.60	1.50
1R308 Power According to His Stature	2.50	6.00
1R310 Sam, Faithful Companion	.60	1.50
1R313 Sting	1.25	3.00
1R314 Stone Trolls	.60	1.50
1R318 Thror's Map	.60	1.50
1U105 Foes of Mordor	.30	.75
1U108 No Stranger to the Shadows	.30	.75
1U109 One Whom Men Would Follow	.30	.75
1U112 Ranger's Sword	.30	.75
1U113 A Ranger's Versatility	.30	.75.
1U126 Hunt Them Down!	.30	.75
1U130 No Ordinary Storm	.30	.75
1U135 Saruman's Frost	.30	.75
1U136 Saruman's Power	.30	.75
1U142 Traitor's Voice	.30	.75
1U153 Uruk Slayer	.30	.75
1U159 Uruk-hai Rampage	.30	.75
1U161 Wariness	.30	.75
1U162 Worry	.30	.75
1U164 Bitter Hatred	.30	.75
1U178 Goblin Runner	.30	.75
1U181 Goblin Sneak	.30	.75
1U188 The Long Dark	.30	.75
1U194 Relentless	.30	.75
1U198 Through the Misty Mountains	.30	.75
1U202 What Is This New Devilry?	.30	.75
1U203 All Blades Perish	.30	.75
1U207 Black Breath	.30	.75
1U209 Blade Tip	.30	.75
1U211 Drawn to Its Power	.30	.75
1U213 Frozen by Fear	.30	.75
1U215 The Master's Will	.30	.75
1U218 Nazgul Sword	.30	.75
1U219 The Nine Servants of Sauron	.30	.75
1U220 Not Easily Destroyed	.30	.75
1U222 Paths Seldom Trodden	.30	.75
1U223 Relentless Charge	.30	.75
1U225 Sword of Minas Morgul	.30	.75
1U226 Their Power Is in Terror	.30	.75
1U227 Threshold of Shadow	.30	.75
1U231a Ulaire Enquea, Lieutenant of Morgul	.30	.75
1U231b Ulaire Enquea		
Lieutenant of Morgul TENGWAR		
1U232 Ulaire Lemenya, Lieutenant of Morgul	.30	.75
1U233 Ulaire Nelya, Lieutenant of Morgul	.30	.75
1U234 Ulaire Nertea, Messenger of Dol Guldur	.30	.75
1U235 Ulaire Otsea, Lieutenant of Morgul	.30	.75
1U238 Wreathed in Shadow	.30	.75
1U239 All Thought Bent on It	.30	.75
1U241 Curse From Mordor	.30	.75
1U242 The Dark Lord's Summons	.30	.75
1U249 Gleaming Spires Will Crumble	.30	.75
1U251 A Host Avails Little	.30	.75
1U257 Morgul Skirmisher	.30	.75
1U258 Morgul Skulker	.30	.75
1U260 The Number Must Be Few	.30	.75
1U262 Orc Assassin	.30	.75
1U267 Orc Hunters	.30	.75
1U270 Orc Scouting Band	.30	.75
1U274 Sauron's Defenses	.30	.75
1U275 Seeking It Always	.30	.75
1U280 Tower Lieutenant	.30	.75
1U285 Bilbo's Pipe	.30	.75
1U292 The Gaffer's Pipe	.30	.75
1U293 Halfling Deftness	.30	.75
1U301 Master Proudfoot, Distant Relative of Bilbo	.30	.75
1U309 Rosie Cotton, Hobbiton Lass	.30	.75
1U316 A Talent for Not Being Seen	.30	.75
1U319 Bag End	.30	.75
1U320 East Road	.30	.75
1U321 Farmer Maggot's Fields	.30	.75
1U322 Green Dragon Inn	.30	.75
1U323 Green Hill Country	.30	.75
1U324 The Prancing Pony	.30	.75
1U325 Shire Lookout Point	.30	.75
1U327 Bree Gate	.30	.75
1U328 Bree Streets	.30	.75
1U329 Breeland Forest	.30	.75
1U330 Buckleberry Ferry	.30	.75
1U332 Midgewater Marshes	.30	.75
1U333 Midgewater Moors	.30	.75
1U334 Trollshaw Forest	.30	.75
1U335 Weatherhills	.30	.75
1U336 Weathertop	.30	.75
1U338 Ford of Bruinen	.30	.75
1U339 Frodo's Bedroom	.30	.75
1U340 Rivendell Terrace	.30	.75
1U341 Rivendell Valley	.30	.75
1U342 Rivendell Waterfall	.30	.75
1U343 Balin's Tomb	.30	.75
1U344 Dwarrowdelf Chamber	.30	.75
1U345 Mithril Mine	.30	.75
1U347 Moria Stairway	.30	.75
1U348 Pass of Caradhras	.30	.75
1U350 Dimrill Dale	.30	.75
1U352 Lothlorien Woods	.30	.75
1U353 Anduin Confluence	.30	.75
1U355 Silverlode Banks	.30	.75
1U357 Brown Lands	.30	.75
1U358 Pillars of the Kings	.30	.75
1U359 Shores of Nen Hithoel	.30	.75
1U360 Emyn Muil	.30	.75
1U361 Slopes of Amon Hen	.30	.75
1U363 Tol Brandir	.30	.75

2002 Lord of the Rings Mines of Moria

Card	Low	High
COMPLETE SET (122)	15.00	30.00
BOOSTER BOX (36 PACKS)	20.00	40.00
BOOSTER PACK (11 CARDS)	1.00	2.00
RELEASED ON MARCH 6, 2002		
2C2 Disquiet of Our People	.12	.30
2C5 Flurry of Blows	.12	.30
2C6 Fror, Gimli's Kinsman	.12	.30
2C9 Great Works Begun There	.12	.30
2R1 Beneath the Mountains	.60	1.50
2R7 Gloin, Friend to Thorin	.60	1.50
2U3 Dwarven Bracers	.30	.75
2U4 Endurance of Dwarves	.30	.75
2U8 Golden Light on the Land	.30	.75
2C10 Hand Axe	.12	.30
2C14 Till Durin Wakes Again	.12	.30
2C21 Erland, Advisor to Brand	.12	.30
2C23 Gandalf's Wisdom	.12	.30
2C24 Hugin, Emissary from Laketown	.12	.30
2C26 Speak Friend and Enter	.12	.30
2C29 Wizard Staff	.12	.30
2C35 Natural Cover	.12	.30
2C37 Sentinels of Numenor	.12	.30
2C40 Demands of the Sackville-Bagginses	.12	.30
2C42 Goblin Man	.12	.30
2C44 No Business of Ours	.12	.30
2C47 Uruk Scout	.12	.30
2C51 The Balrog, Durin's Bane	.12	.30
2C55 Dark Places	.12	.30
2C58 Foul Tentacle	.12	.30
2C60 Goblin Bowman	.12	.30
2C61 Goblin Flankers	.12	.30
2C62 Goblin Pursuer	.12	.30
2C63 Goblin Reinforcements	.12	.30
2C64 Goblin Scrabbler	.12	.30
2C65 Goblin Spearman	.12	.30
2C69 Old Differences	.12	.30
2C88 Memory of Many Things	.12	.30
2C89 Orc Scout	.12	.30
2C90 Orc Taskmaster	.12	.30
2C91 Southern Spies	.12	.30
2C95 Vile Blade	.12	.30
2C99 Deft in Their Movements	.12	.30
2R11 Make Light of Burdens	.60	1.50
2R12 Realm of Dwarrowdelf	.60	1.50
2R15 What Are We Waiting For?	.60	1.50
2R19 Release the Angry Flood	.60	1.50
2R20 Secret Sentinels	.60	1.50
2R22 Gandalf's Staff	.60	1.50
2R25 Jarnsmid, Merchant from Dale	.60	1.50
2R27 Staff Asunder	.60	1.50
2R32 Flaming Brand	1.25	3.00
2R36 No Mere Ranger	.60	1.50
2R38 Shield of Boromir	.60	1.50
2R39 Beyond the Height of Men	.60	1.50
2R43 Lurtz's Sword	.60	1.50
2R45 Too Much Attention	.60	1.50
2R46 Uruk Captain	.60	1.50
2R49 Archer Commander	.75	2.00
2R50 The Balrog's Sword	.60	1.50
2R52a The Balrog, Flame of Udun	.60	1.50
2R52b The Balrog, Flame of Udun		
TENGWAR		
2R53 Cave Troll's Chain	.60	1.50
2R57 Final Cry	.60	1.50
2R66 Huge Tentacle	.60	1.50
2R73 Watcher in the Water	.75	2.00
Keeper of Westgate		
2R74 Whip of Many Thongs	.60	1.50
2R75 Bill Ferny, Swarthy Sneering Fellow	1.00	2.50
2R77 His Terrible Servants	.60	1.50
2R80 Stricken Dumb	.60	1.50
2R84 Ulaire Nelya, Ringwraith in Twilight	.60	1.50
2R85 The Witch-king, Lord of the Nazgul	1.50	4.00
2R86 Wraith-world	.60	1.50
2R93 Tower Assassin	.60	1.50
2R94 Verily I Come	.60	1.50
2R97 Consorting With Wizards	.60	1.50
2U13 Tidings of Erebor	.30	.75
2U16 A Blended Race	.30	.75
2U17 Dismay Our Enemies	.30	.75
2U18 Hosts of the Last Alliance	.30	.75
2U28 Wielder of the Flame	.30	.75
2U30 You Cannot Pass!	.30	.75
2U31 Blood of Numenor	.30	.75
2U33 Flee in Terror	.30	.75
2U34 Gondor Will See It Done	.30	.75
2U41 Evil Afoot	.30	.75
2U48 Wizard Storm	.30	.75
2U54 Dark Fire	.30	.75
2U56 Fill With Fear	.30	.75
2U59 Foul Things	.30	.75
2U67 Moria Archer Troop	.30	.75
2U68 Must Do Without Hope	.30	.75
2U70 Power and Terror	.30	.75
2U71 Throw Yourself in Next Time	.30	.75
2U72 Troubled Mountains	.30	.75
2U76 Helpless	.30	.75
2U78 It Wants to be Found	.30	.75
2U79 Resistance Becomes Unbearable	.30	.75
2U81 They Will Find the Ring	.30	.75
2U82 Ulaire Attea, The Easterling	.30	.75
2U83 Ulaire Enquea, Ringwraith in Twilight	.30	.75
2U87 The Eye of Sauron	.30	.75
2U92 Spies of Mordor	.30	.75
2U96 Bilbo, Well-spoken Gentlehobbit	.30	.75
2U98 Dear Friends	.30	.75
2C101 Filibert Bolger, Wily Rascal	.12	.30
2C102a Frodo, Reluctant Adventurer	.12	.30
2C102b Frodo, Reluctant Adventurer		
TENGWAR		
2C104 Merry, Horticulturalist	.12	.30
2C110 Pippin, Mr. Took	.12	.30
2C114 Sam, Proper Poet	.12	.30
2C117 Town Center	.12	.30
2C119 Hollin	.12	.30
2P121 Gimli, Dwarf of the Mountain-race	.40	1.00
2P122 Gandalf, The Grey Pilgrim	.40	1.00
2R100 Fearing the Worst	.60	1.50
2R105a Mithril-coat	.75	2.00
2R105b Mithril-coat TENGWAR		
2R108 O Elbereth! Gilthoniel!	.75	2.00
2R109 Orc-bane	.60	1.50
2R112 A Promise	2.50	6.00
2R113 Red Book of Westmarch	.60	1.50
2U103 Hobbit Sword-play	.30	.75
2U106 Nice Imitation	.30	.75
2U107 Not Feared in Sunlight	.30	.75
2U111 Practically Everyone Was Invited	.30	.75
2U115 Hobbiton Party Field	.30	.75
2U116 Hobbiton Woods	.30	.75
2U118 Great Chasm	.30	.75
2U120 Valley of the Silverlode	.30	.75

2002 Lord of the Rings Realms of the Elf-Lords

Card	Low	High
COMPLETE SET (122)	20.00	40.00
BOOSTER BOX (36 PACKS)	20.00	40.00
BOOSTER PACK (11 CARDS)	1.00	2.00
RELEASED ON JUNE 19, 2002		
3C6 Storm of Argument	.12	.30
3R1 Book of Mazarbul	.60	1.50
3R3 Mines of Khazad-Dum	.60	1.50
3R8 Arwen, Lady Undomiel	.60	1.50
3U2 Gimli's Pipe	.30	.75
3U4 A Royal Welcome	.30	.75
3U5 Song of Durin	.30	.75
3U7 Arwen, Elven Rider	.30	.75
3U9 Beren and Luthien	.30	.75
3C11 Cast It Into the Fire!	.12	.30
3C14 Erestor, Chief Advisor to Elrond	.12	.30
3C16 Friends of Old	.12	.30
3C22 Master of Healing	.12	.30
3C28 Voice of Nimrodel	.12	.30
3C30 Deep in Thought	.12	.30
3C31 Depart Silently	.12	.30
3C32 Fireworks	.12	.30
3C33 His First Serious Check	.12	.30
3C36 Unknown Perils	.12	.30
3C37 Answering the Cries	.12	.30
3C43 Might of Numenor	.12	.30
3C48 We Must Go Warily	.12	.30
3C49 Abandoning Reason for Madness	.12	.30
3C51 Coming for the Ring	.12	.30
3C55 Isengard Axe	.12	.30
3C56 Isengard Forger	.12	.30
3C59 Isengard Shaman	.12	.30
3C62 Isengard Worker	.12	.30
3C63 One of You Must Do This	.12	.30
3C69 Saruman, Servant of the Eye	.12	.30
3C70 Servants to Saruman	.12	.30
3C74 Uruk Raider	.12	.30
3C76 Dangerous Gamble	.12	.30
3C78 Hide and Seek	.12	.30
3C84 They Will Never Stop Hunting You	.12	.30
3C87 The Dark Lord Advances	.12	.30

3C90 Hand of Sauron .12 .30
3C94 Orc Butcher .12 .30
3C95 Orc Guard .12 .30
3C98 Orc Swordsman .12 .30
3R13 Elrond, Herald to Gil-galad 1.25 3.00
3R15 Forests of Lothlorien .60 1.50
3R17 Galadriel, Lady of the Golden Wood .60 1.50
3R19 Gift of the Evenstar .60 1.50
3R21 Long-knives of Legolas 2.00 5.00
3R23 Nenya .60 1.50
3R27 Vilya .60 1.50
3R29 Betrayal of Isengard .60 1.50
3R34 Narya 1.00 2.50
3R38 Aragorn, Heir to the White City .60 1.50
3R39 Banner of the White Tree .75 2.00
3R40 Citadel of Minas Tirith .75 2.00
3R41 Gondor Bowmen 2.00 5.00
3R42 Horn of Boromir .60 1.50
3R44 The Shards of Narsil .75 2.00
3R50 Can You Protect Me From Yourself? .60 1.50
3R52 A Fell Voice on the Air .60 1.50
3R54 Hollowing of Isengard .60 1.50
3R64 Orc Commander .60 1.50
3R65 Orc Overseer .60 1.50
3R66 Orthanc Berserker .60 1.50
3R67 The Palantir of Orthanc .60 1.50
3R68 Saruman, Keeper of Isengard .60 1.50
3R71 Tower of Orthanc .60 1.50
3R77 Depths of Moria .60 1.50
3R80 Such a Little Thing .60 1.50
3R81 Gates of the Dead City .60 1.50
3R85 Too Great and Terrible .60 1.50
3R91 His Cruelty and Malice .60 1.50
3R93 Morgul Slayer .60 1.50
3R99 Orc Trooper .60 1.50
3U10 Calaglin, Elf of Lorien .30 .75
3U12 Dinendal, Silent Scout .30 .75
3U18 Galdor, Councilor From the West .30 .75
3U20 Golradir, Councilor of Imladris .30 .75
3U24 Phial of Galadriel .30 .75
3U25 Saelbeth, Elven Councilor .30 .75
3U26 Something Draws Near .30 .75
3U35 Trust Me as You Once Did .30 .75
3U45 Some Who Resisted .30 .75
3U46 Still Sharp .30 .75
3U47 Voice of Rauros .30 .75
3U53 Hate and Anger .30 .75
3U57 Isengard Retainer .30 .75
3U58 Isengard Servant .30 .75
3U60 Isengard Smith .30 .75
3U61 Isengard Warrior .30 .75
3U72 Trapped and Alone .30 .75
3U73 The Trees Are Strong .30 .75
3U75 Uruk Ravager .30 .75
3U79 Malice .30 .75
3U82 News of Mordor .30 .75
3U83 The Ring Draws Them .30 .75
3U86 Ulaire Otsea, Ringwraith in Twilight .30 .75
3U88 Get Off the Road! .30 .75
3U89 Gleaming in the Snow .30 .75
3U92 Massing in the East .30 .75
3U96 Orc Pillager .30 .75
3U97 Orc Slayer .30 .75
3C101 Orc Warrior .12 .30
3C108 Frying Pan .12 .30
3C109 Meant to Be Alone .12 .30
3C111 Old Noakes, Purveyor of Wisdoms .12 .30
3C112 Seek and Hide .12 .30
3C114 Three Monstrous Trolls .12 .30
3C117 Gates of Argonath .12 .30
3C118 The Great River .12 .30
3P121 Legolas, Son of Thranduil .40 1.00
3P122 Boromir, Defender of Minas Tirith .40 1.00
3R102 Our List of Allies Grows Thin .60 1.50
3R103 Terrible as the Dawn .60 1.50
3R104 Tower of Barad-dur .75 2.00
3R105 Why Shouldn't I Keep It? .60 1.50
3R110 Melilot Brandybuck, Merry Dancer .60 1.50
3R113 The Shire Countryside 1.00 2.50
3U100 Orc Veteran .30 .75
3U106 Bill the Pony .30 .75
3U107 Frodo's Pipe .30 .75
3U115 Caras Galadhon .30 .75
3U116 Eregion Hills .30 .75
3U119 House of Elrond .30 .75
3U120 Wastes of Emyn Muil .30 .75

2002 Lord of the Rings The Two Towers

COMPLETE SET (365) 50.00 100.00
BOOSTER BOX (36 PACKS) 25.00 50.00
BOOSTER PACK (11 CARDS) 1.00 2.00
RELEASED ON NOVEMBER 6, 2002
4C2 The One Ring, The Ruling Ring .12 .30
4C3 Anger .12 .30
4C4 Band of Wild Men .12 .30
4C5 Burn Every Village .12 .30
4C7 Dark Fury .12 .30
4R1A The One Ring, Answer To All Riddles 7.50 15.00
4R1B The One Ring
Answer To All Riddles TENGWAR
4R6 Constantly Threatening .60 1.50
4U8 Death to the Strawheads .30 .75
4U9 Dunlending Arsonist .30 .75
4C10 Dunlending Brigand .12 .30
4C12 Dunlending Madman .12 .30
4C14 Dunlending Ransacker .12 .30
4C15 Dunlending Ravager .12 .30
4C16 Dunlending Robber .12 .30
4C17 Dunlending Savage .12 .30
4C18 Dunlending Warrior .12 .30
4C21 Hillman Band .12 .30
4C25 Hillman Tribe .12 .30
4C26 Iron Axe .12 .30
4C37 War Cry of Dunland .12 .30
4C42 Best Company .12 .30
4C44 Courtesy of My Hall .12 .30
4C49 Gimli, Unbidden Guest .12 .30
4C50 Here Is Good Rock .12 .30
4C51 Khazad Ai-menu .12 .30
4C56 Search Far and Wide .12 .30
4C64 Elven Sword .12 .30
4C67 Fereveldir, Son of Thandronen .12 .30
4C68 Ferevellon, Son of Thandronen .12 .30
4C70 Flashing Steel .12 .30
4C71 Haldir, Emissary of the Galadhrim .12 .30
4C74 Legolas, Elven Comrade .12 .30
4C76 Lorien Guardian .12 .30
4C78 Lorien Swordsman .12 .30
4C83 Supporting Fire .12 .30
4C85 Thandronen, Veteran Protector .12 .30
4C87 Valor .12 .30
4C90a Gandalf, The White Wizard .12 .30
4C90b Gandalf, The White Wizard
TENGWAR
4C93 Have Patience .12 .30
4C97 Long I Fell .12 .30
4C98 Mithrandir, Mithrandir! .12 .30
4R19A Hides 3.00 8.00
4R19B Hides TENGWAR
4R20 Hill Chief .60 1.50
4R22 Hillman Horde .60 1.50
4R23 Hillman Mob .60 1.50
4R29 No Refuge .60 1.50
4R30 No Retreat .60 1.50
4R32 Ravage the Defeated .60 1.50
4R33 Saruman, Rabble-rouser 1.50 4.00
4R35 Wake of Destruction .60 1.50
4R39 Wild Man Raid .60 1.50
4R40 Wulf, Dunlending Chieftain .60 1.50
4R41 Axe of Erebor .75 2.00
4R45 Dwarven Foresight .60 1.50
4R46 Ever My Heart Rises .60 1.50
4R48 Gimli, Lockbearer .60 1.50
4R52 My Axe Is Notched .60 1.50
4R54 Rest by Blind Night .60 1.50
4R55 Restless Axe .60 1.50
4R58 Alliance Reforged .60 1.50
4R61 Company of Archers 1.25 3.00
4R65 Erethon, Naith Lieutenant .60 1.50
4R69 Final Count .60 1.50
4R72 Killing Field .60 1.50
4R73A Legolas, Dauntless Hunter .60 1.50
4R73B Legolas, Dauntless Hunter
TENGWAR
4R75 Lembas 1.00 2.50
4R79 Night Without End .60 1.50
4R84 Sword-wall .60 1.50
4R89 Gandalf, Greyhame .75 2.00
4R91 Gandalf's Staff, Walking Stick .60 1.50
4R92 Grown Suddenly Tall .60 1.50
4R94 Hearken to Me 1.00 2.50
4R95 Into Dark Tunnels .60 1.50
4U11 Dunlending Looter .30 .75
4U13 Dunlending Pillager .30 .75
4U24 Hillman Rabble .30 .75
4U27 Living Off Rock .30 .75
4U28 No Defense .30 .75
4U31 Over the Isen .30 .75
4U34 Secret Folk .30 .75
4U36 War Club .30 .75
4U38 Wild Man of Dunland .30 .75
4U43 Come Here Lad .30 .75
4U47 From the Armory .30 .75
4U53 Quick As May Be .30 .75
4U57 Stout and Strong .30 .75
4U59 Arrow and Blade .30 .75
4U60 Blades Drawn .30 .75
4U62 Elven Bow .30 .75
4U63 Elven Brooch .30 .75
4U66 Feathered .30 .75
4U77 Lorien Is Most Welcome .30 .75
4U80 Ordulus, Young Warrior .30 .75
4U81 Pengedhel, Naith Warrior .30 .75
4U82 Strength of Arms .30 .75
4U86 Thonnas, Naith Captain .30 .75
4U88 Behold the White Rider .30 .75
4U96 Keep Your Forked Tongue .30 .75
4U99 Roll of Thunder .30 .75
4C102 Task Was Not Done .12 .30
4C104 Treebeard, Oldest Living Thing .12 .30
4C105 Under the Living Earth .12 .30
4C109 Aragorn, Heir of Elendil .12 .30
4C112 Boromir's Gauntlets .12 .30
4C113 Curse Them .12 .30
4C115 Defend It and Hope .12 .30
4C117 Faramir, Son of Denethor .12 .30
4C122 Gondorian Ranger .12 .30
4C128 New Errand .12 .30
4C129 Pathfinder .12 .30
4C130 Ranger of Ithilien .12 .30
4C131 Ranger's Bow .12 .30
4C134 Sword of Gondor .12 .30
4C135 War and Valor .12 .30
4C137 Attack on Helm's Deep .12 .30
4C141 Beyond Dark Mountains .12 .30
4C142 Broad-bladed Sword .12 .30
4C145 Cloud of Arrows .12 .30
4C151 Ferocity .12 .30
4C153 Grima, Son of Galmod .12 .30
4C156 Kill Them Now .12 .30
4C165 Orthanc Warrior .12 .30
4C175 Still They Came .12 .30
4C178 Unferth, Grima's Bodyguard .12 .30
4C180 Uruk Besieger .12 .30
4C181 Uruk Chaser .12 .30
4C183 Uruk Crossbowman .12 .30
4C184 Uruk Defender .12 .30
4C185 Uruk Fanatic .12 .30
4C187 Uruk Foot Soldier .12 .30
4C189 Uruk Plains Runner .12 .30
4C190 Uruk Pursuer .12 .30
4C191 Uruk Rear Guard .12 .30
4C192 Uruk Regular .12 .30
4C193 Uruk Runner .12 .30
4C195 Uruk Seeker .12 .30
4C196 Uruk Spear .12 .30
4C197 Uruk Stalker .12 .30
4C198 Uruk Stormer .12 .30
4C204 Uruk-hai Marauder .12 .30
4C206 Uruk-hai Patrol .12 .30
4C207 Uruk-hai Raiding Party .12 .30
4C210 We Are the Fighting Uruk-hai .12 .30
4C212 Weary .12 .30
4C221 Desert Spearman .12 .30
4C222 Desert Warrior .12 .30
4C224 Easterling Axeman .12 .30
4C226 Easterling Guard .12 .30
4C227 Easterling Infantry .12 .30
4C228 Easterling Lieutenant .12 .30
4C235 Gathering to the Summons .12 .30
4C239 Men of Rhun .12 .30
4C241 On the March .12 .30
4C248 Southron Bowman .12 .30
4C252 Southron Scout .12 .30
4C254 Southron Soldier .12 .30
4C255 Southron Spear .12 .30
4C258 Southron Wanderer .12 .30
4C260 Whirling Strike .12 .30
4C265 Elite Rider .12 .30
4C266 Eomer, Sister-son of Theoden .12 .30
4C270 Eowyn, Lady of Rohan .12 .30
4C273 Fight for the Villagers .12 .30
4C277 Guma, Plains Farmer .12 .30
4C278 Heavy Chain .12 .30
4C281 Hlafwine, Village Farmhand .12 .30
4C283 Horse of Rohan .12 .30
4C286 Rider of Rohan .12 .30
4C287 Rider's Mount .12 .30
4C288 Rider's Spear .12 .30
4C291 Sword of Rohan .12 .30
4C292 Theoden, Son of Thengel .12 .30
4C297 Work for the Sword .12 .30
4C298 Brace of Coneys .12 .30
4C302 Frodo, Tired Traveller .12 .30
4C306 Hobbit Sword .12 .30
4C308 Knocked on the Head .12 .30
4C310 Merry, Learned Guide .12 .30
4C314 Pippin, Woolly-footed Rascal .12 .30
4C316 Sam, Samwise the Brave .12 .30
4C319 Severed His Bonds .12 .30
4C321 Swiftly and Softly .12 .30
4C322 Warmed Up a Bit .12 .30
4P364A Aragorn, Wingfoot .40 1.00
4P364B Aragorn, Wingfoot
TENGWAR
4P365 Theoden, Lord of the Mark .40 1.00
4R100A Shadowfax .60 1.50
4R100B Shadowfax TENGWAR
4R103A Treebeard, Earthborn .60 1.50
4R103B Treebeard, Earthborn
TENGWAR
4R106 Well Met Indeed .60 1.50
4R107 Windows in a Stone Wall .60 1.50
4R111 Boromir, My Brother .60 1.50
4R116 Faramir, Captain of Gondor .60 1.50
4R118 Faramir's Bow 2.00 5.00
4R119 Faramir's Cloak .60 1.50
4R120 Forbidden Pool .60 1.50
4R121 Forests of Ithilien .60 1.50
4R124 Help in Doubt and Need .60 1.50
4R125 Henneth Annun .60 1.50
4R133 Ruins of Osgiliath .60 1.50
4R139 Banished .60 1.50
4R140 Beyond All Hope .60 1.50
4R144 Burning of Westfold .60 1.50
4R146 Come Down .60 1.50
4R149 Driven Back .60 1.50
4R150 Elite Crossbowmen .75 2.00
4R154A Grima, Wormtongue 1.25 3.00
4R154B Grima, Wormtongue TENGWAR
4R157 Leechcraft .60 1.50
4R158 Lieutenant of Orthanc .60 1.50
4R160 Mauhur, Patrol Leader .60 1.50
4R162 New Power Rising .60 1.50
4R163 No Dawn for Men .60 1.50
4R164 Orthanc Champion .75 2.00
4R166 The Palantir of Orthanc .60 1.50
Seventh Seeing-stone
4R167 Pillage of Rohan .60 1.50
4R168 Race Across the Mark .60 1.50
4R169 Ranged Commander .60 1.50
4R171 Rest While You Can .60 1.50
4R172 Rohan Is Mine .60 1.50
4R173A Saruman, Black Traitor 1.00 2.50
4R173B Saruman, Black Traitor TENGWAR
4R174 Saruman's Staff, Wizard's Device .75 2.00
4R176A Ugluk, Servant of Saruman .75 2.00
4R176B Ugluk, Servant of Saruman TENGWAR
4R177 Ugluk's Sword .60 1.50
4R179 Uruk Assault Band .60 1.50
4R186 Uruk Follower .60 1.50
4R199 Uruk Trooper .60 1.50
4R200 Uruk Vanguard .75 2.00
4R203 Uruk-hai Horde .60 1.50
4R209 Volley Fire .60 1.50
4R211 Weapons of Isengard 1.50 4.00
4R213 What Did You Discover? .60 1.50
4R214 Where Has Grima Stowed It? .60 1.50
4R215 Wounded .60 1.50
4R218 Desert Legion .75 2.00
4R219A Desert Lord 2.50 6.00
4R219B Desert Lord TENGWAR
4R223 Discovered .60 1.50
4R225A Easterling Captain .75 2.00
4R225B Easterling Captain TENGWAR
4R229 Easterling Skirmisher .60 1.50
4R231 Eastern Emyn Muil .60 1.50
4R237 Ithilien Wilderness .60 1.50
4R238 Men of Harad .60 1.50
4R240 New Fear 1.00 2.50
4R243 Rapid Fire .75 2.00
4R244 Regiment of Haradrim .60 1.50
4R245 Southron Archer .75 2.00
4R246 Southron Assassin .60 1.50
4R247 Southron Bow .75 2.00
4R251 Southron Fighter .60 1.50
4R256 Southron Troop .60 1.50
4R257 Southron Veterans .60 1.50
4R259 Vision From Afar 2.00 5.00
4R261 Wrath of Harad .60 1.50
4R262 Aldor, Soldier of Edoras .60 1.50
4R267 Eomer, Third Marshal of Riddermark 1.50 4.00
4R269 Eothain, Scout of the Mark .60 1.50

4R271 Eowyn, Sister-daughter of Theoden	.60	1.50
4R272 Eowyn's Sword	.75	2.00
4R274 Firefoot	1.00	2.50
4R279 Helm! Helm!	.60	1.50
4R284 King's Mail	.60	1.50
4R289A Simbelmyne	1.50	4.00
4R289B Simbelmyne TENGWAR		
4R290 Supplies of the Mark	.60	1.50
4R293 Valleys of the Mark	.60	1.50
4R294 Weapon Store	.75	2.00
4R299 Cliffs of Emyn Muil	.75	2.00
4R300 Escape	1.00	2.50
4R301A Frodo, Courteous Halfling	.60	1.50
4R301B Frodo, Courteous Halfling TENGWAR		
4R303 Frodo's Cloak	.60	1.50
4R304 Get On and Get Away	.60	1.50
4R307 Impatient and Angry	.60	1.50
4R311 Merry, Unquenchable Hobbit	.60	1.50
4R313 Pippin, Just a Nuisance	.60	1.50
4R315 Sam, Frodo's Gardener	.60	1.50
4R317 Sam's Pack	.60	1.50
4U101 Stump and Bramble	.30	.75
4U108 Wizardry Indeed	.30	.75
4U110 Arrows Thick in the Air	.30	.75
4U114 Damrod, Ranger of Ithilien	.30	.75
4U123 Hard Choice	.30	.75
4U126 Ithilien Trap	.30	.75
4U127 Mablung, Soldier of Gondor	.30	.75
4U132 Ranger's Sword, Blade of Aragorn	.30	.75
4U136 Advance Uruk Patrol	.30	.75
4U138 Band of Uruk Bowmen	.30	.75
4U143 Brought Back Alive	.30	.75
4U147 Covering Fire	.30	.75
4U148 Down to the Last Child	.30	.75
4U152 Get Back	.30	.75
4U155 Haunting Her Steps	.30	.75
4U159 Many Riddles	.30	.75
4U161 Men Will Fall	.30	.75
4U170 Ranks Without Number	.30	.75
4U182 Uruk Crossbow Troop	.30	.75
4U188 Uruk Hunter	.30	.75
4U194 Uruk Searcher	.30	.75
4U201 Uruk Veteran	.30	.75
4U202 Uruk-hai Band	.30	.75
4U205 Uruk-hai Mob	.30	.75
4U208 Vengeance	.30	.75
4U216 Arrow From the South	.30	.75
4U217 Desert Lancers	.30	.75
4U220 Desert Soldier	.30	.75
4U230 Easterling Trooper	.30	.75
4U232 Elite Archer	.30	.75
4U233 Fearless	.30	.75
4U234 Flanking Attack	.30	.75
4U236 Howl of Harad	.30	.75
4U242 Raiders From the East	.30	.75
4U249 Southron Commander	.30	.75
4U250 Southron Explorer	.30	.75
4U253 Southron Sentry	.30	.75
4U263 Brego	.30	.75
4U264 Ceorl, Weary Horseman	.30	.75
4U268 Eomer's Spear	.30	.75
4U275 Forth Eorlingas!	.30	.75
4U276 Fortress Never Fallen	.30	.75
4U280 Herugrim	.30	.75
4U282 An Honorable Charge	.30	.75
4U285 Leod, Westfold Herdsman	.30	.75
4U295 Weland, Smith of the Riddermark	.30	.75
4U296 Well Stored	.30	.75
4U305 Good Work	.30	.75
4U309 Light Shining Faintly	.30	.75
4U312 Mind Your Own Affairs	.30	.75
4U318 Seven We Had	.30	.75
4U320 Store-room	.30	.75
4U323 East Wall of Rohan	.30	.75
4U324 Eastemnet Downs	.30	.75
4U325 Eastemnet Gullies	.30	.75
4U326 Horse-country	.30	.75
4U327 Plains of Rohan	.30	.75
4U328 The Riddermark	.30	.75
4U329 Western Emyn Muil	.30	.75
4U330 Derndingle	.30	.75
4U331 Eastfold	.30	.75
4U332 Fangorn Forest	.30	.75
4U333 Plains of Rohan Camp	.30	.75
4U334 Rohirrim Village	.30	.75
4U335 Uruk Camp	.30	.75
4U336 Wold of Rohan	.30	.75
4U337 Barrows of Edoras	.30	.75
4U338 Golden Hall	.30	.75
4U339 Stables	.30	.75
4U340 Streets of Edoras	.30	.75
4U341 Throne Room	.30	.75
4U342 Westemnet Plains	.30	.75
4U343 Ered Nimrais	.30	.75
4U344 Westemnet Hills	.30	.75
4U345 White Mountains	.30	.75
4U346 White Rocks	.30	.75
4U347 Deep of Helm	.30	.75
4U348 Deeping Wall	.30	.75
4U349 Helm's Gate	.30	.75
4U350 Hornburg Courtyard	.30	.75
4U351 Hornburg Parapet	.30	.75
4U352 Caves of Aglarond	.30	.75
4U353 Great Hall	.30	.75
4U354 Hornburg Armory	.30	.75
4U355 Cavern Entrance	.30	.75
4U356 Hornburg Causeway	.30	.75
4U357 King's Room	.30	.75
4U358 Ring of Isengard	.30	.75
4U359 Wizard's Vale	.30	.75
4U360 Fortress of Orthanc	.30	.75
4U361 Orthanc Balcony	.30	.75
4U362 Orthanc Library	.30	.75
4U363 Palantir Chamber	.30	.75

2003 Lord of the Rings Battle of Helm's Deep

COMPLETE SET (128)	25.00	50.00
BOOSTER BOX (36 PACKS)	25.00	50.00
BOOSTER PACK (11 CARDS)	1.00	2.00
RELEASED ON MARCH 12, 2003		
5C6 Defending the Keep	.12	.30
5R3 Leaping Blaze	.60	1.50
5R4 Wild Men of the Hills	.60	1.50
5R5 Baruk Khazad	.60	1.50
5R7 Gimli, Skilled Defender	.60	1.50
5U1 Dunlending Rampager	.30	.75
5U2 Dunlending Renegade	.30	.75
5U8 Horn of Helm	.30	.75
5U9 More to My Liking	.30	.75
5C14 That Is No Orc Horn	.12	.30
5C17 Forest Guardian	.12	.30
5C24 Gollum, Nasty Treacherous Creature	.12	.30
5C27 Poor Wretch	.12	.30
5C28 Smeagol, Old Noser	.12	.30
5C30 We Must Have It	.12	.30
5C32 Citadel of the Stars	.12	.30
5C33 City Wall	.12	.30
5C35 Gondorian Knight	.12	.30
5C36 Knight of Gondor	.12	.30
5C37 Men of Numenor	.12	.30
5C40 Take Cover	.12	.30
5C43 War Must Be	.12	.30
5C52 Isengard Flanker	.12	.30
5C53 Isengard Rider	.12	.30
5C61 Uruk Engineer	.12	.30
5C62 Uruk Sapper	.12	.30
5C65 Warg	.12	.30
5C66 Warg-master	.12	.30
5C67 Warg-rider	.12	.30
5C68 Wolf-voices	.12	.30
5C73 Mumak	.12	.30
5C74 Southron Marcher	.12	.30
5C75 Southron Runner	.12	.30
5C76 Southron Traveler	.12	.30
5C81 Ecglaf, Courageous Farmer	.12	.30
5C83 Household Guard	.12	.30
5C85 Let Us Be Swift	.12	.30
5C88 Rohirrim Bow	.12	.30
5C90 Rohirrim Scout	.12	.30
5C91 Rohirrim Shield	.12	.30
5C93 Theoden, King of the Golden Hall	.12	.30
5C97 Gate Soldier	.12	.30
5C98 Gate Trooper	.12	.30
5C99 Gate Veteran	.12	.30
5R11 Break the Charge	.60	1.50
5R16 Down From the Hills	.60	1.50
5R18 Fury of the White Rider	.60	1.50
5R19 Lindenroot, Elder Shepherd	.60	1.50
5R21 Be Back Soon	.60	1.50
5R25A Gollum, Stinker	2.00	5.00
5R25B Gollum, Stinker TENGWAR		
5R29A Smeagol, Slinker	.60	1.50
5R29B Smeagol, Slinker TENGWAR		
5R31 Alcarin, Warrior of Lamedon	.60	1.50
5R39 Stone Tower	.60	1.50
5R41 These Are My People	.60	1.50
5R46 Berserk Savage	.60	1.50
5R47 Berserk Slayer	.60	1.50
5R49 Devilry of Orthanc	.60	1.50
5R50 Foul Horde	.60	1.50
5R51 Grima, Chief Counselor	.60	1.50
5R56 Saruman, Master of Foul Folk	.60	1.50
5R58 Sharku, Warg-captain	.60	1.50
5R59 Sharku's Warg	.75	2.00
5R69 Wolves of Isengard	.60	1.50
5R70 Army of Haradrim	.60	1.50
5R71 Company of Haradrim	.60	1.50
5R72 Desert Stalker	.60	1.50
5R78 War Mumak	1.25	3.00
5R82 Gamling, Warrior of Rohan	.60	1.50
5R84 I Am Here	.60	1.50
5R86 No Rest for the Weary	.60	1.50
5R89 Rohirrim Helm	.60	1.50
5R94 Thundering Host	.60	1.50
5R95 Dead Marshes	.60	1.50
5R96 Eye of Barad-Dur	.60	1.50
5U10 Balglin, Elven Warrior	.30	.75
5U12 Legolas' Sword	.30	.75
5U13 Taurnil, Sharp-eyed Bowman	.30	.75
5U15 Birchseed, Tall Statesman	.30	.75
5U20 Turn of the Tide	.30	.75
5U22 Evil-smelling Fens	.30	.75
5U23 Follow Smeagol	.30	.75
5U26 Look at Him	.30	.75
5U34 Fall Back	.30	.75
5U38 Rally Point	.30	.75
5U42 Turgon, Man of Belfalas	.30	.75
5U44 Battering Ram	.30	.75
5U45 Berserk Rager	.30	.75
5U48 Black Shapes Crawling	.30	.75
5U54 Isengard Scimitar	.30	.75
5U55 Isengard Scout Troop	.30	.75
5U57 Scaling Ladder	.30	.75
5U60 Siege Engine	.30	.75
5U63 Uruk-hai Berserker	.30	.75
5U64 War-warg	.30	.75
5U77 Strength in Numbers	.30	.75
5U79 Armory	.30	.75
5U80 Arrow-slits	.30	.75
5U87 Parapet	.30	.75
5U92 Sigewulf, Brave Volunteer	.30	.75
5C106 Orc Infantry	.12	.30
5C108 Orc Pursuer	.12	.30
5C109 Orc Runner	.12	.30
5C117 You Must Help Us	.12	.30
5P121 Legolas, Archer of Mirkwood	.40	1.00
5P122 Eowyn, Daughter of Eomund	.40	1.00
5R100A Grishnakh, Orc Captain	2.00	5.00
5R100B Grishnakh, Orc Captain TENGWAR		
5R102 Morannon	.60	1.50
5R103 Orc Captain	.60	1.50
5R112 No Help for It	.60	1.50
5R113 No Use That Way	.60	1.50
5R116A Sting, Baggins Heirloom	1.50	4.00
5R116B Sting, Baggins Heirloom TENGWAR		
5R123 Baruk Khazad	.40	1.00
5R124 Break the Charge	.40	1.00
5R125 Foul Horde	.40	1.00
5R126 Army of Haradrim	.40	1.00
5R127 Rohirrim Helm	.40	1.00
5R128 Thundering Host	.40	1.00
5U101 I'd Make You Squeak	.30	.75
5U104 Orc Cutthroat	.30	.75
5U105 Orc Fighter	.30	.75
5U107 Orc Patrol	.30	.75
5U110 Teeth of Mordor	.30	.75
5U111 Frodo, Master of the Precious	.30	.75
5U114 Rare Good Ballast	.30	.75
5U115 Sam, Nice Sensible Hobbit	.30	.75
5U118 Hornburg Wall	.30	.75
5U119 Nan Curunir	.30	.75
5U120 Caverns of Isengard	.30	.75

2003 Lord of the Rings Ents of Fagorn

COMPLETE SET (128)	15.00	30.00
BOOSTER BOX (36 PACKS)	20.00	40.00
BOOSTER PACK (11 CARDS)	1.00	2.00
RELEASED ON JULY 2, 2003		
6C1 Bound By Rage	.12	.30
6C2 Dunlending Elder	.12	.30
6C3 Dunlending Footmen	.12	.30
6C4 Dunlending Headman	.12	.30
6C5 Dunlending Reserve	.12	.30
6R6 Hill Clan	.60	1.50
6R7 Ready to Fall	.75	2.00
6U8 Too Long Have These Peasants Stood	.30	.75
6U9 Lend Us Your Aid	.30	.75
6C10 Suspended Palaces	.12	.30
6C12 Agility	.12	.30
6C17 Forewarned	.12	.30
6C21 Naith Longbow	.12	.30
6C27 Ent Avenger	.12	.30
6C29 Ent Moot	.12	.30
6C33 Quickbeam, Bregalad	.12	.30
6C34 Roused	.12	.30
6C37 Treebeard, Guardian of the Forest	.12	.30
6C38 Don't Follow the Lights	.12	.30
6C40 Gollum, Old Villain	.12	.30
6C42 Nasty, Foul Hobbitses	.12	.30
6C43 Not Listening	.12	.30
6C45 Smeagol, Poor Creature	.12	.30
6C47 You're a Liar and a Thief	.12	.30
6C48 Anborn, Skilled Huntsman	.12	.30
6C52 Garrison of Osgiliath	.12	.30
6C53 Mortal Men	.12	.30
6C56 Trust	.12	.30
6C59 Banner of Isengard	.12	.30
6C65 Isengard Artisan	.12	.30
6C67 Isengard Journeyman	.12	.30
6C69 Isengard Plodder	.12	.30
6C71 Isengard Tinker	.12	.30
6C72 Rohirrim Traitor	.12	.30
6C81 Southron Invaders	.12	.30
6C95 Hrethel, Rider of Rohan	.12	.30
6C97 We Left None Alive	.12	.30
6C98 Banner of the Eye	.12	.30
6C99 Corpse Lights	.12	.30
6R11 Toss Me	.60	1.50
6R15 Elrond, Keeper of Vilya	.60	1.50
6R18 Galadriel, Keeper of Nenya	.60	1.50
6R23 Naith Warband	.60	1.50
6R26 Enraged	.75	2.00
6R28 Ent Horde	.60	1.50
6R30 Gandalf, Mithrandir	.60	1.50
6R31 Glamdring, Lightning Brand	.60	1.50
6R35 Skinbark, Fladrif	.60	1.50
6R39 Don't Look at Them	.75	2.00
6R41 Master Broke His Promise	.60	1.50
6R44 Safe Paths	.60	1.50
6R46 They Stole It	.75	2.00
6R49 Ancient Roads	.60	1.50
6R50 Aragorn, Defender of Free Peoples	.75	2.00
6R55 Ring of Barahir	.60	1.50
6R57 Agents of Orthanc	.60	1.50
6R60 Berserk Butcher	.60	1.50
6R62 Fires and Foul Fumes	.60	1.50
6R68 Isengard Mechanics	.60	1.50
6R74 Sharku, Vile Marauder	.60	1.50
6R76 The Balrog, Terror of Flame and Shadow	1.25	3.00
6R77 Durin's Tower	.60	1.50
6R78 Easterling Army	1.00	2.50
6R80 Southron Archer Legion	.60	1.50
6R82 Trample	.60	1.50
6R85 Sword of Dol Guldur	.60	1.50
6R88A Ulaire Toldea, Winged Sentry	1.00	2.50
6R88B Ulaire Toldea, Winged Sentry TENGWAR		
6R89 Winged and Ominous	.60	1.50
6R92 Eomer, Rohirrim Captain	.60	1.50
6R94 Hama, Doorward of Theoden	.60	1.50
6R96 News From the Mark	.60	1.50
6U13 Arwen, Evenstar of Her People	.30	.75
6U14 Banner of Elbereth	.30	.75
6U16 Forearmed	.30	.75
6U19 Gift of Foresight	.30	.75
6U20 Must Be a Dream	.30	.75
6U22 Naith Troop	.30	.75
6U24 Boomed and Trumpeted	.30	.75
6U25 Crack Into Rubble	.30	.75
6U32 Host of Fangorn	.30	.75
6U36 Threw Down My Enemy	.30	.75
6U51 Banner of Westernesse	.30	.75
6U54 Perilous Ventures	.30	.75
6U58 Assault Ladder	.30	.75
6U61 Desertion	.30	.75
6U63 Gnawing, Biting, Hacking, Burning	.30	.75
6U64 Iron Fist of the Orc	.30	.75
6U66 Isengard Builder	.30	.75
6U70 Isengard Tender	.30	.75
6U73 Scaffolding	.30	.75
6U75 Twisted Tales	.30	.75
6U79 Easterling Polearm	.30	.75
6U83 Fell Beast	.30	.75
6U84 Spied From Above	.30	.75
6U86 Ulaire Lemenya, Winged Hunter	.30	.75
6U87 Ulaire Nertea, Winged Hunter	.30	.75
6U90 Banner of the Mark	.30	.75
6U91 Blood Has Been Spilled	.30	.75
6U93 Ever the Hope of Men	.30	.75
6C100 Dead Ones	.12	.30
6C102 Gate Sentry	.12	.30
6C108 Wisp of Pale Sheen	.12	.30
6C111 Kept Safe	.12	.30

Card	Low	High
6C112 Long Slow Wrath	.12	.30
6P121 Faramir, Ithilien Ranger	.60	1.50
6P122 The Witch-king, Deathless Lord	.60	1.50
6R101 Gate Picket	.60	1.50
6R103 Gate Troll	.60	1.50
6R106 Troll of Udun	.60	1.50
6R109 Held	.60	1.50
6R113 Merry, Impatient Hobbit	.60	1.50
6R114 Pippin, Hastiest of All	.60	1.50
6R123 Enraged	1.00	2.50
6R124 Skinbark, Fladrif	.60	1.50
6R125 Don't Look at Them	1.50	4.00
6R126 Ancient Roads	.75	2.00
6R127 Isengard Mechanics	.60	1.50
6R128 Gate Troll	.60	1.50
6U104 Orc Insurgent	.30	.75
6U105 Peril	.30	.75
6U107 Troll's Chain	.30	.75
6U110 It Burns Us	.30	.75
6U115 Rocks of Emyn Muil	.30	.75
6U116 Westfold	.30	.75
6U117 Meduseld	.30	.75
6U118 Hornburg Hall	.30	.75
6U119 Valley of Saruman	.30	.75
6U120 Saruman's Laboratory	.30	.75

2003 Lord of the Rings The Return of the King

Card	Low	High
COMPLETE SET (367)	75.00	150.00
BOOSTER BOX (36 PACKS)	25.00	50.00
BOOSTER PACK (11 CARDS)	1.00	2.00
RELEASED ON NOVEMBER 5, 2003		
7C1 The One Ring, The Ruling Ring	.12	.30
7C4 Calculated Risk	.12	.30
7C6 Gimli, Faithful Companion	.12	.30
7R5 Dark Ways	.75	2.00
7R7 Gimli, Feared Axeman	.60	1.50
7R9 Gimli's Battle Axe, Trusted Weapon	1.00	2.50
7U3 Battle Tested	.30	.75
7U8 Gimli's Armor	.30	.75
7C11 Out of Darkness	.12	.30
7C20 Defiance	.12	.30
7C23 Into the West	.12	.30
7C26 Legolas, Nimble Warrior	.12	.30
7C29 Still Needed	.12	.30
7C30 Uncertain Paths	.12	.30
7C31 All Save One	.12	.30
7C34 Echoes of Valinor	.12	.30
7C36 Gandalf, Defender of the West	.12	.30
7C40 Have Patience	.12	.30
7C41 Intimidate	.12	.30
7C46 Peace of Mind	.12	.30
7C51 Undaunted	.12	.30
7C52 Wizard Staff	.12	.30
7C53 Captured by the Ring	.12	.30
7C59 Gollum, Vile Creature	.12	.30
7C62 It's Mine	.12	.30
7C65 Never	.12	.30
7C72 Smeagol, Hurried Guide	.12	.30
7C75 Sweeter Meats	.12	.30
7C76 Very Nice Friends	.12	.30
7C81 Aragorn, Captain of Gondor	.12	.30
7C82 Cirion	.12	.30
7C83 City of Men	.12	.30
7C84 Dagger Strike	.12	.30
7C86 Denethor, Wizened Steward	.12	.30
7C89 Duty of Two	.12	.30
7C90 Faramir, Stout Captain	.12	.30
7C92 First Level	.12	.30
7C96 Gondorian Captain	.12	.30
7C99 Great Gale	.12	.30
7R10 Loyalty Unshaken	1.00	2.50
7R12 Preparations	1.00	2.50
7R16 Arwen, Fair Elf Maiden	.60	1.50
7R17 Asfaloth, Elven Steed	1.00	2.50
7R18 Bow of the Galadhrim, Gift of Galadriel	.60	1.50
7R21 Elrond, Elven Lord	.75	2.00
7R22 Hope Comes	.60	1.50
7R24 Leaving Forever	.60	1.50
7R25 Legolas, Fearless Marksman	.60	1.50
7R27 Mirkwood Bowman	.60	1.50
7R28 Shadow Between	1.25	3.00
7R2a The One Ring, Such a Weight to Carry	3.00	8.00
7R2b The One Ring, Such A Weight To Carry TENGWAR		
7R32 The Board Is Set	.60	1.50
7R33 Citadel to Gate	.60	1.50
7R37 Gandalf, Manager of Wizards	1.50	4.00
7R38 Gandalf's Staff, Focus of Power	1.25	3.00
7R39 Glamdring, Elven Blade	1.25	3.00
7R43 Light the Beacons	.60	1.50
7R44 Moment of Respite	1.25	3.00
7R48 Stay This Madness	.60	1.50
7R50 Terrible and Evil	1.50	4.00
7R56 The Dead City	.60	1.50
7R57 Fat One Wants It	.60	1.50
7R58 Gollum, Plotting Deceiver	.60	1.50
7R61 Hobbitses Are Dead	1.25	3.00
7R63 Let Her Deal With Them	1.25	3.00
7R66 No Safe Places	.60	1.50
7R67 Plotting	1.25	3.00
7R68 Scouting	.60	1.50
7R69 Secret Paths	.60	1.50
7R70 Serving the Precious	.60	1.50
7R71 Smeagol, Always Helps	1.25	3.00
7R73 Sneaking!	1.25	3.00
7R74 So Polite	.60	1.50
7R80 Anduril, King's Blade	1.00	2.50
7R85 Denethor, Steward of the City	.60	1.50
7R87 Derufin	.60	1.50
7R91 Faramir, Wizard's Pupil	.60	1.50
7R95 Gondor Still Stands	.60	1.50
7R97 Gondorian Merchant	.60	1.50
7U13 Reckless Pride	.30	.75
7U14 Slaked Thirsts	.30	.75
7U15 Ancient Blade	.30	.75
7U19 Careful Study	.30	.75
7U35 Fool's Hope	.30	.75
7U42 King's Advisor	.30	.75
7U45 Numenor's Pride	.30	.75
7U47 Sharpen Your Swords	.30	.75
7U49 Steadfast Champion	.30	.75
7U54 Clever Hobbits	.30	.75
7U55 Days Growing Dark	.30	.75
7U60 Heavy Burden	.30	.75
7U64 Nasty	.30	.75
7U77 We Hates Them	.30	.75
7U78 Where Shall We Go	.30	.75
7U88 Dervorin	.30	.75
7U93 Footman's Armor	.30	.75
7U94 Gondor Bow	.30	.75
7U98 Gondorian Sword	.30	.75
7C105 I Will Go	.12	.30
7C106 Ingold	.12	.30
7C108 Knight's Spear	.12	.30
7C111 Man the Walls	.12	.30
7C115 Ranger of Minas Tirith	.12	.30
7C116 Ranger of Osgiliath	.12	.30
7C117 Reckless Counter	.12	.30
7C118 Second Level	.12	.30
7C121 Stout Resistance	.12	.30
7C124 Targon	.12	.30
7C130 Dark Tidings	.12	.30
7C131 Desert Fighter	.12	.30
7C132 Desert Nomad	.12	.30
7C133 Desert Runner	.12	.30
7C135 Desert Sneak	.12	.30
7C137 Desert Spearman	.12	.30
7C139 Easterling Aggressor	.12	.30
7C140 Easterling Assailant	.12	.30
7C141 Easterling Attacker	.12	.30
7C142 Easterling Blademaster	.12	.30
7C144 Easterling Ransacker	.12	.30
7C149 Great Beasts	.12	.30
7C150 Harsh Tongues	.12	.30
7C153 Mumakil of the Harad	.12	.30
7C154 New Strength Came Now	.12	.30
7C155 Raider Bow	.12	.30
7C156 Raider Halberd	.12	.30
7C161 Southron Brigand	.12	.30
7C172 Troop of Haradrim	.12	.30
7C173 War Towers	.12	.30
7C184 More Unbearable	.12	.30
7C186 Morgul Axe	.12	.30
7C189 Morgul Cur	.12	.30
7C192 Morgul Hound	.12	.30
7C193 Morgul Lackey	.12	.30
7C194 Morgul Mongrel	.12	.30
7C196 Morgul Predator	.12	.30
7C198 Morgul Ruffian	.12	.30
7C199 Morgul Soldier	.12	.30
7C200 Morgul Spawn	.12	.30
7C201 Morgul Spearman	.12	.30
7C208 There Came a Cry	.12	.30
7C209 Too Late	.12	.30
7C220 War Long Planned	.12	.30
7C222 Deor	.12	.30
7C225 Elite Rider	.12	.30
7C226 Enraged Horseman	.12	.30
7C229 Eowyn, Restless Maiden	.12	.30
7C235 Guthlaf, Herald	.12	.30
7C237 His Golden Shield	.12	.30
7C240 Long Spear	.12	.30
7C243 Morning Came	.12	.30
7C246 Rohirrim Guard	.12	.30
7C247 Rohirrim Herdsman	.12	.30
7C248 Rohirrim Javelin	.12	.30
7C253 Swift Steed	.12	.30
7C256 They Sang as They Slew	.12	.30
7C257 Veteran Horseman	.12	.30
7C259 Wind in His Face	.12	.30
7C262 Above the Battlement	.12	.30
7C263 Anguish	.12	.30
7C265 Besieging Pike	.12	.30
7C273 Gorgoroth Garrison	.12	.30
7C275 Gorgoroth Pillager	.12	.30
7C276 Gorgoroth Ransacker	.12	.30
7C277 Gorgoroth Sapper	.12	.30
7C285 Mordor Defender	.12	.30
7C287 Mordor Guard	.12	.30
7C288 Mordor Regular	.12	.30
7C290 Mordor Soldier	.12	.30
7C291 Mordor Trooper	.12	.30
7C296 Orc Brood	.12	.30
7C297 Orc Butcher	.12	.30
7C298 Orc Chaser	.12	.30
7C299 Orc Destroyer	.12	.30
7C300 Orc Fanatic	.12	.30
7C303 Orc Pursuer	.12	.30
7C304 Orc Rager	.12	.30
7C312 Siegecraft	.12	.30
7C313 Some Secret Art of Flame	.12	.30
7C315 Tower Walkway	.12	.30
7C317 Frodo, Hope of Free Peoples	.12	.30
7C319 Hobbit Sword	.12	.30
7C320 Merry, Rohirrim Squire	.12	.30
7C322 Noble Intentions	.12	.30
7C323 Pippin, Sworn to Service	.12	.30
7C326 Sam, Needer of Vittles	.12	.30
7P364 Aragorn, Driven by Need	1.00	2.50
7P365 Eomer, Valiant Warchief	.40	1.00
7R100 Greatest Stronghold	.60	1.50
7R101 Guarded	.60	1.50
7R103 Hearts Raised	.75	2.00
7R104 Hidden Knowledge	.60	1.50
7R112 Noble Leaders	3.00	8.00
7R113 Pippin's Armor	.60	1.50
7R114 Pippin's Sword	.60	1.50
7R119 Seventh Level	.60	1.50
7R122 Strong and Old	.60	1.50
7R127 Vorondil	.60	1.50
7R129 Bold Men and Grim	1.00	2.50
7R143 Easterling Footman	.60	1.50
7R145 Easterling Regiment	.60	1.50
7R148 Fierce in Despair	1.00	2.50
7R152 Mumak Commander	.60	1.50
7R158 Rout	.60	1.50
7R159 Small Hope	2.00	5.00
7R163 Southron Chieftain	.60	1.50
7R164 Southron Conqueror	.60	1.50
7R165 Southron Intruder	.60	1.50
7R166 Southron Leader	.60	1.50
7R167 Southron Marksmen	.75	2.00
7R169 Surging Up	.60	1.50
7R170 Suzerain of Harad	.60	1.50
7R177 Feel His Blade	.60	1.50
7R179 Ghastly Host	.60	1.50
7R180 Gorbag, Lieutenant of Cirith Ungol	1.00	2.50
7R181 Held Ground	.60	1.50
7R182 Loathsome	.60	1.50
7R183 Mind and Body	.75	2.00
7R188 Morgul Brute	5.00	10.00
7R191 Morgul Detachment	.75	2.00
7R197 Morgul Regiment	.60	1.50
7R204 Out of Sight and Shot	1.25	3.00
7R205 Put Forth His Strength	.60	1.50
7R206 Stronghold of Minas Morgul	.75	2.00
7R210 Ulaire Attea, Wraith on Wings	1.25	3.00
7R211a Ulaire Cantea, Faster Than Winds	.75	2.00
7R211b Ulaire Cantea, Faster Than Winds TENGWAR		
7R213 Ulaire Lemenya, Assailing Minion	.60	1.50
7R215 Ulaire Nelya, Assailing Minion	.60	1.50
7R219 Ulaire Toldea, Wraith on Wings	1.00	2.50
7R221a The Witch-king, Morgul King	.75	2.00
7R221b The Witch-king, Morgul King TENGWAR		
7R223 Death They Cried	.60	1.50
7R227a Eomer, Skilled Tactician	.75	2.00
7R227b Eomer, Skilled Tactician TENGWAR		
7R228 Eowyn, Dernhelm	.60	1.50
7R230 Eowyn's Sword, Dernhelm's Blade	1.25	3.00
7R232 Firefoot, Eomer's Steed	.60	1.50
7R233 Grimbold, Marshal of Rohan	1.00	2.50
7R236 Herugrim, Sword of the Mark	.60	1.50
7R239 Leowyn	.60	1.50
7R241 Merry's Armor	.75	2.00
7R242 Merry's Sword	.75	2.00
7R249 Seeking New Foes	.60	1.50
7R250 Snowmane	.60	1.50
7R251 Stern People	.60	1.50
7R255 Theoden, Rekindled King	.60	1.50
7R260 Windfola	.60	1.50
7R261 With Strength to Fight	1.00	2.50
7R266 Breached	.60	1.50
7R267 Din of Arms	1.00	2.50
7R268 Encirclement	.60	1.50
7R269 Fires Raged Unchecked	.60	1.50
7R274 Gorgoroth Officer	.60	1.50
7R279 Gorgoroth Troop	1.25	3.00
7R283 Legions of Morgul	.60	1.50
7R284 Mordor Assassin	.60	1.50
7R286 Mordor Fighter	.60	1.50
7R306 Orc Seeker	.60	1.50
7R308 Rally the Host	.60	1.50
7R311 Siege Commander	.60	1.50
7R314 Stronghold of Cirith Ungol	.60	1.50
7R316 Troop Tower	2.00	5.00
7R318 Frodo, Wicked Masster!	.60	1.50
7R321a Merry, Swordthain	.75	2.00
7R321b Merry, Swordthain TENGWAR		
7R324a Pippin, Wearer of Black and Silver	1.00	2.50
7R324b Pippin, Wearer of Black and Silver TENGWAR		
7R325 Pressing On	.60	1.50
7R327 Sam, Resolute Halfling	.60	1.50
7R79a Anduril, Flame of the West	5.00	10.00
7R79b Anduril, Flame of the West TENGWAR		
7U102 Hasty Repairs	.30	.75
7U107 Iorlas	.30	.75
7U109 Long Prepared	.30	.75
7U110 Madril, Faramir's Aide	.30	.75
7U120 Stand to Arms	.30	.75
7U123 Support of the City	.30	.75
7U125 Third Level	.30	.75
7U126 Unexpected Visitor	.30	.75
7U128 While We Yet Live	.30	.75
7U134 Desert Scout	.30	.75
7U136 Desert Soldier	.30	.75
7U138 Desert Villain	.30	.75
7U146 Easterling Sergeant	.30	.75
7U147 Easterling Veteran	.30	.75
7U151 Hosts Still Unfought	.30	.75
7U157 Red Wrath	.30	.75
7U160 Southron Bandit	.30	.75
7U162 Southron Captain	.30	.75
7U168 Southron Thief	.30	.75
7U171 Thrice Outnumbered	.30	.75
7U174 Called	.30	.75
7U175 Corrupt	.30	.75
7U176 Disposable Servants	.30	.75
7U178 Foul Clutches	.30	.75
7U185 Morgul Answers	.30	.75
7U187 Morgul Brawler	.30	.75
7U190 Morgul Destroyer	.30	.75
7U195 Morgul on the March	.30	.75
7U202 Morgul Whelp	.30	.75
7U203 Nazgul Scimitar	.30	.75
7U207 Their Power Is in Terror	.30	.75
7U212 Ulaire Enquea, Faster Than Winds	.30	.75
7U214 Ulaire Lemenya, Wraith on Wings	.30	.75
7U216 Ulaire Nelya, Black-Mantled Wraith	.30	.75
7U217 Ulaire Nertea, Black-Mantled Wraith	.30	.75
7U218 Ulaire Otsea, Black-Mantled Wraith	.30	.75
7U224 Elfhelm, Marshal of Rohan	.30	.75
7U231 Fey He Seemed	.30	.75
7U234 Guarded Fastness	.30	.75
7U238 Knights of His House	.30	.75
7U244 Mustering for Battle	.30	.75
7U245 Riding Armor	.30	.75
7U252 Strong Arms	.30	.75
7U254 Theoden, Leader of Spears	.30	.75
7U258 White Hot Fury	.30	.75
7U264 Army of Udun	.30	.75
7U270 Gorgoroth Attacker	.30	.75
7U271 Gorgoroth Axeman	.30	.75
7U272 Gorgoroth Engineer	.30	.75
7U278 Gorgoroth Soldier	.30	.75
7U280 Great Peril of Fire	.30	.75
7U281 Great Siege-towers	.30	.75
7U282 Host of Udun	.30	.75
7U289 Mordor Savage	.30	.75
7U292 Mordor Veteran	.30	.75
7U293 Mordor Warrior	.30	.75

7U294 Orc Archer Troop	.30	.75
7U295 Orc Assault Band	.30	.75
7U301 Orc Marauder	.30	.75
7U302 Orc Officer	.30	.75
7U305 Orc Savage	.30	.75
7U307 Orc Stalker	.30	.75
7U309 Rope and Winch	.30	.75
7U310 Sauron's Hatred	.30	.75
7U328 Slow-kindled Courage	.30	.75
7U329 Dunharrow Plateau	.30	.75
7U330 Edoras Hall	.30	.75
7U331 Isengard Ruined	.30	.75
7U332 Rohirrim Road	.30	.75
7U333 Sleeping Quarters	.30	.75
7U334 Steps of Edoras	.30	.75
7U335 King's Tent	.30	.75
7U336 Rohirrim Camp	.30	.75
7U337 West Road	.30	.75
7U338 Beacon of Minas Tirith	.30	.75
7U339 Hall of the Kings	.30	.75
7U340 Tower of Ecthelion	.30	.75
7U341 Anduin Banks	.30	.75
7U342 Osgiliath Fallen	.30	.75
7U343 Pelennor Plain	.30	.75
7U344 City Gates	.30	.75
7U345 Pelennor Flat	.30	.75
7U346 Minas Tirith Fifth Circle	.30	.75
7U347 Minas Tirith First Circle	.30	.75
7U348 Minas Tirith Fourth Circle	.30	.75
7U349 Minas Tirith Second Circle	.30	.75
7U350 Minas Tirith Seventh Circle	.30	.75
7U351 Minas Tirith Sixth Circle	.30	.75
7U352 Minas Tirith Third Circle	.30	.75
7U353 Osgiliath Crossing	.30	.75
7U354 Pelennor Grassland	.30	.75
7U355 Ruined Capitol	.30	.75
7U356 Cross Roads	.30	.75
7U357 Morgul Vale	.30	.75
7U358 Morgulduin	.30	.75
7U359 Northern Ithilien	.30	.75
7U360 Dagorlad	.30	.75
7U361 Haunted Pass	.30	.75
7U362 Narchost	.30	.75
7U363 Slag Mounds	.30	.75

2004 Lord of the Rings Mount Doom

COMPLETE SET (124)	20.00	40.00
BOOSTER BOX (36 PACKS)	25.00	50.00
BOOSTER PACK (11 CARDS)	1.00	2.00
RELEASED ON JULY 14, 2004		
10R1 Great Day, Great Hour	.60	1.50
10R3 More Yet to Come	.60	1.50
10R7 Celeborn, Lord of the Galadhrim	.60	1.50
10R8 Cirdan, The Shipwright	2.00	5.00
10U2 Memories of Darkness	.30	.75
10U4 Aegnor, Elven Escort	.30	.75
10U5 Arwen, Echo of Luthien	.30	.75
10C10 Fleet-footed	.12	.30
10C16 Gathering Wind	.12	.30
10C24 Unabated in Malice	.12	.30
10C27 Dead Man of Dunharrow	.12	.30
10C30 End of the Game	.12	.30
10C31 Every Little is a Gain	.12	.30
10C34 Last Throw	.12	.30
10C36 Cast Unto the Winds	.12	.30
10C37 Corsair Boatswain	.12	.30
10C41 Easterling Pillager	.12	.30
10C42 Far Harad Mercenaries	.12	.30
10C49 Southron Fanatic	.12	.30
10C50 Southron Savage	.12	.30
10C52 Under Foot	.12	.30
10C55 Cirith Ungol Soldier	.12	.30
10C56 Cirith Ungol Warrior	.12	.30
10C61 Houses of Lamentation	.12	.30
10C62 Morgul Banner-bearer	.12	.30
10C64 Stooping to the Kill	.12	.30
10C65 Swarming Like Beetles	.12	.30
10C66 Ten Times Outnumbered	.12	.30
10C76 Advance Marauder	.12	.30
10C77 Advance Regular	.12	.30
10C79 Barren Land	.12	.30
10C80 Beaten Back	.12	.30
10C81 Cirith Ungol Guard	.12	.30
10C84 Cirith Ungol Sentry	.12	.30
10C85 Flames Within	.12	.30
10C86 Gorgoroth Keeper	.12	.30
10C87 Gorgoroth Swarm	.12	.30
10C90 Mordor Brute	.12	.30
10C91 Mordor Fiend	.12	.30
10R11 Galadriel, Lady Redeemed	.60	1.50
10R13 Phial of Galadriel, Star-glass	.60	1.50
10R14 Borne Far Away	.60	1.50
10R17 Out of the High Airs	1.25	3.00
10R18 Treebeard, Keeper of the Watchwood	.60	1.50
10R19 A Dark Shape Sprang	.60	1.50
10R21 Gollum, Mad Thing	.60	1.50
10R23 Shelob, Her Ladyship	2.50	6.00
10R25a Aragorn, Elessar Telcontar	.75	2.00
10R25b Aragorn, Elessar Telcontar TENGWAR		
10R28 Denethor, Lord of Minas Tirith	.60	1.50
10R29 Drawing His Eye	.60	1.50
10R38 Corsair Brute	.60	1.50
10R40 Easterling Berserker	.60	1.50
10R45 Mumak Chieftain	1.25	3.00
10R46 Quelled	.60	1.50
10R48 Seasoned Leader	1.25	3.00
10R51 Stampeded	.60	1.50
10R58 Dark Swooping Shadows	.60	1.50
10R59 Gorbag, Covetous Captain	.60	1.50
10R60 Gorbag's Sword	.60	1.50
10R63 Morgul Vanguard	.60	1.50
10R67 Ulaire Cantea, Thrall of the One	.60	1.50
10R68 Ulaire Enquea, Thrall of the One	5.00	10.00
10R6a Arwen, Queen of Elves and Men	.75	2.00
10R6b Arwen, Queen of Elves and Men TENGWAR		
10R71 Ulaire Toldea, Thrall of the One	.60	1.50
10R72 Eowyn, Lady of Ithilien	.60	1.50
10R75 Advance Captain	.75	2.00
10R88a Gothmog, Lieutenant of Morgul	1.25	3.00
10R88b Gothmog, Lieutenant of Morgul TENGWAR		
10R89 Gothmog's Warg	.60	1.50
10R94 Orc Ravager	.60	1.50
10R95 Orc Slaughterer	.60	1.50
10R99 Shagrat, Captain of Cirith Ungol	.60	1.50
10R9a Elrond, Venerable Lord	.60	1.50
10R9b Elrond, Venerable Lord TENGWAR		
10U12 Glimpse of Fate	.30	.75
10U15 Brooding on Tomorrow	.30	.75
10U20 Final Strike	.30	.75
10U22 Reclaim the Precious	.30	.75
10U26 Cursed of Erech	.30	.75
10U32 Fifth Level	.30	.75
10U33 Hardy Garrison	.30	.75
10U35 Suffered Much Loss	.30	.75
10U39 Corsair Ruffian	.30	.75
10U43 Field of the Fallen	.30	.75
10U44 High Vantage	.30	.75
10U47 Rallying Call	.30	.75
10U53 Black Marshal	.30	.75
10U54 Cirith Ungol Scavenger	.30	.75
10U57 Cirith Ungol Watchman	.30	.75
10U69 Ulaire Lemenya, Thrall of the One	.30	.75
10U70 Ulaire Nelya, Thrall of the One	.30	.75
10U73 Fell Deeds Awake	.30	.75
10U74 Unyielding	.30	.75
10U78 Advance Scout	.30	.75
10U82 Cirith Ungol Patroller	.30	.75
10U83 Cirith Ungol Sentinel	.30	.75
10U92 Mordor Pillager	.30	.75
10U93 Mordor Wretch	.30	.75
10U96 Rank and File	.30	.75
10U97 The Ring is Mine!	.30	.75
10U98 Ruinous Hail	.30	.75
10C102 Uruk Axe	.12	.30
10C103 Window of the Eye	.12	.30
10C106 Chance Observation	.12	.30
10C107 Great Heart	.12	.30
10C109 Make Haste	.12	.30
10C110 A Marvel	.12	.30
10C112 Nine-fingered Frodo and the Ring of Doom	.12	.30
10C113 Orc Armor	.12	.30
10P121 Frodo, Resolute Hobbit	2.00	5.00
10P122a Sam, Great Elf Warrior	.75	2.00
10P122b Sam, Great Elf Warrior TENGWAR		
10R100 Speak No More to Me	.60	1.50
10R101 Troll of Cirith Gorgor	2.00	5.00
10R104 Birthday Present	.75	2.00
10U105 Brave and Loyal	.30	.75
10U108 A Light in His Mind	.30	.75
10U111 Narrow Escape	.30	.75
10U114 Shadowplay	.30	.75
10U115 Slunk Out of Sight	.30	.75
10U116 The Tale of the Great Ring	.30	.75
10U117 Base of Mindolluin	.30	.75
10U118 Pelennor Prairie	.30	.75
10U119 Steward's Tomb	.30	.75
10U120 Watchers of Cirith Ungol	.30	.75

2004 Lord of the Rings Reflections

COMPLETE SET (52)	40.00	80.00
BOOSTER BOX (24 PACKS)	50.00	100.00
BOOSTER PACK (11 CARDS)	2.50	5.00
RELEASED ON MAY 12, 2004		
9R1 The One Ring, The Binding Ring	1.25	3.00
9R2 Freca, Hungry Savage	2.00	5.00
9R3 Durin III, Dwarven Lord	5.00	10.00
9R4 Gimli, Bearer of Grudges	1.50	4.00
9R5 Linnar, Dwarven Lord	.40	1.00
9R6 Ring of Accretion	.40	1.00
9R7 Ring of Fury	3.00	8.00
9R8 Ring of Guile	.40	1.00
9R9 Ring of Retribution	.40	1.00
9R10 Sindri, Dwarven Lord	.40	1.00
9R11 Uri, Dwarven Lord	.40	1.00
9R12 Aiglos	2.50	6.00
9R13 Elven Rope	.40	1.00
9R14 Galadriel, Bearer of Wisdom	1.50	4.00
9R15 Gil-galad, Elven High King	5.00	10.00
9R16 Glorfindel, Revealed in Wrath	1.25	3.00
9R17 Knife of the Galadhrim	1.25	3.00
9R18 Merry's Dagger	.40	1.00
9R19 Narya, Ring of Fire	.40	1.00
9R20 Nenya, Ring of Adamant	.40	1.00
9R21 Pippin's Dagger	.40	1.00
9R22 Strands of Elven Hair	.40	1.00
9R23 Vilya, Ring of Air	.40	1.00
9R24 Ent Draught	.40	1.00
9R25 Huorn	.40	1.00
9R26 Radagast, The Brown	5.00	10.00
9R27 Sent Back	.40	1.00
9R28 Gollum, Dark as Darkness	1.25	3.00
9R29 Slippery as Fishes	2.00	5.00
9R30 Smeagol, Bearer of Great Secrets	1.25	3.00
9R31 Boromir, Bearer of Council	2.00	5.00
9R32 Elendil, The Tall	1.00	2.50
9R33 Isildur, Bearer of Heirlooms	1.50	4.00
9R34 Narsil, Blade of the Faithful	2.00	5.00
9R35 Sapling of the White Tree	.40	1.00
9R36 Scroll of Isildur	.40	1.00
9R37 Seeing Stone of Minas Anor	.40	1.00
9R38 Seeing Stone of Orthanc	.40	1.00
9R39 Library of Orthanc	.40	1.00
9R40 Sack of the Shire	.40	1.00
9R41 Host of Moria, Legion of the Underdeeps	2.50	6.00
9R42 Ring of Asperity	.40	1.00
9R43 Ring of Ire	.75	2.00
9R44 Ring of Rancor	.40	1.00
9R45 Horn of the Mark	.40	1.00
9R46 The Red Arrow	.40	1.00
9R47 Ithil Stone	2.50	6.00
9R48 Sauron, The Lord of the Rings	5.00	10.00
9R49 Bilbo, Bearer of Things Burgled	.75	2.00
9R50 Everyone Knows	.40	1.00
9R51 Goldberry, River-daughter	.40	1.00
9R52 Tom Bombadil, The Master	.75	2.00

2004 Lord of the Rings Seige of Gondor

COMPLETE SET (122)	20.00	40.00
BOOSTER BOX (36 PACKS)	25.00	50.00
BOOSTER PACK (11 CARDS)	1.00	2.00
RELEASED ON MARCH 10, 2004		
8C1 Aggression	.12	.30
8C5 Gimli, Counter of Foes	.12	.30
8C6 Honed	.12	.30
8R2 Battle in Earnest	.60	1.50
8R3 Blood Runs Chill	2.50	6.00
8R7 Unheard of	.60	1.50
8U4 Counts But One	.30	.75
8U8 Wish For Our Kinfolk	.30	.75
8U9 A Grey Ship	.30	.75
8C10 Legolas, Elven Stalwart	.12	.30
8C14 A Fool	.12	.30
8C22 Hidden Even From Her	.12	.30
8C26 Shelob, Last Child of Ungoliant	.12	.30
8C28 Spider Poison	.12	.30
8C30 Web	.12	.30
8C31 At His Command	.12	.30
8C34 Faramir, Defender of Osgiliath	.12	.30
8C35 Fourth Level	.12	.30
8C39 Knight of Dol Amroth	.12	.30
8C40 Knight's Mount	.12	.30
8C41 Oathbreaker	.12	.30
8C47 Stronger and More Terrible	.12	.30
8C48 Swept Away	.12	.30
8C50 Black Sails of Umbar	.12	.30
8C52 Corsair Ballista	.12	.30
8C53 Corsair Buccaneer	.12	.30
8C54 Corsair Freebooter	.12	.30
8C55 Corsair Gunners	.12	.30
8C58 Corsair Plunderer	.12	.30
8C61 Haradwaith	.12	.30
8C63 Line of Defense	.12	.30
8C66 Wind That Sped Ships	.12	.30
8C74 Morgul Ambusher	.12	.30
8C75 Morgul Creeper	.12	.30
8C76 Morgul Lurker	.12	.30
8C87 Eomer, Keeper of Oaths	.12	.30
8C89 Fury of the Northmen	.12	.30
8C90 No Living Man	.12	.30
8R11 Life of the Eldar	.60	1.50
8R12 Reckless We Rode	.60	1.50
8R15a Gandalf, Leader of Men	1.25	3.00
8R15b Gandalf, Leader of Men TENGWAR		
8R20 Saved From the Fire	5.00	10.00
8R21 Shadowfax, Greatheart	.60	1.50
8R24 Promise Keeping	1.25	3.00
8R25a Shelob, Eater of Light	1.25	3.00
8R25b Shelob, Eater of Light TENGWAR		
8R27 Smeagol, Slippery Sneak	.60	1.50
8R32 Catapult	.60	1.50
8R33 Elessar's Edict	.60	1.50
8R36 Garrison of Gondor	1.50	4.00
8R37 Imrahil, Prince of Dol Amroth	.60	1.50
8R38a King of the Dead, Oathbreaker	1.25	3.00
8R38b King of the Dead, Oathbreaker TENGWAR		
8R43 Shadow Host	.75	2.00
8R49 Black Numenorean	1.50	4.00
8R51a Castamir of Umbar	1.50	4.00
8R51b Castamir of Umbar TENGWAR		
8R57a Corsair Marauder	3.00	8.00
8R57b Corsair Marauder TENGWAR		
8R62 Heavy Axeman	.60	1.50
8R65 Ships of Great Draught	3.00	8.00
8R67 Between Nazgul and Prey	2.00	5.00
8R68 Beyond All Darkness	.75	2.00
8R70 Black Flail	.75	2.00
8R72 Gothmog, Morgul Commander	1.00	2.50
8R77 Morgul Squealer	.75	2.00
8R81 Ulaire Otsea, Thrall of the One	.60	1.50
8R84 The Witch-king, Black Captain	1.00	2.50
8R88 Eowyn's Shield	.60	1.50
8R91 Rohirrim Army	.75	2.00
8R92 Theoden, Tall and Proud	1.00	2.50
8R93 Called Away	.60	1.50
8R95 Gorgoroth Assassin	1.00	2.50
8R96 Gorgoroth Berserker	.60	1.50
8U100 Gorgoroth Servitor	.30	.75
8U107 Their Marching Companies	.30	.75
8U110 Morgai Foothills	.30	.75
8U112 Song of the Shire	.30	.75
8U117 The Dimholt	.30	.75
8U118 City of the Dead	.30	.75
8U119 Crashed Gate	.30	.75
8U120 Osgiliath Channel	.30	.75
8U13 Shake Off the Shadow	.30	.75
8U16 Let Us Not Tarry	.30	.75
8U17 Mighty Steed	.30	.75
8U18 Not the First Halfling	.30	.75
8U19 On Your Doorstep	.30	.75
8U23 Larder	.30	.75
8U29 Still Far Ahead	.30	.75
8U42 A Path Appointed	.30	.75
8U44 Sixth Level	.30	.75
8U45 Sleepless Dead	.30	.75
8U46 Spectral Sword	.30	.75
8U56 Corsair Lookout	.30	.75
8U59 Corsair War Galley	.30	.75
8U60 Haradrim Marksman	.30	.75
8U64 Mumakil	.30	.75
8U69 Black Dart	.30	.75
8U71 Flung Into the Fray	.30	.75
8U73 Mastered By Madness	.30	.75
8U78 Streaming to the Field	.30	.75
8U79 Ulaire Attea, Thrall of the One	.30	.75
8U80 Ulaire Nertea, Thrall of the One	.30	.75
8U82 Unhindered	.30	.75
8U83 Winged Mount	.30	.75
8U85 Charged Headlong	.30	.75
8U86 Doom Drove Them	.30	.75
8U94 Gorgoroth Agitator	.30	.75
8U97 Gorgoroth Breaker	.30	.75
8U98 Gorgoroth Looter	.30	.75
8U99 Gorgoroth Patrol	.30	.75
8C101 Gorgoroth Stormer	.12	.30
8C102 Great Hill Troll	.12	.30
8C104 Morgai	.12	.30
8C106 Siege Troop	.12	.30
8C109 Closer and Closer He Bent	.12	.30
8C111 So Fair, So Desperate	.12	.30
8C114 Straining Towards Us	.12	.30
8C116 We Shall Meet Again Soon	.12	.30
8P121 Merry, Noble Warrior	.40	1.00

8P122 Pippin, Guard of Minas Tirith .40 1.00
8R103a Grond, Hammer of the Underworld 1.00 2.50
8R103b Grond, Hammer of the Underworld TENGWAR
8R105 Olog-hai of Mordor .75 2.00
8R108 Troll of Gorgoroth, Abomination of Sauron .75 2.00
8R113 Sling, Bane of the Eight Legs 1.25 3.00
8R115 Unheeded .75 2.00

2004 Lord of the Rings Shadows

COMPLETE SET (266) 20.00 40.00
BOOSTER BOX (36 PACKS) 20.00 40.00
BOOSTER PACK (11 CARDS) 1.00 2.00
RELEASED ON NOVEMBER 3, 2004
11C4 Battle to the Last .12 .30
11C5 Dwarven Embassy .12 .30
11C7 Farin, Emissary of Erebor .12 .30
11R1a The One Ring, The Ring of Rings 2.50 6.00
11R1b The One Ring, The Ring of Rings TENGWAR
11R9 Gimli's Battle Axe, Vicious Weapon .60 1.50
11S2 The One Ring, The Ruling Ring .40 1.00
11U3 Axe of Khazad-dum .30 .75
11U6 Fallen Lord .30 .75
11U8 Gimli, Lively Combatant .30 .75
11C13 On Guard .12 .30
11C19 Farewell to Lorien .12 .30
11C27 Woodland Sentinel .12 .30
11C31 Final Account .12 .30
11C36 Inspiration .12 .30
11C39 Prolonged Struggle .12 .30
11C46 Master Commands It .12 .30
11C62 Madril, Ranger of Ithilien .12 .30
11C63 Much-needed Rest .12 .30
11C71 Bold and Cunning .12 .30
11C72 Column of Easterlings .12 .30
11C73 Corps of Harad .12 .30
11C76 Easterling Shield Wall .12 .30
11C79 Fearsome Dunlending .12 .30
11C83 Force of Harad .12 .30
11C85 Horde of Harad .12 .30
11C86 Invading Haradrim .12 .30
11C88 Legion of Harad .12 .30
11C89 Long Battle Bow .12 .30
11C93 Patroller of Haradrim .12 .30
11C94 Pavise .12 .30
11C98 Rampaging Easterling .12 .30
11R10 Grimir, Dwarven Emissary .60 1.50
11R11 Hall of Our Fathers .60 1.50
11R14 Well-equipped .60 1.50
11R17 Elven Marksmanship .60 1.50
11R22 Legolas, Woodland Emissary .60 1.50
11R23 Legolas' Bow .60 1.50
11R24 Might of the Elf-lords .60 1.50
11R30 Erland, Dale Counselor .75 2.00
11R34 Gandalf's Staff, Ash-Staff .60 1.50
11R35 Glamdring, Foe-hammer 1.25 3.00
11R42 Gollum, Skulker .60 1.50
11R43 Horribly Strong .75 2.00
11R44 Incited .60 1.50
11R48 Not Yet Vanquished .60 1.50
11R50 Safe Passage .60 1.50
11R51 Smeagol, Scout and Guide .60 1.50
11R54a Aragorn, Strider 2.50 6.00
11R54b Aragorn, Strider TENGWAR
11R57a Boromir, Hero of Osgiliath 1.25 3.00
11R57b Boromir, Hero of Osgiliath TENGWAR
11R60 The Highest Quality .60 1.50
11R66 Well-traveled 1.00 2.50
11R68 Armored Easterling .60 1.50
11R70 Bloodthirsty .60 1.50
11R75 Easterling Host .60 1.50
11R78 Elevated Fire 1.50 4.00
11R81 Fletcher of Harad .60 1.50
11R91 Oath Sworn .60 1.50
11R96 Precision Targeting .75 2.00
11S18 Elven Scout .40 1.00
11S20 The Lady's Blessing .40 1.00
11S21 Legolas, Companion of the Ring .40 1.00
11S32 G for Grand .40 1.00
11S33a Gandalf, Leader of the Company .75 2.00
11S33b Gandalf, Leader of the Company TENGWAR
11S53 Aragorn, Guide and Protector .40 1.00
11S56 Battle Cry .40 1.00
11S64 Pledge of Loyalty .60 1.50
11S65 Ranger of Westernesse .40 1.00
11S77 Elder of Dunland .40 1.00
11S82 Footman of Dunland .40 1.00
11S84 Harad Standard-bearer .40 1.00
11S90 Man of Bree .40 1.00
11S92 Overrun .40 1.00
11S95 Poleaxe .40 1.00
11S97 Raging Dunlending .40 1.00
11U12 Mountain Homestead .30 .75
11U15 Arwen, Staunch Defender .30 .75
11U16 Blade of Lindon .30 .75
11U25 Nocked .30 .75
11U26 Uncertain Future .30 .75
11U28 The Art of Gandalf .30 .75
11U29 Ease the Burden .30 .75
11U37 New Authority .30 .75
11U38 New-awakened .30 .75
11U40 Shadowfax, Unequaled Steed .30 .75
11U41 Frenzied Attack .30 .75
11U45 Led Astray .30 .75
11U47 No End of Wickedness .30 .75
11U49 One Good Turn Deserves Another .30 .75
11U52 Strange and Terrible .30 .75
11U55 Armor of the Citadel .30 .75
11U58 Bow of Minas Tirith .30 .75
11U59 Gondorian Blade .30 .75
11U61 Houses of Healing .30 .75
11U67 Archer of Harad .30 .75
11U69 Axeman of Harad .30 .75
11U74 Detachment of Haradrim .30 .75
11U80 Ferocious Haradrim .30 .75
11U87 Lathspell .30 .75
11U99 Squad of Haradrim .30 .75
11C101 Swarthy Bree-lander .12 .30
11C102 Throng of Harad .12 .30
11C103 Warrior of Dunland .12 .30
11C107 Barbarous Orc .12 .30
11C111 Champion Orc .12 .30
11C113 Cutthroat Orc .12 .30
11C120 Entrapping Orc .12 .30
11C121 Foraging Orc .12 .30
11C122 Frenzied Orc .12 .30
11C125 Isengard Underling .12 .30
11C127 Mocking Goblin .12 .30
11C128 Mordor Scimitar .12 .30
11C129 Mountain Orc .12 .30
11C131 Orc Miscreant .12 .30
11C132 Orkish Smith .12 .30
11C136 Prowling Orc .12 .30
11C140 Strength in Shadows .12 .30
11C148 Hrothlac, Man of Rohan .12 .30
11C155 Riding Like the Wind .12 .30
11C157 Rush of Steeds .12 .30
11C162 Crouched Down .12 .30
11C167 Incognito .12 .30
11C168 Merry, Loyal Companion .12 .30
11C169 The More, The Merrier .12 .30
11C192 Isengard Sword .12 .30
11C195 Murderous Uruk .12 .30
11C196 Our Foes Are Weak .12 .30
11C198 Patrol of Uruk-hai .12 .30
11C199 Relentless Uruk .12 .30
11C200 Ruthless Uruk .12 .30
11C201 Sentinel Uruk .12 .30
11C202 Squad of Uruk-hai .12 .30
11C203 Swarming Uruk .12 .30
11C204 Tyrannical Uruk .12 .30
11C206 Watchman Uruk .12 .30
11R100 Strange-looking Men .60 1.50
11R108 Beastly Olog-hai 1.25 3.00
11R119 Emboldened Orc 1.00 2.50
11R123a Goblin Hordes 6.00 12.00
11R123b Goblin Hordes TENGWAR
11R133 Orkish Worker .60 1.50
11R134 Persistent Orc .60 1.50
11R135 Porter Troll 1.00 2.50
11R141 Undisciplined .60 1.50
11R143 Watchful Orc .75 2.00
11R147 Gamling, Defender of the Hornburg .60 1.50
11R154 Riders of the Mark .60 1.50
11R158 Sword Rack .60 1.50
11R165 Habits of Home .60 1.50
11R170 Pippin, Brave Decoy .60 1.50
11R171 Salt from the Shire .60 1.50
11R173 Sting, Weapon of Heritage .75 2.00
11R177 Army of Uruk-hai .60 1.50
11R179 Brawling Uruk .60 1.50
11R181 Determined Uruk .60 1.50
11R184 Force of Uruk-hai .60 1.50
11R186 Furious Uruk .60 1.50
11R194 Lurtz, Minion of the White Wizard .75 2.00
11R205 Vigilant Uruk .60 1.50
11R207 Dark Powers Strengthen .60 1.50
11R211 Keening Wail 1.25 3.00
11R214 The Pale Blade, Sword of Flame .60 1.50
11R216 A Shadow Rises .60 1.50
11R217 Shapes Slowly Advancing .75 2.00
11R219 Ulaire Attea, Second of the Nine Riders .60 1.50
11R224 Ulaire Otsea, Seventh of the Nine Riders .75 2.00
11R226a The Witch-king, Captain of the Nine Riders 3.00 8.00
11R226b The Witch-king, Captain of the Nine Riders TENGWAR
11S112 Conquered Halls .40 1.00
11S115 Denizen of Khazad-dum .40 1.00
11S116 Denizen of Moria .40 1.00
11S117 Denizen of the Black Pit .40 1.00
11S126 Marauding Orcs .40 1.00
11S130 Orc Hammer .40 1.00
11S138 Skulking Goblin .40 1.00
11S142 Unyielding Goblin .40 1.00
11S146 Eowyn, Shieldmaiden of Rohan .40 1.00
11S150 Rally Cry .40 1.00
11S152 Riddermark Soldier .40 1.00
11S153 Rider's Spear .40 1.00
11S160 War Now Calls Us .40 1.00
11S161 Concerning Hobbits .40 1.00
11S164 Frodo, Protected by Many .40 1.00
11S166 Hobbit Sword .40 1.00
11S174 Sworn Companion .40 1.00
11S176 Unharmed .40 1.00
11S178 Bloodthirsty Uruk .40 1.00
11S180 Brutality .40 1.00
11S183 Feral Uruk .40 1.00
11S187 Furor .40 1.00
11S188 Hounding Uruk .40 1.00
11S190 Invincible Uruk .40 1.00
11S193 Lookout Uruk .40 1.00
11S209 Drawn to its Power .40 1.00
11S213 Moving This Way .40 1.00
11S215 Riders in Black .40 1.00
11S220 Ulaire Cantea, Fourth of the Nine Riders .40 1.00
11S221 Ulaire Lemenya, Fifth of the Nine Riders .40 1.00
11S222 Ulaire Nelya, Third of the Nine Riders .60 1.50
11S223 Ulaire Nertea, Ninth of the Nine Riders .40 1.00
11S225 Ulaire Toldea, Eighth of the Nine Riders .40 1.00
11S228 Anduin Confluence .60 1.50
11S229 Barazinbar .40 1.00
11S230 Buckland Homestead .40 1.00
11S231 Caras Galadhon .40 1.00
11S232 Cavern Entrance .40 1.00
11S233 Chamber of Mazarbul .40 1.00
11S234 Crags of Emyn Muil .40 1.00
11S236 East Road .40 1.00
11S237 Ettenmoors .40 1.00
11S238 Expanding Marshland .40 1.00
11S239 Fangorn Glade .40 1.00
11S240 Flats of Rohan .40 1.00
11S241 Fortress of Orthanc .40 1.00
11S242 Green Dragon Inn .40 1.00
11S243 Harrowdale .40 1.00
11S245 Helm's Gate .40 1.00
11S247 Moria Guardroom .40 1.00
11S248 Moria Stairway .40 1.00
11S249 Neekerbreekers' Bog .75 2.00
11S250 North Undeep .40 1.00
11S251 Old Forest Road .40 1.00
11S252 Osgiliath Reclaimed .40 1.00
11S253 Pelennor Fields .40 1.00
11S254 Pelennor Flat .40 1.00
11S255 Pinnacle of Zirakzigil .40 1.00
11S256 The Prancing Pony .40 1.00
11S257 Rohan Uplands .40 1.00
11S258 Slag Mounds .40 1.00
11S259 Stables .40 1.00
11S260 Trollshaw Forest .40 1.00
11S261 Valley of the Silverlode .40 1.00
11S262 Watch-tower of Cirith Ungol .40 1.00
11S263 West Gate of Moria .40 1.00
11S264 Westernnet Village .40 1.00
11S265 Window on the West .40 1.00
11S266 Woody-End .60 1.50
11U104 Whistling Death .30 .75
11U105 Wielding the Ring .30 .75
11U106 Armed for Battle .30 .75
11U109 Bladed Gauntlets .30 .75
11U110 Bound to its Fate .30 .75
11U114 Demoralized .30 .75
11U118 Dread and Despair .30 .75
11U124 Hill Orc .30 .75
11U137 Scurrying Goblin .30 .75
11U139 Spurred to Battle .30 .75
11U144 Border Patrol .30 .75
11U145 Eomer, Guardian of the Eastmark .30 .75
11U149 Protecting the Hall .30 .75
11U151 Riddermark Javelin .30 .75
11U156 Rohirrim Mount .30 .75
11U159 Theoden, King of the Eorlingas .30 .75
11U163 Farmer Maggot, Hobbit of the Marish .30 .75
11U172 Sam, Steadfast Friend .30 .75
11U175 A Task Now to Be Done .30 .75
11U182 Devastation .30 .75
11U185 Fortitude .30 .75
11U189 Intimidating Uruk .30 .75
11U191 Isengard Siege Bow .30 .75
11U197 Overpowering Uruk .30 .75
11U208 Dark Wings .30 .75
11U210 Hatred Stirred .30 .75
11U212 Lost in the Woods .30 .75
11U218 Surrounded by Wraiths .30 .75
11U227 Anduin Banks .30 .75
11U235 Dammed Gate-stream .30 .75
11U244 Heights of Isengard .30 .75
11U246 Mere of Dead Faces .30 .75

2004 Lord of the Rings Shadows Foil

COMPLETE SET (18) 15.00 30.00
RELEASED ON NOVEMBER 3, 2004
11RF1 The One Ring, The Ring of Rings F 2.00 5.00
11RF2 Elven Marksmanship F 1.25 3.00
11RF3 Legolas, Woodland Emissary F .60 1.50
11RF4 Glamdring, Foe-hammer F 1.50 4.00
11RF5 Gollum, Skulker F .60 1.50
11RF6 Smeagol, Scout and Guide F .75 2.00
11RF7 Aragorn, Strider F 2.00 5.00
11RF8 Bloodthirsty F .60 1.50
11RF9 Fletcher of Harad F .75 2.00
11RF10 Porter Troll F 1.00 2.50
11RF11 Undisciplined F .60 1.50
11RF12 Gamling, Defender of the Hornburg F .60 1.50
11RF13 Sword Rack F .60 1.50
11RF14 Salt from the Shire F .75 2.00
11RF15 Brawling Uruk F .60 1.50
11RF16 Lurtz, Minion of the White Wizard F .75 2.00
11RF17 The Pale Blade, Sword of Flame F .75 2.00
11RF18 The Witch-king, Captain of the Nine Riders F 3.00 8.00

2005 Lord of the Rings Black Rider

COMPLETE SET (194) 20.00 40.00
BOOSTER BOX (36 PACKS) 20.00 40.00
BOOSTER PACK (11 CARDS) 1.00 2.00
RELEASED ON MARCH 18, 2005
12C4 Durability .12 .30
12C6 Dwarven Skill .12 .30
12C7 Dwarven Warrior .12 .30
12C8 His Father's Charge .12 .30
12R9 Loud and Strong .60 1.50
12U1 Argument Ready to Hand .30 .75
12U2 Belt of Erebor .30 .75
12U3 A Clamour of Many Voices .30 .75
12U5 Dwarven Bracers .30 .75
12C16 Attunement .12 .30
12C20 Orophin, Brother of Haldir .12 .30
12C22 Rumil, Brother of Haldir .12 .30
12C31 Mysterious Wizard .12 .30
12C32 Salve .12 .30
12C33 The Terror of His Coming .12 .30
12C34 Traveled Leader .12 .30
12C40 There's Another Way .12 .30
12C44 Concealment .12 .30
12C45 Confronting the Eye .12 .30
12C46 Elendil's Valor .12 .30
12C52 Tireless .12 .30
12C53 Valorous Leader .12 .30
12C59 Covetous Easterling .12 .30
12C60 Crazed Hillman .12 .30
12C61 Crooked Townsman .12 .30
12C64 Enraged Southron .12 .30
12C67 Goaded to War .12 .30
12C70 Hemmed In .12 .30
12C77 War Trident .12 .30
12C78 Wrathful Hillman .12 .30
12C84 Bloodstained Field .12 .30
12C87 Goblin Aggressor .12 .30
12C88 Great Cost .12 .30
12C92 Orc Dreg .12 .30
12C93 Orc Footman .12 .30
12C95 Orc Skulker .12 .30
12C96 Orc Spear .12 .30
12C98 Orc Tormentor .12 .30
12R10 No Pauses, No Spills 5.00 10.00
12R17a Elrond, Witness to History 1.25 3.00
12R17b Elrond, Witness to History TENGWAR
12R18 Hadafang 1.25 3.00
12R19 Long-knives of Legolas .60 1.50
12R26 Discoveries .60 1.50
12R27 Gandalf, The White Rider .60 1.50
12R28 Gandalf's Hat .60 1.50
12R30 Jarnsmid, Barding Emissary .60 1.50
12R35a Watch and Wait 1.50 4.00
12R35b Watch and Wait TENGWAR
12R37 Come Away .60 1.50

2005 Lord of the Rings Black Rider

12R38 From Deep in Shadow	.60	1.50
12R42 Blade of Gondor, Sword of Boromir	.75	2.00
12R47 Faramir, Dunadan of Gondor	.60	1.50
12R48 Faramir's Sword	.75	2.00
12R54a Saruman, of Many Colours	.75	2.00
12R54b Saruman, of Many Colours TENGWAR		
12R56 Castamir of Umbar, Corsair Vandal	.75	2.00
12R57 Corrupted Spy	.60	1.50
12R68 Grima, Betrayer of Rohan	.60	1.50
12R69 Harrying Hillman	.60	1.50
12R72 Messenger's Mount	.60	1.50
12R74 Mumak Rider	2.00	5.00
12R75 Poisonous Words	.60	1.50
12R79 The Balrog, The Terror of Khazad-dum	1.00	2.50
12R80 Whip of Many Thongs, Weapon of Flame and Shadow	1.25	3.00
12R81 Abiding Evil	.75	2.00
12R82 Barrage	.75	2.00
12R83 The Beckoning Shadow	.60	1.50
12R85 Cave Troll of Moria, Savage Menace	1.25	3.00
12R86 Cave Troll's Hammer, Unwieldy Cudgel	.60	1.50
12R91 Orc Artisan	.60	1.50
12S55 Brutal Easterling	.40	1.00
12S65 Frenzied Dunlending	.40	1.00
12S73a The Mouth of Sauron, Messenger of Mordor	.40	1.00
12S73b The Mouth of Sauron, Messenger of Mordor TENGWAR		
12U11 Nobody Tosses a Dwarf	.30	.75
12U12 Proud and Able	.30	.75
12U13 Sharp Defense	.30	.75
12U14 Stalwart Support	.30	.75
12U15 Thrarin, Smith of Erebor	.30	.75
12U21 Refuge	.30	.75
12U23 Seclusion	.30	.75
12U24 Taking the High Ground	.30	.75
12U25 Betrayal of Isengard	.30	.75
12U29 Introspection	.30	.75
12U36 With Doom We Come	.30	.75
12U39 Not Alone	.30	.75
12U41 Treacherous Little Toad	.30	.75
12U43 Boromir, Defender of Minas Tirith	.30	.75
12U49 Gondorian Steed	.30	.75
12U50 Guardian	.30	.75
12U51 Invigorated	.30	.75
12U58 Countless Companies	.30	.75
12U62 Dunlending Zealot	.30	.75
12U63 Easterling Banner-bearer	.30	.75
12U66 Gathering Strength	.30	.75
12U71 Last Days	.30	.75
12U76 Trail of Terror	.30	.75
12U79 The Balrog, The Terror of Khazad-dum TENGWAR	.30	.75
12U89 Mordor Aggressor	.30	.75
12U90 Morgul Tormentor	.30	.75
12U94 Orc Sapper	.30	.75
12U97 Orc Strategist	.30	.75
12U99 Pitiless Orc	.30	.75
12C102 Scavenging Goblins	.12	.30
12C106 Vile Goblin	.12	.30
12C107 Aldred, Eored Soldier	.12	.30
12C109 Challenging the Orc-host	.12	.30
12C110 Cleaving a Path	.12	.30
12C114 For the Mark	.12	.30
12C115 Golden Glimmer	.12	.30
12C121 Flotsam and Jetsam	.12	.30
12C122 Home and Hearth	.12	.30
12C123 Hope is Kindled	.12	.30
12C134 Advancing Uruk	.12	.30
12C137 Breeding Pit Conscript	.12	.30
12C142 Merciless Uruk	.12	.30
12C143 Quelling Force	.12	.30
12C145 Shingle in a Storm	.12	.30
12C146 Strange Device	.12	.30
12C149 Uruk Common	.12	.30
12C153 Uruk Pikeman	.12	.30
12C159 Weapon of Opportunity	.12	.30
12C160 Worthy of Mordor	.12	.30
12C164 Echo of Hooves	.12	.30
12C168 Nazgul Blade	.12	.30
12C172 Steed of Mordor	.12	.30
12C177 Ulaire Nelya, Black Hunter	.12	.30
12C178 Ulaire Nertea, Black Horseman	.12	.30
12C181 Unending Life	.12	.30
12C182 Unimpeded	.12	.30
12R100 Rallying Orc	3.00	8.00
12R101 Retribution	2.00	5.00
12R105 Troll's Keyward, Keeper of the Beast	1.00	2.50
12R108 Cast Out	.60	1.50
12R111 Coif	.75	2.00
12R116 Haethen, Veteran Fighter	.75	2.00
12R118 The Mouth of Sauron, Lieutenant of Barad-dur	1.25	3.00
12R119 Bilbo, Melancholy Hobbit	.60	1.50
12R120 Diversion	.60	1.50
12R124 Long Live the Halflings	.60	1.50
12R127 Pippin, Hobbit of Some Intelligence	.60	1.50
12R128 A Promise	1.00	2.50
12R129 Rosie Cotton, Barmaid	.75	2.00
12R139 Broken in Defeat	.60	1.50
12R141 Dark Alliance	.60	1.50
12R150 Uruk Decimator	.60	1.50
12R154 Uruk Slaughterer	.60	1.50
12R155 Uruk Zealot	.60	1.50
12R156 Uruk-hai Guard	.60	1.50
12R157 Uruk-hai Troop	.60	1.50
12R162 Dark Approach	7.50	15.00
12R163 Dark Temptation	1.00	2.50
12R169 Sauron's Gaze	.60	1.50
12R171 Shadowy Mount	1.25	3.00
12R173 Ulaire Attea, Black Predator	.60	1.50
12R174a Ulaire Cantea, Black Assassin	1.50	4.00
12R174b Ulaire Cantea, Black Assassin TENGWAR		
12R175 Ulaire Enquea, Black Threat	.75	2.00
12R179 Ulaire Otsea, Black Specter	.60	1.50
12R183 The Witch-king, Black Lord	1.25	3.00
12S113 Eored Warrior	.40	1.00
12S125 Measure of Comfort	.40	1.00
12S126 No Worse for Wear	.40	1.00
12S133 Tolman Cotton, Farmer of Bywater	.40	1.00
12S144 Saruman, Agent of the Dark Lord	.40	1.00
12S151 Uruk Desecrator	.40	1.00
12S152 Uruk Dominator	.40	1.00
12S187 Emyn Muil	.40	1.00
12S188 Hill of Sight	.40	1.00

12S189 Hobbiton Market	.40	1.00
12S190 Northern Pelennor	.40	1.00
12U103 Storming the Ramparts	.30	.75
12U104 Taunt	.30	.75
12U112 Eomer, Eored Leader	.30	.75
12U117 Leofric, Defender of the Mark	.30	.75
12U130 Simple Living	.30	.75
12U131 Stand Together	.30	.75
12U132 Sudden Fury	.30	.75
12U135 Barbaric Uruk	.30	.75
12U136 Berserker Torch	.30	.75
12U138 Broken Heirloom	.30	.75
12U140 Crushing Uruk	.30	.75
12U147 Suppressing Uruk	.30	.75
12U148 Tempest of War	.30	.75
12U158 Vicious Uruk	.30	.75
12U161 Black Rider	.30	.75
12U165 In the Ringwraith's Wake	.30	.75
12U166 Lingering Shadow	.30	.75
12U167 Minas Morgul Answers	.30	.75
12U170 Sense of Obligation	.30	.75
12U176 Ulaire Lemenya, Black Enemy	.30	.75
12U180 Ulaire Toldea, Black Shadow	.30	.75
12U184 The Witch-king's Beast, Fell Creature	.30	.75
12U185 The Angle	.30	.75
12U186 The Bridge of Khazad-dum	.30	.75
12U191 Shores of Nen Hithoel	.30	.75
12U192 Slopes of Orodruin	.30	.75
12U193 Starkhorn	.30	.75
12U194 Wold Battlefield	.30	.75

2005 Lord of the Rings Black Rider Legends Foil

COMPLETE SET (18)	20.00	40.00
RELEASED ON MARCH 18, 2005		
12RF1 Elrond, Witness to History F	1.50	4.00
12RF2 Hadafang F	2.50	6.00
12RF3 Gandalf, The White Rider F	.75	2.00
12RF4 Faramir, Dunadan of Gondor F	1.00	2.50
12RF5 Faramir's Sword F	1.25	3.00
12RF6 Castamir of Umbar, Corsair Vandal F	2.00	5.00
12RF7 Grima, Betrayer of Rohan F	.60	1.50
12RF8 The Balrog, The Terror of Khazad-dum F	1.50	4.00
12RF9 Cave Troll of Moria, Savage Menace F	5.00	10.00
12RF10 Orc Artisan F	1.25	3.00
12RF11 The Mouth of Sauron, Lieutenant of Barad-dur F	1.25	3.00
12RF12 Bilbo, Melancholy Hobbit F	.60	1.50
12RF13 Uruk Zealot F	.60	1.50
12RF14 Dark Approach F	7.50	15.00
12RF15 Ulaire Attea, Black Predator F	.60	1.50
12RF16 Ulaire Cantea, Black Assassin F	3.00	8.00
12RF17 Ulaire Enquea, Black Threat F	1.00	2.50
12RF18 The Witch-king, Black Lord F	2.50	6.00

2005 Lord of the Rings Black Rider Legends Masterworks Foil

COMPLETE SET (9)	25.00	50.00
RELEASED ON MARCH 18, 2005		
12O1 Gandalf, The White Rider O	5.00	10.00
12O2 Faramir, Dunadan of Gondor O	5.00	10.00
12O3 Faramir's Sword O	3.00	8.00
12O4 The Balrog, The Terror of Khazad-dum O	5.00	10.00
12O5 Dark Approach O	7.50	15.00
12O6 Ulaire Attea, Black Predator O	3.00	8.00
12O7 Ulaire Cantea, Black Assassin O	6.00	12.00
12O8 Ulaire Enquea, Black Threat O	3.00	8.00
12O9 The Witch-king, Black Lord O	7.50	15.00

2005 Lord of the Rings Bloodlines

COMPLETE SET (194)	100.00	200.00
BOOSTER BOX (36 PACKS)	30.00	60.00
BOOSTER PACK (11 CARDS)	1.25	2.50
RELEASED ON AUGUST 12, 2005		
13C2 Awkward Moment	.12	.30
13C6 Honoring His Kinfolk	.12	.30
13C7 Sorrow Shared	.12	.30
13R1 Arod, Rohirrim Steed	1.50	4.00
13R5a Gimli, Lord of the Glittering Caves	2.00	5.00
13R5b Gimli, Lord of the Glittering Caves TENGWAR		
13R8 Subterranean Homestead	.60	1.50
13S9 Arwen, Reflection of Luthien	.40	1.00
13U3 Deep Hatred	.30	.75
13U4 Dwarf-lords	.30	.75
13C12 City of the Trees	.12	.30
13C13 Crashing Cavalry	.12	.30
13C14 Final Shot	.12	.30
13C16 Inside a Song	.12	.30
13C21 Many Miles	.12	.30
13C23 Shrouded Elf	.12	.30
13C24 Sprang Forth Nimbly	.12	.30
13C25 Standing Tall	.12	.30
13C29 Dasron, Merchant from Dorwinion	.12	.30
13C30 Fear and Great Wonder	.12	.30
13C32 For a While Less Dark	.12	.30
13C35 No Colour Now	.12	.30
13C39 Return to Us	.12	.30
13C41 Strange Meeting	.12	.30
13C47 Duality	.12	.30
13C51 It's My Birthday	.12	.30
13C54 Out of All Knowledge	.12	.30
13C66 Faramir, Prince of Ithilien	.12	.30
13C68 Guarded City	.12	.30
13C69 Heirs of Gondor	.12	.30
13C73 Kingsfoil	.12	.30
13C77 Tradesman From Lebennin	.12	.30
13C82 Bring Down the Wall	.12	.30
13C83 Caravan From the South	.12	.30
13C87 Driven From the Plains	.12	.30
13C90 Easterling Runner	.12	.30
13C96 Merciless Dunlending	.12	.30
13C97 Pirate Cutthroat	.12	.30
13R10 Asfaloth, Swift Blossom	.60	1.50
13R11 Celeborn, The Wise	1.00	2.50
13R15 Galadriel, Sorceress of the Hidden Land	.75	2.00
13R18 Legolas, of the Grey Company	1.25	3.00
13R22 Secluded Homestead	.75	2.00
13R26 Take Up the Bow	1.00	2.50
13R33 Gandalf, Bearer of Obligation	2.00	5.00
13R36 The Palantir of Orthanc, Recovered Seeing Stone	1.25	3.00
13R37 Pallando, Far-travelling One	5.00	10.00
13R38 Radagast, Tender of Beasts	2.00	5.00
13R40 Shadowfax, Roaring Wind	.60	1.50
13R42 Traveler's Homestead	.75	2.00
13R44 Chasm's Edge	1.25	3.00

13R46a Deagol, Fateful Finder	.75	2.00
13R46b Deagol, Fateful Finder TENGWAR		
13R48 Fishing Boat	.75	2.00
13R49 Gladden Homestead	1.25	3.00
13R57 Trap Is Sprung	.75	2.00
13R58 Wild Light of Madness	1.25	3.00
13R59 Aragorn, Isildur's Heir	1.00	2.50
13R63 Brego, Loyal Steed	1.25	3.00
13R64 Denethor, Last Ruling Steward	1.00	2.50
13R65 Elendil, High-King of Gondor	6.00	12.00
13R76 Storied Homestead	1.00	2.50
13R78 Alatar Deceived	.75	2.00
13R80 Radagast Deceived	.60	1.50
13R81 Staff of Saruman, Fallen Istar's Stave	1.25	3.00
13R84 Corsair Champion	.75	2.00
13R86 Desert Wind	1.00	2.50
13R93 Harmless	1.25	3.00
13S20 Lorien Protector	.40	1.00
13S62 Boromir, Doomed Heir	.40	1.00
13S74 Rally the Company	.40	1.00
13S85 Cruel Dunlending	.40	1.00
13S99 Stragglers	.40	1.00
13U17 Kindreds Estranged	.30	.75
13U19 Let Fly	.30	.75
13U27 Wells of Deep Memory	.30	.75
13U28 Alatar, Final Envoy	.30	.75
13U31 The Flame of Anor	.30	.75
13U34 Look to My Coming	.30	.75
13U43 Vapour and Steam	.30	.75
13U45 Cunningly Hidden	.30	.75
13U50 Gollum, Her Sneak	.30	.75
13U52 Little Snuffler	.30	.75
13U53 Naked Waste	.30	.75
13U55 Smeagol, Simple Stoor	.30	.75
13U56 Softly Up Behind	.30	.75
13U60 Away on the Wind	.30	.75
13U61 Banners Blowing	.30	.75
13U67 Guard of the White Tree	.30	.75
13U70 Hope Renewed	.30	.75
13U71 Isildur, Heir of Elendil	.30	.75
13U72 Kings' Legacy	.30	.75
13U75 Stewards' Legacy	.30	.75
13U79 Pallando Deceived	.30	.75
13U88 Dunlending Patriarch	.30	.75
13U89 Dunlending Trapper	.30	.75
13U91 Fires Brightly Burning	.30	.75
13U92 Grima, Footman of Saruman	.30	.75
13U94 Howdah	.30	.75
13U95 Lying in Wait	.30	.75
13U98 Southron Murderer	.30	.75
13C102 Worn Battleaxe	.12	.30
13C107 Expendable Servants	.12	.30
13C111 Massing Strength	.12	.30
13C113 Orc Line-breaker	.12	.30
13C116 Orc Reaper	.12	.30
13C119 Underdeeps Denizen	.12	.30
13C120 Unforgiving Depths	.12	.30
13C121 Whatever Means	.12	.30
13C125 Ferthu Theoden Hal	.12	.30
13C127 Freely Across Our Land	.12	.30
13C129 Hamstrung	.12	.30
13C132 Merchant of Westfold	.12	.30
13C133 Riddermark Tactician	.12	.30
13C134 Ride With Me	.12	.30
13C145 Don't Let Go	.12	.30
13C147 Faith in Friendship	.12	.30
13C157 Westfarthing Businessman	.12	.30
13C159 Assault Denizen	.12	.30
13C160 Cavern Denizen	.12	.30
13C161 Endless Assault	.12	.30
13C162 Enemy Without Number	.12	.30
13C163 Entranced Uruk	.12	.30
13C164 Fearless Approach	.12	.30
13C168 Uruk Aggressor	.12	.30
13C172 Uruk Outrider	.12	.30
13C173 Uruk Reserve	.12	.30
13C175 Uruk Tactician	.12	.30
13C176 War Machine	.12	.30
13C184 Ulaire Nertea, Servant of the Shadow	.12	.30
13R101 Voice of the Desert, Southron Troop	2.00	5.00
13R104 Chamber Patrol	1.00	2.50
13R108 Forced March	.75	2.00
13R112a Orc Crusher	1.50	4.00
13R112b Orc Crusher TENGWAR		
13R115 Orc Raid Commander	.75	2.00
13R117 Ordnance Grunt	3.00	8.00
13R123 Eomer, Heir to Meduseld	1.00	2.50
13R126 Firefoot, Mearas of the Mark	7.50	15.00
13R136 Snowmane, Noble Mearas	1.00	2.50
13R137a Theoden, The Renowned	3.00	8.00
13R137b Theoden, The Renowned TENGWAR		
13R138 Theodred, Second Marshal of the Mark	2.00	5.00
13R139 Wind-swept Homestead	.60	1.50
13R140 Sauron, Dark Lord of Mordor	3.00	8.00
13R141 Sceptre of the Dark Lord	1.50	4.00
13R142 Bilbo, Aged Ring-bearer	2.00	5.00
13R143 Bill the Pony, Dearly-loved	1.00	2.50
13R149 Frodo, Frenzied Fighter	3.00	8.00
13R152 Humble Homestead	1.00	2.50
13R153 Mithril-coat, Dwarf-mail	1.00	2.50
13R155 Phial of Galadriel, The Light of Earendil	1.00	2.50
13R156a Sam, Bearer of Great Need	.75	2.00
13R156b Sam, Bearer of Great Need TENGWAR		
13R158 Assault Commander	.75	2.00
13R169 Uruk Blitz	1.25	3.00
13R171 Uruk Invader	.60	1.50
13R174a Uruk Rogue	1.00	2.50
13R174b Uruk Rogue TENGWAR		
13R178 Dark Fell About Him	.75	2.00
13R180 Shadow in the East	.60	1.50
13R182 Ulaire Enquea, Sixth of the Nine Riders	2.00	5.00
13S100 Vicious Dunlending	.40	1.00
13S109 Howling Orc	.40	1.00
13S114 Orc Plains Runner	.40	1.00
13S118 Picket Denizen	.40	1.00
13S186 Caves of Aglarond	.75	2.00
13S189 Crossroads of the Fallen Kings	.75	2.00
13S191 Fords of Isen	.40	1.00
13S192 The Great Gates	.40	1.00
13U103 Always Threatening	.30	.75

Card	Low	High
13U105 Defiled	.30	.75
13U106 Enemy Upon Enemy	.30	.75
13U110 Isengard Informant	.30	.75
13U122 Bitter Tidings	.30	.75
13U124 Eowyn, Restless Warrior	.30	.75
13U128 Hama, Captain of the King's Guard	.30	.75
13U130 Hurried Barrows	.30	.75
13U131 King's Board	.30	.75
13U135 Rider's Bow	.30	.75
13U144 Daddy Twofoot, Next-door Neighbor	.30	.75
13U146 Everything but My Bones	.30	.75
13U148 Fates Entwined	.30	.75
13U150 Frodo Gamgee, Son of Samwise	.30	.75
13U151 The Gaffer, Master Gardener	.30	.75
13U154 New Chapter	.30	.75
13U165 Isengard Infiltrator	.30	.75
13U166 New Enemy	.30	.75
13U167 Signs of War	.30	.75
13U170 Uruk Distractor	.30	.75
13U177 Weapons of Control	.30	.75
13U179 From Hideous Eyrie	.30	.75
13U181 They Came From Mordor	.30	.75
13U183 Ulaire Lemenya, Servant of the Shadow	.30	.75
13U185 Abandoned Mine Shaft	.30	.75
13U187 City of Kings	.30	.75
13U188 Courtyard Parapet	.30	.75
13U190 Doors of Durin	.30	.75
13U193 Isenwash	.30	.75
13U194 Redhorn Pass	.30	.75

2005 Lord of the Rings Bloodlines Legends Foil

Card	Low	High
COMPLETE SET (18)	30.00	60.00
RELEASED ON AUGUST 12, 2005		
13RF1 Celeborn, The Wise F	2.00	5.00
13RF2 Galadriel, Sorceress of the Hidden Land F	.75	2.00
13RF3 Legolas, of the Grey Company F	3.00	8.00
13RF4 Gandalf, Bearer of Obligation F	2.50	6.00
13RF5 Pallando, Far-travelling One F	3.00	8.00
13RF6 Deagol, Fateful Finder F	1.25	3.00
13RF7 Aragorn, Isildur's Heir F	.75	2.00
13RF8 Denethor, Last Ruling Steward F	1.50	4.00
13RF9 Voice of the Desert, Southron Troop F	1.50	4.00
13RF10 Chamber Patrol F	1.00	2.50
13RF11 Orc Crusher F	1.50	4.00
13RF12 Eomer, Heir to Meduseld F	.75	2.00
13RF13 Theoden, The Renowned F	1.25	3.00
13RF14 Sauron, Dark Lord of Mordor F	6.00	12.00
13RF15 Frodo, Frenzied Fighter F	3.00	8.00
13RF16 Sam, Bearer of Great Need F	2.50	6.00
13RF17 Uruk Blitz F	.75	2.00
13RF18 Uruk Rogue F	1.50	4.00

2005 Lord of the Rings Bloodlines Legends Masterworks Foil

Card	Low	High
COMPLETE SET (9)	50.00	100.00
RELEASED ON AUGUST 12, 2005		
13O1 Celeborn, The Wise O	7.50	15.00
13O2 Galadriel, Sorceress of the Hidden Land O	10.00	20.00
13O3 Legolas, of the Grey Company O	15.00	30.00
13O4 Gandalf, Bearer of Obligation O	10.00	20.00
13O5 Pallando, Far-traveling One O	12.00	25.00
13O6 Aragorn, Isildur's Heir O	10.00	20.00
13O7 Denethor, Last Ruling Steward O	7.50	15.00
13O8 Eomer, Heir to Meduseld O	7.50	15.00
13O9 Theoden, The Renowned O	10.00	20.00

2006 Lord of the Rings Expanded Middle-Earth

Card	Low	High
COMPLETE SET (15)	20.00	40.00
14R1 Dain Ironfoot, King Under the Mountain	2.00	5.00
14R2 Elladan, Son of Elrond	5.00	10.00
14R3 Elrohir, Son of Elrond	6.00	12.00
14R4 Gildor Inglorion, of the House of Finrod	1.25	3.00
14R5 Brand, King of Dale	2.00	5.00
14R6 Grimbeorn, Beorning Chieftain	5.00	10.00
14R7 Duilin, Ranger from Blackroot Vale	1.25	3.00
14R8 Duinhir, Tall Man of Blackroot Vale	1.25	3.00
14R9 Halbarad, Ranger of the North	2.50	6.00
14R10 Furious Hillman	1.25	3.00
14R11 Swarming Hillman	1.25	3.00
14R12 Half-troll of Far Harad	1.50	4.00
14R13 Horror of Harad	1.25	3.00
14R14 Uruk-hai Healer	1.25	3.00
14R15 Uruk-hai Scout	1.25	3.00

2006 Lord of the Rings The Hunters

Card	Low	High
COMPLETE SET (194)	200.00	300.00
BOOSTER BOX (36 PACKS)	50.00	100.00
BOOSTER PACK (11 CARDS)	2.00	4.00
RELEASED ON JUNE 9, 2006		
15C5 Gimli, Eager Hunter	.12	.30
15C8 Sturdy Stock	.12	.30
15R1 The One Ring, The Ring of Doom	12.00	25.00
15R6 Gloin, Son of Groin	3.00	8.00
15R9 Well-crafted Armor	1.25	3.00
15S2 The One Ring, The Ruling Ring	.40	1.00
15U3 Chamber of Records	.30	.75
15U4 The Fortunes of Balin's Folk	.30	.75
15U7 Heavy Axe	.30	.75
15C10 Whatever End	.12	.30
15C13 Elven Bow	.12	.30
15C14 Elven Warrior	.12	.30
15C15 Focus	.12	.30
15C23 Point Blank Range	.12	.30
15C25 Sword of the Fallen	.12	.30
15C28 Ent Avenger	.12	.30
15C45 Hurry Hobbitses	.12	.30
15C46 Nice Fish	.12	.30
15C48 Release Them	.12	.30
15C59 Dunedain of the South	.12	.30
15C60a Forth the Three Hunters! DWARVEN	.12	.30
15C60b Forth the Three Hunters! ELVEN	.12	.30
15C60c Forth the Three Hunters! GONDOR	.12	.30
15C62 Ithilien Blade	.12	.30
15C65 No Quicker Path	.12	.30
15C68 Ranger's Cloak	.12	.30
15C69 Silent Traveler	.12	.30
15C71 Unyielding Ranger	.12	.30
15C73 Bold Easterling	.12	.30
15C75 Courageous Easterling	.12	.30
15C77 Easterling Scout	.12	.30
15C80 Great Axe	.12	.30
15C82 Grousing Hillman	.12	.30
15C83 Hunting Herdsman	.12	.30
15C91 Ravaging Wild Man	.12	.30
15C93 Swarthy Hillman	.12	.30
15C97 Beasts of Burden	.12	.30
15R11 Arwen, She-Elf	5.00	10.00
15R12 Dinendal, Mirkwood Archer	5.00	10.00
15R19 Legolas, of the Woodland Realm	6.00	12.00
15R22 The Mirror of Galadriel, Dangerous Guide	2.00	5.00
15R24 Spied From Afar	1.25	3.00
15R29 Gandalf, Powerful Guide	7.50	15.00
15R29P Gandalf, Powerful Guide PROMO	5.00	10.00
15R30 Leaflock, Finglas	6.00	12.00
15R33 One Last Surprise	1.50	4.00
15R34 Quickbeam, Hastiest of All Ents	2.50	6.00
15R36 Shepherd of the Trees	5.00	10.00
15R38 Treebeard, Enraged Shepherd	6.00	12.00
15R40 Connected by Fate	.75	2.00
15R42 Desperate Move	1.50	4.00
15R43 Gollum, Hopeless	2.50	6.00
15R47 Not This Time!	5.00	10.00
15R49 Smeagol, Wretched and Hungry	1.25	3.00
15R53 Unseen Foe	3.00	8.00
15R55 Aragorn, Thorongil	6.00	12.00
15R56 Aragorn's Bow, Ranger's Longbow	12.00	25.00
15R58 Decorated Barricade	2.00	5.00
15R64 Madril, Defender of Osgiliath	1.50	4.00
15R70 Tremendous Wall	1.00	2.50
15R72 Bill Ferny, Agent of Saruman	6.00	12.00
15R74 Chieftain of Dunland	2.00	5.00
15R76 Destroyed Homestead	1.00	2.50
15R84 Last Gasp	1.50	4.00
15R86 Mumak Commander, Giant Among the Swertings	6.00	12.00
15R87 Primitive Savage	1.50	4.00
15R99 Black Land Chieftain	1.50	4.00
15S18 Legolas, Fleet-footed Hunter	.40	1.00
15S54 Aragorn, Swift Hunter	.40	1.00
15S95 Battlefield Recruit	.40	1.00
15S96 Battlefield Veteran	.40	1.00
15U16 Gift of the Evenstar, Blessed Light	.30	.75
15U17 Haldir, Sentry of the Golden Wood	.30	.75
15U20 Lorien's Blessing	.30	.75
15U21 Mighty Shot	.30	.75
15U26 Uruviel, Woodland Maid	.30	.75
15U27 Be Gone!	.30	.75
15U31 Mellon!	.30	.75
15U32 Momentous Gathering	.30	.75
15U35 Shadow of the Wood	.30	.75
15U37 Skinbark, Elder Ent	.30	.75
15U39 Called to Mordor	.30	.75
15U41 Controlled by the Ring	.30	.75
15U44 Herbs and Stewed Rabbit	.30	.75
15U50 Something Slimy	.30	.75
15U51 Sudden Strike	.30	.75
15U52 Swear By the Precious	.30	.75
15U57 Damrod, Dunadan of Gondor	.30	.75
15U61 Gondorian Prowler	.30	.75
15U63 Mablung, Ranger of Ithilien	.30	.75
15U66 No Travellers In This Land	.30	.75
15U69 Portico	.30	.75
15U78 Engrossed Hillman	.30	.75
15U79 Enraged Herdsman	.30	.75
15U81 Grieving the Fallen	.30	.75
15U85 Lying Counsel	.30	.75
15U88 Pursuing Horde	.30	.75
15U89 Rapid Reload	.30	.75
15U90 Rapt Hillman	.30	.75
15U92 Savage Southron	.30	.75
15U94 Wandering Hillman	.30	.75
15U98 Black Gate Sentry	.30	.75
15C100 Black Land Commander	.12	.30
15C101 Black Land Observer	.12	.30
15C103 Black Land Runner	.12	.30
15C105 Black Land Spy	.12	.30
15C107 Desolation Orc	.12	.30
15C108 Destructive Orc	.12	.30
15C110 Isengard Marauder	.12	.30
15C116 Scouting Orc	.12	.30
15C120 Veteran War Chief	.12	.30
15C121 Brilliant Light	.12	.30
15C125 Eowyn, Willing Fighter	.12	.30
15C127 Grim Trophy	.12	.30
15C130 Horseman of the North	.12	.30
15C131 Our Inspiration	.12	.30
15C133 Rider's Mount	.12	.30
15C136 Rohirrim Axe	.12	.30
15C143 Community Living	.12	.30
15C144 Frodo, Weary From the Journey	.12	.30
15C145 Hobbit Sword	.12	.30
15C147 Hobbiton Farmer, Lover of Pipeweed	.12	.30
15C149 Merry, The Tall One	.12	.30
15C150 No Visitors	.12	.30
15C151 Pippin, The Short One	.12	.30
15C156 Charging Uruk	.12	.30
15C157 Chasing Uruk	.12	.30
15C158 Covetous Uruk	.12	.30
15C161 Hunting Uruk	.12	.30
15C167 Pursuing Uruk	.12	.30
15C169 Seeking Uruk	.12	.30
15C176 Uruk Village Assassin	.12	.30
15C178 Uruk Village Stormer	.12	.30
15C179 Violent Hurl	.12	.30
15R104 Black Land Shrieker	2.50	6.00
15R109 Gorbag, Filthy Rebel	2.50	6.00
15R112 Mountain-troll	7.50	15.00
15R117 Tower Troll	3.00	8.00
15R119 Unreasonable Choice	1.25	3.00
15R122 Burial Mounds	1.25	3.00
15R123 Eomer, Horsemaster	3.00	8.00
15R124 Eomer's Spear, Trusty Weapon	3.00	8.00
15R135 Rohan Worker	1.00	2.50
15R141 Sturdy Shield	1.25	3.00
15R146 Hobbiton Brewer, Maker of Fine Ales	5.00	10.00
15R148 Little Golden Flower	2.00	5.00
15R152 Relaxation	2.00	5.00
15R154 Second Breakfast	1.25	3.00
15R155 Advancing Horde	2.00	5.00
15R162 Lurtz, Now Perfected	2.00	5.00
15R163 Lurtz's Sword, Mighty Longsword	1.00	2.50
15R165 Merciless Berserker	1.25	3.00
15R170 Sentry Uruk	1.50	4.00
15R172 Ugluk, Ugly Fellow	7.50	15.00
15R173 Ugluk's Sword, Weapon of Command	1.50	4.00
15R174 Uruk Cavern Striker	.75	2.00
15R180 With All Possible Speed	1.50	4.00
15R182 A Shadow Fell Over Them	1.50	4.00
15R184 Ulaire Attea, Desirous of Power	1.25	3.00
15R185 Ulaire Lemenya, Eternally Threatening	5.00	10.00
15R186 Ulaire Nelya, Fell Rider	.75	2.00
15R193 Mount Doom	3.00	8.00
15S126 Gamling, The Old	.40	1.00
15S138 Rohirrim Soldier	.40	1.00
15S164 Mauhur, Relentless Hunter	.40	1.00
15S171 Tracking Uruk	.40	1.00
15U102 Black Land Overlord	.30	.75
15U106 Coordinated Effort	.30	.75
15U111 Moria Menace	.30	.75
15U113 Orkish Camp	.30	.75
15U114 Orkish Hunting Spear	.30	.75
15U115 Pummeling Blow	.30	.75
15U118 Unmistakable Omen	.30	.75
15U128 Haleth, Son of Hama	.30	.75
15U129 Horse of Great Stature	.30	.75
15U132 Last Days of My House	.30	.75
15U134 Rohan Stable Master	.30	.75
15U137 Rohirrim Doorwarden	.30	.75
15U139 Rohirrim Warrior	.30	.75
15U140 Spear of the Mark	.30	.75
15U142 Swift Stroke	.30	.75
15U153 Sam, Innocent Traveler	.30	.75
15U159 Defensive Rush	.30	.75
15U160 Following Uruk	.30	.75
15U166 Poised for Assault	.30	.75
15U168 Searching Uruk	.30	.75
15U175 Uruk Infantry	.30	.75
15U177 Uruk Village Rager	.30	.75
15U181 Later Than You Think	.30	.75
15U183 They Feel the Precious	.30	.75
15U187 Anduin River	.30	.75
15U188 Breeding Pit of Isengard	.30	.75
15U189 City Gates	.30	.75
15U190 East Wall of Rohan	.30	.75
15U191 Gate of Mordor	.30	.75
15U192 Isengard Ruined	.30	.75
15U194 Westfold Village	.30	.75

2006 Lord of the Rings The Hunters Legends Foil

Card	Low	High
COMPLETE SET (18)	50.00	100.00
RELEASED ON JUNE 9, 2006		
15RF1 The One Ring, The Ring of Doom F	30.00	60.00
15RF2 Well-crafted Armor F	2.00	5.00
15RF3 Legolas, of the Woodland Realm F	3.00	8.00
15RF4 The Mirror of Galadriel, Dangerous Guide F	1.25	3.00
15RF5 Gandalf, Powerful Guide F	7.50	15.00
15RF6 One Last Surprise F	.75	2.00
15RF7 Quickbeam, Hastiest of All Ents F	5.00	10.00
15RF8 Smeagol, Wretched and Hungry F	2.50	6.00
15RF9 Aragorn, Thorongil F	10.00	20.00
15RF10 Madril, Defender of Osgiliath F	2.00	5.00
15RF11 Black Land Chieftain F	1.25	3.00
15RF12 Gorbag, Filthy Rebel F	2.00	5.00
15RF13 Eomer, Horsemaster F	3.00	8.00
15RF14 Sentry Uruk F	1.00	2.50
15RF15 Ulaire Attea, Desirous of Power F	2.50	6.00
15RF16 Ulaire Lemenya, Eternally Threatening F	5.00	10.00
15RF17 Ulaire Nelya, Fell Rider F	1.00	2.50
15RF18 Mount Doom F	7.50	15.00

2006 Lord of the Rings The Hunters Legends Masterworks Foil

Card	Low	High
COMPLETE SET (9)	125.00	200.00
RELEASED ON JUNE 9, 2006		
15O1 Legolas, of the Woodland Realm O	25.00	50.00
15O2 Gandalf, Powerful Guide O	15.00	30.00
15O3 Quickbeam, Hastiest of All Ents O	12.00	25.00
15O4 Aragorn, Thorongil O	30.00	60.00
15O5 Madril, Defender of Osgiliath O	15.00	30.00
15O6 Eomer, Horsemaster O	10.00	20.00
15O7 Ulaire Attea, Desirous of Power O	12.00	25.00
15O8 Ulaire Lemenya, Eternally Threatening O	10.00	20.00
15O9 Ulaire Nelya, Fell Rider O	10.00	20.00

2006 Lord of the Rings The Wraith Collection

Card	Low	High
COMPLETE SET (6)	7.50	15.00
16R1 Barrow-wight Stalker	1.50	4.00
16R2 Candle Corpses	1.50	4.00
16R3 Covetous Wisp	1.50	4.00
16R4 Dead Faces	1.50	4.00
16R5 Spirit of Dread	1.50	4.00
16R6 Undead of Angmar	1.50	4.00

2007 Lord of the Rings Rise of Saruman

Card	Low	High
COMPLETE SET (148)	200.00	300.00
BOOSTER BOX (36 PACKS)		
BOOSTER BOX (11 CARDS)		
RELEASED ON MARCH 1, 2007		
17R2 Balin Avenged	1.50	4.00
17R4 Ring of Artifice	6.00	12.00
17R6 Thorin III, Stonehelm	6.00	12.00
17S7 Elven Guardian	.60	1.50
17U1 Armor of Khazad	.40	1.00
17U3 Dwarven Stratagem	.40	1.00
17U5 Axe- Work	.40	1.00
17U8 Hearth and Hall	.40	1.00
17U9 Lothlorien Guides	.40	1.00
17C46 Pandemonium	.12	.30
17C51 Stampeding Madman	.12	.30
17C53 Stampeding Savage	.12	.30
17C54 Stampeding Shepherd	.12	.30
17C55 Sunland Guard	.12	.30
17C57 Sunland Skirmisher	.12	.30
17C59 Sunland Trooper	.12	.30
17C60 Sunland Warrior	.12	.30
17C62 Vengeful Savage	.12	.30
17C63 Vengeful Wild Man	.12	.30
17C64 Vengeful Pillager	.12	.30
17C66 Wildman's Oath	.12	.30
17C68 Chaotic Clash	.12	.30
17C69 Cry and Panic	.12	.30
17C70 Feral Ride	.12	.30
17C72 Orkish Assassin	.12	.30
17C75 Orkish Dreg	.12	.30
17C78 Orkish Footman	.12	.30
17C80 Orkish Lackey	.12	.30
17C81 Orkish Maurader	.12	.30
17C83 Orkish Runner	.12	.30

17C85 Orkish Traveler	.12	.30
17C92 Vicious Warg	.12	.30
17R13 The World Ahead	5.00	10.00
17R17 Gandalf, Returned	12.00	25.00
17R18 Glamdring, Orc Beater	2.00	5.00
17R20 Gwaihir, The Windlord	6.00	12.00
17R23 Scintillating Bird	.75	2.00
17R24 Shadowfax, Greatest of the Mearas	6.00	12.00
17R27 Anduril, Sword That Was Broken	6.00	12.00
17R28 Faramir, Bearer of Quality	7.50	15.00
17R29 Faramir's Bow, Ithilien Longbow	3.00	8.00
17R31 Narsil, Forged by Telchar	5.00	10.00
17R36 Throne of Minas Tirith	5.00	10.00
17R37 Saruman, Instigator of Insurrection	5.00	10.00
17R38 Saruman, Servant of Sauron	6.00	12.00
17R39 Throne of Isengard	1.25	3.00
17R41 Ceremonial Armor	2.50	6.00
17R43 Easterling Sneak	1.50	4.00
17R44 Grima's Dagger	1.25	3.00
17R45 In the Wild Men's Wake	2.50	6.00
17R49 Stampeding Chief	3.00	8.00
17R52 Stampeding Ransacker	2.00	5.00
17R56 Sunland Scout	1.50	4.00
17R58 Sunland Sneak	2.00	5.00
17R61 Sunland Weaponmaster	5.00	10.00
17R65 Vengeful Primitive	.75	2.00
17R67 A Defiled Charge	3.00	8.00
17R71 Grishnakh, Treacherous Captain	6.00	12.00
17R73 Orkish Berserker	1.25	3.00
17R74 Orkish Cavalry	2.50	6.00
17R76 Orkish Fiend	2.00	5.00
17R79 Orkish Invader	2.50	6.00
17R82 Orkish Rider	2.00	5.00
17R84 Orkish Scout	2.50	6.00
17R86 Orkish Veteran	3.00	8.00
17R87 Orkish Warg-master	2.50	6.00
17R89 Relentless Warg	6.00	12.00
17R93 Aragorn, Defender of Rohan	6.00	12.00
17R95 Eomer, Northman	6.00	12.00
17R96 Eowyn, Northwoman	6.00	12.00
17R98 Throne of the Golden Hall	3.00	8.00
17R99 Hama, Northman	1.50	4.00
17S11 Orophin, Silvan Elf	.60	1.50
17S12 Rumil, Silvan Elf	.60	1.50
17S30 Madril, Loyal Lieutenant	.60	1.50
17S33 Ranger of the White Tree	.60	1.50
17S35 Soldier's Cache	.60	1.50
17S48 Saruman, Coldly Still	.60	1.50
17U10 Namarie	.40	1.00
17U14 Weapons of Lothlorien	.40	1.00
17U15 A New Light	.40	1.00
17U16 Barliman Butterbur, Red-Faced Landlord	.40	1.00
17U19 Guidance of the Istari	.40	1.00
17U21 Long-stemmed Pipe	.40	1.00
17U22 Meneldor, Misty Mountain Eagle	.40	1.00
17U25 The Sap is in the Bough	.40	1.00
17U26 Woodland Onod	.40	1.00
17U32 Nimble Attack	.40	1.00
17U34 Spirit of the White Tree	.40	1.00
17U40 Beast of War	.40	1.00
17U42 Easterling Dispatcher	.40	1.00
17U47 Primitive Brand	.40	1.00
17U50 Stampeding Hillsman	.40	1.00
17U77 Orkish Flanker	.40	1.00
17U88 Orkish Warrior	.40	1.00
17U90 Rider's Gear	.40	1.00
17U91 Threatening Warg	.40	1.00
17U94 Dispatched with Haste	.40	1.00
17U97 For Death and Glory	.40	1.00
17C113 Deathly Roar	.12	.30
17C118 Vile Pit	.12	.30
17C119 White Hand Aggressor	.12	.30
17C120 White Hand Attacker	.12	.30
17C122 White Hand Butcher	.12	.30
17C125 White Hand Enforcer	.12	.30
17C126 White Hand Guard	.12	.30
17C127 White Hand Intruder	.12	.30
17C128 White Hand Invader	.12	.30
17C130 White Hand Scout	.12	.30
17C131 White Hand Slayer	.12	.30
17C133 White Hand Trooper	.12	.30
17C134 White Hand Vanquisher	.12	.30
17C136 White Hand Warrior	.12	.30
17R102 Theoden, Northman, King of Rohan	1.50	4.00
17R105 Throne of the Dark Lord	3.00	8.00
17R114 Land Had Changed	2.00	5.00
17R116 Saruman, Master of the White Hand	3.00	8.00
17R121 White Hand Berserker	2.00	5.00
17R123 White Hand Captain	1.50	4.00
17R124 White Hand Destroyer	2.50	6.00
17R129 White Hand Legion	1.50	4.00
17R132 White Hand Taskmaster	2.00	5.00
17R135 White Hand Veteran	2.50	6.00
17R137 You Do Not Know Fear	5.00	10.00
17R139 Ulaire Cantea, Duplicitous Assassin	6.00	12.00
17R140 Ulaire Enquea, Duplicitous Lieutenant	3.00	8.00
17R141 Ulaire Otsea, Duplicitous Specter	5.00	10.00
17R142 Ring of Savagery	2.50	6.00
17R143 Ring of Terror	6.00	12.00
17R144 The Witch-king, Conqueror of Arthedain	3.00	8.00
17S115 Saruman, Curunir	.60	1.50
17U100 Into the Caves	.40	1.00
17U101 Soldier of Rohan	.40	1.00
17U103 Where Now the Horse	.40	1.00
17U104 Warrior of Rohan	.40	1.00
17U106 Halfling Leaf	.40	1.00
17U107 Merry, In the Bloom of Health	.40	1.00
17U108 Hornblower Leaf	.40	1.00
17U109 Pippin, In the Bloom of Health	.40	1.00
17U110 Southfarthing Leaf	.40	1.00
17U111 Southlinch Leaf	.40	1.00
17U112 Blade of the White Hand	.40	1.00
17U117 Spear of the White Hand	.40	1.00
17U138 You Do Not Know Pain	.40	1.00
17U145 Dol Guldur	.40	1.00
17U146 Falls of Rauros	.40	1.00
17U147 Imladris	.40	1.00
17U148 Num	.40	1.00

2007 Lord of the Rings Rise of Saruman Legends Foil

COMPLETE SET (18)	120.00	250.00
RELEASED ON MARCH 1, 2007		
17RF1 Ring of Artifice F	7.50	15.00
17RF2 Glamdring, Orc Beater F	7.50	15.00
17RF3 Shadowfax, Greatest of the Mearas F	20.00	40.00
17RF4 Gwaihir, The Windlord F	10.00	20.00
17RF5 Anduril, Sword That Was Broken F	12.00	25.00
17RF6 Faramir, Bearer of Quality F	30.00	60.00
17RF7 Narsil, Forged by Telchar F	12.00	25.00
17RF8 Throne of Minas Tirith F	7.50	15.00
17RF9 Throne of Isengard F	15.00	30.00
17RF10 Stampeding Chief F	10.00	20.00
17RF11 Orkish Invader F	12.00	25.00
17RF12 Aragorn, Defender of Rohan F	10.00	20.00
17RF13 Throne of the Golden Hall F	12.00	25.00
17RF14 Theoden, Northman, King of Rohan F	15.00	30.00
17RF15 Throne of the Dark Lord F	15.00	30.00
17RF16 Ulaire Otsea, Duplicitous Specter F	15.00	30.00
17RF17 Ring of Savagery F	15.00	30.00
17RF18 Ring of Terror F	7.50	15.00

2007 Lord of the Rings Treachery and Deceit

COMPLETE SET (140)	200.00	350.00
BOOSTER BOX (36 PACKS)		
BOOSTER PACK (11 CARDS)		
RELEASED IN MAY 2007		
18C3 Thorin's Harp	.25	.60
18C9 Elven Defender	.25	.60
18R1 Gimli, Sprinter	3.00	8.00
18R4 Arwen's Bow	3.00	8.00
18R5 Arwen's Dagger	3.00	8.00
18R6 Back to the Light	5.00	10.00
18R7 Celebring, Elven-smith	2.50	6.00
18U2 Run Until Found	.40	1.00
18U8 Elven Armaments	.40	1.00
18C16 Miruvore	.25	.60
18C17 Woodhall Elf, Exile	.25	.60
18C19 Drawn to Full Height	.25	.60
18C20 Ents Marching	.25	.60
18C22 Librarian, Keeper of Ancient Texts	.25	.60
18C36 Time for Food	.25	.60
18C39 Armor of the White City	.25	.60
18C44 Defenses Long Held	.25	.60
18C49 Faramir's Company	.25	.60
18C51 For Gondor!	.25	.60
18C56 Ranger of the South	.25	.60
18C57 Shield of the White Tree	.25	.60
18C65 Declined Business	.25	.60
18C68 Harry Goatleaf	.25	.60
18C70 Ill News Is An Ill Guest	.25	.60
18C72 Ruffian	.25	.60
18C73 Rough Man of the South	.25	.60
18C74 Squint-eyed Southerner	.25	.60
18C77 Whisper in the Dark	.25	.60
18C84 Orkish Ax	.25	.60
18C85 Orkish Aggressor	.25	.60
18C87 Orkish Breeder	.25	.60
18C88 Orkish Defender	.25	.60
18C89 Orkish Headsman	.25	.60
18C90 Orkish Skirmisher	.25	.60
18C91 Orkish Sneak	.25	.60
18C94 Cast From the Hall	.25	.60
18R11 Galadriel's Silver Ewer	7.50	15.00
18R12 Gil-galad, High King of the Noldor	15.00	30.00
18R13 Glorfindel, Eldarin Lord	6.00	12.00
18R14 Haldir, Warrior Messenger	2.50	6.00
18R15 Lembas Bread	3.00	8.00
18R18 Beorning Axe	6.00	12.00
18R24 Our Time	3.00	8.00
18R26 Radagast's Herb Bag	6.00	12.00
18R28 Countless Cords	2.50	6.00
18R29 Deceit	3.00	8.00
18R31 It Draws Him	2.50	6.00
18R32 Not Easily Avoided	5.00	10.00
18R34 Shelob, Menace	6.00	12.00
18R35 Sting of Shelob	3.00	8.00
18R38 Aragorn, Heir to the Throne of Gondor	7.50	15.00
18R40 Boromir, Proud and Noble Man	6.00	12.00
18R41 Crown of Gondor	3.00	8.00
18R42 Denethor, On the Edge of Madness	2.00	5.00
18R43 Denethor's Sword	2.00	5.00
18R47 Elendil's Army	3.00	8.00
18R48 Faramir, Captain of Ithilien	6.00	12.00
18R50 The Faithful Stone	5.00	10.00
18R52 Gondorian Servant, Denethor's Handman	2.50	6.00
18R53 Horn of Boromir, The Great Horn	5.00	10.00
18R54 Isildur, Sword-Bearer	6.00	12.00
18R55 Ranger of the North	2.00	5.00
18R59 Watcher at Sarn Ford, Ranger of the North	3.00	8.00
18R66 Fleet of Corsair Ships	2.50	6.00
18R67 Grima, Witless Worm	6.00	12.00
18R69 Henchman's Dagger	2.00	5.00
18R71 Mumakil Commander, Bold and Grim	2.50	6.00
18R76 Treachery	2.50	6.00
18R80 Gothmog, Morgul Leader	7.50	15.00
18R81 Gothmog's Warg, Leader's Mount	3.00	8.00
18R82 Grond, Forged With Black Steel	5.00	10.00
18R83 Gruesome Meal	3.00	8.00
18R95 Eomer's Bow	2.50	6.00
18R96 Erkenbrand's Horn	3.00	8.00
18R97 Erkenbrand's Shield	6.00	12.00
18R98 Fall back to Helm's Deep	3.00	8.00
18R99 Gamling, Dutiful Marshal	2.50	6.00
18U10 Elven Supplies	.40	1.00
18U21 Last Stand	.40	1.00
18U23 One-Upsmanship	.40	1.00
18U25 Perspective	.40	1.00
18U27 Ship of Smoke	.40	1.00
18U30 Enemy in Your Midst	.40	1.00
18U33 Set Up	.40	1.00
18U37 Trusted Promise	.40	1.00
18U45 Dunadan's Bow	.40	1.00
18U46 Disarmed	.40	1.00
18U58 Soldier's Cache	.40	1.00
18U60 Corsair Boarding Axe	.40	1.00
18U61 Corsair Bow	.40	1.00
18U62 Corsair Grappling Hook	.40	1.00
18U63 Corsair Halberd	.40	1.00
18U64 Corsair Scimitar	.40	1.00
18U75 Ted Sandyman, Chief's Men's Ally	.40	1.00
18U78 Destroyers and Usurpers	.40	1.00
18U79 Frenzy of Arrows	.40	1.00
18U86 Orkish Archer Troop	.40	1.00
18U92 War Preparations	.40	1.00
18U93 Wary Orc	.40	1.00
18C101 Precise Attack	.25	.60
18C103 Rohirrim Recruit	.25	.60
18C106 A Dragon's Tale	.25	.60
18C109 Make a Run For It	.25	.60
18C116 Fury of the Evil Army	.25	.60
18C117 Ghastly Wound	.25	.60
18C124 White Hand Attacker	.25	.60
18C125 White Hand Exorciser	.25	.60
18C128 White Hand Mystic	.25	.60
18C129 White Hand Sieger	.25	.60
18C131 White Hand Uruk	.25	.60
18R100 Gamling's Horn	3.00	8.00
18R102 Rohirrim Diadem	2.50	6.00
18R105 Theoden, Ednew	3.00	8.00
18R107 Fredegar Bolger, Fatty	5.00	10.00
18R112 Scouring of the Shire	7.50	15.00
18R113 Sting, Elven Long Knife	5.00	10.00
18R114 Cleaved	3.00	8.00
18R115 Final Triumph	3.00	8.00
18R118 Lurtz, Halfling Hunter	5.00	10.00
18R119 Lurtz's Bow, Black-Fletch Bow	5.00	10.00
18R122 Shagrat, Tower Captain	5.00	10.00
18R126 White Hand Marchers	2.00	5.00
18R127 White Hand Marshal	6.00	12.00
18R133 Pull of the Ring	2.50	6.00
18U104 Surrendered Weapons	.40	1.00
18U108 Golden Perch Ale	.40	1.00
18U110 Prized Lagan	.40	1.00
18U111 Robin Smallburrow, Shirriff Cock-Robin	.40	1.00
18U120 New Forges Built	.40	1.00
18U121 Pikes Upon Pikes	.40	1.00
18U123 Tracking the Prize	.40	1.00
18U130 White Hand Traveler	.40	1.00
18U132 All Life Flees	.40	1.00
18U134 Doorway to Doom	.40	1.00
18U135 Foot of Mount Doom	.40	1.00
18U136 Mithlond	.40	1.00
18U137 Morannon Plains	.40	1.00
18U138 Sirannon Ruins	.40	1.00
18U139 Steward's Tomb	.40	1.00
18U140 Streets of Bree	.40	1.00

2007 Lord of the Rings Treachery and Deceit Legends Foil

COMPLETE SET (18)	120.00	200.00
RELEASED IN MAY 2007		
18RF1 Arwen's Bow F	10.00	20.00
18RF2 Arwen's Dagger F	7.50	15.00
18RF3 Galadriel's Silver Ewer F	10.00	20.00
18RF4 Beorning Axe F	15.00	30.00
18RF5 Radagast's Herb Bag F	10.00	20.00
18RF6 Shelob, Menace F	7.50	15.00
18RF7 Crown of Gondor F	7.50	15.00
18RF8 Denethor's Sword F	7.50	15.00
18RF9 Watcher at Sarn Ford, Ranger of the North F	7.50	15.00
18RF10 Gothmog, Morgul Leader F	10.00	20.00
18RF11 Erkenbrand's Horn F	10.00	20.00
18RF12 Erkenbrand's Shield F	7.50	15.00
18RF13 Rohirrim Diadem F	7.50	15.00
18RF14 Theoden, Ednew F	7.50	15.00
18RF15 Fredegar Bolger, Fatty F	7.50	15.00
18RF16 Sting, Elven Long Knife F	10.00	20.00
18RF17 Shagrat, Tower Captain F	7.50	15.00
18RF18 Pull of the Ring F	10.00	20.00

2007 Lord of the Rings Treachery and Deceit Legends Masterworks Foil

COMPLETE SET (9)	150.00	300.00
RELEASED IN MAY 2007		
1801 Beorning Axe O	25.00	50.00
1802 Radagast's Herb Bag O	25.00	50.00
1803 Crown of Gondor O	25.00	50.00
1804 Denethor's Sword O	25.00	50.00
1805 Watcher at Sarn Ford, Ranger of the North O	20.00	40.00
1806 Erkenbrand's Horn O	20.00	40.00
1807 Erkenbrand's Shield O	25.00	50.00
1808 Rohirrim Diadem O	20.00	40.00
1809 Pull of the Ring O	20.00	40.00

1995 Marvel OverPower

COMPLETE SET (346)	65.00	80.00
BOOSTER BOX (36 PACKS)	20.00	35.00
BOOSTER PACK (9 CARDS)	1.25	1.50
RELEASED IN AUGUST 1995		
1 Apocalypse R	2.00	3.50
2 Beast U	.40	.60
3 Bishop C	.10	.15
4 Cable R	2.00	3.50
5 Captain America R	2.00	3.50
6 Carnage C	.10	.15
7 Colossus U	.40	.60
8 Cyclops C	.10	.15
9 Deadpool C	.10	.15
10 Dr. Doom C	.10	.15
11 Dr. Octopus C	.10	.15
12 Elektra R	2.00	3.50
13 Gambit C	.10	.15
14 Hobgoblin C	.10	.15
15 Hulk U	.40	.60
16 Human Torch R	2.00	3.50
17 Invisible Woman R	2.00	3.50
18 Iron Man R	2.00	3.50
19 Jean Grey C	.10	.15
20 Jubilee C	.10	.15
21 Magneto R	2.00	3.50
22 Mr. Fantastic R	2.00	3.50
23 Mystique R	2.00	3.50
24 Omega Red U	.40	.60
25 Professor X C	.10	.15
26 Psylocke R	2.00	3.50
27 Punisher U	.40	.60
28 Rhino C	.10	.15
29 Rogue C	.10	.15

30 Sabretooth C .10 .15
31 Silver Surfer U .40 .60
32 Spider-Man R 5.00 8.00
33 Spider-Woman C .10 .15
34 Storm C .10 .15
35 Thing C .10 .15
36 Thor C .10 .15
37 Venom R 2.00 3.50
38 War Machine C .10 .15
39 Wolverine R 3.50 6.00
40 Apocalypse - Shape Shift C .10 .15
41 Apocalypse - Megamorph R 2.00 3.50
42 Apocalypse - Survival of the Fittest U .40 .60
43 Apocalypse - Enhance Strength U .40 .60
44 Apocalypse - Genetic Engineering U .40 .60
45 Beast - Beastial Brawn C .10 .15
46 Beast - Animal Dexterity C .10 .15
47 Beast - Analyze C .10 .15
48 Beast - Biochemist U .40 .60
49 Beast - Drop Kick U .40 .60
50 Bishop - XSE Tactics C .10 .15
51 Bishop - Draw Enemy Fire C .10 .15
52 Bishop - Absorb Energy C .10 .15
53 Bishop - Spectrum Blast R 2.00 3.50
54 Bishop - Plasma Gun U .40 .60
55 Cable - Bodyslide C .10 .15
56 Cable - Custom Firearms U .40 .60
57 Cable - Cover Fire U .40 .60
58 Cable - Bionic Eye U .40 .60
59 Cable - Battle Tactics U .40 .60
60 Captain America - Ricochet Shield U .40 .60
61 Captain America - Avenger U .40 .60
62 Captain America - Mighty Shield U .40 .60
63 Captain America - Stars & Stripes U .40 .60
64 Captain America - Super Soldier U .40 .60
65 Carnage - Insane Rage C .10 .15
66 Carnage - Climb C .10 .15
67 Carnage - Blade Hand C .10 .15
68 Carnage - Symbiotic Web R 2.00 3.50
69 Carnage - Ruthless R 2.00 3.50
70 Colossus - Metal Barrier C .10 .15
71 Colossus - Smash Object C .10 .15
72 Colossus - Haymaker C .10 .15
73 Colossus - Skin of Steel U .40 .60
74 Colossus - Fastball Special U .40 .60
75 Cyclops - Visual Sweep C .10 .15
76 Cyclops - Optic Obliteration C .10 .15
77 Cyclops - Fearless Leader C .10 .15
78 Cyclops - Wide Beam C .10 .15
79 Cyclops - Ground Blast R 2.00 3.50
80 Deadpool - Killing Machine C .10 .15
81 Deadpool - Super Spy C .10 .15
82 Deadpool - Regeneration C .10 .15
83 Deadpool - Assassin R 2.00 3.50
84 Deadpool - High Threshold of Pain R 2.00 3.50
85 Dr. Doom - Concussion Beams C .10 .15
86 Dr. Doom - Energy Dampening Field C .10 .15
87 Dr. Doom - Time Machine C .10 .15
88 Dr. Doom - Super Genius R 2.00 3.50
89 Dr. Doom - Villainous Plot R 2.00 3.50
90 Dr. Octopus - Multi-Armed Menace C .10 .15
91 Dr. Octopus - Villainous Shield C .10 .15
92 Dr. Octopus - Criminal Mastermind C .10 .15
93 Dr. Octopus - Grasping Tentacles R 2.00 3.50
94 Dr. Octopus - Evasive Action U .40 .60
95 Elektra - Martial Artist R 2.00 3.50
96 Elektra - Ninja Master U .40 .60
97 Elektra - Sai U .40 .60
98 Elektra - Anticipate U .40 .60
99 Elektra - Resurrection U .40 .60
100 Gambit - 52 Card Pickup C .10 .15
101 Gambit - Intercept Object C .10 .15
102 Gambit - Charge Object C .10 .15
103 Gambit - Charm R 2.00 3.50
104 Gambit - Staff Attack U .40 .60
105 Hobgoblin - Razor Bats C .10 .15
106 Hobgoblin - Concussion Grenade C .10 .15
107 Hobgoblin - Pumpkin Bomb C .10 .15
108 Hobgoblin - Stun Gas R 2.00 3.50
109 Hobgoblin - Goblin Glider U .40 .60
110 Hulk - Shrug Off C .10 .15
111 Hulk - Hulk Smash C .10 .15
112 Hulk - Enraged R 2.50 4.00
113 Hulk - Intimidate R 2.00 3.50
114 Hulk - Green Goliath U .40 .60
115 Human Torch - Fire Storm C .10 .15
116 Human Torch - Nova Burst R 2.00 3.50
117 Human Torch - Inferno U .40 .60
118 Human Torch - Searing Heat U .40 .60
119 Human Torch - Fire Shield U .40 .60
120 Invisible Woman - Invisible Ram R 2.00 3.50
121 Invisible Woman - Unseen Assailant U .40 .60
122 Invisible Woman - Force Field U .40 .60
123 Invisible Woman - Invisibility U .40 .60
124 Invisible Woman - Bubble Shield U .40 .60
125 Iron Man - Heat Seeking Missile R 2.00 3.50
126 Iron Man - Tactical Computer R 2.00 3.50
127 Iron Man - Concealed Arsenal U .40 .60
128 Iron Man - In the Line of Fire U .40 .60
129 Iron Man - Radar Warning U .40 .60
130 Jean Grey - Mental Deflection C .10 .15
131 Jean Grey - Mind Scan C .10 .15
132 Jean Grey - Telekinesis C .10 .15
133 Jean Grey - Telepathic Unity R 2.00 3.50
134 Jean Grey - Mind Over Matter U .40 .60
135 Jubilee - Fireworks C .10 .15
136 Jubilee - Spectrum Tease C .10 .15
137 Jubilee - Blinding Flare C .10 .15
138 Jubilee - Distracting Burst C .10 .15
139 Jubilee - Plasmoid Flash R 2.00 3.50
140 Magneto - Paralyze Opponent R 2.00 3.50
141 Magneto - Repel Object U .40 .60
142 Magneto - Evil Genius U .40 .60
143 Magneto - Gravity Alteration U .40 .60
144 Magneto - Magnetic Shield U .40 .60
145 Mr. Fantastic - Ingenuity C .10 .15
146 Mr. Fantastic - Stretch Attack U .40 .60
147 Mr. Fantastic - Team Leader U .40 .60
148 Mr. Fantastic - Protect Teammate U .40 .60
149 Mr. Fantastic - Python Hold U .40 .60
150 Mystique - Infiltration C .10 .15
151 Mystique - Surprise Attack R 2.00 3.50
152 Mystique - Cool Under Fire U .40 .60
153 Mystique - Commando Raid U .40 .60
154 Mystique - Illusion of Ally U .40 .60
155 Omega Red - KGB Training C .10 .15
156 Omega Red - Sacrificial Lamb C .10 .15
157 Omega Red - Drain Lifeforce C .10 .15
158 Omega Red - Carbonadium Coils C .10 .15
159 Omega Red - Tendril Tactics R 2.00 3.50
160 Professor X - Cerebro C .10 .15
161 Professor X - X-Men Founder C .10 .15
162 Professor X - Psychic Scan C .10 .15
163 Professor X - Psionic Hold R 2.00 3.50
164 Professor X - Telepathic Coordination R 2.00 3.50
165 Psylocke - Mental Hold R 2.00 3.50
166 Psylocke - Psychic Knife R 2.00 3.50
167 Psylocke - Combat Prowess U .40 .60
168 Psylocke - Psi-Fighting U .40 .60
169 Psylocke - Thought Probe U .40 .60
170 Punisher - Full Auto C .10 .15
171 Punisher - Smoke Screen C .10 .15
172 Punisher - Sniper C .10 .15
173 Punisher - Secret Weapon R 2.00 3.50
174 Punisher - Vendetta R 2.00 3.50
175 Rhino - Pinball Blow C .10 .15
176 Rhino - Romp n' Stomp C .10 .15
177 Rhino - Bowl Over C .10 .15
178 Rhino - Rhino Charge C .10 .15
179 Rhino - Rhino Hide U .40 .60
180 Rogue - Intercept Attack C .10 .15
181 Rogue - Sky Soar C .10 .15
182 Rogue - Power Transfer C .10 .15
183 Rogue - Mutagenic Drain R 2.00 3.50
184 Rogue - Super Strength U .40 .60
185 Sabretooth - Bloodlust C .10 .15
186 Sabretooth - Danger Scent C .10 .15
187 Sabretooth - Healing Factor C .10 .15
188 Sabretooth - Wildcat Attack C .10 .15
189 Sabretooth - Blood Hunt R 2.00 3.50
190 Silver Surfer - Energy Protection C .10 .15
191 Silver Surfer - Force Shield C .10 .15
192 Silver Surfer - Rearrange Matter C .10 .15
193 Silver Surfer - Cosmic Healing C .10 .15
194 Silver Surfer - Power Cosmic R 2.00 3.50
195 Spider-Man - Wall Crawl C .10 .15
196 Spider-Man - Web R 2.50 4.00
197 Spider-Man - Arachnid Agility U .40 .60
198 Spider-Man - Web Shield U .40 .60
199 Spider-Man - Spider Sense U .40 .60
200 Spider-Woman - Spider Strength C .10 .15
201 Spider-Woman - Spider Attack C .10 .15
202 Spider-Woman - Web Lines C .10 .15
203 Spider-Woman - Arachnophobia C .10 .15
204 Spider-Woman - Psi-Web R 2.00 3.50
205 Storm - Chain Lightning C .10 .15
206 Storm - Flight C .10 .15
207 Storm - Hurricane Winds C .10 .15
208 Storm - Emotional Outburst R 2.00 3.50
209 Storm - Summon Elemental Power R 2.00 3.50
210 Thing - Temper Tantrum C .10 .15
211 Thing - Rock Skin C .10 .15
212 Thing - Bear Hug C .10 .15
213 Thing - Clobberin' Time R 2.00 3.50
214 Thing - Revoltin' Development R 2.00 3.50
215 Thor - Mystic Uru Metal C .10 .15
216 Thor - Protect Teammate C .10 .15
217 Thor - God of Thunder C .10 .15
218 Thor - Power of Asgard R 2.00 3.50
219 Thor - Mjolnir Speaks U .40 .60
220 Venom - Alien Webbing C .10 .15
221 Venom - Symbiotic Snare R 2.00 3.50
222 Venom - Panic Attack R 2.00 3.50
223 Venom - Rampage U .40 .60
224 Venom - Creepy Crawler U .40 .60
225 War Machine - Hidden Weapon C .10 .15
226 War Machine - Guided Missile C .10 .15
227 War Machine - Energy Shield C .10 .15
228 War Machine - Battle Computer R 2.00 3.50
229 War Machine - Unleash Arsenal U .40 .60
230 Wolverine - Fighting Instinct C .10 .15
231 Wolverine - Wounded Animal R 2.00 3.50
232 Wolverine - Berserk Attack U .40 .60
233 Wolverine - Snikt U .40 .60
234 Wolverine - Heal U .40 .60
235 Bishop - Age of Apocalypse 1 of 7 U .40 .60
236 Weapon X, Jean Grey - Age of Apocalypse 2 of 7 U .40 .60
237 Sue Storm - Age of Apocalypse 3 of 7 U .40 .60
238 Beast - Age of Apocalypse 4 of 7 U .40 .60
239 Colossus - Age of Apocalypse 5 of 7 U .40 .60
240 Holocaust - Age of Apocalypse 6 of 7 U .40 .60
241 Apocalypse - Age of Apocalypse 7 of 7 U .40 .60
242 Deadpool - Annihilation Affair 1 of 7 U .40 .60
243 Thunderbolt - Annihilation Affair 2 of 7 U .40 .60
244 Captain America - Annihilation Affair 3 of 7 U .40 .60
245 Dr. Octopus - Annihilation Affair 4 of 7 U .40 .60
246 Doc Samson - Annihilation Affair 5 of 7 U .40 .60
247 Omega Red - Annihilation Affair 6 of 7 U .40 .60
248 Hulk - Annihilation Affair 7 of 7 U .40 .60
249 Exodus - Fatal Attractions 1 of 7 C .10 .15
250 Cable - Fatal Attractions 2 of 7 C .10 .15
251 Storm - Fatal Attractions 3 of 7 C .10 .15
252 Magneto - Fatal Attractions 4 of 7 C .10 .15
253 Wolverine - Fatal Attractions 5 of 7 C .10 .15
254 Colossus - Fatal Attractions 6 of 7 C .10 .15
255 Professor X - Fatal Attractions 7 of 7 C .10 .15
256 Brood Swarm - Infestation Incident 1 of 7 U .40 .60
257 Punisher - Infestation Incident 2 of 7 U .40 .60
258 Captain America - Infestation Incident 3 of 7 U .40 .60
259 Nick Fury - Infestation Incident 4 of 7 U .40 .60
260 Cyclops - Infestation Incident 5 of 7 U .40 .60
261 Wolverine - Infestation Incident 6 of 7 U .40 .60
262 Brood Queen - Infestation Incident 7 of 7 U .40 .60
263 Dr. Strange - Infinity Gauntlet 1 of 7 C .10 .15
264 Adam Warlock - Infinity Gauntlet 2 of 7 C .10 .15
265 Dr. Doom - Infinity Gauntlet 3 of 7 C .10 .15
266 Galactus - Infinity Gauntlet 4 of 7 C .10 .15
267 Thor - Infinity Gauntlet 5 of 7 C .10 .15
268 Silver Surfer - Infinity Gauntlet 6 of 7 C .10 .15
269 Thanos - Infinity Gauntlet 7 of 7 C .10 .15
270 Cletus Kasady - Maximum Carnage 1 of 7 C .10 .15
271 Venom - Maximum Carnage 2 of 7 C .10 .15
272 Demogoblin - Maximum Carnage 3 of 7 C .10 .15
273 Carrion - Maximum Carnage 4 of 7 C .10 .15
274 Doppelganger - Maximum Carnage 5 of 7 C .10 .15
275 Shriek - Maximum Carnage 6 of 7 C .10 .15
276 Carnage - Maximum Carnage 7 of 7 C .10 .15
277 Century - Energy 1 - Fighting 1 - Strength 1 C .10 .15
278 Iron Man - Energy 2 - Fighting 2 - Strength 2 C .10 .15
279 Nightcrawler - Energy 3 - Fighting 3 - Strength 3 C .10 .15
280 Super Skrull - Energy 4 - Fighting 4 - Strength 4 C .10 .15
281 Nebula - Energy 1 C .10 .15
282 Black Cat - Energy 2 C .10 .15
283 Sauron - Energy 3 C .10 .15
284 Electro - Energy 4 C .10 .15
285 Century - Energy 5 C .10 .15
286 Storm - Energy 6 C .10 .15
287 Cyclops - Energy 7 C .10 .15
288 Professor X - Energy 8 C .10 .15
289 Bloody Mary - Fighting 1 C .10 .15
290 Black Widow - Fighting 2 C .10 .15
291 Longshot - Fighting 3 C .10 .15
292 Nightcrawler - Fighting 4 C .10 .15
293 Venom - Fighting 5 C .10 .15
294 Wolverine - Fighting 6 C .10 .15
295 Domino - Fighting 7 C .10 .15
296 Cyber - Fighting 8 C .10 .15
297 Archangel - Strength 1 C .10 .15
298 Spider-Man - Strength 2 C .10 .15
299 War Machine - Strength 3 C .10 .15
300 Loki - Strength 4 C .10 .15
301 Cyber - Strength 5 C .10 .15
302 Super Skrull - Strength 6 C .10 .15
303 Thing - Strength 7 C .10 .15
304 Abomination - Strength 8 C .10 .15
305 Professor X - Alien Technology C .10 .15
306 Cyber - Booster Shot C .10 .15
307 Sabretooth - Chain C .10 .15
308 Hulk - City Bus U .40 .60
309 Wolverine - Crossbow U .40 .60
310 Loki - Divine Intervention C .10 .15
311 Iron Man - Dumpster U .40 .60
312 Magneto - EM Force Lines U .40 .60
313 Storm - Energy Booster C .10 .15
314 Gambit - Energy Enhancer U .40 .60
315 Cyclops - Energy Maximizer C .10 .15
316 Electro - Generator C .10 .15
317 Abomination - Girder C .10 .15
318 Black Widow - Hand Grenade C .10 .15
319 Venom - Hot Dog Cart C .10 .15
320 Rhino - Hunk of Asphalt C .10 .15
321 Thing - Lamp Post C .10 .15
322 Nebula - Laser Pistol U .40 .60
323 Domino - Machine Gun C .10 .15
324 Spider-Woman - Manhole Cover C .10 .15
325 Silver Surfer - Power Cosmic C .10 .15
326 Bishop - Power Lines C .10 .15
327 Punisher - Rocket Launcher C .10 .15
328 Bloody Mary - Sword C .10 .15
329 Colossus - Taxi Cab C .10 .15
330 Magneto, Juggernaut, Sabretooth - Teamwork - 6 to use C .10 .15
331 Magneto, Juggernaut, Sabretooth - Teamwork - 7 to use R 2.00 3.50
332 Magneto, Juggernaut, Sabretooth - Teamwork - 8 to use R 2.00 3.50
333 Wolverine, Cyclops, Beast - Teamwork - 6 to use C .10 .15
334 Wolverine, Cyclops, Beast - Teamwork - 7 to use R 2.00 3.50
335 Wolverine, Cyclops, Beast - Teamwork - 8 to use R 2.00 3.50
336 Thing, Mr. Fantastic, Human Torch - Teamwork - 6 to use C .10 .15
337 Thing, Mr. Fantastic, Human Torch - Teamwork - 7 to use R 2.00 3.50
338 Thing, Mr. Fantastic, Human Torch - Teamwork - 8 to use R 2.00 3.50
339 Longshot - Throwing Blades C .10 .15
340 Archangel - Training C .10 .15
341 Black Cat - Training C .10 .15
342 Century - Training C .10 .15
343 Human Torch - Training C .10 .15
344 Jubilee - Training C .10 .15
345 Sauron - Training C .10 .15
346 Rogue - Tree C .10 .15

Meta X

2017 Meta X Green Lantern

COMPLETE SET (150) 225.00 375.00
BOOSTER BOX (24 PACKS) 70.00 95.00
BOOSTER PACK (12 CARDS) 4.00 6.00
RELEASED ON DECEMBER 22, 2017
C1GL Superman C .15 .25
C2GL Saint Walker C .15 .25
C3GL Warth C .15 .25
C4GL Mogo C .15 .25
C5GL Iroque C .15 .25
C6GL Munk C .15 .25
C7GL Larfleeze C .15 .25
C8GL Dex-Starr C .15 .25
C9GL Mongul C .15 .25
C10GL Scarecrow C .15 .25
C11GL Carol Ferris C .15 .25
C12GL Star Sapphire C .15 .25
C13GL Deadman C .15 .25
C14GL Sinestro C .15 .25
C15GL Assault C .15 .25
C16GL Devastating Thoughts C .15 .25
C17GL Gathering Strength C .15 .25
C18GL Heralds of the Corps C .15 .25
C19GL Lantern Synergy C .15 .25
C20GL Love Conquers All C .15 .25
C21GL Meta Superiority C .15 .25
C22GL Moment Of Peace C .15 .25
C23GL Preparations C .15 .25
C24GL Recharge C .15 .25
C25GL Transformation C .15 .25
C26GL Triumph C .15 .25
C27GL Uncommon Allies C .15 .25
C28GL United C .15 .25
C29GL Upper Hand C .15 .25
C30GL Willpower C .15 .25
C31GL Strength 1 C .15 .25
C32GL Strength 1 C .15 .25
C33GL Strength 2 C .15 .25
C34GL Strength 2 C .15 .25
C35GL Strength 3 C .15 .25
C36GL Strength 4 C .15 .25
C37GL Strength 5 C .15 .25

C38GL Strength 5 C	.15	.25
C39GL Strength 6 C	.15	.25
C40GL Strength 7 C	.15	.25
C41GL Intelligence 1 C	.15	.25
C42GL Intelligence 2 C	.15	.25
C43GL Intelligence 2 C	.15	.25
C44GL Intelligence 3 C	.15	.25
C45GL Intelligence 3 C	.15	.25
C46GL Intelligence 4 C	.15	.25
C47GL Intelligence 5 C	.15	.25
C48GL Intelligence 5 C	.15	.25
C49GL Intelligence 6 C	.15	.25
C50GL Intelligence 7 C	.15	.25
C51GL Special 1 C	.15	.25
C52GL Special 2 C	.15	.25
C53GL Special 3 C	.15	.25
C54GL Special 4 C	.15	.25
C55GL Special 4 C	.15	.25
C56GL Special 5 C	.15	.25
C57GL Special 5 C	.15	.25
C58GL Special 6 C	.15	.25
C59GL Special 7 C	.15	.25
C60GL Special 7 C	.15	.25
U61GL Hal Jordan U	.25	.40
U62GL Saint Walker U	.25	.40
U63GL Nekron U	.25	.40
U64GL Green Lantern U	.25	.40
U65GL Green Lantern U	.25	.40
U66GL Green Lantern U	.25	.40
U67GL Green Lantern U	.25	.40
U68GL Green Lantern U	.25	.40
U69GL Green Lantern U	.25	.40
U70GL Green Lantern U	.25	.40
U71GL Kilowogg U	.25	.40
U72GL Green Lantern U	.25	.40
U73GL Larfleeze U	.25	.40
U74GL Atrocitus U	.25	.40
U75GL Bleez U	.25	.40
U76GL Guy Gardner U	.25	.40
U77GL Beware Your Fears U	.25	.40
U78GL Blood and Rage U	.25	.40
U79GL Burn You All U	.25	.40
U80GL Communion U	.25	.40
U81GL Green Lantern's Light U	.25	.40
U82GL Hope Burns Bright U	.25	.40
U83GL In Blackest Night U	.25	.40
U84GL In Brightest Day U	.25	.40
U85GL In Raging Night U	.25	.40
U86GL Man Beyond Tomorrow U	.25	.40
U87GL Not Yours! U	.25	.40
U88GL Power Players U	.25	.40
U89GL Sifting Through the Wreckage U	.25	.40
U90GL The Darkness Grows U	.25	.40
U91GL What's Mine is Mine U	.25	.40
U92GL Strength 2 U	.25	.40
U93GL Strength 3 U	.25	.40
U94GL Strength 4 U	.25	.40
U95GL Intelligence 1 U	.25	.40
U96GL Intelligence 3 U	.25	.40
U97GL Intelligence 5 U	.25	.40
U98GL Special 4 U	.25	.40
U99GL Special 5 U	.25	.40
R101GL Sinestro R	2.00	3.50
R102GL Green Arrow R	2.00	3.50
R103GL Black Hand R	2.00	3.50
R104GL Kyle Rayner R	2.00	3.50
R105GL Saint Walker R	2.00	3.50
R106GL Green Lantern R	2.00	3.50
R107GL Atom R	2.00	3.50
R108GL Iroque R	2.00	3.50
R109GL Agent Orange R	2.00	3.50
R110GL Hal Jordan R	2.00	3.50
R111GL Atrocitus R	2.00	3.50
R112GL Lyssa Drak R	2.00	3.50
R113GL The Anti-Monitor R	2.00	3.50
R114GL Star Sapphire R	2.00	3.50
R115GL Wonder Woman R	2.00	3.50
R116GL Kyle Rayner R	2.00	3.50
R117GL Beware My Power R	2.00	3.50
R118GL Black Hole R	2.00	3.50
R119GL Burst of Power R	2.00	3.50
R120GL Coming Storm R	2.00	3.50
R121GL Endless Brawl R	2.00	3.50
R122GL Heroism R	2.00	3.50
R123GL Join Our Fight R	2.00	3.50
R124GL Legion of Doom R	2.00	3.50
R125GL Power Ring R	2.00	3.50
R126GL Purifying Shield R	2.00	3.50
R127GL Shifting the Meta R	2.00	3.50
R128GL The Dead Shall Rise R	2.00	3.50
R129GL Strength 5 R	2.00	3.50
R130GL Strength 6 R	2.00	3.50
R131GL Strength 7 R	2.00	3.50
R132GL Intelligence 4 R	2.00	3.50
R133GL Intelligence 7 R	2.00	3.50
R134GL Intelligence 7 R	2.00	3.50
R135GL Special 4 R	2.00	3.50
R136GL Special 6 R	2.00	3.50
R137GL Special 7 R	2.00	3.50
R138GL STR/INT/SP 5 R	2.00	3.50
R139GL STR/INT/SP 6 R	2.00	3.50
R140GL STR/INT/SP 7 R	2.00	3.50
U100GL Special 6 U	2.00	3.50
UR145GL Superboy-Prime UR	25.00	40.00
UR146GL Green Lantern UR	25.00	40.00
XR141GL Batman XR	15.00	25.00
XR142GL Parallax XR	15.00	25.00
XR143GL Sinestro XR	15.00	25.00
XR144GL Superman XR	15.00	25.00
NNO Active Player Card NR	3.00	5.00
NNO Active Player Card NR	3.00	5.00
NNO Active Player Card NR	3.00	5.00
NNO Active Player Card NR	3.00	5.00

2017 Meta X Green Lantern Foil

COMPLETE SET (140)	200.00	300.00
C1GL Superman C	.60	1.00
C2GL Saint Walker C	.60	1.00
C3GL Warth C	.60	1.00
C4GL Mogo C	.60	1.00
C5GL Iroque C	.60	1.00
C6GL Munk C	.60	1.00
C7GL Larfleeze C	.60	1.00
C8GL Dex-Starr C	.60	1.00
C9GL Mongul C	.60	1.00
C10GL Scarecrow C	.60	1.00
C11GL Carol Ferris C	.60	1.00
C12GL Star Sapphire C	.60	1.00
C13GL Deadman C	.60	1.00
C14GL Sinestro C	.60	1.00
C15GL Assault C	.60	1.00
C16GL Devastating Thoughts C	.60	1.00
C17GL Gathering Strength C	.60	1.00
C18GL Heralds of the Corps C	.60	1.00
C19GL Lantern Synergy C	.60	1.00
C20GL Love Conquers All C	.60	1.00
C21GL Meta Superiority C	.60	1.00
C22GL Moment Of Peace C	.60	1.00
C23GL Preparations C	.60	1.00
C24GL Recharge C	.60	1.00
C25GL Transformation C	.60	1.00
C26GL Triumph C	.60	1.00
C27GL Uncommon Allies C	.60	1.00
C28GL United C	.60	1.00
C29GL Upper Hand C	.60	1.00
C30GL Willpower C	.60	1.00
C31GL Strength 1 C	.60	1.00
C32GL Strength 1 C	.60	1.00
C33GL Strength 2 C	.60	1.00
C34GL Strength 2 C	.60	1.00
C35GL Strength 3 C	.60	1.00
C36GL Strength 4 C	.60	1.00
C37GL Strength 5 C	.60	1.00
C38GL Strength 5 C	.60	1.00
C39GL Strength 6 C	.60	1.00
C40GL Strength 7 C	.60	1.00
C41GL Intelligence 1 C	.60	1.00
C42GL Intelligence 2 C	.60	1.00
C43GL Intelligence 2 C	.60	1.00
C44GL Intelligence 3 C	.60	1.00
C45GL Intelligence 3 C	.60	1.00
C46GL Intelligence 4 C	.60	1.00
C47GL Intelligence 5 C	.60	1.00
C48GL Intelligence 5 C	.60	1.00
C49GL Intelligence 6 C	.60	1.00
C50GL Intelligence 7 C	.60	1.00
C51GL Special 1 C	.60	1.00
C52GL Special 2 C	.60	1.00
C53GL Special 3 C	.60	1.00
C54GL Special 4 C	.60	1.00
C55GL Special 4 C	.60	1.00
C56GL Special 5 C	.60	1.00
C57GL Special 5 C	.60	1.00
C58GL Special 6 C	.60	1.00
C59GL Special 7 C	.60	1.00
C60GL Special 7 C	.60	1.00
U61GL Hal Jordan U	.75	2.00
U62GL Saint Walker U	.75	2.00
U63GL Nekron U	.75	2.00
U64GL Green Lantern U	.75	2.00
U65GL Green Lantern U	.75	2.00
U66GL Green Lantern U	.75	2.00
U67GL Green Lantern U	.75	2.00
U68GL Green Lantern U	.75	2.00
U69GL Green Lantern U	.75	2.00
U70GL Green Lantern U	.75	2.00
U71GL Kilowogg U	.75	2.00
U72GL Green Lantern U	.75	2.00
U73GL Larfleeze U	.75	2.00
U74GL Atrocitus U	.75	2.00
U75GL Bleez U	.75	2.00
U76GL Guy Gardner U	.75	2.00
U77GL Beware Your Fears U	.75	2.00
U78GL Blood and Rage U	.75	2.00
U79GL Burn You All U	.75	2.00
U80GL Communion U	.75	2.00
U81GL Green Lantern's Light U	.75	2.00
U82GL Hope Burns Bright U	.75	2.00
U83GL In Blackest Night U	.75	2.00
U84GL In Brightest Day U	.75	2.00
U85GL In Raging Night U	.75	2.00
U86GL Man Beyond Tomorrow U	.75	2.00
U87GL Not Yours! U	.75	2.00
U88GL Power Players U	.75	2.00
U89GL Sifting Through the Wreckage U	.75	2.00
U90GL The Darkness Grows U	.75	2.00
U91GL What's Mine is Mine U	.75	2.00
U92GL Strength 2 U	.75	2.00
U93GL Strength 3 U	.75	2.00
U94GL Strength 4 U	.75	2.00
U95GL Intelligence 1 U	.75	2.00
U96GL Intelligence 3 U	.75	2.00
U97GL Intelligence 5 U	.75	2.00
U98GL Special 4 U	.75	2.00
U99GL Special 5 U	.75	2.00
R101GL Sinestro R	3.00	5.00
R102GL Green Arrow R	3.00	5.00
R103GL Black Hand R	3.00	5.00
R104GL Kyle Rayner R	3.00	5.00
R105GL Saint Walker R	3.00	5.00
R106GL Green Lantern R	3.00	5.00
R107GL Atom R	3.00	5.00
R108GL Iroque R	3.00	5.00
R109GL Agent Orange R	3.00	5.00
R110GL Hal Jordan R	3.00	5.00
R111GL Atrocitus R	3.00	5.00
R112GL Lyssa Drak R	3.00	5.00
R113GL The Anti-Monitor R	3.00	5.00
R114GL Star Sapphire R	3.00	5.00
R115GL Wonder Woman R	3.00	5.00
R116GL Kyle Rayner R	3.00	5.00
R117GL Beware My Power R	3.00	5.00
R118GL Black Hole R	3.00	5.00
R119GL Burst of Power R	3.00	5.00
R120GL Coming Storm R	3.00	5.00
R121GL Endless Brawl R	3.00	5.00
R122GL Heroism R	3.00	5.00
R123GL Join Our Fight R	3.00	5.00
R124GL Legion of Doom R	3.00	5.00
R125GL Power Ring R	3.00	5.00
R126GL Purifying Shield R	3.00	5.00
R127GL Shifting the Meta R	3.00	5.00
R128GL The Dead Shall Rise R	3.00	5.00
R129GL Strength 5 R	3.00	5.00
R130GL Strength 6 R	3.00	5.00
R131GL Strength 7 R	3.00	5.00
R132GL Intelligence 4 R	3.00	5.00
R133GL Intelligence 7 R	3.00	5.00
R134GL Intelligence 7 R	3.00	5.00
R135GL Special 4 R	3.00	5.00
R136GL Special 6 R	3.00	5.00
R137GL Special 7 R	3.00	5.00
R138GL STR/INT/SP 5 R	3.00	5.00
R139GL STR/INT/SP 6 R	3.00	5.00
R140GL STR/INT/SP 7 R	3.00	5.00
U100GL Special 6 U	3.00	5.00

2017 Meta X Justice League

COMPLETE SET (146)	160.00	250.00
BOOSTER BOX (24 PACKS)	65.00	95.00
BOOSTER PACK (12 CARDS)	3.00	5.00
RELEASED ON AUGUST 4, 2017		
C1JL Alfred Pennyworth - Butler C	.15	.25
C2JL Amanda Waller - The Wall C	.15	.25
C3JL Black Canary - Dinah Lance C	.15	.25
C4JL Hawkgirl - Gravity-defying Nth C	.15	.25
C5JL Deadman - Boston Brand C	.15	.25
C6JL Firestorm - Nuclear Man C	.15	.25
C7JL Hawkman - Carter Hall C	.15	.25
C8JL Martian Manhunter - J'onn J'onzz C	.15	.25
C9JL Red Tornado - John Smith C	.15	.25
C10JL Starfire - Koriand'r C	.15	.25
C11JL Superboy - Kon-El C	.15	.25
C12JL Mister Freeze - Victor Fries C	.15	.25
C13JL Bane - Professional Criminal C	.15	.25
C14JL Scarecrow - Jonathan Crane C	.15	.25
C15JL General Zod - Dru-Zod C	.15	.25
C16JL Poison Ivy - Pamela Isley C	.15	.25
C17JL Ra's Al Ghul - The Demons Head C	.15	.25
C18JL Absence of Fear C	.15	.25
C19JL Leap Into Action C	.15	.25
C20JL Birds of a Feather C	.15	.25
C21JL Disgraced C	.15	.25
C22JL Echolocation C	.15	.25
C23JL Rise From the Ashes C	.15	.25
C24JL Injustice C	.15	.25
C25JL Battle Frenzy C	.15	.25
C26JL Lose the Battle to Win the War C	.15	.25
C27JL Overboard C	.15	.25
C28JL Combat Mastery C	.15	.25
C29JL Resurrection of Power C	.15	.25
C30JL Reinforcements C	.15	.25
C31JL 1 Strength C	.15	.25
C32JL 1 Intelligence C	.15	.25
C33JL 1 Special C	.15	.25
C34JL 1 Special C	.15	.25
C35JL 2 Strength C	.15	.25
C36JL 2 Strength C	.15	.25
C37JL 2 Strength C	.15	.25
C38JL 2 Intelligence C	.15	.25
C39JL 2 Special C	.15	.25
C40JL 3 Strength C	.15	.25
C41JL 7 Special C	.15	.25
C42JL 3 Intelligence C	.15	.25
C43JL 3 Intelligence C	.15	.25
C44JL 3 Special C	.15	.25
C45JL 4 Strength C	.15	.25
C46JL 4 Intelligence C	.15	.25
C47JL 4 Special C	.15	.25
C48JL 4 Special C	.15	.25
C49JL 4 Special C	.15	.25
C50JL 5 Strength C	.15	.25
C51JL 5 Intelligence C	.15	.25
C52JL 5 Intelligence C	.15	.25
C53JL 5 Special C	.15	.25
C54JL 6 Strength C	.15	.25
C55JL 6 Intelligence C	.15	.25
C56JL 6 Special C	.15	.25
C57JL 7 Strength C	.15	.25
C58JL 7 Intelligence C	.15	.25
C59JL 3 Strength C	.15	.25
C60JL 7 Special C	.15	.25
U61JL Batgirl - Barbara Gordon U	.25	.40
U62JL Batman - Dark Knight U	.25	.40
U63JL Blue Beetle - Ted Kord U	.25	.40
U64JL Vixen - Mari McCabe U	.25	.40
U65JL Cyborg - Victor Stone U	.25	.40
U66JL Green Arrow - Emerald Archer U	.25	.40
U67JL Green Lantern - Hal Jordan U	.25	.40
U68JL Nightwing - Dick Grayson U	.25	.40
U69JL Krypto - The Super Dog U	.25	.40
U70JL Robin - Boy Wonder U	.25	.40
U71JL Supergirl - Kara Zor-El U	.25	.40
U72JL Superman - Man of Steel U	.25	.40
U73JL Brainiac - Collector of Worlds U	.25	.40
U74JL Harley Quinn - Former Psychiatrist U	.25	.40
U75JL Sinestro - Intergalactic Criminal U	.25	.40
U76JL Solomon Grundy - Cyrus Gold U	.25	.40
U77JL Victorious U	.25	.40
U78JL Unexpected Turnaround U	.25	.40
U79JL Transfer of Power U	.25	.40
U80JL Don't Go It Alone U	.25	.40
U81JL Point Blank U	.25	.40
U82JL Joke's On You U	.25	.40
U83JL Passion For The Hunt U	.25	.40
U84JL Power Corrupts U	.25	.40
U85JL Push and Pull U	.25	.40
U86JL Rebirth U	.25	.40
U87JL Upper Hand U	.25	.40
U88JL Sleight of Hand U	.25	.40
U89JL Paralysis U	.25	.40
U90JL Strength in Numbers U	.25	.40
U91JL Meta Superiority U	.25	.40
U92JL 1 STR/INT/SP U	.25	.40
U93JL 4 Intelligence U	.25	.40
U94JL 4 STR/INT/SP U	.25	.40
U95JL 5 STR/INT/SP U	.25	.40
U96JL 6 Intelligence U	.25	.40
U97JL 6 Special U	.25	.40
U98JL 7 Strength U	.25	.40
U99JL 7 Intelligence U	.25	.40
U100JL 7 Special U	.25	.40

Card	Low	High
R101JL Aquaman - Arthur Curry R	.60	1.00
R102JL Atom - Ray Palmer R	.60	1.00
R103JL Doctor Fate - Agent of the Lords of Order R	.60	1.00
R104JL John Constantine - Occult Detective R	.60	1.00
R105JL Shazam - Captain Marvel R	.60	1.00
R106JL The Flash - Scarlet Speedster R	.60	1.00
R107JL Wonder Woman - Amazon Princess R	.60	1.00
R108JL Zatanna - Magician R	.60	1.00
R109JL Bizarro - Imperfect Duplicate R	.60	1.00
R110JL Black Adam - Teth Adam R	.60	1.00
R111JL Darkseid - Uxas R	.60	1.00
R112JL Deathstroke - Slade Wilson R	.60	1.00
R113JL Doomsday - Destroyer R	.60	1.00
R114JL Lex Luthor - CEO of LexCorp R	.60	1.00
R115JL The Joker - Clown Prince of Crime R	.60	1.00
R116JL Against the Current R	.60	1.00
R117JL Come and Take It R	.60	1.00
R118JL Evil Parade R	.60	1.00
R119JL Knockout R	.60	1.00
R120JL Microscopic Victory R	.60	1.00
R121JL Showdown R	.60	1.00
R122JL Right on Target R	.60	1.00
R123JL Ingenuity R	.60	1.00
R124JL Teleportation R	.60	1.00
R125JL With Friends Like These R	.60	1.00
R126JL Inherent Weakness R	.60	1.00
R127JL 1 Intelligence R	.60	1.00
R128JL 2 Special R	.60	1.00
R129JL 3 Intelligence R	.60	1.00
R130JL 3 Special R	.60	1.00
R131JL 4 Strength R	.60	1.00
R132JL 5 Strength R	.60	1.00
R133JL 5 STR/INT R	.60	1.00
R134JL 5 STR/SP R	.60	1.00
R135JL 5 INT/SP R	.60	1.00
R136JL 6 Strength R	.60	1.00
R137JL 7 Strength R	.60	1.00
R138JL 7 Intelligence R	.60	1.00
R139JL 7 Special R	.60	1.00
R140JL 7 STR/INT/SP R	.60	1.00
XR141JL Wonder Woman - Princess Diana of Themyscira XR	15.00	20.00
XR142JL Darkseid - Ruler of Apokolips XR	15.00	20.00
XR143JL Harley Quinn - Dr. Harleen Quinzel XR	15.00	20.00
XR144JL The Joker - Certifiably Insane XR	15.00	20.00
UR145JL Batman - The Caped Crusader UR	30.00	50.00
UR146JL Superman - Last Son of Krypton UR	30.00	50.00

2017 Meta X Justice League Foil

Card	Low	High
COMPLETE SET (146)	280.00	450.00
BOOSTER BOX (24 PACKS)	65.00	95.00
BOOSTER PACK (12 CARDS)	3.00	5.00
RELEASED ON AUGUST 4, 2017		
C1JL Alfred Pennyworth - Butler C	.25	.40
C2JL Amanda Waller - The Wall C	.25	.40
C3JL Black Canary - Dinah Lance C	.25	.40
C4JL Hawkgirl - Gravity-defying Nth C	.25	.40
C5JL Deadman - Boston Brand C	.25	.40
C6JL Firestorm - Nuclear Man C	.25	.40
C7JL Hawkman - Carter Hall C	.25	.40
C8JL Martian Manhunter - J'onn J'onzz C	.25	.40
C9JL Red Tornado - John Smith C	.25	.40
C10JL Starfire - Koriand'r C	.25	.40
C11JL Superboy - Kon-El C	.25	.40
C12JL Mister Freeze - Victor Fries C	.25	.40
C13JL Bane - Professional Criminal C	.25	.40
C14JL Scarecrow - Jonathan Crane C	.25	.40
C15JL General Zod - Dru-Zod C	.25	.40
C16JL Poison Ivy - Pamela Isley C	.25	.40
C17JL Ra's Al Ghul - The Demons Head C	.25	.40
C18JL Absence of Fear C	.25	.40
C19JL Leap Into Action C	.25	.40
C20JL Birds of a Feather C	.25	.40
C21JL Disgraced C	.25	.40
C22JL Echolocation C	.25	.40
C23JL Rise From the Ashes C	.25	.40
C24JL Injustice C	.25	.40
C25JL Battle Frenzy C	.25	.40
C26JL Lose the Battle to Win the War C	.25	.40
C27JL Overboard C	.25	.40
C28JL Combat Mastery C	.25	.40
C29JL Resurrection of Power C	.25	.40
C30JL Reinforcements C	.25	.40
C31JL 1 Strength C	.25	.40
C32JL 1 Intelligence C	.25	.40
C33JL 1 Special C	.25	.40
C34JL 1 Special C	.25	.40
C35JL 2 Strength C	.25	.40
C36JL 2 Strength C	.25	.40
C37JL 2 Strength C	.25	.40
C38JL 2 Intelligence C	.25	.40
C39JL 2 Special C	.25	.40
C40JL 3 Strength C	.25	.40
C41JL 7 Special C	.25	.40
C42JL 3 Intelligence C	.25	.40
C43JL 3 Intelligence C	.25	.40
C44JL 3 Special C	.25	.40
C45JL 4 Strength C	.25	.40
C46JL 4 Intelligence C	.25	.40
C47JL 4 Special C	.25	.40
C48JL 4 Special C	.25	.40
C49JL 4 Special C	.25	.40
C50JL 5 Strength C	.25	.40
C51JL 5 Intelligence C	.25	.40
C52JL 5 Intelligence C	.25	.40
C53JL 5 Special C	.25	.40
C54JL 6 Strength C	.25	.40
C55JL 6 Intelligence C	.25	.40
C56JL 6 Special C	.25	.40
C57JL 7 Strength C	.25	.40
C58JL 7 Intelligence C	.25	.40
C59JL 3 Strength C	.25	.40
C60JL 7 Special C	.25	.40
U61JL Batgirl - Barbara Gordon U	.60	1.00
U62JL Batman - Dark Knight U	.60	1.00
U63JL Blue Beetle - Ted Kord U	.60	1.00
U64JL Vixen - Mari McCabe U	.60	1.00
U65JL Cyborg - Victor Stone U	.60	1.00
U66JL Green Arrow - Emerald Archer U	.60	1.00
U67JL Green Lantern - Hal Jordan U	.60	1.00
U68JL Nightwing - Dick Grayson U	.60	1.00
U69JL Krypto - The Super Dog U	.60	1.00
U70JL Robin - Boy Wonder U	.60	1.00
U71JL Supergirl - Kara Zor-El U	.60	1.00
U72JL Superman - Man of Steel U	.60	1.00
U73JL Brainiac - Collector of Worlds U	.60	1.00
U74JL Harley Quinn - Former Psychiatrist U	.60	1.00
U75JL Sinestro - Intergalactic Criminal U	.60	1.00
U76JL Solomon - Grundy Cyrus Gold U	.60	1.00
U77JL Victorious U	.60	1.00
U78JL Unexpected Turnaround U	.60	1.00
U79JL Transfer of Power U	.60	1.00
U80JL Don't Go It Alone U	.60	1.00
U81JL Point Blank U	.60	1.00
U82JL Joke's On You U	.60	1.00
U83JL Passion For The Hunt U	.60	1.00
U84JL Power Corrupts U	.60	1.00
U85JL Push and Pull U	.60	1.00
U86JL Rebirth U	.60	1.00
U87JL Upper Hand U	.60	1.00
U88JL Sleight of Hand U	.60	1.00
U89JL Paralysis U	.60	1.00
U90JL Strength in Numbers U	.60	1.00
U91JL Meta Superiority U	.60	1.00
U92JL 1 STR/INT/SP U	.60	1.00
U93JL 4 Intelligence U	.60	1.00
U94JL 4 STR/INT/SP U	.60	1.00
U95JL 5 STR/INT/SP U	.60	1.00
U96JL 6 Intelligence U	.60	1.00
U97JL 6 Special U	.60	1.00
U98JL 7 Strength U	.60	1.00
U99JL 7 Intelligence U	.60	1.00
U100JL 7 Special U	.60	1.00
R101JL Aquaman - Arthur Curry R	3.00	5.00
R102JL Atom - Ray Palmer R	3.00	5.00
R103JL Doctor Fate - Agent of the Lords of Order R	3.00	5.00
R104JL John Constantine - Occult Detective R	3.00	5.00
R105JL Shazam - Captain Marvel R	3.00	5.00
R106JL The Flash - Scarlet Speedster R	3.00	5.00
R107JL Wonder Woman - Amazon Princess R	3.00	5.00
R108JL Zatanna - Magician R	3.00	5.00
R109JL Bizarro - Imperfect Duplicate R	3.00	5.00
R110JL Black Adam - Teth Adam R	3.00	5.00
R111JL Darkseid - Uxas R	3.00	5.00
R112JL Deathstroke - Slade Wilson R	3.00	5.00
R113JL Doomsday - Destroyer R	3.00	5.00
R114JL Lex Luthor - CEO of LexCorp R	3.00	5.00
R115JL The Joker - Clown Prince of Crime R	3.00	5.00
R116JL Against the Current R	3.00	5.00
R117JL Come and Take It R	3.00	5.00
R118JL Evil Parade R	3.00	5.00
R119JL Knockout R	3.00	5.00
R120JL Microscopic Victory R	3.00	5.00
R121JL Showdown R	3.00	5.00
R122JL Right on Target R	3.00	5.00
R123JL Ingenuity R	3.00	5.00
R124JL Teleportation R	3.00	5.00
R125JL With Friends Like These R	3.00	5.00
R126JL Inherent Weakness R	3.00	5.00
R127JL 1 Intelligence R	3.00	5.00
R128JL 2 Special R	3.00	5.00
R129JL 3 Intelligence R	3.00	5.00
R130JL 3 Special R	3.00	5.00
R131JL 4 Strength R	3.00	5.00
R132JL 5 Strength R	3.00	5.00
R133JL 5 STR/INT R	3.00	5.00
R134JL 5 STR/SP R	3.00	5.00
R135JL 5 INT/SP R	3.00	5.00
R136JL 6 Strength R	3.00	5.00
R137JL 7 Strength R	3.00	5.00
R138JL 7 Intelligence R	3.00	5.00
R139JL 7 Special R	3.00	5.00
R140JL 7 STR/INT/SP R	3.00	5.00
XR141JL Wonder Woman - Princess Diana of Themyscira XR	15.00	20.00
XR142JL Darkseid - Ruler of Apokolips XR	15.00	20.00
XR143JL Harley Quinn - Dr. Harleen Quinzel XR	15.00	20.00
XR144JL The Joker - Certifiably Insane XR	15.00	20.00
UR145JL Batman - The Caped Crusader UR	30.00	50.00
UR146JL Superman - Last Son of Krypton UR	30.00	50.00

2017 Meta X Justice League Starter Deck

Card	Low	High
COMPLETE SET (72)	10.00	20.00
STARTER DECK (50 CARDS)	15.00	20.00
RELEASED ON AUGUST 4, 2017		
S1JL Harley Quinn - Former Psychiatrist	.75	1.25
S2JL Brainiac - Collector of Worlds	.60	1.00
S3JL Sinestro - Intergalactic Criminal	.60	1.00
S4JL Solomon Grundy - Cyrus Gold	.15	.25
S5JL Joke's On You	1.25	2.00
S6JL Push and Pull	.60	1.00
S7JL Transfer of Power	.60	1.00
S8JL 6 Strength	.15	.25
S9JL 3 Strength	.15	.25
S10JL 2 Strength	.15	.25
S11JL 1 Strength	.15	.25
S12JL 7 Intelligence	.15	.25
S13JL 4 Intelligence	.15	.25
S14JL 2 Intelligence	.15	.25
S15JL 1 Intelligence	.15	.25
S16JL 6 Special	.15	.25
S17JL 5 Special	.15	.25
S18JL 3 Special	.15	.25
S19JL Superman - Man of Steel	.15	.25
S20JL Supergirl - Kara Zor-El	.15	.25
S21JL Krypto - The Super Dog	.15	.25
S22JL Green Arrow - Emerald Archer	.15	.25
S23JL Rebirth	.15	.25
S24JL Passion For The Hunt	.15	.25
S25JL Power Corrupts	.15	.25
S26JL 7 Strength	.15	.25
S27JL 6 Strength	.15	.25
S28JL 3 Strength	.15	.25
S29JL 2 Strength	.15	.25
S30JL 1 Strength	.15	.25
S31JL 3 Intelligence	.15	.25
S32JL 2 Intelligence	.15	.25
S33JL 1 Intelligence	.15	.25
S34JL 5 Special	.15	.25
S35JL 4 Special	.15	.25
S36JL 1 Special	.15	.25
S37JL Cyborg - Victor Stone	.15	.25
S38JL Green Lantern - Hal Jordan	.15	.25
S39JL Blue Beetle - Ted Kord	.15	.25
S40JL Vixen - Mari McCabe	.15	.25
S41JL Sleight of Hand	.15	.25
S42JL Strength in Numbers	.15	.25
S43JL Meta Superiority	.15	.25
S44JL 4 Strength	.15	.25
S45JL 3 Strength	.15	.25
S46JL 2 Strength	.15	.25
S47JL 1 Strength	.15	.25
S48JL 5 Intelligence	.15	.25
S49JL 3 Intelligence	.15	.25
S50JL 1 Intelligence	.15	.25
S51JL 6 Special	.15	.25
S52JL 5 Special	.15	.25
S53JL 4 Special	.15	.25
S54JL 3 Special	.15	.25
S55JL Batman - Dark Knight	.15	.25
S56JL Batgirl - Barbara Gordon	.15	.25
S57JL Nightwing - Dick Grayson	.75	1.25
S58JL Robin - Boy Wonder	.15	.25
S59JL Don't Go It Alone	.15	.25
S60JL Point Blank	.15	.25
S61JL Upper Hand	.60	1.00
S62JL 4 Strength	.15	.25
S63JL 3 Strength	.15	.25
S64JL 2 Strength	.15	.25
S65JL 1 Strength	.15	.25
S66JL 7 Intelligence	.15	.25
S67JL 5 Intelligence	.75	1.25
S68JL 4 Intelligence	.15	.25
S69JL 1 Intelligence	.75	1.25
S70JL 6 Special	.15	.25
S71JL 4 Special	.15	.25
S72JL 1 Special	.15	.25

2017 Meta X Justice League Starter Deck Foil

Card	Low	High
COMPLETE SET (72)	40.00	70.00
STARTER DECK (50 CARDS)	15.00	20.00
RELEASED ON AUGUST 4, 2017		
S1JL Harley Quinn - Former Psychiatrist S	.60	1.00
S2JL Brainiac - Collector of Worlds S	.60	1.00
S3JL Sinestro - Intergalactic Criminal S	.60	1.00
S4JL Solomon Grundy - Cyrus Gold S	.60	1.00
S5JL Joke's On You S	.60	1.00
S6JL Push and Pull S	.60	1.00
S7JL Transfer of Power S	.60	1.00
S8JL 6 Strength S	.60	1.00
S9JL 3 Strength S	.60	1.00
S10JL 2 Strength S	.60	1.00
S11JL 1 Strength S	.60	1.00
S12JL 7 Intelligence S	.60	1.00
S13JL 4 Intelligence S	.60	1.00
S14JL 2 Intelligence S	.60	1.00
S15JL 1 Intelligence S	.60	1.00
S16JL 6 Special S	.60	1.00
S17JL 5 Special S	.60	1.00
S18JL 3 Special S	.60	1.00
S19JL Superman - Man of Steel S	.60	1.00
S20JL Supergirl - Kara Zor-El S	.60	1.00
S21JL Krypto - The Super Dog S	.60	1.00
S22JL Green Arrow - Emerald Archer S	.60	1.00
S23JL Rebirth S	.60	1.00
S24JL Passion For The Hunt S	.60	1.00
S25JL Power Corrupts S	.60	1.00
S26JL 7 Strength S	.60	1.00
S27JL 6 Strength S	.60	1.00
S28JL 3 Strength S	.60	1.00
S29JL 2 Strength S	.60	1.00
S30JL 1 Strength S	.60	1.00
S31JL 3 Intelligence S	.60	1.00
S32JL 2 Intelligence S	.60	1.00
S33JL 1 Intelligence S	.60	1.00
S34JL 5 Special S	.60	1.00
S35JL 4 Special S	.60	1.00
S36JL 1 Special S	.60	1.00
S37JL Cyborg - Victor Stone S	.60	1.00
S38JL Green Lantern - Hal Jordan S	.60	1.00
S39JL Blue Beetle - Ted Kord S	.60	1.00
S40JL Vixen - Mari McCabe S	.60	1.00
S41JL Sleight of Hand S	.60	1.00
S42JL Strength in Numbers S	.60	1.00
S43JL Meta Superiority S	.60	1.00
S44JL 4 Strength S	.60	1.00
S45JL 3 Strength S	.60	1.00
S46JL 2 Strength S	.60	1.00
S47JL 1 Strength S	.60	1.00
S48JL 5 Intelligence S	.60	1.00
S49JL 3 Intelligence S	.60	1.00
S50JL 1 Intelligence S	.60	1.00
S51JL 6 Special S	.60	1.00
S52JL 5 Special S	.60	1.00
S53JL 4 Special S	.60	1.00
S54JL 3 Special S	.60	1.00
S55JL Batman - Dark Knight S	.60	1.00
S56JL Batgirl - Barbara Gordon S	.60	1.00
S57JL Nightwing - Dick Grayson S	.60	1.00
S58JL Robin - Boy Wonder S	.60	1.00
S59JL Don't Go It Alone S	.60	1.00
S60JL Point Blank S	.60	1.00
S61JL Upper Hand S	.60	1.00
S62JL 4 Strength S	.60	1.00
S63JL 3 Strength S	.60	1.00
S64JL 2 Strength S	.60	1.00
S65JL 1 Strength S	.60	1.00
S66JL 7 Intelligence S	.60	1.00
S67JL 5 Intelligence S	.60	1.00
S68JL 4 Intelligence S	.60	1.00
S69JL 1 Intelligence S	.60	1.00
S70JL 6 Special S	.60	1.00
S71JL 4 Special S	.60	1.00
S72JL 1 Special S	.60	1.00

2017 Meta X Justice League Promos

Card	Low	High
P1JL 1 STR/INT/SP		
P2JL Victorious		
P3JL 4 STR/INT/SP		
P4JL Unexpected Turnaround		
P5JL Batman - Dark Knight		
P6JL Superman - Man of Steel		
P7JL Green Lantern - Hal Jordan		
P8JL Harley Quinn - Former Psychiatrist		
P9JL Aquaman - Arthur Curry	10.00	15.00

(2017 SDCC Exclusive)		
P10JL The Joker - Clown Prince of Crime	10.00	15.00
(2017 SDCC Exclusive)		
P11JL Wonder Woman - Amazon Princess	10.00	15.00
(2017 SDCC Exclusive)		
P12JL Lex Luthor - CEO of LexCorp	10.00	15.00
(2017 SDCC Exclusive)		
P13JL Shazam - Captain Marvel		
P14JL Darkseid - Uxas		
P15JL The Flash - Scarlet Speedster		
P16JL Doomsday - Destroyer		
P17JL Paralysis		
P18JL 5 STR/INT/SP		
P19JL Battle Frenzy		
P20JL Disgraced	1.50	2.50

2018 Meta X Attack on Titan

RELEASED ON MARCH 30, 2018		
C1AT Armin Arlelt – Young Genius C	.15	.25
C2AT Christa Lenz – Noble Daughter C	.15	.25
C3AT Ymir – Freckles C	.15	.25
C4AT Hannes – Family Friend C	.15	.25
C5AT Kitz Woermann – Paranoid C	.15	.25
C6AT Rico Brzenska – Composed Leader C	.15	.25
C7AT Hitch Dreyse – Persuasive C	.15	.25
C8AT Marlo Freudenberg – Bowl Cut C	.15	.25
C9AT Eld Gin – Adept Slayer C	.15	.25
C10AT Eren Jaeger – Suicidal Bastard C	.15	.25
C11AT Jean Kirschtein – Confident C	.15	.25
C12AT Oruo Bozad – Outspoken C	.15	.25
C13AT Petra Rall – Kind Scout C	.15	.25
C14AT Grisha Jaeger – Doctor C	.15	.25
C15AT Towering Titan – Hungry C	.15	.25
C16AT Backup C	.15	.25
C17AT Camaraderie C	.15	.25
C18AT Devastation C	.15	.25
C19AT Devour C	.15	.25
C20AT Elite Scout Regiment C	.15	.25
C21AT Exhaustion C	.15	.25
C22AT Finisher C	.15	.25
C23AT Frightened C	.15	.25
C24AT Hearty Meal C	.15	.25
C25AT Joke's On You C	.15	.25
C26AT Machinations C	.15	.25
C27AT Open War C	.15	.25
C28AT Rank and File C	.15	.25
C29AT Recruitment C	.15	.25
C30AT Tension C	.15	.25
C31AT Training C	.15	.25
C32AT Triple Threat C	.15	.25
C33AT 1 Intelligence C	.15	.25
C34AT 1 Intelligence C	.15	.25
C35AT 1 Special C	.15	.25
C36AT 1 Strength C	.15	.25
C37AT 2 Intelligence C	.15	.25
C38AT 2 Special C	.15	.25
C39AT 2 Special C	.15	.25
C40AT 2 Strength C	.15	.25
C41AT 3 Intelligence C	.15	.25
C42AT 3 Strength C	.15	.25
C43AT 3 Strength C	.15	.25
C44AT 4 Intelligence C	.15	.25
C45AT 4 Intelligence C	.15	.25
C46AT 4 Special C	.15	.25
C47AT 4 Special C	.15	.25
C48AT 4 Strength C	.15	.25
C49AT 5 Intelligence C	.15	.25
C50AT 5 Special C	.15	.25
C51AT 5 Strength C	.15	.25
C52AT 5 Strength C	.15	.25
C53AT 6 INT/SP C	.15	.25
C54AT 6 Intelligence C	.15	.25
C55AT 6 Intelligence C	.15	.25
C56AT 6 Strength C	.15	.25
C57AT 6 Strength C	.15	.25
C58AT 7 Intelligence C	.15	.25
C59AT 7 Special C	.15	.25
C60AT 7 Strength C	.15	.25
U61AT Conny Springer – Outgoing Cadet U	.25	.40
U62AT Jean Kirschtein – Hot Head U	.25	.40
U63AT Bertholdt Hoover – Quiet Teammate U	.25	.40
U64AT Captain Levi – Humanity's Strongest Soldier U	.25	.40
U65AT Erwin Smith – Commanding Presence U	.25	.40
U66AT Hange Zoe – Quirky Scientist U	.25	.40
U67AT Miche Zacharius – Section Commander U	.25	.40
U68AT Mikasa Ackermann – Lethal Force U	.25	.40
U69AT Reiner Braun – Reliable U	.25	.40
U70AT Proud Titan – Posing U	.25	.40
U71AT Cunning Plot U	.25	.40
U72AT Flanking U	.25	.40
U73AT Painful Choice U	.25	.40
U74AT Perseverance U	.25	.40
U75AT Potato U	.25	.40
U76AT Preparations U	.25	.40
U77AT Diversity U	.25	.40
U78AT Synchronicity U	.25	.40
U79AT Teamwork U	.25	.40
U80AT Wall Breach U	.25	.40
U81AT 1 Special U	.25	.40
U82AT 1 STR/INT U	.25	.40
U83AT 1 Strength U	.25	.40
U84AT 2 Intelligence U	.25	.40
U85AT 2 Special U	.25	.40
U86AT 2 Strength U	.25	.40
U87AT 3 Intelligence U	.25	.40
U88AT 3 Intelligence U	.25	.40
U89AT 3 Strength U	.25	.40
U90AT 4 Intelligence U	.25	.40
U91AT 4 Strength U	.25	.40
U92AT 5 Intelligence U	.25	.40
U93AT 5 Special U	.25	.40
U94AT 5 Strength U	.25	.40
U95AT 6 Special U	.25	.40
U96AT 6 Strength U	.25	.40
U97AT 7 Intelligence U	.25	.40
U98AT 7 Special U	.25	.40
U99AT 7 STR/INT/SP U	.25	.40
R101AT Eren Jaeger – Determined Trainee R	.60	1.00
R102AT Commander Pyxis – Eccentric R	.60	1.00
R103AT Dhalis Zachary – Commander-in-Chief R	.60	1.00
R104AT Annie Leonhart – Solemn Warrior R	.60	1.00
R105AT Nile Dawk – Military Police Commander R	.60	1.00
R106AT Armin Arlelt – Strategist R	.60	1.00
R107AT Mikasa Ackermann – Stoic R	.60	1.00
R108AT Sasha Braus – Potato Girl R	.60	1.00
R109AT Big Mouth Titan – Rampaging R	.60	1.00
R110AT Crawling Titan – Surprisingly Quick R	.60	1.00
R111AT Sullen Titan – Drooling R	.60	1.00
R112AT Brutality R	.60	1.00
R113AT Discipline R	.60	1.00
R114AT Standstill R	.60	1.00
R115AT Epic Battle R	.60	1.00
R116AT If You Don't Fight, You Can't Win! R	.60	1.00
R117AT Omni-Directional Mobility Gear R	.60	1.00
R118AT Rampage R	.60	1.00
R119AT Research R	.60	1.00
R120AT Retreat R	.60	1.00
R121AT Stability R	.60	1.00
R122AT Steam R	.60	1.00
R123AT Titanic Transformation R	.60	1.00
R124AT Volley R	.60	1.00
R125AT 1 Special R	.60	1.00
R126AT 1 Strength R	.60	1.00
R127AT 2 Intelligence R	2.00	3.00
R128AT 2 Strength R	.60	1.00
R129AT 3 Intelligence R	.60	1.00
R130AT 3 Special R	.60	1.00
R131AT 3 STR/INT/SP R	4.00	6.00
R132AT 4 Special R	.60	1.00
R133AT 4 STR/SP R	.60	1.00
R134AT 5 Special R	.60	1.00
R135AT 5 Special R	.60	1.00
R136AT 6 Intelligence R	.60	1.00
R137AT 6 Special R	.60	1.00
R138AT 7 Intelligence R	.60	1.00
R139AT 7 Special R	.60	1.00
R140AT 7 Strength R	.60	1.00
U100AT 7 Strength R	.60	1.00
UR145AT Captain Levi – Juggernaut UR	30.00	50.00
UR146AT Mikasa Ackermann – Battle Genius UR	30.00	50.00
XR141AT Armored Titan – Wallbreaker XR	25.00	40.00
XR142AT Colossal Titan – God of Destruction XR	30.00	50.00
XR143AT Eren Jaeger – Mysterious Titan XR	20.00	30.00
XR144AT Female Titan – Hardened Warrior XR	25.00	40.00

2018 Meta X Batman

COMPLETE SET (146)		
COMPLETE SET W/O SP (100)		
BOOSTER BOX (24 PACKS)		
BOOSTER PACK (12 CARDS)		
*FOIL: X TO X BASIC CARDS		
RELEASED ON JUNE 29, 2018		
C1BM Killer Croc – Waylon Jones C	.20	.30
C2BM Mad Hatter – Jervis Tetch C	.20	.30
C3BM Poison Ivy – Botanist C	.20	.30
C4BM Arsenal – Roy Harper C	.20	.30
C5BM Batwoman – Kate Kane C	.20	.30
C6BM Catwoman – Selina Kyle C	1.25	2.00
C7BM Oracle – Barbara Gordon C	.20	.30
C8BM Terry McGinnis – Batman of the Future C	.20	.30
C9BM GCPD Officers – Gotham City's Finest C	.20	.30
C10BM Harvey Bullock – Detective C	.20	.30
C11BM Deathstroke – Expert Tactician C	.20	.30
C12BM Harley Quinn – Skilled Gymnast C	.20	.30
C13BM Mr. Freeze – King of Cold C	.20	.30
C14BM Batman – Bruce Wayne C	.20	.30
C15BM Dick Grayson – Master Martial Artist C	.20	.30
C16BM Zatanna – Expert Illusionist C	.20	.30
C17BM Bat-Mite – Interdimensional Imp C	.20	.30
C18BM Deathstroke – Ultimate Assassin C	.20	.30
C19BM Hush – Dr. Thomas Elliot C	.20	.30
C20BM Selfie C	1.25	2.00
C21BM Card Burst C	.20	.30
C22BM Conceal C	1.25	2.00
C23BM Confidence C	.20	.30
C24BM Detect C	.20	.30
C25BM Electrify C	.20	.30
C26BM Entangled C	.20	.30
C27BM Hand to Hand C	.20	.30
C28BM Identification C	.20	.30
C29BM Infighting C	.20	.30
C30BM Insanity C	1.25	2.00
C31BM Party Time C	1.25	2.00
C32BM Preen C	.20	.30
C33BM Rogues Gallery C	.20	.30
C34BM Surprise Visit C	.20	.30
C35BM Theatricality C	.20	.30
C36BM Tracking C	1.50	2.50
C37BM 1 Intelligence C	.20	.30
C38BM 1 Special C	.20	.30
C39BM 1 Strength C	.20	.30
C40BM 1 STR/INT/SP C	1.50	2.50
C41BM 2 Intelligence C	.20	.30
C42BM 2 Special C	.20	.30
C43BM 2 Strength C	.20	.30
C44BM 2 STR/INT/SP C	.20	.30
C45BM 3 Intelligence C	.20	.30
C46BM 3 Intelligence C	.20	.30
C47BM 3 Strength C	1.25	2.00
C48BM 3 INT/SP C	.20	.30
C49BM 3 STR/SP C	.20	.30
C50BM 4 Intelligence C	.20	.30
C51BM 4 Special C	.20	.30
C52BM 4 Special C	.20	.30
C53BM 5 Intelligence C	1.75	3.00
C54BM 5 Special C	.20	.30
C55BM 5 Strength C	.20	.30
C56BM 6 Intelligence C	.20	.30
C57BM 6 Special C	1.25	2.00
C58BM 6 Strength C	1.25	2.00
C59BM 7 Intelligence C	1.25	2.00
C60BM 7 Strength C	.20	.30
U61BM Bane – Venom U	.25	.40
U62BM Mr. Zsasz – Victor Zsasz U	.25	.40
U63BM Talon – William Cobb U	.25	.40
U64BM Batgirl – Cassandra Cain U	.25	.40
U65BM Nightwing – Fearless Acrobat U	1.75	3.00
U66BM Robin – Damian Wayne U	.25	.40
U67BM Spoiler – Stephanie Brown U	1.75	3.00
U68BM James Gordon – GCPD Officer U	.25	.40
U69BM Ra's Al Ghul – Assassin U	.25	.40
U70BM Two-Face – Harvey Dent U	.25	.40
U71BM Red Hood – Freelance Mercenary U	.25	.40
U72BM Catwoman – Thief U	.25	.40
U73BM Red Hood – Jason Todd U	.25	.40
U74BM Crime Spree U	.25	.40
U75BM Dynamic Duo U	1.75	3.00
U76BM Frustration U	.25	.40
U77BM Gifts U	.25	.40
U78BM Jail Break U	.25	.40
U79BM Mastermind U	.25	.40
U80BM Peer U	.25	.40
U81BM Power Players U	1.75	3.00
U82BM Prison Cycle U	1.75	3.00
U83BM Teamwork U	.25	.40
U84BM The World's Finest U	.25	.40
U85BM 1 Strength U	.25	.40
U86BM 1 STR/INT U	.25	.40
U87BM 2 Intelligence U	.25	.40
U88BM 2 Special U	.25	.40
U89BM 2 Strength U	.25	.40
U90BM 2 INT/SP U	.25	.40
U91BM 2 STR/SP U	.25	.40
U92BM 3 Special U	.25	.40
U93BM 3 Strength U	.25	.40
U94BM 4 Intelligence U	.25	.40
U95BM 4 Strength U	.25	.40
U96BM 4 STR/INT/SP U	.25	.40
U97BM 3 STR/INT/SP U	.40	.60
U98BM 6 Intelligence U	.25	.40
U99BM 6 INT/SP U	.25	.40
R101BM Scarecrow – Scarebeast R	1.00	1.50
R102BM The Joker – Ruthless R	1.00	1.50
R103BM Alfred Pennyworth – Loyal Servant R	.60	1.00
R104BM Batgirl – Exceptional Detective R	.60	1.00
R105BM Batman – Detective R	1.75	3.00
R106BM Batwoman – Vigilante R	1.00	1.50
R107BM James Gordon – Commissioner R	1.00	1.50
R108BM Poison Ivy – Chlorokinetic R	1.00	1.50
R109BM The Joker – Romantic R	1.75	3.00
R110BM Black Canary – Dinah Drake R	.60	1.00
R111BM Harley Quinn – Heartbreaker R	.60	1.00
R112BM Superman – Big Blue Boy Scout R	1.00	1.50
R113BM Blackfire – Komand'r R	.60	1.00
R114BM Assume the Mantle R	1.00	1.50
R115BM Bat-Signal R	.60	1.00
R116BM Cat and Bat R	1.00	1.50
R117BM Death in the Family R	.60	1.00
R118BM Endless Waltz R	.60	1.00
R119BM Gotham City's Finest R	1.00	1.50
R120BM Heroic Charge R	1.00	1.50
R121BM Killing Blow R	.60	1.00
R122BM Pick a Card R	.75	1.25
R123BM Rage R	1.00	1.50
R124BM Research R	.60	1.00
R125BM Surrounded R	.60	1.00
R126BM 1 Intelligence R	.75	1.25
R127BM 1 Special R	.75	1.25
R128BM 3 Intelligence R	.60	1.00
R129BM 3 Special R	1.00	1.50
R130BM 4 Strength R	.60	1.00
R131BM 5 Intelligence R	1.00	1.50
R132BM 5 Special R	.75	1.25
R133BM 5 Strength R	.60	1.00
R134BM 6 Special R	.60	1.00
R135BM 6 Strength R	2.50	4.00
R136BM 7 Intelligence R	.75	1.25
R137BM 7 Special R	.60	1.00
R138BM 7 Special R	.75	1.25
R139BM 7 Strength R	.75	1.25
R140BM 7 STR/INT/SP R	.60	1.00
U100BM 7 Special U	1.25	2.50
UR145BM Batman – Prepared UR	25.00	40.00
UR146BM The Joker – Unpredictable UR	25.00	40.00
XR141BM Catwoman – Burglar Extraordinaire XR	20.00	35.00
XR142BM Harley Quinn – Queen of Arkham XR	20.00	35.00
XR143BM Nightwing – Adopted Son XR	20.00	35.00
XR144BM Robin – Carrie Kelley XR	20.00	35.00

2018 Munchkin Season 1

BOOSTER BOX (24 PACKS)		
BOOSTER PACK (12 CARDS)		
RELEASED IN FEBRUARY 2018		
1 Barbarian the Librarian C	.10	.15
2 Bertha C	.10	.15
3 BOD-E Guard C	.10	.15
4 Sword Caddy C	.10	.15
5 Red Tunic U	.15	.25
6 Fizbandantelminster R	1.25	2.00
7 Eric the Jerk R	1.25	2.00
8 Offices of Dewey, Cheatem & Howe U	.15	.25
9 Cowardly Canyon U	.15	.25
10 Land C	.10	.15
11 Dungeon of Dragons R	1.25	2.00
12 Flaming Foyer R	1.25	2.00
13 Goldman Stacks U	.15	.25
14 Wight Bros. Dungeon R	1.25	2.00
15 School of Badassery W	15.00	25.00
16 Boots of Butt-Kicking C	.25	.40
17 Nonstick Plate U	.15	.25
18 Boots of Butt-Kicking (Alt 1) X	2.50	4.00
19 Flaming Armor C	.10	.15
20 Flaming Armor (Alt 1) X	2.00	3.00
21 Purple Loot-us C	.10	.15
22 Hot Potato U	.15	.25
23 Liar's Dice U	.15	.25
24 Big Baby Bandage U	.50	.75
25 Geekstone R	1.25	2.00
26 Silver Bullet U	.15	.25
27 Locket of Fleeting Fortune R	1.25	2.00
28 Eleven-Foot Pole C	.10	.15
29 Spiked Blade U	.15	.25
30 Eleven-Foot Pole (Alt 1) X	2.50	4.00
31 Chainsaw of Bloody Dismemberment C	.10	.15
32 Bane of the Planes U	.15	.25
33 Staff of SRS BSNS U	.15	.25
34 Chainsaw of Bloody Dismemberment (Alt 1) X	1.50	2.50
35 Clobberknocker C	.10	.15
36 Hammer Time C	.10	.15
37 Collector's Edition Blade R	1.25	2.00

38 Kova R	1.25	2.00
39 Combo Rat C	.10	.15
40 Wombo Bat C	.10	.15
41 Aggro-Bat U	.30	.50
42 Glassjaw C	.10	.15
43 Drop Bear C	.10	.15
44 Dynomites C	.10	.15
45 Rage-in-the-Cage R	1.25	2.00
46 Bank Demon U	.15	.25
47 Relentless Slobberbeast U	.15	.25
48 Peigh'Toowyn U	.15	.25
49 Squidzilla C	.10	.15
50 Squidzilla (Alt 1) X	4.00	6.00
51 Mnemonic Tudor VR	10.00	15.00
52 Plutonium Dragon C	.10	.15
53 Plutonium Dragon (Alt 1) X	1.50	2.50
54 Vanillamental C	.10	.15
55 Explodia's Pinky R	1.25	2.00
56 Explodia's Index Finger U	.15	.25
57 Explodia's Thumb R	1.25	2.00
58 Explodia's Middle Finger U	.15	.25
59 Explodia's Ring Finger U	.15	.25
60 Walking Dreads C	.10	.15
61 Crusty Disgusty C	.10	.15
62 Wring Wraith C	.10	.15
63 Leperchaun U	.15	.25
64 Blandy McBlanderson C	.10	.15
65 Lame Goblin C	.10	.15
66 Used Card Dealer C	.10	.15
67 Blandy McBlanderson (Alt 1) X	2.00	3.00
68 Goblin Kaboomer C	.10	.15
69 Pied Piper U	.15	.25
70 Landwar Elf C	.10	.15
71 Card Shark C	.10	.15
72 Ferrous Oxide Monster C	.10	.15
73 Gazebo U	.15	.25
74 Hipstaur U	.15	.25
75 The 1 Percent U	.15	.25
76 Gazebo (Alt 1) X	3.00	5.00
77 Budget Sasquatch C	.10	.15
78 RNGesus C	.10	.15
79 RNGesus (Alt 1) X	2.00	3.00
80 Explodia, The Trademarked One VR	15.00	25.00
81 3,872 Orcs C	.10	.15
82 3,872 Orcs (Alt 1) X	3.00	5.00
83 Hillbilly Ogre U	.15	.25
84 Even Steven R	1.25	2.00
85 Mr. Suitcase R	1.25	2.00
86 The X Monster W	15.00	25.00
87 Hot Poker W	15.00	25.00
88 Painata U	.15	.25
89 Centaur Warrior H	4.00	6.00
90 Centaur Warrior (Alt 1) R	1.25	2.00
91 Inhumane Society C	.10	.15
92 Epic Loot, Inc. R	1.25	2.00
93 Brawlhalla VR	6.00	10.00
94 Belt Buckler C	.10	.15
95 Rear Deflector U	.15	.25
96 Belt Buckler (Alt 1) X	2.50	4.00
97 Pwn Pole U	.15	.25
98 Shiny Manipulator U	.15	.25
99 Discount Cudgel C	.10	.15
100 Dead Weights R	1.25	2.00
101 Hydraxe C	.10	.15
102 Unnatural Axe VR	8.00	12.00
103 Whacka-Maul C	.10	.15
104 The Banhammer VR	6.00	10.00
105 Uber-Blade X	2.50	4.00
106 Weenie Buffet U	.15	.25
107 Crushinate! C	.10	.15
108 All Teh Blades U	.50	.75
109 Crushinate! (Alt 1) X	2.50	4.00
110 DING!! C	.10	.15
111 Tavern Brawl C	.10	.15
112 Thwack! C	.10	.15
113 Stomp, Stomp, Stomp! R	1.25	2.00
114 Spin Kick C	.10	.15
115 Inflatable Dragon C	.10	.15
116 Face Elemental C	.10	.15
117 Punch McFacey C	.10	.15
118 Field Armorer C	.10	.15
119 Hanz U	.15	.25
120 Field Armorer (Alt 1) X	1.50	2.50
121 Franz C	.10	.15
122 Kobold Blademaster R	1.25	2.00
123 The Pain Train R	1.25	2.00
124 Dr. Meow Practice C	.10	.15
125 Avenging Apostle U	.15	.25
126 Good Samaritan U	.15	.25
127 Dr. Meow Practice (Alt 1) X	2.50	4.00
128 Dwarf Cleric H	4.00	6.00
129 Dwarf Cleric (Alt 1) R	1.25	2.00
130 The Just Desert U	.15	.25
131 Home of the Brave R	1.25	2.00
132 Tax Heaven U	.15	.25
133 House of Indulgences R	1.25	2.00
134 The One Bling VR	8.00	12.00
135 Robe of Retribution C	.10	.15
136 Holier Symbol C	.10	.15
137 Censer of Censoring R	1.25	2.00
138 Holiest Symbol R	1.25	2.00
139 Suction Cup C	.10	.15
140 Holy Roller C	.10	.15
141 Book of Axe U	.15	.25
142 Final Judgment VR	8.00	12.00
143 Stuff Shaming C	.10	.15
144 Tragedy of the Commons U	.15	.25
145 Nun Slap! U	.15	.25
146 Alms for the Poor C	.10	.15
147 Cheaters Never Win C	.10	.15
148 Smite Unseen C	.10	.15
149 Healing Salvo C	.10	.15
150 Healing Salvo (Alt 1) X	1.50	2.50
151 Plea Bargain C	.10	.15
152 Angel of Awesomeness R	1.25	2.00
153 Pygmy Suckophant C	.10	.15
154 Holey Ghost C	.10	.15
155 Holey Ghost (Alt 1) X	2.00	3.00
156 Hairy Tick C	.10	.15
157 Leecher C	.10	.15
158 The Spanish Inquisition X	1.50	2.50
159 False Prophet VR	6.00	10.00
160 Pilfergeist U	.15	.25
161 Repeat Offender U	.15	.25
162 Chunky Flunky C	.10	.15
163 Elf Thief H	3.00	5.00
164 Elf Thief (Alt 1) R	1.25	2.00
165 Honest Al's Casino C	.10	.15
166 Mark Market U	.15	.25
167 Hurtnasium VR	8.00	12.00
168 Charm of Cheating VR		
169 Lucky Giant's Toe VR	10.00	15.00
170 Platinum Lockpicks R	1.25	2.00
171 Mugsy's Sap C	.10	.15
172 Automatic Machinebow C	.10	.15
173 Dagger of Treachery C	.10	.15
174 Long Shot R	1.25	2.00
175 Cutlass of Cloning U	.15	.25
176 Skewer C	.10	.15
177 Skewer (Alt 1) X	2.00	3.00
178 Stabbity Stab! C	.10	.15
179 Nope! C	.10	.15
180 Nope! (Alt 1) X	1.50	2.50
181 Whacked! C	.10	.15
182 Silent but Deadly U	.15	.25
183 Up My Sleeve… U	.15	.25
184 Amscray C	.10	.15
185 Dogpile C	.10	.15
186 Yoink! R	1.25	2.00
187 Bling Beastie R	2.50	4.00
188 Deckogorgon R	1.25	2.00
189 Salt Elemental U	.15	.25
190 Ex-ecutioner C	.10	.15
191 Ex-ecutioner (Alt 1) X	1.50	2.50
192 Mugsy C	.10	.15
193 Vampire Cat C	.10	.15
194 Legbreaker Joe C	.10	.15
195 Rules Lawyer X	3.00	5.00
196 Trollinator U	.15	.25
197 Human Wizard H	2.50	4.00
198 Human Wizard (Alt 1) R	1.25	2.00
199 Unfairgrounds C	.10	.15
200 Pity Party U	.15	.25
201 The Last Ditch R	1.25	2.00
202 Sequined Robes C	.10	.15
203 Amulet of Ridiculous Power VR	2.50	4.00
204 Stick of Suffering C	.10	.15
205 Staff of Magic VR	8.00	12.00
206 Magic Missile C	.10	.15
207 Rod of Owies X	2.00	3.00
208 Spiky Bit U	.15	.25
209 Curse of Quack C	.10	.15
210 Bodius Odiferus VR	8.00	12.00
211 Forked! R	1.25	2.00
212 Jazz Hands C	.10	.15
213 Portal Kombat U	.15	.25
214 Jazz Hands (Alt 1) X	3.00	5.00
215 Disappearing Act C	.10	.15
216 Zorch! C	.10	.15
217 Spell-Caption R	1.25	2.00
218 Blood Geyser C	.10	.15
219 Crash and Burn C	.10	.15
220 Blood Geyser (Alt 1) X	1.50	2.50
221 Kaboom! C	.10	.15
222 Rain of Death U	.15	.25
223 Beezlebob C	.10	.15
224 Dr. Feelbad R	1.25	2.00
225 Beezlebob (Alt 1) X	2.00	3.00
226 Hack-in-the-Box C	.10	.15
227 Smug C	.10	.15
228 Toll Dragon U	.15	.25
229 Coin Elemental U	.15	.25
230 Re-Animator R	1.25	2.00
231 Heart of the Cards C	.10	.15
232 Backup Dancers C	.10	.15
233 DJ Tim U	.15	.25
234 Orc Bard H	2.50	4.00
235 Orc Bard (Alt 1) R	1.25	2.00
236 Mosh Pit R	1.25	2.00
237 The Howling Mimes R	1.25	2.00
238 Stairway to Heaven VR	8.00	12.00
239 Blue Suede Shoes U	.50	.75
240 Whammy Bar R	1.25	2.00
241 Cool Shades VR	6.00	10.00
242 Chopsticks C	.10	.15
243 Chopsticks (Alt 1) X	3.00	5.00
244 Vuvuzela C	.10	.15
245 Brass Kicker U	.15	.25
246 Elvish Impersonator C	.10	.15
247 Elvish Impersonator (Alt 1) X	2.50	4.00
248 Starstruck C	.10	.15
249 Jam Session C	.10	.15
250 Trom-Boned C	.10	.15
251 Trom-Boned (Alt 1) X	2.00	3.00
252 The Final Countdown X	4.00	6.00
253 Trololol C	.10	.15
254 99 Bottles… C	.40	.60
255 Irresistible Disco C	.10	.15
256 YOLO! U	.15	.25
257 The Danger Zone C	.10	.15
258 Can't Touch This C	.10	.15
259 I Want It All U	.15	.25
260 Master of Puppets VR	8.00	12.00
261 Yelling Goat! R	1.25	2.00
262 One Hit Wonder R	1.25	2.00
263 Groupies U	.15	.25
264 Freebird C	.10	.15
265 Grody Roadies C	.10	.15
266 Earworm U	.15	.25
267 Shrieking Fans C	.10	.15
268 Beagle Scout C	.10	.15
269 Stumpy U	.15	.25
270 Recycle Ben R	1.25	2.00
271 Beagle Scout (Alt 1) X	2.00	3.00
272 Halfling Ranger H	1.50	2.50
273 Halfling Ranger (Alt 1) R	1.25	2.00
274 Woodland Workout C	.10	.15
275 Comeback Cove U	.15	.25
276 Elf Commune R	1.25	2.00
277 Biodegradable Armor C	.10	.15
278 Aura of the Wilderness U	.50	.75
279 Crown of Crazy VR	8.00	12.00
280 Cattle Prod C	.10	.15
281 Bull Whip C	.10	.15
282 Bow of Called Shots U	.15	.25
283 Reseeding Rifle C	.10	.15
284 Cat-a-pult R	1.25	2.00
285 Tree Hugger VR	4.00	6.00
286 Doge! C	.10	.15
287 Doge! (Alt 1) X	1.50	2.50
288 Ooh, Shiny! C	.10	.15
289 Rawr! C	.10	.15
290 Tracking U	.15	.25
291 Compost C	.10	.15
292 Timber! U	.15	.25
293 Pole Cat R	1.25	2.00
294 Alpha Alpha Alpha Wolf C	.30	.50
295 Bumbles U	.15	.25
296 Squirrel C	.10	.15
297 Squirrel (Alt 1) X	2.00	3.00
298 Hairy Scary Bear C	.10	.15
299 Moose C	.10	.15
300 My Little Pawny R	1.25	2.00
301 Rash Barkbelly X	1.50	2.50
302 Salvage Salamander C	.10	.15
303 Dumpster of Doom VR		
304 Ace of Spades X	10.00	15.00
305 Potted Plant F	2.00	3.00
306 Goldfish Wanderer (Alt 1) P		
307 Goldfish Wanderer (Alt 2) P		
308 Halfling Ranger (Alt 2) H	6.00	10.00
309 Elf Thief (Alt 2) H	6.00	10.00
310 Orc Bard (Alt 2) H	6.00	10.00
311 Human Wizard (Alt 2) H	6.00	10.00
312 Centaur Warrior (Alt 2) H	6.00	10.00
313 Dwarf Cleric (Alt 2) H	6.00	10.00
163B Elf Thief H		

2018 Munchkin Season 1 Organized Play

OA1 Goldfish Wanderer	1.25	2.00
OA2 Ferrous Oxide Monster	4.00	6.00
OA3 Blandy McBlanderson	4.00	6.00
OA4 Aggro-Bat	4.00	6.00

2018 Munchkin Season 1 Oversized Promos

NNO Centaur Warrior	20.00	30.00
NNO Dwarf Cleric	20.00	30.00
NNO Elf Thief	20.00	30.00
NNO Halfling Ranger	20.00	30.00
NNO Human Wizard	20.00	30.00
NNO Orc Bard	20.00	30.00

2018 Munchkin The Desolation of Blarg

COMPLETE SET (125)
BOOSTER BOX (24 PACKS)
BOOSTER PACK (12 CARDS)
RELEASED ON MAY 30, 2018

1 Ambulance Chaser C	.20	.35
2 Meercenaries C	.20	.35
3 Spirit Guide R	.60	1.00
4 Bob C	.20	.35
5 Ice-Filled Bathtub C	.20	.35
6 Expensive Care Unit U	.40	.60
7 The Plains of Pain C	.20	.35
8 Inn of Improbable Rooms W	8.00	12.00
9 Gambeson of Gambling U	.40	.60
10 Second Aid Kit C	.20	.35
11 Scepter of Schadenfreude R	1.25	2.00
12 Miserstone VR		
13 Me Too Medallion U	.40	.60
14 Sticky Shield VR		
15 Beast-B-Gone C	.20	.35
16 Angry Catana C	.20	.35
17 The Shredder C	.20	.35
18 High Roller U	.40	.60
19 Boring Beetle C	.20	.35
20 Cute-o-saurus C	.20	.35
21 Haardvark C	.20	.35
22 Beast E. Bois R	.60	1.00
23 Vengeance Most Fowl R	.60	1.00
24 Honey Badger C	.20	.35
25 Trash Panda C	.20	.35
26 Wounded Pride C	.20	.35
27 Bullrog C	.20	.35
28 Blarg U	.40	.60
29 Building Inspectre C	.20	.35
30 Gold Finch C	.20	.35
31 Spyder U	.40	.60
32 Potato Bug C	.20	.35
33 Allygator R	.60	1.00
34 Dragomancer R	.60	1.00
35 Hunting Guide C	.20	.35
36 Lodge of Complaints U	.40	.60
37 Meat Shield C	.20	.35
38 Net Benefit U	.40	.60
39 Elephant Gun R	.60	1.00
40 Dibs! C	.20	.35
41 Denied! U	.40	.60
42 Flail Flail C	.20	.35
43 Axe-ident R	.60	1.00
44 Analysis Paralysis VR		
45 Bearer C	.20	.35
46 Overcharging Rhino U	.40	.60
47 Spirit Hunter C	.20	.35
48 Craven R	.60	1.00
49 Hippopede C	.20	.35
50 Missionary Impossible C	.20	.35
51 Holy Ground U	.40	.60
52 Monster Juicer U	.50	.75
53 Manual of Health C	.20	.35
54 Virtuous Vacuum R	.60	1.00
55 Boop C	.20	.35
56 Prophet Profit U	.40	.60
57 Ally-Oop R	.60	1.00
58 House Hunting U	.50	.75
59 The Tithes Have Turned VR		
60 Savannah Lyin' R	2.50	4.00
61 Wight Knight C	.20	.35
62 Clampire C	.20	.35
63 Banal-ish Hero C	.20	.35
64 Bluebirds of Bitterness U	.40	.60
65 Robbin Hoodlum C	.20	.35
66 Cheaty McCheaterson R	.60	1.00
67 Monte's Roadside Carnival U	.40	.60

68 Blackmail VR		
69 Contingency Plank C	.20	.35
70 Surreptitious Scythe R	.60	1.00
71 Rehoming Stick U	.50	.75
72 All in the Reflexes C	.20	.35
73 Smoke Bomb! C	.20	.35
74 Finders Keepers R	2.50	4.00
75 Boot to the Head U	.40	.60
76 Litterbug C	.20	.35
77 Cheatah C	.20	.35
78 Perret U	.40	.60
79 Monte 3-Cards C	.20	.35
80 Shrimpy Imp C	.20	.35
81 Edifice of Enervation U	.40	.60
82 Enchanted Coat Rack C	.20	.35
83 Ring of Zotz R	.60	1.00
84 Copyright Protection Device VR		
85 Violent Vivification C	.20	.35
86 Upgrade! C	.20	.35
87 Kracka-DOOM! C	.20	.35
88 Ouchian Bargain R	.60	1.00
89 Rain of Brains U	.50	.75
90 Asplode U	.40	.60
91 Hairy Brimstone U	.40	.60
92 Sarsaparillamental C	.20	.35
93 Off-Centaur R	.60	1.00
94 Claire Voyant C	.20	.35
95 Chopin' C	.20	.35
96 Cheap Seats U	.40	.60
97 Sonic Shield U	.40	.60
98 Tiny Unicycle C	.20	.35
99 Air Guitar VR	8.00	12.00
100 Whakety Sax U	1.00	1.50
101 Bleed It Out C	.20	.35
102 I'll Be Bach… U	.40	.60
103 Fight Song R	.60	1.00
104 Roar! C	.20	.35
105 Fire R	.60	1.00
106 Concert Security R	.60	1.00
107 Maneater C	.20	.35
108 Orcupine U	.50	.75
109 Lucy in the Sky C	.20	.35
110 Branchlandian R	.60	1.00
111 Branchlandia U	1.25	2.00
112 Health Elixir Mixer C	.20	.35
113 Back Lash C	.20	.35
114 Mr. Wuffles U	.50	.75
115 Beast Mode! R	.60	1.00
116 Here, Boy! U	1.50	2.50
117 Interrupting Cow C	.20	.35
118 Nature's Call C	.20	.35
119 Law of the Jungle C	.20	.35
120 Makin' Bacon VR	4.00	6.00
121 Snakes on a Plain C	.20	.35
122 Rampaging Barkbelly U	.40	.60
123 MacDuff The Tragic Dragon R	.60	1.00
124 Grabby C	.20	.35
125 Dorksteel Hat P	6.00	10.00

2018 Munchkin The Desolation of Blarg Organized Play

OB1 Flamingo Wanderer	2.50	4.00
OB2 Tiny Unicycle (Alt 1)	3.00	5.00
OB3 Bearer (Alt 1)	3.00	5.00
OB4 Wounder Pride (Alt 1)	5.00	8.00

2018 Munchkin The Desolation of Blarg Promo

NNO Tardigrade Wanderer

Naruto

2009 Naruto Emerging Alliance

COMPLETE SET (145)	50.00	100.00
BOOSTER BOX (24 PACKS)	50.00	100.00
BOOSTER PACK (10 CARDS)	2.00	5.00
RELEASED IN OCTOBER 2009		
J496 Art of Ink Mist U	.20	.50
J497 Ninja Art: Super Beast Scroll R	.75	2.00
J498 Fire Style: Phoenix Flower Jutsu R	.75	2.00
J499 Self-Destruct Doppelganger R	.75	2.00
J500 Water Style: Water Shark Bomb Jutsu SR	10.00	25.00
J501 Detonating Kunai C	.10	.25
J502 Sealing Jutsu: Breaking the Lions Roar SR	3.00	8.00
J503 Flamethrower U	.20	.50
J504 Secret White Move: Chikamatsu?s Ten Puppets R	.75	2.00
J505 Partial Expansion Jutsu U	.20	.50
J506 Ninja Art: Shadow Stitching SR	3.00	8.00
J507 Reanimation Ninjutsu U	.20	.50
J508 Secret Red Move: Performance of a Hundred Puppets R	.75	2.00
J509 Critical Wound C	.10	.25
J510 Getting Ready U	.20	.50
J511 Sense of Fear SR	4.00	10.00
J512 Assimilation C	.10	.25
J513 Tricky Move C	.10	.25
J514 Ninja Art: Super Beast Scroll Rat U	.20	.50
J515 Wood Style Transformation C	.10	.25
J516 Striking Multi Shadow Snakes Jutsu U	.20	.50
J517 Formation! R	.75	2.00
J518 Revealing the True Face C	.10	.25
J519 Earth Style: Rending Piercing Fang SR	3.00	8.00
J520 Ultimate Art U	.20	.50
J521 Ten Thousand Snakes Wave U	.20	.50
J522 Wood Style Jutsu: Wooden Lock Wall C	.10	.25
J523 Wood Clone Jutsu C	.10	.25
J524 Summoning Jutsu: Triple Rashomon R	.75	2.00
J525 Chakra Cannon U	.20	.50
J526 Thunder Funeral: Feast of Lightning U	.20	.50
J527 Unique Skill U	.20	.50
J528 Razor Chain C	.10	.25
J529 Sonic Attack C	.10	.25
J530 Super Sonic Slicing Wave C	.10	.25
J531 Stealing Chakra R	.75	2.00
J532 Twining Limbs C	.10	.25
J533 Bone Transformation C	.10	.25
J534 Bone Guard C	.10	.25
J535 Supplement of Energy U	.20	.50
J536 Wood Style Jutsu: Four Pillars Prison Jutsu U	.20	.50
J537 Visual Jutsu R	.75	2.00
J538 Giant Rasengan R	.75	2.00
J539 Crow Clone Jutsu R	.75	2.00
J540 Long Sword Shark Skin U	.20	.50
M455 Rules for Medical Ninjas R	.75	2.00
M456 Search Party C	.10	.25
M457 Piggyback C	.10	.25
M458 Filling Up the Open Spot R	.75	2.00
M459 100 Hot-Blooded C	.10	.25
M460 Fellowship C	.10	.25
M461 Tears for a Friend C	.10	.25
M462 Constricting Bind U	.20	.50
M463 Bad Dream R	.75	2.00
M464 Control by Fear C	.10	.25
M465 Transmitter U	.20	.50
M466 Lunchbox U	.20	.50
M467 Shake Hands U	.20	.50
M468 Meaning of Comrade C	.10	.25
M469 Tenchi Bridge C	.10	.25
M470 Releasing the Sealed Power U	.20	.50
M471 Compressed Chakra C	.10	.25
M472 A Sign of Revival U	.20	.50
M473 The best pair C	.10	.25
M474 Hiding U	.20	.50
M475 Check U	.20	.50
M476 Fateful Encounter C	.10	.25
M477 Super Bushy-Brow C	.10	.25
M478 Ninja Info Card R	.75	2.00
M479 Pressure R	.75	2.00
M480 Captivity R	.75	2.00
M481 Precious Student C	.10	.25
M482 The Ones Who Have the Same Eyes U	.20	.50
M483 Meaning of Life C	.10	.25
M484 Impersonation U	.20	.50
M485 Medical Ninja U	.20	.50
M486 Sealing Barrier R	.75	2.00
M487 A New Squad R	.75	2.00
M488 Surprise Training C	.10	.25
M489 Invitation to the Darkness U	.20	.50
M490 Picture Book C	.10	.25
M491 Discord C	.10	.25
M492 Secret Meeting C	.10	.25
M493 Commemorative Photo U	.20	.50
M494 Pledge under a Starry Sky C	.10	.25
M495 Respective Dreams C	.10	.25
M496 Underground Organization U	.20	.50
M497 Advisors U	.20	.50
M498 Prelude to an End U	.20	.50
M499 Intellectual Strategy R	.75	2.00
N590 Kakashi Hatake & Might Guy U	.20	.50
N591 Naruto Uzumaki (Tailed Beast Mode) SR	10.00	25.00
N592 Naruto Uzumaki C	.10	.25
N593 Sakura Haruno C	.10	.25
N594 Sai R	1.00	2.50
N595 Ino Yamanaka C	.10	.25
N596 Shikamaru Nara C	.10	.25
N597 Choji Akimichi C	.10	.25
N598 Yamato R	.75	2.00
N599 Shizune C	.10	.25
N600 Danzo R	.75	2.00
N601 Chiyo U	.20	.50
N602 Matsuri C	.10	.25
N603 Mikoshi C	.10	.25
N604 Tobi R	1.50	4.00
N605 Sasori (Possesion Mode) R	.75	2.00
N606 Kabuto Yakushi SR	5.00	12.00
N607 Orochimaru SR	5.00	12.00
N608 Naruto Uzumaki & Sai R	.75	2.00
N609 Anbu (The Foundation) R	.75	2.00
N610 Homura Mitomon U	.20	.50
N611 Koharu Utatane U	.20	.50
N612 The First Hokage SR	5.00	12.00
N613 The Second Hokage SR	5.00	12.00
N614 Haku (Childhood) C	.10	.25
N615 Kabuto Yakushi R	.75	2.00
N616 Naruto Uzumaki & Yamato SR	4.00	10.00
N617 Dosu Kinuta C	.10	.25
N618 Zaku Abumi C	.10	.25
N619 Kin Tsuchi C	.10	.25
N620 Kimimaro (Childhood) U	.20	.50
N621 Dosu Kinuta, Zaku Abumi & Kin Tsuchi U	.20	.50
N622 Anko Mitarashi C	.10	.25
N623 Ranmaru C	.10	.25
N624 Manda R	.75	2.00
N625 Raiga Kurosuki R	.75	2.00
N626 The Demon Brothers Gouzu C	.10	.25
N627 The Demon Brothers Meizu C	.10	.25
N628 Shimon Hijiri U	.20	.50
N629 Misumi Tsurugi C	.10	.25
N630 Yoroi Akado C	.10	.25
N631 Ino Yamanaka C	.10	.25
N632 Naruto Uzumaki R	.75	2.00
N633 Rock Lee & Tortoise Ninja U	.20	.50
N634 Shikamaru Nara SR	10.00	25.00
N635 Choji Akimichi C	.10	.25
N636 Shizune & Tonton U	.20	.50
N637 Sasuke Uchiha C	.10	.25
N638 Gaara of the Desert (Possessed Mode) SR	4.00	10.00
N639 Sakura Haruno & Sai R	.75	2.00
N640 Might Guy SR	3.00	8.00
N641 Kankuro & Black Ant U	.20	.50
N642 Temari R	.75	2.00
N643 Itachi Uchiha R	1.50	4.00
N644 Kisame Hoshigaki R	.75	2.00

2009 Naruto Fateful Reunion

COMPLETE SET (156)	60.00	120.00
BOOSTER BOX (24 PACKS)	60.00	120.00
BOOSTER PACK (10 CARDS)	3.00	6.00
RELEASED IN MAY 2009		
C047 Teuchi C	.10	.25
C048 Takamaru C	.10	.25
J450 Radio C	.10	.25
J451 A Thousand Years of Death R	.75	2.00
J452 Snatching the Weapon C	.10	.25
J453 Giant Shuriken U	.20	.50
J454 Multi Shadow Clone Taijutsu U	.20	.50
J455 Copy Ninjutsu C	.10	.25
J456 Mirror Reflection Jutsu R	.75	2.00
J457 Button Hook Entry C	.10	.25
J458 Detonating Clay Centipede C	.10	.25
J459 Mangekyo Sharingan SR	3.00	8.00
J460 Water Style: Five Hungry Sharks SR	3.00	8.00
J461 Five-Seal Barrier U	.20	.50
J462 Sealing Jutsu: Nine Phantom Dragons C	.10	.25
J463 Simultaneous Attacks U	.20	.50
J464 Assault Blade R	.75	2.00
J465 Medical Ninjutsu U	.20	.50
J466 Iron Sand: Scattered Showers C	.10	.25
J467 Iron Sand: Unleash C	.10	.25
J468 Body Manipulation C	.10	.25
J469 Concealed Weapon C	.10	.25
J470 Chakra Shield C	.10	.25
J471 Poison Smoke U	.20	.50
J472 Power of the Cursed Blood C	.10	.25
J473 8 Trigrams Palms Rotation C	.10	.25
J474 Scope C	.10	.25
J475 Fire Style: Fire Ball Jutsu U	.20	.50
J476 Illusion by Genjutsu U	.20	.50
J477 A Treasure Puppet U	.20	.50
J478 Continuous Firing of Poison Needles R	.75	2.00
J479 Hallucination by Genjutsu R	.75	2.00
J480 Perfect Defense R	.75	2.00
J481 Continuous Shuriken Attacks C	.10	.25
J482 Water Style: Exploding Water Shock Wave R	.75	2.00
J483 Clean Hit R	.75	2.00
J484 Clay Clone C	.10	.25
J485 Shadow Clone Jutsu U	.20	.50
J486 Genjutsu: Sylvan Fetters R	.75	2.00
J487 Crescent Moon Dance C	.10	.25
J488 Human Boulder C	.10	.25
J489 Genjutsu Negation U	.20	.50
J490 Ino-Shika-Cho Formation R	.75	2.00
J491 Trap C	.10	.25
J492 Spinning Kick C	.10	.25
J493 Demon Illusion: Death Mirage Jutsu R	.75	2.00
J494 Detonating Clay Signature Technique R	.75	2.00
J495 Rasengan SR	3.00	8.00
M412 Mission of Capturing the Missing Pet Tora R	.75	2.00
M413 Lottery C	.10	.25
M414 Fulfilling the Quota C	.10	.25
M415 Buying Time R	.75	2.00
M416 Cruel Irony C	.10	.25
M417 Eliminating the Alliance U	.20	.50
M418 Weak Remembrance C	.10	.25
M419 Uncovered Trick C	.10	.25
M420 Control of the Nine-Tailed C	.10	.25
M421 Ubiquitous U	.20	.50
M422 Evil Spirit U	.20	.50
M423 Whim U	.20	.50
M424 Puppet Show R	.75	2.00
M425 Quota U	.20	.50
M426 The Ones Wriggling in the Dark C	.10	.25
M427 Messenger C	.10	.25
M428 Eight Ninja Dogs R	.75	2.00
M429 Sealing the Tailed Beast U	.20	.50
M430 Threat of the Tailed Beasts C	.10	.25
M431 Successive Kazekage U	.20	.50
M432 Detecting the Enemy C	.10	.25
M433 Unhealed Wound R	.75	2.00
M434 Bad Omen U	.20	.50
M435 Kazekage in Custody C	.10	.25
M436 Hidden Village of the Wind R	.75	2.00
M437 Long Awaited Reunion C	.10	.25
M438 Overflowing Fighting Spirits C	.10	.25
M439 New Hokage Rock C	.10	.25
M440 Misunderstanding U	.20	.50
M441 Dark Ritual U	.20	.50
M442 Reinforcement from Sand C	.10	.25
M443 Substitute R	3.00	8.00
M444 Tactic against Genjutsu C	.10	.25
M445 Unstable Ground R	.75	2.00
M446 Report C	.10	.25
M447 4 Times Faster U	.20	.50
M448 Fellow and Loneliness SR	3.00	8.00
M449 Losing Control of Chakra C	.10	.25
M450 Eternal Rivalry R	.75	2.00
M451 Beginning of the New Chronicle R	.75	2.00
M452 Corps in Black U	.20	.50
M453 Successive Hokage U	.20	.50
M454 Sleeping in the Open U	.20	.50
N522 Naruto Uzumaki (Tailed Beast Mode) SR	8.00	20.00
N523 Sakura Haruno R	.75	2.00
N527 Kakashi Hatake R	.75	2.00
N528 Kiba Inuzuka R	.75	2.00
N529 Shino Aburame R	.75	2.00
N530 Hinata Hyuga U	.20	.50
N531 Ino Yamanaka U	.20	.50
N532 Choji Akimichi U	.20	.50
N533 Kotetsu Hagane U	.20	.50
N534 Izumo Kamizuki U	.20	.50
N535 Kidomaru C	.10	.25
N536 Jirobo C	.10	.25
N537 Sakon C	.10	.25
N538 Tayuya C	.10	.25
N539 Chiyo SR	5.00	12.00
N540 Father and Mother U	.20	.50
N541 Deidara U	.20	.50
N542 Sasori SR	8.00	20.00
N543 The 3rd Kazekage SR	6.00	15.00
N544 Sasori (Puppet Mode) SR	3.00	8.00
N545 Hanabi Hyuga C	.10	.25
N546 Neji Hyuga U	.20	.50
N547 Sasuke Uchiha N-548	.10	.25
N548 Sasuke Uchiha SR	10.00	25.00
N549 Neji Hyuga & Hinata Hyuga R	.75	2.00
N550 Sasuke Uchiha & Orochimaru SR	10.00	25.00
N551 Shino Aburame & Kiba Inuzuka R	2.50	6.00
N552 Sasori & Deidara R	.75	2.00
N553 Ino Yamanaka U	.20	.50
N554 Anko Mitarashi R	.75	2.00
N555 Jiraiya C	.10	.25
N556 Shizune R	.75	2.00
N557 Rock Lee N-558	.20	.50
N558 Orochimaru U	.20	.50
N559 Naruto Uzumaki U	.20	.50
N560 Neji Hyuga SR	10.00	25.00
N561 Hinata Hyuga U	.20	.50
N562 Tenten R	.75	2.00
N563 Naruto Uzumaki U	.20	.50
N564 Sasuke Uchiha U	.20	.50
N565 Rock Lee R	.75	2.00

N566 Naruto Uzumaki U .20 .50
N567 Kakashi Hatake (Anbu Days) U .20 .50
N568 Neji Hyuga U .20 .50
N569 Temari R .75 2.00
N570 Tsunade U .20 .50
N571 Rock Lee U .20 .50
N572 Kakashi Hatake & Might Guy R .75 2.00
N573 Kakashi Hatake & Pakkun R .75 2.00
N574 Kiba Inuzuka & Akamaru R 1.50 4.00
N575 Naruto Uzumaki C .10 .25
N576 Neji Hyuga R .75 2.00
N577 Tenten U .20 .50
N578 Shikamaru Nara SR 5.00 12.00
N579 Sakura Haruno ST .40 1.00
N580 Kakashi Hatake ST .40 1.00
N581 Itachi Uchiha ST .40 1.00
N582 Rock Lee ST .40 1.00
N583 Ninja Dog Squad (All Gathered) ST .40 1.00
N584 The 5th Kazekage ST .40 1.00
N585 Jiraiya ST .40 1.00
N586 The 5th Hokage ST .40 1.00
N587 Orochimaru ST .40 1.00
N588 Naruto Uzumaki STSR 2.00 5.00
N589 Sasuke Uchiha STSR 2.00 5.00

2009 Naruto Foretold Prophecy

COMPLETE SET (177) 60.00 120.00
BOOSTER BOX (24 PACKS) 40.00 80.00
BOOSTER PACK (10 CARDS) 2.00 4.00
RELEASED IN DECEMBER 2009
C049 Taruho U .20 .50
C050 Susuki U .20 .50
C051 Miroku R 1.25 3.00
J541 Tongla C .10 .25
J542 Dynamic Action U .20 .50
J543 Storm by Rasengan ST .40 1.00
J544 Destructive Swing C .10 .25
J545 Fast Capture R 1.00 2.50
J546 Power of Sharingan U .20 .50
J547 Fire Style: Fire Ball Jutsu C .10 .25
J548 Burst of Lightning Blade U .20 .50
J549 Assault of Snakes C .10 .25
J550 Ecdysis C .10 .25
J551 Sand Arm R 1.00 2.50
J552 Giant Sand Shield C .10 .25
J553 Heaven Kick of Pain U .20 .50
J554 Chakra Thread C .10 .25
J555 Leaf Hurricane R 1.25 3.00
J556 Priestess's Bell C .10 .25
J557 Chocolate Bomb!! U .20 .50
J558 Hidden Lotus U .20 .50
J559 Super Chakra Rasengan R 1.25 3.00
J560 Shadow Mirror Body Transfer Art U .20 .50
J561 Monstrous Warriors U .20 .50
J562 Water Style: Surface Slicer U .20 .50
J563 Combination Ninjutsu C .10 .25
J564 Chakra Infusion R 1.00 2.50
J565 Wind Style: Divine Down-Current C .10 .25
J566 Earth Style: Petrifying Jutsu U .20 .50
J567 Youth at Full Power! C .10 .25
J569 Great Leaf Flash U .20 .50
J570 Radiant Energy C .10 .25
J571 Ninja Art: Super Beast Scroll Falcon C .10 .25
J572 Ninja Art: Super Beast Scroll Snake U .20 .50
J573 Snake Sword ST .40 1.00
J574 Mulitple Striking Shadow Snake R 1.50 4.00
J575 Chidori Stream SR 5.00 12.00
J576 Sickle Chain C .10 .25
J577 Weapon Control! Tensasai U .20 .50
J578 Antidote C .10 .25
J579 8 Trigrams Hazan Strike C .10 .25
J580 Fist of Anger C .10 .25
J581 Cherry Blossom Impact SR 5.00 12.00
J582 Detonating Clay C .10 .25
J583 Gentle Fist U .20 .50
J584 Emergency Meeting U .20 .50
J585 Giving Ones Best C .10 .25
J586 Thousand Arms Manipulation U .20 .50
J587 Wood Style: Four Pillars House Jutsu C .10 .25
J588 Massive Iron Sand Attack U .20 .50
J589 Kamui SR 5.00 12.00
J590 8 Trigrams Air Palm C .10 .25
J591 Glare of Snake U .20 .50
J592 Power of the Evil C .10 .25
J593 Special Power C .10 .25
J594 Sealing the Evil U .20 .50
J595 Ink Clone Jutsu C .10 .25
J596 Running on the Water U .20 .50
J597 Stock C .10 .25
J598 Chakra Knife U .20 .50
J599 Wood Style: Domed Wall C .10 .25
J600 Revival of the Dead R 1.00 2.50
J601 Interrogation C .10 .25
M500 Leaf Academy U .20 .50
M501 Reunion of Destiny C .10 .25
M502 Betrayal R 1.25 3.00
M503 Sacrifice C .10 .25
M504 Target of the Vengeance C .10 .25
M505 Lack of Sensitivity R 1.25 3.00
M506 Luxurious Meal C .10 .25
M507 Temporary Squad C .10 .25
M508 The Priestess Who Seals the Evil ST .40 1.00
M509 Beyond the Time C .10 .25
M510 Changed Prophecy C .10 .25
M511 Competition R 1.00 2.50
M512 Retiring Character R 1.00 2.50
M513 Surprise Attack from a Mysterious Enemy R 1.00 2.50
M514 Powerless C .10 .25
M515 Punishment U .20 .50
M516 Not Again U .20 .50
M517 Cold Eyes U .20 .50
M518 Heart-to-Heart Communication C .10 .25
M519 Weird Picture Book U .20 .50
M520 Fake Smile R 1.00 2.50
M521 Internal Trouble U .20 .50
M522 Secret Mission U .20 .50
M523 Buddy System R 1.00 2.50
M524 Search for a Member U .20 .50
M525 A Tail C .10 .25
M526 Necklace of the First Hokage U .20 .50
M527 Master of the Weapons R 1.00 2.50
M528 Inherited Kekkei Genkai C .10 .25
M529 Dummy U .20 .50
M530 Member List R 1.00 2.50
M531 Impatient Feeling U .20 .50
M532 Earth Style: Hidden Mole Jutsu C .10 .25
M533 Jealousy C .10 .25
M534 Bashfulness SR 6.00 15.00
M535 Deep-Rooted Organization R 1.00 2.50
M536 Deeply Cut Wound U .20 .50
M537 Approaching Shadow of a Snake R 1.00 2.50
M538 Crying in Vain R 1.00 2.50
M539 The Power to Seal the Disaster U .20 .50
M540 Not Another Step! R 1.00 2.50
M541 Firm Union U .20 .50
M542 Will of the Third Hokage C .10 .25
M543 Sharpening the Blade C .10 .25
M544 Big Help C .10 .25
M545 Leaf Hospital SR 5.00 12.00
M546 Destiny of the Clan U .20 .50
M547 Approaching Showdown SR 5.00 12.00
M548 Threat of the State 2 R 1.00 2.50
M549 Leaf Police Force ST .40 1.00
N645 Shion (Awakened) ST .40 1.00
N646 Kusuna R 1.50 4.00
N647 Shizuku U .20 .50
N648 Setsuna U .20 .50
N649 Gitai C .10 .25
N650 The Nine-Tailed Fox Spirit R 1.25 3.00
N651 Naruto Uzumaki C .10 .25
N652 Sakura Haruno U .20 .50
N653 Sasuke Uchiha R 5.00 12.00
N654 Sai R 1.25 3.00
N655 Yamato SR 10.00 25.00
N656 Kiba Inuzuka U .20 .50
N657 Shino Aburame C .10 .25
N658 Hinata Hyuga U .20 .50
N659 Hiashi Hyuga U .20 .50
N660 Akamaru U .20 .50
N661 The 5th Kazekage R 1.00 2.50
N662 Kankuro R 1.00 2.50
N663 Ebizo U .20 .50
N664 Sasori (Childhood) U .20 .50
N665 Deidara U .20 .50
N666 Orochimaru SR 6.00 15.00
N667 Kabuto Yakushi R 1.25 3.00
N668 Sasuke Uchiha SR 10.00 25.00
N669 Naruto Uzumaki STSR 2.00 5.00
N670 Sasuke Uchiha STSR 2.00 5.00
N671 Sai ST .40 1.00
N672 Sakura Haruno C .10 .25
N673 Sasori & The 3rd Kazekage R 1.25 3.00
N674 Shikamaru Nara U .20 .50
N675 Kakashi Hatake R 1.00 2.50
N676 Itachi Uchiha ST .40 1.00
N677 Yamato R 1.25 3.00
N678 Baki R 3.00 8.00
N679 Temari C .10 .25
N680 Jiraiya ST .40 1.00
N681 Tsunade C .10 .25
N682 Orochimaru U .20 .50
N683 Konohamaru ST .40 1.00
N684 Naruto Uzumaki & Jiraiya R 2.00 5.00
N685 Sakura Haruno & Tsunade SR 6.00 15.00
N686 Naruto Uzumaki & Yamato C .10 .25
N687 Naruto Uzumaki & Sai ST .40 1.00
N688 Naruto Uzumaki & Shion R 1.25 3.00
N689 Shion ST .40 1.00
N690 Yomi ST .40 1.00
N691 The Fourth Kazekage SR 6.00 15.00
N692 Giant Ninja Toad ST .40 1.00
N693 Giant Snake U .20 .50
N694 Tonton C .10 .25
N695 Tortoise Ninja C .10 .25
N696 Giant Tiger C .10 .25
N697 Kakashi Hatake (Childhood) C .10 .25
N698 The Third Hokage (Childhood) U .20 .50
N699 Koharu Utatane (Childhood) C .10 .25
N700 Homura Mitomon (Childhood) C .10 .25
N701 The Fourth Hokage (Childhood) C .10 .25
N702 The Fourth Hokage (Younger Days) SR 10.00 25.00
N703 Neji Hyuga (Childhood) C .10 .25
N704 Tekka Uchiha ST .40 1.00
N705 Inabi Uchiha ST .40 1.00
N706 Yashiro Uchiha ST .40 1.00
N707 Elder of Hyuga Clan U .20 .50
N708 Iruka Umino (Childhood) C .10 .25

2009 Naruto A New Chronicle

COMPLETE SET (172) 75.00 150.00
BOOSTER BOX (24 PACKS) 50.00 100.00
BOOSTER PACK (10 CARDS) 2.50 5.00
RELEASED IN FEBRUARY 2009
J387 Sexy Jutsu R .75 2.00
J388 New Pervy Ninjutsu R .75 2.00
J389 Revealing the Ending C .10 .25
J390 Make-Out Tactics C .10 .25
J391 Brainwash Jutsu U .20 .50
J392 Forbidden Word C .10 .25
J393 Iron-Armed U .20 .50
J394 Wind Scythe Jutsu R .75 2.00
J395 Sand Shield C .10 .25
J396 Leaf Rising Wind U .20 .50
J397 Nunchaku C .10 .25
J398 Opening the Eight Inner Gates R .75 2.00
J399 Asakujaku SR 10.00 25.00
J400 Giant Rasengan SR 6.00 15.00
J401 Genjutsu C .10 .25
J402 Mission File C .10 .25
J403 Detonating Clay Eagle U .20 .50
J404 Detonating Clay Bird U .20 .50
J405 Detonating Clay Spider U .20 .50
J406 Detonating Clay Signature Technique R 1.50 4.00
J407 Cleanup U .20 .50
J408 Water Style: Exploding Water Shock Wave U .20 .50
J409 Water Prison Jutsu R .75 2.00
J410 Shark Skin R .75 2.00
J411 Impersonation Jutsu U .20 .50
J412 Explosive Blade C .10 .25
J413 Puppet Master Jutsu U .20 .50
J414 Absolute Defense U .20 .50
J415 Sand Prison U .20 .50
J416 Sand Coffin SR 5.00 12.00
J417 Detoxification C .10 .25
J418 Deadly Poison R 1.50 4.00
J419 Emission of Chakra R .75 2.00
J420 Compound Jutsu C .10 .25
J421 8 Trigrams Air Palm R 2.50 6.00
J422 Arhat Fist R .75 2.00
J423 Spider Bow: Fierce Rip R .75 2.00
J424 Deadly Combination Attack R .75 2.00
J425 Demon Flute: Chains of Fantasia U .20 .50
J426 Threat of the Puppets C .10 .25
J427 Substitution by Insects C .10 .25
J428 Concealed Weapon U .20 .50
J429 Gentle Fist Style: 8 Trigrams 64 Palms R .75 2.00
J430 Shadow Strangle Jutsu U .20 .50
J431 Poison Needles U .20 .50
J432 Dispatch of Anbu U .20 .50
J433 Angry Fist U .20 .50
J434 Striking Shadow Snake U .20 .50
J435 Reaper Death Seal R .75 2.00
J436 Shadow Clone Jutsu R .75 2.00
J437 Summoning Jutsu C .10 .25
J438 Playing Possum Jutsu C .10 .25
J439 Liquid Bullets R .75 2.00
J440 Air Bullets R .75 2.00
J441 Sealing Jutsu: Fire Seal C .10 .25
J442 Anbu Mask U .20 .50
J443 Knockout Blow U .20 .50
J444 Opening the Byakugan C .10 .25
J445 Wolf Fang Over Fang C .10 .25
J446 Larch Dance U .20 .50
J447 Substitution by Puppet R .75 2.00
J448 Capture C .10 .25
J449 Fire Style: Fire Ball Jutsu C .10 .25
M364 Dangerous Intruder U .20 .50
M365 New leader of the Village U .20 .50
M366 Round-Table Conference C .10 .25
M367 Sending Off C .10 .25
M368 Growth of the Two R .60 1.50
M369 Existence of Tailed Beast U .20 .50
M370 Powerful Help C .10 .25
M371 Art is an explosion! R .60 1.50
M372 Akatsuki Gathered C .10 .25
M373 The ones who interrupt C .10 .25
M374 Revenge for My Son C .10 .25
M375 Sasori of the Red Sand R 3.00 8.00
M376 Playing Dead U .20 .50
M377 Heroic Whirl Wind R .60 1.50
M378 Tyrannical Storm R .60 1.50
M379 West Gate, North Gate C .10 .25
M380 South Gate, East Gate C .10 .25
M381 The one who lives within SR 6.00 15.00
M382 Raid By Anbu U .20 .50
M383 Teacher and pupils C .10 .25
M384 Great Memory C .10 .25
M385 A Mark U .20 .50
M386 Arbitration R .60 1.50
M387 Oath of Vengeance U .20 .50
M388 Welling Up Red Chakra C .10 .25
M389 Secret of Uchiha Clan U .20 .50
M390 On the Stump C .10 .25
M391 Debt R 1.25 3.00
M392 A Preach C .10 .25
M393 Found You! C .10 .25
M394 Wonderful Days U .20 .50
M395 Wager C .10 .25
M396 A Gift U .20 .50
M397 BBQ R 3.00 8.00
M398 Preparation C .10 .25
M399 Ino-Shika-Cho Trio U .20 .50
M400 Inuzuka Clan U .20 .50
M401 Ichiraku Noodle Shop R .60 1.50
M402 Chase U .20 .50
M403 Creeping Up Dark Clouds U .20 .50
M404 Agony of the Strong C .10 .25
M405 Numbness U .20 .50
M406 Archrival U .20 .50
M407 Ultimate Two-Step Program C .10 .25
M408 Invitation to the Evil U .20 .50
M409 Escape C .10 .25
M410 Apology C .10 .25
M411 Long Awaited Reinforcements R 1.50 4.00
N461 Kankuro SR 12.00 30.00
N462 Temari R .50 1.25
N463 Yura C .10 .25
N464 Baki U .20 .50
N465 The Fifth Kazekage SR 8.00 20.00
N466 Naruto Uzumaki U .20 .50
N467 Sakura Haruno R 1.25 3.00
N468 Iruka Umino U .20 .50
N469 Konohamaru C .10 .25
N470 Moegi C .10 .25
N471 Udon C .10 .25
N472 Ebisu C .10 .25
N473 Kakashi Hatake SR 8.00 20.00
N474 Might Guy R 1.25 3.00
N475 Rock Lee R 1.25 3.00
N476 Neji Hyuga U .20 .50
N477 Tenten U .20 .50
N478 Itachi Uchiha SR 8.00 20.00
N479 Kisame Hoshigaki R 1.25 3.00
N480 Deidara SR 12.00 30.00
N481 Sasori SR 12.00 30.00
N482 Zetsu SR 6.00 15.00
N483 Gaara of the Desert U .20 .50
N484 Crow U .20 .50
N485 Black Ant U .20 .50
N486 Salamander U .20 .50
N487 Ebizo U .20 .50
N488 Chiyo R 1.50 4.00
N489 Cipher Corps U .20 .50
N490 Naruto Uzumaki C .10 .25
N491 Sakura Haruno C .10 .25
N492 Rock Lee U .20 .50
N493 Hinata Hyuga C .10 .25
N494 Naruto Uzumaki & Gaara of the Desert SR 8.00 20.00
N495 Temari & Kankuro SR 10.00 25.00
N496 Sasuke Uchiha U .20 .50
N497 Naruto Uzumaki U .20 .50
N498 Kiba Inuzuka C .10 .25
N499 Ninja Dog Squad C .10 .25

N500 Hinata Hyuga & Hiashi Hyuga U .20 .50
N501 Sasori & Kisame Hoshigaki SR 8.00 20.00
N502 Itachi Uchiha & Deidara SR 6.00 15.00
N503 Double Headed Wolf R 1.25 3.00
N504 Kiba Inuzuka & Akamaru R 1.25 3.00
N505 Kotetsu Hagane C .10 .25
N506 Kurenai Yuhi U .20 .50
N507 Genma Shiranui C .10 .25
N508 Hayate Gekko U .20 .50
N509 Hanabi Hyuga C .10 .25
N510 Kankuro U .20 .50
N511 Shino Aburame R 4.00 10.00
N512 Ninja Dog Squad (All Gathered) C .10 .25
N513 Neji Hyuga C .10 .25
N514 Inoichi Yamanaka R 1.25 3.00
N515 Shikaku Nara R 2.50 6.00
N516 Choza Akimichi R 1.25 3.00
N517 Gen Aburame R 1.25 3.00
N518 Hiashi Hyuga R 1.25 3.00
N519 Choji Akimichi C .10 .25
N520 Deidara U .20 .50
N521 Sasori U .20 .50

2010 Naruto Broken Promise

COMPLETE SET (157) 50.00 100.00
BOOSTER BOX (24 PACKS) 50.00 100.00
BOOSTER PACK (10 CARDS) 2.50 5.00
RELEASED IN MARCH 2010
C052 Lady Haruna R .40 1.00
C053 Momiji R .40 1.00
C054 Chikara U .20 .50
C055 Uroko U .20 .50
J602 Summoning Jutsu: Ninja Dogs C .10 .25
J603 Special Kunai C .10 .25
J604 Chidori SR FOIL 8.00 20.00
J605 White Fang's Blade C .10 .25
J606 Sharingan Kunai R 1.00 2.50
J607 Detonating Clay: Mysterious Bird C .10 .25
J608 Tsukuyomi U .20 .50
J609 Chakra Slice U .20 .50
J610 Mental Fatigue R .40 1.00
J611 Water Style: Water Dragon Jutsu R 1.00 2.50
J612 Striking Shadow Snake R .40 1.00
J613 Counter R 1.00 2.50
J614 Infuriation R .40 1.00
J615 Wood Style: Tree Bind Eternal Burial U .20 .50
J616 Sharpness of the Weapon U .20 .50
J617 Intrustion C .10 .25
J618 Sharingan of Tears C .10 .25
J619 Change in Chakra Form C .10 .25
J620 Change in Chakra Nature R .40 1.00
J621 Power of the Clones C .10 .25
J622 Power of the Meteorite U .20 .50
J623 Summoning Jutsu: Air Fish C .10 .25
J624 Magnetic Power C .10 .25
J625 Rasengan R .40 1.00
J626 Genjutsu U .20 .50
J627 Space Created by Genjutsu R .40 1.00
J628 Canceling Tone C .10 .25
J629 Dragon Eyes: Fang Release: Dark Sword U .20 .50
J630 Wind Slicer C .10 .25
J631 Wind Scythe Jutsu U .20 .50
J632 Soaring Shot Sword C .10 .25
J633 Wood Style: Great Forest Jutsu SR 3.00 8.00
J634 Inflow of Chakra U .20 .50
J635 Chidori Stream R 1.25 3.00
J636 Water Style: Bubbling Water C .10 .25
J637 Flower Shuriken: Burning Petals and Fallen Leaves C .10 .25
J638 Exposing the Hideout R .40 1.00
J639 High Speed Hand Signs C .10 .25
J640 Fear by Genjutsu SR 12.00 30.00
J641 Release of Fury SR FOIL 2.50 6.00
J642 Trump card R .40 1.00
J643 Beast Transformation C .10 .25
J644 Beast Mimicry Ninja Art: Man Beast Clone C .10 .25
M585 Succeeded Will of Fire R .40 1.00
M586 Beauty and Intelligence R .40 1.00
M587 Chakra Paper C .10 .25
M588 Earth Style: Rampart of Flowing Soil C .10 .25
M589 BBQ House "Barbe-Q" C .10 .25
M590 Recollection C .10 .25
M591 Restricted Jutsu U .20 .50
M592 Tears of Determination R .40 1.00
M593 Shogi Match SR 5.00 12.00
M594 A Snake Hiding in the Dark R .40 1.00
M595 Infiltration C .10 .25
M596 Reconfirmation of the Mission R .40 1.00
M597 Skeleton Key U .20 .50
M598 Smile of the Two C .10 .25
M599 Retreat C .10 .25
M600 Fire Temple C .10 .25
M601 Group Lesson R .75 2.00
M602 Messenger Ninjas C .10 .25
M603 Lullaby U .20 .50
M604 Showy Entrance U .20 .50
M605 Tracking Mission C .10 .25
M606 Clear Tone Carries in the Sunset C .10 .25
M607 Picture of Their Dreams C .10 .25
M608 My First Fellow C .10 .25
M609 Favor to Ask U .20 .50
M610 Visiting Kakashi in the Hospital U .20 .50
M611 Narrow Escape R .40 1.00
M612 Seeing Through Distance U .20 .50
M613 A Gift from a Friend U .20 .50
M614 Pressing R .40 1.00
M615 Imaginary Monster C .10 .25
M616 Last Message U .20 .50
M617 Efficient Training SR FOIL 5.00 12.00
M618 Determination of Men SR 3.00 8.00
M619 Water Style: Watefall Basin Jutsu C .10 .25
M620 Reconnoitering Party C .10 .25
N709 Kakashi Hatake (Boyhood) SR FOIL 10.00 25.00
N710 Rin U .20 .50
N711 Obito Uchiha SR FOIL 12.00 30.00
N712 The Fourth Hokage SR 10.00 25.00
N713 Kakkou U .20 .50
N714 Taiseki C .10 .25
N715 Mahiru C .10 .25
N716 Zetsu U .20 .50
N717 Tobi U .20 .50
N718 Orochimaru (Childhood) R 1.50 4.00
N719 Jiraiya (Childhood) R 1.25 3.00
N720 Tsunade (Childhood) R 1.50 4.00
N721 Chiriku C .10 .25
N722 Hana Inuzuka U .20 .50
N723 Haimaru Brothers C .10 .25
N724 Yoshino Nara R 1.25 3.00
N725 Shin C .10 .25
N726 Naruto Uzumaki (Student) U .20 .50
N727 Sasuke Uchiha (Student) U .20 .50
N728 Sakura Haruno (Student) U .20 .50
N729 Sakura Haruno & Hinata Hyuga R .40 1.00
N730 Shikamaru Nara & Kakashi Hatake SR 5.00 12.00
N731 Kakashi Hatake (Teacher) U .20 .50
N732 Asuma Sarutobi C .10 .25
N733 Yugito Ni'i R .40 1.00
N734 Two Tails SR 5.00 12.00
N735 Sasori & Zetsu U .20 .50
N736 Deidara & Tobi U .20 .50
N737 Itachi Uchiha SR FOIL 4.00 10.00
N738 Kankuro R .75 2.00
N739 Temari R .40 1.00
N740 Yugao Uzuki U .20 .50
N741 Kakashi Hatake C .10 .25
N742 Kakashi Hatake & Pakkun C .10 .25
N743 Kiba Inuzuka C .10 .25
N744 Kiba Inuzuka & Akamaru C .10 .25
N745 The First Hokage & Yamato R .40 1.00
N746 Naruto Uzumaki U .20 .50
N747 Naruto Uzumaki (Tailed Beast Form) SR FOIL 4.00 10.00
N748 Sasuke Uchiha U .20 .50
N749 The Third Hokage C .10 .25
N750 Advisor of the Sand C .10 .25
N751 Rock Lee & Neji Hyuga U .20 .50
N752 Ino Yamanka C .10 .25
N753 Ziga C .10 .25
N754 Ruiga U .20 .50
N755 Renga R .40 1.00
N756 Mizuki (Transformed) C .10 .25
N757 Raiga Kurosuki U .20 .50
N758 Ranmaru C .10 .25
N759 Lord Sagi C .10 .25
N760 Chishima C .10 .25
N761 Amachi (Sea Monster) U .20 .50
N762 Anko Mitarashi & Orochimaru U .20 .50
N763 Isaribi (Sea Monster) U .20 .50
N764 Rampageous Pig C .10 .25
N765 Hotarubi C .10 .25
N767 Natsuhi U .20 .50
N768 The 3rd Hoshikage U .20 .50
N769 Shiso C .10 .25
N770 Yotaka C .10 .25
N771 Naruto Uzumaki C .10 .25
N772 Hinata Hyuga C .10 .25
N773 Choji Akimichi C .10 .25
N774 Ino Yamanaka U .20 .50
N775 Might Guy (Afro) R .40 1.00
N776 Anbu U .20 .50
N777 Yakumo Kurama U .20 .50
N778 Gantetsu C .10 .25
N779 Menma C .10 .25
N780 Hoki U .20 .50
N781 Kujaku C .10 .25
N782 Ryugan C .10 .25
N783 Suiko C .10 .25

2010 Naruto Fangs of the Snake

COMPLETE SET (132) 50.00 100.00
BOOSTER BOX (24 PACKS) 50.00 100.00
BOOSTER PACK (10 CARDS) 2.50 5.00
RELEASED IN AUGUST 2010
J706 Hokage Style: Elder Jutsu R .40 1.00
J707 Explosive Kunai U .20 .50
J708 Summoning Jutsu: Projectile Weapons U .20 .50
J709 Wood Style: Tree Bind Eternal Burial SR 5.00 12.00
J710 Shikamaru's Judgement U .20 .50
J711 Flying Swallow C .10 .25
J712 Awakening the Byakugan U .20 .50
J713 Genjutsu of Pain! R .40 1.00
J714 Following the Trail C .10 .25
J715 Veterinary Meds U .20 .50
J716 Take Down U .20 .50
J717 Backed into a Corner R .40 1.00
J718 Quick Reflex U .20 .50
J719 Revenge C .10 .25
J720 Reading Movement U .20 .50
J721 Expert Kunai C .10 .25
J722 Wind Style: Toad Water Pistol U .20 .50
J723 Collaboration Ninjutsu! Wind Style: Toad Flame Bombs! R .40 1.00
J724 Multi Shadow Clone Jutsu U .20 .50
J725 Summoning Jutsu SR 5.00 12.00
J726 Collateral Damage U .20 .50
J727 Clone Tactics U .20 .50
J728 Snake Transformation Jutsu C .10 .25
J729 Transference Ritual U .20 .50
J730 Curse Mark Activation U .20 .50
J731 Sword Charge C .10 .25
J732 Chidori Lance U .20 .50
J733 Multi Striking Shadow Snake R .40 1.00
J734 Chidori Sword U .20 .50
J735 Snake Bind U .20 .50
J736 Elemental Defense R .40 1.00
J737 Sand Cocoon U .20 .50
J738 Puppet Master Jutsu U .20 .50
J739 Iron-Armed Punch C .10 .25
J740 Iron Sand: Unleash! R .40 1.00
J741 Wind Style: Rasen Shuriken U .20 .50
J742 Flamethrower U .20 .50
M670 Team Asuma C .10 .25
M671 Master of Weapons U .20 .50
M672 Comparative Strengths C .10 .25
M673 Student and Sensei R .40 1.00
M674 Kakuzu's Abilities R .40 1.00
M675 Shelter from the Shifting Sands R .40 1.00
M676 Surprise Help R .40 1.00
M677 Rapid Communication U .20 .50
M678 Scouting Party R .40 1.00
M679 Master of Genjutsu U .20 .50
M680 Hidden Leaf Veterinary Hospital U .20 .50
M681 Sync Dance U .20 .50
M682 Desperate Training U .20 .50
M683 Relaxation U .20 .50
M684 Silent Prayer R .40 1.00
M685 Well Fed U .20 .50
M686 Enveloping Chakra U .20 .50
M687 Animal Contract U .20 .50
M688 Chakra Molding U .20 .50
M689 Spread Talons U .20 .50
M690 Friendship from Sorrow U .20 .50
M691 Formation of Hebi R .40 1.00
M692 Controlling the Curse U .20 .50
M693 Sasori's Feelings U .20 .50
M694 Puppet Fight: 10 VS 100! R .40 1.00
M695 Kankuro's Puppet Show R .40 1.00
M696 Shinobi of the Sand U .20 .50
M697 Sakura's Desire R .40 1.00
M698 Battle over the Barrier R .40 1.00
N883 Neji Hyuga C .10 .25
N884 Hanabi Hyuga C .10 .25
N885 Choji Akimichi C .10 .25
N886 Shikamaru Nara C .10 .25
N887 Hinata Hyuga C .10 .25
N888 Ino Yamanaka C .10 .25
N889 Neji Hyuga R .40 1.00
N890 Zetsu C .10 .25
N891 Asuma Sarutobi SR 6.00 15.00
N892 Yamato R .40 1.00
N893 Deidara R .40 1.00
N894 The First Hokage SR 6.00 15.00
N895 Neji Hyuga & Hinata Hyuga R .40 1.00
N896 Urushi C .10 .25
N897 Guruko C .10 .25
N898 Kiba Inuzuka C .10 .25
N899 Sasuke Uchiha C .10 .25
N900 Big Bark Bull C .10 .25
N901 Obito Uchiha C .10 .25
N902 Biscuit C .10 .25
N903 Kotetsu Hagane C .10 .25
N904 Hayate Gekko C .10 .25
N905 Tobi C .10 .25
N906 Kakashi Hatake (Anbu Days) SR 10.00 25.00
N907 Itachi Uchiha SR 8.00 20.00
N908 Gamakichi C .10 .25
N909 Gamatatsu C .10 .25
N910 Gamariki C .10 .25
N911 Naruto Uzumaki C .10 .25
N912 Gama C .10 .25
N913 Rock Lee C .10 .25
N914 The Fourth Hokage R .40 1.00
N915 Might Guy U .20 .50
N916 Sai R .40 1.00
N917 Konohamaru Ninja Squad C .10 .25
N918 Anko Mitarashi C .10 .25
N919 Naruto Uzumaki SR 6.00 15.00
N920 Kidomaru C .10 .25
N921 Jirobo C .10 .25
N922 Tayuya C .10 .25
N923 Kabuto Yakushi SR 6.00 15.00
N924 Suigetsu Hozuki R 1.50 4.00
N925 Karin C .10 .25
N926 Jugo C .10 .25
N927 Kimimaro C .10 .25
N928 Kimimaro (Childhood) C .10 .25
N929 Sakon C .10 .25
N930 Anko Mitarashi (Childhood) C .10 .25
N931 Sasuke Uchiha R .40 1.00
N932 Orochimaru (Snake Form) SR 6.00 15.00
N933 Kimimaro & Jugo R .40 1.00
N934 Sasuke Uchiha (State 2) SR 12.00 30.00
N935 Gaara of the Desert C .10 .25
N936 Kankuro C .10 .25
N937 Matsuri (Childhood) C .10 .25
N938 Temari C .10 .25
N939 Advisor of the Sand C .10 .25
N940 Sakura Haruno C .10 .25
N941 Black Ant, Crow, & Salamander R .40 1.00
N942 Chiyo R .40 1.00
N943 Kurenai Yuhi R .40 1.00
N944 Unkai Kurama U .20 .50
N945 Hiruko SR 6.00 15.00
N946 Katsuyu SR 6.00 15.00
N947 Sasori (Puppet Mode) R .40 1.00
N948 Gaara of the Desert & Temari R .40 1.00

2010 Naruto Fierce Ambitions Tin

N145 Gaara of the Desert .30 .75
N370 The Third Hokage .30 .75
N372 The Fifth Hokage .30 .75
N453 Itachi Uchiha .50 1.25
N461 Kankuro .50 1.25
N473 Kakashi Hatake .30 .75
N480 Deidara .30 .75
N495 Temari & Kankuro .30 .75
NUS020 Rock Lee .50 1.25
NUS040 Shikamaru Nara & Asuma Sarutobi .30 .75

2010 Naruto Path of Pain

COMPLETE SET (112) 50.00 100.00
BOOSTER BOX 50.00 100.00
BOOSTER PACK 2.50 5.00
J743 Detonating Clay: C2 Dragon U .20 .50
J744 Detonating Clay: Snake C .10 .25
J745 Detonating Clay: Mines U .20 .50
J746 Detonating Clay: C3 Ohako U .20 .50
J747 Detonating Clay: C4 Karura SR 5.00 12.00
J748 Clay Clone Jutsu U .20 .50
J749 Lightning Blade F 2.00 5.00
J750 Mangekyou Sharingan SR 6.00 15.00
J751 Anticipation U .20 .50
J752 Fatigue C .10 .25
J753 Tracking Orders U .20 .50
J754 Animal Transformation U .20 .50
J755 Leaf Hurricane U .20 .50
J756 Eight Inner Gates R .40 1.00
J757 Primary Lotus SR 6.00 15.00
J758 Severe Leaf Hurricane C .10 .25
J759 Toad Mouth Trap U .20 .50
J760 Piggyback R .40 1.00

J761 Fire Style: Searing Migraine U	.20	.50
J762 Striking Shadow Snake U	.20	.50
J763 Striking Multi Shadow Snakes Jutsu R	.40	1.00
J764 Chidori C	.10	.25
J765 Chakra Punch C	.10	.25
J766 Righteous Anger U	.20	.50
J767 Kick of Anger! U	.20	.50
J768 Palm Healing R	.40	1.00
J769 Coordination R	.40	1.00
J770 The Fangs of Pain U	.20	.50
J771 The Wings of Pain R	.40	1.00
J772 Rinnegan SR	5.00	12.00
M699 Intellectual Strategy U	.20	.50
M700 Sharpened Skills R	.40	1.00
M701 Strategy Scroll U	.20	.50
M702 Rooftop Standoff U	.20	.50
M703 Past Lessons C	.10	.25
M704 Reaper Death Seal R	.40	1.00
M705 Sacrifice U	.20	.50
M706 Supervised Training U	.20	.50
M707 Denka & Hina U	.20	.50
M708 Burst of Power R	.40	1.00
M709 Tailed Beast Unleashed U	.20	.50
M710 Surprise Ability C	.10	.25
M711 Promise to Return U	.20	.50
M712 Kakashi's Test U	.20	.50
M713 The Great Naruto Bridge R	.40	1.00
M714 Suigetsu's Joy R	.40	1.00
M715 Power of State 2 U	.20	.50
M716 Pledge under a Setting Sun F	2.00	5.00
M717 Barrier Preparation R	.40	1.00
M718 Perfect Chakra Control C	.10	.25
M719 Delicate Operation U	.20	.50
M720 Reflection R	.40	1.00
M721 The Time of Pain R	.40	1.00
M722 The City of Pain R	.40	1.00
N949 Detonating Clay Minion C	.10	.25
N950 Ino Yamanaka C	.10	.25
N951 Kikunojou C	.10	.25
N952 Yurinojou C	.10	.25
N953 Shikamaru Nara C	.10	.25
N954 Tenten U	.20	.50
N955 Chiriku U	.20	.50
N956 Yamato U	.20	.50
N957 Deidara SR•	6.00	15.00
N958 Deidara & Tobi R	.40	1.00
N959 Pakkun U	.20	.50
N960 Uhei C	.10	.25
N961 Shiba C	.10	.25
N962 Akino C	.10	.25
N963 Sasuke Uchiha C	.10	.25
N964 Kotetsu Hagane C	.10	.25
N965 Monkey King Enma R	.40	1.00
N966 Kakashi Hatake F	2.00	5.00
N967 Itachi Uchiha C	.10	.25
N968 The Third Hokage SR	5.00	12.00
N969 Might Guy R	.40	1.00
N970 Rock Lee & Might Guy R	.40	1.00
N971 Naruto Uzumaki (Taijutsu) C	.10	.25
N972 Izumo Kamizuki C	.10	.25
N973 Iruka Umino C	.10	.25
N974 Ninja Tortoise U	.20	.50
N975 Naruto Uzumaki C	.10	.25
N976 Naruto Uzumaki (Nine-Tail's Cloak) R	.40	1.00
N977 Jiraiya U	.20	.50
N978 The Fourth Hokage R	.40	1.00
N979 Doki C	.10	.25
N980 Karin C	.10	.25
N981 Tayuya (State 1) C	.10	.25
N982 Suigetsu Hozuki C	.10	.25
N983 Jugo (State 1) C	.10	.25
N984 Anko Mitarashi F	2.00	5.00
N985 Orochimaru R•	.40	1.00
N986 Sasuke Uchiha U	.20	.50
N987 Kabuto Yakushi (Possessed Mode) R	.40	1.00
N988 Tayuya (State 2) U	.20	.50
N989 Kakuzu (Soul Form) SR	6.00	15.00
N990 Kamatari C	.10	.25
N991 Sakura Haruno C	.10	.25
N992 Rin C	.10	.25
N993 Temari C	.10	.25
N994 Chiyo U	.20	.50
N995 Shizune U	.20	.50
N996 Kurenai Yuhi R	.40	1.00
N997 Tsunade U	.20	.50
N998 Shukaku SR	6.00	15.00
N999 Konan C	.10	.25
N1000 Pain (Deva Path) SR	12.00	25.00
N1001 Giant Chameleon C	.10	.25
N1002 Giant Chimera C	.10	.25
N1003 Pain (Animal Path) C	.10	.25
N1004 Pain (Petra Path) U	.20	.50
N1005 Sasuke Uchiha STSR		
N1006 Naruto Uzumaki STSR		

2010 Naruto Tournament Pack 1

COMPLETE SET (60)	40.00	80.00
BOOSTER BOX (24 PACKS)	60.00	120.00
BOOSTER PACK	3.00	6.00
RELEASED IN AUGUST 2010		
J697 Expansion Jutsu: Super Slap!	.20	.50
J698 Fire Style: Fireball Jutsu	.50	1.25
J699 Lightning Blade Single Slash	.75	2.00
J700 Ninja Art: Super Beast Scroll Lion	.40	1.00
J701 Severe Leaf Hurricane	.20	.50
J702 Water Clone Jutsu	.20	.50
J703 Water Prison Jutsu	.40	1.00
J704 Medical Jutsu: Reanimation	.20	.50
J705 Wind Nature: Chakra Blades	.40	1.00
M665 Shogi Lesson	.20	.50
M666 Make-Out Tactics	.50	1.25
M667 Fierce Rivals	2.50	6.00
M668 Dehydration	.50	1.25
M669 Bonds of Friendship	1.00	2.50
N019 Naruto Uzumaki	.50	1.25
N024 Zabuza Momochi	.50	1.25
N114 Temari	.10	.25
N122 Hayate Gekko	.10	.25
N202 Kisame Hoshigaki	.20	.50
N209 Nawaki	.20	.50
N333 Kakashi Hatake	.10	.25
N336 Tsubaki	.20	.50
N371 The Fourth Hokage	.10	.25
N382 Toki	.75	2.00
N384 Isaribi	.20	.50
N451 Shizune	.10	.25
N511 Shino Aburame	.40	1.00
N547 Sasuke Uchiha	.50	1.25
N571 Rock Lee	.10	.25
N595 Ino Yamanaka	.10	.25
N600 Danzo	.10	.25
N622 Anko Mitarashi	.10	.25
N631 Ino Yamanaka	.10	.25
N640 Might Guy	.10	.25
N864 Choji Akimichi (Childhood)	2.50	6.00
N865 Hinata Hyuga (Childhood)	.10	.25
N866 Shikamaru Nara (Childhood)	.10	.25
N867 Anbu (Captain)	.10	.25
N868 Itachi Uchiha (Anbu Days)	.20	.50
N869 Kiba Inuzuka (Childhood)	8.00	20.00
N870 Gamabunta	.10	.25
N871 Konohamaru Ninja Squad	8.00	20.00
N872 Rock Lee (Childhood)	.10	.25
N873 Giant Spider	.10	.25
N874 Rashomon	.10	.25
N875 Zabuza Momochi (Younger Days)	.40	1.00
N876 Ebisu	6.00	15.00
N877 Gaara of the Desert (Childhood)	.10	.25
N878 Sasori	.10	.25
N879 Hinata Hyuga	25.00	50.00
N880 Yamato	.10	.25
N881 Iruka Umino	8.00	20.00
N882 Konohamaru	.10	.25
J696B Byakugan	.10	.25
NUS006 Sakura Haruno	.20	.50
NUS015 Shikamaru Nara	4.00	10.00
NUS027 Jiraiya	.20	.50
NUS035 Haku	.10	.25
NUS072 Gamakichi	.20	.50
NUS106 Kurenai Yuhi	.20	.50

2010 Naruto Tournament Pack 2

COMPLETE SET (64)	20.00	40.00
BOOSTER BOX (24 PACKS)	25.00	50.00
BOOSTER PACK (10 CARDS)	2.00	3.00
RELEASED IN FEBRUARY 2011		
J696 Byakugan U	.20	.50
J697 Expansion Jutsu: Super Slap! R	.40	1.00
J698 Fire Style: Fireball Jutsu R	.40	1.00
J699 Lightning Blade Single Slash R	.40	1.00
J700 Ninja Art: Super Beast Scroll Lion U	.20	.50
J701 Severe Leaf Hurricane U	.20	.50
J702 Water Clone Jutsu R	.40	1.00
J703 Water Prison Jutsu U	.20	.50
J704 Reanimation Ninjutsu R	.40	1.00
J705 Chakra Blades U	.20	.50
M665 Shogi Lesson R	.40	1.00
M666 Make-Out Tactics R	.40	1.00
M667 Fierce Rivals R	.40	1.00
M668 Dehydration R	.40	1.00
M669 Bonds of Friendship R	.40	1.00
N864 Choji Akimichi (Childhood) C	.10	.25
N865 Hinata Hyuga (Childhood) C	.10	.25
N866 Shikamaru Nara (Childhood) C	.10	.25
N867 Anbu (Captain) R	.40	1.00
N868 Itachi Uchiha (Anbu Days) SR	6.00	15.00
N869 Kiba Inuzuka (Childhood) C	.10	.25
N870 Gamabunta SR	5.00	12.00
N871 Konohamaru Ninja Squad U	.20	.50
N872 Rock Lee (Childhood) C	.10	.25
N873 Giant Spider C	.10	.25
N874 Rashomon R	.40	1.00
N875 Zabuza Momochi (Younger Days) SR	5.00	12.00
N876 Ebisu U	.20	.50
N877 Gaara of the Desert (Childhood) C	.10	.25
N878 Sasori SR	5.00	12.00
N879 Hinata Hyuga U	.20	.50
N880 Yamato SR	6.00	15.00
N881 Iruka Umino C	.10	.25
N882 Konohamaru C	.10	.25
N1007 Neji Hyuga C	.10	.25
N1008 Shikamaru Nara U	.20	.50
N1009 Zetsu C	.10	.25
N1010 Deidara U	.20	.50
N1011 Ibiki Morino U	.20	.50
N1012 Shikaku Nara R	.40	1.00
N1013 Hidan SR	6.00	15.00
N1014 Tobi C	.10	.25
N1015 Itachi Uchiha R	.40	1.00
N1016 Kiba Inuzuka U	.20	.50
N1017 Sasuke Uchiha C	.10	.25
N1018 Raido Namiashi C	.10	.25
N1019 Naruto Uzumaki C	.10	.25
N1020 Iruka Umino C	.10	.25
N1021 Naruto Uzumaki C	.10	.25
N1022 Sai R	.40	1.00
N1023 Ink Summon U	.20	.50
N1024 Jiraiya U	.20	.50
N1025 Kisame Hoshigaki SR	5.00	12.00
N1026 Kakuzu SR	5.00	12.00
N1027 Karin U	.20	.50
N1028 Haku C	.10	.25
N1029 Kimimaro R	.40	1.00
N1030 Sasuke Uchiha R	.40	1.00
N1031 Mizuki U	.20	.50
N1032 Shizune C	.10	.25
N1033 Rin C	.10	.25
N1034 Gaara of the Desert C	.10	.25
N1035 Konan R	.40	1.00
N1036 The Fifth Hokage R	.40	1.00

2010 Naruto Untouchables Tin

N086 Sasuke Uchiha	.40	1.00
N146 Temari	.75	2.00
N168 The Second Hokage	1.00	2.50
N224 Naruto Uzumaki	.30	.75
N311 Tenten	.30	.75
N324 Kisame Hoshigaki	.50	1.25
N531 Ino Yamanaka	.75	2.00
N567 Kakashi Hatake (Anbu Days)	1.25	3.00
PR063 Kakashi Hatake & Itachi Uchiha	1.25	3.00
PR064 Naruto Uzumaki & Sasuke Uchiha	1.00	2.50
PR065 Jiraiya & The Fourth Hokage	1.50	4.00
NUS005 Sakura Haruno	1.00	2.50

2010 Naruto Will of Fire

COMPLETE SET (177)	60.00	120.00
BOOSTER BOX (24 PACKS)	40.00	80.00
BOOSTER PACK (10 CARDS)	2.50	5.00
RELEASED IN JUNE 2010		
C056 Princess Koto U	.20	.50
C057 Lord Owashi U	.20	.50
C058 Murakumo R	.40	1.00
C059 Giant Eagle R	.40	1.00
J645 Wind Style: Rasen Shuriken SR	4.00	10.00
J646 Raigo! Thousand Hand Strike! U	.20	.50
J647 Burning Ash U	.20	.50
J648 Anger of the Tailed Beast U	.20	.50
J649 Water Style: Syrup Trap C	.10	.25
J650 Earth Style: Earth Pike R	.40	1.00
J651 Three-Bladed Scythe C	.10	.25
J652 Black Strings U	.20	.50
J653 Ritual Circle U	.20	.50
J654 High Speed Thinking U	.20	.50
J655 Shadow Possession Jutsu U	.20	.50
J656 Water Clone Jutsu U	.20	.50
J657 Howl U	.20	.50
J658 Scattered Thousand Birds Jutsu U	.20	.50
J659 Black Sword C	.10	.25
J660 Sharing the Pain U	.20	.50
J661 Shadow Stitching Jutsu U	.20	.50
J662 Attacking on Both Sides C	.10	.25
J663 Change in Chakra Nature: Rasengan U	.20	.50
J664 Kiss of Death U	.20	.50
J665 Combination Jutsu C	.10	.25
J666 Super Strength U	.20	.50
J667 Transporting the Bodies U	.20	.50
J668 Beast Wave: Palm Hurricane U	.20	.50
J669 Giant Spider U	.20	.50
J670 Labyrinth R	.40	1.00
J671 Sharingan Activated R	.40	1.00
J672 Illusion caused by the Poisonous Moths R	.40	1.00
J673 Super Expansion Jutsu U	.20	.50
J674 Fatal Blow U	.20	.50
J675 Five Pronged Seal Release C	.10	.25
J676 Power of the Red Chakra R	.40	1.00
J677 War Cry U	.20	.50
J678 Giant Club C	.10	.25
J679 Chakra Blade C	.10	.25
J680 Shuriken C	.10	.25
J681 Art of the Raging Lion's Mane U	.20	.50
J682 Concentration U	.20	.50
J683 Booby-Trap R	.40	1.00
J684 Kunai C	.10	.25
J685 Piercing Chidori SR	6.00	15.00
J686 Water Style: Water Shark Bomb Jutsu U	.20	.50
J687 Attack from Behind U	.20	.50
J688 Hellfire U	.20	.50
J689 Exposing the Real Face U	.20	.50
J690 Killer Shot U	.20	.50
J691 Burst of Shots U	.20	.50
J692 Sharp Shooting U	.20	.50
J693 Earth Style: Stone Plate Coffin U	.20	.50
J694 Earth Style Revival Jutsu: Soil Bodies R	.40	1.00
J695 Lightning Style: Earth Slide R	.40	1.00
J696 Rasengan R	.40	1.00
M624 Bounty C	.10	.25
M625 Invasion of the Akatsuki R	1.25	3.00
M626 Ritual R	.40	1.00
M627 Scream U	.20	.50
M628 Just Like That Hero SR	3.00	8.00
M629 Tragic Destiny SR	4.00	10.00
M630 The Last Moment R	.40	1.00
M631 The Top Priority U	.20	.50
M632 In the Rain C	.10	.25
M633 Loss R	.40	1.00
M634 Distraction R	.40	1.00
M635 Entrustment U	.20	.50
M636 Emergency Call-Up U	.20	.50
M637 Reading U	.20	.50
M638 The Next Target U	.20	.50
M639 Argument U	.20	.50
M640 Capture U	.20	.50
M641 Strong Bond C	.10	.25
M642 Approaching Shadow of Death R	.40	1.00
M643 Sudden Entry R	.40	1.00
M644 Strategy Meeting R	.40	1.00
M645 Stolen Bodies U	.20	.50
M646 Fierce Clash U	.20	.50
M647 Interruption U	.20	.50
M648 Present for the Promotion R	.40	1.00
M649 Mid-Night Shogi Match R	.40	1.00
M650 Under the Drifting Clouds U	.20	.50
M651 Farewell C	.10	.25
M652 Taking Over the World R	.40	1.00
M653 Violent Emotion U	.20	.50
M654 Clue U	.20	.50
M655 Scary Story U	.20	.50
M656 Rebellion U	.20	.50
M657 Shout of Victory U	.20	.50
M658 Backup C	.10	.25
M659 Hate U	.20	.50
M660 Flash Back U	.20	.50
M661 Hard Ones to Deal With R	.40	1.00
M662 Additional Team Member R	.40	1.00
M663 Shock R	.40	1.00
M664 Eight Gate Lock Up U	.20	.50
N784 Hidan (Cursed Mode) R	.40	1.00
N785 Hidan SR	10.00	25.00
N786 Kakuzu SR	8.00	20.00
N787 Kotetsu Hagane C	.10	.25
N788 Izumo Kamizuki C	.10	.25
N789 Sai C	.10	.25
N790 Kurenai Yuhi C	.10	.25
N791 Shikamaru Nara SR	6.00	15.00
N792 Ino Yamanaka C	.10	.25
N793 Choji Akimichi C	.10	.25
N794 Naruto Uzumaki (Childhood) C	.10	.25
N795 Sasuke Uchiha (Childhood) C	.10	.25

N796 Sakura Haruno (Childhood) C .10 .25
N797 Hinata Hyuga (Student) C .10 .25
N798 Sora C .10 .25
N799 Gozu C .10 .25
N800 Guren R .40 1.00
N801 Kigiri C .10 .25
N802 Kihou C .10 .25
N803 Nurari C .10 .25
N804 Rinji C .10 .25
N805 Yukimaru C .10 .25
N806 Seimei R .40 1.00
N807 Fudo C .10 .25
N808 Fuen C .10 .25
N809 Furido R .40 1.00
N810 Fouka C .10 .25
N811 Kazuma C .10 .25
N812 Tatsuji C .10 .25
N813 Roshi SR 6.00 15.00
N814 Three Tails SR 5.00 12.00
N815 Naruto Uzumaki C .10 .25
N816 Naruto Uzumaki & Jiraiya SR 5.00 12.00
N817 Rock Lee C .10 .25
N818 Gaara of the Desert C .10 .25
N819 Shikamaru Nara & Choji Akmichi R .40 1.00
N820 Hinata Hyuga C .10 .25
N821 Kisame Hoshigaki R .40 1.00
N822 The Second Hokage SR 5.00 12.00
N823 Asuma Sarutobi C .10 .25
N824 Shino Aburame C .10 .25
N825 The First Hokage SR 8.00 20.00
N826 Might Guy C .10 .25
N827 Jiraiya U .20 .50
N828 Kabuto Yakushi R .40 1.00
N829 Sasuke Uchiha C .10 .25
N830 Kakashi Hatake R .40 1.00
N831 Tenten C .10 .25
N832 Kiba Inuzuka C .10 .25
N833 Temari C .10 .25
N834 Tracking Ninja C .10 .25
N835 Ino Yamanaka C .10 .25
N836 Anko Mitrashi C .10 .25
N837 The Fifth Kazekage R .40 1.00
N838 The Third Hokage R .40 1.00
N839 Rock Lee C .10 .25
N840 Sakura Haruno SR 4.00 10.00
N841 Four Souls of Kakuzu R .40 1.00
N842 Tenzo C .10 .25
N843 Tsunade SR 3.00 8.00
N844 Yugito Ni'i R .40 1.00
N845 Fujin C .10 .25
N846 Raijin C .10 .25
N847 Mizuki (Childhood) C .10 .25
N848 Queen Bee C .10 .25
N849 Cursed Warrior C .10 .25
N850 Sea Monster C .10 .25
N851 Shiin C .10 .25
N852 Agira R .40 1.00
N853 Gensho R .40 1.00
N854 Rokkaku C .10 .25
N855 Yagura C .10 .25
N856 Jako C .10 .25
N857 Monju C .10 .25
N858 Shura C .10 .25
N859 Todoroki C .10 .25
N860 Shikamaru Nara & Asuma Sarutobi R .40 1.00
N861 Naruto Uzumaki SR 2.00 5.00
N862 Sakura Haruno C .10 .25
N863 Kakashi Hatake SR 1.50 4.00

2011 Naruto Invasion

COMPLETE SET (120) 40.00 80.00
BOOSTER BOX (24 PACKS) 40.00 80.00
BOOSTER PACK (10 CARDS) 2.50 4.00
RELEASED ON
J865 Human Boulder U .20 .50
J866 Earth Style, Mud Wall C .10 .25
J867 Partial Expansion Jutsu U .20 .50
J868 Smoke Pellet Kunai C .10 .25
J869 Shadow Stitching R .40 1.00
J870 Lightning Blade SR 2.00 5.00
J871 Kamui SR 2.50 6.00
J872 Fire Style, Biscuit Firing Jutsu C .10 .25
J873 Fang over Fang R .40 1.00
J874 Lightning Beast Running Jutsu U .20 .50
J875 Sage Art, Amphibian Jutsu U .20 .50
J876 Iron Chain C .10 .25
J877 Lightning Style Shadow Clone R .40 1.00
J878 Lightning Style, Four-Pillar Trap U .20 .50
J879 Rasengan SR 10.00 25.00
J880 Chakra Liquid U .20 .50
J881 Water Whip ST .10 .25
J882 Sticky Webbing C .10 .25
J883 Ninja Art, Grudge Rain R .40 1.00
J884 Wind Blade C .10 .25
J885 Mind Scan C .10 .25
J886 Healing Chakra Transmission R .40 1.00
J887 Finishing Blow U .20 .50
J888 Almighty Push SR 6.00 15.00
J889 Absorption Barrier U .20 .50
M817 Cornered U .20 .50
M818 Information Extraction U .20 .50
M819 Brooding Mood U .20 .50
M820 Betrayal R .40 1.00
M821 Decoding the Message R .40 1.00
M822 Defensive Posture C .10 .25
M823 The Man Who Died Twice U .20 .50
M824 Patriarch R .40 1.00
M825 Lifeflash U .20 .50
M826 Final Moments U .20 .50
M827 The Warhawk R .40 1.00
M828 Heated Argument C .10 .25
M829 Motionless R .40 1.00
M830 The Sage Returns R .40 1.00
M831 Ichiraku Ramen U .20 .50
M832 Hero's Welcome U .20 .50
M833 Feudal Lord's Treasure ST .10 .25
M834 Wager U .20 .50
M835 Struggle U .20 .50
M836 Suspicious Characters R .40 1.00
M837 Hiding C .10 .25
M838 Contemplation ST .10 .25
M839 Outlaws Converge U .20 .50
M840 Revenge R .40 1.00
M841 Floating U .20 .50
M842 Regret R .40 1.00
M843 A Master's Death R .40 1.00
M844 Autopsy Report C .10 .25
M845 The Six Paths U .20 .50
M846 Invasion R .40 1.00
N1270 Shikamaru Nara C .10 .25
N1271 Choji Akimichi C .10 .25
N1272 Shiho C .10 .25
N1273 Hinata Hyuga C .10 .25
N1274 Ino Yamanaka C .10 .25
N1275 Neji Hyuga C .10 .25
N1276 Ibiki Morino U .20 .50
N1277 Tenten SR 2.00 5.00
N1278 Shikamaru Nara R .40 1.00
N1279 Inoichi Yamanaka R .40 1.00
N1280 Choza Akimichi U .20 .50
N1281 Deidara SR 3.00 8.00
N1282 Asuma Sarutobi R .40 1.00
N1283 Kisuke Maboroshi C .10 .25
N1284 Sasuke Uchiha (Childhood) C .10 .25
N1285 Tsukado C .10 .25
N1286 Genma Shiranui C .10 .25
N1287 Monkey King Enma C .10 .25
N1288 Tobi U .20 .50
N1289 Hidan U .20 .50
N1290 Anbu Elite R .40 1.00
N1291 Kakashi Hatake (Boyhood) R .40 1.00
N1292 Sakumo Hatake SR 2.50 6.00
N1293 Kakashi Hatake R .40 1.00
N1294 Ink Leech C .10 .25
N1295 Akaboshi C .10 .25
N1296 Rock Lee C .10 .25
N1297 Ink Snake C .10 .25
N1298 Naruto Uzumaki STSR .75 2.00
N1299 Rock Lee C .10 .25
N1300 Sai U .20 .50
N1301 Shima U .20 .50
N1302 Fukasaku R .40 1.00
N1303 Killer Bee SR 2.50 6.00
N1304 Might Guy ST .10 .25
N1305 Jiraiya SR 3.00 8.00
N1306 Samidare C .10 .25
N1307 Jako C .10 .25
N1308 Karin C .10 .25
N1309 Jugo C .10 .25
N1310 Suigetsu Hozuki C .10 .25
N1311 Haku C .10 .25
N1312 Tayuya C .10 .25
N1313 Sasuke Uchiha STSR .75 2.00
N1314 Jirobo (State 2) R .40 1.00
N1315 Kisame Hoshigaki R .40 1.00
N1316 Kabuto Yakushi R .40 1.00
N1317 Kakuzu R .40 1.00
N1318 Orochimaru R .40 1.00
N1319 Yaoki C .10 .25
N1320 Sakura Haruno (Childhood) C .10 .25
N1321 Crow C .10 .25
N1322 Black Ant C .10 .25
N1323 Shino Aburame SR 3.00 8.00
N1324 Temari C .10 .25
N1325 Salamander U .20 .50
N1326 Sakura Haruno C .10 .25
N1327 Gaara of the Desert R .40 1.00
N1328 Kankuro U .20 .50
N1329 Konan U .20 .50
N1330 Sasori (Puppet Mode) SR 4.00 10.00
N1331 Giant Centipede C .10 .25
N1332 Pain (Animal Path) C .10 .25
N1333 Heretical Icon R .40 1.00
N1334 Pain (Asura Path) R .40 1.00

2011 Naruto Shattered Truth

COMPLETE SET (120) 50.00 100.00
BOOSTER BOX (24 PACKS) 50.00 100.00
BOOSTER PACK (10 CARDS) 2.50 5.00
RELEASED IN APRIL 2011
J802 Ninja Art: Tile Shuriken C .10 .25
J803 Earth Style: Earth Dragon Bomb R .40 1.00
J804 Flying Swallow U .20 .50
J805 Self-Destructing Clay Clone R .40 1.00
J806 Headhunter Jutsu U .20 .50
J807 Fire Style: Fireball Jutsu R .40 1.00
J808 Dispatch of Anbu U .20 .50
J809 Madara's Eye U .20 .50
J810 Fire Style: Great Dragon Flame Jutsu U .20 .50
J811 Overwhelming Power U .20 .50
J812 Feral Rage R .40 1.00
J813 Wire Trap C .10 .25
J814 Kirin SR 6.00 15.00
J815 Chidori R .40 1.00
J816 Snake Sword U .20 .50
J817 Water Style: Raging Waves C .10 .25
J818 Tsuchigumo Style: Forbidden Jutsu Release - Big Bang U .20 .50
J819 Chameleon Jutsu C .10 .25
J820 Infinite Embrace R .40 1.00
J821 Bubble Barrier Jutsu R .40 1.00
J822 Poison Senbon Stream U .20 .50
J823 Amaterasu C .10 .25
J824 Tsukuyomi R .40 1.00
J825 Hologram C .10 .25
J826 Sealing Jutsu: Nine Phantom Dragons R .40 1.00
M749 Raigo's Blessing U .20 .50
M750 Clear Sky R .40 1.00
M751 Team Guy U .20 .50
M752 Senju vs. Uchiha SR 6.00 15.00
M753 World of Earth R .40 1.00
M754 Anbu Assault U .20 .50
M755 World of Fire R .40 1.00
M756 Make-Out Paradise R .40 1.00
M757 Throne of the Uchiha U .20 .50
M758 Last Words U .20 .50
M759 World of Lightning R .40 1.00
M760 Baneful Gaze SR 5.00 12.00
M761 Passing Fates C .10 .25
M762 Cursed Existence R .40 1.00
M763 New Members U .20 .50
M764 Rashomon's Defense U .20 .50
M765 Sasuke's Curse C .10 .25
M766 Eight-Headed Serpent Jutsu U .20 .50
M767 Orochimaru's Goal U .20 .50
M768 World of Water R .40 1.00
M769 World of Wind R .40 1.00
M770 Slug Infestation! U .20 .50
M771 Daydreaming C .10 .25
M772 Dreams of the Past C .10 .25
M773 Void World R .40 1.00
M774 Symbol of the Rogue Ninja R .40 1.00
M775 Chakra Seal U .20 .50
N1102 Choji Akimichi C .10 .25
N1103 Deidara (Younger Days) U .20 .50
N1104 Tenzo (Anbu Days) U .20 .50
N1105 Deidara (C0 Form) R .40 1.00
N1106 Denka C .10 .25
N1107 Hina C .10 .25
N1108 Anbu C .10 .25
N1109 The Thrid Hokage (Younger Days) R .40 1.00
N1110 Anbu U .20 .50
N1111 Madara Uchiha SR 5.00 12.00
N1112 Kakashi Hatake (Anbu Days) U .20 .50
N1113 Itachi Uchiha R .40 1.00
N1114 Susano'o SR 5.00 12.00
N1115 Sai SR 6.00 15.00
N1116 Kushina Uzumaki C .10 .25
N1117 Rock Lee C .10 .25
N1118 Naruto Uzumaki U .20 .50
N1119 Jiraiya U .20 .50
N1120 Anko Mitarashi C .10 .25
N1121 Konohamaru Ninja Corp. C .10 .25
N1122 Minato Namikaze SR 5.00 12.00
N1123 Ninja Art: Tile Shuriken C .40 1.00
N1124 Karin C .10 .25
N1125 Suigetsu C .10 .25
N1126 Jugo C .10 .25
N1127 Sakon (State 1) U .20 .50
N1128 Ukon (State 1) R .40 1.00
N1129 Sasuke Uchiha SR 5.00 12.00
N1130 Rashomon U .20 .50
N1131 Sakon & Ukon (State 2) R .40 1.00
N1132 Harusame C .10 .25
N1133 Utakata R .40 1.00
N1134 Hotaru Katsuragi C .10 .25
N1135 Sakura Haruno C .10 .25
N1136 Konan (Childhood) C .10 .25
N1137 Salamander C .10 .25
N1138 Temari U .20 .50
N1139 Hiruko R .40 1.00
N1140 Sasori U .20 .50
N1141 The 3rd Kazekage R .40 1.00
N1142 Sasori & Hiruko R .40 1.00
N1143 Six Tails SR 6.00 15.00
N1144 Giant Panda C .10 .25
N1145 Zetsu F 2.00 5.00
N1146 Tobi F 2.00 5.00
N1147 Konan F 2.00 5.00
N1148 Sasori F 2.00 5.00
N1149 Deidara F 2.00 5.00
N1150 Kisame Hoshigaki F 2.00 5.00
N1151 Itachi Uchiha STSR .40 1.00
N1152 Pain (Deva Path) STSR .40 1.00
N1153 Kakuzu F 2.00 5.00
N1154 Hidan F 2.00 5.00
N1155 Neji Hyuga C .10 .25
N1156 Hinata Hyuga C .10 .25
N1157 Ino Yamanaka C .10 .25
N1158 Tenten C .10 .25
N1159 Shikamaru Nara U .20 .50
N1160 Yamato C .10 .25
N1161 Asuma Sarutobi C .10 .25
N1162 The 1st Hokage U .20 .50
N1163 Tsume Inuzuka C .10 .25
N1164 Kuromaru C .10 .25
N1165 Kiba Inuzuka C .10 .25
N1166 Akamaru C .10 .25
N1167 Rock Lee C .10 .25
N1168 Naruto Uzumaki C .10 .25
N1169 Might Guy U .20 .50

2011 Naruto Tales of the Gallant Sage

COMPLETE SET (140) 50.00 100.00
BOOSTER BOX (24 PACKS) 50.00 100.00
BOOSTER PACK (10 CARDS) 2.50 5.00
RELEASED IN FEBRUARY 2011
J773 Protective 8 Trigrams 64 Palms U .20 .50
J774 8 Trigrams Palms Rotation C .10 .25
J775 Gentle Fist Style: 8 Trigrams 64 R .40 1.00
J776 8 Trigrams Air Palm U .20 .50
J777 Detonating Kunai C .10 .25
J778 Fire Style: Dragon Flame Jutsu C .10 .25
J779 Eyes of the Betrayer U .20 .50
J780 Echoes of Pain U .20 .50
J781 Sage Art: Bath of Boiling Oil R .40 1.00
J782 Shield Block C .10 .25
J783 Toad Subjugation: Art of the Manipulated Shadow U .20 .50
J784 Sage Art: Kebari Senbon R .40 1.00
J785 Demonic Illusion: Toad Confrontation Singing SR 4.00 10.00
J786 Snake Sword R .40 1.00
J787 Summoning Jutsu: Reanimation SR 6.00 15.00
J788 Digital Phalanx Shrapnel U .20 .50
J789 Spider Bow: Fierce Rip U .20 .50
J790 Spider Armor C .10 .25
J791 Crystal Style: Burst Crystal Dragon C .10 .25
J792 Acid Shot C .10 .25
J793 First-Aid C .10 .25
J794 Ferocious Punch! U .20 .50
J795 Puppet Shield U .20 .50
J796 Puppet Summoning R .40 1.00
J797 Hydro-pump SR 4.00 10.00
J798 Summoning Jutsu: Pain R .40 1.00
J799 The Eyes of Pain C .10 .25
J800 The Hand of Pain R .40 1.00
J801 The Soul of Pain U .20 .50
M723 Training in the Moonlight R .40 1.00
M724 Gentle Fist Style: Eight Trigrams U .20 .50

M725 End of the Immortal R .40 1.00
M726 Mover's Jacket C .10 .25
M727 Follower of Jashin C .10 .25
M728 Past and Future R .40 1.00
M729 Scornful Eyes U .20 .50
M730 Gathering Intel U .20 .50
M731 Another Mask... U .20 .50
M732 Doppelganger U .20 .50
M733 Mount Myoboku R .40 1.00
M734 Jiraya's Hermit Dance R .40 1.00
M735 Tale of the Gallent Jiraya C .10 .25
M736 Vessel for Dreams R .40 1.00
M737 Orochimaru's Forbidden Jutsu U .20 .50
M738 Anko's Memory C .10 .25
M739 Karin's Anger U .20 .50
M740 Monster Research R .40 1.00
M741 Katsuyu's Division R .40 1.00
M742 Ino's Tears R .40 1.00
M743 Puppet Master in Training R .40 1.00
M744 Kankuro's Tenacity U .20 .50
M745 Rash Decision U .20 .50
M746 The Ame Orphans R .40 1.00
M747 A Gift of Pain U .20 .50
M748 Chakra Paper C .10 .25
N1037 Neji Hyuga R .40 1.00
N1037 Neji Hyuga P
N1038 Hinata Hyuga U .20 .50
N1039 Ino Yamanaka C .10 .25
N1039 Ino Yamanaka P
N1040 Choji Akimichi C .10 .25
N1041 The First Hokage R .40 1.00
N1041 The First Hokage P
N1042 Asuma Sarutobi SR 6.00 15.00
N1042 Asuma Sarutobi P
N1043 Shikamaru Nara (Suit) C .10 .25
N1044 Tenten C .10 .25
N1044 Tenten P
N1045 Hanabi Hyuga C .10 .25
N1046 Choji Akimichi & Shikamaru Nara R .40 1.00
N1047 Hinata Hyuga (Awakened) C .10 .25
N1047 Hinata Hyuga (Awakened) P
N1048 Hiashi Hyuga R .40 1.00
N1049 Protective 8 Trigrams 64 Palms U .10 .25
N1050 Sasuke Uchiha C .10 .25
N1051 Hidan U .20 .50
N1051 Hidan P
N1052 Akamaru C .10 .25
N1053 Kakashi Hatake & Yamato R .40 1.00
N1053 Kakashi Hatake & Yamato P
N1054 The Third Hokage U .20 .50
N1054 The Third Hokage P
N1055 Itachi Uchiha & Sasuke Uchiha R .40 1.00
N1056 Sasuke Uchiha (Suit) C .10 .25
N1057 Kakashi Hatake R .40 1.00
N1057 Kakashi Hatake P
N1058 Itachi Uchiha U .20 .50
N1059 Kiba Inuzuka & Akamaru R .40 1.00
N1060 Kakashi Hatake &
The 4th Hokage SR 5.00 12.00
N1060 Kakashi Hatake & The 4th Hokage P
N1061 Naruto Uzumaki (Tailed Beast Form) R .40 1.00
N1062 Naruto Uzumaki (Four Tails) R .40 1.00
N1062 Naruto Uzumaki (Four Tails) P
N1063 Fukasaku U .20 .50
N1064 Shima C .10 .25
N1065 Gamaken C .10 .25
N1066 Great Toad Sage C .10 .25
N1067 Jiraiya (Sage Mode) SR 5.00 12.00
N1067 Jiraiya (Sage Mode) P
N1068 Jiraiya U .20 .50
N1068 Jiraiya P
N1069 Rock Lee C .10 .25
N1070 Killer Bee C .10 .25
N1071 Naruto Uzumaki (Suit) C .10 .25
N1072 Sai (Suit) C .10 .25
N1073 Yahiko (Childhood) C .10 .25
N1074 Giant Spider C .10 .25
N1075 Kidomaru (State 1) U .20 .50
N1075 Kidomaru (State 1) P
N1076 Karin C .10 .25
N1077 Suigetsu Hozuki C .10 .25
N1078 Jugo C .10 .25
N1079 Kimimaro (State 1) U .20 .50
N1080 Sasuke Uchiha U .20 .50
N1080 Sasuke Uchiha P
N1081 Orochimaru SR 6.00 15.00
N1082 Hanzo the Salamander R .40 1.00
N1083 Manda U .20 .50
N1083 Manda P
N1084 Kidomaru (State 2) R .40 1.00
N1085 Mini Katsuyu C .10 .25
N1086 Crow C .10 .25
N1087 Black Ant C .10 .25
N1088 Gaara of the Desert (Suit) C .10 .25
N1089 Father and Mother C .10 .25
N1090 Chiyo U .20 .50
N1090 Chiyo P
N1091 Ebizo C .10 .25
N1092 Kankuro C .10 .25
N1093 Monzaemon Chikamatsu SR 5.00 12.00
N1094 Sakura Haruno R .40 1.00
N1094 Sakura Haruno P
N1095 Ino Yamanaka C .10 .25
N1096 Pain & Itachi Uchiha SR 5.00 12.00
N1096 Pain & Itachi Uchiha P
N1097 Giant Rhino C .10 .25
N1098 Nagato (Childhood) C .10 .25
N1099 Pain (Human Path) U .20 .50
N1100 Pain (Naraka Path) C .10 .25
N1101 Pain (Asura Path) R .40 1.00

2011 Naruto Tournament Pack 3

COMPLETE SET (60) 20.00 40.00
BOOSTER BOX (24 PACKS) 50.00 100.00
BOOSTER PACK (10 CARDS) 2.50 5.00
RELEASED IN JULY 2011
J827 Tree Climbing Training U .20 .50
J828 Standing Alone U .20 .50
J829 Fire Style: Fireball Jutsu R 4.00 1.00
J830 Chidori SR 5.00 12.00
J831 Wind Style: Rasen Shuriken SR 4.00 10.00
J832 Barrier Battle Arts R .40 1.00
J833 Deformable Body U• .20 .50
J834 Blade of the Thunder God R .40 1.00
J835 Stunning Strike U .20 .50
J836 Fear of Blood R .40 1.00
J837 Chakra Manipulation Training U .20 .50
J838 Money Style: Shadow Clone Jutsu R .40 1.00
M776 Summoning Weapons R .40 1.00
M777 After the Battle R .40 1.00
M778 Old Faces, New Problems R .40 1.00
M779 Demon's Eyes R .40 1.00
M780 Clone Training U .20 .50
M781 Awkward Thinking SR 6.00 15.00
M782 Low Stamina R .40 1.00
M783 Observer U .20 .50
M784 Under the Rising Moon U .20 .50
M785 Fond Memories R .40 1.00
M786 The Fool & The Elite R .40 1.00
M787 Money Style: Help Me Jutsu R .40 1.00
N1170 Hinata Hyuga C .10 .25
N1171 Shikamaru Nara C .10 .25
N1172 Neji Hyuga C .10 .25
N1173 Asuma Sarutobi C .10 .25
N1174 The 1st Hokage U .20 .50
N1175 Sasuke Uchiha C .10 .25
N1176 Kakashi Hatake C .10 .25
N1177 Itachi Uchiha U .20 .50
N1178 The 3rd Hokage R .40 1.00
N1179 Naruto Uzumaki C .10 .25
N1180 Rock Lee C .10 .25
N1181 Kushina Uzumaki C .10 .25
N1182 Killer Bee C .10 .25
N1183 Sai C .10 .25
N1184 Naruto Uzumaki
(Tailed Beast Form) SR 6.00 15.00
N1185 A R .40 1.00
N1186 Eight Tails U .20 .50
N1187 Suigetsu Hozuki C .10 .25
N1188 Jugo C .10 .25
N1189 Karin C .10 .25
N1190 Suigetsu Hozuki C .10 .25
N1191 Jugo C .10 .25
N1192 Sasuke Uchiha C .10 .25
N1193 Orochimaru U .20 .50
N1194 Sasuke Uchiha (State 2) R .40 1.00
N1195 Sakura Haruno C .10 .25
N1196 Gaara of the Desert C .10 .25
N1197 Kurenai Yuhi C .10 .25
N1198 Konan U .20 .50
N1199 Pain (Animal Path) C .10 .25
N1200 Pain (Preta Path) C .10 .25
N1201 Pain (Naraka Path) C .10 .25
N1202 Pain (Human Path) U .20 .50
N1203 Pain (Asura Path) U .20 .50
N1204 Pain (Deva Path) U .20 .50
N1205 Nagato SR 5.00 12.00

2011 Naruto Ultimate Battle Tin

PR069 Sasori .30 .75
PR070 Deidara .30 .75
PR071 Kakashi Hatake .30 .75
PR072 Naruto Uzumaki .30 .75
PR073 Itachi Uchiha .30 .75
PR074 Sasuke Uchiha .30 .75

2011 Naruto Weapons of War

COMPLETE SET (119) 50.00 100.00
BOOSTER BOX (24 PACKS) 50.00 100.00
BOOSTER PACK (10 CARDS) 2.50 5.00
RELEASED IN OCTOBER 2011
J839 Byakugan R .40 1.00
J840 Deflection C .10 .25
J841 Mind Transfer Jutsu U .20 .50
J842 Partial Expansion Jutsu R .40 1.00
J843 Shadow Possession Jutsu C .10 .25
J844 Shuriken C .10 .25
J845 Smash C .10 .25
J846 Sharingan Eye C .10 .25
J847 Mangekyo Sharingan R .40 1.00
J848 Fire Style: Dragon Flame Jutsu R .40 1.00
J849 Needle Jizo C .10 .25
J850 Double Impact U .20 .50
J851 Seven Swords Dance R .40 1.00
J852 Lariat SR 6.00 15.00
J853 Chakra Cannon U .20 .50
J854 Severe Leaf Hurricane U .20 .50
J855 Water Style: Demon Wave R .40 1.00
J856 Walking on Water C .10 .25
J857 Chidori Lance R .40 1.00
J858 Snake Sword SR 8.00 20.00
J859 Earth Style Barrier:
Earth Dome Prison U .20 .50
J860 Parasitic Insect Jutsu R .40 1.00
J861 Mind Scour C .10 .25
J862 Finger Flick R .40 1.00
J863 Puppet Master Jutsu C .10 .25
J864 Flamethrower U .20 .50
M788 Wrath of the Two Tails U .20 .50
M789 Leaf Squad Organized! R .40 1.00
M790 Sweet Treat U .20 .50
M791 Weapons of War R .40 1.00
M792 12 Shinobi Guardians R .40 1.00
M793 Quicksand C .10 .25
M794 Pad C .10 .25
M795 Guidance U .20 .50
M796 Naruto vs. Sasuke SR 4.00 10.00
M797 Hokage Rocks U .20 .50
M798 Fading Touch R .40 1.00
M799 Brotherhood R .40 1.00
M800 Sage Training R .40 1.00
M801 A Good Book U .20 .50
M802 Mad Skillz R .40 1.00
M803 Ditched C .10 .25
M804 Disaster of the
Nine-Tailed Fox Spirit R .40 1.00
M805 Just Like That Hero R .40 1.00
M806 Fierce Clash U .20 .50
M807 Flashback U .20 .50
M808 Ambush C .10 .25
M809 Right of Succession SR 4.00 10.00
M810 Teacher and Pupil R .40 1.00
M811 Research U .20 .50
M812 The Blank Page C .10 .25
M813 Sealing Barrier R .40 1.00
M814 Ignorance U .20 .50
M815 A Gift R .40 1.00
M816 Kage of the Leaf U• .20 .50
N1206 Choji Akimichi C .10 .25
N1207 Hinata Hyuga (Kimono) C .10 .25
N1208 Tenten (Kimono) C .10 .25
N1209 Ino Yamanaka (Kimono) U .20 .50
N1210 Neji Hyuga C .10 .25
N1211 Shikamaru Nara C .10 .25
N1212 Chiriku R .40 1.00
N1213 Hinata Hyuga C .10 .25
N1214 Deidara R .40 1.00
N1215 Yamato R .40 1.00
N1216 The 1st Hokage SR 6.00 15.00
N1217 Akamaru C .10 .25
N1218 Kiba Inuzuka C .10 .25
N1219 Sasuke Uchiha C .10 .25
N1220 Pakkun C .10 .25
N1221 Yugao Uzuki U .20 .50
N1222 Sasuke Uchiha C .10 .25
N1223 Obito Uchiha R .40 1.00
N1224 Tobi C .10 .25
N1225 Danzo R .40 1.00
N1226 Hidan R .40 1.00
N1227 Kakashi Hatake U .20 .50
N1228 Itachi Uchiha U .20 .50
N1229 The 3rd Hokage SR 4.00 10.00
N1230 Konohamaru C .10 .25
N1231 Naruto Uzumaki C .10 .25
N1232 Ink Lion C .10 .25
N1233 Rock Lee C .10 .25
N1234 Naruto Uzumaki (Clone) C .10 .25
N1235 Iruka Umino C .10 .25
N1236 Sai R .40 1.00
N1237 Killer Bee U• .20 .50
N1238 Anko Mitarashi (Kimono) U .20 .50
N1239 Might Guy R .40 1.00
N1240 Jiraiya R .40 1.00
N1241 The 4th Hokage SR 10.00 25.00
N1242 Eight Tails R .40 1.00
N1243 Orochimaru C .10 .25
N1244 Sakon C .10 .25
N1245 Karin C .10 .25
N1246 Anko Mitarashi R .40 1.00
N1247 Suigetsu Hozuki U .20 .50
N1248 Jugo (State 1) U .20 .50
N1249 Zabuza Momochi SR 5.00 12.00
N1250 Sasuke Uchiha SR 15.00 30.00
N1251 The 2nd Hokage SR 4.00 10.00
N1252 Sakura Haruno (Kimono) C .10 .25
N1253 Kankuro C .10 .25
N1254 Tonton C .10 .25
N1255 Shino Aburame C .10 .25
N1256 Sakura Haruno R .40 1.00
N1257 Shizune (Kimono) U .20 .50
N1258 Kurenai Yuhi R .40 1.00
N1259 The 5th Hokage SR 4.00 10.00
N1260 Kurenai Yuhi (Kimono) R .40 1.00
N1261 Tsunade (Kimono) R .40 1.00
N1262 Jirobo (State 1) C .10 .25
N1263 Kabuto Yakushi C .10 .25
N1264 Tayuya C .10 .25
N1265 Haku U .20 .50
N1266 Temari C .10 .25
N1267 Gaara of the Desert C .10 .25
N1268 Chiyo U .20 .50
N1269 Baki U .20 .50

2012 Naruto Avenger's Wrath

COMPLETE SET (120) 75.00 150.00
BOOSTER BOX (24 PACKS) 40.00 80.00
BOOSTER PACK (10 CARDS) 2.50 4.00
RELEASED ON SEPTEMBER 7, 2012
J946 Earth Style: Hidden in Stones U .20 .50
J947 Earth Style: Mud Wave R .40 1.00
J948 Paper Bomb C .10 .25
J949 Spontaneous Tree Summoning SR 12.00 30.00
J950 Narrow Dodge C .10 .25
J951 Summoning Jutsu U .20 .50
J952 Simulstrike R .40 1.00
J953 Izanagi SR 8.00 20.00
J954 Taking a Hostage U .20 .50
J955 Panic Attack C .10 .25
J956 Art of the Raging Lion's Mane R .40 1.00
J957 Shadow Clone Jutsu U .20 .50
J958 Naruto Uzumaki Barrage U .20 .50
J959 Chidori Sword R .40 1.00
J960 Sacrifice U .20 .50
J961 Chakra Transference C .10 .25
J962 Mystic Fog Prison C .10 .25
J963 Savior R .40 1.00
J964 Wind Style: Vacuum Blade U .20 .50
J965 Wind Style: Vacuum Bullets R .40 1.00
J966 Enhanced Shuriken C .10 .25
J967 Paralyzing Seal C .10 .25
J968 Wind Style: Vacuum Blast U .20 .50
J969 Reverse Tetragram Sealing Jutsu SR 10.00 25.00
J970 Chakra Stream U .20 .50
J971 Unorthodox Weaponry R .40 1.00
M914 A Quiet Day C .10 .25
M915 Konoha's Strongest Genin SR 3.00 8.00
M916 Intriguing Story R .40 1.00
M917 The Ultimate Weapon U .20 .50
M918 Self Conversation U .20 .50
M919 Desperate Power R .40 1.00
M920 Pocket Dimension R .40 1.00
M921 Face-off U .20 .50
M922 The Fire Lord C .10 .25
M923 A Rival's Challenge SR 3.00 8.00
M924 Differing Emotions C .10 .25
M925 An Old Friend R .40 1.00
M926 Medicinal Pills C .10 .25
M927 Stuffed U .20 .50
M928 Inari's Decision R .40 1.00
M929 Moment of Weakness U .20 .50
M930 Turn of Phrase SR 3.00 8.00
M931 Seasick U .20 .50
M932 Skeleton Panic R .40 1.00

M933 A Fisherman's Quarry C	.10	.25
M934 The Rogue Jinchuriki C	.10	.25
M935 Sakura's Confession SR	6.00	15.00
M936 Shameful Actions R	.40	1.00
M937 Present from Students C	.10	.25
M938 Kakashi Hatake's Date U	.20	.50
M939 Jofuku Flower R	.40	1.00
M940 Ex-Samurai R	.40	1.00
M941 Strength in Numbers U	.20	.50
M942 The Mediator R	.40	1.00
N1488 Choji Akimichi C	.10	.25
N1489 Hinata Hyuga (Childhood) C	.10	.25
N1490 Neji Hyuga C	.10	.25
N1491 Ino Yamanaka (Childhood) C	.10	.25
N1492 Chushin C	.10	.25
N1493 Tenten C	.10	.25
N1494 Shikamaru Nara U	.20	.50
N1495 Tonbei U	.20	.50
N1496 Ko Hyuga U	.20	.50
N1497 Neji Hyuga U	.20	.50
N1498 Asuma Sarutobi R	.40	1.00
N1499 Yamato R	.40	1.00
N1500 The 1st Hokage SR	8.00	20.00
N1501 Hibachi C	.10	.25
N1502 Akane C	.10	.25
N1503 Tamaki (Childhood) C	.10	.25
N1504 Kiba Inuzuka C	.10	.25
N1505 Nango C	.10	.25
N1506 Sasuke Uchiha U	.20	.50
N1507 Tobi C	.10	.25
N1508 Sasuke Uchiha R	.40	1.00
N1509 Hidan U	.20	.50
N1510 Kakashi Hatake U	.20	.50
N1511 Itachi Uchiha R	.40	1.00
N1512 Madara Uchiha SR	8.00	2.00
N1513 The 6th Hokage SR	12.00	30.00
N1514 The Sage U	.20	.50
N1515 Gameru C	.10	.25
N1516 Kusune C	.10	.25
N1517 Naruto Uzumaki C	.10	.25
N1518 Izumo Kamizuki C	.10	.25
N1519 Rock Lee U	.20	.50
N1520 Naruto Uzumaki U	.20	.50
N1521 Anko Mitarashi U	.20	.50
N1522 Sai U	.20	.50
N1523 Jiraiya R	.40	1.00
N1524 Might Guy R	.40	1.00
N1525 Might Guy and Kakashi Hatake SR	3.00	8.00
N1526 Kanabun C	.10	.25
N1527 Tanishi C	.10	.25
N1528 Karin C	.10	.25
N1529 Haku C	.10	.25
N1530 Suigetsu Hozuki U	.20	.50
N1531 Jugo U	.20	.50
N1532 Kabuto Yakushi U	.20	.50
N1533 Zabuza Momochi R	.40	1.00
N1534 Kisame Hoshigaki R	.40	1.00
N1535 Jugo (State 2) R	.40	1.00
N1536 Orochimaru R	.40	1.00
N1537 Susano'o (Sasuke) SR	25.00	50.00
N1538 Shino Aburame (Childhood) C	.10	.25
N1539 Sakura Haruno U	.20	.50
N1540 Hotaru Katsuragi C	.10	.25
N1541 Temari C	.10	.25
N1542 Gaara of the Desert C	.10	.25
N1543 Inner Sakura R	.40	1.00
N1544 Father and Mother U	.20	.50
N1545 Hiruko U	.20	.50
N1546 Kurenai Yuhi U	.20	.50
N1547 Sasori R	.40	1.00
N1548 Kurenai Yuhi and Asuma Sarutobi R	.40	1.00
N1549 Sakura Haruno and Chiyo R	.40	1.00
N1550 En no Gyoja R	.40	1.00
N1551 Samurai Warrior C	.10	.25
N1552 Mifune R	.40	1.00

2012 Naruto Hero's Ascension

COMPLETE SET (132)	80.00	150.00
BOOSTER BOX (24 PACKS)	50.00	80.00
BOOSTER PACK (10 CARDS)	2.50	4.00
RELEASED ON DECEMBER 17, 2012		
C060 Madara Uchiha ST	2.50	6.00
J1000 Wind Style: Rasen Shuriken ST	.40	1.00
J1001 The Mind of Pain ST	.20	.50
J972 Mind Transfer, Puppet Curse Jutsu SR	1.25	3.00
J973 Barrier Ninjutsu U	.20	.50
J974 Interrogation R	.50	1.25
J975 Overwhelming Hunger C	.10	.25
J976 Chidori R	.40	1.00
J977 Threaten C	.10	.25
J978 Body Flicker U	.20	.50
J979 Reaper Death Seal SR	2.00	5.00
J980 Backstab U	.30	.75
J981 Role Reversal R	.40	1.00
J982 Pencil Toss U	.20	.50
(Mull to Four Exclusive Preview)		
J983 Double Lariat SR	2.50	6.00
J984 Unlocking the Seal C	.10	.25
J985 Special Kunai U	.20	.50
J986 Rasengan R	1.50	4.00
J987 Water Prison Shark Dance Jutsu SR	1.25	3.00
J988 Skeletal Control U	.20	.50
J989 Summoning Jutsu: Reanimation SR	4.00	10.00
J990 Water Prison Jutsu C	.10	.25
J991 Voracious Appetite C	.10	.25
J992 Simple Disguise C	.10	.25
J993 Gigantic Fan C	.10	.25
J994 Palm Healing R	.40	1.00
J995 Fungal Power U	.20	.50
J996 Shark Skin C	.10	.25
(Pojo Exclusive Preview)		
J997 The Passion of Youth C	.10	.25
(Pojo Exclusive Preview)		
J998 Almighty Push ST	.50	1.25
J999 Eyes of the Sage ST	.20	.50
M943 Rebuilding the Village U	.20	.50
M944 Great Praise C	.10	.25
M945 The Power of the Trio R	.40	1.00
M946 A Hard Bargain R	.40	1.00
M947 The Future Hokage? U	.20	.50
M948 Out of Control Curse Mark C	.10	.25
M949 Path of the Avenger R	.40	1.00
M950 Shadow of the Leaf U	.30	.75
M951 Jonin's Intervention R	1.50	4.00
M952 Exhaustion U	.20	.50
M953 A Master's Treat U	.20	.50
M954 Disaster of the Nine-Tailed Fox Spirit R	.40	1.00
M955 A Parent's Love R	.40	1.00
M956 Unlocking the Power C	.10	.25
(Mull to Four Exclusive Preview)		
M957 The Evil Within U	.20	.50
M958 The Tailless Beast R	.40	1.00
M959 A New Master U	.20	.50
M960 Dark Aspirations R	.40	1.00
M961 Alliance of Evil U	.20	.50
M962 A Show of Power U	.20	.50
M963 Forceful Persuasion R	.40	1.00
M964 Sakura's Tears R	.40	1.00
M965 Idle Comrades U	.20	.50
M966 What Could Have Been U	.20	.50
M967 Tinker R	.40	1.00
M968 Gathering Herbs R	.40	1.00
M969 Outcast R	.40	1.00
(Pojo Exclusive Preview)		
M970 The Lord's Convene C	.10	.25
(Pojo Exclusive Preview)		
M971 Sparring U	.20	.50
(Pojo Exclusive Preview)		
M972 The Spiral of Pain ST	.40	1.00
M973 Sage's Training Ground ST	.20	.50
M974 Exhaustive Battle ST	.20	.50
M975 The Herald of Pain ST	.20	.50
N1553 Choji Akimichi C	.10	.25
N1554 Ino Yamanaka C	.10	.25
N1555 Tenten C	.10	.25
N1556 Tofu C	.10	.25
N1557 Mikage C	.10	.25
N1558 Shikamaru Nara U	.20	.50
N1559 Hinata Hyuga C	.10	.25
N1560 Zetsu U	.20	.50
N1561 Asuma Sarutobi U	.20	.50
N1562 Neji Hyuga U	.20	.50
N1563 Deidara R	.40	1.00
N1564 The 3rd Tsuchikage SR	1.50	4.00
N1565 Hanabi Hyuga C	.10	.25
N1566 Gentleman Cat C	.10	.25
N1567 Suguro C	.10	.25
N1568 Mr. Ostrich C	.10	.25
N1569 Kiba Inuzuka C	.10	.25
N1570 Sasuke Uchiha C	.10	.25
N1571 Obito Uchiha U	.20	.50
N1572 Tobi C	.10	.25
N1573 Hidan U	.20	.50
N1574 Sasuke Uchiha R	.75	2.00
N1575 Kakashi Hatake (Boyhood) U	.20	.50
N1576 Kakashi Hatake R	1.25	3.00
N1577 Itachi Uchiha R	.40	1.00
N1578 Masked Man SR	8.00	20.00
N1579 Konohamaru C	.10	.25
N1580 Naruto Uzumaki C	.10	.25
N1581 Pakkun C	.10	.25
N1582 Rock Lee U	.20	.50
(Mull to Four Exclusive Preview)		
N1583 Kushina Uzumaki R	.40	1.00
N1584 Izumo Kamizuki U	.20	.50
N1585 Sora R	.40	1.00
N1586 Naruto Uzumaki U	.20	.50
N1587 Sai U	.20	.50
N1588 Killer Bee R	.40	1.00
N1589 Killer Bee (Version 2) SR	10.00	25.00
N1590 The 4th Hokage SR	12.00	30.00
N1591 Gamabunta R	.50	1.25
N1592 Jirobo C	.10	.25
N1593 Karin C	.10	.25
N1594 Suigetsu C	.10	.25
N1595 Jugo U	.20	.50
N1596 Haku R	.40	1.00
N1597 Utakata U	.20	.50
N1598 Kabuto Yakushi U	.20	.50
N1599 Zabuza Momochi R	.40	1.00
N1600 Kisame Hoshigaki C	.10	.25
N1601 Kimimaro R	.40	1.00
N1602 Kabuto Yakushi SR	10.00	25.00
N1603 Kisame Hoshigaki SR	12.00	30.00
N1604 Gaara of the Desert C	.10	.25
N1605 Sakura Haruno C	.10	.25
N1606 Kankuro C	.10	.25
N1607 Temari C	.10	.25
N1608 Rin C	.10	.25
N1609 Shino Aburame U	.20	.50
N1610 Temari U	.20	.50
N1611 Sakura Haruno U	.20	.50
N1612 Hiruko R	.40	1.00
N1613 Chiyo U	.20	.50
N1614 Shizune R	.40	1.00
N1615 Kurenai Yuhi R	.40	1.00
N1616 Tsunade SR	3.00	8.00
N1617 Kakuzu R	.40	1.00
(Pojo Exclusive Preview)		
N1618 Naruto Uzumaki (Sage Mode) STSR	4.00	10.00
N1619 Pain (Deva Path) STSR	4.00	10.00
N1620 Jiraiya ST	.20	.50

2012 Naruto Kage Summit

COMPLETE SET (120)	150.00	250.00
BOOSTER BOX (24 PACKS)	40.00	80.00
BOOSTER PACK (10 CARDS)	2.50	4.00
RELEASED ON JUNE 22, 2012		
J921 Sporulation Jutsu U	.20	.50
J922 Wood Style: Four Pillar Prison R	.40	1.00
J923 Lava Style: Lava Monster R	.40	1.00
J924 Golem Technique R	.40	1.00
J925 Earth Style: Weighted Boulder C	.10	.25
J926 Particle Style: Atomic Dismantling SR	6.00	15.00
J927 Danzo's Seal C	.10	.25
J928 Lightning Blade U	.20	.50
J929 Genjutsu SR	8.00	20.00
J930 Amaterasu Shield U	.20	.50
J931 Inferno Style: Flame Control R	.40	1.00
J932 Gale Style: Laser Circus R	.40	1.00
J933 Lightning Illusion: Flash Pillar C	.10	.25
J934 Liger Bomb SR	4.00	10.00
J935 Lightning Style Armor R	.40	1.00
J936 Lightning Style: Emotion Wave R	.40	1.00
J937 Water Style: Water Wall C	.10	.25
J938 Cursed Seal Chakra Blast U	.20	.50
J939 Hiramekarei Unleash: Hammer R	.40	1.00
J940 Vapor Style: Solid Fog SR	2.50	6.00
J941 Sand Shield C	.10	.25
J942 Wind Scythe Jutsu R	.40	1.00
J943 Secret Red Technique: Puppet Triad SR	6.00	15.00
J944 Sand Shower Barrage R	.40	1.00
J945 Sand Wall U	.20	.50
M884 Messengers U	.20	.50
M885 The Stone Council SR	6.00	15.00
M886 Five Kage Summit R	.40	1.00
M887 Spoils of War C	.10	.25
M888 Exhaustion R	.40	1.00
M889 Untold Destruction R	.40	1.00
M890 Battle of Attrition R	.40	1.00
M891 New Orders U	.20	.50
M892 The Leaf Council SR	6.00	15.00
M893 Tense Negotiations U	.20	.50
M894 An Honest Discussion C	.10	.25
M895 Power of Suggestion C	.10	.25
M896 Bodyguard's Protection C	.10	.25
M897 Exaggeration R	.40	1.00
M898 For Vengeance U	.20	.50
M899 The Cloud Council SR	6.00	15.00
M900 A Unique Exit U	.20	.50
M901 A Plea U	.20	.50
M902 A Dark Message C	.10	.25
M903 The Mist Council SR	3.00	8.00
M904 Massacre U	.20	.50
M905 The Kage Assassins U	.20	.50
M906 Arrogance R	.40	1.00
M907 Leader of the Bloody Mist U	.20	.50
M908 Grossed Out U	.20	.50
M909 Personal Guard R	.40	1.00
M910 The Sand Council SR	6.00	15.00
M911 Pure of Heart R	.40	1.00
M912 Sneak Attack U	.20	.50
M913 Village Heroes C	.10	.25
N1423 Neji Hyuga C	.10	.25
N1424 Ino Yamanaka C	.10	.25
N1425 Shikamaru Nara C	.10	.25
N1426 Tenten C	.10	.25
N1427 Choji Akimichi ST	.10	.25
N1428 Shikamaru Nara ST	.40	1.00
N1429 Hinata Hyuga ST	.75	2.00
N1430 Zetsu U	.20	.50
N1431 Deidara U	.20	.50
N1432 Akatsuchi R	.40	1.00
N1433 Yamato R	.40	1.00
N1434 Kurotsuchi R	.40	1.00
N1435 The 3rd Tsuchikage SR	8.00	20.00
N1436 Bartender Cat C	.10	.25
N1437 Chainya C	.10	.25
N1438 Sabiru R	.40	1.00
N1439 Sasuke Uchiha C	.10	.25
N1440 Kiba Inuzuka C	.10	.25
N1441 Tobi C	.10	.25
N1442 Hidan U	.20	.50
N1443 Sasuke Uchiha U	.20	.50
N1444 Kakashi Hatake R	.40	1.00
N1445 Itachi Uchiha R	.40	1.00
N1446 The 3rd Hokage SR	12.00	30.00
N1447 Four Tails R	.40	1.00
N1448 Io C	.10	.25
N1449 Shoseki C	.10	.25
N1450 Rock Lee C	.10	.25
N1451 Mabui U	.20	.50
N1452 Ink Mouse U	.20	.50
N1453 Naruto Uzumaki ST	.10	.25
N1454 Sai U	.20	.50
N1455 Cee U	.20	.50
N1456 Might Guy U	.20	.50
N1457 Darui R	.40	1.00
N1458 Ink Bat R	.40	1.00
N1459 The 4th Raikage SR	10.00	25.00
N1460 The Nine-Tailed Fox Spirit R	.40	1.00
N1461 Mist Anbu C	.10	.25
N1462 Suiu C	.10	.25
N1463 Jirobo C	.10	.25
N1464 Tayuya C	.10	.25
N1465 Kidomaru C	.10	.25
N1466 Sakon C	.10	.25
N1467 Jugo (State 1) C	.10	.25
N1468 Suigetsu Hozuki U	.20	.50
N1469 Chojuro U	.20	.50
N1470 Ao R	.40	1.00
N1471 The 5th Mizukage SR	15.00	40.00
N1472 Orochimaru R	.40	1.00
N1473 Zhandou C	.10	.25
N1474 Epidemic Prevention Officer C	.10	.25
N1475 Tonton C	.10	.25
N1476 Shino Aburame C	.10	.25
N1477 Sakura Haruno C	.10	.25
N1478 Temari C	.10	.25
N1479 Sand Anbu U	.20	.50
N1480 Shizune U	.20	.50
N1481 Kankuro ST	.20	.50
N1482 Scorpion R	.40	1.00
N1483 Seven Tails R	.40	1.00
N1484 Temari ST	.40	1.00
N1485 The 5th Kazekage SR	12.00	30.00
N1486 Ino Yamanaka, Shikamaru Nara, and Choji Akimichi STSR	2.00	5.00
N1487 Kankuro, Temari, and Gaara of the Desert STSR	1.50	4.00

2012 Naruto Sage's Legacy

COMPLETE SET (120)	100.00	150.00
BOOSTER BOX (24 PACKS)	30.00	50.00
BOOSTER PACK (10 CARDS)	1.00	2.00
RELEASED ON FEBRUARY 10, 2012		
J895 Tailed Beast Sealing R	.40	1.00
J896 Gentle Fist U	.20	.50
J897 Bravery C	.10	.25
J898 Gentle Step: Twin Lion Fists SR	.40	1.00
J899 Mangekyo Sharingan R	.40	1.00
J900 Shadow Windmill C	.10	.25

J901 Crow Clone U .20 .50
J902 Amaterasu SR 4.00 10.00
J903 Sage Art: Frog Call C .10 .25
J904 Sage Jutsu: Rasengan Barrage R .75 2.00
J905 Frog Kumite U .20 .50
J906 Sage Art: Giant Rasengan R 1.00 2.50
J907 Wind Style: Rasen-Shuriken SR 4.00 10.00
J908 Chidori Lance U .20 .50
J909 Striking Shadow Snake C .10 .25
J910 Water Style .10 .25
Exploding Water Shockwave C
J911 Chakra Stealing C .10 .25
J912 Bug Shield U .20 .50
J913 Chakra Scalpel C .10 .25
J914 Wind Style: Pressure Damage R .40 1.00
J915 Palm Healing U .20 .50
J916 Pinned Down U .20 .50
J917 Chakra Disturbance U .20 .50
J918 Chakra Drain C .10 .25
J919 Catastrophic Planetary Devastation SR 5.00 12.00
J920 Demonic Dragon R .40 1.00
M855 The Hyuga Clan R 1.00 2.50
M856 Determination to Protect U .20 .50
M857 A Matter of Love R .40 1.00
M858 Troubling Sign U .20 .50
M859 The Nara Clan R .75 2.00
M860 Hyuga Training C .10 .25
M861 The Inuzuka Clan R .40 1.00
M862 Leader of the Cats U .20 .50
M863 The Uchiha Clan R .40 1.00
M864 Insanity R .40 1.00
M865 The Strongest One R .40 1.00
M866 Guardians of the Village R .40 1.00
M867 Musings of a Hermit U .20 .50
M868 Nice Guy Pose U .20 .50
M869 Burden of Hatred C .10 .25
M870 A Father In Dark Times U .20 .50
M871 Shadows of the Past SR 3.00 8.00
M872 Angering the Beast R 1.00 2.50
M873 Organization of Peace R .40 1.00
M874 An Impossible Situation R .40 1.00
M875 Final Goodbye U .20 .50
M876 Training in the Rain U .20 .50
M877 Reminisce R .75 2.00
M878 The Aburame Clan R .40 1.00
M879 Chakra Transmission U .20 .50
M880 Secret Book U .20 .50
M881 Gedo: Art of Rinne Rebirth SR 3.00 8.00
M882 The True Pain U .20 .50
M883 Awakening U .20 .50
N1358 Choji Akimichi C .10 .25
N1359 Shikamaru Nara C .10 .25
N1360 Hinata Hyuga C .10 .25
N1361 Ino Yamanaka C .10 .25
N1362 TenTen C .10 .25
N1363 Shikamaru Nara R .75 2.00
N1364 Zetsu C .10 .25
N1365 Two Tails U .20 .50
N1366 Foo U .20 .50
N1367 Hinata Hyuga SR 10.00 25.00
N1368 Yamato R 1.00 2.50
N1369 Deidara R .75 2.00
N1370 The First Hokage R .40 1.00
N1371 Cat Guard C .10 .25
N1372 Katazu C .10 .25
N1373 Sasuke Uchiha C .10 .25
N1374 Kiba Inuzuka C .10 .25
N1375 Akamaru C .10 .25
N1376 Pakkun R .40 1.00
N1377 Tobi C .10 .25
N1378 Sasuke Uchiha U .20 .50
N1379 Double Headed Wolf R .40 1.00
N1380 Kakashi Hatake U .20 .50
N1381 Itachi Uchiha R .75 2.00
N1382 Hidan R .40 1.00
N1383 The 6th Hokage SR .40 1.00
N1384 Naruto Uzumaki C .10 .25
N1385 Sekiei C .10 .25
N1386 Ink Fish C .10 .25
N1387 Konohamaru C .10 .25
N1388 Naruto Uzumaki C .10 .25
N1389 Karui C .10 .25
N1390 Omoi U .20 .50
N1391 Ink Eagle U .20 .50
N1392 Samui R 2.00 5.00
N1393 Gamahiro R .40 1.00
N1394 Naruto Uzumaki and Jiraiya R 1.50 4.00
N1395 Naruto Uzumaki SR 35.00 70.00
N1396 Naruto Uzumaki R 3.00 8.00
N1397 Unagi C .10 .25
N1398 Kandachi C .10 .25
N1399 Karin C .10 .25
N1400 Jirobo C .10 .25
N1401 Jugo C .10 .25
N1402 Suigetsu C .10 .25
N1403 Haku U .20 .50
N1404 Five-Tails R 2.50 6.00
N1405 Kimimaro SR 4.00 10.00
N1406 Kisame Hoshigaki U .20 .50
N1407 Zabuza Momochi U .20 .50
N1408 Kisame Hoshigaki and Zetsu R 1.50 4.00
N1409 The Second Hokage R .40 1.00
N1410 Hanare C .10 .25
N1411 Furufuki C .10 .25
N1412 Shino Aburame C .10 .25
N1413 Sakura Haruno C .10 .25
N1414 Temari C .10 .25
N1415 Father and Mother C .10 .25
N1416 Shizune C .10 .25
N1417 Torune U .20 .50
N1418 Chiyo R .75 2.00
N1419 Kurenai Yuhi R .40 1.00
N1420 Sasori R .75 2.00
N1421 Tsunade SR 6.00 15.00
N1422 Pain SR 3.00 8.00

2012 Naruto Tournament Pack 4

COMPLETE SET (60) 20.00 40.00
BOOSTER BOX (24 PACKS) 40.00 80.00
BOOSTER PACK (10 CARDS) 3.00 5.00
RELEASED IN DECEMBER 2011

C019 Futaba C .10 .25
C032 Teyaki Uchiha U .20 .50
C046 Takamaru C .10 .25
C059 Giant Eagle R .40 1.00
J021 Earth Style: Headhunter Jutsu C .10 .25
J214 Application of the First Stage U .20 .50
J268 Sand Tsunami R .40 1.00
J462 Sealing Jutsu: .10 .25
Nine Phantom Dragons C
J890 Formidable Team U .20 .50
J891 Subdue C .10 .25
J892 Taijutsu Suit U .10 .25
J893 Chakra Eater Sword U .20 .50
J894 Healing U .20 .50
M080 Sakura's Decision R .60 1.50
M092 Tide of the Deadly Combat R .40 1.00
M847 Generations U .20 .50
M848 Shikamaru's Decision R 5.00 12.00
M849 Eyes of the Betrayer U .20 .50
M850 Race! C .10 .25
M851 Dango U 1.50 4.00
M852 Mysterious Warrior SR 2.50 6.00
M853 Twining Limbs C .10 .25
M854 Genjutsu Adept U .20 .50
N320 Orochimaru R .40 1.00
N365 Itachi Uchiha R .40 1.00
N424 Konohamaru C .10 .25
N454 Kisame Hoshigaki R .40 1.00
N488 Chiyo R .40 1.00
N560 Neji Hyuga R .40 1.00
N595 Ino Yamanaka C .10 .25
N635 Choji Akimichi C .10 .25
N657 Shino Aburame C .10 .25
N658 Hinata Hyuga C .10 .25
N675 Kakashi Hatake R .40 1.00
N711 Obito Uchiha SR 5.00 12.00
N1335 Tenten C .10 .25
N1336 Neji Hyuga C .10 .25
N1337 Deidara SR 1.25 3.00
N1338 Sasuke Uchiha C .10 .25
N1339 Tobi U .20 .50
N1340 Naruto Uzumaki SR 2.50 6.00
N1341 Rock Lee U .20 .50
N1342 Iruka Umino C .10 .25
N1343 Sai U .20 .50
N1344 Jiraiya R .40 1.00
N1345 The 4th Hokage R .40 1.00
N1346 Yukimaru C .10 .25
N1347 Kabuto Yakushi U .30 .75
N1348 Gozu C .10 .25
N1349 Rinji C .10 .25
N1350 Guren SR 3.00 8.00
N1351 Sasuke Uchiha C .10 .25
N1352 Rin C .10 .25
N1353 Utakata C .10 .25
N1354 Ebisu C .10 .25
N1355 Sakura Haruno SR 12.00 30.00
N1356 Shizune U .20 .50
N1357 Gaara of the Desert R .40 1.00
JUS065 Chidori R .40 1.00
PRUS010 Sakura Haruno U .20 .50

2013 Naruto Ultimate Ninja Storm 3

COMPLETE SET (120) 120.00 200.00
BOOSTER BOX (24 PACKS) 60.00 90.00
BOOSTER PACK (10 CARDS) 3.50 4.50
RELEASED ON MARCH 9, 2013
J1002 Golem Technique C .10 .25
J1003 Lava Style: Quicklime Congealing Jutsu C .10 .25
J1004 Particle Style: Atomic Dismantling C .10 .25
J1005 8 Trigrams 64 Palms C .10 .25
J1006 Cat Fire Bowl R 1.00 2.50
J1007 Shattered Heaven SR 3.00 8.00
J1008 Great Blazing Eruption R 1.00 2.50
J1009 Flame Control Sword R 1.00 2.50
J1010 Yasaka Magatama C .10 .25
J1011 Summoning: Gedo Statue R .40 1.00
J1012 Hirudora C .10 .25
J1013 Hell Stab: One-Finger Spear Hand U .20 .50
J1014 Tailed Beast Bomb SR 25.00 50.00
J1015 Gale Style: Black Hunting C .10 .25
J1016 Bashosen's Power C .10 .25
J1017 Benihisago's Power C .10 .25
J1018 Five-Mountain Jump U .20 .50
J1019 Rough Sea Spume U .20 .50
J1020 Ninja Art: Sickle Fog Jutsu C .10 .25
J1021 Summoning: Reanimation SR 4.00 10.00
J1022 Freight Bubbles U .20 .50
J1023 Phosphorus Blast U .20 .50
J1024 Sand Tsunami C .10 .25
J1025 Hidden Jutsu: Insect Bog C .10 .25
J1026 Full Blossom: Cherry Blossom Clash R .60 1.50
J1027 Spirit of the Samurai U .20 .50
J1028 Helmetsplitter's Rush C .10 .25
J1029 Fang's Rush C .10 .25
J1030 Sewing Needle's Rush U .20 .50
J1031 Master of the 7 Swords R .75 2.00
J1032 Needle Senbon C .10 .25
J1033 Spatter's Rush C .10 .25
M976 Zetsu Army C .20 .50
M977 Super Sized C .10 .25
M978 Bloodline Selection U .20 .50
M979 Masterful User R .40 1.00
M980 Digging One's Grave C .10 .25
M981 Strength of Conviction U .20 .50
M982 Destructive Duo R .60 1.50
M983 Vengeful Spirit C .10 .25
M984 Heroic Spirit C .10 .25
M985 Eight Inner Gates R .60 1.50
M986 Clash of Ideals SR 5.00 12.00
M987 Lightning Speed U .20 .50
M988 Axis of Evil U .20 .50
M989 Bloodline Limit C .10 .25
M990 Hiding in the Mist U .20 .50
M991 Indomitable Strength C .20 .50
M992 Empassioned Speech R .40 1.00
M993 4 Man Squad C .10 .25
M994 Furious Tempest R 1.00 2.50
M995 Tailed Beast Transformation R .75 2.00
M996 Gathering the Beasts U .40 1.00
M997 Mist's Greatest Swordsmen C .20 .50
M998 Ninja Alliance SR 3.00 8.00
N1621 Choji Akimichi C .20 .50
N1622 Ino Yamanaka C .10 .25
N1623 Tenten C .10 .25
N1624 Hinata Hyuga C .10 .25
N1625 Shikamaru Nara C .10 .25
N1626 Two Tails C .10 .25
N1627 Neji Hyuga C .10 .25
N1628 Akatsuchi C .10 .25
N1629 Kurotsuchi U .20 .50
N1630 The 3rd Tsuchikage R .50 1.25
N1631 Kakashi Hatake (Boyhood) C .20 .50
N1632 Kiba Inuzuka C .10 .25
N1633 Obito Uchiha C .10 .25
N1634 Four Tails U .20 .50
N1635 Kakashi Hatake R .50 1.25
N1636 Sasuke Uchiha R 2.00 5.00
N1637 Danzo U .20 .50
N1638 Tobi SR 10.00 25.00
N1639 Rock Lee C .10 .25
N1640 Cee C .10 .25
N1641 Naruto Uzumaki C .10 .25
N1642 Sai C .10 .25
N1643 Killer Bee R .50 1.25
N1644 Darui U .20 .50
N1645 The 4th Raikage R .60 1.50
N1646 Naruto Uzumaki (9 Tails Cloak) SR 25.00 50.00
N1647 Kabuto Yakushi R 2.00 5.00
N1648 Three Tails U .40 1.00
N1649 Chojuro U .20 .50
N1650 Kisame Hoshigaki U .20 .50
N1651 Ao C .10 .25
N1652 Five Tails U .20 .50
N1653 The 5th Mizukage R 1.00 2.50
N1654 Shino Aburame C .10 .25
N1655 Sakura Haruno SR 6.00 15.00
N1656 Kankuro C .10 .25
N1657 Six Tails R 1.00 2.50
N1658 Seven Tails R 1.25 3.00
N1659 Temari U .20 .50
N1660 The 5th Kazekage R .75 2.00
N1661 Haku C .10 .25
N1662 Utakata C .10 .25
N1663 Fuu C 1.00 2.50
N1664 Jinin Akebino C .20 .50
N1665 Jinpachi Munashi C .20 .50
N1666 Ameyuri Ringo C .20 .50
N1667 Kushimaru Kuriarare U .20 .50
N1668 Mangetsu Hozuki SR 8.00 20.00
N1669 Zabuza Momochi U .20 .50
N1670 Fuguki Suikazan R .40 1.00
N1671 Kinkaku C .10 .25
N1672 Ginkaku C .10 .25
N1673 Asuma Sarutobi C .10 .25
N1674 Yugito Ni'i C .10 .25
N1675 Han C .20 .50
N1676 Roshi C .10 .25
N1677 Itachi Uchiha U .20 .50
N1678 Mifune SR 12.00 30.00
N1679 The 2nd Tsuchikage U .40 1.00
N1680 The 3rd Raikage R .75 2.00
N1681 The 4th Kazekage U .20 .50
N1682 Yagura C .20 .50
N1683 Nagato SR 12.00 30.00
N1684 Hanzo The Salamander U .20 .50
N1685 Madara Uchiha SR 10.00 25.00

Star Trek

1994 Star Trek Premiere Black Border

COMPLETE SET (363) 120.00 200.00
BOOSTER BOX (36 PACKS) 50.00 100.00
BOOSTER PACK (15 CARDS) 2.00 4.00
RELEASED ON NOVEMBER 10, 1994
1 Albert Einstein R 1.25 3.00
14 Anti-Time Anomaly R .75 2.00
27 B'Etor R .60 1.50
28 Beverly Crusher R .60 1.50
33 Borg Ship R 1.50 4.00
34 Bynars Weapon Enhancement R .60 1.50
43 Crosis R 1.25 3.00
48 Data R 2.00 5.00
50 Deanna Troi R 2.00 5.00
52 Devoras R .75 2.00
60 Dr. Leah Brahms R .60 1.50
99 Geordi LaForge R 3.00 8.00
106 Haakona R .60 1.50
111 Horga'hn R .75 2.00
138 Investigate Rogue Comet R .60 1.50
140 Investigate Time Continuum R .60 1.50
145 Jean-Luc Picard R 5.00 10.00
175 Kurak R .60 1.50
176 Kurlan Naiskos R .60 1.50
188 Lwaxanna Troi R .75 2.00
205 Morgan Bateson R .60 1.50
237 Q R 1.50 4.00
253 Roga Danar R 2.00 5.00
259 Sarek R .75 2.00
260 Sarjenka R .75 2.00
274 Sir Isaac Newton R 1.25 3.00
290 Supernova R .75 2.00
297 Tam Elbrun R 1.25 3.00
300 Tasha Yar R 2.00 5.00
313 Thomas Riker R 1.50 4.00
325 Tox Uthat R .60 1.50
336 U.S.S. Enterprise R 4.00 10.00
355 Wesley Crusher R 1.25 3.00
357 William T. Riker R 3.00 8.00
359 Worf R 2.00 5.00
361 Wormhole Negotiations R .60 1.50

1994 Star Trek Premiere White Border

COMPLETE SET (363) 60.00 120.00
BOOSTER BOX (36 PACKS)
BOOSTER PACK (15 CARDS)
RELEASED ON DECEMBER 12, 1994
ALSO KNOWN AS ALPHA VERSION
1 Albert Einstein R .75 2.00
14 Anti-Time Anomaly R .50 1.25
27 B'Etor R .40 1.00

28 Beverly Crusher R	.40	1.00
33 Borg Ship R	1.00	2.50
34 Bynars Weapon Enhancement R	.40	1.00
43 Crosis R	.75	2.00
48 Data R	1.25	3.00
50 Deanna Troi R	1.25	3.00
52 Devoras R	.50	1.25
60 Dr. Leah Brahms R	.40	1.00
99 Geordi LaForge R	2.00	5.00
106 Haakona R	.40	1.00
111 Horga'hn R	.50	1.25
138 Investigate Rogue Comet R	.40	1.00
140 Investigate Time Continuum R	.40	1.00
145 Jean-Luc Picard R	2.50	6.00
175 Kurak R	.40	1.00
176 Kurlan Naiskos R	.40	1.00
188 Lwaxanna Troi R	.50	1.25
205 Morgan Bateson R	.40	1.00
237 Q R	1.00	2.50
253 Roga Danar R	1.25	3.00
259 Sarek R	.50	1.25
260 Sarjenka R	.50	1.25
274 Sir Isaac Newton R	.75	2.00
290 Supernova R	.50	1.25
297 Tam Elbrun R	.75	2.00
300 Tasha Yar R	1.25	3.00
313 Thomas Riker R	1.00	2.50
325 Tox Uthat R	.40	1.00
336 U.S.S. Enterprise R	2.50	6.00
355 Wesley Crusher R	.75	2.00
357 William T. Riker R	2.00	5.00
359 Worf R	1.25	3.00
361 Wormhole Negotiations R	.40	1.00

1995 Star Trek Alternate Universe

COMPLETE SET (122)	50.00	100.00
BOOSTER BOX (36 PACKS)	15.00	30.00
BOOSTER PACK (15 CARDS)	1.00	1.50
RELEASED ON DECEMBER 8, 1995		
7 Berlingoff Rasmussen R	1.25	3.00
8 Beverly Picard R	2.00	5.00
15 Commander Tomalak R	2.00	5.00
16 Compromised Mission R	1.50	4.00
19 Cryosatellite R	1.25	3.00
20 Data's Head R	1.50	4.00
25 Devidian Door R	1.50	4.00
29 Echo Papa 607 Killer Drone R	1.50	4.00
40 Future Enterprise UR	30.00	60.00
42 Governor Worf R	1.25	3.00
51 Ian Andrew Troi R	1.25	3.00
58 Jack Crusher R	1.25	3.00
68 Major Rakal R	1.25	3.00
86 Rachel Garrett R	1.50	4.00
98 Samuel Clemens' Pocketwatch R	1.25	3.00
105 Tasha Yar - Alternate R	1.50	4.00
114 U.S.S. Enterprise-C R	1.50	4.00
117 Warped Space R	1.25	3.00

1995 Star Trek Premiere White Border

COMPLETE SET (363)	80.00	150.00
BOOSTER BOX		
BOOSTER PACK		
RELEASED IN JUNE 1995		
ALSO KNOWN AS BETA VERSION		
1 Albert Einstein R	1.25	3.00
14 Anti-Time Anomaly R	.75	2.00
27 B'Etor R	.60	1.50
28 Beverly Crusher R	.60	1.50
33 Borg Ship R	1.50	4.00
34 Bynars Weapon Enhancement R	.60	1.50
43 Crosis R	1.25	3.00
48 Data R	2.00	5.00
50 Deanna Troi R	2.00	5.00
52 Devoras R	.75	2.00
60 Dr. Leah Brahms R	.60	1.50
99 Geordi LaForge R	3.00	8.00
106 Haakona R	.60	1.50
111 Horga'hn R	.75	2.00
138 Investigate Rogue Comet R	.60	1.50
140 Investigate Time Continuum R	.60	1.50
145 Jean-Luc Picard R	5.00	10.00
175 Kurak R	.60	1.50
176 Kurlan Naiskos R	.60	1.50
188 Lwaxanna Troi R	.75	2.00
205 Morgan Bateson R	.60	1.50
237 Q R	1.50	4.00
253 Roga Danar R	2.00	5.00
259 Sarek R	.75	2.00
260 Sarjenka R	.75	2.00
274 Sir Isaac Newton R	1.25	3.00
290 Supernova R	.75	2.00
297 Tam Elbrun R	1.25	3.00
300 Tasha Yar R	2.00	5.00
313 Thomas Riker R	1.50	4.00
325 Tox Uthat R	.60	1.50
336 U.S.S. Enterprise R	4.00	10.00
355 Wesley Crusher R	1.25	3.00
357 William T. Riker R	3.00	8.00
359 Worf R	2.00	5.00
361 Wormhole Negotiations R	.60	1.50

1996 Star Trek Introductory Two-Player Game

1 A Good Place to Die C
2 Admiral McCoy P
3 Admiral Picard P
4 Avert Danger C
5 Cargo Rendezvous C
6 Commander Data P
7 Commander Troi P
8 Data Laughing P
9 Distress Mission C
10 Gault C
11 Gi'ral P
12 Gravesworld C
13 Homeward C
14 Hostage Situation C
15 Ja'rod P
16 Mogh P
17 Reopen Dig C
18 Reported Activity C
19 Sensitive Search C
20 Spock P
21 Survey Instability C

1996 Star Trek Q Continuum

COMPLETE SET (121)	25.00	60.00
BOOSTER BOX (36 PACKS)	20.00	40.00
BOOSTER PACK (18 CARDS)	1.00	2.00
RELEASED IN OCTOBER 1996		
15 Data's Body R	1.25	3.00
19 Doppelganger R	1.25	3.00
25 Galen R	1.25	3.00
43 Juliana Tainer R	1.25	3.00
46 Katherine Pulaski R	1.25	3.00
48 Keiko O'Brien R	1.25	3.00
54 Lal R	1.25	3.00
56 Madam Guinan R	1.25	3.00
65 Mortal Q R	1.50	4.00
112 U.S.S. Stargazer R	1.50	4.00
118 Yuta R	1.25	3.00

1997 Star Trek The Fajo Collection

COMPLETE SET (18)	30.00	60.00
COMMON CARD	2.00	5.00
RELEASED ON DECEMBER 31, 1997		

1997 Star Trek First Anthology

COMPLETE SET (6)	8.00	20.00
COMMON CARD	2.00	5.00
RELEASED IN JUNE 1997		

1997 Star Trek First Contact

COMPLETE SET (130)	40.00	80.00
BOOSTER BOX (30 PACKS)	30.00	60.00
BOOSTER PACK (9 CARDS)	2.00	3.00
RELEASED ON DECEMBER 17, 1997		
6 Admiral Hayes R	.75	2.00
8 Alyssa Ogawa R	.75	2.00
13 Assimilate Homeworld R	1.00	2.50
21 Beverly Crusher R	1.50	4.00
27 Borg Queen R	.75	2.00
32 Data R	2.00	5.00
35 Deanna Troi R	1.25	3.00
44 Espionage Mission R	.75	2.00
50 Geordi LaForge R	1.50	4.00
56 Jean-Luc Picard R	2.00	5.00
62 Lily Sloane R	.75	2.00
79 Phoenix R	.75	2.00
82 Primitive Culture R	1.00	2.50
83 Queen's Borg Cube R	1.50	4.00
84 Queen's Borg Sphere R	.75	2.00
86 Regenerate R	2.00	5.00
87 Reginald Barclay R	.75	2.00
89 Retask R	1.00	2.50
93 Scout Encounter R	1.00	2.50
96 Shipwreck R	.75	2.00
103 Stop First Contact R	.75	2.00
104 Strict Dress Code R	.75	2.00
109 Theta-Radiation Poisoning R	.75	2.00
121 U.S.S. Enterprise-E R	3.00	8.00
122 Undetected Beam-In R	.75	2.00
123 Visit Cochrane Memorial R	.75	2.00
125 Wall of Ships R	1.00	2.50
127 William T. Riker R	1.50	4.00
128 Worf R	1.50	4.00
129 Zefram Cochrane R	1.00	2.50

1998 Star Trek Deep Space Nine

COMPLETE SET (277)	80.00	150.00
BOOSTER BOX (30 PACKS)		
BOOSTER PACK (9 CARDS)		
RELEASED ON JULY 23, 1998		
1 Aamin Marritza R	.60	1.50
6 Airlock R	.60	1.50
7 Aldara R	.60	1.50
11 Altovar R	.60	1.50
20 Automated Security System R	.75	2.00
21 Bajoran Civil War R	1.00	2.50
30 Bareil Antos R	.75	2.00
31 Baseball R	.75	2.00
32 Benjamin Sisko R	2.00	5.00
34 Boheeka R	.60	1.50
35 Borad R	.60	1.50
36 Bo'Rak R	.60	1.50
38 Camping Trip R	.60	1.50
44 Central Command R	.75	2.00
45 Cha'Joh R	1.00	2.50
46 Chamber of Ministers R	.60	1.50
47 Changeling Research R	.60	1.50
50 Colonel Day R	.60	1.50
56 Cure Blight R	.60	1.50
59 Danar R	.75	2.00
60 Deep Space Nine / Terok Nor R	6.00	15.00
61 Defiant Dedication Plaque R	1.25	3.00
64 D'Ghor R	.60	1.50
65 DNA Clues R	.60	1.50
72 Dukat R	2.00	5.00
74 Duranja R	.60	1.50
75 Elim Garak R	2.00	5.00
77 Enabran Tain R	1.00	2.50
79 Entek R	.60	1.50
88 Establish Tractor Lock R	.60	1.50
99 Garak Has Some Issues R	1.00	2.50
100 Garak's Tailor Shop R	.60	1.50
102 General Krim R	.60	1.50
104 Gilora Rejal R	.60	1.50
105 Going to the Top R	2.00	5.00
107 Grilka R	1.00	2.50
108 Groumall R	.75	2.00
110 Harvester Virus R	.75	2.00
115 HQ: Return Orb to Bajor R	1.00	2.50
120 I.K.C. Toh'Kaht R	1.00	2.50
126 Investigate Rumors R	.60	1.50
130 Jadzia Dax R	2.00	5.00
132 Jake and Nog R	1.50	4.00
133 Jaro Essa R	.60	1.50
135 Julian Bashir R	2.00	5.00
137 Kai Opaka R	.60	1.50
141 Karina R	.75	2.00
143 Kira Nerys R	1.50	4.00
145 Korinas R	.75	2.00
147 Kovat R	.75	2.00
149 Lenaris Holem R	.60	1.50
151 Li Nalas R	.60	1.50
155 Makbar R	1.00	2.50
156 Martus Mazur R	.60	1.50
162 Mora Pol R	.60	1.50
163 Morka R	.60	1.50
164 Mysterious Orb R	.75	2.00
166 Natima Lang R	.75	2.00
168 Neela R	.75	2.00
169 No Loose Ends R	.60	1.50
172 Odo R	2.00	5.00
177 Orb Fragment R	.60	1.50
181 Pallra R	.60	1.50
185 Plain, Simple Garak R	1.00	2.50
186 Plans of the Obsidian Order R	.75	2.00
187 Plans of the Tal Shiar R	.75	2.00
188 Prakesh R	.60	1.50
192 Protouniverse R	.60	1.50
195 Pup R	.60	1.50
199 Razka Karn R	.60	1.50
202 Recruit Mercenaries R	.60	1.50
208 Rescue Personnel R	.60	1.50
210 Retaya R	.60	1.50
216 Ruwon R	.60	1.50
217 Sakonna R	.60	1.50
218 Saltah'na Clock R	.60	1.50
224 Secret Compartment R	.60	1.50
226 Seismic Quake R	.60	1.50
227 Selveth R	.60	1.50
228 Shakaar Edon R	.60	1.50
232 Sorus R	.60	1.50
236 Surmak Ren R	.75	2.00
238 Symbiont Diagnosis R	.60	1.50
239 System 5 Disruptors R	.60	1.50
240 Tahna Los R	.60	1.50
242 Tekeny Ghemor R	.75	2.00
243 The Three Vipers R	.60	1.50
244 The Walls Have Ears R	1.00	2.50
248 Tora Ziyal R	.60	1.50
249 Toran R	.60	1.50
250 Trauma R	.60	1.50
256 Turrel R	.60	1.50
259 U.S.S. Yangtzee Kiang R	.60	1.50
263 Vakis R	.75	2.00
267 Vedek Winn R	.60	1.50
275 Yeto R	.60	1.50
276 Zef'No R	.60	1.50
277 U.S.S. Defiant PREVIEW	6.00	15.00

1998 Star Trek Official Tournament Sealed Deck

COMPLETE SET (20)	10.00	20.00
COMMON CARD	.75	2.00
RELEASED ON MAY 14, 1998		

1998 Star Trek Starter Deck II

COMPLETE SET (8)	4.00	8.00
COMMON CARD	.75	2.00
RELEASED ON DECEMBER 16, 1998		

1999 Star Trek Blaze of Glory

COMPLETE SET (130)	30.00	60.00
BOOSTER BOX (30 PACKS)	100.00	150.00
BOOSTER PACK (9 CARDS)	4.00	6.00
RELEASED ON AUGUST 18, 1998		
3 Admiral Ross R	.75	2.00
11 Blood Oath R	.75	2.00
16 Chief O'Brien R	1.25	3.00
31 E-Band Emissions R	.75	2.00
32 Elim R	1.00	2.50
48 I.K.C. Koraga R	1.00	2.50
49 I.K.C. Lukara R	1.00	2.50
50 I.K.C. Negh'Var R	1.00	2.50
52 Impersonate Captive R	.75	2.00
56 Jadzia Dax R	1.50	4.00
62 Koloth R	.75	2.00
63 Kor R	.75	2.00
68 Locutus' Borg Cube R	1.25	3.00
69 Long Live the Queen R	.75	2.00
71 Maximum Firepower R	1.50	4.00
73 Miles O'Brien R	1.50	4.00
78 Odo Founder R	.75	2.00
86 Picard Maneuver R	.75	2.00
95 Quark Son of Keldar R	.75	2.00
96 Riker Wil R	.75	2.00
98 Ro Laren R	.75	2.00
110 Sword of Kahless R	.75	2.00
114 Target These Coordinates R	1.25	3.00
121 Torture R	.75	2.00
122 U.S.S. Thunderchild R	1.25	3.00
129 Worf Son of Mogh R	1.25	3.00

1999 Star Trek Blaze of Glory Foil

COMPLETE SET (18)	40.00	80.00
RELEASED ON AUGUST 18, 1998		
2 Elim URF	6.00	15.00
7 Jadzia Dax URF	6.00	15.00
10 Kor SRF	3.00	8.00
12 La Forge Impersonator SRF	3.00	8.00
13 Locutus' Borg Cube URF	6.00	15.00
14 Maximum Firepower SRF	3.00	8.00
15 Odo Founder SRF	3.00	8.00
16 Riker Wil URF	6.00	15.00
17 Sword of Kahless SRF	3.00	8.00
18 U.S.S. Thunderchild SRF	3.00	8.00

1999 Star Trek The Dominion

COMPLETE SET (130)	50.00	100.00
BOOSTER BOX (30 PACKS)	50.00	100.00
BOOSTER PACK (9 CARDS)	2.50	5.00
RELEASED ON JANUARY 20, 1999		
1 10 and 01 R	.75	2.00
24 D'deridex Advanced R	1.50	4.00
27 Empok Nor R	.75	2.00
36 Founder Leader R	.75	2.00
42 Goran'Agar R	.75	2.00
44 I.K.C. Rotarran R	.75	2.00
61 Keldon Advanced R	1.25	3.00
65 Kira Founder R	.75	2.00
73 Martok Founder R	.75	2.00

74 Martok R	1.50	4.00
76 Michael Eddington R	.75	2.00
80 O'Brien Founder R	.75	2.00
81 Office of the President R	.75	2.00
82 Office of the Proconsul R	.75	2.00
111 The Great Hall R	.75	2.00
112 The Great Link R	.75	2.00
119 U.S.S. Defiant R	3.00	8.00
124 Weyoun R	1.25	3.00

1999 Star Trek Enhanced First Contact

COMPLETE SET (16)	30.00	60.00
COMMON CARD	2.00	5.00
RELEASED ON JANUARY 13, 1999		

1999 Star Trek Rules of Acquisition

COMPLETE SET (130)	20.00	40.00
BOOSTER BOX (30 PACKS)	15.00	30.00
BOOSTER PACK (9 CARDS)	1.00	1.50
RELEASED ON DECEMBER 1, 1999		
9 Aluura R	1.25	3.00
11 Apnex R	1.25	3.00
12 Arandis R	1.25	3.00
21 Brunt R	1.25	3.00
26 Chula: The Door R	.75	2.00
28 Continuing Committee R	.75	2.00
32 Deyos R	.75	2.00
37 Elizabeth Lense R	1.00	2.50
50 Gaila R	1.00	2.50
51 George Primmin R	1.00	2.50
54 Gral R	.75	2.00
55 Grand Nagus Gint R	1.25	3.00
56 Grand Nagus Zek R	1.25	3.00
58 Hagath R	1.00	2.50
61 Ikat'Ika R	.75	2.00
65 Ishka R	.75	2.00
69 Kasidy Yates R	.75	2.00
71 Krajensky Founder R	.75	2.00
77 Kukalaka R	.75	2.00
79 Leeta R	1.25	3.00
83 Maihar'du R	1.00	2.50
85 Margh R	1.00	2.50
87 Morn R	.75	2.00
89 Naprem R	1.00	2.50
93 Nog R	1.25	3.00
96 Orion Syndicate Bomb R	.75	2.00
107 Quark R	2.50	6.00
108 Quark's Bar R	1.25	3.00
110 Quark's Treasure R	.75	2.00
112 Rom R	1.25	3.00
116 Senator Cretak R	1.25	3.00
128 U.S.S. Sao Paulo R	1.25	3.00
130 Writ of Accountability R	.75	2.00

2000 Star Trek Enhanced Premiere

COMPLETE SET (21)	20.00	40.00
COMMON CARD	2.00	5.00
RELEASED IN NOVEMBER 2000		

2000 Star Trek Mirror Mirror

COMPLETE SET (131)	30.00	60.00
BOOSTER BOX (30 PACKS)	20.00	40.00
BOOSTER PACK (11 CARDS)	1.00	2.00
RELEASED ON DECEMBER 6, 2000		
2 A Fast Ship Would be Nice R	.75	2.00
10 Kelvan Show of Force R	.75	2.00
14 The Guardian of Forever R	.75	2.00
27 Mirror Terok Nor (Front) | (Reverse) R+	2.00	5.00
29 Terran Rebellion HQ R	.75	2.00
46 Construct Starship R	.75	2.00
49 Bareil R+	1.25	3.00
53 Overseer Odo R+	1.50	4.00
56 The Intendant R+	1.25	3.00
57 Weyoun of Borg R+	1.50	4.00
61 Security Chief Garak R+	1.50	4.00
64 Captain Bashir R+	1.25	3.00
65 Captain Dax R+	1.25	3.00
66 Chief Engineer Scott R+	1.25	3.00
67 Chief Navigator Chekov R+	1.25	3.00
68 Chief Surgeon McCoy R+	1.25	3.00
69 Comm Officer Uhura R+	1.25	3.00
74 First Officer Spock UR	20.00	40.00
75 Jake Sisko R+	1.25	3.00
76 James Tiberius Kirk R+	2.00	5.00
80 Marlena Moreau R+	1.25	3.00
82 Mr. Tuvok R	1.00	2.50
83 Nurse Chapel R+	1.25	3.00
85 Security Chief Sulu R+	1.25	3.00
86 Smiley R+	1.25	3.00
88 Mr. Brunt R+	1.25	3.00
89 Mr. Nog R+	1.25	3.00
90 Mr. Quark R+	1.25	3.00
91 Mr. Rom R+	1.25	3.00
94 Regent Worf R+	1.25	3.00
102 Ezri R+	1.25	3.00
103 Fontaine R+	1.25	3.00
104 Mr. Sisko R+	1.50	4.00
105 Professor Sisko R+	1.25	3.00
107 Thomas Paris R	.75	2.00
109 Commander Charvanek R+	1.25	3.00
115 Bajoran Warship R	.75	2.00
118 Defiant R+	2.00	5.00
120 I.S.S. Enterprise R+	1.50	4.00
127 Regency 1 R	.75	2.00

2000 Star Trek Reflections

COMPLETE SET (105)	200.00	400.00
COMMON CARD	.40	1.00
BOOSTER BOX (36 PACKS)	40.00	80.00
BOOSTER PACK (18 CARDS)	2.00	4.00
1 Borg Queen URF	25.00	50.00
2 D'deridex Advanced SRF	2.00	5.00
3 Keldon Advanced SRF	2.00	5.00
4 10 and 01 SRF	1.25	3.00
5 100,000 Tribbles (Clone) BTF	3.00	8.00
6 Admiral Riker BTF	6.00	15.00
10 Barclay's Protomorphosis Disease SRF	1.00	2.50
12 Benjamin Sisko SRF	3.00	8.00
14 B'Etor SRF	1.25	3.00
15 Beverly Crusher SRF	2.00	5.00
16 Beverly Picard SRF	1.50	4.00
17 Borg Ship SRF	2.50	6.00
18 Bynars Weapon Enhancement SRF	1.50	4.00
19 Central Command SRF	1.00	2.50
21 Chamber of Ministers SRF	1.25	3.00
24 Cytherians SRF	1.00	2.50
26 Data SRF	2.50	6.00
27 Data's Head SRF	1.00	2.50
28 Dathon SRF	1.00	2.50
29 Deanna Troi SRF	2.50	6.00
31 Devidian Door SRF	2.00	5.00
33 Dr. Telek R'Mor BTF	2.50	6.00
34 Dukat SRF	2.00	5.00
35 Elim Garak SRF	1.00	2.50
36 Espionage Mission SRF	1.00	2.50
37 Founder Leader SRF	1.00	2.50
38 Future Enterprise URF	50.00	100.00
39 Galen SRF	1.25	3.00
41 Geordi La Forge SRF	1.50	4.00
43 Governor Worf SRF	1.00	2.50
44 Gowron SRF	1.00	2.50
45 Gowron of Borg BTF	2.50	6.00
46 Horga'hn SRF	1.00	2.50
54 Jadzia Dax SRF	2.00	5.00
55 Jean-Luc Picard URF	30.00	60.00
56 Julian Bashir SRF	2.00	5.00
60 Kira Nerys SRF	2.50	6.00
62 Kurlan Naiskos SRF	1.00	2.50
64 Lursa SRF	1.00	2.50
65 Madam Guinan SRF	1.00	2.50
67 Major Rakal SRF	1.00	2.50
68 Martok SRF	1.50	4.00
72 Odo SRF	1.50	4.00
73 Office of the President SRF	1.00	2.50
74 Office of the Proconsul SRF	1.00	2.50
78 Q SRF	1.00	2.50
79 Queen's Borg Cube SRF	1.25	3.00
80 Regenerate SRF	1.25	3.00
84 Roga Danar SRF	1.00	2.50
86 Sela SRF	1.00	2.50
87 Seven of Nine CTF	4.00	10.00
92 Tasha Yar-Alternate SRF	1.25	3.00
93 The Great Hall SRF	1.00	2.50
94 The Great Link SRF	1.00	2.50
97 U.S.S Defiant URF	20.00	40.00
98 U.S.S. Enterprise SRF	1.25	3.00
101 Weyoun SRF	1.50	4.00
102 William T. Riker SRF	1.50	4.00
103 Worf SRF	1.00	2.50

2000 Star Trek Second Anthology

COMPLETE SET (6)	2.50	6.00
COMMON CARD	.75	2.00
RELEASED ON MARCH 15, 2000		

2000 Star Trek The Trouble with Tribbles

COMPLETE SET (141)	30.00	60.00
BOOSTER BOX (30 PACKS)	20.00	40.00
BOOSTER PACK (11 CARDS)	1.00	2.00
RELEASED ON AUGUST 9, 2000		
4 Executive Authorization R	.75	2.00
22 Deep Space Station K-7 R	.75	2.00
40 Council of Warriors R	.75	2.00
43 First Minister Shakaar R+	1.25	3.00
46 Third of Five R+	1.25	3.00
48 Kira R+	1.50	4.00
51 Thot Gor R+	1.25	3.00
55 Captain Kirk R+	2.00	5.00
56 Dr. McCoy UR	2.50	6.00
57 Dulmer R+	1.25	3.00
58 Ensign Checkov R+	1.50	4.00
59 Ensign O'Brien R+	1.25	3.00
60 Lt. Bailey R+	1.25	3.00
61 Lt. Bashir R+	1.50	4.00
63 Lt. Dax R+	1.50	4.00
67 Lt. Sulu R+	1.50	4.00
68 Lt. Uhura R+	1.50	4.00
70 Lucsly R+	1.25	3.00
71 Mr. Scott R+	1.50	4.00
72 Mr. Spock R+	2.00	5.00
75 Lumba R+	1.25	3.00
77 Arne Darvin R+	1.25	3.00
85 Barry Waddle R+	1.25	3.00
88 Grebnedlog R+	1.25	3.00
90 Odo R+	1.25	3.00
92 Worf R+	1.25	3.00
96 Keras R+	1.25	3.00
97 The Centurion R+	1.25	3.00
98 Velal R+	1.25	3.00
102 Stolen Attack Ship R	1.00	2.50
103 Breen Warship R	1.00	2.50
104 Dominion Battleship R	1.00	2.50
105 Weyoun's Warship R	1.00	2.50
108 Starship Enterprise R+	2.00	5.00
110 I.K.C. Gr'oth R+	1.25	3.00
111 I.K.C. Ning'tao R	.75	2.00
117 Breen Energy-Dampening Weapon R	1.00	2.50
132 10,000 Tribbles (Go) R+	.75	2.00
133 10,000 Tribbles (Poison) R+	.75	2.00
134 10,000 Tribbles (Rescue) R+	.75	2.00
135 100,000 Tribbles (Clone) R+	.75	2.00
136 100,000 Tribbles (Discard) R+	.75	2.00
137 100,000 Tribbles (Rescue) R+	.75	2.00

2000 Star Trek The Trouble with Tribbles Federation Starter Deck

COMPLETE SET (13)	1.50	4.00
RELEASED ON AUGUST 9, 2000		
1 Alyssa Ogawa (FC) R	.75	2.00
2 Archer (Prem) C	.10	.25
3 Chula: The Abyss (BoG) R	.60	1.50
4 Chula: The Lights (BoG) C	.10	.25
5 Fleet Admiral Shanthi (Prem) U	.20	.50
6 Hazardous Duty (BoG) C	.10	.25
7 Male's Love Interest (Prem) C	.10	.25
8 Medical Kit (Prem) C	.10	.25
9 Montgomery Scott (AU) C	.10	.25
10 Plasmadyne Relay (QC) C	.10	.25
11 Security Precautions (QC) C	.10	.25
12 Starfleet Type I Phaser (BoG) C	.10	.25
13 Thomas McClure (FC) U	.20	.50

2000 Star Trek The Trouble with Tribbles Klingon Starter Deck

COMPLETE SET (14)	1.50	4.00
RELEASED ON AUGUST 9, 2000		

2000 Star Trek Voyager

COMPLETE SET (201)	125.00	175.00
BOOSTER BOX (30 PACKS)	25.00	50.00
BOOSTER PACK (11 CARDS)	1.25	2.50
UNLISTED C	.10	.25
UNLISTED U	.20	.50
UNLISTED R	.60	1.50
RELEASED ON MAY 23, 2001		
13 Hull Breach R	.75	2.00
30 Barzan Wormhole R	1.25	3.00
59 Caretaker's Array R	.75	2.00
66 Vidiian Boarding Claw R	.75	2.00
67 War Council R	.75	2.00
74 Quinn R	1.25	3.00
112a Tabor BLUE R	1.25	3.00
112b Tabor PLUM R	1.25	3.00
113a Seska DK RED R	1.25	3.00
113b Seska PURPLE R	1.25	3.00
115a B'Elanna Torres BLUE R	3.00	8.00
115b B'Elanna Torres GOLD R	3.00	8.00
117a Chakotay BLUE R	3.00	8.00
117b Chakotay GOLD R	3.00	8.00
120 Harry Kim R	1.50	4.00
122 Kathryn Janeway R	2.50	6.00
123a Lon Suder BLUE R	2.00	5.00
123b Lon Suder GOLD R	2.00	5.00
126a Maxwell Burke BLUE R	2.00	5.00
126b Maxwell Burke GOLD R	2.00	5.00
131a Rudolph Ransom BLUE R	2.00	5.00
131b Rudolph Ransom GOLD R	2.00	5.00
132 Samantha Wildman R	.75	2.00
134 The Doctor R	1.50	4.00
136 Tom Paris R	1.50	4.00
137 Tuvok R	1.50	4.00
138 Vorik R	.75	2.00
143 Culluh R	.75	2.00
148 Karden R	1.25	3.00
164a Kes BLUE R	1.50	4.00
164b Kes GOLD R	1.50	4.00
167a Neelix BLUE R	1.50	4.00
167b Neelix GOLD R	1.50	4.00
170 Penk R	1.25	3.00
171a Seven of Nine BLUE R	6.00	15.00
171b Seven of Nine GOLD R	25.00	50.00
173 The Pendari Champion UR	15.00	30.00
174 Dr. Telek R'Mor R	.75	2.00
192a U.S.S. Equinox BLUE R	1.25	3.00
192b U.S.S. Equinox GOLD R	1.25	3.00
194 U.S.S. Voyager R	2.50	6.00
197 Kazon Warship R	1.25	3.00
199 Vidiian Cruiser R	1.25	3.00

2001 Star Trek The Borg

COMPLETE SET (131)	80.00	150.00
BOOSTER BOX (30 PACKS)	15.00	30.00
BOOSTER PACK (11 CARDS)	1.00	1.50
RELEASED ON SEPTEMBER 19, 2001		
9 The Weak Will Perish R	.75	2.00
24 Unicomplex R+	.75	2.00
50 Borg Queen R+	3.00	8.00
55 Fifth R+	.75	2.00
56 First R+	.75	2.00
57 Four of Nine R+	.75	2.00
60 Second R+	.75	2.00
61 Seven of Nine R+	1.50	4.00
64 Third and Fourth R+	.75	2.00
65 Three of Nine R+	.75	2.00
66 Two of Nine R+	.75	2.00
69 Deanna Troi R+	1.25	3.00
70a Equinox Doctor BLUE R+	3.00	8.00
70b Equinox Doctor GOLD R+	3.00	8.00
72 Reginald Barclay UR	10.00	20.00
78 Donik R+	.75	2.00
80a Hajur DK BLUE R+	3.00	8.00
80b Hajur GOLD R+	3.00	8.00
86 Karr R+	.75	2.00
88 Netek R+	1.00	2.50
101 B'Elanna R+	1.25	3.00
102 Captain Chakotay R+	1.25	3.00
104a Icheb BLUE R+	2.00	5.00
104b Icheb GOLD R+	2.00	5.00
105 Kes R+	.75	2.00
108a Marika BLUE R+	1.50	4.00
108b Marika GOLD R+	1.50	4.00
109a Mezoti BLUE R+	1.50	4.00
109b Mezoti GOLD R+	1.50	4.00
110 One R+	1.00	2.50
111a Orum GOLD R+	2.00	5.00
111b Orum GREEN R+	2.00	5.00
113a Rebi and Azan BLUE R+	1.50	4.00
113b Rebi and Azan GOLD R+	1.50	4.00
114a Riley Frasier BLUE R+	1.50	4.00
114b Riley Frasier GOLD R+	1.50	4.00
122 Borg Queen's Ship R	.75	2.00
123 Borg Tactical Cube R	.75	2.00
124a U.S.S. Prometheus BLUE R+	10.00	20.00
124b U.S.S. Prometheus GREEN R+	10.00	20.00
128 I.K.C. Voq'leng R+	.75	2.00
129 Liberty R+	.75	2.00
131a U.S.S. Dauntless BLUE R+	6.00	15.00
131b U.S.S. Dauntless GOLD R+	6.00	15.00

2001 Star Trek Holodeck Adventures

COMPLETE SET (131)	60.00	125.00
BOOSTER BOX (30 PACKS)	25.00	50.00
BOOSTER PACK (11 CARDS)	1.25	2.50
RELEASED ON DECEMBER 21, 2001		
12 Your Galaxy is Impure R	.75	2.00
51a Iden DK BLUE R+	2.50	6.00
51b Iden PLUM R+	2.50	6.00
53 Crell Moset R+	.75	2.00
57a Kejal DK BLUE R+	2.50	6.00
57b Kejal PURPLE R+	2.50	6.00
64 Admiral J.P. Hanson R+	.75	2.00
65 Boothby R+	1.25	3.00

67 Edward Jellico R+	.75	2.00
68 Ezri Dax R+	2.00	5.00
69 Lewis Zimmerman R+	.75	2.00
73 The E.C.H. R+	.75	2.00
74a Weiss BLUE R+	2.50	6.00
74b Weiss DK BLUE R+	2.50	6.00
76 B'Elanna Daughter of Miral R+	1.25	3.00
77 Chancellor Gowron R+	.75	2.00
81 Anastasia Komananov R+	1.25	3.00
82 Arachnia R+	1.25	3.00
84 Buster Kincaid R	.75	2.00
85 Captain Proton R+	1.25	3.00
87 Chaotica R	.75	2.00
91 Dixon Hill UR	25.00	50.00
92 Dr. Noah R+	1.25	3.00
93 Duchamps R+	1.25	3.00
94 Durango R+	.75	2.00
96 Falcon R+	1.25	3.00
98 Frank Hollander R+	.75	2.00
99 John Watson R+	1.25	3.00
100 Leonardo da Vinci R	.75	2.00
106 Mr. Garak R+	.75	2.00
110 Professor Honey Bare R+	1.50	4.00
111 Professor Moriarty R+	.75	2.00
113 Secret Agent Julian Bashir R+	1.25	3.00
114 Sheriff Worf R+	1.25	3.00
115 Sherlock Holmes R+	1.25	3.00
119 Vic Fontaine R+	.75	2.00
121 Praetor Neral R+	.75	2.00
129a Olarra DK BLUE R+	6.00	15.00
129b Olarra GOLD R+	6.00	15.00

2002 Star Trek The Motion Pictures

COMPLETE SET (131)	100.00	200.00
BOOSTER BOX (30 PACKS)	100.00	200.00
BOOSTER PACK (11 CARDS)	4.00	8.00
RELEASED ON APRIL 17, 2002		
1 The Genesis Device R	.60	1.50
2 Engine Imbalance U	.20	.50
3 God R	.60	1.50
4 Hero Worship R	.60	1.50
5 I Hate You C	.10	.25
6 Linguistic Legerdemain C	.10	.25
7 Now Would Be A Good Time U	.20	.50
8 Subspace Shock Wave C	.10	.25
9 The Whale Probe R	.60	1.50
10 V'Ger R	.60	1.50
11 The Nexus U	.20	.50
12 Transport Inhibitor C	.10	.25
13 Transporter Drones U	.20	.50
14 Duj Saq C	.10	.25
15 Fal-tor-pan C	.10	.25
16 I Just Love Scanning for Life-forms R	.60	1.50
17 Isomagnetic Disintegrator U	.20	.50
18 To Be Or Not To Be U	.20	.50
19 Ceti Eel C	.10	.25
20 Release This Pain C	.10	.25
21 I Do Not Take Orders From You! U	.20	.50
22 Lure of the Nexus C	.10	.25
23 No, Kirk... The Game's Not Over C	.10	.25
24 Prefix Code Transmission C	.10	.25
25 Smooth as an Android's BottomU	.20	.50
26 The Needs of the Many... C	.10	.25
27 What Does God Need With A StarshipR	.75	2.00
28 Analyze Radiation C	.10	.25
29 Insurrection C	.10	.25
30 Observe Ritual C	.10	.25
31 The Discovery of Sha Ka Ree C	.10	.25
32 Collect Metaphasic Particles U	.20	.50
33 Revenge is a Dish Best Served Cold U	.20	.50
34 Admiral Cartwright U	.20	.50
35 Admiral Kirk R+	3.00	8.00
36 Amanda Grayson R+	.75	2.00
37 Ambassador Sarek R+	.75	2.00
38 Captain Spock R+	1.50	4.00
39 Captain Styles U	.20	.50
40 Captain Sulu R+	1.25	3.00
41 Carol Marcus R	.75	2.00
42 Clark Terrell U	.20	.50
43 Commander Chekov R+	1.25	3.00
44 Commander Rand R	.60	1.50
45 Commander Uhura R+	1.25	3.00
46 David Marcus R	.75	2.00
47 Demora Sulu U	.20	.50
48 Dmitri Valtane U	.20	.50
49 Dr. Chapel R+	1.25	3.00
50 Dr. McCoy R+	1.25	3.00
51 Ensign Tuvok R	.75	2.00
52 Henreid C	.10	.25
53 Ilia U	.20	.50
54 J.T. Esteban U	.20	.50
55 Jacobson C	.10	.25
56 James T. Kirk UR	30.00	60.00
57 John Harriman R+	.75	2.00
58 Lojur C	.10	.25
59 Mark Tobiaston C	.10	.25
60 Matthew Dougherty U	.20	.50
61 Mr. Scott R+	1.25	3.00
62 Saavik R+	1.25	3.00
63 St. John Talbot U	.20	.50
64 T'Lar U	.20	.50
65 Tahglio C	.10	.25
66 Valeris R	.60	1.50
67 Voight C	.10	.25
68 Willard Decker R+	.75	2.00
69 Azetbur U	.20	.50
70 Brigadier Kerla R	.60	1.50
71 Captain Kang R+	1.25	3.00
72 Ch'dak C	.10	.25
73 Chancellor Gorkon R+	.75	2.00
74 Colonel Worf R+	1.25	3.00
75 General Chang R+	1.50	4.00
76 General Korrd U	.20	.50
77 Kamarag U	.20	.50
78 Karnog C	.10	.25
79 Klaa U	.20	.50
80 Komal C	.10	.25
81 Kor'choth C	.10	.25
82 Koth U	.20	.50
83 Krase R+	.75	2.00
84 Kruge R+	.75	2.00
85 Maltz U	.20	.50
86 Regnor C	.10	.25
87 Torg R	.60	1.50
88 Valkris U	.20	.50
89 Vixis U	.20	.50
90 Wotelin C	.10	.25
91 Gracie and George U	.20	.50
92a Dr. Gillian Taylor BLUE R+	10.00	20.00
92b Dr. Gillian Taylor GOLD R+	10.00	20.00
93 Dr. Tolian Soran R+	1.25	3.00
94 Gallatin R	.60	1.50
95 J'Onn U	.20	.50
96 Joachim R	.60	1.50
97 Khan R+	1.50	4.00
98 Martia U	.20	.50
99 Mas'ud C	.10	.25
100 Pa'rena C	.10	.25
101 Rae'alin C	.10	.25
102 Ru'afo R+	1.25	3.00
103 Sam'po C	.10	.25
104 Sarod C	.10	.25
105 Sharic C	.10	.25
106 Sybok U	.20	.50
107 Wajahut C	.10	.25
108 Caithlin Dar U	.20	.50
109 Nanclus R	.60	1.50
110a H.M.S. Bounty BLUE R+	15.00	30.00
110b H.M.S. Bounty RED R+	15.00	30.00
111 Starship Constitution C	.10	.25
112 Starship Enterprise R+	1.50	4.00
113 Starship Excelsior R+	1.25	3.00
114 U.S.S. Enterprise-A R+	1.50	4.00
115 U.S.S. Enterprise-B U	.20	.50
116 I.K.C. Amar R	.60	1.50
117 I.K.C. Chontay U	.20	.50
118 I.K.C. K'elric U	.20	.50
119 I.K.C. K't'inga C	.10	.25
120 I.K.C. Kla'Diyus R+	1.25	3.00
121 Kronos One R+	1.25	3.00
122 Injector Assembly One U	.20	.50
123 Li'seria U	.20	.50
124 Son'a Battleship R	.60	1.50
125 Son'a Shuttle C	.10	.25
126a U.S.S. Reliant BLUE R+	20.00	40.00
126b U.S.S. Reliant GOLD R+	20.00	40.00
127 Isolytic Burst U	.20	.50
128 Riker Maneuver U	.20	.50
129 Target Warp Field Coils C	.10	.25
130 Camp Khitomer R	.60	1.50
131 Cetacean Institute C	.10	.25

2002 Star Trek Premiere

COMPLETE SET (415)	200.00	500.00
BOOSTER BOX (30 PACKS)	40.00	80.00
BOOSTER PACK (11 CARDS)	2.00	4.00
RELEASED ON DECEMBER 8, 2002		
ALSO KNOWN AS SECOND EDITION		
1C2 Aggressive Behavior	.12	.30
1C3 Alien Abduction	.12	.30
1C5 Armus Roulette	.12	.30
1C7 Assassination Attempt (1E)	.12	.30
1C8 Authenticate Artifacts (1E)	.12	.30
1R1 A Living Death	1.50	4.00
1R4 Antedean Assassins (1E)	1.50	4.00
1R6 Assassin's Blade	1.50	4.00
1R9 Automated Weapons (1E)	1.50	4.00
1C11 Blended	.12	.30
1C12 Bynars' Password	.12	.30
1C13 Captain's Holiday (1E)	.12	.30
1C14 Center of Attention	.12	.30
1C15 Chula: Echoes	.12	.30
1C17 Command Decisions (1E)	.12	.30
1C18 Console Overload	.12	.30
1C20 Damaged Reputation (1E)	.12	.30
1C21 Dangerous Liaisons	.12	.30
1C28 Graviton Ellipse (1E)	.12	.30
1C30 Impressive Trophies	.12	.30
1C35 Maglock	.12	.30
1C36 Magnetic Field Disruptions (1E)	.12	.30
1C37 Microbrain (1E)	.12	.30
1C39 Nanite Attack (1E)	.12	.30
1C40 None Shall Pass	.12	.30
1C43 Pinned Down (1E)	.12	.30
1C47 Quarren Labor Shortage	.12	.30
1C49 Skullduggery	.12	.30
1C51 Sympathetic Magic (1E)	.12	.30
1C53 Temptation (1E)	.12	.30
1C55 The Moon's a Window to Heaven	.12	.30
1C56 Trabe Grenade	.12	.30
1C59 Vastly Outnumbered (1E)	.12	.30
1C63 Cardassian Phaser Pistol	.12	.30
1C64 Engineering Kit	.12	.30
1C66 Klingon Disruptor Pistol	.12	.30
1C67 Medical Kit	.12	.30
1C69 Romulan Disruptor Pistol	.12	.30
1C71 Starfleet Type-2 Phaser	.12	.30
1C74 A Treasure Beyond Comparison	.12	.30
1C78 BaH! (1E)	.12	.30
1C80 Battle Drills (1E)	.12	.30
1C85 Days of Atonement	.12	.30
1C87 Engage Cloak	.12	.30
1C94 Let Honor Guide You (1E)	.12	.30
1R22 Debris Field	1.50	4.00
1R23 Drumhead	1.50	4.00
1R25 Equipment Malfunction	1.50	4.00
1R26 Explosive Decompression (1E)	1.50	4.00
1R27 Gravimetric Distortion	1.50	4.00
1R29 Hunter Gangs	1.50	4.00
1R31 Invidium Leak (1E)	1.50	4.00
1R34 Limited Welcome	1.50	4.00
1R38 Misguided Activist	1.50	4.00
1R41 Omaran Threat (1E)	1.50	4.00
1R45 Primitive Culture	1.50	4.00
1R50 Stellar Core Fragment (1E)	1.50	4.00
1R54 Tense Negotiations (1E)	1.50	4.00
1R57 Triage (1E)	1.50	4.00
1R60 Wavefront (1E)	1.50	4.00
1R72 Tricorder	1.50	4.00
1R73 A Chance for Glory (1E)	1.50	4.00
1R75 Astrometrics Lab (1E)	1.50	4.00
1R79 Bajoran Gratitude Festival	1.50	4.00
1R86 Diplomatic Overture (1E)	1.50	4.00
1R88 Feast on the Dying	1.50	4.00
1R89 For All Our Sons	1.50	4.00
1R90 How Would You Like a Trip to Romulus?	1.50	4.00
1R95 Line of Defense (1E)	1.50	4.00
1R97 No Love for the Spoon Heads	1.50	4.00
1S16 Chula: Pick One to Save Two	.12	.30
1S24 Enemy Boarding Party	.12	.30
1S32 Kelvan Show of Force	.12	.30
1S33 Kolaran Raiders (1E)	.12	.30
1S42 Personal Duty (1E)	.12	.30
1S82 Brutal Struggle (1E)	.12	.30
1S83 Cry "Havoc!" (1E)	.12	.30
1U10 Berserk Changeling	.12	.30
1U19 Contamination	.12	.30
1U44 Planetary Survey (1E)	.12	.30
1U46 Pursuit Just Behind (1E)	.12	.30
1U48 Recurring Injury (1E)	.12	.30
1U52 Systems Diagnostic (1E)	.12	.30
1U58 Unscientific Method	.12	.30
1U61 Alien Gambling Device	.12	.30
1U62 Bajoran Phaser Pistol	.12	.30
1U65 Engineering PADD	.12	.30
1U68 Medical Tricorder	.12	.30
1U70 Science PADD	.12	.30
1U76 Awaiting Trial (1E)	.12	.30
1U77 Back-flush Bussard Collectors	.12	.30
1U81 Blind Spot (1E)	.12	.30
1U84 D'Arsay Archive	.12	.30
1U91 Inspiring Leader	.12	.30
1U92 Just Like Old Times (1E)	.12	.30
1U93 Labor Camp (1E)	.12	.30
1U96 Nelvana Trap (1E)	.12	.30
1U98 No Peace in Our Time (1E)	.12	.30
1U99 Nothing That Happens is Truly Random	.12	.30
1C101 Order of the Bat'leth	.12	.30
1C118 To Boldly Go	.12	.30
1C129 Kevin Uxbridge	.12	.30
1C134 Pursuit Course	.12	.30
1C140 Shady Resources	.12	.30
1C206 Wormhole Negotiations	.12	.30
1C209 Benjamin Sisko, The Emissary of the Prophets (1E)	.12	.30
1C210 Brilgar (1E)	.12	.30
1C213 Hazar	.12	.30
1C214 Jabara (1E)	.12	.30
1C224 Shakaar Edon, Resistance Leader (1E)	.12	.30
1C226 Trazko, Hired Muscle (1E)	.12	.30
1C233 Darhe'el, The Butcher of Gallitep (1E)	.12	.30
1C236 Elim Garak, Agent of the Obsidian Order (1E)	.12	.30
1C240 Gilora Rejal, Subspace Researcher (1E)	.12	.30
1C246 Makbar, Chief Archon (1E)	.12	.30
1C248 Ocett, Dogged Rival (1E)	.12	.30
1C249 Parn (1E)	.12	.30
1C250 Rogesh (1E)	.12	.30
1C253 Andrea Brand, Academy Superintendent (1E)	.12	.30
1C254 Bandee (1E)	.12	.30
1C257 Beverly Crusher, Chief Medical Officer (1E)	.12	.30
1C259 Data, Aspirer (1E)	.12	.30
1C264 Gideon Seyetik, Great Terraformer (1E)	.12	.30
1C272 Leyton, Chief of Starfleet Operations	.12	.30
1C273 Lian T'su (1E)	.12	.30
1C275 Luther Sloan, Man of Secrets	.12	.30
1C277 Miles O'Brien, Chief of Operations	.12	.30
1C279 Nog, Eager Cadet	.12	.30
1C280 Paulson (1E)	.12	.30
1C282 Robin Lefler, Mission Specialist	.12	.30
1C283 Seth Mendoza (1E)	.12	.30
1C284 T'Lara (1E)	.12	.30
1C286 Tasha Yar, Chief of Security (1E)	.12	.30
1C291 Worf, Strategic Operations Officer	.12	.30
1C294 Bo'rak, Klingon Intelligence Agent	.12	.30
1C297 Gowron, Leader of the High Council	.12	.30
1C300 Kahlest, GhojmoH of Worf (1E)	.12	.30
1C306 Koroth, High Cleric of Boreth (1E)	.12	.30
1C311 Martok, Soldier of the Empire	.12	.30
1C314 Nu'Daq, Tenacious Rival (1E)	.12	.30
1C315 T'vis (1E)	.12	.30
1C316 Vorax (1E)	.12	.30
1C318 Altovar, Vindictive Criminal (1E)	.12	.30
1C319 Berild (1E)	.12	.30
1C322 Chorgan, Leader of the Gatherers (1E)	.12	.30
1C324 Dathon, Speaker of Tama (1E)	.12	.30
1C326 Etana Jol, Ktarian Operative (1E)	.12	.30
1C328 Grathon Tolar, Hologram Forger (1E)	.12	.30
1C329 Grenis (1E)	.12	.30
1C332 Kamala, The Perfect Mate (1E)	.12	.30
1C333 Kolos (1E)	.12	.30
1C335 Marouk, Sovereign of Acamar (1E)	.12	.30
1C338 Nel Apgar, Temperamental Researcher (1E)	.12	.30
1C339 Pran Tainer, Atrean Seismologist (1E)	.12	.30
1C340 Rabal (1E)	.12	.30
1C344 Serova, Warp Field Theorist (1E)	.12	.30
1C345 Soto	.12	.30
1C346 Sunad (1E)	.12	.30
1C348 The Albino, Killer of Children (1E)	.12	.30
1C352 Vash, Treasure Hunter (1E)	.12	.30
1C354 Alidar Jarok, Conscientious Admiral (1E)	.12	.30
1C357 Donatra, Compassionate Patriot (1E)	.12	.30
1C359 Hiren, Romulan Praetor (1E)	.12	.30
1C361 Lovok, Tal Shiar Colonel	.12	.30
1C364 N'Vek, Soldier of the Underground	.12	.30
1C365 Noram (1E)	.12	.30
1C372 Tal'Aura, Impatient Senator (1E)	.12	.30
1C380 Assault Vessel	.12	.30
1C381 Bajoran Interceptor	.12	.30
1C383 Bralek (1E)	.12	.30
1C384 Galor	.12	.30
1C392 U.S.S. Enterprise-E, Federation Envoy (1E)	.12	.30
1C393 U.S.S. Excelsior	.12	.30
1C397 I.K.S. Hegh'ta	.12	.30
1C403 I.K.S. Vor'cha	.12	.30
1C404 Flaxian Scout Vessel	.12	.30
1C405 Miradorn Raider	.12	.30
1C406 T'Lani Munitions Ship	.12	.30
1C411 Haakona (1E)	.12	.30
1R108 Rescue Captives	1.50	4.00
1R113 Taken Prisoner (1E)	1.50	4.00
1R114 Tapestry (1E)	1.50	4.00
1R119 Warrior's Birthright (1E)	1.50	4.00
1R120 Alternate Identity	1.50	4.00

1R121 Amanda Rogers	1.50	4.00
1R123 Comfort Women	1.50	4.00
1R124 Condition Captive	1.50	4.00
1R125 Dimensional Shifting (1E)	1.50	4.00
1R126 Empathic Touch (1E)	1.50	4.00
1R128 Evasive Maneuvers	1.50	4.00
1R133 Protection of the Tal Shiar	1.50	4.00
1R136 Render Assistance	1.50	4.00
1R138 Sensor Sweep	1.50	4.00
1R146 Torture	1.50	4.00
1R207 Anara	1.50	4.00
1R208 Bareil Antos, Esteemed Vedek (1E)	1.50	4.00
1R215 Keeve Falor	1.50	4.00
1R219 Mora Pol, Pioneering Scientist (1E)	1.50	4.00
1R220 Odo, Constable (1E)	1.50	4.00
1R222 Ranjen Koral, Student of B'hala (1E)	1.50	4.00
1R223 Rom, Diagnostic and Repair Technician (1E)	1.50	4.00
1R225 Shandor (1E)	1.50	4.00
1R229 Ari	1.50	4.00
1R234 Daro	1.50	4.00
1R235 Dukat, Military Advisor	1.50	4.00
1R237 Emok (1E)	1.50	4.00
1R238 Enabran Tain, Head of the Obsidian Order	1.50	4.00
1R241 Jerax (1E)	1.50	4.00
1R244 Lemec, Posturing Negotiator (1E)	1.50	4.00
1R245 Madred, Calculating Captor (1E)	1.50	4.00
1R247 Megar (1E)	1.50	4.00
1R251 Altman (1E)	1.50	4.00
1R256 Benjamin Sisko, Defiant Captain	1.50	4.00
1R258 Daniel Kwan (1E)	1.50	4.00
1R260 Davies (1E)	1.50	4.00
1R262 Elizabeth Shelby, Formidable Presence	1.50	4.00
1R265 Hoya (1E)	1.50	4.00
1R266 Jadzia Dax, Science Officer (1E)	1.50	4.00
1R268 Jean-Luc Picard, Explorer	1.50	4.00
1R270 Kalandra, Battlefield Surgeon (1E)	1.50	4.00
1R271 Kathryn Janeway, Wry Admiral	1.50	4.00
1R274 Lopez (1E)	1.50	4.00
1R276 Martin (1E)	1.50	4.00
1R278 Mills (1E)	1.50	4.00
1R285 T'Lor	1.50	4.00
1R287 Van Orton (1E)	1.50	4.00
1R292 B'amara (1E)	1.50	4.00
1R293 B'Etor, Sister of Duras	1.50	4.00
1R295 Dokar (1E)	1.50	4.00
1R301 Kahmis (1E)	1.50	4.00
1R303 Kitrik, "The Tyrant Molor" (1E)	1.50	4.00
1R304 Koloth, D'akturak (1E)	1.50	4.00
1R307 Kroval (1E)	1.50	4.00
1R308 Kurak, Warp Field Specialist	1.50	4.00
1R309 Kurn, Squadron Commander	1.50	4.00
1R310 Lursa, Sister of Duras	1.50	4.00
1R312 Meraht (1E)	1.50	4.00
1R313 Morka, Klingon Intelligence Agent	1.50	4.00
1R317 Acost Jared (1E)	1.50	4.00
1R323 Dallan (1E)	1.50	4.00
1R330 Inad (1E)	1.50	4.00
1R331 Jo'Bril, Patient Schemer (1E)	1.50	4.00
1R336 Marshor	1.50	4.00
1R341 Regana Tosh (1E)	1.50	4.00
1R343 Riva, Respected Mediator (1E)	1.50	4.00
1R347 Temarek (1E)	1.50	4.00
1R349 Togaran (1E)	1.50	4.00
1R351 Ty Kajada, Relentless Investigator	1.50	4.00
1R356 Cretak, Supporter of the Alliance	1.50	4.00
1R360 Jorvas (1E)	1.50	4.00
1R363 Movar, Political General	1.50	4.00
1R366 Sabrun (1E)	1.50	4.00
1R368 Selveth, Tal Shiar Pilot (1E)	1.50	4.00
1R370 Shinzon, Romulan Praetor (1E)	1.50	4.00
1R371 Suran, Ambitious Commander (1E)	1.50	4.00
1R374 Taris, Deceitful Subcommander	1.50	4.00
1R375 Telek R'Mor, Astrophysical Researcher	1.50	4.00
1R377 Thexor (1E)	1.50	4.00
1R378 Tomalak, Beguiling Adversary (1E)	1.50	4.00
1R382 Bajoran Scout Vessel	1.50	4.00
1R387 Prakesh (1E)	1.50	4.00
1R388 Reklar (1E)	1.50	4.00
1R390 U.S.S. Akira	1.50	4.00
1R391 U.S.S. Defiant, Prototype Warship (1E)	1.50	4.00
1R396 U.S.S. Sovereign (1E)	1.50	4.00
1R400 I.K.S. Lukara (1E)	1.50	4.00
1R401 I.K.S. Maht-H'a (1E)	1.50	4.00
1R410 Deranas (1E)	1.50	4.00
1R412 Romulan Scout Vessel	1.50	4.00
1R413 Scimitar, Predator (1E)	1.50	4.00
1R414 Serrola (1E)	1.50	4.00
1R415 Valdore (1E)	1.50	4.00
1S130 Lasting Peace (1E)	.12	.30
1S135 Quantum Slipstream Drive	.12	.30
1S139 Sermon	.12	.30
1S142 Symbol of Devotion	.12	.30
1S144 The Tides of Fortune	.12	.30
1S147 Twist of Fate (1E)	.12	.30
1S160 Deliver Supplies	.12	.30
1S166 Excavation	.12	.30
1S169 Feldomite Rush	.12	.30
1S170 Fissure Research	.12	.30
1S171 Geological Survey	.12	.30
1S175 Intercept Maquis	.12	.30
1S177 Investigate Alien Probe	.12	.30
1S179 Investigate Massacre	.12	.30
1S182 Investigate Sighting	.12	.30
1S186 Military Exercises	.12	.30
1S187 Mining Survey	.12	.30
1S190 Plague Planet	.12	.30
1S194 Rescue Prisoners	.12	.30
1S197 Search and Rescue	.12	.30
1S198 Search for Survivors	.12	.30
1S199 Security Briefing	.12	.30
1S200 Sensitive Search	.12	.30
1S201 Study Cometary Cloud	.12	.30
1S202 Supervise Dilithium Mine (1E)	.12	.30
1S216 Kira Nerys, Colonel Kira (1E)	.12	.30
1S255 Barron (1E)	.12	.30
1S261 Deanna Troi, Guide and Conscience	.12	.30
1S267 Jean-Luc Picard, Argo Pilot	.12	.30
1S288 Wesley Crusher, Prodigy (1E)	.12	.30
1S289 William T. Riker, Number One (1E)	.12	.30
1S290 Worf, Security Detail Leader	.12	.30
1S296 Duras, Son of a Traitor (1E)	.12	.30
1S298 J'Dan	.12	.30
1S299 K'nera, Klingon Defense Force Commander (1E)	.12	.30
1S302 Kang, Honored Warrior	.12	.30
1S350 Tosk, The Hunted (1E)	.12	.30
1S355 Chagrith (1E)	.12	.30
1S362 Mopak	.12	.30
1S369 Shinzon, Capable Commander	.12	.30
1S376 The Viceroy, Shinzon's Protector (1E)	.12	.30
1S389 Vetar (1E)	.12	.30
1S394 U.S.S. Galaxy	.12	.30
1S402 I.K.S. Rotarran, Ship of Tears	.12	.30
1S407 Tamarian Vessel	.12	.30
1U100 Observer from the Obsidian Order	.12	.30
1U102 Peacemaker or Predator? (1E)	.12	.30
1U103 Pierce Their Defenses	.12	.30
1U104 Point Blank Strike	.12	.30
1U105 Precise Attack	.12	.30
1U106 Prejudice and Politics (1E)	.12	.30
1U107 Process Identification (1E)	.12	.30
1U109 Resistance Tactics (1E)	.12	.30
1U110 Romulan Intelligence Network (1E)	.12	.30
1U111 Standard Cardassian Procedure (1E)	.12	.30
1U112 Tactical Planning	.12	.30
1U115 The Orion Underworld (1E)	.12	.30
1U116 The Pillage of Bajor (1E)	.12	.30
1U117 The Reman Mines (1E)	.12	.30
1U122 Arrest Order	.12	.30
1U127 Escape	.12	.30
1U131 Mission Briefing	.12	.30
1U132 Power to the Shields (1E)	.12	.30
1U137 Secret Conspiracy	.12	.30
1U141 Souls of the Dead (1E)	.12	.30
1U143 The Promise	.12	.30
1U145 Ties of Blood and Water	.12	.30
1U148 Abduction Plot (1E)	.12	.30
1U149 Access Relay Station	.12	.30
1U150 Acquire Illicit Explosives	.12	.30
1U151 Amnesty Talks (1E)	.12	.30
1U152 Bajor, Gift of the Prophets	.12	.30
1U153 Cardassia Prime, Hardscrabble World	.12	.30
1U154 Cargo Rendezvous	.12	.30
1U155 Changeling Research	.12	.30
1U156 Chart Stellar Cluster	.12	.30
1U157 Collect Sample	.12	.30
1U158 Colony Preparations	.12	.30
1U159 Cure Blight	.12	.30
1U161 Earth, Cradle of the Federation	.12	.30
1U162 Earth, Home of Starfleet Command	.12	.30
1U163 Eliminate Harvesters	.12	.30
1U164 Encounter at Farpoint (1E)	.12	.30
1U165 Evacuate Colony	.12	.30
1U167 Explore Black Cluster	.12	.30
1U168 Extraction	.12	.30
1U172 Host Metaphasic Shielding Test (1E)	.12	.30
1U173 Hunt for DNA Program	.12	.30
1U174 Iconia Investigation	.12	.30
1U176 Intercept Renegade	.12	.30
1U178 Investigate Coup	.12	.30
1U180 Investigate Rogue Comet	.12	.30
1U181 Investigate Rumors	.12	.30
1U183 Khitomer Investigation	.12	.30
1U184 Kressari Rendezvous	.12	.30
1U185 Medical Relief	.12	.30
1U188 Mouth of the Wormhole, Deep Space 9	.12	.30
1U189 Pegasus Search	.12	.30
1U191 Qo'noS, Heart of the Empire	.12	.30
1U192 Qualor II Rendezvous	.12	.30
1U193 Quest for the Sword of Kahless	.12	.30
1U195 Romulus, Seat of Power	.12	.30
1U196 Runabout Search	.12	.30
1U203 Surgery Under Fire (1E)	.12	.30
1U204 Uncover DNA Clues	.12	.30
1U205 Verify Evidence	.12	.30
1U211 Dohlem (1E)	.12	.30
1U212 Furel, Resistance Fighter (1E)	.12	.30
1U217 Li Nalas, Legend of Bajor (1E)	.12	.30
1U218 Lupaza, Resistance Fighter (1E)	.12	.30
1U221 Opaka, Kai of Bajor	.12	.30
1U227 Weld Ram	.12	.30
1U228 Winn Adami, Kai of Bajor (1E)	.12	.30
1U230 Corbin Entek, Undercover Operations Supervisor	.12	.30
1U231 Damar, Loyal Glinn (1E)	.12	.30
1U232 Danar, Irascible Gul (1E)	.12	.30
1U239 Evek, Attaché to the Demilitarized Zone (1E)	.12	.30
1U242 Joret Dal, Patriotic Visionary	.12	.30
1U243 Kovat, Public Conservator	.12	.30
1U252 Alyssa Ogawa, Enterprise Medical Assistant (1E)	.12	.30
1U263 Geordi La Forge, Chief Engineer	.12	.30
1U269 Julian Bashir, "Frontier" Physician	.12	.30
1U281 Rixx (1E)	.12	.30
1U305 Kor, Dahar Master	.12	.30
1U320 Bhavani (1E)	.12	.30
1U321 Brull, Encampment Leader (1E)	.12	.30
1U325 Durg (1E)	.12	.30
1U327 Galnar (1E)	.12	.30
1U334 Leyor (1E)	.12	.30
1U337 Morn, Barfly	.12	.30
1U342 Retaya, Urbane Poisoner	.12	.30
1U353 Volnoth (1E)	.12	.30
1U358 Dralvak (1E)	.12	.30
1U367 Sela, Mysterious Operative	.12	.30
1U373 Talvin (1E)	.12	.30
1U379 Vreenak, Tal Shiar Chairman	.12	.30
1U385 Keldon	.12	.30
1U386 Keldon Advanced	.12	.30
1U395 U.S.S. Nebula	.12	.30
1U398 I.K.S. K't'inga	.12	.30
1U399 I.K.S. K'Vort	.12	.30
1U408 D'deridex	.12	.30
1U409 D'deridex Advanced	.12	.30

2003 Star Trek All Good Things

COMPLETE SET (40)	600.00	1200.00
COMMON CARD	10.00	25.00
RELEASED ON JULY 16, 2003		
7 Kobayashi Maru Scenario P	25.00	40.00
8 Strategema P	25.00	40.00
9 Changeling Sweep P	20.00	35.00
14 Colonel Kira P	50.00	80.00
18 Christopher Pike P	60.00	100.00
24 Yeoman Rand P	30.00	50.00
25 Uri'lash P	30.00	50.00
36 U.S.S. Grissom P	30.00	50.00

2003 Star Trek Call to Arms

COMPLETE SET (208)	30.00	80.00
BOOSTER BOX (30 PACKS)	25.00	50.00
BOOSTER PACK (11 CARDS)	1.25	2.50
COMMON CARD	.08	.20
RELEASED ON SEPTEMBER 10, 2003		
3R5 Dangerous Climb (1E)	.40	1.00
3S2 An Old Debt	.20	.50
3S7 DNA Analysis (1E)	.20	.50
3U9 Dressing Down	.20	.50
3R11 Forsaken (1E)	.75	2.00
3R12 Gomtuu Shock Wave (1E)	1.25	3.00
3R19 Overwhelmed	.75	2.00
3R22 Quantum Filament (1E)	.40	1.00
3R31 The Demands of Duty (1E)	.40	1.00
3R34 Abduction	.40	1.00
3R37 Bred For Battle (1E)	.40	1.00
3R38 Building a Bridge (1E)	.40	1.00
3R39 Cavalry Raid	1.00	2.50
3R44 I Don't Like to Lose	.40	1.00
3R46 Jem'Hadar Birthing Chamber	.40	1.00
3R49 Psychological Pressure (1E)	1.25	3.00
3R54 Set Up (1E)	.75	2.00
3R56 Sluggo	.40	1.00
3R57 Steeled By Loss	.40	1.00
3R59 The Blight	.40	1.00
3R60 The Crystalline Entity	.40	1.00
3R61 The Enterprise Incident	.40	1.00
3R62 The Manheim Effect	.40	1.00
3R72 Founder Trap	.60	1.50
3R74 Our Death is Glory To the Founders	1.50	4.00
3R75 Parting Shot	.40	1.00
3R76 Pseudopod	1.50	4.00
3S10 Failure To Communicate (1E)	.20	.50
3S15 Inside Collaborators (1E)	.20	.50
3S16 Justice or Vengeance (1E)	.20	.50
3S21 Psycho-Kinetic Attack (1E)	.20	.50
3S30 Sokath, His Eyes Uncovered	.20	.50
3S36 Borg Cutting Beam	.20	.50
3S70 Analyze	.20	.50
3S82 Assault On Species 8472	.20	.50
3S83 Battle Reconnaissance (1E)	.20	.50
3S86 Destroy Iconian Gateway (1E)	.20	.50
3S92 Founders' Homeworld, Home of the Great Link	.20	.50
3S94 Hunt Alien	.20	.50
3U20 Psychic Receptacle (1E)	.20	.50
3U23 Restricted Area (1E)	.20	.50
3U25 Rogue Borg Ambush	.20	.50
3U26 Secret Identity (1E)	.20	.50
3U28 Skeleton Crew (1E)	.20	.50
3U32 Jem'Hadar Disruptor Pistol	.20	.50
3U35 Adding to Our Perfection	.20	.50
3U40 Changeling Sabotage	.20	.50
3U42 Dissolving the Senate	.20	.50
3U47 Jem'Hadar Strike Force (1E)	.20	.50
3U48 One With the Borg	.20	.50
3U52 Sabotage Program	.20	.50
3U53 Sensing a Trap	.20	.50
3U63 The Trial Never Ended	.20	.50
3U64 The Will of the Collective	.20	.50
3U65 Trial of Faith (1E)	.20	.50
3U66 Under Suspicion	.20	.50
3U68 We're Mutants	.20	.50
3U69 Adapt	.20	.50
3U73 Insult	.20	.50
3U77 Security Sweep (1E)	.20	.50
3U80 You Could Be Invaluable (1E)	.20	.50
3U81 Archanis Dispute	.20	.50
3U84 Camping Trip	.20	.50
3U85 Clash at Chin'toka (1E)	.20	.50
3U87 Destroy Transwarp Hub	.20	.50
3U88 Evade Borg Vessel	.20	.50
3U89 Evade Dominion Squadron (1E)	.20	.50
3U90 Expose Changeling Influence	.20	.50
3U91 Extract Defector	.20	.50
3U93 Harness Omega Particle	.20	.50
3U95 Instruct Advanced Drone	.20	.50
3U96 Mouth of the Wormhole, Terok Nor	.20	.50
3U97 Pacify Warring Factions	.20	.50
3U98 Peaceful Contact	.20	.50
3U99 Plot Invasion	.20	.50
3R112 Kira Nerys, Reformed Collaborator (1E)	.75	2.00
3R113 Odo, Wayward Link (1E)	.60	1.50
3R114 Porta, Advisor to the Emissary	.40	1.00
3R116 Yassim, Zealous Protester	.40	1.00
3R123 Borg Queen, Guardian of the Hive	1.50	4.00
3R132 Locutus, Voice of the Borg	1.50	4.00
3R138 Seven of Nine, Part of the Greater Whole	1.50	4.00
3R141 Damar, Useful Adjutant	.40	1.00
3R143 Dukat, Liberator and Protector (1E)	.60	1.50
3R149 Tora Ziyal, Beloved Daughter (1E)	1.25	3.00
3R150 Bashir Founder, Nefarious Saboteur	.40	1.00
3R151 Borath, Psychological Researcher	.40	1.00
3R155 Ikat'ika, Honorable Warrior (1E)	1.25	3.00
3R159 Kira Founder, Examiner	1.00	2.50
3R166 Remata'Klan, Unit Leader (1E)	.60	1.50
3R171 Weyoun, Loyal Subject of the Dominion (1E)	.75	2.00
3R173 Yelgrun, Blunt Negotiator	.40	1.00
3R174 B'Elanna Torres, Creative Engineer (1E)	.75	2.00
3R175 Jack, Maladjusted Misfit (1E)	.60	1.50
3R176 Lauren, Seductress	.40	1.00
3R177 Michael Eddington, Traitor to Starfleet (1E)	1.25	3.00
3R180 Reginald Barclay, Reclusive Engineer	.60	1.50
3R182 Quark, Resistance Informant (1E)	.75	2.00
3R183 Rom, Undercover Spy (1E)	.60	1.50
3R184 Alexander Rozhenko, Good Luck Charm (1E)	.40	1.00
3R185 Darok, Martok's Aide	.40	1.00
3R186 Kor, Noble Warrior to the End	.40	1.00
3R191 Kasidy Yates, Maquis Smuggler	.40	1.00
3R196 Pardek, Betrayer (1E)	.40	1.00
3R197 Ruwon, Intelligence Analyst (1E)	.40	1.00
3R200 Locutus' Borg Cube	1.25	3.00
3R204 Tenak'talar, Weyoun's Warship (1E)	1.50	4.00
3R205 U.S.S. Defiant, Stolen Warship	2.00	5.00
3R206 I.K.S. Pagh (1E)	.40	1.00
3R207 Xhosa	.40	1.00

3R208 Soterus (1E)	.60	1.50
3S101 Rescue Prisoners of War	.20	.50
3S103 Salvage Borg Ship (1E)	.20	.50
3S104 Salvage Dominion Ship	.20	.50
3S108 Survey Star System	.20	.50
3S110 Unicomplex, Root of the Hive Mind	.20	.50
3S122 Borg Queen, Bringer of Order	.40	1.00
3S124 Calibration Drone (1E)	.40	1.00
3S139 Seven of Nine, Representative of the Hive (1E)	.40	1.00
3S154 Founder Leader, Forbidding Judge	.20	.50
3S158 Kilana, Dissembling Envoy (1E)	.20	.50
3S162 Martok Founder, Poison of the Empire	.20	.50
3S163 Noret'ikar (1E)	.20	.50
3S199 Borg Sphere	.40	1.00
3S202 Jem'Hadar Attack Ship	.20	.50
3U100 Political Intrigue	.20	.50
3U102 Restock Ketracel-White	.20	.50
3U105 Signal for Rescue (1E)	.20	.50
3U106 Stage Bombardment	.20	.50
3U107 Study Rare Phenomenon (1E)	.20	.50
3U109 The Siege of AR-558 (1E)	.20	.50
3U115 Tahna Los, Voice of the Kohn-ma (1E)	.20	.50
3U136 Reclamation Drone (1E)	.20	.50
3U144 Elim Garak, Plain, Simple Taylor (1E)	.20	.50
3U146 Mavek, Science Officer (1E)	.20	.50
3U153 Founder Leader, Beguiling Teacher (1E)	.20	.50
3U157 Keevan, Conniving Liar (1E)	.20	.50
3U160 Limara'Son, Fierce Soldier	.20	.50
3U161 Lovok Founder, Puppet Master	.20	.50
3U170 Weyoun, Instrument of the Founders	.20	.50
3U172 Yak'Talon, Deadly Patroller	.20	.50
3U178 Norah Satie, Starfleet Investigator	.20	.50
3U179 Patrick, Idiot Savant (1E)	.20	.50
3U181 Sarina Douglas, Cataleptic Conundrum (1E)	.20	.50
3U187 Larg, Piece of Baktag (1E)	.20	.50
3U188 Martok, Leader of Destiny (1E)	.20	.50
3U194 Karina, Intelligence Analyst (1E)	.20	.50

2003 Star Trek Energize

COMPLETE SET (180)	30.00	80.00
BOOSTER BOX (30 PACKS)	100.00	200.00
BOOSTER PACK (11 CARDS)	4.00	8.00
COMMON CARD	.10	.20
RELEASED ON MAY 21, 2003		
2R2 Casualties of War	.50	1.25
2R9 Face to Face (1E)	.75	2.00
2U1 A Klingon Matter	.20	.50
2U3 Crippling Attack (1E)	.20	.50
2U8 Exposed Power Relay (1E)	.20	.50
2R11 Head to Head (1E)	.50	1.25
2R26 Training Accident	.50	1.25
2R30 Ak'voh	.50	1.25
2R31 Assassination Plot (1E)	1.25	3.00
2R35 Common Ground	.50	1.25
2R36 Complications	.50	1.25
2R37 Confessions in the Pale Moonlight	.50	1.25
2R38 Conscription	.50	1.25
2R40 Deep Roots	.50	1.25
2R41 Disable Sensors (1E)	1.00	2.50
2R49 Machinations	.50	1.25
2R59 Retaliation	.50	1.25
2R61 Shadow Operation	.50	1.25
2R65 Straying from the Path (1E)	.50	1.25
2R67 The Text of the Kosst Amojan	.50	1.25
2R68 Under Scrutiny (1E)	.50	1.25
2R72 Visionary (1E)	.50	1.25
2R81 If Wishes Were Horses	.50	1.25
2R82 Ja'chuq	1.25	3.00
2R83 Powerful Example	.50	1.25
2R85 Relentless	.75	2.00
2R91 Vile Deception	.50	1.25
2U10 Flim-Flam Artist (1E)	.20	.50
2U12 Hired Muscle (1E)	.20	.50
2U17 Picking Up the Pieces (1E)	.20	.50
2U18 Plasma Shock (1E)	.20	.50
2U19 Quaint Technology (1E)	.20	.50
2U22 Stolen Computer Core	.20	.50
2U32 Born for Conquest (1E)	.20	.50
2U33 Brief Reunion	.20	.50
2U42 Ferocity (1E)	.20	.50
2U44 For the Sisko (1E)	.20	.50
2U46 Kotra (1E)	.20	.50
2U50 Mental Discipline (1E)	.20	.50
2U51 Peldor Jol	.20	.50
2U53 Picking Up the Basics	.20	.50
2U55 Political Leverage (1E)	.20	.50
2U62 Sickbay (1E)	.20	.50
2U63 Smuggling Run	.20	.50
2U64 Staunch Determination	.20	.50
2U66 Temba, His Arms Wide	.20	.50
2U70 Unseen Manipulations	.20	.50
2U71 Vast Resources	.20	.50
2U73 We Will Not Surrender (1E)	.20	.50
2U74 Bank Heist	.20	.50
2U76 Diplomatic Masquerade	.20	.50
2U77 Discreet Inquiry	.20	.50
2U80 Honorable Death	.20	.50
2U84 Precautionary Measures (1E)	.20	.50
2U86 Shared Delicacy (1E)	.20	.50
2U87 Stricken Dumb	.20	.50
2U93 We Are Klingon	.20	.50
2U94 Well-Crafted Lure	.20	.50
2U95 Aid Clone Colony	.20	.50
2U96 Athos IV, Maquis Base	.20	.50
2U97 Avert Danger	.20	.50
2U98 Brute Force	.20	.50
2U99 Cargo Haul	.20	.50
2R104 Borum, Selfless Hero (1E)	.50	1.25
2R105 Jaro Essa, Leader of the Circle	.50	1.25
2R106 Kira Nerys, Impassioned Major (1E)	1.25	3.00
2R107 Kurn, Bajoran Security Officer (1E)	.50	1.25
2R108 Leeta, Dabo Girl (1E)	1.25	3.00
2R112 Winn Adami, Devious Manipulator	.50	1.25
2R114 Enabran Tain, Retired Mastermind (1E)	.50	1.25
2R115 Evek, Harsh Interrogator (1E)	.50	1.25
2R120 Chakotay, Freedom Fighter	1.25	3.00
2R121 Ezri Dax, Station Counselor	.75	2.00
2R122 Jake Sisko, Temporal Anchor	.50	1.25
2R125 Keiko O'Brien, School Teacher	.50	1.25
2R127 Michael Eddington, Noble Hero (1E)	.75	2.00
2R128 Miles O'Brien, Transporter Chief	.75	2.00
2R130 Rebecca Sullivan, Resistance Fighter (1E)	1.50	4.00
2R131 Thomas Riker, Defiant Leader (1E)	1.00	2.50
2R135 Drex, Arrogant Warrior	.50	1.25
2R136 K'mpec, Klingon Supreme Commander	.50	1.25
2R138 Kahless, The Unforgettable	.50	1.25
2R139 Kargan, Rash Captain (1E)	.50	1.25
2R142 Konmel, Renegade Warrior	.50	1.25
2R144 Korris, Renegade Captain (1E)	.50	1.25
2R157 Roga Danar, Decorated Subhadar	.75	2.00
2R158 Sakonna, Gunrunner (1E)	.50	1.25
2R161 Galathon, Steadfast Rival	.75	2.00
2R163 Neral, Senate Proconsul	.50	1.25
2R165 Sirol, Diplomatic Adversary (1E)	.50	1.25
2R168 Toreth, Cautious Commander (1E)	.50	1.25
2R169 Kitara (1E)	1.00	2.50
2R170 Aldara (1E)	.75	2.00
2R173 Valjean	.60	1.50
2R174 I.K.S. Qam-Chee (1E)	.75	2.00
2R175 Fortune	.50	1.25
2R178 Khazara (1E)	.75	2.00
2R179 Terix (1E)	.75	2.00
2R180 Trolarak (1E)	.75	2.00
2U100 Investigate Maquis Activity (1E)	.20	.50
2U101 Mine Nebula	.20	.50
2U102 Treat Plague Ship (1E)	.20	.50
2U103 Akorem Laan, Revered Poet (1E)	.20	.50
2U110 The Sirah, The Storyteller	.20	.50
2U111 Varis Sul, Tetrarch of the Paqu (1E)	.20	.50
2U113 Boheeka, Clandestine Connection	.20	.50
2U117 Natima Lang, Professor of Political Ethics (1E)	.20	.50
2U118 Benjamin Sisko, Man of Resolve (1E)	.20	.50
2U119 Cal Hudson, Attache to the Demilitarized Zone	.20	.50
2U123 Joseph Sisko, Creole Chef (1E)	.20	.50
2U124 Julian Bashir, Unnatural Freak	.20	.50
2U132 William Patrick Samuels, Maquis Saboteur (1E)	.20	.50
2U137 Kahless, The Greatest Warrior of Them All (1E)	.20	.50
2U146 M'vil	.20	.50
2U147 Amaros, Earnest Vanguard	.20	.50
2U156 Raimus, Criminal Master	.20	.50
2U162 Mirok, Interphase Researcher (1E)	.20	.50
2U166 T'Rul, Curt Subcommander (1E)	.20	.50
2U171 Guingouin (1E)	.20	.50
2U177 Tama (1E)	.20	.50

2004 Star Trek Fractured Time

COMPLETE SET (40)	30.00	80.00
COMMON CARD	.75	2.00
RELEASED ON OCTOBER 13, 2004		
5P2 The Clown: Bitter Medicine (1E)	1.50	4.00
5P3 Tragic Turn	5.00	10.00
5P4 Cardassian Protectorate	1.25	3.00
5R5 Expand the Collective	1.25	3.00
5P10 Quantum Incursions (1E)	1.25	3.00
5P12 Security Drills (1E)	1.50	4.00
5P18 Unyielding	2.00	5.00
5P19 Explicit Orders (1E)	1.50	4.00
5P20 Fitting In (1E)	2.00	5.00
5P22 Kira Nerys, The Intendant	1.25	3.00
5P24 Dukat, Prefect of Bajor	1.25	3.00
5P25 Elim Garak, First Officer of Terok Nor	1.25	3.00
5P28 James T. Kirk, Living Legend	2.00	5.00
5P29 Tasha Yar, Tactical Officer	1.50	4.00
5P30 Worf, First Officer	1.50	4.00
5P31 Korath, Duplicitous Tinkerer	1.25	3.00
5P32 Worf, Regent of the Alliance	1.50	4.00
5P33 Benjamin Sisko, Outlaw (1E)	1.50	4.00
5P34 Daniels, Temporal Enforcers	1.25	3.00
5P35 Miles O'Brien, Smiley	2.50	6.00
5P39 Sphere 634	2.00	5.00
5P40 U.S.S. Enterprise-D, Personal Flagship	3.00	8.00

2004 Star Trek Necessary Evil

COMPLETE SET (180)	120.00	200.00
BOOSTER BOX (30 PACKS)	200.00	300.00
BOOSTER PACK (11 CARDS)	6.00	12.00
COMMON CARD	.10	.20
RELEASED ON MARCH 17, 2004		
4R7 Biochemical Hyperacceleration	1.50	4.00
4R9 Broken Captive (1E)	1.25	3.00
4U8 Bleeding to Death (1E)	.20	.50
4R11 Counterinsurgency Program	1.25	3.00
4R18 In Training	1.25	3.00
4R25 Talosian Trial	1.25	3.00
4R27 The Dreamer and the Dream	1.50	4.00
4R28 Tsiolkovsky Infection	2.00	5.00
4R30 Whisper in the Dark	1.25	3.00
4R34 The Sword of Kahless	1.25	3.00
4R35 Accepting the Past	1.50	4.00
4R36 All-Out War	3.00	8.00
4R37 Anything or Anyone	3.00	8.00
4R40 At What Cost?	6.00	12.00
4R44 Caught in the Act	2.00	5.00
4R49 Endangered	3.00	8.00
4R51 Far-Seeing Eyes	2.50	6.00
4R52 Field Studies	1.25	3.00
4R59 Militia Patrol (1E)	1.25	3.00
4R65 Organized Terrorist Activities	7.50	15.00
4R68 Prison Compound (1E)	2.50	6.00
4R70 Ressikan Flute	2.50	6.00
4R71 Running a Tight Ship	1.25	3.00
4R74 Storage Compartment	2.00	5.00
4R78 The Perfect Tool	1.25	3.00
4R79 Thought Maker	2.50	6.00
4R83 You've Always Been My Favorite	5.00	10.00
4R85 Allies on the Inside	2.50	6.00
4R86 Brainwashing	1.25	3.00
4R89 Knowledge and Experience	1.25	3.00
4R94 Outlining the Stakes	1.25	3.00
4R98 The Rite of Emergence	1.25	3.00
4U10 Cave-In	.20	.50
4U12 Dealing With Pressure	.20	.50
4U14 Formal Hearing	.20	.50
4U16 Harsh Conditions	.20	.50
4U22 Renegade Ambush	.20	.50
4U23 Short Circuit (1E)	.20	.50
4U24 Side by Side (1E)	.20	.50
4U29 Ungracious Hosts (1E)	.20	.50
4U33 The Stone of Gol	.20	.50
4U38 Apprehended	.20	.50
4U39 At An Impasse	.20	.50
4U41 Battle Lust	.20	.50
4U42 Biological Distinctiveness	.20	.50
4U47 Deploy the Fleet	.20	.50
4U48 Desperate Sacrifice	.20	.50
4U50 Escaping Detection	.20	.50
4U53 Forcing Their Hand (1E)	.20	.50
4U54 Forever Linked (1E)	.20	.50
4U55 Getting Under Your Skin (1E)	.20	.50
4U60 Misdirection (1E)	.20	.50
4U61 Mission Accomplished (1E)	.20	.50
4U62 More Than Meets the Eye	.20	.50
4U67 Power Shift	.20	.50
4U75 Targeted for Assimilation	.20	.50
4U76 Tempted By Flesh	.20	.50
4U80 Undercover Resource	.20	.50
4U84 Your Fear Will Destroy You	.20	.50
4U88 Indomitable	.20	.50
4U90 Lying in Wait	.20	.50
4U91 Natural Instincts	.20	.50
4U92 One-Upmanship	.20	.50
4U93 Operational Necessity	.20	.50
4U95 Reborn	.20	.50
4R100 Bareil Antos, Opaka's Protector	1.25	3.00
4R102 Dukat, Anjohl Tennan	1.50	4.00
4R103 Kira Meru, Comfort Woman (1E)	1.50	4.00
4R104 Krim, Thoughtful Tactician	1.25	3.00
4R106 Leeta, Rebel Supporter (1E)	2.00	5.00
4R108 Solbor, Faithful Attendant (1E)	2.00	5.00
4R119 Kira Nerys, Iliana Ghemor	2.00	5.00
4R121 Odo, Impartial Investigator	2.00	5.00
4R124 Toran, Ambitious Brute (1E)	1.25	3.00
4R126 Founder Architect (1E)	1.50	4.00
4R130 Odo Founder, Adept Imposter	1.50	4.00
4R131 Rodek'koden (1E)	1.25	3.00
4R133 Beverly Crusher, Chief Physician (1E)	2.50	6.00
4R134 Data, Pinocchio (1E)	2.50	6.00
4R138 Guinan, Listener	1.50	4.00
4R139 Jadzia Dax, Problem Solver (1E)	3.00	8.00
4R140 Jake Sisko, Reporter Behind the Lines	3.00	8.00
4R149 William T. Riker, First Officer (1E)	2.50	6.00
4R150 Worf, Conn Officer	2.50	6.00
4R151 B'Etor, Ambitious Renegade	1.25	3.00
4R152 Jadzia Dax, Sworn Ally (1E)	2.50	6.00
4R154 Lursa, Ambitious Renegade	1.25	3.00
4R155 William T. Riker, Exchange Officer	2.00	5.00
4R157 Crosis, Fanatical Lieutenant	1.25	3.00
4R158 Data, Loyal Brother (1E)	1.25	3.00
4R161 Lore, The One	2.50	6.00
4R165 B'Etor, Romulan Conspirator	1.25	3.00
4R168 Koval, Chairman of the Tal Shiar	1.25	3.00
4R169 Lursa, Romulan Conspirator	1.25	3.00
4R173 Sela, Devious Schemer (1E)	1.25	3.00
4R180 I.K.S. Ning'tao	2.50	6.00
4U101 Day Kannu	.20	.50
4U109 Surmak Ren, Medical Administrator	.20	.50
4U113 Facilitation Drone	.20	.50
4U114 Five of Twelve, Secondary Adjunct of Trimatrix 942	.20	.50
4U115 Reconnaissance Drone (1E)	.20	.50
4U116 Aamin Marritza, Honorable Patriot (1E)	.20	.50
4U117 Broca, Groveling Lackey	.20	.50
4U120 Mila, Trusted Confidante	.20	.50
4U122 Rusot, Proud Nationalist (1E)	.20	.50
4U123 Seskal, Comrade in Arms	.20	.50
4U128 Luaran, Cautious Inspector	.20	.50
4U129 O'Brien Founder, Agent Provocateur	.20	.50
4U132 Weyoun, Warship Commander	.20	.50
4U135 Deanna Troi, Ship's Counselor (1E)	.20	.50
4U137 Geordi La Forge, Conn Officer (1E)	.20	.50
4U141 Kalita, Maquis Pilot	.20	.50
4U143 Lenara Kahn, Wormhole Theorist (1E)	.20	.50
4U144 Miles O'Brien, Repair Chief	.20	.50
4U148 Tim Watters, Valiant Captain (1E)	.20	.50
4U159 Goval, Follower of the One	.20	.50
4U166 Bochra, Loyal Centurion	.20	.50
4U171 Parem, Special Security (1E)	.20	.50
4U176 Tamarith, Reformist (1E)	.20	.50
4U178 Talnot	.20	.50
4U179 U.S.S. Valiant, Red Squad Training Ship (1E)	.20	.50

2004 Star Trek Necessary Evil Foil

COMPLETE SET (18)	150.00	250.00
COMMON CARD	10.00	25.00
RELEASED ON MARCH 17, 2004		

2004 Star Trek Reflections 2.0

COMPLETE SET (61)	40.00	80.00
COMMON CARD	.10	.30
BOOSTER BOX (24 PACKS)	30.00	60.00
BOOSTER PACK (18 CARDS)	1.50	3.00
6P2 Dignitaries and Witnesses (1E)	.60	1.50
6P3 Eye to Eye (1E)	.60	1.50
6P6 Hard Time (1E)	.60	1.50
6P7 Helpless (1E)	.60	1.50
6P8 Mr. Tricorder (1E)	.60	1.50
6P9 Shipboard Fire (1E)	.60	1.50
6P11 Unknown Microorganism (1E)	.60	1.50
6P17 Changed History (1E)	.60	1.50
6P20 Friction (1E)	.60	1.50
6P26 Maquis Raid	1.50	4.00
6P29 Stalling for Time (1E)	.60	1.50
6P33 Change of Heart (1E)	.60	1.50
6P40 Odo, Curzon Odo (1E)	.60	1.50
6P43 Requisitions Drone (1E)	.60	1.50
6P46 Gelnon, Aloof Tactician	1.50	4.00
6P47 Ixtana'Rax, Honored Elder (1E)	.60	1.50
6P50 Kira Nerys, Starfleet Emissary (1E)	.60	1.50
6P51 Santos, Squad Leader	.75	2.00
6P53 William T. Riker, Wistful Admiral	3.00	8.00
6P55 Worf, Son of Mogh (1E)	1.50	4.00
6P56 Jean-Luc Picard, Galen (1E)	15.00	30.00
6P57 Vina, Orion Slave Girl (1E)	.60	1.50
6P59 Mendak, Duplicitous Admiral	1.50	4.00
6P60 Dominion Battleship (1E)	.60	1.50

2004 Star Trek Tenth Anniversary Collection

COMPLETE SET (18)	45.00	100.00
RELEASED ON MAY 3, 2004		
0P6 Benjamin Sisko, Shipwright (1E)	2.50	6.00
0P7 Borg Queen, Perfectionist	2.50	6.00
0P8 Dukat, True Cardassian	2.50	6.00
0P9 Kudak'Etan, Arrogant First (1E)	2.50	6.00
0P10 Data, Commanding Officer	2.50	6.00

0P11 Jean-Luc Picard, Starship Captain (1E) 2.50 6.00
0P12 Gowron, Sole Leader of the Empire (1E) 2.50 6.00
0P13 Arctus Baran, Treasure Seeker 2.50 6.00
0P14 Velal, Reluctant Aggressor 2.50 6.00
0P15 Baraka (1E) 2.50 6.00
0P16 Queen's Borg Cube 2.50 6.00
0P17 Naprem 2.50 6.00
0P18 U.S.S. Defiant, Commandeered Warship 2.50 6.00
0P19 U.S.S. Enterprise-D, Explorer 2.50 6.00
0P20 U.S.S. Sutherland 2.50 6.00
0P21 I.K.S. Bortas 2.50 6.00
0P22 Fortune, Raider for Hire (1E) 2.50 6.00
0P23 Rovaran (1E) 2.50 6.00

2005 Star Trek Strange New Worlds

COMPLETE SET (120) 40.00 100.00
BOOSTER BOX (30 PACKS) 25.00 50.00
BOOSTER PACK (11 CARDS) 1.00 2.00
RELEASED ON MAY 13, 2005
7R2 Code of Honor .75 2.00
7R4 Entanglement .75 2.00
7R8 Molecular Reversion Field (1E) .75 2.00
7R10 Proximity-Actuated Field .75 2.00
7R15 Where No One Has Gone Before .75 2.00
7R18 Brinkmanship .75 2.00
7R20 Exceed Engine Output .75 2.00
7R23 Provoked Attack .75 2.00
7R25 Rule of Acquisition #6 .75 2.00
7R26 Rule of Acquisition #22 .75 2.00
7R28 Rule of Acquisition #141 .75 2.00
7R29 Rule of Acquisition #144 .75 2.00
7R32 Temporal Incursion .75 2.00
7R36 Ascertain .75 2.00
7R40 Delegated Assignment .75 2.00
7R59 Tekeny Ghemor, Prominent Official .75 2.00
7R61 Goran'Agar, Trusted Commander .75 2.00
7R62 Omet'iklan, Steely Disciplinarian .75 2.00
7R67 Leonard H. McCoy, Remarkable Man .75 2.00
7R69 Montgomery Scott, Relic .75 2.00
7R70 Arridor, Great Sage .75 2.00
7R74 Brunt, FCA Liquidator .75 2.00
7R77 Ishka, Moogie .75 2.00
7R78 Kazago, First Officer .75 2.00
7R81 Leck, Eliminator .75 2.00
7R83 Lurin, Renegade DaiMon .75 2.00
7R89 Quark, True Ferengi .75 2.00
7R92 Sovak, Treasure Hunter .75 2.00
7R93 Taar, Bristling DaiMon .75 2.00
7R94 Zek, The Grand Nagus .75 2.00
7R95 Jean-Luc Picard, Worf's cha'Dich .75 2.00
7R98 B-4, Dangerous Simpleton (1E) .75 2.00
7R101 Ira Graves, Noted Molecular Cyberneticist .75 2.00
7R102 Kivas Fajo, Collector .75 2.00
7R104 Noonien Soong, Often-Wrong .75 2.00
7R109 Tolian Soran, Renegade Scientist .75 2.00
7R111 Vic Fontaine, Vegas Crooner .75 2.00
7R113 Spock, Celebrated Ambassador .75 2.00
7R116 Aurulent .75 2.00
7R118 Kurdon .75 2.00
7R120 Devoras .75 2.00

2006 Star Trek Captain's Log

COMPLETE SET (120) 100.00 200.00
BOOSTER BOX (30 PACKS) 30.00 60.00
BOOSTER PACK (11 CARDS) 1.25 2.50
RELEASED ON OCTOBER 27, 2006
10R2 An Issue of Trust 2.50 6.00
10R3 Armed Search Party (1E) 2.50 6.00
10R6 Contaminating a Culture (1E) 2.50 6.00
10R14 Psionic Attack (1E) 2.50 6.00
10R19 Thermokinetic Explosion 2.50 6.00
10R23 A Sight for Sore Eyes (1E) 2.50 6.00
10R25 Dark Pursuit 2.50 6.00
10R31 Parallel Course 2.50 6.00
10R32 Political Putsch 2.50 6.00
10R33 Rule of Acquisition #16 2.50 6.00
10R35 The Dominion Will Prevail 2.50 6.00
10R36 The Long Journey Home 2.50 6.00
10R37 The Spirit of Kahless 2.50 6.00
10R42 Surprise Snag 2.50 6.00
10R45 Warp Speed Transfer (1E) 2.50 6.00
10R53 Basso Tromac, Smug Subordinate 2.50 6.00
10R56 Second, Neonatal Drone (1E) 2.50 6.00
10R58 Macet, Skeptical Commander (1E) 2.50 6.00
10R66 Harry Kim, Eager to Please (1E) 2.50 6.00
10R70 Kathryn Janeway, Forceful Captain 2.50 6.00
10R75 Matthew Dougherty, Misguided Admiral 2.50 6.00
10R83 The Doctor, Emergency Medical Hologram 2.50 6.00
10R84 Tom Paris, Best Pilot You Could Have 2.50 6.00
10R85 Tuvok, Chief of Security (1E) 2.50 6.00
10R86 Quark, Little Green Man (1E) 2.50 6.00
10R94 Lal, Beloved (1E) 2.50 6.00
10R96 Neelix, Morale Officer (1E) 2.50 6.00
10R98 Tam Elbrun, Prodigal Telepath 2.50 6.00
10R99 Thon 2.50 6.00

2006 Star Trek Captain's Log Foil

COMPLETE SET (18) 50.00 100.00
RELEASED ON OCTOBER 27, 2006
10A1 An Issue of Trust 2.50 6.00
10A2 Armed Search Party (1E) 2.50 6.00
10A3 Thermokinetic Explosion 2.50 6.00
10A4 A Sight for Sore Eyes (1E) 2.50 6.00
10A5 Dark Pursuit 2.50 6.00
10A6 The Long Journey Home 2.50 6.00
10A7 Warp Speed Transfer (1E) 2.50 6.00
10A8 Second, Neonatal Drone (1E) 2.50 6.00
10A9 Kathryn Janeway, Forceful Captain 2.50 6.00
10A10 The Doctor, Emergency Medical Hologram 2.50 6.00
10A11 The Viceroy, Advisor to the Praetor (1E) 2.50 6.00
10A12 Charles Tucker III, Chief Engineer 2.50 6.00
10A13 U.S.S. Defiant, Patrolling Warship (1E) 2.50 6.00
10A14 U.S.S. Enterprise-C, Yesterday's Enterprise (1E) 2.50 6.00
10A15 U.S.S. Enterprise-E, Flagship of the Federation 2.50 6.00
10A16 U.S.S. Yangtzee Kiang, Modified Transport 2.50 6.00
10A17 Quark's Treasure, Sabotaged Shuttle 2.50 6.00
10A18 Columbia, The Second Warp Five Ship 2.50 6.00

2006 Star Trek Dangerous Missions

COMPLETE SET (19) 20.00 40.00
RELEASED ON SEPTEMBER 1, 2006
9R1 Bio-neural Computer Core .75 2.00
9R2 Shields Up! (1E) .75 2.00
9R3 Maquis Vendetta (1E) .75 2.00
9R4 Revelry .75 2.00
9R5 Avert Solar Implosion (1E) .75 2.00
9R6 Deliver Ancient Artifact (1E) .75 2.00
9R7 Deliver Evidence .75 2.00
9R8 Bareil Antos, Escort .75 2.00
9R9 Kira Nerys, Hero of Bajor (1E) .75 2.00
9R10 Jadzia Dax, Elder .75 2.00
9R11 James T. Kirk, Irrational Human Being (1E) .75 2.00
9R12 Jean-Luc Picard, Captain of the Enterprise (1E) .75 2.00
9R13 William T. Riker, Skilled Commander .75 2.00
9R14 Charles Tucker III, Standing In .75 2.00
9R15 Jonathan Archer, Bearer of Surak's Katra .75 2.00
9R16 T'Pol, Non-believer .75 2.00
9R17 Vedek Assembly Transport .75 2.00
9R18 U.S.S. Enterprise-D, Federation Flagship .75 2.00
9R19 Enterprise, Battle Hardened .75 2.00

2006 Star Trek The Enterprise Collection

COMPLETE SET (18) 20.00 40.00
RELEASED ON AUGUST 26, 2006
41P Starfleet Phaser Pistol .75 2.00
42P Revisionist History .75 2.00
43P Temporal Shifting .75 2.00
44P Seat of Starfleet .75 2.00
45P Charles Tucker III .75 2.00
46P Elizabeth Cutler .75 2.00
47P Emory Erickson .75 2.00
48P Ethan Novakovich .75 2.00
49P Hoshi Sato .75 2.00
50P Jeremy Lucas .75 2.00
51P Jonathan Archer .75 2.00
52P Malcolm Reed .75 2.00
53P Maxwell Forrest .75 2.00
54P Phlox .75 2.00
55P T'Pol .75 2.00
56P Travis Mayweather .75 2.00
57P Enterprise .75 2.00
58P T'Pol/Soong Maneuver .75 2.00

2006 Star Trek Genesis

COMPLETE SET (27) 20.00 40.00
RELEASED ON NOVEMBER 13, 2006
11P1 Accelerated Aging (1E) .75 2.00
11P2 Destined Journey (1E) .75 2.00
11P3 Final Triumph (1E) .75 2.00
11P4 Not Quite Domesticated Pets (1E) .75 2.00
11P5 Subterranean Barrier (1E) .75 2.00
11P6 The Caretaker's Guests (1E) .75 2.00
11P7 Unbelievable Emergency (1E) .75 2.00
11P8 Blow You Out of the Stars (1E) .75 2.00
11P9 Cellular Peptide Cake (1E) .75 2.00
11P10 Learning Curve (1E) .75 2.00
11P11 No-Win Situation (1E) .75 2.00
11P12 The Genesis Effect (1E) .75 2.00
11P13 Khan! (1E) .75 2.00
11P14 Genesis Planet (1E) .75 2.00
11P15 Kira Nerys, Outspoken Major (1E) .75 2.00
11P16 Jasad (1E) .75 2.00
11P17 James T. Kirk, Original Thinker (1E) .75 2.00
11P18 Spock, Trainee Instructor (1E) .75 2.00
11P19 Tom Paris, Starfleet Observer (1E) .75 2.00
11P20 Tuvok, Undercover (1E) .75 2.00
11P21a Saavik, Protegee (1E) .75 2.00
11P21b Saavik, Protegee (1E) .75 2.00
11P22 Kruge, Instinctive Commander (1E) .75 2.00
11P23 Carol Marcus, Intelligent Scientist (1E) .75 2.00
11P24 David Marcus, Young Scientist (1E) .75 2.00
11P25 Khan Noonien Singh, Genetically-Engineered Nemesis (1E) .75 2.00
11P26 Queen's Borg Sphere, Contingency Vessel (1E) .75 2.00
11P27 U.S.S. Enterprise, Earth's Savior (1E) .75 2.00

2006 Star Trek To Boldly Go

COMPLETE SET (120) 100.00 250.00
BOOSTER BOX (30 PACKS) 40.00 80.00
BOOSTER PACK (11 CARDS) 1.50 3.00
RELEASED ON AUGUST 18, 2006
8C8 Cultural Differences (1E) .10 .30
8R1 Agonizing Encounter 2.50 6.00
8R4 Bre'Nan Ritual 2.50 6.00
8R5 Cardassian Processing (1E) 2.50 6.00
8U2 Assist Rescue Operation .10 .30
8U3 Between Duty and Respect (1E) .10 .30
8U6 Chula: Move Along Home (1E) .10 .30
8U7 Covert Insertion .10 .30
8U9 Dangerous Standoff .10 .30
8C19 Warp Bubble Mishap (1E) .10 .30
8C22 Phase Pistol .10 .30
8C24 Aggressive Solutions .10 .30
8C25 Assimilation Technique (1E) .10 .30
8C26 Bound by Addiction (1E) .10 .30
8C27 Continuing Committee Hearing .10 .30
8C29 Defend Our People (1E) .10 .30
8C30 Destined To Be .10 .30
8C34 First-hand Experience .10 .30
8C36 Not Easily Destroyed .10 .30
8C40 Restorative Responsibility .10 .30
8C42 Seal the Temple's Door .10 .30
8C44 Target Practice (1E) .10 .30
8C47 Transporter Buffer .10 .30
8C63 Mardah, Quite a Writer .10 .30
8C64 Borg Queen, The One Who is Many .10 .30
8C69 Ulani Belor, Senior Cardassian Scientist .10 .30
8C70 Turan'Ekan .10 .30
8C72 Boothby, Groundskeeper (1E) .10 .30
8C73 Jean Hejar, Nova Squadron Navigator (1E) .10 .30
8C75 Sito Jaxa, Nova Squadron Pilot .10 .30
8C77 Frool, Old and Fragile .10 .30
8C80 Aluura, Nice to Everyone .10 .30
8C82 Cyrus Redblock, Civil Criminal (1E) .10 .30
8C85 Miss Sarda, Not a Legal Expert (1E) .10 .30
8C89 T'Pol, Subcommander .10 .30
8C92 Shinzon, Reman Leader (1E) .10 .30
8C93 Burrows, Diagnostic Tech (1E) .10 .30
8C95 Charles Tucker III, Trip .10 .30
8C96 Cunningham, Assigned to the Gallery .10 .30
8C97 Dallas (1E) .10 .30
8C99 Elizabeth Cutler, Eager Entomologist (1E) .10 .30
8R11 Molecular Mishap 2.50 6.00
8R13 Outclassed 2.50 6.00
8R14 Parallels (1E) 2.50 6.00
8R16 Tactical Disadvantage (1E) 2.50 6.00
8R18 Up The Ante 2.50 6.00
8R20 Zero Hour 2.50 6.00
8R21 Data's Emotion Chip 2.50 6.00
8R28 Dabo! 2.50 6.00
8R32 Distracting Exhibition 2.50 6.00
8R33 Escape Pod 2.50 6.00
8R35 Latinum Storage 2.50 6.00
8R38 Reman Subterfuge 2.50 6.00
8R39 Remarkable Regeneration 2.50 6.00
8R43 Strafing Fire 2.50 6.00
8R46 The Muse 2.50 6.00
8R49 Disinterested Visitant 2.50 6.00
8R51 Temporal Delineation 2.50 6.00
8R65 First, Unstable 2.50 6.00
8R67 Third, Neonatal Drone 2.50 6.00
8R68 Thrax, Chief of Security 2.50 6.00
8R76 Wesley Crusher, Nova Squadron Pilot (1E) 2.50 6.00
8R83 Kieran MacDuff, Executive Officer 2.50 6.00
8R86 Raakin, Dominant Augment 2.50 6.00
8R87 Shran, In Archer's Debt 2.50 6.00
8R88 Silik, Chameleon 2.50 6.00
8R90 Zefram Cochrane, Ready to Make History 2.50 6.00
8R91 Jean-Luc Picard, Bearer of Ill Tidings 2.50 6.00
8U10 Deuterium Plunderers .10 .30
8U12 Opportunity for Profits .10 .30
8U15 Profitable Venture .10 .30
8U17 Telepathic Invasion .10 .30
8U23 Vulcan Tricorder (1E) .10 .30
8U31 Diplomatic Offer (1E) .10 .30
8U37 Preeminent Precision (1E) .10 .30
8U41 Rule of Acquisition #102 (1E) .10 .30
8U45 That's the Last Time .10 .30
8U48 We're All On Strike .10 .30
8U50 He Speaks in Shale .10 .30
8U52 Assist Cloaked Ship (1E) .10 .30
8U53 Automated Repair Station (1E) .10 .30
8U54 Control Plague (1E) .10 .30
8U55 Earth, Humanity's Home .10 .30
8U56 Escape Gulag (1E) .10 .30
8U57 Investigate Stalled Ship (1E) .10 .30
8U58 Navigate Minefield .10 .30
8U59 Practice Orbital Maneuvers (1E) .10 .30
8U60 Retrieve Material (1E) .10 .30
8U61 Traverse Ion Storm (1E) .10 .30
8U62 Survey New World (1E) .10 .30
8U66 Fourth, Neonatal Drone .10 .30
8U71 Benjamin Sisko, First Officer .10 .30
8U74 Nicolas Locarno, Nova Squadron Leader .10 .30
8U78 Grimp, Pessimist (1E) .10 .30
8U79 Quark, Son of Keldar .10 .30
8U81 Arik Soong, Father of Many (1E) .10 .30
8U84 Malik, Dangerous Augment (1E) .10 .30
8U94 Callaghan (1E) .10 .30
8U98 Daniels, Temporal Agent (1E) .10 .30
8C101 Gaeta (1E) .10 .30
8C102 Garrid (1E) .10 .30
8C104 Jeffery Pierce, On The Edge (1E) .10 .30
8C110 McDermott (1E) .10 .30
8C112 T'Pol, Austere Commander (1E) .10 .30
8C118 Sarajevo, Starfleet Vessel .10 .30
8R106 Jonathan Archer, Headstrong Captain (1E) 2.50 6.00
8R108 Malcolm Reed, Weapon Expert (1E) 2.50 6.00
8R109 Maxwell Forrest, Starfleet Executive (1E) 2.50 6.00
8R111 Phlox, Alien Physiologist (1E) 2.50 6.00
8R113 Travis Mayweather, Space Boomer (1E) 2.50 6.00
8R115 U.S.S. Ganges, One of the First 2.50 6.00
8R116 U.S.S. Rio Grande, Built to Last 2.50 6.00
8R117 Enterprise, Finally Ready to Swim 2.50 6.00
8R119 Shuttlepod One, Reliable Transport 2.50 6.00
8R120 Shuttlepod Two, Landing Craft .10 .30
8U100 Emory Erickson, father of the Transporter (1E) .10 .30
8U103 Hoshi Sato, Uneasy Educator (1E) .10 .30
8U105 Jeremy Lucas, Phlox's Colleague .10 .30
8U107 Kelby, Arrogant Engineer (1E) .10 .30
8U114 Williams, Starfleet Commander (1E) .10 .30

2006 Star Trek To Boldly Go Foil

COMPLETE SET (18) 75.00 180.00
RELEASED ON AUGUST 18, 2006
8A1 Cardassian Processing (1E) 4.00 10.00
8A2 Outclassed 4.00 10.00
8A3 Zero Hour 4.00 10.00
8A4 Distracting Exhibition 4.00 10.00
8A5 Latinum Storage 4.00 10.00
8A6 Reman Subterfuge 4.00 10.00
8A7 Remarkable Regeneration 4.00 10.00
8A8 Strafing Fire 4.00 10.00
8A9 Temporal Delineation 4.00 10.00
8A10 First, Unstable 4.00 10.00
8A11 Thrax, Chief of Security 4.00 10.00
8A12 Wesley Crusher, Nova Squadron Pilot (1E) 4.00 10.00
8A13 Shran, In Archer's Debt 4.00 10.00
8A14 Silik, Chameleon 4.00 10.00
8A15 Jonathan Archer, Headstrong Captain (1E) 4.00 10.00
8A16 U.S.S. Ganges, One of the First 4.00 10.00
8A17 U.S.S. Rio Grande, Built to Last 4.00 10.00
8A18 Enterprise, Finally Ready to Swim 4.00 10.00

2007 Star Trek In a Mirror Darkly

COMPLETE SET (122) 100.00 250.00
BOOSTER BOX (30 PACKS) 200.00 300.00
BOOSTER PACK (11 CARDS) 1.50 3.00
RELEASED ON JUNE 15, 2007
13C1 Aftereffects .10 .30
13C2 Alien Conspiracy (1E) .10 .30
13C5 Crew Advancement (1E) .10 .30
13C7 Disarming Dream .10 .30
13C8 Distraction .10 .30
13C9 Fractured Time (1E) .10 .30
13R4 Chula: The Dice .10 .30
13U3 Captured by the Breen .10 .30
13U6 Dangerous Missions .10 .30
13C11 Interphasic Effects .10 .30
13C16 Preventative Repercussions .10 .30
13C17 Reflections (1E) .10 .30
13C18 Security Weapons .10 .30
13C22 Multidimensional Transporter Device (1E) .10 .30
13C24 Call of the Nagus .10 .30
13C30 One Man Cannot Summon the Future (1E) .10 .30

Card	Low	High
13C33 Seasoned Leader	.10	.30
13C37 These Are The Voyages	.10	.30
13C38 To Be A Warrior	.10	.30
13C41 Watchdog (1E)	.10	.30
13C57 Lam	.10	.30
13C59 Beverly Crusher, Battleship Doctor	.10	.30
13C60 Data, Battleship Officer	.10	.30
13C62 Farrell	.10	.30
13C63 Hikaru Sulu, Savage Security Chief	.10	.30
13C64 Jean-Luc Picard, Battleship Captain	.10	.30
13C68 Lwaxana Troi, Extravagant Ambassador	.10	.30
13C69 Marlena Moreau	.10	.30
13C71 Pavel A. Chekov, Treacherous Underling	.10	.30
13C81 Uhura, Unprincipled Technician	.10	.30
13C82 Wesley Crusher, Battleship Helmsman	.10	.30
13C83 William T. Riker, Battleship First Officer	.10	.30
13C92 Ezri Tigan, Soldier of Fortune	.10	.30
13C93 Jadzia Dax, Soldier of Fortune	.10	.30
13C94 Julian Bashir, Rebel Captain	.10	.30
13R14 Paradan Replicant	3.00	8.00
13R15 Paranoid Escape (1E)	3.00	8.00
13R20 The Dal'Rok	3.00	8.00
13R23 Bigger Tattoo	3.00	8.00
13R26 Captain's Log	3.00	8.00
13R28 Guardians Advice	3.00	8.00
13R29 Necessary Evil (1E)	3.00	8.00
13R32 Sabotaged Transporter	3.00	8.00
13R34 Strange New Worlds (1E)	3.00	8.00
13R35 Temporal Flux Energy Ribbon	3.00	8.00
13R36 The Inner Light (1E)	3.00	8.00
13R39 Unimatrix Zero	3.00	8.00
13R42 Brutal Experiments	3.00	8.00
13R47 Bareil Antos, Petty Thief	3.00	8.00
13R49 Kira Nerys, Resourceful Prisoner (1E)	3.00	8.00
13R50 Odo, Efficient Overseer	3.00	8.00
13R53 Elim Garak, Crafty Underling	3.00	8.00
13R56 Gor, Thot	3.00	8.00
13R58 Pran, Thot	3.00	8.00
13R61 Erika Benteen, Leyton's Adjunct	3.00	8.00
13R65 James T. Kirk, Brutal Barbarian	3.00	8.00
13R67 Leonard H. McCoy, Fiendish Physician	3.00	8.00
13R80 Spock, Man of Integrity	3.00	8.00
13R84 Worf, Defiant Commander	3.00	8.00
13R88 Quark, Simple Barkeep	3.00	8.00
13R90 Grilka, Glorious Lady	3.00	8.00
13R95 Laas, One of the 100	3.00	8.00
13R96 Slar, Gorn Slave Master (1E)	3.00	8.00
13R97 Tuvok, Coldly Logocal Soldier (1E)	3.00	8.00
13R99 Data, From the City of Rateg (1E)	3.00	8.00

2007 Star Trek In a Mirror Darkly Foil

Card	Low	High
COMPLETE SET (18)	80.00	140.00
RELEASED ON JUNE 15, 2007		
13A1 Chula: The Dice	3.00	8.00
13A2 Paranoid Escape (1E)	3.00	8.00
13A3 The Dal'Rok	3.00	8.00
13A4 Temporal Flux Energy Ribbon	3.00	8.00
13A5 Elim Garak, Crafty Underling	3.00	8.00
13A6 Gor, Thot	3.00	8.00
13A7 Pran, Thot	3.00	8.00
13A8 James T. Kirk, Brutal Barbarian	3.00	8.00
13A9 Spock, Man of Integrity	3.00	8.00
0AP11 Stripped Down	3.00	8.00
0AP12 Neras, Slave Girl	3.00	8.00
13A10 Worf, Defiant Commander	3.00	8.00
13A11 Slar, Gorn Slave Master (1E)	3.00	8.00
13A12 Jonathan Archer, Covetous Commander (1E)	3.00	8.00
13A13 T'Pol, Not a Slave	3.00	8.00
13A14 Tykk	3.00	8.00
13A15 U.S.S. Lakota, Modified Starship	3.00	8.00
13A16 Defiant, Mirror Warship	3.00	8.00
13A17 Phoenix, Risen From the Ashes	3.00	8.00
13A18 I.S.S. Enterprise, Terran Flagship (1E)	3.00	8.00

2007 Star Trek These Are the Voyages

Card	Low	High
COMPLETE SET (122)	150.00	350.00
BOOSTER BOX (30 PACKS)	40.00	80.00
BOOSTER PACK (11 CARDS)	1.50	3.00
RELEASED ON MARCH 6, 2007		
12A1 No Kill I	.15	.40
12A2 Psychokinetic Control	.15	.40
12A3 Swashbuckler at Heart	.15	.40
12A4 Vian Test	.15	.40
12A5 James T. Kirk, Highly-Decorated Captain	.15	.40
12A6 Leonard H. McCoy, Chief Medical Officer	.15	.40
12A7 Seven of Nine, Efficient Analyst	.15	.40
12A8 Spock, Science Officer	.15	.40
12A9 Kang, Vigilant Commander	.15	.40
12C1 Arena (1E)	.15	.40
12C2 Barrier's Effect	.15	.40
12C5 Excalbian Drama (1E)	.15	.40
12C6 Fesarius Bluff (1E)	.15	.40
12C7 Gangster's Welcome	.15	.40
12C8 Gorgan	.15	.40
12R3 Casualties	.15	.40
12R4 Distress Call	.15	.40
12U9 Lawgivers (1E)	.15	.40
12A10 Koloth, Ingratiating Captain	.15	.40
12A11 Kor, Courageous Governor	.15	.40
12A12 Dukat, Pah-Wraith Puppet	.15	.40
12A13 Khan Noonien Singh, Bold Man	.15	.40
12A14 Charvanek, Neutral Zone Commander	.15	.40
12A15 Keras, Creature of Duty	.15	.40
12A16 Delta Flyer, Innovative Vessel	.15	.40
12A17 U.S.S. Enterprise, Beautiful Lady	.15	.40
12A18 Gal Gath'thong, Pride of the Praetor	.15	.40
12C10 Mark of Gideon (1E)	.15	.40
12C11 Moment of Doubt	.15	.40
12C12 Mugato	.15	.40
12C16 Silent Attack	.15	.40
12C18 Trelane's Trial (1E)	.15	.40
12C54 Angela Martine	.15	.40
12C55 Areel Shaw	.15	.40
12C59 Carolyn Palamas	.15	.40
12C61 Christine Chapel, Medical Assistant	.15	.40
12C62 Evans	.15	.40
12C63 Gary Mitchell, Godlike Mutant	.15	.40
12C64 George Stocker, Starbase Commodore	.15	.40
12C65 Hikaru Sulu, Senior Helmsman	.15	.40
12C68 James T. Kirk, Youngest Captain in Starfleet	.15	.40
12C69 Janice Rand, Captain's Yeoman	.15	.40
12C70 Josephs	.15	.40
12C73 Mark Piper	.15	.40
12C74 Marlena Moreau	.15	.40
12C75 Mathews	.15	.40
12C80 Palmer	.15	.40
12C81 Pavel A. Chekov, Young Navigator	.15	.40
12C82 Richard Daystrom, Influential Scientist	.15	.40
12C83 Robert Tomlinson	.15	.40
12C86 Uhura, Skilled Technician	.15	.40
12C97 Ambassador Gral, High-Ranking Official (1E)	.15	.40
12C99 Gaard	.15	.40
12R13 Neural Parasites	4.00	10.00
12R14 No Kill I	4.00	10.00
12R15 Psychokinetic Control (1E)	4.00	10.00
12R17 Swashbuckler at Heart (1E)	4.00	10.00
12R20 Vian Test	4.00	10.00
12R21 Tox Uthat	4.00	10.00
12R31 The Circle	4.00	10.00
12R33 Cascade Virus	4.00	10.00
12R37 Grav-Plating Trap	4.00	10.00
12R45 Four of Nine, Heuristics Drone	4.00	10.00
12R47 Three of Nine, Tactician Drone (1E)	4.00	10.00
12R48 Two of Nine, Translator Drone	4.00	10.00
12R50 Parek, Privileged Legate (1E)	4.00	10.00
12R51 Bashir Founder, Imperturbable Infiltrator	4.00	10.00
12R52 Krajensky Founder, Adversary	4.00	10.00
12R56 B'Elanna Torres, Chief Engineer	4.00	10.00
12R58 Benjamin Sisko, Command Staffer	4.00	10.00
12R60 Chakotay, First Officer	4.00	10.00
12R66 Jadzia Dax, Communications Staffer (1E)	4.00	10.00
12R67 James T. Kirk, Highly-Decorated Captain	4.00	10.00
12R71 Julian Bashir, Medical Staffer (1E)	4.00	10.00
12R72 Leonard H. McCoy, Chief Medical Officer	4.00	10.00
12R78 Montgomery Scott, Chief Engineer	4.00	10.00
12R84 Seven of Nine, Efficient Analyst	4.00	10.00
12R85 Spock, Science Officer	4.00	10.00
12R89 Kang, Vigilant Commander	4.00	10.00
12R91 Koloth, Ingratiating Captain	4.00	10.00
12R92 Kor, Courageous Governor	4.00	10.00
12R98 Dukat, Pah-Wraith Puppet (1E)	4.00	10.00
12U19 Vault of Tomorrow	.15	.40
12U22 Condition Red (1E)	.15	.40
12U23 Discovered	.15	.40
12U24 Final Cry (1E)	.15	.40
12U25 Hurried Departure	.15	.40
12U26 Not Easily Avoided	.15	.40
12U27 Obstacle to Opportunity	.15	.40
12U28 Optimism	.15	.40
12U29 Plasma Energy Weapon	.15	.40
12U30 Rule of Acquisition #18	.15	.40
12U32 You Have a Disease (1E)	.15	.40
12U34 Covert Relationship	.15	.40
12U35 Dominion Hierarchy (1E)	.15	.40
12U36 Driven (1E)	.15	.40
12U38 Neural Transceiver (1E)	.15	.40
12U39 Assimilate Resistance	.15	.40
12U40 Earth, Lush and Beautiful Home	.15	.40
12U41 Navigate Argolis Cluster (1E)	.15	.40
12U42 Secure Strategic Base (1E)	.15	.40
12U43 Kira Nerys, Bit of a Fighter (1E)	.15	.40
12U44 Mullibok, Gnarled and Battered Old Tree	.15	.40
12U46 Four of Twelve, Standardization Drone (1E)	.15	.40
12U49 Oran, Irritable Gul (1E)	.15	.40
12U53 Lovok Founder, Effective Changeling	.15	.40
12U57 Bejal Otner, Wormhole Theorist	.15	.40
12U76 Matt Decker, Vengeful Commodore	.15	.40
12U77 Miles O'Brien, Engineering Staffer (1E)	.15	.40
12U79 Orfil Quinteros	.15	.40
12U87 Krax, Arrogant Heir (1E)	.15	.40
12U88 Qol, Lascivious Lackey (1E)	.15	.40
12U90 Khod, Conniving Captain	.15	.40
12U93 Korax, Instigator	.15	.40
12U94 Kras, Merciless Officer	.15	.40
12U95 Mara, Science Officer	.15	.40
12U96 Ro'suv	.15	.40
12C100 Gav, Diplomat	.15	.40
12C101 Gem	.15	.40
12C104 Skalaar, Bounty Hunter (1E)	.15	.40
12C110 Amanda Cole (1E)	.15	.40
12C111 Hideaki Chang, Conscientious Corporal (1E)	.15	.40
12C113 Nelson Kemper (1E)	.15	.40
12C114 Sascha Money (1E)	.15	.40
12C115 Sean Hawkins (1E)	.15	.40
12C118 U.S.S. Constitution	.15	.40
12C121 Kumari, A Fine Ship	.15	.40
12R102 Khan Noonien Singh, Bold Man	.15	.40
12R103 S'salk, Gorn Captain	.15	.40
12R106 Charvanek, Neutral Zone Commander	.15	.40
12R107 Keras, Creature of Duty	.15	.40
12R108 T'Auethn, Obedient Centurion	.15	.40
12R112 Jeremiah Hayes, Diligent Major (1E)	.15	.40
12R116 Delta Flyer, Innovative Vessel	.15	.40
12R119 U.S.S. Enterprise, Beautiful Lady	.15	.40
12R122 Gal Gath'thong, Pride of the Praetor	.15	.40
12U105 Charvanek, Fleet Commander	.15	.40
12U109 Tal, Alert Subcommander	.15	.40
12U117 U.S.S. Constellation, Dead Hulk	.15	.40
12U120 D-7 Battlecruiser (1E)	.15	.40

2007 Star Trek These Are the Voyages Foil

Card	Low	High
COMPLETE SET (18)	50.00	100.00
RELEASED ON MARCH 6, 2007		
12A1 No Kill I	2.50	6.00
12A2 Psychokinetic Control	2.50	6.00
12A3 Swashbuckler at Heart	2.50	6.00
12A4 Vian Test	2.50	6.00
12A5 James T. Kirk, Highly-Decorated Captain	2.50	6.00
12A6 Leonard H. McCoy, Chief Medical Officer	2.50	6.00
12A7 Seven of Nine, Efficient Analyst	2.50	6.00
12A8 Spock, Science Officer	2.50	6.00
12A9 Kang, Vigilant Commander	2.50	6.00
12A10 Koloth, Ingratiating Captain	2.50	6.00
12A11 Kor, Courageous Governor	2.50	6.00
12A12 Dukat, Pah-Wraith Puppet	2.50	6.00
12A13 Khan Noonien Singh, Bold Man	2.50	6.00
12A14 Charvanek, Neutral Zone Commander	2.50	6.00
12A15 Keras, Creature of Duty	2.50	6.00
12A16 Delta Flyer, Innovative Vessel	2.50	6.00
12A17 U.S.S. Enterprise, Beautiful Lady	2.50	6.00
12A18 Gal Gath'thong, Pride of the Praetor	2.50	6.00

2007 Star Trek What You Leave Behind

Card	Low	High
COMPLETE SET (122)	75.00	200.00
BOOSTER BOX (30 PACKS)	40.00	80.00
BOOSTER PACK (11 CARDS)	1.50	3.00
RELEASED ON DECEMBER 20, 2007		
14C2 Caretaker's Wave (1E)	.10	.30
14C3 Cargo Pirates (1E)	.10	.30
14C7 Moral Choice (1E)	.10	.30
14R1 Back to Basics (1E)	2.50	6.00
14U4 Chula: The Chandra	.10	.30
14U5 Inferiority	.10	.30
14U6 Juxtaposition	.10	.30
14U8 Neutrogenic Field	.10	.30
14U9 Night Terrors	.10	.30
14C10 Old Differences	.10	.30
14C11 Prefix Codes	.10	.30
14C19 Toe to Toe	.10	.30
14C21 Vascular Pad	.10	.30
14C22 A Few Minor Difficulties	.10	.30
14C23 Are You Offering Me ... a Bribe?	.10	.30
14C25 Deja Q	.10	.30
14C28 Five Year Mission	.10	.30
14C29 Gatherer's Raid (1E)	.10	.30
14C31 Good Shepherd (1E)	.10	.30
14C32 Hall of Warriors (1E)	.10	.30
14C33 Improvised Modifications	.10	.30
14C36 One Man Can Summon the Future	.10	.30
14C38 Reclaim Terok Nor	.10	.30
14C40 Straight and Steady	.10	.30
14C41 The New Occupation	.10	.30
14C45 Walk the Line	.10	.30
14C46 Advanced Tactical Training	.10	.30
14C73 Talak'talan, Keen Third	.10	.30
14C74 Benjamin Finney, Bitter Records Officer	.10	.30
14C76 Beverly Crusher, Captain Picard (1E)	.10	.30
14C77 Clark Terrell, Reliant Captain	.10	.30
14C80 Geordi La Forge, Retired Engineer	.10	.30
14C82 Mot, The Barber	.10	.30
14C84 Sarek, Vulcan Delegate	.10	.30
14C85 Sirna Kolrami, Famed Strategist	.10	.30
14C87 Leosa, Grifter (1E)	.10	.30
14C93 Worf, Governor of H'atoria	.10	.30
14C94 D'Nesh, Manipulative Gift (1E)	.10	.30
14C95 Harrad-Sar, Slave of the Situation (1E)	.10	.30
14C98 Maras	.10	.30
14C99 Navaar, Experienced Gift (1E)	.10	.30
14R12 Prisoner of the Exile	2.50	6.00
14R14 Spatial Distortions	2.50	6.00
14R15 Stripped Down	2.50	6.00
14R16 Sylvia	2.50	6.00
14R17 The Clown: Guillotine	2.50	6.00
14R18 The Phage	2.50	6.00
14R24 Clarity	2.50	6.00
14R26 Distant Control (1E)	2.50	6.00
14R30 Ghost Stories	2.50	6.00
14R34 In a Mirror, Darkly	2.50	6.00
14R35 Military Assault Command Operations (1E)	2.50	6.00
14R43 U.S.S. Enterprise-J (1E)	2.50	6.00
14R47 Covenant (1E)	2.50	6.00
14R64 Leeta, Union Member	2.50	6.00
14R66 Borg Queen, Obsessed	2.50	6.00
14R67 Data, Tempted by Flesh (1E)	2.50	6.00
14R68 Crell Moset, Notorious Exobiologist	2.50	6.00
14R71 Founder Leader, Single Minded (1E)	2.50	6.00
14R72 Odo, The Great Link's Saviour (1E)	2.50	6.00
14R78 Data, Lucasian Chair	2.50	6.00
14R79 Ezri Dax, Resourceful Counselor	2.50	6.00
14R83 Sarek, Logical Being	2.50	6.00
14R86 The Doctor, Emergency Command Hologram (1E)	2.50	6.00
14R91 Gorkon, Visionary Chancellor	2.50	6.00
14R92 Gowron, Celebrated Leader	2.50	6.00
14R97 Kasidy Yates, Conflicted Captain (1E)	2.50	6.00
14U13 Shocking Betrayal (1E)	.10	.30
14U20 Kir'Shara	.10	.30
14U27 Disruptive Presence	.10	.30
14U37 Quark's Advice	.10	.30
14U39 Standard Orbit (1E)	.10	.30
14U42 The Reckoning	.10	.30
14U44 Vacation from the Continuum	.10	.30
14U48 Dear Friends	.10	.30
14U49 Rule of Acquisition #33 (1E)	.10	.30
14U50 Silent Strike	.10	.30
14U51 Aid Lost Colony	.10	.30
14U52 Commandeer Prototype	.10	.30
14U53 Eliminate Sphere Network	.10	.30
14U54 Elude Federation Forces	.10	.30
14U55 Expand Business Opportunities	.10	.30
14U56 Find Lifeless World	.10	.30
14U57 Follow Homing Beacon	.10	.30
14U58 Navigate Xindi Corridor	.10	.30
14U59 Patrol Neutral Zone	.10	.30
14U60 Purchase Moon	.10	.30
14U61 Restore Errant Moon	.10	.30
14U62 Risa Shore Leave	.10	.30
14U63 Kira Nerys, First Officer	.10	.30
14U65 Winn Adami, Religious Opportunist	.10	.30
14U69 Silaran Prin, Between Darkness and Light (1E)	.10	.30
14U70 Eris, Duplicitous Vorta	.10	.30
14U75 Benjamin Sisko, Bold Captain (1E)	.10	.30
14U81 Katherine Pulaski, Chief Medical Officer (1E)	.10	.30
14U88 Nog, Little Green Man	.10	.30
14U89 Rom, Little Green Man (1E)	.10	.30
14U90 Chang, Gorkon's Chief of Staff (1E)	.10	.30
14U96 Hugh, Rogue Borg	.10	.30
14C101 Persis, Loyal Daughter (1E)	.10	.30
14C105 Nevala (1E)	.10	.30
14C108 D'Vela (1E)	.10	.30
14C109 Kelby, Industrious Engineer	.10	.30
14C110 Stewart Rivers, Patriotic Engineer	.10	.30
14C120 U.S.S. Reliant, Part of One Big Happy Fleet (1E)	.10	.30
14R103 Tallera, Covert Isolationist	.10	.30
14R107 Sela, Cunning Strategist (1E)	.10	.30
14R111 Borg Queen's Vessel, Borg Flagship	.10	.30
14R112 I.K.S. Qel'Poh, H.M.S. Bounty (1E)	.10	.30
14R113 U.S.S. Pasteur, Medical Ship	.10	.30
14R114 U.S.S. Prometheus, Experimental Prototype	.10	.30
14R115 U.S.S. Reliant, Searching for Lifeless Planets	.10	.30
14R116 I.K.S. Kla'Diyus, Prototype	.10	.30
14R117 I.K.S. Qel'poh, Clandestine Vessel (1E)	.10	.30
14R118 Kronos One	.10	.30

14R119 Devna-Lev, Harrad-Sar's Barge .10 .30
14R121 Scimitar, Built for Only One Purpose .10 .30
14R122 U.S.S. Prometheus, Stolen Prototype .10 .30
14U100 Neras, Slave Girl (1E) .10 .30
14U102 Soval, Vulcan Ambassador .10 .30
14U104 Tuvix, Symbiogenesis (1E) .10 .30
14U106 Nanclus, Co-Conspirator (1E) .10 .30

2007 Star Trek What You Leave Behind Foil

COMPLETE SET (18) 50.00 100.00
RELEASED ON DECEMBER 20, 2007
14A1 The Clown: Guillotine 2.50 6.00
14A2 Clarity 2.50 6.00
14A3 Ghost Stories 2.50 6.00
14A4 U.S.S. Enterprise-J (1E) 2.50 6.00
14A5 Data, Tempted by Flesh (1E) 2.50 6.00
14A6 Odo, The Great Link's Savior (1E) 2.50 6.00
14A7 Data, Lucasian Chair 2.50 6.00
14A8 Borg Queen's Vessel, Borg Flagship 2.50 6.00
14A9 I.K.S. Qel'Poh, H.M.S. Bounty (1E) 2.50 6.00
14A10 U.S.S. Pasteur, Medical Ship 2.50 6.00
14A11 U.S.S. Prometheus, Experimental Prototype 2.50 6.00
14A12 U.S.S. Reliant, Searching for Lifeless Planets 2.50 6.00
14A13 I.K.S. Kla'Diyus, Prototype 2.50 6.00
14A14 I.K.S. Qel'poh, Clandestine Vessel (1E) 2.50 6.00
14A15 Kronos One 2.50 6.00
14A16 Devna-Lev, Harrad-Sar's Barge 2.50 6.00
14A17 Scimitar, Built for Only One Purpose 2.50 6.00
14A18 U.S.S. Prometheus, Stolen Prototype 2.50 6.00

Star Wars

1995 Star Wars Premiere

COMPLETE SET (324) 75.00 150.00
BOOSTER BOX (36 PACKS) 75.00 150.00
BOOSTER PACK (15 CARDS) 3.00 6.00
RELEASED IN DECEMBER 1995
1 5D6-RA-7 (Fivedesix) R1 2.00 3.00
2 Admiral Motti R2 1.25 2.00
3 Chief Bast U1 .50 .75
4 Colonel Wullf Yularen U1 .50 .75
5 Commander Praji U2 .50 .75
6 Darth Vader R1 .50 .75
7 Dathcha U1 5.00 8.00
8 Death Star Trooper C2 15.00 25.00
9 Djas Puhr R2 .50 .75
10 Dr. Evazan R2 .20 .30
11 DS-61-2 U1 1.25 2.00
12 DS-61-3 R1 1.25 2.00
13 EG-6 (Eegee-Six) U2 .50 .75
14 Feltipern Trevagg U1 .50 .75
15 Garindan R2 1.25 2.00
16 General Tagge R2 1.25 2.00
17 Grand Moff Tarkin R1 5.00 8.00
18 Imperial Pilot C2 .20 .30
19 Imperial Trooper Guard C2 .20 .30
20 Jawa DARK C2 .20 .30
21 Kitik Keed'kak R1 2.00 3.00
22 Labria R2 .20 .30
23 Lieutenant Tanbris U2 1.25 2.00
24 LIN-V8M (Elleyein-Veeateemm) C1 .50 .75
25 M'iiyoom Onith U2 .50 .75
26 MSE-6 'Mouse' Droid U1 .50 .75
27 Myo R2 1.25 2.00
28 Ponda Baba U1 .50 .75
29 Prophetess U1 .50 .75
30 R1-G4 (Arone-Geefour) C2 .20 .30
31 R4-M9 (Arfour-Emmnine) C2 .20 .30
32 Stormtrooper C3 .20 .30
33 Tonnika Sisters R1 2.00 3.00
34 Tusken Raider C2 .20 .30
35 WED-9-M1 'Bantha' Droid R2 1.25 2.00
36 Wuher U2 .50 .75
37 Blaster Scope U1 .50 .75
38 Caller DARK U2 .50 .75
39 Comlink C1 .20 .30
40 Droid Detector C2 .20 .30
41 Fusion Generator Supply Tanks DARK C2 .20 .30
42 Observation Holocam U2 .50 .75
43 Restraining Bolt DARK C2 .20 .30
44 Stormtrooper Backpack C2 .20 .30
45 Stormtrooper Utility Belt C2 .20 .30
46 A Disturbance In The Force U1 .50 .75
47 Baniss Keeg C2 .20 .30
48 Blast Door Controls U2 .50 .75
49 Blaster Rack U1 .50 .75
50 Dark Hours U2 .50 .75
51 Death Star Sentry U1 .50 .75
52 Disarmed DARK R1 2.00 3.00
53 Expand The Empire R1 2.00 3.00
54 Fear Will Keep Them In Line R2 1.25 2.00
55 I Find Your Lack Of Faith Disturbing R1 2.00 3.00
56 I've Lost Artoo! U1 .50 .75
57 Jawa Pack U1 .50 .75
58 Juri Juice R2 1.25 2.00
59 Ket Maliss C2 .20 .30
60 Lateral Damage R2 1.25 2.00
61 Luke? Luuuuke! U1 .50 .75
62 Macroscan C2 .20 .30
63 Molator R1 2.00 3.00
64 Organa's Ceremonial Necklace R1 2.00 3.00
65 Presence Of The Force R1 2.00 3.00
66 Reactor Terminal U2 .50 .75
67 Send A Detachment Down R1 2.00 3.00
68 Sunsdown U1 .50 .75
69 Tactical Re-Call R2 1.25 2.00
70 Wrong Turn U1 .50 .75
71 Your Eyes Can Deceive You U1 .50 .75
72 Alter DARK U1 .50 .75
73 Boring Conversation Anyway R1 2.00 3.00
74 Charming To The Last R2 1.25 2.00
75 Collateral Damage C2 .20 .30
76 Counter Assault C1 .20 .30
77 Dark Collaboration R1 2.00 3.00
78 Dark Jedi Presence R1 6.00 10.00
79 Dark Maneuvers C2 .20 .30
80 Dead Jawa C2 .20 .30
81 Elis Helrot U2 .50 .75
82 Emergency Deployment U1 .50 .75
83 Evacuate? U2 .50 .75
84 Full Scale Alert U2 .50 .75
85 Gravel Storm U2 .50 .75
86 I Have You Now R2 1.25 2.00
87 I've Got A Problem Here C2 .20 .30
88 Imperial Reinforcements C1 .20 .30
89 Imperial Code Cylinder C2 .20 .30
90 It's Worse C2 .20 .30
91 Imperial Barrier DARK C2 .20 .30
92 Kintan Strider C1 .20 .30
93 Limited Resources U2 .50 .75
94 Local Trouble R1 2.00 3.00
95 Lone Pilot R2 1.25 2.00
96 Lone Warrior R2 1.25 2.00
97 Look Sir, Droids R1 2.00 3.00
98 Moment Of Triumph R2 1.25 2.00
99 Nevar Yalnal R2 1.25 2.00
100 Ommni Box C2 .20 .30
101 Overload C2 .20 .30
102 Physical Choke R1 2.00 3.00
103 Precise Attack C2 .20 .30
104 Scanning Crew C2 .20 .30
105 Sense DARK U1 .50 .75
106 Set For Stun C2 .20 .30
107 Takeel C2 .20 .30
108 Tallon Roll C2 .20 .30
109 The Circle Is Now Complete R1 2.00 3.00
110 The Empire's Back U1 .50 .75
111 Trinto Duaba U1 .50 .75
112 Trooper Charge U2 .50 .75
113 Tusken Scavengers C2 .20 .30
114 Utinni! DARK R1 2.00 3.00
115 Vader's Eye R1 2.00 3.00
116 We're All Gonna Be A Lot Thinner! R1 2.00 3.00
117 You Overestimate Their Chances C1 .50 .75
118 Your Powers Are Weak, Old Man R1 .20 .30
119 Alderaan DARK R1 2.00 3.00
120 Dantooine DARK U1 .50 .75
121 Death Star: Central Core U2 .50 .75
122 Death Star: Detention Block Corridor C1 .20 .30
123 Death Star: Docking Bay 327 DARK C2 .20 .30
124 Death Star: Level 4 Military Corridor U1 .50 .75
125 Death Star: War Room U2 .50 .75
126 Kessel U2 1.25 2.00
127 Tatooine DARK C2 .20 .30
128 Tatooine: Cantina DARK R2 1.25 2.00
129 Tatooine: Docking Bay 94 DARK C2 .20 .30
130 Tatooine: Jawa Camp DARK C1 .20 .30
131 Tatooine: Jundland Wastes C1 .20 .30
132 Tatooine: Lars' Moisture Farm DARK C1 .20 .30
133 Tatooine: Mos Eisley DARK C1 .20 .30
134 Yavin 4 DARK C2 .20 .30
135 Yavin 4: Docking Bay DARK C2 .20 .30
136 Yavin 4: Jungle DARK U2 .50 .75
137 Black 2 R1 4.00 6.00
138 Black 3 U1 .50 .75
139 Devastator R1 4.00 6.00
140 Imperial-Class Star Destroyer U1 1.25 2.00
141 TIE Advanced x1 U2 .50 .75
142 TIE Fighter C2 .20 .30
143 TIE Scout C2 .20 .30
144 Vader's Custom TIE R1 6.00 10.00
145 Bantha U2 .50 .75
146 Lift Tube DARK C2 .20 .30
147 Sandcrawler DARK R2 1.25 2.00
148 Ubrikkian 9000 Z001 C2 .20 .30
149 Assault Rifle R2 1.25 2.00
150 Blaster Rifle DARK C1 .20 .30
151 Boosted TIE Cannon U1 .50 .75
152 Dark Jedi Lightsaber U1 .60 1.00
153 Gaderffii Stick C2 .20 .30
154 Han Seeker R2 1.25 2.00
155 Imperial Blaster DARK C2 .20 .30
156 Ion Cannon U1 .50 .75
157 Laser Projector U2 .50 .75
158 Light Repeating Blaster Rifle R1 2.00 3.00
159 Luke Seeker R2 1.25 2.00
160 Timer Mine DARK C2 .20 .30
161 Turbolaser Battery R2 1.25 2.00
162 Vader's Lightsaber R1 5.00 8.00
163 2X-3KPR (Tooex) U1 .50 .75
164 Beru Lars U2 .50 .75
165 Biggs Darklighter R2 1.25 2.00
166 BoShek U1 .50 .75
167 C-3PO (See-Threepio) R1 5.00 8.00
168 CZ-3 (Seezee-Three) C1 .20 .30
169 Dice Ibegon R2 1.25 2.00
170 Dutch R1 4.00 6.00
171 Figrin D'an U2 .50 .75
172 General Dodonna U1 .50 .75
173 Han Solo R1 8.00 12.00
174 Jawa LIGHT C2 .20 .30
175 Jek Porkins U1 .50 .75
176 Kabe U1 .50 .75
177 Kal'Falnl C'ndros R1 2.00 3.00
178 Leesub Sirln R2 .20 .30
179 Leia Organa R1 1.25 2.00
180 LIN-V8K (Elleyein-Veeatekay) C1 6.00 10.00
181 Luke Skywalker R1 10.00 15.00
182 Momaw Nadon U2 .50 .75
183 Obi-Wan Kenobi R1 6.00 10.00
184 Owen Lars U1 .50 .75
185 Pops U1 .50 .75
186 R2-X2 (Artoo-Extoo) C2 .20 .30
187 R4-E1 (Arfour-Eeone) C2 .20 .30
188 Rebel Guard C2 .20 .30
189 Rebel Pilot C2 .20 .30
190 Rebel Trooper C3 .20 .30
191 Red Leader R1 4.00 6.00
192 Shistavanen Wolfman C2 .20 .30
193 Talz C2 .20 .30
194 WED-9-M1 'Bantha' Droid R2 1.25 2.00
195 Wioslea U1 .50 .75
196 Caller LIGHT U2 .50 .75
197 Electrobinoculars C2 .20 .30
198 Fusion Generator Supply Tanks LIGHT C2 .20 .30
199 Hydroponics Station U2 .50 .75
200 Restraining Bolt LIGHT C2 .20 .30
201 Targeting Computer U1 .50 .75
202 Tatooine Utility Belt C2 .20 .30
203 Vaporator C2 .20 .30
204 A Tremor In The Force U1 .50 .75
205 Affect Mind R1 2.00 3.00
206 Beggar R1 2.00 3.00
207 Crash Site Memorial U1 .50 .75
208 Death Star Plans R1 2.00 3.00
209 Demotion R2 1.25 2.00
210 Disarmed Light R1 2.00 3.00
211 Ellorrs Madak C2 .20 .30
212 Eyes In The Dark U1 .50 .75
213 Jawa Siesta U1 .50 .75
214 Kessel LIGHT U2 2.00 3.00
215 K'lor'slug R1 .50 .75
216 Lightsaber Proficiency R1 2.00 3.00
217 Mantellian Savrip R2 1.25 2.00
218 Nightfall U1 .50 .75
219 Obi-Wan's Cape R1 2.00 3.00
220 Our Most Desperate Hour R1 2.00 3.00
221 Plastoid Armor U2 .50 .75
222 Rebel Planners R2 1.25 2.00
223 Restricted Deployment U1 .50 .75
224 Revolution R1 2.00 3.00
225 Rycar Ryjerd U1 .50 .75
226 Sai'torr Kal Fas C2 .20 .30
227 Special Modifications U1 .50 .75
228 Traffic Control U2 .50 .75
229 Tusken Breath Mask U1 .50 .75
230 Yavin Sentry U2 .50 .75
231 Yerka Mig U1 .20 .30
232 A Few Maneuvers C2 .20 .30
233 Alter LIGHT U1 .50 .75
234 Beru Stew U2 .50 .75
235 Cantina Brawl R1 2.00 3.00
236 Collision! C2 .20 .30
237 Combined Attack C2 .20 .30
238 Don't Get Cocky R1 2.00 3.00
239 Don't Underestimate Our Chances C1 .20 .30
240 Droid Shutdown C2 .20 .30
241 Escape Pod U2 .50 .75
242 Friendly Fire C2 .20 .30
243 Full Throttle R2 1.25 2.00
244 Gift Of The Mentor R1 2.00 3.00
245 Han's Back U2 .50 .75
246 Han's Dice C2 .20 .30
247 Hear Me Baby, Hold Together C2 .20 .30
248 Help Me Obi-Wan Kenobi R1 2.00 3.00
249 How Did We Get Into This Mess? U2 .50 .75
250 Hyper Escape C2 .20 .30
251 I've Got A Bad Feeling About This C2 .20 .30
252 It Could Be Worse C2 1.25 2.00
253 Into The Garbage Chute, Flyboy R2 .20 .30
254 Jedi Presence R1 2.00 3.00
255 Krayt Dragon Howl R1 2.00 3.00
256 Leia's Back U2 .50 .75
257 Luke's Back U2 .50 .75
258 Move Along... R1 2.00 3.00
259 Nabrun Leids U2 .50 .75
260 Narrow Escape C2 .20 .30
261 Noble Sacrifice R2 1.25 2.00
262 Old Ben C2 .20 .30
263 On The Edge R2 1.25 2.00
264 Out Of Nowhere U2 .50 .75
265 Panic U1 .50 .75
266 Radar Scanner C2 .20 .30
267 Rebel Barrier C2 .20 .30
268 Rebel Reinforcements C1 .20 .30
269 Return Of A Jedi U2 .50 .75
270 Scomp Link Access C2 .20 .30
271 Sense LIGHT U1 .50 .75
272 Skywalkers R1 2.00 3.00
273 Solo Han R2 1.25 2.00
274 Spaceport Speeders U2 .50 .75
275 Surprise Assault C1 .20 .30
276 Thank The Maker R2 1.25 2.00
277 The Bith Shuffle C2 .20 .30
278 The Force Is Strong With This One R2 1.25 2.00
279 This Is All Your Fault U1 .50 .75
280 Utinni! LIGHT R1 2.00 3.00
281 Warrior's Courage R2 1.25 2.00
282 We're Doomed C2 .20 .30
283 Alderaan LIGHT U2 1.25 2.00
284 Dantooine LIGHT U1 .50 .75
285 Death Star: Detention Block Control Room U2 .50 .75
286 Death Star: Docking Bay 327 LIGHT C2 .20 .30
287 Death Star: Trash Compactor U1 .50 .75
288 Kessel LIGHT U2 .50 .75
289 Tatooine LIGHT C2 .20 .30
290 Tatooine: Cantina LIGHT R2 1.25 2.00
291 Tatooine: Docking Bay 94 LIGHT C2 .20 .30
292 Tatooine: Dune Sea C1 .20 .30
293 Tatooine: Jawa Camp LIGHTC1 .20 .30
294 Tatooine: Lars' Moisture Farm LIGHT U2 .50 .75
295 Tatooine: Mos Eisley LIGHT C1 .20 .30
296 Tatooine: Obi-Wan's Hut R1 2.00 3.00
297 Yavin 4: LIGHT C2 .20 .30
298 Yavin 4: Docking Bay LIGHT C1 .20 .30
299 Yavin 4: Jungle LIGHT C2 2.00 3.00
300 Yavin 4: Massassi Throne Room R1 .50 .75
301 Yavin 4: Massassi War Room U2 .50 .75
302 Corellian Corvette U2 .60 1.00
303 Gold 1 R2 1.25 2.00
304 Gold 5 R2 1.25 2.00
305 Millenium Falcon R1 5.00 8.00
306 Red 1 U1 .50 .75
307 Red 3 R2 1.25 2.00
308 X-wing C2 .20 .30
309 Y-wing C2 .20 .30
310 Lift Tube LIGHT C2 .20 .30
311 Luke's X-34 Landspeeder U2 .50 .75
312 Sandcrawler LIGHT R2 1.25 2.00
313 SoroSuub V-35 Landspeeder C2 .20 .30
314 Blaster C2 .20 .30
315 Blaster Rifle LIGHT C2 .20 .30
316 Han's Heavy Blaster Pistol R2 1.25 2.00
317 Jedi Lightsaber U1 .50 .75
318 Leia's Sporting Blaster U1 .50 .75
319 Obi-Wan's Lightsaber R1 4.00 6.00
320 Proton Torpedoes C2 .20 .30
321 Quad Laser Cannon U1 .50 .75
322 Tagge Seeker R2 1.25 2.00
323 Tarkin Seeker R2 1.25 2.00
324 Timer Mine LIGHT C2 .20 .30

1996 Star Wars Hoth

COMPLETE SET (163)	50.00	100.00
BOOSTER BOX (36 PACKS)	50.00	100.00
BOOSTER PACK (15 CARDS)	2.00	4.00
RELEASED IN NOVEMBER 1996		
1 AT-AT Driver C2	.20	.30
2 Admiral Ozzel R1	2.00	3.00
3 Captain Lennox U1	.60	1.00
4 Captain Piett R2	2.00	3.00
5 FX-10 (Effex-ten) C2	.20	.30
6 General Veers R1	5.00	8.00
7 Imperial Gunner C2	.20	.30
8 Lieutenant Cabbel U2	.60	1.00
9 Probe Droid C2	.20	.30
10 Snowtrooper C3	.20	.30
11 Snowtrooper Officer C1	.20	.30
12 Wampa R2	2.00	3.00
13 Deflector Shield Generators U2	.60	1.00
14 Evacuation Control U1	.60	1.00
15 Portable Fusion Generator C2	.20	.30
16 Probe Antennae U2	.60	1.00
17 Breached Defenses U2	.60	1.00
18 Death Mark R1	2.00	3.00
19 Death Squadron U1	.60	1.00
20 Frostbite LIGHT C2	.20	.30
21 Frozen Dinner R1	2.00	3.00
22 High Anxiety R1	2.00	3.00
23 Ice Storm LIGHT U1	.60	1.00
24 Image Of The Dark Lord R2	2.00	3.00
25 Imperial Domination U1	.60	1.00
26 Meteor Impact? R1	2.00	3.00
27 Mournful Roar R1	2.00	3.00
28 Responsibility Of Command R1	2.00	3.00
29 Silence Is Golden U2	.60	1.00
30 The Shield Doors Must Be Closed U1	.60	1.00
31 This Is Just Wrong R1	2.00	3.00
32 Too Cold For Speeders U1	.60	1.00
33 Weapon Malfunction R1	2.00	3.00
34 Target The Main Generator R2	2.00	3.00
35 A Dark Time For The Rebellion C1	.20	.30
36 Cold Feet C2	.20	.30
37 Collapsing Corridor R2	2.00	3.00
38 ComScan Detection C2	.20	.30
39 Crash Landing U1	.60	1.00
40 Debris Zone R2	2.00	3.00
41 Direct Hit U1	.60	1.00
42 Exhaustion U2	.60	1.00
43 Exposure U1	.60	1.00
44 Furry Fury R2	2.00	3.00
45 He Hasn't Come Back Yet C2	.20	.30
46 I'd Just As Soon Kiss A Wookiee C2	.20	.30
47 Imperial Supply C1	.20	.30
48 Lightsaber Deficiency U1	.60	1.00
49 Oh, Switch Off C2	.20	.30
50 Our First Catch Of The Day C2	.20	.30
51 Probe Telemetry C2	.20	.30
52 Scruffy-Looking Nerf Herder R2	2.00	3.00
53 Self-Destruct Mechanism U1	.60	1.00
54 Stop Motion C2	.20	.30
55 Tactical Support R2	2.00	3.00
56 That's It, The Rebels Are There! U2	.60	1.00
57 Trample R1	2.00	3.00
58 Turn It Off! Turn It Off! C1	.20	.30
59 Walker Barrage U1	.60	1.00
60 Wall Of Fire U1	.60	1.00
61 Yaggle Gakkle R2	2.00	3.00
62 Hoth DARK U2	.60	1.00
63 Hoth: Defensive Perimeter LIGHT C2	.20	.30
64 Hoth: Echo Command Center (War Room) LIGHT U2	.60	1.00
65 Hoth: Echo Corridor DARK U2	.60	1.00
66 Hoth: Echo Docking Bay LIGHT C2	.20	.30
67 Hoth: Ice Plains C2	.20	.30
68 Hoth: North Ridge LIGHT C2	.20	.30
69 Hoth: Wampa Cave R2	2.00	3.00
70 Ord Mantell LIGHT U2	.60	1.00
71 Stalker R1	6.00	10.00
72 Tyrant R1	5.00	8.00
73 Blizzard 1 R1	4.00	6.00
74 Blizzard 2 R2	2.00	3.00
75 Blizzard Scout 1 R1	4.00	6.00
76 Blizzard Walker U2	.60	1.00
77 AT-AT Cannon U1	.60	1.00
78 Echo Base Operations R2	2.00	3.00
79 Infantry Mine LIGHT C2	.20	.30
80 Probe Droid Laser U2	.60	1.00
81 Vehicle Mine LIGHT C2	.20	.30
82 2-1B (Too-Onebee) R1	2.00	3.00
83 Cal Alder U2	.60	1.00
84 Commander Luke Skywalker R1	10.00	15.00
85 Dack Ralter R2	2.00	3.00
86 Derek 'Hobbie' Klivian U1	.60	1.00
87 Electro-Rangefinder U1	.60	1.00
88 Echo Base Trooper Officer C1	.20	.30
89 Echo Trooper Backpack C2	.20	.30
90 FX-7 (Effex-Seven) C2	.20	.30
91 General Carlist Rieekan R2	2.00	3.00
92 Jeroen Webb U1	.60	1.00
93 K-3PO (Kay-Threepio) R1	2.00	3.00
94 Major Bren Derlin R2	2.00	3.00
95 R2 Sensor Array C2	.20	.30
96 R5-M2 (Arfive-Emmtoo) C2	.20	.30
97 Rebel Scout C1	.20	.30
98 Rogue Gunner C2	.20	.30
99 Romas Lock Navander U2	.60	1.00
100 Shawn Valdez U1	.60	1.00
101 Tamizander Rey U2	.60	1.00
102 Tauntaun Handler C2	.20	.30
103 Tigran Jamiro U1	.60	1.00
104 Toryn Farr U1	.60	1.00
105 WED-1016 'Techie' Droid C1	.20	.30
106 Wes Janson R2	2.00	3.00
107 Wyron Serper U2	.60	1.00
108 Zev Senesca R2	2.00	3.00
109 Artillery Remote R2	2.00	3.00
110 EG-4 (Eegee-Four) C1	.20	.30
111 Hoth LIGHT U2	.60	1.00
112 R-3PO (Ar-Threepio) DARK R2	2.00	3.00
112 R-3PO (Ar-Threepio) LIGHT R2	2.00	3.00
113 Bacta Tank R2	3.00	5.00
114 Disarming Creature R1	2.00	3.00
115 Echo Base Trooper C3	.20	.30
116 E-web Blaster C1	.20	.30
117 Frostbite DARK C2	.20	.30
118 Ice Storm DARK U1	.60	1.00
119 Tauntaun Bones U1	.60	1.00
120 The First Transport Is Away! R1	2.00	3.00
121 Attack Pattern Delta U1	.60	1.00
122 Dark Dissension R1	2.00	3.00
123 Fall Back! C2	.20	.30
124 I Thought They Smelled Bad On The Outside R1	2.00	3.00
125 It Can Wait C2	.20	.30
126 Lucky Shot U1	.60	1.00
127 Nice Of You Guys To Drop By C2	.20	.30
128 One More Pass U1	.60	1.00
129 Perimeter Scan C2	.20	.30
130 Rug Hug R1	2.00	3.00
131 Under Attack U1	.60	1.00
132 Walker Sighting U2	.60	1.00
133 Who's Scruffy-Looking? R1	2.00	3.00
134 You Have Failed Me For The Last Time R1	2.00	3.00
135 You Will Go To The Dagobah System R1	2.00	3.00
136 Hoth Survival Gear C2	.20	.30
137 Hoth: Defensive Perimeter DARK C2	.20	.30
138 Hoth: Echo Command Center (War Room) DARK U2	.60	1.00
139 Hoth: Echo Corridor LIGHT C2	.20	.30
140 Hoth: Echo Docking Bay DARK C2	.20	.30
141 Hoth: Echo Med Lab C2	.20	.30
142 Hoth: Main Power Generators U2	.60	1.00
143 Hoth: North Ridge DARK C2	.20	.30
144 Hoth: Snow Trench C2	.20	.30
145 Ord Mantell DARK C2	.20	.30
146 Medium Transport U2	.60	1.00
147 Rogue 1 R1	4.00	6.00
148 Rogue 2 R2	2.00	3.00
149 Rogue 3 R1	4.00	6.00
150 Snowspeeder U2	.60	1.00
151 Tauntaun C2	.20	.30
152 Anakin's Lightsaber R1	10.00	15.00
153 Atgar Laser Cannon U2	.60	1.00
154 Concussion Grenade R1	2.00	3.00
155 Dual Laser Cannon U1	.60	1.00
156 Golan Laser Battery U1	.60	1.00
157 Infantry Mine DARK C2	.20	.30
158 Medium Repeating Blaster Cannon C1	.20	.30
159 Planet Defender Ion Cannon R2	2.00	3.00
160 Power Harpoon U1	.60	1.00
161 Surface Defense Cannon R2	2.00	3.00
162 Vehicle Mine DARK C2	.20	.30

1996 Star Wars Jedi Pack

COMPLETE SET (11)	3.00	8.00
RELEASED IN 1996		
1 Hyperoute Navigation Chart PM	.60	1.00
2 Dark Forces PM	.60	1.00
3 Eriadu PM	.60	1.00
4 For Luck PM	.60	1.00
5 Gravity Shadow PM	.60	1.00
6 Han PM	.60	1.00
7 Leia PM	.60	1.00
8 Luke's T-16 Skyhopper PM	.60	1.00
9 Motti PM	.60	1.00
10 Tarkin PM	.60	1.00
11 Tedn Dahai PM	.60	1.00

1996 Star Wars A New Hope

COMPLETE SET (162)	50.00	100.00
BOOSTER BOX (36 PACKS)	50.00	100.00
BOOSTER PACK (15 CARDS)	2.00	4.00
RELEASED IN JULY 1996		
1 Advosze C2	.20	.30
2 Captain Khurgee U1	.60	1.00
3 DS-61-4 R2	2.00	3.00
4 Dannik Jerriko R1	2.00	3.00
5 Danz Borin U2	.60	1.00
6 Death Star R2	6.00	10.00
7 Defel C2	.20	.30
8 Greedo R1	5.00	8.00
9 Hem Dazon R1	2.00	3.00
10 IT-O (Eyetee-Oh) R1	2.00	3.00
11 Imperial Commander C2	.20	.30
12 Imperial Squad Leader C3	.20	.30
13 Lirin Car'n U2	.60	1.00
14 Lt. Pol Treidum C1	.20	.30
15 Lt. Shann Childsen U1	.60	1.00
16 Mosep U2	.60	1.00
17 Officer Evax C1	.20	.30
18 R2-Q2 (Artoo-Kyootoo) C2	.20	.30
19 R3-T6 (Arthree-Teesix) R1	2.00	3.00
20 R5-A2 (Arfive-Aytoo) C2	.20	.30
21 Reegesk U2	.60	1.00
22 Reserve Pilot U1	.60	1.00
23 Rodian C2	.20	.30
24 Tech Mo'r U2	.60	1.00
25 Trooper Davin Felth R2	2.00	3.00
26 U-3PO (Yoo-Threepio) R1	2.00	3.00
27 URoRRuR'R'R U2	.60	1.00
28 WED15-I7 'Septoid' Droid U2	.60	1.00
29 Dianoga R2	2.00	3.00
30 Death Star Tractor Beam R2	2.00	3.00
31 Hypo R1	2.00	3.00
32 Laser Gate U2	.60	1.00
33 Maneuver Check R2	2.00	3.00
34 Tractor Beam U1	.60	1.00
35 Astromech Shortage U2	.60	1.00
36 Besieged R2	2.00	3.00
37 Come With Me C2	.20	.30
38 Dark Waters R2	2.00	3.00
39 Hyperwave Scan U1	.60	1.00
40 Imperial Justice C2	.20	.30
41 Krayt Dragon Bones U1	.60	1.00
42 Merc Sunlet C2	.20	.30
43 Program Trap U1	.60	1.00
44 Spice Mines Of Kessel R1	2.00	3.00
45 Swilla Corey C2	.20	.30
46 Tentacle C2	.20	.30
47 There'll Be Hell To Pay U2	.60	1.00
48 Undercover LIGHT U2	.60	1.00
49 Commence Primary Ignition R2	2.00	3.00
50 Evader U1	.60	1.00
51 Ghhhk C2	.20	.30
52 I'm On The Leader R1	2.00	3.00
53 Informant U1	.60	1.00
54 Monnok C2	.20	.30
55 Ng'ok C2	.20	.30
56 Oo-ta Goo-ta, Solo? C2	.20	.30
57 Retract the Bridge R1	2.00	3.00
58 Sniper U1	.60	1.00
59 Stunning Leader C2	.20	.30
60 This Is Some Rescue! U1	.60	1.00
61 We Have A Prisoner C2	.20	.30
62 Death Star Gunner C1	.20	.30
63 Death Star: Conference Room U1	.60	1.00
64 Imperial Holotable R1	2.00	3.00
65 Kashyyyk LIGHTC1	.20	.30
66 Kiffex R1	2.00	3.00
67 Ralltiir LIGHT C1	.20	.30
68 Sandcrawler: Droid Junkheap R1	2.00	3.00
69 Tatooine: Bluffs R1	2.00	3.00
70 Black 4 U2	.60	1.00
71 Conquest R1	6.00	10.00
72 TIE Assault Squadron U1	.60	1.00
73 TIE Vanguard C2	.20	.30
74 Victory-Class Star Destroyer U1	.60	1.00
75 Bespin Motors Void Spider THX 1138 C2	.20	.30
76 Mobquet A-1 Deluxe Floater C2	.20	.30
77 Enhanced TIE Laser Cannon C2	.20	.30
78 Jawa Blaster C2	.20	.30
79 Leia Seeker R2	2.00	3.00
80 Superlaser R2	3.00	5.00
81 URoRRuR'R'R's Hunting Rifle U1	.60	1.00
82 Arcona C2	.20	.30
83 Brainiac R1	4.00	6.00
84 Chewbacca R2	10.00	15.00
85 Commander Evram Lajaie C1	.20	.30
86 Commander Vanden Willard U2	.60	1.00
87 Corellian C2	.20	.30
88 Doikk Na'ts U2	.60	1.00
89 Garouf Lafoe U2	.60	1.00
90 Het Nkik U2	.60	1.00
91 Hunchback R1	2.00	3.00
92 Ickabel G'ont U2	.60	1.00
93 Magnetic Suction Tube DARK R2	2.00	3.00
94 Nalan Cheel U2	.60	1.00
95 R2-D2 (Artoo-Detoo) R2	10.00	15.00
96 R5-D4 (Arfive-Defour) C2	.20	.30
97 RA-7 (Aray-Seven) C2	.20	.30
98 Rebel Commander C2	.20	.30
99 Rebel Squad Leader C3	.20	.30
100 Rebel Tech C1	.20	.30
101 Saurin C2	.20	.30
102 Tiree U2	.60	1.00
103 Tzizvvt R2	2.00	3.00
104 Wedge Antilles R1	10.00	15.00
105 Zutton C1	.20	.30
106 Fire Extinguisher U2	.60	1.00
107 Magnetic Suction Tube LIGHT R2	2.00	3.00
108 Rectenna C2	.20	.30
109 Remote C2	.20	.30
110 Sensor Panel U1	.60	1.00
111 Cell 2187 R1	2.00	3.00
112 Commence Recharging R2	2.00	3.00
113 Eject! Eject! C2	.20	.30
114 Grappling Hook C2	.20	.30
115 Logistical Delay U2	.60	1.00
116 Luke's Cape R1	2.00	3.00
117 M-HYD 'Binary' Droid U1	.60	1.00
118 Scanner Techs U1	.60	1.00
119 Solomahal C2	.20	.30
120 They're On Dantooine R1	2.00	3.00
121 Undercover DARK U2	.60	1.00
122 What're You Tryin' To Push On Us? U2	.60	1.00
123 Attack Run R2	2.00	3.00
124 Advance Preparation U1	.60	1.00
125 Alternatives To Fighting U1	.60	1.00
126 Blast The Door, Kid! C2	.20	.30
127 Blue Milk C2	.20	.30
128 Corellian Slip C2	.20	.30
129 Double Agent R2	2.00	3.00
130 Grimtaash C2	.20	.30
131 Houjix C2	.20	.30
132 I Have A Very Bad Feeling About This C2	.20	.30
133 I'm Here To Rescue You U1	.60	1.00
134 Let The Wookiee Win R1	8.00	12.00
135 Out Of Commission U2	.60	1.00
136 Quite A Mercenary C2	.20	.30
137 Sabotage U1	.60	1.00
138 Sorry About The Mess U1	.60	1.00
139 Wookiee Roar R1	2.00	3.00
140 Y-wing Assault Squadron U1	.60	1.00
141 Clak'dor VII R2	2.00	3.00
142 Corellia R1	2.00	3.00
143 Death Star: Trench R2	2.00	3.00
144 Dejarik Hologameboard R1	2.00	3.00
145 Kashyyyk DARK C1	.20	.30
146 Ralltiir DARK C1	.20	.30
147 Sandcrawler: Loading Bay R1	2.00	3.00
148 Yavin 4: Massassi Ruins U1	.60	1.00
149 You're All Clear Kid! R1	2.00	3.00
150 Gold 2 U1	.60	1.00
151 Red 2 R1	2.00	3.00
152 Red 5 R1	5.00	8.00
153 Red 6 U1	.60	1.00
154 Tantive IV R1	6.00	10.00
155 Yavin 4: Briefing Room U1	.60	1.00
156 Incom T-16 Skyhopper C2	.20	.30
157 Rogue Bantha U1	.60	1.00
158 Bowcaster R2	2.00	3.00
159 Jawa Ion Gun C2	.20	.30
160 Luke's Hunting Rifle U1	.60	1.00
161 Motti Seeker R2	2.00	3.00
162 SW-4 Ion Cannon R2	2.00	3.00

1997 Star Wars Cloud City

COMPLETE SET (180)	50.00	100.00
BOOSTER BOX (60 PACKS)	50.00	100.00
BOOSTER PACK (9 CARDS)	2.00	4.00
RELEASED IN NOVEMBER 1997		
1 Ability, Ability, Ability C	.20	.30

2 Abyss U	.60	1.00
3 Access Denied C	.20	.30
4 Advantage R	2.00	3.00
5 Aiiii! Aaa! Agggggggggg! R	2.00	3.00
6 All My Urchins R	2.00	3.00
7 All Too Easy R	2.00	3.00
8 Ambush R	2.00	3.00
9 Armed And Dangerous U	.60	1.00
10 Artoo, Come Back At Once! R	2.00	3.00
11 As Good As Gone C	.20	.30
12 Atmospheric Assault R	2.00	3.00
13 Beldon's Eye R	2.00	3.00
14 Bespin DARK U	.60	1.00
15 Bespin LIGHT U	.60	1.00
16 Bespin: Cloud City DARK U	.60	1.00
17 Bespin: Cloud City LIGHT U	.60	1.00
18 Binders C	.20	.30
19 Bionic Hand R	2.00	3.00
20 Blasted Droid C	.20	.30
21 Blaster Proficiency C	.20	.30
22 Boba Fett R	12.00	20.00
23 Boba Fett's Blaster Rifle R	5.00	8.00
24 Bounty C	.20	.30
25 Brief Loss Of Control R	2.00	3.00
26 Bright Hope R	2.00	3.00
27 Captain Bewil R	2.00	3.00
28 Captain Han Solo R	12.00	20.00
29 Captive Fury U	.60	1.00
30 Captive Pursuit C	.20	.30
31 Carbon-Freezing U	.60	1.00
32 Carbonite Chamber Console U	.60	1.00
33 Chasm U	.60	1.00
34 Chief Retwin R	2.00	3.00
35 Civil Disorder C	.20	.30
36 Clash Of Sabers U	.60	1.00
37 Cloud Car DARK C	.20	.30
38 Cloud Car LIGHT C	.20	.30
39 Cloud City Blaster DARK C	.20	.30
40 Cloud City Blaster LIGHT C	.20	.30
41 Cloud City Engineer C	.20	.30
42 Cloud City Sabacc DARK U	.60	1.00
43 Cloud City Sabacc LIGHT U	.60	1.00
44 Cloud City Technician C	.20	.30
45 Cloud City Trooper DARK C	.20	.30
46 Cloud City Trooper LIGHT C	.20	.30
47 Cloud City: Carbonite Chamber DARK U	.60	1.00
48 Cloud City: Carbonite Chamber LIGHT U	.60	1.00
49 Cloud City: Chasm Walkway DARK C	.20	.30
50 Cloud City: Chasm Walkway LIGHT C	.20	.30
51 Cloud City: Dining Room R	2.00	3.00
52 Cloud City: East Platform (Docking Bay) C	.20	.30
53 Cloud City: Guest Quarters R	2.00	3.00
54 Cloud City: Incinerator DARK C	.20	.30
55 Cloud City: Incinerator LIGHT C	.20	.30
56 Cloud City: Lower Corridor DARK U	.60	1.00
57 Cloud City: Lower Corridor LIGHT U	.60	1.00
58 Cloud City: Platform 327 (Docking Bay) C	.20	.30
59 Cloud City: Security Tower C	.20	.30
60 Cloud City: Upper Plaza Corridor DARK C	.20	.30
61 Cloud City: Upper Plaza Corridor LIGHT U	.60	1.00
62 Clouds DARK C	.20	.30
63 Clouds LIGHT C	.20	.30
64 Commander Desanne U	.60	1.00
65 Computer Interface C	.20	.30
66 Courage Of A Skywalker R	2.00	3.00
67 Crack Shot U	.60	1.00
68 Cyborg Construct U	.60	1.00
69 Dark Approach R	2.00	3.00
70 Dark Deal R	2.00	3.00
71 Dark Strike C	.20	.30
72 Dash C	.20	.30
73 Despair R	2.00	3.00
74 Desperate Reach U	.60	1.00
75 Dismantle On Sight R	2.00	3.00
76 Dodge C	.20	.30
77 Double Back U	.60	1.00
78 Double-Crossing, No-Good Swindler C	.20	.30
79 E Chu Ta C	.20	.30
80 E-3PO R	2.00	3.00
81 End This Destructive Conflict R	2.00	3.00
82 Epic Duel R	3.00	5.00
83 Fall Of The Empire U	.60	1.00
84 Fall Of The Legend U	.60	1.00
85 Flight Escort R	2.00	3.00
86 Focused Attack R	2.00	3.00
87 Force Field R	2.00	3.00
88 Forced Landing R	2.00	3.00
89 Frozen Assets R	2.00	3.00
90 Gambler's Luck R	2.00	3.00
91 Glancing Blow R	2.00	3.00
92 Haven R	2.00	3.00
93 He's All Yours, Bounty Hunter R	2.00	3.00
94 Heart Of The Chasm U	.60	1.00
95 Hero Of A Thousand Devices U	.60	1.00
96 Higher Ground R	2.00	3.00
97 Hindsight R	2.00	3.00
98 Hopping Mad R	2.00	3.00
99 Human Shield C	.20	.30
100 I Am Your Father R	2.00	3.00
101 I Don't Need Their Scum, Either R	2.00	3.00
102 I Had No Choice R	2.00	3.00
103 Imperial Decree U	.60	1.00
104 Imperial Trooper Guard Dainsom U	.60	1.00
105 Impressive, Most Impressive R	2.00	3.00
106 Innocent Scoundrel U	.60	1.00
107 Interrogation Array R	2.00	3.00
108 Into The Ventilation Shaft, Lefty R	2.00	3.00
109 It's A Trap! U	.60	1.00
110 Kebyc U	.60	1.00
111 Keep Your Eyes Open C	.20	.30
112 Lando Calrissian DARK R	8.00	12.00
113 Lando Calrissian LIGHT R	8.00	12.00
114 Lando's Wrist Comlink U	.60	1.00
115 Leia Of Alderaan R	3.00	5.00
116 Levitation Attack U	.60	1.00
117 Lieutenant Cecius U	.60	1.00
118 Lieutenant Sheckil R	2.00	3.00
119 Lift Tube Escape C	.20	.30
120 Lobot R	4.00	6.00
121 Luke's Blaster Pistol R	2.00	3.00
122 Mandalorian Armor R	3.00	5.00
123 Mostly Armless R	2.00	3.00
124 NOOOOOOOOOOOO! R	2.00	3.00
125 Obsidian 7 R	3.00	5.00
126 Obsidian 8 R	3.00	5.00
127 Off The Edge R	2.00	3.00
128 Old Pirates R	2.00	3.00
129 Out Of Somewhere U	.60	1.00
130 Path Of Least Resistance C	.20	.30
131 Point Man R	2.00	3.00
132 Prepare The Chamber U	.60	1.00
133 Princess Leia R	6.00	10.00
134 Projective Telepathy U	.60	1.00
135 Protector R	2.00	3.00
136 Punch It! R	2.00	3.00
137 Put That Down C	.20	.30
138 Redemption R	4.00	6.00
139 Release Your Anger R	2.00	3.00
140 Rendezvous Point On Tatooine R	2.00	3.00
141 Rescue In The Clouds C	.20	.30
142 Restricted Access C	.20	.30
143 Rite Of Passage C	.20	.30
144 Shattered Hope U	.60	1.00
145 Shocking Information C	.20	.30
146 Shocking Revelation C	.20	.30
147 Slave I R	6.00	10.00
148 Slip Sliding Away R	2.00	3.00
149 Smoke Screen R	2.00	3.00
150 Somersault C	.20	.30
151 Sonic Bombardment U	.60	1.00
152 Special Delivery C	.20	.30
153 Surprise R	2.00	3.00
154 Surreptitious Glance R	2.00	3.00
155 Swing-And-A-Miss U	.60	1.00
156 The Emperor's Prize R	2.00	3.00
157 This Is Even Better R	2.00	3.00
158 This Is Still Wrong R	2.00	3.00
159 Tibanna Gas Miner DARK C	.20	.30
160 Tibanna Gas Miner LIGHT C	.20	.30
161 TIE Sentry Ships C	.20	.30
162 Treva Horme U	.60	1.00
163 Trooper Assault C	.20	.30
164 Trooper Jerrol Blendin U	.60	1.00
165 Trooper Utris M'toc U	.60	1.00
166 Ugloste R	2.00	3.00
167 Ugnaught C	.20	.30
168 Uncontrollable Fury R	2.00	3.00
169 Vader's Bounty R	2.00	3.00
170 Vader's Cape R	2.00	3.00
171 We'll Find Han R	2.00	3.00
172 We're The Bait R	2.00	3.00
173 Weapon Levitation U	.60	1.00
174 Weapon Of An Ungrateful Son U	.60	1.00
175 Weather Vane DARK U	.60	1.00
176 Weather Vane LIGHT U	.60	1.00
177 Why Didn't You Tell Me? R	2.00	3.00
178 Wiorkettle U	.60	1.00
179 Wookiee Strangle R	2.00	3.00
180 You Are Beaten U	.60	1.00

1997 Star Wars Dagobah

COMPLETE SET (181)	50.00	100.00
BOOSTER BOX (60 PACKS)	50.00	100.00
BOOSTER PACK (9 CARDS)	1.50	3.00
RELEASED ON APRIL 23, 1997		
1 3,720 To 1 C	.20	.30
2 4-LOM R	4.00	6.00
3 4-LOM's Concussion Rifle R	3.00	5.00
4 A Dangerous Time C	.20	.30
5 A Jedi's Strength U	.60	1.00
6 Anger, Fear, Aggression C	.20	.30
7 Anoat DARK U	.60	1.00
8 Anoat LIGHT U	.60	1.00
9 Apology Accepted C	.20	.30
10 Asteroid Field DARK C	.20	.30
11 Asteroid Field LIGHT C	.20	.30
12 Asteroid Sanctuary C	.20	.30
13 Asteroids Do Not Concern Me R	2.00	3.00
14 Astroid Sanctuary C	.20	.30
15 Astromech Translator C	.20	.30
16 At Peace R	2.00	3.00
17 Avenger R	6.00	10.00
18 Away Put Your Weapon U	.60	1.00
19 Awwww, Cannot Get Your Ship Out C	.20	.30
20 Bad Feeling Have I R	2.00	3.00
21 Big One DARK U	.60	1.00
22 Big One LIGHT U	.60	1.00
23 Big One: Asteroid Cave or Space Slug Belly DARK U	.60	1.00
24 Big One: Asteroid Cave or Space Slug Belly LIGHT U	.60	1.00
25 Blasted Varmints C	.20	.30
26 Bog-wing DARK C	.20	.30
27 Bog-wing LIGHT C	.20	.30
28 Bombing Run R	2.00	3.00
29 Bossk R	5.00	8.00
30 Bossk's Mortar Gun R	3.00	5.00
31 Broken Concentration R	2.00	3.00
32 Captain Needa R	3.00	5.00
33 Close Call C	.20	.30
34 Closer?! U	.60	1.00
35 Comm Chief C	.20	.30
36 Commander Brandei U	.60	1.00
37 Commander Gherant U	.60	1.00
38 Commander Nemet U	.60	1.00
39 Control DARK U	.60	1.00
40 Control LIGHT U	.60	1.00
41 Corporal Derdram U	.60	1.00
42 Corporal Vandolay U	.60	1.00
43 Corrosive Damage R	2.00	3.00
44 Dagobah U	.60	1.00
45 Dagobah: Bog Clearing R	2.00	3.00
46 Dagobah: Cave R	2.00	3.00
47 Dagobah: Jungle U	.60	1.00
48 Dagobah: Swamp U	.60	1.00
49 Dagobah: Training Area C	.20	.30
50 Dagobah: Yoda's Hut R	3.00	5.00
51 Defensive Fire C	.20	.30
52 Dengar R	2.00	3.00
53 Dengar's Blaster Carbine R	2.00	3.00
54 Descent Into The Dark R	2.00	3.00
55 Do, Or Do Not C	.20	.30
56 Domain Of Evil U	.60	1.00
57 Dragonsnake R	2.00	3.00
58 Droid Sensorscope C	.20	.30
59 Effective Repairs R	2.00	3.00
60 Egregious Pilot Error R	2.00	3.00
61 Encampment C	.20	.30
62 Executor R	12.00	20.00
63 Executor: Comm Station U	.60	1.00
64 Executor: Control Station U	.60	1.00
65 Executor: Holotheatre R	2.00	3.00
66 Executor: Main Corridor C	.20	.30
67 Executor: Meditation Chamber R	2.00	3.00
68 Failure At The Cave R	2.00	3.00
69 Fear C	.20	.30
70 Field Promotion R	2.00	3.00
71 Flagship R	2.00	3.00
72 Flash Of Insight U	.60	1.00
73 Found Someone You Have U	.60	1.00
74 Frustration R	2.00	3.00
75 Great Warrior C	.20	.30
76 Grounded Starfighter U	.60	1.00
77 Han's Toolkit R	2.00	3.00
78 He Is Not Ready C	.20	.30
79 Hiding In The Garbage R	2.00	3.00
80 HoloNet Transmission U	.60	1.00
81 Hound's Tooth R	4.00	6.00
82 I Have A Bad Feeling About This R	2.00	3.00
83 I Want That Ship R	2.00	3.00
84 IG-2000 R	3.00	5.00
85 IG-88 R	6.00	10.00
86 IG-88's Neural Inhibitor R	3.00	5.00
87 IG-88's Pulse Cannon R	3.00	5.00
88 Imbalance U	.60	1.00
89 Imperial Helmsman C	.20	.30
90 Ineffective Maneuver U	.60	1.00
91 It Is The Future You See R	2.00	3.00
92 Jedi Levitation R	2.00	3.00
93 Knowledge And Defense C	.20	.30
94 Landing Claw R	2.00	3.00
95 Lando System? R	2.00	3.00
96 Levitation U	.60	1.00
97 Lieutenant Commander Ardan U	.60	1.00
98 Lieutenant Suba R	2.00	3.00
99 Lieutenant Venka U	.60	1.00
100 Light Maneuvers R	2.00	3.00
101 Location, Location, Location R	2.00	3.00
102 Lost In Space R	2.00	3.00
103 Lost Relay C	.20	.30
104 Luke's Backpack R	2.00	3.00
105 Mist Hunter R	3.00	5.00
106 Moving To Attack Position C	.20	.30
107 Much Anger In Him R	2.00	3.00
108 Mynock DARK C	.20	.30
109 Mynock LIGHT C	.20	.30
110 Never Tell Me The Odds C	.20	.30
111 No Disintegrations! R	2.00	3.00
112 Nudj C	.20	.30
113 Obi-Wan's Apparition R	2.00	3.00
114 Order To Engage R	2.00	3.00
115 Polarized Negative Power Coupling R	2.00	3.00
116 Portable Fusion Generator C	.20	.30
117 Precision Targeting U	.60	1.00
118 Proton Bombs U	.60	1.00
119 Punishing One R	3.00	5.00
120 Quick Draw C	.20	.30
121 Raithal DARK R	2.00	3.00
122 Raithal LIGHT U	.60	1.00
123 Rebel Flight Suit C	.20	.30
124 Recoil In Fear C	.20	.30
125 Reflection R	2.00	3.00
126 Report To Lord Vader R	2.00	3.00
127 Res Luk Ra'auf R	2.00	3.00
128 Retractable Arm C	.20	.30
129 Rogue Asteroid DARK C	.20	.30
130 Rogue Asteroid LIGHT C	.20	.30
131 Rycar's Run R	2.00	3.00
132 Scramble U	.60	1.00
133 Shoo! Shoo! U	.60	1.00
134 Shot In The Dark U	.60	1.00
135 Shut Him Up Or Shut Him Down U	.60	1.00
136 Size Matters Not R	2.00	3.00
137 Sleen C	.20	.30
138 Smuggler's Blues R	2.00	3.00
139 Something Hit Us! U	.60	1.00
140 Son of Skywalker R	12.00	20.00
141 Space Slug DARK R	2.00	3.00
142 Space Slug LIGHT U	.60	1.00
143 Star Destroyer: Launch Bay C	.20	.30
144 Starship Levitation U	.60	1.00
145 Stone Pile R	2.00	3.00
146 Sudden Impact U	.60	1.00
147 Take Evasive Action C	.20	.30
148 The Dark Path R	2.00	3.00
149 The Professor R	2.00	3.00
150 There Is No Try C	.20	.30
151 They'd Be Crazy To Follow Us C	.20	.30
152 This Is More Like It R	2.00	3.00
153 This Is No Cave R	2.00	3.00
154 Those Rebels Won't Escape Us C	.20	.30
155 Through The Force Things You Will See R	2.00	3.00
156 TIE Avenger C	.20	.30
157 TIE Bomber U	.60	1.00
158 Tight Squeeze R	2.00	3.00
159 Transmission Terminated U	.60	1.00
160 Tunnel Vision U	.60	1.00
161 Uncertain Is The Future C	.20	.30
162 Unexpected Interruption R	2.00	3.00
163 Vine Snake DARK C	.20	.30
164 Vine Snake LIGHT C	.20	.30
165 Visage Of The Emperor R	2.00	3.00
166 Visored Vision C	.20	.30
167 Voyeur C	.20	.30
168 Warrant Officer M'Kae U	.60	1.00
169 Wars Not Make One Great U	.60	1.00
170 We Can Still Outmaneuver Them R	2.00	3.00
171 We Don't Need Their Scum R	2.00	3.00

172 WHAAAAAAAAAOOOOW! R	2.00	3.00
173 What Is Thy Bidding, My Master? R	2.00	3.00
174 Yoda R	12.00	20.00
175 Yoda Stew U	.60	1.00
176 Yoda, You Seek Yoda R	2.00	3.00
177 Yoda's Gimer Stick R	2.00	3.00
178 Yoda's Hope U	.60	1.00
179 You Do Have Your Moments U	.60	1.00
180 Zuckuss R	3.00	5.00
181 Zuckuss' Snare Rifle R	2.00	3.00

1997 Star Wars First Anthology

COMPLETE SET (6)	3.00	8.00
RELEASED IN 1997		
1 Boba Fett PV	1.25	2.00
2 Commander Wedge Antilles PV	1.25	2.00
3 Death Star Assault Squadron PV	1.25	2.00
4 Hit And Run PV	1.25	2.00
5 Jabba's Influence PV	1.25	2.00
6 X-wing Assault Squadron PV	1.25	2.00

1997 Star Wars Rebel Leaders

COMPLETE SET (2)	1.25	3.00
RELEASED IN 1997		
1 Gold Leader In Gold 1 PM	1.50	2.50
2 Red Leader In Red 1 PM	1.50	2.50

1998 Star Wars Enhanced Premiere

COMPLETE SET (6)	3.00	8.00
RELEASED IN 1998		
1 Boba Fett With Blaster Rifle PM	1.25	2.00
2 Darth Vader With Lightsaber PM	1.25	2.00
3 Han With Heavy Blaster Pistol PM	1.25	2.00
4 Leia With Blaster Rifle PM	1.25	2.00
5 Luke With Lightsaber PM	1.25	2.00
6 Obi-Wan With Lightsaber PM	1.25	2.00

1998 Star Wars Jabba's Palace

COMPLETE SET (180)	40.00	80.00
BOOSTER BOX (60 PACKS)	40.00	80.00
BOOSTER PACK (9 CARDS)	1.00	2.00
RELEASED IN MAY 1998		
1 8D8 R	2.00	3.00
2 A Gift U	.60	1.00
3 Abyssin C	.20	.30
4 Abyssin Ornament U	.60	1.00
5 All Wrapped Up U	.60	1.00
6 Amanaman R	2.00	3.00
7 Amanin C	.20	.30
8 Antipersonnel Laser Cannon U	.60	1.00
9 Aqualish C	.20	.30
10 Arc Welder U	.60	1.00
11 Ardon Vapor Crell R	2.00	3.00
12 Artoo R	5.00	8.00
13 Artoo, I Have A Bad Feeling About This U	.60	1.00
14 Attark R	2.00	3.00
15 Aved Luun R	2.00	3.00
16 B'omarr Monk C	.20	.30
17 Bane Malar R	2.00	3.00
18 Bantha Fodder C	.20	.30
19 Barada R	2.00	3.00
20 Baragwin C	.20	.30
21 Bargaining Table U	.60	1.00
22 Beedo R	2.00	3.00
23 BG-J38 R	2.00	3.00
24 Bib Fortuna R	2.00	3.00
25 Blaster Deflection R	2.00	3.00
26 Bo Shuda U	.60	1.00
27 Bubo U	.60	1.00
28 Cane Adiss U	.60	1.00
29 Chadra-Fan C	.20	.30
30 Chevin C	.20	.30
31 Choke C	.20	.30
32 Corellian Retort U	.60	1.00
33 CZ-4 C	.20	.30
34 Den Of Thieves U	.60	1.00
35 Dengar's Modified Riot Gun R	2.00	3.00
36 Devaronian C	.20	.30
37 Don't Forget The Droids C	.20	.30
38 Double Laser Cannon R	2.00	3.00
39 Droopy McCool R	2.00	3.00
40 Dune Sea Sabacc DARK U	.60	1.00
41 Dune Sea Sabacc LIGHT U	.60	1.00
42 Elom C	.20	.30
43 Ephant Mon R	2.00	3.00
44 EV-9D9 R	2.00	3.00
45 Fallen Portal U	.60	1.00
46 Florn Lamproid C	.20	.30
47 Fozec R	2.00	3.00
48 Gailid R	2.00	3.00
49 Gamorrean Ax C	.20	.30
50 Gamorrean Guard C	.20	.30
51 Garon Nas Tal R	2.00	3.00
52 Geezum R	2.00	3.00
53 Ghoel R	2.00	3.00
54 Giran R	2.00	3.00
55 Gran C	.20	.30
56 H'nemthe C	.20	.30
57 Herat R	2.00	3.00
58 Hermi Odle R	2.00	3.00
59 Hidden Compartment U	.60	1.00
60 Hidden Weapons U	.60	1.00
61 Holoprojector U	.60	1.00
62 Hutt Bounty R	2.00	3.00
63 Hutt Smooch U	.60	1.00
64 I Must Be Allowed To Speak R	2.00	3.00
65 Information Exchange U	.60	1.00
66 Ishi Tib C	.20	.30
67 Ithorian C	.20	.30
68 J'Quille R	2.00	3.00
69 Jabba the Hutt R	6.00	10.00
70 Jabba's Palace Sabacc DARK U	.60	1.00
71 Jabba's Palace Sabacc LIGHT U	.60	1.00
72 Jabba's Palace: Audience Chamber DARK U	.60	1.00
73 Jabba's Palace: Audience Chamber LIGHT U	.60	1.00
74 Jabba's Palace: Droid Workshop U	.60	1.00
75 Jabba's Palace: Dungeon U	.60	1.00
76 Jabba's Palace: Entrance Cavern DARK U	.60	1.00
77 Jabba's Palace: Entrance Cavern LIGHT U	.60	1.00
78 Jabba's Palace: Rancor Pit U	.60	1.00
79 Jabba's Sail Barge R	4.00	6.00
80 Jabba's Sail Barge: Passenger Deck R	2.00	3.00
81 Jedi Mind Trick R	2.00	3.00
82 Jess R	2.00	3.00
83 Jet Pack U	.60	1.00
84 Kalit R	2.00	3.00
85 Ke Chu Ke Kakuta? C	.20	.30
86 Kiffex R	2.00	3.00
87 Kirdo III R	2.00	3.00
88 Kithaba R	2.00	3.00
89 Kitonak C	.20	.30
90 Klaatu R	2.00	3.00
91 Klatooinian Revolutionary C	.20	.30
92 Laudica R	2.00	3.00
93 Leslomy Tacema R	2.00	3.00
94 Life Debt R	2.00	3.00
95 Loje Nella R	2.00	3.00
96 Malakili R	2.00	3.00
97 Mandalorian Mishap U	.60	1.00
98 Max Rebo R	2.00	3.00
99 Mos Eisley Blaster DARK C	.20	.30
100 Mos Eisley Blaster LIGHT C	.20	.30
101 Murttoc Yine R	2.00	3.00
102 Nal Hutta R	2.00	3.00
103 Nar Shaddaa Wind Chimes U	.60	1.00
104 Nikto C	.20	.30
105 Nizuc Bek R	2.00	3.00
106 None Shall Pass C	.20	.30
107 Nysad R	2.00	3.00
108 Oola R	2.00	3.00
109 Ortolan C	.20	.30
110 Ortugg R	2.00	3.00
111 Palejo Reshad R	2.00	3.00
112 Pote Snitkin R	2.00	3.00
113 Princess Leia Organa R	5.00	8.00
114 Projection Of A Skywalker U	.60	1.00
115 Pucumir Thryss R	2.00	3.00
116 Quarren C	.20	.30
117 Quick Reflexes C	.20	.30
118 R'kik D'nec, Hero Of The Dune Sea R	2.00	3.00
119 Rancor R	4.00	6.00
120 Rayc Ryjerd R	2.00	3.00
121 Ree-Yees R	2.00	3.00
122 Rennek R	2.00	3.00
123 Resistance U	.60	1.00
124 Revealed U	.60	1.00
125 Saelt-Marae R	2.00	3.00
126 Salacious Crumb R	2.00	3.00
127 Sandwhirl DARK U	.60	1.00
128 Sandwhirl LIGHT U	.60	1.00
129 Scum And Villainy R	2.00	3.00
130 Sergeant Doallyn R	2.00	3.00
131 Shasa Tiel R	2.00	3.00
132 Sic-Six C	.20	.30
133 Skiff DARK C	.20	.30
134 Skiff LIGHT C	.20	.30
135 Skrilling C	.20	.30
136 Skull U	.60	1.00
137 Snivvian C	.20	.30
138 Someone Who Loves You U	.60	1.00
139 Strangle R	2.00	3.00
140 Tamtel Skreej R	4.00	6.00
141 Tanus Spijek R	2.00	3.00
142 Tatooine: Desert DARK C	.20	.30
143 Tatooine: Desert LIGHT C	.20	.30
144 Tatooine: Great Pit Of Carkoon U	.60	1.00
145 Tatooine: Hutt Canyon U	.60	1.00
146 Tatooine: Jabba's Palace U	.60	1.00
147 Taym Dren-garen R	2.00	3.00
148 Tessek R	2.00	3.00
149 The Signal C	.20	.30
150 Thermal Detonator R	3.00	5.00
151 Thul Fain R	2.00	3.00
152 Tibrin R	2.00	3.00
153 Torture C	.20	.30
154 Trandoshan C	.20	.30
155 Trap Door U	.60	1.00
156 Twi'lek Advisor C	.20	.30
157 Ultimatum U	.60	1.00
158 Unfriendly Fire R	2.00	3.00
159 Vedain R	2.00	3.00
160 Velken Tezeri R	2.00	3.00
161 Vibro-Ax DARK C	.20	.30
162 Vibro-Ax LIGHT C	.20	.30
163 Vizam R	2.00	3.00
164 Vul Tazaene R	2.00	3.00
165 Weapon Levitation U	.60	1.00
166 Weequay Guard C	.20	.30
167 Weequay Hunter C	.20	.30
168 Weequay Marksman U	.60	1.00
169 Weequay Skiff Master C	.20	.30
170 Well Guarded U	.60	1.00
171 Whiphid C	.20	.30
172 Wittin R	2.00	3.00
173 Wooof R	2.00	3.00
174 Worrt U	.60	1.00
175 Wounded Wookiee U	.60	1.00
176 Yarkora C	.20	.30
177 Yarna d'al' Gargan U	.60	1.00
178 You Will Take Me To Jabba Now C	.20	.30
179 Yoxgit R	2.00	3.00
180 Yuzzum C	.20	.30

1998 Star Wars Official Tournament Sealed Deck

COMPLETE SET (18)	4.00	10.00
RELEASED IN 1998		
1 Arleil Schous PM	.60	1.00
2 Black Squadron TIE PM	.60	1.00
3 Chall Bekan PM	.60	1.00
4 Corulag DARK PM	.60	1.00
5 Corulag LIGHT PM	.60	1.00
6 Dreadnaught-Class Heavy Cruiser PM	.60	1.00
7 Faithful Service PM	.60	1.00
8 Forced Servitude PM	.60	1.00
9 Gold Squadron Y-wing PM	.60	1.00
10 It's a Hit! PM	.60	1.00
11 Obsidian Squadron TIE PM	.60	1.00
12 Rebel Trooper Recruit PM	.60	1.00
13 Red Squadron X-wing PM	.60	1.00
14 Stormtrooper Cadet PM	.60	1.00
15 Tarkin's Orders PM	.60	1.00
16 Tatooine: Jundland Wastes PM	.60	1.00
17 Tatooine: Tusken Canyon PM	.60	1.00
18 Z-95 Headhunter PM	.60	1.00

1998 Star Wars Second Anthology

COMPLETE SET (6)	4.00	10.00
RELEASED IN 1998		
1 Flagship Operations PV	1.50	2.50
2 Mon Calamari Star Cruiser PV	1.50	2.50
3 Mon Mothma PV	1.50	2.50
4 Rapid Deployment PV	1.50	2.50
5 Sarlacc PV	1.50	2.50
6 Thunderflare PV	1.50	2.50

1998 Star Wars Special Edition

COMPLETE SET (324)	75.00	150.00
BOOSTER BOX (30 PACKS)	60.00	120.00
BOOSTER PACK (9 CARDS)	3.00	6.00
RELEASED IN NOVEMBER 1998		
1 ISB Operations / Empire's Sinister Agents R	1.50	2.50
2 2X-7KPR (Tooex) C	.20	.30
3 A Bright Center To The Universe U	.60	1.00
4 A Day Long Remembered U	.60	1.00
5 A Real Hero R	1.50	2.50
6 Air-2 Racing Swoop C	.20	.30
7 Ak-rev U	.60	1.00
8 Alderaan Operative C	.20	.30
9 Alert My Star Destroyer! C	.20	.30
10 All Power To Weapons C	.20	.30
11 All Wings Report In R	1.50	2.50
12 Anoat Operative DARK C	.20	.30
13 Anoat Operative LIGHT C	.20	.30
14 Antilles Maneuver C	.20	.30
15 ASP-707 (Ayesspee) F	1.00	1.50
16 Balanced Attack U	.60	1.00
17 Bantha Herd R	1.25	2.00
18 Barquin D'an U	.60	1.00
19 Ben Kenobi R	3.00	5.00
20 Blast Points C	.20	.30
21 Blown Clear U	.60	1.00
22 Boba Fett R	2.50	4.00
23 Boelo R	1.50	2.50
24 Bossk In Hound's Tooth R	1.50	2.50
25 Bothan Spy C	.20	.30
26 Bothawui F	1.00	1.50
27 Bothawui Operative C	.20	.30
28 Brangus Glee R	1.25	2.00
29 Bren Quersey U	.60	1.00
30 Bron Burs R	1.25	2.00
31 B-wing Attack Fighter F	1.00	1.50
32 Camie R	1.50	2.50
33 Carbon Chamber Testing My Favorite Decoration R	1.50	2.50
34 Chyler U	.60	1.00
35 Clak'dor VII Operative U	.60	1.00
36 Cloud City Celebration R	1.50	2.50
37 Cloud City Occupation R	2.00	3.00
38 Cloud City: Casino DARK U	.60	1.00
39 Cloud City: Casino LIGHT U	.60	1.00
40 Cloud City: Core Tunnel U	.60	1.00
41 Cloud City: Downtown Plaza DARK R	1.50	2.50
42 Cloud City: Downtown Plaza LIGHT R	1.50	2.50
43 Cloud City: Interrogation Room C	.20	.30
44 Cloud City: North Corridor C	.20	.30
45 Cloud City: Port Town District U	.60	1.00
46 Cloud City: Upper Walkway C	.20	.30
47 Cloud City: West Gallery DARK C	.20	.30
48 Cloud City: West Gallery LIGHT C	.20	.30
49 Colonel Feyn Gospic R	1.50	2.50
50 Combat Cloud Car F	1.00	1.50
51 Come Here You Big Coward! C	.20	.30
52 Commander Wedge Antilles R	1.50	2.50
53 Coordinated Attack C	.20	.30
54 Corellia Operative U	.60	1.00
55 Corellian Engineering Corporation R	1.50	2.50
56 Corporal Grenwick R	1.25	2.00
57 Corporal Prescott U	.60	1.00
58 Corulag Operative C	.20	.30
59 Coruscant Celebration R	1.25	2.00
60 Coruscant DARK R	4.00	6.00
61 Coruscant LIGHT R	1.50	2.50
62 Coruscant: Docking Bay C	.20	.30
63 Coruscant: Imperial City U	.60	1.00
64 Coruscant: Imperial Square R	2.00	3.00
65 Counter Surprise Assault R	1.50	2.50
66 Dagobah U	.60	1.00
67 Dantooine Base Operations More Dangerous Than You Realize R	1.25	2.00
68 Dantooine Operative C	.20	.30
69 Darklighter Spin C	.20	.30
70 Darth Vader, Dark Lord Of The Sith R	10.00	15.00
71 Death Squadron Star Destroyer R	1.50	2.50
72 Death Star Assault Squadron R	1.50	2.50
73 Death Star R	2.00	3.00
74 Death Star: Detention Block Control Room C	.20	.30
75 Death Star: Detention Block Corridor C	.20	.30
76 Debnoli R	1.50	2.50
77 Desert DARK F	1.00	1.50
78 Desert LIGHT F	1.00	1.50
79 Desilijic Tattoo U	.60	1.00
80 Desperate Tactics C	.20	.30
81 Destroyed Homestead R	1.50	2.50
82 Dewback C	.20	.30
83 Direct Assault C	.20	.30
84 Disruptor Pistol DARK F	1.00	1.50
85 Disruptor Pistol LIGHT F	1.00	1.50
86 Docking And Repair Facilities R	1.50	2.50
87 Dodo Bodonawieedo U	.60	1.00
88 Don't Tread On Me R	1.50	2.50
89 Down With The Emperor! U	.60	1.00
90 Dr. Evazan's Sawed-off Blaster U	.60	1.00
91 Draw Their Fire U	.60	1.00
92 Dreaded Imperial Starfleet R	2.00	3.00
93 Droid Merchant C	.20	.30

94 Dune Walker R	2.00	3.00
95 Echo Base Trooper Rifle C	.20	.30
96 Elyhek Rue U	.60	1.00
97 Entrenchment R	1.25	2.00
98 Eriadu Operative C	.20	.30
99 Executor: Docking Bay U	.60	1.00
100 Farm F	1.00	1.50
101 Feltipern Trevagg's Stun Rifle U	.60	1.00
102 Firepower C	.20	.30
103 Firin Morett U	.60	1.00
104 First Aid F	1.00	1.50
105 First Strike U	.60	1.00
106 Flare-S Racing Swoop C	.20	.30
107 Flawless Marksmanship C	.20	.30
108 Floating Refinery C	.20	.30
109 Fondor U	.60	1.00
110 Forest DARK F	1.00	1.50
111 Forest LIGHT F	1.00	1.50
112 Gela Yeens U	.60	1.00
113 General McQuarrie R	1.25	2.00
114 Gold 3 U	.60	1.00
115 Gold 4 U	.60	1.00
116 Gold 6 U	.60	1.00
117 Goo Nee Tay R	1.50	2.50
118 Greeata U	.60	1.00
119 Grondorn Muse R	1.25	2.00
120 Harc Seff U	.60	1.00
121 Harvest R	2.00	3.00
122 Heavy Fire Zone C	.20	.30
123 Heroes Of Yavin R	1.25	2.00
124 Heroic Sacrifice U	.60	1.00
125 Hidden Base Systems Will Slip Through Your Fingers R	2.50	4.00
126 Hit And Run R	1.25	2.00
127 Hol Okand U	.60	1.00
128 Homing Beacon R	1.50	2.50
129 Hoth Sentry U	.60	1.00
130 Hunt Down And Destroy The Jedi Their Fire Has Gone Out Of The Universe R	2.50	4.00
131 Hunting Party R	1.50	2.50
132 I Can't Shake Him! C	.20	.30
133 Iasa, The Traitor Of Jawa Canyon R	1.25	2.00
134 IM4-099 F	1.00	1.50
135 Imperial Atrocity R	5.00	8.00
136 Imperial Occupation / Imperial Control R	1.50	2.50
137 Imperial Propaganda R	5.00	8.00
138 In Range C	.20	.30
139 Incom Corporation R	1.25	2.00
140 InCom Engineer C	.20	.30
141 Intruder Missile DARK F	1.00	1.50
142 Intruder Missile LIGHT F	1.00	1.50
143 It's Not My Fault! F	1.00	1.50
144 Jabba R	1.50	2.50
145 Jabba's Influence R	1.25	2.00
146 Jabba's Space Cruiser R	2.00	3.00
147 Jabba's Through With You U	.60	1.00
148 Jabba's Twerps U	.60	1.00
149 Joh Yowza R	1.25	2.00
150 Jungle DARK F	1.00	1.50
151 Jungle LIGHT F	1.00	1.50
152 Kalit's Sandcrawler R	1.50	2.50
153 Kashyyyk Operative DARK U	.60	1.00
154 Kashyyyk Operative LIGHT U	.60	1.00
155 Kessel Operative U	.60	1.00
156 Ketwol R	1.25	2.00
157 Kiffex Operative DARK U	.60	1.00
158 Kiffex Operative LIGHT U	.60	1.00
159 Kirdo III Operative C	.20	.30
160 Koensayr Manufacturing R	1.50	2.50
161 Krayt Dragon R	1.50	2.50
162 Kuat Drive Yards R	2.00	3.00
163 Kuat U	.60	1.00
164 Lando's Blaster Rifle R	1.50	2.50
165 Legendary Starfighter C	.20	.30
166 Leia's Blaster Rifle R	1.50	2.50
167 Lieutenant Lepira U	.60	1.00
168 Lieutenant Naytaan U	.60	1.00
169 Lieutenant Tarn Mison R	1.50	2.50
170 Lobel C	.20	.30
171 Lobot R	1.50	2.50
172 Local Defense U	.60	1.00
173 Local Uprising / Liberation R	1.50	2.50
174 Lyn Me U	.60	1.00
175 Major Palo Torshan R	1.50	2.50
176 Makurth F	1.00	1.50
177 Maneuvering Flaps C	.20	.30
178 Masterful Move C	.20	.30
179 Mechanical Failure R	1.25	2.00
180 Meditation R	2.00	3.00
181 Medium Bulk Freighter U	.60	1.00
182 Melas R	1.50	2.50
183 Mind What You Have Learned Save You It Can R	2.00	3.00
184 Moisture Farmer C	.20	.30
185 Nal Hutta Operative C	.20	.30
186 Neb Dulo U	.60	1.00
187 Nebit R	1.50	2.50
188 Niado Duegad U	.60	1.00
189 Nick Of Time U	.60	1.00
190 No Bargain U	.60	1.00
191 Old Times R	1.25	2.00
192 On Target C	.20	.30
193 One-Arm R	1.50	2.50
194 Oppressive Enforcement U	.60	1.00
195 Ord Mantell Operative C	.20	.30
196 Organized Attack C	.20	.30
197 OS-72-1 In Obsidian 1 R	1.50	2.50
198 OS-72-10 R	1.50	2.50
199 OS-72-2 In Obsidian 2 R	1.50	2.50
200 Outer Rim Scout R	2.50	4.00
201 Overwhelmed C	.20	.30
202 Patrol Craft DARK C	.20	.30
203 Patrol Craft LIGHT C	.20	.30
204 Planetary Subjugation U	.60	1.00
205 Ponda Baba's Hold-out Blaster U	.60	1.00
206 Portable Scanner C	.20	.30
207 Power Pivot C	.20	.30
208 Precise Hit C	.20	.30
209 Pride Of The Empire C	.20	.30
210 Princess Organa R	2.00	3.00
211 Put All Sections On Alert C	.20	.30
212 R2-A5 (Artoo-Ayfive) U	.60	1.00
213 R3-A2 (Arthree-Aytoo) U	.60	1.00
214 R3-T2 (Arthree-Teetoo) R	1.50	2.50
215 Raithal Operative C	.20	.30
216 Ralltiir Freighter Captain F	1.00	1.50
217 Ralltiir Operations In The Hands Of The Empire R	2.50	4.00
218 Ralltiir Operative C	.20	.30
219 Rapid Fire C	.20	.30
220 Rappertunie U	.60	1.00
221 Rebel Ambush C	.20	.30
222 Rebel Base Occupation R	1.25	2.00
223 Rebel Fleet R	1.50	2.50
224 Red 10 U	.60	1.00
225 Red 7 U	.60	1.00
226 Red 8 U	.60	1.00
227 Red 9 U	.60	1.00
228 Relentless Pursuit C	.20	.30
229 Rendezvous Point R	1.50	2.50
230 Rendili F	1.00	1.50
231 Rendili StarDrive R	1.25	2.00
232 Rescue The Princess Sometimes I Amaze Even Myself R	1.50	2.50
233 Return To Base R	1.50	2.50
234 Roche U	.60	1.00
235 Rock Wart F	1.00	1.50
236 Rogue 4 R	2.50	4.00
237 Ronto DARK C	.20	.30
238 Ronto LIGHT C	.20	.30
239 RR'uruurrr R	1.50	2.50
240 Ryle Torsyn U	.60	1.00
241 Rystall R	2.50	4.00
242 Sacrifice F	1.00	1.50
243 Sandspeeder F	1.00	1.50
244 Sandtrooper F	1.00	1.50
245 Sarlacc R	1.50	2.50
246 Scrambled Transmission U	.60	1.00
247 Scurrier F	1.00	1.50
248 Secret Plans U	.60	1.00
249 Sentinel-Class Landing Craft F	1.00	1.50
250 Sergeant Edian U	.60	1.00
251 Sergeant Hollis R	1.50	2.50
252 Sergeant Major Bursk U	.60	1.00
253 Sergeant Major Enfield R	1.25	2.00
254 Sergeant Merril U	.60	1.00
255 Sergeant Narthax R	1.50	2.50
256 Sergeant Torent R	1.50	2.50
257 S-Foils C	.20	.30
258 SFS L-s9.3 Laser Cannons C	.20	.30
259 Short-Range Fighters R	1.50	2.50
260 Sienar Fleet Systems R	1.50	2.50
261 Slayn and Korpil Facilities R	1.25	2.00
262 Slight Weapons Malfunction C	.20	.30
263 Soth Petikkin R	1.25	2.00
264 Spaceport City DARK F	1.00	1.50
265 Spaceport City LIGHT F	1.00	1.50
266 Spaceport Docking Bay DARK F	1.00	1.50
267 Spaceport Docking Bay LIGHT F	1.00	1.50
268 Spaceport Prefect's Office F	1.00	1.50
269 Spaceport Street DARK F	1.00	1.50
270 Spaceport Street LIGHT F	1.00	1.50
271 Spiral R	2.00	3.00
272 Star Destroyer! R	1.50	2.50
273 Stay Sharp! U	.60	1.00
274 Steady Aim C	.20	.30
275 Strategic Reserves R	1.50	2.50
276 Suppressive Fire C	.20	.30
277 Surface Defense R	1.50	2.50
278 Swamp DARK F	1.00	1.50
279 Swamp LIGHT F	1.00	1.50
280 Swoop Mercenary F	1.00	1.50
281 Sy Snootles R	1.50	2.50
282 T-47 Battle Formation R	1.50	2.50
283 Tarkin's Bounty U	.60	1.00
284 Tatooine Celebration R	2.00	3.00
285 Tatooine Occupation R	2.50	4.00
286 Tatooine: Anchorhead F	1.00	1.50
287 Tatooine: Beggar's Canyon R	1.25	2.00
288 Tatooine: Jabba's Palace C	.20	.30
289 Tatooine: Jawa Canyon DARK U	.60	1.00
290 Tatooine: Jawa Canyon LIGHT U	.60	1.00
291 Tatooine: Krayt Dragon Pass F	1.00	1.50
292 Tatooine: Tosche Station C	.20	.30
293 Tauntaun Skull C	.20	.30
294 Tawss Khaa R	1.25	2.00
295 The Planet That It's Farthest From U	.60	1.00
296 Thedit R	1.50	2.50
297 Theron Nett U	.60	1.00
298 They're Coming In Too Fast! C	.20	.30
299 They're Tracking Us C	.20	.30
300 They've Shut Down The Main Reactor C	.20	.30
301 Tibrin Operative C	.20	.30
302 TIE Defender Mark I F	1.00	1.50
303 TK-422 R	1.50	2.50
304 Trooper Sabacc DARK F	1.00	1.50
305 Trooper Sabacc LIGHT F	1.00	1.50
306 Uh-oh! U	.60	1.00
307 Umpass-stay R	1.25	2.00
308 Ur'Ru'r R	1.50	2.50
309 URoRRuR'R'R's Bantha R	1.50	2.50
310 Uutkik R	1.50	2.50
311 Vader's Personal Shuttle R	1.50	2.50
312 Vengeance R	1.50	2.50
313 Wakeelmui U	.60	1.00
314 Watch Your Back! C	.20	.30
315 Weapons Display C	.20	.30
316 Wise Advice U	.60	1.00
317 Wittin's Sandcrawler R	1.50	2.50
318 Womp Rat C	.20	.30
319 Wookiee F	1.00	1.50
320 Wrist Comlink C	.20	.30
321 X-wing Assault Squadron R	1.50	2.50
322 X-wing Laser Cannon C	.20	.30
323 Yavin 4 Trooper F	1.00	1.50
324 Yavin 4: Massassi Headquarters R	1.50	2.50

1999 Star Wars Endor

COMPLETE SET (180)	75.00	150.00
BOOSTER BOX (30 PACKS)	75.00	150.00
BOOSTER PACK (9 CARDS)	3.50	7.00
RELEASED IN JUNE 1999		
1 AT-ST Pilot C	.20	.30
2 Biker Scout Trooper C	.20	.30
3 Colonel Dyer R	2.00	3.00
4 Commander Igar R	2.00	3.00
5 Corporal Avarik U	.60	1.00
6 Corporal Drazin U	.60	1.00
7 Corporal Drelosyn R	2.00	3.00
8 Corporal Misik R	1.50	2.50
9 Corporal Oberk R	2.00	3.00
10 Elite Squadron Stormtrooper C	.20	.30
11 Lieutenant Arnet U	.60	1.00
12 Lieutenant Grond U	.60	1.00
13 Lieutenant Renz R	1.25	2.00
14 Lieutenant Watts R	2.00	3.00
15 Major Hewex R	1.25	2.00
16 Major Marquand R	2.50	4.00
17 Navy Trooper C	.20	.30
18 Navy Trooper Fenson R	1.50	2.50
19 Navy Trooper Shield Technician C	.20	.30
20 Navy Trooper Vesden U	.60	1.00
21 Sergeant Barich R	3.00	5.00
22 Sergeant Elsek U	.60	1.00
23 Sergeant Irol R	2.50	4.00
24 Sergeant Tarl U	.60	1.00
25 Sergeant Wallen R	2.50	4.00
26 An Entire Legion Of My Best Troops U	.60	1.00
27 Aratech Corporation R	1.50	2.50
28 Battle Order U	.40	1.00
29 Biker Scout Gear U	.60	1.00
30 Closed Door R	1.25	2.00
31 Crossfire R	5.00	8.00
32 Early Warning Network R	1.25	2.00
33 Empire's New Order R	1.25	2.00
34 Establish Secret Base R	2.50	4.00
35 Imperial Academy Training C	.20	.30
36 Imperial Arrest Order U	.60	1.00
37 Ominous Rumors R	1.25	2.00
38 Perimeter Patrol R	1.50	2.50
39 Pinned Down U	.60	1.00
40 Relentless Tracking R	1.25	2.00
41 Search And Destroy U	.60	1.00
42 Security Precautions R	4.00	6.00
43 Well-earned Command R	1.25	2.00
44 Accelerate C	.20	.30
45 Always Thinking With Your Stomach R	4.00	6.00
46 Combat Readiness C	.20	.30
47 Compact Firepower C	.20	.30
48 Counterattack R	1.25	2.00
49 Dead Ewok C	.20	.30
50 Don't Move! C	.20	.30
51 Eee Chu Wawa! C	.20	.30
52 Endor Scout Trooper C	.20	.30
53 Freeze! U	.60	1.00
54 Go For Help! C	.20	.30
55 High-speed Tactics U	.60	1.00
56 Hot Pursuit C	.20	.30
57 Imperial Tyranny C	.20	.30
58 It's An Older Code R	1.25	2.00
59 Main Course U	.60	1.00
60 Outflank C	.20	.30
61 Pitiful Little Band C	.20	.30
62 Scout Recon C	.20	.30
63 Sneak Attack C	.20	.30
64 Wounded Warrior R	2.50	4.00
65 You Rebel Scum R	1.50	2.50
66 Carida U	.60	1.00
67 Endor Occupation R	1.25	2.00
68 Endor: Ancient Forest U	.60	1.00
69 Endor: Back Door LIGHT U	.60	1.00
70 Endor: Bunker LIGHT U	.60	1.00
71 Endor: Dark Forest R	4.00	6.00
72 Endor: Dense Forest LIGHT C	.20	.30
73 Endor: Ewok Village LIGHT U	.60	1.00
74 Endor: Forest Clearing U	.60	1.00
75 Endor: Great Forest LIGHT C	.20	.30
76 Endor: Landing Platform (Docking Bay) LIGHT C	.20	.30
77 Endor DARK U	.60	1.00
78 Lambda-class Shuttle C	.20	.30
79 Speeder Bike LIGHT C	.20	.30
80 Tempest 1 R	1.25	2.00
81 Tempest Scout 1 R	1.50	2.50
82 Tempest Scout 2 R	3.00	5.00
83 Tempest Scout 3 R	1.25	2.00
84 Tempest Scout 4 R	4.00	6.00
85 Tempest Scout 5 R	3.00	5.00
86 Tempest Scout 6 R	4.00	6.00
87 Tempest Scout U	.60	1.00
88 AT-ST Dual Cannon R	10.00	15.00
89 Scout Blaster C	.20	.30
90 Speeder Bike Cannon U	.60	1.00
91 Captain Yutani U	.60	1.00
92 Chewbacca of Kashyyyk R	1.25	2.00
93 Chief Chirpa R	1.50	2.50
94 Corporal Beezer U	.60	1.00
95 Corporal Delevar U	.60	1.00
96 Corporal Janse U	.60	1.00
97 Corporal Kensaric R	2.00	3.00
98 Daughter of Skywalker R	12.00	20.00
99 Dresselian Commando C	.20	.30
100 Endor LIGHT U	.60	1.00
101 Ewok Sentry C	.20	.30
102 Ewok Spearman C	.20	.30
103 Ewok Tribesman C	.20	.30
104 General Crix Madine R	1.50	2.50
105 General Solo R	1.25	2.00
106 Graak R	1.25	2.00
107 Kazak R	1.50	2.50
108 Lieutenant Greeve R	1.25	2.00
109 Lieutenant Page R	2.50	4.00
110 Logray R	1.25	2.00
111 Lumat U	.60	1.00
112 Mon Mothma R	2.00	3.00
113 Orrimaarko R	1.25	2.00
114 Paploo U	.60	1.00

115 Rabin U .60 1.00
116 Romba R 1.25 2.00
117 Sergeant Brooks Carlson R 1.25 2.00
118 Sergeant Bruckman R 1.25 2.00
119 Sergeant Junkin U .60 1.00
120 Teebo R 1.25 2.00
121 Threepio R 2.00 3.00
122 Wicket R 1.25 2.00
123 Wuta U .60 1.00
124 Aim High R 1.50 2.50
125 Battle Plan U .60 1.00
126 Commando Training C .20 .30
127 Count Me In R 1.25 2.00
128 I Hope She's All Right U .60 1.00
129 I Wonder Who They Found U .60 1.00
130 Insurrection U .60 1.00
131 That's One R 1.25 2.00
132 Wokling R 10.00 15.00
133 Deactivate The Shield Generator R 2.00 3.00
134 Careful Planning C .20 .30
135 Covert Landing U .60 1.00
136 Endor Operations / Imperial Outpost R 4.00 6.00
137 Ewok And Roll C .20 .30
138 Ewok Log Jam C .20 .30
139 Ewok Rescue C .20 .30
140 Firefight C .20 .30
141 Fly Casual R 1.25 2.00
142 Free Ride U .60 1.00
143 Get Alongside That One U .60 1.00
144 Here We Go Again R 1.25 2.00
145 I Have A Really Bad .20 .30
Feeling About This C
146 I Know R 2.00 3.00
147 Lost In The Wilderness R 1.25 2.00
148 Rapid Deployment R 1.25 2.00
149 Sound The Attack C .20 .30
150 Surprise Counter Assault R 1.25 2.00
151 Take The Initiative C .20 .30
152 This Is Absolutely Right R 1.25 2.00
153 Throw Me Another Charge U .60 1.00
154 Were You Looking For Me? R 6.00 10.00
155 Wookiee Guide C .20 .30
156 Yub Yub! C .20 .30
157 Chandrila U .60 1.00
158 Endor Celebration R 1.25 2.00
159 Endor: Back Door DARK U .60 1.00
160 Endor: Bunker DARK U .60 1.00
161 Endor: Chief Chirpa's Hut R 5.00 8.00
162 Endor: Dense Forest DARK C .20 .30
163 Endor: Ewok Village DARK U .60 1.00
164 Endor: Great Forest DARK C .20 .30
165 Endor: Hidden Forest Trail U .60 1.00
166 Endor: Landing Platform .20 .30
(Docking Bay) DARK C
167 Endor: Rebel Landing Site (Forest) R 4.00 6.00
168 Rebel Strike Team 2.00 3.00
Garrison Destroyed R
169 Tydirium R 2.00 3.00
170 YT-1300 Transport C .20 .30
171 Chewie's AT-ST R 5.00 8.00
172 Ewok Glider C .20 .30
173 Speeder Bike DARK C .20 .30
174 A280 Sharpshooter Rifle R 4.00 6.00
175 BlasTech E-11B Blaster Rifle C .20 .30
176 Chewbacca's Bowcaster R 4.00 6.00
177 Ewok Bow C .20 .30
178 Ewok Catapult U .60 1.00
179 Ewok Spear C .20 .30
180 Explosive Charge U .60 1.00

1999 Star Wars Enhanced Cloud City

COMPLETE SET (12) 12.00 25.00
RELEASED IN 1999
1 4-LOM With Concussion Rifle PM 2.50 4.00
2 Any Methods Necessary PM 3.00 5.00
3 Boba Fett in Slave I PM 1.50 2.50
4 Chewie With Blaster Rifle PM 1.50 2.50
5 Crush The Rebellion PM 2.00 3.00
6 Dengar In Punishing One PM 1.50 2.50
7 IG-88 With Riot Gun PM 5.00 8.00
8 Lando In Millennium Falcon PM 1.50 2.50
9 Lando With Blaster Pistol PM 1.50 2.50
10 Quiet Mining Colony 1.50 2.50
Independent Operation PM
11 This Deal Is Getting Worse All The Time 1.50 2.50
Pray I Don't Alter It Any Further
12 Z-95 Bespin Defense Fighter PM 1.50 2.50

1999 Star Wars Enhanced Jabba's Palace

COMPLETE SET (12) 20.00 40.00
RELEASE IN 1999
1 Bossk With Mortar Gun PM 1.50 2.50
2 Boushh PM 2.00 3.00
3 Court Of The Vile Gangster 1.50 2.50
I Shall Enjoy Watching You Die PM
4 Dengar With Blaster Carbine PM 1.50 2.50
5 IG-88 In IG-2000 PM 1.50 2.50
6 Jodo Kast PM 2.50 4.00
7 Mara Jade, The Emperor's Hand PM 12.00 20.00
8 Mara Jade's Lightsaber PM 2.50 4.00
9 Master Luke PM 4.00 6.00
10 See-Threepio PM 1.50 2.50
11 You Can Either Profit By This... 1.50 2.50
Or Be Destroyed PM
12 Zuckuss In Mist Hunter PM 2.00 3.00

2000 Star Wars Death Star II

COMPLETE SET (182) 200.00 300.00
BOOSTER BOX (30 PACKS) 150.00 250.00
BOOSTER PACK (11 CARDS) 5.00 9.00
RELEASED IN JULY 2000
1 Accuser R 2.00 3.00
2 Admiral Ackbar XR 2.00 3.00
3 Admiral Chiraneau R 2.50 4.00
4 Admiral Piett XR 1.50 2.50
5 Anakin Skywalker R 1.50 2.50
6 Aquaris C .20 .30
7 A-wing C .20 .30
8 A-wing Cannon C .20 .30
9 Baron Soontir Fel R 2.50 4.00
10 Battle Deployment R 2.00 3.00
11 Black 11 R 1.50 2.50
12 Blue Squadron 5 U .60 1.00
13 Blue Squadron B-wing R 2.50 4.00
14 Bring Him Before Me 1.50 2.50
Take Your Father's Place R
15 B-wing Attack Squadron R 1.50 2.50
16 B-wing Bomber C .20 .30
17 Capital Support R 1.50 2.50
18 Captain Godherdt U .60 1.00
19 Captain Jonus U .60 1.00
20 Captain Sarkli R 1.50 2.50
21 Captain Verrack U .60 1.00
22 Captain Yorr U .60 1.00
23 Chimaera R 4.00 6.00
24 Close Air Support C .20 .30
25 Colonel Cracken R 1.50 2.50
26 Colonel Davod Jon U .60 1.00
27 Colonel Jendon R 1.50 2.50
28 Colonel Salm U .60 1.00
29 Combat Response C .20 .30
30 Combined Fleet Action R 1.50 2.50
31 Commander Merrejk R 2.00 3.00
32 Concentrate All Fire R 1.50 2.50
33 Concussion Missiles DARK C .20 .30
34 Concussion Missiles LIGHT C .20 .30
35 Corporal Marmor U .60 1.00
36 Corporal Midge U .60 1.00
37 Critical Error Revealed C .20 .30
38 Darth Vader's Lightsaber R 1.50 2.50
39 Death Star II R 2.00 3.00
40 Death Star II: Capacitors C .20 .30
41 Death Star II: Coolant Shaft C .20 .30
42 Death Star II: Docking Bay C .20 .30
43 Death Star II: Reactor Core C .20 .30
44 Death Star II: Throne Room R 1.50 2.50
45 Defiance R 2.00 3.00
46 Desperate Counter C .20 .30
47 Dominator R 1.50 2.50
48 DS-181-3 U .60 1.00
49 DS-181-4 U .60 1.00
50 Emperor Palpatine UR 40.00 60.00
51 Emperor's Personal Shuttle R 1.50 2.50
52 Emperor's Power U .60 1.00
53 Endor Shield U .60 1.00
54 Enhanced Proton Torpedoes C .20 .30
55 Fighter Cover R 3.00 5.00
56 Fighters Coming In R 1.50 2.50
57 First Officer Thaneespi R 1.50 2.50
58 Flagship Executor R 2.00 3.00
59 Flagship Operations R 1.50 2.50
60 Force Lightning R 3.00 5.00
61 Force Pike C .20 .30
62 Gall C .20 .30
63 General Calrissian R 1.50 2.50
64 General Walex Blissex U .60 1.00
65 Gold Squadron 1 R 1.50 2.50
66 Gray Squadron 1 U .60 1.00
67 Gray Squadron 2 U .60 1.00
68 Gray Squadron Y-wing Pilot C .20 .30
69 Green Leader R 1.50 2.50
70 Green Squadron 1 R 1.50 2.50
71 Green Squadron 3 R 1.50 2.50
72 Green Squadron A-wing R 2.00 3.00
73 Green Squadron Pilot C .20 .30
74 Head Back To The Surface C .20 .30
75 Heading For The Medical Frigate C .20 .30
76 Heavy Turbolaser Battery DARK C .20 .30
77 Heavy Turbolaser Battery LIGHT C .20 .30
78 Home One R 6.00 10.00
79 Home One: Docking Bay C .20 .30
80 Home One: War Room R 2.00 3.00
81 Honor Of The Jedi U .60 1.00
82 I Feel The Conflict U .60 1.00
83 I'll Take The Leader R 4.00 6.00
84 I'm With You Too R 2.50 4.00
85 Imperial Command R 6.00 10.00
86 Inconsequential Losses C .20 .30
87 Independence R 2.00 3.00
88 Insertion Planning C .20 .30
89 Insignificant Rebellion U .60 1.00
90 Intensify The Forward Batteries R 1.50 2.50
91 Janus Greejatus R 1.50 2.50
92 Judicator R 2.50 4.00
93 Karie Neth U .60 1.00
94 Keir Santage U .60 1.00
95 Kin Kian U .60 1.00
96 Launching The Assault R 1.50 2.50
97 Leave Them To Me C .20 .30
98 Let's Keep A Little Optimism Here C .20 .30
99 Liberty R 2.00 3.00
100 Lieutenant Blount R 1.50 2.50
101 Lieutenant Endicott U .60 1.00
102 Lieutenant Hebsly U .60 1.00
103 Lieutenant s'Too Vees U .60 1.00
104 Lieutenant Telsij U .60 1.00
105 Lord Vader R 12.00 20.00
106 Luke Skywalker, Jedi Knight UR 40.00 60.00
107 Luke's Lightsaber R 2.50 4.00
108 Luminous U .60 1.00
109 Major Haash'n U .60 1.00
110 Major Mianda U .60 1.00
111 Major Olander Brit U .60 1.00
112 Major Panno U .60 1.00
113 Major Rhymer U .60 1.00
114 Major Turr Phennir U .60 1.00
115 Masanya R 2.50 4.00
116 Menace Fades C .20 .30
117 Mobilization Points C .20 .30
118 Moff Jerjerrod R 1.50 2.50
119 Mon Calamari DARK C .20 .30
120 Mon Calamari LIGHT C .20 .30
121 Mon Calamari Star Cruiser R 2.00 3.00
122 Myn Kyneugh R 1.50 2.50
123 Nebulon-B Frigate U .60 1.00
124 Nien Nunb R 2.00 3.00
125 Obsidian 10 U .60 1.00
126 Onyx 1 R 2.00 3.00
127 Onyx 2 U .60 1.00
128 Operational As Planned C .20 .30
129 Orbital Mine C .20 .30
130 Our Only Hope U .60 1.00
131 Overseeing It Personally R 1.50 2.50
132 Prepared Defenses C .20 .30
133 Rebel Leadership R 5.00 8.00
134 Red Squadron 1 R 1.50 2.50
135 Red Squadron 4 U .60 1.00
136 Red Squadron 7 U .60 1.00
137 Rise, My Friend R 1.50 2.50
138 Royal Escort C .20 .30
139 Royal Guard C .20 .30
140 Saber 1 R 10.00 15.00
141 Saber 2 U .60 1.00
142 Saber 3 U .60 1.00
143 Saber 4 U .60 1.00
144 Scimitar 1 U .60 1.00
145 Scimitar 2 U .60 1.00
146 Scimitar Squadron TIE C .20 .30
147 Scythe 1 U .60 1.00
148 Scythe 3 U .60 1.00
149 Scythe Squadron TIE C .20 .30
150 SFS L-s7.2 TIE Cannon C .20 .30
151 Sim Aloo R 1.50 2.50
152 Something Special Planned For Them C .20 .30
153 Squadron Assignments C .20 .30
154 Staging Areas C .20 .30
155 Strike Planning R 1.50 2.50
156 Strikeforce C .20 .30
157 Sullust DARK C .20 .30
158 Sullust LIGHT C .20 .30
159 Superficial Damage C .20 .30
160 Superlaser Mark II U .60 1.00
161 Taking Them With Us R 2.00 3.00
162 Tala 1 R 1.50 2.50
163 Tala 2 R 1.50 2.50
164 Ten Numb R 1.50 2.50
165 That Thing's Operational R 1.50 2.50
166 The Emperor's Shield R 1.50 2.50
167 The Emperor's Sword R 1.50 2.50
168 The Time For Our Attack Has Come C .20 .30
169 The Way Of Things U .60 1.00
170 There Is Good In Him 1.50 2.50
I Can Save Him R
171 Thunderflare R 1.50 2.50
172 TIE Interceptor C .20 .30
173 Twilight Is Upon Me R 1.50 2.50
174 Tycho Celchu R 2.00 3.00
175 Visage R 1.50 2.50
176 We're In Attack Position Now R 4.00 6.00
177 Wedge Antilles, Red Squadron Leader R 2.50 4.00
178 You Cannot Hide Forever U .60 1.00
179 You Must Confront Vader R 2.50 4.00
180 Young Fool R 1.50 2.50
181 Your Destiny C .20 .30
182 Your Insight Serves You Well U .60 1.00

2000 Star Wars Jabba's Palace Sealed Deck

COMPLETE SET (20) 5.00 12.00
RELEASE DATE FALL, 2000
1 Agents In The Court .60 1.00
No Love For The Empire PM
2 Hutt Influence PM .60 1.00
3 Jabba's Palace: Antechamber PM .60 1.00
4 Jabba's Palace: Lower Passages PM .60 1.00
5 Lando With Vibro-Ax PM .60 1.00
6 Let Them Make The First Move / My Kind Of Scum .60 1.00
Fearless And Inventive PM
7 Mercenary Pilot PM .60 1.00
8 Mighty Jabba PM .60 1.00
9 No Escape PM .60 1.00
10 Ounee Ta PM .60 1.00
11 Palace Raider PM .60 1.00
12 Power Of The Hutt PM .60 1.00
13 Racing Skiff DARK PM .60 1.00
14 Racing Skiff LIGHT PM .60 1.00
15 Seeking An Audience PM .60 1.00
16 Stun Blaster DARK PM .60 1.00
17 Stun Blaster LIGHT PM .60 1.00
18 Tatooine: Desert Heart PM .60 1.00
19 Tatooine: Hutt Trade Route (Desert) PM .60 1.00
20 Underworld Contacts PM .60 1.00

2000 Star Wars Reflections II

COMPLETE SET (54) 20.00 50.00
BOOSTER BOX (30 PACKS) 150.00 250.00
BOOSTER PACK (11 CARDS) 5.00 10.00
RELEASED IN DECEMBER 2000
1 There Is No Try and 1.00 1.50
Oppressive Enforcement PM
2 Abyssin Ornament and .60 1.00
Wounded Wookiee PM
3 Agents Of Black Sun .60 1.00
Vengence Of The Dark Prince PM
4 Alter and Collateral Damage PM 1.00 1.50
5 Alter and Friendly Fire PM 1.00 1.50
6 Arica PM 3.00 5.00
7 Artoo and Threepio PM 1.00 1.50
8 Black Sun Fleet PM .60 1.00
9 Captain Gilad Pellaeon PM 1.00 1.50
10 Chewbacca, Protector PM 1.00 1.50
11 Control and Set For Stun PM 1.00 1.50
12 Control and Tunnel Vision PM 1.50 2.50
13 Corran Horn PM 2.50 4.00
14 Dark Maneuvers and Tallon Roll PM 1.50 2.50
15 Dash Rendar PM 2.00 3.00
16 Defensive Fire and Hutt Smooch PM .60 1.00
17 Do, Or Do Not and Wise Advice PM .60 1.00
18 Dr Evazan and Ponda Baba PM .60 1.00
19 Evader and Monnok PM 1.00 1.50
20 Ghhhk and Those Rebels .60 1.00
Won't Escape Us PM
21 Grand Admiral Thrawn PM 4.00 6.00
22 Guri PM 2.00 3.00
23 Houjix and Out Of Nowhere PM 1.00 1.50
24 Jabba's Prize PM .60 1.00
25 Kir Kanos PM .60 1.00
26 LE-BO2D9 [Leebo] PM .60 1.00
27 Luke Skywalker, Rebel Scout PM 1.50 2.50
28 Mercenary Armor PM .60 1.00
29 Mirax Terrik PM 1.00 1.50
30 Nar Shaddaa Wind Chimes .60 1.00
and Out Of Somewhere PM

31 No Questions Asked PM .60 1.00
32 Obi-Wan's Journal PM .60 1.00
33 Ommni Box and It's Worse PM .60 1.00
34 Out of Commission and Transmission Terminated PM 1.50 2.50
35 Outrider PM 1.00 1.50
36 Owen Lars and Beru Lars PM .60 1.00
37 Path Of Least Resistance and Revealed PM .60 1.00
38 Prince Xizor PM 2.50 4.00
39 Pulsar Skate PM .60 1.00
40 Sense and Recoil In Fear PM 1.00 1.50
41 Sense and Uncertain Is The Future PM 1.00 1.50
42 Shocking Information and Grimtaash PM .60 1.00
43 Sniper and Dark Strike PM .60 1.00
44 Snoova PM 1.50 2.50
45 Sorry About The Mess and Blaster Proficiency PM 1.00 1.50
46 Stinger PM .60 1.00
47 Sunsdown and Too Cold For Speeders PM .60 1.00
48 Talon Karrde PM 1.00 1.50
49 The Bith Shuffle and Desperate Reach PM .60 1.00
50 The Emperor PM 2.50 4.00
51 Vigo PM 2.50 4.00
52 Virago PM .60 1.00
53 Watch Your Step This Place Can Be A Little Rough PM .60 1.00
54 Yoda Stew and You Do Have Your Moments PM .60 1.00

2000 Star Wars Third Anthology

COMPLETE SET (6) 4.00 10.00
RELEASED IN 2000
1 A New Secret Base PM 1.50 2.50
2 Artoo-Detoo In Red 5 PM 1.50 2.50
3 Echo Base Garrison PM 1.50 2.50
4 Massassi Base Operations One In A Million PM 1.50 2.50
5 Prisoner 2187 PM 1.50 2.50
6 Set Your Course For Alderaan The Ultimate Power In The Universe PM 1.50 2.50

2001 Star Wars Coruscant

COMPLETE SET (188) 120.00 250.00
BOOSTER BOX (30 PACKS) 300.00 400.00
BOOSTER PACK (11 CARDS) 12.00 15.00
RELEASED IN AUGUST 2001
1 A Tragedy Has Occurred U .60 1.00
2 A Vergence In The Force U .60 1.00
3 Accepting Trade Federation Control U .60 1.00
4 Aks Moe R 2.00 3.00
5 All Wings Report In and Darklighter Spin R 10.00 15.00
6 Allegations Of Corruption U .60 1.00
7 Alter DARK U .60 1.00
8 Alter LIGHT U .60 1.00
9 Another Pathetic Lifeform U .60 1.00
10 Are You Brain Dead?! R 2.50 4.00
11 Ascertaining The Truth U .60 1.00
12 Baseless Accusations C .20 .30
13 Baskol Yeesrim U .60 1.00
14 Battle Droid Blaster Rifle C .20 .30
15 Battle Order and First Strike R 1.50 2.50
16 Battle Plan and Draw Their Fire R 2.50 4.00
17 Begin Landing Your Troops U .60 1.00
18 Blockade Flagship: Bridge R 5.00 8.00
19 Captain Madakor R 1.50 2.50
20 Captain Panaka R 1.50 2.50
21 Chokk U .60 1.00
22 Control DARK U .60 1.00
23 Control LIGHT U .60 1.00
24 Coruscant DARK C .20 .30
25 Coruscant LIGHT C .20 .30
26 Coruscant Guard DARK C .20 .30
27 Coruscant Guard LIGHT C .20 .30
28 Coruscant: Docking Bay DARK C .20 .30
29 Coruscant: Docking Bay LIGHT C .20 .30
30 Coruscant: Galactic Senate DARK C .20 .30
31 Coruscant: Galactic Senate LIGHT C .20 .30
32 Coruscant: Jedi Council Chamber R 5.00 8.00
33 Credits Will Do Fine C .20 .30
34 Darth Maul, Young Apprentice R 20.00 30.00
35 Daultay Dofine R 2.00 3.00
36 Depa Billaba R 2.00 3.00
37 Destroyer Droid R 15.00 25.00
38 Dioxis R 1.50 2.50
39 Do They Have A Code Clearance? R 1.50 2.50
40 Droid Starfighter C .20 .30
41 Drop! U .60 1.00
42 Edcel Bar Gane C .20 .30
43 Enter The Bureaucrat U .60 1.00
44 Establish Control U .60 1.00
45 Free Ride and Endor Celebration R 2.50 4.00
46 Freon Drevan U .60 1.00
47 Gardulla The Hutt U .60 1.00
48 Graxol Kelvyyn U .60 1.00
49 Grotto Werribee R 2.00 3.00
50 Gungan Warrior C .20 .30
51 Horox Ryyder C .20 .30
52 I Will Not Defer U .60 1.00
53 I've Decided To Go Back C .20 .30
54 Imperial Arrest Order and Secret Plans R 5.00 8.00
55 Imperial Artillery R 5.00 8.00
56 Inconsequential Barriers C .20 .30
57 Insurrection and Aim High R 4.00 6.00
58 Jawa DARK C .20 .30
59 Jawa LIGHT C .20 .30
60 Keder The Black R 1.50 2.50
61 Ki-Adi-Mundi U .60 1.00
62 Kill Them Immediately C .20 .30
63 Lana Dobreed U .60 1.00
64 Laser Cannon Battery U .60 1.00
65 Liana Merian U .60 1.00
66 Lieutenant Williams U .60 1.00
67 Little Real Power C .20 .30
68 Lott Dod R 2.00 3.00
69 Mace Windu R 12.00 20.00
70 Malastare DARK U .60 1.00
71 Malastare LIGHT U .60 1.00
72 Mas Amedda U .60 1.00
73 Master Qui-Gon R 5.00 8.00
74 Masterful Move and Endor Occupation R 3.00 5.00
75 Maul Strikes R 3.00 5.00
76 Maul's Sith Infiltrator R 5.00 8.00
77 Might Of The Republic R 4.00 6.00
78 Mind Tricks Don't Work On Me U .60 1.00
79 Mindful Of The Future C .20 .30
80 Motion Supported U .60 1.00
81 Murr Danod R 1.50 2.50
82 My Lord, Is That Legal? I Will Make It Legal U .60 1.00
83 My Loyal Bodyguard U .60 1.00
84 Naboo Blaster C .20 .30
85 Naboo Blaster Rifle DARK C .20 .30
86 Naboo Blaster Rifle LIGHT C .20 .30
87 Naboo Defense Fighter C .20 .30
88 Naboo Fighter Pilot C .20 .30
89 Naboo Security Officer Blaster C .20 .30
90 Naboo DARK U .60 1.00
91 Naboo LIGHT U .60 1.00
92 Naboo: Battle Plains DARK C .20 .30
93 Naboo: Battle Plains LIGHT C .20 .30
94 Naboo: Swamp DARK C .20 .30
95 Naboo: Swamp LIGHT C .20 .30
96 Naboo: Theed Palace Courtyard DARK C .20 .30
97 Naboo: Theed Palace Courtyard LIGHT C .20 .30
98 Naboo: Theed Palace Docking Bay DARK C .20 .30
99 Naboo: Theed Palace Docking Bay LIGHT C .20 .30
100 Naboo: Theed Palace Throne Room DARK C .20 .30
101 Naboo: Theed Palace Throne Room LIGHT C .20 .30
102 Neimoidian Advisor U .60 1.00
103 Neimoidian Pilot C .20 .30
104 New Leadership Is Needed C .20 .30
105 No Civility, Only Politics C .20 .30
106 No Money, No Parts, No Deal! You're A Slave? U .60 1.00
107 Nute Gunray R 1.50 2.50
108 Odin Nesloor U .60 1.00
109 On The Payroll Of The Trade Federation C .20 .30
110 Orn Free Taa C .20 .30
111 Our Blockade Is Perfectly Legal U .60 1.00
112 P-59 R 5.00 8.00
113 P-60 R 2.50 4.00
114 Panaka's Blaster R 2.00 3.00
115 Passel Argente C .20 .30
116 Phylo Gandish R 2.50 4.00
117 Plea To The Court U .60 1.00
118 Plead My Case To The Senate Sanity And Compassion U .60 1.00
119 Plo Koon R 5.00 8.00
120 Queen Amidala, Ruler Of Naboo R 6.00 10.00
121 Queen's Royal Starship R 2.00 3.00
122 Radiant VII R 2.50 4.00
123 Rebel Artillery R 5.00 8.00
124 Republic Cruiser C .20 .30
125 Reveal Ourselves To The Jedi C .20 .30
126 Ric Olie R 1.50 2.50
127 Rune Haako R 1.50 2.50
128 Sabe R 2.00 3.00
129 Sache U .60 1.00
130 Secure Route U .60 1.00
131 Security Battle Droid C .20 .30
132 Security Control U .60 1.00
133 Sei Taria U .60 1.00
134 Senator Palpatine (head and shoulders) R 5.00 8.00
135 Senator Palpatine (head shot) R 20.00 30.00
136 Sense DARK U .60 1.00
137 Sense LIGHT U .60 1.00
138 Short Range Fighters and Watch Your Back! R 4.00 6.00
139 Speak With The Jedi Council R 5.00 8.00
140 Squabbling Delegates R 2.00 3.00
141 Stay Here, Where It's Safe C .20 .30
142 Supreme Chancellor Valorum R 1.50 2.50
143 Tatooine DARK U .60 1.00
144 Tatooine LIGHT U .60 1.00
145 Tatooine: Marketplace DARK C .20 .30
146 Tatooine: Marketplace LIGHT C .20 .30
147 Tatooine: Mos Espa Docking Bay DARK C .20 .30
148 Tatooine: Mos Espa Docking Bay LIGHT C .20 .30
149 Tatooine: Watto's Junkyard DARK C .20 .30
150 Tatooine: Watto's Junkyard LIGHT C .20 .30
151 TC-14 R 1.50 2.50
152 Televan Koreyy R 1.50 2.50
153 Tendau Bendon U .60 1.00
154 Tey How U .60 1.00
155 The Gravest Of Circumstances U .60 1.00
156 The Hyperdrive Generator's Gone We'll Need A New One U .60 1.00
157 The Phantom Menace R 6.00 10.00
158 The Point Is Conceded C .20 .30
159 They Will Be No Match For You R 1.50 2.50
160 They're Still Coming Through! U .60 1.00
161 This Is Outrageous! U .60 1.00
162 Thrown Back C .20 .30
163 Tikkes C .20 .30
164 Toonbuck Toora U .60 1.00
165 Trade Federation Battleship U .60 1.00
166 Trade Federation Droid Control Ship R 2.00 3.00
167 Tusken Raider C .20 .30
168 Vote Now! DARK R 1.50 2.50
169 Vote Now! LIGHT R 2.00 3.00
170 We Must Accelerate Our Plans R 12.00 20.00
171 We Wish To Board At Once R 3.00 5.00
172 We're Leaving C .20 .30
173 Wipe Them Out, All Of Them U .60 1.00
174 Yade M'rak U .60 1.00
175 Yané U .60 1.00
176 Yarua U .60 1.00
177 Yeb Yeb Adem'thorn C .20 .30
178 Yoda, Senior Council Member R 4.00 6.00
179 You Cannot Hide Forever and Mobilization Points R 4.00 6.00
180 You've Got A Lot Of Guts Coming Here R 2.00 3.00
181 Your Insight Serves You Well and Staging Areas R 1.50 2.50
182 Coruscant Dark Side List 1 .20 .30
183 Coruscant Dark Side List 2 .20 .30
184 Coruscant Light Side List 1 .20 .30
185 Coruscant Light Side List 2 .20 .30
186 Coruscant Rule Card 1 .20 .30
187 Coruscant Rule Card 2 .20 .30
188 Coruscant Rule Card 3 .20 .30

2001 Star Wars Reflections III

COMPLETE SET (96) 80.00 150.00
BOOSTER BOX (30 PACKS) 250.00 350.00
BOOSTER PACK (11 CARDS) 7.50 15.00
RELEASED IN 2001
1 A Close Race PM 1.50 2.50
2 A Remote Planet PM 1.50 2.50
3 A Tragedy Has Occured PM 2.00 3.00
4 A Useless Gesture PM 1.50 2.50
5 Aim High PM 2.00 3.00
6 Allegations of Coruption PM 1.50 2.50
7 An Unusual Amount Of Fear PM 1.50 2.50
8 Another Pathetic Lifeform PM 1.50 2.50
9 Armament Dismantled PM 1.50 2.50
10 Battle Order PM 1.50 2.50
11 Battle Plan PM 2.00 3.00
12 Bib Fortuna PM 1.50 2.50
13 Blizzard 4 PM 3.00 5.00
14 Blockade Flagship: Hallway PM 1.50 2.50
15 Blow Parried PM 1.50 2.50
16 Boba Fett, Bounty Hunter PM 8.00 12.00
17 Chewie, Enraged PM 2.50 4.00
18 Clinging To The Edge PM 1.50 2.50
19 Colo Claw Fish DARK PM 1.50 2.50
20 Colo Claw Fish LIGHT PM 1.50 2.50
21 Come Here You Big Coward PM 2.00 3.00
22 Conduct Your Search PM 2.00 3.00
23 Crossfire PM 1.50 2.50
24 Dark Rage PM 1.50 2.50
25 Darth Maul's Demise PM 1.50 2.50
26 Deep Hatred PM 1.50 2.50
27 Desperate Times PM 1.50 2.50
28 Diversionary Tactics PM 1.50 2.50
29 Do They Have A Code Clearance? PM 2.00 3.00
30 Do, Or Do Not PM 1.50 2.50
31 Don't Do That Again PM 1.50 2.50
32 Echo Base Sensors PM 2.00 3.00
33 Energy Walls DARK PM 1.50 2.50
34 Energy Walls LIGHT PM 1.50 2.50
35 Ewok Celebration PM 1.50 2.50
36 Fall Of A Jedi PM 1.50 2.50
37 Fanfare PM 1.50 2.50
38 Fear Is My Ally PM 1.50 2.50
39 Force Push PM 2.00 3.00
40 Han, Chewie, and The Falcon PM 8.00 12.00
41 He Can Go About His Business PM 1.50 2.50
42 Horace Vancil PM 1.50 2.50
43 Inner Strength PM 1.50 2.50
44 Jabba Desilijic Tiure PM 1.50 2.50
45 Jar Jar's Electropole PM 1.50 2.50
46 Jedi Leap PM 1.50 2.50
47 Lando Calrissian, Scoundrel PM 3.00 5.00
48 Lando's Not A System, He's A Man PM 1.50 2.50
49 Leave them to Me PM 1.50 2.50
50 Leia, Rebel Princess PM 4.00 6.00
51 Let's Keep A Little Optimism Here PM 1.50 2.50
52 Lord Maul PM 10.00 15.00
53 Maul's Double-Bladed Lightsaber PM 3.00 5.00
54 Naboo: Theed Palace Generator Core DARK PM 1.50 2.50
55 Naboo: Theed Palace Generator Core LIGHT PM 1.50 2.50
56 Naboo: Theed Palace Generator DARK PM 1.50 2.50
57 Naboo: Theed Palace Generator LIGHT PM 1.50 2.50
58 No Escape PM 1.50 2.50
59 No Match For A Sith PM 1.50 2.50
60 Obi-Wan Kenobi, Jedi Knight PM 2.50 4.00
61 Obi-Wan's Lightsaber PM 1.50 2.50
62 Only Jedi Carry That Weapon PM 1.50 2.50
63 Opee Sea Killer DARK PM 1.50 2.50
64 Opee Sea Killer LIGHT PM 1.50 2.50
65 Oppressive Enforcement PM 1.50 2.50
66 Ounee Ta PM 1.50 2.50
67 Planetary Defenses PM 1.50 2.50
68 Prepare For A Surface Attack PM 1.50 2.50
69 Qui-Gon Jinn, Jedi Master PM 4.00 6.00
70 Qui-Gon's End PM 2.00 3.00
71 Reistance PM 1.50 2.50
72 Sando Aqua Monster DARK PM 1.50 2.50
73 Sando Aqua Monster LIGHT PM 1.50 2.50
74 Secret Plans PM 1.50 2.50
75 Sio Bibble PM 1.50 2.50
76 Stormtrooper Garrison PM 6.00 10.00
77 Strike Blockaded PM 1.50 2.50
78 The Ebb Of Battle PM 1.50 2.50
79 The Hutts Are Gangsters PM 1.50 2.50
80 There Is No Try PM 2.00 3.00
81 They Must Never Again Leave This City PM 1.50 2.50
82 Thok and Thug PM 1.50 2.50
83 Through The Corridor PM 1.50 2.50
84 Ultimatum PM 1.50 2.50
85 Unsalvageable PM 1.50 2.50
86 We'll Let Fate-a Decide, Huh? PM 1.50 2.50
87 Weapon Of A Fallen Mentor PM 1.50 2.50
88 Weapon Of A Sith PM 1.50 2.50
89 Where Are Those Droidekas?! PM 1.50 2.50
90 Wipe Them Out, All Of Them PM 1.50 2.50
91 Wise Advice PM 1.50 2.50
92 Yoda, Master Of The Force PM 6.00 10.00
93 You Cannot Hide Forever PM 1.50 2.50
94 You've Never Won A Race? PM 1.50 2.50
95 Your Insight Serves You Well PM 1.50 2.50
96 Your Ship? PM 2.00 3.00

2001 Star Wars Tatooine

COMPLETE SET (95)	25.00	60.00
BOOSTER BOX (30 PACKS)	50.00	100.00
BOOSTER PACK (11 CARDS)	2.50	5.00
RELEASED IN MAY 2001		
1 A Jedi's Concentration C	.20	.30
2 A Jedi's Focus C	.20	.30
3 A Jedi's Patience C	.20	.30
4 A Jedi's Resilience U	.60	1.00
5 A Million Voices Crying Out R	1.25	2.00
6 A Step Backward U	.60	1.00
7 Anakin's Podracer R	1.25	2.00
8 Aurra Sing R	2.50	4.00
9 Ben Quadinaros' Podracer C	.20	.30
10 Boonta Eve Podrace DARK R	1.50	2.50
11 Boonta Eve Podrace LIGHT R	1.25	2.00
12 Brisky Morning Munchen R	1.25	2.00
13 Caldera Righim C	.20	.30
14 Changing The Odds C	.20	.30
15 Daroe R	1.25	2.00
16 Darth Maul R	2.50	4.00
17 Deneb Both U	.60	1.00
18 Don't Do That Again C	.20	.30
19 Dud Bolt's Podracer C	.20	.30
20 Either Way, You Win U	.60	1.00
21 End Of A Reign R	1.25	2.00
22 Entering The Arena U	.60	1.00
23 Eopie C	.20	.30
24 Eventually You'll Lose U	.60	1.00
25 Fanfare C	.20	.30
26 Gamall Wironicc U	.60	1.00
27 Ghana Gleemort U	.60	1.00
28 Gragra U	.60	1.00
29 Great Shot, Kid! R	1.25	2.00
30 Grugnak U	.60	1.00
31 His Name Is Anakin C	.20	.30
32 Hit Racer U	.60	1.00
33 I Can't Believe He's Gone C	.20	.30
34 I Did It! R	1.25	2.00
35 I Will Find Them Quickly, Master R	1.25	2.00
36 I'm Sorry R	1.25	2.00
37 If The Trace Was Correct U	.60	1.00
38 Jar Jar Binks R	1.25	2.00
39 Jedi Escape C	.20	.30
40 Join Me! U	.60	1.00
41 Keeping The Empire Out Forever R	1.25	2.00
42 Lathe U	.60	1.00
43 Lightsaber Parry C	.20	.30
44 Loci Rosen U	.60	1.00
45 Losing Track C	.20	.30
46 Maul's Electrobinoculars C	.20	.30
47 Maul's Lightsaber R	1.25	2.00
48 Neck And Neck U	.60	1.00
49 Ni Chuba Na?? C	.20	.30
50 Obi-wan Kenobi, Padawan Learner R	1.50	2.50
51 Padme Naberrie R	3.00	5.00
52 Pit Crews U	.60	1.00
53 Pit Droid C	.20	.30
54 Podrace Prep U	.60	1.00
55 Podracer Collision U	.60	1.00
56 Quietly Observing U	.60	1.00
57 Qui-Gon Jinn R	2.50	4.00
58 Qui-Gon Jinn's Lightsaber R	1.50	2.50
59 Rachalt Hyst U	.60	1.00
60 Sebulba R	1.25	2.00
61 Sebulba's Podracer R	1.25	2.00
62 Shmi Skywalker R	1.25	2.00
63 Sith Fury C	.20	.30
64 Sith Probe Droid R	1.50	2.50
65 Start Your Engines! U	.60	1.00
66 Tatooine: City Outskirts U	.60	1.00
67 Tatooine: Desert Landing Site R	1.25	2.00
68 Tatooine: Mos Espa DARK C	.20	.30
69 Tatooine: Mos Espa LIGHT C	.20	.30
70 Tatooine: Podrace Arena DARK C	.20	.30
71 Tatooine: Podrace Arena LIGHT C	.20	.30
72 Tatooine: Podracer Bay C	.20	.30
73 Tatooine: Slave Quarters U	.60	1.00
74 Teemto Pagalies' Podracer C	.20	.30
75 The Camp C	.20	.30
76 The Shield Is Down! R	1.25	2.00
77 There Is No Conflict C	.20	.30
78 Threepio With His Parts Showing R	2.00	3.00
79 Too Close For Comfort U	.60	1.00
80 Vader's Anger C	.20	.30
81 Watto R	2.00	3.00
82 Watto's Box C	.20	.30
83 Watto's Chance Cube U	.60	1.00
84 We Shall Double Our Efforts! R	1.25	2.00
85 What Was It U	.60	1.00
86 Yotts Orren U	.60	1.00
87 You May Start Your Landing R	1.25	2.00
88 You Swindled Me! U	.60	1.00
89 You Want This, Don't You? C	.20	.30
90 You'll Find I'm Full Of Surprises U	.60	1.00
91 Tatooine Dark Side List	.20	.30
92 Tatooine Light Side List	.20	.30
93 Tatooine Rule Card 1	.20	.30
94 Tatooine Rule Card 2	.20	.30
95 Tatooine Rule Card 3	.20	.30

2001 Star Wars Theed Palace

COMPLETE SET (121)	80.00	150.00
BOOSTER BOX (30 PACKS)	400.00	500.00
BOOSTER PACK (11 CARDS)	15.00	20.00
RELEASED IN DECEMBER 2001		
FINAL EXPANSION PRODUCT BY DECIPHER		
1 3B3-10 U	.50	.75
2 3B3-1204 U	.50	.75
3 3B3-21 U	.50	.75
4 3B3-888 U	.50	.75
5 AAT Assault Leader R	1.50	2.50
6 AAT Laser Cannon U	.50	.75
7 Activate The Droids C	.20	.30
8 After Her! R	1.25	2.00
9 Amidala's Blaster R	1.25	2.00
10 Armored Attack Tank U	.50	.75
11 Artoo, Brave Little Droid R	2.50	4.00
12 Ascension Guns U	.50	.75
13 At Last We Are Getting Results C	.20	.30
14 Battle Droid Officer C	.20	.30
15 Battle Droid Pilot C	.20	.30
16 Big Boomers! C	.20	.30
17 Blockade Flaghip R	2.50	4.00
18 Blockade Flagship: Docking Bay DARK U	.50	.75
19 Blockade Flagship: Docking Bay LIGHT U	.50	.75
20 Bok Askol U	.50	.75
21 Booma C	.20	.30
22 Boss Nass R	2.00	3.00
23 Bravo 1 R	1.25	2.00
24 Bravo 2 U	.50	.75
25 Bravo 3 U	.50	.75
26 Bravo 4 U	.50	.75
27 Bravo 5 U	.50	.75
28 Bravo Fighter R	1.25	2.00
29 Captain Tarpals R	1.25	2.00
30 Captain Tarpals' Electropole C	.20	.30
31 Captian Daultay Dofine R	1.25	2.00
32 Cease Fire! C	.20	.30
33 Corporal Rushing U	.50	.75
34 Dams Denna U	.50	.75
35 Darth Maul With Lightsaber R	15.00	25.00
36 Darth Sidious R	30.00	50.00
37 DFS Squadron Starfighter C	.20	.30
38 DFS-1015 U	.50	.75
39 DFS-1308 R	1.25	2.00
40 DFS-327 C	.20	.30
41 Droid Racks R	2.00	3.00
42 Droid Starfighter Laser Cannons C	.20	.30
43 Drop Your Weapons C	.20	.30
44 Electropole C	.20	.30
45 Energy Shell Launchers C	.20	.30
46 Fambaa C	.20	.30
47 Fighters Straight Ahead U	.50	.75
48 General Jar Jar R	2.00	3.00
49 Get To Your Ships! C	.20	.30
50 Gian Speeder C	.20	.30
51 Gimme A Lift! R	1.25	2.00
52 Gungan Energy Shield C	.20	.30
53 Gungan General C	.20	.30
54 Gungan Guard C	.20	.30
55 Halt! C	.20	.30
56 I'll Try Spinning R	1.25	2.00
57 Infantry Battle Droid C	.20	.30
58 Invasion / In Complete Control U	.50	.75
59 It's On Automatic Pilot C	.20	.30
60 Jerus Jannick U	.50	.75
61 Kaadu C	.20	.30
62 Let's Go Left R	1.25	2.00
63 Lieutenant Arven Wendik U	.50	.75
64 Lieutenant Chamberlyn U	.50	.75
65 Lieutenant Rya Kirsch U	.50	.75
66 Mace Windu, Jedi Master R	10.00	15.00
67 Master, Destroyers! R	1.50	2.50
68 Multi Troop Transport U	.50	.75
69 Naboo Celebration R	1.25	2.00
70 Naboo Occupation R	1.50	2.50
71 Naboo: Boss Nass's Chambers U	.50	.75
72 Naboo: Otoh Gunga Entrance U	.50	.75
73 Naboo: Theed Palace Hall U	.50	.75
74 Naboo: Theed Palace Hallway U	.50	.75
75 No Giben Up, General Jar Jar! R	1.25	2.00
76 Nothing Can Get Through Are Shield R	1.50	2.50
77 Nute Gunray, Neimoidian Viceroy R	3.00	5.00
78 Officer Dolphe U	.50	.75
79 Officer Ellberger U	.50	.75
80 Officer Perosei U	.50	.75
81 OOM-9 U	.50	.75
82 Open Fire! C	.20	.30
83 OWO-1 With Backup R	2.00	3.00
84 Panaka, Protector Of The Queen R	4.00	6.00
85 Proton Torpedoes C	.20	.30
86 Queen Amidala R	12.00	20.00
87 Qui-Gon Jinn With Lightsaber R	10.00	15.00
88 Rayno Vaca U	.50	.75
89 Rep Been U	.50	.75
90 Ric Olie, Bravo Leader R	1.25	2.00
91 Rolling, Rolling, Rolling R	1.50	2.50
92 Royal Naboo Security Officer C	.20	.30
93 Rune Haako, Legal Counsel R	2.00	3.00
94 Senate Hovercam DARK R	1.50	2.50
95 Senate Hovercam LIGHT R	1.50	2.50
96 Sil Unch U	.50	.75
97 Single Trooper Aerial Platform C	.20	.30
98 SSA-1015 U	.50	.75
99 SSA-306 U	.50	.75
100 SSA-719 R	2.00	3.00
101 STAP Blaster Cannons C	.20	.30
102 Steady, Steady C	.20	.30
103 Take Them Away C	.20	.30
104 Take This! C	.20	.30
105 Tank Commander C	.20	.30
106 The Deflector Shield Is Too Strong R	1.25	2.00
107 There They Are! U	.50	.75
108 They Win This Round R	1.25	2.00
109 This Is Not Good C	.20	.30
110 Trade Federation Landing Craft C	.20	.30
111 TT-6 R	1.50	2.50
112 TT-9 R	1.25	2.00
113 We Didn't Hit It C	.20	.30
114 We Don't Have Time For This R	1.50	2.50
115 We Have A Plan They Will Be Lost And Confused C	.20	.30
116 We're Hit Artoo C	.20	.30
117 Wesa Gotta Grand Army C	.20	.30
118 Wesa Ready To Do Our-sa Part C	.20	.30
119 Whoooo! C	.20	.30
120 Theed Palace Dark Side List	.20	.30
121 Theed Palace Light Side List	.20	.30

2002 Star Wars Attack of the Clones

COMPLETE SET (180)	30.00	80.00
BOOSTER BOX (36 PACKS)	20.00	40.00
BOOSTER PACK (11 CARDS)	1.00	1.50
*FOIL: .75X TO 2X BASIC CARDS		
RELEASED IN APRIL 2002		
1 Anakin Skywalker (A) R	1.00	1.50
2 Anakin Skywalker (B) R	1.00	1.50
3 Assassin Droid ASN-121 (A) R	1.00	1.50
4 Bail Organa (A) R	1.00	1.50
5 Battle Fatigue R	1.00	1.50
6 Boba Fett (A) R	1.00	1.50
7 Captain Typho (A) R	1.00	1.50
8 Clear the Skies R	1.00	1.50
9 Clone Officer R	1.00	1.50
10 Dark Rendezvous R	1.00	1.50
11 Dark Side's Command R	1.00	1.50
12 Dark Side's Compulsion R	1.00	1.50
13 Darth Sidious (A) R	1.00	1.50
14 Darth Tyranus (A) R	1.00	1.50
15 Destruction of Hope R	1.00	1.50
16 Dexter Jettster (A) R	1.00	1.50
17 Geonosian Sentry R	1.00	1.50
18 Hero's Duty R	1.00	1.50
19 Hero's Flaw R	1.00	1.50
20 Interference in the Senate R	1.00	1.50
21 Jango Fett (A) R	1.00	1.50
22 Jango Fett (B) R	1.00	1.50
23 Jar Jar Binks (A) R	1.00	1.50
24 Jedi Call for Help R	1.00	1.50
25 Jedi Council Summons R	1.00	1.50
26 Jedi Knight's Deflection R	1.00	1.50
27 Lama Su (A) R	1.00	1.50
28 Luxury Airspeeder U	.30	.50
29 A Moment's Rest R	1.00	1.50
30 Naboo Defense Station R	1.00	1.50
31 Obi-Wan Kenobi (A) R	1.00	1.50
32 Obi-Wan's Starfighter (A) R	1.00	1.50
33 Order Here R	1.00	1.50
34 Padmé Amidala (A) R	1.00	1.50
35 Padmé Amidala (B) R	1.00	1.50
36 Padmé's Yacht (A) R	1.00	1.50
37 Plo Koon (A) R	1.00	1.50
38 Plot the Secession R	1.00	1.50
39 Power Dive R	1.00	1.50
40 Queen Jamillia (A) R	1.00	1.50
41 R2-D2 (A) R	1.00	1.50
42 San Hill (A) U	.30	.50
43 Second Effort R	1.00	1.50
44 Seek the Council's Wisdom R	1.00	1.50
45 Shu Mai (A) U	.30	.50
46 Slave I (A) R	1.00	1.50
47 Spirit of the Fallen R	1.00	1.50
48 Target the Senator R	1.00	1.50
49 Taun We (A) R	1.00	1.50
50 Trade Federation Battleship Core R	1.00	1.50
51 Tyranus's Edict R	1.00	1.50
52 Tyranus's Geonosian Speeder (A) R	1.00	1.50
53 Tyranus's Solar Sailer (A) R	1.00	1.50
54 Tyranus's Wrath R	1.00	1.50
55 War Will Follow R	1.00	1.50
56 Ward of the Jedi R	1.00	1.50
57 Windu's Solution R	1.00	1.50
58 Yoda (A) R	1.00	1.50
59 Yoda's Intervention R	1.00	1.50
60 Zam Wesell (A) R	1.00	1.50
61 Acklay U	.30	.50
62 Anakin Skywalker (C) U	.30	.50
63 Anakin's Inspiration U	.30	.50
64 AT-TE Walker 23X U	.30	.50
65 AT-TE Walker 71E R	1.00	1.50
66 Attract Enemy Fire U	.30	.50
67 C-3PO (A) U	.30	.50
68 Capture Obi-Wan U	.30	.50
69 Chancellor Palpatine (A) R	1.00	1.50
70 Chase the Villain U	.30	.50
71 Cheat the Game U	.30	.50
72 Cliegg Lars (A) U	.30	.50
73 Clone Warrior 4/163 U	.30	.50
74 Clone Warrior 5/373 U	.30	.50
75 Commerce Guild Droid Platoon U	.30	.50
76 Cordé (A) U	.30	.50
77 Coruscant Freighter AA-9 (A) U	.30	.50
78 Dark Speed U	.30	.50
79 Darth Tyranus (B) U	.30	.50
80 Departure Time U	.30	.50
81 Destroyer Droid, P Series U	.30	.50
82 Down in Flames U	.30	.50
83 Droid Control Ship U	.30	.50
84 Elan Sleazebaggano (A) R	1.00	1.50
85 Geonosian Guard U	.30	.50
86 Geonosian Warrior U	.30	.50
87 Go to the Temple U	.30	.50
88 Infantry Battle Droid, B1 Series U	.30	.50
89 Jango Fett (C) U	.30	.50
90 Jawa Sandcrawler U	.30	.50
91 Jedi Patrol U	.30	.50
92 Kaminoan Guard U	.30	.50
93 Kit Fisto (A) U	.30	.50
94 Master and Apprentice U	.30	.50
95 Naboo Security Guard U	.30	.50
96 Naboo Spaceport U	.30	.50
97 Nexu U	.30	.50
98 Nute Gunray (A) U	.30	.50
99 Obi-Wan Kenobi (B) U	.30	.50
100 Padmé Amidala (C) U	.30	.50
101 Poggle the Lesser (A) U	.30	.50
102 Reek U	.30	.50
103 Republic Assault Ship U	.30	.50
104 Republic Cruiser C	.15	.25
105 Shaak Ti (A) U	.30	.50
106 Ship Arrival U	.30	.50
107 Splinter the Republic U	.30	.50
108 Strength of Hate U	.30	.50
109 Subtle Assassination U	.30	.50
110 Super Battle Droid 8EX U	.30	.50
111 Trade Federation Battleship U	.30	.50
112 Trade Federation C-9979 U	.30	.50
113 Tyranus's Gift U	.30	.50
114 Underworld Connections U	.30	.50
115 Wat Tambor (A) U	.30	.50
116 Watto (A) U	.30	.50
117 Weapon Response U	.30	.50
118 Wedding of Destiny U	.30	.50
119 Yoda (B) U	.30	.50
120 Zam's Airspeeder (A) U	.30	.50
121 Anakin Skywalker (D) C	.15	.25
122 Battle Droid Squad C	.15	.25
123 Bravo N-1 Starfighter C	.15	.25

124 Chancellor's Guard Squad C .15 .25
125 Clone Platoon C .15 .25
126 Clone Squad C .15 .25
127 Commerce Guild Droid 81 C .15 .25
128 Commerce Guild Starship C .15 .25
129 Corellian Star Shuttle C .15 .25
130 Darth Tyranus (C) C .15 .25
131 Destroyer Droid Squad C .15 .25
132 Droid Starfighter DFS-4CT C .15 .25
133 Droid Starfighter Squadron C .15 .25
134 Droid Starfighter Wing C .15 .25
135 Elite Jedi Squad C .15 .25
136 Flying Geonosian Squad C .15 .25
137 Geonosian Defense Platform C .15 .25
138 Geonosian Fighter C .15 .25
139 Geonosian Squad C .15 .25
140 Gozanti Cruiser C .15 .25
141 Hatch a Clone C .15 .25
142 Hero's Dodge C .15 .25
143 High-Force Dodge C .15 .25
144 Hyperdrive Ring C .15 .25
145 InterGalactic Banking Clan Starship C .15 .25
146 Jango Fett (D) C .15 .25
147 Jedi Starfighter 3R3 C .15 .25
148 Knockdown C .15 .25
149 Lost in the Asteroids C .15 .25
150 Lull in the Fighting C .15 .25
151 Mending C .15 .25
152 N-1 Starfighter C .15 .25
153 Naboo Cruiser C .15 .25
154 Naboo Royal Starship C .15 .25
155 Naboo Senatorial Escort C .15 .25
156 Naboo Starfighter Squadron C .15 .25
157 Obi-Wan Kenobi (C) C .15 .25
158 Padawan's Deflection C .15 .25
159 Padmé Amidala (D) C .15 .25
160 Patrol Speeder C .15 .25
161 Peace on Naboo C .15 .25
162 Pilot's Dodge C .15 .25
163 Recon Speeder U .15 .25
164 Republic Attack Gunship UH-478 C .15 .25
165 Repulsorlift Malfunction C .15 .25
166 Return to Spaceport C .15 .25
167 Rickshaw C .15 .25
168 Slumming on Coruscant C .15 .25
169 Sonic Shockwave C .15 .25
170 Speeder Bike Squadron C .15 .25
171 Starship Refit C .15 .25
172 Surge of Power C .15 .25
173 Swoop Bike C .15 .25
174 Take the Initiative C .15 .25
175 Target Locked C .15 .25
176 Taylander Shuttle C .15 .25
177 Techno Union Starship C .15 .25
178 Trade Federation War Freighter C .15 .25
179 Walking Droid Fighter C .15 .25
180 Zam Wesell (B) C .15 .25

2002 Star Wars A New Hope

COMPLETE SET (180) 30.00 80.00
BOOSTER BOX (36 PACKS) 25.00 50.00
BOOSTER PACK (11 CARDS) 1.50 3.00
*FOIL: .75X TO 2X BASIC CARDS
RELEASED IN OCTOBER 2002
1 Admiral Motti (A) R 1.00 1.50
2 Beru Lars (A) R 1.00 1.50
3 Blaster Barrage R 1.00 1.50
4 Capture the Falcon R 1.00 1.50
5 Contingency Plan R 1.00 1.50
6 Dannik Jerriko (A) R 1.00 1.50
7 Darth Vader (A) R 2.00 3.00
8 Desperate Confrontation R 1.25 2.00
9 Destroy Alderaan R 1.00 1.50
10 Dianoga (A) R 1.00 1.50
11 Disturbance in the Force R 1.00 1.50
12 It's Not Over Yet R 1.00 1.50
13 EG-6 Power Droid R 1.00 1.50
14 Elite Stormtrooper Squad R 1.00 1.50
15 Figrin D'an (A) R 1.25 2.00
16 Greedo (A) R 1.00 1.50
17 Hold 'Em Off R 1.00 1.50
18 Imperial Blockade R 1.00 1.50
19 Imperial Navy Helmsman R 1.00 1.50
20 Imperial Sentry Droid R 1.00 1.50
21 IT-0 Interrogator Droid R 1.25 2.00
22 Jawa Leader R 1.00 1.50
23 Krayt Dragon R 1.00 1.50
24 Leia's Kiss R 1.00 1.50
25 Luke Skywalker (B) R 1.00 1.50
26 Luke Skywalker (A) R 1.00 1.50
27 Luke's Speeder (A) R 1.00 1.50
28 Luke's X-Wing (A) R 1.00 1.50
29 Momaw Nadon (A) R 1.50 2.50
30 Most Desperate Hour R 1.00 1.50
31 No Escape R 1.00 1.50
32 Obi-Wan Kenobi (E) R 1.00 1.50
33 Obi-Wan's Prowess R 1.00 1.50
34 Obi-Wan's Task R 1.00 1.50
35 Our Only Hope R 1.00 1.50
36 Owen Lars (A) R 1.00 1.50
37 Plan of Attack R 1.00 1.50
38 Princess Leia (A) R 1.00 1.50
39 Protection of the Master R 1.00 1.50
40 R5-D4 (A) R 1.00 1.50
41 Rebel Crew Chief R 1.00 1.50
42 Rebel Lieutenant R 1.00 1.50
43 Regroup on Yavin R 1.00 1.50
44 Sandtrooper R 1.00 1.50
45 Starfighter's End R 1.00 1.50
46 Stormtrooper TK-421 R 1.00 1.50
47 Strategy Session R 1.00 1.50
48 Strike Me Down R 1.00 1.50
49 Surprise Attack R 1.00 1.50
50 Tantive IV (A) R 1.00 1.50
51 Tarkin's Stench R 1.00 1.50
52 TIE Fighter Elite Pilot U .30 .50
53 Tiree (A) R 1.00 1.50
54 Tractor Beam R 1.00 1.50
55 URoRRuR'R'R (A) R 1.00 1.50
56 Imperial Manipulation R 1.00 1.50
57 Vader's Leadership R 1.00 1.50
58 Vader's TIE Fighter (A) R 1.00 1.50
59 Wedge Antilles (A) R 1.00 1.50
60 Yavin 4 Hangar Base R 1.00 1.50
61 Astromech Assistance U .30 .50
62 Benefits of Training U .30 .50
63 Biggs Darklighter (A) U .30 .50
64 C-3PO (C) U .30 .50
65 Commander Praji (A) U .30 .50
66 Tatooine Sandcrawler U .30 .50
67 Darth Vader (B) U .30 .50
68 Death Star Hangar Bay U .30 .50
69 Death Star Plans U .30 .50
70 Death Star Scanning Technician U .30 .50
71 Death Star Superlaser Gunner U .30 .50
72 Death Star Turbolaser Gunner U .30 .50
73 Demonstration of Power U .30 .50
74 Devastator (A) U .30 .50
75 Dissolve the Senate U .30 .50
76 Error in Judgment U .30 .50
77 Fate of the Dragon U .30 .50
78 General Dodonna (A) U .30 .50
79 General Tagge (A) U .30 .50
80 Han's Courage U .30 .50
81 Imperial Control Station U .30 .50
82 Imperial Navy Lieutenant U .30 .50
83 Insignificant Power U .30 .50
84 Into the Garbage Chute C .15 .25
85 Jawa U .30 .50
86 Jawa Collection Team U .30 .50
87 Jedi Extinction U .30 .50
88 Jon Dutch Vander (A) U .30 .50
89 Learning the Force U .30 .50
90 Lieutenant Tanbris (A) U .30 .50
91 LIN Demolitionmech U .30 .50
92 Luke Skywalker (C) U .30 .50
93 Luke's Warning U .30 .50
94 Mounted Stormtrooper U .30 .50
95 Mouse Droid U .30 .50
96 Obi-Wan Kenobi (F) U .30 .50
97 Oil Bath U .30 .50
98 Princess Leia (B) U .30 .50
99 R2-D2 (C) U .30 .50
100 Rebel Blockade Runner U .30 .50
101 Rebel Control Officer U .30 .50
102 Rebel Control Post U .30 .50
103 Rebel Marine U .30 .50
104 Rebel Surrender U .30 .50
105 Rebel Trooper U .30 .50
106 Remote Seeker Droid U .30 .50
107 Press the Advantage U .30 .50
108 Stabilize Deflectors U .30 .50
109 Star Destroyer Commander U .30 .50
110 Stormtrooper Charge U .30 .50
111 Stormtrooper DV-692 U .30 .50
112 Stormtrooper Squad Leader U .30 .50
113 Stormtrooper TK-119 U .30 .50
114 Support in the Senate U .30 .50
115 Disrupt the Power System U .30 .50
116 Tatooine Speeder U .30 .50
117 Tusken Sharpshooter U .30 .50
118 Vader's Interference U .30 .50
119 Vader's TIE Fighter (B) U 1.00 1.50
120 Wuher (A) U .30 .50
121 Air Cover C .15 .25
122 Precise Blast C .15 .25
123 Stay Sharp C .15 .25
124 Carrack Cruiser C .15 .25
125 Darth Vader (C) C .15 .25
126 Death Star Cannon Tower C .15 .25
127 Death Star Guard Squad C .15 .25
128 Domesticated Bantha C .15 .25
129 Flare-S Swoop C .15 .25
130 Ground Support C .15 .25
131 Imperial Detention Block C .15 .25
132 Imperial Star Destroyer C .15 .25
133 Incom T-16 Skyhopper C .15 .25
134 Into Hiding C .15 .25
135 Jawa Squad C .15 .25
136 Jawa Supply Trip C .15 .25
137 Jump to Lightspeed C .15 .25
138 Luke Skywalker (D) C .15 .25
139 Luke's Repairs C .15 .25
140 Moisture Farm C .15 .25
141 Planetary Defense Turret C .15 .25
142 Nowhere to Run C .15 .25
143 Obi-Wan Kenobi (G) C .15 .25
144 Jedi Intervention C .15 .25
145 Obi-Wan's Plan C .15 .25
146 Penetrate the Shields C .15 .25
147 Preemptive Shot C .15 .25
148 Princess Leia (C) C .15 .25
149 Rebel Fighter Wing C .15 .25
150 Rebel Honor Company C .15 .25
151 Rebel Marine Squad C .15 .25
152 Rebel Pilot C .15 .25
153 Rebel Squad C .15 .25
154 Rescue C .15 .25
155 Slipping Through C .15 .25
156 SoruSuub V-35 Courier C .15 .25
157 Synchronized Assault C .15 .25
158 Stormtrooper Assault Team C .15 .25
159 Stormtrooper DV-523 C .15 .25
160 Stormtrooper Patrol C .15 .25
161 Stormtrooper Squad C .15 .25
162 TIE Fighter DS-3-12 C .15 .25
163 TIE Fighter DS-73-3 C .15 .25
164 TIE Fighter DS-55-6 C .15 .25
165 TIE Fighter DS-61-9 C .15 .25
166 TIE Fighter Pilot C .15 .25
167 TIE Fighter Squad C .15 .25
168 Tusken Squad C .15 .25
169 Vader's Grip U .15 .25
170 Victory-Class Star Destroyer C .15 .25
171 Well-Aimed Shot C .15 .25
172 X-wing Red One C .15 .25
173 X-wing Red Three C .15 .25
174 X-wing Red Two C .15 .25
175 X-wing Attack Formation C .15 .25
176 Y-wing Gold One C .15 .25
177 Y-wing Gold Squadron C .15 .25
178 YT-1300 Transport C .15 .25
179 YV-664 Light Freighter C .15 .25
180 Z-95 Headhunter C .15 .25

2002 Star Wars Sith Rising

COMPLETE SET (90) 15.00 40.00
BOOSTER BOX (36 PACKS) 25.00 50.00
BOOSTER PACK (11 CARDS) 1.00 2.00
*FOIL: .75X TO 2X BASIC CARDS
RELEASED IN JULY 2002
1 Aayla Secura (A) R 1.00 1.50
2 Anakin Skywalker (E) R 1.00 1.50
3 Aurra Sing (A) R 1.00 1.50
4 Chancellor Palpatine (B) R 1.00 1.50
5 Clone Captain R 1.00 1.50
6 Clone Facility R 1.00 1.50
7 Darth Maul (A) R 1.00 1.50
8 Darth Maul (C) R 1.00 1.50
9 Darth Sidious (B) R 1.00 1.50
10 Darth Tyranus (D) R 1.00 1.50
11 Geonosian Picadors R 1.00 1.50
12 Impossible Victory R 1.00 1.50
13 Jango Fett (E) R 1.00 1.50
14 Jedi Bravery R 1.00 1.50
15 Jedi Starfighter Wing R 1.00 1.50
16 Jocasta Nu (A) R 1.00 1.50
17 Mace Windu (A) R 1.00 1.50
18 Mace Windu (C) R 1.00 1.50
19 Massiff R 1.00 1.50
20 Nute Gunray (B) R 1.00 1.50
21 Republic Drop Ship R 1.00 1.50
22 Sio Bibble (A) R 1.00 1.50
23 Sith Infiltrator (A) R 1.00 1.50
24 Slave I (B) R 1.00 1.50
25 Super Battle Droid 5TE R 1.00 1.50
26 Trade Federation Control Core R 1.00 1.50
27 Tusken Camp R 1.00 1.50
28 Twilight of the Republic R 1.00 1.50
29 Unfriendly Fire R 1.00 1.50
30 Yoda (C) R 1.00 1.50
31 Aiwha Rider U .30 .50
32 C-3PO (B) U .30 .50
33 Careful Targeting U .30 .50
34 Clever Escape U .30 .50
35 Clone Trooper 6/298 U .30 .50
36 Darth Maul (B) U .30 .50
37 Darth Tyranus (E) U .30 .50
38 Destroyer Droid, W Series U .30 .50
39 Female Tusken Raider U .30 .50
40 Fog of War U .30 .50
41 Geonosian Scout U .30 .50
42 Hailfire Droid U .30 .50
43 Homing Spider Droid U .30 .50
44 Infantry Battle Droid U .30 .50
45 Jedi Heroes U .30 .50
46 Jedi Starfighter Scout U .30 .50
47 Mace Windu (B) U .30 .50
48 Moment of Truth U .30 .50
49 Obi_Wan Kenobi (D) U .30 .50
50 Out of His Misery U .30 .50
51 Padmé Amidala (E) U .30 .50
52 Passel Argente (A) U .30 .50
53 Price of Failure U .30 .50
54 R2-D2 (B) U .30 .50
55 Recognition of Valor U .30 .50
56 Sun Fac (A) U .30 .50
57 Techno Union Warship U .30 .50
58 Trade Federation Offensive U .30 .50
59 Tusken Raider U .30 .50
60 Visit the Lake Retreat U .30 .50
61 Acclamator-Class Assault Ship C .15 .25
62 Aggressive Negotiations C .15 .25
63 Anakin Skywalker (F) C .15 .25
64 AT-TE Troop Transport C .15 .25
65 Battle Droid Assault Squad C .15 .25
66 Brutal Assault C .15 .25
67 Clone Trooper Legion C .15 .25
68 Commerce Guild Cruiser C .15 .25
69 Commerce Guild Spider Droid C .15 .25
70 Concentrated Fire C .15 .25
71 Corsucant Speeder C .15 .25
72 Darth Maul (D) C .15 .25
73 Diplomatic Cruiser C .15 .25
74 Droid Starfighter DFS-1VR C .15 .25
75 Geonosian Artillery Battery C .15 .25
76 Geonosian Defense Fighter C .15 .25
77 Maul's Strategy C .15 .25
78 Mobile Assault Cannon C .15 .25
79 Naboo Starfighter Wing C .15 .25
80 Nubian Yacht C .15 .25
81 Padawan and Senator C .15 .25
82 Reassemble C-3PO C .15 .25
83 Republic LAAT/i Gunship C .15 .25
84 Retreat Underground R .15 .25
85 Run the Gauntlet C .15 .25
86 Senatorial Cruiser C .15 .25
87 Shoot Her or Something C .15 .25
88 Super Battle Droid Squad C .15 .25
89 Suppressing Fire C .15 .25
90 Trade Federation Warship C .15 .25

2003 Star Wars Battle of Yavin

COMPLETE SET (105) 60.00 120.00
BOOSTER BOX (36 PACKS) 30.00 50.00
BOOSTER PACK (11 CARDS) 2.50 5.00
*FOIL: .75X TO 2X BASIC CARDS
RELEASED IN MARCH 2003
1 Artoo's Repairs R 3.00 5.00
2 Blow This Thing R 2.50 4.00
3 Celebrate the Victory R 1.25 2.00
4 Chariot Light Assault Vehicle R 1.25 2.00
5 Chewbacca (B) R 6.00 10.00
6 Chewbacca (A) R 6.00 10.00
7 Chief Bast (A) R 3.00 5.00
8 Colonel Wulff Yularen (A) R 3.00 5.00
9 Darth Vader (D) R 6.00 10.00
10 Death Star (A) R 5.00 8.00
11 Death Star (C) R 5.00 8.00
12 Garven Dreis (A) R 2.00 3.00
13 Grand Moff Tarkin (A) R 5.00 8.00

14 Han Solo (B) R	8.00	12.00
15 Han Solo (A) R	6.00	10.00
16 Hero's Potential R	.30	.50
17 Jek Porkins (A) R	1.00	1.50
18 Lieutenant Shann Childsen (A) R	2.00	3.00
19 Luke Skywalker (E) R	6.00	10.00
20 Luke's Skyhopper (A) R	.30	.50
21 Luke's X-wing (B) R	3.00	5.00
22 Millennium Falcon (A) R	3.00	5.00
23 Millennium Falcon (B) R	3.00	5.00
24 Millennium Falcon (C) R	3.00	5.00
25 Obi-Wan Kenobi (H) R	6.00	10.00
26 Obi-Wan's Guidance R	1.25	2.00
27 Princess Leia (D) R	2.00	3.00
28 R2-X2 (A) R	2.00	3.00
29 R2-Q5 (A) R	2.00	3.00
30 Rebel Ground Crew Chief R	1.25	2.00
31 Second Wave R	2.00	3.00
32 Stormtrooper Commander R	6.00	10.00
33 Vader's Fury R	3.00	5.00
34 X-wing Squadron R	3.00	5.00
35 Your Powers Are Weak R	2.00	3.00
36 Alien Rage U	.60	1.00
37 C-3PO (D) U	.60	1.00
38 Chewbacca (C) U	.60	1.00
39 Commander Willard (A) U	.60	1.00
40 Countermeasures U	.60	1.00
41 Darth Vader (E) U	.60	1.00
42 Death Star (B) U	.60	1.00
43 Death Star Trooper U	.60	1.00
44 Deflectors Activated U	.60	1.00
45 Grand Moff Tarkin (B) U	.60	1.00
46 Grand Moff Tarkin (C) U	.60	1.00
47 Han Solo (C) U	.60	1.00
48 Heavy Fire Zone U	.60	1.00
49 Imperial Dewback U	.60	1.00
50 Interrogation Droid U	.60	1.00
51 Jawa Crawler U	.60	1.00
52 Jawa Scavenger U	.60	1.00
53 Labria (A) U	.60	1.00
54 Let the Wookiee Win U	.60	1.00
55 Luke Skywalker (F) U	.60	1.00
56 Luke's Speeder (B) U	.60	1.00
57 Mobile Command Base U	.60	1.00
58 Obi-Wan's Handiwork U	.60	1.00
59 Princess Leia (E) U	.60	1.00
60 R2-D2 (D) U	.60	1.00
61 Rebel Armored Freerunner U	.60	1.00
62 Refit on Yavin U	.60	1.00
63 Sabers Locked U	.60	1.00
64 Stormtrooper KE-829 U	.60	1.00
65 Tatooine Hangar U	.60	1.00
66 Tusken Raider Squad U	.60	1.00
67 Tusken War Party U	.60	1.00
68 Untamed Ronto U	.60	1.00
69 WED Treadwell U	.60	1.00
70 Womp Rat U	.60	1.00
71 Accelerate C	.30	.50
72 Blast It! C	.30	.50
73 Chewbacca (D) C	.30	.50
74 Corellian Corvette C	.30	.50
75 Creature Attack C	.30	.50
76 Luke Skywalker (G) C	.30	.50
77 Darth Vader (F) C	.30	.50
78 Death Star Turbolaser Tower C	.30	.50
79 Dewback Patrol C	.30	.50
80 Escape Pod C	.30	.50
81 Greedo's Marksmanship C	.30	.50
82 Han Solo (D) C	.30	.50
83 Han's Evasion C	.30	.50
84 Imperial Landing Craft C	.30	.50
85 Jawa Salvage Team C	.30	.50
86 Juggernaut U	.30	.50
87 Star Destroyer C	.30	.50
88 Malfunction C	.30	.50
89 Outrun C	.30	.50
90 Pilot's Speed C	.30	.50
91 Rebel Defense Team C	.30	.50
92 Sandtrooper Squad C	.30	.50
93 Stormtrooper Assault C	.30	.50
94 Stormtrooper TK-875 C	.30	.50
95 Stormtrooper Platoon C	.30	.50
96 Stormtrooper Regiment C	.30	.50
97 TIE Defense Squadron C	.30	.50
98 TIE Fighter DS-73-5 C	.30	.50
99 TIE Fighter DS-29-4 C	.30	.50
100 TIE Fighter DS-55-2 C	.30	.50
101 Trust Your Feelings C	.30	.50
102 Visit to Mos Eisley C	.30	.50
103 X-wing Red Squadron C	.30	.50
104 X-wing Red Ten C	.30	.50
105 Y-wing Gold Two C	.30	.50

2003 Star Wars The Empire Strikes Back

COMPLETE SET (210)	100.00	200.00
BOOSTER BOX (36 PACKS)	400.00	550.00
BOOSTER PACK (11 CARDS)	1.25	2.50
*FOIL: .75X TO 2X BASIC CARDS		
RELEASED IN NOVEMBER 2003		
1 2-1B Medical Droid (A) R	2.00	3.00
2 Admiral Firmus Piett (B) R	2.00	3.00
3 AT-AT Assault Group R	2.00	3.00
4 Avenger (A) R	6.00	10.00
5 Blizzard Force Snowtrooper R	2.00	3.00
6 Blizzard One (A) R	2.00	3.00
7 C-3PO (E) R	2.00	3.00
8 Captain Lorth Needa (A) R	2.00	3.00
9 Carbon Freezing Chamber R	8.00	12.00
10 Chewbacca (E) U	2.00	3.00
11 Chewbacca (G) R	2.00	3.00
12 Dack Ralter (A) R	2.00	3.00
13 Dangerous Gamble R	2.00	3.00
14 Dark Cave R	2.00	3.00
15 Darth Vader (H) R	3.00	5.00
16 Darth Vader (I) R	5.00	8.00
17 Decoy Tactics R	2.00	3.00
18 Desperate Times R	2.00	3.00
19 Echo Base R	5.00	8.00
20 Emperor's Bidding R	2.00	3.00
21 Emperor's Prize R	2.00	3.00
22 Executor (A) R	2.00	3.00
23 Failed for the Last Time R	2.00	3.00
24 Future Sight R	2.00	3.00
25 FX-7 Medical Droid (A) R	2.00	3.00
26 General Carlist Rieekan (A) R	2.00	3.00
27 General Maximilian Veers (B) R	2.00	3.00
28 Go for the Legs R	2.00	3.00
29 Han Solo (G) R	3.00	5.00
30 Jedi Test R	2.00	3.00
31 Jedi's Failure R	2.00	3.00
32 K-3PO (A) R	2.00	3.00
33 Kiss From Your Sister R	2.00	3.00
34 Lando Calrissian (A) R	4.00	6.00
35 Lando Calrissian (D) R	4.00	6.00
36 Lieutenant Wes Janson (A) R	3.00	5.00
37 Lobot (A) R	2.00	3.00
38 Luke Skywalker (J) R	10.00	15.00
39 Luke Skywalker (K) R	8.00	12.00
40 Luke's Snowspeeder (A) R	6.00	10.00
41 Luke's Wrath R	2.00	3.00
42 Luke's X-wing (c) R	3.00	5.00
43 Major Bren Derlin (A) R	2.00	3.00
44 Mara Jade (A) R	2.00	3.00
45 Millennium Falcon (E) R	3.00	5.00
46 Millennium Falcon (F) R	3.00	5.00
47 Millennium Falcon (G) R	3.00	5.00
48 Obi-Wan's Spirit (A) R	2.00	3.00
49 Occupation R	2.00	3.00
50 Parting of Heroes R	2.00	3.00
51 Planetary Ion Cannon R	2.00	3.00
52 Princess Leia (G) R	3.00	5.00
53 Quest for Truth R	2.00	3.00
54 R2-D2 (G) R	2.00	3.00
55 R2-D2's Heroism R	2.00	3.00
56 Rally the Defenders R	2.00	3.00
57 Sacrifice R	2.00	3.00
58 Search for the Rebels R	2.00	3.00
59 Stormtrooper Swarm R	2.00	3.00
60 Streets of Cloud City R	2.00	3.00
61 Toryn Farr (A) R	2.00	3.00
62 Vader's Imperial Shuttle (A) R	3.00	5.00
63 Wampa Cave R	2.00	3.00
64 Wedge Antilles (B) R	6.00	10.00
65 Wedge's Snowspeeder (A) R	6.00	10.00
66 Yoda (F) R	2.00	3.00
67 Yoda (G) R	2.00	3.00
68 Yoda (H) R	2.00	3.00
69 Yoda's Training R	2.00	3.00
70 Zev Senesca (A) R	2.00	3.00
71 3,720 to 1 U	.60	1.00
72 Admiral Firmus Piett (A) U	.60	1.00
73 Admiral Kendal Ozzel (A) U	.60	1.00
74 Outmaneuver Them U	.60	1.00
75 All Terrain Troop Transport U	.60	1.00
76 Anti-Infantry Laser Battery U	.60	1.00
77 Asteroid Field U	.60	1.00
78 AT-AT Driver U	.60	1.00
79 Blizzard Force AT-ST U	.60	1.00
80 Battle the Wampa U	.60	1.00
81 Cloud City Penthouse U	.60	1.00
82 Cloud City Prison U	.60	1.00
83 Bespin Twin-Pod Cloud Car U	.60	1.00
84 Blockade U	.60	1.00
85 Bright Hope (A) U	.60	1.00
86 C-3PO (F) U	.60	1.00
87 Change in Destiny U	.60	1.00
88 Chewbacca (F) R	.60	1.00
89 Darth Vader (G) R	.60	1.00
90 Darth Vader (K) U	.60	1.00
91 Death Mark U	.60	1.00
92 Derek Hobbie Klivian (A) U	.60	1.00
93 Don't Get All Mushy U	.60	1.00
94 Dragonsnake U	.60	1.00
95 Emergency Repairs U	.60	1.00
96 Carbon Freeze U	.60	1.00
97 Executor Bridge U	.60	1.00
98 Executor Hangar U	.60	1.00
99 Quicker Easier More Seductive U	.60	1.00
100 General Maximilian Veers (A) U	.60	1.00
101 Han Enchained U	.60	1.00
102 Han Solo (F) U	.60	1.00
103 Hoth Icefields U	.60	1.00
104 Imperial Fleet U	.60	1.00
105 Imperial Misdirection U	.60	1.00
106 Jungles of Dagobah U	.60	1.00
107 Lambda-Class Shuttle U	.60	1.00
108 Lando Calrissian (C) U	.60	1.00
109 Leia's Warning U	.60	1.00
110 Luke Skywalker (I) U	.60	1.00
111 Medical Center U	.60	1.00
112 Millennium Falcon (D) U	.60	1.00
113 Mynock U	.60	1.00
114 Painful Reckoning U	.60	1.00
115 Princess Leia (H) U	.60	1.00
116 Probe Droid U	.60	1.00
117 Probot U	.60	1.00
118 R2-D2 (F) U	.60	1.00
119 Rebel Fleet U	.60	1.00
120 Rebel Hoth Army U	.60	1.00
121 Rebel Trenches U	.60	1.00
122 Rebel Troop Cart U	.60	1.00
123 Redemption (A) U	.60	1.00
124 See You In Hell U	.60	1.00
125 Self Destruct U	.60	1.00
126 Shield Generator U	.60	1.00
127 Snowspeeder Rogue Ten U	.60	1.00
128 Snowspeeder Squad U	.60	1.00
129 Snowtrooper Elite Squad U	.60	1.00
130 Stormtrooper Sentry U	.60	1.00
131 Surprise Reinforcements U	.60	1.00
132 TIE Bomber Pilot U	.60	1.00
133 TIE Bomber Squad U	.60	1.00
134 TIE Pursuit Pilot U	.60	1.00
135 Torture Room U	.60	1.00
136 Vader's Call U	.60	1.00
137 Vicious Attack U	.60	1.00
138 Wampa U	.60	1.00
139 Yoda's Hut U	.60	1.00
140 725 to 1 C	.30	.50
141 All Terrain Armored Transport C	.30	.50
142 All Terrain Scout Transport C	.30	.50
143 Alter the Deal C	.30	.50
144 Antivehicle Laser Cannon C	.30	.50
145 Armor Plating C	.30	.50
146 Space Slug C	.30	.50
147 Blizzard Force AT-AT C	.30	.50
148 Precise Attack C	.30	.50
149 Belly of the Beast C	.30	.50
150 Cloud City Battleground C	.30	.50
151 Cloud City Dining Hall C	.30	.50
152 Cloud City Landing Platform C	.30	.50
153 Bespin System C	.30	.50
154 Blizzard C	.30	.50
155 Bogwing C	.30	.50
156 Close the Shield Doors C	.30	.50
157 Darth Vader (J) C	.30	.50
158 Vader's Vengeance C	.30	.50
159 Dagobah System C	.30	.50
160 Explore the Swamps C	.30	.50
161 Float Away C	.30	.50
162 Force Throw C	.30	.50
163 Gallofree Medium Transport C	.30	.50
164 Ground Assault C	.30	.50
165 Han Solo (E) C	.30	.50
166 Han's Attack U	.30	.50
167 Han's Promise C	.30	.50
168 Hanging Around C	.30	.50
169 Hope of Another C	.30	.50
170 Hoth Battle Plains C	.30	.50
171 Hoth System C	.30	.50
172 Imperial II-Class Star Destroyer C	.30	.50
173 Jedi Master's Meditation C	.30	.50
174 Jedi Trap C	.30	.50
175 Kuat Lancer-Class Frigate C	.30	.50
176 Kuat Nebulon-B Frigate C	.30	.50
177 Lando Calrissian (B) C	.30	.50
178 Lando's Repairs C	.30	.50
179 Leap into the Chasm C	.30	.50
180 Luke Skywalker (H) C	.30	.50
181 Meditation Chamber C	.30	.50
182 Navy Trooper C	.30	.50
183 Princess Leia (F) C	.30	.50
184 Probe the Galaxy C	.30	.50
185 Rebel Command Center C	.30	.50
186 Rebel Escape Squad C	.30	.50
187 Rebel Hangar C	.30	.50
188 Rebel Trench Defenders C	.30	.50
189 Rebel Assault Frigate C	.30	.50
190 Dreadnaught Heavy Cruiser C	.30	.50
191 Snowspeeder Rogue Two C	.30	.50
192 Snowstorm C	.30	.50
193 Snowtrooper Heavy Weapons Team C	.30	.50
194 Snowtrooper Squad C	.30	.50
195 Snowtrooper Guard C	.30	.50
196 Imperial II Star Destroyer C	.30	.50
197 Strange Lodgings C	.30	.50
198 Swamps of Dagobah C	.30	.50
199 Tauntaun C	.30	.50
200 Tauntaun Mount C	.30	.50
201 TIE Bomber EX-1-2 C	.30	.50
202 TIE Bomber EX-1-8 C	.30	.50
203 TIE Fighter EX-4-9 C	.30	.50
204 TIE Fighter OS-72-8 C	.30	.50
205 TIE Pursuit Squad C	.30	.50
206 Trust Her Instincts C	.30	.50
207 Visions of the Future C	.30	.50
208 Well-Earned Meal C	.30	.50
209 X-wing Rogue Seven C	.30	.50
210 Y-wing Gold Six C	.30	.50

2003 Star Wars Jedi Guardians

COMPLETE SET (105)	60.00	120.00
BOOSTER BOX (36 PACKS)	120.00	250.00
BOOSTER PACK (11 CARDS)	5.00	7.00
*FOIL: .75X TO 2X BASIC CARDS		
RELEASED IN JULY 2003		
1 Adi Gallia (A) R	2.00	3.00
2 Anakin Skywalker (H) R	2.00	3.00
3 Aurra Sing (B) R	2.00	3.00
4 Boba Fett (B) R	2.00	3.00
5 Coup de Grace U	2.00	3.00
6 Dark Dreams R	2.00	3.00
7 Darth Maul (E) R	5.00	8.00
8 Darth Sidious (C) R	2.00	3.00
9 Darth Tyranus (F) R	3.00	5.00
10 Eeth Koth (A) R	2.00	3.00
11 Even Piell (A) R	2.00	3.00
12 Furious Charge C	2.00	3.00
13 Gather the Council R	2.00	3.00
14 Guidance of the Chancellor C	2.00	3.00
15 Homing Missile R	2.00	3.00
16 Jango Fett (G) R	2.00	3.00
17 Jedi Council Quorum R	2.00	3.00
18 Jedi Youngling R	2.00	3.00
19 Ki-Adi-Mundi (A) R	2.00	3.00
20 Kouhun R	2.00	3.00
21 Mace Windu (D) R	4.00	6.00
22 Trade Federation Battle Freighter C	2.00	3.00
23 Obi-Wan Kenobi (I) R	2.00	3.00
24 Obi-Wan's Starfighter (B) R	3.00	5.00
25 Oppo Rancisis (A) R	2.00	3.00
26 Padme Amidala (F) R	3.00	5.00
27 Plo Koon (B) R	2.00	3.00
28 R2-D2 (E) R	2.00	3.00
29 Remember the Prophecy R	2.00	3.00
30 Saesee Tiin (A) R	3.00	5.00
31 Senator Tikkes (A) R	2.00	3.00
32 Shaak Ti (B) R	3.00	5.00
33 Shmi Skywalker (A) R	3.00	5.00
34 Slave I (C) R	2.00	3.00
35 Trade Federation Blockade Ship C	2.00	3.00
36 Rapid Recovery R	2.00	3.00
37 Tipoca Training Ground R	2.00	3.00
38 Trade Federation Core Ship C	2.00	3.00
39 Tyranus's Geonosis Speeder (B) C	2.00	3.00
40 Unified Attack U	2.00	3.00
41 Yoda (D) R	8.00	12.00
42 Zam Wesell (D) R	2.00	3.00
43 Zam's Airspeeder (B) R	2.00	3.00
44 Battle Droid Division U	.60	1.00
45 Battle Protocol Droid (A) U	.60	1.00
46 Call for Reinforcements U	.60	1.00

47 Tyranus's Power C .60 1.00
48 Clone Cadet U .60 1.00
49 Coleman Trebor (A) U .60 1.00
50 Corporate Alliance Tank Droid U .60 1.00
51 Coruscant Air Bus U .60 1.00
52 Depa Billaba (A) U .60 1.00
53 Executioner Cart U .60 1.00
54 FA-4 (A) U .60 1.00
55 Jango Fett (F) U .60 1.00
56 Jedi Arrogance U .60 1.00
57 Jedi Training Exercise U .60 1.00
58 Jedi Knight's Survival U .60 1.00
59 Jedi Superiority U .60 1.00
60 Lightsaber Gift U .60 1.00
61 Lightsaber Loss U .60 1.00
62 Neimoidian Shuttle (A) U .60 1.00
63 Obi-Wan Kenobi (J) U .60 1.00
64 Orray U .60 1.00
65 Padme's Yacht (B) U .60 1.00
66 Underworld Investigations C .60 1.00
67 Protocol Battle Droid (A) U .60 1.00
68 Qui-Gon Jinn (B) U .60 1.00
69 Republic Communications Tower U .60 1.00
70 RIC-920 U .60 1.00
71 Sun-Fac (B) U .60 1.00
72 Tactical leadership U .60 1.00
73 Tame the Beast U .60 1.00
74 Train For War U .60 1.00
75 Tyranus's Return U .60 1.00
76 Tyranus's Solar Sailer (B) U .60 1.00
77 Yoda (E) U .60 1.00
78 Zam Wesell (C) U .60 1.00
79 Anakin Skywalker (I) C .30 .50
80 Mobile Artillery Division C .30 .50
81 Captured Reek C .30 .50
82 Clone Fire Team C .30 .50
83 Close Pursuit C .30 .50
84 Darth Tyranus (G) C .30 .50
85 Destroyer Droid Team U .30 .50
86 Diplomatic Barge C .30 .50
87 Droid Deactivation C .30 .50
88 Droid Starfighter Assault Wing C .30 .50
89 Trade Federation Droid Bomber C .30 .50
90 Forward Command Center C .30 .50
91 Geonosian Fighter Escort C .30 .50
92 Gondola Speeder C .30 .50
93 Gunship Offensive C .30 .50
94 Jedi Starfighter Squadron C .30 .50
95 Obi-Wan's Maneuver C .30 .50
96 Plan for the Future C .30 .50
97 Republic Assault Transport C .30 .50
98 Republic Attack Gunship C .30 .50
99 Republic Light Assault Cruiser C .30 .50
100 Republic Hyperdrive Ring C .30 .50
101 Sabaoth Starfighter C .30 .50
102 Scurrier C .30 .50
103 Separatist Battle Droid C .30 .50
104 Shaak C .30 .50
105 Synchronized Systems C .30 .50

2004 Star Wars The Phantom Menace

COMPLETE SET (90) 50.00 100.00
BOOSTER BOX (36 PACKS) 200.00 250.00
BOOSTER PACK (11 CARDS) 1.50 3.00
*FOIL: .75X TO 2X BASIC CARDS
RELEASED IN JULY 2004
1 Ann and Tann Gella (A) R 3.00 5.00
2 Aurra Sing (C) R 2.00 3.00
3 Bongo Sub R 2.00 3.00
4 Boss Nass (A) R 2.00 3.00
5 C-9979 R 2.00 3.00
6 Corridors of Power R 2.00 3.00
7 Dark Woman (A) R 3.00 5.00
8 Darth Maul (F) R 3.00 5.00
9 Duel of the Fates R 2.00 3.00
10 Fambaa Shield Beast R 2.00 3.00
11 Fight on All Fronts R 2.00 3.00
12 Gardulla the Hutt (A) R 2.00 3.00
13 Gas Attack R 2.00 3.00
14 Gungan Grand Army R 2.50 4.00
15 Guardian Mantis (A) R 2.00 3.00
16 In Disguise R 2.00 3.00
17 Jar Jar Binks (B) R 2.00 3.00
18 Jedi Temple R 2.00 3.00
19 Ki-Adi-Mundi (B) R 3.00 5.00
20 Marauder-Class Corvette R 2.00 3.00
21 Negotiate the Peace R 2.00 3.00
22 Nute Gunray (C) R 2.00 3.00
23 Orn Free Taa (A) R 2.00 3.00
24 Otoh Gunga R 2.00 3.00
25 Podracing Course R 2.00 3.00
26 Quinlan Vos (A) R 2.00 3.00
27 Sando Aqua Monster R 2.00 3.00
28 Sith Infiltrator (B) R 2.00 3.00
29 Walking Droid Starfighter R 2.00 3.00
30 Watto's Shop R 2.00 3.00
31 A'Sharad Hett (A) U 2.00 3.00
32 Anakin Skywalker (J) U 5.00 8.00
33 Anakin's Podracer (A) U 3.00 5.00
34 Bravo Starfighter U .60 1.00
35 Captain Panaka (A) U .60 1.00
36 Captain Tarpals (A) U .60 1.00
37 Citadel Cruiser U .60 1.00
38 Colo Claw Fish U .60 1.00
39 Discuss It in Committee U .60 1.00
40 Durge (A) U .60 1.00
41 Falumpaset U .60 1.00
42 Gungan Battle Wagon U .60 1.00
43 Gungan Catapult U .60 1.00
44 Inferno (A) U .60 1.00
45 Kaadu Scout U .60 1.00
46 Let the Cube Decide U .60 1.00
47 Modified YV-330 (A) U .60 1.00
48 Naboo System U .60 1.00
49 Qui-Gon Jinn (D) U .60 1.00
50 Ric Olié (A) U .60 1.00
51 Royal Cruiser U .60 1.00
52 Rune Haako (A) U .60 1.00
53 Sebulba (A) U .60 1.00
54 Sebulba's Podracer (A) U .60 1.00
55 Streets of Theed U .60 1.00
56 Trade Federation Hangar U .60 1.00
57 Trade Federation MTT U .60 1.00
58 Vilmarh Grahrk (A) U .60 1.00
59 Watto (B) U .60 1.00
60 Yaddle (A) U .60 1.00
61 A Bigger Fish C .30 .50
62 Aayla Secura (B) C .30 .50
63 Blockade (TPM) C .30 .50
64 Blockade Battleship C .30 .50
65 CloakShape Fighter C .30 .50
66 Darth Sidious (D) C .30 .50
67 Delta Six Jedi Starfighter C .30 .50
68 Eopie C .30 .50
69 Finis Valorum (B) C .30 .50
70 Flash Speeder C .30 .50
71 Gian Speeder C .30 .50
72 Gungan Kaadu Squad C .30 .50
73 Jedi Transport C .30 .50
74 Melt Your Way In C .30 .50
75 Mos Espa C .30 .50
76 Naboo Pilot C .30 .50
77 Obi-Wan Kenobi (K) C .30 .50
78 Opee Sea Killer C .30 .50
79 Podrace C .30 .50
80 Qui-Gon Jinn (C) C .30 .50
81 Sith Probe Droid C .30 .50
82 Sneak Attack C .30 .50
83 Swamps of Naboo C .30 .50
84 TC-14 (A) C .30 .50
85 Theed Power Generator C .30 .50
86 Theed Royal Palace C .30 .50
87 Trade Federation AAT C .30 .50
88 Trade Federation STAP C .30 .50
89 Unconventional Maneuvers C .30 .50
90 Yinchorri Fighter C .30 .50

2004 Star Wars Return of the Jedi

COMPLETE SET (109) 50.00 100.00
BOOSTER BOX (36 PACKS) 100.00 200.00
BOOSTER PACK (11 CARDS) 3.00 5.00
*FOIL: .75X TO 2X BASIC CARDS
RELEASED IN OCTOBER 2004
1 Admiral Ackbar (A) R 2.00 3.00
2 Anakin Skywalker (K) R 2.00 3.00
3 Anakin's Spirit (A) R 2.00 3.00
4 Bargain with Jabba R 2.00 3.00
5 Bib Fortuna (A) R 2.00 3.00
6 Chewbacca (J) R 2.00 3.00
7 Darth Vader (P) R 2.00 3.00
8 Death Star II (B) R 2.00 3.00
9 Emperor Palpatine (E) R 2.00 3.00
10 Endor Imperial Fleet R 2.00 3.00
11 Endor Rebel Fleet R 2.00 3.00
12 Endor Shield Generator R 2.00 3.00
13 Ephant Mon (A) R 2.00 3.00
14 Endor Regiment R 2.00 3.00
15 Free Tatooine R 2.00 3.00
16 Han Solo (K) R 2.00 3.00
17 Home One (A) R 2.00 3.00
18 Honor the Fallen R 2.00 3.00
19 Jabba the Hutt (A) R 2.00 3.00
20 Jabba's Dancers R 2.00 3.00
21 Jabba's Palace R 2.00 3.00
22 Jabba's Spies R 2.00 3.00
23 Lando Calrissian (H) R 2.00 3.00
24 Luke Skywalker (N) R 2.00 3.00
25 Malakili (A) R 2.00 3.00
26 Max Rebo Band (A) R 2.00 3.00
27 Mixed Battlegroup R 2.00 3.00
28 Mon Mothma (A) R 2.00 3.00
29 Nien Nunb (A) R 2.00 3.00
30 Occupied Tatooine R 2.00 3.00
31 Progress Report R 2.00 3.00
32 Rancor R 2.00 3.00
33 Reactor Core R 2.00 3.00
34 Salacious B. Crumb (A) R 2.00 3.00
35 Sarlacc (A) R 2.00 3.00
36 Scythe Squadron (A) R 2.00 3.00
37 Throne Room R 2.00 3.00
38 Trap Door! R 2.00 3.00
39 Vader's Guile R 2.00 3.00
40 Yoda's Spirit (A) R 2.00 3.00
41 Baited Trap U .60 1.00
42 Boba Fett (H) U .60 1.00
43 C-3PO (H) U .60 1.00
44 Captain Lennox (A) U .60 1.00
45 Chief Chirpa (A) U .60 1.00
46 Darth Vader (N) U .60 1.00
47 Desperate Bluff U .60 1.00
48 Emperor Palpatine (D) U .60 1.00
49 Ewok Village U .60 1.00
50 Free Bespin U .60 1.00
51 Free Endor U .60 1.00
52 Han Solo (J) U .60 1.00
53 Ionization Weapons U .60 1.00
55 Jabba the Hutt (C) U .60 1.00
56 Jabba's Sail Barge (A) U .60 1.00
57 Lando Calrissian (I) U .60 1.00
58 Luke Skywalker (O) U .60 1.00
59 Millennium Falcon (J) U .60 1.00
60 Occupied Bespin U .60 1.00
61 Occupied Endor U .60 1.00
62 Princess Leia (J) U .60 1.00
63 R2-D2 (I) U .60 1.00
64 Rancor Pit U .60 1.00
65 Red Squadron X-wing U .60 1.00
66 Skiff U .60 1.00
67 Vader's Summons U .60 1.00
68 Wicket W. Warrick (A) U .60 1.00
69 Wookiee Hug U .60 1.00
70 Worrt U .60 1.00
71 A-wing C .30 .50
72 B-wing C .30 .50
73 Cantina Bar Mob C .30 .50
74 Chewbacca (K) C .30 .50
75 Close Quarters C .30 .50
76 Elite Royal Guard C .30 .50
77 Darth Vader (O) C .30 .50
78 Death Star Battalion C .30 .50
79 Death Star II (A) C .30 .50
80 Decoy C .30 .50
81 Dune Sea C .30 .50
82 Elite Squad C .30 .50
83 Emperor Palpatine (C) C .30 .50
84 Ewok Artillery C .30 .50
85 Ewok Glider C .30 .50
86 Fly Casual C .30 .50
87 Force Lightning C .30 .50
88 Forest AT-AT C .30 .50
89 Forest AT-ST C .30 .50
90 Endor Attack Squad C .30 .50
91 Forests of Endor C .30 .50
92 Free Coruscant C .30 .50
93 Gray Squadron Y-wing C .30 .50
94 High-Speed Dodge C .30 .50
95 Imperial Speeder Bike C .30 .50
96 Imperial-Class Star Destroyer C .30 .50
97 Jabba's Guards C .30 .50
98 Lightsaber Throw C .30 .50
99 Log Trap C .30 .50
100 Luke Skywalker (M) C .30 .50
101 Mon Calamari Cruiser C .30 .50
102 Occupied Coruscant C .30 .50
103 Oola (A) C .30 .50
104 Princess Leia (K) C .30 .50
105 Rebel Scouts C .30 .50
106 Royal Guards C .30 .50
107 Scout Trooper C .30 .50
108 Surprising Strength C .30 .50
109 TIE Interceptor C .30 .50
110 Savage Attack C .30 .50

2004 Star Wars Rogues and Scoundrels

COMPLETE SET (105) 50.00 100.00
BOOSTER BOX (36 PACKS) 40.00 80.00
BOOSTER PACK (11 CARDS) 1.50 3.00
*FOIL: .75X TO 2X BASIC CARDS
RELEASED IN APRIL 2004
1 Admiral Firmus Piett (C) R 2.00 3.00
2 Boba Fett (G) R 2.00 3.00
3 Bossk (A) R 2.00 3.00
4 Call For Hunters R 2.00 3.00
5 Chewbacca (I) R 2.00 3.00
6 Commander Nemet (A) R 2.00 3.00
7 Dantooine System R 2.00 3.00
8 Dark Sacrifice R 2.00 3.00
9 Dengar (A) R 2.00 3.00
10 Doctor Evazan (A) R 2.00 3.00
11 Guri (A) R 2.00 3.00
12 Han Solo (I) R 2.00 3.00
13 Het Nkik (A) R 2.00 3.00
14 Hounds Tooth (A) R 2.00 3.00
15 IG-2000 (A) R 2.00 3.00
16 IG-88 (A) R 2.00 3.00
17 Dune Sea Krayt Dragon R 2.00 3.00
18 Lando Calrissian (F) R 2.00 3.00
19 Lando Calrissian (G) R 2.00 3.00
20 Lando's Influence R 2.00 3.00
21 Lobot (B) R 2.00 3.00
22 Mara Jade (B) R 2.00 3.00
23 Millennium Falcon (I) R 2.00 3.00
24 Mist Hunter (A) R 2.00 3.00
25 Modal Nodes (A) R 2.00 3.00
26 Prince Xizor (A) R 2.00 3.00
27 Princess Leia (I) R 2.00 3.00
28 Slave 1 (F) R 2.00 3.00
29 Stinger (A) R 2.00 3.00
30 Take A Prisoner R 2.00 3.00
31 Trash Compactor R 2.00 3.00
32 Virago (A) R 2.00 3.00
33 Yoda (I) R 2.00 3.00
34 Yoda's Lesson R 2.00 3.00
35 Zuckuss (A) R 2.00 3.00
36 4 Lom (A) U .60 1.00
37 AT-AT U .60 1.00
38 Bespin Cloud Car Squad U .60 1.00
39 Big Asteroid U .60 1.00
40 Boba Fett (F) U .60 1.00
41 C 3PO (G) U .60 1.00
42 Chewbacca (H) U .60 1.00
43 Cloud City Wing Guard U .60 1.00
44 Darth Vader (M) U .60 1.00
45 Death Star Control Room U .60 1.00
46 Garindan (A) U .60 1.00
47 Greedo (B) U .60 1.00
48 Han Solo (H) U .60 1.00
49 Han's Sacrifice U .60 1.00
50 Holoprojection Chamber U .60 1.00
51 Human Shield U .60 1.00
52 Kessel System U .60 1.00
53 Lando Calrissian (E) U .60 1.00
54 Lando's Trickery U .60 1.00
55 Luke Skywalker (L) U .60 1.00
56 Luke's X-wing (D) U .60 1.00
57 Millennium Falcon (H) U .60 1.00
58 Ponda Baba (A) U .60 1.00
59 Punishing One (A) U .60 1.00
60 R2-D2 (H) U .60 1.00
61 Redoubled Effort U .60 1.00
62 E-3PO (A) U .60 1.00
63 Slave 1 (E) U .60 1.00
64 Slave 1 (D) U .60 1.00
65 Space Slug (RaS) U .60 1.00
66 Outrider (A) U .60 1.00
67 Ugnaught U .60 1.00
68 Vendetta U .60 1.00
69 Enraged Wampa U .60 1.00
70 Lars Homestead U .60 1.00
71 2-1B's Touch C .30 .50
72 Bantha Herd C .30 .50
73 Base Guards C .30 .50
74 Bespin Patrol Cloud Car C .30 .50
75 Boba Fett (C) C .30 .50
76 Boba Fett (D) C .30 .50
77 Boba Fett (E) C .30 .50
78 Darth Vader (L) C .30 .50
79 Dash Rendar (A) C .30 .50
80 Disrupting Strike C .30 .50
81 Falcon's Needs C .30 .50
82 Jabba's Death Mark C .30 .50
83 Kabe (A) C .30 .50
84 Kyle Katarn (A) C .30 .50

85 Lando System? C	.30	.50
86 Leebo (A) C	.30	.50
87 Luke's Garage C	.30	.50
88 Luke's Vow C	.30	.50
89 Medium Asteroid C	.30	.50
90 Mos Eisley C	.30	.50
91 Mos Eisley Cantina C	.30	.50
92 Muftak C	.30	.50
93 No Good To Me Dead C	.30	.50
94 Ord Mantell System C	.30	.50
95 Sleen C	.30	.50
96 Small Asteroid C	.30	.50
97 Zutton (A) C	.30	.50
98 Star Destroyer (RaS) C	.30	.50
99 Stormtrooper Detachment C	.30	.50
100 Streets Of Tatooine C	.30	.50
101 Tatooine Desert C	.30	.50
102 Tie Fighter C	.30	.50
103 Tusken Warrior C	.30	.50
104 Unmodified Snowspeeder C	.30	.50
105 X Wing Escort C	.30	.50

2005 Star Wars Revenge of the Sith

COMPLETE SET (110)	50.00	100.00
BOOSTER BOX (36 PACKS)	30.00	60.00
BOOSTER PACK (11 CARDS)	1.25	2.50
*FOIL: .75X TO 2X BASIC CARDS		
RELEASED IN MAY 2005		
1 Anakin Skywalker (M) R	2.00	3.00
2 Bail Organa (B) R	2.00	3.00
3 Chewbacca (M) R	2.00	3.00
4 Commerce Guild Droid 81-X R	2.00	3.00
5 Commerce Guild Starship (ROTS) R	2.00	3.00
6 Coruscant Shuttle R	2.00	3.00
7 Darth Sidious (G) R	2.00	3.00
8 Darth Tyranus (I) R	2.00	3.00
9 Darth Vader (R) R	2.00	3.00
10 Darth Vader (S) R	2.00	3.00
11 Dismiss R	2.00	3.00
12 Droid Security Escort R	2.00	3.00
13 Engine Upgrade R	2.00	3.00
14 Foil R	2.00	3.00
15 Palpatine's Sanctum R	2.00	3.00
16 Grand Moff Tarkin (D) R	2.00	3.00
17 It Just Might Work R	2.00	3.00
18 Jar Jar Binks (C) R	2.00	3.00
19 Lightsaber Quick Draw R	2.00	3.00
20 Mace Windu (F) R	2.00	3.00
21 Mas Amedda (A) R	2.00	3.00
22 Mustafar Battle Grounds R	2.00	3.00
23 Mustafar System R	2.00	3.00
24 Nos Monster R	2.00	3.00
25 Obi-Wan Kenobi (N) R	2.00	3.00
26 Padmé Amidala (G) R	2.00	3.00
27 R4-P17 (A) R	2.00	3.00
28 Rage of Victory R	2.00	3.00
29 Recusant-Class Light Destroyer R	2.00	3.00
30 Republic Fighter Wing R	2.00	3.00
31 Sacrifice the Expendable R	2.00	3.00
32 Separatist Fleet R	2.00	3.00
33 Spinning Slash R	2.00	3.00
34 Strike with Impunity R	2.00	3.00
35 Stubborn Personality R	2.00	3.00
36 Super Battle Droid 7EX R	2.00	3.00
37 Theta-Class Shuttle R	2.00	3.00
38 Unexpected Attack R	2.00	3.00
39 Venator-Class Destroyer R	2.00	3.00
40 Yoda (K) R	2.00	3.00
41 Acclamator II-Class Assault Ship U	.60	1.00
42 AT-AP U	.60	1.00
43 C-3PO (I) U	.60	1.00
44 Chancellor's Office U	.60	1.00
45 Combined Squadron Tactics U	.60	1.00
46 Confusion U	.60	1.00
47 Darth Sidious (F) U	.60	1.00
48 Darth Vader (Q) U	.60	1.00
49 Destroyer Droid, Q Series U	.60	1.00
50 Droid Missiles U	.60	1.00
51 Elite Guardian U	.60	1.00
52 Hardcell-Class Transport U	.60	1.00
53 Jedi Concentration U	.60	1.00
54 Jedi Master's Deflection U	.60	1.00
55 Kashyyyk System U	.60	1.00
56 Naboo Star Skiff U	.60	1.00
57 Nute Gunray (D) U	.60	1.00
58 Obi-Wan Kenobi (L) U	.60	1.00
59 Padmé Amidala (H) U	.60	1.00
60 Patrol Mode Vulture Droid U	.60	1.00
61 GH-7 Medical Droid U	.60	1.00
62 R2-D2 (J) U	.60	1.00
63 Thread The Needle U	.60	1.00
64 Thwart U	.60	1.00
65 Treachery U	.60	1.00
66 Techno Union Interceptor U	.60	1.00
67 Utapau System U	.60	1.00
68 Vehicle Shields Package U	.60	1.00
69 Vehicle Weapons Package U	.60	1.00
70 Yoda (J) U	.60	1.00
71 Anakin Skywalker (L) C	.30	.50
72 Anakin's Starfighter (A) C	.30	.50
73 ARC-170 Starfighter C	.30	.50
74 AT-RT C	.30	.50
75 BARC Speeder C	.30	.50
76 Blaster Pistol C	.30	.50
77 Blaster Rifle C	.30	.50
78 Buzz Droid C	.30	.50
79 Chewbacca (L) C	.30	.50
80 Coruscant Emergency Ship C	.30	.50
81 Darth Sidious (E) C	.30	.50
82 Darth Tyranus (H) C	.30	.50
83 DC0052 Intergalactic Airspeeder C	.30	.50
84 Diving Attack C	.30	.50
85 Droid Battlestaff C	.30	.50
86 Droid Tri-Fighter C	.30	.50
87 Force Dodge C	.30	.50
88 HAVw A6 Juggernaut C	.30	.50
89 Homing Missiles Salvo C	.30	.50
90 IBC Hailfire Droid C	.30	.50
91 Instill Doubt C	.30	.50
92 InterGalactic Banking Clan Cruiser C	.30	.50
93 Jedi Lightsaber C	.30	.50
94 Jedi Piloting C	.30	.50
95 Meditate C	.30	.50
96 Obi-Wan Kenobi (M) C	.30	.50
97 Plo Koon's Starfighter (A) C	.30	.50
98 Power Attack C	.30	.50
99 Republic Assault Gunboat C	.30	.50
100 Security Droid C	.30	.50
101 Sith Lightsaber C	.30	.50
102 STAP Squad C	.30	.50
103 Surge of Strength C	.30	.50
104 Tank Droid C	.30	.50
105 TF Battle Droid Army C	.30	.50
106 Trade Federation Cruiser C	.30	.50
107 Unity of the Jedi C	.30	.50
108 Utapau Sinkhole C	.30	.50
109 Vulture Droid Starfighter C	.30	.50
110 V-wing Clone Starfighter C	.30	.50

2015 Star Wars Between the Shadows

12710633 A Hero's Trial	1.25	2.00
12720634 Luke Skywalker	1.25	2.00
12730635 Speeder Bike	1.25	2.00
12740636 Luke's Lightsaber	1.25	2.00
12750637 I Am a Jedi	1.25	2.00
12760065 Heat of Battle	1.25	2.00
12810638 The Master's Domain	1.25	2.00
12820639 Yoda	1.25	2.00
12830640 Bogwing	1.25	2.00
12840641 Yoda's Hut	1.25	2.00
12850089 Lightsaber Deflection	1.25	2.00
12860642 The Jedi's Resolve	1.25	2.00
12910643 Following Fate	1.25	2.00
12920644 Obi-Wan Kenobi	1.25	2.00
12930106 R2-D2	1.25	2.00
12940645 Obi-Wan's Lightsaber	1.25	2.00
12950646 Noble Sacrifice	1.25	2.00
12960133 Target of Opportunity	1.25	2.00
13010647 Journey Through the Swamp	1.25	2.00
13020648 Jubba Bird	1.25	2.00
13030648 Jubba Bird	1.25	2.00
13040649 Knobby White Spider	1.25	2.00
13050650 Life Creates It	1.25	2.00
13060651 Size Matters Not	1.25	2.00
13110652 Sacrifice at Endor	1.25	2.00
13120653 Ewok Hunter	1.25	2.00
13130653 Ewok Hunter	1.25	2.00
13140654 Funeral Pyre	1.25	2.00
13150655 Unexpected Assistance	1.25	2.00
13160656 Retreat to the Forest	1.25	2.00
13210657 Commando Raid	1.25	2.00
13220658 Lieutenant Judder Page	1.25	2.00
13230659 Page's Commandos	1.25	2.00
13240659 Page's Commandos	1.25	2.00
13250065 Heat of Battle	1.25	2.00
13260133 Target of Opportunity	1.25	2.00
13310660 Calling In Favors	1.25	2.00
13320661 Talon Karrde	1.25	2.00
13330662 Skipray Blastboat	1.25	2.00
13340662 Skipray Blastboat	1.25	2.00
13350663 Dirty Secrets	1.25	2.00
13360664 Clever Ruse	1.25	2.00
13410665 No Disintegrations	1.25	2.00
13420666 Boba Fett	1.25	2.00
13430667 Freelance Hunter	1.25	2.00
13440668 Flamethrower	1.25	2.00
13450378 Prized Possession	1.25	2.00
13460669 Entangled	1.25	2.00
13510670 Masterful Manipulation	1.25	2.00
13520671 Prince Xizor	1.25	2.00
13530672 Black Sun Headhunter	1.25	2.00
13540673 Debt Collector	1.25	2.00
13550674 Shadows of the Empire	1.25	2.00
13560675 The Prince's Scheme	1.25	2.00
13610676 All Out Brawl	1.25	2.00
13620677 Zekka Thyne	1.25	2.00
13630673 Debt Collector	1.25	2.00
13640678 Armed to the Teeth	1.25	2.00
13650669 Entangled	1.25	2.00
13660169 Heat of Battle	1.25	2.00
13710679 The Best That Credits Can Buy	1.25	2.00
13720680 Virago	1.25	2.00
13730672 Black Sun Headhunter	1.25	2.00
13740681 Rise of the Black Sun	1.25	2.00
13750682 Warning Shot	1.25	2.00
13760170 Target of Opportunity	1.25	2.00
13810683 The Hunters	1.25	2.00
13820684 Boushh	1.25	2.00
13830685 Snoova	1.25	2.00
13840686 A Better Offer	1.25	2.00
13850542 Pay Out	1.25	2.00
13860687 Show of Force	1.25	2.00
13910688 The Investigation	1.25	2.00
13920689 Ysanne Isard	1.25	2.00
13930690 Imperial Intelligence Officer	1.25	2.00
13940690 Imperial Intelligence Officer	1.25	2.00
13950691 Confiscation	1.25	2.00
13960692 Official Inquiry	1.25	2.00
14010693 Family Connections	1.25	2.00
14020694 General Tagge	1.25	2.00
14030695 Security Task Force	1.25	2.00
14040695 Security Task Force	1.25	2.00
14050696 Imperial Discipline	1.25	2.00
14060697 Precision Fire	1.25	2.00

2015 Star Wars Chain of Command

1611 A Hero's Beginning	1.25	2.00
1612 Luke's X-34 Landspeeder	1.25	2.00
1613 Owen Lars	1.25	2.00
1614 Moisture Vaporator	1.25	2.00
1615 Unfinished Business	1.25	2.00
1616 Supporting Fire	1.25	2.00
1621 Breaking the Blockade	1.25	2.00
1622 Smuggling Freighter	1.25	2.00
1623 Smuggling Freighter	1.25	2.00
1624 Duros Smuggler	1.25	2.00
1625 Duros Smuggler	1.25	2.00
1626 Surprising Maneuver	1.25	2.00
1631 The Imperial Bureaucracy	1.25	2.00
1632 Sate Pestage	1.25	2.00
1633 Advisor to the Emperor	1.25	2.00
1634 Quarren Bureaucrat	1.25	2.00
1635 Endless Bureaucracy	1.25	2.00
1636 Supporting Fire	1.25	2.00
1641 The Last Grand Admiral	1.25	2.00
1642 Grand Admiral Thrawn	1.25	2.00
1643 Noghri Bodyguard	1.25	2.00
1644 Noghri Bodyguard	1.25	2.00
1645 Chain of Command	3.00	5.00
1646 Supporting Fire	1.25	2.00
1651 Nar Shaddaa Drift	1.25	2.00
1652 Race Circut Champion	1.25	2.00
1653 Racing Swoop	1.25	2.00
1654 Racing Swoop	1.25	2.00
1655 Black Market Exchange	1.25	2.00
1656 Cut Off	1.25	2.00

2015 Star Wars Draw Their Fire

14610722 The Survivors	1.25	2.00
14620723 Qu Rahn	1.25	2.00
14630724 Sulon Sympathizer	1.25	2.00
14640725 Shien Training	1.25	2.00
14650061 Force Rejuvenation	1.25	2.00
14660256 Protection	1.25	2.00
14710726 Called to Arms	1.25	2.00
14720727 Gray Squadron Gunner	1.25	2.00
14730728 Gray Squadron Y-Wing	1.25	2.00
14740729 Advanced Proton Torpedoes	1.25	2.00
14750730 Desperation	1.25	2.00
14760133 Target of Opportunity	1.25	2.00
14810731 The Daring Escape	1.25	2.00
14820732 LE-B02D9	1.25	2.00
14830733 Outrider	1.25	2.00
14840734 Spacer Cantina	1.25	2.00
14850735 Punch It	1.25	2.00
14860702 Stay on Target	1.25	2.00
14910736 The Emperor's Sword	1.25	2.00
14920737 Maarek Stele	1.25	2.00
14930738 Delta One	1.25	2.00
14940739 Advanced Concussion Missiles	1.25	2.00
14950740 Hand of the Emperor	1.25	2.00
14960169 Heat of Battle	1.25	2.00
15010741 Guarding the Wing	1.25	2.00
15020742 DS-61-3	1.25	2.00
15030743 Black Squadron Fighter	1.25	2.00
15040743 Black Squadron Fighter	1.25	2.00
15050744 Elite Pilot Training	1.25	2.00
15060170 Target of Opportunity	1.25	2.00

2015 Star Wars Imperial Entanglement

17110838 House Edge	1.25	2.00
17120839 Lando Calrissian	1.25	2.00
17130840 Herglic Sabacc Addict	1.25	2.00
17140022 Cloud City Casino	1.25	2.00
17150841 Sabacc Shift	1.25	2.00
17160842 The Gambler's Trick	1.25	2.00
17210843 Debt of Honor	1.25	2.00
17220844 Chewbacca	1.25	2.00
17230845 Wookiee Defender	1.25	2.00
17240846 Kashyyyk Resistance Hideout	1.25	2.00
17250847 Wookiee Rage	1.25	2.00
17260256 Protection	1.25	2.00
17310848 Fortune and Fate	1.25	2.00
17320849 Lady Luck	1.25	2.00
17330850 Cloud City Technician	1.25	2.00
17340850 Cloud City Technician	1.25	2.00
17350851 Central Computer	1.25	2.00
17360133 Target of Opportunity	1.25	2.00
17410852 Honor Among Thieves	1.25	2.00
17420853 Mirax Terrik	1.25	2.00
17430854 Fringer Captain	1.25	2.00
17440854 Fringer Captain	1.25	2.00
17450855 Special Discount	1.25	2.00
17460856 One Last Trick	1.25	2.00
17510857 Renegade Reinforcements	1.25	2.00
17520858 Corporal Dansra Beezer	1.25	2.00
17530210 Renegade Squadron Operative	1.25	2.00
17540859 Hidden Backup	1.25	2.00
17550860 Directed Fire	1.25	2.00
17560861 Last Minute Reinforcements	1.25	2.00
17610862 Mysteries of the Rim	1.25	2.00
17620863 Outer Rim Mystic	1.25	2.00
17630863 Outer Rim Mystic	1.25	2.00
17640864 Niman Training	1.25	2.00
17650864 Niman Training	1.25	2.00
17660865 Force Illusion	1.25	2.00
17710866 Planning the Rescue	1.25	2.00
17720867 General Airen Cracken	1.25	2.00
17730868 Alliance Infiltrator	1.25	2.00
17740869 Superior Intelligence	1.25	2.00
17750870 Undercover	1.25	2.00
17760117 Rescue Mission	1.25	2.00
17810871 The Tarkin Doctrine	1.25	2.00
17820872 Grand Moff Tarkin	1.25	2.00
17830873 Stormtrooper Assault Team	1.25	2.00
17840874 Rule by Fear	1.25	2.00
17850875 Moment of Triumph	1.25	2.00
17860171 Twist of Fate	1.25	2.00
17910876 Might of the Empire	1.25	2.00
17920877 Chimaera	1.25	2.00
17930878 DP20 Corellian Gunship	1.25	2.00
17940879 Fleet Staging Area	1.25	2.00
17950392 Tractor Beam	1.25	2.00
17960880 The Empire Strikes Back	1.25	2.00
18010881 Enforced Loyalty	1.25	2.00
18020882 Colonel Yularen	1.25	2.00
18030883 Lieutenant Mithel	1.25	2.00
18040884 MSE-6 "Mouse" Droid	1.25	2.00
18050024 Control Room	1.25	2.00
18060885 The Imperial Fist	1.25	2.00
18110886 Imperial Entanglements	1.25	2.00
18120887 Imperial Raider	1.25	2.00
18130888 VT-49 Decimator	1.25	2.00
18140888 VT-49 Decimator	1.25	2.00
18150889 Customs Blockade	1.25	2.00
18160890 Ion Cannon	1.25	2.00
18210891 Phantoms of Imdaar	1.25	2.00
18220892 TIE Phantom	1.25	2.00
18230892 TIE Phantom	1.25	2.00
18240893 Enhanced Laser Cannon	1.25	2.00
18250894 Fighters Coming In!	1.25	2.00
18260169 Heat of Battle	1.25	2.00
18310895 Brothers of the Sith	1.25	2.00

18320896 Gorc	1.25	2.00
18330897 Pic	1.25	2.00
18340898 Telepathic Connection	1.25	2.00
18350062 Force Stasis	1.25	2.00
18360899 Force Invisibility	1.25	2.00
18410900 The Hutt's Menagerie	1.25	2.00
18420901 Malakili	1.25	2.00
18430902 Jabba's Rancor	1.25	2.00
18440903 Bubo	1.25	2.00
18450904 Underground Entertainment	1.25	2.00
18460905 Jabba's Summons	1.25	2.00

2015 Star Wars Jump to Lightspeed

1661 The Forgotten Masters	1.25	2.00
1662 T'ra Saa	1.25	2.00
1663 Lost Master	1.25	2.00
1664 Lost Master	1.25	2.00
1665 A Gift from the Past	1.25	2.00
1666 Echoes of the Force	1.25	2.00
1671 Heroes of the Rebellion	1.25	2.00
1672 Tycho Celchu	1.25	2.00
1673 Wes Janson	1.25	2.00
1674 Rogue Six	1.25	2.00
1675 Rogue Nine	1.25	2.00
1676 Ready for Takeoff	1.25	2.00
1681 That Bucket o' Bolts	1.25	2.00
1682 Han Solo	1.25	2.00
1683 Millennium Falcon	1.25	2.00
1684 Well Paid	1.25	2.00
1685 Well Paid	1.25	2.00
1686 Heat of Battle	1.25	2.00
1691 The Reawakening	1.25	2.00
1692 Arden Lyn	1.25	2.00
1693 Dark Side Apprentice	1.25	2.00
1694 Return to Darkness	1.25	2.00
1695 Give in to Your Anger	1.25	2.00
1696 Give in to Your Anger	1.25	2.00
1701 Behind the Black Sun	1.25	2.00
1702 Guri	1.25	2.00
1703 Freelance Assassin	1.25	2.00
1704 Hidden Vibroknife	1.25	2.00
1705 Threat Removal	1.25	2.00
1706 Heat of Battle	1.25	2.00

2015 Star Wars Ready for Takeoff

14110698 Rogue Squadron Assault	1.25	2.00
14120699 Derek "Hobbie" Klivian	1.25	2.00
14130700 Rogue Squadron X-Wing	1.25	2.00
14140700 Rogue Squadron X-Wing	1.25	2.00
14150701 Pilot Ready Room	1.25	2.00
14160702 Stay on Target	1.25	2.00
14210703 Memories of Taanab	1.25	2.00
14220704 Lando Calrissian	1.25	2.00
14230705 System Patrol Craft	1.25	2.00
14240705 System Patrol Craft	1.25	2.00
14250706 Conner Net	1.25	2.00
14260707 A Little Maneuver	1.25	2.00
14310708 Black Squadron Formation	1.25	2.00
14320709 "Mauler" Mithel	1.25	2.00
14330710 Black Two	1.25	2.00
14340146 TIE Advanced	1.25	2.00
14350711 Death Star Ready Room	1.25	2.00
14360712 Stay on Target	1.25	2.00
14410713 The Empire's Elite	1.25	2.00
14420714 Baron Fel	1.25	2.00
14430715 181st TIE Interceptor	1.25	2.00
14440715 181st TIE Interceptor	1.25	2.00
14450716 Flight Academy	1.25	2.00
14460712 Stay on Target	1.25	2.00
14510717 The Grand Heist	1.25	2.00
14520718 Niles Ferrier	1.25	2.00
14530719 Novice Starship Thief	1.25	2.00
14540719 Novice Starship Thief	1.25	2.00
14550720 Pirate Hideout	1.25	2.00
14560721 Salvage Operation	1.25	2.00

2016 Star Wars Destiny Awakening

COMPLETE SET (174)	450.00	650.00
BOOSTER BOX (36 PACKS)	80.00	120.00
BOOSTER PACK (5 CARDS AND 1 DICE)	4.00	6.00
RELEASED IN NOVEMBER, 2016		
1 Captain Phasma L	10.00	15.00
2 First Order Stormtrooper R	3.00	5.00
3 General Grievous R	3.00	5.00
4 General Veers R	3.00	5.00
5 AT ST L	8.00	12.00
6 First Order TIE Fighter R	3.00	5.00
7 Commanding Presence L	10.00	15.00
8 F 11D Rifle S	2.00	3.00
9 Count Dooku R	3.00	5.00
10 Darth Vader L	20.00	30.00
11 Kylo Ren S	1.50	2.50
12 Nightsister R	3.00	5.00
13 Force Choke L	12.00	20.00
14 Immobilize R	3.00	5.00
15 Kylo Rens Lightsaber L	12.00	20.00
16 Sith Holocron R	10.00	13.00
17 Infantry Grenades R	3.00	5.00
18 Speeder Bike Scout R	3.00	5.00
19 Bala Tik R	3.00	5.00
20 Jabba the Hutt L	15.00	25.00
21 Jango Fett R	3.00	5.00
22 Tusken Raider R	3.00	5.00
23 Crime Lord L	10.00	15.00
24 Flame Thrower R	3.00	5.00
25 Gaffi Stick R	3.00	5.00
26 On the Hunt R	3.00	5.00
27 Admiral Ackbar R	3.00	5.00
28 Leia Organa R	3.00	5.00
29 Poe Dameron L	15.00	25.00
30 Rebel Trooper R	3.00	5.00
31 Launch Bay L	6.00	10.00
32 Black One L	5.00	8.00
33 Scout R	3.00	5.00
34 Survival Gear R	3.00	5.00
35 Luke Skywalker L	15.00	25.00
36 Padawan R	3.00	5.00
37 Qui Gon Jinn R	3.00	5.00
38 Rey S	2.00	3.00
39 Force Protection R	3.00	5.00
40 Jedi Robes R	3.00	5.00
41 Luke Skywalkers Lightsaber L	10.00	15.00
42 One With the Force L	15.00	25.00
43 BB 8 R	3.00	5.00
44 Reys Staff R	3.00	5.00
45 Finn S	2.00	3.00
46 Han Solo L	12.00	20.00
47 Hired Gun R	3.00	5.00
48 Padme Amidala R	3.00	5.00
49 Millennium Falcon L	10.00	15.00
50 Diplomatic Immunity R	3.00	5.00
51 DL 44 Heavy Blaster Pistol R	3.00	5.00
52 Infiltrate R	3.00	5.00
53 Outpost R	3.00	5.00
54 DH 17 Blaster Pistol R	3.00	5.00
55 IQA 11 Blaster Rifle R	3.00	5.00
56 Promotion R	3.00	5.00
57 Force Throw S	6.00	10.00
58 Force Training R	3.00	5.00
59 Lightsaber S	2.00	3.00
60 Mind Probe S	5.00	8.00
61 Comlink R	3.00	5.00
62 Datapad R	3.00	5.00
63 Holdout Blaster R	12.00	20.00
64 Black Market R	3.00	5.00
65 Cunning R	3.00	5.00
66 Jetpack R	3.00	5.00
67 Thermal Detonator L	15.00	25.00
68 Cannon Fodder C	.15	.20
69 Closing the Net C	.15	.20
70 Endless Ranks U	1.25	2.00
71 Occupation C	.15	.20
72 Probe C	.15	.20
73 Sweep the Area C	.15	.20
74 Tactical Mastery U	2.00	3.00
75 The Best Defense U	.25	.40
76 Drudge Work C	.15	.20
77 Local Garrison U	.25	.40
78 Personal Escort C	.15	.20
79 Abandon All Hope U	.25	.40
80 Boundless Ambition C	.15	.20
81 Enrage C	.15	.20
82 Feel Your Anger C	.15	.20
83 Force Strike U	.75	1.25
84 Intimidate C	.15	.20
85 Isolation C	.15	.20
86 No Mercy U	2.00	3.00
87 Pulling the Strings C	.15	.20
88 Emperors Favor U	.25	.40
89 Power of the Dark Side S	.40	.60
90 Hidden in Shadow U	.25	.40
91 Nowhere to Run U	.25	.40
92 Ace in the Hole U	.75	1.25
93 Armed to the Teeth C	.15	.20
94 Confiscation U	.25	.40
95 Fight Dirty U	.25	.40
96 Go for the Kill C	.15	.20
97 He Doesnt Like You C	.15	.20
98 Lying in Wait C	.15	.20
99 Backup Muscle C	.15	.20
100 My Kind of Scum C	.15	.20
101 Underworld Connections U	1.00	1.50
102 Prized Possession U	.25	.40
103 Commando Raid U	.25	.40
104 Defensive Position C	.15	.20
105 Field Medic C	.15	.20
106 Hit and Run C	.15	.20
107 Its a Trap U	.75	1.25
108 Natural Talent C	.15	.20
109 Rearm U	.25	.40
110 Retreat U	.25	.40
111 Strategic Planning C	.15	.20
112 Surgical Strike C	.15	.20
113 Resistance HQ U	.25	.40
114 Anticipate U	.25	.40
115 Defensive Stance C	.15	.20
116 Force Misdirection C	.15	.20
117 Heroism C	.15	.20
118 Noble Sacrifice C	.15	.20
119 Patience C	.15	.20
120 Return of the Jedi U	.25	.40
121 Riposte C	.15	.20
122 Willpower U	.40	.60
123 Jedi Council U	.25	.40
124 Awakening S	.60	1.00
125 The Force is Strong C	.15	.20
126 Daring Escape U	.25	.40
127 Dont Get Cocky C	.15	.20
128 Draw Attention C	.15	.20
129 Hyperspace Jump U	.25	.40
130 Let the Wookiee Win U	.25	.40
131 Negotiate C	.15	.20
132 Scavenge C	.15	.20
133 Shoot First U	.25	.40
134 Smuggling C	.15	.20
135 Play the Odds U	.25	.40
136 Street Informants C	.15	.20
137 Second Chance U	1.50	2.50
138 Award Ceremony C	.15	.20
139 Dug In U	2.00	3.00
140 Firepower C	.15	.20
141 Leadership U	.40	.60
142 Logistics C	.15	.20
143 Squad Tactics C	.15	.20
144 Supporting Fire U	.25	.40
145 Deflect C	.15	.20
146 Disturbance in the Force C	.15	.20
147 Mind Trick U	.40	.60
148 The Power of the Force C	.15	.20
149 Use the Force S	.75	1.25
150 It Binds All Things U	1.25	2.00
151 Aim S	.50	.75
152 All In U	1.25	2.00
153 Block C	.15	.20
154 Close Quarters Assault S	1.00	1.50
155 Dodge C	.15	.20
156 Flank U	.25	.40
157 Take Cover C	.15	.20
158 Disarm C	.15	.20
159 Electroshock U	4.00	6.00
160 Reversal U	1.00	1.50
161 Scramble C	.15	.20
162 Unpredictable C	.15	.20
163 Infamous U	1.50	2.50
164 Hunker Down C	.15	.20
165 Command Center U	.25	.40
166 Echo Base U	.25	.40
167 Emperors Throne Room U	.25	.40
168 Frozen Wastes S	.60	1.00
169 Imperial Armory C	.15	.20
170 Jedi Temple C	.15	.20
171 Rebel War Room C	.15	.20
172 Mos Eisley Spaceport C	.15	.20
173 Separatist Base C	.15	.20
174 Starship Graveyard S	1.50	2.50

1999 Young Jedi Menace of Darth Maul

COMPLETE SET (140)	10.00	25.00
BOOSTER BOX (30 PACKS)	30.00	50.00
BOOSTER PACK (11 CARDS)	1.00	2.00
RELEASED ON MAY 12, 1999		
1 Obi-Wan Kenobi, Young Jedi R	3.00	5.00
2 Qui-Gon Jinn, Jedi Master R	2.50	4.00
3 Jar Jar Binks, Gungan Chuba Thief R	1.50	2.50
4 Anakin Skywalker, Podracer Pilot R	1.25	2.00
5 Padme Naberrie, Handmaiden R	2.00	3.00
6 Captain Panaka, Protector of the Queen R	1.25	2.00
7 Mace Windu, Jedi Master R	1.50	2.50
8 Queen Amidala, Ruler of Naboo R	2.00	3.00
9 Queen Amidala, Royal Leader R	2.00	3.00
10 Yoda, Jedi Master R	2.00	3.00
11 R2-D2, Astromech Droid R	1.50	2.50
12 C-3PO, Anakin's Creation R	1.50	2.50
13 Boss Nass, Leader of the Gungans U	.50	.75
14 Ric Olie, Ace Pilot U	.50	.75
15 Captain Tarpals, Gungan Guard U	.50	.75
16 Rabe, Handmaiden U	.50	.75
17 Rep Been, Gungan U	.50	.75
18 Mas Amedda, Vice Chancellor U	.50	.75
19 Naboo Officer, Battle Planner U	.50	.75
20 Naboo Security, Guard C	.15	.25
21 Bravo Pilot, Veteran Flyer C	.15	.25
22 Gungan Official, Bureaucrat C	.15	.25
23 Gungan Soldier, Scout C	.15	.25
24 Gungan Guard C	.15	.25
25 Gungan Warrior, Infantry C	.15	.25
26 Gungan Soldier, Veteran C	.15	.25
27 Ishi Tib, Warrior C	.15	.25
28 Ithorian, Merchant C	.15	.25
29 Jawa, Thief C	.15	.25
30 Jawa, Bargainer S	.15	.25
31 Royal Guard, Leader C	.15	.25
32 Royal Guard, Veteran C	.15	.25
33 Obi-Wan Kenobi, Jedi Padawan S	.15	.25
34 Obi-Wan Kenobi's Lightsaber R	1.50	2.50
35 Jedi Lightsaber	.50	.75
Constructed by Ki-Adi-Mundi U		
36 Anakin Skywalker's Podracer R	1.25	2.00
37 Captain Panaka's Blaster C	.15	.25
38 Jar Jar Binks' Electropole U	.50	.75
39 Electropole C	.15	.25
40 Eopie C	.15	.25
41 Kaadu C	.15	.25
42 Flash Speeder C	.15	.25
43 Jawa Ion Blaster C	.15	.25
44 Naboo Blaster C	.15	.25
45 Blaster C	.15	.25
46 Blaster Rifle C	.15	.25
47 Anakin Skywalker	.50	.75
Meet Obi-Wan Kenobi U		
48 Are You An Angel? U	.50	.75
49 Cha Skrunee Da Pat, Sleemo C	.15	.25
50 Counterparts U	.50	.75
51 Da Beings Hereabouts Cawazy C	.15	.25
52 Enough Of This Pretense U	.50	.75
53 Fear Attracts The Fearful U	.50	.75
54 Gungan Curiosity C	.15	.25
55 He Was Meant To Help You U	.50	.75
56 I Have A Bad Feeling About This U	.50	.75
57 I've Been Trained In Defense U	.50	.75
58 Security Volunteers C	.15	.25
59 Shmi's Pride U	.50	.75
60 The Federation Has Gone Too Far C	.15	.25
61 The Negotiations Were Short C	.15	.25
62 The Queen's Plan C	.15	.25
63 We're Not In Trouble Yet U	.50	.75
64 Yousa Guys Bombad! R	1.00	1.50
65 Tatooine Podrace Arena S	.15	.25
66 Coruscant Capital City S	.15	.25
67 Naboo Theed Palace S	.15	.25
68 Bravo 1, Naboo Starfighter U	.50	.75
69 Naboo Starfighter C	.15	.25
70 Republic Cruiser, Transport C	.15	.25
71 Darth Maul, Sith Apprentice R	4.00	6.00
72 Darth Sidious, Sith Master R	2.50	4.00
73 Sebulba, Bad-Tempered Dug R	1.50	2.50
74 Watto, Slave Owner R	1.25	2.00
75 Aurra Sing, Bounty Hunter R	2.00	3.00
76 Jabba the Hutt, Vile Crime Lord R	1.50	2.50
77 Gardulla the Hutt, Crime Lord U	.50	.75
78 Destroyer Droid Squad	1.00	1.50
Security Division R		
79 Battle Droid Squad, Assault Unit R	1.25	2.00
80 Ben Quadinaros, Podracer Pilot U	.50	.75
81 Gasgano, Podracer Pilot U	.50	.75
82 Mawhonic, Podracer Pilot U	.50	.75
83 Teemto Pagalies, Podracer Pilot U	.50	.75
84 Bib Fortuna, Twi'lek Advisor U	.50	.75
85 Ann and Tann Gella	.50	.75
Sebulba's Attendants U		
86 Gragra, Chuba Peddler C	.15	.25
87 Passel Argente, Senator C	.15	.25
88 Trade Federation Tank	1.25	2.00
Armored Division R		
89 Destroyer Droid, Wheel Droid C	.15	.25
90 Destroyer Droid, Defense Droid C	.15	.25
91 Sith Probe Droid, Spy Drone C	.15	.25
92 Pit Droid, Engineer C	.15	.25
93 Pit Droid, Heavy Lifter C	.15	.25
94 Pit Droid, Mechanic C	.15	.25
95 Tusken Raider, Nomad C	.15	.25
96 Tusken Raider, Marksman C	.15	.25
97 Battle Droid: Pilot, MTT Division C	.15	.25

98 Battle Droid: Security, MTT Division C .15 .25
99 Battle Droid: Infantry, MTT Division C .15 .25
100 Battle Droid: Officer, MTT Division C .15 .25
101 Battle Droid: Pilot, AAT Division C .15 .25
102 Battle Droid: Security, AAT Division C .15 .25
103 Battle Droid: Infantry, AAT Division C .15 .25
104 Battle Droid: Officer, AAT Division C .15 .25
105 Neimoidian, Trade Federation Pilot S .15 .25
106 Darth Maul, Sith Lord S .60 1.00
107 Sith Lightsaber R 1.25 2.00
108 Aurra Sing's Blaster Rifle R 1.00 1.50
109 Sebulba's Podracer R 1.00 1.50
110 Ben Quadinaros' Podracer U .50 .75
111 Gasgano's Podracer U .50 .75
112 Mawhonic's Podracer U .50 .75
113 Teemto Pagalies' Podracer U .50 .75
114 Trade Federation Tank Laser Cannon U .50 .75
115 Multi Troop Transport U .50 .75
116 STAP U .50 .75
117 Tatooine Thunder Rifle C .15 .25
118 Battle Droid Blaster Rifle C .15 .25
119 Blaster C .15 .25
120 Blaster Rifle C .15 .25
121 At Last We Will Have Revenge R 1.00 1.50
122 Begin Landing Your Troops C .15 .25
123 Boonta Eve Podrace U .50 .75
124 Grueling Contest U .50 .75
125 In Complete Control C .15 .25
126 Kaa Bazza Kundee Hodrudda! U .50 .75
127 Opee Sea Killer C .15 .25
128 Podrace Preparation U .50 .75
129 Sandstorm C .15 .25
130 Sniper C .15 .25
131 The Invasion Is On Schedule C .15 .25
132 Vile Gangsters U .50 .75
133 Watto's Wager U .50 .75
134 You Have Been Well Trained R 1.00 1.50
135 Tatooine Desert Landing Site S .15 .25
136 Coruscant Jedi Council Chamber S .15 .25
137 Naboo Gungan Swamp S .15 .25
138 Darth Maul's Starfighter
Sith Infiltrator R 1.50 2.50
139 Droid Starfighter C .15 .25
140 Battleship
Trade Federation Transport C .15 .25

1999 Young Jedi Menace of Darth Maul Foil

COMPLETE SET (18) 6.00 15.00
RELEASED ON MAY 12, 1999
F1 Obi-Wan Kenobi, Young Jedi R 4.00 6.00
F2 Jar-Jar Binks, Gungan Chuba Thief R 2.00 3.00
F3 Mace Windu, Jedi Master U 2.00 3.00
F4 Queen Amidala, Ruler of Naboo U 3.00 5.00
F5 C-3PO, Anakin's Creation U 2.00 3.00
F6 Obi-Wan Kenobi's Lightsaber C 1.50 2.50
F7 Anakin Skywalker's Podracer C 1.25 2.00
F8 Bravo 1, Naboo Starfighter C .60 1.00
F9 Republic Cruiser, Transport C .60 1.00
F10 Darth Maul, Sith Apprentice R 5.00 8.00
F11 Darth Sidious, Sith Master R 3.00 5.00
F12 Destroyer Droid Squad
Security Division U 1.00 1.50
F13 Battle Droid Squad, Assault Unit U 1.00 1.50
F14 Sebulba's Podracer U 1.00 1.50
F15 Ben Quadinaros' Podracer C .60 1.00
F16 Gasgano's Podracer C .60 1.00
F17 Mawhonic's Podracer C .60 1.00
F18 Teemto Pagalies' Podracer C .60 1.00

1999 Young Jedi The Jedi Council

COMPLETE SET (140) 8.00 20.00
BOOSTER BOX (30 PACKS) 20.00 30.00
BOOSTER BOX (11 CARDS) .75 1.25
RELEASED ON OCTOBER 27, 1999
1 Obi-Wan Kenobi, Jedi Apprentice R 2.50 4.00
2 Qui-Gon Jinn, Jedi Protector R 2.00 3.00
3 Jar Jar Binks, Gungan Outcast R 1.25 2.00
4 Anakin Skywalker, Child of Prophecy R 1.25 2.00
5 Padme Naberrie, Queen's Handmaiden R 1.50 2.50
6 Captain Panaka, Amidala's Bodyguard R 1.00 1.50
7 Mace Windu
Senior Jedi Council Member R 1.25 2.00
8 Queen Amidala, Representative of Naboo R 1.50 2.50
9 Queen Amidala, Voice of Her People R 1.50 2.50
10 Yoda, Jedi Council Member R 1.50 2.50
11 R2-D2, Loyal Droid R 1.25 2.00
12 Ki-Adi-Mundi, Cerean Jedi Knight R 1.25 2.00
13 Adi Gallia, Corellian Jedi Master U .50 .75
14 Depa Billaba, Jedi Master U .50 .75
15 Eeth Koth, Zabrak Jedi Master U .50 .75
16 Even Piell, Lannik Jedi Master U .50 .75
17 Oppo Rancisis, Jedi Master U .50 .75
18 Plo Koon, Jedi Master U .50 .75
19 Saesee Tiin, Iktotchi Jedi Master U .50 .75
20 Yaddle, Jedi Master U .50 .75
21 Yarael Poof, Quermian Jedi Master U .50 .75
22 Boss Nass, Gungan Leader U .50 .75
23 Ric Olié, Chief Pilot U .50 .75
24 Captain Tarpals, Gungan Battle Leader U .50 .75
25 Eirtae, Handmaiden U .50 .75
26 Valorum, Supreme Chancellor C .15 .25
27 Sci Taria, Chancellor's Aide C .15 .25
28 Naboo Officer, Liberator C .15 .25
29 Bravo Pilot, Naboo Volunteer C .15 .25
30 Naboo Security, Amidala's Guard C .15 .25
31 Republic Captain, Officer C .15 .25
32 Republic Pilot, Veteran C .15 .25
33 Coruscant Guard
Coruscant Detachment C .15 .25
34 Coruscant Guard, Peacekeeper C .15 .25
35 Coruscant Guard, Officer C .15 .25
36 Coruscant Guard, Chancellor's Guard C .15 .25
37 Wookiee Senator, Representative C .15 .25
38 Galactic Senator, Delegate S .15 .25
39 Obi-Wan Kenobi, Jedi Warrior S .15 .25
40 Qui-Gon Jinn's Lightsaber R 1.00 1.50
41 Amidala's Blaster R 1.00 1.50
42 Adi Gallia's Lightsaber U .50 .75
43 Coruscant Guard Blaster Rifle U .50 .75
44 Ascension Gun C .15 .25
45 Electropole C .15 .25
46 Kaadu C .15 .25
47 Flash Speeder C .15 .25
48 Gian Speeder C .15 .25
49 Naboo Blaster C .15 .25
50 Blaster C .15 .25
51 Blaster Rifle C .15 .25
52 Balance To The Force U .50 .75
53 Brave Little Droid U .50 .75
54 Dos Mackineeks No Comen Here! C .15 .25
55 Galactic Chancellor C .15 .25
56 Hate Leads To Suffering U .50 .75
57 I Will Not Cooperate U .50 .75
58 Invasion! C .15 .25
59 May The Force Be With You C .15 .25
60 Senator Palpatine C .15 .25
61 The Might Of The Republic C .15 .25
62 We Don't Have Time For This C .15 .25
63 We Wish To Board At Once C .15 .25
64 Wisdom Of The Council R 1.00 1.50
65 Tatooine Mos Espa S .15 .25
66 Coruscant Jedi Council Chamber S .15 .25
67 Naboo Gungan Swamp S .15 .25
68 Bravo 2, Naboo Starfighter U .50 .75
69 Naboo Starfighter C .15 .25
70 Radiant VII, Republic Cruiser Transport C .15 .25
71 Darth Maul, Master of Evil R 3.00 5.00
72 Darth Sidious, Lord of the Sith R 2.00 3.00
73 Sebulba, Podracer Pilot R 1.25 2.00
74 Watto, Junk Merchant R 1.00 1.50
75 Jabba the Hutt, Gangster R 1.25 2.00
76 Nute Gunray, Neimoidian Viceroy R 1.00 1.50
77 Rune Haako, Neimoidian Advisor R 1.00 1.50
78 Destroyer Droid Squad, Defense Division R 1.00 1.50
79 Battle Droid Squad, Escort Unit R 1.00 1.50
80 Trade Federation Tank, Assault Division R 1.00 1.50
81 Lott Dod, Neimoidian Senator R 1.00 1.50
82 Fode and Beed, Podrace Announcer R 1.00 1.50
83 Clegg Holdfast, Podracer Pilot U .50 .75
84 Dud Bolt, Podracer Pilot U .50 .75
85 Mars Guo, Podracer Pilot U .50 .75
86 Ody Mandrell, Podracer Pilot U .50 .75
87 Ratts Tyerell, Podracer Pilot U .50 .75
88 Aks Moe, Senator C .15 .25
89 Horox Ryyder, Senator C .15 .25
90 Edcel Bar Gane, Roona Senator C .15 .25
91 Galactic Delegate, Representative C .15 .25
92 Destroyer Droid, Assault Droid C .15 .25
93 Destroyer Droid, Battleship Security C .15 .25
94 Sith Probe Droid, Hunter Droid C .15 .25
95 Rodian, Mercenary C .15 .25
96 Battle Droid: Pilot, Assault Division C .15 .25
97 Battle Droid: Security, Assault Division C .15 .25
98 Battle Droid: Infantry, Assault Division C .15 .25
99 Battle Droid: Officer, Assault Division C .15 .25
100 Battle Droid: Pilot, Guard Division C .15 .25
101 Battle Droid: Security, Guard Division C .15 .25
102 Battle Droid: Infantry, Guard Division C .15 .25
103 Battle Droid: Officer, Guard Division C .15 .25
104 Neimoidian Aide
Trade Federation Delegate S .15 .25
105 Darth Maul, Sith Warrior S .15 .25
106 Darth Maul's Lightsaber R 1.00 1.50
107 Darth Maul's Sith Speeder R 1.00 1.50
108 Clegg Holdfast's Podracer U .50 .75
109 Dud Bolt's Podracer U .50 .75
110 Mars Guo's Podracer U .50 .75
111 Ody Mandrell's Podracer U .50 .75
112 Ratts Tyerell's Podracer U .50 .75
113 Trade Federation Tank Laser Cannon U .50 .75
114 Multi Troop Transport U .50 .75
115 STAP U .50 .75
116 Thermal Detonator U .50 .75
117 Battle Droid Blaster Rifle C .15 .25
118 Blaster C .15 .25
119 Blaster Rifle C .15 .25
120 I Object! C .15 .25
121 I Will Deal With Them Myself C .15 .25
122 Let Them Make The First Move R 1.00 1.50
123 Move Against The Jedi First C .15 .25
124 Open Fire! U .50 .75
125 Seal Off The Bridge U .50 .75
126 Start Your Engines! U .50 .75
127 Switch To Bio C .15 .25
128 Take Them To Camp Four C .15 .25
129 Very Unusual C .15 .25
130 Vote Of No Confidence C .15 .25
131 We Are Meeting No Resistance C .15 .25
132 We Have Them On The Run U .50 .75
133 Yoka To Bantha Poodoo C .15 .25
134 Your Little Insurrection Is At An End U .50 .75
135 Tatooine Podrace Arena S .15 .25
136 Coruscant Galactic Senate S .15 .25
137 Naboo Battle Plains S .15 .25
138 Sith Infiltrator, Starfighter U .50 .75
139 Droid Starfighter C .15 .25
140 Battleship, Trade Federation Transport C .15 .25

1999 Young Jedi The Jedi Council Foil

COMPLETE SET (18) 4.00 10.00
RELEASED ON OCTOBER 27, 1999
F1 Obi-Wan Kenobi, Jedi Apprentice UR 3.00 5.00
F2 Qui-Gon Jinn, Jedi Protector SR 1.25 2.00
F3 Padmé Naberrie
Queen's Handmaiden SR 1.25 2.00
F4 Captain Panaka
Amidala's Bodyguard SR 1.00 1.50
F5 Mace Windu
Senior Jedi Council Member SR 1.50 2.50
F6 Queen Amidala
Representative of Naboo VR 2.00 3.00
F7 R2-D2, Loyal Droid VR 2.00 3.00
F8 Qui-Gon Jinn's Lightsaber VR .60 1.00
F9 Amidala's Blaster VR .60 1.00
F10 Darth Maul, Master of Evil UR 3.00 5.00
F11 Darth Sidious, Lord of the Sith UR 2.00 3.00
F12 Watto, Junk Merchant SR 1.00 1.50
F13 Jabba the Hutt, Gangster SR 1.00 1.50
F14 Nute Gunray, Neimoidian Viceroy SR 1.00 1.50
F15 Rune Haako, Neimoidian Advisor VR .60 1.00
F16 Lott Dod, Neimoidian Senator VR .60 1.00
F17 Darth Maul's Lightsaber VR .60 1.00
F18 Darth Maul's Sith Speeder VR .60 1.00

2000 Young Jedi Battle of Naboo

COMPLETE SET (140) 8.00 20.00
BOOSTER BOX (30 PACKS) 15.00 30.00
BOOSTER PACK (11 CARDS) .75 1.25
RELEASED ON APRIL 5, 2000
1 Obi-Wan Kenobi, Jedi Knight R 2.50 4.00
2 Qui-Gon Jinn, Jedi Ambassador R 2.00 3.00
3 Jar Jar Binks, Bombad Gungan General R 1.25 2.00
4 Anakin Skywalker, Padawan R 1.25 2.00
5 Padme Naberrie, Amidala's Handmaiden R 1.50 2.50
6 Captain Panaka, Veteran Leader R 1.00 1.50
7 Mace Windu, Jedi Speaker R 1.25 2.00
8 Queen Amidala, Resolute Negotiator R 1.50 2.50
9 Queen Amidala, Keeper of the Peace R 1.50 2.50
10 Yoda, Jedi Elder R 1.50 2.50
11 R2-D2, The Queen's Hero R 1.25 2.00
12 Boss Nass, Gungan Chief U .50 .75
13 Ric Olie, Bravo Leader U .50 .75
14 Captain Tarpals, Gungan Officer U .50 .75
15 Sio Bibble, Governor of Naboo U .50 .75
16 Sabe, Handmaiden Decoy Queen U .50 .75
17 Sache, Handmaiden U .50 .75
18 Yane, Handmaiden U .50 .75
19 Naboo Officer, Squad Leader U .50 .75
20 Naboo Officer, Commander C .15 .25
21 Naboo Bureaucrat, Official C .15 .25
22 Naboo Security, Trooper C .15 .25
23 Naboo Security, Defender C .15 .25
24 Bravo Pilot, Ace Flyer C .15 .25
25 Coruscant Guard, Chancellor's Escort C .15 .25
26 Alderaan Diplomat, Senator C .15 .25
27 Council Member, Naboo Governor C .15 .25
28 Gungan Warrior, Veteran C .15 .25
29 Gungan Guard, Lookout C .15 .25
30 Gungan General, Army Leader C .15 .25
31 Gungan Soldier, Infantry C .15 .25
32 Rep Officer, Gungan Diplomat S .15 .25
33 Obi-Wan Kenobi, Jedi Negotiator S .15 .25
34 Mace Windu's Lightsaber R 1.00 1.50
35 Eeth Koth's Lightsaber U .50 .75
36 Captain Tarpals' Electropole U .50 .75
37 Planetary Shuttle C .15 .25
38 Fambaa C .15 .25
39 Electropole C .15 .25
40 Kaadu C .15 .25
41 Flash Speeder C .15 .25
42 Blaster C .15 .25
43 Heavy Blaster C .15 .25
44 Capture The Viceroy C .15 .25
45 Celebration C .15 .25
46 Guardians Of The Queen U .50 .75
47 Gunga City C .15 .25
48 Gungan Battle Cry U .50 .75
49 How Wude! U .50 .75
50 I Will Take Back What Is Ours C .15 .25
51 Jedi Force Push U .50 .75
52 Meeeesa Lika Dis! C .15 .25
53 NOOOOOOOOOOO! R 1.00 1.50
54 Thanks, Artoo! U .50 .75
55 The Chancellor's Ambassador U .50 .75
56 The Will Of The Force R 1.00 1.50
57 Young Skywalker U .50 .75
58 Your Occupation Here Has Ended C .15 .25
59 Bombad General U .50 .75
60 Kiss Your Trade Franchise Goodbye U .50 .75
61 There's Always A Bigger Fish C .15 .25
62 Uh-Oh! C .15 .25
63 We Wish To Form An Alliance C .15 .25
64 Tatooine Desert Landing Site S .15 .25
65 Coruscant Galactic Senate S .15 .25
66 Naboo Battle Plains S .15 .25
67 Amidala's Starship, Royal Transport R 1.00 1.50
68 Bravo 3, Naboo Starfighter U .50 .75
69 Naboo Starfighter C .15 .25
70 Republic Cruiser, Transport C .15 .25
71 Darth Maul, Dark Lord of the Sith R 3.00 5.00
72 Darth Sidious, Sith Manipulator R 2.00 3.00
73 Sebulba, Dangerous Podracer Pilot R 1.00 1.50
74 Watto, Toydarian Gambler R 1.00 1.50
75 Aurra Sing, Mercenary R 1.25 2.00
76 Jabba The Hutt, Crime Lord R 1.00 1.50
77 Nute Gunray, Neimoidian Despot R 1.00 1.50
78 Rune Haako, Neimoidian Deputy R 1.00 1.50
79 Destroyer Droid Squad, Guard Division R 1.00 1.50
80 Battle Droid Squad, Guard Unit R 1.00 1.50
81 Trade Federation Tank, Guard Division R 1.00 1.50
82 Trade Federation Tank, Patrol Division R 1.00 1.50
83 P-59, Destroyer Droid Commander U .50 .75
84 OOM-9, Battle Droid Commander U .50 .75
85 Daultay Dofine, Neimoidian Attendant U .50 .75
86 Diva Shaliqua, Singer U .50 .75
87 Diva Funquita, Dancer U .50 .75
88 Bith, Musician U .50 .75
89 Quarren, Smuggler U .50 .75
90 Toonbuck Toora, Senator U .50 .75
91 Aqualish, Galactic Senator C .15 .25
92 Twi'lek Diplomat, Senator C .15 .25
93 Weequay, Enforcer C .15 .25
94 Nikto, Slave C .15 .25
95 Pacithhip, Prospector C .15 .25
96 Destroyer Droid, Vanguard Droid C .15 .25
97 Destroyer Droid, MTT Infantry C .15 .25
98 Sith Probe Droid, Remote Tracker C .15 .25
99 Battle Droid: Pilot, Patrol Division C .15 .25
100 Battle Droid: Security, Patrol Division C .15 .25
101 Battle Droid: Infantry, Patrol Division C .15 .25
102 Battle Droid: Officer, Patrol Division C .15 .25
103 Battle Droid: Pilot, Defense Division C .15 .25
104 Battle Droid: Security, Defense Division C .15 .25
105 Battle Droid: Infantry, Defense Division C .15 .25
106 Battle Droid: Officer, Defense Division C .15 .25
107 Neimoidian Advisor, Bureaucrat S .15 .25
108 Darth Maul, Evil Sith Lord S .15 .25
109 Darth Maul's Lightsaber R 1.25 2.00
110 Sith Lightsaber R 1.00 1.50
111 Darth Maul's Electrobinoculars U .50 .75

112 Trade Federation Tank Laser Cannon U .50 .75
113 Multi Troop Transport U .50 .75
114 STAP U .50 .75
115 Battle Droid Blaster Rifle C .15 .25
116 Blaster C .15 .25
117 Blaster Rifle C .15 .25
118 A Thousand Terrible Things C .15 .25
119 Armored Assault C .15 .25
120 Death From Above C .15 .25
121 Don't Spect A Werm Welcome C .15 .25
122 I Will Make It Legal C .15 .25
123 Not For A Sith R 1.00 1.50
124 Now There Are Two Of Them U .50 .75
125 Sith Force Push U .50 .75
126 The Phantom Menace U .50 .75
127 They Win This Round C .15 .25
128 We Are Sending All Troops C .15 .25
129 After Her! C .15 .25
130 Da Dug Chaaa! U .50 .75
131 Sando Aqua Monster C .15 .25
132 They Will Not Stay Hidden For Long C .15 .25
133 This Is Too Close! U .50 .75
134 Tatooine Mos Espa S .15 .25
135 Coruscant Capital City S .15 .25
136 Naboo Theed Palace S .15 .25
137 Droid Control Ship .50 .75
Trade Federation Transport U
138 Sith Infiltrator, Starfighter U .50 .75
139 Droid Starfighter C .15 .25
140 Battleship, Trade Federation Transport C .15 .25

2000 Young Jedi Battle of Naboo Foil

COMPLETE SET (18) 4.00 10.00
F1 Obi-Wan Kenobi, Jedi Knight UR 2.50 4.00
F2 Qui-Gon Jinn, Jedi Ambassador UR 1.25 2.00
F3 Queen Amidala, Keeper of the Peace SR 1.25 2.00
F4 Yoda, Jedi Elder SR 1.25 2.00
F5 R2-D2, The Queen's Hero SR 1.25 2.00
F6 Queen Amidala, Resolute Negotiator VR 1.00 1.50
F7 Mace Windu's Lightsaber VR .60 1.00
F8 The Will Of The Force VR .60 1.00
F9 Amidala's Starship, Royal Transport VR .60 1.00
F10 Darth Maul, Dark Lord of the Sith UR 2.50 4.00
F11 Aurra Sing, Mercenary UR 1.25 2.00
F12 Nute Gunray 1.00 1.50
Neimoidian Despot SR
F13 Destroyer Droid Squad 1.00 1.50
Guard Division SR
F14 Trade Federation Tank 1.00 1.50
Guard Division SR
F15 Battle Droid Squad, Guard Unit VR .60 1.00
F16 Trade Federation Tank .60 1.00
Patrol Division VR
F17 Darth Maul's Lightsaber VR .60 1.00
F18 Not For A Sith VR .60 1.00

2000 Young Jedi Duel of the Fates

COMPLETE SET (60) 5.00 12.00
BOOSTER BOX (30 PACKS) 30.00 40.00
BOOSTER PACK (11 CARDS) 1.00 1.50
RELEASED ON NOVEMBER 8, 2000
1 Obi-Wan Kenobi, Jedi Student R 2.50 4.00
2 Qui-Gon Jinn, Jedi Mentor UR 2.00 3.00
3 Anakin Skywalker, Rookie Pilot R 1.25 2.00
4 Captain Panaka, Security Commander R 1.00 1.50
5 Mace Windu, Jedi Councilor R 1.25 2.00
6 Queen Amidala, Young Leader R 1.50 2.50
7 Yoda, Jedi Philosopher R 1.50 2.50
8 R2-D2, Repair Droid R 1.25 2.00
9 Ric Olie, Starship Pilot R 1.00 1.50
10 Bravo Pilot, Flyer C .15 .25
11 Valorum, Leader of the Senate C .15 .25
12 Qui-Gon Jinn's Lightsaber 1.00 1.50
Wielded by Obi-Wan Kenobi R
13 Booma U .50 .75
14 A Powerful Opponent C .15 .25
15 Come On, Move! U .50 .75
16 Critical Confrontation C .15 .25
17 Gungan Mounted Troops U .50 .75
18 Naboo Fighter Attack C .15 .25
19 Qui-Gon's Final Stand C .15 .25
20 Run The Blockade C .15 .25
21 Twist Of Fate C .15 .25
22 You Are Strong With The Force U .50 .75
23 Gungan Energy Shield U .50 .75
24 He Can See Things Before They Happen U .50 .75
25 Jedi Meditation U .50 .75
26 Jedi Training U .50 .75
27 Naboo Royal Security Forces U .50 .75
28 Pounded Unto Death C .15 .25
29 Senate Guard C .15 .25
30 Naboo Starfighter C .15 .25
31 Darth Maul, Student of the Dark Side UR 2.50 4.00
32 Darth Sidious, Master of the Dark Side R 1.50 2.50
33 Aurra Sing, Trophy Collector R 1.25 2.00
34 Tey How, Neimoidian Command Officer R 1.00 1.50
35 OWO-1, Battle Droid Command Officer R 1.00 1.50
36 Rayno Vaca, Taxi Driver R 1.00 1.50
37 Baskol Yeesrim, Gran Senator R 1.00 1.50
38 Starfighter Droid, DFS-327 R 1.00 1.50
39 Starfighter Droid, DFS-1104 R 1.00 1.50
40 Starfighter Droid, DFS-1138 R 1.00 1.50
41 Jedi Lightsaber, Stolen by Aurra Sing U .50 .75
42 Coruscant Taxi U .50 .75
43 Neimoidian Viewscreen C .15 .25
44 Battle Droid Patrol U .50 .75
45 Change In Tactics C .15 .25
46 Dangerous Encounter C .15 .25
47 Darth Maul Defiant C .15 .25
48 Impossible! C .15 .25
49 It's A Standoff! U .50 .75
50 Mobile Assassin U .50 .75
51 Power Of The Sith C .15 .25
52 Starfighter Screen C .15 .25
53 To The Death C .15 .25
54 Use Caution U .50 .75
55 Blockade U .50 .75
56 End This Pointless Debate U .50 .75
57 The Duel Begins U .50 .75
58 The Jedi Are Involved U .50 .75
59 Where Are Those Droidekas? U .50 .75
60 Droid Starfighter C .15 .25

2000 Young Jedi Enhanced Menace of Darth Maul

P1 Qui-Gon Jinn, Jedi Protector 3.00 5.00
P2 Mace Windu, Jedi Warrior 2.00 3.00
P3 Queen Amidala, Cunning Warrior 6.00 10.00
P4 Darth Maul, Sith Assassin 3.00 5.00
P5 Sebulba, Champion Podracer Pilot 6.00 10.00
P6 Trade Federation Tank, Assault Leader 4.00 6.00

2001 Young Jedi Boonta Eve Podrace

COMPLETE SET (63) 4.00 10.00
BOOSTER BOX (30 PACKS) 30.00 40.00
BOOSTER PACK (11 CARDS) 1.00 1.50
RELEASED ON SEPTEMBER 5, 2001
1 Anakin Skywalker, Boonta Eve Podracer Pilot UR 1.25 2.00
2 Yoda, Jedi Instructor R 1.50 2.50
3 C-3PO, Human-Cyborg Relations Droid R 1.25 2.00
4 Jira, Pallie Vendor R 1.00 1.50
5 Kitster, Anakin's Friend R 1.00 1.50
6 Wald, Anakin's Friend R 1.00 1.50
7 Seek, Anakin's Friend U .50 .75
8 Amee, Anakin's Friend U .50 .75
9 Melee, Anakin's Friend U .50 .75
10 Captain Tarpals, Gungan Leader R 1.00 1.50
11 Boles Roor, Podracer Pilot U .50 .75
12 Elan Mak, Podracer Pilot U .50 .75
13 Neva Kee, Podracer Pilot U .50 .75
14 Wan Sandage, Podracer Pilot U .50 .75
15 Shmi Skywalker, Anakin's Mother R 1.00 1.50
16 Boles Roor's Podracer U .50 .75
17 Elan Mak's Podracer U .50 .75
18 Neva Kee's Podracer U .50 .75
19 Wan Sandage's Podracer U .50 .75
20 Comlink C .15 .25
21 Hold-Out Blaster C .15 .25
22 Dis Is Nutsen C .15 .25
23 Masquerade C .15 .25
24 No Giben Up, General Jar Jar C .15 .25
25 What Does Your Heart Tell You? C .15 .25
26 All-Out Defense U .50 .75
27 Bravo Squadron C .15 .25
28 Hologram Projector C .15 .25
29 Boonta Eve Classic R 1.00 1.50
30 Amidala's Starship R 1.00 1.50
31 Sebulba, Dug Podracer Pilot UR 1.00 1.50
32 Watto, Podrace Sponsor R 1.00 1.50
33 Aurra Sing, Formidable Adversary R 1.25 2.00
34 Jabba The Hutt, O Grandio Lust R 1.00 1.50
35 TC-14, Protocol Droid R 1.00 1.50
36 Orr'UrRuuR'R, Tusken Raider Leader Rare R 1.00 1.50
37 UrrOr'RuuR, Tusken Raider Warrior U .50 .75
38 RuuR'Ur, Tusken Raider Sniper C .15 .25
39 Sil Unch, Neimoidian Comm Officer U .50 .75
40 Graxol Kelvyyn and Shakka U .50 .75
41 Corix Venne, Bith Musician C .15 .25
42 Reike Th'san, Arms Smuggler R 1.00 1.50
43 Meddun, Nikto Mercenary U .50 .75
44 Rum Sleg, Bounty Hunter R 1.00 1.50
45 Aehrrley Rue, Freelance Pilot U .50 .75
46 Jedwar Seelah, Explorer Scout U .50 .75
47 Chokk, Klatooinian Explosives Expert C .15 .25
48 Tatooine Backpack C .15 .25
49 Gaderffii Stick C .15 .25
50 Hold-Out Blaster C .15 .25
51 Watto's Datapad U .50 .75
52 Colo Claw Fish C .15 .25
53 He Always Wins! C .15 .25
54 Bounty Hunter C .15 .25
55 Two-Pronged Attack C .15 .25
56 All-Out Attack U .50 .75
57 Eventually You'll Lose U .50 .75
58 Gangster's Paradise U .50 .75
59 Boonta Eve Classic R 1.00 1.50
60 Viceroy's Battleship R 1.00 1.50
R1 Rule Card 1 .15 .20
R2 Rule Card 2 .15 .20
R3 Rule Card 3 .15 .25

2001 Young Jedi Enhanced Battle of Naboo

COMPLETE SET (12) 30.00 80.00
RELEASED IN 2001
P8 Obi-Wan Kenobi, Jedi Avenger 6.00 10.00
P9 Anakin Skywalker, Tested By The Jedi Council 15.00 25.00
P10 Padmé Naberrie, Loyal Handmaiden 20.00 30.00
P11 Captain Panaka, Royal Defender 3.00 5.00
P12 Yoda, Wise Jedi 6.00 10.00
P13 R2-D2, Starship Maintenance Droid 8.00 12.00
P14 Darth Sidious, The Phantom Menace 3.00 5.00
P15 Watto, Risk Taker 6.00 10.00
P16 Aurra Sing, Scoundrel 6.00 10.00
P17 Jabba The Hutt 6.00 10.00
P18 Nute Gunray, Neimoidean Bureaucrat 4.00 6.00
P19 Rune Haako, Neimoidean Lieutenant 8.00 12.00

2001 Young Jedi Reflections

COMPLETE SET (106) 200.00 350.00
RELEASED ON JULY 18, 2001
A1 Jar Jar Binks, Bombad Gungan General 2.00 3.00
Jar Jar Binks' Electropole
A2 Boss Nass, Gungan Chief 3.00 5.00
Fambaa
A3 Adi Gallia, Corellian Jedi Master 2.50 4.00
Adi Gallia's Lightsaber
A4 Eeth Koth, Zabrak Jedi Master 3.00 5.00
Eeth Koth's Lightsaber
A5 Ki-Adi-Mundi, Cerean Jedi Knight 3.00 5.00
Jedi Lightsaber, Constructed by Ki-Adi-Mundi
A6 Valorum, Supreme Chancellor 2.00 3.00
Planetary Shuttle
A7 Aurra Sing, Trophy Collector 3.00 5.00
Jedi Lightsaber, Stolen by Aurra Sing
A8 Nute Gunray, Neimoidian Viceroy 2.50 4.00
Neimoidian Viewscreen
A9 OOM-9, Battle Droid Commander 2.50 4.00
Battle Droid Blaster Rifle
A10 OWO-1, Battle Droid Command Officer 3.00 5.00
STAP
A11 P-59, Destroyer Droid Commander 2.50 4.00
Multi Troop Transport
A12 Toonbuck Toora, Senator 3.00 5.00
Coruscant Taxi
C1 Are You An Angel? 1.25 2.00
I've Been Trained In Defense
C2 Brave Little Droid 1.00 1.50
Counterparts
C3 Celebration 1.25 2.00
Gungan Mounted Trooops
C4 Enough Of This Pretense 1.00 1.50
I Will Not Cooperate
C5 Fear Attracts The Fearful 1.25 2.00
How Wude!
C6 I Have A Bad Feeling About This 1.25 2.00
NOOOOOOOOOO!
C7 Jedi Force Push 1.25 2.00
We're Not In Trouble Yet
C8 Dos Mackineeks No Comen Here! 1.25 2.00
Bombad General
C9 At last we will have revenge .60 1.00
Sith force push
C10 The Queen's Plan 1.25 2.00
Naboo Royal Security Forces
C11 The Might Of The Republic 1.25 2.00
Senate Guard
C12 The Negotiations Were Short 1.25 2.00
Qui-Gon's Final Stand
C13 Wisdom Of The Council 1.25 2.00
Jedi Training
C14 Yousa Guys Bombad! 1.25 2.00
Uh-Oh!
C15 A Thousand Terrible Things & We Are Sending All Troops 1.00 1.50
C16 Battle Droid Patrol & In Complete Control 1.00 1.50
C17 Boonta Eve Podrace & Kaa Bazza Kundee Hodrudda! 1.00 1.50
C18 Podrace Preparation & Yoka To Bantha Poodoo 1.25 2.00
C19 Switch To Bio & Your Little Insurrection Is At An End .60 1.00
C20 The Phantom Menace & Use Caution 1.25 2.00
D1 Dos Mackineeks No Comen Here! 1.25 2.00
Bombad General
D2 Gunga City 1.25 2.00
Gungan Energy Shield
D3 The Queen's Plan 1.25 2.00
Naboo Royal Security Forces
D4 The Might Of The Republic 1.25 2.00
Senate Guard
D5 The Negotiations Were Short 1.25 2.00
Qui-Gon's Final Stand
D6 Wisdom Of The Council 1.25 2.00
Jedi Training
D7 Yousa Guys Bombad! 1.25 2.00
Uh-Oh!
D8 Grueling Contest 1.25 2.00
Da Dug Chaaa!
D9 Let Them Make The First Move .60 1.00
Very Unusual
D10 Now There Are Two Of Them 1.00 1.50
The Duel Begins
D11 Opee Sea Killer 1.25 2.00
To The Death
D12 Starfighter Screen 1.25 2.00
Blockade
D13 We Have Them On The Run 1.25 2.00
Where Are Those Droidekas?
D14 You Have Been Well Trained .60 1.00
After Her!
2BEP Yoda, Jedi Instructor (foil) 4.00 6.00
2MDM Qui-Gon Jinn, Jedi Master (foil) 15.00 25.00
3BEP C-3PO, Human-Cyborg Relations Droid (foil) 4.00 6.00
4BEP Jira, Pallie Vendor (foil) 2.00 3.00
4BON Anakin Skywalker, Padawan (foil) 5.00 8.00
4TJC Anakin Skywalker, Child of Prophecy (foil) 10.00 15.00
5BEP Kitster, Anakin's Friend (foil) 3.00 5.00
6BEP Wald, Anakin's Friend (foil) 2.50 4.00
7BON Mace Windu, Jedi Speaker (foil) 15.00 25.00
9MDM Queen Amidala, Royal Leader (foil) 5.00 8.00
9TJC Queen Amidala, Voice of Her People (foil) 6.00 10.00
10MDM Yoda, Jedi Master (foil) 3.00 5.00
1DOTF Obi-Wan Kenobi, Jedi Student (foil) 10.00 15.00
2DOTF Qui-Gon Jinn, Jedi Mentor (foil) 5.00 8.00
30BEP Amidala's Starship, Queen's Transport (foil) 3.00 5.00
32BEP Watto, Podrace Sponsor (foil) 3.00 5.00
33BEP Aurra Sing, Formidable Adversary (foil) 6.00 10.00
34BEP Jabba The Hutt, O Grandio Lust (foil) 3.00 5.00
35BEP TC-14, Protocol Droid (foil) 3.00 5.00
36BEP Orr'UrRuuR'R, Tusken Raider Leader (foil) 3.00 5.00
3DOTF Anakin Skywalker, Rookie Pilot (foil) 5.00 8.00
4DOTF Captain Panaka, Security Commander (foil) 3.00 5.00
5DOTF Mace Windu, Jedi Councilor (foil) 4.00 6.00
60BEP Viceroy's Battleship, Trade Federation Transport (foil) 2.50 4.00
6DOTF Queen Amidala, Young Leader (foil) 5.00 8.00
72BON Darth Sidious, Sith Manipulator (foil) 5.00 8.00
73BON Sebulba, Dangerous Podracer Pilot (foil) 12.00 20.00
73TJC Sebulba, Podracer Pilot (foil) 2.50 4.00
74BON Watto, Toydarian Gambler (foil) 1.50 2.50
74MDM Watto, Slave Owner (foil) 3.00 5.00
75MDM Aurra Sing, Bounty Hunter (foil) 6.00 10.00
76BON Jabba The Hutt, Crime Lord (foil) 3.00 5.00
78BON Rune Haako, Neimoidian Deputy (foil) 3.00 5.00
78TJC Destroyer Droid Squad, Defense Division (foil) 5.00 8.00
79TJC Battle Droid Squad, Escort Unit (foil) 3.00 5.00
7DOTF Yoda, Jedi Philosopher (foil) 6.00 10.00
80TJC Trade Federation Tank, Assault Division (foil) 10.00 15.00
88MDM Trade Federation Tank, Armored Division (foil) 3.00 5.00
31DOTF Darth Maul, Student of the Dark Side (foil) 5.00 8.00
32DOTF Darth Sidious, Master of the Dark Side (foil) 15.00 25.00
33DOTF Aurra Sing, Trophy Collector (foil) 2.50 4.00
P1EMDM Qui-Gon Jinn, Jedi Protector (foil) 6.00 10.00
P2EMDM Mace Windu, Jedi Warrior (foil) 6.00 10.00
P3EMDM Queen Amidala, Cunning Warrior (foil) 12.00 20.00
P4EMDM Darth Maul, Sith Assassin (foil) 12.00 20.00
P5EMDM Sebulba, Champion Podracer Pilot (foil) 3.00 5.00
P6EMDM Trade Federation Tank, Assault Leader (foil) 2.50 4.00
P7PREM Shmi Skywalker, Anakin's Mother (foil) 2.50 4.00
P8EBON Obi-Wan Kenobi, Jedi Avenger (foil) 5.00 8.00
P9EBON Anakin Skywalker, Tested by the Jedi Council (foil) 5.00 8.00
P10EBON Padmé Naberrie, Loyal Handmaiden (foil) 3.00 5.00
P11EBON Captain Panaka, Royal Defender (foil) 3.00 5.00

P12EBON Yoda, Wise Jedi (foil)	6.00	10.00
P13EBON R2-D2, Starship Maintenance Droid (foil)	5.00	8.00
P14EBON Darth Sidious, The Phantom Menace (foil)	5.00	8.00
P15EBON Watto, Risk Taker (foil)	3.00	5.00
P16EBON Aurra Sing, Scoundrel (foil)	2.50	4.00
P17EBON Jabba The Hutt, Tatooine Tyrant (foil)	3.00	5.00
P18EBON Nute Gunray, Neimoidian Bureaucrat (foil)	2.50	4.00
P19EBON Rune Haako, Neimoidian Lieutenant (foil)	3.00	5.00

2018 Transformers

BOOSTER BOX (30 PACKS)		
BOOSTER PACK (8 CARDS)		
RELEASED ON SEPTEMBER 28, 2018		
1 Aerial Recon U	.15	.25
2 Agility of Bumblebee R	.30	.50
3 Armed Hovercraft U	.75	1.25
4 Armored Plating C	.10	.15
5 Backup Plan U	.15	.25
6 Battle Ready C	.10	.15
7 Blast Shield U	.15	.25
8 Body Armor U	.15	.25
9 Bombing Run R	.75	1.25
10 Brainstorm C	.10	.15
11 Bug Bomb U	.15	.25
12 Cargo Trailer R	.40	.60
13 Collateral Damage U	.15	.25
14 Combat Training R	.30	.50
15 Computer Sabotage U	.30	.50
16 Crushing Size C	.10	.15
17 Crushing Treads U	.15	.25
18 Cybertonium Bow R	.30	.50
19 Data Bank R	1.25	2.00
20 Data Pad C	.10	.15
21 Debilitating Crystal U	.15	.25
22 Dino-Chomp! R	.60	1.00
23 Disarm U	.15	.25
24 Disruption U	.20	.30
25 Disruptive Entrance U	.40	.60
26 Drill Arms C	.10	.15
27 Emergency Maintenance U	.15	.25
28 Energon Axe R	6.00	10.00
29 Equipment Enthusiast U	.15	.25
30 Flamethrower C	.10	.15
31 Force Field C	.10	.15
32 Fusion Cannon of Megatron R	.60	1.00
33 Grenade Launcher U	.60	1.00
34 Handheld Blaster C	.10	.15
35 Heroism R	.30	.50
36 Hunker Down R	.75	1.25
37 I Still Function! R	3.00	5.00
38 Improvised Shield C	.10	.15
39 Incoming Transmission C	.10	.15
40 Inspiring Leadership C	.10	.15
41 Ion Blaster of Optimus Prime R	1.00	1.50
42 Jaws of Steel U	.15	.25
43 Leap into Battle C	.10	.15
44 Matrix of Leadership R	6.00	10.00
45 Medic! C	.10	.15
46 Multi-Mission Gear U	.15	.25
47 Multi-Tool U	.15	.25
48 New Designs C	.10	.15
49 Null-Ray of Starscream R	.30	.50
50 One Shall Stand, One Shall Fall R	2.50	4.00
51 Peace Through Tyranny R	12.00	20.00
52 Photon Bomb R	.30	.50
53 Piercing Blaster C	.10	.15
54 Plasma Burst U	.15	.25
55 Power Sword U	.25	.40
56 Primary Laser C	.10	.15
57 Ramming Speed U	.15	.25
58 Rapid Ascent U	.15	.25
59 Rapid Conversion C	.10	.15
60 Ready for Action C	.10	.15
61 Reinforced Plating C	.10	.15
62 Repair Bay C	.10	.15
63 Roll Out! R	8.00	12.00
64 Salvage for Parts R	.30	.50
65 Scrapper Gauntlets C	.10	.15
66 Security Checkpoint R	12.00	20.00
67 Shock Absorbers R	.30	.50
68 Start Your Engines R	2.50	4.00
69 Static Laser of Ironhide R	.30	.50
70 Strafing Run U	.15	.25
71 Supercharge C	.10	.15
72 Swap Missions U	.15	.25
73 Swap Parts R	.30	.50
74 Swarm! R	1.25	2.00
75 System Reboot R	1.00	1.50
76 Team-Up Tactics R	.30	.50
77 The Bigger They Are... R	6.00	10.00
78 Thermal Weaponry R	.60	1.00
79 Treasure Hunt U	.60	1.00
80 Turbo Boosters U	.30	.50
81 Zap C	.10	.15
T1 Arcee R FOIL	15.00	25.00
T2 Autobot Cosmos R FOIL	8.00	12.00
T3 Autobot Hound C FOIL	.10	.15
T4 Autobot Jazz U FOIL	.25	.40
T5 Autobot Mirage U FOIL	.15	.25
T6 Barrage C FOIL	.10	.15
T7 Bombshell C FOIL	.10	.15
T8 Bumblebee C FOIL	.10	.15
T9 Bumblebee SR FOIL	30.00	50.00
T10 Chop Shop U FOIL	.50	.75
T11 Chromia R FOIL	6.00	10.00
T12 Darkmount R FOIL	10.00	15.00
T13 Deadlock U FOIL	.15	.25
T14 Decepticon Shockwave R FOIL	12.00	20.00
T15 Demolisher U FOIL	.30	.50
T16 Dinobot Sludge U FOIL	.25	.40
T17 Dinobot Slug C FOIL	.10	.15
T18 Dinobot Snarl U FOIL	.25	.40
T19 Dinobot Swoop C FOIL	.10	.15
T20 Flamewar C FOIL	.10	.15
T21 Grimlock R FOIL	20.00	30.00
T22 Inferno U FOIL	.30	.50
T23 Insecticon Skrapnel R FOIL	12.00	20.00
T24 Jetfire U FOIL	.20	.30
T25 Kickback U FOIL	.40	.60
T26 Megatron C FOIL	.10	.15
T27 Megatron R FOIL	10.00	15.00
T28 Nemesis Prime SR FOIL	40.00	60.00
T29 Optimus Prime R FOIL	30.00	50.00
T30 Optimus Prime C FOIL	.10	.15
T31 Prowl U FOIL	.30	.50
T32 Ramjet C FOIL	.10	.15
T33 Ransack U FOIL	.20	.30
T34 Sergeant Kup C FOIL	.10	.15
T35 Skywarp U FOIL	.20	.30
T36 Starscream U FOIL	.50	.75
T37 Starscream C FOIL	.10	.15
T38 Sunstorm R FOIL	6.00	10.00
T39 Thundercracker U FOIL	.40	.60
T40 Wheeljack U FOIL	.15	.25

2017 Universal Fighting System Capcom Platinum

COMPLETE SET (247)	500.00	750.00
BOOSTER BOX (24 PACKS)	100.00	150.00
BOOSTER PACK (10 CARDS)	4.00	6.00
RELEASED ON NOVEMBER 21, 2017		
1 Bubble Man C	.20	.35
2 Demitri C	.20	.35
3 Drill Man C	.20	.35
4 Gemini Man C	.20	.35
5 Huitzil C	.20	.35
6 Napalm Man C	.20	.35
7 Plant Man C	.20	.35
8 Shadow Man C	.20	.35
9 Sheep Man C	4.00	6.00
10 Skull Man C	.20	.35
11 Splash Woman C	.20	.35
12 Stone Man C	.20	.35
13 Wood Man C	.20	.35
14 Aura of Protection C	.20	.35
15 Bounce and Roll C	.20	.35
16 Dodge! R	10.00	15.00
17 Ghostly Maneuvers C	.20	.35
18 Jealousy and Fake R	3.00	5.00
19 Ki Aura C	.20	.35
20 Mega Slide R	3.00	5.00
21 Not over Yet R	10.00	15.00
22 Ominous Whistle R	3.00	5.00
23 Polar Warp R	3.00	5.00
24 Reprogramming C	.20	.35
25 Sacrifice R	3.00	5.00
26 Self Destruct! R	3.00	5.00
27 Tama Yose R	3.00	5.00
28 Waves of Blood R	3.00	5.00
29 Air Tikki R	3.00	5.00
30 Cossack Citadel R	3.00	5.00
31 E-Tank R	3.00	5.00
32 Egyptian Pyraid R	3.00	5.00
33 Felicity House R	3.00	5.00
34 Hannya R	3.00	5.00
35 Homemade Explosives C	.20	.35
36 Kien C	.20	.35
37 Le Malta C	.20	.35
38 Majigen R	3.00	5.00
39 Moon Base R	3.00	5.00
40 Roll R	3.00	5.00
41 Saw Blades R	3.00	5.00
42 Swarm of Bats C	.20	.35
43 Up Her Sleeves R	3.00	5.00
44 Yellow Scarf C	.20	.35
45 Zeltzereich R	3.00	5.00
46 Aerial Ring Boomerang R	3.00	5.00
47 Bat Spin C	.20	.35
48 Beast Cannon C	.20	.35
49 Big Blow C	.20	.35
50 Big Cyclone R	10.00	15.00
51 Blizzard Sword R	3.00	5.00
52 Bubble Lead R	10.00	15.00
53 Cat Spike C	.20	.35
54 Chireitou R	3.00	5.00
55 Cossack Buster C	.20	.35
56 Crash Bomber C	.20	.35
57 Crash Slasm C	.20	.35
58 Crawling Strike C	.20	.35
59 Dancing Flash R	3.00	5.00
60 Danger Zone R	3.00	5.00
61 Darkside Master R	3.00	5.00
62 Delta Kick C	.20	.35
63 Double Gemini Slam R	3.00	5.00
64 Dragon Cannon R	3.00	5.00
65 Drill Bomb R	10.00	15.00
66 Dust Crusher C	.20	.35
67 Finale Rosso R	3.00	5.00
68 Fire Storm C	3.00	5.00
69 Flying Fortress Buster R	3.00	5.00
70 Gamma Crusher C	.20	.35
71 Gemini Beam R	3.00	5.00
72 Gemini Slam C	.20	.35
73 Gravity Hold C	.20	.35
74 Guts Cannon C	.20	.35
75 Hell Dunk R	3.00	5.00
76 Holographic Buster C	.20	.35
77 Hyper Bomb R	10.00	15.00
78 Hyper Mega Buster C	.20	.35
79 Iaigiri C	.20	.35
80 Ice Slasher R	3.00	5.00
81 Innocent Hug C	.20	.35
82 Karame Dama R	3.00	5.00
83 Laser Trident R	15.00	20.00
84 Leaf Shield C	.20	.35
85 Magnet Missile R	3.00	5.00
86 Magnet Slam C	.20	.35
87 Mecha Dragon Blast C	.20	.35
88 Mega Ball C	.20	.35
89 Mega Crush C	.20	.35
90 Merry Turn C	.20	.35
91 Metal Blade C	.20	.35
92 MM:\Copy C	.20	.35
93 Mukuro Fuuji C	.20	.35
94 Negative Stolen C	.20	.35
95 Oil Slider R	3.00	5.00
96 Omnidirectional Blade Strike R	3.00	5.00
97 Pharaoh Salvation R	3.00	5.00
98 Pharaoh Shot C	.20	.35
99 Pharaoh Wave R	3.00	5.00
100 Pinbot Strike C	.20	.35
101 Plant Barrier R	3.00	5.00
102 Power Stone R	10.00	15.00
103 Quick Boomerang R	3.00	5.00
104 Quick Charge C	.20	.35
105 Quick Slam C	.20	.35
106 Rain Flush R	15.00	20.00
107 Ring Boomerang C	.20	.35
108 Rolling Cutter C	.20	.35
109 Rolling Uppercut R	10.00	15.00
110 Scorch Wheel R	15.00	20.00
111 Search Snake C	.20	.35
112 Shadow Blade C	.20	.35
113 Shadow Blade Shuriken R	3.00	5.00
114 Shell Kick C	.20	.35
115 Shield Ram C	.20	.35
116 Shining Blade C	.20	.35
117 Skull Barrier R	20.00	25.00
118 Skull Buster C	.20	.35
119 Smile and Missile R	3.00	5.00
120 Soul Flash C	.20	.35
121 Splendor Love C	.20	.35
122 Spreggio R	3.00	5.00
123 Super Arm C	.20	.35
124 Tenrai Ha R	3.00	5.00
125 Thunder Wool R	3.00	5.00
126 Time Slow R	20.00	25.00
127 Top Spin R	3.00	5.00
128 Tsurane Giri R	3.00	5.00
129 Turbo Charge R	3.00	5.00
130 Ultimate Undead R	15.00	20.00
131 Wing Slash C	.20	.35
132 Wood Man's Leaf Shield R	20.00	25.00
133 88 M.P.H. C	.20	.35
134 200 Below Zero C	.20	.35
135 8000 Degrees C	.20	.35
136 A Big Job C	.20	.35
137 A Fighting Robot C	.20	.35
138 A New Ally C	.20	.35
139 A World Unprepared C	.20	.35
140 Agile C	.20	.35
141 Agile Warrior C	.20	.35
142 Always on the Move C	.20	.35
143 Always Watching C	.20	.35
144 Balanced Fighter C	.20	.35
145 Basic Training C	.20	.35
146 Beauty Can Overcome C	4.00	6.00
147 Big Spender C	.20	.35
148 Black Justice R	3.00	5.00
149 Body of Spirits C	.20	.35
150 Briding the Races C	.20	.35
151 Buddhist Devotion C	.20	.35
152 Built for Speed C	.20	.35
153 Ceratanium Blades C	.20	.35
154 Changing Directions C	.20	.35
155 Clever Strategist R	3.00	5.00
156 Concerned for the Future C	.20	.35
157 Conflicting Ambitions C	.20	.35
158 Conqueror of Night and Day R	3.00	5.00
159 Copyright Dr.Light: 20XX C	.20	.35
160 Curiosity C	.20	.35
161 Cursed Fate C	.20	.35
162 Dauntless Hero C	.20	.35
163 Deadly Needle C	.20	.35
164 Deforester C	.20	.35
165 Design Flaws C	.20	.35
166 Designed for Combat C	.20	.35
167 Deligent Worker R	3.00	5.00
168 DLN 001 C	.20	.35
169 Double Crosser C	.20	.35
170 Dream Thief C	.20	.35
171 Driven by Hatred C	.20	.35
172 Dust in the Wind C	.20	.35
173 Egotistical C	.20	.35
174 Ever Hopeful C	.20	.35
175 Expert Swimmer C	4.00	6.00
176 Feral R	3.00	5.00
177 Fighting as One R	3.00	5.00
178 First Class Materials C	.20	.35
179 Flawed Energy Core R	3.00	5.00
180 Focused and Patient C	.20	.35
181 Forgotten C	.20	.35
182 Fulfilled in Battle C	.20	.35
183 Garden Mascot C	.20	.35
184 Genius Architect C	.20	.35
185 Glacial Assault C	.20	.35
186 Granted Body C	.20	.35
187 Gymnastic Techniques C	.20	.35
188 Hatred of Autumn C	.20	.35
189 Hidden in His Shadow C	.20	.35
190 Hunters Once More C	.20	.35
191 Improved Design C	.20	.35
192 Impulsive R	40.00	50.00
193 Intelligent and Shrewd R	3.00	5.00
194 Jiang Shi C	.20	.35
195 Ki Techniques C	.20	.35
196 Killing Dinosaurs C	.20	.35
197 Kreutz Bloodline C	.20	.35
198 Lesser Half C	.20	.35
199 Like Watching a Nightmare R	3.00	5.00
200 Malicious Heart C	.20	.35
201 Master of Magnetism C	.20	.35
202 Mechanical Maniac C	.20	.35
203 Merciless Master C	.20	.35
204 Merry C	4.00	6.00
205 Motivation C	.20	.35
206 Narcissist C	.20	.35
207 New Experiences C	.20	.35
208 No Other Purpose R	3.00	5.00
209 Nobel Prize C	.20	.35
210 One With Nature C	4.00	6.00
211 Ophidiophobia C	.20	.35
212 Peaceful Coexistence C	.20	.35
213 Pity for a Traitor R	3.00	5.00
214 Power Struggles C	.20	.35
215 Powers Split C	.20	.35
216 Preparing the Curse C	.20	.35
217 Prototype R	3.00	5.00
218 Proud Nose C	.20	.35
219 Pulled to Majigen C	.20	.35

220 Quick and Precise C	.20	.35
221 Reactive Style C	.20	.35
222 Reformed Scientist C	.20	.35
223 Repaying a Debt C	.20	.35
224 Rescuer C	.20	.35
225 Robot Masters C	.20	.35
226 S Class Hunter R	3.00	5.00
227 Sense of Justice C	.20	.35
228 Short Fuse R	3.00	5.00
229 Siverian Scientist C	.20	.35
230 Slithering Serpent C	.20	.35
231 Soul Beats C	.20	.35
232 Static Build Up C	.20	.35
233 Strength of Tail C	.20	.35
234 Surveyor C	.20	.35
235 Tainted Blood C	.20	.35
236 The Land of Makai C	.20	.35
237 The Year 200X C	.20	.35
238 Thundering Assault C	.20	.35
239 To Cleanse All Souls R	20.00	25.00
240 Tough as Bricks C	.20	.35
241 Tribal Protector C	.20	.35
242 Walking Weapon C	.20	.35
243 Weapons Upgrade R	3.00	5.00
244 Where the Seas Meet C	.20	.35
245 Wings and Claws C	.20	.35
246 Wisdom of Castor R	3.00	5.00
247 Without a Master C	.20	.35

2017 Universal Fighting System Street Fighter

COMPLETE SET (190)	400.00	600.00
BOOSTER BOX (24 PACKS)	65.00	80.00
BOOSTER PACK (10 CARDS)	4.00	6.00
UNLISTED C	.15	.25
UNLISTED U	.25	.40
UNLISTED R	.60	1.00
RELEASED ON MAY 26, 2017		
1 Akuma UC	.25	.40
2 Gohadoken C	.15	.25
3 Goshoryuken R	2.50	4.00
4 Tatsumaki Zankukyaku C	.15	.25
5 Wrath of the Raging Demon UR	6.00	10.00
6 Master of the Fist C	.15	.25
7 Power Made Flesh UC	.25	.40
8 Shun Goku Satsu C	.15	.25
9 True Path of Ansatsuken R	2.50	4.00
10 Balrog UC	.25	.40
11 Charging Turn Punch C	.15	.25
12 Crazy Buffalo UR	6.00	10.00
13 Dash Low Smash C	.15	.25
14 Dash Uppercut UC	.25	.40
15 Buffalo Strength UC	.25	.40
16 Chasing the Fight Money C	.15	.25
17 Hired Muscle R	2.50	4.00
18 Sadistic Boxer C	.15	.25
19 Blanka UC	.15	.25
20 Electric Thunder R	2.50	4.00
21 Lightning Cannonball UR	6.00	10.00
22 Rolling Attack C	.15	.25
23 Vertical Rolling Attack UC	.25	.40
24 Fight Like a Beast UC	.25	.40
25 Savage Style C	.15	.25
26 Unpredictable Movement C	.15	.25
27 Victory Howl UC	.25	.40
29 Cannon Spike C	.15	.25
30 Cannon Strike UC	.25	.40
31 Gyro Drive Smasher UR	20.00	30.00
32 Spiral Arrow R	2.50	4.00
33 Beginning Mission! C	.15	.25
34 Delta Blue Team Leader R	2.50	4.00
35 Mutual Contempt UC	.25	.40
36 Rescue Mission R	2.50	4.00
37 Chun-Li SE	.40	.60
38 Hyakuretsukyaku SE	.40	.60
39 Kikoken SE	.40	.60
40 Kikosho SE	3.00	5.00
41 Senenshu SE	.40	.60
42 Spinning Bird Kick SE	.40	.60
43 Tenkukyaku SE	.40	.60
44 Yosokyaku SE	.40	.60
45 Devotion to Justice SE	.40	.60
46 First Lady of Fighting SE	.40	.60
47 Interpol Agent SE	.40	.60
48 Legendary Legs SE	.40	.60
49 Like Father Like Daughter SE	.40	.60
50 Off Duty Officer SE	.40	.60
51 Personal Tragedy SE	.40	.60
52 Strongest Woman in the World SE	.40	.60
53 To Avenge a Loved One SE	.40	.60
54 United Against Terrorism SE	.40	.60
55 Deejay UC	.25	.40
56 Air Slasher UC	.25	.40
57 Climax Beat UR	10.00	15.00
58 Double Rolling Sobat C	.15	.25
59 Sobat Carnival R	2.50	4.00
60 Maximum Rhythm UC	.15	.25
61 Meaning Business C	.15	.25
62 Rhythmic Fighting Style R	5.00	7.00
63 The Southern Comet C	.15	.25
64 Dhalsim UC	.25	.40
65 Stretch Kick C	.15	.25
66 Yoga Fire C	.15	.25
67 Yoga Flame R	2.50	4.00
68 Yoga Inferno UR	6.00	10.00
69 Esoteric Yoga R	2.50	4.00
70 Expanded Spirituality UC	.25	.40
71 Inner Neutrality R	2.50	4.00
72 Mind Becomes Flame UC	.25	.40
73 E. Honda UC	.25	.40
74 Hundred Hand Slap R	2.50	4.00
75 Oicho Throw C	.15	.25
76 Sumo Headbutt UC	.25	.40
77 Ultimate Killer Head Ram UR	6.00	10.00
78 Battle Royale C	.15	.25
79 Blue Tsunami UC	.25	.40
80 Ozeki R	2.50	4.00
81 Well-Earned Relaxation R	2.50	4.00
82 Fei Long UC	.25	.40
83 Rekkaken C	.15	.25
84 Rekkashingeki UR	6.00	10.00
85 Rekkashinken C	.15	.25
86 Shien Kyaku R	2.50	4.00
87 Action Superstar UC	.25	.40
88 Despise All Evil C	.15	.25
89 Hitenryu Training C	.15	.25
90 Intriguing Challenge R	2.50	4.00
91 Guile UC	.25	.40
92 Double Flash Kick UR	6.00	10.00
93 Flash Kick R	2.50	4.00
94 Reverse Spin Kick C	.15	.25
95 Sonic Boom UC	.25	.40
96 Career Soldier C	.15	.25
97 Cool and Focused UC	.25	.40
98 Pursuing a Vendetta R	2.50	4.00
99 Refusing to Let Go R	2.50	4.00
100 Ken UC	.25	.40
101 Ken's Hadoken C	.15	.25
102 Ken's Shoryuken C	.15	.25
103 Ken's Tatsumaki R	2.50	4.00
104 Shoryureppa UR	6.00	10.00
105 Alpha Male R	2.50	4.00
106 Flashy Fighting Style UC	.25	.40
107 Friendly Rivalry C	.15	.25
108 United States Champion UC	.25	.40
109 M. Bison UC	.25	.40
110 Devil Reverse UC	.25	.40
111 Double Knee Press C	.15	.25
112 Nightmare Booster UR	6.00	10.00
113 Psycho Crusher R	2.50	4.00
114 Demanding Submission R	2.50	4.00
115 Psycho Powered UC	.25	.40
116 Ruthless Dictator UC	.25	.40
117 Sinister Malevolence C	.15	.25
118 Ryu SE	.40	.60
119 Collarbone Breaker SE	.40	.60
120 Joudan Sokutogeri SE	.40	.60
121 Ryu's Hadoken SE	.40	.60
122 Ryu's Shinku Hadoken SE	3.00	5.00
123 Ryu's Shoryuken SE	.40	.60
124 Ryu's Tatsumaki SE	.40	.60
125 Shoulder Throw SE	.40	.60
126 Adopted by a Sensei SE	.40	.60
127 Brothers in Arts SE	.40	.60
128 Destiny's Path SE	.40	.60
129 Fallen Master SE	.40	.60
130 Forbidden Ansatsuken SE	.40	.60
131 Look the Devil in the Eye SE	.40	.60
132 Reluctant Icon SE	.40	.60
133 Satsui no Hado SE	.40	.60
134 Wanted Man SE	.40	.60
135 Way of a True Warrior SE	.40	.60
136 Sagat UC	.25	.40
137 Tiger Destruction UR	10.00	15.00
138 Tiger Knee C	.15	.25
139 Tiger Shot C	.15	.25
140 Tiger Uppercut R	.15	.25
141 Emperor of Muay Thai UC	.25	.40
142 Proud Fighter C	.15	.25
143 Securing His Destiny R	2.50	4.00
144 Towering Over Rivals C	.15	.25
145 Sakura UC	.25	.40
146 Sakura Otoshi UC	.25	.40
147 Sakura's Hadoken C	.15	.25
148 Sakura's Shinku Hadoken UR	15.00	20.00
149 Shououken R	2.50	4.00
150 Eager to Train C	.15	.25
151 Personal Rivalry C	.15	.25
152 Summer Vacation UR	6.00	10.00
153 Youthful Enthusiasm R	2.50	4.00
154 T. Hawk UC	.25	.40
155 Condor Dive C	.15	.25
156 Heavy Body Press UC	.25	.40
157 Mexican Typhoon UR	10.00	15.00
158 Tomahawk Buster C	.15	.25
159 Forced into Exile UC	.25	.40
160 Haunted by Loss C	.15	.25
161 Pride of the Tribe R	2.50	4.00
162 Strength of the Land C	.15	.25
163 Vega UC	.25	.40
164 Bloody High Claw UR	10.00	15.00
165 Flying Barcelona Attack C	.15	.25
166 Izuna Drop R	2.50	4.00
167 Matador Turn C	.15	.25
168 Beauty is Power UC	.25	.40
169 Cage Fighter C	.15	.25
170 Masked Assassin R	2.50	4.00
171 My Beautiful Face is Ruined UC	.25	.40
172 Zangief UC	.25	.40
173 Banishing Flat C	.15	.25
174 Double Lariat R	2.50	4.00
175 Spinning Piledriver C	.15	.25
176 Ultimate Atomic Buster UR	10.00	15.00
177 Borscht Aficionado C	.15	.25
178 For Mother Russia! R	2.50	4.00
179 Invincible Iron Body R	2.50	4.00
180 Muscle Spirit C	.15	.25
181 Juri BT	2.00	3.50
182 Focus UR	6.00	10.00
183 Prepare to Fight UR	50.00	65.00
184 Strongest Style UR	10.00	15.00
185 Surprise Reunion UR	6.00	10.00
186 Chikara no Hado UR	6.00	10.00
187 Dedicated Teacher UR	6.00	10.00
188 Kanzuki Dojo UR	6.00	10.00
189 Pink Gi UR	6.00	10.00
28A Cammy UC	.25	.40
28B Cammy Alt Art UR	50.00	60.00

2018 Universal Fighting System Cowboy Bebop 1st Edition

COMPLETE SET (145)	400.00	600.00
BOOSTER BOX (24 PACKS)	70.00	100.00
BOOSTER PACK (10 CARDS)	4.00	6.00
RELEASED ON JANUARY 26, 2018		
1 Asimov & Katerina UC	.30	.50
2 Asimov's Frenzy UC	.30	.50
3 Bloody Eye Rampage C	.20	.35
4 Bloody Eye Rushdown C	.20	.35
5 Katerina's Shot R	3.00	5.00
6 Dreaming of Mars C	.20	.35
7 Red Eye Capsule C	.20	.35
8 Secret Stash R	3.00	5.00
9 Tijuana Groceries UR	10.00	15.00
10 Edward & Ein UC	.30	.50
11 Here We Go! UR	10.00	15.00
12 Codename: Julia UR	15.00	20.00
13 Digital Manipulation UR	10.00	15.00
14 Ein's Brain Scratch UC	.30	.50
15 Leaping Neck Chomp R	3.00	5.00
16 Leg Crunch C	.20	.35
17 Samba Slam C	.20	.35
18 Stink Gas R	3.00	5.00
19 Cowgirl Edward C	.20	.35
20 Curious Magnetism R	3.00	5.00
21 Data Dog C	.20	.35
22 Faye-Faye! C	.20	.35
23 Funky Tomato UC	.30	.50
24 Hacker Extraordinaire R	3.00	5.00
25 Loyal Friend R	3.00	5.00
26 Mushroom Experimentation UC	.30	.50
27 Radical Edward R	3.00	5.00
28 Faye UC	.30	.50
29 Gateway Shuffle UR	40.00	60.00
30 Faye's Cover Fire R	3.00	5.00
31 Getaway Fire UR	10.00	15.00
32 Lights Out Bounty UC	.30	.50
33 NPYUU Distraction R	3.00	5.00
34 Red Tail Gunfire UC	.30	.50
35 Red Tail Missiles C	.20	.35
36 Surprising Shower C	.20	.35
37 An Evening With Gren C	.20	.35
38 Emergency Rations R	3.00	5.00
39 Feigned Interest UR	5.00	8.00
40 Funny Valentine C	.20	.35
41 Honky Tonk Woman R	3.00	5.00
42 Not My Problem C	.20	.35
43 Poker Alice C	.20	.35
44 Useless Futility UC	.30	.50
45 Welcome to Woody's UC	.30	.50
46 Jet UC	.30	.50
47 Armed Vengeance R	3.00	5.00
48 Black Dog's Aim C	.20	.35
49 Black Dog's Fangs UR	30.00	40.00
50 Hammerhead Assault R	3.00	5.00
51 ISSP Grapple UC	.30	.50
52 Missile Launcher UR	20.00	30.00
53 Relentless Pursuit C	.20	.35
54 Bonsai Enthusiast R	3.00	5.00
55 Captian's Discontent C	.20	.35
56 Feng Shui 101 C	.20	.35
57 Folk Tale Storyteller UC	.30	.50
58 Marshall Banana UC	.30	.50
59 Overly Dramatic R	3.00	5.00
60 Police Connections C	.20	.35
61 Presidente on the House UC	.30	.50
62 Unhealthy Diet C	.20	.35
63 Wounded Dog UC	.30	.50
64 Mad Pierrot UC	.30	.50
65 Ailurophobia C	.20	.35
66 ISSP Execution C	.20	.35
67 Let's Party! UR	15.00	20.00
68 Tongpu's Assault UC	.30	.50
69 Explosive Acrobatics C	.20	.35
70 Kinetic Energy Shield UC	.30	.50
71 Section 13's Failed Experiment UC	.30	.50
72 Space Land R	3.00	5.00
73 Spike (Hand-to-Hand) SE	.30	.50
74 Cross Punch SE	.30	.50
75 Falling Heel Strike SE	.30	.50
76 High Roundhouse Kick SE	.30	.50
77 Jaw Jammer SE	.30	.50
78 Kickback Crescendo SE	.30	.50
79 Swimming Bird SE	.30	.50
80 Vengeance of the Fallen Angel SE	.30	.50
81 Ending the Dream SE	.30	.50
82 Finally Awake SE	.30	.50
83 Generous Gambler SE	.30	.50
84 Habitual Smoker SE	.30	.50
85 Light it Up SE	.30	.50
86 Nothing Like Andy SE	.30	.50
87 Red Dragon Assassin SE	.30	.50
88 Sing for Me SE	.30	.50
89 Specialized Ammunition SE	.30	.50
90 Syndicate Target SE	.30	.50
91 Spike (Pilot) UC	.30	.50
92 Swordfish II UR	15.00	20.00
93 Ace Maneuver R	3.00	5.00
94 M3C Devastator Plasma Cannon UR	25.00	40.00
95 Space Salvo C	.20	.35
96 Swordfish Gunfire UC	.30	.50
97 Swordfish Plasma Cannon UR	20.00	25.00
98 Tijuana Takeoff C	.20	.35
99 Urban Shower C	.20	.35
100 Carrying the Weight UC	.30	.50
101 Cleaning the Fish C	.20	.35
102 Coordinating Position R	3.00	5.00
103 Finding What Was Lost C	.20	.35
104 Fueling Up UC	.30	.50
105 Graffiti Job R	3.00	5.00
106 New Shipmate R	3.00	5.00
107 One Who Wanders R	3.00	5.00
108 Tank! UR	8.00	12.00
109 Twinkle Murdock UC	.30	.50
110 Distraction Destruction UR	10.00	15.00
111 Ganymede Terrorists C	.20	.35
112 Space Warrior Squad UC	.30	.50
113 Virus Unchained UR	10.00	15.00
114 Harrison's Lucky Day C	.20	.35
115 Peaceful Beginnings R	3.00	5.00
116 Save the Sea Rats R	3.00	5.00
117 Unmet Demands UC	.30	.50
118 Vicious SE	.30	.50
119 Cormorant SE	.30	.50
120 Cathedral Standoff SE	.30	.50
121 Disarm SE	.30	.50
122 Grip of a Ravenous Beast SE	.30	.50
123 Scorpion Stab SE	.30	.50
124 Settling the Score SE	.30	.50
125 Tears of Scarlet SE	.30	.50
126 Unsheathing Slash SE	.30	.50
127 Arranging a Deal SE	.30	.50
128 Avoiding Assassination SE	.30	.50

Card	Low	High
129 Caught by the Past SE	.30	.50
130 Failed Coup SE	.30	.50
131 Eliminating the Van SE	.30	.50
132 Unbridled Arrogance SE	.30	.50
133 Syndicate Allies SE	.30	.50
134 Fallen Angels SE	.30	.50
135 The Snake Becomes the Dragon SE	.30	.50
136 Big Shot: Judy R	3.00	5.00
137 Big Shot: Punch R	3.00	5.00
138 Teddy Bomber UR	10.00	15.00
139 Psychedelic Mushroom R	10.00	15.00
140 Coffee Samba UR	8.00	12.00
141 Jupiter Jazz UR	10.00	15.00
142 Meifa's Assault R	3.00	5.00
143 Syndicate Slice C	.20	.35
144 Bebop Blues R	3.00	5.00
145 Bang! BT	3.00	5.00

2004 Vs System DC Origins

Card	Low	High
COMPLETE SET (165)	30.00	60.00
BOOSTER BOX (24 PACKS)	15.00	30.00
BOOSTER PACK (14 CARDS)	.75	1.25
*FOIL: .75X TO 2X BASIC CARDS		
RELEASED IN JULY 2004		
1 Alfred Pennyworth, Faithful Friend R	3.00	5.00
2 Azrael, Jean Paul Valley C	.15	.25
3 Barbara Gordon Oracle, Information Network R	2.00	3.00
4 Batman, Caped Crusader C	.15	.25
5 Batman, The Dark Knight R	3.00	5.00
6 Batman, World's Greatest Detective U	.30	.50
7 Cassandra Cain Batgirl, Martial Artist C	.15	.25
8 Catwoman, Selina Kyle C	.15	.25
9 Commissioner Gordon, James Gordon U	.30	.50
10 Dick Grayson Nightwing, High-Flying Acrobat R	2.50	4.00
11 Dick Grayson Nightwing, Defender of Bludhaven C	.15	.25
12 Dick Grayson Robin, Sidekick R	2.00	3.00
13 Dinah Laurel Lance Black Canary, Canary Cry C	.15	.25
14 GCPD Officer, Army C	.15	.25
15 Harvey Bullock, GCPD Detective U	.30	.50
16 Huntress, Helena Rosa Bertinelli C	.15	.25
17 Lady Shiva, Sandra Woosan C	.15	.25
18 Lucius Fox, Wayne Enterprises Executive R	.60	1.00
19 Spoiler, Stephanie Brown U	.30	.50
20 Superman, Big Blue Boy Scout R	4.00	6.00
21 Tim Drake Robin, Young Detective C	.15	.25
22 Batarang U	.30	.50
23 Batcave R	1.25	2.00
24 Batmobile R	2.00	3.00
25 Batplane U	.30	.50
26 Bat-Signal U	.30	.50
27 Clocktower C	.15	.25
28 Dynamic Duo U	.30	.50
29 Fizzle R	3.00	5.00
30 GCPD Headquarters U	.30	.50
31 Utility Belt U	.30	.50
32 Wayne Enterprises R	.60	1.00
33 Wayne Manor U	.30	.50
34 Bart Allen Kid Flash, Speedster C	.15	.25
35 Beast Boy, Garfield Logan R	.60	1.00
36 Cassie Sandsmark Wonder Girl, Zeus's Chosen C	.15	.25
37 Connor Kent Superboy, Tactile Telekinetic C	.15	.25
38 Dick Grayson Nightwing, Titan Leader C	.15	.25
39 Donna Troy Wonder Girl, Amazon Warrior R	2.50	4.00
40 Dawn Granger Dove, Agent of Order C	.15	.25
41 Garth Tempest, Atlantean Sorcerer R	3.00	5.00
42 Hank Hall Hawk, Agent of Chaos C	.15	.25
43 Kole, Kole Weathers U	.30	.50
44 Koriand'r Starfire, Alien Princess C	.15	.25
45 Mirage, Miriam Delgado U	.30	.50
46 Omen, Lilith Clay R	.60	1.00
47 Pantha, Subject X-24 C	.15	.25
48 Phantasm, Danny Chase R	1.25	2.00
49 Raven, Daughter of Trigon R	2.00	3.00
50 Red Star, Leonid Kovar U	.30	.50
51 Roy Harper Arsenal, Sharpshooter C	.15	.25
52 Terra, Tara Markov R	1.50	2.50
53 Tim Drake Robin, The Boy Wonder C	.15	.25
54 Vic Stone Cyborg, Human Machine C	.15	.25
55 Circle Defense U	.30	.50
56 Heroic Sacrifice R	1.25	2.00
57 Liberty Island Base U	.30	.50
58 Optitron R	1.25	2.00
59 Tamaran U	.30	.50
60 Teen Titans Go! C	.15	.25
61 Titans Tower U	.30	.50
62 T-Jet U	.30	.50
63 USS Argus R	.60	1.00
64 Bane, The Man Who Broke the Bat C	.15	.25
65 Charaxes, Drury Walker C	.15	.25
66 Firefly, Garfield Lynns R	1.00	1.50
67 Harley Quinn, Dr. Harleen Quinzel C	.15	.25
68 Killer Croc, Waylon Jones C	.15	.25
69 Mad Hatter, Jervis Tetch R	1.00	1.50
70 Man-Bat, Dr. Robert Langstrom C	.15	.25
71 Matt Hagen Clayface, Man of Clay C	.15	.25
72 Mr. Freeze, Dr. Victor Fries C	.15	.25
73 Mr. Zsasz, Victor Zsasz R	1.00	1.50
74 Poison Ivy, Pamela Isley R	1.25	2.00
75 Professor Hugo Strange, Psycho-Analyst C	.15	.25
76 Query and Echo, Double Trouble U	.30	.50
77 Ratcatcher, Otis Flannegan U	.30	.50
78 Scarecrow, Professor Jonathan Crane R	1.50	2.50
79 The Joker, Joker's Wild R	2.50	4.00
80 The Joker, Laughing Lunatic C	.15	.25
81 The Joker, The Clown Prince of Crime R	2.00	3.00
82 The Penguin, Oswald Chesterfield Cobblepot C	.15	.25
83 The Riddler, Edward Nygma U	.30	.50
84 Two-Face, Harvey Dent U	.30	.50
85 Ventriloquist Scarface, Arnold Wesker R	1.00	1.50
86 Arkham Asylum U	.30	.50
87 Blackgate Prison R	1.00	1.50
88 Cracking the Vault R	.60	1.00
89 Fear and Confusion C	.15	.25
90 Kidnapping U	.30	.50
91 No Man's Land U	.30	.50
92 Paralyzing Kiss U	.30	.50
93 Prison Break U	.30	.50
94 Riddle Me This U	.30	.50
95 Rigged Elections R	1.00	1.50
96 Assassin Initiate, Army C	.15	.25
97 Bane, Ubu C	.15	.25
98 Dr. Tzin-Tzin, Master of Hypnosis C	.15	.25
99 Hassim, Loyal Retainer U	.30	.50
100 Josef Witschi, Talia's Assistant U	.30	.50
101 Kyle Abbot, Wolf in Man's Clothing C	.15	.25
102 Lady Shiva, Master Assassin R	1.00	1.50
103 Malaq, Money Man U	.30	.50
104 Ra's al Ghul, Immortal Villain C	.15	.25
105 Ra's al Ghul, Master Swordsman C	.15	.25
106 Ra's al Ghul, The Demon's Head R	1.00	1.50
107 Talia, Daughter of the Demon's Head R	1.00	1.50
108 Thuggee, Army C	.15	.25
109 Ubu, Ra's al Ghul's Bodyguard C	.15	.25
110 Whisper A'Daire, Cold-Blooded Manipulator C	.15	.25
111 Clench Virus U	.30	.50
112 Dual Nature R	.60	1.00
113 Flying Fortress U	.30	.50
114 Lazarus Pit C	.15	.25
115 Mountain Stronghold U	.30	.50
116 Remake the World R	.60	1.00
117 The Shrike R	.60	1.00
118 Tower of Babel R	1.00	1.50
119 Wheel of Plagues R	.60	1.00
120 Dr. Light, Arthur Light U	.30	.50
121 Gizmo, Mikron O'Jeneus U	.30	.50
122 Jinx, Elemental Sorceress U	.30	.50
123 Mammoth, Baran Flinders R	.60	1.00
124 Neutron, Nat Tryon R	.60	1.00
125 Psimon, Dr. Simon Jones R	.60	1.00
126 Shimmer, Selinda Flinders U	.30	.50
127 The Underworld Star U	.30	.50
128 Deathstroke the Terminator, Slade Wilson R	1.25	2.00
129 Black Mask, Roman Sionis U	.30	.50
130 Blackfire, Komand'r R	.60	1.00
131 Brother Blood, Leader of the Church of Blood C	.15	.25
132 Ferak, Army C	.15	.25
133 King Snake, Sir Edmund Dorrance U	.30	.50
134 Lady Vic, Lady Elaine Marsh-Morton U	.30	.50
135 Lightning, Travis Williams U	.30	.50
136 Lockup, Lyle Bolton U	.30	.50
137 The Demon, Jason Blood R	1.00	1.50
138 The Demon, Etrigan R	1.00	1.50
139 Thunder, Gan Williams U	.30	.50
140 Trigon, The Terrible R	.60	1.00
141 Wildebeest, Army C	.15	.25
142 A Death in the Family R	.60	1.00
143 Airborne Assault U	.30	.50
144 Break You C	.15	.25
145 Combat Reflexes C	.15	.25
146 Concrete Jungle R	.60	1.00
147 Crossbow C	.15	.25
148 Escrima Sticks U	.30	.50
149 Fast Getaway C	.15	.25
150 From the Shadows C	.15	.25
151 Gone But Not Forgotten U	.30	.50
152 GothCorp R	.60	1.00
153 Have a Blast! R	2.00	3.00
154 Hidden Surveillance R	.60	1.00
155 Home Surgery U	.30	.50
156 Last Laugh U	.30	.50
157 Mega-Blast C	.15	.25
158 Museum Heist R	.60	1.00
159 My Beloved U	.30	.50
160 Shape Change U	.30	.50
161 Tag Team C	.15	.25
162 The Brave and the Bold U	.30	.50
163 Total Anarchy R	.60	1.00
164 Twin Firearms U	.30	.50
165 World's Finest C	.15	.25

2004 Vs System Marvel Origins

Card	Low	High
COMPLETE SET (220)	40.00	80.00
BOOSTER BOX (24 PACKS)	20.00	40.00
BOOSTER PACK (14 CARDS)	1.00	2.00
*FOIL: .75X TO 2X BASIC CARDS		
RELEASED IN APRIL 2004		
1 Archangel, Warren Worthington III C	.15	.25
2 Banshee, Sean Cassidy C	.15	.25
3 Beast, Dr. Henry McCoy U	.30	.50
4 Bishop, Lucas Bishop C	.15	.25
5 Colossus, Peter Rasputin C	.15	.25
6 Cyclops, Scott Summers C	.15	.25
7 Cyclops, Slim C	.15	.25
8 Dazzler, Alison Blaire C	.15	.25
9 Forge, Cheyenne Mystic R	.60	1.00
10 Gambit, Remy LeBeau U	.30	.50
11 Havok, Alex Summers R	.60	1.00
12 Iceman, Bobby Drake U	.30	.50
13 Jean Grey, Marvel Girl C	.15	.25
14 Jean Grey, Phoenix Force R	1.50	2.50
15 Longshot, Rebel Freedom Fighter R	1.25	2.00
16 Moira MacTaggert, World-Renowned Geneticist R	.60	1.00
17 Nightcrawler, Fuzzy Elf R	1.50	2.50
18 Nightcrawler, Kurt Wagner U	.30	.50
19 Professor X, Charles Xavier C	.15	.25
20 Professor X, World's Most Powerful Telepath R	.75	1.25
21 Psylocke, Betsy Braddock C	.15	.25
22 Rogue, Power Absorption R	1.25	2.00
23 Rogue, Powerhouse U	.30	.50
24 Shadowcat, Kitty Pryde C	.15	.25
25 Storm, Ororo Munroe C	.15	.25
26 Storm, Weather Witch R	2.00	3.00
27 Wolverine, Berserker Rage R	1.50	2.50
28 Wolverine, James Howlett U	.30	.50
29 Wolverine, Logan C	.15	.25
30 Cerebro R	1.50	2.50
31 Children of the Atom R	1.25	2.00
32 Danger Room U	.30	.50
33 Fastball Special U	.30	.50
34 Muir Island U	.30	.50
35 Professor Xavier's Mansion R	.75	1.25
36 The Blackbird R	.60	1.00
37 X-Corporation U	.30	.50
38 Xavier's Dream R	.75	1.25
39 Xavier's School for Gifted Youngsters U	.30	.50
40 Alicia Masters, Blind Sculptress R	.60	1.00
41 Ant Man, Scott Lang C	.15	.25
42 Crystal, Inhuman C	.15	.25
43 Frankie Raye, Herald of Galactus U	.30	.50
44 Franklin Richards, Child Prodigy R	.75	1.25
45 Ghost Rider, New Fantastic Four R	1.50	2.50
46 Hulk, New Fantastic Four R	1.50	2.50
47 Human Torch, Johnny Storm C	.15	.25
48 Human Torch, Hotshot R	1.00	1.50
49 Human Torch, Super Nova U	.30	.50
50 Invisible Woman, The Invisible Girl U	.30	.50
51 Invisible Woman, Sue Storm C	.15	.25
52 Invisible Woman, Sue Richards R	.60	1.00
53 Luke Cage, Hero for Hire U	.30	.50
54 Medusa, Inhuman C	.15	.25
55 Mr. Fantastic, Reed Richards C	.15	.25
56 Mr. Fantastic, Stretch U	.30	.50
57 Mr. Fantastic, Scientific Genius R	1.25	2.00
58 She-Hulk, Jennifer Walters U	.30	.50
59 She-Hulk, Green Jeans C	.15	.25
60 She-Thing, Sharon Ventura C	.15	.25
61 Spider-Man, New Fantastic Four R	1.50	2.50
62 Thing, Ben Grimm C	.15	.25
63 Thing, Heavy Hitter R	1.50	2.50
64 Thing, The Ever-Lovin' Blue-Eyed Thing U	.30	.50
65 Wolverine, New Fantastic Four R	2.00	3.00
66 A Child Named Valeria R	.60	1.00
67 Antarctic Research Base R	.60	1.00
68 Baxter Building U	.30	.50
69 Cosmic Radiation R	.75	1.25
70 Fantasticar R	.75	1.25
71 Four Freedoms Plaza R	.60	1.00
72 It's Clobberin' Time! R	2.50	4.00
73 Signal Flare R	.60	1.00
74 The Pogo Plane R	.60	1.00
75 Yancy Street U	.30	.50
76 Avalanche, Dominic Petros U	.30	.50
77 Blob, Fred Dukes C	.15	.25
78 Destiny, Irene Adler C	.15	.25
79 Lorelei, Savage Land Mutate C	.15	.25
80 Magneto, Eric Lehnsherr U	.30	.50
81 Magneto, Master of Magnetism R	1.50	2.50
82 Magneto, Lord Magnus R	1.50	2.50
83 Mastermind, Jason Wyngarde U	.30	.50
84 Mystique, Raven Darkholme U	.30	.50
85 Mystique, Shape-Changing Assassin C	.15	.25
86 Phantazia, Eileen Harsaw C	.15	.25
87 Pyro, St. John Allerdyce C	.15	.25
88 Quicksilver, Pietro Maximoff C	.15	.25
89 Quicksilver, Speed Demon R	1.25	2.00
90 Rogue, Anna Raven C	.15	.25
91 Sabretooth, Feral Rage R	.75	1.25
92 Sabretooth, Victor Creed C	.15	.25
93 Sauron, Dr. Karl Lykos C	.15	.25
94 Scarlet Witch, Wanda Maximoff C	.15	.25
95 Toad, Mortimer Toynbee C	.15	.25
96 Unus, Angelo Unuscione U	.30	.50
97 Asteroid M U	.30	.50
98 Avalon Space Station U	.30	.50
99 Genosha R	1.50	2.50
100 Global Domination R	.60	1.00
101 Lost City U	.30	.50
102 Mutant Supremacy R	.75	1.25
103 Savage Land U	.30	.50
104 The Mutant Menace U	.30	.50
105 The New Brotherhood U	.30	.50
106 War On Humanity U	.30	.50
107 Boris, Personal Servant of Dr. Doom R	2.50	4.00
108 Darkoth, Major Desmund Pitt U	.30	.50
109 Doom Guards, Army C	.15	.25
110 Doom-Bot, Army U	.60	1.00
111 Dr. Doom, Diabolic Genius U	.30	.50
112 Dr. Doom, Victor Von Doom C	.15	.25
113 Dr. Doom, Lord of Latveria R	2.00	3.00
114 Dragon Man, Experimental Monster C	.15	.25
115 Kristoff Von Doom, The Boy Who Would Be Doom U	.30	.50
116 Rama-Tut, Pharaoh from the 30th Century R	.60	1.00
117 Robot Destroyer, Army R	.60	1.00
118 Robot Enforcer, Army C	.15	.25
119 Robot Seeker, Army C	.15	.25
120 Robot Sentry, Army C	.15	.25
121 Sub-Mariner, Ally of Doom R	1.25	2.00
122 Tibetan Monks, Army C	.15	.25
123 Titania, Mary MacPherran C	.15	.25
124 Victor Von Doom II, Son of Doom U	.30	.50
125 Volcana, Marsha Rosenberg U	.30	.50
126 Bitter Rivals U	.30	.50
127 Doom Triumphant R	.75	1.25
128 Doom's Throne Room R	.30	.50
129 Doomstadt C	.15	.25
130 Faces of Doom U	.30	.50
131 Latveria R	.60	1.00
132 Micro-Size C	.15	.25
133 Mystical Paralysis U	.30	.50
134 Power Compressor R	.60	1.00
135 Reign of Terror R	.75	1.25
136 The Power Cosmic R	.75	1.25
137 Bastion, Leader of Operation: Zero Tolerance R	1.25	2.00
138 Boliver Trask, Creator of the Sentinel Program R	1.25	2.00
139 Master Mold, Sentinel Supreme R	1.25	2.00
140 Nimrod, Mutant Hunter U	.30	.50
141 Senator Kelly, Anti-Mutant Advocate U	.30	.50
142 Sentinel Mark I, Army C	.15	.25
143 Sentinel Mark II, Army C	.15	.25
144 Sentinel Mark IV, Army U	.30	.50
145 Wild Sentinel, Army C	.15	.25
146 Combat Protocols U	.30	.50
147 Micro-Sentinels R	.75	1.25

Card	Low	High
148 Orbital Sentinel Base U	.30	.50
149 Primary Directive R	.60	1.00
150 Prime Sentinels U	.30	.50
151 Project: Wide Awake U	.30	.50
152 Reconstruction Program C	.15	.25
153 Search and Destroy U	.30	.50
154 South American Sentinel Base U	.30	.50
155 Underground Sentinel Base R	.75	1.25
156 Annihilus, Destroyer of Life R	.60	1.00
157 Blastaar, King of Baluur R	.75	1.25
158 Negative Zone U	.30	.50
159 Skrull Soldier, Army C	.15	.25
160 Super Skrull, Engineered Super-Soldier R	1.25	2.00
161 Apocalypse, En Sabah Nur R	1.50	2.50
162 Arcade, Master of Murderworld U	.30	.50
163 Black Tom, Thomas Cassidy C	.15	.25
164 Dark Phoenix, Cosmic Entity R	3.00	5.00
165 Juggernaut, Cain Marko R	2.00	3.00
166 Lady Deathstrike, Yuriko Oyama R	.75	1.25
167 Mojo, Ruler of Mojoworld U	.30	.50
168 Mr. Sinister, Dr. Nathaniel Essex R	1.25	2.00
169 Onslaught, Psionic Spawn of Xavier and Magneto R	2.00	3.00
170 Puppet Master, Philip Masters C	.15	.25
171 Random Punks, Army C	.15	.25
172 Spiral, Ricochet Rita C	.15	.25
173 Acrobatic Dodge C	.15	.25
174 Advanced Hardware C	.15	.25
175 Backfire C	.15	.25
176 Base of Operations C	.15	.25
177 Betrayal R	.75	1.25
178 Blind Sided R	.60	1.00
179 Borrowed Blade C	.15	.25
180 Burn Rubber C	.15	.25
181 Charge! U	.30	.50
182 Common Enemy U	.30	.50
183 Cover Fire C	.15	.25
184 Dual Sidearms C	.15	.25
185 Entangle U	.30	.50
186 Fall Back! U	.30	.50
187 Finishing Move C	.15	.25
188 Flame Trap R	1.00	1.50
189 Flying Kick C	.15	.25
190 Focused Blast U	.30	.50
191 Foiled R	1.25	2.00
192 Friendly Fire U	.30	.50
193 Gamma Bomb R	1.50	2.50
194 Greater of Two Evils R	.75	1.25
195 Heroes United U	.30	.50
196 Ka-Boom! R	2.00	3.00
197 Kevlar Body Armor U	.30	.50
198 Last Stand C	.15	.25
199 Marvel Team-Up U	.30	.50
200 Medical Attention C	.15	.25
201 Mutant Nation U	.30	.50
202 Nasty Surprise C	.15	.25
203 Night Vision U	.30	.50
204 Not So Fast U	.30	.50
205 One-Two Punch C	.15	.25
206 Overload U	.30	.50
207 Overpowered U	.30	.50
208 Personal Force Field U	.30	.50
209 Political Pressure R	.75	1.25
210 Press the Attack U	.30	.50
211 Reconnaissance U	.30	.50
212 Relocation R	.75	1.25
213 Salvage R	1.00	1.50
214 Savage Beatdown R	6.00	10.00
215 Surprise Attack C	.15	.25
216 Swift Escape U	.30	.50
217 Team Tactics C	.15	.25
218 Tech Upgrade C	.15	.25
219 Unlikely Allies U	.30	.50
220 Unstable Molecules C	.15	.25

2004 Vs System Superman Man of Steel

Card	Low	High
COMPLETE SET (165)	20.00	40.00
BOOSTER BOX (24 PACKS)	15.00	30.00
BOOSTER PACK (14 CARDS)	.75	1.25
*FOIL: .75X TO 2X BASIC CARDS		
RELEASED IN NOVEMBER 2004		
1 Alpha Centurion, Marcus Aelius C	.15	.25
2 Cir-El Supergirl, Daughter of Tomorrow C	.15	.25
3 Connor Kent Superboy, Kon-El U	.30	.50
4 Dubbilex, DNAlien U	.30	.50
5 Eradicator, Soul of Krypton C	.15	.25
6 Gangbuster, Jose Delgado C	.15	.25
7 Girl 13, Traci Thirteen U	.30	.50
8 Jimmy Olsen, Superman's Pal U	.30	.50
9 John Henry Irons Steel, Peerless Engineer C	.15	.25
10 Kara Zor-El Supergirl, Last Daughter of Krypton C	.15	.25
11 Krypto, Superdog R	.60	1.00
12 Lana Lang, Smallville Sweetheart U	.30	.50
13 Linda Danvers Supergirl, Matrix R	1.25	2.00
14 Lois Lane, Star Reporter U	.30	.50
15 Perry White, Chief R	1.00	1.50
16 Professor Emil Hamilton, Garrulous Genius C	.15	.25
17 Rose Thorn, Rose Forrest U	.30	.50
18 Scorn, Ceritak C	.15	.25
19 Strange Visitor, Sharon Vance R	.60	1.00
20 Superman, Blue R	.15	.25
21 Superman, Clark Kent C	.60	1.00
22 Superman, Kal-El U	2.50	4.00
23 Superman, Man of Steel R	.15	.25
24 Superman, Red C	.15	.25
25 Superman, Robots Army C	2.00	3.00
26 Cadmus Labs U	.30	.50
27 Daily Planet R	1.00	1.50
28 Entropy Aegis Armor R	.60	1.00
29 Fortress of Solitude U	.30	.50
30 Kandor R	.60	1.00
31 Last Son of Krypton R	1.00	1.50
32 Man of Tomorrow U	.30	.50
33 Super Speed U	.30	.50
34 X-Ray Vision R	1.00	1.50
35 Beautiful Dreamer, Forever People U	.30	.50
36 Big Barda, Barda Free C	.15	.25
37 Big Bear, Forever People C	.15	.25
38 Fastbak, Sky Scorcher C	.15	.25
39 Forager, Bug Warrior C	.15	.25
40 Himon, Enigmatic Researcher U	.30	.50
41 Infinity Man, Drax R	.60	1.00
42 Izaya Highfather, The Inheritor C	.15	.25
43 Lightray, Solis C	.15	.25
44 Lonar, Explorer U	.30	.50
45 Mark Moonrider, Forever People C	.15	.25
46 Metron, Time Traveler C	.15	.25
47 Orion, Dog of War R	.60	1.00
48 Orion, True Son of Darkseid C	.15	.25
49 Scott Free Mister Miracle, Escape Artist R	1.00	1.50
50 Serifan, Forever People C	.15	.25
51 Takion Highfather, Josh Saunders R	.60	1.00
52 Vykin, Forever People U	.30	.50
53 Astro Force R	1.25	2.00
54 Dog of War U	.30	.50
55 Escape Artist U	.30	.50
56 Forever People R	1.25	2.00
57 New Genesis R	1.25	2.00
58 Supercycle U	.30	.50
59 The Prophecy Fulfilled R	1.00	1.50
60 The Source R	3.00	5.00
61 Atomic Skull, Joe Martin U	.30	.50
62 Bizarro, Imperfect Duplicate R	1.50	2.50
63 Brainiac 2.5, Vrill Dox C	.15	.25
64 Dominus, Tuoni R	1.00	1.50
65 Doomsday, Armageddon Creature R	.60	1.00
66 Encantadora, Lourdes Lucero C	.15	.25
67 Eradicator, Doctor David Connor C	.15	.25
68 General Zod, Ruler of Pokolistan R	.60	1.00
69 Gog, Nemesis C	.15	.25
70 Hank Henshaw Cyborg, Evil Imposter R	1.00	1.50
71 Hope, Amazon Bodyguard U	.30	.50
72 Intergang, Army U	.30	.50
73 Lex Luthor, Power Armor C	.15	.25
74 Lex Luthor, President Luthor R	1.50	2.50
75 Massacre, Alien Bounty Hunter U	.30	.50
76 Mercy, Amazon Bodyguard C	.15	.25
77 Metallo, John Corben C	.15	.25
78 Mongal, Ruler of Almerac C	.15	.25
79 Mongul, Tyrant of Warworld C	.15	.25
80 Mr. Mxyzptlk, Fifth Dimension Imp U	.30	.50
81 Parasite, Rudy Jones C	.15	.25
82 Prankster, Oswald Loomis U	.30	.50
83 Satanus, Evil Incarnate R	.60	1.00
84 Silver Banshee, Siobhan McDougal C	.15	.25
85 Talia, LexCorp CEO U	.30	.50
86 Winslow Schott Toyman, Crooked Craftsman U	.30	.50
87 Bizarro World R	.60	1.00
88 Brainiac's Ship R	1.00	1.50
89 Feeding Time! U	.30	.50
90 Kryptonite R	1.00	1.50
91 LexCorp U	.30	.50
92 Revenge Pact R	1.00	1.50
93 State of the Union R	.60	1.00
94 Suicide Slums U	.30	.50
95 Toy Soldiers U	.30	.50
96 Warworld R	.60	1.00
97 Amazing Grace, Manipulator R	.60	1.00
98 Bernadeth, Leader of Female Furies C	.15	.25
99 Brimstone, Engine of Destruction R	.60	1.00
100 Darkseid, Lord of Apokolips R	1.50	2.50
101 Darkseid, Uxas U	.30	.50
102 Desaad, Royal Torturer C	.15	.25
103 Devilance, The Pursuer C	.15	.25
104 Glorious Godfrey, Persuader U	.30	.50
105 Gole, Deep Six U	.30	.50
106 Granny Goodness, Everyone's Favorite Granny C	.15	.25
107 Hunger Dogs, Army U	.30	.50
108 Jaffar, Deep Six U	.30	.50
109 Kalibak, Unworthy Son C	.15	.25
110 Kanto, Darkseid's Assassin C	.15	.25
111 Kurin, Deep Six U	.30	.50
112 Shaligo, Deep Six C	.15	.25
113 Slig, Deep Six C	.15	.25
114 Steppenwolf, Darkseid's General C	.15	.25
115 Superman, False Son R	.30	.50
116 Topkick, Parademon Drill Instructor U	.30	.50
117 Trok, Deep Six C	.15	.25
118 Anti-Life Equation R	.60	1.00
119 Apokolips R	.60	1.00
120 Armagetto U	.30	.50
121 Beta Club U	.30	.50
122 Firepits of Apokolips U	.30	.50
123 Granny Loves You U	.30	.50
124 Happiness Home R	.60	1.00
125 Hordes of Apokolips U	.30	.50
126 Omega Beams R	.60	1.00
127 Ride of the Black Racer R	.60	1.00
128 Blood Feud U	.30	.50
129 Phantom Zone U	.30	.50
130 The Exchange R	.60	1.00
131 Barbara Gordon Batgirl, Guardian of Gotham R	1.25	2.00
132 Jason Todd Robin, Crime Fighter R	1.25	2.00
133 Spoiler Robin, The Girl Wonder U	.30	.50
134 Detective Work R	1.50	2.50
135 Donna Troy Troia, Child of Myth R	1.25	2.00
136 Roy Harper Speedy, Mercurial Marksman R	.60	1.00
137 Wally West Kid Flash, Fastest Teen Alive R	.60	1.00
138 New Teen Titans R	1.50	2.50
139 Blockbuster, Roland Desmond U	.30	.50
140 Maxie Zeus, God Complex U	.30	.50
141 The Joker, Emperor Joker R	1.25	2.00
142 Smiles, Everyone! R	.60	1.00
143 Bronze Tiger, Benjamin Turner U	.30	.50
144 Merlyn, Deadly Archer U	.30	.50
145 Pit of Madness R	.60	1.00
146 The Demon's Head R	.60	1.00
147 Charger, Power Conduit U	.30	.50
148 Deuce, Miss Perception U	.30	.50
149 Imperiex, The Beginning and The End R	.60	1.00
150 Back to Back C	.15	.25
151 Boom Tube C	.15	.25
152 Female Furies C	.15	.25
153 Heat Vision C	.15	.25
154 I Hate Magic! C	.15	.25
155 Men of Steel C	.15	.25
156 Metropolis C	.15	.25
157 Mother Box U	.30	.50
158 Narrow Escape C	.15	.25
159 Path of Destruction C	.15	.25
160 Phantom Zone Projector U	.30	.50
161 Play Time C	.15	.25
162 Royal Decree U	.30	.50
163 Stopped Cold C	.15	.25
164 Super Strength C	.15	.25
165 Up, Up, and Away C	.15	.25

2004 Vs System Web of Spider-Man

Card	Low	High
COMPLETE SET (165)	25.00	50.00
BOOSTER BOX (24 PACKS)	20.00	40.00
BOOSTER PACK (14 CARDS)	.75	1.50
*FOIL: .75X TO 2X BASIC CARDS		
RELEASED IN SEPTEMBER 2004		
1 Black Cat, Felicia Hardy C	.15	.25
2 Daredevil, The Man Without Fear C	.15	.25
3 Madame Web, Cassandra Webb C	.15	.25
4 Prowler, Hobie Brown C	.15	.25
5 Punisher, Vigilante U	.30	.50
6 Solo, James Bourne C	.15	.25
7 Spider-Man, Friendly Neighborhood Spider-Man C	.15	.25
8 Spider-Man, The Amazing Spider-Man R	2.00	3.00
9 Nova, Richard Rider U	.30	.50
10 Daily Bugle U	.30	.50
11 ESU Science Lab U	.30	.50
12 Spider Senses U	.30	.50
13 Twist of Fate U	.30	.50
14 Dr. Octopus, Doc Ock R	2.00	3.00
15 Dr. Octopus, Otto Octavius C	.15	.25
16 Electro, Maxwell Dillon U	.30	.50
17 Green Goblin, Norman Osborn C	.15	.25
18 Kraven the Hunter, Sergei Kravinoff C	.15	.25
19 Lizard, Dr. Curtis Connors C	.15	.25
20 Rhino, Alex O'Hirn C	.15	.25
21 Venom, Eddie Brock U	.30	.50
22 Vulture, Adrian Toomes C	.15	.25
23 Doc Ock's Lab U	.30	.50
24 Osborn Industries U	.30	.50
25 Sadistic Choice U	.30	.50
26 Sinister Salvo U	.30	.50
27 Alley-Oop! C	.15	.25
28 Crushing Blow C	.15	.25
29 Jetpack C	.15	.25
30 No Fear C	.15	.25
31 Smoke Screen C	.15	.25
32 Aunt May, May Parker U	.30	.50
33 Black Cat, Master Thief U	.30	.50
34 Cardiac, Elias Wirtham U	.30	.50
35 Cloak, Tyrone Johnson C	.15	.25
36 Dagger, Tandy Bowen U	.30	.50
37 Dusk, Cassie St. Commons C	.15	.25
38 Ezekiel, Spirit of the Spider C	.15	.25
39 Firestar, Hot Stuff R	.75	1.25
40 Hornet, Eddie McDonough C	.15	.25
41 Human Torch, Friendly Rival C	.15	.25
42 Iceman, Cool Customer C	.15	.25
43 Jessica Drew Spider-Woman, Venom Blast U	.30	.50
44 Julia Carpenter Spider-Woman, Web Weaver R	1.25	2.00
45 Mary Jane Watson, MJ R	2.00	3.00
46 Mattie Franklin Spider-Woman, Gift of Power U	.30	.50
47 Prodigy, Richie Gilmore C	.15	.25
48 Puma, Thomas Fireheart C	.15	.25
49 Ricochet, Johnny Gallo C	.15	.25
50 Rocket Racer, Robert Farrell C	.15	.25
51 Scarlet Spider, Ben Reilly C	.15	.25
52 Silver Sable, Silver Sablinovia C	.15	.25
53 Spider-Man, Alien Symbiote C	.15	.25
54 Spider-Man, Cosmic Spider-Man R	4.00	6.00
55 Wild Pack, Army C	.15	.25
56 Will O' The Wisp, Jackson Arvad R	.75	1.25
57 Ace Reporter R	.75	1.25
58 Armored Spider Suit U	.30	.50
59 Costume Change U	.30	.50
60 Fun and Games R	.75	1.25
61 Going My Way? U	.30	.50
62 Midtown High School C	.15	.25
63 My Hero U	.30	.50
64 Nice Try! R	.75	1.25
65 Spider-Tracer R	.75	1.25
66 Sticky Situation U	.30	.50
67 Tragic Loss U	.30	.50
68 Unexpected Mutation U	.30	.50
69 Alistair Smythe, Ultimate Spider Slayer R	.75	1.25
70 Beetle, Abner Jenkins C	.15	.25
71 Boomerang, Fred Myers C	.15	.25
72 Carnage, Cletus Kasady R	1.50	2.50
73 Chameleon, Dmitri Smerdyakov C	.15	.25
74 Green Goblin, Altered Ego C	.15	.25
75 Hammerhead, Gangster C	.15	.25
76 Hobgoblin, Roderick Kingsley C	.15	.25
77 Hydro-Man, Morris Bench C	.15	.25
78 Jackal, Dr. Miles Warren C	.15	.25
79 Kaine, Imperfect Clone C	.15	.25
80 Kingpin, Crime Boss R	1.50	2.50
81 Man-Wolf, John Jameson C	.15	.25
82 Morbius, Dr. Michael Morbius R	1.50	2.50
83 Mysterio, Quentin Beck R	.75	1.25
84 Sandman, William Baker R	1.50	2.50
85 Scorpion, MacDonald Gargan C	.15	.25
86 Shocker, Herman Schultz C	.15	.25
87 Shriek, Frances Barrison U	.30	.50
88 Silvermane, Silvio Manfredi C	.15	.25
89 Speed Demon, James Sanders C	.15	.25
90 The Rose, Richard Fisk R	.75	1.25
91 Tinkerer, Phineas Mason R	.75	1.25
92 Tombstone, Lonnie Lincoln R	1.25	2.00
93 Venom, Alien Symbiote R	3.00	5.00
94 Dangerous Experiment R	1.25	2.00
95 Fisk Towers R	.75	1.25
96 Get Him My Petsss R	.75	1.25
97 Goblin Glider U	.30	.50

98 Hired Goons C .15 .25
99 Lion's Den C .15 .25
100 Oscorp Board Room U .30 .50
101 Rejuvenation U .30 .50
102 Spider Slayers U .30 .50
103 Archangel, Angel of Death U .30 .50
104 Emma Frost, Headmistress of Xavier's Academy R 2.50 4.00
105 John Proudstar Thunderbird, Apache Warrior U .30 .50
106 Shadowcat, Pride of the X-Men U .30 .50
107 Sunfire, Shiro Yoshida R .75 1.25
108 Aerial Supremacy U .30 .50
109 Bamf! R 2.00 3.00
110 Madripoor U .30 .50
111 Power Nexus R 1.25 2.00
112 Siege Perilous R .75 1.25
113 Ultimate Sacrifice R 2.00 3.00
114 Silver Surfer, Norrin Radd R 4.00 6.00
115 Wyatt Wingfoot, Keewazi Adventurer U .30 .50
116 Marvel's First Family R 1.25 2.00
117 Pier 4 R .75 1.25
118 Supernova U .30 .50
119 Mimic, Calvin Rankin R 1.50 2.50
120 Post, Kevin Tremain R .75 1.25
121 Thornn, Feral Hunter U .30 .50
122 Insignificant Threat R .75 1.25
123 Misappropriation U .30 .50
124 Rise to Power R 1.25 2.00
125 Volcanic Base R .75 1.25
126 Dr. Hauptmann, Diabolic Inventor U .30 .50
127 Purple Man, Zebediah Killgrave U .30 .50
128 Terrax, Tyros R .75 1.25
129 Decoy Program R .75 1.25
130 Devil's Due R 1.25 2.00
131 Latverian Embassy R .75 1.25
132 Mark II, Number II, Leader Unit R 1.50 2.50
133 Sentinel Mark V, Army C .15 .25
134 Sentinel Mark III, Army C .15 .25
135 Tri-Sentinel, Super Sentinel R .75 1.25
136 Next Generation Technology R 1.25 2.00
137 Termination Sequence R 1.25 2.00
138 Wave of Sentinels R .75 1.25
139 Lyja, The Lazerfist U .30 .50
140 Deathlok, Luther Manning R 1.50 2.50
141 J. Jonah Jameson, Sensationalist R 1.25 2.00
142 Mole Man, Leader of the Moloids U .30 .50
143 Bad Press R .75 1.25
144 Big Bully C .15 .25
145 Breaking Story U .30 .50
146 Clone Saga U .30 .50
147 Com Link U .30 .50
148 Crowd Control C .15 .25
149 Fight to the Finish U .30 .50
150 Flamethrower R .75 1.25
151 Forced Allegiance U .30 .50
152 Grounded C .15 .25
153 Mojoverse C .15 .25
154 Murderworld R 1.50 2.50
155 Pinned U .30 .50
156 Pleasant Distraction U .30 .50
157 Rapier U .30 .50
158 Rise from the Grave R .75 1.25
159 Sinister Six U .30 .50
160 Sonic Gun U .30 .50
161 Sucker Punch U .30 .50
162 Surrounded C .15 .25
163 Thinking Outside the Box R .75 1.25
164 Time Platform R .75 1.25
165 Unmasked U .30 .50

2005 Vs System The Avengers

COMPLETE SET (220) 25.00 50.00
BOOSTER BOX (24 PACKS) 20.00 40.00
BOOSTER PACK (14 CARDS) 1.00 2.00
*FOIL: .75X TO 2X BASIC CARDS
RELEASED IN AUGUST 2005
1 Beast, Furry Blue Scientist C .15 .25
2 Black Panther, T'challa U .30 .50
3 Captain America, Steve Rogers C .15 .25
4 Captain America, Super Soldier R 1.50 2.50
5 Carol Danvers Warbird, Galactic Adventurer C .15 .25
6 Dane Whitman Black Knight, Heroic Paladin C .15 .25
7 Falcon, Sam Wilson C .15 .25
8 Hank Pym Ant Man, Diminutive Hero C .15 .25
9 Hank Pym Giant Man, Towering Titan U .30 .50
10 Hank Pym Goliath, Giant Genius C .15 .25
11 Hank Pym Yellowjacket, Pym Particle Creator C .15 .25
12 Hawkeye, Clinton Barton C .15 .25
13 Hercules, Son of Zeus U .30 .50
14 Hulk, Gamma Rage R .75 1.25
15 Iron Man, Invincible C .15 .25
16 Iron Man, Tony Stark C .15 .25
17 Jarvis, Honorary Avenger R 1.50 2.50
18 Monica Rambeau Captain Marvel, Lady of Light R 1.50 2.50
19 Natasha Romanoff Black Widow, Super Spy U .30 .50
20 Quicksilver, Mutant Avenger C .15 .25
21 Rick Jones, A Hero's Best Friend U .30 .50
22 Scarlet Witch, Mistress of Chaos Magic C .15 .25
23 She-Hulk, Gamma Bombshell C .15 .25
24 Thor, God of Thunder R 2.50 4.00
25 Thor, Odinson R 2.50 4.00
26 Vision, Synthetic Humanoid C .15 .25
27 Wasp, Janet Van Dyne-Pym C .15 .25
28 Wonder Man, Simon Williams U .30 .50
29 Avengers Assemble! R 3.00 5.00
30 Avengers Mansion R 1.50 2.50
31 Call Down the Lightning C .15 .25
32 Chaos Magic R .60 1.00
33 Earth's Mightiest Heroes R 2.00 3.00
34 Legendary Battles C .15 .25
35 Mjolnir R .75 1.25
36 Playroom C .15 .25
37 Pym Laboratories U .30 .50
38 Quinjet C .15 .25
39 Repel Attack C .15 .25
40 Repulsor Ray C .15 .25
41 Two Worlds, Team-Up C .15 .25
42 Walk Through Walls R .60 1.00
43 Albert Gaines Nuke, Atomic Powerhouse C .15 .25
44 Amphibian, Kingsley Rice R .60 1.00
45 Ape X, Xina C .15 .25
46 Arcanna, Arcanna Jones C .15 .25
47 Blue Eagle, James Dore Jr. C .15 .25
48 Doctor Decibel, Anton Decibel C .15 .25
49 Doctor Spectrum, Joe Ledger R .75 1.25
50 Foxfire, Olivia Underwood U .30 .50
51 Golden Archer, Wyatt McDonald C .15 .25
52 Haywire, Harold Danforth C .15 .25
53 Hyperion, Mark Milton C .15 .25
54 Hyperion, Sun God R .60 1.00
55 Inertia, Edith Freiberg C .15 .25
56 Lady Lark, Linda Lewis U .30 .50
57 Lamprey, Donald McQuiggan C .15 .25
58 Moonglow, Melissa Hanover C .15 .25
59 Nighthawk, Kyle Richmond C .15 .25
60 Power Princess, The Last Utopian R .60 1.00
61 Power Princess, Zarda C .15 .25
62 Quagmire, Jerome Meyers U .30 .50
63 Redstone, Michael Redstone U .30 .50
64 Shape, Malleable Mutant U .30 .50
65 Skymax, Skrullian Skymaster C .15 .25
66 Thermite, Sam Yurimoto C .15 .25
67 Tom Thumb, Thomas Thompson C .15 .25
68 Whizzer, Stanley Stewart U .30 .50
69 AIDA R .60 1.00
70 Airskimmer C .15 .25
71 Answer the Call C .15 .25
72 Behavior Modification Device, Team-Up C .15 .25
73 Eldritch Power C .15 .25
74 Hibernaculum C .15 .25
75 Other-Earth R .75 1.25
76 Panacea Potion U .30 .50
77 Peace in Our Time U .30 .50
78 Project Utopia R .60 1.00
79 Rocket Central R .60 1.00
80 Squadron City R .60 1.00
81 Supply Line U .30 .50
82 Utopia Isle U .30 .50
83 Beetle Mach 1, Reluctant Hero C .15 .25
84 Beetle Mach 2, Matthew Davis C .15 .25
85 Beetle Mach 3, Repentant Villain U .30 .50
86 Beetle Mach 4, New Team Leader C .15 .25
87 Blizzard, Donny Gill C .15 .25
88 Charcoal, Charles Burlingame C .15 .25
89 Dallas Riordan, Mayoral Aide C .15 .25
90 Dallas Riordan Vantage, Ionic Inheritor C .15 .25
91 Erik Josten Atlas, Ionic Powerhouse R .60 1.00
92 Erik Josten Atlas, Kosmos Convict U .30 .50
93 Genis-Vell Captain Marvel, Son of Mar-Vell R .75 1.25
94 Hawkeye, Leader by Example R 1.00 1.50
95 Helmut Zemo Citizen V, Tactician C .15 .25
96 Helmut Zemo Citizen V, Warmonger C .15 .25
97 Iron Man Cobalt Man, Avenger in Disguise C .15 .25
98 Jolt, Helen Takahama C .15 .25
99 Joystick, Janice Yanizesh U .30 .50
100 Karla Sofen Meteorite, Celestial Power R .60 1.00
101 Karla Sofen Meteorite, Twin Moonstones R .60 1.00
102 Melissa Gold Songbird, Heroine Unbound C .15 .25
103 Melissa Gold Songbird, Sonic Carapace U .30 .50
104 Ogre, Weaponsmith U .30 .50
105 Paul Ebersol Techno, Gadgeteer C .15 .25
106 Paul Ebersol Techno, Man of Metal C .15 .25
107 Plant Man Blackheath, Samuel Smithers C .15 .25
108 Radioactive Man, Reformed Renegade U .30 .50
109 Speed Demon, Second Chance Speedster U .30 .50
110 A Second Chance U .30 .50
111 Biomodem Satellite U .30 .50
112 Combat Maneuvers C .15 .25
113 Deadly Conspiracy C .15 .25
114 Justice, Like Lightning C .15 .25
115 Marvel's Most Wanted R .60 1.00
116 Mt. Charteris R .60 1.00
117 New Identity R 2.00 3.00
118 Project Liberator R .60 1.00
119 Stormfront-1, Team-Up C .15 .25
120 Thunder Jet C .15 .25
121 Thunderbolts Plaza R .60 1.00
122 V-Wing U .30 .50
123 Win-Lose Deal U .30 .50
124 Beetle, Armorsmith C .15 .25
125 Bulldozer, Wrecking Crew C .15 .25
126 Egghead, Elihas Starr C .15 .25
127 Enchantress, Amora C .15 .25
128 Erik Josten Goliath, Growing Menace C .15 .25
129 Executioner, Scourge of Jotunheim R .60 1.00
130 Grey Gargoyle, Paul Pierre Duval U .30 .50
131 Heinrich Zemo Baron Zemo, Baron of Zeulniz C .15 .25
132 Helmut Zemo Baron Zemo, Uber Enemy U .30 .50
133 Karla Sofen Moonstone, Master Manipulator U .30 .50
134 Klaw, Ulysses Klaw R .75 1.25
135 Marcus Daniels Blackout, Darkbringer C .15 .25
136 Melissa Gold Screaming Mimi, Mimi Schwartz C .15 .25
137 Melter, Bruno Horgan C .15 .25
138 Mr. Hyde, Engine of Destruction C .15 .25
139 Nathan Garrett Black Knight, Corrupt Crusader C .15 .25
140 Paul Ebersol Fixer, Problem Solver R .60 1.00
141 Piledriver, Wrecking Crew C .15 .25
142 Radioactive Man, Chen Lu C .15 .25
143 Scorpion, Fatal Sting U .30 .50
144 Shocker, Vibro-Shock Villain R .60 1.00
145 The Wrecker, Wrecking Crew C .15 .25
146 Thunderball, Wrecking Crew C .15 .25
147 Tiger Shark, Todd Arliss C .15 .25
148 Titania, Vengeful Vixen C .15 .25
149 Ultron Crimson Cowl, Dark Disguise U .30 .50
150 Ultron Ultron 5, Ultimate Evil R .60 1.00
151 Whirlwind, David Cannon U .30 .50
152 Yellowjacket, Rita DeMara C .15 .25
153 Adhesive X U .30 .50
154 Crime Spree C .15 .25
155 Evil Reborn C .15 .25
156 Hard Sound Construct, Construct R .75 1.25
157 Hero's Demise R .75 1.25
158 Mystic Summons C .15 .25
159 Sonic Disruption C .15 .25
160 Stolen Power C .15 .25
161 The Wrecking Crew C .15 .25
162 Under Siege R .60 1.00
163 Unfair Advantage C .15 .25
164 Amenhotep, Dark Pharaoh U .30 .50
165 Baltag, Hand of the Conqueror C .15 .25
166 Growing Man, Kinetic Stimuloid U .30 .50
167 Kang Kross-roads U .30 .50
168 Kang, Earth Mesozoic-24 U .30 .50
169 Kang, Immortus R .60 1.00
170 Kang, Kang Cobra C .15 .25
171 Kang, Kang Kong R .60 1.00
172 Kang, Kang Ransom R .75 1.25
173 Kang, Lord Kang R .60 1.00
174 Kang, Lord of Limbo C .15 .25
175 Kang, Master of Time C .15 .25
176 Kang, Rama Tut U .30 .50
177 Kang, The Conqueror R .60 1.00
178 Kang's Guards, Army U .30 .50
179 Macrobots, Army C .15 .25
180 Tempus, Menace out of Time C .15 .25
181 Game of the Galaxy R .60 1.00
182 Kang, Ultimate Kang C .15 .25
183 Null Time Zone R 1.50 2.50
184 Psyche-Globe U .30 .50
185 Spheres of Solitude U .30 .50
186 The Time Keepers C .15 .25
187 Faces of Evil, Team-Up C .15 .25
188 Justice for All, Team-Up C .15 .25
189 Supreme Sanction, Team-Up C .15 .25
190 A Day Unlike Any Other, Team-Up C .15 .25
191 Avengers Disassembled R .60 1.00
192 Call to Arms C .15 .25
193 Force Field Belt C .15 .25
194 Heroes in Reserve C .15 .25
195 Insect Swarm C .15 .25
196 Might Makes Right C .15 .25
197 Prismatic Shield, Construct C .15 .25
198 Seek Cover C .15 .25
199 Shrink U .30 .50
200 System Failure R 1.25 2.00
201 United We Stand C .15 .25
202 War of Attrition R .60 1.00
203 Windstorm C .15 .25
204 Polaris, Lorna Dane U .30 .50
205 Framistat U .30 .50
206 Mammomax, Elephant Boy U .30 .50
207 Zorba, Deposed Leader of Latveria R .60 1.00
208 Ahab, Houndkeeper U .30 .50
209 Spider-Man, Peter Parker R 2.00 3.00
210 White Tiger, Hector Ayala U .30 .50
211 Basilisk, Basil Elks U .30 .50
212 Vermin, Sewer Rat U .30 .50
213 Lady Punisher, Lynn Michaels U .30 .50
214 Bring Down the House R .60 1.00
215 Phat, Liv'n Large U .30 .50
216 Mutant of the Year R .75 1.25
217 Hitman, Burt Kenyon U .30 .50
218 Hired Hit R .75 1.25
219 Mortician, Toussaint Morrow U .30 .50
220 Spirits of Vengeance R .60 1.00

2005 Vs System Green Lantern Corps

COMPLETE SET (220) 30.00 60.00
BOOSTER BOX (24 PACKS) 30.00 60.00
BOOSTER PACK (14 CARDS) 1.50 2.50
*FOIL: .75X TO 2X BASIC CARDS
RELEASED IN MAY 2005
1 Abin Sur, Green Lantern of Ungara U .30 .50
2 Alan Scott, Keeper of the Starheart C .15 .25
3 Anti-Green Lantern, Army C .30 .50
4 Anti-Matter Cannon R .15 .25
5 Anti-Matter Universe R .30 .50
6 Anti-Monitor, Architect of Destruction R .15 .25
7 Apokoliptian Hospitality U .15 .25
8 Appa Ali Apsa, Mad God R .15 .25
9 Arisia, Green Lantern of Graxos IV U .15 .25
10 Armies of Qward R 2.50 4.00
11 Azrael Batman, Knightfall U 1.50 2.50
12 Banished to the Anti-Matter Universe U .30 .50
13 Bart Allen Impulse, Hyper-Accelerated U .15 .25
14 Bat's Belfry R .15 .25
15 Battered and Broken U .15 .25
16 Battle of Wills C .15 .25
17 Birthing Chamber U .15 .25
18 Black Hand, Dark-Hearted Villain C .15 .25
19 Blood in the Dark U 1.50 2.50
20 Boodikka, Green Lantern of Bellatrix C .30 .50
21 Book of Oa C .15 .25
22 Breaking Ground, Construct R .15 .25
23 Brik, Green Lantern of Dryad U .30 .50
24 Carol Ferris Star Sapphire, Beloved Enemy C 3.00 5.00
25 Catcher's Mitt, Construct C .30 .50
26 Central Power Battery C .15 .25
27 Ch'p, Green Lantern of H'lven C .15 .25
28 Children of Forever R .15 .25
29 Chopping Block, Construct C .15 .25
30 Coast City C .30 .50
31 Commander, Military Leader of New Genesis R .30 .50
32 Cosmic Conflict C .15 .25
33 Council of Power R .30 .50
34 Damsel in Distress, Construct C .75 1.25
35 Darkseid Undenied R 2.00 3.00
36 Dead-Eye, Qwardian Conglomerate U .30 .50
37 Death of Superman R .50 .75
38 Dimming of the Starheart C .15 .25

Card	Low	High
39 Dr. Bedlam, Psionic Being R	.15	.25
40 Dr. Ebenezer Darrk, Original Leader of the League U	.30	.50
41 Dr. Light, Master of Holograms U	.15	.25
42 Dr. Polaris, Dr. Neal Emerson C	.15	.25
43 Dr. Ub'X, Galactic Conqueror C	1.25	2.00
44 Elasti-Man, Qwardian Conglomerate C	.50	.75
45 Element Man, Qwardian Conglomerate C	.15	.25
46 Emerald City, Construct R	.15	.25
47 Emerald Dawn U	2.50	4.00
48 Emerald Twilight U	.15	.25
49 Empire of Tears U	.30	.50
50 Evil Star, Servant of the Star-Band R	.15	.25
51 Fatality, Yrra Cynril R	.15	.25
52 Femme Fatality U	.15	.25
53 Fiero, Qwardian Conglomerate C	.30	.50
54 Fifth Dimension R	.15	.25
55 Fire Support C	.15	.25
56 Fists of the Guardians, Oan Enforcers U	.15	.25
57 Force Sphere, Construct C	.15	.25
58 From Qward With Hate R	2.00	3.00
59 Frostbite, Qwardian Conglomerate C	.15	.25
60 G'Nort, Green Lantern of G'Newt C	.30	.50
61 Ganthet, Last Guardian C	.30	.50
62 Garth Aqualad, Atlantean Ambassador U	.15	.25
63 Gnaxos, Arena Robot C	.30	.50
64 Golden Death C	.15	.25
65 Goldface, Keith Kenyon C	.30	.50
66 Governor Tozad, Planetary Commander U	.30	.50
67 Grandmaster, Manhunter Leader R	.30	.50
68 Grayven, Son of Darkseid C	.15	.25
69 Green Lantern Ring U	.30	.50
70 Guardians Reborn U	.50	.75
71 Guy Gardner, Strong Arm of the Corps C	.50	.75
72 Guy Gardner, Warrior C	.50	.75
73 Hal Jordan, Green Lantern of Earth C	.15	.25
74 Hal Jordan, Green Lantern of Sector 2814 R	.15	.25
75 Hal Jordan, Reborn R	1.25	2.00
76 Hal Jordan, Parallax R	.30	.50
77 Hal Jordan Spectre, Mortal Avatar R	.15	.25
78 Hard-Traveling Heroes C	.15	.25
79 Harlequin, Molly Mayne-Scott C	.15	.25
80 Hector Hammond, Super-Futuristic Mind C	.15	.25
81 Helping Hand, Construct C	.15	.25
82 Henry King Jr. Brainwave, Psionic Manipulator U	1.50	2.50
83 Highmaster, Supreme Leader C	.30	.50
84 Hostage Situation R	1.25	2.00
85 House of El U	.15	.25
86 Hush, Mystery Man R	.15	.25
87 In Darkest Night U	.30	.50
88 In Evil Star's Evil Clutches C	.15	.25
89 In Remembrance C	.30	.50
90 In the Hands of Qward R	.30	.50
91 Invisible Destroyer, Subconscious Entity C	.15	.25
92 Jack T. Chance, Green Lantern of Garnet U	.15	.25
93 Jackhammer, Construct C	.15	.25
94 Jade, Jennifer-Lynn Hayden C	.15	.25
95 Jailbird, Construct R	.15	.25
96 Jericho, Joseph Wilson R	.15	.25
97 John Stewart, Green Lantern of Earth C	.15	.25
98 Johnny Quick, Crime Syndicate R	.30	.50
99 Katma Tui, Green Lantern of Korugar C	1.50	2.50
100 Kilowog, Green Lantern of Bolovax Vik C	.75	1.25
101 Kiman, Chief Weaponer U	.30	.50
102 Korugar R	.50	.75
103 Kreon, Green Lantern of Tebis C	.50	.75
104 Krona, Creator of the Anti-Matter Universe C	.15	.25
105 Kyle Rayner, Green Lantern of the Universe C	.30	.50
106 Kyle Rayner, Ion R	.15	.25
107 Kyle Rayner, Last Green Lantern U	.50	.75
108 Lana Lang, Manhunter Sleeper U	.50	.75
109 Lantern's Light C	.15	.25
110 Lanterns in Love, Construct C	.30	.50
111 Legion, He Who Is Many C	.30	.50
112 Light Armor, Construct C	.50	.75
113 Light Brigade, Construct C	.15	.25
114 Living Ink, Construct C	.15	.25
115 Locked in Combat C	.30	.50
116 Major Disaster, Paul Booker U	.15	.25
117 Major Force, Clifford Zmeck C	.15	.25
118 Malvolio, Lord of the Green Flame C	.15	.25
119 Manhunter Engineer, Army C	.15	.25
120 Manhunter Excavator, Army C	.15	.25
121 Manhunter Giant, Army C	.15	.25
122 Manhunter Guardsman, Army C	.15	.25
123 Manhunter Infiltrator, Army C	.15	.25
124 Manhunter Lantern, Power Ring Thief C	.15	.25
125 Manhunter Protector, Army C	.15	.25
126 Manhunter Science C	.50	.75
127 Manhunter Sniper, Army C	.15	.25
128 Manhunter Soldier, Army C	.15	.25
129 Manhunter Spacecraft R	.15	.25
130 Manhunter Transphere C	.50	.75
131 Mark Shaw, Manhunter C	.15	.25
132 Mean Green Machine, Construct U	.15	.25
133 Millennium C	.75	1.25
134 Mogo R	.15	.25
135 Mosaic World C	.15	.25
136 Mouse Trap, Construct U	.75	1.25
137 Myrwhydden, Mightiest of Mages C	.15	.25
138 Nero, Qwardian Puppet R	1.25	2.00
139 Nero Unleashed C	1.25	2.00
140 No Evil Shall Escape Our Sight, Construct C	.75	1.25
141 No Man Escapes the Manhunters C	.30	.50
142 Oa R	.30	.50
143 Olapet, Green Lantern of Southern Goldstar C	.30	.50
144 Ole!, Construct C	.75	1.25
145 Only a Friend Can Betray You C	1.25	2.00
146 Orinda R	.75	1.25
147 Owlman, Crime Syndicate C	.30	.50
148 Pan, Manhunter Duplicate R	.50	.75
149 Parademons, Army U	.50	.75
150 Pest Control, Construct C	.30	.50
151 Plans Within Plans C	2.00	3.00
152 Power Armor Elite, Army U	.75	1.25
153 Power Ring, Crime Syndicate C	.50	.75
154 Power Surge U	.50	.75
155 Prison Planet R	.30	.50
156 Prisoner of a Mad God R	.30	.50
157 Q Energy U	.30	.50
158 Q Field C	.75	1.25
159 Qward R	.30	.50
160 Qwardian Council Hall R	.75	1.25
161 Qwardian Pincer C	.30	.50
162 Qwardian Watchdog, Gatekeeper U	.30	.50
163 Qwardians, Army C	.30	.50
164 Ragman, Rory Regan R	.50	.75
165 Rain of Acorns, Construct U	.50	.75
166 Rebellion on Oa R	.75	1.25
167 Recharging the Ring C	.75	1.25
168 Reciting the Oath U	.30	.50
169 Reign of Terra R	.30	.50
170 Remoni-Notra Star Sapphire, Obsessed Warrior Princess C	.50	.75
171 Rocket Red, Manhunter Sleeper C	.75	1.25
172 Rot Lop Fan, F-Sharp Bell of the Obsidian Deeps C	.30	.50
173 S.T.A.R. Labs R	.15	.25
174 Salakk, Green Lantern of Slyggia U	.15	.25
175 Scarab, Qwardian Conglomerate U	2.00	3.00
176 Sector 2814 U	.15	.25
177 Sensei, Martial Arts Master U	.30	.50
178 Shadow Creatures, Army U	.15	.25
179 Shadows of the Past R	.15	.25
180 Shock Troops C	.50	.75
181 Sinestro, Lantern in Exile C	.15	.25
182 Sinestro, Green Lantern of Korugar R	.30	.50
183 Sinestro, Enemy of the Corps R	.15	.25
184 Sinestro Defiant C	.50	.75
185 Sleeper Agent, Manhunter Sleeper C	.15	.25
186 Slipstream, Qwardian Conglomerate C	.15	.25
187 Soldiers of New Genesis, Army U	.15	.25
188 Solomon Grundy, Born on a Monday C	.15	.25
189 Sonar, Dastardly Discord C	.15	.25
190 Space Bears, Construct C	.30	.50
191 St'nlli, Super-Qwardian C	.15	.25
192 Starlings, Army U	.15	.25
193 Stealing the Light C	.15	.25
194 Sturmer, War Dog R	.15	.25
195 Superman, Returned U	.50	.75
196 Supermanhunter, Kryptonite Armor C	.15	.25
197 Superwoman, Crime Syndicate C	.15	.25
198 Sweeping Up, Construct C	.15	.25
199 Tattooed Man, Abel Tarrant U	.15	.25
200 The Fall of Oa R	.15	.25
201 The Kent Farm R	.15	.25
202 The Manhunters are a Myth R	.15	.25
203 The Ring Has Chosen U	.15	.25
204 The Shark, T. S. Smith C	.15	.25
205 Thunderous Onslaught C	.15	.25
206 Tomar Re, Green Lantern of Xudar U	.15	.25
207 Tomar Tu, Green Lantern of Xudar C	.30	.50
208 Trapped in the Sciencells U	.15	.25
209 Two-Face, Split Personality R	.30	.50
210 Ultraman, Crime Syndicate C	.15	.25
211 Underground Complex U	.30	.50
212 Uppercut, Construct C	.15	.25
213 Virman Vundabar, Military Leader of Apokolips U	.15	.25
214 Weaponers of Qward, Army C	.15	.25
215 Willworld R	.30	.50
216 Xallarap, Anti-Green Lantern Corps C	.30	.50
217 Yellow Impurity C	.15	.25
218 Yellow Power Ring U	.50	.75
219 Yokal, The Atrocious U	.15	.25
220 Zero Hour R	1.50	2.50

2005 Vs System Justice League of America

Card	Low	High
COMPLETE SET (220)	25.00	50.00
BOOSTER BOX (24 PACKS)	25.00	50.00
BOOSTER PACK (14 CARDS)	1.00	2.00
*FOIL: .75X TO 2X BASIC CARDS		
RELEASED IN NOVEMBER 2005		
1 Aquaman, Arthur Curry C	.15	.25
2 Aquaman, King of the Seven Seas U	.30	.50
3 Barry Allen The Flash, Scarlet Speedster R	.50	.75
4 Batman, Avatar of Justice C	.15	.25
5 Connor Hawke Green Arrow, Son of the Archer U	.30	.50
6 Dinah Laurel Lance Black Canary, Blonde Bombshell C	.15	.25
7 Elongated Man, Ralph Dibny C	.15	.25
8 Faith, The Fat Lady U	.30	.50
9 Firestorm, The Nuclear Man U	.30	.50
10 Gypsy, Cynthia Reynolds C	.15	.25
11 Hal Jordan, Hard-Traveling Hero C	.15	.25
12 John Henry Irons Steel, Steel-Drivin' Man C	.15	.25
13 John Stewart, Emerald Architect C	.15	.25
14 Katar Hol Hawkman, Thanagarian Enforcer C	.15	.25
15 Martian Manhunter, Manhunter from Mars R	.50	.75
16 Oliver Queen Green Arrow, Hard-Traveling Hero C	.15	.25
17 Plastic Man, Eel O'Brian R	.50	.75
18 Ray Palmer The Atom, World's Smallest Hero R	.50	.75
19 Red Tornado, John Smith C	.15	.25
20 Shayera Thal Hawkwoman, Thanagarian Enforcer C	.15	.25
21 Snapper Carr, Cool Daddy-O U	.30	.50
22 Superman, Avatar of Peace R	2.00	3.00
23 Wonder Woman, Princess Diana C	.15	.25
24 Wonder Woman, Avatar of Truth R	.60	1.00
25 Zatanna, Zatanna Zatara R	.60	1.00
26 Zauriel, Guardian Angel C	.15	.25
27 Disband the League U	.30	.50
28 Field of Honor U	.30	.50
29 Hero's Welcome R	.60	1.00
30 Monitor Womb Station R	.50	.75
31 New Era R	.50	.75
32 Reform the League C	.15	.25
33 Roll Call! C	.15	.25
34 Satellite HQ C	.15	.25
35 Secret Sanctuary U	.30	.50
36 Teleport Tube R	.50	.75
37 Wall of Will, Construct C	.15	.25
38 The Watchtower R	.60	1.00
39 Batman, Hidden Crusader C	.15	.25
40 Bluejay, Jay Abrams C	.15	.25
41 Booster Gold, Michael Jon Carter C	.15	.25
42 Captain Atom, Nathaniel Adam C	.15	.25
43 Captain Marvel, Billy Batson R	.50	.75
44 Catherine Cobert, Embassy Chief U	.30	.50
45 Crimson Fox, Vivian and Constance D'Aramis U	.30	.50
46 Dinah Laurel Lance Black Canary, Pretty Bird C	.15	.25
47 Dr. Fate, Kent Nelson R	.50	.75
48 Fire, Beatriz DaCosta C	.15	.25
49 Guy Gardner, Egomaniac C	.15	.25
50 Ice, Tora Olafsdotter C	.15	.25
51 Joseph Jones General Glory, Lady Liberty's Champion C	.15	.25
52 Kimiyo Hoshi Dr. Light, Starlight Sentinel C	.15	.25
53 L-Ron, Robot Companion U	.30	.50
54 Martian Manhunter, J'onn J'onzz U	.30	.50
55 Maxwell Lord, Financier C	.15	.25
56 Metamorpho, Rex Mason C	.15	.25
57 Oberon, Micro Manager U	.30	.50
58 Power Girl, Karen Starr R	.50	.75
59 Rocket Red #4, Dmitri Pushkin C	.15	.25
60 Scott Free Mister Miracle, Man of a Thousand Escapes U	.30	.50
61 Silver Sorceress, Laura Cynthia Neilsen C	.15	.25
62 Sue Dibny, Charismatic Coordinator C	.15	.25
63 Tasmanian Devil, Hugh Dawkins C	.15	.25
64 Ted Kord Blue Beetle, Heir of the Scarab C	.15	.25
65 BWA HA HA HA HA! R	1.50	2.50
66 The Castle U	.30	.50
67 JLI Embassy C	.15	.25
68 Justice League Task Force, Team-Up C	.15	.25
69 Kooey Kooey Kooey R	1.50	2.50
70 Plasma Blast C	.15	.25
71 Running Interference U	.30	.50
72 Safety in Numbers U	.30	.50
73 Staged Attack C	.15	.25
74 UN General Assembly R	.60	1.00
75 UN Recognition C	.15	.25
76 Abra Kadabra, Citizen Abra U	.30	.50
77 Captain Boomerang, George Harkness C	.15	.25
78 Circe, Immortal Sorceress C	.15	.25
79 Creeping Doom, Army C	.15	.25
80 David Clinton Chronos, The Time Thief C	.15	.25
81 Dr. Light, Light Shaper R	.50	.75
82 Evan McCulloch Mirror Master, Smoke and Mirrors C	.15	.25
83 Floronic Man, Alien Hybrid U	.30	.50
84 The General, Wade Eiling R	.50	.75
85 Illusionary Warriors, Army C	.15	.25
86 Infernal Minions, Army C	.15	.25
87 Insectoid Troopers, Army C	.15	.25
88 IQ, Ira Quimby C	.15	.25
89 The Joker, Headline Stealer C	.15	.25
90 Lex Luthor, Nefarious Philanthropist U	.30	.50
91 Lex Luthor, Evil Incorporated C	.15	.25
92 Libra, Alien Conqueror R	.50	.75
93 Ocean Master, Son of Atlan C	.15	.25
94 Poison Ivy, Deadly Rose R	2.00	3.00
95 Prometheus, Darker Knight C	.15	.25
96 Sam Scudder Mirror Master, Reflective Rogue U	.30	.50
97 Scarecrow, Psycho Psychologist C	.15	.25
98 Shadow-Thief, Carl Sands C	.15	.25
99 The Shark, Karshon C	.15	.25
100 Tattooed Man, Living Ink C	.15	.25
101 Zazzala Queen Bee, Royal Genetrix C	.15	.25
102 All Too Easy C	.15	.25
103 Criminal Mastermind C	.15	.25
104 Gang-Up, Team-Up C	.15	.25
105 Hard-Light Storage Tank R	.75	1.25
106 Infestation U	.30	.50
107 Injustice Gang Satellite R	.50	.75
108 Philosopher's Stone R	.50	.75
109 Power Siphon R	1.25	2.00
110 Royal Egg-Matrix U	.30	.50
111 Secret Files C	.15	.25
112 World War III R	.50	.75
113 Captain Boomerang, Digger U	.30	.50
114 Captain Cold, Leonard Snart U	.30	.50
115 Charaxes, Killer Moth C	.15	.25
116 Copperhead, Slithering Assassin C	.15	.25
117 Crystal Frost Killer Frost, Cold-Hearted Killer U	.30	.50
118 Darkseid, Heart of Darkness C	.15	.25
119 Deadshot, Floyd Lawton R	.50	.75
120 Dr. Sivana, Thaddeus Bodog Sivana C	.15	.25
121 Floronic Man, Jason Woodrue C	.15	.25
122 Funky Flashman, Salesman Supreme U	.30	.50
123 Gorilla Grodd, Simian Mastermind C	.15	.25
124 Hector Hammond, Mind Over Matter C	.15	.25
125 Henry King Brainwave, Sinister Psionic C	.15	.25
126 James Jesse Trickster, Giovanni Giuseppe C	.15	.25
127 Lex Luthor, Criminal Genius R	.50	.75
128 Manhunter Clone, Clone of Paul Kirk C	.15	.25
129 Mark Desmond Blockbuster, Mindless Brute U	.30	.50
130 The Mist, Jonathan Smythe C	.15	.25
131 Poison Ivy, Kiss of Death C	.15	.25
132 Psycho-Pirate, Roger Hayden R	.50	.75
133 Quakemaster, Robert Coleman U	.30	.50
134 Remoni-Notra Star Sapphire, Zamoran Champion U	.30	.50
135 Scarecrow, Fearmonger C	.15	.25
136 Sinestro, Corrupted by the Ring R	.50	.75
137 Solomon Grundy, Buried on Sunday R	.50	.75
138 Ultra-Humanite, Evolutionary Antecedent C	.15	.25
139 The Wizard, William Zard C	.15	.25
140 Attend or Die! R	.50	.75
141 Divided We Fall R	.50	.75
142 Funky's Big Rat Code, Team-Up C	.15	.25
143 Gorilla City C	.15	.25
144 Mysterious Benefactor U	.30	.50
145 The Plunder Plan C	.15	.25
146 Quadromobile U	.30	.50
147 Sinister Citadel U	.30	.50
148 Slaughter Swamp C	.15	.25
149 Sorcerer's Treasure R	.50	.75
150 Straight to the Grave R	4.00	6.00
151 With Prejudice C	.15	.25
152 Justice League Signal Device C	.15	.25

153 Magnificent Seven C .15 .25
154 World's Greatest Heroes, Team-Up C .15 .25
155 Amazo, Ivo's Android R .50 .75
156 Despero, Master of the Third Eye C .15 .25
157 Dr. Destiny, John Dee C .15 .25
158 Felix Faust, Infernal Dealmaker U .30 .50
159 Kanjar Ro, Kylaq Defense Minister C .15 .25
160 Mageddon, Weapon of Universal Destruction R .50 .75
161 Neron, Soul Collector R .50 .75
162 Professor Ivo, Anthony Ivo C .15 .25
163 Queen of Fables, Wickedest Witch C .15 .25
164 Rama Khan, Elemental Magician C .15 .25
165 Starro the Conqueror, Intergalactic Starfish R .50 .75
166 T. O. Morrow, Thomas Oscar Morrow U .30 .50
167 Tomorrow Woman, Trojan Telepath R .50 .75
168 Air Strike C .15 .25
169 Atlantean Trident U .30 .50
170 Balance of Power C .15 .25
171 Bulletproof C .15 .25
172 Counterstrike C .15 .25
173 Counterterrorism U .30 .50
174 Crisis on Infinite Earths, Team-Up R 2.50 4.00
175 Death Times Five C .15 .25
176 Death Trap C .15 .25
177 Funeral For a Friend U .30 .50
178 Glass Jaw C .15 .25
179 High-Tech Flare Gun U .30 .50
180 H'ronmeer's Curse R .50 .75
181 Identity Crisis R .50 .75
182 Lair of the Mastermind C .15 .25
183 Lead by Example C .15 .25
184 Membership Drive C .15 .25
185 Midnight Cravings C .15 .25
186 Not on My Watch U .30 .50
187 Nth Metal C .15 .25
188 Rallying Cry! C .15 .25
189 Resistance is Useless C .15 .25
190 Secret Origins R 1.25 2.00
191 Shake it Off C .15 .25
192 S.T.A.R. Labs Orbital Platform C .15 .25
193 Token Resistance C .15 .25
194 Trial by Fire C .15 .25
195 UN Building, Team-Up C .15 .25
196 Vicarious Living U .30 .50
197 Wheel of Misfortune U .30 .50
198 Mogo, The Living Planet R .50 .75
199 Oliver Queen Green Arrow, Emerald Archer U .30 .50
200 Recharge the Sun R .50 .75
201 Controller Sanction U .30 .50
202 Fatality, Emerald Assassin R .50 .75
203 Chomin, Qwardian Spy U .30 .50
204 General Fabrikant, Qwardian General U .30 .50
205 Matter Convergence R .50 .75
206 Conscription R .50 .75
207 Manhunter Conqueror, Grandmaster U .30 .50
208 War Without End R .50 .75
209 Kelex, Faithful Servant U .30 .50
210 Look-Alike Squad R 1.50 2.50
211 Bizarro Ray U .30 .50
212 Maxima, Empress of Almerac R .50 .75
213 Mobius Chair U .30 .50
214 Valkyra, Valkyrie of New Genesis U .30 .50
215 Die for Darkseid! U .30 .50
216 Mantis, Power Parasite R .50 .75
217 Justice League of Arkham, Team-Up U .30 .50
218 The Creeper, Jack Ryder R 1.25 2.00
219 Poisoned! U .30 .50
220 Bumblebee, Karen Beecher-Duncan U .30 .50

2005 Vs System Marvel Knights

COMPLETE SET (220) 25.00 50.00
BOOSTER BOX (24 PACKS) 15.00 30.00
BOOSTER PACK (14 CARDS) .75 1.25
*FOIL: .75X TO 2X BASIC CARDS
RELEASED IN FEBRUARY 2005
1 Blade, Eric Brooks R .75 1.25
2 Brother Voodoo, Jericho Drumm C .15 .25
3 Caretaker, Nomadic Mentor C .15 .25
4 Cloak, Child of Darkness C .15 .25
5 Dagger, Child of Light U .30 .50
6 Daredevil, Guardian Devil C .15 .25
7 Daredevil, Matt Murdock R 1.50 2.50
8 Daredevil, Protector of Hell's Kitchen C .15 .25
9 Dr. Strange, Stephen Strange R .60 1.00
10 Elektra, Assassin U .30 .50
11 Elektra, Elektra Natchios C .15 .25
12 Ghost Rider, Danny Ketch R 1.00 1.50
13 Ghost Rider, Johnny Blaze C .15 .25
14 Hannibal King, Occult Investigator C .15 .25
15 Iron Fist, Danny Rand C .15 .25
16 Iron Fist, Living Weapon C .15 .25
17 Luke Cage, Power Man R .60 1.00
18 Luke Cage, Street Enforcer C .15 .25
19 Micro-Chip, Linus Lieberman C .15 .25
20 Mikado and Mosha, Angels of Destruction C .15 .25
21 Moon Knight, Marc Spector C .15 .25
22 Natasha Romanoff Black Widow, KGB Killer U .30 .50
23 Punisher, Executioner C .15 .25
24 Punisher, Judge R .60 1.00
25 Punisher, Jury U .30 .50
26 Shang Chi, Master of Kung Fu U .30 .50
27 Spider-Man, The Spectacular Spider-Man C .15 .25
28 Stick, Leader of the Chaste U .30 .50
29 Yelena Belova Black Widow, Enemy Agent R .60 1.00
30 Blind Justice R .60 1.00
31 Bring the Pain C .15 .25
32 Crime and Punishment C .15 .25
33 Deposed C .15 .25
34 Head Shot C .15 .25
35 Hell's Kitchen U .30 .50
36 Judge, Jury, and Executioner C .15 .25
37 Midnight Sons C .15 .25
38 Penance Stare U .30 .50
39 Punisher's Armory U .30 .50
40 Quentin Carnival U .30 .50
41 Quick Kill C .15 .25
42 Swan Dive U .30 .50
43 Titanium Sword U .30 .50
44 War Wagon C .15 .25
45 Wild Ride R 4.00 6.00
46 Anarchist, Man of the People R .60 1.00
47 Anarchist, Tike Alicar U .30 .50
48 Battering Ram, Short-Lived Strongman C .15 .25
49 Bloke, Mickey Tork U .30 .50
50 Coach, Manipulative Mentor C .15 .25
51 Corkscrew, Twisted Trainee C .15 .25
52 Dead Girl, Crafty Cadaver C .15 .25
53 Doop, Forward Observer C .15 .25
54 Doop, Ultimate Weapon R .60 1.00
55 El Guapo, Robbie Rodriguez U .30 .50
56 Gin Genie, Beckah Parker C .15 .25
57 La Nuit, Pierre Truffaut C .15 .25
58 Mysterious Fan Boy, Arthur Lundberg C .15 .25
59 Orphan, Good Guy C .15 .25
60 Orphan, Guy Smith C .15 .25
61 Orphan, Mr. Sensitive R .60 1.00
62 Phat, William Reilly R .60 1.00
63 Plazm, Protoplasmic Protagonist C .15 .25
64 Saint Anna, Sympathetic Healer C .15 .25
65 Sluk, Byron Spencer C .15 .25
66 The Spike, Angry Young Mutant C .15 .25
67 U-Go-Girl, Eddie Sawyer U .30 .50
68 U-Go-Girl, Tragic Teleporter U .30 .50
69 Venus Dee Milo, Dee Milo R .60 1.00
70 Venus Dee Milo, Telegenic Teleporter U .30 .50
71 Vivisector, Lunatic Lycanthrope C .15 .25
72 Vivisector, Myles Alfred C .15 .25
73 Zeitgeist, Axel Cluney C .15 .25
74 Dead Weight U .30 .50
75 Doop Cam C .15 .25
76 Falling Stars C .15 .25
77 Glory Hound C .15 .25
78 Go in Swinging U .30 .50
79 Grandstanding U .30 .50
80 Mind Over Matter U .30 .50
81 Missed Drop C .15 .25
82 Nerve Strike C .15 .25
83 Never Give Up! U .30 .50
84 Overexposed C .15 .25
85 Spin Doctoring R 1.25 2.00
86 Star of the Show R 1.00 1.50
87 Supporting Role C .15 .25
88 Training Theatre U .30 .50
89 X-Statix Cafe C .15 .25
90 X-Statix HQ R .60 1.00
91 Bullseye, Deadly Marksman R .75 1.25
92 Bullseye, Master of Murder C .15 .25
93 Carbone's Assassins, Army C .15 .25
94 Cobra, Klaus Vorhees C .15 .25
95 Deadpool, Wade Wilson R .75 1.25
96 Death-Stalker, Phillip Sterling C .15 .25
97 Echo, Maya Lopez C .15 .25
98 Jaime Ortiz Damage, Cybernetic Enforcer C .15 .25
99 Jester, Jonathan Powers U .30 .50
100 Jigsaw, Billy Russo U .30 .50
101 Kingpin, The Kingpin of Crime R .60 1.00
102 Kingpin, Wilson Fisk C .15 .25
103 Kirigi, Master Assassin U .30 .50
104 Masked Marauder, Frank Farnum C .15 .25
105 Mr. Code, Masked Malcontent U .30 .50
106 Mr. Fear, Zoltan Drago C .15 .25
107 Mr. Hyde, Calvin Zabo C .15 .25
108 Nuke, Renegade Super Soldier C .15 .25
109 Owl, Leland Owlsley R .75 1.25
110 Roscoe Sweeny, Fixer U .30 .50
111 Saracen, Muzzafar Lambert C .15 .25
112 Sniper, Rich van Burian C .15 .25
113 Stilt-Man, Wilbur Day R .60 1.00
114 The Hand, Army C .15 .25
115 The Rose, Shadowy Lieutenant U .30 .50
116 The Russian, Contract Killer C .15 .25
117 Typhoid Mary, Mary Walker R .60 1.00
118 Vanessa Fisk, Mob Matron C .15 .25
119 Armed Escort C .15 .25
120 Boss of Bosses U .30 .50
121 Drive-by Shooting C .15 .25
122 Face the Master U .30 .50
123 Geraci Family Estate U .30 .50
124 Good Night, Sweet Prince C .15 .25
125 Hand Dojo U .30 .50
126 King Takes Knight R .60 1.00
127 Made Men C .15 .25
128 Marked for Death U .30 .50
129 No Rest for the Wicked C .15 .25
130 Rough House C .15 .25
131 Shakedown C .15 .25
132 Sold Out R .60 1.00
133 The Family C .15 .25
134 Untouchable R .60 1.00
135 Uprising U .30 .50
136 Anton Hellgate, Thanatologist C .15 .25
137 Asmodeus, Duke of Hell U .30 .50
138 Blackheart, Son of Mephisto C .15 .25
139 Blackout, Master of Darkness U .30 .50
140 Centurious, The Soulless Man C .15 .25
141 Deacon Frost, Vampire Master R .75 1.25
142 Dracula, Lord of the Damned C .15 .25
143 Dracula, Vlad Dracula R .75 1.25
144 Lilith, Daughter of Dracula R .60 1.00
145 Marie Laveau, Voodoo Priestess U .30 .50
146 Mephisto, Father of Lies R .60 1.00
147 Mephisto, Soulstealer U .30 .50
148 Morbius, The Living Vampire C .15 .25
149 Nekra, Nekra Sinclair U .30 .50
150 New Blood, Army C .15 .25
151 Nightmare, Dark Lord of Dreams C .15 .25
152 Orb, Drake Shannon R 1.00 1.50
153 Reaper, Vampire Armageddon C .15 .25
154 Shelob, Queen of Spiders U .30 .50
155 Skinner, Psychotic Shredder C .15 .25
156 Steel Wind, Cyborg Cyclist C .15 .25
157 Suicide, Chris Daniels C .15 .25
158 Tryks, Army C .15 .25
159 Varnae, First Vampire R .60 1.00
160 Vengeance, Michael Badilino C .15 .25
161 Werewolf by Night, Jack Russell C .15 .25
162 Zarathos, Spirit of Vengeance C .15 .25
163 Zodiak, Norman Harrison C .15 .25
164 Black Magic C .15 .25
165 Blood Hunt R .60 1.00
166 Children of the Night C .15 .25
167 Dark Embrace R .60 1.00
168 Dracula's Castle U .30 .50
169 Evil Awakens U .30 .50
170 Gravesite U .30 .50
171 Hypnotic Charms C .15 .25
172 Infernal Gateway U .30 .50
173 Mist Form U .30 .50
174 Shadow Step C .15 .25
175 Strength of the Grave C .15 .25
176 The Darkhold C .15 .25
177 Club Dead C .15 .25
178 Wake the Dead U .30 .50
179 Witching Hour R .60 1.00
180 Blade, The Daywalker C .15 .25
181 Professor X, Mutant Mentor R .75 1.25
182 Elektra, Agent of the Hand C .15 .25
183 Deathwatch, Unrepentant Killer C .15 .25
184 Moving Target C .15 .25
185 Hell's Fury C .15 .25
186 Day of the Dead C .15 .25
187 Blown to Pieces C .15 .25
188 Team X-change R .60 1.00
189 Coalition of Heroes R .60 1.00
190 Honor Among Thieves R .60 1.00
191 Professor X, Mental Master R .75 1.25
192 Outback Stronghold R .60 1.00
193 Valeria, Daughter of Doom R .60 1.00
194 Lockjaw, Inhuman U .30 .50
195 Scarlet Witch, Eldritch Enchantress R .60 1.00
196 Monument to a Madman R .60 1.00
197 Diplomatic Immunity R .60 1.00
198 Hounds of Ahab, Army U .30 .50
199 Mekanix R .60 1.00
200 Frog Man, Eugene Patilio U .30 .50
201 Scarlet Spider Spider-Man, Successor R .75 1.25
202 Swing into Action R .60 1.00
203 The Slingers R .60 1.00
204 Web Shooters R .60 1.00
205 Carrion, Cadaverous Clone U .30 .50
206 Mendel Stromm, Robot Master R .60 1.00
207 Scorpia, Elaine Colls U .30 .50
208 Inside Job R .60 1.00
209 Lacuna, Media Darling C .15 .25
210 Sharon Ginsberg, Corrupt Counsel C .15 .25
211 Advance Recon C .15 .25
212 Marvel Team-Up C .15 .25
213 Medallion of Power R .60 1.00
214 Meltdown C .15 .25
215 Mystic Chain R .75 1.25
216 Mystical Sigil U .30 .50
217 Out of the Darkness C .15 .25
218 Psychoville C .15 .25
219 Team Spirit U .30 .50
220 Weapon of Choice R .75 1.25

2006 Vs System Heralds of Galactus

COMPLETE SET (220) 35.00 75.00
BOOSTER BOX (24 PACKS) 25.00 50.00
BOOSTER PACK (14 CARDS) 1.00 2.00
*FOIL: .75X TO 2X BASIC CARDS
RELEASED IN SEPTEMBER 2006
1 Air-Walker, Gabriel Lan R 4.00 6.00
2 Air-Walker, Harbinger of Despair U .30 .50
3 Destroyer, Soulless Juggernaut C .15 .25
4 Destroyer, Harbinger of Devastation C .15 .25
5 Firelord, Pyreus Kril C .15 .25
6 Firelord, Harbinger of Havoc C .15 .25
7 Frankie Raye Nova, Optimistic Youth C .15 .25
8 Frankie Raye Nova, Soul Searcher C .15 .25
9 Frankie Raye Nova, Harbinger of Death C .15 .25
10 Galactus, The Maker U .30 .50
11 Galactus, Devourer of Worlds R 5.00 8.00
12 Galan, Famished C .15 .25
13 Human Torch, The Invisible Man C .15 .25
14 Morg, Slayer C .15 .25
15 Morg, Corrupt Destroyer C .15 .25
16 Morg, Harbinger of Extinction C .15 .25
17 Plasma, Replacement Herald C .15 .25
18 Red Shift, Rift Walker R 3.00 5.00
19 Silver Surfer, Skyrider of the Spaceways U 1.25 2.00
20 Silver Surfer, Righteous Protector C .15 .25
21 Silver Surfer, Harbinger of Oblivion R 2.50 4.00
22 Stardust, Merciless Warrior C .15 .25
23 Terrax, The Tamer R 1.00 1.50
24 Terrax, Harbinger of Ruin R .75 1.25
25 The Fallen One, The Forgotten C .15 .25
26 The Punishers, Army C .15 .25
27 Tyrant, The Original Herald U .30 .50
28 Absorba Shield R 1.25 2.00
29 Cosmic Necessity U .30 .50
30 Creation of a Herald R 5.00 8.00
31 Elemental Battle C .15 .25
32 Elemental Converters U .30 .50
33 I Hunger R 1.00 1.50
34 I Must Obey R .60 1.00
35 Inspiring Demise R 2.50 4.00
36 Kindred Spirits U .30 .50
37 Pacification U .30 .50
38 Relentless Onslaught C .15 .25
39 Taa II R .60 1.00
40 The Herald Ordeal, Team-Up C .15 .25
41 The Power Cosmic Unleashed C .15 .25
42 Ultimate Nullifier R .75 1.25
43 Worldeater Apparatus U .30 .50

44 Worldship U .30 .50
45 Admiral Galen Kor, Lunatic Legion C .15 .25
46 Bron Char, Lunatic Legion R .75 1.25
47 Captain Att-Lass, Starforce C .15 .25
48 Clumsy Foulup, Puppet Dictator C .15 .25
49 Colonel Yon-Rogg, Commander of the Helion R 1.00 1.50
50 Commander Dylon Cir, Lunatic Legion C .15 .25
51 Dr. Minerva, Starforce C .15 .25
52 Korath the Pursuer, Starforce C .15 .25
53 Kree Commandos, Army U .30 .50
54 Kree Public Accusers, Army U .30 .50
55 Kree Soldiers, Army U .30 .50
56 Lieutenant Kona Lor, Lunatic Legion C .15 .25
57 Lunatic Legionnaires, Army U .30 .50
58 Mar-Vell Captain Marvel, Soldier of the Empire C .15 .25
59 Mar-Vell Captain Marvel, Enemy of the Empire C .15 .25
60 Nenora, Skrull Usurper C .15 .25
61 Ronan the Accuser, Starforce C .15 .25
62 Ronan the Accuser, Supreme Public Accuser R .60 1.00
63 Ruul Warrior, Army C .15 .25
64 Sentry #459, Advance Guard C .15 .25
65 Shatterax, Starforce C .15 .25
66 Sintariis, High Kronamaster R .60 1.00
67 Supreme Intelligence, Kree Collective R .60 1.00
68 Supremor, Starforce C .15 .25
69 Talla Ron, Lunatic Legion C .15 .25
70 Ultimus, Starforce C .15 .25
71 Conquered Planet C .15 .25
72 Enemy of the Empire U .30 .50
73 Genetic Destiny U .30 .50
74 Hala C .15 .25
75 Improper Burial U .30 .50
76 Live Kree . . . or Die! U .30 .50
77 Nega-Bands U .30 .50
78 Nega-Bomb R .60 1.00
79 Penal Colony C .15 .25
80 Planet Weapon R 1.00 1.50
81 Pressed into Service, Team-Up C .15 .25
82 Remnant Fleet C .15 .25
83 Starforce Strike C .15 .25
84 Stargate R 4.00 6.00
85 Strategic Retreat R .60 1.00
86 The Infamous Seven U .30 .50
87 The Lunatic Legion U .30 .50
88 Universal Weapon C .15 .25
89 Ahura, Heir to Attilan C .15 .25
90 Alaris, The Outgoing One C .15 .25
91 Alpha Primitives, Army C .15 .25
92 Black Bolt, Illuminati C .15 .25
93 Black Bolt, King of the Inhumans C .15 .25
94 Black Bolt, Devastating Decree R .75 1.25
95 Crystal, Elementelle C .15 .25
96 Dewoz, Dark Reflection C .15 .25
97 Dinu, Face of Terror C .15 .25
98 Franklin Richards, Creator of Counter-Earth C .15 .25
99 Gorgon, Thundering Hooves R .60 1.00
100 Human Torch, Sparky C .15 .25
101 Invisible Woman, Flame On! C .15 .25
102 Jolen, The Treacherous One U .30 .50
103 Karnak, The Shatterer R 1.25 2.00
104 Lockjaw, Inhuman's Best Friend U 1.25 2.00
105 Luna Maximoff, Only Human C .15 .25
106 Maximus the Mad, Mental Manipulator C .15 .25
107 Medusa, Queen of the Inhumans U .30 .50
108 Mr. Fantastic, Illuminati U .30 .50
109 Nahrees, The Negative One C .15 .25
110 Quicksilver, Inhuman by Marriage C .15 .25
111 San, The Alienated One C .15 .25
112 Thing, Rockhead C .15 .25
113 Tonaja, The Responsible One C .15 .25
114 Triton, Aquatic Ambassador R .60 1.00
115 Attilan R 1.25 2.00
116 Blue Area of the Moon C .15 .25
117 Exploiting the Flaw R .75 1.25
118 Extended Family, Team-Up C .15 .25
119 Final Decree R .60 1.00
120 Himalayan Enclave C .15 .25
121 It's Slobberin' Time! C .15 .25
122 Power Struggle U .30 .50
123 Terragenesis U .30 .50
124 The Great Refuge R 5.00 8.00
125 The Outside World C .15 .25
126 The Royal Guard R 2.50 4.00
127 The Substructure C .15 .25
128 Waking the Ancestors C .15 .25
129 Divinity, Vampiric General U .30 .50
130 Doom-Bot Dr. Doom, Cosmic Thief C .15 .25
131 Doom-Bot Corps, Army C .15 .25
132 Dorma, Atlantean General C .15 .25
133 Dr. Doom, Richards's Rival C .15 .25
134 Dr. Doom, Sorcerous Savant C .15 .25
135 Dr. Doom, Latverian Monarch R 1.00 1.50
136 Elite Doom Guards, Army C .15 .25
137 Invisible Woman, Baroness Von Doom C .15 .25
138 Iron Man, Illuminati C .15 .25
139 Kang, One of Many U .30 .50
140 Kang, Destiny Warrior R 1.25 2.00
141 Klaw, Sonic Construct R .60 1.00
142 Lancer, Samantha Dunbar C .15 .25
143 Magneto, Acts of Vengeance C .15 .25
144 Mole Man, Moloid Master U .30 .50
145 Molecule Man, Owen Reece R .60 1.00
146 Moloids, Army C .15 .25
147 Mr. Fantastic, Doom's Adversary U .30 .50
148 Purple Man, Subtle Manipulator U .30 .50
149 Shakti, Mage General C .15 .25
150 Sub-Mariner, Illuminati C .15 .25
151 Technarx, Cyborg General C .15 .25
152 Titania, Temper Tantrum C .15 .25
153 Ultron Ultron 11, Army C .15 .25
154 Valeria Von Doom, Heir to Latveria C .15 .25
155 Armies of Doom U .30 .50
156 Arsenal of Doom C .15 .25
157 Astral Suppression U .30 .50
158 Doom Needs Only Doom C .15 .25
159 Doomed Earth R 2.50 4.00
160 Doomstadt, Castle Doom R 2.00 3.00
161 Expendable Ally R 2.00 3.00
162 For the Glory of Doom!; Team-Up C .15 .25
163 Lust for Power R .60 1.00
164 Mask of Doom U .30 .50
165 Master of Puppets U .30 .50
166 Super Genius C .15 .25
167 The Devil We Know C .15 .25
168 The Enemy Within R .60 1.00
169 Time Thief R 5.00 8.00
170 Unthinkable R .60 1.00
171 Adam Warlock, Protector of the Soul Gem U .30 .50
172 Drax the Destroyer, Protector of the Power Gem R .60 1.00
173 Gamora, Protector of the Time Gem U .30 .50
174 Moondragon, Protector of the Mind Gem C .15 .25
175 Pip the Troll, Protector of the Space Gem U .30 .50
176 Thanos, Protector of the Reality Gem R .60 1.00
177 Gathering the Watch U .30 .50
178 Mind Gem, Infinity Gem C .15 .25
179 Power Gem, Infinity Gem C .15 .25
180 Reality Gem, Infinity Gem R 2.50 4.00
181 Soul Gem, Infinity Gem U .30 .50
182 Soul World U .30 .50
183 Space Gem, Infinity Gem U .30 .50
184 The Infinity Gauntlet R .75 1.25
185 Time Gem, Infinity Gem R .75 1.25
186 Captain America, Skrull Impostor U .30 .50
187 Ethan Edwards, Visitor from Another World C .15 .25
188 Paibok, The Power Skrull C .15 .25
189 Rogue, Total Transformation R .75 1.25
190 Titannus, Alien Conqueror C .15 .25
191 Warskrull, Skrull Infiltrator U .30 .50
192 Wolverine, Skrunucklehead C .15 .25
193 Act of Defiance, Team-Up C .15 .25
194 Alien Insurrection C .15 .25
195 Interstellar Offensive C .15 .25
196 Armageddon R 1.25 2.00
197 Assault and Battery U .30 .50
198 Barbaric Brawl C .15 .25
199 Battleworld C .15 .25
200 Cannibal Tech C .15 .25
201 Cosmic Order C .15 .25
202 Ego the Living Planet R .60 1.00
203 Intergalactic Summit C .15 .25
204 Sworn Enemies C .15 .25
205 The Kyln C .15 .25
206 The Rapture U .30 .50
207 The Uni-Power C .15 .25
208 Thanos, Alpha and Omega R .60 1.00
209 Barnacle, Acolyte U .30 .50
210 Negative Zone, Shadow Dimension U .30 .50
211 Syphonn, Energy Leech R .75 1.25
212 Carnage, Symbiote Surfer R 1.00 1.50
213 Dr. Strange, Illuminati U .30 .50
214 Mephisto, Lord of Hell U .30 .50
215 Taskmaster, Mnemonic Assassin U .30 .50
216 O-Force R .60 1.00
217 Katrina Luisa Van Horne Amazon, Unrepentant Hero U .30 .50
218 Haywire, Suicidal Lover R 1.00 1.50
219 Litterbug, Killer Cockroach U .30 .50
220 Mr. Sinister, Supreme Geneticist U .30 .50

2006 Vs System Infinite Crisis

COMPLETE SET (220) 25.00 50.00
BOOSTER BOX (24 PACKS) 20.00 40.00
BOOSTER PACK (14 CARDS) 1.00 2.00
*FOIL: .75X TO 2X BASIC CARDS
RELEASED IN APRIL 2006
1 Alan Scott Sentinel, Golden Age Guardian R .60 1.00
2 Atom Smasher, Al Rothstein U .30 .50
3 Batman, Earth 2 C .15 .25
4 Black Adam, Ruthless Hero C .15 .25
5 Captain Marvel, Earth's Mightiest Mortal R .60 1.00
6 Carter Hall Hawkman, Eternal Champion C .15 .25
7 Charles McNider Dr. Mid-Nite, Golden Age Academic U .30 .50
8 Chay-Ara Hawkgirl, Eternal Companion C .15 .25
9 Dr. Fate, Lord of Order R .60 1.00
10 Hourman III Hourman, Time Machine U .30 .50
11 Huntress, Earth 2 C .15 .25
12 Jakeem Williams, JJ Thunder U .30 .50
13 Jay Garrick The Flash, Golden Age Speedster R .60 1.00
14 Katar Hol Hawkman, Eternal Hero C .15 .25
15 Kate Spencer Manhunter, Fearless Renegade U .30 .50
16 Kendra Saunders Hawkgirl, Eternal Heroine C .15 .25
17 Michael Holt Mr. Terrific, Renaissance Man C .15 .25
18 Power Girl, Earth 2 C .15 .25
19 Prince Khufu Hawkman, Eternal Warrior C .15 .25
20 Rex Tyler Hourman, Inventor of Miraclo R .60 1.00
21 Richard Tyler Hourman, Man of the Hour U .30 .50
22 Sand, Sanderson Hawkins C .15 .25
23 Stargirl, Courtney Whitmore C .15 .25
24 Superman, Earth 2 C .15 .25
25 Ted Grant Wildcat, Golden Age Pugilist C .15 .25
26 Terry Sloane Mr. Terrific, Golden Age Gold Medalist C .15 .25
27 The Phantom Stranger, Wandering Hero U .30 .50
28 Thunderbolt, Yz R .60 1.00
29 Wesley Dodds The Sandman, Golden Age Gunman U .30 .50
30 Wonder Woman, Earth 2 C .15 .25
31 A Moment of Crisis C .15 .25
32 Advance Warning R .60 1.00
33 Allied Against the Dark C .15 .25
34 Brothers in Arms U .30 .50
35 Double Play U .30 .50
36 Heroic Rescue C .15 .25
37 JSA Headquarters R .60 1.00
38 Justice United, Team-Up C .15 .25
39 Living Legacy U .30 .50
40 Taking Up the Mantle C .15 .25
41 The Rock of Eternity R 1.25 2.00
42 T-Spheres C .15 .25
43 Black Alice, Lori Zechlin U .30 .50
44 Blackbriar Thorn, Druid of Cymru U .30 .50
45 Blue Devil, Dan Cassidy C .15 .25
46 Blue Devil, Big Blue C .15 .25
47 Captain Marvel, Champion of Magic R .60 1.00
48 Detective Chimp, Bobo T. Chimpanzee C .15 .25
49 Detective Chimp, Shoeless Gumshoe R .60 1.00
50 Dr. Fate, Hector Hall C .15 .25
51 Dr. Occult, Richard Occult C .15 .25
52 Ibis, Prince Amentep C .15 .25
53 June Moon Enchantress, Good Witch R .60 1.00
54 June Moon Enchantress, Bad Witch R .60 1.00
55 Madame Xanadu, Cartomancer U .30 .50
56 Manitou Dawn, Spirit Shaman C .15 .25
57 Nightmaster, Jim Rook C .15 .25
58 Nightmaster, Demon Slayer R .60 1.00
59 Nightshade, Eve Eden C .15 .25
60 Nightshade, Shadow Siren C .15 .25
61 Ragman, Patchmonger U .30 .50
62 Ragman, Redeemer of Souls C .15 .25
63 Rose Psychic, Ghost Detective C .15 .25
64 Shazam, The Sorcerer R .60 1.00
65 The Phantom Stranger, Fallen Angel C .15 .25
66 Witchfire, Rebecca Carstairs C .15 .25
67 Zatanna, Magical Manipulator C .15 .25
68 Zatanna, Showstopper C .15 .25
69 Abjuration, Magic U .30 .50
70 Chimp Detective Agency R .60 1.00
71 Collecting Souls, Magic C .15 .25
72 Conjuration, Magic R .60 1.00
73 Divination, Magic C .15 .25
74 Magical Conduit, Magic U .30 .50
75 Mystical Binding, Magic C .15 .25
76 Spectral Slaughter, Magic R .60 1.00
77 Stepping Between Worlds, Magic C .15 .25
78 The Conclave, Magic R 2.00 3.00
79 The Oblivion Bar U .30 .50
80 True Name, Magic C .15 .25
81 Adrian Chase Vigilante, Street Justice R .60 1.00
82 Ahmed Samsarra, White King U .30 .50
83 Amanda Waller, Queen C .15 .25
84 Annihilation Protocol OMAC Robot, Army C .15 .25
85 Arthur Kendrick, Knight C .15 .25
86 Aspiring Pawn, Army C .15 .25
87 Black Thorn, Elizabeth Thorne U .30 .50
88 Christopher Smith Peacemaker, Obsessed Outlaw U .30 .50
89 Connie Webb, Knight U .30 .50
90 Elimination Protocol OMAC Robot, Army C .15 .25
91 Graziella Reza, Knight C .15 .25
92 Harry Stein, King in Check U .30 .50
93 Huntress, Reluctant Queen C .15 .25
94 Jacob Lee, Knight U .30 .50
95 Maxwell Lord, Black King R .60 1.00
96 Neutralization Protocol OMAC Robot, Army C .15 .25
97 Retrieval Protocol OMAC Robot, Army C .15 .25
98 Roy Harper Arsenal, Knight C .15 .25
99 Sarge Steel, Knight U .30 .50
100 Sasha Bordeaux, Knight C .15 .25
101 Sasha Bordeaux, Autonomous Prototype C .15 .25
102 Surveillance Pawn, Army C .15 .25
103 Valentina Vostok Negative Woman, Bishop C .15 .25
104 Brother Eye U .30 .50
105 Brother I Satellite U .30 .50
106 Check and Mate! R .60 1.00
107 Checkmate Armory C .15 .25
108 Checkmate Safe House, Team-Up C .15 .25
109 Knight Armor U .30 .50
110 Knightmare Scenario U .30 .50
111 Knights' Gambit R .60 1.00
112 Laser Watch C .15 .25
113 Pawn of the Black King R .60 1.00
114 Rook Control U .30 .50
115 Secret Checkmate HQ C .15 .25
116 Target Acquired C .15 .25
117 Threat Neutralized U .30 .50
118 Traitor to the Cause C .15 .25
119 Alexander Luthor, Duplicitous Doppelganger U .30 .50
120 Alexander Luthor, Insidious Impostor R .60 1.00
121 Alexander Luthor, Diabolical Double C .15 .25
122 Bizarro, ME AM BIZARRO #1 C .15 .25
123 Black Adam, Teth-Adam C .15 .25
124 Black Adam, Lord of Kahndaq R .60 1.00
125 Cheetah, Feral Feline C .15 .25
126 Count Vertigo, Werner Vertigo C .15 .25
127 Deathstroke the Terminator, Lethal Weapon C .15 .25
128 Deathstroke the Terminator, Ultimate Assassin R .60 1.00
129 Dr. Polaris, Force of Nature C .15 .25
130 Dr. Light, Furious Flashpoint U .30 .50
131 Dr. Psycho, Mental Giant C .15 .25
132 Dr. Psycho, Twisted Telepath C .15 .25
133 Fatality, Flawless Victory R .60 1.00
134 Hunter Zolomon Professor Zoom, Sinister Speedster R .60 1.00
135 Ishmael Gregor Sabbac, Malevolent Marvel C .15 .25
136 Mr. Freeze, Brutal Blizzard C .15 .25
137 Sinestro, Villain Reborn C .15 .25
138 Talia, Beloved Betrayer U .30 .50
139 Talia, Daughter of Madness R .60 1.00
140 The Calculator, Noah Kuttler C .15 .25
141 The Calculator, Evil Oracle C .15 .25
142 The Calculator, Crime Broker C .15 .25
143 Weather Wizard, Mark Mardon C .15 .25
144 Zazzala Queen Bee, Mistress of the Hive C .15 .25
145 3 . . . 2 . . . 1 . . . R .60 1.00
146 Arms Deal R .60 1.00
147 Baddest of the Bad U .30 .50
148 Coercion, Team-Up C .15 .25
149 Grand Gesture C .15 .25
150 Join Us or Die U .30 .50

151 No Hope R	.60	1.00
152 No Mercy C	.15	.25
153 Return Fire! C	.15	.25
154 Systematic Torture C	.15	.25
155 The Science Spire R	1.25	2.00
156 Catman, Thomas Blake C	.15	.25
157 Cheshire, Jade C	.15	.25
158 Deadshot, Dead Aim C	.15	.25
159 Fiddler, Isaac Bowin C	.15	.25
160 Lex Luthor Mockingbird, Evil Exile U	.30	.50
161 Parademon, Apokoliptian Ally C	.15	.25
162 Ragdoll, Resilient Rogue C	.15	.25
163 Scandal, Savage Spawn C	.15	.25
164 Dodge the Bullet R	.60	1.00
165 Help Wanted, Team-Up U	.30	.50
166 House of Secrets U	.30	.50
167 It's Not Over Yet U	.30	.50
168 Secret Six Victorious R	.60	1.00
169 Harbinger, Multiverse Messenger R	.60	1.00
170 Pariah, Herald of Doom R	.60	1.00
171 Superboy, Earth Prime R	.60	1.00
172 The Monitor, Guardian of the Multiverse R	.60	1.00
173 Bart Allen The Flash, Impulsive Speedster R	.60	1.00
174 Amulet of Nabu, Fate Artifact C	.15	.25
175 Cloak of Nabu, Fate Artifact C	.15	.25
176 Helm of Nabu, Fate Artifact C	.15	.25
177 Dr. Fate's Tower U	.30	.50
178 Fate Has Spoken, Magic R	.60	1.00
179 Eclipso, Jean Loring R	.60	1.00
180 Jaime Reyes Blue Beetle, High-Tech Hero U	.30	.50
181 Mordru, Dark Lord C	.15	.25
182 The Spectre, Soulless R	.60	1.00
183 Absolute Dominance R	.60	1.00
184 Blinding Rage R	1.50	2.50
185 Burning Gaze C	.15	.25
186 Death from Above C	.15	.25
187 Defend Yourself! C	.15	.25
188 Deflection C	.15	.25
189 End of All That Is R	.60	1.00
190 Epic Battle C	.15	.25
191 Forbidden Loyalties, Team-Up C	.15	.25
192 I Still Hate Magic! C	.15	.25
193 Magical Lobotomy, Magic U	.30	.50
194 Multiverse Power Battery U	.30	.50
195 Rann C	.15	.25
196 Relentless Pursuit C	.15	.25
197 Removed from Continuity R	.60	1.00
198 Revitalize C	.15	.25
199 Thanagar C	.15	.25
200 Thanagarian Invasion C	.15	.25
201 Transmutation, Magic R	.60	1.00
202 Tricked-Out Sports Car C	.15	.25
203 Watch the Birdie! C	.15	.25
204 Barbara Gordon Oracle, Data Broker R	.60	1.00
205 Leslie Thompkins's Clinic U	.30	.50
206 Mourn for the Lost U	.30	.50
207 Return of Donna Troy U	.30	.50
208 Amadeus Arkham, Architect of Insanity U	.30	.50
209 The Joker, Permanent Vacation R	1.00	1.50
210 The Penguin, Arms Merchant U	.30	.50
211 Seiobo's Garden R	.60	1.00
212 Lois Lane, Earth 2 U	.30	.50
213 Lex Luthor, Champion of the Common Man U	.30	.50
214 Kilowog, Drill Sergeant U	.30	.50
215 Brainiac, Earth 2 U	.30	.50
216 Obsidian, Todd James Rice U	.30	.50
217 Adam Strange, Champion of Rann R	.60	1.00
218 Animal Man, Buddy Baker U	.30	.50
219 Mr. Mxyzptlk, Troublesome Trickster R	.60	1.00
220 Ultra-Humanite, Metahuman Manipulator R	.60	1.00

2006 Vs System Legion of Super-Heroes

COMPLETE SET (220)	30.00	60.00
BOOSTER BOX (24 PACKS)	25.00	50.00
BOOSTER PACK (14 CARDS)	1.00	2.00

*FOIL: .75X TO 2X BASIC CARDS
RELEASED IN DECEMBER 2006

1 Andromeda, Laurel Gand C	.15	.25
2 Apparition, Tinya Wazzo C	.15	.25
3 Bouncing Boy, Chuck Taine C	.15	.25
4 Brainiac 5.1, Querl Dox R	1.25	2.00
5 Chameleon, Reep Daggle U	.30	.50
6 Colossal Boy Leviathan, Gim Allon C	.15	.25
7 Cosmic Boy, Rokk Krinn R	1.25	2.00
8 Dream Girl, Nura Nal R	1.50	2.50
9 Element Lad, Jan Arrah C	.15	.25
10 Ferro Lad, Andrew Nolan C	.15	.25
11 Jazmin Cullen Kid Quantum, Hero of Xanthu C	.15	.25
12 Kara Zor-El Supergirl, Lost in Time U	.30	.50
13 Karate Kid, Val Armorr C	.15	.25
14 Kinetix, Zoe Saugin C	.15	.25
15 Live Wire, Garth Ranzz C	.15	.25
16 Mon-el Valor, Lar Gand R	.60	1.00
17 R.J. Brande, Philanthropist U	.30	.50
18 Saturn Girl, Imra Ardeen R	1.00	1.50
19 Sensor, Jeka Wynzorr U	.30	.50
20 Shrinking Violet Leviathan, Salu Digby U	.30	.50
21 Spark, Ayla Ranzz C	.15	.25
22 Star Boy, Thom Kallor C	.15	.25
23 Sun Boy, Dirk Morgna C	.15	.25
24 Timber Wolf, Brin Londo C	.15	.25
25 Triad, Luornu Durgo U	.30	.50
26 Ultra Boy, Jo Nah U	.30	.50
27 Umbra, Tasmia Mallor C	.15	.25
28 Wildfire, Drake Burroughs C	.15	.25
29 XS, Jenni Ognats C	.15	.25
30 Celebrity Status R	1.00	1.50
31 Flight Ring C	.15	.25
32 Foiled Assassination U	.30	.50
33 Legion Headquarters C	.15	.25
34 Legion of Super-Pets C	.15	.25
35 Legion World C	.15	.25
36 Let's Go, Legionnaires! C	.15	.25
37 Long Live the Legion U	.30	.50
38 Many Worlds C	.15	.25
39 New Recruits R	1.25	2.00
40 Past, Present, and Future, Team-Up C	.15	.25
41 Science Police Central R	1.00	1.50
42 Terror Incognita R	1.25	2.00
43 We Are Legion U	.30	.50
44 Youth of Tomorrow, Team-Up C	.15	.25
45 Atrophos, Chief Blight Scientist U	.30	.50
46 Brainiac 4, Dark Circle Leader C	.15	.25
47 Composite Man, Living Weapon R	.60	1.00
48 Computo, Rogue Program C	.15	.25
49 Computo Mr. Venge, Hidden File C	.15	.25
50 Cosmic King, Legion of Super Villains C	.15	.25
51 Daxamites, Army C	.15	.25
52 Dominators, Alien Invaders C	.15	.25
53 Emerald Empress, Fatal Five U	.30	.50
54 Emerald Eye, Sentient Artifact C	.15	.25
55 Glorith, Seductive Sorceress C	.15	.25
56 Lightning Lord, Legion of Super Villains C	.15	.25
57 Mano, Fatal Five C	.15	.25
58 Mordru, The Merciless C	.15	.25
59 Ol-Vir, Legion of Super Villains C	.15	.25
60 Ra's al Ghul, Engine of Change C	.15	.25
61 Ra's al Ghul Leland McCauley, U.P. President C	.15	.25
62 Saturn Queen, Legion of Super Villains C	.15	.25
63 Shrinking Violet Emerald Empress, Emerald Vi C	.15	.25
64 Starfinger, Char Burrane R	1.25	2.00
65 Tarik the Mute, Legion of Super Villains C	.15	.25
66 Tharok, Fatal Five C	.15	.25
67 The Blight, Army U	.30	.50
68 The Persuader, Fatal Five R	1.50	2.50
69 Time Trapper, Temporal Manipulator R	2.00	3.00
70 Universo, Vidar R	1.25	2.00
71 Validus, Fatal Five C	.15	.25
72 Altered History C	.15	.25
73 Asteroid JS-1967 U	.30	.50
74 Chain Lightning C	.15	.25
75 Dark Circle Rising U	.30	.50
76 Dominated R	.60	1.00
77 Earth Enslaved U	.30	.50
78 Fatal Five Hundred C	.15	.25
79 Five Against One C	.15	.25
80 For Khundia! C	.15	.25
81 Khundian Warship U	.30	.50
82 Legion of the Damned C	.15	.25
83 Mutual Enemies U	.30	.50
84 Return of the Demon's Head R	2.00	3.00
85 Sorcerous Suppression C	.15	.25
86 Tempus Fugit U	.30	.50
87 The Sun-Eater R	1.00	1.50
88 Apokoliptian Zealots, Army C	.15	.25
89 Bernadeth, Female Fury U	.30	.50
90 Dark Champion, Mockery C	.15	.25
91 Dark Firestorm, Mockery C	.15	.25
92 Dark Kryptonian Dark Superboy, Mockery R	1.25	2.00
93 Dark Lantern, Mockery C	.15	.25
94 Dark Martian, Mockery C	.15	.25
95 Dark Superboy, Mockery R	1.25	2.00
96 Dark Thanagarian, Mockery C	.15	.25
97 Dark Warrior, Mockery C	.15	.25
98 Darkseid, 8th Century C	.15	.25
99 Darkseid, Apokolips Now R	1.25	2.00
100 Darkseid, Apokoliptian Oppressor C	.15	.25
101 Darkseid, Evil Reborn C	.15	.25
102 Darkseid, Nemesis R	1.25	2.00
103 Gilotina, Female Fury C	.15	.25
104 Kara Zor-El Supergirl, Female Fury C	.15	.25
105 Knockout, Female Fury C	.15	.25
106 Lashina, Female Fury C	.15	.25
107 Mad Harriet, Female Fury C	.15	.25
108 Malice Vundabar, Female Fury C	.15	.25
109 Parademon Elite, Army C	.15	.25
110 Speed Queen, Female Fury C	.15	.25
111 Stompa, Female Fury R	1.00	1.50
112 31st Century Apokolips R	.75	1.25
113 All Hail Darkseid! U	.30	.50
114 Ancient Evils, Team-Up C	.15	.25
115 Ancient Throne U	.30	.50
116 Created from Hate R	4.00	6.00
117 Curse of Darkness R	.60	1.00
118 Dark Fury C	.15	.25
119 Dark Matter Drain R	.60	1.00
120 Joining the Darkseid, Team-Up C	.15	.25
121 No Match for Darkseid R	1.25	2.00
122 Omega Effect C	.15	.25
123 Price of Treason C	.15	.25
124 Prophetic Battle C	.15	.25
125 Servants of Darkness C	.15	.25
126 Shock and Awe U	.30	.50
127 Unravel Reality U	.30	.50
128 Bart Allen Kid Flash, Heir to the Mantle U	.30	.50
129 Bart Allen The Flash, Titans Tomorrow West U	.30	.50
130 Beast Boy, Party Animal C	.15	.25
131 Beast Boy Animal Man, Titans Tomorrow West C	.15	.25
132 Bette Kane Batwoman, Titans Tomorrow East U	.30	.50
133 Bumblebee, Titans Tomorrow East C	.15	.25
134 Cassie Sandsmark Wonder Girl, Ares's Chosen C	.15	.25
135 Cassie Sandsmark Wonder Woman, Titans Tomorrow West C	.15	.25
136 Connor Kent Superboy, Inspiration to the Legion C	.15	.25
137 Connor Kent Superman, Titans Tomorrow West R	.60	1.00
138 Dawn Granger Dove, Avatar of Order C	.15	.25
139 Duela Dent Harlequin, The Joker's Daughter C	.15	.25
140 Freddy Freeman Captain Marvel, Titans Tomorrow East C	.15	.25
141 Holly Granger Hawk, Avatar of Chaos C	.15	.25
142 Kid Devil, Eddie Bloomberg C	.15	.25
143 Koriand'r Starfire, Tamaranian Princess C	.15	.25
144 Lorena Marquez Aquawoman, Titans Tomorrow West R	.75	1.25
145 Mia Dearden Speedy, Deadly Aim C	.15	.25
146 Raven, Rachel Roth R	.75	1.25
147 Raven Dark Raven, Titans Tomorrow West R	1.25	2.00
148 Rose Wilson The Ravager, Daughter of Deathstroke R	.60	1.00
149 Rose Wilson The Ravager, Titans Tomorrow East U	.30	.50
150 Terra, Titans Tomorrow East U	.30	.50
151 The Herald, Malcolm Duncan C	.15	.25
152 Tim Drake Batman, Titans Tomorrow West U	.30	.50
153 Tim Drake Robin, Sidekick No More C	.15	.25
154 Vic Stone Cyborg, Titans Veteran C	.15	.25
155 Vic Stone Cyborg 2.0, Titans Tomorrow East U	.30	.50
156 Born of Blood U	.30	.50
157 Clash of the Titans C	.15	.25
158 First Date C	.15	.25
159 Generation Next, Team-Up C	.15	.25
160 Hall of Mentors U	.30	.50
161 Now You See Me R	.60	1.00
162 Order and Chaos U	.30	.50
163 Pour It On R	1.50	2.50
164 Tamaranian Garden R	.60	1.00
165 Titans Communicator C	.15	.25
166 Titans Memorial U	.30	.50
167 Titans, Together! R	.75	1.25
168 T-Jet, Tamaranian Fighter U	.30	.50
169 Donna Troy, Born Again C	.15	.25
170 Superboy, Yellow Sun Armor U	.30	.50
171 Jason Todd Red Hood, Revived R	.60	1.00
172 31st Century Metropolis, Team-Up C	.15	.25
173 Awestruck C	.15	.25
174 Blinding Light C	.15	.25
175 Busted Knee C	.15	.25
176 Contact! U	.30	.50
177 Cosmic Tuning Fork R	2.50	4.00
178 Death of a Legionnaire C	.15	.25
179 Earth 2 U	.30	.50
180 Forged in Crisis U	.30	.50
181 Furious Assault C	.15	.25
182 Furnace of Apokolips C	.15	.25
183 Girls' Night Out C	.15	.25
184 Legion Lost C	.15	.25
185 Level 12 Intelligence R	2.00	3.00
186 Lost in Translation U	.30	.50
187 Mobilize R	20.00	30.00
188 Need for Speed R	1.50	2.50
189 Ravaged! U	.30	.50
190 Steely Resolve R	.60	1.00
191 Substitute Heroes C	.15	.25
192 The Future Is Changing C	.15	.25
193 Titans of Tomorrow U	.30	.50
194 United Planets HQ, Team-Up C	.15	.25
195 Crimson Avenger, Jill Carlyle U	.30	.50
196 Jack Knight Starman, Knight Past U	.30	.50
197 Power Girl, Child of Crisis R	2.00	3.00
198 S.T.R.I.P.E., Pat Dugan U	.30	.50
199 Alan Scott, White King U	.30	.50
200 Director Bones, D.E.O. U	.30	.50
201 Fire, Knight U	.30	.50
202 Girl 13 Traci Thirteen, Hex and the City R	.60	1.00
203 Mary Marvel, World's Mightiest Girl U	.30	.50
204 Otherworldly Battle, Magic R	.60	1.00
205 Blüdhaven Destroyed R	.60	1.00
206 Chemo, Chemical Golem U	.30	.50
207 High Society C	.15	.25
208 Harvey Bullock, Bishop R	1.25	2.00
209 The Riddler, Brain Teaser R	.60	1.00
210 Nyssa Raatko, Daughter of the Demon R	1.00	1.50
211 Solar Powered R	1.50	2.50
212 Brainiac 2.5, Future Intelligence R	1.00	1.50
213 Shiloh Norman Mister Miracle, Soldier of Victory R	.75	1.25
214 Kyle Rayner Ion, Torch Bearer R	2.50	4.00
215 Mongul, Intergalactic Menace R	.60	1.00
216 Alexander Luthor, Earth 3 U	.30	.50
217 Kate Spencer Manhunter, Vigilante Justice U	.30	.50
218 Wally West The Flash, The Fastest Man Alive R	1.00	1.50
219 Peter Merkel Ragdoll, Malleable Miscreant U	.30	.50
220 Owen Mercer Captain Boomerang, Digger's Son U	.30	.50

2006 Vs System X-Men

COMPLETE SET (220)	30.00	60.00
BOOSTER BOX (24 PACKS)	30.00	60.00
BOOSTER PACK (14 CARDS)	1.50	2.50

*FOIL: .75X TO 2X BASIC CARDS
RELEASED IN FEBRUARY 2006

1 Archangel, Angel C	.15	.25
2 Beast, Feline Geneticist U	.30	.50
3 Bishop, XSE Commando C	.15	.25
4 Cannonball, Blast Field C	.15	.25
5 Changeling, Kevin Sidney R	.60	1.00
6 Colossus, Organic Steel U	.30	.50
7 Cyclops, Blue Leader C	.15	.25
8 Dazzler, Rock Star C	.15	.25
9 Emma Frost, Friend or Foe R	1.50	2.50
10 Gambit, Ragin' Cajun U	.30	.50
11 Havok, Critical Mass C	.15	.25
12 Iceman, Deep Freeze C	.15	.25
13 Jean Grey, Red R	.60	1.00
14 Jubilee, Jubilation Lee U	.30	.50
15 Juggernaut, The Unstoppable U	1.25	2.00
16 Lockheed, Saurian Sidekick C	.15	.25
17 Longshot, Hero of Mojoworld U	.30	.50
18 Nightcrawler, Swashbuckler C	.15	.25
19 Professor X, Headmaster R	2.50	4.00
20 Psylocke, Armored Empath C	.15	.25
21 Rachel Summers Phoenix, Phoenix of the Future R	.60	1.00
22 Rogue, Anna Marie C	.15	.25
23 Sage, Xavier's Secret Weapon C	.15	.25
24 Shadowcat, Katya C	.15	.25
25 Storm, Gold Leader C	.15	.25
26 Wolverine, The Best at What He Does C	.15	.25
27 Xorn, Shen Xorn C	.15	.25
28 Angel of Mercy U	.30	.50
29 Blackbird Blue U	.30	.50
30 Harry's Hideaway U	.30	.50
31 Phoenix Rising R	.60	1.00
32 Rebirth C	.15	.25
33 SNIKT! R	1.00	1.50
34 Time Breach R	.60	1.00
35 Turnabout C	.15	.25
36 Worthington Industries, X-Corp R	2.00	3.00
37 X-Corp: Amsterdam, X-Corp C	.15	.25
38 X-Corp: Hong Kong, X-Corp C	.15	.25
39 X-Corp: Paris, X-Corp C	.15	.25
40 X-Men United, Team-Up C	.15	.25
41 X-Treme Maneuver U	.30	.50
42 Angel Dust, Adrenaline Junkie U	.30	.50
43 Annalee, Mother Hen C	.15	.25
44 Ape, Metamorph R	.60	1.00
45 Artie, Arthur Maddicks C	.15	.25
46 Blow Hard, Windbag U	.30	.50
47 Caliban, Mutant Bloodhound C	.15	.25
48 Callisto, Morlock Queen C	.15	.25
49 Cybelle, Meltdown R	.60	1.00
50 Electric Eve, Live Wire C	.15	.25
51 Erg, Electric Eye C	.15	.25
52 Feral, Maria Callasantos C	.15	.25

Card	Low	High
53 Healer, Life Giver C	.15	.25
54 Hemingway, Gene Nation C	.15	.25
55 Hump, Servant of Masque U	.30	.50
56 Leech, Inhibitor U	.30	.50
57 Marrow, Gene Nation C	.15	.25
58 Masque, Flesh Shaper U	.30	.50
59 Mikhail Rasputin, Morlock Messiah R	.60	1.00
60 Piper, Rat Charmer C	.15	.25
61 Plague, Deathwalker C	.15	.25
62 Postman, Memory Thief U	.30	.50
63 Scaleface, Dragon Lady C	.15	.25
64 Storm, Leader of the Morlocks C	.15	.25
65 Sunder, Callisto's Enforcer C	.15	.25
66 Tar Baby, Adhesive Ally C	.15	.25
67 The Beautiful Dreamer, Dreamweaver C	.15	.25
68 Thornn, Lucia Callasantos R	.60	1.00
69 Tommy, Runaway C	.15	.25
70 Backs Against the Wall R	.60	1.00
71 Bloodhound U	.30	.50
72 Bum's Rush C	.15	.25
73 Good Samaritan R	.60	1.00
74 Morlock Justice U	.30	.50
75 Neutralized C	.15	.25
76 Retribution C	.15	.25
77 Sewer System U	.30	.50
78 Shrapnel Blast U	.30	.50
79 Subterranean Sanctuary R	.60	1.00
80 The Alley U	.30	.50
81 The Forsaken, Team-Up C	.15	.25
82 The Hill C	.15	.25
83 Amelia Voght, Acolyte R	1.25	2.00
84 Anne-Marie Cortez, Acolyte C	.15	.25
85 Avalanche, Freedom Force R	.60	1.00
86 Blob, Freedom Force C	.15	.25
87 Chrome, Acolyte C	.15	.25
88 Colossus, Acolyte U	.30	.50
89 Crimson Commando, Freedom Force C	.15	.25
90 Destiny, Freedom Force C	.15	.25
91 Exodus, Acolyte C	.15	.25
92 Fabian Cortez, Acolyte U	.30	.50
93 Harry Delgado, Acolyte C	.15	.25
94 Joanna Cargill, Acolyte C	.15	.25
95 Julia Carpenter, Freedom Force C	.15	.25
96 Kleinstock Brothers, Acolyte U	.30	.50
97 Magneto, Ruler of Avalon R	.75	1.25
98 Mystique, Freedom Force U	.30	.50
99 Polaris, Acolyte C	.15	.25
100 Pyro, Freedom Force C	.15	.25
101 Rem-Ram, Acolyte C	.15	.25
102 Sabretooth, Savage Killer R	.75	1.25
103 Scanner, Acolyte C	.15	.25
104 Senyaka, Acolyte C	.15	.25
105 Silver Sabre, Freedom Force C	.15	.25
106 Spiral, Freedom Force R	.60	1.00
107 Spoor, Acolyte C	.15	.25
108 Stonewall, Freedom Force U	.30	.50
109 Toad, Hopalong C	.15	.25
110 Unuscione, Acolyte U	.30	.50
111 Acolyte Body Armor U	.30	.50
112 Boot to the Head R	.75	1.25
113 Freedom Force C	.15	.25
114 Go Down Fighting C	.15	.25
115 Hellhound U	.30	.50
116 Kill the Flatscans U	.30	.50
117 Lying in Wait C	.15	.25
118 Planet X, Team-Up C	.15	.25
119 Ruins of Avalon R	.60	1.00
120 Shake, Rattle, and Roll R	.60	1.00
121 Sovereign Superior U	.30	.50
122 The Acolytes R	.60	1.00
123 Wundagore Citadel C	.15	.25
124 Beef, Hellion C	.15	.25
125 Bevatron, Hellion C	.15	.25
126 Catseye, Hellion U	.30	.50
127 Courtney Ross, Once and Future Queen U	.30	.50
128 Dark Phoenix, Alien Life Force R	.75	1.25
129 Donald Pierce, White Bishop C	.15	.25
130 Emma Frost, White Queen C	.15	.25
131 Empath, Hellion C	.15	.25
132 Firestar, Hellion C	.15	.25
133 Friedrich Von Roehm, Black Rook C	.15	.25
134 Harry Leland, Black Bishop R	.60	1.00
135 Hellfire Club Initiate, Army C	.15	.25
136 Hellfire Club Mercenary, Army C	.15	.25
137 James Proudstar Thunderbird, Hellion R	.60	1.00
138 Jetstream, Hellion C	.15	.25
139 Madelyne Pryor, Black Rook C	.15	.25
140 Magneto, Black Lord R	.60	1.00
141 Mastermind, Dark Dreamer C	.15	.25
142 Roberto Da Costa, Heir to the Throne C	.15	.25
143 Roulette, Hellion R	.60	1.00
144 Sage, Tessa C	.15	.25
145 Sebastian Shaw, Black King R	.60	1.00
146 Selene, Black Queen C	.15	.25
147 Shinobi Shaw, White King C	.15	.25
148 Tarot, Hellion C	.15	.25
149 Trevor Fitzroy, White Rook R	.60	1.00
150 Viper, White Warrior Princess C	.15	.25
151 Absolute Power U	.30	.50
152 Army of One C	.15	.25
153 Cardinal Law C	.15	.25
154 Deadly Game R	.60	1.00
155 Eminent Domain R	.60	1.00
156 Evil Alliance, Team-Up C	.15	.25
157 Inner Circle R	.60	1.00
158 Join the Club! U	.30	.50
159 Massachusetts Academy U	.30	.50
160 Power and Wealth R	1.25	2.00
161 Power Play R	.60	1.00
162 Raising Hell C	.15	.25
163 Shaw Industries U	.30	.50
164 The Hellfire Club C	.15	.25
165 Above and Below, Team-Up U	.30	.50
166 Blow the Man Down R	.75	1.25
167 Chill Out! R	.60	1.00
168 Drain Essence C	.15	.25
169 Feel the Burn C	.15	.25
170 Magnetic Force U	.30	.50
171 The Evil Eye C	.15	.25
172 Phase Shift C	.15	.25
173 Memory Probe C	.15	.25
174 Mental Domination U	.30	.50
175 Mind Control C	.15	.25
176 Psi-Link R	.60	1.00
177 Psionic Storm C	.15	.25
178 Psychic Armor C	.15	.25
179 Psychic Struggle R	.60	1.00
180 Immovable C	.15	.25
181 Kidney Punch C	.15	.25
182 Kill or be Killed C	.15	.25
183 Mob Mentality R	.60	1.00
184 Momentary Distraction R	.60	1.00
185 Pack Tactics C	.15	.25
186 Special Delivery U	.30	.50
187 Krakoa, Island Monster C	.15	.25
188 Multiple Man Jamie Madrox, Army U	2.50	4.00
189 Wolverine, Patch R	.60	1.00
190 X-23, Laura Kinney R	.75	1.25
191 Alter Density C	.15	.25
192 Brave New World, Team-Up C	.15	.25
193 District X U	.30	.50
194 Enemy of My Enemy R	15.00	25.00
195 Homo Superior C	.15	.25
196 Image Inducer C	.15	.25
197 Leadership Challenge C	.15	.25
198 Mindtap Mechanism U	.30	.50
199 Mutant Massacre U	.30	.50
200 Mutopia, Team-Up C	.15	.25
201 Super Hero Showdown C	.15	.25
202 Teamwork U	.30	.50
203 Franklin Richards, Trapped in Time R	.60	1.00
204 Kristoff Von Doom, Pretender to the Throne R	.60	1.00
205 Sentinel Mark VI, Army U	.30	.50
206 Toxin, Patrick Mulligan U	.30	.50
207 Man-Bull, William Taurens R	.60	1.00
208 Black Panther, King of Wakanda U	.30	.50
209 Henrietta Hunter, X-Celebrity U	.30	.50
210 Doctor Sun, Creator of Project: Mind R	.60	1.00
211 Witch Woman, Linda Littletrees U	.30	.50
212 Doctor Druid, Anthony Druid U	.30	.50
213 Sub-Mariner, Namor U	.30	.50
214 Lady Lark, Skylark R	.60	1.00
215 Mysterium, Joseph Lightner R	.60	1.00
216 Genis-Vell Photon, Transformed U	.30	.50
217 Mech Bay R	.60	1.00
218 Absorbing Man, Carl Creel R	.60	1.00
219 Gargantua, Edward Cobert R	.60	1.00
220 Kang, Scarlet Centurion U	.30	.50

2007 Vs System DC Legends

Card	Low	High
COMPLETE SET (273)	50.00	100.00
BOOSTER BOX (24 PACKS)	50.00	100.00
BOOSTER PACK (14 CARDS)	3.00	4.00
*FOIL: .75X TO 2X BASIC CARDS		
RELEASED IN DECEMBER 2007		
1 Aquaman, Founding Member C	.15	.25
2 Aquaman, Lord of Atlantis U	.30	.50
3 Aztek, Champion of Quetzalcoatl C	.15	.25
4 Barry Allen The Flash, Crimson Tornado R	5.00	8.00
5 Barry Allen The Flash, Founding Member R	2.00	3.00
6 Batman, Founding Member R	8.00	12.00
7 Batman, Justice's Shadow C	.15	.25
8 Big Barda, Furious Fatale C	.15	.25
9 Black Lightning, Energetic Hero U	.30	.50
10 Dinah Laurel Lance Black Canary, New Wings C	.15	.25
11 Elongated Man, Stretchable Sleuth U	.30	.50
12 Firehawk, Flaming Justice C	.15	.25
13 Firestorm, Ronnie Raymond U	.30	.50
14 Hal Jordan, Founding Member R	5.00	8.00
15 Hal Jordan, Fearless R	4.00	6.00
16 John Henry Irons Steel, Working Man C	.15	.25
17 John Stewart, The Master Builder C	.15	.25
18 Katar Hol Hawkman, Death from Above C	.15	.25
19 Kendra Saunders Hawkgirl, Thanagarian Heroine C	.15	.25
20 Kyle Rayner, Guardian of the Universe U	.30	.50
21 Martian Manhunter, Founding Member C	.15	.25
22 Martian Manhunter, The Last Martian R	2.00	3.00
23 Oliver Queen Green Arrow, Bullseye C	.15	.25
24 Plastic Man, Plastic Fantastic U	.30	.50
25 Ray Palmer The Atom, World's Smallest Hero R	.60	1.00
26 Red Tornado, Elemental Android C	.15	.25
27 Roy Harper Red Arrow, Coming of Age R	1.25	2.00
28 Superman, Metropolis Marvel R	3.00	5.00
29 Superman, Founding Member R	2.50	4.00
30 Vixen, Tantu Totem C	.15	.25
31 Wally West The Flash, Keystone Cop C	.15	.25
32 Wonder Woman, Ambassador of Peace R	3.00	5.00
33 Wonder Woman, Founding Member C	.15	.25
34 Zatanna, Sucoh Sucop! C	.15	.25
35 Sea Creatures, Army R	2.50	4.00
36 Lasso of Truth R	.75	1.25
37 Batcomputer, Criminal Database U	.30	.50
38 Cadmus Labs U	.30	.50
39 Hall of Justice U	.30	.50
40 Keystone City U	.30	.50
41 Poseidonis R	1.25	2.00
42 The Watchtower R	.60	1.00
43 Atomize R	1.25	2.00
44 Battle Training C	.15	.25
45 Crisis Averted C	.15	.25
46 Emerald Rebirth U	.30	.50
47 Fearless R	1.00	1.50
48 From the Darkness R	5.00	8.00
49 Full Throttle R	2.00	3.00
50 Fury of the Amazons R	2.00	3.00
51 Indestructible R	6.00	10.00
52 Intangible R	.60	1.00
53 Magnificent Seven C	.15	.25
54 Mightiest Heroes R	6.00	10.00
55 New Era R	.60	1.00
56 Recharge! R	2.00	3.00
57 Reform the League C	.15	.25
58 Stalwart Defense U	.30	.50
59 Telepathic Link R	.60	1.00
60 Terminal Velocity R	1.50	2.50
61 Truth, Justice, and Peace R	1.25	2.00
62 Argent, Toni Monetti C	.15	.25
63 Bart Allen Kid Flash, Generation Fourth U	.30	.50
64 Beast Boy, Garfield Logan R	1.25	2.00
65 Beast Boy, Freak of Nature C	.15	.25
66 Bette Kane Flamebird, Reflex Action C	.15	.25
67 Bumblebee, Sonic Sting U	.30	.50
68 Cassie Sandsmark Wonder Girl, Might of Atlas C	.15	.25
69 Dawn Granger Dove, Terataya's Chosen C	.15	.25
70 Dick Grayson Nightwing, Going it Alone C	.15	.25
71 Donna Troy Wonder Girl, Amazon Warrior R	.60	1.00
72 Freddy Freeman Captain Marvel Jr., Third in Line C	.15	.25
73 Holly Granger Hawk, T'Charr's Chosen U	.30	.50
74 Hot Spot, Isaiah Crockett C	.15	.25
75 Jericho, Contact! R	.60	1.00
76 Kid Devil, Teen Hellion C	.15	.25
77 Koriand'r Starfire, Fiery Temper U	.30	.50
78 Koriand'r Starfire, X'Hal's Fury R	6.00	10.00
79 Mia Dearden Speedy, Archer's Apprentice C	.15	.25
80 Miss Martian, M'gann M'orzz R	2.00	3.00
81 Pantha, Subject X-24 C	.15	.25
82 Raven, Demon Spawn C	.15	.25
83 Ray Palmer The Atom, Tiny Titan C	.15	.25
84 Red Star, Russian Roulette C	.15	.25
85 Rose Wilson The Ravager, Redemption Earned U	.30	.50
86 Roy Harper Speedy, Mercurial Marksman R	.60	1.00
87 Roy Harper Arsenal, Additional Firepower R	2.00	3.00
88 Tim Drake Robin, Titan in Command U	.30	.50
89 Tim Drake Robin, Leader of the Pack R	1.25	2.00
90 Vic Stone Cyborg, Mechanized Mentor C	.15	.25
91 Vic Stone Cyborg, Titans Warhorse U	.30	.50
92 Zatara, Teen Magician U	.30	.50
93 Cybernetic Laser U	.30	.50
94 T-Jet, Unique * Titans Transport R	.60	1.00
95 Weapon Upgrade R	.60	1.00
96 Optitron R	.60	1.00
97 Solar Tower C	.15	.25
98 Titans Tower U	.30	.50
99 Best Friends Forever R	.60	1.00
100 Call of the Wild U	.30	.50
101 Cunning Strategy R	1.00	1.50
102 Follow the Leader U	.30	.50
103 Graduation Day U	.30	.50
104 Headstrong Charge R	.60	1.00
105 More Than Just Sidekicks C	.15	.25
106 Prodigies U	.30	.50
107 Starbolts R	.75	1.25
108 Teen Titans Go! C	.15	.25
109 Abra Kadabra, Magical Rogue C	.15	.25
110 Agamemno, Interplanetary Conqueror R	.60	1.00
111 Barracuda, Earth 3 C	.15	.25
112 Black Manta, Deepwater Denizen C	.15	.25
113 Captain Boomerang, George Harkness C	.15	.25
114 Catwoman, Cat o' Nine Tails C	.15	.25
115 Circe, Evil Enchantress C	.15	.25
116 David Clinton Chronos, Timetwister R	.60	1.00
117 Dr. Light, Blinding Flash R	.60	1.00
118 Felix Faust, Soulless Mystic C	.15	.25
119 Jemm, Son of Saturn U	.30	.50
120 Johnny Quick, Earth 3 C	.15	.25
121 The Joker, Headline Stealer C	.15	.25
122 The Joker, Killer Smile R	1.25	2.00
123 Lex Luthor, Megalomaniac R	2.50	4.00
124 Lex Luthor, Metropolis Mogul C	.15	.25
125 Lex Luthor, The Everyman R	.60	1.00
126 Ocean Master, Son of Atlan C	.15	.25
127 Owlman, Earth 3 C	.15	.25
128 The Penguin, Gentleman of Crime C	.15	.25
129 Power Ring, Earth 3 C	.15	.25
130 Prometheus, New Year's Evil U	.30	.50
131 Scarecrow, Chiroptophobic R	1.25	2.00
132 The Shade, Ageless Enigma U	.30	.50
133 Sinestro, Korugaran Despot C	.15	.25
134 Superwoman, Earth 3 C	.15	.25
135 Tattooed Man, Art Imitates Life R	.60	1.00
136 Ultraman, Earth 3 C	.15	.25
137 Vandal Savage, Cro-Magnon Man R	.60	1.00
138 White Martian, Earth 3 C	.15	.25
139 Zazzala Queen Bee, H.I.V.E. Monarch R	1.00	1.50
140 Laughing Gas U	.30	.50
141 Earth 3 U	.30	.50
142 Injustice Gang Satellite R	.60	1.00
143 All Too Easy C	.15	.25
144 Crime Syndicate of Amerika R	2.50	4.00
145 Criminal Mastermind C	.15	.25
146 Evil Genius U	.30	.50
147 Gang-Up, Team-Up C	.15	.25
148 Injustice for All R	.60	1.00
149 The Joke's on You! R	.75	1.25
150 Power Siphon R	.60	1.00
151 Research and Development R	.60	1.00
152 Secret Files C	.15	.25
153 Sunburst R	.75	1.25
154 Amazo, Power Duplication C	.15	.25
155 Basil Karlo Clayface, Slimy Shapeshifter U	.30	.50
156 Bizarro, Dark Mirror U	.30	.50
157 Black Manta, Underwater Marauder R	2.00	3.00
158 The Calculator, Q.E.D. C	.15	.25
159 Charaxes, Moth Monster R	3.00	5.00
160 Cheetah, Barbara Minerva U	.30	.50
161 Chemo, Toxic Waste R	4.00	6.00
162 Darkseid, Destroyer of Life C	.15	.25
163 Darkseid, Dark God R	2.50	4.00
164 Deadshot, Floyd Lawton R	.60	1.00
165 Deathstroke the Terminator, Killing Machine C	.15	.25
166 Desaad, Dark Side Therapy R	.75	1.25
167 Doomsday, Engine of Destruction R	.75	1.25
168 Dr. Polaris, Polar Opposite C	.15	.25

169 Dr. Psycho, Demented Dwarf C	.15	.25
170 Dr. Sivana, Mad Scientist C	.15	.25
171 Fatality, Okaaran Warrior R	1.50	2.50
172 Felix Faust, Dark Bargain U	.30	.50
173 Floronic Man, Jason Woodrue C	.15	.25
174 Giganta, Rampaging U	.30	.50
175 Gorilla Grodd, Grodd Awful C	.15	.25
176 Gorilla Grodd, Psionic Simian C	.15	.25
177 Ishmael Gregor Sabbac, Deadly Sin R	.60	1.00
178 King Shark, Jaws of Death R	1.50	2.50
179 Mark Desmond Blockbuster, Mindless Brute U	.30	.50
180 Mr. Freeze, Cold Blooded R	1.25	2.00
181 Poison Ivy, Intoxicating U	.30	.50
182 Psycho-Pirate, Medusa Mask C	.15	.25
183 The Riddler, Riddle Me This R	2.00	3.00
184 Shadow-Thief, Umbral Burglar C	.15	.25
185 Sinestro, Yellow Lantern R	2.00	3.00
186 Solomon Grundy, Died on a Saturday R	1.00	1.50
187 Gorilla City C	.15	.25
188 Hidden HQ R	1.50	2.50
189 Remote Facility, Non-Unique C	.15	.25
190 Acceptable Loss C	.15	.25
191 Anger and Hate R	1.25	2.00
192 Anti-Life R	1.00	1.50
193 Coup d'Etat R	.60	1.00
194 Endgame R	.75	1.25
195 Forced Conscription C	.15	.25
196 Going Ape U	.30	.50
197 Lord of Apokolips U	.30	.50
198 Maleficent Meeting C	.15	.25
199 Master Plan U	.30	.50
200 Monkey See, Monkey Do R	1.25	2.00
201 Shadow Strike C	.15	.25
202 Straight to the Grave R	1.50	2.50
203 Unnatural Selection U	.30	.50
204 Cassandra Cain, Daughter of Shiva U	.30	.50
205 David Cain, World Class Assassin R	.60	1.00
206 Hassim, Loyal Retainer U	.30	.50
207 Lady Shiva, Master Assassin R	.60	1.00
208 The Mad Dog, Rabid Killer C	.15	.25
209 Merlyn, Direct Hit Man R	1.50	2.50
210 Novice Assassin, Army C	.15	.25
211 Nyssa Raatko, Maiden of Death C	.15	.25
212 Ra's al Ghul, Demon's Head Rising C	.15	.25
213 Ra's al Ghul, The Demon's Head R	2.00	3.00
214 Shadow Assassin, Army C	.15	.25
215 Shrike, Boone C	.15	.25
216 Talia, Heir Apparent C	.15	.25
217 Ubu, Ra's al Ghul's Bodyguard C	.15	.25
218 The Demon's Quarters R	.60	1.00
219 Flying Fortress U	.30	.50
220 Lazarus Pit, Non-Unique * Death's Door R	1.00	1.50
221 Mountain Stronghold, Non-Unique U	.30	.50
222 Plague Zone, Non-Unique U	.30	.50
223 The Demon's Head R	.60	1.00
224 Demonfang C	.15	.25
225 Divide and Conquer R	.75	1.25
226 Harsh Judgment R	.60	1.00
227 Tower of Babel R	.60	1.00
228 The Chief, Niles Caulder U	.30	.50
229 Elasti-Girl, Rita Farr R	1.00	1.50
230 Mento, Steve Dayton U	.30	.50
231 Negative Man, Larry Trainor U	.30	.50
232 Robotman, Cliff Steele C	.15	.25
233 Dayton Manor R	1.50	2.50
234 Freak Out R	1.00	1.50
235 Misfits R	.75	1.25
236 Strange Days R	.60	1.00
237 Captain Atom, Quantum Energy R	.60	1.00
238 The Demon, Etrigan R	.75	1.25
239 Imperiex, The Beginning and The End R	.60	1.00
240 Lobo, The Main Man R	2.50	4.00
241 Supernova, Daniel Carter R	1.50	2.50
242 Terra, Earth Mover R	.75	1.25
243 Twin Firearms U	.30	.50
244 Nth Metal C	.15	.25
245 Birthing Chamber U	.30	.50
246 Coast City C	.15	.25
247 Metropolis Reborn, Non-Unique * Team-Up C	.15	.25
248 A Better World, Team-Up C	.15	.25
249 Blind Sided R	2.00	3.00
250 Blinding Rage R	1.50	2.50
251 Break You C	.15	.25
252 Changing Minds, Team-Up C	.15	.25
253 Chaos and Villainy, Team-Up C	.15	.25
254 Combat Reflexes C	.15	.25
255 Death Trap C	.15	.25
256 Dirty Tricks R	.60	1.00
257 Duty Calls C	.15	.25
258 From the Shadows C	.15	.25
259 Have a Blast! R	1.50	2.50
260 Hero's Best Friend C	.15	.25
261 Heroes of Two Worlds R	4.00	6.00
262 Heroic Effort C	.15	.25
263 Home Surgery C	.15	.25
264 Judgment Day R	.60	1.00
265 Mirror Image R	.75	1.25
266 The Multiverse, Team-Up C	.15	.25
267 Nasty Surprise C	.15	.25
268 Overwhelming Odds C	.15	.25
269 Path of Destruction C	.15	.25
270 Shape Change U	.30	.50
271 Tag Team C	.15	.25
272 Total Anarchy R	.60	1.00
273 Total Recall, Team-Up U	.30	.50

2007 Vs System Marvel Legends

COMPLETE SET (273)	50.00	100.00
BOOSTER BOX (24 PACKS)	30.00	60.00
BOOSTER PACK (14 CARDS)	1.50	2.50
*FOIL: .75X TO 2X BASIC CARDS		
RELEASED IN AUGUST 2007		
1 Archangel, Aeroballistic C	.15	.25
2 Beast, Bookworm R	1.25	2.00
3 Bishop, Time Cop C	.15	.25
4 Blink, Exile C	.15	.25
5 Cable, Nathan Summers C	.15	.25
6 Cable, Askani'Son U	.30	.50
7 Colossus, Tin Man C	.15	.25
8 Cyclops, Fearless Leader C	.15	.25
9 Domino, Neena Thurman R	2.50	4.00
10 Emma Frost, Ice Queen R	4.00	6.00
11 Forge, Inventor Extraordinaire U	.30	.50
12 Gambit, Swamp Rat U	.30	.50
13 Havok, Unstable Son C	.15	.25
14 Iceman, Frosty C	.15	.25
15 Jean Grey, Teen Telepath C	.15	.25
16 Jean Grey, Phoenix Rising C	.15	.25
17 Jean Grey, Phoenix Force R	1.00	1.50
18 Jubilee, Mallrat C	.15	.25
19 Mimic, Exile R	1.50	2.50
20 Morph, Exile U	.30	.50
21 Multiple Man, Army MadroX C	.15	.25
22 Nightcrawler, Man of the Cloth C	.15	.25
23 Professor X, Idealistic Dreamer C	.15	.25
24 Professor X, World's Most Powerful Telepath R	1.00	1.50
25 Psylocke, Second Skin C	.15	.25
26 Rogue, Power Absorption R	1.50	2.50
27 Shadowcat, Phase Shifter R	2.00	3.00
28 Storm, Elemental Goddess C	.15	.25
29 Sunfire, Rising Sun C	.15	.25
30 Wolverine, Logan C	.15	.25
31 Wolverine, Bub R	3.00	5.00
32 Wolverine, Bloodlust U	.30	.50
33 X-Man, Nate Grey C	.15	.25
34 Cerebro R	.60	1.00
35 Muir Island U	.30	.50
36 Xavier's Institute of Higher Learning R	6.00	10.00
37 Adamantium Claws R	5.00	8.00
38 Battle Tactics C	.15	.25
39 Berserker Rage R	6.00	10.00
40 Bodyslide R	5.00	8.00
41 Children of the Atom R	1.25	2.00
42 Cleansing Flame R	1.25	2.00
43 Commanding Nature C	.15	.25
44 Fastball Special U	.30	.50
45 Healing Factor U	.30	.50
46 Sneak Attack R	2.00	3.00
47 Splintering Consciousness U	.30	.50
48 Telepathic Suppression R	1.25	2.00
49 To Me, My X-Men! R	2.00	3.00
50 Turnabout C	.15	.25
51 Avalanche, Earthmover R	1.00	1.50
52 Black Tom, Callous Opportunist C	.15	.25
53 Blob, Fred Dukes C	.15	.25
54 Blob, Immovable Object U	.30	.50
55 Dark Beast, Sinister Reflection R	1.25	2.00
56 Destiny, Doomsday Diarist U	.30	.50
57 Exodus, Bennet du Paris C	.15	.25
58 Juggernaut, Champion of Cyttorak C	.15	.25
59 Juggernaut, Walking Disaster U	.30	.50
60 Juggernaut, Weapon of Mass Destruction R	1.25	2.00
61 Magneto, Mutant Terrorist C	.15	.25
62 Magneto, Mutant Supreme R	2.00	3.00
63 Magneto, Master of Magnetism R	.75	1.25
64 Mammomax, Maximus Jensen C	.15	.25
65 Mystique, Shapely Shifter U	.30	.50
66 Mystique, Shape-Changing Assassin C	.15	.25
67 Nocturne, Talia Wagner R	1.50	2.50
68 Phantazia, Eileen Harsaw C	.15	.25
69 Post, Harbinger of Onslaught C	.15	.25
70 Pyro, St. John Allerdyce C	.15	.25
71 Quicksilver, Mercurial Speedster C	.15	.25
72 Quicksilver, Speed Demon R	1.25	2.00
73 Random, Marshall Evan Stone III R	1.50	2.50
74 Rogue, Southern Belle C	.15	.25
75 Sabretooth, Genocidal Savage C	.15	.25
76 Sabretooth, Feral Rage R	1.25	2.00
77 Sauron, Mutant Vampire R	1.25	2.00
78 Scarlet Witch, Mistress of Magic C	.15	.25
79 Scarlet Witch, Brotherhood Sister C	.15	.25
80 Sentinel Mark VII, Repurposed R	2.00	3.00
81 Toad, Court Jester C	.15	.25
82 Unus, Angelo Unuscione U	.30	.50
83 Xorn, Champion of Mutantkind R	1.25	2.00
84 Juggernaut's Helmet U	.30	.50
85 Asteroid M U	.30	.50
86 Genosha R	1.50	2.50
87 Underground Resistance R	4.00	6.00
88 A Human Juggernaut R	1.00	1.50
89 Avalanched! C	.15	.25
90 Betrayal Most Foul R	.75	1.25
91 Eviscerate C	.15	.25
92 Immovable Object C	.15	.25
93 Insignificant Threat R	1.00	1.50
94 Iron Extraction R	2.00	3.00
95 Metallic Assault R	1.00	1.50
96 Pecking Order U	.30	.50
97 Sibling Support C	.15	.25
98 The Next Brotherhood R	4.00	6.00
99 Unstoppable R	2.50	4.00
100 Xorn's Takeover R	.60	1.00
101 Black Cat, Thrillseeker C	.15	.25
102 Black Panther, Silent Stalker C	.15	.25
103 Black Widow, Femme Fatale R	2.00	3.00
104 Blade, Vampire Slayer R	2.00	3.00
105 Captain America, Loyal Patriot R	3.00	5.00
106 Cloak, Shadowmaster R	.75	1.25
107 Dagger, Lightbringer C	.15	.25
108 Daredevil, Fearless Survivor C	.15	.25
109 Daredevil, Hornhead C	.15	.25
110 Deadgirl, Dead Again? U	.30	.50
111 Dr. Strange, Master of the Mystic Arts C	.15	.25
112 Echo, Masterless Samurai R	1.50	2.50
113 Elektra, Masterless Assassin R	4.00	6.00
114 Ghost Rider, The Devil's Rider C	.15	.25
115 Ghost Rider, Spirit of Vengeance U	.30	.50
116 Ghost Rider, Danny Ketch R	1.25	2.00
117 Hulk, Savage Hulk R	2.50	4.00
118 Iron Fist, Hired Hero C	.15	.25
119 Luke Cage, Hired Hero C	.15	.25
120 Marvel Boy, Noh-Varr U	.30	.50
121 Moon Knight, Knight of Khonshu C	.15	.25
122 Morbius, Biochemical Bloodsucker U	.30	.50
123 Nick Fury, Col. Nicholas Fury R	1.50	2.50
124 Punisher, Suicide Run C	.15	.25
125 Punisher, Guns Blazing U	.30	.50
126 Punisher, Angel of Death R	3.00	5.00
127 Shang Chi, Martial Master R	.75	1.25
128 Spider-Man, Webhead C	.15	.25
129 Spider-Man, Outlaw C	.15	.25
130 The Sentry, Forgotten Hero U	.30	.50
131 Vengeance, Spirit of Vengeance C	.15	.25
132 White Tiger, Angela Del Toro C	.15	.25
133 Wolverine, Covert Predator C	.15	.25
134 Brass Grill C	.15	.25
135 Desert Eagle C	.15	.25
136 M60s U	.30	.50
137 Scattergun R	1.25	2.00
138 Wheels of Vengeance R	1.25	2.00
139 Dark Alley C	.15	.25
140 Anguish of the Innocent R	1.00	1.50
141 Bring the Pain C	.15	.25
142 Chain of Vengeance U	.30	.50
143 Defensive Formation R	1.50	2.50
144 Encircle R	1.25	2.00
145 Neighborhood Watch, Team-Up C	.15	.25
146 Penance Stare U	.30	.50
147 Quick Kill C	.15	.25
148 Reload R	1.25	2.00
149 Sniper Shot R	2.00	3.00
150 Wild Ride R	3.00	5.00
151 Ant-Man, King of the Hill C	.15	.25
152 Crystal, Inhuman Elemental C	.15	.25
153 Dr. Strange, Ally of The Four R	2.00	3.00
154 Frankie Raye, Johnny's Flame C	.15	.25
155 Franklin Richards, Child of the Cosmos C	.15	.25
156 Ghost Rider, Rider on the Storm C	.15	.25
157 H.E.R.B.I.E., Robot Nanny R	1.25	2.00
158 Hulk, The Fantastic Hulk C	.15	.25
159 Human Torch, Matchstick U	.30	.50
160 Human Torch, Nova Blast C	.15	.25
161 Human Torch, Flame On! R	1.25	2.00
162 Invisible Woman, Walking on Air C	.15	.25
163 Invisible Woman, First Lady of the Fantastic Four C	.15	.25
164 Invisible Woman, Sight Unseen U	.30	.50
165 Invisible Woman, Shield of The Four R	1.25	2.00
166 Luke Cage, Steel-Hard Skin R	2.00	3.00
167 Luke Cage, Paid in Full C	.15	.25
168 Lyja, Mrs. Johnny Storm R	1.00	1.50
169 Medusa, Red R	1.25	2.00
170 Mr. Fantastic, Stringbean C	.15	.25
171 Mr. Fantastic, Critical Thinker U	.30	.50
172 Mr. Fantastic, Dimensional Explorer C	.15	.25
173 Namorita, Atlantean Warrior Princess R	1.25	2.00
174 Nathaniel Richards, Temporal Traveler R	1.25	2.00
175 She-Hulk, Single Green Lawyer C	.15	.25
176 Silver Surfer, Norrin Radd R	1.25	2.00
177 Spider-Man, Power and Responsibility U	.30	.50
178 Sub-Mariner, Uncertain Ally U	.30	.50
179 Thing, Idol O'Millions C	.15	.25
180 Thing, Heavy Hitter R	.75	1.25
181 Thing, The Ever-Lovin' Blue-Eyed Thing U	.30	.50
182 Uatu the Watcher , He Who Watches U	.30	.50
183 Valeria Richards, Child of Light and Darkness U	.30	.50
184 Fantasticar 2.0 R	1.00	1.50
185 Future Technology R	1.00	1.50
186 Unstable Molecular Suit C	.15	.25
187 Four Freedoms Plaza R	1.25	2.00
188 Pier 4 R	.75	1.25
189 Clobberin' Pine! R	1.25	2.00
190 Eureka! R	1.00	1.50
191 Family of Four R	2.00	3.00
192 Firewall U	.30	.50
193 Force Field Projection R	2.50	4.00
194 Heat Wave R	1.25	2.00
195 Invisibility U	.30	.50
196 It's Clobberin' Time! R	1.25	2.00
197 Reed and Sue C	.15	.25
198 Signal Flare R	1.25	2.00
199 Stretch Out U	.30	.50
200 Torch and Thing C	.15	.25
201 Boris, Personal Servant of Dr. Doom R	1.50	2.50
202 Doom-Bot, Army U	.30	.50
203 Doom-Bot II, Army C	.15	.25
204 Dr. Doom, Diabolic Genius U	.30	.50
205 Dr. Doom, Gypsy King C	.15	.25
206 Dr. Doom, Fearsome Monarch U	.30	.50
207 Dr. Doom, Lord of Latveria R	.75	1.25
208 Dragon Man, Experimental Monster C	.15	.25
209 Dreadnought Tank, Arsenal of Doom R	1.25	2.00
210 Pacifier Robot, Army C	.15	.25
211 Puppet Master, Overprotective Father R	1.25	2.00
212 Swarm Bots, Army C	.15	.25
213 Ultron, Army C	.15	.25
214 Armor of Doom R	1.25	2.00
215 Faces of Doom U	.30	.50
216 Fervent Research R	2.00	3.00
217 Mystical Paralysis U	.30	.50
218 Robotic Offensive U	.30	.50
219 Sacrificial Pawn C	.15	.25
220 Supersize C	.15	.25
221 The Power Cosmic R	.60	1.00
222 Gladiator, Praetor of the Imperial Guard R	.75	1.25
223 Lilandra, Majestrix of the Shi'ar R	1.25	2.00
224 Shi'ar Soldier, Army C	.15	.25
225 Apocalypse, The Fittest R	1.25	2.00
226 Bullseye, #1 with a Bullet U	.30	.50
227 Deadpool, Interminable Terminator U	.30	.50
228 Holocaust, Nemesis R	1.25	2.00
229 Mr. Sinister, Visionary Geneticist U	.30	.50
230 Omega Red, Cold War Commando R	1.25	2.00
231 Onslaught, Psionic Spawn of Xavier and Magneto R	1.25	2.00
232 Random Punks, Army C	.15	.25
233 Stryfe, X-Cutioner C	.15	.25
234 Frag Grenade C	.15	.25
235 Katana C	.15	.25
236 Mandroid Prototype R	.75	1.25
237 Med Kit U	.30	.50
238 Steel Girder R	1.25	2.00
239 Three-Ton Boulder R	.60	1.00
240 Construction Site C	.15	.25
241 Evil Lair U	.30	.50

Card	Low	High
242 Research Facility C	.15	.25
243 Unstable Ground R	.75	1.25
244 Assorted Aliases R	2.00	3.00
245 Burn Rubber C	.15	.25
246 Combat Veteran U	.30	.50
247 Crushing Blow C	.15	.25
248 Dealing with the Devil, Team-Up U	.30	.50
249 Devastating Blow C	.15	.25
250 Finishing Move C	.15	.25
251 For Great Justice! C	.15	.25
252 Fortify C	.15	.25
253 Forward Assault C	.15	.25
254 Gamma Bomb R	.60	1.00
255 Heroes of the City, Team-Up C	.15	.25
256 Marvel Crossover, Team-Up C	.15	.25
257 Mental Blast C	.15	.25
258 Mobilize R	10.00	15.00
259 Monkey Business R	2.00	3.00
260 New and Improved R	3.00	5.00
261 New Mutations U	1.25	2.00
262 Only Human R	4.00	6.00
263 Overwhelming Force U	1.25	2.00
264 RAT-TAT-TAT R	.75	1.25
265 Reset R	2.50	4.00
266 Rigged Explosives R	2.00	3.00
267 Savage Beatdown R	8.00	12.00
268 Secret Identity R	1.50	2.50
269 Shrink U	.30	.50
270 Strange Bedfellows, Team-Up U	.30	.50
271 Swift Escape U	.30	.50
272 The 198, Team-Up C	.15	.25
273 The Greater Threat, Team-Up C	.15	.25

2007 Vs System Marvel Team-Up

Card	Low	High
COMPLETE SET (220)	30.00	60.00
BOOSTER BOX (24 PACKS)	20.00	40.00
BOOSTER PACK (14 CARDS)	1.00	2.00
*FOIL: .75X TO 2X BASIC CARDS		
RELEASED IN FEBRUARY 2007		
1 Aunt May, Golden Oldie U	.30	.50
2 Black Cat, Nine Lives C	.15	.25
3 Blade, Nightstalker U	.30	.50
4 Captain America, Heroic Paragon C	.15	.25
5 Daredevil, New Kingpin C	.15	.25
6 Darkhawk, Chris Powell C	.15	.25
7 Elektra, Leader of the Hand C	.15	.25
8 Frank Drake, Nightstalker C	.15	.25
9 Ka-Zar, Lord Kevin Plunder C	.15	.25
10 Luke Cage, Neighborhood Watch C	.15	.25
11 Man-Thing, Theodore Sallis U	.30	.50
12 Mattie Franklin, Reserve Webhead C	.15	.25
13 Michael Collins Deathlok, Schizophrenic Cyborg C	.15	.25
14 Night Thrasher, Dwayne Michael Taylor C	.15	.25
15 Phil Urich Green Goblin, Lunatic Laugh U	.30	.50
16 Punisher, Frank Castle U	.30	.50
17 The Sentry, Golden Guardian of Good R	.60	1.00
18 Shanna the She-Devil, Shanna O'Hara Plunder C	.15	.25
19 Sleepwalker, Rick Sheridan R	.60	1.00
20 Speedball, Robert Baldwin C	.15	.25
21 Spider-Man, Stark's Protege R	2.00	3.00
22 Spider-Man, The Sensational Spider-Man R	1.25	2.00
23 Spider-Man, Parasitic Host C	.15	.25
24 Spider-Man, Spider-Hulk C	.15	.25
25 Spider-Man, The Amazing Bag-Man C	.15	.25
26 Venom, Lethal Protector C	.15	.25
27 Wolverine, Canucklehead C	.15	.25
28 Zabu, Constant Companion C	.15	.25
29 Catch You Later! U	.30	.50
30 Down, but Not Out U	.30	.50
31 Drink This! R	.60	1.00
32 Empire State University R	2.00	3.00
33 Feminine Wiles U	.30	.50
34 Gift Wrapped R	2.50	4.00
35 Indebted R	2.50	4.00
36 Need a Lift? U	.30	.50
37 Ring of Fire U	.30	.50
38 Spider-Sense Tingling! C	.15	.25
39 Spider-Signal U	.30	.50
40 Spider-Mobile, Unique C	.15	.25
41 Stark Tower, Team-Up C	.15	.25
42 Target Practice C	.15	.25
43 Trial by Jury R	.75	1.25
44 Archangel, New Defender C	.15	.25
45 Beast, New Defender U	.30	.50
46 Brunnhilde Valkyrie, Barbara Norriss C	.15	.25
47 Devil-Slayer, Eric Simon Payne R	.60	1.00
48 Dr. Strange, Founding Father R	1.25	2.00
49 Dr. Strange, Sorcerer Supreme R	1.00	1.50
50 Gargoyle, Isaac Christians C	.15	.25
51 Hawkeye, Loud Mouth R	1.00	1.50
52 Hellcat, Patsy Walker C	.15	.25
53 Howard the Duck, Master of Quack-Fu C	.15	.25
54 Hulk, Grumpy Green Goliath C	.15	.25
55 Hulk, Strongest One There Is R	.75	1.25
56 Iceman, New Defender U	.30	.50
57 Jack of Hearts, Jack Hart C	.15	.25
58 John Walker U.S. Agent, Loose Cannon C	.15	.25
59 Johnny Blaze Ghost Rider, Damned C	.15	.25
60 Kyle Richmond Nighthawk, Heart of the Team C	.15	.25
61 Professor X, Illuminati C	.15	.25
62 Richard Rider Nova, Xandarian Nova Corps C	.15	.25
63 Samantha Parrington Valkyrie, Chooser of the Slain R	2.50	4.00
64 Silver Surfer, Prodigal Herald U	.30	.50
65 Silver Surfer, Earthbound C	.15	.25
66 Sub-Mariner, Neptune's Fist C	.15	.25
67 Sub-Mariner, King of Atlantis C	.15	.25
68 Tania Belinskya Red Guardian, Cold Warrior C	.15	.25
69 Wendell Vaughn Quasar, Protector of the Universe C	.15	.25
70 Wong, Mystical Manservant R	2.50	4.00
71 Astral Projection U	.30	.50
72 Banished to the Abyss U	.30	.50
73 The Arrival R	3.00	5.00
74 The Book of the Vishanti U	.30	.50
75 Consulting the Orb U	.30	.50
76 Crimson Bands of Cyttorak R	.75	1.25
77 Defenders Defend! U	.30	.50
78 Eye of Agamotto, Unique R	.60	1.00
79 Imperius Rex! C	.15	.25
80 One-Man Rampage R	.75	1.25
81 The Order R	1.25	2.00
82 Sanctum Sanctorum U	.30	.50
83 Secret Defenders, Team-Up C	.15	.25
84 Soul Survival U	.30	.50
85 Star-Crossed C	.15	.25
86 Teleportation Ring, Unique C	.15	.25
87 Zzzax Attax! C	.15	.25
88 Albert Malik Red Skull, Axis of Evil C	.15	.25
89 Answer, Aaron Nicholson R	1.25	2.00
90 Black Tarantula, Carlos LaMuerto U	.30	.50
91 Bullseye, Assassin for Hire C	.15	.25
92 Carnage, Psychopath R	1.25	2.00
93 Chameleon, Man of Many Faces C	.15	.25
94 Dr. Octopus, Master of Evil R	1.00	1.50
95 Electro, Shock Jock U	.30	.50
96 Francis Klum Mysterio, Mutant Magician C	.15	.25
97 Fusion, Markley C	.15	.25
98 Gog, Alien Menace R	.60	1.00
99 Harry Osborn Green Goblin, Unfortunate Son C	.15	.25
100 Jason Macendale Hobgoblin, Possessed Lunatic C	.15	.25
101 Lizard, Voracious Predator R	1.00	1.50
102 Maguire Beck Mad Jack, Jack o' Lantern C	.15	.25
103 Nitro, Robert Hunter R	.60	1.00
104 Razorfist, Sociopathic Mercenary C	.15	.25
105 Rhino, Unstoppable Force C	.15	.25
106 Slyde, Jalome Beacher C	.15	.25
107 Spider-Man Robot, Timespinner C	.15	.25
108 Spider-Slayer V.X., Arachnid Hunter C	.15	.25
109 Spot, Dr. Jonathan Ohnn C	.15	.25
110 Swarm, Fritz von Meyer U	.30	.50
111 Trapster, Peter Petruski C	.15	.25
112 Venom, Mac Gargan C	.15	.25
113 Venom, The Hunger C	.15	.25
114 Vulture, Aerial Stalker C	.15	.25
115 Alien Symbiote, Unique C	.15	.25
116 Breakout U	.30	.50
117 The Contract, Team-Up C	.15	.25
118 Demonic Association U	.30	.50
119 The Enforcers R	.60	1.00
120 Gotcha! C	.15	.25
121 The Great Game U	.30	.50
122 Hidden Cache R	.60	1.00
123 Legacy of Evil U	.30	.50
124 Legion of Losers C	.15	.25
125 Planet of the Symbiotes U	.30	.50
126 Ravencroft Institute R	.60	1.00
127 Sand Trap U	.30	.50
128 Spider Hunt R	1.00	1.50
129 Suffocation C	.15	.25
130 The Vault U	.30	.50
131 Baron Mordo, Karl Amadeus Mordo C	.15	.25
132 Black Rose, Roxanne Simpson U	.30	.50
133 Blackheart, Black King R	1.00	1.50
134 Chthon, Demon of the Darkhold U	.30	.50
135 Doppelganger, Killer Clone C	.15	.25
136 Dormammu, Dread Dormammu C	.15	.25
137 The Dwarf, Soul Broker U	.30	.50
138 Dweller-in-Darkness, Fear Lord C	.15	.25
139 Ebenezer Laughton Scarecrow, Undead Lunatic C	.15	.25
140 Illyana Rasputin Magik, Queen of Limbo C	.15	.25
141 Madelyne Pryor, Goblyn Queen U	.30	.50
142 Meatmarket, Lilin C	.15	.25
143 Mephisto, pheles C	.15	.25
144 The Mindless Ones, Army C	.15	.25
145 Modred the Mystic, Servant of Chthon C	.15	.25
146 Morlun, Totem Hunter C	.15	.25
147 N'astirh, Liege of Limbo C	.15	.25
148 The N'Garai, Army C	.15	.25
149 Noble Kale, Lord of Hell R	.60	1.00
150 Pilgrim, Lilin C	.15	.25
151 Queen Lilith, Den Mother C	.15	.25
152 Satana, Hellstrom C	.15	.25
153 Shathra, Sharon Keller C	.15	.25
154 Shuma-Gorath, He Who Sleeps but Shall Awake R	.60	1.00
155 Thanos, Courting Death R	.60	1.00
156 Umar, Sorceress Sublime R	.60	1.00
157 Zarathos, Demon of Fire C	.15	.25
158 Book of Cagliostro U	.30	.50
159 Dark Bargain R	.60	1.00
160 Dark Designs C	.15	.25
161 The Dark Dimension, Non-Unique C	.15	.25
162 Death's Embrace R	2.50	4.00
163 Demonic Embryo C	.15	.25
164 Dimensional Rift R	1.00	1.50
165 In Limbo U	.30	.50
166 Mausoleum, Non-Unique C	.15	.25
167 Midnight Massacre R	.75	1.25
168 Netherworld Gift U	.30	.50
169 Ritual Sacrifice, Team-Up C	.15	.25
170 Siege of Darkness C	.15	.25
171 Strange Love U	.30	.50
172 Surtur's Anvil U	.30	.50
173 Transformation C	.15	.25
174 Undead Legions R	.75	1.25
175 Battlestar, Lemar Hoskins R	.60	1.00
176 Chen, Amy Chen C	.15	.25
177 Crippler, Carl Striklan C	.15	.25
178 Dominic Fortune, Soldier of Fortune U	.30	.50
179 Fin, Intruders C	.15	.25
180 Man-Eater, Intruders C	.15	.25
181 Paladin, Intruders R	.60	1.00
182 Powell, Southern Charm U	.30	.50
183 Quentino, Raul Quentino U	.30	.50
184 Sandman, Intruders U	.30	.50
185 Silver Sable, World's Deadliest Mercenary R	.60	1.00
186 Wild Pack Recruit, Army U	.30	.50
187 Bounty Hunt U	.30	.50
188 Capture Net U	.30	.50
189 Stealthcraft, Team-Up C	.15	.25
190 Alyosha Kravinoff, Son of Kraven C	.15	.25
191 Deadpool, Merc With a Mouth R	1.00	1.50
192 Demogoblin, Disembodied Demon C	.15	.25
193 Dr. Doom, Just Reward R	.60	1.00
194 Hellstorm, Son of Satan C	.15	.25
195 Moon Knight, Fist of Khonshu C	.15	.25
196 Morbius, Shadow of the Vampire R	.60	1.00
197 Against All Odds R	1.25	2.00
198 Big Leagues R	6.00	10.00
199 Burns at the Touch C	.15	.25
200 He Who Watches U	.30	.50
201 The Illuminati C	.15	.25
202 Justice Is Served! C	.15	.25
203 Marvel Crossover, Team-Up C	.15	.25
204 Poker Night C	.15	.25
205 Rabbit Fire C	.15	.25
206 We Had a Team-Up, Team-Up C	.15	.25
207 What Are Friends For? C	.15	.25
208 Cassandra Nova, Genocidal Tendencies U	.30	.50
209 Damocles Base R	1.50	2.50
210 Dark Beast, McCoy U	.30	.50
211 Ego Gem, Unique ? Infinity Gem U	.30	.50
212 Hulk, Joe Fixit U	.30	.50
213 Monster Island R	.60	1.00
214 New Baxter Building U	.30	.50
215 Quicksilver, Terrigenesis Rebirth U	.30	.50
216 Ronan the Accuser, Exiled U	.30	.50
217 Super Skrull, Kl'rt R	.60	1.00
218 The B Team R	.60	1.00
219 The Annihilation Wave R	.60	1.00
220 The Void, Robert Reynolds R	.60	1.00

2007 Vs System World's Finest

Card	Low	High
COMPLETE SET (220)	30.00	60.00
BOOSTER BOX (24 PACKS)	40.00	80.00
BOOSTER PACK (14 CARDS)	2.00	3.00
*FOIL: .75X TO 2X BASIC CARDS		
RELEASED IN JULY 2007		
1 Bibbo Bibbowski, Barroom Brawler U	.30	.50
2 Brahma, Supermen of America C	.15	.25
3 The Guardian, Jim Harper U	.30	.50
4 Hiro Okamura Toyman, Whiz-Kid C	.15	.25
5 John Henry Irons Steel, Armor Aura C	.15	.25
6 John Henry Irons Steel, Steel Works U	.30	.50
7 Kara Zor-El Flamebird Kandorian Vigilante C	.15	.25
8 Kara Zor-El Supergirl, Claire Connors R	1.50	2.50
9 Kelex, Caretaker of the Fortress C	.15	.25
10 Krypto, Guard Dog of El C	.15	.25
11 Lois Lane, Reporter Extraordinaire U	.30	.50
12 Loser, Supermen of America C	.15	.25
13 Maximum, Supermen of America C	.15	.25
14 Natasha Irons Steel, Unlikely Alloy C	.15	.25
15 The Newsboy Legion, Army C	.15	.25
16 Outburst, Supermen of America C	.15	.25
17 Power Girl Nightwing, Kandorian Vigilante C	.15	.25
18 Pyrogen, Supermen of America R	1.25	2.00
19 Superman, Man of Tomorrow C	.15	.25
20 Superman, Deterrent Force R	3.00	5.00
21 Superman, Last Son of Krypton R	3.00	5.00
22 Superman, Bulletproof R	2.00	3.00
23 Vartox, Hero of Tynola U	.30	.50
24 White Lotus, Supermen of America C	.15	.25
25 Wonder Woman, Deflection Diva R	1.25	2.00
26 City of Tomorrow, Team-Up C	.15	.25
27 Kandor, City in a Bottle U	.30	.50
28 Smallville U	.30	.50
29 Desperate Sacrifice U	.30	.50
30 Double Team C	.15	.25
31 Early Edition R	1.00	1.50
32 For the Man Who Has Everything R	1.00	1.50
33 Future Friends C	.15	.25
34 Good Boy! C	.15	.25
35 Home Sweet Home U	.30	.50
36 Impervious U	.30	.50
37 Iron Will C	.15	.25
38 Soaring to New Heights C	.15	.25
39 Alfred Pennyworth, Faithful Friend R	1.00	1.50
40 Batman, Problem Solver U	.30	.50
41 Batman, Twilight Vigilante C	.15	.25
42 Bat-Mite, #1 Fan R	1.25	2.00
43 Batmobile, Burn Rubber U	.30	.50
44 Commissioner Gordon, Gotham Central U	.30	.50
45 Crispus Allen, Gotham Central C	.15	.25
46 Gotham Central S.W.A.T., Army C	.15	.25
47 Harvey Bullock, Gotham Central C	.15	.25
48 Kate Kane Batwoman, Katherine the Younger R	1.50	2.50
49 Maggie Sawyer, Gotham Central C	.15	.25
50 The Question, Victor Sage U	.30	.50
51 Renee Montoya, Gotham Central U	.30	.50
52 Tim Drake Robin, Flying Solo C	.15	.25
53 Two-Face, Jekyll and Hyde C	.15	.25
54 Batman and the Outsiders R	2.00	3.00
55 Bat-Signal U	.30	.50
56 Batman, Cape and Cowl R	1.25	2.00
57 Gotham Central U	.30	.50
58 Bat Got Your Tongue? R	1.00	1.50
59 Batcave, Crime-Fighting Lab U	.30	.50
60 Good Cop, Good Cop C	.15	.25
61 The Hook-Up, Team-Up C	.15	.25
62 Interrogate R	1.00	1.50
63 Nine Lives U	.30	.50
64 Taking Aim R	1.00	1.50
65 Barbara Gordon Oracle, Hacker Elite C	.15	.25
66 Barbara Gordon Oracle, Inside Information U	.30	.50
67 Cassandra Cain, Death's Daughter C	.15	.25
68 Catwoman, Feline Fatale C	.15	.25
69 Dinah Laurel Lance Black Canary, Cry in the Dark C	.15	.25
70 Gypsy, Illusionary Operative U	.30	.50
71 Huntress, Vicious Vigilante C	.15	.25
72 Lady Blackhawk, Zinda Blake R	1.00	1.50
73 Lady Shiva, Jade Canary C	.15	.25

74 Savant, Brian Durlin C .15 .25
75 Ted Grant Wildcat, Nine Lives C .15 .25
76 Vixen, Mari Jiwe McCabe C .15 .25
77 Aerie One U .30 .50
78 Birds of a Feather C .15 .25
79 Cry for Blood C .15 .25
80 Black Lightning, Jefferson Pierce C .15 .25
81 Dick Grayson Nightwing, Renegade C .15 .25
82 Dick Grayson Nightwing, Rough Justice U .30 .50
83 Faust, Sebastian Faust U .30 .50
84 Freddy Freeman Captain Marvel Jr. , CM3 C .15 .25
85 Geo-Force, Brion Markov C .15 .25
86 Grace, Grace Choi C .15 .25
87 Grace, The Bouncer U .30 .50
88 Halo, Gabrielle Doe C .15 .25
89 Huntress, Harsh Mistress C .15 .25
90 Indigo, Paranoid Android C .15 .25
91 Jade, Emerald Beacon C .15 .25
92 Katana, Tatsu Yamashiro U .30 .50
93 Katana, Soultaker R 1.00 1.50
94 Kimiyo Hoshi Dr. Light, Sunburst R 1.25 2.00
95 Koriand'r Starfire, Royal Temper C .15 .25
96 Looker, Emily Briggs C .15 .25
97 Metamorpho, The Element Man C .15 .25
98 Owen Mercer Captain Boomerang Jr., Prodigal Son C .15 .25
99 Roy Harper Arsenal, Ladies' Man C .15 .25
100 Shift, Knockoff R 1.00 1.50
101 Technocrat, Geoffrey Barron C .15 .25
102 Terra, Little Sis R 1.50 2.50
103 Thunder, Anissa Pierce C .15 .25
104 Thunder, Heavy Duty C .15 .25
105 Wylde, Charlie Wylde C .15 .25
106 Pequod, Unique U .30 .50
107 Brooklyn HQ R 1.00 1.50
108 Markovia U .30 .50
109 Optitron Corporation U .30 .50
110 Batman, Dark Knight Returned U .30 .50
111 Betrayal of Trust U .30 .50
112 Booze Elementals C .15 .25
113 Fighting the Liar C .15 .25
114 Get It Done U .30 .50
115 Hell Breaks Loose C .15 .25
116 Incognito C .15 .25
117 The Insiders, Team-Up C .15 .25
118 Recruiting Drive R 1.25 2.00
119 Scorched Earth C .15 .25
120 Soul Slicer U .30 .50
121 Taking Out the Trash U .30 .50
122 Anarky, Lonnie Machin U .30 .50
123 Basil Karlo Ultimate Clayface, Mud Pack R 1.00 1.50
124 Batarang, Cutting Edge R 1.50 2.50
125 Batzarro, World's Worst Detective U .30 .50
126 Calendar Man, Julian Gregory Day U .30 .50
127 Catwoman, Jewel Thief C .15 .25
128 Charaxes, Drury Walker C .15 .25
129 Crime Doctor, Bradford Thorne C .15 .25
130 Firefly, Burning Desire C .15 .25
131 Great White, Warren White C .15 .25
132 Harley Quinn, Mr. J's Girl C .15 .25
133 The Joker, Crazy for You R 1.25 2.00
134 The Joker, Out of His Mind R 2.00 3.00
135 The Joker Red Hood, The Man Who Laughs U .30 .50
136 KGBeast, Anatoli Knyazev C .15 .25
137 Killer Croc, Cannibal C .15 .25
138 Mad Hatter, Mad as a Hatter U .30 .50
139 Matt Hagen Clayface, Mud Pack C .15 .25
140 Mr. Freeze, Cold Shoulder C .15 .25
141 Mr. Zsasz, Scar Tissue C .15 .25
142 The Penguin, Crime's Early Bird C .15 .25
143 Poison Ivy, Venomous Vixen C .15 .25
144 The Riddler, Multiple Choice U .30 .50
145 Scarecrow, Fear and Loathing R 1.00 1.50
146 Sondra Fuller Clayface, Mud Pack C .15 .25
147 Tally Man, Tax Time R 1.00 1.50
148 Two-Face, Heads or Tails C .15 .25
149 Arkham Asylum, Team-Up R 1.00 1.50
150 Blackgate Prison, Maximum Security U .30 .50
151 All Locked Up C .15 .25
152 Beside Myself R 1.00 1.50
153 Burn Baby Burn C .15 .25
154 Hush Baby C .15 .25
155 It's a Hard Life R 1.00 1.50
156 Money Talks R 1.00 1.50
157 Pick a Card R 1.25 2.00
158 Usual Suspects U .30 .50
159 Alexandra Allston Parasite, Power Drain C .15 .25
160 Atomic Skull, Cursed R 1.00 1.50
161 Bizarro, Bizarro World's Finest R 1.25 2.00
162 Brainiac 12, Upgrade Complete C .15 .25
163 Brainiac 13, B-13 C .15 .25
164 Darkseid, The Omega U .30 .50
165 Doomsday, Evolution Advanced C .15 .25
166 Hank Henshaw Cyborg, Manhunter Grandmaster U .30 .50
167 Indigo, Brainiac 8 R 1.25 2.00
168 Kryptonite Man, K. Russell Abernathy C .15 .25
169 Lex Luthor, Master Manipulator R 2.00 3.00
170 Lex Luthor, Sinister Scientist C .15 .25
171 Livewire, Leslie Willis C .15 .25
172 Manchester Black, Union Jack C .15 .25
173 Maxima, Warrior Queen C .15 .25
174 Metallo, Kryptonite Heart C .15 .25
175 Mongul, Son of the Tyrant C .15 .25
176 Mr. Mxyzptlk, Felonious Fiend R 1.00 1.50
177 Natasha Irons Starlight, Everyman Project U .30 .50
178 Preus, Citizen's Patrol C .15 .25
179 Professor Emil Hamilton Ruin, Power Suit R 1.00 1.50
180 Satanus, Colin Thornton U .30 .50
181 Solaris, Tyrant Sun R 1.50 2.50
182 Terra-Man, Toby Manning C .15 .25
183 Ultraman, Despot of Kandor C .15 .25
184 Winslow Schott Toyman, Child's Play C .15 .25
185 Graveyard of Solitude U .30 .50
186 Battle for Metropolis U .30 .50
187 Bizarro Brawl R 1.00 1.50
188 Dimensional Deal, Team-Up C .15 .25
189 Executive Privilege R 1.25 2.00
190 Fatal Weakness R 1.50 2.50
191 Future Shock C .15 .25
192 Hidden Agenda R 1.00 1.50
193 Hostile Takeover C .15 .25
194 Imprisoned in the Source R 1.00 1.50
195 Knowledge Is Power U .30 .50
196 Never-Ending Battle C .15 .25
197 Obey or Die! R 1.25 2.00
198 World's Worstest, Team-Up C .15 .25
199 At Their Finest R 1.00 1.50
200 Best of the Best R 2.00 3.00
201 Brains and Brawn R 1.50 2.50
202 Phantom Zone U .30 .50
203 Power Armor C .15 .25
204 Stryker's Island R 1.00 1.50
205 Batter Up! C .15 .25
206 Batzarro Beatdown R 1.00 1.50
207 Certifiable R 1.00 1.50
208 Chilly Reception R 1.00 1.50
209 Crackshot C .15 .25
210 Engine of Change U .30 .50
211 Gorilla Warfare C .15 .25
212 Jack-in-the-Box R 1.25 2.00
213 SKREEEEEEE! C .15 .25
214 Spirit of Nabu, Magic U .30 .50
215 Standoff U .30 .50
216 Tied Down C .15 .25
217 Training Day, Team-Up C .15 .25
218 Truth and Justice, Team-Up C .15 .25
219 Matter-Eater Lad, Tenzil Kem U .30 .50
220 Deathstroke the Terminator, Wolf in Bat's Clothing U .30 .50

2008 Vs System Marvel Universe

COMPLETE SET (330) 50.00 100.00
BOOSTER BOX (24 PACKS) 30.00 60.00
BOOSTER PACK (14 CARDS) 2.00 3.00
*FOIL: .75X TO 2X BASIC CARDS
RELEASED IN JUNE 2008
1 Bill Foster Goliath, Secret Avenger R 1.25 2.00
2 Black Panther, Secret Avenger C .15 .25
3 Cable, Secret Avenger R 1.25 2.00
4 Captain America, The Patriot Secret Avenger C .15 .25
5 Captain America, Champion License R 3.00 5.00
6 Captain America, Living Legend R 2.50 4.00
7 Captain America, Sentinel of Liberty R 2.50 4.00
8 Cloak, Secret Avenger U .30 .50
9 Dagger, Secret Avenger C .15 .25
10 Dr. Strange, Secret Avenger R 2.50 4.00
11 Echo Ronin, Secret Avenger C .15 .25
12 Falcon, Secret Avenger C .15 .25
13 Hawkeye Ronin, Secret Avenger U .30 .50
14 Hercules, Secret Avenger C .15 .25
15 Hulkling, Teddy Altman Young Avenger C .15 .25
16 Human Torch, Secret Avenger C .15 .25
17 Invisible Woman, Secret Avenger C .15 .25
18 Iron Fist Daredevil, Imposter Secret Avenger U .30 .50
19 Iron Fist, Secret Avenger C .15 .25
20 Jessica Drew Spider-Woman Secret Avenger U .30 .50
21 Kate Bishop Hawkeye, Young Avenger R 1.25 2.00
22 Luke Cage, Secret Avenger U .30 .50
23 Patriot, Elijah Bradley - Young Avenger C .15 .25
24 Punisher, Secret Avenger R 1.50 2.50
25 Speed, Thomas Shepard Young Avenger U .30 .50
26 Spider-Man, Secret Avenger R 2.50 4.00
27 Stature, Cassandra Lang Young Avenger U .30 .50
28 Storm, Secret Avenger C .15 .25
29 Vision, Young Avenger R 1.25 2.00
30 Wiccan, William Kaplan Young Avenger U .30 .50
31 Wolverine, Secret Avenger R 2.50 4.00
32 Captain America's Shield, Null R 2.50 4.00
33 Electron Scrambler, Null R 1.25 2.00
34 Safe House No. 23, Team-Up U .30 .50
35 Above the Law, Null U .30 .50
36 Atlantis, Null R 1.25 2.00
37 Avengers Forever, Null U .30 .50
38 Avengers Reassembled, Null R 3.00 5.00
39 The Big Three, Null C .15 .25
40 Charging Star, Null R 2.50 4.00
41 Final Justice, Null U .30 .50
42 Hard to Kill, Null C .15 .25
43 Liberating Number 42, Null C .15 .25
44 Reckless Youth, Null R 1.25 2.00
45 Secret Avengers, Team-Up C .15 .25
46 Shield Slash, Null C .15 .25
47 Stars and Stripes, Null U .30 .50
48 Switching Sides, Null U .30 .50
49 Thou Art No Thor!, Null R 1.25 2.00
50 Young Avengers, Null C .15 .25
51 Beetle Mach, Discharged C .15 .25
52 Blizzard, Frosty Friend U .30 .50
53 Bullseye, Lester R 2.00 3.00
54 Bullseye, Closer to God R 2.00 3.00
55 Genis-Vell Photon, Cosmic Threat C .15 .25
56 Green Goblin, Insanity Unleashed C .15 .25
57 Green Goblin, Director of the Thunderbolts C .15 .25
58 Helmut Zemo Baron Zemo Master of the Moonstones R 1.25 2.00
59 Joystick, Fun and Games U .30 .50
60 Karla Sofen Moonstone Uncertain Loyalty C .15 .25
61 Karla Sofen Moonstone Field Commander U .30 .50
62 Lady Deathstrike, Opportunistic Killer C .15 .25
63 Melissa Gold Songbird, Caged Angel C .15 .25
64 Radioactive Man, Containment Suit R 1.50 2.50
65 Radioactive Man Sheep in Wolf's Clothing U .30 .50
66 Speed Demon, Whizzer U .30 .50
67 Speedball Penance, Pain Monger C .15 .25
68 Speedball Penance Repentant Masochist R 1.25 2.00
69 Swordsman, Andreas Von Strucker C .15 .25
70 Taskmaster, Super Hero Trainer C .15 .25
71 Venom, Faithless Monster U .30 .50
72 Venom, Brain-Eater C .15 .25
73 The T-Wagon, Null U .30 .50
74 The Zeus, Unique R 1.25 2.00
75 Thunderbolts Mountain, Null R 1.25 2.00
76 Collect Them All!, Null R 1.50 2.50
77 Dangerous Liason, Null R 1.25 2.00
78 Faith In Monsters, Null U .30 .50
79 Ruthless Agression, Null C .15 .25
80 Sanctioned Killers, Team-Up C .15 .25
81 Speedball Is Dead, Null U .30 .50
82 Unregistered Combatants, Null R 1.25 2.00
83 The Wrong Stuff, Team-Up C .15 .25
84 Ares, Mighty Avenger R 1.50 2.50
85 Bishop, Agent of S.H.I.E.L.D. U .30 .50
86 Blade, Independant Contractor U .30 .50
87 Cape-Killers Unit, Army Agent of S.H.I.E.L.D. U .30 .50
88 Carol Danvers Ms. Marvel, Mighty Avenger C .15 .25
89 Daisy Johnson, Agent of S.H.I.E.L.D. C .15 .25
90 Deadpool, Independant Contractor C .15 .25
91 Doc Samson, Agent of S.H.I.E.L.D. C .15 .25
92 Dum-Dum Dugan, Howling Commando C .15 .25
93 Eric O'Grady Ant Man, Fugitive at Large C .15 .25
94 Hank Pym Yellowjacket, Initiative Instructor U .30 .50
95 Iron Man, Mighty Avenger R 3.00 5.00
96 Iron Man, Director of S.H.I.E.L.D. U .30 .50
97 Jessica Drew Spider-Woman, Agent of S.H.I.E.L.D. - HYDRA C .15 .25
98 Justice, Vance Astrovik C .15 .25
99 Life Model Decoy, More Human Than Human R 1.50 2.50
100 Maria Hill, Deputy Commander of S.H.I.E.L.D. C .15 .25
101 Mar-Vell Captain Marvel, Warden of Prison Alpha C .15 .25
102 Mr. Fantastic, Haunted Genius C .15 .25
103 Natasha Romanoff Black Widow, Mighty Avenger U .30 .50
104 Nick Fury, Director of S.H.I.E.L.D. R 1.50 2.50
105 S.H.I.E.L.D. Agents, Army Agent of S.H.I.E.L.D. C .15 .25
106 Sentinel Squad O*N*E*, Army U .30 .50
107 The Sentry, Mighty Avenger R 1.25 2.00
108 Sharon Carter, Agent 13 Agent of S.H.I.E.L.D. C .15 .25
109 She-Hulk, Agent of S.H.I.E.L.D. C .15 .25
110 Spider-Man, Unmasked R 1.50 2.50
111 Squirrel Girl, Doreen Green U .30 .50
112 Thing, Conscientious Objector R 1.25 2.00
113 Thor, Cyborg Clone R 1.25 2.00
114 Tigra, Greer Grant Nelson C .15 .25
115 War Machine Director of the Initiative C .15 .25
116 Wasp, Mighty Avenger U .30 .50
117 Wolverine, Agent of S.H.I.E.L.D. HYDRA U .30 .50
118 Wonder Man, Mighty Avenger R 1.25 2.00
119 Yelena Belova Black Widow, Agent of S.H.I.E.L.D. - HYDRA R 1.25 2.00
120 Extremis Upgrade, Null U .30 .50
121 Hulkbuster Armor, Null R 1.50 2.50
122 Power Dampeners, Null U .30 .50
123 S.H.I.E.L.D. Flying Car, Null U .30 .50
124 Godseye Satellite, Null U .30 .50
125 Negative Zone, Non-Unique Prison Alpha R 1.25 2.00
126 S.H.I.E.L.D. Helicarrier, Null R 1.50 2.50
127 Stark Armory, Null R 1.25 2.00
128 Company of Heroes, Null U .30 .50
129 I'm a Futurist, Null R 1.25 2.00
130 The Intiative, Team-Up C .15 .25
131 License to Kill, Null R 1.25 2.00
132 Out for Justice, Null C .15 .25
133 S.T.A.R. Squad, Null U .30 .50
134 Scarlet Spiders, Null U .30 .50
135 Secret War, Team-Up C .15 .25
136 Security Clearance, Null R 1.25 2.00
137 You're Under Arrest!, Null R 1.25 2.00
138 A.I.M. Agents, Army - A.I.M. C .15 .25
139 Arnim Zola, The Bio-Fanatic Raid U .30 .50
140 Baron Strucker, Baron Wolfgang Von Strucker - HYDRA C .15 .25
141 Crossbones, Brock Rumlow - Raid C .15 .25
142 Doctor Faustus, Johann Fennhoff - Raid U .30 .50
143 Elektra, Pawn of the Gorgon - HYDRA U .30 .50
144 The Gorgon, Tomi Shishido - HYDRA R 1.25 2.00
145 The Hand, Army - HYDRA U .30 .50
146 Head Case, Sean Madigan - A.I.M. R 1.25 2.00
147 The Hood, Prince of Pistols C .15 .25
148 HYDRA Recruit, Army - HYDRA C .15 .25
149 James Barnes Winter Soldier, Communist Puppet - Raid R 1.50 2.50
150 Kingpin, War Profiteer - HYDRA U .30 .50
151 M.O.D.O.K., Mobile Organism Designed Only for Killing - A.I.M. C .15 .25
152 Mandarin, Tem Borjigan R 1.25 2.00
153 Master Man, Max Lohmer - Raid U .30 .50
154 MODOC Squad, Army - A.I.M. C .15 .25
155 Red Skull, Aleksander Lukin - Raid C .15 .25
156 Red Skull, Johann Shmidt - HYDRA C .15 .25
157 Red Skull, Master of Creation C .15 .25
158 Scientist Supreme, Monica Rappaccini - A.I.M. U .30 .50
159 Silver Samurai, Kenuichio Harada - HYDRA R 1.25 2.00
160 Sin, Synthia Schmidt - Raid C .15 .25
161 The Sleeper, Doomsday Device - Raid R 1.25 2.00
162 Viper, Madame Hydra - HYDRA U .30 .50
163 Cosmic Cube, Null R 1.25 2.00
164 Death Warrant, Null R 1.50 2.50
165 Satan Claw, Null U .30 .50
166 Fortress Yashida, Null U .30 .50

167 HYDRA Armageddon Carrier, Null R	1.25	2.00
168 Underground Laboratory, Null R	1.25	2.00
169 Acts of Vengeance, Null U	.30	.50
170 Assault on Hellicarrier 13, Null U	.30	.50
171 Cold Storage, Null R	1.25	2.00
172 Cut Off One Head..., Null R	1.25	2.00
173 Double Agent!, Team-Up C	.15	.25
174 Enemies of the State, Null C	.15	.25
175 Hail Hydra!, Team-Up C	.15	.25
176 New King in Town, Null U	.30	.50
177 Ninjas! Ninjas! Ninjas!, Null R	1.25	2.00
178 Radically Advanced, Null U	.30	.50
179 Archangel, Champion U	.30	.50
180 Brood, Brood Creature 2 of 6 C	.15	.25
181 Caiera, The Oldstrong U	.30	.50
182 Elloe Kaifi, Slave of the Empire U	.30	.50
183 Hiroim, The Shamed C	.15	.25
184 Hulk, Exile C	.15	.25
185 Hulk, Green Scar R	2.50	4.00
186 Hulk, Gladiator C	.15	.25
187 Hulk, The Green King C	.15	.25
188 Hulk, Sakaar'Son C	.15	.25
189 Hulk, Worldbreaker R	1.50	2.50
190 Korg, Kronan Warrior U	.30	.50
191 Mastermind Excello, Amadeus Cho R	1.50	2.50
192 Miek, The Unhived C	.15	.25
193 Rick Jones, Monster's Best Friend C	.15	.25
194 The Great Arena, Null R	1.25	2.00
195 Imperial Dreadnaught, Null C	.15	.25
196 Sakaar, Null R	1.25	2.00
197 Bloodsport, Null U	.30	.50
198 The End of the World, Null R	1.25	2.00
199 Fight or Die!, Null U	.30	.50
200 Hulk Red, Null U	.30	.50
201 Hulk Smash, Null R	8.00	12.00
202 Righteous Anger, Null R	1.25	2.00
203 The Strongest One There Is, Null U	.30	.50
204 Warbound to the End, Null R	1.50	2.50
205 World War Hulk, Team-Up	.30	.50
206 Annihilus, Anti-Matter Master C	.15	.25
207 Annihilus, The Living Death That Walks R	1.25	2.00
208 Blastaar, The Living Bomb Burst R	1.25	2.00
209 The Centurians, Army C	.15	.25
210 Currs, Army U	.30	.50
211 Ravenous, Steward of Annihilus U	.30	.50
212 Seekers, Army C	.15	.25
213 Skreet, Chaos Mite C	.15	.25
214 Thanos, The Mad Titan R	1.50	2.50
215 Cosmic Control Rod, Unique U	.30	.50
216 Negative Zone, Non-Unique - Gateway R	1.25	2.00
217 Negative Zone, Non-Unique - Harvester of Sorrows C	.15	.25
218 Negative Zone, Non-Unique - Seat of Annihilation C	.15	.25
219 Gift for Death, Null R	1.25	2.00
220 Swarm of Annihilus, Null R	1.25	2.00
221 Wave of Destruction, Null R	1.25	2.00
222 Beta Ray Bill, Simon Walters - Omega Flight R	2.50	4.00
223 John Walker U.S. Agent, Omega Flight R	1.25	2.00
224 Julia Carpenter Arachne, Omega Flight C	.15	.25
225 Sasquatch, Walter Langrowski - Omega Flight C	.15	.25
226 Talisman, Elizabeth Twoyoungmen - Omega Flight C	.15	.25
227 Weapon Omega, Michael Pointer - Omega Flight R	1.25	2.00
228 Alpha Flight: Reborn, Null R	2.00	3.00
229 Omega Flight, Team-Up C	.15	.25
230 Black Bolt, Protector of the Space Gem U	.30	.50
231 Dr. Strange, Protector of the Soul Gem U	.30	.50
232 Iron Man, Protector of the Reality Gem U	.30	.50
233 Mr. Fantastic, Protector of the Power Gem C	.15	.25
234 Professor X, Protector of the Mind Gem U	.30	.50
235 Sub-Mariner, Protector of the Time Gem U	.30	.50
236 Atlantis Attacks!, Null C	.15	.25
237 Undisclosed Location, Non-Unique U	.30	.50
238 The 100 Ideas, Null U	.30	.50
239 Clandestine Operations, Null R	2.50	4.00
240 The Elektra Situation, Null R	1.50	2.50
241 Essence of Zom, Null R	1.25	2.00
242 The Infinity Gauntlet, Null R	1.50	2.50
243 Realm of the Mind, Null U	.30	.50
244 Secret Government, Null U	.30	.50
245 Silent War, Null R	1.25	2.00
246 Loki, Loki Laufeyson R	1.25	2.00
247 Thor, Donald Blake R	1.25	2.00
248 The Reckoning, Null U	.30	.50
249 Sub-Mariner, The Avenging Son U	.30	.50
250 Atlantean Warriors, Army U	.30	.50
251 Magneto, House of M C	.15	.25
252 Quicksilver, House of M R	1.50	2.50
253 Scarlet Witch, House of M R	1.25	2.00
254 Dr. Doom, Future Perfect U	.30	.50
255 Torture Chamber, Null U	.30	.50
256 I Am Doom, Null C	.15	.25
257 Silver Surfer, The Silver Savage U	.30	.50
258 Black Bolt, Enemy Within C	.15	.25
259 James Barnes Bucky, Kid Commando R	1.50	2.50
260 Kang, Non-Unique - Time Warrior U	.30	.50
261 Kang Iron Lad, Non-Unique - Young Avenger R	1.25	2.00
262 Punisher, Captain America R	1.50	2.50
263 Aaron Stack, Hater of Fleshy Ones U	.30	.50
264 The Captain, Can't Remember His Real Name U	.30	.50
265 Elsa Bloodstone, Foulmouthed Bombshell U	.30	.50
266 Monica Rambeau, I Was An Avenger U	.30	.50
267 Tabitha Smith, Zomg! U	.30	.50
268 Ultron, Ultron Prime R	1.25	2.00
269 Spider-Girl, Daughter of Spider-Man U	.30	.50
270 Cammi, Annoying Sidekick U	.30	.50
271 Drax the Destroyer, Titan Slayer U	.30	.50
272 Phyla-Vell Quasar, Protector of the Universe C	.15	.25
273 Richard Rider Nova Centurion, Keeper of the Worldmind U	.30	.50
274 Ronan the Accuser, Kree Emporer U	.30	.50
275 Star-Lord, Peter Quill R	1.25	2.00
276 Super Skrull, Noble Sacrifice U	.30	.50
277 Maverick, Christoph Nord R	1.25	2.00
278 Sabretooth, Government Assassin U	.30	.50
279 Wolverine, Weapon 10 U	.30	.50
280 Professor X, Mutant Benefactor U	.30	.50
281 Abomination, Emil Blonsky U	.30	.50
282 Adam Warlock, Savior of the Universe R	1.25	2.00
283 Aegis, Lady of All Sorrows R	1.25	2.00
284 The Beyonder, Inhuman R	1.25	2.00
285 Death, The Second Force of the Universe R	1.25	2.00
286 Fin Fang Foom, He Whose Limbs Shatter Mountains R	1.25	2.00
287 James Barnes Captain America, Legacy Reborn U	.30	.50
288 James Barnes Winter Soldier, Out in the Cold R	1.50	2.50
289 Layla Miller, She Knows Stuff U	.30	.50
290 Nick Fury, Off the Grid U	.30	.50
291 Skaar, Son of Hulk U	.30	.50
292 Tenebrous, Of the Darkness R	1.25	2.00
293 Quantum Bands, Unique C	.15	.25
294 Alias Investigations, Null U	.30	.50
295 Asgard, Null C	.15	.25
296 The Raft, Null U	.30	.50
297 Agents of H.A.T.E., Null C	.15	.25
298 Annihilating Conquest, Null U	.30	.50
299 Carrying the Torch, Null R	3.00	5.00
300 Casualty of War, Null C	.15	.25
301 Code White, Null U	.30	.50
302 Collateral Damage, Null C	.15	.25
303 Death of the Dream, Null U	.30	.50
304 Empire's End, Null U	.30	.50
305 Flattened, Null C	.15	.25
306 Frog of Thunder, Null R	1.25	2.00
307 Grudge Match, Null C	.15	.25
308 Heroes for Hire, Team-Up C	.15	.25
309 House of M, Null C	.15	.25
310 Hunt for Nitro, Null C	.15	.25
311 I Got 'Em All, Null R	1.25	2.00
312 Invasion Plans, Null C	.15	.25
313 Lay Down With Dogs, Null U	.30	.50
314 Losing the Argument, Null C	.15	.25
315 Messiah Complex, Null C	.15	.25
316 My Name is Peter Parker..., Null R	2.50	4.00
317 No Retreat, No Surrender, Null C	.15	.25
318 Now I'm Fighting Dirty, Null C	.15	.25
319 Outmatched, Null C	.15	.25
320 Public Outcry, Null C	.15	.25
321 Rogue Squadron, Null U	.30	.50
322 She-Hulk Smash!, Null U	.30	.50
323 Sleeper Cells, Null R	1.25	2.00
324 Slobberknocker, Null C	.15	.25
325 The Stamford Incident, Null U	.30	.50
326 Superhuman Registration Act, Team-Up R	3.00	5.00
327 Trouble With Dinosaurs, Null R	1.50	2.50
328 Uncertain Legacy, Null R	1.50	2.50
329 Underground Movement, Team-Up R	1.25	2.00
330 What If?, Team-Up C	.15	.25

World of Warcraft

2008 World of Warcraft Drums of War

COMPLETE SET (268)	100.00	180.00
BOOSTER BOX (24 PACKS)	80.00	100.00
BOOSTER PACK (19 CARDS)	3.00	4.00
RELEASED IN NOVEMBER 2008		
1 Grand Marshall Goldensword U	.30	.50
2 Lord Benjamin Tremendouson U	.30	.50
3 Martiana the Mindwrench U	.30	.50
4 Oakenclaw U	.30	.50
5 Pidge Filthfinder U	.30	.50
6 Shaii, Strategist Supreme U	.30	.50
7 Spellweaver Jihan U	.30	.50
8 Umbrage U	.30	.50
9 Zorin of the Thunderhead U	.30	.50
10 Boarguts the Impaler U	.30	.50
11 Justice Blindburn U	.30	.50
12 The Longeye U	.30	.50
13 Maleo the Blur U	.30	.50
14 Shalu Stormshatter U	.30	.50
15 Sinthya Flabberghast U	.30	.50
16 Spiritualist Sunshroud U	.30	.50
17 Turane Soulpact U	.30	.50
18 Velindra Sepulchre U	.30	.50
19 Aquatic Form R	.60	1.00
20 Celestial Communion U	.30	.50
21 Cower U	.30	.50
22 Feral Charge R	2.50	4.00
23 Hibernate C	.12	.20
24 Life of the Land R	.60	1.00
25 Master Instinct C	.12	.20
26 Moonflare U	.30	.50
27 Empty the Stables R	.60	1.00
28 Hissy R	.60	1.00
29 Hunter's Mark U	.30	.50
30 Resourcefulness R	.60	1.00
31 Snipe C	.12	.20
32 Sudden Shot U	.30	.50
33 Turn the Blade C	.12	.20
34 Zip U	.30	.50
35 Conjured Cinnamon Roll U	.30	.50
36 Ice Lance C	.12	.20
37 Mystic Denial R	4.00	6.00
38 Presence of Mind R	.60	1.00
39 Pyroclastic Consumption R	.60	1.00
40 Spell Suppression C	.12	.20
41 Temporary Dissipation U	.30	.50
42 Transfigure U	.30	.50
43 Aura of Accuracy R	.60	1.00
44 Blessing of Trials U	.30	.50
45 Crusader Strike R	.60	1.00
46 Inspiring Light C	.12	.20
47 Penance R	.60	1.00
48 Reprisal U	.30	.50
49 Seal of Justice U	.30	.50
50 Seal of Righteousness C	.12	.20
51 Dawn's Grace U	.30	.50
52 Equalize R	4.00	6.00
53 Exasperate U	.30	.50
54 Misery R	2.50	4.00
55 Precognition R	.60	1.00
56 Shadow Word: Anguish C	.12	.20
57 Sublimate U	.30	.50
58 Vampiric Tendrils C	.12	.20
59 Deathblow U	.30	.50
60 Detect Traps R	2.50	4.00
61 Gang Up C	.12	.20
62 Nerves of Steel R	1.25	2.00
63 Pernicious Poison U	.30	.50
64 Ransack R	.60	1.00
65 Slay the Feeble C	.12	.20
66 Surge of Adrenaline U	.30	.50
67 Energized C	.12	.20
68 Greater Chain Lightning R	.60	1.00
69 Grounding Totem U	.30	.50
70 Lightning Overload R	.60	1.00
71 Natural Conduit C	.12	.20
72 Primal Totem U	.30	.50
73 Water Breathing R	.60	1.00
74 Winterstorm Totem U	.30	.50
75 Curse of Fatigue U	.30	.50
76 Drain Will C	.12	.20
77 Enslaved Abyssal R	.60	1.00
78 Gakmat U	.30	.50
79 Rain of Shadow U	.30	.50
80 Suspended Curse C	.12	.20
81 Unending Breath R	.60	1.00
82 Unholy Power R	.60	1.00
83 Absolute Poise U	.30	.50
84 Battle Tactics R	.60	1.00
85 Behead C	.12	.20
86 Enduring Shout U	.30	.50
87 Menace C	.12	.20
88 Taunt U	.30	.50
89 War of Attrition R	.60	1.00
90 Weapon Mastery R	.60	1.00
91 Arcane Spikes C	.12	.20
92 Bloody Ritual C	.12	.20
93 Courageous Defense C	.12	.20
94 Creeping Shadow C	.12	.20
95 Demolish C	.12	.20
96 Eagle Sight C	.12	.20
97 Engulfing Blaze C	.12	.20
98 Fire and Ice C	.12	.20
99 Immobilize C	.12	.20
100 Lose Control C	.12	.20
101 Natural Disaster C	.12	.20
102 Nature Unleashed C	.12	.20
103 Revitalize C	.12	.20
104 Revival Stone C	.12	.20
105 Spell Ricochet C	.12	.20
106 Sphere of Divinity C	.12	.20
107 Thud C	.12	.20
108 Topple C	.12	.20
109 Owned R	.60	1.00
110 Pandamonium R	.60	1.00
111 Slashdance U	.30	.50
112 Al'lanora U	.30	.50
113 Angur Frostbeard C	.12	.20
114 Braeden Nightblade C	.12	.20
115 Brelnor Mindbender U	.30	.50
116 Catarina Clark C	.12	.20
117 Chief Researcher Kartos R	.60	1.00
118 Consul Rhys Lorgrand R	2.50	4.00
119 Cymbre Shadowdrifter C	.12	.20
120 Daniel Soortan C	.12	.20
121 Durgrin Ironedge C	.12	.20
122 Elementalist Psyrin C	.12	.20
123 Envoy Aiden LeNoir C	.12	.20
124 Envoy Samantha Dillon C	.12	.20
125 Errzig Cogflicker C	.12	.20
126 Falcore C	.12	.20
127 Gryth Thurden, Gryphon Master U	.30	.50
128 The Hammerhand Brothers C	.12	.20
129 Helena Demonfire R	.60	1.00
130 High Tinker Mekkatorque E	4.00	6.00
131 Keward Rocksalt C	.12	.20
132 Kinivus C	.12	.20
133 Lanthus of the Forest C	.12	.20
134 Lolly the Unsuspecting R	.60	1.00
135 Loraala C	.12	.20
136 Magnus Longbarrel C	.12	.20
137 Meganna Callaghan C	.12	.20
138 Mollie Brightheart C	.12	.20
139 Ninoo of the Light C	.12	.20
140 Rayne Savageboon C	.12	.20
141 Ryno the Short C	.12	.20
142 Swordsmith Hanso C	.12	.20
143 Tinker Art Seaclock C	.12	.20
144 Tinker Bixy Blue C	.12	.20
145 Tinker Burnfizzle C	.12	.20
146 Tinker Casey Springlock C	.12	.20
147 Tonks the Tenacious C	.12	.20
148 Treewarden Tolven C	.12	.20
149 Tully Fiddlewit U	.30	.50
150 Virkaltor C	.12	.20
151 Weldon Barov E	12.00	20.00
152 Woodsie Leafsong C	.12	.20
153 Wyler Surestrike C	.12	.20
154 Zempre, Grace of Elune R	2.50	4.00
155 Zophos C	.12	.20
156 Alamo R	.60	1.00
157 Alexi Barov E	5.00	8.00
158 Boum Headshot C	.12	.20
159 Cairne Bloodhoof E	5.00	8.00
160 Centurion Addisyn C	.12	.20
161 Chief Researcher Amereldine R	.60	1.00
162 Cromarius Blackfist C	.12	.20
163 Darbun Steppeheart C	.12	.20
164 Defender Kaniya C	.12	.20

Card	Low	High
165 Doomsayer Din'ju R	.60	1.00
166 Elizabeth Crowley C	.12	.20
167 Erindae Firestrider C	.12	.20
168 Gatlin Clouds-the-Sky C	.12	.20
169 Geoffrey Kimble C	.12	.20
170 Himul Longstrider C	.12	.20
171 Horkin Figluster C	.12	.20
172 Jack Coor C	.12	.20
173 Jee'zee C	.12	.20
174 Jil'ti U	.30	.50
175 Johnny Rotten U	.30	.50
176 Kileana Darkblaze C	.12	.20
177 Kirga Earthguard C	.12	.20
178 Kray'zin Firetusk R	.60	1.00
179 Lifemender Dorn C	.12	.20
180 Logor Blackfist C	.12	.20
181 Malicious Mallina U	.30	.50
182 Michael Garrett, Bat Handler U	.30	.50
183 Mistress Naila Flameburst C	.12	.20
184 Mortok C	.12	.20
185 Munkin Blackfist C	.12	.20
186 Nok'tal the Savage C	.12	.20
187 Orion C	.12	.20
188 Quakelord Razek Warhoof R	2.50	4.00
189 Rensarth Shadowsun C	.12	.20
190 Roktar Blackfist C	.12	.20
191 Rula Blackfist C	.12	.20
192 Sanva C	.12	.20
193 Sarn Earthtrembler C	.12	.20
194 Sepirion U	.30	.50
195 Skumm Bag'go C	.12	.20
196 Sorga the Swift C	.12	.20
197 Tormentor Emek C	.12	.20
198 Zari'zari C	.12	.20
199 Zi'mo C	.12	.20
200 Dagg'um Ty'gor U	.30	.50
201 The Red Bearon R	1.25	2.00
202 Vixton Pinchwhistle E	4.00	6.00
203 Amani Mask of Death R	.60	1.00
204 Blue Suede Shoes U	.30	.50
205 Boots of the Resilient U	.30	.50
206 Cloak of Subjugated Power R	.60	1.00
207 Forest Stalker's Bracers U	.30	.50
208 Girdle of the Blasted Reaches U	.30	.50
209 Gladiator's Regalia E	5.00	7.00
210 Masquerade Gown R	.60	1.00
211 Merciless Gladiator's Battlegear E	4.00	6.00
212 Mok'Nathal Wildercloak U	.30	.50
213 Nyn'jah's Tabi Boots R	.60	1.00
214 Scaled Breastplate of Carnage R	.60	1.00
215 Vengeful Gladiator's Vestments E	5.00	8.00
216 Arcanite Dragonling U	.30	.50
217 Rune of Metamorphosis U	.30	.50
218 Veteran's Pendant R	.60	1.00
219 Medallion of the Alliance U	.30	.50
220 Medallion of the Horde U	.30	.50
221 Black Amnesty R	2.50	4.00
222 Bloodseeker R	.60	1.00
223 Blue Diamond Witchwand U	.30	.50
224 Cold Forged Hammer R	.60	1.00
225 Continuum Blade R	.60	1.00
226 Frostguard U	.30	.50
227 Gladiator's Spellblade R	.60	1.00
228 Ice Barbed Spear R	.60	1.00
229 Light's Justice U	.30	.50
230 Lohn'goron, Bow of the Torn-heart U	.30	.50
231 Merciless Gladiator's Greatsword R	.60	1.00
232 Netherbane U	.30	.50
233 The Oathkeeper E	4.00	6.00
234 The Staff of Twin Worlds E	5.00	8.00
235 Vengeful Gladiator's Bonecracker R	.60	1.00
236 Wand of Biting Cold U	.30	.50
237 Electrified Dagger U	.30	.50
238 Glacial Blade U	.30	.50
239 Establishing New Outposts C	.12	.20
240 In Defense of Halaa C	.12	.20
241 Order Must Be Restored C	.12	.20
242 Bolstering Our Defenses C	.12	.20
243 Enemies, Old and New C	.12	.20
244 The Final Message to the Wildhammer C	.12	.20
245 Arena Master C	.12	.20
246 Corruption of Earth and Seed C	.12	.20
247 The Last Barov C	.12	.20
248 Oshu'gun Crystal Powder C	.12	.20
249 Outland Sucks C	.12	.20
250 A Rare Bean C	.12	.20
251 Revenge is Tasty C	.12	.20
252 Scouring the Desert C	.12	.20
253 Someone Else's Hard Work Pays Off R	.60	1.00
254 Soup for the Soul C	.12	.20
255 Spirits of Auchindoun C	.12	.20
256 Super Hot Stew C	.12	.20
257 Darnassus R	.60	1.00
258 Southshore U	.30	.50
259 Stormwind City R	4.00	6.00
260 Sen'jin Village R	.60	1.00
261 Tarren Mill U	.30	.50
262 Thunder Bluff R	.60	1.00
263 Auchindoun Spirit Towers U	.30	.50
264 Halaa U	.30	.50
265 Hellfire Citadel C	.12	.20
266 Silithus R	.60	1.00
267 Towers of Eastern Plaguelands C	.12	.20
268 Twin Spire Ruins C	.12	.20

2008 World of Warcraft Drums of War Loot

Card	Low	High
1 Slashdance	2.50	4.00
2 Owned	40.00	60.00
3 The Red Bearon	100.00	200.00

2008 World of Warcraft Hunt for Illidan

Card	Low	High
COMPLETE SET (252)	120.00	200.00
BOOSTER BOX (24 PACKS)	50.00	100.00
BOOSTER PACK (19 CARDS)	3.00	4.00
RELEASED IN JULY 2008		
1 Black Ice Fizzlefreeze U	.30	.50
2 Blaine Roberts U	.30	.50
3 Durga Gravestone U	.30	.50
4 Elumeria Wildershot U	.30	.50
5 Eriun Moonglow U	.30	.50
6 Kamboozle, Bringer of Doom U	.30	.50
7 Marta Spires U	.30	.50
8 Vakeron U	.30	.50
9 Zaritha U	.30	.50
10 Grindel Hellbringer U	.30	.50
11 Joren the Martyr U	.30	.50
12 Koth, Caller of the Hunt U	.30	.50
13 Phosphus the Everburning U	.30	.50
14 Ravenna U	.30	.50
15 Ringleader Kuma U	.30	.50
16 Tahanu Brinkrunner U	.12	.20
17 Valterus U	.30	.50
18 Warmaster Bo'jo U	.30	.50
19 Kurzon the False U	.30	.50
20 Famish the Binder U	.30	.50
21 Imp Lord Pinprik U	.30	.50
22 Mother Misery U	.30	.50
23 Obliveron U	.30	.50
24 Xia, Queen of Suffering U	.30	.50
25 Brace or Mace U	.30	.50
26 Energize C	.12	.20
27 Feral Energy R	.60	1.00
28 Ferociousness C	.12	.20
29 Furor R	.60	1.00
30 Insect Swarm R	3.00	5.00
31 Rebirth U	.30	.50
32 Rotten to the Spore R	.60	1.00
33 Stormfire C	.12	.20
34 Typhoon U	.30	.50
35 Bait the Trap U	.30	.50
36 The Beast Within R	.12	.20
37 Ice Trap C	.12	.20
38 Patient Shot C	.12	.20
39 Shadow C	.12	.20
40 Stable Master U	.30	.50
41 Trueshot Aura R	2.50	4.00
42 Viper Sting R	.60	1.00
43 Webster R	.60	1.00
44 Wipe or Snipe U	.30	.50
45 Arcane Research C	.12	.20
46 Astral Grief C	.12	.20
47 Blast Wave R	6.00	10.00
48 Brain Lock C	.12	.20
49 Flickers from the Past R	.60	1.00
50 Mage Armor U	.30	.50
51 The More, the Scarier R	.60	1.00
52 Smoke or Croak U	.30	.50
53 Supernova U	.30	.50
54 Water Elemental R	10.00	15.00
55 Blessing of Salvation U	3.00	5.00
56 Blessing of Sanctuary R	2.00	3.00
57 Crusader's Sweep C	.12	.20
58 Divine Plea R	.60	1.00
59 Exemplar's Shield U	.30	.50
60 Full Circle R	.60	1.00
61 Holy Shock R	6.00	10.00
62 Righteousness Aura C	.12	.20
63 Seal of Retribution C	.12	.20
64 Shield or Wield U	.30	.50
65 Circle of Healing R	.60	1.00
66 Divine Spirit R	3.00	5.00
67 Equal Opportunity C	.12	.20
68 Faces from the Past R	1.25	2.00
69 Lesser Heal C	.12	.20
70 Levitate C	.12	.20
71 Mana Burst U	.30	.50
72 Mindflip R	2.00	3.00
73 Shadow Word: Agony U	.30	.50
74 Woe or Grow U	.30	.50
75 Dirty Work R	1.25	2.00
76 Disassemble C	.12	.20
77 Feint C	.12	.20
78 Fight or Blight U	.30	.50
79 Knock Out U	.30	.50
80 Massacre U	.30	.50
81 Overkill R	.60	1.00
82 Sap C	.12	.20
83 Shadowstep R	.60	1.00
84 Vigor R	2.50	4.00
85 Crackling Purge U	3.00	5.00
86 Exemplar's Blades U	.30	.50
87 Far Sight C	.12	.20
88 Gifts from the Past R	.60	1.00
89 Lightning Arc C	.12	.20
90 Magma Totem C	.12	.20
91 Mend or End U	.30	.50
92 Raise from the Ashes R	.60	1.00
93 Spirit Weapons R	.60	1.00
94 Totemic Mastery R	.60	1.00
95 Aftermath R	.60	1.00
96 Clinging Curse C	.12	.20
97 Crush Soul C	.12	.20
98 Curse of Exhaustion R	.60	1.00
99 Demon Armor U	.30	.50
100 Enslave Demon U	.30	.50
101 Rain or Pain U	.30	.50
102 Sarlia R	.60	1.00
103 Velnoth C	.12	.20
104 Vicious Circle R	2.00	3.00
105 Disarm C	.12	.20
106 Duty Bound U	.30	.50
107 Finishing Shout U	.30	.50
108 Infuriate R	.60	1.00
109 Pummel R	3.00	5.00
110 Slay or Stay U	.30	.50
111 Sweeping Strikes R	.30	.50
112 Taste for Blood C	.12	.20
113 Taunting Blows C	.12	.20
114 Vitality R	.60	1.00
115 Disco Inferno R	1.25	2.00
116 The Footsteps of Illidan U	.12	.20
117 Acolyte Kemistra U	.30	.50
118 Alamira Grovetender C	.12	.20
119 Bimble Blackout U	.30	.50
120 Brodien U	.30	.50
121 Dashel Stonefist U	.30	.50
122 Defender Nagalaas C	.12	.20
123 Elaar R	.60	1.00
124 First Responder Avaressa C	.12	.20
125 First Responder Margan C	.12	.20
126 Harnum Firebelly C	.12	.20
127 High Inspector Campbell R	2.00	3.00
128 Kathia the Quick C	.12	.20
129 Kindara Mindflayer C	.12	.20
130 Kurdran Wildhammer E	2.00	3.00
131 Liandra Rustshadow C	.12	.20
132 Lord Cindervein C	.12	.20
133 Luumon C	.12	.20
134 Madison Alters U	.30	.50
135 Master Marksman McGee R	.60	1.00
136 Ol' Stonewall C	.12	.20
137 Raena the Unpredictable C	.12	.20
138 Ripley Spellfizzle C	.12	.20
139 Scrapper Ironbane C	.12	.20
140 Spirit of Stormrage E	4.00	6.00
141 Talian Bladebender C	.30	.50
142 Wildwatcher Elandra C	.12	.20
143 Wimbly Tinkerton U	.30	.50
144 Zorus the Judicator R	.60	1.00
145 Alecia Hall C	.12	.20
146 Blood Guard Gulmok E	2.00	3.00
147 Blood Knight Kyria C	.12	.20
148 Brok Bloodcaller U	.30	.50
149 Chief Apothecary Hildagard E	2.50	4.00
150 Dawn Ravensdale C	.12	.20
151 Deathgrip Jones C	.12	.20
152 Elder Huntsman Swiftshot R	.60	1.00
153 Eyeball Jones U	.30	.50
154 Flame Bender Ta'jin U	.30	.50
155 Forager Cloudbloom U	.30	.50
156 Forager Hoofbeat C	.12	.20
157 Illia the Bitter C	.12	.20
158 Kaelos Sunscream C	.12	.20
159 Kam'pah C	.12	.20
160 Lu'ka de Wall C	.12	.20
161 Natasha Hutchins C	.12	.20
162 Offender Gora U	.30	.50
163 Overlord Or'barokh R	.60	1.00
164 The Painsaw C	2.00	3.00
165 Ra'waza Stonetusk C	.12	.20
166 Roger Mortis C	.12	.20
167 Roon Plainswalker C	.12	.20
168 Skronk Skullseeker C	.12	.20
169 The Soul Conductor R	.12	.20
170 Tusk U	.30	.50
171 Xela the Tormentor R	.60	1.00
172 Ya'za the Vandal C	.12	.20
173 Anchorite Ceyla R	.60	1.00
174 Anchorite Kilandra C	.12	.20
175 Exarch Onaala E	5.00	8.00
176 Instructor Giralo C	.12	.20
177 Thief Catcher Norun C	.12	.20
178 Vindicator Aluumen R	.60	1.00
179 Vindicator Falaan R	.60	1.00
180 Vindicator Javlo C	.12	.20
181 Vindicator Kentho U	.30	.50
182 Vindicator Lorin U	.30	.50
183 Vindicator Vasha U	.30	.50
184 Arcanist Bartis C	.12	.20
185 Arcanist Renaan C	.12	.20
186 Arcanist Thelis R	.60	1.00
187 Battlemage Vyara R	.60	1.00
188 Historian Firana C	.12	.20
189 Magistrix Valthin U	.30	.50
190 Retainer Alashon R	.60	1.00
191 Retainer Faryn U	.30	.50
192 Retainer Kai C	.12	.20
193 Retainer Marcus U	.12	.20
194 Varen the Reclaimer E	2.00	3.00
195 Akama E	6.00	10.00
196 Ambassador Jerrikar R	.60	1.00
197 Azaloth E	6.00	10.00
198 Collidus the Warp-Watcher E	4.00	6.00
199 Doomwalker E	4.00	6.00
200 Edward the Odd E	2.50	4.00
201 Ethereal Plunderer R	1.25	2.00
202 Maiev Shadowsong E	8.00	12.00
203 Xi'ri E	4.00	6.00
204 Akama's Sash R	.60	1.00
205 A'tor's Mainstay R	.60	1.00
206 Borak's Belt of Bravery U	.30	.50
207 Coif of the Wicked R	.60	1.00
208 Doomplate Shoulderguards U	.30	.50
209 Gloves of the High Magus E	6.00	10.00
210 Greaves of Desolation R	.60	1.00
211 The Hands of Fate R	.30	.50
212 Hauberk of Karabor R	.60	1.00
213 Mana-Etched Spaulders U	.30	.50
214 Naaru Belt of Precision R	.60	1.00
215 Netherwing Protector's Shield U	.30	.50
216 Pauldrons of Desolation R	.60	1.00
217 Wastewalker Shoulderpads U	.30	.50
218 Band of the Inevitable R	4.00	6.00
219 Lightwarden's Band R	2.50	4.00
220 Medallion of the Lightbearer U	.30	.50
221 Scryer's Bloodgem U	.30	.50
222 Seer's Signet R	.60	1.00
223 Ashtongue Blade U	.30	.50
224 Bloodwarder's Rifle R	.60	1.00
225 Felstel Whisper Knives R	2.00	3.00
226 Hammer of the Naaru E	8.00	12.00
227 Illidari-Bane Mageblade U	.30	.50
228 Lucky Strike Axe R	.60	1.00
229 Staff of the Ashtongue Deathsworn R	.60	1.00
230 Tirisfal Wand of Ascendancy U	.30	.50
231 Vindicator's Brand R	2.50	4.00
232 Retainer's Blade R	5.00	8.00
233 Return to the Aldor C	.12	.20
234 Return to the Scryers C	.12	.20
235 Against the Illidari C	.12	.20
236 Akama's Promise C	.12	.20
237 Bane of the Illidari C	.12	.20
238 Battle of the Crimson Watch C	.12	.20
239 The Cipher of Damnation C	.60	1.00
240 The Deathforge U	.12	.20
241 The Fel and the Furious C	.30	.50
242 I Was a Lot of Things C	.12	.20
243 The Lexicon Demonica R	.60	1.00
244 Minions of the Shadow Council R	4.00	6.00
245 The Path of Conquest C	.12	.20
246 Reclaiming Holy Grounds U	.30	.50

247 The Secret Compromised C	.12	.20
248 Skywing R	.60	1.00
249 The Summoning Chamber U	.60	1.00
250 Tabards of the Illidari C	.60	1.00
251 Teron Gorefiend, I Am C	.12	.20
252 What Illidan Wants, Illidan Gets U	.30	.50

2008 World of Warcraft Hunt for Illidan Loot

1 The Footsteps of Illidan	4.00	6.00
2 Disco Inferno	40.00	60.00
3 Ethereal Plunderer	150.00	300.00

2008 World of Warcraft Servants of the Betrayer

COMPLETE SET (264)	100.00	150.00
BOOSTER BOX (24 PACKS)	40.00	80.00
BOOSTER PACK (19 CARDS)	2.00	3.00
RELEASED IN APRIL 2008		
1 Commander Michael Goodchilde U	.30	.50
2 Fallingstar U	.30	.50
3 Ixamos the Redeemed U	.30	.50
4 Marlowe Christophers U	.30	.50
5 Mythen of the Wild U	.30	.50
6 Obora the Wise U	.30	.50
7 Ressa Shadeshine U	.30	.50
8 Sharpshooter Nally U	.30	.50
9 Sister Remba U	.30	.50
10 Crusader Michael Goodchilde U	.30	.50
11 Fallenstar U	.30	.50
12 Ixamos the Corrupted U	.30	.50
13 Marlowe the Felsworn U	.30	.50
14 Mythen of the Fang U	.30	.50
15 Obora the Mad U	.30	.50
16 Ressa the Leper Queen U	.30	.50
17 Seadog Nally U	.30	.50
18 Remba, Abbess of Ash U	.30	.50
19 Jonas White U	.30	.50
20 Kil'zin of the Darkspear U	.30	.50
21 Lelora Sunlancer U	.30	.50
22 Lionar, Unbound U	.30	.50
23 Morn Walks-the-Path U	.30	.50
24 Plague Fleshbane U	.30	.50
25 Runetusk U	.30	.50
26 Vor'na the Disciplined U	.30	.50
27 Warden Stormclaw U	.30	.50
28 Jonas the Red U	.30	.50
29 Kil'zin of the Bloodscalp U	.30	.50
30 Lelora the Dawnslayer U	.30	.50
31 Lionar the Blood Cursed U	.30	.50
32 Morn Salts-the-Land U	.30	.50
33 Plague Demonsoul U	.30	.50
34 Bloodtusk U	.30	.50
35 Vor'na the Wretched U	.30	.50
36 Desecrator Stormclaw U	.30	.50
37 Chew Toy U	.30	.50
38 Earth Mother's Blessing C	.12	.20
39 Form of the Serpent R	6.00	10.00
40 Gift of Nature R	.60	1.00
41 King of the Jungle R	.60	1.00
42 Lacerate C	.12	.20
43 The Natural Order C	.12	.20
44 Savage Fury R	.60	1.00
45 Tainted Earth U	.30	.50
46 Tranquility U	.30	.50
47 Bogspike C	.12	.20
48 Death Trap R	.60	1.00
49 Feeding Frenzy U	.30	.50
50 Feign Death R	4.00	6.00
51 King Khan U	.30	.50
52 Rain of Arrows C	.12	.20
53 Ranged Weapon Specialization R	2.00	3.00
54 Run to Ground C	.12	.20
55 Snake Trap U	.30	.50
56 Survival Instincts R	1.25	2.00
57 Arcane Focus R	.60	1.00
58 Blaze C	.12	.20
59 Frost Armor U	.30	.50
60 Frostbite R	.60	1.00
61 Invisibility U	.30	.50
62 Invocation R	1.25	2.00
63 Living Pyre C	.12	.20
64 Metalmorph C	.12	.20
65 Murderous Torment U	.30	.50
66 Tomb of Ice R	.60	1.00
67 Aura of Fanaticism U	.30	.50
68 Avenging Wrath U	.30	.50
69 Blessed Life R	1.25	2.00
70 Blessing of the Martyr C	.12	.20
71 Crusade R	.60	1.00
72 Divine Riposte U	.30	.50
73 Flash of Light C	.12	.20
74 Seal of Betrayal R	2.00	3.00
75 Seal of Redemption C	.12	.20
76 Wrath of Turalyon R	.60	1.00
77 Castigate U	.30	.50
78 Darkness R	.60	1.00
79 Eclipse U	.30	.50
80 Enlightenment R	.60	1.00
81 Fade U	.30	.50
82 Melt Face C	.12	.20
83 Prayer of Mending C	.12	.20
84 Salvation C	.12	.20
85 Shadow Silhouettes R	.60	1.00
86 Spiritual Domination R	2.00	3.00
87 Blade Twisting R	.60	1.00
88 Cloak of Shadows C	.12	.20
89 Cut to the Chase U	.30	.50
90 Diversion C	.12	.20
91 Evasion R	.60	1.00
92 Find Weakness R	.60	1.00
93 Gut Shot R	.60	1.00
94 Pilfer U	.30	.50
95 Sacrificial Poison U	.30	.50
96 Unbalance C	.12	.20
97 Death Shock U	.30	.50
98 Elemental Precision R	.60	1.00
99 Life Cycle C	.12	.20
100 Maelstrom Weapon C	.12	.20
101 Shamanistic Dual Wield R	1.25	2.00
102 Stoneskin Totem U	.30	.50
103 Storm Shock C	.12	.20
104 Totemic Recovery R	.60	1.00
105 Totem of Decay R	.60	1.00
106 Water Shield U	.30	.50
107 Apocanon U	.30	.50
108 Banish to the Nether C	.12	.20
109 Curse of Frenzy U	.30	.50
110 Demonic Knowledge R	.60	1.00
111 Dread Infernal R	2.50	4.00
112 Fel Fire C	.12	.20
113 Gobloz C	.12	.20
114 Ripped through the Portal R	5.00	8.00
115 Ritual of Souls U	.30	.50
116 Shadow and Flame R	.60	1.00
117 Armed to the Teeth C	.12	.20
118 Bloodbath R	.60	1.00
119 Champion Stance C	.12	.20
120 Deafening Shout R	.60	1.00
121 Shield Slam R	.60	1.00
122 Smash C	.30	.50
123 Sudden Death U	.30	.50
124 Titan's Grip U	.30	.50
125 Unbridled Wrath R	.60	1.00
126 Whirlwind U	.30	.50
127 Papa Hummel's Old-Fashioned Pet Biscuit U	.30	.50
128 Personal Weather Maker R	.60	1.00
129 Angelista C	.12	.20
130 Antikron the Unyielding U	.30	.50
131 Barous the Storm Baron R	1.25	2.00
132 Bearlady Brala R	.60	1.00
133 Breen Toestubber C	.12	.20
134 Domona the Ever-Watchful U	.30	.50
135 Falana of the Glen C	.12	.20
136 Highlord Bolvar Fordragon E	3.00	5.00
137 Horace Shadowfall R	.60	1.00
138 Inventor Dorbin Callus E	3.00	5.00
139 Jezbella of Karabor C	.12	.20
140 Justicar Brace U	.30	.50
141 Kronore R	.60	1.00
142 Llyras Keeneye C	.12	.20
143 Lunen the Moon Baron R	.60	1.00
144 Miner Steelwhiskers C	.12	.20
145 Myriam Starcaller C	.12	.20
146 Narthadus C	.12	.20
147 Orderkeeper Calister C	.12	.20
148 Orderkeeper Henley C	.12	.20
149 Orderkeeper Vesra U	.30	.50
150 Quigley Slipshade C	.12	.20
151 Rames the Purifier C	.12	.20
152 Razak Ironsides E	5.00	8.00
153 Roke the Ice Baron R	.60	1.00
154 Rysa the Earthcaller C	.12	.20
155 Sampron the Banisher R	.60	1.00
156 Stella Forgebane C	.12	.20
157 Aesadonna Al'mere R	.60	1.00
158 Alchemist Norrin'thal C	.12	.20
159 Cerrik Blooddawn C	.12	.20
160 David Smythe C	.12	.20
161 Delrach the Vile C	.12	.20
162 Gok Stormhammer R	.60	1.00
163 Hulok Trailblazer C	.12	.20
164 Icemistress Gal'ha R	.60	1.00
165 Jae'va the Relentless C	.12	.20
166 Jessup Smythe C	.12	.20
167 Leoroxx E	4.00	6.00
168 Lifemistress Tanagra R	.60	1.00
169 Lilith Smythe C	.12	.20
170 Matalo Trailfinder U	.30	.50
171 Mojo Doctor Zin'tar U	.30	.50
172 Ras'fari Bloodfrenzy U	.30	.50
173 Roena Trailmaker C	.12	.20
174 Rogg Dreadnock U	.30	.50
175 Saurfang the Younger E	2.00	3.00
176 Scholar Krosiss C	.12	.20
177 Sek Grimlash R	.60	1.00
178 Sha'kar C	.60	1.00
179 Skymistress Taranna R	.60	1.00
180 Tarn Darkwalker C	.12	.20
181 Tatulla the Reclaimer C	.12	.20
182 Ulrac Bloodshadow R	.60	1.00
183 Vexmaster Nar'jo C	.12	.20
184 Anchorite Fareena U	.30	.50
185 Anchorite Karja E	1.25	2.00
186 Anchorite Onkoth U	.30	.50
187 Atani of the Watch C	.12	.20
188 Bulvai of the Watch C	.12	.20
189 Exarch Orelis E	2.50	4.00
190 Marksman Eowan U	.30	.50
191 Marksman Glous R	12.00	20.00
192 Niyore of the Watch R	3.00	5.00
193 Vindicator Agran C	.12	.20
194 Vindicator Ostakron C	.12	.20
195 Xanata the Lightsworn U	.30	.50
196 Arcanist Alathana U	.30	.50
197 Arcanist Atikan R	.60	1.00
198 Arcanist Dayvana U	.30	.50
199 Arcanist Lyronia C	.12	.20
200 Magistrix Dianas C	.12	.20
201 Magistrix Larynna E	3.00	5.00
202 Retainer Athan U	.30	.50
203 Retainer Cara C	.12	.20
204 Retainer Eteron R	.60	1.00
205 Retainer Ryn U	.30	.50
206 Retainer Zian C	.12	.20
207 Spymaster Thalodien E	4.00	6.00
208 Coilfang Myrmidon C	.12	.20
209 Lady Katrana Prestor E	2.50	4.00
210 Lady Vashj E	6.00	10.00
211 Millhouse Manastorm E	2.00	3.00
212 Pathaleon the Calculator R	.60	1.00
213 Prince Kael'thas Sunstrider E	8.00	12.00
214 Sunseeker Astromage C	.12	.20
215 Warlord Kalithresh R	.60	1.00
216 X-51 Nether-Rocket R	.60	1.00
217 Arcanium Signet Bands U	.30	.50
218 Armwraps of Disdain U	.30	.50
219 Azure-Shield of Coldarra R	.60	1.00
220 Barbaric Legstraps U	.30	.50
221 Doomplate Warhelm U	.30	.50
222 Fanblade Pauldrons U	.30	.50
223 Helm of Desolation U	.30	.50
224 Legguards of the Shattered Hand R	.60	1.00
225 Mana-Etched Crown R	.60	1.00
226 Mana-Sphere Shoulderguards R	.60	1.00
227 Wastewalker Helm U	.30	.50
228 Wastewalker Leggings R	2.00	3.00
229 Choker of Vile Intent R	.60	1.00
230 Hourglass of the Unraveller R	.60	1.00
231 Quagmirran's Eye R	2.00	3.00
232 Ring of the Shadow Deeps U	.30	.50
233 Ring of the Silver Hand R	.60	1.00
234 Blade of Wizardry E	6.00	10.00
235 Bloodskull Destroyer U	.30	.40
236 Essence Gatherer U	.30	.50
237 Plasma Rat's Hyper-Scythe U	.30	.50
238 Quantum Blade E	3.00	5.00
239 Reflex Blades U	.30	.50
240 Terokk's Shadowstaff R	1.25	2.00
241 Vileblade of the Betrayer R	.60	1.00
242 Voidfire Wand R	8.00	12.00
243 Wand of the Seer R	.60	1.00
244 Wrathtide Longbow U	.30	.50
245 Marks of Kil'jaeden C	.12	.20
246 Sunfury Briefings C	.12	.20
247 Firewing Signets C	.12	.20
248 Manaforge B'naar C	.60	1.00
249 Deep Sea Salvage C	.12	.20
250 Dr. Boom C	.12	.20
251 An Improper Burial C	.12	.20
252 Information Gathering C	.12	.20
253 Kim'jael Indeed U	.30	.50
254 Leader of the Darkcrest C	.12	.20
255 Meeting with the Master C	.12	.20
256 Needs More Cowbell R	1.25	2.00
257 Orders From Lady Vashj C	.12	.20
258 Potential Energy Source U	.30	.50
259 Preparing for War C	.12	.20
260 Shutting Down Manaforge Ara C	.12	.20
261 The Sigil of Krasus C	.12	.20
262 The Unending Invasion C	.12	.20
263 A Warm Welcome R	1.25	2.00
264 You, Robot U	.30	.50

2008 World of Warcraft Servants of the Betrayer Loot

1 Papa Hummel's Old-Fashioned Pet Biscuit	6.00	10.00
2 Personal Weather Maker	60.00	100.00
3 X-51 Nether-Rocket	250.00	350.00

2009 World of Warcraft Blood of Gladiators

COMPLETE SET (208)	50.00	100.00
BOOSTER BOX (24 PACKS)	30.00	60.00
BOOSTER PACK (19 CARDS)	1.50	3.00
RELEASED IN MARCH 2009		
1 Bronson Greatwhisker U	.30	.50
2 Chloe Mithrilbolt U	.30	.50
3 Feera Quickshot U	.30	.50
4 Gwon Strongbark U	.30	.50
5 Gyro of the Ring U	.30	.50
6 Kalatine Carmichael U	.30	.50
7 Kristoff Manchester U	.30	.50
8 Nicholas Merrick U	.30	.50
9 Statia the Preserver U	.30	.50
10 Andarius the Damned U	.30	.50
11 Bonewall Simms U	.30	.50
12 Brahu Starsear U	.30	.50
13 Cerripha Sunstreak U	.30	.50
14 Savitir Skullsmasher U	.30	.50
15 Sharpeye Yan'ja U	.30	.50
16 Thoros the Savior U	.30	.50
17 Tribemother Torra U	.30	.50
18 Witch Doctor Koo'zar U	.30	.50
19 Friends in High Places C	.12	.20
20 Nature's Reach R	1.00	1.50
21 Reforestation U	.30	.50
22 The Sowing of Seeds U	.30	.50
23 Starshot C	.12	.20
24 Tiger's Fury R	.60	1.00
25 Utopia R	.60	1.00
26 The Aim of Eagles U	.30	.50
27 Bolton U	.30	.50
28 Clutch Shot C	.12	.20
29 Improvised Weaponry R	.60	1.00
30 Quickdraw C	.12	.20
31 Scatter Shot R	1.00	1.50
32 Volley R	1.00	1.50
33 Blizzard R	.60	1.00
34 Combustion R	.60	1.00
35 Heartburn C	.12	.20
36 Mana Ruby R	.60	1.00
37 Meltdown U	.30	.50
38 Sear C	.12	.20
39 The Taste of Arcana U	.30	.50
40 Atonement C	.12	.20
41 Divine Favor R	1.00	1.50
42 Divine Justice C	.12	.20
43 Glimmer of Hope U	.30	.50
44 Reckoning of the Light R	1.00	1.50
45 The Rewards of Faith U	.30	.50
46 Sacred Moment R	1.00	1.50
47 Darkest Before the Light R	.60	1.00
48 Disperse Magic C	.12	.20
49 Focused Will R	.60	1.00
50 Horrify C	.12	.20
51 The Omens of Terror U	.30	.50
52 Power Word: Restore U	.30	.50
53 Splinter Mind R	.60	1.00
54 Deadliness R	.60	1.00
55 The Depth of Shadows U	.30	.50
56 Intuition C	.12	.20
57 Slash and Dash C	.12	.20
58 Stab in the Dark U	.30	.50
59 Surgical Strikes R	.60	1.00
60 Yoink! R	1.00	1.50
61 The Crash of Tides U	.30	.50
62 Echo Totem R	.60	1.00
63 Fork Lightning C	.12	.20
64 Greater Chain Heal U	.30	.50
65 Strength of Earth Totem C	.12	.20
66 Tidal Mastery R	1.00	1.50

67 Tremor Shock R	2.00	3.00
68 Curse of Endless Suffering C	.12	.20
69 Curse of Midnight U	.30	.50
70 Dark Justice C	.12	.20
71 Grim Reach R	1.25	2.00
72 Kreedom R	1.00	1.50
73 The Promises of Darkness U	.30	.50
74 Ritual of Summoning R	.60	1.00
75 The Benefits of Practice U	.30	.50
76 Cowering Shout C	.12	.20
77 Defiance R	.60	1.00
78 A Final Sacrifice C	.12	.20
79 A Flawless Advance R	.60	1.00
80 Pulverize U	.30	.50
81 Shield Wall R	1.00	1.50
82 Blessing of the Heavens C	.12	.20
83 Burly Bellow C	.12	.20
84 Disappear C	.12	.20
85 Double Time C	.12	.20
86 Optimize C	.12	.20
87 Phase Hound C	.12	.20
88 Poof! C	.12	.20
89 Recall from the Brink C	.12	.20
90 Victimize C	.12	.20
91 Center of Attention R	.60	1.00
92 Foam Sword Rack R	.60	1.00
93 Anduin Wrynn E	2.00	3.00
94 Chillhands Spigotgulp U	.30	.50
95 Cracklehands Spigotgulp C	.12	.20
96 Elder Achillia C	.12	.20
97 Elder Tomas C	.12	.20
98 Elder Valdar of the Exodar C	.12	.20
99 Elder Zeez C	.12	.20
100 Gladiator Katianna C	.12	.20
101 Gladiator Keward C	.12	.20
102 Gladiator Kinivus C	.12	.20
103 Gladiator Lanthus C	.12	.20
104 Gladiator Loraala C	.12	.20
105 Gladiator Magnus C	.12	.20
106 Gladiator Meganna C	.12	.20
107 Gladiator Ryno C	.12	.20
108 Gladiator Zophos C	.12	.20
109 Huntress Xenia C	.12	.20
110 Kristina Soulcinder C	.12	.20
111 Kurdoc Greybeard U	.30	.50
112 Mikael the Blunt U	.30	.50
113 Miranda McMiserson R	.60	1.00
114 Ossus the Ancient R	2.50	4.00
115 Pappy Ironbane U	.30	.50
116 Quickhands Spigotgulp C	.12	.20
117 Trakas C	.12	.20
118 Tyrus Lionheart C	.12	.20
119 Wynnd the Spry C	.12	.20
120 Aknot Whetstone C	.12	.20
121 Canissa the Shadow C	.12	.20
122 Edward Hack Robinson C	.12	.20
123 Furious Kalla U	.30	.50
124 Gladiator Addisyn C	.12	.20
125 Gladiator Boum C	.12	.20
126 Gladiator Dorn C	.12	.20
127 Gladiator Emek C	.12	.20
128 Gladiator Kaniya C	.12	.20
129 Gladiator Kileana C	.12	.20
130 Gladiator Sepirion C	.12	.20
131 Gladiator Skumm C	.12	.20
132 Gladiator Zi'mo C	.12	.20
133 Grismare U	.30	.50
134 Hex Doctor No'jin C	.12	.20
135 Karina of Silvermoon C	.12	.20
136 Karta Foultongue C	.12	.20
137 Kazamon Steelskin R	6.00	10.00
138 Kino the Cold C	.12	.20
139 Melissa Gerrard C	.12	.20
140 Naliss the Silencer R	1.00	1.50
141 Nea Sunmark C	.12	.20
142 Rorga Trueshot C	.12	.20
143 Thomas Slash Robinson C	.12	.20
144 Tor'gor Darkfire U	.30	.50
145 Vol'jin E	1.25	2.00
146 Voltrinnia U	.30	.50
147 Broll Bearmantle E	1.25	2.00
148 Lo'Gosh E	1.50	2.50
149 Rehgar Earthfury E	6.00	10.00
150 Valeera Sanguinar E	1.50	2.50
151 Krixel Pinchwhistle R	.60	1.00
152 Mogor R	1.00	1.50
153 Sandbox Tiger U	.30	.50
154 Short John Mithril R	1.00	1.50
155 Skarr the Unbreakable R	.60	1.00
156 Amice of Brilliant Light U	.30	.50
157 Antonidas's Aegis of Rapt Concentration R	3.00	5.00
158 Bloodsea Brigand's Vest U	.30	.50
159 Cloak of the Shrouded Mists R	.60	1.00
160 Cowl of the Guiltless U	.30	.50
161 Cuffs of Devastation U	.30	.50
162 Fists of Mukoa U	.30	.50
163 Gladiator's Aegis E	1.25	2.00
164 Merciless Gladiator's Pursuit E	1.25	2.00
165 Quickstrider Moccasins R	.60	1.00
166 Slayer's Waistguard U	.30	.50
167 Vengeful Gladiator's Felshroud E	4.00	6.00
168 Band of Vile Aggression R	.60	1.00
169 The Seal of Danzalar R	1.00	1.50
170 Talisman of the Alliance U	.30	.50
171 Talisman of the Horde U	.30	.50
172 Battle Mage's Baton R	1.00	1.50
173 Boggspine Knuckles U	.30	.50
174 Boundless Agony R	.60	1.00
175 The Decapitator R	1.00	1.50
176 Emerald Ripper R	1.00	1.50
177 Gladiator's Salvation R	1.00	1.50
178 Gorehowl E	3.00	5.00
179 King's Defender U	.30	.50
180 Merciless Gladiator's Crossbow of the Phoenix R	.60	1.00
181 Mogor's Anointing Club R	.60	1.00
182 Nethershard R	1.00	1.50
183 Seth's Graphite Fishing Pole R	.60	1.00
184 Shuriken of Negation R	1.50	2.50
185 Tempest of Chaos R	1.00	1.50
186 Twinblade of the Phoenix R	3.00	5.00
187 Vengeful Gladiator's Piercing Touch R	.60	1.00
188 Wand of the Forgotten Star U	.30	.50
189 World Breaker R	1.00	1.50
190 Arena Grandmaster C	.12	.20
191 The Challenge C	.12	.20
192 Mark V Is Alive! R	.60	1.00
193 A Question of Gluttony C	.12	.20
194 The Ring of Blood: The Blue Brothers C	.12	.20
195 The Ring of Blood: Brokentoe C	.12	.20
196 The Ring of Blood: The Final Challenge C	.12	.20
197 The Ring of Blood: Rokdar the Sundered Lord C	.12	.20
198 The Ring of Blood: Skra'gath C	.12	.20
199 The Ring of Blood: The Warmaul Champion C	.12	.20
200 Uncatalogued Species C	.12	.20
201 Gurubashi Arena U	.30	.50
202 The Ring of Blood U	.30	.50
203 The Circle of Blood C	.12	.20
204 Ring of Trials C	.12	.20
205 The Ruins of Lordaeron C	.12	.20
206 The Exodar R	.60	1.00
207 Orgrimmar R	6.00	10.00
208 Silvermoon City R	4.00	6.00

2009 World of Warcraft Blood of Gladiators Loot

1 Sandbox Tiger	3.00	5.00
2 Center of Attention	30.00	50.00
3 Foam Sword Rack	50.00	75.00

2009 World of Warcraft Fields of Honor

COMPLETE SET (208)	50.00	100.00
BOOSTER BOX (24 PACKS)	40.00	80.00
BOOSTER PACK (19 CARDS)	2.00	4.00
RELEASED IN JUNE 2009		
1 Katianna the Shrouded U	.30	.50
2 Keward the Ravager U	.30	.50
3 Kinivus the Focused U	.30	.50
4 Lanthus the Restorer U	.30	.50
5 Loraala the Frigid U	.30	.50
6 Magnus the Depriver U	.30	.50
7 Meganna the Stalker U	.30	.50
8 Ryno the Wicked U	.30	.50
9 Zophos the Vengeful U	.30	.50
10 Addisyn the Untouchable U	.30	.50
11 Boum the Bloodseeker U	.30	.50
12 Dorn the Tranquil U	.30	.50
13 Emek the Equalizer U	.30	.50
14 Kaniya the Steadfast U	.30	.50
15 Kileana the Inferno U	.30	.50
16 Sepirion the Poised U	.30	.50
17 Skumm the Pillager U	.30	.50
18 Zi'mo the Empowered U	.30	.50
19 Celestial Shard U	.30	.50
20 Convocation R	.60	1.00
21 Grizzly Defender R	.60	1.00
22 Omen of Clarity R	.60	1.00
23 Pack Tactics U	.30	.50
24 Regrowth C	.12	.20
25 Tanglevine C	.12	.20
26 Crusty C	.12	.20
27 Dundee R	.60	1.00
28 Explosive Trap U	.30	.50
29 Intimidation R	.60	1.00
30 Planned Assault R	.60	1.00
31 Reload U	.30	.50
32 Track Hidden C	.12	.20
33 Brittilize C	.12	.20
34 Everlasting Cold C	.12	.20
35 Ice Barbs R	.60	1.00
36 Icy Veins R	.60	1.00
37 Nether Fissure U	.30	.50
38 Roaring Blaze U	.30	.50
39 Set Ablaze R	.60	1.00
40 Blessed Defense C	.12	.20
41 Blessing of Kings R	.60	1.00
42 Concentration Aura U	.30	.50
43 Convert U	.30	.50
44 Holy Strike C	.12	.20
45 Resolute Aura R	.60	1.00
46 Uplifting Prayer R	.60	1.00
47 Blind Faith R	.60	1.00
48 Mist of Corrosion C	.12	.20
49 Searing Light R	.60	1.00
50 A Taste of Divinity R	.60	1.00
51 Tithe U	.30	.50
52 United Front C	.12	.20
53 Vampiric Dominance U	.30	.50
54 Burgle R	.60	1.00
55 Carnage U	.30	.50
56 Hidden Weaponry C	.12	.20
57 Kidney Shot R	.60	1.00
58 Lead Astray C	.12	.20
59 Rupture U	.30	.50
60 Ruthlessness R	.60	1.00
61 Chain Purge U	.30	.50
62 Earthen Flurry C	.12	.20
63 Elemental Weapons R	.60	1.00
64 Hatchet Totem R	.60	1.00
65 Spark U	.30	.50
66 Wavestorm Totem C	.12	.20
67 Windfury Infusion R	.60	1.00
68 Backlash R	.60	1.00
69 Cremate C	.12	.20
70 Curse of the Elements R	.60	1.00
71 Curse of Weakness C	.12	.20
72 Dominate U	.30	.50
73 Hesriana E	6.00	10.00
74 Soulstone U	.30	.50
75 Bleed C	.12	.20
76 Blood Frenzy R	.60	1.00
77 Collateral Damage U	.30	.50
78 Keys to the Armory R	.60	1.00
79 Overpower R	.60	1.00
80 Reckless Abandon U	.30	.50
81 Split Open C	.12	.20
82 Arcane Warding C	.12	.20
83 Celerity C	.12	.20
84 Essence of Mending C	.12	.20
85 Fortifying Shout C	.12	.20
86 Frigid Winds C	.12	.20
87 No Man's Land C	.12	.20
88 Pin C	.12	.20
89 Sacrificial Vengeance C	.12	.20
90 Screeching Shot C	.12	.20
91 Path of Centarius U	.30	.50
92 Adam Eternum R	.60	1.00
93 Baelgond Soulgrace U	.30	.50
94 Bladehands Spigotgulp C	.12	.20
95 Corvus Promaethon C	.12	.20
96 Darok Steelstrike C	.12	.20
97 Dimzer the Prestidigitator R	.60	1.00
98 Durgle Wizzledab C	.12	.20
99 Endina the Hunted C	.12	.20
100 Gromble the Apt U	.30	.50
101 Grudum, Trove Guardian C	.12	.20
102 Illiyana Moonblaze E	1.25	2.00
103 Iravar U	.30	.50
104 Jonas Targan C	.12	.20
105 Lairin the Grounded C	.12	.20
106 Larrington Zarus R	.60	1.00
107 Maeryl Leafstrike C	.12	.20
108 Marundal the Kindred R	.60	1.00
109 Mayla Finksputter C	.12	.20
110 Modric Sternbeard C	.12	.20
111 Naan the Selfless C	.12	.20
112 Noxel Shroudhaggle C	.12	.20
113 Orlund C	.12	.20
114 Quenlan Lifeboon C	.12	.20
115 Royal Guardian Jameson R	.60	1.00
116 Skaduzzle C	.12	.20
117 Spelunker Maddocks R	.60	1.00
118 Vanndar Stormpike E	3.00	5.00
119 Vurkeran C	.12	.20
120 Zumbly Fiddlespark C	.12	.20
121 Blood Knight Haeleth C	.12	.20
122 Bloodwatcher Denissa C	.12	.20
123 Charkov C	.12	.20
124 Dannon Spellsurge C	.12	.20
125 Dark Archon Farrum U	.30	.50
126 Deathstalker Leanna C	.12	.20
127 Dethvir The Malignant R	.60	1.00
128 Drek'Thar E	2.50	4.00
129 Elder Narando C	.12	.20
130 Grugthar Sharpblade C	.12	.20
131 Iku'tak C	.12	.20
132 Keldor the Lost R	.60	1.00
133 Kelm Hargunth E	2.00	3.00
134 Mojo Masher Shakko C	.12	.20
135 Mojo Masher Ven'dango C	.12	.20
136 Morkad Sharptooth C	.12	.20
137 Nathaniel Voran C	.12	.20
138 Nazguk Sharptongue R	.60	1.00
139 Plainsrunner Marun C	.12	.20
140 Plainswatcher Taro R	.60	1.00
141 Rakasa Mournewind C	.12	.20
142 Samuel Harrison C	.12	.20
143 Scout Kurgo C	.12	.20
144 Sergeant Pugg U	.30	.50
145 Siaranna the Fickle R	.60	1.00
146 Sivandra Darklust C	.12	.20
147 Windstriker Larun R	.60	1.00
148 Yula the Fair U	.30	.50
149 Zalan Ragewind C	.12	.20
150 Backstab Bindo E	2.50	4.00
151 El Pollo Grande R	.60	1.00
152 Treebole E	2.00	3.00
153 Berserker Bracers R	.60	1.00
154 Bonefist Gauntlets U	.30	.50
155 Bulwark of the Amani Empire R	.60	1.00
156 Don Alejandro's Money Belt R	.60	1.00
157 Dryad's Wrist Bindings U	.30	.50
158 Gladiator's Sanctuary E	2.00	3.00
159 Grips of Damnation U	.30	.50
160 Marksman's Legguards U	.30	.50
161 Merciless Gladiator's Raiment E	2.50	4.00
162 Vengeful Gladiator's Earthshaker E	2.00	3.00
163 Veteran's Dreadweave Belt R	.60	1.00
164 Windtalker's Wristguards R	.60	1.00
165 Bangle of Endless R	.60	1.00
166 Pinata R	.60	1.00
167 Stormpike Insignia U	.30	.50
168 Frostwolf Insignia U	.30	.50
169 Apostle of Argus U	.30	.50
170 Arcanite Steam-Pistol U	.30	.50
171 Blackout Truncheon R	.60	1.00
172 Firemaul of Destruction U	.30	.50
173 Gladiator's Maul R	.60	1.00
174 Heartless U	.30	.50
175 Heartrazor U	.30	.50
176 Hope Ender R	.60	1.00
177 Jin'rohk, The Great Apocalypse E	10.00	15.00
178 Merciless Gladiator's Gavel R	.60	1.00
179 Steelhawk Crossbow R	.60	1.00
180 Vengeful Gladiator's Cleaver R	.60	1.00
181 Wand of Prismatic Focus U	.30	.50
182 Wub's Cursed Hexblade R	.60	1.00
183 Crackling Staff U	.30	.50
184 Hellforged Halberd R	.60	1.00
185 Blackened Spear R	.60	1.00
186 Whiteout Staff U	.30	.50
187 Call to Arms: Alterac Valley C	.12	.20
188 Call to Arms: Arathi Basin C	.12	.20
189 Call to Arms: Eye of the Storm C	.12	.20
190 Call to Arms: Warsong Gulch C	.12	.20
191 Capture a Mine C	.12	.20
192 Defusing the Threat C	.12	.20
193 The Eye of Command C	.12	.20
194 In Nightmares U	.30	.50
195 Legendary Heroes C	.12	.20
196 Proving Grounds C	.12	.20
197 Rise and Be Recognized C	.12	.20
198 Showdown R	.60	1.00
199 Towers and Bunkers C	.12	.20
200 Concerted Efforts C	.12	.20
201 For Great Honor C	.12	.20
202 Alterac Valley C	.12	.20
203 Arathi Basin C	.12	.20
204 Eye of the Storm C	.12	.20
205 Warsong Gulch C	.12	.20
206 Gnomeregan R	.60	1.00
207 Ironforge R	.60	1.00
208 Undercity R	.60	1.00

2009 World of Warcraft Fields of Honor Loot

1 Path of Cenarius 4.00 6.00
2 Pinata 25.00 40.00
3 El Pollo Grande 150.00 250.00

2009 World of Warcraft Scourgewar

COMPLETE SET (270) 80.00 120.00
BOOSTER BOX (24 PACKS) 50.00 100.00
BOOSTER PACK (19 CARDS) 3.00 5.00
RELEASED IN NOVEMBER 2009
1 Auryna the Lightsworn U .30 .50
2 Bordrak Barrelblast U .30 .50
3 Erondra Frostmoon U .30 .50
4 Felbender Lara U .30 .50
5 Ivan, Bladewind Brute U .30 .50
6 Nylaith, Guardian of the Wild U .30 .50
7 Prometha U .30 .50
8 Riley Sizzleswitch U .30 .50
9 Rordag the Sly U .30 .50
10 Xerandaal, Shade Servitor U .30 .50
11 Blythe the Pyromaniac U .30 .50
12 Emerson Zantides U .30 .50
13 Kaerie, Defender of the Sunwell U .30 .50
14 Levander of the Sanguine Shot U .30 .50
15 Maloduri U .30 .50
16 Souldrinker Bogmara U .30 .50
17 Teina Cloudstalker U .30 .50
18 Triton the Sacrilegious U .30 .50
19 Zagrun Wolfeye U .30 .50
20 Zorak'tul U .30 .50
21 Kel'Thuzad E 6.00 10.00
22 Army of the Dead R 2.50 4.00
23 Corpse Explosion R 2.00 3.00
24 Death and Decay U .30 .50
25 Deathcharger R 2.00 3.00
26 Death Pact U .30 .50
27 Icy Torment C .12 .20
28 Obliterate C .12 .20
29 Suffocating Grip C .12 .20
30 Unholy Presence C .12 .20
31 Unholy Rune C .12 .20
32 Berserk R .60 1.00
33 Blessing of Cenarius C .12 .20
34 Call of the Grove U .30 .50
35 Feline Grace C .12 .20
36 Hurricane R 3.00 5.00
37 Natural Repossession U .30 .50
38 Nature's Focus C .12 .20
39 Nourish R 1.25 2.00
40 Ursoc's Fury C .12 .20
41 Bombard R 1.25 2.00
42 Buzz U .30 .50
43 Chimera Shot R .60 1.00
44 Conflagration Trap C .12 .20
45 Fang C .12 .20
46 Master's Call U .30 .50
47 Raptor Strike C .12 .20
48 Scorpid Sting C .12 .20
49 Spoils of the Hunt R .60 1.00
50 Arcane Burst C .12 .20
51 Arcane Tactics C .12 .20
52 Astral Denial U .30 .50
53 Freeze U .30 .50
54 Living Bomb R .60 1.00
55 Mana Sapphire R 1.00 1.50
56 Mirror Image R .60 1.00
57 Polymorph: Penguin C .12 .20
58 Smoldering Blast C .12 .20
59 Blessing of Liberty U .30 .50
60 Boon of Light C .12 .20
61 Divine Storm R .60 1.00
62 Hammer of the Divine R 1.00 1.50
63 Seal of Divinity R .60 1.00
64 Shadow Resistance Aura C .12 .20
65 Stifling Decree C .12 .20
66 Vengeance of the Light U .30 .50
67 Vindictive Strike C .12 .20
68 Dark Penance C .12 .20
69 Delusions of Grandeur C .12 .20
70 Devouring Plague R 1.00 1.50
71 Dispersion R 1.00 1.50
72 Gathering of Wits R .60 1.00
73 Power Word: Sanctuary U .30 .50
74 Power Word: Vigor C .12 .20
75 Prayer of Shadow Protection U .30 .50
76 Shadow Word: Chaos C .12 .20
77 Aggressive Infiltration C .12 .20
78 Belligerence U .30 .50
79 Dead Weight C .12 .20
80 Deadly Throw R .60 1.00
81 Disarm Trap C .12 .20
82 Enveloping Shadows R .60 1.00
83 Perforation Poison C .12 .20
84 Plunder R .60 1.00
85 Sinister Set-up C .12 .20
86 Feral Spirit R 3.00 5.00
87 Incendiary Totem U .30 .50
88 Mass Purge C .12 .20
89 Soothing Wave C .12 .20
90 Squall Totem R 4.00 6.00
91 Surge of Lightning C .12 .20
92 Tidal Infusion C .12 .20
93 Water Walking U .30 .50
94 Wind Shear R 2.00 3.00
95 Detonate Soul R 1.00 1.50
96 Dreadsteed R 2.00 3.00
97 Haunt R 2.00 3.00
98 Jek'kresh U .30 .50
99 Offering to the Nether C .12 .20
100 Rhuunom C .12 .20
101 Shadow Burst C .12 .20
102 Shadow Ward C .12 .20
103 Terrifying Visage C .12 .20
104 Death Wish R 1.50 2.50
105 Debilitating Shout U .30 .50
106 Gushing Wound C .12 .20
107 Human Shield C .12 .20
108 Provoke C .12 .20
109 Recklessness R .60 1.00
110 Reconstruct R 1.25 2.00
111 Ruination C .12 .20
112 Shield Block C .12 .20
113 Tuskarr Kite U .30 .50
114 Bloody Grip U .30 .50
115 Crippling Strike U .30 .50
116 Frost Burst U .30 .50
117 Galvanize U .30 .50
118 Putrefying Poison U .30 .50
119 Shadows of Death U .30 .50
120 Shield of Distortion U .30 .50
121 Staunch Reprisal U .30 .50
122 Word of Blight U .30 .50
123 Next Stop, Menethil Harbor! C .12 .20
124 All Aboard for Undercity! C .12 .20
125 Anarchist Bladewalker U .30 .50
126 Anduros Silversong C .12 .20
127 Archduke Franklin Pearce C .12 .20
128 Corruptor Mimi Whippleshade U .30 .50
129 Danyssa Stillheart C .12 .20
130 Earthshaper Javuun C .12 .20
131 Ferandus Duskfall C .12 .20
132 Field Commander Foggo C .12 .20
133 Flint Shadowmore E 5.00 8.00
134 Great Elekk R 1.00 1.50
135 Gregory Flamewaker C .12 .20
136 High Magus Euli C .12 .20
137 Horatio Plaguetouch C .12 .20
138 Hulstom, Servant of the Light C .12 .20
139 Justicar Andaer Ragepaw U .30 .50
140 Justicar Broxlo Frostnuggle U .30 .50
141 Justicar Gavin Shadesticker U .30 .50
142 Justicar Maxwell Forthright U .30 .50
143 Kaale C .12 .20
144 King Varian Wrynn E 4.00 6.00
145 Mardun Valorhearth C .12 .20
146 Mioma Shadowflint C .12 .20
147 Mooncaller Jynalla Nightpath U .30 .50
148 Myrodan Silversong C .12 .20
149 Nakistis, Exodar Armorer C .12 .20
150 Olaf Steelbreaker C .12 .20
151 Petreus Roffe C .12 .20
152 Plasu C .12 .20
153 Skaala of the Somber Watch C .12 .20
154 Soulseeker Huulo C .12 .20
155 Starli C .12 .20
156 Swift Nightsaber R .60 1.00
157 Swift Ram R .60 1.00
158 Trixie Boltclunker C .12 .20
159 Varah, Fury of the Stars C .12 .20
160 Vesperia Silversong C .12 .20
161 Voidmaven Christie Noone U .30 .50
162 Zealot Kalinov R .60 1.00
163 Azamoth Deathfang C .12 .20
164 Besora Galeleather C .12 .20
165 Broderick Langforth R 12.00 20.00
166 Claemora Amberglare C .12 .20
167 Conqueror Gurzom U .30 .50
168 Conqueror Jarano U .30 .50
169 Conqueror Neusuada U .30 .50
170 Conqueror Yun'zon U .30 .50
171 Drandus the Deathcaller U .30 .50
172 Emelia Darkhand C .12 .20
173 Farander Shadesurge C .12 .20
174 Firewarden Wyland Kaslinth C .12 .20
175 Garrosh Hellscream E 2.50 4.00
176 Ginza Darktusk C .12 .20
177 Great Kodo R .60 1.00
178 Grovemender Ash'lon C .12 .20
179 Haranto Darkstrider C .12 .20
180 Huro'shal Gutwrench C .12 .20
181 Huzrula C .12 .20
182 Jaroth Lightguard C .12 .20
183 Kurao Stormheart C .12 .20
184 Makta the Rumbler U .30 .50
185 Mojo Mistress Zurania C .12 .20
186 Nathanos Blightcaller E 6.00 10.00
187 Raztu'jor C .12 .20
188 Rukdara Dreadhand C .12 .20
189 Sindo'zur the Toxifier U .30 .50
190 Swift Raptor R 1.50 2.50
191 Tanzuri C .12 .20
192 Teresa Voidheart C .12 .20
193 Thag Big Bounty Cragshot C .12 .20
194 Thurgood Steelwall C .12 .20
195 Twilight Vanquisher Knolan R 1.00 1.50
196 Verzuk Bloodfist C .12 .20
197 Vindron the Impure U .30 .50
198 Whitney Gravecaller C .12 .20
199 Winston Duskhaven C .12 .20
200 Alard Schmied R .60 1.00
201 Azjol-anak Acidslinger C .12 .20
202 Azjol-anak Acidspewer C .12 .20
203 Azjol-anak Battleguard C .12 .20
204 Azjol-anak Broodguard C .12 .20
205 Azjol-anak Webspinner C .12 .20
206 Azjol-anak Webweaver C .12 .20
207 Charles Worth R .60 1.00
208 Diane Cannings R .60 1.00
209 Kilix the Unraveler R .60 1.00
210 Klannoc Macleod E 1.00 1.50
211 Lord Darion Mograine E 1.00 1.50
212 Lord Jorach Ravenholdt E 1.50 2.50
213 Mor'zul Bloodbringer E 1.00 1.50
214 Spectral Kitten R 1.25 2.00
215 Tiny U .30 .50
216 Bloodbane's Fall C .12 .20
217 Boots of the Whirling Mist R .60 1.00
218 Breastplate of Undeath U .30 .50
219 The Darkspeaker's Footpads C .12 .20
220 Greaves of Ancient Evil R 1.00 1.50
221 Incursion Vestments R .60 1.00
222 King Dred's Helm R .60 1.00
223 Riot Shield U .30 .50
224 Shoulderpads of Fleshwerks C .12 .20
225 Spaulders of Lost Secrets C .12 .20
226 Vengeance Wrap U .30 .50
227 Oracle Talisman of Ablution U .30 .50
228 Dragonflight Great-Ring E 1.25 2.00
229 Extract of Necromantic Power R 2.00 3.00
230 Mighty Shadow Protection Potion C .12 .20
231 Arm Blade of Augelmir U .30 .50
232 Blade of the Empty Void R .60 1.00
233 Crimson Cranium Crusher R .60 1.00
234 Dagger of Betrayal R .60 1.00
235 Edge of Oblivion R 1.25 2.00
236 Encrusted Zombie Finger R .60 1.00
237 Fleshwerk Throwing Glaive R .60 1.00
238 Gavel of the Fleshcrafter U .30 .50
239 Life-Staff of the Web Lair R .60 1.00
240 Netherbreath Spellblade R 1.00 1.50
241 Reanimator's Hacker U .30 .50
242 Reaper of Dark Souls U .30 .50
243 Saliva Corroded Pike U .30 .50
244 Staff of Sinister Claws U .30 .50
245 Touch of Unlife U .30 .50
246 Trapper's Rifle R .60 1.00
247 Trophy Gatherer U .30 .50
248 Unearthed Broadsword C .12 .20
249 Death to the Traitor King C .12 .20
250 A Voice in the Dark C .12 .20
251 Brothers in Death U .30 .50
252 Culling the Damned C .12 .20
253 Dark Horizon C .12 .20
254 Death's Gaze C .12 .20
255 Defiling the Defilers C .12 .20
256 Dreadsteed of Xoroth U .30 .50
257 Junkboxes Needed U .30 .50
258 Pure Evil C .12 .20
259 Sacrifices Must Be Made C .12 .20
260 Scourge Tactics C .12 .20
261 Tales of Destruction C .12 .20
262 The Overseer's Shadow C .12 .20
263 The Restless Dead C .12 .20
264 Under the Shadow C .12 .20
265 Unfit for Death C .12 .20
266 Whirlwind Weapon U .30 .50
267 World of Shadows C .12 .20
268 Legendary Leathers, Dalaran R .60 1.00
269 Talismanic Textiles, Dalaran R .60 1.00
270 Tanks for Everything, Dalaran R .60 1.00

2009 World of Warcraft Scourgewar Loot

1 Tiny 5.00 8.00
2 Tuskarr Kite 60.00 100.00
3 Spectral Kitten 100.00 175.00

2010 World of Warcraft Icecrown

COMPLETE SET (220) 50.00 100.00
BOOSTER BOX (24 PACKS) 50.00 100.00
BOOSTER PACK (19 CARDS) 3.00 5.00
RELEASED IN SEPTEMBER 2010
1 Arch Druid Lilliandra U .30 .50
2 Argent Confessor Paletress U .30 .50
3 Eadric the Pure U .30 .50
4 Rimblat Earthshatter U .30 .50
5 Dalronn the Controller U .30 .50
6 General Lightsbane U .30 .50
7 Overseer Savryn U .30 .50
8 Queen Angerboda U .30 .50
9 Syreian the Bonecarver U .30 .50
10 Thane Ufrang the Mighty U .30 .50
11 Turov the Risen U .30 .50
12 Askalti Darksteel U .30 .50
13 Blood Lord Vorath U .30 .50
14 Deathseer Zuk'raj U .30 .50
15 Kjaran the Callous U .30 .50
16 Lich King, The E 6.00 10.00
17 Arctic Blast C .15 .25
18 Blood Plague C .15 .25
19 Death Gate R .60 1.00
20 Entomb C .15 .25
21 Frost Rune U .30 .50
22 Frost Strike R .60 1.00
23 Mark of Undeath U .30 .50
24 Rune Strike C .15 .25
25 Feral Dominance U .30 .50
26 Gale Winds R .60 1.00
27 Mark of Life C .15 .25
28 Natural Reclamation R .60 1.00
29 Predatory Sense C .15 .25
30 Ravage C .15 .25
31 Savage Roar U .30 .50
32 Bestial Resurgence U .30 .50
33 Cold Bones C .15 .25
34 Deuce R 2.50 4.00
35 Freezing Arrow C .15 .25
36 Penetrating Shots R .60 1.00
37 Primal Focus U .30 .50
38 Sharp Eye C .15 .25
39 Arcane Binding R .60 1.00
40 Arcane Essence U .30 .50
41 Cone of Cold C .15 .25
42 Fingers of Frost R .60 1.00
43 Flame Burst C .15 .25
44 Frost Ward C .15 .25
45 Whiteout U .30 .50
46 Blessing of the Templar R .60 1.00
47 Deliberate Heal C .15 .25
48 Deliberate Vengeance C .15 .25
49 Frost Resistance Aura C .15 .25
50 Reckoning R .60 1.00
51 Restitution U .30 .50
52 Seal of Purity U .30 .50
53 Desperate Condemnation C .15 .25
54 Desperate Plea C .15 .25
55 Mind Sear U .30 .50
56 Power Infusion R .60 1.00
57 Prayer of Spirit U .30 .50
58 Prayer of Vitality C .15 .25
59 Psychic Shriek R .60 1.00
60 Butcher U .30 .50
61 Close Quarters Combat R .60 1.00
62 Divert C .15 .25
63 Fan of Knives R 1.00 1.50
64 Instant Poison C .15 .25
65 Paralyze U .30 .50
66 Poach C .15 .25
67 Colossal Totem U .30 .50
68 Elemental Shield C .15 .25
69 Frost Resistance Totem U .30 .50
70 Hex C .15 .25
71 Lava Burst C .15 .25

72 Spiritual Awakening R .60 1.00
73 Thunderstorm R 1.00 1.50
74 Demonic Accord C .15 .25
75 Embrace of the Nether C .15 .25
76 Fel Fury U .30 .50
77 Fel Infernal U .30 .50
78 Jaktip C .15 .25
79 Metamorphosis R .60 1.00
80 Nether Rift R .60 1.00
81 Command Decision C .15 .25
82 Conquering Shout C .15 .25
83 Fit of Rage R .60 1.00
84 Heroic Throw U .30 .50
85 Payment of Blood U .30 .50
86 Pierce C .15 .25
87 Warbringer R .60 1.00
88 Bloody Slaughter U .30 .50
89 Boundless Concentration U .30 .50
90 Embolism U .30 .50
91 Fortify U .30 .50
92 Frost Surge U .30 .50
93 Inner Rage U .30 .50
94 Necessary Sacrifice U .30 .50
95 Primal Taming U .30 .50
96 Torment of Shadows U .30 .50
97 Paint Bomb U .30 .50
98 Akiko the Alert U .30 .50
99 Ashnaar, Frost Herald R 3.00 5.00
100 Bronwyn Lightborn C .15 .25
101 Cynthia Masters C .15 .25
102 Darktwister Kern C .15 .25
103 Hazlow Mudshuggle C .15 .25
104 Jaina, Lady of Theramore E 8.00 12.00
105 Justicar Andra Goldblast U .30 .50
106 Justicar Johanna Rastol U .30 .50
107 Justicar Nordar Stonegrave U .30 .50
108 Kylanda the Harmonious U .30 .50
109 Kysa Shadowstalker C .15 .25
110 Lissie Spizfrat C .15 .25
111 Madrea Bluntbrew C .15 .25
112 Pathfinder Fansal R .60 1.00
113 Phantrich C .15 .25
114 Rhyllor of the Glade C .15 .25
115 Sparkington the Abrupt U .30 .50
116 Swift Palomino R .60 1.00
117 Tani Bixtix C .15 .25
118 Thassarian R .60 1.00
119 Vanora Moonshot C .15 .25
120 Vishala C .15 .25
121 Vylar Whitepaw C .15 .25
122 Wesley Shadowsworn C .15 .25
123 Adenda Lighthaven C .15 .25
124 Bradford the Frozen U .30 .50
125 Buma Sharpstride C .15 .25
126 Conqueror Edge U .30 .50
127 Conqueror Nairi U .30 .50
128 Conqueror Tristos U .30 .50
129 Deathlord Jones R .60 1.00
130 Doom C .15 .25
131 Frostweaver Dakar'sith R .60 1.00
132 Hansi Wildcoat C .15 .25
133 Indauma Bloodfire C .15 .25
134 Jasmine von Ludrow C .15 .25
135 Koltira Deathweaver R .60 1.00
136 Kozik Skullcracker C .15 .25
137 Kuz'vun C .15 .25
138 Loate Grimtusk C .15 .25
139 Savuka the Acute U .30 .50
140 Skeletal Warhorse R .60 1.00
141 Stephen Hathrow C .15 .25
142 Thrall, Warchief E 10.00 15.00
143 Torashu Stronghoof C .15 .25
144 Treewatcher Kursha U .30 .50
145 Uh'gali the Elementalist U .30 .50
146 Vukora Netherflame C .15 .25
147 Zaduru C .15 .25
148 Banshee Soulclaimer C .15 .25
149 Crypt Fiend C .15 .25
150 Hulking Abomination U .30 .50
151 King Ymiron R .60 1.00
152 Malefic Necromancer C .15 .25
153 Marauding Geist C .15 .25
154 Orbaz Bloodbane R .60 1.00
155 Overlord Drakuru R .60 1.00
156 Plague Eruptor U .30 .50
157 Shade of Arugal R .60 1.00
158 Sindragosa, Frost Queen E 2.00 3.00
159 Stonespine Gargoyle C .15 .25
160 Underking Talonox R .60 1.00
161 Ymirheim Chosen Warrior C .15 .25
162 Azjol-anak Deathwatcher R .60 1.00
163 Azjol-anak Skirmisher U .30 .50
164 Alchemist Finklestein U .30 .50
165 Babagahnoosh, Grumpy E 2.50 4.00
166 Bath'rah the Windwatcher E 1.25 2.00
167 Hemet Nesingwary E 5.00 8.00
168 Rhonin E 1.00 1.50
169 Wooly White Rhino R .60 1.00
170 Bitter Cold Armguards C .15 .25
171 Frost-bound Chain Bracers R .60 1.00
172 Gloves of the Frozen Glade R .60 1.00
173 Hero's Surrender R 1.00 1.50
174 Iceshear Mantle C .15 .25
175 Icy Scale Chestguard C .15 .25
176 Legplates of the Endless Void R .60 1.00
177 Shawl of Haunted R .60 1.00
178 Winter's Icy Embrace C .15 .25
179 Flare of the Heavens R .60 1.00
180 Frostbridge Orb R .60 1.00
181 Frostweave Bandage U .30 .50
182 Glacial Bag R .60 1.00
183 Portal Stone R .60 1.00
184 Sigil of the Vengeful Heart R .60 1.00
185 Soul of the Dead R .60 1.00
186 Super Simian Sphere R .60 1.00
187 Titan-forged Rune R .60 1.00
188 Totem of Splintering R .60 1.00
189 Avalanche R .60 1.00
190 Black Ice U .30 .50
191 Chilly Slobberknocker R .60 1.00
192 Hailstorm R .60 1.00
193 Iceshrieker's Touch U .30 .50
194 Journey's End R .60 1.00
195 Kel'Thuzad's Reach E 1.00 1.50
196 Kingsbane R .60 1.00
197 Nesingwary 4000 U .30 .50
198 Spinning Fate R .60 1.00
199 Stormstrike Mace R .60 1.00
200 Stormtip R .60 1.00
201 Val'anyr, Hammer of Ancient E 1.50 2.50
202 Voldrethar, Dark Blade R .60 1.00
203 Proper String, A U .30 .50
204 Rituals of Power U .30 .50
205 Spirit Totem U .30 .50
206 Army of the Damned C .15 .25
207 All Things in Good Time U .30 .50
208 Tirion's Gambit U .30 .50
209 Boon of A'dal, The C .15 .25
210 Boon of Alexstrasza, The C .15 .25
211 Boon of Remulos, The C .15 .25
212 Cold Hearted C .15 .25
213 Everfrost C .15 .25
214 Hero's Burden, A C .15 .25
215 Last Line of Defense, The C .15 .25
216 Rider of Frost, The C .15 .25
217 Storm King's Vengeance, The C .15 .25
218 That's Abominable! C .15 .25
219 Orgrim's Hammer R .60 1.00
220 Skybreaker, The R .60 1.00

2010 World of Warcraft Icecrown Loot

1 Paint Bomb 1.50 2.50
2 Portal Stone 30.00 50.00
3 Wooly White Rhino 100.00 150.00

2010 World of Warcraft Wrathgate

COMPLETE SET (220) 50.00 100.00
BOOSTER BOX (24 PACKS) 50.00 100.00
BOOSTER PACK (19 CARDS) 3.00 5.00
RELEASED IN MAY 2010
1 Archmage Barstow U .30 .50
2 Durzion, Champion of A'dal U .30 .50
3 Earthmender Vaaki U .30 .50
4 Esonea U .30 .50
5 Gramm Thunderjaw U .30 .50
6 Krunkle Deadspark U .30 .50
7 Lunira Swiftbreath U .30 .50
8 Rinni Gloomtrik U .30 .50
9 Sarina the Immaculate U .30 .50
10 Tysandri Duskstrike U .30 .50
11 Crusader Farisa U .30 .50
12 Harona Proudmane U .30 .50
13 Jeremiah Karvok U .30 .50
14 Krog the Deathfist U .30 .50
15 Kungen the Thunderer U .30 .50
16 Mojo Master Zandum U .30 .50
17 Nuvon Dawnfury U .30 .50
18 Spiritwalker Kavi'je U .30 .50
19 Sunstalker Andora U .30 .50
20 Thaka Deadeye U .30 .50
21 Highlord Tirion Fordring E 5.00 8.00
22 Anti-Magic Shell U .30 .50
23 Blood Rune U .30 .50
24 Dark Command C .15 .25
25 Frost Fever C .15 .25
26 Hysteria R .60 1.00
27 Lesson of the Grave C .15 .25
28 Pestilence R .60 1.00
29 Surge of Blood C .15 .25
30 Blustering Winds C .15 .25
31 Dire Bear Form U .30 .50
32 Gift of the Earthmother R 1.50 2.50
33 Lesson of the Wild C .15 .25
34 Nature's Vengeance R .60 1.00
35 Scent of Nature C .15 .25
36 Stranglevine U .30 .50
37 Banzai U .30 .50
38 Explosive Shot R .60 1.00
39 Eyes of the Beast U .30 .50
40 Hail of Arrows R .60 1.00
41 Lesson of the Beast C .15 .25
42 Mongoose Bite C .15 .25
43 Mothra C .15 .25
44 Explosive Flames C .15 .25
45 Flash of Brilliance R .60 1.00
46 Frozen Solid U .30 .50
47 Ice Nova U .30 .50
48 Lesson of the Arcane C .15 .25
49 Netherwind Presence R .60 1.00
50 Scald C .15 .25
51 Charger R .60 1.00
52 Holy Fury C .15 .25
53 Lesson of the Divine C .15 .25
54 Presence of the Divine U .30 .50
55 Seal of Sanctity U .30 .50
56 Shelter C .15 .25
57 Unyielding Faith R .60 1.00
58 Dementia U .30 .50
59 Fright C .15 .25
60 Holy Guardian R .60 1.00
61 Lesson of the Light C .15 .25
62 Power Word: Faith C .15 .25
63 Sacred Circle U .30 .50
64 Spirit of Redemption R .60 1.00
66 Annihilate U .30 .50
66 Flesh Eating Poison U .30 .50
67 Lesson of the Shadow C .15 .25
68 Master Poisoner R .60 1.00
69 Pick Lock C .15 .25
70 Raze R .60 1.00
71 Weakening Poison U .30 .50
72 Ancestral Awakening R .60 1.00
73 Astral Recall R .60 1.00
74 Fusion Totem U .30 .50
75 Gushing Totem U .30 .50
76 Infusion of Earth C .15 .25
77 Lesson of the Elements C .15 .25
78 Surge of Life C .15 .25
79 Curse of Doom U .30 .50
80 Devastation R .60 1.00
81 Drain Essence C .15 .25
82 Dread Doomguard R .60 1.00
83 Lesson of the Nether C .15 .25
84 Lynxia U .30 .50
85 Void Pact C .15 .25
86 Expertise of Steel R .60 1.00
87 Flawless Defense U .30 .50
88 Impede U .30 .50
89 Lesson of the Call C .15 .25
90 Mortal Slash C .15 .25
91 Requite C .15 .25
92 Wrecking Crew R .60 1.00
93 Bestial Rage U .30 .50
94 Feast of Flame U .30 .50
95 Gift of the Pious U .30 .50
96 Hit and Run U .30 .50
97 Holy Barrier U .30 .50
98 Kick Thinking U .30 .50
99 Master's Stable U .30 .50
100 Nurturing Spirit U .30 .50
101 Strength of Battle U .30 .50
102 Landro's Gift U .30 .50
103 Tubs Klankbopple C .15 .25
104 Antyr C .15 .25
105 Arlen the Untamed U .30 .50
106 Armored Snowy Gryphon R .60 1.00
107 Ayluro Nightwind C .15 .25
108 Bantham, Jadefist Apprentice C .15 .25
109 Blazemistress Lindsey C .15 .25
110 Bolvar, Highlord E 1.00 1.50
111 Bronthea the Resolute U .30 .50
112 Burly Berta R 5.00 8.00
113 Devona Berkshire R .60 1.00
114 Grumdur Bladebane C .15 .25
115 High Commander Halford E 1.00 1.50
116 Hurdan the Everlasting U .30 .50
117 Ixiya the Attuned C .15 .25
118 Justicar Drathnea U .30 .50
119 Justicar Nimzi Banedrizzle U .30 .50
120 Justicar Ularu U .30 .50
121 Kaelyn Vineminder C .15 .25
122 Lady Bancroft C .15 .25
123 Lyshala Ravenshot C .15 .25
124 Mithran the Sniper C .15 .25
125 Nethermaven Donna Chastain C .15 .25
126 Nurgle Tinkfrost C .15 .25
127 Swift Mechanostrider R .60 1.00
128 Wyndarr Shadefist C .15 .25
129 Armored Blue Wind Rider R .60 1.00
130 Astani Dawngrace C .15 .25
131 Bluffstalker Honovi C .15 .25
132 Cedric Darwin C .15 .25
133 Conqueror Hashkon U .30 .50
134 Conqueror Vun'jin U .30 .50
135 Conqueror Zaala U .30 .50
136 Daralis the Sanctifier U .30 .50
137 Dhoros Ravestrike C .15 .25
138 Dorzok Shadowhand C .15 .25
139 Goru Thornmane C .15 .25
140 Hanthal Lightward C .15 .25
141 Katoka Dreadblade R .60 1.00
142 Murphy Watson C .15 .25
143 Muruna the Savage U .30 .50
144 Roanauk Icemist E 1.00 1.50
145 Roshen the Oathsworn U .30 .50
146 Saurfang the Younger E 6.00 10.00
147 Soram Wildbark C .15 .25
148 Sullivan Holmes C .15 .25
149 Sunguard Cersie C .15 .25
150 Swift Hawkstrider R .60 1.00
151 Swift Timber Wolf R .60 1.00
152 Tuskmender Jan'zu C .15 .25
153 Uruka the Cutthroat R 1.50 2.50
154 Vuz'din C .15 .25
155 Zugna, Windseer Apprentice C .15 .25
156 Blazing Hippogryph R .60 1.00
157 Brother Keltan U .30 .50
158 Commander Falstaav C .15 .25
159 Crusade Commander Entari R .60 1.00
160 Crusade Engineer Spitzpatrick C .15 .25
161 Crusader Lord Dalfors C .15 .25
162 Eitrigg E 1.00 1.50
163 Father Gustav C .15 .25
164 Sister Colleen Tulley C .15 .25
165 Veteran Crusader Aliocha Segard C .15 .25
166 Azjol-anak Champion R 1.50 2.50
167 Aurius E 1.00 1.50
168 Eris Havenfire E 1.00 1.50
169 Keeper Remulos E 1.00 1.50
170 Boots of the Renewed Flight U .30 .50
171 Cloak of the Shadowed Sun R .60 1.00
172 Gloves of Token Respect R .60 1.00
173 Helm of Vital Protection R .60 1.00
174 Hood of the Exodus R .60 1.00
175 Leggings of the Honored U .30 .50
176 Protective Barricade of the Light R .60 1.00
177 Sun-Emblazoned Chestplate R .60 1.00
178 Sympathy U .30 .50
179 Upstanding Spaulders R .60 1.00
180 Gigantique Bag R .60 1.00
181 Idol of the Shooting Star R .60 1.00
182 Libram of Radiance R .60 1.00
183 Life-Binder's Locket R .60 1.00
184 Platinium Disks of Swiftness R .60 1.00
185 Statue Generator R .60 1.00
186 Angry Dread C .15 .25
187 Colossal Skull-Clad Cleaver U .30 .50
188 Fading Glow C .15 .25
189 Final Voyage R .60 1.00
190 Fist of the Deity R .60 1.00
191 Haunting Call R .60 1.00
192 Life and Death R .60 1.00
193 Lifeblade of Belgaristrasz R .60 1.00
194 Nerubian Conqueror R .60 1.00
195 Silent Crusader R .60 1.00
196 Spire of Sunset R .60 1.00
197 Staff of Trickery C .15 .25
198 Sword of Justice R .60 1.00
199 Torch of Holy Fire R .60 1.00
200 Wraith Spear R .60 1.00
201 No Mere Dream U .30 .50

202 Paladin Training U .30 .50
203 The Ichor of Undeath U .30 .50
204 The Call of the Crusade C .15 .25
205 Apply This Twice Daily C .15 .25
206 Conversing With the Depths C .15 .25
207 Cycle of Life C .15 .25
208 I'm Not Dead Yet! R .60 1.00
209 Light Within the Darkness C .15 .25
210 No One to Save You C .15 .25
211 On Ruby Wings R .60 1.00
212 Planning for the Future C .15 .25
213 Really Big Worm C .15 .25
214 Return to Angrathar C .15 .25
215 Seeds of the Lashers C .15 .25
216 A Tale of Valor C .15 .25
217 Wanton Warlord C .15 .25
218 Fordragon Hold R .60 1.00
219 Kor'kron Vanguard R 1.50 2.50
220 Angrathar the Wrathgate E 1.00 1.50

2010 World of Warcraft Wrathgate Loot

1 Landro's Gift 12.00 20.00
2 Statue Generator 25.00 40.00
3 Blazing Hippogryph 150.00 250.00

2010 World of Warcraft Worldbreaker

COMPLETE SET (270) 50.00 100.00
BOOSTER BOX (24 PACKS) 40.00 80.00
BOOSTER PACK (19 CARDS) 3.00 4.00
RELEASED IN DECEMBER 2010
1 Amaria Kelsur U .30 .50
2 Arturius Hathrow U .30 .50
3 Bragvi Stormstein U .30 .50
4 Caleb Pavish U .30 .50
5 Haedis U .30 .50
6 Jaenel U .30 .50
7 Kadus Frosthand U .30 .50
8 Peter Hottelet U .30 .50
9 Tilly Fiddlelight U .30 .50
10 Victor Baltus U .30 .50
11 Ayaka Winterhoof U .30 .50
12 Grizlik Sparkhex U .30 .50
13 Jai Dawnsteel U .30 .50
14 Jumo'zin U .30 .50
15 Malaxia Wizwhirl U .30 .50
16 Rekwa Proudhorn U .30 .50
17 Suvok Frozeneye U .30 .50
18 Valerie Worfield U .30 .50
19 Vorix Zorbuzz U .30 .50
20 Yuna Sunridge U .30 .50
21 Alexstrasza the Life-Binder E 8.00 12.00
22 Ysera the Dreamer E 1.50 2.50
23 Black Blood C .15 .25
24 Blood Chill C .15 .25
25 Chains of Ice R .60 1.00
26 Dancing Rune Weapon R .60 1.00
27 Frenzy U .30 .50
28 Grip of the Damned C .15 .25
29 Path of Frost C .15 .25
30 Strangulate U .30 .50
31 Unholy Ground R .60 1.00
32 Withering Decay U .30 .50
33 Earth and Moon R .60 1.00
34 Entangling Growth C .15 .25
35 Faerie Fire U .30 .50
36 Flourish U .30 .50
37 Mark of the Untamed U .30 .50
38 Nature's Fury R .60 1.00
39 Reawakening R .60 1.00
40 Rejuvenation C .15 .25
41 Savage Bear Form C .15 .25
42 Wrath C .15 .25
43 Aspect of the Wild R .60 1.00
44 Blast Trap U .30 .50
45 Boomer R 2.00 3.00
46 Detect Prey U .30 .50
47 Flare C .15 .25
48 Steady Shot U .30 .50
49 Tesla C .15 .25
50 Track Dragonkin C .15 .25
51 Wing Clip C .15 .25
52 Wyvern Sting R .60 1.00
53 Enduring Winter R .60 1.00
54 Extinguish U .30 .50
55 Fire Blast C .15 .25
56 Frost Wave C .15 .25
57 Frostfire Bolt U .30 .50
58 Frozen Nerves C .15 .25
59 Mana Diamond R .60 1.00
60 Mana Shift R .60 1.00
61 Ripple U .30 .50
62 Unstable Infusion C .15 .25
63 Blessing of Defense C .15 .25
64 Blessing of the Kindred R .60 1.00
65 Blessing of Virtue U .30 .50
66 Censure C .15 .25
67 Divine Cleansing U .30 .50
68 Holy Light C .15 .25
69 Repentance R .60 1.00
70 Sacred Shield U .30 .50
71 Seal of Wrath R .60 1.00
72 Stasis C .15 .25
73 Dark Extortion R .60 1.00
74 Divine Fury R .60 1.00
75 Divine Hymn U .30 .50
76 Flash Heal C .15 .25
77 Oppress C .15 .25
78 Power Word: Preservation C .15 .25
79 Power Word: Shelter U .30 .50
80 Psychic Wail U .30 .50
81 Seeping Shadows R .60 1.00
82 Spiritual Harmony C .15 .25
83 Aggressive Exploitation C .15 .25
84 Bully C .15 .25
85 Contagious Poison R .60 1.00
86 Daze U .30 .50
87 Draining Poison U .30 .50
88 Excessive Force C .15 .25
89 Gouge C .15 .25
90 Incapacitate U .30 .50
91 Seal Fate R .60 1.00
92 Steal Steel R .60 1.00
93 Ancestral Purge C .15 .25
94 Breath of the Elements R .60 1.00
95 Earthen Blast U .30 .50
96 Earthen Embrace C .15 .25
97 Elemental Vision C .15 .25
98 Lightning Bolt C .15 .25
99 Nature Resistance Totem U .30 .50
100 Rolling Thunder R .60 1.00
101 Spiritual Return R .60 1.00
102 Thunderstrike Weapon U .30 .50
103 Demonic Reclamation U .30 .50
104 Demonic Soulstone C .15 .25
105 Fear C .15 .25
106 Fel Blaze U .30 .50
107 Jhuunash R .60 1.00
108 Muddle U .30 .50
109 Nether Inversion C .15 .25
110 Sardok C .15 .25
111 Searing Pain R .60 1.00
112 Summoning Portal R .60 1.00
113 Chaotic Rush U .30 .50
114 Crushing Strike C .15 .25
115 Defender's Vigil C .15 .25
116 Execute C .15 .25
117 Heroic Impulse C .15 .25
118 Juggernaut R .60 1.00
119 Onslaught R .60 1.00
120 Raging Shout U .30 .50
121 Stance Mastery R .60 1.00
122 Thunderous Challenge U .30 .50
123 Avatar of the Wild E 6.00 10.00
124 Vigil of the Light E 1.50 2.50
125 Viciousness U .30 .50
126 Rocket Barrage U .30 .50
127 Adrienne the Inspiring U .30 .50
128 Aileen the Thunderblessed R .60 1.00
129 Alador Stonebrew C .15 .25
130 Alister Cooper C .15 .25
131 Andrew Ulric C .15 .25
132 Aresha Thorncaller U .30 .50
133 Arisa Sarum U .30 .50
134 Bayner Cogbertson C .15 .25
135 Bella Wilder C .15 .25
136 Fenton Guardmont C .15 .25
137 Furan Rookbane C .15 .25
138 Garet Vice C .15 .25
139 Gerana Sparkfist C .15 .25
140 Hira C .15 .25
141 Jarrod Gravon U .30 .50
142 Jinie Swizzleshade C .15 .25
143 Kalek Deepearth C .15 .25
144 Kentro Slade R .60 1.00
145 King Genn Greymane E 1.50 2.50
146 Kirjen Fizzgar C .15 .25
147 Koeus C .15 .25
148 Laenthor Shademoon C .15 .25
149 Loriam Argos C .15 .25
150 Magni, the Mountain King E 2.00 3.00
151 Marcus Dominar C .15 .25
152 Marius Jator U .30 .50
153 Nami Dabpox C .15 .25
154 Nightstalker Austen C .15 .25
155 Pixia Darkmist C .15 .25
156 Pyromancer Davins R .60 1.00
157 Rolan Phoenix R 1.00 1.50
158 Savis Cindur C .15 .25
159 Shanis Bladefall C .15 .25
160 Terina Calin C .15 .25
161 Varandas Silverleaf U .30 .50
162 Watchman Visi C .15 .25
163 Wazix Blonktop C .15 .25
164 Zuur C .15 .25
165 Boki Earthgaze C .15 .25
166 Cadon Thundershade C .15 .25
167 Cairne, Earthmother's E 8.00 12.00
168 Ceraka U .30 .50
169 Dorladris Spellfire C .15 .25
170 Drizzie Steelslam C .15 .25
171 Exxi the Windshaper R .60 1.00
172 Frek Snipelix U .30 .50
173 Gispax the Mixologist R .60 1.00
174 Gorz Blazefist C .15 .25
175 Grazzle Grubhook C .15 .25
176 Guardian Steelhoof C .15 .25
177 Huruk Lightvow C .15 .25
178 Jezziki Shinebog C .15 .25
179 Kerzok Plixboom U .30 .50
180 Kistix Shockvat C .15 .25
181 Kloxx Dedrix C .15 .25
182 Landon Dunavin C .15 .25
183 Mahna Lightsky U .30 .50
184 Neboz Tombwex U .30 .50
185 Onnekra Bloodfang C .15 .25
186 Orkahn of Orgrimmar U .30 .50
187 Oruk Starstorm C .15 .25
188 Rosalyne von Erantor U .30 .50
189 Ruon Wildhoof C .15 .25
190 Sava'gin the Reckless R .60 1.00
191 Sura Lightningheart C .15 .25
192 Telor Sunsurge C .15 .25
193 Thrandis the Venomous R .60 1.00
194 Toz'jun C .15 .25
195 Trade Prince Gallywix E 1.50 2.50
196 Traxel Emberklik C .15 .25
197 Vala Carville C .15 .25
198 Veline Bladestar C .15 .25
199 Zakis Trickstab C .15 .25
200 Zerzu C .15 .25
201 Zulanji C .15 .25
202 Zulbraka C .15 .25
203 Emerald Acidspewer C .15 .25
204 Emerald Captain C .15 .25
205 Emerald Emissary U .30 .50
206 Emerald Lifewarden U .30 .50
207 Emerald Soldier C .15 .25
208 Emerald Tree Warder C .15 .25
209 Emerald Wanderer C .15 .25
210 Eranikus R .60 1.00
211 Korialstrasz R .60 1.00
212 Ruby Blazewing U .30 .50
213 Ruby Emissary U .30 .50
214 Ruby Enforcer C .15 .25
215 Ruby Flameblade C .15 .25
216 Ruby Protector C .15 .25
217 Ruby Skyrazor C .15 .25
218 Ruby Stalker C .15 .25
219 Mottled Drake E 1.25 2.00
220 Landro's Lil' XT U .30 .50
221 Etched Dragonbone Girdle U .30 .50
222 Polished Breastplate of Valor R .60 1.00
223 Prized Beastmaster's Mantle R .60 1.00
224 Robe of the Waking Nightmare U .30 .50
225 Skinned Whelp Shoulders U .30 .50
226 Stained Shadowcraft Tunic R .60 1.00
227 Tattered Dreadmist Mantle R .60 1.00
228 Wyrmwing Treads U .30 .50
229 Discerning Eye of the Beast U .30 .50
230 Dread Pirate Ring U .30 .50
231 Grim Campfire R .60 1.00
232 Swift Hand of Justice U .30 .50
233 Abomination Knuckles C .15 .25
234 Abracadaver R .60 1.00
235 Balanced Heartseeker R .60 1.00
236 Bloodied Arcanite Reaper R .60 1.00
237 Charmed Ancient Bone Bow R .60 1.00
238 Citadel Enforcer's Claymore C .15 .25
239 Devout Aurastone Hammer R .60 1.00
240 Dignified Headmaster's Charge R .60 1.00
241 Gutbuster R .60 1.00
242 Hersir's Greatspear U .30 .50
243 Lockjaw U .30 .50
244 Ramaladni's Blade of Culling R .60 1.00
245 Repurposed Lava Dredger R .60 1.00
246 Stakethrower U .30 .50
247 Troggbane, Axe King E 1.00 1.50
248 Venerable Mass of McGowan R .60 1.00
249 Wand of Ruby Claret C .15 .25
250 Warmace of Menethil R .60 1.00
251 Leader of the Pack R .60 1.00
252 Warchief's Revenge R .60 1.00
253 Challenge to the Black Flight C .15 .25
254 Cleansing Witch Hill C .15 .25
255 Corrosion Prevention C .15 .25
256 Counting Out Time C .15 .25
257 Crystals of Power C .15 .25
258 Essence of Enmity, The C .15 .25
259 Finding the Source C .15 .25
260 Grimtotem Weapon, The C .15 .25
261 Key to Freedom, The C .15 .25
262 Locked Away C .15 .25
263 Matter of Time, A C .15 .25
264 Mighty U'cha, The C .15 .25
265 Mystery Goo C .15 .25
266 Torch of Retribution, The C .15 .25
267 What's Haunting Witch Hill? C .15 .25
268 Witch's Bane, The C .15 .25
269 Gilneas R .60 1.00
270 Lost Isles R .60 1.00

2010 World of Warcraft Worldbreaker Loot

1 Landro's Lil' XT 8.00 12.00
2 Grim Campfire 25.00 40.00
3 Mottled Drake 125.00 200.00

2011 World of Warcraft Throne of the Tides

COMPLETE SET (263) 80.00 120.00
BOOSTER BOX (36 PACKS) 50.00 100.00
BOOSTER PACK (16 CARDS) 3.00 4.00
RELEASED IN OCTOBER 2011
1 Anaka the Light's Bulwark U .30 .50
2 Barathex, Undeath's Hand U .30 .50
3 High Magus Olvek U .30 .50
4 Janvaru the Thunderspeaker U .30 .50
5 Master Sniper Simon McKey U .30 .50
6 Sana the Black Blade U .30 .50
7 Skodis the Nethertwister C .15 .25
8 Steelguard Adamson U .30 .50
9 Tinker Priest Cassie U .30 .50
10 Wildseer Varel U .30 .50
11 Drazul the Molten U .30 .50
12 Fama'sin the Lifeseer U .30 .50
13 Gaxtro, Bilgewater Marksman U .30 .50
14 Ghoulmaster Kalisa U .30 .50
15 High Priestess Neeri U .30 .50
16 Jak the Bilgewater Bruiser U .30 .50
17 Joleera U .30 .50
18 Rohashu, Zealot of the Sun U .30 .50
19 Samaku, Hand of the Tempest U .30 .50
20 Voidbringer Jindal'an U .30 .50
21 Deathbringer Kor'ush C .15 .25
22 Grglmrgl U .30 .50
23 Lady Sira'kess U .30 .50
24 Rawrbrgle U .30 .50
25 Neptulon E 1.50 2.50
26 Brittle Bones R .60 1.00
27 Claws of the Dead U .30 .50
28 Death's Duo R 1.00 1.50
29 Infestation U .30 .50
30 Monstrous Essence R .60 1.00
31 Plagued Mind U .30 .50
32 Skullchewer U .30 .50
33 Boundless Wild R 1.25 2.00
34 Fungal Growth R 1.00 1.50
35 Mark of Goldrinn C .15 .25
36 Stalwart Bear Form U .30 .50
37 Verdant Boon U .30 .50
38 Wild Roots U .30 .50
39 Bestial Revival R .60 1.00
40 Chompers U .30 .50
41 Clamps C .15 .25
42 Concussive Barrage R 1.50 2.50
43 Monstrous Mark R .60 1.00
44 Roar of the Beast U .30 .50
45 Track Enemy U .30 .50
46 Char R 1.00 1.50
47 Focus Magic R 1.25 2.00
48 Glacial Tomb C .15 .25
49 Molten Scorch U .30 .50
50 Monstrous Frostbolt Volley R .60 1.00
51 Touch of Brilliance U .30 .50
52 Vortex U .30 .50

53 Blessing of the Light C .15 .25
54 Blessing of the Righteous U .30 .50
55 Boundless Might R 1.00 1.50
56 Grand Crusader R 3.00 5.00
57 Hammer of the Zealot U .30 .50
58 Righteous Cleanse U .30 .50
59 Boundless Shadows R .60 1.00
60 Chakra R 1.25 2.00
61 Power Word: Purity C .15 .25
62 Power Word: Vitality U .30 .50
63 Psychic Screech U .30 .50
64 Tendrils of Darkness U .30 .50
65 Disorienting Blow U .30 .50
66 Distraction Technique U .30 .50
67 Poison Bomb R 1.00 1.50
68 Sleeping Poison R 1.00 1.50
69 Vendetta R 1.00 1.50
70 Boundless Life R .60 1.00
71 Earthen Might C .15 .25
72 Lava Shock U .30 .50
73 Shock of the Elements C .15 .25
74 Spark of Life R .60 1.00
75 Windguard Totem U .30 .50
76 Fel Summon U .30 .50
77 Grimnar U .30 .50
78 Hellisa C .15 .25
79 Nether Balance R 1.00 1.50
80 Soul Cleave U .30 .50
81 Soul Swap R 1.25 2.00
82 Armsman U .30 .50
83 Augment Steel R .60 1.00
84 Bloodsurge R 1.00 1.50
85 Furious Strike U .30 .50
86 Monstrous Cleave U .30 .50
87 Rallying Swarm R 1.00 1.50
88 Monstrous Strike C .15 .25
89 Monstrous Upheaval C .15 .25
90 RwlRwlRwlRwl! U .30 .50
91 Unleash the Swarm! U .30 .50
92 Face of Fear C .15 .25
93 Rallying Cry of the Dragonslayer C .15 .25
94 Strength of Will C .15 .25
95 Surge of Power R 1.25 2.00
96 Arcanomage Misti R 1.25 2.00
97 Ardon Almastor C .15 .25
98 Balrak Stoutstone C .15 .25
99 Braeo Darkpaw C .15 .25
100 Burdok Brewshot C .15 .25
101 Corin Stallnorth C .15 .25
102 Dastrin Bowman C .15 .25
103 Davius, Herald of Nature U .30 .50
104 Dradam Chillblade C .15 .25
105 Dulvar, Hand of the Light E 1.00 1.50
106 Evaax, Herald of Death U .30 .50
107 Faenis the Tranquil R .60 1.00
108 Faithseer Jasmina R .60 1.00
109 Fumdol Mountainfrost C .15 .25
110 Funken Fusemissile C .15 .25
111 Grumdak, Herald of the Hunt U .30 .50
112 Hadrack the Devoted R 1.00 1.50
113 Hunrik Blackiron C .15 .25
114 Jaerna, Herald of the Light R 1.00 1.50
115 Kaelon, Herald of the Flame U .30 .50
116 Kara Vesstal C .15 .25
117 Kieron the Loaner R 1.00 1.50
118 Laetho Moonbranch C .15 .25
119 Larrisa Valorshield C .15 .25
120 Lodur, Herald of the Elements U .30 .50
121 Malar Silverfrost U .30 .50
122 Maloc, Herald of Trickery C .15 .25
123 Mekkatorque, King E 1.25 2.00
124 Militia Commander Balor R 1.00 1.50
125 Sebastian Malak C .15 .25
126 Shanla, Herald of Faith C .15 .25
127 Shaylith Swiftblade U .30 .50
128 Tallie Sprinklelight C .15 .25
129 Trista, Herald of the Fel U .30 .50
130 Vaakia C .15 .25
131 Valak the Vortex R .60 1.00
132 Vandos, Herald of War U .30 .50
133 Vindicator Saaris R 1.00 1.50
134 Wuzlo Grindergear C .15 .25
135 Xuurvis C .15 .25
136 Zintix the Frostbringer R 1.25 2.00
137 Akasi, Herald of Nature U .30 .50
138 Alana the Woebringer R .60 1.00
139 Alethia Brightsong C .15 .25
140 Amano, Herald of the Sun U .30 .50
141 Anastina, Herald of the Fel U .30 .50
142 Asoren Darksnout C .15 .25
143 Baxtan, Herald of the Flame U .30 .50
144 Daroka Venomfist C .15 .25
145 Déatheater Stroud U .30 .50
146 Draga'zal C .15 .25
147 Eralysa Sunshot C .15 .25
148 Hagtrix the Mindsifter R 1.00 1.50
149 Hesawa Stormwalker C .15 .25
150 Izzy Quizfiz C .15 .25
151 Jagrok, Herald of Trickery U .30 .50
152 Jaron, Herald of the Hunt U .30 .50
153 Jex'ali C .15 .25
154 Jumahko Thundersky C .15 .25
155 Kalam'ti R .60 1.00
156 Kazbaz C .15 .25
157 Kelena Ashford C .15 .25
158 Kinza, Mistress R 1.25 2.00
159 Krezza the Explosive R 1.00 1.50
160 Kromdar, Herald of War U .30 .50
161 Lordann the Bloodreaver R 1.25 2.00
162 Mazu'kon E 5.00 8.00
163 Moro Wildmesa C .15 .25
164 Nazuk Darkblood C .15 .25
165 Parexia, Herald of the Shadows U .30 .50
166 Prazo Whiptrick C .15 .25
167 Runzik Shrapnelwhiz C .15 .25
168 Samantha Galvington C .15 .25
169 Shala'zum R 1.00 1.50
170 Treespeaker Onaha R 1.25 2.00
171 Vol'jin, Darkspear Chieftain E 1.00 1.50
172 Vuza'jin C .15 .25
173 Yana'mi C .15 .25
174 Zarixx, Herald of Death U .30 .50
175 Zizzlix Drizzledrill C .15 .25
176 Zudzo, Herald of the Elements U .30 .50
177 Gilblin Bully C .15 .25
178 Gilblin Deathscrounger R .60 1.00
179 Gilblin Hoarder U .30 .50
180 Gilblin Plunderer U .30 .50
181 Gilblin Trickster U .30 .50
182 Bobbler U .30 .50
183 Brighteye C .15 .25
184 Bubblegil U .30 .50
185 Chumly U .30 .50
186 Crabbyfin U .30 .50
187 Gobbler R .60 1.00
188 Murloc Coastrunner C .15 .25
189 Nibbler C .15 .25
190 Slippyfist R 1.00 1.50
191 Snurky C .15 .25
192 Swarmtooth U .30 .50
193 Buldrug C .15 .25
194 Drugush the Crusher C .15 .25
195 Neph'lahim R 1.00 1.50
196 Tar'gak the Felcrazed U .30 .50
197 Thrug the Hurler U .30 .50
198 Zor'chal the Shadowseer U .30 .50
199 Commander Ulthok E 5.00 8.00
200 Faceless Sapper C .15 .25
201 Faceless Watcher R .60 1.00
202 Deep Subjugator U .30 .50
203 Mindbender Ghur'sha R .60 1.00
204 Idra'kess Enchantress U .30 .50
205 Idra'kess Mistress U .30 .50
206 Lady Naz'jar E 1.00 1.50
207 Naz'jar Harpooner C .15 .25
208 Naz'jar Myrmidon C .15 .25
209 Naz'jar Sorceress C .15 .25
210 Sira'kess Tide Priestess U .30 .50
211 Abyssal Seahorse R 1.00 1.50
212 Gnash R 1.25 2.00
213 Kolorath E 1.00 1.50
214 Nespirah R 1.00 1.50
215 Ozumat E 1.50 2.50
216 Revenant of Neptulon U .30 .50
217 Servant of Neptulon U .30 .50
218 Unstable Corruption R .60 1.00
219 Wasteland Tallstrider E 1.00 1.50
220 Bloat the Bubble Fish U .30 .50
221 Erunak Stonespeaker R .60 1.00
222 Toshe Chaosrender R 1.25 2.00
223 Periwinkle Cloak U .30 .50
224 Shroud of Cooperation U .30 .50
225 Triton Legplates R 1.25 2.00
226 Wentletrap Vest C .15 .25
227 Big Cauldron of Battle R 1.00 1.50
228 Blessing of the Old God C .15 .25
229 Bottled Cunning C .15 .25
230 Bottled Death C .15 .25
231 Bottled Elements C .15 .25
232 Bottled Knowledge C .15 .25
233 Bottled Life C .15 .25
234 Bottled Light C .15 .25
235 Bottled Mind C .15 .25
236 Bottled Rage C .15 .25
237 Bottled Spite C .15 .25
238 Bottled Void C .15 .25
239 Bottled Wild C .15 .25
240 Nautilus Ring U .30 .50
241 Ring of the Great Whale U .30 .50
242 Severed Visionary Tentacle U .30 .50
243 Throwing Starfish R 1.25 2.00
244 Breathstone-Infused Longbow U .30 .50
245 Cerith Spire Staff R 1.25 2.00
246 Dawnblaze Blade U .30 .50
247 Dirk's Command C .15 .25
248 Downfall Hammer U .30 .50
249 Eel Cutter C .15 .25
250 Lightning Whelk Axe C .15 .25
251 Potentate's Letter Opener U .30 .50
252 Sorrow's End R .60 1.00
253 Throat Slasher C .15 .25
254 The Culmination of Our Efforts C .15 .25
255 The Last Living Lorekeeper C .15 .25
256 Reoccupation U .30 .50
257 Rescue the Earthspeaker! C .15 .25
258 Seeds of Their Demise C .15 .25
259 Setting an Example C .15 .25
260 Wake of Destruction U .30 .50
261 Waking the Beast C .15 .25
262 Waters of Elune C .15 .25
263 Throne of the Tides R 1.00 1.50

2011 World of Warcraft Throne of the Tides Loot

1 Bloat the Bubble Fish 6.00 10.00
2 Throwing Starfish 8.00 12.00
3 Wasteland Tallstrider 60.00 100.00

2011 World of Warcraft Twilight of the Dragons

COMPLETE SET (220) 100.00 150.00
BOOSTER BOX (24 PACKS) 40.00 80.00
BOOSTER PACK (19 CARDS) 3.00 4.00
RELEASED IN JULY 2011
1 Auralyn the Light of Dawn U .30 .50
2 Bladesinger Alyssa U .30 .50
3 Deragor the Earthsworn U .30 .50
4 Jasmia, Nature's Chosen U .30 .50
5 Kavar the Bloodthirsty U .30 .50
6 Nomak the Blazingclaw U .30 .50
7 Soul-Eater Morgania U .30 .50
8 Trilik the Light's Spark U .30 .50
9 Vad of the Four Winds U .30 .50
10 Zane the Sniper U .30 .50
11 Amah the Sun's Grace U .30 .50
12 Amaxi the Cruel U .30 .50
13 Dar'thael the Bloodsworn U .30 .50
14 Dragonslayer Drux U .30 .50
15 Earthseer Nakza U .30 .50
16 Flame Keeper Rizzli U .30 .50
17 Samael the Bloodpoint U .30 .50
18 Sumi'jin, Guardian of Cenarius U .30 .50
19 Suncaller Haruh U .30 .50
20 Zazel the Greedy U .30 .50
21 Deathwing the Destroyer E 15.00 25.00
22 Black Death U .30 .50
23 Dark Simulacrum R .60 1.00
24 Favor of Undeath C .15 .25
25 Frozen Core C .15 .25
26 Glacial Strike C .15 .25
27 Hungering Cold R 1.00 1.50
28 Necrotic Strike U .30 .50
29 Twisted Death Pact U .30 .50
30 Favor of Nature C .15 .25
31 Fierce Cat Form U .30 .50
32 Living Roots C .15 .25
33 Rebirth U .30 .50
34 Tears of Aessina C .15 .25
35 Twisted Wrath U .30 .50
36 Wild Growth R .60 1.00
37 Wild Mushroom R .60 1.00
38 Camouflage R .60 1.00
39 Cinder C .15 .25
40 Disengage C .15 .25
41 Explosive Hunt U .30 .50
42 Favor of the Hunt C .15 .25
43 Immolation Trap U .30 .50
44 Master Marksman R 1.00 1.50
45 Nag the Twisted U .30 .50
46 Blazing Debris C .15 .25
47 Favor of the Arcane C .15 .25
48 Fireball U .30 .50
49 Flame Orb R 1.00 1.50
50 Glaciate C .15 .25
51 Pyromaniac R 1.25 2.00
52 Ring of Frost U .30 .50
53 Twisted Arcana U .30 .50
54 Beacon of Light R 1.50 2.50
55 Blessing of Might U .30 .50
56 Favor of the Light C .15 .25
57 Guardian of Ancient Kings R 3.00 5.00
58 Hammer of Retribution C .15 .25
59 Hand of Protection C .15 .25
60 Twisted Light U .30 .50
61 Word of Glory U .30 .50
62 Favor of Spirit C .15 .25
63 Heal U .30 .50
64 Holy Blaze U .30 .50
65 Inner Will R .60 1.00
66 Power Word: Absorb C .15 .25
67 Power Word: Barrier R 1.25 2.00
68 Psychic Melt C .15 .25
69 Twisted Mind Spike U .30 .50
70 Break Steel C .15 .25
71 Favor of Mischief C .15 .25
72 Mind-Numbing Poison U .30 .50
73 Revealing Strike R 1.50 2.50
74 Smoke Bomb R 1.25 2.00
75 Swindle U .30 .50
76 Twisted Massacre U .30 .50
77 Vicious Strike C .15 .25
78 Burning Winds R .60 1.00
79 Cleanse Spirit C .15 .25
80 Favor of the Elements C .15 .25
81 Flametongue Weapon U .30 .50
82 Inferno Totem U .30 .50
83 Primal Strike C .15 .25
84 Riptide R 1.50 2.50
85 Twisted Fire Nova U .30 .50
86 Chaos Bolt R 2.50 4.00
87 Demonic Corruption R 4.00 6.00
88 Favor of the Nether C .15 .25
89 Fel Immolation C .15 .25
90 Incinerate U .30 .50
91 Selora C .15 .25
92 Twisted Infernal U .30 .50
93 Void Rip U .30 .50
94 Colossus Smash R .60 1.00
95 Demoralizing Strike C .15 .25
96 Executioner's Mark C .15 .25
97 Favor of Steel C .15 .25
98 Heroic Leap U .30 .50
99 Shockwave R 1.00 1.50
100 Slam U .30 .50
101 Twisted Rampage U .30 .50
102 Frozen Frenzy E 3.00 5.00
103 Council of Three Hammers E 4.00 6.00
104 Fool's Gold R 1.00 1.50
105 Abbie Whizzleblade C .15 .25
106 Alrak Stonecrack C .15 .25
107 Brel Blazebeard C .15 .25
108 Chandra Marlight C .15 .25
109 Frizzle Stumbleshade C .15 .25
110 Gardos Gravefang U .30 .50
111 Haratha Hammerflame C .15 .25
112 Javeer C .15 .25
113 Jerrak Krandle U .30 .50
114 Jessa the Lifebound U .30 .50
115 Kalan Howland C .15 .25
116 Kelsa Wildfire C .15 .25
117 Knight Karia C .15 .25
118 Lord Darius Crowley U .30 .50
119 Lyrana of Eldre'Thalas R .60 1.00
120 Maurice Steelson U .30 .50
121 Prince Anduin Wrynn E 4.00 6.00
122 Roger Ulric C .15 .25
123 Stacia Markton U .30 .50
124 Stargazer Ronal C .15 .25
125 Tania Falan U .30 .50
126 Vakus the Inferno R 10.00 15.00
127 Windspeaker Nuvu C .15 .25
128 Abysswalker Rakax U .30 .50
129 Azami'tal the Flamebender R 1.00 1.50
130 Azizi Daggerflick C .15 .25
131 Banok Sunrock C .15 .25
132 Blood Knight Adrenna U .30 .50
133 Commander Molotov R .60 1.00
134 Dagax the Butcher R 8.00 12.00
135 Falixia Frizzleblast C .15 .25
136 Flamebringer Gaxix U .30 .50

137 Gavin Haverston C	.15	.25
138 Gerwixicks C	.15	.25
139 Gollom Skybang C	.15	.25
140 Gordash Firetooth C	.15	.25
141 High Chieftain Baine E	3.00	5.00
142 High Guard Braxx C	.15	.25
143 Jaga'zul the Wild's Fury R	1.25	2.00
144 Kraxos Chizzlecoin U	.30	.50
145 Kyroth Steelspite C	.15	.25
146 Rakala Deathsmash C	.15	.25
147 Sahama Brighthorn C	.15	.25
148 Shade Emissary Vaxxod U	.30	.50
149 Warchief Garrosh E	6.00	10.00
150 Wildweaver Masa'zun C	.15	.25
151 Yazli Earthspark C	.15	.25
152 Zor'dul Deathbinder C	.15	.25
153 Nefarian U	.30	.50
154 Obsidia R	.60	1.00
155 Obsidian Drakonid C	.15	.25
156 Obsidian Drudge C	.15	.25
157 Obsidian Enforcer C	.15	.25
158 Obsidian Pyrewing C	.15	.25
159 Obsidian Skyterror C	.15	.25
160 Sinestra R	3.00	5.00
161 Twilight Corruptor U	.30	.50
162 Twilight Drake U	.30	.50
163 Twilight Emissary U	.30	.50
164 Twilight Shadowdrake U	.30	.50
165 Twilight Wyrmkiller U	.30	.50
166 Caelestrasz R	2.50	4.00
167 Merithra R	.60	1.00
168 Arygos R	1.50	2.50
169 Anachronos R	.60	1.00
170 Ignacious R	.60	1.00
171 Feludius R	.60	1.00
172 Arion R	1.00	1.50
173 Terrastra R	.60	1.00
174 Cho'gall E	2.50	4.00
175 Amani Dragonhawk E	4.00	6.00
176 Nightsaber Cub U	.30	.50
177 Thrall, Guardian E	5.00	8.00
178 Battleplate of the Apocalypse U	.30	.50
179 Double Attack Handguards U	.30	.50
180 Flame Pillar Leggings C	.15	.25
181 Polished Helm of Valor R	1.00	1.50
182 Proto-Handler's Gauntlets C	.15	.25
183 Stained Shadowcraft Cap R	1.25	2.00
184 Tarnished Raging Helm R	1.00	1.50
185 Tattered Dreadmist Mask R	1.00	1.50
186 Corrupted Egg Shell U	.30	.50
187 Darkmoon Card: Hurricane R	1.25	2.00
188 Akirus the Worm-Breaker R	3.00	5.00
189 Axe of the Eclipse U	.30	.50
190 Blade of the Burning Sun R	.60	1.00
191 Blade of the Witching Hour C	.15	.25
192 Chelley's Staff of Mending R	1.25	2.00
193 Claws of Torment C	.15	.25
194 Cookie's Stirring Rod R	.60	1.00
195 Crul'korak, the Lightning R	4.00	6.00
196 Darklight Torch U	.30	.50
197 Dragonheart Piercer U	.30	.50
198 Elementium Poleaxe U	.30	.50
199 Lava Spine U	.30	.50
200 Obsidium Executioner C	.15	.25
201 Organic Lifeform Inverter U	.30	.50
202 Shalug'doom, the Axe E	5.00	8.00
203 Twilight's Hammer R	2.50	4.00
204 Volatile Thunderstick U	.30	.50
205 Battle of Life and Death C	.15	.25
206 Blackout U	.30	.50
207 The Crucible of Carnage: The Twilight Terror C	.15	.25
208 Devoured C	.15	.25
209 Enter the Dragon Queen C	.15	.25
210 Far from the Nest C	.15	.25
211 Fire the Cannon C	.15	.25
212 A Fiery Reunion C	.15	.25
213 Last of Her Kind C	.15	.25
214 The Maw of Iso'rath C	.15	.25
215 Mercy for the Bound C	.15	.25
216 Mr. Goldmine's Wild Ride C	.15	.25
217 Twilight Extermination C	.15	.25
218 Unbinding C	.15	.25
219 The Worldbreaker R	1.25	2.00
220 Twilight Citadel R	25.00	40.00

2011 World of Warcraft Twilight of the Dragons Loot

1 Nightsaber Cub	10.00	15.00
2 Fool's Gold	15.00	25.00
3 Amani Dragonhawk	125.00	200.00

2011 World of Warcraft War of the Elements

COMPLETE SET (220)	100.00	150.00
BOOSTER BOX (24 PACKS)	40.00	80.00
BOOSTER PACK (19 CARDS)	3.00	4.00
RELEASED IN APRIL 2011		
1 Almia Moonwhisper U	.30	.50
2 Aric Stonejack U	.30	.50
3 Edwin Blademark U	.30	.50
4 Grayson Steelworth U	.30	.50
5 Gundek Hammerguard U	.30	.50
6 Huntsman Gorwal U	.30	.50
7 Merissa Firebrew U	.30	.50
8 Olivia Demascas U	.30	.50
9 Thira Anvilash U	.30	.50
10 Vanira Raventhorne U	.30	.50
11 Baxxel Geartooth U	.30	.50
12 Fraznak the Furious U	.30	.50
13 Jinxy Blastwheel U	.30	.50
14 Kanga the Primal U	.30	.50
15 Mindtwister Quimtrix U	.30	.50
16 Sunwalker Nahano U	.30	.50
17 Tazrik Crankrust U	.30	.50
18 Uzak'zim U	.30	.50
19 Zimzi the Trickster U	.30	.50
20 Zin'sul U	.30	.50
21 Kalecgos E	10.00	15.00
22 Nozdormu the Timeless E	6.00	10.00
23 Blight Bringers C	.15	.25
24 Command of Undeath C	.15	.25
25 Death Strike U	.30	.50
26 Frozen Blight U	.30	.50
27 Gargoyle R	10.00	15.00
28 Horn of Winter C	.15	.25
29 Outbreak R	.60	1.00
30 Sanguine Presence R	.60	1.00
31 Brutal Bear Form U	.30	.50
32 Celestial Moonfire R	2.50	4.00
33 Healing Touch U	.30	.50
34 Maim C	.15	.25
35 Moonshard C	.15	.25
36 Rend and Tear R	1.25	2.00
37 Savage Cat Form C	.15	.25
38 Starburst R	3.00	5.00
39 Arcane Shot C	.15	.25
40 Cobra Shot R	1.25	2.00
41 Donatello C	.15	.25
42 Loque R	3.00	5.00
43 Noxious Trap R	1.25	2.00
44 Warning Shot C	.15	.25
45 Widow Venom U	.30	.50
46 Wild Fervor U	.30	.50
47 Arcane Barrage R	6.00	10.00
48 Arcane Foresight C	.15	.25
49 Arcane Inferno R	.60	1.00
50 Arcane Missiles C	.15	.25
51 Draconic Flames U	.30	.50
52 Flash Freeze C	.15	.25
53 Mystical Refreshment R	.60	1.00
54 Tidal Elemental U	.30	.50
55 Blessing of Faith U	.30	.50
56 Flash of Light C	.15	.25
57 Holy Vengeance R	.60	1.00
58 Holy Wrath R	.60	1.00
59 Inquisition C	.15	.25
60 Light of Reckoning C	.15	.25
61 Shield of the Righteous R	.60	1.00
62 Vengeful Crusader Strike U	.30	.50
63 Dark Embrace R	.60	1.00
64 Expel C	.15	.25
65 Focused Dispel C	.15	.25
66 Hymn of Hope U	.30	.50
67 Leap of Faith R	5.00	8.00
68 Mind Melt R	2.50	4.00
69 Power Word: Endurance U	.30	.50
70 Shadow Word: Death C	.15	.25
71 Agonizing Poison U	.30	.50
72 Coated Blades R	.60	1.00
73 Infiltrate C	.15	.25
74 Invigorate U	.30	.50
75 Sap C	.15	.25
76 Shadow Dance R	3.00	5.00
77 Tormenting Gouge C	.15	.25
78 Tricksters Gambit R	3.00	5.00
79 Ancestral Recovery C	.15	.25
80 Blazing Elemental Totem U	.30	.50
81 Chain Heal C	.15	.25
82 Elemental Flames C	.15	.25
83 Primal Dexterity U	.30	.50
84 Tempest Totem R	1.50	2.50
85 Totemic Vigor R	.60	1.00
86 Unleash Elements R	3.00	5.00
87 Dread Touch C	.15	.25
88 Everlasting Affliction R	2.50	4.00
89 Fel Covenant C	.15	.25
90 Fel Flame R	2.50	4.00
91 Grimdron U	.30	.50
92 Grim Harvest R	.60	1.00
93 Maazhum C	.15	.25
94 Seed of Corruption U	.30	.50
95 Burning Rage R	.60	1.00
96 Dauntless Defender C	.15	.25
97 Enraged Regeneration R	.60	1.00
98 Intercept C	.15	.25
99 Merciless Strikes U	.30	.50
100 Peerless Guard C	.15	.25
101 Shattering Throw U	.30	.50
102 Intensify E	5.00	8.00
103 To Arms! E	6.00	10.00
104 Firelord's Gift, The U	.30	.50
105 Stonemother's Gift, The U	.30	.50
106 Tidehunter's Gift, The U	.30	.50
107 Windlord's Gift, The U	.30	.50
108 Arvos Jadestone C	.15	.25
109 Axar C	.15	.25
110 Brimi Tinkerblade C	.15	.25
111 Cadric Talworth C	.15	.25
112 Dagin Bootzap C	.15	.25
113 Dominic Kandor C	.15	.25
114 Elmira Moonsurge R	.60	1.00
115 Erama C	.15	.25
116 Gully Rustinax C	.15	.25
117 Jeniva Prescott C	.15	.25
118 Jerrick Valder C	.15	.25
119 Kane the Arcanist U	.30	.50
120 Nathar Wilderson C	.15	.25
121 Nessera Gildenrose C	.15	.25
122 Patricia Potter C	.15	.25
123 Rufus Claybourne R	6.00	10.00
124 Shadowseer Calista U	.30	.50
125 Shaytha Lumenira U	.30	.50
126 Stevrona Forgemender R	1.25	2.00
127 Tidus the Relentless R	3.00	5.00
128 Vincent Brayden C	.15	.25
129 Xeris C	.15	.25
130 Zooti Fizzlefury U	.30	.50
131 Burom Bladeseer C	.15	.25
132 Caera Sunforge C	.15	.25
133 Drax Fellfuse C	.15	.25
134 Hanu Skyhorn U	.30	.50
135 Kark Baneblood C	.15	.25
136 Kizzli Grinderstub C	.15	.25
137 Korlix Grimvik C	.15	.25
138 Kuatha Mornhoof C	.15	.25
139 Lena Naville C	.15	.25
140 Maxie the Blaster R	.60	1.00
141 Nikka Blastbor C	.15	.25
142 Rakzi the Earthgraced R	1.25	2.00
143 Razo'jun U	.30	.50
144 Rumu Moonhaze C	.15	.25
145 Shaera Strikewing C	.15	.25
146 Talaan Solaras C	.15	.25
147 Timriv the Enforcer C	.15	.25
148 Tharuk Foulblade U	.30	.50
149 Tol'zin R	3.00	5.00
150 Valytha Colton C	.15	.25
151 Yoza'tsu C	.15	.25
152 Zarvix the Tormentor R	.60	1.00
153 Zeni'vun U	.30	.50
154 Azure Captain C	.15	.25
155 Azure Drake C	.15	.25
156 Azure Emissary U	.30	.50
157 Azure Enforcer C	.15	.25
158 Azure Magus C	.15	.25
159 Azure Skyrazor U	.30	.50
160 Tyrygosa R	2.50	4.00
161 Bronze Drake C	.15	.25
162 Bronze Drakonid U	.30	.50
163 Bronze Emissary U	.30	.50
164 Bronze Guardian C	.15	.25
165 Bronze Skyrazor C	.15	.25
166 Bronze Warden C	.15	.25
167 Soridormi R	2.50	4.00
168 Al'Akir the Windlord E	5.00	8.00
169 Bound Vortex U	.30	.50
170 Bound Rumbler U	.30	.50
171 Therazane Stonemother E	4.00	6.00
172 Bound Inferno U	.30	.50
173 Ragnaros the Firelord E	4.00	6.00
174 Bound Torrent U	.30	.50
175 Neptulon the Tidehunter E	4.00	6.00
176 Landro's Lichling U	.30	.50
177 Malfurion Stormrage E	6.00	10.00
178 Savage Raptor E	4.00	6.00
179 Champions Dthdlr Brstplte R	1.25	2.00
180 Crown of Chelonian Freedom U	.30	.50
181 God Grinding Grips U	.30	.50
182 Helm of Terrorizing Fangs R	.60	1.00
183 Leggings of the Vanquished Usurper U	.30	.50
184 Polished Spaulders of Valor R	.60	1.00
185 Stained Shadowcraft Spaulders R	.60	1.00
186 Tattered Dreadmist Robe R	1.25	2.00
187 Wildlife Defender R	.60	1.00
188 Darkmoon Card: Volcano R	.60	1.00
189 Landros Hitching Post R	.60	1.00
190 Axe of Grounded Flame R	.60	1.00
191 Barnacle Coated Greataxe R	.60	1.00
192 Blacksoul Polearm R	.60	1.00
193 Crusher of Bonds C	.15	.25
194 Fire Etched Dagger U	.30	.50
195 Glyphtrace Ritual Knife R	2.50	4.00
196 Kickback 5000 R	.60	1.00
197 Lightningflash U	.30	.50
198 Lordbane Scepter R	.60	1.00
199 Poisonfire Greatsword R	.60	1.00
200 Perforator, The R	.60	1.00
201 Wild Hammer R	.60	1.00
202 Aessina's Miracle C	.15	.25
203 All That Rises C	.15	.25
204 Bird In Hand, A C	.15	.25
205 Breaking the Bonds C	.15	.25
206 Defending the Rift C	.15	.25
207 Dragon, Unchained C	.15	.25
208 Elemental Energy C	.15	.25
209 End of the Supply Line C	.15	.25
210 Entrenched C	.15	.25
211 Forged of Shadow and Flame C	.15	.25
212 Head Full of Wind, A U	.30	.50
213 Lightning in a Bottle C	.15	.25
214 Putting the Pieces Together U	.30	.50
215 Sea Legs U	.30	.50
216 Something That Burns U	.30	.50
217 Abyssal Maw R	2.50	4.00
218 Deepholm R	1.25	2.00
219 Firelands R	3.00	5.00
220 Skywall R	1.50	2.50

2011 World of Warcraft War of the Elements Loot

1 Landro's Lichling	5.00	8.00
2 War Party Hitching Post	25.00	40.00
3 Savage Raptor	125.00	200.00

2012 World of Warcraft Crown of the Heavens

COMPLETE SET (202)	120.00	200.00
BOOSTER BOX (36 PACKS)	60.00	90.00
BOOSTER PACK (16 CARDS)	2.00	3.00
RELEASED IN JUNE 2012		
1 Arisella, Daughter of Cenarius U	.30	.50
2 Iso'rath U	.30	.50
3 Tyrus Blackhorn U	.30	.50
4 Warlord Grok'thol U	.30	.50
5A Cenarius, Lord of the Forest E	3.00	5.00
5B Cenarius, Lord (Ext. Art)	6.00	10.00
6 Crimson Guard C	.15	.25
7 Dark Transformation R	1.00	1.50
8 Despair of Undeath U	.30	.50
9 Leeching Fever U	.30	.50
10 Vampiric Siphon R	1.00	1.50
11 Ferocious Cat Form U	.30	.50
12 Malfurion's Gift R	1.00	1.50
13 Mark of Elderlimb U	.30	.50
14 Mark of the Ancients C	.15	.25
15 Monstrous Boon R	2.50	4.00
16 Wild Cascade R	.60	1.00
17 McCloud the Fox C	.15	.25
18 Quick Trap U	.30	.50
19 Sniper Training R	1.50	2.50
20 Yertle R	6.00	10.00
21 Flame Lance C	.15	.25
22 Frost Blast U	.30	.50
23 Ice Barrier R	6.00	10.00
24 Overload U	.30	.50
25 Shroud of the Archmage R	3.00	5.00
26 The Art of War R	.60	1.00
27 Blessing of the Devoted C	.15	.25

28 Divine Bulwark R .60 1.00
29 Light of the Naaru U .30 .50
30 Vindicator's Shock U .30 .50
31 Borrowed Time R 2.50 4.00
32 Faithful Heat U .30 .50
33 Shadow Word: Despair U .30 .50
34 Shroud of the High Priest R .60 1.00
35 Spiritual Imbalance C .15 .25
36 Assassin's Strike C .15 .25
37 Boundless Thievery R 1.50 2.50
38 Hemorrhage R .60 1.00
39 Poison the Well U .30 .50
40 Earthquake R .60 1.00
41 Frost Arc C .15 .25
42 Monstrous Totem R 1.50 2.50
43 Rage of the Elements U .30 .50
44 Tidal Totem U .30 .50
45 Unleash Inferno R 2.00 3.00
46 Banish Soul U .30 .50
47 Fire and Brimstone R 1.50 2.50
48 Gakuri U .30 .50
49 Monstrous Void R 2.00 3.00
50 Shaafun C .15 .25
51 Shroud of the Nethermancer R 1.00 1.50
52 Bladestorm R 5.00 8.00
53 Boundless Rage R 1.50 2.50
54 Brutal Strike C .15 .25
55 Destructive Disarm U .30 .50
56 Infectious Brutality U .30 .50
57 Hexamorph U .30 .50
58 The Light's Gaze U .30 .50
59 Master's Embrace U .30 .50
60 Overwhelm U .30 .50
61 Paralyzing Strike U .30 .50
62 Essence of Aggression U .30 .50
63 Essence of Defense U .30 .50
64 Essence of Focus U .30 .50
65 Essence of Light U .30 .50
66 Essence of Rage U .30 .50
67 Essence of War U .30 .50
68 Bark and Bite R 1.00 1.50
69 Bash and Slash R 2.00 3.00
70 Fear and Loathing R .60 1.00
71 Preserve and Protect R 2.50 4.00
72 Rime and Freezin' R 2.50 4.00
73 Aeshia Moonstreak C .15 .25
74 Aleksei Brandal U .30 .50
75 Anathel the Eagle-Eye R 2.00 3.00
76 Andrews the Just C .15 .25
77 Archdruid Malfurion E 4.00 6.00
78 Bromor the Shadowblade R .60 1.00
79 Dar the Beastmaster C .15 .25
80 Emree U .30 .50
81 Esala U .30 .50
82 Father Charles C .15 .25
83 Flamesinger Zara C .15 .25
84 Frimzy Fuzzbum U .30 .50
85 Gerrunge the Sadist R .60 1.00
86 Graddis Battlebeard R .60 1.00
87 Grovewarden Daviak U .30 .50
88 Jeishal U .60 1.00
89 Kalam Blacksteel C .15 .25
90 Kaldric Stoutwhisker U .30 .50
91 Lucy Elizabeth C .15 .25
92 Shalyssa Groveshaper C .15 .25
93 Targus Roughblade C .15 .25
94 Thadrus, Shield of Teldrassil R 5.00 8.00
95 Tharal Wildbreeze C .15 .25
96 Tommi Spazzratchet C .15 .25
97 Tyrande, High Priestess E 6.00 10.00
98 Velkin Gray U .30 .50
99 Wendy Anne C .15 .25
100 Zazzo Dizzleflame R 1.50 2.50
101 Abasha Windstorm U .30 .50
102 Alyna Sunshower C .15 .25
103 Baru Gravehorn U .30 .50
104 Drotara the Bloodpoint C .15 .25
105 Elderguard Brennan U .30 .50
106 Grak Foulblade C .15 .25
107 Gravelord Adams R 1.50 2.50
108 Hamuul Runetotem E 1.50 2.50
109 Horngrim U .30 .50
110 Ian Lanstrick U .30 .50
111 Icaros the Sunward C .15 .25
112 Kraznix Smolderpain C .15 .25
113 Lazarus Marrowbane C .15 .25
114 Moharu the Skyseer R .60 1.00
115 Muluno Sunbreath U .30 .50
116 Nox the Lifedrainer R .60 1.00
117 Raezi C .15 .25
118 Soulde the Earthshaker R 2.00 3.00
119 Sylvanas, Queen E 3.00 5.00
120 Thespius Bloodblaze C .15 .25
121 Thunderpetal U .30 .50
122 Tor Earthwalker C .15 .25
123 Tristani the Sunblade R .60 1.00
124 Vazu'jin C .15 .25
125 Vizo Arctwister C .15 .25
126 Vor'zun C .15 .25
127 Witch Doctor Ka'booma R 5.00 8.00
128 Zaza'jun U .30 .50
129 Brogre U .30 .50
130 Deathsmasher Mogdar C .15 .25
131 Drak'narr C .15 .25
132 Dro'gash R .60 1.00
133 Grag'tok C .15 .25
134 Grug the Bonecrusher C .15 .25
135 High Warlord Zogar E 4.00 6.00
136 Krogar the Colossal R 5.00 8.00
137 Krum'shal U .30 .50
138 Throk the Conqueror C .15 .25
139 Torr'nag U .30 .50
140 Trag'ush C .15 .25
141 Jadefire Felsworn U .30 .50
142 Jadefire Hellcaller C .15 .25
143 Jadefire Rogue U .30 .50
144 Jadefire Satyr C .15 .25
145 Jadefire Scout C .15 .25
146 Jadefire Trickster C .15 .25
147 Prince Xavalis E 8.00 12.00
148 Vylokx R 4.00 6.00
149 Baby Murloc U 1.50 2.50
150 Bubblesmash C .15 .25
151 Gutfin C .15 .25
152 King Bagurgle, Terror E 5.00 8.00
153 Splashtooth C .15 .25
154 Keeper Alinar C .15 .25
155 Keeper Balos C .15 .25
156 Keeper Sharus R 6.00 10.00
157 Remulos, Son of Cenarius R 4.00 6.00
158 Ashroot, Ancient of Lore U .30 .50
159 Stonebranch, Ancient of War U .30 .50
160 High Prophet Barim R .60 1.00
161 Neferset Darkcaster C .15 .25
162 Aessina R .60 1.00
163 Gronn Skullcracker R 4.00 6.00
164 Harpy Matriarch C .15 .25
165 Vicious Grell U .30 .50
166 Corrupted Hippogryph E 1.50 2.50
167 Farseer Nobundo R .60 1.00
168 Hyjal Stag C .15 .25
169 Muln Earthfury R 2.50 4.00
170 Belt of Absolute Zero C .15 .25
171 Crown of the Ogre King R 3.00 5.00
172 Gravitational Pull R 2.50 4.00
173 Power Generator Hood C .15 .25
174 Spaulders of the Scarred Lady U .30 .50
175 Magical Ogre Idol R 2.50 4.00
176 Miniature Voodoo Mask R 8.00 12.00
177 Vial of Stolen Memories R 2.50 4.00
178 Brainsplinter U .30 .50
179 Branch of Nordrassil R .60 1.00
180 Dragonwrath, Tarecgosa's Rest E 2.50 4.00
181 Gurubashi Punisher U .30 .50
182 Irontree Knives U .30 .50
183 Legacy of Arlokk U .30 .50
184 Lumbering Ogre Axe C .15 .25
185 Maimgor's Bite R 2.50 4.00
186 Mandible of Beth'tilac C .15 .25
187 Mandokir's Tribute U .30 .50
188 Reclaimed Ashkandi R 2.50 4.00
189 Skullstealer Greataxe C .15 .25
190 Sulfuras, Extinguished R 2.00 3.00
191 An Ancient Awakens C .15 .25
192 As Hyjal Burns C .15 .25
193 The Battle Is Won, the War Goes On C .15 .25
194 Black Heart of Flame C .15 .25
195 Cleaning House C .15 .25
196 If You're Not Against Us... C .15 .25
197 Signed in Blood C .15 .25
198 Nordrassil, the World Tree R 2.50 4.00

2012 World of Warcraft Crown of the Heavens Loot

1 Vicious Grell 8.00 12.00
2 Magical Ogre Idol 25.00 40.00
3 Corrupted Hippogryph 125.00 200.00

2012 World of Warcraft Tomb of the Forgotten

COMPLETE SET (202) 50.00 100.00
BOOSTER BOX (36 PACKS) 50.00 80.00
BOOSTER PACK (16 CARDS) 2.00 3.00
RELEASED IN JUNE 2012
1 Dark Pharaoh Tekahn U .30 .50
2 The Forgotten U .30 .50
3 Nexus-Thief Asar U .30 .50
4 Augh U .30 .50
5 High Guardian Malosun U .30 .50
6 Jasani, Shrine Keeper U .30 .50
7 Mistress Nesala U .30 .50
8 Mogdar the Frozenheart U .30 .50
9 Thrall the Earth-Warder E 6.00 10.00
9EA Thrall the Earth-Warder EA
10 Blood Parasite R .60 1.00
11 Boundless Winter R .60 1.00
12 Frozen Strength U .30 .50
13 Raise the Dead C .15 .25
14 Siphon of Undeath U .30 .50
15 Mark of Restoration U .30 .50
16 Natural Purification R .60 1.00
17 Primal Madness R .60 1.00
18 Wild Rejuvenation U .30 .50
19 Wild Wrath C .15 .25
20 Cobra Sting R .60 1.00
21 Hunter's Focus C .15 .25
22 Interfering Shot U .30 .50
23 Obliterating Trap U .30 .50
24 Uberserc R .60 1.00
25 Boundless Magic R .60 1.00
26 Firestarter R .60 1.00
27 Polymorph: Pig U .30 .50
28 Spark of Brilliance C .15 .25
29 Wildfire U .30 .50
30 Blessing of Resolution U .30 .50
31 Divine Redemption R .60 1.00
32 Hammer of Vengeance U .30 .50
33 Hand of Devotion U .30 .50
34 Monstrous Vengeance R .60 1.00
35 Tower of Radiance R .60 1.00
36 Faithful Dispel U .30 .50
37 Mind Shatter C .15 .25
38 Monstrous Intervention R .60 1.00
39 Power Word: Resurrection R .60 1.00
40 Shadow Word: Corruption U .30 .50
41 Shadowy Apparition R 1.25 2.00
42 Decisive Strike C .15 .25
43 Extortion U .30 .50
44 Monstrous Rush R .60 1.00
45 Restless Blades R 1.25 2.00
46 Slaughter R .60 1.00
47 Trickster's Reflex U .30 .50
48 Ancestral Revival R .60 1.00
49 Arc Heal U .30 .50
50 Call of Lightning U .30 .50
51 Force of Earth C .15 .25
52 Unleashed Rage R .60 1.00
53 Boundless Hellfire R 2.50 4.00
54 Dark Intent U .30 .50
55 Drain Soul C .15 .25
56 Frenzied Doomguard U .30 .50
57 Hand of Gul'dan R .60 1.00
58 Champion's Shout R .60 1.00
59 Concussion Blow R .60 1.00
60 Fearless Strike U .30 .50
61 Guardian's Endurance U .30 .50
62 Terrifying Shout C .15 .25
63 Thrall's Desire R .60 1.00
64 Thrall's Doubt R .60 1.00
65 Thrall's Fury R .60 1.00
66 Thrall's Patience R .60 1.00
67 Courage C .15 .25
68 Monstrous Heal C .15 .25
69 Monstrous Regeneration C .15 .25
70 Monstrous Strength C .15 .25
71 Power C .15 .25
72 Wisdom C .15 .25
73 Aaron Goodchilde R .60 1.00
74 Alaria the Huntress C .15 .25
75 Ashton Barstow C .15 .25
76 Baradis Darkstone C .15 .25
77 Bishop Ketodo C .15 .25
78 Crankston Deathspark C .15 .25
79 Darkstalker Soran E 1.25 2.00
80 Earthseer Dambrak R .60 1.00
81 Elementalist Arax U .30 .50
82 Goetia C .15 .25
83 Gretta Grindstone U .30 .50
84 Jaelen the Ripper R 1.25 2.00
85 Jarius Blackwood U .30 .50
86 Kalaan C .15 .25
87 Kedan Burstbeard C .15 .25
88 Kraven the Gravebound U .30 .50
89 Naasi C .15 .25
90 Philosopher Kirlenko U .30 .50
91 Renzo Soulfang R .60 1.00
92 Sergeant Corsetti C .15 .25
93 Shadowseer Thraner U .30 .50
94 Taliax the Ironjaw R .60 1.00
95 Velen, Prophet of the Naaru E 1.00 1.50
96 Zalabar the Dark Tinkerer R .60 1.00
97 Amara Kells C .15 .25
98 Brulu Breaks-the-Land U .30 .50
99 Daedak the Graveborne R 3.00 5.00
100 Dakturak C .15 .25
101 Deathguard Ashleigh R .60 1.00
102 Galvano the Beast Lord E 1.00 1.50
103 Grok Goreblade C .15 .25
104 Harudu Cloudshot C .15 .25
105 Ishael Bloodlight C .15 .25
106 Kaelzin C .15 .25
107 Lor'themar Theron, Regent Lord E 1.25 2.00
108 Nadina the Red R 1.25 2.00
109 Raso'jin U .30 .50
110 Seraxa Brightmix R .60 1.00
111 Sludgelauncher Krillzix R .60 1.00
112 Soulstealer Adams U .30 .50
113 Sunstalker Maelan C .15 .25
114 Thanu Sunhorn U .30 .50
115 Trickster Tesslah C .15 .25
116 Veliana Felblood U .30 .50
117 Wrex C .15 .25
118 Yunzo the Hexer U .30 .50
119 Zanrix Steelboot C .15 .25
120 Zindalan R .60 1.00
121 General Husam E 5.00 8.00
122 Harbinger Sefu R .60 1.00
123 High Oracle Naseem R .60 1.00
124 Neferset Bladelord C .15 .25
125 Neferset Champion C .15 .25
126 Neferset Darkcaster C .15 .25
127 Neferset Frostbringer C .15 .25
128 Neferset Runecaster C .15 .25
129 Neferset Scorpid Keeper C .15 .25
130 Neferset Sentry U .30 .50
131 Neferset Shadowlancer C .15 .25
132 Neferset Shadowstalker U .30 .50
133 Neferset Shieldguard U .30 .50
134 Okumet, Herald of the Light U .30 .50
135 Taluret, Herald of Faith U .30 .50
136 Dun'zarg C .15 .25
137 Gorlash, Herald of the Elements U .30 .50
138 Korbash the Devastator R .60 1.00
139 Mok'drul U .30 .50
140 Zog, Herald of Death U .30 .50
141 Zores, Herald of War U .30 .50
142 Zuglisch C .15 .25
143 Frizzlight C .15 .25
144 Nargle, Fang of the Swarm E 1.00 1.50
145 Ragespike C .15 .25
146 Shiverspine U .30 .50
147 Slimefin U .30 .50
148 Swifteye R .60 1.00
149 Kresss, Herald of the Hunt U .30 .50
150 Pythisss, Herald of Frost U .30 .50
151 Araxian, Herald of Trickery U .30 .50
152 Bazul, Herald of the Fel U .30 .50
153 Akhet R .60 1.00
154 Lockmaw R .60 1.00
155 Obsidian Colossus R .60 1.00
156 Pygmy Firebreather C .15 .25
157 Pygmy Pyramid E 10.00 15.00
158 Renshol, Herald of Nature U .30 .50
159 Siamat, Lord of the South Wind E 1.00 1.50
160 Sand Scarab U .30 .50
161 Aggra R 3.00 5.00
162 Harrison Jones R .60 1.00
163 White Camel E 1.00 1.50
164 Anraphet's Regalia C .15 .25
165 Bulwark of the Primordial Mound U .30 .50
166 Flickering Cowl U .30 .50
167 Flickering Shoulders C .15 .25
168 Gloves of Dissolving Smoke U .30 .50
169 Helm of Blazing Glory R .60 1.00

170 Helm of Setesh U .30 .50
171 Mantle of Master Cho U .30 .50
172 Pauldrons of Roaring Flame C .15 .25
173 Poison Fang Bracers U .30 .50
174 Scalp of the Bandit Prince R .60 1.00
175 Ammunae, Construct of Life R .60 1.00
176 Isiset, Construct of Magic R .60 1.00
177 Rajh, Construct of the Sun R .60 1.00
178 Setesh, Construct of Destruction R .60 1.00
179 Apparatus of Khaz'goroth C .15 .25
180 Rune of Zeth C .15 .25
181 Spurious Sarcophagus R .60 1.00
182 Variable Pulse Lightning Capacitor R .60 1.00
183 Barim's Main Cauche U .30 .50
184 Biting Wind U .30 .50
185 Fandral's Flamescythe C .15 .25
186 Feeding Frenzy R .60 1.00
187 Hammer of Sparks U .30 .50
188 Ko'gun, Hammer of the Firelord R .60 1.00
189 Lava Bolt Crossbow U .30 .50
190 Obsidim Cleaver C .15 .25
191 Overpowered Chicken Splitter C .15 .25
192 Ruthless Gladiator's Decapitator R .60 1.00
193 Scepter of Power U .30 .50
194 Spire of Scarlet Pain U .30 .50
195 Zoid's Firelit Greatsword U .30 .50
196 The Defense of Nahom C .15 .25
197 The Fall of Neferst City C .15 .25
198 Gnomebliteration C .15 .25
199 Tailgunner C .15 .25
200 Thieving Little Pluckers C .15 .25
201 Traitors! C .15 .25
202 Uldum R .60 1.00

2012 World of Warcraft Tomb of the Forgotten Loot

1 Sand Scarab 5.00 8.00
2 Spurious Sarcophagus 8.00 12.00
3 White Camel 60.00 100.00

2012 World of Warcraft War of the Ancients

COMPLETE SET (240) 100.00 150.00
BOOSTER BOX (36 PACKS) 50.00 80.00
BOOSTER PACK (15 CARDS) 2.00 3.00
RELEASED IN OCTOBER 2012
1EA Malorne the White Stag (Ext.Art) 2.50 4.00
1 Malorne the White Stag E 2.50 4.00
2 Beyond the Grave R 1.00 1.50
3 Crushing Death U .30 .50
4 Death's Decree U .30 .50
5 Despair of Winter R .60 1.00
6 Ebon Plague R .60 1.00
7 Festering Disease U .30 .50
8 Frigid Frailty C .15 .25
9 Ancient Bear Form U .30 .50
10 Euphoria R 1.00 1.50
11 Lions, Tigers, and Bears R 1.00 1.50
12 Mark of Growth U .30 .50
13 Mark of Malorne C .15 .25
14 Wild Attunement R 1.00 1.50
15 Wild Seeds U .30 .50
16 Arrowstorm C .15 .25
17 Bear Trap U .30 .50
18 Beast Mastery R .60 1.00
19 Endure R 1.00 1.50
20 Furious George U .30 .50
21 Skitter R 1.00 1.50
22 Arcane Potency R 1.25 2.00
23 Arcane Unraveling U .30 .50
24 Conjure Elementals R 1.00 1.50
25 Firestorm U .30 .50
26 Ice Prison C .15 .25
27 Manaflow R 1.00 1.50
28 Reckless Fireball U .30 .50
29 Blessing of Vigilance U .30 .50
30 Crusader's Might R 1.00 1.50
31 Divinity R 1.00 1.50
32 Guardian of the Light R .60 1.00
33 Hammer of Sanctity U .30 .50
34 Holy Ground U .30 .50
35 Shield of Light C .15 .25
36 Gifted Heal U .30 .50
37 Guardian Spirit R 1.00 1.50
38 Mind Crush U .30 .50
39 Power Word: Tenacity R 1.00 1.50
40 Redeeming Dispel C .15 .25
41 Shadow Word: Devour R 1.00 1.50
42 Spirit Shield U .30 .50
43 Devious Dismantle U .30 .50
44 Guise of the Stalker U .30 .50
45 Hands of Deceit R .60 1.00
46 Hidden Strike C .15 .25
47 Kiss of Death R .60 1.00
48 Opportunity R 1.00 1.50
49 Volatile Poison U .30 .50
50 Elemental Echo R 1.00 1.50
51 Elemental Purge U .30 .50
52 Gale Force C .15 .25
53 Lava Strike U .30 .50
54 Scalding Totem U .30 .50
55 Spark of Rage R 1.00 1.50
56 Spirit Link Totem R 1.00 1.50
57 Call the Void U .30 .50
58 Demonic Infusion U .30 .50
59 Gaktai C .15 .25
60 Netherpocalypse R .60 1.00
61 Nightfall R .60 1.00
62 Nimanda R 1.00 1.50
63 Soul Trap U .30 .50
64 Blind Rage U .30 .50
65 Bloodthirsty Shout C .15 .25
66 Combat Stance R .60 1.00
67 Decimate U .30 .50
68 Raging Blow R 1.00 1.50
69 Ruthless Execution U .30 .50
70 Strife R .60 1.00
71 Blitz C .15 .25
72 Focused Heal C .15 .25
73 Legacy of Stormrage E 1.00 1.50
74 Legacy of the Legion E 6.00 10.00
75 Vigilant Guard C .15 .25
76 Glory to the Alliance! C .15 .25
77 Blood and Thunder! C .15 .25
78 Burn Away C .15 .25
79 Elune's Blessing C .15 .25
80 Shattering Blow C .15 .25
81 Strike C .15 .25
82 Alpha Prime R 1.00 1.50
83 Ansem, Timewalker Deathblade R .60 1.00
84 Bolin Moonflare U .30 .50
85 Darkshire Deathsworn C .15 .25
86 Darlon Blacksoul U .30 .50
87 Darnassus Mooncaller C .15 .25
88 Darnassus Shadowblade C .15 .25
89 Darnassus Warrior C .15 .25
90 Delinar Silvershot U .30 .50
91 Eldre'Thalas Sorceress C .15 .25
92 Elysa Lockewood U .30 .50
93 Fimlet Sparklight U .30 .50
94 Hugh Mann U .30 .50
95 Ian Barus U .30 .50
96 Jaal U .30 .50
97 Jarod Shadowsong R .60 1.00
98 Lady Bancroft C .15 .25
99 Lara, Timewalker Commander R 1.00 1.50
100 Lexie Silverblade U .30 .50
101 Lord Kur'talos Ravencrest E 10.00 15.00
101EA Lord Kur'talos (Ext.Art) 20.00 30.00
102 Nalisa Nightbreeze U .30 .50
103 Northshire Cleric C .15 .25
104 Northshire Crusader C .15 .25
105 Nyala Shadefury U .30 .50
106 Rhonin the Time-Lost E 1.25 2.00
107 Shadowglen Stalker C .15 .25
108 Shandris Feathermoon R .60 1.00
109 SI:7 Assassin C .15 .25
110 Stella Bellamy U .30 .50
111 Stormwind Summoner C .15 .25
112 Tarwila Gladespring C .15 .25
113 Teldrassil Tracker C .15 .25
114 Teldrassil Wildguard C .15 .25
115 Tessa Black E 2.00 3.00
116 Timewalker Guard C .15 .25
117 Timewalker Lightsworn C .15 .25
118 Timewalker Sentinel C .15 .25
119 Toraan, Eye of O'ros R 1.00 1.50
120 Virgil, Timewalker Marshal R 1.00 1.50
121 Ahul Moonspeaker U .30 .50
122 Baine, Son of Cairne E 1.00 1.50
123 Belmaril, Timewalker Bloodmage R 1.00 1.50
124 Bhenn Checks-the-Sky C .15 .25
125 Bloodsoul C .15 .25
126 Dawnhoof Brightcaller C .15 .25
127 Drom'kor, Timewalker Necrolyte R 1.00 1.50
128 Durotar Flamecaster C .15 .25
129 Durotar Frostblade C .15 .25
130 Ellen Burroughs U .30 .50
131 Garrosh, Son of Grom E 3.00 5.00
131EA Garrosh, Son (Ext.Art) 20.00 30.00
132 Garyk Stormcrier U .30 .50
133 Jevan Grimtotem R 1.00 1.50
134 Kahul the Sunseer R 2.00 3.00
135 Klandark U .30 .50
136 Mulgore Deathwalker C .15 .25
137 Mulgore Guardian C .15 .25
138 Orgrimmar Heartstriker C .15 .25
139 Orgrimmar Killblade C .15 .25
140 Orgrimmar Marksman C .15 .25
141 Orox Darkhorn U .30 .50
142 Razor Hill Assassin C .15 .25
143 Razor Hill Spiritseer C .15 .25
144 Ror Tramplehoof U .30 .50
145 Shaka Deadmark U .30 .50
146 Soulrender Keldah U .30 .50
147 Stala'jul U .30 .50
148 Takara, Timewalker Warlord R 2.00 3.00
149 Thunder Bluff Spiritwalker C .15 .25
150 Thunder Bluff Steelsnout C .15 .25
151 Thunder Bluff Sunwalker C .15 .25
152 Thunder Bluff Wildheart C .15 .25
153 Tilu Plainstalker U .30 .50
154 Timewalker Grunt C .15 .25
155 Timewalker Sunguard C .15 .25
156 Toho Bloomhorn U .30 .50
157 Torzuk Soulfang E 2.00 3.00
158 Vorgo, Timewalker Stormlord R .60 1.00
159 Xarantaur R 1.00 1.50
160 Zarim Redskull U .30 .50
161 Agamaggan R 1.00 1.50
162 Aviana the Reborn R 1.00 1.50
163 Azgalor the Pit Lord E 2.00 3.00
164 Azzinoth R 1.00 1.50
165 Blazing Infernal C .15 .25
166 Child of Agamaggan C .15 .25
167 Child of Aviana C .15 .25
168 Child of Goldrinn C .15 .25
169 Child of Tortolla C .15 .25
170 Child of Ursoc C .15 .25
171 Child of Ursol C .15 .25
172 Corrupted Furbolg U .30 .50
173 Eye of the Legion C .15 .25
174 Feldrake R .60 1.00
175 Felguard Marauder C .15 .25
176 Frenzied Felhound C .15 .25
177 Frenzyfin U .30 .50
178 Furbolg Avenger C .15 .25
179 Furbolg Chieftain U .30 .50
180 Furbolg Firecaller C .15 .25
181 Goldrinn R .60 1.00
182 Hulking Helboar C .15 .25
183 Jadefire Netherseer U .30 .50
184 Jadefire Soulstealer U .30 .50
185 Keening Shivarra U .30 .50
186 Keeper Yarashal C .15 .25
187 Leafbeard, Ancient of Lore U .30 .50
188 Legion Fel Reaver U .30 .50
189 Mo'arg Doomsmith U .30 .50
190 Monstrous Terrorguard U .30 .50
191 Mossbark, Ancient of War C .15 .25
192 Neltharion the Earth-Warder E 1.00 1.50
193 Peroth'arn R 1.00 1.50
194 Rampaging Furbolg C .15 .25
195 Scheming Dreadlord C .15 .25
196 Sinister Watcher C .15 .25
197 Strongroot, Ancient of War U .30 .50
198 Tortolla R .60 1.00
199 Trogg Earthrager C .15 .25
200 Unstoppable Abyssal C .15 .25
201 Ursoc the Mighty R 1.00 1.50
202 Ursol the Wise R 1.00 1.50
203 Void Terror C .15 .25
204 Volatile Terrorfiend U .30 .50
205 Warmaul Ogre C .15 .25
206 Dungard Ironcutter R 1.00 1.50
207 Earthen Crusher C .15 .25
208 Girdle of the Queen's Champion C .15 .25
209 Helm of Thorns C .15 .25
210 Historian's Sash U .30 .50
211 Legguards of the Legion R .60 1.00
212 Spaulders of Eternity C .15 .25
213 Darnassus Tabard U .30 .50
214 Demon Hunter's Aspect U .30 .50
215 Grand Marshal's Tome of Power U .30 .50
216 Orgrimmar Tabard U .30 .50
217 Signet of the Timewalker U .30 .50
218 Stormwind Tabard U .30 .50
219 Tabard of the Legion U .30 .50
220 Thunder Bluff Tabard U .30 .50
221 Arathar, the Eye of Flame U .30 .50
222 Axe of Cenarius E 3.00 5.00
223 Axe of the Tauren Chieftains C .15 .25
224 Crescent Wand R 1.00 1.50
225 Gavel of Peroth'arn R 1.00 1.50
226 High Warlord's Cleaver U .30 .50
227 Pit Lord's Destroyer C .15 .25
228 Scepter of Azshara R 1.00 1.50
229 Stalk of Corruption U .30 .50
230 Trickster's Edge R 1.00 1.50
231 Wand of the Demonsoul C .15 .25
232 Archival Purposes C .15 .25
233 The Caverns of Time U .30 .50
234 Documenting the Timeways C .15 .25
235 The End Time U .30 .50
236 In Unending Numbers U .30 .50
237 The Path to the Dragon Soul C .15 .25
238 The Vainglorious C .15 .25
239 The Well of Eternity C .15 .25
240 Zin-Azshari R 1.00 1.50
T1 Human Warrior TOKEN .15 .25
T2 Orc Warrior TOKEN .15 .25

2012 World of Warcraft War of the Ancients Loot

1 Eye of the Legion 5.00 8.00
2 Demon Hunter's Aspect 20.00 30.00
3 Feldrake 150.00 250.00

2013 World of Warcraft Betrayal of the Guardian

COMPLETE SET (202) 50.00 100.00
BOOSTER BOX (36 PACKS) 50.00 80.00
BOOSTER PACK (16 CARDS) 1.50 2.50
RELEASED IN FEBRUARY 2013
1 Aegwynn, Guardian of Tirisfal E 1.00 1.50
1EA Aegwynn, Guardian (Ext.Art) 15.00 25.00
2 Bone Shield R 1.00 1.50
3 Corruption of the Ages R .60 1.00
4 Grim Touch R .60 1.00
5 Hand of Dread C .15 .25
6 Soul Pox U .30 .50
7 Timeless Undeath U .30 .50
8 Ancient Moonkin Form R .60 1.00
9 Feral Prowess C .15 .25
10 Living Seed R .75 1.25
11 Roar of the Ages R .60 1.00
12 Thorns of Nordrassil U .30 .50
13 Timeless Bounty U .30 .50
14 Bitey C .15 .25
15 Gahz'rilla E 1.25 2.00
16 Intervening Shot U .30 .50
17 Piercing Shots R .60 1.00
18 Timeless Aim U .30 .50
19 Wrath of the Ages R .75 1.25
20 Arcane Shock U .30 .50
21 Critical Mass R .60 1.00
22 Flame Volley C .15 .25
23 Frost Stasis R .60 1.00
24 Secrets of the Ages R .75 1.25
25 Timeless Arcana U .30 .50
26 Blessing of the Pure C .15 .25
27 Crusade of Kings R .60 1.00
28 Guardian of the Ages R 1.00 1.50
29 Light of Dawn R .60 1.00
30 Light's Vengeance U .30 .50
31 Timeless Light U .30 .50
32 Dark Deliverance C .15 .25
33 Holy Word: Hope U .30 .50
34 Power Word: Spirit R .60 1.00
35 Prayer of the Ages R .75 1.25
36 Psychic Horror R .60 1.00
37 Timeless Agony U .30 .50
38 Fast-Acting Poison U .30 .50
39 No Mercy R .60 1.00
40 Timeless Deception U .30 .50
41 Venomous Wounds R .60 1.00
42 Cloudburst R .75 1.25
43 Freezing Rain Totem U .30 .50
44 Magma Blast C .15 .25
45 Static Shock R .60 1.00
46 Storm of the Ages R .75 1.25
47 Timeless Winds U .30 .50
48 Curse of the Fel R .60 1.00
49 Demonic Rebirth R 1.00 1.50
50 Fel Inversion C .15 .25
51 Ritual of the Ages R .75 1.25
52 Thoglos U .30 .50

53 Timeless Shadow U .30 .50
54 Bastion of Defense R .60 1.00
55 Brutal Steel R .75 1.25
56 Fortified Defenses U .30 .50
57 Fury of the Ages R .60 1.00
58 Timeless Resilience U .30 .50
59 Legacy of Betrayal E 12.00 20.00
60 More Work? C .15 .25
61 Sigil of the Legion C .15 .25
62 Archdruid Fandral Staghelm R 2.50 4.00
63 Belthira the Black Thorn E 3.00 5.00
64 Danath Trollbane R .60 1.00
65 Darris Leafshade U .30 .50
66 Dwarf Demolitionist U .30 .50
67 Elistari Silverwind U .30 .50
68 General Turalyon E 1.00 1.50
69 Gnomish Flying Machine U .30 .50
70 Human Darkweaver C .15 .25
71 Human Footman C .15 .25
72 Human Knight C .15 .25
73 Human Operative C .15 .25
74 Human Peasant C .15 .25
75 Human Sniper C .15 .25
76 Khadgar R .60 1.00
77 Lady Voltaire R .60 1.00
78 Loremaster Pooth R .75 1.25
79 Myro Lumastis U .30 .50
80 Night Elf Arcanist C .15 .25
81 Night Elf Bladedancer C .15 .25
82 Night Elf Grovewalker C .15 .25
83 Night Elf Moon Priestess C .15 .25
84 Night Elf Ranger C .15 .25
85 Night Elf Swiftblade C .15 .25
86 Thane Kurdran Wildhammer R .60 1.00
87 Virendra Moonglow U .30 .50
88 Xander Blackcrow U .30 .50
89 Blood Knight Lynesta R .60 1.00
90 Chora Cloudspeaker U .30 .50
91 Dohna Darksky U .30 .50
92 Draka R .60 1.00
93 Durotan R .75 1.25
94 Farseer Horgath R .60 1.00
95 Goblin Sapper U .30 .50
96 Korah Icefang U .30 .50
97 Korgen Skullcleaver U .30 .50
98 Magatha Grimtotem R .60 1.00
99 Makuna Hatada E 2.00 3.00
100 Orc Blackblade C .15 .25
101 Orc Flamecaller C .15 .25
102 Orc Grunt C .15 .25
103 Orc Necrolyte C .15 .25
104 Orc Peon C .15 .25
105 Orgrim Doomhammer E 1.00 1.50
106 Tauren Deathwalker C .15 .25
107 Tauren Lightcaller C .15 .25
108 Tauren Mystic C .15 .25
109 Tauren Plainsrider C .15 .25
110 Tauren Sunhoof C .15 .25
111 Tauren Tracker C .15 .25
112 Tauren Wildmender C .15 .25
113 Troll Axethrower U .30 .50
114 Zafira Ragebolt U .30 .50
115 Zul'jin R .60 1.00
116 Bianca, Timewalker Mage U .30 .50
117 Enabrin, Timewalker Druid U .30 .50
118 Lyra, Timewalker Embermage U .30 .50
119 Moro, Timewalker Druid U .30 .50
120 Nazzik, Timewalker Trickster R .60 1.00
121 Nehru, Timewalker Hunter U .30 .50
122 Timewalker Juggernaut C .15 .25
123 Timewalker Shadowseer C .15 .25
124 Timewalker Smasher C .15 .25
125 Timewalker Vanguard C .15 .25
126 Watsun, Timewalker Lightshield R .60 1.00
127 Zor'ka, Timewalker Shaman U .30 .50
128 Arcane Anomaly C .15 .25
129 Arcane Protector U .30 .50
130 The Big Bad Wolf R 1.00 1.50
131 Bigbelly, Furbolg Chieftain R .60 1.00
132 Blackfang Tarantula C .15 .25
133 Darkwater Crocolisk C .15 .25
134 Doom Commander Zaakuul E 8.00 12.00
135 Doomguard Soldier C .15 .25
136 Durnholde Tracking Hound C .15 .25
137 Enslaved Red Dragon U .30 .50
138 Eredar Deathbringer C .15 .25
139 Ethereal Spellfilcher U .30 .50
140 Ethereal Thief U .30 .50
141 Felguard Annihilator C .15 .25
142 Frostwolf C .15 .25
143 Furbolg Shaman C .15 .25
144 Ghostly Charger R .75 1.25
145 Greater Fleshbeast C .15 .25
146 Highland Lion C .15 .25
147 Karazhan Concubine C .15 .25
148 Kil'rek R .60 1.00
149 Moroes R 1.00 1.50
150 Nightbane E 1.00 1.50
151 Prince Malchezaar E 1.25 2.00
152 Ravenous Furbolg C .15 .25
153 Servant of Terestian C .15 .25
154 Shade of Aran R 1.00 1.50
155 Shadowmoon Mage C .15 .25
156 Shivarra Deathspeaker C .15 .25
157 Snappyfin R .75 1.25
158 Spawn of Hyakiss U .30 .50
159 Spawn of Rokad U .30 .50
160 Spawn of Shadikith U .30 .50
161 Terestian Illhoof R .60 1.00
162 Vile Watcher C .15 .25
163 Voidshrieker C .15 .25
164 Wildhammer Gryphon U .30 .50
165 Wrathguard Defender C .15 .25
166 Floating Spellbook C .15 .25
167 Don Carlos' Famous Hat U .30 .50
168 Durotan's Battle Harness U .30 .50
169 Gauntlets of the Ancient Frostwolf U .30 .50
170 Khadgar's Kilt of Abjuration U .30 .50
171 Mantle of Abrahmis R .60 1.00
172 Royal Crest of Lordaeron R .60 1.00
173 VanCleef's Boots R .60 1.00
174 Dark Portal Hearthstone U .30 .50
175 Time-Bending Gem C .15 .25
176 Moroes' Lucky Pocket Watch U .30 .50
177 Atiesh, Greatstaff of the Guardian E 1.00 1.50
178 Bloodfire Greatstaff C .15 .25
179 Despair R .60 1.00
180 Fool's Bane R .60 1.00
181 Hellscream Slicer U .30 .50
182 Lothar's Edge U .30 .50
183 Millennium Blade C .15 .25
184 Quel'Serrar C .15 .25
185 Riftmaker R .60 1.00
186 Shard of the Virtuous U .30 .50
187 Staff of Infinite Mysteries R .60 1.00
188 Time-Shifted Dagger C .15 .25
189 Vagaries of Time C .15 .25
190 Warglaive of Azzinoth E 6.00 10.00
191 Windrunner's Bow R .60 1.00
192 Assault on Blackrock Spire U .30 .50
193 The Fall of Lordaeron U .30 .50
194 The Black Morass C .15 .25
195 A Demonic Presence U .30 .50
196 Escape from Durnholde C .15 .25
197 The Master's Touch C .15 .25
198 Medivh's Journal C .15 .25
199 The Opening of the Dark Portal C .15 .25
200 Taretha's Diversion C .15 .25
201 Capital City, Lordaeron R .60 1.00
202 Blackrock Spire R .60 1.00

2013 World of Warcraft Betrayal of the Guardian Loot

1 Floating Spellbook 6.00 10.00
2 Dark Portal Hearthstone 25.00 40.00
3 Ghostly Charger 125.00 200.00

2013 World of Warcraft Reign of Fire

COMPLETE SET (197) 80.00 120.00
BOOSTER BOX (36 PACKS) 100.00 150.00
BOOSTER PACK (16 CARDS) 3.00 5.00
RELEASED IN JULY 2013
1 Medivh the Prophet E 5.00 8.00
1EA Medivh the Prophet EA 10.00 15.00
2 Kil'jaeden the Deceiver E 3.00 5.00
3 Gravebound C .15 .25
4 Howling Blast R 4.00 6.00
5 Numbing Cold U .25 .40
6 Rune of Vengeance R .50 .75
7 Vilegut R 2.50 4.00
8 Will from Beyond U .25 .40
9 Agile Cat Form U .25 .40
10 Blood in the Water R .60 1.00
11 Lunar Barrage R 1.25 2.00
12 Nurture R 1.00 1.50
13 Snare from Beyond U .25 .40
14 Wild Harmony C .15 .25
15 Counterattack R .60 1.00
16 Dakota R 1.50 2.50
17 Disrupting Shot U .25 .40
18 Ravenous Frenzy C .15 .25
19 Track from Beyond U .25 .40
20 Unleash the Beasts R .50 .75
21 Arcane Breach U .25 .40
22 Flames from Beyond U .25 .40
23 Mass Teleport R .50 .75
24 Permafrost R .50 .75
25 Phoenix R 2.50 4.00
26 Temporal Shift C .15 .25
27 Blaze of Light C .15 .25
28 Blessing from Beyond U .25 .40
29 Blinding Word R 3.00 5.00
30 Heroic Bulwark U .25 .40
31 Mass Redemption R .50 .75
32 Zealotry R .60 1.00
33 Lightlance U .25 .40
34 Power Word: Bravery R .50 .75
35 Shadows from Beyond U .25 .40
36 Soul Warding R 1.00 1.50
37 Splintered Thought R 1.25 2.00
38 Spook C .15 .25
39 Bounty Hunt C .15 .25
40 Malice From Beyond U .25 .40
41 Savage Combat R 1.00 1.50
42 Smoke Screen U .25 .40
43 Torturous Poison R .50 .75
44 Ancestral Renewal R .50 .75
45 Feedback R .60 1.00
46 Lust for Battle C .15 .25
47 Magnetic Totem R 1.25 2.00
48 Tempest Elemental U .25 .40
49 Totem from Beyond U .40 .60
50 Curse from Beyond U .25 .40
51 Havoc R .60 1.00
52 Life Drain C .15 .25
53 Nether Rip R 1.50 2.50
54 Soulbond U .25 .40
55 Zhar'doom R 1.50 2.50
56 Bladewhirl R .60 1.00
57 Blade Strike U .25 .40
58 Howl from Beyond C .15 .25
59 Impale R .50 .75
60 Tactical Mastery R .50 .75
61 Thundercrash C .15 .25
62 Call of C'Thun R .50 .75
63 Call of Yogg-Saron R .50 .75
64 Dodge C .15 .25
65 Legacy of the Horde E 5.00 8.00
66 Legacy of Lordaeron E 2.50 4.00
67 Savage Beatdown C .15 .25
68 Alana the Hopebringer E 2.50 4.00
69 Alethar the Blightspreader R 1.50 2.50
70 Ashenvale Acolyte C .15 .25
71 Ashenvale Archer C .15 .25
72 Ashenvale Illusionist C .15 .25
73 Daniel Darkheart U .25 .40
74 Disciple of the Light C .15 .25
75 Druid of the Talon U .25 .40
76 Elwynn Burglar C .15 .25
77 Elwynn Huntsman C .15 .25
78 Emora Delwin U .25 .40
79 Felwood Grovestalker C .15 .25
80 Goran, Timewalker Lavacaller U .25 .40
81 Grand Admiral Daelin Proudmoore R .75 1.25
82 Huntress C .15 .25
83 Jaina, Apprentice of Antonidas R 1.25 2.00
84 Johnny B. Goode U .25 .40
85 Komma, Timewalker Graveguard U .25 .40
86 Ky'lai Darkblood U .25 .40
87 Lunaris Silverfrost U .25 .40
88 Mias the Fair C .15 .25
89 Muradin, Bronzebeard Adventurer R 1.25 2.00
90 Naisha R 5.00 8.00
91 Stormwind Recruit C .15 .25
92 Warden Maiev E 6.00 10.00
93 The Widow Deadsie R .60 1.00
94 Adonal Brokenhoof U .25 .40
95 Blackrock Shooter C .15 .25
96 Blurg Firekin U .25 .40
97 Bor Breakfist U .25 .40
98 Dawnstrider Sunward C .15 .25
99 Drek'Thar, Frostwolf General R .50 .75
100 Grom Hellscream R .60 1.00
101 Haro Setting-Sun U .25 .40
102 High Chieftain Cairne Bloodhoof E 2.00 3.00
103 High Warlord Gorebelly E 6.00 10.00
104 Joru the Blinding Light R 2.50 4.00
105 Kurala Deadshot U .25 .40
106 Nuada Windwaker U .25 .40
107 Orc Raider C .15 .25
108 Orc Shaman C .15 .25
109 Rokhan R .75 1.25
110 Roza the Star-Mother R .50 .75
111 Runetotem Guardian C .15 .25
112 Seres, Timewalker Assassin U .25 .40
113 Shattered Hand Cutthroat C .15 .25
114 Sixto the Earth-Blessed R 2.50 4.00
115 Sunwalker Lighthorn C .15 .25
116 Thunderhorn Windwalker C .15 .25
117 Valik, Timewalker Sharpshooter U .25 .40
118 Warsong Deadblade C .15 .25
119 Winterhoof Frostheart C .15 .25
120 Abomination U .25 .40
121 Anub'arak, The Traitor King E 6.00 10.00
122 Banshee U .25 .40
123 Blackhorn Fearmonger C .15 .25
124 Bleakheart Hellcaller C .15 .25
125 Brood Mother R .50 .75
126 Cult Master Kel'Thuzad R 1.25 2.00
127 Cunning Crypt Fiend C .15 .25
128 Darkflame Dreadlord C .15 .25
129 Doomguard Invader C .15 .25
130 Dreadhound C .15 .25
131 Eredar Chaosbringer U .25 .40
132 Eredar Strategist U .40 .60
133 Fel Imp U .25 .40
134 Felguard Basher C .15 .25
135 Frost Wyrm R .60 1.00
136 Furbolg Champion U .25 .40
137 Furbolg Spiritbinder C .15 .25
138 Hateful Darkweaver U .25 .40
139 Hateful Fiend U .25 .40
140 Hateful Infernal U .25 .40
141 Hateful Seductress U .25 .40
142 Hungry Ghoul C .15 .25
143 Mal'Ganis E 3.00 5.00
144 Mo'arg Punisher C .15 .25
145 Naga Royal Guard U .25 .40
146 Naga Siren U .25 .40
147 Necromancer U .25 .40
148 Priestess of Horror C .15 .25
149 Priestess of Ruin C .15 .25
150 Quillbeast C .15 .25
151 Savage Wrathguard C .15 .25
152 Scheming Watcher C .15 .25
153 Sister of Seduction C .15 .25
154 Sogoridon the Savage R .60 1.00
155 Terror Hound C .15 .25
156 Terrorguard Detonator C .15 .25
157 Thunder Hawk C .15 .25
158 Torrid Abyssal C .15 .25
159 Varimathras, Dreadlord Insurgent R 3.00 5.00
160 Void Brute C .15 .25
161 Zalekor the Ferocious R 1.00 1.50
162 Bloodmage Kael'thas R .50 .75
163 Goblin Tinkerer R .75 1.25
164 Pandaren Brewmaster R 1.25 2.00
165 Rexxar the Wanderer R 2.00 3.00
166 Belt of Giant Strength R .60 1.00
167 Boots of Quel'Thalas U .25 .40
168 Boots of Speed U .25 .40
169 Circlet of Nobility C .15 .25
170 Cloak of Flames U .25 .40
171 Mask of Death U .25 .40
172 Robe of the Magi R .50 .75
173 Amulet of Spell Shield U .25 .40
174 Anti-magic Potion C .15 .25
175 Glyph of Omniscience C .15 .25
176 Healing Wards U .25 .40
177 Health Stone C .15 .25
178 Orb of Darkness U .25 .40
179 Ring of Protection C .15 .25
180 Scroll of Town Portal C .15 .25
181 Claws of Attack R .50 .75
182 Corrupted Ashbringer R .60 1.00
183 Doomhammer E 2.00 3.00
184 Frostmourne E 4.00 6.00
185 Kelen's Dagger of Escape C .15 .25
186 Rod of Necromancy R .50 .75
187 Staff of Silence U .25 .40
188 Wand of Mana Stealing U .25 .40
189 Eternity's End U .25 .40
190 The Founding of Durotar U .25 .40
191 The Invasion of Kalimdor C .15 .25
192 Legacy of the Damned C .15 .25
193 Path of the Damned C .15 .25
194 The Scourge of Lordaeron C .15 .25
195 Terror of the Tides C .15 .25
196 Ashenvale R 8.00 12.00
197 Mulgore R .50 .75

Pokemon

Pokémon price guide brought to you by Hill's Wholesale Gaming www.wholesalegaming.com

1999 Pokemon Base 1st Edition Thick Stamp

COMPLETE SET (102)	2500.00	4100.00
BOOSTER BOX (36 PACKS)	50000.00	55000.00
BOOSTER PACK (11 CARDS)	600.00	1000.00
RELEASED ON JANUARY 9, 1999		
1 Alakazam HOLO R	80.00	120.00
2 Blastoise HOLO R	120.00	250.00
3 Chansey HOLO R	30.00	60.00
4 Charizard HOLO R	800.00	1100.00
5 Clefairy HOLO R	30.00	60.00
6 Gyarados HOLO R	50.00	100.00
7 Hitmonchan HOLO R	80.00	120.00
8 Machamp HOLO R	30.00	60.00
9 Magneton HOLO R	30.00	80.00
10 Mewtwo HOLO R	75.00	150.00
11 Nidoking HOLO R	30.00	60.00
12 Ninetales HOLO R	80.00	120.00
13 Poliwrath HOLO R	50.00	100.00
14 Raichu HOLO R	80.00	120.00
15 Venusaur HOLO R	250.00	400.00
16 Zapdos HOLO R	50.00	100.00
17 Beedrill R	15.00	30.00
18 Dragonair R	20.00	40.00
19 Dugtrio R	20.00	40.00
20 Electabuzz R	20.00	40.00
21 Electrode R	15.00	30.00
22 Pidgeotto R	15.00	30.00
23 Arcanine U	10.00	20.00
24 Charmeleon U	15.00	30.00
25 Dewgong U	3.00	8.00
26 Dratini U	4.00	10.00
27 Farfetch'd U	4.00	10.00
28 Growlithe U	4.00	10.00
29 Haunter U	4.00	10.00
30 Ivysaur U	15.00	30.00
31 Jynx U	3.00	8.00
32 Kadabra U	8.00	15.00
33 Kakuna (UER) U	3.00	8.00
34 Machoke U	5.00	12.00
35 Magikarp U	5.00	12.00
36 Magmar U	3.00	8.00
37 Nidorino U	3.00	8.00
38 Poliwhirl U	3.00	8.00
39 Porygon U	3.00	8.00
40 Raticate U	3.00	8.00
41 Seel U	3.00	8.00
42 Wartortle U	15.00	30.00
43 Abra C	2.00	5.00
44 Bulbasaur (UER) C	15.00	30.00
45 Caterpie (UER) C	6.00	15.00
46 Charmander C	15.00	30.00
47 Diglett C	3.00	8.00
48 Doduo C	3.00	8.00
49 Drowzee C	2.00	5.00
50 Gastly C	3.00	8.00
51 Koffing C	3.00	8.00
52 Machop C	3.00	8.00
53 Magnemite C	2.50	6.00
54 Metapod (UER) C	3.00	8.00
55 Nidoran-M C	2.50	6.00
56 Onix C	2.50	6.00
57 Pidgey C	2.50	6.00
58 Pikachu (Red cheeks Error) C	15.00	30.00
58 Pikachu (Yellow cheeks Corr.) C	15.00	30.00
59 Poliwag C	2.50	6.00
60 Ponyta C	2.50	6.00
61 Rattata C	2.50	6.00
62 Sandshrew C	2.50	6.00
63 Squirtle C	10.00	20.00
64 Starmie C	2.50	6.00
65 Staryu C	2.50	6.00
66 Tangela C	2.50	6.00
67 Voltorb (UER) C	2.50	6.00
68 Vulpix (UER) C	2.50	6.00
69 Weedle C	2.50	6.00
70 Clefairy Doll R	6.00	15.00
71 Computer Search R	12.00	25.00
72 Devolution Spray R	6.00	15.00
73 Impostor Professor Oak R	6.00	15.00
74 Item Finder R	10.00	20.00
75 Lass R	15.00	30.00
76 Pokemon Breeder R	15.00	30.00
77 Pokemon Trader R	6.00	15.00
78 Scoop Up R	6.00	15.00
79 Super Energy Removal R	8.00	15.00
80 Defender U	2.50	6.00
81 Energy Retrieval U	3.00	8.00
82 Full Heal U	1.50	4.00
83 Maintenance U	3.00	8.00
84 Plus Power U	3.00	8.00
85 Pokemon Center U	3.00	8.00
86 Pokemon Flute U	3.00	8.00
87 PokÃ©dex U	3.00	8.00
88 Professor Oak U	3.00	8.00
89 Revive U	3.00	8.00
90 Super Potion U	3.00	8.00
91 Bill C	3.00	8.00
92 Energy Removal C	3.00	8.00
93 Gust of Wind C	3.00	8.00
94 Potion C	3.00	8.00
95 Switch C	3.00	8.00
96 Double Colorless Energy U	6.00	15.00
97 Fighting Energy	2.50	6.00
98 Fire Energy	2.50	6.00
99 Grass Energy	2.50	6.00
100 Lightning Energy	2.50	6.00
101 Psychic Energy	2.50	6.00
102 Water Energy	2.50	6.00

1999 Pokemon Base Unlimited

COMPLETE SET (102)	335.00	525.00
BOOSTER BOX (36 PACKS)	1300.00	1600.00
BOOSTER PACK (11 CARDS)	30.00	40.00
STARTER SET (60 CARDS)	45.00	60.00
BLACKOUT DECK (60 CARDS)	30.00	40.00
BRUSHFIRE DECK (60 CARDS)	35.00	50.00
OVERGROWTH DECK (60 CARDS)	35.00	45.00
ZAP DECK (60 CARDS)	30.00	40.00
RELEASED ON JANUARY 9, 1999		
1 Alakazam HOLO R	9.00	12.00
2 Blastoise HOLO R	25.00	35.00
3 Chansey HOLO R	7.00	10.00
4 Charizard HOLO R	50.00	75.00
5 Clefairy HOLO R	7.00	10.00
6 Gyarados HOLO R	7.00	10.00
7 Hitmonchan HOLO R	7.00	10.00
8 Machamp HOLO R 1st Ed. Only	7.00	10.00
9 Magneton HOLO R	7.00	10.00
10 Mewtwo HOLO R	10.00	15.00
11 Nidoking HOLO R	8.00	11.00
12 Ninetales HOLO R	7.00	10.00
13 Poliwrath HOLO R	7.00	10.00
14 Raichu HOLO R	8.00	11.00
15 Venusaur HOLO R	25.00	35.00
16 Zapdos HOLO R	10.00	15.00
17 Beedrill R	1.25	2.25
18 Dragonair R	3.00	5.00
19 Dugtrio R	1.50	2.50
20 Electabuzz R	2.00	3.50
21 Electrode R	1.25	2.25
22 Pidgeotto R	2.50	4.00
23 Arcanine U	2.50	4.00
24 Charmeleon U	2.50	4.00
25 Dewgong U	1.50	2.50
26 Dratini U	1.50	2.50
27 Farfetch'd U	1.50	2.50
28 Growlithe U	1.50	2.50
29 Haunter U	1.50	2.50
30 Ivysaur U	2.50	4.00
31 Jynx U	1.50	2.50
32 Kadabra U	1.50	2.50
33 Kakuna (Length/Length Error) U	1.50	2.50
33 Kakuna (Length/Weight Corr.) U	1.50	2.50
34 Machoke U	1.50	2.50
35 Magikarp U	1.50	2.50
36 Magmar U	1.50	2.50
37 Nidorino U	1.50	2.50
38 Poliwhirl U	1.50	2.50
39 Porygon U	1.50	2.50
40 Raticate U	1.50	2.50
41 Seel U	1.50	2.50
42 Wartortle U	1.50	2.50
43 Abra C	1.50	2.50
44 Bulbasaur (Length/Length Error) C	1.25	2.25
44 Bulbasaur (Length/Weight Corr.) C	1.25	2.25
45 Caterpie (HP 40 Error) C	1.25	2.25
45 Caterpie (40 HP Corr.) C	1.25	2.25
46 Charmander C	1.25	2.25
47 Diglett C	1.25	2.25
48 Doduo C	1.25	2.25
49 Drowzee C	1.25	2.25
50 Gastly C	1.25	2.25
51 Koffing C	1.25	2.25
52 Machop C	1.25	2.25
53 Magnemite C	1.25	2.25
54 Metapod (HP 70 Error) C	1.25	2.25
54 Metapod (70 HP Corr.) C	1.25	2.25
55 Nidoran C	1.25	2.25
56 Onix C	1.25	2.25
57 Pidgey C	1.25	2.25
58 Pikachu (Red cheeks Error) C	1.25	2.25
58 Pikachu (Yellow cheeks Corr.)C	1.25	2.25
59 Poliwag C	1.25	2.25
60 Ponyta C	1.25	2.25
61 Rattata C	1.25	2.25
62 Sandshrew C	1.25	2.25
63 Squirtle C	1.25	2.25
64 Starmie C	1.25	2.25
65 Staryu C	1.25	2.25
66 Tangela C	1.25	2.25
67 Voltorb (Monster Ball Error) C	1.25	2.25
67 Voltorb (PokÃ© Ball Corr.) C	1.25	2.25
68 Vulpix (UER) C	1.25	2.25
69 Weedle C	1.25	2.25
70 Clefairy Doll R	2.00	3.00
71 Computer Search R	3.50	5.00
72 Devolution Spray R	2.50	3.50
73 Impostor Professor Oak R	1.50	2.25
74 Item Finder R	2.00	3.00
75 Lass R	2.00	3.00
76 PokÃ©mon Breeder R	3.00	5.00
77 PokÃ©mon Trader R	3.00	5.00
78 Scoop Up R	2.00	3.00
79 Super Energy Removal R	2.00	3.00
80 Defender U	1.25	2.25
81 Energy Retrieval U	1.25	2.25
82 Full Heal U	1.25	2.25
83 Maintenance U	1.25	2.25
84 Plus Power U	1.25	2.25
85 PokÃ©mon Center U	1.25	2.25
86 PokÃ©mon Flute U	1.25	2.25
87 PokÃ©dex U	1.25	2.25
88 Professor Oak U	1.25	2.25
89 Revive U	1.25	2.25
90 Super Potion U	1.25	2.25
91 Bill C	1.25	2.25
92 Energy Removal C	1.25	2.25
93 Gust of Wind C	1.25	2.25
94 Potion C	1.25	2.25
95 Switch C	1.25	2.25
96 Double Colorless Energy U	1.25	2.25
97 Fighting Energy C	.75	1.25
98 Fire Energy C	.75	1.25
99 Grass Energy C	.75	1.25
100 Lightning Energy C	.75	1.25
101 Psychic Energy C	.75	1.25
102 Water Energy C	.75	1.25

1999 Pokemon Jungle 1st Edition

COMPLETE SET (64)	425.00	600.00
BOOSTER BOX (36 PACKS)	900.00	1100.00
BOOSTER PACK (11 CARDS)	20.00	25.00
RELEASED ON JUNE 16, 1999		
1 Clefable HOLO R	15.00	20.00
2 Electrode HOLO R	15.00	20.00
3 Flareon HOLO R	25.00	35.00
4 Jolteon HOLO R	25.00	35.00
5 Kangaskhan HOLO R	15.00	20.00
6 Mr. Mime HOLO R	15.00	20.00
7 Nidoqueen HOLO R	15.00	20.00
8 Pidgeot HOLO R	15.00	20.00
9 Pinsir HOLO R	15.00	20.00
10 Scyther HOLO R	20.00	25.00
11 Snorlax HOLO R	25.00	30.00
12 Vaporeon HOLO R	25.00	35.00
13 Venomoth HOLO R	15.00	20.00
14 Victreebel HOLO R	15.00	20.00
15 Vileplume HOLO R	15.00	20.00
16 Wigglytuff HOLO R	15.00	20.00
17 Clefable R	7.00	10.00
18 Electrode (UER) R	5.00	8.00
19 Flareon R	7.00	10.00
20 Jolteon R	7.00	10.00
21 Kangaskhan R	2.50	4.00
22 Mr. Mime R	3.00	5.00
23 Nidoqueen R	5.00	7.00
24 Pidgeot R	4.00	6.00
25 Pinsir R	4.00	6.00
26 Scyther R	5.00	8.00
27 Snorlax R	5.00	8.00
28 Vaporeon R	7.00	10.00
29 Venomoth R	4.00	6.00
30 Victreebel R	3.00	5.00
31 Vileplume R	3.00	5.00
32 Wigglytuff R	3.00	5.00
33 Butterfree ("d" Edition Error) U	6.00	10.00
33 Butterfree (1 Edition Corr.) U	2.00	3.50
34 Dodrio U	2.00	3.50
35 Exeggutor U	2.00	3.50
36 Fearow U	2.00	3.50
37 Gloom U	2.00	3.50
38 Lickitung U	2.00	3.50
39 Marowak U	2.00	3.50
40 Nidorina U	2.00	3.50
41 Parasect U	2.00	3.50
42 Persian U	2.00	3.50
43 Primeape U	2.00	3.50
44 Rapidash U	2.00	3.50
45 Rhydon U	2.00	3.50
46 Seaking U	2.00	3.50
47 Tauros U	2.00	3.50
48 Weepinbell U	2.00	3.50
49 Bellsprout C	1.75	2.50
50 Cubone C	1.75	2.50
51 Eevee C	1.75	2.50
52 Exeggcute C	1.75	2.50
53 Goldeen C	1.75	2.50
54 Jigglypuff C	1.75	2.50
55 Mankey C	1.75	2.50
56 Meowth C	1.75	2.50
57 Nidoran-F C	1.75	2.50
58 Oddish C	1.75	2.50
59 Paras C	1.75	2.50
60 Pikachu C	1.75	2.50
61 Rhyhorn C	1.75	2.50
62 Spearow C	1.75	2.50
63 Venonat C	1.75	2.50
64 Trainer: PokÃ© Ball C	1.75	2.50

1999 Pokemon Jungle Unlimited

COMPLETE SET (64)	50.00	100.00
BOOSTER BOX (36 PACKS)	300.00	400.00
BOOSTER PACK (11 CARDS)	8.00	20.00
POWER RESERVE DECK (60 CARDS)	15.00	25.00
WATER BLAST DECK (60 CARDS)	20.00	40.00
HOLO ERRORS ARE MISSING JUNGLE LOGO	8.00	15.00
RELEASED ON JUNE 16, 1999		
1A Clefable HOLO R	2.00	4.00
1B Clefable HOLO R ERR	6.00	12.00
2A Electrode HOLO R	2.00	5.00
2B Electrode HOLO R ERR	6.00	12.00
3A Flareon HOLO R	2.00	5.00
3B Flareon HOLO R ERR	8.00	20.00
4A Jolteon HOLO R	2.00	5.00
4B Jolteon HOLO R ERR	8.00	20.00
5A Kangaskhan HOLO R	2.00	4.00
5B Kangaskhan HOLO R ERR	8.00	20.00
6A Mr. Mime HOLO R	2.00	4.00
6B Mr Mime HOLO R ERR	8.00	20.00
7A Nidoqueen HOLO R	2.00	5.00
7B Nidoqueen HOLO R ERR	8.00	20.00
8A Pidgeot HOLO R	2.00	4.00
8B Pidgeot HOLO R ERR	8.00	20.00
9A Pinsir HOLO R	2.00	4.00
9B Pinsir HOLO R ERR	8.00	20.00
10A Scyther HOLO R	2.00	4.00
10B Scyther HOLO R ERR	8.00	20.00
11A Snorlax HOLO R	2.00	5.00
11B Snorlax HOLO R ERR	8.00	20.00
12A Vaporeon HOLO R	2.00	4.00
12B Vaporeon HOLO R ERR	8.00	20.00
13A Venomoth HOLO R	2.00	5.00
13B Venomoth HOLO R ERR	8.00	20.00
14A Victreebel HOLO R	2.00	4.00
14B Victreebel HOLO R ERR	8.00	20.00
15A Vileplume HOLO R	2.00	4.00
15B Vileplume HOLO R ERR	8.00	20.00
16A Wigglytuff HOLO R	3.00	6.00
16B Wigglytuff HOLO R ERR	8.00	20.00
17 Clefable R	3.00	8.00
18 Electrode R	3.00	8.00
19 Flareon R	3.00	8.00
20 Jolteon R	3.00	8.00
21 Kangaskhan R	3.00	8.00
22 Mr. Mime R	3.00	8.00
23 Nidoqueen R	3.00	8.00
24 Pidgeot R	3.00	8.00
25 Pinsir R	3.00	8.00
26 Scyther R	3.00	8.00
27 Snorlax R	3.00	8.00
28 Vaporeon R	3.00	8.00
29 Venomoth R	3.00	8.00
30 Victreebel R	3.00	8.00
31 Vileplume R	3.00	8.00
32 Wigglytuff R	3.00	8.00
33 Butterfree U	1.00	2.50
34 Dodrio U	1.00	2.50
35 Exeggutor U	1.00	2.50
36 Fearow U	1.00	2.50
37 Gloom U	1.00	2.50
38 Lickitung U	1.00	2.50
39 Marowak U	1.00	2.50

Card	Low	High
40 Nidorina U	1.00	2.50
41 Parasect U	1.00	2.50
42 Persian U	1.00	2.50
43 Primeape U	1.00	2.50
44 Rapidash U	1.00	2.50
45 Rhydon U	1.00	2.50
46 Seaking U	1.00	2.50
47 Tauros U	1.00	2.50
48 Weepinbell U	1.00	2.50
49 Bellsprout C	1.00	2.50
50 Cubone C	1.00	2.50
51 Eevee C	1.00	2.50
52 Exeggcute C	1.00	2.50
53 Goldeen C	1.00	2.50
54 Jigglypuff C	1.00	2.50
55 Mankey C	1.00	2.50
56 Meowth C	1.00	2.50
57 Nidoran-F C	1.00	2.50
58 Oddish C	1.00	2.50
59 Paras C	1.00	2.50
60 Pikachu C	1.00	2.50
61 Rhyhorn C	1.00	2.50
62 Spearow C	1.00	2.50
63 Venonat C	1.00	2.50
64 Trainer: Poke Ball C	1.00	2.50

1999 Pokemon Fossil 1st Edition

Card	Low	High
COMPLETE SET (62)	375.00	550.00
BOOSTER BOX (36 PACKS)	750.00	900.00
BOOSTER PACK (11 CARDS)	20.00	25.00
RELEASED ON OCTOBER 10, 1999		
1 Aerodactyl HOLO R	20.00	25.00
2 Articuno HOLO R	20.00	25.00
3 Ditto HOLO R	15.00	20.00
4 Dragonite HOLO R	45.00	60.00
5 Gengar HOLO R	30.00	40.00
6 Haunter HOLO R	10.00	15.00
7 Hitmonlee HOLO R	15.00	20.00
8 Hypno HOLO R	10.00	15.00
9 Kabutops HOLO R	15.00	20.00
10 Lapras HOLO R	15.00	20.00
11 Magneton HOLO R	8.00	12.00
12 Moltres HOLO R	20.00	30.00
13 Muk HOLO R	10.00	15.00
14 Raichu HOLO R	10.00	15.00
15 Zapdos HOLO R	25.00	35.00
16 Aerodactyl R	3.00	5.00
17 Articuno R	5.00	8.00
18 Ditto R	3.00	5.00
19 Dragonite R	5.00	8.00
20 Gengar R	7.00	10.00
21 Haunter R	1.00	1.50
22 Hitmonlee R	2.50	4.00
23 Hypno R	5.00	8.00
24 Kabutops R	3.00	5.00
25 Lapras R	3.00	5.00
26 Magneton R	3.00	5.00
27 Moltres R	5.00	8.00
28 Muk R	2.50	4.00
29 Raichu R	2.50	4.00
30 Zapdos R	5.00	8.00
31 Arbok U	2.00	3.50
32 Cloyster U	2.00	3.50
33 Gastly U	2.00	3.50
34 Golbat U	2.00	3.50
35 Golduck U	2.00	3.50
36 Golem U	2.00	3.50
37 Graveler U	2.00	3.50
38 Kingler U	2.00	3.50
39 Magmar (U)	2.00	3.50
40 Omastar U	2.00	3.50
41 Sandslash U	2.00	3.50
42 Seadra U	2.00	3.50
43 Slowbro U	2.00	3.50
44 Tentacruel U	2.00	3.50
45 Weezing U	2.00	3.50
46 Ekans C	1.25	2.50
47 Geodude C	1.25	2.50
48 Grimer C	1.25	2.50
49 Horsea C	1.25	2.50
50 Kabuto C	1.25	2.50
51 Krabby C	1.25	2.50
52 Omanyte C	1.25	2.50
53 Psyduck C	1.25	2.50
54 Shellder C	1.25	2.50
55 Slowpoke C	1.25	2.50
56 Tentacool C	1.25	2.50
57 Zubat C	1.25	2.50
58 Mr. Fuji U	1.25	2.50
59 Energy Search C	1.25	2.50
60 Gambler C	1.25	2.50
61 Recycle C	1.25	2.50
62 Mysterious Fossil C	1.25	2.50

1999 Pokemon Fossil Unlimited

Card	Low	High
COMPLETE SET (62)	50.00	100.00
BOOSTER BOX (36 PACKS)	300.00	500.00
BOOSTER PACK (11 CARDS)	6.00	15.00
BODYGUARD DECK (60)	8.00	20.00
LOCK DOWN DECK (60)	15.00	30.00
RELEASED ON OCTOBER 10, 1999		
1 Aerodactyl HOLO R	2.00	6.00
2 Articuno HOLO R	4.00	10.00
3 Ditto HOLO R	3.00	8.00
4 Dragonite HOLO R	5.00	15.00
5 Gengar HOLO R	5.00	12.00
6 Haunter HOLO R	2.00	6.00
7 Hitmonlee HOLO R	3.00	8.00
8 Hypno HOLO R	3.00	8.00
9 Kabutops HOLO R	3.00	8.00
10 Lapras HOLO R	2.00	5.00
11 Magneton HOLO R	1.25	4.00
12 Moltres HOLO R	5.00	10.00
13 Muk HOLO R	1.50	4.00
14 Raichu HOLO R	2.00	7.00
15 Zapdos HOLO R	2.00	4.00
16 Aerodactyl R	1.00	2.00
17 Articuno R	2.00	4.00
18 Ditto R	1.00	3.00
19 Dragonite R	3.00	8.00
20 Gengar R	1.00	3.00
21 Haunter R	1.00	3.00
22 Hitmonlee R	2.00	5.00
23 Hypno R	1.00	3.00
24 Kabutops R	1.00	3.00
25 Lapras R	1.00	3.00
26 Magneton R	1.00	3.00
27 Moltres R	1.00	3.00
28 Muk R	1.00	3.00
29 Raichu R	1.00	3.00
30 Zapdos R	1.00	3.00
31 Arbok U	1.00	3.00
32 Cloyster U	1.00	3.00
33 Gastly U	1.00	3.00
34 Golbat U	1.00	3.00
35 Golduck U	1.00	3.00
36 Golem U	1.00	3.00
37 Graveler U	1.00	3.00
38 Kingler U	1.00	3.00
39 Magmar U	1.00	3.00
40 Omastar U	1.00	3.00
41 Sandslash U	1.00	3.00
42 Seadra U	1.00	3.00
43 Slowbro U	1.00	3.00
44 Tentacruel U	1.00	3.00
45 Weezing U	1.00	3.00
46 Ekans C	1.00	3.00
47 Geodude C	1.00	3.00
48 Grimer C	1.00	3.00
49 Horsea C	1.00	3.00
50 Kabuto C	1.00	3.00
51 Krabby C	1.00	3.00
52 Omanyte C	1.00	3.00
53 Psyduck C	1.00	3.00
54 Shellder C	1.00	3.00
55 Slowpoke C	1.00	3.00
56 Tentacool C	1.00	3.00
57 Zubat C	1.00	3.00
58 Old Man Fuji U	1.00	3.00
59 Energy Search C	1.00	3.00
60 Gambler C	1.00	3.00
61 Recycle C	1.00	3.00
62 Mysterious Fossil C	1.00	3.00

2000 Pokemon Base 2 Unlimited

Card	Low	High
COMPLETE SET (130)	160.00	240.00
BOOSTER BOX (36 PACKS)	550.00	700.00
BOOSTER PACK (11 CARDS)	15.00	22.00
GRASS CHOPPER DECK (60)	25.00	40.00
HOT WATER DECK (60)	20.00	35.00
LIGHTNING BUG DECK (60)	20.00	30.00
PSYCH OUT DECK (60)	20.00	30.00
RELEASED ON FEBRUARY 24, 2000		
1 Alakazam HOLO R	4.00	6.00
2 Blastoise HOLO R	15.00	20.00
3 Chansey HOLO R	3.00	5.00
4 Charizard HOLO R	25.00	30.00
5 Clefable HOLO R	2.50	4.00
6 Clefairy HOLO R	2.50	4.00
7 Gyarados HOLO R	3.00	5.00
8 Hitmonchan HOLO R	3.00	5.00
9 Magneton HOLO R	2.00	3.50
10 Mewtwo HOLO R	4.00	6.00
11 Nidoking HOLO R	4.00	6.00
12 Nidoqueen HOLO R	4.00	6.00
13 Ninetales HOLO R	3.00	5.00
14 Pidgeot HOLO R	4.00	6.00
15 Poliwrath HOLO R	4.00	6.00
16 Raichu HOLO R	4.00	6.00
17 Scyther HOLO R	5.00	8.00
18 Venusaur HOLO R	12.00	16.00
19 Wigglytuff HOLO R	2.50	4.00
20 Zapdos HOLO R	5.00	7.00
21 Beedrill R	1.25	2.00
22 Dragonair R	1.75	3.50
23 Dugtrio R	.75	1.25
24 Electabuzz R	1.50	2.50
25 Electrode R	.40	.60
26 Kangaskhan R	.40	.75
27 Mr. Mime R	3.00	4.00
28 Pidgeotto R	1.25	2.00
29 Pinsir R	.75	1.25
30 Snorlax R	2.00	3.00
31 Venomoth R	1.25	2.00
32 Victreebel R	1.25	2.00
33 Arcanine U	1.25	2.00
34 Butterfree U	.75	1.00
35 Charmeleon U	.30	.50
36 Dewgong U	.30	.50
37 Dodrio U	.30	.50
38 Dratini U	.30	.50
39 Exeggutor U	.30	.50
40 Farfetch'd U	.30	.50
41 Fearow U	.30	.50
42 Growlithe U	.30	.50
43 Haunter U	1.00	1.50
44 Ivysaur (U)	1.00	1.50
45 Jynx U	.30	.50
46 Kadabra U	.30	.50
47 Kakuna U	.30	.50
48 Lickitung U	1.00	1.50
49 Machoke U	.30	.50
50 Magikarp U	.30	.50
51 Magmar U	.75	1.25
52 Marowak U	.30	.50
53 Nidorina U	.30	.50
54 Nidorino U	.30	.50
55 Parasect U	.30	.50
56 Persian U	.75	1.25
57 Poliwhirl U	.30	.50
58 Raticate U	.30	.50
59 Rhydon U	.30	.50
60 Seaking U	.30	.50
61 Seel U	.30	.50
62 Tauros U	.30	.50
63 Wartortle U	.30	.50
64 Weepinbell U	.30	.50
65 Abra C	.25	.40
66 Bellsprout C	.25	.40
67 Bulbasaur C	.25	.40
68 Caterpie C	.25	.40
69 Charmander C	.25	.40
70 Cubone C	.25	.40
71 Diglett C	.25	.40
72 Doduo C	.25	.40
73 Drowzee C	.25	.40
74 Exeggcute C	.25	.40
75 Gastly C	.25	.40
76 Goldeen C	.25	.40
77 Jigglypuff C	.25	.40
78 Machop C	.25	.40
79 Magnemite C	.25	.40
80 Meowth C	.25	.40
81 Metapod C	.25	.40
82 Nidoran-F C	.25	.40
83 Nidoran-M C	.25	.40
84 Onix C	.25	.40
85 Paras C	.25	.40
86 Pidgey C	.25	.40
87 Pikachu C	.25	.40
88 Poliwag C	.25	.40
89 Rattata C	.25	.40
90 Rhyhorn C	.25	.40
91 Sandshrew C	.25	.40
92 Spearow C	.25	.40
93 Squirtle C	.25	.40
94 Starmie C	.25	.40
95 Staryu C	.25	.40
96 Tangela C	.25	.40
97 Venonat C	.25	.40
98 Voltorb C	.25	.40
99 Vulpix C	.25	.40
100 Weedle C	.25	.40
101 Computer Search R	1.50	2.50
102 Imposter Professor Oak R	.40	.60
103 Item Finder R	2.00	3.00
104 Lass R	.40	.60
105 PokÃ©mon Breeder R	1.75	2.25
106 PokÃ©mon Trader R	.40	.60
107 Scoop Up R	1.25	2.00
108 Super Energy Removal R	.75	1.25
109 Defender U	.30	.50
110 Energy Retrieval U	.30	.50
111 Full Heal U	.30	.50
112 Maintenance U	.30	.50
113 PlusPower U	.30	.50
114 PokÃ©mon Center U	.30	.50
115 PokÃ©dex U	.30	.50
116 Professor Oak U	.30	.50
117 Super Potion U	.30	.50
118 Bill C	.25	.40
119 Energy Removal C	.25	.40
120 Gust of Wind C	.25	.40
121 PokÃ© Ball C	.25	.40
122 Potion C	.25	.40
123 Switch C	.25	.40
124 Double Colorless Energy U	.25	.40
125 Fighting Energy C	.25	.40
126 Fire Energy C	.25	.40
127 Grass Energy C	.25	.40
128 Lightning Energy C	.25	.40
129 Psychic Energy C	.25	.40
130 Water Energy C	.25	.40

2000 Pokemon Team Rocket 1st Edition

Card	Low	High
COMPLETE SET (82)	240.00	400.00
COMPLETE SET W/RAICHU (83)	600.00	800.00
BOOSTER BOX (36 PACKS)	400.00	500.00
BOOSTER PACK (11 CARDS)	15.00	20.00
RELEASED ON APRIL 24, 2000		
1 Dark Alakazam HOLO R	10.00	15.00
2 Dark Arbok HOLO R ERR	4.00	7.00
3 Dark Blastoise HOLO R	15.00	20.00
4 Dark Charizard HOLO R	20.00	30.00
5 Dark Dragonite HOLO R	15.00	20.00
6 Dark Dugtrio HOLO R	7.00	12.00
7 Dark Golbat HOLO R	6.00	11.00
8 Dark Gyarados HOLO R	4.00	7.00
9 Dark Hypno HOLO R	6.00	10.00
10 Dark Machamp HOLO R	7.00	12.00
11 Dark Magneton HOLO R	7.00	12.00
12 Dark Slowbro HOLO R	7.00	12.00
13 Dark Vileplume HOLO R	7.00	12.00
14 Dark Weezing HOLO R	3.00	5.00
15 Here Comes Team Rocket HOLO R	5.00	8.00
16 Rocket's Sneak Attack HOLO R	4.00	7.00
17 Rainbow Energy HOLO R	3.00	5.00
18 Dark Alakazam R	2.00	3.00
19 Dark Arbok R ERR	2.00	3.00
20 Dark Blastoise R	3.00	5.00
21 Dark Charizard R	7.00	12.00
22 Dark Dragonite R	2.50	4.00
23 Dark Dugtrio R	2.00	3.00
24 Dark Golbat R	2.00	3.00
25 Dark Gyarados R	2.00	3.00
26 Dark Hypno R	2.00	3.00
27 Dark Machamp R	2.00	3.00
28 Dark Magneton R	2.00	3.00
29 Dark Slowbro R	2.00	3.00
30 Dark Vileplume R	2.00	3.00
31 Dark Weezing R	2.00	3.00
32 Dark Charmeleon U	2.50	4.00
33 Dark Dragonair U	1.50	2.50
34 Dark Electrode U	1.50	2.50
35 Dark Flareon U	1.50	2.50
36 Dark Gloom U	1.50	2.50
37 Dark Golduck U	1.50	2.50
38 Dark Jolteon U	1.50	2.50
39 Dark Kadabra U	1.50	2.50
40 Dark Machoke U	1.50	2.50
41 Dark Muk U	1.50	2.50
42 Dark Persian U	1.50	2.50
43 Dark Primeape U	1.50	2.50
44 Dark Rapidash U ERR	1.50	2.50
45 Dark Vaporeon U	1.50	2.50
46 Dark Wartortle U	1.50	2.50
47 Magikarp U	1.50	2.50
48 Porygon U	1.50	2.50
49 Abra C	1.00	1.75
50 Charmander C	1.00	1.75
51 Dark Raticate C	1.00	1.75
52 Diglett C	1.00	1.75
53 Dratini C	1.00	1.75
54 Drowzee C	1.00	1.75
55 Eevee C	1.00	1.75
56 Ekans C	1.00	1.75
57 Grimer C	1.00	1.75
58 Koffing C	1.00	1.75
59 Machop C	1.00	1.75
60 Magnemite C	1.00	1.75
61 Mankey C	1.00	1.75
62 Meowth C	1.00	1.75
63 Oddish C	1.00	1.75
64 Ponyta C	1.00	1.75
65 Psyduck C	1.00	1.75
66 Rattata C	1.00	1.75
67 Slowpoke C	1.00	1.75
68 Squirtle C	1.00	1.75
69 Voltorb C	1.00	1.75
70 Zubat C	1.00	1.75
71 Here Comes Team Rocket R	2.00	3.00
72 Rocket's Sneak Attack R	2.00	3.00
73 The Boss's Way U	1.50	2.50
74 Challenge U	1.50	2.50
75 Digger U	1.50	2.50
76 Imposter Oak's Revenge U	1.50	2.50
77 Nightly Garbage Run U	1.50	2.50
78 Gas Attack C	1.00	1.75
79 Sleep C	1.00	1.75
80 Rainbow Energy R	2.00	3.00
81 Full Heal Energy U	1.00	1.75
82 Potion Energy U	1.00	1.75
83 Dark Raichu HOLO R ERR	25.00	35.00

2000 Pokemon Team Rocket Unlimited

Card	Low	High
COMPLETE SET (82)	95.00	150.00
BOOSTER BOX (36 PACKS)	400.00	550.00
BOOSTER PACK (11 CARDS)	15.00	20.00
THEME DECK (60 CARDS)	20.00	30.00
RELEASED ON APRIL 24, 2000		
1 Dark Alakazam HOLO R	3.00	5.00
2 Dark Arbok HOLO R ERR	1.00	1.50
3 Dark Blastoise HOLO R	10.00	15.00
4 Dark Charizard HOLO R	15.00	20.00
5 Dark Dragonite HOLO R	8.00	12.00
6 Dark Dugtrio HOLO R	2.00	3.50
7 Dark Golbat HOLO R	2.00	3.50
8 Dark Gyarados HOLO R	3.00	5.00
9 Dark Hypno HOLO R	2.50	4.00
10 Dark Machamp HOLO R	2.00	3.50
11 Dark Magneton HOLO R	2.50	4.00
12 Dark Slowbro HOLO R	2.50	4.00
13 Dark Vileplume HOLO R	3.00	5.00
14 Dark Weezing HOLO R	.75	1.25
15 Here Comes Team Rocket HOLO R	3.00	5.00
16 Rocket's Sneak Attack HOLO R	2.00	3.50
17 Rainbow Energy HOLO R	4.00	7.00
18 Dark Alakazam R	1.00	1.50
19 Dark Arbok R ERR	.50	.80
20 Dark Blastoise R	1.25	2.00
21 Dark Charizard R	3.00	5.00
22 Dark Dragonite R	1.25	2.00
23 Dark Dugtrio R	.50	.80
24 Dark Golbat R	.40	.75
25 Dark Gyarados R	.60	1.00
26 Dark Hypno R	.60	1.00
27 Dark Machamp R	.40	.75
28 Dark Magneton R	.50	.80
29 Dark Slowbro R	.60	1.00
30 Dark Vileplume R	.50	.75
31 Dark Weezing R	.40	.75
32 Dark Charmeleon U	.30	.50
33 Dark Dragonair U	.30	.50
34 Dark Electrode U	.30	.50
35 Dark Flareon U	.30	.50
36 Dark Gloom U	.30	.50
37 Dark Golduck U	.30	.50
38 Dark Jolteon U	.30	.50
39 Dark Kadabra U	.30	.50
40 Dark Machoke U	.30	.50
41 Dark Muk U	.30	.50
42 Dark Persian U	.30	.50
43 Dark Primeape U	.30	.50
44 Dark Rapidash U ERR	.30	.50
45 Dark Vaporeon U	.30	.50
46 Dark Wartortle U	.30	.50
47 Magikarp U	.30	.50
48 Porygon U	.30	.50
49 Abra C	.20	.35
50 Charmander C	.20	.35
51 Dark Raticate C	.20	.35
52 Diglett C	.20	.35
53 Dratini C	.20	.35
54 Drowzee C	.20	.35
55 Eevee C	.20	.35
56 Ekans C	.20	.35
57 Grimer C	.20	.35
58 Koffing C	.20	.35
59 Machop C	.20	.35
60 Magnemite C	.20	.35
61 Mankey C	.20	.35

62 Meowth C .20 .35
63 Oddish C .20 .35
64 Ponyta C .20 .35
65 Psyduck C .20 .35
66 Rattata C .20 .35
67 Slowpoke C .20 .35
68 Squirtle C .20 .35
69 Voltorb C .20 .35
70 Zubat C .20 .35
71 Here Comes Team Rocket R .40 .75
72 Rocket's Sneak Attack R 1.25 2.00
73 The Boss's Way U .30 .50
74 Challenge U .30 .50
75 Digger U .30 .50
76 Imposter Oak's Revenge U .30 .50
77 Nightly Garbage Run U .30 .50
78 Gas Attack C .20 .35
79 Sleep C .20 .35
80 Rainbow Energy R 1.50 4.00
81 Full Heal Energy U .20 .35
82 Potion Energy U .20 .35
83 Dark Raichu HOLO R ERR 5.00 8.00

2000 Pokemon Gym Heroes 1st Edition

COMPLETE SET (132) 375.00 600.00
UNOPENED BOX (36 PACKS) 650.00 800.00
UNOPENED PACK (11 CARDS) 20.00 25.00
RELEASED ON AUGUST 14, 2000
1 Blaine's Moltres HOLO R 20.00 25.00
2 Brock's Rhydon HOLO R 10.00 15.00
3 Erika's Clefable HOLO R 8.00 15.00
4 Erika's Dragonair HOLO R 15.00 20.00
5 Erika's Vileplume HOLO R 7.00 12.00
6 Lt. Surge's Electabuzz HOLO R 8.00 13.00
7 Lt. Surge's Fearow HOLO R 10.00 15.00
8 Lt. Surge's Magneton HOLO R 7.00 12.00
9 Misty's Seadra (holo) (R) 7.00 12.00
10 Misty's Tentacruel HOLO R 10.00 15.00
11 Rocket's Hitmonchan HOLO R 8.00 13.00
12 Rocket's Moltres HOLO R 12.00 16.00
13 Rocket's Scyther HOLO R 15.00 20.00
14 Sabrina's Gengar HOLO R 25.00 35.00
15 Brock HOLO R 7.00 12.00
16 Erika HOLO R 10.00 15.00
17 Lt. Surge HOLO R 7.00 12.00
18 Misty HOLO R 7.00 12.00
19 The Rocket's Trap HOLO R 7.00 12.00
20 Brock's Golem R 5.00 8.00
21 Brock's Onix R 2.00 3.00
22 Brock's Rhyhorn R 1.25 2.00
23 Brock's Sandslash R 2.00 3.00
24 Brock's Zubat R 2.00 3.00
25 Erika's Clefairy R 4.00 7.00
26 Erika's Victreebel R 3.50 6.00
27 Lt. Surge's Electabuzz R 2.50 4.00
28 Lt. Surge's Raichu R 7.00 10.00
29 Misty's Cloyster R 3.00 5.00
30 Misty's Goldeen R 3.00 5.00
31 Misty's Poliwrath R 2.00 3.50
32 Misty's Tentacool R 3.00 5.00
33 Rocket's Snorlax R 4.00 7.00
34 Sabrina's Venomoth R 3.00 4.50
35 Blaine's Growlithe U 1.25 2.00
36 Blaine's Kangaskhan U 1.25 2.00
37 Blaine's Magmar U 1.25 2.00
38 Brock's Geodude U 1.25 2.00
39 Brock's Golbat U 1.25 2.00
40 Brock's Graveler U 1.25 2.00
41 Brock's Lickitung U 1.25 2.00
42 Erika's Dratini U 1.25 2.00
43 Erika's Exeggcute U 1.25 2.00
44 Erika's Exeggutor U 1.25 2.00
45 Erika's Gloom U 1.25 2.00
46 Erika's Gloom U 1.25 2.00
47 Erika's Oddish U 1.25 2.00
48 Erika's Weepinbell U 1.25 2.00
49 Erika's Weepinbell U 1.25 2.00
50 Lt. Surge's Magnemite U 1.25 2.00
51 Lt. Surge's Raticate U 1.25 2.00
52 Lt. Surge's Spearow U 1.25 2.00
53 Misty's Poliwhirl U 1.25 2.00
54 Misty's Psyduck U 1.25 2.00
55 Misty's Seaking U 1.25 2.00
56 Misty's Starmie U 1.25 2.00
57 Misty's Tentacool U 1.25 2.00
58 Sabrina's Haunter U 1.25 2.00
59 Sabrina's Jynx U 1.25 2.00
60 Sabrina's Slowbro U 1.25 2.00
61 Blaine's Charmander C 1.25 2.00
62 Blaine's Growlithe C 1.25 2.00
63 Blaine's Ponyta C 1.25 2.00
64 Blaine's Tauros C 1.25 2.00
65 Blaine's Vulpix C 1.25 2.00
66 Brock's Geodude C 1.25 2.00
67 Brock's Mankey C 1.25 2.00
68 Brock's Mankey C 1.25 2.00
69 Brock's Onix C 1.25 2.00
70 Brock's Rhyhorn C 1.25 2.00
71 Brock's Sandshrew C 1.25 2.00
72 Brock's Sandshrew C 1.25 2.00
73 Brock's Vulpix C 1.25 2.00
74 Brock's Zubat C 1.25 2.00
75 Erika's Bellsprout C 1.25 2.00
76 Erika's Bellsprout C 1.25 2.00
77 Erika's Exeggcute C 1.25 2.00
78 Erika's Oddish C 1.25 2.00
79 Erika's Tangela C 1.25 2.00
80 Lt. Surge's Magnemite C 1.25 2.00
81 Lt. Surge's Pikachu C 1.25 2.00
82 Lt. Surge's Rattata C 1.25 2.00
83 Lt. Surge's Spearow C 1.25 2.00
84 Lt. Surge's Voltorb C 1.25 2.00
85 Misty's Goldeen C 1.25 2.00
86 Misty's Horsea C 1.25 2.00
87 Misty's Poliwag C 1.25 2.00
88 Misty's Seel C 1.25 2.00
89 Misty's Shellder C 1.25 2.00
90 Misty's Staryu C 1.25 2.00
91 Sabrina's Abra C 1.25 2.00
92 Sabrina's Drowzee C 1.25 2.00
93 Sabrina's Gastly C 1.25 2.00
94 Sabrina's Mr. Mime C 1.25 2.00
95 Sabrina's Slowpoke C 1.25 2.00
96 Sabrina's Venonat C 1.25 2.00
97 Blaine's Quiz #1 R 3.00 5.00
98 Brock R 2.00 3.00
99 Charity R 1.50 2.50
100 Erika R 2.50 4.00
101 Lt. Surge R 1.25 2.00
102 Misty R 2.00 3.00
103 No Removal Gym R 3.00 5.00
104 The Rocket's Gym R 1.25 2.00
105 Blaine's Last Resort U 1.25 2.00
106 Brock's Training Method U 1.25 2.00
107 Celadon City Gym U 1.25 2.00
108 Cerulean City Gym U 1.25 2.00
109 Erika's Maids U 1.25 2.00
110 Erika's Perfume U 1.25 2.00
111 Good Manners U 1.25 2.00
112 Lt. Surge's Treaty U 1.25 2.00
113 Minion of Team Rocket U 1.25 2.00
114 Misty's Wrath U 1.25 2.00
115 Pewter City Gym U 1.25 2.00
116 Recall U 1.25 2.00
117 Sabrina's ESP U 1.25 2.00
118 Secret Mission U 1.25 2.00
119 Tickling Machine U 1.25 2.00
120 Vermillion City Gym U 1.25 2.00
121 Blaine's Gamble C 1.25 2.00
122 Energy Flow C 1.25 2.00
123 Misty's Duel C 1.25 2.00
124 Narrow Gym C 1.25 2.00
125 Sabrina's Gaze C 1.25 2.00
126 Trash Exchange C 1.25 2.00
127 Fighting Energy C 1.25 2.00
128 Fire Energy C 1.25 2.00
129 Grass Energy C 1.25 2.00
130 Lightning Energy C 1.25 2.00
131 Psychic Energy C 1.25 2.00
132 Water Energy C 1.25 2.00

2000 Pokemon Gym Heroes Unlimited

COMPLETE SET (132) 150.00 250.00
BOOSTER BOX (36 PACKS) 600.00 700.00
BOOSTER PACK (11 CARDS) 15.00 20.00
RELEASED ON AUGUST 14, 2000
1 Blaine's Moltres HOLO R 6.00 10.00
2 Brock's Rhydon HOLO R 2.00 3.50
3 Erika's Clefable HOLO R 3.00 5.00
4 Erika's Dragonair HOLO R 5.00 8.00
5 Erika's Vileplume HOLO R 2.00 3.50
6 Lt. Surge's Electabuzz HOLO R 5.00 8.00
7 Lt. Surge's Fearow HOLO R 4.00 6.00
8 Lt. Surge's Magneton HOLO R 2.00 3.50
9 Misty's Seadra HOLO R 2.00 3.50
10 Misty's Tentacruel HOLO R 2.50 4.00
11 Rocket's Hitmonchan HOLO R 4.00 6.00
12 Rocket's Moltres HOLO R 6.00 10.00
13 Rocket's Scyther HOLO R 6.00 10.00
14 Sabrina's Gengar HOLO R 5.00 8.00
15 Brock HOLO R 4.00 6.00
16 Erika HOLO R 6.00 10.00
17 Lt. Surge HOLO R 4.00 6.00
18 Misty HOLO R 4.00 6.00
19 The Rocket's Trap HOLO R 3.00 5.00
20 Brock's Golem R 1.25 2.00
21 Brock's Onix R .75 1.25
22 Brock's Rhyhorn R 1.25 2.00
23 Brock's Sandslash R 1.25 2.00
24 Brock's Zubat R 1.00 1.75
25 Erika's Clefairy R .75 1.25
26 Erika's Victreebel R 2.50 4.00
27 Lt. Surge's Electabuzz R .75 1.25
28 Lt. Surge's Raichu R 2.50 4.00
29 Misty's Cloyster R 1.25 2.00
30 Misty's Goldeen R .75 1.25
31 Misty's Poliwrath R 1.00 1.75
32 Misty's Tentacool R .75 1.25
33 Rocket's Snorlax R 1.25 2.00
34 Sabrina's Venomoth R 1.25 2.00
35 Blaine's Growlithe U .75 1.25
36 Blaine's Kangaskhan U .75 1.25
37 Blaine's Magmar U .75 1.25
38 Brock's Geodude U .75 1.25
39 Brock's Golbat U .75 1.25
40 Brock's Graveler U .75 1.25
41 Brock's Lickitung U .75 1.25
42 Erika's Dratini U .75 1.25
43 Erika's Exeggcute U .75 1.25
44 Erika's Exeggutor U .75 1.25
45 Erika's Gloom U .75 1.25
46 Erika's Gloom U .75 1.25
47 Erika's Oddish U .75 1.25
48 Erika's Weepinbell U .75 1.25
49 Erika's Weepinbell U .75 1.25
50 Lt. Surge's Magnemite U .75 1.25
51 Lt. Surge's Raticate U .75 1.25
52 Lt. Surge's Spearow U .75 1.25
53 Misty's Poliwhirl U .75 1.25
54 Misty's Psyduck U .75 1.25
55 Misty's Seaking U .75 1.25
56 Misty's Starmie U .75 1.25
57 Misty's Tentacool U .75 1.25
58 Sabrina's Haunter U .75 1.25
59 Sabrina's Jynx U .75 1.25
60 Sabrina's Slowbro U .75 1.25
61 Blaine's Charmander C .40 .75
62 Blaine's Growlithe C .40 .75
63 Blaine's Ponyta C .40 .75
64 Blaine's Tauros C .40 .75
65 Blaine's Vulpix C .40 .75
66 Brock's Geodude C .40 .75
67 Brock's Mankey C .40 .75
68 Brock's Mankey C .40 .75
69 Brock's Onix C .40 .75
70 Brock's Rhyhorn C .40 .75
71 Brock's Sandshrew C .40 .75
72 Brock's Sandshrew C .40 .75
73 Brock's Vulpix C .40 .75
74 Brock's Zubat C .40 .75
75 Erika's Bellsprout C .40 .75
76 Erika's Bellsprout C .40 .75
77 Erika's Exeggcute C .40 .75
78 Erika's Oddish C .40 .75
79 Erika's Tangela C .40 .75
80 Lt. Surge's Magnemite C .40 .75
81 Lt. Surge's Pikachu C .40 .75
82 Lt. Surge's Rattata C .40 .75
83 Lt. Surge's Spearow C .40 .75
84 Lt. Surge's Voltorb C .40 .75
85 Misty's Goldeen C .40 .75
86 Misty's Horsea C .40 .75
87 Misty's Poliwag C .40 .75
88 Misty's Seel C .40 .75
89 Misty's Shellder C .40 .75
90 Misty's Staryu C .40 .75
91 Sabrina's Abra C .40 .75
92 Sabrina's Drowzee C .40 .75
93 Sabrina's Gastly C .40 .75
94 Sabrina's Mr. Mime C .40 .75
95 Sabrina's Slowpoke C .40 .75
96 Sabrina's Venonat C .40 .75
97 Blaine's Quiz #1 R 1.25 2.00
98 Brock R .75 1.25
99 Charity R .75 1.25
100 Erika R 1.50 2.50
101 Lt. Surge R .75 1.25
102 Misty R .75 1.25
103 No Removal Gym R 2.00 3.00
104 The Rocket's Gym R 1.25 1.75
105 Blaine's Last Resort U .75 1.25
106 Brock's Training Method U .75 1.25
107 Celadon City Gym U .75 1.25
108 Cerulean City Gym U .75 1.25
109 Erika's Maids U .75 1.25
110 Erika's Perfume U .75 1.25
111 Good Manners U .75 1.25
112 Lt. Surge's Treaty U .75 1.25
113 Minion of Team Rocket U .75 1.25
114 Misty's Wrath U .75 1.25
115 Pewter City Gym U .75 1.25
116 Recall U .75 1.25
117 Sabrina's ESP U .75 1.25
118 Secret Mission U .75 1.25
119 Tickling Machine U .75 1.25
120 Vermillion City Gym U .75 1.25
121 Blaine's Gamble C .40 .75
122 Energy Flow C .40 .75
123 Misty's Duel C .40 .75
124 Narrow Gym C .40 .75
125 Sabrina's Gaze C .40 .75
126 Trash Exchange C .40 .75
127 Fighting Energy C .40 .75
128 Fire Energy C .40 .75
129 Grass Energy C .40 .75
130 Lightning Energy C .40 .75
131 Psychic Energy C .40 .75
132 Water Energy C .40 .75

2000 Pokemon Gym Challenge 1st Edition

COMPLETE SET (132) 500.00 765.00
BOOSTER BOX (36 PACKS) 700.00 850.00
BOOSTER PACK (11 CARDS) 20.00 25.00
RELEASED ON OCTOBER 16, 2000
1 Blaine's Arcanine HOLO R 20.00 30.00
2 Blaine's Charizard HOLO R 50.00 80.00
3 Brock's Ninetales HOLO R 10.00 15.00
4 Erika's Venusaur HOLO R 20.00 30.00
5 Giovanni's Gyarados HOLO R 15.00 20.00
6 Giovanni's Machamp HOLO R 10.00 15.00
7 Giovanni's Nidoking HOLO R 10.00 15.00
8 Giovanni's Persian HOLO R 8.00 15.00
9 Koga's Beedrill HOLO R 8.00 12.00
10 Koga's Ditto HOLO R 15.00 20.00
11 Lt. Surge's Raichu HOLO R 10.00 15.00
12 Misty's Golduck HOLO R 10.00 15.00
13 Misty's Gyarados HOLO R 20.00 25.00
14 Rocket's Mewtwo HOLO R 20.00 30.00
15 Rocket's Zapdos HOLO R 15.00 20.00
16 Sabrina's Alakazam HOLO R 15.00 20.00
17 Blaine HOLO R 8.00 12.00
18 Giovanni HOLO R 8.00 12.00
19 Koga HOLO R 10.00 15.00
20 Sabrina HOLO R 10.00 15.00
21 Blaine's Ninetales R 4.00 6.00
22 Brock's Dugtrio R 4.00 6.00
23 Giovanni's Nidoqueen R 3.00 5.00
24 Giovanni's Pinsir R 3.00 5.00
25 Koga's Arbok R 3.00 5.00
26 Koga's Muk R 3.00 5.00
27 Koga's Pidgeotto R 3.00 5.00
28 Lt. Surge's Jolteon R 5.00 8.00
29 Sabrina's Gengar R 6.00 10.00
30 Sabrina's Golduck R 2.50 4.00
31 Blaine's Charmeleon U 2.00 3.50
32 Blaine's Dodrio U 2.00 3.50
33 Blaine's Rapidash U 2.00 3.50
34 Brock's Graveler U 2.00 3.50
35 Brock's Primeape U 2.00 3.50
36 Brock's Sandslash U 2.00 3.50
37 Brock's Vulpix U 2.00 3.50
38 Erika's Bellsprout U 2.00 3.50
39 Erika's Bulbasaur U 2.00 3.50
40 Erika's Clefairy U 2.00 3.50
41 Erika's Ivysaur U 2.00 3.50
42 Giovanni's Machoke U 2.00 3.50
43 Giovanni's Meowth U 2.00 3.50
44 Giovanni's Nidorina U 2.00 3.50
45 Giovanni's Nidorino U 2.00 3.50
46 Koga's Golbat U 2.00 3.50
47 Koga's Kakuna U 2.00 3.50
48 Koga's Koffing U 2.00 3.50
49 Koga's Pidgey U 2.00 3.50
50 Koga's Weezing U 2.00 3.50
51 Lt. Surge's Eevee U 2.00 3.50
52 Lt. Surge's Electrode U 2.00 3.50
53 Lt. Surge's Raticate U 2.00 3.50
54 Misty's Dewgong U 2.00 3.50
55 Sabrina's Haunter U 2.00 3.50
56 Sabrina's Hypno U 2.00 3.50
57 Sabrina's Jynx U 2.00 3.50
58 Sabrina's Kadabra U 2.00 3.50
59 Sabrina's Mr. Mime U 2.00 3.50
60 Blaine's Charmander C 1.25 2.00
61 Blaine's Doduo C 1.25 2.00
62 Blaine's Growlithe C 1.25 2.00
63 Blaine's Mankey C 1.25 2.00
64 Blaine's Ponyta C 1.25 2.00
65 Blaine's Rhyhorn C 1.25 2.00
66 Blaine's Vulpix C 1.25 2.00
67 Brock's Diglett C 1.25 2.00
68 Brock's Geodude C 1.25 2.00
69 Erika's Jigglypuff C 1.25 2.00
70 Erika's Oddish C 1.25 2.00
71 Erika's Paras C 1.25 2.00
72 Giovanni's Machop C 1.25 2.00
73 Giovanni's Magikarp (C) 1.25 2.00
74 Giovanni's Meowth C 1.25 2.00
75 Giovanni's Nidoran (Fem) C 1.25 2.00
76 Giovanni's Nidoran (Male) C 1.25 2.00
77 Koga's Ekans C 1.25 2.00
78 Koga's Grimer C 1.25 2.00
79 Koga's Koffing C 1.25 2.00
80 Koga's Pidgey C 1.25 2.00
81 Koga's Tangela C 1.25 2.00
82 Koga's Weedle C 1.25 2.00
83 Koga's Zubat C 1.25 2.00
84 Lt. Surge's Pikachu C 1.25 2.00
85 Lt. Surge's Rattata C 1.25 2.00
86 Lt. Surge's Voltorb C 1.25 2.00
87 Misty's Horsea C 1.25 2.00
88 Misty's Magikarp C 1.25 2.00
89 Misty's Poliwag C 1.25 2.00
90 Misty's Psyduck C 1.25 2.00
91 Misty's Seel C 1.25 2.00
92 Misty's Staryu C 1.25 2.00
93 Sabrina's Abra C 1.25 2.00
94 Sabrina's Abra C 1.25 2.00
95 Sabrina's Drowzee C 1.25 2.00
96 Sabrina's Gastly C 1.25 2.00
97 Sabrina's Gastly C 1.25 2.00
98 Sabrina's Porygon C 1.25 2.00
99 Sabrina's Psyduck C 1.25 2.00
100 Blaine R 3.00 5.00
101 Brock's Protection R 2.00 3.00
102 Chaos Gym R 3.00 4.00
103 Erika's Kindness R 2.00 3.00
104 Giovanni R 3.00 4.00
105 Giovanni's Last Resort R 2.00 3.00
106 Koga R 3.00 5.00
107 Lt. Surge's Secret Plan R 2.00 3.00
108 Misty's Wish R 3.00 5.00
109 Resistance Gym R 2.00 3.00
110 Sabrina R 3.00 5.00
111 Blaine's Quiz #2 U 1.50 2.50
112 Blaine's Quiz #3 U 1.50 2.50
113 Cinnabar City Gym U 1.25 2.00
114 Fuchsia City Gym U 1.25 2.00
115 Koga's Ninja Trick U 2.00 3.00
116 Master Ball U 2.00 3.50
117 Max Revive U 1.50 2.50
118 Misty's Tears U 3.00 4.00
119 Rocket's Minefield Gym U 1.50 2.50
120 Rocket's Secret Experiment U 2.00 3.00
121 Sabrina's Psychic Control U 1.25 2.00
122 Saffron City Gym U 1.25 2.00
123 Viridian City Gym U 1.25 2.00
124 Fervor C 1.25 2.00
125 Transparent Walls C 1.25 2.00
126 Warp Point C 1.25 2.00
127 Fighting Energy C 1.25 1.50
128 Fire Energy C 1.25 1.50
129 Grass Energy C 1.25 1.50
130 Lightning Energy C 1.25 1.50
131 Psychic Energy C 1.25 1.50
132 Water Energy C 1.25 1.50

2000 Pokemon Gym Challenge Unlimited

COMPLETE SET (132) 225.00 350.00
BOOSTER BOX (36 PACKS) 600.00 700.00
BOOSTER PACK (11 CARDS) 15.00 20.00
RELEASED ON OCTOBER 16, 2000
1 Blaine's Arcanine HOLO R 6.00 10.00
2 Blaine's Charizard HOLO R 25.00 35.00
3 Brock's Ninetales HOLO R 6.00 10.00
4 Erika's Venusaur HOLO R 10.00 15.00
5 Giovanni's Gyarados HOLO R 6.00 10.00
6 Giovanni's Machamp HOLO R 5.00 8.00
7 Giovanni's Nidoking HOLO R 7.00 11.00
8 Giovanni's Persian HOLO R 3.00 5.00
9 Koga's Beedrill HOLO R 3.00 5.00
10 Koga's Ditto HOLO R 4.00 6.00
11 Lt. Surge's Raichu HOLO R 6.00 10.00
12 Misty's Golduck HOLO R 5.00 8.00
13 Misty's Gyarados HOLO R 7.00 11.00
14 Rocket's Mewtwo HOLO R 10.00 15.00
15 Rocket's Zapdos HOLO R 7.00 11.00
16 Sabrina's Alakazam HOLO R 5.00 8.00
17 Blaine HOLO R 3.00 5.00
18 Giovanni HOLO R 4.00 6.00
19 Koga HOLO R 3.00 5.00
20 Sabrina HOLO R 5.00 8.00
21 Blaine's Ninetales R 2.00 3.00
22 Brock's Dugtrio R 2.00 3.00

23 Giovanni's Nidoqueen R 2.00 3.00
24 Giovanni's Pinsir R 2.00 3.00
25 Koga's Arbok R 2.00 3.00
26 Koga's Muk R 2.00 3.00
27 Koga's Pidgeotto R 2.00 3.00
28 Lt. Surge's Jolteon R 2.00 3.00
29 Sabrina's Gengar R 2.00 3.00
30 Sabrina's Golduck R 2.00 3.00
31 Blaine's Charmeleon U .75 1.25
32 Blaine's Dodrio U .75 1.25
33 Blaine's Rapidash U .75 1.25
34 Brock's Graveler U .75 1.25
35 Brock's Primeape U .75 1.25
36 Brock's Sandslash U .75 1.25
37 Brock's Vulpix U .75 1.25
38 Erika's Bellsprout U .75 1.25
39 Erika's Bulbasaur U .75 1.25
40 Erika's Clefairy U .75 1.25
41 Erika's Ivysaur U .75 1.25
42 Giovanni's Machoke U .75 1.25
43 Giovanni's Meowth U .75 1.25
44 Giovanni's Nidorina U .75 1.25
45 Giovanni's Nidorino U .75 1.25
46 Koga's Golbat U .75 1.25
47 Koga's Kakuna U .75 1.25
48 Koga's Koffing U .75 1.25
49 Koga's Pidgey U .75 1.25
50 Koga's Weezing U .75 1.25
51 Lt. Surge's Eevee U .75 1.25
52 Lt. Surge's Electrode U .75 1.25
53 Lt. Surge's Raticate U .75 1.25
54 Misty's Dewgong U .75 1.25
55 Sabrina's Haunter U .75 1.25
56 Sabrina's Hypno U .75 1.25
57 Sabrina's Jynx U .75 1.25
58 Sabrina's Kadabra U .75 1.25
59 Sabrina's Mr. Mime U .75 1.25
60 Blaine's Charmander C .40 .75
61 Blaine's Doduo C .40 .75
62 Blaine's Growlithe C .40 .75
63 Blaine's Mankey C .40 .75
64 Blaine's Ponyta C .40 .75
65 Blaine's Rhyhorn C .40 .75
66 Blaine's Vulpix C .40 .75
67 Brock's Diglett C .40 .75
68 Brock's Geodude C .40 .75
69 Erika's Jigglypuff C .40 .75
70 Erika's Oddish C .40 .75
71 Erika's Paras C .40 .75
72 Giovanni's Machop C .40 .75
73 Giovanni's Magikarp C .40 .75
74 Giovanni's Meowth C .40 .75
75 Giovanni's Nidoran (Fem) C .40 .75
76 Giovanni's Nidoran (Male) C .40 .75
77 Koga's Ekans C .40 .75
78 Koga's Grimer C .40 .75
79 Koga's Koffing C .40 .75
80 Koga's Pidgey C .40 .75
81 Koga's Tangela C .40 .75
82 Koga's Weedle C .40 .75
83 Koga's Zubat C .40 .75
84 Lt. Surge's Pikachu C .40 .75
85 Lt. Surge's Rattata C .40 .75
86 Lt. Surge's Voltorb C .40 .75
87 Misty's Horsea C .40 .75
88 Misty's Magikarp C .40 .75
89 Misty's Poliwag C .40 .75
90 Misty's Psyduck C .40 .75
91 Misty's Seel C .40 .75
92 Misty's Staryu C .40 .75
93 Sabrina's Abra C .40 .75
94 Sabrina's Abra C .40 .75
95 Sabrina's Drowzee C .40 .75
96 Sabrina's Gastly C .40 .75
97 Sabrina's Gastly C .40 .75
98 Sabrina's Porygon C .40 .75
99 Sabrina's Psyduck C .40 .75
100 Blaine R 2.00 3.00
101 Brock's Protection R 2.00 3.00
102 Chaos Gym R 2.00 3.00
103 Erika's Kindness R 2.00 3.00
104 Giovanni R 2.00 3.00
105 Giovanni's Last Resort R 2.00 3.00
106 Koga R 2.00 3.00
107 Lt. Surge's Secret Plan R 2.00 3.00
108 Misty's Wish R 2.00 3.00
109 Resistance Gym R 2.00 3.00
110 Sabrina R 2.00 3.00
111 Blaine's Quiz #2 U .75 1.25
112 Blaine's Quiz #3 U .75 1.25
113 Cinnabar City Gym U .75 1.25
114 Fuchsia City Gym U .75 1.25
115 Koga's Ninja Trick U .75 1.25
116 Master Ball U .75 1.25
117 Max Revive U .75 1.25
118 Misty's Tears U .75 1.25
119 Rocket's Minefield Gym U .75 1.25
120 Rocket's secret Experiment U .75 1.25
121 Sabrina's Psychic Control U .75 1.25
122 Saffron City Gym U .75 1.25
123 Viridian City Gym U .75 1.25
124 Fervor C .40 .75
125 Transparent Walls C .40 .75
126 Warp Point C .40 .75
127 Fighting Energy C .40 .75
128 Fire Energy C .40 .75
129 Grass Energy C .40 .75
130 Lightning Energy C .40 .75
131 Psychic Energy C .40 .75
132 Water Energy C .40 .75

2000 Pokemon Neo Genesis 1st Edition

COMPLETE SET (111) 375.00 600.00
BOOSTER BOX (36 PACKS) 1000.00 1500.00
BOOSTER PACK (11 CARDS) 30.00 35.00
RELEASED ON DECEMBER 16, 2000
1 Ampharos HOLO R 7.00 12.00
2 Azumarill HOLO R 7.00 12.00
3 Bellossom HOLO R 6.00 10.00
4 Feraligatr Lv.56 HOLO R 15.00 25.00
5 Feraligatr Lv.69 HOLO R 15.00 25.00
6 Heracross HOLO R 10.00 15.00
7 Jumpluff HOLO R 6.00 10.00
8 Kingdra HOLO R 7.00 12.00
9 Lugia HOLO R 40.00 60.00
10 Meganium Lv.54 HOLO R 15.00 25.00
11 Meganium Lv.57 HOLO R 15.00 25.00
12 Pichu HOLO R 20.00 30.00
13 Skarmory HOLO R 7.00 12.00
14 Slowking HOLO R 10.00 15.00
15 Steelix HOLO R 15.00 20.00
16 Togetic HOLO R 7.00 12.00
17 Typhlosion Lv.55 HOLO R 25.00 40.00
18 Typhlosion Lv.57 HOLO R 20.00 35.00
19 Metal Energy HOLO R 6.00 10.00
20 Cleffa R 8.00 13.00
21 Donphan R 2.50 4.00
22 Elekid R 3.00 5.00
23 Magby R 2.50 4.00
24 Murkrow R 2.50 4.00
25 Sneasel R 2.50 4.00
26 Aipom U 1.00 1.75
27 Ariados U 1.00 1.75
28 Bayleef Lv.22 U 1.00 1.75
29 Bayleef Lv.39 U 1.00 1.75
30 Clefairy U 1.00 1.75
31 Croconaw Lv.34 U 1.00 1.75
32 Croconaw Lv.41 U 1.00 1.75
33 Electabuzz U 1.00 1.75
34 Flaaffy U 1.00 1.75
35 Furret U 1.00 1.75
36 Gloom U 1.00 1.75
37 Granbull U 1.00 1.75
38 Lanturn U 1.00 1.75
39 Ledian U 1.00 1.75
40 Magmar U 1.00 1.75
41 Miltank U 1.00 1.75
42 Noctowl U 1.00 1.75
43 Phanpy U 1.00 1.75
44 Piloswine U 1.00 1.75
45 Quagsire U 1.00 1.75
46 Quilava Lv.28 U 1.00 1.75
47 Quilava Lv.35 U 1.00 1.75
48 Seadra U 1.00 1.75
49 Skiploom U 1.00 1.75
50 Sunflora U 1.00 1.75
51 Togepi U 1.00 1.75
52 Xatu U 1.00 1.75
53 Chikorita Lv.12 C 1.00 1.75
54 Chikorita Lv.19 C 1.00 1.75
55 Chinchou C 1.00 1.75
56 Cyndaquil Lv.14 C 1.00 1.75
57 Cyndaquil Lv.21 C 1.00 1.75
58 Girafarig C 1.00 1.75
59 Gligar C 1.00 1.75
60 Hoothoot C 1.00 1.75
61 Hoppip C 1.00 1.75
62 Horsea C 1.00 1.75
63 Ledyba C 1.00 1.75
64 Mantine C 1.00 1.75
65 Mareep C 1.00 1.75
66 Marill C 1.00 1.75
67 Natu C 1.00 1.75
68 Oddish C 1.00 1.75
69 Onix C 1.00 1.75
70 Pikachu C 1.00 1.75
71 Sentret C 1.00 1.75
72 Shuckle C 1.00 1.75
73 Slowpoke C 1.00 1.75
74 Snubbull C 1.00 1.75
75 Spinarak C 1.00 1.75
76 Stantler C 1.00 1.75
77 Sudowoodo C 1.00 1.75
78 Sunkern C 1.00 1.75
79 Swinub C 1.00 1.75
80 Totodile Lv.13 C 1.00 1.75
81 Totodile Lv.20 C 1.00 1.75
82 Wooper C 1.00 1.75
83 Arcade Game R 2.00 3.00
84 Ecogym R 1.75 3.00
85 Energy Charge R 2.00 3.00
86 Focus Band R 4.00 6.00
87 Mary R 1.75 3.00
88 PokeGear R 2.00 3.50
89 Super Energy Retrieval R 2.50 4.00
90 Time Capsule R 1.50 2.50
91 Bill's Teleporter U 1.00 1.75
92 Card-Flip Game U 1.00 1.75
93 Gold Berry U 1.00 1.75
94 Miracle Berry U 1.00 1.75
95 New Pokedex U 1.00 1.75
96 Professor Elm U 1.00 1.75
97 Sprout Tower U 1.00 1.75
98 Super Scoop Up U 1.00 1.75
99 Berry C 1.00 1.75
100 Double Gust C 1.00 1.75
101 Moo-Moo Milk C 1.00 1.75
102 Pokemon March C 1.00 1.75
103 Super Rod C 1.00 1.75
104 Darkness Energy R 2.50 4.00
105 Recycle Energy R 2.00 3.50
106 Fighting Energy 1.00 1.75
107 Fire Energy 1.00 1.75
108 Grass Energy 1.00 1.75
109 Lightning Energy 1.00 1.75
110 Psychic Energy 1.00 1.75
111 Water Energy 1.00 1.75

2000 Pokemon Neo Genesis Unlimited

COMPLETE SET (111) 165.00 260.00
BOOSTER BOX (36 PACKS) 800.00 1100.00
BOOSTER PACK (11 CARDS) 20.00 25.00
HOTFOOT DECK (60 CARDS) 15.00 25.00
COLD FUSION DECK (60 CARDS) 20.00 25.00
RELEASED ON DECEMBER 16, 2000
1 Ampharos HOLO R 2.00 3.50
2 Azumarill HOLO R 3.00 5.00
3 Bellossom HOLO R 2.50 4.00
4 Feraligatr Lv.56 HOLO R 6.00 10.00
5 Feraligatr Lv.69 HOLO R 7.00 12.00
6 Heracross HOLO R 4.00 6.00
7 Jumpluff HOLO R 1.25 2.00
8 Kingdra HOLO R 1.50 2.50
9 Lugia HOLO R 15.00 20.00
10 Meganium Lv.54 HOLO R 6.00 10.00
11 Meganium Lv.57 HOLO R 6.00 10.00
12 Pichu HOLO R 7.00 12.00
13 Skarmory HOLO R 2.50 4.00
14 Slowking HOLO R 5.00 8.00
15 Steelix HOLO R 4.00 6.00
16 Togetic HOLO R 4.00 6.00
17 Typhlosion Lv.55 HOLO R 12.00 17.00
18 Typhlosion Lv.57 HOLO R 12.00 17.00
19 Metal Energy HOLO R 5.00 8.00
20 Cleffa R 6.00 10.00
21 Donphan R .75 1.25
22 Elekid R .50 .75
23 Magby R .50 .75
24 Murkrow R .75 1.00
25 Sneasel R 1.25 2.00
26 Aipom U .75 1.25
27 Ariados U .75 1.25
28 Bayleef Lv.22 U .75 1.25
29 Bayleef Lv.39 U .75 1.25
30 Clefairy U .75 1.25
31 Croconaw Lv.34 U .75 1.25
32 Croconaw Lv.41 U .75 1.25
33 Electabuzz U .75 1.25
34 Flaaffy U .75 1.25
35 Furret U .75 1.25
36 Gloom U .75 1.25
37 Granbull U .75 1.25
38 Lanturn U .75 1.25
39 Ledian U .75 1.25
40 Magmar U .75 1.25
41 Miltank U .75 1.25
42 Noctowl U .75 1.25
43 Phanpy U .75 1.25
44 Piloswine U .75 1.25
45 Quagsire U .75 1.25
46 Quilava Lv.28 U .75 1.25
47 Quilava Lv.35 U .75 1.25
48 Seadra U .75 1.25
49 Skiploom U .75 1.25
50 Sunflora U .75 1.25
51 Togepi U .75 1.25
52 Xatu U .75 1.25
53 Chikorita Lv.12 C .30 .50
54 Chikorita Lv.19 C .30 .50
55 Chinchou C .30 .50
56 Cyndaquil Lv.14 C .30 .50
57 Cyndaquil Lv.21 C .30 .50
58 Girafarig C .30 .50
59 Gligar C .30 .50
60 Hoothoot C .30 .50
61 Hoppip C .30 .50
62 Horsea C .30 .50
63 Ledyba C .30 .50
64 Mantine C .30 .50
65 Mareep C .30 .50
66 Marill C .30 .50
67 Natu C .30 .50
68 Oddish C .30 .50
69 Onix C .30 .50
70 Pikachu C .30 .50
71 Sentret C .30 .50
72 Shuckle C .30 .50
73 Slowpoke C .30 .50
74 Snubbull C .30 .50
75 Spinarak C .30 .50
76 Stantler C .30 .50
77 Sudowoodo C .30 .50
78 Sunkern C .30 .50
79 Swinub C .30 .50
80 Totodile Lv.13 C .30 .50
81 Totodile Lv.20 C .30 .50
82 Wooper C .30 .50
83 Arcade Game R .50 .75
84 Ecogym R 1.25 1.75
85 Energy Charge R .75 1.25
86 Focus Band R 2.50 4.00
87 Mary R .50 .75
88 PokeGear R .50 .75
89 Super Energy Retrieval R .75 1.25
90 Time Capsule R .50 .75
91 Bill's Teleporter U .75 1.25
92 Card-Flip Game U .75 1.25
93 Gold Berry U .75 1.25
94 Miracle Berry U .75 1.25
95 New Pokedex U .75 1.25
96 Professor Elm U .75 1.25
97 Sprout Tower U .75 1.25
98 Super Scoop Up U .75 1.25
99 Berry C .30 .50
100 Double Gust C .30 .50
101 Moo-Moo Milk C .30 .50
102 Pokemon March C .30 .50
103 Super Rod C .30 .50
104 Darkness Energy R 2.00 3.50
105 Recycle Energy R 2.50 4.00
106 Fighting Energy .30 .50
107 Fire Energy .30 .50
108 Grass Energy .30 .50
109 Lightning Energy .30 .50
110 Psychic Energy .30 .50
111 Water Energy .30 .50

2001 Pokemon Neo Discovery 1st Edition

COMPLETE SET (75) 440.00 650.00
BOOSTER BOX (36 PACKS) 1800.00 2200.00
BOOSTER PACK (11 CARDS) 25.00 30.00
RELEASED ON JUNE 1, 2001
1 Espeon HOLO R 55.00 70.00
2 Forretress HOLO R 6.00 10.00
3 Hitmontop HOLO R 15.00 20.00
4 Houndoom HOLO R 10.00 15.00
5 Houndour HOLO R 25.00 35.00
6 Kabutops HOLO R 10.00 15.00
7 Magnemite HOLO R 8.00 12.00
8 Politoed HOLO R 20.00 30.00
9 Poliwrath HOLO R 10.00 15.00
10 Scizor HOLO R 15.00 25.00
11 Smeargle HOLO R 6.00 10.00
12 Tyranitar HOLO R 35.00 50.00
13 Umbreon HOLO R 65.00 80.00
14 Unown A HOLO R 8.00 12.00
15 Ursaring HOLO R 8.00 12.00
16 Wobbuffet HOLO R 8.00 12.00
17 Yanma HOLO R 10.00 15.00
18 Beedrill R 2.00 3.50
19 Butterfree R 2.00 3.50
20 Espeon R 6.00 10.00
21 Forretress R 3.00 5.00
22 Hitmontop R 2.00 3.50
23 Houndoom R 3.00 5.00
24 Houndour R 2.00 3.50
25 Kabutops R 3.00 5.00
26 Magnemite R 3.00 5.00
27 Politoed R 4.00 7.00
28 Poliwrath R 2.00 3.50
29 Scizor R 3.00 5.00
30 Smeargle R 3.00 5.00
31 Tyranitar R 10.00 15.00
32 Umbreon R 6.00 10.00
33 Unown A R 3.00 5.00
34 Ursaring R 2.50 4.00
35 Wobbuffet R 3.00 5.00
36 Yanma R 2.50 4.00
37 Corsola U 2.00 3.50
38 Eevee U 2.00 3.50
39 Houndour U 2.00 3.50
40 Igglybuff U 2.00 3.50
41 Kakuna U 2.00 3.50
42 Metapod U 2.00 3.50
43 Omastar U 2.00 3.50
44 Poliwhirl U 2.00 3.50
45 Pupitar U 2.00 3.50
46 Scyther U 2.00 3.50
47 Unown D U 2.00 3.50
48 Unown F U 2.00 3.50
49 Unown M U 2.00 3.50
50 Unown N U 2.00 3.50
51 Unown U U 2.00 3.50
52 Xatu U 2.00 3.50
53 Caterpie C 1.25 2.00
54 Dunsparce C 1.25 2.00
55 Hoppip C 1.25 2.00
56 Kabuto C 1.25 2.00
57 Larvitar C 1.25 2.00
58 Mareep C 1.25 2.00
59 Natu C 1.25 2.00
60 Omanyte C 1.25 2.00
61 Pineco C 1.25 2.00
62 Poliwag C 1.25 2.00
63 Sentret C 1.25 2.00
64 Spinarak C 1.25 2.00
65 Teddiursa C 1.25 2.00
66 Tyrogue C 1.25 2.00
67 Unown E C 1.25 2.00
68 Unown I C 1.25 2.00
69 Unown O C 1.25 2.00
70 Weedle C 1.25 2.00
71 Wooper C 1.25 2.00
72 Trainer: Fossil Egg U 2.00 3.50
73 Trainer: Hyper Devolution Spray U 2.00 3.50
74 Trainer: Ruin Wall U 2.00 3.50
75 Trainer: Energy Ark C 1.25 2.00

2001 Pokemon Neo Discovery Unlimited

COMPLETE SET (75) 170.00 260.00
BOOSTER BOX (36 PACKS) 800.00 1200.00
BOOSTER PACK (11 CARDS) 20.00 25.00
BRAINWAVE DECK 10.00 25.00
WALLOP DECK 10.00 25.00
RELEASED ON JUNE 1, 2001
1 Espeon HOLO R 15.00 20.00
2 Forretress HOLO R 4.00 6.00
3 Hitmontop HOLO R 2.00 3.50
4 Houndoom HOLO R 6.00 10.00
5 Houndour HOLO R 5.00 8.00
6 Kabutops HOLO R 4.00 6.00
7 Magnemite HOLO R 2.00 3.50
8 Politoed HOLO R 6.00 10.00
9 Poliwrath HOLO R 4.00 6.00
10 Scizor HOLO R 4.00 6.00
11 Smeargle HOLO R 4.00 6.00
12 Tyranitar HOLO R 10.00 15.00
13 Umbreon HOLO R 20.00 25.00
14 Unown A HOLO R 3.00 5.00
15 Ursaring HOLO R 4.00 6.00
16 Wobbuffet HOLO R 3.00 5.00
17 Yanma HOLO R 3.00 5.00
18 Beedrill R 1.25 2.00
19 Butterfree R 1.25 2.00
20 Espeon R 3.00 5.00
21 Forretress R 1.25 2.00
22 Hitmontop R 1.25 2.00
23 Houndoom R 1.25 2.00
24 Houndour R 3.00 5.00

25 Kabutops R	1.25	2.00
26 Magnemite R	1.25	2.00
27 Politoed R	1.25	2.00
28 Poliwrath R	1.25	2.00
29 Scizor R	1.25	2.00
30 Smeargle R	1.25	2.00
31 Tyranitar R	5.00	8.00
32 Umbreon R	3.00	5.00
33 Unown A R	1.25	2.00
34 Ursaring R	1.25	2.00
35 Wobbuffet R	1.25	2.00
36 Yanma R	1.25	2.00
37 Corsola U	1.25	2.00
38 Eevee U	1.25	2.00
39 Houndour U	1.25	2.00
40 Igglybuff U	1.25	2.00
41 Kakuna U	1.25	2.00
42 Metapod U	1.25	2.00
43 Omastar U	1.25	2.00
44 Poliwhirl U	1.25	2.00
45 Pupitar U	1.25	2.00
46 Scyther U	1.25	2.00
47 Unown D U	1.25	2.00
48 Unown F U	1.25	2.00
49 Unown M U	1.25	2.00
50 Unown N U	1.25	2.00
51 Unown U U	1.25	2.00
52 Xatu U	1.25	2.00
53 Caterpie C	.75	1.25
54 Dunsparce C	.75	1.25
55 Hoppip C	.75	1.25
56 Kabuto C	.75	1.25
57 Larvitar C	.75	1.25
58 Mareep C	.75	1.25
59 Natu C	.75	1.25
60 Omanyte C	.75	1.25
61 Pineco C	.75	1.25
62 Poliwag C	.75	1.25
63 Sentret C	.75	1.25
64 Spinarak C	.75	1.25
65 Teddiursa C	.75	1.25
66 Tyrogue C	.75	1.25
67 Unown E C	.75	1.25
68 Unown I C	.75	1.25
69 Unown O C	.75	1.25
70 Weedle C	.75	1.25
71 Wooper C	.75	1.25
72 Trainer: Fossil Egg U	1.25	2.00
73 Trainer: Hyper Devolution Spray U	1.25	2.00
74 Trainer: Ruin Wall U	1.25	2.00
75 Trainer: Energy Ark C	.75	1.25

2001 Pokemon Neo Revelation 1st Edition

COMPLETE SET (66)	500.00	700.00
BOOSTER BOX (36 PACKS)	1500.00	1800.00
BOOSTER PACK (11 CARDS)	40.00	50.00
RELEASED ON SEPTEMBER 21, 2001		
1 Ampharos HOLO R	10.00	15.00
2 Blissey HOLO R	15.00	25.00
3 Celebi HOLO R	20.00	30.00
4 Crobat HOLO R	10.00	15.00
5 Delibird HOLO R	10.00	15.00
6 Entei HOLO R	30.00	40.00
7 Ho-oh HOLO R	40.00	60.00
8 Houndoom HOLO R	15.00	20.00
9 Jumpluff HOLO R	15.00	20.00
10 Magneton HOLO R	10.00	15.00
11 Misdreavus HOLO R	25.00	30.00
12 Porygon 2 HOLO R	15.00	20.00
13 Raikou HOLO R	30.00	40.00
14 Suicune HOLO R	45.00	60.00
15 Aerodactyl R	3.00	5.00
16 Celebi R	4.00	6.00
17 Entei R	7.00	10.00
18 Ho-oh R	4.00	7.00
19 Kingdra R	2.00	3.50
20 Lugia R	4.00	6.00
21 Raichu R	3.00	5.00
22 Raikou R	5.00	8.00
23 Skarmory R	2.00	3.50
24 Sneasel R	2.50	4.00
25 Starmie R	4.00	6.00
26 Sudowoodo R	2.00	3.50
27 Suicune R	5.00	8.00
28 Flaaffy U	1.25	2.00
29 Golbat U	1.25	2.00
30 Graveler U	1.25	2.00
31 Jynx U	1.25	2.00
32 Lanturn U	1.25	2.00
33 Magcargo U	1.25	2.00
34 Octillery U	1.25	2.00
35 Parasect U	1.25	2.00
36 Piloswine U	1.25	2.00
37 Seaking U	1.25	2.00
38 Stantler U	1.25	2.00
39 Unown B U	1.25	2.00
40 Unown Y U	1.25	2.00
41 Aipom C	1.25	2.00
42 Chinchou C	1.25	2.00
43 Farfetch'd C	1.25	2.00
44 Geodude C	1.25	2.00
45 Goldeen C	1.25	2.00
46 Murkrow C	1.25	2.00
47 Paras C	1.25	2.00
48 Quagsire C	1.25	2.00
49 Qwilfish C	1.25	2.00
50 Remoraid C	1.25	2.00
51 Shuckle C	1.25	2.00
52 Skiploom C	1.25	2.00
53 Slugma C	1.25	2.00
54 Smoochum C	1.25	2.00
55 Snubbull C	1.25	2.00
56 Staryu C	1.25	2.00
57 Swinub C	1.25	2.00
58 Unown K C	1.25	2.00
59 Zubat C	1.25	2.00
60 Balloon Berry U	1.25	2.00
61 Healing Field U	1.25	2.00
62 Pokemon Breeder Fields U	1.25	2.00
63 Rocket's Hideout U	1.25	2.00
64 Old Rod C	1.25	2.00
65 Shining Gyarados HOLO R	80.00	100.00
66 Shining Magikarp HOLO R	40.00	60.00

2001 Pokemon Neo Revelation Unlimited

COMPLETE SET (66)	180.00	275.00
BOOSTER BOX (36 PACKS)	1000.00	1200.00
BOOSTER PACK (11 CARDS)	25.00	30.00
*CARD VALUES ARE 50% OF 1ST EDITION PRICING.		
RELEASED ON SEPTEMBER 21, 2001		
1 Ampharos HOLO R	6.00	10.00
2 Blissey HOLO R	5.00	8.00
3 Celebi HOLO R	7.00	10.00
4 Crobat HOLO R	5.00	8.00
5 Delibird HOLO R	4.00	6.00
6 Entei HOLO R	10.00	15.00
7 Ho-oh HOLO R	20.00	25.00
8 Houndoom HOLO R	10.00	15.00
9 Jumpluff HOLO R	2.00	3.50
10 Magneton HOLO R	2.00	3.50
11 Misdreavus HOLO R	7.00	10.00
12 Porygon 2 HOLO R	4.00	6.00
13 Raikou HOLO R	10.00	15.00
14 Suicune HOLO R	10.00	15.00
15 Aerodactyl R	1.25	2.00
16 Celebi R	2.00	3.50
17 Entei R	2.00	3.50
18 Ho-oh R	3.00	5.00
19 Kingdra R	1.25	2.00
20 Lugia R	3.00	5.00
21 Raichu R	2.00	3.50
22 Raikou R	2.00	3.50
23 Skarmory R	.75	1.25
24 Sneasel R	.75	1.00
25 Starmie R	.75	1.00
26 Sudowoodo R	.50	.75
27 Suicune R	3.00	5.00
28 Flaaffy U	.40	.60
29 Golbat U	.40	.60
30 Graveler U	.40	.60
31 Jynx U	.40	.60
32 Lanturn U	.40	.60
33 Magcargo U	.40	.60
34 Octillery U	.40	.60
35 Parasect U	.40	.60
36 Piloswine U	.40	.60
37 Seaking U	.40	.60
38 Stantler U	.40	.60
39 Unown B U	.40	.60
40 Unown Y U	.40	.60
41 Aipom C	.30	.50
42 Chinchou C	.30	.50
43 Farfetch'd C	.30	.50
44 Geodude C	.30	.50
45 Goldeen C	.30	.50
46 Murkrow C	.30	.50
47 Paras C	.30	.50
48 Quagsire C	.30	.50
49 Qwilfish C	.30	.50
50 Remoraid C	.30	.50
51 Shuckle C	.30	.50
52 Skiploom C	.30	.50
53 Slugma C	.30	.50
54 Smoochum C	.30	.50
55 Snubbull C	.30	.50
56 Staryu C	.30	.50
57 Swinub C	.30	.50
58 Unown K C	.30	.50
59 Zubat C	.30	.50
60 Balloon Berry U	.40	.60
61 Healing Field U	.75	1.00
62 Pokemon Breeder Fields U	.40	.60
63 Rocket's Hideout U	.40	.60
64 Old Rod C	.30	.50
65 Shining Gyarados HOLO R	25.00	40.00
66 Shining Magikarp HOLO R	20.00	30.00

2002 Pokemon Neo Destiny 1st Edition

COMPLETE SET (113)	1400.00	1800.00
BOOSTER BOX (36 PACKS)	2000.00	3000.00
BOOSTER PACK (11 CARDS)	65.00	80.00
RELEASED ON FEBRUARY 28, 2001		
1 Dark Ampharos HOLO R	20.00	30.00
2 Dark Crobat HOLO R	15.00	20.00
3 Dark Donphan HOLO R	20.00	25.00
4 Dark Espeon HOLO R	60.00	80.00
5 Dark Feraligatr HOLO R	25.00	35.00
6 Dark Gengar HOLO R	20.00	25.00
7 Dark Houndoom HOLO R	25.00	35.00
8 Dark Porygon2 HOLO R	20.00	25.00
9 Dark Scizor HOLO R	20.00	30.00
10 Dark Typhlosion HOLO R	20.00	25.00
11 Dark Tyranitar HOLO R	20.00	30.00
12 Light Arcanine HOLO R	35.00	45.00
13 Light Azumarill HOLO R	10.00	15.00
14 Light Dragonite HOLO R	30.00	40.00
15 Light Togetic HOLO R	15.00	20.00
16 Miracle Energy HOLO R	13.00	18.00
17 Dark Ariados R	2.50	4.00
18 Dark Magcargo R	2.00	3.50
19 Dark Omastar R	2.00	3.50
20 Dark Slowking R	3.00	5.00
21 Dark Ursaring R	4.00	6.00
22 Light Dragonair R	4.00	7.00
23 Light Lanturn R	3.00	5.00
24 Light Ledian R	2.00	3.50
25 Light Machamp R	2.00	3.50
26 Light Piloswine R	2.00	3.50
27 Unown G R	2.00	3.50
28 Unown H R	2.00	3.50
29 Unown W R	2.00	3.50
30 Unown X R	2.00	3.50
31 Chansey U	2.00	3.00
32 Dark Croconaw U	2.00	3.00
33 Dark Exeggutor U	2.00	3.00
34 Dark Flaaffy U	2.00	3.00
35 Dark Forretress U	2.00	3.00
36 Dark Haunter U	2.00	3.00
37 Dark Omanyte U	2.00	3.00
38 Dark Pupitar U	2.00	3.00
39 Dark Quilava U	2.00	3.00
40 Dark Wigglytuff U	2.00	3.00
41 Heracross U	2.00	3.00
42 Hitmonlee U	2.00	3.00
43 Houndour U	2.00	3.00
44 Jigglypuff U	2.00	3.00
45 Light Dewgong U	2.00	3.00
46 Light Flareon U	4.00	6.00
47 Light Golduck U	2.00	3.00
48 Light Jolteon U	5.00	8.00
49 Light Machoke U	2.00	3.00
50 Light Ninetales U	4.00	6.00
51 Light Slowbro U	2.00	3.00
52 Light Vaporeon U	4.00	6.00
53 Light Venomoth U	2.00	3.00
54 Light Wigglytuff U	2.00	3.00
55 Scyther U	2.00	3.00
56 Togepi U	2.00	3.00
57 Unown C U	2.00	3.00
58 Unown P U	2.00	3.00
59 Unown Q U	2.00	3.00
60 Unown Z U	2.00	3.00
61 Cyndaquil C	1.25	2.00
62 Dark Octillery C	1.25	2.00
63 Dratini C	1.25	2.00
64 Exeggcute C	1.25	2.00
65 Gastly C	1.25	2.00
66 Girafarig C	1.25	2.00
67 Gligar C	1.25	2.00
68 Growlithe C	1.25	2.00
69 Hitmonchan C	1.25	2.00
70 Larvitar C	1.25	2.00
71 Ledyba C	1.25	2.00
72 Light Sunflora C	1.25	2.00
73 Machop C	1.25	2.00
74 Mantine C	1.25	2.00
75 Mareep C	1.25	2.00
76 Phanpy C	1.25	2.00
77 Pineco C	1.25	2.00
78 Porygon C	1.25	2.00
79 Psyduck C	1.25	2.00
80 Remoraid C	1.25	2.00
81 Seel C	1.25	2.00
82 Slugma C	1.25	2.00
83 Sunkern C	1.25	2.00
84 Swinub C	1.25	2.00
85 Totodile C	1.25	2.00
86 Unown L C	1.25	2.00
87 Unown S C	1.25	2.00
88 Unown T C	1.25	2.00
89 Unown V C	1.25	2.00
90 Venonat C	1.25	2.00
91 Vulpix C	1.25	2.00
92 Broken Ground Gym R	2.00	3.50
93 EXP.ALL R	2.00	3.50
94 Impostor Professor Oak's Invention R	2.00	3.50
95 Radio Tower R	2.00	3.50
96 Thought Wave Machine R	2.00	3.50
97 Counterattack Claws U	2.00	3.00
98 Energy Amplifier U	2.00	3.00
99 Energy Stadium U	2.00	3.00
100 Lucky Stadium U	2.00	3.00
101 Pigmented Lens U	2.00	3.00
102 Pokemon Personality Test U	2.00	3.00
103 Team Rockets Evil Deeds U	2.00	3.00
104 Heal Powder C	1.25	2.00
105 Mail from Bill C	1.25	2.00
106 Shining Celebi HOLO R	80.00	100.00
107 Shining Charizard HOLO R	250.00	300.00
108 Shining Kabutops HOLO R	80.00	100.00
109 Shining Mewtwo HOLO R	90.00	120.00
110 Shining Noctowl HOLO R	50.00	65.00
111 Shining Raichu HOLO R	100.00	130.00
112 Shining Steelix HOLO R	70.00	80.00
113 Shining Tyranitar HOLO R	150.00	160.00

2002 Pokemon Neo Destiny Unlimited

COMPLETE SET (113)	550.00	750.00
BOOSTER BOX (36 PACKS)	1500.00	2000.00
BOOSTER PACK (11 CARDS)	30.00	40.00
RELEASED ON FEBRUARY 8, 2001		
1 Dark Ampharos HOLO R	5.00	8.00
2 Dark Crobat HOLO R	8.00	12.00
3 Dark Donphan HOLO R	5.00	8.00
4 Dark Espeon HOLO R	15.00	20.00
5 Dark Feraligatr HOLO R	8.00	12.00
6 Dark Gengar HOLO R	10.00	15.00
7 Dark Houndoom HOLO R	8.00	12.00
8 Dark Porygon2 HOLO R	7.00	10.00
9 Dark Scizor HOLO R	8.00	12.00
10 Dark Typhlosion HOLO R	5.00	8.00
11 Dark Tyranitar HOLO R	10.00	15.00
12 Light Arcanine HOLO R	15.00	20.00
13 Light Azumarill HOLO R	3.00	5.00
14 Light Dragonite HOLO R	15.00	20.00
15 Light Togetic HOLO R	7.00	10.00
16 Miracle Energy HOLO R	5.00	8.00
17 Dark Ariados R	1.25	2.00
18 Dark Magcargo R	1.25	2.00
19 Dark Omastar R	1.25	2.00
20 Dark Slowking R	1.25	2.00
21 Dark Ursaring R	1.25	2.00
22 Light Dragonair R	1.25	2.00
23 Light Lanturn R	1.25	2.00
24 Light Ledian R	1.25	2.00
25 Light Machamp R	1.25	2.00
26 Light Piloswine R	1.25	2.00
27 Unown G R	1.25	2.00
28 Unown H R	1.25	2.00
29 Unown W R	1.25	2.00
30 Unown X R	1.25	2.00
31 Chansey U	1.00	1.50
32 Dark Croconaw U	1.00	1.50
33 Dark Exeggutor U	1.00	1.50
34 Dark Flaaffy U	1.00	1.50
35 Dark Forretress U	1.00	1.50
36 Dark Haunter U	1.00	1.50
37 Dark Omanyte U	1.00	1.50
38 Dark Pupitar U	1.00	1.50
39 Dark Quilava U	1.00	1.50
40 Dark Wigglytuff U	1.00	1.50
41 Heracross U	1.00	1.50
42 Hitmonlee U	1.00	1.50
43 Houndour U	1.00	1.50
44 Jigglypuff U	1.00	1.50
45 Light Dewgong U	1.00	1.50
46 Light Flareon U	2.50	4.00
47 Light Golduck U	1.00	1.50
48 Light Jolteon U	3.00	5.00
49 Light Machoke U	1.00	1.50
50 Light Ninetales U	2.50	4.00
51 Light Slowbro U	1.00	1.50
52 Light Vaporeon U	2.50	4.00
53 Light Venomoth U	1.00	1.50
54 Light Wigglytuff U	1.00	1.50
55 Scyther U	1.00	1.50
56 Togepi U	1.00	1.50
57 Unown C U	1.00	1.50
58 Unown P U	1.00	1.50
59 Unown Q U	1.00	1.50
60 Unown Z U	1.00	1.50
61 Cyndaquil C	.75	1.25
62 Dark Octillery C	.75	1.25
63 Dratini C	.75	1.25
64 Exeggcute C	.75	1.25
65 Gastly C	.75	1.25
66 Girafarig C	.75	1.25
67 Gligar C	.75	1.25
68 Growlithe C	.75	1.25
69 Hitmonchan C	.75	1.25
70 Larvitar C	.75	1.25
71 Ledyba C	.75	1.25
72 Light Sunflora C	.75	1.25
73 Machop C	.75	1.25
74 Mantine C	.75	1.25
75 Mareep C	.75	1.25
76 Phanpy C	.75	1.25
77 Pineco C	.75	1.25
78 Porygon C	.75	1.25
79 Psyduck C	.75	1.25
80 Remoraid C	.75	1.25
81 Seel C	.75	1.25
82 Slugma C	.75	1.25
83 Sunkern C	.75	1.25
84 Swinub C	.75	1.25
85 Totodile C	.75	1.25
86 Unown L C	.75	1.25
87 Unown S C	.75	1.25
88 Unown T C	.75	1.25
89 Unown V C	.75	1.25
90 Venonat C	.75	1.25
91 Vulpix C	.75	1.25
92 Broken Ground Gym R	1.25	2.00
93 EXP.ALL R	1.25	2.00
94 Impostor Prof.Oak's Invent.R	1.25	2.00
95 Radio Tower R	1.25	2.00
96 Thought Wave Machine R	1.25	2.00
97 Counterattack Claws U	1.00	1.50
98 Energy Amplifier U	1.00	1.50
99 Energy Stadium U	1.00	1.50
100 Lucky Stadium U	1.00	1.50
101 Pigmented Lens U	1.00	1.50
102 Pokemon Personality Test U	1.00	1.50
103 Team Rockets Evil Deeds U	1.00	1.50
104 Heal Powder C	.75	1.25
105 Mail from Bill C	.75	1.25
106 Shining Celebi HOLO R	30.00	40.00
107 Shining Charizard HOLO R	100.00	120.00
108 Shining Kabutops HOLO R	25.00	40.00
109 Shining Mewtwo HOLO R	40.00	60.00
110 Shining Noctowl HOLO R	30.00	35.00
111 Shining Raichu HOLO R	35.00	45.00
112 Shining Steelix HOLO R	25.00	35.00
113 Shining Tyranitar HOLO R	35.00	50.00

2002 Pokemon Legendary Collection

COMPLETE SET (110)	260.00	380.00
BOOSTER BOX (36 PACKS)	3000.00	4000.00
BOOSTER PACK (11 CARDS)	60.00	75.00
RELEASED ON MAY 24, 2002		
1 Alakazam HOLO R	10.00	15.00
2 Articuno HOLO R	8.00	12.00
3 Charizard HOLO R	50.00	65.00
4 Dark Blastoise HOLO R	10.00	15.00
5 Dark Dragonite HOLO R	5.00	8.00
6 Dark Persian HOLO R	5.00	8.00
7 Dark Raichu HOLO R	8.00	12.00
8 Dark Slowbro HOLO R	5.00	8.00
9 Dark Vaporeon HOLO R	7.00	10.00
10 Flareon HOLO R	7.00	10.00
11 Gengar HOLO R	8.00	12.00
12 Gyarados HOLO R	5.00	8.00
13 Hitmonlee HOLO R	5.00	8.00
14 Jolteon HOLO R	8.00	12.00
15 Machamp HOLO R	4.00	6.00
16 Muk HOLO R	3.00	5.00
17 Ninetales HOLO R	5.00	8.00
18 Venusaur HOLO R	10.00	15.00
19 Zapdos HOLO R	8.00	12.00
20 Beedrill R	2.00	3.00
21 Butterfree R	2.00	3.00
22 Electrode R	1.50	2.50
23 Exeggutor R	1.50	2.50
24 Golem R	2.00	3.00

25 Hypno R	1.50	2.50
26 Jynx R	1.50	2.50
27 Kabutops R	2.00	3.00
28 Magneton R	1.50	2.50
29 Mewtwo R	4.00	6.00
30 Moltres R	4.00	6.00
31 Nidoking R	5.00	8.00
32 Nidoqueen R	1.50	2.50
33 Pidgeot R	1.50	2.50
34 Pidgeotto R	2.50	4.00
35 Rhydon R	1.50	2.50
36 Arcanine U	1.50	2.50
37 Charmeleon U	1.00	1.50
38 Dark Dragonair U	.75	1.25
39 Dark Wartortle U	.75	1.25
40 Dewgong U	.75	1.25
41 Dodrio U	.75	1.25
42 Fearow U	.75	1.25
43 Golduck U	.75	1.25
44 Graveler U	.75	1.25
45 Growlithe U	.75	1.25
46 Haunter U	.75	1.25
47 Ivysaur U	.75	1.25
48 Kabuto U	.75	1.25
49 Kadabra U	1.50	2.50
50 Kakuna U	.75	1.25
51 Machoke U	.75	1.25
52 Magikarp U	.75	1.25
53 Meowth U	.75	1.25
54 Metapod U	.75	1.25
55 Nidorina U	.75	1.25
56 Nidorino U	.75	1.25
57 Omanyte U	.75	1.25
58 Omastar U	.75	1.25
59 Primeape U	.75	1.25
60 Rapidash U	.75	1.25
61 Raticate U	.75	1.25
62 Sandslash U	.75	1.25
63 Seadra U	.75	1.25
64 Snorlax U	.75	1.25
65 Tauros U	.75	1.25
66 Tentacruel U	.75	1.25
67 Abra C	.40	.60
68 Bulbasaur C	.40	.60
69 Caterpie C	.40	.60
70 Charmander C	.40	.60
71 Doduo C	.40	.60
72 Dratini C	.40	.60
73 Drowzee C	.40	.60
74 Eevee C	.40	.60
75 Exeggcute C	.40	.60
76 Gastly C	.40	.60
77 Geodude C	.40	.60
78 Grimer C	.40	.60
79 Machop C	.40	.60
80 Magnemite C	.40	.60
81 Mankey C	.40	.60
82 Nidoran (F) C	.40	.60
83 Nidoran (M) C	.40	.60
84 Onix C	.40	.60
85 Pidgey C	.40	.60
86 Pikachu C	.40	.60
87 Ponyta C	.40	.60
88 Psyduck C	.40	.60
89 Rattata C	.40	.60
90 Rhyhorn C	.40	.60
91 Sandshrew C	.40	.60
92 Seel C	.40	.60
93 Slowpoke C	.40	.60
94 Spearow C	.40	.60
95 Squirtle C	.40	.60
96 Tentacool C	.40	.60
97 Voltorb C	.40	.60
98 Vulpix C	.40	.60
99 Weedle C	.40	.60
100 Full Heal Energy U	.75	1.25
101 Potion Energy U	.75	1.25
102 Pokemon Breeder R	3.00	5.00
103 Pokemon Trader R	1.50	2.50
104 Scoop Up R	2.00	3.00
105 Boss's Way U	.75	1.25
106 Challenge! U	.75	1.25
107 Energy Retrieval U	.75	1.25
108 Bill C	.40	.60
109 Mysterious Fossil C	.40	.60
110 Potion C	.40	.60

2002 Pokemon Legendary Collection Reverse Foil

COMPLETE SET (110)	1100.00	1600.00
BOOSTER BOX (36 PACKS)	3000.00	4000.00
1 Alakazam HOLO R	15.00	20.00
2 Articuno HOLO R	15.00	20.00
3 Charizard HOLO R	60.00	80.00
4 Dark Blastoise HOLO R	15.00	20.00
5 Dark Dragonite HOLO R	15.00	25.00
6 Dark Persian HOLO R	8.00	10.00
7 Dark Raichu HOLO R	10.00	15.00
8 Dark Slowbro HOLO R	7.00	10.00
9 Dark Vaporeon HOLO R	15.00	20.00
10 Flareon HOLO R	20.00	25.00
11 Gengar HOLO R	15.00	20.00
12 Gyarados HOLO R	15.00	20.00
13 Hitmonlee HOLO R	8.00	12.00
14 Jolteon HOLO R	15.00	20.00
15 Machamp HOLO R	10.00	15.00
16 Muk HOLO R	7.00	10.00
17 Ninetales HOLO R	10.00	15.00
18 Venusaur HOLO R	25.00	40.00
19 Zapdos HOLO R	15.00	20.00
20 Beedrill R	10.00	12.00
21 Butterfree R	8.00	12.00
22 Electrode R	4.00	7.00
23 Exeggutor R	10.00	12.00
24 Golem R	10.00	15.00
25 Hypno R	7.00	10.00
26 Jynx R	5.00	8.00
27 Kabutops R	5.00	8.00
28 Magneton R	5.00	8.00
29 Mewtwo R	20.00	25.00
30 Moltres R	10.00	12.00
31 Nidoking R	10.00	15.00
32 Nidoqueen R	7.00	10.00
33 Pidgeot R	7.00	10.00
34 Pidgeotto R	10.00	12.00
35 Rhydon R	10.00	15.00
36 Arcanine U	20.00	25.00
37 Charmeleon U	10.00	15.00
38 Dark Dragonair U	8.00	12.00
39 Dark Wartortle U	10.00	15.00
40 Dewgong U	7.00	10.00
41 Dodrio U	7.00	10.00
42 Fearow U	7.00	10.00
43 Golduck U	8.00	12.00
44 Graveler U	7.00	10.00
45 Growlithe U	7.00	10.00
46 Haunter U	15.00	20.00
47 Ivysaur U	10.00	15.00
48 Kabuto U	4.00	7.00
49 Kadabra U	7.00	10.00
50 Kakuna U	5.00	8.00
51 Machoke U	7.00	10.00
52 Magikarp U	5.00	8.00
53 Meowth U	7.00	10.00
54 Metapod U	10.00	12.00
55 Nidorina U	7.00	10.00
56 Nidorino U	7.00	10.00
57 Omanyte U	5.00	8.00
58 Omastar U	10.00	15.00
59 Primeape U	4.00	7.00
60 Rapidash U	15.00	20.00
61 Raticate U	10.00	15.00
62 Sandslash U	8.00	12.00
63 Seadra U	7.00	10.00
64 Snorlax U	10.00	15.00
65 Tauros U	8.00	12.00
66 Tentacruel U	8.00	12.00
67 Abra C	7.00	10.00
68 Bulbasaur C	10.00	15.00
69 Caterpie C	5.00	8.00
70. Charmander C	10.00	15.00
71 Doduo C	7.00	10.00
72 Dratini C	15.00	20.00
73 Drowzee C	5.00	8.00
74 Eevee C	5.00	8.00
75 Exeggcute C	4.00	7.00
76 Gastly C	10.00	15.00
77 Geodude C	5.00	8.00
78 Grimer C	4.00	7.00
79 Machop C	5.00	8.00
80 Magnemite C	10.00	15.00
81 Mankey C	8.00	12.00
82 Nidoran (F) C	5.00	8.00
83 Nidoran (M) C	5.00	8.00
84 Onix C	8.00	12.00
85 Pidgey C	8.00	12.00
86 Pikachu C	30.00	40.00
87 Ponyta C	8.00	12.00
88 Psyduck C	7.00	10.00
89 Rattata C	7.00	10.00
90 Rhyhorn C	10.00	15.00
91 Sandshrew C	10.00	15.00
92 Seel C	7.00	10.00
93 Slowpoke C	8.00	12.00
94 Spearow C	5.00	8.00
95 Squirtle C	10.00	15.00
96 Tentacool C	8.00	12.00
97 Voltorb C	5.00	8.00
98 Vulpix C	5.00	8.00
99 Weedle C	3.00	5.00
100 Full Heal Energy U	8.00	12.00
101 Potion Energy U	8.00	12.00
102 Pokemon Breeder R	5.00	8.00
103 Pokemon Trader R	5.00	8.00
104 Scoop Up R	8.00	12.00
105 Boss's Way U	5.00	8.00
106 Challenge! U	10.00	15.00
107 Energy Retrieval U	5.00	8.00
108 Bill C	8.00	12.00
109 Mysterious Fossil C	8.00	12.00
110 Potion C	8.00	12.00
S1 Charizard Oversized P	45.00	55.00
S2 Dark Blastoise Oversized P	20.00	30.00
S3 Dark Raichu Oversized P	15.00	20.00
S4 Mewtwo Oversized P	15.00	20.00

2002 Pokemon Expedition

COMPLETE SET (165)	310.00	475.00
BOOSTER BOX (36 PACKS)	1700.00	2000.00
BOOSTER PACK (11 CARDS)	30.00	40.00
ELECTRIC GARDEN THEME DECK	10.00	25.00
*BOX TOPPER 1.5X REGULAR VERSION		
*REV.FOIL: .75X TO 2X BASIC CARDS		
RELEASED ON SEPTEMBER 15, 2002		
1 Alakazam HOLO R	5.00	8.00
2 Ampharos HOLO R	3.00	5.00
3 Arbok HOLO R	3.00	5.00
4 Blastoise HOLO R	10.00	15.00
5 Butterfree HOLO R	5.00	8.00
6 Charizard HOLO R	15.00	20.00
7 Clefable HOLO R	2.00	3.50
8 Cloyster HOLO R	5.00	8.00
9 Dragonite HOLO R	7.00	10.00
10 Dugtrio HOLO R	4.00	6.00
11 Fearow HOLO R	4.00	6.00
12 Feraligatr HOLO R	9.00	12.00
13 Gengar HOLO R	7.00	10.00
14 Golem HOLO R	5.00	8.00
15 Kingler HOLO R	3.00	5.00
16 Machamp HOLO R	5.00	8.00
17 Magby HOLO R	4.00	6.00
18 Meganium HOLO R	7.00	10.00
19 Mew HOLO R	15.00	20.00
20 Mewtwo HOLO R	10.00	15.00
21 Ninetales HOLO R	7.00	10.00
22 Pichu HOLO R	9.00	12.00
23 Pidgeot HOLO R	4.00	6.00
24 Poliwrath HOLO R	4.00	6.00
25 Raichu HOLO R	4.00	6.00
26 Rapidash HOLO R	4.00	6.00
27 Skarmory HOLO R	7.00	10.00
28 Typhlosion HOLO R	5.00	8.00
29 Tyranitar HOLO R	7.00	10.00
30 Venusaur HOLO R	5.00	8.00
31 Vileplume HOLO R	2.00	3.50
32 Weezing HOLO R	5.00	8.00
33 Alakazam R	.75	1.25
34 Ampharos R	.75	1.25
35 Arbok R	.75	1.25
36 Blastoise R	4.00	6.00
37 Blastoise R	4.00	6.00
38 Butterfree R	.75	1.25
39 Charizard R	5.00	8.00
40 Charizard R	5.00	8.00
41 Clefable R	.75	1.25
42 Cloyster R	.75	1.25
43 Dragonite R	2.00	3.50
44 Dugtrio R	.75	1.25
45 Fearow R	.75	1.25
46 Feraligatr R	.75	1.25
47 Feraligatr R	.75	1.25
48 Gengar R	2.00	3.50
49 Golem R	.75	1.25
50 Kingler R	.75	1.25
51 Machamp R	.75	1.25
52 Magby R	1.50	2.50
53 Meganium R	.75	1.25
54 Meganium R	1.25	2.00
55 Mew R	5.00	8.00
56 Mewtwo R	4.00	6.00
57 Ninetales R	4.00	6.00
58 Pichu R	4.00	6.00
59 Pidgeot R	.75	1.25
60 Poliwrath R	1.50	2.50
61 Raichu R	.75	1.25
62 Rapidash R	.75	1.25
63 Skarmory R	.75	1.25
64 Typhlosion R	1.25	2.00
65 Typhlosion R	1.25	2.00
66 Tyranitar R	2.50	4.00
67 Venusaur R	3.00	5.00
68 Venusaur R	3.00	5.00
69 Vileplume R	.75	1.25
70 Weezing R	.75	1.25
71 Bayleef U	.50	.75
72 Chansey U	.50	.75
73 Charmeleon U	1.00	1.50
74 Croconaw U	.50	.75
75 Dragonair U	.50	.75
76 Electabuzz U	.50	.75
77 Flaafy U	.50	.75
78 Gloom U	.50	.75
79 Graveler U	1.25	2.00
80 Haunter U	.50	.75
81 Hitmonlee U	.50	.75
82 Ivysaur U	3.00	5.00
83 Jynx U	.50	.75
84 Kadabra U	.50	.75
85 Machoke U	.50	.75
86 Magmar U	.50	.75
87 Metapod U	.50	.75
88 Pidgeotto U	.50	.75
89 Poliwhirl U	.50	.75
90 Pupitar U	.50	.75
91 Quilava U	.50	.75
92 Wartortle U	1.00	1.50
93 Abra C	.40	.60
94 Bulbasaur C	.40	.60
95 Bulbasaur C	.40	.60
96 Caterpie C	.40	.60
97 Charmander C	.40	.60
98 Charmander C	.40	.60
99 Chikorita C	.40	.60
100 Chikorita C	.40	.60
101 Clefairy C	.40	.60
102 Corsola C	.40	.60
103 Cubone C	1.25	2.00
104 Cyndaquil C	.40	.60
105 Cyndaquil C	.40	.60
106 Diglett C	.40	.60
107 Dratini C	1.00	1.50
108 Ekans C	.40	.60
109 Gastly C	.40	.60
110 Geodude C	.40	.60
111 Goldeen C	.40	.60
112 Hoppip C	.40	.60
113 Houndour C	.40	.60
114 Koffing C	.40	.60
115 Krabby C	.40	.60
116 Larvitar C	.40	.60
117 Machop C	.40	.60
118 Magikarp C	.40	.60
119 Mareep C	.40	.60
120 Marill C	.40	.60
121 Meowth C	.40	.60
122 Oddish C	.40	.60
123 Pidgey C	.40	.60
124 Pikachu C	.40	.60
125 Poliwag C	.40	.60
126 Ponyta C	.40	.60
127 Qwilfish C	.40	.60
128 Rattata C	.40	.60
129 Shellder C	.40	.60
130 Spearow C	.40	.60
131 Squirtle C	.40	.60
132 Squirtle C	.40	.60
133 Tauros C	.40	.60
134 Totodile C	.40	.60
135 Totodile C	.40	.60
136 Vulpix C	.75	1.25
137 Bill's Maintenance C	.40	.60
138 Copycat C	.40	.60
139 Dual Ball C	.40	.60
140 Energy Removal 2 U	.50	.75
141 Energy Restore U	.50	.75
142 Mary's Impulse U	.50	.75
143 Master Ball U	.75	1.25
144 Multi Technical U	.50	.75
145 Pokemon Nurse U	1.00	1.50
146 Pokemon Reversal U	.50	.75
147 Power Charge U	.50	.75
148 Professor Elm's U	.50	.75
149 Professor Oak's U	.50	.75
150 Strength Charm U	.50	.75
151 Super Scoop Up U	1.50	2.50
152 Warp Point U	.50	.75
153 Energy Search C	.40	.60
154 Full Heal C	.40	.60
155 Moo-moo Milk C	.40	.60
156 Potion C	.40	.60
157 Switch C	.40	.60
158 Darkness Energy R	.75	1.25
159 Metal Energy R	.75	1.25
160 Fire Energy	.40	.60
161 Rock Energy	.40	.60
162 Grass Energy	.40	.60
163 Lightning Energy	.40	.60
164 Psychic Energy	.40	.60
165 Water Energy	.40	.60

2002 Pokemon Expedition Reverse Foil

COMPLETE SET (165)	370.00	590.00
BOOSTER BOX (36 PACKS)	1700.00	2000.00
BOOSTER PACK (11 CARDS)	30.00	40.00
ELECTRIC GARDEN THEME DECK	15.00	20.00
*BOX TOPPER 1.5X REGULAR VERSION		
*REV.FOIL: .75X TO 2X BASIC CARDS		
1 Alakazam HOLO R	4.00	6.00
2 Ampharos HOLO R	3.00	5.00
3 Arbok HOLO R	2.00	3.00
4 Blastoise HOLO R	8.00	12.00
5 Butterfree HOLO R	4.00	6.00
6 Charizard HOLO R	15.00	20.00
7 Clefable HOLO R	2.00	3.50
8 Cloyster HOLO R	2.00	3.50
9 Dragonite HOLO R	4.00	6.00
10 Dugtrio HOLO R	2.00	3.50
11 Fearow HOLO R	1.50	2.50
12 Feraligatr HOLO R	2.00	3.50
13 Gengar HOLO R	4.00	6.00
14 Golem HOLO R	2.00	3.50
15 Kingler HOLO R	2.00	3.00
16 Machamp HOLO R	3.00	5.00
17 Magby HOLO R	2.00	3.50
18 Meganium HOLO R	3.00	5.00
19 Mew HOLO R	8.00	12.00
20 Mewtwo HOLO R	8.00	12.00
21 Ninetales HOLO R	3.00	5.00
22 Pichu HOLO R	4.00	6.00
23 Pidgeot HOLO R	2.00	3.50
24 Poliwrath HOLO R	2.00	3.50
25 Raichu HOLO R	2.00	3.50
26 Rapidash HOLO R	2.00	3.50
27 Skarmory HOLO R	2.00	3.50
28 Typhlosion HOLO R	3.00	5.00
29 Tyranitar HOLO R	5.00	8.00
30 Venusaur HOLO R	4.00	6.00
31 Vileplume HOLO R	2.00	3.50
32 Weezing HOLO R	4.00	6.00
33 Alakazam R	3.00	5.00
34 Ampharos R	1.50	2.50
35 Arbok R	1.50	2.50
36 Blastoise R	2.00	3.00
37 Blastoise R	10.00	13.00
38 Butterfree R	1.50	2.50
39 Charizard R	10.00	13.00
40 Charizard R	10.00	15.00
41 Clefable R	1.50	2.50
42 Cloyster R	1.50	2.50
43 Dragonite R	4.00	6.00
44 Dugtrio R	1.00	1.50
45 Fearow R	1.50	2.00
46 Feraligatr R	2.00	3.00
47 Feraligatr R	1.25	2.00
48 Gengar R	2.00	3.00
49 Golem R	.50	.75
50 Kingler R	3.00	4.00
51 Machamp R	1.50	2.50
52 Magby R	1.50	2.50
53 Meganium R	3.00	5.00
54 Meganium R	3.00	5.00
55 Mew R	8.00	12.00
56 Mewtwo R	8.00	12.00
57 Ninetales R	3.00	5.00
58 Pichu R	1.50	2.50
59 Pidgeot R	1.50	2.50
60 Poliwrath R	1.50	2.50
61 Raichu R	1.50	2.50
62 Rapidash R	1.50	2.50
63 Skarmory R	1.50	2.50
64 Typhlosion R	1.50	2.50
65 Typhlosion R	1.50	2.50
66 Tyranitar R	3.00	5.00
67 Venusaur R	3.00	5.00
68 Venusaur R	3.00	5.00
69 Vileplume R	1.50	2.50
70 Weezing R	3.00	5.00
71 Bayleef U	1.50	2.50
72 Chansey U	1.50	2.50
73 Charmeleon U	1.50	2.50
74 Croconaw U	1.50	2.50

75 Dragonair U	1.50	2.50
76 Electabuzz U	1.50	2.50
77 Flaafy U	1.50	2.50
78 Gloom U	1.50	2.50
79 Graveler U	1.50	2.50
80 Haunter U	1.50	2.50
81 Hitmonlee U	1.50	2.50
82 Ivysaur U	1.50	2.50
83 Jynx U	1.50	2.50
84 Kadabra U	1.50	2.50
85 Machoke U	1.50	2.50
86 Magmar U	1.50	2.50
87 Metapod U	1.50	2.50
88 Pidgeotto U	1.50	2.50
89 Poliwhirl U	1.50	2.50
90 Pupitar U	1.50	2.50
91 Quilava U	1.50	2.50
92 Wartortle U	1.50	2.50
93 Abra C	1.50	2.50
94 Bulbasaur C	1.50	2.50
95 Bulbasaur C	1.50	2.50
96 Caterpie C	1.50	2.50
97 Charmander C	1.50	2.50
98 Charmander C	1.50	2.50
99 Chikorita C	1.50	2.50
100 Chikorita C	1.50	2.50
101 Clefairy C	1.50	2.50
102 Corsola C	1.50	2.50
103 Cubone C	1.50	2.50
104 Cyndaquil C	1.50	2.50
105 Cyndaquil C	1.50	2.50
106 Diglett C	1.50	2.50
107 Dratini C	1.50	2.50
108 Ekans C	1.50	2.50
109 Gastly C	1.50	2.50
110 Geodude C	1.50	2.50
111 Goldeen C	1.50	2.50
112 Hoppip C	1.50	2.50
113 Houndour C	1.50	2.50
114 Koffing C	1.50	2.50
115 Krabby C	1.50	2.50
116 Larvitar C	1.50	2.50
117 Machop C	1.50	2.50
118 Magikarp C	1.50	2.50
119 Mareep C	1.50	2.50
120 Marill C	1.50	2.50
121 Meowth C	1.50	2.50
122 Oddish C	1.50	2.50
123 Pidgey C	1.50	2.50
124 Pikachu C	1.50	2.50
125 Poliwag C	1.50	2.50
126 Ponyta C	1.50	2.50
127 Qwilfish C	1.50	2.50
128 Rattata C	1.50	2.50
129 Shellder C	1.50	2.50
130 Spearow C	1.50	2.50
131 Squirtle C	1.50	2.50
132 Squirtle C	1.50	2.50
133 Tauros C	1.50	2.50
134 Totodile C	1.50	2.50
135 Totodile C	1.50	2.50
136 Vulpix C	1.50	2.50
137 Bill's Maintenance C	1.50	2.50
138 Copycat C	1.50	2.50
139 Dual Ball C	1.50	2.50
140 Energy Removal 2 U	1.50	2.50
141 Energy Restore U	1.50	2.50
142 Mary's Impulse U	1.50	2.50
143 Master Ball U	1.50	2.50
144 Multi Technical U	1.50	2.50
145 Pokemon Nurse U	1.50	2.50
146 Pokemon Reversal U	1.50	2.50
147 Power Charge U	1.50	2.50
148 Professor Elm's U	1.50	2.50
149 Professor Oak's U	1.50	2.50
150 Strength Charm U	1.50	2.50
151 Super Scoop Up U	1.50	2.50
152 Warp Point U	1.50	2.50
153 Energy Search C	1.50	2.50
154 Full Heal C	1.50	2.50
155 Moo-moo Milk C	1.50	2.50
156 Potion C	1.50	2.50
157 Switch C	1.50	2.50
158 Darkness Energy R	.75	2.00
159 Metal Energy R	.75	2.00
160 Fire Energy	1.50	2.50
161 Rock Energy	1.50	2.50
162 Grass Energy	1.50	2.50
163 Lightning Energy	1.50	2.50
164 Psychic Energy	1.50	2.50
165 Water Energy	1.50	2.50

2003 Pokemon Aquapolis

COMPLETE SET (186)	750.00	1100.00
BOOSTER BOX (36 PACKS)	1600.00	2100.00
BOOSTER PACK (11 CARDS)	25.00	50.00
*REV.FOIL: .75X TO 2X BASIC CARDS		
THEME DECK	20.00	40.00
*BOX TOPPER: .75X TO 2X BASIC TOPPER		
RELEASED ON JANUARY 15, 2003		
1 Ampharos R	3.00	5.00
2 Arcanine R	3.00	5.00
3 Ariados R	3.00	5.00
4 Azumarill R	3.00	5.00
5 Bellossom R	3.00	5.00
6 Blissey R	3.00	5.00
7 Donphan R	3.00	5.00
8 Electrode R	3.00	5.00
9 Elekid R	3.00	5.00
10 Entei R	3.00	5.00
11 Espeon R	5.00	8.00
12 Exeggutor R	3.00	5.00
13 Exeggutor R	3.00	5.00
14 Houndoom R	3.00	5.00
15 Houndoom R	3.00	5.00
16 Hypno R	3.00	5.00
17 Jumpluff R	3.00	5.00
18 Jynx R	3.00	5.00
19 Kingdra R	3.00	5.00
20 Lanturn R	3.00	5.00
21 Lanturn R	3.00	5.00
22 Magneton R	3.00	5.00
23 Muk R	3.00	5.00
24 Nidoking R	3.00	5.00
25 Ninetales R	3.00	5.00
26 Octillery R	3.00	5.00
27 Parasect R	3.00	5.00
28 Porygon2 R	3.00	5.00
29 Primeape R	3.00	5.00
30 Quagsire R	3.00	5.00
31 Rapidash R	3.00	5.00
32 Scizor R	3.00	5.00
33 Slowbro R	3.00	5.00
34 Slowking R	3.00	5.00
35 Steelix R	3.00	5.00
36 Sudowoodo R	3.00	5.00
37 Suicune R	3.00	5.00
38 Tentacruel R	3.00	5.00
39 Togetic R	3.00	5.00
40 Tyranitar R	4.00	7.00
41 Umbreon R	5.00	8.00
42 Victreebel R	3.00	5.00
43 Vileplume R	3.00	5.00
44 Zapdos R	3.00	5.00
45 Bellsprout U	1.25	2.00
46 Dodrio U	1.25	2.00
47 Flaaffy U	1.25	2.00
48 Furret U	2.00	3.00
49 Gloom U	1.25	2.00
50A Golduck U	2.00	3.00
50B Golduck U	2.00	3.00
51 Growlithe U	1.25	2.00
52 Magnemite U	1.25	2.00
53 Marill U	2.00	3.00
54 Marowak U	1.25	2.00
55 Nidorino U	1.25	2.00
56 Pupitar U	1.25	2.00
57 Scyther U	3.00	5.00
58 Seadra U	1.25	2.00
59 Seaking U	1.25	2.00
60 Skiploom U	1.25	2.00
61 Smoochum U	1.25	2.00
62 Spinarak U	1.25	2.00
63 Tyrogue U	1.25	2.00
64 Voltorb U	1.25	2.00
65 Weepinbell U	1.25	2.00
66 Wooper U	1.25	2.00
67 Aipom C	.40	.60
68 Bellsprout C	.40	.60
69 Chansey C	.40	.60
70 Chinchou C	.75	1.00
71 Chinchou C	.40	.60
72 Cubone C	.40	.60
73 Doduo C	.40	.60
74A Drowzee C	.40	.60
74B Drowzee C	.40	.60
75 Eevee C	3.00	5.00
76 Exeggcute C	.40	.60
77 Exeggcute C	.40	.60
78 Goldeen C	.40	.60
79 Grimer C	.40	.60
80 Growlithe C	.40	.60
81 Hitmonchan C	1.00	1.25
82 Hitmontop C	.40	.60
83 Hoppip C	.50	.75
84 Horsea C	.40	.60
85 Horsea C	.40	.60
86 Houndour C	.40	.60
87 Houndour C	.50	.75
88 Kangaskhan C	.60	1.00
89 Larvitar C	.40	.60
90 Lickitung C	.40	.60
91 Magnemite C	.40	.60
92 Mankey C	.40	.60
93 Mareep C	.40	.60
94 Miltank C	.40	.60
95A Mr. Mime C	.40	.60
95B Mr. Mime C	.40	.60
96 Nidoran C	.40	.60
97 Oddish C	.40	.60
98 Onix C	.50	.75
99 Paras C	.75	1.00
100 Phanpy C	.40	.60
101 Pinsir C	.40	.60
102 Ponyta C	.40	.60
103A Porygon C	.40	.60
103B Porygon C	.60	1.00
104 Psyduck C	.40	.60
105 Remoraid C	.40	.60
106 Scyther C	.40	.60
107 Sentret C	.40	.60
108 Slowpoke C	.40	.60
109 Smeargle C	1.25	2.00
110 Sneasel C	.50	.75
111 Spinarak C	.50	.75
112 Tangela C	.40	.60
113 Tentacool C	.40	.60
114 Togepi C	2.00	3.00
115 Voltorb C	.40	.60
116 Vulpix C	.40	.60
117 Wooper C	.40	.60
118 Apricorn Forest R	1.25	2.00
119 Darkness Cube U	1.25	2.00
120 Energy Switch U	2.75	3.50
121 Fighting Cube 01 U	1.25	2.00
122 Fire Cube 01 U	1.25	2.00
123 Forest Guardian U	1.25	2.00
124 Grass Cube 01 U	1.25	2.00
125 Healing Berry U	1.25	2.00
126 Juggler U	1.25	2.00
127 Lightning Cube 01 U	1.25	2.00
128 Memory Berry U	1.25	2.00
129 Metal Cube 01 U	1.25	2.00
130 Pokemon Fan Club U	1.25	2.00
131 Pokemon Park U	1.25	2.00
132 Psychic Cube 01 U	1.25	2.00
133 Seer U	1.25	2.00
134 Super Energy Removal 2 U	1.25	2.00
135 Time Shard U	1.25	2.00
136 Town Volunteers U	1.25	2.00
137 Traveling Salesman U	1.25	2.00
138 Undersea Ruins U	1.25	2.00
139 Power Plant U	1.25	2.00
140 Water Cube 1 U	1.25	2.00
141 Weakness Guard U	1.25	2.00
142 Darkness Energy R	.75	1.25
143 Metal Energy R	.75	1.25
144 Rainbow Energy R	.75	1.25
145 Boost Energy U	.75	1.25
146 Crystal Energy U	2.00	3.00
147 Warp Energy U	1.25	2.00
148 Kingdra HOLO R	45.00	60.00
149 Lugia HOLO R	80.00	100.00
150 Nidoking HOLO R	75.00	100.00
H1 Ampharos HOLO R	7.00	12.00
H2 Arcanine HOLO R	15.00	20.00
H3 Ariados HOLO R	7.00	10.00
H4 Azumarill HOLO R	10.00	15.00
H5 Bellossom HOLO R	6.00	10.00
H6 Blissey HOLO R	10.00	15.00
H7 Electrode HOLO R	5.00	8.00
H8 Entei HOLO R	15.00	20.00
H9 Espeon HOLO R	20.00	30.00
H10 Exeggutor HOLO R	10.00	15.00
H11 Houndoom HOLO R	20.00	30.00
H12 Hypno HOLO R	5.00	8.00
H13 Jumpluff HOLO R	5.00	8.00
H14 Kingdra HOLO R	14.00	18.00
H15 Lanturn HOLO R	5.00	8.00
H16 Magneton HOLO R	5.00	8.00
H17 Muk HOLO R	6.00	10.00
H18 Nidoking HOLO R	15.00	20.00
H19 Ninetales HOLO R	15.00	20.00
H20 Octillery HOLO R	5.00	8.00
H21 Scizor HOLO R	10.00	15.00
H22 Slowking HOLO R	10.00	15.00
H23 Steelix HOLO R	10.00	15.00
H24 Sudowoodo HOLO R	4.00	7.00
H25 Suicune HOLO R	15.00	20.00
H26 Tentacruel HOLO R	6.00	10.00
H27 Togetic HOLO R	8.00	12.00
H28 Tyranitar HOLO R	15.00	20.00
H29 Umbreon HOLO R	25.00	35.00
H30 Victreebel HOLO R	4.00	7.00
H31 Vileplume HOLO R	14.00	18.00
H32 Zapdos HOLO R	14.00	18.00

2003 Pokemon Skyridge

REGULAR SET (150)	1500.00	2100.00
COMPLETE SET (182)	1800.00	2500.00
BOOSTER BOX (36 PACKS)	1800.00	2500.00
BOOSTER PACK (11 CARDS)	40.00	50.00
*JUMBO BOX TOPPERS: 6X TO 1.5X BASIC	40.00	80.00
RELEASED ON MAY 12, 2003		
1 Aerodactyl R	2.00	2.50
2 Alakazam R	3.00	5.00
3 Arcanine R	3.00	5.00
4 Articuno R	5.00	8.00
5 Beedrill R	3.00	5.00
6 Crobat R	5.00	8.00
7 Dewgong R	3.00	4.00
8 Flareon R	3.00	5.00
9 Forretress R	3.00	4.00
10 Gengar R	8.00	12.00
11 Gyarados R	4.00	6.00
12 Houndoom R	3.00	5.00
13 Jolteon R	3.00	4.00
14 Kabutops R	3.00	5.00
15 Ledian R	3.00	4.00
16 Machamp R	2.00	3.00
17 Magcargo R	3.00	4.00
18 Magcargo R	1.00	1.50
19 Magneton R	3.00	4.00
20 Magneton R	3.00	4.00
21 Moltres R	3.00	5.00
22 Nidoqueen R	3.00	4.00
23 Omastar R	3.00	4.00
24 Piloswine R	2.00	3.00
25 Politoed R	4.00	6.00
26 Poliwrath R	3.00	5.00
27 Raichu R	2.50	4.00
28 Raikou R	4.00	6.00
29 Rhydon R	2.00	3.00
30 Starmie R	3.00	5.00
31 Steelix R	3.00	5.00
32 Umbreon R	15.00	20.00
33 Vaporeon R	3.00	4.00
34 Wigglytuff R	2.50	4.00
35 Xatu R	2.00	3.50
36 Electrode U	3.00	4.00
37 Kabuto U	3.00	4.00
38 Machoke U	3.00	4.00
39 Misdreavus U	3.00	4.00
40 Noctowl U	3.00	4.00
41 Omanyte U	3.00	4.00
42 Persian U	3.00	4.00
43 Piloswine U	3.00	4.00
44 Starmie U	3.00	4.00
45 Wobbuffet U	3.00	4.00
46 Abra C	2.00	3.00
47 Buried Fossil C	2.00	3.00
48 Cleffa C	2.00	3.00
49 Delibird C	2.00	3.00
50 Diglett C	2.00	3.00
51 Ditto C	2.00	3.00
52 Dugtrio C	2.00	3.00
53 Dunsparce C	2.00	3.00
54 Eevee C	2.00	3.00
55 Farfetch'd C	2.00	3.00
56 Forretress C	2.00	3.00
57 Gastly C	2.00	3.00
58 Girafarig C	2.00	3.00
59 Gligar C	2.00	3.00
60 Golbat C	2.00	3.00
61 Granbull C	2.00	3.00
62 Growlithe C	2.00	3.00
63 Haunter C	2.00	3.00
64 Heracross C	2.00	3.00
65 Hoothoot C	2.00	3.00
66 Houndour C	2.00	3.00
67 Igglybuff C	2.00	3.00
68 Jigglypuff C	2.00	3.00
69 Kadabra C	2.00	3.00
70 Kakuna C	2.00	3.00
71 Lapras C	2.00	3.00
72 Ledyba C	2.00	3.00
73 Ledyba C	2.00	3.00
74 Machop C	2.00	3.00
75 Magikarp C	2.00	3.00
76 Magnemite C	2.00	3.00
77 Mantine C	2.00	3.00
78 Meowth C	2.00	3.00
79 Murkrow C	2.00	3.00
80 Natu C	2.00	3.00
81 Nidoran F C	2.00	3.00
82 Nidoran F C	2.00	3.00
83 Nidorina C	2.00	3.00
84 Pikachu C	2.00	3.00
85 Pineco C	2.00	3.00
86 Pineco C	2.00	3.00
87 Poliwag C	2.00	3.00
88 Poliwhirl C	2.00	3.00
89 Raticate C	2.00	3.00
90 Rattata C	2.00	3.00
91 Rhyhorn C	2.00	3.00
92 Sandshrew C	2.00	3.00
93 Sandslash C	2.00	3.00
94 Seel C	2.00	3.00
95 Seel C	2.00	3.00
96 Shuckle C	2.00	3.00
97 Skarmory C	2.00	3.00
98 Slugma C	2.00	3.00
99 Slugma C	2.00	3.00
100 Snorlax C	2.00	3.00
101 Snubbull C	2.00	3.00
102 Stantler C	2.00	3.00
103 Staryu C	2.00	3.00
104 Staryu C	2.00	3.00
105 Sunflora C	2.00	3.00
106 Sunkern C	2.00	3.00
107 Swinub C	2.00	3.00
108 Swinub C	2.00	3.00
109 Teddiursa C	2.00	3.00
110 Ursaring C	3.00	4.00
111 Venomoth C	2.00	3.00
112 Venonat C	2.00	3.00
113 Voltorb C	2.00	3.00
114 Weedle C	2.00	3.00
115 Weedle C	1.25	2.00
116 Yanma C	2.00	3.00
117 Zubat C	2.00	3.00
118 Zubat C	2.00	3.00
119 Ancient Ruins U	2.00	3.00
120 Relic Hunter U	1.25	2.00
121 Apricorn U	1.25	2.00
122 Crystal Shard U	1.25	2.00
123 Desert Shaman U	2.00	3.00
124 Fast Ball U	1.25	2.00
125 Fisherman U	3.00	4.00
126 Friend Ball U	2.00	3.00
127 Hyper Potion U	2.00	3.00
128 Lure Ball U	2.00	3.00
129 Miracle Sphere (Alpha) U	2.00	3.00
130 Miracle Sphere (Beta) U	2.00	3.00
131 Miracle Sphere (Gamma) U	2.00	3.00
132 Mirage Stadium U	2.00	3.00
133 Mystery Plate (Alpha) U	2.00	3.00
134 Mystery Plate (Beta) U	2.00	3.00
135 Mystery Plate (Gamma) U	2.00	3.00
136 Mystery Plate (Delta) U	2.00	3.00
137 Mystery Zone U	2.00	3.00
138 Oracle U	7.00	10.00
139 Star Piece U	2.00	3.00
140 Underground Expedition U	2.00	3.00
141 Underground Lake U	1.75	2.00
142 Bounce Energy U	1.25	2.00
143 Cyclone Energy U	1.25	2.00
144 Retro Energy U	1.50	2.50
145 Celebi HOLO R	90.00	115.00
146 Charizard HOLO R	225.00	300.00
147 Crobat HOLO R	40.00	60.00
148 Golem HOLO R	40.00	60.00
149 Ho-Oh HOLO R	80.00	100.00
150 Kabutops HOLO R	60.00	80.00
H1 Alakazam HOLO R	30.00	40.00
H2 Arcanine HOLO R	20.00	30.00
H3 Articuno HOLO R	35.00	45.00
H4 Beedrill HOLO R	14.00	18.00
H5 Crobat HOLO R	20.00	30.00
H6 Dewgong HOLO R	15.00	20.00
H7 Flareon HOLO R	30.00	40.00
H8 Forretress HOLO R	14.00	18.00
H9 Gengar HOLO R	20.00	30.00
H10 Gyarados HOLO R	25.00	35.00
H11 Houndoom HOLO R	20.00	30.00
H12 Jolteon HOLO R	30.00	40.00
H13 Kabutops HOLO R	15.00	20.00
H14 Ledian HOLO R	10.00	15.00
H15 Machamp HOLO R	20.00	25.00
H16 Magcargo HOLO R	14.00	18.00
H17 Magcargo HOLO R	10.00	15.00
H18 Magneton HOLO R	10.00	15.00

H19 Magneton HOLO R 15.00 20.00
H20 Moltres HOLO R 20.00 30.00
H21 Nidoqueen HOLO R 20.00 25.00
H22 Piloswine HOLO R 7.00 10.00
H23 Politoed HOLO R 13.00 18.00
H24 Poliwrath HOLO R 13.00 18.00
H25 Raichu HOLO R 20.00 25.00
H26 Raikou HOLO R 25.00 35.00
H27 Rhydon HOLO R 13.00 18.00
H28 Starmie HOLO R 13.00 18.00
H29 Steelix HOLO R 15.00 20.00
H30 Umbreon HOLO R 70.00 100.00
H31 Vaporeon HOLO R 40.00 60.00
H32 Xatu HOLO R 10.00 15.00
9 Charizard Crystal Oversized P
10 Crobat Crystal Oversized P
11 Ho-Oh Crystal Oversized P
12 Kabutops Crystal Oversized P

2003 Pokemon EX Ruby and Sapphire

COMPLETE SET (109) 100.00 150.00
BOOSTER BOX (36 PACKS) 350.00 450.00
BOOSTER PACK (9 CARDS) 7.00 18.00
*REV.FOIL: .75X TO 2X BASIC CARDS
RUBY THEME DECK 8.00 20.00
SAPPHIRE THEME DECK 8.00 20.00
RELEASED ON JUNE 18, 2003
1 Aggron HOLO R 2.00 4.00
2 Beautifly HOLO R 2.00 4.00
3 Blaziken HOLO R 2.00 4.00
4 Camerupt HOLO R 2.00 6.00
5 Delcatty HOLO R 2.00 6.00
6 Dustox HOLO R 2.00 4.00
7 Gardevoir HOLO R 2.00 4.00
8 Hariyama HOLO R 2.00 4.00
9 Manectric HOLO R 2.00 4.00
10 Mightyena HOLO R 2.00 4.00
11 Sceptile HOLO R 2.00 4.00
12 Slaking HOLO R 2.00 4.00
13 Swampert HOLO R 2.00 4.00
14 Wailord HOLO R 2.00 4.00
15 Blaziken R .75 2.00
16 Breloom R .75 2.00
17 Donphan R .75 2.00
18 Nosepass R .75 2.00
19 Pelipper R .75 2.00
20 Sceptile R .75 2.00
21 Seaking R .75 2.00
22 Sharpedo R .75 2.00
23 Swampert R .75 2.00
24 Weezing R .75 2.00
25 Aron U .75 2.00
26 Cascoon U .75 2.00
27 Combusken U .75 2.00
28 Combusken U .75 2.00
29 Delcatty U .75 2.00
30 Electrike U .75 2.00
31 Grovyle U .75 2.00
32 Grovyle U .75 2.00
33 Hariyama U .75 2.00
34 Kirlia U .75 2.00
35 Kirlia U .75 2.00
36 Lairon U .75 2.00
37 Lairon U .75 2.00
38 Linoone U .75 2.00
39 Manectric U .75 2.00
40 Marshtomp U .75 2.00
41 Marshtomp U .75 2.00
42 Mightyena U .75 2.00
43 Silcoon U .75 2.00
44 Skitty U .75 2.00
45 Slakoth U .75 2.00
46 Swellow U .75 2.00
47 Vigoroth U .75 2.00
48 Wailmer U .75 2.00
49 Aron C .75 2.00
50 Aron C .75 2.00
51 Carvanha C .75 2.00
52 Electrike C .75 2.00
53 Electrike C .75 2.00
54 Koffing C .75 2.00
55 Goldeen C .75 2.00
56 Makuhita C .75 2.00
57 Makuhita C .75 2.00
58 Makuhita C .75 2.00
59 Mudkip C .75 2.00
60 Mudkip C .75 2.00
61 Numel C .75 2.00
62 Phanpy C .75 2.00
63 Poochyena C .75 2.00
64 Poochyena C .75 2.00
65 Poochyena C .75 2.00
66 Ralts C .75 2.00
67 Ralts C .75 2.00
68 Ralts C .75 2.00
69 Shroomish C .75 2.00
70 Skitty C .75 2.00
71 Skitty C .75 2.00
72 Taillow C .75 2.00
73 Torchic C .75 2.00
74 Torchic C .75 2.00
75 Treecko C .75 2.00
76 Treecko C .75 2.00
77 Wingull C .75 2.00
78 Wurmple C .75 2.00
79 Zigzagoon C .75 2.00
80 Trainer: Energy Removal 2 U .75 2.00
81 Trainer: Energy Restore U .75 2.00
82 Trainer: Energy Switch U .75 2.00
83 Trainer: Lady Outing U .75 2.00
84 Trainer: Lum Berry U .75 2.00
85 Trainer: Oran Berry U .75 2.00
86 Trainer: Poke Ball U .75 2.00
87 Trainer: Pokemon Reversal U .75 2.00
88 Trainer: PokeNav U .75 2.00
89 Trainer: Professor Birch U .75 2.00
90 Trainer: Energy Search C .75 2.00
91 Trainer: Potion C .75 2.00
92 Trainer: Switch C .75 2.00
93 Darkness Energy R .75 2.00
94 Metal Energy R .75 2.00
95 Rainbow Energy R .75 2.00
96 Chansey EX HOLO R 2.00 6.00
97 Electabuzz EX HOLO R 2.00 6.00
98 Hitmonchan EX HOLO R 2.00 6.00
99 Lapras EX HOLO R 2.00 6.00
100 Magmar EX HOLO R 2.00 6.00
101 Mewtwo EX HOLO R 3.00 8.00
102 Scyther EX HOLO R 2.00 6.00
103 Sneasel EX HOLO R 2.00 6.00
104 Grass Energy C .75 2.00
105 Fighting Energy C .75 2.00
106 Water Energy C .75 2.00
107 Psychic Energy C .75 2.00
108 Fire Energy C .75 2.00
109 Lightning Energy C .75 2.00

2003 Pokemon EX Sandstorm

COMPLETE SET (100) 90.00 150.00
REVERSE HOLOFOIL SET (100) 150.00 200.00
BOOSTER BOX (36 PACKS) 350.00 550.00
BOOSTER PACK (9 CARDS) 10.00 25.00
*REV.FOIL: .75X TO 2X BASIC CARDS
RELEASED ON SEPTEMBER 17, 2003
1 Armaldo HOLO R 2.00 4.00
2 Cacturne HOLO R 2.00 4.00
3 Cradily HOLO R 2.00 4.00
4 Dusclops HOLO R 2.00 4.00
5 Flareon HOLO R 2.00 6.00
6 Jolteon HOLO R 2.00 6.00
7 Ludicolo HOLO R 2.00 4.00
8 Lunatone HOLO R 2.00 4.00
9 Mawile HOLO R 2.00 4.00
10 Sableye HOLO R 2.00 4.00
11 Seviper HOLO R 2.00 4.00
12 Shiftry HOLO R 2.00 4.00
13 Solrock HOLO R 3.00 6.00
14 Zangoose HOLO R 2.00 4.00
15 Arcanine R .75 2.00
16 Espeon R .75 2.00
17 Golduck R .75 2.00
18 Kecleon R .75 2.00
19 Omastar R .75 2.00
20 Pichu R .75 2.00
21 Sandslash R .75 2.00
22 Shiftry R .75 2.00
23 Steelix R .75 2.00
24 Umbreon R .75 2.00
25 Vaporeon R .75 2.00
26 Wobbuffet R .75 2.00
27 Anorith U .50 1.50
28 Anorith U .50 1.50
29 Arbok U .50 1.50
30 Azumarill U .50 1.50
31 Azurill U .50 1.50
32 Baltoy U .50 1.50
33 Breloom U .50 1.50
34 Delcatty U .50 1.50
35 Electabuzz U .50 1.50
36 Elekid U .50 1.50
37 Fearow U .50 1.50
38 Illumise U .50 1.50
39 Kabuto U .50 1.50
40 Kirlia U .50 1.50
41 Lairon U .50 1.50
42 Lileep U .50 1.50
43 Lileep U .50 1.50
44 Linoone U .50 1.50
45 Lombre U .50 1.50
46 Lombre U .50 1.50
47 Murkrow U .50 1.50
48 Nuzleaf U .50 1.50
49 Nuzleaf U .50 1.50
50 Pelipper U .50 1.50
51 Quilava U .50 1.50
52 Vigoroth U .50 1.50
53 Volbeat U .50 1.50
54 Wynaut U .50 1.50
55 Xatu U .50 1.50
56 Aron C .50 1.50
57 Cacnea C .50 1.50
58 Cacnea C .50 1.50
59 Cyndaquil C .50 1.50
60 Dunsparce C .50 1.50
61 Duskull C .50 1.50
62 Duskull C .50 1.50
63 Eevee C .50 1.50
64 Ekans C .50 1.50
65 Growlithe C .50 1.50
66 Lotad C .50 1.50
67 Lotad C .50 1.50
68 Marill C .50 1.50
69 Natu C .50 1.50
70 Omanyte C .50 1.50
71 Onix C .50 1.50
72 Pikachu C .50 1.50
73 Psyduck C .50 1.50
74 Ralts C .50 1.50
75 Sandshrew C .50 1.50
76 Seedot C .50 1.50
77 Seedot C .50 1.50
78 Shroomish C .50 1.50
79 Skitty C .50 1.50
80 Slakoth C .50 1.50
81 Spearow C .50 1.50
82 Trapinch C .50 1.50
83 Wailmer C .50 1.50
84 Wingull C .50 1.50
85 Zigzagoon C .50 1.50
86 Double Full Heal U .50 1.50
87 Lanette's Net Search U .50 1.50
88 Rare Candy U .50 1.50
89 Wally's Training U .50 1.50
90 Claw Fossil C .50 1.50
91 Mysterious Fossil C .50 1.50
92 Root Fossil C .50 1.50
93 Multi Energy R .50 1.50
94 Aerodactyl EX HOLO R 3.00 8.00
95 Aggron EX HOLO R 3.00 8.00
96 Gardevoir EX HOLO R 3.00 8.00
97 Kabutops EX HOLO R 3.00 8.00
98 Raichu EX HOLO R 5.00 12.00
99 Typhlosion EX HOLO R 3.00 8.00
100 Wailord EX HOLO R 3.00 8.00

2003 Pokemon EX Dragon

COMPLETE SET (100) 175.00 260.00
BOOSTER BOX (36 PACKS) 1000.00 1200.00
BOOSTER PACK (9 CARDS) 20.00 30.00
FIREFANG DECK 20.00 25.00
WINDBLAST DECK 20.00 25.00
RELEASED ON NOVEMBER 24, 2003
1 Absol HOLO R 5.00 8.00
2 Altaria HOLO R 4.00 6.00
3 Crawdaunt HOLO R 1.50 2.50
4 Flygon HOLO R 2.00 3.50
5 Golem HOLO R 2.00 3.50
6 Grumpig HOLO R 2.00 3.50
7 Minun HOLO R 5.00 8.00
8 Plusle HOLO R 4.00 6.00
9 Roselia HOLO R 2.00 3.50
10 Salamence HOLO R 2.50 4.00
11 Shedinja HOLO R 3.00 5.00
12 Torkoal HOLO R 1.50 2.50
13 Crawdaunt R 1.25 2.00
14 Dragonair R 1.25 2.00
15 Flygon R 1.25 2.00
16 Girafarig R 1.25 2.00
17 Magneton R 1.25 2.00
18 Ninjask R 1.25 2.00
19 Salamence R 1.25 2.00
20 Shelgon R 1.25 2.00
21 Skarmory R 1.25 2.00
22 Vibrava R 1.25 2.00
23 Bagon U .50 .75
24 Camerupt U .50 .75
25 Combusken U .50 .75
26 Dratini U .50 .75
27 Flaaffy U .50 .75
28 Forretress U .50 .75
29 Graveler U .50 .75
30 Graveler U .50 .75
31 Grovyle U .50 .75
32 Gyarados U .50 .75
33 Horsea U .50 .75
34 Houndoom U .50 .75
35 Magneton U .50 .75
36 Marshtomp U .50 .75
37 Meditite U .50 .75
38 Ninjask U .50 .75
39 Seadra U .50 .75
40 Seadra U .50 .75
41 Shelgon U .50 .75
42 Shelgon U .50 .75
43 Shuppet U .50 .75
44 Snorunt U .50 .75
45 Swellow U .50 .75
46 Vibrava U .50 .75
47 Vibrava U .50 .75
48 Whiscash U .50 .75
49 Bagon C .30 .50
50 Bagon C .30 .50
51 Barboach C .30 .50
52 Corphish C .30 .50
53 Corphish C .30 .50
54 Corphish C .30 .50
55 Geodude C .30 .50
56 Geodude C .30 .50
57 Grimer C .30 .50
58 Horsea U .30 .50
59 Houndour C .30 .50
60 Magikarp C .30 .50
61 Magnemite C .30 .50
62 Magnemite C .30 .50
63 Magnemite C .30 .50
64 Mareep C .30 .50
65 Mudkip C .30 .50
66 Nincada C .30 .50
67 Nincada C .30 .50
68 Nincada C .30 .50
69 Numel C .30 .50
70 Numel C .30 .50
71 Pineco C .30 .50
72 Slugma C .30 .50
73 Spoink C .30 .50
74 Spoink C .30 .50
75 Swablu C .30 .50
76 Taillow C .30 .50
77 Torchic C .30 .50
78 Trapinch C .30 .50
79 Trapinch C .30 .50
80 Treecko C .30 .50
81 Wurmple C .30 .50
82 Balloon Berry C .30 .50
83 Buffer Piece C .30 .50
84 Energy Recycle System C .30 .50
85 High Pressure System C .30 .50
86 Low Pressure System C .30 .50
87 Mr. Briney's Compassion C .30 .50
88 TV Reporter U .30 .50
89 Ampharos EX HOLO R 7.00 10.00
90 Dragonite EX HOLO R 10.00 15.00
91 Golem EX HOLO R 5.00 8.00
92 Kingdra EX HOLO R 4.00 6.00
93 Latias EX HOLO R 8.00 12.00
94 Latios EX HOLO R 8.00 12.00
95 Magcargo EX HOLO R 4.00 6.00
96 Muk EX HOLO R 4.00 6.00
97 Rayquaza EX HOLO R 10.00 15.00
98 Charmander HOLO R 10.00 15.00
99 Charmeleon HOLO R 8.00 12.00
100 Charizard HOLO R 25.00 35.00

2003 Pokemon EX Dragon Reverse Foil

COMPLETE SET (100) 100.00 160.00
BOOSTER BOX (36 PACKS) 1000.00 1200.00
*REV.FOIL: .75X TO 2X BASIC CARDS
1 Absol HOLO R 2.50 4.00
2 Altaria HOLO R 2.00 2.50
3 Crawdaunt HOLO R 2.00 2.50
4 Flygon HOLO R 2.00 3.00
5 Golem HOLO R 2.00 3.00
6 Grumpig HOLO R 2.00 3.00
7 Minun HOLO R 3.00 5.00
8 Plusle HOLO R 2.00 3.00
9 Roselia HOLO R 2.00 3.00
10 Salamence R 2.00 3.00
11 Shedinja HOLO R 2.00 3.00
12 Torkoal HOLO R 2.00 3.00
13 Crawdaunt R 1.50 2.50
14 Dragonair R 1.50 2.50
15 Flygon R 1.50 2.50
16 Girafarig R 1.50 2.50
17 Magneton R 1.50 2.50
18 Ninjask R 1.50 2.50
19 Salamence R 1.50 2.50
20 Shelgon R 1.50 2.50
21 Skarmory R 1.50 2.50
22 Vibrava R 1.50 2.50
23 Bagon U 1.25 2.00
24 Camerupt U 1.25 2.00
25 Combusken U 1.25 2.00
26 Dratini U 1.25 2.00
27 Flaaffy U 1.25 2.00
28 Forretress U 1.25 2.00
29 Graveler U 1.25 2.00
30 Graveler U 1.25 2.00
31 Grovyle U 1.25 2.00
32 Gyarados U 1.25 2.00
33 Horsea U 1.25 2.00
34 Houndoom U 1.25 2.00
35 Magneton U 1.25 2.00
36 Marshtomp U 1.25 2.00
37 Meditite U 1.25 2.00
38 Ninjask U 1.25 2.00
39 Seadra U 1.25 2.00
40 Seadra U 1.25 2.00
41 Shelgon U 1.25 2.00
42 Shelgon U 1.25 2.00
43 Shuppet U 1.25 2.00
44 Snorunt U 1.25 2.00
45 Swellow U 1.25 2.00
46 Vibrava U 1.25 2.00
47 Vibrava U 1.25 2.00
48 Whiscash U 1.25 2.00
49 Bagon C .75 1.25
50 Bagon C .75 1.25
51 Barboach C .75 1.25
52 Corphish C .75 1.25
53 Corphish C .75 1.25
54 Corphish C .75 1.25
55 Geodude C .75 1.25
56 Geodude C .75 1.25
57 Grimer C .75 1.25
58 Horsea U .75 1.25
59 Houndour C .75 1.25
60 Magikarp C .75 1.25
61 Magnemite C .75 1.25
62 Magnemite C .75 1.25
63 Magnemite C .75 1.25
64 Mareep C .75 1.25
65 Mudkip C .75 1.25
66 Nincada C .75 1.25
67 Nincada C .75 1.25
68 Nincada C .75 1.25
69 Numel C .75 1.25
70 Numel C .75 1.25
71 Pineco C .75 1.25
72 Slugma C .75 1.25
73 Spoink C .75 1.25
74 Spoink C .75 1.25
75 Swablu C .75 1.25
76 Taillow C .75 1.25
77 Torchic C .75 1.25
78 Trapinch C .75 1.25
79 Trapinch C .75 1.25
80 Treecko C .75 1.25
81 Wurmple C .75 1.25
82 Balloon Berry C .75 1.25
83 Buffer Piece C .75 1.25
84 Energy Recycle System C .75 1.25
85 High Pressure System C .75 1.25
86 Low Pressure System C .75 1.25
87 Mr. Briney's Compassion C .75 1.25
88 TV Reporter U .75 1.25
88R TV Reporter UR .75 1.25

2004 Pokemon EX Team Magma vs. Team Aqua

COMPLETE SET (97) 60.00 120.00
BOOSTER BOX (36 PACKS) 400.00 600.00
BOOSTER PACK (9 CARDS) 15.00 30.00
*REV.FOIL: .75X TO 2X BASIC CARDS
RELEASED ON MARCH 15, 2004
1 Team Aqua's Cacturne HOLO R 1.50 3.00
2 Team Aqua's Crawdaunt HOLO R .75 2.00
3 Team Aqua's Kyogre HOLO R 2.00 5.00
4 Team Aqua's Manectric HOLO R 1.00 2.50
5 Team Aqua's Sharpedo HOLO R 2.50 6.00
6 Team Aqua's Walrein HOLO R .75 2.00
7 Team Magma's Aggron HOLO R 1.00 2.50

8 Team Magma's Claydol HOLO R	.75	2.00
9 Team Magma's Groudon HOLO R	3.00	8.00
10 Team Magma's Houndoom HOLO R	2.00	5.00
11 Team Magma's Rhydon HOLO R	.75	2.00
12 Team Magma's Torkoal HOLO R	.75	2.00
13 Raichu R	.50	1.00
14 Team Aqua's Crawdaunt R	.50	1.00
15 Team Aqua's Mightyena R	.50	1.00
16 Team Aqua's Sealeo R	.50	1.00
17 Team Aqua's Seviper R	.50	1.00
18 Team Aqua's Sharpedo R	.50	1.00
19 Team Magma's Camerupt R	.50	1.00
20 Team Magma's Lairon R	.50	1.00
21 Team Magma's Mightyena R	.50	1.00
22 Team Magma's Rhydon R	.50	1.00
23 Team Magma's Zangoose R	.50	1.00
24 Team Aqua's Cacnea U	.20	.50
25 Team Aqua's Carvanha U	.20	.50
26 Team Aqua's Corphish U	.20	.50
27 Team Aqua's Electrike U	.20	.50
28 Team Aqua's Lanturn U	.20	.50
29 Team Aqua's Manectric U	.20	.50
30 Team Aqua's Mightyena U	.20	.50
31 Team Aqua's Sealeo U	.20	.50
32 Team Magma's Baltoy U	.20	.50
33 Team Magma's Claydol U	.20	.50
34 Team Magma's Houndoom U	.20	.50
35 Team Magma's Houndour U	.20	.50
36 Team Magma's Lairon U	.20	.50
37 Team Magma's Mightyena U	.20	.50
38 Team Magma's Rhyhorn U	.20	.50
39 Bulbasaur C	.10	.20
40 Cubone C	.10	.20
41 Jigglypuff C	.10	.20
42 Meowth C	.10	.20
43 Pikachu C	.10	.20
44 Psyduck C	.10	.20
45 Slowpoke C	.10	.20
46 Squirtle C	.10	.20
47 Team Aqua's Carvanha C	.10	.20
48 Team Aqua's Carvanha C	.10	.20
49 Team Aqua's Chinchou C	.10	.20
50 Team Aqua's Corphish C	.10	.20
51 Team Aqua's Corphish C	.10	.20
52 Team Aqua's Electrike C	.10	.20
53 Team Aqua's Electrike C	.10	.20
54 Team Aqua's Poochyena C	.10	.20
55 Team Aqua's Poochyena C	.10	.20
56 Team Aqua's Spheal C	.10	.20
57 Team Aqua's Spheal C	.10	.20
58 Team Magma's Aron C	.10	.20
59 Team Magma's Aron C	.10	.20
60 Team Magma's Baltoy C	.10	.20
61 Team Magma's Baltoy C	.10	.20
62 Team Magma's Houndour C	.10	.20
63 Team Magma's Houndour C	.10	.20
64 Team Magma's Numel C	.10	.20
65 Team Magma's Poochyena C	.10	.20
66 Team Magma's Poochyena C	.10	.20
67 Team Magma's Rhyhorn C	.10	.20
68 Team Magma's Rhyhorn C	.10	.20
69 Team Aqua Schemer U	.20	.50
70 Team Magma Schemer U	.20	.50
71 Archie U	.20	.50
72 Dual Ball U	.20	.50
73 Maxie U	.20	.50
74 Strength Charm U	.20	.50
75 Team Aqua Ball U	.20	.50
76 Team Aqua Belt U	.20	.50
77 Team Aqua Conspirator U	.20	.50
78 Team Aqua Hideout U	.20	.50
79 Team Aqua Technical Machine 01 U	.20	.50
80 Team Magma Ball U	.20	.50
81 Team Magma Belt U	.20	.50
82 Team Magma Conspirator U	.20	.50
83 Team Magma Hideout U	.20	.50
84 Team Magma Tech. Machine 01 U	.20	.50
85 Warp Point U	.20	.50
86 Aqua Energy U	.25	.75
87 Magma Energy U	.75	2.00
88 Double Rainbow Energy R	1.50	4.00
89 Blaziken EX HOLO R	8.00	20.00
90 Cradily EX HOLO R	6.00	15.00
91 Entei EX HOLO R	10.00	25.00
92 Raikou EX HOLO R	6.00	15.00
93 Sceptile EX HOLO R	8.00	20.00
94 Suicune EX HOLO R	8.00	20.00
95 Swampert EX HOLO R	8.00	20.00
96 Absol HOLO R	6.00	15.00
97 Jirachi HOLO R	4.00	10.00

2004 Pokemon EX Hidden Legends

COMPLETE SET (102)	150.00	250.00
BOOSTER BOX (36 PACKS)	700.00	800.00
BOOSTER PACK (9 CARDS)	8.00	20.00
*REV.FOIL: .75X TO 2X BASIC CARDS		
RELEASED ON JUNE 14, 2004		
1 Banette HOLO R	2.00	6.00
2 Claydol HOLO R	2.00	6.00
3 Crobat HOLO R	2.00	6.00
4 Dark Celebi HOLO R	2.00	6.00
5 Electrode HOLO R	2.00	6.00
6 Exploud HOLO R	2.00	6.00
7 Heracross HOLO R	2.00	6.00
8 Jirachi HOLO R	2.00	6.00
9 Machamp HOLO R	2.00	6.00
10 Medicham HOLO R	2.00	6.00
11 Metagross HOLO R	2.00	6.00
12 Milotic HOLO R	2.00	6.00
13 Pinsir HOLO R	2.00	6.00
14 Shiftry HOLO R	2.00	6.00
15 Walrein HOLO R	2.00	6.00
16 Bellossom R	.75	2.00
17 Chimecho R	.75	2.00
18 Gorebyss R	.75	2.00
19 Huntail R	.75	2.00
20 Masquerain R	.75	2.00
21 Metang R	.75	2.00
22 Ninetales R	.75	2.00
23 Rain Castform R	.75	2.00
24 Relicanth R	.75	2.00
25 Snow-cloud Castform R	.75	2.00
26 Sunny Castform R	.75	2.00
27 Tropius R	.75	2.00
28 Beldum U	.25	.75
29 Beldum U	.25	.75
30 Castform U	.25	.75
31 Claydol U	.25	.75
32 Corsola U	.25	.75
33 Dodrio U	.25	.75
34 Glalie U	.25	.75
35 Gloom U	.25	.75
36 Golbat U	.25	.75
37 Igglybuff U	.25	.75
38 Lanturn U	.25	.75
39 Loudred U	.25	.75
40 Luvdisc U	.25	.75
41 Machoke U	.25	.75
42 Medicham U	.25	.75
43 Metang U	.25	.75
44 Metang U	.25	.75
45 Nuzleaf U	.25	.75
46 Rhydon U	.25	.75
47 Sealeo U	.25	.75
48 Spinda U	.25	.75
49 Starmie U	.25	.75
50 Swalot U	.25	.75
51 Tentacruel U	.25	.75
52 Baltoy C	.25	.75
53 Baltoy C	.25	.75
54 Beldum C	.25	.75
55 Chikorita C	.25	.75
56 Chinchou C	.25	.75
57 Chinchou C	.25	.75
58 Clamperl C	.25	.75
59 Cyndaquil C	.25	.75
60 Doduo C	.25	.75
61 Feebas C	.25	.75
62 Gulpin C	.25	.75
63 Jigglypuff C	.25	.75
64 Machop C	.25	.75
65 Meditite C	.25	.75
66 Meditite C	.25	.75
67 Minun C	.25	.75
68 Oddish C	.25	.75
69 Plusle C	.25	.75
70 Rhyhorn C	.25	.75
71 Seedot C	.25	.75
72 Shuppet C	.25	.75
73 Snorunt C	.25	.75
74 Spheal C	.25	.75
75 Staryu C	.25	.75
76 Surskit C	.25	.75
77 Tentacool C	.25	.75
78 Togepi C	.25	.75
79 Totodile C	.25	.75
80 Voltorb C	.25	.75
81 Vulpix C	.25	.75
82 Whismur C	.25	.75
83 Zubat C	.25	.75
84 Ancient Technical Machine [Ice] U	.25	.75
85 Ancient Technical Machine [Rock] U	.25	.75
86 Ancient Technical Machine [Steel] U	.25	.75
87 Ancient Tomb U	.25	.75
88 Desert Ruins U	.25	.75
89 Island Cave U	.25	.75
90 Life Herb U	.25	.75
91 Magnetic Storm U	.25	.75
92 Steven's Advice U	.25	.75
93 Groudon EX HOLO R	4.00	10.00
94 Kyogre EX HOLO R	5.00	12.00
95 Metagross EX HOLO R	3.00	8.00
96 Ninetales EX HOLO R	6.00	15.00
97 Regice EX HOLO R	5.00	12.00
98 Regirock EX HOLO R	5.00	12.00
99 Registeel EX HOLO R	5.00	12.00
100 Vileplume EX HOLO R	3.00	8.00
101 Wigglytuff EX HOLO R	4.00	10.00
102 Groudon HOLO R	2.00	6.00

2004 Pokemon EX Fire Red Leaf Green

COMPLETE SET (116)	280.00	400.00
BOOSTER BOX (36 PACKS)	650.00	900.00
BOOSTER PACK (9 CARDS)	15.00	30.00
*REV.FOIL: .75X TO 2X BASIC CARDS		
RELEASED ON AUGUST 30, 2004		
1 Beedrill HOLO R	1.50	4.00
2 Butterfree HOLO R	2.00	6.00
3 Dewgong HOLO R	1.50	4.00
4 Ditto HOLO R	1.50	4.00
5 Exeggutor HOLO R	1.50	4.00
6 Kangaskhan HOLO R	1.50	4.00
7 Marowak HOLO R	1.50	4.00
8 Nidoking HOLO R	1.50	4.00
9 Nidoqueen HOLO R	1.50	4.00
10 Pidgeot HOLO R	1.50	4.00
11 Poliwrath HOLO R	1.50	4.00
12 Raichu HOLO R	4.00	10.00
13 Rapidash HOLO R	1.50	4.00
14 Slowbro HOLO R	1.50	4.00
15 Snorlax HOLO R	1.50	4.00
16 Tauros HOLO R	1.50	4.00
17 Victreebel HOLO R	1.50	4.00
18 Arcanine R	1.25	3.00
19 Chansey R	1.25	3.00
20 Cloyster R	1.25	3.00
21 Dodrio R	1.25	3.00
22 Dugtrio R	1.25	3.00
23 Farfetch'd R	1.25	3.00
24 Fearow R	1.25	3.00
25 Hypno R	1.25	3.00
26 Kingler R	1.25	3.00
27 Magneton R	1.25	3.00
28 Primeape R	1.25	3.00
29 Scyther R	1.25	3.00
30 Tangela R	1.25	3.00
31 Charmeleon U	.25	.75
32 Drowzee U	.25	.75
33 Exeggcute U	.25	.75
34 Haunter U	.25	.75
35 Ivysaur U	.25	.75
36 Kakuna U	.25	.75
37 Lickitung U	.25	.75
38 Mankey U	.25	.75
39 Metapod U	.25	.75
40 Nidorina U	.25	.75
41 Nidorino U	.25	.75
42 Onix U	.25	.75
43 Parasect U	.25	.75
44 Persian U	.25	.75
45 Pidgeotto U	.25	.75
46 Poliwhirl U	.25	.75
47 Porygon U	.25	.75
48 Raticate U	.25	.75
49 Venomoth U	.25	.75
50 Wartortle U	.25	.75
51 Weepinbell U	.25	.75
52 Wigglytuff U	.25	.75
53 Bellsprout C	.25	.75
54 Bulbasaur C	.25	.75
55 Bulbasaur C	.25	.75
56 Caterpie C	.25	.75
57 Charmander C	.25	.75
58 Charmander C	.25	.75
59 Clefairy C	.25	.75
60 Cubone C	.25	.75
61 Diglett C	.25	.75
62 Doduo C	.25	.75
63 Gastly C	.25	.75
64 Growlithe C	.25	.75
65 Jigglypuff C	.25	.75
66 Krabby C	.25	.75
67 Magikarp C	.25	.75
68 Magnemite C	.25	.75
69 Meowth C	.25	.75
70 Nidoran F C	.25	.75
71 Nidoran M C	.25	.75
72 Paras C	.25	.75
73 Pidgey C	.25	.75
74 Pikachu C	.25	.75
75 Poliwag C	.25	.75
76 Ponyta C	.25	.75
77 Rattata C	.25	.75
78 Seel C	.25	.75
79 Shellder C	.25	.75
80 Slowpoke C	.25	.75
81 Spearow C	.25	.75
82 Squirtle C	.25	.75
83 Squirtle C	.25	.75
84 Venonat C	.25	.75
85 Voltorb C	.25	.75
86 Weedle C	.25	.75
87 Bill's Maintenance U	.25	.75
88 Celio's Network U	.25	.75
89 Energy Removal 2 U	.25	.75
90 Energy Switch U	.25	.75
91 EXP.ALL U	.25	.75
92 Great Ball U	.25	.75
93 Life Herb U	.25	.75
94 Mt. Moon U	.25	.75
95 Poke Ball U	.25	.75
96 PokeDEX HANDY 909 U	.25	.75
97 Pokemon Reversal U	.25	.75
98 Professor Oak's Research U	.25	.75
99 Super Scoop Up U	.25	.75
100 VS Seeker U	6.00	15.00
101 Potion C	.25	.75
102 Switch C	.25	.75
103 Multi Energy HOLO R	.75	2.00
104 Blastoise EX HOLO R	15.00	30.00
105 Charizard EX HOLO R	60.00	100.00
106 Clefable EX HOLO R	3.00	8.00
107 Electrode EX HOLO R	3.00	8.00
108 Gengar EX HOLO R	8.00	20.00
109 Gyarados EX HOLO R	8.00	20.00
110 Mr. Mime EX HOLO R	3.00	8.00
111 Mr. Mime EX HOLO R	3.00	8.00
112 Venusaur EX HOLO R	15.00	30.00
113 Charmander HOLO R	4.00	10.00
114 Articuno EX HOLO R	5.00	12.00
115 Moltres EX HOLO R	5.00	12.00
116 Zapdos EX HOLO R	6.00	15.00

2004 Pokemon EX Team Rocket Returns

COMPLETE SET (111)	400.00	700.00
BOOSTER BOX (36 PACKS)	800.00	1100.00
BOOSTER PACK (9 CARDS)	15.00	30.00
*REV.FOIL: .75X TO 2X BASIC CARDS		
RELEASED ON NOVEMBER 4, 2004		
1 Azumarill HOLO R	2.00	6.00
2 Dark Ampharos HOLO R	2.00	6.00
3 Dark Crobat HOLO R	2.00	6.00
4 Dark Electrode HOLO R	2.00	6.00
5 Dark Houndoom HOLO R	2.00	6.00
6 Dark Hypno HOLO R	2.00	6.00
7 Dark Marowak HOLO R	2.00	6.00
8 Dark Octillery HOLO R	2.00	6.00
9 Dark Slowking HOLO R	2.00	6.00
10 Dark Steelix HOLO R	2.00	6.00
11 Jumpluff HOLO R	2.00	6.00
12 Kingdra HOLO R	2.00	6.00
13 Piloswine HOLO R	2.00	6.00
14 Togetic HOLO R	2.00	6.00
15 Dark Dragonite R	1.50	4.00
16 Dark Muk R	.75	2.00
17 Dark Raticate R	.75	2.00
18 Dark Sandslash R	.75	2.00
19 Dark Tyranitar R	.75	2.00
20 Dark Tyranitar R	.75	2.00
21 Delibird R	.75	2.00
22 Furret R	.75	2.00
23 Ledian R	.75	2.00
24 Magby R	.75	2.00
25 Misdreavus R	.75	2.00
26 Quagsire R	.75	2.00
27 Qwilfish R	.75	2.00
28 Yanma R	.75	2.00
29 Dark Arbok U	.75	2.00
30 Dark Ariados U	.75	2.00
31 Dark Dragonair U	1.50	4.00
32 Dark Dragonair U	1.50	4.00
33 Dark Flaaffy U	.75	2.00
34 Dark Golbat U	.75	2.00
35 Dark Golduck U	.75	2.00
36 Dark Gyarados U	1.50	4.00
37 Dark Houndoom U	.75	2.00
38 Dark Magcargo U	.75	2.00
39 Dark Magneton U	.75	2.00
40 Dark Pupitar U	.75	2.00
41 Dark Pupitar U	.75	2.00
42 Dark Weezing U	.75	2.00
43 Heracross U	.75	2.00
44 Magmar U	.75	2.00
45 Mantine U	.75	2.00
46 Rocket's Meowth U	.75	2.00
47 Rocket's Wobbuffet U	.75	2.00
48 Seadra U	.75	2.00
49 Skiploom U	.75	2.00
50 Togepi U	.75	2.00
51 Cubone C	.25	.75
52 Dratini C	.25	2.00
53 Dratini C	.25	2.00
54 Drowzee C	.25	2.00
55 Ekans C	.25	2.00
56 Grimer C	.25	2.00
57 Hoppip C	.25	2.00
58 Horsea C	.25	2.00
59 Houndour C	.25	2.00
60 Houndour C	.25	2.00
61 Koffing C	.25	2.00
62 Larvitar C	.25	2.00
63 Larvitar C	.25	2.00
64 Ledyba C	.25	2.00
65 Magikarp C	.25	2.00
66 Magnemite C	.25	2.00
67 Mareep C	.25	2.00
68 Marill C	.25	2.00
69 Onix C	.25	2.00
70 Psyduck C	.25	2.00
71 Rattata C	.25	2.00
72 Rattata C	.25	2.00
73 Remoraid C	.25	2.00
74 Sandshrew C	.25	2.00
75 Sentret C	.25	2.00
76 Slowpoke C	.25	2.00
77 Slugma C	.25	2.00
78 Spinarak C	.25	2.00
79 Swinub C	.25	2.00
80 Voltorb C	.25	2.00
81 Wooper C	.25	2.00
82 Zubat C	.25	2.00
83 Copycat U	.25	2.00
84 Pokemon Retriever U	.25	2.00
85 Pow! Hand Extension U	.25	2.00
86 Rocket's Admin. U	2.00	6.00
87 Rocket's Hideout U	.25	2.00
88 Rocket's Mission U	.25	2.00
89 Rocket's Poke Ball U	.25	2.00
90 Rocket's Tricky Gym U	.25	2.00
91 Surprise! Time Machine U	.25	2.00
92 Swoop! Teleporter U	.25	2.00
93 Venture Bomb U	.25	2.00
94 Dark Metal Energy U	.25	2.00
95 R Energy U	.25	2.00
96 Rocket's Articuno EX HOLO R	10.00	25.00
97 Rocket's Entei EX HOLO R	15.00	30.00
98 Rocket's Hitmonchan EX HOLO R	8.00	20.00
99 Rocket's Mewtwo EX HOLO R	20.00	40.00
100 Rocket's Moltres EX HOLO R	15.00	30.00
101 Rocket's Scizor EX HOLO R	8.00	20.00
102 Rocket's Scyther EX HOLO R	15.00	30.00
103 Rocket's Sneasel EX HOLO R	6.00	15.00
104 Rocket's Snorlax EX HOLO R	10.00	25.00
105 Rocket's Suicune EX HOLO R	10.00	25.00
106 Rocket's Zapdos EX HOLO R	15.00	30.00
107 Mudkip Gold Star HOLO R	50.00	100.00
108 Torchic Gold Star HOLO R	60.00	120.00
109 Treecko Gold Star HOLO R	50.00	100.00
110 Charmeleon SCR	3.00	8.00
111 Here Comes Team Rocket! SCR	10.00	25.00

2004 Pokemon EX Trainer Kit

COMPLETE SET (60)	7.00	12.00
RELEASED ON MARCH 15, 2005		
2 Latios HOLO R	2.00	5.00
4 Latias HOLO R	2.00	5.00

2005 Pokemon EX Deoxys

COMPLETE SET (108)	400.00	700.00
BOOSTER BOX (36 PACKS)	1000.00	1600.00
BOOSTER PACK (9 CARDS)	8.00	20.00
*REV.FOIL: .75X TO 2X BASIC CARDS		
RELEASED ON FEBRUARY 14, 2005		
1 Altaria HOLO R	2.00	6.00
2 Beautifly HOLO R	2.00	6.00
3 Breloom HOLO R	2.00	6.00
4 Camerupt HOLO R	2.00	6.00
5 Claydol HOLO R	2.00	6.00
6 Crawdaunt HOLO R	2.00	6.00
7 Dusclops HOLO R	2.00	6.00
8 Gyarados HOLO R	2.00	6.00
9 Jirachi HOLO R	2.00	6.00
10 Ludicolo HOLO R	2.00	6.00
11 Metagross HOLO R	2.00	6.00

12 Mightyena HOLO R	2.00	6.00
13 Ninjask HOLO R	2.00	6.00
14 Shedinja HOLO R	2.00	6.00
15 Slaking HOLO R	2.00	6.00
16 Deoxys (Normal) R	1.50	3.00
17 Deoxys (Attack) R	1.50	3.00
18 Deoxys (Defense) R	1.50	3.00
19 Ludicolo R	1.50	3.00
20 Magcargo R	1.50	3.00
21 Pelipper R	1.50	3.00
22 Rayquaza R	1.50	3.00
23 Sableye R	1.50	3.00
24 Seaking R	1.50	3.00
25 Shiftry R	1.50	3.00
26 Skarmory R	1.50	3.00
27 Tropius R	1.50	3.00
28 Whiscash R	1.50	3.00
29 Xatu R	1.50	3.00
30 Donphan U	.25	.75
31 Golbat U	.25	.75
32 Grumpig U	.25	.75
33 Lombre U	.25	.75
34 Lombre U	.25	.75
35 Lotad U	.25	.75
36 Lunatone U	.25	.75
37 Magcargo U	.25	.75
38 Manectric U	.25	.75
39 Masquerain U	.25	.75
40 Metang U	.25	.75
41 Minun U	.25	.75
42 Nosepass U	.25	.75
43 Nuzleaf U	.25	.75
44 Plusle U	.25	.75
45 Shelgon U	.25	.75
46 Silcoon U	.25	.75
47 Solrock U	.25	.75
48 Starmie U	.25	.75
49 Swellow U	.25	.75
50 Vigoroth U	.25	.75
51 Weezing U	.25	.75
52 Bagon C	.25	.75
53 Baltoy C	.25	.75
54 Barboach C	.25	.75
55 Beldum C	.25	.75
56 Carvanha C	.25	.75
57 Corphish C	.25	.75
58 Duskull C	.25	.75
59 Electrike C	.25	.75
60 Electrike C	.25	.75
61 Goldeen C	.25	.75
62 Koffing C	.25	.75
63 Lotad C	.25	.75
64 Magikarp C	.25	.75
65 Makuhita C	.25	.75
66 Natu C	.25	.75
67 Nincada C	.25	.75
68 Numel C	.25	.75
69 Phanpy C	.25	.75
70 Poochyena C	.25	.75
71 Seedot C	.25	.75
72 Shroomish C	.25	.75
73 Slakoth C	.25	.75
74 Slugma C	.25	.75
75 Slugma C	.25	.75
76 Spoink C	.25	.75
77 Staryu C	.25	.75
78 Surskit C	.25	.75
79 Swablu C	.25	.75
80 Taillow C	.25	.75
81 Wingull C	.25	.75
82 Wurmple C	.25	.75
83 Zubat C	.25	.75
84 Balloon Berry U	.25	.75
85 Crystal Shard U	.25	.75
86 Energy Charge U	.25	.75
87 Lady Outing U	.25	.75
88 Master Ball U	.25	.75
89 Meteor Falls U	.25	.75
90 Professor Cozmo's Discovery U	.25	.75
91 Space Center U	.25	.75
92 Strength Charm U	.25	.75
93 Boost Energy U	.25	.75
94 Healing Energy U	.25	.75
95 Scramble Energy U	.75	2.00
96 Crobat EX HOLO R	3.00	8.00
97 Deoxys EX (Normal) HOLO R	5.00	12.00
98 Deoxys EX (Attack) HOLO R	4.00	10.00
99 Deoxys EX (Defense) HOLO R	3.00	8.00
100 Hariyama EX HOLO R	3.00	8.00
101 Manectric EX HOLO R	3.00	8.00
102 Rayquaza EX HOLO R	3.00	8.00
103 Salamence EX HOLO R	8.00	20.00
104 Sharpedo EX HOLO R	5.00	12.00
105 Latias Gold Star HOLO R	80.00	140.00
106 Latios Gold Star HOLO R	80.00	140.00
107 Rayquaza Gold Star HOLO R	200.00	300.00
108 Rocket's Raikou EX HOLO R	6.00	15.00

2005 Pokemon EX Emerald

COMPLETE SET (107)	150.00	250.00
BOOSTER BOX (36 PACKS)	600.00	800.00
BOOSTER PACK (9 CARDS)	8.00	20.00
*REV.FOIL: .75X TO 2X BASIC CARDS		
RELEASED ON MAY 9, 2005		
1 Blaziken HOLO R	1.50	4.00
2 Deoxys HOLO R	1.50	4.00
3 Exploud HOLO R	1.50	4.00
4 Gardevoir HOLO R	1.50	4.00
5 Groudon HOLO R	1.50	4.00
6 Kyogre HOLO R	1.50	4.00
7 Manectric HOLO R	1.50	4.00
8 Milotic HOLO R	1.50	4.00
9 Rayquaza HOLO R	1.50	4.00
10 Sceptile HOLO R	1.50	4.00
11 Swampert HOLO R	1.50	4.00
12 Chimecho R	.75	2.00
13 Glalie R	.75	2.00
14 Groudon R	.75	2.00
15 Kyogre R	.75	2.00
16 Manectric R	.75	2.00
17 Nosepass R	.75	2.00
18 Relicanth R	.75	2.00
19 Rhydon R	.75	2.00
20 Seviper R	.75	2.00
21 Zangoose R	.75	2.00
22 Breloom U	.75	2.00
23 Camerupt U	.75	2.00
24 Claydol U	.75	2.00
25 Combusken U	.75	2.00
26 Dodrio U	.75	2.00
27 Electrode U	.75	2.00
28 Grovyle U	.75	2.00
29 Grumpig U	.75	2.00
30 Grumpig U	.75	2.00
31 Hariyama U	.75	2.00
32 Illumise U	.75	2.00
33 Kirlia U	.75	2.00
34 Linoone U	.75	2.00
35 Loudred U	.75	2.00
36 Marshtomp U	.75	2.00
37 Minun U	.75	2.00
38 Ninetales U	.75	2.00
39 Plusle U	.75	2.00
40 Swalot U	.75	2.00
41 Swellow U	.75	2.00
42 Volbeat U	.75	2.00
43 Baltoy C	.75	2.00
44 Cacnea C	.75	2.00
45 Doduo C	.75	2.00
46 Duskull C	.75	2.00
47 Electrike C	.75	2.00
48 Electrike C	.75	2.00
49 Feebas C	.75	2.00
50 Feebas C	.75	2.00
51 Gulpin C	.75	2.00
52 Larvitar C	.75	2.00
53 Luvdisc C	.75	2.00
54 Makuhita C	.75	2.00
55 Meditite C	.75	2.00
56 Mudkip C	.75	2.00
57 Numel C	.75	2.00
58 Numel C	.75	2.00
59 Pichu C	.75	2.00
60 Pikachu C	.75	2.00
61 Ralts C	.75	2.00
62 Rhyhorn C	.75	2.00
63 Shroomish C	.75	2.00
64 Snorunt C	.75	2.00
65 Spoink C	.75	2.00
66 Spoink C	.75	2.00
67 Swablu C	.75	2.00
68 Taillow C	.75	2.00
69 Torchic C	.75	2.00
70 Treecko C	.75	2.00
71 Voltorb C	.75	2.00
72 Vulpix C	.75	2.00
73 Whismur C	.75	2.00
74 Zigzagoon C	.75	2.00
75 Battle Frontier U	.75	2.00
76 Double Full Heal U	.75	2.00
77 Lanette's Net Search U	.75	2.00
78 Lum Berry U	.75	2.00
79 Mr. Stone's Project U	.75	2.00
80 Oran Berry U	.75	2.00
81 Pokenav U	.75	2.00
82 Professor Birch U	.75	2.00
83 Rare Candy U	.75	2.00
84 Scott U	.75	2.00
85 Wally's Training U	.75	2.00
86 Darkness Energy R	.75	2.00
87 Double Rainbow Energy R	.75	2.00
88 Metal Energy R	.75	2.00
89 Mutli Energy R	.75	2.00
90 Altaria EX HOLO R	5.00	12.00
91 Cacturne EX HOLO R	4.00	10.00
92 Camerupt EX HOLO R	3.00	8.00
93 Deoxys EX HOLO R	6.00	15.00
94 Dusclops EX HOLO R	6.00	15.00
95 Medicham EX HOLO R	6.00	15.00
96 Milotic EX HOLO R	10.00	25.00
97 Raichu EX HOLO R	10.00	25.00
98 Regice EX HOLO R	6.00	15.00
99 Regirock HOLO R	6.00	15.00
100 Registeel HOLO R	6.00	15.00
101 Grass Energy HOLO	3.00	8.00
102 Fire Energy HOLO	3.00	8.00
103 Water Energy HOLO	3.00	8.00
104 Lightning Energy HOLO	3.00	8.00
105 Psychic Energy HOLO	3.00	8.00
106 Fighting Energy HOLO	3.00	8.00
107 Farfetch'd SCR	3.00	8.00

2005 Pokemon EX Unseen Forces

COMPLETE SET (117)	400.00	600.00
BOOSTER BOX (36 PACKS)	500.00	650.00
BOOSTER PACK (9 CARDS)	10.00	25.00
*REV.FOIL: .75X TO 2X BASIC CARDS		
RELEASED ON AUGUST 22, 2005		
1 Ampharos HOLO R	2.00	6.00
2 Ariados HOLO R	2.00	6.00
3 Bellossom HOLO R	2.00	6.00
4 Feraligatr HOLO R	2.00	6.00
5 Flareon HOLO R	2.00	6.00
6 Forretress HOLO R	2.00	6.00
7 Houndoom HOLO R	2.00	6.00
8 Jolteon HOLO R	2.00	6.00
9 Meganium HOLO R	2.00	6.00
10 Octillery HOLO R	2.00	6.00
11 Poliwrath HOLO R	2.00	6.00
12 Porygon 2 HOLO R	2.00	6.00
13 Slowbro HOLO R	2.00	6.00
14 Slowking HOLO R	2.00	6.00
15 Sudowoodo HOLO R	2.00	6.00
16 Sunflora HOLO R	2.00	6.00
17 Typhlosion HOLO R	2.00	6.00
18 Ursaring HOLO R	2.00	6.00
19 Vaporeon HOLO R	2.00	6.00
20 Chansey R	1.25	3.00
21 Cleffa R	1.25	3.00
22 Electabuzz R	1.25	3.00
23 Elekid R	1.25	3.00
24 Hitmonchan R	1.25	3.00
25 Hitmonlee R	1.25	3.00
26 Hitmontop R	1.25	3.00
27 Ho-Oh R	1.25	3.00
28 Jynx R	1.25	3.00
29 Lugia R	1.25	3.00
30 Murkrow R	1.25	3.00
31 Smoochum R	1.25	3.00
32 Stantler R	1.25	3.00
33 Tyrogue R	1.25	3.00
34 Aipom U	.25	.75
35 Bayleef U	.25	.75
36 Clefable U	.25	.75
37 Corsola U	.25	.75
38 Croconaw U	.25	.75
39 Granbull U	.25	.75
40 Lanturn U	.25	.75
41 Magcargo U	.25	.75
42 Miltank U	.25	.75
43 Noctowl U	.25	.75
44 Quagsire U	.25	.75
45 Quilava U	.25	.75
46 Scyther U	.25	.75
47 Shuckle U	.25	.75
48 Smeargle U	.25	.75
49 Xatu U	.25	.75
50 Yanma U	.25	.75
51 Chikorita C	.25	.75
52 Chinchou C	.25	.75
53 Clefairy C	.25	.75
54 Cyndaquil C	.25	.75
55 Eevee C	.25	.75
56 Flaaffy C	.25	.75
57 Gligar C	.25	.75
58 Gloom C	.25	.75
59 Hoothoot C	.25	.75
60 Houndour C	.25	.75
61 Larvitar C	.25	.75
62 Mareep C	.25	.75
63 Natu C	.25	.75
64 Oddish C	.25	.75
65 Onix C	.25	.75
66 Pineco C	.25	.75
67 Poliwag C	.25	.75
68 Poliwhirl C	.25	.75
69 Porygon C	.25	.75
70 Pupitar C	.25	.75
71 Remoraid C	.25	.75
72 Slowpoke C	.25	.75
73 Slugma C	.25	.75
74 Snubbull C	.25	.75
75 Spinarak C	.25	.75
76 Sunkern C	.25	.75
77 Teddiursa C	.25	.75
78 Totodile C	.25	.75
79 Wooper C	.25	.75
80 Curse Powder U	.25	.75
81 EnergyRecycle System U	.25	.75
82 EnergyRemoval 2 U	.25	.75
83 EnergyRoot U	.25	.75
84 Energy Switch U	.25	.75
85 Fluffy Berry U	.25	.75
86 Mary'sRequest U	.25	.75
87 Poke Ball U	.25	.75
88 PokemonReversal U	.25	.75
89 Professor Elm's Training Method U	.25	.75
90 Protective Orb U	.25	.75
91 Sitrus Berry U	.25	.75
92 SolidRage U	.25	.75
93 Warp Point U	.25	.75
94 Energy Search C	.25	.75
95 Potion C	.25	.75
96 Darkness Energy R	.75	2.00
97 Metal Energy R	.75	.75
98 Boost Energy U	.25	.75
99 Cyclone Energy U	.25	.75
100 Warp Energy U	.25	.75
101 Blissey EX UR HOLO	6.00	15.00
102 Espeon EX UR HOLO	8.00	20.00
103 Feraligatr EX UR HOLO	4.00	10.00
104 Ho-Oh EX UR HOLO	6.00	15.00
105 Lugia EX UR HOLO	25.00	50.00
106 Meganium EX UR HOLO	4.00	10.00
107 Politoed EX UR HOLO	5.00	12.00
108 Scizor EX UR HOLO	6.00	15.00
109 Steelix EX UR HOLO	4.00	10.00
110 Typhlosion EX UR HOLO	4.00	10.00
111 Tyranitar EX UR HOLO	8.00	20.00
112 Umbreon EX UR HOLO	8.00	20.00
113 Entei Gold Star HOLO R	25.00	50.00
114 Raikou Gold Star HOLO R	25.00	50.00
115 Suicune Gold Star HOLO R	25.00	50.00
116 Rocket's Persian EX HOLO R	3.00	8.00
117 Celebi EX SCR	20.00	40.00

2005 Pokemon EX Unseen Forces Unown

COMPLETE SET (28)	30.00	60.00
RELEASED ON AUGUST 22, 2005		
A Unown	1.50	4.00
B Unown	1.50	4.00
C Unown	1.50	4.00
D Unown	1.50	4.00
E Unown	1.50	4.00
F Unown	1.50	4.00
G Unown	1.50	4.00
H Unown	1.50	4.00
I Unown	1.50	4.00
J Unown	1.50	4.00
K Unown	1.50	4.00
L Unown	1.50	4.00
M Unown	1.50	4.00
N Unown	1.50	4.00
O Unown	1.50	4.00
P Unown	1.50	4.00
Q Unown	1.50	4.00
R Unown	1.50	4.00
S Unown	1.50	4.00
T Unown	1.50	4.00
U Unown	1.50	4.00
V Unown	1.50	4.00
W Unown	1.50	4.00
X Unown	1.50	4.00
Y Unown	1.50	4.00
Z Unown	1.50	4.00
QM Unown	3.00	8.00
EP Unown	5.00	12.00

2005 Pokemon EX Delta Species

COMPLETE SET (113)	300.00	450.00
BOOSTER BOX (36 PACKS)	700.00	1000.00
BOOSTER PACK (9 CARDS)	15.00	30.00
*REV.FOIL: .75X TO 2X BASIC CARDS		
RELEASED ON OCTOBER 31, 2005		
1 Beedrill DS HOLO R	2.00	6.00
2 Crobat DS HOLO R	2.00	6.00
3 Dragonite DS HOLO R	2.00	6.00
4 Espeon DS HOLO R	2.00	6.00
5 Flareon DS HOLO R	2.00	6.00
6 Gardevoir DS HOLO R	2.00	6.00
7 Jolteon DS HOLO R	2.00	6.00
8 Latias DS HOLO R	2.00	6.00
9 Latios HOLO R	2.00	6.00
10 Marowak DS HOLO R	2.00	6.00
11 Metagross DS HOLO R	2.00	6.00
12 Mewtwo DS HOLO R	5.00	12.00
13 Rayquaza DS HOLO R	2.00	6.00
14 Salamence DS HOLO R	2.00	6.00
15 Starmie DS HOLO R	2.00	6.00
16 Tyranitar DS HOLO R	2.00	6.00
17 Umbreon DS HOLO R	2.00	6.00
18 Vaporeon DS HOLO R	2.00	6.00
19 Azumarill DS R	.75	2.00
20 Azurill R	.75	2.00
21 Holon's Electrode R	.75	2.00
22 Holon's Magneton R	.75	2.00
23 Hypno R	.75	2.00
24 Mightyena DS R	.75	2.00
25 Porygon2 R	.75	2.00
26 Rain Castform R	.75	2.00
27 Sandslash DS R	.75	2.00
28 Slowking R	.75	2.00
29 Snow-cloud Castform R	.75	2.00
30 Starmie DS R	.75	2.00
31 Sunny Castform R	.75	2.00
32 Swellow R	.75	2.00
33 Weezing R	.75	2.00
34 Castform U	.30	1.00
35 Ditto U	.30	1.00
36 Ditto U	.30	1.00
37 Ditto U	.30	1.00
38 Ditto U	.30	1.00
39 Ditto (U)	.30	1.00
40 Ditto U	.30	1.00
41 Dragonair DS U	.30	1.00
42 Dragonair DS U	.30	1.00
43 Golbat U	.30	1.00
44 Hariyama U	.30	1.00
45 Illumise U	.30	1.00
46 Kakuna U	.30	1.00
47 Kirlia U	.30	1.00
48 Magneton U	.30	1.00
49 Metang DS U	.30	1.00
50 Persian U	.30	1.00
51 Pupitar DS U	.30	1.00
52 Rapidash U	.30	1.00
53 Shelgon DS U	.30	1.00
54 Shelgon DS U	.30	1.00
55 Skarmory U	.30	1.00
56 Volbeat U	.30	1.00
57 Bagon DS C	.30	1.00
58 Bagon DS C	.30	1.00
59 Beldum DS C	.30	1.00
60 Cubone C	.30	1.00
61 Ditto C	.30	1.00
62 Ditto C	.30	1.00
63 Ditto C	.30	1.00
64 Ditto C	.30	1.00
65 Dratini DS C	.30	1.00
66 Dratini DS C	.30	1.00
67 Drowzee C	.30	1.00
68 Eevee DS C	.30	1.00
69 Eevee C	.30	1.00
70 Holon's Magnemite C	.30	1.00
71 Holon's Voltorb C	.30	1.00
72 Koffing C	.30	1.00
73 Larvitar DS C	.30	1.00
74 Magnemite C	.30	1.00
75 Makuhita C	.30	1.00
76 Marill C	.30	1.00
77 Meowth C	.30	1.00
78 Ponyta C	.30	1.00
79 Poochyena C	.30	1.00
80 Porygon C	.30	1.00
81 Ralts C	.30	1.00
82 Sandshrew C	.30	1.00
83 Slowpoke C	.30	1.00
84 Staryu C	.30	1.00
85 Staryu C	.30	1.00
86 Taillow C	.30	1.00

87 Weedle C .30 1.00
88 Zubat C .30 1.00
89 Dual Ball U .30 1.00
90 Great Ball U .30 1.00
91 Holon Farmer U .30 1.00
92 Holon Lass U .30 1.00
93 Holon Mentor U .30 1.00
94 Holon Research Tower U .30 1.00
95 Holon Researcher U .30 1.00
96 Holon Ruins U .30 1.00
97 Holon Scientist U .30 1.00
98 Holon Transceiver U .30 1.00
99 Master Ball U .30 1.00
100 Super Scoop Up U .30 1.00
101 Potion C .30 1.00
102 Switch C .30 1.00
103 Darkness Energy R .30 1.00
104 Holon Energy FF R .30 1.00
105 Holon Energy GL R .30 1.00
106 Holon Energy WP R .30 1.00
107 Metal Energy R .30 1.00
108 Flareon EX HOLO R 5.00 12.00
109 Jolteon EX HOLO R 5.00 12.00
110 Vaporeon EX HOLO R 5.00 12.00
111 Groudon Gold Star HOLO R 40.00 80.00
112 Kyogre Gold Star HOLO R 40.00 80.00
113 Metagross Gold Star HOLO R 35.00 70.00
114 Azumarill SCR 2.00 6.00

2006 Pokemon EX Legend Maker

COMPLETE SET (93) 300.00 500.00
BOOSTER BOX (36 PACKS) 700.00 900.00
BOOSTER PACK (9 CARDS) 15.00 30.00
*REV.FOIL: .75X TO 2X BASIC CARDS
RELEASED ON FEBRUARY 13, 2006
1 Aerodactyl HOLO R 2.00 6.00
2 Aggron HOLO R 2.00 6.00
3 Cradily HOLO R 2.00 6.00
4 Delcatty HOLO R 2.00 6.00
5 Gengar HOLO R 2.00 6.00
6 Golem HOLO R 2.00 6.00
7 Kabutops HOLO R 2.00 6.00
8 Lapras HOLO R 2.00 6.00
9 Machamp HOLO R 2.00 6.00
10 Mew HOLO R 2.00 6.00
11 Muk HOLO R 2.00 6.00
12 Shiftry HOLO R 2.00 6.00
13 Victreebel HOLO R 2.00 6.00
14 Wailord HOLO R 2.00 6.00
15 Absol R .75 2.00
16 Girafarig R .75 2.00
17 Gorebyss R .75 2.00
18 Huntail R .75 2.00
19 Lanturn R .75 2.00
20 Lunatone R .75 2.00
21 Magmar R .75 2.00
22 Magneton R .75 2.00
23 Omastar R .75 2.00
24 Pinsir R .75 2.00
25 Solrock R .75 2.00
26 Spinda R .75 2.00
27 Torkoal R .75 2.00
28 Wobbuffet R .75 2.00
29 Anorith U .20 .50
30 Cascoon U .20 2.00
31 Dunsparce U .20 2.00
32 Electrode U .20 2.00
33 Furret U .20 2.00
34 Graveler U .20 2.00
35 Haunter U .20 2.00
36 Kabuto U .20 2.00
37 Kecleon U .20 2.00
38 Lairon U .20 2.00
39 Machoke U .20 2.00
40 Misdreavus U .20 2.00
41 Nuzleaf U .20 2.00
42 Roselia U .20 2.00
43 Sealeo U .20 2.00
44 Tangela U .20 2.00
45 Tentacruel U .20 2.00
46 Vibrava U .20 2.00
47 Weepinbell U .20 2.00
48 Aron C .20 .50
49 Bellsprout C .20 .50
50 Chinchou C .20 .50
51 Clamperl C .20 .50
52 Gastly C .20 .50
53 Geodude C .20 .50
54 Grimer C .20 .50
55 Growlithe C .20 .50
56 Lileep C .20 .50
57 Machop C .20 .50
58 Magby C .20 .50
59 Magnemite C .20 .50
60 Omanyte C .20 .50
61 Seedot C .20 .50
62 Sentret C .20 .50
63 Shuppet C .20 .50
64 Skitty C .20 .50
65 Spheal C .20 .50
66 Tentacool C .20 .50
67 Trapinch C .20 .50
68 Voltorb C .20 .50
69 Wailmer C .20 .50
70 Wurmple C .20 .50
71 Wynaut C .20 .50
72 Cursed Stone U .20 .50
73 Fieldworker U .20 .50
74 Full Flame U .20 .50
75 Giant Stump U .20 .50
76 Power Tree U .20 .50
77 Strange Cave U .20 .50
78 Claw Fossil C .20 .50
79 Mysterious Fossil C .20 .50
80 Root Fossil C .20 .50
81 Rainbow Energy R .75 2.00
82 React Energy U .20 .50
83 Arcanine EX HOLO R 10.00 25.00
84 Armaldo EX HOLO R 6.00 15.00
85 Banette EX HOLO R 4.00 10.00
86 Dustox EX HOLO R 4.00 10.00
87 Flygon EX HOLO R 5.00 12.00
88 Mew EX HOLO R 10.00 25.00
89 Walrein EX HOLO R 3.00 8.00
90 Regice Gold Star HOLO R 30.00 60.00
91 Regirock Gold Star HOLO R 30.00 60.00
92 Registeel Gold Star HOLO R 30.00 60.00
93 Pikachu DS HOLO R 5.00 12.00

2006 Pokemon EX Holon Phantoms

COMPLETE SET (111) 100.00 150.00
BOOSTER BOX (36 PACKS) 400.00 500.00
BOOSTER PACK (9 CARDS) 10.00 15.00
THEME DECK 7.00 10.00
*REV.FOIL: .75X TO 2X BASIC CARDS
RELEASED ON MAY 3, 2006
1 Armaldo HOLO R 2.00 6.00
2 Cradily HOLO R 2.00 6.00
3 Deoxys Attack HOLO R 2.00 6.00
4 Deoxys Defense HOLO R 2.00 6.00
5 Deoxys Normal HOLO R 2.00 6.00
6 Deoxys Speed HOLO R 2.00 6.00
7 Flygon HOLO R 2.00 6.00
8 Gyarados HOLO R 2.00 6.00
9 Kabutops HOLO R 2.00 6.00
10 Kingdra HOLO R 2.00 6.00
11 Latias HOLO R 2.00 6.00
12 Latios HOLO R 2.00 6.00
13 Omastar HOLO R 2.00 6.00
14 Pidgeot HOLO R 2.00 6.00
15 Raichu HOLO R 2.00 6.00
16 Rayquaza HOLO R 2.00 6.00
17 Vileplume HOLO R 2.00 6.00
18 Absol R .75 2.00
19 Bellossom R .75 2.00
20 Blaziken R .75 2.00
21 Latias R .75 2.00
22 Latios R .75 2.00
23 Mawile R .75 2.00
24 Mewtwo R 2.00 6.00
25 Nosepass R .75 2.00
26 Rayquaza R .75 2.00
27 Regice R .75 2.00
28 Regirock R .75 2.00
29 Registeel R .75 2.00
30 Relicanth R .75 2.00
31 Sableye R .75 2.00
32 Seviper R .75 2.00
33 Torkoal R .75 2.00
34 Zangoose R .75 2.00
35 Aerodactyl U .20 .50
36 Camerupt U .20 .50
37 Chimecho U .20 .50
38 Claydol U .20 .50
39 Combusken U .20 .50
40 Donphan U .20 .50
41 Exeggutor U .20 .50
42 Gloom U .20 .50
43 Golduck U .20 .50
44 Holon's Castform U .50 1.50
45 Lairon U .20 .50
46 Manectric U .20 .50
47 Masquerain U .20 .50
48 Persian U .20 .50
49 Pidgeotto U .20 .50
50 Primeape U .20 .50
51 Raichu U .20 .50
52 Seadra U .20 .50
53 Sharpedo U .20 .50
54 Vibrava U .20 .50
55 Whiscash U .20 .50
56 Wobbuffet U .20 .50
57 Anorith C .10 .20
58 Aron C .10 .20
59 Baltoy C .10 .20
60 Barboach C .10 .20
61 Carvanha C .10 .20
62 Corphish C .10 .20
63 Corphish C .10 .20
64 Electrike C .10 .20
65 Exeggcute C .10 .20
66 Horsea C .10 .20
67 Kabuto C .10 .20
68 Lileep C .10 .20
69 Magikarp C .10 .20
70 Mankey C .10 .20
71 Meowth C .10 .20
72 Numel C .10 .20
73 Oddish C .10 .20
74 Omanyte C .10 .20
75 Phanpy C .10 .20
76 Pichu C .20 .50
77 Pidgey C .10 .20
78 Pikachu C .20 .50
79 Pikachu C .20 .50
80 Poochyena C .10 .20
81 Psyduck C .10 .20
82 Surskit C .10 .20
83 Torchic C .10 .20
84 Trapinch C .10 .20
85 Holon Adventurer U .20 .50
86 Holon Fossil U .20 .50
87 Holon Lake U .20 .50
88 Mr. Stone's Project U .20 .50
89 Professor Cozmo's Discovery U .20 .50
90 Rare Candy U 3.00 5.00
91 Claw Fossil C .10 .20
92 Mysterious Fossil C .10 .20
93 Root Fossil C .10 .20
94 Darkness Energy R .50 1.00
95 Metal Energy R .50 1.00
96 Multi Energy R .50 1.00
97 d Rainbow Energy U .20 .50
98 Dark Metal Energy U .20 .50
99 Crawdaunt EX HOLO R 3.00 8.00
100 Mew EX HOLO R 8.00 20.00
101 Mightyena EX HOLO R 3.00 8.00
102 Gyarados Gold Star HOLO R 100.00 150.00
103 Mewtwo Gold Star HOLO R 60.00 100.00
104 Pikachu Gold Star HOLO R 60.00 100.00
105 Grass Energy HOLO R 2.00 6.00
106 Fire Energy HOLO R 2.00 6.00
107 Water Energy HOLO R 2.00 6.00
108 Lightning Energy HOLO R 2.00 6.00
109 Psychic Energy HOLO R 2.00 6.00
110 Fighting Energy HOLO R 2.00 6.00
111 Mew HOLO R 5.00 12.00

2006 Pokemon EX Crystal Guardians

COMPLETE SET (100) 200.00 300.00
BOOSTER BOX (36 PACKS) 800.00 1000.00
BOOSTER PACK (9 CARDS) 6.00 15.00
*REV.FOIL: .75X TO 2X BASIC CARDS
1 Banette HOLO R 3.00 6.00
2 Blastoise DS HOLO R 2.00 6.00
3 Camerupt HOLO R 3.00 6.00
4 Charizard DS HOLO R 8.00 20.00
5 Dugtrio HOLO R 3.00 6.00
6 Ludicolo DS HOLO R 3.00 6.00
7 Luvdisc HOLO R 3.00 6.00
8 Manectric HOLO R 3.00 6.00
9 Mawile HOLO R 3.00 6.00
10 Sableye HOLO R 3.00 6.00
11 Swalot HOLO R 3.00 5.00
12 Tauros HOLO R 3.00 6.00
13 Wigglytuff HOLO R 3.00 6.00
14 Blastoise R 1.00 2.00
15 Cacturne DS R .50 1.00
16 Combusken R .50 1.00
17 Dusclops R .50 1.00
18 Fearow DS R .50 1.00
19 Grovyle DS R .50 1.00
20 Grumpig R .50 1.00
21 Igglybuff R .50 1.00
22 Kingler DS R .50 1.00
23 Loudred R .50 1.00
24 Marshtomp R .50 1.00
25 Medicham R .50 1.00
26 Pelipper DS R .50 1.00
27 Swampert R .50 1.00
28 Venusaur R .50 1.00
29 Charmeleon U .20 .50
30 Charmeleon DS U .20 .50
31 Combusken U .20 .50
32 Grovyle U .20 .50
33 Gulpin U .20 .50
34 Ivysaur U .20 .50
35 Ivysaur U .20 .50
36 Lairon U .20 .50
37 Lombre U .20 .50
38 Marshtomp U .20 .50
39 Nuzleaf U .20 .50
40 Shuppet U .20 .50
41 Skitty U .20 .50
42 Wartortle U .20 .50
43 Wartortle U .20 .50
44 Aron C .10 .20
45 Bulbasaur C .10 .20
46 Bulbasaur C .10 .20
47 Cacnea C .10 .20
48 Charmander C .10 .20
49 Charmander DS C .10 .20
50 Diglett C .10 .20
51 Duskull C .10 .20
52 Electrike C .10 .20
53 Jigglypuff C .10 .20
54 Krabby C .10 .20
55 Lotad C .10 .20
56 Meditite C .10 .20
57 Mudkip C .10 .20
58 Mudkip C .10 .20
59 Numel C .10 .20
60 Seedot C .10 .20
61 Spearow C .10 .20
62 Spoink C .10 .20
63 Squirtle C .10 .20
64 Squirtle C .10 .20
65 Torchic C .10 .20
66 Torchic C .10 .20
67 Treecko C .10 .20
68 Treecko DS C .10 .20
69 Whismur C .10 .20
70 Wingull C .10 .20
71 Bill's Maintenance U .20 .50
72 Castaway U .20 .50
73 Celio's Network U .20 .50
74 Cessation Crystal U .20 .50
75 Crystal Beach U .20 .50
76 Crystal Shard U .20 .50
77 Double Full Heal U .20 .50
78 Dual Ball U .20 .50
79 Holon Circle U .20 .50
80 Memory Berry U .20 .50
81 Mysterious Shard U .20 .50
82 Poke Ball U .20 .50
83 PokeNav U .20 .50
84 Warp Point U .20 .50
85 Windstorm U .20 .50
86 Energy Search C .10 .20
87 Potion C .10 .20
88 Double Rainbow Energy R 3.00 5.00
89 Aggron EX HOLO R 4.00 10.00
90 Blaziken EX HOLO R 6.00 15.00
91 Delcatty EX HOLO R 3.00 8.00
92 Exploud EX HOLO R 2.00 6.00
93 Groudon EX HOLO R 5.00 12.00
94 Jirachi EX HOLO R 3.00 8.00
95 Kyogre EX HOLO R 3.00 8.00
96 Sceptile EX DS HOLO R 6.00 15.00
97 Shiftry EX HOLO R 2.00 6.00
98 Swampert EX HOLO R 6.00 15.00
99 Alakazam GOLD STAR HOLO R 30.00 60.00
100 Celebi GOLD STAR HOLO R 30.00 60.00

2006 Pokemon EX Dragon Frontiers

COMPLETE SET (101) 400.00 600.00
BOOSTER BOX (36 PACKS) 2000.00 2500.00
BOOSTER PACK (9 CARDS) 15.00 30.00
THEME DECK 10.00 25.00
*REV.FOIL: .75X TO 2X BASIC CARDS
RELEASED ON NOVEMBER 8, 2006
1 Ampharos DS HOLO R 1.50 4.00
2 Feraligatr DS HOLO R 1.50 4.00
3 Heracross DS HOLO R 1.50 4.00
4 Meganium DS HOLO R 1.50 4.00
5 Milotic DS HOLO R 1.50 4.00
6 Nidoking DS HOLO R 1.50 4.00
7 Nidoqueen DS HOLO R 1.50 4.00
8 Ninetales DS HOLO R 1.50 4.00
9 Pinsir DS HOLO R 1.50 4.00
10 Snorlax DS HOLO R 1.50 4.00
11 Togetic DS HOLO R 1.50 4.00
12 Typhlosion DS HOLO R 1.50 4.00
13 Arbok DS R .50 1.00
14 Cloyster DS R .50 1.00
15 Dewgong DS R .50 1.00
16 Gligar DS R .50 1.00
17 Jynx DS R .50 1.00
18 Ledian DS R .50 1.00
19 Lickitung DS R .50 1.00
20 Mantine DS R .50 1.00
21 Quagsire DS R .50 1.00
22 Seadra DS R .50 1.00
23 Tropius DS R .50 1.00
24 Vibrava DS R .50 1.00
25 Xatu DS R .50 1.00
26 Bayleef DS U .20 .50
27 Croconaw DS U .20 .50
28 Dragonair DS U .20 .50
29 Electabuzz DS U .20 .75
30 Flaaffy DS U .20 .50
31 Horsea DS U .20 .50
32 Kirlia U .20 .50
33 Kirlia DS U .20 .50
34 Nidorina DS U .20 .50
35 Nidorino DS U .20 .50
36 Quilava DS U .20 .50
37 Seadra DS U .20 .50
38 Shelgon DS U .20 .50
39 Smeargle DS U .20 .50
40 Swellow DS U .20 .50
41 Togepi DS U .20 .50
42 Vibrava DS U .20 .50
43 Bagon DS C .10 .20
44 Chikorita DS C .10 .20
45 Cyndaquil DS C .10 .20
46 Dratini DS C .10 .20
47 Ekans DS C .10 .20
48 Elekid DS C .10 .20
49 Feebas DS C .10 .20
50 Horsea DS C .10 .20
51 Larvitar C .10 .20
52 Larvitar DS C .10 .20
53 Ledyba DS C .10 .20
54 Mareep DS C .10 .20
55 Natu DS C .10 .20
56 Nidoran DS C .10 .20
57 Nidoran DS C .10 .20
58 Pupitar C .10 .20
59 Pupitar DS .10 .20
60 Ralts C .10 .20
61 Ralts DS C .10 .20
62 Seel DS C .10 .20
63 Shellder DS C .10 .20
64 Smoochum DS C .10 .20
65 Swablu DS C .10 .20
66 Taillow DS C .10 .20
67 Totodile DS C .10 .20
68 Trapinch DS C .10 .20
69 Trapinch DS C .10 .20
70 Vulpix DS C .10 .20
71 Wooper DS C .10 .20
72 Buffer Piece U .20 .50
73 Copycat U .20 .50
74 Holon Legacy U .20 .50
75 Holon Mentor U .20 .50
76 Island Hermit U .20 .50
77 Mr. Stone's Project U .20 .50
78 Old Rod U .20 .50
79 Professor Elm's Training Method U .20 .50
80 Professor Oak's Research U .20 .50
81 Strength Charm U .20 .50
82 TV Reporter U .20 .50
83 Switch C .10 .20
84 Holon Energy FF R .50 1.00
85 Holon Energy GL R .50 1.00
86 Holon Energy WP R .50 1.00
87 Boost Energy U .20 .50
88 Rainbow Energy U .20 .50
89 Scramble Energy U .20 .50
90 Altaria EX DS HOLO R 4.00 10.00
91 Dragonite EX DS HOLO R 6.00 15.00
92 Flygon EX DS HOLO R 6.00 15.00
93 Gardevoir EX DS HOLO R 5.00 12.00
94 Kingdra EX DS HOLO R 4.00 10.00
95 Latias EX DS HOLO R 6.00 15.00
96 Latios EX DS HOLO R 6.00 15.00
97 Rayquaza EX DS HOLO R 6.00 15.00
98 Salamence EX DS HOLO R 6.00 15.00
99 Tyranitar EX DS HOLO R 8.00 20.00
100 Charizard Gold Star DS HOLO R 150.00 250.00
101 Mew Gold Star DS HOLO R 60.00 120.00

2007 Pokemon EX Power Keepers

COMPLETE SET (108) 300.00 500.00
BOOSTER BOX (36 PACKS) 400.00 600.00
BOOSTER PACK (9 CARDS) 6.00 15.00
*REV.FOIL: .75X TO 2X BASIC CARDS
RELEASED ON FEBRUARY 14, 2007
1 Aggron HOLO R 1.00 2.50
2 Altaria HOLO R 1.00 2.50
3 Armaldo HOLO R 1.00 2.50
4 Banette HOLO R 1.00 2.50
5 Blaziken HOLO R 1.00 2.50
6 Charizard HOLO R 6.00 15.00
7 Cradily HOLO R 1.00 2.50
8 Delcatty HOLO R 1.00 2.50
9 Gardevoir HOLO R 1.00 2.50
10 Kabutops HOLO R 1.00 2.50
11 Machamp HOLO R 1.00 2.50
12 Raichu HOLO R 1.00 2.50
13 Slaking HOLO R 1.00 2.50
14 Dusclops R .60 1.50
15 Lanturn R .60 1.50
16 Magneton R .60 1.50
17 Mawile R .60 1.50
18 Mightyena R .60 1.50
19 Ninetales R .60 1.50
20 Omastar R .60 1.50
21 Pichu R .60 1.50
22 Sableye R .60 1.50
23 Seviper R .60 1.50
24 Wobbuffet R .60 1.50
25 Zangoose R .60 1.50
26 Anorith U .30 .75
27 Cacturne U .30 .75
28 Charmeleon U .30 .75
29 Combusken U .30 .75
30 Glalie U .30 .75
31 Kirlia U .30 .75
32 Lairon U .30 .75
33 Machoke U .30 .75
34 Medicham U .30 .75
35 Metang U .30 .75
36 Nuzleaf U .30 .75
37 Sealeo U .30 .75
38 Sharpedo U .30 .75
39 Shelgon U .30 .75
40 Vibrava U .30 .75
41 Vigoroth U .30 .75
42 Aron C .30 .75
43 Bagon C .30 .75
44 Baltoy C .30 .75
45 Beldum C .30 .75
46 Cacnea C .30 .75
47 Carvanha C .30 .75
48 Charmander C .30 .75
49 Chinchou C .30 .75
50 Duskull C .30 .75
51 Kabuto C .30 .75
52 Lileep C .30 .75
53 Machop C .30 .75
54 Magnemite C .30 .75
55 Meditite C .30 .75
56 Omanyte C .30 .75
57 Pikachu C .30 .75
58 Poochyena C .30 .75
59 Ralts C .30 .75
60 Seedot C .30 .75
61 Shuppet C .30 .75
62 Skitty C .30 .75
63 Slakoth C .30 .75
64 Snorunt C .30 .75
65 Spheal C .30 .75
66 Swablu C .30 .75
67 Torchic C .30 .75
68 Trapinch C .30 .75
69 Vulpix C .30 .75
70 Wynaut C .30 .75
71 Battle Frontier U .30 .75
72 Drake's Stadium U .30 .75
73 Energy Recycle System U .30 .75
74 Energy Removal 2 U .30 .75
75 Energy Switch U .30 .75
76 Glacia's Stadium U .50 1.25
77 Great Ball U .30 .75
78 Master Ball U .30 .75
79 Phoebe's Stadium U .30 .75
80 Professor Birch U .30 .75
81 Scott U .30 .75
82 Sidney's Stadium U .30 .75
83 Steven's Advice U .50 1.25
84 Claw Fossil C .30 .75
85 Mysterious Fossil C .30 .75
86 Root Fossil C .30 .75
87 Darkness Energy R .30 .75
88 Metal Energy R .30 .75
89 Multi Energy R .30 .75
90 Cyclone Energy U .30 .75
91 Warp Energy U .30 .75
92 Absol EX HOLO R 3.00 8.00
93 Claydol EX HOLO R 3.00 8.00
94 Flygon EX HOLO R 2.00 6.00
95 Metagross EX HOLO R 2.00 6.00
96 Salamence EX HOLO R 5.00 12.00
97 Shiftry EX HOLO R 2.00 6.00
98 Skarmory EX HOLO R 2.00 6.00
99 Walrein EX HOLO R 3.00 8.00
100 Flareon Gold Star HOLO R 30.00 60.00
101 Jolteon Gold Star HOLO R 30.00 60.00
102 Vaporeon Gold Star HOLO R 30.00 60.00
103 Grass Energy HOLO R 1.50 4.00
104 Fire Energy HOLO R 1.50 4.00
105 Water Energy HOLO R 2.50 6.00
106 Lightning Energy HOLO R 1.50 4.00
107 Psychic Energy HOLO R 1.50 4.00
108 Fighting Energy HOLO R 1.50 4.00

2007 Pokemon Diamond and Pearl

COMPLETE SET (130) 50.00 100.00
BOOSTER BOX (36 PACKS) 150.00 300.00
BOOSTER PACK (9 CARDS) 2.00 6.00
*REV.FOIL: .75X TO 2X BASIC CARDS
COLLECTOR'S TIN 18.00 22.00
RELEASED ON MAY 23, 2007
1 Dialga HOLO R 1.25 3.00
2 Dusknoir HOLO R 1.25 3.00
3 Electivire HOLO R 1.25 3.00
4 Empoleon HOLO R 1.25 3.00
5 Infernape HOLO R 1.25 3.00
6 Lucario HOLO R 1.25 3.00
7 Luxray HOLO R 1.25 3.00
8 Magnezone HOLO R 1.25 3.00
9 Manaphy HOLO R 1.25 3.00
10 Mismagius HOLO R 1.25 3.00
11 Palkia HOLO R 1.25 3.00
12 Rhyperior HOLO R 1.25 3.00
13 Roserade HOLO R 1.25 3.00
14 Shiftry HOLO R 1.25 3.00
15 Skuntank HOLO R 1.25 3.00
16 Staraptor HOLO R 1.25 3.00
17 Torterra HOLO R 1.25 3.00
18 Azumarill R .60 1.50
19 Beautifly R .60 1.50
20 Bibarel R .60 1.50
21 Carnivine R .60 1.50
22 Clefable R .60 1.50
23 Drapion R .60 1.50
24 Drifblim R .60 1.50
25 Dustox R .60 1.50
26 Floatzel R .60 1.50
27 Gengar R .60 1.50
28 Heracross R .60 1.50
29 Hippowdon R .60 1.50
30 Lopunny R .60 1.50
31 Machamp R .60 1.50
32 Medicham R .60 1.50
33 Munchlax R .60 1.50
34 Noctowl R .60 1.50
35 Pachirisu R .60 1.50
36 Purugly R .60 1.50
37 Snorlax R .60 1.50
38 Steelix R .60 1.50
39 Vespiquen R .60 1.50
40 Weavile R .60 1.50
41 Wobbuffet R .60 1.50
42 Wynaut R .60 1.50
43 Budew U .25 .60
44 Cascoon U .25 .60
45 Cherrim U .25 .60
46 Drifloon U .25 .60
47 Dusclops U .25 .60
48 Elekid U .25 .60
49 Grotle U .25 .60
50 Haunter U .25 .60
51 Hippopotas U .25 .60
52 Luxio (U) .25 .60
53 Machoke U .25 .60
54 Magneton U .25 .60
55 Mantyke U 1.75 5.00
56 Monferno U .25 .60
57 Nuzleaf U .25 .60
58 Prinplup U .25 .60
59 Rapidash U .25 .60
60 Rhydon U .25 .60
61 Riolu U .25 .60
62 Seaking U .25 .60
63 Silcoon U .25 .60
64 Staravia U .25 .60
65 Unown A U .25 .60
66 Unown B U .25 .60
67 Unown C U .25 .60
68 Unown D U .25 .60
69 Azurill C .50 .75
70 Bidoof C .15 .25
71 Bonsly C 1.00 1.50
72 Buizel C .15 .25
73 Buneary C .15 .25
74 Chatot C .15 .25
75 Cherubi C .15 .25
76 Chimchar C .15 .25
77 Clefairy C .15 .25
78 Cleffa C .30 .50
79 Combee C .15 .25
80 Duskull C .15 .25
81 Electabuzz C .15 .25
82 Gastly C .15 .25
83 Glameow C .15 .25
84 Goldeen C .15 .25
85 Hoothoot C .15 .25
86 Machop C .15 .25
87 Magnemite C .15 .25
88 Marill C .15 .25
89 Meditite C .15 .25
90 Mime Jr. C .15 .25
91 Misdreavus C .15 .25
92 Onix C .15 .25
93 Piplup C .15 .25
94 Ponyta C .15 .25
95 Rhyhorn C .15 .25
96 Roselia C .15 .25
97 Seedot C .15 .25
98 Shinx C .15 .25
99 Skorupi C .15 .25
100 Sneasel C .15 .25
101 Starly C .15 .25
102 Stunky C .15 .25
103 Turtwig C .15 .25
104 Wurmple C .15 .25
105 Double Full Heal U .25 .60
106 Energy Restore U .25 .60
107 Energy Switch U .25 .60
108 Night Pokemon Center U .25 .60
109 PlusPower U .25 .60
110 Poke Ball U .25 .60
111 Pokedex HANDY910s U .25 .60
112 Professor Rowan U .25 .60
113 Rival U .25 .60
114 Speed Stadium U .25 .60
115 Super Scoop Up U .25 .60
116 Warp Point U .25 .60
117 Energy Search C .15 .25
118 Potion C .15 .25
119 Switch C .15 .25
120 Empoleon Lv.X HOLO R 2.00 6.00
121 Infernape Lv.X HOLO R 3.00 8.00
122 Torterra Lv.X HOLO R 2.00 6.00
123 Grass Energy .40 .60
124 Fire Energy .40 .60
125 Water Energy .40 .60
126 Lightning Energy .75 1.00
127 Fighting Energy .40 .60
128 Psychic Energy .40 .60
129 Darkness Energy .40 .60
130 Metal Energy 1.00 1.50

2007 Pokemon DP Mysterious Treasures

COMPLETE SET (124) 80.00 120.00
BOOSTER BOX (36 PACKS) 150.00 200.00
BOOSTER PACK (10 CARDS) 3.00 7.00
*REV.FOIL: .75X TO 2X BASIC CARDS
RELEASED ON AUGUST 22, 2007
1 Aggron HOLO R 1.00 2.50
2 Alakazam HOLO R 1.00 2.50
3 Ambipom HOLO R 1.00 2.50
4 Azelf HOLO R 1.00 2.50
5 Blissey HOLO R 1.00 2.50
6 Bronzong HOLO R 1.00 2.50
7 Celebi HOLO R 1.00 2.50
8 Feraligatr HOLO R 1.00 2.50
9 Garchomp HOLO R 1.00 2.50
10 Honchkrow HOLO R 1.00 2.50
11 Lumineon HOLO R 1.00 2.50
12 Magmortar HOLO R 1.00 2.50
13 Meganium HOLO R 1.00 2.50
14 Mesprit HOLO R 1.00 2.50
15 Raichu HOLO R 1.00 2.50
16 Typhlosion HOLO R 1.00 2.50
17 Tyranitar HOLO R 1.00 2.50
18 Uxie HOLO R 1.00 2.50
19 Abomasnow R .40 1.00
20 Ariados R .40 1.00
21 Bastiodon R .40 1.00
22 Chimecho R .40 1.00
23 Crobat R .40 1.00
24 Exeggutor R .40 1.00
25 Glalie R .40 1.00
26 Gyarados R .40 1.00
27 Kricketune R .40 1.00
28 Manectric R .40 1.00
29 Mantine R .40 1.00
30 Mr. Mime R .40 1.00
31 Nidoqueen R .40 1.00
32 Ninetales R .40 1.00
33 Rampardos R .40 1.00
34 Slaking R .40 1.00
35 Sudowoodo R .40 1.00
36 Toxicroak R .40 1.00
37 Unown R .40 1.00
38 Ursaring R .40 1.00
39 Walrein R .40 1.00
40 Whiscash R .40 1.00
41 Bayleef U .25 .60
42 Chingling U .25 .60
43 Cranidos U .25 .60
44 Croconaw U .25 .60
45 Dewgong U .25 .60
46 Dodrio U .25 .60
47 Dunsparce U .25 .60
48 Gabite U .25 .60
49 Girafarig U .25 .60
50 Golbat U .25 .60
51 Graveler U .25 .60
52 Happiny U .25 .60
53 Lairon U .25 .60
54 Magmar U .25 .60
55 Masquerain U .25 .60
56 Nidorina U .25 .60
57 Octillery U .25 .60
58 Parasect U .25 .60
59 Pupitar U .25 .60
60 Quilava U .25 .60
61 Sandslash U .25 .60
62 Sealeo U .25 .60
63 Shieldon U .25 .60
64 Tropius U .25 .60
65 Unown E U .25 .60
66 Unown M U .25 .60
67 Unown T U .25 .60
68 Vigoroth U .25 .60
69 Abra C .25 .60
70 Aipom C .25 .60
71 Aron C .25 .60
72 Barboach C .25 .60
73 Bidoof C .25 .60
74 Bronzor C .25 .60
75 Buizel C .25 .60
76 Chansey C .25 .60
77 Chikorita C .25 .60
78 Croagunk C .25 .60
79 Cyndaquil C .25 .60
80 Doduo C .25 .60
81 Electrike C .25 .60
82 Exeggcute C .25 .60
83 Finneon C .25 .60
84 Geodude C .25 .60
85 Gible C .25 .60
86 Kricketot C .25 .60
87 Larvitar C .25 .60
88 Magby C .25 .60
89 Magikarp C .25 .60
90 Murkrow C .25 .60
91 Nidoran C .25 .60
92 Paras C .25 .60
93 Pichu C .25 .60
94 Pikachu C .25 .60
95 Remoraid C .25 .60
96 Sandshrew C .25 .60
97 Seel C .25 .60
98 Shinx C .25 .60
99 Slakoth C .25 .60
100 Snorunt C .25 .60
101 Snover C .25 .60
102 Spheal C .25 .60
103 Spinarak C .25 .60
104 Surskit C .25 .60
105 Teddiursa C .25 .60
106 Totodile C .25 .60
107 Vulpix C .25 .60
108 Zubat C .25 .60
109 Bebe's Search U .25 .60
110 Dusk Ball U .25 .60
111 Fossil Excavator U .25 .60
112 Lake Boundary U .25 .60
113 Night Maintenance U .25 .60
114 Quick Ball U .25 .60
115 Team Galactic's Wager U .25 .60
116 Armor Fossil C .25 .60
117 Skull Fossil C .25 .60
118 Multi Energy R .25 .60
119 Darkness Energy U .25 .60
120 Metal Energy U .25 .60
121 Electivire Lv.X HOLO R 2.00 6.00
122 Lucario Lv.X HOLO R 2.00 6.00
123 Magmortar Lv.X HOLO R 3.00 8.00
124 Time Space Distortion HOLO SCR 2.00 6.00

2007 Pokemon DP Secret Wonders

COMPLETE SET (132) 60.00 100.00
BOOSTER BOX (36 PACKS) 150.00 200.00
BOOSTER PACK (9 CARDS) 2.50 6.00
*REV.FOIL: .75X TO 2X BASIC CARDS
RELEASED ON NOVEMBER 7, 2007
1 Ampharos HOLO R 1.50 4.00
2 Blastoise HOLO R 1.50 4.00
3 Charizard HOLO R 4.00 10.00
4 Entei HOLO R 1.50 4.00
5 Flygon HOLO R 1.50 4.00
6 Gallade HOLO R 1.50 4.00
7 Gardevoir HOLO R 2.00 6.00
8 Gastrodon East Sea HOLO R 1.50 4.00
9 Gastrodon West Sea HOLO R 1.50 4.00
10 Ho-Oh HOLO R 1.50 4.00
11 Jumpluff HOLO R 1.50 4.00
12 Lickilicky HOLO R 1.50 4.00
13 Ludicolo HOLO R 1.50 4.00
14 Lugia HOLO R 4.00 10.00
15 Mew HOLO R 3.00 8.00
16 Raikou HOLO R 2.00 6.00
17 Roserade HOLO R 1.50 4.00
18 Salamence HOLO R 1.50 4.00
19 Suicune HOLO R 1.50 4.00
20 Venusaur HOLO R 1.50 4.00
21 Absol R .75 2.00
22 Arcanine R .75 2.00
23 Banette R .75 2.00
24 Dugtrio R .75 2.00
25 Electivire R .75 2.00
26 Electrode R .75 2.00
27 Furret R .75 2.00
28 Golduck R .75 2.00
29 Golem R .75 2.00
30 Jynx R .75 2.00
31 Magmortar R .75 2.00
32 Minun R .75 2.00
33 Mothim R .75 2.00
34 Nidoking R .75 2.00
35 Pidgeot R .75 2.00
36 Plusle R .75 2.00
37 Sharpedo R .75 2.00
38 Sunflora R .75 2.00
39 Unown S R .75 2.00
40 Weavile R .75 2.00
41 Wormadam Plant Cloak R .75 2.00
42 Wormadam Sandy Cloak R .75 2.00
43 Wormadam Trash Cloak R .75 2.00
44 Xatu R .75 2.00
45 Breloom U .25 .60
46 Charmeleon U .25 .60
47 Cloyster U .25 .60
48 Donphan U .25 .60
49 Farfetch'd U .25 .60
50 Flaaffy U .25 .60
51 Ivysaur U .25 .60
52 Kecleon U .25 .60
53 Kirlia U .25 .60
54 Lombre U .25 .60
55 Miltank U .25 .60
56 Muk U .25 .60
57 Nidorino U .25 .60
58 Pidgeotto U .25 .60
59 Pinsir U .25 .60
60 Quagsire U .25 .60
61 Raticate U .25 .60
62 Roselia U .25 .60
63 Sableye U .25 .60
64 Shelgon U .25 .60
65 Skiploom U .25 .60
66 Smeargle U .25 .60
67 Smoochum U .25 .60
68 Unown K U .25 .60
69 Unown N U .25 .60
70 Unown O U .25 .60

71 Unown X U .25 .60
72 Unown Z U .25 .60
73 Venomoth U .25 .60
74 Vibrava U .25 .60
75 Wartortle U .25 .60
76 Bagon C .25 .60
77 Bulbasaur C .25 .60
78 Burmy Plant Cloak C .25 .60
79 Burmy Sandy Cloak C .25 .60
80 Burmy Trash Cloak C .25 .60
81 Carvanha C .25 .60
82 Charmander C .25 .60
83 Clefairy C .25 .60
84 Corsola C .25 .60
85 Diglett C .25 .60
86 Duskull C .25 .60
87 Electabuzz C .25 .60
88 Grimer C .25 .60
89 Growlithe C .25 .60
90 Hoppip C .25 .60
91 Lickitung C .25 .60
92 Lotad C .25 .60
93 Magmar C .25 .60
94 Mareep C .25 .60
95 Murkrow C .25 .60
96 Natu C .25 .60
97 Nidoran C .25 .60
98 Phanpy C .25 .60
99 Pidgey C .25 .60
100 Psyduck C .25 .60
101 Qwilfish C .25 .60
102 Ralts C .25 .60
103 Rattata C .25 .60
104 Sentret C .25 .60
105 Shellder C .25 .60
106 Shellos East Sea C .25 .60
107 Shellos West Sea C .25 .60
108 Shroomish C .25 .60
109 Shuckle C .25 .60
110 Shuppet C .25 .60
111 Spinda C .25 .60
112 Squirtle C .25 .60
113 Stantler C .25 .60
114 Sunkern C .25 .60
115 Trapinch C .25 .60
116 Venonat C .25 .60
117 Voltorb C .25 .60
118 Wooper C .25 .60
119 Bebe's Search U .50 1.25
120 Night Maintenance U .25 .60
121 PlusPower U .25 .60
122 Professor Oak's Visit U .25 .60
123 Professor Rowan U .25 .60
124 Rival U .25 .60
125 Roseanne's Research U .75 2.00
126 Team Galactic's Mars U .25 .60
127 Potion C .25 .60
128 Switch C .25 .60
129 Darkness Energy U .25 .60
130 Metal Energy U .25 .60
131 Gardevoir LV.X HOLO R 2.50 6.00
132 Honchkrow LV.X HOLO R 2.50 6.00

2008 Pokemon DP Great Encounters

COMPLETE SET (106) 70.00 100.00
BOOSTER BOX (36 PACKS) 150.00 200.00
BOOSTER PACK (10 CARDS) 2.00 6.00
*REV.FOIL: .75X TO 2X BASIC CARDS
RELEASED ON FEBRUARY 13, 2008
1 Blaziken HOLO R 1.25 2.00
2 Cresselia HOLO R 1.75 2.25
3 Darkrai HOLO R 1.75 2.25
4 Darkrai HOLO R 2.00 2.50
5 Pachirisu HOLO R .75 1.00
6 Porygon-Z HOLO R .60 1.00
7 Rotom HOLO R .40 .60
8 Sceptile HOLO R 2.00 2.50
9 Swampert HOLO R 2.00 3.00
10 Tangrowth HOLO R .50 .75
11 Togekiss HOLO R .75 1.00
12 Altaria R .50 .75
13 Beedrill R .50 .75
14 Butterfree R .50 .75
15 Claydol R 1.25 2.00
16 Dialga R .50 .75
17 Exploud R .50 .75
18 Houndoom R .50 .75
19 Hypno R .50 .75
20 Kingler R .50 .75
21 Lapras R .50 .75
22 Latias R 1.25 2.00
23 Latios R 1.00 1.50
24 Mawile R .50 .75
25 Milotic R .50 .75
26 Palkia R .50 .75
27 Primeape R .50 .75
28 Slowking R .50 .75
29 Unown H R .50 .75
30 Wailord R 1.25 2.00
31 Weezing R .50 .75
32 Wigglytuff R .50 .75
33 Arbok U .20 .35
34 Cacturne U .20 .35
35 Combusken U .20 .35
36 Delibird U .20 .35
37 Floatzel U .20 .35
38 Gorebyss U .20 .35
39 Granbull U .20 .35
40 Grovyle U .20 .35
41 Hariyama U .20 .35
42 Huntail U .40 .75
43 Linoone U .20 .35
44 Loudred U .20 .35
45 Magcargo U .20 .35
46 Marshtomp U .20 .35
47 Metapod U .20 .35
48 Pelipper U .20 .35
49 Porygon2 U .30 .50
50 Purugly U .20 .35
51 Relicanth U .20 .35
52 Seviper U .20 .35
53 Skarmory U .20 .35
54 Slowbro U .20 .35
55 Togetic U .20 .35
56 Unown F U .20 .35
57 Unown G U 1.00 1.25
58 Wailmer U .20 .35
59 Zangoose U .20 .35
60 Baltoy C .75 1.00
61 Buizel C .20 .35
62 Cacnea C .20 .35
63 Caterpie C .20 .35
64 Clamperl C .20 .35
65 Drowzee C .20 .35
66 Ekans C .20 .35
67 Feebas C .20 .35
68 Glameow C .20 .35
69 Houndour C .20 .35
70 Igglybuff C .20 .35
71 Illumise C .20 .35
72 Jigglypuff C .60 1.00
73 Kakuna C .20 .35
74 Koffing C .20 .35
75 Krabby C .20 .35
76 Lunatone C .20 .35
77 Luvdisc C .20 .35
78 Makuhita C .20 .35
79 Mankey C .20 .35
80 Mudkip C .40 .60
81 Porygon C .20 .35
82 Slowpoke C .20 .35
83 Slugma C .20 .35
84 Snubbull C .20 .35
85 Solrock C .20 .35
86 Swablu C .20 .35
87 Tangela C .20 .35
88 Togepi C .40 .60
89 Torchic C .20 .35
90 Treecko C .20 .35
91 Unown L C .20 .35
92 Volbeat C .20 .35
93 Weedle C .20 .35
94 Whismur C .20 .35
95 Wingull C .20 .35
96 Zigzagoon C .20 .35
97 Amulet Coin U .30 .50
98 Felicity's Drawing U .20 .35
99 Leftovers U .20 .35
100 Moonlight Stadium U 2.50 3.25
101 Premier Ball U .40 .60
102 Rare Candy U 1.25 2.00
103 Cresselia LV.X HOLO R 2.50 3.50
104 Darkrai LV.X HOLO R 6.00 8.00
105 Dialga LV.X HOLO R 6.00 8.00
106 Palkia LV.X HOLO R 7.00 10.00

2008 Pokemon DP Majestic Dawn

COMPLETE SET (100) 130.00 180.00
BOOSTER BOX (36 PACKS) 200.00 300.00
BOOSTER PACK (10 CARDS) 2.50 6.00
*REV.FOIL: .75X TO 2X BASIC CARDS
RELEASED ON MAY 21, 2008
1 Articuno HOLO R 1.50 2.50
2 Cresselia HOLO R 1.25 2.00
3 Darkrai HOLO R 4.00 6.00
4 Dialga HOLO R 2.00 3.00
5 Glaceon HOLO R 4.00 7.00
6 Kabutops HOLO R 2.00 3.00
7 Leafeon HOLO R 2.00 3.50
8 Manaphy HOLO R .40 .60
9 Mewtwo HOLO R 6.00 8.00
10 Moltres HOLO R 2.00 3.00
11 Palkia HOLO R 2.00 3.00
12 Phione HOLO R 1.25 2.00
13 Rotom HOLO R .75 1.00
14 Zapdos HOLO R 1.25 2.00
15 Aerodactyl R .60 1.00
16 Bronzong R .60 1.00
17 Empoleon R .60 1.00
18 Espeon R .60 1.00
19 Flareon R .60 1.00
20 Glaceon R .60 1.00
21 Hippowdon R .60 1.00
22 Infernape R .60 1.00
23 Jolteon R .60 1.00
24 Leafeon R .60 1.00
25 Minun R .60 1.00
26 Omastar R .60 1.00
27 Phione R .60 1.00
28 Plusle R .60 1.00
29 Scizor R .60 1.00
30 Torterra R .60 1.00
31 Toxicroak R .60 1.00
32 Umbreon R 3.00 5.00
33 Unown P R .60 1.00
34 Vaporeon R 1.25 2.00
35 Ambipom U .25 .40
36 Fearow U .25 .40
37 Grotle U .25 .40
38 Kangaskhan U .25 .40
39 Lickitung U .25 .40
40 Manectric U .25 .40
41 Monferno U .25 .40
42 Mothim U .25 .40
43 Pachirisu U .25 .40
44 Prinplup U .25 .40
45 Raichu U .25 .40
46 Scyther U .25 .40
47 Staravia U .25 .40
48 Sudowoodo U .25 .40
49 Unown Q U .60 1.00
50 Aipom C .20 .35
51 Aipom C .20 .35
52 Bronzor C .20 .35
53 Buneary C .30 .50
54 Burmy Sand Cloak C .20 .35
55 Chatot C .20 .35
56 Chimchar C .20 .35
57 Chimchar C .30 .50
58 Chingling C .20 .35
59 Combee C .20 .35
60 Croagunk C .20 .35
61 Drifloon C .20 .35
62 Eevee C .30 .50
63 Eevee C .30 .50
64 Electrike C .20 .35
65 Glameow C .20 .35
66 Hippopotas C .20 .35
67 Kabuto C .20 .35
68 Munchlax C .20 .35
69 Omanyte C .20 .35
70 Pikachu C .30 .50
71 Piplup C .20 .35
72 Piplup C .20 .35
73 Shellos East Sea C .20 .35
74 Spearow C .20 .35
75 Starly C .20 .35
76 Stunky C .20 .35
77 Turtwig C .20 .35
78 Turtwig C .20 .35
79 Dawn Stadium U 1.25 2.00
80 Dusk Ball U .25 .40
81 Energy Restore U .25 .40
82 Fossil Excavator U .25 .40
83 Mom's Kindness U .25 .40
84 Old Amber U .25 .40
85 Poke Ball U .25 .40
86 Quick Ball U .25 .40
87 Super Scoop Up U .75 1.00
88 Warp Point C .20 .35
89 Dome Fossil C .20 .35
90 Energy Search C .20 .35
91 Helix Fossil C .20 .35
92 Call Energy U 4.00 6.00
93 Darkness Energy U .25 .40
94 Health Energy U .40 .60
95 Metal Energy U .25 .40
96 Recover Energy U .25 .40
97 Garchomp Lv X HOLO R 8.00 10.00
98 Glaceon LV.X HOLO R 25.00 30.00
99 Leafeon LV.X HOLO R 20.00 25.00
100 Porygon-Z LV.X HOLO R 10.00 15.00

2008 Pokemon DP Legends Awakened

COMPLETE SET (146) 140.00 200.00
BOOSTER BOX (36 PACKS) 180.00 250.00
BOOSTER PACK (10 CARDS) 2.00 6.00
*REV.FOIL: .75X TO 2X BASIC CARDS
RELEASED ON AUGUST 20, 2008
1 Deoxys Normal Form HOLO R .75 1.00
2 Dragonite HOLO R 3.00 5.00
3 Froslass HOLO R .75 1.00
4 Giratina HOLO R 2.00 2.50
5 Gliscor HOLO R .75 1.00
6 Heatran HOLO R 1.25 2.00
7 Kingdra HOLO R 1.00 1.50
8 Luxray HOLO R 1.25 2.00
9 Mamoswine HOLO R .75 1.00
10 Metagross HOLO R 1.00 1.50
11 Mewtwo HOLO R 2.00 6.00
12 Politoed HOLO R 1.75 2.25
13 Probopass HOLO R .40 .60
14 Rayquaza HOLO R 2.00 2.50
15 Regigigas HOLO R 1.25 2.00
16 Spiritomb HOLO R .60 1.00
17 Yanmega HOLO R .50 .75
18 Armaldo R 1.25 2.00
19 Azelf R 3.00 5.00
20 Bellossom R .40 .60
21 Cradily R .60 1.00
22 Crawdaunt R 1.00 1.50
23 Delcatty R .60 1.00
24 Deoxys Attack Form R 1.25 2.00
25 Deoxys Defense Form R 1.25 2.00
26 Deoxys Speed Form R .75 1.00
27 Ditto R 1.25 2.00
28 Forretress R 1.00 1.50
29 Groudon R 1.25 2.00
30 Heatran R 2.00 3.00
31 Jirachi R .75 1.00
32 Kyogre R 1.25 2.00
33 Lopunny R .75 1.00
34 Mesprit R 2.00 3.00
35 Poliwrath R 1.00 1.50
36 Regice R 5.00 6.00
37 Regigigas R .75 1.00
38 Regirock R 2.00 2.50
39 Registeel R 2.00 3.00
40 Shedinja R .60 1.00
41 Torkoal R .60 1.00
42 Unown ! R .75 1.00
43 Uxie R 3.00 5.00
44 Victreebel R .75 1.00
45 Vileplume R .75 1.00
46 Anorith U .25 .40
47 Camerupt U .25 .40
48 Castform U .25 .40
49 Castform Rain Form U .25 .40
50 Castform Snow-Cloud Form U .25 .40
51 Castform Sunny Form U .50 .75
52 Dragonair U 2.00 3.00
53 Drifblim U .25 .40
54 Exeggutor U .25 .40
55 Gliscor U .25 .40
56 Grumpig U .25 .40
57 Houndoom U .25 .40
58 Lanturn U .25 .40
59 Lanturn U .25 .40
60 Ledian U .25 .40
61 Lucario U .60 1.00
62 Luxio U .25 .40
63 Marowak U .25 .40
64 Metang U .25 .40
65 Metang U .25 .40
66 Mightyena U .25 .40
67 Ninjask U .25 .40
68 Persian U .25 .40
69 Piloswine U .25 .40
70 Seadra U .25 .40
71 Starmie U .25 .40
72 Swalot U .25 .40
73 Swellow U .25 .40
74 Tauros U .25 .40
75 Tentacruel U .25 .40
76 Unown J U .25 .40
77 Unown R U .60 1.00
78 Unown U U .25 .40
79 Unown V U .25 .40
80 Unown W U .25 .40
81 Unown Y U .25 .40
82 Unown ? U .25 .40
83 Beldum C .20 .35
84 Beldum C .20 .35
85 Bellsprout C .20 .35
86 Buneary C .20 .35
87 Chinchou C .20 .35
88 Chinchou C .20 .35
89 Corphish C .20 .35
90 Cubone C .20 .35
91 Dratini C .20 .35
92 Drifloon C .20 .35
93 Exeggcute C .20 .35
94 Gligar C .20 .35
95 Gligar C .20 .35
96 Gloom C .20 .35
97 Gloom C .20 .35
98 Gulpin C .20 .35
99 Hitmonchan C .20 .35
100 Hitmonlee C .20 .35
101 Hitmontop C .20 .35
102 Horsea C .20 .35
103 Houndour C .20 .35
104 Ledyba C .20 .35
105 Lileep C .20 .35
106 Meowth C .20 .35
107 Misdreavus C .20 .35
108 Nincada C .20 .35
109 Nosepass C .20 .35
110 Numel C .20 .35
111 Oddish C .20 .35
112 Oddish C .20 .35
113 Pineco C .20 .35
114 Poliwag C .20 .35
115 Poliwhirl C .20 .35
116 Poochyena C .20 .35
117 Riolu C .20 .35
118 Shinx C .20 .35
119 Skitty C .20 .35
120 Sneasel C .20 .35
121 Spoink C .20 .35
122 Staryu C .20 .35
123 Swinub C .20 .35
124 Taillow C .20 .35
125 Tentacool C .20 .35
126 Tyrogue C .20 .35
127 Weepinbell C .20 .35
128 Yanma C .20 .35
129 Bubble Coat U .25 .40
130 Buck's Training U .25 .40
131 Cynthia's Feelings U .25 .40
132 Energy Pickup U .25 .40
133 Poke Radar U .25 .40
134 Snowpoint Temple U .25 .40
135 Stark Mountain U .25 .40
136 Technical Machine TS-1 U .25 .40
137 Technical Machine TS-2 U .25 .40
138 Claw Fossil C .20 .35
139 Root Fossil C .20 .35
140 Azelf LV.X HOLO R 9.00 11.00
141 Gliscor LV.X HOLO R 5.00 7.00
142 Magnezone LV.X HOLO R 3.00 5.00
143 Mesprit LV.X HOLO R 12.00 15.00
144 Mewtwo LV.X HOLO R 10.00 12.00
145 Rhyperior LV.X HOLO R 3.00 5.00
146 Uxie LV.X HOLO R 15.00 20.00

2008 Pokemon DP Stormfront

COMPLETE SET (103) 130.00 200.00
BOOSTER BOX (36 PACKS) 200.00 300.00
BOOSTER PACK (10 CARDS) 6.00 8.00
*REV.FOIL: .75X TO 2X BASIC CARDS
RELEASED ON NOVEMBER 5, 2008
1 Dusknoir HOLO R .75 1.00
2 Empoleon HOLO R .75 1.00
3 Infernape HOLO R 1.25 2.00
4 Lumineon HOLO R .75 1.00
5 Magnezone HOLO R .75 1.00
6 Magnezone HOLO R .60 1.00
7 Mismagius HOLO R .60 1.00
8 Raichu HOLO R 2.25 3.00
9 Regigigas HOLO R 1.00 1.50
10 Sceptile HOLO R .60 1.00
11 Torterra HOLO R 1.25 1.75
12 Abomasnow R .75 1.00
13 Bronzong R .40 .60
14 Cherrim R .40 .60
15 Drapion R .50 .75
16 Drifblim R .40 .60
17 Dusknoir R .60 1.00
18 Gengar R 3.00 4.00
19 Gyarados R 2.00 3.00
20 Machamp R 2.50 3.50
21 Mamoswine R .50 .75
22 Rapidash R .50 .75

23 Roserade R	.50	.75
24 Salamence R	1.00	1.50
25 Scizor R	.75	1.00
26 Skuntank R	.40	.60
27 Staraptor R	.50	.75
28 Steelix R	8.00	10.00
29 Tangrowth R	.75	1.00
30 Tyranitar R	.75	1.00
31 Vespiquen R	.50	.75
32 Bibarel U	.30	.50
33 Budew U	.40	.60
34 Dusclops U	.30	.50
35 Dusclops U	.30	.50
36 Electrode U	.30	.50
37 Electrode U	.30	.50
38 Farfetch'd U	.30	.50
39 Grovyle U	.30	.50
40 Haunter U	.30	.50
41 Machoke U	.30	.50
42 Magneton U	.30	.50
43 Magneton U	.30	.50
44 Miltank U	.30	.50
45 Pichu U	2.00	3.00
46 Piloswine U	.30	.50
47 Pupitar U	.30	.50
48 Sableye U	1.00	1.50
49 Scyther U	.30	.50
50 Shelgon U	.30	.50
51 Skarmory U	.30	.50
52 Staravia U	.30	.50
53 Bagon C	.20	.35
54 Bidoof C	.20	.35
55 Bronzor C	.20	.35
56 Cherubi C	.20	.35
57 Combee C	.20	.35
58 Drifloon C	.20	.35
59 Duskull C	.20	.35
60 Duskull C	.20	.35
61 Finneon C	.20	.35
62 Gastly C	.20	.35
63 Larvitar C	.20	.35
64 Machop C	.20	.35
65 Magikarp C	.20	.35
66 Magnemite C	.20	.35
67 Magnemite C	.20	.35
68 Misdreavus C	.20	.35
69 Onix C	.20	.35
70 Pikachu C	.75	1.00
71 Ponyta C	.20	.35
72 Roselia C	.20	.35
73 Skorupi C	.20	.35
74 Snover C	.20	.35
75 Starly C	.20	.35
76 Stunky C	.20	.35
77 Swinub C	.20	.35
78 Tangela C	.20	.35
79 Treecko C	.20	.35
80 Voltorb C	.20	.35
81 Voltorb C	.20	.35
82 Conductive Quarry U	.30	.50
83 Energy Link U	.30	.50
84 Energy Switch U	.30	.50
85 Great Ball U	.30	.50
86 Luxury Ball U	.75	1.00
87 Marley's Request U	.30	.50
88 Poke Blower U	.30	.50
89 Poke Drawer U	.40	.60
90 Poke Healer U	.30	.50
91 Premier Ball U	.30	.50
92 Potion C	.20	.35
93 Switch C	.20	.35
94 Cyclone Energy U	.30	.50
95 Warp Energy U	.30	.50
96 Dusknoir LVX HOLO R	5.00	7.00
97 Heatran LVX HOLO R	3.00	5.00
98 Machamp LVX HOLO R	4.00	6.00
99 Raichu LVX HOLO R	8.00	10.00
100 Regigigas LVX HOLO R	4.00	6.00
101 Charmander HOLO R	6.00	10.00
102 Charmeleon HOLO R	6.00	10.00
103 Charizard HOLO R	20.00	30.00
SH1 Drifloon UR	6.00	10.00
SH2 Duskull UR	10.00	15.00
SH3 Voltorb	4.00	6.00

2009 Pokemon Platinum

COMPLETE SET (130)	100.00	150.00
BOOSTER BOX (36 PACKS)	150.00	200.00
BOOSTER PACK (10 CARDS)	5.00	8.00
*REV.FOIL: .75X TO 2X BASIC CARDS		
RELEASED ON FEBRUARY 11, 2009		
1 Ampharos HOLO R	1.25	1.75
2 Blastoise HOLO R	2.00	3.00
3 Blaziken HOLO R	1.50	2.00
4 Delcatty HOLO R	.50	.75
5 Dialga HOLO R	.50	.75
6 Dialga HOLO R	.50	.75
7 Dialga G HOLO R	1.50	2.00
8 Gardevoir HOLO R	.50	.75
9 Giratina HOLO R	1.25	2.00
10 Giratina HOLO R	3.00	5.00
11 Manectric HOLO R	.50	.75
12 Palkia G HOLO R	1.50	2.00
13 Rampardos HOLO R	.75	1.25
14 Shaymin HOLO R	.60	1.00
15 Shaymin HOLO R	1.50	2.00
16 Slaking HOLO R	.75	1.00
17 Weavile G HOLO R	.75	1.00
18 Altaria R	.60	1.00
19 Banette R	.30	.50
20 Bastiodon R	.60	1.00
21 Beautifly R	.30	.50
22 Blissey R	.30	.50
23 Dialga R	1.00	1.25
24 Dugtrio R	.30	.50
25 Dustox R	.30	.50
26 Empoleon R	.50	.75
27 Giratina R	.60	1.00
28 Giratina R	.30	.50
29 Golduck R	.30	.50
30 Gyarados G R	.60	1.00
31 Infernape R	.30	.50
32 Kricketune R	.30	.50
33 Lickilicky R	.30	.50
34 Ludicolo R	.30	.50
35 Luvdisc R	.60	1.00
36 Ninetales R	.60	1.00
37 Palkia R	.75	1.00
38 Shaymin R	.30	.50
39 Torterra R	1.25	2.00
40 Toxicroak G R	.30	.50
41 Bronzong G U	.20	.35
42 Cacturne U	.20	.35
43 Carnivine U	.20	.35
44 Cascoon U	.20	.35
45 Combusken U	.20	.35
46 Cranidos U	.40	.60
47 Crobat G U	.75	1.25
48 Flaaffy U	.20	.35
49 Grotle U	.20	.35
50 Houndoom G U	.20	.35
51 Kirlia U	.20	.35
52 Lombre U	.20	.35
53 Lucario U	.20	.35
54 Mightyena U	.30	.50
55 Mismagius U	.20	.35
56 Monferno U	.20	.35
57 Muk U	.20	.35
58 Octillery U	.20	.35
59 Prinplup U	.20	.35
60 Probopass U	.20	.35
61 Seviper U	.20	.35
62 Shieldon U	.20	.35
63 Silcoon (U)	.20	.35
64 Vigoroth U	.20	.35
65 Wartortle U	.40	.60
66 Zangoose U	.60	1.00
67 Cacnea C	.15	.25
68 Carnivine C	.15	.25
69 Chansey C	.15	.25
70 Chimchar C	.15	.25
71 Combee C	.15	.25
72 Diglett C	.15	.25
73 Dunsparce C	.15	.25
74 Electrike C	.15	.25
75 Grimer C	.15	.25
76 Happiny C	.15	.25
77 Honchkrow G C	.15	.25
78 Kricketot C	.15	.25
79 Lapras C	.15	.25
80 Lickitung C	.15	.25
81 Lotad C	.15	.25
82 Mareep C	.15	.25
83 Misdreavus C	.15	.25
84 Nosepass C	.15	.25
85 Piplup C	.15	.25
86 Poochyena C	.15	.25
87 Psyduck C	.15	.25
88 Purugly G C	.15	.25
89 Ralts C	.15	.25
90 Remoraid C	.15	.25
91 Riolu C	.15	.25
92 Shuppet C	.15	.25
93 Skitty C	.15	.25
94 Skuntank G C	.15	.25
95 Slakoth C	.15	.25
96 Squirtle C	.15	.25
97 Swablu C	.15	.25
98 Tauros C	.15	.25
99 Torchic C	.15	.25
100 Torkoal C	.15	.25
101 Turtwig C	.15	.25
102 Vulpix C	.15	.25
103 Wurmple C	.15	.25
104 Broken Time-Space U	1.50	2.00
105 Cyrus's Conspiracy U	1.75	2.00
106 Galactic HQ U	.20	.35
107 Level Max U	.20	.35
108 Life Herb U	.20	.35
109 Looker's Investigation U	.20	.35
110 Memory Berry U	.20	.35
111 Miasma Valley U	.40	.60
112 Pluspower U	.20	.35
113 Poke Ball U	.20	.35
114 Pokedex Handy 910s U	.20	.35
115 Pokemon Rescue U	.50	.75
116 Energy Gain U	.50	.75
117 Power Spray U	.30	.50
118 Poke Turn U	1.00	1.50
119 Armor Fossil C	.15	.25
120 Skull Fossil C	.15	.25
121 Rainbow Energy U	1.00	1.25
122 Dialga G LV.X HOLO R	4.00	6.00
123 Drapion LV.X HOLO R	4.00	6.00
124 Giratina LV.X HOLO R	7.00	9.00
125 Palkia G LV.X HOLO R	3.00	5.00
126 Shaymin LV.X HOLO R	7.00	9.00
127 Shaymin LV.X HOLO R	4.50	6.00
128 Electabuzz HOLO R	3.00	4.00
129 Hitmonchan HOLO R	3.00	5.00
130 Scyther HOLO R	3.00	5.00
SH4 Lotad HOLO R	3.00	4.00
SH5 Swablu HOLO R	5.00	7.00
SH6 Vulpix HOLO R	6.00	8.00

2009 Pokemon Platinum Rising Rivals

COMPLETE SET (114)	160.00	220.00
BOOSTER BOX (36 PACKS)	250.00	350.00
BOOSTER PACK (10 CARDS)	3.00	8.00
*REV.FOIL: .75X TO 2X BASIC CARDS		
RELEASED ON MAY 20, 2009		
1 Arcanine HOLO R	1.25	2.00
2 Bastiodon GL HOLO R	.75	1.00
3 Darkrai G HOLO R	1.50	2.00
4 Floatzel GL HOLO R	.50	.75
5 Flygon HOLO R	1.25	2.00
6 Froslass GL HOLO R	.75	1.00
7 Jirachi HOLO R	2.00	2.50
8 Lucario GL HOLO R	.75	1.00
9 Luxray GL HOLO R	2.00	3.00
10 Mismagius GL HOLO R	.75	1.00
11 Rampardos GL HOLO R	1.50	2.00
12 Roserade GL HOLO R	.60	1.00
13 Shiftry HOLO R	.75	1.00
14 Aggron R	.75	1.00
15 Beedrill R	.60	1.00
16 Bronzong 4 R	.40	.60
17 Drapion 4 R	.50	.75
18 Espeon 4 R	.50	.75
19 Flareon R	.40	.60
20 Gallade 4 R	.50	.75
21 Gastrodon East Sea R	.50	.75
22 Gastrodon West Sea R	.30	.50
23 Golem 4 R	.40	.75
24 Heracross 4 R	.40	.60
25 Hippowdon R	.40	.60
26 Jolteon R	.60	1.00
27 Mamoswine GL R	.60	1.00
28 Mr. Mime 4 R	.40	.60
29 Nidoking R	.60	1.00
30 Nidoqueen R	.60	1.00
31 Raichu GL R	.75	1.00
32 Rhyperior 4 R	.60	1.00
33 Snorlax R	.50	.75
34 Vaporeon R	.75	1.25
35 Vespiquen 4 R	.50	.75
36 Walrein R	.50	.75
37 Yanmega 4 R	.30	.50
38 Alakazam 4 U	.60	1.00
39 Electrode G U	.20	.35
40 Gengar GL U	.30	.50
41 Glaceon U	1.00	1.25
42 Hippowdon 4 U	.25	.35
43 Infernape 4 U	.50	.75
44 Lairon U	.20	.35
45 Leafeon U	.40	.60
46 Machamp GL U	.20	.35
47 Rapidash 4 U	.20	.35
48 Scizor 4 U	.20	.35
49 Sharpedo U	.20	.35
50 Starmie U	.20	.35
51 Steelix GL U	.20	.35
52 Tropius U	.20	.35
53 Vibrava U	.20	.35
54 Whiscash 4 U	.20	.35
55 Aerodactyl GL C	.15	.25
56 Ambipom G C	.15	.25
57 Aron C	.15	.25
58 Carvanha C	.15	.25
59 Eevee C	.40	.60
60 Flareon 4 C	.20	.35
61 Forretress G C	.20	.35
62 Gliscor 4 C	.15	.25
63 Growlithe C	.15	.25
64 Hippopotas C	.15	.25
65 Houndoom 4 C	.15	.25
66 Kakuna C	.15	.25
67 Kecleon C	.15	.25
68 Koffing C	.15	.25
69 Munchlax C	.15	.25
70 Munchlax C	.15	.25
71 Nidoran F C	.15	.25
72 Nidoran M C	.15	.25
73 Nidorina C	.15	.25
74 Nidorino C	.15	.25
75 Nuzleaf C	.15	.25
76 Quagsire GL C	.15	.25
77 Sealeo C	.15	.25
78 Seedot C	.15	.25
79 Shellos East Sea C	.15	.25
80 Shellos West Sea C	.15	.25
81 Snorlax C	.40	.60
82 Spheal C	.15	.25
83 Staryu C	.15	.25
84 Trapinch C	.15	.25
85 Turtwig GL C	.15	.25
86 Weedle C	.15	.25
87 Weezing C	.20	.35
88 Aaron's Collection U	.20	.35
89 Bebe's Search U	.30	.50
90 Bertha's Warmth U	.20	.35
91 Flint's Willpower U	.20	.35
92 Lucian's Assignment U	.20	.35
93 Pokemon Contest Hall U	.20	.35
94 Sunyshore City Gym U	.20	.35
95 Technical Machine G U	.20	.35
96 SP-Radar U	.30	.50
97 Underground Expedition U	.20	.35
98 Volkner's Philosophy U	2.00	.35
99 Darkness Energy U	.20	.35
100 Metal Energy U	.30	.50
101 SP Energy U	.20	.35
102 Upper Energy U	.20	.35
103 Alakazam 4 LV.X HOLO R	7.00	10.00
104 Floatzel GL LV.X HOLO R	6.00	7.00
105 Flygon LV.X HOLO R	10.00	13.00
106 Gallade 4 LV.X HOLO R	7.00	9.00
107 Hippowdon LV.X HOLO R	5.00	7.00
108 Infernape 4 LV.X HOLO R	8.00	10.00
109 Luxray GL LV.X HOLO R	15.00	18.00
110 Mismagius GL LV.X HOLO R	4.00	6.00
111 Snorlax LV.X HOLO R	13.00	16.00
112 Pikachu HOLO R	8.00	10.00
113 Flying Pikachu HOLO R	10.00	12.00
114 Surfing Pikachu HOLO R	10.00	13.00
RT1 Fan Rotom HOLO R	8.00	10.00
RT2 Frost Rotom HOLO R	4.00	6.00
RT3 Heat Rotom HOLO R	2.00	3.00
RT4 Mow Rotom HOLO R	2.00	3.00
RT5 Wash Rotom HOLO R	2.00	3.00
RT6 Charons Choice HOLO R	2.50	3.50

2009 Pokemon Platinum Supreme Victors

COMPLETE SET (150)	150.00	200.00
BOOSTER BOX (36 PACKS)	200.00	250.00
BOOSTER PACK (10 CARDS)	6.00	8.00
*REV.FOIL: .75X TO 2X BASIC CARDS		
RELEASED ON AUGUST 19, 2009		
1 Absol G HOLO R	2.00	3.00
2 Blaziken FB HOLO R	.75	1.25
3 Drifblim FB HOLO R	.60	1.00
4 Electivire FB HOLO R	.75	1.00
5 Garchomp HOLO R	1.25	2.00
6 Magmortar HOLO R	.60	1.00
7 Metagross HOLO R	.75	1.00
8 Rayquaza C HOLO R	3.00	4.00
9 Regigigas FB HOLO R	.60	1.00
10 Rhyperior HOLO R	.60	1.00
11 Staraptor FB HOLO R	.75	1.00
12 Swampert HOLO R	1.25	2.00
13 Venusaur HOLO R	3.00	4.00
14 Yanmega HOLO R	.60	1.00
15 Arcanine G R	.75	1.00
16 Articuno R	.75	1.00
17 Butterfree FB R	.60	1.00
18 Camerupt R	.60	1.00
19 Camerupt G R	.40	.60
20 Charizard R	4.00	5.00
21 Chimecho R	1.00	1.50
22 Claydol R	.40	.60
23 Crawdaunt R	.60	1.00
24 Dewgong R	.60	1.00
25 Dodrio R	.60	1.00
26 Dusknoir FB R	.60	1.00
27 Empoleon FB R	1.00	1.00
28 Exploud R	.40	.60
29 Honchkrow R	.60	1.00
30 Lickilicky C R	.40	.60
31 Lucario C R	.75	1.00
32 Lunatone R	.60	1.00
33 Mawile R	.60	1.00
34 Medicham R	.60	1.00
35 Milotic C R	.60	1.00
36 Moltres R	.75	1.00
37 Mr. Mime R	.60	1.00
38 Parasect R	.60	1.00
39 Primeape R	.60	1.00
40 Roserade C R	.60	1.00
41 Sableye R	.60	1.00
42 Sandslash R	.60	1.00
43 Seaking R	.60	1.00
44 Shedinja R	.60	1.00
45 Solrock R	.60	1.00
46 Spinda R	.40	.60
47 Wailord R	1.25	2.00
48 Zapdos R	1.00	1.25
49 Altaria C U	.20	.35
50 Arcanine U	.20	.35
51 Bibarel U	.20	.35
52 Breloom U	.20	.35
53 Carnivine U	.20	.35
54 Chatot G U	.30	.50
55 Cherrim U	.20	.35
56 Dragonite FB U	.50	.75
57 Drifblim U	.20	.35
58 Floatzel U	.20	.35
59 Gabite U	.40	.60
60 Garchomp C U	1.25	2.00
61 Hippopotas U	.20	.35
62 Ivysaur U	.30	.50
63 Lopunny U	.20	.35
64 Loudred U	.20	.35
65 Magmar U	.20	.35
66 Manectric G U	.20	.35
67 Marshtomp U	.20	.35
68 Masquerain U	.20	.35
69 Metang U	.20	.35
70 Milotic U	.40	.60
71 Minun U	.20	.35
72 Murkrow U	.20	.35
73 Ninjask U	.20	.35
74 Numel U	.20	.35
75 Pinsir U	.20	.35
76 Plusle U	.20	.35
77 Raichu U	.30	.50
78 Raticate U	.20	.35
79 Relicanth U	.20	.35
80 Rhydon U	.20	.35
81 Roserade U	.20	.35
82 Rotom U	.20	.35
83 Skarmory U	.25	.40
84 Spiritomb U	.20	.35
85 Staravia U	.20	.35
86 Togekiss C U	.75	1.00
87 Wailmer U	.40	.60
88 Yanma U	.20	.35
89 Baltoy C	.20	.35
90 Beldum C	.20	.35
91 Bidoof C	.20	.35
92 Buizel C	.20	.35
93 Bulbasaur C	.20	.35
94 Buneary C	.20	.35
95 Chatot C	.20	.35
96 Cherubi C	.20	.35
97 Chimchar C	.20	.35
98 Chingling C	.20	.35
99 Combee C	.20	.35
100 Corphish C	.20	.35
101 Croagunk C	.20	.35
102 Doduo C	.20	.35

103 Drifloon C	.20	.35
104 Feebas C	.20	.35
105 Geodude C	.20	.35
106 Gible C	.20	.35
107 Goldeen C	.20	.35
108 Growlithe C	.20	.35
109 Kricketot C	.20	.35
110 Magikarp C	.20	.35
111 Magnemite C	.20	.35
112 Mankey C	.20	.35
113 Meditite C	.20	.35
114 Meowth C	.20	.35
115 Mime Jr C	.20	.35
116 Mudkip C	.20	.35
117 Nincada C	.20	.35
118 Pachirisu C	.20	.35
119 Paras C	.20	.35
120 Pikachu C	.20	.35
121 Piplup C	.20	.35
122 Rhyhorn C	.20	.35
123 Roselia C	.20	.35
124 Sandshrew C	.20	.35
125 Seel C	.20	.35
126 Shinx C	.20	.35
127 Shroomish C	.20	.35
128 Skorupi C	.20	.35
129 Starly C	.20	.35
130 Surskit C	.20	.35
131 Turtwig C	.20	.35
132 Whismur C	.20	.35
133 Zubat C	.20	.35
134 Battle Tower U	.20	.35
135 Champion Room U	.20	.35
136 Cynthia's Guidance U	.20	.35
137 Cyrus's Initiative U	.20	.35
138 Night Teleporter U	.20	.35
139 Palmer's Contribution U	.75	1.00
140 VS. Seeker U	8.00	10.00
141 Absol G LV.X HOLO R	4.00	5.00
142 Blaziken FB LV.X HOLO R	4.00	6.00
143 Charizard G LV.X HOLO R	10.00	12.00
144 Electivire FB LV.X HOLO R	4.00	5.00
145 Garchomp C LV.X HOLO R	3.50	4.50
146 Rayquaza C LV.X HOLO R	15.00	17.00
147 Staraptor FB LV.X HOLO R	2.00	3.00
148 Articuno HOLO R	7.00	9.00
149 Moltres HOLO R	7.00	9.00
150 Zapdos HOLO R	7.00	9.00
SH7 Milotic HOLO R	7.00	9.00
SH8 Yanma HOLO R	5.00	6.00
SH9 Relicanth HOLO R	3.00	4.00

2009 Pokemon Platinum Arceus

COMPLETE SET (99)	110.00	160.00
BOOSTER BOX (36 PACKS)	200.00	300.00
BOOSTER PACK (10 CARDS)	6.00	8.00
*REV.FOIL: .75X TO 2X BASIC CARDS		
RELEASED ON NOVEMBER 4, 2009		
1 Charizard HOLO R	3.00	4.00
2 Froslass HOLO R	.75	1.00
3 Heatran HOLO R	.75	1.00
4 Kabutops HOLO R	1.00	1.25
5 Luxray HOLO R	.50	.75
6 Mothim HOLO R	.50	.75
7 Probopass HOLO R	.40	.60
8 Salamence HOLO R	.60	1.00
9 Swalot HOLO R	.40	.60
10 Tangrowth HOLO R	.40	.60
11 Toxicroak HOLO R	.50	.75
12 Zapdos HOLO R	.75	1.00
13 Aerodactyl R	.50	.75
14 Bronzong R	.50	.75
15 Cherrim R	.40	.60
16 Gengar R	2.00	3.00
17 Gengar R	2.00	3.00
18 Glalie R	.50	.75
19 Golem R	.60	1.00
20 Hariyama R	.25	.40
21 Lopunny R	.30	.50
22 Manectric R	.40	.60
23 Omastar R	.60	1.00
24 Pelipper R	.25	.40
25 Pichu R	1.50	2.00
26 Porygon Z R	.50	.75
27 Raichu R	.50	.75
28 Rapidash R	.50	.75
29 Raticate R	.40	.60
30 Sceptile R	.50	.75
31 Sceptile R	.50	.75
32 Spiritomb R	1.50	2.00
33 Bronzong U	.20	.35
34 Bronzor U	.20	.35
35 Charmeleon U	.20	.35
36 Gastly U	.40	.60
37 Graveler U	.20	.35
38 Grovyle U	.20	.35
39 Grovyle U	.20	.35
40 Gulpin U	.20	.35
41 Haunter U	.20	.35
42 Haunter U	.20	.35
43 Luxio U	.20	.35
44 Manectric U	.20	.35
45 Pelipper U	.20	.35
46 Ponyta U	.20	.35
47 Rapidash U	.20	.35
48 Shelgon U	.20	.35
49 Wormadam U	.20	.35
50 Wormadam U	.20	.35
51 Wormadam U	.20	.35
52 Bagon C	.15	.25
53 Beedrill C	.15	.25
54 Bronzor C	.15	.25
55 Buneary C	.15	.25
56 Burmy C	.15	.25
57 Burmy C	.15	.25
58 Burmy C	.15	.25
59 Charmander C	.15	.25
60 Cherubi C	.15	.25
61 Croagunk C	.15	.25
62 Electrike C	.15	.25
63 Electrike C	.15	.25
64 Gastly C	.15	.25
65 Geodude C	.15	.25
66 Gulpin C	.15	.25
67 Kabuto C	.15	.25
68 Makuhita C	.15	.25
69 Nosepass C	.15	.25
70 Omanyte C	.15	.25
71 Pikachu C	.15	.25
72 Ponyta C	.15	.25
73 Rattata C	.15	.25
74 Shinx C	.15	.25
75 Snorunt (C)	.15	.25
76 Tangela C	.15	.25
77 Tangela C	.15	.25
78 Treecko C	.15	.25
79 Treecko C	.15	.25
80 Wingull C	.15	.25
81 Wingull C	.15	.25
82 Beginning Door U	.20	.35
83 Bench Shield U	.20	.35
84 Buffer Piece U	.20	.35
85 Department Store Girl U	.20	.35
86 Energy Restore U	.20	.35
87 Expert Belt U	.50	.75
88 Lucky Egg U	.20	.35
89 Old Amber U	.20	.35
90 Professor Oak's Visit U	.20	.35
91 Ultimate Zone U	.20	.35
92 Dome Fossil C	.15	.25
93 Helix Fossil C	.15	.25
94 Arceus LV.X HOLO R	4.00	6.00
95 Arceus LV.X HOLO R	5.00	7.00
96 Arceus LV.X HOLO R	5.00	7.00
97 Gengar LV.X HOLO R	5.00	6.00
98 Salamence LV.X HOLO R	4.00	6.00
99 Tangrowth LV.X HOLO R	2.00	3.00
SH10 Bagon Rev H R	4.00	6.00
SH11 Ponyta (Rev H) R	15.00	20.00
SH12 Shinx (Rev H) R	8.00	12.00
AR1 Arceus HOLO R	4.00	6.00
AR2 Arceus HOLO R	3.00	4.00
AR3 Arceus HOLO R	1.75	3.00
AR4 Arceus HOLO R	2.00	3.00
AR5 Arceus HOLO R	4.00	6.00
AR6 Arceus HOLO R	1.00	1.50
AR7 Arceus HOLO R	2.50	3.50
AR8 Arceus HOLO R	3.00	4.00
AR9 Arceus HOLO R	3.00	4.00

2010 Pokemon HeartGold SoulSilver

COMPLETE SET (123)	145.00	200.00
BOOSTER BOX (36 PACKS)	250.00	350.00
BOOSTER PACK (10 CARDS)	2.50	6.00
*REV.FOIL: .75X TO 2X BASIC CARDS		
RELEASED ON FEBRUARY 10, 2010		
1 Arcanine HOLO R	4.00	7.00
2 Azumarill HOLO R	.40	.60
3 Clefable HOLO R	.40	.75
4 Gyarados HOLO R	2.50	4.00
5 Hitmontop HOLO R	.40	.75
6 Jumpluff HOLO R	.75	1.25
7 Ninetales HOLO R	4.00	7.00
8 Noctowl HOLO R	.60	1.00
9 Quagsire HOLO R	.40	.60
10 Raichu HOLO R	1.00	1.50
11 Shuckle HOLO R	.60	1.00
12 Slowking HOLO R	.60	1.00
13 Wobbuffet HOLO R	.40	.60
14 Ampharos R	.60	1.00
15 Ariados R	.50	.75
16 Butterfree R	.50	.75
17 Cleffa R	.75	1.25
18 Exeggutor R	.30	.50
19 Farfetch'd R	.25	.40
20 Feraligatr R	.60	1.00
21 Furret R	.60	1.00
22 Granbull R	.30	.50
23 Hypno R	.40	.75
24 Lapras R	.30	.50
25 Ledian R	.30	.50
26 Meganium R	.50	.75
27 Persian R	.50	.75
28 Pichu R	4.00	5.00
29 Sandslash R	.25	.40
30 Smoochum R	.40	.60
31 Sunflora R	.50	.75
32 Typhlosion R	1.25	2.00
33 Tyrogue R	.60	1.00
34 Weezing R	.30	.50
35 Bayleef U	.75	1.00
36 Blissey U	.20	.35
37 Corsola U	.20	.35
38 Croconaw U	.20	.35
39 Delibird U	.20	.35
40 Donphan U	.20	.35
41 Dunsparce U	.20	.35
42 Flaaffy U	.20	.35
43 Heracross U	.20	.35
44 Igglybuff U	1.00	1.50
45 Mantine U	.20	.35
46 Metapod U	.20	.35
47 Miltank U	.20	.35
48 Parasect U	.20	.35
49 Quilava U	.60	1.00
50 Qwilfish U	.20	.35
51 Skiploom U	.20	.35
52 Slowbro U	.20	.35
53 Starmie U	.20	.35
54 Unown U	.20	.35
55 Unown U	.20	.35
56 Wigglytuff U	.20	.35
57 Caterpie C	.15	.25
58 Chansey C	.15	.25
59 Chikorita C	.15	.25
60 Clefairy C	.15	.25
61 Cyndaquil C	.50	.75
62 Drowzee C	.15	.25
63 Exeggcute C	.15	.25
64 Girafarig C	.15	.25
65 Growlithe C	.15	.25
66 Hoothoot C	.15	.25
67 Hoppip C	.15	.25
68 Jigglypuff C	.15	.25
69 Jynx C	.15	.25
70 Koffing C	.15	.25
71 Ledyba C	.15	.25
72 Magikarp C	.15	.25
73 Mareep C	.15	.25
74 Marill C	.15	.25
75 Meowth C	.15	.25
76 Paras C	.15	.25
77 Phanpy C	.15	.25
78 Pikachu C	.60	.80
79 Sandshrew C	.15	.25
80 Sentret C	.15	.25
81 Slowpoke C	.15	.25
82 Snubbull C	.15	.25
83 Spinarak C	.15	.25
84 Staryu C	.15	.25
85 Sunkern C	.15	.25
86 Totodile C	.25	.40
87 Vulpix C	.40	.60
88 Wooper C	.15	.25
89 Bill U	.20	.35
90 Copycat U	.20	.35
91 Energy Switch U	.30	.50
92 Fisherman U	.20	.35
93 Full Heal U	.20	.35
94 Moomoo Milk U	.20	.35
95 Poke Ball U	.20	.35
96 Pokegear 3.0 U	.30	.50
97 Pokemon Collector U	3.00	5.00
98 Pokemon Communication U	.75	.35
99 Pokemon Reversal U	.20	.35
100 Professor Elm's Training Method U	.20	.35
101 Professor Oak's New Theory U	.50	.75
102 Switch U	.30	.50
103 Double Colorless Energy U	3.00	4.00
104 Rainbow Energy U	1.00	1.50
105 Ampharos Prime HOLO R	1.75	3.00
106 Blissey Prime HOLO R	1.75	3.00
107 Donphan Prime HOLO R	3.50	5.00
108 Feraligatr Prime HOLO R	2.50	4.00
109 Meganium (Prime) HOLO R	1.75	3.00
110 Typhlosion (Prime) HOLO R	2.00	3.00
111 HoOh LEGEND Top HOLO R	7.00	9.00
112 HoOh LEGEND Bottom HOLO R	8.00	10.00
113 Lugia LEGEND Top HOLO R	12.00	15.00
114 Lugia LEGEND Bottom HOLO R	15.00	18.00
115 Grass Energy C	2.00	3.50
116 Fire Energy C	4.00	6.00
117 Water Energy C	3.00	4.50
118 Lightning Energy C	2.00	3.00
119 Psychic Energy C	3.00	4.50
120 Fighting Energy C	1.50	2.50
121 Darkness Energy C	5.00	6.50
122 Metal Energy C	3.00	4.50
123 Gyarados HOLO R	8.00	10.00
124 Alph Lithograph UR	4.50	6.00

2010 Pokemon HS Triumphant

COMPLETE SET (102)	85.00	125.00
BOOSTER BOX (36 PACKS)	150.00	200.00
BOOSTER PACK (10 CARDS)	2.50	6.00
*REV.FOIL: .75X TO 2X BASIC CARDS		
RELEASED ON NOVEMBER 3, 2010		
1 Aggron HOLO R	.75	1.00
2 Altaria HOLO R	.40	.60
3 Celebi HOLO R	1.00	1.50
4 Drapion HOLO R	.40	.60
5 Mamoswine HOLO R	.50	.75
6 Nidoking HOLO R	1.25	2.00
7 PorygonZ HOLO R	.40	.60
8 Rapidash HOLO R	.40	.60
9 Solrock HOLO R	.40	.50
10 Spiritomb HOLO R	.40	.50
11 Venomoth HOLO R	.40	.60
12 Victreebel HOLO R	.50	.75
13 Ambipom R	.30	.50
14 Banette R	.30	.50
15 Bronzong R	.30	.50
16 Carnivine R	.25	.40
17 Ditto R	.75	1.25
18 Dragonite R	.60	1.00
19 Dugtrio R	.30	.50
20 Electivire R	.60	1.00
21 Elekid R	.60	1.00
22 Golduck R	.25	.40
23 Grumpig R	.25	.40
24 Kricketune R	.20	.35
25 Lunatone R	.25	.40
26 Machamp R	.30	.50
27 Magmortar R	.25	.40
28 Nidoqueen R	.30	.50
29 Pidgeot R	.25	.40
30 Sharpedo R	.30	.50
31 Wailord R	1.00	1.50
32 Dragonair U	.20	.35
33 Electabuzz U	.20	.35
34 Electrode U	.20	.35
35 Haunter U	1.00	1.50
36 Kangaskhan U	.20	.35
37 Lairon U	.20	.35
38 Lickilicky U	.20	.35
39 Luvdisc U	.20	.35
40 Machoke U	.20	.35
41 Magby U	.20	.35
42 Magmar U	.20	.35
43 Magneton U	.20	.35
44 Marowak U	.20	.35
45 Nidorina U	.20	.35
46 Nidorino U	.20	.35
47 Pidgeotto U	.20	.35
48 Piloswine U	.20	.35
49 Porygon2 U	.20	.35
50 Tentacruel U	.20	.35
51 Unown U	.20	.35
52 Wailmer U	.20	.35
53 Weepinbell U	.20	.35
54 Yanmega U	.20	.35
55 Aipom C	.15	.25
56 Aron C	.15	.25
57 Bellsprout C	.15	.25
58 Bronzor C	.15	.25
59 Carvanha C	.15	.25
60 Cubone C	.15	.25
61 Diglett C	.15	.25
62 Dratini C	.15	.25
63 Gastly C	.15	.25
64 Illumise C	.15	.25
65 Kricketot C	.15	.25
66 Lickitung C	.15	.25
67 Machop C	.15	.25
68 Magnemite C	.15	.25
69 Nidoran F C	.15	.25
70 Nidoran M C	.15	.25
71 Pidgey C	.15	.25
72 Ponyta C	.15	.25
73 Porygon C	.15	.25
74 Psyduck C	.15	.25
75 Shuppet C	.15	.25
76 Skorupi C	.15	.25
77 Spoink C	.15	.25
78 Swablu C	.15	.25
79 Swinub C	.15	.25
80 Tentacool C	.15	.25
81 Venonat C	.15	.25
82 Volbeat C	.15	.25
83 Voltorb C	.15	.25
84 Yanma C	.15	.25
85 Black Belt U	.20	.35
86 Indigo Plateau U	.20	.35
87 Junk Arm U	2.00	3.00
88 Seeker U	.60	1.00
89 Twins U	.40	.60
90 Rescue Energy U	.30	.50
91 Absol Prime HOLO R	3.00	4.25
92 Celebi Prime HOLO R	2.00	2.50
93 Electrode Prime HOLO R	2.00	2.50
94 Gengar Prime HOLO R	10.00	15.00
95 Machamp Prime HOLO R	2.50	3.00
96 Magnezone Prime HOLO R	3.00	4.50
97 Mew Prime HOLO R	8.00	10.00
98 Yanmega Prime HOLO R	1.50	2.00
99 Darkrai & Cresselia LEGEND R	5.00	8.00
100 Darkrai & Cresselia LEGEND R	6.00	9.00
101 Palkia & Dialga LEGEND HOLO R	5.00	7.00
102 Palkia & Dialga LEGEND HOLO R	5.00	7.00
SP Alph Lithograph UR	4.00	6.00

2010 Pokemon HS Unleashed

COMPLETE SET (96)	95.00	140.00
BOOSTER BOX (36 PACKS)	200.00	250.00
BOOSTER PACK (10 CARDS)	6.00	8.00
*REV.FOIL: .75X TO 2X BASIC CARDS		
RELEASED ON MAY 12, 2010		
1 Jirachi HOLO R	1.00	1.50
2 Magmortar HOLO R	.50	.75
3 Manaphy HOLO R	.75	1.00
4 Metagross HOLO R	.75	1.00
5 Mismagius HOLO R	.40	.60
6 Octillery HOLO R	.40	.60
7 Politoed HOLO R	.75	1.00
8 Shaymin HOLO R	2.00	3.00
9 Sudowoodo HOLO R	.50	.75
10 Torterra HOLO R	1.25	2.00
11 Xatu HOLO R	.40	.60
12 Beedrill R	.40	.60
13 Blastoise R	1.50	2.00
14 Crobat R	.50	.75
15 Fearow R	.30	.50
16 Floatzel R	.25	.40
17 Kingdra R	.60	1.00
18 Lanturn R	.25	.40
19 Lucario R	.40	.60
20 Ninetales R	.50	.75
21 Poliwrath R	.60	1.00
22 Primeape R	.25	.40
23 Roserade R	.25	.40
24 Steelix R	1.25	2.00
25 Torkoal R	.30	.50
26 Tyranitar R	1.25	2.00
27 Ursaring R	.50	.75
28 Cherrim U	.20	.35
29 Dunsparce U	.20	.35
30 Golbat U	.20	.35
31 Grotle U	.20	.35
32 Kakuna U	.20	.35
33 Metang U	.20	.35
34 Minun U	.20	.35
35 Numel U	.20	.35
36 Plusle U	.20	.35
37 Poliwhirl U	.20	.35
38 Pupitar U	.20	.35
39 Pupitar U	.20	.35
40 Seadra U	.20	.35
41 Tauros U	.20	.35
42 Wartortle U	.20	.35
43 Aipom C	.15	.25
44 Beldum C	.15	.25
45 Buizel C	.15	.25
46 Carnivine C	.15	.25
47 Cherubi C	.15	.25

48 Chinchou C .15 .25
49 Horsea C .15 .25
50 Larvitar C .15 .25
51 Larvitar C .15 .25
52 Magmar C .15 .25
53 Mankey C .15 .25
54 Misdreavus C .15 .25
55 Natu C .15 .25
56 Onix C .15 .25
57 Onix C .15 .25
58 Poliwag C .15 .25
59 Remoraid C .15 .25
60 Riolu C .15 .25
61 Roselia C .15 .25
62 Spearow C .15 .25
63 Squirtle C .15 .25
64 Stantler C .15 .25
65 Teddiursa C .15 .25
66 Tropius C .15 .25
67 Turtwig C .15 .25
68 Vulpix C .15 .25
69 Weedle C .15 .25
70 Zubat C .15 .25
71 Cheerleader's Cheer U .20 .35
72 Dual Ball U .20 .35
73 Emcee's Chatter U .20 .35
74 Energy Returner U .20 .35
75 Engineer's Adjustments U .20 .35
76 Good Rod U .20 .35
77 Interviewer's Questions U .20 .35
78 Judge U 1.50 2.00
79 Life Herb U .20 .35
80 Plus Power U .20 .35
81 Pokemon Circulator U .20 .35
82 Rare Candy U 1.00 1.50
83 Super Scoop Up U .60 1.00
84 Crobat Prime HOLO R 3.00 5.00
85 Kingdra Prime HOLO R 3.00 4.00
86 Lanturn Prime HOLO R 1.75 2.25
87 Steelix Prime HOLO R 3.00 4.00
88 Tyranitar (Prime) HOLO R 4.00 6.00
89 Ursaring (Prime) HOLO R 3.00 4.00
90 Entei & Raikou LEGEND HOLO R 8.00 12.00
91 Entei & Raikou LEGEND HOLO R 8.00 12.00
92 Raikou & Suicune LEGEND HOLO R 8.00 12.00
93 Raikou & Suicune LEGEND HOLO R 8.00 12.00
94 Suicune & Entei LEGEND HOLO R 8.00 12.00
95 Suicune & Entei LEGEND HOLO R 6.00 8.00
96 Alph Lithograph R 2.00 3.00

2010 Pokemon HS Undaunted

COMPLETE SET (90) 90.00 130.00
BOOSTER BOX (36 PACKS) 200.00 250.00
BOOSTER PACK (10 CARDS) 6.00 8.00
*REV.FOIL: .75X TO 2X BASIC CARDS
RELEASED ON AUGUST 18, 2010
1 Bellossom HOLO R .40 .75
2 Espeon HOLO R 3.00 5.00
3 Forretress HOLO R .40 .75
4 Gliscor HOLO R .75 1.00
5 Houndoom HOLO R .60 1.00
6 Magcargo HOLO R .40 .75
7 Scizor HOLO R 1.00 1.50
8 Smeargle HOLO R 1.00 1.50
9 Togekiss HOLO R .60 1.00
10 Umbreon HOLO R 4.00 6.00
11 Dodrio R .30 .50
12 Drifblim R .30 .50
13 Forretress R .30 .50
14 Hariyama R .30 .50
15 Honchkrow R .30 .50
16 Honchkrow R .30 .50
17 Leafeon R .60 1.00
18 Metagross R .30 .50
19 Mismagius R .30 .50
20 Rotom R .30 .50
21 Skarmory R .30 .50
22 Tropius R .30 .50
23 Vespiquen R .30 .50
24 Vileplume R .75 1.25
25 Weavile R .30 .50
26 Flareon U .50 .75
27 Gloom U .20 .35
28 Jolteon U .30 .50
29 Lairon U .20 .35
30 Metang U .20 .35
31 Muk U .20 .35
32 Pinsir U .20 .35
33 Raichu U .20 .35
34 Raticate U .20 .35
35 Sableye U .20 .35
36 Scyther U .40 .75
37 Skuntank U .20 .35
38 Slowbro U .20 .35
39 Togetic U .20 .35
40 Unown U .20 .35
41 Vaporeon U .40 .60
42 Aron C .15 .25
43 Beldum C .15 .25
44 Combee C .15 .25
45 Doduo C .15 .25
46 Drifloon C .15 .25
47 Eevee C .15 .25
48 Eevee C .15 .25
49 Gligar C .15 .25
50 Grimer C .15 .25
51 Hitmonchan C .15 .25
52 Hitmonlee C .15 .25
53 Houndour C .15 .25
54 Houndour C .15 .25
55 Makuhita C .15 .25
56 Mawile C .15 .25
57 Misdreavus C .15 .25
58 Murkrow C .15 .25
59 Murkrow C .15 .25
60 Oddish C .15 .25
61 Pikachu C .50 .75
62 Pineco C .15 .25
63 Pineco C .15 .25
64 Rattata C .15 .25
65 Scyther C .15 .25
66 Slowpoke C .15 .25
67 Slugma C .15 .25
68 Sneasel C .15 .25
69 Stunky C .15 .25
70 Togepi C .15 .25
71 Burned Tower U .20 .35
72 Defender U .20 .35
73 Energy Exchanger U .20 .35
74 Flower Shop Lady U .20 .35
75 Legend Box U .20 .35
76 Ruins of Alph U .20 .35
77 Sage's Training U .20 .35
78 Team Rocket's Trickery U .20 .35
79 Darkness Energy U .30 .50
80 Metal Energy U .30 .50
81 Espeon Prime HOLO R 2.75 3.50
82 Houndoom Prime HOLO R 2.00 3.50
83 Raichu Prime HOLO R 6.00 8.00
84 Scizor Prime HOLO R 3.50 5.00
85 Slowking Prime HOLO R 1.75 2.50
86 Umbreon Prime HOLO R 4.00 6.00
87 Kyogre & Groudon LEGEND HOLO R 12.00 15.00
88 Kyogre & Groudon LEGEND HOLO R 12.00 15.00
89 Rayquaza & Deoxys LEGEND HOLO R 8.00 12.00
90 Rayquaza & Deoxys LEGEND HOLO R 8.00 12.00
SP Alph Lithograph UR 4.00 6.00

2011 Pokemon Black and White

COMPLETE SET (115) 40.00 70.00
BOOSTER BOX (36 PACKS) 100.00 120.00
BOOSTER PACK (10 CARDS) 3.00 5.00
*REV.FOIL: .75X TO 2X BASIC CARDS
RELEASED ON APRIL 25, 2011
1 Snivy C .15 .25
2 Snivy C .15 .25
3 Servine U .25 .40
4 Servine U .25 .40
5 Serperior HOLO R .60 1.00
6 Serperior HOLO R .50 .75
7 Pansage C .15 .25
8 Simisage U .25 .40
9 Petilil C .15 .25
10 Lilligant R .30 .50
11 Maractus U .25 .40
12 Maractus R .20 .35
13 Deerling C .15 .25
14 Sawsbuck R .30 .50
15 Tepig C .15 .25
16 Tepig C .15 .25
17 Pignite U .25 .40
18 Pignite U .25 .40
19 Emboar HOLO R 1.25 2.00
20 Emboar HOLO R .75 1.25
21 Pansear C .15 .25
22 Simisear U .25 .40
23 Darumaka C .15 .25
24 Darumaka U .25 .40
25 Darmanitan R .20 .35
26 Reshiram HOLO R .60 1.00
27 Oshawott C .15 .25
28 Oshawott C .15 .25
29 Dewott U .25 .40
30 Dewott U .25 .40
31 Samurott HOLO R .60 1.00
32 Samurott HOLO R .75 1.25
33 Panpour C .15 .25
34 Simipour U .25 .40
35 Basculin U .25 .40
36 Ducklett C .15 .25
37 Swanna R .20 .35
38 Alomomola U .25 .40
39 Alomomola R .20 .35
40 Blitzle C .15 .25
41 Blitzle C .15 .25
42 Zebstrika U .25 .40
43 Zebstrika R .20 .35
44 Joltik C .15 .25
45 Joltik C .15 .25
46 Galvantula R .20 .35
47 Zekrom HOLO R .60 1.00
48 Munna U .25 .40
49 Musharna R .20 .35
50 Woobat C .15 .25
51 Swoobat U .25 .40
52 Venipede C .15 .25
53 Whirlipede U .25 .40
54 Scolipede R .30 .50
55 Solosis C .15 .25
56 Duosion U .25 .40
57 Reuniclus HOLO R .60 1.00
58 Timburr C .15 .25
59 Timburr C .15 .25
60 Gurdurr U .25 .40
61 Throh R .20 .35
62 Sawk R .20 .35
63 Sandile (C) .15 .25
64 Krokorok U .25 .40
65 Krookodile HOLO R .50 .75
66 Purrloin C .15 .25
67 Liepard R .40 .60
68 Scraggy C .15 .25
69 Scrafty R .20 .35
70 Zorua C .15 .25
71 Zoroark HOLO R 1.00 1.50
72 Vullaby C .15 .25
73 Mandibuzz R .20 .35
74 Klink C .15 .25
75 Klang U .25 .40
76 Klinklang HOLO R .60 1.00
77 Patrat C .15 .25
78 Patrat C .15 .25
79 Watchog U .25 .40
80 Lillipup C .15 .25
81 Lillipup C .15 .25
82 Herdier U .25 .40
83 Stoutland R .30 .50
84 Pidove C .15 .25
85 Tranquill U .25 .40
86 Unfezant R .20 .35
87 Audino U .25 .40
88 Minccino C .15 .25
89 Cinccino R .20 .35
90 Bouffalant U .25 .40
91 Bouffalant R .20 .35
92 Energy Retrieval U .25 .40
93 Energy Search C .15 .25
94 Energy Switch U .25 .40
95 Full Heal U .25 .40
96 PlusPower U .25 .40
97 Poke Ball U .25 .40
98 Pokedex U .25 .40
99 Pokemon Communication U .25 .40
100 Potion C .15 .25
101 Professor Juniper U .25 .40
102 Revive U .25 .40
103 Super Scoop Up U .25 .40
104 Switch U .25 .40
105 Grass Energy C .15 .25
106 Fire Energy C .15 .25
107 Water Energy C .15 .25
108 Lightning Energy C .15 .25
109 Psychic Energy C .15 .25
110 Fighting Energy C .15 .25
111 Darkness Energy C .15 .25
112 Metal Energy C .15 .25
113 Reshiram HOLO SR 3.00 5.00
114 Zekrom HOLO SR 5.00 8.00
115 Pikachu UR 10.00 13.00

2011 Pokemon Black and White Emerging Powers

COMPLETE SET (98) 40.00 100.00
BOOSTER BOX (36 PACKS) 100.00 120.00
BOOSTER PACK (10 CARDS) 3.00 5.00
*REV.FOIL: .75X TO 2X BASIC CARDS
RELEASED ON AUGUST 31, 2011
1 Pansage C .10 .25
2 Simisage R .40 1.00
3 Sewaddle C .10 .25
4 Sewaddle C .10 .25
5 Swadloon U .20 .50
6 Swadloon U .20 .50
7 Leavanny R .75 2.00
8 Leavanny R .75 2.00
9 Cottonee C .10 .25
10 Cottonee C .10 .25
11 Whimsicott U .20 .50
12 Whimsicott R .40 1.00
13 Petilil C .10 .25
14 Lilligant U .20 .50
15 Deerling C .10 .25
16 Sawsbuck R .40 1.00
17 Virizion HOLO R 2.00 5.00
18 Pansear C .10 .25
19 Simisear R .40 1.00
20 Darumaka C .10 .25
21 Darmanitan R .60 1.50
22 Panpour C .10 .25
23 Simipour R .40 1.00
24 Basculin C .10 .25
25 Basculin U .20 .50
26 Ducklett C .10 .25
27 Swanna R .40 1.00
28 Cubchoo C .10 .25
29 Cubchoo C .10 .25
30 Beartic HOLO R .50 1.00
31 Beartic R .75 2.00
32 Emolga C .10 .25
33 Joltik C .10 .25
34 Galvantula U .20 .50
35 Thundurus HOLO R .50 1.00
36 Woobat C .10 .25
37 Swoobat R .40 1.00
38 Venipede C .10 .25
39 Whirlipede U .20 .50
40 Scolipede R .40 1.00
41 Sigilyph U .20 .50
42 Sigilyph U .20 .50
43 Gothita C .10 .25
44 Gothita C .10 .25
45 Gothorita U .20 .50
46 Gothorita U .20 .50
47 Gothitelle HOLO R .50 1.00
48 Gothitelle R .40 1.00
49 Roggenrola C .10 .25
50 Roggenrola C .10 .25
51 Boldore U .20 .50
52 Boldore U .20 .50
53 Gigalith R .40 1.00
54 Drilbur (U) .20 .50
55 Drilbur C .10 .25
56 Excadrill HOLO R .50 1.00
57 Excadrill R .50 1.00
58 Throh U .20 .50
59 Sawk U .20 .50
60 Sandile C .10 .25
61 Krokorok U .20 .50
62 Krookodile R .60 1.50
63 Terrakion HOLO R 1.00 2.50
64 Purrloin C .10 .25
65 Liepard R 1.50 4.00
66 Zorua U .20 .50
67 Zoroark HOLO R .50 1.00
68 Vullaby C .10 .25
69 Mandibuzz R .60 1.50
70 Ferroseed C .10 .25
71 Ferroseed C .10 .25
72 Ferrothorn R .40 1.00
73 Ferrothorn U .20 .50
74 Klink C .10 .25
75 Klang U .20 .50
76 Klinklang R .75 2.00
77 Cobalion HOLO R .50 1.00
78 Patrat C .10 .25
79 Watchog U .20 .50
80 Pidove C .10 .25
81 Tranquill U .20 .50
82 Unfezant R .60 1.50
83 Audino U .20 .50
84 Minccino C .10 .25
85 Cinccino U .20 .50
86 Rufflet C .10 .25
87 Rufflet C .10 .25
88 Braviary HOLO R .50 1.00
89 Tornadus HOLO R .50 1.00
90 Bianca U .50 1.25
91 Cheren U .20 .50
92 Crushing Hammer U .20 .50
93 Great Ball U .20 .50
94 Max Potion U .50 1.50
95 Pokemon Catcher U .50 1.50
96 Recycle U .20 .50
97 Thundurus Full Art UR 2.00 4.00
98 Tornadus Full Art UR 2.00 4.00

2011 Pokemon Black and White Noble Victories

COMPLETE SET (102) 150.00 200.00
BOOSTER BOX (36 PACKS) 100.00 120.00
BOOSTER PACK (10 CARDS) 3.00 5.00
*REV.FOIL: .75X TO 2X BASIC CARDS
RELEASED ON NOVEMBER 16, 2011
1 Sewaddle C .05 .15
2 Swadloon U .05 .15
3 Leavanny HOLO R .40 .75
4 Petilil C .05 .15
5 Lilligant R .25 .40
6 Dwebble C .05 .15
7 Crustle U .05 .15
8 Karrablast C .05 .15
9 Foongus C .05 .15
10 Amoonguss U .05 .15
11 Shelmet C .05 .15
12 Accelgor R .30 .50
13 Virizion HOLO R .75 1.00
14 Victini HOLO R .75 1.00
15 Victini HOLO R 1.25 1.75
16 Pansear C .05 .15
17 Simisear U .05 .15
18 Heatmor U .05 .15
19 Larvesta C .05 .15
20 Larvesta C .05 .15
21 Volcarona R .30 .50
22 Tympole C .05 .15
23 Palpitoad U .25 .40
24 Seismitoad R .40 .75
25 Tirtouga U .20 .35
26 Carracosta R 1.00 1.50
27 Vanillite C .05 .15
28 Vanillish U .05 .15
29 Vanilluxe R .40 .75
30 Frillish C .05 .15
31 Jellicent R .30 .50
32 Cryogonal U .05 .15
33 Cryogonal R .30 .50
34 Kyurem HOLO R 1.25 2.00
35 Blitzle C .05 .15
36 Zebstrika R .30 .50
37 Emolga U .05 .15
38 Tynamo C .20 .35
39 Tynamo C .05 .15
40 Eelektrik U .50 .75
41 Eelektross HOLO R .40 .75
42 Stunfisk C .05 .15
43 Victini R .75 1.00
44 Yamask C .05 .15
45 Yamask C .05 .15
46 Cofagrigus R .30 .50
47 Cofagrigus R .30 .50
48 Trubbish C .20 .35
49 Garbodor U .05 .15
50 Solosis C .05 .15
51 Duosion U .05 .15
52 Reuniclus R .30 .50
53 Reuniclus R .30 .50
54 Elgyem C .05 .15
55 Elgyem C .05 .15
56 Beheeyem R .30 .50
57 Litwick C .05 .15
58 Litwick C .05 .15
59 Lampent U .20 .35
60 Chandelure R .75 1.25
61 Gigalith R .30 .50
62 Timburr C .05 .15
63 Gurdurr U .05 .15
64 Conkeldurr HOLO R .75 1.00
65 Conkeldurr R .30 .50
66 Archen U .30 .50
67 Archeops R 11.00 14.00
68 Stunfisk U .05 .15
69 Mienfoo C .05 .15
70 Mienshao U .05 .15
71 Golett C .05 .15
72 Golurk R .30 .50
73 Terrakion HOLO R .75 1.00
74 Landorus HOLO R .75 1.00
75 Pawniard C .05 .15
76 Bisharp U .05 .15
77 Deino C .05 .15

78 Zweilous U	.20	.35
79 Hydreigon HOLO R	.75	1.00
80 Escavalier R	.25	.40
81 Pawniard C	.05	.15
82 Bisharp HOLO R	.40	.75
83 Durant U	.60	1.00
84 Cobalion HOLO R	.75	1.00
85 Audino U	.05	.15
86 Axew C	.05	.15
87 Fraxure U	.20	.35
88 Haxorus HOLO R	.75	1.00
89 Druddigon R	.30	.50
90 Cover Fossil U	.05	.15
91 Eviolite U	.05	.15
92 N U	2.50	4.00
93 Plume Fossil U	.05	.15
94 Rocky Helmet U	.05	.15
95 Super Rod U	3.00	5.00
96 Xtransceiver U	.05	.15
97 Virizion Full Art UR	4.00	7.00
98 Victini Full Art UR	8.00	12.00
99 Terrakion Full Art UR	2.00	5.00
100 Cobalion Full Art UR	4.00	7.00
101 N Full Art UR	90.00	110.00
102 Meowth UR	7.00	10.00

2011 Pokemon Call of Legends

COMPLETE SET (95)	40.00	80.00
BOOSTER BOX (36 PACKS)	200.00	250.00
BOOSTER PACK (10 CARDS)	6.00	8.00
*REV.FOIL: .75X TO 2X BASIC CARDS		
RELEASED ON FEBRUARY 9, 2011		
1 Clefable HOLO R	.40	.75
2 Deoxys HOLO R	.75	1.25
3 Dialga HOLO R	.75	1.25
4 Espeon HOLO R	2.75	3.25
5 Forretress HOLO R	.40	.75
6 Groudon HOLO R	1.00	1.50
7 Gyarados HOLO R	1.00	1.50
8 Hitmontop HOLO R	.40	.75
9 Ho-Oh HOLO R	2.50	4.00
10 Houndoom HOLO R	1.00	1.50
11 Jirachi HOLO R	1.00	1.50
12 Kyogre HOLO R	.75	1.25
13 Leafeon HOLO R	1.25	2.00
14 Lucario HOLO R	1.00	1.50
15 Lugia HOLO R	3.50	5.00
16 Magmortar HOLO R	.40	.75
17 Ninetales HOLO R	4.00	6.00
18 Pachirisu HOLO R	.75	1.25
19 Palkia HOLO R	1.25	2.00
20 Rayquaza HOLO R	1.50	2.50
21 Smeargle HOLO R	1.75	3.00
22 Umbreon HOLO R	2.50	4.00
23 Ampharos R	.30	.75
24 Cleffa R	.40	1.00
25 Feraligatr R	.30	.75
26 Granbull R	.30	.75
27 Meganium R	.30	.75
28 Mismagius R	.30	.75
29 Mr. Mime R	.30	.75
30 Pidgeot R	.30	.75
31 Skarmory R	.30	.75
32 Slowking R	.30	.75
33 Snorlax R	.30	.75
34 Tangrowth R	.30	.75
35 Typhlosion R	.30	.75
36 Tyrogue R	.30	.75
37 Ursaring R	.30	.75
38 Weezing R	.30	.75
39 Zangoose R	.30	.75
40 Bayleef U	.20	.35
41 Croconaw U	.20	.35
42 Donphan (U)	.20	.35
43 Flaaffy U	.20	.35
44 Flareon U	.20	.35
45 Jolteon U	.20	.35
46 Magby U	.20	.35
47 Mime Jr. U	.20	.35
48 Pidgeotto U	.20	.35
49 Quilava U	.20	.35
50 Riolu U	.20	.35
51 Seviper U	.20	.35
52 Vaporeon U	.20	.35
53 Chikorita C	.15	.25
54 Clefairy C	.15	.25
55 Cyndaquil C	.15	.25
56 Eevee C	.15	.25
57 Hitmonchan C	.15	.25
58 Hitmonlee C	.15	.25
59 Houndour C	.15	.25
60 Koffing C	.15	.25
61 Magikarp C	.15	.25
62 Magmar C	.15	.25
63 Mareep C	.15	.25
64 Mawile C	.15	.25
65 Misdreavus C	.15	.25
66 Phanpy C	.15	.25
67 Pidgey C	.15	.25
68 Pineco C	.15	.25
69 Relicanth C	.15	.25
70 Slowpoke C	.15	.25
71 Snubbull C	.15	.25
72 Tangela C	.15	.25
73 Teddiursa C	.15	.25
74 Totodile C	.15	.25
75 Vulpix C	.15	.25
76 Cheerleader's Cheer U	.20	.35
77 Copycat U	.20	.35
78 Dual Ball U	.20	.35
79 Interviewer's Questions U	.20	.35
80 Lost Remover U	.20	.35
81 Lost World U	.20	.35
82 Professor Elm's Training Method U	.20	.35
83 Professor Oak's New Theory U	.20	.35
84 Research Record U	.20	.35
85 Sage's Training U	.20	.35
86 Darkness Energy U	.20	.35
87 Metal Energy U	.20	.35
88 Grass Energy C	.15	.25
89 Fire Energy C	.15	.25
90 Water Energy C	.15	.25
91 Lightning Energy C	.15	.25
92 Psychic Energy C	.15	.25
93 Fighting Energy C	.15	.25
94 Darkness Energy C	.15	.25
95 Metal Energy C	.15	.25

2011 Pokemon Call of Legends Shiny

COMPLETE SET (11)	40.00	80.00
SL1 Deoxys HOLO R	3.00	8.00
SL2 Dialga HOLO R	4.00	10.00
SL3 Entei HOLO R	3.00	8.00
SL4 Groudon HOLO R	4.00	10.00
SL5 Ho-Oh HOLO R	6.00	15.00
SL6 Kyogre HOLO R	4.00	10.00
SL7 Lugia HOLO R	5.00	12.00
SL8 Palkia HOLO R	3.00	8.00
SL9 Raikou HOLO R	3.00	8.00
SL10 Rayquaza HOLO R	6.00	15.00
SL11 Suicune HOLO R	4.00	10.00

2012 Pokemon Black and White Boundaries Crossed

COMPLETE SET (153)	250.00	350.00
BOOSTER BOX (36 PACKS)	120.00	150.00
BOOSTER PACK (10 CARDS)	4.00	6.00
*REV.FOIL: .75X TO 2X BASIC CARDS		
RELEASED ON NOVEMBER 11, 2012		
1 Oddish C	.15	.25
2 Gloom U	.20	.35
3 Vileplume HOLO R	.60	1.00
4 Bellossom R	.20	.35
5 Tangela C	.15	.25
6 Tangrowth HOLO R	.40	.60
7 Scyther C	.15	.25
8 Heracross U	.20	.35
9 Celebi EX UR	5.00	8.00
10 Shaymin R	.40	.60
11 Snivy C	.15	.25
12 Servine U	.20	.35
13 Serperior HOLO R	1.00	1.50
14 Cottonee C	.15	.25
15 Whimsicott R	.20	.35
16 Petilil U	.20	.35
17 Lilligant R	.25	.40
18 Charmander C	.15	.25
19 Charmeleon U	.20	.35
20 Charizard HOLO R	4.00	5.00
21 Numel C	.15	.25
22 Camerupt R	.25	.40
23 Victini R	.30	.50
24 Tepig C	.15	.25
25 Pignite U	.20	.35
26 Emboar HOLO R	1.00	2.00
27 Darumaka C	.15	.25
28 Darmanitan U	.20	.35
29 Squirtle C	.15	.25
30 Wartortle U	.20	.35
31 Blastoise HOLO R	3.50	4.50
32 Psyduck C	.15	.25
33 Psyduck C	.15	.25
34 Golduck U	.20	.35
35 Golduck R	.25	.40
36 Marill C	.15	.25
37 Azumarill U	.20	.35
38 Delibird U	.20	.35
39 Oshawott C	.15	.25
40 Dewott U	.20	.35
41 Samurott HOLO R	.75	1.25
42 Ducklett C	.15	.25
43 Swanna U	.20	.35
44 Frillish C	.15	.25
45 Jellicent R	.20	.35
46 Cryogonal U	.20	.35
47 Keldeo HOLO R	.50	.75
48 Keldeo R	.40	.60
49 Keldeo EX UR	2.50	4.00
50 Pikachu C	.15	.25
51 Voltorb C	.15	.25
52 Electrode U	.20	.35
53 Electabuzz C	.15	.25
54 Electivire HOLO R	.40	.75
55 Chinchou C	.15	.25
56 Blitzle C	.15	.25
57 Zebstrika HOLO R	.40	.75
58 Wobbuffet U	.20	.35
59 Spoink C	.15	.25
60 Grumpig R	.20	.35
61 Duskull C	.15	.25
62 Dusclops U	.20	.35
63 Dusknoir HOLO R	2.00	3.00
64 Croagunk C	.15	.25
65 Croagunk U	.20	.35
66 Toxicroak R	.20	.35
67 Cresselia EX UR	3.00	4.00
68 Munna U	.20	.35
69 Musharna R	.20	.35
70 Woobat C	.15	.25
71 Swoobat R	.25	.40
72 Venipede C	.15	.25
73 Whirlipede U	.20	.35
74 Scolipede HOLO R	1.00	1.50
75 Gothita C	.15	.25
76 Gothorita U	.20	.35
77 Meloetta (Holo) (R)	.75	1.25
78 Sandshrew C	.15	.25
79 Sandslash U	.20	.35
80 Gligar C	.15	.25
81 Gliscor HOLO R	.40	.75
82 Makuhita C	.15	.25
83 Trapinch C	.15	.25
84 Dwebble C	.15	.25
85 Crustle HOLO R	.40	.75
86 Mienfoo C	.15	.25
87 Mienfoo U	.20	.35
88 Mienshao U	.20	.35
89 Landorus EX UR	5.00	8.00
90 Purrloin C	.15	.25
91 Liepard HOLO R	.40	.60
92 Vullaby C	.15	.25
93 Mandibuzz U	.20	.35
94 Scizor HOLO R	1.50	2.50
95 Skarmory U	.20	.35
96 Skarmory U	.20	.35
97 Klink U	.20	.35
98 Vibrava U	.20	.35
99 Flygon HOLO R	1.50	2.00
100 Black Kyurem R	.60	1.00
101 Black Kyurem EX UR	5.00	8.00
102 White Kyurem R	.60	1.00
103 White Kyurem EX UR	4.00	6.00
104 Rattata C	.15	.25
105 Raticate U	.20	.35
106 Meowth C	.15	.25
107 Farfetch'd U	.20	.35
108 Ditto HOLO R	2.50	3.50
109 Snorlax U	.20	.35
110 Togepi C	.15	.25
111 Dunsparce C	.15	.25
112 Taillow C	.15	.25
113 Skitty C	.15	.25
114 Delcatty U	.20	.35
115 Spinda C	.15	.25
116 Buneary C	.15	.25
117 Lopunny U	.20	.35
118 Patrat C	.15	.25
119 Watchog U	.20	.35
120 Lillipup C	.15	.25
121 Herdier U	.20	.35
122 Stoutland HOLO R	.50	.75
123 Pidove C	.15	.25
124 Tranquill U	.20	.35
125 Unfezant R	.20	.35
126 Audino R	.75	1.00
127 Aspertia City Gym U	.20	.35
128 Energy Search C	.15	.25
129 Great Ball U	.20	.35
130 Hugh U	.20	.35
131 Poke Ball C	.15	.25
132 Potion C	.15	.25
133 Rocky Helmet U	.20	.35
134 Skyla U	.20	.35
135 Switch C	.15	.25
136 Town Map U	.20	.35
137 Computer Search UR	20.00	25.00
138 Crystal Edge HOLO R	.50	.75
139 Crystal Wall HOLO R	.75	1.25
140 Gold Potion HOLO R	2.75	3.50
141 Celebi EX Full Art UR	12.00	15.00
142 Keldeo EX Full Art UR	25.00	30.00
143 Cresselia EX Full Art UR	8.00	10.00
144 Landorus EX Full Art UR	13.00	16.00
145 Black Kyurem EX Full Art UR	13.00	16.00
146 White Kyurem EX Full Art UR	15.00	18.00
147 Bianca Full Art UR	16.00	20.00
148 Cheren Full Art UR	8.00	10.00
149 Skyla Full Art UR	18.00	22.00
150 Golurk UR	10.00	13.00
151 Terrakion UR	8.00	11.00
152 Altaria UR	10.00	13.00
153 Rocky Helmet UR	5.00	8.00

2012 Pokemon Black and White Dark Explorers

COMPLETE SET (111)	300.00	400.00
BOOSTER BOX (36 PACKS)	300.00	400.00
BOOSTER PACK (10 CARDS)	8.00	10.00
*REV.FOIL: .75X TO 2X BASIC CARDS		
RELEASED ON MAY 9, 2012		
1 Bulbasaur C	.15	.25
2 Ivysaur U	1.75	3.00
3 Venusaur HOLO R	2.00	3.00
4 Scyther U	.25	.40
5 Carnivine R	.30	.50
6 Leafeon R	.40	.60
7 Dwebble C	.15	.25
8 Crustle U	.15	.25
9 Karrablast C	.15	.25
10 Shelmet C	.15	.25
11 Accelgor R	2.00	3.50
12 Flareon U	.30	.50
13 Entei EX HOLO R	12.00	15.00
14 Torchic C	.15	.25
15 Torchic C	.15	.25
16 Combusken U	.15	.25
17 Blaziken HOLO R	1.25	2.00
18 Torkoal U	.15	.25
19 Heatmor R	.25	.40
20 Larvesta C	.15	.25
21 Larvesta C	.15	.25
22 Volcarona HOLO R	.60	1.00
23 Slowpoke C	.15	.25
24 Slowbro U	.15	.25
25 Vaporeon U	.60	1.00
26 Kyogre EX HOLO R	8.00	10.00
27 Piplup C	.15	.25
28 Prinplup U	.15	.25
29 Empoleon HOLO R	2.00	3.00
30 Glaceon R	.40	.60
31 Tympole C	.15	.25
32 Palpitoad U	.15	.25
33 Vanillite C	.15	.25
34 Vanillish U	.15	.25
35 Ducklett (C)	.15	.25
36 Swanna R	.25	.45
37 Jolteon U	.50	.75
38 Raikou EX HOLO R	15.00	20.00
39 Plusle C	.15	.25
40 Minun C	.15	.25
41 Joltik C	.15	.25
42 Joltik C	.15	.25
43 Galvantula R	.30	.50
44 Tynamo C	.15	.25
45 Tynamo C	.15	.25
46 Eelektrik U	.15	.25
47 Eelektross HOLO R	.60	1.00
48 Espeon R	2.50	4.00
49 Slowking R	.60	1.00
50 Woobat C	.15	.25
51 Yamask U	.15	.25
52 Cofagrigus R	.30	.50
53 Aerodactyl R	.40	.60
54 Groudon EX HOLO R	8.00	12.00
55 Drilbur C	.15	.25
56 Excadrill R	.30	.50
57 Excadrill R	.30	.50
58 Timburr C	.15	.25
59 Gurdurr U	.15	.25
60 Umbreon U	3.00	5.00
61 Umbreon U	3.00	5.00
62 Sableye U	1.00	1.50
63 Darkrai EX HOLO R	3.00	5.00
64 Sandile C	.15	.25
65 Krokorok U	.15	.25
66 Krookodile HOLO R	.40	.75
67 Scraggy C	.15	.25
68 Scrafty R	.25	.40
69 Zorua C	.15	.25
70 Zorua C	.15	.25
71 Zoroark R	.60	1.00
72 Bisharp R	.20	.35
73 Vullaby U	.15	.25
74 Escavalier R	.30	.50
75 Klink C	.15	.25
76 Klang U	.15	.25
77 Klinklang HOLO R	.40	.60
78 Pawniard C	.15	.25
79 Bisharp R	.60	1.00
80 Chansey C	.15	.25
81 Chansey C	.15	.25
82 Blissey HOLO R	.40	.60
83 Eevee C	.15	.25
84 Eevee C	.15	.25
85 Chatot U	.15	.25
86 Lillipup C	.15	.25
87 Herdier U	.15	.25
88 Stoutland R	.30	.50
89 Haxorus HOLO R	.50	.75
90 Tornadus EX HOLO R	4.50	6.50
91 Cheren U	.20	.35
92 Dark Claw U	.20	.35
93 Dark Patch U	.15	.25
94 Enhanced Hammer U	.20	.35
95 Hooligans Jim & Cas U	.15	.25
96 N U	5.00	7.00
97 Old Amber Aerodactyl U	.15	.25
98 Professor Juniper U	.40	.60
99 Random Receiver U	.40	.60
100 Rare Candy U	1.00	1.75
101 Twist Mountain U	.20	.35
102 Ultra Ball U	.60	1.00
103 Entei EX HOLO SR	30.00	35.00
104 Kyogre EX HOLO SR	18.00	22.00
105 Raikou EX HOLO SR	25.00	35.00
106 Groudon EX HOLO SR	20.00	25.00
107 Darkrai EX HOLO SR	40.00	50.00
108 Tornadus EX HOLO SR	10.00	15.00
109 Gardevoir UR	20.00	30.00
110 Archeops UR	25.00	35.00
111 Pokemon Catcher UR	10.00	20.00

2012 Pokemon Black and White Dragons Exalted

COMPLETE SET (128)	225.00	300.00
BOOSTER BOX (36 PACKS)	100.00	120.00
BOOSTER PACK (10 CARDS)	3.00	5.00
*REV.FOIL: .75X TO 2X BASIC CARDS		
RELEASED ON AUGUST 15, 2012		
1 Hoppip C	.05	.15
2 Skiploom U	.15	.25
3 Jumpluff R	.25	.40
4 Yanma C	.05	.15
5 Yanmega R	.25	.40
6 Wurmple C	.05	.15
7 Silcoon U	.15	.25
8 Beautifly R	.25	.40
9 Cascoon U	.15	.25
10 Nincada C	.05	.15
11 Ninjask U	.15	.25
12 Roselia U	.15	.25
13 Roselia C	.05	.15
14 Roserade U	.15	.25
15 Roserade R	.25	.40
16 Maractus U	.15	.25
17 Foongus C	.05	.15
18 Vulpix C	.05	.15
19 Ninetales HOLO R	.75	1.25
20 Magmar C	.05	.15
21 Magmortar R	.25	.40
22 Ho-Oh EX UR	10.00	13.00
23 Magikarp C	.05	.15
24 Gyarados R	.25	.40
25 Wailmer U	.20	.35
26 Wailord HOLO R	1.50	2.00
27 Feebas C	.05	.15
28 Milotic HOLO R	.60	1.00
29 Spheal (C)	.05	.15
30 Sealeo U	.15	.25
31 Walrein R	.25	.40
32 Buizel C	.05	.15
33 Floatzel U	.15	.25

34 Tympole C	.05	.15
35 Palpitoad U	.15	.25
36 Seismitoad R	.30	.50
37 Alomomola R	.25	.40
38 Mareep C	.05	.15
39 Flaaffy U	.15	.25
40 Ampharos HOLO R	.60	1.00
41 Electrike C	.05	.15
42 Electrike C	.05	.15
43 Manectric R	.40	.60
44 Manectric R	.25	.40
45 Emolga U	.15	.25
46 Mew EX UR	15.00	20.00
47 Dustox R	.25	.40
48 Shedinja R	.25	.40
49 Drifloon C	.05	.15
50 Drifloon C	.05	.15
51 Drifblim R	.40	.60
52 Sigilyph HOLO R	.75	1.25
53 Trubbish C	.05	.15
54 Garbodor HOLO R	.75	1.25
55 Gothita C	.05	.15
56 Gothorita U	.15	.25
57 Gothitelle R	.25	.40
58 Golett C	.05	.15
59 Golurk HOLO R	.30	.50
60 Cubone C	.05	.15
61 Marowak R	.25	.40
62 Nosepass C	.05	.15
63 Baltoy C	.05	.15
64 Claydol R	.25	.40
65 Roggenrola C	.05	.15
66 Boldore U	.15	.25
67 Gigalith HOLO R	.40	.60
68 Throh U	.15	.25
69 Sawk U	.15	.25
70 Stunfisk U	.15	.25
71 Terrakion EX UR	4.00	6.00
72 Murkrow C	.05	.15
73 Honchkrow R	.25	.40
74 Houndour C	.05	.15
75 Houndoom R	.25	.40
76 Stunky C	.05	.15
77 Skuntank U	.15	.25
78 Aron C	.05	.15
79 Lairon U	.15	.25
80 Aggron HOLO R	.60	1.00
81 Registeel EX UR	5.00	7.00
82 Probopass R	.25	.40
83 Durant U	.15	.25
84 Altaria HOLO R	1.25	2.00
85 Rayquaza EX UR	2.00	3.50
86 Gible C	.05	.15
87 Gible C	.05	.15
88 Gabite U	.15	.25
89 Gabite U	.40	.60
90 Garchomp HOLO R	1.00	1.25
91 Garchomp R	.40	.60
92 Giratina EX UR	5.00	7.00
93 Deino C	.05	.15
94 Deino C	.05	.15
95 Zweilous U	.15	.25
96 Zweilous U	.15	.25
97 Hydreigon HOLO R	.75	1.00
98 Hydreigon R	.40	.60
99 Aipom C	.05	.15
100 Ambipom R	.25	.40
101 Slakoth C	.05	.15
102 Vigoroth U	.15	.25
103 Slaking HOLO R	.50	.75
104 Swablu U	.15	.25
105 Swablu C	.05	.15
106 Bidoof C	.05	.15
107 Bibarel U	.15	.25
108 Audino U	.15	.25
109 Minccino C	.05	.15
110 Bouffalant U	.30	.50
111 Rufflet C	.05	.15
112 Braviary R	.25	.40
113 Devolution Spray U	.20	.35
114 Giant Cape U	.15	.25
115 Rescue Scarf U	.15	.25
116 Tool Scrapper U	.20	.35
117 Blend Energy GFPD U	1.25	1.75
118 Blend Energy WLFM U	.75	1.00
119 Ho-oh EX Full Art UR	20.00	25.00
120 Mew EX Full Art UR	40.00	50.00
121 Terrakion EX Full Art UR	7.00	9.00
122 Registeel EX Full Art UR	8.00	12.00
123 Rayquaza EX Full Art UR	18.00	22.00
124 Giratina EX Full Art UR	14.00	20.00
125 Serperior UR	10.00	12.00
126 Reuniclus UR	8.00	10.00
127 Krookodile UR	12.00	15.00
128 Rayquaza UR	20.00	25.00

2012 Pokemon Black and White Next Destinies

COMPLETE SET (105)	175.00	260.00
BOOSTER BOX (36 PACKS)	100.00	120.00
BOOSTER PACK (10 CARDS)	3.00	5.00
*REV.FOIL: .75X TO 2X BASIC CARDS		
RELEASED ON FEBRUARY 8, 2012		
1 Pinsir R	.40	.60
2 Seedot C	.05	.15
3 Kricketot C	.05	.15
4 Kricketune U	.05	.15
5 Shaymin EX HOLO R	2.00	3.50
6 Pansage C	.05	.15
7 Simisage R	.20	.35
8 Foongus (C)	.05	.15
9 Amoonguss R	.40	.60
10 Growlithe C	.05	.15
11 Growlithe C	.05	.15
12A Arcanine R	.60	1.00
12B Arcanine STAFF	10.00	20.00
13 Arcanine U	.05	.15
14 Moltres HOLO R	.75	1.25
15 Pansear C	.05	.15
16 Simisear R	.20	.35
17 Darumaka C	.05	.15
18 Litwick C	.05	.15
19 Lampent U	.05	.15
20 Chandelure HOLO R	.50	.75
21 Reshiram R	.60	1.00
22 Reshiram EX HOLO R	3.00	5.00
23 Staryu C	.05	.15
24 Starmie U	.05	.15
25 Lapras R	.25	.40
26 Lapras U	.05	.15
27 Articuno HOLO R	.50	.75
28 Panpour C	.05	.15
29 Simipour R	.30	.50
30 Basculin U	.05	.15
31 Vanillite C	.05	.15
32 Vanillish U	.05	.15
33 Vanilluxe HOLO R	.40	.60
34 Frillish U	.05	.15
35 Jellicent R	.20	.35
36 Cubchoo C	.05	.15
37 Beartic R	.25	.40
38 Kyurem EX HOLO R	2.50	4.00
39 Pikachu C	.05	.15
40 Raichu U	.20	.35
41 Zapdos HOLO R	.60	1.00
42 Shinx C	.05	.15
43 Shinx C	.05	.15
44 Luxio U	.05	.15
45 Luxio U	.05	.15
46 Luxray HOLO R	.60	1.00
47 Blitzle C	.05	.15
48 Zebstrika R	.25	.40
49 Emolga U	.05	.15
50 Zekrom R	1.25	2.00
51 Zekrom EX HOLO R	3.00	5.00
52 Grimer C	.05	.15
53 Muk R	.40	.60
54 Mewtwo EX HOLO R	3.00	5.00
54B Mewtwo EX HOLO JUMBO	4.00	10.00
55 Ralts C	.05	.15
56 Kirlia U	.05	.15
57 Gardevoir HOLO R	1.25	2.00
58 Munna C	.05	.15
59 Musharna R	.30	.50
60 Darmanitan R	.25	.40
61 Elgyem C	.05	.15
62 Beheeyem R	.20	.35
63 Riolu C	.05	.15
64 Lucario HOLO R	.60	1.00
65 Hippopotas C	.05	.15
66 Hippowdon U	.05	.15
67 Mienfoo C	.05	.15
68 Mienshao U	.05	.15
69 Sneasel C	.05	.15
70 Weavile R	.25	.40
71 Nuzleaf U	.05	.15
72 Shiftry R	.60	1.00
73 Scraggy U	.05	.15
74 Scrafty HOLO R	.30	.50
75 Bronzor C	.05	.15
76 Bronzong R	.30	.50
77 Ferroseed C	.05	.15
78 Jigglypuff U	.05	.15
79 Wigglytuff R	.25	.40
80 Meowth C	.05	.15
81 Persian R	.20	.35
82 Regigigas EX HOLO R	3.00	5.00
83 Pidove C	.05	.15
84 Minccino U	.05	.15
85 Cinccino HOLO R	.40	.60
86 Cilan U	.15	.25
87 Exp. Share U	.05	.15
88 Heavy Ball U	.05	.15
89 Level Ball U	.40	.60
90 Pokemon Center U	.05	.15
91 Skyarrow Bridge U	.05	.15
92 Double Colorless Energy U	1.25	2.00
93 Prism Energy U	.60	1.00
94 Shaymin EX HOLO SR	6.00	10.00
95 Reshiram EX HOLO SR	10.00	15.00
96 Kyurem EX HOLO SR	5.00	8.00
97 Zekrom EX HOLO SR	15.00	20.00
98 Mewtwo EX HOLO SR	30.00	35.00
99 Regigigas EX HOLO SR	15.00	20.00
100 Emboar UR	10.00	13.00
101 Chandelure UR	8.00	11.00
102 Zoroark UR	20.00	25.00
103 Hydreigon UR	10.00	15.00

2012 Pokemon Dragon Vault

COMPLETE SET	20.00	40.00
PROMO CARDS ISSUED ONE PER BLISTER PACK		
1 Dratini	.40	.75
2 Dratini	.40	.75
3 Dragonair	.40	.75
4 Dragonair	.60	1.00
5 Dragonite	.60	1.00
6 Bagon	.40	.75
7 Shelgon	.40	.75
8 Salamence	.75	1.00
9a Latias	.75	1.25
9b Latias PROMO	.40	.75
10a Latios	1.00	1.50
10b Latios PROMO	.40	.75
11a Rayquaza	2.00	3.00
11b Rayquaza PROMO	.40	.75
12 Axew	.40	.75
13 Axew	.40	.75
14 Fraxure	.40	.75
15 Fraxure	.40	.75
16b Haxorus	1.00	1.50
16a Haxorus PROMO	.40	.75
17b Druddigon	.40	.75
17a Druddigon PROMO	.40	.75
18 Exp. Share	.40	.75
19 First Ticket	.40	.75
20 Super Rod	4.00	6.00
21 Kyurem	6.00	10.00
NNO Code Card	.40	.75

2013 Pokemon Black and White Legendary Treasures

COMPLETE SET (115)	125.00	170.00
BOOSTER BOX (36 PACKS)	100.00	120.00
BOOSTER PACK (10 CARDS)	3.00	5.00
*REV.FOIL: .75X TO 2X BASIC CARDS		
RELEASED ON NOVEMBER 8, 2013		
1 Tangela C	.05	.15
2 Tangrowth R	.20	.35
3 Shuckle U	.05	.15
4 Cherubi U	.05	.15
5 Carnivine U	.05	.15
6 Snivy C	.05	.15
7 Servine U	.05	.15
8 Serperior HOLO R	.40	.60
9 Sewaddle C	.05	.15
10 Sewaddle C	.05	.15
11 Swadloon U	.05	.15
12 Leavanny HOLO R	.40	.60
13 Dwebble C	.05	.15
14 Crustle U	.05	.15
15 Virizion HOLO R	.40	.60
16 Genesect HOLO R	.50	.75
17 Charmander C	.05	.15
18 Charmeleon U	.20	.35
19 Charizard HOLO R	4.00	5.00
20 Vulpix C	.05	.15
21 Ninetales R	.20	.35
22 Moltres HOLO R	1.25	1.75
23 Victini HOLO R	.50	.75
24 Victini EX UR	3.00	3.50
25 Tepig C	.05	.15
26 Pignite U	.05	.15
27 Emboar HOLO R	.60	1.00
28 Reshiram HOLO R	.50	.75
29 Reshiram EX UR	3.50	4.15
30 Magikarp C	.05	.15
31 Gyarados R	.30	.50
32 Articuno HOLO R	.40	.60
33 Piplup C	.05	.15
34 Prinplup U	.05	.15
35 Empoleon R	.20	.35
36 Phione R	.20	.35
37 Oshawott C	.05	.15
38 Dewott U	.05	.15
39 Samurott HOLO R	.50	.75
40 Tympole C	.05	.15
41 Palpitoad U	.05	.15
42 Seismitoad R	.20	.35
43 Kyurem HOLO R	.50	.75
44 Kyurem EX UR	3.00	4.00
45 Keldeo EX UR	3.50	4.25
46 Zapdos HOLO R	.60	1.00
47 Plusle U	.05	.15
48 Minun U	.05	.15
49 Emolga U	.05	.15
50 Thundurus HOLO R	.30	.50
51 Zekrom HOLO R	.60	1.00
52 Zekrom EX UR	4.50	5.50
53 Mewtwo HOLO R	3.00	3.50
54 Mewtwo EX UR	3.50	4.25
55 Natu C	.05	.15
56 Xatu R	.20	.35
57 Misdreavus C	.05	.15
58 Mismagius R	.20	.35
59 Ralts C	.05	.15
60 Kirlia U	.05	.15
61 Sableye U	.05	.15
62 Croagunk C	.05	.15
63 Toxicraok R	.20	.35
64 Woobat C	.05	.15
65 Swoobat U	.05	.15
66 Sigilyph HOLO R	.75	1.15
67 Trubbish C	.05	.15
68 Garbodor HOLO R	.50	.75
69 Gothita C	.05	.15
70 Gothita C	.05	.15
71 Gothorita U	.05	.15
72 Gothitelle HOLO R	.30	.50
73 Solosis C	.05	.15
74 Solosis C	.05	.15
75 Duosion U	.05	.15
76 Reuniclus R	.20	.35
77 Chandelure EX HOLO R	4.75	5.50
78 Meloetta HOLO R	.60	1.00
79 Riolu U	.05	.15
80 Lucario HOLO R	.30	.50
81 Gallade R	.20	.35
82 Excadrill EX HOLO R	2.75	3.50
83 Stunfisk U	.05	.15
84 Terrakion HOLO R	.50	.75
85 Landorus HOLO R	.30	.50
86 Meloetta R	.20	.35
87 Spiritomb U	.05	.15
88 Darkrai EX UR	3.25	4.00
89 Zorua C	.05	.15
90 Zoroark HOLO R	.40	.60
91 Cobalion HOLO R	.60	1.00
92 Altaria U	.05	.15
93 Rayquaza HOLO R	1.00	1.50
94 Gible C	.05	.15
95 Gabite U	.05	.15
96 Garchomp HOLO R	.40	.60
97 Deino C	.05	.15
98 Zweilous U	.05	.15
99 Hydreigon HOLO R	.50	.75
100 Black Kyurem EX UR	5.50	7.00
101 White Kyurem EX UR	4.00	5.00
102 Lugia EX UR	3.00	4.00
103 Swablu C	.05	.15
104 Minccino C	.05	.15
105 Cinccino HOLO R	.40	.60
106 Druddigon U	.05	.15
107 Bouffalant U	.05	.15
108 Tornadus HOLO R	.40	.60
109 Bianca U	.05	.15
110 Cedric Juniper U	.05	.15
111 Crushing Hammer U	.30	.50
112 Energy Switch U	.05	.15
113 Double Colorless Energy U	1.25	1.75
114 Reshiram Full Art UR	25.00	30.00
115 Zekrom Full Art UR	30.00	40.00

2013 Pokemon Black and White Legendary Treasures Radiant Collection

COMPLETE SET (25)	8.00	20.00
RELEASED ON NOVEMBER 3, 2013		
RC1 Snivy C	.10	.25
RC2 Servine C	.10	.25
RC3 Serperior U	.15	.40
RC4 Growlithe U	.15	.40
RC5 Torchic C	.10	.25
RC6 Piplup U	.15	.40
RC7 Pikachu U	.25	.60
RC8 Ralts C	.10	.25
RC9 Kirlia C	.10	.25
RC10 Gardevoir U	.15	.40
RC11 Meloetta EX UR	1.25	3.00
RC12 Stunfisk U	.15	.40
RC13 Purrloin U	.15	.40
RC14 Eevee U	.15	.40
RC15 Teddiursa C	.10	.25
RC16 Ursaring C	.10	.25
RC17 Audino C	.10	.25
RC18 Minccino C	.10	.25
RC19 Cinccino U	.15	.40
RC20 Elesa C	.10	.25
RC21 Shaymin EX Full Art UR	1.50	4.00
RC22 Reshiram Full Art UR	2.00	5.00
RC23 Emolga Full Art UR	1.50	4.00
RC24 Mew EX Full Art UR	5.00	10.00
RC25 Meloetta EX Full Art UR	2.00	5.00

2013 Pokemon Black and White Plasma Blast

COMPLETE SET (105)	190.00	170.00
BOOSTER BOX (36 PACKS)	100.00	120.00
BOOSTER PACK (10 CARDS)	3.00	5.00
*REV.FOIL: .75X TO 2X BASIC CARDS		
RELEASED ON AUGUST 14, 2013		
1 Surskit C	.05	.15
2 Masquerain R	.20	.35
3 Lileep U	.05	.15
4 Cradily R	.40	.75
5 Tropius U	.05	.15
6 Karrablast C	.05	.15
7 Shelmet C	.05	.15
8 Accelgor R	.20	.35
9 Virizion EX UR	7.00	9.00
10 Genesect R	.40	.60
11 Genesect EX UR	5.00	7.00
12 Larvesta C	.05	.15
13 Volcarona R	.20	.35
14 Squirtle C	.05	.15
15 Wartortle U	.50	.75
16 Blastoise HOLO R	2.75	4.00
17 Lapras C	.05	.15
18 Remoraid C	.05	.15
19 Octillery U	.05	.15
20 Suicune R	1.25	1.75
21 Snorunt C	.05	.15
22 Glalie U	.05	.15
23 Froslass R	.20	.35
24 Relicanth U	.05	.15
25 Snover C	.05	.15
26 Abomasnow U	.20	.30
27 Tirtouga U	.05	.15
28 Carracosta R	.40	.60
29 Ducklett C	.05	.15
30 Kyurem EX HOLO R	2.75	4.00
31 Tynamo C	.05	.15
32 Eelektrik U	.05	.15
33 Eelektross HOLO R	.60	1.00
34 Drifloon C	.05	.15
35 Drifblim R	.20	.35
36 Uxie R	.20	.35
37 Mesprit HOLO R	.60	1.00
38 Azelf R	.20	.35
39 Munna C	.05	.15
40 Musharna U	.05	.15
41 Sigilyph HOLO R	.40	.75
42 Solosis C	.05	.15
43 Duosion U	.05	.15
44 Reuniclus (R)	.20	.35
45 Golett C	.05	.15
46 Golurk HOLO R	.40	.60
47 Machop C	.05	.15
48 Machoke U	.05	.15
49 Machamp HOLO R	.60	1.00
50 Machamp R	.20	.35
51 Throh C	.05	.15
52 Sawk C	.05	.15
53 Archen U	.05	.15
54 Archeops HOLO R	.25	.60
55 Houndour C	.05	.15
56 Houndoom HOLO R	.40	.75
57 Aron C	.05	.15
58 Lairon U	.25	.40
59 Aggron R	.40	.60
60 Jirachi EX UR	13.00	18.00
61 Escavalier R	.20	.35

62 Bagon C	.05	.15
63 Shelgon U	.05	.15
64 Salamence HOLO R	.60	1.00
65 Dialga EX UR	3.00	5.00
66 Palkia EX UR	2.00	3.00
67 Axew C	.05	.15
68 Fraxure U	.20	.35
69 Haxorus HOLO R	.50	.75
70 Druddigon C	.05	.15
71 Kangaskhan C	.05	.15
72 Porygon C	.05	.15
73 Porygon2 U	.05	.15
74 Porygon-Z HOLO R	.40	.75
75 Teddiursa C	.05	.15
76 Ursaring U	.05	.15
77 Chatot U	.05	.15
78 Caitlin U	.05	.15
79 Cover Fossil U	.05	.15
80 Energy Retrieval U	.20	.30
81 Iris U	.05	.15
82 Plume Fossil U	.05	.15
83 PokÃ©mon Catcher U	.25	.40
84 Professor Juniper U	.50	.75
85 Rare Candy U	1.25	2.00
86 Reversal Trigger U	.05	.15
87 Root Fossil Lileep U	.05	.15
88 Silver Bangle U	.15	.25
89 Silver Mirror U	.05	.15
90 Ultra Ball U	.75	1.15
91 Plasma Energy U	.20	.30
92 G Booster HOLO R	2.00	5.00
93 G Scope HOLO R	1.00	2.50
94 Master Ball HOLO R	2.00	5.00
95 Scoop Up Cyclone HOLO R	1.50	4.00
96 Virizion EX Full Art UR	10.00	13.00
97 Genesect EX Full Art UR	12.00	15.00
98 Jirachi EX Full Art UR	24.00	27.00
99 Dialga EX Full Art UR	10.00	12.00
100 Palkia EX Full Art UR	8.00	10.00
101 Iris Full Art UR	8.00	10.00
102 Exeggcute UR	15.00	25.00
103 Virizion UR	10.00	17.00
104 Dusknoir UR	6.00	12.00
105 Rare Candy UR	30.00	40.00

2013 Pokemon Black and White Plasma Freeze

COMPLETE SET (122)	400.00	525.00
BOOSTER BOX (36 PACKS)	150.00	200.00
BOOSTER PACK (10 CARDS)	4.00	6.00
*REV.FOIL: .75X TO 2X BASIC CARDS		
RELEASED ON MAY 8, 2013		
1 Weedle C	.05	.15
2 Kakuna U	.05	.15
3 Beedrill R	.40	.60
4 Exeggcute U	1.00	2.00
5 Exeggutor R	1.00	1.50
6 Treecko C	.05	.15
7 Grovyle U	.05	.15
8 Sceptile HOLO R	.40	1.00
9 Cacnea C	.05	.15
10 Cacturne R	.20	.35
11 Leafeon R	2.00	3.00
12 Flareon U	2.00	3.00
13 Heatran EX HOLO R	3.00	4.50
14 Litwick C	.05	.15
15 Lampent U	.05	.15
16 Chandelure HOLO R	.60	1.50
17 Reshiram HOLO R	.40	1.00
18 Horsea C	.05	.15
19 Seadra U	.05	.15
20 Vaporeon U	.30	.50
21 Wooper C	.05	.15
22 Quagsire R	.25	.40
23 Glaceon R	1.00	1.50
24 Tympole C	.05	.15
25 Palpitoad U	.05	.15
26 Seismitoad R	.25	.40
27 Vanillite C	.05	.15
28 Vanillish U	.05	.15
29 Vanilluxe R	.30	.50
30 Cryogonal U	.05	.15
31 Kyurem HOLO R	4.00	10.00
32 Voltorb C	.05	.15
33 Electrode HOLO R	.40	1.00
34 Jolteon U	.40	.75
35 Chinchou C	.05	.15
36 Lanturn U	.05	.15
37 Pachirisu C	.05	.15
38 Thundurus EX HOLO R	2.00	3.00
39 Zekrom HOLO R	.40	1.00
40 Nidoran F C	.05	.15
41 Nidorina U	.05	.15
42 Nidoqueen R	.20	.35
43 Nidoran M C	.05	.15
44 Nidorino U	.05	.15
45 Grimer C	.05	.15
46 Muk R	.40	.60
47 Mr. Mime R	1.00	2.00
48 Espeon U	.75	1.25
49 Sableye R	.25	.40
50 Beldum C	.05	.15
51 Metang U	.05	.15
52 Metagross HOLO R	.30	.75
53 Deoxys EX HOLO R	3.00	4.00
54 Yamask C	.05	.15
55 Yamask C	.05	.15
56 Cofagrigus HOLO R	.30	.75
57 Cofagrigus R	.20	.35
58 Nidoking R	.60	1.00
59 Mankey C	.05	.15
60 Primeape C	.05	.15
61 Onix U	.20	.35
62 Makuhita C	.05	.15
63 Hariyama R	.30	.50
64 Umbreon HOLO R	4.00	6.00
65 Sneasel (C)	.05	.15
66 Weavile R	.50	.75
67 Absol HOLO R	1.25	3.00
68 Sandile C	.05	.15
69 Krokorok U	.05	.15
70 Krookodile R	.30	.50
71 Pawniard C	.05	.15
72 Pawniard C	.05	.15
73 Bisharp R	.40	.60
74 Bisharp U	.05	.15
75 Deino C	.05	.15
76 Deino C	.05	.15
77 Zweilous U	.05	.15
78 Hydreigon HOLO R	.30	.75
79 Steelix R	.60	1.00
80 Mawile U	.05	.15
81 Dratini C	.05	.15
82 Dragonair U	.25	.40
83 Dragonite HOLO R	.60	1.50
84 Kingdra HOLO R	.60	1.50
85 Latias EX HOLO R	4.00	5.50
86 Latios EX HOLO R	3.00	4.00
87 Rattata C	.05	.15
88 Raticate R	.20	.35
89 Eevee C	.20	.35
90 Eevee C	.20	.35
91 Hoothoot C	.05	.15
92 Noctowl U	.05	.15
93 Miltank U	.05	.15
94 Kecleon R	.30	.50
95 Starly C	.05	.15
96 Staravia U	.05	.15
97 Staraptor R	.40	.75
98 Tornadus EX HOLO R	2.50	4.00
99 Float Stone U	3.00	4.00
100 Frozen City U	.15	.25
101 Ghetsis HOLO R	1.50	4.00
102 Shadow Triad U	.15	.25
103 Superior Energy Retrieval U	.60	1.00
104 Team Plasma Badge U	.05	.15
105 Team Plasma Ball U	.15	.25
106 Plasma Energy U	.20	.35
107 Life Dew HOLO R	4.00	6.00
108 Rock Guard HOLO R	4.00	6.00
109 Heatran EX HOLO SR	4.75	6.00
110 Thundurus EX HOLO SR	4.50	6.00
111 Deoxys EX HOLO SR	8.00	10.00
112 Latias EX HOLO SR	14.00	18.00
113 Latios EX HOLO SR	8.00	11.00
114 Tornadus EX HOLO SR	4.00	5.50
115 Ghetsis HOLO SR	10.00	12.00
116 Professor Juniper HOLO SR	18.00	22.00
117 Empoleon UR	20.00	25.00
118 Sigilyph UR	10.00	13.00
119 Garbodor UR	14.00	18.00
120 Garchomp UR	14.00	18.00
121 Max Potion UR	35.00	50.00
122 Ultra Ball UR	180.00	200.00

2013 Pokemon Black and White Plasma Storm

COMPLETE SET (138)	100.00	250.00
BOOSTER BOX (36 PACKS)	200.00	250.00
BOOSTER PACK (10 CARDS)	6.00	8.00
*REV.FOIL: .75X TO 2X BASIC CARDS		
RELEASED ON FEBRUARY 6, 2013		
1 Turtwig C	.15	.25
2 Grotle U	.05	.15
3 Torterra R	.30	.75
4 Combee C	.05	.15
5 Vespiquen R	.30	.75
6 Cherubi C	.05	.15
7 Cherrim R	.30	.75
8 Sewaddle C	.05	.15
9 Swadloon U	.05	.15
10 Leavanny R	.30	.75
11 Maractus U	.05	.15
12 Foongus C	.05	.15
13 Amoonguss U	.05	.15
14 Moltres EX UR	4.00	8.00
15 Chimchar C	.05	.15
16 Monferno U	.05	.15
17 Infernape HOLO R	.75	2.00
18 Victini EX UR	4.00	6.00
19 Pansear (C)	.05	.15
20 Simisear U	.05	.15
21 Litwick C	.05	.15
22 Lampent U	.05	.15
23 Heatmor U	.05	.15
24 Squirtle C	.05	.15
25 Articuno EX UR	6.00	10.00
26 Swinub C	.05	.15
27 Piloswine U	.05	.15
28 Mamoswine R	.30	.75
29 Lotad C	.05	.15
30 Lombre U	.05	.15
31 Ludicolo R	.30	.75
32 Carvanha C	.05	.15
33 Sharpedo R	.30	.75
34 Manaphy HOLO R	.60	1.50
35 Vanillite C	.05	.15
36 Vanillish U	.05	.15
37 Vanilluxe R	.30	.75
38 Frillish C	.05	.15
39 Jellicent R	.30	.75
40 Cubchoo C	.05	.15
41 Beartic R	.30	.75
42 Magnemite C	.05	.15
43 Magnemite C	.05	.15
44 Magneton U	.05	.15
45 Magneton U	.05	.15
46 Magnezone HOLO R	.50	1.50
47 Magnezone R	.30	.75
48 Zapdos EX UR	5.00	8.00
49 Rotom U	.05	.15
50 Joltik C	.05	.15
51 Galvantula U	.05	.15
52 Zubat C	.05	.15
53 Zubat C	.50	.75
54 Golbat U	.05	.15
55 Crobat HOLO R	.75	2.00
56 Koffing C	.05	.15
57 Koffing U	.05	.15
58 Weezing HOLO R	.60	1.50
59 Ralts C	.05	.15
60 Kirlia U	.05	.15
61 Gallade HOLO R	.60	1.50
62 Giratina R	.40	1.00
63 Trubbish U	.05	.15
64 Trubbish C	.05	.15
65 Trubbish C	.25	.40
66 Garbodor HOLO R	.40	1.00
67 Garbodor R	.30	.75
68 Elgyem C	.05	.15
69 Elgyem U	.05	.15
70 Beheeyem R	.30	.75
71 Phanpy C	.20	.35
72 Donphan U	.05	.15
73 Lunatone U	.05	.15
74 Solrock U	.05	.15
75 Riolu C	.05	.15
76 Riolu C	.05	.15
77 Lucario U	.05	.15
78 Lucario HOLO R	.60	1.50
79 Timburr C	.05	.15
80 Gurdurr U	.05	.15
81 Conkeldurr R	.30	.75
82 Purrloin C	.05	.15
83 Purrloin C	.05	.15
84 Liepard R	.30	.75
85 Scraggy C	.05	.15
86 Scrafty R	.30	.75
87 Skarmory R	.30	.75
88 Klink C	.15	.25
89 Klang U	.05	.15
90 Klinklang HOLO R	.50	1.50
91 Durant U	.05	.15
92 Durant U	.05	.15
93 Cobalion EX UR	2.00	5.00
94 Druddigon R	.30	.75
95 Black Kyurem EX HOLO R	14.00	20.00
96 White Kyurem EX UR	4.00	8.00
97 Clefairy C	.05	.15
98 Clefable R	.30	.75
99 Doduo C	.05	.15
100 Dodrio R	.30	.75
101 Snorlax R	.40	1.00
102 Togepi C	.05	.15
103 Togetic U	.05	.15
104 Togekiss HOLO R	.60	1.50
105 Whismur C	.05	.15
106 Loudred U	.05	.15
107 Exploud R	.30	.75
108 Lugia EX UR	3.00	6.00
109 Skitty C	.05	.15
110 Patrat C	.05	.15
111 Patrat C	.05	.15
112 Watchog U	.05	.15
113 Watchog R	.30	.75
114 Bouffalant R	.30	.75
115 Rufflet C	.05	.15
116 Braviary R	.30	.75
117 Bicycle U	.05	.15
118 Colress U	.05	.15
119 Colress Machine U	.05	.15
120 Escape Rope U	.05	.15
121 Ether U	.05	.15
122 Eviolite U	.05	.15
123 Hypnotoxic Laser U	.05	.15
124 Plasma Frigate U	.05	.15
125 Team Plasma Grunt U	.05	.15
126 Virbank City Gym U	.05	.15
127 Plasma Energy U	.05	.15
128 Dowsing Machine HOLO R	2.00	4.00
129 Scramble Switch HOLO R	2.00	5.00
130 Victory Piece HOLO R	.50	2.00
131 Victini EX Full Art UR	8.00	12.00
132 Articuno EX Full Art UR	10.00	15.00
133 Cobalion EX Full Art UR	5.00	10.00
134 Lugia EX Full Art UR	8.00	12.00
135 Colress Full Art UR	8.00	15.00
136 Charizard UR	60.00	80.00
137 Blastoise UR	35.00	45.00
138 Random Receiver UR	10.00	15.00

2014 Pokemon XY

COMPLETE SET (146)	130.00	170.00
BOOSTER BOX (36 PACKS)	100.00	120.00
BOOSTER PACK (10 CARDS)	3.00	5.00
*REV.FOIL: .75X TO 2X BASIC CARDS		
RELEASED ON FEBRUARY 5, 2014		
1 Venusaur EX UR	2.00	3.00
2 M Venusaur EX UR	11.00	13.00
3 Weedle C	.10	.20
4 Kakuna U	.05	.15
5 Beedrill R	.30	.50
6 Ledyba C	.05	.15
7 Ledian U	.05	.15
8 Volbeat U	.05	.15
9 Illumise U	.05	.15
10 Pansage C	.05	.15
11 Simisage R	.20	.30
12 Chespin C	.05	.15
13 Quilladin U	.15	.25
14 Chesnaught HOLO R	.50	.75
15 Scatterbug C	.05	.15
16 Spewpa U	.05	.15
17 Vivillon HOLO R	.40	.60
18 Skiddo C	.05	.15
19 Gogoat HOLO R	.30	.50
20 Slugma C	.05	.15
21 Magcargo R	.25	.30
22 Pansear C	.05	.15
23 Simisear R	.20	.30
24 Fennekin C	.05	.15
25 Braixen U	.15	.25
26 Delphox HOLO R	1.25	2.00
27 Fletchinder U	.05	.15
28 Talonflame HOLO R	.40	.60
29 Blastoise EX UR	3.00	4.00
30 M Blastoise EX UR	13.00	15.00
31 Shellder C	.05	.15
32 Cloyster R	.20	.30
33 Staryu C	.05	.15
34 Starmie R	.20	.30
35 Lapras HOLO R	.75	1.00
36 Corsola U	.05	.15
37 Panpour C	.05	.15
38 Simipour R	.20	.30
39 Froakie C	.05	.15
40 Frogadier U	.05	.15
41 Greninja HOLO R	2.00	3.00
42 Pikachu C	.20	.30
43 Raichu HOLO R	1.25	2.00
44 Voltorb C	.05	.15
45 Electrode U	.05	.15
46 Emolga EX UR	2.00	3.00
47 Ekans C	.05	.15
48 Arbok R	.20	.30
49 Spoink C	.05	.15
50 Grumpig R	.20	.30
51 Venipede C	.05	.15
52 Whirlipede (U)	.05	.15
53 Scolipede R	.20	.30
54 Phantump C	.20	.30
55 Trevenant HOLO R	8.00	9.00
56 Pumpkaboo C	.05	.15
57 Gourgeist HOLO R	.40	.60
58 Diglett C	.05	.15
59 Dugtrio R	.20	.30
60 Rhyhorn C	.05	.15
61 Rhydon R	.20	.30
62 Rhyperior HOLO R	.40	.60
63 Lunatone U	.05	.15
64 Solrock U	.05	.15
65 Timburr C	.05	.15
66 Gurdurr U	.05	.15
67 Conkeldurr R	.20	.30
68 Sableye U	.10	.20
69 Sandile C	.05	.15
70 Krokorok U	.05	.15
71 Krookodile R	.20	.30
72 Zorua C	.05	.15
73 Zoroark HOLO R	.40	.60
74 Inkay U	.05	.15
75 Inkay C	.05	.15
76 Malamar R	.20	.30
77 Malamar R	.20	.30
78 Yveltal R	.75	1.25
79 Yveltal EX UR	5.00	6.00
80 Skarmory EX UR	2.75	3.25
81 Pawniard C	.05	.15
82 Bisharp R	.20	.30
83 Honedge C	.05	.15
84 Doublade U	.10	.20
85 Aegislash R	.25	.40
86 Aegislash HOLO R	.40	.60
87 Jigglypuff C	.05	.15
88 Jigglypuff C	.20	.30
89 Wigglytuff R	.25	.40
90 Wigglytuff R	.25	.40
91 Mr. Mime U	.05	.15
92 Spritzee C	.10	.20
93 Aromatisse HOLO R	4.00	5.00
94 Swirlix C	.05	.15
95 Slurpuff HOLO R	.40	.60
96 Xerneas R	1.75	2.00
97 Xerneas EX UR	3.00	4.00
98 Doduo C	.05	.15
99 Dodrio U	.05	.15
100 Tauros R	.20	.30
101 Dunsparce U	.05	.15
102 Taillow C	.05	.15
103 Swellow R	.20	.30
104 Skitty C	.05	.15
105 Delcatty U	.05	.15
106 Bidoof C	.05	.15
107 Bibarel R	.20	.30
108 Lillipup C	.05	.15
109 Herdier U	.05	.15
110 Stoutland R	.20	.30
111 Bunnelby C	.05	.15
112 Diggersby U	.10	.20
113 Fletchling C	.05	.15
114 Furfrou HOLO R	.30	.50
115 Cassius U	.05	.15
116 Evosoda U	.30	.50
117 Fairy Garden U	.15	.25
118 Great Ball U	.05	.15
119 Hard Charm U	.25	.40
120 Max Revive U	.05	.15
121 Muscle Band U	1.50	2.00
122 Professor Sycamore U	.75	1.25
123 Professor's Letter U	.20	.30
124 Red Card U	.20	.30
125 Roller Skates U	.05	.15
126 Shadow Circle U	.15	.25
127 Shauna U	.20	.30
128 Super Potion U	.05	.15
129 Team Flare Grunt U	.20	.30
130 Double Colorless Energy U	1.50	2.00
131 Rainbow Energy U	.35	.50
132 Grass Energy C	.20	.35
133 Fire Energy C	.30	.50
134 Water Energy C	.30	.50

135 Lightning Energy C .25 .40
136 Psychic Energy C .25 .40
137 Fighting Energy C .25 .40
138 Darkness Energy C .50 .75
139 Metal Energy C .40 .60
140 Fairy Energy C .25 .40
141 Venusaur EX HOLO UR 8.00 10.00
142 Blastoise EX Full Art UR 8.00 11.00
143 Emolga EX HOLO UR 3.00 4.00
144 Yveltal EX HOLO UR 15.00 18.00
145 Skarmory EX HOLO UR 4.00 5.00
146 Xerneas EX HOLO UR 9.00 11.00

2014 Pokemon XY Flashfire

COMPLETE SET (109) 260.00 325.00
BOOSTER BOX (36 PACKS) 100.00 120.00
BOOSTER PACK (10 CARDS) 3.00 5.00
*REV.FOIL: .75X TO 2X BASIC CARDS
RELEASED ON MAY 7, 2014
1 Caterpie C .05 .15
2 Metapod U .05 .15
3 Butterfree R .30 .50
4 Pineco C .05 .15
5 Seedot C .05 .15
6 Nuzleaf U .05 .15
7 Shiftry HOLO R .40 .60
8 Roselia C .05 .15
9 Roserade U .05 .15
10 Maractus U .05 .15
11 Charizard EX HOLO R 3.75 4.50
12 Charizard EX HOLO R 4.50 5.00
13 M Charizard EX HOLO R 35.00 45.00
14 Ponyta C .05 .15
15 Rapidash U .05 .15
16 Torkoal U .05 .15
17 Fletchinder U .05 .15
18 Litleo C .05 .15
19 Litleo C .05 .15
20 Pyroar HOLO R 1.25 2.00
21 Qwilfish R .20 .30
22 Feebas C .05 .15
23 Milotic HOLO R .30 .50
24 Spheal C .05 .15
25 Sealeo U .05 .15
26 Walrein R .20 .35
27 Luvdisc U .05 .15
28 Buizel C .05 .15
29 Floatzel R .20 .30
30 Bergmite C .05 .15
31 Avalugg U .05 .15
32 Shinx C .05 .15
33 Luxio U .05 .15
34 Luxray R .30 .50
35 Magnezone EX HOLO R 2.00 4.00
36 Helioptile C .05 .15
37 Heliolisk R .20 .35
38 Duskull C .05 .15
39 Dusclops U .05 .15
40 Dusknoir HOLO R .30 .50
41 Toxicroak EX HOLO R 2.75 3.25
42 Espurr C .05 .15
43 Meowstic R .30 .50
44 Skrelp C .05 .15
45 Geodude C .05 .15
46 Graveler U .05 .15
47 Golem R .20 .35
48 Binacle C .05 .15
49 Barbaracle R .20 .35
50 Sneasel U .05 .15
51 Sneasel C .05 .15
52 Weavile (R) .20 .35
53 Stunky C .05 .15
54 Stunky C .05 .15
55 Skuntank R .20 .30
56 Sandile C .05 .15
57 Krokorok U .05 .15
58 Scraggy C .05 .15
59 Scrafty R .20 .30
60 Forretress R .40 .60
61 Durant R .20 .35
62 FlabÃ©bÃ© C .05 .15
63 FlabÃ©bÃ© C .05 .15
64 Floette R .25 .40
65 Floette U .05 .15
66 Florges HOLO R .30 .50
67 Spritzee C .05 .15
68 Carbink HOLO R .25 .40
69 M Charizard EX HOLO R 40.00 50.00
70 Druddigon HOLO R .30 .50
71 Dragalge R .30 .50
72 Goomy C .05 .15
73 Sliggoo U .05 .15
74 Goodra HOLO R .30 .50
75 Pidgey C .05 .15
76 Pidgeotto U .05 .15
77 Pidgeot R .20 .35
78 Kangaskhan EX HOLO R 2.75 3.25
79 M Kangaskhan EX HOLO R 6.00 7.00
80 Snorlax R .20 .35
81 Sentret C .05 .15
82 Furret R .20 .30
83 Miltank U .25 .40
84 Buneary C .05 .15
85 Lopunny R .20 .30
86 Fletchling C .05 .15
87 Furfrou U .05 .15
88 Blacksmith U 1.75 2.25
89 Fiery Torch U .15 .25
90 Lysandre U .60 1.00
91 Magnetic Storm U .05 .15
92 Pal Pad U .10 .20
93 PokÃ©mon Center Lady U .20 .35
94 PokÃ©mon Fan Club U .20 .30
95 Protection Cube U .05 .15
96 Sacred Ash U .30 .50
97 Startling Megaphone U .25 .40
98 Trick Shovel U .05 .15
99 Ultra Ball U .60 1.00
100 Charizard EX Full Art UR 12.00 16.00
101 Magnezone EX HOLO UR 3.00 4.00
102 Toxicroak EX HOLO UR 4.00 5.00
103 Kangaskhan EX HOLO UR 4.00 5.00
104 Lysandre Full Art UR 20.00 25.00
105 Pokemon Center Lady Full Art UR 7.50 9.00
106 Pokemon Fan Club Full Art UR 5.00 5.50
107 M Charizard EX UR 40.00 43.00
108 M Charizard EX UR 46.00 52.00
109 M Kangaskhan UR 9.00 11.00

2014 Pokemon XY Furious Fists

COMPLETE SET (113) 120.00 170.00
BOOSTER BOX (36 PACKS) 100.00 120.00
BOOSTER PACK (10 CARDS) 3.00 5.00
*REV.FOIL: .75X TO 2X BASIC CARDS
RELEASED ON AUGUST 13, 2014
1 Bellsprout C .05 .15
2 Weepinbell U .05 .15
3 Victreebel HOLO R .40 .60
4 Heracross EX HOLO R 2.00 3.00
5 MegaHeracross EX HOLO R 4.00 6.00
6 Shroomish C .05 .15
7 Leafeon R .50 .75
8 Shelmet C .05 .15
9 Accelgor U .05 .15
10 Magmar C .05 .15
11 Magmortar R .30 .50
12 Torchic C .05 .15
13 Combusken U .05 .15
14 Blaziken HOLO R .60 1.00
15 Poliwag C .05 .15
16 Poliwhirl U .15 .25
17 Poliwrath HOLO R .50 .75
18 Politoed R .20 .35
19 Glaceon R .60 1.00
20 Seismitoad EX HOLO R 6.00 8.00
21 Cubchoo C .05 .15
22 Beartic R .20 .30
23 Clauncher C .05 .15
24 Clawitzer HOLO R .40 .60
25 Amaura U .05 .15
26 Aurorus R .30 .50
27 Pikachu C .05 .15
28 Raichu U .20 .35
29 Electabuzz C .05 .15
30 Electivire R .30 .50
31 Plusle C .05 .15
32 Minun (C) .05 .15
33 Thundurus R .30 .40
34 Dedenne U .05 .15
35 Drowzee C .05 .15
36 Hypno R .20 .30
37 Jynx R .20 .30
38 Skorupi C .05 .15
39 Gothita C .05 .15
40 Gothorita U .05 .15
41 Gothitelle R .20 .30
42 Golett C .05 .15
43 Golurk R .20 .30
44 Machop C .05 .15
45 Machoke U .05 .15
46 Machamp HOLO R .60 1.00
47 Hitmonlee U .05 .15
48 Hitmonchan U .05 .15
49 Hitmontop U .05 .15
50 Breloom R .15 .25
51 Makuhita C .05 .15
52 Hariyama R .15 .25
53 Trapinch C .05 .15
54 Lucario EX HOLO R 7.00 10.00
55 MegaLucario EX HOLO R 14.00 16.00
56 Mienfoo C .05 .15
57 Mienshao U .05 .15
58 Landorus HOLO R 1.50 2.00
59 Pancham U .05 .15
60 Pancham C .05 .15
61 Tyrunt U .05 .15
62 Tyrantrum R .75 1.00
63 Hawlucha HOLO R .75 1.00
64 Hawlucha EX HOLO R 2.00 5.00
65 Drapion R .20 .30
66 Scraggy C .05 .15
67 Scrafty U .05 .15
68 Pangoro R .20 .35
69 Clefairy C .05 .15
70 Clefairy C .05 .15
71 Clefable U .05 .15
72 Sylveon R 1.50 2.25
73 Klefki U .05 .15
74 Dragonite EX HOLO R 3.00 4.00
75 Vibrava U .05 .15
76 Flygon R .25 .40
77 Noivern HOLO R 1.00 1.25
78 Lickitung C .05 .15
79 Lickilicky U .05 .15
80 Eevee C .20 .30
81 Slakoth C .05 .15
82 Vigoroth U .05 .15
83 Slaking HOLO R .40 .60
84 Patrat C .05 .15
85 Watchog U .05 .15
86 Tornadus R .20 .35
87 Noibat C .05 .15
88 Battle Reporter U .05 .15
89 Energy Switch U .05 .15
90 Fighting Stadium U .20 .35
91 Focus Sash U .15 .25
92 Fossil Researcher U .05 .15
93 Full Heal U .05 .15
94 Jaw Fossil U .05 .15
95 Korrina U .40 .60
96 Maintenance U .05 .15
97 Mountain Ring U .05 .15
98 Sail Fossil U .05 .15
99 Sparkling Robe U .05 .15
100 Super Scoop Up U .50 .75
101 Tool Retriever U .05 .15
102 Training Center U .05 .15
103 Herbal Energy U .20 .30
104 Strong Energy U .75 1.15
105 Heracross HOLO SR 3.00 4.00
106 Seismitoad HOLO SR 9.00 11.00
107 Lucario HOLO SR 10.00 15.00
108 Dragonite HOLO SR 7.00 8.00
109 Battle Reporter HOLO SR 3.00 4.00
110 Fossil Researcher HOLO SR 2.00 3.00
111 Korrina HOLO SR 6.00 8.00
112 MegaHeracross UR 7.00 10.00
113 MegaLucario UR 18.00 23.00

2014 Pokemon XY Phantom Forces

COMPLETE SET (122) 150.00 200.00
BOOSTER BOX (36 PACKS) 100.00 120.00
BOOSTER PACK (10 CARDS) 3.00 5.00
*REV.FOIL: .75X TO 2X BASIC CARDS
RELEASED ON NOVEMBER 5, 2014
1 Venonat C .05 .15
2 Venomoth R .20 .35
3 Yanma C .05 .15
4 Yanmega R .25 .60
5 Sewaddle C .05 .15
6 Swadloon U .05 .15
7 Leavanny R .20 .30
8 Karrablast C .05 .15
9 Fletchinder U .05 .15
10 Talonflame R .20 .35
11 Litleo C .05 .15
12 Pyroar HOLO R .30 .50
13 Krabby C .05 .15
14 Kingler U .05 .15
15 Totodile C .05 .15
16 Croconaw U .05 .15
17 Feraligatr HOLO R .50 .75
18 Finneon C .05 .15
19 Lumineon U .05 .15
20 Frillish C .05 .15
21 Jellicent R .20 .35
22 Alomomola C .05 .15
23 Manectric EX HOLO R 3.00 4.00
24 MegaManectric EX HOLO R 5.00 7.00
25 Pachirisu R .25 .60
26 Joltik C .05 .15
27 Galvantula R .25 .60
28 Helioptile C .05 .15
29 Helioptile C .05 .15
30 Heliolisk HOLO R .30 .50
31 Zubat C .15 .25
32 Golbat U .20 .30
33 Crobat R 1.25 2.00
34 Gengar EX HOLO R 6.00 8.00
35 MegaGengar EX HOLO R 10.00 13.00
36 Wobbuffet U .20 .30
37 Gulpin C .05 .15
38 Swalot R .25 .60
39 Munna C .05 .15
40 Musharna R .25 .60
41 Litwick C .05 .15
42 Lampent U .20 .30
43 Chandelure HOLO R .40 .60
44 Pumpkaboo C .05 .15
45 Gourgeist HOLO R .40 .60
46 Gligar C .05 .15
47 Gliscor R .25 .60
48 Roggenrola C .05 .15
49 Boldore U .05 .15
50 Gigalith HOLO R .30 .50
51 Murkrow C .05 .15
52 Honchkrow R .20 .35
53 Poochyena C .05 .15
54 Mightyena R .25 .60
55 Spiritomb R .25 .60
56 Purrloin C .05 .15
57 Liepard U .05 .15
58 Malamar EX HOLO R 2.50 3.50
59 Skarmory C .05 .15
60 Bronzor C .05 .15
61 Bronzong R .60 1.00
62 Dialga EX HOLO R 3.50 4.50
63 Heatran HOLO R .40 .60
64 Escavalier R .25 .60
65 Aegislash EX HOLO R 3.50 4.50
66 Klefki U .05 .15
67 Florges EX HOLO R 2.00 2.50
68 Swirlix C .05 .15
69 Slurpuff HOLO R .40 .60
70 Dedenne C .05 .15
71 Diancie HOLO R .30 .50
72 Deino C .05 .15
73 Zweilous U .05 .15
74 Hydreigon HOLO R .30 .50
75 Goomy C .05 .15
76 Sliggoo U .05 .15
77 Goodra HOLO R .30 .50
78 Spearow C .05 .15
79 Fearow U .05 .15
80 Chansey C .05 .15
81 Blissey R .20 .35
82 Girafarig U .05 .15
83 Whismur C .05 .15
84 Loudred U .05 .15
85 Exploud R .25 .60
86 Regigigas HOLO R .50 .75
87 Bunnelby C .05 .15
88 Diggersby R .25 .60
89 Fletchling C .05 .15
90 Furfrou U .05 .15
91 AZ U .20 .30
92 Battle Compressor U 1.25 2.00
93 Dimension Valley U 1.00 1.50
94 Enhanced Hammer U .20 .30
95 Gengar Spirit Link U .05 .15
96 Hand Scope U .05 .15
97 Head Ringer HOLO R 2.00 3.00
98 Jamming Net HOLO R .40 .60
99 Lysandre's Trump Card U .15 .25
100 Manectric Spirit Link U .05 .15
101 Professor Sycamore U .75 1.15
102 Robo Substitute U .15 .25
103 Roller Skates U .05 .15
104 Shauna U .20 .30
105 Steel Shelter U .15 .25
106 Target Whistle U .10 .20
107 Tierno U .20 .30
108 Trick Coin U .15 .25
109 VS Seeker U 10.00 12.00
110 Xerosic U .20 .30
111 Double Colorless Energy U 1.25 1.75
112 Mystery Energy U .30 .50
113 Manectric EX UR 4.00 6.00
114 Gengar EX UR 10.00 12.00
115 Malamar EX UR 4.00 6.00
116 Florges EX UR 2.50 3.50
117 AZ UR 4.00 6.00
118 Lysandre's Trump Card UR 3.00 4.00
119 Xerosic UR 3.50 4.50
120 MegaManectric EX HOLO SR 8.00 10.00
121 MegaGengar EX HOLO SR 15.00 17.00
122 Dialga EX HOLO SR 28.00 32.00

2015 Pokemon XY Primal Clash

COMPLETE SET (164) 270.00 340.00
BOOSTER BOX (36 PACKS) 100.00 120.00
BOOSTER PACK (10 CARDS) 3.00 5.00
*REV.FOIL: .75X TO 2X BASIC CARDS
RELEASED ON FEBRUARY 4, 2015
1 Weedle C .05 .15
2 Kakuna U .05 .15
3 Beedrill R .25 .40
4 Tangela C .05 .15
5 Tangrowth R .20 .30
6 Treecko C .05 .15
7 Grovyle U .10 .20
8 Sceptile R .30 .50
9 Sceptile HOLO R .60 1.00
10 Lotad C .05 .15
11 Lombre U .05 .15
12 Ludicolo HOLO R .30 .50
13 Surskit C .05 .15
14 Masquerain U .05 .15
15 Shroomish C .05 .15
16 Breloom R .15 .25
17 Volbeat C .05 .15
18 Illumise C .05 .15
19 Trevenant EX HOLO R 2.25 3.00
20 Vulpix C .05 .15
21 Ninetales R .40 .60
22 Slugma C .05 .15
23 Magcargo U .05 .15
24 Magcargo R .25 .40
25 Torchic C .05 .15
26 Torchic U .20 .30
27 Combusken U .05 .15
28 Blaziken HOLO R .60 1.00
29 Camerupt EX HOLO R 2.25 2.75
30 Horsea C .05 .15
31 Seadra U .05 .15
32 Staryu C .05 .15
33 Mudkip C .05 .15
34 Marshtomp U .20 .30
35 Swampert R .25 .40
36 Swampert HOLO R 2.00 2.50
37 Ludicolo R .25 .40
38 Wailord EX HOLO R 7.00 8.50
39 Barboach C .05 .15
40 Whiscash U .05 .15
41 Whiscash R .20 .35
42 Corphish C .05 .15
43 Feebas C .05 .15
44 Milotic HOLO R 1.75 2.25
45 Spheal C .05 .15
46 Spheal C .05 .15
47 Sealeo U .05 .15
48 Walrein R .20 .30
49 Clamperl C .05 .15
50 Huntail HOLO R .60 .80
51 Gorebyss U .05 .15
52 Gorebyss R .15 .25
53 Kyogre R .40 .60
54 Kyogre EX HOLO R 3.00 4.00
55 Primal Kyogre EX HOLO R 10.00 12.00
56 Manaphy HOLO R .50 .75
57 Chinchou C .05 .15
58 Lanturn U .05 .15
59 Electrike C .05 .15
60 Electrike U .05 .15
61 Manectric HOLO R .30 .50
62 Tynamo C .05 .15
63 Eelektrik U .05 .15
64 Eelektrik R .25 .40
65 Eelektross HOLO R .40 .60
66 Nidoran C .05 .15
67 Nidorina U .05 .15
68 Nidoqueen U .05 .15
69 Nidoqueen R .30 .50
70 Tentacool C .05 .15
71 Tentacool U .05 .15
72 Tentacruel R .20 .35
73 Starmie R .15 .25
74 Rhyhorn C .05 .15
75 Rhydon U .05 .15
76 Rhyperior R .20 .35

Card	Low	High
77 Rhyperior HOLO R	.60	1.00
78 Nosepass C	.05	.15
79 Meditite C	.05	.15
80 Medicham HOLO R	.30	.50
81 Medicham R	.40	.60
82 Trapinch C	.05	.15
83 Solrock C	.05	.15
84 Groudon R	.30	.50
85 Groudon EX HOLO R	4.00	5.00
86 Primal Groudon EX HOLO R	15.00	17.00
87 Hippopotas C	.05	.15
88 Hippowdon HOLO R	.40	.60
89 Drilbur C	.05	.15
90 Diggersby R	.20	.30
91 Sharpedo EX HOLO R	3.75	4.25
92 Crawdaunt HOLO R	.75	1.00
93 Aggron EX HOLO R	3.00	4.00
94 MegaAggron EX HOLO R	7.75	9.00
95 Probopass R	.15	.25
96 Excadrill R	.20	.30
97 Excadrill HOLO R	.60	.80
98 Honedge C	.05	.15
99 Doublade U	.10	.20
100 Aegislash HOLO R	.30	.50
101 Mr. Mime U	.05	.15
102 Marill C	.05	.15
103 Azumarill R	.15	.25
104 Azumarill HOLO R	.40	.60
105 Gardevoir EX HOLO R	3.75	4.50
106 MegaGardevoir EX HOLO R	5.75	7.00
107 Kingdra R	.20	.35
108 Kingdra HOLO R	.75	1.25
109 Vibrava U	.05	.15
110 Flygon HOLO R	.40	.60
111 Zigzagoon C	.05	.15
112 Linoone U	.05	.15
113 Skitty C	.05	.15
114 Delcatty R	.20	.30
115 Spinda C	.05	.15
116 Bidoof C	.05	.15
117 Bidoof U	.15	.25
118 Bibarel U	.05	.15
119 Bouffalant U	.05	.15
120 Bunnelby C	.05	.15
121 Bunnelby U	.20	.30
122 Acro Bike U	1.25	1.75
123 Aggron Spirit Link U	.05	.15
124 Archie's Ace in the Hole U	.20	.30
125 Dive Ball U	2.00	2.50
126 Energy Retrieval U	.20	.30
127 Escape Rope U	.30	.50
128 Exp. Share U	.15	.25
129 Fresh Water Set U	.10	.20
130 Gardevoir Spirit Link U	.10	.20
131 Groudon Spirit Link U	.05	.15
132 Kyogre Spirit Link U	.05	.15
133 Maxie's Hidden Ball Trick U	.20	.30
134 Professor Birch's Observations U	1.25	1.75
135 Rare Candy U	1.75	2.25
136 Repeat Ball U	.10	.20
137 Rough Seas U	3.00	4.00
138 Scorched Earth U	.20	.35
139 Shrine of Memories U	.30	.50
140 Silent Lab U	.20	.30
141 Teammates U	.30	.50
142 Weakness Policy U	.15	.25
143 Shield Energy U	.20	.30
144 Wonder Energy U	.20	.35
145 Trevenant EX UR FULL ART	4.75	6.00
146 Camerupt EX UR FULL ART	4.00	5.00
147 Wailord EX UR FULL ART	10.00	13.00
148 Kyogre EX UR FULL ART	7.00	10.00
149 Primal Kyogre EX UR FULL ART	14.00	16.00
150 Groudon EX UR FULL ART	8.00	10.00
151 Primal Groudon EX UR FULL ART	15.00	17.00
152 Sharpedo EX UR FULL ART	6.50	7.50
153 Aggron EX UR FULL ART	5.00	6.00
154 MegaAggron EX UR FULL ART	12.00	14.00
155 Gardevoir EX UR FULL ART	10.00	12.00
156 MegaGardevoir EX UR FULL ART	8.00	10.00
157 Archie's Ace in the Hole UR FULL ART	4.50	5.25
158 Maxie's Hidden Ball Trick UR FULL ART	6.25	7.25
159 Professor Birch's Observations UR FULL ART	6.50	7.50
160 Teammates UR FULL ART	8.00	10.00
161 Dive Ball UR	15.00	18.00
162 Enhanced Hammer UR	9.00	11.00
163 Switch UR	12.00	13.00
164 Weakness Policy UR	4.75	6.00

2015 Pokemon XY Double Crisis

Card	Low	High
COMPLETE SET (34)	20.00	30.00
BOOSTER BOX (36 PACKS)	100.00	120.00
BOOSTER PACK (10 CARDS)	3.00	4.00
*REV.FOIL: .75X TO 2X BASIC CARDS		
RELEASED ON MARCH 25, 2015	3.00	5.00
1 Team Magma's Numel C	1.00	1.25
2 Team Magma's Camerupt HOLO R	2.25	3.00
3 Team Aqua's Spheal C	.10	.20
4 Team Aqua's Sealeo C	.10	.20
5 Team Aqua's Walrein HOLO R	.30	.50
6 Team Aqua's Kyogre EX HOLO R	5.00	6.00
7 Team Aqua's Grimer C	.10	.20
8 Team Aqua's Muk HOLO R	.60	1.00
9 Team Aqua's Seviper C	.10	.20
10 Team Magma's Baltoy C	.10	.20
11 Team Magma's Claydol HOLO R	.30	.50
12 Team Magma's Aron C	.10	.20
13 Team Magma's Lairon C	.10	.20
14 Team Magma's Aggron HOLO R	.50	.75
15 Team Magma's Groudon EX HOLO R	5.25	6.50
16 Team Aqua's Poochyena C	.10	.20
17 Team Magma's Poochyena C	.10	.20
18 Team Aqua's Mightyena C	.10	.20
19 Team Magma's Mightyena C	.10	.20
20 Team Aqua's Carvanha C	.10	.20
21 Team Aqua's Sharpedo HOLO R	.50	.75
22 Team Magma's Zangoose C	.10	.20
23 Aqua Diffuser U	.20	.30
24 Magma Pointer U	.20	.30
25 Team Aqua Admin U	.20	.30
26 Team Aqua Grunt U	.20	.30
27 Team Aqua's Great Ball U	.20	.30
28 Team Aqua's Secret Base U	2.00	2.25
29 Team Magma Admin U	.25	.40
30 Team Magma Grunt U	.20	.30
31 Team Magma's Great Ball U	.20	.30
32 Team Magma's Secret Base U	1.25	1.75
33 Double Aqua Energy U	.40	.60
34 Double Magma Energy U	.40	.60

2015 Pokemon XY Roaring Skies

Card	Low	High
COMPLETE SET (110)	345.00	440.00
BOOSTER BOX (36 PACKS)	100.00	120.00
BOOSTER PACK (10 CARDS)	3.00	5.00
*REV.FOIL: .75X TO 2X BASIC CARDS		
RELEASED ON MAY 6, 2015		
1 Exeggcute C	.05	.15
2 Exeggutor U	.05	.15
3 Wurmple C	.05	.15
4 Silcoon U	.05	.15
5 Beautifly HOLO R	.40	1.00
6 Cascoon C	.05	.15
7 Dustox U	.05	.15
8 Dustox R	.15	.25
9 Nincada C	.05	.15
10 Ninjask U	.05	.15
11 Shedinja R	.15	.25
12 Tropius U	.05	.15
13 Victini R	.15	.25
14 Fletchinder U	.05	.15
15 Talonflame R	.15	.25
16 Articuno R	.50	.75
17 Articuno R	.40	.60
18 Wingull C	.05	.15
19 Pelipper U	.05	.15
20 Pikachu C	.05	.15
21 Voltorb C	.05	.15
22 Electrode U	.05	.15
23 Zapdos R	.20	.35
24 Electrike C	.05	.15
25 Manectric U	.05	.15
26 Thundurus EX HOLO R	2.75	3.50
27 Natu C	.05	.15
28 Natu C	.05	.15
29 Xatu R	.15	.25
30 Shuppet C	.05	.15
31 Banette R	.15	.25
32 Banette R	.20	.30
33 Deoxys HOLO R	.75	1.50
34 Gallade EX HOLO R	2.75	3.25
35 MegaGallade EX HOLO R	4.75	5.50
36 Gligar C	.05	.15
37 Gliscor U	.05	.15
38 Binacle C	.05	.15
39 Hawlucha C	.05	.15
40 Absol HOLO R	.75	2.00
41 Inkay C	.05	.15
42 Jirachi HOLO R	.75	2.00
43 Togepi C	.05	.15
44 Togetic U	.05	.15
45 Togekiss R	.15	.25
46 Togekiss HOLO R	.75	2.00
47 Carbink R	.15	.25
48 Klefki R	.15	.25
49 Dratini C	.05	.15
50 Dragonair U	.05	.15
51 Dragonite R	.25	.40
52 Dragonite HOLO R	.75	1.50
53 Altaria U	.05	.15
54 Bagon C	.05	.15
55 Bagon C	.05	.15
56 Shelgon U	.05	.15
57 Salamence HOLO R	.50	1.50
58 Latios EX HOLO R	2.25	3.00
59 MegaLatios EX HOLO R	4.50	5.25
60 Rayquaza EX HOLO R	3.75	4.25
61 MegaRayquaza EX HOLO R	23.00	28.00
62 Hydreigon EX HOLO R	3.00	3.75
63 Reshiram HOLO R	.75	2.00
64 Zekrom HOLO R	.75	2.00
65 Spearow C	.05	.15
66 Fearow U	.05	.15
67 Meowth C	.05	.15
68 Dunsparce C	.05	.15
69 Skarmory R	.20	.30
70 Taillow C	.05	.15
71 Swellow R	.15	.25
72 Swellow HOLO R	.75	2.00
73 Swablu C	.05	.15
74 Altaria R	.20	.30
75 Rayquaza EX HOLO R	6.00	7.50
76 MegaRayquaza EX HOLO R	14.00	16.00
77 Shaymin EX HOLO R	70.00	80.00
78 Pidove C	.05	.15
79 Tranquill U	.05	.15
80 Unfezant U	.05	.15
81 Unfezant R	.20	.30
82 Fletchling C	.05	.15
83 Gallade Spirit Link U	.05	.15
84 Healing Scarf U	.05	.15
85 Latios Spirit Link U	.05	.15
86 Mega Turbo U	.30	.50
87 Rayquaza Spirit Link U	.05	.15
88 Revive U	.05	.15
89 Sky Field U	.20	.35
90 Steven U	.15	.25
91 Switch U	.15	.25
92 Trainers' Mail U	4.00	4.50
93 Ultra Ball U	.50	.75
94 Wally U	.20	.30
95 Wide Lens U	.05	.15
96 Winona U	.10	.20
97 Double Dragon Energy U	1.25	1.75
98 Thundurus EX UR FULL ART	3.75	4.25
99 Gallade EX UR FULL ART	3.50	4.00
100 MegaGallade EX UR FULL ART	6.75	7.50
101 Latios EX UR FULL ART	4.50	5.25
102 MegaLatios EX UR FULL ART	5.00	6.50
103 Hydreigon EX UR FULL ART	5.00	6.00
104 Rayquaza EX UR FULL ART	12.00	14.00
105 MegaRayquaza EX UR FULL ART	23.00	28.00
106 Shaymin EX UR FULL ART	90.00	110.00
107 Wally UR	4.00	7.00
108 Winona UR	3.00	6.00
109 Energy Switch UR	3.00	5.00
110 VS Seeker UR	25.00	35.00

2015 Pokemon XY Ancient Origins

Card	Low	High
COMPLETE SET (100)	300.00	375.00
BOOSTER BOX (36 PACKS)	100.00	120.00
BOOSTER PACK (10 CARDS)	3.00	5.00
*REV.FOIL: .75X TO 2X BASIC CARDS		
RELEASED ON AUGUST 12, 2015		
1 Oddish C	.05	.15
2 Gloom U	.10	.20
3 Vileplume R	.40	.75
4 Bellossom U	.10	.20
5 Spinarak C	.05	.15
6 Ariados U	.20	.30
7 Sceptile EX HOLO R	8.00	10.00
8 MegaSceptile EX HOLO R	6.00	9.00
9 Combee C	.05	.15
10 Vespiquen (Intelligence Gathering) U	.20	.30
11 Vespiquen (Double) R	.10	.20
12 Virizion HOLO R	.40	.60
13 Flareon U	.10	.20
14 Entei (Burning Roar) R	.30	.50
15 Entei (Double) HOLO R	1.25	1.75
16 Larvesta C	.05	.15
17 Volcarona (Sun Birth) HOLO R	.40	.60
18 Volcarona (Stop) R	.20	.30
19 Magikarp C	.05	.15
20 Gyarados (Berserker Splash) R	.20	.30
21 Gyarados (Double) HOLO R	.50	.75
22 Vaporeon U	.15	.25
23 Relicanth C	.05	.15
24 Regice R	.40	.75
25 Kyurem EX HOLO R	2.75	3.25
26 Jolteon HOLO R	.60	1.00
27 Ampharos EX HOLO R	2.25	3.00
28 MegaAmpharos EX HOLO R	5.50	6.50
29 Rotom U	.10	.20
30 Unown C	.20	.30
31 Baltoy (Spinning Attack) C	.05	.15
32 Baltoy (Stop) C	.05	.15
33 Claydol R	.15	.25
34 Golett C	.05	.15
35 Golurk (Stop) R	.25	.40
36 Hoopa EX HOLO R	12.00	15.00
37 Machamp EX HOLO R	2.50	3.00
38 Wooper C	.05	.15
39 Quagsire C	.05	.15
40 Regirock R	.20	.30
41 Golurk (Dig Out) C	.05	.15
42 Tyranitar EX HOLO R	3.00	4.00
43 MegaTyranitar EX HOLO R	7.00	8.00
44 Sableye U	.10	.20
45 Inkay C	.05	.15
46 Malamar C	.05	.15
47 Beldum C	.05	.15
48 Metang U	.10	.20
49 Metagross (Magnetic Warp) R	.15	.25
50 Metagross (Double) R	.20	.30
51 Registeel R	.20	.30
52 Ralts C	.05	.15
53 Kirlia U	.10	.20
54 Gardevoir HOLO R	.50	.75
55 Cottonee C	.05	.15
56 Whimsicott U	.10	.20
57 Giratina EX HOLO R	18.00	20.00
58 Goomy C	.05	.15
59 Sliggoo U	.10	.20
60 Goodra HOLO R	.25	.40
61 Meowth C	.05	.15
62 Persian C	.05	.15
63 Eevee C	.05	.15
64 Porygon C	.05	.15
65 Porygon2 U	.10	.20
66 Porygon-Z (Cyber Crush) R	.10	.20
67 Porygon-Z (Stop) HOLO R	.40	.60
68 Lugia EX HOLO R	5.50	6.50
69 Ace Trainer U	.10	.20
70 Ampharos Spirit Link U	.10	.20
71 Eco Arm U	.10	.20
72 Energy Recycler U	.10	.20
73 Faded Town U	.10	.20
74 Forest of Giant Plants U	.25	.40
75 Hex Maniac U	.20	.30
76 Level Ball U	.50	.75
77 Lucky Helmet U	.10	.20
78 Lysandre U	.75	1.00
79 Paint Roller U	.10	.20
80 Sceptile Spirit Link U	.10	.20
81 Tyranitar Spirit Link U	.10	.20
82 Dangerous Energy U	.15	.25
83 Flash Energy U	.10	.20
84 Sceptile EX UR FULL ART	12.00	15.00
85 MegaSceptile EX UR FULL ART	15.00	18.00
86 Kyurem EX UR FULL ART	3.00	4.00
87 Ampharos EX UR FULL ART	6.00	8.00
88 MegaAmpharos EX UR FULL ART	5.00	6.00
89 Hoopa EX UR FULL ART	35.00	40.00
90 Machamp EX UR FULL ART	5.00	6.00
91 Tyranitar EX UR FULL ART	7.00	8.00
92 MegaTyranitar EX UR FULL ART	9.00	11.00
93 Giratina EX UR FULL ART	30.00	35.00
94 Lugia EX UR FULL ART	15.00	18.00
95 Steven UR FULL ART	4.75	5.50
96 Primal Kyogre EX UR FULL ART	15.00	18.00
97 Primal Groudon EX UR FULL ART	15.00	18.00
98 MegaRayquaza EX UR FULL ART	15.00	20.00
99 Energy Retrieval SCR	4.50	7.00
100 Trainers' Mail SCR	18.00	20.00

2015 Pokemon XY Breakthrough

Card	Low	High
COMPLETE SET (164)	250.00	325.00
BOOSTER BOX (36 PACKS)	80.00	100.00
BOOSTER PACK (10 CARDS)	2.50	6.00
*REV.FOIL: .75X TO 2X BASIC CARDS		
RELEASED ON NOVEMBER 4, 2015		
1 Paras C	.05	.15
2 Parasect R	.15	.25
3 Pinsir U	.10	.20
4 Cacnea C	.05	.15
5 Pansage C	.05	.15
6 Simisage R	.15	.25
7 Chespin (Nosh) C	.05	.15
8 Chespin (Work) C	.05	.15
9 Chespin (Tree Climb) C	.05	.15
10 Quilladin U	.10	.20
11 Chesnaught HOLO R	.50	.75
12 Chesnaught BREAK	2.75	3.25
13 Scatterbug C	.05	.15
14 Spewpa U	.10	.20
15 Vivillon HOLO R	.30	.50
16 Skiddo C	.05	.15
17 Gogoat U	.10	.20
18 Cyndaquil C	.05	.15
19 Quilava U	.10	.20
20 Typhlosion HOLO R	2.00	3.00
21 Houndoom EX HOLO R	2.50	3.50
22 MHoundoom EX HOLO R	4.00	6.00
23 Pansear C	.05	.15
24 Simisear R	.15	.25
25 Fennekin C	.05	.15
26 Braixen U	.10	.20
27 Goldeen C	.05	.15
28 Seaking U	.10	.20
29 Staryu C	.05	.15
30 Starmie U	.10	.20
31 Remoraid (Wild River) C	.20	.30
32 Remoraid (Ion Pool) C	.20	.35
33 Octillery HOLO R	2.00	3.50
34 Glalie EX HOLO R	2.00	2.50
35 MGlalie EX HOLO R	3.00	5.00
36 Piplup C	.05	.15
37 Prinplup U	.10	.20
38 Empoleon HOLO R	.60	1.00
39 Snover C	.05	.15
40 Abomasnow R	.20	.30
41 Panpour C	.05	.15
42 Simipour R	.15	.25
43 Vanillite C	.05	.15
44 Vanillish U	.10	.20
45 Vanilluxe R	.20	.30
46 Froakie C	.05	.15
47 Frogadier U	.10	.20
48 Pikachu C	.05	.15
49 Raichu R	.30	.50
50 Raichu BREAK R	3.00	5.00
51 Magnemite (Glittering Guidance) C	.05	.15
52 Magnemite (Sparking Generator) C	.05	.15
53 Magneton U	.10	.20
54 Magnezone HOLO R	1.75	2.25
55 Raikou HOLO R	3.00	4.00
56 Stunfisk U	.10	.20
57 Dedenne U	.10	.20
58 Gastly C	.05	.15
59 Haunter U	.10	.20
60 Gengar HOLO R	1.25	1.75
61 Mewtwo EX (Photon Wave) EX HOLO R	1.50	2.50
62 Mewtwo EX (Shatter Shot) EX HOLO R	4.00	6.00
63 M Mewtwo EX (Vanishing Strike) EX HOLO R	9.00	12.00
64 M Mewtwo EX (Psychic Infinity) EX HOLO R	11.00	13.00
65 Misdreavus C	.05	.15
66 Mismagius HOLO R	.50	.75
67 Wobbuffet U	.10	.20
68 Ralts C	.05	.15
69 Kirlia U	.10	.20
70 Cresselia R	.25	.40
71 Woobat C	.05	.15
72 Swoobat U	.10	.20
73 Elgyem C	.05	.15
74 Beheeyem U	.10	.20
75 Sandshrew C	.05	.15
76 Sandslash U	.10	.20
77 Cubone C	.05	.15
78 Marowak R	.20	.30
79 Marowak BREAK R	1.00	1.25
80 Swinub C	.05	.15
81 Piloswine U	.10	.20
82 Mamoswine HOLO R	.30	.50
83 Hippopotas C	.05	.15
84 Gallade HOLO R	1.25	1.75
85 Meloetta HOLO R	.50	.75
86 Pancham C	.05	.15
87 Hawlucha R	.15	.25
88 Cacturne U	.10	.20
89 Zorua (Moonlight Madness) C	.20	.30
90 Zorua (Whiny Voice) C	.05	.15
91 Zoroark HOLO R	3.00	4.00
92 Zoroark BREAK R	2.00	3.00
93 Inkay C	.05	.15
94 Yveltal HOLO R	4.00	6.00
95 Bronzor C	.05	.15
96 Bronzong R	.15	.25
97 Mr. Mime R	.25	.40
98 Snubbull C	.05	.15
99 Granbull U	.10	.20
100 Ralts (Magical Shot) C	.05	.15
101 Flabebe C	.05	.15
102 Floette U	.10	.20
103 Florges R	.30	.50
104 Florges BREAK R	1.00	1.50

105 Spritzee C .05 .15
106 Aromatisse R .20 .30
107 Xerneas HOLO R 1.50 2.50
108 Axew (Brat Snack) C .05 .15
109 Axew (Extra Chop) C .05 .15
110 Fraxure U .10 .20
111 Haxorus HOLO R 1.25 1.75
112 Noivern R .30 .50
113 Noivern BREAK R 1.75 2.25
114 Meowth C .05 .15
115 Doduo (Simultaneous Peck) C .05 .15
116 Doduo (Double Stab) C .05 .15
117 Dodrio R .15 .25
118 Snorlax U .10 .20
119 Hoothoot C .05 .15
120 Noctowl R .20 .30
121 Teddiursa C .05 .15
122 Ursaring U .10 .20
123 Smeargle R .25 .40
124 Swablu C .05 .15
125 Starly C .05 .15
126 Staravia U .10 .20
127 Staraptor R .20 .30
128 Chatot R .15 .25
129 Rufflet C .05 .15
130 Braviary R .20 .30
131 Noibat C .05 .15
132 Noibat (Mysterious Beam) C .05 .15
133 Assault Vest U .20 .30
134 Brigette U .40 .75
135 Buddy-Buddy Rescue U .10 .20
136 Fisherman U .50 .75
137 Float Stone U 2.75 3.25
138 Giovanni's Scheme U .20 .30
139 Glalie Spirit Link U .10 .20
140 Heavy Ball U .20 .30
141 Heavy Boots U .10 .20
142 Houndoom Spirit Link U .10 .20
143 Judge U .30 .50
144 Mewtwo Spirit Link U .40 .60
145 Parallel City U .40 .60
146 Professor's Letter U .20 .30
147 Reserved Ticket U .10 .20
148 Skyla U .60 1.00
149 Super Rod U 2.25 3.00
150 Town Map U .20 .35
151 Burning Energy U .60 1.00
152 Rainbow Energy U .30 .50
153 Houndoom EX UR FULL ART 4.00 6.00
154 MHoundoom EX UR FULL ART 6.00 8.00
155 Glalie EX UR FULL ART 3.00 4.00
156 MGlalie EX UR FULL ART 5.00 7.00
157 Mewtwo EX (Photon Wave) UR FULL ART 3.00 5.00
158 Mewtwo EX (Shatter Shot) UR FULL ART 8.00 10.00
159 Mewtwo EX (Vanishing Strike) UR FULL ART 13.00 15.00
160 Mewtwo EX (Psychic Infinity) UR FULL ART 14.00 17.00
161 Brigette UR FULL ART 5.00 6.00
162 Giovanni's Scheme UR FULL ART 2.50 4.00
163 Mewtwo EX (Photon Wave) SCR 7.00 10.00
164 Mewtwo EX (Shatter Shot) SCR 10.00 12.00

2016 Pokemon Generations

COMPLETE SET (83) 100.00 130.00
*REV.FOIL: .75X TO 2X BASIC CARDS
RELEASED ON FEBRUARY 22, 2016
1 Venusaur EX HOLO R 2.00 3.00
2 M Venusaur EX HOLO R 4.00 5.00
3 Caterpie C .15 .25
4 Metapod U .20 .35
5 Butterfree HOLO R .60 1.00
6 Paras C .15 .25
7 Parasect R .30 .50
8 Tangela C .15 .25
9 Pinsir R .30 .50
10 Leafeon EX HOLO R 7.00 10.00
11 Charizard EX HOLO R 3.00 4.50
12 MCharizard EX HOLO R 18.00 21.00
13 Ninetales EX HOLO R 3.00 4.00
14 Ponyta C .15 .25
15 Rapidash R .30 .50
16 Magmar C .15 .25
17 Blastoise EX HOLO R 3.00 4.50
18 MBlastoise EX HOLO R 9.00 11.00
19 Shellder C .15 .25
20 Cloyster U .20 .35
21 Krabby C .15 .25
22 Magikarp C .15 .25
23 Gyarados R .30 .50
24 Vaporeon EX HOLO R 4.00 5.00
25 Articuno HOLO R FULL ART 5.00 6.50
26 Pikachu C .15 .25
27 Raichu HOLO R .60 1.00
28 Jolteon EX HOLO R 10.00 15.00
29 Zapdos HOLO R FULL ART 6.00 8.00
30 Zubat C .15 .25
31 Golbat U .20 .35
32 Slowpoke C .15 .25
33 Gastly C .15 .25
34 Haunter U .20 .35
35 Gengar HOLO R .60 1.00
36 Jynx R .30 .50
37 Meowstic EX HOLO R 2.50 4.00
38 Diglett C .15 .25
39 Dugtrio R .30 .50
40 Machop C .15 .25
41 Machoke U .20 .35
42 Machamp HOLO R .60 1.00
43 Geodude C .15 .25
44 Graveler U .20 .35
45 Golem HOLO R .60 1.00
46 Golem EX HOLO R 3.00 4.00
47 Hitmonlee R .30 .50
48 Hitmonchan R .30 .50
49 Rhyhorn C .15 .25
50 Clefairy C .15 .25
51 Clefable U .20 .35
52 Mr. Mime U .20 .35
53 Meowth C .15 .25
54 Persian U .20 .35
55 Doduo C .15 .25
56 Dodrio R .30 .50
57 Tauros R .30 .50
58 Snorlax R .30 .50
59 Clemont U .20 .35
60 Crushing Hammer U .20 .35
61 Energy Switch U .20 .35
62 Evosoda U .20 .35
63 Imakuni? U .20 .35
64 Maintenance U .20 .35
65 Max Revive U .20 .35
66 Olympia U .20 .35
67 Poke Ball U .20 .35
68 Pokemon Center Lady U .20 .35
69 Pokemon Fan Club U .20 .35
70 Revitalizer U .20 .35
71 Red Card U .20 .35
72 Shauna U .20 .35
73 Team Flare Grunt U .20 .35
74 Double Colorless Energy U .20 .35
75 Grass Energy C .15 .25
76 Fire Energy C .15 .25
77 Water Energy C .15 .25
78 Lightning Energy C .15 .25
79 Psychic Energy C .15 .25
80 Fighting Energy C .15 .25
81 Darkness Energy C .15 .25
82 Metal Energy C .15 .25
83 Fairy Energy C .15 .25

2016 Pokemon Generations Radiant Collection

COMPLETE SET (32) 20.00 35.00
RC1 Chikorita C .15 .25
RC2 Shroomish C .15 .25
RC3 Charmander C .15 .25
RC4 Charmeleon C .25 .40
RC5 Charizard U 1.50 2.00
RC6 Flareon EX HOLO R 2.25 3.25
RC7 Snorunt C .15 .25
RC8 Froslass U .20 .35
RC9 Raichu C .40 .60
RC10 Dedenne U .20 .35
RC11 Wobbuffet C .15 .25
RC12 Gulpin C .15 .25
RC13 Jirachi U .20 .35
RC14 Espurr C .15 .25
RC15 Meowstic U .20 .35
RC16 Yveltal U .50 .75
RC17 Flabebe C .15 .25
RC18 Floette U .20 .35
RC19 Swirlix U .20 .35
RC20 Slurpuff U .20 .35
RC21 Sylveon EX HOLO R 3.00 4.00
RC22 Diancie U .20 .35
RC23 Swablu C .15 .25
RC24 Altaria U .20 .35
RC25 Fletchling C .15 .25
RC26 Floral Crown C .15 .25
RC27 Wally U .30 .50
RC28 Flareon EX UR FULL ART 3.00 4.00
RC29 Pikachu FULL ART UR 3.00 4.00
RC30 Gardevoir EX UR FULL ART 3.00 4.00
RC31 M Gardevoir EX FULL ART UR 4.00 5.00
RC32 Sylveon EX FULL ART UR 3.00 3.50

2016 Pokemon XY Breakpoint

COMPLETE SET (123) 200.00 250.00
BOOSTER BOX (36 PACKS) 80.00 100.00
BOOSTER PACK (10 CARDS) 2.50 6.00
*REV.FOIL: .75X TO 2X BASIC CARDS
1 Chikorita C .05 .15
2 Bayleef U .10 .20
3 Meganium HOLO R .75 1.00
4 Seedot C .05 .15
5 Kricketot C .05 .15
6 Kricketune U .10 .20
7 Petilil C .05 .15
8 Lilligant R .15 .25
9 Durant U .10 .20
10 Growlithe C .05 .15
11 Arcanine U .10 .20
12 Numel C .05 .15
13 Camerupt R .15 .25
14 Emboar EX HOLO R 2.00 3.00
15 Heatmor U .10 .20
16 Psyduck C .05 .15
17 Golduck R .15 .25
18 Golduck BREAK R 1.50 2.00
19 Slowpoke C .05 .15
20 Slowbro U .10 .20
21 Slowking HOLO R .30 .50
22 Shellder .05 .15
Razor Shell C
23 Shellder .05 .15
Clamp C
24 Cloyster U .10 .20
25 Staryu C .05 .15
26 Gyarados EX HOLO R 3.00 4.00
27 M Gyarados EX HOLO R 7.00 9.00
28 Lapras U .10 .20
29 Corsola C .05 .15
30 Suicune HOLO R .40 .60
31 Palkia EX HOLO R 5.00 6.00
32 Manaphy EX HOLO R 4.00 5.00
33 Tympole C .05 .15
34 Palpitoad U .10 .20
35 Seismitoad R .15 .25
36 Ducklett C .05 .15
37 Swanna U .10 .20
38 Froakie C .05 .15
39 Frogadier U .20 .30
40 Greninja R 1.25 1.75
41 Greninja BREAK R 8.00 10.00
42 Electabuzz C .05 .15
43 Electivire U .10 .20
44 Shinx C .05 .15
45 Luxio U .10 .20
46 Luxray R .15 .25
47 Luxray BREAK R 2.00 2.50
48 Blitzle C .05 .15
49 Zebstrika R .30 .50
50 Drowzee C .05 .15
51 Hypno R .15 .25
52 Espeon EX HOLO R 3.75 4.50
53 Skorupi C .05 .15
54 Drapion R .15 .25
55 Sigilyph U .10 .20
56 Trubbish C .20 .30
57 Garbodor HOLO R 2.00 3.00
58 Espurr C .05 .15
59 Meowstic R .15 .25
60 Honedge C .05 .15
61 Doublade U .10 .20
62 Aegislash HOLO R .30 .50
63 Skrelp C .05 .15
64 Phantump C .05 .15
65 Trevenant R .30 .50
66 Trevenant BREAK R 1.75 2.25
67 Sudowoodo U .10 .20
68 Gible C .05 .15
69 Gabite U .10 .20
70 Garchomp HOLO R .75 1.15
71 Pancham C .05 .15
72 Nuzleaf U .10 .20
73 Shiftry R .15 .25
74 Darkrai EX HOLO R 7.00 9.00
75 Pangoro R .15 .25
76 Scizor EX HOLO R 3.00 4.50
77 M Scizor EX HOLO R 5.00 7.00
78 Mawile U .10 .20
79 Ferroseed C .05 .15
80 Ferrothorn R .15 .25
81 Clefairy C .05 .15
82 Clefable R .15 .25
83 Togekiss EX HOLO R 2.00 2.50
84 Spritzee C .05 .15
85 Aromatisse U .10 .20
86 Dragalge HOLO R .30 .40
87 Rattata C .05 .15
88 Raticate R .30 .50
89 Raticate BREAK R 2.00 2.50
90 Dunsparce U .10 .20
91 Stantler U .10 .20
92 Ho-Oh EX HOLO R 3.00 3.50
93 Glameow C .05 .15
94 Purugly U .10 .20
95 Furfrou C .05 .15
96 All-Night Party U .10 .20
97 Bursting Balloon U 1.00 1.50
98 Delinquent U .20 .30
99 Fighting Fury Belt U 2.00 3.00
100 Great Ball U .10 .20
101 Gyarados Spirit Link U .10 .20
102 Max Elixir U 3.50 5.00
103 Max Potion U .30 .50
104 Misty's Determination U .10 .20
105 Pokemon Catcher U .10 .20
106 Potion U .10 .20
107 Professor Sycamore U .75 1.15
108 Psychic's Third Eye U .10 .20
109 Puzzle of Time U .75 1.15
110 Reverse Valley U .10 .20
111 Scizor Spirit Link U .10 .20
112 Tierno U .15 .25
113 Splash Energy U .20 .30
114 Gyarados EX UR 4.00 6.00
115 M Gyarados EX UR 11.00 13.00
116 Manaphy EX UR 5.00 7.00
117 Espeon EX UR 6.00 8.00
118 Darkrai EX UR 13.00 15.00
119 Scizor EX UR 5.00 7.00
120 M Scizor EX UR 7.00 9.00
121 Ho-Oh EX UR 5.00 7.00
122 Skyla UR 9.00 11.00
123 Gyarados EX SCR 5.00 7.00

2016 Pokemon XY Fates Collide

COMPLETE SET (124) 140.00 200.00
*REV.FOIL: .75X TO 2X BASIC CARDS
RELEASED ON MAY 2, 2016
1 Shuckle U .15 .25
2 Burmy C .10 .20
3 Wormadam (Solar Ray) U .15 .25
4 Mothim R .20 .35
5 Snivy C .10 .20
6 Servine U .15 .25
7 Serperior R .20 .35
8 Deerling C .10 .20
9 Moltres R .20 .35
10 Fennekin (Will-O-) C .10 .20
11 Fennekin (Invite Out) C .10 .20
12 Braixen U .15 .25
13 Delphox HOLO R .50 .75
14 Delphox BREAK R 2.00 3.00
15 Seel C .10 .20
16 Dewgong U .15 .25
17 Omanyte U .15 .25
18 Omastar R .10 .20
19 Omastar BREAK R .60 1.00
20 Glaceon EX HOLO R 7.00 10.00
21 White Kyurem HOLO R .40 .60
22 Binacle C .10 .20
23 Barbaracle R .20 .35
24 Rotom R .20 .35
25 Alakazam EX HOLO R 3.00 5.00
26MAlakazam EX HOLO R 6.00 8.00
27 Koffing C .10 .20
28 Weezing U .15 .25
29 Mew HOLO R 2.00 2.50
30 Spoink C .10 .20
31 Grumpig R .20 .35
32 Gothita C .10 .20
33 Solosis C .10 .20
34 Duosion U .15 .25
35 Reuniclus R .20 .35
36 Diglett C .10 .20
37 Marowak R .20 .35
38 Kabuto U .15 .25
39 Kabutops R .20 .35
40 Larvitar C .10 .20
41 Larvitar C .10 .20
42 Pupitar U .15 .25
43 Regirock EX HOLO R 4.00 6.00
44 Wormadam (Sand Spray) U .15 .25
45 Riolu C .10 .20
46 Riolu C .10 .20
47 Lucario (Beatdown) R .20 .35
48 Hawlucha U .15 .25
49 Carbink R .20 .35
50 Carbink (Safeguard) C .10 .20
51 CarbinkBREAK R 2.00 3.00
52 Zygarde (Lookout) U .15 .25
53 Zygarde (Rumble) R .20 .35
54 Zygarde EX HOLO R 6.00 8.00
55 Umbreon EX HOLO R 6.00 8.00
56 Tyranitar HOLO R .40 .60
57 Vullaby C .10 .20
58 Mandibuzz R .20 .35
59 Wormadam (Return Attack) U .15 .25
60 Bronzor C .10 .20
61 Bronzong R .20 .35
62 BronzongBREAK R 1.00 1.50
63 Lucario (Vacuum Wave) HOLO R .60 .80
64 Genesect EX HOLO R 1.75 2.25
65 Jigglypuff C .10 .20
66 Wigglytuff U .15 .25
67 Mr. Mime R .20 .35
68 Snubbull C .10 .20
69 MAltaria EX HOLO R 3.00 5.00
70 Cottonee C .10 .20
71 Whimsicott U .15 .25
72 Diancie EX HOLO R 2.25 3.00
73 Kingdra EX HOLO R 1.75 2.25
74 Meowth C .10 .20
75 Kangaskhan U .15 .25
76 Aerodactyl R .20 .35
77 Snorlax R .20 .35
78 Lugia R .20 .35
79 LugiaBREAK R 1.75 2.25
80 Whismur C .10 .20
81 Loudred U .15 .25
82 Exploud R .20 .35
83 Altaria EX HOLO R 2.00 3.00
84 Audino EX HOLO R 2.50 4.00
85 MAudino EX HOLO R 5.00 7.00
86 Minccino (Cleaning Up) C .10 .20
87 Minccino (Tail Smack) C .10 .20
88 Cinccino (Sweeping Cure) U .15 .25
90 Alakazam Spirit Link U .15 .25
91 Altaria Spirit Link U .15 .25
92 Audino Spirit Link U .15 .25
93 Bent Spoon U .15 .25
94 Chaos Tower U .15 .25
95 Devolution Spray U .15 .25
96 Dome Fossil Kabuto U .15 .25
97 Energy Pouch U .15 .25
98 Energy Reset U .15 .25
99 Fairy Drop U .15 .25
100 Fairy Garden U .15 .25
101 Fossil Excavation Kit U .15 .25
102 Helix Fossil Omanyte U .15 .25
103 Lass's Special U .15 .25
104 MCatcher U .15 .25
105 N U .15 .25
106 Old Amber Aerodactyl U .15 .25
107 PokÃ©mon Fan Club U .15 .25
108 Power Memory U .15 .25
109 Random Receiver U .15 .25
110 Scorched Earth U .15 .25
111 Shauna U .15 .25
112 Team Rocket's Handiwork U .15 .25
113 Ultra Ball U .15 .25
114 Double Colorless Energy U .15 .25
115 Strong Energy U .15 .25
116 Glaceon EX UR 10.00 13.00
117 Alakazam EX UR 4.00 6.00
118 MAlakazam EX UR 12.00 15.00
119 Umbreon EX UR 10.00 13.00
120 Genesect EX UR 4.00 6.00
121 MAltaria EX UR 5.00 7.00
122 Kingdra EX UR 3.00 4.00
123 Altaria EX UR 3.00 5.00
124 Team Rocket's Handiwork UR 3.00 5.00
125 Alakazam EX SR 7.00 8.00

2016 Pokemon XY Steam Siege

COMPLETE SET (116) 140.00 190.00
RELEASED ON AUGUST 3, 2016
1 Tangela C .10 .20
2 Tangrowth U .15 .25
3 Hoppip C .10 .20
4 Skiploom U .15 .25
5 Jumpluff R .30 .50
6 Yanma C .10 .20
7 Yanmega R .30 .50
8 Yanmega BREAK HOLO R .60 1.00
9 Seedot C .10 .20
10 Nuzleaf U .10 .20
11 Shiftry HOLO R .60 1.00
12 Foongus C .10 .20
13 Amoonguss R .30 .50
14 Larvesta C .10 .20

15 Volcarona R .30 .50
16 Ponyta C .10 .20
17 Rapidash U .15 .25
18 Chimchar C .10 .20
19 Monferno U .15 .25
20 Infernape HOLO R .60 1.00
21 Talonflame BREAK HOLO R .60 1.00
22 Litleo C .10 .20
23 Pyroar R .30 .50
24 PyroarBREAK HOLO R .60 1.00
25 Volcanion R .30 .50
26 Volcanion EX HOLO R 4.00 6.00
27 Mantine C .10 .20
28 Shellos C .10 .20
29 Gastrodon R .30 .50
30 Oshawott C .10 .20
31 Dewott U .15 .25
32 Samurott R .30 .50
33 Clauncher C .10 .20
34 Clawitzer R .30 .50
35 ClawitzerBREAK HOLO R .60 1.00
36 Bergmite C .10 .20
37 Avalugg R .30 .50
38 Mareep C .10 .20
39 Flaaffy U .15 .25
40 Ampharos HOLO R .60 1.00
41 Joltik C .10 .20
42 Galvantula R .30 .50
43 Nidoran C .10 .20
44 Nidorino U .15 .25
45 Nidoking R .30 .50
46 Drifloon C .10 .20
47 Drifblim U .15 .25
48 Litwick C .10 .20
49 Lampent U .15 .25
50 Chandelure HOLO R .60 1.00
51 Hoopa R .30 .50
52 Mankey C .10 .20
53 Primeape R .30 .50
54 Nosepass C .10 .20
55 Probopass R .30 .50
56 Anorith U .15 .25
57 Armaldo R .30 .50
58 Croagunk C .10 .20
59 Toxicroak R .30 .50
60 Sneasel C .10 .20
61 Weavile R .30 .50
62 Spiritomb R .30 .50
63 Pawniard C .10 .20
64 Bisharp HOLO R .60 1.00
65 Yveltal HOLO R .60 1.00
66 Yveltal BREAK HOLO R .60 1.00
67 Steelix EX HOLO R 1.25 2.00
68 MegaSteelixEX HOLO R 4.00 6.00
69 Shieldon U .15 .25
70 Bastiodon R .30 .50
71 Klink C .10 .20
72 Klang U .15 .25
73 Klinklang HOLO R .60 1.00
74 Cobalion R .30 .50
75 MagearnaEX HOLO R 1.25 2.00
76 Marill C .10 .20
77 Azumarill U .15 .25
78 GardevoirEX HOLO R 1.50 2.50
79 MegaGardevoirEX HOLO R 2.00 3.50
80 Klefki U .15 .25
81 Xerneas HOLO R .60 1.00
82 Xerneas BREAK HOLO R 4.00 6.00
83 Druddigon R .30 .50
84 Deino C .10 .20
85 Zweilous U .15 .25
86 Hydreigon HOLO R .60 1.00
87 HydreigonBREAK HOLO R .60 1.00
88 Meowth C .10 .20
89 Persian U .15 .25
90 Aipom C .10 .20
91 Ambipom U .15 .25
92 Rufflet C .10 .20
93 Braviary U .15 .25
94 Fletchling C .10 .20
95 Fletchinder U .15 .25
96 Talonflame R .30 .50
97 Hawlucha U .15 .25
98 Armor Fossil Shieldon U .15 .25
99 Captivating Poke Puff U .15 .25
100 Claw Fossil Anorith U .15 .25
101 Gardevoir Spirit Link U .15 .25
102 Greedy Dice U .15 .25
103 Ninja Boy U .15 .25
104 Pokemon Ranger U .15 .25
105 Special Charge U .15 .25
106 Steelix Spirit Link U .15 .25
107 Volcanion EX FULL ART UR 5.00 7.00
108 Steelix EX FULL ART UR 2.00 3.50
109 MegaSteelixEX UR Full Art 5.00 7.00
110 MagearnaEX UR Full Art 2.50 4.00
111 GardevoirEX UR Full Art 3.00 5.00
112 MegaGardevoirEX UR Full Art 4.00 6.00
113 Pokemon Ranger UR Full Art 3.00 5.00
114 Professor Sycamore UR Full Art 20.00 25.00
115 Volcanion EX SCR 8.00 11.00
116 GardevoirEX SCR 7.00 10.00

2016 Pokemon Evolutions

COMPLETE SET (113) 160.00 230.00
RELEASED ON NOVEMBER 2, 2016
1 Venusaur EX UR 1.50 2.50
2 Mega Venusaur EX UR 2.50 4.00
3 Caterpie C .15 .25
4 Metapod U .15 .25
5 Weedle C .15 .25
6 Kakuna U .15 .25
7 Beedrill R .20 .35
8 Tangela C .15 .25
9 Charmander C .15 .25
10 Charmeleon U .15 .25
11 Charizard HOLO R 10.00 13.00
12 Charizard EX UR 2.50 4.00
13 Mega Charizard EX UR 14.00 17.00
14 Vulpix C .15 .25
15 Ninetales HOLO R .75 1.25
16 Ninetales BREAK HOLO BREAK 1.00 1.50
17 Growlithe C .15 .25
18 Arcanine R .20 .35
19 Ponyta C .15 .25
20 Magmar U .15 .25
21 Blastoise EX UR 2.50 4.00
22 Mega Blastoise EX UR 4.00 6.00
23 Poliwag C .15 .25
24 Poliwhirl U .15 .25
25 Poliwrath HOLO R 1.00 1.50
26 Slowbro EX UR 2.00 3.00
27 Mega Slowbro EX UR 4.00 6.00
28 Seel C .15 .25
29 Dewgong R .20 .35
30 Staryu C .15 .25
31 Starmie R .20 .35
32 Starmie BREAK HOLO BREAK .60 1.00
33 Magikarp C .15 .25
34 Gyarados HOLO R .75 1.25
35 Pikachu C .15 .25
36 Raichu HOLO R .75 1.25
37 Magnemite C .15 .25
38 Magneton HOLO R 1.00 1.50
39 Voltorb C .15 .25
40 Electrode R .20 .35
41 Electabuzz C .15 .25
42 Zapdos HOLO R 1.00 1.50
43 Nidoran C .15 .25
44 Nidorino U .15 .25
45 Nidoking HOLO R 1.25 1.75
46 Nidoking BREAK HOLO BREAK 1.00 1.50
47 Gastly C .15 .25
48 Haunter U .15 .25
49 Drowzee C .15 .25
50 Koffing U .15 .25
51 Mewtwo R .50 .75
52 Mewtwo EX UR 2.00 3.00
53 Mew HOLO R 2.00 3.00
54 Sandshrew C .15 .25
55 Diglett C .15 .25
56 Dugtrio R .20 .35
57 Machop C .15 .25
58 Machoke U .15 .25
59 Machamp HOLO R .75 1.25
60 Machamp BREAK HOLO BREAK 1.25 1.75
61 Onix C .15 .25
62 Hitmonchan HOLO R 1.00 1.50
63 Clefairy HOLO R .75 1.25
64 Pidgeot EX UR 2.00 3.00
65 Mega Pidgeot EX UR 3.00 5.00
66 Rattata C .15 .25
67 Raticate R .20 .35
68 Farfetch'd R .15 .25
69 Doduo C .15 .25
70 Chansey HOLO R .75 1.25
71 Porygon U .15 .25
72 Dragonite EX UR 4.00 6.00
73 Blastoise Spirit Link U .25 .40
74 Brocks Grit U .30 .50
75 Charizard Spirit Link U .25 .40
76 Devolution Spray U .15 .25
77 Energy Retrieval U .15 .25
78 Full Heal U .15 .25
79 Maintenance U .15 .25
80 Misty's Determination U .15 .25
81 Pidgeot Spirit Link U .15 .25
82 Pokedex U .15 .25
83 Potion U .15 .25
84 Professor Oak's Hint U .15 .25
85 Revive U .15 .25
86 Slowbro Spirit Link U .15 .25
87 Super Potion U .15 .25
88 Switch U .15 .25
89 Venusaur Spirit Link U .25 .40
90 Double Colorless Energy U .75 1.00
91 Grass Energy C .25 .40
92 Fire Energy C .25 .40
93 Water Energy C .25 .40
94 Lightning Energy C .25 .40
95 Psychic Energy C .25 .40
96 Fighting Energy C .25 .40
97 Darkness Energy C .25 .40
98 Metal Energy C .25 .40
99 Fairy Energy C .25 .40
100 Mega Venusaur EX FULL ART UR 7.00 10.00
101 Mega Charizard EX FULL ART UR 23.00 26.00
102 Mega Blastoise EX FULL ART UR 8.00 10.00
103 Mewtwo EX FULL ART UR 5.00 8.00
104 Pidgeot EX FULL ART UR 4.00 6.00
105 Mega Pidgeot EX FULL ART UR 5.00 8.00
106 Dragonite EX FULL ART UR 8.00 10.00
107 Brocks Grit FULL ART UR 5.00 8.00
108 Misty's Determination FULL ART SR 10.00 13.00
109 Exeggutor SCR 1.25 1.75
110 Flying Pikachu SCR 2.00 2.50
111 Surfing Pikachu SCR 1.75 2.25
112 Imakuni's Doduo SCR 1.00 1.50
113 Here Comes Team Rocket! SCR 1.75 2.25

2016 Pokemon Evolutions Reverse Foil

COMPLETE SET (83) 75.00 115.00
RELEASED ON NOVEMBER 2, 2016
3 Caterpie C .25 .40
4 Metapod U .30 .50
5 Weedle C .25 .40
6 Kakuna U .30 .50
7 Beedrill R .75 1.00
8 Tangela C .25 .40
9 Charmander C .25 .40
10 Charmeleon U .30 .50
11 Charizard HOLO R 8.00 12.00
14 Vulpix C .25 .40
15 Ninetales HOLO R 1.50 2.00
17 Growlithe C .25 .40
18 Arcanine R .75 1.00
19 Ponyta C .25 .40
20 Magmar U .30 .50
23 Poliwag C .25 .40
24 Poliwhirl U .30 .50
25 Poliwrath HOLO R 1.25 1.75
28 Seel C .25 .40
29 Dewgong R .75 1.00
30 Staryu C .25 .40
31 Starmie R .75 1.00
33 Magikarp C .25 .40
34 Gyarados HOLO R 1.00 1.50
35 Pikachu C .25 .40
36 Raichu HOLO R 1.00 1.50
37 Magnemite C .25 .40
38 Magneton HOLO R 1.00 1.50
39 Voltorb C .25 .40
40 Electrode R .75 1.00
41 Electabuzz C .25 .40
42 Zapdos HOLO R 1.50 2.50
43 Nidoran C .25 .40
44 Nidorino U .30 .50
45 Nidoking HOLO R 1.00 1.50
47 Gastly C .25 .40
48 Haunter U .30 .50
49 Drowzee C .25 .40
50 Koffing U .30 .50
51 Mewtwo R 1.50 2.00
53 Mew HOLO R 2.50 3.50
54 Sandshrew C .25 .40
55 Diglett C .25 .40
56 Dugtrio R .75 1.00
57 Machop C .25 .40
58 Machoke U .30 .50
59 Machamp HOLO R 1.00 1.50
61 Onix C .25 .40
62 Hitmonchan HOLO R 1.00 1.50
63 Clefairy HOLO R 1.00 1.50
66 Rattata C .30 .50
67 Raticate R .75 1.00
68 Farfetch'd R .75 1.00
69 Doduo C .25 .40
70 Chansey HOLO R 1.00 1.50
71 Porygon U .30 .50
73 Blastoise Spirit Link U .60 1.00
74 Brock's Grit U 1.00 1.50
75 Charizard Spirit Link U .60 1.00
76 Devolution Spray U .30 .50
77 Energy Retrieval U .30 .50
78 Full Heal U .30 .50
79 Maintenance U .30 .50
80 Misty's Determination U .60 1.00
81 Pidgeot Spirit Link U .30 .50
82 Pokedex U .30 .50
83 Potion U .30 .50
84 Professor Oak's Hint U .30 .50
85 Revive U .30 .50
86 Slowbro Spirit Link U .30 .50
87 Super Potion U .30 .50
88 Switch U .50 .75
89 Venusaur Spirit Link U .60 1.00
90 Double Colorless Energy U 4.00 6.00
91 Grass Energy C .25 .40
92 Fire Energy C 3.00 5.00
93 Water Energy C 3.00 5.00
94 Lightning Energy C 3.00 5.00
95 Psychic Energy C 3.00 5.00
96 Fighting Energy C 3.00 5.00
97 Darkness Energy C 3.00 5.00
98 Metal Energy C 3.00 5.00
99 Fairy Energy C 3.00 5.00

2016 Pokemon Evolutions Pre-Release

RELEASED ON OCTOBER 22, 2016
11 Charizard HOLO R 50.00 65.00
11 Charizard STAFF HOLO R 250.00 500.00
34 Gyarados STAFF HOLO R 35.00 50.00
34 Gyarados HOLO R 15.00 20.00
51 Mewtwo HOLO R 20.00 30.00
51 Mewtwo STAFF HOLO R 40.00 60.00
59 Machamp STAFF HOLO R 30.00 50.00
59 Machamp HOLO R 15.00 20.00

2017 Pokemon Sun and Moon

COMPLETE SET (163) 500.00 665.00
BOOSTER BOX (36 PACKS) 85.00 120.00
BOOSTER PACK (11 CARDS) 3.00 5.00
RELEASED ON FEBRUARY 3, 2017
1 Caterpie C .10 .20
2 Metapod U .20 .30
3 Butterfree R .30 .50
4 Paras C .10 .20
5 Parasect R .30 .50
6 Pinsir U .20 .30
7 Surskit C .10 .20
8 Masquerain R .30 .50
9 Rowlet C .10 .20
10 Dartrix U .20 .30
11 Decidueye R .30 .50
12 Decidueye GX UR 15.00 20.00
13 Grubbin C .10 .20
14 Fomantis C .10 .20
15 Lurantis GX UR 7.00 10.00
16 Morelull C .10 .20
17 Shiinotic HOLO R 1.00 1.50
18 Bounsweet C .10 .20
19 Steenee U .20 .30
20 Tsareena HOLO R 1.50 2.50
21 Growlithe C .10 .20
22 Arcanine HOLO R .50 .75
23 Torkoal C .10 .20
24 Litten C .10 .20
25 Torracat U .20 .30
26 Incineroar R .30 .50
27 Incineroar GX UR 3.00 5.00
28 Psyduck C .10 .20
29 Golduck R .30 .50
30 Poliwag C .10 .20
31 Poliwhirl U .20 .30
32 Poliwrath HOLO R .50 .75
33 Shellder C .10 .20
34 Cloyster R .30 .50
35 Lapras GX UR 2.50 4.00
36 Corsola U .20 .30
37 Wingull C .10 .20
38 Pelipper U .20 .30
39 Popplio C .10 .20
40 Brionne U .20 .30
41 Primarina R .30 .50
42 Primarina GX UR 2.50 4.00
43 Crabominable R .30 .50
44 Wishiwashi U .20 .30
45 Dewpider C .10 .20
46 Araquanid U .20 .30
47 Pyukumuku U .20 .30
48 Bruxish R .30 .50
49 Chinchou C .10 .20
50 Lanturn R .30 .50
51 Charjabug U .20 .30
52 Vikavolt HOLO R .75 1.25
53 Togedemaru C .10 .20
54 Zubat C .10 .20
55 Golbat U .20 .30
56 Crobat HOLO R .50 .75
57 Alolan Grimer C .10 .20
58 Alolan Muk HOLO R 1.00 1.50
59 Drowzee C .10 .20
60 Hypno U .20 .30
61 Espeon GX UR 3.00 5.00
62 Mareanie C .10 .20
63 Toxapex HOLO R .50 .75
64 Cosmog C .10 .20
65 Cosmoem R .30 .50
66 Lunala GX UR 3.00 5.00
67 Makuhita C .10 .20
68 Hariyama R .30 .50
69 Roggenrola C .10 .20
70 Boldore U .20 .30
71 Gigalith HOLO R .50 .75
72 Crabrawler C .10 .20
73 Passimian U .20 .30
74 Sandygast C .10 .20
75 Palossand R .30 .50
76 Alolan Rattata C .10 .20
77 Alolan Raticate U .20 .30
78 Alolan Meowth C .10 .20
79 Alolan Persian U .20 .30
80 Umbreon GX UR 7.00 10.00
81 Carvanha C .10 .20
82 Sharpedo HOLO R .75 1.25
83 Sandile C .10 .20
84 Krokorok U .20 .30
85 Krookodile HOLO R .50 .75
86 Alolan Diglett C .10 .20
87 Alolan Dugtrio HOLO R .50 .75
88 Skarmory C .10 .20
89 Solgaleo GX UR 4.00 7.00
90 Snubbull C .10 .20
91 Granbull U .20 .30
92 Cutiefly C .10 .20
93 Ribombee HOLO R .50 .75
94 Dratini C .10 .20
95 Dragonair U .20 .30
96 Dragonite HOLO R .50 .75
97 Spearow C .10 .20
98 Fearow C .10 .20
99 Kangaskhan HOLO R .50 .75
100 Tauros GX UR 3.00 5.00
101 Eevee C .10 .20
102 Spinda U .20 .30
103 Lillipup C .10 .20
104 Herdier U .20 .30
105 Stoutland R .30 .50
106 Pikipek C .10 .20
107 Trumbeak U .20 .30
108 Toucannon R .30 .50
109 Yungoos C .10 .20
110 Gumshoos GX UR 2.00 3.50
111 Stufful C .10 .20
112 Bewear U .20 .30
113 Oranguru HOLO R 2.00 3.50
114 Big Malasada U .20 .30
115 Crushing Hammer U .20 .30
116 Energy Retrieval U .20 .30
117 Energy Switch U .20 .30
118 Exp. Share U .20 .30
119 Great Ball U .20 .30
120 Hau U .20 .30
121 Ilima U .20 .30
122 Lillie U .20 .30
123 Nest Ball U .40 .60
124 Poison Barb U .20 .30
125 Poke Ball U .20 .30
126 Pokemon Catcher U .20 .30
127 Potion U .20 .30
128 Professor Kukui U .40 .60
129 Rare Candy U .30 .50
130 Repel U .20 .30
131 Rotom Dex U .20 .30
132 Switch U .20 .30
133 Team Skull Grunt U .25 .40
134 Timer Ball U .30 .50
135 Ultra Ball U .20 .30
136 Double Colorless Energy U .50 .75
137 Rainbow Energy U .20 .30
138 Lurantis GX FULL ART UR 10.00 15.00
139 Lapras GX FULL ART UR 4.00 7.00
140 Espeon GX FULL ART UR 6.00 8.00

141 Lunala GX FULL ART UR 6.00 8.00
142 Umbreon GX FULL ART UR 10.00 15.00
143 Solgaleo GX FULL ART UR 8.00 12.00
144 Tauros GX FULL ART UR 6.00 8.00
145 Gumshoos GX FULL ART UR 3.00 5.00
146 Ilima FULL ART UR 5.00 8.00
147 Lillie FULL ART UR 13.00 16.00
148 Professor Kukui FULL ART UR 10.00 15.00
149 Team Skull Grunt FULL ART UR 7.00 10.00
150 Lurantis GX SCR 15.00 20.00
151 Lapras GX SCR 15.00 20.00
152 Espeon GX SCR 20.00 25.00
153 Lunala GX SCR 20.00 25.00
154 Umbreon GX SCR 25.00 30.00
155 Solgaleo GX SCR 20.00 25.00
156 Tauros GX SCR 15.00 20.00
157 Gumshoos GX SCR 10.00 15.00
158 Nest Ball SCR 20.00 25.00
159 Rotom Dex SCR 10.00 15.00
160 Switch SCR 15.00 20.00
161 Ultra Ball SCR 100.00 120.00
162 Psychic Energy SCR 20.00 25.00
163 Metal Energy SCR 20.00 25.00

2017 Pokemon Sun and Moon Reverse Foil

COMPLETE SET (126) 45.00 70.00
1 Caterpie C .25 .40
2 Metapod U .25 .40
3 Butterfree R .50 .75
4 Paras C .25 .40
5 Parasect R .50 .75
6 Pinsir U .25 .40
7 Surskit C .25 .40
8 Masquerain R .50 .75
9 Rowlet C .25 .40
10 Dartrix U .25 .40
11 Decidueye R .50 .75
13 Grubbin C .25 .40
14 Fomantis C .25 .40
16 Morelull C .25 .40
17 Shiinotic HOLO R 1.50 2.50
18 Bounsweet C .25 .40
19 Steenee U .25 .40
20 Tsareena HOLO R .75 1.25
21 Growlithe C .25 .40
22 Arcanine HOLO R .50 .75
23 Torkoal C .25 .40
24 Litten C .25 .40
25 Torracat U .25 .40
26 Incineroar R .50 .75
28 Psyduck C .25 .40
29 Golduck R .50 .75
30 Poliwag C .25 .40
31 Poliwhirl U .25 .40
32 Poliwrath HOLO R .50 .75
33 Shellder C .25 .40
34 Cloyster R .50 .75
36 Corsola U .25 .40
37 Wingull C .25 .40
38 Pelipper U .25 .40
39 Popplio C .25 .40
40 Brionne U .25 .40
41 Primarina R .50 .75
43 Crabominable R .50 .75
44 Wishiwashi U .25 .40
45 Dewpider C .25 .40
46 Araquanid U .25 .40
47 Pyukumuku U .25 .40
48 Bruxish R .50 .75
49 Chinchou C .25 .40
50 Lanturn R .50 .75
51 Charjabug U .25 .40
52 Vikavolt HOLO R .75 1.25
53 Togedemaru C .25 .40
54 Zubat C .25 .40
55 Golbat U .25 .40
56 Crobat HOLO R .50 .75
57 Alolan Grimer C .25 .40
58 Alolan Muk HOLO R 1.50 2.50
59 Drowzee C .25 .40
60 Hypno U .25 .40
62 Mareanie C .25 .40
63 Toxapex HOLO R .75 1.25
64 Cosmog C .25 .40
65 Cosmoem R .50 .75
67 Makuhita C .25 .40
68 Hariyama R .50 .75
69 Roggenrola C .25 .40
70 Boldore U .25 .40
71 Gigalith HOLO R .50 .75
72 Crabrawler C .25 .40
73 Passimian U .25 .40
74 Sandygast C .25 .40
75 Palossand R .50 .75
76 Alolan Rattata C .25 .40
77 Alolan Raticate U .25 .40
78 Alolan Meowth C .25 .40
79 Alolan Persian U .25 .40
81 Carvanha C .25 .40
82 Sharpedo HOLO R .75 1.25
83 Sandile C .25 .40
84 Krokorok U .25 .40
85 Krookodile HOLO R .50 .75
86 Alolan Diglett C .25 .40
87 Alolan Dugtrio HOLO R .50 .75
88 Skarmory C .25 .40
90 Snubbull C .25 .40
91 Granbull U .25 .40
92 Cutiefly C .25 .40
93 Ribombee HOLO R .50 .75
94 Dratini C .25 .40
95 Dragonair U .25 .40
96 Dragonite HOLO R .50 .75
97 Spearow C .25 .40
98 Fearow C .25 .40
99 Kangaskhan HOLO R .50 .75
101 Eevee C .25 .40
102 Spinda U .25 .40
103 Lillipup C .25 .40
104 Herdier U .25 .40
105 Stoutland R .50 .75
106 Pikipek C .25 .40
107 Trumbeak U .25 .40
108 Toucannon R .50 .75
109 Yungoos C .25 .40
111 Stufful C .25 .40
112 Bewear U .25 .40
113 Oranguru HOLO R 2.00 3.00
114 Big Malasada U .25 .40
115 Crushing Hammer U .25 .40
116 Energy Retrieval U .25 .40
117 Energy Switch U .25 .40
118 Exp. Share U .25 .40
119 Great Ball U .25 .40
120 Hau U .25 .40
121 Ilima U .25 .40
122 Lillie U .25 .40
123 Nest Ball U .75 1.25
124 Poison Barb U .25 .40
125 Poke Ball U .25 .40
126 Pokemon Catcher U .25 .40
127 Potion U .25 .40
128 Professor Kukui U .50 .75
129 Rare Candy U .60 1.00
130 Repel U .25 .40
131 Rotom Dex U .25 .40
132 Switch U .25 .40
133 Team Skull Grunt U .40 .60
134 Timer Ball U .50 .75
135 Ultra Ball U .25 .40
136 Double Colorless Energy U .75 1.25
137 Rainbow Energy U .25 .40

2017 Pokemon Sun and Moon Guardians Rising

COMPLETE SET (166) 700.00 950.00
RELEASED ON MAY 5, 2017
1 Bellsprout C .15 .25
2 Weepinbell U .25 .40
3 Victreebel R .30 .50
4 Petilil C .15 .25
5 Lilligant R .30 .50
6 Phantump C .15 .25
7 Trevenant R .30 .50
8 Wimpod C .15 .25
9 Golisopod HOLO R .50 .80
10 Victini HOLO R .50 .80
11 Litwick C .15 .25
12 Lampent U .25 .40
13 Chandelure HOLO R .50 .80
14 Oricorio R .30 .50
15 Salandit C .15 .25
16 Salazzle R .30 .50
17 Turtonator R .30 .50
18 Turtonator GX UR 2.00 3.50
19 Alolan Sandshrew C .15 .25
20 Alolan Sandslash U .25 .40
21 Alolan Vulpix C .15 .25
22 Alolan Ninetales GX UR 2.00 3.50
23 Tentacool C .15 .25
24 Tentacruel U .25 .40
25 Politoed HOLO R .50 .80
26 Delibird C .15 .25
27 Carvanha C .15 .25
28 Sharpedo R .30 .50
29 Wailmer C .15 .25
30 Wailord R .30 .50
31 Snorunt C .15 .25
32 Glalie U .25 .40
33 Vanillite C .15 .25
34 Vanillish U .25 .40
35 Vanilluxe R .30 .50
36 Alomomola U .25 .40
37 Wishiwashi C .15 .25
38 Wishiwashi GX UR 1.50 2.50
39 Mareanie C .15 .25
40 Alolan Geodude C .15 .25
41 Alolan Graveler U .25 .40
42 Alolan Golem HOLO R .50 .80
43 Helioptile C .15 .25
44 Heliolisk R .30 .50
45 Vikavolt GX UR 2.00 3.50
46 Oricorio R .30 .50
47 Tapu Koko GX UR 6.00 8.00
48 Slowpoke C .15 .25
49 Slowbro U .25 .40
50 Trubbish C .15 .25
51 Garbodor R .30 .50
52 Gothita C .15 .25
53 Gothorita U .25 .40
54 Gothitelle R .30 .50
55 Oricorio R .30 .50
56 Oricorio R .30 .50
57 Toxapex GX UR 3.00 5.00
58 Mimikyu HOLO R .50 .80
59 Dhelmise HOLO R .50 .80
60 Tapu Lele GX UR 40.00 45.00
61 Lunala R .30 .50
62 Machop C .15 .25
63 Machop C .15 .25
64 Machoke U .25 .40
65 Machamp HOLO R .50 .80
66 Sudowoodo U .25 .40
67 Gligar C .15 .25
68 Gliscor U .25 .40
69 Nosepass C .15 .25
70 Barboach C .15 .25
71 Whiscash R .30 .50
72 Pancham C .15 .25
73 Rockruff C .15 .25
74 Lycanroc GX UR 1.50 2.50
75 Mudbray C .15 .25
76 Mudsdale HOLO R .50 .80
77 Minior HOLO R .50 .80
78 Murkrow C .15 .25
79 Honchkrow R .30 .50
80 Sableye U .25 .40
81 Absol HOLO R .50 .80
82 Pangoro R .30 .50
83 Beldum C .15 .25
84 Metang U .25 .40
85 Metagross GX UR 2.00 3.50
86 Probopass R .30 .50
87 Solgaleo R .30 .50
88 Clefairy C .15 .25
89 Clefable U .25 .40
90 Cottonee C .15 .25
91 Whimsicott U .25 .40
92 Sylveon GX UR 2.00 3.50
93 Comfey HOLO R .50 .80
94 Goomy C .15 .25
95 Sliggoo U .25 .40
96 Goodra HOLO R .50 .80
97 Drampa HOLO R .50 .80
98 Jangmo o C .15 .25
99 Hakamo o U .25 .40
100 Kommo-O GX UR 1.25 2.00
101 Chansey C .15 .25
102 Blissey HOLO R .50 .80
103 Taillow C .15 .25
104 Swellow R .30 .50
105 Castform C .15 .25
106 Rayquaza R .30 .50
107 Patrat C .15 .25
108 Watchog U .25 .40
109 Fletchling C .15 .25
110 Fletchinder U .25 .40
111 Talonflame R .30 .50
112 Stufful C .15 .25
113 Bewear U .25 .40
114 Komala U .25 .40
115 Drampa GX UR 2.50 4.00
116 Aether Paradise Conservation Area U .25 .40
117 Altar of the Moone U .25 .40
118 Altar of the Sunne U .25 .40
119 Aqua Patch U .25 .40
120 Brooklet Hill U .25 .40
121 Choice Band U .25 .40
122 Energy Loto U .25 .40
123 Energy Recycler U .25 .40
124 Enhanced Hammer U .25 .40
125 Field Blower U .25 .40
126 Hala U .25 .40
127 Mallow U .25 .40
128 Max Potion U .25 .40
129 Multi Switch U .25 .40
130 Rescue Stretcher U .25 .40
131 Turtonator GX FULL ART UR 3.00 5.00
132 Alolan Ninetales GX FULL ART UR 5.00 7.00
133 Wishiwashi GX FULL ART UR 3.00 5.00
134 Vikavolt GX FULL ART UR 1.50 2.50
135 Tapu Koko GX FULL ART UR 3.00 5.00
136 Toxapex GX FULL ART UR 1.50 2.50
137 Tapu Lele GX FULL ART UR 50.00 55.00
138 Lycanroc GX FULL ART UR 3.00 5.00
139 Metagross GX FULL ART UR 5.00 7.00
140 Sylveon GX FULL ART UR 4.00 6.00
141 Kommo-O GX FULL ART UR 1.25 2.00
142 Drampa GX FULL ART UR 3.00 5.00
143 Hala FULL ART UR 3.00 5.00
144 Hau FULL ART UR 3.00 5.00
145 Mallow FULL ART UR 8.00 12.00
146 Decidueye GX FULL ART SCR 10.00 15.00
147 Inciniroar GX FULL ART SCR 6.00 8.00
148 Turtonator GX FULL ART SCR 10.00 15.00
149 Primarina GX FULL ART SCR 6.00 8.00
150 Alolan Ninetales GX FULL ART SCR 15.00 20.00
151 Wishiwashi GX FULL ART SCR 4.00 6.00
152 Vikavolt GX FULL ART SCR 4.00 6.00
153 Tapu Koko GX FULL ART SCR 8.00 12.00
154 Toxapex GX FULL ART SCR 4.00 6.00
155 Tapu Lele GX FULL ART SCR 60.00 65.00
156 Lycanroc GX FULL ART SCR 7.00 10.00
157 Metagross GX FULL ART SCR 10.00 15.00
158 Sylveon GX FULL ART SCR 15.00 20.00
159 Kommo-O GX FULL ART SCR 4.00 6.00
160 Drampa GX FULL ART SCR 8.00 12.00
161 Aqua Patch FULL ART SCR 10.00 15.00
162 Enhanced Hammer FULL ART SCR 6.00 8.00
163 Field Blower FULL ART SCR 20.00 25.00
164 Max Potion FULL ART SCR 10.00 15.00
165 Rare Candy FULL ART SCR 25.00 30.00
166 Double Colorless Energy FULL ART SCR 50.00 55.00
167 Grass Energy FULL ART SCR 15.00 20.00
168 Lightning Energy FULL ART SCR 10.00 15.00
169 Fighting Energy FULL ART SCR 10.00 15.00

2017 Pokemon Sun and Moon Guardians Rising Reverse Foil

COMPLETE SET (169) 600.00 900.00
RELEASED ON MAY 5, 2017
1 Bellsprout C .20 .35
2 Weepinbell U .25 .40
3 Victreebel R .30 .50
4 Petilil C .20 .35
5 Lilligant R .30 .50
6 Phantump C .20 .35
7 Trevenant R .30 .50
8 Wimpod C .20 .35
9 Golisopod HOLO R .40 .75
10 Victini HOLO R .40 .75
11 Litwick C .20 .35
12 Lampent U .25 .40
13 Chandelure HOLO R .40 .75
14 Oricorio R .30 .50
15 Salandit C .20 .35
16 Salazzle R .30 .50
17 Turtonator R .30 .50
18 Turtonator GX UR 3.00 5.00
19 Alolan Sandshrew C .20 .35
20 Alolan Sandslash U .25 .40
21 Alolan Vulpix C .20 .35
22 Alolan Ninetales GX UR 5.00 7.00
23 Tentacool C .20 .35
24 Tentacruel U .25 .40
25 Politoed HOLO R .40 .75
26 Delibird C .20 .35
27 Carvanha C .20 .35
28 Sharpedo R .30 .50
29 Wailmer C .20 .35
30 Wailord R .30 .50
31 Snorunt C .20 .35
32 Glalie U .25 .40
33 Vanillite C .20 .35
34 Vanillish U .25 .40
35 Vanilluxe R .30 .50
36 Alomomola U .25 .40
37 Wishiwashi C .20 .35
38 Wishiwashi GX UR 1.50 2.50
39 Mareanie C .20 .35
40 Alolan Geodude C .20 .35
41 Alolan Graveler U .25 .40
42 Alolan Golem HOLO R .40 .75
43 Helioptile C .20 .35
44 Heliolisk R .30 .50
45 Vikavolt GX UR 2.00 3.50
46 Oricorio R .30 .50
47 Tapu Koko GX UR 6.00 8.00
48 Slowpoke C .20 .35
49 Slowbro U .25 .40
50 Trubbish C .20 .35
51 Garbodor R .30 .50
52 Gothita C .20 .35
53 Gothorita U .25 .40
54 Gothitelle R .30 .50
55 Oricorio R .30 .50
56 Oricorio R .30 .50
57 Toxapex GX UR 3.00 5.00
58 Mimikyu HOLO R .40 .75
59 Dhelmise HOLO R .40 .75
60 Tapu Lele GX UR 35.00 40.00
61 Lunala R .30 .50
62 Machop C .20 .35
63 Machop C .20 .35
64 Machoke U .25 .40
65 Machamp HOLO R .40 .75
66 Sudowoodo U .25 .40
67 Gligar C .20 .35
68 Gliscor U .25 .40
69 Nosepass C .20 .35
70 Barboach C .20 .35
71 Whiscash R .30 .50
72 Pancham C .20 .35
73 Rockruff C .20 .35
74 Lycanroc GX UR 4.00 6.00
75 Mudbray C .20 .35
76 Mudsdale HOLO R .40 .75
77 Minior HOLO R .40 .75
78 Murkrow C .20 .35
79 Honchkrow R .30 .50
80 Sableye U .25 .40
81 Absol HOLO R .40 .75
82 Pangoro R .30 .50
83 Beldum C .20 .35
84 Metang U .25 .40
85 Metagross GX UR 2.00 3.50
86 Probopass R .30 .50
87 Solgaleo R .30 .50
88 Clefairy C .20 .35
89 Clefable U .25 .40
90 Cottonee C .20 .35
91 Whimsicott U .25 .40
92 Sylveon GX UR 7.00 10.00
93 Comfey HOLO R .40 .75
94 Goomy C .20 .35
95 Sliggoo U .25 .40
96 Goodra HOLO R .40 .75
97 Drampa HOLO R .40 .75
98 Jangmo o C .20 .35
99 Hakamo o U .25 .40
100 Kommo o GX UR 2.00 3.50
101 Chansey C .20 .35
102 Blissey HOLO R .40 .75
103 Taillow C .20 .35
104 Swellow R .30 .50
105 Castform C .20 .35
106 Rayquaza R .30 .50
107 Patrat C .20 .35
108 Watchog U .25 .40
109 Fletchling C .20 .35
110 Fletchinder U .25 .40
111 Talonflame R .30 .50
112 Stufful C .20 .35
113 Bewear U .25 .40
114 Komala U .25 .40
115 Drampa GX UR 3.00 5.00
116 Aether Paradise Conservation Area U .25 .40
117 Altar of the Moone U .25 .40
118 Altar of the Sunne U .25 .40
119 Aqua Patch U .75 1.25
120 Brooklet Hill U .25 .40
121 Choice Band U .50 .75
122 Energy Loto U .25 .40
123 Energy Recycler U .25 .40
124 Enhanced Hammer U .25 .40
125 Field Blower U .25 .40
126 Hala U .25 .40
127 Mallow U .25 .40
128 Max Potion U .25 .40

129 Multi Switch U .25 .40
130 Rescue Stretcher U .25 .40
131 Turtonator GX FULL ART UR 6.00 9.00
132 Alolan Ninetales GX FULL ART UR 10.00 15.00
133 Wishiwashi GX FULL ART UR 3.00 5.00
134 Vikavolt GX FULL ART UR 5.00 7.00
135 Tapu Koko GX FULL ART UR 10.00 15.00
136 Toxapex GX FULL ART UR 7.00 10.00
137 Tapu Lele GX FULL ART UR 40.00 45.00
138 Lycanroc GX FULL ART UR 7.00 10.00
139 Metagross GX FULL ART UR 5.00 7.00
140 Sylveon GX FULL ART UR 10.00 15.00
141 Kommo o GX FULL ART UR 4.00 6.00
142 Drampa GX FULL ART UR 7.00 10.00
143 Hala FULL ART UR 7.00 10.00
144 Hau FULL ART UR 6.00 8.00
145 Mallow FULL ART UR 8.00 12.00
146 Decidueye GX FULL ART SCR 30.00 35.00
147 Incinirroar GX FULL ART SCR 15.00 20.00
148 Turtonator GX FULL ART SCR 10.00 15.00
149 Primarina GX FULL ART SCR 13.00 16.00
150 Alolan Ninetales GX FULL ART SCR 20.00 25.00
151 Wishiwashi GX FULL ART SCR 10.00 15.00
152 Vikavolt GX FULL ART SCR 10.00 15.00
153 Tapu Koko GX FULL ART SCR 20.00 25.00
154 Toxapex GX FULL ART SCR 10.00 15.00
155 Tapu Lele GX FULL ART SCR 60.00 70.00
156 Lycanroc GX FULL ART SCR 15.00 20.00
157 Metagross GX FULL ART SCR 13.00 16.00
158 Sylveon GX FULL ART SCR 25.00 30.00
159 Kommo-O GX FULL ART SCR 15.00 20.00
160 Drampa GX FULL ART SCR 15.00 20.00
161 Aqua Patch FULL ART SCR 25.00 30.00
162 Enhanced Hammer FULL ART SCR 15.00 20.00
163 Field Blower FULL ART SCR 25.00 30.00
164 Max Potion FULL ART SCR 15.00 20.00
165 Rare Candy FULL ART SCR 20.00 25.00
166 Double Colorless Energy FULL ART SCR 70.00 80.00
167 Grass Energy FULL ART SCR
168 Lightning Energy FULL ART SCR
169 Fighting Energy FULL ART SCR

2017 Pokemon Sun and Moon Burning Shadows

COMPLETE SET (169) 750.00 1000.00
RELEASED ON AUGUST 4, 2017
1 Caterpie C .10 .20
2 Metapod U .25 .40
3 Butterfree R .30 .50
4 Oddish C .10 .20
5 Gloom U .25 .40
6 Vileplume HOLO R .50 .80
7 Tangela C .10 .20
8 Tangrowth R .30 .50
9 Ledyba C .10 .20
10 Ledian R .30 .50
11 Heracross R .30 .50
12 Pansage C .10 .20
13 Simisage U .25 .40
14 Dewpider C .10 .20
15 Araquanid R .30 .50
16 Wimpod C .10 .20
17 Golisopod GX UR 6.00 8.00
18 Charmander C .10 .20
19 Charmeleon U .25 .40
20 Charizard GX UR 7.00 10.00
21 Ho Oh GX UR 2.00 3.50
22 Pansear C .10 .20
23 Simisear U .25 .40
24 Heatmor U .25 .40
25 Salazzle GX UR 2.00 3.50
26 Turtonator R .30 .50
27 Alolan Vulpix C .10 .20
28 Alolan Ninetales R .30 .50
29 Horsea C .10 .20
30 Seadra U .10 .20
31 Kingdra HOLO R .50 .80
32 Magikarp C .10 .20
33 Gyarados HOLO R .50 .80
34 Marill C .10 .20
35 Azumarill R .30 .50
36 Panpour C .10 .20
37 Simipour U .25 .40
38 Bruxish R .30 .50
39 Tapu Fini GX UR 1.50 2.50
40 Pikachu C .10 .20
41 Raichu HOLO R .50 .80
42 Electabuzz U .25 .40
43 Electivire R .30 .50
44 Tynamo C .10 .20
45 Eelektrik U .25 .40
46 Eelektross R .30 .50
47 Togedemaru C .10 .20
48 Slowking R .30 .50
49 Wobbuffet U .25 .40
50 Seviper U .25 .40
51 Duskull C .10 .20
52 Dusclops U .25 .40
53 Dusknoir HOLO R .50 .80
54 Croagunk C .10 .20
55 Toxicroak R .30 .50
56 Venipede C .10 .20
57 Whirlipede U .25 .40
58 Scolipede R .30 .50
59 Espurr C .10 .20
60 Meowstic R .30 .50
61 Sandygast C .10 .20
62 Palossand HOLO R .50 .80
63 Necrozma GX UR 2.00 3.50
64 Machamp GX UR 1.25 2.00
65 Rhyhorn C .10 .20
66 Rhydon U .25 .40
67 Rhyperior HOLO R .50 .80
68 Lunatone U .25 .40
69 Solrock U .25 .40
70 Riolu C .10 .20
71 Lucario HOLO R .50 .80
72 Sawk C .10 .20
73 Crabrawler C .10 .20
74 Crabominable R .30 .50
75 Lycanroc HOLO R .50 .80
76 Lycanroc R .30 .50
77 Mudbray C .10 .20
78 Mudsdale R .30 .50
79 Passimian R .30 .50
80 Marshadow GX UR 1.50 2.50
81 Alolan Rattata C .10 .20
82 Alolan Raticate R .30 .50
83 Alolan Grimer C .10 .20
84 Alolan Muk GX UR 1.50 2.50
85 Sneasel C .10 .20
86 Weavile R .30 .50
87 Darkrai HOLO R .50 .80
88 Darkrai GX UR 2.00 3.50
89 Inkay C .10 .20
90 Malamar R .30 .50
91 Ralts C .10 .20
92 Kirlia U .25 .40
93 Gardevoir GX UR 7.00 10.00
94 Diancie HOLO R .50 .80
95 Cutiefly C .10 .20
96 Ribombee U .25 .40
97 Morelull C .10 .20
98 Shiinotic R .30 .50
99 Noivern GX UR 1.25 2.00
100 Zygarde HOLO R .50 .80
101 Meowth C .10 .20
102 Persian R .30 .50
103 Porygon C .10 .20
104 Porygon2 U .25 .40
105 Porygon Z HOLO R .50 .80
106 Hoothoot C .10 .20
107 Noctowl U .25 .40
108 Bouffalant U .25 .40
109 Noibat C .10 .20
110 Stufful C .10 .20
111 Bewear R .30 .50
112 Acerola U .25 .40
113 Bodybuilding Dumbbells U .25 .40
114 Escape Rope U .25 .40
115 Guzma U 1.50 2.50
116 Kiawe U .25 .40
117 Lana U .25 .40
118 Mount Lanakila U .25 .40
119 Olivia U .25 .40
120 Plumeria U .25 .40
121 Po Town U .25 .40
122 Rotom Dex Poke Finder Mode U .25 .40
123 Sophocles U .25 .40
124 Super Scoop Up U .25 .40
125 Tormenting Spray U .25 .40
126 Weakness Policy U .25 .40
127 Wicke U .25 .40
128 Wishful Baton U .25 .40
129 Golisopod GX FULL ART UR 8.00 12.00
130 Tapu Bulu GX FULL ART UR 5.00 7.00
131 Ho Oh GX FULL ART UR 5.00 7.00
132 Salazzle GX FULL ART UR 4.00 6.00
133 Tapu Fini GX FULL ART UR 4.00 6.00
134 Necrozma GX FULL ART UR 5.00 7.00
135 Machamp GX FULL ART UR 1.50 2.50
136 Lycanroc GX FULL ART UR 1.50 2.50
137 Marshadow GX FULL ART UR 3.00 5.00
138 Alolan Muk GX FULL ART UR 2.00 3.50
139 Darkrai GX FULL ART UR 5.00 8.00
140 Gardevoir GX FULL ART UR 15.00 20.00
141 Noivern GX FULL ART UR 3.00 5.00
142 Acerola FULL ART UR 20.00 25.00
143 Guzma FULL ART UR 40.00 45.00
144 Kiawe FULL ART UR 8.00 12.00
145 Plumeria FULL ART UR 5.00 7.00
146 Sophocles FULL ART UR 4.00 6.00
147 Wicke FULL ART UR 5.00 8.00
148 Golisopod GX SCR 10.00 15.00
149 Tapu Bulu GX SCR 8.00 10.00
150 Charizard GX SCR 70.00 80.00
151 Salazzle GX SCR 6.00 8.00
152 Tapu Fini GX SCR 5.00 8.00
153 Necrozma GX SCR 8.00 12.00
154 Machamp GX SCR 4.00 6.00
155 Lycanroc GX SCR 6.00 8.00
156 Marshadow GX SCR 10.00 15.00
157 Alolan Muk GX SCR 4.00 6.00
158 Darkrai GX SCR 10.00 15.00
159 Gardevoir GX SCR 15.00 20.00
160 Noivern GX SCR 6.00 8.00
161 Bodybuilding Dumbbells SCR 6.00 8.00
162 Choice Band SCR 30.00 35.00
163 Escape Rope SCR 6.00 8.00
164 Multi Switch SCR 5.00 7.00
165 Rescue Stretcher SCR 15.00 20.00
166 Super Scoop Up SCR 5.00 8.00
167 Fire Energy SCR 15.00 20.00
168 Darkness Energy SCR 25.00 30.00
169 Fairy Energy SCR 35.00 40.00

2017 Pokemon Sun and Moon Burning Shadows Reverse Foil

COMPLETE SET (116)
RELEASED ON AUGUST 4, 2017
1 Caterpie C .20 .35
2 Metapod U .30 .50
3 Butterfree R .40 .60
4 Oddish C .20 .35
5 Gloom U .20 .35
6 Vileplume HOLO R .60 1.00
7 Tangela C .20 .35
8 Tangrowth R .40 .60
9 Ledyba C .20 .35
10 Ledian R .40 .60
11 Heracross R .40 .60
12 Pansage C .20 .35
13 Simisage U .30 .50
14 Dewpider C .20 .35
15 Araquanid R .40 .60
16 Wimpod C .20 .35
18 Charmander C .20 .35
19 Charmeleon U .30 .50
22 Pansear C .20 .35
23 Simisear U .30 .50
24 Heatmor U .30 .50
26 Turtonator R .40 .60
27 Alolan Vulpix C .20 .35
28 Alolan Ninetales R .40 .60
29 Horsea C .20 .35
30 Seadra U .30 .50
31 Kingdra HOLO R .60 1.00
32 Magikarp C .20 .35
33 Gyarados HOLO R .60 1.00
34 Marill C .20 .35
35 Azumarill R .40 .60
36 Panpour C .20 .35
37 Simipour U .30 .50
38 Bruxish R .40 .60
40 Pikachu C .20 .35
41 Raichu HOLO R .60 1.00
42 Electabuzz U .30 .50
43 Electivire R .40 .60
44 Tynamo C .20 .35
45 Eelektrik U .30 .50
46 Eelektross R .40 .60
47 Togedemaru C .20 .35
48 Slowking R .40 .60
49 Wobbuffet U .30 .50
50 Seviper U .30 .50
51 Duskull C .20 .35
52 Dusclops U .30 .50
53 Dusknoir HOLO R .60 1.00
54 Croagunk C .20 .35
55 Toxicroak R .40 .60
56 Venipede C .20 .35
57 Whirlipede U .30 .50
58 Scolipede R .40 .60
59 Espurr C .20 .35
60 Meowstic R .40 .60
61 Sandygast C .20 .35
62 Palossand HOLO R .60 1.00
65 Rhyhorn C .20 .35
66 Rhydon U .30 .50
67 Rhyperior HOLO R .60 1.00
68 Lunatone U .30 .50
69 Solrock U .30 .50
70 Riolu C .20 .35
71 Lucario HOLO R .60 1.00
72 Sawk C .20 .35
73 Crabrawler C .20 .35
74 Crabominable R .40 .60
75 Lycanroc HOLO R .60 1.00
76 Lycanroc R .40 .60
77 Mudbray C .20 .35
78 Mudsdale R .40 .60
79 Passimian R .40 .60
81 Alolan Rattata C .20 .35
82 Alolan Raticate R .40 .60
83 Alolan Grimer C .20 .35
85 Sneasel C .20 .35
86 Weavile R .40 .60
87 Darkrai HOLO R .60 1.00
89 Inkay C .20 .35
90 Malamar R .40 .60
91 Ralts C .20 .35
92 Kirlia U .30 .50
94 Diancie HOLO R .60 1.00
95 Cutiefly C .20 .35
96 Ribombee U .30 .50
97 Morelull C .20 .35
98 Shiinotic R .40 .60
100 Zygarde HOLO R .60 1.00
101 Meowth C .20 .35
102 Persian R .40 .60
103 Porygon C .20 .35
104 Porygon2 U .30 .50
105 Porygon Z HOLO R .60 1.00
106 Hoothoot C .20 .35
107 Noctowl U .30 .50
108 Bouffalant U .30 .50
109 Noibat C .20 .35
110 Stufful C .20 .35
111 Bewear R .40 .60
112 Acerola U .30 .50
113 Bodybuilding Dumbbells U .30 .50
114 Escape Rope U .30 .50
115 Guzma U .30 .50
116 Kiawe U .30 .50
117 Lana U .30 .50
118 Mount Lanakila U .30 .50
119 Olivia U .30 .50
120 Plumeria U .30 .50
121 Po Town U .30 .50
122 Rotom Dex Poke Finder Mode U .30 .50
123 Sophocles U .30 .50
124 Super Scoop Up U .30 .50
125 Tormenting Spray U .30 .50
126 Weakness Policy U .30 .50
127 Wicke U .30 .50
128 Wishful Baton U .30 .50

2017 Pokemon Shining Legends

COMPLETE SET (87) 400.00 500.00
RELEASED ON OCTOBER 6, 2017
1 Bulbasaur C .10 .20
2 Ivysaur C .10 .20
3 Venusaur U .20 .35
4 Shroomish C .10 .20
5 Breloom C .10 .20
6 Carnivine U .20 .35
7 Shaymin HOLO R .30 .50
8 Virizion HOLO R .20 .35
9 Shining Genesect HOLO R 10.00 15.00
10 Entei GX UR 1.25 2.00
11 Torkoal C .10 .20
12 Larvesta C .10 .20
13 Volcarona U .20 .35
14 Reshiram HOLO R .20 .35
15 Litten C .10 .20
16 Torracat C .10 .20
17 Incineroar U .20 .35
18 Totodile C .10 .20
19 Croconaw C .10 .20
20 Feraligatr U .20 .35
21 Qwilfish C .10 .20
22 Buizel C .10 .20
23 Floatzel U .20 .35
24 Palkia HOLO R .20 .35
25 Manaphy HOLO R .20 .35
26 Keldeo HOLO R .20 .35
27 Shining Volcanion HOLO R 5.00 7.00
28 Pikachu C .10 .20
29 Raichu GX UR 6.00 8.00
30 Voltorb C .10 .20
31 Electrode U .20 .35
32 Raikou HOLO R .20 .35
33 Plusle C .10 .20
34 Minun C .10 .20
35 Zekrom Holo R .20 .35
36 Ekans C .10 .20
37 Arbok U .20 .35
38 Jynx C .10 .20
39 Mewtwo GX UR 2.00 3.50
40 Shining Mew HOLO R 20.00 25.00
41 Latios HOLO R .20 .35
42 Shining Jirachi HOLO R 8.00 10.00
43 Golett C .10 .20
44 Golurk U .20 .35
45 Marshadow HOLO R .40 .60
46 Stunfisk C .10 .20
47 Spiritomb U .20 .35
48 Purrloin C .10 .20
49 Liepard U .20 .35
50 Scraggy C .10 .20
51 Scrafty U .20 .35
52 Zorua C .10 .20
53 Zoroark GX UR 15.00 20.00
54 Yveltal Holo R .30 .50
55 Hoopa HOLO R 1.00 1.50
56 Shining Rayquaza HOLO R 8.00 10.00
57 Shining Arceus HOLO R 4.00 6.00
58 Damage Mover U .20 .35
59 Energy Retrieval U .20 .35
60 Great Ball U .20 .35
61 Hau U .20 .35
62 Lillie U .20 .35
63 Pokemon Breeder U .20 .35
64 Pokemon Catcher U .20 .35
65 Sophocles U .20 .35
66 Super Scoop Up U .20 .35
67 Switch U .20 .35
68 Ultra Ball U .20 .35
69 Double Colorless Energy U .20 .35
70 Warp Energy U .20 .35
71 Entei GX FULL ART UR 3.00 5.00
72 Mewtwo GX FULL ART UR 4.00 6.00
73 Pokemon Breeder FULL ART UR 4.00 6.00
74 Entei GX SCR 10.00 15.00
75 Raichu GX SCR 25.00 30.00
76 Mewtwo GX SCR 20.00 25.00
77 Zoroark GX SCR 30.00 35.00
78 Shining Mewtwo GX SCR 25.00 30.00
NNO Grass Energy .05 .15
NNO Fire Energy .05 .15
NNO Water Energy .05 .15
NNO Lightning Energy .05 .15
NNO Psychic Energy .05 .15
NNO Fighting Energy .05 .15
NNO Darkness Energy .05 .15
NNO Metal Energy .05 .15
NNO Fairy Energy .05 .15

2017 Pokemon Shining Legends Reverse Foil

COMPLETE SET (69) 20.00 35.00
RELEASED ON OCTOBER 6, 2017
1 Bulbasaur C .20 .35
2 Ivysaur C .20 .35
3 Venusaur U .40 .60
4 Shroomish C .20 .35
5 Breloom C .20 .35
6 Carnivine U .40 .60
7 Shaymin HOLO R .40 .60
8 Virizion HOLO R .40 .60
11 Torkoal C .20 .35
12 Larvesta C .20 .35
13 Volcarona U .40 .60
14 Reshiram HOLO R .40 .60
15 Litten C .20 .35
16 Torracat C .20 .35
17 Incineroar U .40 .60
18 Totodile C .20 .35
19 Croconaw C .20 .35
20 Feraligatr U .40 .60
21 Qwilfish C .20 .35
22 Buizel C .20 .35
23 Floatzel U .40 .60
24 Palkia HOLO R .40 .60
25 Manaphy HOLO R .40 .60
26 Keldeo HOLO R .40 .60
28 Pikachu C .20 .35
30 Voltorb C .20 .35
31 Electrode U .40 .60
32 Raikou HOLO R .40 .60
33 Plusle C .20 .35

34 Minun C .20 .35
35 Zekrom Holo R .40 .60
36 Ekans C .20 .35
37 Arbok U .40 .60
38 Jynx C .20 .35
41 Latios HOLO R .40 .60
43 Golett C .20 .35
44 Golurk U .40 .60
45 Marshadow HOLO R .40 .60
46 Stunfisk C .20 .35
47 Spiritomb U .40 .60
48 Purrloin C .20 .35
49 Liepard U .40 .60
50 Scraggy C .20 .35
51 Scrafty U .40 .60
52 Zorua C .20 .35
54 Yveltal Holo R .40 .60
55 Hoopa HOLO R .40 .60
58 Damage Mover U .40 .60
59 Energy Retrieval U .40 .60
60 Great Ball U .40 .60
61 Hau U .40 .60
62 Lillie U .40 .60
63 Pokemon Breeder U .40 .60
64 Pokemon Catcher U .40 .60
65 Sophocles U .40 .60
66 Super Scoop Up U .40 .60
67 Switch U .40 .60
68 Ultra Ball U .40 .60
69 Double Colorless Energy U .40 .60
70 Warp Energy U .40 .60
NNO Grass Energy .20 .35
NNO Fire Energy .20 .35
NNO Water Energy .20 .35
NNO Lightning Energy .20 .35
NNO Psychic Energy .20 .35
NNO Fighting Energy .20 .35
NNO Darkness Energy .20 .35
NNO Metal Energy .20 .35
NNO Fairy Energy .20 .35

2017 Pokemon Sun and Moon Crimson Invasion

COMPLETE SET (124) 300.00 450.00
RELEASED ON NOVEMBER 3, 2017
1 Weedle C .15 .25
2 Kakuna U .20 .35
3 Beedrill R .30 .50
4 Exeggcute C .15 .25
5 Cacnea C .15 .25
6 Cacturne R .30 .50
7 Karrablast C .15 .25
8 Shelmet C .15 .25
9 Accelgor U .20 .35
10 Skiddo C .15 .25
11 Gogoat HOLO R .50 .80
12 Alolan Marowak HOLO R .50 .80
13 Numel C .15 .25
14 Camerupt R .30 .50
15 Staryu C .15 .25
16 Starmie R .30 .50
17 Magikarp C .15 .25
18 Gyarados GX UR 2.50 4.00
19 Swinub C .15 .25
20 Piloswine U .20 .35
21 Mamoswine R .30 .50
22 Remoraid C .15 .25
23 Octillery R .30 .50
24 Corphish C .15 .25
25 Crawdaunt R .30 .50
26 Feebas C .15 .25
27 Milotic HOLO R .50 .80
28 Regice HOLO R .50 .80
29 Shellos C .15 .25
30 Pikachu C .15 .25
31 Alolan Raichu HOLO R .50 .80
32 Alolan Geodude C .15 .25
33 Alolan Graveler U .20 .35
34 Alolan Golem GX UR 1.50 2.50
35 Emolga U .20 .35
36 Gastly C .15 .25
37 Haunter U .20 .35
38 Gengar HOLO R .50 .80
39 Misdreavus C .15 .25
40 Mismagius R .30 .50
41 Spoink C .15 .25
42 Grumpig U .20 .35
43 Chimecho C .15 .25
44 Pumpkaboo C .15 .25
45 Gourgeist R .30 .50
46 Salandit C .15 .25
47 Salazzle HOLO R .50 .80
48 Oranguru R .30 .50
49 Nihilego GX UR 4.00 6.00
50 Mankey C .15 .25
51 Primeape R .30 .50
52 Cubone C .15 .25
53 Regirock R .30 .50
54 Gastrodon U .20 .35
55 Stufful C .15 .25
56 Bewear HOLO R .50 .80
57 Buzzwole GX UR 8.00 12.00
58 Houndour C .15 .25
59 Houndoom R .30 .50
60 Deino C .15 .25
61 Zweilous U .20 .35
62 Hydreigon R .30 .50
63 Guzzlord GX UR 4.00 6.00
64 Mawile U .20 .35
65 Aron C .15 .25
66 Lairon U .20 .35
67 Aggron HOLO R .50 .80
68 Registeel R .30 .50
69 Escavalier R .30 .50
70 Kartana GX UR 4.00 6.00
71 Jigglypuff C .15 .25
72 Wigglytuff R .15 .25
73 Xerneas HOLO R .50 .80
74 Alolan Exeggutor GX UR 2.00 3.50
75 Jangmo o C .15 .25
76 Hakamo o U .20 .35
77 Kommo o R .30 .50
78 Miltank U .20 .35
79 Swablu C .15 .25
80 Altaria R .30 .50
81 Starly C .15 .25
82 Staravia U .20 .35
83 Staraptor R .30 .50
84 Regigigas HOLO R .50 .80
85 Minccino C .15 .25
86 Cinccino U .15 .25
87 Bunnelby C .15 .25
88 Diggersby U .20 .35
89 Type Null HOLO R 6.00 8.00
90 Silvally GX UR 7.00 10.00
91 Counter Catcher U .20 .35
92 Dashing Pouch U .20 .35
93 Devoured Field U .20 .35
94 Fighting Memory U .20 .35
95 Gladion U .20 .35
96 Lusamine U .20 .35
97 Peeking Red Card U .20 .35
98 Psychic Memory U .20 .35
99 Sea of Nothingness U .20 .35
100 Counter Energy U .20 .35
101 Gyarados GX FULL ART UR 5.00 7.00
102 Alolan Golem GX FULL ART UR 3.00 5.00
103 Nihilego GX FULL ART UR 8.00 10.00
104 Buzzwole GX FULL ART UR 15.00 20.00
105 Guzzlord GX FULL ART UR 4.00 6.00
106 Kartana GX FULL ART UR 6.00 8.00
107 Alolan Exeggutor GX FULL ART UR 4.00 6.00
108 Silvally GX FULL ART UR 10.00 15.00
109 Gladion FULL ART UR 15.00 20.00
110 Lusamine FULL ART UR 20.00 25.00
111 Olivia FULL ART UR 10.00 15.00
112 Gyarados GX SCR 10.00 15.00
113 Alolan Golem GX SCR 8.00 12.00
114 Nihilego GX SCR 10.00 15.00
115 Buzzwole GX SCR 15.00 20.00
116 Guzzlord GX SCR 10.00 15.00
117 Kartana GX SCR 10.00 15.00
118 Alolan Exeggutor GX SCR 8.00 12.00
119 Silvally GX SCR 18.00 22.00
120 Counter Catcher SCR 10.00 15.00
121 Wishful Baton SCR 6.00 8.00
122 Counter Energy SCR 15.00 20.00
123 Warp Energy SCR 10.00 15.00
124 Water Energy SCR 15.00 20.00

2018 Pokemon Sun and Moon Ultra Prism

COMPLETE SET (173) 600.00 750.00
RELEASED ON FEBRUARY 2, 2018
1 Exeggcute C .15 .25
2 Yanma C .15 .25
3 Yanmega U .20 .35
4 Roselia C .15 .25
5 Roserade R .25 .40
6 Turtwig C .15 .25
7 Turtwig C .15 .25
8 Grotle U .20 .35
9 Torterra HOLO R .40 .60
10 Cherubi C .15 .25
11 Cherrim U .20 .35
12 Carnivine C .15 .25
13 Leafeon GX UR 6.00 8.00
14 Mow Rotom R .25 .40
15 Shaymin HOLO R .40 .60
16 Dewpider C .15 .25
17 Araquanid R .25 .40
18 Magmar C .15 .25
19 Magmortar HOLO R .40 .60
20 Chimchar C .15 .25
21 Chimchar C .15 .25
22 Monferno U .20 .35
23 Infernape HOLO R .40 .60
24 Heat Rotom R .25 .40
25 Salandit C .15 .25
26 Salazzle R .25 .40
27 Turtonator U .20 .35
28 Alolan Sandshrew C .15 .25
29 Alolan Sandslash R .25 .40
30 Alolan Vulpix C .15 .25
31 Piplup C .15 .25
32 Piplup C .15 .25
33 Prinplup U .20 .35
34 Empoleon R .25 .40
35 Buizel C .15 .25
36 Floatzel U .20 .35
37 Snover C .15 .25
38 Abomasnow R .25 .40
39 Glaceon GX UR 10.00 15.00
40 Wash Rotom R .25 .40
41 Frost Rotom R .25 .40
42 Manaphy U .20 .35
43 Electabuzz C .15 .25
44 Electivire R .25 .40
45 Shinx C .15 .25
46 Shinx C .15 .25
47 Luxio U .20 .35
48 Luxray HOLO R .40 .60
49 Pachirisu C .15 .25
50 Rotom U .20 .35
51 Drifloon C .15 .25
52 Drifblim U .20 .35
53 Spiritomb U .20 .35
54 Skorupi C .15 .25
55 Drapion R .25 .40
56 Croagunk C .15 .25
57 Toxicroak R .25 .40
58 Giratina Prism HOLO R .40 .60
59 Cresselia HOLO R .40 .60
60 Cosmog C .15 .25
61 Cosmoem U .20 .35
62 Lunala Prism HOLO R .40 .60
63 Dawn Wings Necrozma GX UR 2.00 3.50
64 Cranidos U .20 .35
65 Rampardos HOLO R .40 .60
66 Riolu C .15 .25
67 Lucario HOLO R .40 .60
68 Hippopotas C .15 .25
69 Hippowdon R .25 .40
70 Passimian C .15 .25
71 Murkrow C .15 .25
72 Honchkrow U .20 .35
73 Sneasel C .15 .25
74 Weavile HOLO R .40 .60
75 Stunky C .15 .25
76 Skuntank U .20 .35
77 DarkraiÂ•Prism HOLO R .40 .60
78 Alolan Diglett C .15 .25
79 Alolan Dugtrio U .20 .35
80 Magnemite C .15 .25
81 Magnemite C .15 .25
82 Magneton U .20 .35
83 Magnezone HOLO R .40 .60
84 Shieldon U .20 .35
85 Bastiodon HOLO R .40 .60
86 Bronzor C .15 .25
87 Bronzong U .20 .35
88 Heatran HOLO R .40 .60
89 Solgaleo Prism HOLO R .40 .60
90 Dusk Mane Necrozma GX UR 13.00 16.00
91 Magearna R .25 .40
92 Morelull C .15 .25
93 Shiinotic R .25 .40
94 Tapu Lele R .25 .40
95 Alolan Exeggutor R .25 .40
96 Gible C .15 .25
97 Gible C .15 .25
98 Gabite U .20 .35
99 Garchomp R .25 .40
100 Dialga GX UR 4.00 6.00
101 Palkia GX UR 1.50 2.50
102 Lickitung C .15 .25
103 Lickilicky R .25 .40
104 Eevee C .15 .25
105 Eevee C .15 .25
106 Buneary C .15 .25
107 Lopunny U .20 .35
108 Glameow C .15 .25
109 Purugly U .20 .35
110 Fan Rotom R .25 .40
111 Shaymin R .25 .40
112 Yungoos C .15 .25
113 Gumshoos U .20 .35
114 Oranguru U .20 .35
115 Type: Null R .25 .40
116 Silvally GX UR 1.50 2.50
117 Drampa HOLO R .40 .60
118 Ancient Crystal U .20 .35
119 Cynthia U .20 .35
120 Cyrus Prism HOLO R .40 .60
121 Electric Memory U .20 .35
122 Escape Board U .20 .35
123 Fire Memory U .20 .35
124 Gardenia U .20 .35
125 Lillie U .20 .35
126 Looker U .20 .35
127 Looker Whistle U .20 .35
128 Mars U .20 .35
129 Missing Clover U .20 .35
130 Mt. Coronet U .20 .35
131 Order Pad U .20 .35
132 Pal Pad U .20 .35
133 Pokemon Fan Club U .20 .35
134 Unidentified Fossil U .20 .35
135 Volkner U .20 .35
136 Super Boost Energy Prism HOLO R .40 .60
137 Unit Energy GFW U .20 .35
138 Unit Energy LPM U .20 .35
139 Leafeon GX UR 10.00 15.00
140 Pheromosa GX UR 5.00 7.00
141 Glaceon GX UR 20.00 25.00
142 Xurkitree GX UR 6.00 8.00
143 Dawn Wings Necrozma GX UR 7.00 10.00
144 Celesteela GX UR 8.00 12.00
145 Dusk Mane Necrozma GX UR 20.00 25.00
146 Dialga GX UR 8.00 12.00
147 Palkia GX UR 5.00 8.00
148 Cynthia UR 70.00 80.00
149 Gardenia UR 8.00 11.00
150 Lana UR 7.00 10.00
151 Lillie UR 20.00 25.00
152 Looker UR 6.00 8.00
153 Lusamine UR 10.00 15.00
154 Mars UR 8.00 12.00
155 Pokemon Fan Club UR 8.00 11.00
156 Volkner UR 10.00 15.00
157 Leafeon GX SCR 18.00 22.00
158 Pheromosa GX SCR 5.00 7.00
159 Glaceon GX SCR 25.00 30.00
160 Xurkitree GX SCR 10.00 15.00
161 Dawn Wings Necrozma GX SCR 10.00 15.00
162 Celesteela GX SCR 10.00 15.00
163 Dusk Mane Necrozma GX SCR 18.00 22.00
164 Dialga GX SCR 10.00 15.00
165 Palkia GX SCR 10.00 15.00
166 Crushing Hammer SCR 10.00 15.00
167 Escape Board SCR 8.00 12.00
168 Missing Clover SCR 7.00 10.00
169 Peeking Red Card SCR 6.00 8.00
170 Unit Energy GFW SCR 14.00 16.00
171 Unit Energy LPM SCR 14.00 16.00
172 Lunala GX SCR 40.00 45.00
173 Solgaleo GX SCR 60.00 65.00

2018 Pokemon Sun and Moon Ultra Prism Reverse Foil

COMPLETE SET (125) 30.00 50.00
1 Exeggcute C .20 .35
2 Yanma C .20 .35
3 Yanmega U .25 .40
4 Roselia C .20 .35
5 Roserade R .30 .50
6 Turtwig C .20 .35
7 Turtwig C .20 .35
8 Grotle U .25 .40
9 Torterra HOLO R .40 .60
10 Cherubi C .20 .35
11 Cherrim U .25 .40
12 Carnivine C .20 .35
14 Mow Rotom R .30 .50
15 Shaymin HOLO R .40 .60
16 Dewpider C .20 .35
17 Araquanid R .30 .50
18 Magmar C .20 .35
19 Magmortar HOLO R .40 .60
20 Chimchar C .20 .35
21 Chimchar C .20 .35
22 Monferno U .25 .40
23 Infernape HOLO R .40 .60
24 Heat Rotom R .30 .50
25 Salandit C .20 .35
26 Salazzle R .30 .50
27 Turtonator U .25 .40
28 Alolan Sandshrew C .20 .35
29 Alolan Sandslash R .30 .50
30 Alolan Vulpix C .20 .35
31 Piplup C .20 .35
32 Piplup C .20 .35
33 Prinplup U .25 .40
34 Empoleon R .30 .50
35 Buizel C .20 .35
36 Floatzel U .25 .40
37 Snover C .20 .35
38 Abomasnow R .30 .50
40 Wash Rotom R .30 .50
41 Frost Rotom R .30 .50
42 Manaphy U .25 .40
43 Electabuzz C .20 .35
44 Electivire R .30 .50
45 Shinx C .20 .35
46 Shinx C .20 .35
47 Luxio U .25 .40
48 Luxray HOLO R .40 .60
49 Pachirisu C .20 .35
50 Rotom U .25 .40
51 Drifloon C .20 .35
52 Drifblim U .25 .40
53 Spiritomb U .25 .40
54 Skorupi C .20 .35
55 Drapion R .30 .50
56 Croagunk C .20 .35
57 Toxicroak R .30 .50
59 Cresselia HOLO R .40 .60
60 Cosmog C .20 .35
61 Cosmoem U .25 .40
63 Cranidos U .25 .40
65 Rampardos HOLO R .40 .60
66 Riolu C .20 .35
67 Lucario HOLO R .40 .60
68 Hippopotas C .20 .35
69 Hippowdon R .30 .50
70 Passimian C .20 .35
71 Murkrow C .20 .35
72 Honchkrow U .25 .40
73 Sneasel C .20 .35
74 Weavile HOLO R .40 .60
75 Stunky C .20 .35
76 Skuntank U .25 .40
78 Alolan Diglett C .20 .35
79 Alolan Dugtrio U .25 .40
80 Magnemite C .20 .35
81 Magnemite C .20 .35
82 Magneton U .25 .40
83 Magnezone HOLO R .40 .60
84 Shieldon U .25 .40
85 Bastiodon HOLO R .40 .60
86 Bronzor C .20 .35
87 Bronzong U .25 .40
88 Heatran HOLO R .40 .60
91 Magearna R .30 .50
92 Morelull C .20 .35
93 Shiinotic R .30 .50
94 Tapu Lele R .30 .50
95 Alolan Exeggutor R .30 .50
96 Gible C .20 .35
97 Gible C .20 .35
98 Gabite U .25 .40
99 Garchomp R .30 .50
102 Lickitung C .20 .35
103 Lickilicky R .30 .50
104 Eevee C .20 .35
105 Eevee C .20 .35
106 Buneary C .20 .35
107 Lopunny U .25 .40
108 Glameow C .20 .35
109 Purugly U .25 .40
110 Fan Rotom R .30 .50
111 Shaymin R .30 .50
112 Yungoos C .20 .35
113 Gumshoos U .25 .40
114 Oranguru U .25 .40
115 Type: Null R .30 .50
117 Drampa HOLO R .40 .60
118 Ancient Crystal U .25 .40
119 Cynthia U .25 .40
121 Electric Memory U .25 .40
122 Escape Board U .25 .40
123 Fire Memory U .25 .40
124 Gardenia U .25 .40
125 Lillie U .25 .40
126 Looker U .25 .40
127 Looker Whistle U .25 .40
128 Mars U .25 .40
129 Missing Clover U .25 .40
130 Mt. Coronet U .25 .40
131 Order Pad U .25 .40
132 Pal Pad U .25 .40
133 Pokemon Fan Club U .25 .40
134 Unidentified Fossil U .25 .40
135 Volkner U .25 .40
137 Unit Energy GFW U .25 .40
138 Unit Energy LPM U .25 .40

2018 Pokemon Sun and Moon Forbidden Light

Card	Low	High
COMPLETE SET (146)	400.00	500.00
RELEASED ON MAY 4, 2018		
1 Exeggcute C	.15	.25
2 Alolan Exeggutor R	.40	.60
3 Snover C	.15	.25
4 Abomasnow R	.40	.60
5 Scatterbug C	.15	.25
6 Scatterbug C	.15	.25
7 Spewpa U	.30	.50
8 Vivillon R	.40	.60
9 Skiddo C	.15	.25
10 Gogoat U	.30	.50
11 Pheromosa HOLO R	.60	1.00
12 Alolan Marowak R	.40	.60
13 Heatran R	.40	.60
14 Fennekin C	.15	.25
15 Fennekin C	.15	.25
16 Braixen U	.30	.50
17 Delphox HOLO R	.60	1.00
18 Litleo C	.15	.25
19 Pyroar HOLO R	.60	1.00
20 Palkia GX UR	.60	1.00
21 Froakie C	.15	.25
22 Froakie C	.15	.25
23 Frogadier U	.30	.50
24 Greninja GX UR	6.00	8.00
25 Clauncher C	.15	.25
26 Clawitzer R	.40	.60
27 Amaura U	.30	.50
28 Aurorus HOLO R	.60	1.00
29 Bergmite C	.15	.25
30 Avalugg R	.40	.60
31 Volcanion Prism Star HOLO R	.60	1.00
32 Dewpider C	.15	.25
33 Araquanid U	.30	.50
34 Magnemite C	.15	.25
35 Magneton U	.30	.50
36 Magnezone HOLO R	.60	1.00
37 Helioptile C	.15	.25
38 Heliolisk U	.30	.50
39 Xurkitree R	.40	.60
40 Rotom R	.40	.60
41 Uxie U	.30	.50
42 Mesprit U	.30	.50
43 Azelf U	.30	.50
44 Espurr C	.15	.25
45 Meowstic R	.40	.60
46 Honedge C	.15	.25
47 Honedge C	.15	.25
48 Doublade U	.30	.50
49 Aegislash R	.40	.60
50 Inkay C	.15	.25
51 Malamar R	1.50	2.00
52 Skrelp C	.15	.25
53 Dragalge R	.40	.60
54 Hoopa U	.30	.50
55 Poipole U	.30	.50
56 Naganadel GX UR	5.00	7.00
57 Cubone C	.15	.25
58 Torterra R	.40	.60
59 Infernape HOLO R	.60	1.00
60 Gible C	.15	.25
61 Gabite U	.30	.50
62 Garchomp HOLO R	.60	1.00
63 Croagunk C	.15	.25
64 Toxicroak R	.40	.60
65 Pancham C	.15	.25
66 Binacle C	.15	.25
67 Barbaracle R	.40	.60
68 Tyrunt U	.30	.50
69 Tyrantrum HOLO R	.60	1.00
70 Hawlucha U	.30	.50
71 Zygarde U	.30	.50
72 Zygarde R	.40	.60
73 Zygarde GX UR	3.00	5.00
74 Diancie Prism Star HOLO R	2.50	4.00
75 Rockruff C	.15	.25
76 Lycanroc R	.40	.60
77 Buzzwole R	.40	.60
78 Pangoro R	.40	.60
79 Yveltal GX UR	1.50	2.50
80 Guzzlord HOLO R	.60	1.00
81 Empoleon HOLO R	.60	1.00
82 Dialga GX UR	1.50	2.00
83 Flabebe C	.15	.25
84 Flabebe C	.15	.25
85 Floette U	.30	.50
86 Florges R	.40	.60
87 Sylveon R	.40	.60
88 Dedenne U	.30	.50
89 Klefki U	.30	.50
90 Xerneas GX UR	1.50	2.00
91 Goomy C	.15	.25
92 Goomy C	.15	.25
93 Sliggoo U	.30	.50
94 Goodra HOLO R	.60	1.00
95 Ultra Necrozma GX UR	20.00	30.00
96 Arceus Prism Star HOLO R	.60	1.00
97 Bunnelby C	.15	.25
98 Diggersby U	.30	.50
99 Furfrou C	.15	.25
100 Noibat C	.15	.25
101 Noivern R	.40	.60
102 Beast Ring R	2.00	3.50
103 Bonnie U	.30	.50
104 Crasher Wake U	.30	.50
105 Diantha HOLO R	.60	1.00
106 Eneporter U	.30	.50
107 Fossil Excavation Map U	.30	.50
108 Judge U	.30	.50
109 Lady U	.30	.50
110 Lysandre Prism Star HOLO R	.60	1.00
111 Lysandre Labs U	.30	.50
112 Metal Frying Pan U	.30	.50
113 Mysterious Treasure U	.30	.50
114 Ultra Recon Squad U	.30	.50
115 Ultra Space U	.30	.50
116 Unidentified Fossil U	.30	.50
117 Beast Energy Prism Star HOLO R	2.50	4.00
118 Unit Energy FDF U	.30	.50
119 Palkia GX UR Full Art	3.00	5.00
120 Greninja GX UR Full Art	10.00	15.00
121 Naganadel GX UR Full Art	10.00	15.00
122 Lucario GX UR Full Art	7.00	10.00
123 Zygarde GX UR Full Art	7.00	10.00
124 Yveltal GX UR Full Art	3.00	5.00
125 Dialga GX UR Full Art	3.00	5.00
126 Xerneas GX UR Full Art	3.00	5.00
127 Ultra Necrozma GX UR Full Art	25.00	30.00
128 Bonnie UR Full Art	7.00	10.00
129 Crasher Wake UR Full Art	6.00	8.00
130 Diantha UR Full Art	10.00	15.00
131 Ultra Recon Squad UR Full Art	6.00	8.00
132 Palkia GX SCR	6.00	8.00
133 Greninja GX SCR	15.00	20.00
134 Naganadel GX SCR	15.00	20.00
135 Lucario GX SCR	15.00	20.00
136 Zygarde GX SCR	15.00	20.00
137 Yveltal GX SCR	7.00	10.00
138 Dialga GX SCR	6.00	8.00
139 Xerneas GX SCR	8.00	11.00
140 Ultra Necrozma GX SCR	30.00	35.00
141 Beast Ring SCR	45.00	55.00
142 Eneporter SCR	5.00	7.00
143 Energy Recycler SCR	7.00	10.00
144 Metal Frying Pan SCR	5.00	7.00
145 Mysterious Treasure SCR	35.00	40.00
146 Unit Energy FDF SCR	8.00	12.00

2018 Pokemon Sun and Moon Forbidden Light Reverse Foil

Card	Low	High
COMPLETE SET (106)	35.00	50.00
1 Exeggcute C	.20	.35
2 Alolan Exeggutor R	.40	.60
3 Snover C	.20	.35
4 Abomasnow R	.40	.60
5 Scatterbug C	.20	.35
6 Scatterbug C	.20	.35
7 Spewpa U	.30	.50
8 Vivillon R	.40	.60
9 Skiddo C	.20	.35
10 Gogoat U	.30	.50
11 Pheromosa HOLO R	.60	1.00
12 Alolan Marowak R	.40	.60
13 Heatran R	.40	.60
14 Fennekin C	.20	.35
15 Fennekin C	.20	.35
16 Braixen U	.30	.50
17 Delphox HOLO R	.60	1.00
18 Litleo C	.20	.35
19 Pyroar HOLO R	.60	1.00
21 Froakie C	.20	.35
22 Froakie C	.20	.35
23 Frogadier U	.30	.50
25 Clauncher C	.20	.35
26 Clawitzer R	.40	.60
27 Amaura U	.30	.50
28 Aurorus HOLO R	.60	1.00
29 Bergmite C	.20	.35
30 Avalugg R	.40	.60
32 Dewpider C	.20	.35
33 Araquanid U	.30	.50
34 Magnemite C	.20	.35
35 Magneton U	.30	.50
36 Magnezone HOLO R	.60	1.00
37 Helioptile C	.20	.35
38 Heliolisk U	.30	.50
39 Xurkitree R	.40	.60
40 Rotom R	.40	.60
41 Uxie U	.30	.50
42 Mesprit U	.30	.50
43 Azelf U	.30	.50
44 Espurr C	.20	.35
45 Meowstic R	.40	.60
46 Honedge C	.20	.35
47 Honedge C	.20	.35
48 Doublade U	.30	.50
49 Aegislash R	.40	.60
50 Inkay C	.20	.35
51 Malamar R	.40	.60
52 Skrelp C	.20	.35
53 Dragalge R	.40	.60
54 Hoopa U	.30	.50
55 Poipole U	.30	.50
57 Cubone C	.20	.35
58 Torterra R	.20	.35
59 Infernape HOLO R	.60	1.00
60 Gible C	.20	.35
61 Gabite U	.30	.50
62 Garchomp HOLO R	.60	1.00
63 Croagunk C	.20	.35
64 Toxicroak R	.40	.60
65 Pancham C	.20	.35
66 Binacle C	.20	.35
67 Barbaracle R	.40	.60
68 Tyrunt U	.30	.50
69 Tyrantrum HOLO R	.60	1.00
70 Hawlucha U	.30	.50
71 Zygarde U	.30	.50
72 Zygarde R	.40	.60
75 Rockruff C	.20	.35
76 Lycanroc R	.40	.60
77 Buzzwole R	.40	.60
78 Pangoro R	.40	.60
80 Guzzlord HOLO R	.60	1.00
81 Empoleon HOLO R	.60	1.00
83 Flabebe C	.20	.35
84 Flabebe C	.20	.35
85 Floette U	.30	.50
86 Florges R	.40	.60
87 Sylveon R	.40	.60
88 Dedenne U	.30	.50
89 Klefki U	.30	.50
91 Goomy C	.20	.35
92 Goomy C	.20	.35
93 Sliggoo U	.30	.50
94 Goodra HOLO R	.60	1.00
97 Bunnelby C	.20	.35
98 Diggersby U	.30	.50
99 Furfrou C	.20	.35
100 Noibat C	.20	.35
101 Noivern R	.40	.60
102 Beast Ring R	.40	.60
103 Bonnie U	.30	.50
104 Crasher Wake U	.30	.50
105 Diantha HOLO R	.60	1.00
106 Eneporter U	.30	.50
107 Fossil Excavation Map U	.30	.50
108 Judge U	.30	.50
109 Lady U	.30	.50
111 Lysandre Labs U	.30	.50
112 Metal Frying Pan U	.30	.50
113 Mysterious Treasure U	.30	.50
114 Ultra Recon Squad U	.30	.50
115 Ultra Space U	.30	.50
116 Unidentified Fossil U	.30	.50
117 Beast Energy Prism Star HOLO R	.60	1.00
118 Unit Energy FDF U	.30	.50

2018 Pokemon Sun and Moon Celestial Storm

Card	Low	High
COMPLETE SET (183)	90.00	100.00
RELEASED ON AUGUST 3, 2018		
1 Bellsprout C	.10	.20
2 Weepinbell U	.25	.40
3 Victreebel HOLO R	.60	1.00
4 Scyther U	.25	.40
5 Spinarak C	.10	.20
6 Ariados HOLO R	.60	1.00
7 Treecko C	.10	.20
8 Treecko C	.10	.20
9 Grovyle U	.25	.40
10 Sceptile R	.40	.60
11 Seedot C	.10	.20
12 Seedot C	.10	.20
13 Nuzleaf U	.25	.40
14 Shiftry GX UR	4.00	6.00
15 Surskit C	.10	.20
16 Masquerain U	.25	.40
17 Volbeat U	.25	.40
18 Illumise U	.25	.40
19 Cacnea C	.10	.20
20 Cacturne U	.25	.40
21 Tropius U	.25	.40
22 Dhelmise R	.40	.60
23 Slugma C	.10	.20
24 Magcargo R	.40	.60
25 Torchic C	.10	.20
26 Torchic C	.10	.20
27 Combusken U	.25	.40
28 Blaziken GX UR	1.50	2.00
29 Torkoal U	.25	.40
30 Oricorio U	.25	.40
31 Articuno GX UR	2.00	3.50
32 Mudkip C	.10	.20
33 Mudkip C	.10	.20
34 Marshtomp U	.25	.40
35 Swampert R	.40	.60
36 Lotad C	.10	.20
37 Lombre U	.25	.40
38 Ludicolo HOLO R	.60	1.00
39 Wailmer C	.10	.20
40 Wailord R	.40	.60
41 Clamperl C	.10	.20
42 Huntail U	.25	.40
43 Gorebyss U	.25	.40
44 Luvdisc C	.10	.20
45 Regice R	.40	.60
46 Kyogre HOLO R	.60	1.00
47 Voltorb C	.10	.20
48 Electrode GX UR	2.00	3.00
49 Chinchou C	.10	.20
50 Lanturn U	.25	.40
51 Electrike C	.10	.20
52 Manectric R	.40	.60
53 Plusle U	.25	.40
54 Minun U	.25	.40
55 Oricorio U	.25	.40
56 Mr. Mime GX UR	2.00	3.00
57 Gulpin C	.10	.20
58 Swalot U	.25	.40
59 Spoink C	.10	.20
60 Grumpig R	.40	.60
61 Lunatone HOLO R	.60	1.00
62 Solrock U	.25	.40
63 Shuppet C	.10	.20
64 Shuppet C	.10	.20
65 Banette R	.40	.60
66 Banette GX UR	4.00	6.00
67 Deoxys HOLO R	.60	1.00
68 Deoxys R	.40	.60
69 Deoxys R	.40	.60
70 Lunala HOLO R	.60	1.00
71 Onix C	.10	.20
72 Phanpy C	.10	.20
73 Donphan U	.25	.40
74 Larvitar C	.10	.20
75 Pupitar U	.25	.40
76 Meditite C	.10	.20
77 Medicham R	.40	.60
78 Baltoy C	.10	.20
79 Claydol R	.40	.60
80 Regirock R	.40	.60
81 Groudon HOLO R	.60	1.00
82 Palossand GX UR	2.00	3.00
83 Minior U	.25	.40
84 Alolan Rattata C	.10	.20
85 Alolan Raticate GX UR	2.50	4.00
86 Sneasel C	.10	.20
87 Tyranitar HOLO R	.60	1.00
88 Sableye U	.25	.40
89 Steelix HOLO R	.60	1.00
90 Scizor GX UR	4.00	6.00
91 Mawile U	.25	.40
92 Beldum C	.10	.20
93 Beldum C	.10	.20
94 Metang U	.25	.40
95 Metagross HOLO R	.60	1.00
96 Registeel R	.40	.60
97 Jirachi Prism Star HOLO R	.60	1.00
98 Heatran HOLO R	.60	1.00
99 Solgaleo HOLO R	.60	1.00
100 Celesteela HOLO R	.60	1.00
101 Kartana R	.40	.60
102 Stakataka GX UR	7.00	10.00
103 Bagon C	.10	.20
104 Bagon C	.10	.20
105 Shelgon U	.25	.40
106 Salamence HOLO R	.60	1.00
107 Latias Prism Star HOLO R	.60	1.00
108 Latios Prism Star HOLO R	.60	1.00
109 Rayquaza GX UR	20.00	25.00
110 Dunsparce U	.25	.40
111 Wingull C	.10	.20
112 Pelipper U	.25	.40
113 Slakoth C	.10	.20
114 Vigoroth U	.25	.40
115 Slaking HOLO R	.60	1.00
116 Whismur C	.10	.20
117 Whismur C	.10	.20
118 Loudred U	.25	.40
119 Exploud R	.10	.20
120 Skitty C	.10	.20
121 Delcatty HOLO R	.60	1.00
122 Kecleon U	.25	.40
123 Acro Bike U	.25	.40
124 Apricorn Maker U	.25	.40
125 Beast Ball U	.25	.40
126 Bill's Maintenance U	.25	.40
127 Copycat U	.25	.40
128 Energy Recycle System U	.25	.40
129 Energy Switch U	.25	.40
130 Fisherman U	.25	.40
131 Friend Ball U	.25	.40
132 Hau U	.25	.40
133 Hiker U	.25	.40
134 Hustle Belt U	.25	.40
135 Last Chance Potion U	.25	.40
136 Life Herb U	.25	.40
137 Lisia U	.25	.40
138 Lure Ball U	.25	.40
139 The Masked Royal U	.25	.40
140 PokÃ©Nav U	.25	.40
141 Rainbow Brush U	.25	.40
142 Rare Candy U	.25	.40
143 Shrine of Punishments U	.25	.40
144 Sky Pillar U	.25	.40
145 Steven's Resolve HOLO R	.60	1.00
146 Super Scoop Up U	.25	.40
147 Switch U	.25	.40
148 Tate & Liza U	.25	.40
149 TV Reporter U	.25	.40
150 Underground Expedition U	.25	.40
151 Rainbow Energy U	.25	.40
152 Shiftry GX FULL ART UR	8.00	11.00
153 Blaziken GX FULL ART UR	8.00	11.00
154 Articuno GX FULL ART UR	7.00	10.00
155 Electrode GX FULL ART UR	6.00	8.00
156 Mr. Mime GX FULL ART UR	7.00	10.00
157 Banette GX FULL ART UR	10.00	15.00
158 Scizor GX FULL ART UR	8.00	11.00
159 Stakataka GX FULL ART UR	15.00	20.00
160 Rayquaza GX FULL ART UR	35.00	40.00
161 Apricorn Maker FULL ART UR	10.00	15.00
162 Bill's Maintenance FULL ART UR	8.00	11.00
163 Copycat FULL ART UR	25.00	30.00
164 Lisia FULL ART UR	15.00	20.00
165 Steven's Resolve FULL ART UR	15.00	20.00
166 Tate & Liza FULL ART UR	15.00	20.00
167 TV Reporter FULL ART UR	8.00	11.00
168 Underground Expedition FULL ART UR	10.00	15.00
169 Shiftry GX SCR	20.00	25.00
170 Blaziken GX SCR	15.00	20.00
171 Articuno GX SCR	20.00	25.00
172 Electrode GX SCR	10.00	15.00
173 Mr. Mime GX SCR	10.00	15.00
174 Banette GX SCR	25.00	30.00
175 Scizor GX SCR	10.00	15.00
176 Stakataka GX SCR	20.00	25.00
177 Rayquaza GX SCR	55.00	60.00
178 Acro Bike SCR	30.00	35.00
179 Hustle Belt SCR	10.00	15.00
180 Life Herb SCR	7.00	10.00
181 PokÃ©Nav SCR	.40	.60
182 Rainbow Brush SCR	8.00	12.00
183 Rainbow Energy SCR	35.00	40.00

2018 Pokemon Sun and Moon Celestial Storm Reverse Foil

Card	Low	High
COMPLETE SET (142)	20.00	35.00
RELEASED ON AUGUST 3, 2018		
1 Bellsprout C	.20	.35
2 Weepinbell U	.25	.40
3 Victreebel HOLO R	.50	.75
4 Scyther U	.25	.40
5 Spinarak C	.20	.35
6 Ariados HOLO R	.50	.75
7 Treecko C	.20	.35

8 Treecko C .20 .35
9 Grovyle U .25 .40
10 Sceptile R .30 .50
11 Seedot C .20 .35
12 Seedot C .20 .35
13 Nuzleaf U .25 .40
15 Surskit C .20 .35
16 Masquerain U .25 .40
17 Volbeat U .25 .40
18 Illumise U .25 .40
19 Cacnea C .20 .35
20 Cacturne U .25 .40
21 Tropius U .25 .40
22 Dhelmise R .30 .50
23 Slugma C .20 .35
24 Magcargo R .30 .50
25 Torchic C .20 .35
26 Torchic C .20 .35
27 Combusken U .25 .40
29 Torkoal U .25 .40
30 Oricorio U .25 .40
32 Mudkip C .20 .35
33 Mudkip C .20 .35
34 Marshtomp U .25 .40
35 Swampert R .30 .50
36 Lotad C .20 .35
37 Lombre U .25 .40
38 Ludicolo HOLO R .50 .75
39 Wailmer C .20 .35
40 Wailord R .30 .50
41 Clamperl C .20 .35
42 Huntail U .25 .40
43 Gorebyss U .25 .40
44 Luvdisc C .20 .35
45 Regice R .30 .50
46 Kyogre HOLO R .50 .75
47 Voltorb C .20 .35
49 Chinchou C .20 .35
50 Lanturn U .25 .40
51 Electrike C .20 .35
52 Manectric R .30 .50
53 Plusle U .25 .40
54 Minun U .25 .40
55 Oricorio U .25 .40
57 Gulpin C .20 .35
58 Swalot U .25 .40
59 Spoink C .20 .35
60 Grumpig R .30 .50
61 Lunatone HOLO R .50 .75
62 Solrock U .25 .40
63 Shuppet C .20 .35
64 Shuppet C .20 .35
65 Banette R .30 .50
67 Deoxys HOLO R .50 .75
68 Deoxys R .30 .50
69 Deoxys R .30 .50
70 Lunala HOLO R .50 .75
71 Onix C .20 .35
72 Phanpy C .20 .35
73 Donphan U .25 .40
74 Larvitar C .20 .35
75 Pupitar U .25 .40
76 Meditite C .20 .35
77 Medicham R .30 .50
78 Baltoy C .20 .35
79 Claydol R .30 .50
80 Regirock R .30 .50
81 Groudon HOLO R .50 .75
83 Minior U .25 .40
84 Alolan Rattata C .20 .35
86 Sneasel C .20 .35
87 Tyranitar HOLO R .50 .75
88 Sableye U .25 .40
89 Steelix HOLO R .50 .75
91 Mawile U .25 .40
92 Beldum C .20 .35
93 Beldum C .20 .35
94 Metang U .25 .40
95 Metagross HOLO R .50 .75
96 Registeel R .30 .50
97 Jirachi Prism Star HOLO R .50 .75
98 Heatran HOLO R .50 .75
99 Solgaleo HOLO R .50 .75
100 Celesteela HOLO R .50 .75
101 Kartana R .30 .50
103 Bagon C .20 .35
104 Bagon C .20 .35
105 Shelgon U .25 .40
106 Salamence HOLO R .50 .75
107 Latias Prism Star HOLO R .50 .75
108 Latios Prism Star HOLO R .50 .75
110 Dunsparce U .25 .40
111 Wingull C .20 .35
112 Pelipper U .25 .40
113 Slakoth C .20 .35
114 Vigoroth U .25 .40
115 Slaking HOLO R .50 .75
116 Whismur C .20 .35
117 Whismur C .20 .35
118 Loudred U .25 .40
119 Exploud R .30 .50
120 Skitty C .20 .35
121 Delcatty HOLO R .50 .75
122 Kecleon U .25 .40
123 Acro Bike U .25 .40
124 Apricorn Maker U .25 .40
125 Beast Ball U .25 .40
126 Bill's Maintenance U .25 .40
127 Copycat U .25 .40
128 Energy Recycle System U .25 .40
129 Energy Switch U .25 .40
130 Fisherman U .25 .40
131 Friend Ball U .25 .40
132 Hau U .25 .40
133 Hiker U .25 .40
134 Hustle Belt U .25 .40
135 Last Chance Potion U .25 .40
136 Life Herb U .25 .40
137 Lisia U .25 .40
138 Lure Ball U .25 .40
139 The Masked Royal U .25 .40
140 PokÃ©Nav U .25 .40
141 Rainbow Brush U .25 .40
142 Rare Candy U .25 .40
143 Shrine of Punishments U .25 .40
144 Sky Pillar U .25 .40
145 Steven's Resolve HOLO R .50 .75
146 Super Scoop Up U .25 .40
147 Switch U .25 .40
148 Tate & Liza U .25 .40
149 TV Reporter U .25 .40
150 Underground Expedition U .25 .40
151 Rainbow Energy U .25 .40

2018 Pokemon Dragon Majesty

RELEASED ON SEPTEMBER 7, 2018
1 Charmander C .10 .20
2 Charmeleon U .40 .60
3 Charizard HOLO R 5.00 7.00
4 Torchic C .10 .20
5 Combusken U .40 .60
6 Blaziken HOLO R 1.50 2.50
7 Victini Prism Star HOLO R 1.50 2.50
8 Darumaka C .10 .20
9 Darmanitan U .40 .60
10 Heatmor U .40 .60
11 Reshiram GX UR 10.00 15.00
12 Litten C .10 .20
13 Salandit C .10 .20
14 Salazzle U .40 .60
15 Horsea C .10 .20
16 Horsea C .10 .20
17 Seadra U .40 .60
18 Kingdra GX UR 6.00 8.00
19 Magikarp C .10 .20
20 Gyarados HOLO R 1.50 2.50
21 Lapras U .40 .60
22 Totodile C .10 .20
23 Croconaw U .40 .60
24 Feraligatr HOLO R 1.50 2.50
25 Wooper C .10 .20
26 Quagsire U .40 .60
27 Corsola C .10 .20
28 Feebas C .10 .20
29 Milotic U .40 .60
30 Phione U .40 .60
31 Wishiwashi C .10 .20
32 Trapinch C .10 .20
33 Hydreigon HOLO R 1.50 2.50
34 Dratini C .10 .20
35 Dratini C .10 .20
36 Dragonair U .40 .60
37 Dragonite GX UR 6.00 8.00
38 Vibrava C .10 .20
39 Flygon U .40 .60
40 Altaria HOLO R 1.50 2.50
41 Altaria GX UR 10.00 15.00
42 Bagon C .10 .20
43 Shelgon U .40 .60
44 Salamence GX UR 8.00 12.00
45 Druddigon U .40 .60
46 Zekrom HOLO R 1.50 2.50
47 Kyurem HOLO R 1.50 2.50
48 White Kyurem GX UR 6.00 8.00
49 Zygarde U .40 .60
50 Turtonator U .40 .60
51 Drampa U .40 .60
52 Jangmo-o C .10 .20
53 Hakamo-o C .10 .20
54 Kommo-o HOLO R 1.50 2.50
55 Kangaskhan C .10 .20
56 Swablu C .10 .20
57 Swablu C .10 .20
58 Blaine's Last Stand HOLO R 1.50 2.50
59 Dragon Talon U .40 .60
60 Fiery Flint U .40 .60
61 Lance Prism Star HOLO R 1.50 2.50
62 Switch Raft U .40 .60
63 Wela Volcano Park U .40 .60
64 Zinnia U 1.50 2.50
65 Reshiram GX FULL ART UR 20.00 25.00
66 Kingdra GX FULL ART UR 15.00 20.00
67 Dragonite GX FULL ART UR 20.00 25.00
68 Altaria GX FULL ART UR 20.00 25.00
69 Blaine's Last Stand FULL ART UR 15.00 20.00
70 Zinnia FULL ART UR 90.00 100.00
71 Reshiram GX SCR 30.00 35.00
72 Altaria GX SCR 25.00 30.00
73 Salamence GX SCR 30.00 35.00
74 White Kyurem GX SCR 30.00 35.00
75 Dragon Talon SCR 25.00 30.00
76 Fiery Flint SCR 30.00 35.00
77 Switch Raft SCR 30.00 35.00
78 Ultra Necrozma GX SCR 100.00 125.00

2018 Pokemon Sun and Moon Lost Thunder

RELEASED ON NOVEMBER 2, 2018
1 Tangela C .10 .25
2 Tangrowth R .30 .50
3 Scyther C .10 .25
4 Pinsir U .25 .40
5 Chikorita C .10 .25
6 Chikorita C .10 .25
7 Bayleef U .25 .40
8 Meganium HOLO R .30 .50
9 Spinarak C .10 .25
10 Ariados U .25 .40
11 Hoppip C .10 .25
12 Hoppip C .10 .25
13 Skiploom U .25 .40
14 Jumpluff HOLO R 5.00 8.00
15 Pineco C .10 .25
16 Shuckle U .25 .40
17 Shuckle GX UR 3.00 5.00
18 Heracross U .25 .40
19 Celebi PRISM HOLO R .30 .50
20 Treecko C .10 .25
21 Grovyle U .25 .40
22 Sceptile GX UR 4.00 7.50
23 Wurmple C .10 .25
24 Wurmple C .10 .25
25 Silcoon U .25 .40
26 Beautifly R .30 .50
27 Cascoon U .25 .40
28 Dustox R .30 .50
29 Nincada C .10 .25
30 Ninjask U .25 .40
31 Combee C .10 .25
32 Vespiquen U .25 .40
33 Shaymin HOLO R .30 .50
34 Virizion GX UR 1.50 2.50
35 Skiddo C .10 .25
36 Gogoat U .25 .40
37 Tapu Bulu HOLO R .30 .50
38 Moltres R .30 .50
39 Cyndaquil C .10 .25
40 Cyndaquil C .10 .25
41 Quilava U .25 .40
42 Typhlosion HOLO R .30 .50
43 Slugma C .10 .25
44 Magcargo GX UR 2.50 4.00
45 Houndour C .10 .25
46 Houndoom R .30 .50
47 Entei R .30 .50
48 Heatran HOLO R .30 .50
49 Victini R .30 .50
50 Litleo C .10 .25
51 Pyroar R .30 .50
52 Blacephalon GX UR 20.00 30.00
53 Alolan Vulpix C .10 .25
54 Slowpoke C .10 .25
55 Slowking R .30 .50
56 Lapras R .30 .50
57 Delibird U .25 .40
58 Mantine U .25 .40
59 Suicune HOLO R .30 .50
60 Suicune GX UR 2.00 3.50
61 Cubchoo C .10 .25
62 Beartic R .30 .50
63 White Kyurem HOLO R .75 1.50
64 Popplio C .10 .25
65 Popplio C .10 .25
66 Brionne U .25 .40
67 Primarina R .30 .50
68 Mareanie C .10 .25
69 Toxapex R .30 .50
70 Bruxish C .10 .25
71 Electabuzz U .25 .40
72 Electivire R .30 .50
73 Chinchou C .10 .25
74 Lanturn R .30 .50
75 Mareep C .10 .25
76 Mareep C .10 .25
77 Flaaffy U .25 .40
78 Ampharos HOLO R .30 .50
79 Raikou R .30 .50
80 Pachirisu C .10 .25
81 Blitzle C .10 .25
82 Zebstrika R .30 .50
83 Stunfisk C .10 .25
84 Dedenne C .10 .25
85 Tapu Koko HOLO R .30 .50
86 Zeraora GX UR 10.00 15.00
87 Natu C .10 .25
88 Xatu U .25 .40
89 Espeon R .30 .50
90 Unown R .30 .50
91 Unown R .30 .50
92 Unown R .30 .50
93 Wobbuffet R .30 .50
94 Girafarig U .25 .40
95 Shedinja R .30 .50
96 Sableye U .25 .40
97 Giratina HOLO R 3.50 6.00
98 Sigilyph GX UR 1.50 2.50
99 Yamask C .10 .25
100 Cofagrigus R .30 .50
101 Litwick C .10 .25
102 Lampent U .25 .40
103 Chandelure HOLO R .30 .50
104 Meloetta R .30 .50
105 Mareanie C .10 .25
106 Nihilego HOLO R .30 .50
107 Poipole C .10 .25
108 Naganadel HOLO R 5.00 8.00
109 Onix C .10 .25
110 Sudowoodo U .25 .40
111 Phanpy C .10 .25
112 Donphan R .30 .50
113 Hitmontop U .25 .40
114 Larvitar C .10 .25
115 Larvitar C .10 .25
116 Pupitar U .25 .40
117 Carbink C .10 .25
118 Alolan Meowth C .10 .25
119 Alolan Persian R .30 .50
120 Umbreon R .30 .50
121 Tyranitar GX UR 1.50 2.50
122 Alolan Diglett C .10 .25
123 Alolan Dugtrio U .25 .40
124 Forretress R .30 .50
125 Steelix R .30 .50
126 Scizor HOLO R .30 .50
127 Dialga HOLO R .40 .60
128 Durant C .10 .25
129 Cobalion HOLO R .30 .50
130 Genesect GX UR 1.50 2.50
131 Magearna U .25 .40
132 Alolan Ninetales GX UR 25.00 40.00
133 Jigglypuff C .10 .25
134 Wigglytuff R .30 .50
135 Marill C .10 .25
136 Azumarill R .30 .50
137 Snubbull C .10 .25
138 Granbull R .30 .50
139 Ralts C .10 .25
140 Kirlia U .25 .40
141 Gardevoir HOLO R .40 .60
142 Dedenne U .25 .40
143 Carbink U .25 .40
144 Xerneas PRISM HOLO R .30 .50
145 Cutiefly C .10 .25
146 Ribombee R .30 .50
147 Morelull C .10 .25
148 Shiinotic U .25 .40
149 Mimikyu GX UR 2.00 3.50
150 Tapu Lele HOLO R .30 .50
151 Tapu Fini HOLO R .30 .50
152 Chansey C .10 .25
153 Blissey HOLO R .30 .50
154 Ditto PRISM HOLO R 3.00 5.00
155 Eevee C .10 .25
156 Stantler U .25 .40
157 Smeargle R .30 .50
158 Miltank R .30 .50
159 Lugia GX UR 2.50 4.00
160 Ho-Oh R .30 .50
161 Kecleon U .25 .40
162 Kecleon U .25 .40
163 Pikipek C .10 .25
164 Pikipek C .10 .25
165 Trumbeak U .25 .40
166 Toucannon R .30 .50
167 Adventure Bag U .25 .40
168 Aether Foundation Employee U .25 .40
169 Choice Helmet U .25 .40
170 Counter Gain U .25 .40
171 Custom Catcher U .25 .40
172 Electropower U .25 .40
173 Faba U .25 .40
174 Fairy Charm G U .25 .40
175 Fairy Charm P U .25 .40
176 Fairy Charm F U .25 .40
177 Fairy Charm D U .25 .40
178 Heat Factory PRISM HOLO R .50 .75
179 Kahili U .25 .40
180 Life Forest PRISM HOLO R .30 .50
181 Lost Blender U .25 .40
182 Lusamine PRISM HOLO R .30 .50
183 Mina U .25 .40
184 Mixed Herbs U .25 .40
185 Moomoo Milk U .25 .40
186 Morty U .25 .40
187 Net Ball U .25 .40
188 Professor Elm's Lecture U .25 .40
189 Sightseer U .25 .40
190 Spell Tag U .25 .40
191 Thunder Mountain PRISM HOLO R .50 .75
192 Wait and See U .25 .40
193 Whitney U .25 .40
194 Memoray Energy U .25 .40
195 Shuckle GX FULL ART UR 5.00 8.00
196 Sceptile GX FULL ART UR 6.00 10.00
197 Virizion GX FULL ART UR 3.00 5.00
198 Magcargo GX FULL ART UR 4.00 7.50
199 Blacephalon GX FULL ART UR 25.00 35.00
200 Suicune GX UR 3.00 5.00
201 Zeraora GX FULL ART UR 15.00 20.00
202 Sigilyph GX FULL ART UR 2.50 4.00
203 Tyranitar GX FULL ART UR 5.00 8.00
204 Genesect GX FULL ART UR 2.50 4.00
205 Alolan Ninetales GX FULL ART UR 30.00 45.00
206 Mimikyu GX FULL ART UR 5.00 8.00
207 Lugia GX FULL ART UR 5.00 8.00
208 Faba FULL ART UR 6.00 10.00
209 Judge FULL ART UR 12.00 20.00
210 Kahili FULL ART UR 5.00 8.00
211 Mina FULL ART UR 8.00 12.00
212 Morty FULL ART UR 3.50 6.00
213 Professor Elm's Lecture FULL ART UR 30.00 45.00
214 Whitney FULL ART UR 8.00 12.00
215 Shuckle GX SCR 8.00 12.00
216 Sceptile GX SCR 8.00 12.00
217 Virizion GX SCR 5.00 8.00
218 Magcargo GX SCR 8.00 12.00
219 Blacephalon GX SCR 25.00 40.00
220 Suicune GX SCR 10.00 15.00
221 Zeraora GX SCR 20.00 25.00
222 Sigilyph GX SCR 5.00 8.00
223 Tyranitar GX SCR 10.00 15.00
224 Genesect GX SCR 5.00 8.00
225 Alolan Ninetales GX SCR 35.00 50.00
226 Mimikyu GX SCR 10.00 15.00
227 Lugia GX SCR 15.00 25.00
228 Adventure Bag SCR 8.00 12.00
229 Choice Helmet SCR 6.00 10.00
230 Counter Gain SCR 10.00 15.00
231 Custom Catcher SCR 8.00 12.00
232 Electropower SCR 10.00 15.00
233 Lost Blender SCR 15.00 25.00
234 Net Ball SCR 15.00 25.00
235 Spell Tag SCR 10.00 15.00
236 Wait and See Hammer SCR 4.00 6.00

2019 Pokemon Detective Pikachu

COMPLETE SET (18) 12.00 20.00
RELEASED ON MARCH 29, 2019
1 Bulbasaur C .20 .30
2 Ludicolo R .60 1.00
3 Morelull C .15 .25

4 Charmander C .15 .25
5 Charizard HOLO R 4.00 6.00
6 Arcanine R .60 1.00
7 Psyduck C .25 .40
8 Magikarp C .25 .40
9 Greninja HOLO R 2.50 4.00
10 Detective Pikachu R 1.50 2.50
11 Mr. Mime R .50 .75
12 Mewtwo HOLO R 2.50 4.00
13 Machamp R .35 .50
14 Jigglypuff C .15 .25
15 Snubbull C .15 .25
16 Lickitung C .15 .25
17 Ditto HOLO R 1.50 2.50
18 Slaking R .50 .75

2019 Pokemon Sun and Moon Team Up

COMPLETE SET (196)
*REV.FOIL: .75X TO 2X BASIC CARDS
RELEASED ON FEBRUARY 1, 2019
1 Celebi & Venusaur GX URR 4.00 6.00
2 Weedle C .10 .20
3 Weedle C .10 .20
4 Kakuna U .20 .30
5 Beedrill R .25 .40
6 Paras C .10 .20
7 Parasect R .25 .40
8 Exeggcute C .10 .20
9 Pinsir R .25 .40
10 Shaymin Prism Star HOLO R .50 .75
11 Charmander C .10 .20
12 Charmander C .10 .20
13 Charmeleon U .20 .30
14 Charizard R 1.50 2.50
15 Vulpix C .10 .20
16 Ninetales R 3.50 5.00
17 Ponyta C .10 .20
18 Rapidash U .20 .30
19 Moltres HOLO R .50 .75
20 Litten C .10 .20
21 Torracat U .20 .30
22 Squirtle C .10 .20
23 Squirtle C .10 .20
24 Wartortle U .20 .30
25 Blastoise R 1.50 2.50
26 Psyduck C .10 .20
27 Golduck U .20 .30
28 Staryu C .10 .20
29 Magikarp C .10 .20
30 Gyarados HOLO R 1.50 2.50
31 Lapras R .25 .40
32 Articuno HOLO R 1.00 1.50
33 Pikachu & Zekrom GX URR 6.00 15.00
34 Alolan Geodude C .10 .20
35 Alolan Geodude C .10 .20
36 Alolan Graveler U .20 .30
37 Alolan Golem R .25 .40
38 Voltorb C .10 .20
39 Electrode HOLO R .40 .60
40 Zapdos HOLO R 3.50 5.00
41 Mareep C .10 .20
42 Flaaffy U .20 .30
43 Ampharos GX URR 2.00 3.00
44 Blitzle C .10 .20
45 Zebstrika R .25 .40
46 Emolga C .10 .20
47 Joltik C .10 .20
48 Galvantula R .25 .40
49 Helioptile C .10 .20
50 Heliolisk U .20 .30
51 Tapu Koko Prism Star HOLO R 1.00 1.50
52 Zeraora HOLO R .40 .60
53 Gengar & Mimikyu GX URR 4.00 6.00
54 Nidoran? C .10 .20
55 Nidorina U .20 .30
56 Nidoqueen R .25 .40
57 Nidoran? C .10 .20
58 Nidorino U .20 .30
59 Nidoking R .25 .40
60 Tentacool C .10 .20
61 Tentacruel U .20 .30
62 Grimer C .10 .20
63 Muk R .25 .40
64 Alolan Marowak R .25 .40
65 Starmie R .25 .40
66 Mr. Mime R .25 .40
67 Mr. Mime GX URR 2.00 3.00
68 Jynx U .20 .30
69 Cosmog C .10 .20
70 Cosmoem U .20 .30
71 Mankey C .10 .20
72 Primeape R .25 .40
73 Hitmonlee U .20 .30
74 Hitmonchan U .20 .30
75 Omanyte U .20 .30
76 Omastar HOLO R .75 1.25
77 Kabuto U .20 .30
78 Kabutops R .25 .40
79 Larvitar C .10 .20
80 Pupitar U .20 .30
81 Pancham C .10 .20
82 Lycanroc GX URR 1.50 2.50
83 Alolan Grimer C .10 .20
84 Alolan Muk R .25 .40
85 Tyranitar HOLO R .50 .75
86 Poochyena C .10 .20
87 Mightyena R .25 .40
88 Absol HOLO R .75 1.25
89 Spiritomb U .20 .30
90 Zorua C .10 .20
91 Zoroark HOLO R .50 .75
92 Vullaby C .10 .20
93 Mandibuzz R .25 .40
94 Pangoro R .25 .40
95 Yveltal HOLO R .40 .60
96 Hoopa GX URR 2.00 3.00
97 Incineroar GX URR 3.00 4.00
98 Skarmory R .25 .40
99 Jirachi HOLO R 25.00 40.00
100 Bronzor C .10 .20
101 Bronzong R .25 .40
102 Ferroseed C .10 .20
103 Ferrothorn R .25 .40
104 Pawniard C .10 .20
105 Bisharp R .25 .40
106 Cobalion GX URR 2.00 3.00
107 Honedge C .10 .20
108 Doublade U .20 .30
109 Aegislash HOLO R .40 .60
110 Klefki C .10 .20
111 Alolan Ninetales HOLO R 1.25 2.00
112 Mimikyu R .25 .40
113 Latias & Latios GX URR 3.00 4.00
114 Alolan Exeggutor R .25 .40
115 Alolan Exeggutor R .25 .40
116 Dratini C .10 .20
117 Dratini C .10 .20
118 Dragonair U .20 .30
119 Dragonite HOLO R .60 1.00
120 Eevee & Snorlax GX URR 4.00 6.00
121 Pidgey C .10 .20
122 Pidgey C .10 .20
123 Pidgeotto C .10 .20
124 Pidgeot R .25 .40
125 Meowth C .10 .20
126 Persian U .20 .30
127 Farfetch'd U .20 .30
128 Kangaskhan U .20 .30
129 Tauros U .20 .30
130 Aerodactyl R .25 .40
131 Lugia HOLO R .60 1.00
132 Zangoose HOLO R .40 .60
133 Bill's Analysis HOLO R 8.00 12.00
134 Black Market Prism Star HOLO R .60 1.00
135 Brock's Grit U .20 .30
136 Buff Padding U .20 .30
137 Dana U .20 .30
138 Dangerous Drill U .20 .30
139 Electrocharger U .20 .30
140 Erika's Hospitality HOLO R 2.50 4.00
141 Evelyn U .20 .30
142 Fairy Charm UB U .20 .30
143 Grass Memory U .20 .30
144 Ingo & Emmet U .20 .30
145 Jasmine U .20 .30
146 Judge Whistle U .35 .50
147 Lavender Town U .20 .30
148 Metal Goggles U .20 .30
149 Morgan U .20 .30
150 Nanu U .20 .30
151 Nita U .20 .30
152 Pokemon Communication U .50 .75
153 Return Label U .20 .30
154 Sabrina's Suggestion U .20 .30
155 Unidentified Fossil U .20 .30
156 Viridian Forest U 2.00 3.00
157 Water Memory U .20 .30
158 Wondrous Labyrinth Prism Star HOLO R 1.00 1.50
159 Celebi & Venusaur GX UR 4.00 6.00
160 Magikarp & Wailord GX UR 8.00 12.00
161 Magikarp & Wailord GX UR 10.00 15.00
162 Pikachu & Zekrom GX UR 15.00 20.00
163 AmpharosGX UR 3.00 4.00
164 Gengar & Mimikyu GX UR 10.00 15.00
165 Gengar & Mimikyu GX UR 10.00 15.00
166 HoopaGX UR 3.00 4.00
167 IncineroarGX UR 3.50 5.00
168 CobalionGX UR 2.00 3.00
169 Latias & Latios GX UR 4.00 6.00
170 Latias & Latios GX UR 25.00 35.00
171 Eevee & Snorlax GX UR 8.00 12.00
172 Brock's Grit UR 5.00 8.00
173 Dana UR 5.00 8.00
174 Erika's Hospitality UR 25.00 35.00
175 Evelyn UR 5.00 8.00
176 Ingo & Emmet UR 4.00 6.00
177 Jasmine UR 6.00 10.00
178 Morgan UR 4.00 6.00
179 Nanu UR 5.00 8.00
180 Nita UR 5.00 8.00
181 Sabrina's Suggestion UR 10.00 15.00
182 Celebi & Venusaur GX SCR 10.00 15.00
183 Magikarp & Wailord GX SCR 10.00 15.00
184 Pikachu & Zekrom GX SCR 30.00 40.00
185 AmpharosGX SCR 6.00 10.00
186 Gengar & Mimikyu GX SCR 15.00 25.00
187 HoopaGX SCR 5.00 8.00
188 IncineroarGX SCR 5.00 8.00
189 CobalionGX SCR 5.00 8.00
190 Latias & Latios GX SCR 10.00 15.00
191 Eevee & Snorlax GX SCR 15.00 25.00
192 Dangerous Drill SCR 2.50 4.00
193 Electrocharger SCR 2.50 4.00
194 Judge Whistle SCR 5.00 8.00
195 Metal Goggles SCR 2.50 4.00
196 Pokemon Communication SCR 12.00 20.00

2019 Pokemon Sun and Moon Unbroken Bonds

RELEASED ON MAY 3, 2019
1 Pheromosa & Buzzwole GX URR 3.00 4.00
2 Caterpie C .10 .15
3 Metapod U .15 .25
4 Butterfree R .20 .30
5 Oddish C .10 .15
6 Oddish C .10 .15
7 Gloom U .15 .25
8 Vileplume HOLO R .40 .60
9 Venonat C .10 .15
10 Venonat C .10 .15
11 Venomoth R .20 .30
12 Venomoth GX URR 1.50 2.50
13 Bellsprout C .10 .15
14 Weepinbell U .15 .25
15 Victreebel R .20 .30
16 Tangela C .10 .15
17 Tangrowth R .20 .30
18 Grubbin C .10 .15
19 Kartana HOLO R .50 .75
20 Reshiram & Charizard GX URR 12.00 20.00
21 Growlithe C .10 .15
22 Arcanine HOLO R 1.00 1.50
23 Darumaka C .10 .15
24 Darmanitan R .20 .30
25 Volcanion HOLO R 5.00 8.00
26 Litten C .10 .15
27 Litten C .10 .15
28 Torracat U .15 .25
29 Incineroar R .20 .30
30 Salandit C .10 .15
31 Salazzle R .40 .60
32 Blacephalon R .40 .60
33 Squirtle C .10 .15
34 Wartortle U .15 .25
35 Blastoise GX URR 2.50 4.00
36 Poliwag C .10 .15
37 Poliwag C .10 .15
38 Poliwhirl U .15 .25
39 Poliwrath R .20 .30
40 Tentacool C .10 .15
41 Tentacruel U .15 .25
42 Slowpoke C .10 .15
43 Slowbro HOLO R .35 .50
44 Seel C .10 .15
45 Dewgong R .35 .50
46 Krabby C .10 .15
47 Kingler R .20 .30
48 Goldeen C .10 .15
49 Seaking R .20 .30
50 Kyurem HOLO R .40 .60
51 Froakie C .10 .15
52 Frogadier U .15 .25
53 Pyukumuku U .15 .25
54 Pikachu C .10 .15
55 Raichu R .20 .30
56 Stunfisk R .20 .30
57 Dedenne GX URR 25.00 35.00
58 Charjabug U .15 .25
59 Vikavolt HOLO R .40 .60
60 Zeraora R .20 .30
61 Muk & Alolan Muk GX URR 2.50 4.00
62 Ekans C .10 .15
63 Arbok R .20 .30
64 Zubat C .10 .15
65 Golbat U .15 .25
66 Crobat HOLO R .35 .50
67 Gastly C .10 .15
68 Gastly C .10 .15
69 Haunter U .15 .25
70 Gengar R .25 .40
71 Drowzee C .10 .15
72 Hypno R .20 .30
73 Koffing C .10 .15
74 Weezing R .50 .75
75 Mewtwo R .20 .30
76 Mew HOLO R 3.00 4.00
77 Misdreavus C .10 .15
78 Mismagius R .40 .60
79 Espurr C .10 .15
80 Meowstic R .20 .30
81 Marshadow HOLO R 1.00 1.50
82 Marshadow & Machamp GX URR 2.50 4.00
83 Sandshrew C .10 .15
84 Sandslash R .20 .30
85 Diglett C .10 .15
86 Dugtrio R .20 .30
87 Geodude C .10 .15
88 Graveler U .15 .25
89 Golem HOLO R .35 .50
90 Cubone C .10 .15
91 Marowak R .20 .30
92 Rhyhorn C .10 .15
93 Rhyhorn C .10 .15
94 Rhydon U .15 .25
95 Rhyperior R .20 .30
96 Wooper C .10 .15
97 Quagsire R .20 .30
98 Gligar C .10 .15
99 Gliscor U .15 .25
100 Tyrogue U .15 .25
101 Hitmontop U .15 .25
102 Riolu C .10 .15
103 Landorus HOLO R .35 .50
104 Crabrawler C .10 .15
105 Crabominable R .20 .30
106 Stakataka HOLO R .40 .60
107 Greninja & Zoroark GX URR 4.00 6.00
108 Murkrow C .10 .15
109 Honchkrow GX URR 1.50 2.50
110 Carvanha C .10 .15
111 Sharpedo R .35 .50
112 Spiritomb HOLO R 1.25 2.00
113 Sandile C .10 .15
114 Sandile C .10 .15
115 Krokorok U .15 .25
116 Krookodile R .20 .30
117 Greninja HOLO R .50 .75
118 Inkay C .10 .15
119 Malamar HOLO R .35 .50
120 Lucario & Melmetal GX URR 2.50 4.00
121 Alolan Diglett C .10 .15
122 Alolan Dugtrio R .20 .30
123 Aron C .10 .15
124 Lairon U .15 .25
125 Aggron R .20 .30
126 Lucario HOLO R .35 .50
127 Genesect R .20 .30
128 Meltan C .10 .15
129 Melmetal HOLO R .40 .60
130 Gardevoir & Sylveon GX URR 6.00 10.00
131 Cleffa U .15 .25
132 Clefairy C .10 .15
133 Clefable R .20 .30
134 Jigglypuff C .10 .15
135 Wigglytuff R .20 .30
136 Togepi C .10 .15
137 Togetic U .15 .25
138 Togekiss HOLO R .35 .50
139 Cottonee C .10 .15
140 Whimsicott GX URR 2.50 4.00
141 Spritzee C .10 .15
142 Aromatisse R .20 .30
143 Rattata C .10 .15
144 Raticate U .15 .25
145 Spearow C .10 .15
146 Fearow U .15 .25
147 Meowth C .10 .15
148 Persian R .20 .30
149 Persian GX URR 2.00 3.00
150 Doduo C .10 .15
151 Dodrio U .15 .25
152 Lickitung C .10 .15
153 Lickilicky R .20 .30
154 Porygon C .10 .15
155 Porygon C .10 .15
156 Porygon2 U .15 .25
157 Porygon-Z HOLO R 2.00 3.00
158 Snorlax HOLO R .40 .60
159 Glameow C .10 .15
160 Purugly R .20 .30
161 Happiny U .15 .25
162 Chatot U .15 .25
163 Celesteela GX URR 1.50 2.50
164 Beast Bringer U .15 .25
165 Chip-Chip Ice Axe U .15 .25
166 Devolution Spray Z U .15 .25
167 Dusk Stone U .15 .25
168 Dust Island U .15 .25
169 Electromagnetic Radar U .15 .25
170 Energy Spinner U .15 .25
171 Fairy Charm Ability U .15 .25
172 Fairy Charm L U .15 .25
173 Fire Crystal U .15 .25
174 Giovanni's Exile U .15 .25
175 Green's Exploration U .15 .25
176 Janine U .15 .25
177 Koga's Trap U .15 .25
178 Lt. Surge's Strategy U .15 .25
179 Martial Arts Dojo U .15 .25
180 Metal Core Barrier U .15 .25
181 Molayne U .15 .25
182 Pokegear 3.0 U .15 .25
183 Power Plant U .15 .25
184 Red's Challenge HOLO R 1.00 1.50
185 Samson Oak U .15 .25
186 Stealthy Hood U .15 .25
187 Surprise Box U .15 .25
188 Ultra Forest Kartenvoy U .15 .25
189 Welder U .15 .25
190 Triple Acceleration Energy U .15 .25
191 Pheromosa & Buzzwole GX UR 4.00 6.00
192 Pheromosa & Buzzwole GX UR 8.00 12.00
193 Venomoth GX UR 2.50 4.00
194 Reshiram & Charizard GX UR 25.00 30.00
195 Dedenne GX UR 30.00 40.00
196 Muk & Alolan Muk GX UR 2.50 4.00
197 Muk & Alolan Muk GX UR 5.00 8.00
198 Marshadow & Machamp GX UR 4.00 6.00
199 Marshadow & Machamp GX UR 5.00 8.00
200 Greninja & Zoroark GX UR 6.00 10.00
201 Greninja & Zoroark GX UR 10.00 15.00
202 Honchkrow GX UR 3.50 5.00
203 Lucario & Melmetal GX UR 4.00 6.00
204 Gardevoir & Sylveon GX UR 6.00 10.00
205 Gardevoir & Sylveon GX UR 20.00 25.00
206 Whimsicott GX UR 4.00 6.00
207 Persian GX UR 3.00 5.00
208 Celesteela GX UR 2.00 3.00
209 Green's Exploration UR 20.00 30.00
210 Janine UR 4.00 6.00
211 Koga's Trap UR 5.00 8.00
212 Molayne UR 2.50 4.00
213 Red's Challenge UR 12.00 20.00
214 Welder UR 15.00 25.00
215 Pheromosa & Buzzwole GX SCR 8.00 12.00
216 Venomoth GX SCR 4.00 6.00
217 Reshiram & Charizard GX SCR 150.00 200.00
218 Blastoise GX SCR 40.00 50.00
219 Dedenne GX SCR 25.00 35.00
220 Muk & Alolan Muk GX SCR 6.00 10.00
221 Marshadow & Machamp GX SCR 8.00 12.00
222 Greninja & Zoroark GX SCR 10.00 15.00
223 Honchkrow GX SCR 5.00 8.00
224 Lucario & Melmetal GX SCR 8.00 12.00
225 Gardevoir & Sylveon GX SCR 10.00 15.00
226 Whimsicott GX SCR 6.00 10.00
227 Persian GX SCR 4.00 6.00
228 Celesteela GX SCR 5.00 8.00
229 Beast Bringer SCR 3.50 5.00
230 Electromagnetic Radar SCR 10.00 15.00
231 Fire Crystal SCR 10.00 15.00
232 Metal Core Barrier SCR 2.50 4.00
233 Pokegear 3.0 SCR 10.00 15.00
234 Triple Acceleration Energy SCR 12.00 20.00

2019 Pokemon Sun and Moon Unified Minds

COMPLETE SET (258)
RELEASED ON AUGUST 2, 2019
1 Rowlet & Alolan ExeggutorTag Team GX URR 3.00 5.00
2 Yanma C .10 .15
3 Yanmega U .12 .20
4 Celebi HOLO R .30 .50

5 Shroomish C .10 .15
6 Sewaddle C .10 .15
7 Sewaddle C .10 .15
8 Swadloon U .12 .20
9 Leavanny R .20 .30
10 Dwebble C .10 .15
11 Crustle R .20 .30
12 Karrablast C .10 .15
13 Foongus C .10 .15
14 Amoonguss R .20 .30
15 Fomantis C .10 .15
16 Lurantis U .12 .20
17 Bounsweet C .10 .15
18 Steenee U .12 .20
19 Tsareena HOLO R .20 .30
20 Dhelmise U .12 .20
21 Magmar C .10 .15
22 Magmortar R .20 .30
23 Numel C .10 .15
24 Camerupt R .20 .30
25 HeatranGX URR 2.50 4.00
26 Victini HOLO R .25 .40
27 Litwick C .10 .15
28 Litwick C .10 .15
29 Lampent U .12 .20
30 Chandelure HOLO R .40 .60
31 Fletchinder C .10 .15
32 Talonflame R .20 .30
33 Salandit C .10 .15
34 Salazzle R .20 .30
35 Slowpoke & PsyduckTag Team GX URR 4.00 6.00
36 Lapras U .12 .20
37 Snorunt C .10 .15
38 Froslass HOLO R .20 .30
39 Finneon C .10 .15
40 Lumineon U .12 .20
41 Snover C .10 .15
42 Abomasnow R .20 .30
43 Basculin U .12 .20
44 Tirtouga U .12 .20
45 Carracosta U .12 .20
46 Cryogonal C .10 .15
47 KeldeoGX URR 2.50 4.00
48 Dewpider C .10 .15
49 Araquanid R .20 .30
50 Wimpod C .10 .15
51 Golisopod HOLO R .20 .30
52 Pyukumuku U .12 .20
53 Tapu Fini R .20 .30
54 Raichu & Alolan RaichuTag Team GX URR 8.00 12.00
55 Pikachu C .10 .15
56 Pikachu C .10 .15
57 Alolan Raichu HOLO R .20 .30
58 Magnemite C .10 .15
59 Magneton U .12 .20
60 Magnezone HOLO R .20 .30
61 Joltik C .10 .15
62 Galvantula R .20 .30
63 Tynamo C .10 .15
64 Tynamo C .10 .15
65 Eelektrik U .12 .20
66 Eelektross HOLO R .25 .40
67 Stunfisk C .10 .15
68 Thundurus U .12 .20
69 Tapu Koko HOLO R .20 .30
70 Xurkitree R .20 .30
71 Mewtwo & MewTag Team GX URR 20.00 35.00
72 Espeon & DeoxysTag Team GX URR 3.00 5.00
73 Exeggcute C .10 .15
74 Exeggutor R .20 .30
75 Alolan Marowak R .20 .30
76 Jynx U .12 .20
77 Wynaut U .12 .20
78 LatiosGX URR 2.50 4.00
79 JirachiGX URR 2.50 4.00
80 Drifloon C .10 .15
81 Drifblim R .20 .30
82 Skorupi C .10 .15
83 Uxie HOLO R .20 .30
84 Mesprit U .12 .20
85 Azelf U .12 .20
86 Giratina HOLO R .20 .30
87 Cresselia U .12 .20
88 Munna C .10 .15
89 Musharna U .12 .20
90 Elgyem U .15 .25
91 Beheeyem R 1.50 2.50
92 Honedge C .10 .15
93 Honedge C .10 .15
94 Doublade U .12 .20
95 Aegislash HOLO R .20 .30
96 Mareanie C .10 .15
97 Toxapex R .20 .30
98 Salandit C .10 .15
99 Salazzle R .20 .30
100 Cosmog C .10 .15
101 Necrozma R .20 .30
102 Poipole C .10 .15
103 Onix C .10 .15
104 Steelix R .20 .30
105 Cubone C .10 .15
106 AerodactylGX URR 2.50 4.00
107 Heracross U .12 .20
108 Breloom U .12 .20
109 Meditite C .10 .15
110 Medicham R .20 .30
111 Relicanth U .12 .20
112 Gible C .10 .15
113 Gabite U .12 .20
114 Garchomp HOLO R .20 .30
115 Riolu C .10 .15
116 Riolu C .10 .15
117 Lucario R .20 .30
118 Drilbur C .10 .15
119 Excadrill R .20 .30
120 Archen U .12 .20
121 Archeops R .20 .30
122 Terrakion HOLO R .20 .30
123 Meloetta R .20 .30
124 Zygarde R .20 .30
125 Umbreon & DarkraiTag Team GX URR 8.00 12.00
126 Mega Sableye & TyranitarTag Team GX URR 4.00 6.00
127 Alolan Grimer C .10 .15
128 Murkrow C .10 .15
129 Murkrow C .10 .15
130 Honchkrow R .20 .30
131 Sneasel C .10 .15
132 WeavileGX URR 8.00 12.00
133 Sableye U .12 .20
134 Drapion R .20 .30
135 Purrloin C .10 .15
136 Liepard R .20 .30
137 Scraggy C .10 .15
138 Scrafty R .20 .30
139 Yveltal HOLO R .25 .40
140 Hoopa HOLO R 1.50 2.00
141 MawileGX URR 1.50 2.50
142 Escavalier R .20 .30
143 Cottonee C .10 .15
144 Whimsicott R .20 .30
145 Dedenne U .12 .20
146 Garchomp & GiratinaTag Team GX URR 10.00 15.00
147 Dratini C .10 .15
148 Dratini C .10 .15
149 Dragonair U .12 .20
150 Dragonair U .12 .20
151 Dragonite R .20 .30
152 DragoniteGX URR 1.75 3.00
153 Latias R .20 .30
154 Axew C .10 .15
155 Fraxure U .12 .20
156 Haxorus HOLO R .20 .30
157 Druddigon C .10 .15
158 Noibat C .10 .15
159 Noivern R .20 .30
160 NaganadelGX URR 6.00 10.00
161 Lickitung C .10 .15
162 Lickilicky R .20 .30
163 Kangaskhan HOLO R .20 .30
164 Tauros U .12 .20
165 Hoothoot C .10 .15
166 Noctowl U .12 .20
167 Slakoth C .10 .15
168 Slakoth C .10 .15
169 Vigoroth U .12 .20
170 Slaking HOLO R .20 .30
171 Bidoof C .10 .15
172 Bibarel U .12 .20
173 Munchlax U .12 .20
174 Pidove C .10 .15
175 Tranquill U .12 .20
176 Unfezant R .20 .30
177 Audino U .12 .20
178 Tornadus U .12 .20
179 Fletchling C .10 .15
180 Yungoos C .10 .15
181 Gumshoos R .20 .30
182 Oranguru U .12 .20
183 Type: Null U .12 .20
184 Silvally HOLO R .20 .30
185 Komala U .12 .20
186 Blaine's Quiz Show U .12 .20
187 Blizzard Town U .12 .20
188 Blue's Tactics U .20 .30
189 Bug Catcher U .12 .20
190 Channeler U .12 .20
191 Cherish Ball U 2.50 4.00
192 Coach Trainer U .50 .75
193 Dark City U .12 .20
194 Ear-Ringing Bell U .12 .20
195 Flyinium Z: Air Slash U .12 .20
196 Giant Bomb U .25 .40
197 Giant Hearth U 1.50 2.00
198 Great Potion U 1.75 3.00
199 Grimsley U .12 .20
200 Hapu U .50 .75
201 Karate Belt U .15 .25
202 Misty's Favor U .20 .30
203 Normalium Z: Tackle U .12 .20
204 Poke Maniac U .12 .20
205 Pokemon Research Lab U .20 .30
206 Reset Stamp U .60 1.00
207 Slumbering Forest U .12 .20
208 Stadium Nav U .50 .75
209 Tag Switch U .60 1.00
210 Unidentified Fossil U .12 .20
211 U-Turn Board U .20 .30
212 Recycle Energy U .30 .50
213 Weakness Guard Energy U .25 .40
214 Rowlet & Alolan ExeggutorTag Team GX UR 4.00 6.00
215 Rowlet & Alolan ExeggutorTag Team GX UR 8.00 12.00
216 HeatranGX UR 4.00 6.00
217 Slowpoke & PsyduckTag Team GX UR 4.00 6.00
218 Slowpoke & PsyduckTag Team GX UR 6.00 10.00
219 KeldeoGX UR 4.00 6.00
220 Raichu & Alolan RaichuTag Team GX UR 8.00 12.00
221 Raichu & Alolan RaichuTag Team GX UR 15.00 25.00
222 Mewtwo & MewTag Team GX UR 25.00 40.00
223 LatiosGX UR 4.00 6.00
224 AerodactylGX UR 2.50 4.00
225 Mega Sableye & TyranitarTag Team GX UR 4.00 6.00
226 Mega Sableye & TyranitarTag Team GX UR 8.00 12.00
227 MawileGX UR 1.75 3.00
228 Garchomp & GiratinaTag Team GX UR 10.00 15.00
229 DragoniteGX UR 2.50 4.00
230 NaganadelGX UR 6.00 10.00
231 Blue's Tactics UR 8.00 12.00
232 Channeler UR 4.00 6.00
233 Coach Trainer UR 10.00 15.00
234 Grimsley UR 2.50 4.00
235 Misty's Favor UR 15.00 25.00
236 Poke Maniac UR 4.00 6.00
237 Rowlet & Alolan ExeggutorTag Team GX SCR 8.00 12.00
238 HeatranGX SCR 6.00 10.00
239 Slowpoke & PsyduckTag Team GX SCR 8.00 12.00
240 KeldeoGX SCR 8.00 12.00
241 Raichu & Alolan RaichuTag Team GX SCR 20.00 35.00
242 Mewtwo & MewTag Team GX SCR 75.00 125.00
243 LatiosGX SCR 8.00 12.00
244 AerodactylGX SCR 4.00 6.00
245 Mega Sableye & TyranitarTag Team GX SCR 10.00 15.00
246 MawileGX SCR 5.00 8.00
247 Garchomp & GiratinaTag Team GX SCR 12.00 20.00
248 DragoniteGX SCR 10.00 15.00
249 NaganadelGX SCR 8.00 12.00
250 Cherish Ball SCR 30.00 50.00
251 Giant Bomb SCR 8.00 12.00
252 Karate Belt SCR 6.00 10.00
253 Reset Stamp SCR 20.00 35.00
254 Tag Switch SCR 8.00 12.00
255 U-Turn Board SCR 6.00 10.00
256 Viridian Forest SCR 25.00 40.00
257 Recycle Energy SCR 10.00 15.00
258 Weakness Guard Energy SCR 8.00 12.00

2004 Pokemon Organized Play Series 1

COMPLETE SET (17)
RELEASED IN SEPT. 2004 8.00 20.00
BOOSTER PACK (2 CARDS) 2.00 3.00
1 Blaziken R .50 1.00
2 Metagross R .50 1.00
3 Rayquaza R .50 1.00
4 Sceptile R .50 1.00
5 Swampert R .50 1.00
6 Beautifly U .20 .50
7 Masquerain U .20 .50
8 Murkrow U .20 .50
9 Pupitar U .20 .50
10 Torkoal U .20 .50
11 Larvitar C .10 .20
12 Minun C .20 .50
13 Plusle C .20 .50
14 Surskit C .10 .50
15 Swellow C .10 .20
16 Armaldo EX R 4.00 10.00
17 Tyranitar EX R 5.00 10.00

2005 Pokemon Organized Play Series 2

BOOSTER PACK (2 CARDS) 2.00 3.00
RELEASED IN AUG. 2005
1 Entei R .50 1.00
2 Pidgeot R .50 1.00
3 Raikou R .50 1.00
4 Suicune R 1.00 2.00
5 Tauros R .50 1.00
6 Venusaur R 2.00 2.00
7 Ivysaur U .20 .50
8 Mr. Briney's Compassion U .20 .50
9 Multi Technical Machine 01 U .20 .50
10 PokÃ©mon Park U .20 .50
11 TV Reporter U .20 .50
12 Bulbasaur C .10 .20
13 Cacnea C .10 .20
14 Luvdisc C .10 .20
15 Phanpy C .10 .20
16 Pikachu C .20 .50
17 Celebi EX R 4.00 8.00

2006 Pokemon Organized Play Series 3

BOOSTER PACK (2 CARDS) 2.00 3.00
RELEASED IN APRIL 2006
1A Blastoise R 1.00 2.00
1B Blastoise HOLO R 10.00 20.00
2A Flareon R 1.00 2.00
2B Flareon HOLO R 4.00 10.00
3A Jolteon R .50 1.00
3B Jolteon HOLO R 4.00 10.00
4A Minun R 1.00 2.00
4B Minun HOLO R 4.00 10.00
5A Plusle R 1.00 2.00
5B Plusle HOLO R 4.00 10.00
6A Vaporeon R 1.00 2.00
6B Vaporeon HOLO R 4.00 10.00
7 Combusken U .20 .50
8 Donphan U .20 .50
9 Forretress U .20 .50
10 High Pressure System U .20 .50
11 Low Pressure System U .20 .50
12 Ditto (Mr. Mime) C .10 .20
13 Eevee C .10 .20
14 Ivysaur C .10 .20
15 Marshtomp C .10 .20
16 Pichu Bros. C 2.00 4.00
17A Ho-oh EX R 1.00 2.00
17B Ho-oh EX HOLO R 5.00 12.00

2006 Pokemon Organized Play Series 4

BOOSTER PACK (2 CARDS) 2.00 3.00
RELEASED IN AUGUST 2006
1 Chimecho R 1.00 2.00
2A Deoxys R 1.00 2.00
2B Deoxys HOLO R 4.00 10.00
3A Flygon R 1.00 2.00
3B Flygon HOLO R 3.00 6.00
4A Mew R 1.00 2.00
4B Mew HOLO R 4.00 10.00
5 Sceptile R 1.00 2.00
6A Combusken U .20 .50
6B Combusken HOLO R 3.00 6.00
7 Grovyle U .20 .50
8 Heal Energy U .20 .50
9 PokÃ©mon Fan Club U .20 .50
10 Scramble Energy U .20 .50
11A Mudkip C .10 .20
11B Mudkip HOLO R 3.00 7.00
12 Pidgey C .10 .20
13A Pikachu C .50 1.00
13B Pikachu HOLO R 4.00 10.00
14 Squirtle C .10 .20
15 Treecko C .10 .20
16A Wobbuffet C .10 .20
16B Wobbuffet HOLO R 3.00 6.00
17 Deoxys EX R 1.00 2.00

2007 Pokemon Organized Play Series 5

BOOSTER PACK (2 CARDS) 2.00 3.00
RELEASED IN MARCH 2007
1A Ho-Oh R 1.00 2.00
1B Ho-Oh HOLO R 7.00 15.00
2B Lugia R 1.00 2.00
2A Lugia HOLO R 7.00 15.00
3B Mew R 1.00 2.00
3A Mew HOLO R 4.00 10.00
4 Double Rainbow Energy R .50 1.00
5 Charmeleon U .20 .50
6 Billâ•™s Maintenance U .20 .50
7 Rare Candy U 1.00 2.00
8 Boost Energy U .20 .50
9 Delta Rainbow Energy U .20 .50
10 Charmander C .10 .20
11 Meowth C .10 .20
12B Pikachu C .50 1.00
12A Pikachu HOLO R 4.00 10.00
13 Pikachu C .50 1.00
14B Pelipper C .10 .20
14A Pelipper HOLO R 3.00 6.00
15B Zangoose C .10 .20
15A Zangoose HOLO R 3.00 6.00
16 Espeon Gold Star R 400.00 500.00
17 Umbreon Gold Star R 400.00 500.00

2007 Pokemon Organized Play Series 6

BOOSTER PACK 2.00 3.00
RELEASED IN SEPT. 2007
1 Bastiodon R 1.00 2.00
2 Lucario R 1.00 2.00
3A Manaphy R .50 1.00
3B Manaphy HOLO R 3.00 6.00
4 Pachirisu R 1.00 2.00
5 Rampardos R .50 1.00
6 Drifloon U .20 .50
7A Gible U .20 .50
7B Gible HOLO R 3.00 6.00
8A Riolu U .20 .50
8B Riolu HOLO R 3.00 6.00
9A Pikachu U .20 .50
9B Pikachu HOLO R 4.00 10.00
10 Staravia U .20 .50
11 Bidoof C .10 .20
12 Buneary C .10 .20
13 Cherubi C .10 .20
14A Chimchar C .10 .20
14B Chimchar HOLO R 4.00 8.00
15B Piplup HOLO R 5.00 10.00
15A Piplup C .10 .20
16 Starly C .10 .20
17 Turtwig C .10 .20

2008 Pokemon Organized Play Series 7

BOOSTER PACK (2 CARDS) 2.00 3.00
RELEASED IN FEB. 2008
1 Ampharos R 2.00 5.00
2 Gallade R 4.00 8.00
3 Latias R 2.00 5.00
4 Latios R 2.00 4.00
5 Mothim R 2.00 4.00
6 Delibird U .20 .50
7 Flaaffy U .20 .50
8 Kirlia U .20 .50
8 Kirlia HOLO R 5.00 10.00
9 Stantler U .20 .50
10 Wormadam U .20 .50
11 Burmy C .20 .50
12 Burmy C .10 .20
13 Corsola C .10 .20
14 Mareep C .20 .50
15 Ralts C .20 .50
16 Sentret C .20 .50
17 Spinda C .20 .50

2008 Pokemon Organized Play Series 8

1 Heatran R 2.00 4.00
2 Lucario R 5.00 10.00
3 Luxray HOLO R 4.00 8.00
4 Probopass HOLO R 4.00 8.00
5 Yanmega R 2.00 4.00
6 Cherrim U .20 .50
7 Carnivine U .20 .50
8 Luxio U .20 .50
9 Night Maintenance U .20 .50
10 Rare Candy U 2.00 4.00
11 Roseanne's Research U 2.00 4.00
12 Chimchar C .10 .20
13 Croagunk C .10 .20
14 Happiny C .10 .20
15 Piplup C .10 .20
16 Riolu C .10 .20
17 Turtwig C .10 .20

2009 Pokemon Organized Play Series 9

1 Garchomp 2.00 4.00
2 Manaphy .20 .50
3 Raichu .50 1.00
4 Regigigas 1.00 2.00
5 Rotom (Holo) 5.00 10.00
6 Buizel .20 .50
7 Croagunk .20 .50
8 Gabite .20 .50
9 Lopunny .20 .50
10 Pachirisu .50 1.00
11 Pichu .20 .50
12 Buneary .20 .50
13 Chimchar .20 .50
14 Gible .20 .50
15 Pikachu .50 1.00
16 Piplup .20 .50
17 Turtwig .20 .50

YU-GI-OH!

Beckett Yu-Gi-Oh! price guide sponsored by YugiohMint.com

TCG Booster

2002 Yu-Gi-Oh Legend of Blue Eyes White Dragon 1st Edition

COMPLETE SET (126)	800.00	1000.00
BOOSTER BOX (24 PACKS)	1100.00	1300.00
BOOSTER PACK (9 CARDS)	40.00	80.00
*UNLIMITED: .4X TO .8X 1ST EDITION		
RELEASED ON MARCH 8, 2002		
LOB0 Tri-Horned Dragon SCR	40.00	80.00
LOB1 Blue-Eyes White Dragon UR	80.00	120.00
LOB2 Hitotsu-Me Giant C	.60	1.50
LOB3 Flame Swordsman SR	25.00	50.00
LOB4 Skull Servant C	.60	1.50
LOB5 Dark Magician UR	80.00	130.00
LOB6 Gaia The Fierce Knight UR	25.00	50.00
LOB7 Celtic Guardian SR	10.00	25.00
LOB8 Basic Insect C	.60	1.50
LOB9 Mammoth Graveyard C	.60	1.50
LOB10 Silver Fang C	.60	1.50
LOB11 Dark Gray C	.60	1.50
LOB12 Trial of Hell C	.60	1.50
LOB13 Nemuriko C	.60	1.50
LOB14 The 13th Grave C	.60	1.50
LOB15 Charubin Fire Knight R	1.50	4.00
LOB16 Flame Manipulator C	.60	1.50
LOB17 Monster Egg C	.60	1.50
LOB18 Firegrass C	.60	1.50
LOB19 Darkfire Dragon R	2.00	5.00
LOB20 Dark King of Abyss C	.60	1.50
LOB21 Fiend Reflection #2 C	.60	1.50
LOB22 Fusionist R	1.50	4.00
LOB23 Turtle Tiger C	.60	1.50
LOB24 Petit Dragon C	.60	1.50
LOB25 Petit Angel C	.60	1.50
LOB26 Hinotama Soul C	.60	1.50
LOB27 Aqua Madoor R	.75	2.00
LOB28 Kagemusha of Blue Flame C	.60	1.50
LOB29 Flame Ghost R	1.25	3.00
LOB30 Two-Mouth Darkruler C	.60	1.50
LOB31 Dissolverock C	.60	1.50
LOB32 Root Water C	.60	1.50
LOB33 The Furious Sea King C	.60	1.50
LOB34 Green Phantom King C	.60	1.50
LOB35 Ray & Temperature C	.60	1.50
LOB36 King Fog C	.60	1.50
LOB37 Mystical Sheep #2 C	.60	1.50
LOB38 Masaki Legendary Swordsman C	.60	1.50
LOB39 Kurama C	.60	1.50
LOB40 Legendary Sword SP	.60	1.50
LOB41 Beast Fangs SP	.60	1.50
LOB42 Violet Crystal SP	.60	1.50
LOB43 Book of Secret Arts SP	.60	1.50
LOB44 Power of Kaishin SP	.60	1.50
LOB45 Dragon Capture Jar R	1.50	4.00
LOB46 Forest C	.60	1.50
LOB47 Wasteland C	.60	1.50
LOB48 Mountain C	.60	1.50
LOB49 Sogen C	.60	1.50
LOB50 Umi C	.60	1.50
LOB51 Yami C	.60	1.50
LOB52 Dark Hole SR	10.00	25.00
LOB53 Raigeki SR	25.00	50.00
LOB54 Red Medicine C	.60	1.50
LOB55 Sparks C	.60	1.50
LOB56 Hinotama C	.60	1.50
LOB57 Fissure R	1.00	2.50
LOB58 Trap Hole SR	5.00	12.00
LOB59 Polymerization SR	10.00	25.00
LOB60 Remove Trap C	.60	1.50
LOB61 Two-Pronged Attack R	.75	2.00
LOB62 Mystical Elf SR	8.00	20.00
LOB63 Tyhone C	.60	1.50
LOB64 Beaver Warrior C	.60	1.50
LOB65 Gravedigger Ghoul R	.75	2.00
LOB66 Curse of Dragon SR	8.00	20.00
LOB67 Karbonala Warrior R	1.50	4.00
LOB68 Giant Soldier of Stone R	1.50	4.00
LOB69 Uraby C	.60	1.50
LOB70 Red Eyes B Dragon UR	180.00	220.00
LOB71 Reaper of the Cards R	1.00	2.50
LOB72 Witty Phantom C	.60	1.50
LOB73 Larvas C	.60	1.50
LOB74 Hard Armor C	.60	1.50
LOB75 Man Eater C	.60	1.50
LOB76 M-Warrior #1 C	.60	1.50
LOB77 M-Warrior #2 C	.60	1.50
LOB78 Spirit of the Harp R	.75	2.00
LOB79 Armaill C	.60	1.50
LOB80 Terra the Terrible C	.60	1.50
LOB81 Frenzied Panda C	.60	1.50
LOB82 Kumootoko C	.60	1.50
LOB83 Meda Bat C	.60	1.50
LOB84 Enchanting Mermaid C	.60	1.50
LOB85 Fireyarou C	.60	1.50
LOB86 Dragoness The Wicked R	1.25	3.00
LOB87 One-Eyed Shield Dragon C	.60	1.50
LOB88 Dark Energy SP	.60	1.50
LOB89 Laser Cannon Armor SP	.60	1.50
LOB90 Vile Germs SP	.60	1.50
LOB91 Silver Bow and Arrow SP	.60	1.50
LOB92 Dragon Treasure SP	.60	1.50
LOB93 Electro-Whip	.60	1.50
LOB94 Mystical Moon SP	.60	1.50
LOB95 Stop Defense R	.75	2.00
LOB96 Machine Convers. Factory SP	.60	1.50
LOB97 Raise Body Heat SP	.60	1.50
LOB98 Follow Wind SP	.60	1.50
LOB99 Goblin's Secret Remedy R	.75	2.00
LOB100 Final Flame R	1.25	3.00
LOB101 Swords of Rev. Light SR	4.00	10.00
LOB102 Metal Dragon R	1.25	3.00
LOB103 Spike Seadra C	.60	1.50
LOB104 Tripwire Beast C	.60	1.50
LOB105 Skull Red Bird C	.60	1.50
LOB106 Armed Ninja R	.75	2.00
LOB107 Flower Wolf R	.75	2.00
LOB108 Man-Eater Bug SR	8.00	20.00
LOB109 Sand Stone C	.60	1.50
LOB110 Hane-Hane R	.75	2.00
LOB111 Misairuzame C	.60	1.50
LOB112 Steel Ogre Grotto #1 C	.60	1.50
LOB113 Lesser Dragon C	.60	1.50
LOB114 Darkworld Thorns C	.60	1.50
LOB115 Drooling Lizard C	.60	1.50
LOB116 Armored Starfish C	.60	1.50
LOB117 Succubus Knight C	.60	1.50
LOB118 Monster Reborn UR	40.00	80.00
LOB119 Pot of Greed R	3.00	8.00
LOB120 Right Leg of Forbid.One UR	80.00	120.00
LOB121 Left Leg of Forbidden One UR	80.00	120.00
LOB122 Right Arm of Forbid.One UR	80.00	120.00
LOB123 Left Arm of Forbid.One UR	80.00	120.00
LOB124 Exodia the Forbidden One UR	150.00	200.00
LOB125 Gaia the Dragon Champion SCR	80.00	120.00

2002 Yu-Gi-Oh Metal Raiders 1st Edition

COMPLETE SET (144)	200.00	400.00
BOOSTER BOX (24 PACKS)	350.00	500.00
BOOSTER PACK (9 CARDS)	8.00	20.00
*UNLIMITED: .4X TO .8X 1ST EDITION		
RELEASED ON JUNE 26, 2002		
MRD0 Gate Guardian SCR	25.00	50.00
MRD1 Feral Imp SP	.75	2.00
MRD2 Winged Dragon C	.40	1.00
MRD3 Summoned Skull UR	30.00	60.00
MRD4 Rock Ogre Grotto 1 C	.30	.75
MRD5 Armored Lizard C	.30	.75
MRD6 Killer Needle C	.30	.75
MRD7 Larvae Moth C	.40	1.00
MRD8 Harpie Lady C	1.25	3.00
MRD9 Harpie Lady Sisters SR	8.00	20.00
MRD10 Kojikocy C	.30	.75
MRD11 Cocoon of Evolution SP	.60	1.50
MRD12 Crawling Dragon C	.30	.75
MRD13 Armored Zombie C	.30	.75
MRD14 Mask of Darkness R	1.00	2.50
MRD15 Doma the Angel of Silence C	.30	.75
MRD16 White Magical Hat R	.40	1.00
MRD17 Big Eye C	.30	.75
MRD18 B Skull Dragon UR	30.00	60.00
MRD19 Masked Sorcerer R	.40	1.00
MRD20 Roaring Ocean Snake C	.30	.75
MRD21 Water Omotics C	.30	.75
MRD22 Ground Attacker Bugroth C	.40	1.00
MRD23 Petit Moth C	.30	.75
MRD24 Elegant Egotist R	.75	2.00
MRD25 Sanga of Thunder SR	2.50	6.00
MRD26 Kazejin SR	4.00	10.00
MRD27 Suijin SR	4.00	10.00
MRD28 Mystic Lamp SP	.30	.75
MRD29 Steel Scorpion C	.30	.75
MRD30 Ocubeam C	.30	.75
MRD31 Leghul SP	.30	.75
MRD32 Ooguchi SP	.30	.75
MRD33 Leogun C	.30	.75
MRD34 Blast Juggler C	.30	.75
MRD35 Jinzo #7 SP	.60	1.50
MRD36 Magician of Faith R	1.50	4.00
MRD37 Ancient Elf C	.30	.75
MRD38 Deepsea Shark C	.30	.75
MRD39 Bottom Dweller C	.30	.75
MRD40 Destroyer Golem C	.40	1.00
MRD41 Kaminari Attack C	.40	1.00
MRD42 Rainbow Flower SP	.40	1.00
MRD43 Morinphen C	.30	.75
MRD44 Mega Thunderball C	.30	.75
MRD45 Tongyo C	.30	.75
MRD46 Empress Judge C	.30	.75
MRD47 Pale Beast C	.30	.75
MRD48 Electric Lizard C	.30	.75
MRD49 Hunter Spider C	.30	.75
MRD50 Ancient Lizard Warrior C	.30	.75
MRD51 Queen's Double SP	.75	2.00
MRD52 Trent C	.30	.75
MRD53 Disk Magician C	.30	.75
MRD54 Hyosube C	.30	.75
MRD55 Hibikime C	.40	1.00
MRD56 Fake Trap R	.60	1.50
MRD57 Tribute to the Doomed SR	1.50	4.00
MRD58 Soul Release C	.75	2.00
MRD59 Cheerful Coffin C	.40	1.00
MRD60 Change of Heart UR	15.00	30.00
MRD61 Baby Dragon SP	.40	1.00
MRD62 Blackland Fire Dragon C	.30	.75
MRD63 Swamp Battleguard C	.40	1.00
MRD64 Battle Steer C	.30	.75
MRD65 Time Wizard UR	35.00	70.00
MRD66 Saggi the Dark Clown C	.30	.75
MRD67 Dragon Piper C	.40	1.00
MRD68 Illusionist Faceless Mage C	.30	.75
MRD69 Sangan R	1.50	4.00
MRD70 Great Moth R	1.25	3.00
MRD71 Kuriboh SR	8.00	20.00
MRD72 Jellyfish C	.30	.75
MRD73 Castle of Dark Illusions C	1.25	3.00
MRD74 King of Yamimakai C	.30	.75
MRD75 Catapult Turtle SR	2.00	5.00
MRD76 Mystic Horseman C	.30	.75
MRD77 Rabid Horseman C	.40	1.00
MRD78 Crass Clown SP	.75	2.00
MRD79 Pumpking King of Ghosts C	.30	.75
MRD80 Dream Clown SP	.75	2.00
MRD81 Tainted Wisdom C	.30	.75
MRD82 Ancient Brain C	.40	1.00
MRD83 Guardian of Labyrinth C	.30	.75
MRD84 Prevent Rat C	.30	.75
MRD85 Little Swordsman of Aile C	.30	.75
MRD86 Princess of Tsurugi R	.50	1.25
MRD87 Protector of the Throne C	.30	.75
MRD88 Tremendous Fire C	.40	1.00
MRD89 Jirai Gumo C	.30	.75
MRD90 Shadow Ghoul R	.75	2.00
MRD91 Labyrinth Tank C	.30	.75
MRD92 Ryu-Kishin Powered C	.30	.75
MRD93 Bickuribox C	.30	.75
MRD94 Giltia the D Knight C	.60	1.50
MRD95 Launcher Spider C	.30	.75
MRD96 Giga-Tech Wolf C	.30	.75
MRD97 Thunder Dragon SP	2.00	5.00
MRD98 7 Colored Fish C	.30	.75
MRD99 Immortal of Thunder C	.30	.75
MRD100 Punished Eagle C	.30	.75
MRD101 Insect Soldiers of the Sky C	.30	.75
MRD102 Hoshiningen R	.40	1.00
MRD103 Musician King C	.40	1.00
MRD104 Yado Karu C	.30	.75
MRD105 Cyber Saurus C	1.50	4.00
MRD106 Cannon Soldier R	.40	1.00
MRD107 Muka Muka R	.40	1.00
MRD108 The Bistro Butcher C	.30	.75
MRD109 Star Boy R	.60	1.50
MRD110 Milus Radiant R	.40	1.00
MRD111 Flame Cerebus C	.30	.75
MRD112 Niwatori C	.30	.75
MRD113 Dark Elf R	.40	1.00
MRD114 Mushroom Man #2 C	.30	.75
MRD115 Lava Battleguard C	.30	.75
MRD116 Witch of Black Forest R	.75	2.00
MRD117 Little Chimera R	.40	1.00
MRD118 Bladefly R	.40	1.00
MRD119 Lady of Faith C	.30	.75
MRD120 Twin-Headed Thunder Dragon SR	1.00	3.00
MRD121 Witch's Apprentice R	.40	1.00
MRD122 Blue-Winged Crown C	.30	.75
MRD123 Skull Knight C	.30	.75
MRD124 Gazelle King of Myth Beasts SP	.40	1.00
MRD125 Garnecia Elefantis SR	.75	2.00
MRD126 Barrel Dragon UR	20.00	40.00
MRD127 Solemn Judgment UR	20.00	40.00
MRD128 Magic Jammer UR	5.00	12.00
MRD129 Seven Tools of the Bandit UR	5.00	12.00
MRD130 Horn of Heaven UR	10.00	25.00
MRD131 Shield and Sword R	.40	1.00
MRD132 Sword of Deep-Seated C	.30	.75
MRD133 Block Attack C	.30	.75
MRD134 The Unhappy Maiden SP	.40	1.00
MRD135 Robbin Goblin R	.40	1.00
MRD136 Germ Infection C	.30	.75
MRD137 Paralyzing Potion C	.30	.75
MRD138 Mirror Force UR	60.00	100.00
MRD139 Ring of Magnetism C	.40	1.00
MRD140 Share the Pain C	.30	.75
MRD141 Stim-pack SP	.30	.75
MRD142 Heavy Storm SR	8.00	20.00
MRD143 Thousand Dragon SCR	8.00	20.00

2002 Yu-Gi-Oh Magic Ruler 1st Edition

COMPLETE SET (104)	100.00	175.00
BOOSTER BOX (24 PACKS)	100.00	150.00
RETAIL BOOSTER BOX (36 PACKS)	100.00	150.00
BOOSTER PACK (9 CARDS)	3.00	8.00
*UNLIMITED: .4X TO .8X 1ST EDITION		
RELEASED ON SEPTEMBER 16, 2002		
MRL0 Blue Eyes Toon Dragon SCR	20.00	40.00
MRL1 Penguin Knight C	.30	.75
MRL2 Axe of Despair UR	4.00	10.00
MRL3 Black Pendant SR	.75	2.00
MRL4 Horn of Light C	.30	.75
MRL5 Malevolent Nuzzler C	.30	.75
MRL6 Spellbinding Circle UR	15.00	30.00
MRL8 Electric Snake C	.30	.75
MRL9 Queen Bird C	.30	.75
MRL-7 Metal Fish C	.30	.75
MRL10 Ameba R	.40	1.00
MRL11 Peacock C	.30	.75
MRL12 Maha Vailo SR	.75	2.00
MRL13 Guardian of Throne Room C	.30	.75
MRL14 Fire Kraken C	.30	.75
MRL15 Minar C	.30	.75
MRL16 Griggle C	.30	.75
MRL17 Tyhone #2 C	.60	1.50
MRL18 Ancient One of Deep Forest C	.30	.75
MRL19 Dark Witch C	.30	.75
MRL20 Weather Report C	.30	.75
MRL21 Mechanical Snail C	.30	.75
MRL22 Giant Turtle Feeds on Flames C	.30	.75
MRL23 Liquid Beast C	.30	.75
MRL24 Hiro's Shadow Scout R	.40	1.00
MRL25 High Tide Gyojin C	.30	.75
MRL26 Invader of the Throne SR	.75	2.00
MRL27 Whiptail Crow C	.30	.75
MRL28 Slot Machine C	.30	.75
MRL29 Relinquished UR	8.00	20.00
MRL30 Red Archery Girl C	.30	.75
MRL31 Gravekeeper's Servant C	1.50	4.00
MRL32 Curse of Fiend C	.40	1.00
MRL33 Upstart Goblin C	1.50	4.00
MRL34 Toll C	.30	.75
MRL35 Final Destiny C	.30	.75
MRL36 Snatch Steal UR	6.00	15.00
MRL37 Chorus of Sanctuary C	.30	.75
MRL38 Confiscation SR	6.00	15.00
MRL39 Delinquent Duo UR	8.00	20.00
MRL40 Darkness Approaches C	.30	.75
MRL41 Fairy's Hand Mirror C	.40	1.00
MRL42 Tailor of the Fickle C	.30	.75
MRL43 Rush Recklessly R	.40	1.00
MRL44 The Reliable Guardian C	.30	.75
MRL45 The Forceful Sentry UR	6.00	15.00
MRL46 Chain Energy C	.40	1.00
MRL47 Mystical Space Typhoon UR	30.00	60.00
MRL48 Giant Trunade SR	3.00	8.00
MRL49 Painful Choice SR	4.00	10.00
MRL50 Snake Fang C	.30	.75
MRL51 Black Illusion Ritual SR	2.50	6.00
MRL52 Octoberser C	.30	.75
MRL53 Psychic Kappa C	.30	.75
MRL54 Horn of the Unicorn R	.40	1.00
MRL55 Labyrinth Wall C	.30	.75
MRL56 Wall Shadow C	.30	.75
MRL57 Twin Long Rods #2 C	.30	.75
MRL58 Stone Ogre Grotto C	.30	.75
MRL59 Magical Labyrinth C	.30	.75
MRL60 Eternal Rest C	.30	.75
MRL61 Megamorph UR	3.00	8.00
MRL62 Commencement Dance C	.30	.75
MRL63 Hamburger Recipe C	.40	1.00
MRL64 House of Adhesive Tape C	.30	.75
MRL65 Eatgaboon C	.30	.75
MRL66 Turtle Oath C	.30	.75
MRL67 Performance of Sword C	.30	.75
MRL68 Hungry Burger C	.30	.75
MRL69 Crab Turtle C	.30	.75
MRL70 Ryu-Ran C	.30	.75
MRL71 Manga Ryu-Ran R	.40	1.00
MRL72 Toon Mermaid UR	5.00	12.00
MRL73 Toon Summoned Skull UR	8.00	20.00
MRL74 Jigen Bakudan C	.30	.75
MRL75 Hyozanryu R	.40	1.00
MRL76 Toon World SR	6.00	15.00
MRL77 Cyber Jar R	.75	2.00
MRL78 Banisher of the Light SR	.75	2.00
MRL79 Giant Rat R	.40	1.00
MRL80 Senju of Thousand Hands R	.40	1.00
MRL81 UFO Turtle R	.40	1.00
MRL82 Flash Assailant C	.30	.75
MRL83 Karate Man R	.30	.75
MRL84 Dark Zebra C	.30	.75
MRL85 Giant Germ R	.75	2.00
MRL86 Nimble Momonga R	.75	2.00
MRL87 Spear Cretin C	.30	.75
MRL88 Shining Angel R	.60	1.50
MRL89 Boar Soldier C	.30	.75
MRL90 Mother Grizzly R	.40	1.00
MRL91 Flying Kamakiri #1 R	.40	1.00
MRL92 Ceremonial Bell C	.30	.75
MRL93 Sonic Bird C	.30	.75
MRL94 Mystic Tomato R	.40	1.00
MRL95 Kotodama C	.30	.75
MRL96 Gaia Power C	.30	.75
MRL97 Umiiruka C	.40	1.00
MRL98 Molten Destruction C	.40	1.00
MRL99 Rising Air Current C	.40	1.00
MRL100 Luminous Spark C	.60	1.50
MRL101 Mystic Plasma Zone C	.60	1.50
MRL102 Messenger of Peace SR	3.00	8.00
MRL103 Serpent Night Dragon SCR	6.00	15.00

2002 Yu-Gi-Oh Pharaoh's Servant 1st Edition

COMPLETE SET (105)	100.00	150.00
BOOSTER BOX (24 PACKS)	200.00	300.00
RETAIL BOOSTER BOX (36 PACKS)	550.00	700.00
BOOSTER PACK (9 CARDS)	3.00	8.00
*UNLIMITED: .4X TO .8X 1ST EDITION		
RELEASED ON OCTOBER 20, 2002		
PSV0 Jinzo SCR	45.00	80.00
PSV1 Steel Ogre Grotto #2 C	.30	.75
PSV2 Three-Headed Geedo C	.30	.75
PSV3 Parasite Paracide SR	.75	2.00
PSV4 7 Completed C	.30	.75
PSV5 Lightforce Sword R	.30	.75
PSV6 Chain Destruction UR	1.50	4.00
PSV7 Time Seal SP	.30	.75
PSV8 Graverobber SR	.75	2.00
PSV9 Gift of the Mystical Elf SP	.30	.75
PSV10 The Eye of Truth SP	.30	.75
PSV11 Dust Tornado SR	1.50	4.00
PSV12 Call of the Haunted UR	10.00	25.00
PSV13 Solomon's Lawbook C	.30	.75
PSV14 Earthshaker C	.30	.75
PSV15 Enchanted Javelin C	.30	.75
PSV16 Mirror Wall SR	.75	2.00
PSV17 Gust C	.30	.75
PSV18 Driving Snow C	.30	.75
PSV19 Armored Glass C	.30	.75
PSV20 World Suppression C	.30	.75
PSV21 Mystic Probe C	.30	.75
PSV22 Metal Detector C	.30	.75
PSV23 Numinous Healer SP	.30	.75
PSV24 Appropriate R	1.00	2.00
PSV25 Forced Requisition R	.75	2.00
PSV26 DNA Surgery SP	3.00	6.00
PSV27 The Regulation of Tribe C	.30	.75
PSV28 Backup Soldier SR	.75	2.00
PSV29 Major Riot SP	.30	.75
PSV30 Ceasefire UR	1.50	4.00
PSV31 Light of Intervention C	.30	.75
PSV32 Respect Play C	.30	.75
PSV33 Magical Hats SR	1.50	4.00
PSV34 Nobleman of Crossout SR	1.00	2.50
PSV35 Nobleman of Extermination R	.75	2.00
PSV36 The Shallow Grave R	.75	2.00
PSV37 Premature Burial UR	5.00	12.00
PSV38 Inspection SP	.40	1.00
PSV39 Prohibition R	1.00	2.50
PSV40 Morphing Jar #2 R	1.25	3.00
PSV41 Flame Champion C	.30	.75
PSV42 Twin-Headed Fire Dragon C	.30	.75
PSV43 Darkfire Soldier C	.30	.75
PSV44 Mr.Volcano C	.30	.75
PSV45 Darkfire Soldier #2 C	.30	.75
PSV46 Kiseitai SP	.30	.75
PSV47 Cyber Falcon C	.30	.75
PSV48 Flying Kamakiri #2 C	.30	.75
PSV49 Harpie's Brother C	.30	.75
PSV50 Buster Blader UR	20.00	40.00
PSV51 Michizure R	.40	1.00
PSV52 Minor Goblin Official SP	.30	.75
PSV53 Gamble C	.30	.75
PSV54 Attack and Receive C	.30	.75
PSV55 Solemn Wishes SP	1.50	4.00
PSV56 Skull Invitation R	.40	1.00
PSV57 Bubonic Vermin C	.30	.75
PSV58 Dark Bat C	.30	.75
PSV59 Oni Tank T-34 C	.30	.75
PSV60 Overdrive C	.30	.75
PSV61 Burning Land C	.30	.75
PSV62 Cold Wave C	.30	.75
PSV63 Fairy Meteor Crush SR	.75	2.00
PSV64 Limiter Removal SR	.75	2.00
PSV65 Rain of Mercy C	.30	.75
PSV66 Monster Recovery R	.40	1.00
PSV67 Shift R	.40	1.00
PSV68 Insect Imitation C	.60	1.50
PSV69 Dimensionhole R	.30	.75
PSV70 Ground Collapse C	.30	.75
PSV71 Magic Drain R	.60	1.50
PSV72 Infinite Dismissal C	.30	.75
PSV73 Gravity Bind R	1.25	3.00
PSV74 Type Zero Magic Crusher C	.30	.75
PSV75 Shadow of Eyes C	.30	.75
PSV76 The Legendary Fisherman UR	6.00	15.00
PSV77 Sword Hunter SP	.30	.75
PSV78 Drill Bug C	.30	.75
PSV79 Deepsea Warrior C	.30	.75
PSV80 Bite Shoes C	.30	.75
PSV81 Spikebot C	.30	.75
PSV82 Invitation to a Dark Sleep C	.30	.75
PSV83 Thousand-Eyes Idol SP	.40	1.00
PSV84 Thousand-Eyes Restrict UR	20.00	40.00
PSV85 Girochin Kuwagata C	.30	.75
PSV86 Hayabusa Knight R	.40	1.00
PSV87 Bombardment Beetle SP	.30	.75
PSV88 4-Starred Ladybug of Doom SP	.30	.75
PSV89 Gradius SP	.30	.75
PSV90 Red-Moon Baby R	.40	1.00
PSV91 Mad Sword Beast R	.30	.75
PSV92 Skull Mariner C	.30	.75
PSV93 The All-Seeing White Tiger C	.30	.75
PSV94 Goblin Attack Force UR	2.50	6.00
PSV95 Island Turtle SP	.30	.75
PSV96 Wingweaver C	.30	.75
PSV97 Science Soldier C	.30	.75
PSV98 Souls of the Forbidden C	.30	.75
PSV99 Dokuroyaiba C	.30	.75
PSV100 The Fiend Megacyber UR	2.00	5.00
PSV101 Gearfried the Iron Knight SR	.75	2.00
PSV102 Insect Barrier C	.30	.75
PSV103 Beast of Talwar UR	2.00	5.00
PSV104 Imperial Order SCR	8.00	20.00

2003 Yu-Gi-Oh Labyrinth of Nightmare 1st Edition

COMPLETE SET (105)	100.00	150.00
BOOSTER BOX (24 PACKS)	200.00	300.00
RETAIL BOOSTER BOX (36 PACKS)	250.00	350.00
BOOSTER PACK (9 CARDS)	3.00	8.00
*UNLIMITED: .4X TO .8X 1ST EDITION		
RELEASED ON MARCH 1, 2003		
LON0 Gemini Elf SCR	10.00	25.00
LON1 The Masked Beast UR	3.00	8.00
LON2 Swordsman of Landstar C	.30	.75
LON3 Humanoid Slime SP	.40	1.00
LON4 Worm Drake C	.30	.75
LON5 Humanoid Worm Drake C	.30	.75
LON6 Revival Jam SR	2.00	5.00
LON7 Flying Fish C	.30	.75
LON8 Amphibian Beast R	.40	1.00
LON9 Shining Abyss C	.30	.75
LON10 Gadget Soldier C	.30	.75
LON11 Grand Tiki Elder C	.30	.75
LON12 Melchid the Four-Face Beast C	.30	.75
LON13 Nuvia the Wicked R	.40	1.00
LON14 Chosen One C	.30	.75
LON15 Mask of Weakness C	.30	.75
LON16 Curse of the Masked Beast C	.40	1.00
LON17 Mask of Dispel SR	.75	2.00
LON18 Mask of Restrict UR	10.00	25.00
LON19 Mask of the Accursed SR	1.00	2.50
LON20 Mask of Brutality R	.40	1.00
LON21 Return of the Doomed R	.30	.75
LON22 Lightning Blade C	.30	.75
LON23 Tornado Wall C	.40	1.00
LON24 Fairy Box C	.40	1.00
LON25 Torrential Tribute UR	6.00	15.00
LON26 Jam Breeding Machine R	.40	1.00
LON27 Infinite Cards R	.75	2.00
LON28 Jam Defender SP	.30	.75
LON29 Card of Safe Return UR	3.00	8.00
LON30 Lady Panther C	.30	.75
LON31 The Unfriendly Amazon C	.30	.75
LON32 Amazon Archer C	.30	.75
LON33 Crimson Sentry C	.30	.75
LON34 Fire Princess SR	.75	2.00
LON35 Lady Assailant of Flames C	.30	.75
LON36 Fire Sorcerer C	.30	.75
LON37 Spirit of the Breeze R	.40	1.00
LON38 Dancing Fairy C	.30	.75
LON39 Fairy Guardian C	.30	.75
LON40 Empress Mantis C	.30	.75
LON41 Cure Mermaid C	.30	.75
LON42 Hysteric Fairy C	.30	.75
LON43 Bio-Mage C	.30	.75
LON44 The Forgiving Maiden C	.30	.75
LON45 St. Joan C	.30	.75
LON46 Marie the Fallen One R	.40	1.00
LON47 Jar of Greed SR	1.25	3.00
LON48 Scroll of Bewitchment C	.30	.75
LON49 United We Stand UR	6.00	15.00
LON50 Mage Power UR	4.00	10.00
LON51 Offerings to the Doomed C	.30	.75
LON52 The Portrait's Secret C	.30	.75
LON53 The Gross Ghost of Fled Dreams C	.30	.75
LON54 Headless Knight C	.30	.75
LON55 Earthbound Spirit C	.30	.75
LON56 The Earl of Demise C	.30	.75
LON57 Boneheimer C	.30	.75
LON58 Flame Dancer C	.30	.75
LON59 Spherous Lady C	.30	.75
LON60 Lightning Conger C	.30	.75
LON61 Jowgen the Spiritualist R	1.50	4.00
LON62 Kycoo the Ghost Destroyer SR	1.50	4.00
LON63 Summoner of Illusions C	.30	.75
LON64 Bazoo the Soul-Eater SR	.75	2.00
LON65 Dark Necrofear UR	2.00	5.00
LON66 Soul of Purity and Light C	.30	.75
LON67 Spirit of Flames C	.30	.75
LON68 Aqua Spirit C	.30	.75
LON69 The Rock Spirit C	.30	.75
LON70 Garuda the Wind Spirit C	.30	.75
LON71 Gilasaurus R	.40	1.00
LON72 Tornado Bird R	.40	1.00
LON73 Dreamsprite C	.30	.75
LON74 Zombyra the Dark C	.40	1.00
LON75 Supply C	.30	.75
LON76 Maryokutai C	.30	.75
LON77 The Last Warrior (UR)	1.50	4.00
LON78 Collected Power C	.30	.75
LON79 Dark Spirit of the Silent SR	.60	1.50
LON80 Royal Command UR	.75	2.00
LON81 Riryoku Field SR	.75	2.00
LON82 Skull Lair C	.60	1.50
LON83 Graverobber's Retribution C	.30	.75
LON84 Deal of Phantom C	.40	1.00
LON85 Destruction Punch R	.40	1.00
LON86 Blind Destruction C	.30	.75
LON87 The Emperor's Holiday C	.30	.75
LON88 Destiny Board UR	6.00	15.00
LON89 Spirit Message I R	.40	1.00
LON90 Spirit Message N R	.40	1.00
LON91 Spirit Message A R	.40	1.00
LON92 Spirit Message L R	.40	1.00
LON93 The Dark Door C	.30	.75
LON94 Spiritualism R	.40	1.00
LON95 Cyclon Laser C	.30	.75
LON96 Bait Doll C	.30	.75
LON97 De-Fusion SR	.75	2.00
LON98 Fusion Gate C	3.00	8.00
LON99 Ekibyo Drakmord C	.30	.75
LON100 Miracle Dig C	.30	.75
LON101 Dragonic Attack C	.30	.75
LON102 Spirit Elimination C	.30	.75
LON103 Vengeful Bog Spirit SP	.40	1.00
LON104 Magic Cylinder SCR	5.00	12.00

2003 Yu-Gi-Oh Legacy of Darkness 1st Edition

COMPLETE SET (101)	100.00	150.00
BOOSTER BOX (24 PACKS)	100.00	140.00
RETAIL BOOSTER BOX (36 PACKS)	140.00	180.00
BOOSTER PACK (9 CARDS)	3.00	8.00
*UNLIMITED: .4X TO .8X 1ST EDITION		
RELEASED ON JUNE 6, 2003		

LOD0 Yata-Garasu SCR 10.00 25.00
LOD2 Dark Balter the Terrible SR 1.50 4.00
LOD3 Lesser Fiend R .40 1.00
LOD4 Possessed Dark Soul C .30 .75
LOD5 Winged Minion C .30 .75
LOD6 Skull Knight #2 C .30 .75
LOD7 Ryu-Kishin Clown C .30 .75
LOD8 Twin-Headed Wolf C .30 .75
LOD9 Opticlops R .40 1.00
LOD1 Dark Ruler Ha Des UR 2.00 5.00
LOD10 Bark of Dark Ruler C .30 .75
LOD11 Fatal Abacus R .40 1.00
LOD12 Life Absorbing Machine C .30 .75
LOD13 The Puppet Magic of Dark Ruler C .30 .75
LOD14 Soul Demolition C .30 .75
LOD15 Double Snare C .30 .75
LOD16 Freed the Matchless General UR .75 2.00
LOD17 Throwstone Unit C .30 .75
LOD18 Marauding Captain UR 2.50 6.00
LOD19 Ryu Senshi SR .60 1.50
LOD20 Warrior Dai Grepher C .30 .75
LOD21 Mysterious Guard C .30 .75
LOD22 Frontier Wiseman C .30 .75
LOD23 Exiled Force SR .60 1.50
LOD24 The Hunter with 7 Weapons C .30 .75
LOD25 Shadow Tamer R .40 1.00
LOD26 Dragon Manipulator C .30 .75
LOD27 The A Forces R .75 2.00
LOD28 Reinforcements of the Army SR 2.50 6.00
LOD29 Array of Revealing Light R .40 1.00
LOD30 The Warrior Returning Alive R .60 1.50
LOD31 Ready for Intercepting C .30 .75
LOD32 A Feint Plan C .30 .75
LOD33 Emergency Provisions C .40 1.00
LOD34 Tyrant Dragon UR 6.00 15.00
LOD35 Spear Dragon SR 1.50 4.00
LOD36 Spirit Ryu C .30 .75
LOD37 The Dragon Dwelling in the Cave C .30 .75
LOD38 Lizard Soldier C .30 .75
LOD39 Fiend Skull Dragon SR .75 2.00
LOD40 Cave Dragon SP .60 1.50
LOD41 Gray Wing C .30 .75
LOD42 Troop Dragon C .30 .75
LOD43 The Dragon's Bead R .40 1.00
LOD44 A Wingbeat of Giant Dragon C .40 1.00
LOD45 Dragon's Gunfire C .30 .75
LOD46 Stamping Destruction C .30 .75
LOD47 Super Rejuvenation C .50 1.00
LOD48 Dragon's Rage C .50 1.00
LOD49 Burst Breath C .30 .75
LOD50 Luster Dragon SR .75 2.00
LOD51 Robotic Knight C .30 .75
LOD52 Wolf Axwielder C .30 .75
LOD53 The Illusory Gentleman C .30 .75
LOD54 Robolady C .30 .75
LOD55 Roboyarou C .30 .75
LOD56 Fiber Jar UR 3.00 8.00
LOD57 Serpentine Princess C .30 .75
LOD58 Patrician of Darkness C .30 .75
LOD59 Thunder Nyan Nyan R .40 1.00
LOD60 Gradius Option C .30 .75
LOD61 Woodland Sprite C .30 .75
LOD62 Airknight Parshath UR 2.00 5.00
LOD63 Twin-Headed Behemoth SR .60 1.50
LOD64 Maharaghi SP .30 .75
LOD65 Inaba White Rabbit SP .60 1.50
LOD66 Susa Soldier R .40 1.00
LOD67 Yamata Dragon UR 5.00 12.00
LOD68 Great Long Nose SP .30 .75
LOD69 Otohime SP .40 1.00
LOD70 Hino-Kagu-Tsuchi UR 4.00 10.00
LOD71 Asura Priest SR 1.25 3.00
LOD72 Fushi No Tori C .30 .75
LOD73 Super Robolady C .30 .75
LOD74 Super Roboyarou C .30 .75
LOD75 Fengsheng Mirror C .30 .75
LOD76 Spring of Rebirth C .30 .75
LOD77 Heart of Clear Water C .50 1.25
LOD78 A Legendary Ocean C .30 .75
LOD79 Fusion Sword Murasame Blade R .40 1.00
LOD80 Smoke Grenade of the Thief SP .60 1.50
LOD81 Creature Swap UR 3.00 8.00
LOD82 Spiritual Energy Settle Machine C .30 .75
LOD83 Second Coin Toss R .60 1.50
LOD84 Convulsion of Nature C .30 .75
LOD85 The Secret of the Bandit C .30 .75
LOD86 After Genocide R .40 1.00
LOD87 Magic Reflector R .40 1.00
LOD88 Blast with Chain R .40 1.00
LOD89 Disppear SP .30 .75
LOD90 Bubble Crash C .30 .75
LOD91 Royal Oppression R .75 2.00
LOD92 Bottomless Trap Hole R 1.50 4.00
LOD93 Bad Reaction to Simochi C .60 1.50
LOD94 Omnious Fortunetelling C .30 .75
LOD95 Spirit's Invitation C .30 .75
LOD96 Nutrient Z C .40 1.00
LOD97 Drop Off SR .75 2.00
LOD98 Fiend Comedian C .30 .75
LOD99 Last Turn UR 2.50 6.00
LOD100 Injection Fairy Lily SCR 5.00 12.00

2003 Yu-Gi-Oh Pharaonic Guardian 1st Edition

COMPLETE SET (108) 60.00 150.00
BOOSTER BOX (24 PACKS) 140.00 180.00
RETAIL BOOSTER BOX (36 PACKS) 150.00 200.00
BOOSTER PACK (9 CARDS) 3.00 8.00
*UNLIMITED: .4X TO .8X 1ST EDITION
RELEASED ON JULY 18, 2003
PGD0 Ring of Destruction SCR 3.00 8.00
PGD1 Molten Behemoth C .30 .75
PGD2 Shapesnatch C .30 .75
PGD3 Souleater C .30 .75
PGD4 King Tiger Wanghu R .60 1.50
PGD5 Birdface C .30 .75
PGD6 Kryuel C .30 .75
PGD7 Arsenal Bug C .30 .75
PGD8 Maiden of the Aqua C .40 1.00
PGD9 Jowl of Dark Demise R .40 1.00
PGD10 Timeater C .30 .75
PGD11 Mucus Yolk C .30 .75
PGD12 Servant of Catabolism C .30 .75
PGD13 Moisture Creature R .40 1.00
PGD14 Gora Turtle R .40 1.00
PGD15 Sasuke Samurai SR .60 1.50
PGD16 Poison Mummy C .30 .75
PGD17 Dark Dust Spirit C .30 .75
PGD18 Royal Keeper C .30 .75
PGD19 Wandering Mummy R .40 1.00
PGD20 Great Dezard UR .60 1.50
PGD21 Swarm of Scarabs C .30 .75
PGD22 Swarm of Locusts C .30 .75
PGD23 Giant Axe Mummy C .30 .75
PGD24 8-Claws Scorpion C .30 .75
PGD25 Guardian Sphinx UR .60 1.50
PGD26 Pyramid Turtle R .40 1.00
PGD27 Dice Jar C .75 2.00
PGD28 Dark Scorpion Burglars C .30 .75
PGD29 Don Zaloog UR 1.00 2.50
PGD30 Des Lacooda C .30 .75
PGD31 Fushioh Richie UR .60 1.50
PGD32 Cobraman Sakuzy C .30 .75
PGD33 Book of Life SR 1.25 3.00
PGD34 Book of Taiyou C .75 2.00
PGD35 Book of Moon R 1.25 3.00
PGD36 Mirage of Nightmare SR .60 1.50
PGD37 Secret Pass to the Treasure C .30 .75
PGD38 Call of the Mummy C .30 .75
PGD39 Timidity C .30 .75
PGD40 Pyramid Energy C .30 .75
PGD41 Tutan Mask C .30 .75
PGD42 Ordeal of a Traveler SP .60 1.50
PGD43 Bottomless Shifting Sand C .30 .75
PGD44 Curse of Royal R .40 1.00
PGD45 Needle Ceiling C .30 .75
PGD46 Statue of the Wicked SR .60 1.50
PGD47 Dark Coffin C .30 .75
PGD48 Needle Wall C .30 .75
PGD49 Trap Dustshoot C .40 1.00
PGD50 Pyro Clock of Destiny C .30 .75
PGD51 Reckless Greed R .60 1.50
PGD52 Pharaoh's Treasure R .40 1.00
PGD53 Master Kyonshee C .30 .75
PGD54 Kabazauls C 1.00 2.50
PGD55 Inpachi C .30 .75
PGD56 Dark Jeroid R .40 1.00
PGD57 Newdoria R .40 1.00
PGD58 Helpoemer UR 4.00 10.00
PGD59 Gravekeeper's Spy C .30 .75
PGD60 Gravekeeper's Curse C .30 .75
PGD61 Gravekeeper's Guard C .30 .75
PGD62 Gravekeepers's Spear Soldier C .30 .75
PGD63 Gravekeeper's Vassal C .60 1.50
PGD64 Gravekeeper's Watcher R .40 1.00
PGD65 Gravekeeper's Chief SR .60 1.50
PGD66 Gravekeeper's Cannonholder C .30 .75
PGD67 Gravekeeper's Assailant C .30 .75
PGD68 A Man with Wdjat C .30 .75
PGD69 Mystical Knight of Jackal UR 1.50 4.00
PGD70 A Cat of Ill Omen C .30 .75
PGD71 Yomi Ship C .40 1.00
PGD72 Winged Sage Falcos R .40 1.00
PGD73 An Owl of Luck C .30 .75
PGD74 Charm of Shabti C .30 .75
PGD75 Cobra Jar SP .30 .75
PGD76 Spirit Reaper R 1.25 3.00
PGD77 Nightmare Horse SP .40 1.00
PGD78 Reaper on the Nightmare SR 1.25 3.00
PGD79 Dark Designator R .40 1.00
PGD80 Card Shuffle C .30 .75
PGD81 Reasoning C .30 .75
PGD82 Dark Room of Nightmare SR .60 1.50
PGD83 Different Dimension Capsule C .30 .75
PGD84 Necrovalley SR .75 2.00
PGD85 Buster Rancher C .30 .75
PGD86 Hieroglyph Lithograph C .30 .75
PGD87 Dark Snake Syndrome C .30 .75
PGD88 Terraforming C .40 1.00
PGD89 Banner of Courage C .30 .75
PGD90 Metamorphosis C .30 .75
PGD91 Royal Tribute C .60 1.50
PGD92 Reversal Quiz SP .60 1.50
PGD93 Coffin Seller R .40 1.00
PGD94 Curse of Aging C .30 .75
PGD95 Barrel Behind the Door SR .60 1.50
PGD96 Raigeki Break C .40 1.00
PGD97 Narrow Pass C .30 .75
PGD98 Disturbance Strategy C .30 .75
PGD99 Trap of Board Eraser SR .60 1.50
PGD100 Rite of Spirit C .30 .75
PGD101 Non Aggression Area C .30 .75
PGD102 D. Tribe C .30 .75
PGD103 Byser Shock UR .60 1.50
PGD104 Question UR 1.25 3.00
PGD105 Rope of Life UR .60 1.50
PGD106 Nightmare Wheel UR 2.00 5.00
PGD107 Lava Golem SCR 2.50 6.00

2003 Yu-Gi-Oh Magician's Force 1st Edition

COMPLETE SET (108) 225.00 350.00
BOOSTER BOX (24 PACKS) 500.00 800.00
BOOSTER PACK (9 CARDS) 7.00 10.00
*UNLIMITED: .4X TO .8X 1ST EDITION
RELEASED ON OCTOBER 10, 2003
MFC0 Dark Magician Girl SCR 80.00 120.00
MFC1 People Running About C .30 .75
MFC2 Oppressed People C .50 1.00
MFC3 United Resistance C .30 .75
MFC4 X-Head Cannon SR 2.00 5.00
MFC5 Y-Dragon Head SR 2.00 5.00
MFC6 Z-Metal Tank SR 2.00 5.00
MFC7 Dark Blade R .60 1.50
MFC8 Pitch-Dark Dragon C .30 .75
MFC9 Kiryu C .30 .75
MFC10 Decayed Commander C .30 .75
MFC11 Zombie Tiger C .30 .75
MFC12 Giant Orc C .30 .75
MFC13 Second Goblin C .30 .75
MFC14 Vampire Orchis C .30 .75
MFC15 Des Dendle C .30 .75
MFC16 Burning Beast C .30 .75
MFC17 Freezing Beast C .30 .75
MFC18 Union Rider C .30 .75
MFC19 D.D. Crazy Beast R .40 1.00
MFC20 Spell Canceller UR 4.00 10.00
MFC21 Neko Mane King C .50 1.00
MFC22 Helping Robo For Combat R .40 1.00
MFC23 Dimension Jar SP .30 .75
MFC24 Great Phantom Thief R .40 1.00
MFC25 Roulette Barrel C .30 .75
MFC26 Paladin of White Dragon UR 2.00 5.00
MFC27 White Dragon Ritual C .30 .75
MFC28 Frontline Base C .30 .75
MFC29 Demotion SP .30 .75
MFC30 Combination Attack R .40 1.00
MFC31 Kaiser Colosseum C .40 1.00
MFC32 Autonomous Action Unit C .30 .75
MFC33 Poison of the Old Man C .30 .75
MFC34 Ante R .40 1.00
MFC35 Dark Core R 1.00 2.00
MFC36 Raregold Armor C .40 1.00
MFC37 Metalsilver Armor C .30 .75
MFC38 Kishido Spirit C .30 .75
MFC39 Tribute Doll R .40 1.00
MFC40 Wave-Motion Cannon SP 4.00 8.00
MFC41 Huge Revolution C .30 .75
MFC42 Thunder of Ruler C .50 1.00
MFC43 Spell Shield Type-8 SR .75 2.00
MFC44 Meteorain C .30 .75
MFC45 Pineapple Blast C .30 .75
MFC46 Secret Barrel SP 1.25 3.00
MFC47 Physical Double C .30 .75
MFC48 Rivalry of Warlords C .40 1.00
MFC49 Formation Union C .30 .75
MFC50 Adhesion Trap Hole C .50 1.00
MFC51 XY-Dragon Cannon UR 8.00 20.00
MFC52 XYZ-Dragon Cannon UR 10.00 25.00
MFC53 XZ-Tank Cannon SR 5.00 12.00
MFC54 YZ-Tank Dragon SR 2.00 5.00
MFC55 Great Angus C .30 .75
MFC56 Aitsu C .30 .75
MFC57 Sonic Duck C .30 .75
MFC58 Luster Dragon UR 6.00 15.00
MFC59 Amazoness Paladin C .30 .75
MFC60 Amazoness Fighter SP .40 1.00
MFC61 Amazoness Swords Woman UR 3.00 8.00
MFC62 Amazoness Blowpiper C .30 .75
MFC63 Amazoness Tiger R .40 1.00
MFC64 Skilled White Magician SR 2.00 5.00
MFC65 Skilled Dark Magician SR 2.00 5.00
MFC66 Apprentice Magician R .50 1.25
MFC67 Old Vindictive Magician C .30 .75
MFC68 Chaos Command Magician UR 6.00 15.00
MFC69 Magical Marionette C .30 .75
MFC70 Pixie Knight C .30 .75
MFC71 Breaker the Magical Warrior UR 6.00 15.00
MFC72 Magical Plant Mandragola C .30 .75
MFC73 Magical Scientist C .30 .75
MFC74 Royal Magical Library C .30 .75
MFC75 Armor Exe R .40 1.00
MFC76 Tribe-Infecting Virus SR 1.50 4.00
MFC77 Des Koala R .60 1.50
MFC78 Cliff the Trap Remover SP .40 1.00
MFC79 Magical Merchant C .60 1.50
MFC80 Koitsu C .30 .75
MFC81 Cat's Ear Tribe R .40 1.00
MFC82 Ultimate Obedient Fiend SP .75 2.00
MFC83 Dark Cat with White Tail C .30 .75
MFC84 Amazoness Spellcaster C .30 .75
MFC85 Continuous Destruction Punch R .40 1.00
MFC86 Big Bang Shot R .40 1.00
MFC87 Gather Your Mind C .30 .75
MFC88 Mass Driver C .30 .75
MFC89 Senri Eye SP .30 .75
MFC90 Emblem of Dragon Destroyer C .50 1.00
MFC91 Jar Robber C .30 .75
MFC92 My Body as a Shield C .30 .75
MFC93 Pigeonholing Books of Spell SP .30 .75
MFC94 Mega Ton Magical Cannon R .40 1.00
MFC95 Pitch-Black Power Stone SP .40 1.00
MFC96 Amazoness Archers SR .75 2.00
MFC97 Dramatic Rescue R .40 1.00
MFC98 Exhausting Spell C .30 .75
MFC99 Hidden Book of Spell C .30 .75
MFC100 Miracle Restoring C .30 .75
MFC101 Remove Brainwashing C .50 1.00
MFC102 Disarmament C .30 .75
MFC103 Anti-Spell C .30 .75
MFC104 The Spell Absorbing Life C .30 .75
MFC105 Dark Paladin Misprint UR 40.00 80.00
MFC105 Dark Paladin Correct Art UR 50.00 100.00
MFC106 Double Spell UR 2.00 5.00
MFC107 Diffussion Wave-Motion SCR .60 1.50

2003 Yu-Gi-Oh Dark Crisis 1st Edition

COMPLETE SET (106) 125.00 175.00
BOOSTER BOX (24 PACKS) 250.00 350.00
RETAIL BOOSTER BOX (36 PACKS) 350.00 450.00
BOOSTER PACK (9 CARDS) 3.00 8.00
*UNLIMITED: .4X TO .8X 1ST EDITION
RELEASED ON DECEMBER 1, 2003
DCR0 Vampire Lord SCR 6.00 15.00
DCR1 Battle Footballer C .30 .75
DCR2 Nin-Ken Dog C 1.00 2.50
DCR3 Acrobat Monkey C .30 .75

DCR4 Arsenal Summoner C .30 .75
DCR5 Guardian Elma C .30 .75
DCR6 Guardian Ceal UR .60 1.50
DCR7 Guardian Grarl UR 1.25 3.00
DCR8 Guardian Baou R .40 1.00
DCR9 Guardian Kay'est C .30 .75
DCR10 Guardian Tryce R .40 1.00
DCR11 Cyber Raider SP .30 .75
DCR12 Reflect Bounder UR 3.00 8.00
DCR13 Little-Winguard SP .30 .75
DCR14 Des Feral Imp R .40 1.00
DCR15 Different Dimension Dragon SR .60 1.50
DCR16 Shinato, King of a Higher Plane UR 2.50 6.00
DCR17 Dark Flare Knight SR 1.25 3.00
DCR18 Mirage Knight SR 1.25 3.00
DCR19 Berserk Dragon SR 1.50 4.00
DCR20 Exodia Necross UR 20.00 40.00
DCR21 Gyaku-Gire Panda SP .30 .75
DCR22 Blindly Loyal Goblin C .30 .75
DCR23 Despair from the Dark SP .30 .75
DCR24 Maju Garzett SP .30 .75
DCR25 Fear from the Dark R .40 1.00
DCR26 Dark Scorpion - Chick the Yellow C .30 .75
DCR27 D. D. Warrior Lady SR 1.00 2.50
DCR28 Thousand Needles C .30 .75
DCR29 Shinato's Ark SP .40 1.00
DCR30 A Deal with Dark Ruler SP .50 1.25
DCR31 Contract with Exodia SP .75 2.00
DCR32 Butterfly Dagger - Elma SR .60 1.50
DCR33 Shooting Star Bow - Ceal C .20 .75
DCR34 Gravity Axe - Grarl C .20 .75
DCR35 Wicked-Breaking Flamberge R .40 1.00
DCR36 Rod of Silence - Kay'est C .30 .75
DCR37 Twin Swords of Flashing Light C .30 .75
DCR38 Precious Cards from Beyond C .30 .75
DCR39 Rod of the Mind's Eye C .30 .75
DCR40 Fairy of the Spring C .30 .75
DCR41 Token Thanksgiving C .30 .75
DCR42 Morale Boost C .30 .75
DCR43 Non-Spellcasting Area C .30 .75
DCR44 Different Dimension Gate R .40 1.00
DCR45 Final Attack Orders C .30 .75
DCR46 Staunch Defender C .30 .75
DCR47 Ojama Trio SP 1.00 2.00
DCR48 Arsenal Robber C .30 .75
DCR49 Skill Drain R 2.00 5.00
DCR50 Really Eternal Rest C .30 .75
DCR51 Kaiser Glider UR 1.25 3.00
DCR52 Interdimensional Matter Trans. UR 1.25 3.00
DCR53 Cost Down UR 1.50 4.00
DCR54 Gagagigo C .30 .75
DCR55 D. D. Trainer C .30 .75
DCR56 Ojama Green C .30 .75
DCR57 Archfiend Soldier R 1.25 3.00
DCR58 Pandemonium Watchbear C .30 .75
DCR59 Sasuke Samurai #2 C .30 .75
DCR60 Dark Scorpion - Gorg C .30 .75
DCR61 Dark Scorpion - Meanae C .30 .75
DCR62 Outstanding Dog Marron SP .30 .75
DCR63 Great Maju Garzett R 1.50 4.00
DCR64 Iron Blacksmith Kotetsu C .30 .75
DCR65 Goblin of Greed C .30 .75
DCR66 Mefist the Infernal General R .40 1.00
DCR67 Vilepawn Archfiend C .30 .75
DCR68 Shadowknight Archfiend C .30 .75
DCR69 Darkbishop Archfiend R .40 1.00
DCR70 Desrook Archfiend C .30 .75
DCR71 Infernalqueen Archfiend R .40 1.00
DCR72 Terrorking Archfiend SR 1.50 4.00
DCR73 Skull Archfiend of Lightning UR 1.50 4.00
DCR74 Metallizing Parasite - Lunatite R .40 1.00
DCR75 Tsukuyomi R 1.50 4.00
DCR76 Mudora SR .40 1.00
DCR77 Keldo C .30 .75
DCR78 Kelbek C .30 .75
DCR79 Zolga C .30 .75
DCR80 Agido C .30 .75
DCR81 Legendary Flame Lord R .40 1.00
DCR82 Dark Master - Zorc SR .60 1.50
DCR83 Spell Reproduction C .30 .75
DCR84 Dragged Down into Grave C 1.25 3.00
DCR85 Incandescent Ordeal SP .30 .75
DCR86 Contract with the Abyss R .40 1.00
DCR87 Contract with the Dark Master SP .30 .75
DCR88 Falling Down SP .50 1.00
DCR89 Checkmate C .30 .75
DCR90 Cestus of Dagla C .30 .75
DCR91 Final Countdown SP .75 2.00
DCR92 Archfiend's Oath C .30 .75
DCR93 Mustering of Dark Scorpions C .30 .75
DCR94 Pandemonium SP .60 1.50
DCR95 Altar for Tribute C .30 .75
DCR96 Frozen soul C .30 .75
DCR97 Battle-Scarred C .30 .75
DCR98 Dark Scorpion Combination R .40 1.00
DCR99 Archfiend's Roar C .75 2.00
DCR100 Dice Re-Roll SP .40 1.00
DCR101 Spell Vanishing SR .30 .75
DCR102 Sakuretsu Armor C .50 1.25
DCR103 Ray of Hope C .30 .75
DCR104 Blast Held by a Tribute UR 2.00 5.00
DCR105 Judgment of Anubis SCR 1.50 4.00

2004 Yu-Gi-Oh Invasion of Chaos 1st Edition

COMPLETE SET (112) 100.00 225.00
BOOSTER BOX (24 PACKS) 1000.00 1500.00
RETAIL BOOSTER BOX (24 PACKS) 1000.00 1500.00
BOOSTER PACK (9 CARDS) 8.00 20.00
SPECIAL EDITION BOX (3 PACKS 1 VAR. CARD) 10.00 25.00
*UNLIMITED: .4X TO .8X 1ST EDITION
RELEASED ON MARCH 1, 2004
IOC0 Chaos Emperor Dragon - Envoy of the End SCR 100.00 150.00
IOC1 Ojama Yellow C .20 .50
IOC2 Ojama Black C .20 .50
IOC3 Soul Tiger C .20 .50
IOC4 Big Koala C .20 .50
IOC5 Des Kangaroo C .20 .50
IOC6 Crimson Ninja C .20 .50
IOC7 Strike Ninja UR 2.50 6.00
IOC8 Gale Lizard C .20 .50
IOC9 Spirit of the Pot of Greed SP .20 .50
IOC10 Chopman the Desperate Outlaw C .20 .50
IOC11 Sasuke Samurai #3 R .30 .75
IOC12 D.D. Scout Plane SR .60 1.50
IOC13 Beserk Gorilla R .40 1.00
IOC14 Freed the Brave Wanderer SR .40 1.00
IOC15 Coach Goblin C .20 .50
IOC16 Witch Doctor of Chaos SP .20 .50
IOC17 Chaos Necromancer SP .30 .75
IOC18 Chaosrider Gustaph SR .60 1.50
IOC19 Inferno C .20 .50
IOC20 Fenrir C .20 .50
IOC21 Gigantes C .20 .50
IOC22 Silpheed C .20 .50
IOC23 Chaos Sorcerer C .30 .75
IOC24 Gren Maju Da Eiza C .40 1.00
IOC25 Black Luster Soldier - Envoy of the Beginning UR 95.00 105.00
IOC26 Drillago R .30 .75
IOC27 Lekunga R .30 .75
IOC28 Lord Poison SP .40 1.00
IOC29 Bowganian SP .20 .50
IOC30 Granadora SP .20 .50
IOC31 Fuhma Shuriken R .30 .75
IOC32 Heart of the Underdog SP 1.50 4.00
IOC33 Wild Nature's Release SR .30 .75
IOC34 Ojama Delta Hurricane SP .20 .50
IOC35 Stumbling SP .60 1.50
IOC36 Chaos End C .20 .50
IOC37 Yellow Luster Shield C .20 .50
IOC38 Chaos Greed C .20 .50
IOC39 D.D. Designator SR .60 1.50
IOC40 D.D. Borderline C .20 .50
IOC41 Recycle C .20 .50
IOC42 Primal Seed C .20 .50
IOC43 Thunder Crash SP .20 .50
IOC44 Dimension Distortion SP .20 .50
IOC45 Reload SR .50 1.25
IOC46 Soul Absorption C .60 1.50
IOC47 Big Burn SR .40 1.00
IOC48 Blasting the Ruins C .20 .50
IOC49 Cursed Seal of Forbidden Spell C .75 2.00
IOC50 Tower of Babel C .20 .50
IOC51 Spatial Collapse C .20 .50
IOC52 Chain Disappearance R .75 2.00
IOC53 Zero Gravity C .20 .50
IOC54 Dark Mirror Force UR 2.00 5.00
IOC55 Energy Drain C .20 .50
IOC56 Giga Gagagigo SP 1.25 3.00
IOC57 Mad Dog of Darkness R .30 .75
IOC58 Neo Bug C .20 .50
IOC59 Sea Serpent Warrior of Darkness C .20 .50
IOC60 Terrorking Salmon C .20 .50
IOC61 Blazing Inpachi C .20 .50
IOC62 Burning Algae C .20 .50
IOC63 The Thing in the Crater C .20 .50
IOC64 Molten Zombie C .20 .50
IOC65 Dark Magician of Chaos UR 40.00 50.00
IOC66 Gora Turtle of Illusion C .20 .50
IOC67 Manticore of Darkness UR 1.25 3.00
IOC68 Stealth Bird SP .30 .75
IOC69 Sacred Crane C .40 1.00
IOC70 Enraged Battle Ox R .30 .75
IOC71 Don Turtle SP .20 .50
IOC72 Balloon Lizard C .20 .50
IOC73 Dark Dricreratops R .30 .75
IOC74 Hyper Hammerhead SP .20 .50
IOC75 Black Tyranno UR 1.00 2.50
IOC76 Anti-Aircraft Flower SP .20 .50
IOC77 Prickle Fairy C .20 .50
IOC78 Pinch Hopper SP 1.25 3.00
IOC79 Skull-Mark Ladybug SP .20 .50
IOC80 Insect Princess UR .60 1.50
IOC81 Amphibious Bugroth MK-3 C .20 .50
IOC82 Torpedo Fish SP .20 .50
IOC83 Levia-Dragon Daedalus UR 2.00 5.00
IOC84 Orca Mega-Fortress of Darkness SR .40 1.00
IOC85 Cannonball Spear Shellfish SP .30 .75
IOC86 Mataza the Zapper R .30 .75
IOC87 Guardian Angel Joan UR 1.50 4.00
IOC88 Manju of Ten Thousand Hands SP 7.00 10.00
IOC89 Getsu Fuhma R .30 .75
IOC90 Ryu Kokki C .20 .50
IOC91 Gryphon's Feather Duster C .20 .50
IOC92 Stray Lambs R .20 .50
IOC93 Smashing Ground SP .60 1.50
IOC94 Dimension Fusion UR 12.00 16.00
IOC95 Dedication through Light & Darkness SR 2.00 5.00
IOC96 Salvage C .50 1.25
IOC97 Ultra Evolution Pill R .30 .75
IOC98 Multiplication of Ants C .20 .50
IOC99 Earth Chant SP .20 .50
IOC100 Jade Insect Whistle C .20 .50
IOC101 Destruction Ring R .30 .75
IOC102 Fiend's Hand Mirror C .20 .50
IOC103 Compulsory Evacuation Device R 2.00 5.00
IOC104 A Hero Emerges C .20 .50
IOC105 Self-Destruct Button SP .50 1.25
IOC106 Curse of Darkness R 2.00 5.00
IOC107 Begone, Knave! C .20 .50
IOC108 DNA Transplant C .20 .50
IOC109 Robbin' Zombie R .30 .75
IOC110 Trap Jammer SR .75 2.00
IOC111 Invader of Darkness SCR 2.00 5.00

2004 Yu-Gi-Oh Ancient Sanctuary 1st Edition

COMPLETE SET (112) 60.00 140.00
BOOSTER BOX (24 PACKS) 90.00 110.00
BOOSTER PACK (9 CARDS) 3.00 6.00
*UNLIMITED: .4X TO .8X 1ST EDITION
RELEASED ON JUNE 1, 2004
AST0 The End of Anubis SCR 3.00 8.00
AST1 Gogiga Gagagigo C .20 .50
AST2 Warrior of Zera C .30 .75
AST3 Sealmaster Meisei R .30 .75
AST4 Mystical Shine Ball C .50 1.25
AST5 Metal Armored Bug C .20 .50
AST6 The Agent of Judgment Saturn UR .75 2.00
AST7 The Agent of Wisdom Mercury R .30 .75
AST8 The Agent of Creation Venus R .75 2.00
AST9 The Agent of Force Mars SR .40 1.00
AST10 The Unhappy Girl C .20 .50
AST11 Soul-Absorbing Bone Tower R 1.00 2.50
AST12 The Kick Man C .20 .50
AST13 Vampire Lady C .20 .50
AST14 Stone Statue of the Aztecs SR .40 1.00
AST15 Rocket Jumper C .20 .50
AST16 Avatar of the Pot R .30 .75
AST17 Legendary Jujitsu Master C .30 .75
AST18 Gear Golem the Moving Fortress UR .75 2.00
AST19 KA-2 Des Scissors C .20 .50
AST20 Needle Burrower SR .30 .75
AST21 Sonic Jammer C .20 .50
AST22 Blowback Dragon UR 1.50 4.00
AST23 Zaborg the Thunder Monarch SR 1.50 4.00
AST24 Atomic Firefly C .20 .50
AST25 Mermaid Knight C .20 .50
AST26 Piranha Army C .20 .50
AST27 Two Thousand Needles C .20 .50
AST28 Disc Fighter C .20 .50
AST29 Arcane Archer of the Forest C .20 .50
AST30 Lady Ninja Yae C .60 1.50
AST31 Goblin King C .20 .50
AST32 Solar Flare Dragon C .20 .50
AST33 White Magician Pikeru C .20 .50
AST34 Archlord Zerato UR 2.00 5.00
AST35 Opti-Camouflage Armor C 1.50 4.00
AST36 Mystik Wok C .20 .50
AST37 Enemy Controller UR 3.00 8.00
AST38 Burst Stream of Destruction UR 8.00 20.00
AST39 Monster Gate C .20 .50
AST40 Amplifier SR 2.50 6.00
AST41 Weapon Change C .20 .50
AST42 The Sanctuary in the Sky SR 1.50 4.00
AST43 Earthquake C .20 .50
AST44 Talisman of Trap Sealing R .30 .75
AST45 Goblin Thief C .20 .50
AST46 Backfire C .20 .50
AST47 Micro Ray C .20 .50
AST48 Light of Judgment C .20 .50
AST49 Talisman of Spell Sealing R .30 .75
AST50 Wall of Revealing Light C .40 1.00
AST51 Solar Ray C .20 .50
AST52 Ninjitsu Art of Transformation C .50 1.25
AST53 Beckoning Light C .20 .50
AST54 Draining Shield R .75 2.00
AST55 Armor Break C .20 .50
AST56 Gigobyte C .20 .50
AST57 Mokey Mokey C 1.00 2.50
AST58 Kozaky C .20 .50
AST59 Fiend Scorpion C .20 .50
AST60 Pharaoh's Servant C .20 .50
AST61 Pharaonic Protector C .20 .50
AST62 Spirit of the Pharaoh UR .75 2.00
AST63 Theban Nightmare R .30 .75
AST64 Aswan Apparition C .20 .50
AST65 Protector of the Sanctuary C .20 .50
AST66 Nubian Guard C .20 .50
AST67 Legacy Hunter SR .40 1.00
AST68 Desertapir C .20 .50
AST69 Sand Gambler C .20 .50
AST70 3-Hump Lacooda C .20 .50
AST71 Ghost Knight of Jackal UR .50 1.25
AST72 Absorbing Kid from the Sky C .20 .50
AST73 Elephant Statue of Blessing C .20 .50
AST74 Elephant Statue of Disaster C .20 .50
AST75 Spirit Caller C .20 .50
AST76 Emissary of the Afterlife SR 1.00 2.50
AST77 Grave Protector R .30 .75
AST78 Double Coston R .30 .75
AST79 Regenerating Mummy C .20 .50
AST80 Night Assailant C .40 1.00
AST81 Man-Thro' Tho' C .20 .50
AST82 King of the Swamp R 4.00 10.00
AST83 Emissary of the Oasis C .20 .50
AST84 Special Hurricane R .30 .75
AST85 Order to Charge C .20 .50
AST86 Sword of the Soul-Eater C .20 .50
AST87 Dust Barrier C .20 .50
AST88 Soul Reversal C .20 .50
AST89 Spell Economics R .30 .75
AST90 Blessings of the Nile C .20 .50
AST91 7 C .20 .50
AST92 Level Limit - Area B SP 2.00 5.00
AST93 Enchanting Fitting Room C .20 .50
AST94 The Law of the Normal C .20 .50
AST95 Dark Magic Attack UR 15.00 30.00
AST96 Delta Attacker C .20 .50
AST97 Thousand Energy R .30 .75
AST98 Triangle Power R .30 .75
AST99 The Third Sarcophagus C .20 .50
AST100 The Second Sarcophagus C .20 .50
AST101 The First Sarcophagus SR .40 1.00
AST102 Dora of Fate C .20 .50
AST103 Judgment of the Desert C .20 .50
AST104 Human-Wave Tactics C .20 .50
AST105 Curse of Anubis UR .75 2.00
AST106 Desert Sunlight C .20 .50
AST107 Des Counterblow SR .30 .75
AST108 Labyrinth of Nightmare C .20 .50
AST109 Soul Resurrection R .30 .75
AST110 Order to Smash C .20 .50
AST111 Mazera Deville SCR 1.50 4.00

2004 Yu-Gi-Oh Soul of the Duelist 1st Edition

COMPLETE SET (60)	50.00	100.00
COMPLETE MASTER SET (85)	200.00	400.00
BOOSTER BOX (24 PACKS)	60.00	120.00
BOOSTER PACK (9 CARDS)	2.50	6.00
*UNLIMITED: .4X TO .8X 1ST EDITION		
RELEASED ON OCTOBER 1, 2004		
SODEN01 Charcoal Inpachi R	.30	.75
SODEN01 Charcoal Inpachi UTR	1.25	3.00
SODEN02 Neo Aqua Madoor C	.20	.50
SODEN03 Skull Dog Marron C	.20	.50
SODEN04 Goblin Calligrapher C	.20	.50
SODEN05 Ultimate Insect LV1 R	.30	.75
SODEN05 Ultimate Insect LV1 UTR	.75	2.00
SODEN06 Horus the Black Flame Dragon LV4 UTR	3.00	8.00
SODEN06 Horus the Black Flame Dragon LV4 R	1.50	4.00
SODEN07 Horus the Black Flame Dragon LV6 SR	3.00	8.00
SODEN07 Horus the Black Flame Dragon LV6 UTR	3.00	8.00
SODEN08 Horus the Black Flame Dragon LV8 UTR	25.00	50.00
SODEN08 Horus the Black Flame Dragon LV8 UR	8.00	20.00
SODEN09 Dark Mimic LV1 C	.20	.50
SODEN10 Dark Mimic LV3 R	.30	.75
SODEN10 Dark Mimic LV3 (UTR)	2.00	5.00
SODEN11 Mystic Swordsman LV2 R	.30	.75
SODEN11 Mystic Swordsman LV2 UTR	1.50	4.00
SODEN12 Mystic Swordsman LV4 UR	.75	2.00
SODEN12 Mystic Swordsman LV4 UTR	2.50	6.00
SODEN13 Armed Dragon LV3 C	.20	.50
SODEN14 Armed Dragon LV5 R	.30	.75
SODEN14 Armed Dragon LV5 UTR	4.00	10.00
SODEN15 Armed Dragon LV7 UR	4.00	10.00
SODEN15 Armed Dragon LV7 UTR	10.00	25.00
SODEN16 Horus' Servant C	.20	.50
SODEN17 Red-Eyes B. Chick C	.30	.75
SODEN18 Malice Doll of Demise C	.20	.50
SODEN19 Ninja Grandmaster Sasuke R	.40	1.00
SODEN19 Ninja Grandmaster Sasuke UTR	3.00	8.00
SODEN20 Rafflesia Seduction R	.30	.75
SODEN20 Rafflesia Seduction UTR	.75	2.00
SODEN21 Ultimate Baseball Kid C	.20	.50
SODEN22 Mobius the Frost Monarch SR	.75	2.00
SODEN22 Mobius the Frost Monarch UTR	8.00	20.00
SODEN23 Element Dragon C	.20	.50
SODEN24 Element Soldier C	.20	.50
SODEN25 Howling Insect C	.20	.50
SODEN26 Masked Dragon C	.30	.75
SODEN27 Mind on Air R	.30	.75
SODEN27 Mind on Air UTR	1.00	2.50
SODEN28 Unshaven Angler C	.20	.50
SODEN29 The Trojan Horse C	.20	.50
SODEN30 Nobleman-Eater Bug C	.20	.50
SODEN31 Enraged Muka Muka C	.20	.50
SODEN32 Hade-Hane C	.20	.50
SODEN33 Penumbral Soldier Lady SR	.40	1.00
SODEN33 Penumbral Soldier Lady UTR	.75	2.00
SODEN34 Ojama King UTR	2.00	5.00
SODEN34 Ojama King R	.40	1.00
SODEN35 Master of Oz R	.30	.75
SODEN35 Master of Oz UTR	6.00	15.00
SODEN36 Sanwitch C	.20	.50
SODEN37 Dark Factory of Mass Production C	.60	1.50
SODEN38 Hammer Shot R	.30	.75
SODEN38 Hammer Shot UTR	2.50	6.00
SODEN39 Mind Wipe C	.20	.50
SODEN40 Abyssal Designator C	.20	.50
SODEN41 Level Up!	.30	.75
SODEN42 Inferno Fire Blast UR	3.00	8.00
SODEN42 Inferno Fire Blast UTR	10.00	25.00
SODEN43 Ectoplasmer UTR	.60	1.50
SODEN43 Ectoplasmer SR	.40	1.00
SODEN44 The Graveyard in the Fourth Dimension C	.20	.50
SODEN45 Two-Man Cell Battle C	.20	.50
SODEN46 Big Wave Small Wave C	.20	.50
SODEN47 Fusion Weapon C	.20	.50
SODEN48 Ritual Weapon C	.20	.50
SODEN49 Taunt C	.20	.50
SODEN50 Absolute End C	.20	.50
SODEN51 Spirit Barrier R	1.50	4.00
SODEN51 Spirit Barrier UTR	4.00	10.00
SODEN52 Ninjitsu Art of Decoy C	.20	.50
SODEN53 Enervating Mist R	.30	.75
SODEN53 Enervating Mist UTR	2.50	6.00
SODEN54 Heavy Slump C	.30	.75
SODEN55 Greed SR	.40	1.00
SODEN55 Greed UTR	.60	1.50
SODEN56 Mind Crush C	.60	1.50
SODEN57 Null and Void SR	.40	1.00
SODEN57 Null and Void UTR	.60	1.50
SODEN58 Gorgon's Eye C	.20	.50
SODEN59 Cemetary Bomb C	.20	.50
SODEN60 Hallowed Life Barrier SR	.40	1.00
SODEN60 Hallowed Life Barrier UTR	.75	2.00

2004 Yu-Gi-Oh Rise of Destiny 1st Edition

COMPLETE SET (60)	30.00	60.00
COMPLETE MASTER SET (85)	60.00	100.00
BOOSTER BOX (24 PACKS)	50.00	75.00
BOOSTER PACK (9 CARDS)	2.50	6.00
SE BOX (3 PACKS, 1 VARIANT)	6.00	15.00
*UNLIMITED: .4X TO .8X 1ST EDITION		
RELEASED ON NOVEMBER 24, 2004		
RDSEN01 Woodborg Inpachi	.20	.50
RDSEN02 Mighty Guard	.20	.50
RDSEN03 Bokoichi the Freightening Car	.20	.50
RDSEN04 Harpie Girl	.20	.50
RDSEN05 The Creator UR	1.25	3.00
RDSEN05 The Creator UTR	2.00	5.00
RDSEN06 The Creator Incarnate	.20	.50
RDSEN07 Ultimate Insect LV3 R	.30	.75
RDSEN07 Ultimate Insect LV3 UTR	.60	1.50
RDSEN08 Mystic Swordsman LV6 UTR	3.00	8.00
RDSEN08 Mystic Swordsman LV6 UR	2.50	6.00
RDSEN09 Silent Swordsman LV3 UR	1.50	4.00
RDSEN09 Silent Swordsman LV3 UTR	2.00	5.00
RDSEN10 Nightmare Penguin	.20	.50
RDSEN11 Heavy Mech Support Platform	.20	.50
RDSEN12 Perfect Machine King UR	2.50	6.00
RDSEN12 Perfect Machine King UTR	3.00	8.00
RDSEN13 Element Magician C	.20	.50
RDSEN14 Element Saurus C	.20	.50
RDSEN15 Roc from the Valley of Haze C	.20	.50
RDSEN16 Sasuke Samurai #4 R	.30	.75
RDSEN16 Sasuke Samurai #4 UTR	.60	1.50
RDSEN17 Harpie Lady 1 C	.40	1.00
RDSEN18 Harpie Lady 2 C	.20	.50
RDSEN19 Harpie Lady 3 C	.20	.50
RDSEN20 Raging Flame Sprite C	.20	.50
RDSEN21 Thestalos the Firestorm Monarch SR	.40	1.00
RDSEN21 Thestalos the Firestorm Monarch UTR	5.00	12.00
RDSEN22 Eagle Eye C	.20	.50
RDSEN23 Tactical Espionage Expert C	.20	.50
RDSEN24 Invasion of Flames C	.20	.50
RDSEN25 Creeping Doom Manta C	.20	.50
RDSEN26 Pitch-Black Warwolf C	.20	.50
RDSEN27 Mirage Dragon C	.30	.75
RDSEN28 Gaia Soul (R)	.30	.75
RDSEN28 Gaia Soul (UTR)	.60	1.50
RDSEN29 Fox Fire C	.20	.50
RDSEN30 Big Core SR	.30	.75
RDSEN30 Big Core UTR	.60	1.50
RDSEN31 Fusilier Dragon (UTR)	1.25	3.00
RDSEN31 Fusilier Dragon (R)	.50	1.00
RDSEN32 Dekoichi (R)	.30	.75
RDSEN32 Dekoichi (UTR)	1.50	4.00
RDSEN33 A-Team: Trap Disposal Unit UTR	.60	1.50
RDSEN33 A-Team: Trap Disposal Unit R	.30	.75
RDSEN34 Homunculus the Alchemic Being C	.20	.50
RDSEN35 Dark Blade The Dragon Knight R	.30	.75
RDSEN35 Dark Blade The Dragon Knight UTR	1.00	2.50
RDSEN36 Mokey Mokey King C	.20	.50
RDSEN37 Serial Spell R	.30	.75
RDSEN37 Serial Spell UTR	.60	1.50
RDSEN38 Harpies' Hunting Ground C	.20	.50
RDSEN39 Triangle Ecstasy Spark UR	.40	1.00
RDSEN39 Triangle Ecstasy Spark UTR	2.00	5.00
RDSEN40 Necklace of Command UTR	.60	1.50
RDSEN40 Necklace of Command R	.30	.75
RDSEN41 Machine Duplication R	.30	.75
RDSEN41 Machine Duplication UTR	1.25	3.00
RDSEN42 Flint UTR	.60	1.50
RDSEN42 Flint R	.30	.75
RDSEN43 Mokey Mokey Smackdown C	.20	.50
RDSEN44 Back to Square One C	.20	.50
RDSEN45 Monster Reincarnation SR	.75	2.00
RDSEN45 Monster Reincarnation UTR	6.00	15.00
RDSEN46 Ballista of Rampart Smashing C	.20	.50
RDSEN47 Lighten the Load C	.20	.50
RDSEN48 Malice Dispersion C	.20	.50
RDSEN49 Tragedy SR	.30	.75
RDSEN49 Tragedy UTR	.60	1.50
RDSEN50 Divine Wrath UTR	3.00	8.00
RDSEN50 Divine Wrath SR	.60	1.50
RDSEN51 Xing Zhen Hu C	.20	.50
RDSEN52 Rare Metalmorph R	.30	.75
RDSEN52 Rare Metalmorph UTR	.60	1.50
RDSEN53 Fruits of Kozaky's Studies C	.20	.50
RDSEN54 Mind Haxorz C	.20	.50
RDSEN55 Fuh-Rin-Ka-Zan C	.20	.50
RDSEN56 Chain Burst R	.30	.75
RDSEN56 Chain Burst UTR	.60	1.50
RDSEN57 Pikeru's Circle of Enchantment UTR	.75	2.00
RDSEN57 Pikeru's Circle of Enchantment SR	.30	.75
RDSEN58 Spell Purification C	.20	.50
RDSEN59 Astral Barrier C	.20	.50
RDSEN60 Covering Fire R	.30	.75
RDSEN60 Covering Fire UTR	.60	1.50

2005 Yu-Gi-Oh Flaming Eternity 1st Edition

COMP.SET W/O UTR (60)	100.00	150.00
COMPLETE SET (85)	150.00	300.00
BOOSTER BOX (24 PACKS)	80.00	120.00
BOOSTER PACK (9 CARDS)	2.50	6.00
*UNLIMITED: .4X TO .8X 1ST EDITION		
RELEASED ON MARCH 3, 2005		
FETEN1 Space Mambo C	.10	.30
FETEN2 Divine Dragon Ragnarok C	.75	2.00
FETEN3 Chu-Ske The Mouse Fighter C	.10	.30
FETEN4 Insect Knight C	.10	.30
FETEN5 Sacred Phoenix of Nephthys UR	1.50	4.00
FETEN5 Sacred Phoenix of Nephthys UTR	4.00	10.00
FETEN6 Hand of Nephthys C	.10	.30
FETEN7 Ultimate Insect LV5 R	.40	1.00
FETEN7 Ultimate Insect LV5 UTR	3.00	8.00
FETEN8 Silent Swordsman LV5 UTR	3.00	8.00
FETEN8 Silent Swordsman LV5 UR	1.25	3.00
FETEN9 Granmarg the Rock Monarch SR	.75	2.00
FETEN9 Granmarg the Rock Monarch UTR	6.00	15.00
FETEN10 Element Valkyrie C	.10	.30
FETEN11 Element Doom C	.10	.30
FETEN12 Maji-Gire Panda C	.10	.30
FETEN13 Catnipped Kitty C	.10	.30
FETEN14 Behemoth the King of all Animals SR	.75	2.00
FETEN14 Behemoth the King of all Animals UTR	1.25	3.00
FETEN15 Big-Tusked Mammoth UTR	1.25	3.00
FETEN15 Big-Tusked Mammoth R	.40	1.00
FETEN16 Kangaroo Champ C	.10	.30
FETEN17 Hyena C	.10	.30
FETEN18 Blade Rabbit C	.10	.30
FETEN19 Mecha-Dog Marron C	.10	.30
FETEN20 Blast Magician SR	.75	2.00
FETEN20 Blast Magician UTR	2.00	6.00
FETEN21 Chiron the Mage UTR	1.50	4.00
FETEN21 Chiron the Mage R	.40	1.00
FETEN22 Gearfried the Swordsmaster UR	2.00	5.00
FETEN22 Gearfried the Swordsmaster UTR	4.00	10.00
FETEN23 Armed Samurai - Ben Kei C	.10	.30
FETEN24 Shadowslayer R	.40	1.00
FETEN24 Shadowslayer UTR	1.25	3.00
FETEN25 Golem Sentry C	.10	.30
FETEN26 Abare Ushioni C	.10	.30
FETEN27 The Light - Hex-Sealed Fusion C	.10	.30
FETEN28 The Dark - Hex-Sealed Fusion C	.10	.30
FETEN29 The Earth - Hex-Sealed Fusion C	.10	.30
FETEN30 Whirlwind Prodigy C	.10	.30
FETEN31 Flame Ruler C	.10	.30
FETEN32 Firebird C	.10	.30
FETEN33 Rescue Cat C	.10	.30
FETEN34 Brain Jacker R	.40	1.00
FETEN34 Brain Jacker UTR	1.25	3.00
FETEN35 Gatling Dragon UTR	6.00	15.00
FETEN35 Gatling Dragon UR	2.00	5.00
FETEN36 King Dragun SR	4.00	10.00
FETEN36 King Dragun UTR	8.00	20.00
FETEN37 A Feather of the Phoenix UTR	6.00	15.00
FETEN37 A Feather of the Phoenix SR	.75	2.00
FETEN38 Poison Fangs C	.10	.30
FETEN39 Spell Absorption R	1.25	3.00
FETEN39 Spell Absorption UTR	4.00	10.00
FETEN40 Lightning Vortex UTR	10.00	25.00
FETEN40 Lightning Vortex SR	1.50	4.00
FETEN41 Meteor of Destruction R	.40	1.00
FETEN41 Meteor of Destruction UTR	1.25	3.00
FETEN42 Swords of Concealing Light UTR	10.00	25.00
FETEN42 Swords of Concealing Light R	.50	1.25
FETEN43 Spiral Spear Strike R	.40	1.00
FETEN43 Spiral Spear Strike UTR	3.00	8.00
FETEN44 Release Restraint C	.10	.30
FETEN45 Centrifugal Field C	.10	.30
FETEN46 Fulfillment of the Contract C	.10	.30
FETEN47 Re-Fusion C	.75	2.00
FETEN48 The Big March of Animals C	.10	.30
FETEN49 Cross Counter R	.40	1.00
FETEN49 Cross Counter UTR	1.25	3.00
FETEN50 Pole Position C	.10	.30
FETEN51 Penalty Game! R	.40	1.00
FETEN51 Penalty Game! UTR	2.00	5.00
FETEN52 Threatening Roar C	.25	.75
FETEN53 Phoenix Wing Wind Blast R	.50	1.25
FETEN53 Phoenix Wing Wind Blast UTR	15.00	30.00
FETEN54 Good Goblin Housekeeping C	.10	.30
FETEN55 Beast Soul Swap C	.10	.30
FETEN56 Assault on GHQ R	.40	1.00
FETEN56 Assault on GHQ UTR	1.25	3.00
FETEN57 D.D. Dynamite C	.25	.75
FETEN58 Deck Devastation Virus SR	2.50	6.00
FETEN58 Deck Devastation Virus UTR	20.00	40.00
FETEN59 Elemental Burst C	.10	.30
FETEN60 Forced Ceasefire R	.40	1.00
FETEN60 Forced Ceasefire UTR	1.25	3.00

2005 Yu-Gi-Oh The Lost Millennium 1st Edition

COMPLETE SET (85)	115.00	225.00
BOOSTER BOX (24 PACKS)	60.00	100.00
BOOSTER PACK (9 CARDS)	2.50	6.00
SE PACK	8.00	20.00
*UNLIMITED: .4X TO .8X 1ST EDITION		
RELEASED ON JUNE 1, 2005		
TLM1 Elemental Hero Avian C	.50	1.25
TLM2 Elemental Hero Burstinatrix C	.50	1.25
TLM3 Elemental Hero Clayman C	.50	1.25
TLM4 Elemental Hero Sparkman C	.50	1.25
TLM5 Winged Kuriboh SR	1.50	4.00
TLM6 Ancient Gear Golem UR	3.00	8.00
TLM6 Ancient Gear Golem UTR	10.00	25.00
TLM7 Ancient Gear Beast UTR	1.50	4.00
TLM7 Ancient Gear Beast R	.40	1.00
TLM8 Ancient Gear Soldier C	.20	.50
TLM9 Millennium Scorpion R	.40	1.00
TLM9 Millennium Scorpion UTR	1.50	4.00
TLM-5 Winged Kuriboh UTR	5.00	12.00
TLM10 Ultimate Insect LV7 SR	.75	2.00
TLM10 Ultimate Insect LV7 UTR	3.00	8.00
TLM11 Lost Guardian C	.20	.50
TLM12 Hieracosphinx SR	.75	2.00
TLM12 Hieracosphinx UTR	1.50	4.00
TLM13 Criosphinx UTR	1.50	4.00
TLM13 Criosphinx R	.40	1.00
TLM14 Moai Interceptor Cannons C	.20	.50
TLM15 Megarock Dragon SR	.75	2.00
TLM15 Megarock Dragon UTR	3.00	8.00
TLM16 Dummy Golem C	.20	.50
TLM17 Grave Ohja R	.40	1.00
TLM17 Grave Ohja UTR	1.50	4.00
TLM18 Mine Golem C	.20	.50
TLM19 Monk Fighter C	.20	.50
TLM20 Master Monk SR	.75	2.00
TLM20 Master Monk UTR	1.50	4.00
TLM21 Guardian Statue C	.20	.50
TLM22 Medusa Worm C	.20	.50
TLM23 D.D. Survivor R	.40	1.00
TLM23 D.D. Survivor UTR	3.00	8.00
TLM24 Mid Shield Gardna UTR	1.50	4.00
TLM24 Mid Shield Gardna R	.40	1.00
TLM25 White Ninja C	.20	.50
TLM26 Aussa the Earth Charmer C	.20	.50
TLM27 Eria the Water Charmer C	.20	.50
TLM28 Hiita the Fire Charmer C	.20	.50
TLM29 Wynn the Wind Charmer C	.20	.50
TLM30 Batteryman AA C	.20	.50
TLM31 Des Wombat C	.20	.50
TLM32 King of the Skull Servants C	.50	1.25
TLM33 Reshef the Dark Being UR	2.00	5.00
TLM33 Reshef the Dark Being UTR	5.00	12.00
TLM34 Elemental Mistress Doriado UTR	1.50	4.00

TLM34 Elemental Mistress Doriado R	.40	1.00
TLM35 Elemental Hero Flame Wingman UR	3.00	8.00
TLM35 Elemental Hero Flame Wingman UTR	5.00	12.00
TLM36 Elemental Hero Thunder Giant UTR	5.00	12.00
TLM36 Elemental Hero Thunder Giant UR	2.50	6.00
TLM37 Card of Sanctity SR	.75	2.00
TLM37 Card of Sanctity UTR	1.50	4.00
TLM38 Brain Control UTR	10.00	25.00
TLM38 Brain Control SR	.75	2.00
TLM39 Gift of the Martyr C	.20	.50
TLM40 Double Attack C	.20	.50
TLM41 Battery Charger C	.20	.50
TLM42 Kaminote Blow C	.20	.50
TLM43 Doriado's Blessing C	.20	.50
TLM44 Final Ritual of the Ancients C	.20	.50
TLM45 Legendary Black Belt R	.40	1.00
TLM45 Legendary Black Belt UTR	1.50	4.00
TLM46 Nitro Unit UTR	1.50	4.00
TLM46 Nitro Unit R	.40	1.00
TLM47 Shifting Shadows C	.20	.50
TLM48 Impenetrable Formation C	.20	.50
TLM49 Hero Signal R	.40	1.00
TLM49 Hero Signal UTR	1.50	4.00
TLM50 Pikeru's Second Sight C	.20	.50
TLM51 Minefield Eruption C	.20	.50
TLM52 Kozaky's Self-Destruct Button R	.40	1.00
TLM52 Kozaky's Self-Destruct Button UTR	1.50	4.00
TLM53 Mispolymerization C	.20	.50
TLM54 Level Conversion Lab C	.20	.50
TLM55 Rock Bombardment C	.20	.50
TLM56 Grave Lure C	.20	.50
TLM57 Token Feastevil R	.40	1.00
TLM57 Token Feastevil UTR	1.50	4.00
TLM58 Spell-Stopping Statute UTR	1.50	4.00
TLM58 Spell-Stopping Statute R	.40	1.00
TLM59 Royal Surrender R	.40	1.00
TLM59 Royal Surrender UTR	1.50	4.00
TLM60 Lone Wolf C	.20	.50

2005 Yu-Gi-Oh Cybernetic Revolution 1st Edition

COMPLETE SET (60)	180.00	350.00
BOOSTER BOX (24 PACKS)	90.00	110.00
BOOSTER PACK (9 CARDS)	2.50	6.00
*UNLIMITED: .4X TO .8X 1ST EDITION		
RELEASED ON AUGUST 6, 2005		
CRV1 Cycloid C	.10	.30
CRV2 Soitsu C	.10	.30
CRV3 Mad Lobster C	.10	.30
CRV4 Jelly Beans Man C	.10	.30
CRV5 Winged Kuriboh LV 10 UR	3.00	8.00
CRV5 Winged Kuriboh LV 10 UTR	10.00	25.00
CRV6 Patroid C	.10	.30
CRV7 Gyroid C	.10	.30
CRV8 Steamroid C	.10	.30
CRV9 Drillroid C	.10	.30
CRV11 Jetroid C	.10	.30
CRV17 Cybernetic Cyclops C	.10	.30
CRV18 Mechanical Hound C	.10	.30
CRV19 Cyber Archfiend C	.10	.30
CRV22 Giant Kozaky C	.10	.30
CRV23 Indomitable Fighter Lei Lei C	.10	.30
CRV24 Protective Soul Ailin C	.10	.30
CRV25 Doitsu C	.10	.30
CRV26 Des Frog C	.10	.30
CRV27 T.A.D.P.O.L.E. C	.10	.30
CRV28 Poison Draw Frog C	.10	.30
CRV29 Tyranno Infinity C	.10	.30
CRV30 Batteryman C	.10	.30
CRV31 Ebon Magician Curran C	.10	.30
CRV33 Steam Gyroid C	.10	.30
CRV38 Fusion Recovery C	.10	.30
CRV40 Dragon's Mirror C	.10	.30
CRV42 Des Croaking C	.10	.30
CRV43 Pot of Generosity C	.10	.30
CRV44 Shien's Spy C	.10	.30
CRV50 Spiritual Earth Art - Kurogane C	.10	.30
CRV51 Spiritual Water Art - Aoi C	.10	.30
CRV52 Spiritual Fire Art - Kurenai C	.10	.30
CRV53 Spiritual Wind Art - Miyabi C	.10	.30
CRV54 A Rival Appears! C	.10	.30
CRV55 Magical Explosion R	.40	1.00
CRV55 Magical Explosion UTR	3.00	8.00
CRV58 Conscription C	.10	.30
CRV60 Prepare to Strike Back C	.10	.30
CRV10A UFOroid SR	.75	2.00
CRV10B UFOroid UTR	.75	2.00
CRV12A Wroughtweiler R	.40	1.00
CRV12B Wroughtweiler UTR	1.50	4.00
CRV13B Dark Catapulter UTR	.40	1.00
CRV13B Dark Catapulter UTR	.75	2.00
CRV14A Elemental Hero Bubbleman R	.40	3.00
CRV14B Elemental Hero Bubbleman UTR	15.00	30.00
CRV15A Cyber Dragon SR	3.00	8.00
CRV15B Cyber Dragon UTR	30.00	60.00
CRV16A Cybernetic Magician SR	.75	2.00
CRV16B Cybernetic Magician UTR	.75	2.00
CRV20A Goblin Elite Attack Force SR	.75	2.00
CRV20B Goblin Elite Attack Force UTR	1.50	4.00
CRV21A B.E.S. Crystal Core SR	.75	2.00
CRV21B B.E.S. Crystal Core UTR	1.00	2.50
CRV32A D.D.M. Different Dimension (R)	.40	1.00
CRV32B D.D.M. Different Dimension UTR	1.00	2.50
CRV34A UFOroid Fighter UR	1.00	2.50
CRV34B UFOroid Fighter UTR	2.50	6.00
CRV35A Cyber Twin Dragon SR	2.50	6.00
CRV35B Cyber Twin Dragon UTR	10.00	25.00
CRV36A Cyber End Dragon UR	6.00	15.00
CRV36B Cyber End Dragon UTR	25.00	50.00
CRV37A Power Bond UR	3.00	8.00
CRV37B Power Bond UTR	15.00	30.00
CRV39A Miracle Fusion R	.40	1.00
CRV39B Miracle Fusion UTR	8.00	20.00
CRV41A System Down R	.40	1.00
CRV41B System Down UTR	10.00	25.00
CRV45A Transcendant Wings R	.40	1.00
CRV45B Transcendent Wings UTR	3.00	8.00
CRV46A Bubble Shuffle R	.40	1.00
CRV46B Bubble Shuffle UTR	.75	2.00
CRV47A Spark Blaster R	.40	1.00
CRV47B Spark Blaster UTR	.75	2.00
CRV48A Skyscraper SR	1.00	2.50
CRV48B Skyscraper UTR	3.00	8.00
CRV49A Fire Darts R	.40	1.00
CRV49B Fire Darts UTR	.75	2.00
CRV56A Rising Energy R	.40	1.00
CRV56B Rising Energy UTR	1.00	2.50
CRV57A D.D. Trap Hole R	.40	1.00
CRV57B D.D. Trap Hole UTR	.75	2.00
CRV59A Dimension Wall R	.40	1.00
CRV59B Dimension Wall UTR	2.50	6.00

2005 Yu-Gi-Oh Elemental Energy 1st Edition

COMPLETE SET (60)	200.00	400.00
BOOSTER BOX (24 PACKS)	80.00	120.00
BOOSTER PACK (9 CARDS)	2.50	6.00
*UNLIMITED: .4X TO .8X 1ST EDITION		
RELEASED ON NOVEMBER 30, 2005		
EEN1 Zure, Knight of Dark World C	.20	.50
EEN2 V-Tiger Jet C	.20	.50
EEN3 Blade Skater C	.20	.50
EEN4 Queen's Knight R	.40	1.00
EEN4 Queen's Knight UTR	3.00	8.00
EEN5 Jack's Knight UTR	15.00	30.00
EEN5 Jack's Knight R	.40	1.00
EEN6 King's Knight R	.40	1.00
EEN6 King's Knight UTR	3.00	8.00
EEN7 Elemental Hero Bladedge UTR	4.00	10.00
EEN7 Elemental Hero Bladedge SR	.75	2.00
EEN8 Elemental Hero Wildheart C	.20	.50
EEN9 Reborn Zombie C	.20	.50
EEN10 Chthonian Soldier R	.40	1.00
EEN10 Chthonian Soldier UTR	.75	2.00
EEN11 W-Wing Catapult C	.20	.50
EEN12 Infernal Incinerator C	.20	.50
EEN13 Hydrogeddon C	.20	.50
EEN14 Oxygeddon C	.20	.50
EEN15 Water Dragon SR	.75	2.00
EEN15 Water Dragon UTR	2.50	6.00
EEN16 Etoile Cyber C	.20	.50
EEN17 B.E.S. Tetran SR	.75	2.00
EEN17 B.E.S. Tetran UTR	.75	2.00
EEN18 Nanobreaker C	.20	.50
EEN19 Rapid-Fire Magician R	.40	1.00
EEN19 Rapid-Fire Magician UTR	.75	2.00
EEN20 Beiige, Vanguard of Dark World C	.20	.50
EEN21 Broww, Huntsman of Dark World R	.40	1.00
EEN21 Broww, Huntsman of Dark World UTR	5.00	12.00
EEN22 Brron, Mad King of Dark World UTR	.75	2.00
EEN22 Brron, Mad King of Dark World R	.40	1.00
EEN23 Sillva, Warlord of Dark World R	.40	1.00
EEN23 Sillva, Warlord of Dark World UTR	2.50	6.00
EEN24 Goldd, Wu-Lord of Dark World UTR	2.50	6.00
EEN24 Goldd, Wu-Lord of Dark World SR	.75	2.00
EEN25 Scarr, Scout of Dark World C	.20	.50
EEN26 Familiar-Possessed - Aussa C	.20	.50
EEN27 Familiar-Possessed - Eria C	.20	.50
EEN28 Familiar-Possessed - Hiita C	.20	.50
EEN29 Familiar-Possessed - Wynn C	.20	.50
EEN30 VW-Tiger Catapult C	.20	.50
EEN31 VWXYZ-Dragon Catapult Cannon SR	.75	2.00
EEN31 VWXYZ-Dragon Catapult Cannon UTR	3.00	8.00
EEN32 Cyber Blader UTR	1.50	4.00
EEN32 Cyber Blader SR	.75	2.00
EEN33 Elemental Hero Rampart Blaster UR	2.00	5.00
EEN33 Elem.Hero Rampart Blast. UTR	8.00	20.00
EEN34 Elemental Hero Tempest UTR	20.00	40.00
EEN34 Elemental Hero Tempest UR	2.50	6.00
EEN35 Elemental Hero Wildedge UR	2.50	6.00
EEN35 Elemental Hero Wildedge UTR	40.00	80.00
EEN36 Elem. Hero Shining Flare UTR	60.00	100.00
EEN36 Elem. Hero Shining Flare UR	6.00	15.00
EEN37 Pot of Avarice SR	.75	2.00
EEN37 Pot of Avarice UTR	15.00	30.00
EEN38 Dark World Lightning C	.20	.50
EEN39 Level Modulation C	.20	.50
EEN40 Ojamagic C	.20	.50
EEN41 Ojamuscle C	.20	.50
EEN42 Feather Shot R	.40	1.00
EEN42 Feather Shot UTR	.75	2.00
EEN43 Bonding - H2O C	.20	.50
EEN44 Chthonian Alliance R	.40	1.00
EEN44 Chthonian Alliance UTR	.75	2.00
EEN45 Armed Changer UTR	.75	2.00
EEN45 Armed Changer R	.40	1.00
EEN46 Branch! C	.20	.50
EEN47 Boss Rush C	.20	.50
EEN48 Gateway to Dark World C	.20	.50
EEN49 Hero Barrier R	.40	1.00
EEN49 Hero Barrier UTR	.75	2.00
EEN50 Chthonian Blast UTR	.75	2.00
EEN50 Chthonian Blast R	.40	1.00
EEN51 The Forces of Darkness C	.20	.50
EEN52 Dark Deal C	.20	.50
EEN53 Simultaneous Loss C	.20	.50
EEN54 Weed Out C	.20	.50
EEN55 The League of Uniform Nomenclature C	.20	.50
EEN56 Roll Out! C	.20	.50
EEN57 Chthonian Polymer C	.20	.50
EEN58 Feather Wind C	.20	.50
EEN59 Non-Fusion Area C	.20	.50
EEN60 Level Limit - Area A R	.40	1.00
EEN60 Level Limit - Area A UTR	.75	2.00

2006 Yu-Gi-Oh Shadow of Infinity 1st Edition

COMPLETE SET (60)	200.00	400.00
BOOSTER BOX (24 PACKS)	80.00	110.00
BOOSTER PACK (9 CARDS)	2.50	6.00
*UNLIMITED: .4X TO .8X 1ST EDITION		
RELEASED ON FEBRUARY 18, 2006		
SOI1 Uria, Lord of Searing Flames UR	3.00	8.00
SOI1 Uria, Lord of Searing Flames UTR	70.00	100.00
SOI2 Hamon, Lord of Striking Thunder UTR	40.00	70.00
SOI2 Hamon, Lord of Striking Thunder UR	3.00	8.00
SOI3 Raviel, Lord of Phantasms UR	3.00	8.00
SOI3 Raviel, Lord of Phantasms UTR	30.00	60.00
SOI4 Elemental Hero Neo Bubbleman C	.10	.30
SOI5 Hero Kid C	.10	.30
SOI6 Cyber Barrier Dragon SR	.60	1.50
SOI6 Cyber Barrier Dragon UTR	2.50	6.00
SOI7 Cyber Laser Dragon UTR	8.00	20.00
SOI7 Cyber Laser Dragon UR	3.00	8.00
SOI8 Ancient Gear C	.10	.30
SOI9 Ancient Gear Cannon C	.10	.30
SOI10 Proto-Cyber Dragon R	.40	1.00
SOI10 Proto-Cyber Dragon UTR	3.00	8.00
SOI11 Adhesive Explosive UTR	1.00	2.50
SOI11 Adhesive Explosive R	.40	1.00
SOI12 Machine King Prototype C	.10	.30
SOI13 B.E.S. Covered Core SR	.60	1.50
SOI13 B.E.S. Covered Core UTR	1.25	3.00
SOI14 D.D. Guide C	.10	.30
SOI15 Chain Thrasher C	.10	.30
SOI16 Disciple of the Forbidden Spell C	.10	.30
SOI17 Tenkabito Shien C	.10	.30
SOI18 Parasitic Ticky C	.10	.30
SOI19 Gokipon C	.10	.30
SOI20 Silent Insect C	.10	.30
SOI21 Chainsaw Insect R	.40	1.00
SOI21 Chainsaw Insect UTR	2.50	6.00
SOI22 Anteatereatingant C	.10	.30
SOI23 Saber Beetle C	.10	.30
SOI24 Doom Dozer R	.60	1.50
SOI24 Doom Dozer UTR	3.00	8.00
SOI25 Treeborn Frog UTR	8.00	20.00
SOI25 Treeborn Frog R	.60	1.50
SOI26 Beelze Frog C	.10	.30
SOI27 Princess Pikeru R	.40	1.00
SOI27 Princess Pikeru UTR	2.50	6.00
SOI28 Princess Curran UTR	2.50	6.00
SOI28 Princess Curran R	.40	1.00
SOI29 Memory Crusher R	.40	1.00
SOI29 Memory Crusher UTR	.75	2.00
SOI30 Malice Ascendant C	.10	.30
SOI31 Grass Phantom C	.10	.30
SOI32 Sand Moth C	.10	.30
SOI33 Divine Dragon - Excelion SR	.60	1.50
SOI33 Divine Dragon-Excelion UTR	1.00	2.50
SOI34 Ruin, Queen of Oblivion UTR	3.00	8.00
SOI34 Ruin, Queen of Oblivion SR	.60	1.50
SOI35 Demise, King of Armageddon SR	3.00	8.00
SOI35 Demise, King of Armageddon UTR	4.00	10.00
SOI36 D.3.S. Frog C	.10	.30
SOI37 Hero Heart C	.10	.30
SOI38 Magnet Circle LV2 C	.10	.30
SOI39 Ancient Gear Factory C	.10	.30
SOI40 Ancient Gear Drill C	.10	.30
SOI41 Phantasmal Martyrs R	.40	1.00
SOI41 Phantasmal Martyrs UTR	1.00	2.50
SOI42 Cyclone Bommerang UTR	1.00	2.50
SOI42 Cyclone Boomerang R	.40	1.00
SOI43 Symbol of Heritage C	.10	.30
SOI44 Trial of the Princesses C	.10	.30
SOI45 Photon Generator Unit C	.10	.30
SOI46 End of the World C	.10	.30
SOI47 Ancient Gear Castle SR	.60	1.50
SOI47 Ancient Gear Castle UTR	1.00	2.50
SOI48 Samsara C	.10	.30
SOI49 Super Junior Confrontation C	.10	.30
SOI50 Miracle Kids C	.10	.30
SOI51 Attack Reflector Unit C	.10	.30
SOI52 Damage Condenser SR	.60	1.50
SOI52 Damage Condenser UTR	2.00	5.00
SOI53 Karma Cut UTR	6.00	15.00
SOI53 Karma Cut R	.75	2.00
SOI54 Next to be Lost C	.10	.30
SOI55 Generation Shift C	.10	.30
SOI56 Full Salvo C	.10	.30
SOI57 Success Probability 0% C	.10	.30
SOI58 Option Hunter R	.40	1.00
SOI58 Option Hunter UTR	1.00	2.50
SOI59 Goblin Out of the Frying Pan UTR	1.00	2.50
SOI59 Goblin Out of the Frying Pan R	.40	1.00
SOI60 Malfunction R	.40	1.00
SOI60 Malfunction UTR	1.00	2.50

2006 Yu-Gi-Oh Enemy of Justice 1st Edition

COMPLETE SET (60)	100.00	175.00
BOOSTER BOX (24 PACKS)	60.00	80.00
BOOSTER PACK (9 CARDS)	2.50	6.00
*UNLIMITED: .4X TO .8X 1ST EDITION		
RELEASED ON MAY 17, 2006		
EOJ1 Destiny Hero - Doom Lord C	.10	.30
EOJ2 Destiny Hero - Captain Tenacious C	.10	.30
EOJ3A Destiny Hero - Diamond Dude R	.40	1.00
EOJ3B Destiny Hero - Diamond Dude UTR	8.00	20.00
EOJ4A Destiny Hero - Dreadmaster UR	1.00	2.50
EOJ4B Destiny Hero - Dreadmaster UTR	5.00	12.00
EOJ5 Cyber Tutu C	.10	.30
EOJ6 Cyber Gymnast C	.10	.30
EOJ7A Cyber Prima SR	.60	1.50
EOJ7B Cyber Prima UTR	1.00	2.50
EOJ8 Cyber Kirin C	.10	.30
EOJ9A Cyber Phoenix SR	.75	2.00
EOJ9B Cyber Phoenix UTR	3.00	8.00
EOJ10 Searchlightman C	.10	.30
EOJ11A Victory Viper XX03 SR	.60	1.50
EOJ11B Victory Viper XX03 UTR	1.25	3.00
EOJ12 Swift Birdman Joe C	.10	.30
EOJ13A Harpie's Pet Baby Dragon R	.50	1.25
EOJ13B Harpie's Pet Baby Dragon UTR	4.00	10.00
EOJ14 Majestic Mech - Senku C	.10	.30
EOJ15A Majestic Mech - Ohka R	.40	1.00
EOJ15B Majestic Mech - Ohka UTR	1.00	2.50
EOJ16A Majestic Mech - Goryu SR	.60	1.50
EOJ16B Majestic Mech - Goryu UTR	1.00	2.50
EOJ17 Royal Knight C	.10	.30

EOJ18A Herald of Green Light R .40 1.00
EOJ18B Herald of Green Light UTR 1.50 4.00
EOJ19A Herald of Purple Light R .40 1.00
EOJ19B Herald of Purple Light UTR 1.50 4.00
EOJ20 Bountiful Artemis C .10 .30
EOJ21 Layard the Liberator C .10 .30
EOJ22A Banisher of the Radiance R .60 1.50
EOJ22B Banisher of Radiance UTR 4.00 10.00
EOJ23A Voltanis the Adjudicator UR 1.50 4.00
EOJ23B Voltanis the Adjudicator UTR 2.50 6.00
EOJ24 Guard Dog C .10 .30
EOJ25 Whirlwind Weasel C .10 .30
EOJ26 Avalanching Aussa C .10 .30
EOJ27 Raging Eria C .10 .30
EOJ28 Blazing Hiita C .10 .30
EOJ29 Storming Wynn C .10 .30
EOJ30 Batteryman D C .10 .30
EOJ31A Super-Electromagnetic SR .60 1.50
EOJ31B Super-Electromagnetic UTR 1.25 3.00
EOJ32A Elem. Hero Phoenix UR 2.00 5.00
EOJ32B Elem. Hero Phoenix UTR 20.00 40.00
EOJ33A Elem. Hero Shining Phoenix UR 2.00 5.00
EOJ33B Elem. Hero Shining Phoenix UTR 20.00 40.00
EOJ34 Elemental Hero Mariner C .10 .30
EOJ35A Elemental Hero Wild Wingman SR .60 1.50
EOJ35B Elemental Hero Wild Wingman UTR 1.50 4.00
EOJ36 Elemental Hero Necroid Shaman C .10 .30
EOJ37 Misfortune C .10 .30
EOJ38 H - Heated Heart C .10 .30
EOJ39 E - Emergency Call C .10 .30
EOJ40 R - Righteous Justice C .10 .30
EOJ41 O - Oversoul C .10 .30
EOJ42A HERO Flash!! R .40 1.00
EOJ42B HERO Flash!! UTR 1.00 2.50
EOJ43 Power Capsule C .10 .30
EOJ44 Celestial Transformation C .10 .30
EOJ45A Guard Penalty R .40 1.00
EOJ45B Guard Penalty UTR 1.00 2.50
EOJ46 Grand Convergence C .10 .30
EOJ47 Dimensional Fissure C .10 .30
EOJ48A Clock Tower Prison SR .60 1.50
EOJ48B Clock Tower Prison UTR 1.50 4.00
EOJ49A Life Equalizer R .75 2.00
EOJ49B Life Equilizer UTR 4.00 10.00
EOJ50 Elemental Recharge C .10 .30
EOJ51A Destruction of Destiny R .40 1.00
EOJ51B Destruction of Destiny UTR 1.00 2.50
EOJ52 Destiny Signal C .10 .30
EOJ53A D - Time R .40 1.00
EOJ53B D - Time UTR 1.00 2.50
EOJ54 D - Shield C .10 .30
EOJ55 Icarus Attack C .50 1.25
EOJ56A Elemental Absorber R .40 1.00
EOJ56B Elemental Absorber UTR 1.00 2.50
EOJ57 Macro Cosmos C .40 1.00
EOJ58A Miraculous Descent R .40 1.00
EOJ58B Miraculous Descent UTR 1.25 3.00
EOJ59 Shattered Axe C .10 .30
EOJ60A Forced Back R 1.50 4.00
EOJ60B Forced Back UTR 4.00 10.00

2006 Yu-Gi-Oh Power of the Duelist 1st Edition

COMPLETE SET (60) 80.00 150.00
BOOSTER BOX (24 PACKS) 50.00 80.00
BOOSTER PACK (9 CARDS) 2.50 6.00
*UNLIMITED: .4X TO .8X 1ST EDITION
RELEASED ON AUGUST 16, 2006
POTD1 Elemental Hero Neos C .10 .30
POTD2 Sabersaurus C .10 .30
POTD3 Neo-Spacian Aqua Dolphin SR 2.50 6.00
POTD3 Neo-Spacian Aqua Dolphin UTR 1.50 4.00
POTD4 Neo Spacian Flare Scarab UTR 2.50 6.00
POTD4 Neo-Spacian Flare Scarab SR .60 1.50
POTD5 Neo-Spacian Dark Panther SR .60 1.50
POTD5 Neo-Spacian Dark Panther UTR 3.00 8.00
POTD6 Chrysalis Dolphin C .10 .30
POTD7 Rallis The Star Bird C .10 .30
POTD8 Submarineroid R .40 1.00
POTD8 Submarineroid UTR 1.50 4.00
POTD9 Ambulanceroid C .10 .30
POTD10 Decoyroid C .10 .30
POTD11 Rescueroid C .10 .30
POTD12 Destiny Hero-Double Dude SR .60 1.50
POTD12 Destiny Hero-Double Dude UTR 1.50 4.00
POTD13 Destiny Hero-Defender C .10 .30
POTD14 Destiny Hero-Dogma SR .60 1.50
POTD14 Destiny Hero-Dogma UTR 4.00 10.00
POTD15 Destiny Hero-Blade Master C .10 .30
POTD16 Destiny Hero-Fear Monger C .10 .30
POTD17 Destiny Hero-Dasher R .40 1.00
POTD17 Destiny Hero Dasher UTR 1.50 4.00
POTD18 Black Ptera C .10 .30
POTD19 Black Stego C .10 .30
POTD20 Ultimate Tyranno SR .60 1.50
POTD20 Ultimate Tyranno UTR 2.00 5.00
POTD21 Miracle Jurassic Egg C .10 .30
POTD22 Babycerasaurus C .10 .30
POTD23 Bitelon C .10 .30
POTD24 Alien Grey C .10 .30
POTD25 Alien Skull C .10 .30
POTD26 Alien Hunter C .10 .30
POTD27 Alien Warrior R .40 1.00
POTD27 Alien Warrior UTR 2.00 5.00
POTD28 Alien Mother UTR 1.50 4.00
POTD28 Alien Mother R .40 1.00
POTD29 Cosmic Horror Gangi'el R .40 1.00
POTD29 Cosmic Horror Gangi'el UTR 1.50 4.00
POTD30 Flying Saucer Muusik'I C .10 .30
POTD31 Elemental Hero Aqua Neos UR 1.50 4.00
POTD31 Elemental Hero Aqua Neos UTR 1.50 4.00
POTD32 Elemental Hero Flare Neos UTR 4.00 10.00
POTD32 Elemental Hero Flare Neos UR 1.50 4.00
POTD33 Elemental Hero Dark Neos UR 1.50 4.00
POTD33 Elemental Hero Dark Neos UTR 5.00 12.00
POTD34 Chimeratech Overdragon UTR 8.00 20.00
POTD34 Chimeratech Overdragon UR 1.50 4.00
POTD35 Ambulance Rescueroid C .10 .30
POTD36 Super Vehicroid Jumbo Drill SR .60 1.50
POTD36 Super Vehicroid Jumbo Drill UTR 1.50 4.00
POTD37 Contact C .10 .30
POTD38 Fake Hero C .10 .30
POTD39 Spell Calling R .40 1.00
POTD39 Spell Calling UTR 1.50 4.00
POTD40 Vehicroid Connection Zone C .10 .30
POTD41 D-Spirit C .10 .30
POTD42 Overload Fusion R .60 1.50
POTD42 Overload Fusion UTR 5.00 12.00
POTD43 Cyclone Blade UTR 1.50 4.00
POTD43 Cyclone Blade R .40 1.00
POTD44 Future Fusion R .75 2.00
POTD44 Future Fusion UTR 5.00 12.00
POTD45 Common Soul C .10 .30
POTD46 Neo Space R .40 1.00
POTD46 Neo Space UTR 3.00 8.00
POTD47 Mausoleum of the Emperor C .10 .30
POTD48 Dark City R .40 1.00
POTD48 Dark City UTR 1.50 4.00
POTD49 Destiny Mirage C .10 .30
POTD50 D-Chain R .40 1.00
POTD50 D-Chain UTR 1.50 4.00
POTD51 Crop Circles C .10 .30
POTD52 The Paths of Destiny C .50 1.25
POTD53 Orbital Bombardment C .10 .30
POTD54 Royal Writ of Taxation C .10 .30
POTD55 Wonder Garage C .10 .30
POTD56 Supercharge R .40 1.00
POTD56 Supercharge UTR 1.50 4.00
POTD57 Cyber Summon Blaster R .40 1.00
POTD57 Cyber Summon Blaster UTR 1.50 4.00
POTD58 Fossil Excavation C .10 .30
POTD59 Synthetic Seraphim C .10 .30
POTD60 Brainwashing Beam C .10 .30

2006 Yu-Gi-Oh Cyberdark Impact 1st Edition

COMPLETE SET (60) 100.00 200.00
BOOSTER BOX (24 PACKS) 50.00 80.00
BOOSTER PACK (9 CARDS) 2.50 6.00
*UNLIMITED: .4X TO .8X 1ST EDITION
RELEASED ON NOVEMBER 15, 2006
CDIP1A Cyberdark Horn SR 1.25 3.00
CDIP1B Cyberdark Horn ULT 2.50 6.00
CDIP2A Cyberdark Edge SR 1.50 4.00
CDIP2B Cyberdark Edge ULT 4.00 10.00
CDIP3A Cyberdark Keel SR 1.25 3.00
CDIP3B Cyberdark Keel ULT 2.00 5.00
CDIP4 Cyber Ogre C .10 .30
CDIP5A Cyber Esper SR 1.00 2.50
CDIP5B Cyber Esper ULT 1.00 2.50
CDIP6 Allure Queen LV3 C .10 .30
CDIP7A Allure Queen LV5 R .40 1.00
CDIP7B Allure Queen LV5 ULT 2.00 5.00
CDIP8A Allure Queen LV7 UR 2.00 5.00
CDIP8B Allure Queen LV7 ULT 6.00 15.00
CDIP9 Dark Lucius LV4 C .10 .30
CDIP10A Dark Lucius LV6 R .40 1.00
CDIP10B Dark Lucius LV6 ULT 1.00 2.50
CDIP11A Dark Lucius LV8 UR 1.00 2.50
CDIP11B Dark Lucius LV8 ULT 2.50 6.00
CDIP12 Stray Asmodian C .10 .30
CDIP13 Abaki C .10 .30
CDIP14 Flame Ogre C .10 .30
CDIP15 Snipe Hunter C .40 1.00
CDIP16 Blast Asmodian C .10 .30
CDIP17 Vanity's Fiend R .40 1.00
CDIP17 Vanity's Fiend ULT 25.00 50.00
CDIP18 Barrier Statue of the Abyss C .10 .30
CDIP19 Barrier Statue of the Torrent C .10 .30
CDIP20 Barrier Statue of the Inferno C .10 .30
CDIP21 Barrier Statue of the Stormwinds C .10 .30
CDIP22 Barrier Statue of the Drought C .10 .30
CDIP23 Barrier Statue of the Heavens C .10 .30
CDIP24A Vanity's Ruler R 3.00 8.00
CDIP24B Vanity's Ruler ULT 6.00 15.00
CDIP25A Iris, the Earth Mother R .40 1.00
CDIP25B Iris, the Earth Mother ULT 1.00 2.50
CDIP26A Lightning Punisher R .40 1.00
CDIP26B Lightning Punisher ULT 1.00 2.50
CDIP27 Queen's Bodyguard C .10 .30
CDIP28 Combo Fighter C .10 .30
CDIP29A Combo Master R .40 1.00
CDIP29B Combo Master ULT 1.00 2.50
CDIP30 Man Beast of Ares C .10 .30
CDIP31A Rampaging Rhynos R .40 1.00
CDIP31B Rampaging Rhynos ULT 1.00 2.50
CDIP32A Storm Shooter SR .60 1.50
CDIP32B Storm Shooter ULT 1.00 2.50
CDIP33 Alien Infiltrator C .10 .30
CDIP34 Alien Mars C .10 .30
CDIP35A Cyberdark Dragon UR 2.00 5.00
CDIP35B Cyberdark Dragon ULT 15.00 30.00
CDIP36A Cyber Ogre 2 UR 1.25 3.00
CDIP36B Cyber Ogre 2 ULT 3.00 8.00
CDIP37 Corruption Cell A C .10 .30
CDIP38A Flash of the Forbidden Spell R .40 1.00
CDIP38B Flash of the Forbidden Spell ULT 1.00 2.50
CDIP39 Ritual Foregone C .10 .30
CDIP40 Instant Fusion C 2.50 6.00
CDIP41 Counter Cleaner C .10 .30
CDIP42 Linear Accelerator Cannon C .10 .30
CDIP43 Chain Strike C .10 .30
CDIP44A Miraculous Rebirth R .40 1.00
CDIP44B Miraculous Rebirth ULT 1.00 2.50
CDIP45 Mystical Wind Typhoon C .10 .30
CDIP46 Level Down!? C .10 .30
CDIP47A Degenerate Circuit R .40 1.00
CDIP47B Degenerate Circuit ULT 1.00 2.50
CDIP48 Senet Switch C .10 .30
CDIP49A Blasting Fuse R .40 1.00
CDIP49B Blasting Fuse ULT 1.00 2.50
CDIP50 Straight Flush C .10 .30
CDIP51 Justi-Break C .10 .30
CDIP52A Dimensional Inversion R .40 1.00
CDIP52B Dimensional Inversion ULT 1.00 2.50
CDIP53 Chain Healing C .10 .30
CDIP54 Chain Detonation C .10 .30
CDIP55 Byroad Sacrifice C .10 .30
CDIP56A Trojan Blast SR .60 1.50
CDIP56B Trojan Blast ULT 1.00 2.50
CDIP57 Accumulated Fortune C .10 .30
CDIP58A Cyber Shadow Gardna SR 1.00 2.50
CDIP58B Cyber Shadow Gardna ULT 3.00 8.00
CDIP59 Vanity's Call C .10 .30
CDIP60A Black Horn of Heaven R .50 1.25
CDIP60B Black Horn of Heaven ULT 5.00 12.00

2007 Yu-Gi-Oh Strike of Neos 1st Edition

COMPLETE SET (94) 150.00 300.00
BOOSTER BOX (24 PACKS) 80.00 120.00
BOOSTER PACK (9 CARDS) 2.50 6.00
*UNLIMITED: .4X TO .8X 1ST EDITION
RELEASED ON FEBRUARY 28, 2007
STON1A Gene-Warped Warwolf SR .75 2.00
STON1B Gene-Warped Warwolf UTR 1.50 4.00
STON2A Frostosaurus R .40 1.00
STON2B Frostosaurus UTR 2.00 5.00
STON3A Spiral Serpent R .40 1.00
STON3B Spiral Serpent UTR 1.00 2.50
STON4A Neo-Spacian Air Hummingbird SR .75 2.00
STON4B Neo-Spacian Air Hummingbird UTR 2.50 6.00
STON5A Neo-Spacian Grand Mole R .75 2.00
STON5B Neo-Spacian Grand Mole UTR 6.00 15.00
STON6 Neo-Spacian Glow Moss C .10 .30
STON7 The Six Samurai - Yaichi C .10 .30
STON8 The Six Samurai - Kamon C .10 .30
STON9 The Six Samurai - Yariza C .10 .30
STON10 The Six Samurai - Nisashi C .10 .30
STON11 The Six Samurai - Zanji C .10 .30
STON12 The Six Samurai - Irou C .10 .30
STON13A Great Shogun Shien SR .60 1.50
STON13B Great Shogun Shien UTR 3.00 8.00
STON14 Shien's Footsoldier C .10 .30
STON15A Sage of Silence R .40 1.00
STON15B Sage of Silence UTR 1.25 3.00
STON16 Sage of Stillness C .10 .30
STON17A Reign-Beaux, Overlord of Dark World UR 1.00 2.50
STON17B Reign-Beaux, Overlord of Dark World UTR 2.00 5.00
STON18 Kahkki, Guerilla of Dark World C .10 .30
STON19 Gren, Tactician of Dark World C .10 .30
STON20A Fusion Devourer R .40 1.00
STON20B Fusion Devourer UTR 1.00 2.50
STON21 Electric Virus C .10 .30
STON22 Puppet Plant C .10 .30
STON23 Marionette Mite C .10 .30
STON24A D.D. Crow R .40 1.00
STON24B D.D. Crow UTR 6.00 15.00
STON25 Silent Abyss C .10 .30
STON26 Firestorm Prominence C .10 .30
STON27 Raging Earth C .10 .30
STON28 Destruction Cyclone C .10 .30
STON29 Radiant Spirit C .10 .30
STON30 Umbral Soul C .10 .30
STON31 Alien Psychic C .10 .30
STON32 Lycanthrope C .10 .30
STON33 CÃ° Chulainn the Awakened C .10 .30
STON34A Elemental Hero Air Neos UR 8.00 20.00
STON34B Elemental Hero Air Neos UTR 15.00 30.00
STON35A Elemental Hero Grand Neos UR 1.00 2.50
STON35B Elemental Hero Grand Neos UTR 5.00 12.00
STON36A Elemental Hero Glow Neos UR 1.50 4.00
STON36B Elemental Hero Glow Neos UTR 3.00 8.00
STON37A Ancient Rules R 2.00 5.00
STON37B Ancient Rules UTR 6.00 15.00
STON38A Dark World Dealings SR 2.00 5.00
STON38B Dark World Dealings UTR 8.00 20.00
STON39A Neos Force R .40 1.00
STON39B Neos Force UTR 1.00 2.50
STON40 Legendary Ebon Steed C .10 .30
STON41 A Cell Scatter Burst C .10 .30
STON42A Twister R .40 1.00
STON42B Twister UTR 2.50 6.00
STON43 Synthesis Spell C .10 .30
STON44 Emblem of the Awakening C .10 .30
STON45 Advanced Ritual Art C .10 .30
STON46A Card Trader SR .60 1.50
STON46B Card Trader UTR 1.25 3.00
STON47 Shienâ•™s Castle of Mist C .10 .30
STON48A Skyscraper 2 - Hero City SR 1.25 3.00
STON48B Skyscraper 2 - Hero City UTR 2.00 5.00
STON49 Change of Hero - Reflector Ray C .10 .30
STON50A Hero Medal R .40 1.00
STON50B Hero Medal UTR 1.00 2.50
STON51 Return of the Six Samurai C .10 .30
STON52A Eliminating the League R .40 1.00
STON52B Eliminating the League UTR 1.00 2.50
STON53 Flashbang C .10 .30
STON54A The Transmigration Prophecy R .40 1.00
STON54B The Transmigration Prophecy UTR 2.00 5.00
STON55 Anti-Fusion Device C .10 .30
STON56 Ritual Sealing C .10 .30
STON57A Birthright SR .60 1.50
STON57B Birthright UTR 1.00 2.50
STON58 Swift Samurai Storm! .10 .30
STON59A Cloak and Dagger R .40 1.00
STON59B Cloak and Dagger UTR 1.50 4.00
STON60A Pulling the Rug R .40 1.00
STON60B Pulling the Rug UTR 2.00 5.00
STON61 Neo-Parshath, Sky Paladin SCR 2.00 5.00
STON62 Meltiel, Sage of the Sky SCR 4.00 10.00
STON63 Harvest Angel of Wisdom SCR 2.00 5.00
STON64 Freya, Spirit of Victory SCR 6.00 15.00
STON65 Nova Summoner SCR 2.50 6.00
STON66 Radiant Jeral SCR 1.50 4.00
STON67 Gellenduo SCR 5.00 12.00
STON68 Aegis of Gaia SCR 1.25 3.00
STON0 Grandmaster of Six Samurai SCR 8.00 20.00

2007 Yu-Gi-Oh Force of the Breaker 1st Edition

COMPLETE SET (94) 150.00 400.00
BOOSTER BOX (24 PACKS) 140.00 200.00
BOOSTER PACK (9 CARDS) 2.50 6.00
*UNLIMITED: .4X TO .8X 1ST EDITION
RELEASED ON MAY 16, 2007
FOTB00 Volcanic Rocket SCR 15.00 30.00
FOTB01 Crystal Beast Ruby Carbuncle C .20 .50
FOTB02 Crystal Beast Amethyst Cat C .20 .50
FOTB03 Crystal Beast Emerald Tortoise C .20 .50
FOTB04 Crystal Beast Topaz Tiger R .60 1.50
FOTB04 Crystal Beast Topaz Tiger UTR 8.00 20.00
FOTB05 Crystal Beast Amber Mammoth C .20 .50
FOTB06 Crystal Beast Cobalt Eagle C .20 .50
FOTB07 Crystal Beast Sapphire Pegasus UR 2.00 5.00
FOTB07 Crystal Beast Sapphire Pegasus UTR 15.00 30.00
FOTB08 Volcanic Doomfire UR 1.25 3.00
FOTB08 Volcanic Doomfire UTR 2.50 6.00
FOTB09 Volcanic Shell R 1.50 4.00
FOTB09 Volcanic Shell UTR 5.00 12.00
FOTB10 Volcanic Scattershot C .20 .50
FOTB11 Volcanic Blaster C .20 .50
FOTB12 Volcanic Slicer R .60 1.50
FOTB12 Volcanic Slicer UTR 2.50 6.00
FOTB13 Volcanic Hammerer C .20 .50
FOTB14 Elemental Hero Captain Gold UR .75 2.00
FOTB14 Elemental Hero Captain Gold UTR 2.00 5.00
FOTB15 Gravekeeper's Commandant R .75 2.00
FOTB15 Gravekeeper's Commandant UTR 3.00 8.00
FOTB16 Warrior of Atlantis R .40 1.00
FOTB16 Warrior of Atlantis UTR 1.25 3.00
FOTB17 Destroyersaurus R .60 1.50
FOTB17 Destroyersaurus UTR .75 2.00
FOTB18 Zeradias, Herald of Heaven R .60 1.50
FOTB18 Zeradias, Herald of Heaven UTR 5.00 12.00
FOTB19 Archfiend General R .75 2.00
FOTB19 Archfiend General UTR 1.50 4.00
FOTB20 Harpie Queen R 1.50 4.00
FOTB20 Harpie Queen UTR 20.00 40.00
FOTB21 Sky Scourge Enrise SR .60 1.50
FOTB21 Sky Scourge Enrise UTR 1.00 2.50
FOTB22 Sky Scourge Norleras SR .60 1.50
FOTB22 Sky Scourge Norleras UTR 8.00 20.00
FOTB23 Sky Scourge Invicil SR .60 1.50
FOTB23 Sky Scourge Invicil UTR 1.25 3.00
FOTB24 Goe Goe the Gallant Ninja R .40 1.00
FOTB24 Goe Goe the Gallant Ninja UTR .75 2.00
FOTB25 Mei-Kou, Master of Barriers C .20 .50
FOTB26 Raiza the Storm Monarch SR 1.25 3.00
FOTB26 Raiza the Storm Monarch UTR 6.00 15.00
FOTB27 Seismic Crasher C .20 .50
FOTB28 Dweller in the Depths C .20 .50
FOTB29 Magna-Slash Dragon C .20 .50
FOTB30 Gravi-Crush Dragon C .20 .50
FOTB31 Soul of Fire SR .60 1.50
FOTB31 Soul of Fire UTR .75 2.00
FOTB32 Crystal Beacon C .20 .50
FOTB33 Rare Value UR .75 2.00
FOTB33 Rare Value UTR 3.00 8.00
FOTB34 Crystal Blessing C .20 .50
FOTB35 Crystal Abundance C .20 .50
FOTB36 Crystal Promise C .20 .50
FOTB37 Lucky Iron Axe R .40 1.00
FOTB37 Lucky Iron Axe UTR 1.00 2.50
FOTB38 Tornado C .20 .50
FOTB39 Wild Fire C .20 .50
FOTB40 Blaze Accelerator C .20 .50
FOTB41 Tri-Blaze Accelerator SR 1.00 2.50
FOTB41 Tri-Blaze Accelerator UTR 2.00 5.00
FOTB42 Field Barrier C .20 .50
FOTB43 A Cell Breeding Device C .20 .50
FOTB44 Otherworld - The A Zone C .20 .50
FOTB45 Ancient City - Rainbow Ruins R .40 1.00
FOTB45 Ancient City - Rainbow Ruins UTR 8.00 20.00
FOTB46 Triggered Summon UTR 1.00 2.50
FOTB46 Triggered Summon R .40 1.00
FOTB47 Last Resort C .20 .50
FOTB48 Crystal Raigeki C .20 .50
FOTB49 Volcanic Recharge C .20 .50
FOTB50 Terrible Deal C .20 .50
FOTB51 Breakthrough! C .20 .50
FOTB52 Backs to the Wall C .20 .50
FOTB53 Introduction to Gallantry C .20 .50
FOTB54 Secrets of the Gallant C .20 .50
FOTB55 Radiant Mirror Force SR .75 2.00
FOTB55 Radiant Mirror Force UTR 3.00 8.00
FOTB56 Hard-sellin' Goblin C .20 .50
FOTB57 Hard-sellin' Zombie C .20 .50
FOTB58 Mass Hypnosis C .20 .50
FOTB59 Gem Flash Energy C .20 .50
FOTB60 Firewall R .40 1.00
FOTB60 Firewall UTR 1.00 2.50
FOTB61 Diabolos, King of the Abyss SCR 3.00 8.00
FOTB62 Lich Lord, King SCR 1.25 3.00
FOTB63 Prometheus, King of the Shadows SCR 1.50 4.00
FOTB64 Mist Archfield SCR 2.00 5.00
FOTB65 Plague Wolf SCR 1.00 2.50
FOTB66 Recurring Nightmare SCR 5.00 12.00
FOTB67 Sword of Dark Rites SCR 1.25 3.00
FOTB68 Eradicator Epidemic SCR 8.00 20.00

2007 Yu-Gi-Oh Tactical Evolution 1st Edition

COMPLETE SET (103) 150.00 300.00
BOOSTER BOX (24 PACKS) 80.00 120.00
BOOSTER PACK (9 CARDS) 2.50 6.00
*UNLIMITED: .4X TO .8X 1ST EDITION
RELEASED ON AUGUST 15, 2007
TAEV01 Alien Shocktrooper C .10 .30
TAEV02 Volcanic Rat C .10 .30
TAEV03 Renge Gatekeeper Dark World C .10 .30
TAEV04 Hunter Dragon R .40 1.00
TAEV05 Venom Cobra C .10 .30
TAEV06 Rainbow Dragon SCR 6.00 15.00
TAEV06 Rainbow Dragon GR 40.00 80.00
TAEV07 Chrysalis Pantail C .10 .30
TAEV08 Chrysalis Chicky C .10 .30
TAEV09 Chrysalis Pinny C .10 .30
TAEV10 Chrysalis Larva C .10 .30
TAEV11 Chrysalis Mole C .10 .30
TAEV12 Necro Gardna SR .75 2.00
TAEV12 Necro Gardna UTR 2.50 6.00
TAEV13 Vennominaga Deity of Pois.Snakes SCR 30.00 60.00
TAEV14 Vennominon King of Pois.Snakes UR .75 2.00
TAEV14 Vennominon King of Pois. Snakes UTR 2.00 5.00
TAEV15 Venom Snake C .10 .30
TAEV16 Venom Boa C .10 .30
TAEV17 Venom Serpent C .10 .30
TAEV18 Elemental Hero Neos Alius SR 1.00 2.50
TAEV18 Elemental Hero Neos Alius UTR 4.00 10.00
TAEV19 Chthonian Emperor Dragon UTR 1.50 4.00
TAEV19 Chthonian Emperor Dragon UR 1.25 3.00
TAEV20 Aquarian Alessa SR .60 1.50
TAEV20 Aquarian Alessa UTR 1.00 2.50
TAEV21 Lucky Pied Piper UTR 1.00 2.50
TAEV21 Lucky Pied Piper SR 1.50 4.00
TAEV22 Grasschopper R .40 1.00
TAEV23 Goggle Golem C .10 .30
TAEV24 Dawnbreak Gardna C .10 .30
TAEV25 Doom Shaman SR .60 1.50
TAEV25 Doom Shaman UTR 1.00 2.50
TAEV26 King Pyron C .10 .30
TAEV27 Shadow Delver C .10 .30
TAEV28 Flint Lock C .10 .30
TAEV29 Gravitic Orb C .10 .30
TAEV30 Phantom Cricket C .10 .30
TAEV31 Crystal Seer UR .75 2.00
TAEV31 Crystal Seer UTR .75 2.00
TAEV32 Neo Space Pathfinder R .60 1.50
TAEV33 Frost and Flame Dragon SCR 2.00 5.00
TAEV34 Desert Twister UR .75 2.00
TAEV34 Desert Twister UTR .75 2.00
TAEV35 Ritual Raven C .10 .30
TAEV36 Razor Lizard C .10 .30
TAEV37 Light Effigy C .10 .30
TAEV38 Dark Effigy C .10 .30
TAEV39 Zombie Master SR 1.25 3.00
TAEV39 Zombie Master UTR 15.00 30.00
TAEV40 Neo-Spacian Marine Dolphin C .10 .30
TAEV41 Elemental Hero Marine Neos R .40 1.00
TAEV42 Elemental Hero Darkbright UR 1.25 3.00
TAEV42 Elemental Hero Darkbright UTR 4.00 10.00
TAEV43 Elemental Hero Magma Neos SCR 8.00 20.00
TAEV44 Ojama Knight C .10 .30
TAEV45 Fifth Hope SR .75 2.00
TAEV45 Fifth Hope UTR 1.50 4.00
TAEV46 Reverse of Neos C .10 .30
TAEV47 Convert Contract C .10 .30
TAEV48 Cocoon Party C .10 .30
TAEV49 NEX C .10 .30
TAEV50 Cocoon Rebirth C .10 .30
TAEV52 Snake Rain R .75 2.00
TAEV53 Venom Shot C .10 .30
TAEV54 Cyberdark Impact! SCR 15.00 30.00
TAEV55 Flint Missile C .10 .30
TAEV56 Double Summon R 1.25 3.00
TAEV57 Summoner's Art R .40 1.00
TAEV58 Creature Seizure C .10 .30
TAEV59 Phalanx Pike R 1.25 3.00
TAEV60 Symbols of Duty R .40 1.00
TAEV61 Amulet of Ambition C .10 .30
TAEV62 Broken Bamboo Sword C 1.25 3.00
TAEV63 Mirror Gate SR .60 1.50
TAEV63 Mirror Gate UTR 1.00 2.50
TAEV64 Hero Counterattack C .10 .30
TAEV65 Cocoon Veil C .10 .30
TAEV66 Snake Whistle C .10 .30
TAEV67 Damage = Reptile R .40 1.00
TAEV68 Snake Deity's Command R .40 1.00
TAEV69 Rise of the Snake Deity C .10 .30
TAEV70 Ambush Fangs C .10 .30
TAEV71 Venom Burn C .10 .30
TAEV72 Common Charity R .40 1.00
TAEV73 Destructive Draw C .10 .30
TAEV74 Shield Spear C .10 .30
TAEV75 Strike Slash C .10 .30
TAEV76 Spell Reclamation R .40 1.00
TAEV77 Trap Reclamation R .40 1.00
TAEV78 Gift Card C 1.50 4.00
TAEV79 The Gift of Greed C .10 .30
TAEV80 Counter Counter C .10 .30
TAEV81 Ocean's Keeper R .40 1.00
TAEV82 Thousand-Eyes Jellyfish R .40 1.00
TAEV83 Cranium Fish SCR 1.50 4.00
TAEV84 Abyssal Kingshark SCR 1.25 3.00
TAEV85 Mormolith SCR .75 2.00
TAEV86 Fossil Tusker R .40 1.00
TAEV87 Phantom Dragonray Bronto R .40 1.00
TAEV88 Il Blud SCR 4.00 10.00
TAEV89 Blazewing Butterfly SR .60 1.50
TAEV89 Blazewing Butterfly UTR 1.00 2.50
TAEV000 Gemini Summoner SCR 1.25 3.00
TAEV000 Gemini Summoner SR 2.00 5.00

2007 Yu-Gi-Oh Gladiator's Assault 1st Edition

COMPLETE SET (110) 300.00 600.00
BOOSTER BOX (24 PACKS) 125.00 200.00
BOOSTER PACK (9 CARDS) 2.50 6.00
*UNLIMITED: .4X TO .8X 1ST EDITION
RELEASED ON NOVEMBER 14, 2007
GLAS0 Gladiator Beast Octavius SCR 1.50 4.00
GLAS1 Chamberlain of Six Samurai C .20 .50
GLAS2 Cloudian Smoke Ball C .20 .50
GLAS3 Evil Hero Malicious Edge SR .60 1.50
GLAS3 Evil Hero Malicious Edge UTR 2.00 5.00
GLAS4 Evil Hero Infernal Gainer R .40 1.00
GLAS5 Cloudian Eye of Typhoon SR .60 1.50
GLAS5 Cloudian Eye of Typhoon UTR 1.00 2.50
GLAS6 Cloudian Ghost Fog C .20 .50
GLAS7 Cloudian Nimbusman C .20 .50
GLAS8 Cloudian Sheep Cloud SR .60 1.50
GLAS8 Cloudian Sheep Cloud UTR 1.00 2.50
GLAS9 Cloudian Poison Cloud C .20 .50
GLAS10 Cloudian Acid Cloud R .40 1.00
GLAS11 Cloudian Cirrostratus R .75 2.00
GLAS12 Cloudian Altus R .40 1.00
GLAS13 Cloudian Turbulence C .20 .50
GLAS14 Truckroid C .20 .50
GLAS15 Stealthroid C .20 .50
GLAS16 Expressroid R .40 1.00
GLAS17 Gladiator Beast Alexander SR .60 1.50
GLAS17 Gladiator Beast Alexander UTR 1.00 2.50
GLAS18 Gladiator Beast Spartacus R .40 1.00
GLAS19 Gladiator Beast Murmillo R .40 1.00
GLAS20 Gladiator Beast Bestiari C .20 .50
GLAS21 Gladiator Beast Laquari R .60 1.50
GLAS22 Gladiator Beast Hoplomus C .20 .50
GLAS23 Gladiator Beast Dimacari C .20 .50
GLAS24 Gladiator Beast Secutor C .20 .50
GLAS25 Test Ape C .20 .50
GLAS26 Witch Doctor of Sparta C .20 .50
GLAS27 Infinity Dark C .20 .50
GLAS28 Magical Reflect Slime C .20 .50
GLAS29 Ancient Gear Knight C .20 .50
GLAS30 Goblin Black Ops R .40 1.00
GLAS31 Gambler of Legend C .20 .50
GLAS32 Enishi, Shiens Chancellor UR .75 2.00
GLAS32 Enishi, Shiens Chancellor UTR 1.50 4.00
GLAS33 Spirit of the Six Samurai C .20 .50
GLAS34 Alien Telepath R .40 1.00
GLAS35 Alien Hypno C .20 .50
GLAS36 Elemental Hero Chaos Neos SCR 2.00 5.00
GLAS36 Elemental Hero Chaos Neos GR 8.00 20.00
GLAS36 Elemental Hero Chaos Neos (Rainbow Dragon Err) GR 100.00 150.00
GLAS37 Elemental Hero Plasma Vice SCR 2.50 6.00
GLAS38 Evil Hero Inferno Wing UR .75 2.00
GLAS38 Evil Hero Inferno Wing UTR 2.00 5.00
GLAS39 Evil Hero Lightning Golem UR .75 2.00
GLAS39 Evil Hero Lightning Golem UTR 1.25 3.00
GLAS40 Evil Hero Dark Gaia R .40 1.00
GLAS41 Super Vehicroid Stealth Union SCR 4.00 10.00
GLAS42 Superalloy Beast Raptinus C .20 .50
GLAS43 Gladiator Beast Gaiodiaz R .40 1.00
GLAS44 Gladiator Beast Heraklinos SCR 4.00 10.00
GLAS45 Contact Out C .20 .50
GLAS46 Swing of Memories C .20 .50
GLAS47 Dark Fusion R 1.50 4.00
GLAS48 Diamond-Dust Cyclone R .40 1.00
GLAS49 Summon Cloud C .20 .50
GLAS50 Lucky Cloud C .20 .50
GLAS51 Fog Control C .20 .50
GLAS52 Cloudian Squall C .20 .50
GLAS53 Super Double Summon C .20 .50
GLAS54 Colosseum Cage Gladiatr Beasts R 1.25 3.00
GLAS55 Glad.Beasts Bttle Halberd C .20 .50
GLAS56 Glad. Beasts Battle Gladius C .20 .50
GLAS57 Glad.Beasts Battle Manica R .40 1.00
GLAS58 Gladiator Beasts Respite R .40 1.00
GLAS59 Gladiators Return C .20 .50
GLAS60 Soul Devouring Bamboo Sword C .20 .50
GLAS61 Cunning of the Six Samurai SR .60 1.50
GLAS61 Cunning of the Six Samurai UTR 1.50 4.00
GLAS62 A Cell Incubator C .20 .50
GLAS63 Over Limit C .20 .50
GLAS64 No Entry!! C .20 .50
GLAS65 Natural Disaster C .20 .50
GLAS66 Rain Storm C .20 .50
GLAS67 Updraft SR .60 1.50
GLAS67 Updraft UTR 1.00 2.50
GLAS68 Release from Stone C .20 .50
GLAS69 Light-Imprisoning Mirror C .60 1.50
GLAS70 Shadow-Imprisoning Mirror C .60 1.50
GLAS71 Disarm C .20 .50
GLAS72 Parry C .20 .50
GLAS73 Swiftstrike Armor C .20 .50
GLAS74 DoubleEdged Sword Tech C .20 .50
GLAS75 Energy-Absorbing Monolith SR .60 1.50
GLAS75 Energy-Absorbing Monolith UTR 1.00 2.50
GLAS76 Cell Explosion Virus R .40 1.00
GLAS77 Detonator Circle A C .20 .50
GLAS78 Interdimensional Warp C .20 .50
GLAS79 Foolish Revival C .20 .50
GLAS80 An Unfortunate Report C .20 .50
GLAS81 Gladiator Beast Torax SR .60 1.50
GLAS81 Gladiator Beast Torax UTR 1.00 2.50
GLAS82 Test Tiger UR .75 2.00
GLAS82 Test Tiger UTR 4.00 10.00
GLAS83 Defensive Tactics SR .60 1.50
GLAS83 Defensive Tactics UTR 1.00 2.50
GLAS84 Dragon Ice SCR 4.00 10.00
GLAS85 Tongue Twister SCR 4.00 10.00
GLAS86 Skreech SCR 1.50 4.00
GLAS87 Royal Firestorm Guards SCR 15.00 30.00
GLAS88 Veil of Darkness SCR 2.00 5.00
GLAS89 Security Orb UR .75 2.00
GLAS89 Security Orb UTR 25.00 50.00
GLAS90 Necroface SCR 40.00 80.00
GLAS91 Gil Garth SCR 8.00 20.00
GLAS92 Soul Taker SCR 20.00 40.00
GLAS93 Magic Formula SCR 40.00 80.00
GLAS94 Silent Doom SCR 15.00 30.00

2008 Yu-Gi-Oh Phantom Darkness 1st Edition

COMPLETE SET (109) 200.00 400.00
BOOSTER BOX (24 PACKS) 300.00 500.00
BOOSTER PACK (9 CARDS) 3.00 8.00
*UNLIMITED: .4X TO .8X 1ST EDITION
RELEASED ON FEBRUARY 13, 2008
PTDN0 Dark Grepher SCR 6.00 15.00
PTDN2 Atlantean Pikeman C .10 .30
PTDN3 Rainbow Dark Dragon SCR 5.00 12.00
PTDN4 Samsara Lotus C .10 .30
PTDN5 Regenerating Rose C .10 .30
PTDN6 Yubel SR 1.00 2.50
PTDN7 Yubel - Terror Incarnate UR 1.00 2.50
PTDN7 Yubel - Terror Incarnate UTR 1.25 3.00

PTDN8 Yubel - The Ultimate Nightmare SCR 4.00 10.00
PTDN9 Armored Cybern C .10 .30
PTDN10 Cyber Valley SR 1.00 2.50
PTDN11 Cyber Ouroboros C .10 .30
PTDN12 Volcanic Counter SR .60 1.50
PTDN13 Fire Trooper C .10 .30
PTDN14 Destiny Hero - Dunker C .10 .30
PTDN15 Destiny Hero - Departed C .10 .30
PTDN16 Dark Horus UR 1.00 2.50
PTDN16 Dark Horus UTR 1.25 3.00
PTDN17 The Dark Creator SCR 3.00 8.00
PTDN18 Dark Nephthys UR .75 2.00
PTDN18 Dark Nephthys UTR 1.00 2.50
PTDN19 Dark Armed Dragon SCR 25.00 50.00
PTDN20 Dark Crusader C .10 .30
PTDN21 Armageddon Knight SR 1.50 4.00
PTDN22 Doomsday Horror SR .60 1.50
PTDN23 Obsidian Dragon C .10 .30
PTDN24 Shadowpriestess of Ohm R .40 1.00
PTDN25 Gemini Lancer C .10 .30
PTDN26 Gigaplant R 2.00 5.00
PTDN27 Future Samurai R .40 1.00
PTDN28 Vengeful Shinobi C .10 .30
PTDN29 The Immortal Bushi C .10 .30
PTDN30 Field-Commander Rahz SR .60 1.50
PTDN31 Gladiator Beast Darius C .10 .30
PTDN32 Imprisoned Queen Archfiend C .10 .30
PTDN33 Black Veloci C .10 .30
PTDN34 Superancient Deepsea King Coelacanth UR .75 2.00
PTDN34 Superancient Deepsea King Coelacanth UTR 1.25 3.00
PTDN35 Cannon Soldier MK-2 C .10 .30
PTDN36 The Calculator C .10 .30
PTDN37 Sea Koala C .10 .30
PTDN38 Blue Thunder T-45 C .10 .30
PTDN39 Magnetic Mosquito C .10 .30
PTDN40 Earth Effigy C .10 .30
PTDN41 Wind Effigy C .10 .30
PTDN42 Neo-Spacian Twinkle Moss C .10 .30
PTDN43 Elemental Hero Storm Neos SR .75 2.00
PTDN44 Rainbow Neos SCR 3.00 8.00
PTDN44 Rainbow Neos GR 10.00 25.00
PTDN45 Rainbow Veil C .10 .30
PTDN46 Super Polymerization R .75 2.00
PTDN47 Vicious Claw C .10 .30
PTDN48 Instant Neo Space C .10 .30
PTDN49 Mirage Tube C .10 .30
PTDN50 Spell Chronicle C .10 .30
PTDN51 Dimension Explosion C .10 .30
PTDN52 Cybernetic Zone C .10 .30
PTDN53 The Beginning of the End UR .75 2.00
PTDN53 The Beginning of the End UTR 2.50 6.00
PTDN54 Dark Eruption SR .75 2.00
PTDN55 Fires of Doomsday R 1.25 3.00
PTDN56 Unleash Your Power! C .10 .30
PTDN57 Chain Summoning C .10 .30
PTDN58 Acidic Downpour C .10 .30
PTDN59 Six Samurai United R .75 2.00
PTDN60 Gladiator Beast's Battle Archf.Shield C .10 .30
PTDN61 Gladiator Proving Ground C .10 .30
PTDN62 Dark World Grimoire C .10 .30
PTDN63 Rainbow Path C .10 .30
PTDN64 Rainbow Life R .75 2.00
PTDN65 Sinister Seeds C .10 .30
PTDN66 Hate Buster R .40 1.00
PTDN67 Chain Material C .10 .30
PTDN68 Alchemy Cycle C .10 .30
PTDN69 Cybernetic Hidden Technology C .10 .30
PTDN70 Dark Spirit Art - Greed R .40 1.00
PTDN71 Dark Illusion R 1.00 2.50
PTDN72 Escape from Dark Dimension SR 1.50 4.00
PTDN73 Gemini Trap Hole C .10 .30
PTDN74 Drastic Drop Off UR 1.25 3.00
PTDN74 Drastic Drop Off UTR 6.00 15.00
PTDN75 All-Out Attacks C .10 .30
PTDN76 Double Tag Team C .10 .30
PTDN77 Offering to the Snake Deity R .40 1.00
PTDN78 Cry Havoc! R .40 1.00
PTDN79 Transmigration Break C .10 .30
PTDN80 Fine C .10 .30
PTDN81 Darklord Zerato SCR 2.00 5.00
PTDN82 Darknight Parshath UR .75 2.00
PTDN82 Darknight Parshath UTR 1.00 2.50
PTDN83 Deepsea Macrotrema R .40 1.00
PTDN84 Allure of Darkness UTR 30.00 60.00
PTDN84 Allure of Darkness UR 8.00 20.00
PTDN85 Metabo Globster R .40 1.00
PTDN86 Golden Flying Fish SR .60 1.50
PTDN87 Prime Material Dragon SR 1.00 2.50
PTDN88 Lonefire Blossom R 1.50 4.00
PTDN89 Aztekipede, the Worm Warrior R .40 1.00
PTDN90 Vampire's Curse UR 1.00 2.50
PTDN90 Vampire's Curse UTR 1.00 2.50
PTDN91 Castle Gate R .40 1.00
PTDN92 Dark-Eyes Illusionist R .40 1.00
PTDN93 Legendary Fiend R .40 1.00
PTDN94 Metal Reflect Slime UR 2.00 5.00
PTDN94 Metal Reflect Slime UTR 2.50 6.00
PTDN95 Zoma the Spirit SR .75 2.00
PTDN96 Call of the Earthbound R .40 1.00
PTDN97 Dark Red Enchanter SCR 3.00 8.00
PTDN98 Goblin Zombie SCR 8.00 20.00
PTDN99 Belial Marquis of Darkness SCR 1.50 4.00

2008 Yu-Gi-Oh Light of Destruction 1st Edition

COMPLETE SET (100) 150.00 400.00
BOOSTER BOX (24 PACKS) 200.00 400.00
BOOSTER PACK (9 CARDS) 3.00 8.00
*UNLIMITED: .4X TO .8X 1ST EDITION
RELEASED ON MAY 13, 2008
LODT1 Honest SCR 10.00 25.00
LODT1 Honest GR 30.00 60.00
LODT2 Cross Porter C .15 .25
LODT3 Miracle Flipper C .15 .25
LODT4 Destiny Hero - Dread Servant C .15 .25
LODT5 Volcanic Queen C .15 .25
LODT6 Jinzo - Returner R 1.50 4.00
LODT7 Jinzo - Lord SR 1.50 4.00
LODT8 Arcana Force 0 - The Fool C .15 .25
LODT9 Arcana Force I - The Magician C .15 .25
LODT00 Guardian of Order SCR 4.00 10.00
LODT10 Arcana Force III - The Empress C .15 .25
LODT11 Arcana Force IV - The Emperor C .15 .25
LODT12 Arcana Force VI - The Lovers C .15 .25
LODT13 Arcana Force VII - The Chariot C .15 .25
LODT14 Arcana Force XIV - Temperance R .40 1.00
LODT15 Arcana Force XVIII - The Moon C .15 .25
LODT16 Arcana Force XXI - The World UR 1.50 4.00
LODT16 Arcana Force XXI - The World UTR 2.50 6.00
LODT17 Arcana Force EX - The Dark Ruler SCR 2.00 5.00
LODT19 Lyla, Lightsworn Sorceress UR 3.00 8.00
LODT19 Lyla, Lightsworn Sorceress UTR 8.00 20.00
LODT20 Garoth, Lightsworn Warrior C .15 .25
LODT21 Lumina, Lightsworn Summoner R .40 1.00
LODT22 Ryko, Lightsworn Hunter SR .40 1.00
LODT23 Wulf, Lightsworn Beast SR .40 1.00
LODT24 Celestia, Lightsworn Angel UR .75 2.00
LODT24 Celestia, Lightsworn Angel UTR 1.50 4.00
LODT25 Gragonith, Lightsworn Dragon C .15 .25
LODT26 Judgment Dragon SCR 15.00 30.00
LODT27 Dark Valkyria R .40 1.00
LODT28 Substitoad R .15 .25
LODT29 Unifrog C .15 .25
LODT30 Batteryman Charger C .15 .25
LODT31 Batteryman Industrial Strength R .50 1.25
LODT32 Batteryman Micro-Cell C .15 .25
LODT33 Goblin Recon Squad C .15 .25
LODT34 Interplanetary Invader A C .15 .25
LODT35 Diskblade Rider R .40 1.00
LODT36 Golden Ladybug R 1.25 3.00
LODT37 DUCKER Mobile Cannon SR .75 2.00
LODT38 The Lady in Wight C .15 .25
LODT39 Simorgh, Bird of Ancestry R .40 1.00
LODT40 Cloudian - Storm Dragon C .15 .25
LODT41 Phantom Dragon UR .40 1.00
LODT41 Phantom Dragon UTR .40 1.00
LODT42 Destiny End Dragoon UTR 2.50 6.00
LODT42 Destiny End Dragoon UR 1.25 3.00
LODT43 Ultimate Ancient Gear Golem UR 5.00 12.00
LODT43 Ultimate Ancient Gear Golem UTR 5.00 12.00
LODT44 Gladiator Beast Gyzarus SR .40 1.00
LODT45 Hero Mask C .15 .25
LODT46 Space Gift C .15 .25
LODT47 Demise of the Land C .15 .25
LODT48 D - Formation C .15 .25
LODT49 Spell Gear C .15 .25
LODT50 Cup of Ace C .15 .25
LODT51 Light Barrier R .15 .25
LODT52 Solar Recharge UR 2.00 5.00
LODT52 Solar Recharge UTR 8.00 20.00
LODT53 Realm of Light C .15 .25
LODT54 Wetlands C .15 .25
LODT55 Quick Charger C .15 .25
LODT56 Short Circuit C .15 .25
LODT57 Light of Redemption SR .40 1.00
LODT58 Mystical Cards of Light C .15 .25
LODT59 Level Tuning C .15 .25
LODT60 Deck Lockdown R .75 2.00
LODT61 Ribbon of Rebirth R .20 .50
LODT62 Golden Bamboo Sword C .15 .25
LODT63 Limit Reverse C .15 .25
LODT64 Hero Blast R .20 .50
LODT65 Rainbow Gravity C .15 .25
LODT66 D - Fortune C .15 .25
LODT67 Reversal of Fate C .15 .25
LODT68 Tour of Doom C .15 .25
LODT69 Arcana Call C .15 .25
LODT70 Light Spiral C .15 .25
LODT71 Glorious Illusion R .20 .50
LODT72 Destruction Jammer R 1.25 3.00
LODT73 Froggy Forcefield R .20 .50
LODT74 Portable Battery Pack C .15 .25
LODT75 Gladiator Lash C .15 .25
LODT76 Raging Cloudian C .15 .25
LODT77 Sanguine Swamp C .15 .25
LODT78 Lucky Chance C .15 .25
LODT79 Summon Limit C .15 .25
LODT80 Dice Try! C .15 .25
LODT81 Aurkus, Lightsworn Druid SR .75 2.00
LODT82 Ehren, Lightsworn Monk SCR 4.00 10.00
LODT83 Dark General Freed SCR 1.25 3.00
LODT84 Magical Exemplar SR 1.25 3.00
LODT85 Maniacal Servant R .20 .50
LODT86 Nimble Musasabi R .20 .50
LODT87 Flame Spirit Ignis R .20 .50
LODT88 Super-Ancient Dinobeast UR 1.25 3.00
LODT88 Super-Ancient Dinobeast UTR 1.25 3.00
LODT89 Vanquishing Light SR .60 1.50
LODT90 Tualatin SCR 2.00 5.00
LODT91 Divine Knight Ishzark SR .40 1.00
LODT92 Angel O7 SCR 2.00 5.00
LODT93 Union Attack SR .60 1.50
LODT94 Owner's Seal R 4.00 10.00
LODT95 Helios Trice Megistus SR .60 1.50
LODT96 Dangerous Machine Type-6 UR .40 1.00
LODT96 Dangerous Machine Type-6 UTR .40 1.00
LODT97 Maximum Six UTR .40 1.00
LODT97 Maximum Six UR .40 1.00
LODT98 Fog King SCR 10.00 25.00
LODT99 Fossil Dyna Pachycephalo SCR 6.00 15.00

2008 Yu-Gi-Oh The Duelist Genesis 1st Edition

COMPLETE SET (100) 200.00 400.00
BOOSTER BOX (24 PACKS) 70.00 100.00
BOOSTER PACK (9 CARDS) 3.00 8.00
*UNLIMITED: .4X TO .8X 1ST EDITION
RELEASED ON SEPTEMBER 2, 2008
TDGS000 Avenging Knight Parshath SCR 1.50 4.00
TDGS001 Turbo Booster C .10 .30
TDGS002 Nitro Synchron SR .40 1.00
TDGS003 Quillbolt Hedgehog C .10 .30
TDGS004 Ghost Gardna C .10 .30
TDGS005 Shield Warrior R .40 1.00
TDGS006 Small Piece Golem C .10 .30
TDGS007 Medium Piece Golem C .10 .30
TDGS008 Big Piece Golem R .40 1.00
TDGS009 Sinister Sprocket SR .30 .75
TDGS010 Dark Resonator R .40 1.00
TDGS011 Twin-Shield Defender C .10 .30
TDGS012 Jutte Fighter C .10 .30
TDGS013 Handcuffs Dragon R .40 1.00
TDGS014 Montage Dragon UR 1.50 4.00
TDGS014 Montage Dragon UTR 2.50 6.00
TDGS015 Gonogo C .10 .30
TDGS016 Mind Master R .40 1.00
TDGS017 Doctor Cranium C .10 .30
TDGS018 Krebons C .10 .30
TDGS019 Mind Protector C .10 .30
TDGS020 Psychic Commander C .50 1.25
TDGS021 Psychic Snail C .10 .30
TDGS022 Telekinetic Shocker C .10 .30
TDGS023 Destructotron C .10 .30
TDGS024 Gladiator Beast Equeste C .10 .30
TDGS025 Jenis, Lightsworn Mender C .50 1.25
TDGS026 Dharc the Dark Charmer C .10 .30
TDGS027 Mecha Bunny C .10 .30
TDGS028 Oyster Meister C .10 .30
TDGS029 Twin-Barrel Dragon SR .30 .75
TDGS030 Izanagi SR .30 .75
TDGS031 Kunoichi C .10 .30
TDGS032 Beast of the Pharaoh C .10 .30
TDGS033 Dark Hunter UR .40 1.00
TDGS033 Dark Hunter UTR .75 2.00
TDGS034 Kinka-byo SR 2.50 6.00
TDGS035 Yamato-no-Kami R .40 1.00
TDGS036 Silent Strider C .10 .30
TDGS037 Noisy Gnat C .10 .30
TDGS038 Multiple Piece Golem UR .40 1.00
TDGS038 Multiple Piece Golem UTR .75 2.00
TDGS039 Nitro Warrior UR .50 1.25
TDGS039 Nitro Warrior UTR 1.00 2.50
TDGS040 Stardust Dragon UR 3.00 8.00
TDGS040 Stardust Dragon UTR 15.00 30.00
TDGS040 Stardust Dragon GR 70.00 100.00
TDGS041 Red Dragon Archfiend UR 3.00 8.00
TDGS041 Red Dragon Archfiend UTR 4.00 10.00
TDGS042 Goyo Guardian UR 2.50 6.00
TDGS042 Goyo Guardian UTR 6.00 15.00
TDGS043 Magical Android SR 1.25 3.00
TDGS044 Thought Ruler Archfiend UR 2.00 5.00
TDGS044 Thought Ruler Archfiend UTR 4.00 10.00
TDGS045 Fighting Spirit R .40 1.00
TDGS046 Domino Effect C .10 .30
TDGS047 Junk Barrage C .10 .30
TDGS048 Battle Tuned C .10 .30
TDGS049 De-Synchro R .40 1.00
TDGS050 Lightwave Tuning C .10 .30
TDGS051 Psi-Station C .10 .30
TDGS052 Psi-Impulse C .10 .30
TDGS053 Emergency Teleport UR 5.00 12.00
TDGS053 Emergency Teleport UTR 20.00 40.00
TDGS054 Sword of Kusanagi C .10 .30
TDGS055 Orb of Yasaka C .40 1.00
TDGS056 Mirror of Yata C .10 .30
TDGS057 Geartown C .10 .30
TDGS058 Power Filter SR .50 1.25
TDGS059 Lightsworn Sabre SR 1.00 2.50
TDGS060 Unstable Evolution SR .30 .75
TDGS061 Recycling Batteries .40 1.00
TDGS062 Book of Eclipse C .40 1.00
TDGS063 Equip Shot C .10 .30
TDGS064 Graceful Revival R .40 1.00
TDGS065 Defense Draw R .40 1.00
TDGS066 Remote Revenge C .10 .30
TDGS067 Spacegate C .10 .30
TDGS068 Synchro Deflector C .10 .30
TDGS069 Broken Blocker SR .30 .75
TDGS070 Psychic Overload UR .40 1.00
TDGS070 Psychic Overload UTR 1.50 4.00
TDGS071 Psychic Rejuvenation C .10 .30
TDGS072 Telepathic Power C .10 .30
TDGS073 Mind Over Matter R .40 1.00
TDGS074 Gladiator Beast War Chariot SR .75 2.00
TDGS075 Lightsworn Barrier C .10 .30
TDGS076 Intercept SR 2.50 6.00
TDGS077 Judgment of Thunder C .10 .30
TDGS078 Fish Depth Charge C .10 .30
TDGS079 Needlebug Nest C .60 1.50
TDGS080 Overworked C .10 .30
TDGS081 Counselor Lily SR .40 1.00
TDGS082 Herald of Orange Light R .40 1.00
TDGS083 Izanami R .40 1.00
TDGS084 Maiden of Macabre R .40 1.00
TDGS085 Hand of the Six Samurai SCR 1.25 3.00
TDGS086 Cyber Shark SCR 1.25 3.00
TDGS087 Grapple Blocker R .40 1.00
TDGS088 Telekinetic Charging Cell R .40 1.00
TDGS089 Charge of the Light Brigade SCR 20.00 40.00
TDGS090 The Tricky R .40 1.00
TDGS091 Tricky Spell 4 C .10 .30
TDGS092 Trap of Darkness R .40 1.00
TDGS093 The Selection R .40 1.00
TDGS094 Splendid Venus SCR 1.25 3.00
TDGS095 Fiendish Engine W SCR .50 1.25
TDGS096 Cold Enchanter R .40 1.00
TDGS097 Ice Master SCR 1.50 4.00
TDGS098 Kunai with Chain SR .40 1.00
TDGS099 Toy Magician SCR 1.50 4.00
TDGSSE2 Gladiator Beast Heraklinos SR .30 .75
TDGSSP1 Avenging Knight Parshath SR 2.00 5.00

2008 Yu-Gi-Oh Crossroads of Chaos 1st Edition

COMPLETE SET (111) 200.00 400.00
BOOSTER BOX (24 PACKS) 80.00 120.00
BOOSTER PACK (9 CARDS) 2.50 6.00
*UNLIMITED: .4X TO .8X 1ST EDITION .40 1.00

RELEASED ON NOVEMBER 18, 2009

CSOC0 Rose, Warrior of Revenge UR	2.00	5.00
CSOC0 Rose, Warrior of Revenge UTR	2.50	6.00
CSOC1 Healing Wave Generator C	.15	.25
CSOC2 Turbo Synchron R	1.00	2.50
CSOC3 Mad Archfiend R	.75	2.00
CSOC4 Wall of Ivy C	.15	.25
CSOC5 Copy Plant C	.15	.25
CSOC6 Morphtronic Celfon C	.15	.25
CSOC7 Morphtronic Magnen C	.15	.25
CSOC8 Morphtronic Datatron C	.15	.25
CSOC9 Morphtronic Boomboxen R	.60	1.50
CSOC10 Morphtronic Cameran C	.15	.25
CSOC11 Morphtronic Radion R	.75	2.00
CSOC12 Morphtronic Clocken C	.15	.25
CSOC13 Gadget Hauler C	.15	.25
CSOC14 Gadget Driver C	.15	.25
CSOC15 Search Striker R	.75	2.00
CSOC16 Pursuit Chaser C	.15	.25
CSOC17 Iron Chain Repairman R	.60	1.50
CSOC18 Iron Chain Snake C	.15	.25
CSOC19 Iron Chain Blaster C	.15	.25
CSOC20 Iron Chain Coil C	.15	.25
CSOC21 Power Injector C	.15	.25
CSOC22 Storm Caller R	.75	2.00
CSOC23 Psychic Jumper C	.15	.25
CSOC24 Nettles C	.15	.25
CSOC25 Gigantic Cephalotus C	.15	.25
CSOC26 Horseytail C	.15	.25
CSOC27 Botanical Girl C	.15	.25
CSOC28 Cursed Fig C	.15	.25
CSOC29 Tytannial, Princess of Camellias UR	4.00	10.00
CSOC29 Tytannial, Princess of Camellias UTR	1.50	4.00
CSOC30 Zombie Mammoth C	.15	.25
CSOC31 Plaguespreader Zombie UR	2.00	5.00
CSOC31 Plaguespreader Zombie UTR	10.00	25.00
CSOC32 Goblin Decoy Squad C	.15	.25
CSOC33 Comrade Swordsman of Landstar C	.15	.25
CSOC34 Hanewata SR	1.25	3.00
CSOC35 The White Stone of Legend C	.15	.25
CSOC36 Tiger Dragon R	1.25	3.00
CSOC37 Jade Knight C	.15	.25
CSOC38 Turbo Warrior UR	3.00	8.00
CSOC38 Turbo Warrior UTR	1.00	2.50
CSOC39 Black Rose Dragon UR	4.00	10.00
CSOC39 Black Rose Dragon UTR	15.00	30.00
CSOC39 Black Rose Dragon GR	70.00	110.00
CSOC40 Iron Chain Dragon R	1.50	4.00
CSOC41 Psychic Lifetrancer R	1.50	4.00
CSOC42 Queen of Thorns SR	2.00	5.00
CSOC43 Doomkaiser Dragon UR	1.50	4.00
CSOC43 Doomkaiser Dragon UTR	2.50	6.00
CSOC44 Revived King Ha Des UR	2.00	5.00
CSOC44 Revived King Ha Des UTR	3.00	8.00
CSOC45 Card Rotator C	.15	.25
CSOC46 Seed of Deception C	.15	.25
CSOC47 Mark of the Rose UR	1.50	4.00
CSOC47 Mark of the Rose UTR	1.50	4.00
CSOC48 Black Garden SR	1.25	3.00
CSOC49 Factory of 100 Machines C	.15	.25
CSOC50 Morphtronic Accelerator R	.60	1.50
CSOC51 Morphtronic Cord C	.15	.25
CSOC52 Morphtronic Engine C	.15	.25
CSOC53 Poison Chain C	.15	.25
CSOC54 Paralyzing Chain R	.60	1.50
CSOC55 Teleport C	.15	.25
CSOC56 Psychokinesis UR	1.50	4.00
CSOC56 Psychokinesis UTR	1.00	2.50
CSOC57 Miracle Fertilizer R	.75	2.00
CSOC58 Fragrance Storm C	.15	.25
CSOC59 The World Tree R	.75	2.00
CSOC60 Everliving Underworld Cannon C	.15	.25
CSOC61 Secret Village of the Spellcasters SR	10.00	25.00
CSOC62 Omega Goggles C	.15	.25
CSOC63 Battle Mania SR	.75	2.00
CSOC64 Confusion Chaff C	.15	.25
CSOC65 Urgent Tuning SR	1.25	3.00
CSOC66 Synchro Strike C	.15	.25
CSOC67 Prideful Roar R	.75	2.00
CSOC68 Revival Gift C	.15	.25
CSOC69 Lineage of Destruction C	.15	.25
CSOC70 Doppelganger C	.15	.25
CSOC71 Morphtransition C	.15	.25
CSOC72 Morphtronic Monitron C	.15	.25
CSOC73 Psychic Trigger SR	1.00	2.50
CSOC74 Pollinosis R	.40	1.00
CSOC75 Bamboo Scrap C	.15	.25
CSOC76 Plant Food Chain C	.15	.25
CSOC77 Trap of the Imperial Tomb R	.40	1.00
CSOC78 DNA Checkup C	.15	.25
CSOC79 Gozen Match C	.15	.25
CSOC80 Giant Trap Hole C	.15	.25
CSOC81 Seed of Flame UR	1.50	4.00
CSOC81 Seed of Flame UTR	3.00	8.00
CSOC82 Cactus Fighter R	.60	1.50
CSOC83 Overdrive Teleporter SCR	10.00	25.00
CSOC84 Rai-Jin SR	.75	2.00
CSOC85 Rai-Mei SR	2.00	5.00
CSOC86 Gladiator Beast Retiari SCR	2.50	6.00
CSOC87 Night's End Sorcerer SR	2.50	6.00
CSOC88 Tempest Magician SCR	3.00	8.00
CSOC89 Treacherous Trap Hole SCR	10.00	25.00
CSOC90 Puppet Master SR	.75	2.00
CSOC91 Time Machine SCR	1.50	4.00
CSOC92 Virus Cannon R	.60	1.50
CSOC93 Machine Lord Ur SCR	1.50	4.00
CSOC94 Mosaic Manticore R	.40	1.00
CSOC95 Goka, the Pyre of Malice SR	.75	2.00
CSOC96 Red Ogre SR	.15	.25
CSOC97 Neos Wiseman SCR	2.50	6.00
CSOC98 Elem. Hero Divine SCR	2.00	5.00
CSOC99 Botanical Lion SR	3.00	8.00

2009 Yu-Gi-Oh Crimson Crisis 1st Edition

COMPLETE SET (100)	75.00	150.00
BOOSTER BOX (24 PACKS)	40.00	80.00
BOOSTER PACK (9 CARDS)	2.50	6.00

*UNLIMITED: .4X TO .8X 1ST EDITION

RELEASED ON MARCH 3, 2009

CRMS0 Colossal Fighter/Assault Mode SCR	1.25	3.00
CRMS1 Turret Warrior SR	.75	2.00
CRMS2 Debris Dragon R	.40	1.00
CRMS3 Hyper Synchron R	.40	1.00
CRMS4 Red Dragon Archfiend UR	2.50	6.00
CRMS4 Red Dragon Archfiend UTR	3.00	8.00
CRMS4 Red Dragon Archfiend GR	6.00	15.00
CRMS5 Trap Eater C	.15	.25
CRMS6 Twin-Sword Marauder C	.15	.25
CRMS7 Dark Tinker C	.15	.25
CRMS8 Blackwing - Gale the Whirlwind R	.40	1.00
CRMS9 Blackwing - Bora the Spear C	.15	.25
CRMS10 Blackwing - Sirocco the Dawn C	.15	.25
CRMS11 Twilight Rose Knight SR	1.00	2.50
CRMS12 Summon ReactorÂ·SK C	.15	.25
CRMS13 Trap ReactorÂ·Y FI C	.15	.25
CRMS14 Spell ReactorÂ·RE C	.15	.25
CRMS15 Black Salvo SR	.75	2.00
CRMS16 Flying Fortress SKY FIRE R	.40	1.00
CRMS17 Morphtronic Boarden C	.15	.25
CRMS18 Morphtronic Slingen C	.15	.25
CRMS19 Doomkaiser Dragon UR	.75	2.00
CRMS19 Doomkaiser Dragon UTR	.75	2.00
CRMS20 Hyper Psychic Blaster UR	.75	2.00
CRMS20 Hyper Psychic Blaster UTR	1.00	2.50
CRMS21 Arcanite Magician UR	2.00	5.00
CRMS21 Arcanite Magician UTR	2.00	5.00
CRMS22 Arcane Apprentice R	.40	1.00
CRMS23 Assault Mercenary C	.15	.25
CRMS24 Assault Beast R	.60	1.50
CRMS25 Night Wing Sorceress C	.15	.25
CRMS26 Lifeforce Harmonizer UR	.75	2.00
CRMS26 Lifeforce Harmonizer UTR	.75	2.00
CRMS27 Gladiator Beast Samnite R	.40	1.00
CRMS28 Dupe Frog C	.15	.25
CRMS29 Flip Flop Frog C	.15	.25
CRMS30 B.E.S. Big Core MK-2 R	.40	1.00
CRMS31 Inmato R	.40	1.00
CRMS32 Scanner SR	.75	2.00
CRMS33 Dimension Fortress Weapon SR	.75	2.00
CRMS34 Desert Protector C	.15	.25
CRMS35 Cross-Sword Beetle C	.15	.25
CRMS36 Bee List Soldier C	.15	.25
CRMS37 Hydra Viper C	.15	.25
CRMS38 Alien Overlord R	.40	1.00
CRMS39 Alien Ammonite R	.40	1.00
CRMS40 Dark Strike Fighter SR	.75	2.00
CRMS41 Blackwing Armor Master UR	1.00	2.50
CRMS41 Blackwing Armor Master UTR	2.50	6.00
CRMS42 Hyper Psychic Blaster UR	2.50	6.00
CRMS42 Hyper Psychic Blaster UTR	1.50	4.00
CRMS43 Arcanite Magician SR	.75	2.00
CRMS44 Cosmic Fortress Gol'gar UR	3.00	8.00
CRMS44 Cosmic Fortress Gol'gar UTR	4.00	10.00
CRMS45 Prevention Star C	.15	.25
CRMS46 Vengeful Servant C	.15	.25
CRMS47 Star Blast R	.40	1.00
CRMS48 Raptor Wing Strike C	.15	.25
CRMS49 Morphtronic Rusty Engine C	.15	.25
CRMS50 Morphtronic Map C	.15	.25
CRMS51 Assault Overload C	.15	.25
CRMS52 Assault Teleport C	.15	.25
CRMS53 Assault Revival C	.15	.25
CRMS54 Psychic Sword C	.15	.25
CRMS55 Telekinetic Power Well C	.15	.25
CRMS56 Indomitable Gladiator Beast C	.15	.25
CRMS57 Seed Cannon C	.15	.25
CRMS58 Super Solar Nutrient C	.15	.25
CRMS59 Six Scrolls of the Samurai C	.15	.25
CRMS60 Verdant Sanctuary C	.15	.25
CRMS61 Arcane Barrier R	.40	1.00
CRMS62 Mysterious Triangle C	.15	.25
CRMS63 Assault Mode Activate C	.15	.25
CRMS64 Spirit Force SR	.75	2.00
CRMS65 Descending Lost Star C	.15	.25
CRMS66 Shining Silver Force R	.40	1.00
CRMS67 Half or Nothing C	.15	.25
CRMS68 Nightmare Archfiends C	.15	.25
CRMS69 Ebon Arrow C	.15	.25
CRMS70 Ivy Shackles C	.15	.25
CRMS71 Fake Explosion C	.15	.25
CRMS72 Morphtronic Forcefield C	.15	.25
CRMS73 Morphtronic Mix-up C	.15	.25
CRMS74 Assault Slash C	.15	.25
CRMS75 Assault Counter C	.15	.25
CRMS76 Psychic Tuning R	.40	1.00
CRMS77 Metaphysical Regeneration C	.15	.25
CRMS78 Trojan Gladiator Beast C	.15	.25
CRMS79 Wall of Thorns R	.50	1.25
CRMS80 Planet Pollutant Virus R	.40	1.00
CRMS81 Dark Voltanis SCR	3.00	8.00
CRMS82 Prime Material Falcon SCR	.40	1.00
CRMS83 Bone Crusher UR	.75	2.00
CRMS83 Bone Crusher UTR	.75	2.00
CRMS84 Alien Kid SR	.75	2.00
CRMS85 Totem Dragon SR	2.00	5.00
CRMS86 Royal Swamp Eel SR	.75	2.00
CRMS87 Submarine Frog C	.15	.25
CRMS88 Code A Ancient Ruins SR	1.25	3.00
CRMS89 Synchro Change R	.40	1.00
CRMS90 Multiply SR	1.50	4.00
CRMS91 Makiu, the Magical Mist R	.40	1.00
CRMS92 Assault Armor R	.40	1.00
CRMS93 Puppet King SCR	.40	1.00
CRMS94 Zeta Reticulant SCR	.40	1.00
CRMS95 Tethys, Goddess of Light SCR	2.00	5.00
CRMS96 Ido the Supreme Magical Force SCR	.40	1.00
CRMS97 Violet Witch UR	.75	2.00
CRMS97 Violet Witch UTR	.50	1.25
CRMS98 Greed Quasar SCR	1.25	3.00
CRMS99 Armoroid SR	.75	2.00

2009 Yu-Gi-Oh Raging Battle 1st Edition

COMPLETE SET (100)	150.00	250.00
BOOSTER BOX (24 PACKS)	40.00	80.00
BOOSTER PACK (9 CARDS)	2.00	5.00

*UNLIMITED: .4X TO .8X 1ST EDITION

RELEASED ON MAY 12, 2009

RGBT00 Battlestorm SCR	1.50	4.00
RGBT01 Rockstone Warrior SR	.75	2.00
RGBT02 Level Warrior SR	1.00	2.50
RGBT03 Strong Wind Dragon UR	2.00	5.00
RGBT03 Strong Wind Dragon UTR	2.00	5.00
RGBT04 Dark Verger R	.40	1.00
RGBT05 Phoenixian Seed C	.15	.25
RGBT06 Phoenixian Cluster Amaryllis SR	.50	1.25
RGBT07 Rose Tentacles C	.15	.25
RGBT08 Hedge Guard C	.15	.25
RGBT09 Evil Thorn C	.15	.25
RGBT10 Blackwing - Blizzard the Far North R	.75	2.00
RGBT11 Blackwing - Shura the Blue Flame C	.15	.25
RGBT12 Blackwing - Kalut the Moon Shadow C	.15	.25
RGBT13 Blackwing - Elphin the Raven UR	.40	1.00
RGBT13 Blackwing - Elphin the Raven UTR	.75	2.00
RGBT14 Morphtronic Remoten R	1.00	2.50
RGBT15 Morphtronic Videon C	.15	.25
RGBT16 Morphtronic Scopen C	.15	.25
RGBT17 Gadget Arms C	.15	.25
RGBT18 Torapart R	.40	1.00
RGBT19 Earthbound Immortal Aslla Piscu UR	1.50	4.00
RGBT19 Earthbound Immortal Aslla Piscu UTR	1.50	4.00
RGBT20 Earthbound Immortal Ccapac UR	6.00	15.00
RGBT20 Earthbound Immortal Ccapac UTR	3.00	8.00
RGBT21 Koa'ki Meiru Valafar SR	.75	2.00
RGBT22 Koa'ki Meiru Powerhand SR	.40	1.00
RGBT23 Koa'ki Meiru Guardian C	.15	.25
RGBT24 Koa'ki Meiru Drago UR	8.00	20.00
RGBT24 Koa'ki Meiru Drago UTR	20.00	40.00
RGBT25 Koa'ki Meiru Ice R	.40	1.00
RGBT26 Koa'ki Meiru Doom C	.15	.25
RGBT27 Brain Golem R	.40	1.00
RGBT28 Minoan Centaur C	.15	.25
RGBT29 Reinforced Human Psychic Borg SR	.75	2.00
RGBT30 Master Gig C	.15	.25
RGBT31 Emissary from Pandemonium C	.15	.25
RGBT32 Gigastone Omega C	.15	.25
RGBT33 Alien Dog C	.15	.25
RGBT34 Spined Gillman C	.15	.25
RGBT35 Deep Sea Diva R	.40	1.00
RGBT36 Mermaid Archer C	.15	.25
RGBT37 Lava Dragon C	.15	.25
RGBT38 Vanguard of the Dragon C	.15	.25
RGBT39 G.B. Hunter C	.15	.25
RGBT40 Exploder Dragonwing UR	2.00	5.00
RGBT40 Exploder Dragonwing UTR	2.00	5.00
RGBT41 Blackwing Armed Wing SR	.50	1.25
RGBT42 Power Tool Dragon UR	2.00	5.00
RGBT42 Power Tool Dragon UTR	2.50	6.00
RGBT42 Power Tool Dragon GR	6.00	15.00
RGBT43 Trident Dragion UR	1.25	3.00
RGBT43 Trident Dragion UTR	2.00	5.00
RGBT44 Sea Dragon Lord Gishilnodon SR	1.25	3.00
RGBT45 One for One R	.75	2.00
RGBT46 Mind Trust C	.15	.25
RGBT47 Thorn of Malice C	.15	.25
RGBT48 Magic Planter SR	4.00	10.00
RGBT49 Wonder Clover C	.15	.25
RGBT50 Against the Wind R	.40	1.00
RGBT51 Black Whirlwind C	.15	.25
RGBT52 Junk Box C	.15	.25
RGBT53 Double Tool C&D C	.15	.25
RGBT54 Morphtronic Repair Unit C	.15	.25
RGBT55 Iron Core of Koa'ki Meiru R	.40	1.00
RGBT56 Iron Core Immediate Disposal C	.15	.25
RGBT57 Urgent Synthesis C	.15	.25
RGBT58 Psychic Path C	.15	.25
RGBT59 Natural Tune C	.15	.25
RGBT60 Supremacy Berry C	.15	.25
RGBT61 Forbidden Chalice UR	3.00	8.00
RGBT61 Forbidden Chalice UTR	10.00	25.00
RGBT62 Calming Magic R	.40	1.00
RGBT63 Miracle Locus C	.15	.25
RGBT64 Crimson Fire C	.15	.25
RGBT65 Tuner Capture C	.15	.25
RGBT66 Overdoom Line C	.15	.25
RGBT67 Wicked Rebirth C	.15	.25
RGBT68 Delta Crow - Anti Reverse SR	1.25	3.00
RGBT69 Level Retuner C	.15	.25
RGBT70 Fake Feather C	.15	.25
RGBT71 Trap Stun C	.15	.25
RGBT72 Morphtronic Bind C	.15	.25
RGBT73 Reckoned Power C	.15	.25
RGBT74 Automatic Laser C	.15	.25
RGBT75 Attack of the Cornered Rat C	.15	.25
RGBT76 Proof of Powerlessness C	.15	.25
RGBT77 Bone Temple Block C	.15	.25
RGBT78 Grave of the Super UR	6.00	15.00
RGBT78 Grave of the Super UTR	6.00	15.00
RGBT79 Swallow Flip SR	.40	1.00
RGBT80 Mirror of Oaths C	.15	.25
RGBT81 Koa'ki Meiru War Arms SR	.75	2.00
RGBT82 Immortal Ruler SCR	4.00	10.00
RGBT83 Hardened Armed Dragon SCR	3.00	8.00
RGBT84 Moja R	.40	1.00
RGBT85 Beast Striker SR	.40	1.00
RGBT86 King of the Beasts SCR	1.50	4.00
RGBT87 Swallow's Nest SR	5.00	12.00
RGBT88 Overwhelm SCR	3.00	8.00
RGBT89 Berserking R	.40	1.00
RGBT90 Spell of Pain R	.40	1.00
RGBT91 Light End Dragon SCR	1.50	4.00
RGBT92 Chaos-End Master SCR	4.00	10.00
RGBT93 Sphere of Chaos SCR	8.00	20.00
RGBT94 Snowman Eater R	.40	1.00

RGBT95 Tree Otter R	.40	1.00
RGBT96 Ojama Red R	1.00	2.50
RGBT97 Ojama Blue R	1.50	4.00
RGBT98 Ojama Country R	1.50	4.00
RGBT99 Emperor Sem R	.40	1.00

2009 Yu-Gi-Oh Ancient Prophecy 1st Edition

COMPLETE SET (100)	115.00	200.00
BOOSTER BOX (24 PACKS)	50.00	90.00
BOOSTER PACK (9 CARDS)	2.50	6.00
RELEASED ON SEPTEMBER 1, 2009		
ANPR0 XX-Saber Gardestrike SCR	1.50	4.00
ANPR1 Kuribon R	.40	1.00
ANPR2 Sunny Pixie C	.15	.25
ANPR3 Sunlight Unicorn C	.15	.25
ANPR4 Blackwing - Mistral the Silver Shield C	.15	.25
ANPR5 Blackwing - Vayu UR	.75	2.00
ANPR5 Blackwing - Vayu UTR	1.50	4.00
ANPR6 Blackwing - Fane the Steel Chain C	.15	.25
ANPR7 Morphtronic Magnen Bar C	.15	.25
ANPR8 Jester Lord R	.40	1.00
ANPR9 Jester Confit SR	1.50	4.00
ANPR10 Fortune Lady Light R	.50	1.25
ANPR11 Fortune Lady Fire R	.40	1.00
ANPR12 Infernity Beast C	.15	.25
ANPR13 Darksea Rescue R	.40	1.00
ANPR14 Darksea Float C	.15	.25
ANPR15 Turbo Rocket R	.40	1.00
ANPR16 Earthbound Immortal Cusillu UR	1.00	2.50
ANPR16 Earthbound Immortal Cusillu UTR	1.50	4.00
ANPR17 Earthbound Immortal Chacu UR	1.50	4.00
ANPR17 Earthboudn Immortal Chacu UTR	3.00	8.00
ANPR18 Koa'ki Meiru Boulder C	.15	.25
ANPR19 Koa'ki Meiru Crusader SR	1.00	2.50
ANPR20 Koa'ki Meiru Speeder R	.40	1.00
ANPR21 Koa'ki Meiru Tornado R	.40	1.00
ANPR22 Koa'ki Meiru Hydro Barrier C	.15	.25
ANPR23 Scary Moth C	.15	.25
ANPR24 Shiny Black C C	.15	.25
ANPR25 Armed Sea Hunter C	.15	.25
ANPR26 Divine Dragon Aquabizarre C	.15	.25
ANPR27 Fishborg Blaster C	.15	.25
ANPR28 Shark Cruiser C	.15	.25
ANPR29 Armored Axon Kicker C	.15	.25
ANPR30 Genetic Woman C	.15	.25
ANPR31 Magicat R	.40	1.00
ANPR32 Cyborg Doctor C	.15	.25
ANPR33 White Potan C	.15	.25
ANPR34 Minefieldriller SR	.60	1.50
ANPR35 XX-Saber Faultroll SR	1.50	4.00
ANPR36 XX-Saber Ragigura C	.15	.25
ANPR37 Flamvell Firedog R	.40	1.00
ANPR38 Ancient Crimson Ape C	.15	.25
ANPR39 Falchion R	.40	1.00
ANPR40 Ancient Fairy Dragon UR	2.00	5.00
ANPR40 Ancient Fairy Dragon UTR	6.00	15.00
ANPR40 Ancient Fairy Dragon GR	15.00	30.00
ANPR41 Turbo Cannon SR	.75	2.00
ANPR42 Archfiend Zombie-Skull SR	8.00	20.00
ANPR43 Ancient Sacred Wyvern UR	3.00	8.00
ANPR43 Ancient Sacred Wyvern UTR	6.00	15.00
ANPR44 XX-Saber Gottoms UR	.75	2.00
ANPR44 XX-Saber Gottoms UTR	1.50	4.00
ANPR45 Release Restraint Wave C	.15	.25
ANPR46 Silver Wing C	.15	.25
ANPR47 Advance Draw C	.15	.25
ANPR48 Ancient Forest SR	.75	2.00
ANPR49 Emergency Assistance C	.15	.25
ANPR50 Spirit Burner C	.15	.25
ANPR51 Future Visions SR	3.00	8.00
ANPR52 Core Compression SR	1.00	2.50
ANPR53 Core Blaster C	.15	.25
ANPR54 Solidarity R	1.25	3.00
ANPR55 Hydro Pressure Cannon C	.15	.25
ANPR56 Water Hazard C	.15	.25
ANPR57 Brain Research Lab C	.15	.25
ANPR58 Saber Slash SR	.75	2.00
ANPR59 Sword of Sparkles C	.15	.25
ANPR60 Rekindling C	.15	.25
ANPR61 Ancient Leaf C	.15	.25
ANPR62 Fossil Dig C	.15	.25
ANPR63 Skill Successor SR	.75	2.00
ANPR64 Reinforce Truth R	.40	1.00
ANPR65 Pixie Ring C	.15	.25
ANPR66 Fairy Wind C	.15	.25
ANPR67 Imperial Custom C	.15	.25
ANPR68 Discord SR	.40	1.00
ANPR69 Slip of Fortune C	.15	.25
ANPR70 Depth Amulet C	.15	.25
ANPR71 Damage Translation C	.15	.25
ANPR72 Battle Teleportation C	.15	.25
ANPR73 Core Reinforcement R	.40	1.00
ANPR74 Iron Core Luster C	.15	.25
ANPR75 Battle of the Elements C	.15	.25
ANPR76 Aegis of the Ocean Dragon Lord C	.15	.25
ANPR77 Psychic Soul C	.15	.25
ANPR78 Flamvell Counter C	.15	.25
ANPR79 At One With the Sword C	.15	.25
ANPR80 A Major Upset C	.15	.25
ANPR81 XX-Saber Fulhelmknight R	.40	1.00
ANPR82 Koa'ki Meiru Ghoulungulate UR	.75	2.00
ANPR82 Koa'ki Meiru Ghoulungulate UTR	.50	1.25
ANPR83 Koa'ki Meiru Gravirose UR	.75	2.00
ANPR83 Koa'ki Meiru Gravirose UTR	.75	2.00
ANPR84 Psychic Emperor R	.40	1.00
ANPR85 Card Guard SCR	4.00	10.00
ANPR86 Flamvell Commando UR	.75	2.00
ANPR86 Flamvell Commando UTR	.75	2.00
ANPR87 Pseudo Space R	3.00	8.00
ANPR88 Greed Grado SCR	1.50	4.00
ANPR89 Revival of the Immortals SR	.60	1.50
ANPR90 Arcana Knight Joker R	1.50	4.00
ANPR91 Armityle the Chaos Phantom SCR	10.00	25.00
ANPR92 White Night Dragon SCR	3.00	8.00
ANPR93 Card Blocker SCR	.50	1.25
ANPR94 Gaia Plate the Earth Giant UR	1.50	4.00
ANPR94 Gaia Plate the Earth Giant UTR	3.00	8.00
ANPR95 Sauropod Brachion R	.40	1.00
ANPR96 Gaap the Divine Soldier R	.40	1.00
ANPR97 Beast Machine King Barbaros Ur SR	.75	2.00
ANPR98 Kasha SCR	1.00	2.50
ANPR99 Elemental Hero Gaia SCR	4.00	10.00

2009 Yu-Gi-Oh Stardust Overdrive 1st Edition

COMPLETE SET (100)	175.00	300.00
BOOSTER BOX (24 PACKS)	80.00	120.00
BOOSTER PACK (9 CARDS)	2.50	6.00
*UNLIMITED: .4X TO .8X 1ST EDITION		
RELEASED ON NOVEMBER 17, 2009		
SOVR0 Koa'ki Meiru Beetle SR	.75	2.00
SOVR1 Majestic Dragon SR	1.25	3.00
SOVR2 Stardust Xiaolong R	.60	1.50
SOVR3 Max Warrior SR	.75	2.00
SOVR4 Quickdraw Synchron C	.15	.25
SOVR5 Level Eater C	.15	.25
SOVR6 Zero Gardna R	.60	1.50
SOVR7 Regulus C	.15	.25
SOVR8 Infernity Necromancer C	.15	.25
SOVR9 Fortune Lady Wind R	.75	2.00
SOVR10 Fortune Lady Water R	.75	2.00
SOVR11 Fortune Lady Dark R	1.00	2.50
SOVR12 Fortune Lady Earth R	.75	2.00
SOVR13 Solitaire Magician C	.15	.25
SOVR14 Catoblepas and the Witch of Fate R	.40	1.00
SOVR15 Dark Spider C	.15	.25
SOVR16 Ground Spider C	.15	.25
SOVR17 Relinquished Spider C	.15	.25
SOVR18 Spyder Spider C	.15	.25
SOVR19 Mother Spider R	.40	1.00
SOVR20 Reptilianne Gorgon C	.15	.25
SOVR21 Reptilianne Medusa C	.15	.25
SOVR22 Reptilianne Scylla C	.15	.25
SOVR23 Reptilianne Viper C	.15	.25
SOVR24 Earthbound Immortal Ccarayhua UR	1.50	4.00
SOVR24 Earthbound Immortal Ccarayhua UTR	3.00	8.00
SOVR25 Earthbound Immortal Uru UR	2.50	6.00
SOVR25 Earthbound Immortal Uru UTR	3.00	8.00
SOVR26 Earth. Immortal Wiraqocha UR	1.50	4.00
SOVR26 Earth. Immortal Wiraqocha UTR	1.25	3.00
SOVR27 Koa'ki Meiru Sea Panther C	.15	.25
SOVR28 Koa'ki Meiru Rooklord SR	.75	2.00
SOVR29 Tuned Magician C	.15	.25
SOVR30 Crusader of Endymion UR	1.50	4.00
SOVR30 Crusader of Endymion UTR	6.00	15.00
SOVR31 Woodland Archer C	.15	.25
SOVR32 Knight of the Red Lotus SR	2.50	6.00
SOVR33 Energy Bravery C	.15	.25
SOVR34 Swap Frog C	.15	.25
SOVR35 Lord British Space Fighter R	.60	1.50
SOVR36 Oshaleon C	.15	.25
SOVR37 Djinn Releaser of Rituals R	.60	1.50
SOVR38 Djinn Presider of Rituals R	.40	1.00
SOVR39 Divine Grace - Northwemko UR	1.50	4.00
SOVR39 Divine Grace - Northwemko UTR	2.00	5.00
SOVR40 Majestic Star Dragon UR	1.50	4.00
SOVR40 Majestic Star Dragon UTR	2.00	5.00
SOVR40 Majestic Star Dragon GR	8.00	20.00
SOVR41 Blackwing - Silverwind UR	1.50	4.00
SOVR41 Blackwing - Silverwind UTR	1.25	3.00
SOVR42 Reptilianne Hydra SR	.75	2.00
SOVR43 Black Brutdrago SR	.75	2.00
SOVR44 Explosive Magician UR	2.00	5.00
SOVR44 Explosive Magician UTR	3.00	8.00
SOVR45 Spider Web C	.15	.25
SOVR46 Earthbound Whirlwind SR	.60	1.50
SOVR47 Savage Colosseum C	.15	.25
SOVR48 Attack Pheromones C	.15	.25
SOVR49 Molting Escape C	.15	.25
SOVR50 Reptilianne Spawn C	.15	.25
SOVR51 Fortune's Future SR	2.00	5.00
SOVR52 Time Passage C	.15	.25
SOVR53 Iron Core Armor C	.15	.25
SOVR54 Herculean Power C	.15	.25
SOVR55 Gemini Spark C	.15	.25
SOVR56 Ritual of Grace C	.15	.25
SOVR57 Preparation of Rites SR	1.25	3.00
SOVR58 Moray of Greed C	.15	.25
SOVR59 Spiritual Forest C	.15	.25
SOVR60 Raging Mad Plants R	.40	1.00
SOVR61 Insect Neglect C	.15	.25
SOVR62 Faustian Bargain C	.15	.25
SOVR63 Slip Summon C	.15	.25
SOVR64 Synchro Barrier C	.15	.25
SOVR65 Enlightenment C	.15	.25
SOVR66 Bending Destiny C	.15	.25
SOVR67 Inherited Fortune R	.40	1.00
SOVR68 Spider Egg C	.15	.25
SOVR69 Wolf in Sheep's Clothing C	.15	.25
SOVR70 Earthbound Wave C	.15	.25
SOVR71 Roar of the Earthbound C	.15	.25
SOVR72 Limit Impulse C	.15	.25
SOVR73 Infernity Force C	.15	.25
SOVR74 Nega-Ton Corepanel R	.40	1.00
SOVR75 Gemini Counter C	.15	.25
SOVR76 Gemini Booster C	.15	.25
SOVR77 Ritual Buster C	.15	.25
SOVR78 Stygian Dirge C	.15	.25
SOVR79 Seal of Wickedness SR	.75	2.00
SOVR80 Appointer of the Red Lotus C	.15	.25
SOVR81 Koa'ki Meiru Maximus UR	1.50	4.00
SOVR81 Koa'ki Meiru Maximus UTR	1.25	3.00
SOVR82 Shire, Lightsworn Spirit SR	.75	2.00
SOVR83 Rinyan, Lightsworn Rogue R	.60	1.50
SOVR84 Yellow Baboon, Archer UR	1.50	4.00
SOVR84 Yellow Baboon, Archer UTR	1.25	3.00
SOVR85 Gemini Scorpion R	.40	1.00
SOVR86 Metabo-Shark SR	.75	2.00
SOVR87 Earthbound Revival R	.40	1.00
SOVR88 Reptilianne Poison R	.40	1.00
SOVR89 Gateway of the Six SR	2.50	6.00
SOVR90 Dark Rabbit R	.40	1.00
SOVR91 Shine Palace R	.60	1.50
SOVR92 Dark Simorgh SCR	15.00	30.00
SOVR93 Victoria SCR	10.00	25.00
SOVR94 Ice Queen SCR	1.50	4.00
SOVR95 Shutendoji SCR	4.00	10.00
SOVR96 Archlord Kristya SCR	20.00	40.00
SOVR97 Guardian Eatos SCR	50.00	100.00
SOVR98 Clear Vice Dragon SCR	1.50	4.00
SOVR99 Clear World SCR	1.00	2.50

2010 Yu-Gi-Oh Absolute Powerforce 1st Edition

COMPLETE SET (100)	100.00	200.00
BOOSTER BOX (24 PACKS)	40.00	80.00
BOOSTER PACK (9 CARDS)	2.00	5.00
*UNLIMITED: .4X TO .8X 1ST EDITION		
RELEASED ON FEBRUARY 16, 2010		
ABPF0 Grvkpr's Prstss SR	.75	2.00
ABPF1 Unicycular C	.15	.25
ABPF2 Bicular C	.15	.25
ABPF3 Tricular C	.15	.25
ABPF4 Drill Synchron R	.40	1.00
ABPF5 Ogre Scarlet Sorrow SR	.75	2.00
ABPF6 Battle Fader UR	2.00	5.00
ABPF6 Battle Fader UTR	8.00	20.00
ABPF7 Power Supplier C	.15	.25
ABPF8 Magic Hole Golem C	.15	.25
ABPF9 Power Invader C	.15	.25
ABPF10 Dark Bug R	.40	1.00
ABPF11 Sword Master	.15	.25
ABPF12 Witch Black Rose UR	1.50	4.00
ABPF12 Witch Black Rose UTR	2.00	5.00
ABPF13 Rose Fairy C	.15	.25
ABPF14 Dragon Queen SR	.75	2.00
ABPF15 Reptilianne Servant C	.15	.25
ABPF16 Reptilianne Gardna C	.15	.25
ABPF17 Reptilianne Naga C	.15	.25
ABPF18 Reptilianne Vaskii R	.40	1.00
ABPF19 Oracle of the Sun SR	.75	2.00
ABPF20 Fire Ant Ascator C	.15	.25
ABPF21 Weeping Idol C	.15	.25
ABPF22 Apocatequil C	.15	.25
ABPF23 Supay C	.15	.25
ABPF24 Informer Spider C	.15	.25
ABPF25 Koa Mei Urnight UR	1.50	4.00
ABPF25 Koa Mei Urnight UTR	1.50	4.00
ABPF26 XX-Saber Garsem R	.40	1.00
ABPF27 Grvkpr's Visionary SR	.75	2.00
ABPF28 Grvkpr's Dscndnt R	.40	1.00
ABPF29 Black Potan C	.15	.25
ABPF30 Shreddder C	.15	.25
ABPF31 Pandaborg C	.15	.25
ABPF32 Codarus C	.15	.25
ABPF33 Consecrated Light C	.15	.25
ABPF34 Gundari C	.15	.25
ABPF35 Cyber Dragon Zwei R	.40	1.00
ABPF36 Oilman C	.15	.25
ABPF37 Djinn Cursenchanter R	.40	1.00
ABPF38 Djinn Prognosticator R	.40	1.00
ABPF39 Garlandolf, King UR	1.50	4.00
ABPF39 Garlandolf, King UTR	1.50	4.00
ABPF40 Maj Red Dragon UR	1.50	4.00
ABPF40 Maj Red Dragon UTR	1.50	4.00
ABPF40 Maj Red Dragon GR	5.00	12.00
ABPF41 Drill Warrior UR	1.50	4.00
ABPF41 Drill Warrior UTR	1.50	4.00
ABPF42 Sun Dragon Inti UR	1.50	4.00
ABPF42 Sun Dragon Inti UTR	1.50	4.00
ABPF43 Moon Dragon UR	1.50	4.00
ABPF43 Moon Dragon UTR	1.50	4.00
ABPF44 XX-Saber Hyunlei UR	2.50	6.00
ABPF44 XX-Saber Hyunlei UTR	3.00	8.00
ABPF45 Cards Consonance SR	2.50	6.00
ABPF46 Variety Comes Out C	.15	.25
ABPF47 Reptilianne Rage C	.15	.25
ABPF48 Advance Force C	.15	.25
ABPF49 Viper's Rebirth C	.15	.25
ABPF50 Temple of the Sun C	.15	.25
ABPF51 Rocket Pilder C	.15	.25
ABPF52 Break! Draw! C	.15	.25
ABPF53 Power Pickaxe R	.40	1.00
ABPF54 Spider's Lair C	.15	.25
ABPF55 Iron Core SR	.75	2.00
ABPF56 Gravekeeper's Stele C	.15	.25
ABPF57 Machine Assembly Line C	.15	.25
ABPF58 Ritual of Destruction C	.15	.25
ABPF59 Ascending Soul R	.40	1.00
ABPF60 Ritual Cage R	.40	1.00
ABPF61 Pot of Benevolence C	.15	.25
ABPF62 Synchro Control SR	.75	2.00
ABPF63 Changing Destiny C	.15	.25
ABPF64 Fiendish Chain SR	3.00	8.00
ABPF65 Nature's Reflection C	.15	.25
ABPF66 Serpent Suppression C	.15	.25
ABPF67 Meteor Flare C	.15	.25
ABPF68 Offering Immortals R	.40	1.00
ABPF69 Destruct Potion C	.15	.25
ABPF70 Call of the Reaper C	.15	.25
ABPF71 Lair Wire C	.15	.25
ABPF72 Core Blast R	.40	1.00
ABPF73 Saber Hole SR	1.50	4.00
ABPF74 Machine King - 3000 B.C. C	.15	.25
ABPF75 Alien Brain C	.15	.25
ABPF76 Forgotten Temple of the Deep C	.15	.25
ABPF77 Tuner's Scheme SR	.75	2.00
ABPF78 Psi-Curse C	.15	.25
ABPF79 Widespread Dud C	.15	.25
ABPF80 Inverse Universe C	.15	.25
ABPF81 XX-Saber Emrsblde SCR	2.00	5.00
ABPF82 Alchemist Blk Splls UR	1.50	4.00
ABPF82 Alchemist Blk Splls UTR	2.00	5.00
ABPF83 Super-Nimble Mega SR	.75	2.00
ABPF84 Cactus Bouncer SCR	8.00	20.00
ABPF85 Dragonic Guard SR	.75	2.00
ABPF86 The Dragon Dwlling SR	.75	2.00

ABPF87 Djinn Disserere SCR 1.50 4.00
ABPF88 Earthbound Linewalker SCR 2.00 5.00
ABPF89 Core Transport SCR 1.50 4.00
ABPF90 Gale Dogra R .40 1.00
ABPF91 Berfomet R .40 1.00
ABPF92 Chimera Flying R .40 1.00
ABPF93 Viser Des R .40 1.00
ABPF94 Evil Blast R .40 1.00
ABPF95 Shield Wing SCR 1.50 4.00
ABPF96 Undrgrnd Archnd SCR 1.50 4.00
ABPF97 Zeman the Ape SCR 1.50 4.00
ABPF98 Skull Conductor R .40 1.00
ABPF99 Shield Worm R .40 1.00

2010 Yu-Gi-Oh The Shining Darkness 1st Edition

COMPLETE SET (111) 100.00 200.00
BOOSTER BOX (24 PACKS) 60.00 90.00
BOOSTER PACK (9 CARDS) 3.00 4.00
RELEASED ON MAY 11, 2010
TSHD0 XX-Saber Boggart SR .75 2.00
TSHD1 Blackwing - Ghibli the Searing Wind .15 .25
TSHD2 Blackwing Gust R .40 1.00
TSHD3 Blackwing Breeze UR 1.00 2.50
TSHD3 Blackwing Breeze UR 1.50 4.00
TSHD4 Changer Synchron .15 .25
TSHD5 Card Breaker .15 .25
TSHD6 Second Booster .15 .25
TSHD7 Archfiend Interceptor .15 .25
TSHD8 Dread Dragon R .50 1.25
TSHD9 Trust Guardian SR .40 1.00
TSHD10 Flare Resonator .15 .25
TSHD11 Synchro Magnet .15 .25
TSHD12 Infernity Mirage SR 1.25 3.00
TSHD13 Infernity Randomizer .15 .25
TSHD14 Infernity Beetle R .75 2.00
TSHD15 Infernity Avenger (R) .40 1.00
TSHD16 Revival Rose R .40 1.00
TSHD17 Morphtronic Vacuumen .15 .25
TSHD18 Bird of Roses SR .75 2.00
TSHD19 Spore .15 .25
TSHD20 Fairy Archer .15 .25
TSHD21 Biofalcon .15 .25
TSHD22 Cherry Inmato R .40 1.00
TSHD23 Magidog R .40 1.00
TSHD24 Lyna the Light Charmer .15 .25
TSHD25 Wattgiraffe SR 4.00 10.00
TSHD26 Wattfox .15 .25
TSHD27 Wattwoodpecker .15 .25
TSHD28 Koa'ki Meiru Sandman .15 .25
TSHD29 Memory Crush King .15 .25
TSHD30 Delta Tri R .40 1.00
TSHD31 Trigon .15 .25
TSHD32 Testudo Erat SP 1.00 2.50
TSHD33 Ronintoadin .15 .25
TSHD34 Batteryman AAA .15 .25
TSHD35 Batteryman Fuel Cell R 1.25 3.00
TSHD36 Key Mouse .15 .25
TSHD37 Core Destroyer R .40 1.00
TSHD38 Hunter of Black SP .20 .50
TSHD39 Herald Perfect UR .75 2.00
TSHD39 Herald Perfect UTR 5.00 12.00
TSHD40 Black-Winged UR 1.00 2.50
TSHD40 Black-Winged UTR 1.00 2.50
TSHD40 Black-Winged GR 6.00 15.00
TSHD41 Chaos King UR 1.25 3.00
TSHD41 Chaos King UTR 1.00 2.50
TSHD42 Infernity Doom UR 1.50 4.00
TSHD42 Infernity Doom UTR 2.00 5.00
TSHD43 Splendid Rose UR .50 1.25
TSHD43 Splendid Rose UTR .75 2.00
TSHD44 Chaos Goddess SCR 3.00 8.00
TSHD45 Black-Winged Strafe .15 .25
TSHD46 Cards for Black UR 1.00 2.50
TSHD46 Cards for Black UTR .75 2.00
TSHD47 ZERO-MAX SR .40 1.00
TSHD48 Infernity Launcher SR 1.00 2.50
TSHD49 Into The Void UR 20.00 35.00
TSHD49 Into The Void UTR 25.00 40.00
TSHD50 Intercept Wave UR .75 2.00
TSHD50 Intercept Wave UTR .40 1.00
TSHD51 Pyramid of Wonders R .40 1.00
TSHD52 The Fountain R .40 1.00
TSHD53 Dragon Laser .15 .25
TSHD54 Wattcube .15 .25
TSHD55 Electromagnetic R .40 1.00
TSHD56 Worm Call .15 .25
TSHD57 Magic Triangle of the Ice Barrier .15 .25
TSHD58 Koa'ki Meiru Initialize .15 .25
TSHD59 Dawn of the Herald .15 .25
TSHD60 Forbidden Graveyard .15 .25
TSHD61 Leeching the Light .15 .25
TSHD62 Corridor of Agony SP .20 .50
TSHD63 Power Frame SR .40 1.00
TSHD64 Blackwing Bcklsh R .40 1.50
TSHD65 Blackwing - Bombardment .15 .25
TSHD66 Black Thunder .15 .25
TSHD67 Guard Mines R .40 1.00
TSHD68 Infernity Reflector .15 .25
TSHD69 Infernity Break .15 .25
TSHD70 Damage Gate SR .40 1.00
TSHD71 Infernity Inferno R .40 1.00
TSHD72 Phantom Hand .15 .25
TSHD73 Assault Spirits .15 .25
TSHD74 Blossom Bombardment .15 .25
TSHD75 Morphtronics, Scramble! .15 .25
TSHD76 Power Break .15 .25
TSHD77 Koa'ki Meiru Shield R .40 1.00
TSHD78 Crevice into the Different Dimension .15 .25
TSHD79 Synchro Ejection SR .40 1.00
TSHD80 Chaos Trap Hole SP 4.00 10.00
TSHD81 XX-Saber Drksl UR .50 1.25
TSHD81 XX-Saber Drksl UTR 2.50 6.00
TSHD82 Koa Mei Prttype R .40 1.00
TSHD83 Snyffus SCR .40 1.00
TSHD84 Nimble Sunfish SR .50 1.25
TSHD85 Akz, the Pumer R .40 1.00
TSHD86 Saber Vault SCR .40 1.00
TSHD87 Core Overclock SR .40 1.00
TSHD88 Wave-Motion SCR .40 1.00
TSHD89 Infernity Barrier SCR 2.50 6.00
TSHD90 Genex Controller .15 .25
TSHD91 Genex Undine .15 .25
TSHD92 Genex Searcher R .40 1.00
TSHD93 X-Saber Palomuro .15 .25
TSHD94 X-Saber Pashuul .15 .25
TSHD95 Hydro Genex SR .40 1.00
TSHD96 Light Gazer SR .40 1.00
TSHD97 Genex Neutron SCR .40 1.00
TSHD98 Infernity Dstryr SCR .40 1.00
TSHD99 Koa Mei Bergzak SCR 1.50 4.00

2010 Yu-Gi-Oh Duelist Revolution 1st Edition

COMPLETE SET (110) 175.00 300.00
BOOSTER BOX (24 PACKS) 150.00 300.00
BOOSTER PACK (9 CARDS) 3.00 8.00
RELEASED ON AUGUST 17, 2010
DREV0 Scrap Archfiend SR 1.25 3.00
DREV1 Earthquake Giant .15 .25
DREV2 Effect Veiler UR 8.00 20.00
DREV2 Effect Veiler UTR 50.00 80.00
DREV3 Dash Warrior .15 .25
DREV4 Damage Eater .15 .25
DREV5 A/D Changer .15 .25
DREV6 Stronghold Guardian .15 .25
DREV7 Playful Possum R .40 1.00
DREV8 Egotistical Ape R .40 1.00
DREV9 Uni-Horned Familiar .15 .25
DREV10 Monoceros .15 .25
DREV11 D.D. Unicorn Knight R .40 1.00
DREV12 Unibird SR .40 1.00
DREV13 Bicorn Re'em .15 .25
DREV14 Mine Mole .15 .25
DREV15 Trident Warrior SR .40 1.00
DREV16 Delta Flyer R 2.00 5.00
DREV17 Rhinotaurus .15 .25
DREV18 Hypnocorn R .40 1.00
DREV19 Scrap Chimera SR .50 1.25
DREV20 Scrap Goblin .15 .25
DREV21 Scrap Beast R .40 1.00
DREV22 Scrap Hunter R .40 1.00
DREV23 Scrap Golem R .40 1.00
DREV24 Wattbetta .15 .25
DREV25 Wattlemur .15 .25
DREV26 Wattpheasant .15 .25
DREV27 Naturia Mosquito .15 .25
DREV28 Naturia Beans .15 .25
DREV29 Naturia Bamboo (UR) 2.00 5.00
DREV29 Naturia Bamboo (UTR) 2.50 6.00
DREV30 Amazoness Sage .15 .25
DREV31 Amazoness Trainee .15 .25
DREV32 Amazoness Queen SR 3.00 8.00
DREV33 Lock Cat .15 .25
DREV34 Elephun .15 .25
DREV35 Synchro Fusionist R .40 1.00
DREV36 Ambitious Gofer R .40 1.00
DREV37 Final Psychic Ogre .15 .25
DREV38 Dragon Knight (UR) .50 1.25
DREV38 Dragon Knight (UR) .75 2.00
DREV38 Dragon Knight Draco-Equiste GR 2.50 6.00
DREV39 Ultimate Axon Kick (SR) 1.25 3.00
DREV40 Thunder Unicorn UR .50 1.25
DREV40 Thunder Unicorn UTR .75 2.00
DREV41 Voltic Bicorn UR .50 1.25
DREV41 Voltic Bicorn UTR .75 2.00
DREV42 Lightning Tricorn UR .50 1.25
DREV42 Lightning Tricorn UTR .75 2.00
DREV43 Scrap Dragon UR 2.00 5.00
DREV43 Scrap Dragon UTR 5.00 12.00
DREV44 Wattchimera UR .50 1.25
DREV44 Wattchimera UTR .75 2.00
DREV45 Blind Spot Strike .15 .25
DREV46 Double Cyclone .15 .25
DREV47 Scrapyard SR .40 1.00
DREV48 Scrapstorm SR .40 1.00
DREV49 Scrap Sheen .15 .25
DREV50 Wattcine .15 .25
DREV51 Naturia Forest .15 .25
DREV52 Landoise's Luminous (R) .40 1.00
DREV53 Amazoness Village R .40 1.00
DREV54 Amazoness Fighting .15 .25
DREV55 Unicorn Beacon SR .40 1.00
DREV56 Beast Rage .15 .25
DREV57 Miracle Synchro Fusion .15 .25
DREV58 Pestilence .15 .25
DREV59 Cursed Armaments .15 .25
DREV60 Wiseman's Chalice SR .40 1.00
DREV61 Summoning Curse .15 .25
DREV62 Pot of Duality SCR 8.00 20.00
DREV63 Desperate Tag .15 .25
DREV64 Battle Instinct .15 .25
DREV65 Howl of the Wild .15 .25
DREV66 Parallel Selection R .40 1.00
DREV67 Reanimation Wave R .40 1.00
DREV68 Barrier Wave .15 .25
DREV69 Chain Whirlwind .15 .25
DREV70 Scrap Rage .15 .25
DREV71 Wattcannon .15 .25
DREV72 Amazoness Wllpwr (R) .40 1.00
DREV73 Queen's Pawn .15 .25
DREV74 Beast Rising .15 .25
DREV75 Horn of Phantom (R) .40 1.00
DREV76 Paradox Fusion SR 1.00 2.50
DREV77 Solemn Warning UR 6.00 15.00
DREV77 Solemn Warning UTR 40.00 60.00
DREV78 Anti-Magic Prism .15 .25
DREV79 Chivalry UR 1.00 2.50
DREV79 Chivalry UTR 2.00 5.00
DREV80 Light of Destruction .15 .25
DREV81 Amazoness Scouts R .40 1.00
DREV82 Naturia Pnpple (SCR) .75 2.00
DREV83 D.D. Destroyer R .40 1.00
DREV84 Dark Desertapir R .40 1.00
DREV85 Psychic Nghtmre (SCR) 1.50 4.00
DREV86 Guts of Steel R .40 1.00
DREV87 Amznss Hrlm (SR) 1.00 2.50
DREV88 Amznss Shmnsm (SR) .40 1.00
DREV89 Super Rush (SR) .40 1.00
DREV90 Mystical Refpanel SCR 8.00 20.00
DREV91 Fabled Raven SCR 2.50 6.00
DREV92 Cyclone Creator (SCR) .75 2.00
DREV93 Miracle's Wake SCR .75 2.00
DREV94 Flamvell Poun .15 .25
DREV95 Flamvell Archer .15 .25
DREV96 Flamvell Fiend .15 .25
DREV97 Genex Worker .15 .25
DREV98 Genex Power Planner .15 .25
DREV99 Stygian Street (SCR) 2.00 5.00

2010 Yu-Gi-Oh Starstrike Blast 1st Edition

COMPLETE SET (100) 200.00 275.00
BOOSTER BOX (24 PACKS) 75.00 125.00
BOOSTER PACK (9 CARDS) 3.50 6.00
RELEASED ON NOVEMBER 16, 2010
STBLEN000 Archfiend Empress SR .75 2.00
STBLEN001 Swift Scarecrow .15 .25
STBLEN002 Mirror Ladybug .15 .25
STBLEN003 Reed Butterfly .15 .25
STBLEN004 Needle Soldier .15 .25
STBLEN005 Necro Linker .15 .25
STBLEN006 Rescue Warrior .15 .25
STBLEN007 Power Giant UTR 1.50 4.00
STBLEN007 Power Giant UR .75 2.00
STBLEN008 Vice Berserker .15 .25
STBLEN009 Lancer Archfiend R .40 1.00
STBLEN010 Power Breaker SR 1.00 2.50
STBLEN011 Extra Veiler .15 .25
STBLEN012 Synchro Soldier .15 .25
STBLEN013 Creation Resonator R .40 1.00
STBLEN014 Attack Gainer .15 .25
STBLEN015 Blackwing - Etesian of Two Swords .15 .25
STBLEN016 Blackwing - Aurora the Northern Lights R .40 1.00
STBLEN017 Blackwing - Abrolhos the Megaquake R .40 1.00
STBLEN018 Glow-Up Bulb UTR 10.00 25.00
STBLEN018 Glow Up Bulb UR 3.00 8.00
STBLEN019 Karakuri Soldier mdl 236 Nisamu .15 .25
STBLEN020 Karakuri Merchant mdl 177 Inashichi R .40 1.00
STBLEN021 Karakuri Strategist mdl 248 Nishipachi .15 .25
STBLEN022 Karakuri Ninja mdl 339 Sazank SR .50 1.25
STBLEN023 Karakuri Bushi mdl 6318 Muzanichiha R .40 1.00
STBLEN024 Scrap Soldier R .40 1.00
STBLEN025 Scrap Searcher .15 .25
STBLEN026 Wattkiwi .15 .25
STBLEN027 Watthopper .15 .25
STBLEN028 Wattdragonfly .15 .25
STBLEN029 Wattsquirrel R .40 1.00
STBLEN030 Naturia Cherries SR 5.00 12.00
STBLEN031 Naturia Pumpkin .15 .25
STBLEN032 Naturia Stag Beetle .15 .25
STBLEN033 Dance Princess of the Ice Barrier SR 3.00 8.00
STBLEN034 Chain Dog R .40 1.00
STBLEN035 Wightmare .15 .25
STBLEN036 Anarchist Monk Ranshin SR 1.00 2.50
STBLEN037 Delg the Dark Monarch SR 3.00 8.00
STBLEN038 Supreme Arcanite Magician UTR 3.00 8.00
STBLEN038 Supreme Arcanite Magician UR 3.00 8.00
STBLEN039 Gaia Drake, the Universal Force UTR 6.00 15.00
STBLEN039 Gaia Drake the Universal Force UR 5.00 12.00
STBLEN040 Shooting Star Dragon GR 10.00 25.00
STBLEN040 Shooting Star Dragon UTR 4.00 10.00
STBLEN040 Shooting Star Dragon UR 3.00 8.00
STBLEN041 Formula Synchron R 2.00 5.00
STBLEN042 Red Nova Dragon UTR 3.00 8.00
STBLEN042 Red Nova Dragon UR 1.50 4.00
STBLEN043 Karakuri Shogun mdl 00 Burei UR .75 2.00
STBLEN043 Karakuri Shogun mdl 00 Burei UTR 2.00 5.00
STBLEN044 Scrap Twin Dragon UTR 2.00 5.00
STBLEN044 Scrap Twin Dragon UR 1.50 4.00
STBLEN045 Tuning UTR 5.00 12.00
STBLEN045 Tuning UR 2.00 5.00
STBLEN046 Karakuri Showdown Castle R .40 1.00
STBLEN047 Golden Gearbox .15 .25
STBLEN048 Karakuri Anatomy .15 .25
STBLEN049 Scrap Lube .15 .25
STBLEN050 Wattcastle R .40 1.00
STBLEN051 Wattjustment .15 .25
STBLEN052 Barkion's Bark .15 .25
STBLEN053 Leodrake's Mane .15 .25
STBLEN054 Medallion of the Ice Barrier .15 .25
STBLEN055 Mirror of the Ice Barrier .15 .25
STBLEN056 Koa'ki Ring .15 .25
STBLEN057 Darkworld Shackles .15 .25
STBLEN058 Axe of Fools .15 .25
STBLEN059 Cursed Bill .15 .25
STBLEN060 Tokkosho of Ghost Destroying R .40 1.00
STBLEN061 Heat Wave R .40 1.00
STBLEN062 White Elephant's Gift .15 .25
STBLEN063 D2 Shield SR .75 2.00
STBLEN064 Red Screen .15 .25
STBLEN065 Blackback SR .75 2.00
STBLEN066 Defenders Intersect .15 .25
STBLEN067 Gravity Collapse R .40 1.00
STBLEN068 Blackwing - Boobytrap .15 .25
STBLEN069 Star Siphon .15 .25
STBLEN070 Half Counter .15 .25
STBLEN071 Karakuri Trick House .15 .25
STBLEN072 Karakuri Klock SR .50 1.25
STBLEN073 Scrap Crash .15 .25
STBLEN074 Wattkeeper .15 .25
STBLEN075 Exterio's Fang .15 .25
STBLEN076 Vanity's Emptiness .15 .25
STBLEN077 Different Dimension Ground SR 1.25 3.00
STBLEN078 Powersink Stone .15 .25
STBLEN079 Tyrant's Temper SR 1.50 4.00
STBLEN080 Dark Trap Hole .15 .25
STBLEN081 Skull Meister SCR 8.00 20.00

STBLEN082 Droll & Lock Bird R	1.00	2.50
STBLEN083 Spellstone Sorcerer Karood SCR	1.00	2.50
STBLEN084 Scrap Mind Reader SCR	.50	1.25
STBLEN085 Gravekeeper's Recruiter R	2.50	6.00
STBLEN086 Psi-Blocker SCR	2.50	6.00
STBLEN087 Koa'ki Meiru Wall R	.40	1.00
STBLEN088 Karakuri Barrel mdl 96 Shinkuro R	.40	1.00
STBLEN089 Mischief of the Yokai UTR	1.50	4.00
STBLEN089 Mischief of the Yokai UR	1.00	2.50
STBLEN090 Karakuri Spider	.15	.25
STBLEN091 Royal Knight of the Ice Barrier SR	.75	2.00
STBLEN092 Ally Salvo R	.40	1.00
STBLEN093 Ally of Justice Thousand Arms	.15	.25
STBLEN094 Ally of Justice Unknown Crusher	.15	.25
STBLEN095 Genex Ally Duradark SCR	.75	2.00
STBLEN096 The Fabled Rubyruda SCR	1.00	2.50
STBLEN097 Dragunity Knight - Vajrayana SR	2.00	5.00
STBLEN098 Dragunity Knight - Gae Dearg SCR	25.00	50.00
STBLEN099 Genex Ally Axel SCR	1.00	2.50

2011 Yu-Gi-Oh Storm of Ragnarok 1st Edition

COMPLETE SET (111)	100.00	200.00
BOOSTER BOX (24 PACKS)	60.00	90.00
BOOSTER PACK (9 CARDS)	2.50	4.00
RELEASED ON FEBRUARY 8, 2011		
STOR000 Vortex Whrlwnd SR	.20	.60
STOR001 Cosmic Compass C	.15	.25
STOR002 Doppelwarrior R	.20	.60
STOR003 Stardust Phantom R	.20	.60
STOR004 D.D. Sprite SR	.20	.60
STOR005 Top Runner C	.15	.25
STOR006 Barrier Resonator C	.15	.25
STOR007 Blackwing - Boreas the Sharp R	.20	.60
STOR008 Blackwing - Brisote the Tailwind C	.15	.25
STOR009 Blackwing - Calima the Haze C	.15	.25
STOR010 Tanngrisnir of the Nordic Beasts SR	.20	.60
STOR011 Guldfaxe of the Nordic Beasts R	.20	.60
STOR012 Garmr of the Nordic Beasts C	.15	.25
STOR013 Tanngnjostr of the Nordic Beasts R	.20	.60
STOR014 Ljosalf of the Nordic Alfar C	.15	.25
STOR015 Svartalf of the Nordic Alfar SR	.20	.60
STOR016 Dverg of the Nordic Alfar R	.20	.60
STOR017 Valkyrie of the Nordic Ascendant SR	.75	2.00
STOR018 Mimir of the Nordic Ascendant C	.15	.25
STOR019 Tyr of the Nordic Champions R	.20	.60
STOR020 Legendary Six Samurai - Kizan SR	2.50	6.00
STOR021 Legendary Six Samurai - Enishi UR	.50	1.25
STOR021 Legendary Six Samurai - Enishi UTR	2.00	5.00
STOR022 Legendary Six Samurai - Kageki R	.20	.60
STOR023 Legendary Six Samurai - Shinai C	.15	.25
STOR024 Legendary Six Samurai - Mizuho C	.15	.25
STOR025 Kagemusha of the Six Samurai C	.15	.25
STOR026 Shien's Squire C	.15	.25
STOR027 Karakuri Watchdog mdl 313 Saizan C	.15	.25
STOR028 Karakuri Ninja mdl 919 Kuick C	.15	.25
STOR029 Scrap Worm R	.20	.60
STOR030 Scrap Shark C	.15	.25
STOR031 Wattberyx R	.20	.60
STOR032 Wattmole C	.15	.25
STOR033 Symphonic Warrior Basses SR	.20	.60
STOR034 Symphonic Warrior Drumss SR	.20	.60
STOR035 Symphonic Warrior Piaano R	.20	.60
STOR036 Majioshaleon C	.15	.25
STOR037 Yaksha C	.15	.25
STOR038 Thor, Lord of the Aesir UR	1.00	2.50
STOR038 Thor, Lord of the Aesir UTR	2.00	5.00
STOR039 Loki, Lord of the Aesir UR	1.00	2.50
STOR039 Loki, Lord of the Aesir UTR	1.25	3.00
STOR040 Odin, Father of the Aesir UR	1.00	2.50
STOR040 Odin, Father of the Aesir UTR	1.00	2.50
STOR040 Odin, Father of the Aesir GR	3.00	8.00
STOR041 Legendary Six Samurai - Shi En UR	4.00	10.00
STOR041 Legendary Six Samurai - Shi En UTR	8.00	20.00
STOR042 Karakuri Steel Shogun mdl 00X Bureido UR	.75	2.00
STOR042 Karakuri Steel Shogun mdl 00X Bureido UTR	2.00	5.00
STOR043 Atomic Scrap Dragon UR	.50	1.25
STOR043 Atomic Scrap Dragon UTR	.50	1.25
STOR044 Watthydra SR	.20	.60
STOR045 Nordic Relic Draupnir C	.15	.25
STOR046 Gotterdammerung C	.15	.25
STOR047 March Towards Ragnarok R	.20	.60
STOR048 Shien's Smoke Signal R	.20	.60
STOR049 Six Strike - Triple Impact C	.15	.25
STOR050 Asceticism of the Six Samurai R	2.50	6.00
STOR051 Temple of the Six SR	.20	.60
STOR052 Karakuri Cash Cache C	.15	.25
STOR053 Karakuri Gold Dust C	.15	.25
STOR054 Wattkey C	.15	.25
STOR055 Stardust Shimmer SR	1.50	4.00
STOR056 Resonator Engine C	.15	.25
STOR057 Token Sundae C	.15	.25
STOR058 Foolish Return R	.20	.60
STOR059 Divine Wind of Mist Valley C	.15	.25
STOR060 Vylon Matter C	.15	.25
STOR061 Forbidden Lance SR	1.50	4.00
STOR062 Terminal World C	.15	.25
STOR063 Hope for Escape R	.60	1.50
STOR064 Zero Force C	.15	.25
STOR065 Blackboost C	.15	.25
STOR066 Divine Relic Mjollnir C	.15	.25
STOR067 Solemn Authority C	.15	.25
STOR068 Nordic Relic Brisingamen C	.15	.25
STOR069 Nordic Relic Laevateinn C	.15	.25
STOR070 Nordic Relic Gungnir R	.20	.60
STOR071 The Golden Apples SCR	.75	2.00
STOR072 Odin's Eye C	.15	.25
STOR073 Gleipnir, the Fetters of Fenrir UR	.75	2.00
STOR073 Gleipnir, the Fetters of Fenrir UTR	1.25	3.00
STOR074 Musakani Magatama R	.20	.60
STOR075 Shien's Scheme C	.15	.25
STOR076 Token Stampede C	.15	.25
STOR077 Xing Zhen Hu Replica C	.15	.25
STOR078 Tyrant's Tirade C	.15	.25
STOR079 Tiki Curse C	.15	.25
STOR080 Tiki Soul C	.15	.25
STOR081 Vanadis of the Nordic Ascendant SCR	3.00	8.00
STOR082 Shien's Daredevil R	.20	.60
STOR083 Karakuri Muso mdl 818 Haipa UR	.50	1.25
STOR083 Karakuri Muso mdl 818 Haipa UTR	.50	1.25
STOR084 Scrap Breaker SCR	.50	1.25
STOR085 Chaos Hunter SCR	5.00	12.00
STOR086 Maxx C SCR	20.00	40.00
STOR087 The Nordic Lights UR	.50	1.25
STOR087 The Nordic Lights UTR	.50	1.25
STOR088 Nordic Relic Megingjord SCR	.50	1.25
STOR089 Six Strike - Thunder Blast SCR	.50	1.25
STOR090 Cyber Shield C	.15	.25
STOR091 Hourglass of Courage C	.15	.25
STOR092 Needle Ball C	.15	.25
STOR093 Blood Sucker C	.15	.25
STOR094 Overpowering Eye R	.20	.60
STOR095 Worm Illidan C	.15	.25
STOR096 Worm Jetelikpse C	.15	.25
STOR097 Worm King SR	.20	.60
STOR098 Elemental Hero Ice Edge SR	.75	2.00
STOR099 Vylon Delta SCR	1.50	4.00

2011 Yu-Gi-Oh Extreme Victory 1st Edition

COMPLETE SET (110)	125.00	250.00
BOOSTER BOX (24 PACKS)	50.00	75.00
BOOSTER PACK (9 CARDS)	2.50	4.00
RELEASED ON MAY 10, 2011		
EXVC000 Reborn Tengu SR	1.00	2.50
EXVC001 Junk Servant R	.50	1.25
EXVC002 Unknown Synchron	.15	.25
EXVC003 Salvage Warrior R	.30	.75
EXVC004 Necro Defender R	.30	.75
EXVC005 Mystic Piper SCR	8.00	20.00
EXVC006 Force Resonator	.15	.25
EXVC007 Clock Resonator	.15	.25
EXVC008 Hillen Tengu SR	.40	1.00
EXVC009 Kogarashi UR	.75	2.00
EXVC009 Kogarashi UTR	1.50	4.00
EXVC010 Morphtronic Lantron	.15	.25
EXVC011 Morphtronic Staplen	.15	.25
EXVC012 Meklord Army of Wisel	.15	.25
EXVC013 Meklord Army of Skiel	.15	.25
EXVC014 Meklord Army Granel R	.30	.75
EXVC015 Dragon Asterisk SR	.40	1.00
EXVC016 Cyber Magician SR	.40	1.00
EXVC017 T.G. Striker R	.50	1.25
EXVC018 T.G. Jet Falcon	.15	.25
EXVC019 T.G. Catapult Dragon	.15	.25
EXVC020 T.G. Warwolf	.15	.25
EXVC021 T.G. Rush Rhino R	.40	1.00
EXVC022 Buster Blaster R	.50	1.25
EXVC023 Esper Girl	.15	.25
EXVC024 Mental Seeker	.15	.25
EXVC025 Silent Psych Wiz SR	.40	1.00
EXVC026 Serene Psychic Witch	.15	.25
EXVC027 Hushed Psych Cleric R	.75	2.00
EXVC028 Elder of Six Samurai	.15	.25
EXVC029 Shien's Advisor SR	.40	1.00
EXVC030 Karakuri Komachi	.15	.25
EXVC031 Karakuri Ninja	.15	.25
EXVC032 Scrap Kong	.15	.25
EXVC033 Tradetoad R	.30	.75
EXVC034 Gladiator Tygerius	.15	.25
EXVC035 Jar Turtle	.15	.25
EXVC036 Aurora Paragon	.15	.25
EXVC037 Junk Berserker UTR	2.00	5.00
EXVC037 Junk Berserker GR	2.50	6.00
EXVC037 Junk Berserker UR	1.00	2.50
EXVC038 Life Strm Dragon UR	1.50	4.00
EXVC038 Life Strm Dragon UTR	2.00	5.00
EXVC039 Recipro Dragonfly R	.75	2.00
EXVC040 Wonder Magician UR	.75	2.00
EXVC040 Wonder Magician UTR	1.25	3.00
EXVC041 Power Gladiator SR	.40	1.00
EXVC042 Blade Blaster UR	.75	2.00
EXVC042 Blade Blaster UTR	1.00	2.50
EXVC043 Halberd Cannon UR	.75	2.00
EXVC043 Halberd Cannon UTR	1.00	2.50
EXVC044 Ovrmnd Archfnd UR	1.50	4.00
EXVC044 Ovrmnd Archfnd UTR	1.25	3.00
EXVC045 Scarlet Security	.15	.25
EXVC046 Red Dragon Vase	.15	.25
EXVC047 Resonator Call R	.60	1.50
EXVC048 Resonant Destruction	.15	.25
EXVC049 Fortissimo the Mobile	.15	.25
EXVC050 Boon of the Meklord	.15	.25
EXVC051 Resolute Meklord Army	.15	.25
EXVC052 Reboot	.15	.25
EXVC053 TGX1-HL	.15	.25
EXVC054 TGX300	.15	.25
EXVC055 ESP Amplifier	.15	.25
EXVC056 Psychic Feel Zone R	1.25	3.00
EXVC057 Shien's Dojo SR	.40	1.00
EXVC058 Runaway Karakuri	.15	.25
EXVC059 Contact Aquamirror	.15	.25
EXVC060 Soundproofed R	.30	.75
EXVC061 Out of the Blue	.15	.25
EXVC062 Self-Mummification	.15	.25
EXVC063 Red Carpet	.15	.25
EXVC064 Power-Up Adapter	.15	.25
EXVC065 Chaos Infinity R	.50	1.25
EXVC066 Mektimed Blast	.15	.25
EXVC067 Meklord Factory	.15	.25
EXVC068 TGX3-DX2 R	.50	1.25
EXVC069 TG-SX1	.15	.25
EXVC070 TG1-EM1	.15	.25
EXVC071 Psychic Reactor	.15	.25
EXVC072 Brain Hazard R	.50	1.25
EXVC073 Six Style - Dual Wield	.15	.25
EXVC074 Karakuri Cash SR	.40	1.00
EXVC075 Tyrant's Tantrum	.15	.25
EXVC076 Debunk SR	1.00	2.50
EXVC077 Sealing Ceremony	.15	.25
EXVC078 Safe Zone SR	1.50	4.00
EXVC079 Localized Tornado	.15	.25
EXVC080 W Nebula Meteorite	.15	.25
EXVC081 Vampire Dragon SCR	1.25	3.00
EXVC082 Dodger Dragon SR	1.50	4.00
EXVC083 Mara Alfar UR	.75	2.00
EXVC083 Mara Alfar UTR	1.25	3.00
EXVC084 Tour Guide Undrwrld SCR	8.00	20.00
EXVC085 Psi-Beast R	.60	1.50
EXVC086 Gladiator Beast UR	1.25	3.00
EXVC086 Gladiator Beast UTR	1.50	4.00
EXVC087 Gladiator Taming SCR	.40	1.00
EXVC088 Full House R	.50	1.25
EXVC089 Psych Shckwve SCR	3.00	8.00
EXVC090 Axe Dragonute	.15	.25
EXVC091 Lancer Dragonute SR	.40	1.00
EXVC092 Lancer Lindwurm	.15	.25
EXVC093 EH Neos Knight UR	3.00	8.00
EXVC093 EH Neos Knight UTR	3.00	8.00
EXVC094 Meklord Emperor SCR	1.50	4.00
EXVC095 Meklord Fortress R	.40	1.00
EXVC096 Blackwing Rain Shadow R	.60	1.50
EXVC097 Scrap Orthros SCR	1.25	3.00
EXVC098 Naturia Eggplant SR	.40	1.00
EXVC099 Blue Rose SCR	1.50	4.00

2011 Yu-Gi-Oh Generation Force 1st Edition

COMPLETE SET (111)	100.00	200.00
BOOSTER BOX (24 PACKS)	60.00	90.00
BOOSTER PACK (9 CARDS)	2.50	4.00
RELEASED ON AUGUST 16, 2011		
GENFEN000 Xyz Veil SR	.25	.75
GENFEN001 Gagaga Magician SR	.20	.60
GENFEN002 Gogogo Golem	.15	.25
GENFEN003 Achacha Archer	.15	.25
GENFEN004 Goblindbergh	.15	.25
GENFEN005 Big Jaws R	.20	.60
GENFEN006 Skull Kraken	.15	.25
GENFEN007 Drill Barnacle	.15	.25
GENFEN008 Jawsman R	.20	.60
GENFEN009 Crashbug X	.15	.25
GENFEN010 Crashbug Y	.15	.25
GENFEN011 Crashbug Z	.15	.25
GENFEN012 Super Crashbug SR	.20	.60
GENFEN013 Wind-Up Soldier	.15	.25
GENFEN014 Wind-Up Magician R	.20	.60
GENFEN015 Wind-Up Juggler SR	.20	.60
GENFEN016 Wind-Up Dog	.15	.25
GENFEN017 Wind-Up Snail R	.20	.60
GENFEN018 Spearfish Soldier	.15	.25
GENFEN019 Flyfang	.15	.25
GENFEN020 Skystarray R	.20	.60
GENFEN021 Airorca R	.20	.60
GENFEN022 Wingtortoise R	.20	.60
GENFEN023 Space-Time Police UR	.20	.60
GENFEN023 Space-Time Police UTR	.40	1.00
GENFEN024 Time Escaper SR	.20	.60
GENFEN025 Gem-Elephant	.15	.25
GENFEN026 Laval Magma Cannoneer	.15	.25
GENFEN027 Gishki Diviner R	.20	.60
GENFEN028 Gusto Codor	.15	.25
GENFEN029 Saambell the Summoner	.15	.25
GENFEN030 Geargiano	.15	.25
GENFEN031 Poki Draco	.15	.25
GENFEN032 Master of the Flaming Dragonswords	.15	.25
GENFEN033 Perditious Puppeteer	.15	.25
GENFEN034 Blue-Blooded Oni SR	.25	.75
GENFEN035 Ghost Ship R	.20	.60
GENFEN036 Absolute Crusader SR	.20	.60
GENFEN037 Big Emperor Penguin	.15	.25
GENFEN038 Milla the Temporal Magician	.15	.25
GENFEN039 17: Leviathan Dragon UR	.50	1.25
GENFEN039 17: Leviathan Dragon UTR	.75	2.00
GENFEN039 17: Leviathan Dragon GR	3.00	8.00
GENFEN040 Submersible Carrier SR	.20	.60
GENFEN041 Number 34: Terror-Byte UR	.20	.60
GENFEN041 Number 34: Terror-Byte UTR	.40	1.00
GENFEN042 Wind-Up Zenmaister UR	.20	.60
GENFEN042 Wind-Up Zenmaister UTR	.50	1.25
GENFEN043 Leviair the Sea Dragon UR	6.00	15.00
GENFEN043 Leviair the Sea Dragon UTR	15.00	30.00
GENFEN044 Tiras, Keeper of Genesis SCR	4.00	10.00
GENFEN045 Wonder Wand UR	2.50	6.00
GENFEN045 Wonder Wand UTR	4.00	10.00
GENFEN046 Double Up Chance	.15	.25
GENFEN047 Thunder Short	.15	.25
GENFEN048 Aqua Jet	.15	.25
GENFEN049 Surface SR	1.25	3.00
GENFEN050 Crashbug Road	.15	.25
GENFEN051 Infected Mail SR	.20	.60
GENFEN052 Cracking	.15	.25
GENFEN053 Legendary Wind-Up	.15	.25
GENFEN054 Wind-Up Factory SR	1.00	2.50
GENFEN055 Fish and Kicks	.15	.25
GENFEN056 Future Glow	.15	.25
GENFEN057 Vylon Filament	.15	.25
GENFEN058 Quill Pen of Gulldos SR	1.25	3.00
GENFEN059 Star Changer R	.20	.60
GENFEN060 Oni-Gami Combo	.15	.25
GENFEN061 Resonance Device R	.20	.60
GENFEN062 Peeking Goblin	.15	.25
GENFEN063 Asleep at the Switch	.15	.25
GENFEN064 Poseidon Waves	.15	.25
GENFEN065 Explosive Urchin	.15	.25
GENFEN066 Damage Vaccine MAX	.15	.25
GENFEN067 Overwind	.15	.25
GENFEN068 Underworld Egg Clutch	.15	.25
GENFEN069 Oh FIsh! R	.20	.60
GENFEN070 Bright Future R	.20	.60
GENFEN071 Past Image	.15	.25
GENFEN072 Burgeoning Whirlflame	.15	.25
GENFEN073 Treaty on Uniform Nomenclature	.15	.25
GENFEN074 Utopian Aura	.15	.25
GENFEN075 United Front R	.20	.60
GENFEN076 Curse of the Circle R	.20	.60
GENFEN077 Tyrant's Tummyache	.15	.25
GENFEN078 Attention! R	.20	.60

GENFEN079 Raigeki Bottle UR	.20	.60
GENFEN079 Raigeki Bottle UTR	.40	1.00
GENFEN080 Gravelstorm	.15	.25
GENFEN081 Sea Lancer R	.20	.60
GENFEN082 Piercing Moray UR	.20	.60
GENFEN082 Piercing Moray UTR	.40	1.00
GENFEN083 Lost Blue Breaker SCR	.40	1.00
GENFEN084 Pain Painter SCR	3.00	8.00
GENFEN085 Orient Dragon SCR	.75	2.00
GENFEN086 Adreus, Keeper SCR	15.00	30.00
GENFEN087 Fish and Swaps R	.20	.60
GENFEN088 Painful Return R	.20	.60
GENFEN089 Smashing Horn SCR	1.50	4.00
GENFEN090 Elemental HERO Flash	.15	.25
GENFEN091 Vision HERO Trinity SR	2.50	6.00
GENFEN092 Phantom Magician	.15	.25
GENFEN093 Elemental HERO Nova UR	8.00	20.00
GENFEN093 Elemental HERO Nova UTR	8.00	20.00
GENFEN094 Masked HERO Goka R	1.00	2.50
GENFEN095 Masked HERO Vapor SR	3.00	8.00
GENFEN096 Vision HERO Adoration SCR	8.00	20.00
GENFEN097 Mask Change	.15	.25
GENFEN098 A Hero Lives UR	3.00	8.00
GENFEN098 A Hero Lives UTR	8.00	20.00
GENFEN099 Steelswarm Roach SCR	2.50	6.00

2011 Yu-Gi-Oh Photon Shockwave 1st Edition

COMPLETE SET (111)	100.00	200.00
BOOSTER BOX (24 PACKS)	50.00	80.00
BOOSTER PACK (9 CARDS)	2.50	4.00
RELEASED ON NOVEMBER 15, 2011		
PHSW000 Alexandrite Dragon SR	.75	2.00
PHSW001 Bunilla C	.15	.25
PHSW002 Rabidragon C	.15	.25
PHSW003 Rai Rider C	.15	.25
PHSW004 Stinging Swordsman C	.15	.25
PHSW005 Kagetokage R	.25	.60
PHSW006 Acorno C	.15	.25
PHSW007 Pinecono C	.15	.25
PHSW008 Friller Rabca SR	.20	.60
PHSW009 Shark Stickers C	.15	.25
PHSW010 Needle Sunfish C	.15	.25
PHSW011 Galaxy-Eyes Photon Dragon UR	2.50	6.00
PHSW011 Galaxy-Eyes Photon Dragon UTR	3.00	8.00
PHSW011 Galaxy-Eyes Photon Dragon GR	8.00	20.00
PHSW012 Daybreaker R	.25	.60
PHSW013 Lightserpent SR	.20	.60
PHSW014 Plasma Ball C	.15	.25
PHSW015 Photon Cerberus R	.25	.60
PHSW016 Evoltile Gephyro C	.15	.25
PHSW017 Evoltile Westlo SR	.75	2.00
PHSW018 Evoltile Odonto C	.15	.25
PHSW019 Evolsaur Vulcano R	.25	.60
PHSW020 Evolsaur Cerato UR	.60	1.50
PHSW020 Evolsaur Cerato UTR	1.00	2.50
PHSW021 Evolsaur Diplo R	.25	.60
PHSW022 Wind-Up Warrior C	.15	.25
PHSW023 Wind-Up Knight R	.25	.60
PHSW024 Wind-Up Hunter SR	.20	.60
PHSW025 Wind-Up Bat C	.15	.25
PHSW026 Wind-Up Kitten (UR)	1.25	3.00
PHSW026 Wind-Up Kitten UTR	1.50	4.00
PHSW027 D.D. Telepon R	.25	.60
PHSW028 Wattcobra C	.15	.25
PHSW029 Naturia Marron C	.15	.25
PHSW030 Prior of the Ice Barrier C	.15	.25
PHSW031 Senior Silver Ninja C	.15	.25
PHSW032 Rodenut C	.15	.25
PHSW033 Fenghuang SR	.20	.60
PHSW034 Tribe-Shocking Virus R	.25	.60
PHSW035 Goblin Pothole Squad C	.15	.25
PHSW036 Creepy Coney C	.15	.25
PHSW037 Rescue Rabbit SCR	6.00	15.00
PHSW038 Baby Tiragon R	.40	1.00
PHSW039 Number 83: Galaxy Queen SR	.40	1.00
PHSW040 Black Ray Lancer SR	.20	.60
PHSW041 Number 10: Illumiknight UR	.40	1.00
PHSW041 Number 10: Illumiknight UTR	.60	1.50
PHSW042 Number 20: Giga-Brilliant SR	.20	.60
PHSW043 Evolzar Laggia UR	.50	1.25
PHSW043 Evolzar Laggia UTR	1.50	4.00
PHSW044 Thunder End Dragon UR	4.00	10.00
PHSW044 Thunder End Dragon UTR	5.00	12.00
PHSW045 Attraffic Control C	.15	.25
PHSW046 Ego Boost C	.15	.25
PHSW047 Monster Slots C	.15	.25
PHSW048 Cross Attack C	.15	.25
PHSW049 Xyz Gift UR	.20	.60
PHSW049 Xyz Gift UTR	.40	1.00
PHSW050 Photon Veil UR	.50	1.25
PHSW050 Photon Veil UTR	1.50	4.00
PHSW051 Photon Lead C	.15	.25
PHSW052 Photon Booster R	.25	.60
PHSW053 Evo-Karma C	.15	.25
PHSW054 Evo-Miracle C	.15	.25
PHSW055 Zenmailfunction C	.15	.25
PHSW056 Extra Gate SR	.20	.60
PHSW057 Shard of Greed SCR	.75	2.00
PHSW058 Murmur of the Forest R	.25	.60
PHSW059 Tri-Wight C	.15	.25
PHSW060 One Day of Peace C	.15	.25
PHSW061 Space Cyclone C	.15	.25
PHSW062 Poisonous Winds C	.15	.25
PHSW063 Heartfelt Appeal C	.15	.25
PHSW064 Fiery Fervor C	.15	.25
PHSW065 Damage Diet C	.15	.25
PHSW066 Copy Knight R	.25	.60
PHSW067 Mirror Mail C	.15	.25
PHSW068 Fish Rain C	.15	.25
PHSW069 Icy Crevasse C	.15	.25
PHSW070 Lumenize C	.15	.25
PHSW071 Evolutionary Bridge C	.15	.25
PHSW072 Zenmairch C	.15	.25
PHSW073 Wattcancel C	.15	.25
PHSW074 Champion's Vigilance C	.15	.25
PHSW075 Darklight SR	.20	.60
PHSW076 Tyrant's Throes R	.75	2.00
PHSW077 Sound the Retreat! C	.15	.25
PHSW078 Deep Dark Trap Hole R	.40	1.00
PHSW079 Eisbahn R	.40	1.00
PHSW080 Sealing Ceremony of Suiton C	.15	.25
PHSW081 Photon Sabre Tiger SR	.40	1.00
PHSW082 Evolsaur Pelta R	.25	.60
PHSW083 Wind-Up Rabbit SCR	.75	2.00
PHSW084 D-Boyz SCR	.75	2.00
PHSW085 Latinum, Exarch of Dark World UTR	.60	1.50
PHSW085 Latinum, Exarch of Dark World UR	.20	.60
PHSW086 Evolzar Dolkka SCR	.75	2.00
PHSW087 Wind-Up Zenmaines SCR	.75	2.00
PHSW088 Xyz Territory R	.25	.60
PHSW089 Dark Smog SCR	.75	2.00
PHSW090 Sergeant Electro UR	.20	.60
PHSW090 Sergeant Electro UTR	.40	1.00
PHSW091 Vylon Ohm C	.15	.25
PHSW092 Laval Dual Slasher C	.15	.25
PHSW093 Gem-Turtle SR	.40	1.00
PHSW094 Laval Lancelord C	.15	.25
PHSW095 Gishki Beast R	.25	.60
PHSW096 Gem-Knight Emerald R	.25	.60
PHSW097 Junk Defender R	.25	.60
PHSW098 Metaion, the Timelord SCR	.75	2.00
PHSW099 Infernity Knight SR	.20	.60

2012 Yu-Gi-Oh Order of Chaos 1st Edition

COMPLETE SET (113)	250.00	350.00
BOOSTER BOX (24 PACKS)	50.00	80.00
BOOSTER PACK (9 CARDS)	2.50	4.00
RELEASED ON JANUARY 24, 2012		
ORCS000 Axe - Zektahawk SR	.25	.75
ORCS000 Axe - Zektahawk UR	.50	1.25
ORCS001 Kurivolt	.15	.25
ORCS002 Darklon	.15	.25
ORCS003 Gagaga Girl SCR	2.00	5.00
ORCS004 Gogogo Giant R	.10	.30
ORCS005 ZW - Unicorn Spear R	.10	.30
ORCS006 Shocktopus	.15	.25
ORCS007 Photon Lizard R	.10	.30
ORCS008 Photon Thrasher R	.50	1.25
ORCS009 Photon Crusher	.15	.25
ORCS010 Photon Leo	.15	.25
ORCS011 Photon Circle	.15	.25
ORCS012 Reverse Buster R	.10	.30
ORCS013 Flame Armor Ninja	.15	.25
ORCS014 Air Armor Ninja	.15	.25
ORCS015 Aqua Armor Ninja	.15	.25
ORCS016 Earth Armor Ninja	.15	.25
ORCS017 Inzektor Hornet SR	1.50	4.00
ORCS018 Inzektor Ant	.15	.25
ORCS019 Inzektor Centipede	.15	.25
ORCS020 Inzektor Dragonfly R	.10	.30
ORCS021 Inzekt Giga-Mantis UR	.50	1.25
ORCS021 Inzekt Giga-Mantis UTR	.50	1.25
ORCS022 Inzektor Giga-Weevil	.15	.25
ORCS023 Wind-Up Rat SR	.50	1.25
ORCS024 Wind-Up Honeybee	.15	.25
ORCS025 Evoltile Pleuro	.15	.25
ORCS026 Evoltile Casinerio R	.10	.30
ORCS027 Evolsaur Elias	.15	.25
ORCS028 Evolsaur Terias	.15	.25
ORCS029 Grandmaster Hanzo UR	.50	1.25
ORCS029 Grandmaster Hanzo UTR	1.50	4.00
ORCS030 Masked Ninja Ebisu	.15	.25
ORCS031 Upstart Golden Ninja	.15	.25
ORCS032 Chow Len the Prophet	.15	.25
ORCS033 Familiar-Possessed - Dharc	.15	.25
ORCS034 Dark Blade the Captain R	.10	.30
ORCS035 Trance Archfiend SP	.10	.30
ORCS036 Divine Dragon Apocralyph	.15	.25
ORCS037 Darkstorm Dragon SR	.25	.75
ORCS038 Numen erat Testudo	.15	.25
ORCS039 Twin Photon Lizard UR	.50	1.25
ORCS039 Twin Photon Lizard UTR	.50	1.25
ORCS040 C39: Utopia Ray UR	.50	1.25
ORCS040 C39: Utopia Ray UTR	.75	2.00
ORCS040 C39: Utopia Ray GR	2.50	6.00
ORCS041 Blade Armor Ninja SR	.75	2.00
ORCS042 12: Crimson Shadow UR	.50	1.25
ORCS042 12: Crimson Shadow UTR	.50	1.25
ORCS043 96: Dark Mist UR	.75	2.00
ORCS043 96: Dark Mist UTR	.75	2.00
ORCS044 Wind-Up Carrier UR	2.50	6.00
ORCS044 Wind-Up Carrier UTR	2.50	6.00
ORCS045 Evolzar Solda UR	1.25	3.00
ORCS045 Evolzar Solda UTR	.50	1.25
ORCS046 Inzektor Exa-Beetle SCR	1.50	4.00
ORCS047 Full-Force Strike	.15	.25
ORCS048 Gagagabolt R	.10	.30
ORCS049 Double Defender	.15	.25
ORCS050 Galaxy Storm	.15	.25
ORCS051 Ninjitsu Alchemy SR	.25	.75
ORCS052 Star Light, Star Bright	.15	.25
ORCS053 Armor Blast SR	.25	.75
ORCS054 Sword - Zektkaliber UR	1.00	2.50
ORCS054 Sword - Zektkaliber UTR	.50	1.25
ORCS055 Weights & Zenmaisures R	.10	.30
ORCS056 Primordial Soup	.15	.25
ORCS057 Evo-Force SR	.25	.75
ORCS058 Dark Mambele	.15	.25
ORCS059 Creeping Darkness SR	.25	.75
ORCS060 Shrine of Mist Valley R	.10	.30
ORCS061 Xyz Burst	.15	.25
ORCS062 Galaxy Wave	.15	.25
ORCS063 Dicephoon	.15	.25
ORCS064 Counterforce	.15	.25
ORCS065 Gagagaguard R	.10	.30
ORCS066 Xyz Reflect UR	.50	1.25
ORCS066 Xyz Reflect UTR	.50	1.25
ORCS067 Splash Capture	.15	.25
ORCS068 Armor Ninjitsu Freezing	.15	.25
ORCS069 Armor Ninjitsu Freezing	.25	.75
ORCS070 Inzektor Orb R	.10	.30
ORCS071 Variable Form	.15	.25
ORCS072 Zenmailstrom	.15	.25
ORCS073 Degen-Force	.15	.25
ORCS074 Evo-Branch	.15	.25
ORCS075 Ninjitsu Super-Trans SR	1.00	2.50
ORCS076 Xyz Reborn SCR	2.50	6.00
ORCS077 Over Capacity R	.10	.30
ORCS078 The Huge Revolution is Over	.15	.25
ORCS079 Royal Prison R	.10	.30
ORCS080 Sealing Ceremony of Katon	.15	.25
ORCS081 Inzektor Hopper R	.10	.30
ORCS082 Wind-Up Shark SR	.25	.75
ORCS083 Evoltile Najasho SR	.25	.75
ORCS084 White Dragon Ninja SCR	3.00	8.00
ORCS085 Interplanet. Dragon	.15	.25
ORCS086 Tour Bus Undrwrld SCR	1.25	3.00
ORCS087 Photon Trident	.15	.25
ORCS088 Evo-Instant R	.10	.30
ORCS089 Ninjitsu Duplication R	.10	.30
ORCS090 White Night Queen R	.10	.30
ORCS091 Danipon	.15	.25
ORCS092 Sweet Corn	.15	.25
ORCS093 Vampire Koala	.15	.25
ORCS094 Koalo-Koala	.15	.25
ORCS095 Dark Diviner SR	.25	.75
ORCS096 Dark Flattop R	.10	.30
ORCS097 Driven Daredevil SCR	.60	1.50
ORCS098 Arsenal Zenmaioh SCR	10.00	25.00
ORCS099 M-X-Saber Invoker SCR	5.00	12.00
ORCSSP1 Axe - Zektahawk PROMO	.10	.30

2012 Yu-Gi-Oh Galactic Overlord 1st Edition

COMPLETE SET (111)	250.00	350.00
BOOSTER BOX (24 PACKS)	60.00	90.00
BOOSTER PACK (9 CARDS)	3.00	4.00
RELEASED ON MAY 8, 2012		
GAOV000 Noble Knight SR	.20	.60
GAOV001 Wattaildragon	.15	.25
GAOV002 Hieratic Seal of the Sun Dragon Overlord	.15	.25
GAOV003 Overlay Owl	.15	.25
GAOV004 Tasuke Knight SR	.20	.60
GAOV005 Gagaga Gardna R	.25	.75
GAOV006 Cardcar D SCR	2.50	6.00
GAOV007 Overlay Eater	.15	.25
GAOV008 Hammer Shark R	.25	.75
GAOV009 Hammer Bounzer SR	.20	.60
GAOV010 Blade Bounzer	.15	.25
GAOV011 Phantom Bounzer	.15	.25
GAOV012 Morpho Butterspy	.15	.25
GAOV013 Swallowtail Butterspy	.15	.25
GAOV014 Moonlit Papillon	.15	.25
GAOV015 Jumbo Drill SR	.20	.60
GAOV016 Rocket Arrow Express R	.25	.75
GAOV017 Cameraclops	.15	.25
GAOV018 Hieratic Dragon of Nuit	.15	.25
GAOV019 Dragon of Gebeb SR	1.00	2.50
GAOV020 Hieratic Dragon of Eset	.15	.25
GAOV021 Hieratic Dragon of Nebthet	.15	.25
GAOV022 Dragon of Tefnuit R	.25	.75
GAOV023 Hieratic Dragon of Su	.15	.25
GAOV024 Hieratic Dragon of Asar R	.25	.75
GAOV025 Dragon of Sutekh UR	.60	1.50
GAOV025 Dragon of Sutekh UTR	.60	1.50
GAOV026 Evoltile Lagosucho	.15	.25
GAOV027 Evolsaur Darwino	.15	.25
GAOV028 Inzektor Firefly	.15	.25
GAOV029 Inzektor Ladybug	.15	.25
GAOV030 Inzektor Earwig	.15	.25
GAOV031 Inzektor Giga-Cricket R	.25	.75
GAOV032 Lightray Sorcerer R	.25	.75
GAOV033 Lightray Daedalus	.15	.25
GAOV034 Lightray Gearfried R	.25	.75
GAOV035 Lightray Diabolos R	.25	.75
GAOV036 Lady of D.	.15	.25
GAOV037 Absorbing Jar R	.25	.75
GAOV038 Red-Headed Oni	.15	.25
GAOV039 Flame Tiger	.15	.25
GAOV040 Nomadic Force	.15	.25
GAOV041 Neo Galaxy-Eyes UR	5.00	12.00
GAOV041 Neo Galaxy-Eyes UTR	5.00	12.00
GAOV041 Neo Galaxy-Eyes (GR)	8.00	20.00
GAOV042 Shark Drake UR	1.00	2.50
GAOV042 Shark Drake UTR	.60	1.50
GAOV043 Photon Strike SCR	1.50	4.00
GAOV044 Photon Papilloperative R	.25	.75
GAOV045 Force Focus UR	.60	1.50
GAOV045 Force Focus UTR	.60	1.50
GAOV046 Gaia Dragon SR	8.00	20.00
GAOV047 Dragon King of Atum SR	3.00	8.00
GAOV048 Dragon Overlord SCR	4.00	10.00
GAOV049 Dragun Djinn SR	5.00	12.00
GAOV050 Inzektor Exa-Stag UR	.60	1.50
GAOV050 Inzektor Exa-Stag UTR	.60	1.50
GAOV051 Bound Wand (SR)	.75	2.00
GAOV052 Mini-Guts	.15	.25
GAOV053 Falling Current	.15	.25
GAOV054 Berserk Scales	.15	.25
GAOV055 Night Beam UR	1.25	3.00
GAOV055 Night Beam UTR	2.00	5.00
GAOV056 Seal of Convocation R	1.00	2.50
GAOV057 Hieratic Seal of Supremacy	.15	.25
GAOV058 Evo-Diversity R	.25	.75
GAOV059 Evo-Price R	.25	.75
GAOV060 Final Inzektion R	.25	.75
GAOV061 Crossbow - Zektarrow R	.25	.75
GAOV062 Xyz Unit UR	.60	1.50
GAOV062 Xyz Unit UTR	.60	1.50
GAOV063 That Wacky Magic	.15	.25
GAOV064 Constellar Belt	.15	.25
GAOV065 Storm	.15	.25
GAOV066 Nitwit Outwit	.15	.25
GAOV067 Gamushara	.15	.25
GAOV068 Commander of Swords	.15	.25
GAOV069 Bounzer Guard	.15	.25

GAOV070 Butterflyoke	.15	.25
GAOV071 Hieratic Seal of Banishment	.15	.25
GAOV072 Seal of Reflection SR	.40	1.00
GAOV073 Zekt Conversion UR	.60	1.50
GAOV073 Zekt Conversion UTR	.60	1.50
GAOV074 Inzektor Gauntlet	.15	.25
GAOV075 Return	.15	.25
GAOV076 Dimension Slice R	.25	.75
GAOV077 Light Art - Hijiri SR	.20	.60
GAOV078 Sealing Ceremony of Raiton	.15	.25
GAOV079 Aquamirror Cycle	.15	.25
GAOV080 Double Payback	.15	.25
GAOV081 Ancient Dragon R	.25	.75
GAOV082 Hieratic Seal of the Dragon King	.15	.25
GAOV083 Evoltile Elginero SR	.20	.60
GAOV084 Lightray Grepher R	.25	.75
GAOV085 Tardy Orc SCR	.40	1.00
GAOV086 Draconnection UR	3.00	8.00
GAOV086 Draconnection UTR	5.00	12.00
GAOV087 Trial and Tribulation SCR	1.50	4.00
GAOV088 Seal From Ashes SCR	1.50	4.00
GAOV089 Xyz Wrath	.15	.25
GAOV090 Big Eye SCR	5.00	12.00
GAOV091 Lucky Straight SCR	1.50	4.00
GAOV092 Beetron UR	.60	1.50
GAOV092 Beetron UTR	.60	1.50
GAOV093 Influence Dragon	.15	.25
GAOV094 Bright Star Dragon	.15	.25
GAOV095 Buten	.15	.25
GAOV096 Doom Donuts	.15	.25
GAOV097 Nimble Manta	.15	.25
GAOV098 Shining Elf SR	.20	.60
GAOV099 Flelf SR	.20	.60

2012 Yu-Gi-Oh Return of the Duelist 1st Edition

COMPLETE SET (111)	250.00	350.00
BOOSTER BOX (24 PACKS)	70.00	100.00
BOOSTER PACK (9 CARDS)	3.00	5.00
RELEASED ON AUGUST 28, 2012		
REDU000 Noble Knight Gawayn SR	.25	.75
REDU001 Trance the Magic Swordsman C	.15	.25
REDU002 Damage Mage C	.15	.25
REDU003 ZW - Phoenix Bow R	.15	.40
REDU004 Photon Caesar C	.15	.25
REDU005 Heroic Challenger - Spartan C	.15	.25
REDU006 Heroic Challenger - War Hammer C	.15	.25
REDU007 Heroic Challenger - Swordshield C	.15	.25
REDU008 Heroic Challenger - Double Lance R	.15	.40
REDU009 Chronomaly Mayan Machine C	.15	.25
REDU010 Chronomaly Colossal Head R	.15	.40
REDU011 Chronomaly Golden Jet C	.15	.25
REDU012 Chronomaly Crystal Bones R	.15	.40
REDU013 Chronomaly Crystal Skull R	.15	.40
REDU014 Chronomaly Moai C	.15	.25
REDU015 Spellbook Magician of Prophecy UR	4.00	10.00
REDU015 Spellbook Magician of Prophecy UTR	5.00	12.00
REDU016 Amores of Prophecy C	.15	.25
REDU017 Temperance of Prophecy SR	1.50	4.00
REDU018 Strength of Prophecy C	.15	.25
REDU019 Charioteer of Prophecy C	.15	.25
REDU020 High Priestess of Prophecy SCR	6.00	15.00
REDU021 Madolche Mewfeuille C	.15	.25
REDU022 Madolche Baaple C	.15	.25
REDU023 Madolche Chouxvalier R	.15	.40
REDU024 Madolche Magileine SR	6.00	15.00
REDU025 Madolche Butlerusk C	.15	.25
REDU026 Madolche Puddingcess UR	2.00	5.00
REDU026 Madolche Puddingcess UTR	2.50	6.00
REDU027 Geargiano Mk-II R	.15	.40
REDU028 Geargiaccelerator C	.15	.25
REDU029 Geargiarsenal R	.15	.40
REDU030 Geargiarmor SR	.60	1.50
REDU031 Uniflora, Mystical Beast of the Forest C	.15	.25
REDU032 Little Trooper C	.15	.25
REDU033 Silver Sentinel UR	.20	.60
REDU033 Silver Sentinel UTR	.40	1.00
REDU034 Dust Knight R	.15	.40
REDU035 Block Golem C	.15	.25
REDU036 Atlantean Attack Squad C	.15	.25
REDU037 Illusory Snatcher SR	.25	.75
REDU038 Grandsoil the Elemental Lord SCR	1.25	3.00
REDU039 Three Thousand Needles SP	.15	.40
REDU040 Goblin Marauding Squad SP	.15	.40
REDU041 Heroic Champion - Excalibur UR	1.25	3.00
REDU041 Heroic Champion - Excalibur UTR	1.50	4.00
REDU041 Heroic Champion - Excalibur GR	3.00	8.00
REDU042 Chronomaly Crystal Chrononaut SR	.75	2.00
REDU043 Number 33: Chronomaly Machu Mech UR	2.00	5.00
REDU043 Number 33: Chronomaly Machu Mech UTR	2.00	5.00
REDU044 Superdimensional Robot Galaxy Destroyer UR	.75	2.00
REDU044 Superdimensional Robot Galaxy Destroyer UTR	.60	1.50
REDU045 Hierophant of Prophecy UR	.60	1.50
REDU045 Hierophant of Prophecy UTR	.60	1.50
REDU046 Gear Gigant X SCR	3.00	8.00
REDU047 Alchemic Magician SR	1.25	3.00
REDU048 Soul of Silvermountain SR	.25	.75
REDU049 Fairy King Albverdich R	.15	.40
REDU050 Sword Breaker SR	.25	.75
REDU051 Gagagarevenge SR	.50	1.25
REDU052 Overlay Regen C	.15	.25
REDU053 Heroic Chance C	.15	.25
REDU054 Chronomaly Technology C	.15	.25
REDU055 Chronomaly Pyramid Eye Tablet C	.15	.25
REDU056 Galaxy Queen's Light C	.15	.25
REDU057 Spellbook of Secrets UR	5.00	12.00
REDU057 Spellbook of Secrets UTR	6.00	15.00
REDU058 Spellbook of Power C	.15	.25
REDU059 Spellbook of Life SR	1.25	3.00
REDU060 Spellbook of Wisdom R	.15	.40
REDU061 Madolche Chateau C	.15	.25
REDU062 Where Art Thou? C	.15	.25
REDU063 Generation Force C	.15	.25
REDU064 Catapult Zone C	.15	.25
REDU065 Cold Feet SP	.15	.40
REDU066 Impenetrable Attack C	.15	.25
REDU067 Gagagarush C	.15	.25
REDU068 Heroic Retribution Sword C	.15	.25
REDU069 Stonehenge Methods C	.15	.25
REDU070 Madolche Lesson C	.15	.25
REDU071 Madolche Waltz C	.15	.25
REDU072 Madolche Tea Break R	.15	.40
REDU073 Xyz Soul C	.15	.25
REDU074 Compulsory Escape Device C	.15	.25
REDU075 Turnabout C	.15	.25
REDU076 Void Trap Hole SR	1.25	3.00
REDU077 Three of a Kind C	.15	.25
REDU078 Soul Drain R	.15	.40
REDU079 Rebound SR	.25	.75
REDU080 Lucky Punch SP	.15	.40
REDU081 Prophecy Destroyer UR	.20	.60
REDU081 Prophecy Destroyer UTR	.40	1.00
REDU082 Lightray Madoor C	.15	.25
REDU083 Blue Dragon Ninja SR	.25	.75
REDU084 Imairuka R	.15	.40
REDU085 Revival Golem R	.15	.40
REDU086 Noble Arms - Gallatin C	.15	.25
REDU087 Spellbook Library of the Crescent R	.15	.40
REDU088 Advance Zone SCR	1.00	2.50
REDU089 Ninjitsu Art of Shadow Sealing C	.15	.25
REDU090 Chewbone C	.15	.25
REDU091 Eco, Mystical Spirit of the Forest R	.15	.40
REDU092 Number 6: Chronomaly Atlandis SCR	.75	2.00
REDU093 Miracle Contact SCR	6.00	15.00
REDU094 Advanced Dark SCR	1.50	4.00
REDU095 Pahunder R	.15	.40
REDU096 Mahunder R	.15	.40
REDU097 Sishunder R	.15	.40
REDU098 Number 91: Thunder Spark Dragon UR	1.25	3.00
REDU098 Number 91: Thunder Spark Dragon UTR	1.25	3.00
REDU099 Spirit Converter SCR	.40	1.00

2012 Yu-Gi-Oh Abyss Rising 1st Edition

COMPLETE SET (111)	300.00	500.00
BOOSTER BOX (24 PACKS)	50.00	80.00
BOOSTER PACK (9 CARDS)	3.00	4.50
RELEASED ON NOVEMBER 9, 2012		
ABYR000 Ignoble Knight SR	.25	.75
ABYR001 Gagaga Caesar R	.25	.60
ABYR002 Bull Blader C	.15	.25
ABYR003 Achacha Chanbara C	.15	.25
ABYR004 Mogmole C	.15	.25
ABYR005 Grandram C	.15	.25
ABYR006 Tripod Fish C	.15	.25
ABYR007 Deep Sweeper C	.15	.25
ABYR008 Heroic Challenger - Extra Sword C	.15	.25
ABYR009 Heroic Challenger - Night Watchman C	.15	.25
ABYR010 Planet Pathfinder C	.15	.25
ABYR011 Solar Wind Jammer C	.15	.25
ABYR012 Heraldic Beast Aberconway C	.15	.25
ABYR013 Heraldic Beast Berners Falcon C	.15	.25
ABYR014 Mermail Abysslinde UR	2.50	6.00
ABYR014 Mermail Abysslinde UTR	2.50	6.00
ABYR015 Mermail Abyssgunde R	.25	.60
ABYR016 Mermail Abysshilde C	.15	.25
ABYR017 Mermail Abyssturge R	.25	.60
ABYR018 Mermail Abysspike R	.40	1.00
ABYR019 Mermail Abysslung C	.15	.25
ABYR020 Mermail Abyssmegalo SCR	6.00	15.00
ABYR021 Stoic of Prophecy C	.15	.25
ABYR022 Hermit of Prophecy C	.15	.25
ABYR023 Justice of Prophecy R	.60	1.50
ABYR024 Emperor of Prophecy R	.25	.60
ABYR025 Madolche Croiwanssant C	.15	.25
ABYR026 Madolche Marmalmaid C	.15	.25
ABYR027 Madolche Messengelato R	1.00	2.50
ABYR028 Abyss Warrior C	.15	.25
ABYR029 Snowman Creator C	.15	.25
ABYR030 Fishborg Planter C	.15	.25
ABYR031 Nimble Angler C	.15	.25
ABYR032 Shore Knight R	.25	.60
ABYR033 Mecha Sea Dragon Plesion C	.15	.25
ABYR034 Metalizing Parasite - Soltite C	.15	.25
ABYR035 Moulinglacia SCR	5.00	12.00
ABYR036 House Duston C	.15	.25
ABYR037 Puny Penguin SP	.10	.30
ABYR038 Missing Force SP	.10	.30
ABYR039 No.32 Shark Drake UR	.75	2.00
ABYR039 No.32 Shark Drake UTR	1.00	2.50
ABYR039 No.32 Shark Drake GR	2.00	5.00
ABYR040 One-Eyed Skill Gainer SR	.40	1.00
ABYR041 Gagaga Cowboy SR	.75	2.00
ABYR042 Heroic Champion - Gandiva UR	1.00	2.50
ABYR042 Heroic Champion - Gandiva UTR	1.50	4.00
ABYR043 Heroic Champion - Kusanagi SR	1.25	3.00
ABYR044 Number 9: Dyson Sphere UR	1.50	4.00
ABYR044 Number 9: Dyson Sphere UTR	1.50	4.00
ABYR045 No.8 Heraldic King SR	.60	1.50
ABYR046 Mermail Abyssgaios UR	1.00	2.50
ABYR046 Mermail Abyssgaios UTR	1.50	4.00
ABYR047 Empress of Prophecy UR	.25	.75
ABYR047 Empress of Prophecy UTR	.40	1.00
ABYR048 Madolche Queen Tiaramisu UR	1.00	2.50
ABYR048 Madolche Queen Tiaramisu UTR	2.50	6.00
ABYR049 Snowdust Giant R	.25	.60
ABYR050 Gagagigo the Risen R	.25	.60
ABYR051 One-Shot Wand C	.15	.25
ABYR052 Different Dimension Deepsea Trench C	.15	.25
ABYR053 Tannhauser Gate SR	.25	.75
ABYR054 Gravity Blaster C	.15	.25
ABYR055 Advanced Heraldry Art R	.25	.60
ABYR056 Abyss-scale of the Kraken C	.15	.25
ABYR057 Lemuria, the Forgotten City C	.15	.25
ABYR058 Spellbook of Eternity R	.25	.60
ABYR059 Spellbook of Fate UR	2.00	5.00
ABYR059 Spellbook of Fate UTR	2.50	6.00
ABYR060 The Grand Spellbook Tower SCR	2.00	5.00
ABYR061 Madolche Ticket C	.15	.25
ABYR062 Forbidden Dress SR	.25	.75
ABYR063 Final Gesture C	.15	.25
ABYR064 Mind Pollutant R	.25	.60
ABYR065 The Humble Sentry SP	.10	.30
ABYR066 Battle Break C	.15	.25
ABYR067 Bubble Bringer SR	.25	.75
ABYR068 Heroic Gift C	.15	.25
ABYR069 Heroic Advance C	.15	.25
ABYR070 Xyz Xtreme !! C	.15	.25
ABYR071 Abyss-squall SR	.25	.75
ABYR072 Abyss-sphere UR	2.00	5.00
ABYR072 Abyss-sphere UTR	2.00	5.00
ABYR073 Abyss-strom R	.25	.60
ABYR074 Madolchepalooza SR	1.00	2.50
ABYR075 Memory of an Adversary SR	.25	.75
ABYR076 Magic Deflector C	.15	.25
ABYR077 That Wacky Alchemy! UR	.15	.40
ABYR077 That Wacky Alchemy! UTR	.25	.75
ABYR078 Cash Back SP	.75	2.00
ABYR079 Unification C	.15	.25
ABYR080 Retort SCR	1.25	3.00
ABYR081 Mermail Abyssmander R	.25	.60
ABYR082 Red Dragon Ninja SR	.25	.75
ABYR083 Slushy R	.25	.60
ABYR084 Abyss Dweller SR	1.00	2.50
ABYR085 Giant Soldier of Steel SCR	.40	1.00
ABYR086 Noble Arms - Arfeudutyr R	.25	.60
ABYR087 Spellbook Library SCR	.50	1.25
ABYR088 Spellbook Star Hall R	.25	.60
ABYR089 Attack the Moon! SR	.25	.75
ABYR090 Electromagnetic Bagworm C	.15	.25
ABYR091 Rage of the Deep Sea C	.15	.25
ABYR092 Ape Magician C	.15	.25
ABYR093 Snowdust Dragon C	.15	.25
ABYR094 Snow Dragon C	.15	.25
ABYR095 Uminotaurus R	.25	.60
ABYR096 Fishborg Launcher C	.15	.25
ABYR097 Papa-Corn R	.25	.60
ABYR098 Thunder Sea Horse SCR	1.00	2.50
ABYR099 Bahamut Shark SCR	2.00	5.00

2013 Yu-Gi-Oh Cosmo Blazer 1st Edition

COMPLETE SET (111)	350.00	500.00
BOOSTER BOX (24 PACKS)	80.00	100.00
BOOSTER PACK (9 CARDS)	3.00	4.00
RELEASED ON JANUARY 25, 2013		
CBLZ000 Noble Arms - Caliburn SR	.25	.75
CBLZ001 Dododo Bot C	.15	.25
CBLZ002 Gogogo Ghost C	.15	.25
CBLZ003 Bacon Saver C	.15	.25
CBLZ004 Amarylease C	.15	.25
CBLZ005 ZW - Lightning Blade R	.15	.40
CBLZ006 ZW - Tornado Bringer R	.15	.40
CBLZ007 ZW - Ultimate Shield C	.15	.25
CBLZ008 Gagaga Clerk SR	1.00	2.50
CBLZ009 Spear Shark C	.15	.25
CBLZ010 Double Shark C	.15	.25
CBLZ011 Xyz Remora C	.15	.25
CBLZ012 Hyper-Ancient Shark Megalodon R	.15	.40
CBLZ013 Heraldic Beast Basilisk C	.15	.25
CBLZ014 Heraldic Beast Eale C	.15	.25
CBLZ015 Heraldic Beast Twin-Headed Eagle R	.15	.40
CBLZ016 Heraldic Beast Unicorn C	.15	.25
CBLZ017 Heraldic Beast Leo R	.15	.40
CBLZ018 Garbage Ogre C	.15	.25
CBLZ019 Garbage Lord C	.15	.25
CBLZ020 Orbital 7 SR	.25	.75
CBLZ021 Brotherhood of the Fire Fist - Hawk C	.15	.25
CBLZ022 Brotherhood of the Fire Fist - Raven C	.15	.25
CBLZ023 Brotherhood of the Fire Fist - Gorilla R	.15	.40
CBLZ024 Brotherhood of the Fire Fist - Bear UR	.60	1.50
CBLZ024 Brotherhood of the Fire Fist - Bear UTR	1.50	4.00
CBLZ025 Brotherhood of the Fire Fist - Dragon SR	1.00	2.50
CBLZ026 Brotherhood of the Fire Fist - Snake SR	.25	.75
CBLZ027 Brotherhood of the Fire Fist - Swallow SR	.25	.75
CBLZ028 Hazy Flame Cerbereus C	.15	.25
CBLZ029 Hazy Flame Griffin C	.15	.25
CBLZ030 Hazy Flame Sphynx C	.15	.25
CBLZ031 Hazy Flame Peryton R	.15	.40
CBLZ032 Mermail Abyssdine SR	.25	.75
CBLZ033 Mermail Abyssnose C	.15	.25
CBLZ034 Mermail Abyssleed SCR	2.50	6.00
CBLZ035 Fool of Prophecy SR	.25	.75
CBLZ036 Reaper of Prophecy SR	.25	.75
CBLZ037 Brushfire Knight R	.15	.40
CBLZ038 Inari Fire C	.15	.25
CBLZ039 Valkyrian Knight SR	1.00	2.50
CBLZ040 Pyrorex the Elemental SCR	.50	1.25
CBLZ041 Pyrotech Mech - Shiryu C	.15	.25
CBLZ042 Leotaur C	.15	.25
CBLZ043 Star Drawing SP	.40	1.00
CBLZ044 Red Duston SP	.10	.30
CBLZ045 Heart-eartH Dragon UR	1.25	3.00
CBLZ045 Heart-eartH Dragon UTR	1.50	4.00
CBLZ045 Heart-eartH Dragon GR	2.50	6.00
CBLZ046 No. 53: Heart-eartH UR	.60	1.50
CBLZ046 No. 53: Heart-eartH UTR	1.00	2.50
CBLZ047 ZW - Leo Arms UR	.60	1.50
CBLZ047 ZW - Leo Arms UTR	.60	1.50
CBLZ048 Brohood - Tiger King UR	.60	1.50
CBLZ048 Brohood - Tiger King UTR	1.25	3.00
CBLZ049 Hazy Flame Basiltrice R	.15	.40
CBLZ050 Mermail Abysstrite SR	.60	1.50
CBLZ051 Diamond Dire Wolf SCR	4.00	10.00
CBLZ052 Lightning Chidori UR	2.50	6.00
CBLZ052 Lightning Chidori UTR	4.00	10.00
CBLZ053 Slacker Magician R	.40	1.00
CBLZ054 Zerozerock C	.15	.25
CBLZ055 Gagagadraw SR	.25	.75
CBLZ056 Xyz Double Back C	.15	.25
CBLZ057 Heraldry Reborn R	.15	.40
CBLZ058 Fire Formation - Tensu C	.15	.25
CBLZ059 Fire Formation - Tenki C	.15	.25
CBLZ060 Hazy Pillar C	.15	.25
CBLZ061 Abyss-scale of Cetus C	.15	.25
CBLZ062 Spellbook of Master SCR	1.50	4.00
CBLZ063 The Big Cattle Drive C	.15	.25
CBLZ064 March of the Monarchs C	.15	.25

CBLZ065 Quick Booster UR	.60	1.50
CBLZ065 Quick Booster UTR	.60	1.50
CBLZ066 After the Storm C	.15	.25
CBLZ067 Goblin Circus SP	.10	.30
CBLZ068 Dimension Gate C	.15	.25
CBLZ069 Xyz Dimension Splash C	.15	.25
CBLZ070 Heraldry Change C	.15	.25
CBLZ071 Fire Formation - Tensen C	.15	.25
CBLZ072 Fire Formation - Tenken C	.15	.25
CBLZ073 Ultimate Fire Formation - Seito R	.15	.40
CBLZ074 Hazy Glory C	.15	.25
CBLZ075 Abyss-scorn C	.15	.25
CBLZ076 Spikeshield with Chain C	.15	.25
CBLZ077 Xyz Tribalrivals C	.15	.25
CBLZ078 Breakthrough Skill UR	2.50	6.00
CBLZ078 Breakthrough Skill UTR	8.00	20.00
CBLZ079 Jurrac Impact C	.15	.25
CBLZ080 Dice-nied SP	.10	.30
CBLZ081 Knight Medraut SCR	3.00	8.00
CBLZ082 Hazy Flame Mantikor R	.15	.40
CBLZ083 Mermail Abyssteus UR	8.00	20.00
CBLZ083 Mermail Abyssteus UTR	15.00	30.00
CBLZ084 Bonfire Colossus SCR	.20	.60
CBLZ085 Fairy Elfuria SCR	1.25	3.00
CBLZ086 Artorigus, King UR	.60	1.50
CBLZ086 Artorigus, King UTR	.60	1.50
CBLZ087 Infernal Flame Vixen R	.15	.40
CBLZ088 Spell Wall C	.15	.25
CBLZ089 Kickfire SCR	.75	2.00
CBLZ090 Crimson Sunbird C	.15	.25
CBLZ091 Ignition Beast Volcannon C	.15	.25
CBLZ092 Noble Knight Joan R	.15	.40
CBLZ093 Crimson Blader R	.60	1.50
CBLZ094 Infernity Archer R	.25	.75
CBLZ095 Blackwing - Gladius the Midnight Sun R	.15	.40
CBLZ096 Blackwing - Damascus the Polar Night R	.15	.40
CBLZ097 Brohood - Horse Prince SR	1.25	3.00
CBLZ098 Brohood - Spirit R	.15	.40
CBLZ099 Brohood - Lion Emperor SR	.75	2.00

2013 Yu-Gi-Oh Lord of the Tachyon Galaxy 1st Edition

COMPLETE SET (111)	100.00	250.00
BOOSTER BOX (24 PACKS)	80.00	100.00
BOOSTER PACK (9 CARDS)	4.00	5.00
RELEASED ON MAY 17, 2013		
LTGY000 MPB Turtleracer SR	.20	.60
LTGY001 Bachibachibachi C	.15	.25
LTGY002 Gogogo Gigas R	.15	.40
LTGY003 Mimimic C	.15	.25
LTGY004 Dotedotengu C	.15	.25
LTGY005 Tatakawa Knight C	.15	.25
LTGY006 Little Fairy C	.15	.25
LTGY007 Sharkraken C	.15	.25
LTGY008 Big Whale R	.15	.40
LTGY009 Starfish C	.15	.25
LTGY010 Panther Shark C	.15	.25
LTGY011 Eagle Shark C	.15	.25
LTGY012 Blizzard Falcon C	.15	.25
LTGY013 Aurora Wing C	.15	.25
LTGY014 Radius, the Half-Moon Dragon C	.15	.25
LTGY015 Parsec, the Interstellar Dragon C	.15	.25
LTGY016 Battlin' Boxer Headgeared C	.15	.25
LTGY017 Battlin' Boxer Glassjaw C	.15	.25
LTGY018 Battlin' Boxer Sparrer C	.15	.25
LTGY019 Battlin' Boxer Switchitter C	.15	.25
LTGY020 Battlin' Boxer Counterpunch C	.15	.25
LTGY021 MPB Megaraptor SR	.20	.60
LTGY022 MPB Tetherwolf R	.15	.40
LTGY023 MPB Blackfalcon	.15	.25
LTGY024 MPB Stealthray	.15	.25
LTGY025 MPB Hamstrat UR	.20	.75
LTGY025 MPB Hamstrat UTR	.60	1.50
LTGY026 BFF - Wolf	.15	.25
LTGY027 BFF - Leopard	.15	.25
LTGY028 BFF - Rhino R	.15	.40
LTGY029 BFF - Buffalo R	.15	.40
LTGY030 Mermail Abyssocea C	.15	.25
LTGY031 Wheel of Prophecy R	.15	.40
LTGY032 Madolche Hootcake SR	.75	2.00
LTGY033 Legendary Atlantean Tridon C	.15	.25
LTGY034 Fire King Avatar Garunix C	.15	.25
LTGY035 Harpie Channeler UR	2.00	5.00
LTGY035 Harpie Channeler UTR	2.50	6.00
LTGY036 Altitude Knight R	.15	.40
LTGY037 Windrose the Elemental SCR	.40	1.00
LTGY038 Redox, Dragon Ruler R	.25	.75
LTGY039 Tidal, Dragon Rule R	.25	.75
LTGY040 Blaster, Dragon Ruler R	.40	1.00
LTGY041 Tempest, Dragon Rule R	.25	.75
LTGY042 Risebell the Star Adjuster SP	.10	1.00
LTGY043 Green Duston SP	.10	.30
LTGY044 No.107: Galaxy-Eyes GR	20.00	40.00
LTGY044 No.107: Galaxy-Eyes UR	8.00	20.00
LTGY044 No.107: Galaxy-Eyes UTR	15.00	30.00
LTGY045 Gauntlet Launcher UR	.20	.75
LTGY045 Gauntlet Launcher UTR	.60	1.50
LTGY046 Fairy Cheer Girl R	.15	.40
LTGY047 CXyz Dark Fairy Cheer Girl R	.15	.40
LTGY048 Shark Fortress C	.15	.25
LTGY049 Ice Beast Zerofyne R	1.25	3.00
LTGY050 Battlin' Boxer Lead Yoke R	.15	.40
LTGY051 No.105: Star Cestus SR	.60	1.50
LTGY052 No.105: Comet Cestus UR	.20	.75
LTGY052 No.105: Comet Cestus UTR	.60	1.50
LTGY053 MPB Dracossack SCR	5.00	12.00
LTGY054 BFF - Cardinal SCR	.40	1.00
LTGY055 Harpie's Pet Phantasmal Dragon R	.20	.60
LTGY056 King of the Feral Imps C	.15	.25
LTGY057 Gagagawind C	.15	.25
LTGY058 Magnum Shield C	.15	.25
LTGY059 Xyz Revenge R	.15	.40
LTGY060 RUM Barian's Force UR	.20	.75
LTGY060 RUM Barian's Force UTR	.60	1.50
LTGY061 Scramble!! Scramble!! UR	.20	.75
LTGY061 Scramble!! Scramble!! UTR	.60	1.50
LTGY062 Fire Formation - Gyokkou SR	.50	1.25
LTGY063 Spellbook of Judgment SCR	1.25	3.00
LTGY064 Abyss-scale of the Mizuchi C	.15	.25
LTGY065 Hysteric Sign SR	1.50	4.00
LTGY066 Sacred Sword SR	.75	2.00
LTGY067 Jewels of the Valiant C	.15	.25
LTGY068 Summon Breaker SP	.10	.30
LTGY069 Pinpoint Guard SCR	1.00	2.50
LTGY070 Memory Loss C	.15	.25
LTGY071 Torrential Reborn SCR	.40	1.00
LTGY072 Xyz Block C	.15	.25
LTGY073 Aerial Recharge C	.15	.25
LTGY074 Do a Barrel Roll R	.15	.40
LTGY075 Fire Formation - Kaiyo C	.15	.25
LTGY076 Madolche Nights SR	.20	.60
LTGY077 Geargiagear SR	.20	.60
LTGY078 High Tide on Fire Island C	.15	.25
LTGY079 Mind Drain C	.15	.25
LTGY080 Dragoncarnation SP	.20	.60
LTGY081 Noble Knight Gwalchavad UR	.20	.75
LTGY081 Noble Knight Gwalchavad UTR	.60	1.50
LTGY082 BFF - Coyote SCR	.40	1.00
LTGY083 Mermail Abyssbalaen UR	.20	.75
LTGY083 Mermail Abyssbalaen UTR	.60	1.50
LTGY084 Trifortressops R	.15	.40
LTGY085 Ghost Fairy Elfobia SR	.20	.60
LTGY086 Totem Bird SCR	.75	2.00
LTGY087 Noble Arms of Destiny SR	.20	.60
LTGY088 Spellbook of Miracles C	.15	.25
LTGY089 Five Brothers Explosion C	.15	.25
LTGY090 Sonic Warrior C	.15	.25
LTGY091 Constellar Omega UR	.50	1.25
LTGY091 Constellar Omega UTR	.60	1.50
LTGY092 Number 69: Heraldry Crest R	.15	.40
LTGY093 Constellar Sombre SR	.20	.60
LTGY094 Evilswarm Kerykeion SR	.75	2.00
LTGY095 Reactan, Dragon Ruler of Pebbles C	.15	.25
LTGY096 Stream, Dragon Ruler of Droplets C	.15	.25
LTGY097 Burner, Dragon Ruler of Sparks C	.15	.25
LTGY098 Lightning, Dragon Ruler of Drafts C	.15	.25
LTGY099 Duck Fighter SR	.20	.60

2013 Yu-Gi-Oh Number Hunters 1st Edition

COMPLETE SET (60)	40.00	80.00
BOOSTER BOX (24 PACKS)	40.00	50.00
BOOSTER PACK (5 CARDS)	3.00	4.00
RELEASED ON JULY 12, 2013		
NUMH001 Chronomaly Aztec Mask Golem SR	.10	.30
NUMH002 Chronomaly Cabrera Trebuchet SR	.10	.30
NUMH003 Chronomaly Mud Golem SR	.10	.30
NUMH004 Chronomaly Sol Monolith SR	.10	.30
NUMH005 Gimmick Puppet Egg Head SR	.50	1.25
NUMH006 Gimmick Puppet Gear Changer SR	.20	.60
NUMH007 Gimmick Puppet Twilight Joker SR	.10	.30
NUMH008 Gimmick Puppet Scissor Arms SR	.20	.60
NUMH009 Gimmick Puppet Nightmare SR	.10	.30
NUMH010 Heroic Challenger - Ambush Soldier SCR	.20	.60
NUMH011 Heroic Challenger - Clasp Sword SR	.10	.30
NUMH012 Blue Mountain Butterspy SR	.40	1.00
NUMH013 Box of Friends SCR	1.25	3.00
NUMH014 Zombowwow SR	.10	.30
NUMH015 Gash the Dust Lord SR	.10	.30
NUMH016 Zubaba Knight SR	.10	.30
NUMH017 Gogogo Golem SR	.10	.30
NUMH018 Kagetokage SR	.25	.75
NUMH019 Kurivolt SR	.10	.30
NUMH020 Gogogo Giant SR	.10	.30
NUMH021 Gagaga Gardna SR	.10	.30
NUMH022 Photon Cerberus SR	.10	.30
NUMH023 Photon Lizard SR	.10	.30
NUMH024 Rocket Arrow Express SR	.10	.30
NUMH025 Battle Warrior SR	.10	.30
NUMH026 Number 54: Lion Heart SCR	1.50	4.00
NUMH027 Number 15: Gimmick Puppet Giant Grinder SCR	2.50	6.00
NUMH028 Number 44: Sky Pegasus SCR	1.00	2.50
NUMH029 Number 49: Fortune Tune SCR	1.50	4.00
NUMH030 Number 57: Tri-Head Dust Dragon SCR	.60	1.50
NUMH031 Number 63: Shamoji Soldier SR	.10	.30
NUMH032 Number 74: Master of Blades SCR	1.50	4.00
NUMH033 Number 85: Crazy Box SR	.40	1.00
NUMH034 Number 87: Queen of the Night SR	.60	1.50
NUMH035 Mechquipped Angineer SR	.40	1.00
NUMH036 CXyz Mechquipped Djinn Angeneral SR	.10	.30
NUMH037 Coach King Giantrainer SCR	.20	.60
NUMH038 CXyz Coach Lord Ultimatrainer SCR	1.50	4.00
NUMH039 Norito the Moral Leader SCR	1.50	4.00
NUMH040 CXyz Simon the Great Moral Leader SCR	.20	.60
NUMH041 Comics Hero King Arthur SCR	1.50	4.00
NUMH042 CXyz Comics Hero Legend Arthur SCR	.20	.60
NUMH043 Battlecruiser Dianthus SR	.10	.30
NUMH044 CXyz Battleship Cherry Blossom SCR	.20	.60
NUMH045 Skypalace Gangaridai SCR	.50	1.25
NUMH046 CXyz Skypalace Babylon SCR	.20	.60
NUMH047 Photon Alexandra Queen SCR	.20	.60
NUMH048 Night Papilloperative SR	.10	.30
NUMH049 Unformed Void SR	.10	.30
NUMH050 Princess Cologne SCR	.20	.60
NUMH051 Baby Tiragon SR	.10	.30
NUMH052 Chakra SR	.10	.30
NUMH053 Resurrection of Chakra SR	.10	.30
NUMH054 Gimmick Puppet Ritual SR	.10	.30
NUMH055 Stoic Challenge SR	.10	.30
NUMH056 Overlay Capture SR	.10	.30
NUMH057 Insect Armor with Laser Cannon SR	.10	.30
NUMH058 Number Wall SCR	.60	1.50
NUMH059 Heraldry Record SR	.10	.30
NUMH060 Butterspy Protection SR	.10	.30

2013 Yu-Gi-Oh Judgment of the Light 1st Edition

COMPLETE SET (106)	100.00	250.00
BOOSTER BOX (24 PACKS)	60.00	80.00
BOOSTER PACK (9 CARDS)	3.00	4.00
RELEASED ON AUGUST 9, 2013		
JOTL000 Galaxy Serpent SR	.50	1.25
JOTL001 DZW - Chimera Clad R	.10	.30
JOTL002 V Salamander R	.10	.30
JOTL003 Interceptomato C	.15	.25
JOTL004 Spell Recycler C	.15	.25
JOTL005 Xyz Agent C	.15	.25
JOTL006 Super Defense Robot Lio C	.15	.25
JOTL007 Super Defense Robot Elephan C	.15	.25
JOTL008 Super Defense Robot Monki C	.15	.25
JOTL009 Star Seraph Scout C	.15	.25
JOTL010 Star Seraph Sage C	.15	.25
JOTL011 Star Seraph Sword C	.15	.25
JOTL012 Umbral Horror Ghoul C	.15	.25
JOTL013 Umbral Horror Unform C	.15	.25
JOTL014 Umbral Horror Will o' the Wisp C	.15	.25
JOTL015 Schwarzschild Limit Dragon C	.15	.25
JOTL016 Bujin Yamato UR	.60	1.50
JOTL017 Bujingi Quilin SR	.25	.75
JOTL018 Bujingi Turtle C	.15	.25
JOTL019 Bujingi Wolf C	.15	.25
JOTL020 Bujingi Crane R	.10	.30
JOTL021 Bujingi Ophidian C	.15	.25
JOTL022 Mecha Phantom Beast Warbluran R	.10	.30
JOTL023 Mecha Phantom Beast Blue Impala UR	.25	.75
JOTL024 Mecha Phantom Beast Coltwing C	.15	.25
JOTL025 Mecha Phantom Beast Harrliard C	.15	.25
JOTL026 Brotherhood of the Fire Fist - Boar R	.10	.30
JOTL027 Brotherhood of the Fire Fist - Caribou C	.15	.25
JOTL028 World of Prophecy SCR	.40	1.00
JOTL029 Archfiend Heiress R	.10	.30
JOTL030 Archfiend Cavalry R	.10	.30
JOTL031 Archfiend Emperor, the First Lord of Horror R	.10	.30
JOTL032 Traptrix Atrax R	.10	.30
JOTL033 Traptrix Myrmeleo R	.50	1.25
JOTL034 Traptrix Nepenthes C	.15	.25
JOTL035 The Calibrator C	.15	.25
JOTL036 Talaya, Princess of Cherry Blossoms SR	.40	1.00
JOTL037 Cheepcheepcheep C	.15	.25
JOTL038 Masked Chameleon UR	1.50	4.00
JOTL039 Flying C SP	.40	1.00
JOTL040 Yellow Duston SP	.10	.30
JOTL041 Mecha Phantom Beast Concoruda SR	.25	.75
JOTL042 Brotherhood of the Fire Fist - Kirin R	.10	.30
JOTL043 Mist Bird Clausolas SR	.75	2.00
JOTL044 Underworld Fighter Balmung R	.10	.30
JOTL045 Armades, Keeper of Boundaries SCR	2.00	5.00
JOTL046 HTS Psyhemuth SR	.25	.75
JOTL047 Star Eater GR	8.00	20.00
JOTL047 Star Eater SCR	.40	10.00
JOTL047 Star Eater UTR	4.00	10.00
JOTL048 Number C39: Utopia Ray Victory SR	2.50	6.00
JOTL048 Number C39: Utopia Ray Victory UTR	2.50	6.00
JOTL049 Shark Caesar C	.15	.25
JOTL050 Starliege Lord Galaxion SR	.25	.75
JOTL051 Googly-Eyes Drum Dragon C	.15	.25
JOTL052 Ice Princess Zereort C	.15	.25
JOTL053 Number 102: Star Seraph Sentry R	.10	.30
JOTL054 Number 66: Master Key Beetle SR	.75	2.00
JOTL055 Number 104: Masquerade R	.50	1.25
JOTL056 Number C104: Umbral Horror SR	.40	1.00
JOTL056 Number C104: Umbral Horror UTR	.75	2.00
JOTL057 Bujintei Susanowo UR	.25	.75
JOTL057 Bujintei Susanowo UTR	.75	2.00
JOTL058 Herald of Pure Light SR	2.50	6.00
JOTL059 Rank-Up-Magic Numeron Force UR	.25	.75
JOTL059 Rank-Up-Magic Numeron Force UTR	.40	1.00
JOTL060 Xyz Reception C	.15	.25
JOTL061 Sargasso the D.D. Battlefield C	.15	.25
JOTL062 Sargasso Lighthouse C	.15	.25
JOTL063 Bujincarnation R	.10	.30
JOTL064 Vertical Landing C	.15	.25
JOTL065 Fire Formation - Yoko SR	.25	.75
JOTL066 Archfiend Palabyrinth R	.10	.30
JOTL067 Transmodify SCR	10.00	25.00
JOTL068 Black and White Wave C	.15	.25
JOTL069 Single Purchase SP	.10	.30
JOTL070 Reverse Glasses C	.15	.25
JOTL071 Xyz Revenge Shuffle C	.15	.25
JOTL072 Corrupted Keys R	.10	.30
JOTL073 Vain Betrayer C	.15	.25
JOTL074 Bujin Regalia - The Sword C	.15	.25
JOTL075 Bujinfidel C	.15	.25
JOTL076 Sonic Boom C	.15	.25
JOTL077 Traptrix Trap Hole Nightmare SR	.60	1.50
JOTL078 Xyz Reversal C	.15	.25
JOTL079 Shapesister UR	.25	.75
JOTL080 Armageddon Designator SP	.10	.30
JOTL081 Bujingi Warg C	.15	.25
JOTL082 Mecha Phantom Beast Aerosguin UR	.25	.75
JOTL083 Cockadoodledoo UR	2.50	6.00
JOTL084 Noble Knight Drystan SCR	.40	1.00
JOTL085 Tour Bus To Forbidden Realms R	.10	.30
JOTL086 Confronting the C R	.10	.30
JOTL087 Angel of Zera SCR	.50	1.25
JOTL088 Xyz Encore UR	.60	1.50
JOTL089 Moon Dance Ritual R	.10	.30
JOTL090 The Atmosphere C	.15	.25
JOTL091 Junk Blader C	.15	.25
JOTL092 Coach Captain Bearman UR	.25	.75
JOTL093 Coach Soldier Wolfbark SCR	2.00	5.00
JOTL094 Brotherhood Fire Fist - Rooster SCR	1.00	2.50
JOTL095 Fire King Avatar Yaksha SR	1.50	4.00
JOTL096 Fishborg Archer C	.15	.30
JOTL097 Fencing Fire Ferret C	.15	.25
JOTL098 Kujakujaku C	.15	.25
JOTL099 Madolche Chickolates C	.15	.25

2013 Yu-Gi-Oh Judgment of the Light Deluxe Edition

JOTLENDE1 Archfiend Emperor, the First Lord of Horror UR	1.25	3.00
JOTLENDE2 Flying C UR	.75	2.00
JOTLENDE3 Dragon Shield J SR	1.00	2.50
JOTLENDE4 Vampire Kingdom SR	1.25	3.00

2013 Yu-Gi-Oh Shadow Specters 1st Edition

COMPLETE SET (107)	75.00	200.00
BOOSTER BOX (24 PACKS)	60.00	80.00
BOOSTER PACK (9 CARDS)	3.00	4.00
RELEASED ON NOVEMBER 8, 2013		
SHSP000 Ghostrick Ghoul SR	.20	.60

SHSP001 Labradorite Dragon SR 2.50 6.00
SHSP002 Chow Chow Chan C .15 .25
SHSP003 Malicevorous Spoon C .15 .25
SHSP004 Malicevorous Fork C .15 .25
SHSP005 Malicevorous Knife C .15 .25
SHSP006 Battlin' Boxer Rib Gardna C .15 .25
SHSP007 Battlin' Boxer Rabbit Puncher C .15 .25
SHSP008 Secret Sect Druid Wid C .15 .25
SHSP009 Secret Sect Druid Dru C .15 .25
SHSP010 Mythic Tree Dragon C .15 .25
SHSP011 Mythic Water Dragon C .15 .25
SHSP012 Armed Protector Dragon C .15 .25
SHSP013 Soul Drain Dragon C .15 .25
SHSP014 Baby Raccoon Ponpoko C .15 .25
SHSP015 Baby Raccoon Tantan C .15 .25
SHSP016 Ghostrick Lantern SR 2.50 6.00
SHSP017 Ghostrick Specter C .15 .25
SHSP018 Ghostrick Witch C .15 .25
SHSP019 Ghostrick Yuki-onna C .15 .25
SHSP020 Ghostrick Jiangshi C .15 .25
SHSP021 Ghostrick Stein C .15 .25
SHSP022 Bujin Mikazuchi UR 1.00 2.50
SHSP023 Bujingi Crow R .10 .30
SHSP024 Bujingi Ibis C .15 .25
SHSP025 Bujingi Boar C .15 .25
SHSP026 Bujingi Centipede C .15 .25
SHSP027 Mecha Phantom Beast Sabre Hawk C .15 .25
SHSP028 Mecha Phantom Beast Kalgriffin R .10 .30
SHSP029 Vampire Sorcerer UR 2.00 5.00
SHSP030 Shadow Vampire SCR .50 1.25
SHSP031 Vampire Grace C .15 .25
SHSP032 Pumprincess the Princess of Ghosts C .15 .25
SHSP033 Yellow-Bellied Oni C .15 .25
SHSP034 Vampire Hunter SR .20 .60
SHSP035 Aratama R .10 .30
SHSP036 Rasetsu C .15 .25
SHSP037 Skelesaurus C .15 .25
SHSP038 Knight Day Grepher C .15 .25
SHSP039 Genomix Fighter UR .15 .40
SHSP040 Marina, Princess of Sunflowers SR .20 .60
SHSP041 Granmarg the Mega Monarch SCR .50 1.25
SHSP042 Swarm of Crows R .10 .30
SHSP043 Terrene Toothed Tsuchinoko C .15 .25
SHSP044 Risebell the Star Psycher SP .10 .30
SHSP045 Blue Duston SP .10 .30
SHSP046 Number C96: Dark Storm SR .20 .60
SHSP046 Number C96: Dark Storm UTR .40 1.00
SHSP047 Number 65: Djinn Buster R .10 .30
SHSP048 Number C65: King Overfiend R .10 .30
SHSP049 Battlin' Boxer Cheat Commissioner R .10 .30
SHSP050 Number 46: Dragluon SR 2.50 6.00
SHSP050 Number 46: Dragluon UTR 5.00 12.00
SHSP051 Number 64: Ronin Raccoon Sandayu R .40 1.00
SHSP052 Ghostrick Alucard UR 1.50 4.00
SHSP052 Ghostrick Alucard UTR 2.50 6.00
SHSP053 Bujintei Kagutsuchi UR .60 1.50
SHSP053 Bujintei Kagutsuchi UTR .75 2.00
SHSP054 Crimson Knight Vampire Bram UR 1.25 3.00
SHSP055 Meliae of the Trees SCR .50 1.25
SHSP056 Divine Dragon Knight Felgrand GR 8.00 20.00
SHSP056 Divine Dragon Knight Felgrand SCR 6.00 15.00
SHSP056 Divine Dragon Knight Felgrand UTR 6.00 15.00
SHSP057 Puralis, the Purple Pyrotile R .10 .30
SHSP058 Giganticastle R .10 .30
SHSP059 Gagagatag C .15 .25
SHSP060 Battlin' Boxing Spirits SR .60 1.50
SHSP061 Dragon Shield C .15 .25
SHSP062 Ghostrick Mansion C .15 .25
SHSP063 Bujin Regalia - The Mirror R .10 .30
SHSP064 Vampire Kingdom C .15 .25
SHSP065 Pot of Dichotomy SCR 1.00 2.50
SHSP066 Swords at Dawn R .10 .30
SHSP067 Return of the Monarchs UR 2.50 6.00
SHSP068 Sacred Serpent's Wake C .15 .25
SHSP069 Magicalized Duston Mop SP .10 .30
SHSP070 Burst Rebirth R .10 .30
SHSP071 Numbers Overlay Boost C .15 .25
SHSP072 Intrigue Shield C .15 .25
SHSP073 Ghostrick Vanish C .15 .25
SHSP074 Ghostrick Scare C .15 .25
SHSP075 Vampire Takeover SR .20 .60
SHSP076 Mistake SCR 1.00 2.50
SHSP077 Chain Ignition C .15 .25
SHSP078 Grisaille Prison R .50 1.25
SHSP079 Survival of the Fittest C .15 .25
SHSP080 BIG Win!! SP .10 .30
SHSP081 Bujingi Raven R .10 .30
SHSP082 Vampire Duke R .10 .30
SHSP083 Archfiend Giant R .10 .30
SHSP084 Lady of the Lake SCR .50 1.25
SHSP085 Noble Knight Borz SR .20 .60
SHSP086 Ignoble Knight of High Laundsallyn SCR .50 1.25
SHSP087 Sacred Noble Knight of King Artorigus UR .75 2.00
SHSP088 Noble Arms - Excaliburn SR .20 .60
SHSP089 Sinister Yorishiro UR .60 1.50
SHSP090 Celestial Wolf Lord, Blue Sirius UR .60 1.50
SHSP091 Mira the Star-Bearer C .15 .25
SHSP092 Dragard SR .60 1.50
SHSP093 White Dragon Wyverburster C .15 .25
SHSP094 Kidmodo Dragon SR 1.50 4.00
SHSP095 Secret Sanctuary of the Spellcasters R .10 .30
SHSP096 Black Dragon Collapserpent C .15 .25
SHSP097 Armored Kappa SR .20 .60
SHSP098 Oh Tokenbaum! R .10 .30
SHSP099 Vivid Knight R .10 .30
SHSPSP1 Ghostrick Ghoul UR .60 1.50

2014 Yu-Gi-Oh Legacy of the Valiant 1st Edition

COMPLETE SET (107) 95.00 140.00
BOOSTER BOX (24 PACKS) 80.00 100.00
BOOSTER PACK (9 CARDS) 4.00 5.00
RELEASED ON JANUARY 24, 2014
LVAL000 Sylvan Bladefender SR .15 .25
LVAL001 White Duston SP .10 .20
LVAL002 ZW - Asura Strike R .10 .20
LVAL003 Gillagillancer C .15 .25
LVAL004 Rainbow Kuriboh SCR 1.25 1.75
LVAL005 Overlay Sentinel C .15 .25
LVAL006 Overlay Booster C .15 .25
LVAL007 Photon Chargeman C .15 .25
LVAL008 Chronomaly Moai Carrier C .15 .25
LVAL009 Chronomaly Winged Sphinx C .15 .25
LVAL010 Deep-Space Cruiser IX C .15 .25
LVAL011 Gorgonic Golem C .15 .25
LVAL012 Gorgonic Gargoyle C .15 .25
LVAL013 Gorgonic Ghoul C .15 .25
LVAL014 Gorgonic Cerberus C .15 .25
LVAL015 Sylvan Peaskeeper R .10 .20
LVAL016 Sylvan Komushroomo R .20 .35
LVAL017 Sylvan Marshalleaf UR .50 .75
LVAL018 Sylvan Flowerknight SR .25 .40
LVAL019 Sylvan Guardioak C .15 .25
LVAL020 Sylvan Hermitree UR 1.25 2.00
LVAL021 Ghostrick Jackfrost C .15 .25
LVAL022 Ghostrick Mary SR 3.50 4.00
LVAL023 Ghostrick Nekomusume C .15 .25
LVAL024 Ghostrick Skeleton C .15 .25
LVAL025 Ghostrick Mummy C .15 .25
LVAL026 Bujin Arasuda UR .50 .75
LVAL027 Bujingi Peacock R .10 .20
LVAL028 Bujingi Swallow C .15 .25
LVAL029 Bujingi Fox R .10 .20
LVAL030 Bujingi Hare SR 1.00 1.50
LVAL031 Gravekeeper's Nobleman UR 2.25 3.00
LVAL032 Gravekeeper's Ambusher C .15 .25
LVAL033 Gravekeeper's Shaman SR .50 .75
LVAL034 Gravekeeper's Oracle UR 1.00 1.25
LVAL035 Mystic Macrocarpa Seed C .15 .25
LVAL036 Kalantosa, Mystical Beast of the Forest C .15 .25
LVAL037 Nikitama R .20 .35
LVAL038 Black Brachios C .15 .25
LVAL039 ChirubimÃ©, Princess of Autumn Leaves SR .30 .50
LVAL040 Mobius the Mega Monarch GR 3.50 5.00
LVAL040 Mobius the Mega Monarch SCR 1.25 2.00
LVAL041 Sirenorca C .15 .25
LVAL042 Xyz Avenger C .15 .25
LVAL043 Tackle Crusader C .15 .25
LVAL044 Majiosheldon SP .10 .20
LVAL045 Paladin of Photon Dragon R .10 .20
LVAL046 Number C101: Silent Honor DARK UR 2.00 3.00
LVAL046 Number C101: Silent Honor DARK UTR 2.00 3.00
LVAL047 Number 101: Silent Honor ARK UR 2.50 4.00
LVAL047 Number 101: Silent Honor ARK UTR 7.00 9.00
LVAL048 Number 39: Utopia Roots R .50 .75
LVAL048 Number 39: Utopia Roots UTR 2.50 3.50
LVAL049 Number C69: Heraldry Crest of Horror R .30 .50
LVAL050 Number C92: Heart-eartH Chaos Dragon R .10 .20
LVAL051 Gorgonic Guardian C .15 .25
LVAL052 Alsei, the Sylvan High Protector UR 3.50 5.00
LVAL053 Ghostrick Dullahan R 2.50 3.00
LVAL054 Bujintei Tsukuyomi UR 8.00 10.00
LVAL054 Bujintei Tsukuyomi UTR 20.00 25.00
LVAL055 Fairy Knight Ingunar SR .30 .50
LVAL056 Evilswarm Exciton Knight SCR 9.00 12.00
LVAL057 Downerd Magician SCR 1.25 2.00
LVAL058 Leo, the Keeper of the Sacred Tree R .75 1.25
LVAL059 Rank-Up-Magic Astral Force UR .75 1.25
LVAL059 Rank-Up-Magic Astral Force UTR 4.00 5.00
LVAL060 Rank-Down-Magic Numeron Fall R .10 .20
LVAL061 Xyz Shift C .15 .25
LVAL062 Luminous Dragon Ritual C .15 .25
LVAL063 Mount Sylvania SR .30 .50
LVAL064 Ghostrick Museum C .15 .25
LVAL065 Bujinunity R .10 .20
LVAL066 Hidden Temples of Necrovalley R .10 .20
LVAL067 Onomatopaira R .60 1.00
LVAL068 Xyz Override C .15 .25
LVAL069 Stand-Off SP .10 .20
LVAL070 Shared Ride SCR .60 1.00
LVAL071 Release, Reverse, Burst C .15 .25
LVAL072 Purge Ray C .15 .25
LVAL073 Sylvan Blessing C .15 .25
LVAL074 Ghostrick-Go-Round R .75 1.25
LVAL075 Bujin Regalia - The Jewel C .15 .25
LVAL076 Imperial Tombs of Necrovalley SCR 2.00 2.50
LVAL077 The Monarchs Awaken C .15 .25
LVAL078 Skill Prisoner SR .30 .50
LVAL079 Oath of Companionship R .10 .20
LVAL080 Duston Roller SP .10 .20
LVAL081 Sylvan Mikorange R .10 .20
LVAL082 Ghostrick Yeti C .15 .25
LVAL083 Bujingi Pavo SR .20 .30
LVAL084 Gravekeeper's Heretic R .20 .30
LVAL085 Noble Knight Peredur SR .20 .30
LVAL086 Gwenhwyfar, Queen of Noble Arms SCR 1.00 1.50
LVAL087 Powered Inzektron SR .40 .75
LVAL088 Obedience Schooled SR .60 1.00
LVAL089 The First Monarch SCR .60 1.00
LVAL090 Dark Artist C .15 .25
LVAL091 Swordsman from a Distant Land C .15 .25
LVAL092 Queen Angel of Roses SR .20 .30
LVAL093 Rose Witch C .15 .25
LVAL094 Snapdragon C .15 .25
LVAL095 Alpacaribou, Mystical Beast of the Forest C .15 .25
LVAL096 Mighty Warrior C .15 .25
LVAL097 Dododo Buster C .15 .25
LVAL098 Interplanetarypurplythorny Beast C .15 .25
LVAL099 Starship Spy Plane C .15 .25
LVALSP1 Sylvan Bladefender UR .60 1.50

2014 Yu-Gi-Oh Legacy of the Valiant Deluxe Edition

COMPLETE SET (4) 5.00 10.00
ONE SET PER DELUXE EDITION BOX
LVALENDE1 Sylvan Peaskeeper UR .15 .40
LVALENDE2 Ghostric Jackfrost UR .50 1.25
LVALENDE3 Sylvan Cherubsprout SR .40 1.00
LVALENDE4 Bujintervention SR .15 .40

2014 Yu-Gi-Oh Dragons of Legend 1st Edition

COMPLETE SET (51) 115.00 150.00
BOOSTER BOX (24 PACKS) 200.00 350.00
BOOSTER PACK (9 CARDS) 3.00 8.00
RELEASED ON APRIL 25, 2014
DRLGEN001 Legendary Knight Timaeus SCR 4.00 6.00
DRLGEN002 Kuribandit SCR .75 1.25
DRLGEN003 Amulet Dragon SCR 6.00 8.00
DRLGEN004 Dark Magician Girl the Dragon Knight SCR 12.00 16.00
DRLGEN005 The Eye of Timaeus SCR 10.00 15.00
DRLGEN006 Legend of Heart SCR 1.50 2.50
DRLGEN007 Berserker Soul SCR .20 .35
DRLGEN008 Relay Soul SR .25 .40
DRLGEN009 Guardian Eatos SR .25 .40
DRLGEN010 Guardian Dreadscythe SCR 1.00 1.50
DRLGEN011 Celestial Sword Eatos SR .25 .40
DRLGEN012 Reaper Scythe Dreadscythe SR .25 .40
DRLGEN013 Guarded Treasure SCR .40 .60
DRLGEN014 Soul Charge SR 2.00 2.50
DRLGEN015 Sabatiel The Philosopher's Stone SR .25 .40
DRLGEN016 Flash Fusion SR .25 .40
DRLGEN017 Battle Fusion SR .25 .40
DRLGEN018 Final Fusion SR .25 .40
DRLGEN019 Pair Cycroid SR .25 .40
DRLGEN020 Ayers Rock Sunrise SR .25 .40
DRLGEN021 Doble Passe SCR .60 1.00
DRLGEN022 Carboneddon SR .25 .40
DRLGEN023 Mathematician SCR 1.00 1.50
DRLGEN024 Ra's Disciple SCR 2.00 3.50
DRLGEN025 Mound of the Bound Creator SCR 1.00 1.50
DRLGEN026 Shooting Star SCR .20 .35
DRLGEN027 Blackwing Oroshi the Squall SR .25 .40
DRLGEN028 Blackwing Steam the Cloak SR .25 .40
DRLGEN029 Blackwing Hurricane the Tornado SR .25 .40
DRLGEN030 Black Sonic SCR 4.00 6.00
DRLGEN031 Black Wing Revenge SR .25 .40
DRLGEN032 Shadow Impulse SR .25 .40
DRLGEN033 Assault Dog SR .25 .40
DRLGEN034 Gate Blocker SCR .10 .20
DRLGEN035 Wiretap SR .25 .40
DRLGEN036 Lionhearted Locomotive SR .25 .40
DRLGEN037 Express Train Trolley Olley SCR .20 .30
DRLGEN038 Construction Train Signal Red SR .25 .40
DRLGEN039 Train Connection SR .25 .40
DRLGEN040 Abyss Splash SR .25 .40
DRLGEN041 Abyss Supra Splash SR .25 .40
DRLGEN042 Rank Up Magic Quick Chaos SCR 1.00 1.50
DRLGEN043 Chaos Chimera Dragon SR .25 .40
DRLGEN044 Rank Up Magic Admiration of the Thousands SCR .20 .35
DRLGEN045 Magic Hand SR .25 .40
DRLGEN046 Fire Hand SCR .75 1.25
DRLGEN047 Ice Hand SCR .75 1.25
DRLGEN048 Prominence Hand SR .25 .40
DRLGEN049 Giant Red Hand SR .25 .40
DRLGEN050 Lillybot SR .25 .40
DRLGEN051 Rising Sun Slash SR .25 .40

2014 Yu-Gi-Oh Dragons of Legend Unlimited

COMPLETE SET (51)
BOOSTER BOX
BOOSTER PACK
RELEASED ON
DRLGEN001 Legendary Knight Timaeus SCR 6.00 15.00
DRLGEN002 Kuribandit SCR 2.00 5.00
DRLGEN003 Amulet Dragon SCR 15.00 30.00
DRLGEN004 Dark Magician Girl the Dragon Knight SCR 25.00 50.00
DRLGEN005 The Eye of Timaeus SCR 30.00 60.00
DRLGEN006 Legend of Heart SCR 4.00 10.00
DRLGEN007 Berserker Soul SCR .15 .40
DRLGEN008 Relay Soul SR .10 .30
DRLGEN009 Guardian Eatos SR .10 .30
DRLGEN010 Guardian Dreadscythe SCR 1.50 4.00
DRLGEN011 Celestial Sword Eatos SR .10 .30
DRLGEN012 Reaper Scythe Dreadscythe SR .10 .30
DRLGEN013 Guarded Treasure SCR 1.00 2.50
DRLGEN014 Soul Charge SR 2.00 5.00
DRLGEN015 Sabatiel The Philosopher's Stone SR .10 .30
DRLGEN016 Flash Fusion SR .10 .30
DRLGEN017 Battle Fusion SR .40 1.00
DRLGEN018 Final Fusion SR .10 .30
DRLGEN019 Pair Cycroid SR .10 .30
DRLGEN020 Ayers Rock Sunrise SR .10 .30
DRLGEN021 Doble Passe SCR .75 2.00
DRLGEN022 Carboneddon SR .10 .30
DRLGEN023 Mathematician SCR .75 2.00
DRLGEN024 Ra's Disciple SCR 5.00 12.00
DRLGEN025 Mound of the Bound Creator SCR 4.00 10.00
DRLGEN026 Shooting Star SCR .10 .30
DRLGEN027 Blackwing Oroshi the Squall SR .25 .75
DRLGEN028 Blackwing Steam the Cloak SR .10 .30
DRLGEN029 Blackwing Hurricane the Tornado SR .10 .30
DRLGEN030 Black Sonic SCR 2.50 6.00
DRLGEN031 Black Wing Revenge SR .10 .30
DRLGEN032 Shadow Impulse SR .10 .30
DRLGEN033 Assault Dog SR .10 .30
DRLGEN034 Gate Blocker SCR .10 .30
DRLGEN035 Wiretap SR .50 1.25
DRLGEN036 Lionhearted Locomotive SR .10 .30
DRLGEN037 Express Train Trolley Olley SCR .10 .30
DRLGEN038 Construction Train Signal Red SR .10 .30
DRLGEN039 Train Connection SR .10 .30
DRLGEN040 Abyss Splash SR .10 .30
DRLGEN041 Abyss Supra Splash SR .10 .30
DRLGEN042 Rank Up Magic Quick Chaos SCR .75 2.00
DRLGEN043 Chaos Chimera Dragon SR .10 .30
DRLGEN044 Rank Up Magic Admiration of the Thousands SCR .15 .40
DRLGEN045 Magic Hand SR .10 .30
DRLGEN046 Fire Hand SCR .75 2.00
DRLGEN047 Ice Hand SCR .75 2.00
DRLGEN048 Prominence Hand SR .10 .30
DRLGEN049 Giant Red Hand SR .10 .30
DRLGEN050 Lillybot SR .10 .30
DRLGEN051 Rising Sun Slash SR .10 .30

2014 Yu-Gi-Oh Primal Origin 1st Edition

COMPLETE SET (111) 60.00 150.00
BOOSTER BOX (24 PACKS) 60.00 80.00
BOOSTER PACK (9 CARDS) 3.00 4.00
RELEASED ON MAY 16, 2014
PRIOEN000A Artifact Scythe SR .40 1.00
PRIOEN000B Artifact Scythe UR 1.25 3.00

PRIOEN001 ZS - Vanish Sage C	.15	.25
PRIOEN002 Galaxy Mirror Sage C	.15	.25
PRIOEN003 Galaxy Tyranno R	.15	.40
PRIOEN004 Heliosphere Dragon C	.15	.25
PRIOEN005 Mermaid Shark R	.15	.40
PRIOEN006 Gazer Shark C	.15	.25
PRIOEN007 Blizzard Thunderbird C	.15	.25
PRIOEN008 Battlin' Boxer Big Bandage C	.15	.25
PRIOEN009 Battlin' Boxer Veil C	.15	.25
PRIOEN010 Umbral Horror Ghost C	.15	.25
PRIOEN011 Artifact Moralltach SR	.75	2.00
PRIOEN012 Artifact Beagalltach C	.15	.25
PRIOEN013 Artifact Failnaught C	.15	.25
PRIOEN014 Artifact Aegis C	.15	.25
PRIOEN015 Artifact Achilleshield C	.15	.25
PRIOEN016 Artifact Labrys C	.15	.25
PRIOEN017 Artifact Caduceus R	.15	.40
PRIOEN018 Sylvan Cherubsprout C	.15	.25
PRIOEN019A Sylvan Snapdrassinagon R	.15	.40
PRIOEN019B Sylvan Snapdrassinagon UR	.20	.75
PRIOEN020 Sylvan Lotuswain C	.15	.25
PRIOEN021 Sylvan Sagequoia UR	.50	1.25
PRIOEN022 Ghostrick Doll C	.15	.25
PRIOEN023 Ghostrick Warwolf C	.15	.25
PRIOEN024 Bujin Hirume UR	1.00	2.50
PRIOEN025 Traptrix Dionaea R	.15	.40
PRIOEN026 Mecha Phantom Beast O-Lion R	.15	.40
PRIOEN027 Hazy Flame Hydra C	.15	.25
PRIOEN028 Madolche Anjelly UR	3.00	8.00
PRIOEN029 Pilica, Descendant of Gusto SR	1.50	4.00
PRIOEN030 Gladiator Beast Augustus R	.15	.40
PRIOEN031 Lucent, Netherlord of Dark World SR	2.00	5.00
PRIOEN032 Ancient Gear Box C	.15	.25
PRIOEN033 Dawn Knight R	.15	.40
PRIOEN034 Majesty's Fiend SCR	5.00	12.00
PRIOEN035 Thestalos the Mega Monarch SCR	5.00	12.00
PRIOEN036 Beautunaful Princess R	.15	.40
PRIOEN037 Nopenguin C	.15	.25
PRIOEN038 Condemned Maiden C	.15	.25
PRIOEN039 Starduston C	.15	.25
PRIOEN040A Number 62: Galaxy-Eyes Prime Photon Dragon UR	5.00	12.00
PRIOEN040B Number 62: Galaxy-Eyes Prime Photon Dragon UTR	8.00	20.00
PRIOEN041 Number C107: Neo Galaxy-Eyes Tachyon Dragon SR	.75	2.00
PRIOEN041 Number C107: Neo Galaxy-Eyes Tachyon Dragon UTR	1.25	3.00
PRIOEN042 Number 103: Ragnazero R	.75	2.00
PRIOEN043 Number C103: Ragnafinity R	.15	.40
PRIOEN044A Number C102: Archfiend Seraph SR	.40	1.00
PRIOEN044B Number C102: Archfiend Seraph UTR	.40	1.00
PRIOEN045 Number 80: Rhapsody in Berserk R	.40	1.00
PRIOEN046 Number C80: Requiem in Berserk R	.15	.40
PRIOEN047 Number 43: Manipulator of Souls C	.15	.25
PRIOEN048 Number C43: High Manipulator of Chaos R	.15	.40
PRIOEN049 Artifact Durendal UR	2.00	5.00
PRIOEN049 Artifact Durendal UTR	3.00	8.00
PRIOEN050 Orea, the Sylvan High Arbiter SCR	.75	2.00
PRIOEN051 Ghostrick Socuteboss R	.60	1.50
PRIOEN052A Bujinki Amaterasu SCR	.75	2.00
PRIOEN052B Bujinki Amaterasu GR	2.00	5.00
PRIOEN052C Bujinki Amaterasu UTR	1.00	2.50
PRIOEN053 Phantom Fortress Enterblathnir R	.15	.40
PRIOEN054 Cairngorgon, Antiluminescent Knight SR	.40	1.00
PRIOEN055 Phonon Pulse Dragon R	.15	.40
PRIOEN056 Reverse Breaker C	.15	.25
PRIOEN057 Galactic Charity C	.15	.25
PRIOEN058 Rank-Up-Magic - The Seventh One SCR	.75	2.00
PRIOEN059 Don Thousand's Throne R	.15	.40
PRIOEN060 Artifact Ignition UR	2.00	5.00
PRIOEN061 Artifacts Unleashed C	.15	.25
PRIOEN062 Sylvan Charity UR	.20	.75
PRIOEN063 Ghostrick Parade C	.15	.25
PRIOEN064 Bujintervention C	.15	.25
PRIOEN065 Diamond Core of Koa'ki Meiru C	.15	.25
PRIOEN066 Scrap Factory C	.15	.25
PRIOEN067 Forbidden Scripture SCR	.75	2.00
PRIOEN068 Jackpot 7 C	.15	.25
PRIOEN069 Double Dragon Descent C	.15	.25
PRIOEN070 Tachyon Chaos Hole SR	.40	1.00
PRIOEN071 Last Counter UR	.20	.75
PRIOEN072 Artifact Sanctum UR	3.00	8.00
PRIOEN073 Sylvan Waterslide C	.15	.25
PRIOEN074 Ghostrick Night C	.15	.25
PRIOEN075 Bujincident C	.15	.25
PRIOEN076 The Monarchs Erupt SR	.40	1.00
PRIOEN077 Evo-Singularity C	.15	.25
PRIOEN078 Xyz Universe R	.50	1.25
PRIOEN079A And the Band Played On C	.15	.25
PRIOEN079B And the Band Played On UR	.20	.75
PRIOEN080 Tri-and-Guess C	.15	.25
PRIOEN081 Noble Knight Brothers SCR	2.00	5.00
PRIOEN082 Noble Knight Eachtar SR	.40	1.00
PRIOEN083 Sylvan Princessprout SR	.40	1.00
PRIOEN084 Bujingi Sinyou UR	.20	.75
PRIOEN085 Vampire Vamp SR	.75	2.00
PRIOEN086 Gladiator Beast Nerokius SCR	1.25	3.00
PRIOEN087 Noble Knights of the Round Table UR	.20	.75
PRIOEN088 Avalon SR	.40	1.00
PRIOEN089 Escalation of the Monarchs SR	.60	1.50
PRIOEN090 Bolt Penguin C	.15	.25
PRIOEN091 Phantom King Hydride C	.15	.25
PRIOEN092 Number 42: Galaxy Tomahawk C	.15	.25
PRIOEN093 Rose Archer R	.15	.40
PRIOEN094 Shogi Knight C	.15	.25
PRIOEN095 Gimmick Puppet Des Troy C	.15	.25
PRIOEN096 ZW - Sleipnir Mail C	.15	.25
PRIOEN097 Number 48: Shadow Lich C	.15	.25
PRIOEN098 Galaxy Dragon C	.15	.25
PRIOEN099 Hundred-Footed Horror C	.15	.25
PRIOENDE3 Agent of Entropy - Uranus R	.50	1.25
PRIOENDE4 Re-Cover R	.15	.40

2014 Yu-Gi-Oh Duelist Alliance 1st Edition

COMPLETE SET (105)	140.00	200.00
BOOSTER BOX (24 PACKS)	100.00	120.00
BOOSTER PACK (9 CARDS)		5.00
RELEASED ON AUGUST 15, 2014		
DUEAEN000 Dragon Horn Hunter SR	.60	1.00
DUEAEN001 Flash Knight R	.30	.50
DUEAEN002 Foucault's Cannon SR	.30	.50
DUEAEN003 Metaphys Armed Dragon C	.10	.20
DUEAEN004 Odd-Eyes Pendulum Dragon SCR	5.00	7.00
DUEAEN004u Odd-Eyes Pendulum Dragon UTR	7.00	9.00
DUEAEN005 Performapal Skeeter Skimmer C	.10	.20
DUEAEN006 Performapal Whip Snake R	.30	.50
DUEAEN007 Performapal Sword Fish C	.10	.20
DUEAEN008 Performapal Hip Hippo C	.10	.20
DUEAEN009 Performapal Kaleidoscorp R	.30	.50
DUEAEN010 Performapal Turn Toad R	.30	.50
DUEAEN011 Superheavy Samurai Blue Brawler C	.10	.20
DUEAEN012 Superheavy Samurai Swordsman C	.10	.20
DUEAEN013 Superheavy Samurai Big Benkei R	.30	.50
DUEAEN014 Aria the Melodious Diva C	.10	.20
DUEAEN015 Sonata the Melodious Diva C	.10	.20
DUEAEN016 Mozarta the Melodious Maestra R	.30	.50
DUEAEN017 Battleguard King C	.10	.20
DUEAEN018 Satellarknight Deneb UR	3.00	5.00
DUEAEN019 Satellarknight Altair R	.30	.50
DUEAEN020 Satellarknight Vega C	.10	.20
DUEAEN021 Satellarknight Alsahm SR	1.25	2.00
DUEAEN022 Satellarknight Unukalhai C	.10	.20
DUEAEN023 Shaddoll Falco R	.30	.50
DUEAEN024 Shaddoll Hedgehog C	.10	.20
DUEAEN025 Shaddoll Squamata C	.10	.20
DUEAEN026 Shaddoll Dragon R	.30	.50
DUEAEN027 Shaddoll Beast R	.30	.50
DUEAEN028 Suanni, Fire of the Yang Zing SR	4.00	6.00
DUEAEN029 Bi'an, Earth of the Yang Zing SR	1.50	2.50
DUEAEN030 Bixi, Water of the Yang Zing SR	.60	1.00
DUEAEN031 Pulao, Wind of the Yang Zing SR	.20	.35
DUEAEN032 Chiwen, Light of the Yang Zing UR	7.00	10.00
DUEAEN033 Artifact Chakram C	.10	.20
DUEAEN034 Artifact Lancea C	.10	.20
DUEAEN035 Nefarious Archfiend Eater of Nefariousness C	.10	.20
DUEAEN036 The Agent of Entropy - Uranus C	.10	.20
DUEAEN037 Djinn Demolisher of Rituals C	.10	.20
DUEAEN038 Batteryman 9-Volt C	.10	.20
DUEAEN039 Resonance Insect C	.10	.20
DUEAEN040 Breaker the Dark Magical Warrior C	.10	.20
DUEAEN041 Raiza the Mega Monarch SCR	.75	1.25
DUEAEN042 Dogu C	.10	.20
DUEAEN043 Hypnosister SR	.30	.50
DUEAEN044 Re-Cover C	.10	.20
DUEAEN045 Deskbot 001 C	.10	.20
DUEAEN046 Spy-C-Spy C	.10	.20
DUEAEN047 Wightprince C	.10	.20
DUEAEN048 El Shaddoll Winda UR	3.00	5.00
DUEAEN049 El Shaddoll Construct UR	2.50	4.00
DUEAEN049u El Shaddoll Construct UTR	15.00	20.00
DUEAEN050 Saffira, Queen of Dragons UR	1.50	2.00
DUEAEN050 Saffira, Queen of Dragons UTR	2.50	4.00
DUEAEN051 Baxia, Brightness of the Yang Zing SCR	1.25	2.00
DUEAEN051u Baxia, Brightness of the Yang Zing UTR	3.00	5.00
DUEAEN052 Samsara, Dragon of Rebirth SR	1.00	1.50
DUEAEN053 Stellarknight Delteros SCR	1.00	1.50
DUEAEN053g Stellarknight Delteros GR	6.00	8.00
DUEAEN053u Stellarknight Delteros UTR	1.50	2.50
DUEAEN054 Castel, the Skyblaster Musketeer SR	2.00	3.50
DUEAEN055 Hippo Carnival C	.10	.20
DUEAEN056 Feast of the Wild LV5 C	.10	.20
DUEAEN057 Stellarknight Alpha C	.10	.20
DUEAEN058 Satellarknight Skybridge R	.30	.50
DUEAEN059 Shaddoll Fusion SR	5.00	7.00
DUEAEN060 Curse of the Shadow Prison C	.10	.20
DUEAEN061 Yang Zing Path SCR	2.00	3.50
DUEAEN062 Yang Zing Prana C	.10	.20
DUEAEN063 Hymn of Light C	.10	.20
DUEAEN064 Dracocension C	.10	.20
DUEAEN065 Magical Spring SCR	.75	1.25
DUEAEN066 The Monarchs Stormforth C	.10	.20
DUEAEN067 Pop-Up C	.10	.20
DUEAEN068 Battleguard Rage C	.10	.20
DUEAEN069 Battleguard Howling C	.10	.20
DUEAEN070 Stellarnova Wave C	.10	.20
DUEAEN071 Stellarnova Alpha UR	1.50	2.50
DUEAEN072 Sinister Shadow Games UR	.75	1.25
DUEAEN073 Shaddoll Core SR	.60	1.00
DUEAEN074 Yang Zing Creation UR	.60	1.00
DUEAEN075 Yang Zing Unleashed C	.10	.20
DUEAEN076 Chain Dispel C	.10	.20
DUEAEN077 Face-Off R	.30	.50
DUEAEN078 Pendulum Back SR	.30	.50
DUEAEN079 Time-Space Trap Hole SCR	1.00	1.50
DUEAEN080 That Six C	.10	.20
DUEAEN081 Doomstar Magician UR	.40	.60
DUEAEN082 Scarm, Malebranche of the Burning Abyss R	.30	.50
DUEAEN083 Graff, Malebranche of the Burning Abyss R	.30	.50
DUEAEN084 Cir, Malebranche of the Burning Abyss R	.30	.50
DUEAEN085 Dante, Traveler of the Burning Abyss SCR	4.00	6.00
DUEAEN086 The Traveler and the Burning Abyss SR	.30	.50
DUEAEN087 U.A. Mighty Slugger R	.30	.50
DUEAEN088 U.A. Perfect Ace R	.30	.50
DUEAEN089 U.A. Stadium C	.10	.20
DUEAEN090 Gaia, the Polar Knight C	.10	.20
DUEAEN091 Gaia, the Mid-Knight Sun C	.10	.20
DUEAEN092 Chaos Seed C	.10	.20
DUEAEN093 Exchange of Night and Day C	.10	.20
DUEAEN094 Number 58: Burner Visor C	.10	.20
DUEAEN095 Felis, Lightsworn Archer UR	3.00	5.00
DUEAEN096 Fishborg Doctor C	.10	.20
DUEAEN097 Panzer Dragon R	.30	.50
DUEAEN098 Cloudcastle C	.10	.20
DUEAEN099 Pilgrim Reaper C	.10	.20

2014 Yu-Gi-Oh The New Challengers 1st Edition

COMPLETE SET (119)	120.00	250.00
BOOSTER BOX (24 PACKS)	60.00	70.00
BOOSTER PACK (9 CARDS)	3.00	4.00
RELEASED ON NOVEMBER 7, 2014		
NECHEN000 Lancephorhynchus SR	.15	.40
NECHEN001 Performapal Cheermole R	.10	.30
NECHEN002 Performapal Trampolynx R	.10	.30
NECHEN003 Block Spider C	.15	.25
NECHEN004 Canon the Melodious Diva C	.15	.25
NECHEN005 Serenade the Melodious Diva C	.15	.25
NECHEN006 Elegy the Melodious Diva C	.15	.25
NECHEN007 Shopina the Melodious Maestra R	.10	.30
NECHEN008 Superheavy Samurai Kabuto C	.15	.25
NECHEN009 Superheavy Samurai Scales R	.10	.30
NECHEN010 Superheavy Samurai Soulfire Suit C	.15	.25
NECHEN011 Superheavy Samurai Soulshield Wall C	.15	.25
NECHEN012 Superheavy Samurai Soulbreaker Armor C	.15	.25
NECHEN013 Superheavy Samurai Soulbang Cannon C	.15	.25
NECHEN014 Edge Imp Sabres SR	2.00	5.00
NECHEN015 Fluffal Leo C	.15	.25
NECHEN016 Fluffal Bear C	.15	.25
NECHEN017 Fluffal Dog R	.50	1.25
NECHEN018 Fluffal Owl R	.40	1.00
NECHEN019 Fluffal Cat C	.15	.25
NECHEN020 Fluffal Rabbit C	.15	.25
NECHEN021 Qliphort Scout UR	.50	1.25
NECHEN022 Qliphort Carrier SR	.50	1.25
NECHEN023 Qliphort Helix SR	1.25	3.00
NECHEN024 Qliphort Disk SCR	.75	2.00
NECHEN025 Qliphort Shell R	.10	.30
NECHEN026 Apoqliphort Towers R	.10	.30
NECHEN027 Satellarknight Sirius R	.10	.30
NECHEN028 Satellarknight Procyon C	.15	.25
NECHEN029 Satellarknight Betelgeuse C	.15	.25
NECHEN030 Shaddoll Hound C	.15	.25
NECHEN031 Taotie, Shadow of the Yang Zing SR	.15	.40
NECHEN032 Jiaotu, Darkness of the Yang Zing UR	6.00	15.00
NECHEN033 Lindbloom C	.15	.25
NECHEN034 Night Dragolich UR	.60	1.50
NECHEN035 Unmasked Dragon R	.10	.30
NECHEN036 Machina Megaform SR	.15	.40
NECHEN037 Zaborg the Mega Monarch UR	1.00	2.50
NECHEN038 Valerifawn, Mystical Beast of the Forest C	.15	.25
NECHEN039 Rescue Hamster SR	1.50	4.00
NECHEN040 Watch Dog C	.15	.25
NECHEN041 Denko Sekka UR	3.00	8.00
NECHEN042 Deskbot 002 C	.15	.25
NECHEN043 Ms. Judge NR	.10	.30
NECHEN044 Scrounging Goblin NR	.10	.30
NECHEN045 Herald of Ultimateness UR	.40	1.00
NECHEN046 Frightfur Bear R	.10	.30
NECHEN046u Frightfur Bear UTR	.75	2.00
NECHEN047 Frightfur Wolf R	.50	1.25
NECHEN048 El Shaddoll Grysta SCR	.75	2.00
NECHEN049 El Shaddoll Shekhinaga SCR	.75	2.00
NECHEN049u El Shaddoll Shekhinaga UTR	2.00	5.00
NECHEN050 First of the Dragons SR	1.00	2.50
NECHEN051 Yazi, Evil of the Yang Zing SCR	.75	2.00
NECHEN051u Yazi, Evil of the Yang Zing UTR	1.50	4.00
NECHEN052 Herald of the Arc Light SR	.75	2.00
NECHEN053 Dark Rebellion Xyz Dragon SCR	2.00	5.00
NECHEN053u Dark Rebellion Xyz Dragon UTR	3.00	8.00
NECHEN054 Stellarknight Triverr UR	.15	.40
NECHEN054u Stellarknight Triverr UTR	.60	1.50
NECHEN055 Wonder Balloons C	.15	.25
NECHEN056 Mimiclay C	.15	.25
NECHEN057 Draw Muscle R	.10	.30
NECHEN058 Magical Star Illusion C	.15	.25
NECHEN059 1st Movement Solo SR	.60	1.50
NECHEN060 Toy Vendor C	.15	.25
NECHEN061 Saqlifice UR	.20	.60
NECHEN062 Laser Qlip C	.15	.25
NECHEN063 Hexatellarknight C	.15	.25
NECHEN064 El Shaddoll Fusion SR	.40	1.00
NECHEN065 Celestia C	.15	.25
NECHEN066 Oracle of the Herald C	.15	.25
NECHEN067 Strike of the Monarchs C	.15	.25
NECHEN068 Cursed Bamboo Sword C	.15	.25
NECHEN069 Command Performance C	.15	.25
NECHEN070 Performapal Revival C	.15	.25
NECHEN071 Punch-in-the-Box C	.15	.25
NECHEN072 The Phantom Knights of Shadow Veil C	.15	.25
NECHEN073 Qlimate Change C	.15	.25
NECHEN074 Qlipper Launch C	.15	.25
NECHEN075 Yang Zing Brutality C	.15	.25
NECHEN076 Naturia Sacred Tree R	.10	.30
NECHEN077 Oasis of Dragon Souls R	.75	2.00
NECHEN078 Fusion Reserve UR	2.50	6.00
NECHEN079 Solemn Scolding SCR	3.00	8.00
NECHEN080 Different Dimension Encounter C	.15	.25
NECHEN081 Fusion Substitute C	.15	.25
NECHEN082 Rubic, Malebranche of the Burning Abyss UR	1.25	3.00
NECHEN083 Alich, Malebranche of the Burning Abyss R	.10	.30
NECHEN084 Calcab, Malebranche of the Burning Abyss R	.10	.30
NECHEN085 Virgil, Rock Star of the Burning Abyss SCR	.75	2.00
NECHEN086 Fire Lake of the Burning Abyss SR	.40	1.00
NECHEN087 U.A. Midfielder R	.50	1.25
NECHEN088 U.A. Goalkeeper R	.10	.30
NECHEN089 U.A. Powered Jersey C	.15	.25
NECHEN090 Ruffian Railcar C	.15	.25
NECHEN091 SZW - Fenrir Sword C	.15	.25
NECHEN092 Gogogo Goram C	.15	.25
NECHEN093 Dododo Driver C	.15	.25
NECHEN094 Xyz Change Tactics R	.10	.30
NECHEN095 Number 39: Utopia Beyond SR	1.25	3.00
NECHEN096 CXyz Barian Hope SR	.15	.40
NECHEN097 Shogi Lance C	.15	.25
NECHEN098 Guiding Light C	.15	.25
NECHEN099 Number 99: Utopic Dragon SCR	2.00	5.00
NECHENS01 Lancephorhynchus SR	.15	.40
NECHENS02 Edge Imp Sabres SR	2.00	5.00
NECHENS03 Qliphort Carrier SR	.50	1.25
NECHENS04 Qliphort Helix SR	1.25	3.00
NECHENS05 Taotie, Shadow of the Yang Zing SR	.15	.40
NECHENS06 Machina Megaform SR	.15	.40
NECHENS07 Rescue Hamster SR	1.50	4.00
NECHENS08 First of the Dragons SR	1.00	2.50
NECHENS09 Herald of the Arc Light SR	.75	2.00
NECHENS10 1st Movement Solo SR	.50	1.25
NECHENS11 El Shaddoll Fusion SR	.40	1.00
NECHENS12 Fire Lake of the Burning Abyss SR	.40	1.00
NECHENS13 Number 39: Utopia Beyond SR	1.25	3.00
NECHENS14 CXyz Barian Hope SR	.15	.40

2015 Yu-Gi-Oh Secrets of Eternity 1st Edition

COMPLETE SET (105)	95.00	125.00
BOOSTER BOX (24 PACKS)	50.00	60.00
BOOSTER PACK (9 CARDS)	3.00	4.00
RELEASED ON JANUARY 16, 2015		
SECEEN000 Dragons of Draconia R	.30	.50
SECEEN001 Performapal Fire Mufflerlion C	.10	.20
SECEEN002 Performapal Partnaga C	.10	.20
SECEEN003 Performapal Friendonkey C	.10	.20
SECEEN004 Performapal Spikeagle C	.10	.20
SECEEN005 Performapal Stamp Turtle C	.10	.20
SECEEN006 Performapal Trump Witch R	.10	.20
SECEEN007 Superheavy Samurai Flutist SR	2.00	3.50
SECEEN008 Superheavy Samurai Trumpeter SR	.75	1.25
SECEEN009 Superheavy Samurai Soulpiercer C	.10	.20
SECEEN010 Superheavy Samurai Soulbeads C	.10	.20
SECEEN011 Raidraptor - Vanishing Lanius C	.10	.20
SECEEN012 Gem-Knight Lapis C	.10	.20
SECEEN013 Infernoid Antra SR	.30	.50
SECEEN014 Infernoid Harmadik UR	1.25	2.00
SECEEN015 Infernoid Patrulea R	.20	.35
SECEEN016 Infernoid Piaty C	.10	.20
SECEEN017 Infernoid Seitsemas C	.10	.20
SECEEN018 Infernoid Attondel C	.10	.20
SECEEN019 Infernoid Onuncu SCR	.60	1.00
SECEEN019u Infernoid Onuncu UTR	1.50	2.50
SECEEN020 Qliphort Monolith SCR	5.00	7.00
SECEEN021 Qliphort Cephalopod SR	.30	.50
SECEEN022 Qliphort Stealth UR	.30	.50
SECEEN023 Apoqliphort Skybase UR	.75	1.25
SECEEN024 Satellarknight Capella C	.10	.20
SECEEN025 Satellarknight Rigel SR	.30	.50
SECEEN026 Yosenju Magat C	.10	.20
SECEEN027 Yosenju Tsujik C	.10	.20
SECEEN028 Dance Princess of the Nekroz R	.15	.25
SECEEN029 Spiritual Beast Rampengu C	.10	.20
SECEEN030 Morphtronic Smartfon C	.10	.20
SECEEN031 Jinzo - Jector SR	.75	1.25
SECEEN032 Skilled Blue Magician SR	.40	.60
SECEEN033 Koa'ki Meiru Overload R	.25	.40
SECEEN034 Jigabyte C	.10	.20
SECEEN035 Caius the Mega Monarch UR	5.00	8.00
SECEEN036 Thunderclap Skywolf SR	.10	.20
SECEEN037 Lightning Rod Lord SR	.10	.20
SECEEN038 Dragon Dowser R	.10	.20
SECEEN039 Frontline Observer R	.15	.25
SECEEN040 Uni-Zombie C	.40	.60
SECEEN041 Deskbot 003 C	.60	1.00
SECEEN042 Legendary Maju Garzett C	.10	.20
SECEEN043 Marmiting Captain C	.10	.20
SECEEN044 Nekroz of Gungnir SCR	1.00	1.50
SECEEN044u Nekroz of Gungnir UTR	2.00	3.50
SECEEN045 Rune-Eyes Pendulum Dragon UR	1.00	1.50
SECEEN046 Gem-Knight Lady Lapis Lazuli R	.15	.25
SECEEN047 El Shaddoll Wendigo SR	.30	.50
SECEEN048 Superheavy Samurai Warlord Susanowo SR	2.00	3.50
SECEEN048u Superheavy Samurai Warlord Susanowo UTR	2.50	4.00
SECEEN049 Metaphys Horus UR	1.00	1.50
SECEEN049u Metaphys Horus UTR	3.00	5.00
SECEEN050 Raidraptor - Rise Falcon C	.10	.20
SECEEN051 Stellarknight Constellar Diamond UR	.60	1.00
SECEEN051u Stellarknight Constellar Diamond UTR	2.00	3.50
SECEEN052 Sky Cavalry Centaurea UR	5.00	6.50
SECEEN053 Illusion Balloons C	.10	.20
SECEEN054 Raidraptor - Nest R	.10	.20
SECEEN055 Constellar Twinkle C	.10	.20
SECEEN056 Gottoms' Second Call R	.15	.25
SECEEN057 Void Seer SR	.40	.60
SECEEN058 Void Expansion R	.10	.20
SECEEN059 Nephe Shaddoll Fusion SCR	.75	1.25
SECEEN060 Nekroz Cycle R	.15	.25
SECEEN061 Tenacity of the Monarchs R	.40	.60
SECEEN062 Dragunity Divine Lance C	.10	.20
SECEEN063 Pot of Riches SCR	2.00	3.50
SECEEN064 A Wild Monster Appears! SCR	1.00	1.50
SECEEN065 Pendulum Shift C	.10	.20
SECEEN066 Extra Net C	.10	.20
SECEEN067 Performapal Call C	.10	.20
SECEEN068 Wall of Disruption C	.10	.20
SECEEN069 Last Minute Cancel C	.10	.20
SECEEN070 Raidraptor - Readiness C	.10	.20
SECEEN071 Eye of the Void UR	.25	.40
SECEEN072 Void Launch SR	.10	.20
SECEEN073 Re-qliate C	.10	.20
SECEEN074 Ritual Beast Ambush C	.10	.20
SECEEN075 Zenmaiday C	.10	.20
SECEEN076 Unpossessed C	.10	.20
SECEEN077 Blaze Accelerator Reload C	.10	.20
SECEEN078 Soul Transition SCR	1.25	2.00
SECEEN079 Echo Oscillation C	.10	.20
SECEEN080 Double Trap Hole C	.10	.20
SECEEN081 Mischief of the Gnomes C	.10	.20
SECEEN082 Farfa, Malebranche of the Burning Abyss R	.75	1.25
SECEEN083 Libic, Malebranche of the Burning Abyss R	.10	.25
SECEEN084 Cagna, Malebranche of the Burning Abyss R	.10	.20
SECEEN085 Malacoda, Netherlord of the Burning Abyss SCR	3.00	4.50
SECEEN085 Malacoda Netherlord of the Burning Abyss GR	5.00	7.00
SECEEN086 Good & Evil in the Burning Abyss SR	.75	1.25
SECEEN087 U.A. Playmaker R	.10	.20
SECEEN088 U.A. Blockbacker R	.10	.20
SECEEN089 U.A. Turnover Tactics R	.10	.20
SECEEN090 Gogogo Golem - Golden Form C	.10	.20
SECEEN091 Dododo Witch C	.10	.20
SECEEN092 Dododo Swordsman C	.10	.20
SECEEN093 Toy Knight C	.10	.20
SECEEN094 Explossum C	.10	.20
SECEEN095 Swordsman of Revealing Light UR	1.50	2.50
SECEEN096 Doggy Diver R	.10	.20
SECEEN097 Level Lifter C	.10	.20
SECEEN098 Gogogo Talisman C	.10	.20
SECEEN099 Soul Strike C	.10	.20

2015 Yu-Gi-Oh Secrets of Eternity Unlimited

COMPLETE SET (106)	95.00	125.00
BOOSTER BOX (24 PACKS)	50.00	60.00
BOOSTER PACK (9 CARDS)	3.00	4.00
RELEASED ON JANUARY 16, 2015		
SECEEN000 Dragons of Draconia R	.30	.50
SECEEN001 Performapal Fire Mufflerlion C	.10	.20
SECEEN002 Performapal Partnaga C	.10	.20
SECEEN003 Performapal Friendonkey C	.10	.20
SECEEN004 Performapal Spikeagle C	.10	.20
SECEEN005 Performapal Stamp Turtle C	.10	.20
SECEEN006 Performapal Trump Witch R	.10	.20
SECEEN007 Superheavy Samurai Flutist SR	2.00	3.50
SECEEN008 Superheavy Samurai Trumpeter SR	.75	1.25
SECEEN009 Superheavy Samurai Soulpiercer C	.10	.20
SECEEN010 Superheavy Samurai Soulbeads C	.10	.20
SECEEN011 Raidraptor - Vanishing Lanius C	.10	.20
SECEEN012 Gem-Knight Lapis C	.10	.20
SECEEN013 Infernoid Antra SR	.30	.50
SECEEN014 Infernoid Harmadik UR	1.25	2.00
SECEEN015 Infernoid Patrulea R	.20	.35
SECEEN016 Infernoid Piaty C	.10	.20
SECEEN017 Infernoid Seitsemas C	.10	.20
SECEEN018 Infernoid Attondel C	.10	.20
SECEEN019 Infernoid Onuncu SCR	.60	1.00
SECEEN019u Infernoid Onuncu UTR	1.50	2.50
SECEEN020 Qliphort Monolith SCR	5.00	7.00
SECEEN021 Qliphort Cephalopod SR	.30	.50
SECEEN022 Qliphort Stealth UR	.30	.50
SECEEN023 Apoqliphort Skybase UR	.75	1.25
SECEEN024 Satellarknight Capella C	.10	.20
SECEEN025 Satellarknight Rigel SR	.30	.50
SECEEN026 Yosenju Magat C	.10	.20
SECEEN027 Yosenju Tsujik C	.10	.20
SECEEN028 Dance Princess of the Nekroz R	.15	.25
SECEEN029 Spiritual Beast Rampengu C	.10	.20
SECEEN030 Morphtronic Smartfon C	.10	.20
SECEEN031 Jinzo - Jector SR	.75	1.25
SECEEN032 Skilled Blue Magician SR	.40	.60
SECEEN033 Koa'ki Meiru Overload R	.25	.40
SECEEN034 Jigabyte C	.10	.20
SECEEN035 Caius the Mega Monarch UR	5.00	8.00
SECEEN036 Thunderclap Skywolf SR	.10	.20
SECEEN037 Lightning Rod Lord SR	.10	.20
SECEEN038 Dragon Dowser R	.10	.20
SECEEN039 Frontline Observer R	.15	.25
SECEEN040 Uni-Zombie C	.40	.60
SECEEN041 Deskbot 003 C	.60	1.00
SECEEN042 Legendary Maju Garzett C	.10	.20
SECEEN043 Marmiting Captain C	.10	.20
SECEEN044 Nekroz of Gungnir SCR	1.00	1.50
SECEEN044u Nekroz of Gungnir UTR	2.00	3.50
SECEEN045 Rune-Eyes Pendulum Dragon UR	1.00	1.50
SECEEN046 Gem-Knight Lady Lapis Lazuli R	.15	.25
SECEEN047 El Shaddoll Wendigo SR	.30	.50
SECEEN048 Superheavy Samurai Warlord Susanowo SR	2.00	3.50
SECEEN048u Superheavy Samurai Warlord Susanowo UTR	2.50	4.00
SECEEN049 Metaphys Horus UR	1.00	1.50
SECEEN049u Metaphys Horus UTR	3.00	5.00
SECEEN050 Raidraptor - Rise Falcon C	.10	.20
SECEEN051 Stellarknight Constellar Diamond UR	.60	1.00
SECEEN051u Stellarknight Constellar Diamond UTR	2.00	3.50
SECEEN052 Sky Cavalry Centaurea UR	5.00	6.50
SECEEN053 Illusion Balloons C	.10	.20
SECEEN054 Raidraptor - Nest R	.10	.20
SECEEN055 Constellar Twinkle C	.10	.20
SECEEN056 Gottoms' Second Call R	.15	.25
SECEEN057 Void Seer SR	.40	.60
SECEEN058 Void Expansion R	.10	.20
SECEEN059 Nephe Shaddoll Fusion SCR	.75	1.25
SECEEN060 Nekroz Cycle R	.15	.25
SECEEN061 Tenacity of the Monarchs R	.40	.60
SECEEN062 Dragunity Divine Lance C	.10	.20
SECEEN063 Pot of Riches SCR	2.00	3.50
SECEEN064 A Wild Monster Appears! SCR	1.00	1.50
SECEEN065 Pendulum Shift C	.10	.20
SECEEN066 Extra Net C	.10	.20
SECEEN067 Performapal Call C	.10	.20
SECEEN068 Wall of Disruption C	.10	.20
SECEEN069 Last Minute Cancel C	.10	.20
SECEEN070 Raidraptor - Readiness C	.10	.20
SECEEN071 Eye of the Void UR	.25	.40
SECEEN072 Void Launch SR	.10	.20
SECEEN073 Re-qliate C	.10	.20
SECEEN074 Ritual Beast Ambush C	.10	.20
SECEEN075 Zenmaiday C	.10	.20
SECEEN076 Unpossessed C	.10	.20
SECEEN077 Blaze Accelerator Reload C	.10	.20
SECEEN078 Soul Transition SCR	1.25	2.00
SECEEN079 Echo Oscillation C	.10	.20
SECEEN080 Double Trap Hole C	.10	.20
SECEEN081 Mischief of the Gnomes C	.10	.20
SECEEN082 Farfa, Malebranche of the Burning Abyss R	.75	1.25
SECEEN083 Libic, Malebranche of the Burning Abyss R	.10	.20
SECEEN084 Cagna, Malebranche of the Burning Abyss R	.10	.20
SECEEN085 Malacoda, Netherlord of the Burning Abyss SCR	3.00	4.50
SECEEN085 Malacoda Netherlord of the Burning Abyss GR	5.00	7.00
SECEEN086 Good & Evil in the Burning Abyss SR	.75	1.25
SECEEN087 U.A. Playmaker R	.10	.20
SECEEN088 U.A. Blockbacker R	.10	.20
SECEEN089 U.A. Turnover Tactics R	.10	.20
SECEEN090 Gogogo Golem - Golden Form C	.10	.20
SECEEN091 Dododo Witch C	.10	.20
SECEEN092 Dododo Swordsman C	.10	.20
SECEEN093 Toy Knight C	.10	.20
SECEEN094 Explossum C	.10	.20
SECEEN095 Swordsman of Revealing Light UR	1.50	2.50
SECEEN096 Doggy Diver R	.10	.20
SECEEN097 Level Lifter C	.10	.20
SECEEN098 Gogogo Talisman C	.10	.20
SECEEN099 Soul Strike C	.10	.20

2015 Yu-Gi-Oh The Secret Forces 1st Edition

COMPLETE SET (60)	80.00	100.00
BOOSTER BOX (24 PACKS)	80.00	100.00
BOOSTER PACK (9 CARDS)	4.00	5.00
RELEASED ON FEBRUARY 13, 2015		
THSFEN001 Mayosenju Daibak SCR	3.50	4.15
THSFEN002 Yosenju Misak SCR	.15	.25
THSFEN003 Yosenju Kama 1 SCR	.75	1.00
THSFEN004 Yosenju Kama 2 SCR	.80	1.00
THSFEN005 Yosenju Kama 3 SCR	.75	1.15
THSFEN006 Yosenju Shinchu L SR	.10	.20
THSFEN007 Yosenju Shinchu R SR	.15	.25
THSFEN008 Yosen Training Grounds SR	.05	.15
THSFEN009 Yosenjus' Secret Move SR	.15	.25
THSFEN010 Shurit, Strategist of the Nekroz SR	.15	.25
THSFEN011 Great Sorcerer of the Nekroz SR	.05	.15
THSFEN012 Exa, Enforcer of the Nekroz SR	.05	.15
THSFEN013 Nekroz of Clausolas SCR	.50	.75
THSFEN014 Nekroz of Brionac SCR	10.00	12.00
THSFEN015 Nekroz of Trishula SCR	14.00	16.00
THSFEN016 Nekroz of Unicore SCR	.50	.75
THSFEN017 Nekroz of Valkyrus SCR	25.00	28.00
THSFEN018 Nekroz of Catastor SCR	.20	.30
THSFEN019 Nekroz of Decisive Armor SCR	.20	.30
THSFEN020 Nekroz Mirror SCR	.30	.50
THSFEN021 Nekroz Kaleidoscope SCR	1.00	1.50
THSFEN022 Ritual Beast Tamer Lara SCR	.40	.60
THSFEN023 Ritual Beast Tamer Elder SCR	1.25	1.75
THSFEN024 Ritual Beast Tamer Wen SCR	.30	.50
THSFEN025 Spiritual Beast Apelio SR	.60	1.00
THSFEN026 Spiritual Beast Pettlephin SR	.05	.15
THSFEN027 Spiritual Beast Cannahawk SR	.20	.30
THSFEN028 Ritual Beast Ulti-Apelio SCR	1.75	2.15
THSFEN029 Ritual Beast Ulti-Pettlephin SCR	.75	1.15
THSFEN030 Ritual Beast Ulti-Cannahawk SCR	.30	.50
THSFEN031 Ritual Beast's Bond SR	.05	.15
THSFEN032 Ritual Beast Steeds SR	.25	.40
THSFEN033 Manju of the Ten Thousand Hands SR	5.00	5.75
THSFEN034 Necro Gardna SR	.05	.15
THSFEN035 Armageddon Knight SR	.60	1.00
THSFEN036 Djinn Releaser of Rituals SR	.05	.15
THSFEN037 Djinn Presider of Rituals SR	.05	.15
THSFEN038 Djinn Cursenchanter of Rituals SR	.05	.15
THSFEN039 Djinn Prognosticator of Rituals SR	.05	.15
THSFEN040 Djinn Disserere of Rituals SR	.15	.25
THSFEN041 Gishki Chain SR	.05	.15
THSFEN042 Gishki Shadow SR	.05	.15
THSFEN043 Gishki Noellia SR	.05	.15
THSFEN044 Cardcar D SR	.20	.30
THSFEN045 Gishki Vision SR	.05	.15
THSFEN046 Altitude Knight SR	.05	.15
THSFEN047 Abyss Dweller SR	1.00	1.50
THSFEN048 Soul Release SR	.20	.30
THSFEN049 Soul Absorption SR	.10	.20
THSFEN050 Ritual Weapon SR	.05	.15
THSFEN051 Burial from a Different Dimension SR	.75	1.25
THSFEN052 Advanced Ritual Art SR	.60	1.00
THSFEN053 Preparation of Rites SR	.20	.30
THSFEN054 Ascending Soul SR	.05	.15
THSFEN055 Ritual Cage SR	.05	.15
THSFEN056 Divine Wind of Mist Valley SR	.05	.15
THSFEN057 Fire Formation - Tenki SR	1.25	1.75
THSFEN058 Royal Decree SR	1.00	1.50
THSFEN059 Vanity's Emptiness SR	2.00	2.75
THSFEN060 Aquamirror Cycle SR	.05	.15

2015 Yu-Gi-Oh The Secret Forces Unlimited

COMPLETE SET (60)	80.00	100.00
BOOSTER BOX (24 PACKS)	80.00	100.00
BOOSTER PACK (5 CARDS)	4.00	5.00
RELEASED ON FEBRUARY 13, 2015		
THSFEN001 Mayosenju Daibak SCR	3.50	4.15
THSFEN002 Yosenju Misak SCR	.15	.25
THSFEN003 Yosenju Kama 1 SCR	.75	1.00
THSFEN004 Yosenju Kama 2 SCR	.80	1.00
THSFEN005 Yosenju Kama 3 SCR	.75	1.15
THSFEN006 Yosenju Shinchu L SR	.10	.20
THSFEN007 Yosenju Shinchu R SR	.15	.25
THSFEN008 Yosen Training Grounds SR	.05	.15
THSFEN009 Yosenjus' Secret Move SR	.15	.25
THSFEN010 Shurit, Strategist of the Nekroz SR	.15	.25
THSFEN011 Great Sorcerer of the Nekroz SR	.05	.15
THSFEN012 Exa, Enforcer of the Nekroz SR	.05	.15
THSFEN013 Nekroz of Clausolas SCR	.50	.75
THSFEN014 Nekroz of Brionac SCR	10.00	12.00
THSFEN015 Nekroz of Trishula SCR	14.00	16.00
THSFEN016 Nekroz of Unicore SCR	.50	.75
THSFEN017 Nekroz of Valkyrus SCR	25.00	28.00
THSFEN018 Nekroz of Catastor SCR	.20	.30
THSFEN019 Nekroz of Decisive Armor SCR	.20	.30
THSFEN020 Nekroz Mirror SCR	.30	.50
THSFEN021 Nekroz Kaleidoscope SCR	1.00	1.50
THSFEN022 Ritual Beast Tamer Lara SCR	.40	.60
THSFEN023 Ritual Beast Tamer Elder SCR	1.25	1.75
THSFEN024 Ritual Beast Tamer Wen SCR	.30	.50
THSFEN025 Spiritual Beast Apelio SR	.60	1.00
THSFEN026 Spiritual Beast Pettlephin SR	.05	.15
THSFEN027 Spiritual Beast Cannahawk SR	.20	.30
THSFEN028 Ritual Beast Ulti-Apelio SCR	1.75	2.15
THSFEN029 Ritual Beast Ulti-Pettlephin SCR	.75	1.15
THSFEN030 Ritual Beast Ulti-Cannahawk SCR	.30	.50
THSFEN031 Ritual Beast's Bond SR	.05	.15
THSFEN032 Ritual Beast Steeds SR	.25	.40
THSFEN033 Manju of the Ten Thousand Hands SR	5.00	5.75
THSFEN034 Necro Gardna SR	.05	.15
THSFEN035 Armageddon Knight SR	.60	1.00
THSFEN036 Djinn Releaser of Rituals SR	.05	.15
THSFEN037 Djinn Presider of Rituals SR	.05	.15
THSFEN038 Djinn Cursenchanter of Rituals SR	.05	.15
THSFEN039 Djinn Prognosticator of Rituals SR	.05	.15
THSFEN040 Djinn Disserere of Rituals SR	.15	.25
THSFEN041 Gishki Chain SR	.05	.15
THSFEN042 Gishki Shadow SR	.05	.15
THSFEN043 Gishki Noellia SR	.05	.15
THSFEN044 Cardcar D SR	.20	.30
THSFEN045 Gishki Vision SR	.05	.15
THSFEN046 Altitude Knight SR	.05	.15
THSFEN047 Abyss Dweller SR	1.00	1.50
THSFEN048 Soul Release SR	.20	.30
THSFEN049 Soul Absorption SR	.10	.20
THSFEN050 Ritual Weapon SR	.05	.15
THSFEN051 Burial from a Different Dimension SR	.75	1.25
THSFEN052 Advanced Ritual Art SR	.60	1.00
THSFEN053 Preparation of Rites SR	.20	.30

THSFEN054 Ascending Soul SR	.05	.15
THSFEN055 Ritual Cage SR	.05	.15
THSFEN056 Divine Wind of Mist Valley SR	.05	.15
THSFEN057 Fire Formation - Tenki SR	1.25	1.75
THSFEN058 Royal Decree SR	1.00	1.50
THSFEN059 Vanity's Emptiness SR	2.00	2.75
THSFEN060 Aquamirror Cycle SR	.05	.15

2015 Yu-Gi-Oh World Superstars

COMPLETE SET (52)	55.00	70.00
BOOSTER BOX (24 PACKS)	40.00	60.00
BOOSTER PACK (9 CARDS)	3.00	4.00
RELEASED ON APRIL 17, 2015		
WSUPEN001 Chronomaly Nebra Disk SCR	.15	.25
WSUPEN002 Number 36: Chronomaly Chateau Huyuk SR	.20	.35
WSUPEN003 Heraldic Beast Amphisbaena SR	.20	.35
WSUPEN004 Number 18: Heraldry Patriarch SR	.20	.35
WSUPEN005 Augmented Heraldry SR	.20	.35
WSUPEN006 Gagaga Sister SCR	.50	.80
WSUPEN007 Number 55: Gogogo Goliath SR	.20	.35
WSUPEN008 Dodododraw SR	.20	.35
WSUPEN009 Galaxy-Eyes Cloudragon SR	.40	.60
WSUPEN010 Galaxy Soldier SCR	10.00	12.00
WSUPEN011 Photon Stream of Destruction SR	.20	.35
WSUPEN012 Tachyon Transmigration SCR	.75	1.25
WSUPEN013 Battlin' Boxer Shadow SR	.20	.35
WSUPEN014 Number 79: Battlin' Boxer Nova Kaiser SR	.20	.35
WSUPEN015 Jolt Counter SR	.20	.35
WSUPEN016 Heroic Challenger - Assault Halberd SR	.20	.35
WSUPEN017 Heroic Challenger - Thousand Blades SR	.20	.35
WSUPEN018 Star Seraph Scepter SCR	.50	.80
WSUPEN019 Star Seraph Scale SR	.20	.35
WSUPEN020 Star Seraph Sovereignty SCR	5.00	7.00
WSUPEN021 Numeral Hunter SCR	.10	.20
WSUPEN022 Number 86: Heroic Champion - Rhongomyniad SCR	1.50	2.50
WSUPEN023 Humhumming the Key Djinn SR	.20	.35
WSUPEN024 Onomatopia SCR	.10	.20
WSUPEN025 Marshalling Field SCR	.15	.25
WSUPEN026 Number F0: Utopic Future SCR	3.00	4.00
WSUPEN027 Gagaga Samurai SR	.75	1.25
WSUPEN028 Gagaga Mancer SR	.20	.35
WSUPEN029 Guard Go! SR	.20	.35
WSUPEN030 Hi-Five the Sky SCR	.10	.20
WSUPEN031 The Door of Destiny SCR	.10	.20
WSUPEN032 Elemental HERO Blazeman SCR	3.00	5.00
WSUPEN033 Naturia Gaiastrio SR	.20	.35
WSUPEN034 Mecha Phantom Beast Jaculuslan SR	.20	.35
WSUPEN035 Ghostrick Angel of Mischief SR	1.25	2.00
WSUPEN036 Flowerbot SR	.20	.35
WSUPEN037 Humpty Grumpty SR	.20	.35
WSUPEN038 Dragoroar SR	.20	.35
WSUPEN039 Planckton SR	.20	.35
WSUPEN040 Guerilla Kite SR	.20	.35
WSUPEN041 Wattsychic Fighter SR	.20	.35
WSUPEN042 Earthshattering Event SCR	.10	.20
WSUPEN043 Ghostrick Break SR	.20	.35
WSUPEN044 P.M. Captor SR	.05	.15
WSUPEN045 Spiritual Whisper SR	.20	.35
WSUPEN046 Xyz-Raypierce SR	.20	.35
WSUPEN047 Heavy Knight of the Flame SR	.20	.35
WSUPEN048 BOXer SR	.20	.35
WSUPEN049 Kabuki Dragon SR	.20	.35
WSUPEN050 Pendulum Impenetrable SCR	.10	.20
WSUPEN051 Legendary Dragon of White SCR	6.00	8.00
WSUPEN052 Legendary Magician of Dark SCR	6.00	8.00

2015 Yu-Gi-Oh Crossed Souls 1st Edition

COMPLETE SET (105)	180.00	230.00
BOOSTER BOX (24 PACKS)	50.00	75.00
BOOSTER PACK (9 CARDS)	2.00	5.00
RELEASED ON MAY 15, 2015		
CROSEN000 Sea Dragoons of Draconia R	.15	.25
CROSEN001 Phantom Gryphon C	.10	.20
CROSEN002 Performapal Elephammer R	.10	.20
CROSEN003 Performapal Bowhopper C	.10	.20
CROSEN004 Performapal Lizardraw C	.10	.20
CROSEN005 Performapal Springoose C	.10	.20
CROSEN006 Superheavy Samurai Big Waraji C	.10	.20
CROSEN007 Superheavy Samurai Gigagloves C	.10	.20
CROSEN008 Superheavy Samurai Battleball SR	1.00	1.50
CROSEN009 Superheavy Samurai Soulbuster Gauntlet C	.10	.20
CROSEN010 Soprano the Melodious Songstress C	.10	.20
CROSEN011 Fluffal Sheep C	.10	.20
CROSEN012 Edge Imp Saw C	.10	.20
CROSEN013 Edge Imp Chain C	.10	.20
CROSEN014 Edge Imp Tomahawk R	.10	.20
CROSEN015 Edge Imp Frightfuloid C	.10	.20
CROSEN016 Raidraptor - Sharp Lanius C	.10	.20
CROSEN017 Raidraptor - Mimicry Lanius C	.10	.20
CROSEN018 Yosenju Kodam C	.10	.20
CROSEN019 Yosenju Oyam R	.05	.15
CROSEN020 Satellarknight Zefrathuban UR	1.50	2.50
CROSEN021 Stellarknight Zefraxciton R	.10	.20
CROSEN022 Shaddoll Zefranaga C	.10	.20
CROSEN023 Shaddoll Zefracore C	.10	.20
CROSEN024 Zefraxi, Treasure of the Yang Zing UR	2.50	4.00
CROSEN025 Zefraniu, Secret of the Yang Zing R	.40	.60
CROSEN026 Zefrasaber, Swordmaster of the Nekroz C	.10	.20
CROSEN027 Zefraxa, Flame Beast of the Nekroz C	.10	.20
CROSEN028 Ritual Beast Tamer Zeframpilica C	.10	.20
CROSEN029 Ritual Beast Tamer Zefrawendi R	.10	.20
CROSEN030 Infernoid Pirmais UR	.75	1.25
CROSEN031 Infernoid Sjette C	.10	.20
CROSEN032 Infernoid Devyaty UR	3.00	5.00
CROSEN033 Ghost Ogre & Snow Rabbit SCR	30.00	35.00
CROSEN034 Magma Dragon C	.10	.20
CROSEN035 Deskbot 004 C	.10	.20
CROSEN036 Doomdog Octhros C	.10	.20
CROSEN037 Putrid Pudding Body Buddies C	.10	.20
CROSEN038 Nekroz of Sophia SCR	1.50	2.50
CROSEN038u Nekroz of Sophia UTR	1.50	2.50
CROSEN039 Schuberta the Melodious Maestra R	.15	.25
CROSEN040 Bloom Diva the Melodious Choir UR	.20	.35
CROSEN041 Frightfur Leo SR	1.50	2.50
CROSEN042 Frightfur Sheep SR	.40	.60
CROSEN043 Frightfur Chimera R	.05	.15
CROSEN043u Frightfur Chimera UTR	1.50	2.50
CROSEN044 El Shaddoll Anoyatyllis SCR	4.00	6.00
CROSEN045 Ritual Beast Ulti-Gaiapelio UR	3.00	5.00
CROSEN045u Ritual Beast Ulti-Gaiapelio UTR	3.00	5.00
CROSEN046 Clear Wing Synchro Dragon SCR	5.00	8.00
CROSEN046 Clear Wing Synchro Dragon GR	10.00	15.00
CROSEN046u Clear Wing Synchro Dragon UTR	5.00	8.00
CROSEN047 Chaofeng, Phantom of the Yang Zing SR	4.00	6.00
CROSEN048 Raidraptor - Blaze Falcon R	.30	.50
CROSEN049 Raidraptor - Revolution Falcon R	.10	.20
CROSEN050 Tellarknight Ptolemaeus UR	1.00	1.50
CROSEN050u Tellarknight Ptolemaeus UTR	2.00	3.50
CROSEN051 Madolche Puddingcess Chocolat-a-la-Mode UR	3.00	5.00
CROSEN052 Performapal Recasting C	.10	.20
CROSEN053 Fusion Conscription R	.30	.50
CROSEN054 Frightfur Factory C	.10	.20
CROSEN055 Suture Rebirth R	.10	.20
CROSEN056 Frightfur Fusion R	.40	.60
CROSEN057 Rank-Up-Magic Revolution Force R	.10	.20
CROSEN058 Yosen Whirlwind C	.10	.20
CROSEN059 Zefra Path C	.10	.20
CROSEN060 Oracle of Zefra SCR	4.00	6.00
CROSEN061 Void Vanishment SR	1.50	2.50
CROSEN062 Galaxy Cyclone SCR	2.00	3.50
CROSEN063 Harmonic Oscillation C	.10	.20
CROSEN064 Pendulum Rising C	.10	.20
CROSEN065 Unexpected Dai SR	2.50	3.50
CROSEN066 Performapal Pinch Helper C	.10	.20
CROSEN067 Melodious Illusion R	.20	.35
CROSEN068 Fluffal Crane C	.10	.20
CROSEN069 Designer Frightfur C	.10	.20
CROSEN070 Dizzying Winds of Yosen Village C	.10	.20
CROSEN071 Chosen of Zefra C	.10	.20
CROSEN072 Zefra Divine Strike SR	.40	.60
CROSEN073 Void Purification R	.10	.20
CROSEN074 Jar of Avarice SCR	2.00	3.50
CROSEN075 Lose 1 Turn UR	1.50	2.50
CROSEN076 Fiend Griefing C	.10	.20
CROSEN077 Abyss Stungray C	.10	.20
CROSEN078 Statue of Anguish Pattern C	.10	.20
CROSEN079 Monster Rebone SR	.10	.20
CROSEN080 Diceversity C	.10	.20
CROSEN081 Moon Mirror Shield R	1.00	1.50
CROSEN082 Draghig, Malebranche of the Burning Abyss SR	.15	.25
CROSEN083 Barbar, Malebranche of the Burning Abyss R	.10	.20
CROSEN084 Dante, Pilgrim of the Burning Abyss SCR	1.50	2.50
CROSEN085 The Terminus of the Burning Abyss UR	.20	.35
CROSEN086 U.A. Dreadnought Dunker C	.10	.20
CROSEN087 U.A. Rival Rebounder C	.10	.20
CROSEN088 U.A. Signing Deal C	.10	.20
CROSEN089 U.A. Penalty Box C	.10	.20
CROSEN090 Half Unbreak C	.10	.20
CROSEN091 The Melody of Awakening Dragon SR	1.25	2.00
CROSEN092 Cybernetic Fusion Support C	.10	.20
CROSEN093 Powerful Rebirth SR	.50	.75
CROSEN094 Number S39: Utopia Prime SR	.75	1.25
CROSEN095 Galaxy-Eyes Full Armor Photon Dragon SR	2.00	3.50
CROSEN096 Performapal Thunderhino C	.10	.20
CROSEN097 Primitive Butterfly C	.10	.20
CROSEN098 Junk Anchor R	.10	.20
CROSEN099 Harpie Harpist SR	1.00	1.75

2015 Yu-Gi-Oh Crossed Souls Unlimited

COMPLETE SET (106)	180.00	230.00
BOOSTER BOX (24 PACKS)	50.00	75.00
BOOSTER PACK (9 CARDS)	3.00	5.00
RELEASED ON MAY 15, 2016		
CROSEN000 Sea Dragoons of Draconia R	.05	.15
CROSEN001 Phantom Gryphon C	.05	.15
CROSEN002 Performapal Elephammer R	.10	.20
CROSEN003 Performapal Bowhopper C	.05	.15
CROSEN004 Performapal Lizardraw C	.15	.25
CROSEN005 Performapal Springoose C	.05	.15
CROSEN006 Superheavy Samurai Big Waraji C	.05	.15
CROSEN007 Superheavy Samurai Gigagloves C	.05	.15
CROSEN008 Superheavy Samurai Battleball SR	2.25	3.00
CROSEN009 Superheavy Samurai Soulbuster Gauntlet C	.05	.15
CROSEN010 Soprano the Melodious Songstress C	.05	.15
CROSEN011 Fluffal Sheep C	.05	.15
CROSEN012 Edge Imp Saw C	.05	.15
CROSEN013 Edge Imp Chain C	.05	.15
CROSEN014 Edge Imp Tomahawk R	.10	.20
CROSEN015 Edge Imp Frightfuloid C	.05	.15
CROSEN016 Raidraptor - Sharp Lanius C	.05	.15
CROSEN017 Raidraptor - Mimicry Lanius C	.05	.15
CROSEN018 Yosenju Kodam C	.05	.15
CROSEN019 Yosenju Oyam R	.05	.15
CROSEN020 Satellarknight Zefrathuban UR	.75	1.15
CROSEN021 Stellarknight Zefraxciton R	.10	.20
CROSEN022 Shaddoll Zefranaga C	.05	.15
CROSEN023 Shaddoll Zefracore C	.05	.15
CROSEN024 Zefraxi, Treasure of the Yang Zing UR	8.75	10.00
CROSEN025 Zefraniu, Secret of the Yang Zing R	1.00	1.75
CROSEN026 Zefrasaber, Swordmaster of the Nekroz C	.05	.15
CROSEN027 Zefraxa, Flame Beast of the Nekroz C	.05	.15
CROSEN028 Ritual Beast Tamer Zeframpilica C	.05	.15
CROSEN029 Ritual Beast Tamer Zefrawendi R	.05	.15
CROSEN030 Infernoid Pirmais UR	1.50	2.00
CROSEN031 Infernoid Sjette C	.05	.15
CROSEN032 Infernoid Devyaty UR	4.00	4.75
CROSEN033 Ghost Ogre & Snow Rabbit SCR	15.00	18.00
CROSEN034 Magma Dragon C	.05	.15
CROSEN035 Deskbot 004 C	.20	.30
CROSEN036 Doomdog Octhros C	.05	.15
CROSEN037 Putrid Pudding Body Buddies C	.10	.30
CROSEN038 Nekroz of Sophia SCR	1.00	1.50
CROSEN039 Nekroz of Sophia UTR	1.25	1.75
CROSEN040 Schuberta the Melodious Maestra R	.15	.25
CROSEN041 Bloom Diva the Melodious Choir UR	5.00	6.00
CROSEN042 Frightfur Leo SR	1.50	2.00
CROSEN043 Frightfur Sheep SR	4.00	4.75
CROSEN044 Frightfur Chimera R	.05	.15
CROSEN045 Frightfur Chimera UTR	1.00	1.50
CROSEN046 El Shaddoll Anoyatyllis SCR	7.00	9.00
CROSEN047 Ritual Beast Ulti-Gaiapelio UR	3.50	4.25
CROSEN048 Ritual Beast Ulti-Gaiapelio UTR	4.00	6.00
CROSEN049 Clear Wing Synchro Dragon SCR	15.00	18.00
CROSEN050 Clear Wing Synchro Dragon GR	23.00	26.00
CROSEN051 Clear Wing Synchro Dragon UTR	16.00	20.00
CROSEN052 Chaofeng, Phantom of the Yang Zing SR	2.00	2.75
CROSEN053 Raidraptor - Blaze Falcon R	.10	.20
CROSEN054 Raidraptor - Revolution Falcon R	.10	.20
CROSEN055 Tellarknight Ptolemaeus UR	2.00	2.50
CROSEN056 Tellarknight Ptolemaeus UTR	2.25	3.00
CROSEN057 Madolche Puddingcess Chocolat-a-la-Mode UR	2.00	2.50
CROSEN058 Performapal Recasting C	.10	.30
CROSEN059 Fusion Conscription R	.40	.60
CROSEN060 Frightfur Factory C	.10	.30
CROSEN061 Suture Rebirth R	.05	.15
CROSEN062 Frightfur Fusion R	.40	.60
CROSEN063 Rank-Up-Magic Revolution Force R	.15	.25
CROSEN064 Yosen Whirlwind C	.10	.30
CROSEN065 Zefra Path C	.10	.30
CROSEN066 Oracle of Zefra SCR	4.75	5.75
CROSEN067 Void Vanishment SR	.25	.40
CROSEN068 Galaxy Cyclone SCR	5.00	6.50
CROSEN069 Harmonic Oscillation C	.10	.30
CROSEN070 Pendulum Rising C	.10	.30
CROSEN071 Unexpected Dai SR	2.75	3.50
CROSEN072 Performapal Pinch Helper C	.10	.30
CROSEN073 Melodious Illusion R	.15	.25
CROSEN074 Fluffal Crane C	.10	.30
CROSEN075 Designer Frightfur C	.10	.30
CROSEN076 Dizzying Winds of Yosen Village C	.10	.30
CROSEN077 Chosen of Zefra C	.10	.30
CROSEN078 Zefra Divine Strike SR	1.25	2.00
CROSEN079 Void Purification R	.05	.15
CROSEN080 Jar of Avarice SCR	6.75	2.75
CROSEN081 Lose 1 Turn UR	3.75	4.50
CROSEN082 Fiend Griefing C	.10	.30
CROSEN083 Abyss Stungray C	.10	.30
CROSEN084 Statue of Anguish Pattern C	.10	.30
CROSEN085 Monster Rebone SR	.20	.30
CROSEN086 Diceversity C	.10	.30
CROSEN087 Moon Mirror Shield R	.30	.50
CROSEN088 Draghig, Malebranche of the Burning Abyss SR	.20	.30
CROSEN089 Barbar, Malebranche of the Burning Abyss R	.10	.20
CROSEN090 Dante, Pilgrim of the Burning Abyss SCR	2.25	2.75
CROSEN091 The Terminus of the Burning Abyss UR	.30	.50
CROSEN092 U.A. Dreadnought Dunker C	.10	.30
CROSEN093 U.A. Rival Rebounder C	.10	.30
CROSEN094 U.A. Signing Deal C	.10	.30
CROSEN095 U.A. Penalty Box C	.10	.30
CROSEN096 Half Unbreak C	.05	.15
CROSEN097 The Melody of Awakening Dragon SR	9.00	11.00
CROSEN098 Cybernetic Fusion Support C	.05	.15
CROSEN099 Powerful Rebirth SR	.50	.75
CROSEN038u Number S39: Utopia Prime SR	2.75	3.25
CROSEN043u Galaxy-Eyes Full Armor Photon Dragon SR	7.00	8.00
CROSEN045u Performapal Thunderhino C	.10	.30
CROSEN046u Primitive Butterfly C	.10	.30
CROSEN050u Junk Anchor R	.05	.15
CROSEN046 Harpie Harpist SR	1.00	1.75

2015 Yu-Gi-Oh Dragons of Legend 2 1st Edition

COMPLETE SET (45)	80.00	100.00
BOOSTER BOX (24 PACKS)	60.00	80.00
BOOSTER PACK (9 CARDS)	3.00	4.00
RELEASED ON JULY 17, 2015		
DRL2EN001 Timaeus the Knight of Destiny SCR	.20	.35
DRL2EN002 Legendary Knight Critias SCR	.10	.20
DRL2EN003 Doom Virus Dragon SCR	2.50	3.50
DRL2EN004 Tyrant Burst Dragon SCR	.20	.35
DRL2EN005 Mirror Force Dragon SCR	4.00	6.00
DRL2EN006 The Fang of Critias SCR	3.00	5.00
DRL2EN007 Tyrant Wing SR	.10	.20
DRL2EN008 Legendary Knight Hermos SCR	.10	.20
DRL2EN009 Time Magic Hammer SCR	.15	.25
DRL2EN010 Rocket Hermos Cannon SCR	.10	.20
DRL2EN011 Goddess Bow SCR	.15	.25
DRL2EN012 Red-Eyes Black Dragon Sword SCR	.60	1.00
DRL2EN013 The Claw of Hermos SCR	2.50	4.00
DRL2EN014 Roulette Spider SR	.10	.20
DRL2EN015 Double Magical Arm Bind SR	.10	.20
DRL2EN016 Lord of the Red SCR	.60	1.00
DRL2EN017 Red-Eyes Transmigration SR	.10	.20
DRL2EN018 Paladin of Dark Dragon SCR	1.50	2.50
DRL2EN019 Dark Dragon Ritual SR	.30	.50
DRL2EN020 Red-Eyes Spirit SR	.10	.20
DRL2EN021 Red-Eyes Burn SR	.50	.80
DRL2EN022 Toon Ancient Gear Golem SR	.60	1.00
DRL2EN023 Toon Kingdom SCR	25.00	30.00
DRL2EN024 Toon Rollback SR	.30	.50
DRL2EN025 Shadow Toon SR	.60	1.00
DRL2EN026 Comic Hand SCR	1.50	2.00
DRL2EN027 Mimicat SCR	17.00	20.00
DRL2EN028 Toon Mask SCR	1.00	1.50
DRL2EN029 Toon Briefcase SR	.60	1.00
DRL2EN030 Prediction Princess Coinorma SR	.10	.20
DRL2EN031 Prediction Princess Petalelf SR	.10	.20
DRL2EN032 Prediction Princess Astromorrigan SR	.10	.20
DRL2EN033 Prediction Princess Arrowsylph SR	.10	.20
DRL2EN034 Prediction Princess Crystaldine SR	.10	.20
DRL2EN035 Prediction Princess Tarotrei SCR	.60	1.00
DRL2EN036 Prediction Ritual SR	.10	.20
DRL2EN037 Black Cat-astrophe SR	.10	.20
DRL2EN038 Reverse Reuse SR	.10	.20
DRL2EN039 Aquaactress Tetra SR	.10	.20
DRL2EN040 Aquaactress Guppy SR	.10	.20
DRL2EN041 Aquaactress Arowana SR	.10	.20
DRL2EN042 Aquarium Stage SR	.10	.20
DRL2EN043 Aquarium Set SR	.10	.20
DRL2EN044 Aquarium Lighting SR	.10	.20
DRL2EN045 Aqua Story - Urashima SR	.10	.20

2015 Yu-Gi-Oh Clash of Rebellions 1st Edition

COMPLETE SET (105)	180.00	230.00
BOOSTER BOX (24 PACKS)	60.00	80.00
BOOSTER PACK (9 CARDS)	3.00	4.00
RELEASED ON AUGUST 7, 2015		
COREEN000 Sky Dragoons of Draconia R	.20	.35

COREEN001 Mystery Shell Dragon C	.10	.20
COREEN002 Risebell the Summoner C	.10	.20
COREEN003 Xiangke Magician SR	1.00	1.50
COREEN004 Xiangsheng Magician SR	.40	.60
COREEN005 Performapal Camelump C	.10	.20
COREEN006 Performapal Drummerilla C	.10	.20
COREEN007 Superheavy Samurai Blowtorch C	.10	.20
COREEN008 Opera the Melodious Diva C	.10	.20
COREEN009 Tamtam the Melodious Diva C	.10	.20
COREEN010 Fluffal Mouse SR	1.00	1.50
COREEN011 D/D Pandora C	.10	.20
COREEN012 Crystal Rose R	.20	.35
COREEN013 Raidraptor - Fuzzy Lanius C	.10	.20
COREEN014 Raidraptor - Singing Lanius C	.10	.20
COREEN015 Performage Damage Juggler C	.10	.20
COREEN016 Performage Flame Eater C	.10	.20
COREEN017 Performage Hat Tricker C	.10	.20
COREEN018 Performage Trick Clown C	.10	.20
COREEN019 Performage Stilts Launcher C	.10	.20
COREEN020 Red-Eyes Black Flare Dragon SR	6.00	8.00
COREEN021 The Black Stone of Legend SCR	10.00	15.00
COREEN022 Black Metal Dragon C	.10	.20
COREEN023 Red-Eyes Archfiend of Lightning SR	1.50	2.50
COREEN024 Keeper of the Shrine C	.10	.20
COREEN025 Luster Pendulum, the Dracoslayer SR	1.00	1.50
COREEN026 Igknight Squire C	.10	.20
COREEN027 Igknight Crusader SR	2.00	3.00
COREEN028 Igknight Templar UR	.40	.60
COREEN029 Igknight Paladin C	.10	.20
COREEN030 Igknight Margrave C	.10	.20
COREEN031 Igknight Gallant C	.10	.20
COREEN032 Igknight Lancer R	.20	.35
COREEN033 Igknight Champion R	.20	.35
COREEN034 Aromage Jasmine SCR	8.00	10.00
COREEN035 Aromage Cananga C	.10	.20
COREEN036 Aromage Rosemary UR	3.00	5.00
COREEN037 Aromage Bergamot R	.20	.35
COREEN038 Aroma Jar C	.10	.20
COREEN039 Infernoid Decatron SR	1.00	1.50
COREEN040 Bird of Paradise Lost C	.10	.20
COREEN041 Magical Abductor R	.20	.35
COREEN042 Archfiend Eccentrick SCR	5.00	7.00
COREEN043 Toon Cyber Dragon R	.75	1.25
COREEN044 Deskbot 005 C	.10	.20
COREEN045 Retaliating C NR	.10	.20
COREEN046 D/D/D Oracle King d'Arc R	.60	.35
COREEN047 Gem-Knight Lady Brilliant Diamond UR	1.00	1.50
COREEN048 Archfiend Black Skull Dragon UR	3.00	5.00
COREEN048u Archfiend Black Skull Dragon UTR	4.00	6.00
COREEN049 Infernoid Tierra UR	.75	1.25
COREEN049u Infernoid Tierra UTR	1.00	1.50
COREEN050 Ignister Prominence, the Blasting Dracoslayer UR	1.00	1.50
COREEN050u Ignister Prominence, the Blasting Dracoslayer UTR	3.00	4.25
COREEN051 Odd-Eyes Rebellion Dragon SCR	1.50	2.50
COREEN051u Odd-Eyes Rebellion Dragon UTR	3.00	5.00
COREEN052 D/D/D Marksman King Tell R	.20	.35
COREEN053 Performage Trapeze Magician R	.20	.35
COREEN054 Red-Eyes Flare Metal Dragon SCR	3.00	5.00
COREEN054 Red Eyes Flare Metal Draogn GR	10.00	15.00
COREEN054u Red-Eyes Flare Metal Dragon UTR	5.50	7.00
COREEN055 Pianissimo C	.10	.20
COREEN056 Brilliant Fusion SR	5.00	7.00
COREEN057 Rank-Up-Magic Raptor's Force C	.10	.20
COREEN058 Bubble Barrier C	.10	.20
COREEN059 Red-Eyes Fusion SR	3.00	5.00
COREEN060 Cards of the Red Stone UR	3.00	5.00
COREEN061 Ignition Phoenix C	.10	.20
COREEN062 Aroma Garden C	.10	.20
COREEN063 Void Imagination SR	.30	.50
COREEN064 Back-Up Rider C	.10	.20
COREEN065 Mistaken Arrest SCR	1.00	1.50
COREEN066 Wavering Eyes C	.10	.20
COREEN067 Chicken Game C	.10	.20
COREEN068 Brilliant Spark C	.10	.20
COREEN069 Raidraptor - Return C	.10	.20
COREEN070 Raptor's Gust C	.10	.20
COREEN071 Trick Box C	.10	.20
COREEN072 Return of the Red-Eyes C	.10	.20
COREEN073 Igknight Burst R	.20	.35
COREEN074 Humid Winds C	.10	.20
COREEN075 Dried Winds SR	.25	.35
COREEN076 Storming Mirror Force SCR	8.00	12.00
COREEN077 Ferret Flames C	.10	.20
COREEN078 Balance of Judgment C	.10	.20
COREEN079 Extra Buck R	.20	.35
COREEN080 Side Effects? NR	.10	.20
COREEN081 Extinction on Schedule C	.10	.20
COREEN082 Kozmo Farmgirl UR	2.00	2.50
COREEN083 Kozmo Goodwitch SR	.50	.75
COREEN084 Kozmo Sliprider R	.20	.35
COREEN085 Kozmo Forerunner R	.20	.35
COREEN086 Kozmotown R	.20	.35
COREEN087 Dogoran, the Mad Flame Kaiju R	1.50	2.50
COREEN088 Kumongous, the Sticky String Kaiju R	.60	1.00
COREEN089 Kyoutou Waterfront C	.10	.20
COREEN090 Performapal Silver Claw C	.10	.20
COREEN091 Escher the Frost Vassal C	.10	.20
COREEN092 Absorb Fusion UR	1.50	2.50
COREEN093 Performapal Salutiger C	.10	.20
COREEN094 Superheavy Samurai Ogre Shutendoji SR	.75	1.25
COREEN095 Hi-Speedroid Kendama UR	.25	.40
COREEN096 Dragong R	.20	.35
COREEN097 Mandragon R	.20	.35
COREEN098 Tatsunoko SCR	1.00	1.50
COREEN099 Secret Blast C	.10	.20
COREENSE1 Ultimaya Tzolkin SR	2.75	3.25
COREENSE2 Frightfur Tiger SR	.30	.50
COREENSE3 Engraver of the Mark SR	.05	.15
COREENSE4 Destruction Sword Flash SR	.10	.20

2015 Yu-Gi-Oh Clash of Rebellions Unlimited

COMPLETE SET (110)	180.00	230.00
BOOSTER BOX (24 PACKS)	60.00	80.00
BOOSTER PACK (9 CARDS)	3.00	5.00
RELEASED ON AUGUST 7, 2015		
COREEN000 Sky Dragoons of Draconia UR	.05	.15
COREEN001 Mystery Shell Dragon C	.05	.15
COREEN002 Risebell the Summoner C	.05	.15
COREEN003 Xiangke Magician SR	4.00	5.00
COREEN004 Xiangsheng Magician SR	1.50	1.75
COREEN005 Performapal Camelump C	.05	.15
COREEN006 Performapal Drummerilla C	.05	.15
COREEN007 Superheavy Samurai Blowtorch C	.05	.15
COREEN008 Opera the Melodious Diva C	.05	.15
COREEN009 Tamtam the Melodious Diva C	.05	.15
COREEN010 Fluffal Mouse SR	2.75	3.50
COREEN011 D/D Pandora C	.05	.15
COREEN012 Crystal Rose R	.10	.20
COREEN013 Raidraptor - Fuzzy Lanius C	.05	.15
COREEN014 Raidraptor - Singing Lanius C	.05	.15
COREEN015 Performage Damage Juggler C	.15	.25
COREEN016 Performage Flame Eater C	.05	.15
COREEN017 Performage Hat Tricker C	.05	.15
COREEN018 Performage Trick Clown C	.10	.20
COREEN019 Performage Stilts Launcher C	.05	.15
COREEN020 Red-Eyes Black Flare Dragon SR	7.50	8.50
COREEN021 The Black Stone of Legend SCR	33.00	37.00
COREEN022 Black Metal Dragon C	.20	.30
COREEN023 Red-Eyes Archfiend of Lightning SR	1.50	1.75
COREEN024 Keeper of the Shrine C	.05	.15
COREEN025 Luster Pendulum, the Dracoslayer SR	.75	1.25
COREEN026 Igknight Squire C	.05	.15
COREEN027 Igknight Crusader SR	1.00	1.25
COREEN028 Igknight Templar UR	5.25	6.00
COREEN029 Igknight Paladin C	.05	.15
COREEN030 Igknight Margrave C	.05	.15
COREEN031 Igknight Gallant C	.05	.15
COREEN032 Igknight Lancer R	.05	.15
COREEN033 Igknight Champion R	.05	.15
COREEN034 Aromage Jasmine SCR	8.75	9.50
COREEN035 Aromage Cananga C	.05	.15
COREEN036 Aromage Rosemary UR	2.00	2.50
COREEN037 Aromage Bergamot R	.05	.15
COREEN038 Aroma Jar C	.05	.15
COREEN039 Infernoid Decatron SR	.75	1.00
COREEN040 Bird of Paradise Lost C	.05	.15
COREEN041 Magical Abductor R	1.00	1.25
COREEN042 Archfiend Eccentrick SCR	10.00	11.50
COREEN043 Toon Cyber Dragon R	1.00	1.15
COREEN044 Deskbot 005 C	.20	.30
COREEN045 Retaliating C NR	.10	.30
COREEN046 D/D/D Oracle King d'Arc R	.60	.80
COREEN047 Gem-Knight Lady Brilliant Diamond UR	.40	.60
COREEN048 Archfiend Black Skull Dragon UR	5.00	6.50
COREEN048u Archfiend Black Skull Dragon UTR	4.25	5.50
COREEN049 Infernoid Tierra UR	.30	.50
COREEN049u Infernoid Tierra UTR	.75	1.25
COREEN050 Ignister Prominence, the Blasting Dracoslayer UR	1.00	1.50
COREEN050u Ignister Prominence, the Blasting Dracoslayer UTR	3.00	4.25
COREEN051 Odd-Eyes Rebellion Dragon SCR	10.00	12.00
COREEN051u Odd-Eyes Rebellion Dragon UTR	11.00	13.00
COREEN052 D/D/D Marksman King Tell R	.10	.20
COREEN053 Performage Trapeze Magician R	.20	.30
COREEN054 Red-Eyes Flare Metal Dragon SCR	5.00	6.00
COREEN054 Red Eyes Flare Metal Draogn GR	10.00	13.00
COREEN054u Red-Eyes Flare Metal Dragon UTR	5.50	7.00
COREEN055 Pianissimo C	.05	.15
COREEN056 Brilliant Fusion SR	7.00	9.00
COREEN057 Rank-Up-Magic Raptor's Force C	.05	.15
COREEN058 Bubble Barrier C	.05	.15
COREEN059 Red-Eyes Fusion SR	3.25	3.75
COREEN060 Cards of the Red Stone UR	5.00	6.00
COREEN061 Ignition Phoenix C	.05	.15
COREEN062 Aroma Garden C	.05	.15
COREEN063 Void Imagination SR	.30	.50
COREEN064 Back-Up Rider C	.05	.15
COREEN065 Mistaken Arrest SCR	.60	1.00
COREEN066 Wavering Eyes C	.15	.25
COREEN067 Chicken Game C	.75	1.25
COREEN068 Brilliant Spark C	.05	.15
COREEN069 Raidraptor - Return C	.05	.15
COREEN070 Raptor's Gust C	.15	.25
COREEN071 Trick Box C	.05	.15
COREEN072 Return of the Red-Eyes C	.05	.15
COREEN073 Igknight Burst R	.05	.15
COREEN074 Humid Winds C	.05	.15
COREEN075 Dried Winds SR	.25	.35
COREEN076 Storming Mirror Force SCR	6.50	8.50
COREEN077 Ferret Flames C	.05	.15
COREEN078 Balance of Judgment C	.05	.15
COREEN079 Extra Buck R	.05	.15
COREEN080 Side Effects? NR	.10	.30
COREEN081 Extinction on Schedule C	.05	.15
COREEN082 Kozmo Farmgirl UR	2.00	2.50
COREEN083 Kozmo Goodwitch SR	.50	.75
COREEN084 Kozmo Sliprider R	.20	.30
COREEN085 Kozmo Forerunner R	.10	.20
COREEN086 Kozmotown R	.20	.30
COREEN087 Dogoran, the Mad Flame Kaiju R	.60	1.00
COREEN088 Kumongous, the Sticky String Kaiju R	.50	.75
COREEN089 Kyoutou Waterfront C	.20	.30
COREEN090 Performapal Silver Claw C	.05	.15
COREEN091 Escher the Frost Vassal C	.05	.15
COREEN092 Kozmotown R	.75	1.25
COREEN093 Performapal Salutiger C	.05	.15
COREEN094 Superheavy Samurai Ogre Shutendoji SR	2.00	2.50
COREEN095 Hi-Speedroid Kendama UR	.25	.40
COREEN096 Dragong R	.05	.15
COREEN097 Mandragon R	.05	.15
COREEN098 Tatsunoko SCR	9.00	10.00
COREEN099 Secret Blast C	.05	.15
COREENSE1 Ultimaya Tzolkin SR	2.75	3.25
COREENSE2 Frightfur Tiger SR	.30	.50
COREENSE3 Engraver of the Mark SR	.05	.15
COREENSE4 Destruction Sword Flash SR	.05	.15

2015 Yu-Gi-Oh High-Speed Riders 1st Edition

COMPLETE SET (60)	140.00	165.00
BOOSTER BOX (24 PACKS)	55.00	75.00
BOOSTER PACK	3.00	5.00
RELEASED ON OCTOBER 2, 2015		
HSRDEN001 Speedroid Terrortop SR	12.00	15.00
HSRDEN002 Speedroid Tri-Eyed Dice C	.10	.20
HSRDEN003 Speedroid Double Yoyo C	.10	.20
HSRDEN004 Speedroid Razorang R	.20	.35
HSRDEN005 Speedroid Menko C	.10	.20
HSRDEN006 Speedroid Taketomborg SR	.75	1.25
HSRDEN007 Speedroid Ohajikid R	.20	.35
HSRDEN008 Speedroid Red-Eyed Dice SR	.25	.40
HSRDEN009 Hi-Speedroid Kendama R	.20	.35
HSRDEN010 Hi-Speedroid Chanbara SCR	15.00	20.00
HSRDEN011 Speed Recovery SR	.20	.35
HSRDEN012 Shock Surprise R	.20	.35
HSRDEN013 Synchro Cracker C	.10	.20
HSRDEN014 Dice Roll Battle R	.20	.35
HSRDEN015 Red Sprinter SR	.40	.60
HSRDEN016 Red Resonator C	.10	.20
HSRDEN017 Synkron Resonator C	.10	.20
HSRDEN018 Chain Resonator C	.10	.20
HSRDEN019 Mirror Resonator SR	.10	.20
HSRDEN020 Dark Resonator C	.10	.20
HSRDEN021 Vice Dragon C	.10	.20
HSRDEN022 Red Wyvern SCR	4.50	5.50
HSRDEN023 Red Dragon Archfiend C	.10	.20
HSRDEN024 Red Nova Dragon R	.20	.35
HSRDEN025 Resonator Call C	.10	.20
HSRDEN026 Red Cocoon C	.10	.20
HSRDEN027 Red Carpet R	.20	.35
HSRDEN028 PSY-Frame Driver R	.20	.35
HSRDEN029 PSY-Framegear Alpha C	.10	.20
HSRDEN030 PSY-Framegear Beta UR	1.00	1.50
HSRDEN031 PSY-Framegear Gamma UR	10.00	15.00
HSRDEN032 PSY-Framegear Delta R	.20	.35
HSRDEN033 PSY-Framegear Epsilon C	.10	.20
HSRDEN034 PSY-Framelord Zeta SR	.20	.35
HSRDEN035 PSY-Framelord Omega SCR	10.00	15.00
HSRDEN036 PSY-Frame Circuit R	.40	.60
HSRDEN037 PSY-Frame Overload R	.20	.35
HSRDEN038 Goyo Chaser UR	.15	.25
HSRDEN039 Goyo Predator UR	.25	.40
HSRDEN040 Hot Red Dragon Archfiend SR	1.00	1.50
HSRDEN041 Hot Red Dragon Archfiend Abyss UR	10.00	12.00
HSRDEN042 Hot Red Dragon Archfiend Bane SCR	10.00	12.00
HSRDEN043 Stardust Spark Dragon SR	3.00	3.75
HSRDEN044 Black Rose Moonlight Dragon SR	4.00	6.00
HSRDEN045 Expressroid C	.10	.20
HSRDEN046 Krebons C	.10	.20
HSRDEN047 Armoroid C	.10	.20
HSRDEN048 Silent Psychic Wizard C	.10	.20
HSRDEN049 Serene Psychic Witch C	.10	.20
HSRDEN050 Hushed Psychic Cleric C	.10	.20
HSRDEN051 Cardcar D C	.10	.20
HSRDEN052 Trishula, Dragon of the Ice Barrier SCR	24.00	28.00
HSRDEN053 Mystical Space Typhoon C	.50	.80
HSRDEN054 Emergency Teleport UR	.75	1.25
HSRDEN055 Psychokinesis C	.10	.20
HSRDEN056 Pot of Duality R	1.50	2.00
HSRDEN057 Future Glow C	.10	.20
HSRDEN058 Compulsory Evacuation Device C	.10	.20
HSRDEN059 Supercharge C	.10	.20
HSRDEN060 Psychic Overload C	.10	.20

2015 Yu-Gi-Oh Dimension of Chaos 1st Edition

COMPLETE SET (106)	250.00	300.00
BOOSTER BOX (24 PACKS)	100.00	120.00
BOOSTER PACK (9 CARDS)	5.00	8.00
RELEASED ON NOVEMBER 6, 2015		
DOCSEN000 Samurai Cavalry of Reptier R	.20	.30
DOCSEN001 Performapal Secondonkey R	.40	.60
DOCSEN002 Performapal Splashmammoth R	.20	.30
DOCSEN003 Performapal Helpprincess R	.20	.30
DOCSEN004 Superheavy Samurai Thief C	.15	.25
DOCSEN005 Superheavy Samurai Transporter C	.15	.25
DOCSEN006 Superheavy Samurai Drum C	.15	.25
DOCSEN007 Superheavy Samurai Soulhorns C	.15	.25
DOCSEN008 Superheavy Samurai Soulclaw C	.15	.25
DOCSEN088 Gameciel, the Sea Turtle Kaiju R	4.00	4.50
DOCSEN009 Fluffal Wings C	.15	.25
DOCSEN010 D/D Berfomet R	.60	1.00
DOCSEN011 D/D Swirl Slime C	.15	.25
DOCSEN012 D/D Necro Slime C	.15	.25
DOCSEN013 Raidraptor - Wild Vulture C	.15	.25
DOCSEN014 Raidraptor - Skull Eagle C	.15	.25
DOCSEN015 Performage Mirror Conductor C	.15	.25
DOCSEN016 Performage Plushfire C	.15	.25
DOCSEN017 The Legendary Fisherman III SR	.40	.75
DOCSEN018 Assault Blackwing - Kunai the Drizzle R	.15	.25
DOCSEN019 Charging Gaia the Fierce Knight UR	4.75	5.25
DOCSEN020 Sphere Kuriboh R	.25	.35
DOCSEN021 Super Soldier Soul C	.15	.25
DOCSEN022 Beginning Knight SR	1.00	1.75
DOCSEN023 Evening Twilight Knight SR	2.50	3.50
DOCSEN024 Vector Pendulum, the Dracoverlord SR	1.50	2.00
DOCSEN025 Majespecter Cat - Nekomata SR	1.25	2.00
DOCSEN026 Majespecter Raccoon - Bunbuku UR	15.00	18.00
DOCSEN027 Majespecter Crow - Yata C	.15	.25
DOCSEN028 Majespecter Fox - Kyubi C	.15	.25
DOCSEN029 Majespecter Unicorn - Kirin R	2.00	2.75
DOCSEN030 Igknight Cavalier C	.15	.25
DOCSEN031 Igknight Veteran C	.15	.25
DOCSEN032 Graydle Slime R	.30	.50
DOCSEN033 Graydle Alligator C	.15	.25
DOCSEN034 Graydle Cobra C	.15	.25
DOCSEN035 Graydle Eagle C	.15	.25
DOCSEN036 Skilled Red Magician R	.10	.20
DOCSEN037 Giant Pairfish R	.10	.20
DOCSEN038 Toon Barrel Dragon R	.25	.35
DOCSEN039 Deskbot 006 C	.15	.25
DOCSEN040 Pot of The Forbidden SP	1.25	2.00
DOCSEN041 Dr. Frankenderp SP	.05	.15
DOCSEN042 Black Luster Soldier - Super Soldier UR	6.50	7.25
DOCSEN042 Black Luster Soldier - Super Soldier UTR	8.00	9.00
DOCSEN043 Frightfur Sabre-Tooth UR	10.00	12.00
DOCSEN044 D/D/D Wave Oblivion King Caesar Ragnarok SR	4.00	6.00
DOCSEN045 Odd-Eyes Vortex Dragon SCR	10.00	13.00

DOCSEN045 Odd-Eyes Vortex Dragon UTR	15.00	16.50
DOCSEN046 Scarlight Red Dragon Archfiend SCR	18.00	20.00
DOCSEN046 Scarlight Red Dragon Archfiend UTR	20.00	23.00
DOCSEN046 Scarlight Red Dragon Archfiend GR	23.00	25.00
DOCSEN047 Assault Blackwing - Raikiri the Rain Shower UR	7.00	8.00
DOCSEN047 Assault Blackwing - Raikiri the Rain Shower UTR	8.00	9.00
DOCSEN048 Graydle Dragon SR	2.75	3.50
DOCSEN049 Deskbot Jet C	.15	.25
DOCSEN050 D/D/D Duo-Dawn King Kali Yuga SR	2.25	3.00
DOCSEN051 Raidraptor - Fiend Eagle R	.15	.25
DOCSEN052 Majester Paladin, the Ascending Dracoslayer UR	1.25	1.75
DOCSEN052 Majester Paladin, the Ascending Dracoslayer UTR	2.75	3.50
DOCSEN053 Shuffle Reborn C	.15	.25
DOCSEN054 Rank-Up-Magic Raid Force R	.25	.35
DOCSEN055 Raptor's Ultimate Mace C	.15	.25
DOCSEN056 Super Soldier Ritual R	.30	.50
DOCSEN057 Gateway to Chaos SR	2.00	2.50
DOCSEN058 Majesty's Pegasus SR	.75	1.00
DOCSEN059 Majespecter Storm C	.15	.25
DOCSEN060 Majespecter Cyclone SR	.50	.75
DOCSEN061 Igknight Reload UR	5.50	7.00
DOCSEN062 Graydle Impact C	.15	.25
DOCSEN063 Odd-Eyes Fusion SCR	15.00	18.00
DOCSEN064 Psychic Blade C	.15	.25
DOCSEN065 Painful Decision SCR	12.00	15.00
DOCSEN066 Super Rush Headlong SP	.05	.15
DOCSEN067 Frightfur March C	.15	.25
DOCSEN068 D/D/D Contract Change C	.15	.25
DOCSEN069 Dark Contract with Errors C	.15	.25
DOCSEN070 Super Soldier Rebirth C	.15	.25
DOCSEN071 Super Soldier Shield UR	1.25	2.00
DOCSEN072 Majespecter Tornado UR	2.50	3.25
DOCSEN073 Majespecter Tempest C	.15	.25
DOCSEN074 Graydle Parasite SR	1.25	1.75
DOCSEN075 Graydle Split C	.15	.25
DOCSEN076 Blazing Mirror Force SCR	2.00	2.50
DOCSEN077 Pendulum Area R	.05	.15
DOCSEN078 Urgent Ritual Art SCR	1.25	1.75
DOCSEN079 Grand Horn of Heaven C	.15	.25
DOCSEN080 First-Aid Squad SP	.05	.15
DOCSEN081 Painful Escape SCR	1.25	1.75
DOCSEN082 Kozmo Strawman UR	2.25	3.00
DOCSEN083 Kozmoll Wickedwitch C	.15	.25
DOCSEN084 Kozmo DOG Fighter SR	.30	.50
DOCSEN085 Kozmo Dark Destroyer SCR	8.00	10.00
DOCSEN086 Kozmo Lightsword C	.15	.25
DOCSEN087 Radian, the Multidimensional Kaiju R	1.25	1.75
DOCSEN089 Kaiju Capture Mission C	.15	.25
DOCSEN090 D/D/D Wave King Caesar R	.30	.50
DOCSEN091 D/D Savant Galilei C	.15	.25
DOCSEN092 D/D Savant Kepler C	.15	.25
DOCSEN093 Dark Contract with the Gate C	.15	.25
DOCSEN094 Dark Contract with the Swamp King C	.15	.25
DOCSEN095 Dark Contract with the Witch C	.15	.25
DOCSEN096 Contract Laundering C	.15	.25
DOCSEN097 D/D/D Human Resources C	.15	.25
DOCSEN098 D/D/D Rebel King Leonidas SR	5.00	6.50
DOCSEN099 D/D/D Oblivion King Abyss Ragnarok R	3.25	4.25

2016 Yu-Gi-Oh Breakers of Shadow 1st Edition

COMPLETE SET (100)	115.00	160.00
BOOSTER BOX	70.00	90.00
BOOSTER PACK	2.50	6.00
RELEASED ON JANUARY 15, 2016		
BOSHEN000 Steel Cavalry of Dinon R	.10	.30
BOSHEN001 Tuning Magician SR	.10	.20
BOSHEN002 Timebreaker Magician R	.10	.30
BOSHEN003 Performapal Monkeyboard C	.15	.25
BOSHEN004 Performapal Guitartle R	.10	.30
BOSHEN005 Performapal Bit Bite Turtle C	.15	.25
BOSHEN006 Performapal Rain Goat C	.15	.25
BOSHEN007 Performapal Trump Girl C	.15	.25
BOSHEN008 Superheavy Samurai Magnet C	.15	.25
BOSHEN009 Superheavy Samurai Prepped Defense C	.15	.25
BOSHEN010 Superheavy Samurai General Jade C	.15	.25
BOSHEN011 Superheavy Samurai General Coral C	.15	.25
BOSHEN012 Solo the Melodious Songstress C	.15	.25
BOSHEN013 Score the Melodious Diva C	.15	.25
BOSHEN014 Blackwing - Harmattan the Dust C	.15	.25
BOSHEN015 Twilight Ninja Shingetsu C	.15	.25
BOSHEN016 Twilight Ninja Nichirin, the Chunin C	.15	.25
BOSHEN017 Twilight Ninja Getsuga, the Shogun R	.10	.30
BOSHEN018 Buster Blader, the Destruction Swordmaster UR	1.25	2.00
BOSHEN019 Buster Whelp of the Destruction Swordsman SR	.20	.30
BOSHEN020 Dragon Buster Destruction Sword C	.15	.25
BOSHEN021 Wizard Buster Destruction Sword C	.15	.25
BOSHEN022 Robot Buster Destruction Sword C	.15	.25
BOSHEN023 Master Pendulum, the Dracoslayer SR	.60	1.00
BOSHEN024 Dinomist Stegosaur C	.15	.25
BOSHEN025 Dinomist Plesios C	.15	.25
BOSHEN026 Dinomist Pteran R	.10	.30
BOSHEN027 Dinomist Brachion C	.15	.25
BOSHEN028 Dinomist Ceratops C	.15	.25
BOSHEN029 Dinomist Rex SR	.20	.35
BOSHEN030 Majespecter Toad - Ogama SR	.05	.15
BOSHEN031 Shiranui Spectralsword UR	1.00	1.50
BOSHEN032 Shiranui Smith C	.15	.25
BOSHEN033 Shiranui Spiritmaster R	.10	.30
BOSHEN034 Shiranui Samurai C	.15	.25
BOSHEN035 Dark Doriado C	.15	.25
BOSHEN036 Guiding Ariadne SR	.15	.25
BOSHEN037 Al-Lumi'raj C	.15	.25
BOSHEN038 Toon Buster Blader R	.10	.30
BOSHEN039 Deskbot 007 C	.15	.25
BOSHEN040 Deskbot 008 C	.15	.25
BOSHEN041 Engraver of the Mark SP	.05	.15
BOSHEN042 Zany Zebra SP	.05	.15
BOSHEN043 Odd-Eyes Gravity Dragon UR	.75	1.00
BOSHEN044 Goyo Emperor R	.10	.30
BOSHEN045 Buster Blader, the Dragon Destroyer Swordsman SCR	.10	.30
BOSHEN045 Buster Blader, the Dragon Destroyer Swordsman SCR	5.00	7.00
BOSHEN046 Dinoster Power, the Mighty Dracoslayer R	.30	.50
BOSHEN047 Enlightenment Paladin UR	.60	1.15
BOSHEN048 Superheavy Samurai Beast Kyubi R	.10	.30
BOSHEN049 Hi-Speedroid Hagoita R	.10	.30
BOSHEN050 Goyo Defender R	.10	.30
BOSHEN051 Goyo King R	.10	.30
BOSHEN052 Buster Dragon UR	2.75	4.00
BOSHEN053 Shiranui Samuraisaga C	.15	.25
BOSHEN054 Shiranui Shogunsaga UR	.60	1.00
BOSHEN055 Aegaion the Sea Castrum C	.15	.25
BOSHEN056 Performance Hurricane C	.15	.25
BOSHEN057 Pendulum Storm SR	.10	.20
BOSHEN058 Hi-Speed Re-Level C	.15	.25
BOSHEN059 Destruction Swordsman Fusion C	.15	.25
BOSHEN060 Karma of the Destruction Swordsman C	.15	.25
BOSHEN061 Draco Face-Off C	.15	.25
BOSHEN062 Dinomic Powerload C	.15	.25
BOSHEN063 Dinomist Charge C	.15	.25
BOSHEN064 Majespecter Sonics C	.15	.25
BOSHEN065 Shiranui Style Synthesis C	.15	.25
BOSHEN066 Odd-Eyes Advent R	.10	.30
BOSHEN067 Twin Twisters SR	10.00	12.00
BOSHEN068 Mistaken Accusation SP	.05	.15
BOSHEN069 Dragon's Bind C	.15	.25
BOSHEN070 Follow Wing C	.15	.25
BOSHEN071 Reject Reborn R	.10	.30
BOSHEN072 Destruction Sword Flash C	.15	.25
BOSHEN073 Dinomist Rush C	.15	.25
BOSHEN074 Majespecter Supercell SR	.05	.15
BOSHEN075 Shiranui Style Swallow's Slash C	.15	.25
BOSHEN076 Quaking Mirror Force UR	10.00	13.00
BOSHEN077 Pendulum Reborn R	.10	.30
BOSHEN078 Forbidden Apocrypha C	.15	.25
BOSHEN079 Solemn Strike SCR	28.00	33.00
BOSHEN080 Bad Luck Blast SP	.05	.15
BOSHEN081 Ultimate Providence SCR	2.00	3.00
BOSHEN082 Kozmo Tincan UR	5.00	6.50
BOSHEN083 Kozmo Soartroopers SR	.20	.30
BOSHEN084 Kozmo Delta Shuttle C	.15	.25
BOSHEN085 Kozmo Dark Eclipser SCR	2.75	3.50
BOSHEN086 Kozmojo SCR	10.00	12.00
BOSHEN087 Gadarla, the Mystery Dust Kaiju R	.10	.30
BOSHEN088 Jizukiru, the Star Destroying Kaiju R	1.00	1.75
BOSHEN089 Interrupted Kaiju Slumber SR	.60	1.00
BOSHEN090 Performapal Pendulum Sorcerer SCR	6.75	8.00
BOSHEN091 Fiendish Rhino Warrior R	.40	.60
BOSHEN092 Neptabyss, the Atlantean Prince UR	1.00	1.50
BOSHEN093 Chimeratech Rampage Dragon SR	.20	.35
BOSHEN094 Cyber Dragon Infinity SCR	14.00	17.00
BOSHEN095 Red-Eyes Retro Dragon SR	.20	.35
BOSHEN096 Dharma-Eye Magician SR	.05	.15
BOSHEN097 Black Luster Soldier - Sacred Soldier UR	.75	1.15
BOSHEN098 Arisen Gaia the Fierce Knight R	.10	.30
BOSHEN099 Traptrix Rafflesia SCR	4.75	6.00
BOSHENSE1 Beast-Eyes Pendulum Dragon SR	.10	.30
BOSHENSE2 Number 23: Lancelot Dark Knight of the Underworld SR	.10	.30
BOSHENSE3 Beacon of White SR	.10	.30
BOSHENSE4 Forge of the True Dracos SR	.10	.30

2016 Yu-Gi-Oh Breakers of Shadow Unlimited

BOSHEN000 Steel Cavalry of Dinon R	.20	.35
BOSHEN001 Tuning Magician SR	.10	.30
BOSHEN002 Timebreaker Magician R	.20	.35
BOSHEN003 Performapal Monkeyboard C	.15	.25
BOSHEN004 Performapal Guitartle R	.20	.35
BOSHEN005 Performapal Bit Bite Turtle C	.15	.25
BOSHEN006 Performapal Rain Goat C	.15	.25
BOSHEN007 Performapal Trump Girl C	.15	.25
BOSHEN008 Superheavy Samurai Magnet C	.15	.25
BOSHEN009 Superheavy Samurai Prepped Defense C	.15	.25
BOSHEN010 Superheavy Samurai General Jade C	.15	.25
BOSHEN011 Superheavy Samurai General Coral C	.15	.25
BOSHEN012 Solo the Melodious Songstress C	.15	.25
BOSHEN013 Score the Melodious Diva C	.15	.25
BOSHEN014 Blackwing Harmattan the Dust C	.15	.25
BOSHEN015 Twilight Ninja Shingetsu C	.15	.25
BOSHEN016 Twilight Ninja Nichirin, the Chunin C	.15	.25
BOSHEN017 Twilight Ninja Getsuga, the Shogun R	.20	.35
BOSHEN018 Buster Blader, the Destruction Swordmaster UR	2.50	6.00
BOSHEN019 Buster Whelp of the Destruction Swordsman SR	.10	.30
BOSHEN020 Dragon Buster Destruction Sword C	.15	.25
BOSHEN021 Wizard Buster Destruction Sword C	.15	.25
BOSHEN022 Robot Buster Destruction Sword C	.15	.25
BOSHEN023 Master Pendulum, the Dracoslayer SR	.10	.30
BOSHEN024 Dinomist Stegosaur C	.15	.25
BOSHEN025 Dinomist Plesios C	.15	.25
BOSHEN026 Dinomist Pteran R	.20	.35
BOSHEN027 Dinomist Brachion C	.15	.25
BOSHEN028 Dinomist Ceratops C	.15	.25
BOSHEN029 Dinomist Rex SR	.40	1.00
BOSHEN030 Majespecter Toad Ogama SR	.10	.30
BOSHEN031 Shiranui Spectralsword UR	.75	2.00
BOSHEN032 Shiranui Smith C	.15	.25
BOSHEN033 Shiranui Spiritmaster R	.20	.35
BOSHEN034 Shiranui Samurai C	.15	.25
BOSHEN035 Dark Doriado C	.15	.25
BOSHEN036 Guiding Ariadne SR	.10	.30
BOSHEN037 AlLumiraj C	.15	.25
BOSHEN038 Toon Buster Blader R	.20	.35
BOSHEN039 Deskbot 007 C	.15	.25
BOSHEN040 Deskbot 008 C	.15	.25
BOSHEN041 Engraver of the Mark SP	.10	.30
BOSHEN042 Zany Zebra SP	.10	.30
BOSHEN043 OddEyes Gravity Dragon UR	.50	1.25
BOSHEN044 Goyo Emperor R	.20	.35
BOSHEN045 Buster Blader, the Dragon Destroyer Swordsman SCT	.20	.35
BOSHEN045 Buster Blader, the Dragon Destroyer Swordsman SCR	2.50	6.00
BOSHEN046 Dinoster Power, the Mighty Dracoslayer R	.20	.35
BOSHEN047 Enlightenment Paladin UR	.50	1.25
BOSHEN048 Superheavy Samurai Beast Kyubi R	.20	.35
BOSHEN049 HiSpeedroid Hagoita R	.20	.35
BOSHEN050 Goyo Defender R	.20	.35
BOSHEN051 Goyo King R	.20	.35
BOSHEN052 Buster Dragon UR	.50	1.25
BOSHEN053 Shiranui Samuraisaga C	.15	.25
BOSHEN054 Shiranui Shogunsaga UR	.75	2.00
BOSHEN055 Aegaion the Sea Castrum C	.15	.25
BOSHEN056 Performance Hurricane C	.15	.25
BOSHEN057 Pendulum Storm SR	.10	.30
BOSHEN058 HiSpeed ReLevel C	.15	.25
BOSHEN059 Destruction Swordsman Fusion C	.15	.25
BOSHEN060 Karma of the Destruction Swordsman C	.15	.25
BOSHEN061 Draco FaceOff C	.15	.25
BOSHEN062 Dinomic Powerload C	.15	.25
BOSHEN063 Dinomist Charge C	.15	.25
BOSHEN064 Majespecter Sonics C	.15	.25
BOSHEN065 Shiranui Style Synthesis C	.15	.25
BOSHEN066 OddEyes Advent R	.20	.35
BOSHEN067 Twin Twisters SR	5.00	12.00
BOSHEN068 Mistaken Accusation SP	.10	.30
BOSHEN069 Dragons Bind C	.15	.25
BOSHEN070 Follow Wing C	.15	.25
BOSHEN071 Reject Reborn R	.20	.35
BOSHEN072 Destruction Sword Flash C	.15	.25
BOSHEN073 Dinomist Rush C	.15	.25
BOSHEN074 Majespecter Supercell SR	.10	.30
BOSHEN075 Shiranui Style Swallows Slash C	.15	.25
BOSHEN076 Quaking Mirror Force UR	.40	1.00
BOSHEN077 Pendulum Reborn R	.20	.35
BOSHEN078 Forbidden Apocrypha C	.15	.25
BOSHEN079 Solemn Strike SCT	30.00	45.00
BOSHEN080 Bad Luck Blast SP	.10	.30
BOSHEN081 Ultimate Providence SCT	1.50	4.00
BOSHEN082 Kozmo Tincan UR	5.00	12.00
BOSHEN083 Kozmo Soartroopers SR	.10	.30
BOSHEN084 Kozmo Delta Shuttle C	.15	.25
BOSHEN085 Kozmo Dark Eclipser SCT	1.25	3.00
BOSHEN086 Kozmojo SCT	8.00	20.00
BOSHEN087 Gadarla, the Mystery Dust Kaiju R	.20	.35
BOSHEN088 Jizukiru, the Star Destroying Kaiju R	.20	.35
BOSHEN089 Interrupted Kaiju Slumber SR	.40	1.00
BOSHEN090 Performapal Pendulum Sorcerer SCT	8.00	20.00
BOSHEN091 Fiendish Rhino Warrior R	.20	.35
BOSHEN092 Neptabyss, the Atlantean Prince UR	.60	1.50
BOSHEN093 Chimeratech Rampage Dragon SR	.10	.30
BOSHEN094 Cyber Dragon Infinity SCT	20.00	35.00
BOSHEN095 RedEyes Retro Dragon SR	.10	.30
BOSHEN096 DharmaEye Magician SR	.10	.30
BOSHEN097 Black Luster Soldier Sacred Soldier UR	.40	1.00
BOSHEN098 Arisen Gaia the Fierce Knight R	.20	.35
BOSHEN099 Traptrix Rafflesia SCT	3.00	8.00
BOSHENSE1 Beast-Eyes Pendulum Dragon SR	.10	.30
BOSHENSE2 Number 23: Lancelot Dark Knight of the Underworld SR	.10	.30
BOSHENSE3 Beacon of White SR	.10	.30
BOSHENSE4 Forge of the True Dracos SR	.10	.30

2016 Yu-Gi-Oh Wing Raiders 1st Edition

COMPLETE SET (60)	110.00	140.00
BOOSTER BOX	50.00	75.00
BOOSTER PACK	2.00	5.00
RELEASED ON FEBRUARY 12, 2016		
WIRAEN001 The Phantom Knights of Ancient Cloak UR	7.00	10.00
WIRAEN002 The Phantom Knights of Silent Boots SR	.50	.80
WIRAEN003 The Phantom Knights of Ragged Gloves C	.10	.25
WIRAEN004 The Phantom Knights of Cloven Helm R	.10	.30
WIRAEN005 The Phantom Knights of Fragile Armor SR	.10	.20
WIRAEN006 The Phantom Knights of Break Sword SCR	40.00	45.00
WIRAEN007 Dark Rebellion Xyz Dragon R	1.00	1.50
WIRAEN008 Phantom Knights' Spear R	.10	.30
WIRAEN009 Phantom Knights' Fog Blade UR	10.00	15.00
WIRAEN010 Phantom Knights' Sword R	.10	.30
WIRAEN011 Phantom Knights' Wing C	.10	.25
WIRAEN012 The Phantom Knights of Shadow Veil C	.10	.25
WIRAEN013 Booby Trap E SR	.20	.35
WIRAEN014 Raidraptor - Necro Vulture SR	.10	.20
WIRAEN015 Raidraptor - Last Strix C	.10	.25
WIRAEN016 Raidraptor - Vanishing Lanius C	.10	.25
WIRAEN017 Raidraptor - Fuzzy Lanius C	.10	.25
WIRAEN018 Raidraptor - Singing Lanius C	.10	.25
WIRAEN019 Raidraptor - Sharp Lanius C	.10	.25
WIRAEN020 Raidraptor - Mimicry Lanius C	.10	.25
WIRAEN021 Raidraptor - Tribute Lanius UR	3.00	4.00
WIRAEN022 Raidraptor - Force Strix SCR	14.00	17.00
WIRAEN023 Raidraptor - Revolution Falcon C	.10	.25
WIRAEN024 Raidraptor - Satellite Cannon Falcon SCR	8.00	10.00
WIRAEN025 Raidraptor - Call UR	1.00	1.50
WIRAEN026 Raidraptor - Nest C	.10	.25
WIRAEN027 Rank-Up-Magic Doom Double Force R	.10	.30
WIRAEN028 Rank-Up-Magic Soul Shave Force SR	.20	.35
WIRAEN029 Raidraptor - Readiness C	.10	.25
WIRAEN030 Super Quantum Red Layer UR	7.00	8.50
WIRAEN031 Super Quantum Green Layer SR	.20	.35
WIRAEN032 Super Quantum Blue Layer R	.30	.50
WIRAEN033 Super Quantal Fairy Alphan C	.10	.25
WIRAEN034 Super Quantal Mech Beast Grampulse R	.60	1.00
WIRAEN035 Super Quantal Mech Beast Aeroboros SR	.20	.30
WIRAEN036 Super Quantal Mech Beast Magnaliger UR	1.00	1.50
WIRAEN037 Super Quantal Mech King Great Magnus SCR	1.75	2.25
WIRAEN038 Super Quantal Mech Ship Magnacarrier R	.10	.30
WIRAEN039 Super Quantal Mech Sword - Magnaslayer C	.10	.25
WIRAEN040 Crane Crane C	.10	.25
WIRAEN041 Harpie Harpist R	.10	.30
WIRAEN042 Gem-Knight Pearl C	.10	.25
WIRAEN043 Gagaga Cowboy R	.30	.50
WIRAEN044 Zubaba General C	.10	.25
WIRAEN045 Number 66: Master Key Beetle C	.10	.25
WIRAEN046 Ghostrick Alucard R	.30	.50
WIRAEN047 Number 101: Silent Honor ARK SR	1.75	2.15
WIRAEN048 Bujinki Amaterasu C	.10	.25
WIRAEN049 Cairngorgon, Antiluminescent Knight C	.10	.25
WIRAEN050 Number 52: Diamond Crab King SCR	1.75	2.25
WIRAEN051 Mystical Space Typhoon C	.30	.50
WIRAEN052 Reinforcement of the Army C	.10	.25
WIRAEN053 Forbidden Chalice C	.10	.25
WIRAEN054 Swallow's Nest R	.10	.30
WIRAEN055 Rank-Up-Magic Astral Force C	.10	.25
WIRAEN056 Bottomless Trap Hole C	.40	.60
WIRAEN057 Call of the Haunted C	.10	.25
WIRAEN058 Icarus Attack SR	.20	.35
WIRAEN059 Needlebug Nest C	.10	.25
WIRAEN060 Xyz Reborn SR	.40	.60

2016 Yu-Gi-Oh Shining Victories 1st Edition

COMPLETE SET (100)	175.00	225.00
BOOSTER BOX (24 PACKS)	65.00	90.00
BOOSTER PACK (9 CARDS)	2.00	5.00
RELEASED ON MAY 6, 2016		
SHVIEN000 Magical Cavalry of Cxulub R	.20	.35
SHVIEN001 Angel Trumpeter C	.10	.20
SHVIEN002 Performapal Sellshell Crab C	.10	.20
SHVIEN003 Performapal Odd-Eyes Light Phoenix R	.20	.35
SHVIEN004 Performapal Odd-Eyes Unicorn R	.20	.35
SHVIEN005 Performapal Fireflux C	.10	.20
SHVIEN006 Speedroid Den-Den Daiko Duke R	.20	.35
SHVIEN007 Speedroid Pachingo-Kart R	.20	.35
SHVIEN008 Lunalight Blue Cat R	.20	.35
SHVIEN009 Lunalight Purple Butterfly C	.10	.20
SHVIEN010 Lunalight White Rabbit C	.10	.20
SHVIEN011 Lunalight Black Sheep C	.10	.20
SHVIEN012 Lunalight Wolf C	.10	.20
SHVIEN013 Lunalight Tiger C	.10	.20
SHVIEN014 Raidraptor - Avenge Vulture C	.10	.20
SHVIEN015 Raidraptor - Pain Lanius C	.10	.20
SHVIEN016 Raidraptor - Booster Strix C	.10	.20
SHVIEN017 Blackwing - Decay the Ill Wind C	.10	.20
SHVIEN018 Dragon Spirit of White UR	.10	.20
SHVIEN019 Protector with Eyes of Blue C	.10	.20
SHVIEN020 Sage with Eyes of Blue UR	.10	.20
SHVIEN021 Master with Eyes of Blue C	.10	.20
SHVIEN022 The White Stone of Ancients UR	.10	.20
SHVIEN023 Lector Pendulum, the Dracoverlord UR	.10	.20
SHVIEN024 Amorphage Gluttony R	.20	.35
SHVIEN025 Amorphage Lechery UR	.10	.20
SHVIEN026 Amorphage Greed R	.20	.35
SHVIEN027 Amorphage Envy R	.20	.35
SHVIEN028 Amorphage Wrath C	.10	.20
SHVIEN029 Amorphage Pride C	.10	.20
SHVIEN030 Amorphage Sloth SCT	4.50	5.50
SHVIEN031 Amorphage Goliath SR	.10	.20
SHVIEN032 Dinomist Spinos C	.10	.20
SHVIEN033 Digital Bug Cocoondenser C	.10	.20
SHVIEN034 Digital Bug Centibit C	.10	.20
SHVIEN035 Digital Bug Websolder C	.10	.20
SHVIEN036 Red-Eyes Toon Dragon SR	.10	.20
SHVIEN037 Ryu Okami C	.10	.20
SHVIEN038 Tenmataitei R	.20	.35
SHVIEN039 Spirit of the Fall Wind R	.10	.20
SHVIEN040 Ghost Reaper & Winter Cherries SCT	25.00	30.00
SHVIEN041 Gendo the Ascetic Monk C	.10	.20
SHVIEN042 Deskbot 009 C	.10	.20
SHVIEN043 Dicelops C	.10	.20
SHVIEN044 Amorphactor Pain, the Imagination Dracoverlord SR	.10	.20
SHVIEN045 Bloom Prima the Melodious Choir R	.20	.35
SHVIEN046 Lunalight Cat Dancer R	.20	.35
SHVIEN047 Lunalight Panther Dancer UR	.10	.20
SHVIEN048 Lunalight Leo Dancer SR	.10	.20
SHVIEN049 Crystal Wing Synchro Dragon SCT	55.00	65.00
SHVIEN050 Hi-Speedroid Puzzle R	.20	.35
SHVIEN051 Assault Blackwing - Chidori the Rain Sprinkling SR	.10	.20
SHVIEN052 Blue-Eyes Spirit Dragon SCT	14.00	16.00
SHVIEN053 Raidraptor - Ultimate Falcon SR	.10	.20
SHVIEN054 Digital Bug Scaradiator C	.10	.20
SHVIEN055 Digital Bug Corebage C	.10	.20
SHVIEN056 Digital Bug Rhinosebus SR	.10	.20
SHVIEN057 Fortissimo C	.10	.20
SHVIEN058 Rank-Up-Magic Skip Force R	.20	.35
SHVIEN059 Mausoleum of White R	.20	.35
SHVIEN060 Beacon of White C	.10	.20
SHVIEN061 Forge of the True Dracos C	.10	.20
SHVIEN062 Amorphous Persona UR	.10	.20
SHVIEN063 Amorphage Infection SR	.10	.20
SHVIEN064 Bug Matrix C	.10	.20
SHVIEN065 Pre-Preparation of Rites SR	.10	.20
SHVIEN066 Fusion Tag R	.20	.35
SHVIEN067 Tuner's High SR	.10	.20
SHVIEN068 Deskbot Base C	.10	.20
SHVIEN069 Finite Cards C	.10	.20
SHVIEN070 Re-dyce-cle C	.10	.20
SHVIEN071 Lunalight Reincarnation Dance C	.10	.20
SHVIEN072 Amorphage Lysis R	.20	.35
SHVIEN073 Dinomist Eruption C	.10	.20
SHVIEN074 Bug Emergency C	.10	.20
SHVIEN075 Drowning Mirror Force SCT	12.00	15.00
SHVIEN076 Wonder Xyz C	.10	.20
SHVIEN077 Rise to Full Height C	.10	.20
SHVIEN078 Bad Aim C	.10	.20
SHVIEN079 Unwavering Bond UR	.10	.20
SHVIEN080 Graceful Tear C	.10	.20
SHVIEN081 Cattle Call SR	.10	.20
SHVIEN082 Kozmo Scaredy Lion SR	.10	.20
SHVIEN083 Kozmoll Dark Lady SCT	7.00	9.00
SHVIEN084 Kozmo Landwalker SR	.10	.20
SHVIEN085 Kozmo Dark Planet SCT	4.00	4.75
SHVIEN086 Kozmourning C	.10	.20
SHVIEN087 Thunder King, the Lightningstrike Kaiju R	.20	.35
SHVIEN088 Super Anti-Kaiju War Machine Mecha-Dogoran R	.20	.35
SHVIEN089 The Kaiju Files C	.10	.20
SHVIEN090 Cuben C	.10	.20
SHVIEN091 World Carrotweight Champion C	.10	.20
SHVIEN092 Fire King Island C	.10	.20
SHVIEN093 Dwarf Star Dragon Planeter C	.10	.20
SHVIEN094 Geargianchor C	.10	.20
SHVIEN095 Geargia Change C	.10	.20
SHVIEN096 Stardust Sifr Divine Dragon UR	.10	.20
SHVIEN097 Hot Red Dragon Archfiend King Calamity UR	.10	.20
SHVIEN098 Priestess with Eyes of Blue SR	.10	.20
SHVIEN099 Blue-Eyes Twin Burst Dragon SCT	10.00	12.00
SHVIENSE1 Ebon Illusion Magician SR	.10	.20
SHVIENSE2 Elemental HERO Core SR	.10	.20
SHVIENSE3 Magician's Rob SR	.10	.20
SHVIENSE4 Scapeghost SR	.10	.20

2016 Yu-Gi-Oh Shining Victories Unlimited

COMPLETE SET (104)	100.00	200.00
BOOSTER BOX (24 PACKS)	5.00	85.00
BOOSTER PACK (9 CARDS)	2.50	6.00
RELEASED ON MAY 6, 2016		
SHVIEN000 Magical Cavalry of Cxulub R	.10	.25
SHVIEN001 Angel Trumpeter C	.10	.25
SHVIEN002 Performapal Sellshell Crab C	.10	.25
SHVIEN003 Performapal Odd-Eyes Light Phoenix R	.20	.50
SHVIEN004 Performapal Odd-Eyes Unicorn R	.25	.75
SHVIEN005 Performapal Fireflux C	.10	.25
SHVIEN006 Speedroid Den-Den Daiko Duke R	.10	.25
SHVIEN007 Speedroid Pachingo-Kart R	.10	.25
SHVIEN008 Lunalight Blue Cat R	.20	.50
SHVIEN009 Lunalight Purple Butterfly C	.10	.25
SHVIEN010 Lunalight White Rabbit C	.10	.25
SHVIEN011 Lunalight Black Sheep C	.10	.25
SHVIEN012 Lunalight Wolf C	.10	.25
SHVIEN013 Lunalight Tiger C	.10	.25
SHVIEN014 Raidraptor - Avenge Vulture C	.10	.25
SHVIEN015 Raidraptor - Pain Lanius C	.10	.25
SHVIEN016 Raidraptor - Booster Strix C	.10	.25
SHVIEN017 Blackwing - Decay the Ill Wind C	.10	.25
SHVIEN018 Dragon Spirit of White UR	5.00	12.00
SHVIEN019 Protector with Eyes of Blue C	.10	.25
SHVIEN020 Sage with Eyes of Blue UR	10.00	25.00
SHVIEN021 Master with Eyes of Blue C	.10	.25
SHVIEN022 The White Stone of Ancients UR	8.00	20.00
SHVIEN023 Lector Pendulum, the Dracoverlord UR	.75	2.00
SHVIEN024 Amorphage Gluttony R	.10	.25
SHVIEN025 Amorphage Lechery UR	.60	1.50
SHVIEN026 Amorphage Greed R	.10	.25
SHVIEN027 Amorphage Envy R	.10	.25
SHVIEN028 Amorphage Wrath C	.10	.25
SHVIEN029 Amorphage Pride C	.10	.25
SHVIEN030 Amorphage Sloth SCT	2.50	6.00
SHVIEN031 Amorphage Goliath SR	.10	.30
SHVIEN032 Dinomist Spinos C	.10	.25
SHVIEN033 Digital Bug Cocoondenser C	.10	.25
SHVIEN034 Digital Bug Centibit C	.10	.25
SHVIEN035 Digital Bug Websolder C	.10	.25
SHVIEN036 Red-Eyes Toon Dragon SR	.10	.30
SHVIEN037 Ryu Okami C	.10	.25
SHVIEN038 Tenmataitei R	.10	.25
SHVIEN039 Spirit of the Fall Wind R	.10	.25
SHVIEN040 Ghost Reaper & Winter Cherries SCT	8.00	20.00
SHVIEN041 Gendo the Ascetic Monk C	.10	.25
SHVIEN042 Deskbot 009 C	.10	.25
SHVIEN043 Dicelops C	.10	.25
SHVIEN044 Amorphactor Pain, the Imagination Dracoverlord SR	.10	.30
SHVIEN045 Bloom Prima the Melodious Choir R	.10	.25
SHVIEN046 Lunalight Cat Dancer R	.50	1.25
SHVIEN047 Lunalight Panther Dancer UR	1.50	4.00
SHVIEN048 Lunalight Leo Dancer SR	.10	.30
SHVIEN049 Crystal Wing Synchro Dragon SCT	15.00	30.00
SHVIEN050 Hi-Speedroid Puzzle R	.10	.25
SHVIEN051 Assault Blackwing - Chidori the Rain Sprinkling SR	.10	.30
SHVIEN052 Blue-Eyes Spirit Dragon SCT	15.00	30.00
SHVIEN053 Raidraptor - Ultimate Falcon SR	.10	.30
SHVIEN054 Digital Bug Scaradiator C	.10	.25
SHVIEN055 Digital Bug Corebage C	.10	.25
SHVIEN056 Digital Bug Rhinosebus SR	.10	.30
SHVIEN057 Fortissimo C	.10	.25
SHVIEN058 Rank-Up-Magic Skip Force R	.20	.50
SHVIEN059 Mausoleum of White R	.20	.50
SHVIEN060 Beacon of White C	.10	.25
SHVIEN061 Forge of the True Dracos C	.10	.25
SHVIEN062 Amorphous Persona UR	.60	1.50
SHVIEN063 Amorphage Infection SR	.10	.30
SHVIEN064 Bug Matrix C	.10	.25
SHVIEN065 Pre-Preparation of Rites SR	.50	1.25
SHVIEN066 Fusion Tag R	.20	.50
SHVIEN067 Tuner's High SR	.10	.30
SHVIEN068 Deskbot Base C	.10	.25
SHVIEN069 Finite Cards C	.10	.25
SHVIEN070 Re-dyce-cle C	.10	.25
SHVIEN071 Lunalight Reincarnation Dance C	.10	.25
SHVIEN072 Amorphage Lysis R	.10	.25
SHVIEN073 Dinomist Eruption C	.10	.25
SHVIEN074 Bug Emergency C	.10	.25
SHVIEN075 Drowning Mirror Force SCT	8.00	20.00
SHVIEN076 Wonder Xyz C	.10	.25
SHVIEN077 Rise to Full Height C	.10	.25
SHVIEN078 Bad Aim C	.10	.25
SHVIEN079 Unwavering Bond UR	.75	2.00
SHVIEN080 Graceful Tear C	.10	.25
SHVIEN081 Cattle Call SR	.10	.30
SHVIEN082 Kozmo Scaredy Lion SR	.10	.30
SHVIEN083 Kozmoll Dark Lady SCT	6.00	15.00
SHVIEN084 Kozmo Landwalker SR	.10	.30
SHVIEN085 Kozmo Dark Planet SCT	2.50	6.00
SHVIEN086 Kozmourning C	.10	.25
SHVIEN087 Thunder King, the Lightningstrike Kaiju R	.25	.75
SHVIEN088 Super Anti-Kaiju War Machine Mecha-Dogoran R	.25	.75
SHVIEN089 The Kaiju Files C	.10	.25
SHVIEN090 Cuben C	.10	.25
SHVIEN091 World Carrotweight Champion C	.10	.25
SHVIEN092 Fire King Island C	.20	.50
SHVIEN093 Dwarf Star Dragon Planeter C	.10	.25
SHVIEN094 Geargianchor C	.10	.25
SHVIEN095 Geargia Change C	.10	.25
SHVIEN096 Stardust Sifr Divine Dragon UR	.50	1.25
SHVIEN097 Hot Red Dragon Archfiend King Calamity UR	.20	.60
SHVIEN098 Priestess with Eyes of Blue SR	.10	.30
SHVIEN099 Blue-Eyes Twin Burst Dragon SCT	5.00	12.00
SHVIENSE1 Ebon Illusion Magician SR	.10	.30
SHVIENSE2 Elemental HERO Core SR	.10	.30
SHVIENSE3 Magician's Rob SR	.10	.30
SHVIENSE4 Scapeghost SR	.10	.30

2016 Yu-Gi-Oh The Dark Illusion 1st Edition

COMPLETE SET (100)	210.00	275.00
BOOSTER BOX (24 PACKS)	65.00	85.00
BOOSTER PACK (9 CARDS)	2.50	6.00
RELEASED ON AUGUST 5, 2016		
TDILEN000 Magical Something R	.20	.35
TDILEN001 Performapal BotEyes Lizard C	.15	.25
TDILEN002 Performapal Gongato C	.15	.25
TDILEN003 Performapal Extra Slinger C	.15	.25
TDILEN004 Performapal Inflater Tapir C	.15	.25
TDILEN005 Performapal Gumgumouton R	.20	.35
TDILEN006 Performapal Bubblebowwow C	.15	.25
TDILEN007 Performapal Radish Horse C	.15	.25
TDILEN008 Performapal Life Swordsman C	.15	.25
TDILEN009 Acrobatic Magician R	.20	.35
TDILEN010 DD Savant Thomas R	.60	1.00
TDILEN011 DD Savant Nikola C	.15	.25
TDILEN012 Blackwing Tornado the Reverse Wind C	.15	.25
TDILEN013 Blackwing Gofu the Vague Shadow C	.15	.25
TDILEN014 Red Warg C	.15	.25
TDILEN015 Red Gardna C	.15	.25
TDILEN016 Red Mirror C	.15	.25
TDILEN017 Magician of Dark Illusion SR	1.00	1.50
TDILEN018 Magicians Robe C	.15	.25
TDILEN019 Magicians Rod SR	1.50	2.50
TDILEN020 Master Peace the True Dracoslayer UR	.40	.60
TDILEN021 Metalfoes Steelen C	.15	.25
TDILEN022 Metalfoes Silverd C	.15	.25
TDILEN023 Metalfoes Goldriver R	.20	.35
TDILEN024 Metalfoes Volflame R	.20	.35
TDILEN025 True King Agnimazud the Vanisher UR	8.00	10.00
TDILEN026 Dinomist Ankylos C	.15	.25
TDILEN027 Triamid monster C	.15	.25
TDILEN028 Triamid Hunter R	.20	.35
TDILEN029 Triamid Master R	.20	.35
TDILEN030 Triamid Sphinx SR	.10	.20
TDILEN031 Shiranui Solitaire UR	3.00	5.00
TDILEN032 Toon Dark Magician SR	.75	1.25
TDILEN033 Scapeghost C	.15	.25
TDILEN034 Block Dragon UR	.75	1.25
TDILEN035 Amaterasu SR	.10	.20
TDILEN036 Dragon Ninja monster C	.15	.25
TDILEN037 Spell Strider SR	.10	.20
TDILEN038 Zap Mustung C	.15	.25
TDILEN039 Totem Five C	.15	.25
TDILEN040 Tuning Gum R	.20	.35
TDILEN041 Wrecker Panda SP	.15	.25
TDILEN042 Fairy Tail Snow SP	.15	.25
TDILEN043 Metalfoes Adamante R	.20	.35
TDILEN044 Metalfoes Orichalc C	.15	.25
TDILEN045 Metalfoes Crimsonite R	.20	.35
TDILEN046 Nirvana High Paladin SCR	4.00	6.00
TDILEN047 Assault Blackwing Sayo the Rain Hider R	.20	.35
TDILEN048 Assault Blackwing Sohaya the Rain Storm C	.15	.25
TDILEN049 Assault Blackwing Onimaru the Divine Thunder SR	.20	.60
TDILEN050 Tyrant Red Dragon Archfiend UR	1.25	2.00
TDILEN051 Coral Dragon SCR	7.00	10.00
TDILEN052 Ebon High Magician SR	.10	.20
TDILEN053 Super Hippo Carnival C	.15	.25
TDILEN054 Luna Light Perfume SR	.20	.35
TDILEN055 Frightfur Sanctuary C	.15	.25
TDILEN056 Forbidden Dark Contract with the Swamp King C	.15	.25
TDILEN057 Dark Magical Circle SCR	28.00	31.00
TDILEN058 Illusion Magic R	.20	.35
TDILEN059 Dark Magic Expanded C	.15	.25
TDILEN060 Metamorformation SR	.10	.20
TDILEN061 Metalfoes Fusion SR	.15	.25
TDILEN062 Triamid Fortress C	.15	.25
TDILEN063 Triamid Cruiser R	.20	.35
TDILEN064 Triamid Kingolem R	.20	.35
TDILEN065 Cosmic Cyclone SCR	20.00	25.00
TDILEN066 Pot of Desires SCR	28.00	31.00
TDILEN067 Magical MidBreaker Field C	.15	.25
TDILEN068 Card of the Soul SP	.15	.25
TDILEN069 Fusion Fright Waltz C	.15	.25
TDILEN070 King Scarlet C	.15	.25
TDILEN071 Magician Navigation SCR	22.00	26.00
TDILEN072 Metalfoes Counter C	.15	.25
TDILEN073 Metalfoes Combination SR	.30	.50
TDILEN074 Triamid Pulse R	.20	.35
TDILEN075 Destruction Sword Memories C	.15	.25
TDILEN076 Floodgate Trap Hole UR	4.00	6.00
TDILEN077 Premature Return UR	.50	.75
TDILEN078 Unified Front C	.15	.25
TDILEN079 Pendulum Hole C	.15	.25
TDILEN080 The Forceful Checkpoint SCR	1.00	1.50
TDILEN081 Ninjitsu Art Notebook C	.15	.25
TDILEN082 Subterror Nemesis Warrior R	.20	.35
TDILEN083 Subterror Behemoth Umastryx UR	2.00	3.50
TDILEN084 Subterror Behemoth Stalagmo UR	1.50	2.00
TDILEN085 The Hidden City SCR	7.00	10.00
TDILEN086 SPYRAL Super Agent UR	2.50	4.00
TDILEN087 SPYRAL QuikFix R	.20	.35
TDILEN088 SPYRAL GEAR Drone R	.20	.35
TDILEN089 SPYRAL GEAR Big Red R	.20	.35
TDILEN090 Heavy Freight Train Derricrane C	.15	.25
TDILEN091 Number 81 Superdreadnought Rail Cannon Super Dora SR	.25	.40
TDILEN092 Revolving Switchyard C	.15	.25
TDILEN093 Dragodies the Empowered Warrior C	.15	.25
TDILEN094 Empowerment C	.15	.25
TDILEN095 Paleozoic Olenoides C	.15	.25
TDILEN096 Paleozoic Hallucigenia C	.15	.25
TDILEN097 Paleozoic Canadia C	.15	.25
TDILEN098 Paleozoic Pikaia C	.15	.25
TDILEN099 Paleozoic Anomalocaris SR	.30	.50

2016 Yu-Gi-Oh Dragons of Legend Unleashed 1st Edition

COMPLETE SET (73)	60.00	90.00
BOOSTER BOX (24 PACKS)	60.00	75.00
BOOSTER PACK (5 CARDS)	2.50	5.00
RELEASED ON AUGUST 19, 2016		
DRL3EN001 OddEyes Mirage Dragon SCR	1.75	2.25
DRL3EN002 Performapal Uni UR	.10	.30
DRL3EN003 Performapal Corn UR	.10	.30
DRL3EN004 Raidraptor Napalm Dragonius UR	.10	.30
DRL3EN005 Raidraptor Blade Burner Falcon UR	.10	.30
DRL3EN006 The Tripper Mercury SCR	.20	.35
DRL3EN007 The Blazing Mars SCR	.20	.35
DRL3EN008 The Grand Jupiter SCR	.20	.35
DRL3EN009 The Despair Uranus SCR	.20	.35
DRL3EN010 The Suppression Pluto SCR	.20	.35
DRL3EN011 Cyber Petit Angel UR	.40	.75
DRL3EN012 Cyber Angel Benten SCR	7.50	8.50
DRL3EN013 Cyber Angel Idaten SCR	2.25	3.25

DRL3EN014 Cyber Angel Dakini SCR	1.00	1.50
DRL3EN015 Machine Angel Ritual UR	.40	.60
DRL3EN016 Ritual Sanctuary SCR	12.00	15.00
DRL3EN017 Red Nova SCR	.25	.40
DRL3EN018 Zushin the Sleeping Giant UR	.10	.30
DRL3EN019 HandHolding Genie UR	.10	.30
DRL3EN020 Scrum Force UR	.10	.30
DRL3EN021 Number 100 Numeron Dragon SCR	.75	1.25
DRL3EN022 Number 24 Dragulas the Vampiric Dragon SCR	.75	1.25
DRL3EN023 Number 45 Crumble Logos the Prophet of Demolition SCR	1.00	1.50
DRL3EN024 Number 51 Finisher the Strong Arm SCR	.20	.35
DRL3EN025 Number 59 Crooked Cook UR	.30	.50
DRL3EN026 Number 78 Number Archive UR	.10	.30
DRL3EN027 Number 98 Antitopian SCR	.60	1.00
DRL3EN028 Cipher Wing UR	.10	.30
DRL3EN029 GalaxyEyes Cipher Dragon SCR	7.50	9.00
DRL3EN030 Galaxy Stealth Dragon SCR	.60	1.00
DRL3EN031 Flower Cardian Pine SCR	.40	.60
DRL3EN032 Flower Cardian Zebra Grass UR	.10	.30
DRL3EN033 Flower Cardian Willow UR	.10	.30
DRL3EN034 Flower Cardian Paulownia UR	.10	.30
DRL3EN035 Flower Cardian Pine with Crane UR	.10	.30
DRL3EN036 Flower Cardian Zebra Grass with Moon UR	.10	.30
DRL3EN037 Flower Cardian Willow with Calligrapher UR	.10	.30
DRL3EN038 Flower Cardian Paulownia with Phoenix UR	.10	.30
DRL3EN039 Flower Cardian Lightshower SCR	.40	.75
DRL3EN040 Flower Gathering UR	.10	.30
DRL3EN041 Legendary Knight Timaeus UR	.35	.50
DRL3EN042 Kuribandit UR	.40	.75
DRL3EN043 Amulet Dragon UR	1.25	1.75
DRL3EN044 Dark Magician Girl the Dragon Knight UR	2.75	3.50
DRL3EN045 The Eye of Timaeus UR	4.25	5.50
DRL3EN046 Legend of Heart UR	.40	.60
DRL3EN047 Berserker Soul UR	.10	.30
DRL3EN048 Relay Soul UR	.10	.30
DRL3EN049 Guardian Dreadscythe UR	.10	.30
DRL3EN050 Reaper Scythe Dreadscythe UR	.10	.30
DRL3EN051 Soul Charge UR	1.50	2.25
DRL3EN052 Ras Disciple UR	.60	1.00
DRL3EN053 Mound of the Bound Creator UR	.10	.30
DRL3EN054 Wiretap UR	.10	.30
DRL3EN055 Timaeus the Knight of Destiny UR	.30	.50
DRL3EN056 Legendary Knight Critias UR	.10	.30
DRL3EN057 Doom Virus Dragon UR	.60	1.00
DRL3EN058 Tyrant Burst Dragon UR	2.00	3.00
DRL3EN059 Mirror Force Dragon UR	.75	1.25
DRL3EN060 The Fang of Critias UR	.75	1.25
DRL3EN061 Tyrant Wing UR	.10	.30
DRL3EN062 Legendary Knight Hermos UR	.10	.30
DRL3EN063 Time Magic Hammer UR	.10	.30
DRL3EN064 Rocket Hermos Cannon UR	.10	.30
DRL3EN065 Goddess Bow UR	.10	.30
DRL3EN066 RedEyes Black Dragon Sword UR	.10	.30
DRL3EN067 The Claw of Hermos UR	.50	.75
DRL3EN068 Lord of the Red UR	.10	.30
DRL3EN069 RedEyes Transmigration UR	.10	.30
DRL3EN070 The Seal of Orichalcos UR	.25	.40
DRL3EN071 Snow Plow Hustle Rustle UR	.10	.30
DRL3EN072 Night Express Knight UR	2.25	3.25
DRL3EN073 Special Schedule UR	.50	.80

2016 Yu-Gi-Oh Dragons of Legend Unleashed 1st Edition French

DRL3EN001 OddEyes Mirage Dragon SCR	10.00	15.00
DRL3EN002 Performapal Uni UR	8.00	12.00
DRL3EN003 Performapal Corn UR	2.00	3.00
DRL3EN004 Raidraptor Napalm Dragonius UR	2.00	3.00
DRL3EN005 Raidraptor Blade Burner Falcon UR	2.00	3.00
DRL3EN006 The Tripper Mercury SCR	.30	.50
DRL3EN007 The Blazing Mars SCR		
DRL3EN008 The Grand Jupiter SCR		
DRL3EN009 The Despair Uranus SCR		
DRL3EN010 The Suppression Pluto SCR	1.00	1.50
DRL3EN011 Cyber Petit Angel UR	1.00	1.50
DRL3EN012 Cyber Angel Benten SCR	.75	1.00
DRL3EN013 Cyber Angel Idaten SCR	1.00	1.25
DRL3EN014 Cyber Angel Dakini SCR	1.00	1.25
DRL3EN015 Machine Angel Ritual UR	.30	.50
DRL3EN016 Ritual Sanctuary SCR	1.00	1.25
DRL3EN017 Red Nova SCR		
DRL3EN018 Zushin the Sleeping Giant UR	2.00	3.00
DRL3EN019 HandHolding Genie UR		
DRL3EN020 Scrum Force UR	20.00	25.00
DRL3EN021 Number 100 Numeron Dragon SCR	1.00	1.50
DRL3EN022 Number 24 Dragulas the Vampiric Dragon SCR	1.00	1.50
DRL3EN023 Number 45 Crumble Logos the Prophet of Demolition SCR	1.00	1.50
DRL3EN024 Number 51 Finisher the Strong Arm SCR		
DRL3EN025 Number 59 Crooked Cook UR	2.50	3.00
DRL3EN026 Number 78 Number Archive UR	1.00	1.25
DRL3EN027 Number 98 Antitopian SCR	4.00	5.00
DRL3EN028 Cipher Wing UR		
DRL3EN029 GalaxyEyes Cipher Dragon SCR	.75	1.00
DRL3EN030 Galaxy Stealth Dragon SCR		
DRL3EN031 Flower Cardian Pine SCR		
DRL3EN032 Flower Cardian Zebra Grass UR		
DRL3EN033 Flower Cardian Willow UR	.30	.50
DRL3EN034 Flower Cardian Paulownia UR		
DRL3EN035 Flower Cardian Pine with Crane UR		
DRL3EN036 Flower Cardian Zebra Grass with Moon UR	.30	.50
DRL3EN037 Flower Cardian Willow with Calligrapher UR		
DRL3EN038 Flower Cardian Paulownia with Phoenix UR	1.00	1.25
DRL3EN039 Flower Cardian Lightshower SCR		
DRL3EN040 Flower Gathering UR		
DRL3EN041 Legendary Knight Timaeus UR	2.00	3.00
DRL3EN042 Kuribandit UR		
DRL3EN043 Amulet Dragon UR		
DRL3EN044 Dark Magician Girl the Dragon Knight UR	8.00	12.00
DRL3EN045 The Eye of Timaeus UR	10.00	15.00
DRL3EN046 Legend of Heart UR	1.50	2.00
DRL3EN047 Berserker Soul UR		
DRL3EN048 Relay Soul UR		
DRL3EN049 Guardian Dreadscythe UR		
DRL3EN050 Reaper Scythe Dreadscythe UR		
DRL3EN051 Soul Charge UR	1.50	2.00
DRL3EN052 Ras Disciple UR	2.00	2.50
DRL3EN053 Mound of the Bound Creator UR	2.00	3.00
DRL3EN054 Wiretap UR		
DRL3EN055 Timaeus the Knight of Destiny UR		
DRL3EN056 Legendary Knight Critias UR		
DRL3EN057 Doom Virus Dragon UR	2.00	3.00
DRL3EN058 Tyrant Burst Dragon UR	2.00	3.00
DRL3EN059 Mirror Force Dragon UR	5.00	7.00
DRL3EN060 The Fang of Critias UR	1.50	2.00
DRL3EN061 Tyrant Wing UR		
DRL3EN062 Legendary Knight Hermos UR		
DRL3EN063 Time Magic Hammer UR		
DRL3EN064 Rocket Hermos Cannon UR		
DRL3EN065 Goddess Bow UR		
DRL3EN066 RedEyes Black Dragon Sword UR		
DRL3EN067 The Claw of Hermos UR	2.00	3.00
DRL3EN068 Lord of the Red UR		
DRL3EN069 RedEyes Transmigration UR	.30	.50
DRL3EN070 The Seal of Orichalcos UR	.30	.50
DRL3EN071 Snow Plow Hustle Rustle UR	2.00	2.50
DRL3EN072 Night Express Knight UR	3.50	5.00
DRL3EN073 Special Schedule UR	2.00	3.00

2016 Yu-Gi-Oh Dragons of Legend Unleashed 1st Edition German

DRL3EN001 OddEyes Mirage Dragon SCR	10.00	15.00
DRL3EN002 Performapal Uni UR	.30	.50
DRL3EN003 Performapal Corn UR	.30	.50
DRL3EN004 Raidraptor Napalm Dragonius UR	.30	.50
DRL3EN005 Raidraptor Blade Burner Falcon UR	.30	.50
DRL3EN006 The Tripper Mercury SCR	1.00	1.50
DRL3EN007 The Blazing Mars SCR	.75	1.00
DRL3EN008 The Grand Jupiter SCR	1.00	1.25
DRL3EN009 The Despair Uranus SCR	1.00	1.25
DRL3EN010 The Suppression Pluto SCR	1.00	1.25
DRL3EN011 Cyber Petit Angel UR	.30	.50
DRL3EN012 Cyber Angel Benten SCR	1.00	1.50
DRL3EN013 Cyber Angel Idaten SCR	1.00	1.50
DRL3EN014 Cyber Angel Dakini SCR	1.00	1.50
DRL3EN015 Machine Angel Ritual UR	.30	.50
DRL3EN016 Ritual Sanctuary SCR	4.00	5.00
DRL3EN017 Red Nova SCR	.75	1.00
DRL3EN018 Zushin the Sleeping Giant UR	.30	.50
DRL3EN019 HandHolding Genie UR	.30	.50
DRL3EN020 Scrum Force UR	.30	.50
DRL3EN021 Number 100 Numeron Dragon SCR	8.00	12.00
DRL3EN022 Number 24 Dragulas the Vampiric Dragon SCR	2.00	3.00
DRL3EN023 Number 45 Crumble Logos the Prophet of Demolition SCR	2.00	3.00
DRL3EN024 Number 51 Finisher the Strong Arm SCR	2.00	3.00
DRL3EN025 Number 59 Crooked Cook UR	1.00	1.50
DRL3EN026 Number 78 Number Archive UR	.30	.50
DRL3EN027 Number 98 Antitopian SCR	2.00	3.00
DRL3EN028 Cipher Wing UR	.30	.50
DRL3EN029 GalaxyEyes Cipher Dragon SCR	20.00	25.00
DRL3EN030 Galaxy Stealth Dragon SCR	2.50	3.00
DRL3EN031 Flower Cardian Pine SCR	1.00	1.25
DRL3EN032 Flower Cardian Zebra Grass UR	.30	.50
DRL3EN033 Flower Cardian Willow UR	.30	.50
DRL3EN034 Flower Cardian Paulownia UR	.30	.50
DRL3EN035 Flower Cardian Pine with Crane UR	.30	.50
DRL3EN036 Flower Cardian Zebra Grass with Moon UR	.30	.50
DRL3EN037 Flower Cardian Willow with Calligrapher UR	.30	.50
DRL3EN038 Flower Cardian Paulownia with Phoenix UR	.30	.50
DRL3EN039 Flower Cardian Lightshower SCR	1.00	1.25
DRL3EN040 Flower Gathering UR	.30	.50
DRL3EN041 Legendary Knight Timaeus UR	2.00	3.00
DRL3EN042 Kuribandit UR	.30	.50
DRL3EN043 Amulet Dragon UR	.30	.50
DRL3EN044 Dark Magician Girl the Dragon Knight UR	8.00	12.00
DRL3EN045 The Eye of Timaeus UR	10.00	15.00
DRL3EN046 Legend of Heart UR	1.50	2.00
DRL3EN047 Berserker Soul UR	.30	.50
DRL3EN048 Relay Soul UR	.30	.50
DRL3EN049 Guardian Dreadscythe UR	.30	.50
DRL3EN050 Reaper Scythe Dreadscythe UR	.30	.50
DRL3EN051 Soul Charge UR	1.50	2.00
DRL3EN052 Ras Disciple UR	2.00	2.50
DRL3EN053 Mound of the Bound Creator UR	2.00	3.00
DRL3EN054 Wiretap UR	.30	.50
DRL3EN055 Timaeus the Knight of Destiny UR	.30	.50
DRL3EN056 Legendary Knight Critias UR	.30	.50
DRL3EN057 Doom Virus Dragon UR	2.00	3.00
DRL3EN058 Tyrant Burst Dragon UR	2.00	3.00
DRL3EN059 Mirror Force Dragon UR	5.00	7.00
DRL3EN060 The Fang of Critias UR	1.50	2.00
DRL3EN061 Tyrant Wing UR	.30	.50
DRL3EN062 Legendary Knight Hermos UR	.30	.50
DRL3EN063 Time Magic Hammer UR	.30	.50
DRL3EN064 Rocket Hermos Cannon UR	.30	.50
DRL3EN065 Goddess Bow UR	.30	.50
DRL3EN066 RedEyes Black Dragon Sword UR	.30	.50
DRL3EN067 The Claw of Hermos UR	2.00	3.00
DRL3EN068 Lord of the Red UR	.30	.50
DRL3EN069 RedEyes Transmigration UR	.30	.50
DRL3EN070 The Seal of Orichalcos UR	.30	.50
DRL3EN071 Snow Plow Hustle Rustle UR	2.00	2.50
DRL3EN072 Night Express Knight UR	3.50	5.00
DRL3EN073 Special Schedule UR	2.00	3.00

2016 Yu-Gi-Oh Dragons of Legend Unleashed 1st Edition Italian

COMPLETE SET (73)	125.00	150.00
BOOSTER BOX (24 PACKS)	60.00	75.00
BOOSTER PACK (5 CARDS)	2.50	5.00
RELEASED ON AUGUST 19, 2016		
DRL3EN001 OddEyes Mirage Dragon SCR	10.00	15.00
DRL3EN002 Performapal Uni UR	.30	.50
DRL3EN003 Performapal Corn UR	.30	.50
DRL3EN004 Raidraptor Napalm Dragonius UR	.30	.50
DRL3EN005 Raidraptor Blade Burner Falcon UR	.30	.50
DRL3EN006 The Tripper Mercury SCR	1.00	1.50
DRL3EN007 The Blazing Mars SCR	.75	1.00
DRL3EN008 The Grand Jupiter SCR	1.00	1.25
DRL3EN009 The Despair Uranus SCR	1.00	1.25
DRL3EN010 The Suppression Pluto SCR	1.00	1.25
DRL3EN011 Cyber Petit Angel UR	.30	.50
DRL3EN012 Cyber Angel Benten SCR	1.00	1.50
DRL3EN013 Cyber Angel Idaten SCR	1.00	1.50
DRL3EN014 Cyber Angel Dakini SCR	1.00	1.50
DRL3EN015 Machine Angel Ritual UR	.30	.50
DRL3EN016 Ritual Sanctuary SCR	4.00	5.00
DRL3EN017 Red Nova SCR	.75	1.00
DRL3EN018 Zushin the Sleeping Giant UR	.30	.50
DRL3EN019 HandHolding Genie UR	.30	.50
DRL3EN020 Scrum Force UR	.30	.50
DRL3EN021 Number 100 Numeron Dragon SCR	8.00	12.00
DRL3EN022 Number 24 Dragulas the Vampiric Dragon SCR	2.00	3.00
DRL3EN023 Number 45 Crumble Logos the Prophet of Demolition SCR	2.00	3.00
DRL3EN024 Number 51 Finisher the Strong Arm SCR	2.00	3.00
DRL3EN025 Number 59 Crooked Cook UR	1.00	1.50
DRL3EN026 Number 78 Number Archive UR	.30	.50
DRL3EN027 Number 98 Antitopian SCR	2.00	3.00
DRL3EN028 Cipher Wing UR	.30	.50
DRL3EN029 GalaxyEyes Cipher Dragon SCR	20.00	25.00
DRL3EN030 Galaxy Stealth Dragon SCR	2.50	3.00
DRL3EN031 Flower Cardian Pine SCR	1.00	1.25
DRL3EN032 Flower Cardian Zebra Grass UR	.30	.50
DRL3EN033 Flower Cardian Willow UR	.30	.50
DRL3EN034 Flower Cardian Paulownia UR	.30	.50
DRL3EN035 Flower Cardian Pine with Crane UR	.30	.50
DRL3EN036 Flower Cardian Zebra Grass with Moon UR	.30	.50
DRL3EN037 Flower Cardian Willow with Calligrapher UR	.30	.50
DRL3EN038 Flower Cardian Paulownia with Phoenix UR	.30	.50
DRL3EN039 Flower Cardian Lightshower SCR	1.00	1.25
DRL3EN040 Flower Gathering UR	.30	.50
DRL3EN041 Legendary Knight Timaeus UR	2.00	3.00
DRL3EN042 Kuribandit UR	.30	.50
DRL3EN043 Amulet Dragon UR	.30	.50
DRL3EN044 Dark Magician Girl the Dragon Knight UR	8.00	12.00
DRL3EN045 The Eye of Timaeus UR	10.00	15.00
DRL3EN046 Legend of Heart UR	1.50	2.00
DRL3EN047 Berserker Soul UR	.30	.50
DRL3EN048 Relay Soul UR	.30	.50
DRL3EN049 Guardian Dreadscythe UR	.30	.50
DRL3EN050 Reaper Scythe Dreadscythe UR	.30	.50
DRL3EN051 Soul Charge UR	1.50	2.00
DRL3EN052 Ras Disciple UR	2.00	2.50
DRL3EN053 Mound of the Bound Creator UR	2.00	3.00
DRL3EN054 Wiretap UR	.30	.50
DRL3EN055 Timaeus the Knight of Destiny UR	.30	.50
DRL3EN056 Legendary Knight Critias UR	.30	.50
DRL3EN057 Doom Virus Dragon UR	2.00	3.00
DRL3EN058 Tyrant Burst Dragon UR	2.00	3.00
DRL3EN059 Mirror Force Dragon UR	5.00	7.00
DRL3EN060 The Fang of Critias UR	1.50	2.00
DRL3EN061 Tyrant Wing UR	.30	.50
DRL3EN062 Legendary Knight Hermos UR	.30	.50
DRL3EN063 Time Magic Hammer UR	.30	.50
DRL3EN064 Rocket Hermos Cannon UR	.30	.50
DRL3EN065 Goddess Bow UR	.30	.50
DRL3EN066 RedEyes Black Dragon Sword UR	.30	.50
DRL3EN067 The Claw of Hermos UR	2.00	3.00
DRL3EN068 Lord of the Red UR	.30	.50
DRL3EN069 RedEyes Transmigration UR	.30	.50
DRL3EN070 The Seal of Orichalcos UR	.30	.50
DRL3EN071 Snow Plow Hustle Rustle UR	2.00	2.50
DRL3EN072 Night Express Knight UR	3.50	5.00
DRL3EN073 Special Schedule UR	2.00	3.00

2016 Yu-Gi-Oh Dragons of Legend Unleashed 1st Edition Portuguese

COMPLETE SET (73)	125.00	150.00
BOOSTER BOX (24 PACKS)	60.00	75.00
BOOSTER PACK (5 CARDS)	2.50	5.00
RELEASED ON AUGUST 19, 2016		
DRL3EN001 OddEyes Mirage Dragon SCR	10.00	15.00
DRL3EN002 Performapal Uni UR	.30	.50
DRL3EN003 Performapal Corn UR	.30	.50
DRL3EN004 Raidraptor Napalm Dragonius UR	.30	.50
DRL3EN005 Raidraptor Blade Burner Falcon UR	.30	.50
DRL3EN006 The Tripper Mercury SCR	1.00	1.50
DRL3EN007 The Blazing Mars SCR	.75	1.00
DRL3EN008 The Grand Jupiter SCR	1.00	1.25
DRL3EN009 The Despair Uranus SCR	1.00	1.25
DRL3EN010 The Suppression Pluto SCR	1.00	1.25
DRL3EN011 Cyber Petit Angel UR	.30	.50
DRL3EN012 Cyber Angel Benten SCR	1.00	1.50
DRL3EN013 Cyber Angel Idaten SCR	1.00	1.50
DRL3EN014 Cyber Angel Dakini SCR	1.00	1.50
DRL3EN015 Machine Angel Ritual UR	.30	.50
DRL3EN016 Ritual Sanctuary SCR	4.00	5.00
DRL3EN017 Red Nova SCR	.75	1.00
DRL3EN018 Zushin the Sleeping Giant UR	.30	.50
DRL3EN019 HandHolding Genie UR	.30	.50
DRL3EN020 Scrum Force UR	.30	.50
DRL3EN021 Number 100 Numeron Dragon SCR	8.00	12.00
DRL3EN022 Number 24 Dragulas the Vampiric Dragon SCR	2.00	3.00
DRL3EN023 Number 45 Crumble Logos the Prophet of Demolition SCR	2.00	3.00
DRL3EN024 Number 51 Finisher the Strong Arm SCR	2.00	3.00
DRL3EN025 Number 59 Crooked Cook UR	1.00	1.50
DRL3EN026 Number 78 Number Archive UR	.30	.50
DRL3EN027 Number 98 Antitopian SCR	2.00	3.00
DRL3EN028 Cipher Wing UR	.30	.50
DRL3EN029 GalaxyEyes Cipher Dragon SCR	20.00	25.00
DRL3EN030 Galaxy Stealth Dragon SCR	2.50	3.00
DRL3EN031 Flower Cardian Pine SCR	1.00	1.25
DRL3EN032 Flower Cardian Zebra Grass UR	.30	.50
DRL3EN033 Flower Cardian Willow UR	.30	.50
DRL3EN034 Flower Cardian Paulownia UR	.30	.50
DRL3EN035 Flower Cardian Pine with Crane UR	.30	.50
DRL3EN036 Flower Cardian Zebra Grass with Moon UR	.30	.50
DRL3EN037 Flower Cardian Willow with Calligrapher UR	.30	.50
DRL3EN038 Flower Cardian Paulownia with Phoenix UR	.30	.50
DRL3EN039 Flower Cardian Lightshower SCR	1.00	1.25
DRL3EN040 Flower Gathering UR	.30	.50
DRL3EN041 Legendary Knight Timaeus UR	2.00	3.00

DRL3EN042 Kuribandit UR	.30	.50
DRL3EN043 Amulet Dragon UR	.30	.50
DRL3EN044 Dark Magician Girl the Dragon Knight UR	8.00	12.00
DRL3EN045 The Eye of Timaeus UR	10.00	15.00
DRL3EN046 Legend of Heart UR	1.50	2.00
DRL3EN047 Berserker Soul UR	.30	.50
DRL3EN048 Relay Soul UR	.30	.50
DRL3EN049 Guardian Dreadscythe UR	.30	.50
DRL3EN050 Reaper Scythe Dreadscythe UR	.30	.50
DRL3EN051 Soul Charge UR	1.50	2.00
DRL3EN052 Ras Disciple UR	2.00	2.50
DRL3EN053 Mound of the Bound Creator UR	2.00	3.00
DRL3EN054 Wiretap UR	.30	.50
DRL3EN055 Timaeus the Knight of Destiny UR	.30	.50
DRL3EN056 Legendary Knight Critias UR	.30	.50
DRL3EN057 Doom Virus Dragon UR	2.00	3.00
DRL3EN058 Tyrant Burst Dragon UR	2.00	3.00
DRL3EN059 Mirror Force Dragon UR	5.00	7.00
DRL3EN060 The Fang of Critias UR	1.50	2.00
DRL3EN061 Tyrant Wing UR	.30	.50
DRL3EN062 Legendary Knight Hermos UR	.30	.50
DRL3EN063 Time Magic Hammer UR	.30	.50
DRL3EN064 Rocket Hermos Cannon UR	.30	.50
DRL3EN065 Goddess Bow UR	.30	.50
DRL3EN066 RedEyes Black Dragon Sword UR	.30	.50
DRL3EN067 The Claw of Hermos UR	2.00	3.00
DRL3EN068 Lord of the Red UR	.30	.50
DRL3EN069 RedEyes Transmigration UR	.30	.50
DRL3EN070 The Seal of Orichalcos UR	.30	.50
DRL3EN071 Snow Plow Hustle Rustle UR	2.00	2.50
DRL3EN072 Night Express Knight UR	3.50	5.00
DRL3EN073 Special Schedule UR	2.00	3.00

2016 Yu-Gi-Oh Invasion Vengeance 1st Edition

COMPLETE SET (100)	200.00	250.00
BOOSTER BOX (24 PACKS)	65.00	80.00
BOOSTER PACK (9 CARDS)	3.00	4.00
RELEASED ON NOVEMBER 4, 2016		
INOVEN000 Space Dragster R	.20	.35
INOVEN001 Dragon Core Hexer R	.20	.35
INOVEN002 Performapal Whim Witch R	.20	.35
INOVEN003 Performapal Flip Hippo C	.15	.25
INOVEN004 Performapal Seal Eel C	.15	.25
INOVEN005 Performapal Changeraffe C	.15	.25
INOVEN006 Predaplant Flytrap R	.20	.35
INOVEN007 Predaplant Moray Nepenthes C	.15	.25
INOVEN008 Predaplant Squid Drosera C	.15	.25
INOVEN009 Superheavy Samurai Soulpeacemaker R	.20	.35
INOVEN010 Cipher Twin Raptor C	.15	.25
INOVEN011 Cipher Mirror Knight C	.15	.25
INOVEN012 Flower Cardian Clover with Boar C	.15	.25
INOVEN013 Flower Cardian Maple with Deer C	.15	.25
INOVEN014 Flower Cardian Peony with Butterfly C	.15	.25
INOVEN015 Crystron Quan SR	.20	.35
INOVEN016 Crystron Citree UR	1.25	2.00
INOVEN017 Crystron Prasiortle C	.15	.25
INOVEN018 Crystron Smiger C	.15	.25
INOVEN019 Crystron Thystvern C	.15	.25
INOVEN020 Crystron Rosenix C	.15	.25
INOVEN021 True King Bahrastos the Fathomer UR	1.25	2.00
INOVEN022 Raremetalfoes Bismugear C	.15	.25
INOVEN023 Chemicritter Hydron Hawk C	.15	.25
INOVEN024 Chemicritter Carbo Crab C	.15	.25
INOVEN025 Chemicritter Oxy Ox C	.15	.25
INOVEN026 PolyChemicritter Dioxogre R	.20	.35
INOVEN027 PolyChemicritter Hydragon C	.15	.25
INOVEN028 Meteor Dragon RedEyes Impact R	.20	.35
INOVEN029 PSYFrame MultiThreader C	.15	.25
INOVEN030 Graydle Slime Jr C	.15	.25
INOVEN031 Aromaseraphy Angelica C	.15	.25
INOVEN032 Doki Doki C	.15	.25
INOVEN033 Torque Tune Gear SR	.15	.25
INOVEN034 Pandoras Jewelry Box SP	.15	.25
INOVEN035 Fairy Tail Sleeper SP	.15	.25
INOVEN036 Cyber Angel Vrash SR	.20	.35
INOVEN037 Sauravis the Ancient and Ascended SCR	1.25	2.00
INOVEN038 Starving Venom Fusion Dragon SCR	10.00	13.00
INOVEN039 Fullmetalfoes Alkahest SCR	1.50	2.50
INOVEN040 Metalfoes Mithrilium UR	1.25	2.00
INOVEN041 Meteor Black Comet Dragon UR	3.00	4.00
INOVEN042 Superheavy Samurai Ninja Sarutobi R	.20	.35
INOVEN043 Flower Cardian Boardefly R	.20	.35
INOVEN044 Crystron Quandax UR	.60	1.00
INOVEN045 Crystron Ametrix SR	.20	.35
INOVEN046 Crystron Phoenix UR	.60	1.00
INOVEN047 Aromaseraphy Rosemary R	.20	.35
INOVEN048 Denglong First of the Yang Zing UR	3.00	5.00
INOVEN049 Dark Requiem Xyz Dragon SCR	1.50	2.50
INOVEN050 VolaChemicritter Methydraco SR	.20	.35
INOVEN051 Darktellarknight Batlamyus UR	.30	.50
INOVEN052 Toadally Awesome SCR	15.00	20.00
INOVEN053 Amazing Pendulum C	.15	.25
INOVEN054 The Phantom Knights RankUpMagic Launch SR	.20	.35
INOVEN055 Flower Stacking C	.15	.25
INOVEN056 Super Koi Koi R	.20	.35
INOVEN057 Crystolic Potential C	.15	.25
INOVEN058 Fullmetalfoes Fusion SR	.20	.35
INOVEN059 Catalyst Field UR	.60	1.00
INOVEN060 RedEyes Insight R	.20	.35
INOVEN061 Igknights Unite C	.15	.25
INOVEN062 Tellarknight Genesis SR	.20	.35
INOVEN063 A Cell Recombination Device C	.15	.25
INOVEN064 Sprites Blessing C	.15	.25
INOVEN065 Pot of Acquisitiveness SR	.20	.35
INOVEN066 Quarantine SP	.15	.25
INOVEN067 Kings Synchro SR	.20	.35
INOVEN068 Double Cipher C	.15	.25
INOVEN069 Cipher Bit C	.15	.25
INOVEN070 Fraud Freeze C	.15	.25
INOVEN071 Crystron Entry C	.15	.25
INOVEN072 Crystron Impact C	.15	.25
INOVEN073 Burnout R	.15	.25
INOVEN074 PSYFrame Accelerator C	.15	.25
INOVEN075 Graydle Combat C	.15	.25
INOVEN076 Qlifes End R	.20	.35
INOVEN077 Nine Pillars of Yang Zing R	.20	.35
INOVEN078 Dimensional Barrier SCR	25.00	30.00
INOVEN079 Summon Gate C	.15	.25
INOVEN080 Present Card SP	.15	.25
INOVEN081 Vermillion Dragon Mech SCR	2.00	3.50
INOVEN082 Subterror Nemesis Archer SCR	4.00	6.00
INOVEN083 Subterror Behemoth Stygokraken SR	.20	.35
INOVEN084 Subterror Behemoth Ultramafus UR	1.25	2.00
INOVEN085 Subterror Behemoth Burrowing R	.20	.35
INOVEN086 Charming Resort Staff R	.20	.35
INOVEN087 SPYRAL Master Plan SR	.20	.35
INOVEN088 SPYRAL MISSION Assault R	.20	.35
INOVEN089 SPYRAL Resort SR	.20	.35
INOVEN090 Saber Reflection R	.20	.35
INOVEN091 Constellar Tempest R	.20	.35
INOVEN092 Caninetaur C	.15	.25
INOVEN093 DinoSewing C	.15	.25
INOVEN094 Mare Mare C	.15	.25
INOVEN095 Paleozoic Eldonia C	.15	.25
INOVEN096 Paleozoic Dinomischus C	.15	.25
INOVEN097 Paleozoic Marrella C	.15	.25
INOVEN098 Paleozoic Leanchoilia C	.15	.25
INOVEN099 Paleozoic Opabinia SR	.20	.35

2016 Yu-Gi-Oh Destiny Soldiers 1st Edition

COMPLETE SET (60)	90.00	130.00
BOOSTER BOX (24 PACKS)	60.00	75.00
BOOSTER PACK (5 CARDS)	3.00	4.00
RELEASED ON NOVEMBER 18, 2016		
DESOEN001 Destiny HERO Drilldark SR	.15	.25
DESOEN002 Destiny HERO Dynatag SR	.15	.25
DESOEN003 Destiny HERO Decider SCR	.40	.75
DESOEN004 Destiny HERO Dystopia SCR	.40	.75
DESOEN005 Destiny HERO Dark Angel SCR	.40	.75
DESOEN006 Destiny HERO Celestial SCR	4.00	6.00
DESOEN007 D Cubed SCR	.40	.75
DESOEN008 DFusion SCR	.40	.75
DESOEN009 Destiny HERO Diamond Dude SR	.15	.25
DESOEN010 Destiny HERO Malicious SR	.50	.80
DESOEN011 Destiny HERO Dogma SR	.15	.25
DESOEN012 Destiny HERO Plasma SR	.15	.25
DESOEN013 Destiny End Dragoon SR	.15	.25
DESOEN014 Destiny Draw SR	.15	.25
DESOEN015 Over Destiny SR	.15	.25
DESOEN016 Abyss Actor Evil Heel SCR	.40	.75
DESOEN017 Abyss Actor Funky Comedian SR	.15	.25
DESOEN018 Abyss Actor Superstar SCR	.40	.75
DESOEN019 Abyss Actor Sassy Rookie SR	.15	.25
DESOEN020 Abyss Actor Extras SR	.15	.25
DESOEN021 Abyss Actor Leading Lady SCR	.40	.75
DESOEN022 Abyss Actor Wild Hope SCR	.40	.75
DESOEN023 Abyss Script Fantasy Magic SR	.15	.25
DESOEN024 Abyss Script Opening Ceremony SR	.15	.25
DESOEN025 Abyss Script Fire Dragon's Lair SR	.15	.25
DESOEN026 Abyss Prop Wild Wagon SR	.15	.25
DESOEN027 Abyss Script Rise of the Abyss King SCR	.40	.75
DESOEN028 Abyss Actors Back Stage SR	.15	.25
DESOEN029 Darklord Morningstar SCR	.40	.75
DESOEN030 Darklord Ixchel SCR	20.00	25.00
DESOEN031 Darklord Tezcatlipoca SCR	.40	.75
DESOEN032 Darklord Nasten SCR	6.00	8.00
DESOEN033 Darklord Amdusc SCR	.40	.75
DESOEN034 Banishment of the Darklords SCR	1.50	2.00
DESOEN035 Darklord Contact SCR	.40	.75
DESOEN036 Darklord Rebellion SCR	.40	.75
DESOEN037 Darklord Enchantment SCR	.40	.75
DESOEN038 Darklord Asmodeus SR	.15	.25
DESOEN039 Darklord Superbia SR	.15	.25
DESOEN040 Darklord Edeh Arae SR	.15	.25
DESOEN041 Darklord Zerato SR	.15	.25
DESOEN042 Dark Hole SR	1.00	1.50
DESOEN043 Fires of Doomsday SR	.15	.25
DESOEN044 Allure of Darkness SR	3.00	5.00
DESOEN045 Escape from the Dark Dimension SR	.15	.25
DESOEN046 Darklord Marie SR	.15	.25
DESOEN047 Prometheus, King of the Shadows SR	.15	.25
DESOEN048 Darklord Nurse Reficule SR	.15	.25
DESOEN049 Doomsday Horror SR	.15	.25
DESOEN050 Archlord Kristya SR	.15	.25
DESOEN051 Trade In SR	1.50	2.00
DESOEN052 Veil of Darkness SR	.15	.25
DESOEN053 The Beginning of the End SR	.15	.25
DESOEN054 Dark Eruption SR	.15	.25
DESOEN055 Valhalla, Hall of the Fallen SR	.15	.25
DESOEN056 Advance Draw SR	.15	.25
DESOEN057 Dark Mambele SR	.15	.25
DESOEN058 Creeping Darkness SR	.15	.25
DESOEN059 Destiny Signal SR	.15	.25
DESOEN060 Dark Illusion SR	.15	.25

2017 Yu-Gi-Oh Raging Tempest 1st Edition

COMPLETE SET (100)	160.00	225.00
BOOSTER BOX (24 PACKS)	65.00	85.00
BOOSTER PACK (9 CARDS)	3.00	5.00
RELEASED ON FEBRUARY 10, 2017		
RATEEN000 Fusion Recycling Plant R	.10	.20
RATEEN001 Dragoncaller Magician SR	.15	.25
RATEEN002 Performapal Handstandaccoon C	.05	.15
RATEEN003 Performapal Dag Daggerman UR	.15	.25
RATEEN004 Performapal Laugh Maker R	.10	.20
RATEEN005 Speedroid Gum Prize C	.05	.15
RATEEN006 Speedroid Horse Stilts C	.05	.15
RATEEN007 Windwitch Ice Bell UR	8.00	12.00
RATEEN008 Windwitch Snow Bell UR	.50	.80
RATEEN009 Fusion Parasite R	.10	.20
RATEEN010 Cyber Tutubon C	.05	.15
RATEEN011 Cipher Etranger C	.05	.15
RATEEN012 Flower Cardian Cherry Blossom with Curtain C	.05	.15
RATEEN013 Ancient Gear Hunting Hound C	.05	.15
RATEEN014 Zoodiac Ratpier SR	.15	.25
RATEEN015 Zoodiac Bunnyblast C	.05	.15
RATEEN016 Zoodiac Whiptail SR	.15	.25
RATEEN017 Zoodiac Thoroughblade UR	.15	.25
RATEEN018 Zoodiac Ramram C	.05	.15
RATEEN019 True King Lithosagym the Disaster SR	.15	.25
RATEEN020 Crystron Rion C	.05	.15
RATEEN021 Crystron Sulfefnir SR	.15	.25
RATEEN022 Shinobird Crow C	.05	.15
RATEEN023 Shinobird Crane C	.05	.15
RATEEN024 Shinobird Pigeon C	.05	.15
RATEEN025 Envoy of Chaos R	.10	.20
RATEEN026 Spiritual Beast Tamer Winda R	.10	.20
RATEEN027 Tierra Source of Destruction SR	.15	.25
RATEEN028 Miscellaneousaurus C	.05	.15
RATEEN029 Apprentice Piper C	.05	.15
RATEEN030 Hebo Lord of the River C	.05	.15
RATEEN031 Yokotuner C	.05	.15
RATEEN032 Eater of Millions C	.05	.15
RATEEN033 Wightprincess C	.05	.15
RATEEN034 Metrognome SP	.15	.25
RATEEN035 Fairy Tail Rella SP	.15	.25
RATEEN036 Cyber Angel Natasha SR	.15	.25
RATEEN037 Shinobaroness Peacock R	.10	.20
RATEEN038 Shinobaron Peacock R	.10	.20
RATEEN039 Brave Eyes Pendulum Dragon SCR	.40	.60
RATEEN040 Windwitch Crystal Bell R	.10	.20
RATEEN041 Chaos Ancient Gear Giant SR	1.00	1.50
RATEEN042 Ancient Gear Howitzer C	.05	.15
RATEEN043 Windwitch Winter Bell R	.10	.20
RATEEN044 Superheavy Samurai Stealth Ninja R	.10	.20
RATEEN045 Flower Cardian Lightflare R	.10	.20
RATEEN046 Crystron Quariongandrax UR	.15	.25
RATEEN047 Shiranui Sunsaga R	.10	.20
RATEEN048 OddEyes Raging Dragon UR	.40	.60
RATEEN049 Neo Galaxy Eyes Cipher Dragon SR	.15	.25
RATEEN050 Heavy Armored Train Ironwolf SR	.15	.25
RATEEN051 Zoodiac Broadbull SCR	.40	.60
RATEEN052 Zoodiac Tigermortar UR	.15	.25
RATEEN053 Zoodiac Drident SCR	.40	.60
RATEEN054 Zoodiac Boarbow R	.10	.20
RATEEN055 Machine Angel Absolute Ritual C	.05	.15
RATEEN056 RankUpMagic Cipher Ascension C	.05	.15
RATEEN057 Recardination C	.05	.15
RATEEN058 Zodiac Sign C	.05	.15
RATEEN059 Zoodiac Barrage SCR	1.50	2.50
RATEEN060 Shinobirds Calling C	.05	.15
RATEEN061 Shinobird Power Spot C	.05	.15
RATEEN062 Super Soldier Synthesis C	.05	.15
RATEEN063 Super Quantal Alphan Spike C	.05	.15
RATEEN064 Ritual Beast Return C	.05	.15
RATEEN065 Foolish Burial Goods SCR	3.00	5.00
RATEEN066 That Grass Looks Greener SCR	6.00	7.00
RATEEN067 Terminal World NEXT SP	.15	.25
RATEEN068 Lost Wind R	1.00	1.50
RATEEN069 Cipher Spectrum C	.05	.15
RATEEN070 Ancient Gear Reborn R	.10	.20
RATEEN071 Zoodiac Combo C	.05	.15
RATEEN072 Shinobird Salvation C	.05	.15
RATEEN073 Beginning of Heaven and Earth C	.05	.15
RATEEN074 Shiranui Style Samsara C	.05	.15
RATEEN075 Majespecter Gust C	.05	.15
RATEEN076 Void Feast C	.05	.15
RATEEN077 Purushaddoll Aeon C	.05	.15
RATEEN078 Full Force Virus SCR	1.50	2.50
RATEEN079 Switcheroroo R	.10	.20
RATEEN080 Massivemorph SP	.15	.25
RATEEN081 Sea Monster of Theseus SCR	.60	.80
RATEEN082 Subterror Nemesis Defender R	.10	.20
RATEEN083 Subterror Behemoth Dragossuary SR	.15	.25
RATEEN084 Subterror Behemoth Voltelluric R	.10	.20
RATEEN085 Subterror Cave Clash SR	.15	.25
RATEEN086 SPYGAL Misty UR	.15	.25
RATEEN087 SPYRAL Tough R	.10	.20
RATEEN088 SPYRAL GEAR Utility Wire SR	.15	.25
RATEEN089 SPYRAL MISSION Recapture R	.10	.20
RATEEN090 Symphonic Warrior Guitaar C	.05	.15
RATEEN091 Symphonic Warrior Synthess C	.05	.15
RATEEN092 Symph Amplifire C	.05	.15
RATEEN093 Rocket Hand C	.05	.15
RATEEN094 Mekanikal Arkfiend C	.05	.15
RATEEN095 Lightsworn Judgment C	.05	.15
RATEEN096 Symphonic Warrior Miccs C	.05	.15
RATEEN097 Delta The Magnet Warrior SR	.15	.25
RATEEN098 Windwitch Glass Bell UR	.15	.25
RATEEN099 Dark Contract with the Entities UR	.15	.25

2017 Yu-Gi-Oh Raging Tempest Unlimited

COMPLETE SET	315.00	430.00
BOOSTER BOX	65.00	85.00
BOOSTER PACK	3.00	5.00
RELEASED ON FEBRUARY 10, 2017		
RATEEN000 Fusion Recycling Plant R	.30	.50
RATEEN001 Dragoncaller Magician SR	1.50	2.50
RATEEN002 Performapal Handstandaccoon C	.10	.20
RATEEN003 Performapal Dag Daggerman UR	3.00	5.00
RATEEN004 Performapal Laugh Maker R	.30	.50
RATEEN005 Speedroid Gum Prize C	.10	.20
RATEEN006 Speedroid Horse Stilts C	.10	.20
RATEEN007 Windwitch Ice Bell UR	8.00	12.00
RATEEN008 Windwitch Snow Bell UR	7.00	10.00
RATEEN009 Fusion Parasite R	.30	.50
RATEEN010 Cyber Tutubon C	.10	.20
RATEEN011 Cipher Etranger C	.10	.20
RATEEN012 Flower Cardian Cherry Blossom with Curtain C	.10	.20
RATEEN013 Ancient Gear Hunting Hound C	.10	.20
RATEEN014 Zoodiac Ratpier SR	4.00	6.00
RATEEN015 Zoodiac Bunnyblast C	.10	.20
RATEEN016 Zoodiac Whiptail SR	2.00	3.50
RATEEN017 Zoodiac Thoroughblade UR	8.00	12.00
RATEEN018 Zoodiac Ramram C	.75	1.25
RATEEN019 True King Lithosagym the Disaster SR	2.00	3.50
RATEEN020 Crystron Rion C	.10	.20
RATEEN021 Crystron Sulfefnir SR	1.25	2.00
RATEEN022 Shinobird Crow C	.10	.20
RATEEN023 Shinobird Crane C	.10	.20
RATEEN024 Shinobird Pigeon C	.10	.20
RATEEN025 Envoy of Chaos R	.30	.50
RATEEN026 Spiritual Beast Tamer Winda R	.30	.50
RATEEN027 Tierra Source of Destruction SR	2.50	4.00
RATEEN028 Miscellaneousaurus C	.10	.20
RATEEN029 Apprentice Piper C	.10	.20

RATEEN030 Hebo Lord of the River C	.10	.20
RATEEN031 Yokotuner C	.10	.20
RATEEN032 Eater of Millions C	.10	.20
RATEEN033 Wightprincess C	.10	.20
RATEEN034 Metrognome SP	.25	.40
RATEEN035 Fairy Tail Rella SP	.25	.40
RATEEN036 Cyber Angel Natasha SR	1.50	2.50
RATEEN037 Shinobaroness Peacock R	.30	.50
RATEEN038 Shinobaron Peacock R	.30	.50
RATEEN039 BraveEyes Pendulum Dragon SCR	6.00	10.00
RATEEN040 Windwitch Crystal Bell R	.30	.50
RATEEN041 Chaos Ancient Gear Giant SR	2.00	3.00
RATEEN042 Ancient Gear Howitzer C	.10	.20
RATEEN043 Windwitch Winter Bell R	.30	.50
RATEEN044 Superheavy Samurai Stealth Ninja R	.30	.50
RATEEN045 Flower Cardian Lightflare R	.30	.50
RATEEN046 Crystron Quariongandrax UR	3.00	5.00
RATEEN047 Shiranui Sunsaga R	.30	.50
RATEEN048 OddEyes Raging Dragon UR	7.00	10.00
RATEEN049 Neo GalaxyEyes Cipher Dragon SR	2.00	3.00
RATEEN050 Heavy Armored Train Ironwolf SR	1.25	2.00
RATEEN051 Zoodiac Broadbull SCR	40.00	50.00
RATEEN052 Zoodiac Tigermortar UR	10.00	13.00
RATEEN053 Zoodiac Drident SCR	40.00	50.00
RATEEN054 Zoodiac Boarbow R	.30	.50
RATEEN055 Machine Angel Absolute Ritual C	.10	.20
RATEEN056 RankUpMagic Cipher Ascension C	.10	.20
RATEEN057 Recardination C	.10	.20
RATEEN058 Zodiac Sign C	.10	.20
RATEEN059 Zoodiac Barrage SCR	55.00	70.00
RATEEN060 Shinobirds Calling C	.10	.20
RATEEN061 Shinobird Power Spot C	.10	.20
RATEEN062 Super Soldier Synthesis C	.10	.20
RATEEN063 Super Quantal Alphan Spike C	.10	.20
RATEEN064 Ritual Beast Return C	.10	.20
RATEEN065 Foolish Burial Goods SCR	12.00	16.00
RATEEN066 That Grass Looks Greener SCR	30.00	40.00
RATEEN067 Terminal World NEXT SP	.25	.40
RATEEN068 Lost Wind R	.30	.50
RATEEN069 Cipher Spectrum C	.10	.20
RATEEN070 Ancient Gear Reborn R	.30	.50
RATEEN071 Zoodiac Combo C	.10	.20
RATEEN072 Shinobird Salvation C	.10	.20
RATEEN073 Beginning of Heaven and Earth C	.10	.20
RATEEN074 Shiranui Style Samsara C	.10	.20
RATEEN075 Majespecter Gust C	.10	.20
RATEEN076 Void Feast C	.10	.20
RATEEN077 Purushaddoll Aeon C	.10	.20
RATEEN078 Full Force Virus SCR	10.00	15.00
RATEEN079 Switcheroroo R	.30	.50
RATEEN080 Massivemorph SP	.25	.40
RATEEN081 Sea Monster of Theseus SCR	25.00	30.00
RATEEN082 Subterror Nemesis Defender R	.30	.50
RATEEN083 Subterror Behemoth Dragossuary SR	1.25	2.00
RATEEN084 Subterror Behemoth Voltelluric R	.30	.50
RATEEN085 Subterror Cave Clash SR	1.50	2.50
RATEEN086 SPYGAL Misty UR	4.00	7.00
RATEEN087 SPYRAL Tough R	.30	.50
RATEEN088 SPYRAL GEAR Utility Wire SR	1.50	2.50
RATEEN089 SPYRAL MISSION Recapture R	.30	.50
RATEEN090 Symphonic Warrior Guitaar C	.10	.20
RATEEN091 Symphonic Warrior Synthess C	.10	.20
RATEEN092 Symph Amplifire C	.10	.20
RATEEN093 Rocket Hand C	.10	.20
RATEEN094 Mekanikal Arkfiend C	.10	.20
RATEEN095 Lightsworn Judgment C	.10	.20
RATEEN096 Symphonic Warrior Miccs C	.10	.20
RATEEN097 Delta The Magnet Warrior SR	1.25	2.00
RATEEN098 Windwitch Glass Bell UR	8.00	12.00
RATEEN099 Dark Contract with the Entities UR	2.50	4.00

2017 Yu-Gi-Oh Fusion Enforcers 1st Edition

COMPLETE SET (60)	100.00	150.00
BOOSTER BOX	70.00	85.00
BOOSTER PACK	4.00	6.00
RELEASED ON FEBRUARY 24, 2017		
FUENEN001 Predaplant Sarraceniant SR	.15	.25
FUENEN002 Predaplant Drosophyllum Hydra SCR	.15	.25
FUENEN003 Predaplant Pterapenthes SR	.15	.25
FUENEN004 Predaplant Spinodionaea SCR	.30	.50
FUENEN005 Predaplant Chlamydosundew SCR	1.00	1.50
FUENEN006 Predaplant Flytrap SR	.15	.25
FUENEN007 Predaplant Moray Nepenthes SR	.15	.25
FUENEN008 Predaplant Squid Drosera SR	.15	.25
FUENEN009 Predaplant Chimerafflesia SCR	1.00	1.50
FUENEN010 Greedy Venom Fusion Dragon SCR	.40	.60
FUENEN011 Predaponics SCR	.15	.25
FUENEN012 Predapruning SR	.15	.25
FUENEN013 Predaplanet SR	.15	.25
FUENEN014 Fluffal Octopus SCR	.50	.80
FUENEN015 Fluffal Penguin SR	1.00	1.50
FUENEN016 Fluffal Dog SR	.15	.25
FUENEN017 Fluffal Owl SR	.15	.25
FUENEN018 Edge Imp Sabres SR	.15	.25
FUENEN019 Edge Imp Chain SR	.15	.25
FUENEN020 Frightfur Kraken SCR	3.00	4.00
FUENEN021 Frightfur Wolf SR	.15	.25
FUENEN022 Frightfur Tiger SCR	.50	.80
FUENEN023 Frightfur Sheep SR	.15	.25
FUENEN024 Toy Vendor SR	.15	.25
FUENEN025 Frightfur Fusion SR	.15	.25
FUENEN026 Aleister the Invoker SR	.50	.80
FUENEN027 Invoked Caliga SCR	.15	.25
FUENEN028 Invoked Raidjin SCR	1.25	2.00
FUENEN029 Invoked Cocytus SCR	.15	.25
FUENEN030 Invoked Purgatrio SCR	.15	.25
FUENEN031 Invoked Magellanica SCR	.30	.50
FUENEN032 Invoked Mechaba SCR	20.00	25.00
FUENEN033 Invoked Elysium SCR	.15	.25
FUENEN034 Magical Meltdown SCR	1.25	2.00
FUENEN035 Invocation SCR	20.00	25.00
FUENEN036 The Book of the Law SCR	.15	.25
FUENEN037 Omega Summon SCR	.30	.50
FUENEN038 Summoner of Illusions SR	.15	.25
FUENEN039 Summoner Monk SR	.15	.25
FUENEN040 King of the Swamp SR	.75	1.25
FUENEN041 Fusion Substitute SR	.15	.25
FUENEN042 Instant Fusion SR	1.50	2.00
FUENEN043 Fusion Recovery SR	.50	.80
FUENEN044 Phoenix Wing Wind Blast SR	.15	.25
FUENEN045 Homunculus the Alchemic Being SR	.15	.25
FUENEN046 Lonefire Blossom SR	1.00	1.50
FUENEN047 Elemental HERO Prisma SR	.75	1.25
FUENEN048 Performapal Trump Witch SR	.15	.25
FUENEN049 Polymerization SR	1.50	2.00
FUENEN050 Fusion Gate SR	.15	.25
FUENEN051 ReFusion SR	.15	.25
FUENEN052 Branch! SR	.15	.25
FUENEN053 Miracle Fertilizer SR	.15	.25
FUENEN054 Mark of the Rose SR	.15	.25
FUENEN055 Super Solar Nutrient SR	.15	.25
FUENEN056 Battle Fusion SR	.15	.25
FUENEN057 Fusion Conscription SR	.15	.25
FUENEN058 Paradox Fusion SR	.15	.25
FUENEN059 Grisaille Prison SR	.15	.25
FUENEN060 Fusion Reserve SR	.15	.25

2017 Yu-Gi-Oh Fusion Enforcers 1st Edition German

COMPLETE SET (60)	100.00	150.00
RELEASED ON FEBRUARY 24, 2017		
FUENEN001 Predaplant Sarraceniant SR	.15	.25
FUENEN002 Predaplant Drosophyllum Hydra SCR	.15	.25
FUENEN003 Predaplant Pterapenthes SR	.15	.25
FUENEN004 Predaplant Spinodionaea SCR	.30	.50
FUENEN005 Predaplant Chlamydosundew SCR	1.00	1.50
FUENEN006 Predaplant Flytrap SR	.15	.25
FUENEN007 Predaplant Moray Nepenthes SR	.15	.25
FUENEN008 Predaplant Squid Drosera SR	.15	.25
FUENEN009 Predaplant Chimerafflesia SCR	1.00	1.50
FUENEN010 Greedy Venom Fusion Dragon SCR	.40	.60
FUENEN011 Predaponics SCR	.15	.25
FUENEN012 Predapruning SR	.15	.25
FUENEN013 Predaplanet SR	.15	.25
FUENEN014 Fluffal Octopus SCR	.50	.80
FUENEN015 Fluffal Penguin SR	1.00	1.50
FUENEN016 Fluffal Dog SR	.15	.25
FUENEN017 Fluffal Owl SR	.15	.25
FUENEN018 Edge Imp Sabres SR	.15	.25
FUENEN019 Edge Imp Chain SR	.15	.25
FUENEN020 Frightfur Kraken SCR	3.00	4.00
FUENEN021 Frightfur Wolf SR	.15	.25
FUENEN022 Frightfur Tiger SCR	.50	.80
FUENEN023 Frightfur Sheep SR	.15	.25
FUENEN024 Toy Vendor SR	.15	.25
FUENEN025 Frightfur Fusion SR	.15	.25
FUENEN026 Aleister the Invoker SR	.50	.80
FUENEN027 Invoked Caliga SCR	.15	.25
FUENEN028 Invoked Raidjin SCR	1.25	2.00
FUENEN029 Invoked Cocytus SCR	.15	.25
FUENEN030 Invoked Purgatrio SCR	.15	.25
FUENEN031 Invoked Magellanica SCR	.30	.50
FUENEN032 Invoked Mechaba SCR	20.00	25.00
FUENEN033 Invoked Elysium SCR	.15	.25
FUENEN034 Magical Meltdown SCR	1.25	2.00
FUENEN035 Invocation SCR	20.00	25.00
FUENEN036 The Book of the Law SCR	.15	.25
FUENEN037 Omega Summon SCR	.30	.50
FUENEN038 Summoner of Illusions SR	.15	.25
FUENEN039 Summoner Monk SR	.15	.25
FUENEN040 King of the Swamp SR	.75	1.25
FUENEN041 Fusion Substitute SR	.15	.25
FUENEN042 Instant Fusion SR	1.50	2.00
FUENEN043 Fusion Recovery SR	.50	.80
FUENEN044 Phoenix Wing Wind Blast SR	.15	.25
FUENEN045 Homunculus the Alchemic Being SR	.15	.25
FUENEN046 Lonefire Blossom SR	1.00	1.50
FUENEN047 Elemental HERO Prisma SR	.75	1.25
FUENEN048 Performapal Trump Witch SR	.15	.25
FUENEN049 Polymerization SR	1.50	2.00
FUENEN050 Fusion Gate SR	.15	.25
FUENEN051 ReFusion SR	.15	.25
FUENEN052 Branch! SR	.15	.25
FUENEN053 Miracle Fertilizer SR	.15	.25
FUENEN054 Mark of the Rose SR	.15	.25
FUENEN055 Super Solar Nutrient SR	.15	.25
FUENEN056 Battle Fusion SR	.15	.25
FUENEN057 Fusion Conscription SR	.15	.25
FUENEN058 Paradox Fusion SR	.15	.25
FUENEN059 Grisaille Prison SR	.15	.25
FUENEN060 Fusion Reserve SR	.15	.25

2017 Yu-Gi-Oh Maximum Crisis 1st Edition

COMPLETE SET (100)	285.00	355.00
BOOSTER BOX (24 PACKS)	80.00	100.00
BOOSTER PACK (9 CARDS)	4.00	6.00
RELEASED ON MAY 8, 2017		
MACREN000 Pendulum Switch R	.20	.35
MACREN001 Performapal Sky Magician R	.20	.35
MACREN002 Performapal Sky Pupil R	.20	.35
MACREN003 Performapal Revue Dancer C	.15	.25
MACREN004 Performapal U Go Golem R	.20	.35
MACREN005 Performapal Coin Dragon R	.20	.35
MACREN006 Speedroid Skull Marbles C	.15	.25
MACREN007 Speedroid Maliciousmagnet C	.15	.25
MACREN008 Speedroid Rubberband Plane R	.20	.35
MACREN009 Predaplant Ophrys Scorpio R	1.50	2.50
MACREN010 Predaplant Darlingtonia Cobra C	.15	.25
MACREN011 Predaplant Cordyceps C	.15	.25
MACREN012 Lyrilusc Cobalt Sparrow C	.15	.25
MACREN013 Lyrilusc Sapphire Swallow C	.15	.25
MACREN014 Lyrilusc Turquoise Warbler C	.15	.25
MACREN015 DD Ghost C	.15	.25
MACREN016 Double Resonator C	.15	.25
MACREN017 Supreme King Gate Zero SR	.40	.75
MACREN018 Supreme King Gate Infinity SR	.40	.75
MACREN019 Supreme King Dragon Darkwurm C	.15	.25
MACREN020 Majesty Maiden the True Dracocaster UR	2.00	3.50
MACREN021 Ignis Heat the True Dracowarrior UR	1.00	1.50
MACREN022 Dinomight Knight the True Dracofighter UR	5.00	7.00
MACREN023 Dreiath III the True Dracocavalry General UR	.75	1.25
MACREN024 Master Peace the True Dracoslaying King SCR	30.00	35.00
MACREN025 Metaltron XII the True Dracombatant SR	.40	.75
MACREN026 Marianne the True Dracophoenix UR	2.00	3.50
MACREN027 Zoodiac Kataroost C	.15	.25
MACREN028 Phantasm Spiral Dragon R	.20	.35
MACREN029 Digital Bug LEDybug C	.15	.25
MACREN030 Zefraath SR	.40	.75
MACREN031 Ariel Priestess of the Nekroz R	.20	.35
MACREN032 BES Big Core MK 3 R	.20	.35
MACREN033 Pendulumucho SR	.40	.75
MACREN034 Baobaboon C	.15	.25
MACREN035 Fire Cracker C	.15	.25
MACREN036 Ash Blossom and Joyous Spring SCR	80.00	90.00
MACREN037 Familiar Possessed Lyna SP	.15	.25
MACREN038 Fairy Tail Luna SR	.40	.75
MACREN039 Supreme King Z ARC SCR	3.00	5.00
MACREN040 Performapal Gatlinghoul UR	.60	1.00
MACREN041 Lyrilusc Independent Nightingale SR	.40	.75
MACREN042 The Phantom Knights of Cursed Javelin SR	.40	.75
MACREN043 Lyrilusc Assembled Nightingale SR	.40	.75
MACREN044 Raidraptor Stranger Falcon R	.20	.35
MACREN045 DDD Stone King Darius R	.20	.35
MACREN046 True King of All Calamities SR	1.00	1.50
MACREN047 Zoodiac Hammerkong C	.15	.25
MACREN048 Zoodiac Chakanine UR	3.00	5.00
MACREN049 Magicians Right Hand C	.15	.25
MACREN050 Magicians Left Hand C	.15	.25
MACREN051 Magicians Restage R	.20	.35
MACREN052 Ultra Polymerization SCR	5.00	8.00
MACREN053 Dragonic Diagram SCR	90.00	100.00
MACREN054 True Draco Heritage UR	5.00	8.00
MACREN055 Disciples of the True Dracophoenix C	.15	.25
MACREN056 Pacifis the Phantasm City R	.20	.35
MACREN057 Phantasm Spiral Crash C	.15	.25
MACREN058 Phantasm Spiral Grip C	.15	.25
MACREN059 Phantasm Spiral Wave C	.15	.25
MACREN060 Bug Signal C	.15	.25
MACREN061 Zefra Providence R	.20	.35
MACREN062 BEF Zelos C	.15	.25
MACREN063 Duelist Alliance SCR	4.00	6.00
MACREN064 Set Rotation SP	.15	.25
MACREN065 Break Away C	.15	.25
MACREN066 The Phantom Knights of Lost Vambrace C	.15	.25
MACREN067 The Phantom Knights of Wrong Magnetring C	.15	.25
MACREN068 Dark Contract with the Eternal Darkness R	.20	.35
MACREN069 True Kings Return UR	4.00	6.00
MACREN070 True Draco Apocalypse C	.15	.25
MACREN071 Zoodiac Gathering C	.15	.25
MACREN072 Phantasm Spiral Battle R	.20	.35
MACREN073 Phantasm Spiral Power C	.15	.25
MACREN074 Phantasm Spiral Assault C	.15	.25
MACREN075 Prologue of the Destruction Swordsman C	.15	.25
MACREN076 Dinomists Howling C	.15	.25
MACREN077 Zefra War C	.15	.25
MACREN078 Waterfall of Dragon Souls SR	.40	.75
MACREN079 Unending Nightmare SCR	15.00	20.00
MACREN080 Diamond Duston SP	.15	.25
MACREN081 Tornado Dragon SCR	15.00	20.00
MACREN082 Subterror Fiendess SR	.40	.75
MACREN083 Subterror Behemoth Phospheroglacier C	.15	.25
MACREN084 Subterror Behemoth Speleogeist C	.15	.25
MACREN085 Subterror Final Battle R	.20	.35
MACREN086 SPYRAL Sleeper SR	.40	.75
MACREN087 SPYRAL GEAR Last Resort R	.20	.35
MACREN088 SPYRAL GEAR Fully Armed UR	1.50	2.50
MACREN089 SPYRAL MISSION Rescue C	.15	.25
MACREN090 Gift Exchange C	.15	.25
MACREN091 Kaiser Sea Snake C	.15	.25
MACREN092 Bujin Hiruko R	.20	.35
MACREN093 Sylvan Princessprite SR	.40	.75
MACREN094 Artifact Vajra C	.15	.25
MACREN095 Mild Turkey C	.15	.25
MACREN096 Ghost Beef C	.15	.25
MACREN097 Vennu Bright Bird of Divinity C	.15	.25
MACREN098 Primal Cry C	.15	.25
MACREN099 Onikuji C	.15	.25

2017 Yu-Gi-Oh Pendulum Evolution 1st Edition

COMPLETE SET (60)	50.00	80.00
BOOSTER BOX (24 PACKS)	60.00	80.00
BOOSTER PACK (5 CARDS)	3.00	5.00
RELEASED ON JUNE 23, 2017		
PEVOEN001 Astrograph Sorcerer UR	3.00	5.00
PEVOEN002 Chronograph Sorcerer UR	3.00	5.00
PEVOEN003 Double Iris Magician UR	3.00	5.00
PEVOEN004 Black Fang Magician UR	3.00	5.00
PEVOEN005 White Wing Magician UR	3.00	5.00
PEVOEN006 Purple Poison Magician UR	3.00	5.00
PEVOEN007 Star Pendulumgraph UR	3.00	5.00
PEVOEN008 Time Pendulumgraph UR	3.00	5.00
PEVOEN009 Timestar Magician UR	3.00	5.00
PEVOEN010 Harmonizing Magician UR	3.00	5.00
PEVOEN011 Stargazer Magician SR	.40	.60
PEVOEN012 Timegazer Magician SR	.40	.60
PEVOEN013 Dragonpulse Magician SR	.40	.60
PEVOEN014 Dragonpit Magician SR	.40	.60
PEVOEN015 Nobledragon Magician SR	.40	.60
PEVOEN016 Oafdragon Magician SR	.40	.60
PEVOEN017 Wisdom Eye Magician SR	.40	.60
PEVOEN018 Dharma Eye Magician SR	.40	.60
PEVOEN019 Timebreaker Magician SR	.40	.60
PEVOEN020 Tuning Magician SR	.40	.60
PEVOEN021 Doomstar Magician SR	.40	.60
PEVOEN022 Performapal Skullcrobat Joker SR	.40	.60
PEVOEN023 Odd Eyes Pendulum Dragon SR	.40	.60
PEVOEN024 Foucaults Cannon SR	.40	.60
PEVOEN025 Hypnosister SR	.40	.60
PEVOEN026 Archfiend Eccentrick SR	.40	.60
PEVOEN027 Guiding Ariadne SR	.40	.60
PEVOEN028 Rescue Hamster SR	.40	.60
PEVOEN029 Magical Abductor SR	.40	.60
PEVOEN030 Odd Eyes Vortex Dragon SR	.40	.60
PEVOEN031 Enlightenment Paladin SR	.40	.60
PEVOEN032 Odd Eyes Meteorburst Dragon SR	.40	.60
PEVOEN033 Odd Eyes Absolute Dragon SR	.40	.60
PEVOEN034 Amazing Pendulum SR	.40	.60

PEVOEN035 Pendulum Storm SR .40 .60
PEVOEN036 Pendulum Call SR .40 .60
PEVOEN037 Pendulum Shift SR .40 .60
PEVOEN038 Odd Eyes Fusion SR .40 .60
PEVOEN039 Dragons Mirror SR .40 .60
PEVOEN040 Summoners Art SR .40 .60
PEVOEN041 Pendulum Reborn SR .40 .60
PEVOEN042 Echo Oscillation SR .40 .60
PEVOEN043 Unwavering Bond SR .40 .60
PEVOEN044 Satellarknight Zefrathuban SR .40 .60
PEVOEN045 Stellarknight Zefraxciton SR .40 .60
PEVOEN046 Zefraxi Treasure of the Yang Zing SR .40 .60
PEVOEN047 Zefraniu Secret of the Yang Zing SR .40 .60
PEVOEN048 Ritual Beast Tamer Zeframpilica SR .40 .60
PEVOEN049 Ritual Beast Tamer Zefrawendi SR .40 .60
PEVOEN050 Oracle of Zefra SR .40 .60
PEVOEN051 Zefra Divine Strike SR .40 .60
PEVOEN052 Raremetalfoes Bismugear SR .40 .60
PEVOEN053 Metalfoes Crimsonite SR .40 .60
PEVOEN054 Metalfoes Orichalc SR .40 .60
PEVOEN055 Metalfoes Adamante SR .40 .60
PEVOEN056 Metalfoes Counter SR .40 .60
PEVOEN057 Qliphort Scout SR .40 .60
PEVOEN058 Qliphort Monolith SR .40 .60
PEVOEN059 Master Pendulum the Dracoslayer SR .40 .60
PEVOEN060 Lector Pendulum the Dracoverlord SR .40 .60

2017 Yu-Gi-Oh Battles of Legend Light's Revenge 1st Edition

COMPLETE SET (80) 85.00 130.00
BOOSTER BOX (24 PACKS) 70.00 90.00
BOOSTER PACK (5 CARDS) 3.00 5.00
RELEASED ON JULY 7, 2017
BLLREN001 Odd Eyes Lancer Dragon UR .15 .25
BLLREN002 Performapal Odd Eyes Minitaurus UR .15 .25
BLLREN003 Performapal Odd Eyes Dissolver UR .15 .25
BLLREN004 Performapal Odd Eyes Synchron SCR .50 .80
BLLREN005 Performapal Five Rainbow Magician UR .15 .25
BLLREN006 Odd Eyes Venom Dragon SCR 1.25 2.00
BLLREN007 DDD Super Doom King Bright Armageddon UR .15 .25
BLLREN008 DDD Super Doom King Dark Armageddon UR .15 .25
BLLREN009 Superheavy Samurai Helper UR .15 .25
BLLREN010 Superheavy Samurai Fist UR .15 .25
BLLREN011 Superheavy Samurai Steam Train King UR .15 .25
BLLREN012 Abyss Actor Curtain Raiser UR .15 .25
BLLREN013 Abyss Script Abysstainment UR .15 .25
BLLREN014 Raidraptor Rudder Strix UR .15 .25
BLLREN015 Raidraptor Final Fortress Falcon UR .15 .25
BLLREN016 Twilight Ninja Jogen UR .15 .25
BLLREN017 Twilight Ninja Kagen UR .15 .25
BLLREN018 White Moray UR .15 .25
BLLREN019 White Aura Dolphin SCR .40 .60
BLLREN020 White Aura Whale SCR .40 .60
BLLREN021 Gladiator Beast Noxious SCR 1.00 1.50
BLLREN022 Gladiator Beast Andabata UR .15 .25
BLLREN023 Gladiator Beast Tamer Editor SCR .40 .60
BLLREN024 Destiny HERO Dreamer UR .15 .25
BLLREN025 Destiny HERO Dusktopia SCR .40 .60
BLLREN026 Vision HERO Witch Raider SCR .25 .40
BLLREN027 Giant Rex UR .15 .25
BLLREN028 Double Evolution Pill SCR 1.50 2.50
BLLREN029 Spacetime Transcendence UR .15 .25
BLLREN030 Jurassic Impact UR .15 .25
BLLREN031 Lazion the Timelord UR .20 .35
BLLREN032 Zaphion the Timelord UR .40 .60
BLLREN033 Sadion the Timelord UR .20 .35
BLLREN034 Kamion the Timelord UR .20 .35
BLLREN035 Time Maiden SCR .75 1.25
BLLREN036 Lyla Lightsworn Sorceress UR .20 .35
BLLREN037 Garoth Lightsworn Warrior UR .15 .25
BLLREN038 Lumina Lightsworn Summoner UR .20 .35
BLLREN039 Wulf Lightsworn Beast UR .15 .25
BLLREN040 Celestia Lightsworn Angel UR .15 .25
BLLREN041 Judgment Dragon UR .40 .60
BLLREN042 Raiden Hand of the Lightsworn UR .20 .35
BLLREN043 Felis Lightsworn Archer UR .60 1.00
BLLREN044 Minerva the Exalted Lightsworn SCR 15.00 20.00
BLLREN045 Solar Recharge UR .20 .35
BLLREN046 Witch of the Black Forest UR .15 .25
BLLREN047 Vanitys Fiend UR 2.00 3.50
BLLREN048 Crusader of Endymion UR .15 .25
BLLREN049 Cactus Bouncer UR .15 .25
BLLREN050 Spellbook Magician of Prophecy UR 1.00 1.50
BLLREN051 Mermail Abyssteus SCR 2.50 4.00
BLLREN052 Denko Sekka SCR 3.00 5.00
BLLREN053 Galaxy Soldier UR 3.00 5.00
BLLREN054 Infernoid Devyaty UR .15 .25
BLLREN055 Sage with Eyes of Blue SCR 6.00 8.00
BLLREN056 Elemental HERO Nova Master UR .50 .80
BLLREN057 Vision HERO Adoration UR .75 1.25
BLLREN058 Archfiend Zombie Skull UR .20 .35
BLLREN059 Dragunity Knight Gae Dearg UR 1.50 2.50
BLLREN060 Trishula Dragon of the Ice Barrier SCR 3.00 5.00
BLLREN061 PSY Framelord Omega SCR 5.00 7.00
BLLREN062 Crystal Wing Synchro Dragon SCR 6.00 8.00
BLLREN063 M X Saber Invoker SCR 1.50 2.50
BLLREN064 Neo Galaxy Eyes Photon Dragon UR 1.00 1.50
BLLREN065 Gaia Dragon the Thunder Charger UR .60 1.00
BLLREN066 Number 11 Big Eye UR .75 1.25
BLLREN067 Number 107 Galaxy Eyes Tachyon Dragon UR 1.50 2.50
BLLREN068 Evilswarm Exciton Knight UR 1.50 2.50
BLLREN069 Bujintei Tsukuyomi UR .60 1.00
BLLREN070 Number 62 Galaxy Eyes Prime Photon Dragon UR .75 1.25
BLLREN071 The Phantom Knights of Break Sword SCR 3.00 5.00
BLLREN072 Raidraptor Force Strix UR 1.50 2.50
BLLREN073 Raidraptor Satellite Cannon Falcon UR .15 .25
BLLREN074 Into the Void UR 1.25 2.00
BLLREN075 Spellbook of Secrets UR 1.00 1.50
BLLREN076 Miracle Contact UR 1.00 1.50
BLLREN077 Transmodify UR .20 .35
BLLREN078 Anti Spell Fragrance UR 2.00 3.50
BLLREN079 Different Dimension Ground UR 1.50 2.50
BLLREN080 Artifact Sanctum SCR 3.00 5.00

2017 Yu-Gi-Oh Code of the Duelist 1st Edition

COMPLETE SET (101) 160.00 230.00
BOOSTER BOX (24 PACKS) 65.00 95.00
BOOSTER PACK (9 CARDS) 3.00 5.00
RELEASED ON AUGUST 4, 2017
COTDEN000 Vendread Houndhorde UR (Pre-Release) 3.00 5.00
COTDEN000 Vendread Houndhorde R .25 .40
COTDEN001 Cyberse Wizard SR .40 .60
COTDEN002 Backup Secretary C .10 .20
COTDEN003 Stack Reviver C .10 .20
COTDEN004 Launcher Commander C .10 .20
COTDEN005 Salvagent Driver UR 1.00 1.50
COTDEN006 Trickstar Lilybell R .25 .40
COTDEN007 Trickstar Lycoris SR .40 .60
COTDEN008 Trickstar Candina UR 4.00 6.00
COTDEN009 Gouki Twistcobra SR .30 .50
COTDEN010 Gouki Suprex R .25 .40
COTDEN011 Gouki Riscorpio R .25 .40
COTDEN012 Hack Worm C .10 .20
COTDEN013 Jack Wyvern C .10 .20
COTDEN014 Cracking Dragon SR .30 .50
COTDEN015 Supreme King Dragon Odd-Eyes R .25 .40
COTDEN016 Predaplant Banksiogre C .10 .20
COTDEN017 D/D Vice Typhon C .10 .20
COTDEN018 Crowned by the World Chalice C .10 .20
COTDEN019 Chosen by the World Chalice C .10 .20
COTDEN020 Beckoned by the World Chalice C .10 .20
COTDEN021 World Chalice Guardragon UR 6.00 10.00
COTDEN022 Lee the World Chalice Fairy UR 8.00 12.00
COTDEN023 World Legacy - World Chalice R .25 .40
COTDEN024 Jain, Twilightsworn General C .10 .20
COTDEN025 Lyla, Twilightsworn Enchantress SR .50 .80
COTDEN026 Lumina, Twilightsworn Shaman SCR 7.00 10.00
COTDEN027 Ryko, Twilightsworn Fighter R .25 .40
COTDEN028 Punishment Dragon UR 2.50 4.00
COTDEN029 Rescue Ferret SCR 7.00 10.00
COTDEN030 Traptrix Mantis SR .30 .50
COTDEN031 Motivating Captain R .25 .40
COTDEN032 Treasure Panda C .10 .20
COTDEN033 Zombina C .10 .20
COTDEN034 Re: EX R .25 .40
COTDEN035 Orbital Hydralander C .10 .20
COTDEN036 The Ascended of Thunder SP .10 .20
COTDEN037 Parry Knights SP .10 .20
COTDEN038 Supreme King Dragon Starving Venom R .25 .40
COTDEN039 Supreme King Dragon Clear Wing R .25 .40
COTDEN040 D/D/D Gust High King Alexander R .25 .40
COTDEN041 Supreme King Dragon Dark Rebellion R .25 .40
COTDEN042 D/D/D Wave High King Caesar SR .40 .60
COTDEN043 Firewall Dragon SCR 35.00 45.00
COTDEN044 Trickstar Holly Angel UR 2.50 4.00
COTDEN045 Gouki The Great Ogre SR .30 .50
COTDEN046 Topologic Bomber Dragon SCR 10.00 15.00
COTDEN047 Imduk the World Chalice Dragon R .25 .40
COTDEN048 Ib the World Chalice Priestess SR .40 .60
COTDEN049 Auram the World Chalice Blademaster SR .30 .50
COTDEN050 Ningirsu the World Chalice Warrior SCR 10.00 15.00
COTDEN051 Gaia Saber, the Lightning Shadow SCR 6.00 10.00
COTDEN052 Missus Radiant SR 1.50 2.00
COTDEN053 Trickstar Light Stage UR 4.00 6.00
COTDEN054 Gouki Re-Match SR .30 .50
COTDEN055 Air Cracking Storm C .10 .20
COTDEN056 Smile Universe C .10 .20
COTDEN057 World Legacy Discovery R .25 .40
COTDEN058 World Legacy's Heart C .10 .20
COTDEN059 March of the Dark Brigade UR 2.00 3.50
COTDEN060 Twilight Twin Dragons C .10 .20
COTDEN061 Emerging Emergency Rescute Rescue C .10 .20
COTDEN062 Spellbook of Knowledge UR 15.00 20.00
COTDEN063 Gravity Lash C .10 .20
COTDEN064 Boogie Trap C .10 .20
COTDEN065 Castle Link UR .60 1.00
COTDEN066 Defense Zone SP .10 .20
COTDEN067 Three Strikes Barrier C .10 .20
COTDEN068 Trickstar Reincarnation SCR 15.00 20.00
COTDEN069 Pulse Mines C .10 .20
COTDEN070 Supreme Rage C .10 .20
COTDEN071 World Legacy Landmark C .10 .20
COTDEN072 Twilight Eraser R .25 .40
COTDEN073 Twilight Cloth C .10 .20
COTDEN074 Dark World Brainwashing C .10 .20
COTDEN075 Break Off Trap Hole SR .30 .50
COTDEN076 Heavy Storm Duster SR 1.50 2.50
COTDEN077 Back to the Front R 1.00 1.50
COTDEN078 Recall R .25 .40
COTDEN079 Blind Obliteration R .25 .40
COTDEN080 Transmission Gear SP .10 .20
COTDEN081 Samurai Skull C .10 .20
COTDEN082 Revendread Slayer R .25 .40
COTDEN083 Vendread Revenants C .10 .20
COTDEN084 Revendread Origin C .10 .20
COTDEN085 Vendread Reorigin SCR 6.00 10.00
COTDEN086 F.A. Sonic Meister C .10 .20
COTDEN087 F.A. Hang On Mach C .10 .20
COTDEN088 F.A. Circuit Grand Prix C .10 .20
COTDEN089 F.A. Downforce C .10 .20
COTDEN090 Junk Breaker C .10 .20
COTDEN091 Infernity Patriarch C .10 .20
COTDEN092 Gogogo Aristera & Dexia C .10 .20
COTDEN093 Wicked Acolyte Chilam Sabak C .10 .20
COTDEN094 Galaxy Worm C .10 .20
COTDEN095 Performapal Trumpanda C .10 .20
COTDEN096 Destiny HERO - Dangerous C .10 .20
COTDEN097 Abyss Actor - Trendy Understudy C .10 .20
COTDEN098 Speedroid Passinglider C .10 .20
COTDEN099 Ancient Gear Golem - Ultimate Pound C .10 .20

2017 Yu-Gi-Oh Circuit Break 1st Edition

COMPLETE SET (100) 200.00 300.00
BOOSTER BOX (24 PACKS) 60.00 70.00
BOOSTER PACK (9 CARDS) 3.00 5.00
RELEASED ON OCTOBER 20, 2017
CIBREN000 Hallohallo R .20 .35
CIBREN001 Defect Compiler C .15 .25
CIBREN002 Capacitor Stalker C .15 .25
CIBREN003 Link Infra Flier C .15 .25
CIBREN004 Trickstar Narkissus R .20 .35
CIBREN005 Dark Angel C .15 .25
CIBREN006 Gouki Headbatt C .15 .25
CIBREN007 Gateway Dragon SR .60 1.00
CIBREN008 Sniffer Dragon C .15 .25
CIBREN009 Anesthrokket Dragon C .15 .25
CIBREN010 Autorokket Dragon SR .60 1.00
CIBREN011 Magnarokket Dragon UR 2.00 3.50
CIBREN012 Altergeist Marionetter UR 1.25 2.00
CIBREN013 Altergeist Silquitous SR .60 1.00
CIBREN014 Altergeist Meluseek UR 1.25 2.00
CIBREN015 Altergeist Kunquery C .15 .25
CIBREN016 Krawler Spine C .15 .25
CIBREN017 Krawler Axon C .15 .25
CIBREN018 Krawler Glial C .15 .25
CIBREN019 Krawler Receptor C .15 .25
CIBREN020 Krawler Ranvier C .15 .25
CIBREN021 Krawler Dendrite C .15 .25
CIBREN022 World Legacy World Armor R .20 .35
CIBREN023 Metaphys Ragnarok SR .60 1.00
CIBREN024 Metaphys Daedalus R .20 .35
CIBREN025 Metaphys Nephthys SR .60 1.00
CIBREN026 Metaphys Tyrant Dragon R .20 .35
CIBREN027 Metaphys Executor SR .60 1.00
CIBREN028 Mermail Abyssnerei C .15 .25
CIBREN029 Fire King Avatar Arvata R .20 .35
CIBREN030 Mecha Phantom Beast Raiten C .15 .25
CIBREN031 The Accumulator C .15 .25
CIBREN032 Soldier Dragons C .15 .25
CIBREN033 Duck Dummy C .15 .25
CIBREN034 Leng Ling C .15 .25
CIBREN035 Self Destruct Ant C .15 .25
CIBREN036 Amano Iwato C .15 .25
CIBREN037 Fantastic Striborg R .20 .35
CIBREN038 Destrudo the Lost Dragons Frisson R .20 .35
CIBREN039 Elemental Grace Doriado R .20 .35
CIBREN040 Nimble Beaver SP .10 .20
CIBREN041 Muscle Medic SP .10 .20
CIBREN042 Borreload Dragon SCR 20.00 25.00
CIBREN043 Link Bumper SR .60 1.00
CIBREN044 Trickstar Black Catbat UR 1.25 2.00
CIBREN045 Gouki Thunder Ogre UR 1.50 2.00
CIBREN046 Twin Triangle Dragon R .20 .35
CIBREN047 Altergeist Primebanshee UR 1.00 1.50
CIBREN048 X Krawler Synaphysis C .15 .25
CIBREN049 X Krawler Neurogos C .15 .25
CIBREN050 X Krawler Qualiark SR .60 1.00
CIBREN051 Akashic Magician SCR 15.00 20.00
CIBREN052 Mistar Boy C .15 .25
CIBREN053 Security Block R .20 .35
CIBREN054 Dragonoid Generator R .20 .35
CIBREN055 Squib Draw SCR 5.00 8.00
CIBREN056 Quick Launch SCR 5.00 8.00
CIBREN057 World Legacy in Shadow C .15 .25
CIBREN058 World Legacy Clash C .15 .25
CIBREN059 Metaphys Factor C .15 .25
CIBREN060 Asymmetaphys UR 3.00 5.00
CIBREN061 One Time Passcode R .20 .35
CIBREN062 Arrivalrivals UR 2.00 3.50
CIBREN063 Overdone Burial SCR 4.00 6.00
CIBREN064 Temple of the Minds Eye C .15 .25
CIBREN065 Backup Squad R .20 .35
CIBREN066 Burning Bamboo Sword SP .10 .20
CIBREN067 Cyberse Beacon C .15 .25
CIBREN068 Link Restart C .15 .25
CIBREN069 Remote Rebirth?? C .15 .25
CIBREN070 Altergeist Camouflage R .20 .35
CIBREN071 Altergeist Protocol SR .60 1.00
CIBREN072 Personal Spoofing R .20 .35
CIBREN073 World Legacy Pawns C .15 .25
CIBREN074 World Legacy Trap Globe SR .60 1.00
CIBREN075 Metaphys Dimension R .20 .35
CIBREN076 Metaverse R .20 .35
CIBREN077 Evenly Matched SCR 50.00 60.00
CIBREN078 Fuse Line SCR 2.00 3.50
CIBREN079 Broken Line UR 2.00 3.50
CIBREN080 Ojama Duo SP .10 .20
CIBREN081 Samurai Destroyer R .20 .35
CIBREN082 Vendread Chimera SCR 7.00 10.00
CIBREN083 Vendread Striges C .15 .25
CIBREN084 Vendread Nights SR .60 1.00
CIBREN085 Vendread Reunion R .20 .35
CIBREN086 FA Whip Crosser C .15 .25
CIBREN087 FA Turbo Charger C .15 .25
CIBREN088 FA Off Road Grand Prix C .15 .25
CIBREN089 FA Pit Stop C .15 .25
CIBREN090 Lunalight Crimson Fox C .15 .25
CIBREN091 Lunalight Kaleido Chick C .15 .25
CIBREN092 Lyrilusc Recital Starling C .15 .25
CIBREN093 Amazoness Spy C .15 .25
CIBREN094 Amazoness Pet Liger C .15 .25
CIBREN095 Amazoness Empress C .15 .25
CIBREN096 Quiet Life SR .60 1.00
CIBREN097 Number 41 Bagooska the Terribly Tired Tapir SR 2.50 4.00
CIBREN098 Subterror Behemoth Fiendess SR .60 1.00
CIBREN099 SPYRAL Double Helix UR 30.00 40.00

2017 Yu-Gi-Oh Spirit Warriors 1st Edition

COMPLETE SET (60) 85.00 130.00
BOOSTER BOX (24 PACKS) 60.00 70.00
BOOSTER PACK (5 CARDS) 4.00 6.00
RELEASED ON NOVEMBER 17, 2017
SPWAEN001 Secret Six Samurai - Fuma SCR 1.25 2.00
SPWAEN002 Secret Six Samurai - Genba SR .40 .60
SPWAEN003 Secret Six Samurai - Hatsume SCR 1.25 2.00
SPWAEN004 Secret Six Samurai - Doji SCR 1.25 2.00
SPWAEN005 Secret Six Samurai - Kizaru SCR 1.25 2.00
SPWAEN006 Secret Six Samurai - Rihan SCR 1.25 2.00
SPWAEN007 Secret Skills of the Six Samurai SCR 1.25 2.00
SPWAEN008 The Six Shinobi SR .40 .60
SPWAEN009 Grandmaster of the Six Samurai SR .40 .60
SPWAEN010 Legendary Six Samurai - Kizan SR .40 .60
SPWAEN011 Legendary Six Samurai - Shi En SCR 1.25 2.00
SPWAEN012 Shadow of the Six Samurai - Shien SR .40 .60

SPWAEN013 Six Samurai United SR	.40	.60
SPWAEN014 Gateway of the Six SR	.40	.60
SPWAEN015 Shien's Smoke Signal SR	.40	.60
SPWAEN016 Magical Musketeer Caspar SCR	25.00	35.00
SPWAEN017 Magical Musketeer Doc SR	.40	.60
SPWAEN018 Magical Musketeer Kidbrave SR	.40	.60
SPWAEN019 Magical Musketeer Starfire SCR	15.00	20.00
SPWAEN020 Magical Musketeer Calamity SR	.40	.60
SPWAEN021 Magical Musketeer Wild SR	.40	.60
SPWAEN022 Magical Musket Mastermind Zakiel SCR	1.25	2.00
SPWAEN023 Magical Musket - Steady Hands SR	.40	.60
SPWAEN024 Magical Musket - Cross-Domination SCR	1.25	2.00
SPWAEN025 Magical Musket - Desperado SR	.40	.60
SPWAEN026 Magical Musket - Dancing Needle SCR	1.25	2.00
SPWAEN027 Magical Musket - Fiendish Deal SR	.40	.60
SPWAEN028 Magical Musket - Last Stand SCR	1.25	2.00
SPWAEN029 The Weather Painter Snow SCR	10.00	15.00
SPWAEN030 The Weather Painter Rain SR	.40	.60
SPWAEN031 The Weather Painter Cloud SCR	1.25	2.00
SPWAEN032 The Weather Painter Sun SCR	1.25	2.00
SPWAEN033 The Weather Painter Thunder SCR	1.25	2.00
SPWAEN034 The Weather Painter Aurora SCR	1.25	2.00
SPWAEN035 The Weather Painter Rainbow SCR	1.25	2.00
SPWAEN036 The Weather Snowy Canvas SR	.40	.60
SPWAEN037 The Weather Rainy Canvas SR	.40	.60
SPWAEN038 The Weather Cloudy Canvas SR	.40	.60
SPWAEN039 The Weather Sunny Canvas SR	.40	.60
SPWAEN040 The Weather Thundery Canvas SCR	1.25	2.00
SPWAEN041 The Weather Auroral Canvas SR	.40	.60
SPWAEN042 Hand of the Six Samurai SR	.40	.60
SPWAEN043 Legendary Six Samurai - Kageki SR	.40	.60
SPWAEN044 Legendary Six Samurai - Shinai SR	.40	.60
SPWAEN045 Legendary Six Samurai - Mizuho SR	.40	.60
SPWAEN046 Shien's Advisor SR	.40	.60
SPWAEN047 Honest SR	.40	.60
SPWAEN048 Asceticism of the Six Samurai SR	.40	.60
SPWAEN049 Shien's Dojo SR	.40	.60
SPWAEN050 Photon Veil SR	.40	.60
SPWAEN051 Constellar Belt SR	.40	.60
SPWAEN052 Return of the Six Samurai SR	.40	.60
SPWAEN053 Backs to the Wall SR	.40	.60
SPWAEN054 Double-Edged Sword Technique SR	.40	.60
SPWAEN055 Musakani Magatama SR	.40	.60
SPWAEN056 Battleguard Howling SR	.40	.60
SPWAEN057 Beckoning Light SR	.40	.60
SPWAEN058 Scrap-Iron Scarecrow SR	.40	.60
SPWAEN059 Scrap-Iron Statue SR	.40	.60
SPWAEN060 Miraculous Descent SR	.40	.60

2018 Yu-Gi-Oh Extreme Force 1st Edition

COMPLETE SET (100)	200.00	300.00
BOOSTER BOX	60.00	70.00
BOOSTER PACK	3.00	5.00
RELEASED ON FEBRUARY 2, 2018		
EXFOEN000 Yoko-Zuna Sumo Spirit C	.10	.20
EXFOEN001 Zombino C	.10	.20
EXFOEN002 Lockout Gardna C	.10	.20
EXFOEN003 Striping Partner C	.10	.20
EXFOEN004 Flick Clown C	.10	.20
EXFOEN005 Bitrooper C	.10	.20
EXFOEN006 Beltlink Wall Dragon C	.10	.20
EXFOEN007 Shelrokket Dragon R	.30	.50
EXFOEN008 Metalrokket Dragon R	.30	.50
EXFOEN009 Tindangle Angel C	.10	.20
EXFOEN010 Tindangle Base Gardna C	.10	.20
EXFOEN011 Tindangle Hound C	.10	.20
EXFOEN012 Tindangle Protector C	.10	.20
EXFOEN013 Tindangle Intruder C	.10	.20
EXFOEN014 Mekk-Knight Blue Sky SCR	10.00	15.00
EXFOEN015 Mekk-Knight Green Horizon C	.10	.20
EXFOEN016 Mekk-Knight Orange Sunset C	.10	.20
EXFOEN017 Mekk-Knight Yellow Star R	.30	.50
EXFOEN018 Mekk-Knight Red Moon R	.30	.50
EXFOEN019 Mekk-Knight Indigo Eclipse SR	.60	1.00
EXFOEN020 Mekk-Knight Purple Nightfall SCR	10.00	15.00
EXFOEN021 World Legacy - World Shield C	.10	.20
EXFOEN022 Mythical Beast Jackal R	.30	.50
EXFOEN023 Mythical Beast Garuda UR	1.50	2.50
EXFOEN024 Mythical Beast Medusa SR	.60	1.00
EXFOEN025 Mythical Beast Basilisk R	.30	.50
EXFOEN026 Mythical Beast Jackal King UR	1.50	2.50
EXFOEN027 Mythical Beast Master Cerberus SCR	7.00	10.00
EXFOEN028 Artifact Mjollnir C	.10	.20
EXFOEN029 Grappler Angler C	.10	.20
EXFOEN030 Mahjong Munia Maidens C	.10	.20
EXFOEN031 D.D. Seeker C	.10	.20
EXFOEN032 Ghost Bird of Bewitchment R	.30	.50
EXFOEN033 Desmanian Devil R	.30	.50
EXFOEN034 Wattkinetic Puppeteer C	.10	.20
EXFOEN035 Inspector Boarder SCR	10.00	15.00
EXFOEN036 Overtyx Qoatlus SR	.60	1.00
EXFOEN037 Contact C C	.10	.20
EXFOEN038 Excode Talker UR	3.00	5.00
EXFOEN039 Underclock Taker C	.10	.20
EXFOEN040 Vector Scare Archfiend R	.30	.50
EXFOEN041 Flame Administrator C	.10	.20
EXFOEN042 Recovery Sorcerer C	.10	.20
EXFOEN043 Secure Gardna C	.10	.20
EXFOEN044 Three Burst Dragon UR	1.50	2.50
EXFOEN045 Tindangle Acute Cerberus C	.10	.20
EXFOEN046 Altergeist Hexstia SR	.60	1.00
EXFOEN047 Mekk-Knight Spectrum Supreme UR	2.50	4.00
EXFOEN048 Saryuja Skull Dread SCR	45.00	50.00
EXFOEN049 Clara & Rushka, the Ventriloduo UR	3.00	4.00
EXFOEN050 Duelittle Chimera R	.30	.50
EXFOEN051 Link Hole C	.10	.20
EXFOEN052 Fire Prison C	.10	.20
EXFOEN053 Boot Sector Launch UR	1.50	2.50
EXFOEN054 Nagel's Protection C	.10	.20
EXFOEN055 Euler's Circuit C	.10	.20
EXFOEN056 World Legacy Scars R	.30	.50
EXFOEN057 World Legacy Key R	.30	.50
EXFOEN058 Mythical Bestiary UR	1.50	2.50
EXFOEN059 Glory of the Noble Knights R	.30	.50
EXFOEN060 Power of the Guardians SR	.60	1.00
EXFOEN061 Pendulum Paradox SCR	4.00	6.00
EXFOEN062 Hey, Trunade! SCR	15.00	20.00
EXFOEN063 Downbeat SR	.60	1.00
EXFOEN064 Column Switch C	.10	.20
EXFOEN065 Trading Places C	.10	.20
EXFOEN066 Parallel Port Armor C	.10	.20
EXFOEN067 Cynet Refresh C	.10	.20
EXFOEN068 Borrel Cooling C	.10	.20
EXFOEN069 Tindangle Delaunay C	.10	.20
EXFOEN070 Altergeist Manifestation SR	.60	1.00
EXFOEN071 World Legacy Whispers R	.30	.50
EXFOEN072 World Legacy's Secret UR	1.50	2.50
EXFOEN073 Mythical Bestiamorph R	.30	.50
EXFOEN074 Ghostrick Renovation C	.10	.20
EXFOEN075 Call of the Archfiend C	.10	.20
EXFOEN076 There Can Only Be One SR	.60	1.00
EXFOEN077 Dai Dance C	.10	.20
EXFOEN078 Showdown of the Secret Sense Scroll Techniques C	.10	.20
EXFOEN079 Parthian Shot C	.10	.20
EXFOEN080 Oops! C	.10	.20
EXFOEN081 Kuro-Obi Karate Spirit C	.10	.20
EXFOEN082 Vendread Battlelord SR	.60	1.00
EXFOEN083 Vendread Core SR	.60	1.00
EXFOEN084 Vendread Charge R	.30	.50
EXFOEN085 Vendread Revolution SR	.60	1.00
EXFOEN086 F.A. Auto Navigator C	.10	.20
EXFOEN087 F.A. Motorhome Transport C	.10	.20
EXFOEN088 F.A. City Grand Prix C	.10	.20
EXFOEN089 F.A. Test Run C	.10	.20
EXFOEN090 Masterking Archfiend R	.30	.50
EXFOEN091 Curious, the Lightsworn Dominion SR	2.00	2.50
EXFOEN092 Gem-Knight Phantom Quartz SR	.60	1.00
EXFOEN093 Steelswarm Origin R	.30	.50
EXFOEN094 Isolde, Two Tales of the Noble Knights UR	8.00	10.00
EXFOEN095 Qliphort Genius R	.30	.50
EXFOEN096 Ritual Beast Ulti-Kimunfalcos R	.30	.50
EXFOEN097 Zefra Metaltron SR	.60	1.00
EXFOEN098 Heavymetalfoes Electrumite SCR	70.00	80.00
EXFOEN099 Scramble Egg C	.10	.20

2018 Yu-Gi-Oh Flames of Destruction 1st Edition

COMPLETE SET (100)	250.00	350.00
BOOSTER BOX	65.00	80.00
BOOSTER PACK	3.00	5.00
RELEASED ON MAY 4, 2018		
FLODEN000 Kai-Den Kendo Spirit C	.05	.10
FLODEN001 Protron C	.05	.10
FLODEN002 Prompthorn C	.05	.10
FLODEN003 Backup Operator R	.25	.40
FLODEN004 Link Streamer C	.05	.10
FLODEN005 Degrade Buster SR	.60	1.00
FLODEN006 Trickstar Nightshade C	.05	.10
FLODEN007 Trickstar Mandrake C	.05	.10
FLODEN008 Trickstar Rhodode SR	.60	1.00
FLODEN009 Gouki Octostretch C	.05	.10
FLODEN010 Gouki Bearhug C	.05	.10
FLODEN011 Defrag Dragon C	.05	.10
FLODEN012 Background Dragon C	.05	.10
FLODEN013 Tindangle Trinity C	.05	.10
FLODEN014 Altergeist Multifaker UR	13.00	15.00
FLODEN015 Altergeist Pixiel C	.05	.10
FLODEN016 Mekk-Knight Avram C	.05	.10
FLODEN017 Knightmare Corruptor Iblee SCR	40.00	45.00
FLODEN018 World Legacy - World Lance R	.25	.40
FLODEN019 Elementsaber Aina C	.05	.10
FLODEN020 Elementsaber Makani UR	2.00	3.50
FLODEN021 Elementsaber Nalu SR	.60	1.00
FLODEN022 Elementsaber Malo C	.05	.10
FLODEN023 Elementsaber Lapauila SR	.60	1.00
FLODEN024 Elementsaber Molehu UR	2.00	3.50
FLODEN025 Elementsaber Lapauila Mana SR	.60	1.00
FLODEN026 Forceaurage the Elemental Lord SR	.60	1.00
FLODEN027 Solar Batteryman C	.05	.10
FLODEN028 Watch Cat C	.05	.10
FLODEN029 Trancefamiliar C	.05	.10
FLODEN030 Three Trolling Trolls C	.05	.10
FLODEN031 Yajiro Invader C	.05	.10
FLODEN032 Iron Dragon Tiamaton UR	2.00	3.50
FLODEN033 Ghost Belle & Haunted Mansion SCR	35.00	40.00
FLODEN034 Red Hared Hasty Horse SP	.25	.35
FLODEN035 Boycotton SP	.25	.35
FLODEN036 Topologic Trisbaena SCR	8.00	12.00
FLODEN037 Space Insulator C	.05	.10
FLODEN038 Trickstar Bella Madonna UR	2.00	3.50
FLODEN039 Trickstar Bloom C	.05	.10
FLODEN040 Trickstar Delfiendium R	.25	.40
FLODEN041 Gouki The Master Ogre SR	.60	1.00
FLODEN042 Altergeist Kidolga C	.05	.10
FLODEN043 Knightmare Mermaid R	.25	.40
FLODEN044 Knightmare Goblin UR	8.00	10.00
FLODEN045 Knightmare Cerberus SR	.60	1.00
FLODEN046 Knightmare Phoenix SR	.60	1.00
FLODEN047 Knightmare Unicorn SCR	25.00	30.00
FLODEN048 Knightmare Gryphon SCR	25.00	30.00
FLODEN049 Wind-Up Maintenance Zenmaicon SR	.60	1.00
FLODEN050 Vampire Sucker SCR	6.00	8.00
FLODEN051 Fire Fighting Daruma Doll R	.25	.40
FLODEN052 Greatfly R	.25	.40
FLODEN053 Cybersal Cyclone C	.05	.10
FLODEN054 Trickstar Light Arena R	.25	.40
FLODEN055 Trickstar Bouquet R	.25	.40
FLODEN056 Gouki Face Turn R	.25	.40
FLODEN057 World Legacy's Corruption C	.05	.10
FLODEN058 World Legacy Succession UR	2.00	3.50
FLODEN059 World Legacy's Nightmare C	.05	.10
FLODEN060 Palace of the Elemental Lords UR	2.00	3.50
FLODEN061 Restoration of the Monarchs C	.05	.10
FLODEN062 Sekka's Light R	.25	.40
FLODEN063 Link Bound SR	.60	1.00
FLODEN064 Staring Contest C	.05	.10
FLODEN065 Called by the Grave C	.40	.60
FLODEN066 Monster Reborn Reborn C	.05	.10
FLODEN067 Limit Code C	.05	.10
FLODEN068 Red Reboot SR	.60	1.00
FLODEN069 Gergonne's End C	.05	.10
FLODEN070 Altergeist Emulatelf C	.05	.10
FLODEN071 World Legacy Awakens R	.25	.40
FLODEN072 World Legacy Struggle R	.25	.40
FLODEN073 World Legacy's Sorrow SR	.60	1.00
FLODEN074 Elemental Training UR	2.00	3.50
FLODEN075 The Sanctified Darklord R	.25	.40
FLODEN076 Network Trap Hole UR	2.00	3.50
FLODEN077 Infinite Impermanence SCR	70.00	75.00
FLODEN078 Heartless Drop Off R	.25	.40
FLODEN079 Mamemaki SP	.25	.35
FLODEN080 Waking the Dragon SP	1.50	2.00
FLODEN081 Super Team Buddy Force Unite! SCR	2.00	3.50
FLODEN082 Revendread Executor R	.25	.40
FLODEN083 Vendread Anima R	.25	.40
FLODEN084 Revendread Evolution C	.05	.10
FLODEN085 Vendread Nightmare C	.05	.10
FLODEN086 Vendread Daybreak C	.05	.10
FLODEN087 F.A. Dark Dragster R	.25	.40
FLODEN088 F.A. Dawn Dragster R	.25	.40
FLODEN089 F.A. Winners R	.25	.40
FLODEN090 F.A. Dead Heat C	.05	.10
FLODEN091 F.A. Overheat R	.25	.40
FLODEN092 Crystal Master C	.05	.10
FLODEN093 Crystal Keeper C	.05	.10
FLODEN094 Flower Cardian Moonflowerviewing C	.05	.10
FLODEN095 Shaddoll Construct C	.05	.10
FLODEN096 Inzektor Picofalena C	.05	.10
FLODEN097 Madolche Fresh Sistart C	.05	.10
FLODEN098 Rainbow Refraction SR	.60	1.00
FLODEN099 Crystal Conclave C	.05	.10

2018 Yu-Gi-Oh Dark Saviors 1st Edition

COMPLETE SET (60)	150.00	200.00
BOOSTER BOX (24 PACKS)		
BOOSTER PACK (5 CARDS)		
RELEASED ON MAY 25, 2018		
DASAEN001 Vampire Familiar SR	.20	.35
DASAEN002 Vampire Retainer SR	.20	.35
DASAEN003 Vampire FrÄoulein SCR	.40	.60
DASAEN004 Vampire Grimson SR	.20	.35
DASAEN005 Vampire Scarlet Scourge SCR	.40	.60
DASAEN006 Vampire Red Baron SR	.10	.20
DASAEN007 Dhampir Vampire Sheridan SCR	2.00	3.00
DASAEN008 Vampire Desire SCR	.40	.60
DASAEN009 Vampire's Domain SCR	.40	.60
DASAEN010 Vampire Awakening SR	.20	.35
DASAEN011 Vampire Domination SCR	.40	.60
DASAEN012 Shadow Vampire SR	.20	.35
DASAEN013 Crimson Knight Vampire Bram SR	.15	.25
DASAEN014 Donpa, Marksman Fur Hire SR	.10	.20
DASAEN015 Recon, Scout Fur Hire SR	.10	.20
DASAEN016 Helmer, Helmsman Fur Hire SR	.20	.35
DASAEN017 Beat, Bladesman Fur Hire SCR	5.00	8.00
DASAEN018 Seal, Strategist Fur Hire SR	.10	.20
DASAEN019 Bravo, Fighter Fur Hire SR	.15	.25
DASAEN020 Sagitta, Maverick Fur Hire SCR	.15	.20
DASAEN021 Dyna, Hero Fur Hire SCR	.40	.60
DASAEN022 Wiz, Sage Fur Hire SCR	.40	.60
DASAEN023 Rafale, Champion Fur Hire SCR	.40	.60
DASAEN024 Fandora, the Flying Furtress SR	.10	.20
DASAEN025 Mayhem Fur Hire SCR	.60	1.00
DASAEN026 Training Fur Hire, Fur All Your Training Needs SCR	.15	.25
DASAEN027 Sky Striker Ace - Kagari SR	1.00	1.50
DASAEN028 Sky Striker Ace - Shizuku SR	.60	1.00
DASAEN029 Sky Striker Ace - Raye SR	1.00	1.50
DASAEN030 Sky Striker Mobilize - Engage! SCR	80.00	100.00
DASAEN031 Sky Striker Maneuver - Afterburners! SCR	8.00	12.00
DASAEN032 Sky Striker Maneuver - Jamming Waves! SCR	1.50	2.50
DASAEN033 Sky Striker Mecha - Hornet Drones SR	.60	1.00
DASAEN034 Sky Striker Mecha - Widow Anchor SCR	30.00	35.00
DASAEN035 Sky Striker Mecha - Eagle Booster SR	.40	.60
DASAEN036 Sky Striker Mecha - Shark Cannon SCR	1.50	2.50
DASAEN037 Sky Striker Mecharmory - Hercules Base SR	.60	1.00
DASAEN038 Sky Striker Mecha Modules - Multirole SCR	7.00	10.00
DASAEN039 Sky Striker Airspace - Area Zero SR	.40	.60
DASAEN040 Armageddon Knight SR	.15	.25
DASAEN041 Plaguespreader Zombie SR	.10	.20
DASAEN042 Dark Grepher SR	.15	.25
DASAEN043 Toon Table of Contents SR	.60	1.00
DASAEN044 The Monarchs Stormforth SR	.10	.20
DASAEN045 Drowning Mirror Force SR	.10	.20
DASAEN046 Mystic Tomato SR	.10	.20
DASAEN047 Vampiric Orchis SR	.10	.20
DASAEN048 Vampiric Koala SR	.10	.20
DASAEN049 Vampire Sorcerer SR	.20	.35
DASAEN050 Vampire Vamp SR	.10	.20
DASAEN051 Kuribandit SR	.10	.20
DASAEN052 Scapegoat SR	.60	1.00
DASAEN053 Reinforcement of the Army SR	.10	.20
DASAEN054 Allure of Darkness SR	1.50	2.00
DASAEN055 Magical Citadel of Endymion SCR	.60	1.00
DASAEN056 Spell Power Grasp SR	.10	.20
DASAEN057 Quick Booster SR	.10	.20
DASAEN058 Foolish Burial Goods SR	.60	1.00
DASAEN059 Mirror Force SR	.40	.60
DASAEN060 Horn of the Phantom Beast SR	.10	.20

2018 Yu-Gi-Oh Battles of Legend Relentless Revenge 1st Edition

COMPLETE SET (105)	200.00	300.00
RELEASED ON JUNE 29, 2018		
BLRR-EN001 Orgoth the Relentless SCR	2.50	4.00
BLRREN002 Summon Dice UR	.60	1.00
BLRREN003 Flying Elephant SCR	2.50	4.00
BLRREN004 Prinzessin SCR	2.50	4.00
BLRREN005 Pumpkin Carriage UR	.60	1.00
BLRREN006 Iron Hans UR	.60	1.00
BLRREN007 Iron Knight UR	.60	1.00
BLRREN008 Glife the Phantom Bird SCR	2.50	4.00
BLRREN009 Hexe Trude SCR	2.50	4.00
BLRREN010 Golden Castle of Stromberg SCR	30.00	35.00
BLRREN011 Glass Slippers SCR	2.50	4.00
BLRREN012 Iron Cage UR	.60	1.00
BLRREN013 Litmus Doom Swordsman UR	.60	1.00
BLRREN014 Litmus Doom Ritual UR	.60	1.00

BLRREN015 Living Fossil SCR	2.50	4.00
BLRREN016 Cyber Emergency SCR	5.00	7.00
BLRREN017 Born from Draconis UR	.60	1.00
BLRREN018 Cyber Eltanin UR	.60	1.00
BLRREN019 Cyber Larva UR	.60	1.00
BLRREN020 Slash Draw UR	.60	1.00
BLRREN021 Michion, the Timelord UR	.60	1.00
BLRREN022 Hailon, the Timelord UR	.60	1.00
BLRREN023 Raphion, the Timelord UR	.60	1.00
BLRREN024 Gabrion, the Timelord UR	.60	1.00
BLRREN025 Sandaion, the Timelord UR	.60	1.00
BLRREN026 Metaion, the Timelord UR	.60	1.00
BLRREN027 Empty Machine SCR	2.50	4.00
BLRREN028 Infinite Machine SCR	2.50	4.00
BLRREN029 Infinite Light SCR	2.50	4.00
BLRREN030 Number 27: Dreadnought Dreadnoid SCR	8.00	11.00
BLRREN031 Number 67: Pair-a-Dice Smasher SCR	2.50	4.00
BLRREN032 Number 75: Bamboozling Gossip Shadow SCR	10.00	15.00
BLRREN033 Number 90: Galaxy-Eyes Photon Lord SCR	4.00	6.00
BLRREN034 Iron Draw SCR	2.50	4.00
BLRREN035 Glorious Numbers SCR	2.50	4.00
BLRREN036 Hayate the Earth Star UR	.60	1.00
BLRREN037 Tenma the Sky Star UR	.60	1.00
BLRREN038 Kaiki the Unity Star UR	.60	1.00
BLRREN039 Idaten the Conqueror Star UR	.60	1.00
BLRREN040 Shura the Combat Star UR	.60	1.00
BLRREN041 Hibernation Dragon SCR	2.50	4.00
BLRREN042 Triggering Wurm SCR	2.50	4.00
BLRREN043 Topologic Gumblar Dragon SCR	10.00	15.00
BLRREN044 Borrelguard Dragon SCR	7.00	9.00
BLRREN045 Flash Charge Dragon SCR	2.50	4.00
BLRREN046 Monster Reborn SCR	2.50	4.00
BLRREN047 Torrential Tribute UR	.60	1.00
BLRREN048 Cyber Dragon UR	.60	1.00
BLRREN049 Neo-Spacian Aqua Dolphin UR	.60	1.00
BLRREN050 Neo-Spacian Air Hummingbird UR	.60	1.00
BLRREN051 Neo-Spacian Grand Mole UR	.60	1.00
BLRREN052 Neo-Spacian Dark Panther UR	.60	1.00
BLRREN053 Card Trooper SCR	2.50	4.00
BLRREN054 Rainbow Dark Dragon UR	.60	1.00
BLRREN055 Convert Contact UR	.60	1.00
BLRREN056 Sephylon, the Ultimate Timelord UR	.60	1.00
BLRREN057 T.G. Wonder Magician UR	.60	1.00
BLRREN058 Norito the Moral Leader UR	.60	1.00
BLRREN059 Performage Damage Juggler UR	.60	1.00
BLRREN060 Performage Trick Clown UR	.60	1.00
BLRREN061 The Phantom Knights of Ancient Cloak SCR	2.50	4.00
BLRREN062 The Phantom Knights of Silent Boots SCR	2.50	4.00
BLRREN063 Supreme King Dragon Darkwurm SCR	2.50	4.00
BLRREN064 Brilliant Fusion SCR	2.50	4.00
BLRREN065 Phantom Knights' Fog Blade SCR	2.50	4.00
BLRREN066 Altergeist Hexstia UR	.60	1.00
BLRREN067 Altergeist Manifestation UR	.60	1.00
BLRREN068 PSY-Frame Driver UR	.60	1.00
BLRREN069 Pyrorex the Elemental Lord UR	.60	1.00
BLRREN070 Windrose the Elemental Lord UR	.60	1.00
BLRREN071 Noble Knight Medraut UR	.60	1.00
BLRREN072 Noble Knight Brothers UR	.60	1.00
BLRREN073 Merlin SCR	2.50	4.00
BLRREN074 Uni-Zombie UR	.60	1.00
BLRREN075 Gameciel, the Sea Turtle Kaiju SCR	5.00	7.00
BLRREN076 Darklord Ixchel SCR	2.50	4.00
BLRREN077 Darklord Nasten UR	.60	1.00
BLRREN078 Eater of Millions UR	.60	1.00
BLRREN079 Elemental HERO Honest Neos SCR	2.50	4.00
BLRREN080 Trickstar Narkissus UR	.60	1.00
BLRREN081 Fullmetalfoes Alkahest UR	.60	1.00
BLRREN082 Metalfoes Mithrilium SCR	2.50	4.00
BLRREN083 Crystron Quandax SCR	2.50	4.00
BLRREN084 Tornado Dragon SCR	2.50	4.00
BLRREN085 Number 41: Bagooska the Terribly Tired Tapir UR	.60	1.00
BLRREN086 Imduk the World Chalice Dragon UR	.60	1.00
BLRREN087 Gaia Saber, the Lightning Shadow UR	.60	1.00
BLRREN088 Preparation of Rites UR	.60	1.00
BLRREN089 Kyoutou Waterfront UR	.60	1.00
BLRREN090 Pre-Preparation of Rites UR	.60	1.00
BLRREN091 The Kaiju Files UR	.60	1.00
BLRREN092 Union Hangar SCR	2.50	4.00
BLRREN093 Banishment of the Darklords UR	.60	1.00
BLRREN094 Darklord Contact UR	.60	1.00
BLRREN095 Foolish Burial Goods UR	.60	1.00
BLRREN096 Dragonic Diagram SCR	5.00	7.00
BLRREN097 Duelist Alliance UR	.60	1.00
BLRREN098 World Legacy Discovery UR	.60	1.00
BLRREN099 World Legacy's Heart UR	.60	1.00
BLRREN100 Solemn Judgment UR	.60	1.00
BLRREN101 Bottomless Trap Hole UR	.60	1.00
BLRREN102 Solemn Strike UR	2.50	4.00
BLRREN103 Darklord Enchantment UR	.60	1.00
BLRREN104 Unending Nightmare UR	.60	1.00
BLRREN105 Trickstar Reincarnation SCR	6.00	8.00

2018 Yu-Gi-Oh Cybernetic Horizon 1st Edition

COMPLETE SET (100)	300.00	450.00
BOOSTER BOX (24 PACKS)	65.00	80.00
BOOSTER PACK (9 CARDS)	3.00	5.00
RELEASED ON JULY 27, 2018		
CYHOEN000 Contact Gate C	.15	.25
CYHOEN001 SIMM Tablir R	.20	.35
CYHOEN002 Cluster Congester C	.15	.25
CYHOEN003 Gouki Moonsault C	.15	.25
CYHOEN004 Gouki Tagpartner C	.15	.25
CYHOEN005 Gouki Ringtrainer C	.15	.25
CYHOEN006 Crusadia Reclusia C	.15	.25
CYHOEN007 Crusadia Arboria C	.15	.25
CYHOEN008 Crusadia Leonis C	.15	.25
CYHOEN009 Crusadia Draco C	.15	.25
CYHOEN010 Crusadia Maximus SR	.60	1.00
CYHOEN011 World Legacy - World Crown R	.20	.35
CYHOEN012 Impcantation Candoll R	.20	.35
CYHOEN013 Impcantation Talismandra R	.20	.35
CYHOEN014 Cyber Dragon Vier C	.15	.25
CYHOEN015 Cyber Dragon Herz UR	7.00	10.00
CYHOEN016 Dragunity Senatus SR	.60	1.00
CYHOEN017 Dragunity Couse C	.15	.25
CYHOEN018 Metaphys Decoy Dragon C	.15	.25
CYHOEN019 Umbramirage the Elemental Lord SR	.60	1.00
CYHOEN020 Cosmo Brain C	.15	.25
CYHOEN021 Mana Dragon Zirnitron SR	.60	1.00
CYHOEN022 Terrifying Toddler of Torment C	.15	.25
CYHOEN023 Psychic Ace C	.15	.25
CYHOEN024 Cupid Volley C	.15	.25
CYHOEN025 Centerfrog C	.15	.25
CYHOEN026 Cyberse Magician UR	1.00	1.50
CYHOEN027 Ruin, Angel of Oblivion C	.15	.25
CYHOEN028 Demise, Agent of Armageddon C	.15	.25
CYHOEN029 Ruin, Supreme Queen of Oblivion R	.20	.35
CYHOEN030 Demise, Supreme King of Armageddon R	.20	.35
CYHOEN031 Paladin of Storm Dragon R	.20	.35
CYHOEN032 Dragunity Knight - Luin R	.20	.35
CYHOEN033 Dragunity Knight - Ascalon UR	.50	.80
CYHOEN034 Borrelsword Dragon SCR	50.00	60.00
CYHOEN035 Cyberse Witch R	.20	.35
CYHOEN036 Link Devotee C	.15	.25
CYHOEN037 Restoration Point Guard C	.15	.25
CYHOEN038 Gouki Heel Ogre C	.15	.25
CYHOEN039 Gouki The Giant Ogre R	.20	.35
CYHOEN040 Miniborrel Dragon C	.15	.25
CYHOEN041 Vorticular Drumgon SR	.60	1.00
CYHOEN042 Crusadia Magius SR	.60	1.00
CYHOEN043 Crusadia Regulex C	.15	.25
CYHOEN044 Crusadia Equimax UR	7.00	10.00
CYHOEN045 Mekk-Knight of the Morning Star SCR	5.00	7.00
CYHOEN046 Cyber Dragon Zieger UR	7.00	10.00
CYHOEN047 Sky Striker Ace - Hayate SR	.60	1.00
CYHOEN048 Reprodocus R	.20	.35
CYHOEN049 Wee Witch's Apprentice SR	.60	1.00
CYHOEN050 Hip Hoshiningen SR	.60	1.00
CYHOEN051 Cynet Ritual R	.20	.35
CYHOEN052 Zero Extra Link C	.15	.25
CYHOEN053 Borrel Regenerator C	.15	.25
CYHOEN054 Crusadia Revival SR	.60	1.00
CYHOEN055 Crusadia Power C	.15	.25
CYHOEN056 Cycle of the World C	.15	.25
CYHOEN057 Breaking of the World C	.15	.25
CYHOEN058 Turning of the World C	.15	.25
CYHOEN059 Cyber Revsystem SCR	15.00	20.00
CYHOEN060 World Legacy Survivor SR	.60	1.00
CYHOEN061 World Legacy's Memory C	.15	.25
CYHOEN062 Mythical Institution C	.15	.25
CYHOEN063 Beast Magic Attack C	.15	.25
CYHOEN064 Celestial Observatory SCR	3.00	5.00
CYHOEN065 Solitary Sword of Poison C	.15	.25
CYHOEN066 Cross Breed R	.20	.35
CYHOEN067 Ledger of Legerdemain SCR	3.00	5.00
CYHOEN068 Shield Handler C	.15	.25
CYHOEN069 Mirror Force Launcher SR	.60	1.00
CYHOEN070 Link Turret C	.15	.25
CYHOEN071 Crusadia Vanguard C	.15	.25
CYHOEN072 Renewal of the World R	.20	.35
CYHOEN073 Cybernetic Overflow C	.15	.25
CYHOEN074 Dragunity Legion C	.15	.25
CYHOEN075 World Legacy's Mind Meld C	.15	.25
CYHOEN076 Metaphys Ascension C	.15	.25
CYHOEN077 Ballista Squad C	.15	.25
CYHOEN078 The Deep Grave R	.20	.35
CYHOEN079 Universal Adapter C	.15	.25
CYHOEN080 Dealer's Choice SP	.15	.25
CYHOEN081 Pinpoint Landing SCR	6.00	8.00
CYHOEN082 Danger! Bigfoot! SCR	30.00	35.00
CYHOEN083 Danger! Nessie! SCR	35.00	40.00
CYHOEN084 Danger! Chupacabra! UR	6.00	8.00
CYHOEN085 Danger!? Jackalope? UR	8.00	10.00
CYHOEN086 Realm of Danger! UR	.30	.50
CYHOEN087 Danger! Zone UR	1.00	1.50
CYHOEN088 Noble Knight Custennin SR	.60	1.00
CYHOEN089 Sacred Noble Knight of King Custennin UR	1.00	1.50
CYHOEN090 Noble Knight Pellinore SR	.60	1.00
CYHOEN091 Noble Arms - Clarent SR	.60	1.00
CYHOEN092 Divine Serpent Geh C	.15	.25
CYHOEN093 Performapal Handsamuraiger C	.15	.25
CYHOEN094 Performapal Lebellman C	.15	.25
CYHOEN095 Performapal Gold Fang R	.20	.35
CYHOEN096 White Stingray R	.20	.35
CYHOEN097 Interrupt Resistor R	.20	.35
CYHOEN098 Link Disciple R	.20	.35
CYHOEN099 Gladiator Beast Dragacius R	.20	.35

2018 Yu-Gi-Oh Shadows in Valhalla 1st Edition

COMPLETE SET (60)	100.00	150.00
BOOSTER BOX (24 PACKS)	65.00	80.00
BOOSTER PACK (5 CARDS)	3.00	5.00
RELEASED ON AUGUST 17, 2018		
SHVA-EN001 Valkyrie Dritte SR	.10	.20
SHVA-EN002 Valkyrie Zweite SR	.10	.20
SHVA-EN003 Valkyrie Erste SR	.10	.20
SHVA-EN004 Valkyrie Brunhilde SCR	6.00	8.00
SHVA-EN005 Fortune Chariot SR	.10	.20
SHVA-EN006 Ride of the Valkyries SCR	8.00	12.00
SHVA-EN007 Mischief of the Time Goddess SCR	10.00	15.00
SHVA-EN008 Goddess Skuld's Oracle SR	.10	.20
SHVA-EN009 Goddess Verdande's Guidance SR	.10	.20
SHVA-EN010 Goddess Urd's Verdict SR	.10	.20
SHVA-EN011 Ninja Grandmaster Saizo SCR	2.50	3.50
SHVA-EN012 Yellow Ninja SR	.10	.20
SHVA-EN013 Yellow Dragon Ninja SCR	2.00	2.50
SHVA-EN014 Hidden Village of Ninjitsu Arts SCR	1.50	2.00
SHVA-EN015 Ninjitsu Art of Mirage-Transformation SCR	1.00	1.50
SHVA-EN016 Old Entity Chthugua SCR	1.00	1.50
SHVA-EN017 Outer Entity Nyarla SCR	2.00	3.00
SHVA-EN018 Outer Entity Azzathoth SCR	2.00	3.00
SHVA-EN019 Forbidden Trapezohedron SCR	1.00	1.50
SHVA-EN020 Aleister the Meltdown Invoker SCR	25.00	30.00
SHVA-EN021 Strike Ninja SR	.10	.20
SHVA-EN022 Ninja Grandmaster Hanzo SR	.10	.20
SHVA-EN023 Upstart Golden Ninja SR	.10	.20
SHVA-EN024 White Dragon Ninja SR	.10	.20
SHVA-EN025 Red Dragon Ninja SR	.10	.20
SHVA-EN026 Twilight Ninja Jogen SR	.10	.20
SHVA-EN027 Armor Ninjitsu Art of Alchemy SR	.10	.20
SHVA-EN028 Ninjitsu Art of Transformation SR	.10	.20
SHVA-EN029 Ninjitsu Art of Super-Transformation SR	.10	.20
SHVA-EN030 Armor Ninjitsu Art of Rust Mist SR	.10	.20
SHVA-EN031 Elemental HERO Neos SR	.10	.20
SHVA-EN032 Neo-Spacian Glow Moss SR	.10	.20
SHVA-EN033 Neo-Spacian Flare Scarab SR	.10	.20
SHVA-EN034 Elemental HERO Magma Neos SR	.10	.20
SHVA-EN035 Elemental HERO Chaos Neos SR	.10	.20
SHVA-EN036 Vision HERO Trinity SR	.10	.20
SHVA-EN037 Mermail Abyssmegalo SR	1.00	1.50
SHVA-EN038 Mermail Abyssleed SR	.30	.50
SHVA-EN039 Mermail Abyssteus SR	.10	.20
SHVA-EN040 Aleister the Invoker SCR	2.00	3.00
SHVA-EN041 Invoked Mechaba SR	2.50	3.50
SHVA-EN042 Magical Meltdown SR	.10	.20
SHVA-EN043 Invocation SR	2.50	3.50
SHVA-EN044 Omega Summon SR	.10	.20
SHVA-EN045 Mist Valley Apex Avian SR	.10	.20
SHVA-EN046 Windwitch - Ice Bell SCR	2.50	3.00
SHVA-EN047 Ash Blossom & Joyous Spring SR	15.00	20.00
SHVA-EN048 Gem-Knight Seraphinite SCR	2.00	3.00
SHVA-EN049 El Shaddoll Winda SCR	1.00	1.50
SHVA-EN050 Dragunity Knight - Vajrayana SCR	.60	1.00
SHVA-EN051 Hi-Speedroid Chanbara SR	.60	1.00
SHVA-EN052 Akashic Magician SR	.10	.20
SHVA-EN053 Cyberdark Impact! SR	.60	1.00
SHVA-EN054 Golden Bamboo Sword SR	.60	1.00
SHVA-EN055 Magic Planter SR	.10	.20
SHVA-EN056 Advanced Dark SR	.10	.20
SHVA-EN057 Shaddoll Fusion SCR	2.00	3.00
SHVA-EN058 Gateway to Chaos SCR	1.00	1.50
SHVA-EN059 Twin Twisters SCR	2.50	3.50
SHVA-EN060 Urgent Ritual Art SR	.10	.20

2018 Yu-Gi-Oh Soul Fusion 1st Edition

COMPLETE SET (100)	150.00	250.00
RELEASED ON OCTOBER 18, 2018		
SOFUEN000 Alviss of the Nordic Alfar C	.15	.25
SOFUEN001 Clock Wyvern R	.20	.35
SOFUEN002 Salamangreat Meer C	.15	.25
SOFUEN003 Salamangreat Foxy C	.15	.25
SOFUEN004 Salamangreat Falco C	.15	.25
SOFUEN005 Salamangreat Jack Jaguar C	.15	.25
SOFUEN006 Dinowrestler Capoeiraptor C	.15	.25
SOFUEN007 Dinowrestler Capaptera C	.15	.25
SOFUEN008 Dinowrestler Systegosaur C	.15	.25
SOFUEN009 Dinowrestler Pankratops C	.15	.25
SOFUEN010 Galaxy Cleic C	.15	.25
SOFUEN011 Galaxy Brave C	.15	.25
SOFUEN012 Gravekeeper's Headman R	.20	.35
SOFUEN013 Gravekeeper's Spiritualist C	.15	.25
SOFUEN014 Orcust Bass Bombard R	.20	.35
SOFUEN015 Orcust Cymbal Skeleton R	.20	.35
SOFUEN016 Orcust Harp Horro R	.20	.35
SOFUEN017 World Legacy - World Wand C	.15	.25
SOFUEN018 Thunder Dragonmatrix R	.20	.35
SOFUEN019 Thunder Dragondark UR	15.00	25.00
SOFUEN020 Thunder Dragonhawk UR	2.50	4.00
SOFUEN021 Thunder Dragonroar UR	10.00	15.00
SOFUEN022 Thunder Dragonduo SR	.35	.50
SOFUEN023 Impcantation Penciplume C	.15	.25
SOFUEN024 Impcantation Bookstone C	.15	.25
SOFUEN025 Chaos Dragon Levianeer SCR	6.00	10.00
SOFUEN026 Mystrick Hulder SR	.35	.50
SOFUEN027 Diana the Light Spirit C	.15	.25
SOFUEN028 Condemned Witch SCR	3.50	5.00
SOFUEN029 Bearblocker C	.15	.25
SOFUEN030 Gokipole R	.20	.35
SOFUEN031 Token Collector R	.20	.35
SOFUEN032 Two-for-One Team C	.15	.25
SOFUEN033 Salamangreat Emerald Eagle C	.15	.25
SOFUEN034 Cyberse Clock Dragon UR	.60	1.00
SOFUEN035 Gravekeeper's Supernaturalist R	.20	.35
SOFUEN036 Thunder Dragon Colossus SCR	60.00	75.00
SOFUEN037 Thunder Dragon Titan SCR	5.00	8.00
SOFUEN038 Diplexer Chimera C	.15	.25
SOFUEN039 Clock Spartoi R	.20	.35
SOFUEN040 Salamangreat Heatleo R	.20	.35
SOFUEN041 Dinowrestler King T Wrextle C	.15	.25
SOFUEN042 Galaxy-Eyes Solflare Dragon UR	.60	1.00
SOFUEN043 Galatea, the Orcust Automaton SR	.35	.50
SOFUEN044 Longirsu, the Orcust Orchestrator SR	.35	.50
SOFUEN045 Orcustrion UR	.75	1.25
SOFUEN046 Crusadia Soatha C	.15	.25
SOFUEN047 Folgo, Justice Fur Hire SR	.35	.50
SOFUEN048 Agave Dragon C	.15	.25
SOFUEN049 Some Summer Summoner SR	.35	.50
SOFUEN050 Cynet Fusion R	.20	.35
SOFUEN051 Salamangreat Sanctuary C	.15	.25
SOFUEN052 Rise of the Salamangreat C	.15	.25
SOFUEN053 Will of the Salamangreat C	.15	.25
SOFUEN054 World Dino Wrestling C	.15	.25
SOFUEN055 Necrovalley Throne SR	.35	.50
SOFUEN056 Galaxy Trance R	.20	.35
SOFUEN057 Orcustrated Babel R	.20	.35
SOFUEN058 Orcustrated Return SCR	5.00	8.00
SOFUEN059 Orcustrated Einsatz C	.15	.25
SOFUEN060 Thunder Dragon Fusion UR	.50	.75
SOFUEN061 Sky Striker Maneuver - Vector Blast SR	.35	.50
SOFUEN062 Giant Ballpark C	.15	.25
SOFUEN063 Herald of the Abyss SR	.35	.50
SOFUEN064 Concentrating Current C	.15	.25
SOFUEN065 Extra-Foolish Burial SR	.35	.50
SOFUEN066 Parallel Panzer C	.15	.25
SOFUEN067 Salamangreat Gift C	.15	.25
SOFUEN068 Necrovalley Temple R	.20	.35
SOFUEN069 Eternal Galaxy C	.15	.25
SOFUEN070 Orcustrated Attack C	.15	.25
SOFUEN071 Orcustrated Core C	.15	.25
SOFUEN072 Thunder Dragons' Hundred Thunders R	.20	.35
SOFUEN073 Thunder Dragon Discharge R	.20	.35
SOFUEN074 Crusadia Krawler C	.15	.25
SOFUEN075 Necro Fusion C	.15	.25
SOFUEN076 Invincibility Barrier C	.15	.25
SOFUEN077 Toll Hike R	.20	.35

SOFUEN078 Trap Trick SCR	25.00	35.00
SOFUEN079 The Revenge of the Normal C	.15	.25
SOFUEN080 Subsurface Stage Divers C	.15	.25
SOFUEN081 Consolation Prize R	.20	.35
SOFUEN082 Danger! Thunderbird! SCR	3.50	5.00
SOFUEN083 Danger! Dogman! SR	.35	.50
SOFUEN084 Danger! Mothman! SR	.35	.50
SOFUEN085 Danger!? Tsuchinoko? SCR	40.00	50.00
SOFUEN086 Danger! Response Team UR	.60	1.00
SOFUEN087 Second Expedition into Danger! SR	.35	.50
SOFUEN088 Noble Knight Iyvanne SR	.35	.50
SOFUEN089 Morgan, the Enchantress of Avalon UR	1.25	2.50
SOFUEN090 Heritage of the Chalice UR	2.00	3.50
SOFUEN091 Until Noble Arms are Needed Once Again C	.15	.25
SOFUEN092 Fluffal Patchwork C	.15	.25
SOFUEN093 Edge Imp Cotton Eater C	.15	.25
SOFUEN094 Predaplant Dragostapelia C	.15	.25
SOFUEN095 D/D/D Flame High King Genghis C	.15	.25
SOFUEN096 D/D/D Super Doom King Purple Armageddon C	.15	.25
SOFUEN097 Predaplast C	.15	.25
SOFUEN098 Ostinato C	.15	.25
SOFUEN099 Frightfur Patchwork R	.20	.35

2018 Yu-Gi-Oh Hidden Summoners 1st Edition

COMPLETE SET (60)	25.00	40.00
RELEASED ON NOVEMBER 16, 2018		
HISUEN001 Matriarch of Nephthys SR	.12	.25
HISUEN002 Disciple of Nephthys SCR	.50	.75
HISUEN003 Chronicler of Nephthys SR	.12	.25
HISUEN004 Defender of Nephthys SR	.12	.25
HISUEN005 Devotee of Nephthys SCR	.35	.50
HISUEN006 Cerulean Sacred Phoenix of Nephthys SCR	1.25	2.00
HISUEN007 Nephthys, the Sacred Preserver SCR	1.25	2.00
HISUEN008 Nephthys, the Sacred Flame SCR	.50	.75
HISUEN009 Rebirth of Nephthys SR	.12	.25
HISUEN010 Last Hope of Nephthys SR	.12	.25
HISUEN011 Awakening of Nephthys SR	.12	.25
HISUEN012 Sacred Phoenix of Nephthys SR	.12	.25
HISUEN013 Hand of Nephthys SR	.12	.25
HISUEN014 Prank-Kids Fansies SR	.25	.40
HISUEN015 Prank-Kids Lampsies SR	.25	.40
HISUEN016 Prank-Kids Dropsies SR	.25	.40
HISUEN017 Prank-Kids Rocket Ride SR	.25	.40
HISUEN018 Prank-Kids Weather Washer SR	.20	.30
HISUEN019 Prank-Kids Battle Butler SCR	1.25	2.00
HISUEN020 Prank-Kids Dodo-Doodle-Doo SCR	5.00	7.50
HISUEN021 Prank-Kids Bow-Wow-Bark SR	.35	.50
HISUEN022 Prank-Kids Rip-Roarin-Roaster SCR	2.50	4.00
HISUEN023 Prank-Kids Place SCR	15.00	25.00
HISUEN024 Prank-Kids Pranks SR	.75	1.25
HISUEN025 Prank-Kids Pandemonium SR	.25	.40
HISUEN026 Prank-Kids Plan SR	.20	.30
HISUEN027 Dakki, the Graceful Mayakashi SCR	1.25	2.00
HISUEN028 Tsukahagi, the Poisonous Mayakashi SR	.12	.25
HISUEN029 Hajun, the Winged Mayakashi SCR	1.25	2.00
HISUEN030 Shafu, the Wheeled Mayakashi SCR	.50	.75
HISUEN031 Yasha, the Skeletal Mayakashi SR	.12	.25
HISUEN032 Oboro-Guruma, the Wheeled Mayakashi SCR	.35	.50
HISUEN033 Tsuchigumo, the Poisonous Mayakashi SCR	.35	.50
HISUEN034 Tengu, the Winged Mayakashi SCR	.50	.75
HISUEN035 Yoko, the Graceful Mayakashi SCR	1.00	1.50
HISUEN036 Gashadokuro, the Skeletal Mayakashi SCR	1.50	2.50
HISUEN037 Yuki-Onna, the Ice Mayakashi SCR	1.25	2.00
HISUEN038 Mayakashi Return SCR	1.25	2.00
HISUEN039 Mayakashi Metamorphosis SR	.12	.25
HISUEN040 Night's End Sorcerer SR	.12	.25
HISUEN041 Shiranui Spectralsword SR	.12	.25
HISUEN042 Preparation of Rites SR	.12	.25
HISUEN043 Ultra Polymerization SR	.12	.25
HISUEN044 De-Synchro SR	.12	.25
HISUEN045 Phoenix Wing Wind Blast SR	.12	.25
HISUEN046 Thunder Dragon SR	.20	.30
HISUEN047 Manju of the Ten Thousand Hands SR	2.00	3.50
HISUEN048 Shiranui Spiritmaster SR	.20	.30
HISUEN049 Shiranui Samurai SR	.12	.25
HISUEN050 Tatsunoko SR	.12	.25
HISUEN051 Gold Sarcophagus SCR	2.00	3.50
HISUEN052 Fulfillment of the Contract SR	.12	.25
HISUEN053 Re-Fusion SR	.12	.25
HISUEN054 Ritual Foregone SR	.12	.25
HISUEN055 Onslaught of the Fire Kings SR	.12	.25
HISUEN056 Circle of the Fire Kings SR	.12	.25
HISUEN057 Flash Fusion SR	.12	.25
HISUEN058 Fusion Recycling Plant SR	.20	.30
HISUEN059 Rivalry of Warlords SR	2.50	4.00
HISUEN060 Gozen Match SR	2.50	4.00

2019 Yu-Gi-Oh Savage Strike 1st Edition

COMPLETE SET (100)	200.00	300.00
RELEASED ON FEBRUARY 1, 2019		
SASTEN000 Danger! Ogopogo! UR	2.00	3.50
SASTEN001 Catche Eve L2 C	.15	.25
SASTEN002 Cyberse Synchron R	.20	.35
SASTEN003 Salamangreat Wolvie C	.15	.25
SASTEN004 Salamangreat Parro C	.15	.25
SASTEN005 Salamangreat Foxer C	.15	.25
SASTEN006 Speedburst Dragon R	.20	.35
SASTEN007 Rokket Synchron R	.20	.35
SASTEN008 Neo Space Connector C	.15	.25
SASTEN009 T.G. Screw Serpent R	.20	.35
SASTEN010 T.G. Booster Raptor C	.15	.25
SASTEN011 T.G. Tank Grub C	.15	.25
SASTEN012 Guardragon Justicia C	.15	.25
SASTEN013 Guardragon Garmides C	.15	.25
SASTEN014 Guardragon Promineses C	.15	.25
SASTEN015 Guardragon Andrake R	.20	.35
SASTEN016 World Legacy - World Ark"" R	.20	.35
SASTEN017 Shiranui Spectralsword Shade SR	.30	.50
SASTEN018 Shiranui Swordmaster C	.15	.25
SASTEN019 Shiranui Squire SR	.30	.50
SASTEN020 Fantastical Dragon Phantazmay SCR	75.00	100.00
SASTEN021 Orcust Knightmare C	.15	.25
SASTEN022 Prank-Kids Rocksies C	.15	.25
SASTEN023 Madolche Petingcessoeur R	.20	.35
SASTEN024 Psychic Wheeleder SCR	20.00	30.00
SASTEN025 Psychic Tracker C	.15	.25
SASTEN026 Thunderclap Monk SR	.30	.50
SASTEN027 Lappis Dragon R	.20	.35
SASTEN028 Cataclysmic Scorching Sunburner C	.15	.25
SASTEN029 Squirt Squid C	.15	.25
SASTEN030 Aloof Lupine C	.15	.25
SASTEN031 Extraceratops C	.15	.25
SASTEN032 Impcantation Chalislime R	.20	.35
SASTEN033 Trickstar Band Sweet Guitar SR	.30	.50
SASTEN034 Salamangreat Violet Chimera R	.20	.35
SASTEN035 Elemental HERO Brave Neos SR	.30	.50
SASTEN036 Elemental HERO Cosmo Neos SR	.30	.50
SASTEN037 Borreload Savage Dragon UR	.60	30.00
SASTEN038 Cyberse Quantum Dragon UR	.60	1.00
SASTEN039 T.G. Star Guardian UR	.60	1.00
SASTEN040 Shiranui Swordsaga C	.15	.25
SASTEN041 Shiranui Squiresaga C	.15	.25
SASTEN042 Hyper Psychic Riser R	.20	.35
SASTEN043 Cyberse Integrator C	.15	.25
SASTEN044 Cyberse Wicckid C	.15	.25
SASTEN045 Update Jammer C	.15	.25
SASTEN046 Detonate Deleter R	.20	.35
SASTEN047 Clock Lizard C	.15	.25
SASTEN048 Salamangreat Sunlight Wolf R	6.00	10.00
SASTEN049 Trickstar Divaridis UR	.60	1.00
SASTEN050 T.G. Trident Launcher SCR	1.50	2.50
SASTEN051 Guardragon Elpy SR	.30	.50
SASTEN052 Guardragon Pisty SR	.30	.50
SASTEN053 Guardragon Agarpain SR	.30	.50
SASTEN054 Shiranui Skillsaga Supremacy UR	1.50	2.50
SASTEN055 Sky Striker Ace - Kaina SR	.30	.50
SASTEN056 Hiita the Fire Charmer, Ablaze R	.20	.35
SASTEN057 Fusion of Fire R	1.50	2.50
SASTEN058 Trickstar Live Stage SCR	2.50	4.00
SASTEN059 Trickstar Fusion R	.20	.35
SASTEN060 Neos Fusion SR	.30	.50
SASTEN061 Guardragon Shield R	.20	.35
SASTEN062 World Legacy Guardragon UR	5.00	8.00
SASTEN063 Ghost Meets Girl - A Shiranui's Story UR	.60	1.00
SASTEN064 Shiranui Style Solemnity C	.15	.25
SASTEN065 Impcantation Inception C	.15	.25
SASTEN066 Uni-Song Tuning C	.15	.25
SASTEN067 Pot of Extravagance SCR	60.00	75.00
SASTEN068 Edge of the Ring C	.15	.25
SASTEN069 Child's Play C	.15	.25
SASTEN070 Summon Over C	.15	.25
SASTEN071 NEXT SR	.30	.50
SASTEN072 Guardragon Corewakening C	.15	.25
SASTEN073 Guardragon Cataclysm R	.20	.35
SASTEN074 Shiranui Style Success C	.15	.25
SASTEN075 Fateful Hour SR	.30	.50
SASTEN076 Orcustrated Release C	.15	.25
SASTEN077 Subterror Succession C	.15	.25
SASTEN078 Dark Factory of More Production R	.20	.35
SASTEN079 Witch's Strike SCR	10.00	15.00
SASTEN080 Loss Time C	.15	.25
SASTEN081 Super Anti-Kaiju War Machine Mecha-Thunder-King SCR	5.00	8.00
SASTEN082 Time Thief Winder C	.15	.25
SASTEN083 Time Thief Bezel Ship C	.15	.25
SASTEN084 Time Thief Regulator C	.15	.25
SASTEN085 Time Thief Redoer C	.15	.25
SASTEN086 Time Thief Hack C	.15	.25
SASTEN087 Time Thief Flyback C	.15	.25
SASTEN088 Valkyrie Sechste SCR	3.50	5.00
SASTEN089 Valkyrie Vierte? SR	.30	.50
SASTEN090 Final Light UR	.60	1.00
SASTEN091 Apple of Enlightenment?? R	.20	.35
SASTEN092 Cyberse Converter C	.15	.25
SASTEN093 Legendary Secret of the Six Samurai C	.15	.25
SASTEN094 Subterror Guru C	.15	.25
SASTEN095 Trickstar Corobane UR	8.00	12.00
SASTEN096 Performapal Clay Breaker C	.15	.25
SASTEN097 Super Armored Robot Armed Black Iron C"" C	.15	.25
SASTEN098 Shinobi Necro C	.15	.25
SASTEN099 Red Rising Dragon C	.15	.25

2019 Yu-Gi-Oh The Infinity Chasers 1st Edition

COMPLETE SET (60)	75.00	125.00
BOOSTER BOX (24 PACKS)	55.00	70.00
BOOSTER PACK (5 CARDS)	3.00	4.00
RELEASED ON MARCH 22, 2019		
INCHEN001 Infinitrack Harvester SCR	5.00	8.00
INCHEN002 Infinitrack Anchor Drill SCR	6.00	10.00
INCHEN003 Infinitrack Crab Crane SR	.10	.15
INCHEN004 Infinitrack Drag Shovel SR	.10	.15
INCHEN005 Infinitrack Trencher SCR	.30	.50
INCHEN006 Infinitrack Tunneller SR	.10	.15
INCHEN007 Infinitrack River Stormer SCR	.20	.30
INCHEN008 Infinitrack Mountain Smasher SR	.10	.15
INCHEN009 Infinitrack Earth Slicer SCR	.30	.50
INCHEN010 Infinitrack Goliath SR	.10	.15
INCHEN011 Infinitrack Fortress Megaclops SCR	.30	.50
INCHEN012 Outrigger Extension SR	.40	.60
INCHEN013 Spin Turn SR	.10	.15
INCHEN014 Witchcrafter Potterie SR	.20	.30
INCHEN015 Witchcrafter Pittore SCR	.60	1.00
INCHEN016 Witchcrafter Schmietta SR	.15	.25
INCHEN017 Witchcrafter Edel SR	1.25	2.00
INCHEN018 Witchcrafter Haine SR	2.50	4.00
INCHEN019 Witchcrafter Madame Verre SCR	10.00	15.00
INCHEN020 Witchcrafter Creation SCR	25.00	40.00
INCHEN021 Witchcrafter Holiday SCR	.60	1.00
INCHEN022 Witchcrafter Collaboration SR	.12	.20
INCHEN023 Witchcrafter Draping SR	.10	.15
INCHEN024 Witchcrafter Bystreet SCR	.40	.60
INCHEN025 Witchcrafter Scroll SCR	.30	.50
INCHEN026 Witchcrafter Masterpiece SR	.10	.15
INCHEN027 Serziel, Watcher of the Evil Eye SCR	20.00	30.00
INCHEN028 Medusa, Watcher of the Evil Eye SR	.60	1.00
INCHEN029 Catoblepas, Familiar of the Evil Eye SR	.10	.15
INCHEN030 Basilius, Familiar of the Evil Eye SR	.10	.15
INCHEN031 Zerrziel, Ruler of the Evil Eyed SCR	.30	.50
INCHEN032 Evil Eye of Selene SCR	.30	.50
INCHEN033 Evil Eye Domain - Pareidolia SCR	.50	.75
INCHEN034 Evil Eye Awakening SCR	.20	.30
INCHEN035 Evil Eye Confrontation SR	.12	.20
INCHEN036 Evil Eye Repose SCR	.25	.40
INCHEN037 Evil Eye Defeat SR	.25	.40
INCHEN038 Evil Eye Mesmerism SCR	.20	.30
INCHEN039 Evil Eye Retribution SCR	.25	.40
INCHEN040 Confronting the "C" SR	.10	.15
INCHEN041 Juragedo SR	.15	.25
INCHEN042 Hidden Armory SR	.20	.30
INCHEN043 Secret Village of the Spellcasters SR	.60	1.00
INCHEN044 Rank-Up-Magic Astral Force SR	.10	.15
INCHEN045 Marshalling Field SR	.10	.15
INCHEN046 Heavy Freight Train Derricrane SR	.15	.25
INCHEN047 Performapal Sky Magician SR	.10	.15
INCHEN048 Mythical Beast Jackal King SR	2.50	4.00
INCHEN049 Arcanite Magician SR	.12	.20
INCHEN050 Digvorzhak, King of Heavy Industry SR	.12	.20
INCHEN051 Mecha Phantom Beast Dracossack SR	.50	.75
INCHEN052 Phantom Fortress Enterblathnir SR	.15	.25
INCHEN053 Spell Absorption SR	.15	.25
INCHEN054 Wonder Wand SR	.15	.25
INCHEN055 Bound Wand SR	.10	.15
INCHEN056 Tannhauser Gate SR	.10	.15
INCHEN057 Magician's Right Hand SR	.15	.25
INCHEN058 Magician's Left Hand SR	.15	.25
INCHEN059 Spellbook of Knowledge SR	.60	1.00
INCHEN060 Magic Cylinder SR	.15	.25

2019 Yu-Gi-Oh Dark Neostorm 1st Edition

COMPLETE SET (100)	150.00	200.00
BOOSTER BOX		
BOOSTER PACK		
RELEASED ON MAY 3, 2019		
DANEEN000 Gnomaterial SCR	25.00	40.00
DANEEN001 Firewall Guardian C	.15	.25
DANEEN002 Grid Sweeper C	.15	.25
DANEEN003 Salamangreat Fennec C	.15	.25
DANEEN004 Overflow Dragon C	.15	.25
DANEEN005 Altergeist Fifinellag C	.15	.25
DANEEN006 Dinowrestler Eskrimamenchi C	.15	.25
DANEEN007 Dinowrestler Coelasilat C	.15	.25
DANEEN008 Dinowrestler Martial Anga C	.15	.25
DANEEN009 Destiny HERO - Drawhand C	.15	.25
DANEEN010 Psi-Reflector R	.25	.40
DANEEN011 Assault Sentinel C	.15	.25
DANEEN012 T.G. Halberd Cannon/Assault Mode R	.25	.40
DANEEN013 Super Quantum White Layer C	.15	.25
DANEEN014 Neo Flamvell Lady C	.15	.25
DANEEN015 Filo, Messenger Fur Hire R	.25	.40
DANEEN016 Yuki-Musume, the Ice Mayakashi C	.15	.25
DANEEN017 Knightmare Incarnation Idlee SCR	4.00	6.00
DANEEN018 World Legacy Guardragon Mardark R	.25	.40
DANEEN019 Deus X-Krawler C	.15	.25
DANEEN020 Omni Dragon Brotaur SCR	15.00	25.00
DANEEN021 Chaos Betrayer R	.25	.40
DANEEN022 Loud Cloud the Storm Serpent C	.15	.25
DANEEN023 Xyz Slidolphin C	.15	.25
DANEEN024 Star Staring Starling R	.25	.40
DANEEN025 Ghost Sister & Spooky Dogwood SCR	10.00	15.00
DANEEN026 Handigallop C	.15	.25
DANEEN027 Emperor Maju Garzett C	.15	.25
DANEEN028 Cupid Dunk C	.15	.25
DANEEN029 Crealtar, the Impcantation Originator C	.15	.25
DANEEN030 Dinowrestler Chimera T Wrextle C	.15	.25
DANEEN031 Destiny HERO - Dominance SR	.30	.50
DANEEN032 World Chalice Guardragon Almarduke R	.25	.40
DANEEN033 Altergeist Dragvirion C	.15	.25
DANEEN034 Dinowrestler Giga Spinosavate R	.25	.40
DANEEN035 Ib the World Chalice Justiciar SCR	15.00	25.00
DANEEN036 Firewall eXceed Dragon UR	.40	.60
DANEEN037 Super Quantal Mech Beast Lusterrex SR	.30	.50
DANEEN038 Dingirisu, the Orcust of the Evening Star UR	15.00	25.00
DANEEN039 Madolche Teacher Glassoufle R	.25	.40
DANEEN040 Cyberse Reminder C	.15	.25
DANEEN041 Dilingerous Dragon C	.15	.25
DANEEN042 Dinowrestler Terra Parkourio C	.15	.25
DANEEN043 Gouki The Blade Ogre C	.15	.25
DANEEN044 Gouki The Solid Ogre C	.15	.25
DANEEN045 Xtra HERO Cross Crusader R	1.50	2.50
DANEEN046 Neo Super Quantal Mech King Blaster Magna SR	.30	.50
DANEEN047 Mekk-Knight Crusadia Avramax SCR	10.00	15.00
DANEEN048 World Gears of Theurlogical Demiurgy UR	.40	.60
DANEEN049 Puzzlomino, the Drop-n-Deleter C	.15	.25
DANEEN050 Amphibious Swarmship Amblowhale R	.25	.40
DANEEN051 Cynet Mining SCR	30.00	50.00
DANEEN052 Salamangreat Recureance UR	.40	.60
DANEEN053 Tyrant Dino Fusion C	.15	.25
DANEEN054 Fusion Destiny SR	2.00	3.00
DANEEN055 Assault Mode Zero C	.15	.25
DANEEN056 Super Quantal Alphancall Appeal C	.15	.25
DANEEN057 Mayakashi Winter SR	.30	.50
DANEEN058 Cloudian Aerosol C	.15	.25
DANEEN059 World Legacy Monstrosity UR	2.50	4.00
DANEEN060 Guardragon Reincarnation C	.15	.25
DANEEN061 Crusadia Testament C	.15	.25
DANEEN062 Impcantation Thanatosis C	.15	.25
DANEEN063 Dirge of the Lost Dragon SR	.30	.50
DANEEN064 Mystic Mine SR	2.00	3.00
DANEEN065 Mordschlag C	.15	.25
DANEEN066 Stand In C	.15	.25
DANEEN067 Packet Swap C	.15	.25
DANEEN068 Altergeist Haunted Rock C	.15	.25
DANEEN069 D - Tactics R	.25	.40
DANEEN070 Assault Reboot R	.25	.40
DANEEN071 Super Quantal Union - Magnaformation C	.15	.25
DANEEN072 Magical Musket - Crooked Crown C	.15	.25
DANEEN073 The Weather Rainbowed Canvas R	.25	.40
DANEEN074 Orcust Crescendo SR	.30	.50
DANEEN075 World Legacy Collapse C	.15	.25
DANEEN076 World Legacy Cliffhanger C	.15	.25
DANEEN077 Chain Hole SR	.30	.50
DANEEN078 Crackdown SR	2.50	4.00
DANEEN079 Snowman Effect C	.15	.25
DANEEN080 Dice It C	.15	.25
DANEEN081 Muddy Mudragon R	.25	.40
DANEEN082 Saryuja's Shackles C	.15	.25

DANEEN083 Danger! Excitement! Mystery! UR	.40	.60
DANEEN084 Danger! Feets of Strength! R	.25	.40
DANEEN085 You're in Danger! R	.25	.40
DANEEN086 Valkyrie Funfte R	.25	.40
DANEEN087 Valkyrie Erda UR	.40	.60
DANEEN088 Valkyrie Chariot C	.15	.25
DANEEN089 Valkyrie's Embrace UR	.40	.60
DANEEN090 Pegasus Wing C	.15	.25
DANEEN091 Loge's Flame SR	.30	.50
DANEEN092 Number 5: Doom Chimera Dragon SR	.30	.50
DANEEN093 Number XX: Utopic Dark Infinity UR	.40	.60
DANEEN094 Mermail Abyssalacia UR	.40	.60
DANEEN095 Cherubini, Ebon Angel of the Burning Abyss SCR	10.00	15.00
DANEEN096 Speedlift C	.15	.25
DANEEN097 Pendulum Halt SR	.30	.50
DANEEN098 Whitefish Salvage R	.25	.40
DANEEN099 Memories of Hope SR	.30	.50

2019 Yu-Gi-Oh Battles of Legend Hero's Revenge 1st Edition

COMPLETE SET (94)	100.00	150.00
BOOSTER BOX		
BOOSTER PACK		
RELEASED ON JULY 12, 2019		
BLHREN000 Five-Headed Dragon SCR	.75	1.25
BLHREN001 Ipiria SCR	.35	.50
BLHREN002 Water of Life UR	.15	.25
BLHREN003 Gold Moon Coin UR	.15	.25
BLHREN004 Gingerbread House UR	.25	.40
BLHREN005 Vision HERO Minimum Ray UR	.12	.20
BLHREN006 Vision HERO Multiply Guy UR	.12	.20
BLHREN007 Vision HERO Increase SCR	5.00	8.00
BLHREN008 Vision HERO Poisoner UR	.10	.15
BLHREN009 Vision HERO Gravito UR	.15	.25
BLHREN010 Vision HERO Faris SCR	.20	.30
BLHREN011 Vision Release UR	.15	.25
BLHREN012 Vision Fusion SCR	.15	.25
BLHREN013 Apparition UR	.10	.15
BLHREN014 Fortune Fairy Hikari SCR	.35	.50
BLHREN015 Fortune Fairy En UR	.15	.25
BLHREN016 Fortune Fairy Hu UR	.15	.25
BLHREN017 Fortune Fairy Swee UR	.15	.25
BLHREN018 Fortune Fairy Ann UR	.15	.25
BLHREN019 Fortune Fairy Chee UR	.15	.25
BLHREN020 Unacceptable Result UR	.15	.25
BLHREN021 Miracle Stone UR	.15	.25
BLHREN022 Lucky Loan UR	.15	.25
BLHREN023 T.G. Gear Zombie SCR	.15	.25
BLHREN024 T.G. Drill Fish UR	.12	.20
BLHREN025 T.G. Metal Skeleton UR	.15	.25
BLHREN026 Sonic Stun UR	.12	.20
BLHREN027 Number 26: Spaceway Octobypass UR	.15	.25
BLHREN028 Number 60: Dugares the Timeless UR	.75	1.25
BLHREN029 Number 76: Harmonizer Gradielle UR	.40	.60
BLHREN030 Number 97: Draglubion SCR	.60	1.00
BLHREN031 Battlewasp - Pin the Bullseye UR	.10	.15
BLHREN032 Battlewasp - Dart the Hunter UR	.10	.15
BLHREN033 Battlewasp - Sting the Poison UR	.10	.15
BLHREN034 Battlewasp - Twinbow the Attacker UR	.10	.15
BLHREN035 Battlewasp - Arbalest the Rapidfire UR	.10	.15
BLHREN036 Battlewasp - Azusa the Ghost Bow UR	.10	.15
BLHREN037 Battlewasp - Halberd the Charge UR	.10	.15
BLHREN038 Battlewasp - Hama the Conquering Bow SCR	.35	.50
BLHREN039 Battlewasp - Ballista the Armageddon UR	.10	.15
BLHREN040 Summoning Swarm UR	.10	.15
BLHREN041 Revival Swarm UR	.10	.15
BLHREN042 Battlewasp - Nest UR	.10	.15
BLHREN043 All-Eyes Phantom Dragon SCR	.35	.50
BLHREN044 Hi-Speedroid Kitedrake SCR	.60	1.00
BLHREN045 Avendread Savior SCR	.50	.75
BLHREN046 Black Luster Soldier - Soldier of Chaos SCR	35.00	50.00
BLHREN047 Harpie Conductor SCR	.50	.75
BLHREN048 Double Headed Anger Knuckle SCR	.25	.40
BLHREN049 Traptrix Sera SCR	3.00	5.00
BLHREN050 Hi-Speedroid Rubber Band Shooter SCR	.25	.40
BLHREN051 PSY-Framelord Lambda SCR	5.00	8.00
BLHREN052 Magical Musketeer Max UR	.50	.75
BLHREN053 Gimmick Puppet Chimera Doll UR	.10	.15
BLHREN054 Salamangreat Almiraj SCR	.10	.15
BLHREN055 Stardust Mirage SCR	.12	.20
BLHREN056 Dark Sacrifice SCR	.50	.75
BLHREN057 Foolish Burial UR	1.00	1.50
BLHREN058 Symbol of Friendship UR	.10	.15
BLHREN059 Vision HERO Vyon SCR	.60	1.00
BLHREN060 Vision HERO Witch Raider UR	.10	.15
BLHREN061 Elemental HERO Stratos UR	.50	.75
BLHREN062 Vision HERO Trinity UR	.12	.20
BLHREN063 Destiny HERO - Dangerous UR	.15	.25
BLHREN064 Elemental HERO Neos Knight SCR	.12	.20
BLHREN065 Elemental HERO Absolute Zero UR	.25	.40
BLHREN066 Dragonecro Nethersoul Dragon UR	.35	.50
BLHREN067 Lunalight Crimson Fox UR	.12	.20
BLHREN068 Lunalight Kaleido Chick UR	.12	.20
BLHREN069 Predaplast UR	.12	.20
BLHREN070 Dinowrestler Pankratops SCR	4.00	6.00
BLHREN071 Borrelsword Dragon SCR	35.00	50.00
BLHREN072 Salamangreat Sanctuary UR	.15	.25
BLHREN073 Will of the Salamangreat UR	.15	.25
BLHREN074 Cyber-Stein SCR	.60	1.00
BLHREN075 Guardian of Order UR	.10	.15
BLHREN076 White Dragon Wyverburster UR	.25	.40
BLHREN077 Black Dragon Collapserpent UR	.25	.40
BLHREN078 Artifact Scythe UR	.40	.60
BLHREN079 Artifact Lancea SCR	3.00	5.00
BLHREN080 Shaddoll Falco UR	.20	.30
BLHREN081 Shaddoll Hedgehog UR	.20	.30
BLHREN082 Shaddoll Squamata UR	.25	.35
BLHREN083 Shaddoll Beast UR	.15	.25
BLHREN084 Subterror Guru UR	.35	.50
BLHREN085 Herald of the Arc Light UR	.50	.75
BLHREN086 Nekroz Cycle SCR	.50	.75
BLHREN087 Interrupted Kaiju Slumber SCR	1.00	1.50
BLHREN088 Summon Limit UR	2.50	4.00
BLHREN089 Sky Striker Ace - Raye SCR	.60	1.00
BLHREN090 Sky Striker Mobilize - Engage! SCR	12.00	20.00
BLHREN091 Sky Striker Maneuver - Afterburners! UR	.35	.50
BLHREN092 Sky Striker Mecha - Widow Anchor SCR	5.00	8.00
BLHREN093 Number 93: Utopia Kaiser SCR	2.00	3.00

2019 Yu-Gi-Oh Rising Rampage 1st Edition

BOOSTER BOX		
BOOSTER PACK		
RELEASED ON JULY 26, 2019		
RIRAEN000 Capshell SCR	1.25	2.00
RIRAEN001 Rescue Interlacer C	.15	.25
RIRAEN002 Cross Debug C	.15	.25
RIRAEN003 Marincess Sea Horse PRISM SCR	150.00	200.00
RIRAEN003 Marincess Sea Horse UR	8.00	12.00
RIRAEN004 Marincess Sea Star C	.15	.25
RIRAEN005 DMZ Dragon C	.15	.25
RIRAEN006 Dinowrestler Martial Ankylo C	.15	.25
RIRAEN007 Dinowrestler Rambrachio C	.15	.25
RIRAEN008 Fortune Lady Past R	.25	.40
RIRAEN009 Yosenju Sabu C	.15	.25
RIRAEN010 Yosenju Izna C	.15	.25
RIRAEN011 Mayosenju Hitot SR	.35	.50
RIRAEN012 Tenyi Spirit - Adhara R	1.50	2.50
RIRAEN013 Tenyi Spirit - Shthana R	1.25	2.00
RIRAEN014 Tenyi Spirit - Mapura R	.25	.40
RIRAEN015 Tenyi Spirit - Nahata R	.25	.40
RIRAEN016 Tenyi Spirit - Vishuda R	.60	1.00
RIRAEN017 Simorgh, Bird of Beginning C	.15	.25
RIRAEN018 Simorgh, Bird of Bringing R	.25	.40
RIRAEN019 Simorgh, Bird of Calamity C	.15	.25
RIRAEN020 Simorgh, Bird of Protection C	.15	.25
RIRAEN021 Simorgh, Lord of the Storm SR	.35	.50
RIRAEN022 Simorgh of Darkness SR	.35	.50
RIRAEN023 B.E.S. Blaster Cannon Core SR	.35	.50
RIRAEN024 Vic Viper T301 R	.25	.40
RIRAEN025 Reptilianne Lamia C	.15	.25
RIRAEN026 Ranryu C	.15	.25
RIRAEN027 Avida, Rebuilder of Worlds SR	.35	.50
RIRAEN028 Witchcrafter Golem Aruru SCR	3.00	5.00
RIRAEN029 Gizmek Orochi, the Serpentron Sky Slasher SCR	15.00	25.00
RIRAEN030 Cataclysmic Cryonic Coldo C	.15	.25
RIRAEN031 Voltester C	.15	.25
RIRAEN032 Tlakalel, His Malevolent Majesty R	.25	.40
RIRAEN033 Beatraptor C	.15	.25
RIRAEN034 Spirit Sculptor SR	.35	.50
RIRAEN035 Reversible Beetle C	.15	.25
RIRAEN036 Megistric Maginician C	.15	.25
RIRAEN037 Magicalibra C	.15	.25
RIRAEN038 Fortune Lady Every SCR	5.00	8.00
RIRAEN039 Borreload eXcharge Dragon UR	1.00	1.50
RIRAEN040 Marincess Blue Slug UR	5.00	8.00
RIRAEN041 Marincess Coral Anemone SCR	25.00	35.00
RIRAEN042 Marincess Marbled Rock SCR	6.00	10.00
RIRAEN043 Monk of the Tenyi R	.25	.40
RIRAEN044 Shaman of the Tenyi UR	4.00	6.00
RIRAEN045 Berserker of the Tenyi R	.25	.40
RIRAEN046 Wynn the Wind Charmer, Verdant R	.40	.60
RIRAEN046 Wynn the Wind Charmer, Verdant PRISM SCR	150.00	200.00
RIRAEN047 Linkmail Archfiend SR	.35	.50
RIRAEN048 Apollousa, Bow of the Goddess SCR	40.00	60.00
RIRAEN048 Apollousa, Bow of the Goddess PRISM SCR	300.00	400.00
RIRAEN049 Defender of the Labyrinth C	.15	.25
RIRAEN050 Baba Barber C	.15	.25
RIRAEN051 Link Back C	.15	.25
RIRAEN052 Grid Rod C	.15	.25
RIRAEN053 Rising Fire R	.25	.40
RIRAEN054 Fury of Fire C	.15	.25
RIRAEN055 Fortune Vision R	.25	.40
RIRAEN056 Fortune Lady Calling UR	.50	.75
RIRAEN057 Yosenju Wind Worship C	.15	.25
RIRAEN058 Flawless Perfection of the Tenyi R	.25	.40
RIRAEN059 Vessel for the Dragon Cycle R	.25	.40
RIRAEN060 Elborz, the Sacred Lands of Simorgh C	.15	.25
RIRAEN061 Simorgh Onslaught C	.15	.25
RIRAEN062 Simorgh Repulsion C	.15	.25
RIRAEN063 Hypernova Burst SR	.35	.50
RIRAEN064 Psychic Fervor C	.15	.25
RIRAEN065 Blockout Curtain C	.15	.25
RIRAEN066 Sextet Summon C	.15	.25
RIRAEN067 Draw Discharge C	.15	.25
RIRAEN068 Marincess Wave UR	.60	1.00
RIRAEN069 Marincess Current C	.15	.25
RIRAEN070 Fortune Lady Rewind R	.25	.40
RIRAEN071 Yosenjus' Sword Sting C	.15	.25
RIRAEN072 Fists of the Unrivaled Tenyi R	.25	.40
RIRAEN073 Simorgh Sky Battle C	.15	.25
RIRAEN074 World Legacy Bestowal C	.15	.25
RIRAEN075 The Return to the Normal C	.15	.25
RIRAEN076 Get Out! SCR	8.00	12.00
RIRAEN077 Storm Dragon's Return PRISM SCR	60.00	100.00
RIRAEN077 Storm Dragon's Return SR	1.00	1.50
RIRAEN078 Setuppercut C	.15	.25
RIRAEN079 Dwimmered Glimmer C	.15	.25
RIRAEN080 Fighting Dirty C	.15	.25
RIRAEN081 Barricadeborg Blocker C	.15	.25
RIRAEN082 Hraesvelgr, the Desperate Doom Eagle R	.25	.40
RIRAEN083 Star Power!! R	.25	.40
RIRAEN084 Fuhma Wave C	.15	.25
RIRAEN085 Ikelos, the Dream Mirror Sprite UR	.35	1.50
RIRAEN086 Ikelos, the Dream Mirror Mara SR	1.00	1.50
RIRAEN087 Morpheus, the Dream Mirror White Knight SR	1.00	1.50
RIRAEN088 Morpheus, the Dream Mirror Black Knight UR	.35	1.50
RIRAEN089 Dream Mirror of Joy SR	.35	.50
RIRAEN090 Dream Mirror of Terror SR	.35	.50
RIRAEN091 Dream Mirror Fantasy C	.15	.25
RIRAEN092 Yosenju Oroshi Channeling C	.15	.25
RIRAEN093 Number 29: Mannequin Cat C	.15	.25
RIRAEN094 Kikinagashi Fucho C	.15	.25
RIRAEN095 White Aura Monoceros SR	.35	.50
RIRAEN096 White Howling SR	.40	.60
RIRAEN097 F.A. Shining Star GT C	.15	.25
RIRAEN098 Dragunity Knight - Romulus UR	5.00	8.00
RIRAEN099 Rogue of Endymion C	.15	.25

2019 Yu-Gi-Oh Fists of the Gadgets 1st Edition

COMPLETE SET (60)		
BOOSTER BOX		
BOOSTER PACK (5 CARDS)		
RELEASED ON AUGUST 22, 2019		
FIGAEN001 Boot-Up Corporal - Command Dynamo SR	.15	.25
FIGAEN002 Boot-Up Admiral - Destroyer Dynamo SCR	.20	.30
FIGAEN003 Boot-Up Order - Gear Charge SR	.15	.25
FIGAEN004 Boot-Up Order - Gear Force SCR	.20	.30
FIGAEN005 Powerhold the Moving Battery SR	.15	.25
FIGAEN006 Green Gadget SR	.15	.25
FIGAEN007 Red Gadget SR	.15	.25
FIGAEN008 Yellow Gadget SR	.15	.25
FIGAEN009 Gold Gadget SR	.15	.25
FIGAEN010 Silver Gadget SR	.15	.25
FIGAEN011 Brotherhood of the Fire Fist - Ram SCR	.20	.30
FIGAEN012 Brotherhood of the Fire Fist - Elephant SCR	15.00	25.00
FIGAEN013 Brotherhood of the Fire Fist - Panda SCR	12.00	20.00
FIGAEN014 Brotherhood of the Fire Fist - Eland SCR	3.00	5.00
FIGAEN015 Brotherhood of the Fire Fist - Swan SCR	.25	.40
FIGAEN016 Brotherhood of the Fire Fist - Eagle SCR	10.00	15.00
FIGAEN017 Brotherhood of the Fire Fist - Peacock SCR	.75	1.25
FIGAEN018 Fire Fortress atop Liang Peak SCR	.20	.30
FIGAEN019 Fire Formation - Domei SCR	.20	.30
FIGAEN020 Fire Formation - Ingen SCR	.20	.30
FIGAEN021 Ultimate Fire Formation - Sinto SCR	.20	.30
FIGAEN022 Brotherhood of the Fire Fist - Gorilla SR	.15	.25
FIGAEN023 Brotherhood of the Fire Fist - Bear SR	.15	.25
FIGAEN024 Brotherhood of the Fire Fist - Spirit SR	.15	.25
FIGAEN025 Brotherhood of the Fire Fist - Rooster SR	.15	.25
FIGAEN026 Brotherhood of the Fire Fist - Cardinal SR	.15	.25
FIGAEN027 Brotherhood of the Fire Fist - Tiger King SR	.15	.25
FIGAEN028 Fire Formation - Tenki SCR	1.00	1.50
FIGAEN029 Fire Formation - Tensu SR	.15	.25
FIGAEN030 Fire Formation - Yoko SR	.15	.25
FIGAEN031 Archfiend's Awakening SCR	.20	.30
FIGAEN032 Archfiend's Call SCR	.20	.30
FIGAEN033 Archfiend's Ascent SCR	.20	.30
FIGAEN034 Archfiend's Manifestation SCR	.20	.30
FIGAEN035 Latency SR	.15	.25
FIGAEN036 Swap Cleric SR	.15	.25
FIGAEN037 Defcon Bird SR	.15	.25
FIGAEN038 Prohibit Snake SR	.15	.25
FIGAEN039 Code Radiator SCR	8.00	12.00
FIGAEN040 Spool Code? SR	.15	.25
FIGAEN041 Cynet Optimization SR	.15	.25
FIGAEN042 Cynet Conflict SR	.15	.25
FIGAEN043 Code Talker SR	.15	.25
FIGAEN044 Shootingcode Talker SR	.15	.25
FIGAEN045 Elphase SR	.15	.25
FIGAEN046 Talkback Lancer SR	.15	.25
FIGAEN047 Rasterliger SR	.15	.25
FIGAEN048 Subterror Fiendess SR	.15	.25
FIGAEN049 The Hidden City SR	2.50	4.00
FIGAEN050 Subterror Final Battle SR	.15	.25
FIGAEN051 Scrap Recycler SR	4.00	6.00
FIGAEN052 Majesty Maiden, the True Dracocaster SR	.15	.25
FIGAEN053 Ignis Heat, the True Dracowarrior SCR	2.00	3.00
FIGAEN054 Dinomight Knight, the True Dracofighter SR	.15	.25
FIGAEN055 Amorphage Lechery SR	.15	.25
FIGAEN056 Amorphage Sloth SR	.60	1.00
FIGAEN057 Amorphage Goliath SR	.15	.25
FIGAEN058 Chronograph Sorcerer SR	.15	.25
FIGAEN059 Mythical Beast Master Cerberus SR	1.00	1.50
FIGAEN060 Starving Venom Fusion Dragon SR	.50	.75

TCG Decks

2015 Yu-Gi-Oh Yugi's Legendary Decks

COMPLETE SET (133)	80.00	110.00
RELEASED ON DECEMBER 11, 2015		
YGLDENA00 Electromagnetic Turtle SCR	1.00	1.50
YGLDENA01 Black Luster Soldier C	.15	.25
YGLDENA02 Black Luster Soldier - Envoy of the Beginning C	.15	.25
YGLDENA03 Dark Magician C	.15	.25
YGLDENA04 Dark Magician Girl C	.15	.25
YGLDENA05 Gaia The Fierce Knight C	.15	.25
YGLDENA06 Summoned Skull C	.15	.25
YGLDENA07 Curse of Dragon C	.15	.25
YGLDENA08 Catapult Turtle C	.15	.25
YGLDENA09 Celtic Guardian C	.15	.25
YGLDENA10 Winged Dragon, Guardian of the Fortress #1 C	.15	.25
YGLDENA11 Feral Imp C	.15	.25
YGLDENA12 Beaver Warrior C	.15	.25
YGLDENA13 Griffore C	.15	.25
YGLDENA14 Mystical Elf C	.15	.25
YGLDENA15 Giant Soldier of Stone C	.15	.25
YGLDENA16 Mammoth Graveyard C	.15	.25
YGLDENA17 Exodia the Forbidden One UR	2.50	3.00
YGLDENA18 Right Leg of the Forbidden One UR	1.50	2.00
YGLDENA19 Left Leg of the Forbidden One UR	1.50	2.00
YGLDENA20 Right Arm of the Forbidden One UR	1.50	2.00
YGLDENA21 Left Arm of the Forbidden One UR	1.50	2.00
YGLDENA22 Kuriboh C	.15	.25
YGLDENA23 Monster Reborn C	.15	.25
YGLDENA24 Swords of Revealing Light C	.15	.25
YGLDENA25 Mystic Box C	.15	.25
YGLDENA26 Brain Control C	.15	.25
YGLDENA27 Monster Recovery C	.15	.25
YGLDENA28 Spell Shattering Arrow C	.15	.25
YGLDENA29 Horn of the Unicorn C	.15	.25
YGLDENA30 Mystical Moon C	.15	.25
YGLDENA31 Burning Land C	.15	.25
YGLDENA32 Multiply C	.15	.25
YGLDENA33 Detonate C	.15	.25
YGLDENA34 Makiu, the Magical Mist C	.15	.25
YGLDENA35 Polymerization C	.15	.25
YGLDENA36 Black Luster Ritual C	.15	.25
YGLDENA37 Mirror Force C	.15	.25
YGLDENA38 Magical Hats C	.15	.25
YGLDENA39 The Eye of Truth C	.15	.25
YGLDENA40 Shift C	.15	.25

YGLDENA41 Gaia the Dragon Champion C .15 .25
YGLDENB00 Dark Renewal SCR 9.00 10.50
YGLDENB01 Valkyrion the Magna Warrior UR .30 .50
YGLDENB02 Dark Magician UR 3.00 3.50
YGLDENB03 Dark Magician Girl UR 2.25 3.00
YGLDENB04 Buster Blader C .15 .25
YGLDENB05 Archfiend of Gilfer C .15 .25
YGLDENB06 Jack's Knight C .15 .25
YGLDENB07 Queen's Knight C .15 .25
YGLDENB08 King's Knight C .15 .25
YGLDENB09 Berfomet C .15 .25
YGLDENB10 Gazelle the King of Mythical Beasts C .15 .25
YGLDENB11 Alpha The Magnet Warrior C .15 .25
YGLDENB12 Beta The Magnet Warrior C .15 .25
YGLDENB13 Gamma The Magnet Warrior C .15 .25
YGLDENB14 Big Shield Gardna C .15 .25
YGLDENB15 Kuriboh C .15 .25
YGLDENB16 Monster Reborn C .15 .25
YGLDENB17 Swords of Revealing Light UR .20 .30
YGLDENB18 Dark Magic Curtain C .15 .25
YGLDENB19 Thousand Knives C .15 .25
YGLDENB20 Magic Formula C .15 .25
YGLDENB21 Magical Dimension C .15 .25
YGLDENB22 Diffusion Wave-Motion C .15 .25
YGLDENB23 Double Spell C .15 .25
YGLDENB24 Ectoplasmer C .15 .25
YGLDENB25 Soul Taker C .15 .25
YGLDENB26 Pot of Greed C .15 .25
YGLDENB27 Card Destruction C .15 .25
YGLDENB28 Exchange C .15 .25
YGLDENB29 Monster Recovery C .15 .25
YGLDENB30 Polymerization C .15 .25
YGLDENB31 De-Fusion C .15 .25
YGLDENB32 Multiply C .15 .25
YGLDENB33 Mirror Force UR 1.75 2.15
YGLDENB34 Magical Hats C .15 .25
YGLDENB35 Magic Cylinder C .15 .25
YGLDENB36 Spellbinding Circle C .15 .25
YGLDENB37 Lightforce Sword C .15 .25
YGLDENB38 Chain Destruction C .15 .25
YGLDENB39 Soul Rope C .15 .25
YGLDENB40 Tragedy C .15 .25
YGLDENB41 Chimera the Flying Mythical Beast C .15 .25
YGLDENC00 Black Illusion SCR 1.25 1.75
YGLDENC01 Magician of Black Chaos UR .75 1.15
YGLDENC02 Dark Magician of Chaos UR 3.00 3.50
YGLDENC03 Gandora the Dragon of Destruction C .15 .25
YGLDENC04 Silent Magician LV8 UR .40 .60
YGLDENC05 Silent Magician LV4 C .15 .25
YGLDENC06 Silent Swordsman LV7 C .15 .25
YGLDENC07 Silent Swordsman LV5 C .15 .25
YGLDENC08 Silent Swordsman LV3 C .15 .25
YGLDENC09 Dark Magician UR .75 1.25
YGLDENC10 Dark Magician Girl C .15 .25
YGLDENC11 Buster Blader C .15 .25
YGLDENC12 The Tricky C .15 .25
YGLDENC13 Jack's Knight C .15 .25
YGLDENC14 Queen's Knight C .15 .25
YGLDENC15 King's Knight C .15 .25
YGLDENC16 Green Gadget C .15 .25
YGLDENC17 Red Gadget C .15 .25
YGLDENC18 Yellow Gadget C .15 .25
YGLDENC19 Skilled Dark Magician C .15 .25
YGLDENC20 Skilled White Magician C .15 .25
YGLDENC21 Blockman C .15 .25
YGLDENC22 Marshmallon C .15 .25
YGLDENC23 Kuriboh C .15 .25
YGLDENC24 Monster Reborn C .15 .25
YGLDENC25 Swords of Revealing Light C .15 .25
YGLDENC26 Gold Sarcophagus UR 4.00 4.75
YGLDENC27 Card of Sanctity C .15 .25
YGLDENC28 Polymerization C .15 .25
YGLDENC29 Dark Magic Attack C .15 .25
YGLDENC30 Magicians Unite C .15 .25
YGLDENC31 Dedication through Light and Darkness C .15 .25
YGLDENC32 Black Magic Ritual C .15 .25
YGLDENC33 Tricky Spell 4 C .15 .25
YGLDENC34 Emblem of Dragon Destroyer C .15 .25
YGLDENC35 Marshmallon Glasses C .15 .25
YGLDENC36 Mirror Force C .15 .25
YGLDENC37 Magician's Circle C .15 .25
YGLDENC38 Shattered Axe C .15 .25
YGLDENC39 Stronghold the Moving Fortress C .15 .25
YGLDENC40 Miracle Restoring C .15 .25
YGLDENC41 Dark Paladin C .15 .25
YGLDENG01 Slifer the Sky Dragon UR 2.25 3.00
YGLDENG02 Obelisk the Tormentor UR 2.75 3.25
YGLDENG03 The Winged Dragon of Ra UR 2.25 3.00
YGLDENTKN Token UR .50 .75
NNO1 Duelist Kingdom UR .30 .50
NNO2 Glory of the King's Hand UR .30 .50
NNO3 Set Sail for the Kingdom UR .25 .40

2016 Yu-Gi-Oh Legendary Decks II

COMPLETE SET (133) 90.00 110.00
RELEASED ON OCTOBER 7, 2016
LDK2ENJ01 RedEyes B Dragon C .25 .40
LDK2ENJ02 RedEyes Black Flare Dragon C 2.00 3.00
LDK2ENJ03 RedEyes Archfiend of Lightning C .25 .40
LDK2ENJ04 RedEyes Retro Dragon C .25 .40
LDK2ENJ05 The Black Stone of Legend UR 3.00 5.00
LDK2ENJ06 Black Metal Dragon C .25 .40
LDK2ENJ07 Axe Raider C .25 .40
LDK2ENJ08 Alligators Sword C .25 .40
LDK2ENJ09 Baby Dragon C .25 .40
LDK2ENJ10 Jinzo C .25 .40
LDK2ENJ11 Goblin Attack Force C .25 .40
LDK2ENJ12 Gearfried the Iron Knight C .25 .40
LDK2ENJ13 Rocket Warrior C .25 .40
LDK2ENJ14 Blue Flame Swordsman C .25 .40
LDK2ENJ15 Time Wizard C .25 .40
LDK2ENJ16 Phoenix Gearfried C .25 .40
LDK2ENJ17 Gemini Summoner C .25 .40
LDK2ENJ18 Blazewing Butterfly C .25 .40
LDK2ENJ19 Dark Valkyria C .25 .40
LDK2ENJ20 Command Knight C .25 .40
LDK2ENJ21 Valkyrian Knight C .25 .40
LDK2ENJ22 Keeper of the Shrine C .25 .40
LDK2ENJ23 Inferno Fire Blast C .25 .40
LDK2ENJ24 RedEyes Fusion C 1.25 2.00
LDK2ENJ25 Cards of the Red Stone C .60 1.00
LDK2ENJ26 Polymerization C 1.00 1.50
LDK2ENJ27 Salamandra C .25 .40
LDK2ENJ28 Scapegoat C .25 .40
LDK2ENJ29 Foolish Burial C .25 .40
LDK2ENJ30 Roulette Spider C .25 .40
LDK2ENJ31 Supervise C .25 .40
LDK2ENJ32 Mystical Space Typhoon C .60 1.00
LDK2ENJ33 Symbols of Duty C .25 .40
LDK2ENJ34 Return of the RedEyes UR .75 1.25
LDK2ENJ35 RedEyes Spirit C .25 .40
LDK2ENJ36 Kunai with Chain C .25 .40
LDK2ENJ37 Call of the Haunted C .25 .40
LDK2ENJ38 Torrential Tribute C .75 1.00
LDK2ENJ39 Burst Breath C .25 .40
LDK2ENJ40 Curse of Anubis C .25 .40
LDK2ENJ41 RedEyes Flare Metal Dragon UR 1.25 2.00
LDK2ENJ42 Archfiend Black Skull Dragon C .25 .40
LDK2ENJ43 Alligators Sword Dragon C .25 .40
LDK2ENK01 BlueEyes White Dragon (Starter) C 1.00 1.50
LDK2ENK01 BlueEyes White Dragon (LOB) C 1.00 1.50
LDK2ENK01 BlueEyes White Dragon (Tablet) C 1.00 1.50
LDK2ENK02 Dragon Spirit of White C 1.50 2.00
LDK2ENK03 Kaibaman C .25 .40
LDK2ENK04 The White Stone of Legend C .25 .40
LDK2ENK05 The White Stone of Ancients C 5.00 7.00
LDK2ENK06 Maiden with Eyes of Blue UR 1.25 2.00
LDK2ENK07 Protector with Eyes of Blue C .25 .40
LDK2ENK08 Master with Eyes of Blue C .25 .40
LDK2ENK09 Battle Ox C .25 .40
LDK2ENK10 La Jinn the Mystical Genie of the Lamp C .25 .40
LDK2ENK11 Vorse Raider C .25 .40
LDK2ENK12 Alexandrite Dragon C .25 .40
LDK2ENK13 Blade Knight C .25 .40
LDK2ENK14 Ancient Lamp C .25 .40
LDK2ENK15 Tiger Dragon C .25 .40
LDK2ENK16 Kidmodo Dragon C .25 .40
LDK2ENK17 King of the Swamp C .75 1.00
LDK2ENK18 Rider of the Storm Winds C .25 .40
LDK2ENK19 Burst Stream of Destruction C .25 .40
LDK2ENK20 Beacon of White C .25 .40
LDK2ENK21 Mausoleum of White C .25 .40
LDK2ENK22 Polymerization C 1.00 1.50
LDK2ENK23 Enemy Controller C .25 .40
LDK2ENK24 Shrink C .25 .40
LDK2ENK25 Silent Doom C .25 .40
LDK2ENK26 The Melody of Awakening Dragon UR 1.25 2.00
LDK2ENK27 Ancient Rules C .50 .80
LDK2ENK28 Tradeln C .60 1.00
LDK2ENK29 Where Art Thou C .60 1.00
LDK2ENK30 Pot of Dichotomy C .25 .40
LDK2ENK31 Fusion Substitute C .25 .40
LDK2ENK32 Unexpected Dai C .60 1.00
LDK2ENK33 Negate Attack C .25 .40
LDK2ENK34 Final Attack Orders C .25 .40
LDK2ENK35 Shadow Spell C .25 .40
LDK2ENK36 Cloning C .25 .40
LDK2ENK37 Fusion Reserve C .25 .40
LDK2ENK38 Jar of Avarice C .25 .40
LDK2ENK39 AzureEyes Silver Dragon C .50 .80
LDK2ENK40 BlueEyes Ultimate Dragon UR .75 1.25
LDK2ENK41 First of the Dragons C .25 .40
LDK2ENS01 Slifer the Sky Dragon UR .75 1.25
LDK2ENS02 Obelisk the Tormentor UR .75 1.25
LDK2ENS03 The Winged Dragon of Ra UR 2.50 4.00
LDK2ENS04 Dark Burning Attack SCR .75 1.25
LDK2ENS05 Dark Burning Magic SCR .75 1.25
LDK2ENS06 Eternal Soul SCR 3.00 5.00
LDK2ENT01 Token (Yugi) UR .75 1.25
LDK2ENT02 Token (Kaiba) UR .75 1.25
LDK2ENT03 Token (Joey) UR .75 1.25
LDK2ENY01 The Legendary Exodia Incarnate UR 2.00 3.00
LDK2ENY02 Ties of the Brethren UR 3.00 5.00
LDK2ENY03 Obliterate UR .75 1.25
LDK2ENY04 Exodia the Forbidden One C 1.00 1.50
LDK2ENY05 Left Arm of the Forbidden One C .60 1.00
LDK2ENY06 Right Arm of the Forbidden One C .60 1.00
LDK2ENY07 Left Leg of the Forbidden One C .60 1.00
LDK2ENY08 Right Leg of the Forbidden One C .60 1.00
LDK2ENY09 Exodia Necross C .25 .40
LDK2ENY10 Dark Magician C .25 .40
LDK2ENY11 Dark Magician Girl C .25 .40
LDK2ENY12 Buster Blader C .25 .40
LDK2ENY13 Silent Magician LV8 C .25 .40
LDK2ENY14 Silent Magician LV4 C .25 .40
LDK2ENY15 The Tricky C .25 .40
LDK2ENY16 Big Shield Gardna C .25 .40
LDK2ENY17 Magician's Valkyria C .25 .40
LDK2ENY18 Blast Magician C .25 .40
LDK2ENY19 Blockman C .25 .40
LDK2ENY20 Marshmallon C .25 .40
LDK2ENY21 Sangan C .25 .40
LDK2ENY22 Gold Sarcophagus C .75 1.00
LDK2ENY23 Swords of Revealing Light C .25 .40
LDK2ENY24 Magical Dimension C .25 .40
LDK2ENY25 Magicians Unite C .25 .40
LDK2ENY26 Tricky Spell 4 C .25 .40
LDK2ENY27 Thousand Knives C .25 .40
LDK2ENY28 Dark Magic Attack C .25 .40
LDK2ENY29 Contract with Exodia C .25 .40
LDK2ENY30 Messenger of Peace C .25 .40
LDK2ENY31 Dark Factory of Mass Production C .25 .40
LDK2ENY32 Monster Reincarnation C .25 .40
LDK2ENY33 Secret Village of the Spellcasters C 1.50 2.00
LDK2ENY34 Pot of Duality C 1.25 2.00
LDK2ENY35 Mirror Force C 1.00 1.50
LDK2ENY36 Magical Hats C .25 .40
LDK2ENY37 Magic Cylinder C .25 .40
LDK2ENY38 Magician's Circle C .25 .40
LDK2ENY39 Backup Soldier C .25 .40
LDK2ENY40 Gravity Bind C .25 .40

2017 Yu-Gi-Oh Legendary Dragon Decks Cyber Dragon Deck 1st Edition

COMPLETE SET (35)
RELEASED ON
LEDDENB00 Chimeratech Megafleet Dragon UR 1.25 2.00
LEDDENB01 Cyber Dragon C .15 .25
LEDDENB02 Cyber Dragon Zwei C .15 .25
LEDDENB03 Cyber Dragon Drei C .15 .25
LEDDENB04 Cyber Dragon Core C .15 .25
LEDDENB05 Proto Cyber Dragon C .15 .25
LEDDENB06 Cyber Valley C .15 .25
LEDDENB07 Cyber Phoenix C .15 .25
LEDDENB08 Cyber Dinosaur C .15 .25
LEDDENB09 Cyber Eltanin C .15 .25
LEDDENB10 Armored Cybern C .15 .25
LEDDENB11 Machina Fortress C .15 .25
LEDDENB12 Cyber Repair Plant C .15 .25
LEDDENB12 Cyber Repair Plant UR 1.25 2.00
LEDDENB13 Cybernetic Fusion Support C .15 .25
LEDDENB14 Evolution Burst C .15 .25
LEDDENB15 Power Bond C .15 .25
LEDDENB16 Overload Fusion C .15 .25
LEDDENB17 Future Fusion C .15 .25
LEDDENB18 Limiter Removal C .15 .25
LEDDENB19 Machina Armored Unit C .15 .25
LEDDENB20 Cyber Network C .15 .25
LEDDENB20 Cyber Network UR 1.25 2.00
LEDDENB21 Cyber Shadow Gardna C .15 .25
LEDDENB22 Storming Mirror Force C .15 .25
LEDDENB23 Quaking Mirror Force C .15 .25
LEDDENB24 Drowning Mirror Force C .15 .25
LEDDENB25 Cyber End Dragon C .15 .25
LEDDENB26 Cyber Twin Dragon C .15 .25
LEDDENB27 Chimeratech Overdragon C .15 .25
LEDDENB28 Chimeratech Fortress Dragon C .15 .25
LEDDENB29 Chimeratech Rampage Dragon C .15 .25
LEDDENB29 Chimeratech Rampage Dragon UR 1.25 2.00
LEDDENB30 Cyber Dragon Nova C .15 .25
LEDDENB31 Cyber Dragon Infinity UR 1.25 2.00

2017 Yu-Gi-Oh Legendary Dragon Decks Dimensional Dragons Deck 1st Edition

COMPLETE SET (36)
RELEASED ON
LEDDENC00 Odd Eyes Arc Pendulum Dragon UR 1.25 2.00
LEDDENC01 Odd Eyes Pendulum Dragon C .15 .25
LEDDENC01 Odd Eyes Pendulum Dragon UR 1.25 2.00
LEDDENC02 Supreme King Dragon Odd Eyes C .15 .25
LEDDENC03 Odd Eyes Phantom Dragon C .15 .25
LEDDENC04 Odd Eyes Persona Dragon C .15 .25
LEDDENC05 Odd Eyes Mirage Dragon C .15 .25
LEDDENC06 Performapal Odd Eyes Light Phoenix C .15 .25
LEDDENC07 Performapal Odd Eyes Unicorn C .15 .25
LEDDENC08 Performapal Skullcrobat Joker C .15 .25
LEDDENC09 Performapal Rain Goat C .15 .25
LEDDENC10 Performapal U Go Golem C .15 .25
LEDDENC11 Nobledragon Magician C .15 .25
LEDDENC12 Odd Eyes Gravity Dragon C .15 .25
LEDDENC13 Sky Iris C .15 .25
LEDDENC14 Odd Eyes Fusion C .15 .25
LEDDENC15 Odd Eyes Advent C .15 .25
LEDDENC16 Spiral Flame Strike C .15 .25
LEDDENC17 Duelist Alliance C .15 .25
LEDDENC18 Pendulum Impenetrable C .15 .25
LEDDENC19 Pendulum Storm C .15 .25
LEDDENC20 Pot of Riches C .15 .25
LEDDENC21 Terraforming C .15 .25
LEDDENC22 Echo Oscillation C .15 .25
LEDDENC23 Pendulum Reborn C .15 .25
LEDDENC24 Pendulum Switch C .15 .25
LEDDENC25 Starving Venom Fusion Dragon UR 1.25 2.00
LEDDENC26 Supreme King Dragon Starving Venom C .15 .25
LEDDENC27 Odd Eyes Vortex Dragon C .15 .25
LEDDENC28 Performapal Gatlinghoul C .15 .25
LEDDENC29 Clear Wing Synchro Dragon UR 1.25 2.00
LEDDENC30 Supreme King Dragon Clear Wing C .15 .25
LEDDENC31 Odd Eyes Meteorburst Dragon C .15 .25
LEDDENC32 Dark Rebellion Xyz Dragon UR 1.25 2.00
LEDDENC33 Supreme King Dragon Dark Rebellion C .15 .25
LEDDENC34 Odd Eyes Absolute Dragon C .15 .25

2017 Yu-Gi-Oh Legendary Dragon Decks Dragons of Atlantis Deck 1st Edition

COMPLETE SET (44)
RELEASED ON
LEDDENA00 Dark Magician the Dragon Knight UR 1.25 2.00
LEDDENA01 Dark Magician C .15 .25
LEDDENA02 Dark Magician Girl C .15 .25
LEDDENA03 Apprentice Illusion Magician UR 1.25 2.00
LEDDENA04 Magicians Robe C .15 .25
LEDDENA05 Magicians Rod C .15 .25
LEDDENA06 Skilled Dark Magician C .15 .25
LEDDENA07 Legendary Knight Timaeus C .15 .25
LEDDENA08 Legendary Knight Critias C .15 .25
LEDDENA09 Legendary Knight Hermos C .15 .25
LEDDENA10 Breaker the Magical Warrior C .15 .25
LEDDENA11 Magical Exemplar C .15 .25
LEDDENA12 Big Shield Gardna C .15 .25
LEDDENA13 Absolute Crusader C .15 .25
LEDDENA14 Dark Magic Curtain C .15 .25
LEDDENA15 Dark Magical Circle UR 1.25 2.00
LEDDENA16 Illusion Magic C .15 .25
LEDDENA17 Dark Magic Expanded C .15 .25
LEDDENA19 Dark Magic Inheritance C .15 .25
LEDDENA19 Thousand Knives C .15 .25
LEDDENA20 Dark Magic Attack C .15 .25
LEDDENA21 The Eye of Timaeus C .15 .25
LEDDENA22 The Fang of Critias C .15 .25
LEDDENA23 The Claw of Hermos C .15 .25
LEDDENA24 Legend of Heart C .15 .25
LEDDENA25 Swords of Revealing Light C .15 .25
LEDDENA26 Pot of Duality C .15 .25
LEDDENA27 Reinforcement of the Army C .15 .25
LEDDENA28 Eternal Soul UR 1.25 2.00

LEDDENA29 Magician Navigation UR	1.25	2.00
LEDDENA30 Dark Renewal C	.15	.25
LEDDENA31 Crush Card Virus C	.15	.25
LEDDENA32 Mirror Force C	.15	.25
LEDDENA33 Tyrant Wing C	.15	.25
LEDDENA34 Dark Paladin C	.15	.25
LEDDENA35 Amulet Dragon C	.15	.25
LEDDENA36 Dark Magician Girl the Dragon Knight C	.15	.25
LEDDENA37 Doom Virus Dragon C	.15	.25
LEDDENA38 Tyrant Burst Dragon C	.15	.25
LEDDENA39 Mirror Force Dragon C	.15	.25
LEDDENA40 Time Magic Hammer C	.15	.25
LEDDENA41 Rocket Hermos Cannon C	.15	.25
LEDDENA42 Goddess Bow C	.15	.25
LEDDENA43 Red Eyes Black Dragon Sword C	.15	.25

Starter Deck

2002 Yu-Gi-Oh Starter Deck Kaiba 1st Edition

COMPLETE SET (50)	80.00	120.00
RELEASED ON MARCH 29, 2002		
SDK1 Blue Eyes White Dragon UR	50.00	100.00
SDK2 Hitotsu-Me Giant C	.20	.50
SDK3 Ryu-Kishin C	.20	.50
SDK4 Wicked Worm Beast C	.20	.50
SDK5 Battle Ox C	.20	.50
SDK6 Koumori Dragon C	.20	.50
SDK7 Judge Man C	.20	.50
SDK8 Rogue Doll C	.20	.50
SDK9 Kojikocy C	.20	.50
SDK10 Uraby C	.20	.50
SDK11 Gyakutenno Megami C	.20	.50
SDK12 Mystic Horseman C	.20	.50
SDK13 Terra the Terrible C	.20	.50
SDK14 Dark Titan of Terror C	.20	.50
SDK15 Dark Assassin C	.50	1.00
SDK16 Master and Expert C	.20	.50
SDK17 Unknown Warrior of Fiend C	.20	.50
SDK18 Mystic Clown C	.20	.50
SDK19 Ogre of Black Shadow C	.20	.50
SDK20 Dark Energy C	.20	.50
SDK21 Invigoration C	.20	.50
SDK22 Dark Hole C	.50	1.00
SDK23 Ookazi C	.20	.50
SDK24 Ryu-Kishin Powered C	.20	.50
SDK25 Swordstalker C	.20	.50
SDK26 La Jinn the Mystical Genie C	1.00	2.00
SDK27 Rude Kaiser C	.50	1.00
SDK28 Destroyer Golem C	.20	.50
SDK29 Skull Red Bird C	.20	.50
SDK30 D. Human C	.20	.50
SDK31 Pale Beast C	.20	.50
SDK32 Fissure C	.50	1.00
SDK33 Trap Hole C	.20	.50
SDK34 Two-Pronged Attack C	.20	.50
SDK35 De-Spell C	.20	.50
SDK36 Monster Reborn C	2.00	4.00
SDK37 Inexperienced Spy C	.20	.50
SDK38 Reinforcements C	.20	.50
SDK39 Ancient Telescope C	.20	.50
SDK40 Just Desserts C	.20	.50
SDK41 Lord of D. SR	1.25	3.00
SDK42 Flute of Summoning Dragon SR	1.25	3.00
SDK43 Mysterious Puppeteer C	.20	.50
SDK44 Trap Master C	.10	.30
SDK45 Sogen C	.20	.50
SDK46 Hane-Hane C	.20	.50
SDK47 Reverse Trap C	.20	.50
SDK48 Reverse Trap C	.20	.50
SDK49 Castle Walls C	.20	.50
SDK50 Ultimate Offering C	.20	.50

2002 Yu-Gi-Oh Starter Deck Kaiba Unlimited

COMPLETE SET (50)	20.00	40.00
SDK1 Blue Eyes White Dragon UR	15.00	30.00
SDK2 Hitotsu-Me Giant C	.20	.40
SDK3 Ryu-Kishin C	.20	.40
SDK4 Wicked Worm Beast C	.20	.40
SDK5 Battle Ox C	.20	.40
SDK6 Koumori Dragon C	.20	.40
SDK7 Judge Man C	.20	.40
SDK8 Rogue Doll C	.20	.40
SDK9 Kojikocy C	.20	.40
SDK10 Uraby C	.20	.40
SDK11 Gyakutenno Megami C	.20	.40
SDK12 Mystic Horseman C	.20	.40
SDK13 Terra the Terrible C	.20	.40
SDK14 Dark Titan of Terror C	.20	.40
SDK15 Dark Assassin C	.50	1.00
SDK16 Master and Expert C	.20	.40
SDK17 Unknown Warrior of Fiend C	.20	.40
SDK18 Mystic Clown C	.20	.40
SDK19 Ogre of Black Shadow C	.20	.40
SDK20 Dark Energy C	.20	.40
SDK21 Invigoration C	.20	.40
SDK22 Dark Hole C	.50	1.00
SDK23 Ookazi C	.20	.40
SDK24 Ryu-Kishin Powered C	.20	.40
SDK25 Swordstalker C	.20	.40
SDK26 La Jinn the Mystical Genie C	1.25	2.50
SDK27 Rude Kaiser C	.50	1.00
SDK28 Destroyer Golem C	.20	.40
SDK29 Skull Red Bird C	.20	.40
SDK30 D. Human C	.20	.40
SDK31 Pale Beast C	.20	.40
SDK32 Fissure C	.50	1.00
SDK33 Trap Hole C	.20	.40
SDK34 Two-Pronged Attack C	.20	.40
SDK35 De-Spell C	.20	.40
SDK36 Monster Reborn C	1.00	2.50
SDK37 Inexperienced Spy C	.20	.40
SDK38 Reinforcements C	.20	.40
SDK39 Ancient Telescope C	.20	.40
SDK40 Just Desserts C	.20	.40
SDK41 Lord of D. SR	1.00	2.50
SDK42 Flute of Summoning Dragon SR	1.00	2.50
SDK43 Mysterious Puppeteer C	.20	.40
SDK44 Trap Master C	.20	.40
SDK45 Sogen C	.20	.40
SDK46 Hane-Hane C	.30	.75
SDK47 Reverse Trap C	.20	.40
SDK48 Reverse Trap C	.20	.40
SDK49 Castle Walls C	.20	.40
SDK50 Ultimate Offering C	.20	.40

2002 Yu-Gi-Oh Starter Deck Yugi 1st Edition

COMPLETE SET (50)	100.00	150.00
RELEASED ON MARCH 29, 2002		
SDY1 Mystical Elf C	.75	2.00
SDY2 Feral Imp C	.75	2.00
SDY3 Winged Dragon Guardian C	.75	2.00
SDY4 Summoned Skull C	.75	2.00
SDY5 Beaver Warrior C	.75	2.00
SDY6 Dark Magician UR	60.00	100.00
SDY7 Gaia The Fierce Knight C	.75	2.00
SDY8 Curse of Dragon C	.75	2.00
SDY9 Celtic Guardian C	.75	2.00
SDY10 Mammoth Graveyard C	.75	2.00
SDY11 Great White C	.75	2.00
SDY12 Silver Fang C	.75	2.00
SDY13 Giant Soldier of Stone C	.75	2.00
SDY14 Dragon Zombie C	.75	2.00
SDY15 Doma Angel of Silence C	.75	2.00
SDY16 Ansatsu C	.75	2.00
SDY17 Witty Phantom C	.75	2.00
SDY18 Claw Reacher C	.75	2.00
SDY19 Mystic Clown C	.75	2.00
SDY20 Sword of Dark Destruction C	.75	2.00
SDY21 Book of Secret Arts C	.75	2.00
SDY22 Dark Hole C	.75	2.00
SDY23 Dian Keto the Cure Master C	.75	2.00
SDY24 Ancient Elf C	.75	2.00
SDY25 Magical Ghost C	.75	2.00
SDY26 Fissure C	.75	2.00
SDY27 Trap Hole C	.75	2.00
SDY28 Two-Pronged Attack C	.75	2.00
SDY29 De-Spell C	.75	2.00
SDY30 Monster Reborn C	.75	2.00
SDY31 Reinforcements C	.75	2.00
SDY32 Change of Heart C	.75	2.00
SDY33 The Stern Mystic C	.75	2.00
SDY34 Wall of Illusion C	.75	2.00
SDY35 Neo the Magic Swordsman C	.75	2.00
SDY36 Baron of Fiend Sword C	.75	2.00
SDY37 Man-Eating Treasure Chest C	.75	2.00
SDY38 Sorcerer of the Doomed C	.75	2.00
SDY39 Last Will C	.75	2.00
SDY40 Waboku C	.75	2.00
SDY41 Soul Exchange SR	2.50	6.00
SDY42 Card Destruction SR	.75	2.00
SDY43 Trap Master C	.75	2.00
SDY44 Dragon Capture Jar C	.75	2.00
SDY45 Yami C	.75	2.00
SDY46 Man-Eater Bug C	.75	2.00
SDY47 Reverse Trap C	.75	2.00
SDY48 Remove Trap C	.75	2.00
SDY49 Castle Walls C	.75	2.00
SDY50 Ultimate Offering C	.75	2.00

2002 Yu-Gi-Oh Starter Deck Yugi Unlimited

COMPLETE SET (50)	30.00	60.00
SDY1 Mystical Elf C	.50	1.00
SDY2 Feral Imp C	.50	1.00
SDY3 Winged Dragon Guardian C	.50	1.00
SDY4 Summoned Skull C	.50	1.00
SDY5 Beaver Warrior C	.50	1.00
SDY6 Dark Magician UR	8.00	20.00
SDY7 Gaia The Fierce Knight C	.50	1.00
SDY8 Curse of Dragon C	.50	1.00
SDY9 Celtic Guardian C	.50	1.00
SDY10 Mammoth Graveyard C	.50	1.00
SDY11 Great White C	.50	1.00
SDY12 Silver Fang C	.50	1.00
SDY13 Giant Soldier of Stone C	.50	1.00
SDY14 Dragon Zombie C	.50	1.00
SDY15 Doma Angel of Silence C	.50	1.00
SDY16 Ansatsu C	.50	1.00
SDY17 Witty Phantom C	.50	1.00
SDY18 Claw Reacher C	.50	1.00
SDY19 Mystic Clown C	.50	1.00
SDY20 Sword of Dark Destruction C	.50	1.00
SDY21 Book of Secret Arts C	.50	1.00
SDY22 Dark Hole C	.50	1.00
SDY23 Dian Keto the Cure Master C	.50	1.00
SDY24 Ancient Elf C	.50	1.00
SDY25 Magical Ghost C	.50	1.00
SDY26 Fissure C	.50	1.00
SDY27 Trap Hole C	.50	1.00
SDY28 Two-Pronged Attack C	.50	1.00
SDY29 De-Spell C	.50	1.00
SDY30 Monster Reborn C	.50	1.00
SDY31 Reinforcements C	.50	1.00
SDY32 Change of Heart C	.50	1.00
SDY33 The Stern Mystic C	.50	1.00
SDY34 Wall of Illusion C	.50	1.00
SDY35 Neo the Magic Swordsman C	.50	1.00
SDY36 Baron of Fiend Sword C	.50	1.00
SDY37 Man-Eating Treasure Chest C	.50	1.00
SDY38 Sorcerer of the Doomed C	.50	1.00
SDY39 Last Will C	.50	1.00
SDY40 Waboku C	.50	1.00
SDY41 Soul Exchange SR	.75	2.00
SDY42 Card Destruction SR	.75	2.00
SDY43 Trap Master C	.50	1.00
SDY44 Dragon Capture Jar C	.50	1.00
SDY45 Yami C	.50	1.00
SDY46 Man-Eater Bug C	.50	1.00
SDY47 Reverse Trap C	.50	1.00
SDY48 Remove Trap C	.50	1.00
SDY49 Castle Walls C	.50	1.00
SDY50 Ultimate Offering C	.50	1.00

2003 Yu-Gi-Oh Starter Deck Joey 1st Edition

COMPLETE SET (50)	30.00	50.00
RELEASED ON MARCH 30, 2003		
SDJ1 Red-Eyes B. Dragon UR	8.00	20.00
SDJ2 Swordsman of Landstar C	.60	1.50
SDJ3 Baby Dragon C	.60	1.50
SDJ4 Spirit of the Harp C	.60	1.50
SDJ5 Island Turtle C	.60	1.50
SDJ6 Flame Manipulator C	.60	1.50
SDJ7 Masaki The Legendary Swordsman C	.60	1.50
SDJ8 7 Colored Fish C	.60	1.50
SDJ9 Armored Lizard C	.60	1.50
SDJ10 Darkfire Soldier #1 C	.60	1.50
SDJ11 Harpie's Brother C	.60	1.50
SDJ12 Gearfried the Iron Knight C	.60	1.50
SDJ13 Karate Man C	.60	1.50
SDJ14 Milus Radiant C	.60	1.50
SDJ15 Time Wizard C	.60	1.50
SDJ16 Maha Vailo C	.60	1.50
SDJ17 Magician of Faith C	.60	1.50
SDJ18 Big Eye C	.60	1.50
SDJ19 Sangan C	.60	1.50
SDJ20 Princess of Tsurugi C	.60	1.50
SDJ21 White Magical Hat C	.60	1.50
SDJ22 Penguin Soldier SR	.60	1.50
SDJ23 Thousand Dragon C	.60	1.50
SDJ24 Flame Swordsman C	.60	1.50
SDJ25 Malevolent Nuzzler C	.60	1.50
SDJ26 Dark Hole C	.60	1.50
SDJ27 Dian Keto C	.60	1.50
SDJ28 Fissure C	.60	1.50
SDJ29 De-Spell C	.60	1.50
SDJ30 Change of Heart C	.60	1.50
SDJ31 Block Attack C	.60	1.50
SDJ32 Giant Trunade C	.60	1.50
SDJ33 The Reliable Guardian C	.60	1.50
SDJ34 Remove Trap C	.60	1.50
SDJ35 Monster Reborn C	.60	1.50
SDJ36 Polymerization C	.60	1.50
SDJ37 Mountain C	.60	1.50
SDJ38 Dragon Treasure C	.60	1.50
SDJ39 Eternal Rest C	.60	1.50
SDJ40 Shield & Sword C	.60	1.50
SDJ41 Scapegoat SR	.60	1.50
SDJ42 Just Desserts C	.60	1.50
SDJ43 Trap Hole C	.60	1.50
SDJ44 Reinforcements C	.60	1.50
SDJ45 Castle Walls C	.60	1.50
SDJ46 Waboku C	.60	1.50
SDJ47 Ultimate Offering C	.60	1.50
SDJ48 Seven Tools of the Bandit C	.60	1.50
SDJ49 Fake Trap C	.60	1.50
SDJ50 Reverse Trap C	.60	1.50

2003 Yu-Gi-Oh Starter Deck Pegasus 1st Edition

COMPLETE SET (50)	20.00	40.00
RELEASED ON MARCH 30, 2003		
SDP1 Relinquished UR	3.00	8.00
SDP2 Red Archery Girl C	.20	.50
SDP3 Ryu-Ran C	.20	.50
SDP4 Illusionist Faceless Mage C	.20	.50
SDP5 Rogue Doll C	.20	.50
SDP6 Uraby C	.20	.50
SDP7 Giant Soldier of Stone C	.20	.50
SDP8 Aqua Madoor C	.20	.50
SDP9 Toon Alligator C	.75	2.00
SDP10 Hane-Hane C	.20	.50
SDP11 Sonic Bird C	.20	.50
SDP12 Jigen Bakudan C	.20	.50
SDP13 Mask of Darkness C	.20	.50
SDP14 Witch of the Black Forest C	.20	.50
SDP15 Man-Eater Bug C	.20	.50
SDP16 Muka Muka C	.20	.50
SDP17 Dream Clown C	.20	.50
SDP18 Armed Ninja C	.20	.50
SDP19 Hiro's Shadow C	.20	.50
SDP20 Blue-Eyes Toon Dragon C	.50	1.00
SDP21 Toon Summoned Skull C	.20	.50
SDP22 Manga Ryu-Ran C	.20	.50
SDP23 Toon Mermaid C	.20	1.00
SDP24 Toon World C	1.00	2.00
SDP25 Black Pendant C	.20	.50
SDP26 Dark Hole C	.20	1.00
SDP27 Dian Keto The Cure Master C	.20	.50
SDP28 Fissure C	.20	.50
SDP29 De-Spell C	.20	.50
SDP30 Change of Heart C	.20	.50
SDP31 Stop Defense C	.20	.50
SDP32 Mystical Space Typhoon C	.20	.50
SDP33 Rush Recklessly C	.20	.50
SDP34 Remove Trap C	.20	.50
SDP35 Monster Reborn C	.50	1.00
SDP36 Soul Release C	.20	.50
SDP37 Yami C	.20	.50
SDP38 Black Illusion Ritual C	.20	.50
SDP39 Ring of Magnetism C	.20	.50
SDP40 Graceful Charity SR	1.50	4.00
SDP41 Trap Hole C	.20	.50
SDP42 Reinforcements C	.20	.50
SDP43 Castle Walls C	.20	.50
SDP44 Waboku C	.20	.50
SDP45 Seven Tools of the Bandit C	.20	.50
SDP46 Ultimate Offering C	.20	.50
SDP47 Robbin Gobblin C	.20	.50
SDP48 Magic Jammer C	.20	.50
SDP49 Enchanted Javelin C	.20	.50
SDP50 Gryphon Wing SR	.50	1.00

2008 Yu-Gi-Oh Starter Deck 5D's 1st Edition

COMPLETE SET (43)		
RELEASED ON AUGUST 5, 2008		
5DS1-EN001 Tune Warrior C	.20	.75
5DS1-EN002 Water Spirit C	.20	.75
5DS1-EN003 Axe Raider C	.20	.75
5DS1-EN004 Dark Blade C	.20	.75

5DS1-EN005 Charcoal Inpachi C	.20	.75
5DS1-EN006 Woodborg Inpachi C	.20	.75
5DS1-EN007 Spiral Serpent C	.20	.75
5DS1-EN008 Renge, Gatekeeper of Dark World C	.20	.75
5DS1-EN009 Atlantean Pikeman C	.20	.75
5DS1-EN010 Sonic Chick C	.20	.75
5DS1-EN011 Junk Synchron C	.20	.75
5DS1-EN012 Speed Warrior C	.20	.75
5DS1-EN013 Magna Drago C	.20	.75
5DS1-EN014 Frequency Magician C	.20	.75
5DS1-EN015 Copycat C	.20	.75
5DS1-EN016 UFO Turtle C	.20	.75
5DS1-EN017 Mystic Tomato C	.20	.75
5DS1-EN018 Marauding Captain C	.20	.75
5DS1-EN019 Exiled Force C	.20	.75
5DS1-EN020 Synchro Boost C	.20	.75
5DS1-EN021 Synchro Blast Wave C	.20	.75
5DS1-EN022 Synchronized Realm C	.20	.75
5DS1-EN023 The Warrior Returning Alive C	.20	.75
5DS1-EN024 Smashing Ground C	.20	.75
5DS1-EN025 Rush Recklessly C	.20	.75
5DS1-EN026 Monster Reincarnation C	.20	.75
5DS1-EN027 Lightning Vortex C	.20	.75
5DS1-EN028 Twister C	.20	.75
5DS1-EN029 Double Summon C	.75	2.00
5DS1-EN030 Symbols of Duty C	.20	.75
5DS1-EN031 Threatening Roar C	.20	.75
5DS1-EN032 Scrap-Iron Scarecrow C	.20	.75
5DS1-EN033 Miniaturize C	.20	.75
5DS1-EN034 Spellbinding Circle C	.20	.75
5DS1-EN035 Backup Soldier C	.20	.75
5DS1-EN036 Trap Hole C	.20	.75
5DS1-EN037 Sakuretsu Armor C	.20	.75
5DS1-EN038 Divine Wrath C	.20	.75
5DS1-EN039 Seven Tools of the Bandit C	.20	.75
5DS1-EN040 Birthright C	.20	.75
5DS1-EN041 Junk Warrior UR	.20	.75
5DS1-EN042 Gaia Knight, the Force of Earth SR	.20	.75
5DS1-EN043 Colossal Fighter SR	.20	.75

2012 Yu-Gi-Oh Starter Deck Xyz Symphony 1st Edition

COMPLETE SET (43)	4.00	8.00
STARTER DECK	6.00	12.00
RELEASED ON APRIL 17, 2012		
YS12001 Alexandrite Dragon	.10	.30
YS12002 Spirit of the Harp	.10	.30
YS12003 Frostosaurus	.10	.30
YS12004 Zubaba Knight	.10	.30
YS12005 Ganbara Knight	.10	.30
YS12006 Gogogo Golem	.10	.30
YS12007 Gogogo Giant	.10	.30
YS12008 Goblindbergh	.40	1.00
YS12009 Feedback Warrior	.10	.30
YS12010 Shine Knight	.10	.30
YS12011 Cyber Dragon	.20	.60
YS12012 Trident Warrior	.10	.30
YS12013 Chiron the Mage	.10	.30
YS12014 Marauding Captain	.10	.30
YS12015 Penguin Soldier	.10	.30
YS12016 Sangan	.20	.60
YS12017 Giant Rat	.10	.30
YS12018 Shining Angel	.10	.30
YS12019 Blustering Winds	.10	.30
YS12020 Ego Boost	.10	.30
YS12021 Xyz Energy	.10	.30
YS12022 Star Changer	.10	.30
YS12023 Swords of Revealing Light	.10	.30
YS12024 Mystical Space Typhoon	.40	1.00
YS12025 Fissure	.10	.30
YS12026 Gravity Axe - Grarl	.10	.30
YS12027 Reinforcement of the Army	.20	.60
YS12028 Burden of the Mighty	.10	.30
YS12029 Heartfelt Appeal	.10	.30
YS12030 Xyz Effect	.10	.30
YS12031 Raigeki Break	.10	.30
YS12032 Trap Hole	.10	.30
YS12033 Dust Tornado	.10	.30
YS12034 Magic Cylinder	.40	1.00
YS12035 Draining Shield	.40	1.00
YS12036 Call of the Haunted	.10	.30
YS12037 Limit Reverse	.10	.30
YS12038 Seven Tools of the Bandit	.10	.30
YS12039 Number 39: Utopia UR	.75	2.00
YS12040 Muzurhythm the String Djinn SR	.10	.30
YS12041 Temtempo the Percussion Djinn SR	.10	.30
YS12042 Melomelody the Brass Djinn (SR)	.10	.30
YS12043 Maestroke the Symphony Djinn SR	.40	1.00

2013 Yu-Gi-Oh Super Starter Deck V For Victory 1st Edition

COMPLETE SET (42)		
STRUCTURE DECK	6.00	12.00
RELEASED ON JUNE 14, 2013		
YS13001 Cosmo Queen C	.10	.30
YS13002 Trance the Magic Swordsman C	.10	.30
YS13003 Neo the Magic Swordsman C	.10	.30
YS13004 Mystical Elf C	.10	.30
YS13005 Chamberlain of the Six Samurai C	.10	.30
YS13006 Gagaga Child C	.50	1.25
YS13007 Magical Undertaker C	.10	.30
YS13008 Caligo Claw Crow C	.10	.30
YS13009 Gagaga Magician C	.10	.30
YS13010 Gagaga Girl C	.10	.30
YS13011 Gagaga Gardna C	.10	.30
YS13012 Zubaba Knight C	.10	.30
YS13013 Ganbara Knight C	.10	.30
YS13014 Achacha Archer C	.10	.30
YS13015 Goblindbergh C	.10	.30
YS13016 Kagetokage C	.20	.60
YS13017 Tasuke Knight C	.10	.30
YS13018 ZW - Unicorn Spear C	.10	.30
YS13019 Marauding Captain C	.10	.30
YS13020 Old Vindictive Magician C	.10	.30
YS13021 Swords of Burning Light C	.10	.30
YS13022 Blustering Winds C	.10	.30
YS13023 Wonder Wand C	.20	.60
YS13024 Double or Nothing C	.10	.30
YS13025 Ego Boost C	.10	.30
YS13026 Gagagarevenge C	.20	.60
YS13027 Xyz Unit C	.10	.30
YS13028 The A. Forces C	.10	.30
YS13029 Reinforcement of the Army C	.10	.30
YS13030 The Warrior Returning Alive C	.10	.30
YS13031 Puzzle Reborn C	.10	.30
YS13032 Gagagashield C	.10	.30
YS13033 Copy Knight C	.10	.30
YS13034 Impenetrable Attack C	.10	.30
YS13035 Utopian Aura C	.10	.30
YS13036 Xyz Effect C	.10	.30
YS13037 Shadow Spell C	.10	.30
YS13038 Dust Tornado C	.10	.30
YS13039 Call of the Haunted C	.10	.30
YS13040 Dark Bribe C	.75	2.00
YS13041 Number 39: Utopia SR	.60	1.50
YS13042 Number C39: Utopia Ray UR	.25	.75

2013 Yu-Gi-Oh Super Starter Deck V For Victory 1st Edition Power-Up Pack

TWO PACKS PER STARTER DECK		
YS13V01 Number C39: Utopia Ray V UR	.10	.30
YS13V02 Rank-Up-Magic Limited Barian's Force UR	.10	.30
YS13V03 ZW - Eagle Claw C	.10	.30
YS13V04 Ganbara Lancer C	.10	.30
YS13V05 Bite Bug C	.10	.30
YS13V06 Crane Crane C	.10	.30
YS13V07 Gentlemander C	.10	.30
YS13V08 Grenosaurus C	.10	.30
YS13V09 Number 30: Acid Golem of Destruction C	.40	1.00
YS13V10 Shining Elf C	.10	.30
YS13V11 Number 6: Chronomaly Atlandis C	.20	.60
YS13V12 Mystical Space Typhoon SR	1.00	2.50
YS13V13 Swords of Revealing Light SR	.40	1.00
YS13V14 Mirror Force SR	1.00	2.50
YS13V15 Magic Cylinder SR	.50	1.25

2013 Yu-Gi-Oh Starter Deck Kaiba Reloaded 1st Edition

COMPLETE SET (49)		
RELEASED ON DECEMBER 6, 2013		
YSKREN001 Blue Eyes White Dragon UTR	2.00	3.00
YSKREN001 Blue Eyes White Dragon C	.50	.80
YSKREN002 Aqua Madoor C	.15	.25
YSKREN003 La Jinn the Mystical Genie of the Lamp C	.15	.25
YSKREN004 Battle Ox C	.15	.25
YSKREN005 Opticlops C	.15	.25
YSKREN006 The Dragon Dwelling in the Cave C	.15	.25
YSKREN007 Luster Dragon C	.15	.25
YSKREN008 X Head Cannon C	.15	.25
YSKREN009 Mad Dog of Darkness C	.15	.25
YSKREN010 Vorse Raider C	.15	.25
YSKREN011 Alexandrite Dragon C	.15	.25
YSKREN012 Wattaildragon C	.15	.25
YSKREN013 Twin Headed Behemoth C	.15	.25
YSKREN014 Yomi Ship C	.15	.25
YSKREN015 Des Feral Imp C	.15	.25
YSKREN016 Kaiser Sea Horse C	.15	.25
YSKREN017 Chaos Necromancer C	.15	.25
YSKREN018 Blade Knight C	.15	.25
YSKREN019 Horus the Black Flame Dragon LV4 C	.50	.80
YSKREN020 Horus the Black Flame Dragon LV6 C	.50	.80
YSKREN021 Cybernetic Cyclopean C	.15	.25
YSKREN022 Puppet Plant C	.15	.25
YSKREN023 Des Mosquito C	.15	.25
YSKREN024 Tiger Dragon C	.15	.25
YSKREN025 Vanguard of the Dragon C	.15	.25
YSKREN026 Divine Dragon Apocralyph C	.15	.25
YSKREN027 Interplanetarypurplythorny Dragon C	.15	.25
YSKREN028 Dark Hole C	.75	1.25
YSKREN029 Soul Exchange C	.15	.25
YSKREN030 Tribute to The Doomed C	.15	.25
YSKREN031 Rush Recklessly C	.15	.25
YSKREN032 Mystical Space Typhoon C	.15	.25
YSKREN033 Offerings to the Doomed C	.15	.25
YSKREN034 Stamping Destruction C	.15	.25
YSKREN035 Enemy Controller C	.15	.25
YSKREN036 Burst Stream of Destruction C	.15	.25
YSKREN037 Shrink C	.15	.25
YSKREN038 Shield Crush C	.15	.25
YSKREN039 Silent Doom C	.15	.25
YSKREN040 Dragonic Tactics C	.15	.25
YSKREN041 Shard of Greed C	.15	.25
YSKREN042 Trap Hole C	.15	.25
YSKREN043 Sakuretsu Armor C	.15	.25
YSKREN044 Shadow Spell C	.15	.25
YSKREN045 Widespread Ruin C	.15	.25
YSKREN046 Threatening Roar C	.15	.25
YSKREN047 Birthright C	.15	.25
YSKREN048 Damage Gate C	.15	.25

2013 Yu-Gi-Oh Starter Deck Kaiba Reloaded Unlimited

COMPLETE SET (49)		
BOOSTER BOX		
BOOSTER PACK		
RELEASED ON		
YSKREN001 Blue Eyes White Dragon UTR	2.00	3.00
YSKREN001 Blue Eyes White Dragon C	.50	.80
YSKREN002 Aqua Madoor C	.15	.25
YSKREN003 La Jinn the Mystical Genie of the Lamp C	.15	.25
YSKREN004 Battle Ox C	.15	.25
YSKREN005 Opticlops C	.15	.25
YSKREN006 The Dragon Dwelling in the Cave C	.15	.25
YSKREN007 Luster Dragon C	.15	.25
YSKREN008 X Head Cannon C	.15	.25
YSKREN009 Mad Dog of Darkness C	.15	.25
YSKREN010 Vorse Raider C	.15	.25
YSKREN011 Alexandrite Dragon C	.15	.25
YSKREN012 Wattaildragon C	.15	.25
YSKREN013 Twin Headed Behemoth C	.15	.25
YSKREN014 Yomi Ship C	.15	.25
YSKREN015 Des Feral Imp C	.15	.25
YSKREN016 Kaiser Sea Horse C	.15	.25
YSKREN017 Chaos Necromancer C	.15	.25
YSKREN018 Blade Knight C	.15	.25
YSKREN019 Horus the Black Flame Dragon LV4 C	.50	.80
YSKREN020 Horus the Black Flame Dragon LV6 C	.50	.80
YSKREN021 Cybernetic Cyclopean C	.15	.25
YSKREN022 Puppet Plant C	.15	.25
YSKREN023 Des Mosquito C	.15	.25
YSKREN024 Tiger Dragon C	.15	.25
YSKREN025 Vanguard of the Dragon C	.15	.25
YSKREN026 Divine Dragon Apocralyph C	.15	.25
YSKREN027 Interplanetarypurplythorny Dragon C	.15	.25
YSKREN028 Dark Hole C	.75	1.25
YSKREN029 Soul Exchange C	.15	.25
YSKREN030 Tribute to The Doomed C	.15	.25
YSKREN031 Rush Recklessly C	.15	.25
YSKREN032 Mystical Space Typhoon C	.15	.25
YSKREN033 Offerings to the Doomed C	.15	.25
YSKREN034 Stamping Destruction C	.15	.25
YSKREN035 Enemy Controller C	.15	.25
YSKREN036 Burst Stream of Destruction C	.15	.25
YSKREN037 Shrink C	.15	.25
YSKREN038 Shield Crush C	.15	.25
YSKREN039 Silent Doom C	.15	.25
YSKREN040 Dragonic Tactics C	.15	.25
YSKREN041 Shard of Greed C	.15	.25
YSKREN042 Trap Hole C	.15	.25
YSKREN043 Sakuretsu Armor C	.15	.25
YSKREN044 Shadow Spell C	.15	.25
YSKREN045 Widespread Ruin C	.15	.25
YSKREN046 Threatening Roar C	.15	.25
YSKREN047 Birthright C	.15	.25
YSKREN048 Damage Gate C	.15	.25

2013 Yu-Gi-Oh Starter Deck Yugi Reloaded 1st Edition

COMPLETE SET (47)		
RELEASED ON DECEMBER 6, 2013		
YSYREN001 Dark Magician UTR	1.25	2.00
YSYREN001 Dark Magician C	.15	.25
YSYREN002 Mystical Elf C	.15	.25
YSYREN003 Giant Soldier of Stone C	.15	.25
YSYREN004 Summoned Skull C	.15	.25
YSYREN005 Neo the Magic Swordsman C	.15	.25
YSYREN006 Gemini Elf C	.15	.25
YSYREN007 Dark Blade C	.15	.25
YSYREN008 Kuriboh C	.15	.25
YSYREN009 Buster Blader C	.15	.25
YSYREN010 4-Starred Ladybug of Doom C	.15	.25
YSYREN011 Dark Magician Girl C	.15	.25
YSYREN012 Skilled White Magician C	.15	.25
YSYREN013 Skilled Dark Magician C	.15	.25
YSYREN014 Old Vindictive Magician C	.15	.25
YSYREN015 Breaker the Magical Warrior C	.15	.25
YSYREN016 Double Coston C	.15	.25
YSYREN017 Silent Swordsman LV3 C	.15	.25
YSYREN018 Silent Swordsman LV5 C	.15	.25
YSYREN019 Green Gadget C	.15	.25
YSYREN020 Red Gadget C	.15	.25
YSYREN021 Yellow Gadget C	.15	.25
YSYREN022 Electric Virus C	.15	.25
YSYREN023 Magician's Valkyria C	.60	1.00
YSYREN024 The Tricky C	.15	.25
YSYREN025 Dark Hole C	.15	.25
YSYREN026 Swords of Revealing Light C	.15	.25
YSYREN027 Black Pendant C	.15	.25
YSYREN028 Mystical Space Typhoon C	.15	.25
YSYREN029 Mage Power C	.15	.25
YSYREN030 Book of Moon C	.15	.25
YSYREN031 Thousand Knives C	.15	.25
YSYREN032 Dark Magic Attack C	.15	.25
YSYREN033 Magical Dimension C	.15	.25
YSYREN034 Ancient Rules C	.15	.25
YSYREN035 Magicians Unite C	.15	.25
YSYREN036 Soul Taker C	.15	.25
YSYREN037 Shard of Greed C	.15	.25
YSYREN038 Trap Hole C	.15	.25
YSYREN039 Waboku C	.15	.25
YSYREN040 Mirror Force C	.15	.25
YSYREN041 Spellbinding Circle C	.15	.25
YSYREN042 Call of the Haunted C	.15	.25
YSYREN043 Magic Cylinder C	.15	.25
YSYREN044 Miracle Restoring C	.15	.25
YSYREN045 Zero Gravity C	.15	.25
YSYREN046 Rising Energy C	.15	.25

2014 Yu-Gi-Oh Super Starter Deck Space-Time Showdown 1st Edition

COMPLETE SET (40)	8.00	12.00
RELEASED ON JULY 11, 2014		
YS14EN001 Wattaildragon C	.15	.25
YS14EN002 Luster Dragon C	.15	.25
YS14EN003 Hunter Dragon C	.20	.30
YS14EN004 Millennium Shield C	.15	.25
YS14EN005 Dark Blade C	.15	.25
YS14EN006 Warrior Dai Grepher C	.15	.25
YS14EN007 Chamberlain of the Six Samurai C	.15	.25
YS14EN008 Mystical Elf C	.15	.25
YS14EN009 Stargazer Magician SR	.25	.40
YS14EN010 Timegazer Magician SR	.40	.60
YS14EN011 Aether, the Empowering Dragon C	.15	.25
YS14EN012 Ventdra, the Empowered Warrior C	.15	.25
YS14EN013 Arnis, the Empowered Warrior C	.15	.25
YS14EN014 Terratiger, the Empowered Warrior C	.15	.25
YS14EN015 Hydrotortoise, the Empowered Warrior C	.15	.25
YS14EN016 Golden Dragon Summoner C	.15	.25
YS14EN017 Blue Dragon Summoner C	1.00	1.50
YS14EN018 Red Sparrow Summoner C	.15	.25
YS14EN019 White Tiger Summoner C	.15	.25
YS14EN020 Green Turtle Summoner C	.15	.25
YS14EN021 Sorcerous Spell Wall C	.15	.25
YS14EN022 Supply Squad C	.35	.50
YS14EN023 Lightning Vortex C	.60	1.00
YS14EN024 Mystical Space Typhoon C	.20	.30
YS14EN025 Ego Boost C	.15	.25
YS14EN026 Axe of Despair C	.40	.60
YS14EN027 Lucky Iron Axe C	.15	.25
YS14EN028 Monster Reincarnation C	.15	.25

YS14EN029 Dark Factory of Mass Production C	.35	.50
YS14EN030 Poison of the Old Man C	.35	.50
YS14EN031 Trap Hole C	.15	.25
YS14EN032 Sakuretsu Armor C	.25	.40
YS14EN033 Raigeki Break C	.15	.25
YS14EN034 Dust Tornado C	.15	.25
YS14EN035 Shadow Spell C	.15	.25
YS14EN036 A Hero Emerges C	.15	.25
YS14EN037 Soul Resurrection C	.15	.25
YS14EN038 Jar of Greed C	.35	.50
YS14EN039 Magic Jammer C	.20	.30
YS14EN040 Seven Tools of the Bandit C	.15	.25

2014 Yu-Gi-Oh Super Starter Deck Space-Time Showdown 1st Edition Power-Up Pack

COMPLETE SET (15)	5.00	8.00
RELEASED ON JULY 11, 2014		
YS14ENA01 Odd-Eyes Dragon UR	.25	.40
YS14ENA02 Des Volstgalph C	.15	.25
YS14ENA03 Kuraz the Light Monarch C	3.00	5.00
YS14ENA04 D.D. Warrior Lady C	.20	.30
YS14ENA05 Sacred Crane C	.15	.25
YS14ENA06 Amazoness Sage C	.15	.25
YS14ENA07 Injection Fairy Lily C	.15	.25
YS14ENA08 The A. Forces C	.15	.25
YS14ENA09 Reinforcement of the Army C	.15	.25
YS14ENA10 Dark Hole UR	.50	.75
YS14ENA11 Swords of Revealing Light C	.15	.25
YS14ENA12 Mirror Force C	.40	.60
YS14ENA13 Call of the Haunted C	.15	.25
YS14ENA14 Magic Cylinder C	.60	1.00
YS14ENA15 Divine Wrath C	.25	.40

2016 Yu-Gi-Oh Starter Deck Yuya 1st Edition

COMPLETE SET (43)	10.00	20.00
STARTER DECK	8.00	12.00
RELEASED ON MAY 27, 2016		
YS16EN001 Performapal Sleight Hand Magician UR	.30	.50
YS16EN002 Performapal King Bear UR	.30	.50
YS16EN003 Performapal Swincobra C	.10	.30
YS16EN004 Performapal Momoncarpet SR	.20	.30
YS16EN005 Performapal Parrotrio SR	.30	.45
YS16EN006 Performapal Longphone Bull SR	.20	.30
YS16EN007 Performapal Teeter Totter Hopper C	.10	.30
YS16EN008 Odd-Eyes Pendulum Dragon C	.10	.30
YS16EN009 Stargazer Magician C	.10	.30
YS16EN010 Timegazer Magician C	.10	.30
YS16EN011 Performapal Drummerilla C	.10	.30
YS16EN012 Performapal Secondonkey C	.10	.30
YS16EN013 Performapal Hip Hippo C	.10	.30
YS16EN014 Foucault's Cannon C	.10	.30
YS16EN015 Archfiend Eccentrick C	3.00	4.50
YS16EN016 Gene-Warped Warwolf C	.10	.30
YS16EN017 Beast King Barbaros C	.10	.30
YS16EN018 Pitch-Black Warwolf C	.10	.30
YS16EN019 Dragon Dowser C	.10	.30
YS16EN020 Giant Rat C	.10	.30
YS16EN021 Performapal Dramatic Theater C	.10	.30
YS16EN022 Smile World C	.10	.30
YS16EN023 Hippo Carnival C	.10	.30
YS16EN024 Draw Muscle C	.10	.30
YS16EN025 Mystical Space Typhoon C	.50	.75
YS16EN026 Lightning Vortex C	.10	.30
YS16EN027 Book of Moon C	.10	.30
YS16EN028 Lucky Iron Axe C	.10	.30
YS16EN029 Burden of the Mighty C	.10	.30
YS16EN030 Back-Up Rider C	.10	.30
YS16EN031 Performapal Show Down C	.10	.30
YS16EN032 Performapal Pinch Helper C	.10	.30
YS16EN033 Wall of Disruption C	.10	.30
YS16EN034 Ceasefire C	.10	.30
YS16EN035 Raigeki Break C	.10	.30
YS16EN036 Draining Shield C	.10	.30
YS16EN037 Threatening Roar C	.10	.30
YS16EN038 Dark Bribe C	1.25	1.75
YS16EN039 Chaos Burst C	.10	.30
YS16EN040 Pendulum Reborn C	.10	.30
YS16ENT01 Hippo Token Orange T	.10	.30
YS16ENT02 Hippo Token Yellow T	.10	.30
YS16ENT03 Hippo Token Blue T	.10	.30

2017 Yu-Gi-Oh Starter Deck Link Strike 1st Edition

COMPLETE SET (43)	10.00	15.00
RELEASED ON JULY 21, 2017		
YS17EN001 Bitron C	.40	.60
YS17EN002 Draconnet C	.40	.60
YS17EN003 RAM Clouder SR	2.00	3.00
YS17EN004 Linkslayer UR	2.00	3.50
YS17EN005 Galaxy Serpent C	.40	.60
YS17EN006 Mystery Shell Dragon C	.40	.60
YS17EN007 Beast King Barbaros C	.40	.60
YS17EN008 Cyber Dragon C	.40	.60
YS17EN009 Photon Thrasher C	.40	.60
YS17EN010 Exarion Universe C	.40	.60
YS17EN011 Evilswarm Mandragora C	.40	.60
YS17EN012 Marauding Captain C	.40	.60
YS17EN013 Sangan C	.40	.60
YS17EN014 Kuribandit C	.40	.60
YS17EN015 Marshmallon C	.40	.60
YS17EN016 Cardcar D C	.40	.60
YS17EN017 Ryko Lightsworn Hunter C	.40	.60
YS17EN018 Battle Fader C	.40	.60
YS17EN019 Swift Scarecrow C	.40	.60
YS17EN020 Effect Veiler C	.40	.60
YS17EN021 Cynet Universe C	.40	.60
YS17EN022 Monster Reincarnation C	.40	.60
YS17EN023 Dark Hole C	.40	.60
YS17EN024 Mystical Space Typhoon C	.40	.60
YS17EN025 Book of Moon C	.40	.60
YS17EN026 Forbidden Lance C	.40	.60
YS17EN027 United We Stand C	.40	.60
YS17EN028 Pot of Duality C	.40	.60
YS17EN029 Burden of the Mighty C	.40	.60
YS17EN030 Supply Squad C	.40	.60
YS17EN031 Terraforming C	.40	.60
YS17EN032 Jar of Avarice C	.40	.60
YS17EN033 Call of the Haunted C	.40	.60
YS17EN034 Mirror Force C	.40	.60
YS17EN035 Torrential Tribute C	.40	.60
YS17EN036 Ring of Destruction C	.40	.60
YS17EN037 Bottomless Trap Hole C	.40	.60
YS17EN038 Compulsory Evacuation Device C	.40	.60
YS17EN039 Fiendish Chain C	.40	.60
YS17EN040 Dark Bribe C	.40	.60
YS17EN041 Decode Talker UR	3.00	5.00
YS17EN042 Honeybot SR	2.50	4.00
YS17EN043 Link Spider SR	3.00	5.00

2018 Yu-Gi-Oh Starter Deck Codebreaker 1st Edition

COMPLETE SET (45)	10.00	15.00
RELEASED ON JULY 13, 2018		
YS18-EN001 Leotron C	.15	.25
YS18-EN002 Texchanger C	.15	.25
YS18-EN003 Widget Kid SR	.60	1.00
YS18-EN004 Cyberse White Hat UR	.60	1.00
YS18-EN005 Bitron C	.15	.25
YS18-EN006 RAM Clouder C	.15	.25
YS18-EN007 Linkslayer C	.15	.25
YS18-EN008 Backup Secretary C	.15	.25
YS18-EN009 Launcher Commander C	.15	.25
YS18-EN010 Cliant C	.15	.25
YS18-EN011 Bitrooper C	.15	.25
YS18-EN012 Flamvell Guard C	.15	.25
YS18-EN013 Beast King Barbaros C	.15	.25
YS18-EN014 Cyber Dragon C	.15	.25
YS18-EN015 Exarion Universe C	.15	.25
YS18-EN016 Evilswarm Mandragora C	.15	.25
YS18-EN017 Marshmallon C	.15	.25
YS18-EN018 Ryko, Lightsworn Hunter C	.15	.25
YS18-EN019 Battle Fader C	.15	.25
YS18-EN020 Swift Scarecrow C	.15	.25
YS18-EN021 Cynet Recovery SR	.60	1.00
YS18-EN022 Cynet Universe C	.15	.25
YS18-EN023 Scapegoat C	.15	.25
YS18-EN024 Monster Reborn C	.15	.25
YS18-EN025 Dark Hole C	.15	.25
YS18-EN026 Mystical Space Typhoon C	.15	.25
YS18-EN027 Book of Moon C	.15	.25
YS18-EN028 United We Stand C	.15	.25
YS18-EN029 Card Trader C	.15	.25
YS18-EN030 Burden of the Mighty C	.15	.25
YS18-EN031 Ego Boost C	.15	.25
YS18-EN032 Supply Squad C	.15	.25
YS18-EN033 Cynet Regression C	.15	.25
YS18-EN034 Shadow Spell C	.15	.25
YS18-EN035 Call of the Haunted C	.15	.25
YS18-EN036 Mirror Force C	.15	.25
YS18-EN037 Torrential Tribute C	.15	.25
YS18-EN038 Bottomless Trap Hole C	.15	.25
YS18-EN039 Zero Gravity C	.15	.25
YS18-EN040 Compulsory Evacuation Device C	.15	.25
YS18-EN041 Transcode Talker UR	.60	1.00
YS18-EN042 Pentestag SR	.60	1.00
YS18-EN043 Decode Talker C	.15	.25
YS18-EN044 Link Spider C	.15	.25
YS18-EN045 Linkuriboh C	3.00	5.00

Structure Deck

2005 Yu-Gi-Oh Structure Deck Dragon's Roar 1st Edition

COMPLETE SET (28)	8.00	20.00
RELEASED ON JANUARY 1, 2005		
SD1EN001 Red-Eyes Darkness Dragon UR	2.00	5.00
SD1EN002 Red-Eyes B. Dragon C	.50	1.00
SD1EN003 Luster Dragon C	.20	.50
SD1EN004 Twin-Headed Behemoth C	.20	.50
SD1EN005 Armed Dragon LV3 C	.20	.50
SD1EN006 Armed Dragon LV5 C	.20	.50
SD1EN007 Red-Eyes B. Chick C	.20	.50
SD1EN008 Element Dragon C	.20	.50
SD1EN009 Masked Dragon C	.20	.50
SD1EN010 Snatch Steal C	.20	.50
SD1EN011 Mystical Space Typhoon C	.50	1.25
SD1EN012 Nobleman of Crossout C	.20	.50
SD1EN013 Premature Burial C	.20	.50
SD1EN014 Swords of Revealing Light C	.20	.50
SD1EN015 Pot of Greed C	.50	1.25
SD1EN016 Heavy Storm C	.20	.50
SD1EN017 Stamping Destruction C	.20	.50
SD1EN018 Creature Swap C	.20	.50
SD1EN019 Reload C	.20	.50
SD1EN020 The Graveyard in the Fourth Dimension C	.20	.50
SD1EN021 Call of the Haunted C	.20	.50
SD1EN022 Ceasefire C	.20	.50
SD1EN023 The Dragon's Bead C	.20	.50
SD1EN024 Dragon's Rage C	.20	.50
SD1EN025 Reckless Greed C	.40	1.00
SD1EN026 Interdimensional Matter C	.20	.50
SD1EN027 Trap Jammer C	.20	.50
SD1EN028 Curse of Anubis C	.20	.50

2005 Yu-Gi-Oh Structure Deck Zombie Madness 1st Edition

COMPLETE SET (28)	6.00	15.00
RELEASED ON JANUARY 1, 2005		
SD2EN001 Vampire Genesis UR	1.50	4.00
SD2EN002 Master Kyonshee C	.20	.50
SD2EN003 Vampire Lord C	.20	.50
SD2EN004 Dark Dust Spirit C	.20	.50
SD2EN005 Pyramid Turtle C	.20	.50
SD2EN006 Spirit Reaper C	.20	.50
SD2EN007 Despair From The Dark C	.20	.50
SD2EN008 Ryu Kokki C	.20	.50
SD2EN009 Soul-Absorbing Bone Tower C	.20	.50
SD2EN010 Vampire Lady C	.20	.50
SD2EN011 Double Coston C	.20	.50
SD2EN012 Regenerating Mummy C	.20	.50
SD2EN013 Snatch Steal C	.40	1.00
SD2EN014 Mystical Space Typhoon C	.75	2.00
SD2EN015 Giant Trunade C	.20	.50
SD2EN016 Nobleman of Crossout C	.20	.50
SD2EN017 Pot of Greed C	.50	1.25
SD2EN018 Card of Safe Return C	.20	.50
SD2EN019 Heavy Storm C	.20	.50
SD2EN020 Creature Swap C	.20	.50
SD2EN021 Book of Life C	.20	.50
SD2EN022 Call of the Mummy C	.20	.50
SD2EN023 Reload C	.20	.50
SD2EN024 Dust Tornado C	.20	.50
SD2EN025 Torrential Tribute C	.75	2.00
SD2EN026 Magic Jammer C	.20	.50
SD2EN027 Reckless Greed C	.50	1.25
SD2EN028 Compulsory Evacuation Device C	.20	.50

2005 Yu-Gi-Oh Structure Deck Blaze of Destruction 1st Edition

COMPLETE SET (31)	6.00	15.00
STRUCTURE DECK	8.00	20.00
RELEASED ON MAY 9, 2005		
SD3EN001 Infernal Flame Emperor UR	.50	1.50
SD3EN002 Great Angus C	.25	.75
SD3EN003 Blazing Inpachi C	.25	.75
SD3EN004 UFO Turtle- C	.25	.75
SD3EN005 Little Chimera C	.25	.75
SD3EN006 Inferno C	.25	.75
SD3EN007 Molten Zombie C	.25	.75
SD3EN008 Solar Flare Dragon C	.25	.75
SD3EN009 Ultimate Baseball Kid C	.25	.75
SD3EN010 Raging Flame Sprite C	.25	.75
SD3EN011 Thestalos the Firestorm Monarch C	.25	.75
SD3EN012 Gaia Soul the Combustible Collective C	.25	.75
SD3EN013 Fox Fire C	.25	.75
SD3EN014 Snatch Steal C	.25	.75
SD3EN015 Mystical Space Typhoon C	.25	.75
SD3EN016 Molten Destruction C	.25	.75
SD3EN017 Nobleman of Crossout C	.25	.75
SD3EN018 Premature Burial C	.25	.75
SD3EN019 Pot of Greed C	.25	.75
SD3EN020 Tribute to the Doomed C	.25	.75
SD3EN021 Heavy Storm C	.25	.75
SD3EN022 Dark Room of Nightmare C	.25	.75
SD3EN023 Reload C	.25	.75
SD3EN024 Level Limit - Area B C	.25	.75
SD3EN025 Necklace of Command C	.25	.75
SD3EN026 Meteor of Destruction C	.25	.75
SD3EN027 Dust Tornado C	.25	.75
SD3EN028 Call of the Haunted C	.25	.75
SD3EN029 Jar of Greed C	.25	.75
SD3EN030 Spell Shield Type-8 C	.25	.75
SD3EN031 Backfire C	.25	.75

2005 Yu-Gi-Oh Structure Deck Fury from the Deep 1st Edition

COMPLETE SET (32)	8.00	20.00
STRUCTURE DECK	12.00	30.00
RELEASED ON MAY 9, 2005		
SD4EN001 Ocean Dragon Lord - Neo- Daedalus UR	.75	2.00
SD4EN002 7 Colored Fish C	.20	.50
SD4EN003 Sea Serpent Warrior of Darkness C	.20	.50
SD4EN004 Space Mambo C	.20	.50
SD4EN005 Mother Grizzly C	.20	.50
SD4EN006 Star Boy C	.20	.50
SD4EN007 Tribe-Infecting Virus C	.75	2.00
SD4EN008 Fenrir C	.20	.50
SD4EN009 Amphibious Bugroth MK-3 C	.20	.50
SD4EN010 Levia-Dragon - Daedalus C	.50	1.25
SD4EN011 Mermaid Knight C	.20	.50
SD4EN012 Mobius the Frost Monarch C	.20	.50
SD4EN013 Unshaven Angler C	.20	.50
SD4EN014 Creeping Doom Manta C	.20	.50
SD4EN015 Snatch Steal C	.20	.50
SD4EN016 Mystical Space Typhoon C	.50	1.25
SD4EN017 Premature Burial C	.20	.50
SD4EN018 Pot of Greed C	.50	1.25
SD4EN019 Heavy Storm C	.20	.50
SD4EN020 A Legendary Ocean C	.20	.50
SD4EN021 Creature Swap C	.20	.50
SD4EN022 Reload C	.20	.50
SD4EN023 Salvage C	.25	.75
SD4EN024 Hammer Shot C	.20	.50
SD4EN025 Big Wave Small Wave C	.20	.50
SD4EN026 Dust Tornado C	.20	.50
SD4EN027 Call of the Haunted C	.20	.50
SD4EN028 Gravity Bind C	.20	.50
SD4EN029 Tornado Wall C	.20	.50
SD4EN030 Torrential Tribute C	.60	1.50
SD4EN031 Spell Shield Type-8 C	.20	.50
SD4EN032 Xing Zhen Hu C	.20	.50

2005 Yu-Gi-Oh Structure Deck Warrior's Triumph 1st Edition

COMPLETE SET (36)	10.00	25.00
STRUCTURE DECK	12.00	30.00
RELEASED ON OCTOBER 28, 2005		
SD5EN001 Gilford the Legend UR	.75	2.00
SD5EN002 Warrior Lady of the Wasteland C	.25	.75
SD5EN003 Dark Blade C	.25	.75
SD5EN004 Goblin Attack Force C	.25	.75
SD5EN005 Gearfried the Iron Knight C	.25	.75
SD5EN006 Swift Gaia the Fierce Knight C	.25	.75
SD5EN007 Obnoxious Celtic Guard C	.25	.75
SD5EN008 Command Knight C	.40	1.00
SD5EN009 Marauding Captain C	.25	.75
SD5EN010 Exiled Force C	.25	.75
SD5EN011 D.D. Warrior Lady C	.25	.75
SD5EN012 Mataza the Zapper C	.25	.75
SD5EN013 Mystic Swordsman LV2 C	.25	.75
SD5EN014 Mystic Swordsman LV4 C	.25	.75
SD5EN015 Ninja Grandmaster Sasuke C	.25	.75
SD5EN016 Gearfried the Swordmaster C	.25	.75
SD5EN017 Armed Samurai - Ben Kei C	.25	.75
SD5EN018 Divine Sword - Phoenix Blade C	.25	.75
SD5EN019 Snatch Steal C	.25	.75
SD5EN020 Mystical Space Typhoon C	.50	1.25
SD5EN021 Giant Trunade C	.25	.75

SD5EN022 Lightning Blade C	.25	.75
SD5EN023 Heavy Storm C	.25	.75
SD5EN024 Reinforcement of the Army C	.25	.75
SD5EN025 The Warrior Returning Alive C	.25	.75
SD5EN026 Fusion Sword Murasame Blade C	.25	.75
SD5EN027 Wicked-Breaking Flamberge - Baou C	.25	.75
SD5EN028 Fairy of the Spring C	.25	.75
SD5EN029 Reload C	.25	.75
SD5EN030 Lightning Vortex C	.25	.75
SD5EN031 Swords of Concealing Light C	.75	2.00
SD5EN032 Release Restraint C	.25	.75
SD5EN033 Call of the Haunted C	.25	.75
SD5EN034 Magic Jammer C	.25	.75
SD5EN035 Royal Decree C	1.25	3.00
SD5EN036 Blast with Chain C	.25	.75

2006 Yu-Gi-Oh Structure Deck Spellcaster's Judgment 1st Edition

COMPLETE SET (36)	10.00	25.00
STRUCTURE DECK	20.00	40.00
RELEASED ON JANUARY 18, 2006		
SDEN6001 Dark Eradicator Warlock UR	2.00	5.00
SDEN6002 Mythical Beast Cerberus C	.25	.75
SD6EN003 Dark Magician C	.25	.75
SD6EN004 Gemini Elf C	.25	.75
SD6EN005 Magician of Faith C	.25	.75
SD6EN006 Skilled Dark Magician C	.25	.75
SD6EN007 Apprentice Magician C	.25	.75
SD6EN008 Chaos Command Magician C	1.25	3.00
SD6EN009 Breaker the Magical Warrior C	.25	.75
SD6EN010 Royal Magical Library C	.60	1.50
SD6EN011 Tsukuyomi C	.60	1.50
SD6EN012 Chaos Sorcerer C	.25	.75
SD6EN013 White Magician Pikeru C	.25	.75
SD6EN014 Blast Magician C	.25	.75
SD6EN015 Ebon Magician Curran C	.25	.75
SD6EN016 Rapid-Fire Magician C	.25	.75
SD6EN017 Magical Blast C	.25	.75
SD6EN018 Mystical Space Typhoon C	.60	1.50
SD6EN019 Nobleman of Crossout C	.25	.75
SD6EN020 Premature Burial C	.25	.75
SD6EN021 Swords of Revealing Light C	.25	.75
SD6EN022 Mage Power C	.25	.75
SD6EN023 Heavy Storm C	.25	.75
SD6EN024 Diffusion Wave-Motion C	.25	.75
SD6EN025 Reload C	.25	.75
SD6EN026 Dark Magic Attack C	.25	.75
SD6EN027 Spell Absorption C	.75	2.00
SD6EN028 Lightning Vortex C	.25	.75
SD6EN029 Magical Dimension C	.25	.75
SD6EN030 Mystic Box C	.40	1.00
SD6EN031 Nightmare's Steelcage C	.25	.75
SD6EN032 Call of the Haunted C	.25	.75
SD6EN033 Spell Shield Type-8 C	.25	.75
SD6EN034 Pitch-Black Power Stone C	.25	.75
SD6EN035 Divine Wrath C	.25	.75
SD6EN036 Magic Cylinder C	.40	1.00

2006 Yu-Gi-Oh Structure Deck Invincible Fortress 1st Edition

COMPLETE SET (32)	8.00	20.00
STRUCTURE DECK	15.00	30.00
RELEASED ON MAY 15, 2006		
SD7EN001 Exxod, Master of the Guard UR	.60	1.50
SD7EN002 Great Spirit C	.20	.50
SD7EN003 Giant Rat C	.20	.50
SD7EN004 Maharaghi C	.20	.50
SD7EN005 Guardian Sphinx C	.20	.50
SD7EN006 Gigantes C	.20	.50
SD7EN007 Stone Statue of the Aztecs C	.25	.75
SD7EN008 Golem Sentry C	.20	.50
SD7EN009 Hieracosphinx C	.20	.50
SD7EN010 Criosphinx C	.20	.50
SD7EN011 Moai Interceptor Cannons C	.20	.50
SD7EN012 Megarock Dragon C	.20	.50
SD7EN013 Guardian Statue C	.20	.50
SD7EN014 Medusa Worm C	.20	.50
SD7EN015 Sand Moth C	.20	.50
SD7EN016 Canyon C	.40	1.00
SD7EN017 Mystical Space Typhoon C	.60	1.50
SD7EN018 Premature Burial C	.20	.50
SD7EN019 Swords of Revealing Light C	.20	.50
SD7EN020 Shield & Sword C	.20	.50
SD7EN021 Magical Mallet C	.75	2.00
SD7EN022 Hammer Shot C	.20	.50
SD7EN023 Ectoplasmer C	.20	.50
SD7EN024 Brain Control C	.20	.50
SD7EN025 Shifting Shadows C	.20	.50
SD7EN026 Waboku C	.20	.50
SD7EN027 Ultimate Offering C	.20	.50
SD7EN028 Magic Drain C	.20	.50
SD7EN029 Robbin' Goblin C	.20	.50
SD7EN030 Ordeal of a Traveler C	.25	.75
SD7EN031 Reckless Greed C	.40	1.00
SD7EN032 Compulsory Evacuation Device C	.20	.50

2006 Yu-Gi-Oh Structure Deck Lord of the Storm 1st Edition

COMPLETE SET (36)	8.00	20.00
STRUCTURE DECK	8.00	20.00
RELEASED ON JULY 12, 2006		
SD8EN001 Simorgh, Bird of Divinity UR	.20	.50
SD8EN002 Sonic Shooter C	.20	.50
SD8EN003 Sonic Duck C	.20	.50
SD8EN004 Harpie Girl C	.20	.50
SD8EN005 Slate Warrior C	.20	.50
SD8EN006 Flying Kamakiri #1 C	.20	.50
SD8EN007 Harpie Lady Sisters C	.20	.50
SD8EN008 Bladefly C	.20	.50
SD8EN009 Birdface C	.20	.50
SD8EN010 Silpheed C	.20	.50
SD8EN011 Lady Ninja Yae C	.40	1.00
SD8EN012 Roc from the Valley of Haze C	.20	.50
SD8EN013 Harpie Lady 1 C	.20	.50
SD8EN014 Harpie Lady 2 C	.20	.50
SD8EN015 Harpie Lady 3 C	.20	.50
SD8EN016 Swift Birdman Joe C	.20	.50
SD8EN017 Harpie's Pet Baby Dragon C	.50	1.25
SD8EN018 Card Destruction C	.20	.50
SD8EN019 Mystical Space Typhoon C	.50	1.25
SD8EN020 Nobleman of Crossout C	.20	.50
SD8EN021 Elegant Egotist C	.20	.50
SD8EN022 Heavy Storm C	.20	.50
SD8EN023 Reload C	.20	.50
SD8EN024 Harpies' Hunting Ground C	.20	.50
SD8EN025 Triangle Ecstasy Spark C	.20	.50
SD8EN026 Lightning Vortex C	.20	.50
SD8EN027 Hysteric Party C	.40	1.00
SD8EN028 Aqua Chorus C	.20	.50
SD8EN029 Dust Tornado C	.20	.50
SD8EN030 Call of the Haunted C	.20	.50
SD8EN031 Magic Jammer C	.20	.50
SD8EN032 Dark Coffin C	.20	.50
SD8EN033 Reckless Greed C	.40	1.00
SD8EN034 Sakuretsu Armor C	.20	.50
SD8EN035 Ninjitsu Art of Transformation C	.40	1.00
SD8EN036 Icarus Attack C	.60	1.50

2006 Yu-Gi-Oh Dinosaur's Rage

COMPLETE SET (37)	6.00	15.00
STRUCTURE DECK	10.00	25.00
SPECIAL EDITION DECK W/5-HEADED DRAGON	10.00	20.00
5-HEADED DRAGON DECK IS WALMART EXCLUSIVE		
RELEASED ON OCTOBER 20, 2006		
SD9EN001 Super Conductor Tyranno UR	.60	1.50
SD9EN002 Kabazauls C	.20	.50
SD9EN003 Sabersaurus C	.20	.50
SD9EN004 Mad Sword Beast C	.20	.50
SD9EN005 Gilasaurus C	.20	.50
SD9EN006 Dark Driceratops C	.20	.50
SD9EN007 Hyper Hammerhead C	.20	.50
SD9EN008 Black Tyranno C	.20	.50
SD9EN009 Tyranno Infinity C	.20	.50
SD9EN010 Hydrogeddon C	.20	.50
SD9EN011 Oxygeddon C	.20	.50
SD9EN012 Black Ptera C	.20	.50
SD9EN013 Black Stego C	.20	.50
SD9EN014 Ultimate Tyranno C	.20	.50
SD9EN015 Miracle Jurassic Egg C	.20	.50
SD9EN016 Babycerasaurus C	.20	.50
SD9EN017 Big Evolution Pill C	.20	.50
SD9EN018 Tail Swipe C	.20	.50
SD9EN019 Jurassic World C	.20	.50
SD9EN020 Sebek's Blessing C	.20	.50
SD9EN021 Riryoku C	.20	.50
SD9EN022 Mesmeric Control C	.20	.50
SD9EN023 Mystical Space Typhoon C	.60	1.50
SD9EN024 Megamorph C	.20	.50
SD9EN025 Heavy Storm C	.20	.50
SD9EN026 Lightning Vortex C	.25	.75
SD9EN027 Magical Mallet C	.75	2.00
SD9EN028 Hunting Instinct C	.20	.50
SD9EN029 Survival Instinct C	.20	.50
SD9EN030 Volcanic Eruption C	.20	.50
SD9EN031 Seismic Shockwave C	.20	.50
SD9EN032 Magical Arm Shield C	.20	.50
SD9EN033 Negate Attack C	.20	.50
SD9EN034 Goblin Out of the Frying Pan C	.20	.50
SD9EN035 Malfunction C	.20	.50
SD9EN036 Fossil Excavation C	.20	.50
SD9ENSS1 Five-Headed Dragon UR	.75	2.00

2007 Yu-Gi-Oh Structure Deck Machine Re-Volt 1st Edition

COMPLETE SET (37)	8.00	20.00
STRUCTURE DECK	10.00	25.00
RELEASED ON JANUARY 17, 2007		
SD10EN001 Ancient Gear Dragon Gadjiltron UR	.40	1.00
SD10EN002 Ancient Gear Gadjiltron Chimera C	.25	.75
SD10EN003 Ancient Gear Engineer C	.60	1.50
SD10EN004 Boot-Up Soldier - Dread Dynamo C	.25	.75
SD10EN005 Mechanicalchaser C	.25	.75
SD10EN006 Green Gadget C	.25	.75
SD10EN007 Red Gadget C	.25	.75
SD10EN008 Yellow Gadget C	.25	.75
SD10EN009 Cannon Soldier C	.25	.75
SD10EN010 Gear Golem the Moving Fortress C	.25	.75
SD10EN011 Heavy Mech Support Platform C	.25	.75
SD10EN012 Ancient Gear Golem C	.25	.75
SD10EN013 Ancient Gear Beast C	.25	.75
SD10EN014 Ancient Gear Soldier C	.25	.75
SD10EN015 Ancient Gear C	.25	.75
SD10EN016 Ancient Gear Cannon C	.25	.75
SD10EN017 Ancient Gear Workshop C	.40	1.00
SD10EN018 Ancient Gear Tank C	.25	.75
SD10EN019 Ancient Gear Explosive C	.25	.75
SD10EN020 Ancient Gear Fist C	.25	.75
SD10EN021 Ancient Gear Factory C	.25	.75
SD10EN022 Ancient Gear Drill C	.25	.75
SD10EN023 Ancient Gear Castle C	.25	.75
SD10EN024 Mystical Space Typhoon C	.50	1.25
SD10EN025 Limiter Removal C	.25	.75
SD10EN026 Heavy Storm C	.25	.75
SD10EN027 Enemy Controller C	.25	.75
SD10EN028 Weapon Change C	.25	.75
SD10EN029 Machine Duplication C	1.25	3.00
SD10EN030 Pot of Avarice C	.25	.75
SD10EN031 Stronghold the Moving Fortress C	.25	.75
SD10EN032 Ultimate Offering C	.25	.75
SD10EN033 Sakuretsu Armor C	.25	.75
SD10EN034 Micro Ray C	.25	.75
SD10EN035 Rare Metalmorph C	.25	.75
SD10EN036 Covering Fire C	.25	.75
SD10EN037 Roll Out! C	.25	.75

2008 Yu-Gi-Oh Structure Deck Zombie World 1st Edition

STRUCTURE DECK	8.00	20.00
RELEASED ON OCTOBER 21, 2008		
SDZWEN001 Red-Eyes Zombie Dragon UR	.75	2.00
SDZWEN002 Malevolent Mech - Goku En C	.25	.75
SDZWEN003 Paladin of the Cursed Dragon C	.25	.75
SDZWEN004 Gernia C	.25	.75
SDZWEN005 Patrician of Darkness C	.25	.75
SDZWEN006 Royal Keeper C	.25	.75
SDZWEN007 Pyramid Turtle C	.25	.75
SDZWEN008 Master Kyonshee C	.25	.75
SDZWEN009 Spirit Reaper C	.25	.75
SDZWEN010 Getsu Fuhma C	.25	.75
SDZWEN011 Ryu Kokki C	.25	.75
SDZWEN012 Regenerating Mummy C	.25	.75
SDZWEN013 Des Lacooda C	.25	.75
SDZWEN014 Marionette Mite C	.25	.75
SDZWEN015 Plague Wolf C	.25	.75
SDZWEN016 Zombie Master C	.25	.75
SDZWEN017 Zombie World C	1.00	2.50
SDZWEN018 Spell Shattering Arrow C	.50	1.25
SDZWEN019 Cold Wave C	.25	.75
SDZWEN020 Magical Stone Excavation C	.25	.75
SDZWEN021 Card of Safe Return C	.25	.75
SDZWEN022 Creature Swap C	.25	.75
SDZWEN023 Book of Life C	.25	.75
SDZWEN024 Call of the Mummy C	.25	.75
SDZWEN025 Terraforming C	.60	1.50
SDZWEN026 Pot of Avarice C	.25	.75
SDZWEN027 Shrink C	.25	.75
SDZWEN028 Field Barrier C	.25	.75
SDZWEN029 Soul Taker C	.25	.75
SDZWEN030 Ribbon of Rebirth C	.25	.75
SDZWEN031 Card Destruction C	.25	.75
SDZWEN032 Imperial Iron Wall C	.75	2.00
SDZWEN033 Dust Tornado C	.25	.75
SDZWEN034 Bottomless Trap Hole C	1.00	2.50
SDZWEN035 Tutan Mask C	.25	.75
SDZWEN036 Waboku C	.25	.75
SDZWEN037 Magical Arm Shield C	.25	.75

2009 Yu-Gi-Oh Structure Deck Spellcaster's Command 1st Edition

STRUCTURE DECK	10.00	25.00
RELEASED ON MARCH 31, 2009		
SDSC1 Endymion, the Master Magician UR	1.25	3.00
SDSC2 Disenchanter	.15	.25
SDSC3 Defender, the Magical Knight	.15	.25
SDSC4 Hannibal Necromancer	.15	.25
SDSC5 Summoner Monk	.15	.25
SDSC6 Dark Red Enchanter	.15	.25
SDSC7 Skilled Dark Magician	.15	.25
SDSC8 Apprentice Magician	.15	.25
SDSC9 Old Vindictive Magician	.15	.25
SDSC10 Magical Marionette	.15	.25
SDSC11 Breaker the Magical Warrior	.15	.25
SDSC12 Magical Plant Mandragola	.15	.25
SDSC13 Royal Magical Library	.15	.25
SDSC14 Blast Magician	.15	.25
SDSC15 Mythical Beast Cerberus	.15	.25
SDSC16 Mei-Kou, Master of Barriers	.15	.25
SDSC17 Crystal Seer	.15	.25
SDSC18 Magical Exemplar	.15	.25
SDSC19 Magical Citadel of Endymion	.15	.25
SDSC20 Spell Power Grasp	.15	.25
SDSC21 Magicians Unite	.15	.25
SDSC22 Mist Body	.15	.25
SDSC23 Malevolent Nuzzler	.15	.25
SDSC24 Giant Trunade	.15	.25
SDSC25 Fissure	.15	.25
SDSC26 Swords of Revealing Light	.15	.25
SDSC27 Mage Power	.15	.25
SDSC28 Terraforming	.15	.25
SDSC29 Enemy Controller	.15	.25
SDSC30 Book of Moon	.15	.25
SDSC31 Magical Blast	.15	.25
SDSC32 Magical Dimension	.15	.25
SDSC33 Twister	.15	.25
SDSC34 Field Barrier	.15	.25
SDSC35 Magician's Circle	.15	.25
SDSC36 Pitch-Black Power Stone	.15	.25
SDSC37 Tower of Babel	.15	.25
SDSC38 Magic Cylinder	.15	.25

2009 Yu-Gi-Oh Structure Deck Warriors' Strike 1st Edition

STRUCTURE DECK	8.00	12.00
RELEASED ON OCTOBER 27, 2009		
SDWS1 Phoenix Gearfried UR	.40	1.00
SDWS2 Evocator Chevalier SR	.10	.25
SDWS3 Featherizer SR	.10	.25
SDWS4 Gemini Soldier C	.10	.25
SDWS5 Spell Striker C	.40	1.00
SDWS6 Freed the Matchless General C	.10	.25
SDWS7 Marauding Captain C	.10	.25
SDWS8 Exiled Force C	.10	.25
SDWS9 D.D. Warrior Lady C	.60	1.50
SDWS10 Card Trooper C	.10	.25
SDWS11 Gemini Summoner C	.10	.25
SDWS12 Blazewing Butterfly C	.10	.25
SDWS13 D.D. Warrior C	.10	.25
SDWS14 Future Samurai C	.10	.25
SDWS15 Field-Commander Rahz C	.10	.25
SDWS16 Dark Valkyria C	.10	.25
SDWS17 Supervise C	.50	1.25
SDWS18 Mind Control C	.10	.25
SDWS19 Burden of the Mighty C	.75	2.00
SDWS20 Silent Doom C	.10	.25
SDWS21 Hidden Armory C	.60	1.50
SDWS22 Nightmare's Steelcage C	.10	.25
SDWS23 Mystical Space Typhoon C	.10	.25
SDWS24 Ekibyo Drakmord C	.10	.25
SDWS25 Reinforcement of the Army C	.10	.25
SDWS26 Big Bang Shot C	.10	.25
SDWS27 Divine Sword - Phoenix Blade C	.10	.25
SDWS28 Double Summon C	1.25	3.00
SDWS29 Symbols of Duty C	.10	.25
SDWS30 Swing of Memories C	.10	.25
SDWS31 Unleash Your Power! C	.10	.25
SDWS32 Dark Bribe C	.75	2.00

SDWS33 Kunai with Chain C	.10	.25
SDWS34 Sakuretsu Armor C	.60	1.50
SDWS35 Soul Resurrection C	.10	.25
SDWS36 Justi-Break C	.10	.25
SDWS37 Birthright C	.10	.25
SDWS38 Gemini Trap Hole C	.10	.25

2010 Yu-Gi-Oh Structure Deck Marik 1st Edition

COMPLETE SET (38)	8.00	20.00
RELEASED ON OCTOBER 19, 2010		
SDMAEN001 Gil Garth C	.15	.40
SDMAEN002 Mystic Tomato C	.15	.40
SDMAEN003 Viser Des C	.15	.40
SDMAEN004 Legendary Fiend C	.15	.40
SDMAEN005 Dark Jeroid C	.15	.40
SDMAEN006 Newdoria C	.15	.40
SDMAEN007 Gravekeeper's Spy C	.75	2.00
SDMAEN008 Gravekeeper's Curse C	.15	.40
SDMAEN009 Gravekeeper's Guard C	.75	2.00
SDMAEN010 Gravekeeper's Spear Soldier C	.25	.60
SDMAEN011 Gravekeeper's Chief C	.25	.60
SDMAEN012 Gravekeeper's Cannonholder C	.25	.60
SDMAEN013 Gravekeeper's Assailant C	.25	.60
SDMAEN014 Lava Golem UR	.75	2.00
SDMAEN015 Drillago C	.15	.40
SDMAEN016 Bowganian C	.15	.40
SDMAEN017 Gravekeeper's Commandant C	.25	.60
SDMAEN018 Gravekeeper's Visionary C	.25	.60
SDMAEN019 Gravekeeper's Descendant C	.25	.60
SDMAEN020 Mystical Space Typhoon C	.75	2.00
SDMAEN021 Nightmare's Steelcage C	.25	.60
SDMAEN022 Creature Swap C	.25	.60
SDMAEN023 Book of Moon C	2.00	5.00
SDMAEN024 Dark Room of Nightmare C	.15	.40
SDMAEN025 Necrovalley C	.40	1.00
SDMAEN026 Foolish Burial C	.40	1.00
SDMAEN027 Magical Stone Excavation C	.25	.60
SDMAEN028 Allure of Darkness C	1.50	4.00
SDMAEN029 Acid Trap Hole C	.15	.40
SDMAEN030 Mirror Force C	2.50	6.00
SDMAEN031 Skull Invitation C	.15	.40
SDMAEN032 Coffin Seller C	.15	.40
SDMAEN033 Nightmare Wheel C	.30	.75
SDMAEN034 Metal Reflect Slime C	.30	.75
SDMAEN035 Malevolent Catastrophe C	.25	.60
SDMAEN036 Dark Illusion C	.25	.60
SDMAEN037 Mystical Beast of Serket UR	.40	1.00
SDMAEN038 Temple of the Kings UR	.40	1.00

2011 Yu-Gi-Oh Structure Deck Dragunity Legion 1st Edition

COMPLETE SET (39)	8.00	20.00
RELEASED ON MARCH 8, 2011		
SDDL01 Dragunity Arma Leyvaten UTR	.40	1.00
SDDL02 Dragunity Arma Mystletainn SR	.40	1.00
SDDL03 Dragunity Aklys SR	.40	1.00
SDDL04 Dragunity Dux	.25	.60
SDDL05 Dragunity Legionnaire	.15	.40
SDDL06 Dragunity Tribus	.15	.40
SDDL07 Dragunity Darkspear	.15	.40
SDDL08 Dragunity Militum	.15	.40
SDDL09 Dragunity Primus Pilus	.15	.40
SDDL10 Dragunity Brandistock	.15	.40
SDDL11 Dragunity Javelin	.15	.40
SDDL12 Mist Valley Falcon	.15	.40
SDDL13 Hunter Owl	.15	.40
SDDL14 Garuda the Wind Spirit	.15	.40
SDDL15 Flying Kamakiri #1	.15	.40
SDDL16 Spear Dragon	.15	.40
SDDL17 Twin-Headed Behemoth	.15	.40
SDDL18 Armed Dragon LV3	.15	.40
SDDL19 Armed Dragon LV5	.15	.40
SDDL20 Masked Dragon	.25	.60
SDDL21 Dragon Ravine	.75	2.00
SDDL22 Dragon Mastery	.25	.60
SDDL23 United We Stand	1.25	3.00
SDDL24 Mage Power	.40	1.00
SDDL25 Dragon's Gunfire	.15	.40
SDDL26 Stamping Destruction	.15	.40
SDDL27 Creature Swap	.25	.60
SDDL28 Monster Reincarnation	.25	.60
SDDL29 Foolish Burial	.40	1.00
SDDL30 Card Destruction	.15	.40
SDDL31 Windstorm of Etaqua	.15	.40
SDDL32 Relieve Monster	.25	.60
SDDL33 Legacy of Yata-Garasu	.15	.40
SDDL34 Final Attack Orders	.15	.40
SDDL35 Mirror Force	.75	2.00
SDDL36 Dragon's Rage	.15	.40
SDDL37 Bottomless Trap Hole	.75	2.00
SDDL38 Spiritual Wind Art - Miyabi	.15	.40
SDDL39 Icarus Attack	.75	2.00

2011 Yu-Gi-Oh Structure Deck Lost Sanctuary 1st Edition

COMPLETE SET (38)	8.00	20.00
RELEASED ON JUNE 14, 2011		
SDLS01 Master Hyperion UR	2.00	5.00
SDLS02 The Agent of Mystery - Earth SR	1.00	2.50
SDLS03 The Agent of Miracles - Jupiter SR	.75	2.00
SDLS04 The Agent of Judgement - Saturn	.30	.75
SDLS05 The Agent of Wisdom - Mercury	.30	.75
SDLS06 The Agent of Creation - Venus	.30	.75
SDLS07 The Agent of Force - Mars	.30	.75
SDLS08 Mystical Shine Ball	.30	.75
SDLS09 Splendid Venus	.50	1.25
SDLS10 Tethys, Goddess of Light	.75	2.00
SDLS11 Victoria	.60	1.50
SDLS12 Athena	.40	1.00
SDLS13 Marshmallon	1.00	2.50
SDLS14 Hecatrice	.40	1.00
SDLS15 Shining Angel	.60	1.50
SDLS16 Soul of Purity and Light	.60	1.50
SDLS17 Airknight Parshath	.30	.75
SDLS18 Nova Summoner	.60	1.50
SDLS19 Zeradias, Herald of Heaven	.30	.75
SDLS20 Honest	.75	2.00
SDLS21 Hanewata	.30	.75
SDLS22 Consecrated Light	.60	1.50
SDLS23 Cards from the Sky	1.00	2.50
SDLS24 Valhalla, Hall of the Fallen	.50	1.25
SDLS25 Terraforming	.60	1.50
SDLS26 Smashing Ground	1.00	2.50
SDLS27 The Sanctuary in the Sky	.75	2.00
SDLS28 Celestial Transformation	.30	.75
SDLS29 Burial from a Different Dimension	1.50	4.00
SDLS30 Mausoleum of the Emperor	.60	1.50
SDLS31 Solidarity	1.50	4.00
SDLS32 The Fountain in the Sky	.30	.75
SDLS33 Divine Punishment	.60	1.50
SDLS34 Return from the Different Dimension	.60	1.50
SDLS35 Torrential Tribute	1.50	4.00
SDLS36 Beckoning Light	.40	1.00
SDLS37 Miraculous Descent	.30	.75
SDLS38 Solemn Judgment	4.00	10.00

2012 Yu-Gi-Oh Structure Deck Samurai Warlords 1st Edition

COMPLETE SET (41)	6.00	12.00
STRUCTURE DECK	7.50	15.00
RELEASED ON JUNE 26, 2012		
SDWAEN001 Chamberlain of the Six Samurai C	.10	.30
SDWAEN002 Grandmaster of the Six Samurai C	.10	.30
SDWAEN003 The Six Samurai - Yariza C	.10	.30
SDWAEN004 The Six Samurai - Zanji C	.10	.30
SDWAEN005 The Six Samurai - Nisashi C	.10	.30
SDWAEN006 The Six Samurai - Yaichi C	.10	.30
SDWAEN007 The Six Samurai - Kamon C	.10	.30
SDWAEN008 The Six Samurai - Irou C	.10	.30
SDWAEN009 Great Shogun Shien C	.10	.30
SDWAEN010 Shien's Footsoldier C	.10	.30
SDWAEN011 Enishi, Shien's Chancellor C	.10	.30
SDWAEN012 Spirit of the Six Samurai C	.10	.30
SDWAEN013 Future Samurai C	.10	.30
SDWAEN014 The Immortal Bushi C	.10	.30
SDWAEN015 Hand of the Six Samurai C	.10	.30
SDWAEN016 Legendary Six Samurai - Kizan C	1.25	3.00
SDWAEN017 Legendary Six Samurai - Enishi C	15.00	.40
SDWAEN018 Legendary Six Samurai - Kageki SR	.20	.60
SDWAEN019 Shien's Squire C	.10	.30
SDWAEN020 Shien's Daredevil C	.10	.30
SDWAEN021 Elder of the Six Samurai C	.10	.30
SDWAEN022 Shien's Advisor C	.10	.30
SDWAEN023 Dark Hole C	.50	1.25
SDWAEN024 The A. Forces C	.10	.30
SDWAEN025 Reinforcement of the Army C	.20	.60
SDWAEN026 The Warrior Returning Alive C	.10	.30
SDWAEN027 Cunning of the Six Samurai C	.10	.30
SDWAEN028 Six Samurai United C	.40	1.00
SDWAEN029 Gateway of the Six C	.10	.30
SDWAEN030 Shien's Smoke Signal SR	.25	.75
SDWAEN031 Temple of the Six C	.10	.30
SDWAEN032 Shien's Dojo C	.20	.60
SDWAEN033 Rivalry of Warlords C	1.25	3.00
SDWAEN034 Return of the Six Samurai C	.10	.30
SDWAEN035 Double-Edged Sword Technique C	.10	.30
SDWAEN036 Fiendish Chain C	1.25	3.00
SDWAEN037 Musakani Magatama C	.15	.40
SDWAEN038 Shien's Scheme C	.10	.30
SDWAEN039 Six Strike - Thunder Blast C	.10	.30
SDWAEN040 Six Style - Dual Wield C	.10	.30
SDWAEN041 Shadow of the Six Samurai - Shien UR	.10	.30

2012 Yu-Gi-Oh Structure Deck Realm of the Sea Emperor 1st Edition

COMPLETE SET (39)	5.00	10.00
STRUCTURE DECK	5.00	10.00
RELEASED OCTOBER 16, 2012		
SDRE001 Poseidra, the Atlantean UR	.10	.30
SDRE002 Atlantean Dragoons SR	.40	1.00
SDRE003 Atlantean Marksman	.15	.25
SDRE004 Atlantean Heavy Infantry	.15	.25
SDRE005 Atlantean Pikeman	.15	.25
SDRE006 Atlantean Attack Squad	.15	.25
SDRE007 Lost Blue Breaker	.15	.25
SDRE008 Armed Sea Hunter	.15	.25
SDRE009 Spined Gillman	.15	.25
SDRE010 Deep Sea Diva	.15	.25
SDRE011 Mermaid Archer	.15	.25
SDRE012 Codarus	.15	.25
SDRE013 Warrior of Atlantis	.15	.25
SDRE014 Abyss Soldier	.15	.25
SDRE015 Skreech	.15	.25
SDRE016 Snowman Eater	.15	.25
SDRE017 Nightmare Penguin	.15	.25
SDRE018 Penguin Soldier	.15	.25
SDRE019 Deep Diver	.15	.25
SDRE020 Reese the Ice Mistress	.15	.25
SDRE021 Mother Grizzly	.15	.25
SDRE022 Friller Rabca	.15	.25
SDRE023 Call of the Atlanteans SR	.10	.30
SDRE024 A Legendary Ocean	.15	.25
SDRE025 Terraforming	.15	.25
SDRE026 Water Hazard	.15	.25
SDRE027 Aqua Jet	.15	.25
SDRE028 Surface	.15	.25
SDRE029 Moray of Greed	.15	.25
SDRE030 Salvage	.15	.25
SDRE031 Dark Hole	.15	.25
SDRE032 Big Wave Small Wave	.15	.25
SDRE033 Aegis of the Ocean Dragon Lord	.15	.25
SDRE034 Forgotten Temple of the Deep	.15	.25
SDRE035 Tornado Wall	.15	.25
SDRE036 Torrential Tribute	.15	.25
SDRE037 Spiritual Water Art - Aoi	.15	.25
SDRE038 Gravity Bind	.15	.25
SDRE039 Poseidon Wave	.15	.25

2013 Yu-Gi-Oh Structure Deck Onslaught of the Fire Kings 1st Edition

COMPLETE SET (39)	6.00	12.00
STRUCTURE DECK	7.50	15.00
RELEASED ON FEBRUARY 8, 2013		
SDOKEN001 Fire King High Avatar Garunix UR	.75	2.00
SDOKEN002 Fire King Avatar Barong C	1.00	2.50
SDOKEN003 Fire King Avatar Kirin C	.10	.30
SDOKEN004 Sacred Phoenix of Nephthys C	.10	.30
SDOKEN005 Manticore of Darkness C	.10	.30
SDOKEN006 Goka, the Pyre of Malice C	.10	.30
SDOKEN007 Hazy Flame Hyppogrif C	.10	.30
SDOKEN008 Laval Lancelord C	.10	.30
SDOKEN009 Flamvell Firedog C	.10	.30
SDOKEN010 Flamvell Poun C	.10	.30
SDOKEN011 Neo Flamvell Sabre C	.10	.30
SDOKEN012 Royal Firestorm Guards C	.10	.30
SDOKEN013 Volcanic Rocket C	.50	1.25
SDOKEN014 Volcanic Counter C	.10	.30
SDOKEN015 Molten Zombie C	.10	.30
SDOKEN016 Spirit of Flames C	.10	.30
SDOKEN017 Raging Flame Sprite C	.10	.30
SDOKEN018 Fox Fire C	.10	.30
SDOKEN019 Flame Tiger C	.10	.30
SDOKEN020 Little Chimera C	.10	.30
SDOKEN021 UFO Turtle C	.10	.30
SDOKEN022 Onslaught of the Fire Kings SR	1.00	2.50
SDOKEN023 Circle of the Fire Kings SR	.60	1.50
SDOKEN024 Rekindling C	.10	.30
SDOKEN025 Blaze Accelerator C	.10	.30
SDOKEN026 Wild Nature's Release C	.10	.30
SDOKEN027 Pot of Duality C	.75	2.00
SDOKEN028 Hand Destruction C	1.00	2.50
SDOKEN029 Creature Swap C	.10	.30
SDOKEN030 Burden of the Mighty C	.10	.30
SDOKEN031 Backfire C	.10	.30
SDOKEN032 Flamvell Counter C	.10	.30
SDOKEN033 Phoenix Wing Wind Blast C	.50	1.25
SDOKEN034 Horn of the Phantom Beast C	.50	1.25
SDOKEN035 Blast with Chain C	.10	.30
SDOKEN036 Spiritual Fire Art - Kurenai C	.10	.30
SDOKEN037 Regretful Rebirth C	.10	.30
SDOKEN038 Nightmare Wheel C	.10	.30
SDOKEN039 Call of the Haunted C	.10	.30

2013 Yu-Gi-Oh Structure Deck Saga of Blue-Eyes White Dragon 1st Edition

COMPLETE SET (40)	7.50	15.00
STRUCTURE DECK	7.50	15.00
RELEASED ON SEPTEMBER 13, 2013		
SDBE040 Azure-Eyes Silver Dragon UR	1.25	3.00
SDBEEN001 Blue-Eyes White Dragon UR	1.25	3.00
SDBEEN002 Rabidragon C	.15	.40
SDBEEN003 Alexandrite Dragon C	.30	.75
SDBEEN004 Luster Dragon C	.15	.40
SDBEEN005 Flamvell Guard C	.15	.40
SDBEEN006 Maiden with Eyes of Blue SR	2.00	5.00
SDBEEN007 Rider of the Storm Winds C	.15	.40
SDBEEN008 Darkstorm Dragon C	.15	.40
SDBEEN009 Kaiser Glider C	.15	.40
SDBEEN010 Hieratic Dragon of Tefnuit C	.15	.40
SDBEEN011 Mirage Dragon C	.15	.40
SDBEEN012 Divine Dragon Apocralyph C	.15	.40
SDBEEN013 The White Stone of Legend C	.50	1.25
SDBEEN014 Kaibaman C	.15	.40
SDBEEN015 Herald of Creation C	.15	.40
SDBEEN016 Kaiser Sea Horse C	.15	.40
SDBEEN017 Honest C	.15	.40
SDBEEN018 Shining Angel C	.15	.40
SDBEEN019 Dragon Shrine SR	1.25	3.00
SDBEEN020 Silver's Cry C	2.00	5.00
SDBEEN021 Burst Stream of Destruction C	.15	.40
SDBEEN022 Stamping Destruction C	.15	.40
SDBEEN023 A Wingbeat of Giant Dragon C	.15	.40
SDBEEN024 Trade-In C	1.25	3.00
SDBEEN025 Cards of Consonance C	.40	1.00
SDBEEN026 White Elephant's Gift C	.15	.40
SDBEEN027 One for One C	.15	.40
SDBEEN028 Monster Reborn C	.40	1.00
SDBEEN029 Dragonic Tactics C	.15	.40
SDBEEN030 Soul Exchange C	.15	.40
SDBEEN031 Swords of Revealing Light C	.15	.40
SDBEEN032 Enemy Controller C	.15	.40
SDBEEN033 Castle of Dragon Souls C	.15	.40
SDBEEN034 Fiendish Chain C	1.00	2.50
SDBEEN035 Kunai with Chain C	.15	.40
SDBEEN036 Damage Condenser C	.15	.40
SDBEEN037 Call of the Haunted C	.15	.40
SDBEEN038 Compulsory Evacuation Device C	.30	.75
SDBEEN039 Champion's Vigilance C	.15	.40

2014 Yu-Gi-Oh Structure Deck Cyber Dragon Revolution 1st Edition

COMPLETE SET (39)	20.00	35.00
STRUCTURE DECK	5.00	10.00
RELEASED ON FEBRUARY 7, 2014		
SDCR001 Cyber Dragon Core SR	1.75	2.25
SDCR002 Cyber Dragon Drei SR	2.25	3.00
SDCR004 Cyber Dragon Zwei	.15	.25
SDCR005 Proto-Cyber Dragon	.15	.25
SDCR006 Cyber Valley	.15	.25
SDCR007 Cyber Larva	.15	.25
SDCR008 Cyber Phoenix	.15	.25
SDCR009 Cyber Dinosaur	.15	.25
SDCR010 Cyber Eltanin	.15	.25
SDCR011 Armored Cybern	.15	.25
SDCR012 Satellite Cannon	.15	.25
SDCR013 Solar Wind Jammer	.15	.25
SDCR014 Jade Knight	.15	.25
SDCR015 FalchionB	.15	.25
SDCR016 Reflect Bounder	.15	.25
SDCR017 The Light - Hex-Sealed Fusion	.15	.25
SDCR018 Shining Angel	.15	.25
SDCR019 Cyber Repair Plant	3.50	5.00
SDCR020 Evolution Burst	.15	.25
SDCR021 Super Polymerization	1.00	2.00
SDCR022 Power Bond	.40	.75
SDCR023 Limiter Removal	.20	.35
SDCR024 Megamorph	.15	.25
SDCR025 D.D.R. - Different Dimension Reincarnation	.30	.50
SDCR026 Mystical Space Typhoon	.60	1.00

SDCR027 Light of Redemption	.15	.25
SDCR028 Machina Armored Unit	.15	.25
SDCR029 Cyber Network	.25	.45
SDCR030 Cybernetic Hidden Technology	.15	.25
SDCR031 Three of a Kind	.15	.25
SDCR032 Trap Stun	1.00	1.25
SDCR033 Dimensional Prison	1.00	1.50
SDCR034 Malevolent Catastrophe	.15	.25
SDCR035 Waboku	.30	.50
SDCR036 Call of the Haunted	.15	.25
SDCR037 Cyber Twin Dragon UR	.30	.50
SDCR038 Cyber Dragon Nova UR	2.75	3.25
SDCR003a Cyber Dragon (black)	.20	.35
SDCR003b Cyber Dragon (white)	.40	.75

2014 Yu-Gi-Oh Structure Deck Realm of Light 1st Edition

COMPLETE SET (36)	10.00	25.00
RELEASED ON JUNE 27, 2014		
SDLIEN001 Alexandrite Dragon C	.10	.30
SDLIEN002 Minerva, Lightsworn Maiden SR	.50	1.25
SDLIEN003 Raiden, Hand of the Lightsworn SR	1.50	4.00
SDLIEN004 Judgment Dragon C	.20	.60
SDLIEN005 Gragonith, Lightsworn Dragon C	.10	.30
SDLIEN006 Celestia, Lightsworn Angel C	.10	.30
SDLIEN007 Jain, Lightsworn Paladin C	.10	.30
SDLIEN008 Lyla, Lightsworn Sorceress C	.10	.30
SDLIEN009 Garoth, Lightsworn Warrior C	.10	.30
SDLIEN010 Wulf, Lightsworn Beast C	.10	.30
SDLIEN011 Ehren, Lightsworn Monk C	.10	.30
SDLIEN012 Lumina, Lightsworn Summoner C	.10	.30
SDLIEN013 Aurkus, Lightsworn Druid C	.10	.30
SDLIEN014 Shire, Lightsworn Spirit C	.10	.30
SDLIEN015 Ryko, Lightsworn Hunter C	.10	.30
SDLIEN016 Honest C	.20	.60
SDLIEN017 Lightray Diabolos C	.10	.30
SDLIEN018 Lightray Daedalus C	.10	.30
SDLIEN019 Vylon Prism C	.10	.30
SDLIEN020 Fabled Raven C	.10	.30
SDLIEN021 The Fabled Cerburrel C	.10	.30
SDLIEN022 Blackwing - Zephyros the Elite C	.10	.30
SDLIEN023 Necro Gardna C	.10	.30
SDLIEN024 Lightsworn Sanctuary UR	.40	1.00
SDLIEN025 Realm of Light C	.10	.30
SDLIEN026 Solar Recharge C	.20	.60
SDLIEN027 Charge of the Light Brigade C	.10	.30
SDLIEN028 Monster Reincarnation C	.10	.30
SDLIEN029 Foolish Burial C	.25	.75
SDLIEN030 Glorious Illusion C	.10	.30
SDLIEN031 Lightsworn Barrier C	.10	.30
SDLIEN032 Vanquishing Light C	.10	.30
SDLIEN033 Beckoning Light C	.10	.30
SDLIEN034 Skill Successor C	.10	.30
SDLIEN035 Breakthrough Skill C	.60	1.50
SDLIEN036 Michael, the Arch-Lightsworn UR	.40	1.00

2014 Yu-Gi-Oh Structure Deck Geargia Rampage 1st Edition

COMPLETE SET (35)	8.00	15.00
UNLISTED C		
RELEASED ON OCTOBER 17, 2014		
SDGREN001 Geargiano Mk-III SR	.15	.25
SDGREN002 Geargiattacker SR	.10	.20
SDGREN003 Geargiauger UR	.50	.75
SDGREN004 Geargiano C	.10	.20
SDGREN005 Geargiano MK-II C	.10	.20
SDGREN006 Geargiaccelerator C	.20	.30
SDGREN007 Geargiarsenal C	.20	.30
SDGREN008 Geargiarmor C	.20	.35
SDGREN009 Green Gadget C	.10	.20
SDGREN010 Red Gadget C	.10	.20
SDGREN011 Yellow Gadget C	.10	.20
SDGREN012 Ancient Gear Gadjiltron Chimera C	.10	.20
SDGREN013 Ancient Gear Gadjiltron Dragon C	.20	.30
SDGREN014 Jumbo Drill C	.10	.20
SDGREN015 Minefieldriller C	.10	.20
SDGREN016 Card Trooper C	.10	.20
SDGREN017 Swift Scarecrow C	.30	.50
SDGREN018 Oilman C	.10	.20
SDGREN019 Heavy Mech Support Platform C	.10	.20
SDGREN020 Giant Rat C	.10	.20
SDGREN021 Geartown C	.10	.20
SDGREN022 Limiter Removal C	.10	.20
SDGREN023 Machine Assembly Line C	.10	.20
SDGREN024 Fissure C	.10	.20
SDGREN025 Smashing Ground C	.20	.30
SDGREN026 Double Summon C	1.25	2.00
SDGREN027 Creature Swap C	.10	.20
SDGREN028 Terraforming C	.60	1.00
SDGREN029 Geargiagear C	.20	.35
SDGREN030 Stronghold the Moving Fortress C	.10	.20
SDGREN031 Metalmorph C	.10	.20
SDGREN032 Rare Metalmorph C	.10	.20
SDGREN033 Roll Out! C	.10	.20
SDGREN034 Geargiagear Gigant XG UR	.20	.30
SDGREN035 Gear Gigant X C	2.25	3.00

2015 Yu-Gi-Oh Structure Deck Hero Strike 1st Edition

COMPLETE SET (45)	20.00	30.00
STRUCTURE DECK	10.00	15.00
RELEASED ON JANUARY 30, 2015		
SDHSEN001 Elemental HERO Shadow Mist SR	3.75	5.00
SDHSEN002 Elemental HERO Ocean C	.20	.30
SDHSEN003 Elemental HERO Woodsman C	.20	.30
SDHSEN004 Elemental HERO Voltic C	.05	.15
SDHSEN005 Elemental HERO Heat C	.05	.15
SDHSEN006 Elemental HERO Avian C	.05	.15
SDHSEN007 Elemental HERO Neos C	.20	.30
SDHSEN008 Elemental HERO Neos Alius C	.15	.25
SDHSEN009 Elemental HERO Bladedge C	.05	.15
SDHSEN010 Elemental HERO Necroshade C	.15	.25
SDHSEN011 Elemental HERO Wildheart C	.20	.30
SDHSEN012 Elemental HERO Bubbleman C	.60	1.00
SDHSEN013 Neo-Spacian Grand Mole C	.20	.30
SDHSEN014 Honest C	.40	.60
SDHSEN015 Card Trooper C	.05	.15
SDHSEN016 Winged Kuriboh C	.30	.50
SDHSEN017 Summoner Monk C	1.25	1.75
SDHSEN018 Homunculus the Alchemic Being C	.05	.15
SDHSEN019 Mask Change II C	.40	.60
SDHSEN020 Form Change C	.25	.40
SDHSEN021 Mask Charge C	1.00	1.30
SDHSEN022 Mask Charge C	.25	.35
SDHSEN023 Polymerization C	1.25	2.00
SDHSEN024 Miracle Fusion C	.60	1.00
SDHSEN025 Parallel World Fusion C	.05	.15
SDHSEN026 A Hero Lives C	3.00	4.00
SDHSEN027 Hero Mask C	.05	.15
SDHSEN028 H - Heated Heart C	.05	.15
SDHSEN029 E - Emergency Call C	.05	.15
SDHSEN030 R - Righteous Justice C	.05	.15
SDHSEN031 O - Oversoul C	.05	.15
SDHSEN032 Reinforcement of the Army C	.20	.30
SDHSEN033 The Warrior Returning Alive C	.05	.15
SDHSEN034 Pot of Duality C	1.75	2.15
SDHSEN035 Hero Signal C	.05	.15
SDHSEN036 Hero Blast C	.05	.15
SDHSEN037 Call of the Haunted C	.15	.25
SDHSEN038 Bottomless Trap Hole C	.50	.75
SDHSEN039 Compulsory Evacuation Device C	.25	.35
SDHSEN040 Battleguard Howling C	.05	.15
SDHSEN041 Contrast HERO Chaos UR	.15	.25
SDHSEN042 Masked HERO Koga SR	.20	.30
SDHSEN043 Masked HERO Divine Wind SR	.20	.30
SDHSEN044 Masked HERO Dark Law SR	3.00	3.50
SDHSEN045 Elemental HERO Great Tornado C	.05	.15

2015 Yu-Gi-Oh Structure Deck Synchron Extreme 1st Edition

COMPLETE SET (43)	20.00	25.00
RELEASED ON AUGUST 28, 2015		
SDSEEN001 Jet Synchron SR	.60	1.00
SDSEEN002 Rush Warrior C	.15	.25
SDSEEN003 Synchron Carrier C	.15	.25
SDSEEN004 Junk Synchron C	.15	.25
SDSEEN005 Quickdraw Synchron C	.15	.25
SDSEEN006 Drill Synchron C	.15	.25
SDSEEN007 Turbo Synchron C	.15	.25
SDSEEN008 Unknown Synchron C	.15	.25
SDSEEN009 Fleur Synchron C	.15	.25
SDSEEN010 Synchron Explorer C	.15	.25
SDSEEN011 Speed Warrior C	.15	.25
SDSEEN012 Sonic Warrior C	.15	.25
SDSEEN013 Doppelwarrior C	.15	.25
SDSEEN014 Quillbolt Hedgehog C	.15	.25
SDSEEN015 Tuningware C	.15	.25
SDSEEN016 Swift Scarecrow C	.15	.25
SDSEEN017 Level Eater C	.15	.25
SDSEEN018 Effect Veiler C	.15	.25
SDSEEN019 Genex Neutron C	.15	.25
SDSEEN020 Genex Ally Birdman C	.15	.25
SDSEEN021 Plaguespreader Zombie C	.15	.25
SDSEEN022 White Dragon Wyverburster C	.15	.25
SDSEEN023 Black Dragon Collapserpent C	.15	.25
SDSEEN024 Scrap Fist SR	.05	.15
SDSEEN025 Limit Overdrive C	.15	.25
SDSEEN026 Starlight Junktion C	.15	.25
SDSEEN027 Tuning C	.15	.25
SDSEEN028 Reinforcement of the Army C	.15	.25
SDSEEN029 The Warrior Returning Alive C	.15	.25
SDSEEN030 Dark Eruption C	.15	.25
SDSEEN031 One for One C	.15	.25
SDSEEN032 Night Beam C	.15	.25
SDSEEN033 Double Cyclone C	.15	.25
SDSEEN034 Scrap-Iron Statue C	.15	.25
SDSEEN035 Scrap-Iron Scarecrow C	.15	.25
SDSEEN036 Limiter Overload C	.15	.25
SDSEEN037 Call of the Haunted C	.15	.25
SDSEEN038 Imperial Iron Wall C	.15	.25
SDSEEN039 Solemn Warning C	.15	.25
SDSEEN040 Stardust Warrior UR	.30	.50
SDSEEN041 Jet Warrior UR	.20	.35
SDSEEN042 Accel Synchron SR	.60	1.00
SDSEEN043 Junk Warrior C	.15	.25

2015 Yu-Gi-Oh Structure Deck Master of Pendulum 1st Edition

COMPLETE SET (43)	14.00	20.00
STRUCTURE DECK	10.00	15.00
RELEASED ON DECEMBER 4, 2015		
SDMPEN001 Dragonpulse Magician C	.15	.25
SDMPEN009 Odd-Eyes Pendulum Dragon C	.15	.25
SDMPEN017 Fencing Fire Ferret C	.15	.25
SDMPEN025 Sky Iris C	.15	.25
SDMPEN033 Forbidden Dress C	.15	.25
SDMPEN041 Odd-Eyes Meteorburst Dragon UR	.75	1.00
SDMPEN002 Dragonpit Magician C	.15	.25
SDMPEN003 Nobledragon Magician SR	.15	.25
SDMPEN004 Oafdragon Magician SR	.40	.60
SDMPEN005 Wisdom-Eye Magician SR	.25	.40
SDMPEN006 Performapal Skullcrobat Joker C	.15	.25
SDMPEN007 Stargazer Magician C	.15	.25
SDMPEN008 Timegazer Magician C	.15	.25
SDMPEN010 Performapal Silver Claw C	.15	.25
SDMPEN011 Performapal Salutiger C	.15	.25
SDMPEN012 Performapal Trump Witch C	.15	.25
SDMPEN013 Metaphys Armed Dragon C	.15	.25
SDMPEN014 Chaos Hunter C	.15	.25
SDMPEN015 Fusilier Dragon, the Dual-Mode Beast C	.15	.25
SDMPEN016 Lyla, Lightsworn Sorceress C	.15	.25
SDMPEN018 Inari Fire C	.15	.25
SDMPEN019 Nefarious Archfiend Eater of Nefariousness C	.15	.25
SDMPEN020 Jigabyte C	.15	.25
SDMPEN021 Goblindbergh C	.15	.25
SDMPEN022 X-Saber Airbellum C	.15	.25
SDMPEN023 Magna Drago C	.15	.25
SDMPEN024 Re-Cover C	.15	.25
SDMPEN026 Pendulum Call C	.15	.25
SDMPEN027 Pendulum Shift C	.15	.25
SDMPEN028 Pendulum Rising C	.15	.25
SDMPEN029 Sacred Sword of Seven Stars C	.15	.25
SDMPEN030 Summoner's Art C	.15	.25
SDMPEN031 Mystical Space Typhoon C	.15	.25
SDMPEN032 Scapegoat C	.15	.25
SDMPEN034 Polymerization C	.15	.25
SDMPEN035 Terraforming C	.15	.25
SDMPEN036 Pendulum Back C	.15	.25
SDMPEN037 Powerful Rebirth C	.15	.25
SDMPEN038 Traptrix Trap Hole Nightmare C	.15	.25
SDMPEN039 Torrential Tribute C	.15	.25
SDMPEN040 Eradicator Epidemic Virus C	.15	.25
SDMPEN042 Odd-Eyes Absolute Dragon UR	.40	.60
SDMPEN043 Rune-Eyes Pendulum Dragon C	.15	.25

2016 Yu-Gi-Oh Structure Deck Emperor of Darkness 1st Edition

COMPLETE SET (42)	10.00	15.00
RELEASED ON JANUARY 29, 2016		
SR01EN000 Ehther the Heavenly Monarch UR	.40	.70
SR01EN001 Erebus the Underworld Monarch UR	.40	.70
SR01EN002 Eidos the Underworld Squire SR	.50	.75
SR01EN003 Edea the Heavenly Squire SR	.50	.75
SR01EN004 Caius the Shadow Monarch C	.20	.30
SR01EN005 Zaborg the Thunder Monarch C	.10	.25
SR01EN006 Granmarg the Rock Monarch C	.10	.25
SR01EN007 Mobius the Frost Monarch C	.10	.25
SR01EN008 Thestalos the Firestorm Monarch C	.10	.25
SR01EN009 Raiza the Storm Monarch C	.10	.25
SR01EN010 Lucius the Shadow Vassal C	.10	.25
SR01EN011 Mithra the Thunder Vassal C	.10	.25
SR01EN012 Landrobe the Rock Vassal C	.10	.25
SR01EN013 Escher the Frost Vassal C	.10	.25
SR01EN014 Berlineth the Firestorm Vassal C	.10	.25
SR01EN015 Garum the Storm Vassal C	.10	.25
SR01EN016 Illusory Snatcher C	.10	.25
SR01EN017 Tragoedia C	.15	.25
SR01EN018 Dandylion C	.10	.25
SR01EN019 Mathematician C	.20	.30
SR01EN020 Level Eater C	.10	.25
SR01EN021 Battle Fader C	.20	.30
SR01EN022 Rainbow Kuriboh C	.10	.25
SR01EN023 Pantheism of the Monarchs SR	.60	1.00
SR01EN024 Domain of the True Monarchs C	.75	1.15
SR01EN025 March of the Monarchs C	.10	.25
SR01EN026 Return of the Monarchs C	.20	.30
SR01EN027 The Monarchs Stormforth C	.20	.35
SR01EN028 Strike of the Monarchs C	.10	.25
SR01EN029 Tenacity of the Monarchs C	.10	.25
SR01EN030 Soul Exchange C	.10	.25
SR01EN031 Enemy Controller C	.10	.25
SR01EN032 Dicephoon C	.10	.25
SR01EN033 Soul Charge C	1.75	2.15
SR01EN034 The Prime Monarch C	.60	.80
SR01EN035 The First Monarch C	.10	.25
SR01EN036 Escalation of the Monarchs C	.10	.25
SR01EN037 The Monarchs Awaken C	.10	.25
SR01EN038 The Monarchs Erupt C	.10	.25
SR01EN039 By Order of the Emperor C	.10	.25
SR01EN040 Pinpoint Guard C	.10	.25
SR01ENTKN Token C	.20	.30

2016 Yu-Gi-Oh Structure Deck Rise of the True Dragons 1st Edition

COMPLETE SET (42)	13.00	20.00
STRUCTURE DECK	10.00	15.00
RELEASED ON JULY 8, 2016		
SR02EN000 Arkbrave Dragon UR	.30	.50
SR02EN001 Divine Dragon Lord Felgrand UR	.25	.40
SR02EN002 Dragon Knight of Creation SR	.20	.30
SR02EN003 Paladin of Felgrand C	.20	.35
SR02EN004 Guardian of Felgrand C	.20	.35
SR02EN005 Felgrand Dragon C	.20	.35
SR02EN006 Darkblaze Dragon C	.20	.35
SR02EN007 Herald of Creation C	.20	.35
SR02EN008 Decoy Dragon C	.20	.35
SR02EN009 Red-Eyes Darkness Metal Dragon C	.60	1.00
SR02EN010 Red-Eyes Wyvern C	.20	.35
SR02EN011 White Night Dragon C	.20	.35
SR02EN012 Darkstorm Dragon C	.20	.35
SR02EN013 Armed Protector Dragon C	.20	.35
SR02EN014 Evilswarm Zahak C	.20	.35
SR02EN015 Eclipse Wyvern C	.20	.35
SR02EN016 White Dragon Wyverburster C	.20	.35
SR02EN017 Black Dragon Collapserpent C	.20	.35
SR02EN018 Keeper of the Shrine C	.20	.35
SR02EN019 Kidmodo Dragon C	.20	.35
SR02EN020 Jain, Lightsworn Paladin C	.20	.35
SR02EN021 Ehren, Lightsworn Monk C	.20	.35
SR02EN022 Raiden, Hand of the Lightsworn C	.40	.60
SR02EN023 Card Trooper C	.20	.35
SR02EN024 Ruins of the Divine Dragon Lords SR	.10	.20
SR02EN025 Return of the Dragon Lords SR	8.00	10.00
SR02EN026 Dragon Ravine C	.20	.35
SR02EN027 A Wingbeat of Giant Dragon C	.20	.35
SR02EN028 Trade-In C	.75	1.25
SR02EN029 Foolish Burial C	.20	.35
SR02EN030 Hand Destruction C	.60	1.00
SR02EN031 Reinforcement of the Army C	.20	.35
SR02EN032 The Warrior Returning Alive C	.20	.35
SR02EN033 Charge of the Light Brigade C	.20	.35
SR02EN034 Terraforming C	1.00	1.50
SR02EN035 Dragon's Rebirth C	.20	.35
SR02EN036 Burst Breath C	.20	.35
SR02EN037 Needlebug Nest C	.20	.35
SR02EN038 Breakthrough Skill C	.60	1.00
SR02EN039 Call of the Haunted C	.20	.35
SR02EN040 Oasis of Dragon Souls C	.20	.35
SR02ENTKN Dragon Lord Token C	.20	.35

2016 Yu-Gi-Oh Structure Deck Yugi Moto 1st Edition

COMPLETE SET (45)	15.00	20.00
RELEASED ON OCTOBER 21, 2016		
SDMYEN001 Alpha The Electromagnet Warrior SR	1.50	2.00
SDMYEN002 Beta The Electromagnet Warrior SR	1.50	2.00
SDMYEN003 Gamma The Electromagnet Warrior SR	1.50	2.00
SDMYEN004 Berserkion the Electromagna Warrior UR	2.50	3.00

SDMYEN005 Kuribohrn C .15 .25
SDMYEN006 Valkyrion the Magna Warrior C .15 .25
SDMYEN007 Alpha The Magnet Warrior C .15 .25
SDMYEN008 Beta The Magnet Warrior C .15 .25
SDMYEN009 Gamma The Magnet Warrior C .15 .25
SDMYEN010 Dark Magician C .15 .25
SDMYEN011 Dark Magician Girl C .15 .25
SDMYEN012 Buster Blader C .15 .25
SDMYEN013 Jacks Knight C .15 .25
SDMYEN014 Queens Knight C .15 .25
SDMYEN015 Kings Knight C .15 .25
SDMYEN016 Berfomet C .15 .25
SDMYEN017 Gazelle the King of Mythical Beasts C .15 .25
SDMYEN018 Obnoxious Celtic Guard C .15 .25
SDMYEN019 Giant Soldier of Stone C .15 .25
SDMYEN020 Kuriboh C .15 .25
SDMYEN021 Skilled Dark Magician C .15 .25
SDMYEN022 Skilled White Magician C .15 .25
SDMYEN023 TwinHeaded Behemoth C .15 .25
SDMYEN024 Magnetic Field C .15 .25
SDMYEN025 Dark Magic Inheritance C .15 .25
SDMYEN026 Dark Magic Attack C .15 .25
SDMYEN027 Dark Magic Curtain C .15 .25
SDMYEN028 Mystic Box C .15 .25
SDMYEN029 Swords of Revealing Light C .15 .25
SDMYEN030 Spell Shattering Arrow C .15 .25
SDMYEN031 Polymerization C .15 .25
SDMYEN032 DeFusion C .15 .25
SDMYEN033 Swords of Concealing Light C .15 .25
SDMYEN034 Attack the Moon! C .15 .25
SDMYEN035 Magnet Conversion C .15 .25
SDMYEN036 Magicians Circle C .15 .25
SDMYEN037 Mirror Force C .15 .25
SDMYEN038 Magic Cylinder C .15 .25
SDMYEN039 Soul Rope C .15 .25
SDMYEN040 Rock Bombardment C .15 .25
SDMYEN041 Imperion Magnum the Superconductive Battlebot UR 2.50 3.00
SDMYEN042 Arcana Knight Joker C .15 .25
SDMYEN043 Dark Paladin C .15 .25
SDMYEN044 Chimera the Flying Mythical Beast C .15 .25
SDMYEN045 Buster Blader the Dragon Destroyer Swordsman C .15 .25

2016 Yu-Gi-Oh Structure Deck Seto Kaiba 1st Edition

COMPLETE SET (44) 15.00 20.00
RELEASED ON OCTOBER 21, 2016
SDKSEN001 AAssault Core SR 1.75 2.25
SDKSEN002 BBuster Drake SR 1.75 2.25
SDKSEN003 CCrush Wyvern SR 1.75 2.25
SDKSEN004 Heavy Mech Support Armor C .15 .25
SDKSEN005 XHead Cannon C .15 .25
SDKSEN006 YDragon Head C .15 .25
SDKSEN007 ZMetal Tank C .15 .25
SDKSEN008 Heavy Mech Support Platform C .15 .25
SDKSEN009 BlueEyes White Dragon C .15 .25
SDKSEN010 Kaiser Glider C .15 .25
SDKSEN011 Lord of D C .15 .25
SDKSEN012 Vampire Lord C .15 .25
SDKSEN013 Enraged Battle Ox C .15 .25
SDKSEN014 Des Feral Imp C .15 .25
SDKSEN015 Peten the Dark Clown C .15 .25
SDKSEN016 Interplanetarypurplythorny Dragon C .15 .25
SDKSEN017 Blizzard Dragon C .15 .25
SDKSEN018 Keeper of the Shrine C .15 .25
SDKSEN019 Luster Dragon C .15 .25
SDKSEN020 Union Hangar C .15 .25
SDKSEN021 Majesty with Eyes of Blue C .15 .25
SDKSEN022 Burst Stream of Destruction C .15 .25
SDKSEN023 The Flute of Summoning Dragon C .15 .25
SDKSEN024 Silent Doom C .15 .25
SDKSEN025 Shrink C .15 .25
SDKSEN026 Enemy Controller C .15 .25
SDKSEN027 Megamorph C .15 .25
SDKSEN028 Limiter Removal C .15 .25
SDKSEN029 Frontline Base C .15 .25
SDKSEN030 Union Scramble C .15 .25
SDKSEN031 Crush Card Virus C .15 .25
SDKSEN032 Negate Attack C .15 .25
SDKSEN033 Ring of Destruction C .15 .25
SDKSEN034 Interdimensional Matter Transporter C .15 .25
SDKSEN035 Cloning C .15 .25
SDKSEN036 Final Attack Orders C .15 .25
SDKSEN037 Call of the Haunted C .15 .25
SDKSEN038 Roll Out! C .15 .25
SDKSEN039 Fiendish Chain C .15 .25
SDKSEN040 AtoZDragon Buster Cannon UR 2.50 3.00
SDKSEN041 ABCDragon Buster UR 2.50 3.00
SDKSEN042 XYZDragon Cannon C .15 .25
SDKSEN043 XYDragon Cannon C .15 .25
SDKSEN044 XZTank Cannon C .15 .25

2017 Yu-Gi-Oh Structure Deck Pendulum Domination 1st Edition

COMPLETE SET (43) 25.00 35.00
STRUCTURE DECK 10.00 15.00
RELEASED ON JANUARY 20, 2017
SDPDEN001 DDD Chaos King Apocalypse UR 1.50 2.00
SDPDEN002 DD Savant Newton C .15 .25
SDPDEN003 DD Savant Copernicus C .15 .25
SDPDEN004 DD Orthros SR 1.00 1.50
SDPDEN005 DD Lamia SR 3.00 3.50
SDPDEN006 DDD Doom King Armageddon C .15 .25
SDPDEN007 DD Cerberus C .15 .25
SDPDEN008 DD Lilith C .15 .25
SDPDEN009 DD Nighthowl C .15 .25
SDPDEN010 DD Savant Galilei C .15 .25
SDPDEN011 DD Savant Kepler C .15 .25
SDPDEN012 DDD Oblivion King Abyss Ragnarok C .15 .25
SDPDEN013 DDD Supreme King Kaiser C .15 .25
SDPDEN014 DD Proud Ogre C .15 .25
SDPDEN015 DD Proud Chevalier C .15 .25
SDPDEN016 Dark Armed Dragon C .15 .25
SDPDEN017 Dark Grepher C .15 .25
SDPDEN018 Armageddon Knight C .15 .25
SDPDEN019 Trance Archfiend C .15 .25
SDPDEN020 Kuribandit C .15 .25
SDPDEN021 Stygian Street Patrol C .15 .25
SDPDEN022 Stygian Security C .15 .25
SDPDEN023 Dark Contract with the Yamimakai C .15 .25
SDPDEN024 Dark Contract with the Gate C .15 .25
SDPDEN025 Dark Contract with the Swamp King C .15 .25
SDPDEN026 Forbidden Dark Contract with the Swamp King C .15 .25
SDPDEN027 Foolish Burial C .15 .25
SDPDEN028 One for One C .15 .25
SDPDEN029 Allure of Darkness C .15 .25
SDPDEN030 Dark Eruption C .15 .25
SDPDEN031 Emergency Provisions C .15 .25
SDPDEN032 DD Reroll C .15 .25
SDPDEN033 DD Recruits C .15 .25
SDPDEN034 DDD Human Resources C .15 .25
SDPDEN035 Dark Contract with the Witch C .15 .25
SDPDEN036 Dark Contract with Errors C .15 .25
SDPDEN037 Contract Laundering C .15 .25
SDPDEN038 Sinister Yorishiro C .15 .25
SDPDEN039 Escape from the Dark Dimension C .15 .25
SDPDEN040 Hope for Escape C .15 .25
SDPDEN041 DDD Dragonbane King Beowulf UR 3.00 3.50
SDPDEN042 DDD Cursed King Siegfried SR 3.00 3.50
SDPDEN043 DDD Wave King Caesar C .15 .25

2017 Yu-Gi-Oh Structure Deck Machine Reactor 1st Edition

COMPLETE SET (40) 15.00 25.00
RELEASED ON APRIL 14, 2017
SR03EN000 Ancient Gear Gadget UR 1.25 2.00
SR03EN001 Ancient Gear Reactor Dragon UR 1.00 1.50
SR03EN002 Ancient Gear Hydra SR .75 1.25
SR03EN003 Ancient Gear Wyvern SR 1.50 2.50
SR03EN004 Ancient Gear Gadjiltron Dragon C .15 .25
SR03EN005 Ancient Gear Golem C .15 .25
SR03EN006 Ancient Gear Gadjiltron Chimera C .15 .25
SR03EN007 Ancient Gear Beast C .15 .25
SR03EN008 Ancient Gear Engineer C .15 .25
SR03EN009 Ancient Gear Knight C .15 .25
SR03EN010 Ancient Gear Soldier C .15 .25
SR03EN011 Ancient Gear Box C .15 .25
SR03EN012 Geargiauger C .15 .25
SR03EN013 Planet Pathfinder C .15 .25
SR03EN014 Minefieldriller C .15 .25
SR03EN015 Card Trooper C .15 .25
SR03EN016 Gigantes C .15 .25
SR03EN017 BOXer C .15 .25
SR03EN018 Hardened Armed Dragon C .15 .25
SR03EN019 Spell Striker C .15 .25
SR03EN020 Maxx C C .15 .25
SR03EN021 Ancient Gear Catapult SR 1.25 2.00
SR03EN022 Ancient Gear Fortress C .15 .25
SR03EN023 Ancient Gear Castle C .15 .25
SR03EN024 Ancient Gear Workshop C .15 .25
SR03EN025 Geartown C .15 .25
SR03EN026 Mausoleum of the Emperor C .15 .25
SR03EN027 Pseudo Space C .15 .25
SR03EN028 Limiter Removal C .15 .25
SR03EN029 Machine Duplication C .15 .25
SR03EN030 Inferno Reckless Summon C .15 .25
SR03EN031 Galaxy Cyclone C .15 .25
SR03EN032 Terraforming C .15 .25
SR03EN033 Jar of Avarice C .15 .25
SR03EN034 Mischief of the Gnomes C .15 .25
SR03EN035 Machine King 3000 BC C .15 .25
SR03EN036 Fiendish Chain C .15 .25
SR03EN037 Call of the Haunted C .15 .25
SR03EN038 The Huge Revolution is Over C .15 .25
SR03ENTKN Ancient Gear Token C .15 .25

2017 Yu-Gi-Oh Structure Deck Dinosmashers Fury 1st Edition

COMPLETE SET (40) 10.00 15.00
RELEASED ON APRIL 14, 2017
SR04EN000 Petiteranodon UR 2.00 3.00
SR04EN001 Ultimate Conductor Tyranno UR 1.50 2.50
SR04EN002 Souleating Oviraptor SR 4.00 6.00
SR04EN003 Megalosmasher X C .15 .25
SR04EN004 Sabersaurus C .15 .25
SR04EN005 Super Conductor Tyranno C .15 .25
SR04EN006 Ultimate Tyranno C .15 .25
SR04EN007 SuperAncient Dinobeast C .15 .25
SR04EN008 Sauropod Brachion C .15 .25
SR04EN009 Tyranno Infinity C .15 .25
SR04EN010 Black Brachios C .15 .25
SR04EN011 Miracle Jurassic Egg C .15 .25
SR04EN012 Gilasaurus C .15 .25
SR04EN013 Babycerasaurus C .15 .25
SR04EN014 Miscellaneousaurus C .15 .25
SR04EN015 Evilswarm Salamandra C .15 .25
SR04EN016 Stegocyber C .15 .25
SR04EN017 Trilotressops C .15 .25
SR04EN018 Skelesaurus C .15 .25
SR04EN019 Chewbone C .15 .25
SR04EN020 Rescue Rabbit C .15 .25
SR04EN021 Lost World SR 1.50 2.50
SR04EN022 Fossil Dig C .15 .25
SR04EN023 Big Evolution Pill C .15 .25
SR04EN024 Twin Twisters C .15 .25
SR04EN025 Burial from a Different Dimension C .15 .25
SR04EN026 Swords of Concealing Light C .15 .25
SR04EN027 Painful Decision C .15 .25
SR04EN028 Unexpected Dai C .15 .25
SR04EN029 Terraforming C .15 .25
SR04EN030 Survivals End SR .30 .50
SR04EN031 Survival of the Fittest C .15 .25
SR04EN032 Fossil Excavation C .15 .25
SR04EN033 Extinction on Schedule C .15 .25
SR04EN034 Ojama Trio C .15 .25
SR04EN035 Nightmare Archfiends C .15 .25
SR04EN036 Quaking Mirror Force C .15 .25
SR04EN037 Grand Horn of Heaven C .15 .25
SR04EN038 Secret Blast C .15 .25
SR04ENTKN Jurraegg Token C .15 .25

2017 Yu-Gi-Oh Structure Deck Cyberse Link 1st Edition

COMPLETE SET (43) 10.00 15.00
RELEASED ON NOVEMBER 3, 2017
SDCLEN001 Digitron C .15 .25
SDCLEN002 Dotscaper C .15 .25
SDCLEN003 Cliant C .15 .25
SDCLEN004 Backlinker C .15 .25
SDCLEN005 Balancer Lord C .15 .25
SDCLEN006 ROM Cloudia C .15 .25
SDCLEN007 Boot Staggered C .15 .25
SDCLEN008 Dual Assembwurm SR .50 .80
SDCLEN009 Cyberse Wizard C .15 .25
SDCLEN010 Backup Secretary C .15 .25
SDCLEN011 Stack Reviver C .15 .25
SDCLEN012 Launcher Commander C .15 .25
SDCLEN013 Tragoedia C .15 .25
SDCLEN014 Summoner Monk C .15 .25
SDCLEN015 Card Trooper C .15 .25
SDCLEN016 Debris Dragon C .15 .25
SDCLEN017 Mathematician C .15 .25
SDCLEN018 Crane Crane C .15 .25
SDCLEN019 Magician of Faith C .15 .25
SDCLEN020 Jester Confit C .15 .25
SDCLEN021 Glow Up Bulb C .50 .80
SDCLEN022 Kinka byo C .15 .25
SDCLEN023 Cynet Backdoor SR .50 .80
SDCLEN024 Soul Charge C .50 .80
SDCLEN025 Shuffle Reborn C .15 .25
SDCLEN026 DDR Different Dimension Reincarnation C .15 .25
SDCLEN027 Gold Sarcophagus C .50 .80
SDCLEN028 Mind Control C .15 .25
SDCLEN029 Cosmic Cyclone C 2.50 4.00
SDCLEN030 Moon Mirror Shield C .15 .25
SDCLEN031 Where Arf Thou C .15 .25
SDCLEN032 Recoded Alive C .15 .25
SDCLEN033 Miracle's Wake C .15 .25
SDCLEN034 Powerful Rebirth C .15 .25
SDCLEN035 Premature Return C .15 .25
SDCLEN036 Swamp Mirrorer C .15 .25
SDCLEN037 Quantum Cat C .15 .25
SDCLEN038 Storming Mirror Force C .75 1.25
SDCLEN039 Dimensional Barrier C 2.00 3.00
SDCLEN040 Ghosts From the Past C .15 .25
SDCLEN041 Encode Talker UR 1.00 1.50
SDCLEN042 Tri Gate Wizard UR 2.00 3.00
SDCLEN043 Binary Sorceress SR .20 .35

2018 Yu-Gi-Oh Structure Deck Wave of Light 1st Edition

COMPLETE SET (42) 10.00 15.00
RELEASED ON JANUARY 19, 2018
SR05-EN000 Eva UR .60 1.00
SR05-EN001 Sacred Arch-Airknight Parshath UR .50 .80
SR05-EN002 Minerva, Scholar of the Sky C .10 .20
SR05-EN003 Power Angel Valkyria SR .75 1.25
SR05-EN004 Neo-Parshath, the Sky Paladin C .10 .20
SR05-EN005 Airknight Parshath C .10 .20
SR05-EN006 Meltiel, Sage of the Sky C .10 .20
SR05-EN007 Harvest Angel of Wisdom C .10 .20
SR05-EN008 Bountiful Artemis C .10 .20
SR05-EN009 Layard the Liberator C .10 .20
SR05-EN010 Guiding Ariadne C .10 .20
SR05-EN011 Archlord Kristya C .10 .20
SR05-EN012 Splendid Venus C .10 .20
SR05-EN013 Athena C .10 .20
SR05-EN014 Tethys, Goddess of Light C .10 .20
SR05-EN015 Hecatrice C .10 .20
SR05-EN016 Gellenduo C .10 .20
SR05-EN017 Nova Summoner C .10 .20
SR05-EN018 Honest C .10 .20
SR05-EN019 Herald of Orange Light C .10 .20
SR05-EN020 Herald of Green Light C .10 .20
SR05-EN021 Herald of Purple Light C .10 .20
SR05-EN022 Guiding Light C .10 .20
SR05-EN023 D.D. Sprite C .10 .20
SR05-EN024 Hanewata C .10 .20
SR05-EN025 The Sanctum of Parshath SR .75 1.25
SR05-EN026 The Sanctuary in the Sky C .10 .20
SR05-EN027 Cards from the Sky C .10 .20
SR05-EN028 Celestial Transformation C .10 .20
SR05-EN029 Valhalla, Hall of the Fallen C .10 .20
SR05-EN030 Ties of the Brethren C 2.00 3.00
SR05-EN031 Rebirth of Parshath SR .75 1.25
SR05-EN032 Light of Judgment C .10 .20
SR05-EN033 Miraculous Descent C .10 .20
SR05-EN034 Synthetic Seraphim C .10 .20
SR05-EN035 Divine Punishment C .10 .20
SR05-EN036 Dark Bribe C .10 .20
SR05-EN037 Solemn Warning C .75 1.25
SR05-EN038 Ultimate Providence C .10 .20
SR05-EN039 Drastic Drop Off C .10 .20
SR05-EN040 Recall C .10 .20
SR05-ENTKN Synthetic Seraphim Token C .10 .20

2018 Yu-Gi-Oh Structure Deck Lair of Darkness 1st Edition

COMPLETE SET (42) 10.00 15.00
RELEASED ON APRIL 20, 2018
SR06-EN000 Lilith, Lady of Lament UR 1.50 2.00
SR06-EN001 Darkest Diabolos, Lord of the Lair UR 1.50 2.00
SR06-EN002 Ahrima, the Wicked Warden SR .60 1.00
SR06-EN003 Duke Shade, the Sinister Shadow Lord C .15 .25
SR06-EN004 Diabolos, King of the Abyss C .15 .25
SR06-EN005 Lich Lord, King of the Underworld C .15 .25
SR06-EN006 Prometheus, King of the Shadows C .15 .25
SR06-EN007 Archfiend Emperor, the First Lord of Horror C .15 .25
SR06-EN008 Caius the Mega Monarch C .15 .25
SR06-EN009 Legendary Maju Garzett C .15 .25
SR06-EN010 Vanity's Fiend C .15 .25
SR06-EN011 Mist Archfiend C .15 .25
SR06-EN012 Infernal Dragon C .15 .25
SR06-EN013 Archfiend Cavalry C .15 .25
SR06-EN014 Stygian Street Patrol C .15 .25
SR06-EN015 Phantom of Chaos C .15 .25
SR06-EN016 Plague Wolf C .15 .25
SR06-EN017 Fiendish Rhino Warrior C .15 .25

SR06-EN018 Kuribandit C .15 .25
SR06-EN019 Tour Guide From the Underworld C .15 .25
SR06-EN020 Absolute King Back Jack C .15 .25
SR06-EN021 Relinkuriboh C .15 .25
SR06-EN022 Lair of Darkness SR .60 1.00
SR06-EN023 Recurring Nightmare C .15 .25
SR06-EN024 Allure of Darkness C .15 .25
SR06-EN025 Hand Destruction C .15 .25
SR06-EN026 Foolish Burial Goods C .15 .25
SR06-EN027 Boogie Trap C .15 .25
SR06-EN028 Fires of Doomsday C .15 .25
SR06-EN029 Veil of Darkness C .15 .25
SR06-EN030 Grinning Grave Virus SR .60 1.00
SR06-EN031 Crush Card Virus C .15 .25
SR06-EN032 Deck Devastation Virus C .15 .25
SR06-EN033 Eradicator Epidemic Virus C .15 .25
SR06-EN034 Full Force Virus C .15 .25
SR06-EN035 Darklight C .15 .25
SR06-EN036 Trap of Darkness C .15 .25
SR06-EN037 Mind Crush C .15 .25
SR06-EN038 Rise to Full Height C .15 .25
SR06-EN039 Curse of Darkness C .15 .25
SR06-EN040 Sinister Yorishiro C .15 .25
SR06-ENTKN Shadow Token C .15 .25

2018 Yu-Gi-Oh Structure Deck Powercode Link 1st Edition

COMPLETE SET (42) 10.00 15.00
RELEASED ON AUGUST 10, 2018
SDPL-EN001 Datacorn C .10 .20
SDPL-EN002 Garbage Collector C .10 .20
SDPL-EN003 Sea Archiver SR .10 .20
SDPL-EN004 Flame Bufferlo SR .50 .80
SDPL-EN005 Lady Debug SR 1.00 1.50
SDPL-EN006 Antialian C .10 .20
SDPL-EN007 Storm Cipher C .10 .20
SDPL-EN008 Segmental Dragon UR .10 .20
SDPL-EN009 Cyberse Gadget C .10 .20
SDPL-EN010 Juragedo C 1.50 2.00
SDPL-EN011 Mecha Phantom Beast Tetherwolf C .10 .20
SDPL-EN012 Reborn Tengu C .20 .30
SDPL-EN013 Skull Meister C .10 .20
SDPL-EN014 Goblindbergh C .10 .20
SDPL-EN015 Phantom Skyblaster C .20 .35
SDPL-EN016 Genex Ally Birdman C .10 .20
SDPL-EN017 Effect Veiler C 1.00 1.50
SDPL-EN018 Magical Merchant C .10 .20
SDPL-EN019 Cosmic Compass C .10 .20
SDPL-EN020 Launcher Commander C .10 .20
SDPL-EN021 Cynet Storm C .10 .20
SDPL-EN022 Night Beam C .10 .20
SDPL-EN023 Offerings to the Doomed C .10 .20
SDPL-EN024 Forbidden Chalice C .10 .20
SDPL-EN025 Scapegoat C .10 .20
SDPL-EN026 Swords of Revealing Light C .10 .20
SDPL-EN027 Reasoning C .10 .20
SDPL-EN028 Fires of Doomsday C .10 .20
SDPL-EN029 One for One C .10 .20
SDPL-EN030 Terraforming C .40 .60
SDPL-EN031 Packet Link C .10 .20
SDPL-EN032 Wild Tornado C .10 .20
SDPL-EN033 Traptrix Trap Hole Nightmare C .10 .20
SDPL-EN034 Blazing Mirror Force C .10 .20
SDPL-EN035 Trap Stun C .10 .20
SDPL-EN036 Safe Zone C .10 .20
SDPL-EN037 Call of the Haunted C .10 .20
SDPL-EN038 Reckless Greed C .10 .20
SDPL-EN039 Debunk C .10 .20
SDPL-EN040 Powercode Talker UR .10 .20
SDPL-EN041 Traffic Ghost C .20 .30
SDPL-EN042 LANphorhynchus C 1.00 1.50

2019 Yu-Gi-Oh Structure Deck Soulburner 1st Edition

COMPLETE SET (45)
RELEASED ON FEBRUARY 15, 2019
SDSBEN001 Salamangreat Raccoon C .15 .25
SDSBEN002 Salamangreat Mole C .15 .25
SDSBEN003 Salamangreat Gazelle SR .20 .30
SDSBEN004 Salamangreat Spinny SR .35 .50
SDSBEN005 Salamangreat Fowl C .15 .25
SDSBEN006 Salamangreat Beat Bison C .15 .25
SDSBEN007 Salamangreat Meer C .15 .25
SDSBEN008 Salamangreat Foxy C .15 .25
SDSBEN009 Salamangreat Falco C .15 .25
SDSBEN010 Salamangreat Jack Jaguar C .15 .25
SDSBEN011 Salamangreat Wolvie C .15 .25
SDSBEN012 Salamangreat Parro C .15 .25
SDSBEN013 Salamangreat Foxer C .15 .25
SDSBEN014 True King Agnimazud, the Vanisher C .25 .40
SDSBEN015 Dogoran, the Mad Flame Kaiju C .40 .60
SDSBEN016 Flamvell Firedog C .15 .25
SDSBEN017 Fencing Fire Ferret C .15 .25
SDSBEN018 Inferno C .15 .25
SDSBEN019 Ash Blossom & Joyous Spring C 6.00 10.00
SDSBEN020 Red Resonator C .15 .25
SDSBEN021 Volcanic Shell C .15 .25
SDSBEN022 Formud Skipper C .15 .25
SDSBEN023 Salamangreat Circle SR .20 .30
SDSBEN024 Salamangreat Claw C .15 .25
SDSBEN025 Salamangreat Sanctuary C .15 .25
SDSBEN026 Will of the Salamangreat C .15 .25
SDSBEN027 Monster Reincarnation C .15 .25
SDSBEN028 Circle of the Fire Kings C .15 .25
SDSBEN029 Transmodify C .15 .25
SDSBEN030 Link Bound C .15 .25
SDSBEN031 Magic Planter C .15 .25
SDSBEN032 Salamangreat Rage C .15 .25
SDSBEN033 Salamangreat Roar SR .20 .30
SDSBEN034 Salamangreat Gift C .15 .25
SDSBEN035 The Transmigration Prophecy C .15 .25
SDSBEN036 Threatening Roar C .15 .25
SDSBEN037 Break Off Trap Hole C .15 .25
SDSBEN038 Backfire C .15 .25
SDSBEN039 Gozen Match C .25 .40
SDSBEN040 Salamangreat Heatleo (alternate artwork) UR .25 .40
SDSBEN041 Salamangreat Heatleo C .15 .25
SDSBEN042 Salamangreat Miragestallio UR .25 .40
SDSBEN043 Salamangreat Balelynx UR .25 .40
SDSBEN044 Flame Administrator C .15 .25
SDSBEN045 Duelittle Chimera C .15 .25

2019 Yu-Gi-Oh Structure Deck Order of the Spellcasters 1st Edition

COMPLETE SET (41) 12.00 20.00
RELEASED ON APRIL 19, 2019
SR08EN001 Endymion, the Mighty Master of Magic UR .60 1.00
SR08EN002 Reflection of Endymion SR .30 .50
SR08EN003 Magister of Endymion C .15 .25
SR08EN004 Servant of Endymion C 2.50 4.00
SR08EN005 Endymion, the Master Magician C .15 .25
SR08EN006 Crusader of Endymion C .15 .25
SR08EN007 Defender, the Magical Knight C .15 .25
SR08EN008 Mythical Beast Cerberus C .15 .25
SR08EN009 Mythical Beast Medusa C .15 .25
SR08EN010 Magical Something C .15 .25
SR08EN011 Magical Exemplar C .15 .25
SR08EN012 Magical Abductor C .15 .25
SR08EN013 Disenchanter C .15 .25
SR08EN014 Apprentice Magician C .15 .25
SR08EN015 Dark Magician of Chaos C .30 .50
SR08EN016 Fairy Tail - Luna C .15 .25
SR08EN017 Summoner Monk C .15 .25
SR08EN018 Spellbook Magician of Prophecy C .25 .40
SR08EN019 Magical Undertaker C .15 .25
SR08EN020 Magician of Faith C .15 .25
SR08EN021 Droll & Lock Bird C 2.00 3.50
SR08EN022 Spell Power Mastery SR 1.50 2.50
SR08EN023 Endymion's Lab C .15 .25
SR08EN024 Magical Citadel of Endymion C .15 .25
SR08EN025 Spell Power Grasp C .15 .25
SR08EN026 Arcane Barrier C .15 .25
SR08EN027 Spellbook of Secrets C .25 .40
SR08EN028 Spellbook of Power C .15 .25
SR08EN029 Spellbook of Wisdom C .15 .25
SR08EN030 Magical Blast C .15 .25
SR08EN031 Magical Dimension C .15 .25
SR08EN032 Terraforming C .20 .30
SR08EN033 Left Arm Offering C .35 .50
SR08EN034 Pot of Desires C 1.50 2.50
SR08EN035 Mythical Bestiamorph C .15 .25
SR08EN036 Pitch-Black Power Stone C .15 .25
SR08EN037 Extra Buck C .15 .25
SR08EN038 Gagagashield C .15 .25
SR08EN039 Magician's Circle C .15 .25
SR08EN040 Day-Breaker the Shining Magical Warrior UR .30 .50
SR08EN041 Dwimmered Path SR .30 .50

2019 Yu-Gi-Oh Structure Deck Rokket Revolt 1st Edition

COMPLETE SET (46) 10.00 15.00
RELEASED ON AUGUST 16, 2019
SDRREN001 Silverrokket Dragon SR .25 .40
SDRREN002 Rokket Tracer SR .60 1.00
SDRREN003 Rokket Recharger C .15 .25
SDRREN004 Exploderokket Dragon C .15 .25
SDRREN005 Absorouter Dragon SR .60 1.00
SDRREN006 Checksum Dragon C .15 .25
SDRREN007 Anesthrokket Dragon C .15 .25
SDRREN008 Autorokket Dragon C .15 .25
SDRREN009 Magnarokket Dragon C .15 .25
SDRREN010 Shelrokket Dragon C .15 .25
SDRREN011 Metalrokket Dragon C .15 .25
SDRREN012 Rokket Synchron C .15 .25
SDRREN013 Gateway Dragon C .15 .25
SDRREN014 Defrag Dragon C .15 .25
SDRREN015 Background Dragon C .15 .25
SDRREN016 Labradorite Dragon C .15 .25
SDRREN017 Paladin of Felgrand C .15 .25
SDRREN018 Dragon Knight of Creation C .15 .25
SDRREN019 Keeper of the Shrine C .15 .25
SDRREN020 World Chalice Guardragon C .15 .25
SDRREN021 Raiden, Hand of the Lightsworn C .15 .25
SDRREN022 Borrel Supplier C .15 .25
SDRREN023 Rapid Trigger C .15 .25
SDRREN024 Squib Draw C .15 .25
SDRREN025 Quick Launch C .30 .50
SDRREN026 Boot Sector Launch C .15 .25
SDRREN027 Borrel Regenerator C .15 .25
SDRREN028 Dragon Shrine C .15 .25
SDRREN029 Ruins of the Divine Dragon Lords C .15 .25
SDRREN030 Return of the Dragon Lords C .60 1.00
SDRREN031 Polymerization C .40 .60
SDRREN032 Twin Twisters C 1.50 2.50
SDRREN033 Zero-Day Blaster SR .25 .40
SDRREN034 Execute Protocols C .15 .25
SDRREN035 Red Reboot C .30 .50
SDRREN036 Link Turret C .15 .25
SDRREN037 Mirror Force Launcher C .15 .25
SDRREN038 Mirror Force C .15 .25
SDRREN039 Magic Cylinder C .15 .25
SDRREN040 Imperial Order C .40 .60
SDRREN041 Topologic Zeroboros UR .30 .50
SDRREN042 Borreload Furious Dragon UR .30 .50
SDRREN043 Quadborrel Dragon UR .30 .50
SDRREN044 Borreload Dragon C .75 1.25
SDRREN045 Triple Burst Dragon C .60 1.00
SDRREN046 Booster Dragon C .15 .25

TCG Packs

2012 Yu-Gi-Oh Astral Pack 1

AP01EN001 Tsukuyomi UTR 8.00 20.00
AP01EN002 Debris Dragon UTR 8.00 20.00
AP01EN003 Photon Thrasher UTR 8.00 20.00
AP01EN004 Flamvell Firedog SR .40 1.00
AP01EN005 Genex Undine SR .75 2.00
AP01EN006 Kagemusha of the Six Samurai SR 3.00 8.00
AP01EN007 Inzektor Centipede SR .75 2.00
AP01EN008 Hieratic Dragon of Tefnuit SR 2.00 5.00
AP01EN009 Terraforming SR 8.00 20.00
AP01EN010 Moray of Greed SR 1.50 4.00
AP01EN011 Mask Change SR 1.50 4.00
AP01EN012 Hidden Armory SR 1.25 3.00
AP01EN013 The Gates of Dark World SR .40 1.00
AP01EN014 Hyena C
AP01EN015 Dragon Ice C
AP01EN016 Cyber Shark C .75 2.00
AP01EN017 Swift Scarecrow C .50 1.25
AP01EN018 Elemental HERO Ice Edge C .75 2.00
AP01EN019 Mystical Sand C 1.50 4.00
AP01EN020 Spiritual Forest C .15 .40
AP01EN021 Closed Forest C .20 .60
AP01EN022 Shrine of Mist Valley C .15 .40
AP01EN023 Thunder of Ruler C .15 .40
AP01EN024 Fuh-Rin-Ka-Zan C .15 .40
AP01EN025 Astral Barrier C .15 .40

2013 Yu-Gi-Oh Astral Pack 2

COMPLETE SET (25)
BOOSTER BOX
BOOSTER PACK
RELEASED ON
AP02EN001 Atlantean Dragoons UTR 30.00 60.00
AP02EN002 Photon Papilloperative UTR 4.00 10.00
AP02EN003 Spellbook of Power UTR 25.00 50.00
AP02EN004 Interplanetarypurplythorny Dragon SR .40 1.00
AP02EN005 Geargiaccelerator SR 1.00 2.50
AP02EN006 Atlantean Heavy Infantry SR 2.50 6.00
AP02EN007 Slushy SR .20 .60
AP02EN008 Brotherhood of the Fire Fist - Hawk SR .20 .60
AP02EN009 Brotherhood of the Fire Fist - Raven SR .20 .60
AP02EN010 Harpies' Hunting Ground SR .40 1.00
AP02EN011 Gemini Spark SR 3.00 8.00
AP02EN012 Spiritual Water Art - Aoi SR .50 1.25
AP02EN013 Trap Stun SR .75 2.00
AP02EN014 Sky Scout C .20 .60
AP02EN015 Cyber Phoenix C .20 .60
AP02EN016 Light and Darkness Dragon C .75 2.00
AP02EN017 Justice of Prophecy C .40 1.00
AP02EN018 Barox C 1.25 3.00
AP02EN019 Pot of Avarice C .40 1.00
AP02EN020 Instant Fusion C 3.00 8.00
AP02EN021 Recycling Batteries C .20 .60
AP02EN022 Machina Armored Unit C .20 .60
AP02EN023 Photon Veil C .75 2.00
AP02EN024 Hysteric Party C .40 1.00
AP02EN025 Token Stampede C .20 .60

2013 Yu-Gi-Oh Astral Pack 3

COMPLETE SET (26)
BOOSTER BOX
BOOSTER PACK
RELEASED ON
AP03EN001 Atlantean Marksman UTR 20.00 35.00
AP03EN002 Maestroke the Symphony Djinn UTR 3.00 8.00
AP03EN003 Fire Formation - Tenki UTR 20.00 35.00
AP03EN004 Serene Psychic Witch SR .25 .75
AP03EN005 Mermail Abyssgunde SR 1.50 4.00
AP03EN006 Falling Down SR .25 .75
AP03EN007 Miracle Fertilizer SR 1.00 2.50
AP03EN008 Noble Arms - Gallatin SR .25 .75
AP03EN009 Spellbook Library of the Crescent SR 1.00 2.50
AP03EN010 Noble Arms - Arfeudutyr SR .25 .75
AP03EN011 Spellbook Star Hall SR .50 1.25
AP03EN012 Pollinosis SR .25 .75
AP03EN013 Wall of Thorns SR .25 .75
AP03EN014 Curtain of the Dark Ones C 1.00 2.50
AP03EN015 Jowgen the Spiritualist C .50 1.25
AP03EN016 Swarm of Scarabs C .25 .75
AP03EN017 Swarm of Locusts C .25 .75
AP03EN018 Des Lacooda C .25 .75
AP03EN019 Imprisoned Queen Archfiend C .25 .75
AP03EN020 Vampire Dragon C .50 1.25
AP03EN021 Kamionwizard C 2.50 6.00
AP03EN022 Gladiator Beast's Battle Archfiend Shield C .25 .75
AP03EN023 Deck Lockdown C .50 1.25
AP03EN024 Super Solar Nutrient C .25 .75
AP03EN025 Archfiend's Roar C .25 .75
AP03EN026 Heavy Slump C .25 .75

2014 Yu-Gi-Oh Astral Pack 4

COMPLETE SET (26) 130.00 150.00
BOOSTER PACK 2.00 5.00
RELEASED ON FEBRUARY 27, 2014
AP04EN001 Dandylion UTR 10.00 15.00
AP04EN002 Maxx "C" UTR 75.00 80.00
AP04EN003 Necrovalley UTR 18.00 22.00
AP04EN004 Blackwing - Gale the Whirlwind SR 1.00 1.50
AP04EN005 Blackwing - Kalut the Moon Shadow SR 1.00 1.50
AP04EN006 Consecrated Light SR .75 1.25
AP04EN007 Swift Scarecrow SR 1.50 2.00
AP04EN008 Crimson Blader SR 1.50 2.00
AP04EN009 Break! Draw! SR .20 .30
AP04EN010 Spellbook of Wisdom SR 2.00 3.50
AP04EN011 Spellbook of Eternity SR 1.25 2.00
AP04EN012 Fire Formation - Tensu SR 2.00 3.50
AP04EN013 Soul Drain SR 1.00 1.50
AP04EN014 Wings of Wicked Flame C .50 .75
AP04EN015 Morphing Jar #2 C .20 .30
AP04EN016 Magical Merchant C .40 .60
AP04EN017 Lonefire Blossom C .60 1.00
AP04EN018 Fossil Dyna Pachycephalo C 1.00 1.50
AP04EN019 Tytannial, Princess of Camellias C .15 .25
AP04EN020 Scrap Beast C .30 .50
AP04EN021 Ma'at C .10 .20
AP04EN022 Mavelus C 10.00 13.00
AP04EN023 Reasoning C .25 .40
AP04EN024 Archfiend's Oath C .20 .30
AP04EN025 Black Garden C 1.00 1.50
AP04EN026 Scrapstorm C .20 .35

2014 Yu-Gi-Oh Astral Pack 5

COMPLETE SET (26) 60.00 75.00
BOOSTER BOX (100 PACKS) 350.00 400.00
BOOSTER PACK (3 CARDS) 2.00 3.00

RELEASED ON JULY 25, 2014		
AP05EN001 Bujin Yamato UTR	8.00	12.00
AP05EN002 Gagaga Cowboy UTR	10.00	15.00
AP05EN003 Pot of Duality UTR	40.00	45.00
AP05EN004 Card Trooper SR	.20	.35
AP05EN005 Jenis, Lightsworn Mender SR	.50	.80
AP05EN006 Geargiarsenal SR	.30	.50
AP05EN007 Mermail Abysspike SR	.75	1.25
AP05EN008 Star Drawing SR	1.00	1.50
AP05EN009 Bujingi Turtle SR	.20	.35
AP05EN010 Advanced Ritual Art SR	.75	1.25
AP05EN011 Charge of the Light Brigade SR	2.00	3.50
AP05EN012 Overworked SR	.40	.60
AP05EN013 Full House SR	.75	1.00
AP05EN014 Blackland Fire Dragon C	.30	.50
AP05EN015 Copy Plant C	.15	.25
AP05EN016 Hanewata C	.15	.25
AP05EN017 Rinyan, Lightsworn Rogue C	.15	.25
AP05EN018 Skelgon C	1.50	2.00
AP05EN019 Queen of Thorns C	1.00	1.50
AP05EN020 Empress of Prophecy C	.15	.25
AP05EN021 Soul Exchange C	.15	.25
AP05EN022 Book of Moon C	.40	.60
AP05EN023 Lightsworn Sabre C	.60	1.00
AP05EN024 Spiritual Forest C	.15	.25
AP05EN025 Spellbook Library of the Heliosphere C	.40	.60
AP05EN026 Jurrac Impact C	.15	.25

2014 Yu-Gi-Oh Astral Pack 6

COMPLETE SET (28)	70.00	85.00
BOOSTER BOX (100 PACKS)	350.00	400.00
BOOSTER PACK (3 CARDS)	2.00	3.00
RELEASED ON DECEMBER 12, 2014		
AP06EN001 Tour Guide From the Underworld UTR	24.00	26.00
AP06EN002 Number 11: Big Eye UTR	17.00	20.00
AP06EN003 Traptrix Trap Hole Nightmare UTR	6.50	8.00
AP06EN004 Traptrix Myrmeleo SR	.75	1.15
AP06EN005 White Dragon Wyverburster SR	.75	1.00
AP06EN006 Black Dragon Collapserpent SR	.75	1.15
AP06EN007 Superheavy Samurai Big Benkei SR	.50	.80
AP06EN008 Shaddoll Beast SR	2.00	2.25
AP06EN009 Underworld Fighter Balmung SR	.30	.50
AP06EN010 Number 80: Rhapsody in Berserk SR	1.50	2.00
AP06EN011 Summoner's Art SR	5.00	6.00
AP06EN012 Bujincarnation SR	.75	1.15
AP06EN013 Infernity Break SR	.40	.60
AP06EN014 Sea Kamen C	.50	.80
AP06EN015 Gruesome Goo C	.60	.75
AP06EN016 Amazon of the Seas C	.50	.75
AP06EN017 King of the Skull Servants C	.50	.75
AP06EN018 Vanity's Fiend C	2.75	3.15
AP06EN019 Van'Dalgyon the Dark Dragon Lord C	.20	.30
AP06EN020 Machina Fortress C	1.00	1.25
AP06EN021 Man-eating Black Shark C	1.00	1.75
AP06EN022 Madolche Queen Tiaramisu C	.40	.75
AP06EN023 Nobleman of Crossout C	.20	.30
AP06EN024 Thunder Crash C	.20	.30
AP06EN025 The Monarchs Stormforth C	.25	.40
AP06EN026 Ceasefire C	.20	.30
AP06EN027 Royal Command C	.20	.30
AP06EN028 Cursed Seal of the Forbidden Spell C	.75	1.00

2015 Yu-Gi-Oh Astral Pack 7

COMPLETE SET (27)	95.00	115.00
BOOSTER PACK	3.00	5.00
RELEASED ON JUNE 5 2015		
AP07EN001 Gaia Dragon, the Thunder Charger UR	10.00	15.00
AP07EN002 Castel, the Skyblaster Musketeer UR	25.00	30.00
AP07EN003 Spell Shattering Arrow UR	5.00	7.00
AP07EN004 Satellarknight Altair SR	1.00	1.50
AP07EN005 Satellarknight Unukalhai SR	.75	1.25
AP07EN006 Djinn Demolisher of Rituals SR	.40	.60
AP07EN007 Scarm, Malebranche of the Burning Abyss SR	.50	.80
AP07EN008 Leo, the Keeper of the Sacred Tree SR	3.00	5.00
AP07EN009 Number 103: Ragnazero SR	3.00	4.00
AP07EN010 Level Limit - Area B SR	1.50	2.00
AP07EN011 Twister SR	.15	.25
AP07EN012 Dragon Ravine SR	1.50	2.00
AP07EN013 Level Limit - Area A SR	.20	.35
AP07EN014 Invader from Another Dimension C	.60	1.00
AP07EN015 Lord of the Lamp C	.50	.75
AP07EN016 Senju of the Thousand Hands C	1.00	1.50
AP07EN017 Volcanic Scattershot C	.60	1.00
AP07EN018 Gladiator Beast Bestiari C	.40	.60
AP07EN019 Madolche Puddingcess C	1.50	2.00
AP07EN020 Brotherhood of the Fire Fist - Spirit C	.60	1.00
AP07EN021 Soul Hunter C	1.50	2.00
AP07EN022 Dawn of the Herald C	1.50	2.00
AP07EN023 Storm C	.40	.60
AP07EN024 Spiritual Wind Art - Miyabi C	.40	.60
AP07EN025 Light-Imprisoning Mirror C	.60	1.00
AP07EN026 Shadow-Imprisoning Mirror C	.60	1.00
AP07EN027 Fairy Wind C	.10	.20

2015 Yu-Gi-Oh Astral Pack 8

COMPLETE SET (27)	100.00	120.00
BOOSTER PACK (3 CARDS)	3.00	5.00
RELEASED ON DECEMBER 12, 2014		
AP08EN001 Trishula, Dragon of the Ice Barrier UTR	30.00	35.00
AP08EN002 Mystical Space Typhoon UTR	25.00	30.00
AP08EN003 Fiendish Chain UTR	10.00	13.00
AP08EN004 Igknight Margrave SR	.20	.35
AP08EN005 Igknight Gallant SR	.50	.75
AP08EN006 Toon Masked Sorcerer SR	3.00	5.00
AP08EN007 Graff, Malebranche of the Burning Abyss SR	.30	.50
AP08EN008 Black Luster Soldier - Envoy of the Evening Twilight SR	1.00	1.50
AP08EN009 Spiritual Beast Rampengu SR	1.50	2.00
AP08EN010 Instant Fusion SR	1.50	2.00
AP08EN011 Kozmotown SR	.75	1.25
AP08EN012 Book of Eclipse SR	2.50	4.00
AP08EN013 Lose 1 Turn SR	1.50	2.00
AP08EN014 Rhaimundos of the Red Sword C	.75	1.25
AP08EN015 Fireyarou C	.40	.60
AP08EN016 Twin-Headed Behemoth C	.20	.35
AP08EN017 Swift Gaia the Fierce Knight C	.20	.35
AP08EN018 Kinka-byo C	4.00	6.00
AP08EN019 Red-Eyes Wyvern C	.60	1.00
AP08EN020 Gem-Knight Obsidian C	1.25	2.00
AP08EN021 Vermillion Sparrow C	1.25	2.00
AP08EN022 Masked HERO Koga C	.20	.35
AP08EN023 Machine Duplication C	1.25	1.75
AP08EN024 U.A. Stadium C	.20	.35
AP08EN025 Black Horn of Heaven C	.50	.80
AP08EN026 Safe Zone C	1.00	1.50
AP08EN027 Unpossessed C	.30	.50

2012 Yu-Gi-Oh Battle Pack Epic Dawn 1st Edition

COMPLETE SET (220)	75.00	150.00
BOOSTER BOX (36 PACKS)	60.00	80.00
BOOSTER PACK (5 CARDS)	3.00	4.00
*STARFOIL: .6X TO 1.5X BASIC CARDS		
RELEASED ON MAY 28, 2012		
BP01EN001 Witch of the Black R	.25	.75
BP01EN002 Cyber Jar R	.25	.75
BP01EN003 Jinzo R	.50	1.25
BP01EN004 Injection Fairy Lily R	.25	.75
BP01EN005 Dark Dust Spirit R	.25	.75
BP01EN006 Skull Archfiend R	.25	.75
BP01EN007 Dark Magician R	.75	2.00
BP01EN008 Blowback Dragon R	.25	.75
BP01EN009 Mobius the Frost R	.25	.75
BP01EN010 Fox Fire R	.25	.75
BP01EN011 Ancient Gear Golem R	.25	.75
BP01EN012 Treeborn Frog R	.25	.75
BP01EN013 Super Conductor R	.25	.75
BP01EN014 Gorz the Emissary R	.75	2.00
BP01EN015 Raiza the Storm R	.25	.75
BP01EN016 White Night Dragon R	.25	.75
BP01EN017 Deep Diver R	.25	.75
BP01EN018 Caius the Shadow R	.50	1.25
BP01EN019 Krebons R	.25	.75
BP01EN020 Tragoedia R	.50	1.25
BP01EN021 Obelisk the Tormentor R	5.00	12.00
BP01EN022 Machina Fortress R	.75	2.00
BP01EN023 Tour Guide R	1.25	3.00
BP01EN024 Number 39: Utopia R	.50	1.25
BP01EN025 Gachi Gachi Gantetsu R	.25	.75
BP01EN026 Grenosaurus R	.25	.75
BP01EN027 Num. 17: Leviathan R	.25	.75
BP01EN028 Wind-Up Zenmaister R	.25	.75
BP01EN029 Tiras, Keeper R	2.00	5.00
BP01EN030 Adreus, Keeper R	2.50	6.00
BP01EN031 Gem-Knight Pearl R	.25	.75
BP01EN032 Raigeki R	10.00	25.00
BP01EN033 Swords of Revealing R	.25	.75
BP01EN034 Pot of Greed R	.60	1.50
BP01EN035 Harpie's Feather R	2.50	6.00
BP01EN036 Graceful Charity R	.25	.75
BP01EN037 Change of Heart R	.75	2.00
BP01EN038 Heavy Storm R	.25	.75
BP01EN039 Snatch Steal R	.25	.75
BP01EN040 Premature Burial R	.25	.75
BP01EN041 Soul Exchange R	.25	.75
BP01EN042 Scapegoat R	.25	.75
BP01EN043 United We Stand R	1.50	4.00
BP01EN044 Creature Swap R	.25	.75
BP01EN045 Burden of Mighty R	.25	.75
BP01EN046 Pot of Duality R	.60	1.50
BP01EN047 Solemn Judgment R	.25	.75
BP01EN048 Mirror Force R	1.00	2.50
BP01EN049 Call of the Haunted R	.25	.75
BP01EN050 Ring of Destruction R	.75	2.00
BP01EN051 Torrential Tribute R	.75	2.00
BP01EN052 Metal Reflect Slime R	.40	1.00
BP01EN053 Skill Drain R	2.00	5.00
BP01EN054 Divine Wrath R	.25	.75
BP01EN055 Dark Bribe R	.75	2.00
BP01EN056 Greenkappa C	.10	.30
BP01EN057 Penguin Soldier C	.10	.30
BP01EN058 Mysterious Guard C	.10	.30
BP01EN059 Exiled Force C	.10	.30
BP01EN060 Old Vindictive Magician C	.10	.30
BP01EN061 Breaker of the Magical	.10	.30
BP01EN062 Grave Squirmer C	.10	.30
BP01EN063 Ryko, Lightsworn Hunter C	.10	.30
BP01EN064 Snowman Eater C	.10	.30
BP01EN065 Fissure C	.10	.30
BP01EN066 Tribute to the Doomed C	.10	.30
BP01EN067 Axe of Despair C	.10	.30
BP01EN068 Mystical Space Typhoon C	.50	1.25
BP01EN069 Horn of the Unicorn C	.10	.30
BP01EN070 Offerings to the Doomed C	.10	.30
BP01EN071 Bait Doll C	.10	.30
BP01EN072 Book of Moon C	.10	.30
BP01EN073 Autonomous Action Unit C	.10	.30
BP01EN074 Ante C	.10	.30
BP01EN075 Big Bang Shot C	.10	.30
BP01EN076 Fiend's Sanctuary C	.10	.30
BP01EN077 Different Dimension Gate C	.10	.30
BP01EN078 Enemy Controller C	.10	.30
BP01EN079 Monster Gate C	.10	.30
BP01EN080 Shield Crush C	.10	.30
BP01EN081 Fighting Spirit C	.10	.30
BP01EN082 Forbidden Chalice C	.10	.30
BP01EN083 Darkworld Shackles C	.10	.30
BP01EN084 Forbidden Lance C	.75	2.00
BP01EN085 Infected Mail C	.10	.30
BP01EN086 Ego Boost C	.10	.30
BP01EN087 Kunai with Chain C	.10	.30
BP01EN088 Dust Tornado C	.10	.30
BP01EN089 Windstorm of Etaqua C	.10	.30
BP01EN090 Magic Drain C	.10	.30
BP01EN091 Magic Cylinder C	.10	.30
BP01EN092 Shadow Spell C	.10	.30
BP01EN093 Blast with Chain C	.10	.30
BP01EN094 Needle Ceiling C	.10	.30
BP01EN095 Reckless Greed C	.40	1.00
BP01EN096 Nightmare Wheel C	.10	.30
BP01EN097 Spell Shield Type-8 C	.10	.30
BP01EN098 Interdimensional Matter Transporter C	.10	.30
BP01EN099 Compulsory Evacuation	.10	.30
BP01EN100 Prideful Roar C	.10	.30
BP01EN101 Half or Nothing C	.10	.30
BP01EN102 Skill Successor C	.10	.30
BP01EN103 Pixie Ring C	.10	.30
BP01EN104 Changing Destiny C	.10	.30
BP01EN105 Fiendish Chain C	1.00	2.50
BP01EN106 Inverse Universe C	.10	.30
BP01EN107 Miracle's Wake C	.10	.30
BP01EN108 Power Frame C	.10	.30
BP01EN109 Damage Gate C	.10	.30
BP01EN110 Liberty at Last! C	.10	.30
BP01EN111 Luster Dragon C	.10	.30
BP01EN112 Archfiend Soldier C	.10	.30
BP01EN113 Mad Dog of Darkness C	.10	.30
BP01EN114 Charcoal Inpachi C	.10	.30
BP01EN115 Insect Knight C	.10	.30
BP01EN116 Gene-Warped Warwolf C	.10	.30
BP01EN117 Buster Blader C	.10	.30
BP01EN118 Goblin Attack Force C	.10	.30
BP01EN119 Bazoo the Soul-Eater C	.10	.30
BP01EN120 Zombyra the Dark C	.10	.30
BP01EN121 Slate Warrior C	.10	.30
BP01EN122 Dark Ruler Ha Des C	.10	.30
BP01EN123 Freed the Matchless General C	.10	.30
BP01EN124 Airknight Parshath C	.10	.30
BP01EN125 Asura Priest C	.10	.30
BP01EN126 Exarion Universe C	.10	.30
BP01EN127 Vampire Lord C	.10	.30
BP01EN128 Toon Gemini Elf C	.10	.30
BP01EN129 King Tiger Wanghu C	.10	.30
BP01EN130 Guardian Sphinx C	.10	.30
BP01EN131 Skilled White Magician C	.10	.30
BP01EN132 Zaborg the Thunder Monarch C	.10	.30
BP01EN133 D.D. Assailant C	.10	.30
BP01EN134 Theban Nightmare C	.10	.30
BP01EN135 The Tricky C	.10	.30
BP01EN136 Raging Flame Sprite C	.10	.30
BP01EN137 Chiron the Mage C	.10	.30
BP01EN138 Cyber Dragon C	.10	.30
BP01EN139 Cybernetic Magician C	.10	.30
BP01EN140 Goblin Elite Attack Force C	.10	.30
BP01EN141 Doomcaliber Knight C	.10	.30
BP01EN142 Chainsaw Insect C	.10	.30
BP01EN143 Card Trooper C	.10	.30
BP01EN144 Voltic Kong C	.10	.30
BP01EN145 Botanical Lion C	.10	.30
BP01EN146 Ancient Gear Knight C	.10	.30
BP01EN147 Blizzard Dragon C	.40	1.00
BP01EN148 Beast King Barbaros C	.10	.30
BP01EN149 The Calculator C	.10	.30
BP01EN150 Gaap the Divine Soldier C	.10	.30
BP01EN151 Arcana Force XIV - Temperance C	.10	.30
BP01EN152 Dark Valkyria C	.10	.30
BP01EN153 Alector, Sovereign of Birds C	.10	.30
BP01EN154 Twin-Barrel Dragon C	.10	.30
BP01EN155 Abyssal Kingshark C	.10	.30
BP01EN156 Jurrac Protops C	.10	.30
BP01EN157 Hedge Guard C	.10	.30
BP01EN158 Fabled Ashenveil C	.10	.30
BP01EN159 Backup Warrior C	.10	.30
BP01EN160 Ambitious Gofer C	.10	.30
BP01EN161 Power Giant C	.10	.30
BP01EN162 Card Guard C	.10	.30
BP01EN163 Yaksha C	.10	.30
BP01EN164 Gogogo Golem C	.10	.30
BP01EN165 Big Jaws C	.10	.30
BP01EN166 Wind-Up Soldier C	.10	.30
BP01EN167 Wind-Up Dog C	.10	.30
BP01EN168 Milla the Temporal Magician C	.10	.30
BP01EN169 Ape Fighter C	.10	.30
BP01EN170 Wind-Up Warrior C	.10	.30
BP01EN171 Giant Soldier of Stone C	.10	.30
BP01EN172 Mask of Darkness C	.10	.30
BP01EN173 Morphing Jar C	.10	.30
BP01EN174 Muka Muka C	.10	.30
BP01EN175 Blast Sphere C	.10	.30
BP01EN176 Big Shield Gardna C	.10	.30
BP01EN177 Gilasaurus C	.10	.30
BP01EN178 Possessed Dark Soul C	.10	.30
BP01EN179 Twin-Headed Behemoth C	.10	.30
BP01EN180 Makyura the Destructor C	.10	.30
BP01EN181 Helping Robo for Combat C	.10	.30
BP01EN182 Zolga C	.10	.30
BP01EN183 Chaos Necromancer C	.10	.30
BP01EN184 Stealth Bird C	.40	1.00
BP01EN185 Hyper Hammerhead C	.10	.30
BP01EN186 Grave Protector C	.10	.30
BP01EN187 Night Assailant C	.10	.30
BP01EN188 Pitch-Black Warwolf C	.10	.30
BP01EN189 Dekoichi	.10	.30
BP01EN190 Gyroid C	.10	.30
BP01EN191 Drillroid C	.10	.30
BP01EN192 Gravitic Orb C	.10	.30
BP01EN193 Cloudian - Poison Cloud C	.10	.30
BP01EN194 Des Mosquito C	.10	.30
BP01EN195 Mad Reloader C	.10	.30
BP01EN196 Phantom of Chaos C	.50	1.25
BP01EN197 Cyber Valley C	.10	.30
BP01EN198 Blue Thunder T-45 C	.10	.30
BP01EN199 Vortex Trooper C	.10	.30
BP01EN200 DUCKER Mobile Cannon C	.10	.30
BP01EN201 Worm Barses C	.10	.30
BP01EN202 Shield Warrior C	.10	.30
BP01EN203 Dark Resonator C	.10	.30
BP01EN204 Noisy Gnat C	.10	.30
BP01EN205 Fabled Raven C	.10	.30
BP01EN206 Fortress Warrior C	.10	.30
BP01EN207 Twin-Sword Marauder C	.10	.30
BP01EN208 Level Warrior C	.10	.30
BP01EN209 Level Eater C	.10	.30
BP01EN210 Naturia Strawberry C	.10	.30
BP01EN211 Battle Fader C	.50	1.25
BP01EN212 Amazoness Sage C	.10	.30
BP01EN213 Amazoness Trainee C	.10	.30

BP01EN214 Hardened Armed Dragon C	1.00	2.50
BP01EN215 Blackwing - Zephyros	.10	.30
BP01EN216 Tanngrisnir of the Nordic Beasts C	.10	.30
BP01EN217 Shine Knight C	.10	.30
BP01EN218 Gagaga Magician C	.10	.30
BP01EN219 Goblindbergh C	.10	.30
BP01EN220 Psi-Blocker C	.40	1.00

2013 Yu-Gi-Oh Battle Pack 2 War of the Giants 1st Edition

COMPLETE SET (212)	30.00	80.00
BOOSTER BOX (36 PACKS)	40.00	60.00
BOOSTER PACK (5 CARDS)	2.00	3.00
*MOSAIC: .6X TO 1.5X BASIC CARDS		
RELEASED ON JUNE 28, 2013		
BP02EN001 Luster Dragon C	.25	.75
BP02EN002 Gene-Warped Warwolf C	.10	.30
BP02EN003 Frostosaurus R	.25	.75
BP02EN004 Alexandrite Dragon C	.20	.60
BP02EN005 Magician of Faith R	.50	1.25
BP02EN006 Maha Vailo C	.10	.30
BP02EN007 Cyber Jar R	.25	.75
BP02EN008 Goblin Attack Force C	.10	.30
BP02EN009 The Fiend Megacyber R	.25	.75
BP02EN010 Revival Jam C	.10	.30
BP02EN011 Kycoo the Ghost Destroyer C	.10	.30
BP02EN012 Bazoo the Soul-Eater C	.10	.30
BP02EN013 Gilasaurus C	.10	.30
BP02EN014 Zombyra the Dark C	.10	.30
BP02EN015 Sinister Serpent C	.20	.60
BP02EN016 Airknight Parshath R	.25	.75
BP02EN017 Twin-Headed Behemoth C	.10	.30
BP02EN018 Injection Fairy Lily R	.25	.75
BP02EN019 Helping Robo for Combat C	.10	.30
BP02EN020 Little-Winguard C	.10	.30
BP02EN021 D.D. Warrior Lady R	.25	.75
BP02EN022 Zolga C	.10	.30
BP02EN023 Dark Magician of Chaos R	.75	2.00
BP02EN024 Hyper Hammerhead C	.10	.30
BP02EN025 Mataza the Zapper C	.10	.30
BP02EN026 Guardian Angel Joan R	.25	.75
BP02EN027 Slate Warrior R	.25	.75
BP02EN028 D.D. Assailant R	.25	.75
BP02EN029 Ninja Grandmaster Sasuke C	.10	.30
BP02EN030 Pitch-Black Warwolf C	.10	.30
BP02EN031 Mirage Dragon C	.10	.30
BP02EN032 Big Shield Gardna C	.10	.30
BP02EN033 Toon Gemini Elf C	.10	.30
BP02EN034 Chiron the Mage C	.10	.30
BP02EN035 Ancient Gear Golem R	.25	.75
BP02EN036 Gyroid C	.10	.30
BP02EN037 Steamroid C	.10	.30
BP02EN038 Drillroid C	.10	.30
BP02EN039 Cyber Dragon C	.25	.75
BP02EN040 Goblin Elite Attack Force C	.10	.30
BP02EN041 Exarion Universe C	.10	.30
BP02EN042 Mythical Beast Cerberus C	.10	.30
BP02EN043 Treeborn Frog C	.20	.60
BP02EN044 Submarineroid C	.10	.30
BP02EN045 Ultimate Tyranno R	.25	.75
BP02EN046 Super Conductor Tyranno R	.25	.75
BP02EN047 Brain Crusher R	.25	.75
BP02EN048 Card Trooper C	.10	.30
BP02EN049 Blockman C	.10	.30
BP02EN050 Spell Striker C	.50	1.25
BP02EN051 Winged Rhynos C	.10	.30
BP02EN052 Necro Gardna C	.10	.30
BP02EN053 Herald of Creation C	.10	.30
BP02EN054 Evil HERO Malicious Edge R	.25	.75
BP02EN055 Truckroid R	.25	.75
BP02EN056 Ancient Gear Knight C	.10	.30
BP02EN057 Dragon Ice C	.10	.30
BP02EN058 Copycat C	.50	1.25
BP02EN059 Cyber Valley R	.25	.75
BP02EN060 Darklord Zerato R	.25	.75
BP02EN061 Belial - Marquis of Darkness R	.25	.75
BP02EN062 Doomcaliber Knight C	.10	.30
BP02EN063 Exodius the Ultimate Forbidden Lord C	.25	.75
BP02EN064 Dark Valkyria R	.25	.75
BP02EN065 Phantom Dragon R	.25	.75
BP02EN066 Shield Warrior C	.10	.30
BP02EN067 Dark Resonator C	.10	.30
BP02EN068 Krebons R	.25	.75
BP02EN069 The Tricky C	.10	.30
BP02EN070 Splendid Venus R	.25	.75
BP02EN071 Plaguespreader Zombie C	.50	1.25
BP02EN072 Machine Lord Ür C	.10	.30
BP02EN073 Mosaic Manticore R	.25	.75
BP02EN074 Botanical Lion C	.10	.30
BP02EN075 Blizzard Dragon C	.20	.60
BP02EN076 Des Mosquito C	.10	.30
BP02EN077 Dandylion C	.25	.75
BP02EN078 Fortress Warrior C	.10	.30
BP02EN079 Twin-Sword Marauder C	.10	.30
BP02EN080 Beast King Barbaros R	.25	.75
BP02EN081 Hedge Guard C	.10	.30
BP02EN082 Card Guard C	.10	.30
BP02EN083 White Night Dragon R	.25	.75
BP02EN084 Beast Machine King Barbaros Ür R	.25	.75
BP02EN085 Evocator Chevalier C	.10	.30
BP02EN086 Battle Fader C	.60	1.50
BP02EN087 Oracle of the Sun C	.10	.30
BP02EN088 Samurai of the Ice Barrier C	.10	.30
BP02EN089 Jurrac Titano R	.25	.75
BP02EN090 Darklord Desire R	.25	.75
BP02EN091 Power Giant C	.10	.30
BP02EN092 Anarchist Monk Ranshin C	.10	.30
BP02EN093 Ape Fighter C	.10	.30
BP02EN094 Tanngrisnir of the Nordic Beasts C	.10	.30
BP02EN095 Chaos Hunter R	.25	.75
BP02EN096 Axe Dragonute C	.10	.30
BP02EN097 Vylon Soldier C	.10	.30
BP02EN098 Blackwing - Zephyros the Elite C	.20	.60
BP02EN099 Zubaba Knight C	.10	.30
BP02EN100 Gogogo Golem C	.10	.30
BP02EN101 Needle Sunfish C	.10	.30
BP02EN102 Shocktopus C	.10	.30
BP02EN103 Photon Thrasher C	.60	1.50
BP02EN104 Interplanetarypurplythorny Dragon C	.10	.30
BP02EN105 Tour Bus From the Underworld C	.10	.30
BP02EN106 Vylon Tetra C	.10	.30
BP02EN107 Vylon Stella C	.10	.30
BP02EN108 Vylon Prism C	.10	.30
BP02EN109 Photon Wyvern R	.25	.75
BP02EN110 Tasuke Knight C	.10	.30
BP02EN111 Gagaga Gardna C	.10	.30
BP02EN112 Cardcar D R	.25	.75
BP02EN113 Flame Tiger C	.10	.30
BP02EN114 Tardy Orc C	.10	.30
BP02EN115 Bull Blader R	.25	.75
BP02EN116 Solar Wind Jammer C	.10	.30
BP02EN117 Mermail Abyssmegalo R	3.00	8.00
BP02EN118 Dododo Bot C	.10	.30
BP02EN119 Bacon Saver C	.10	.30
BP02EN120 Amarylease C	.10	.30
BP02EN121 Hyper-Ancient Shark Megalodon R	.25	.75
BP02EN122 Pyrotech Mech - Shiryu R	.25	.75
BP02EN123 Aye-Iron C	.10	.30
BP02EN124 Mecha Phantom Beast Hamstrat C	.10	.30
BP02EN125 Obelisk the Tormentor R	6.00	15.00
BP02EN126 The Winged Dragon of Ra R	5.00	12.00
BP02EN127 Slifer the Sky Dragon R	8.00	20.00
BP02EN128 Monster Reborn R	.50	1.25
BP02EN129 Pot of Greed R	.75	2.00
BP02EN130 Shield & Sword C	.10	.30
BP02EN131 Axe of Despair C	.10	.30
BP02EN132 Malevolent Nuzzler C	.10	.30
BP02EN133 Rush Recklessly C	.10	.30
BP02EN134 Horn of the Unicorn C	.10	.30
BP02EN135 Premature Burial R	.25	.75
BP02EN136 Scapegoat C	.20	.60
BP02EN137 Graceful Charity R	.25	.75
BP02EN138 Book of Moon C	.25	.75
BP02EN139 Reasoning C	.75	2.00
BP02EN140 Autonomous Action Unit C	.10	.30
BP02EN141 Big Bang Shot C	.10	.30
BP02EN142 Riryoku C	.10	.30
BP02EN143 Gravity Axe - Grarl C	.10	.30
BP02EN144 Enemy Controller C	.10	.30
BP02EN145 Earthquake C	.10	.30
BP02EN146 Shrink C	.10	.30
BP02EN147 Swords of Concealing Light C	1.00	2.50
BP02EN148 Nightmare's Steelcage C	.10	.30
BP02EN149 Mausoleum of the Emperor C	.10	.30
BP02EN150 Card Trader R	.25	.75
BP02EN151 Fiend's Sanctuary C	.10	.30
BP02EN152 Union Attack C	.10	.30
BP02EN153 Fighting Spirit C	.10	.30
BP02EN154 Star Blast C	.10	.30
BP02EN155 Forbidden Chalice C	.25	.75
BP02EN156 Reptilianne Rage C	.10	.30
BP02EN157 Rocket Pilder C	.10	.30
BP02EN158 Half Shut C	.10	.30
BP02EN159 Cursed Armaments C	.10	.30
BP02EN160 Pot of Duality R	.75	2.00
BP02EN161 Axe of Fools C	.10	.30
BP02EN162 Forbidden Lance C	.75	2.00
BP02EN163 Blustering Winds C	.10	.30
BP02EN164 Ego Boost C	.10	.30
BP02EN165 Shard of Greed R	.25	.75
BP02EN166 Full-Force Strike R	.25	.75
BP02EN167 Photon Sanctuary C	.40	1.00
BP02EN168 Forbidden Dress C	.10	.30
BP02EN169 Reverse Trap C	.10	.30
BP02EN170 Waboku C	.20	.60
BP02EN171 Call of the Haunted R	.40	1.00
BP02EN172 Mirror Wall C	.10	.30
BP02EN173 Metalmorph C	.10	.30
BP02EN174 Mask of Weakness C	.10	.30
BP02EN175 Reckless Greed R	.25	.75
BP02EN176 Rope of Life C	.10	.30
BP02EN177 Windstorm of Etaqua C	.10	.30
BP02EN178 Zero Gravity C	.10	.30
BP02EN179 A Hero Emerges C	.10	.30
BP02EN180 Embodiment of Apophis C	.10	.30
BP02EN181 Draining Shield C	.40	1.00
BP02EN182 Curse of Anubis C	.10	.30
BP02EN183 Labyrinth of Nightmare C	.10	.30
BP02EN184 Threatening Roar C	.25	.75
BP02EN185 Rising Energy C	.10	.30
BP02EN186 Magical Arm Shield C	.10	.30
BP02EN187 Shattered Axe C	.10	.30
BP02EN188 Stronghold the Moving Fortress C	.10	.30
BP02EN189 Strike Slash C	.10	.30
BP02EN190 No Entry!! C	.10	.30
BP02EN191 Cloning C	.10	.30
BP02EN192 Sinister Seeds C	.10	.30
BP02EN193 Metal Reflect Slime C	.50	1.25
BP02EN194 Zoma the Spirit C	.10	.30
BP02EN195 Miniaturize C	.10	.30
BP02EN196 Spacegate C	.10	.30
BP02EN197 Overworked C	.10	.30
BP02EN198 Kunai with Chain C	.10	.30
BP02EN199 Prideful Roar C	.10	.30
BP02EN200 Time Machine C	.25	.75
BP02EN201 Half or Nothing C	.10	.30
BP02EN202 Miracle Locus C	.10	.30
BP02EN203 Skill Successor C	.10	.30
BP02EN204 Power Frame C	.10	.30
BP02EN205 Damage Gate C	.10	.30
BP02EN206 Miracle's Wake C	.10	.30
BP02EN207 Half Counter C	.10	.30
BP02EN208 The Golden Apples R	.25	.75
BP02EN209 Tiki Curse C	.10	.30
BP02EN210 Tiki Soul C	.10	.30
BP02EN211 Impenetrable Attack C	.10	.30
BP02EN212 Memory of an Adversary R	.25	.75
BP02EN213 Dimension Gate C	.10	.30
BP02EN214 Spikeshield with Chain R	.25	.75
BP02EN215 Breakthrough Skill C	.75	2.00

2013 Yu-Gi-Oh Battle Pack 2 War of the Giants 1st Edition Mosaic Rare

*MOSAIC RARE: .6X TO 1.5X BASIC CARDS		
STATED ODDS 1:1		
BP02EN125 Obelisk the Tormentor R	6.00	15.00
BP02EN126 The Winged Dragon of Ra R	6.00	15.00
BP02EN127 Slifer the Sky Dragon R	12.00	30.00

2014 Yu-Gi-Oh Battle Pack 2 War of the Giants Round 2

COMPLETE SET (103)	20.00	60.00
BOOSTER BOX (6 PACKS)	80.00	100.00
BOOSTER PACK (5 CARDS)	15.00	20.00
RELEASED ON JANUARY 17, 2014		
BPR2001 Evilswarm Heliotrope C	.10	.30
BPR2002 Wall of Illusion SR	.25	.75
BPR2003 Big Eye C	.10	.30
BPR2004 Kazejin SR	.25	.75
BPR2005 Otohime C	.10	.30
BPR2006 Yomi Ship SR	.25	.75
BPR2007 Winged Sage Falcos C	.10	.30
BPR2008 Cyber Raider C	.10	.30
BPR2009 Berserk Gorilla C	.10	.30
BPR2010 Invader of Darkness C	.10	.30
BPR2011 Legendary Jujitsu Master SR	.25	.75
BPR2012 Blade Knight C	.10	.30
BPR2013 Big-Tusked Mammoth SR	.25	.75
BPR2014 Golem Sentry SR	.25	.75
BPR2015 Adhesive Explosive SR	.25	.75
BPR2016 Cyber Gymnast SR	.25	.75
BPR2017 Cyber Prima (SR)	.25	.75
BPR2018 Majestic Mech - Goryu C	.10	.30
BPR2019 Destiny HERO - Defender C	.40	1.00
BPR2020 Archfiend of Gilfer SR	.25	.75
BPR2021 Legendary Fiend SR	.25	.75
BPR2022 Lyla, Lightsworn Sorceress SR	1.00	2.50
BPR2023 Montage Dragon C	.75	2.00
BPR2024 Cursed Fig SR	.25	.75
BPR2025 Red Ogre SR	.25	.75
BPR2026 Blackwing - Elphin the Raven SR	.25	.75
BPR2027 Sauropod Brachion C	.10	.30
BPR2028 Worm Apocalypse C	.10	.30
BPR2029 Worm Jetelikpse C	.10	.30
BPR2030 Infernity Destroyer SR	.25	.75
BPR2031 Medium of the Ice Barrier C	.10	.30
BPR2032 A/D Changer C	.10	.30
BPR2033 Playful Possum C	.10	.30
BPR2034 Hypnocorn SR	.25	.75
BPR2035 Wattlemur C	.10	.30
BPR2036 Fabled Soulkius SR	.25	.75
BPR2037 Power Breaker C	.10	.30
BPR2038 Jurrac Gallim C	.10	.30
BPR2039 General Raiho of the Ice Barrier SR	.25	.75
BPR2040 Meklord Army of Granel SR	.25	.75
BPR2041 Skull Kraken C	.10	.30
BPR2042 Skystarray C	.10	.30
BPR2043 Sergeant Electro SR	.25	.75
BPR2044 Chow Len the Prophet SR	.25	.75
BPR2045 White Night Queen C	.10	.30
BPR2046 Junk Forward C	.10	.30
BPR2047 Swallowtail Butterspy C	.10	.30
BPR2048 Cameraclops SR	.25	.75
BPR2049 Madolche Baaple SR	.25	.75
BPR2050 Evilswarm Ketos SR	.25	.75
BPR2051 Evilswarm Mandragora C	.20	.60
BPR2052 Mogmole C	.10	.30
BPR2053 Deep Sweeper C	.10	.30
BPR2054 Heroic Challenger - Night Watchman C	.10	.30
BPR2055 Garbage Lord C	.10	.30
BPR2056 D.D. Esper Star Sparrow C	.10	.30
BPR2057 Evilswarm Obliviwisp C	.10	.30
BPR2058 Evilswarm Salamandra C	.10	.30
BPR2059 Dododo Warrior SR	.25	.75
BPR2060 Mecha Phantom Beast Tetherwolf C	.10	.30
BPR2061 Mecha Phantom Beast Blackfalcon C	.10	.30
BPR2062 Mecha Phantom Beast Stealthray SR	.25	.75
BPR2063 Gentlemander C	.10	.30
BPR2064 Schwarzschild Limit Dragon C	.10	.30
BPR2065 Tribute to The Doomed SR	.25	.75
BPR2066 Share the Pain SR	.25	.75
BPR2067 Slim-Pack C	.10	.30
BPR2068 Black Pendant C	.10	.30
BPR2069 Megamorph SR	.25	.75
BPR2070 Dark Core SR	.50	1.25
BPR2071 Different Dimension Gate SR	.25	.75
BPR2072 Back to Square One SR	.25	.75
BPR2073 Mystic Box SR	.25	.75
BPR2074 Lucky Iron Axe C	.10	.30
BPR2075 Double Summon C	1.00	2.50
BPR2076 Ribbon of Rebirth C	.10	.30
BPR2077 Release Restraint Wave SR	.25	.75
BPR2078 Berserk Scales C	.10	.30
BPR2079 Shift SR	.25	.75
BPR2080 Riryoku Field C	.10	.30
BPR2081 Needle Ceiling C	.25	.75
BPR2082 Pineapple Blast C	.10	.30
BPR2083 Adhesion Trap Hole SR	.25	.75
BPR2084 Covering Fire C	.10	.30
BPR2085 Conscription C	.10	.30
BPR2086 Chthonian Blast C	.10	.30
BPR2087 Dark Bribe SR	1.25	3.00
BPR2088 Nordic Relic Laevateinn SR	.25	.75
BPR2089 Nordic Relic Brisingamen SR	.25	.75
BPR2090 Attention! C	.10	.30
BPR2091 Raigeki Bottle SR	.25	.75
BPR2092 Nitwit Outwit C	.10	.30
BPR2093 Butterflyoke SR	.25	.75
BPR2094 Dimension Slice C	.20	.60
BPR2095 Magical Explosion SR	.25	.75
BPR2096 Memory Loss C	.10	.30
BPR2097 Butterspy Protection C	.10	.30
BPR2098 Reverse Glasses C	.10	.30
BPR2099 Fog King UR	6.00	15.00
BPR2100 High Priestess of Prophecy UR	2.50	6.00
BPR2101 Dragunity Knight - Vajrayana UR	2.00	5.00
BPR2102 Number 11: Big Eye UR	2.50	6.00
BPR2103 Safe Zone UR	1.25	3.00

2014 Yu-Gi-Oh Battle Pack 3 Monster League

COMPLETE SET (220)	40.00	75.00
BOOSTER BOX (36 PACKS)	25.00	40.00
BOOSTER PACK	2.00	4.50
RELEASED ON AUGUST 1, 2014		
BP03EN001 Jerry Beans Man C	.15	.25
BP03EN002 Bazoo the Soul-Eater C	.15	.25
BP03EN003 Frontier Wiseman C	.15	.25
BP03EN004 Arsenal Bug R	.15	.40
BP03EN005 Breaker the Magical Warrior R	.20	.60
BP03EN006 Mudora R	.15	.40
BP03EN007 Gale Lizard C	.15	.25
BP03EN008 Berserk Gorilla R	.15	.40
BP03EN009 Lord Poison C	.15	.25
BP03EN010 Sacred Crane C	.15	.25
BP03EN011 Enraged Battle Ox C	.15	.25
BP03EN012 Hyper Hammerhead C	.15	.25
BP03EN013 Slate Warrior R	.15	.40
BP03EN014 Toon Gemini Elf R	.15	.40
BP03EN015 Chiron the Mage R	.15	.40
BP03EN016 Gyroid C	.15	.25
BP03EN017 Goblin Elite Attack Force R	.15	.40
BP03EN018 Mythical Beast Cerberus C	.15	.25
BP03EN019 Machine King Prototype R	.15	.40
BP03EN020 Cyber Phoenix C	.15	.25
BP03EN021 Victory Viper XX03 C	.15	.25
BP03EN022 Herald of Green Light C	.15	.25
BP03EN023 Herald of Purple Light C	.15	.25
BP03EN024 Submarineroid C	.15	.25
BP03EN025 Black Stego C	.15	.25
BP03EN026 Card Trooper R	.15	.40
BP03EN027 Freya, Spirit of Victory C	.15	.25
BP03EN028 Exploder Dragon C	.30	.50
BP03EN029 Dweller in the Depths C	.15	.25
BP03EN030 Winged Rhynos R	.15	.40
BP03EN031 Blizzard Dragon R	.20	.60
BP03EN032 Evil HERO Infernal Gainer C	.15	.25
BP03EN033 Ancient Gear Knight R	.15	.40
BP03EN034 Royal Firestorm Guards R	.25	.75
BP03EN035 Dark Crusader C	.15	.25
BP03EN036 The Immortal Bushi C	.15	.25
BP03EN037 Black Veloci R	.15	.40
BP03EN038 Sea Koala C	.15	.25
BP03EN039 Blue Thunder T-45 R	.15	.40
BP03EN040 Golden Flying Fish R	.15	.40
BP03EN041 Aztekipede, the Worm Warrior R	.15	.40
BP03EN042 Jain, Lightsworn Paladin R	.15	.40
BP03EN043 Diskblade Rider R	.15	.40
BP03EN044 Magical Exemplar R	.20	.60
BP03EN045 Rigorous Reaver C	.15	.25
BP03EN046 Mezuki R	.60	1.50
BP03EN047 Gonogo C	.15	.25
BP03EN048 Telekinetic Shocker R	.15	.40
BP03EN049 Destructotron C	.15	.25
BP03EN050 Herald of Orange Light R	.40	1.00
BP03EN051 Psychic Jumper C	.15	.25
BP03EN052 Seed of Flame C	.15	.25
BP03EN053 Cross-Sword Beetle R	.60	1.00
BP03EN054 Defender, the Magical Knight C	.15	.25
BP03EN055 Battlestorm R	.15	.40
BP03EN056 Koa'ki Meiru Guardian R	.15	.40
BP03EN057 Koa'ki Meiru Drago R	.75	2.00
BP03EN058 Koa'ki Meiru Doom R	.15	.40
BP03EN059 Spined Gillman R	.15	.40
BP03EN060 Vanguard of the Dragon R	.15	.40
BP03EN061 Koa'ki Meiru War Arms C	.15	.25
BP03EN062 Tree Otter C	.25	.40
BP03EN063 X-Saber Airbellum C	.15	.25
BP03EN064 Sunlight Unicorn R	.15	.40
BP03EN065 Card Guard R	.15	.40
BP03EN066 Koa'ki Meiru Beetle R	.15	.40
BP03EN067 Reptilianne Gorgon C	.15	.25
BP03EN068 Metabo-Shark R	.15	.40
BP03EN069 Shutendoji C	.30	.50
BP03EN070 Gauntlet Warrior C	.15	.25
BP03EN071 Shreddder C	.15	.25
BP03EN072 Koa'ki Meiru Sandman R	.15	.40
BP03EN073 Jurrac Protops C	.15	.25
BP03EN074 Mist Valley Falcon R	.15	.40
BP03EN075 Trident Warrior R	.15	.40
BP03EN076 Rhinotaurus R	.15	.40
BP03EN077 Hypnocorn C	.15	.25
BP03EN078 Stygian Street Patrol C	.40	.60
BP03EN079 Fabled Ashenveil C	.15	.25
BP03EN080 Chain Dog C	.15	.25
BP03EN081 Koa'ki Meiru Wall R	.15	.40
BP03EN082 Genex Ally Bellflame R	.15	.40
BP03EN083 Meklord Army of Granel C	.15	.25
BP03EN084 Silent Psychic Wizard R	.15	.40
BP03EN085 Dodger Dragon R	.50	1.25
BP03EN086 Wind-Up Juggler R	.15	.40
BP03EN087 Airorca C	.15	.25
BP03EN088 Time Escaper C	.15	.25
BP03EN089 Lion Alligator R	.15	.40
BP03EN090 Friller Rabca C	.15	.25
BP03EN091 Vylon Ohm C	.15	.25
BP03EN092 Shocktopus C	.15	.25
BP03EN093 Chow Len the Prophet R	.15	.40
BP03EN094 Vampire Koala R	.15	.40
BP03EN095 Flame Tiger R	.15	.40
BP03EN096 Tardy Orc R	.15	.40
BP03EN097 Madolche Baaple C	.15	.25
BP03EN098 Evilswarm Ketos R	.15	.40
BP03EN099 Evilswarm O'lantern C	.15	.25
BP03EN100 Electromagnetic Bagworm C	.15	.25
BP03EN101 Uminotaurus C	.15	.25
BP03EN102 Leotaur R	.15	.40
BP03EN103 Aye-Iron R	.15	.40
BP03EN104 Evilswarm Thunderbird C	.30	.50
BP03EN105 Magical Undertaker C	.15	.25
BP03EN106 Gentlemander C	.15	.25
BP03EN107 Fencing Fire Ferret R	.15	.40
BP03EN108 Skelesaurus R	.15	.40
BP03EN109 Knight Day Grepher R	.15	.40
BP03EN110 Gorgonic Golem C	.15	.25
BP03EN111 Ghostrick Jackfrost C	.15	.25
BP03EN112 Black Brachios R	.15	.40
BP03EN113 Tackle Crusader C	.15	.25
BP03EN114 Stegocyber C	.15	.25
BP03EN115 Master Craftsman Gamil C	.15	.25
BP03EN133 Swords of Revealing Light C	.15	.25
BP03EN134 Rush Recklessly C	.15	.25
BP03EN135 7 Completed C	.15	.25
BP03EN136 Premature Burial C	.15	.25
BP03EN137 Mask of Brutality C	.15	.25
BP03EN138 Offerings to the Doomed C	.15	.25
BP03EN139 Scapegoat C	.30	.50
BP03EN140 The Warrior Returning Alive C	.15	.25
BP03EN141 Dragon's Gunfire C	.15	.25
BP03EN142 Stamping Destruction C	.15	.25
BP03EN143 Fusion Sword Murasame Blade C	.15	.25
BP03EN144 Creature Swap C	.15	.25
BP03EN145 Book of Life C	.25	.40
BP03EN146 Call of the Mummy C	.15	.25
BP03EN147 Banner of Courage C	.15	.25
BP03EN148 Cestus of Dagla C	.15	.25
BP03EN149 Enemy Controller C	.15	.25
BP03EN150 Earthquake C	.15	.25
BP03EN151 Swords of Concealing Light C	3.75	5.00
BP03EN152 Magicians Unite C	.15	.25
BP03EN153 Ribbon of Rebirth C	.15	.25
BP03EN154 Valhalla, Hall of the Fallen C	1.75	2.25
BP03EN155 Fighting Spirit C	.15	.25
BP03EN156 Psi-Station C	.15	.25
BP03EN157 Unstable Evolution C	.15	.25
BP03EN158 Recycling Batteries C	.20	.30
BP03EN159 Book of Eclipse C	.60	1.00
BP03EN160 Mark of the Rose C	.30	.50
BP03EN161 Psychokinesis C	.15	.25
BP03EN162 Miracle Fertilizer C	.75	1.00
BP03EN163 Psychic Sword C	.15	.25
BP03EN164 Forbidden Chalice C	.30	.50
BP03EN165 Raging Mad Plants C	.15	.25
BP03EN166 Reptilianne Rage C	.15	.25
BP03EN167 Machine Assembly Line C	.15	.25
BP03EN168 Pyramid of Wonders C	.15	.25
BP03EN169 Cursed Armaments C	.15	.25
BP03EN170 Wattjustment C	.15	.25
BP03EN171 Closed Forest C	.15	.25
BP03EN172 Forbidden Lance C	1.00	1.50
BP03EN173 Wonder Wand C	.30	.50
BP03EN174 Murmur of the Forest C	.15	.25
BP03EN175 Bound Wand C	.15	.25
BP03EN176 Night Beam C	.30	.50
BP03EN177 Spellbook of Wisdom C	.50	.75
BP03EN178 Call of the Atlanteans C	.15	.25
BP03EN179 One-Shot Wand C	.15	.25
BP03EN180 Forbidden Dress C	.15	.25
BP03EN181 Noble Arms - Arfeudutyr C	.15	.25
BP03EN182 Noble Arms - Caliburn C	.15	.25
BP03EN183 Ayers Rock Sunrise C	.15	.25
BP03EN184 Forbidden Scripture C	.15	.25
BP03EN185 Card Advance C	5.00	6.00
BP03EN186 Bashing Shield C	.20	.35
BP03EN187 Call of the Haunted C	.15	.25
BP03EN188 Mirror Wall C	.15	.25
BP03EN189 Metalmorph C	.15	.25
BP03EN190 Mask of Weakness C	.15	.25
BP03EN191 Bark of Dark Ruler C	.15	.25
BP03EN192 Ready for Intercepting C	.15	.25
BP03EN193 Burst Breath C	.15	.25
BP03EN194 Blast with Chain C	.15	.25
BP03EN195 Tutan Mask C	.15	.25
BP03EN196 Windstorm of Etaqua C	.15	.25
BP03EN197 Zero Gravity C	.15	.25
BP03EN198 Shadow Spell C	.15	.25
BP03EN199 Curse of Anubis C	.15	.25
BP03EN200 Rare Metalmorph C	.15	.25
BP03EN201 Magical Arm Shield C	.15	.25
BP03EN202 Dark Bribe C	1.00	1.50
BP03EN203 Chaos Burst C	.15	.25
BP03EN204 No Entry!! C	.15	.25
BP03EN205 Hate Buster C	.15	.25
BP03EN206 Miniaturize C	.15	.25
BP03EN207 Psychic Overload C	.15	.25
BP03EN208 Telepathic Power C	.15	.25
BP03EN209 Mind Over Matter C	.20	.30
BP03EN210 Kunai with Chain C	.15	.25
BP03EN211 Pollinosis C	.15	.25
BP03EN212 Plant Food Chain C	.15	.25
BP03EN213 Miracle Locus C	.15	.25
BP03EN214 Skill Successor C	.15	.25
BP03EN215 Alien Brain C	.15	.25
BP03EN216 Forgotten Temple of the Deep C	.15	.25
BP03EN217 Psi-Curse C	.15	.25
BP03EN218 Damage Gate C	.15	.25
BP03EN219 Super Rush Recklessly C	.15	.25
BP03EN220 Miracle's Wake C	.15	.25
BP03EN221 Nordic Relic Laevateinn C	.15	.25
BP03EN222 Psychic Reactor C	.15	.25
BP03EN223 Poseidon Wave C	.15	.25
BP03EN224 Raigeki Bottle C	.15	.25
BP03EN225 Butterflyoke C	.15	.25
BP03EN226 Dimension Gate C	.15	.25
BP03EN227 Breakthrough Skill C	1.00	1.50
BP03EN228 Pinpoint Guard C	.25	.40
BP03EN229 Memory Loss C	.15	.25
BP03EN230 Butterspy Protection C	.15	.25
BP03EN231 Intrigue Shield C	.15	.25
BP03EN232 Inspiration C	.15	.25
BP03EN233 Ghosts From the Past C	.15	.25
BP03EN234 Unbreakable Spirit C	.15	.25
BP03EN235 Typhoon C	.75	1.25
BP03EN236 Swamp Mirrorer C	.25	.40
BP03EN237 Quantum Cat C	.40	.60

2006 Yu-Gi-Oh Champion Pack Game One

COMPLETE SET (20)	200.00	300.00
BOOSTER BOX (20 PACKS)	400.00	500.00
BOOSTER PACK (3 CARDS)	10.00	20.00
RELEASED ON NOVEMBER 11, 2006		
CP01EN001 Satellite Cannon UR	15.00	30.00
CP01EN002 Book of Moon SR	120.00	160.00
CP01EN003 Metamorphosis SR	40.00	80.00
CP01EN004 Sakuretsu Armor SR	10.00	25.00
CP01EN005 Night Assailant SR	10.00	25.00
CP01EN006 Big Shield Gardna R	.75	2.00
CP01EN007 Limiter Removal R	.75	2.00
CP01EN008 Solemn Judgment R	.75	2.00
CP01EN009 Reflect Bounder R	.75	2.00
CP01EN010 Enemy Controller R	.75	2.00
CP01EN011 Pot of Avarice R	.75	2.00
CP01EN012 Thunder Kid C	.60	1.50
CP01EN013 Mysterious Guard C	.60	1.50
CP01EN014 King Tiger Wanghu C	.60	1.50
CP01EN015 My Body as a Shield C	.60	1.50
CP01EN016 Final Countdown C	.60	1.50
CP01EN017 Mudora C	.60	1.50
CP01EN018 Stealth Bird C	.60	1.50
CP01EN019 Emissary of the Afterlife C	.60	1.50
CP01EN020 Threatening Roar C	.60	1.50

2007 Yu-Gi-Oh Champion Pack Game Two

COMPLETE SET (20)	60.00	120.00
BOOSTER BOX (20 PACKS)	400.00	500.00
BOOSTER PACK (3 CARDS)	10.00	20.00
RELEASED ON FEBRUARY 6, 2007		
CP02EN001 Magical Stone Excavation UR	10.00	25.00
CP02EN002 Nimble Momonga SR	5.00	12.00
CP02EN003 Magician of Faith SR	25.00	50.00
CP02EN004 Pyramid Turtle SR	3.00	8.00
CP02EN005 Smashing Ground SR	5.00	12.00
CP02EN006 Kuriboh R	2.00	4.00
CP02EN007 Abyss Solider R	1.00	2.00
CP02EN008 Ring of Destruction R	2.00	5.00
CP02EN009 Morphing Jar R	4.00	7.00
CP02EN010 Dark Master - Zorc R	1.00	2.00
CP02EN011 Magicial Dimension R	1.00	2.50
CP02EN012 Happy Lover C	3.00	8.00
CP02EN013 Rush Recklessly C	.20	.50
CP02EN014 Ceasefire C	.75	2.00
CP02EN015 Thunder Dragon C	.75	2.00
CP02EN016 Twin-Headed Behemoth C	.75	2.00
CP02EN017 Book of Taiyou C	.75	2.00
CP02EN018 Terraforming C	.75	2.00
CP02EN019 Big Bang Shot C	.20	.50
CP02EN020 Stray Lambs C	.20	.50

2007 Yu-Gi-Oh Champion Pack Game Three

COMPLETE SET (7)	45.00	90.00
BOOSTER BOX (20 PACKS)	400.00	500.00
BOOSTER PACK (3 CARDS)	10.00	20.00
RELEASED ON MAY 15, 2007		
CP03EN001 Magicians Unite UR	4.00	10.00
CP03EN002 Spirit Reaper SR	8.00	20.00
CP03EN003 Gravekeeper's Spy SR	15.00	30.00
CP03EN004 Sniper Hunter SR	5.00	12.00
CP03EN005 Dark World Lightning SR	2.50	6.00
CP03EN006 D.D. Assailant R	.50	1.25
CP03EN007 Goldd Wu-Lord of Dark World R	.50	1.25
CP03EN008 Manticore of Darkness R	.50	1.25
CP03EN009 The Agent of Judgment - Saturn R	.50	1.25
CP03EN010 Pikeru's Circle of Enchantment R	.50	1.25
CP03EN011 Widespread Ruin R	.50	1.25
CP03EN012 Fairy Dragon C	.50	1.25
CP03EN013 Chiron the Mage C	.50	1.25
CP03EN014 Kaibaman C	.50	1.25
CP03EN015 B.E.S. Crystal Core C	.50	1.25
CP03EN016 Gravekeeper's Chief C	.50	1.25
CP03EN017 Wild Nature's Release C	.50	1.25
CP03EN018 A Feather of the Phoenix C	.50	1.25
CP03EN019 Contract with the Abyss C	.50	1.25
CP03EN020 Necrovalley C	.50	1.25

2007 Yu-Gi-Oh Champion Pack Game Four

COMPLETE SET (5)	25.00	60.00
BOOSTER BOX (20 PACKS)	400.00	500.00
BOOSTER PACK (3 CARDS)	10.00	20.00
RELEASED ON MAY 15, 2007		
CP04EN001 Germa UR	4.00	10.00
CP04EN002 Ultimate Offering SR	8.00	20.00
CP04EN003 Bottomless Trap Hole SR	90.00	120.00
CP04EN004 Apprentice Magician SR	4.00	10.00
CP04EN005 Hydrogeddon SR	2.50	6.00
CP04EN006 Confiscation R	.75	2.00
CP04EN007 Freed the Brave Wanderer R	.75	2.00
CP04EN008 Divine Sword - Phoenix Blade R	.75	2.00
CP04EN009 Return from the Different Dimension R	.75	2.00
CP04EN010 Kinetic Soldier R	.75	2.00
CP04EN011 Magician's Circle R	.75	2.00
CP04EN012 Soul Exchange C	.50	1.25
CP04EN013 Mother Grizzly C	.50	1.25
CP04EN014 Grand Tiki Elder C	.50	1.25
CP04EN015 Gigantes C	.50	1.25
CP04EN016 Robbin' Goblin C	.50	1.25
CP04EN017 Manju of the Ten Thousand Hands C	.50	1.25
CP04EN018 Hand of Nephthys C	.50	1.25
CP04EN019 D.D. Survivor C	.50	1.25
CP04EN020 Treeborn Frog C	.50	1.25

2008 Yu-Gi-Oh Champion Pack Game Five

COMPLETE SET (20)	60.00	120.00
BOOSTER BOX (20 PACKS)	400.00	500.00
BOOSTER PACK (3 CARDS)	10.00	20.00
RELEASED ON JANUARY 8, 2008		
CP51 Fiend's Sanctuary UR	10.00	25.00
CP520 Spirit Barrier C	.75	2.00
CP05EN002 Giant Germ SR	4.00	10.00
CP05EN003 Magical Merchant SR	6.00	15.00
CP05EN004 Wave Motion Cannon SR	8.00	20.00
CP05EN005 Trap Dustshoot SR	8.00	20.00
CP05EN006 Dark Necrofear R	.75	2.00
CP05EN007 Blowback Dragon R	.40	1.00
CP05EN008 Dark RUler Ha Des R	.75	2.00
CP05EN009 Deck Devastation Virus R	.75	2.00
CP05EN010 Pulling the Rug R	.75	2.00

CP05EN011 Anti Spell Fragrance R	10.00	25.00
CP05EN012 Amazon of the Seas C	.75	2.00
CP05EN013 Protector of the Sanctuary C	.75	2.00
CP05EN014 Double Coston C	.75	2.00
CP05EN015 Rescue Cat C	.40	1.00
CP05EN016 D.D. Crow C	.75	2.00
CP05EN017 Hammer Shot C	.20	.50
CP05EN018 Thousand Knives C	.75	2.00
CP05EN019 Cursed Seal of the Forbidden Spell C	.75	2.00

2008 Yu-Gi-Oh Champion Pack Game Six

COMPLETE SET (20)	40.00	100.00
BOOSTER BOX (20 PACKS)	400.00	500.00
BOOSTER PACK (3 CARDS)	10.00	20.00
RELEASED ON MAY 12, 2008		
CP06EN001 Rigorous Reaver UR	1.50	4.00
CP06EN002 Destiny Hero - Fear Monger SR	4.00	10.00
CP06EN003 Old Vindictive Magician SR	4.00	10.00
CP06EN004 Phoenix Wing Wind Blast SR	10.00	25.00
CP06EN005 Blaze Accelerator SR	4.00	10.00
CP06EN006 Call of Darkness R	.75	2.00
CP06EN007 Blade Knight R	.75	2.00
CP06EN008 Super-Electromagnetic Voltech Dragon R	.75	2.00
CP06EN009 Elemental Hero Stratos R	1.25	3.00
CP06EN010 Helios Duo Megistus R	.75	2.00
CP06EN011 Mage Power R	2.00	5.00
CP06EN012 Sentinel of the Seas C	.75	2.00
CP06EN013 Batteryman AA C	.75	2.00
CP06EN014 Theban Nightmare C	.75	2.00
CP06EN015 Majestic Mech - Ohka C	.75	2.00
CP06EN016 Soul of Purity and Light C	.75	2.00
CP06EN017 Amplifier C	2.00	5.00
CP06EN018 Cold Wave C	.75	2.00
CP06EN019 Magical Hats C	.75	2.00
CP06EN020 Dimension Wall C	2.00	5.00

2008 Yu-Gi-Oh Champion Pack Game Seven

COMPLETE SET (20)	80.00	150.00
BOOSTER BOX (20 PACKS)	400.00	500.00
BOOSTER PACK (3 CARDS)	10.00	20.00
RELEASED ON SEPTEMBER 13, 2008		
CP71 Voltic Kong UR	1.50	4.00
CP07EN002 Legendary Jujitsu Master SR	1.50	4.00
CP07EN003 Threatening Roar SR	5.00	12.00
CP07EN004 Gladiator Beast Bestiari SR	6.00	15.00
CP07EN005 Lonefire Blossom SR	30.00	60.00
CP07EN006 Elemental Hero Ocean R	4.00	10.00
CP07EN007 Fairy King Truesdale R	1.50	4.00
CP07EN008 Spell Striker R	1.25	3.00
CP07EN009 Vanity's Fiend R	6.00	15.00
CP07EN010 Dark World Dealings R	1.50	4.00
CP07EN011 Doom Shaman R	1.25	3.00
CP07EN012 Shovel Crusher C	.75	2.00
CP07EN013 Life Absorbing Machine C	.75	2.00
CP07EN014 Fusilier Dragon, the DualMode Beast C	.75	2.00
CP07EN015 Homunculus the Alchemic Being C	.75	2.00
CP07EN016 Memory Crusher C	.75	2.00
CP07EN017 Instant Fusion C	3.00	8.00
CP07EN018 Dimensional Inversion C	.75	2.00
CP07EN019 Ancient Rules C	4.00	10.00
CP07EN020 Counter Counter C	.75	2.00

2009 Yu-Gi-Oh Champion Pack Game Eight

COMPLETE SET (20)	75.00	150.00
BOOSTER BOX (20 PACKS)	400.00	500.00
BOOSTER PACK (3 CARDS)	10.00	20.00
RELEASED ON MAY 29, 2012		
CP08EN002 Prohibition SR	4.00	10.00
CP08EN003 Mind Crush SR	20.00	40.00
CP08EN004 Dimensional Fissure SR	6.00	15.00
CP08EN005 Lumina, Lightsworn Summoner SR	30.00	60.00
CP08EN006 Magician's Valkyria R	4.00	10.00
CP08EN007 Silent Magician LV4 R	2.00	5.00
CP08EN008 Great Shogun Shien R	.50	1.25
CP08EN009 Herald of Creation R	.40	1.00
CP08EN010 Burial from a Different Dimension R	1.25	3.00
CP08EN011 Necro Gardna R	.40	1.00
CP08EN012 Mushroom Man C	.75	2.00
CP08EN013 Royal Oppression C	3.00	8.00
CP08EN014 Beckoning Light C	.30	1.00
CP08EN015 Neo-Spacian Dark Panther C	.30	1.00
CP08EN016 Alien Warrior C	.30	1.00
CP08EN017 Alien Mother C	.30	1.00
CP08EN018 Vanity's Ruler C	.75	2.00
CP08EN019 Miraculous Rebirth C	.30	1.00
CP08EN020 Cell Explosion Virus C	.30	1.00
CP8EN001 Gravity Behemoth UR	1.50	4.00

2006 Yu-Gi-Oh Duelist Pack Chazz Princeton 1st Edition

COMPLETE SET (30)	40.00	80.00
BOOSTER BOX (30 PACKS)	125.00	200.00
BOOSTER PACK (6 CARDS)	2.50	6.00
RELEASED ON FEBRUARY 8, 2006		
DP2EN001 V-Tiger Jet C	.25	.75
DP2EN002 Ojama Green C	.25	.75
DP2EN003 Ojama Yellow C	.25	.75
DP2EN004 Ojama Black C	.25	.75
DP2EN005 X-Head Cannon C	.25	.75
DP2EN006 Y-Dragon Head C	.25	.75
DP2EN007 Z-Metal Tank C	.25	.75
DP2EN008 W-Wing Catapult C	.25	.75
DP2EN009 Infernal Incinerator R	.25	.75
DP2EN010 Armed Dragon LV3 C	.25	.75
DP2EN011 Armed Dragon LV5 C	.25	.75
DP2EN012 Armed Dragon LV7 SR	2.50	6.00
DP2EN013 Armed Dragon LV10 UR	15.00	30.00
DP2EN014 XYZ-Dragon Cannon R	.25	.75
DP2EN015 Ojama King C	.25	.75
DP2EN016 VW-Tiger Catapult R	.25	.75
DP2EN017 VWXYZ-Dragon Catapult Cannon R	.25	.75
DP2EN018 Ojama Delta Hurricane!! C	.25	.75
DP2EN019 Level Modulation R	.25	.75
DP2EN020 Ojamagic R	.25	.75
DP2EN021 Ojamuscle R	.25	.75
DP2EN022 Chthonian Alliance C	.25	.75
DP2EN023 Armed Changer C	.25	.75
DP2EN024 Magical Mallet SR	1.25	3.00
DP2EN025 Inferno Reckless Summon SR	3.00	8.00
DP2EN026 Ring of Defense UR	3.00	8.00
DP2EN027 Ojama Trio C	.40	1.00
DP2EN028 Chtonian Blast C	.25	.75
DP2EN029 Chthonian Polymer C	.25	.75
DP2EN030 The Grave of Enkindling SR	.25	.75

2006 Yu-Gi-Oh Duelist Pack Jaden Yuki 1st Edition

COMPLETE SET (30)	20.00	50.00
BOOSTER BOX (5 PACKS)	125.00	200.00
BOOSTER PACK (25 CARDS)	2.50	6.00
RELEASED ON FEBRUARY 8, 2006		
DP1EN001 Elemental HERO Avian C	.25	.75
DP1EN002 Elemental HERO Burstinatrix C	.25	.75
DP1EN003 Elemental HERO Clayman C	.25	.75
DP1EN004 Elemental HERO Sparkman C	.25	.75
DP1EN005 Winged Kuriboh R	.75	2.00
DP1EN006 Winged Kuriboh LV10 R	1.25	3.00
DP1EN007 Wroughtweiler C	.25	.75
DP1EN008 Dark Catapulter C	.25	.75
DP1EN009 Elemental HERO Bubbleman C	.25	.75
DP1EN010 Elemental HERO Flame Wingman SR	2.00	5.00
DP1EN011 Elemental HERO Thunder Giant R	.75	2.00
DP1EN012 Elemental HERO Rampart Blaster R	.75	2.00
DP1EN013 Elemental HERO Steam Healer UR	3.00	8.00
DP1EN014 Polymerization C	.75	2.00
DP1EN015 Fusion Sage C	.75	2.00
DP1EN016 The Warrior Returning Alive C	.25	.75
DP1EN017 Feather Shot C	.25	.75
DP1EN018 Transcendent Wings C	.25	.75
DP1EN019 Bubble Shuffle C	.25	.75
DP1EN020 Spark Blaster C	.25	.75
DP1EN021 Skyscraper R	1.50	4.00
DP1EN022 Burst Return SR	.25	.75
DP1EN023 Bubble Blaster SR	.25	.75
DP1EN024 Bubble Illusion UR	1.50	4.00
DP1EN025 A Hero Emerges C	.25	.75
DP1EN026 Draining Shield C	.25	.75
DP1EN027 Negate Attack R	.25	.75
DP1EN028 Hero Signal C	.25	.75
DP1EN029 Feather Wind R	.25	.75
DP1EN030 Clacy Charge SR	.25	.75

2007 Yu-Gi-Oh Duelist Pack Zane Truesdale 1st Edition

COMPLETE SET (30)	20.00	50.00
BOOSTER BOX (30 PACKS)	125.00	200.00
BOOSTER PACK (6 CARDS)	2.50	6.00
RELEASED ON APRIL 17, 2007		
DP04EN001 Cyber Dragon R	1.25	3.00
DP04EN002 Cyber Barrier Dragon R	.25	.75
DP04EN003 Cyber Laser Dragon R	1.25	3.00
DP04EN004 Prot-Cyber Dragon C	.25	.75
DP04EN005 Cyber Kirin C	.25	.75
DP04EN006 Cyber Phoenix C	.25	.75
DP04EN007 Cyberdark Horn C	1.25	3.00
DP04EN008 Cyberdark Edge C	.75	2.00
DP04EN009 Cyberdark Keel C	.75	2.00
DP04EN010 Internal Dragon UR	2.50	6.00
DP04EN011 Cyber Twin Dragon R	.25	.75
DP04EN012 Cyber End Dragon R	2.00	5.00
DP04EN013 Chimeratech Overdragon R	.60	1.50
DP04EN014 Cyberdark Dragon SR	.75	2.00
DP04EN015 Mystical Space Typhoon C	.40	1.00
DP04EN016 Limiter Removal C	.25	.75
DP04EN017 De-Fusion C	.75	2.00
DP04EN018 Creature Swap C	.25	.75
DP04EN019 Different Dimension Capsule C	.50	1.25
DP04EN020 Power Bond R	.25	.75
DP04EN021 Photon Generator Unit C	.25	.75
DP04EN022 Overload Fusion C	.25	.75
DP04EN023 Future Fusion C	.60	1.50
DP04EN024 Ruthless Denial SR	.25	.75
DP04EN025 Call of the Haunted C	.25	.75
DP04EN026 Trap Jammer C	.40	1.00
DP04EN027 Attack Reflector Unit C	.25	.75
DP04EN028 Return Soul SR	.25	.75
DP04EN029 Damage Polarizer UR	1.25	3.00
DP04EN030 Fusion Guard SR	.25	.75

2007 Yu-Gi-Oh Duelist Pack Aster Phoenix 1st Edition

COMPLETE SET (30)	15.00	40.00
BOOSTER BOX (30 PACKS)	125.00	200.00
BOOSTER PACK (6 CARDS)	2.50	6.00
RELEASED ON APRIL 17, 2007		
DP05EN001 Destiny HERO - Doom Lord C	.25	.75
DP05EN002 Destiny HERO - Captain Tenacious C	.25	.75
DP05EN003 Destiny HERO - Diamond Dude C	.25	.75
DP05EN004 Destiny HERO - Dreadmaster R	.25	.75
DP05EN005 Destiny HERO - Double Dude R	.25	.75
DP05EN006 Destiny HERO - Defender R	.25	.75
DP05EN007 Destiny HERO - Dogma R	.25	.75
DP05EN008 Destiny HERO - Blade Master C	.25	.75
DP05EN009 Destiny HERO - Fear Monger R	.25	.75
DP05EN010 Destiny HERO - Dasher C	.25	.75
DP05EN011 Destiny HERO - Malicious UR	4.00	10.00
DP05EN012 Elemental HERO Phoenix Enforcer R	.75	2.00
DP05EN013 Elemental HERO Shining Phoenix Enforcer SR	1.50	4.00
DP05EN014 Misfortune C	.25	.75
DP05EN015 Guard Penalty C	.25	.75
DP05EN016 Clock Tower Prison R	.25	.75
DP05EN017 D - Spirit C	.25	.75
DP05EN018 Cyclone Blade C	.25	.75
DP05EN019 Dark City C	.25	.75
DP05EN020 Destiny Draw UR	4.00	10.00
DP05EN021 Over Destiny SR	.25	.75
DP05EN022 Elemental Recharge C	.25	.75
DP05EN023 Destruction of Destiny C	.25	.75
DP05EN024 Destiny Signal C	.25	.75
DP05EN025 D - Time C	.25	.75
DP05EN026 D - Shield C	.25	.75
DP05EN027 Destiny Mirage C	.25	.75
DP05EN028 D - Chain C	.25	.75
DP05EN029 D - Counter SR	.25	.75
DP05EN030 Eternal Dread SR	.25	.75

2007 Yu-Gi-Oh Duelist Pack Jaden Yuki 2 1st Edition

COMPLETE SET (30)	15.00	40.00
BOOSTER BOX (30 PACKS)	100.00	150.00
BOOSTER PACK (6 CARDS)	2.50	6.00
RELEASED ON FEBRUARY 7, 2007		
DP03EN001 Elemental HERO Neos C	.25	.75
DP03EN002 Elemental HERO Bladedge R	.25	.75
DP03EN003 Elemental HERO Wildheart C	.25	.75
DP03EN004 Hero Kid C	.25	.75
DP03EN005 Neo-Spacian Aqua Dolphin R	.40	1.00
DP03EN006 Neo-Spacian Flare Scarab R	.40	1.00
DP03EN007 Neo-Spacian Dark Panther R	.40	1.00
DP03EN008 Chrysallis Dolphin C	.25	.75
DP03EN009 Card Trooper UR	3.00	8.00
DP03EN010 Elemental HERO Wildedge R	1.25	3.00
DP03EN011 Elemental HERO Wild Wingman C	.25	.75
DP03EN012 Elemental HERO Aqua Neos R	.25	.75
DP03EN013 Elemental HERO Flare Neos R	.25	.75
DP03EN014 Elemental HERO Dark Neos SR	.75	2.00
DP03EN015 Cyclone Boomerang C	.25	.75
DP03EN016 H - Heated Heart C	.25	.75
DP03EN017 E - Emergency Call C	.25	.75
DP03EN018 R - Righteous Justice C	.25	.75
DP03EN019 O - Oversoul C	.25	.75
DP03EN020 Hero Flash!! C	.25	.75
DP03EN021 Contact C	.25	.75
DP03EN022 Fake Hero C	.25	.75
DP03EN023 Common Soul C	.25	.75
DP03EN024 Neo Space C	.25	.75
DP03EN025 Light Laser SR	.25	.75
DP03EN026 Burial from a Different Dimension UR	3.00	8.00
DP03EN027 Hero Barrier C	.25	.75
DP03EN028 Miracle Kids C	.25	.75
DP03EN029 Edge Hammer SR	.25	.75
DP03EN030 Kid Guard SR	.25	.75

2008 Yu-Gi-Oh Duelist Pack Jaden Yuki 3 1st Edition

COMPLETE SET (30)	10.00	30.00
BOOSTER BOX (30 PACKS)	80.00	120.00
BOOSTER PACK (6 CARDS)	2.50	6.00
RELEASED ON JANUARY 22, 2008		
DP06EN001 Neo-Spacian Air Hummingbird C	.50	1.25
DP06EN002 Neo-Spacian Grand Mole R	.40	1.00
DP06EN003 Neo-Spacian Glow Moss C	.10	.30
DP06EN004 Elemental Hero Captain Gold R	.50	1.25
DP06EN005 Elemental Hero Neos Alius C	.10	.30
DP06EN006 Evil Hero Malicious Edge SR	1.50	4.00
DP06EN007 Evil Hero Infernal Gainer C	.10	.30
DP06EN008 Evil Hero Infernal Prodigy SR	.75	2.00
DP06EN009 Armor Breaker R	.40	1.00
DP06EN010 Evil Hero Dark Gaia C	.10	.30
DP06EN011 Evil Hero Wild Cyclone UR	.75	2.00
DP06EN012 Evil Hero Infernal Sniper SR	.25	.75
DP06EN013 Evil Hero Malicious Fiend UR	2.00	5.00
DP06EN014 Skyscraper 2 - Hero City SR	1.50	4.00
DP06EN015 Reverse of Neos C	.10	.30
DP06EN016 Convert Contact C	.10	.30
DP06EN017 Swing of Memories C	.40	1.00
DP06EN018 Dark Fusion C	.75	2.00
DP06EN019 Dark Calling R	.75	2.00
DP06EN020 Revoke Fusion R	.60	1.50
DP06EN021 Hero Medal C	.10	.30
DP06EN022 Mirror Gate C	.10	.30
DP06EN023 Over Limit C	.10	.30
DP06EN024 Hero Counterattack C	.10	.30
DP06EN025 Hero's Rule 2 R	.20	.75

2008 Yu-Gi-Oh Duelist Pack Jesse Anderson 1st Edition

COMPLETE SET (30)	10.00	30.00
BOOSTER BOX (30 PACKS)	80.00	120.00
BOOSTER PACK (6 CARDS)	.25	6.00
RELEASED ON JANUARY 22, 2008		
DP71 Crystal Beast Ruby Carbuncle C	.10	.30
DP72 Crystal Beast Amethyst Cat R	.40	1.00
DP73 Crystal Beast Emerald Tortoise C	.10	.30
DP74 Crystal Beast Topaz Tiger R	.40	1.00
DP75 Crystal Beast Amber Mammoth C	.10	.30
DP76 Crystal Beast Cobalt Eagle C	.10	.30
DP77 Phantom Skyblaster UR	.40	1.00
DP78 Grave Squirmer SR	.60	1.50
DP79 Grinder Golem SR	2.00	5.00
DP710 Magna-Slash Dragon C	.10	.30
DP711 Gravi-Crush Dragon C	.10	.30
DP712 Twister C	.20	.75
DP713 Crystal Beacon C	.10	.30
DP714 Crystal Blessing C	.10	.30
DP715 Crystal Abundance R	.40	1.00
DP716 Crystal Promise C	.10	.30
DP717 Ancient City - Rainbow Ruins R	.40	1.00
DP718 Hand Destruction R	1.25	3.00
DP719 Crystal Release SR	.60	1.50
DP720 Crystal Tree SR	1.25	3.00
DP721 Triggered Summon C	.10	.30
DP722 Last Resort C	.10	.30
DP723 Crystal Raigeki C	.10	.30
DP724 Crystal Counter UR	2.50	6.00
DP725 Crystal Pair R	.50	1.25

2009 Yu-Gi-Oh Duelist Pack Yusei 1st Edition

COMPLETE SET (30)	10.00	25.00
BOOSTER BOX (30 PACKS)	50.00	80.00
BOOSTER PACK (6 CARDS)	2.00	5.00
RELEASED ON FEBRUARY 24, 2009		
DP08EN001 Junk Synchron C	.10	.30
DP08EN002 Speed Warrior C	.10	.30
DP08EN003 Turbo Booster C	.10	.30
DP08EN004 Nitro Synchron R	.40	1.00
DP08EN005 Quillbolt Hedgehog C	.10	.30
DP08EN006 Ghost Gardna C	.10	.30
DP08EN007 Shield Warrior C	.10	.30
DP08EN008 Healing Wave Generator C	.10	.30
DP08EN009 Turbo Synchron R	.40	1.00
DP08EN010 Fortress Warrior SR	.25	.50
DP08EN011 Tuningware UR	1.00	2.50
DP08EN012 Junk Warrior R	.40	1.00

DP08EN013 Nitro Warrior R	.40	1.00
DP08EN014 Stardust Dragon SR	2.00	5.00
DP08EN015 Turbo Warrior R	.40	1.00
DP08EN016 Armory Arm UR	2.00	5.00
DP08EN017 Fighting SPirit C	.10	.30
DP08EN018 Domino Effect C	.10	.30
DP08EN019 Junk Barrage C	.10	.30
DP08EN020 Card Rotator C	.10	.30
DP08EN021 Equip Shot C	.10	.30
DP08EN022 Graceful Revival C	.10	.30
DP08EN023 Defense Draw C	.25	.50
DP08EN024 Remote Revenge C	.10	.30
DP08EN025 Battle Mania R	.40	1.00
DP08EN026 Confusion Chaff C	.10	.30
DP08EN027 Urgent Tuning R	.40	1.00
DP08EN028 Synchro Strike C	.10	.30
DP08EN029 Give and Take SR	.25	.50
DP08EN030 Limiter Overload SR	.25	.50

2009 Yu-Gi-Oh Duelist Pack Yugi 1st Edition

COMPLETE SET (30)	40.00	80.00
BOOSTER BOX (30 PACKS)	150.00	250.00
BOOSTER PACK (6 CARDS)	3.00	8.00
RELEASED ON JULY 7, 2009		
DPYG1 Dark Magician R	.40	1.00
DPYG2 Summoned Skull SR	2.00	5.00
DPYG3 Queen's Knight C	.15	.25
DPYG4 Jack's Knight C	.15	.25
DPYG5 Kuriboh C	.15	.25
DPYG6 Catapult Turtle C	.15	.25
DPYG7 Buster Blader C	.15	.25
DPYG8 Dark Magician Girl SR	2.50	6.00
DPYG9 Big Shield Gardna C	.15	.25
DPYG10 Sorcerer of Dark Magic SR	3.00	8.00
DPYG11 King's Knight C	.15	.25
DPYG12 Green Gadget C	.15	.25
DPYG13 Red Gadget C	.15	.25
DPYG14 Yellow Gadget C	.15	.25
DPYG15 Marshmallon R	1.25	3.00
DPYG16 Dark Paladin UR	8.00	20.00
DPYG17 Black Luster Soldier R	.40	1.00
DPYG18 Swords of Revealing Light C	.15	.25
DPYG19 Monster Reborn R	.40	1.00
DPYG20 Polymerization SR	8.00	20.00
DPYG21 Exchange R	.40	1.00
DPYG22 Black Luster Ritual C	.15	.25
DPYG23 Diffusion Wave-Motion C	.15	.25
DPYG24 Brain Control C	.15	.25
DPYG25 Card of Sanctity R	.40	1.00
DPYG26 Spellbinding Circle C	.15	.25
DPYG27 Mirror Force UR	2.00	5.00
DPYG28 Magical Hats R	.75	2.00
DPYG29 Lightforce Sword C	.15	.25
DPYG30 Stronghold the Moving Fortress C	.15	.25

2009 Yu-Gi-Oh Duelist Pack Yugi Unlimited

DPYGEN001 Dark Magician R	.20	.35
DPYGEN002 Summoned Skull SR	1.50	2.50
DPYGEN003 Queens Knight C	.10	.20
DPYGEN004 Jacks Knight C	.10	.20
DPYGEN005 Kuriboh C	.10	.20
DPYGEN006 Catapult Turtle C	.10	.20
DPYGEN007 Buster Blader C	.10	.20
DPYGEN008 Dark Magician Girl SR	1.50	2.50
DPYGEN009 Big Shield Gardna C	.10	.20
DPYGEN010 Sorcerer of Dark Magic SR	7.00	10.00
DPYGEN011 Kings Knight C	.10	.20
DPYGEN012 Green Gadget C	.10	.20
DPYGEN013 Red Gadget C	.10	.20
DPYGEN014 Yellow Gadget C	.10	.20
DPYGEN015 Marshmallon R	.20	.35
DPYGEN016 Dark Paladin UR	6.00	8.00
DPYGEN017 Black Luster Soldier R	.20	.35
DPYGEN018 Swords of Revealing Light C	.10	.20
DPYGEN019 Monster Reborn R	.20	.35
DPYGEN020 Polymerization SR	3.00	5.00
DPYGEN021 Exchange R	.20	.35
DPYGEN022 Black Luster Ritual C	.10	.20
DPYGEN023 Diffusion Wave Motion C	.10	.20
DPYGEN024 Brain Control C	.10	.20
DPYGEN025 Card of Sanctity R	.20	.35
DPYGEN026 Spellbinding Circle C	.10	.20
DPYGEN027 Mirror Force UR	1.50	2.50
DPYGEN028 Magical Hats R	.20	.35
DPYGEN029 Lightforce Sword C	.10	.20
DPYGEN030 Stronghold the Moving Fortress C	.10	.20

2010 Yu-Gi-Oh Duelist Pack Yusei 2 1st Edition

COMPLETE SET (30)	80.00	120.00
BOOSTER BOX (30 PACKS)	60.00	80.00
BOOSTER PACK (6 CARDS)	3.00	4.00
RELEASED ON JANUARY 26, 2010		
DP09001 Stardust Dragon/Assault Mode SR	.40	1.00
DP09EN002 Road Synchron R	.25	1.50
DP09EN003 Turret Warrior R	.25	1.00
DP09EN004 Debris Dragon	.10	.30
DP09EN005 Hyper Synchron	.10	.35
DP09EN006 Rockstone Warrior R	.25	.30
DP09EN007 Level Warrior	.10	.30
DP09EN008 Majestic Dragon	.75	2.00
DP09EN009 Max Warrior R	.25	.30
DP09EN010 Quickdraw Synchron	.10	.30
DP09EN011 Level Eater	.10	.30
DP09EN012 Zero Gardna	.10	.30
DP09EN013 Gauntlet Warrior UR	.40	1.00
DP09EN014 Eccentric Boy SR	.40	1.00
DP09EN015 Road Warrior R	.75	2.00
DP09EN016 Junk Archer UR	2.50	6.00
DP09EN017 Prevention Star	.10	.30
DP09EN018 One for One R	.25	.30
DP09EN019 Release Restraint Wave	.10	.30
DP09EN020 Silver Wing	.10	.35
DP09EN021 Advance Draw	.10	.30
DP09EN022 Assault Mode Activate	.10	.30
DP09EN023 Spirit Force	.10	.30
DP09EN024 Descending Lost Star	.10	.30
DP09EN025 Miracle Locus	.10	.30
DP09EN026 Skill Successor R	.25	.30
DP09EN027 Reinforce Truth	.10	.30
DP09EN028 Slip Summon	.10	.30
DP09EN029 Scrubbed Raid SR	.40	1.00
DP09EN030 Tuner's Barrier SR	.40	1.00

2011 Yu-Gi-Oh Duelist Pack Yusei 3 1st Edition

COMPLETE SET (30)		
BOOSTER BOX (36 PACKS)	50.00	60.00
BOOSTER PACK (6 CARDS)	3.00	4.00
RELEASED ON JANUARY 21, 2011		
DP10EN001 Sonic Chick	.10	.30
DP10EN002 Shield Wing C	.10	.30
DP10EN003 Stardust Xiaolong C	.10	.30
DP10EN004 Drill Synchron C	.10	.30
DP10EN005 Card Breaker C	.10	.30
DP10EN006 Second Booster C	.10	.30
DP10EN007 Effect Veiler R	2.50	6.00
DP10EN008 Dash Warrior C	.10	.30
DP10EN009 Damage Eater C	.10	.30
DP10EN010 A/D Changer C	.10	.30
DP10EN011 Stronghold Guardian C	.10	.30
DP10EN012 Boost Warrior SR	.60	1.50
DP10EN013 Justice Bringer UR	.40	1.00
DP10EN014 Bri Synchron UR	.40	1.00
DP10EN015 Big One Warrior SR	.40	1.00
DP10EN016 Dragon Knight Draco-Equiste SR	.40	1.00
DP10EN017 Majestic Star Dragon R	.40	1.00
DP10EN018 Drill Warrior R	.40	1.00
DP10EN019 Cards of Consonance C	.50	1.25
DP10EN020 Variety Comes Out C	.10	.30
DP10EN021 Blind Spot Strike C	.10	.30
DP10EN022 Double Cyclone C	.10	.30
DP10EN023 Battle Waltz R	.40	1.00
DP10EN024 Synchro Gift R	.40	1.00
DP10EN025 Starlight Road R	.40	1.00
DP10EN026 Synchro Barrier C	.10	.30
DP10EN027 Power Frame C	.10	.30
DP10EN028 Desperate Tag C	.10	.30
DP10EN029 Cards of Sacrifice R	.40	1.00
DP10EN030 Synchro Material SR	.40	1.00

2011 Yu-Gi-Oh Duelist Pack Crow 1st Edition

COMPLETE SET (30)		
BOOSTER BOX (36 PACKS)	50.00	60.00
BOOSTER PACK (5 CARDS)	3.00	4.00
RELEASED ON MAY 31, 2011		
DP11EN001 Blackwing - Gale the Whirlwind R	.60	1.50
DP11EN002 Blackwing - Bora the Spear R	.50	1.25
DP11EN003 Blackwing - Blizzard the Far North C	.60	1.50
DP11EN004 Blackwing - Shura the Blue Flame R	.40	1.00
DP11EN005 Blackwing - Elphin the Raven R	.40	1.00
DP11EN006 Blackwing - Mistral the Silver Shield C	.10	.30
DP11EN007 Blackwing - Fane the Steel Chain C	.10	.30
DP11EN008 Blackwing - Ghibli the Searing Wind C	.10	.30
DP11EN009 Blackwing - Gust the Backblast C	.10	.30
DP11EN010 Blackwing - Kochi the Daybreak R	.40	1.00
DP11EN011 Blackwing - Jetstream the Blue Sky UR	.75	2.00
DP11EN012 Blackwing - Zephyros the Elite UR	4.00	10.00
DP11EN013 Blackwing Armor Master SR	.50	1.25
DP11EN014 Blackwing Armed Wing R	.40	1.00
DP11EN015 Blackwing - Silverwind the Ascendant R	.40	1.00
DP11EN016 Black-Winged Dragon SR	.50	1.25
DP11EN017 Raptor Wing Strike C	.10	.30
DP11EN018 Against the Wind C	.10	.30
DP11EN019 Black-Winged Strafe C	.10	.30
DP11EN020 Cards for Black Feathers C	.10	.30
DP11EN021 Ebon Arrow C	.10	.30
DP11EN022 Delta Crow - Anti Reverse C	.75	2.00
DP11EN023 Level Retuner C	.10	.30
DP11EN024 Fake Feather C	.10	.30
DP11EN025 Blackwing - Backlash C	.10	.30
DP11EN026 Blackwing - Bombardment C	.10	.30
DP11EN027 Black Thunder C	.10	.30
DP11EN028 Guard Mines C	.10	.30
DP11EN029 Black Feather Beacon SR	.40	1.00
DP11EN030 Black Return SR	.40	1.00

2015 Yu-Gi-Oh Duelist Pack Battle City

COMPLETE SET (47)	45.00	60.00
BOOSTER BOX (36 PACKS)	40.00	60.00
BOOSTER PACK (5 CARDS)	2.00	4.00
RELEASED ON JUNE 19, 2016		
DPBCEN001 The Winged Dragon of Ra - Sphere Mode UR	20.00	25.00
DPBCEN002 Jurageddo SR	4.00	6.00
DPBCEN003 Legion the Fiend Jester SR	3.00	5.00
DPBCEN004 Anti-Magic Arrows UR	3.00	5.00
DPBCEN005 Multiple Destruction UR	.40	.60
DPBCEN006 Black Luster Soldier SR	1.50	2.50
DPBCEN007 Black Luster Ritual C	.10	.20
DPBCEN008 Dark Magician SR	.60	1.00
DPBCEN009 Dark Magician Girl SR	2.00	3.50
DPBCEN010 Buster Blader R	.15	.25
DPBCEN011 Archfiend of Gilfer C	.10	.20
DPBCEN012 Jack's Knight C	.10	.20
DPBCEN013 Queen's Knight C	.10	.20
DPBCEN014 King's Knight C	.10	.20
DPBCEN015 Kuriboh C	.10	.20
DPBCEN016 Blue-Eyes White Dragon UR	2.50	4.00
DPBCEN017 Lord of D. C	.10	.20
DPBCEN018 The Flute of Summoning Dragon C	.10	.20
DPBCEN019 Enemy Controller C	.10	.20
DPBCEN020 Crush Card Virus R	.75	1.25
DPBCEN021 Red-Eyes B. Dragon SR	1.25	1.75
DPBCEN022 Gearfried the Iron Knight C	.10	.20
DPBCEN023 Rocket Warrior C	.10	.20
DPBCEN024 Time Wizard C	.10	.20
DPBCEN025 Foolish Burial R	.20	.35
DPBCEN026 Insect Queen C	.10	.20
DPBCEN027 Jinzo R	.15	.25
DPBCEN028 The Legendary Fisherman C	.10	.20
DPBCEN029 Dragged Down into the Grave C	.10	.20
DPBCEN030 Embodiment of Apophis R	.10	.20
DPBCEN031 The Masked Beast R	.10	.20
DPBCEN032 Curse of the Masked Beast C	.10	.20
DPBCEN033 Dark Necrofear R	.10	.20
DPBCEN034 Lava Golem R	.50	.80
DPBCEN035 Magical Stone Excavation C	.10	.20
DPBCEN036 Malevolent Catastrophe C	.10	.20
DPBCEN037 Harpie Lady C	.10	.20
DPBCEN038 Harpie Lady Sisters C	.10	.20
DPBCEN039 Elegant Egotist C	.10	.20
DPBCEN040 Hysteric Party C	.10	.20
DPBCEN041 Barrel Dragon R	.15	.25
DPBCEN042 Blast Sphere C	.10	.20
DPBCEN043 Blue-Eyes Toon Dragon C	.75	1.25
DPBCEN044 Toon Dark Magician Girl C	.30	.50
DPBCEN045 Toon Gemini Elf C	.10	.20
DPBCEN046 Toon World C	.40	.60
DPBCEN047 Toon Table of Contents R	3.00	5.00

2016 Yu-Gi-Oh Duelist Pack Rivals of the Pharaoh 1st Edition

COMPLETE SET (46)	80.00	100.00
BOOSTER BOX (36 PACKS)	50.00	70.00
BOOSTER PACK (5 CARDS)	2.00	4.00
RELEASED ON SEPTEMBER 16, 2016		
DPRPEN001 Silent Swordsman UR	9.00	12.00
DPRPEN002 Silent Magician UR	10.00	13.00
DPRPEN003 Silent Paladin UR	7.00	10.00
DPRPEN004 Silent Sword Slash SR	2.50	3.00
DPRPEN005 Silent Burning SR	2.50	3.00
DPRPEN006 Magnet Reverse SR	.75	1.00
DPRPEN007 Magnet Force SR	.75	1.00
DPRPEN008 Neutron Blast UR	6.00	8.00
DPRPEN009 Lullaby of Obedience UR	15.00	20.00
DPRPEN010 Tribute Burial SR	3.00	4.00
DPRPEN011 Dark Sanctuary UR	6.50	8.00
DPRPEN012 Dragon Master Knight R	1.00	1.50
DPRPEN013 Dark Magician of Chaos R	1.25	2.00
DPRPEN014 Dedication through Light and Darkness C	.15	.25
DPRPEN015 Fiends Sanctuary R	.75	1.25
DPRPEN016 Silent Swordsman LV3 C	.15	.25
DPRPEN017 Silent Swordsman LV5 C	.15	.25
DPRPEN018 Silent Swordsman LV7 C	.15	.25
DPRPEN019 Silent Magician LV4 C	.15	.25
DPRPEN020 Silent Magician LV8 C	.15	.25
DPRPEN021 Green Gadget C	.15	.25
DPRPEN022 Red Gadget C	.15	.25
DPRPEN023 Yellow Gadget C	.15	.25
DPRPEN024 Stronghold the Moving Fortress C	.15	.25
DPRPEN025 BlueEyes Ultimate Dragon R	1.00	2.00
DPRPEN026 BlueEyes Shining Dragon C	.15	.25
DPRPEN027 YZTank Dragon R	.75	1.25
DPRPEN028 Dragons Mirror R	2.00	2.50
DPRPEN029 Dragon Shrine R	1.25	2.00
DPRPEN030 Silvers Cry SR	3.75	5.00
DPRPEN031 Castle of Dragon Souls R	.75	1.25
DPRPEN032 Helpoemer C	.15	.25
DPRPEN033 Metal Reflect Slime R	.75	1.25
DPRPEN034 Blast Held by a Tribute C	.15	.25
DPRPEN035 Exchange of the Spirit C	.15	.25
DPRPEN036 Mystical Beast of Serket C	.15	.25
DPRPEN037 Temple of the Kings C	.15	.25
DPRPEN038 Sangan C	.15	.25
DPRPEN039 Necroface C	.15	.25
DPRPEN040 Dark Necrofear C	.15	.25
DPRPEN041 Destiny Board C	.15	.25
DPRPEN042 Spirit Message I C	.15	.25
DPRPEN043 Spirit Message N C	.15	.25
DPRPEN044 Spirit Message A C	.15	.25
DPRPEN045 Spirit Message L C	.15	.25
DPRPEN046 ThousandEyes Restrict R	1.25	2.00

2017 Yu-Gi-Oh Duelist Pack Dimensional Guardians 1st Edition

COMPLETE SET (45)	30.00	50.00
BOOSTER BOX (40 PACKS)	35.00	50.00
BOOSTER PACK (5 CARDS)	2.00	3.00
RELEASED ON MAY 26, 2017		
DPDGEN001 Spiral Flame Strike UR	5.00	7.00
DPDGEN002 Performapal Ballad SR	.60	1.00
DPDGEN003 Performapal Barracuda SR	.60	1.00
DPDGEN004 Speedroid Dominobutterfly UR	2.00	3.50
DPDGEN005 Pendulum Fusion SR	5.00	7.00
DPDGEN006 Frightfur Daredevil SR	2.00	3.00
DPDGEN007 Frightfur Reborn UR	4.00	6.00
DPDGEN008 Raidraptor Replica UR	2.00	3.00
DPDGEN009 Cyber Prima C	.10	.20
DPDGEN010 Cyber Tutubon C	.10	.20
DPDGEN011 Etoile Cyber C	.10	.20
DPDGEN012 Cyber Petit Angel R	.20	.35
DPDGEN013 Cyber Angel Vrash C	.10	.20
DPDGEN014 Cyber Angel Dakini R	.20	.35
DPDGEN015 Cyber Angel Benten SR	.60	1.00
DPDGEN016 Cyber Angel Idaten C	.10	.20
DPDGEN017 Machine Angel Ritual C	.10	.20
DPDGEN018 Machine Angel Absolute Ritual R	.20	.35
DPDGEN019 Ritual Sanctuary UR	1.50	2.00
DPDGEN020 Dark Resonator C	.10	.20
DPDGEN021 Synkron Resonator C	.10	.20
DPDGEN022 Chain Resonator C	.10	.20
DPDGEN023 Mirror Resonator C	.10	.20
DPDGEN024 Red Resonator R	.20	.35
DPDGEN025 Red Warg C	.10	.20
DPDGEN026 Red Gardna C	.10	.20
DPDGEN027 Red Sprinter C	.10	.20
DPDGEN028 Red Mirror C	.10	.20
DPDGEN029 Resonator Call R	.20	.35
DPDGEN030 Tyrant Red Dragon Archfiend UR	.60	1.00
DPDGEN031 Scarlight Red Dragon Archfiend R	.50	.80
DPDGEN032 Red Wyvern C	.10	.20
DPDGEN033 Reject Reborn C	.10	.20
DPDGEN034 Kings Synchro R	.20	.35
DPDGEN035 Cipher Wing C	.10	.20
DPDGEN036 Cipher Twin Raptor R	.20	.35
DPDGEN037 Cipher Mirror Knight C	.10	.20
DPDGEN038 Cipher Etranger R	.20	.35
DPDGEN039 Neo Galaxy Eyes Cipher Dragon UR	.30	.50
DPDGEN040 GalaxyEyes Cipher Dragon SR	3.00	5.00

DPDGEN041 Starliege Paladynamo R	.20	.35
DPDGEN042 Rank Up Magic Cipher Ascension C	.10	.20
DPDGEN043 Double Cipher C	.10	.20
DPDGEN044 Cipher Bit C	.10	.20
DPDGEN045 Cipher Spectrum C	.10	.20

2004 Yu-Gi-Oh Exclusive Pack

COMPLETE SET	6.00	15.00
BOOSTER BOX (20 PACKS)	40.00	80.00
BOOSTER PACK (8 CARDS)	2.50	6.00
EP1EN1 Theinen The Great Sphinx UR	1.25	3.00
EP1EN8 Return From The Different Dimension C	.25	.75
EP1EN002 Andro Sphinx UR	1.25	3.00
EP1EN003 Sphinx Teleia UR	1.25	3.00
EP1EN004 Rare Metal Dragon C	.75	2.00
EP1EN005 Peten The Dark Clown C	.75	2.00
EP1EN006 Familiar Knight C	.75	2.00
EP1EN007 Inferno Tempest C	.75	2.00

2017 Yu-Gi-Oh Duelist Saga 1st Edition

COMPLETE SET (100)	150.00	225.00
RELEASED ON MARCH 31, 2017		
DUSAEN001 Double Fin Shark Ultra Rare	.15	.25
DUSAEN002 Silent Angler Ultra Rare	.15	.25
DUSAEN003 Depth Shark Ultra Rare	.15	.25
DUSAEN004 Saber Shark Ultra Rare	.15	.25
DUSAEN005 Guard Penguin Ultra Rare	.15	.25
DUSAEN006 Number 94 Crystalzero Ultra Rare	.15	.25
DUSAEN007 Full Armored Crystalzero Lancer Ultra Rare	.15	.25
DUSAEN008 Full Armored Black Ray Lancer Ultra Rare	.15	.25
DUSAEN009 Sea Lords Amulet Ultra Rare	.15	.25
DUSAEN010 Diamond Dust Ultra Rare	.15	.25
DUSAEN011 Chain Summon Ultra Rare	.15	.25
DUSAEN012 Brohunder Ultra Rare	.15	.25
DUSAEN013 Number 28 Titanic Moth Ultra Rare	.15	.25
DUSAEN014 Number 70 Malevolent Sin Ultra Rare	.15	.25
DUSAEN015 Necroid Synchro Ultra Rare	.15	.25
DUSAEN016 Wandering King Wildwind Ultra Rare	.15	.25
DUSAEN017 Synchro Call Ultra Rare	.15	.25
DUSAEN018 Celestial Double Star Shaman Ultra Rare	.15	.25
DUSAEN019 Legacy of a HERO Ultra Rare	.50	.80
DUSAEN020 Gozuki Ultra Rare	1.00	1.50
DUSAEN021 Vision HERO Vyon Ultra Rare	2.00	2.50
DUSAEN022 Darklord Ukoback Ultra Rare	.15	.25
DUSAEN023 Darklord Descent Ultra Rare	.15	.25
DUSAEN024 Legacy of the Duelist Ultra Rare	.50	.80
DUSAEN025 Chaos Scepter Blast Ultra Rare	.50	.80
DUSAEN026 Diabound Kernel Ultra Rare	.15	.25
DUSAEN027 Harpies Feather Storm Ultra Rare	.40	.60
DUSAEN028 Elemental HERO Honest Neos Ultra Rare	7.00	9.00
DUSAEN029 Skydive Scorcher Ultra Rare	.15	.25
DUSAEN030 Dark Summoning Beast Ultra Rare	.50	.75
DUSAEN031 Fallen Paradise Ultra Rare	.15	.25
DUSAEN032 White Veil Ultra Rare	.15	.25
DUSAEN033 Power Wall Ultra Rare	.15	.25
DUSAEN034 Cosmic Blazar Dragon Ultra Rare	1.25	2.00
DUSAEN035 Clear Effector Ultra Rare	.15	.25
DUSAEN036 Cosmic Flare Ultra Rare	.15	.25
DUSAEN037 Converging Wishes Ultra Rare	.15	.25
DUSAEN038 Clashing Souls Ultra Rare	.15	.25
DUSAEN039 Light Wing Shield Ultra Rare	.15	.25
DUSAEN040 Halfway to Forever Ultra Rare	.15	.25
DUSAEN041 Contract with Don Thousand Ultra Rare	.15	.25
DUSAEN042 Dueltaining Ultra Rare	.15	.25
DUSAEN043 BlueEyes White Dragon Ultra Rare	2.50	3.00
DUSAEN044 Magician of Faith Ultra Rare	1.50	2.00
DUSAEN045 Jinzo Ultra Rare	1.00	1.50
DUSAEN046 Brain Control Ultra Rare	.20	.35
DUSAEN047 Royal Decree Ultra Rare	1.00	1.50
DUSAEN048 Mirror Force Ultra Rare	1.00	1.50
DUSAEN049 Imperial Order Ultra Rare	2.50	3.00
DUSAEN050 Necrovalley Ultra Rare	.50	.80
DUSAEN051 DD Warrior Lady Ultra Rare	.15	.25
DUSAEN052 Tsukuyomi Ultra Rare	.50	.80
DUSAEN053 Black Luster Soldier Envoy of the Beginning Ultra Rare	5.00	7.00
DUSAEN054 Dark Magician of Chaos Ultra Rare	.75	1.25
DUSAEN055 Monster Gate Ultra Rare	.30	.50
DUSAEN056 Doomcaliber Knight Ultra Rare	.15	.25
DUSAEN057 Cyber Dragon Ultra Rare	1.00	1.50
DUSAEN058 Treeborn Frog Ultra Rare	.20	.35
DUSAEN059 Dandylion Ultra Rare	.20	.35
DUSAEN060 Dimensional Fissure Ultra Rare	.60	1.00
DUSAEN061 NeoSpacian Grand Mole Ultra Rare	.15	.25
DUSAEN062 Future Fusion Ultra Rare	.60	1.00
DUSAEN063 Advanced Ritual Art Ultra Rare	2.00	2.50
DUSAEN064 Mezuki Ultra Rare	2.50	3.00
DUSAEN065 Chimeratech Fortress Dragon Ultra Rare	.25	.40
DUSAEN066 Fossil Dyna Pachycephalo Ultra Rare	.50	.80
DUSAEN067 Dark Armed Dragon Ultra Rare	.40	.60
DUSAEN068 RedEyes Darkness Metal Dragon Ultra Rare	1.50	2.00
DUSAEN069 Honest Ultra Rare	2.00	2.50
DUSAEN070 Judgment Dragon Ultra Rare	1.00	1.50
DUSAEN071 Gladiator Beast Gyzarus Ultra Rare	.15	.25
DUSAEN072 Rescue Cat Ultra Rare	1.50	2.00
DUSAEN073 Brionac Dragon of the Ice Barrier Ultra Rare	3.00	4.00
DUSAEN074 Junk Synchron Ultra Rare	.30	.50
DUSAEN075 Goyo Guardian Ultra Rare	.40	.60
DUSAEN076 Plaguespreader Zombie Ultra Rare	.50	.80
DUSAEN077 Black Rose Dragon Ultra Rare	1.00	1.50
DUSAEN078 Blackwing Gale the Whirlwind Ultra Rare	.15	.25
DUSAEN079 Deep Sea Diva Ultra Rare	.30	.50
DUSAEN080 Battle Fader Ultra Rare	.60	1.00
DUSAEN081 Trishula Dragon of the Ice Barrier Ultra Rare	2.00	2.50
DUSAEN082 Infernity Launcher Ultra Rare	.30	.50
DUSAEN083 Effect Veiler Ultra Rare	2.00	2.50
DUSAEN084 Pot of Duality Ultra Rare	3.00	3.50
DUSAEN085 Solemn Warning Ultra Rare	4.00	5.00
DUSAEN086 Formula Synchron Ultra Rare	1.00	1.50
DUSAEN087 A Hero Lives Ultra Rare	1.00	1.50
DUSAEN088 Evolzar Laggia Ultra Rare	1.00	1.50
DUSAEN089 Constellar Ptolemy M7 Ultra Rare	.25	.40
DUSAEN090 Evilswarm Ophion Ultra Rare	.15	.25
DUSAEN091 Tour Guide From the Underworld Ultra Rare	1.00	1.50
DUSAEN092 Soul Charge Ultra Rare	2.50	3.50
DUSAEN093 Castel the Skyblaster Musketeer Ultra Rare	2.50	3.00
DUSAEN094 Masked HERO Dark Law Ultra Rare	4.00	6.00
DUSAEN095 MXSaber Invoker Ultra Rare	.50	.80
DUSAEN096 Uria Lord of Searing Flames Ultra Rare	1.25	2.00
DUSAEN097 Hamon Lord of Striking Thunder Ultra Rare	1.50	2.00
DUSAEN098 Raviel Lord of Phantasms Ultra Rare	.75	1.25
DUSAEN099 Armityle the Chaos Phantom Ultra Rare	1.50	2.50
DUSAEN100 Dark Magician Ultra Rare	.75	1.25

2017 Yu-Gi-Oh Duelist Saga 1st Edition French

COMPLETE SET	150.00	225.00
RELEASED ON		
DUSAFR001 Double Fin Shark Ultra Rare	.15	.25
DUSAFR002 Silent Angler Ultra Rare	.15	.25
DUSAFR003 Depth Shark Ultra Rare	.15	.25
DUSAFR004 Saber Shark Ultra Rare	.15	.25
DUSAFR005 Guard Penguin Ultra Rare	.15	.25
DUSAFR006 Number 94 Crystalzero Ultra Rare	.15	.25
DUSAFR007 Full Armored Crystalzero Lancer Ultra Rare	.15	.25
DUSAFR008 Full Armored Black Ray Lancer Ultra Rare	.15	.25
DUSAFR009 Sea Lords Amulet Ultra Rare	.15	.25
DUSAFR010 Diamond Dust Ultra Rare	.15	.25
DUSAFR011 Chain Summon Ultra Rare	.15	.25
DUSAFR012 Brohunder Ultra Rare	.15	.25
DUSAFR013 Number 28 Titanic Moth Ultra Rare	.15	.25
DUSAFR014 Number 70 Malevolent Sin Ultra Rare	.15	.25
DUSAFR015 Necroid Synchro Ultra Rare	.15	.25
DUSAFR016 Wandering King Wildwind Ultra Rare	.15	.25
DUSAFR017 Synchro Call Ultra Rare	.15	.25
DUSAFR018 Celestial Double Star Shaman Ultra Rare	.15	.25
DUSAFR019 Legacy of a HERO Ultra Rare	.50	.80
DUSAFR020 Gozuki Ultra Rare	1.00	1.50
DUSAFR021 Vision HERO Vyon Ultra Rare	2.00	2.50
DUSAFR022 Darklord Ukoback Ultra Rare	.15	.25
DUSAFR023 Darklord Descent Ultra Rare	.15	.25
DUSAFR024 Legacy of the Duelist Ultra Rare	.50	.80
DUSAFR025 Chaos Scepter Blast Ultra Rare	.50	.80
DUSAFR026 Diabound Kernel Ultra Rare	.15	.25
DUSAFR027 Harpies Feather Storm Ultra Rare	.40	.60
DUSAFR028 Elemental HERO Honest Neos Ultra Rare	7.00	9.00
DUSAFR029 Skydive Scorcher Ultra Rare	.15	.25
DUSAFR030 Dark Summoning Beast Ultra Rare	.50	.75
DUSAFR031 Fallen Paradise Ultra Rare	.15	.25
DUSAFR032 White Veil Ultra Rare	.15	.25
DUSAFR033 Power Wall Ultra Rare	.15	.25
DUSAFR034 Cosmic Blazar Dragon Ultra Rare	1.25	2.00
DUSAFR035 Clear Effector Ultra Rare	.15	.25
DUSAFR036 Cosmic Flare Ultra Rare	.15	.25
DUSAFR037 Converging Wishes Ultra Rare	.15	.25
DUSAFR038 Clashing Souls Ultra Rare	.15	.25
DUSAFR039 Light Wing Shield Ultra Rare	.15	.25
DUSAFR040 Halfway to Forever Ultra Rare	.15	.25
DUSAFR041 Contract with Don Thousand Ultra Rare	.15	.25
DUSAFR042 Dueltaining Ultra Rare	.15	.25
DUSAFR043 BlueEyes White Dragon Ultra Rare	2.50	3.00
DUSAFR044 Magician of Faith Ultra Rare	1.50	2.00
DUSAFR045 Jinzo Ultra Rare	1.00	1.50
DUSAFR046 Brain Control Ultra Rare	.20	.35
DUSAFR047 Royal Decree Ultra Rare	1.00	1.50
DUSAFR048 Mirror Force Ultra Rare	1.00	1.50
DUSAFR049 Imperial Order Ultra Rare	2.50	3.00
DUSAFR050 Necrovalley Ultra Rare	.50	.80
DUSAFR051 DD Warrior Lady Ultra Rare	.15	.25
DUSAFR052 Tsukuyomi Ultra Rare	.50	.80
DUSAFR053 Black Luster Soldier Envoy of the Beginning Ultra Rare	5.00	7.00
DUSAFR054 Dark Magician of Chaos Ultra Rare	.75	1.25
DUSAFR055 Monster Gate Ultra Rare	.30	.50
DUSAFR056 Doomcaliber Knight Ultra Rare	.15	.25
DUSAFR057 Cyber Dragon Ultra Rare	1.00	1.50
DUSAFR058 Treeborn Frog Ultra Rare	.20	.35
DUSAFR059 Dandylion Ultra Rare	.20	.35
DUSAFR060 Dimensional Fissure Ultra Rare	.60	1.00
DUSAFR061 NeoSpacian Grand Mole Ultra Rare	.15	.25
DUSAFR062 Future Fusion Ultra Rare	.60	1.00
DUSAFR063 Advanced Ritual Art Ultra Rare	2.00	2.50
DUSAFR064 Mezuki Ultra Rare	2.50	3.00
DUSAFR065 Chimeratech Fortress Dragon Ultra Rare	.25	.40
DUSAFR066 Fossil Dyna Pachycephalo Ultra Rare	.50	.80
DUSAFR067 Dark Armed Dragon Ultra Rare	.40	.60
DUSAFR068 RedEyes Darkness Metal Dragon Ultra Rare	1.50	2.00
DUSAFR069 Honest Ultra Rare	2.00	2.50
DUSAFR070 Judgment Dragon Ultra Rare	1.00	1.50
DUSAFR071 Gladiator Beast Gyzarus Ultra Rare	.15	.25
DUSAFR072 Rescue Cat Ultra Rare	1.50	2.00
DUSAFR073 Brionac Dragon of the Ice Barrier Ultra Rare	3.00	4.00
DUSAFR074 Junk Synchron Ultra Rare	.30	.50
DUSAFR075 Goyo Guardian Ultra Rare	.40	.60
DUSAFR076 Plaguespreader Zombie Ultra Rare	.50	.80
DUSAFR077 Black Rose Dragon Ultra Rare	1.00	1.50
DUSAFR078 Blackwing Gale the Whirlwind Ultra Rare	.15	.25
DUSAFR079 Deep Sea Diva Ultra Rare	.30	.50
DUSAFR080 Battle Fader Ultra Rare	.60	1.00
DUSAFR081 Trishula Dragon of the Ice Barrier Ultra Rare	2.00	2.50
DUSAFR082 Infernity Launcher Ultra Rare	.30	.50
DUSAFR083 Effect Veiler Ultra Rare	2.00	2.50
DUSAFR084 Pot of Duality Ultra Rare	3.00	3.50
DUSAFR085 Solemn Warning Ultra Rare	4.00	5.00
DUSAFR086 Formula Synchron Ultra Rare	1.00	1.50
DUSAFR087 A Hero Lives Ultra Rare	1.00	1.50
DUSAFR088 Evolzar Laggia Ultra Rare	1.00	1.50
DUSAFR089 Constellar Ptolemy M7 Ultra Rare	.25	.40
DUSAFR090 Evilswarm Ophion Ultra Rare	.15	.25
DUSAFR091 Tour Guide From the Underworld Ultra Rare	1.00	1.50
DUSAFR092 Soul Charge Ultra Rare	2.50	3.50
DUSAFR093 Castel the Skyblaster Musketeer Ultra Rare	2.50	3.00
DUSAFR094 Masked HERO Dark Law Ultra Rare	4.00	6.00
DUSAFR095 MXSaber Invoker Ultra Rare	.50	.80
DUSAFR096 Uria Lord of Searing Flames Ultra Rare	1.25	2.00
DUSAFR097 Hamon Lord of Striking Thunder Ultra Rare	1.50	2.00
DUSAFR098 Raviel Lord of Phantasms Ultra Rare	.75	1.25
DUSAFR099 Armityle the Chaos Phantom Ultra Rare	1.50	2.50
DUSAFR100 Dark Magician Ultra Rare	.75	1.25

2017 Yu-Gi-Oh Duelist Saga 1st Edition German

COMPLETE SET (100)	150.00	225.00
RELEASED ON MARCH 31, 2017		
DUSADE001 Double Fin Shark Ultra Rare	.15	.25
DUSADE002 Silent Angler Ultra Rare	.15	.25
DUSADE003 Depth Shark Ultra Rare	.15	.25
DUSADE004 Saber Shark Ultra Rare	.15	.25
DUSADE005 Guard Penguin Ultra Rare	.15	.25
DUSADE006 Number 94 Crystalzero Ultra Rare	.15	.25
DUSADE007 Full Armored Crystalzero Lancer Ultra Rare	.15	.25
DUSADE008 Full Armored Black Ray Lancer Ultra Rare	.15	.25
DUSADE009 Sea Lords Amulet Ultra Rare	.15	.25
DUSADE010 Diamond Dust Ultra Rare	.15	.25
DUSADE011 Chain Summon Ultra Rare	.15	.25
DUSADE012 Brohunder Ultra Rare	.15	.25
DUSADE013 Number 28 Titanic Moth Ultra Rare	.15	.25
DUSADE014 Number 70 Malevolent Sin Ultra Rare	.15	.25
DUSADE015 Necroid Synchro Ultra Rare	.15	.25
DUSADE016 Wandering King Wildwind Ultra Rare	.15	.25
DUSADE017 Synchro Call Ultra Rare	.15	.25
DUSADE018 Celestial Double Star Shaman Ultra Rare	.15	.25
DUSADE019 Legacy of a HERO Ultra Rare	.50	.80
DUSADE020 Gozuki Ultra Rare	1.00	1.50
DUSADE021 Vision HERO Vyon Ultra Rare	2.00	2.50
DUSADE022 Darklord Ukoback Ultra Rare	.15	.25
DUSADE023 Darklord Descent Ultra Rare	.15	.25
DUSADE024 Legacy of the Duelist Ultra Rare	.50	.80
DUSADE025 Chaos Scepter Blast Ultra Rare	.50	.80
DUSADE026 Diabound Kernel Ultra Rare	.15	.25
DUSADE027 Harpies Feather Storm Ultra Rare	.40	.60
DUSADE028 Elemental HERO Honest Neos Ultra Rare	7.00	9.00
DUSADE029 Skydive Scorcher Ultra Rare	.15	.25
DUSADE030 Dark Summoning Beast Ultra Rare	.50	.75
DUSADE031 Fallen Paradise Ultra Rare	.15	.25
DUSADE032 White Veil Ultra Rare	.15	.25
DUSADE033 Power Wall Ultra Rare	.15	.25
DUSADE034 Cosmic Blazar Dragon Ultra Rare	1.25	2.00
DUSADE035 Clear Effector Ultra Rare	.15	.25
DUSADE036 Cosmic Flare Ultra Rare	.15	.25
DUSADE037 Converging Wishes Ultra Rare	.15	.25
DUSADE038 Clashing Souls Ultra Rare	.15	.25
DUSADE039 Light Wing Shield Ultra Rare	.15	.25
DUSADE040 Halfway to Forever Ultra Rare	.15	.25
DUSADE041 Contract with Don Thousand Ultra Rare	.15	.25
DUSADE042 Dueltaining Ultra Rare	.15	.25
DUSADE043 BlueEyes White Dragon Ultra Rare	2.50	3.00
DUSADE044 Magician of Faith Ultra Rare	1.50	2.00
DUSADE045 Jinzo Ultra Rare	1.00	1.50
DUSADE046 Brain Control Ultra Rare	.20	.35
DUSADE047 Royal Decree Ultra Rare	1.00	1.50
DUSADE048 Mirror Force Ultra Rare	1.00	1.50
DUSADE049 Imperial Order Ultra Rare	2.50	3.00
DUSADE050 Necrovalley Ultra Rare	.50	.80
DUSADE051 DD Warrior Lady Ultra Rare	.15	.25
DUSADE052 Tsukuyomi Ultra Rare	.50	.80
DUSADE053 Black Luster Soldier Envoy of the Beginning Ultra Rare	5.00	7.00
DUSADE054 Dark Magician of Chaos Ultra Rare	.75	1.25
DUSADE055 Monster Gate Ultra Rare	.30	.50
DUSADE056 Doomcaliber Knight Ultra Rare	.15	.25
DUSADE057 Cyber Dragon Ultra Rare	1.00	1.50
DUSADE058 Treeborn Frog Ultra Rare	.20	.35
DUSADE059 Dandylion Ultra Rare	.20	.35
DUSADE060 Dimensional Fissure Ultra Rare	.60	1.00
DUSADE061 NeoSpacian Grand Mole Ultra Rare	.15	.25
DUSADE062 Future Fusion Ultra Rare	.60	1.00
DUSADE063 Advanced Ritual Art Ultra Rare	2.00	2.50
DUSADE064 Mezuki Ultra Rare	2.50	3.00
DUSADE065 Chimeratech Fortress Dragon Ultra Rare	.25	.40
DUSADE066 Fossil Dyna Pachycephalo Ultra Rare	.50	.80
DUSADE067 Dark Armed Dragon Ultra Rare	.40	.60
DUSADE068 RedEyes Darkness Metal Dragon Ultra Rare	1.50	2.00
DUSADE069 Honest Ultra Rare	2.00	2.50
DUSADE070 Judgment Dragon Ultra Rare	1.00	1.50
DUSADE071 Gladiator Beast Gyzarus Ultra Rare	.15	.25
DUSADE072 Rescue Cat Ultra Rare	1.50	2.00
DUSADE073 Brionac Dragon of the Ice Barrier Ultra Rare	3.00	4.00
DUSADE074 Junk Synchron Ultra Rare	.30	.50
DUSADE075 Goyo Guardian Ultra Rare	.40	.60
DUSADE076 Plaguespreader Zombie Ultra Rare	.50	.80
DUSADE077 Black Rose Dragon Ultra Rare	1.00	1.50
DUSADE078 Blackwing Gale the Whirlwind Ultra Rare	.15	.25
DUSADE079 Deep Sea Diva Ultra Rare	.30	.50
DUSADE080 Battle Fader Ultra Rare	.60	1.00
DUSADE081 Trishula Dragon of the Ice Barrier Ultra Rare	2.00	2.50
DUSADE082 Infernity Launcher Ultra Rare	.30	.50
DUSADE083 Effect Veiler Ultra Rare	2.00	2.50
DUSADE084 Pot of Duality Ultra Rare	3.00	3.50
DUSADE085 Solemn Warning Ultra Rare	4.00	5.00
DUSADE086 Formula Synchron Ultra Rare	1.00	1.50
DUSADE087 A Hero Lives Ultra Rare	1.00	1.50
DUSADE088 Evolzar Laggia Ultra Rare	1.00	1.50
DUSADE089 Constellar Ptolemy M7 Ultra Rare	.25	.40
DUSADE090 Evilswarm Ophion Ultra Rare	.15	.25
DUSADE091 Tour Guide From the Underworld Ultra Rare	1.00	1.50
DUSADE092 Soul Charge Ultra Rare	2.50	3.50
DUSADE093 Castel the Skyblaster Musketeer Ultra Rare	2.50	3.00
DUSADE094 Masked HERO Dark Law Ultra Rare	4.00	6.00
DUSADE095 MXSaber Invoker Ultra Rare	.50	.80
DUSADE096 Uria Lord of Searing Flames Ultra Rare	1.25	2.00
DUSADE097 Hamon Lord of Striking Thunder Ultra Rare	1.50	2.00
DUSADE098 Raviel Lord of Phantasms Ultra Rare	.75	1.25
DUSADE099 Armityle the Chaos Phantom Ultra Rare	1.50	2.50
DUSADE100 Dark Magician Ultra Rare	.75	1.25

2017 Yu-Gi-Oh Duelist Saga 1st Edition Italian

COMPLETE SET (100)	150.00	225.00
RELEASED ON MARCH 31, 2017		
DUSAIT001 Double Fin Shark Ultra Rare	.15	.25
DUSAIT002 Silent Angler Ultra Rare	.15	.25
DUSAIT003 Depth Shark Ultra Rare	.15	.25
DUSAIT004 Saber Shark Ultra Rare	.15	.25
DUSAIT005 Guard Penguin Ultra Rare	.15	.25
DUSAIT006 Number 94 Crystalzero Ultra Rare	.15	.25
DUSAIT007 Full Armored Crystalzero Lancer Ultra Rare	.15	.25

DUSAIT008 Full Armored Black Ray Lancer Ultra Rare	.15	.25
DUSAIT009 Sea Lords Amulet Ultra Rare	.15	.25
DUSAIT010 Diamond Dust Ultra Rare	.15	.25
DUSAIT011 Chain Summon Ultra Rare	.15	.25
DUSAIT012 Brohunder Ultra Rare	.15	.25
DUSAIT013 Number 28 Titanic Moth Ultra Rare	.15	.25
DUSAIT014 Number 70 Malevolent Sin Ultra Rare	.15	.25
DUSAIT015 Necroid Synchro Ultra Rare	.15	.25
DUSAIT016 Wandering King Wildwind Ultra Rare	.15	.25
DUSAIT017 Synchro Call Ultra Rare	.15	.25
DUSAIT018 Celestial Double Star Shaman Ultra Rare	.15	.25
DUSAIT019 Legacy of a HERO Ultra Rare	.50	.80
DUSAIT020 Gozuki Ultra Rare	1.00	1.50
DUSAIT021 Vision HERO Vyon Ultra Rare	2.00	2.50
DUSAIT022 Darklord Ukoback Ultra Rare	.15	.25
DUSAIT023 Darklord Descent Ultra Rare	.15	.25
DUSAIT024 Legacy of the Duelist Ultra Rare	.50	.80
DUSAIT025 Chaos Scepter Blast Ultra Rare	.50	.80
DUSAIT026 Diabound Kernel Ultra Rare	.15	.25
DUSAIT027 Harpies Feather Storm Ultra Rare	.40	.60
DUSAIT028 Elemental HERO Honest Neos Ultra Rare	7.00	9.00
DUSAIT029 Skydive Scorcher Ultra Rare	.15	.25
DUSAIT030 Dark Summoning Beast Ultra Rare	.50	.75
DUSAIT031 Fallen Paradise Ultra Rare	.15	.25
DUSAIT032 White Veil Ultra Rare	.15	.25
DUSAIT033 Power Wall Ultra Rare	.15	.25
DUSAIT034 Cosmic Blazar Dragon Ultra Rare	1.25	2.00
DUSAIT035 Clear Effector Ultra Rare	.15	.25
DUSAIT036 Cosmic Flare Ultra Rare	.15	.25
DUSAIT037 Converging Wishes Ultra Rare	.15	.25
DUSAIT038 Clashing Souls Ultra Rare	.15	.25
DUSAIT039 Light Wing Shield Ultra Rare	.15	.25
DUSAIT040 Halfway to Forever Ultra Rare	.15	.25
DUSAIT041 Contract with Don Thousand Ultra Rare	.15	.25
DUSAIT042 Dueltaining Ultra Rare	.15	.25
DUSAIT043 BlueEyes White Dragon Ultra Rare	2.50	3.00
DUSAIT044 Magician of Faith Ultra Rare	1.50	2.00
DUSAIT045 Jinzo Ultra Rare	1.00	1.50
DUSAIT046 Brain Control Ultra Rare	.20	.35
DUSAIT047 Royal Decree Ultra Rare	1.00	1.50
DUSAIT048 Mirror Force Ultra Rare	1.00	1.50
DUSAIT049 Imperial Order Ultra Rare	2.50	3.00
DUSAIT050 Necrovalley Ultra Rare	.50	.80
DUSAIT051 DD Warrior Lady Ultra Rare	.15	.25
DUSAIT052 Tsukuyomi Ultra Rare	.50	.80
DUSAIT053 Black Luster Soldier Envoy of the Beginning Ultra Rare	5.00	7.00
DUSAIT054 Dark Magician of Chaos Ultra Rare	.75	1.25
DUSAIT055 Monster Gate Ultra Rare	.30	.50
DUSAIT056 Doomcaliber Knight Ultra Rare	.15	.25
DUSAIT057 Cyber Dragon Ultra Rare	1.00	1.50
DUSAIT058 Treeborn Frog Ultra Rare	.20	.35
DUSAIT059 Dandylion Ultra Rare	.20	.35
DUSAIT060 Dimensional Fissure Ultra Rare	.60	1.00
DUSAIT061 NeoSpacian Grand Mole Ultra Rare	.15	.25
DUSAIT062 Future Fusion Ultra Rare	.60	1.00
DUSAIT063 Advanced Ritual Art Ultra Rare	2.00	2.50
DUSAIT064 Mezuki Ultra Rare	2.50	3.00
DUSAIT065 Chimeratech Fortress Dragon Ultra Rare	.25	.40
DUSAIT066 Fossil Dyna Pachycephalo Ultra Rare	.50	.80
DUSAIT067 Dark Armed Dragon Ultra Rare	.40	.60
DUSAIT068 RedEyes Darkness Metal Dragon Ultra Rare	1.50	2.00
DUSAIT069 Honest Ultra Rare	2.00	2.50
DUSAIT070 Judgment Dragon Ultra Rare	1.00	1.50
DUSAIT071 Gladiator Beast Gyzarus Ultra Rare	.15	.25
DUSAIT072 Rescue Cat Ultra Rare	1.50	2.00
DUSAIT073 Brionac Dragon of the Ice Barrier Ultra Rare	3.00	4.00
DUSAIT074 Junk Synchron Ultra Rare	.30	.50
DUSAIT075 Goyo Guardian Ultra Rare	.40	.60
DUSAIT076 Plaguespreader Zombie Ultra Rare	.50	.80
DUSAIT077 Black Rose Dragon Ultra Rare	1.00	1.50
DUSAIT078 Blackwing Gale the Whirlwind Ultra Rare	.15	.25
DUSAIT079 Deep Sea Diva Ultra Rare	.30	.50
DUSAIT080 Battle Fader Ultra Rare	.60	1.00
DUSAIT081 Trishula Dragon of the Ice Barrier Ultra Rare	2.00	2.50
DUSAIT082 Infernity Launcher Ultra Rare	.30	.50
DUSAIT083 Effect Veiler Ultra Rare	2.00	2.50
DUSAIT084 Pot of Duality Ultra Rare	3.00	3.50
DUSAIT085 Solemn Warning Ultra Rare	4.00	5.00
DUSAIT086 Formula Synchron Ultra Rare	1.00	1.50
DUSAIT087 A Hero Lives Ultra Rare	1.00	1.50
DUSAIT088 Evolzar Laggia Ultra Rare	1.00	1.50
DUSAIT089 Constellar Ptolemy M7 Ultra Rare	.25	.40
DUSAIT090 Evilswarm Ophion Ultra Rare	.15	.25
DUSAIT091 Tour Guide From the Underworld Ultra Rare	1.00	1.50
DUSAIT092 Soul Charge Ultra Rare	2.50	3.50
DUSAIT093 Castel the Skyblaster Musketeer Ultra Rare	2.50	3.00
DUSAIT094 Masked HERO Dark Law Ultra Rare	4.00	6.00
DUSAIT095 MXSaber Invoker Ultra Rare	.50	.80
DUSAIT096 Uria Lord of Searing Flames Ultra Rare	1.25	2.00
DUSAIT097 Hamon Lord of Striking Thunder Ultra Rare	1.50	2.00
DUSAIT098 Raviel Lord of Phantasms Ultra Rare	.75	1.25
DUSAIT099 Armityle the Chaos Phantom Ultra Rare	1.50	2.50
DUSAIT100 Dark Magician Ultra Rare	.75	1.25

2017 Yu-Gi-Oh Duelist Saga 1st Edition Spanish

COMPLETE SET (100)	150.00	225.00
RELEASED ON MARCH 31, 2017		
DUSASP001 Double Fin Shark Ultra Rare	.15	.25
DUSASP002 Silent Angler Ultra Rare	.15	.25
DUSASP003 Depth Shark Ultra Rare	.15	.25
DUSASP004 Saber Shark Ultra Rare	.15	.25
DUSASP005 Guard Penguin Ultra Rare	.15	.25
DUSASP006 Number 94 Crystalzero Ultra Rare	.15	.25
DUSASP007 Full Armored Crystalzero Lancer Ultra Rare	.15	.25
DUSASP008 Full Armored Black Ray Lancer Ultra Rare	.15	.25
DUSASP009 Sea Lords Amulet Ultra Rare	.15	.25
DUSASP010 Diamond Dust Ultra Rare	.15	.25
DUSASP011 Chain Summon Ultra Rare	.15	.25
DUSASP012 Brohunder Ultra Rare	.15	.25
DUSASP013 Number 28 Titanic Moth Ultra Rare	.15	.25
DUSASP014 Number 70 Malevolent Sin Ultra Rare	.15	.25
DUSASP015 Necroid Synchro Ultra Rare	.15	.25
DUSASP016 Wandering King Wildwind Ultra Rare	.15	.25
DUSASP017 Synchro Call Ultra Rare	.15	.25
DUSASP018 Celestial Double Star Shaman Ultra Rare	.15	.25
DUSASP019 Legacy of a HERO Ultra Rare	.50	.80
DUSASP020 Gozuki Ultra Rare	1.00	1.50
DUSASP021 Vision HERO Vyon Ultra Rare	2.00	2.50
DUSASP022 Darklord Ukoback Ultra Rare	.15	.25
DUSASP023 Darklord Descent Ultra Rare	.15	.25
DUSASP024 Legacy of the Duelist Ultra Rare	.50	.80
DUSASP025 Chaos Scepter Blast Ultra Rare	.50	.80
DUSASP026 Diabound Kernel Ultra Rare	.15	.25
DUSASP027 Harpies Feather Storm Ultra Rare	.40	.60
DUSASP028 Elemental HERO Honest Neos Ultra Rare	7.00	9.00
DUSASP029 Skydive Scorcher Ultra Rare	.15	.25
DUSASP030 Dark Summoning Beast Ultra Rare	.50	.75
DUSASP031 Fallen Paradise Ultra Rare	.15	.25
DUSASP032 White Veil Ultra Rare	.15	.25
DUSASP033 Power Wall Ultra Rare	.15	.25
DUSASP034 Cosmic Blazar Dragon Ultra Rare	1.25	2.00
DUSASP035 Clear Effector Ultra Rare	.15	.25
DUSASP036 Cosmic Flare Ultra Rare	.15	.25
DUSASP037 Converging Wishes Ultra Rare	.15	.25
DUSASP038 Clashing Souls Ultra Rare	.15	.25
DUSASP039 Light Wing Shield Ultra Rare	.15	.25
DUSASP040 Halfway to Forever Ultra Rare	.15	.25
DUSASP041 Contract with Don Thousand Ultra Rare	.15	.25
DUSASP042 Dueltaining Ultra Rare	.15	.25
DUSASP043 BlueEyes White Dragon Ultra Rare	2.50	3.00
DUSASP044 Magician of Faith Ultra Rare	1.50	2.00
DUSASP045 Jinzo Ultra Rare	1.00	1.50
DUSASP046 Brain Control Ultra Rare	.20	.35
DUSASP047 Royal Decree Ultra Rare	1.00	1.50
DUSASP048 Mirror Force Ultra Rare	1.00	1.50
DUSASP049 Imperial Order Ultra Rare	2.50	3.00
DUSASP050 Necrovalley Ultra Rare	.50	.80
DUSASP051 DD Warrior Lady Ultra Rare	.15	.25
DUSASP052 Tsukuyomi Ultra Rare	.50	.80
DUSASP053 Black Luster Soldier Envoy of the Beginning Ultra Rare	5.00	7.00
DUSASP054 Dark Magician of Chaos Ultra Rare	.75	1.25
DUSASP055 Monster Gate Ultra Rare	.30	.50
DUSASP056 Doomcaliber Knight Ultra Rare	.15	.25
DUSASP057 Cyber Dragon Ultra Rare	1.00	1.50
DUSASP058 Treeborn Frog Ultra Rare	.20	.35
DUSASP059 Dandylion Ultra Rare	.20	.35
DUSASP060 Dimensional Fissure Ultra Rare	.60	1.00
DUSASP061 NeoSpacian Grand Mole Ultra Rare	.15	.25
DUSASP062 Future Fusion Ultra Rare	.60	1.00
DUSASP063 Advanced Ritual Art Ultra Rare	2.00	2.50
DUSASP064 Mezuki Ultra Rare	2.50	3.00
DUSASP065 Chimeratech Fortress Dragon Ultra Rare	.25	.40
DUSASP066 Fossil Dyna Pachycephalo Ultra Rare	.50	.80
DUSASP067 Dark Armed Dragon Ultra Rare	.40	.60
DUSASP068 RedEyes Darkness Metal Dragon Ultra Rare	1.50	2.00
DUSASP069 Honest Ultra Rare	2.00	2.50
DUSASP070 Judgment Dragon Ultra Rare	1.00	1.50
DUSASP071 Gladiator Beast Gyzarus Ultra Rare	.15	.25
DUSASP072 Rescue Cat Ultra Rare	1.50	2.00
DUSASP073 Brionac Dragon of the Ice Barrier Ultra Rare	3.00	4.00
DUSASP074 Junk Synchron Ultra Rare	.30	.50
DUSASP075 Goyo Guardian Ultra Rare	.40	.60
DUSASP076 Plaguespreader Zombie Ultra Rare	.50	.80
DUSASP077 Black Rose Dragon Ultra Rare	1.00	1.50
DUSASP078 Blackwing Gale the Whirlwind Ultra Rare	.15	.25
DUSASP079 Deep Sea Diva Ultra Rare	.30	.50
DUSASP080 Battle Fader Ultra Rare	.60	1.00
DUSASP081 Trishula Dragon of the Ice Barrier Ultra Rare	2.00	2.50
DUSASP082 Infernity Launcher Ultra Rare	.30	.50
DUSASP083 Effect Veiler Ultra Rare	2.00	2.50
DUSASP084 Pot of Duality Ultra Rare	3.00	3.50
DUSASP085 Solemn Warning Ultra Rare	4.00	5.00
DUSASP086 Formula Synchron Ultra Rare	1.00	1.50
DUSASP087 A Hero Lives Ultra Rare	1.00	1.50
DUSASP088 Evolzar Laggia Ultra Rare	1.00	1.50
DUSASP089 Constellar Ptolemy M7 Ultra Rare	.25	.40
DUSASP090 Evilswarm Ophion Ultra Rare	.15	.25
DUSASP091 Tour Guide From the Underworld Ultra Rare	1.00	1.50
DUSASP092 Soul Charge Ultra Rare	2.50	3.50
DUSASP093 Castel the Skyblaster Musketeer Ultra Rare	2.50	3.00
DUSASP094 Masked HERO Dark Law Ultra Rare	4.00	6.00
DUSASP095 MXSaber Invoker Ultra Rare	.50	.80
DUSASP096 Uria Lord of Searing Flames Ultra Rare	1.25	2.00
DUSASP097 Hamon Lord of Striking Thunder Ultra Rare	1.50	2.00
DUSASP098 Raviel Lord of Phantasms Ultra Rare	.75	1.25
DUSASP099 Armityle the Chaos Phantom Ultra Rare	1.50	2.50
DUSASP100 Dark Magician Ultra Rare	.75	1.25

2008 Yu-Gi-Oh Gold Series

COMPLETE SET (45)	60.00	120.00
BOOSTER BOX (5 PACKS)	250.00	400.00
BOOSTER PACK (25 CARDS)	40.00	80.00
RELEASED ON APRIL 2, 2008		
GLD1EN001 7 Colored Fish C	.10	.30
GLD1EN002 Sonic Bird C	.10	.30
GLD1EN003 Jinzo GUR	1.50	4.00
GLD1EN004 Summoner Of Illusions C	.10	.30
GLD1EN005 Fire Princess C	.10	.30
GLD1EN006 Needle Worm C	1.25	3.00
GLD1EN007 8-Claws Scorpion C	.10	.30
GLD1EN008 Swarm Of Scarabs C	.20	.60
GLD1EN009 Swarm Of Locusts C	.10	.30
GLD1EN010 Des Lacooda C	.20	.60
GLD1EN011 Newdoria C	.10	.30
GLD1EN012 Don Zaloog GUR	.40	1.00
GLD1EN013 Old Vindictive Magician C	.10	.30
GLD1EN014 Breaker the Magical Warrior GUR	1.00	2.50
GLD1EN015 D.D. Warrior Lady GUR	1.00	2.50
GLD1EN016 Dark Magician of Chaos GUR	8.00	20.00
GLD1EN017 Stealth Bird C	.60	1.50
GLD1EN018 Regenerating Mummy C	.10	.30
GLD1EN019 Solar Flare Dragon C	.10	.30
GLD1EN020 Rare Metal Dragon C	.10	.30
GLD1EN021 Nightmare Penguin C	.10	.30
GLD1EN022 Cyber Dragon GUR	1.25	3.00
GLD1EN023 Sillva, Warlord Of Dark World C	.40	1.00
GLD1EN024 Goldd, Wu-Lord Of Dark World GUR	.40	1.00
GLD1EN025 Doom Dozer C	.10	.30
GLD1EN026 Grandmaster of the Six Samurai GUR	1.25	3.00
GLD1EN027 Prometheus, King Of Shadows GUR	.40	1.00
GLD1EN028 Blue-Eyes Ultimate Dragon GUR	10.00	25.00
GLD1EN029 Chimeratech Overdragon GUR	.75	2.00
GLD1EN030 Swords of Revealing Light GUR	1.00	2.50
GLD1EN031 Heavy Storm GUR	.75	2.00
GLD1EN032 Reinforcement of the Army GUR	1.25	3.00
GLD1EN033 Brain Control GUR	.75	2.00
GLD1EN034 Offerings To The Doomed C	.10	.30
GLD1EN035 Non-Spellcasting Area C	.10	.30
GLD1EN036 Mist Body C	.75	2.00
GLD1EN037 Pandemonium C	.40	1.00
GLD1EN038 Crush Card Virus GUR	8.00	20.00
GLD1EN039 Mirror Force GUR	4.00	10.00
GLD1EN040 Torrential Tribute GUR	1.25	3.00
GLD1EN041 Needle Ceiling C	.40	1.00
GLD1EN042 Royal Command C	.10	.30
GLD1EN043 Rivalry Of Warlords C	1.00	2.50
GLD1EN044 Skill Drain C	1.50	4.00
GLD1EN045 Spell Shield Type-8 C	.10	.30

2009 Yu-Gi-Oh Gold Series 2

COMPLETE SET (100)	30.00	60.00
BOOSTER BOX (5 PACKS)	60.00	100.00
BOOSTER PACK (25 CARDS)	15.00	30.00
RELEASED ON MAY 27, 2009		
GLD21 Sangan GUR	.75	2.00
GLD2EN002 Des Volstgalph GUR	.75	2.00
GLD2EN003 Lekunga C	.20	.50
GLD2EN004 Lord Poison C	.20	.50
GLD2EN005 Rigorous Reaver C	.20	.50
GLD2EN006 Zaborg the Thunder Monarch C	.20	.50
GLD2EN007 Mobius the Frost Monarch C	.20	.50
GLD2EN008 Thestalos the Firestorm Monarch C	.20	.50
GLD2EN009 Granmarg the Rock Monarch C	.20	.50
GLD2EN010 Treeborn Frog C	.20	.50
GLD2EN011 Phantom Beast Cross-Wing C	.20	.50
GLD2EN012 Phantom Beast Wild-Horn C	.20	.50
GLD2EN013 Phantom Beast Thunder-Pegasus C	.20	.50
GLD2EN014 Phantom Beast Rock-Lizard C	.20	.50
GLD2EN015 Winged Rhynos C	.20	.50
GLD2EN016 Snipe Hunter C	.20	.50
GLD2EN017 The Six Samurai - Yaichi C	.20	.50
GLD2EN018 The Six Samurai - Kamon C	.20	.50
GLD2EN019 The Six Samurai - Yariza C	.20	.50
GLD2EN020 The Six Samurai - Nisashi C	.20	.50
GLD2EN021 The Six Samurai - Zanji C	.20	.50
GLD2EN022 The Six Samurai - Irou C	.20	.50
GLD2EN023 Volcanic Rocket GUR	1.00	2.50
GLD2EN024 Volcanic Shell C	1.25	3.00
GLD2EN025 Elemental Hero Captain Gold GUR	1.00	2.50
GLD2EN026 Raiza the Storm Monarch GUR	1.00	2.50
GLD2EN027 Necro Gardna GUR	.75	2.00
GLD2EN028 Elemental Hero Neos Alius C	.20	.50
GLD2EN029 Test Tiger GUR	1.00	2.50
GLD2EN030 Royal Firestorm Guards GUR	1.00	2.50
GLD2EN031 Dark Armed Dragon GUR	2.00	5.00
GLD2EN032 Prime Material Dragon GUR	.75	2.00
GLD2EN033 Caius the Shadow Monarch GUR	1.25	3.00
GLD2EN034 Exile of the Wicked C	.20	.50
GLD2EN035 Warrior Elimination C	.20	.50
GLD2EN036 Giant Trunade C	.20	.50
GLD2EN037 Mind Control GUR	1.00	2.50
GLD2EN038 Skyscraper C	1.25	3.00
GLD2EN039 Future Fusion GUR	1.00	2.50
GLD2EN040 Gold Sarcophagus GUR	1.50	4.00
GLD2EN041 Shien's Castle of Mist C	.20	.50
GLD2EN042 Six Samurai United C	.20	.50
GLD2EN043 Veil of Darkness GUR	.75	2.00
GLD2EN044 Solemn Judgment GUR	1.00	2.50
GLD2EN045 Bottomless Trap Hole GUR	1.25	3.00
GLD2EN046 Compulsory Evacuation Device C	.20	.50
GLD2EN047 Begone, Knave! C	.20	.50
GLD2EN048 Phoenix Wing Wind Blast GUR	1.00	2.50
GLD2EN049 Return of the Six Samurai C	.20	.50
GLD2EN050 Double-Edged Sword Technique C	.20	.50

2010 Yu-Gi-Oh Gold Series 3

COMPLETE SET (50)	30.00	75.00
BOOSTER BOX (5 PACKS)	80.00	120.00
BOOSTER PACK (25 CARDS)	15.00	30.00
RELEASED ON JUNE 23, 2010		
GLD31 Mist Valley Watcher C	.10	.25
GLD3EN002 Amazoness Archer C	.10	.25
GLD3EN003 Amazoness Paladin C	.10	.25
GLD3EN004 Amazoness Fighter C	.10	.25
GLD3EN005 Amazoness Swords Woman C	.20	.50
GLD3EN006 Amazoness Blowpiper C	.10	.25
GLD3EN007 Amazoness Tiger C	.10	.25
GLD3EN008 Destiny Hero - Malicious	1.25	3.00
GLD3EN009 Freya, Spirit of Victory C	.20	.50
GLD3EN010 Nova Summoner C	.20	.50
GLD3EN011 Exploder Dragon GUR	1.00	2.50
GLD3EN012 Goblin Zombie C	.75	2.00
GLD3EN013 Elemental Hero Prisma GUR	2.50	6.00
GLD3EN014 Dimensional Alchemist GUR	1.00	2.50
GLD3EN015 Judgment Dragon GUR	1.50	4.00
GLD3EN016 Amazoness Chain Master C	.10	.25
GLD3EN017 Mezuki GUR	1.00	2.50
GLD3EN018 Plaguespreader Zombie GUR	1.00	2.50
GLD3EN019 Vice Dragon GUR	1.00	2.50
GLD3EN020 Thunder King Rai-Oh GUR	1.25	3.00
GLD3EN021 Blackwing - Gale GUR	1.00	2.50
GLD3EN022 Blackwing - Bora the Spear C	.50	1.25
GLD3EN023 Blackwing - Sirocco the Dawn C	.50	1.25
GLD3EN024 Blackwing - Blizzard the Far North C	.50	1.25
GLD3EN025 Blackwing - Shura the Blue Flame C	.50	1.25
GLD3EN026 Blackwing - Kalut	.50	1.25
GLD3EN027 Infernity Archfiend GUR	1.00	2.50
GLD3EN028 Infernity Dwarf C	.10	.25
GLD3EN029 Infernity Guardian C	.10	.25
GLD3EN030 Reese the Ice Mistress C	.20	.50
GLD3EN031 Numbing Grub in the Ice Barrier C	.10	.25
GLD3EN032 Mist Condor C	.10	.25
GLD3EN033 Mist Valley Windmaster C	.10	.25
GLD3EN034 Worm Falco C	.10	.25

GLD3EN035 Worm Gulse C	.10	.25
GLD3EN036 Worm Hope C	.10	.25
GLD3EN037 Stardust Dragon GUR	2.50	6.00
GLD3EN038 Blackwing Armor Master GUR	1.00	2.50
GLD3EN039 Blackwing Armed Wing GUR	1.00	2.50
GLD3EN040 Mystical Space Typhoon GUR	1.50	4.00
GLD3EN041 My Body as a Shield GUR	1.00	2.50
GLD3EN042 Smashing Ground GUR	1.00	2.50
GLD3EN043 Enemy Controller GUR	1.00	2.50
GLD3EN044 Destiny Draw C	.30	.75
GLD3EN045 Black Whirlwind C	1.25	3.00
GLD3EN046 Amazoness Archers C	.10	.25
GLD3EN047 Dramatic Rescue C	.10	.25
GLD3EN048 Magical Arm Shield C	.10	.25
GLD3EN049 Icarus Attack GUR	1.00	2.50
GLD3EN050 Aegis of Gaia C	.10	.25

2011 Yu-Gi-Oh Gold Series 4

COMPLETE SET (50)	100.00	150.00
BOOSTER BOX (5 PACKS)	60.00	120.00
BOOSTER PACK (25 CARDS)	15.00	30.00
RELEASED ON JULY 1, 2011		
GLD4EN001 Millennium Shield	.25	.75
GLD4EN002 Pendulum Machine	.25	.75
GLD4EN003 The Wicked Worm Beast	.25	.75
GLD4EN004 Goddess with the Third Eye	.25	.75
GLD4EN005 Beastking of the Swamps	.25	.75
GLD4EN006 Versago the Destroyer	.25	.75
GLD4EN007 Morphing Jar GUR	.50	1.25
GLD4EN008 Goddess of Whim	.25	.75
GLD4EN009 Injection Fairy Lily	.25	.75
GLD4EN010 Gravekeeper's Spy GUR	.40	1.00
GLD4EN011 Spirit Reaper GUR	.50	1.25
GLD4EN012 Chaos Sorcerer GUR	1.25	3.00
GLD4EN013 Black Luster Soldier GUR	4.00	10.00
GLD4EN014 White-Horned Dragon	.25	.75
GLD4EN015 Toon Dark Magician Girl	.50	1.25
GLD4EN016 Meltiel, Sage of the Sky	.25	.75
GLD4EN017 Radiant Jeral	.25	.75
GLD4EN018 Diabolos, King of the Abyss	.25	.75
GLD4EN019 Lich Lord, King of the Underworld	.25	.75
GLD4EN020 Prometheus, King of the Shadows	.25	.75
GLD4EN021 Mormolith	.25	.75
GLD4EN022 Darklord Zerato GUR	.25	.75
GLD4EN023 Doomcaliber Knight GUR	.50	1.25
GLD4EN024 Ryko, Lightsworn Hunter GUR	.50	1.25
GLD4EN025 Celestia, Lightsworn Angel GUR	.25	.75
GLD4EN026 Tytannial, Princess GUR	.25	.75
GLD4EN027 Summoner Monk GUR	1.25	3.00
GLD4EN028 Genesis Dragon	1.00	2.50
GLD4EN029 Orichalcos Shunoros	.25	.75
GLD4EN030 Obelisk the Tormentor GUR	6.00	15.00
GLD4EN031 Five-Headed Dragon GUR	1.25	3.00
GLD4EN032 Gladiator Beast Gyzarus GUR	.50	1.25
GLD4EN033 Eternal Drought	.25	.75
GLD4EN034 Eradicating Aerosol	.25	.75
GLD4EN035 Soul Exchange	.25	.75
GLD4EN036 Toon World	.25	.75
GLD4EN037 Graceful Dice	.25	.75
GLD4EN038 Sage's Stone	1.25	3.00
GLD4EN039 Toon Table of Contents GUR	2.50	6.00
GLD4EN040 Pot of Avarice GUR	.50	1.25
GLD4EN041 Recurring Nightmare	1.00	2.50
GLD4EN042 Sword of Dark Rites	.25	.75
GLD4EN043 Trade-In	1.25	3.00
GLD4EN044 Magic Formula	.25	.75
GLD4EN045 Robbin' Goblin	.25	.75
GLD4EN046 Skull Dice	.25	.75
GLD4EN047 Royal Oppression GUR	.50	1.25
GLD4EN048 Xing Zhen Hu	.25	.75
GLD4EN049 Deck Devastation Virus	1.00	2.50
GLD4EN050 Trap Stun GUR	1.25	3.00

2012 Yu-Gi-Oh Gold Series Haunted Mine

COMPLETE SET (55)	50.00	100.00
BOOSTER BOX (5 PACKS)	60.00	80.00
BOOSTER PACK (25 CARDS)	20.00	30.00
RELEASED ON JUNE 12, 2012		
GLD5EN001 Blue-Eyes White GGR	8.00	20.00
GLD5EN002 Patrician of Darkness C	.10	.30
GLD5EN003 Pyramid Turtle C	.10	.30
GLD5EN004 Dark Scorpion Burglars C	.10	.30
GLD5EN005 Don Zaloog C	.20	.60
GLD5EN006 Helpoemer C	.10	.30
GLD5EN007 Dark Scorpion - Cliff the Trap Remover C	.10	.30
GLD5EN008 Despair from the Dark C	.10	.30
GLD5EN009 Fear from the Dark C	.10	.30
GLD5EN010 Dark Scorpion - Chick the Yellow C	.10	.30
GLD5EN011 Dark Scorpion - Gorg the Strong C	.10	.30
GLD5EN012 Dark Scorpion - Meanae the Thorn C	.10	.30
GLD5EN013 Ryu Kokki C	.10	.30
GLD5EN014 Vampire Lady C	.10	.30
GLD5EN015 Double Coston C	.10	.30
GLD5EN016 Regenerating Mummy C	.10	.30
GLD5EN017 Dark Mimic LV1 C	.10	.30
GLD5EN018 Dark Mimic LV3 C	.10	.30
GLD5EN019 Zombie Master C	.40	1.00
GLD5EN020 Gernia C	.10	.30
GLD5EN021 Goblin Zombie C	.75	2.00
GLD5EN022 The Lady in Wight C	.40	1.00
GLD5EN023 Red Ogre C	.10	.30
GLD5EN024 Gorz the Emissary of Darkness GGR	2.50	6.00
GLD5EN025 Bone Crusher C	.10	.30
GLD5EN026 Fabled Grimro GLD	.50	1.25
GLD5EN027 Master Hyperion GLD	.50	1.25
GLD5EN028 Grapha, Dragon Lord GR	.50	1.25
GLD5EN029 Sephylon, the Ultimate GR	.50	1.25
GLD5EN030 Herald of Perfection GGR	2.50	6.00
GLD5EN031 Brionac, Dragon GR	2.50	6.00
GLD5EN032 Naturia Beast GLD	1.50	4.00
GLD5EN033 Naturia Barkion GGR	2.00	5.00
GLD5EN034 Formula Synchron GLD	2.00	5.00
GLD5EN035 Karakuri Steel Shogun GR	.75	2.00
GLD5EN036 Number 39: Utopia GLD	1.50	4.00
GLD5EN037 Dark Hole GLD	1.25	3.00
GLD5EN038 Mystical Space GGR	4.00	10.00
GLD5EN039 Book of Life C	.25	.75
GLD5EN040 Call of the Mummy C	.10	.30
GLD5EN041 Spellbook Organization C	.20	.60
GLD5EN042 Mustering of the Dark Scorpions C	.10	.30
GLD5EN043 Pyramid of Wonders C	.10	.30
GLD5EN044 Dawn of the Herald C	.20	.60
GLD5EN045 Solemn Judgment GGR	2.00	5.00
GLD5EN046 Call of the Haunted GLD	1.25	3.00
GLD5EN047 Physical Double C	.10	.30
GLD5EN048 Hidden Spellbook C	.10	.30
GLD5EN049 Zoma the Spirit C	.40	1.00
GLD5EN050 Embodiment of Apophis C	.10	.30
GLD5EN051 Machine King - 3000 B.C. C	.10	.30
GLD5EN052 Starlight Road GLD	.50	1.25
GLD5EN053 Tiki Curse C	.10	.30
GLD5EN054 Tiki Soul C	.10	.30
GLD5EN055 Copy Knight C	.10	.30

2017 Yu-Gi-Oh Legendary Duelists 1st Edition

COMPLETE SET (52)	45.00	70.00
BOOSTER BOX (36 PACKS)	50.00	65.00
BOOSTER PACK (5 CARDS)	2.00	3.00
RELEASED ON SEPTEMBER 8, 2017		
LEDUEN000 Red Eyes B Dragon C	.15	.25
LEDUEN001 Red Eyes Baby Dragon UR	8.00	10.00
LEDUEN002 Gearfried the Red Eyes Iron Knight UR	5.00	7.00
LEDUEN003 Red Eyes Slash Dragon UR	8.00	10.00
LEDUEN004 Red Eyes Fang with Chain UR	4.00	6.00
LEDUEN005 Red Eyes Retro Dragon C	.15	.25
LEDUEN006 Red Eyes Fusion C	.15	.25
LEDUEN007 Inferno Fire Blast C	.15	.25
LEDUEN008 Amazoness Princess SR	2.00	3.50
LEDUEN009 Amazoness Baby Tiger UR	3.00	5.00
LEDUEN010 Amazoness Call R	.30	.50
LEDUEN011 Amazoness Onslaught R	.30	.50
LEDUEN012 Amazoness Archer C	.15	.25
LEDUEN013 Amazoness Swords Woman C	.15	.25
LEDUEN014 Amazoness Village C	.15	.25
LEDUEN015 The Legendary Fisherman II SR	.50	.80
LEDUEN016 Citadel Whale UR	2.00	3.50
LEDUEN017 Rage of Kairyu Shin R	.30	.50
LEDUEN018 Sea Stealth Attack R	.30	.50
LEDUEN019 The Legendary Fisherman C	.15	.25
LEDUEN020 The Legendary Fisherman III C	.15	.25
LEDUEN021 A Legendary Ocean C	.15	.25
LEDUEN022 Cyberdark Cannon R	.30	.50
LEDUEN023 Cyberdark Claw R	.30	.50
LEDUEN024 Cyberdarkness Dragon SR	1.50	2.50
LEDUEN025 Cyberdark Inferno SR	2.00	3.50
LEDUEN026 Cyberdark Horn C	.15	.25
LEDUEN027 Cyberdark Edge C	.15	.25
LEDUEN028 Cyberdark Keel C	.15	.25
LEDUEN029 Mixeroid R	.30	.50
LEDUEN030 Super Vehicroid Mobile Base SR	.30	.50
LEDUEN031 Megaroid City R	.30	.50
LEDUEN032 Emergeroid Call UR	2.00	3.50
LEDUEN033 Expressroid C	.15	.25
LEDUEN034 Armoroid C	.15	.25
LEDUEN035 Vehicroid Connection Zone C	.15	.25
LEDUEN036 Water Dragon Cluster SR	.75	1.25
LEDUEN037 Duoterion SR	.60	1.00
LEDUEN038 Bonding D2O R	.30	.50
LEDUEN039 Bonding DHO R	.30	.50
LEDUEN040 Hydrogeddon C	.15	.25
LEDUEN041 Oxygeddon C	.15	.25
LEDUEN042 Water Dragon C	.15	.25
LEDUEN043 Sphere Kuriboh C	.15	.25
LEDUEN044 Yomi Ship C	.15	.25
LEDUEN045 Leotaur C	.15	.25
LEDUEN046 Sergeant Electro C	.15	.25
LEDUEN047 Riryoku C	.15	.25
LEDUEN048 Monster Reincarnation C	.15	.25
LEDUEN049 Wonder Balloons C	.15	.25
LEDUEN050 The Golden Apples C	.15	.25
LEDUEN051 Bonding H2O C	.15	.25

2018 Yu-Gi-Oh Legendary Duelists Ancient Millennium 1st Edition

COMPLETE SET (53)	60.00	100.00
BOOSTER BOX (36 PACKS)	45.00	60.00
BOOSTER PACK (5 CARDS)	2.00	3.00
RELEASED ON FEBRUARY 23, 2018		
LED2-EN000 Relinquished C	.15	.25
LED2-EN001 Millennium-Eyes Illusionist UR	15.00	20.00
LED2-EN002 Illusionist Faceless Magician R	.30	.50
LED2-EN003 Millennium-Eyes Restrict UR	15.00	20.00
LED2-EN004 Relinquished Fusion UR	15.00	20.00
LED2-EN005 Thousand-Eyes Restrict C	.15	.25
LED2-EN006 Black Illusion Ritual C	.15	.25
LED2-EN007 Parasite Paranoid R	.30	.50
LED2-EN008 Metamorphosed Insect Queen SR	2.50	4.00
LED2-EN009 Cocoon of Ultra Evolution UR	15.00	20.00
LED2-EN010 Corrosive Scales R	.30	.50
LED2-EN011 Pinch Hopper C	.15	.25
LED2-EN012 Insect Queen C	.15	.25
LED2-EN013 Perfectly Ultimate Great Moth C	.15	.25
LED2-EN014 BM-4 Blast Spider R	.30	.50
LED2-EN015 Desperado Barrel Dragon UR	15.00	20.00
LED2-EN016 Heavy Metal Raiders SR	.15	.25
LED2-EN017 Proton Blast SR	2.50	4.00
LED2-EN018 Blast Sphere C	.15	.25
LED2-EN019 Barrel Dragon C	.15	.25
LED2-EN020 Time Machine C	.15	.25
LED2-EN021 Armed Dragon Catapult Cannon SR	2.50	4.00
LED2-EN022 Ojamassimilation R	.30	.50
LED2-EN023 Ojamatch R	.30	.50
LED2-EN024 Ojama Pajama R	.30	.50
LED2-EN025 Armed Dragon LV3 C	.15	.25
LED2-EN026 Armed Dragon LV5 C	.15	.25
LED2-EN027 Armed Dragon LV7 C	.15	.25
LED2-EN028 VWXYZ-Dragon Catapult Cannon C	.15	.25
LED2-EN029 Ojamagic C	.15	.25
LED2-EN030 Ancient Gear Frame R	.30	.50
LED2-EN031 Ancient Gear Megaton Golem SR	2.50	4.00
LED2-EN032 Ancient Gear Fusion UR	15.00	20.00
LED2-EN033 Corss-Dimensional Duel SR	2.50	4.00
LED2-EN034 Ancient Gear Golem C	.15	.25
LED2-EN035 Ancient Gear Golem-Ultimate Pound C	.15	.25
LED2-EN036 Ultimate Ancient Gear Golem C	.15	.25
LED2-EN037 Rainbow Overdragon SR	2.50	4.00
LED2-EN038 Rainbow Bridge UR	15.00	20.00
LED2-EN039 Crystal Bond UR	15.00	20.00
LED2-EN040 Ultimate Crystal Magic SR	.15	.25
LED2-EN041 Crystal Beast Ruby Carbuncle C	.15	.25
LED2-EN042 Crystal Beast Sapphire Pegasus C	.15	.25
LED2-EN043 Rainbow Dragon C	.15	.25
LED2-EN044 Crystal Release C	.15	.25
LED2-EN045 Crystal Tree C	.15	.25
LED2-EN046 Vortex Trooper C	.15	.25
LED2-EN047 Panzer Dragon C	.15	.25
LED2-EN048 Instant Fusion C	.15	.25
LED2-EN049 Limiter Removal C	.15	.25
LED2-EN050 Worm Bait C	.15	.25
LED2-EN051 Mimicat R	.30	.50
LED2-EN052 Toon Kingdom R	.30	.50

2019 Yu-Gi-Oh Legendary Duelists Sisters of the Rose 1st Edition

COMPLETE SET (56)	80.00	100.00
RELEASED ON JANUARY 11, 2019		
LED4EN000 Harpie's Feather Storm SR	.60	1.00
LED4EN001 Harpie Perfumer UR	12.00	20.00
LED4EN002 Harpie Oracle SR	1.25	2.00
LED4EN003 Alluring Mirror Split UR	3.50	5.00
LED4EN004 Harpie's Feather Rest UR	3.50	5.00
LED4EN005 Harpie Lady Elegance R	.25	.40
LED4EN006 Harpie Lady Sisters C	.15	.25
LED4EN007 Harpie Queen C	.15	.25
LED4EN008 Elegant Egotist C	.15	.25
LED4EN009 Harpies' Hunting Ground C	.15	.25
LED4EN010 Harpie Lady Phoenix Formation C	.15	.25
LED4EN011 Triangle Ecstasy Spark C	.15	.25
LED4EN012 Cyber Angel Izana SR	.60	1.00
LED4EN013 Cyber Egg Angel R	.25	.40
LED4EN014 Merciful Machine Angel SR	.60	1.00
LED4EN015 Incarnated Machine Angel R	.25	.40
LED4EN016 Magnificent Machine Angel R	.25	.40
LED4EN017 Cyber Petit Angel C	.15	.25
LED4EN018 Cyber Angel Benten C	.15	.25
LED4EN019 Cyber Angel Idaten C	.15	.25
LED4EN020 Cyber Angel Dakini C	.15	.25
LED4EN021 Machine Angel Ritual C	.15	.25
LED4EN022 Ritual Sanctuary C	.15	.25
LED4EN023 Garden Rose Maiden UR	4.00	6.00
LED4EN024 Dark Rose Fairy R	.25	.40
LED4EN025 Red Rose Dragon R	.25	.40
LED4EN026 Frozen Rose UR	3.50	5.00
LED4EN027 Blooming of the Darkest Rose R	.25	.40
LED4EN028 Black Rose Dragon C	.15	.25
LED4EN029 Twilight Rose Knight C	.15	.25
LED4EN030 Witch of the Black Rose C	.15	.25
LED4EN031 Blue Rose Dragon C	.15	.25
LED4EN032 Black Garden C	.15	.25
LED4EN033 Mark of the Rose C	.15	.25
LED4EN034 Superdreadnought Rail Cannon Juggernaut Liebe UR	10.00	15.00
LED4EN035 Super Express Bullet Train UR	5.00	8.00
LED4EN036 Flying Pegasus Railroad Stampede SR	1.50	2.50
LED4EN037 Urgent Schedule UR	15.00	25.00
LED4EN038 Barrage Blast UR	.60	1.00
LED4EN039 Superdreadnought Rail Cannon Gustav Max R	.25	.40
LED4EN040 Night Express Knight C	.15	.25
LED4EN041 Snow Plow Hustle Rustle C	.15	.25
LED4EN042 Ruffian Railcar C	.15	.25
LED4EN043 Construction Train Signal Red C	.15	.25
LED4EN044 Special Schedule C	.15	.25
LED4EN045 Lunalight Sabre Dancer SR	2.50	4.00
LED4EN046 Lunalight Emerald Bird R	.25	.40
LED4EN047 Lunalight Yellow Marten R	.25	.40
LED4EN048 Lunalight Fusion SR	4.00	6.00
LED4EN049 Lunalight Serenade Dance SR	3.50	5.00
LED4EN050 Lunalight Blue Cat C	.15	.25
LED4EN051 Lunalight Kaleido Chick C	.15	.25
LED4EN052 Lunalight Cat Dancer C	.15	.25
LED4EN053 Lunalight Panther Dancer C	.15	.25
LED4EN054 Lunalight Leo Dancer C	.15	.25
LED4EN055 Luna Light Perfume C	.15	.25

2014 Yu-Gi-Oh Premium Gold 1st Edition

COMPLETE SET (90)	60.00	150.00
BOOSTER BOX (5 PACKS)	80.00	100.00
BOOSTER PACK (15 CARDS)	20.00	30.00
RELEASED ON MARCH 28, 2014		
PGLD001 Gimmick Puppet Dreary Doll SCR	.60	1.50
PGLD002 Gimmick Puppet Magnet Doll SCR	.40	1.00
PGLD003 Chronomaly Tula Guardian SCR	.20	.60
PGLD004 Big Belly Knight SCR	.20	.60
PGLD005 Power Tool Mecha Dragon SCR	.20	.60
PGLD006 Ancient Pixie Dragon SCR	.75	2.00
PGLD007 Junk Puppet SCR	.20	.60
PGLD008 Chronomaly City Babylon SCR	.20	.60
PGLD009 Utopia Buster SCR	.20	.60
PGLD010 Chronomaly Gordian Knot SCR	.20	.60
PGLD011 Gimmick Puppet Humpty Dumpty SCR	.20	.60
PGLD012 Gimmick Puppet Shadow Feeler SCR	.20	.60
PGLD013 Silent Wobby SCR	.20	.60
PGLD014 Dynatherium SCR	.20	.60
PGLD015 Dragonecro Nethersoul Dragon SCR	1.00	2.50
PGLD016 Beelze of the Diabolic Dragons SCR	8.00	20.00
PGLD017 Blackfeather Darkrage Dragon SCR	.75	2.00
PGLD018 Number C6: Chronomaly Chaos Atlandis SCR	.20	.60
PGLD019 Number C15: Gimmick Puppet Giant Hunter SCR	.20	.60
PGLD020 Number C40: Gimmick Puppet of Dark Strings SCR	.40	1.00
PGLD021 Number C88: Gimmick Puppet Disaster Leo SCR	.40	1.00
PGLD022 Number C9: Chaos Dyson Sphere SCR	.20	.60
PGLD023 Number 13: Embodiment of Crime SCR	.20	.60
PGLD024 Number 31: Embodiment of Punishment SCR	.20	.60
PGLD025 Number 82: Heartlandraco SCR	2.50	6.00
PGLD026 Tri-Edge Levia SCR	.50	1.25
PGLD027 Rank-Up-Magic Argent Chaos Force SCR	1.25	3.00

PGLD028 Gagaga Academy Emergency Network SCR 1.00 2.50
PGLD029 Ghost of a Grudge SCR 1.00 2.50
PGLD030 Obelisk the Tormentor SCR 8.00 20.00
PGLD031 The Winged Dragon of Ra SCR 8.00 20.00
PGLD032 Slifer the Sky Dragon SCR 8.00 20.00
PGLD033 Dark Magician Girl GR 2.00 5.00
PGLD034 Lonefire Blossom GR 1.50 4.00
PGLD035 Honest GR 1.00 2.50
PGLD036 Effect Veiler GR 3.00 8.00
PGLD037 Gagaga Magician GR .50 1.25
PGLD038 Galaxy-Eyes Photon Dragon GR 2.00 5.00
PGLD039 Lightpulsar Dragon GR .75 2.00
PGLD040 Darkflare Dragon GR .50 1.25
PGLD041 Eclipse Wyvern GR .50 1.25
PGLD042 Crane Crane GR .50 1.25
PGLD043 Colossal Fighter GR .20 .60
PGLD044 Number 32: Shark Drake GR .50 1.25
PGLD045 Brotherhood of the Fire Fist - Tiger King GR .50 1.25
PGLD046 Solar Recharge GR .50 1.25
PGLD047 Forbidden Chalice GR 1.00 2.50
PGLD048 Forbidden Lance GR 1.00 2.50
PGLD049 Forbidden Dress GR .50 1.25
PGLD050 Fire Formation - Tenki GR .50 1.25
PGLD051 Jinzo GR 1.00 2.50
PGLD052 Breaker the Magical Warrior GR .50 1.25
PGLD053 Cyber Dragon GR 1.00 2.50
PGLD054 Goldd, Wu-Lord of Dark World GR .15 .40
PGLD055 Blue-Eyes Ultimate Dragon GR 8.00 20.00
PGLD056 Chimeratech Overdragon GR .75 2.00
PGLD057 Swords of Revealing Light GR .50 1.25
PGLD058 Reinforcement of the Army GR .50 1.25
PGLD059 Mirror Force GR 1.25 3.00
PGLD060 Torrential Tribute GR 1.00 2.50
PGLD061 Des Volstgalph GR .50 1.25
PGLD062 Raiza the Storm Monarch GR .50 1.25
PGLD063 Necro Gardna GR .15 .40
PGLD064 Dark Armed Dragon GR 1.50 4.00
PGLD065 Prime Material Dragon GR .50 1.25
PGLD066 Caius the Shadow Monarch GR .50 1.25
PGLD067 Mind Control GR .50 1.25
PGLD068 Gold Sarcophagus GR 1.00 2.50
PGLD069 Bottomless Trap Hole GR 1.00 2.50
PGLD070 Phoenix Wing Wind Blast GR .50 1.25
PGLD071 Exploder Dragon GR .50 1.25
PGLD072 Judgment Dragon GR 1.50 4.00
PGLD073 Mezuki GR .75 2.00
PGLD074 Plaguespreader Zombie GR .75 2.00
PGLD075 Thunder King Rai-Oh GR 1.00 2.50
PGLD076 Stardust Dragon GR 2.00 5.00
PGLD077 Blackwing Armor Master GR .50 1.25
PGLD078 Blackwing Armed Wing GR .15 .40
PGLD079 Mystical Space Typhoon GR 1.25 3.00
PGLD080 Icarus Attack GR .75 2.00
PGLD081 Morphing Jar GR .50 1.25
PGLD082 Gravekeeper's Spy GR .15 .40
PGLD083 Spirit Reaper GR .50 1.25
PGLD084 Chaos Sorcerer GR .75 2.00
PGLD085 Black Luster Soldier - Envoy of the Beginning GR 3.00 8.00
PGLD086 Ryko, Lightsworn Hunter GR .20 .60
PGLD087 Celestia, Lightsworn Angel GR .15 .40
PGLD088 Tytannial, Princess of Camellias GR .15 .40
PGLD089 Summoner Monk GR 1.25 3.00
PGLD090 Trap Stun GR .75 2.00

2015 Yu-Gi-Oh Premium Gold Return of the Bling 1st Edition

COMPLETE SET (91) 115.00 150.00
BOOSTER BOX (5 PACKS) 60.00 80.00
BOOSTER PACK 15.00 20.00
RELEASED ON MARCH 20, 2015
PGL2EN001 Junk Giant GSR .10 .20
PGL2EN002 Absolute King Back Jack GSR .20 .35
PGL2EN003 Rose Lover GSR .50 .80
PGL2EN004 Rose Paladin GSR .20 .35
PGL2EN005 Ghost Charon, the Underworld Boatman GSR .10 .20
PGL2EN006 Blackwing - Kris the Crack of Dawn GSR 4.00 6.00
PGL2EN007 Blackwing - Pinaki the Waxing Moon GSR .50 .80
PGL2EN008 Peropero Cerperus GSR .15 .25
PGL2EN009 Tristan, Knight of the Underworld GSR .40 .60
PGL2EN010 Isolde, Belle of the Underworld GSR .30 .50
PGL2EN011 Masked HERO Anki GSR 1.00 1.50
PGL2EN012 Blackwing Tamer - Obsidian Hawk Joe GSR .50 .80
PGL2EN013 Blackwing - Nothung the Starlight GSR 1.25 2.00
PGL2EN014 Dragocytos Corrupted Nethersoul Dragon GSR .60 1.00
PGL2EN015 Number 95: Galaxy-Eyes Dark Matter Dragon GSR 4.00 6.00
PGL2EN016 Cat Shark GSR .50 .80
PGL2EN017 Number 14: Greedy Sarameya GSR .30 .50
PGL2EN018 Number 21: Frozen Lady Justice GSR .30 .50
PGL2EN019 Parallel Twister GSR .20 .35
PGL2EN020 Stardust Re-Spark GSR .20 .35
PGL2EN021 Santa Claws GSR .30 .50
PGL2EN022 Right Leg of the Forbidden One GDR 1.00 1.50
PGL2EN023 Left Leg of the Forbidden One GDR .75 1.25
PGL2EN024 Right Arm of the Forbidden One GDR 1.00 1.50
PGL2EN025 Left Arm of the Forbidden One GDR .75 1.25
PGL2EN026 Exodia the Forbidden One GDR 2.00 3.00
PGL2EN027 Sinister Serpent GDR .15 .25
PGL2EN028 Card Trooper GDR .20 .35
PGL2EN029 Elemental HERO Neos Alius GDR .25 .40
PGL2EN030 Dandylion GDR .40 .60
PGL2EN031 Debris Dragon GDR .60 1.00
PGL2EN032 Mystical Beast of Serket GDR .10 .20
PGL2EN033 Glow-Up Bulb GDR 10.00 13.00
PGL2EN034 Metaion, the Timelord GDR 2.50 4.00
PGL2EN035 Bujin Yamato GDR .40 .60
PGL2EN036 Traptrix Atrax GDR .30 .50
PGL2EN037 Traptrix Myrmeleo GDR .75 1.25
PGL2EN038 Traptrix Nepenthes GDR .30 .50
PGL2EN039 Mathematician GDR .30 .50
PGL2EN040 Sylvan Sagequoia GDR .20 .35
PGL2EN041 Traptrix Dionaea GDR .30 .50
PGL2EN042 Goyo Guardian GDR 1.00 1.50
PGL2EN043 Armades, Keeper of Boundaries GDR 1.00 1.50
PGL2EN044 Lavalval Chain GDR 2.00 2.50
PGL2EN045 Madolche Queen Tiaramisu GDR .50 .80
PGL2EN046 Number 101: Silent Honor ARK GDR 3.00 5.00
PGL2EN047 Downerd Magician GDR 1.50 2.00
PGL2EN048 Raigeki GDR 20.00 25.00
PGL2EN049 Book of Moon GDR .60 1.00
PGL2EN050 Advanced Ritual Art GDR 1.00 1.50
PGL2EN051 Foolish Burial GDR 1.25 2.00
PGL2EN052 Charge of the Light Brigade GDR .60 1.00
PGL2EN053 Rekindling GDR .20 .35
PGL2EN054 Preparation of Rites GDR .25 .40
PGL2EN055 Pot of Duality GDR 1.50 2.00
PGL2EN056 Temple of the Kings GDR .20 .35
PGL2EN057 The Grand Spellbook Tower GDR .75 1.25
PGL2EN058 Rank-Up-Magic Barian's Force GDR .15 .25
PGL2EN059 Rank-Up-Magic Numeron Force GDR .20 .35
PGL2EN060 Rank-Up-Magic Astral Force GDR .25 .40
PGL2EN061 Sylvan Charity GDR .15 .25
PGL2EN062 Ceasefire GDR .20 .35
PGL2EN063 Ring of Destruction GDR .50 .80
PGL2EN064 Chain Disappearance GDR .75 1.25
PGL2EN065 Compulsory Evacuation Device GDR .30 .50
PGL2EN066 Exchange of the Spirit GDR .15 .25
PGL2EN067 Karma Cut GDR .75 1.25
PGL2EN068 Solemn Warning GDR 2.50 4.00
PGL2EN069 Traptrix Trap Hole Nightmare GDR .50 .80
PGL2EN070 Crush Card Virus GDR 1.00 1.50
PGL2EN071 Veil of Darkness GDR .20 .35
PGL2EN072 Elemental HERO Prisma GDR 1.00 1.50
PGL2EN073 Blackwing - Gale the Whirlwind GDR 1.00 1.50
PGL2EN074 My Body as a Shield GDR 2.00 3.50
PGL2EN075 Smashing Ground GDR .15 .25
PGL2EN076 Enemy Controller GDR .20 .35
PGL2EN077 Doomcaliber Knight GDR .20 .35
PGL2EN078 Five-Headed Dragon GDR 1.00 1.50
PGL2EN079 Gladiator Beast Gyzarus GDR .20 .35
PGL2EN080 Blue-Eyes White Dragon GDR 1.00 1.50
PGL2EN081 Gorz the Emissary of Darkness GDR .75 1.25
PGL2EN082 Master Hyperion GDR .20 .35
PGL2EN083 Grapha, Dragon Lord of Dark World GDR .60 1.00
PGL2EN084 Sephylon, the Ultimate Timelord GDR .40 .60
PGL2EN085 Herald of Perfection GDR 1.25 2.00
PGL2EN086 Naturia Beast GDR 3.00 5.00
PGL2EN087 Naturia Barkion GDR 1.00 1.50
PGL2EN088 Formula Synchron GDR 1.50 2.00
PGL2EN089 Dark Hole GDR 1.00 1.50
PGL2EN090 Call of the Haunted GDR 1.00 1.50
PGL2EN091 Starlight Road GDR 1.00 1.50

2015 Yu-Gi-Oh Premium Gold Return of the Bling Unlimited

COMPLETE SET (91) 75.00 125.00
BOOSTER BOX (5 PACKS) 60.00 80.00
BOOSTER PACK (15 CARDS) 15.00 20.00
RELEASED ON MARCH 20, 2015
PGL2EN001 Junk Giant GSR .10 .20
PGL2EN002 Absolute King Back Jack GSR .20 .35
PGL2EN003 Rose Lover GSR .50 .80
PGL2EN004 Rose Paladin GSR .20 .35
PGL2EN005 Ghost Charon, the Underworld Boatman GSR .10 .20
PGL2EN006 Blackwing - Kris the Crack of Dawn GSR 4.00 6.00
PGL2EN007 Blackwing - Pinaki the Waxing Moon GSR .50 .80
PGL2EN008 Peropero Cerperus GSR .15 .25
PGL2EN009 Tristan, Knight of the Underworld GSR .40 .60
PGL2EN010 Isolde, Belle of the Underworld GSR .30 .50
PGL2EN011 Masked HERO Anki GSR 1.00 1.50
PGL2EN012 Blackwing Tamer - Obsidian Hawk Joe GSR .50 .80
PGL2EN013 Blackwing - Nothung the Starlight GSR 1.25 2.00
PGL2EN014 Dragocytos Corrupted Nethersoul Dragon GSR .60 1.00
PGL2EN015 Number 95: Galaxy-Eyes Dark Matter Dragon GSR 4.00 6.00
PGL2EN016 Cat Shark GSR .50 .80
PGL2EN017 Number 14: Greedy Sarameya GSR .30 .50
PGL2EN018 Number 21: Frozen Lady Justice GSR .30 .50
PGL2EN019 Parallel Twister GSR .20 .35
PGL2EN020 Stardust Re-Spark GSR .20 .35
PGL2EN021 Santa Claws GSR .30 .50
PGL2EN022 Right Leg of the Forbidden One GDR 1.00 1.50
PGL2EN023 Left Leg of the Forbidden One GDR .75 1.25
PGL2EN024 Right Arm of the Forbidden One GDR 1.00 1.50
PGL2EN025 Left Arm of the Forbidden One GDR .75 1.25
PGL2EN026 Exodia the Forbidden One GDR 2.00 3.00
PGL2EN027 Sinister Serpent GDR .15 .25
PGL2EN028 Card Trooper GDR .20 .35
PGL2EN029 Elemental HERO Neos Alius GDR .25 .40
PGL2EN030 Dandylion GDR .40 .60
PGL2EN031 Debris Dragon GDR .60 1.00
PGL2EN032 Mystical Beast of Serket GDR .10 .20
PGL2EN033 Glow-Up Bulb GDR 10.00 13.00
PGL2EN034 Metaion, the Timelord GDR 2.50 4.00
PGL2EN035 Bujin Yamato GDR .40 .60
PGL2EN036 Traptrix Atrax GDR .30 .50
PGL2EN037 Traptrix Myrmeleo GDR .75 1.25
PGL2EN038 Traptrix Nepenthes GDR .30 .50
PGL2EN039 Mathematician GDR .30 .50
PGL2EN040 Sylvan Sagequoia GDR .20 .35
PGL2EN041 Traptrix Dionaea GDR .30 .50
PGL2EN042 Goyo Guardian GDR 1.00 1.50
PGL2EN043 Armades, Keeper of Boundaries GDR 1.00 1.50
PGL2EN044 Lavalval Chain GDR 2.00 2.50
PGL2EN045 Madolche Queen Tiaramisu GDR .50 .80
PGL2EN046 Number 101: Silent Honor ARK GDR 3.00 5.00
PGL2EN047 Downerd Magician GDR 1.50 2.00
PGL2EN048 Raigeki GDR 20.00 25.00
PGL2EN049 Book of Moon GDR .60 1.00
PGL2EN050 Advanced Ritual Art GDR 1.00 1.50
PGL2EN051 Foolish Burial GDR 1.25 2.00
PGL2EN052 Charge of the Light Brigade GDR .60 1.00
PGL2EN053 Rekindling GDR .20 .35
PGL2EN054 Preparation of Rites GDR .25 .40
PGL2EN055 Pot of Duality GDR 1.50 2.00
PGL2EN056 Temple of the Kings GDR .20 .35
PGL2EN057 The Grand Spellbook Tower GDR .75 1.25
PGL2EN058 Rank-Up-Magic Barian's Force GDR .15 .25
PGL2EN059 Rank-Up-Magic Numeron Force GDR .20 .35
PGL2EN060 Rank-Up-Magic Astral Force GDR .25 .40
PGL2EN061 Sylvan Charity GDR .15 .25
PGL2EN062 Ceasefire GDR .20 .35
PGL2EN063 Ring of Destruction GDR .50 .80
PGL2EN064 Chain Disappearance GDR .75 1.25
PGL2EN065 Compulsory Evacuation Device GDR .30 .50
PGL2EN066 Exchange of the Spirit GDR .15 .25
PGL2EN067 Karma Cut GDR .75 1.25
PGL2EN068 Solemn Warning GDR 2.50 4.00
PGL2EN069 Traptrix Trap Hole Nightmare GDR .50 .80
PGL2EN070 Crush Card Virus GDR 1.00 1.50
PGL2EN071 Veil of Darkness GDR .20 .35
PGL2EN072 Elemental HERO Prisma GDR 1.00 1.50
PGL2EN073 Blackwing - Gale the Whirlwind GDR 1.00 1.50
PGL2EN074 My Body as a Shield GDR 2.00 3.50
PGL2EN075 Smashing Ground GDR .15 .25
PGL2EN076 Enemy Controller GDR .20 .35
PGL2EN077 Doomcaliber Knight GDR .20 .35
PGL2EN078 Five-Headed Dragon GDR 1.00 1.50
PGL2EN079 Gladiator Beast Gyzarus GDR .20 .35
PGL2EN080 Blue-Eyes White Dragon GDR 1.00 1.50
PGL2EN081 Gorz the Emissary of Darkness GDR .75 1.25
PGL2EN082 Master Hyperion GDR .20 .35
PGL2EN083 Grapha, Dragon Lord of Dark World GDR .60 1.00
PGL2EN084 Sephylon, the Ultimate Timelord GDR .40 .60
PGL2EN085 Herald of Perfection GDR 1.25 2.00
PGL2EN086 Naturia Beast GDR 3.00 5.00
PGL2EN087 Naturia Barkion GDR 1.00 1.50
PGL2EN088 Formula Synchron GDR 1.50 2.00
PGL2EN089 Dark Hole GDR 1.00 1.50
PGL2EN090 Call of the Haunted GDR 1.00 1.50
PGL2EN091 Starlight Road GDR 1.00 1.50

2016 Yu-Gi-Oh Infinite Gold 1st Edition

COMPLETE SET (100) 120.00 160.00
RELEASED ON MARCH 18, 2016
PGL3EN001 Angmarl the Fiendish Monarch GSCR .30 .50
PGL3EN002 Junk Changer GSCR .30 .50
PGL3EN003 Junkuriboh GSCR .30 .50
PGL3EN004 Magical King Moonstar GSCR .30 .50
PGL3EN005 Stardust Charge Warrior GSCR 2.00 3.50
PGL3EN006 Phantasmal Lord Ultimitl Bishbaalkin GSCR .30 .50
PGL3EN007 Number 37: Hope Woven Dragon Spider Shark GSCR .75 1.25
PGL3EN008 Number 38: Hope Harbinger Dragon Titanic Galaxy GSCR 9.00 .50
PGL3EN009 Number 35: Ravenous Tarantula GSCR .75 1.25
PGL3EN010 Number 84: Pain Gainer GSCR .75 1.25
PGL3EN011 Number 77: The Seven Sins GSCR 2.00 3.00
PGL3EN012 Frost Blast of the Monarchs GSCR .30 .50
PGL3EN013 Tsukumo Slash GSCR .30 .50
PGL3EN014 Shining Hope Road GSCR .30 .50
PGL3EN015 The Phantom Knights of Shade Brigandine GSCR .30 .50
PGL3EN016 The Phantom Knights of Dark Gauntlets GSCR .30 .50
PGL3EN017 The Phantom Knights of Tomb Shield GSCR .30 .50
PGL3EN018 Dark Advance GSCR .30 .50
PGL3EN019 King's Consonance GSCR .30 .50
PGL3EN020 Red Supremacy GSCR .30 .50
PGL3EN021 Beatrice, Lady of the Eternal GSCR 1.25 2.00
PGL3EN022 Fire Hand GSCR .30 .50
PGL3EN023 Ice Hand GSCR .30 .50
PGL3EN024 Kozmo Farmgirl GSCR 1.50 2.50
PGL3EN025 Kozmo Goodwitch GSCR .30 .50
PGL3EN026 Kozmo Sliprider GSCR .75 1.25
PGL3EN027 Kozmo Forerunner GSCR .30 .50
PGL3EN028 Kozmo Strawman GSCR 2.00 3.00
PGL3EN029 Kozmoll Wickedwitch GSCR .30 .50
PGL3EN030 Kozmo DOG Fighter GSCR .30 .50
PGL3EN031 Kozmo Dark Destroyer GSCR .75 1.25
PGL3EN032 Kozmotown GSCR .75 1.25
PGL3EN033 Kozmo Lightsword GSCR .30 .50
PGL3EN034 Horn of Heaven GSCR .30 .50
PGL3EN035 Black Horn of Heaven GSCR .60 1.00
PGL3EN036 Treacherous Trap Hole GSCR .30 .50
PGL3EN037 Deep Dark Trap Hole GSCR .30 .50
PGL3EN038 Void Trap Hole GSCR .30 .50
PGL3EN039 Time-Space Trap Hole GSCR .75 1.25
PGL3EN040 Grand Horn of Heaven GSCR .30 .50
PGL3EN041 Vector Pendulum, the Dracoverlord GLDR .30 .50
PGL3EN042 Maxx "C" GLDR 4.00 6.00
PGL3EN043 Scarm, Malebranche of the Burning Abyss GLDR .75 1.25
PGL3EN044 Graff, Malebranche of the Burning Abyss GLDR .30 .50
PGL3EN045 Cir, Malebranche of the Burning Abyss GLDR .30 .50
PGL3EN046 Rubic, Malebranche of the Burning Abyss GLDR .30 .50
PGL3EN047 Alich, Malebranche of the Burning Abyss GLDR .30 .50
PGL3EN048 Calcab, Malebranche of the Burning Abyss GLDR .30 .50
PGL3EN049 Farfa, Malebranche of the Burning Abyss GLDR .75 1.25
PGL3EN050 Libic, Malebranche of the Burning Abyss GLDR .30 .50
PGL3EN051 Cagna, Malebranche of the Burning Abyss GLDR .30 .50
PGL3EN052 Ghost Ogre & Snow Rabbit GLDR 6.00 8.00
PGL3EN053 Draghig, Malebranche of the Burning Abyss GLDR .30 .50
PGL3EN054 Barbar, Malebranche of the Burning Abyss GLDR .30 .50
PGL3EN055 Luster Pendulum, the Dracoslayer GLDR 1.00 1.50
PGL3EN056 Archfiend Eccentrick GLDR 3.00 4.00
PGL3EN057 Chimeratech Fortress Dragon GLDR .75 1.25
PGL3EN058 Dante, Pilgrim of the Burning Abyss GLDR 3.00 4.00
PGL3EN059 Black Rose Dragon GLDR .75 1.25
PGL3EN060 Arcanite Magician GLDR .30 .50
PGL3EN061 Virgil, Rock Star of the Burning Abyss GLDR .30 .50
PGL3EN062 Ignister Prominence, the Blasting Dracoslayer GLDR .30 .50
PGL3EN063 Number 11: Big Eye GLDR 5.00 7.00
PGL3EN064 Digvorzhak, King of Heavy Industry GLDR .30 .50
PGL3EN065 Daigusto Emeral GLDR 25.00 30.00
PGL3EN066 Constellar Pleiades GLDR .50 .75
PGL3EN067 Gagaga Cowboy GLDR .75 1.25
PGL3EN068 Abyss Dweller GLDR 1.25 2.00
PGL3EN069 Bahamut Shark GLDR 1.00 1.50
PGL3EN070 Lightning Chidori GLDR .75 1.25
PGL3EN071 Constellar Ptolemy M7 GLDR .30 .50
PGL3EN072 Evilswarm Ouroboros GLDR .30 .50
PGL3EN073 Number 61: Volcasaurus GLDR .75 1.25
PGL3EN074 Norito the Moral Leader GLDR .30 .50
PGL3EN075 Number 106: Giant Hand GLDR 4.00 6.00
PGL3EN076 Castel, the Skyblaster Musketeer GLDR 2.50 4.00
PGL3EN077 Dante, Traveler of the Burning Abyss GLDR 3.00 4.00
PGL3EN078 Red-Eyes Flare Metal Dragon GLDR 1.50 2.00
PGL3EN079 Majester Paladin, the Ascending Dracoslayer GLDR .30 .50
PGL3EN080 Reasoning GLDR .30 .50
PGL3EN081 Emergency Teleport GLDR .75 1.25
PGL3EN082 Spell Shattering Arrow GLDR .30 .50
PGL3EN083 Mask Change GLDR .60 1.00

PGL3EN084 Shared Ride GLDR .30 .50
PGL3EN085 The Monarchs Stormforth GLDR .75 1.25
PGL3EN086 Mask Change II GLDR .75 1.25
PGL3EN087 Galaxy Cyclone GLDR 1.25 2.00
PGL3EN088 The Terminus of the Burning Abyss GLDR .30 .50
PGL3EN089 Mistaken Arrest GLDR .30 .50
PGL3EN090 Draco Face-Off GLDR .30 .50
PGL3EN091 Remove Brainwashing GLDR .30 .50
PGL3EN092 Dark Mirror Force GLDR .30 .50
PGL3EN093 Radiant Mirror Force GLDR .30 .50
PGL3EN094 Fairy Wind GLDR .30 .50
PGL3EN095 Breakthrough Skill GLDR 1.00 1.50
PGL3EN096 Mistake GLDR .30 .50
PGL3EN097 The Traveler and the Burning Abyss GLDR .30 .50
PGL3EN098 Fire Lake of the Burning Abyss GLDR .30 .50
PGL3EN099 Storming Mirror Force GLDR 6.00 8.00
PGL3EN100 Blazing Mirror Force GLDR 1.00 1.50

2009 Yu-Gi-Oh Hidden Arsenal Limited Edition

COMPLETE SET (30) 8.00 20.00
BOOSTER BOX (24 PACKS) 80.00 100.00
BOOSTER PACK (5 CARDS) 2.50 6.00
RELEASED ON NOVEMBER 10, 2009
HA01EN001 Blizzed, Defender of the Ice Barrier SCR .10 .30
HA01EN002 Blizzard Warrior SR .10 .30
HA01EN003 Cryomancer of the Ice Barrier SCR .20 .75
HA01EN004 Mist Valley Thunderbird SCR .10 .30
HA01EN005 Mist Valley Shaman SCR .10 1.50
HA01EN006 Mist Valley Soldier SCR .40 1.00
HA01EN007 Flamvell Dragnov SR .10 1.50
HA01EN008 Flamvell Magician SR .10 1.50
HA01EN009 Flamvell Guard SR .20 .75
HA01EN010 X-Saber Axel SR .10 .30
HA01EN011 X-Saber Airbellum SCR .10 .30
HA01EN012 X-Saber Uruz SR .10 .30
HA01EN013 Commander Gottoms SCR .10 1.50
HA01EN014 Ally of Justice Clausolas SR .10 .30
HA01EN015 Ally of Justice Garadholg SR .10 .30
HA01EN016 Ally of Justice Rudra SR .10 1.00
HA01EN017 Worm Apocalypse SR .10 1.00
HA01EN018 Worm Barses SR .10 1.00
HA01EN019 Worm Cartaros SR .10 1.00
HA01EN020 Worm Dimikles SR .10 1.00
HA01EN021 Worm Erokin SCR .10 1.00
HA01EN022 Brionac, Dragon SCR 2.00 5.00
HA01EN023 Mist Wurm SCR 2.00 5.00
HA01EN024 Flamvell Uruquizas SCR .40 1.00
HA01EN025 X-Saber Urbellum SCR .10 .30
HA01EN026 Ally of Justice Catastor SCR 1.25 3.00
HA01EN027 Wrath of Neos SCR .20 .75
HA01EN028 Detonate SR .10 .30
HA01EN029 Berserker Crush SR .10 1.00
HA01EN030 Evolution Burst SCR .20 .75

2010 Yu-Gi-Oh Hidden Arsenal 2 1st Edition

COMPLETE SET (60) 40.00 80.00
BOOSTER BOX (24 PACKS) 30.00 40.00
BOOSTER PACK (5 CARDS) 2.00 3.00
RELEASED ON JULY 20, 2010
HA02EN001 Naturia Beetle SR .40 1.00
HA02EN002 Naturia Rock SR .40 1.00
HA02EN003 Naturia Guardian SCR .60 1.50
HA02EN004 Naturia Vein SR .40 1.00
HA02EN005 Genex Furnace SR .40 1.00
HA02EN006 Genex Gaia SR .40 1.00
HA02EN007 Genex Spare SR .40 1.00
HA02EN008 Genex Turbine SR .40 1.00
HA02EN009 Genex Doctor SR .40 1.00
HA02EN010 Genex Solar SCR .60 1.50
HA02EN011 Dai-sojo of the Ice Barrier SCR .60 1.50
HA02EN012 Medium of the Ice Barrier SR .60 1.50
HA02EN013 Mist Valley Baby Roc SR .40 1.00
HA02EN014 Mist Valley Executor SR .40 1.00
HA02EN015 Flamvell Grunika SR .40 1.00
HA02EN016 Flamvell Baby SR .40 1.00
HA02EN017 Ally Mind SR .40 1.00
HA02EN018 Ally of Justice Nullfier SR .40 1.00
HA02EN019 Ally of Justice Searcher SR .40 1.00
HA02EN020 Ally of Justice Enemy Catcher SR .40 1.00
HA02EN021 Ally of Justice Thunder Armor SR .40 1.00
HA02EN022 Ally of Justice Cosmic SCR .60 1.50
HA02EN023 Worm Linx SR .40 1.00
HA02EN024 Worm Millidith SR .40 1.00
HA02EN025 Worm Noble SR .40 1.00
HA02EN026 Naturia Beast SCR 3.00 8.00
HA02EN027 Dewloren, Tiger King SCR 3.00 8.00
HA02EN028 Thermal Genex SCR .60 1.50
HA02EN029 Geo Genex SCR .60 1.50
HA02EN030 Ally of Justice Field Marshal SCR .75 2.00
HA02EN031 Fabled Lurrie SR .40 1.00
HA02EN032 Fabled Grimro SCR .40 1.00
HA02EN033 Fabled Gallabas SCR .60 1.50
HA02EN034 Fabled Kushano SR .60 1.50
HA02EN035 Jurrac Protops SR .40 1.00
HA02EN036 Jurrac Velo SR 1.00 2.50
HA02EN037 Jurrac Monoloph SR .40 1.00
HA02EN038 Jurrac Tyrannus SCR .75 2.00
HA02EN039 Naturia Antjaw SR .40 1.00
HA02EN040 Naturia Spiderfang SR .40 1.00
HA02EN041 Naturia Rosewhip SR .60 1.50
HA02EN042 Naturia Cosmobeet SR .40 1.00
HA02EN043 Genex Blastfan SR .40 1.00
HA02EN044 Genex Recycled SR .40 1.00
HA02EN045 Genex Army SCR .60 1.50
HA02EN046 Pilgrim of the Ice Barrier SR .40 1.00
HA02EN047 Geomancer of the Ice Barrier SR .40 1.00
HA02EN048 Mist Valley Falcon SR .60 1.50
HA02EN049 Mist Valley Apex Avian SCR 5.00 12.00
HA02EN050 Ally of Justice Reverse Break SR .40 1.00
HA02EN051 Ally of Justice Unlimiter SR .40 1.00
HA02EN052 Worm Opera SR .40 1.00
HA02EN053 Worm Prince SR .40 1.00
HA02EN054 Worm Queen SCR .60 1.50
HA02EN055 Worm Rakuyeh SR .40 1.00
HA02EN056 Fabled Valkyrus SCR 2.00 5.00
HA02EN057 Jurrac Giganoto SCR 1.50 4.00
HA02EN058 Naturia Leodrake SCR .60 1.50
HA02EN059 Windmill Genex SCR .60 1.50
HA02EN060 Mist Valley Thunder Lord SCR .60 1.50

2010 Yu-Gi-Oh Hidden Arsenal 3 1st Edition

COMPLETE SET (60) 40.00 80.00
BOOSTER BOX (24 PACKS) 40.00 50.00
BOOSTER PACK (5 CARDS) 2.00 3.00
RELEASED ON DECEMBER 7, 2010
HA03EN001 Fabled Urustos SR .25 .60
HA03EN002 Fabled Krus SCR 2.00 5.00
HA03EN003 Fabled Topi SR .25 .60
HA03EN004 Fabled Soulkius SCR .50 1.25
HA03EN005 Fabled Miztoji SR .25 .60
HA03EN006 Jurrac Ptera SR .25 .60
HA03EN007 Jurrac Iguanon SR .25 .60
HA03EN008 Jurrac Brachis SR .25 .60
HA03EN009 Jurrac Spinos SR .25 .60
HA03EN010 Naturia Dragonfly SR .25 .60
HA03EN011 Naturia Sunflower SR .25 .60
HA03EN012 Naturia Cliff SCR 1.50 4.00
HA03EN013 Naturia Tulip SR .25 .60
HA03EN014 R-Genex Turbo SR .25 .60
HA03EN015 R-Genex Overseer SR .25 .60
HA03EN016 R-Genex Crusher SR .25 .60
HA03EN017 R-Genex Magma SR .25 .60
HA03EN018 Shock Troops SR .30 .75
HA03EN019 Samurai of the Ice Barrier SR .25 .60
HA03EN020 Dewdark of the Ice Barrier SR .50 1.25
HA03EN021 Caravan of the Ice Barrier SR .25 .60
HA03EN022 Worm Solid SR .25 .60
HA03EN023 Worm Tentacles SR .25 .60
HA03EN024 Worm Ugly SR .25 .60
HA03EN025 Worm Victory SCR .50 1.25
HA03EN026 Fabled Leviathan SCR .60 1.50
HA03EN027 Jurrac Velphito SCR 1.00 2.50
HA03EN028 Naturia Barkion SCR 10.00 25.00
HA03EN029 Locomotion R-Genex SCR .50 1.25
HA03EN030 Gungnir, Dragon of the Ice Barrier SCR 6.00 15.00
HA03EN031 Dragunity Dux SCR 1.00 2.50
HA03EN032 Dragunity Legionnaire SR .25 .60
HA03EN033 Dragunity Tribus SR .25 .60
HA03EN034 Dragunity Darkspear SR .30 .75
HA03EN035 Dragunity Phalanx SCR 5.00 12.00
HA03EN036 Fabled Dyf SR .25 .60
HA03EN037 Fabled Ashenveil SCR .60 1.50
HA03EN038 Fabled Oltro SR .25 .60
HA03EN039 Jurrac Titano SCR .50 1.25
HA03EN040 Jurrac Guaiba SR .25 .60
HA03EN041 Jurrac Stauriko SR .25 .60
HA03EN042 Naturia Horneedle SR .25 .60
HA03EN043 Naturia Fruitfly SR .25 .60
HA03EN044 Naturia Hydrangea SR .25 .60
HA03EN045 R-Genex Accelerator SR .25 .60
HA03EN046 R-Genex Oracle SR .25 .60
HA03EN047 R-Genex Ultimum SR .25 .60
HA03EN048 Spellbreaker of the Ice Barrier SR .25 .60
HA03EN049 General Grunard SCR 1.25 3.00
HA03EN050 Ally of Justice Omni-Weapon SCR .50 1.25
HA03EN051 Ally of Justice Quarantine SR .25 .60
HA03EN052 Ally of Justice Cycle Reader SR .25 .60
HA03EN053 Worm Warlord SR .25 .60
HA03EN054 Worm Xex SR .25 .60
HA03EN055 Worm Yagan SR .25 .60
HA03EN056 Worm Zero SCR .60 1.50
HA03EN057 Dragunity Knight - Gae Bulg SCR 1.00 2.50
HA03EN058 Fabled Ragin SCR 1.50 4.00
HA03EN059 Vindikite R-Genex SCR .50 1.25
HA03EN060 Ally of Justice Decisive SCR 4.00 10.00

2011 Yu-Gi-Oh Hidden Arsenal 4 1st Edition

COMPLETE SET (60) 25.00 50.00
BOOSTER BOX (24 PACKS) 60.00 80.00
BOOSTER PACK (5 CARDS) 3.00 4.00
RELEASED ON APRIL 19, 2011
HA04EN001 Genex Ally Remote SR .15 .40
HA04EN002 Genex Ally Powercell SCR .25 .75
HA04EN003 Genex Ally Changer SR .15 .40
HA04EN004 Genex Ally Volcannon SR .15 .40
HA04EN005 Genex Ally Solid SR .15 .40
HA04EN006 The Fabled Chawa SR .15 .40
HA04EN007 The Fabled Catsith SR .50 1.25
HA04EN008 The Fabled Cerburrel SCR .25 .75
HA04EN009 The Fabled Ganashia SR .15 .40
HA04EN010 The Fabled Nozoochee SR .15 .40
HA04EN011 Dragunity Militum SR .15 .40
HA04EN012 Dragunity Primus Pilus SCR .25 .75
HA04EN013 Dragunity Brandistock SR .15 .40
HA04EN014 Dragunity Javelin SR .15 .40
HA04EN015 Jurrac Dino SR .15 .40
HA04EN016 Jurrac Gallim SR .15 .40
HA04EN017 Jurrac Aeolo SR .15 .40
HA04EN018 Jurrac Herra SR .25 .75
HA04EN019 Naturia Butterfly SR .15 .40
HA04EN020 Naturia Ladybug SR .15 .40
HA04EN021 Naturia Strawberry SR .15 .40
HA04EN022 Defender of the Ice Barrier SR .25 .75
HA04EN023 Warlock of the Ice Barrier SR .15 .40
HA04EN024 Sacred Spirit SR .15 .40
HA04EN025 General Raiho SCR .25 .75
HA04EN026 Genex Ally Triarm SCR .25 .75
HA04EN027 The Fabled Unicore SCR .50 1.25
HA04EN028 Dragunity Knight - Trident SCR .75 2.00
HA04EN029 Jurrac Meteor SCR .25 .75
HA04EN030 Naturia Landoise SCR .25 .75
HA04EN031 Neo Flamvell Origin SR .15 .40
HA04EN032 Neo Flamvell Hedgehog SR .15 .40
HA04EN033 Neo Flamvell Shaman SR .15 .40
HA04EN034 Neo Flamvell Garuda SR .15 .40
HA04EN035 Neo Flamvell Sabre SCR .25 .75
HA04EN036 Genex Ally Chemister SR .15 .40
HA04EN037 Genex Ally Birdman SR .40 1.00
HA04EN038 Genex Ally Bellflame SR .15 .40
HA04EN039 Genex Ally Crusher SR .15 .40
HA04EN040 Genex Ally Reliever SCR .25 .75
HA04EN041 The Fabled Peggulsus SR .15 .40
HA04EN042 The Fabled Kokkator SR .15 .40
HA04EN043 Fabled Dianaira SCR .25 .75
HA04EN044 Dragunity Corsesca SR .15 .40
HA04EN045 Dragunity Partisan SR .15 .40
HA04EN046 Dragunity Pilum SR .15 .40
HA04EN047 Dragunity Angusticlavii SR .15 .40
HA04EN048 Naturia Stinkbug SR .15 .40
HA04EN049 Naturia Mantis SR .15 .40
HA04EN050 Naturia Ragweed SR .15 .40
HA04EN051 Naturia White Oak SCR .25 .75
HA04EN052 Strategist of the Ice Barrier SR .15 .40
HA04EN053 Secret Guards SR .15 .40
HA04EN054 General Gantala SCR .25 .75
HA04EN055 Naturia Exterio SCR .25 .75
HA04EN056 Ancient Flamvell Deity SCR .25 .75
HA04EN057 Genex Ally Triforce SCR .25 .75
HA04EN058 The Fabled Kudabbi SCR .25 .75
HA04EN059 Dragunity Knight - Barcha SCR .75 2.00
HA04EN060 Trishula, Dragon SCR 15.00 30.00

2011 Yu-Gi-Oh Hidden Arsenal 5 1st Edition

COMPLETE SET (60) 100.00 200.00
BOOSTER BOX (24 PACKS) 30.00 40.00
BOOSTER PACK (5 CARDS) 2.00 3.00
RELEASED ON DECEMBER 6, 2011
HA05EN001 Gem Garnet SR 2.00 5.00
HA05EN002 Gem Sapphire SR .40 1.00
HA05EN003 Gem Tourmaline SR .40 1.00
HA05EN004 Gem Alexandrite SCR .75 2.00
HA05EN005 Gem-Armadillo SCR 2.00 5.00
HA05EN006 Gem-Merchant SR .10 .30
HA05EN007 Laval Miller SR .10 .30
HA05EN008 Soaring Eagle Above the Searing Land SR .10 .30
HA05EN009 Laval Warrior SR .10 .30
HA05EN010 Prominence, Molt SR .10 .30
HA05EN011 Laval Forest Sprite SR .10 .30
HA05EN012 Kayenn, the Master SR .10 .30
HA05EN013 Laval Burner SR .10 .30
HA05EN014 Laval Judgment (SCR) .25 .75
HA05EN015 Vylon Cube SR .50 1.25
HA05EN016 Vylon Vanguard SR .10 .30
HA05EN017 Vylon Charger SR .10 .30
HA05EN018 Vylon Soldier SR .10 .30
HA05EN019 Gem-Knight Ruby SCR .75 2.00
HA05EN020 Gem Aquamarine SCR .25 .75
HA05EN021 Gem-Knight Topaz SCR .40 1.00
HA05EN022 Lavalval Dragon SCR .25 .75
HA05EN023 Laval the Greater SCR .25 .75
HA05EN024 Vylon Sigma SCR .25 .75
HA05EN025 Vylon Epsilon SCR 1.50 4.00
HA05EN026 Gem-Knight Fusion SR .40 1.00
HA05EN027 Searing Fire Wall SR .10 .30
HA05EN028 Vylon Material SR .10 .30
HA05EN029 Gem-Enhancement SR .10 .30
HA05EN030 Molten Whirlwind Wall SR .10 .30
HA05EN031 Gishki Abyss SR 1.00 2.50
HA05EN032 Gishki Vanity SR .10 .30
HA05EN033 Gishki Marker SR .10 .30
HA05EN034 Gishki Chain SCR .25 .75
HA05EN035 Gishki Ariel SR .25 .75
HA05EN036 Gishki Shadow SR .40 1.00
HA05EN037 Gusto Gulldo SR .50 1.25
HA05EN038 Gusto Egul SR .40 1.00
HA05EN039 Gusto Thunbolt SR .10 .30
HA05EN040 Winda, Priestess SR .50 1.25
HA05EN041 Caam, Serenity SCR 2.50 6.00
HA05EN042 Windaar, Sage SR .10 .30
HA05EN043 Steelswarm Cell SR .10 .30
HA05EN044 Steelswarm Scout SR .10 .30
HA05EN045 Steelswarm Gatekeeper SR .10 .30
HA05EN046 Steelswarm Caller SR .10 .30
HA05EN047 Steels Mantis SCR .25 .75
HA05EN048 Steels Moth SR .10 .30
HA05EN049 Steels Girastag SCR .25 .75
HA05EN050 Steels Caucastag SCR .50 1.25
HA05EN051 Evigishki Mind SCR .25 .75
HA05EN052 Evigishki Soul SCR .50 1.25
HA05EN053 Daigusto Gulldos SCR .40 1.00
HA05EN054 Daigusto Eguls SCR .25 .75
HA05EN055 Gishki Aquamirror SR 1.50 4.00
HA05EN056 Contact Gusto SCR .60 1.50
HA05EN057 First Step SR .10 .30
HA05EN058 Aquamirror Meditation SR .10 .30
HA05EN059 Blessings for Gusto SR .10 .30
HA05EN060 Infestation Wave SR .10 .30

2012 Yu-Gi-Oh Hidden Arsenal 6 1st Edition

COMPLETE SET (60) 50.00 100.00
BOOSTER BOX (24 PACKS) 40.00 50.00
BOOSTER PACK (5 CARDS) 3.00 4.00
RELEASED ON JULY 24, 2012
HA06EN001 Gem-Knight Crystal SR .20 .60
HA06EN002 Laval Volcano Handmaiden SR .10 .30
HA06EN003 Laval Cannon SCR .25 .75
HA06EN004 Vylon Sphere SR .10 .30
HA06EN005 Vylon Tetra SR .10 .30
HA06EN006 Vylon Stella SR .10 .30
HA06EN007 Vylon Prism SR .15 .40
HA06EN008 Vylon Hept SR .10 .30
HA06EN009 Gishki Reliever SR .10 .30
HA06EN010 Gishki Noellia SR .10 .30
HA06EN011 Gusto Squirro SR .10 .30
HA06EN012 Reeze, Whirlwind of Gusto SR .10 .30
HA06EN013 Steelswarm Genome SR .10 .30
HA06EN014 Steelswarm Sentinel SR .10 .30
HA06EN015 Steelswarm Sting SR .10 .30
HA06EN016 Steelswarm Longhorn SCR .25 .75
HA06EN017 Steelswarm Hercules SCR .25 .75
HA06EN018 Evigishki Tetrogre SCR .25 .75
HA06EN019 Gem-Knight Citrine SCR .75 2.00
HA06EN020 Gem-Knight Prismaura SCR .75 2.00
HA06EN021 Laval Stennon SCR .25 .75
HA06EN022 Vylon Alpha SCR .25 .75
HA06EN023 Vylon Omega SCR .25 .75
HA06EN024 Daigusto Sphreez SCR .75 2.00
HA06EN025 Vylon Component SR .10 .30

Card	Low	High
HA06EN026 Vylon Element SR	.10	.30
HA06EN027 Forbidden Arts of the Gishki SR	.10	.30
HA06EN028 Pyroxene Fusion SR	.10	.30
HA06EN029 Infestation Ripples SR	.10	.30
HA06EN030 Infestation Tool SR	.10	.30
HA06EN031 Gem-Knight Obsidian SR	.40	1.00
HA06EN032 Gem-Knight Iolite SR	.20	.50
HA06EN033 Gem-Knight Amber SR	.20	.60
HA06EN034 Laval Lakeside Lady SCR	.40	1.00
HA06EN035 Laval Coatl SR	.10	.30
HA06EN036 Laval Blaster SR	.10	.30
HA06EN037 Vylon Pentachloro SR	.10	.30
HA06EN038 Vylon Tesseract SR	.10	.30
HA06EN039 Vylon Stigma SR	.10	.30
HA06EN040 Gishki Vision SR	.25	.75
HA06EN041 Gishki Emilia SR	.10	.30
HA06EN042 Gishki Mollusk SR	.10	.30
HA06EN043 Gusto Falco SR	.10	.30
HA06EN044 Kamui, Hope of Gusto SR	.20	.60
HA06EN045 Musto, Oracle of Gusto SR	.10	.30
HA06EN046 Evigishki Gustkraken SCR	.25	.75
HA06EN047 Gem-Knight Amethyst SCR	.40	1.00
HA06EN048 Lavalval Dragun SCR	.25	.75
HA06EN049 Daigusto Falcos SCR	.25	.75
HA06EN050 Gem-Knight Pearl SCR	.50	1.25
HA06EN051 Lavalval Ignis SCR	.25	.75
HA06EN052 Vylon Disigma SCR	1.50	4.00
HA06EN053 Evigishki Merrowgeist SCR	.25	.75
HA06EN054 Daigusto Phoenix SCR	2.00	5.00
HA06EN055 Particle Fusion SR	.10	.30
HA06EN056 Vylon Polytope SR	.10	.30
HA06EN057 Vylon Segment SR	.10	.30
HA06EN058 Dustflame Blast SR	.10	.30
HA06EN059 Aquamirror Illusion SR	.10	.30
HA06EN060 Whirlwind of Gusto SR	.10	.30

2013 Yu-Gi-Oh Hidden Arsenal 7 1st Edition

Card	Low	High
COMPLETE SET (70)	80.00	120.00
BOOSTER BOX (24 PACKS)	100.00	120.00
BOOSTER PACK (5 CARDS)	4.00	5.00
RELEASED ON APRIL 25, 2013		
HA07EN001 Gem-Knight Sardonyx SR	.25	.40
HA07EN002 Laval Phlogis SR	.15	.25
HA07EN003 Gishki Avance SR	.15	.25
HA07EN004 Gusto Griffin SR	.15	.25
HA07EN005 Constellar Sheratan SR	.15	.25
HA07EN006 Constellar Aldebaran SR	.15	.25
HA07EN007 Constellar Algiedi SR	.30	.50
HA07EN008 Constellar Pollux SR	.30	.50
HA07EN009 Constellar Zubeneschamali SCR	.40	.75
HA07EN010 Constellar Virgo SR	.15	.25
HA07EN011 Evilswarm Heliotrope SR	.25	.40
HA07EN012 Evilswarm Zahak SR	.15	.25
HA07EN013 Evilswarm Ketos SR	.15	.25
HA07EN014 Evilswarm O'lantern SR	.15	.25
HA07EN015 Evilswarm Mandragora SR	.30	.50
HA07EN016 Evilswarm Hraesvelg SR	.15	.25
HA07EN017 Evigishki Levianima SCR	.20	.30
HA07EN018 Gem-Knight Zirconia SR	.75	1.00
HA07EN019 Lavalval Chain SCR	4.50	6.00
HA07EN020 Daigusto Emeral SCR	15.00	20.00
HA07EN021 Constellar Hyades SCR	.40	.75
HA07EN022 Constellar Pleiades SCR	.60	1.00
HA07EN023 Evilswarm Nightmare SR	.50	.75
HA07EN024 Evilswarm Bahamut SCR	.60	1.00
HA07EN025 Molten Conduction Field SCR	.20	.30
HA07EN026 Gishki Photomirror SR	.15	.25
HA07EN027 Constellar Star Chart SCR	.30	.50
HA07EN028 Fragment Fusion SR	.15	.25
HA07EN029 Dust Storm of Gusto SR	.15	.25
HA07EN030 Infestation Infection SCR	.30	.50
HA07EN031 D.D. Esper Star Sparrow SCR	.30	.50
HA07EN032 Beast-Warrior Puma SR	.15	.25
HA07EN033 Phoenix Beast Gairuda SR	.15	.25
HA07EN034 Ironhammer the Giant SR	.15	.25
HA07EN035 D.D. Jet Iron SR	.15	.25
HA07EN036 Aye-Iron SR	.15	.25
HA07EN037 Tin Goldfish SR	8.00	10.00
HA07EN038 Gearspring Spirit SR	.50	.75
HA07EN039 Gem-Knight Lazuli SR	1.50	2.50
HA07EN040 Gishki Natalia SR	.15	.25
HA07EN041 Constellar Siat SR	.15	.25
HA07EN042 Constellar Rasalhague SR	.15	.25
HA07EN043 Constellar Leonis SR	.15	.25
HA07EN044 Constellar Acubens SR	.15	.25
HA07EN045 Constellar Kaus SCR	.25	.75
HA07EN046 Constellar Alrescha SR	.15	.25
HA07EN047 Constellar Antares SR	.15	.25
HA07EN048 Evilswarm Castor SR	1.00	1.50
HA07EN049 Evilswarm Obliviwisp SR	.15	.25
HA07EN050 Evilswarm Azzathoth SR	.15	.25
HA07EN051 Evilswarm Thunderbird SCR	.60	1.00
HA07EN052 Evilswarm Salamandra SR	.15	.25
HA07EN053 Evilswarm Golem SR	.15	.25
HA07EN054 Evilswarm Coppelia SR	.15	.25
HA07EN055 Sophia, Goddess of Rebirth SCR	1.00	1.50
HA07EN056 Gishki Psychelone SR	.15	.25
HA07EN057 Gishki Zielgigas SCR	1.50	2.50
HA07EN058 Gem-Knight Seraphinite SR	15.00	20.00
HA07EN059 Gem-Knight Master Diamond SCR	.50	.80
HA07EN060 Tin Archduke SCR	.20	.30
HA07EN061 Constellar Praesepe SCR	.60	1.00
HA07EN062 Constellar Ptolemy M7 SCR	3.50	5.00
HA07EN063 Evilswarm Thanatos SCR	.60	1.00
HA07EN064 Evilswarm Ophion SCR	7.00	10.00
HA07EN065 Evilswarm Ouroboros SCR	3.50	5.00
HA07EN066 Iron Call SCR	2.50	4.00
HA07EN067 Constellar Star Cradle SR	.15	.25
HA07EN068 Infestation Pandemic SCR	2.00	3.00
HA07EN069 Constellar Meteor SR	.15	.25
HA07EN070 Infestation Terminus SR	.15	.25

2011 Yu-Gi-Oh Legendary Collection 2 1st Edition

Card	Low	High
COMPLETE SET (279)	450.00	600.00
BOOSTER BOX (5 PACKS)	50.00	70.00
BOOSTER PACK (25 CARDS)	10.00	15.00
RELEASED ON OCTOBER 4, 2011		
LCGX001 Elemental HERO Avian	.20	.50
LCGX002 HERO Avian (alt) SCR	1.50	4.00
LCGX003 Elemental HERO Burstinatrix	.50	1.25
LCGX004 HERO Burstin (alt) SCR	1.25	3.00
LCGX005 Elemental HERO Clayman	1.25	3.00
LCGX006 Elemental HERO Sparkman	.20	.50
LCGX007 HERO Spark (alt) SCR	1.25	3.00
LCGX008 Elemental HERO Neos	1.00	2.50
LCGX009 Winged Kuriboh	.75	2.00
LCGX010 Winged Kuriboh LV10	1.50	4.00
LCGX011 Wroughtweiler	.20	.50
LCGX012 Elemental HERO Bubbleman	.40	1.00
LCGX013 Elemental HERO Bladedge	.20	.50
LCGX014 Elemental HERO Wildheart	.20	.50
LCGX015 HERO Necroshade R	.40	1.00
LCGX016 Hero Kid	.20	.50
LCGX017 Neo-Spacian Aqua Dolphin	1.00	2.50
LCGX018 Neo-Spacian Flare Scarab	.50	1.25
LCGX019 Neo-Spacian Dark Panther	.20	.50
LCGX020 Card Trooper	.20	.50
LCGX021 Neo-Spacian Air Hummingbird	.60	1.50
LCGX022 Neo-Spacian Grand Mole	.20	.50
LCGX023 Neo-Spacian Glow Moss	.20	.50
LCGX024 Elemental HERO Stratos	.75	2.00
LCGX025 Elemental HERO Ocean R	.50	1.25
LCGX026 Elemental HERO Captain Gold	.75	2.00
LCGX027 Necro Gardna SCR	.75	2.00
LCGX028 HERO Neos Alius SCR	.75	2.00
LCGX029 HERO Malicious SCR	.75	2.00
LCGX030 Evil HERO Infernal Gainer	.20	.50
LCGX031 HERO Infernal Prodigy R	.50	1.25
LCGX032 Card Ejector SR	.75	2.00
LCGX033 Elemental Hero Prisma	2.50	6.00
LCGX034 HERO Woodsman SR	.75	2.00
LCGX035 Elemental HERO Knospe R	.50	1.25
LCGX036 Elemental HERO Poison Rose R	.20	.50
LCGX037 Elemental HERO Heat	.50	1.25
LCGX038 HERO Lady Heat	.75	2.00
LCGX039 Elemental HERO Voltic	.40	1.00
LCGX040 Neos Wiseman UR	1.00	2.50
LCGX041 Gallis Star Beast SCR	.75	2.00
LCGX042 Dandylion SCR	.75	2.00
LCGX043 Winged Kuriboh LV9 SCR	.75	2.00
LCGX044 Card Blocker UR	.50	1.25
LCGX045 HERO Flame SCR	2.50	6.00
LCGX046 HERO Thunder Giant	1.25	3.00
LCGX047 HERO Rampart Blaster SR	.75	2.00
LCGX048 HERO Tempest SR	2.50	6.00
LCGX049 HERO Wildedge	1.50	4.00
LCGX050 HERO Shining SCR	4.00	10.00
LCGX051 HERO Steam Healer R	1.50	4.00
LCGX052 HERO Electrum UR	.75	2.00
LCGX053 HERO Mudballman SR	.75	2.00
LCGX054 Elemental HERO Mariner	.20	.50
LCGX055 HERO Wild Wingman	.20	.50
LCGX056 HERO Necroid Shaman	.20	.50
LCGX057 HERO Aqua Neos SR	.75	2.00
LCGX058 HERO Flare Neos	.20	.50
LCGX059 HERO Dark Neos SCR	.75	2.00
LCGX060 HERO Grand Neos SR	.75	2.00
LCGX061 HERO Glow Neos R	1.25	3.00
LCGX062 HERO Marine Neos	.20	.50
LCGX063 HERO Darkbright SR	1.50	4.00
LCGX064 HERO Magma Neos SR	2.50	6.00
LCGX065 HERO Chaos Neos UR	1.25	3.00
LCGX066 HERO Plasma Vice	2.00	5.00
LCGX067 HERO Inferno Wing SR	.75	2.00
LCGX068 HERO Lightning SR	.75	2.00
LCGX069 HERO Dark Gaia SR	.75	2.00
LCGX070 HERO Wild Cyclone SR	.75	2.00
LCGX071 HERO Infernal Sniper UR	.50	1.25
LCGX072 HERO Malicious Fiend SR	1.25	3.00
LCGX073 HERO Storm Neos	.60	1.50
LCGX074 Rainbow Neos SR	.75	2.00
LCGX075 HERO Terra Firma SR	.75	2.00
LCGX076 HERO Inferno SR	.75	2.00
LCGX077 HERO Divine Neos UR	.50	1.25
LCGX078 Miracle Fusion UR	.75	2.00
LCGX079 Transcendent Wings	.40	1.00
LCGX080 Bubble Shuffle R	.20	.50
LCGX081 Spark Blaster	.20	.50
LCGX082 Skyscraper	1.50	4.00
LCGX083 Feather Shot R	.20	.50
LCGX084 Burst Return R	.20	.50
LCGX085 Hero Heart	.20	.50
LCGX086 Cyclone Boomerang	.20	.50
LCGX087 Flute of Summoning UR	.50	1.25
LCGX088 H - Heated Heart	.20	.50
LCGX089 E - Emergency Call	.20	.50
LCGX090 R - Righteous Justice	.20	.50
LCGX091 O - Oversoul	.20	.50
LCGX092 Hero Flash!! R	.20	.50
LCGX093 Fake Hero R	.20	.50
LCGX094 Neo Space R	.40	1.00
LCGX095 Instant Fusion UR	5.00	12.00
LCGX096 Neos Force	.20	.50
LCGX097 Skyscraper 2 SCR	1.25	3.00
LCGX098 Fifth Hope SCR	1.50	4.00
LCGX099 Dark Fusion UR	2.50	6.00
LCGX100 Dark Calling R	.75	2.00
LCGX101 Super Polymer. SCR	.75	2.00
LCGX102 Instant Neo Space	.20	.50
LCGX103 Hero Mask	.20	.50
LCGX104 Space Gift	.20	.50
LCGX105 Rose Bud R	.20	.50
LCGX106 HERO's Bond	.20	.50
LCGX107 Hero Signal	.20	.50
LCGX108 Hero Barrier	.20	.50
LCGX109 Feather Wind	.20	.50
LCGX110 Hero Ring SR	.75	2.00
LCGX111 Clay Charge	.20	.50
LCGX112 Miracle Kids	.20	.50
LCGX113 Edge Hammer	.20	.50
LCGX114 Kid Guard UR	.50	1.25
LCGX115 Elemental Recharge	.20	.50
LCGX116 Change of Hero - Reflector Ray	.20	.50
LCGX117 Hero Spirit	.20	.50
LCGX118 Hero Counterattack	.20	.50
LCGX119 Mirror Gate UR	.50	1.25
LCGX120 Hero Blast	.20	.50
LCGX121 Terra Firma Gravity R	.20	.50
LCGX122 HERO - Doom Lord	.20	.50
LCGX123 HERO - Captain Tenacious	.20	.50
LCGX124 HERO - Diamond SR	.75	2.00
LCGX125 HERO - Dreadmaster SR	.75	2.00
LCGX126 HERO - Double Dude	.20	.50
LCGX127 HERO - Defender R	.60	1.50
LCGX128 HERO - Dogma SR	.75	2.00
LCGX129 HERO - Blade Master	.20	.50
LCGX130 HERO - Fear Monger	.20	.50
LCGX131 HERO - Dasher	.20	.50
LCGX132 HERO - Malicious	1.50	4.00
LCGX133 HERO - Disk SCR	.75	2.00
LCGX134 HERO - Plasma SR	.75	2.00
LCGX135 HERO - Dunker	.20	.50
LCGX136 HERO - Departed	.20	.50
LCGX137 HERO - Dread Servant	.20	.50
LCGX138 HERO Phoenix SR	.75	2.00
LCGX139 HERO Shining SCR	1.25	3.00
LCGX140 Destiny End Dragoon SR	1.50	4.00
LCGX141 Clock Tower Prison	.20	.50
LCGX142 D - Spirit	.20	.50
LCGX143 Cyclone Blade	.20	.50
LCGX144 Dark City	.20	.50
LCGX145 Destiny Draw SCR	.75	2.00
LCGX146 Over Destiny R	.40	1.00
LCGX147 D - Formation	.20	.50
LCGX148 Destiny Signal	.20	.50
LCGX149 D-Time R	.20	.50
LCGX150 D - Shield	.20	.50
LCGX151 Destiny Mirage R	.20	.50
LCGX152 D - Chain	.20	.50
LCGX153 D - Counter	.20	.50
LCGX154 D - Fortune	.20	.50
LCGX155 Crystal Beast Ruby Carbuncle	.20	.50
LCGX156 Crystal Beast Amethyst Cat	.20	.50
LCGX157 Crystal Beast Emerald Tortoise	.20	.50
LCGX158 Crystal Beast Topaz Tiger	.20	.50
LCGX159 Crystal Beast Amber Mammoth	.50	1.25
LCGX160 Crystal Beast Cobalt Eagle	.20	.50
LCGX161 Crystal Beast Saph SR	2.00	5.00
LCGX162 Rainbow Dragon UR	2.50	6.00
LCGX163 Crystal Beacon R	.20	.50
LCGX164 Rare Value SR	.75	2.00
LCGX165 Crystal Blessing R	.20	.50
LCGX166 Crystal Abundance R	.20	.50
LCGX167 Crystal Promise R	.20	.50
LCGX168 Ancient City - Rainbow	.20	.50
LCGX169 Crystal Release UR	.75	2.00
LCGX170 Crystal Tree UR	1.25	3.00
LCGX171 Crystal Raigeki	.20	.50
LCGX172 Crystal Pair	.75	2.00
LCGX173 Rainbow Path	.20	.50
LCGX174 Rainbow Gravity	.20	.50
LCGX175 Cyber Dragon UR	1.00	2.50
LCGX176 Cyber Dragon (alt) SCR	2.00	5.00
LCGX177 Proto-Cyber Dragon UR	.50	1.25
LCGX178 Cyber Phoenix UR	.50	1.25
LCGX179 Cyber Valley UR	1.00	2.50
LCGX180 Cyber Twin Dragon SCR	.75	2.00
LCGX181 Cyber End Dragon SCR	3.00	8.00
LCGX182 Cyber Dragon (alt) SCR	3.00	8.00
LCGX183 Chimera Over SCR	1.25	3.00
LCGX184 Power Bond SCR	4.00	10.00
LCGX185 Overload Fusion R	.60	1.50
LCGX186 Future Fusion UR	1.00	2.50
LCGX187 Magical Mallet UR	2.00	5.00
LCGX188 Dark End Dragon SCR	.75	2.00
LCGX189 Light End Dragon UR	.50	1.25
LCGX190 Hydrogeddon UR	.50	1.25
LCGX191 Vennominaga Deity UR	.50	1.25
LCGX192 Vennominon the King SR	.75	2.00
LCGX193 Phantom of Chaos SCR	2.00	5.00
LCGX194 Phantom Skyblaster SCR	.75	2.00
LCGX195 Grave Squirmer	.20	.50
LCGX196 Grinder Golem	1.00	2.50
LCGX197 Yubel SCR	2.00	5.00
LCGX198 Yubel - Terror Inc SCR	.75	2.00
LCGX199 Yubel - The Ultimate SCR	2.00	5.00
LCGX200 Mezuki	.50	1.25
LCGX201 Cold Enchanter	.20	.50
LCGX202 Ice Master	.20	.50
LCGX203 Thunder King Rai-Oh	1.00	2.50
LCGX204 Darkness Destroy SCR	.75	2.00
LCGX205 White Night Dragon UR	.50	1.25
LCGX206 Kasha UR	.50	1.25
LCGX207 Ice Queen UR	.50	1.25
LCGX208 Shutendoji UR	.50	1.25
LCGX209 Clear Vice Dragon SR	.75	2.00
LCGX210 Darklord Desire SR	.75	2.00
LCGX211 Armityle the Chaos UR	8.00	20.00
LCGX212 Fusion Recovery	2.50	6.00
LCGX213 System Down	2.00	5.00
LCGX214 Grand Convergence R	.20	.50
LCGX215 Dim Fissure SCR	1.25	3.00
LCGX216 Venom Swamp	.20	.50
LCGX217 Clear World SR	.75	2.00
LCGX218 Macro Cosmos UR	1.25	3.00
LCGX219 Rise of the Snake Deity	.20	.50
LCGX220 Dim Prison UR	1.25	3.00
LCGX221 Offering to the Snake	.20	.50
LCGX222 Chamberlain of the Six	.20	.50
LCGX223 Gladiator Beast Andal	.20	.50
LCGX224 D.D. Survivor	.20	.50
LCGX225 Banisher of Radiance SCR	.75	2.00
LCGX226 Grandmaster of Samurai	.20	.50
LCGX227 Six Samurai - Yaichi	.20	.50
LCGX228 Six Samurai - Kamon	.20	.50
LCGX229 Six Samurai - Yariza	.20	.50

LCGX230 Six Samurai - Nisashi .20 .50
LCGX231 Six Samurai - Zanji .20 .50
LCGX232 Six Samurai - Irou .20 .50
LCGX233 Great Shogun Shien SCR 1.25 3.00
LCGX234 D.D. Crow SR .75 2.00
LCGX235 Beast Octavius UR .50 1.25
LCGX236 Beast Murmillo SCR .75 2.00
LCGX237 Beast Bestiari SCR 2.00 5.00
LCGX238 Beast Laquari SCR .75 2.00
LCGX239 Beast Hoplomus SCR .75 2.00
LCGX240 Beast Secutor SCR .75 2.00
LCGX241 Enishi, Chancellor SR .75 2.00
LCGX242 Test Tiger SCR .75 2.00
LCGX243 Rainbow Dark Dragon UR 1.25 3.00
LCGX244 Beast Darius SCR 1.25 3.00
LCGX245 Jain, Paladin UR .50 1.25
LCGX246 Garoth, Warrior UR 1.00 2.50
LCGX247 Lumina, Summoner UR 1.25 3.00
LCGX248 Wulf, Beast UR .50 1.25
LCGX249 Judgment Dragon .20 .50
LCGX250 Aurkus, Druid UR .50 1.25
LCGX251 Beast Equeste SCR 1.00 2.50
LCGX252 Beast Lanista UR .50 1.25
LCGX253 Beast Heraklinos SR .75 2.00
LCGX254 Beast's Respite R .20 .50
LCGX255 Gladiator's Return R .20 .50
LCGX256 Cunning of the Six Samurai .20 .50
LCGX257 Gladiator Ground R .20 .50
LCGX258 Light of Redemption .20 .50
LCGX259 Gateway of the Six .20 .50
LCGX260 Non-Fusion Area .60 1.50
LCGX261 Success Probability 0 .20 .50
LCGX262 Return of the Six Samurai .20 .50
LCGX263 Swiftstrike Armor R .20 .50
LCGX264 Double-Edged Sword .20 .50
LCGX265 Defensive Tactics UR .50 1.25
LCGX266 Beast War Chariot SCR 1.25 3.00

2012 Yu-Gi-Oh Ra Yellow Mega Pack 1st Edition

COMPLETE SET (113) 60.00 120.00
BOOSTER BOX (24 PACKS) 150.00 200.00
BOOSTER PACK (11 CARDS) 5.00 6.00
RELEASED ON FEBRUARY 21, 2012
RYMPEN001 Elemental HERO Avian ALT .20 .60
RYMPEN002 Elemental HERO Burstinatrix ALT .40 1.00
RYMPEN003 Elemental HERO Sparkman ALT .25 .75
RYMPEN004 Elemental HERO Neos .20 .60
RYMPEN005 Elemental HERO Necroshade .20 .60
RYMPEN006 Card Trooper .15 .40
RYMPEN007 Neo-Spacian Grand SR .25 .75
RYMPEN008 Elemental HERO Stratos .60 1.50
RYMPEN009 Necro Gardna SCR .25 .75
RYMPEN010 Elem HERO Neos SCR .40 1.00
RYMPEN011 Card Ejector .15 .40
RYMPEN012 Elemental HERO Prisma 1.50 4.00
RYMPEN013 Gallis the Star Beast .15 .40
RYMPEN014 Winged Kuriboh LV9 R .25 .60
RYMPEN015 Card Blocker .15 .40
RYMPEN016 Elemental HERO Flame Wingman R 1.25 3.00
RYMPEN017 Elemental HERO Electrum .50 1.25
RYMPEN018 Elemental HERO Mudballman .50 1.25
RYMPEN019 Rainbow Neos .20 .60
RYMPEN020 Elemental HERO Divine Neos .25 .75
RYMPEN021 Miracle Fusion (UR) .60 1.50
RYMPEN022 The Flute of Summoning Kuriboh .20 .60
RYMPEN023 H - Heated Heart SCR .25 .75
RYMPEN024 E - Emergency Call SCR 1.25 3.00
RYMPEN025 R - Right Justice SCR .25 .75
RYMPEN026 O - Oversoul SCR .25 .75
RYMPEN027 Hero Flash!! SCR .25 .75
RYMPEN028 Instant Fusion UR 4.00 10.00
RYMPEN029 Super Polymer SCR .75 2.00
RYMPEN030 Hero Mask .15 .40
RYMPEN031 Hero Signal SR .25 .75
RYMPEN032 Hero Blast SR .25 .75
RYMPEN033 Destiny HERO - Diamond Dude .20 .60
RYMPEN034 HERO - Malicious SCR 2.50 6.00
RYMPEN035 Destiny HERO - Disk Commander R .25 .60
RYMPEN036 Destiny HERO - Plasma .75 2.00
RYMPEN037 Destiny Draw SCR 1.25 3.00
RYMPEN038 Destiny Signal SR .25 .75
RYMPEN039 Destiny Mirage .15 .40
RYMPEN040 Crystal Beast Ruby SR .40 1.00
RYMPEN041 Crystal Beast Ameth SR .25 .75
RYMPEN042 Crystal Beast Emerald SR .25 .75
RYMPEN043 Crystal Beast Topaz SR .60 1.50
RYMPEN044 Crystal Beast Amber SR .50 1.25
RYMPEN045 Crystal Beast Cobalt SR .50 1.25
RYMPEN046 Crystal Beast Sapphire Pegasus 1.50 4.00
RYMPEN047 Rainbow Dragon 1.50 4.00
RYMPEN048 Crystal Beacon SCR .25 .75
RYMPEN049 Rare Value .40 1.00
RYMPEN050 Crystal Blessing SCR .25 .75
RYMPEN051 Crystal Abundance SCR .25 .75
RYMPEN052 Crystal Promise SCR .25 .75
RYMPEN053 Ancient City - Rainbow Ruins .15 .40
RYMPEN054 Crystal Release .40 1.00
RYMPEN055 Crystal Raigeki SR .25 .75
RYMPEN056 Rainbow Path .15 .40
RYMPEN057 Rainbow Gravity .15 .40
RYMPEN058 Cyber Dragon 1.25 3.00
RYMPEN059 Cyber Dragon ALT SCR 1.50 4.00
RYMPEN060 Cyber End Dragon ALT R 1.25 3.00
RYMPEN061 Chimeratech Over R .40 1.00
RYMPEN062 Power Bond .40 1.00
RYMPEN063 Overload Fusion .75 2.00
RYMPEN064 Future Fusion UR .75 2.00
RYMPEN065 Magical Mallet .75 2.00
RYMPEN066 Dark End Dragon SR .25 .75
RYMPEN067 Light End Dragon SR .25 .75
RYMPEN068 Vennominaga the Deity of Poisonous Snakes R .25 .60
RYMPEN069 Vennominon the King of Poisonous Snakes .15 .40
RYMPEN070 Yubel R 1.25 3.00
RYMPEN071 Yubel - Terror Incarnate R .60 1.50
RYMPEN072 Ultimate Nightmare R .75 2.00
RYMPEN073 Mezuki .60 1.50
RYMPEN074 Thunder King Rai-Oh .75 2.00
RYMPEN075 Kasha .15 .40
RYMPEN076 Shutendoji .15 .40
RYMPEN077 Darklord Desire .15 .40
RYMPEN078 Fusion Recovery 2.50 6.00
RYMPEN079 System Down 1.50 4.00
RYMPEN080 Grand Convergence .15 .40
RYMPEN081 Dimensional Fissure SCR .60 1.50
RYMPEN082 Macro Cosmos UR .75 2.00
RYMPEN083 Rise of the Snake Deity .15 .40
RYMPEN084 Dimensional Prison UR .75 2.00
RYMPEN085 Offering to the Snake Deity .15 .40
RYMPEN086 D.D. Survivor .15 .40
RYMPEN087 Grandmaster of the Six Samurai .15 .40
RYMPEN088 The Six - Yaichi UR .25 .75
RYMPEN089 The Six - Kamon UR .25 .75
RYMPEN090 The Six - Yariza UR .25 .75
RYMPEN091 The Six - Nisashi UR .25 .75
RYMPEN092 The Six - Zanji UR .25 .75
RYMPEN093 The Six - Irou UR .25 .75
RYMPEN094 Great Shogun Shien .15 .40
RYMPEN095 D.D. Crow SR .25 .75
RYMPEN096 Gladiator Beast SCR .25 .75
RYMPEN097 Enishi, Shien's Chancellor .15 .40
RYMPEN098 Test Tiger .25 .75
RYMPEN099 Rainbow Dark Dragon .40 1.00
RYMPEN100 Jain, Paladin UR .25 .75
RYMPEN101 Garoth, Warrior R .25 .60
RYMPEN102 Lumina, Summoner UR .75 2.00
RYMPEN103 Wulf, Beast UR .50 1.25
RYMPEN104 Judgement Dragon .15 .40
RYMPEN105 Aurkus, Lightsworn Druid .15 .40
RYMPEN106 Gladiator Beast Lanista .15 .40
RYMPEN107 Gladiator Beast's Respite .15 .40
RYMPEN108 Gladiator's Return .15 .40
RYMPEN109 Cunning of the Six Samurai .15 .40
RYMPEN110 Gladiator Proving UR .25 .75
RYMPEN111 Gateway of the Six .15 .40
RYMPEN112 Double-Edged Sword UR .40 1.00
RYMPEN113 Gladiator Beast Chariot R .40 1.00

2012 Yu-Gi-Oh Legendary Collection 3 Yugi's World 1st Edition

COMPLETE SET (306) 150.00 300.00
BOOSTER BOX (5 PACKS) 30.00 50.00
BOOSTER PACK (25 CARDS) 4.00 5.00
RELEASED ON OCTOBER 2, 2012
LCYWEN001 Dark Magician SCR 1.25 3.00
LCYWEN002 Gaia The Fierce Knight SR .60 1.50
LCYWEN003 Celtic Guardian SR .60 1.50
LCYWEN004 Silver Fang UR .40 1.00
LCYWEN005 Mystical Elf C .15 .40
LCYWEN006 Curse of Dragon R .25 .75
LCYWEN007 Giant Soldier of Stone C .15 .40
LCYWEN008 Feral Imp C .15 .40
LCYWEN009 Winged Dragon, Guardian of the Fortress #1 UR .40 1.00
LCYWEN010 Summoned Skull SR 1.00 2.50
LCYWEN011 Gazelle the King of Mythical Beasts UR .75 2.00
LCYWEN012 Alpha the Magnet Warrior C .15 .40
LCYWEN013 Beta the Magnet Warrior C .20 .60
LCYWEN014 Gamma the Magnet Warrior C .15 .40
LCYWEN015 Queen's Knight UR 1.00 2.50
LCYWEN016 Jack's Knight UR 1.25 3.00
LCYWEN017 King's Knight UR .75 2.00
LCYWEN018 Kuriboh SR .60 1.50
LCYWEN019 Catapult Turtle R .25 .75
LCYWEN020 Buster Blader SCR 2.50 6.00
LCYWEN021 Valkyrion the Magna Warrior SR .60 1.50
LCYWEN022 Dark Magician Girl SCR 4.00 10.00
LCYWEN023 Breaker the Magical Warrior UR .75 2.00
LCYWEN024 Mirage Knight C .15 .40
LCYWEN025 Black Luster Soldier - Envoy of the Beginning SCR 4.00 10.00
LCYWEN026 Dark Magician of Chaos SCR 5.00 12.00
LCYWEN027 Dark Sage C 1.25 3.00
LCYWEN028 Dark Magician Knight C 1.50 4.00
LCYWEN029 Sorcerer of Dark Magic C 1.50 4.00
LCYWEN030 Watapon C .15 .40
LCYWEN031 Swift Gaia the Fierce Knight C .15 .40
LCYWEN032 Big Shield Gardna SCR 1.25 3.00
LCYWEN033 Silent Swordsman LV3 C .15 .40
LCYWEN034 Silent Swordsman LV5 C .15 .40
LCYWEN035 Silent Swordsman LV7 C .50 1.25
LCYWEN036 Obnoxious Celtic Guard C .15 .40
LCYWEN037 Silent Magician LV4 C .50 1.25
LCYWEN038 Silent Magician LV8 C .50 1.25
LCYWEN039 Green Gadget UR .40 1.00
LCYWEN040 Red Gadget UR .40 1.00
LCYWEN041 Yellow Gadget UR .40 1.00
LCYWEN042 Archfiend of Gilfer R .25 .75
LCYWEN043 The Tricky C .15 .40
LCYWEN044 Gorz the Emissary of Darkness UR 1.00 2.50
LCYWEN045 Berfomet SR .60 1.50
LCYWEN046 Black Luster Soldier C .40 1.00
LCYWEN047 Magician of Black Chaos C 1.50 4.00
LCYWEN048 Dark Paladin SCR 8.00 20.00
LCYWEN049 Dark Flare Knight C .40 1.00
LCYWEN050 Dragon Master Knight SR 2.50 6.00
LCYWEN051 Arcana Knight Joker SCR 2.50 6.00
LCYWEN052 Chimera the Flying Mythical Beast SR .60 1.50
LCYWEN053 Dark Hole SCR 1.00 2.50
LCYWEN054 Raigeki SCR 10.00 25.00
LCYWEN055 Fissure SR .60 1.50
LCYWEN056 Polymerization SR 1.25 3.00
LCYWEN057 Swords of Revealing Light UR .40 1.00
LCYWEN058 Monster Reborn UR 1.00 2.50
LCYWEN059 Pot of Greed SCR 1.50 4.00
LCYWEN060 Card Destruction SCR .60 1.50
LCYWEN061 Heavy Storm UR .40 1.00
LCYWEN062 Mystical Space Typhoon SCR 1.50 4.00
LCYWEN063 De-Fusion C .40 1.00
LCYWEN064 Graceful Charity SCR 2.00 5.00
LCYWEN065 Double Spell SR .60 1.50
LCYWEN066 Diffusion Wave-Motion SR .60 1.50
LCYWEN067 Thousand Knives C .15 .40
LCYWEN068 Heart of the Underdog C .15 .40
LCYWEN069 Dedication through Light and Darkness SCR 3.00 8.00
LCYWEN070 Black Luster Ritual C 1.50 4.00
LCYWEN071 Dark Magic Attack C .40 1.00
LCYWEN072 Knight's Title C .15 .40
LCYWEN073 Sage's Stone R 1.50 4.00
LCYWEN074 Brain Control SCR .75 2.00
LCYWEN075 Magical Dimension C .15 .40
LCYWEN076 Mystic Box C .15 .40
LCYWEN077 Magicians Unite C .15 .40
LCYWEN078 Black Magic Ritual C 1.00 2.50
LCYWEN079 Dark Magic Curtain R 1.00 2.50
LCYWEN080 Gold Sarcophagus C 1.00 2.50
LCYWEN081 Soul Taker C .15 .40
LCYWEN082 Magic Formula C .40 1.00
LCYWEN083 Union Attack C .15 .40
LCYWEN084 Tricky Spell 4 C .15 .40
LCYWEN085 Spell Shattering Arrow C .50 1.25
LCYWEN086 Multiply R .75 2.00
LCYWEN087 Makiu, the Magical Mist C .15 .40
LCYWEN088 Detonate C .15 .40
LCYWEN089 Seven Tools of the Bandit SCR .60 1.50
LCYWEN090 Horn of Heaven SCR .60 1.50
LCYWEN091 Mirror Force SCR 1.25 3.00
LCYWEN092 Spellbinding Circle C .15 .40
LCYWEN093 Lightforce Sword SR .60 1.50
LCYWEN094 Chain Destruction C .15 .40
LCYWEN095 Dust Tornado UR .40 1.00
LCYWEN096 Magical Hats C .50 1.25
LCYWEN097 Shift SR .60 1.50
LCYWEN098 Collected Power C .15 .40
LCYWEN099 Magic Cylinder SR .60 1.50
LCYWEN100 Magician's Circle SR 1.00 2.50
LCYWEN101 Stronghold the Moving Fortress UR .40 1.00
LCYWEN102 Soul Rope C .15 .40
LCYWEN103 Blue-Eyes Toon Dragon R .75 2.00
LCYWEN104 Manga Ryu-Ran R .25 .75
LCYWEN105 Toon Mermaid R 1.25 3.00
LCYWEN106 Toon Summoned Skull R .25 .75
LCYWEN107 Toon Gemini Elf R .25 .75
LCYWEN108 Toon Goblin Attack Force R 2.00 5.00
LCYWEN109 Toon Cannon Soldier R 2.00 5.00
LCYWEN110 Toon Masked Sorcerer R 2.00 5.00
LCYWEN111 Toon Dark Magician Girl R .75 2.00
LCYWEN112 Dark-Eyes Illusionist R .25 .75
LCYWEN113 Relinquished R .40 1.00
LCYWEN114 Black Illusion Ritual R .25 .75
LCYWEN115 Toon World R .50 1.25
LCYWEN116 Toon Table of Contents R 1.25 3.00
LCYWEN117 Dragon Capture Jar R .25 .75
LCYWEN118 Toon Defense R .75 2.00
LCYWEN119 Man-Eater Bug C .15 .40
LCYWEN120 Sangan SCR 1.50 4.00
LCYWEN121 Morphing Jar UR .40 1.00
LCYWEN122 Puppet Master C .15 .40
LCYWEN123 Dark Master - Zorc C .15 .40
LCYWEN124 Change of Heart SCR 2.00 5.00
LCYWEN125 Exchange SCR .60 1.50
LCYWEN126 The Dark Door R .25 .75
LCYWEN127 Spiritualism C .15 .40
LCYWEN128 Contract with the Dark Master C .15 .40
LCYWEN129 Guardian Elma C .15 .40
LCYWEN130 Guardian Ceal C .15 .40
LCYWEN131 Guardian Grarl C .40 1.00
LCYWEN132 Guardian Baou C .15 .40
LCYWEN133 Guardian Kay'est C .15 .40
LCYWEN134 Guardian Tryce C .15 .40
LCYWEN135 My Body as a Shield C .15 .40
LCYWEN136 Butterfly Dagger - Elma C .50 1.25
LCYWEN137 Shooting Star Bow - Ceal C .50 1.25
LCYWEN138 Gravity Axe - Grarl C .15 .40
LCYWEN139 Wicked-Breaking Flamberge - Baou C .15 .40
LCYWEN140 Rod of Silence - Kay'est C .40 1.00
LCYWEN141 Twin Swords of Flashing Light - Tryce C .75 2.00
LCYWEN142 Monster Reincarnation R .25 .75
LCYWEN143 Gil Garth UR .40 1.00
LCYWEN144 Bowganian SR .60 1.50
LCYWEN145 Machine Duplication SR 1.50 4.00
LCYWEN146 Hidden Soldiers R .25 .75
LCYWEN147 Rope of Life SCR .60 1.50
LCYWEN148 Malevolent Catastrophe SR .60 1.50
LCYWEN149 Harpie's Feather Duster SCR 4.00 10.00
LCYWEN150 Gravity Bind SR .60 1.50
LCYWEN151 Mechanicalchaser UR .40 1.00
LCYWEN152 Solemn Judgment SCR .60 1.50
LCYWEN153 Magic Jammer SCR .75 2.00
LCYWEN154 Sinister Serpent SCR .60 1.50
LCYWEN155 Mirage of Nightmare SCR .60 1.50
LCYWEN156 Ordeal of a Traveler C .40 1.00
LCYWEN157 Tri-Horned Dragon SR .60 1.50
LCYWEN158 Two-Headed King Rex SCR .75 2.00
LCYWEN159 Millennium Shield SR .60 1.50
LCYWEN160 Cosmo Queen UR .75 2.00
LCYWEN161 Fire Princess UR .40 1.00
LCYWEN162 Command Knight C .40 1.00
LCYWEN163 Malice Doll of Demise R .25 .75
LCYWEN164 White-Horned Dragon SR .60 1.50
LCYWEN165 Green Baboon, Defender of the Forest C .15 .40
LCYWEN166 Summoner Monk UR 1.50 4.00
LCYWEN167 Commander Covington SCR .60 1.50
LCYWEN168 Machina Soldier SCR .60 1.50
LCYWEN169 Machina Sniper SCR .60 1.50
LCYWEN170 Machina Defender SCR .60 1.50
LCYWEN171 Machina Force SCR .60 1.50
LCYWEN172 Limiter Removal UR .75 2.00
LCYWEN173 Reinforcement of the Army SR .60 1.50
LCYWEN174 Dragged Down into the Grave SR 1.00 2.50
LCYWEN175 Ectoplasmer R .25 .75
LCYWEN176 Mind Control UR .40 1.00
LCYWEN177 Trap Hole UR .40 1.00
LCYWEN178 Imperial Order SCR .75 2.00
LCYWEN179 Mask of Restrict C 6.00 15.00
LCYWEN180 Torrential Tribute SCR 1.00 2.50
LCYWEN181 Bottomless Trap Hole UR 1.00 2.50
LCYWEN182 Royal Decree UR 1.00 2.50

Card	Low	High
LCYWEN183 Gravekeeper's Spy UR	.40	1.00
LCYWEN184 Gravekeeper's Guard UR	.40	1.00
LCYWEN185 Gravekeeper's Spear Soldier UR	.40	1.00
LCYWEN186 Gravekeeper's Watcher C	.15	.40
LCYWEN187 Gravekeeper's Chief UR	.40	1.00
LCYWEN188 Gravekeeper's Cannonholder UR	.40	1.00
LCYWEN189 Gravekeeper's Assailant UR	.50	1.25
LCYWEN190 Charm of Shabti C	.15	.40
LCYWEN191 Gravekeeper's Commandant UR	1.25	3.00
LCYWEN192 Gravekeeper's Descendant UR	1.00	2.50
LCYWEN193 Gravekeeper's Recruiter UR	3.00	8.00
LCYWEN194 Necrovalley UR	1.50	4.00
LCYWEN195 Royal Tribute UR	.75	2.00
LCYWEN196 Rite of Spirit C	.50	1.25
LCYWEN197 Horus the Black Flame Dragon LV4 C	.15	.40
LCYWEN198 Horus the Black Flame Dragon LV6 C	.25	.75
LCYWEN199 Horus the Black Flame Dragon LV8 C	1.50	4.00
LCYWEN200 Mystic Swordsman LV2 C	.15	.40
LCYWEN201 Mystic Swordsman LV4 C	.15	.40
LCYWEN202 Mystic Swordsman LV6 C	.40	1.00
LCYWEN203 Armed Dragon LV3 C	.15	.40
LCYWEN204 Armed Dragon LV5 C	.15	.40
LCYWEN205 Armed Dragon LV7 C	1.50	4.00
LCYWEN206 Horus' Servant C	.15	.40
LCYWEN207 Level Up! C	.60	1.50
LCYWEN208 Dark Grepher C	1.50	4.00
LCYWEN209 Dark Horus C	.15	.40
LCYWEN210 The Dark Creator C	.15	.40
LCYWEN211 Dark Nephthys C	.15	.40
LCYWEN212 Darklord Zerato C	.15	.40
LCYWEN213 Darknight Parshath C	.15	.40
LCYWEN214 Dark General Freed C	.15	.40
LCYWEN215 D.D. Warrior Lady R	.25	.75
LCYWEN216 D.D. Scout Plane R	.25	.75
LCYWEN217 D.D. Assailant R	.25	.75
LCYWEN218 D.D. Warrior R	.25	.75
LCYWEN219 Skull Servant UR	2.00	5.00
LCYWEN220 Dark King of the Abyss SCR	.60	1.50
LCYWEN221 Aqua Madoor SCR	.60	1.50
LCYWEN222 Yaranzo SR	.60	1.50
LCYWEN223 Takriminos SR	.60	1.50
LCYWEN224 Megasonic Eye SR	.60	1.50
LCYWEN225 Yamadron SR	.60	1.50
LCYWEN226 Three-Legged Zombie SR	.60	1.50
LCYWEN227 Fairy's Gift SR	.60	1.50
LCYWEN228 Kanan the Swordmistress UR	.40	1.00
LCYWEN229 Mystical Shine Ball SR	.60	1.50
LCYWEN230 Big Eye R	.25	.75
LCYWEN231 Banisher of the Light C	.15	.40
LCYWEN232 Giant Rat SCR	.60	1.50
LCYWEN233 UFO Turtle SCR	.60	1.50
LCYWEN234 Giant Germ C	.40	1.00
LCYWEN235 Nimble Momonga C	.75	2.00
LCYWEN236 Shining Angel SCR	.60	1.50
LCYWEN237 Mother Grizzly SCR	.60	1.50
LCYWEN238 Flying Kamakiri #1 SCR	.60	1.50
LCYWEN239 Mystic Tomato SCR	.60	1.50
LCYWEN240 Morphing Jar #2 SR	.60	1.50
LCYWEN241 Goddess of Whim C	.15	.40
LCYWEN242 Kycoo the Ghost Destroyer SCR	.75	2.00
LCYWEN243 Summoner of Illusions C	.15	.40
LCYWEN244 Needle Worm UR	1.25	3.00
LCYWEN245 Pyramid Turtle SCR	.60	1.50
LCYWEN246 Spirit Reaper UR	.40	1.00
LCYWEN247 Arsenal Summoner C	.15	.40
LCYWEN248 Chaos Sorcerer SR	.60	1.50
LCYWEN249 Levia-Dragon - Daedalus SCR	.60	1.50
LCYWEN250 Manju of the Ten Thousand Hands C	1.25	3.00
LCYWEN251 Invader of Darkness C	.15	.40
LCYWEN252 The Agent of Wisdom - Mercury SR	.60	1.50
LCYWEN253 The Agent of Creation - Venus SR	.60	1.50
LCYWEN254 Solar Flare Dragon SR	.60	1.50
LCYWEN255 Emissary of the Afterlife C	.40	1.00
LCYWEN256 King of the Swamp C	4.00	10.00
LCYWEN257 The Creator C	.15	.40
LCYWEN258 The Creator Incarnate C	.15	.40
LCYWEN259 Sacred Phoenix of Nephthys SR	.60	1.50
LCYWEN260 Hand of Nephthys R	.25	.75
LCYWEN261 Armed Samurai - Ben Kei C	.15	.40
LCYWEN262 The Light - Hex-Sealed Fusion C	.15	.40
LCYWEN263 The Dark - Hex-Sealed Fusion C	.15	.40
LCYWEN264 The Earth - Hex-Sealed Fusion C	.15	.40
LCYWEN265 Upstart Goblin UR	4.00	10.00
LCYWEN266 Messenger of Peace C	1.00	2.50
LCYWEN267 Prohibition SCR	.60	1.50
LCYWEN268 Fusion Gate SR	1.50	4.00
LCYWEN269 Creature Swap UR	.40	1.00
LCYWEN270 Book of Moon SCR	.60	1.50
LCYWEN271 Dark Snake Syndrome R	.25	.75
LCYWEN272 Non-Spellcasting Area C	.15	.40
LCYWEN273 Contract with the Abyss C	.15	.40
LCYWEN274 Stray Lambs C	.15	.40
LCYWEN275 Smashing Ground UR	.40	1.00
LCYWEN276 Salvage SR	1.00	2.50
LCYWEN277 Earth Chant C	.15	.40
LCYWEN278 Spell Economics C	.15	.40
LCYWEN279 Level Limit - Area B C	.75	2.00
LCYWEN280 A Feather of the Phoenix SCR	.60	1.50
LCYWEN281 Swords of Concealing Light UR	4.00	10.00
LCYWEN282 Centrifugal Field C	.15	.40
LCYWEN283 Acid Trap Hole R	.25	.75
LCYWEN284 DNA Surgery C	1.25	3.00
LCYWEN285 Reckless Greed SR	1.25	3.00
LCYWEN286 Raigeki Break SR	.60	1.50
LCYWEN287 Goblin Fan C	.15	.40
LCYWEN288 Sakuretsu Armor SR	1.00	2.50
LCYWEN289 Chain Disappearance C	.40	1.00
LCYWEN290 Dark Mirror Force R	1.00	2.50
LCYWEN291 Compulsory Evacuation Device SCR	.60	1.50
LCYWEN292 DNA Transplant C	.15	.40
LCYWEN293 Beckoning Light UR	.40	1.00
LCYWEN294 Draining Shield C	.50	1.25
LCYWEN295 Mind Crush UR	1.00	2.50
LCYWEN296 Penalty Game! C	.15	.40
LCYWEN297 Threatening Roar SCR	.75	2.00
LCYWEN298 Phoenix Wing Wind Blast SCR	.60	1.50
LCYWEN299 Level Limit - Area A C	.15	.40
LCYWEN300 Black Horn of Heaven SCR	.60	1.50
LCYWEN301 Solemn Warning C	1.50	4.00
LCYWEN302 Right Leg of the Forbidden One SCR	2.50	6.00
LCYWEN303 Left Leg of the Forbidden One SCR	2.50	6.00
LCYWEN304 Right Arm of the Forbidden One SCR	2.50	6.00
LCYWEN305 Left Arm of the Forbidden One SCR	2.50	6.00
LCYWEN306 Exodia the Forbidden One SCR	2.50	6.00

2012 Yu-Gi-Oh Legendary Collection 3 Yugi's World Box Bonus

Card	Low	High
COMPLETE SET (7)	4.00	8.00
ONE SET PER LEGENDARY COLLECTION 3 BOX		
LC03001 The Seal of Orichalcos UR	.60	1.50
LC03002 Dark Necrofear UR	.40	1.00
LC03003 Guardian Eatos UR	.40	1.00
LC03004 Five-Headed Dragon UR	.40	1.00
LC03005 Emissary of Darkness Token UR	.40	1.00
LC03006 Pink Kuriboh Token UR	.40	1.00
LC03007 Orange Kuriboh Token UR	.40	1.00

2013 Yu-Gi-Oh Legendary Collection 4 Joey's World 1st Edition

Card	Low	High
COMPLETE SET (298)	120.00	300.00
BOOSTER BOX (5 PACKS)	20.00	40.00
BOOSTER PACK (9 CARDS)	4.00	5.00
RELEASED ON OCTOBER 11, 2013		
LCJW001 Flame Manipulator C	.30	.50
LCJW002 Masaki the Legendary Swordsman C	.30	.50
LCJW003 Red-Eyes B. Dragon UR	.60	1.50
LCJW004 Rude Kaiser C	.30	.50
LCJW005 Rock Ogre Grotto 1 C	.30	.50
LCJW006 Baby Dragon SR	.15	.50
LCJW007 Axe Raider C	.30	.50
LCJW008 Tiger Axe C	.30	.50
LCJW009 Garoozis C	.30	.50
LCJW010 Swordsman of Landstar C	.30	.50
LCJW011 Cyber-Tech Alligator C	.30	.50
LCJW012 Alligator's Sword C	.30	.50
LCJW013 Meotoko C	.30	.50
LCJW014 Kageningen C	.30	.50
LCJW015 Stone Armadiller C	.30	.50
LCJW016 Anthrosaurus C	.30	.50
LCJW017 Skull Stalker C	.30	.50
LCJW018 Wolf C	.30	.50
LCJW019 Hero of the East C	.30	.50
LCJW020 Swamp Battleguard C	.30	.50
LCJW021 Time Wizard C	.30	.50
LCJW022 Lava Battleguard C	.30	.50
LCJW023 Jinzo R	.40	1.00
LCJW024 The Legendary Fisherman C	.30	.50
LCJW025 Sword Hunter C	.30	.50
LCJW026 Hayabusa Knight C	.30	.50
LCJW027 Mad Sword Beast C	.30	.50
LCJW028 Goblin Attack Force C	.30	.50
LCJW029 The Fiend Megacyber C	.30	.50
LCJW030 Gearfried the Iron Knight C	.30	.50
LCJW031 Red-Eyes Black Metal Dragon C	.30	.50
LCJW032 Marauding Captain C	.30	.50
LCJW033 Fiber Jar C	.30	.50
LCJW034 Sasuke Samurai C	.30	.50
LCJW035 Neko Mane King C	.30	.50
LCJW036 Little-Winguard C	.30	.50
LCJW037 Insect Queen C	.30	.50
LCJW038 Red-Eyes B. Chick SR	.50	1.25
LCJW039 Red-Eyes Darkness Dragon C	.30	.50
LCJW040 Gearfried the Swordmaster C	.30	.50
LCJW041 Gilford the Lightning C	.30	.50
LCJW042 Rocket Warrior C	.30	.50
LCJW043 Panther Warrior C	.30	.50
LCJW044 Gilford the Legend C	.30	.50
LCJW045 Copycat C	.30	.50
LCJW046 Divine Knight Ishzark C	.30	.50
LCJW047 Maximum Six C	.30	.50
LCJW048 Comrade Swordsman of Landstar C	.30	.50
LCJW049 Red-Eyes Wyvern C	.30	.50
LCJW050 Red-Eyes Darkness Metal Dragon SCR	6.00	15.00
LCJW051 Phoenix Gearfried C	.30	.50
LCJW052 Lightray Gearfried C	.30	.50
LCJW053 Flame Swordsman C	.30	.50
LCJW054 B. Skull Dragon R	.75	2.00
LCJW055 Thousand Dragon C	.30	.50
LCJW056 Alligator's Sword Dragon C	.30	.50
LCJW057 Raigeki SCR	10.00	25.00
LCJW058 Hinotama C	.30	.50
LCJW059 Polymerization SR	1.25	3.00
LCJW060 Monster Reborn UR	1.00	2.50
LCJW061 Pot of Greed SCR	1.00	2.50
LCJW062 Salamandra C	.30	.50
LCJW063 Giant Trunade C	.30	.50
LCJW064 Premature Burial C	.30	.50
LCJW065 Graceful Dice C	.30	.50
LCJW066 Scapegoat SCR	.60	1.50
LCJW067 The Warrior Returning Alive C	.30	.50
LCJW068 Meteor of Destruction C	.30	.50
LCJW069 Release Restraint C	.30	.50
LCJW070 Foolish Burial SCR	2.50	6.00
LCJW071 Silent Doom SR	.15	.50
LCJW072 Dangerous Machine Type-6 C	.30	.50
LCJW073 Trap Hole C	.30	.50
LCJW074 Skull Dice C	.30	.50
LCJW075 Metalmorph C	.30	.50
LCJW076 Fairy Box C	.30	.50
LCJW077 Collected Power C	.30	.50
LCJW078 Bottomless Trap Hole SCR	1.50	4.00
LCJW079 Drop Off C	.30	.50
LCJW080 Magical Arm Shield C	.30	.50
LCJW081 Kunai with Chain C	.30	.50
LCJW082 Harpie Lady SR	.15	.50
LCJW083 Harpie Girl C	.30	.50
LCJW084 Dunames Dark Witch UR	.15	.40
LCJW085 Harpie Lady Sisters C	.30	.50
LCJW086 Harpie's Pet Dragon UR	2.00	5.00
LCJW087 Amazoness Paladin SR	.15	.50
LCJW088 Amazoness Fighter C	.30	.50
LCJW089 Amazoness Tiger UR	.10	.30
LCJW090 Harpie Lady 1 SR	.40	1.00
LCJW091 Harpie Lady 2 SR	.15	.50
LCJW092 Harpie Lady 3 SR	.15	.50
LCJW093 Harpie's Pet Baby Dragon C	.30	.50
LCJW094 Harpie Queen UR	1.50	4.00
LCJW095 Amazoness Scouts C	.30	.50
LCJW096 Cyber Harpie Lady C	.30	.50
LCJW097 Harpie Dancer UR	3.00	8.00
LCJW098 Elegant Egotist SR	.15	.50
LCJW099 Harpie's Feather Duster SCR	3.00	8.00
LCJW100 Amazoness Spellcaster C	.30	.50
LCJW101 Spell Reproduction C	.30	.50
LCJW102 Harpies' Hunting Ground SR	.15	.50
LCJW103 Triangle Ecstasy Spark C	.30	.50
LCJW104 Amazoness Village C	.30	.50
LCJW105 Cyber Shield C	.30	.50
LCJW106 Fairy's Hand Mirror C	.30	.50
LCJW107 Mirror Wall C	.30	.50
LCJW108 Gravity Bind C	.30	.50
LCJW109 Shadow of Eyes C	.30	.50
LCJW110 Gryphon Wing C	.30	.50
LCJW111 Trap Jammer SCR	.75	2.00
LCJW112 Hysteric Party SR	.40	1.00
LCJW113 Revival Jam C	.30	.50
LCJW114 Dark Jeroid C	.30	.50
LCJW115 Newdoria C	.30	.50
LCJW116 Helpoemer C	.30	.50
LCJW117 Lava Golem R	.10	.30
LCJW118 Drillago C	.30	.50
LCJW119 Lekunga C	.30	.50
LCJW120 Lord Poison C	.30	.50
LCJW121 Makyura the Destructor C	.30	.50
LCJW122 Legendary Fiend C	.30	.50
LCJW123 Black Pendant C	.30	.50
LCJW124 Jam Breeding Machine C	.30	.50
LCJW125 Vengeful Bog Spirit C	.30	.50
LCJW126 Card of Sanctity C	.30	.50
LCJW127 Magical Stone Excavation C	.30	.50
LCJW128 Spell of Pain C	.30	.50
LCJW129 Magic Jammer C	.30	.50
LCJW130 Mirror Force SCR	1.00	2.50
LCJW131 Jam Defender C	.30	.50
LCJW132 Coffin Seller C	.30	.50
LCJW133 Rope of Life C	.30	.50
LCJW134 Nightmare Wheel C	.30	.50
LCJW135 Judgment of Anubis C	.30	.50
LCJW136 Malevolent Catastrophe C	.30	.50
LCJW137 Relieve Monster C	.30	.50
LCJW138 Metal Reflect Slime C	.30	.50
LCJW139 Serpent Night Dragon C	.30	.50
LCJW140 Two-Headed King Rex C	.30	.50
LCJW141 Crawling Dragon C	.30	.50
LCJW142 Kabazauls SCR	.25	.75
LCJW143 Sabersaurus SCR	.25	.75
LCJW144 Tomozaurus C	.30	.50
LCJW145 Little D C	.30	.50
LCJW146 Sword Arm of Dragon C	.30	.50
LCJW147 Megazowler C	.30	.50
LCJW148 Gilasaurus C	.30	.50
LCJW149 Tyrant Dragon C	.30	.50
LCJW150 Dark Driceratops C	.30	.50
LCJW151 Hyper Hammerhead C	.30	.50
LCJW152 Black Tyranno C	.30	.50
LCJW153 Tyranno Infinity C	.30	.50
LCJW154 Black Ptera C	.30	.50
LCJW155 Black Stego C	.30	.50
LCJW156 Miracle Jurassic Egg C	.30	.50
LCJW157 Babycerasaurus C	.30	.50
LCJW158 Destroyersaurus SCR	.25	.75
LCJW159 Bracchio-Raidus C	.30	.50
LCJW160 Ultra Evolution Pill C	.30	.50
LCJW161 Big Evolution Pill C	.30	.50
LCJW162 Tail Swipe C	.30	.50
LCJW163 Jurassic World C	.30	.50
LCJW164 Fossil Dig C	.30	.50
LCJW165 Fossil Excavation C	.30	.50
LCJW166 Hunting Instinct C	.30	.50
LCJW167 Survival Instinct C	.30	.50
LCJW168 Volcanic Eruption C	.30	.50
LCJW169 Seismic Shockwave C	.30	.50
LCJW170 Seiyaryu C	.30	.50
LCJW171 Launcher Spider C	.30	.50
LCJW172 Slot Machine C	.30	.50
LCJW173 Zoa C	.30	.50
LCJW174 Ancient Tool C	.30	.50
LCJW175 Giganto C	.30	.50
LCJW176 Sword Slasher C	.30	.50
LCJW177 Barrel Dragon C	.30	.50
LCJW178 Metalzoa C	.30	.50
LCJW179 Machine King C	.30	.50
LCJW180 Blast Sphere C	.30	.50
LCJW181 Fiendish Engine O C	.30	.50
LCJW182 Solemn Judgment SCR	.60	1.50
LCJW183 Dragon Zombie C	.30	.50
LCJW184 Armored Zombie C	.30	.50
LCJW185 The Snake Hair C	.30	.50
LCJW186 Vampire Baby C	.30	.50
LCJW187 Patrician of Darkness C	.30	.50
LCJW188 Dark Dust Spirit C	.30	.50
LCJW189 Pyramid Turtle SR	.15	.50
LCJW190 Spirit Reaper UR	.60	1.50
LCJW191 Vampire Lord C	.30	.50
LCJW192 Despair from the Dark C	.30	.50
LCJW193 Fear from the Dark C	.30	.50
LCJW194 Ryu Kokki C	.30	.50
LCJW195 Soul-Absorbing Bone Tower C	.30	.50
LCJW196 Vampire Lady C	.30	.50
LCJW197 Regenerating Mummy C	.30	.50
LCJW198 Vampire Genesis C	.30	.50
LCJW199 Reborn Zombie C	.30	.50
LCJW200 Plague Wolf C	.30	.50
LCJW201 Return Zombie C	.30	.50
LCJW202 Zombie Master C	.30	.50
LCJW203 Il Blud C	.30	.50
LCJW204 Vampire's Curse C	.30	.50

LCJW205 Goblin Zombie C .30 .50
LCJW206 Red-Eyes Zombie Dragon R .10 .30
LCJW207 Malevolent Mech - Goku En C .30 .50
LCJW208 Paladin of the Cursed Dragon C .30 .50
LCJW209 Skull Conductor C .30 .50
LCJW210 Great Mammoth of Goldfine C .30 .50
LCJW211 Book of Life UR .60 1.50
LCJW212 Call of the Mummy SR .15 .50
LCJW213 Zombie World UR 1.25 3.00
LCJW214 Everliving Underworld Cannon C .30 .50
LCJW215 Pyramid of Wonders C .30 .50
LCJW216 Overpowering Eye C .30 .50
LCJW217 Call of the Haunted SR 1.00 2.50
LCJW218 Tutan Mask C .30 .50
LCJW219 Trap of the Imperial Tomb C .30 .50
LCJW220 Labyrinth Wall C .30 .50
LCJW221 Dungeon Worm C .30 .50
LCJW222 Monster Tamer C .30 .50
LCJW223 Gate Guardian C .30 .50
LCJW224 Sanga of the Thunder C .30 .50
LCJW225 Kazejin C .30 .50
LCJW226 Suijin C .30 .50
LCJW227 Jirai Gumo C .30 .50
LCJW228 Shadow Ghoul C .30 .50
LCJW229 Wall Shadow C .30 .50
LCJW230 Labyrinth Tank C .30 .50
LCJW231 Magical Labyrinth C .30 .50
LCJW232 Fairy Meteor Crush C .30 .50
LCJW233 Tribute Doll C .30 .50
LCJW234 Riryoku C .30 .50
LCJW235 Summoned Skull R .40 1.00
LCJW236 Beast of Talwar R .10 .30
LCJW237 Toon Summoned Skull R .10 .30
LCJW238 Lesser Fiend R .10 .30
LCJW239 Shadow Tamer R .10 .30
LCJW240 Fiend Skull Dragon R .10 .30
LCJW241 A Deal with Dark Ruler R .10 .30
LCJW242 Beiige, Vanguard of Dark World UR .60 1.50
LCJW243 Broww, Huntsman of Dark World SCR .75 2.00
LCJW244 Brron, Mad King of Dark World UR .10 .30
LCJW245 Sillva, Warlord of Dark World SCR .25 .75
LCJW246 Goldd, Wu-Lord of Dark World SCR .25 .75
LCJW247 Scarr, Scout of Dark World C .30 .50
LCJW248 Snoww, Unlight of Dark World SCR .50 1.25
LCJW249 Dark World Lightning SCR .25 .75
LCJW250 Gateway to Dark World SCR .25 .75
LCJW251 Dark World Dealings SR 1.25 3.00
LCJW252 Dark World Grimoire C .30 .50
LCJW253 The Gates of Dark World UR .60 1.50
LCJW254 The Forces of Darkness C .30 .50
LCJW255 Gravekeeper's Spy SCR .25 .75
LCJW256 Gravekeeper's Curse C .30 .50
LCJW257 Gravekeeper's Vassal C .30 .50
LCJW258 Gravekeeper's Priestess R .10 .30
LCJW259 Gravekeeper's Visionary R .10 .30
LCJW260 Necrovalley C .30 .50
LCJW261 Gravekeeper's Stele UR .60 1.50
LCJW262 Dice Jar C .30 .50
LCJW263 Roulette Barrel C .30 .50
LCJW264 Blowback Dragon C .30 .50
LCJW265 Snipe Hunter C .30 .50
LCJW266 Twin-Barrel Dragon C .30 .50
LCJW267 Gatling Dragon C .30 .50
LCJW268 Second Coin Toss C .30 .50
LCJW269 Blind Destruction C .30 .50
LCJW270 Needle Wall C .30 .50
LCJW271 Dice Re-Roll C .30 .50
LCJW272 Dice Try C .30 .50
LCJW273 Sixth Sense C .30 .50
LCJW274 Adhesion Trap Hole C .30 .50
LCJW275 D.D. Trap Hole C .30 .50
LCJW276 Giant Trap Hole C .30 .50
LCJW277 Treacherous Trap Hole C .30 .50
LCJW278 Chaos Trap Hole C .30 .50
LCJW279 Cave Dragon C .30 .50
LCJW280 Injection Fairy Lily C .30 .50
LCJW281 Berserk Dragon C .30 .50
LCJW282 Strike Ninja C .30 .50
LCJW283 Dark Hole SCR .75 2.00
LCJW284 Heavy Storm UR .60 1.50
LCJW285 Mystical Space Typhoon SCR 1.50 4.00
LCJW286 Reinforcement of the Army UR .60 1.50
LCJW287 Super Rejuvenation SR .15 .50
LCJW288 Book of Moon SCR .75 2.00
LCJW289 Stray Lambs UR .10 .30
LCJW290 Pot of Avarice SCR .50 1.25
LCJW291 Trade-In UR 4.00 10.00
LCJW292 Horn of Heaven UR .60 1.50
LCJW293 Chain Destruction R .10 .30
LCJW294 Torrential Tribute SCR 1.25 3.00
LCJW295 Compulsory Evacuation Device SCR .50 1.25
LCJW296 Spirit Barrier C .30 .50
LCJW297 Black Horn of Heaven UR .60 1.50
LCJW298 Imperial Iron Wall UR 1.00 2.50

2013 Yu-Gi-Oh Legendary Collection 4 Joey's World Box Bonus

COMPLETE SET (9) 2.00 5.00
ONE SET PER LEGENDARY COLLECTION 4 BOX
LC04001 Blue Flame Swordsman UR .10 .30
LC04002 Harpie Lady Phoenix Formation UR .10 .30
LC04003 Card of Last Will UR .10 .30
LC04004 Blue Sheep Token UR .10 .30
LC04005 Orange Sheep Token UR .10 .30
LC04006 Pink Sheep Token UR .10 .30
LC04007 Yellow Sheep Token UR .10 .30
LC04008 White Lamb Token UR .10 .30
LC04009 Pink Lamb Token UR .10 .30

2014 Yu-Gi-Oh Legendary Collection 5D's

COMPLETE SET (265) 120.00 250.00
BOOSTER BOX (5 PACKS) 20.00 30.00
BOOSTER PACK (9 PACKS) 3.00 4.00
RELEASED ON OCTOBER 24, 2014
LC05EN001 Jormungardr the Nordic Serpent UR .40 1.00
LC05EN002 Fenrir the Nordic Wolf UR .75 2.00
LC05EN003 Stardust Flash UR 1.50 4.00
LC05EN004 Black Rose Dragon UR 1.50 4.00
LC05EN005 Shooting Quasar Dragon UR 1.50 4.00
LC5DEN001 Sonic Chick C .10 .20
LC5DEN002 Junk Synchron SCR 1.25 3.00
LC5DEN003 Speed Warrior C .10 .20
LC5DEN004 Nitro Synchron C .10 .20
LC5DEN005 Quillbolt Hedgehog SCR .75 2.00
LC5DEN006 Turbo Synchron C .10 .20
LC5DEN007 Tuningware SCR 2.00 5.00
LC5DEN008 Turret Warrior R .25 .60
LC5DEN009 Debris Dragon SCR 2.50 6.00
LC5DEN010 Hyper Synchron C .10 .20
LC5DEN011 Road Synchron C .10 .20
LC5DEN012 Majestic Dragon C 2.00 3.00
LC5DEN013 Quickdraw Synchron UR 1.50 4.00
LC5DEN014 Level Eater R .25 .60
LC5DEN015 Drill Synchron SR .40 1.00
LC5DEN016 Shield Wing R .25 .60
LC5DEN017 Synchron Explorer UR 1.25 3.00
LC5DEN018 Effect Veiler C 4.50 5.00
LC5DEN019 Bri Synchron C .10 .20
LC5DEN020 Doppelwarrior SR 1.50 4.00
LC5DEN021 Junk Servant C .10 .20
LC5DEN022 Unknown Synchron SCR 1.25 3.00
LC5DEN023 Junk Defender C .10 .20
LC5DEN024 Junk Forward C .10 .20
LC5DEN025 Junk Blader C .10 .20
LC5DEN026 Mono Synchron R 1.25 3.00
LC5DEN027 Steam Synchron R 1.25 3.00
LC5DEN028 Dragon Knight Draco-Equiste R .25 .60
LC5DEN029 Junk Warrior SR .40 1.00
LC5DEN030 Colossal Fighter SCR .40 1.00
LC5DEN031 Stardust Dragon C 3.00 3.50
LC5DEN031u Stardust Dragon UR 1.25 3.00
LC5DEN032 Nitro Warrior C .10 .20
LC5DEN033 Turbo Warrior C .10 .20
LC5DEN034 Armory Arm SCR 3.00 8.00
LC5DEN035 Road Warrior C 1.25 1.75
LC5DEN036 Majestic Star Dragon SR .25 .60
LC5DEN037 Junk Archer SR .75 2.00
LC5DEN038 Drill Warrior SCR .40 1.00
LC5DEN039 Junk Destroyer SR .40 1.00
LC5DEN040 Shooting Star Dragon SR 2.50 6.00
LC5DEN041 Formula Synchron SCR 3.00 8.00
LC5DEN042 Lightning Warrior UR .60 1.50
LC5DEN043 Junk Berserker SR .50 1.25
LC5DEN044 Junk Barrage C .10 .20
LC5DEN045 One for One UR .60 1.50
LC5DEN046 Silver Wing C .10 .20
LC5DEN047 Advance Draw UR 1.25 3.00
LC5DEN048 Cards of Consonance UR .60 1.50
LC5DEN049 Tuning C .10 .20
LC5DEN050 Battle Waltz C .10 .20
LC5DEN051 Scrap-Iron Scarecrow UR 2.00 5.00
LC5DEN052 Graceful Revival C .10 .20
LC5DEN053 Urgent Tuning C .10 .20
LC5DEN054 Spirit Force C .10 .20
LC5DEN055 Descending Lost Star C .10 .20
LC5DEN056 Starlight Road UR .75 2.00
LC5DEN057 Dark Resonator C .10 .20
LC5DEN058 Trap Eater UR .40 1.00
LC5DEN059 Vice Dragon C .10 .20
LC5DEN060 Strong Wind Dragon R .75 2.00
LC5DEN061 Battle Fader SCR 1.50 4.00
LC5DEN062 Flare Resonator C .10 .20
LC5DEN063 Power Breaker R .25 .60
LC5DEN064 Extra Veiler C .10 .20
LC5DEN065 Creation Resonator C 1.75 2.50
LC5DEN066 Barrier Resonator C .10 .20
LC5DEN067 Force Resonator C .10 .20
LC5DEN068 Clock Resonator C .10 .20
LC5DEN069 Red Dragon Archfiend C .10 .20
LC5DEN069u Red Dragon Archfiend UR 2.00 5.00
LC5DEN070 Exploder Dragonwing R .40 1.00
LC5DEN071 Majestic Red Dragon SR .40 1.00
LC5DEN072 Chaos King Archfiend SR .40 1.00
LC5DEN073 Red Nova Dragon SR 1.25 3.00
LC5DEN074 Crimson Blader SCR 2.00 5.00
LC5DEN075 Resonator Engine C .10 .20
LC5DEN076 Scarlet Security SR .50 1.25
LC5DEN077 Red Dragon Vase R .25 .60
LC5DEN078 Resonator Call C .10 .20
LC5DEN079 Resonant Destruction C .10 .20
LC5DEN080 Crimson Fire R .25 .60
LC5DEN081 Changing Destiny C .10 .20
LC5DEN082 Fiendish Chain SCR 5.00 12.00
LC5DEN083 Red Screen C .10 .20
LC5DEN084 Red Carpet C .10 .20
LC5DEN085 Twilight Rose Knight C 1.00 1.50
LC5DEN086 Violet Witch R .25 .60
LC5DEN087 Dark Verger C .10 .20
LC5DEN088 Rose Tentacles R .25 .60
LC5DEN089 Hedge Guard UR .75 2.00
LC5DEN090 Evil Thorn C .10 .20
LC5DEN091 Rose Fairy C .10 .20
LC5DEN092 Glow-Up Bulb SCR 5.00 12.00
LC5DEN093 Blue Rose Dragon SR .50 1.25
LC5DEN094 Fallen Angel of Roses UR .60 1.50
LC5DEN095 Rosaria, the Stately Fallen Angel UR .60 1.50
LC5DEN096 Queen Angel of Roses UR .60 1.50
LC5DEN097 Rose Witch C .10 .20
LC5DEN098 Rose Archer SR .40 1.00
LC5DEN099 Black Rose Dragon C 1.00 1.50
LC5DEN100 Splendid Rose R .25 .60
LC5DEN101 Black Garden SCR .75 2.00
LC5DEN102 Fragrance Storm UR .40 1.00
LC5DEN103 Thorn of Malice C .10 .20
LC5DEN104 Magic Planter UR 4.00 10.00
LC5DEN105 Ivy Shackles C .10 .20
LC5DEN106 Overdoom Line C .10 .20
LC5DEN107 Wicked Rebirth C .10 .20
LC5DEN108 Blossom Bombardment C .10 .20
LC5DEN109 Star Siphon C .10 .20
LC5DEN110 Blackwing - Gale the Whirlwind UR .40 1.00
LC5DEN111 Blackwing - Bora the Spear UR 1.25 3.00
LC5DEN112 Blackwing - Sirocco the Dawn UR .40 1.00
LC5DEN113 Blackwing - Blizzard the Far North UR .75 2.00
LC5DEN114 Blackwing - Shura the Blue Flame UR .40 1.00
LC5DEN115 Blackwing - Kalut the Moon Shadow UR .40 1.00
LC5DEN116 Blackwing - Elphin the Raven C .10 .20
LC5DEN117 Blackwing - Mistral the Silver Shield C .10 .20
LC5DEN118 Blackwing - Vayu the Emblem of Honor SCR .40 1.00
LC5DEN119 Blackwing - Fane the Steel Chain C .10 .20
LC5DEN120 Blackwing - Ghibli the Searing Wind C .10 .20
LC5DEN121 Blackwing - Gust the Backblast C .10 .20
LC5DEN122 Blackwing - Breeze the Zephyr C .10 .20
LC5DEN123 Blackwing - Elesian of Two Swords C .10 .20
LC5DEN124 Blackwing - Aurora the Northern Lights C .10 .20
LC5DEN125 Blackwing - Abrolhos the Megaquake C .10 .20
LC5DEN126 Blackwing - Boreas the Sharp C .10 .20
LC5DEN127 Blackwing - Brisote the Tailwind C .10 .20
LC5DEN128 Blackwing - Calima the Haze C .10 .20
LC5DEN129 Blackwing - Kogarashi the Wanderer C .10 .20
LC5DEN130 Blackwing - Kochi the Daybreak C .10 .20
LC5DEN131 Blackwing - Gladius the Midnight Sun UR .75 2.00
LC5DEN132 Blackwing Armor Master SCR .40 1.00
LC5DEN133 Blackwing Armed Wing UR .40 1.00
LC5DEN134 Blackwing - Silverwind the Ascendant SR .40 1.00
LC5DEN135 Black-Winged Dragon C 2.00 3.00
LC5DEN135u Black-Winged Dragon UR .50 1.25
LC5DEN136 De-Synchro SR 1.25 3.00
LC5DEN137 Raptor Wing Strike C .10 .20
LC5DEN138 Black Whirlwind UR 2.50 6.00
LC5DEN139 Cards for Black Feathers R .25 .60
LC5DEN140 Delta Crow - Anti Reverse SCR 1.50 4.00
LC5DEN141 Trap Stun SCR 2.50 6.00
LC5DEN142 Blackwing - Backlash C .10 .20
LC5DEN143 Blackback C .10 .20
LC5DEN144 Blackboost C .10 .20
LC5DEN145 Black Return C .10 .20
LC5DEN146 Earthbound Immortal Aslla Piscu SR .40 1.00
LC5DEN147 Earthbound Immortal Ccapac Apu SR .50 1.25
LC5DEN148 Earthbound Immortal Cusillu SR .40 1.00
LC5DEN149 Earthbound Immortal Chacu Challhua SR .40 1.00
LC5DEN150 Earthbound Immortal Wiraqocha Rasca SR .40 1.00
LC5DEN151 Earthbound Immortal Ccarayhua SR .40 1.00
LC5DEN152 Earthbound Immortal Uru SR .40 1.00
LC5DEN153 Earthbound Linewalker SR .40 1.00
LC5DEN154 Hundred Eyes Dragon SR .40 1.00
LC5DEN155 Earthbound Whirlwind R .25 .60
LC5DEN156 Earthbound Revival C .10 .20
LC5DEN157 Revival of the Immortals C .10 .20
LC5DEN158 Earthbound Wave R .25 .60
LC5DEN159 Roar of the Earthbound C .10 .20
LC5DEN160 Offering to the Immortals C .10 .20
LC5DEN161 Meklord Astro Mekanikle SCR .75 2.00
LC5DEN162 Meklord Emperor Granel SR .40 1.00
LC5DEN163 Meklord Army of Wisel R .25 .60
LC5DEN164 Meklord Army of Skiel R .25 .60
LC5DEN165 Meklord Army of Granel C .10 .20
LC5DEN166 Meklord Astro Dragon Asterisk SCR .50 1.25
LC5DEN167 Meklord Emperor Skiel SR 2.00 5.00
LC5DEN168 Meklord Emperor Wisel SR .40 1.00
LC5DEN169 Fortissimo the Mobile Fortress C .10 .20
LC5DEN170 Boon of the Meklord Emperor C .10 .20
LC5DEN171 The Resolute Meklord Army C .10 .20
LC5DEN172 Reboot C .10 .20
LC5DEN173 Meklord Fortress SR .40 1.00
LC5DEN174 Chaos Infinity SR .60 1.50
LC5DEN175 Mektimed Blast C .10 .20
LC5DEN176 Meklord Factory SR .40 1.00
LC5DEN177 Tanngrisnir of the Nordic Beasts SCR .40 1.00
LC5DEN178 Guldfaxe of the Nordic Beasts SCR .40 1.00
LC5DEN179 Garmr of the Nordic Beasts C .10 .20
LC5DEN180 Tanngnjostr of the Nordic Beasts SCR 1.50 4.00
LC5DEN181 Ljosalf of the Nordic Alfar C .10 .20
LC5DEN182 Svartalf of the Nordic Alfar UR 3.00 8.00
LC5DEN183 Dverg of the Nordic Alfar SCR .40 1.00
LC5DEN184 Valkyrie of the Nordic Ascendant SCR .75 2.00
LC5DEN185 Mimir of the Nordic Ascendant C .10 .20
LC5DEN186 Tyr of the Nordic Champions C .10 .20
LC5DEN187 Vanadis of the Nordic Ascendant UR 1.25 3.00
LC5DEN188 Mara of the Nordic Alfar C .10 .20
LC5DEN189 Thor, Lord of the Aesir SCR .75 2.00
LC5DEN190 Loki, Lord of the Aesir SCR .40 1.00
LC5DEN191 Odin, Father of the Aesir SCR .40 1.00
LC5DEN192 Nordic Relic Draupnir R .25 .60
LC5DEN193 Gotterdammerung C .10 .20
LC5DEN194 March Towards Ragnarok C .10 .20
LC5DEN195 The Nordic Lights C .10 .20
LC5DEN196 Divine Relic Mjollnir R .25 .60
LC5DEN197 Solemn Authority C .10 .20
LC5DEN198 Nordic Relic Brisingamen R .25 .60
LC5DEN199 Nordic Relic Laevateinn R .25 .60
LC5DEN200 Nordic Relic Gungnir UR .50 1.25
LC5DEN201 The Golden Apples R .25 .60
LC5DEN202 Odin's Eye C .10 .20
LC5DEN203 Gleipnir, the Fetters of Fenrir SCR .75 2.00
LC5DEN204 Nordic Relic Megingjord R .25 .60
LC5DEN205 T.G. Cyber Magician SCR 2.00 5.00
LC5DEN206 T.G. Striker UR 1.25 3.00
LC5DEN207 T.G. Jet Falcon C .10 .20
LC5DEN208 T.G. Catapult Dragon C .10 .20
LC5DEN209 T.G. Warwolf SCR 1.25 3.00
LC5DEN210 T.G. Rush Rhino UR .40 1.00
LC5DEN211 T.G. Hyper Librarian SCR .40 1.00
LC5DEN212 T.G. Recipro Dragonfly C .10 .20
LC5DEN213 T.G. Wonder Magician SCR 5.00 12.00
LC5DEN214 T.G. Power Gladiator C .10 .20
LC5DEN215 T.G. Blade Blaster SR .40 1.00
LC5DEN216 T.G. Halberd Cannon SR .40 1.00
LC5DEN217 TGX1-HL UR .75 2.00
LC5DEN218 TGX300 C .10 .20
LC5DEN219 TGX3-DX2 UR .50 1.25
LC5DEN220 TG-SX1 C .10 .20
LC5DEN221 TG1-EM1 SCR .75 2.00
LC5DEN222 Black Salvo C .10 .20
LC5DEN223 Oracle of the Sun C .10 .20
LC5DEN224 Fire Ant Ascator R .25 .60
LC5DEN225 Supay R .25 .60

LC5DEN226 Super-Nimble Mega Hamster SCR .75 2.00
LC5DEN227 Maxx "C" UR 3.00 8.00
LC5DEN228 Metaion, the Timelord SR .75 2.00
LC5DEN229 Sephylon, the Ultimate Timelord SR .40 1.00
LC5DEN230 Avenging Knight Parshath C .10 .20
LC5DEN231 Goyo Guardian SR 4.00 10.00
LC5DEN232 Magical Android UR .75 2.00
LC5DEN233 Thought Ruler Archfiend SCR 1.00 2.50
LC5DEN234 Dark Strike Fighter C .10 .20
LC5DEN235 Hyper Psychic Blaster R .25 .60
LC5DEN236 Power Tool Dragon C .60 1.00
LC5DEN237 Trident Dragion SCR 1.25 3.00
LC5DEN238 Ancient Fairy Dragon C 1.25 2.00
LC5DEN238u Ancient Fairy Dragon UR 1.25 3.00
LC5DEN239 Ancient Sacred Wyvern SCR 2.00 5.00
LC5DEN240 Mist Wurm UR 2.00 5.00
LC5DEN241 Sun Dragon Inti C .10 .20
LC5DEN242 Moon Dragon Quilla C .10 .20
LC5DEN243 Stygian Sergeants SCR .40 1.00
LC5DEN244 Naturia Beast UR 2.00 5.00
LC5DEN245 Naturia Barkion UR 2.50 6.00
LC5DEN246 Life Stream Dragon C .40 .60
LC5DEN247 Orient Dragon UR .60 1.50
LC5DEN248 Driven Daredevil R .25 .60
LC5DEN249 Vulcan the Divine SCR 3.00 8.00
LC5DEN250 Synchro Blast Wave C .10 .20
LC5DEN251 Emergency Teleport SCR 10.00 25.00
LC5DEN252 Savage Colosseum C .10 .20
LC5DEN253 Vanity's Emptiness SCR 15.00 40.00
LC5DEN254 Roaring Earth C .10 .20
LC5DEN255 Debunk SCR 2.50 6.00
LC5DEN256 Full House SCR .75 2.00

2016 Yu-Gi-Oh Mega Tin Mega Pack 1st Edition

COMPLETE SET (239) 100.00 150.00
BOOSTER PACK (15 CARDS) 3.00 6.00
RELEASED ON SEPTEMBER 2, 2016
MP16EN001 Phantom Gryphon C .15 .25
MP16EN002 Performapal Elephammer R .30 .50
MP16EN003 Performapal Bowhopper C .15 .25
MP16EN004 Performapal Lizardraw C .15 .25
MP16EN005 Performapal Springoose C .15 .25
MP16EN006 Superheavy Samurai Big Waraji C .15 .25
MP16EN007 Superheavy Samurai Gigagloves C .15 .25
MP16EN008 Superheavy Samurai Soulbuster Gauntlet C .15 .25
MP16EN009 Soprano the Melodious Songstress C .15 .25
MP16EN010 Fluffal Sheep C .15 .25
MP16EN011 Edge Imp Saw C .15 .25
MP16EN012 Edge Imp Chain C .15 .25
MP16EN013 Edge Imp Frightfuloid C .15 .25
MP16EN014 Raidraptor Sharp Lanius C .15 .25
MP16EN015 Raidraptor Mimicry Lanius C .15 .25
MP16EN016 Magma Dragon C .15 .25
MP16EN017 Deskbot 004 C .15 .25
MP16EN018 Doomdog Octhros C .15 .25
MP16EN019 Putrid Pudding Body Buddies C .15 .25
MP16EN020 Bloom Diva the Melodious Choir UR .40 .60
MP16EN021 Frightfur Chimera R .30 .50
MP16EN022 Clear Wing Synchro Dragon SCR 1.00 1.50
MP16EN023 Performapal Recasting C .15 .25
MP16EN024 Fusion Conscription R .30 .50
MP16EN025 Frightfur Factory C .15 .25
MP16EN026 Frightfur Fusion R .30 .50
MP16EN027 Galaxy Cyclone SCR 1.00 1.50
MP16EN028 Harmonic Oscillation C .15 .25
MP16EN029 Pendulum Rising C .15 .25
MP16EN030 Performapal Pinch Helper C .15 .25
MP16EN031 Fluffal Crane C .15 .25
MP16EN032 Designer Frightfur C .15 .25
MP16EN033 Jar of Avarice SCR .30 .50
MP16EN034 Lose 1 Turn UR .75 1.25
MP16EN035 Fiend Griefing C .15 .25
MP16EN036 Abyss Stungray C .15 .25
MP16EN037 Statue of Anguish Pattern C .15 .25
MP16EN038 Diceversity C .15 .25
MP16EN039 Moon Mirror Shield R .75 1.25
MP16EN040 Half Unbreak C .15 .25
MP16EN041 The Melody of Awakening Dragon SR 3.50 4.50
MP16EN042 Cybernetic Fusion Support C .15 .25
MP16EN043 Number S39: Utopia Prime SR .60 1.00
MP16EN044 GalaxyEyes Full Armor Photon Dragon SR 1.75 2.25
MP16EN045 Performapal Thunderhino C .15 .25
MP16EN046 Primitive Butterfly C .15 .25
MP16EN047 Mystery Shell Dragon C .15 .25
MP16EN048 Risebell the Summoner C .15 .25
MP16EN049 Xiangke Magician SR .60 1.00
MP16EN050 Xiangsheng Magician SR .40 .60
MP16EN051 Performapal Camelump C .15 .25
MP16EN052 Performapal Drummerilla C .15 .25
MP16EN053 Superheavy Samurai Blowtorch C .15 .25
MP16EN054 Opera the Melodious Diva C .15 .25
MP16EN055 Tamtam the Melodious Diva C .15 .25
MP16EN056 Fluffal Mouse SR .30 .50
MP16EN057 DD Pandora C .15 .25
MP16EN058 Raidraptor Fuzzy Lanius C .15 .25
MP16EN059 Raidraptor Singing Lanius C .15 .25
MP16EN060 Performage Flame Eater C .15 .25
MP16EN061 Performage Hat Tricker C .15 .25
MP16EN062 Performage Trick Clown C .15 .25
MP16EN063 Performage Stilts Launcher C .15 .25
MP16EN064 Keeper of the Shrine C .15 .25
MP16EN065 Igknight Squire C .15 .25
MP16EN066 Igknight Templar UR 1.50 2.00
MP16EN067 Igknight Paladin C .15 .25
MP16EN068 Igknight Margrave C .15 .25
MP16EN069 Igknight Gallant C .15 .25
MP16EN070 Aromage Cananga C .15 .25
MP16EN071 Aroma Jar C .15 .25
MP16EN072 Bird of Paradise Lost C .15 .25
MP16EN073 Magical Abductor R .30 .50
MP16EN074 Toon Cyber Dragon R 1.25 2.00
MP16EN075 Deskbot 005 C .15 .25
MP16EN076 Retaliating "C" C .15 .25
MP16EN077 DDD Oracle King dArc R 1.00 1.50
MP16EN078 OddEyes Rebellion Dragon SCR .40 .60
MP16EN079 DDD Marksman King Tell R .30 .50
MP16EN080 Performage Trapeze Magician R 2.00 3.50
MP16EN081 Pianissimo C .15 .25
MP16EN082 Brilliant Fusion SR 10.00 15.00
MP16EN083 RankUpMagic Raptors Force C .15 .25
MP16EN084 Bubble Barrier C .15 .25
MP16EN085 Ignition Phoenix C .15 .25
MP16EN086 Aroma Garden C .15 .25
MP16EN087 BackUp Rider C .15 .25
MP16EN088 Brilliant Spark C .15 .25
MP16EN089 Raidraptor Return C .15 .25
MP16EN090 Raptors Gust C .15 .25
MP16EN091 Trick Box C .15 .25
MP16EN092 Humid Winds C .15 .25
MP16EN093 Ferret Flames C .15 .25
MP16EN094 Balance of Judgment C .15 .25
MP16EN095 Extra Buck R .30 .50
MP16EN096 Side Effects? C .15 .25
MP16EN097 Extinction on Schedule C .15 .25
MP16EN098 Dogoran the Mad Flame Kaiju R .60 1.00
MP16EN099 Kumongous the Sticky String Kaiju R 1.50 2.00
MP16EN100 Kyoutou Waterfront C .15 .25
MP16EN101 Performapal Silver Claw C .15 .25
MP16EN102 Performapal Salutiger C .15 .25
MP16EN103 Tatsunoko SCR .20 .35
MP16EN104 Secret Blast C .15 .25
MP16EN105 Performapal Secondonkey R .30 .50
MP16EN106 Performapal Splashmammoth R .30 .50
MP16EN107 Performapal Helpprincess R .30 .50
MP16EN108 Superheavy Samurai Thief C .15 .25
MP16EN109 Superheavy Samurai Transporter C .15 .25
MP16EN110 Superheavy Samurai Drum C .15 .25
MP16EN111 Superheavy Samurai Soulhorns C .15 .25
MP16EN112 Superheavy Samurai Soulclaw C .15 .25
MP16EN113 DD Berfomet R .30 .50
MP16EN114 DD Swirl Slime C .15 .25
MP16EN115 DD Necro Slime C .15 .25
MP16EN116 Raidraptor Wild Vulture C .15 .25
MP16EN117 Raidraptor Skull Eagle C .15 .25
MP16EN118 Performage Mirror Conductor C .15 .25
MP16EN119 Assault Blackwing Kunai the Drizzle R .30 .50
MP16EN120 Charging Gaia the Fierce Knight UR .75 1.25
MP16EN121 Sphere Kuriboh R .60 1.00
MP16EN122 Super Soldier Soul C .15 .25
MP16EN123 Beginning Knight SR 1.25 2.00
MP16EN124 Evening Twilight Knight SR 1.25 2.00
MP16EN125 Majespecter Cat Nekomata SR .30 .50
MP16EN126 Majespecter Raccoon Bunbuku UR .40 .60
MP16EN127 Majespecter Crow Yata C .15 .25
MP16EN128 Majespecter Fox Kyubi C .15 .25
MP16EN129 Majespecter Unicorn Kirin R .30 .50
MP16EN130 Igknight Cavalier C .15 .25
MP16EN131 Igknight Veteran C .15 .25
MP16EN132 Toon Barrel Dragon R .30 .50
MP16EN133 Deskbot 006 C .15 .25
MP16EN134 Pot of The Forbidden C .15 .25
MP16EN135 Dr Frankenderp C .15 .25
MP16EN136 Black Luster Soldier Super Soldier UR 1.00 1.50
MP16EN137 Frightfur SabreTooth UR 1.50 2.00
MP16EN138 DDD Wave Oblivion King Caesar Ragnarok SR .75 1.00
MP16EN139 OddEyes Vortex Dragon SCR .40 .60
MP16EN140 Scarlight Red Dragon Archfiend SCR 2.00 3.00
MP16EN141 Assault Blackwing Raikiri the Rain Shower UR 1.15 1.50
MP16EN142 Deskbot Jet C .15 .25
MP16EN143 DDD DuoDawn King Kali Yuga SR .60 1.00
MP16EN144 Shuffle Reborn C .15 .25
MP16EN145 Raptors Ultimate Mace C .15 .25
MP16EN146 Super Soldier Ritual R 1.00 1.50
MP16EN147 Majespecter Storm C .15 .25
MP16EN148 Igknight Reload UR .75 1.25
MP16EN149 OddEyes Fusion SCR .20 .35
MP16EN150 Psychic Blade C .15 .25
MP16EN151 Painful Decision SCR .30 .50
MP16EN152 Super Rush Headlong C .15 .25
MP16EN153 Frightfur March C .15 .25
MP16EN154 DDD Contract Change C .15 .25
MP16EN155 Dark Contract with Errors C .15 .25
MP16EN156 Super Soldier Rebirth C .15 .25
MP16EN157 Super Soldier Shield UR .30 .50
MP16EN158 Majespecter Tornado UR .50 .75
MP16EN159 Majespecter Tempest C .15 .25
MP16EN160 Grand Horn of Heaven C .15 .25
MP16EN161 FirstAid Squad C .15 .25
MP16EN162 Painful Escape SCR .10 .20
MP16EN163 Radian the Multidimensional Kaiju R 1.50 2.00
MP16EN164 Gameciel the Sea Turtle Kaiju R 9.00 11.00
MP16EN165 Kaiju Capture Mission C .15 .25
MP16EN166 DD Savant Galilei C .15 .25
MP16EN167 DD Savant Kepler C .15 .25
MP16EN168 Dark Contract with the Gate C .15 .25
MP16EN169 Dark Contract with the Swamp King C .15 .25
MP16EN170 Dark Contract with the Witch C .15 .25
MP16EN171 Contract Laundering C .15 .25
MP16EN172 DDD Human Resources C .15 .25
MP16EN173 DDD Rebel King Leonidas SR 1.00 1.50
MP16EN174 Timebreaker Magician R .30 .50
MP16EN175 Performapal Guitartle R .30 .50
MP16EN176 Performapal Bit Bite Turtle C .15 .25
MP16EN177 Performapal Rain Goat C .15 .25
MP16EN178 Performapal Trump Girl C .15 .25
MP16EN179 Superheavy Samurai Magnet C .15 .25
MP16EN180 Superheavy Samurai Prepped Defense C .15 .25
MP16EN181 Superheavy Samurai General Jade C .15 .25
MP16EN182 Superheavy Samurai General Coral C .15 .25
MP16EN183 Solo the Melodious Songstress C .15 .25
MP16EN184 Score the Melodious Diva C .15 .25
MP16EN185 Blackwing Harmattan the Dust C .15 .25
MP16EN186 Twilight Ninja Shingetsu C .15 .25
MP16EN187 Twilight Ninja Nichirin the Chunin C .15 .25
MP16EN188 Twilight Ninja Getsuga the Shogun R .30 .50
MP16EN189 Buster Blader the Destruction Swordmaster UR .40 .60
MP16EN190 Dragon Buster Destruction Sword C .15 .25
MP16EN191 Wizard Buster Destruction Sword C .15 .25
MP16EN192 Robot Buster Destruction Sword C .15 .25
MP16EN193 Dinomist Stegosaur C .15 .25
MP16EN194 Dinomist Plesios C .15 .25
MP16EN195 Dinomist Pteran R .30 .50
MP16EN196 Dinomist Brachion C .15 .25
MP16EN197 Dinomist Ceratops C .15 .25
MP16EN198 Dinomist Rex SR .20 .35
MP16EN199 Shiranui Spectralsword UR .30 .50
MP16EN200 Shiranui Smith C .15 .25
MP16EN201 Shiranui Spiritmaster R 1.25 2.00
MP16EN202 Shiranui Samurai C .15 .25
MP16EN203 Dark Doriado C .15 .25
MP16EN204 AlLumiraj C .15 .25
MP16EN205 Toon Buster Blader R .30 .50
MP16EN206 Deskbot 007 C .15 .25
MP16EN207 Deskbot 008 C .15 .25
MP16EN208 Engraver of the Mark C .15 .25
MP16EN209 Zany Zebra C .15 .25
MP16EN210 Buster Blader the Dragon Destroyer Swordsman SCR .50 .80
MP16EN211 Shiranui Samuraisaga C .15 .25
MP16EN212 Shiranui Shogunsaga UR .25 .40
MP16EN213 Aegaion the Sea Castrum C .15 .25
MP16EN214 Performance Hurricane C .15 .25
MP16EN215 Destruction Swordsman Fusion C .15 .25
MP16EN216 Karma of the Destruction Swordsman C .15 .25
MP16EN217 Dinomic Powerload C .15 .25
MP16EN218 Dinomist Charge C .15 .25
MP16EN219 Majespecter Sonics C .15 .25
MP16EN220 Shiranui Style Synthesis C .15 .25
MP16EN221 Twin Twisters SR 6.00 8.00
MP16EN222 Mistaken Accusation C .15 .25
MP16EN223 Dragons Bind C .15 .25
MP16EN224 Follow Wing C .15 .25
MP16EN225 Reject Reborn R .30 .50
MP16EN226 Destruction Sword Flash C .15 .25
MP16EN227 Dinomist Rush C .15 .25
MP16EN228 Shiranui Style Swallows Slash C .15 .25
MP16EN229 Pendulum Reborn R .30 .50
MP16EN230 Forbidden Apocrypha C .15 .25
MP16EN231 Solemn Strike SCR 8.00 10.00
MP16EN232 Bad Luck Blast C .15 .25
MP16EN233 Ultimate Providence SCR .50 .80
MP16EN234 Gadarla the Mystery Dust Kaiju R 1.00 1.50
MP16EN235 Jizukiru the Star Destroying Kaiju R 3.00 4.00
MP16EN236 Neptabyss the Atlantean Prince UR .40 .60
MP16EN237 Cyber Dragon Infinity SCR 1.50 2.00
MP16EN238 Arisen Gaia the Fierce Knight R .30 .50
MP16EN239 Traptrix Rafflesia SCR 1.00 1.50

2017 Yu-Gi-Oh Mega Tin Mega Pack 1st Edition

COMPLETE SET (239) 130.00 200.00
BOOSTER PACK (16 CARDS) 3.00 5.00
RELEASED ON AUGUST 25, 2017
MP17DE001 Angel Trumpeter C .05 .15
MP17DE002 Performapal Sellshell Crab C .05 .15
MP17DE003 Performapal Fireflux C .05 .15
MP17DE004 Speedroid Den Den Daiko Duke R .15 .25
MP17DE005 Speedroid Pachingo Kart R .15 .25
MP17DE006 Raidraptor Avenge Vulture C .05 .15
MP17DE007 Raidraptor Pain Lanius C .05 .15
MP17DE008 Raidraptor Booster Strix C .05 .15
MP17DE009 Blackwing Decay the Ill Wind C .05 .15
MP17DE010 Dragon Spirit of White UR 1.25 2.00
MP17DE011 Protector with Eyes of Blue C .05 .15
MP17DE012 Master with Eyes of Blue C .05 .15
MP17DE013 The White Stone of Ancients UR 2.00 3.00
MP17DE014 Lector Pendulum the Dracoverlord UR .10 .20
MP17DE015 Dinomist Spinos C .05 .15
MP17DE016 Digital Bug Cocoondenser C .05 .15
MP17DE017 Digital Bug Centibit C .05 .15
MP17DE018 Digital Bug Websolder C .05 .15
MP17DE019 Ryu Okami C .05 .15
MP17DE020 Tenmataitei R .15 .25
MP17DE021 Spirit of the Fall Wind R .15 .25
MP17DE022 Ghost Reaper and Winter Cherries SCR 4.00 5.00
MP17DE023 Gendo the Ascetic Monk C .05 .15
MP17DE024 Deskbot 009 C .05 .15
MP17DE025 Dicelops C .05 .15
MP17DE026 Hi Speedroid Puzzle R .15 .25
MP17DE027 Digital Bug Scaradiator C .05 .15
MP17DE028 Digital Bug Corebage C .05 .15
MP17DE029 Rank Up Magic Skip Force R .15 .25
MP17DE030 Mausoleum of White R .15 .25
MP17DE031 Beacon of White C .05 .15
MP17DE032 Forge of the True Dracos C .05 .15
MP17DE033 Bug Matrix C .05 .15
MP17DE034 Pre Preparation of Rites SR .15 .25
MP17DE035 Fusion Tag R .15 .25
MP17DE036 Deskbot Base C .05 .15
MP17DE037 Finite Cards C .05 .15
MP17DE038 Re dyce cle C .05 .15
MP17DE039 Dinomist Eruption C .05 .15
MP17DE040 Bug Emergency C .05 .15
MP17DE041 Drowning Mirror Force SCR 1.25 2.00
MP17DE042 Wonder Xyz C .05 .15
MP17DE043 Rise to Full Height C .05 .15
MP17DE044 Bad Aim C .05 .15
MP17DE045 Graceful Tear C .05 .15
MP17DE046 Thunder King the Lightningstrike Kaiju R .15 .25
MP17DE047 Super Anti Kaiju War Machine Mecha Dogoran R .15 .25
MP17DE048 The Kaiju Files C .05 .15
MP17DE049 Cuben C .05 .15
MP17DE050 World Carrotweight Champion C .05 .15
MP17DE051 Dwarf Star Dragon Planeter C .05 .15
MP17DE052 Geargianchor C .05 .15
MP17DE053 Geargia Change C .05 .15
MP17DE054 Stardust Sifr Divine Dragon UR .10 .20
MP17DE055 Priestess with Eyes of Blue SR .15 .25
MP17DE056 Blue Eyes Twin Burst Dragon SCR 3.00 4.00
MP17DE057 Magical Something R .15 .25
MP17DE058 Performapal Bot Eyes Lizard C .05 .15
MP17DE059 Performapal Gongato C .05 .15
MP17DE060 Performapal Extra Slinger C .05 .15
MP17DE061 Performapal Inflater Tapir C .05 .15
MP17DE062 Performapal Bubblebowwow C .05 .15
MP17DE063 Performapal Radish Horse C .05 .15
MP17DE064 Performapal Life Swordsman C .05 .15

MP17DE065 DD Savant Thomas R .15 .25
MP17DE066 DD Savant Nikola C .05 .15
MP17DE067 Blackwing Tornado the Reverse Wind C .05 .15
MP17DE068 Blackwing Gofu the Vague Shadow C .05 .15
MP17DE069 Red Warg C .05 .15
MP17DE070 Red Gardna C .05 .15
MP17DE071 Red Mirror C .05 .15
MP17DE072 Magician of Dark Illusion SR .15 .25
MP17DE073 Magicians Robe C .05 .15
MP17DE074 Magicians Rod SR .15 .25
MP17DE075 Master Peace the True Dracoslayer UR .10 .20
MP17DE076 Metalfoes Steelen C .05 .15
MP17DE077 Metalfoes Silverd C .05 .15
MP17DE078 Metalfoes Goldriver R .15 .25
MP17DE079 Metalfoes Volflame R .15 .25
MP17DE080 True King Agnimazud the Vanisher UR 1.00 1.50
MP17DE081 Dinomist Ankylos C .05 .15
MP17DE082 Shiranui Solitaire UR 2.50 4.00
MP17DE083 Toon Dark Magician SR .15 .25
MP17DE084 Scapeghost C .05 .15
MP17DE085 Block Dragon UR .25 .40
MP17DE086 Black Dragon Ninja C .05 .15
MP17DE087 Zap Mustung C .05 .15
MP17DE088 Totem Five C .05 .15
MP17DE089 Tuning Gum R .15 .25
MP17DE090 Wrecker Panda C .05 .15
MP17DE091 Fairy Tail Snow C .05 .15
MP17DE092 Metalfoes Adamante R .15 .25
MP17DE093 Metalfoes Orichalc C .05 .15
MP17DE094 Metalfoes Crimsonite R .15 .25
MP17DE095 Assault Blackwing Sayo the Rain Hider R .15 .25
MP17DE096 Assault Blackwing Sohaya the Rain Storm C .05 .15
MP17DE097 Super Hippo Carnival C .05 .15
MP17DE098 Frightfur Sanctuary C .05 .15
MP17DE099 Forbidden Dark Contract with the Swamp King C .05 .15
MP17DE100 Dark Magical Circle SCR 5.00 6.00
MP17DE101 Illusion Magic R .15 .25
MP17DE102 Dark Magic Expanded C .05 .15
MP17DE103 Metamorformation SR .15 .25
MP17DE104 Metalfoes Fusion SR .15 .25
MP17DE105 Cosmic Cyclone SCR 5.00 6.00
MP17DE106 Magical Mid Breaker Field C .05 .15
MP17DE107 Card of the Soul C .05 .15
MP17DE108 Fusion Fright Waltz C .05 .15
MP17DE109 King Scarlet C .05 .15
MP17DE110 Magician Navigation SCR 5.00 6.00
MP17DE111 Metalfoes Counter C .05 .15
MP17DE112 Metalfoes Combination SR .15 .25
MP17DE113 Destruction Sword Memories C .05 .15
MP17DE114 Floodgate Trap Hole UR 1.25 2.00
MP17DE115 Unified Front C .05 .15
MP17DE116 Pendulum Hole C .05 .15
MP17DE117 Ninjitsu Art Notebook C .05 .15
MP17DE118 Heavy Freight Train Derricrane C .05 .15
MP17DE119 Revolving Switchyard C .05 .15
MP17DE120 Dragodies the Empowered Warrior C .05 .15
MP17DE121 Empowerment C .05 .15
MP17DE122 Paleozoic Olenoides C .05 .15
MP17DE123 Paleozoic Hallucigenia C .05 .15
MP17DE124 Paleozoic Canadia C .05 .15
MP17DE125 Paleozoic Pikaia C .05 .15
MP17DE126 Paleozoic Anomalocaris SR .15 .25
MP17DE127 Dragon Core Hexer R .15 .25
MP17DE128 Performapal Flip Hippo C .05 .15
MP17DE129 Performapal Seal Eel C .05 .15
MP17DE130 Performapal Changeraffe C .05 .15
MP17DE131 Predaplant Flytrap R .15 .25
MP17DE132 Predaplant Moray Nepenthes C .05 .15
MP17DE133 Predaplant Squid Drosera C .05 .15
MP17DE134 Superheavy Samurai Soulpeacemaker R .15 .25
MP17DE135 Cipher Twin Raptor C .05 .15
MP17DE136 Cipher Mirror Knight C .05 .15
MP17DE137 Crystron Prasiortle C .05 .15
MP17DE138 Crystron Smiger C .05 .15
MP17DE139 Crystron Thystvern C .05 .15
MP17DE140 Crystron Rosenix C .05 .15
MP17DE141 True King Bahrastos the Fathomer UR .40 .60
MP17DE142 Raremetalfoes Bismugear C .05 .15
MP17DE143 PSY Frame Multi Threader C .05 .15
MP17DE144 Doki Doki C .05 .15
MP17DE145 Pandoras Jewelry Box C .05 .15
MP17DE146 Fairy Tail Sleeper C .05 .15
MP17DE147 Starving Venom Fusion Dragon SCR 1.00 1.50
MP17DE148 Metalfoes Mithrilium UR .20 .35
MP17DE149 Superheavy Samurai Ninja Sarutobi R .15 .25
MP17DE150 Toadally Awesome SCR 2.50 3.50
MP17DE151 Amazing Pendulum C .05 .15
MP17DE152 The Phantom Knights Rank Up Magic Launch SR .15 .25
MP17DE153 Crystolic Potential C .05 .15
MP17DE154 Fullmetalfoes Fusion SR .15 .25
MP17DE155 Igknights Unite C .05 .15
MP17DE156 Sprites Blessing C .05 .15
MP17DE157 Quarantine C .05 .15
MP17DE158 Double Cipher C .05 .15
MP17DE159 Cipher Bit C .05 .15
MP17DE160 Crystron Entry C .05 .15
MP17DE161 Crystron Impact C .05 .15
MP17DE162 PSY Frame Accelerator C .05 .15
MP17DE163 Dimensional Barrier SCR 5.00 6.00
MP17DE164 Summon Gate C .05 .15
MP17DE165 Caninetaur C .05 .15
MP17DE166 Dino Sewing C .05 .15
MP17DE167 Mare Mare C .05 .15
MP17DE168 Paleozoic Eldonia C .05 .15
MP17DE169 Paleozoic Dinomischus C .05 .15
MP17DE170 Paleozoic Marrella C .05 .15
MP17DE171 Paleozoic Leanchoilia C .05 .15
MP17DE172 Paleozoic Opabinia SR .15 .25
MP17DE173 Fusion Recycling Plant R .15 .25
MP17DE174 Performapal Handstandaccoon C .05 .15
MP17DE175 Speedroid Gum Prize C .05 .15
MP17DE176 Speedroid Horse Stilts C .05 .15
MP17DE177 Fusion Parasite R .15 .25
MP17DE178 Cyber Tutubon C .05 .15
MP17DE179 Cipher Etranger C .05 .15
MP17DE180 Ancient Gear Hunting Hound C .05 .15
MP17DE181 Zoodiac Ratpier SR .15 .25
MP17DE182 Zoodiac Bunnyblast C .05 .15
MP17DE183 Zoodiac Whiptail SR .15 .25
MP17DE184 Zoodiac Thoroughblade UR .20 .35
MP17DE185 Zoodiac Ramram C .05 .15
MP17DE186 True King Lithosagym the Disaster SR .15 .25
MP17DE187 Crystron Rion C .05 .15
MP17DE188 Shinobird Crow C .05 .15
MP17DE189 Shinobird Crane C .05 .15
MP17DE190 Shinobird Pigeon C .05 .15
MP17DE191 Envoy of Chaos R .15 .25
MP17DE192 Spiritual Beast Tamer Winda R .15 .25
MP17DE193 Miscellaneousaurus C .05 .15
MP17DE194 Apprentice Piper C .05 .15
MP17DE195 Hebo Lord of the River C .05 .15
MP17DE196 Eater of Millions C .05 .15
MP17DE197 Wightprincess C .05 .15
MP17DE198 Metrognome C .05 .15
MP17DE199 Fairy Tail Rella C .05 .15
MP17DE200 Shinobaroness Peacock R .15 .25
MP17DE201 Shinobaron Peacock R .15 .25
MP17DE202 Ancient Gear Howitzer C .05 .15
MP17DE203 Superheavy Samurai Stealth Ninja R .15 .25
MP17DE204 Shiranui Sunsaga R .15 .25
MP17DE205 Odd Eyes Raging Dragon UR .30 .50
MP17DE206 Zoodiac Broadbull SCR 1.50 2.50
MP17DE207 Zoodiac Tigermortar UR .20 .35
MP17DE208 Zoodiac Drident SCR 1.00 1.50
MP17DE209 Zoodiac Boarbow R .15 .25
MP17DE210 Rank Up Magic Cipher Ascension C .05 .15
MP17DE211 Zodiac Sign C .05 .15
MP17DE212 Zoodiac Barrage SCR 2.00 3.00
MP17DE213 Shinobirds Calling C .05 .15
MP17DE214 Shinobird Power Spot C .05 .15
MP17DE215 Super Soldier Synthesis C .05 .15
MP17DE216 Super Quantal Alphan Spike C .05 .15
MP17DE217 Ritual Beast Return C .05 .15
MP17DE218 Foolish Burial Goods SCR 2.00 2.50
MP17DE219 Terminal World NEXT C .05 .15
MP17DE220 Lost Wind R .15 .25
MP17DE221 Cipher Spectrum C .05 .15
MP17DE222 Ancient Gear Reborn R .15 .25
MP17DE223 Zoodiac Combo C .05 .15
MP17DE224 Shinobird Salvation C .05 .15
MP17DE225 Beginning of Heaven and Earth C .05 .15
MP17DE226 Shiranui Style Samsara C .05 .15
MP17DE227 Purushaddoll Aeon C .05 .15
MP17DE228 Full Force Virus SCR .60 1.00
MP17DE229 Switcheroroo R .15 .25
MP17DE230 Massivemorph C .05 .15
MP17DE231 Sea Monster of Theseus SCR .75 1.25
MP17DE232 Symphonic Warrior Guitaar C .05 .15
MP17DE233 Symphonic Warrior Synthess C .05 .15
MP17DE234 Symph Amplifire C .05 .15
MP17DE235 Rocket Hand C .05 .15
MP17DE236 Mekanikal Arkfiend C .05 .15
MP17DE237 Lightsworn Judgment C .05 .15
MP17DE238 Symphonic Warrior Miccs C .05 .15
MP17DE239 Dark Contract with the Entities UR .20 .35

2018 Yu-Gi-Oh Mega Tin Mega Pack 1st Edition

COMPLETE SET (223) 130.00 200.00
RELEASED ON AUGUST 31, 2018
MP18-EN001 Speedroid Skull Marbles C .10 .20
MP18-EN002 Speedroid Maliciousmagnet C .10 .20
MP18-EN003 Double Resonator C .10 .20
MP18-EN004 Majesty Maiden, the True Dracocaster UR .60 1.00
MP18-EN005 Mariamne, the True Dracophoenix UR .10 .20
MP18-EN006 Digital Bug LEDybug C .10 .20
MP18-EN007 Ariel, Priestess of the Nekroz R .10 .20
MP18-EN008 Pendulumucho SR .10 .20
MP18-EN009 Baobaboon C .10 .20
MP18-EN010 Familiar-Possessed - Lyna C .10 .20
MP18-EN011 Supreme King Z-ARC SCR 1.00 1.50
MP18-EN012 Magician's Right Hand C .10 .20
MP18-EN013 Magician's Left Hand C .10 .20
MP18-EN014 Ultra Polymerization SCR .50 .80
MP18-EN015 Dragonic Diagram SCR 2.00 2.50
MP18-EN016 True Draco Heritage UR 1.50 2.00
MP18-EN017 Disciples of the True Dracophoenix C .10 .20
MP18-EN018 Bug Signal C .10 .20
MP18-EN019 Set Rotation C .10 .20
MP18-EN020 Break Away C .10 .20
MP18-EN021 The Phantom Knights of Lost Vambrace C .10 .20
MP18-EN022 The Phantom Knights of Wrong Magnetring C .10 .20
MP18-EN023 True Draco Apocalypse C .10 .20
MP18-EN024 Waterfall of Dragon Souls SR .10 .20
MP18-EN025 Kaiser Sea Snake C .10 .20
MP18-EN026 Sylvan Princessprite SR .10 .20
MP18-EN027 Artifact Vajra C .10 .20
MP18-EN028 Mild Turkey C .10 .20
MP18-EN029 Ghost Beef C .10 .20
MP18-EN030 Onikuji C .10 .20
MP18-EN031 Backup Secretary C .10 .20
MP18-EN032 Stack Reviver C .10 .20
MP18-EN033 Launcher Commander C .10 .20
MP18-EN034 Salvagent Driver UR .10 .20
MP18-EN035 Trickstar Lilybell R .10 .20
MP18-EN036 Trickstar Lycoris SR .10 .20
MP18-EN037 Trickstar Candina UR 1.50 2.00
MP18-EN038 Gouki Twistcobra SR .10 .20
MP18-EN039 Gouki Suprex R .10 .20
MP18-EN040 Gouki Riscorpio R .10 .20
MP18-EN041 Hack Worm C .10 .20
MP18-EN042 Jack Wyvern C .10 .20
MP18-EN043 Cracking Dragon SR .10 .20
MP18-EN044 Crowned by the World Chalice C .10 .20
MP18-EN045 Chosen by the World Chalice C .10 .20
MP18-EN046 Beckoned by the World Chalice C .10 .20
MP18-EN047 World Chalice Guardragon UR .25 .40
MP18-EN048 Lee the World Chalice Fairy UR .25 .40
MP18-EN049 World Legacy - World Chalice R .10 .20
MP18-EN050 Jain, Twilightsworn General C .10 .20
MP18-EN051 Lyla, Twilightsworn Enchantress SR .10 .20
MP18-EN052 Lumina, Twilightsworn Shaman SCR .60 1.00
MP18-EN053 Ryko, Twilightsworn Fighter R .10 .20
MP18-EN054 Rescue Ferret SCR .60 1.00
MP18-EN055 Motivating Captain R .10 .20
MP18-EN056 Treasure Panda C .10 .20
MP18-EN057 Zombina C .10 .20
MP18-EN058 Re: EX R .10 .20
MP18-EN059 Orbital Hydralander C .10 .20
MP18-EN060 The Ascended of Thunder C .10 .20
MP18-EN061 Parry Knights C .10 .20
MP18-EN062 Firewall Dragon SCR 10.00 15.00
MP18-EN063 Trickstar Holly Angel UR .10 .20
MP18-EN064 Gouki The Great Ogre SR .10 .20
MP18-EN065 Topologic Bomber Dragon SCR 7.00 10.00
MP18-EN066 Imduk the World Chalice Dragon R .10 .20
MP18-EN067 Ib the World Chalice Priestess SR .10 .20
MP18-EN068 Ningirsu the World Chalice Warrior SCR 1.50 2.00
MP18-EN069 Trickstar Light Stage UR 1.50 2.00
MP18-EN070 Gouki Re-Match SR .10 .20
MP18-EN071 Air Cracking Storm C .10 .20
MP18-EN072 Smile Universe C .10 .20
MP18-EN073 World Legacy Discovery R .10 .20
MP18-EN074 World Legacy's Heart C .10 .20
MP18-EN075 Emerging Emergency Rescute Rescue C .10 .20
MP18-EN076 Spellbook of Knowledge UR 5.00 7.00
MP18-EN077 Gravity Lash C .10 .20
MP18-EN078 Defense Zone C .10 .20
MP18-EN079 Three Strikes Barrier C .10 .20
MP18-EN080 Pulse Mines C .10 .20
MP18-EN081 World Legacy Landmark C .10 .20
MP18-EN082 Twilight Eraser R .10 .20
MP18-EN083 Twilight Cloth C .10 .20
MP18-EN084 Dark World Brainwashing C .10 .20
MP18-EN085 Break Off Trap Hole SR .10 .20
MP18-EN086 Heavy Storm Duster SR .20 .35
MP18-EN087 Back to the Front R .60 1.00
MP18-EN088 Recall R .10 .20
MP18-EN089 Samurai Skull C .10 .20
MP18-EN090 Vendread Reorigin SCR .25 .40
MP18-EN091 F.A. Sonic Meister C .10 .20
MP18-EN092 F.A. Hang On Mach C .10 .20
MP18-EN093 F.A. Circuit Grand Prix C .10 .20
MP18-EN094 F.A. Downforce C .10 .20
MP18-EN095 Junk Breaker C .10 .20
MP18-EN096 Infernity Patriarch C .10 .20
MP18-EN097 Gogogo Aristera & Dexia C .10 .20
MP18-EN098 Wicked Acolyte Chilam Sabak C .10 .20
MP18-EN099 Galaxy Worm C .10 .20
MP18-EN100 Destiny HERO - Dangerous C .10 .20
MP18-EN101 Abyss Actor - Trendy Understudy C .10 .20
MP18-EN102 Speedroid Passinglider C .10 .20
MP18-EN103 Ancient Gear Golem - Ultimate Pound C .10 .20
MP18-EN104 Defect Compiler C .10 .20
MP18-EN105 Capacitor Stalker C .10 .20
MP18-EN106 Link Infra-Flier C .10 .20
MP18-EN107 Trickstar Narkissus R .10 .20
MP18-EN108 Gouki Headbatt C .10 .20
MP18-EN109 Sniffer Dragon C .10 .20
MP18-EN110 Anesthrokket Dragon C .10 .20
MP18-EN111 Autorokket Dragon SR .10 .20
MP18-EN112 Magnarokket Dragon UR .25 .40
MP18-EN113 Altergeist Marionetter UR .60 1.00
MP18-EN114 Altergeist Silquitous SR .10 .20
MP18-EN115 Altergeist Meluseek UR 1.50 2.00
MP18-EN116 Altergeist Kunquery C .10 .20
MP18-EN117 World Legacy - World Armor R .10 .20
MP18-EN118 Mermail Abyssnerei C .10 .20
MP18-EN119 Mecha Phantom Beast Raiten C .10 .20
MP18-EN120 The Accumulator C .10 .20
MP18-EN121 Soldier Dragons C .10 .20
MP18-EN122 Duck Dummy C .10 .20
MP18-EN123 Leng Ling C .10 .20
MP18-EN124 Self-Destruct Ant C .10 .20
MP18-EN125 Amano-Iwato C .10 .20
MP18-EN126 Fantastic Striborg R .10 .20
MP18-EN127 Destrudo the Lost Dragon's Frisson R .30 .50
MP18-EN128 Elemental Grace Doriado R .10 .20
MP18-EN129 Nimble Beaver C .10 .20
MP18-EN130 Muscle Medic C .10 .20
MP18-EN131 Borreload Dragon SCR 15.00 18.00
MP18-EN132 Trickstar Black Catbat UR .10 .20
MP18-EN133 Gouki Thunder Ogre UR .10 .20
MP18-EN134 Twin Triangle Dragon R .10 .20
MP18-EN135 Altergeist Primebanshee UR .10 .20
MP18-EN136 Security Block R .10 .20
MP18-EN137 Dragonoid Generator R .10 .20
MP18-EN138 Squib Draw SCR .10 .20
MP18-EN139 Quick Launch SCR .50 .80
MP18-EN140 World Legacy Clash C .10 .20
MP18-EN141 One-Time Passcode R .10 .20
MP18-EN142 Arrivalrivals UR .15 .25
MP18-EN143 Overdone Burial SCR .10 .20
MP18-EN144 Temple of the Mind's Eye C .10 .20
MP18-EN145 Backup Squad R .10 .20
MP18-EN146 Burning Bamboo Sword C .10 .20
MP18-EN147 Cyberse Beacon C .10 .20
MP18-EN148 Link Restart C .10 .20
MP18-EN149 Remote Rebirth C .10 .20
MP18-EN150 Altergeist Camouflage R .10 .20
MP18-EN151 Altergeist Protocol SR .10 .20
MP18-EN152 Personal Spoofing R .10 .20
MP18-EN153 World Legacy Pawns C .10 .20
MP18-EN154 Evenly Matched SCR 20.00 25.00
MP18-EN155 Fuse Line SCR .10 .20
MP18-EN156 Broken Line UR .10 .20
MP18-EN157 Ojama Duo C .10 .20
MP18-EN158 Vendread Chimera SCR .25 .40
MP18-EN159 F.A. Whip Crosser C .10 .20
MP18-EN160 F.A. Turbo Charger C .10 .20
MP18-EN161 F.A. Off-Road Grand Prix C .10 .20
MP18-EN162 F.A. Pit Stop C .10 .20
MP18-EN163 Lunalight Crimson Fox C .10 .20
MP18-EN164 Lunalight Kaleido Chick C .10 .20
MP18-EN165 Amazoness Spy C .10 .20
MP18-EN166 Amazoness Pet Liger C .10 .20

MP18-EN167 Amazoness Empress C	.10	.20
MP18-EN168 Yoko-Zuna Sumo Spirit C	.10	.20
MP18-EN169 Zombino C	.10	.20
MP18-EN170 Lockout Gardna C	.10	.20
MP18-EN171 Striping Partner C	.10	.20
MP18-EN172 Flick Clown C	.10	.20
MP18-EN173 Bitrooper C	.10	.20
MP18-EN174 Linkbelt Wall Dragon C	.10	.20
MP18-EN175 Shelrokket Dragon R	.10	.20
MP18-EN176 Metalrokket Dragon R	.10	.20
MP18-EN177 Mekk-Knight Blue Sky SCR	6.00	8.00
MP18-EN178 Mekk-Knight Green Horizon C	.10	.20
MP18-EN179 Mekk-Knight Orange Sunset C	.10	.20
MP18-EN180 Mekk-Knight Yellow Star R	.10	.20
MP18-EN181 Mekk-Knight Red Moon R	.10	.20
MP18-EN182 Mekk-Knight Indigo Eclipse SR	.10	.20
MP18-EN183 Mekk-Knight Purple Nightfall SCR	6.00	8.00
MP18-EN184 World Legacy - World Shield C	.10	.20
MP18-EN185 Mythical Beast Master Cerberus SCR	3.00	5.00
MP18-EN186 Artifact Mjollnir C	.10	.20
MP18-EN187 Grappler Angler C	.10	.20
MP18-EN188 Mahjong Munia Maidens C	.10	.20
MP18-EN189 D.D. Seeker C	.10	.20
MP18-EN190 Ghost Bird of Bewitchment R	.10	.20
MP18-EN191 Desmanian Devil R	.10	.20
MP18-EN192 Wattkinetic Puppeteer C	.10	.20
MP18-EN193 Inspector Boarder SCR	2.00	3.00
MP18-EN194 Overtex Qoatlus SR	.10	.20
MP18-EN195 Contact C C	.10	.20
MP18-EN196 Underclock Taker C	.10	.20
MP18-EN197 Flame Administrator C	.10	.20
MP18-EN198 Recovery Sorcerer C	.10	.20
MP18-EN199 Security Block C	.10	.20
MP18-EN200 Altergeist Hexstia SR	.10	.20
MP18-EN201 Mekk-Knight Spectrum Supreme UR	.10	.20
MP18-EN202 Saryuja Skull Dread SCR	15.00	18.00
MP18-EN203 Link Hole C	.10	.20
MP18-EN204 Fire Prison C	.10	.20
MP18-EN205 World Legacy Scars R	.10	.20
MP18-EN206 World Legacy Key R	.10	.20
MP18-EN207 Glory of the Noble Knights R	.10	.20
MP18-EN208 Power of the Guardians SR	.10	.20
MP18-EN209 Pendulum Paradox SCR	.10	.20
MP18-EN210 Hey, Trunade! SCR	1.50	2.00
MP18-EN211 Column Switch C	.10	.20
MP18-EN212 Trading Places C	.10	.20
MP18-EN213 Parallel Port Armor C	.10	.20
MP18-EN214 Cynet Refresh C	.10	.20
MP18-EN215 Borrel Cooling C	.10	.20
MP18-EN216 Altergeist Manifestation SR	.10	.20
MP18-EN217 World Legacy Whispers R	.10	.20
MP18-EN218 World Legacy's Secret UR	.60	1.00
MP18-EN219 Call of the Archfiend C	.10	.20
MP18-EN220 Dai Dance C	.10	.20
MP18-EN221 Showdown of the Secret Sense Scroll Techniques C	.10	.20
MP18-EN222 Parthian Shot C	.10	.20
MP18-EN223 Oops! C	.10	.20
MP18-EN224 Kuro-Obi Karate Spirit C	.10	.20
MP18-EN225 F.A. Auto Navigator C	.10	.20
MP18-EN226 F.A. Motorhome Transport C	.10	.20
MP18-EN227 F.A. City Grand Prix C	.10	.20
MP18-EN228 F.A. Test Run C	.10	.20
MP18-EN229 Heavymetalfoes Electrumite SCR	6.00	8.00
MP18-EN230 Scramble Egg C	.10	.20
MP18-EN231 Ruin, Queen of Oblivion C	.75	1.25
MP18-EN232 Demise, King of Armageddon C	.10	.20
MP18-EN233 End of the World C	.10	.20

2018 Yu-Gi-Oh Legendary Collection Kaiba Mega Pack 1st Edition

COMPLETE SET (113)	400.00	600.00
RELEASED ON MARCH 9, 2018		
LCKC-EN001 Blue-Eyes White Dragon (SDK Art) UR	2.00	3.50
LCKC-EN001 Blue-Eyes White Dragon (World Art) UR	2.00	3.50
LCKC-EN001 Blue-Eyes White Dragon (LOB Art) UR	2.00	3.50
LCKC-EN001 Blue-Eyes White Dragon (Tablet Art) UR	2.00	3.50
LCKC-EN002 La Jinn the Mystical Genie of the Lamp UR	2.00	3.50
LCKC-EN003 Vorse Raider UR	2.00	3.50
LCKC-EN004 Judge Man UR	2.00	3.50
LCKC-EN005 X-Head Cannon UR	2.00	3.50
LCKC-EN006 Y-Dragon Head UR	2.00	3.50
LCKC-EN007 Z-Metal Tank UR	2.00	3.50
LCKC-EN008 Blue-Eyes Shining Dragon SCR	3.00	5.00
LCKC-EN009 Kaibaman UR	2.00	3.50
LCKC-EN010 The White Stone of Legend SCR	3.00	5.00
LCKC-EN011 The White Stone of Ancients SCR	3.00	5.00
LCKC-EN012 Maiden with Eyes of Blue SCR	3.00	5.00
LCKC-EN013 Protector with Eyes of Blue UR	2.00	3.50
LCKC-EN014 Master with Eyes of Blue UR	2.00	3.50
LCKC-EN015 Sage with Eyes of Blue SCR	3.00	5.00
LCKC-EN016 Priestess with Eyes of Blue SCR	3.00	5.00
LCKC-EN017 Rider of the Storm Winds UR	2.00	3.50
LCKC-EN018 Dragon Spirit of White SCR	3.00	5.00
LCKC-EN019 A-Assault Core SCR	3.00	5.00
LCKC-EN020 B-Buster Drake SCR	3.00	5.00
LCKC-EN021 C-Crush Wyvern SCR	3.00	5.00
LCKC-EN022 Heavy Mech Support Platform UR	2.00	3.50
LCKC-EN023 Heavy Mech Support Armor UR	2.00	3.50
LCKC-EN024 Vampire Lord UR	2.00	3.50
LCKC-EN025 Burst Stream of Destruction SCR	3.00	5.00
LCKC-EN026 Polymerization SCR	3.00	5.00
LCKC-EN027 The Flute of Summoning Dragon UR	2.00	3.50
LCKC-EN028 The Melody of Awakening Dragon SCR	3.00	5.00
LCKC-EN029 Card of Demise SCR	15.00	18.00
LCKC-EN030 Fiend's Sanctuary SCR	3.00	5.00
LCKC-EN031 Majesty with Eyes of Blue SCR	3.00	5.00
LCKC-EN032 Enemy Controller SCR	3.00	5.00
LCKC-EN033 Ring of Defense UR	2.00	3.50
LCKC-EN034 Silver's Cry SCR	3.00	5.00
LCKC-EN035 Beacon of White SCR	3.00	5.00
LCKC-EN036 Mausoleum of White UR	2.00	3.50
LCKC-EN037 The Fang of Critias UR	2.00	3.50
LCKC-EN038 Soul Exchange UR	2.00	3.50
LCKC-EN039 Ancient Rules SCR	3.00	5.00
LCKC-EN040 Cost Down SCR	3.00	5.00
LCKC-EN041 Neutron Blast SCR	3.00	5.00
LCKC-EN042 Lullaby of Obedience SCR	3.00	5.00
LCKC-EN043 Shrink UR	2.00	3.50
LCKC-EN044 De-Fusion SCR	3.00	5.00
LCKC-EN045 Spell Reproduction UR	2.00	3.50
LCKC-EN046 Crush Card Virus (Original Art) UR	4.00	6.00
LCKC-EN046 Crush Card Virus (Alt Art) UR	4.00	6.00
LCKC-EN047 Deck Devastation Virus UR	2.00	3.50
LCKC-EN048 Eradicator Epidemic Virus UR	4.00	6.00
LCKC-EN049 Full Force Virus UR	2.00	3.50
LCKC-EN050 Ring of Destruction UR	2.00	3.50
LCKC-EN051 Castle of Dragon Souls UR	2.00	3.50
LCKC-EN052 Interdimensional Matter Transporter SCR	3.00	5.00
LCKC-EN053 Mirror Force UR	2.00	3.50
LCKC-EN054 Tyrant Wing UR	2.00	3.50
LCKC-EN055 Cloning UR	2.00	3.50
LCKC-EN056 Virus Cannon UR	2.00	3.50
LCKC-EN057 Blue-Eyes Ultimate Dragon SCR	3.00	5.00
LCKC-EN058 Blue-Eyes Twin Burst Dragon UR	2.00	3.50
LCKC-EN059 ABC-Dragon Buster SCR	3.00	5.00
LCKC-EN060 VW-Tiger Catapult UR	2.00	3.50
LCKC-EN061 XYZ-Dragon Cannon UR	2.00	3.50
LCKC-EN062 Mirror Force Dragon UR	2.00	3.50
LCKC-EN063 Tyrant Burst Dragon UR	2.00	3.50
LCKC-EN064 Doom Virus Dragon UR	2.00	3.50
LCKC-EN065 Dragon Master Knight SCR	3.00	5.00
LCKC-EN066 Azure-Eyes Silver Dragon SCR	3.00	5.00
LCKC-EN067 Thunder Dragon UR	2.00	3.50
LCKC-EN068 Dark Armed Dragon SCR	3.00	5.00
LCKC-EN069 Tiger Dragon UR	2.00	3.50
LCKC-EN070 Ancient Fairy Dragon UR	4.00	6.00
LCKC-EN071 Beelze of the Diabolic Dragons SCR	10.00	15.00
LCKC-EN072 Dragon Ravine SCR	3.00	5.00
LCKC-EN073 Dragonic Tactics SCR	3.00	5.00
LCKC-EN074 Return of the Dragon Lords SCR	3.00	5.00
LCKC-EN075 Dragon Shrine SCR	3.00	5.00
LCKC-EN076 Trade-In SCR	3.00	5.00
LCKC-EN077 Droll & Lock Bird UR	10.00	15.00
LCKC-EN078 Ghost Ogre & Snow Rabbit UR	10.00	15.00
LCKC-EN079 Ghost Reaper & Winter Cherries UR	4.00	6.00
LCKC-EN080 Ash Blossom & Joyous Spring UR	40.00	45.00
LCKC-EN081 D.D. Crow UR	2.00	3.50
LCKC-EN082 V-Tiger Jet UR	2.00	3.50
LCKC-EN083 W-Wing Catapult UR	2.00	3.50
LCKC-EN084 Dragunity Dux UR	2.00	3.50
LCKC-EN085 Dragunity Legionnaire UR	2.00	3.50
LCKC-EN086 Dragunity Phalanx UR	2.00	3.50
LCKC-EN087 Number S39: Utopia the Lightning SCR	10.00	15.00
LCKC-EN088 Raigeki UR	20.00	25.00
LCKC-EN089 Fusion Sage UR	2.00	3.50
LCKC-EN090 Terraforming SCR	8.00	12.00
LCKC-EN091 Double Summon UR	6.00	10.00
LCKC-EN092 Cards of Consonance SCR	3.00	5.00
LCKC-EN093 The Monarchs Stormforth UR	2.00	3.50
LCKC-EN094 Chain Disappearance SCR	3.00	5.00
LCKC-EN095 Fiendish Chain UR	2.00	3.50
LCKC-EN096 Parrot Dragon UR	2.00	3.50
LCKC-EN097 Giant Red Seasnake UR	2.00	3.50
LCKC-EN098 Mikazukinoyaiba UR	2.00	3.50
LCKC-EN099 Warrior Elimination UR	2.00	3.50
LCKC-EN100 Exile of the Wicked UR	2.00	3.50
LCKC-EN101 Delinquent Duo SCR	3.00	5.00
LCKC-EN102 White Hole SCR	3.00	5.00
LCKC-EN103 Call of the Grave SCR	3.00	5.00
LCKC-EN104 Anti Raigeki SCR	3.00	5.00
LCKC-EN105 Just Desserts UR	2.00	3.50
LCKC-EN106 Goddess of Sweet Revenge SCR	3.00	5.00
LCKC-EN107 The King of D. SCR	3.00	5.00
LCKC-EN108 Destruction Dragon SCR	3.00	5.00
LCKC-EN109 Dragon Revival Rhapsody SCR	3.00	5.00
LCKC-EN110 Loop of Destruction SCR	3.00	5.00

2016 Yu-Gi-Oh Millennium Pack 1st Edition

COMPLETE SET (48)	30.00	40.00
BOOSTER BOX (36 PACKS)	40.00	50.00
BOOSTER PACK (5 CARDS)	1.00	1.50
RELEASED ON APRIL 15, 2016		
MIL1EN001 The Winged Dragon of Ra - Immortal Phoenix UR	3.00	4.00
MIL1EN002 Curse of Dragonfire UR	.20	.35
MIL1EN003 Holding Arms SR	.25	.40
MIL1EN004 Holding Legs SR	.75	1.25
MIL1EN005 Gandora the Dragon of Destruction C	.10	.20
MIL1EN006 Gilford the Lightning C	.10	.20
MIL1EN007 Exodius the Ultimate Forbidden Lord C	.10	.20
MIL1EN008 Relinquished C	.10	.20
MIL1EN009 Dark Master - Zorc C	.10	.20
MIL1EN010 Sky Galloping Gaia the Dragon Champion SR	.30	.50
MIL1EN011 B. Skull Dragon C	.10	.20
MIL1EN012 Five-Headed Dragon C	.10	.20
MIL1EN013 Rebellion UR	.25	.40
MIL1EN014 Card of Demise UR	30.00	35.00
MIL1EN015 Left Arm Offering SR	5.00	7.00
MIL1EN016 The True Name SR	1.25	2.00
MIL1EN017 Symbol of Friendship R	.20	.35
MIL1EN018 Shrink C	.10	.20
MIL1EN019 Scapegoat C	.10	.20
MIL1EN020 Black Illusion Ritual C	.10	.20
MIL1EN021 Contract with the Dark Master C	.10	.20
MIL1EN022 Trap Hole of Spikes SR	.75	1.25
MIL1EN023 Ring of Destruction C	.10	.20
MIL1EN024 Nightmare Wheel C	.10	.20
MIL1EN025 Celtic Guardian R	.20	.35
MIL1EN026 Gaia The Fierce Knight R	.20	.35
MIL1EN027 Red-Eyes B. Dragon C	.10	.20
MIL1EN028 Summoned Skull C	.10	.20
MIL1EN029 La Jinn the Mystical Genie of the Lamp C	.10	.20
MIL1EN030 Launcher Spider C	.10	.20
MIL1EN031 Tiger Axe C	.10	.20
MIL1EN032 Vorse Raider C	.10	.20
MIL1EN033 Pendulum Machine C	.10	.20
MIL1EN034 Kuriboh C	.10	.20
MIL1EN035 Red-Eyes Black Metal Dragon C	.10	.20
MIL1EN036 Panther Warrior R	.20	.35
MIL1EN037 Viser Des C	.10	.20
MIL1EN038 Flame Swordsman R	.20	.35
MIL1EN039 Thousand Dragon R	.20	.35
MIL1EN040 XYZ-Dragon Cannon R	.20	.35
MIL1EN041 Dark Paladin C	.10	.20
MIL1EN042 Toon World C	.10	.20
MIL1EN043 Spiral Spear Strike C	.10	.20
MIL1EN044 Acid Trap Hole R	.20	.35
MIL1EN045 Metalmorph C	.10	.20
MIL1EN046 Widespread Ruin R	.20	.35
MIL1EN047 Crush Card Virus C	.10	.20
MIL1EN048 Kunai with Chain R	.20	.35

2011 Yu-Gi-Oh 3-D Bonds Beyond Time Movie

BOOSTER BOX (20 PACKS)	40.00	75.00
BOOSTER PACK (5 CARDS)	2.50	4.00
YMP1EN001 Malefic Red-Eyes B. Dragon SCR	.75	2.00
YMP1EN002 Malefic Blue-Eyes White Dragon SCR	.75	2.00
YMP1EN003 Malefic Parallel Gear SCR	.75	2.00
YMP1EN004 Malefic Cyber End Dragon SCR	2.00	5.00
YMP1EN005 Malefic Rainbow Dragon SCR	.75	2.00
YMP1EN006 Junk Gardna SCR	.75	2.00
YMP1EN007 Malefic Paradox Dragon SCR	.75	2.00
YMP1EN008 Malefic World SCR	.75	2.00
YMP1EN009 Malefic Claw Stream SCR	.10	.30

2016 Yu-Gi-Oh The Dark Side of Dimensions Movie Pack 1st Edition

COMPLETE SET (57)	40.00	60.00
BOOSTER BOX (24 PACKS)	60.00	80.00
BOOSTER PACK (5 CARDS)	2.00	5.00
RELEASED ON JULY 21, 2016		
MVP1EN001 Neo Blue Eyes Ultimate Dragon UR	1.50	2.50
MVP1EN002 Kaiser Vorse Raider UR	.15	.25
MVP1EN003 Assault Wyvern UR	.15	.25
MVP1EN004 Blue Eyes Chaos MAX Dragon UR	3.00	5.00
MVP1EN005 Deep Eyes White Dragon UR	1.00	1.50
MVP1EN006 Pandemic Dragon UR	.15	.25
MVP1EN007 Dragons Fighting Spirit UR	.15	.25
MVP1EN008 Chaos Form UR	4.00	6.00
MVP1EN009 Induced Explosion UR	.15	.25
MVP1EN010 Counter Gate UR	.15	.25
MVP1EN011 Krystal Avatar UR	.15	.25
MVP1EN012 Sentry Soldier of Stone UR	.15	.25
MVP1EN013 Marshmacaron UR	.15	.25
MVP1EN014 Berry Magician Girl UR	1.00	1.50
MVP1EN015 Apple Magician Girl UR	.60	1.00
MVP1EN016 Kiwi Magician Girl UR	.75	1.25
MVP1EN017 Silver Gadget UR	2.00	3.00
MVP1EN018 Gold Gadget UR	2.00	3.00
MVP1EN019 Dark Magic Veil UR	1.00	1.50
MVP1EN020 Magical Contract Door UR	.15	.25
MVP1EN021 Dimension Reflector UR	.15	.25
MVP1EN022 Dig of Destiny UR	.15	.25
MVP1EN023 Dimension Sphinx UR	.15	.25
MVP1EN024 Dimension Guardian UR	.75	1.25
MVP1EN025 Dimension Mirage UR	.15	.25
MVP1EN026 Dark Horizon UR	.15	.25
MVP1EN027 Metamorphortress UR	.15	.25
MVP1EN028 Magicians Defense UR	.60	1.00
MVP1EN029 Final Geas UR	.15	.25
MVP1EN030 Metalhold the Moving Blockade UR	.15	.25
MVP1EN031 Spiritual Swords of Revealing Light UR	.15	.25
MVP1EN032 Vijam the Cubic Seed UR	.50	.75
MVP1EN033 Dark Garnex the Cubic Beast UR	.15	.25
MVP1EN034 Blade Garoodia the Cubic Beast UR	.15	.25
MVP1EN035 Buster Gundil the Cubic Behemoth UR	.15	.25
MVP1EN036 Geira Guile the Cubic King UR	.15	.25
MVP1EN037 Vulcan Dragni the Cubic King UR	.15	.25
MVP1EN038 Indiora Doom Volt the Cubic Emperor UR	.15	.25
MVP1EN039 Crimson Nova the Dark Cubic Lord UR	.40	.60
MVP1EN040 Crimson Nova Trinity the Dark Cubic Lord UR	.40	.60
MVP1EN041 Cubic Karma UR	.75	1.25
MVP1EN042 Cubic Wave UR	.15	.25
MVP1EN043 Cubic Rebirth UR	.15	.25
MVP1EN044 Cubic Mandala UR	.15	.25
MVP1EN045 Unification of the Cubic Lords UR	.15	.25
MVP1EN046 Blue Eyes Alternative White Dragon UR	10.00	12.00
MVP1EN047 Clear Kuriboh UR	.15	.25
MVP1EN048 Celtic Guard of Noble Arms UR	.15	.25
MVP1EN049 GandoraX the Dragon of Demolition UR	.40	.60
MVP1EN050 Lord Gaia the Fierce Knight UR	.15	.25
MVP1EN051 Lemon Magician Girl UR	.15	.25
MVP1EN052 Chocolate Magician Girl UR	2.00	3.00
MVP1EN053 Palladium Oracle Mahad UR	1.50	2.50
MVP1EN054 Dark Magician UR	.75	1.25
MVP1EN055 BlueEyes White Dragon UR	.75	1.25
MVP1EN056 Dark Magician Girl UR	1.50	2.50
MVP1EN057 Slifer the Sky Dragon UR	.75	1.25

2017 Yu-Gi-Oh The Dark Side of Dimensions Movie Pack Gold Edition

COMPLETE SET (61)	40.00	65.00
BOOSTER BOX (30 PACKS)	70.00	100.00
MINI DISPLAY BOX CONTAINS 3 BOOSTERS WITH 5 CARDS PER BOOSTER	10.00	12.00
RELEASED ON JANUARY 13, 2017		
MVP1ENG01 Neo Blue Eyes Ultimate Dragon GR	1.75	2.50
MVP1ENG02 Kaiser Vorse Raider GR	.30	.50
MVP1ENG03 Assault Wyvern GR	.30	.50
MVP1ENG04 Blue Eyes Chaos MAX Dragon GR	2.00	3.00
MVP1ENG05 Deep Eyes White Dragon GR	.30	.50
MVP1ENG06 Pandemic Dragon GR	.30	.50
MVP1ENG07 Dragon's Fighting Spirit GR	.30	.50
MVP1ENG08 Chaos Form GR	2.00	3.50
MVP1ENG09 Induced Explosion GR	.30	.50
MVP1ENG10 Counter Gate GR	.30	.50
MVP1ENG11 Krystal Avatar GR	.30	.50
MVP1ENG12 Sentry Soldier of Stone GR	.30	.50
MVP1ENG13 Marshmacaron GR	.30	.50
MVP1ENG14 Berry Magician Girl GR	.50	.75
MVP1ENG15 Apple Magician Girl GR	.50	.75
MVP1ENG16 Kiwi Magician Girl GR	.60	1.00
MVP1ENG17 Silver Gadget GR	1.00	1.50
MVP1ENG18 Gold Gadget GR	1.00	1.50
MVP1ENG19 Dark Magic Veil GR	1.25	2.00
MVP1ENG20 Magical Contract Door GR	.30	.50

MVP1ENG21 Dimension Reflector GR .30 .50
MVP1ENG22 Dig of Destiny GR .30 .50
MVP1ENG23 Dimension Sphinx GR .30 .50
MVP1ENG24 Dimension Guardian GR .30 .50
MVP1ENG25 Dimension Mirage GR .30 .50
MVP1ENG26 Dark Horizon GR .30 .50
MVP1ENG27 Metamorphortress GR .30 .50
MVP1ENG28 Magicians' Defense GR .30 .50
MVP1ENG29 Final Geas GR .30 .50
MVP1ENG30 Metalhold the Moving Blockade GR .30 .50
MVP1ENG31 Spiritual Swords of Revealing Light GR .30 .50
MVP1ENG32 Vijam the Cubic Seed GR .30 .50
MVP1ENG33 Dark Garnex the Cubic Beast GR .30 .50
MVP1ENG34 Blade Garoodia the Cubic Beast GR .30 .50
MVP1ENG35 Buster Gundil the Cubic Behemoth GR .30 .50
MVP1ENG36 Geira Guile the Cubic King GR .30 .50
MVP1ENG37 Vulcan Dragni the Cubic King GR .30 .50
MVP1ENG38 Indiora Doom Volt the Cubic Emperor GR .30 .50
MVP1ENG39 Crimson Nova the Dark Cubic Lord GR .30 .50
MVP1ENG40 Crimson Nova Trinity the Dark Cubic Lord GR .30 .50
MVP1ENG41 Cubic Karma GR .30 .50
MVP1ENG42 Cubic Wave GR .30 .50
MVP1ENG43 Cubic Rebirth GR .30 .50
MVP1ENG44 Cubic Mandala GR .30 .50
MVP1ENG45 Unification of the Cubic Lords GR .30 .50
MVP1ENG46 Blue Eyes Alternative White Dragon GR 9.00 11.00
MVP1ENG47 Clear Kuriboh GR .30 .50
MVP1ENG48 Celtic Guard of Noble Arms GR .30 .50
MVP1ENG49 GandoraX the Dragon of Demolition GR .30 .50
MVP1ENG50 Lord Gaia the Fierce Knight GR .30 .50
MVP1ENG51 Lemon Magician Girl GR .50 .75
MVP1ENG52 Chocolate Magician Girl GR .30 .50
MVP1ENG53 Palladium Oracle Mahad GR .75 1.25
MVP1ENG54 Dark Magician GR .60 1.00
MVP1ENG55 BlueEyes White Dragon GR .60 1.00
MVP1ENG56 Dark Magician Girl GR .75 1.25
MVP1ENG57 Slifer the Sky Dragon GR .60 1.00
MVP1ENGV1 Duza the Meteor Cubic Vessel GSR 1.25 2.00
MVP1ENGV2 Krystal Dragon GSR .75 1.25
MVP1ENGV3 Dark Magician GSR 2.00 3.00
MVP1ENGV4 Blue Eyes White Dragon GSR 2.00 3.50

2016 Yu-Gi-Oh OTS Tournament Pack 1

COMPLETE SET (27) 100.00 120.00
BOOSTER BOX (100 PACKS) 350.00 500.00
BOOSTER PACK (3 CARDS) 2.50 6.00
RELEASED ON
OP01EN001 Bountiful Artemis UTR 14.00 17.00
OP01EN002 Vanity's Fiend UTR 20.00 25.00
OP01EN003 Masked HERO Dark Law UTR 20.00 25.00
OP01EN004 Droll & Lock Bird SR 8.00 10.00
OP01EN005 Infernoid Patrulea SR .75 1.25
OP01EN006 Performapal Lizardraw SR .75 1.25
OP01EN007 Performapal Skullcrobat Joker SR 5.00 7.00
OP01EN008 Performapal Monkeyboard SR .50 .75
OP01EN009 Performapal Guitartle SR .60 1.00
OP01EN010 Dinoster Power, the Mighty Dracoslayer SR 1.25 2.00
OP01EN011 Anti-Spell Fragrance SR 10.00 13.00
OP01EN012 Imperial Iron Wall SR 1.25 2.00
OP01EN013 Typhoon SR 2.00 3.00
OP01EN014 Skull Servant C 2.00 3.00
OP01EN015 Battle Warrior C .60 1.00
OP01EN016 Mezuki C 1.25 2.00
OP01EN017 The White Stone of Legend C .75 1.25
OP01EN018 Flying "C" C .75 1.25
OP01EN019 Zombie Warrior C 2.00 3.00
OP01EN020 Michael, the Arch-Lightsworn C 1.25 2.00
OP01EN021 Cyber Dragon Nova C 2.50 4.00
OP01EN022 Mage Power C 1.25 2.00
OP01EN023 Offerings to the Doomed C .15 .25
OP01EN024 Monster Gate C .30 .50
OP01EN025 Allure of Darkness C 3.00 5.00
OP01EN026 Summoning Curse C .50 .75
OP01EN027 Advance Zone C+D2 .40 .60

2016 Yu-Gi-Oh OTS Tournament Pack 2

COMPLETE SET (27) 110.00 135.00
BOOSTER BOX (100 PACKS) 350.00 500.00
BOOSTER PACK (3 CARDS) 2.50 6.00
RELEASED ON JULY 22, 2016
OP02EN001 Fog King UTR 6.00 8.00
OP02EN002 Kuraz the Light Monarch UTR 12.00 16.00
OP02EN003 Raigeki UTR 45.00 50.00
OP02EN004 Gameciel the Sea Turtle Kaiju SR 7.00 10.00
OP02EN005 Fiendish Rhino Warrior SR .75 1.25
OP02EN006 Mithra the Thunder Vassal SR .75 1.25
OP02EN007 The Phantom Knights of Ragged Gloves SR .60 1.00
OP02EN008 Super Quantum Blue Layer SR .60 1.00
OP02EN009 System Down SR 1.00 1.50
OP02EN010 Mask of Restrict SR 4.00 5.00
OP02EN011 Ninjitsu Art of Transformation SR .40 .75
OP02EN012 Armor Ninjitsu Art of Freezing SR .40 .75
OP02EN013 The Prime Monarch SR 2.00 3.00
OP02EN014 Takuhee C .75 1.25
OP02EN015 Temple of Skulls C .60 1.00
OP02EN016 Dark Eradicator Warlock C .60 1.00
OP02EN017 Infernity Archfiend C .30 .50
OP02EN018 Cyber Dragon Core C 1.50 2.50
OP02EN019 Galaxy Dragon C .25 .40
OP02EN020 Prediction Princess Coinorma C .50 .75
OP02EN021 Prediction Princess Tarotrei C .60 1.00
OP02EN022 Skullbird C 1.00 1.50
OP02EN023 United We Stand C 2.00 3.00
OP02EN024 The Melody of Awakening Dragon C 1.00 1.50
OP02EN025 Prediction Ritual C .40 .60
OP02EN026 Ninjitsu Art of SuperTransformation C .40 .75
OP02EN027 Wiretap C .40 .60

2008 Yu-Gi-Oh Retro Pack 1

COMPLETE SET (100) 400.00 500.00
BOOSTER BOX (8 SETS) 150.00 200.00
SET (3 PACKS) 25.00 30.00
BOOSTER PACK (9 CARDS) 5.00 6.00
RELEASED ON JULY 8, 2008
RP010 Blue-Eyes Ultimate Dragon SCR 15.00 30.00
RP011 Blue-Eyes White Dragon UR 30.00 60.00
RP013 Dark Magician UR 15.00 30.00
RP015 Raigeki UR 115.00 140.00
RP016 Fissure R 1.50 4.00
RP0111 Red-Eyes B. Dragon UR 8.00 20.00
RP0112 Swords of Revealing Light SR 2.50 6.00
RP0116 Monster Reborn SR 6.00 15.00
RP0117 Right Leg of the Forbidden One R 5.00 12.00
RP0118 Left Leg of the Forbidden One R 5.00 12.00
RP0119 Right Arm of the Forbidden One R 5.00 12.00
RP0120 Left Arm of the Forbidden One R 5.00 12.00
RP0121 Exodia the Forbidden One UR 10.00 25.00
RP0122 Gaia the Dragon Champion SR 2.00 5.00
RP0123 Gate Guardian UR 10.00 25.00
RP0124 Summoned Skull SR 2.50 6.00
RP0126 Harpie Lady Sisters R 1.00 2.50
RP0128 B. Skull Dragon R 5.00 12.00
RP0130 Sanga of the Thunder R 2.00 5.00
RP0131 Kazejin R 1.50 4.00
RP0132 Suijin R 1.50 4.00
RP0133 Magician of Faith R 1.50 4.00
RP0135 Time Wizard SR 5.00 12.00
RP0136 Sangan SR 8.00 20.00
RP0137 Kuriboh SR 2.00 5.00
RP0138 Catapult Turtle SR 2.00 5.00
RP0144 Barrel Dragon R 2.50 6.00
RP0145 Solemn Judgment SR 8.00 20.00
RP0148 Heavy Storm R 1.25 3.00
RP0150 Blue-Eyes Toon Dragon R 4.00 10.00
RP0151 Axe of Despair R 1.25 3.00
RP0154 Relinquished UR 3.00 8.00
RP0159 Painful Choice R 4.00 10.00
RP0161 Megamorph R 1.00 2.50
RP0182 Messenger of Peace R 2.00 5.00
RP0184 Card Destruction R 2.50 6.00
RP0185 La Jinn the Mystical Genie of the Lamp SR 20.00 35.00
RP0186 Lord of D. R 1.00 2.50
RP0187 The Flute of Summoning Dragon R 1.50 4.00
RP0188 Graceful Charity R 2.00 5.00
RP0190 Scapegoat UR 40.00 70.00
RP0191 Blast Sphere SCR 20.00 40.00
RP0192 Copycat SCR 50.00 80.00
RP0193 Relieve Monster SCR 10.00 25.00
RP0194 Cloning SCR 15.00 30.00
RP0195 Kaibaman SCR 20.00 40.00
RP0196 Cyber Harpie Lady SCR 150.00 250.00
RP0197 Amazoness Chain Master SCR 35.00 70.00
RP0198 Embodiment of Apophis SCR 20.00 40.00
RP0199 Exchange of the Spirit SCR 50.00 80.00
RP01100 Ancient Lamp SCR 25.00 50.00

2009 Yu-Gi-Oh Retro Pack 2

COMPLETE SET (101) 300.00 500.00
BOOSTER BOX (8 SETS) 150.00 300.00
SET (3 PACKS) 10.00 25.00
BOOSTER PACK (9 CARDS) 5.00 12.00
RELEASED ON JULY 28, 2009
RP02EN000 Gorz the Emissary of Darkness SCR 1.25 3.00
RP02EN001 Jinzo UR 2.50 6.00
RP02EN002 Parasite Paracide C .10 .30
RP02EN003 Lightforce Sword C .10 .30
RP02EN004 Chain Destruction R .75 2.00
RP02EN005 Dust Tornado C .10 .30
RP02EN006 Call of the Haunted C .10 .30
RP02EN007 Mirror Wall UR 1.25 3.00
RP02EN008 Appropriate C .10 .30
RP02EN009 Ceasefire R .75 2.00
RP02EN010 Magical Hats R 1.25 3.00
RP02EN011 Nobleman of Crossout C .10 .30
RP02EN012 Premature Burial C .10 .30
RP02EN013 Buster Blader SR 1.25 3.00
RP02EN014 Skull Invitation C .10 .30
RP02EN015 Limiter Removal SR 1.50 4.00
RP02EN016 Insect Imitation C .10 .30
RP02EN017 Magic Drain C .10 .30
RP02EN018 Gravity Bind C .10 .30
RP02EN019 The Legendary Fisherman R .60 1.50
RP02EN020 Thousand-Eyes Idol C .10 .30
RP02EN021 Thousand-Eyes Restrict UR 8.00 20.00
RP02EN022 4 Starred Ladybug of Doom C .10 .30
RP02EN023 Mad Sword Beast C .10 .30
RP02EN024 Goblin Attack Force C .10 .30
RP02EN025 Gearfried the Iron Knight R .60 1.50
RP02EN026 Gemini Elf C .10 .30
RP02EN027 The Masked Beast SR .40 1.00
RP02EN028 Revival Jam R 1.00 2.50
RP02EN029 Melchid the Four-Face Beast C .10 .30
RP02EN030 Curse of the Masked Beast C .10 .30
RP02EN031 Mask of Restrict C 8.00 20.00
RP02EN032 Lightning Blade C .10 .30
RP02EN033 Tornado Wall C .10 .30
RP02EN034 Torrential Tribute C .10 .30
RP02EN035 Infinite Cards R 2.00 5.00
RP02EN036 Jam Defender SR .60 1.50
RP02EN037 Card of Safe Return C .10 .30
RP02EN038 United We Stand UR 2.50 6.00
RP02EN039 Mage Power R .75 2.00
RP02EN040 Kycoo the Ghost Destroyer C .10 .30
RP02EN041 Bazoo the Soul-Eater C .10 .30
RP02EN042 Dark Necrofear SR .40 1.00
RP02EN043 Gilasaurus C .10 .30
RP02EN044 Dark Spirit of the Silent C .10 .30
RP02EN045 Destiny Board SR 2.00 5.00
RP02EN046 Spirit Message I C .10 .30
RP02EN047 Spirit Message N C .10 .30
RP02EN048 Spirit Message A C .10 .30
RP02EN049 Spirit Message L C .10 .30
RP02EN050 Magic Cylinder R .60 1.50
RP02EN051 Yata-Garasu C .10 .30
RP02EN052 Dark Ruler Ha Des UR .75 2.00
RP02EN053 Opticlops C .10 .30
RP02EN054 Freed the Matchless General R .60 1.50
RP02EN055 Emergency Provisions C .10 .30
RP02EN056 Tyrant Dragon SR 1.00 2.50
RP02EN057 Spear Dragon C .10 .30
RP02EN058 Airknight Parshath R 1.25 3.00
RP02EN059 Yamata Dragon R .40 1.00
RP02EN060 Hino-Kagu-Tsuchi SR 2.50 6.00
RP02EN061 Asura Priest C .10 .30
RP02EN062 A Legendary Ocean C .10 .30
RP02EN063 Creature Swap C .10 .30
RP02EN064 Bottomless Trap Hole C .50 1.25
RP02EN065 Injection Fairy Lily UR 1.25 3.00
RP02EN066 Ring of Destruction SCR 6.00 15.00
RP02EN067 Guardian Sphinx C .10 .30
RP02EN068 Don Zaloog R 1.25 3.00
RP02EN069 Book of Taiyou C .10 .30
RP02EN070 Book of Moon C .10 .30
RP02EN071 Reckless Greed C .10 .30
RP02EN072 Dark Jeroid R .40 1.00
RP02EN073 Newdoria R .60 1.50
RP02EN074 Helpoemer UR 1.25 3.00
RP02EN075 Gravekeeper's Spy C .10 .30
RP02EN076 Gravekeeper's Chief C .10 .30
RP02EN077 Gravekeeper's Assailant C .10 .30
RP02EN078 Dark Room of Nightmare C .10 .30
RP02EN079 Necrovalley R 1.50 4.00
RP02EN080 Barrel Behind the Door C .10 .30
RP02EN081 Nightmare Wheel R 1.50 4.00
RP02EN082 Lava Golem SR .75 2.00
RP02EN083 Morphing Jar R 2.50 6.00
RP02EN084 Royal Decree R 1.25 3.00
RP02EN085 Swift Gaia the Fierce Knight UR 1.00 2.50
RP02EN086 Obnoxious Celtic Guardian R .40 1.00
RP02EN087 Kaiser Sea Horse R .40 1.00
RP02EN088 Insect Queen SR .60 1.50
RP02EN089 Alpha The Magnet Warrior R .60 1.50
RP02EN090 Beta The Magnet Warrior R .60 1.50
RP02EN091 Gamma The Magnet Warrior R .60 1.50
RP02EN092 Valkyrion the Magna Warrior SCR 10.00 25.00
RP02EN093 Harpie's Pet Dragon SCR 20.00 40.00
RP02EN094 Archfiend of Gilfer SCR 3.00 8.00
RP02EN095 Light and Darkness Dragon SCR 20.00 45.00
RP02EN096 Blue-Eyes Shining Dragon SCR 150.00 225.00
RP02EN097 Dragon Master Knight SCR 50.00 90.00
RP02EN098 Victory Dragon SCR 8.00 20.00
RP02EN099 Green Baboon, Defender of the Forest SCR 4.00 10.00
RP02EN100 Dreadscythe Harvester SCR 1.00 2.50

2013 Yu-Gi-Oh Star Pack 2013 1st Edition

COMPLETE SET (50)
BOOSTER BOX (50 PACKS) 80.00 100.00
BOOSTER PACK (3 CARDS) 3.00 4.00
*STARFOIL: .6X TO 1.5X BASIC CARDS
SP13001 Zubaba Knight C .25 .75
SP13002 Gagaga Magician C .25 .75
SP13003 Gogogo Golem C .25 .75
SP13004 Achacha Archer C .25 .75
SP13005 Goblindbergh C .60 1.50
SP13006 Big Jaws C .25 .75
SP13007 Skull Kraken C .25 .75
SP13008 Galaxy-Eyes Photon Dragon C 1.50 4.00
SP13009 Kagetokage C 1.25 3.00
SP13010 Friller Rabca C .75 2.00
SP13011 Needle Sunfish C .25 .75
SP13012 Photon Cerberus C .25 .75
SP13013 Kurivolt C .25 .75
SP13014 Darklon C .25 .75
SP13015 Flame Armor Ninja C .25 .75
SP13016 Air Armor Ninja C .25 .75
SP13017 Aqua Armor Ninja C .25 .75
SP13018 Earth Armor Ninja C .25 .75
SP13019 Flelf C .40 1.00
SP13020 Chewbone C .50 1.25
SP13021 Number 39: Utopia C .50 1.25
SP13022 Grenosaurus C .25 .75
SP13023 No. 17: Leviathan Dragon .50 1.25
SP13024 Submersible Aero Shark .25 .75
SP13025 Number 34: Terror-Byte C .75 2.00
SP13026 Number 10: Illumiknight C .75 2.00
SP13027 Baby Tiragon C .25 .75
SP13028 Number 83: Galaxy Queen C .50 1.25
SP13029 Black Ray Lancer C .60 1.50
SP13030 Number 12: Crimson Shadow Armor Ninja C .25 .75
SP13031 Number 96: Dark Mist C .75 2.00
SP13032 Wonder Wand C .40 1.00
SP13033 Infected Mail C .25 .75
SP13034 Ego Boost C .25 .75
SP13035 Monster Slots C .25 .75
SP13036 Heartfelt Appeal C .25 .75
SP13037 Icy Crevasse C .25 .75
SP13038 Nitwit Outwit C .25 .75
SP13039 Faith Bird C .25 .75
SP13040 Gilford the Lightning C .25 .75
SP13041 Gandora the Dragon .25 .75
SP13042 Metalmorph C .25 .75
SP13043 Arcana - Dark Ruler .25 .75
SP13044 Arcana - Light Ruler .60 1.50
SP13045 Barbaroid, Battle Machine 6.00 15.00
SP13046 Elemental HERO Escuridao C 2.00 5.00
SP13047 Meklord Emperor Wisel C .25 .75
SP13048 Seven Swords Warrior C .25 .75
SP13049 Catapult Warrior C .75 2.00
SP13050 One for One C .25 .75

2014 Yu-Gi-Oh Star Pack 2014 1st Edition

COMPLETE SET (50)
BOOSTER BOX (50 PACKS) 30.00 40.00
BOOSTER PACK (3 CARDS) 2.00 3.00
*STARFOIL: .5X TO 1.2X BASIC CARDS
RELEASED ON FEBRUARY 21, 2014
SP14001 Gogogo Golem C .10 .30
SP14002 Daybreaker C .10 .30
SP14003 Gogogo Giant C .10 .30
SP14004 ZW - Unicorn Spear C .10 .30
SP14005 Shocktopus C .10 .30

SP14006 Photon Lizard C	.10	.30
SP14007 Photon Thrasher C	.75	2.00
SP14008 Photon Crusher C	.10	.30
SP14009 Reverse Breaker C	.10	.30
SP14010 Tasuke Knight C	.10	.30
SP14011 Gagaga Gardna C	.10	.30
SP14012 Cardcar D C	.40	1.00
SP14013 Hammer Shark C	.10	.30
SP14014 Jumbo Drill C	.10	.30
SP14015 Rocket Arrow Express C	.10	.30
SP14016 Aye-Iron C	.10	.30
SP14017 Tin Goldfish C	1.25	3.00
SP14018 Dododo Warrior C	.10	.30
SP14019 Zubaba Buster C	.10	.30
SP14020 Twin Photon Lizard C	.10	.30
SP14021 Thunder End Dragon C	2.00	5.00
SP14022 Number C39: Utopia Ray C	.10	.30
SP14023 Number 32: Shark Drake C	.50	1.25
SP14024 Photon Strike Bounzer C	.75	2.00
SP14025 Photon Papilloperative C	.40	1.00
SP14026 Number 25: Force Focus C	.40	1.00
SP14027 Number 7: Lucky Straight C	.50	1.25
SP14028 Muzurhythm the String Djinn C	.10	.30
SP14029 Temtempo the Percussion Djinn C	.10	.30
SP14030 Melomelody the Brass Djinn C	.10	.30
SP14031 Maestroke the Symphony Djinn C	.50	1.25
SP14032 Cross Attack C	.10	.30
SP14033 Gagagabolt C	.10	.30
SP14034 Star Light, Star Bright C	.10	.30
SP14035 Bound Wand C	.10	.30
SP14036 Mini-Guts C	.10	.30
SP14037 Xyz Effect C	.10	.30
SP14038 Xyz Reflect C	.20	.60
SP14039 Morphing Jar #2 C	.10	.30
SP14040 Magical Merchant C	.50	1.25
SP14041 Reasoning C	1.00	2.50
SP14042 Ma'at C	.10	.30
SP14043 Chimeratech Overdragon C	.10	.30
SP14044 Malefic Truth Dragon C	.10	.30
SP14045 Guldfaxe of the Nordic Beasts C	.50	1.25
SP14046 Svartalf of the Nordic Alfar C	.10	.30
SP14047 Valkyrie of the Nordic Ascendant C	1.00	2.50
SP14048 Thor, Lord of the Aesir C	.60	1.50
SP14049 Loki, Lord of the Aesir C	.10	.30
SP14050 Odin, Father of the Aesir C	.50	1.25

2015 Yu-Gi-Oh Star Pack ARC-V

COMPLETE SET (50)	25.00	35.00
BOOSTER BOX	30.00	40.00
BOOSTER PACK (3 CARDS)	1.00	2.50
RELEASED ON JUNE 12, 2015		
SP15EN001 Gem-Knight Tourmaline C	.60	1.00
SP15EN002 Swamp Battleguard C	.10	.20
SP15EN003 Lava Battleguard C	.10	.20
SP15EN004 Mobius the Frost Monarch C	.20	.35
SP15EN005 XX-Saber Fulhelmknight C	.10	.20
SP15EN006 XX-Saber Boggart Knight C	.40	.60
SP15EN007 Constellar Algiedi C	.10	.20
SP15EN008 Constellar Kaus C	.20	.35
SP15EN009 Mobius the Mega Monarch C	1.75	2.15
SP15EN010 Stargazer Magician C	.25	.40
SP15EN011 Timegazer Magician C	.40	.60
SP15EN012 Odd-Eyes Pendulum Dragon C	.10	.20
SP15EN013 Performapal Whip Snake C	.10	.20
SP15EN014 Performapal Sword Fish C	.10	.20
SP15EN015 Performapal Hip Hippo C	.10	.20
SP15EN016 Performapal Kaleidoscorp C	.10	.20
SP15EN017 Superheavy Samurai Big Benkei C	.75	1.15
SP15EN018 Aria the Melodious Diva C	.10	.20
SP15EN019 Mozarta the Melodious Maestra C	.20	.30
SP15EN020 Battleguard King C	.10	.20
SP15EN021 Performapal Trampolynx C	.10	.20
SP15EN022 Edge Imp Sabres C	4.00	4.50
SP15EN023 Fluffal Bear C	.10	.20
SP15EN024 Performapal Fire Mufflerlion C	.10	.20
SP15EN025 Performapal Partnaga C	.10	.20
SP15EN026 Performapal Friendonkey C	.10	.20
SP15EN027 Performapal Trump Witch C	.10	.20
SP15EN028 Superheavy Samurai Trumpeter C	.75	1.15
SP15EN029 Raidraptor - Vanishing Lanius C	.50	.75
SP15EN030 Gem-Knight Master Diamond C	.20	.30
SP15EN031 Frightfur Bear C	.10	.20
SP15EN032 Rune-Eyes Pendulum Dragon C	.50	.75
SP15EN033 X-Saber Souza C	.10	.20
SP15EN034 Superheavy Samurai Warlord Susanowo C	2.75	3.50
SP15EN035 Constellar Pleiades C	.75	1.15
SP15EN036 Dark Rebellion Xyz Dragon C	2.00	5.00
SP15EN037 Raidraptor - Rise Falcon C	.10	.20
SP15EN038 Polymerization C	3.50	4.50
SP15EN039 Gem-Knight Fusion C	.75	1.15
SP15EN040 Hippo Carnival C	.10	.20
SP15EN041 Feast of the Wild LV5 C	.10	.20
SP15EN042 Wonder Balloons C	.10	.20
SP15EN043 Toy Vendor C	.50	.75
SP15EN044 Illusion Balloons C	.10	.20
SP15EN045 Raidraptor - Nest C	.25	.40
SP15EN046 Command Performance C	.10	.20
SP15EN047 Performapal Revival C	.10	.20
SP15EN048 The Phantom Knights of Shadow Veil C	.10	.20
SP15EN049 Wall of Disruption C	.10	.20
SP15EN050 Raidraptor - Readiness C	.10	.20

2015 Yu-Gi-Oh Star Pack ARC-V Shatterfoil

COMPLETE SET (50)	45.00	60.00
BOOSTER BOX	30.00	40.00
BOOSTER PACK (3 CARDS)	1.00	2.50
RELEASED ON JUNE 12, 2015		
SP15EN001s Gem-Knight Tourmaline	.30	.50
SP15EN002s Swamp Battleguard	.20	.30
SP15EN003s Lava Battleguard	.20	.30
SP15EN004s Mobius the Frost Monarch	.30	.50
SP15EN005s XX-Saber Fulhelmknight	.30	.50
SP15EN006s XX-Saber Boggart Knight	.50	.75
SP15EN007s Constellar Algiedi	.20	.35
SP15EN008s Constellar Kaus	.50	.75
SP15EN009s Mobius the Mega Monarch	1.50	2.00
SP15EN010s Stargazer Magician	.30	.50
SP15EN011s Timegazer Magician	.30	.50
SP15EN012s Odd-Eyes Pendulum Dragon	3.00	3.75
SP15EN013s Performapal Whip Snake	.20	.30
SP15EN014s Performapal Sword Fish	.20	.30
SP15EN015s Performapal Hip Hippo	.20	.30
SP15EN016s Performapal Kaleidoscorp	.20	.30
SP15EN017s Superheavy Samurai Big Benkei	.40	.75
SP15EN018s Aria the Melodious Diva	.60	1.00
SP15EN019s Mozarta the Melodious Maestra	.60	1.00
SP15EN020s Battleguard King	.20	.60
SP15EN021s Performapal Trampolynx	.25	.40
SP15EN022s Edge Imp Sabres	3.25	4.00
SP15EN023s Fluffal Bear	4.00	5.00
SP15EN024s Performapal Fire Mufflerlion	.20	.30
SP15EN025s Performapal Partnaga	.60	1.00
SP15EN026s Performapal Friendonkey	.20	.30
SP15EN027s Performapal Trump Witch	.20	.30
SP15EN028s Superheavy Samurai Trumpeter	1.00	1.25
SP15EN029s Raidraptor - Vanishing Lanius	3.00	4.00
SP15EN030s Gem-Knight Master Diamond	.20	.30
SP15EN031s Frightfur Bear	.30	.50
SP15EN032s Rune-Eyes Pendulum Dragon	.60	1.00
SP15EN033s X-Saber Souza	.20	.30
SP15EN034s Superheavy Samurai Warlord Susanowo	3.00	3.75
SP15EN035s Constellar Pleiades	1.00	1.75
SP15EN036s Dark Rebellion Xyz Dragon	3.75	4.15
SP15EN037s Raidraptor - Rise Falcon	3.75	4.15
SP15EN038s Polymerization	2.00	3.00
SP15EN039s Gem-Knight Fusion	.75	1.00
SP15EN040s Hippo Carnival	.20	.30
SP15EN041s Feast of the Wild LV5	.60	1.00
SP15EN042s Wonder Balloons	.20	.60
SP15EN043s Toy Vendor	2.50	3.15
SP15EN044s Illusion Balloons	.25	.40
SP15EN045s Raidraptor - Nest	2.25	3.00
SP15EN046s Command Performance	.20	.30
SP15EN047s Performapal Revival	.20	.30
SP15EN048s The Phantom Knights of Shadow Veil	.30	.50
SP15EN049s Wall of Disruption	.20	.30
SP15EN050s Raidraptor - Readiness	.40	.75

2017 Yu-Gi-Oh Star Pack Battle Royal 1st Edition

COMPLETE SET (99)		
RELEASED ON		
SP17EN001 The Legendary Fisherman C	.10	.20
SP17EN001 The Legendary Fisherman Starfoil R	.20	.35
SP17EN002 Fluffal Leo C	.10	.20
SP17EN002 Fluffal Leo Starfoil R	.20	.35
SP17EN003 Mayosenju Daibak C	.10	.20
SP17EN003 Mayosenju Daibak Starfoil R	.20	.35
SP17EN004 Yosenju Kama 1 C	.10	.20
SP17EN004 Yosenju Kama 1 Starfoil R	.20	.35
SP17EN005 Yosenju Kama 2 C	.10	.20
SP17EN005 Yosenju Kama 2 Starfoil R	.20	.35
SP17EN006 Yosenju Kama 3 C	.10	.20
SP17EN006 Yosenju Kama 3 Starfoil R	.20	.35
SP17EN007 Yosenju Shinchu L C	.10	.20
SP17EN007 Yosenju Shinchu L Starfoil R	.20	.35
SP17EN008 Yosenju Shinchu R C	.10	.20
SP17EN008 Yosenju Shinchu R Starfoil R	.20	.35
SP17EN009 Superheavy Samurai Big Waraji C	.10	.20
SP17EN009 Superheavy Samurai Big Waraji Starfoil R	.20	.35
SP17EN010 Superheavy Samurai Gigagloves C	.10	.20
SP17EN010 Superheavy Samurai Gigagloves Starfoil R	.20	.35
SP17EN011 Superheavy Samurai Battleball C	.10	.20
SP17EN011 Superheavy Samurai Battleball Starfoil R	.20	.35
SP17EN012 Superheavy Samurai Soulbuster Gauntlet C	.10	.20
SP17EN012 Superheavy Samurai Soulbuster Gauntlet Starfoil R	.20	.35
SP17EN013 Soprano the Melodious Songstress C	.10	.20
SP17EN013 Soprano the Melodious Songstress Starfoil R	.20	.35
SP17EN014 Fluffal Sheep C	.10	.20
SP17EN014 Fluffal Sheep Starfoil R	.20	.35
SP17EN015 Edge Imp Saw C	.10	.20
SP17EN015 Edge Imp Saw Starfoil R	.20	.35
SP17EN016 Performapal Thunderhino C	.10	.20
SP17EN016 Performapal Thunderhino Starfoil R	.20	.35
SP17EN017 Xiangke Magician C	.10	.20
SP17EN017 Xiangke Magician Starfoil R	.20	.35
SP17EN018 Xiangsheng Magician C	.10	.20
SP17EN018 Xiangsheng Magician Starfoil R	.20	.35
SP17EN019 Performapal Drummerilla C	.10	.20
SP17EN019 Performapal Drummerilla Starfoil R	.20	.35
SP17EN020 Opera the Melodious Diva C	.10	.20
SP17EN020 Opera the Melodious Diva Starfoil R	.20	.35
SP17EN021 Crystal Rose C	.10	.20
SP17EN021 Crystal Rose Starfoil R	.20	.35
SP17EN022 Speedroid Terrortop C	.10	.20
SP17EN022 Speedroid Terrortop Starfoil R	.20	.35
SP17EN023 Speedroid TriEyed Dice C	.10	.20
SP17EN023 Speedroid TriEyed Dice Starfoil R	.20	.35
SP17EN024 Speedroid Double Yoyo C	.10	.20
SP17EN024 Speedroid Double Yoyo Starfoil R	.20	.35
SP17EN025 Performapal Secondonkey C	.10	.20
SP17EN025 Performapal Secondonkey Starfoil R	.20	.35
SP17EN026 DD Swirl Slime C	.10	.20
SP17EN026 DD Swirl Slime Starfoil R	.20	.35
SP17EN027 DD Necro Slime C	.10	.20
SP17EN027 DD Necro Slime Starfoil R	.20	.35
SP17EN028 The Legendary Fisherman III C	.10	.20
SP17EN028 The Legendary Fisherman III Starfoil R	.20	.35
SP17EN029 DDD Oblivion King Abyss Ragnarok C	.10	.20
SP17EN029 DDD Oblivion King Abyss Ragnarok Starfoil R	.20	.35
SP17EN030 Solo the Melodious Songstress C	.10	.20
SP17EN030 Solo the Melodious Songstress Starfoil R	.20	.35
SP17EN031 Score the Melodious Diva C	.10	.20
SP17EN031 Score the Melodious Diva Starfoil R	.20	.35
SP17EN032 Performapal OddEyes Light Phoenix C	.10	.20
SP17EN032 Performapal OddEyes Light Phoenix Starfoil R	.20	.35
SP17EN033 Performapal OddEyes Unicorn C	.10	.20
SP17EN033 Performapal OddEyes Unicorn Starfoil R	.20	.35
SP17EN034 Performapal Fireflux C	.10	.20
SP17EN034 Performapal Fireflux Starfoil R	.20	.35
SP17EN035 Schuberta the Melodious Maestra C	.10	.20
SP17EN035 Schuberta the Melodious Maestra Starfoil R	.20	.35
SP17EN036 Bloom Diva the Melodious Choir C	.10	.20
SP17EN036 Bloom Diva the Melodious Choir Starfoil R	.20	.35
SP17EN037 Frightfur Leo C	.10	.20
SP17EN037 Frightfur Leo Starfoil R	.20	.35
SP17EN038 Frightfur Sheep C	.10	.20
SP17EN038 Frightfur Sheep Starfoil R	.20	.35
SP17EN039 Frightfur Chimera C	.10	.20
SP17EN039 Frightfur Chimera Starfoil R	.20	.35
SP17EN040 DDD Oracle King dArc C	.10	.20
SP17EN040 DDD Oracle King dArc Starfoil R	.20	.35
SP17EN041 Bloom Prima the Melodious Choir C	.10	.20
SP17EN041 Bloom Prima the Melodious Choir Starfoil R	.20	.35
SP17EN042 Superheavy Samurai Ogre Shutendoji C	.10	.20
SP17EN042 Superheavy Samurai Ogre Shutendoji Starfoil R	.20	.35
SP17EN043 HiSpeedroid Kendama C	.10	.20
SP17EN043 HiSpeedroid Kendama Starfoil R	.20	.35
SP17EN044 OddEyes Rebellion Dragon Starfoil R	.20	.35
SP17EN045 DDD DuoDawn King Kali Yuga C	.10	.20
SP17EN045 DDD DuoDawn King Kali Yuga Starfoil R	.20	.35
SP17EN046 Frightfur Fusion C	.10	.20
SP17EN046 Frightfur Fusion Starfoil R	.20	.35
SP17EN047 Pianissimo C	.10	.20
SP17EN047 Pianissimo Starfoil R	.20	.35
SP17EN048 Speed Recovery C	.10	.20
SP17EN048 Speed Recovery Starfoil R	.20	.35
SP17EN049 Urgent Tuning C	.10	.20
SP17EN049 Urgent Tuning Starfoil R	.20	.35
SP17EN050 Yosenjus Secret Move C	.10	.20
SP17EN050 Yosenjus Secret Move Starfoil R	.20	.35

2002 Yu-Gi-Oh Tournament Pack 1

COMPLETE SET (30)	85.00	150.00
BOOSTER BOX (20 PACKS)	400.00	500.00
BOOSTER PACK (3 CARDS)	10.00	20.00
RELEASED ON SEPTEMBER 21, 2002		
TP1001 Mechanical Chaser UR	30.00	60.00
TP1002 Axe Raider SR	10.00	25.00
TP1003 Kwagar Hercules SR	4.00	10.00
TP1004 Patrol Robo SR	4.00	10.00
TP1005 White Hole SR	15.00	30.00
TP1006 Elf's Light R	8.00	20.00
TP1007 Steel Shell R	5.00	12.00
TP1008 Blue Medicine R	2.50	6.00
TP1009 Raimei R	3.00	8.00
TP1010 Burning Spear R	3.00	8.00
TP1011 Gust Fan R	4.00	10.00
TP1012 Tiger Axe R	3.00	6.00
TP1013 Goddess with Third Eye R	3.00	8.00
TP1014 Beastking of Swamps R	3.00	8.00
TP1015 Versago the Destroyer R	8.00	20.00
TP1016 Oscillo Hero #2 C	1.50	4.00
TP1017 Giant Flea C	1.50	4.00
TP1018 Bean Soldier C	1.50	4.00
TP1019 The Statue of Easter Island C	1.50	4.00
TP1020 Corroding Shark C	1.50	4.00
TP1021 WOW Warrior C	1.50	4.00
TP1022 Winged Dragon C	1.50	4.00
TP1023 Oscillo Hero C	1.50	4.00
TP1024 Shining Friendship C	1.50	4.00
TP1025 Hercules Beetle C	1.50	4.00
TP1026 Judgement Hand C	1.50	4.00
TP1027 Wodan The Resident C	1.50	4.00
TP1028 Cyber Soldier C	1.50	4.00
TP1029 Cockroach Knight C	2.50	6.00
TP1030 Kuwagata Alpha C	1.50	4.00

2002 Yu-Gi-Oh Tournament Pack 2

COMPLETE SET (30)	250.00	300.00
BOOSTER BOX (20 PACKS)	400.00	500.00
BOOSTER PACK (3 CARDS)	4.00	20.00
RELEASED ON DECEMBER 21, 2002		
TP2001 Morphing Jar UR	180.00	220.00
TP2002 Dragon Seeker SR	8.00	20.00
TP2003 Giant Red Seasnake SR	6.00	15.00
TP2004 Exile of the Wicked SR	2.50	6.00
TP2005 Call of the Grave SR	2.50	6.00
TP2006 Mikazukinoyaiba R	15.00	30.00
TP2007 Skull Guardian R	20.00	40.00
TP2008 Novox's Prayer R	3.00	8.00
TP2009 Dokurorider R	6.00	15.00
TP2010 Revival of Dokurorider R	2.50	6.00
TP2011 Beautiful Headhuntress R	8.00	20.00
TP2012 Sonic Maid R	5.00	12.00
TP2013 Mystical Sheep #1 R	2.00	5.00
TP2014 Warrior of Tradition R	6.00	15.00
TP2015 Soul of the Pure R	2.00	5.00
TP2016 Dancing Elf C	1.00	2.50
TP2017 Turu-Purun C	1.00	2.50
TP2018 Dharma Cannon C	1.00	2.50
TP2019 Stuffed Animal C	1.00	2.50
TP2020 Spirit of the Books C	1.00	2.50
TP2021 Faith Bird C	1.00	2.50
TP2022 Takuhee C	1.00	2.50
TP2023 Maiden of the Moonlight C	1.50	4.00
TP2024 Queen of Autumn Leaves C	1.00	2.50
TP2025 Two-Headed King Rex C	1.00	2.50
TP2026 Garoozis C	1.50	4.00
TP2027 Crawling Dragon C	1.00	2.50
TP2028 Parrot Dragon C	1.00	2.50
TP2029 Sky Dragon C	1.00	2.50
TP2030 Water Magician C	1.00	2.50

2003 Yu-Gi-Oh Tournament Pack 3

COMPLETE SET (20)	100.00	200.00
BOOSTER BOX (20 PACKS)	400.00	500.00
BOOSTER PACK (3 CARDS)	10.00	20.00
RELEASED ON MARCH 29, 2003		
TP3001 Needle Worm UR	30.00	50.00
TP3002 Anti Raigeki SR	20.00	40.00
TP3003 Mechanicalchaser SR	3.00	8.00

TP3004 B.Skull Dragon SR	15.00	30.00
TP3005 Horn of Heaven SR	15.00	30.00
TP3006 Axe Raider R	2.00	5.00
TP3007 Kwagar Hercules R	2.00	4.00
TP3008 Patrol Robo R	1.50	4.00
TP3009 White Hole R	2.00	5.00
TP3010 Dragon Capture Jar C	.75	2.00
TP3011 Goblin's Secret Remedy C	.75	2.00
TP3012 Final Flame C	.75	2.00
TP3013 Spirit of the Harp C	.75	2.00
TP3014 Pot of Greed C	.75	2.00
TP3015 Karbonala Warrior C	.75	2.00
TP3016 Darkfire Dragon C	.75	2.00
TP3017 Elegant Egotist C	.75	2.00
TP3018 Dark Elf C	.75	2.00
TP3019 Little Chimera C	.75	2.00
TP3020 Bladefly C	.75	2.00

2003 Yu-Gi-Oh Tournament Pack 4

COMPLETE SET (20)	100.00	150.00
BOOSTER BOX (20 PACKS)	400.00	500.00
BOOSTER PACK (3 CARDS)	10.00	20.00
RELEASED ON NOVEMBER 15, 2003		
TP4001 Royal Decree UR	40.00	80.00
TP4002 Morphing Jar SR	10.00	25.00
TP4003 Megamorph SR	2.00	5.00
TP4004 Chain Destruction SR	2.00	5.00
TP4005 The Fiend Megacyber SR	1.50	4.00
TP4006 Dragon Seeker R	1.25	3.00
TP4007 Giant Red Seasnake R	1.25	3.00
TP4008 Exile of the Wicked R	1.25	3.00
TP4009 Call of the Grave R	2.00	5.00
TP4010 Rush Recklessly C	.75	2.00
TP4011 Giant Rat C	.75	2.00
TP4012 Senju of Thousand Hands C	.75	2.00
TP4013 Karate Man C	.75	2.00
TP4014 Nimble Momonga C	.75	2.00
TP4015 Mystic Tomato C	.75	2.00
TP4016 Nobleman of Extermination C	.75	2.00
TP4017 Magic Drain C	.75	2.00
TP4018 Gravity Bird C	.75	2.00
TP4019 Hayabusa Knight C	.75	2.00
TP4020 Mad Sword Beast C	.75	2.00

2004 Yu-Gi-Oh Tournament Pack 5

COMPLETE SET (20)	25.00	50.00
BOOSTER BOX (20 PACKS)	400.00	500.00
BOOSTER PACK (3 CARDS)	2.50	6.00
RELEASED ON OCTOBER 15, 2004		
TP5EN001 Luminous Soldier UR	2.50	6.00
TP5EN002 Big Shield Gardna SR	2.00	5.00
TP5EN003 Magical Thorn SR	2.00	5.00
TP5EN004 Luster Dragon SR	2.50	6.00
TP5EN005 Needle Worm SR	6.00	15.00
TP5EN006 Kycoo the Ghost Destroyer R	1.00	2.50
TP5EN007 Bazoo the Soul-Eater R	1.00	2.50
TP5EN008 Book of Life R	1.00	2.50
TP5EN009 Trap Board Eraser R	1.00	2.50
TP5EN010 Goddess with the Third Eye C	1.00	2.50
TP5EN011 Jowgen the Spiritualist C	.25	.75
TP5EN012 Tornado Bird C	.25	.75
TP5EN013 Destruction Punch C	.25	.75
TP5EN014 Beastking of the Swamps C	.25	.75
TP5EN015 Versago the Destroyer C	.25	.75
TP5EN016 Mysticak Sheep #1 C	.25	.75
TP5EN017 Pyramid Turtle C	.25	.75
TP5EN018 Curse of Royal C	.25	.75
TP5EN019 Winged Sage Falcos C	.25	.75
TP5EN020 Dark Designator C	.25	.75

2005 Yu-Gi-Oh Tournament Pack 6

COMPLETE SET (20)	50.00	80.00
BOOSTER BOX (20 PACKS)	400.00	500.00
BOOSTER PACK (3 CARDS)	10.00	20.00
RELEASED ON JUNE 1, 2005		
TP6EN001 Toon Cannon Soldier UR	15.00	30.00
TP6EN002 Toon Table of Contents SR	10.00	25.00
TP6EN003 Fusion Sage SR	3.00	8.00
TP6EN004 Royal Decree SR	3.00	8.00
TP6EN005 Restructer Revolution SR	1.00	2.50
TP6EN006 Spear Dragon R	.75	2.00
TP6EN007 Airknight Parshath R	.75	2.00
TP6EN008 Susa Soldier R	.75	2.00
TP6EN009 Yamata Dragon R	.75	2.00
TP6EN010 Dark Balter the Terrible C	.60	1.50
TP6EN011 Ryu Senshi C	.60	1.50
TP6EN012 Emergency Provisions C	.60	1.50
TP6EN013 Fiend Skull Dragon C	.60	1.50
TP6EN014 Thunder Nyan Nyan C	.60	1.50
TP6EN015 Last Turn C	.60	1.50
TP6EN016 Archfiend Marmot of Nefariousness C	.60	1.50
TP6EN017 Sleeping Lion C	.60	1.50
TP6EN018 Nekogal #1 C	.60	1.50
TP6EN019 Burglar C	.60	1.50
TP6EN020 Clown Zombie C	.60	1.50

2006 Yu-Gi-Oh Tournament Pack 7

COMPLETE SET (20)	60.00	140.00
BOOSTER BOX (20 PACKS)	400.00	500.00
BOOSTER PACK (3 CARDS)	10.00	20.00
RELEASED ON NOVEMBER 10, 2005		
TP7EN001 D.D. Warrior UR	6.00	15.00
TP7EN002 Warrior Eliminator SR	3.00	8.00
TP7EN003 Fortress Whale SR	40.00	80.00
TP7EN004 Luminous Soldier SR	2.00	5.00
TP7EN005 Breaker the Magical Warrior SR	10.00	25.00
TP7EN006 Goblin Attack Force R	1.00	3.00
TP7EN007 Amazoness Swords Woman R	2.00	5.00
TP7EN008 Chaos Command Magician R	2.00	5.00
TP7EN009 Scapegoat R	.75	2.00
TP7EN010 Soul Exchange C	.75	2.00
TP7EN011 Fortress Whale's Oath C	.75	2.00
TP7EN012 Skilled Dark Magician C	.75	2.00
TP7EN013 Skilled White Magician C	.75	2.00
TP7EN014 Wall of Illusion C	.75	2.00
TP7EN015 Last Will C	.75	2.00
TP7EN016 Haniwa C	.75	2.00
TP7EN017 Prisman C	.75	2.00
TP7EN018 Millennium Golem C	.75	2.00
TP7EN019 Dig Break C	.75	2.00
TP7EN020 Nekogal #2 C	.75	2.00

2006 Yu-Gi-Oh Tournament Pack 8

COMPLETE SET (7)	180.00	250.00
BOOSTER BOX (20 PACKS)	400.00	500.00
BOOSTER PACK (3 CARDS)	10.00	20.00
RELEASED ON APRIL 28, 2006		
TP8EN001 Magical Arm Shield UR	10.00	25.00
TP8EN002 Harpies Feather Duster SR	100.00	130.00
TP8EN003 Slate Warrior SR	25.00	6.00
TP8EN004 Dunames Dark Witch SR	10.00	25.00
TP8EN005 Garma Sword SR	25.00	50.00
TP8EN006 Zaborg the Thunder Monarch R	.75	2.00
TP8EN007 Granmarg the Rock Monarch R	.75	2.00
TP8EN008 Mobius Frost Monarch R	.75	2.00
TP8EN009 Thestalos the Firestorm Monarch R	.75	2.00
TP8EN010 Garma Sword Oath C	.75	2.00
TP8EN011 Berserk Gorilla C	.75	2.00
TP8EN012 Ultimate Offering C	.75	2.00
TP8EN013 Gatekeeper C	.75	2.00
TP8EN014 Behegon C	.75	2.00
TP8EN015 Violent Rain C	.75	2.00
TP8EN016 Temple of Skulls C	.75	2.00
TP8EN017 Blocker C	.75	2.00
TP8EN018 Wretched Ghost of the Attic C	.75	2.00
TP8EN019 Sectarian of Secrets C	.75	2.00
TP8EN020 Necrolancer the Timelord C	.75	2.00

2009 Yu-Gi-Oh Turbo Pack 1

COMPLETE SET (21)	40.00	100.00
BOOSTER BOX (100 PACKS)	300.00	400.00
BOOSTER PACK (3 CARDS)	3.00	8.00
RELEASED ON AUGUST 15, 2009		
TU10 Judgment Dragon UTR	20.00	40.00
TU120 D.D.R. Different Dimension Reincarnation C	.40	1.00
TU01EN001 Doomcaliber Knight UR	2.50	6.00
TU01EN002 Garoth, Lightsworn Warrior SR	1.25	3.00
TU01EN003 Krebons SR	2.50	6.00
TU01EN004 Gladiator Beast Samnite SR	.75	2.00
TU01EN005 Black Whirlwind SR	5.00	12.00
TU01EN006 Crush Card Virus R	1.25	3.00
TU01EN007 Satellite Cannon R	.60	1.50
TU01EN008 Rescue Cat R	.60	1.50
TU01EN009 Grandmaster of the Six Samurai R	.60	1.50
TU01EN010 TradeIn R	1.50	4.00
TU01EN011 Armageddon Knight R	.75	2.00
TU01EN012 Book of Moon C	.40	1.00
TU01EN013 Terraforming C	.75	2.00
TU01EN014 Hand Destruction C	1.00	2.50
TU01EN015 Gladiator Beast Murmillo C	.40	1.00
TU01EN016 Gladiator Beast Bestiari C	.40	1.00
TU01EN017 Gladiator Beast Laquari C	.40	1.00
TU01EN018 Golden Flying Fish C	.40	1.00
TU01EN019 Ryko, Lightsworn Hunter C	.40	1.00

2010 Yu-Gi-Oh Turbo Pack 2

COMPLETE SET (21)	60.00	140.00
BOOSTER BOX (100 PACKS)	300.00	400.00
BOOSTER PACK (3 CARDS)	10.00	20.00
RELEASED ON JANUARY 9, 2010		
TU20 Gladiator Beast Heraklinos UTR	2.00	5.00
TU02EN001 Chaos Sorcerer UR	8.00	20.00
TU02EN002 Gravekeeper's Assailant SR	1.25	3.00
TU02EN003 Magical Dimension SR	20.00	35.00
TU02EN004 Foolish Burial SR	20.00	40.00
TU02EN005 Beckoning Light SR	1.25	3.00
TU02EN006 Gravekeeper's Spear Soldier R	.75	2.00
TU02EN007 My Body as a Shield R	.50	1.25
TU02EN008 Magical Stone Excavation R	.60	1.50
TU02EN009 Mist Archfiend R	.60	1.50
TU02EN010 Light-Imprisoning Mirror R	1.00	2.50
TU02EN011 Shadow-Imprisoning Mirror R	1.00	2.50
TU02EN012 Anti-Spell Fragrance C	.40	1.00
TU02EN013 Gravekeeper's Cannonholder C	.40	1.00
TU02EN014 Necrovalley C	.40	1.00
TU02EN015 Autonomous Action Unit C	.40	1.00
TU02EN016 Anti-Spell Fragrance C	6.00	15.00
TU02EN017 Reflect Bounder C	.40	1.00
TU02EN018 Mausoleum of the Emperor C	.40	1.00
TU02EN019 Gravekeeper's Commandant C	.75	2.00
TU02EN020 Iron Core of Koa'ki Meiru C	.40	1.00

2010 Yu-Gi-Oh Turbo Pack 3

COMPLETE SET (21)		
BOOSTER BOX		
BOOSTER PACK		
RELEASED ON JULY 12, 2010		
TU03EN000 Caius the Shadow Monarch UTR	15.00	30.00
TU03EN001 Dark Grepher UR	3.00	8.00
TU03EN002 Rescue Cat SR	8.00	20.00
TU03EN003 Morphtronic Celfon SR	2.50	6.00
TU03EN004 Rekindling SR	3.00	8.00
TU03EN005 Treacherous Trap Hole SR	6.00	15.00
TU03EN006 Gladiator Beast Retiari R	1.25	3.00
TU03EN007 XX-Saber Faultroll R	.40	1.00
TU03EN008 XX-Saber Ragigura R	.40	1.00
TU03EN009 Magical Android R	.40	1.00
TU03EN010 Dark Eruption R	.40	1.00
TU03EN011 Saber Slash R	.40	1.00
TU03EN012 Destiny Hero - Diamond Dude C	.10	.30
TU03EN013 D.D. Crow C	.20	.75
TU03EN014 Superancient Deepsea King Coelacanth C	.10	.30
TU03EN015 Koa'ki Meiru Drago C	1.50	4.00
TU03EN016 Kycoo the Ghost Destroyer C	.10	.30
TU03EN017 Nobleman of Crossout C	.10	.30
TU03EN018 Cloak and Dagger C	.10	.30
TU03EN019 Gladiator Beast War Chariot C	.40	1.00
TU03EN020 Pollinosis C	.10	.30

2010 Yu-Gi-Oh Turbo Pack 4

COMPLETE SET	50.00	100.00
BOOSTER BOX		
BOOSTER PACK		
RELEASED ON NOVEMBER 19, 2010		
TU04EN000 Tragoedia UTR	15.00	30.00
TU04EN001 Gottoms' Emergency Call UR	3.00	8.00
TU04EN002 Debris Dragon SR	2.50	6.00
TU04EN003 Blackwing - Sirocco the Dawn SR	1.50	4.00
TU04EN004 Deep Sea Diva SR	15.00	30.00
TU04EN005 Compulsory Evacuation Device SR	8.00	20.00
TU04EN006 Dunames Dark Witch R	.40	1.00
TU04EN007 The End of Anubis R	.60	1.50
TU04EN008 Psychic Commander R	.75	2.00
TU04EN009 Advanced Ritual Art R	.40	1.00
TU04EN010 Bark of Dark Ruler R	.40	1.00
TU04EN011 Swallow Flip R	.40	1.00
TU04EN012 Wattkid C	.25	.75
TU04EN013 Oscillo Hero C	.25	.75
TU04EN014 Mokey Mokey C	.25	.75
TU04EN015 Key Mace C	.25	.75
TU04EN016 King of the Skull Servants C	.50	1.25
TU04EN017 Dark Hole C	.40	1.00
TU04EN018 Amazoness Spellcaster C	.25	.75
TU04EN019 Gladiator Proving Ground C	.25	.75
TU04EN020 White Hole C	.60	1.50

2011 Yu-Gi-Oh Turbo Pack 5

TU05EN000 Colossal Fighter UTR	4.00	10.00
TU05EN001 Dark Hole UR	2.50	6.00
TU05EN002 Gladiator Beast Laquari SR	1.00	2.50
TU05EN003 Snowman Eater SR	1.50	4.00
TU05EN004 Six Samurai United SR	15.00	30.00
TU05EN005 Spell Shattering Arrow SR	2.50	6.00
TU05EN006 Puppet Plant R	.40	1.00
TU05EN007 Wulf, Lightsworn Beast R	.25	.75
TU05EN008 Cyber Eltanin R	.20	.60
TU05EN009 Torrential Tribute R	.75	2.00
TU05EN010 Escape from the Dark Dimension R	.75	2.00
TU05EN011 Zoma the Spirit R	.50	1.25
TU05EN012 Manju of the Ten Thousand Hands C	1.25	3.00
TU05EN013 Abyssal Kingshark C	.15	.40
TU05EN014 Spirit of the Six Samurai C	.15	.40
TU05EN015 Black Salvo C	.15	.40
TU05EN016 Darkness Neosphere C	1.25	3.00
TU05EN017 Miracle Fusion C	.75	2.00
TU05EN018 Shield Crush C	.15	.40
TU05EN019 Seven Tools of the Bandit C	.15	.40
TU05EN020 Royal Command C	.15	.40

2011 Yu-Gi-Oh Turbo Pack 6

TU06EN000 Dark Armed Dragon UTR	25.00	50.00
TU06EN001 Sangan UR	5.00	12.00
TU06EN002 Chain Disappearance SR	5.00	12.00
TU06EN003 Masked Dragon SR	3.00	8.00
TU06EN004 Fishborg Blaster SR	2.00	5.00
TU06EN005 Quickdraw Synchron SR	10.00	25.00
TU06EN006 Zombie Master R	.50	1.25
TU06EN007 Stardust Dragon R	2.00	5.00
TU06EN008 Red Dragon Archfiend R	1.00	2.50
TU06EN009 Black Garden R	.50	1.25
TU06EN010 Armory Arm R	1.25	3.00
TU06EN011 Alector, Sovereign of Birds C	.15	.40
TU06EN012 Fusion Gate C	1.25	3.00
TU06EN013 Kinetic Soldier C	.10	.30
TU06EN014 Greenkappa C	.10	.30
TU06EN015 Creature Swap C	.15	.40
TU06EN016 Magical Dimension C	.20	.60
TU06EN017 Bountiful Artemis C	.50	1.25
TU06EN018 Gemini Spark C	.20	.60
TU06EN019 Golem Dragon C	.75	2.00
TU06EN020 Transforming Sphere C	.10	.30

2012 Yu-Gi-Oh Turbo Pack 7

TU07EN000 Ally of Justice Catastor UTR	4.00	10.00
TU07EN001 Book of Moon UR	5.00	12.00
TU07EN002 Ninja Grandmaster Sasuke SR	.40	1.00
TU07EN003 Yellow Gadget SR	2.00	5.00
TU07EN004 X-Saber Pashuul SR	2.00	5.00
TU07EN005 Horn of the Phantom Beast SR	2.50	6.00
TU07EN006 Dark Horus R	.20	.60
TU07EN007 Lightning Warrior R	.60	1.50
TU07EN008 Primal Seed R	.25	.75
TU07EN009 Big Evolution Pill R	.25	.75
TU07EN010 Tail Swipe R	.25	.75
TU07EN011 Geartown R	.40	1.00
TU07EN012 Seiyaryu C	.25	.75
TU07EN013 Serpent Night Dragon C	.25	.75
TU07EN014 Kotodama C	.10	.30
TU07EN015 Gokipon C	.25	.75
TU07EN016 Goe Goe the Gallant Ninja C	.25	.75
TU07EN017 Herald of Orange Light C	.25	.75
TU07EN018 Blackwing - Sirocco the Dawn C	.25	.75
TU07EN019 Ninjitsu Art of Transformation C	.25	.75
TU07EN020 Ninjitsu Art of Decoy C	.25	.75

2012 Yu-Gi-Oh Turbo Pack 8

TU08EN000 Thunder King Rai-Oh UTR	15.00	30.00
TU08EN001 Skill Drain UR	15.00	30.00
TU08EN002 Green Gadget SR	2.00	5.00
TU08EN003 Red Gadget SR	2.00	5.00
TU08EN004 Upstart Goblin SR	15.00	30.00
TU08EN005 Mirror of Oaths SR	1.00	2.50
TU08EN006 Alligator's Sword R	.50	1.25
TU08EN007 Lost Guardian R	.10	.30
TU08EN008 Alligator's Sword Dragon R	.20	.60
TU08EN009 Magicians Unite R	.10	.30
TU08EN010 Ready for Intercepting R	.10	.30
TU08EN011 Gozen Match R	1.50	4.00
TU08EN012 Elephant Statue of Blessing C	.10	.30
TU08EN013 Elephant Statue of Disaster C	.10	.30
TU08EN014 Gemini Imps C	.10	.30
TU08EN015 Flamvell Firedog C	.10	.30
TU08EN016 Wind-Up Factory C	.50	1.25
TU08EN017 The Emperor's Holiday C	.10	.30
TU08EN018 Really Eternal Rest C	.10	.30
TU08EN019 Rock Bombardment C	.10	.30
TU08EN020 Magician's Circle C	.75	2.00

Graded

Magic The Gathering

1993 Magic The Gathering Alpha

#	Card	NmMt 8	NmMt+ 8.5	MT 9	Gem 9.5/10
1	Air Elemental U :B:	40	▲120	▲175	600
2	Ancestral Recall R :B:	3,500	4,500	▲9,000	▲12,000
3	Animate Artifact U :B:	▲60	▲75	▲100	250
4	Animate Dead U :K:	200	▲350	▲400	▲600
5	Animate Wall R :W:	150	▲300	▲350	500
6	Ankh of Mishra R :A:	300	▲400	▲950	▲2,400
7	Armageddon R :W:	▲800	▲950	▲1,700	
8	Aspect of Wolf R :G:	150	200	▲500	1,800
9	Bad Moon R :K:	200	300	▲1,000	1,300
10	Badlands R :L:	1,500	▲3,800	▲4,000	▲5,300
11	Balance R :W:	800	900	▲2,300	10,000
12	Basalt Monolith U :A:	150	▲300	▲450	▲900
13	Bayou R :L:	▲2,000	▲3,000	▲4,000	▲7,000
15	Berserk U :G:	▼200	▲450	▲700	▲900
16	Birds of Paradise R :G:	1,500	1,800		30,000
17	Black Knight U :K:	200	▲300	▲500	1,200
18	Black Lotus R :A:	18,000	▲45,000	▲80,000	▲120,000
19	Black Vise U :A:	200	500	800	1,000
20	Black Ward U :W:	40	60	▲250	400
21	Blaze of Glory R :W:	300	▲400	▲600	▲2,300
22	Blessing R :W:	200	▲300	▲500	▲1,400
24	Blue Ward U :W:	30	▲60	▲100	▲300
25	Bog Wraith U :K:	▲75	▲100	200	1,500
26	Braingeyser R :B:	▲900	▲1,000	▲2,600	4,300
27	Burrowing U :R:	▲50	▲75	150	300
28	Camouflage U :G:	60	100	▲250	300
29	Castle U :W:	30	50	▲125	▲250
30	Celestial Prism U :A:	30	▲60	▲120	200
31	Channel U :G:	▲120	150	▲400	
32	Chaos Orb R :A:	4,000	4,500	5,000	
33	Chaoslace R :R:	▲200	▲250	500	▲1,000
38	Clockwork Beast R :A:	150	175	▲800	
39	Clone U :B:	100	150	250	400
40	Cockatrice R :G:	150	200	350	
41	Consecrate Land U :W:	30	40	60	
42	Conservator U :A:	40	60	80	300
43	Contract from Below R :K:	250	300	500	
44	Control Magic U :B:	200	250		
45	Conversion U :W:	40	50	75	175
46	Copper Tablet U :A:	100	150	200	250
47	Copy Artifact R :B:	400	500	600	
48	Counterspell U :B:	400	600	900	
51	Crusade R :W:	400	500	600	
52	Crystal Rod U :A:	50	75	100	
53	Cursed Land U :K:	35	50	150	
54	Cyclopean Tomb R :A:	300	400	600	
56	Darkpact R :K:	200	300	400	
58	Deathgrip U :K:	50	80	150	200
59	Deathlace R :K:	150	200	300	900
60	Demonic Attorney R :K:	200	300	500	
61	Demonic Hordes R :K:	150	200	300	650
62	Demonic Tutor U :K:	500	700	900	
63	Dingus Egg R :A:	80	120	250	
66	Disrupting Scepter R :A:	400	600	700	800
67	Dragon Whelp U :R:	80	150	250	
69	Drain Power R :B:	200	300	400	
71	Dwarven Demolition Team U :R:	50	100	200	750
73	Earth Elemental U :R:	40	60	100	200
75	Earthquake R :R:	250	300	400	500
76	Elvish Archers R :G:	200	250	350	
77	Evil Presence U :K:	30	50	85	
79	Farmstead R :W:	300	350	400	450
80	Fastbond R :G:	400	500	700	
82	Feedback U :B:	30	50	200	350
83	Fire Elemental U :R:	30	50	80	
86	Flashfires U :R:	70	125		
89	Force of Nature R :G:	500	700	1,000	
90	Forcefield R :A:	600	800	1,200	▲10,000
93	Fork R :R:	550	700	900	1,000
95	Fungusaur R :G:	200	250		
96	Gaea's Liege R :G:	200	250		
97	Gauntlet of Might R :A:	1,000	1,200		
100	Glasses of Urza U :A:	40	50		
101	Gloom U :K:	60	100	125	
102	Goblin Balloon Brigade U :R:	40	60	80	200
103	Goblin King R :R:	350	500	650	
104	Granite Gargoyle R :R:	250	300	450	600
106	Green Ward U :W:	30	40	60	
110	Helm of Chatzuk R :A:	100	150	400	
112	Hive, The R :A:	300	400	500	
116	Howling Mine R :A:	400	500	700	900
118	Hurricane U :G:	80	100		
119	Hypnotic Specter U :K:	400	500	600	
120	Ice Storm U :G:	100	140	150	300
121	Icy Manipulator U :A:	300	400	500	800
122	Illusionary Mask R :A:	350	400	750	
123	Instill Energy U :G:	150	200	250	
125	Iron Star U :A:	40	60	80	100
128	Island Sanctuary R :W:	200	250	300	1,000
131	Ivory Cup U :A:	20	30	40	200
132	Jade Monolith R :A:	100	150	325	
133	Jade Statue U :A:	100	130		
134	Jayemdae Tome R :A:	500	700	1,100	
135	Juggernaut U :A:	150	200	300	
137	Karma U :W:	50	80	100	200
138	Keldon Warlord U :R:	150	200	300	
139	Kormus Bell R :A:	200	300	500	1,000
140	Kudzu R :G:	150	200		
141	Lance U :W:	60	100	150	
142	Ley Druid U :G:	30	50	100	180
143	Library of Leng U :A:	60	80	100	
144	Lich R :K:	400	500	600	
145	Lifeforce U :G:	30	50	100	175
146	Lifelace R :G:	100	200	300	
147	Lifetap U :B:	40	80	100	125
149	Living Artifact R :G:	100	150	300	800
150	Living Lands R :G:	100	150	200	
151	Living Wall U :A:	30	50	150	450
153	Lord of Atlantis R :B:	300	500	600	
154	Lord of the Pit R :K:	300	500	700	3,000
155	Lure U :G:	60	80	100	
156	Magical Hack R :B:	150	200	500	
157	Mahamoti Djinn R :B:	275	325	500	
158	Mana Flare R :R:	125	180	400	600
159	Mana Short R :B:	300	400	800	
160	Mana Vault R :A:	▲1,400	▲1,500	2,000	▲3,700
161	Manabarbs R :R:	100	150	300	1,300
162	Meekstone R :A:	200	250	400	600
165	Mind Twist R :K:	400	450	750	
169	Mox Emerald R :A:	2,000	▲5,000	▲9,000	▲16,000
170	Mox Jet R :A:	▲2,500	▲6,000	▲9,000	▲40,000
171	Mox Pearl R :A:	▲5,800	▲8,000	▲12,000	▲15,000
172	Mox Ruby R :A:	2,000	3,000	▲10,000	▲20,000
173	Mox Sapphire R :A:	▲3,200	▲7,000	▲13,000	
174	Natural Selection R :G:	150	200	300	
175	Nether Shadow R :K:	150	200	300	500
176	Nettling Imp U :K:	20	30	75	
177	Nevinyrral's Disk R :A:	400	▲1,000	▲1,700	4,000
178	Nightmare R :K:	400	500	600	
179	Northern Paladin R :W:	145	200	500	
180	Obsianus Golem U :A:	15	25	50	
181	Orcish Artillery U :R:	25	30	70	
182	Orcish Oriflamme U :R:	20	35	50	
185	Personal Incarnation R :W:	200	300	500	
187	Phantasmal Forces U :B:	30	50	100	
189	Phantom Monster U :B:	20	30	60	100
190	Pirate Ship R :B:	150	200	500	
194	Plateau R :L:	1,000	▲2,000	▲2,500	▲3,100
197	Power Surge R :R:	100	125	170	
199	Psionic Blast U :B:	80	100	200	
201	Purelace R :W:	75	125	200	500
202	Raging River R :R:	200	250	500	1,000
205	Red Ward U :W:	20	30	60	
207	Regrowth U :G:	50	70	160	
208	Resurrection U :W:	30	45	100	250
209	Reverse Damage R :W:	100	150	500	
210	Righteousness R :W:	150	200	300	400
211	Roc of Kher Ridges R :R:	300	400	500	
212	Rock Hydra R :R:	150	200	250	
213	Rod of Ruin U :A:	20	30	80	
214	Royal Assassin R :K:	300	400	1,100	1,800
215	Sacrifice U :K:	20	30	80	
217	Savannah Lions R :W:	450	600	800	1,000
218	Savannah R :L:	800	1,100	▲2,000	▲5,000
220	Scavenging Ghoul U :K:	20	30	60	
221	Scrubland R :L:	1,000	▲2,500	▲2,700	▲6,300
224	Sedge Troll R :R:	400	500	800	
225	Sengir Vampire U :K:	75	90	200	
226	Serra Angel U :W:	400	600	800	
229	Shivan Dragon R :R:	1,000	1,500	3,000	9,000
230	Simulacrum U :K:	20	35	80	
232	Siren's Call U :B:	20	40	80	180
233	Sleight of Mind R :B:	100	150	300	600
234	Smoke R :R:	100	150	200	
235	Sol Ring U :A:	150	400	1,000	2,000
236	Soul Net U :A:	40	80	200	
238	Stasis R :B:	200	300	400	
239	Steal Artifact U :B:	20	35	50	
240	Stone Giant U :R:	20	35	50	
243	Sunglasses of Urza R :A:	100	150	170	
246	Swords to Plowshares U :W:	200	250	500	
247	Taiga R :L:	1,500	▲2,500	4,000	8,000
249	Thicket Basilisk U :G:	20	30	50	
250	Thoughtlace R :B:	150	180	300	
251	Throne of Bone U :A:	20	30	50	
252	Timber Wolves R :G:	150	200	400	600
253	Time Vault R :A:	900	▲2,000	▲3,000	▲4,000
254	Time Walk R :B:	▲3,000	▲6,200	▲6,000	▲14,000
255	Timetwister R :B:	2,000	▲5,900	▲11,000	▲25,000
257	Tropical Island R :L:	▲3,000	▲3,500	▲4,000	▲6,000
258	Tsunami U :G:	20	35	50	
259	Tundra R :L:	▲2,300	▲2,500	3,000	5,000
260	Tunnel U :R:	20	40	60	
262	Two-Headed Giant of Foriys R :R:	125	180	300	
263	Underground Sea R :L:	▲5,000	▲6,300	▲8,400	▲21,000
266	Uthden Troll U :R:	30	60	100	250
267	Verduran Enchantress R :G:	150	200	500	1,000
268	Vesuvan Doppelganger R :B:	800	1,000	2,000	3,500
269	Veteran Bodyguard R :W:	150	200	250	
270	Volcanic Eruption R :B:	100	150	300	
271	Wall of Air U :B:	20	30	40	120
272	Wall of Bone U :K:	20	30	40	
273	Wall of Brambles U :G:	20	30	40	
274	Wall of Fire U :R:	20	30	40	
275	Wall of Ice U :G:	20	30	40	
276	Wall of Stone U :R:	20	30	40	
277	Wall of Swords U :W:	20	30	40	
278	Wall of Water U :B:	20	30	40	
280	Wanderlust U :G:	20	30	50	
282	Warp Artifact R :K:	100	120	150	
283	Water Elemental U :B:	30	40	60	
285	Web R :G:	100	150	200	
286	Wheel of Fortune R :R:	800	1,000	▲3,500	
287	White Knight U :W:	50	100	150	250
288	White Ward U :W:	20	30	40	180
290	Will-O'-The-Wisp R :K:	150	200	500	700
291	Winter Orb R :A:	300	400	500	
292	Wooden Sphere U :A:	30	40	80	
293	Word of Command R :K:	200	250	400	
294	Wrath of God R :W:	400	600	800	1,200
295	Zombie Master R :K:	250	300	400	500

1993 Magic The Gathering Beta

#	Card	NmMt 8	NmMt+ 8.5	MT 9	Gem 9.5/10
1	Air Elemental U :B:	8	10	15	20
2	Ancestral Recall R :B:	2,000	2,500	3,000	5,000
3	Animate Artifact U :B:	8	15	20	
4	Animate Dead U :K:	20	40	70	90
5	Animate Wall R :W:	15	25	30	75
6	Ankh of Mishra R :A:	50	120	150	350
7	Armageddon R :W:	150	225	300	500
8	Aspect of Wolf R :G:	20	30	40	100
9	Bad Moon R :K:	100	150	200	400
10	Badlands R :L:	800	1,000	1,200	1,500
11	Balance R :W:	150	180	200	500
12	Basalt Monolith U :A:	10	20	30	60
13	Bayou R :L:	1,000	1,300	1,500	2,000
14	Benalish Hero C :W:	5	10	15	25
15	Berserk U :G:	130	150	180	250
16	Birds of Paradise R :G:	400	500	600	800
17	Black Knight U :K:	20	30	50	
18	Black Lotus R :A:	7,500	8,000	12,000	15,000
19	Black Vise U :A:	20	35	50	
20	Black Ward U :W:	8	15	20	
21	Blaze of Glory R :W:	40	100	125	350
22	Blessing R :W:	20	40	60	125
23	Blue Elemental Blast C :B:	8	15	20	30
24	Blue Ward U :W:	8	15	20	30
25	Bog Wraith U :K:	8	15	20	
26	Braingeyser R :B:	130	150	200	350
27	Burrowing U :R:	8	15	20	
28	Camouflage U :G:	12	20	25	
29	Castle U :W:	12	20	25	50
30	Celestial Prism U :A:	8	15	20	
31	Channel U :G:	15	25	30	

32	Chaos Orb R :A:	400	450	500	700
33	Chaoslace R :R:	15	25	30	60
34	Circle of Protection Black C :W:	8	15	20	30
35	Circle of Protection Blue C :W:	8	15	20	40
36	Circle of Protection Green C :W:	8	15	20	30
37	Circle of Protection Red C :W:	8	15	20	30
38	Circle of Protection White C :W:	8	15	20	30
39	Clockwork Beast R :A:	20	30	40	100
40	Clone U :B:	20	40	50	
41	Cockatrice R :G:	25	40	50	
42	Consecrate Land U :W:	15	25	30	75
43	Conservator U :A:	8	15	20	
44	Contract from Below R :K:	40	80	100	250
45	Control Magic U :B:	15	25	30	
46	Conversion U :W:	8	15	20	
47	Copper Tablet U :A:	10	20	30	60
48	Copy Artifact R :B:	50	120	150	400
49	Counterspell U :B:	40	80	100	
50	Craw Wurm C :G:	8	15	20	40
51	Creature Bond C :B:	8	15	20	30
52	Crusade R :W:	50	100	125	500
53	Crystal Rod U :A:	8	15	20	
54	Cursed Land U :K:	8	15	20	30
55	Cyclopean Tomb R :A:	75	125	150	400
56	Dark Ritual C :K:	20	50	60	150
57	Darkpact R :K:	20	40	50	
58	Death Ward C :W:	8	15	20	30
59	Deathgrip U :K:	8	15	20	
60	Deathlace R :K:	20	30	40	100
61	Demonic Attorney R :K:	20	30	40	100
62	Demonic Hordes R :K:	50	100	125	400
63	Demonic Tutor U :K:	100	125	200	300
64	Dingus Egg R :A:	20	40	50	
65	Disenchant C :W:	15	20	25	40
66	Disintegrate C :R:	8	15	20	30
67	Disrupting Scepter R :A:	40	80	100	250
68	Dragon Whelp U :R:	20	40	60	125
69	Drain Life C :K:	8	15	20	30
70	Drain Power R :B:	20	50	60	150
71	Drudge Skeletons C :K:	8	15	20	30
72	Dwarven Demolition Team U :R:	10	20	30	
73	Dwarven Warriors C :R:	8	15	20	30
74	Earth Elemental U :R:	8	15	20	
75	Earthbind C :R:	8	15	20	30
76	Earthquake R :R:	40	80	100	250
77	Elvish Archers R :G:	40	100	125	350
78	Evil Presence U :K:	8	15	20	30
79	False Orders C :R:	8	15	20	30
80	Farmstead R :W:	20	40	50	125
81	Fastbond R :G:	80	150	175	450
82	Fear C :K:	8	15	20	30
83	Feedback U :B:	8	15	20	30
84	Fire Elemental U :R:	8	15	20	30
85	Fireball C :R:	10	20	25	40
86	Firebreathing C :R:	8	15	20	30
87	Flashfires U :R:	10	20	30	60
88	Flight C :B:	8	15	20	30
89	Fog C :G:	8	15	20	
90	Force of Nature R :G:	80	150	175	400
91	Forcefield R :A:	350	400	500	
92	Forest (blue) C :L:	8	15	20	30
93	Forest (black) C :L:	8	15	20	30
94	Forest (with trail) v3 C :L:	8	15	20	30
95	Fork R :R:	80	150	200	350
96	Frozen Shade C :K:	8	15	20	30
97	Fungusaur R :G:	20	30	40	
98	Gaea's Liege R :G:	20	40	50	125
99	Gauntlet of Might R :A:	100	175	225	650
100	Giant Growth C :G:	8	15	20	30
101	Giant Spider C :G:	8	15	20	30
102	Glasses of Urza U :A:	8	15	20	30
103	Gloom U :K:	8	15	20	30
104	Goblin Balloon Brigade U :R:	8	15	20	40
105	Goblin King R :R:	50	100	125	350
106	Granite Gargoyle R :R:	30	50	60	175
107	Gray Ogre C :R:	8	15	20	30
108	Green Ward U :W:	8	15	20	
109	Grizzly Bears C :G:	10	15	25	50
110	Guardian Angel C :W:	8	15	20	30
111	Healing Salve C :W:	8	15	20	30
112	Helm of Chatzuk R :A:	15	25	30	60
113	Hill Giant C :R:	8	15	20	30
114	Hive, The R :A:	20	30	40	100
115	Holy Armor C :W:	8	15	20	30
116	Holy Strength C :W:	8	15	20	30
117	Howl from Beyond C :K:	8	15	20	30
118	Howling Mine R :A:	100	175	200	500
119	Hurloon Minotaur C :R:	8	15	20	30
120	Hurricane U :G:	10	20	25	
121	Hypnotic Specter U :K:	50	80	100	225
122	Ice Storm U :G:	30	60	80	150
123	Icy Manipulator U :A:	50	80	100	350
124	Illusionary Mask R :A:	150	300	400	850
125	Instill Energy U :G:	8	15	20	40
126	Invisibility C :B:	8	15	20	30
127	Iron Star U :A:	8	15	20	30
128	Ironclaw Orcs C :R:	8	15	20	30
129	Ironroot Treefolk C :G:	8	15	20	30
130	Island Sanctuary R :W:	20	50	60	150
131	Island v1 C :L:	8	15	20	30
132	Island v2 C :L:	8	15	20	30
133	Island v3 C :L:	8	15	20	30
134	Ivory Cup U :A:	8	15	20	30
135	Jade Monolith R :A:	20	30	40	100
136	Jade Statue U :A:	15	25	30	75
137	Jayemdae Tome R :A:	25	40	50	125
138	Juggernaut U :A:	25	40	50	125
139	Jump C :B:	8	15	20	30
140	Karma U :W:	8	15	20	
141	Keldon Warlord U :R:	8	15	20	
142	Kormus Bell R :A:	20	30	40	100
143	Kudzu R :G:	20	30	40	100
144	Lance U :W:	8	15	20	
145	Ley Druid U :G:	8	15	20	30
146	Library of Leng U :A:	8	15	20	30
147	Lich R :K:	75	125	150	400
148	Lifeforce U :G:	8	15	20	30
149	Lifelace R :G:	15	25	30	
150	Lifetap U :B:	8	15	20	30
151	Lightning Bolt C :R:	20	50	120	150
152	Living Artifact R :G:	20	30	40	100
153	Living Lands R :G:	20	30	40	100
154	Living Wall U :A:	8	15	20	
155	Llanowar Elves C :G:	20	50	60	150
156	Lord of Atlantis R :B:	50	120	150	350
157	Lord of the Pit R :K:	75	125	150	400
158	Lure U :G:	8	15	20	30
159	Magical Hack R :B:	20	40	50	
160	Mahamoti Djinn R :B:	50	100	125	400
161	Mana Flare R :R:	75	125	150	400
162	Mana Short R :B:	50	100	125	350
163	Mana Vault R :A:	100	200	250	600
164	Manabarbs R :R:	20	30	40	
165	Meekstone R :A:	30	50	60	175
166	Merfolk of the Pearl Trident C :B:	8	15	20	
167	Mesa Pegasus C :W:	8	15	20	30
168	Mind Twist R :K:	125	225	300	750
169	Mons's Goblin Raiders C :R:	8	15	20	30
170	Mountain v1 C :L:	8	15	20	30
171	Mountain v2 C :L:	8	15	20	30
172	Mountain v3 C :L:	8	15	20	30
173	Mox Emerald R :A:	1,500	2,500	4,000	5,000
174	Mox Jet R :A:	1,500	2,500	4,000	10,000
175	Mox Pearl R :A:	1,500	1,800	2,000	4,500
176	Mox Ruby R :A:	1,500	2,000	2,500	4,500
177	Mox Sapphire R :A:	2,000	2,500	3,000	5,000
178	Natural Selection R :G:	50	100	125	350
179	Nether Shadow R :K:	40	80	100	250
180	Nettling Imp U :K:	8	15	20	30
181	Nevinyrral's Disk R :A:	150	275	350	750
182	Nightmare R :K:	50	100	150	400
183	Northern Paladin R :W:	40	80	100	250
184	Obsianus Golem U :A:	8	15	20	
185	Orcish Artillery U :R:	10	20	25	40
186	Orcish Oriflamme U :R:	10	20	25	40
187	Paralyze C :K:	8	15	20	30
188	Pearled Unicorn C :W:	8	15	20	30
189	Personal Incarnation R :W:	20	30	40	
190	Pestilence C :K:	8	15	20	30
191	Phantasmal Forces U :B:	8	15	20	
192	Phantasmal Terrain C :B:	8	15	20	30
193	Phantom Monster U :B:	8	15	20	30
194	Pirate Ship R :B:	20	40	50	125
195	Plague Rats C :K:	8	15	20	30
196	Plains v1 C :L:	8	15	20	30
197	Plains v2 C :L:	8	15	20	30
198	Plains v3 C :L:	8	15	20	30
199	Plateau R :L:	650	800	1,000	2,000
200	Power Leak C :B:	8	15	20	30
201	Power Sink C :B:	8	15	20	30
202	Power Surge R :R:	20	40	60	150
203	Prodigal Sorcerer C :B:	8	15	20	30
204	Psionic Blast U :B:	40	80	100	250
205	Psychic Venom C :B:	8	15	20	
206	Purelace R :W:	12	20	25	50
207	Raging River R :R:	40	80	100	250
208	Raise Dead C :K:	8	15	20	30
209	Red Elemental Blast C :R:	10	20	25	40
210	Red Ward U :W:	8	15	20	30
211	Regeneration C :G:	8	15	20	30
212	Regrowth U :G:	40	80	100	250
213	Resurrection U :W:	8	15	20	30
214	Reverse Damage R :W:	20	40	50	125
215	Righteousness R :W:	20	40	50	125
216	Roc of Kher Ridges R :R:	20	40	50	125
217	Rock Hydra R :R:	30	50	60	175
218	Rod of Ruin U :A:	8	15	20	
219	Royal Assassin R :K:	100	200	250	650
220	Sacrifice U :K:	8	15	20	
221	Samite Healer C :W:	8	15	20	30
222	Savannah Lions R :W:	80	100	150	500
223	Savannah R :L:	800	850	950	1,100
224	Scathe Zombies C :K:	8	15	20	30
225	Scavenging Ghoul U :K:	8	15	20	
226	Scrubland R :L:	800	1,000	1,200	1,500
227	Scryb Sprites C :G:	8	15	20	30
228	Sea Serpent C :B:	8	15	20	30
229	Sedge Troll R :R:	40	80	100	
230	Sengir Vampire U :K:	30	60	70	150
231	Serra Angel U :W:	80	150	175	400
232	Shanodin Dryads C :G:	8	15	20	30
233	Shatter C :R:	8	15	20	30
234	Shivan Dragon R :R:	175	250	300	750
235	Simulacrum U :K:	8	15	20	
236	Sinkhole C :K:	40	100	125	300
237	Siren's Call U :B:	8	15	20	30
238	Sleight of Mind R :B:	20	30	40	100
239	Smoke R :R:	20	40	50	125
240	Sol Ring U :A:	90	150	200	500
241	Soul Net U :A:	8	15	20	30
242	Spell Blast C :B:	8	15	20	30
243	Stasis R :B:	50	100	125	350
244	Steal Artifact U :B:	8	15	20	
245	Stone Giant U :R:	8	15	20	
246	Stone Rain C :R:	8	15	20	30
247	Stream of Life C :G:	8	15	20	30
248	Sunglasses of Urza R :A:	20	30	40	100
249	Swamp v1 C :L:	8	15	20	30
250	Swamp v2 C :L:	8	15	20	30
251	Swamp v3 C :L:	8	15	20	30
252	Swords to Plowshares U :W:	30	75	100	300
253	Taiga R :L:	600	750	900	1,100
254	Terror C :K:	8	15	20	30
255	Thicket Basilisk U :G:	8	15	20	30
256	Thoughtlace R :B:	20	30	40	100
257	Throne of Bone U :A:	8	15	20	30
258	Timber Wolves R :G:	15	25	30	75
259	Time Vault R :A:	600	800	1,000	1,250
260	Time Walk R :B:	1,500	2,000	2,500	3,000
261	Timetwister R :B:	1,000	1,750	2,500	3,000
262	Tranquility C :G:	8	15	20	30
263	Tropical Island R :L:	1,000	1,500	2,000	3,000
264	Tsunami U :G:	8	15	20	30
265	Tundra R :L:	1,800	2,000	2,500	3,500
266	Tunnel U :R:	8	15	20	30
267	Twiddle C :B:	8	15	20	30
268	Two-Headed Giant of Foriys R :R:	50	100	125	350
269	Underground Sea R :L:	3,000	4,000	4,500	5,000
270	Unholy Strength C :K:	8	15	20	30
271	Unsummon C :B:	8	15	20	30
272	Uthden Troll U :R:	8	15	20	
273	Verduran Enchantress R :G:	40	80	100	250
274	Vesuvan Doppelganger R :B:	100	200	250	
275	Veteran Bodyguard R :W:	20	30	40	
276	Volcanic Eruption R :B:	15	25	30	75
277	Volcanic Island R :L:	3,000	4,000	5,000	10,000
278	Wall of Air U :B:	8	15	20	30
279	Wall of Bone U :K:	8	15	20	30
280	Wall of Brambles U :G:	8	15	20	
281	Wall of Fire U :R:	8	15	20	30
282	Wall of Ice U :G:	8	15	20	30
283	Wall of Stone U :R:	8	15	20	
284	Wall of Swords U :W:	8	15	20	30
285	Wall of Water U :B:	8	15	20	
286	Wall of Wood C :G:	8	15	20	
287	Wanderlust U :G:	8	15	20	
288	War Mammoth C :G:	8	15	20	30
289	Warp Artifact R :K:	15	25	30	60
290	Water Elemental U :B:	8	15	20	
291	Weakness C :K:	8	15	20	30
292	Web R :G:	15	25	30	60
293	Wheel of Fortune R :R:	150	300	400	800
294	White Knight U :W:	20	30	40	
295	White Ward U :W:	8	15	20	30
296	Wild Growth C :G:	8	15	20	30
297	Will-O'-The-Wisp R :K:	50	100	125	350
298	Winter Orb R :A:	75	125	175	500
299	Wooden Sphere U :A:	8	15	20	30
300	Word of Command R :K:	75	125	150	400
301	Wrath of God R :W:	300	400	500	600
302	Zombie Master R :K:	50	80	100	250

1993 Magic The Gathering Unlimited

#	Card	NmMt 8	NmMt+ 8.5	MT 9	Gem 9.5/10
1	Air Elemental U :B:	7	10	12	20
2	Ancestral Recall R :B:	1,200	1,500	1,800	2,000
3	Animate Artifact U :B:	7	10	12	20
4	Animate Dead U :K:	10	15	20	30
5	Animate Wall R :W:	8	12	15	25
6	Ankh of Mishra R :A:	10			
7	Armageddon R :W:	15	25	30	
8	Aspect of Wolf R :G:	8	12	15	
9	Bad Moon R :K:	20	30	35	60
10	Badlands R :L:	200	300	350	450
11	Balance R :W:	12	18	20	30
12	Basalt Monolith U :A:	7	10	12	20
13	Bayou R :L:	200	300	350	
14	Benalish Hero C :W:	6	10	12	20
15	Berserk U :G:	60	70	80	150
16	Birds of Paradise R :G:	50	65	75	
17	Black Knight U :K:	8	12	15	25
18	Black Lotus R :A:	4,000	4,750	5,500	7,500
19	Black Vise U :A:	8	12	15	25
20	Black Ward U :W:	6	10	12	20
21	Blaze of Glory R :W:	15	20	25	45
22	Blessing R :W:	8	12	15	25
23	Blue Elemental Blast C :B:	7	10	12	20
24	Blue Ward U :W:	6	10	12	20
25	Bog Wraith U :K:	7	10	12	
26	Braingeyser R :B:	12	18	20	
27	Burrowing U :R:	6	10	12	20
28	Camouflage U :G:	7	10	12	20
29	Castle U :W:	7	10	12	20
30	Celestial Prism U :A:	7	10	12	20
31	Channel U :G:	7	10	12	25
32	Chaos Orb R :A:	150	225	300	350

33	Chaoslace R :R:	8	12	15	25
34	Circle of Protection: Black C :W:	6	10	12	20
35	Circle of Protection: Blue C :W:	6	10	12	20
36	Circle of Protection: Green C :W:	6	10	12	20
37	Circle of Protection: Red C :W:	6	10	12	20
38	Circle of Protection: White C :W:	6	10	12	20
39	Clockwork Beast R :A:	8	12	15	25
40	Clone U :B:	10	15	20	30
41	Cockatrice R :G:	10	15	20	
42	Consecrate Land U :W:	7	10	12	20
43	Conservator U :A:	6	10	12	20
44	Contract from Below R :K:	10	15	20	30
45	Control Magic U :B:	8	12	15	
46	Conversion U :W:	6	10	12	20
47	Copper Tablet U :A:	8	12	15	
48	Copy Artifact R :B:	12	18	20	30
49	Counterspell U :B:	12	18	20	
50	Craw Wurm C :G:	6	10	12	20
51	Creature Bond C :B:	6	10	12	20
52	Crusade R :W:	15	25	30	
53	Crystal Rod U :A:	6	10	12	20
54	Cursed Land U :K:	6	10	12	20
55	Cyclopean Tomb R :A:	30	55	60	90
56	Dark Ritual C :K:	7	10	12	20
57	Darkpact R :K:	7	10	12	
58	Death Ward C :W:	6	10	12	20
59	Deathgrip U :K:	7	10	12	20
60	Deathlace R :K:	8	12	15	25
61	Demonic Attorney R :K:	8	12	15	
62	Demonic Hordes R :K:	15	25	30	
63	Demonic Tutor U :K:	25	35	40	60
64	Dingus Egg R :A:	8	12	15	
65	Disenchant C :W:	7	10	12	20
66	Disintegrate C :R:	6	10	12	20
67	Disrupting Scepter R :A:	8	12	15	25
68	Dragon Whelp U :R:	7	10	12	20
69	Drain Life C :K:	6	10	12	20
70	Drain Power R :B:	10	15	20	
71	Drudge Skeletons C :K:	6	10	12	20
72	Dwarven Demolition Team U :R:	7	10	12	20
73	Dwarven Warriors C :R:	6	10	12	20
74	Earth Elemental U :R:	6	10	12	20
75	Earthbind C :R:	6	10	12	20
76	Earthquake R :R:	10	15	20	30
77	Elvish Archers R :G:	10	15	20	30
78	Evil Presence U :K:	7	10	12	20
79	False Orders C :R:	6	10	12	20
80	Farmstead R :W:	7	10	12	20
81	Fastbond R :G:	15	25	30	
82	Fear C :K:	6	10	12	20
83	Feedback U :B:	6	10	12	20
84	Fire Elemental U :R:	7	10	12	20
85	Fireball C :R:	7	10	12	20
86	Firebreathing C :R:	6	10	12	20
87	Flashfires U :R:	7	10	12	20
88	Flight C :B:	6	10	12	20
89	Fog C :G:	6	10	12	20
90	Force of Nature R :G:	12	18	20	30
91	Forcefield R :A:	100	160	200	
92	Forest v1 C :L:	6	10	12	20
93	Forest v2 C :L:	6	10	12	20
94	Forest v3 C :L:	6	10	12	20
95	Fork R :R:	35	55	65	110
96	Frozen Shade C :K:	7	10	12	20
97	Fungusaur R :G:	8	12	15	25
98	Gaea's Liege R :G:	10	15	20	30
99	Gauntlet of Might R :A:	100	145	175	300
100	Giant Growth C :G:	7	10	12	20
101	Giant Spider C :G:	6	10	12	20
102	Glasses of Urza U :A:	7	10	12	
103	Gloom U :K:	6	10	12	20
104	Goblin Balloon Brigade U :R:	6	10	12	
105	Goblin King R :R:	12	18	20	30
106	Granite Gargoyle R :R:	10	15	20	30
107	Gray Ogre C :R:	6	10	12	20
108	Green Ward U :W:	6	10	12	20
109	Grizzly Bears C :G:	6	10	12	20
110	Guardian Angel C :W:	6	10	12	20
111	Healing Salve C :W:	6	10	12	20
112	Helm of Chatzuk R :A:	8	12	15	25
113	Hill Giant C :R:	6	10	12	20
114	Hive, The R :A:	8	12	15	25
115	Holy Armor C :W:	6	10	12	20
116	Holy Strength C :W:	6	10	12	20
117	Howl from Beyond C :K:	6	10	12	20
118	Howling Mine R :A:	20	30	35	60
119	Hurloon Minotaur C :R:	6	10	12	20
120	Hurricane U :G:	7	10	12	
121	Hypnotic Specter U :K:	15	20	25	45
122	Ice Storm U :G:	20	25	30	60
123	Icy Manipulator U :A:	25	35	40	75
124	Illusionary Mask R :A:	100	130	150	250
125	Instill Energy U :G:	7	10	12	20
126	Invisibility C :B:	6	10	12	20
127	Iron Star U :A:	6	10	12	20
128	Ironclaw Orcs C :R:	6	10	12	20
129	Ironroot Treefolk C :G:	6	10	12	20
130	Island Sanctuary R :W:	8	12	15	25
131	Island v1 C :L:	6	10	12	20
132	Island v2 C :L:	6	10	12	20
133	Island v3 C :L:	6	10	12	20
134	Ivory Cup U :A:	6	10	12	20
135	Jade Monolith R :A:	8	12	15	
136	Jade Statue U :A:	12	18	20	30
137	Jayemdae Tome R :A:	8	12	15	
138	Juggernaut U :A:	10	15	20	30
139	Jump C :B:	6	10	12	20
140	Karma U :W:	7	10	12	20
141	Keldon Warlord U :R:	7	10	12	
142	Kormus Bell R :A:	8	12	15	
143	Kudzu R :G:	8	12	15	25
144	Lance U :W:	6	10	12	20
145	Ley Druid U :G:	6	10	12	20
146	Library of Leng U :A:	7	10	12	20
147	Lich R :K:	40	60	75	150
148	Lifeforce U :G:	6	10	12	20
149	Lifelace R :G:	7	10	12	
150	Lifetap U :B:	6	10	12	20
151	Lightning Bolt C :R:	12	18	20	30
152	Living Artifact R :G:	8	12	15	25
153	Living Lands R :G:	8	12	15	25
154	Living Wall U :A:	7	10	12	
155	Llanowar Elves C :G:	7	10	12	25
156	Lord of Atlantis R :B:	10	15	20	30
157	Lord of the Pit R :K:	10	15	20	30
158	Lure U :G:	7	10	12	20
159	Magical Hack R :B:	8	12	15	
160	Mahamoti Djinn R :B:	15	25	30	50
161	Mana Flare R :R:	12	18	20	35
162	Mana Short R :B:	12	20	25	
163	Mana Vault R :A:	12	18	20	30
164	Manabarbs R :R:	8	12	15	
165	Meekstone R :A:	12	18	20	
166	Merfolk of the Pearl Trident C :B:	6	10	12	20
167	Mesa Pegasus C :W:	6	10	12	20
168	Mind Twist R :K:	15	20	25	
169	Mons's Goblin Raiders C :R:	6	10	12	20
170	Mountain v1 C :L:	6	10	12	20
171	Mountain v2 C :L:	6	10	12	20
172	Mountain v3 C :L:	6	10	12	20
173	Mox Emerald R :A:	900	1,000	1,300	1,400
174	Mox Jet R :A:	1,300	1,400		
175	Mox Pearl R :A:	1,000	1,300		
176	Mox Ruby R :A:	800	1,000	1,300	1,500
177	Mox Sapphire R :A:	2,000	2,250	2,500	3,000
178	Natural Selection R :G:	20	30	35	60
179	Nether Shadow R :K:	10	15	20	30
180	Nettling Imp U :K:	7	10	12	20
181	Nevinyrral's Disk R :A:	20	30	35	60
182	Nightmare R :K:	20	30	35	
183	Northern Paladin R :W:	12	18	20	
184	Obsianus Golem U :A:	7	10	12	20
185	Orcish Artillery U :R:	6	10	12	
186	Orcish Oriflamme U :R:	7	10	12	20
187	Paralyze C :K:	6	10	12	20
188	Pearled Unicorn C :W:	6	10	12	20
189	Personal Incarnation R :W:	8	12	15	
190	Pestilence C :K:	6	10	12	
191	Phantasmal Forces U :B:	7	10	12	
192	Phantasmal Terrain C :B:	6	10	12	20
193	Phantom Monster U :B:	7	10	12	20
194	Pirate Ship R :B:	7	10	12	20
195	Plague Rats C :K:	6	10	12	20
196	Plains v1 C :L:	6	10	12	20
197	Plains v2 C :L:	6	10	12	20
198	Plains v3 C :L:	6	10	12	20
199	Plateau R :L:	250	300	350	
200	Power Leak C :B:	6	10	12	20
201	Power Sink C :B:	6	10	12	20
202	Power Surge R :R:	8	12	15	
203	Prodigal Sorcerer C :B:	6	10	12	20
204	Psionic Blast U :B:	15	20	25	45
205	Psychic Venom C :B:	6	10	12	20
206	Purelace R :W:	7	10	12	
207	Raging River R :R:	25	35	40	60
208	Raise Dead C :K:	6	10	12	20
209	Red Elemental Blast C :R:	7	10	12	20
210	Red Ward U :W:	7	10	12	20
211	Regeneration C :G:	6	10	12	20
212	Regrowth U :G:	10	15	20	30
213	Resurrection U :W:	7	10	12	20
214	Reverse Damage R :W:	8	12	15	25
215	Righteousness R :W:	10	15	20	30
216	Roc of Kher Ridges R :R:	8	12	15	25
217	Rock Hydra R :R:	10	15	20	30
218	Rod of Ruin U :A:	6	10	12	20
219	Royal Assassin R :K:	25	35	40	80
220	Sacrifice U :K:	6	10	12	20
221	Samite Healer C :W:	6	10	12	20
222	Savannah Lions R :W:	20	25	30	60
223	Savannah R :L:	150	175	225	
224	Scathe Zombies C :K:	6	10	12	20
225	Scavenging Ghoul U :K:	7	10	12	20
226	Scrubland R :L:	150	175	200	
227	Scryb Sprites C :G:	6	10	12	20
228	Sea Serpent C :B:	6	10	12	20
229	Sedge Troll R :R:	10	15	20	
230	Sengir Vampire U :K:	10	15	20	30
231	Serra Angel U :W:	12	18	20	40
232	Shanodin Dryads C :G:	6	10	12	20
233	Shatter C :R:	6	10	12	20
234	Shivan Dragon R :R:	30	45	50	100
235	Simulacrum U :K:	6	10	12	
236	Sinkhole C :K:	30	45	50	90
237	Siren's Call U :B:	6	10	12	20
238	Sleight of Mind R :B:	10	15	20	30
239	Smoke R :R:	8	12	15	25
240	Sol Ring U :A:	25	35	40	60
241	Soul Net U :A:	7	10	12	20
242	Spell Blast C :B:	6	10	12	20
243	Stasis R :B:	12	18	20	
244	Steal Artifact U :B:	6	10	12	
245	Stone Giant U :R:	6	10	12	20
246	Stone Rain C :R:	7	10	12	20
247	Stream of Life C :G:	6	10	12	20
248	Sunglasses of Urza R :A:	7	10	12	20
249	Swamp v1 C :L:	6	10	12	20
250	Swamp v2 C :L:	6	10	12	20
251	Swamp v3 C :L:	6	10	12	20
252	Swords to Plowshares U :W:	10	15	20	30
253	Taiga R :L:	250	300	350	
254	Terror C :K:	6	10	12	20
255	Thicket Basilisk U :G:	7	10	12	20
256	Thoughtlace R :B:	8	12	15	
257	Throne of Bone U :A:	7	10	12	20
258	Timber Wolves R :G:	8			
259	Time Vault R :A:	450	500	600	750
260	Time Walk R :B:	1,000	1,200	1,300	1,600
261	Timetwister R :B:	900	1,000	1,100	1,300
262	Tranquility C :G:	6	10	12	20
263	Tropical Island R :L:	350	500	600	900
264	Tsunami U :G:	7	10	12	
265	Tundra R :L:	300	350	400	500
266	Tunnel U :R:	6	10	12	20
267	Twiddle C :B:	6	10	12	20
268	Two-Headed Giant of Foriys R :R:	30	45	50	90
269	Underground Sea R :L:	450	550	750	900
270	Unholy Strength C :K:	6	10	12	20
271	Unsummon C :B:	6	10	12	20
272	Uthden Troll U :R:	6	10	12	
273	Verduran Enchantress R :G:	10	15	20	30
274	Vesuvan Doppelganger R :B:	25	35	40	
275	Veteran Bodyguard R :W:	8	12	15	25
276	Volcanic Eruption R :B:	8	12	15	
277	Volcanic Island R :L:	300	350	400	500
278	Wall of Air U :B:	7	10	12	20
279	Wall of Bone U :K:	7	10	12	20
280	Wall of Brambles U :G:	6	10	12	20
281	Wall of Fire U :R:	7	10	12	20
282	Wall of Ice U :G:	7	10	12	20
283	Wall of Stone U :R:	7	10	12	20
284	Wall of Swords U :W:	6	10	12	20
285	Wall of Water U :B:	6	10	12	
286	Wall of Wood C :G:	6	10	12	20
287	Wanderlust U :G:	6	10	12	20
288	War Mammoth C :G:	6	10	12	20
289	Warp Artifact R :K:	8	12	15	25
290	Water Elemental U :B:	7	10	12	20
291	Weakness C :K:	6	10	12	20
292	Web R :G:	8			
293	Wheel of Fortune R :R:	30	50	60	90
294	White Knight U :W:	8	12	15	25
295	White Ward U :W:	6	10	12	20
296	Wild Growth C :G:	6	10	12	20
297	Will-O'-The-Wisp R :K:	12	18	20	35
298	Winter Orb R :A:	15	20	25	
299	Wooden Sphere U :A:	7	10	12	20
300	Word of Command R :K:	50	70	80	
301	Wrath of God R :W:	50	65	75	150
302	Zombie Master R :K:	12	18	20	30

1993 Magic The Gathering Arabian Nights

		NmMt 8	NmMt+ 8.5	MT 9	Gem 9.5/10
1	Abu Jafar U3 :W:	12	16	20	
2	Aladdin U2 :R:	15	25	35	45
3	Aladdin's Lamp U2 :A:	10	25	50	75
4	Aladdin's Ring U2 :A:	10	25	45	65
5	Ali Baba U3 :R:	10	25	50	70
6	Ali from Cairo U2 :R:	150	200	300	400
7	Army of Allah (dark 1) C3 :W:	12	16	20	40
8	Army of Allah (light 1) C1 :W:	12	16	20	40
9	Bazaar of Baghdad U3 :L:	650	750	800	1,000
10	Bird Maiden (dark 1) C2 :R:	5	8	10	20
11	Bird Maiden (light 1) C2 :R:	5	8	10	20
12	Bottle of Suleiman U2 :A:	12	16	20	40
13	Brass Man U3 :A:	9	12	15	30
14	Camel C5 :W:	5	8	10	20
15	City in a Bottle U2 :A:	125	175	200	350
16	City of Brass U3 :L:	100	150	250	350
17	Cuombajj Witches C4 :K:	10	25	35	50
18	Cyclone U3 :G:	9	12	15	
19	Dancing Scimitar U2 :A:	10	25	35	50
20	Dandan C4 :B:	5	8	10	20
21A	Desert C11 :L:	5	8	10	20
22	Desert Nomads C4 :R:	5	8	10	20
23	Desert Twister U3 :G:	10	15	25	35
24	Diamond Valley U2 :L:	250	300	350	400
25	Drop of Honey U2 :G:	400	450	550	800
26	Ebony Horse U2 :A:	12	16	20	
27	Elephant Graveyard U2 :L:	100	150	300	350
28	El-Hajjaj U2 :K:	10	25	50	100
29	Erg Raiders (dark 1) C3 :K:	9	12	15	30
30	Erg Raiders (light 1) C2 :K:	9	12	15	30
31	Erhnam Djinn U2 :G:	100	150	250	
32	Eye for an Eye U3 :W:	9	12	15	30
33	Fishliver Oil (dark 1) C3 :B:	12	16	20	35

34	Fishliver Oil (light 1) C1 :B:	12	16	20	35
35	Flying Carpet U3 :A:	9	12	15	30
36	Flying Men C5 :B:	12	16	20	35
37	Ghazban Ogre C4 :G:	5	8	10	20
38	Giant Tortoise (dark 1) C3 :B:	12	16	20	35
39	Giant Tortoise (light 1) C1 :B:	12	16	20	35
40	Guardian Beast U2 :K:	150	200	250	700
41	Hasran Ogress (dark mana) C3 :K:	5	8	10	20
42	Hasran Ogress (light mana) C2 :K:	5	8	10	20
43	Hurr Jackal C4 :R:	5	8	10	20
44	Ifh-Biff Efreet U2 :G:	60	80	100	
45	Island Fish Jasconius U2 :B:	12	16	20	35
46	Island of Wak-Wak U2 :L:	100	150	200	400
47	Jandor's Ring U2 :A:	12	16	20	35
48	Jandor's Saddlebags U2 :A:	12	16	20	35
49	Jeweled Bird U3 :A:	12	16	20	35
50	Jihad U2 :W:	40	50	60	80
51	Junun Efreet U2 :K:	10	25	50	70
52	Juzam Djinn U2 :K:	600	650	900	1,200
53	Khabal Ghoul U3 :K:	15	20	25	35
54	King Suleiman U2 :W:	40	50	60	100
55	Kird Ape C5 :R:	10	25	35	50
56	Library of Alexandria U3 :L:	700	800	1,000	1,200
57	Magnetic Mountain U3 :R:	9	12	15	30
58	Merchant Ship U3 :B:	12	16	20	
59	Metamorphosis C4 :G:	5	8	10	20
60	Mijae Djinn U2 :R:	10	20		
61	Moorish Cavalry (dark 2) C4 :W:	5	8	10	20
62	Moorish Cavalry (light 2) C1 :W:	5	8	10	20
63	Mountain C1 :L:	35	50	80	120
64	Naf's Asp (dark 1) C3 :G:	5	8	10	20
65	Naf's Asp (light 1) C2 :G:	5	8	10	20
66	Oasis U4 :L:	9	12	15	30
67	Old Man of the Sea U2 :B:	150	200	250	
68	Oubliette (dark 1) C2 :K:	25	40	60	100
69	Oubliette (light 1) C2 :K:	25	40	60	100
70	Piety (dark 1) C3 :W:	12	16	20	35
71	Piety (light 1) C1 :W:	12	16	20	35
72	Pyramids U2 :A:	20	25	30	65
73	Repentant Blacksmith U2 :W:	12	16	20	
74	Ring of Maruf U2 :A:	20	30	50	80
75	Rukh Egg (dark 3) C3 :R:	12	16	20	40
76	Rukh Egg (light 3) C1 :R:	12	16	20	40
77	Sandals of Abdallah U3 :A:	12	16	20	35
78	Sandstorm C4 :G:	5	8	10	20
79	Serendib Djinn U2 :B:	80	100	150	200
80	Serendib Efreet U2 :B:	200	250	300	550
81	Shahrazad U2 :W:	180	200	250	450
82	Sindbad U3 :B:	9	12	15	
83	Singing Tree U2 :G:	75	100	200	275
84	Sorceress Queen U3 :K:	20	30	35	60
85	Stone-Throwing Devils (dark mana) C3 :K:	15	20	25	50
86	Stone-Throwing Devils (light mana) C1 :K:	15	20	25	50
87	Unstable Mutation C5 :B:	5	8	10	20
88	War Elephant (dark 3) C3 :W:	12	16	20	35
89	War Elephant (light 3) C1 :W:	12	16	20	35
90	Wyluli Wolf (dark 1) C4 :G:	12	16	20	40
91	Wyluli Wolf (light 1) C1 :G:	12	16	20	40
92	Ydwen Efreet U2 :R:	40	60	90	150

Pokemon

1999 Pokemon Base 1st Edition Thick Stamp

		NmMt 8	NmMt+ 8.5	MT 9	Gem 9.5/10
1	Alakazam HOLO R	300	400	500	2,000
2	Blastoise HOLO R	600	800	1,500	7,000
3	Chansey HOLO R	200	250	500	5,000
4	Charizard HOLO R	3,500	4,000	5,500	18,000
5	Clefairy HOLO R	200	300	400	2,000
6	Gyarados HOLO R	250	350	500	2,000
7	Hitmonchan HOLO R	250	350	450	1,800
8	Machamp HOLO R	200	300	400	1,000
9	Magneton HOLO R	200	300	400	1,800
10	Mewtwo HOLO R	200	300	700	6,000
11	Nidoking HOLO R	200	300	400	2,000
12	Ninetales HOLO R	200	300	500	3,000
13	Poliwrath HOLO R	200	300	400	1,800
14	Raichu HOLO R	200	300	500	5,000
15	Venusaur HOLO R	400	500	700	4,500
16	Zapdos HOLO R	200	300	500	2,500
17	Beedrill R	80	100	150	800
18	Dragonair R	40	60	80	800
19	Dugtrio R	30	40	50	450
20	Electabuzz R	30	40	50	400
21	Electrode R	30	40	75	600
22	Pidgeotto R	20	30	40	350
23	Arcanine U	20	30	40	100
24	Charmeleon U	25	40	60	450
25	Dewgong U	15	20	30	65
26	Dratini U	15	20	25	450
27	Farfetch'd U	15	20	30	75
28	Growlithe U	20	30	35	300
29	Haunter U	20	25	30	250
30	Ivysaur U	20	30	40	150
31	Jynx U	15	20	25	300
32	Kadabra U	20	30	40	200
33	Kakuna (UER) U	10	15	20	50
34	Machoke U	15	20	30	70
35	Magikarp U	15	20	30	70
36	Magmar U	15	20	25	70
37	Nidorino U	10	15	20	70
38	Poliwhirl U	15	20	25	75
39	Porygon U	20	25	30	70
40	Raticate U	20	25	30	50
41	Seel U	15	20	25	40
42	Wartortle U	30	40	75	800
43	Abra C	5	10	15	45
44	Bulbasaur (UER) C	30	45	55	200
45	Caterpie (UER) C	10	15	20	80
46	Charmander C	20	25	35	100
47	Diglett C	10	15	20	30
48	Doduo C	10	15	20	40
49	Drowzee C	10	15	20	45
50	Gastly C	10	15	20	45
51	Koffing C	10	15	20	40
52	Machop C	10	15	20	40
53	Magnemite C	10	15	20	40
54	Metapod (UER) C	10	15	20	45
55	Nidoran-M C	10	15	20	35
56	Onix C	10	15	20	40
57	Pidgey C	10	15	20	40
58	Pikachu (Red cheeks Error) C	40	50	75	350
58	Pikachu (Yellow cheeks Corr.) C	20	30	50	150
59	Poliwag C	10	15	20	40
60	Ponyta C	10	15	20	40
61	Rattata C	10	15	20	40
62	Sandshrew C	10	15	20	40
63	Squirtle C	15	20	30	80
64	Starmie C	10	15	20	40
65	Staryu C	10	15	20	40
66	Tangela C	10	15	20	40
67	Voltorb (UER) C	10	15	20	45
68	Vulpix (UER) C	15	20	25	45
69	Weedle C	10	15	20	45
70	Clefairy Doll R	20	30	45	500
71	Computer Search R	60	80	100	450
72	Devolution Spray R	20	30	40	750
73	Impostor Professor Oak R	30	40	60	350
74	Item Finder R	15	20	25	500
75	Lass R	60	80	100	1,000
76	Pokemon Breeder R	20	25	35	300
77	Pokemon Trader R	20	30	40	350
78	Scoop Up R	20	25	35	200
79	Super Energy Removal R	20	30	40	300
80	Defender U	5	10	15	20
81	Energy Retrieval U	10	15	20	200
82	Full Heal U	10	15	20	50
83	Maintenance U	10	15	20	50
84	Plus Power U	10	15	20	120
85	Pokemon Center U	10	15	20	50
86	Pokemon Flute U	10	15	20	300
87	Pokédex U	10	15	20	120
88	Professor Oak U	15	20	30	450
89	Revive U	10	15	25	80
90	Super Potion U	10	15	25	80
91	Bill C	10	15	20	45
92	Energy Removal C	10	15	20	45
93	Gust of Wind C	10	15	25	55
94	Potion C	10	15	25	50
95	Switch C	10	15	25	50
96	Double Colorless Energy U	10	15	25	120
97	Fighting Energy	5	10	15	30
98	Fire Energy	5	10	15	30
99	Grass Energy	5	10	15	30
100	Lightning Energy	5	10	15	30
101	Psychic Energy	5	10	15	30
102	Water Energy	5	10	15	30

Yu-Gi-Oh

2002 Yu-Gi-Oh Legend of Blue Eyes White Dragon 1st Edition

		NmMt 8	NmMt+ 8.5	MT 9	Gem 9.5/10
LOB0	Tri-Horned Dragon SCR			150	400
LOB1	Blue-Eyes White Dragon UR	1,500	1,800	2,800	5,000
LOB2	Hitotsu-Me Giant C				
LOB3	Flame Swordsman SR				
LOB4	Skull Servant C				
LOB5	Dark Magician UR				
LOB6	Gaia The Fierce Knight UR			150	
LOB7	Celtic Guardian SR			50	100
LOB8	Basic Insect C				
LOB9	Mammoth Graveyard C				
LOB10	Silver Fang C				
LOB11	Dark Gray C				
LOB12	Trial of Hell C				
LOB13	Nemuriko C				
LOB14	The 13th Grave C				
LOB15	Charubin Fire Knight R				
LOB16	Flame Manipulator C				
LOB17	Monster Egg C				
LOB18	Firegrass C				
LOB19	Darkfire Dragon R				
LOB20	Dark King of Abyss C				
LOB21	Fiend Reflection #2 C				
LOB22	Fusionist R				
LOB23	Turtle Tiger C				
LOB24	Petit Dragon C				
LOB25	Petit Angel C				
LOB26	Hinotama Soul C				
LOB27	Aqua Madoor R				
LOB28	Kagemusha of Blue Flame C				
LOB29	Flame Ghost R				
LOB30	Two-Mouth Darkruler C				
LOB31	Dissolverock C				
LOB32	Root Water C				
LOB33	The Furious Sea King C				
LOB34	Green Phantom King C				
LOB35	Ray & Temperature C				
LOB36	King Fog C				
LOB37	Mystical Sheep #2 C				
LOB38	Masaki Legendary Swordsman C				
LOB39	Kurama C				
LOB40	Legendary Sword SP				
LOB41	Beast Fangs SP				
LOB42	Violet Crystal SP				
LOB43	Book of Secret Arts SP				
LOB44	Power of Kaishin SP				
LOB45	Dragon Capture Jar R				
LOB46	Forest C				
LOB47	Wasteland C				
LOB48	Mountain C				
LOB49	Sogen C				
LOB50	Umi C				
LOB51	Yami C				
LOB52	Dark Hole SR				
LOB53	Raigeki SR				
LOB54	Red Medicine C				
LOB55	Sparks C				
LOB56	Hinotama C				
LOB57	Fissure R				
LOB58	Trap Hole SR				
LOB59	Polymerization SR			60	
LOB60	Remove Trap C				
LOB61	Two-Pronged Attack R				
LOB62	Mystical Elf SR		60		200
LOB63	Tyhone C				
LOB64	Beaver Warrior C				
LOB65	Gravedigger Ghoul R				
LOB66	Curse of Dragon SR				
LOB67	Karbonala Warrior R				
LOB68	Giant Soldier of Stone R				
LOB69	Uraby C				
LOB70	Red Eyes B Dragon UR				1,200
LOB71	Reaper of the Cards R				
LOB72	Witty Phantom C				
LOB73	Larvas C				
LOB74	Hard Armor C				
LOB75	Man Eater C				
LOB76	M-Warrior #1 C				
LOB77	M-Warrior #2 C				
LOB78	Spirit of the Harp R				
LOB79	Armaill C				
LOB80	Terra the Terrible C				
LOB81	Frenzied Panda C				
LOB82	Kumootoko C				
LOB83	Meda Bat C				
LOB84	Enchanting Mermaid C				
LOB85	Fireyarou C				
LOB86	Dragoness The Wicked R				
LOB87	One-Eyed Shield Dragon C				
LOB88	Dark Energy SP				
LOB89	Laser Cannon Armor SP				
LOB90	Vile Germs SP				
LOB91	Silver Bow and Arrow SP				
LOB92	Dragon Treasure SP				
LOB93	Electro-Whip				
LOB94	Mystical Moon SP				
LOB95	Stop Defense R				
LOB96	Machine Convers. Factory SP				
LOB97	Raise Body Heat SP				
LOB98	Follow Wind SP				
LOB99	Goblin's Secret Remedy R				
LOB100	Final Flame R				
LOB101	Swords of Rev. Light SR				
LOB102	Metal Dragon R				
LOB103	Spike Seadra C				
LOB104	Tripwire Beast C				
LOB105	Skull Red Bird C				
LOB106	Armed Ninja R				
LOB107	Flower Wolf R				
LOB108	Man-Eater Bug SR				
LOB109	Sand Stone C				
LOB110	Hane-Hane R				
LOB111	Misairuzame C				
LOB112	Steel Ogre Grotto #1 C				
LOB113	Lesser Dragon C				
LOB114	Darkworld Thorns C				
LOB115	Drooling Lizard C				
LOB116	Armored Starfish C				
LOB117	Succubus Knight C				
LOB118	Monster Reborn UR			250	350
LOB119	Pot of Greed R				
LOB120	Right Leg of Forbid.One UR	100			325
LOB121	Left Leg of Forbidden One UR			150	
LOB122	Right Arm of Forbid.One UR				
LOB123	Left Arm of Forbid.One UR				
LOB124	Exodia the Forbidden One UR				
LOB125	Gaia the Dragon Champion SCR				